Student's
Oxford
Canadian
Dictionary

Student's
Oxford
Canadian
Dictionary

Edited by
Katherine Barber
Alex Bisset
Robert Pontisso
Eric Sinkins

Editor-in-chief, Canadian Dictionaries
Katherine Barber

OXFORD
UNIVERSITY PRESS

1904 ❦ 2004

100 YEARS OF
CANADIAN PUBLISHING

OXFORD
UNIVERSITY PRESS

70 Wynford Drive, Don Mills, Ontario M3C 1J9

www.oup.com/ca

Oxford University Press is a department of the University of Oxford.
It furthers the University's objective of excellence in research, scholarship,
and education by publishing worldwide in

Oxford New York

Auckland Cape Town Dar es Salaam Hong Kong Karachi
Kuala Lumpur Madrid Melbourne Mexico City Nairobi
New Delhi Shanghai Taipei Toronto

With offices in

Argentina Austria Brazil Chile Czech Republic France Greece
Guatemala Hungary Italy Japan Poland Portugal Singapore
South Korea Switzerland Thailand Turkey Ukraine Vietnam

Oxford is a registered trade mark of Oxford University Press
in the UK and in certain other countries

Published in Canada
by Oxford University Press

Copyright © Oxford University Press Canada 2004

The moral rights of the author have been asserted

Database right Oxford University Press (maker)

First published 2001; reissued 2004

National Library of Canada Cataloguing in Publication

Student's Oxford Canadian dictionary / edited by Katherine Barber ... [et al.].

Previously titled: The Canadian Oxford high school dictionary.

Reprint. Originally published: Don Mills, Ont. : Oxford University Press, 2001.

ISBN-10: 0-19-542076-4   ISBN-13: 978-0-19-542076-0

1. English language—Dictionaries. 2. English language—Canada—Dictionaries.
3. Canadianisms (English)—Dictionaries. I. Barber, Katherine, 1959-

PE3235.C363 2004   423   C2004-902048-X

Cover Design: Brett J. Miller

4 5 6 - 08 07 06

This book is printed on permanent (acid-free) paper ∞.

Printed in Canada

Contents

How to use this dictionary

The words defined (headwords) are listed in alphabetical order.

soggy *adjective* (**soggier**, **soggiest**) **1** sodden, saturated. **2** (of weather) rainy, dank.

Words borrowed from other languages which have not become fully naturalized in English are printed in italics.

canot du nord *noun* (*plural* **canots du nord**) Cdn hist. a birchbark canoe of the fur trade, about 9 m long, used on waterways northwest of Lake Superior. [Say can oh doo NOR]

Alternative spellings of the headword are given before the definition.

adviser *noun* (also **advisor**) a person who advises, esp. one appointed to do so and regularly consulted.

Two or more words with the same spelling but very different meanings are listed as separate entries with different raised numbers.

carp¹ *noun* (*plural* same) a freshwater food fish with large scales and fleshy filaments on either side of its mouth.
carp² *verb* find fault; complain pettily.

The part of speech is printed in italics.

smokie *noun* Cdn a sausage or hot dog.

If a word is used as more than one part of speech, these are defined separately.

airmail • *noun* **1** a system of transporting mail by air. **2** mail carried by air. • *verb* send by airmail.

Meanings are given in ordinary type. If a word has more than one meaning, these meanings are listed separately and numbered.

hairpin *noun* **1** a U-shaped pin for fastening the hair. **2** a sharp curve: *a hairpin turn*.

Example phrases help to clarify the meaning or show how a word is used.

vitriolic *adjective* (of speech or criticism) cruel or bitter: *Stella Duane's critics launched a bitter and vitriolic attack against her.* [Say vitry AWL ick]

Plurals are given if there might be doubt about their spelling.

superhero *noun* (*plural* **superheroes**) a person or fictional character with extraordinary heroic attributes.

Comparative and superlative forms of adjectives are given if they are irregular or their spelling is not obvious.

icy *adjective* (**icier**, **iciest**) **1** very cold. **2** covered with or abounding in ice. **3** (of a tone or manner) unfriendly, hostile: *an icy stare*. **4** like ice: *icy blue eyes*.

Derivatives are included without their definition if their meaning can easily be worked out from the meaning of the headword.

sheepish *adjective* **1** embarrassed through shame or foolishness. **2** bashful, shy, reticent. ▶ **sheepishly** *adverb* **sheepishness** *noun*

Derived forms of verbs are given if they are irregular or there might be doubt about their spelling. Where there are three forms, the first is the third person singular, the second is both the past tense and the past participle, and the third is the present participle; where there are more than three forms the past tense and the past participle are clearly labelled.

refreeze *verb* (**refreezes**; *past* **refroze**; *past participle* **refrozen**; **refreezing**) freeze again.

Phrases based on the headword are grouped together in alphabetical order after the PHRASES symbol.

hilt *noun* **1** the handle of a sword, dagger, etc. **2** the handle of a tool. PHRASES (**to the hilt**) completely.

A label in italics is given if a word is restricted to a particular region, subject area, or style, e.g. *formal* (used in formal and written English), *informal* (used in informal or spoken language), *slang* (very informal or restricted to a particular social group).

beeswax *noun* **1** the wax secreted by bees to make honeycombs. **2** this wax refined and used to make candles, ointments, polishes, etc. **3** (*informal*) business: *mind your own beeswax*.

Entries are sometimes linked by a cross-reference.

garbanzo *noun* (*plural* **garbanzos**) (= CHICKPEA.) [Say gar BON zo]

Pronunciation is given where it may be tricky.

chlorofluorocarbon = CFC. [Say kloro FLORO carbon]

GRAMMAR CHECK boxes provide helpful guidance on points of grammar.

> **GRAMMAR CHECK**
> **between you and me**   ⚠
> ....
> In standard English **between you and me** is correct but **between you and I** is incorrect.

WRITING TIP boxes help you select the right word.

> **WRITING TIP**
> **tortuous, torturous**
> ....
> Do not confuse **torturous**, which describes something considered a torture (*a torturous ordeal*), with **tortuous**, which describes something twisty, complex, or not straightforward (*a tortuous road*).

SPELL CHECK boxes point out potential spelling difficulties.

> **SPELL CHECK**
> **hurdle, hurtle**   ABC
> ....
> To move wildly at a dangerous speed is to **hurtle**.

Aa

A¹ *noun* (also **a**) (*plural* **As** or **A's**) **1** the first letter of the alphabet. **2** *Music* the sixth note of the diatonic scale of C major. **3** the first hypothetical person or example. **4** the highest class or category (of academic marks etc.). **5** (usu. **a**) *Algebra* the first known quantity. **6** a human blood type of the ABO system. PHRASES **from A to B** from one place to another. **from A to Z** over the entire range, completely.

A² *abbreviation* **1** ampere(s). **2** answer. **3** atomic (energy etc.). **4** alto. **5** analog (recording).

Å *abbreviation* angstrom(s).

A1 *adjective informal* excellent; first-rate.

a¹ *indefinite article* (also **an** before a vowel) **1** one, some, any. **2** one like: *a Judas*. **3** one single: *not a thing*. **4** the same: *all of a size*. **5** in, to, or for each: *twice a year*.

a² *abbreviation* are (metric unit).

AA *abbreviation* **1** a size of battery, having a voltage of 1.5 V. **2** *Sport* **a** a level of amateur competition. **b** *Baseball* a minor league directly below AAA. **3** a level of bond rating below AAA. **4** anti-aircraft. **5** ADULT ACCOMPANIMENT.

AAA *abbreviation* **1** a size of battery, having a voltage of 1.5 V. **2** *Sport* **a** a level of amateur sports competition. **b** *Baseball* a minor league directly below the major leagues. **3** the highest level of bond or credit rating.

aardvark *noun* an insect-eating badger-sized mammal with large ears, a long snout, and a long tongue, native to sub-Saharan Africa. [Say ARD vark]

aardwolf *noun* (*plural* **aardwolves**) an African mammal of the hyena family, with grey fur and black stripes, that feeds on insects. [Say ARD wolf]

AB¹ *noun* a human blood type of the ABO system.

AB² *abbreviation* **1** Alberta (in official postal use). **2** *Baseball* (times) at bat. **3** able rating or seaman.

ab *noun* (usu. in *plural*) *slang* an abdominal muscle.

aback *adverb* PHRASES **take aback** surprise.

abacus *noun* (*plural* **abacuses**) an oblong frame with rows of wires or grooves along which beads are slid, used for calculating. [Say ABBA cuss]

abalone *noun* any mollusc of the genus *Haliotis*, with a shallow ear-shaped shell having respiratory holes, and lined with mother-of-pearl. [Say abba LONE ee]

abandon • *verb* **1** give up completely or before completion. **2 a** forsake or desert (a person or a post of responsibility). **b** leave or desert (a motor vehicle or ship). **3 a** give up to another's control or mercy. **b abandon oneself** yield oneself completely to a passion or impulse. • *noun* lack of inhibition or restraint; reckless freedom of manner: *wild abandon*.

abandoned *adjective* **1 a** (of a person) deserted, forsaken. **b** (of a building, vehicle, etc.) left empty or unused. **2** (of a person or behaviour) unrestrained, uninhibited: *a wild, abandoned dance*.

abandonment *noun* **1** the act of leaving a person, thing, or place with no intention of returning: *their childhood abandonment by their mother*. **2** the act of giving up an idea or stopping an activity with no intention of returning to it: *the government's abandonment of its new economic policy*.

abase *verb* (**abases**, **abased**, **abasing**) abase oneself act in a way that shows acceptance of another's power over oneself. ▶ **abasement** *noun*

abashed *adjective* embarrassed and ashamed.

abate *verb* (**abates**, **abated**, **abating**) **1** make or become less strong, severe, intense, etc. **2** *Law* put an end to (a nuisance). ▶ **abatement** *noun*

abattoir *noun* a slaughterhouse. [Say abba TWAR]

abbess *noun* (*plural* **abbesses**) a woman who is the head of certain communities of nuns.

abbey *noun* (*plural* **abbeys**) **1** the building(s) occupied by a community of monks or nuns. **2** the community itself. **3** a church or house that was an abbey.

abbot *noun* the head of an abbey of monks.

abbreviate *verb* (**abbreviates**, **abbreviated**, **abbreviating**) shorten, esp. represent (a word etc.) by a part of it. [Say a BREE vee ate]

abbreviation *noun* **1** an abbreviated form. **2** the process of abbreviating. [Say a bree vee AY sh'n]

ABC *noun* **1** the alphabet. **2** the basics of any subject. **3** an alphabetical guide.

abdicate *verb* (**abdicates**, **abdicated**, **abdicating**) **1** give up or renounce (the throne): *she abdicated in favour of her son*. **2** fail or refuse to perform (a responsibility, duty, etc.): *the government has abdicated its responsibility to ensure a safe water supply*. ▶ **abdication** *noun* [Say ABDA kate, abda KAY sh'n]

abdomen *noun* **1** the part of the body containing the stomach, bowels, reproductive organs, etc. **2** *Zoology* the hinder part of an insect, crustacean, spider, etc.

abdominal • *adjective* of or pertaining to the abdomen. • *noun* (usu. in *plural*) an abdominal muscle. ▶ **abdominally** *adverb* [Say ab DOM in ul]

abduct *verb* carry off or kidnap illegally by force or deception. ▶ **abduction** *noun* **abductor** *noun* [Say ab DUCT]

Abegweit *noun* a member of an Algonquian band living on PEI. [Say ABBA gwit]

Abenaki • *noun* **1** (*plural* **Abenaki** or **Abenakis**) a member of an Algonquian-speaking Aboriginal people now living in S Quebec and Maine. **2** the language of the Abenaki. • *adjective* of or relating to the Abenaki. [Say abba NACK ee]

aberrant *adjective* **1** esp. *Biology* diverging from the normal type: *aberrant chromosomes*. **2** departing from an accepted standard: *aberrant behaviour*. [Say a BEAR'nt]

aberration *noun* **1** a departure from what is normal or accepted or regarded as right: *they described the riots as an aberration in a generally peaceful neighbourhood*. **2** a moral or mental lapse. **3** *Astronomy* the apparent displacement of a celestial body, meteor, etc., caused by the observer's velocity. [Say abba RAY sh'n]

abet *verb* (**abets**, **abetted**, **abetting**) (often in **aid and abet**) encourage or assist (esp. an offender or offence). ▶ **abetment** *noun* **abettor** *noun* [Say a BET]

abhor *verb* (**abhors**, **abhorred**, **abhorring**) detest; regard with disgust and hatred. [Say ab HORE]

abhorrence *noun* a feeling of strong hatred, esp. for moral reasons: *the thought of him filled her with abhorrence* ◊ *society's abhorrence of crime*. [Say ab HORE ince]

abhorrent *adjective* inspiring disgust and loathing:

A

racial discrimination was abhorrent to us all. [Say ab HORE int]

abide *verb* (**abides, abided, abiding**) **1** tolerate: *can't abide him.* **2** (foll. by *by*) **a** act in accordance with: *abide by the rules.* **b** remain faithful to (a promise).

abiding *adjective* enduring. ▶ **abidingly** *adverb*

ability *noun* (*plural* **abilities**) **1** capacity or power. **2** cleverness, talent; mental power.

abiotic *adjective* having to do with the non-living components of an ecosystem, such as water, rocks, light, etc.; physical rather than biological.

abject *adjective* **1** miserable, wretched: *abject poverty.* **2** humble: *abject apology.* ▶ **abjection** *noun* **abjectly** *adverb* [Say AB ject, ab JECK sh'n, AB ject lee]

abjure *verb* (**abjures, abjured, abjuring**) renounce on oath (an opinion, cause, claim, etc.): *was forced to abjure his faith.* [Say ab JOOR]

ablaze *adjective & adverb* **1** on fire: *set it ablaze* ◊ *the house was ablaze.* **2** glittering, glowing. **3** greatly excited.

able *adjective* (**abler, ablest**) **1** having the capacity or power. **2** having great ability: *a very able woman.*

able-bodied *adjective* **1** not physically handicapped. **2** fit, healthy.

abled *adjective* able-bodied, not disabled (also in *combination*: *differently abled.* [Say AY buld]

able seaman *noun* (*plural* **able seamen**) (also **Able Seaman**) a non-commissioned officer of the second-lowest rank in the Canadian Navy, ranking above Ordinary Seaman and below Leading Seaman.

ablution *noun* (usu. in *plural*) **1** the ceremonial washing of parts of the body or sacred vessels etc. **2** *informal* the ordinary washing of the body. [Say ab LOO sh'n]

ably *adverb* skilfully, competently: *Gail has ably demonstrated her point.* [Say ABE lee]

ABM *abbreviation* ANTI-BALLISTIC MISSILE.

Abnaki (*plural* **Abnaki** or **Abnakis**) = ABENAKI. [Say ab NACKY]

abnegation *noun* the action of renouncing or rejecting something: *abnegation of political lawmaking power.* [Say abna GAY sh'n]

abnormal *adjective* **1** deviating from what is normal or usual: *abnormal behaviour.* **2** relating to or dealing with what is abnormal: *abnormal psychology.*

abnormality *noun* (*plural* **abnormalities**) **1 a** an abnormal quality, occurrence, etc. **b** the state of being abnormal. **2** a physical irregularity. [Say ab nor MAL a tee]

abnormally *adverb* unusually, extraordinarily: *abnormally high blood pressure.*

ABO *adjective* of the system in which blood is classified into four types (A, AB, B, and O), based on the presence or absence of certain inherited antigens.

aboard • *adverb* **1** on or into a ship, aircraft, train, etc. **2** onto a horse; on horseback. **3** in or into a group, team, etc. **4** *Baseball* on base. • *preposition* **1** on or into (a ship, aircraft, train, etc.). **2** on or onto (a horse). PHRASES **all aboard!** a call that warns of the imminent departure of a ship, train, etc.

abode¹ *noun* a dwelling place; one's home.

abode² *past of* ABIDE.

aboiteau *noun* (*plural* **aboiteaux**) *Cdn* (*Maritimes*) *hist.* **1** a sluice gate in a dike, which allows flood water to flow out but does not allow sea water to enter. **2** the dike system containing such gates. [Say ab wah TOE for the singular and plural]

abolish *verb* (**abolishes, abolished, abolishing**) put an end to the existence or practice of (esp. a custom or institution). ▶ **abolishment** *noun*

abolition *noun* **1** the act or process of abolishing or being abolished. **2** (**Abolition**) **a** the abolition of

slavery in the British Empire or the US. **b** the abolition of capital punishment. [Say abba LISH un]

abolitionist *noun* a person who favours the abolition of a practice or institution. [Say abba LISH un ist]

abominable *adjective* **1** causing moral disgust. **2** very bad or unpleasant. [Say a BOM in a bull]

abominable snowman *noun* (*plural* **abominable snowmen**) a manlike or bearlike animal said to exist in the Himalaya mountains in southern Asia.

abominably *adverb* in a very bad or unpleasant manner: *he treated her abominably.* [Say a BOM in a blee]

abomination *noun* **1** a thing that causes disgust or hatred: *concrete abominations masquerading as hotels.* **2** loathing: *a Calvinist abomination of self-indulgence.* [Say a bomma NATION]

Aboriginal (also **aboriginal**) • *adjective* **1** (of peoples) inhabiting or existing in a land from the earliest times or from before the arrival of colonists. **2** of or relating to Aboriginal peoples. **3** of the Australian Aboriginals. • *noun* an Aboriginal inhabitant, esp. of Australia. [Say abba RIDGE in ul]

Aboriginal rights *plural noun* rights enjoyed by a people by virtue of the fact that their ancestors inhabited an area from time immemorial.

Aboriginal title *noun* the communal right of Aboriginal peoples to occupy and use the land inhabited by their ancestors from time immemorial.

aborigine *noun* (usu. in *plural*) **1** an Aboriginal inhabitant. **2** (usu. **Aborigine**) an Aboriginal inhabitant of Australia. [Say abba RIDGE in ee]

abort *verb* **1** end a pregnancy early in order to prevent a baby from developing and being born alive: *to abort a child.* **2** cause to end fruitlessly or prematurely. **3** abandon or terminate (a space flight, computer application, etc.) before its completion, usu. because of a fault. **4** *Biology* **a** (of an organism) remain undeveloped; shrink away. **b** cause to do this.

abortion *noun* the deliberate ending of a pregnancy at an early stage.

abortionist *noun* a person who carries out abortions, esp. illegally.

abortive *adjective* unsuccessful, unfinished: *several abortive attempts to paddle across the Atlantic.*

abound *verb* **1** be plentiful: *rumours abound about a gold strike.* **2** have something in great numbers or quantities: *the lakes abound with fish* ◊ *the market area abounds in restaurants.*

about • *preposition* **1** relating to. **2** at a time near to. **3** in, around, surrounding. **4** here and there in: *toys lying about the house.* **5** at a point or points near to: *fighting going on about us.* **6** carried with: *have no money about me.* **7** occupied with: *what's he about?* • *adverb* **1 a** approximately. **b** *informal* used to indicate understatement: *it's about time they came.* **2** here and there: *a lot of flu about.* **3** all around: *look about.* **4** on the move: *out and about.* **5** in partial or alteration from a given position: *the wrong way about.* **6** in rotation or succession: *turn and turn about.* PHRASES **be about to** be on the point of (doing something).

about-face (also **about-turn**) • *noun* **1** a turn made so as to face the opposite direction. **2** a change of opinion or policy etc. • *verb* (**about-faces, about-faced, about-facing**) make an about-face. • *interjection* (**about turn**) *Military* a command to make an about-face.

above • *preposition* **1** over; on the top of; higher (vertically, up a slope or stream etc.) than; over the surface of: *above the din.* **2** more than: *above average.* **3** farther north than. **4** higher in rank, importance, etc., than: *above all.* **5 a** too great or good for: *is not above cheating.* **b** not affected by: *above suspicion.* • *adverb* **1** at

or to a higher point; overhead: *the floor above.*
2 a upstairs. **b** upstream. **3** (of a text reference)
further back on a page or in a book: *as noted above.*
4 higher than zero on the temperature scale. **5** on the
upper side: *above and below.* **6** in addition: *over and
above.* **7** *literary* in heaven. • *adjective* mentioned earlier:
the above argument. • *noun* (**the above**) what is
mentioned above: *the above shows.*
above board *adjective & adverb* without concealment;
fair or fairly; open or openly.
above ground *adjective & adverb* not underground.
above-mentioned *adjective* mentioned earlier.
abracadabra *interjection* a supposedly magic word
used by conjurors.
abrade *verb* (**abrades, abraded, abrading**) scrape
or wear away by rubbing. [Say a BRAID]
abrasion *noun* **1** the scraping or wearing away (of
skin, rock, etc.). **2** a damaged area resulting from this.
[Say a BRAY zh'n]
abrasive • *adjective* **1 a** tending to rub. **b** capable of
polishing by rubbing or grinding. **2** harsh or hurtful in
manner. • *noun* an abrasive substance. [Say a BRAY siv]
abreast *adverb* **1** side by side and facing the same way.
2 (usu. foll. by *of*) well-informed, up to date: *abreast of all
the changes.* **3** (foll. by *of*) alongside; parallel to.
abridge *verb* (**abridges, abridged, abridging**)
1 shorten (a book, film, etc.) by using fewer words or
making deletions. **2** curtail (liberties, rights, etc.).
3 cut short. ▶ **abridgement** *noun*
abroad *adverb* **1** in or to a foreign country or
countries. **2** over a wide area: *scatter abroad.* **3** in
circulation: *there is a rumour abroad.*
abrogate *verb* (**abrogates, abrogated,
abrogating**) repeal or abolish (a law or custom).
▶ **abrogation** *noun* [Say ABRA gate, abra GAY sh'n]
abrupt *adjective* **1** sudden and unexpected; hasty: *her
abrupt departure.* **2** (of speech, manner, etc.) brief to the
point of being rude: *was very abrupt with me.* **3** steep: *an
abrupt fifty-centimetre drop in the lake bed.* ▶ **abruptly**
adverb **abruptness** *noun*
ABS *abbreviation* **1** anti-lock braking system.
2 acrylonitrile butadiene styrene, a hard, lightweight
plastic.
abscess *noun* (*plural* **abscesses**) a swollen area full of
pus within a body tissue. ▶ **abscessed** *adjective* [Say
AB sess]
abscond *verb* depart hurriedly and secretly, typically
to avoid detection of or arrest for an unlawful action
such as theft: *the bartender absconded with the week's
earnings.* [Say ab SKOND]
absence *noun* **1** the state of being away from a place
or person: *fed her cats during her absence ◊ I was in charge in
the absence of the director.* **2** an occasion or period of
being away: *repeated absences from school.* **3** the non-
existence of: *found his total absence of facial expression
unnerving.* [Say AB since]
absent • *adjective* **1** not present in a place or at an
occasion: *most students were absent from school at least once
◊ drink a toast to absent friends.* **2** (of a part or feature of
the body) not forming part of a creature in which it
might be expected: *wings were absent in several species of
crane flies.* **3** inattentive to the matter in hand: *she looked
up with an absent smile.* • *verb* **absent oneself** stay or
go away: *halfway through lunch, he absented himself from the
table.* [Say AB sint for the adjective, ab SENT for the verb]
absentee *noun* a person not present, esp. one who is
absent from work or school. [Say ab sin TEE]
absenteeism *noun* the practice of absenting oneself
from work or school etc., esp. frequently or illicitly. [Say
ab sin TEE ism]
absently *adverb* in a distracted or inattentive manner:

*Dwight stared absently at the magazine, thinking about the
future.* [Say AB sint ly]
absent-minded *adjective* tending to forget things.
▶ **absent-mindedly** *adverb* **absent-mindedness**
noun
absinth *noun* **1** a shrubby plant, *Artemisia absinthium*,
or its essence. **2** (usu. **absinthe**) a green aniseed-
flavoured potent liqueur based on absinth and turning
milky when water is added. [Say AB sinth]
absolute • *adjective* **1** complete, perfect: *absolute bliss.*
2 unconditional, unlimited: *absolute authority.* **3** ruling
arbitrarily or with unrestricted power: *an absolute
monarch.* **4** (of a standard) universally valid; not relative
or comparative. **5** *Grammar* **a** (of a construction)
syntactically independent of the rest of the sentence, as
in *dinner being over, we left the table.* **b** (of an adjective or
transitive verb) used or usable without an expressed
noun or object, e.g. *the hungry; guns kill.* **6** (of a legal
decree etc.) final. • *noun* **1** a value, standard, etc., which
is objective and universally valid, not subjective or
relative. **2** (**the absolute**) **a** *Philosophy* that which can
exist without being related to anything else. **b** *Theology*
God.
absolutely *adverb* **1** completely, utterly: *it was
absolutely marvellous.* **2** independently: *God exists
absolutely.* **3** (no or none) at all: *absolutely nobody.*
4 *informal* in actual fact: *it absolutely exploded.* **5** *Grammar*
(of a verb) without a stated object. **6** *informal* (used in
reply) quite so.
absolute majority *noun* (*plural* **absolute
majorities**) **1** a majority over all others combined.
2 more than half.
absolute pitch *noun Music* the ability to recognize the
pitch of a note or produce any given note.
absolute zero *noun* a theoretical lowest possible
temperature, calculated as −273.15°C (or 0 K).
absolution *noun* **1** a formal release from guilt,
obligation, or punishment. **2** forgiveness, esp. an
ecclesiastical declaration of forgiveness of sins or of the
remission of penance.
absolutism *noun* **1** the acceptance of or belief in
absolute principles in political, philosophical, ethical,
or theological matters. **2** the principle of absolute
government. ▶ **absolutist** *noun & adjective*
absolve *verb* (**absolves, absolved, absolving**)
1 (often foll. by *from*, *of*) **a** set or pronounce free from
blame or obligation etc. **b** acquit; pronounce not
guilty. **2** pardon or give absolution for (a sin etc.).
absorb *verb* **1** include or incorporate as part of itself or
oneself. **2** take in; suck up (liquid, heat, knowledge,
etc.): *absorbed all she was taught.* **3** reduce the effect or
intensity of; deal easily with (an impact, sound,
difficulty, etc.). **4** consume (income, time, resources,
etc.): *debts absorbed half his income.* **5** engross the
attention of: *TV absorbs them completely.* ▶ **absorbable**
adjective **absorber** *noun*
absorbed *adjective* intensely engaged or interested.
absorbency *noun* the quality of being absorbent.
absorbent • *adjective* having a tendency to absorb.
• *noun* a substance that absorbs.
absorbing *adjective* engrossing; intensely interesting.
absorption *noun* **1** the process or action of absorbing
or being absorbed. **2** the process of a smaller group etc.
becoming part of a larger one. **3** mental engrossment.
abstain *verb* **1 a** restrain oneself; refrain from
indulging in: *abstained from meat.* **b** refrain from
drinking alcohol. **2** formally decline to use one's vote.
▶ **abstainer** *noun*
abstention *noun* **1** an act of declining to vote for or
against a proposal or motion: *the resolution passed by
126 votes to one, with six abstentions.* **2** the fact or practice

of restraining oneself from indulging in something: *abstention from alcohol and drugs*.

abstinence *noun* the act of abstaining, esp. from food, drugs, or sexual activity. [Say AB stin ince]

abstinent *adjective* refraining from an activity or from the use or enjoyment of something: *single women were expected to be sexually abstinent*. [Say AB stin int]

abstract • *adjective* **1 a** to do with or existing in thought rather than matter, or in theory rather than practice; not tangible or concrete. **b** (of a word, esp. a noun) denoting a quality or condition or intangible thing rather than a concrete object. **2** (of art) achieving its effect by grouping shapes and colours in satisfying patterns rather than by representing physical reality or by telling a story. • *verb* **1** (often foll. by *from*) take out of; extract; remove. **2** summarize (a book etc.). • *noun* **1** a summary or statement of the contents of a book etc. **2** an abstract work of art. PHRASES **in the abstract** in theory rather than in practice. [Say ABS tract for the adjective and noun, abs TRACT for the verb]

abstracted *adjective* inattentive to the matter in hand. ▶ **abstractedly** *adverb* [Say abs TRACT id]

abstraction *noun* **1** the quality of dealing with ideas rather than events: *topics will vary in degrees of abstraction.* **2 a** an abstract or visionary idea: *the question can no longer be treated as an academic abstraction.* **b** the formation of abstract ideas. **3** freedom from representational qualities in art: *geometric abstraction has been a mainstay in her work.* **4** a state of preoccupation: *she sensed his momentary abstraction.* [Say abs TRACK sh'n]

abstractly *adverb* in an abstract manner.

abstruse *adjective* hard to understand. [Say abs TRUCE]

absurd *adjective* **1** (of an idea, suggestion, etc.) wildly unreasonable, illogical, or inappropriate. **2** (of a person) unreasonable or ridiculous in manner. **3** ludicrous: *an absurd situation*.

absurdism *noun* the belief that human beings exist in a purposeless, chaotic universe.

absurdist *adjective* resembling the characteristics of the theatre of the absurd, where normal conventions of coherent dialogue etc. are abandoned to show that the world is senseless and impossible to explain.

absurdity *noun* (*plural* **absurdities**) the quality or state of being ridiculous or wildly unreasonable: *Melanie laughed at the absurdity of the situation.*

absurdly *adverb* in an absurd or foolish manner.

abundance *noun* **1** a very great quantity, usu. considered to be more than enough: *our national parks boast an abundance of wildlife.* **2** plentifulness of the good things in life; prosperity: *industrial growth promised wealth and abundance.* PHRASES **in abundance** in great quantities: *vines and figs grew in abundance ◊ Bridget was blessed with talent and charm in abundance.*

abundant *adjective* existing in large quantities; plentiful.

abundantly *adverb* **1** in large quantities: *the plant grows abundantly in the wild.* **2** extremely: *my boss made it abundantly clear that I should find another job.*

abuse • *verb* (**abuses, abused, abusing**) **1** misuse: *the judge abused his power by imposing heavy fines.* **2** treat a person or animal with cruelty or violence, esp. regularly or repeatedly: *riders who abuse their horses should be prosecuted.* **3** insult verbally: *the referee was abused by players from both teams.* **4** make excessive and habitual use of alcohol or drugs, esp. illegal ones. **5** assault someone, esp. a woman or child, sexually: *he was a depraved man who had abused his two daughters.* • *noun* **1** incorrect or improper use: *drug abuse ◊ an abuse of power.* **2** unjust or corrupt practice: *political abuses ◊ human rights abuses.* **3** cruel and violent

treatment of a person or animal: *child abuse*. **4** insulting language: *a torrent of abuse ◊ waved his fists and hurled abuse at the driver.* ▶ **abuser** *noun*

abusive *adjective* **1** (of a situation) involving maltreatment. **2** (of a person) tending to abuse others. **3** using insulting language. **4** (of language) insulting. ▶ **abusively** *adverb* **abusiveness** *noun*

abut *verb* (**abuts, abutted, abutting**) **1** (of buildings, sites, etc.) be located next to. **2** (foll. by *on, against*) (of part of a building) touch or lean upon (another) with a projecting end or point. [Say a BUT]

abutment *noun* a structure built to support the lateral pressure of an arch or span, e.g. at the ends of a bridge.

abuzz *adjective* **1** in a state of excitement or activity. **2** buzzing.

abysmal *adjective* **1** extremely bad. **2** profound, utter: *abysmal ignorance.* ▶ **abysmally** *adverb* [Say a BIZ mul]

abyss *noun* (*plural* **abysses**) **1** a deep or seemingly bottomless gap: *a rope led down into the dark abyss.* **2 a** an immeasurable depth: *abyss of despair.* **b** a catastrophic situation seen as likely to occur: *teetering on the edge of the abyss of nuclear war.* **3** a vast difference: *unbridgeable cultural abyss.* **4** (**the abyss**) hell. [Say a BISS]

Abyssinian • *noun* **1** a native or inhabitant of Abyssinia (a former name for Ethiopia). **2** (also **Abyssinian cat**) a cat having a long slender body, long ears, and short brown hair. • *adjective* of Abyssinia or its inhabitants. [Say abba SINNY un]

AC *abbreviation* **1** (also **ac**) ALTERNATING CURRENT. **2** before Christ.

Ac *symbol* actinium.

a/c *abbreviation* **1** = ACCOUNT *noun* 2, 3. **2** = AIR CONDITIONING.

acacia *noun* **1** a usu. thorny tree or shrub with spikes or clusters of white or yellow flowers. **2** (also **false acacia**) = LOCUST 4b. [Say a KAY shuh]

academe *noun* **1** the world of learning. **2** universities collectively. [Say acka DEEM]

academia *noun* the academic world. [Say acka DEEMY un]

academic • *adjective* **1 a** to do with learning. **b** of or relating to a scholarly institution: *academic dress.* **2** not of practical relevance: *the debate was largely academic since the minister had already made her decisions.* • *noun* a teacher or scholar in a university or institute of higher education. ▶ **academically** *adverb*

academics *plural noun* (also treated as *singular*) studies in the humanities or sciences.

academy *noun* (*plural* **academies**) **1** a place of study or training in a special field: *military academy.* **2** (usu. **Academy**) a society or institution of distinguished scholars, artists, etc.: *Royal Academy.* **3** a school (esp. in proper names). **4** (**the academy**) academia.

academic year *noun* a period of nearly a year, going from early September to the following summer, during which a school or university is in session.

Academy Award *noun* any of the annual awards of the Academy of Motion Picture Arts and Sciences.

Acadian • *noun* **1** a native or inhabitant of the former French colony of Acadia, which at its greatest extent occupied the entire region between the St. Lawrence and the Atlantic. **2** esp. *Cdn* a francophone descendant of the early French settlers in Acadia. • *adjective* of or relating to Acadians. [Say a KAY dee un]

a cappella *adjective & adverb* (of singing) unaccompanied. [Say acka PELLA]

accede *verb* (**accedes, acceded, acceding**) (usu. foll. by *to*) **1** assent or agree: *acceded to the request.* **2** take office, esp. become monarch. [Say ack SEED]

accelerate *verb* (**accelerates, accelerated, accelerating**) **1 a** (esp. of a vehicle) move or begin to

move more quickly. **b** (of a process) happen or reach completion more quickly. **2** cause to go or happen more quickly. **3** (often as **accelerated** *adjective*) hasten advancement in (a career, studies, etc.). [Say ack SELLA rate]

acceleration *noun* **1** increase in the rate or speed of something: *the acceleration of industrialization ◊ an acceleration in the rate of economic growth*. **2** a vehicle's capacity to gain speed in a short time: *sports cars have good acceleration*. **3** the rate of change of velocity measured in terms of a unit of time. [Say ack sella RAY sh'n]

accelerator *noun* **1** a device for increasing speed, esp. the pedal that controls the speed of a vehicle's engine. **2** *Physics* an apparatus for imparting high speeds to charged particles. **3** *Chemistry* a substance that speeds up a chemical reaction. [Say ack SELLA rater]

accent • *noun* **1** a particular mode of pronunciation, esp. one associated with a particular region or group. **2** prominence given to a syllable by stress or pitch. **3** a mark on a letter or word to indicate pitch, stress, or the quality of a vowel. **4** emphasis: *an accent on comfort*. **5** a distinctive or contrasting feature: *blue with accents of red ◊ accent colours*. **6** *Music* emphasis on a particular note or chord. • *verb* **1** emphasize (a word or syllable). **2** write or print accents on (words etc.). **3** accentuate or enhance (esp. with a contrasting element).

accentuate *verb* (**accentuates, accentuated, accentuating**) emphasize; make prominent. ▶ **accentuation** *noun* [Say ack SEN choo ate]

SPELL CHECK
accept, except

A word that means "not including" is **except**.

---

accept *verb* **1** consent to receive. **2** give an affirmative answer to (an offer or proposal). **3 a** regard favourably; treat as welcome: *his colleagues never accepted him*. **b** approve for admission: *was accepted by three universities*. **4 a** believe, receive, recognize (an explanation etc.) as adequate or valid. **b** be prepared to subscribe to (a belief, philosophy, etc.). **5** receive as suitable: *accepts traveller's cheques*. **6 a** tolerate; submit to: *accepted the umpire's decision*. **b** be willing to believe: *we accept that you meant well*. **7** undertake (an office or responsibility).

acceptability *noun* the quality of being acceptable.
acceptable *adjective* **1 a** worthy of being accepted. **b** pleasing. **2** adequate. **3** tolerable: *an acceptable risk*. ▶ **acceptably** *adverb*

acceptance *noun* **1** the act or fact of accepting or being accepted: *acceptance to university*. **2** willingness to receive (a gift, payment, duty, etc.). **3** an affirmative answer to an invitation or proposal. **4** a willingness to accept (conditions, a circumstance, etc.). **5 a** approval, belief: *found wide acceptance*. **b** willingness or ability to tolerate.

access • *noun* (*plural* **accesses**) **1** a way of approaching or reaching or entering. **2 a** the right or opportunity to reach or use or visit: *has access to secret files*. **b** the right of a parent without legal custody of a child to visit the child and inquire about his or her welfare. **c** the condition of being readily approached; accessibility. **3** *Computing* the action or process of obtaining stored documents, data, etc. • *verb* (**accesses, accessed, accessing**) gain access to (esp. data, a file, etc.).

accessibility *noun* the quality of being accessible.
accessible *adjective* **1** that can readily be reached, entered, or used. **2** (of a building) posing no obstacles

to handicapped people. **3** (of a person) readily available. **4** easy to understand or appreciate.

accession *noun* **1** entering upon an office (esp. the throne) or a condition (as adulthood). **2** a thing added, e.g. a book to a library. [Say ack SESSION]

accessorize *verb* (**accessorizes, accessorized, accessorizing**) choose or wear accessories to suit (clothing etc.). [Say ack SESSA rise]

accessory • *noun* (*plural* **accessories**) **1** an additional or extra thing. **2** (usu. in *plural*) **a** a small attachment or fitting. **b** a small item of (esp. a woman's) dress, e.g. shoes. **3** (often foll. by *to*) a person who helps in or knows the details of an (esp. illegal) act, esp. one (**accessory before the fact**) who encourages or assists another to commit a crime but is not present when the crime is committed, or one (**accessory after the fact**) who knowingly assists a criminal to escape. • *adjective* additional; contributing or aiding in a minor way. [Say ack SESSA ree]

accident *noun* **1** an event that is without apparent cause, or is unexpected. **2** an unfortunate event, esp. one causing physical harm or damage, brought about unintentionally. **3** an automobile collision or crash. **4** the working of fortune: *accident accounts for much in life*. **5** *euphemism* an occurrence of involuntary urination or defecation. **6** an irregularity in structure.

accidental • *adjective* happening by chance, unintentionally, or unexpectedly. • *noun* *Music* a sign indicating a momentary departure from the key signature by raising or lowering a note. ▶ **accidentally** *adverb*

acclaim • *verb* **1** (often as **acclaimed** *adjective*) praise publicly; welcome or applaud enthusiastically. **2** hail as: *was acclaimed the winner*. **3** *Cdn Politics* elect without opposition. • *noun* public praise.

acclamation *noun* **1** *Cdn Politics* (esp. in **by acclamation**) the act or an instance of election by virtue of being the sole candidate: *if no rival is nominated, the incumbent wins by acclamation*. **2** loud and eager assent to a proposal. **3** a phrase said or sung by the congregation as part of a liturgy: *the Gospel acclamation*. [Say akla MAY sh'n]

acclimatization *noun* the process of making or becoming used to a new place, situation, or climate. [Say a clime a tize AY sh'n]

acclimatize *verb* (**acclimatizes, acclimatized, acclimatizing**) **1** accustom to a new climate or to new conditions: *tomatoes can later be acclimatized to the Canadian summer and moved outdoors*. **2** become acclimatized: *it will take us a while to acclimatize to the new job*. [Say a CLIME a tize]

accolade *noun* the awarding of praise; an acknowledgement of merit. [Say ACKA laid]

accommodate *verb* (**accommodates, accommodated, accommodating**) **1** provide lodging or room for. **2** adapt, harmonize, reconcile: *must accommodate ourselves to new surroundings*.

accommodating *adjective* fitting in with someone's wishes or demands in a helpful way. ▶ **accommodatingly** *adverb*

accommodation *noun* **1** (in *singular* or *plural*) temporary lodging, as at a hotel etc. **2** an adjustment or adaptation to suit a special or different purpose. **3** a convenient arrangement; a compromise: *they were forced to reach an accommodation with the rebels*.

accompaniment *noun* **1** music played to support singing or another instrument. **2** an accompanying thing. **3** the act or fact of accompanying or escorting someone. [Say a COMPANY m'nt]

accompanist *noun* a person who provides a musical accompaniment. [Say a CUMPA nist]

A

accompany *verb* (**accompanies, accompanied, accompanying**) **1** go with. **2 a** be done or found with; supplement: *strong winds accompanied by heavy rain ◊ the textbook comes with an accompanying CD*. **b** have as a result. **3** support or partner a soloist with an instrumental part.

accomplice *noun* a partner in a crime or wrongdoing.

accomplish *verb* (**accomplishes, accomplished, accomplishing**) complete; succeed in doing.

accomplished *adjective* clever, skilled.

accomplishment *noun* **1** the fulfillment or completion (of a task etc.). **2** an acquired skill, esp. a social one. **3** a thing done; an achievement.

accord • *verb* **1** agree with or match something: *these results accord closely with our predictions.* **2** give or grant someone power, status or recognition: *the powers accorded to the head of state ◊ our society accords great importance to the family ◊ accorded them a frosty welcome.* • *noun* **1** agreement, consent: *the government and the rebels are in accord on one point.* **2** harmony or correspondence in pitch, tone, colour, etc. **3** a formal act of agreement; a treaty. PHRASES **of one's own accord** voluntarily. **with one accord** unanimously.

accordance *noun* PHRASES **in accordance with** in a manner corresponding to.

according *adverb* **1** as stated by or in: *according to my sister.* **2** in a manner corresponding to; in proportion to: *lives according to her principles.*

accordingly *adverb* **1** as suggested or required by the (stated) circumstances. **2** consequently, therefore.

accordion *noun* **1** a musical instrument played by means of keys, buttons, and pleated bellows, which are expanded and contracted to force air through metal reeds. **2** (as an *adjective*) having folds like the bellows of an accordion: *accordion pleats.* ▶ **accordionist** *noun*

accost *verb* approach and address (a person), esp. boldly. [Say a COST]

account • *noun* **1** a narration or description. **2 a** an arrangement at a financial institution for transactions, esp. for depositing and withdrawing money. **b** the assets credited by such an arrangement: *has a large account.* **c** an arrangement at a store etc. for buying goods or services on credit. **3** (often in *plural*) a record or statement of money, goods, or services received or expended, with calculation of the balance. **4** a statement of the administration of money in trust. **5** (in *plural*) the department of a firm etc. that deals with accounts. **6** a customer or client having an account with a firm. • *verb* consider, regard as: *it was accounted a poor bargain.* PHRASES **account for 1** serve as or provide an explanation or reason for. **2 a** give a reckoning of (money etc. entrusted). **b** answer for (one's conduct). **3** succeed in killing, destroying, or defeating. **4** supply or make up a specified amount or proportion of. **by all accounts** in everyone's opinion. **call to account** require an explanation from (a person). **give a good** (or **bad**) **account of oneself** make a favourable (or unfavourable) impression; be successful (or unsuccessful). **keep account of** keep a record of; follow closely. **no accounting for tastes** it's impossible to explain why different people like different things, esp. those things which the speaker considers unappealing. **of no account** unimportant. **on account 1** (of goods or services) to be paid for later. **2** (of money) in part payment. **on account of** because of. **on no account** under no circumstances; certainly not. **on one's own account** for one's own purposes; at one's own risk. **settle** (or **square**) **accounts with 1** receive or pay money etc. owed to. **2** have revenge on. **take account of** (or **take into account**) consider along with other factors.

accountability *noun* the quality of being accountable; responsibility: *the accountability of a company's directors to the shareholders.*

accountable *adjective* responsible; required to account for one's conduct.

accountancy *noun* the profession or duties of an accountant.

accountant *noun* a person whose profession is to keep or inspect financial accounts.

accounting *noun* **1** the process of or skill in keeping and verifying accounts. **2** *in senses of* ACCOUNT *verb*.

accounts payable *plural noun* amounts owed by a business to a supplier.

accounts receivable *plural noun* amounts owed by customers to a business.

accoutrement *noun* (usu. in *plural*) additional items of dress or equipment, or other items carried or worn by a person or used for a particular activity: *the accoutrements of religious ritual.* [Say a KOOTRA m'nt, a KOOTER m'nt]

accredit *verb* (**accredits, accredited, accrediting**) **1** officially recognize as meeting certain standards. **2** (foll. by *to*) attribute (a saying etc.) to (a person). ▶ **accreditation** *noun*

accredited *adjective* **1** (of a person or organization) officially recognized. **2** (of a belief) orthodox.

SPELL CHECK	
across	ABC ✔

Warning: **across** is spelled with only one *c*.

accretion *noun* **1** the process of growth or increase, typically by the gradual accumulation of additional layers or matter: *the accretion of sediments in coastal mangroves.* **2** a thing formed or added by such growth: *the city has a historic core surrounded by recent accretions.* [Say a CREE sh'n]

accrue *verb* (**accrues, accrued, accruing**) (often foll. by *to*) **1** come as a natural increase or advantage, esp. financial. **2** accumulate (esp. interest). ▶ **accrued** *adjective* [Say a CREW]

acculturate *verb* (**acculturates, acculturated, acculturating**) assimilate or cause to assimilate a different culture, typically the dominant one: *ethnic minorities acculturated to English as necessary ◊ missionaries' attempts to acculturate native children.* ▶ **acculturation** *noun* [Say a CULTURE ate]

accumulate *verb* (**accumulates, accumulated, accumulating**) **1** gradually get more of something. **2** gradually increase.

accumulation *noun* **1** the acquisition or gradual gathering of something: *the accumulation of wealth.* **2** a mass or quantity of something that has gradually gathered or been acquired: *would she ever get through the accumulation of paperwork on her desk?* **3** the growth of a sum of money by the continued addition of interest.

accumulative *adjective* gathering or growing by gradual increases: *the accumulative effects of pollution.* [Say a CUE myoo luh tiv]

accuracy *noun* (*plural* **accuracies**) **1** the quality of being accurate. **2** exactness or precision.

accurate *adjective* **1** careful, precise; lacking errors. **2** conforming exactly with the truth or with a given standard. **3** able to reach a target or measure a quantity etc. with precision. ▶ **accurately** *adverb*

accursed *adjective* **1** lying under a curse; ill-fated. **2** detestable, annoying. [Say a CUR sed or a CURST]

accusation *noun* **1** a charge or claim that someone has done something wrong or illegal: *accusations of bribery.* **2** the action or process of making such a claim: *there was accusation in Brian's voice.*

accusative • *noun* the case of nouns, pronouns, and adjectives, expressing the object of an action or the goal of motion. • *adjective* of or in this case.

accusatory *adjective* (of language, manner, etc.) of or implying accusation.

accuse *verb* (**accuses, accused, accusing**) **1** (foll. by *of*) charge (a person etc.) with a fault or crime. **2** lay the blame on.

accused • *noun* (*plural* same) a person charged with a crime. • *adjective* charged with a crime, fault, etc.

accuser *noun* a person who accuses someone of something, esp. in a court of law.

accusing *adjective* (of an expression, gesture, or tone of voice) indicating a belief in someone's guilt: *she gave him an accusing look*. ▶ **accusingly** *adverb*

accustom *verb* (foll. by *to*) make (a person or thing or oneself) used to.

accustomed *adjective* **1** used to: *accustomed to hard work*. **2** usual: *took her accustomed route to work*.

AC/DC *abbreviation* designating an appliance etc. that can operate on either alternating or direct current.

ace • *noun* **1** a playing card, domino, etc., with a single spot and generally having the value "one" or in card games the highest value in each suit. **2 a** a person who excels in some activity. **b** a fighter pilot who has shot down many enemy aircraft. **c** *Baseball* the best starting or relief pitcher on a team. **3 a** (in racquet sports, volleyball, etc.) a point scored on a service that an opponent fails to touch. **b** a service that achieves this. **4** *Golf* a hole in one. • *verb* (**aces, aced, acing**) **1** *informal* achieve a high grade in (an exam etc.): *she aced the course*. **2** *Tennis etc.* score an ace against (an opponent). **3** *Golf* complete (a hole) in one stroke. • *adjective* *slang* excellent. PHRASES **ace up one's sleeve** (or **in the hole**) something effective kept in reserve. **play one's ace** use one's best resource. **within an ace of** on the verge of.

acerbic *adjective* critical in a direct and cruel way; biting. ▶ **acerbically** *adverb* [Say a SERB ick]

acetaminophen *noun* a drug used to relieve pain and reduce fever. [Say a seeta MINNA fin]

acetate *noun* **1** a salt or ester of acetic acid, esp. the cellulose ester of acetic acid used to make textiles, plastics, etc. **2** a fabric made from this. **3** a disc coated with this, for direct recording by a cutting stylus; any direct-cut disc. **4** a clear plastic film of this, used for overhead transparencies etc. [Say ASSA tate]

acetic acid *noun* the clear liquid acid that gives vinegar its characteristic taste. [Say a SEAT ick]

acetone *noun* a colourless volatile liquid ketone valuable as a solvent for paints etc. [Say ASSA tone]

acetylene *noun* a colourless hydrocarbon gas, burning with a bright flame, used in welding and formerly in lighting. [Say a SETTA lean]

acetylsalicylic acid *noun* a drug used to relieve pain and reduce fever, the active ingredient in Aspirin. Abbreviation: **ASA**. [Say a seetle salla SILL ick]

ache • *noun* **1** a continuous or prolonged dull pain. **2** mental distress. • *verb* (**aches, ached, aching**) **1** suffer from or be the source of an ache. **2** desire greatly: *we ached to be at home again*. ▶ **achingly** *adverb*

achievable *adjective* that can be achieved.

achieve *verb* (**achieves, achieved, achieving**) **1 a** reach or attain by effort: *achieved victory*. **b** acquire, gain, earn: *achieved notoriety*. **2** accomplish or carry out (a feat or task). **3** attain a desired level of performance.

achievement *noun* **1** a thing done successfully, typically by effort, courage, or skill: *to reach this stage is a great achievement*. **2** the process or fact of achieving something: *the achievement of professional recognition* ◊ *a sense of achievement*. **3** a child's or student's progress in a

course of learning, typically as measured by standardized tests or objectives: *academic achievement*.

achiever *noun* a person who achieves a high or specified level of success: *super-achiever*.

Achilles heel *noun* a person's weak or vulnerable point. [Say a KILL eez]

Achilles tendon *noun* the tendon connecting the heel with the calf muscles. [Say a KILL eez]

achoo *interjection* representing a sneeze.

achy *adjective* (**achier, achiest**) full of or suffering from aches. [Say AKE ee]

acid • *noun* **1 a** any of a class of substances that liberate hydrogen ions in water, are usu. sour and corrosive, and have a pH of less than 7. **b** any compound or atom donating protons. **2** (in general use) any sour substance. **3** *slang* the drug LSD. • *adjective* **1** sour. **2** biting, sharp: *an acid wit*. **3** *Chemistry* having the essential properties of an acid. **4** (of precipitation) containing acids formed in the atmosphere from industrial waste gases: *acid snow*.

acid house *noun* (also **acid rock**) a kind of synthesized music with a simple repetitive beat, often associated with the taking of hallucinogenic drugs.

acidic *adjective* **1** very sour: *some fruit juices are very acidic*. **2** containing acid: *acidic soil*. [Say a SID ick]

acidification *noun* the process of making or becoming acidified. [Say a SID iffa KAY sh'n]

acidify *verb* (**acidifies, acidified, acidifying**) make or become acid. [Say a SIDDA fie]

acidity *noun* (*plural* **acidities**) **1** an acid quality or state. **2** excessive acid in the stomach. [Say a SIDDA tee]

acidly *adverb* in an unpleasant or critical way: *"Thanks for nothing," she said acidly*.

acid rain *noun* acid formed in the atmosphere esp. from industrial waste gases and falling with rain.

acid shock *noun* a sudden increase in the acidity of a body of water caused by the melting of acid snow that has fallen over the winter.

acid test *noun* a severe or conclusive test: *Swan Lake is considered the acid test of a ballerina's classical credentials*.

ackee *noun* **1** a tropical evergreen tree, *Blighia sapida*. **2** the bland, leathery, red or yellow fruit of this tree, edible only when cooked. [Say ACKY]

acknowledge *verb* (**acknowledges, acknowledged, acknowledging**) **1 a** recognize; accept; admit the truth of. **b** recognize as: *acknowledged it to be a success*. **c** admit that something is so: *acknowledged that he was wrong*. **2** confirm the receipt of. **3 a** show that one has noticed: *acknowledged my arrival with a grunt*. **b** express appreciation of (a service etc.). **4** recognize the validity of: *the acknowledged king*.

acknowledgement *noun* **1** acceptance of the truth or existence of something: *there was no acknowledgement of the family's trauma*. **2** the action of expressing or displaying gratitude or appreciation for something: *Gord received an award in acknowledgement of his work*. **3** the action of showing that one has noticed someone or something: *he touched his hat in acknowledgement*. **4** a letter confirming receipt of something: *I received an acknowledgement of my application*. **5** (usu. in *plural*) an author's statement of thanks or indebtedness to others, typically one printed at the beginning of a book.

acme *noun* the highest point or period (of achievement, success, etc.); the peak of perfection: *considered the acme of good taste*. [Say ACK mee]

acne *noun* a skin condition, usu. of the face, characterized by red pimples. [Say ACK nee]

acolyte *noun* **1** a person assisting a priest in a service or procession. **2** an assistant; a beginner. [Say ACKA lite]

A

SPELL CHECK
accommodate   ABC

Warning: **accommodate** is spelled with two *c*'s and two *m*'s.

aconite *noun* **1 a** any poisonous herbaceous plant of the genus *Aconitum*, esp. monkshood. **b** = ACONITINE. **2** = WINTER ACONITE. [Say ACKA nite]

aconitine *noun* a poisonous alkaloid drug obtained from aconite plants, formerly used as a sedative. [Say a CONNA teen]

acorn *noun* the fruit of the oak, with a smooth nut in a rough cup-like base.

acorn squash *noun* = PEPPER SQUASH.

acoustic • *adjective* **1** relating to sound or the sense of hearing. **2** (of music, musicians, or musical instruments) not using electrical amplification: *acoustic guitar*. **3** (of building materials) used for soundproofing or modifying sound: *acoustic tiles*. • *noun* **1** (usu. in *plural*) the properties or qualities (esp. of a room or hall etc.) that determine how sound is transmitted: *good acoustics* ◊ *a poor acoustic*. **2** (in *plural*; usu. treated as *singular*) the science of sound. ▶**acoustical** *adjective* **acoustically** *adverb* [Say a COO stick]

acquaint *verb* (usu. foll. by *with*) make (a person or oneself) aware of or familiar with. PHRASES **acquainted with** having personal knowledge of.

acquaintance *noun* **1** a person one knows slightly. **2** the fact or process of being acquainted: *our acquaintance lasted a year*. **3** (usu. foll. by *with*) knowledge (of a person or thing). PHRASES **make someone's acquaintance** first meet or introduce oneself to another person.

acquaintance rape *noun* = DATE RAPE.

acquiesce *verb* (**acquiesces**, **acquiesced**, **acquiescing**) accept something reluctantly but without protest: *Sara acquiesced in his decision* ◊ *acquiesced to the dismantling of communist regimes*. ▶**acquiescence** *noun* **acquiescent** *adjective* [Say ack wee ESS, ack wee ESSENCE, ack wee ESS'nt]

acquire *verb* (**acquires**, **acquired**, **acquiring**) gain by and for oneself; obtain; come to possess.

acquired immune deficiency syndrome *noun* see AIDS.

acquired taste *noun* **1** a liking gained by experience. **2** the object of such a liking.

acquisition *noun* **1** buying or obtaining assets or objects: *western culture places a high value on material acquisition*. **2** an asset or object bought or obtained, e.g. by a library or museum: *Peng's latest acquisition is a silver sports car* ◊ *acquisitions librarian*. **3** an act of purchase of one company by another. **4** the learning or developing of a skill, habit, or quality: *the acquisition of management skills*. [Say ackwa ZISH un]

acquisitive *adjective* excessively eager to acquire money or material things. ▶**acquisitiveness** *noun* [Say a QUIZZA tiv]

acquit *verb* (**acquits**, **acquitted**, **acquitting**) **1** declare not guilty: *she was acquitted on all counts* ◊ *acquitted of murder*. **2 acquit oneself** conduct oneself or perform in a specified way: *Bryan acquitted himself well*.

acquittal *noun* the process of freeing or being freed from a charge, e.g. by a judgment of not guilty.

acre *noun* **1** a measure of land, 4,840 sq. yds., 0.405 ha. **2** (in *plural*) a large area: *the restaurants feature acres of kitschy decor*.

acreage *noun* **1** a number of acres. **2** an extent of land, esp. farmland. [Say ACRE idge]

acrid *adjective* having an unpleasantly bitter or pungent taste or smell: *acrid smoke from burning tires*. [Say ACK rid]

acrimonious *adjective* extremely bitter in manner or temper: *an acrimonious custody battle over the children*. ▶**acrimoniously** *adverb* [Say ackra MOANY us]

acrimony *noun* (*plural* **acrimonies**) extreme bitterness or ill feeling. [Say ACKRA moany]

acrobat *noun* a performer of feats of agility, esp. in a circus. ▶**acrobatic** *adjective* **acrobatically** *adverb*

acrobatics *plural noun* **1** the feats or skills of an acrobat. **2** (as *singular*) the art of performing these. **3** a skill requiring dexterity: *mental acrobatics*.

acronym *noun* a word, usu. pronounced as such, formed from the initial letters of other words, e.g. *laser*, *NATO*. [Say ACKRA nim]

across • *preposition* **1** to or on the other side of. **2** from one side to another side of. **3** at or forming an angle (esp. a right angle) with. • *adverb* **1** to or on the other side. **2** from one side to another. **3** (of a crossword clue or answer) read horizontally. **4** *Cdn* (*PEI*) in or to Nova Scotia or New Brunswick: *come from across*.

acrostic *noun* a poem or word puzzle in which certain letters in each line form a word or words. [Say a CROSS tick]

acrylic • *adjective* **1** of material made with a synthetic polymer derived from acrylic acid. **2** (of paint) containing acrylic resin. **3** *Chemistry* of or derived from acrylic acid. • *noun* **1** an acrylic plastic, fabric, or paint. **2** a painting in acrylic paints. [Say a CRILL ick]

acrylic acid *noun* a pungent liquid organic acid which can be polymerized to make synthetic resins.

acrylic resin *noun* any of various transparent colourless polymers of acrylic acid.

act • *noun* **1** a deed or action. **2** the process of doing something: *caught in the act*. **3 a** a piece of entertainment, usu. one of a series in a program. **b** the performer(s) of this. **4** a pretense. **5** a main division of a play or opera. **6 a** a written ordinance of a parliament etc. **b** a document attesting a legal transaction. **7** (often in *plural*) the recorded decisions or proceedings of a committee etc. • *verb* **1** behave: *see how they act under stress*. **2** perform actions or functions; operate effectively; take action: *act as referee* ◊ *the brakes failed to act*. **3** exert energy or influence: *the medicine soon began to act*. **4 a** perform a part in a play, film, etc. **b** pretend. **c** embody or portray a character convincingly in a theatrical production. **5 a** perform the part of: *acted Othello*. **b** perform (a play etc.). **c** portray (an incident) by actions. **d** feign: *we acted indifference*. PHRASES **act for** be the (esp. legal) representative of. **act on** (or **upon**) perform or carry out; put into operation. **act out 1** translate (ideas etc.) into action. **2** *Psychology* represent (one's subconscious desires etc.) in action. **act up** *informal* misbehave; give trouble. **get one's act together** *informal* become properly organized. **get in on the act** *informal* become a participant (esp. for profit). **a hard act to follow** *informal* a person or thing difficult to be more impressive or successful than. **put on an act** *informal* carry out a pretense.

acting • *noun* **1** the art or occupation of performing parts in plays, films, etc. **2** in senses of ACT *verb*. • *adjective* serving temporarily or on behalf of another or others: *acting manager*.

acting sub-lieutenant *noun* (also **Acting Sub-Lieutenant**) a commissioned officer ranking below Sub-Lieutenant in the Canadian Navy.

actinium *noun* a radioactive metallic element, occurring naturally in pitchblende. [Say ack TINNY um]

action • *noun* **1** the fact or process of doing or acting. **a** forcefulness or energy as a characteristic: *a woman of action* ◊ *action photograph*. **3** the exertion of energy or

influence. **4** something done; a deed or act. **5 a** a series of events represented in a story, play, etc. **b** *informal* activity: *want some action*. **6 a** armed conflict: *killed in action*. **b** an occurrence of this, esp. a minor military engagement. **7 a** the way in which a machine, instrument, etc. works. **b** the mechanism that makes a musical instrument, gun, etc. work. **c** the mode or style of movement of an animal or human: *a runner with good action*. **8** a legal process; a lawsuit: *bring an action*. **9** (in *imper.*) a word of command to begin, esp. used by a film director etc. • *verb* bring a legal action against. PHRASES **actions speak louder than words** what someone actually does means more than what they say they will do. **go into action** start work. **out of action** not working. **take action** act, esp. against something.

actionable *adjective* giving cause for legal action.

action figure *noun* a doll representing a person or fictional character capable of or known for vigorous action, e.g. a soldier, athlete, superhero, etc.

action film *noun* (also **action movie** etc.) a feature film containing a great deal of fast-moving (esp. violent) action.

action-packed *adjective* full of action or excitement.

action stations *plural noun* positions taken up by troops etc. ready for battle.

activate *verb* (**activates**, **activated**, **activating**) **1** make active; bring into action. **2** *Chemistry* cause reaction in. **3** *Physics* make radioactive.

activated carbon *noun* (also **activated charcoal**, **active carbon**) carbon, esp. charcoal, that has been heated or otherwise treated to increase its power to hold molecules of a gas or liquid as a thin film.

activation *noun* **1** the process of making something active or operative. **2** the process of converting a substance, molecule, etc. into a reactive form.

activator *noun* a thing that activates; a catalyst: *compost activator*.

active *adjective* **1 a** consisting in or marked by action; energetic: *an active life*. **b** able to move about or accomplish practical tasks: *stayed active well into her nineties*. **2** working, operative: *an active volcano*. **3** not merely passive or inert: *active ingredients*. **4** radioactive. **5** of the form of a verb whose grammatical subject is the person or thing that performs the action, e.g. of the verbs in *guns kill; we saw him*. ▶ **actively** *adverb*

active duty *noun* **1** = ACTIVE SERVICE. **2** active involvement in an organization or group.

active layer *noun* the surface layer of soil above permafrost, subject to thawing in summer.

active-matrix *noun* a form of liquid crystal display in which each pixel is controlled by its own transistor, thus improving contrast.

active service *noun* full-time service in the armed forces or police.

activism *noun* the policy or action of using vigorous campaigning to bring about political or social change. ▶ **activist** *noun*

activity *noun* (*plural* **activities**) **1 a** the condition of being active or moving about. **b** the exertion of energy; vigorous action. **2** a particular occupation or pursuit: *outdoor activities*. **3** = RADIOACTIVITY.

act of God *noun* a usu. disastrous event caused by uncontrollable natural forces.

actor *noun* **1** a person who acts a part in a play etc., esp. as a profession. **2** a person skilled at portraying characters in theatrical productions. **3** a participant.

ACTRA *abbreviation* Alliance of Canadian Cinema, Television and Radio Artists.

actress *noun* (*plural* **actresses**) **1** a female who acts a part in a play etc., esp. as a profession. **2** a woman who

is skilled at portraying characters in theatrical productions.

WRITING TIP
actual

Phrases like **the actual facts** are redundant and should be avoided. Simply say **the facts**.

---

actual *adjective* existing in fact; real (often as distinct from ideal). ▶ **actualization** *noun* **actualize** *verb* (**actualizes**, **actualized**, **actualizing**)

actuality *noun* (*plural* **actualities**) **1** reality; what is the case. **2** (in *plural*) existing conditions.

actually *adverb* **1** as a fact, really. **2** as a matter of fact, even (strange as it may seem): *he actually refused!*

actuarial *adjective* relating to the science of calculating insurance risks and premiums. [Say ack choo AIRY ul]

actuary *noun* (*plural* **actuaries**) a person whose job involves calculating insurance risks and payments for insurance companies by studying how frequently accidents, fires, deaths, etc. occur. [Say ACK choo airy]

acuity *noun* (of the mind or the senses, esp. vision) sharpness, acuteness. [Say a CUE a tee]

acumen *noun* the ability to make good judgments and take quick decisions: *business acumen*. [Say ACK you mun]

acupressure *noun* = SHIATSU.

acupuncture *noun* a system of complementary medicine in which fine needles are inserted in the skin at specific points along what are considered to be lines of energy, used in the treatment of various physical and mental conditions. ▶ **acupuncturist** *noun*

acute • *adjective* **1** (of a physical sense or faculty) highly developed; keen: *an acute sense of smell*. **2** shrewd, perceptive: *an acute awareness of changing fashions*. **3** (of a disease) of short duration but typically severe: *acute appendicitis*. **4** (of a bad, difficult, or unwelcome situation or phenomenon) present or experienced to a severe or intense degree: *an acute housing shortage* ◊ *the problem is acute and getting worse*. **5 a** (of an angle) less than 90°. **b** sharp, pointed. **6** (of a sound) high, shrill. • *noun* (also **acute accent**) a mark (´) placed over letters in some languages to show pronunciation (e.g. *rosé*) etc. ▶ **acutely** *adverb* **acuteness** *noun*

AD *abbreviation* (of a date) of the Christian era: *Nero was born in* AD 37 ◊ *Nero was born in the first century* AD.

ad *noun* *informal* an advertisement.

adage *noun* a traditional saying. [Say AD idge]

adagio *Music & Dance* • *adverb & adjective* in slow time. • *noun* (*plural* **adagios**) an adagio movement or passage. [Say a DAZH ee oh or a DADGE ee oh]

Adam¹ *noun* PHRASES **not know a person from Adam** be unable to recognize the person in question.

Adam² *noun* *slang* the hallucinogenic drug MDMA.

adamant *adjective* stubbornly resolute; resistant to persuasion. ▶ **adamantly** *adverb*

Adam's apple *noun* a projection of the thyroid cartilage of the larynx, esp. as prominent in men.

WRITING TIP
adapt, adept

Someone who is highly skilled or talented at something is **adept** at it.

---

adapt *verb* **1 a** fit, adjust (one thing to another). **b** make suitable for a purpose. **c** alter or modify (esp. a text). **d** arrange for broadcasting etc. **2** become adjusted to new conditions.

adaptability *noun* the ability to adapt or be adapted to a new situation or new conditions.

adaptable *adjective* **1** able to adapt oneself to new conditions. **2** that can be adapted.

adaptation *noun* (also **adaption**) **1** the act or process of adapting or being adapted: *the adaptation of teaching strategy to meet students' needs*. **2** a thing made by adapting something else, esp. a text for production on radio etc.: *film adaptations of Jane Austen's novels have been very popular*. **3** *Biology* the process by which an organism or species becomes suited to its environment.

adapter *noun* (also **adaptor**) **1 a** a device for making equipment compatible. **b** a device for changing voltage or current. **2** a device for connecting several electrical plugs to one socket. **3** a person who adapts.

adaptive *adjective* able to change when necessary in order to deal with different situations.

ADD *abbreviation* ATTENTION DEFICIT DISORDER.

add *verb* **1** join (one thing to another) as an increase or supplement. **2** put together (two or more numbers) to find a number denoting their combined value. **3** say in addition: *added a remark*. PHRASES **add in** include. **add to** increase; be a further item among. **add up 1** find the total of. **2** (foll. by *to*) amount to; constitute. **3** *informal* make sense. ▶ **added** *adjective*

addendum *noun* (*plural* **addenda**) **1** a thing (usu. something omitted) to be added, esp. (in *plural*) as additional matter at the end of a book. **2** an appendix; an addition. [Say a DEN dum, a DEN duh]

adder *noun* **1** any of a variety of non-venomous North American snakes, e.g. the hognose snake. **2** any of various small venomous snakes of Europe and Asia.

addict *noun* **1** a person addicted to a habit, esp. one dependent on a (specified) drug. **2** *informal* an enthusiastic devotee of a sport or pastime: *film addict*.

addicted *adjective* (often foll. by *to*) **1** physically and mentally dependent on a particular substance, and unable to stop taking it without incurring adverse effects: *addicted to heroin*. **2** enthusiastically devoted to a particular thing or activity: *addicted to computers*.

addiction *noun* the fact or process of being addicted, esp. the condition of taking a drug habitually and being unable to give it up without adverse effects.

addictive *adjective* (of a drug, habit, etc.) causing addiction or dependence.

addition *noun* **1** the act or process of adding or being added. **2** a person or thing added. PHRASES **in addition** (often foll. by *to*) furthermore; as something added. ▶ **additional** *adjective* **additionally** *adverb*

additive *noun* a thing added, esp. a substance added to another so as to give it specific qualities: *food additive*.

addle-brained *adjective* (also **addle-pated**) silly.

addled *adjective* **1** confused. **2** (of an egg) rotten, producing no chick.

address • *noun* (*plural* **addresses**) **1 a** the place where a person lives or an organization is situated. **b** particulars of this, esp. for postal purposes. **c** *Computing* the location of an item of stored information. **d** the string of codes representing a person's location on an e-mail network. **2** a speech delivered to an audience. • *verb* (**addresses, addressed, addressing**) **1** write the name and address of the intended recipient on (an envelope etc.). **2** direct in speech or writing (remarks, a protest, etc.). **3** speak or write to, esp. formally. **4** direct one's attention to: *addressed my concerns*. PHRASES **address oneself to 1** speak or write to. **2** attend to. ▶ **addressable** *adjective*

addressee *noun* the person to whom something (esp. a letter) is addressed. [Say address EE]

adduce *verb* (**adduces, adduced, adducing**) give as an instance or as evidence: *a number of factors are adduced to explain the situation*. [Say a DYOOSS]

adenine *noun* a purine derivative found in all living tissue as a component base of DNA or RNA. [Say ADDA neen]

adenoidal *adjective* **1** suffering from enlarged adenoids. **2** (of the voice) having the nasal tones of a person with enlarged adenoids. [Say adda NOID ul]

adenoids *plural noun* a mass of lymphatic tissue between the back of the nose and the throat. [Say ADDA noids]

adept • *adjective* (often foll. by *at*, *in*) highly gifted or skilled. • *noun* a skilled performer; an expert. ▶ **adeptly** *adverb* **adeptness** *noun*

adequacy *noun* the quality of being adequate or sufficient for a purpose: *the adequacy of the security arrangements has been questioned*. [Say ADDA kwuh see]

adequate *adjective* **1** sufficient, satisfactory. **2** barely sufficient. ▶ **adequately** *adverb* [Say ADDA quit]

adhere *verb* (**adheres, adhered, adhering**) **1** (of a substance) stick fast to a surface, another substance, etc.: *paint won't adhere well to a greasy surface*. **2** behave according to; follow in detail: *adhered to our plan* ◊ *the people adhere to the Muslim religion*.

adherence *noun* the fact of behaving according to a particular rule etc., or of following a particular set of beliefs or a fixed way of doing something: *strict adherence to the rules*. [Say ad HEAR ince]

adherent *noun* **1** a supporter of a party, person, etc. **2** a devotee of an activity. [Say ad HEAR int]

adhesion *noun* **1** the act or process of adhering. **2** the capacity of a substance to stick fast. **3** *Medical* a union of surfaces due to inflammation. **4** the maintenance of contact between a vehicle's wheels and the road. **5** the giving of support or allegiance. [Say ad HEE zh'n]

adhesive • *adjective* sticky, enabling surfaces or substances to adhere to one another. • *noun* a substance used to stick other substances together. ▶ **adhesiveness** *noun* [Say ad HEE siv]

ad hoc *adverb* & *adjective* for a particular (usu. exclusive) purpose: *an ad hoc committee*.

adieu • *interjection* goodbye. • *noun* (*plural* **adieus** or **adieux**) a goodbye (esp. in *bid adieu to*). [Say ad DYOO (with OO as in FOOT)]

adipose tissue *noun* fatty connective tissue. [Say ADDA pose (POSE rhymes with DOSE or DOZE)]

Adirondack chair *noun* a slatted wooden lawn chair with a fan-shaped back and broad arms; a Muskoka chair. [Say adda RON dack]

adjacent *adjective* **1** lying near or adjoining: *adjacent rooms* ◊ *the area adjacent to the school*. **2** *Math* (of angles) sharing a vertex and one common line. [Say a JAY sunt]

adjectival *adjective* used as an adjective: *an adjectival phrase*. ▶ **adjectivally** *adverb* [Say ad jeck TIVE ul]

adjective *noun* a word or phrase naming an attribute, added to or grammatically related to a noun to modify it or describe it.

adjoin *verb* be close to or joined with (a building, room, or piece of land). ▶ **adjoining** *adjective*

adjourn *verb* **1** stop a meeting or an official process for a period of time with the intention of resuming later, esp. in a court of law: *the court adjourned for lunch* ◊ *the trial has been adjourned until next week* ◊ *the president may adjourn the meeting at any time*. **2** move to another place, esp. for entertainment or refreshment: *they adjourned to the upstairs lounge for a game of Trivial Pursuit*. [Say a JERN]

adjournment *noun* adjourning or being adjourned, esp. the postponement of a court case. [Say a JERN m'nt]

adjudicate *verb* (**adjudicates, adjudicated, adjudicating**) **1** act as judge in a competition, court, etc. **2** decide judicially regarding (a claim etc.). ▶ **adjudication** *noun* **adjudicator** *noun* [Say a JOODA kate, a jooda KAY sh'n]

adjunct • *noun* **1** something added to something else as a supplementary rather than an essential part: *computer technology is an adjunct to learning.* **2** a person who is another's assistant or subordinate: *women no longer wanted to be mere adjuncts to men.* **3** *Grammar* a word or phrase used to explain or amplify the predicate, subject, etc.: *In "She went home yesterday" and "He ran away in a panic", "yesterday" and "in a panic" are adjuncts.* • *adjective* having a subordinate or temporary capacity: *adjunct professor.* [Say AD junct]

adjust *verb* **1 a** arrange; put in the correct order or position. **b** regulate, esp. by a small amount. **2** (usu. foll. by *to*) make suitable. **3** assess (loss or damages). **4** (usu. foll. by *to*) make oneself suited to. **5** (foll. by *for*) alter (a statistic etc.) to allow for circumstances. ▶ **adjustability** *noun* **adjustable** *adjective* **adjuster** *noun* **adjustment** *noun*

adjutant *noun* **1** *Military* An officer who assists superior officers by communicating orders, conducting correspondence, etc. **2** an assistant. [Say AD juh t'nt]

ad lib • *verb* (**ad libs, ad libbed, ad libbing**) speak or perform without formal preparation; improvise. • *adjective* improvised. • *adverb* as one pleases, to any desired extent. • *noun* something spoken or played without preparation, rehearsal, etc.

admin *informal* • *noun* administration. • *adjective* administrative.

administer *verb* **1** attend to the running of (business affairs etc.); manage. **2 a** be responsible for the implementation of (the law, justice, punishment, etc.). **b** *Christianity* give out, or perform the rites of (a sacrament). **c** (usu. foll. by *to*) direct the taking of (an oath). **3 a** give, apply (medication etc.). **b** deliver (a rebuke etc.). **4** have someone undergo (a test etc.). **5** (foll. by *to*) provide what is necessary to satisfy (a person or their needs). **6** act as administrator.

administrate *verb* (**administrates, administrated, administrating**) administer (esp. business affairs); act as an administrator.

administration *noun* **1 a** management of a business, institution, etc. **b** management of public affairs. **2** those responsible for administering a business, institution, etc. **3** the government in power. **4** the term of office of a government or political leader. **5** *Law* the management of another person's estate. **6 a** the administering of justice, an oath, etc. **b** application of medication etc.

administrative *adjective* concerning the management of affairs. ▶ **administratively** *adverb*

administrator *noun* **1** a person who administers a business or public affairs. **2** *Computing* = SYSTEM ADMINISTRATOR. **3** *Law* a person appointed to manage the estate of a person who has died without a will. **4** a person who performs official duties in some sphere, e.g. in religion or justice.

admirable *adjective* **1** deserving admiration: *her dedication to her work was admirable.* **2** excellent: *he made his points with admirable clarity.* ▶ **admirably** *adverb*

admiral *noun* **1** (also **Admiral**) **a** a naval officer of high rank, esp. (in Canada) the highest rank in the Maritime Command. **b** a rear admiral or vice admiral. **2** any of various butterflies.

admiration *noun* **1** respect, warm approval: *I have great admiration for those involved in the project.* **2** pleased contemplation: *they were lost in admiration of the scenery.*

admire *verb* (**admires, admired, admiring**) **1** regard with approval, respect, or satisfaction: *I admire your courage* ◊ *admired the flowering crabapple tree.* **2** express one's admiration of: *they stood around admiring the baby.*

admirer *noun* **1** a person who admires a person or thing. **2** a person who is sexually attracted to another.

admiring *adjective* showing or feeling admiration. ▶ **admiringly** *adverb*

admissibility *noun* the quality of being admissible, esp. in a court of law. [Say ad missa BILLA tee]

admissible *adjective* **1** (of an idea or plan) worth accepting or considering. **2** *Law* allowable as evidence. **3** having the right to be admitted: *admissible immigrants to Canada.* [Say ad MISSA bull]

admission *noun* **1** an acknowledgement or confession. **2 a** the process or right of admitting. **b** a charge for this. **3** (in *plural*) the department (of a university, hospital, etc.) responsible for admitting new students, patients, etc. **4** a person admitted to a hospital.

admit *verb* (**admits, admitted, admitting**) **1** recognize as true. **2** (foll. by *to*) acknowledge responsibility for a deed, fault, etc. **3 a** allow (a person) entrance or access. **b** allow (a person) to be a member of (an institution, group, etc.) or to share in (a privilege etc.). **c** (of a hospital etc.) bring in (a person) for treatment. **4** (foll. by *of*) allow as possible: *the law admits of many interpretations.*

admittance *noun* the right or process of entering or being allowed to enter: *no admittance except on business.*

admittedly *adverb* as an acknowledged fact: *admittedly, there are problems.*

admixture *noun* **1** a combination, esp. of disparate elements: *he felt that his work was an admixture of aggression and creativity.* **2** a thing added, esp. a minor ingredient: *green with an admixture of black.*

admonish *verb* (**admonishes, admonished, admonishing**) **1** reprimand firmly: *she admonished me for appearing at breakfast unshaven.* **2** urge or advise earnestly: *a warning voice admonished him not to drink so much wine.* ▶ **admonition** *noun* **admonitory** *adjective* [Say ad MON ish, adma NISH un, ad MONNA tory]

ad nauseam *adverb* to an excessive or tiresome degree: *TV sports commentators repeat the same phrases ad nauseam.* [Say ad NOZZY um]

ado *noun* fuss: *he was greeted with much ado* ◊ *after much ado, the city finally sent me a cheque to cover the damages.* ▶PHRASES **without further** (or **more**) **ado** immediately. [Say a DOO]

adobe *noun* **1** a sun-dried brick made from clay and straw: *adobe house.* **2** the clay used for making such bricks. [Say a DOE bee]

adolescence *noun* the period following the onset of puberty during which a young person develops from a child into an adult. [Say adda LESS ince]

adolescent • *adjective* **1** between childhood and adulthood. **2** of or characteristic of this age: *adolescent behaviour.* • *noun* an adolescent person. [Say adda LESS int]

Adonis *noun* (*plural* **Adonises**) an extremely handsome young man. [Say a DON niss]

adopt *verb* **1** legally take another's child and raise it as one's own. **2** choose to follow (a course of action etc.): *adopt a new approach.* **3** assume: *adopt an air of indifference.* **4** take over (an idea etc.) from another person. **5** choose as a candidate for office. **6** accept; formally approve (a recommendation, legislation, etc.). ▶ **adoptable** *adjective* **adoption** *noun*

adoptive *adjective* **1** related by adoption: *adoptive parents.* **2** (of a city, country, etc.) chosen as residence by someone born elsewhere.

adorable *adjective* inspiring great affection: *Kate has two adorable cats.* ▶ **adorably** *adverb*

adoration *noun* **1** a feeling of great love or worship: *Vince gazed at Sandra with great adoration.* **2** worship of something divine: *adoration of the Blessed Sacrament.*

adore *verb* (**adores, adored, adoring**) **1** regard with

A

honour and deep affection. **2** worship as divine. **3** *informal* like very much. ▶**adorer** *noun* **adoring** *adjective* **adoringly** *adverb*

adorn *verb* make more beautiful or attractive: *pictures and posters adorned her walls.* ▶**adornment** *noun*

adrenal *adjective* **1** of the adrenal glands. **2** at or near the kidneys. [Say a DREEN ul]

adrenal gland *noun* either of two ductless glands above the kidneys, secreting adrenalin.

adrenalin *noun* (also **adrenaline**) a hormone which makes the heart beat faster and increases energy and the ability to move quickly. [Say a DRENNEL un]

Adriatic *adjective* of or relating to the arm of the Mediterranean Sea between the Balkans and the Italian peninsula. [Say a dree ATTIC]

adrift *adjective* **1** (of a boat etc.) drifting, esp. without direction. **2** away from the intended course. **3** lacking purpose or guidance; detached: *youth adrift in our cities.* **4** *informal* unfastened.

adroit *adjective* skilful and clever, esp. in dealing with people: *an adroit negotiator.* ▶**adroitly** *adverb* **adroitness** *noun* [Say a DROIT]

adsorb *verb* (usu. of a solid) hold (molecules of a gas or liquid or solute) to its surface, causing a thin film to form. ▶**adsorption** *noun*

adulate *verb* (**adulates**, **adulated**, **adulating**) admire and praise very much, esp. excessively. ▶**adulation** *noun* **adulator** *noun* **adulatory** *adjective* [Say AD yuh late, ad yuh LAY sh'n, ADYA luh tory]

adult • *adjective* **1** mature, grown-up. **2 a** of or for adults: *adult education.* **b** *euphemism* sexually explicit: *adult films.* • *noun* **1** an adult person. **2** *Law* a person who has reached the age of majority.

Adult Accompaniment *noun* a film classification which requires viewers under 14 years of age to be accompanied by an adult. Abbreviation: **AA**.

adulterant *noun* a substance used to make food, drink, or drugs less pure: *chicory has long been used as an adulterant of coffee.*

adulterate *verb* (**adulterates**, **adulterated**, **adulterating**) render something (esp. foods) poorer in quality by adding other or inferior ingredients: *the Food and Drug Act prescribes penalties for the sale of any adulterated food.* ▶**adulteration** *noun*

adulterer *noun* a person who commits adultery.

adulteress (*plural* **adulteresses**) *noun* a woman who commits adultery.

adulterous *adjective* involving or involved in adultery: *an adulterous relationship* ◊ *adulterous lovers.* ▶**adulterously** *adverb*

adultery *noun* (*plural* **adulteries**) **1** voluntary sexual intercourse between a married person and a person other than his or her spouse. **2** an adulterous act or relationship: *would no longer tolerate his adulteries.*

adulthood *noun* the state of being an adult: *a child reaching adulthood.*

advance • *verb* (**advances**, **advanced**, **advancing**) **1** move or put forward. **2** make progress. **3 a** pay (money) before it is due. **b** lend (money). **4** give active support to; promote. **5** put forward (a claim or suggestion). **6** cause (an event) to occur at an earlier date: *advanced the meeting three hours.* • *noun* **1** an act of going forward. **2** progress. **3** a payment made before the due time. **4** a loan. **5** (esp. in *plural*) an attempt to start a sexual relationship: *got angry when she rejected his advances.* • *adjective* done or supplied beforehand: *advance warning.* PHRASES **advance on** approach threateningly. **in advance** ahead in place or time.

advanced *adjective* **1** far on in progress. **2** ahead of the times. **3** highly developed, complex.

advance man *noun* (*plural* **advance men**) a person

who arranges security, publicity, etc. before the arrival of a touring politician etc.

advancement *noun* the progression or promotion of a person, cause, or plan.

advance poll *noun Cdn* an early poll for voters who expect to be absent from their riding on election day.

advantage • *noun* **1** a beneficial feature; a favourable circumstance. **2** benefit, profit: *is not to your advantage.* **3** (often foll. by *over*) superiority in a particular respect. **4** *Tennis* the next point won after deuce. **5** *Hockey* numerical superiority over the opposing team, as on a power play: *a two-man advantage.* • *verb* (**advantages**, **advantaged**, **advantaging**) put in a favourable or more favourable position. PHRASES **take advantage of 1** make good use of (a favourable circumstance). **2** exploit or outwit (a person), esp. unfairly. **to advantage** in a way which exhibits the merits: *was seen to advantage.* **turn to advantage** benefit from.

advantaged *adjective* being in a good social or financial situation.

advantageous *adjective* good or useful in a particular situation: *a treaty would be advantageous to both countries.* ▶**advantageously** *adverb* [Say ad van TAY juss]

Advent *noun* **1** *Christianity* the season before Christmas, including the four preceding Sundays. **2** *Christianity* the coming or Second Coming of Christ. **3** (**advent**) the arrival of esp. an important person or thing. [Say AD vent]

Adventist *noun* a member of a Christian group that believes in the imminent Second Coming of Christ. [Say ad VENT ist]

adventure • *noun* **1 a** an unusual and exciting experience. **b** (as an *adjective*) designating a type of tourism to exotic, esp. wilderness destinations usu. combined with hiking, canoeing, etc. **2 a** daring enterprise; a hazardous activity. **3** enterprise: *the spirit of adventure.* • *verb* (**adventures**, **adventured**, **adventuring**) go upon an adventure: *the North is a homeland, not a place for adventuring.*

adventurer *noun* a person who seeks adventure, esp. for gain or enjoyment.

adventuresome *adjective* adventurous.

adventuress *noun* (*plural* **adventuresses**) **1** *derogatory* a woman who pursues financial gain or social advancement, esp. by sexual means. **2** a woman who engages in adventures.

adventurous *adjective* **1** (of a person) willing to take risks and try new ideas; venturesome, enterprising. **2** including new and interesting things, methods, and ideas: *the menu contained traditional favourites as well as more adventurous dishes.* **3** full of new, exciting, and dangerous experiences: *an adventurous lifestyle.* ▶**adventurously** *adverb* **adventurousness** *noun*

adverb *noun* a word or phrase that modifies or qualifies another word (esp. an adjective, verb, or other adverb) or a word group, expressing a relation of place, time, cause, degree, etc. (e.g. *gently*, *here*, *now*, *very*). Some adverbs, called sentence adverbs, can also be used to modify whole sentences, e.g. *fortunately, they had a good dictionary.* ▶**adverbial** *adjective & noun*

adversarial *adjective* **1** involving opposition or conflict: *government and industry had an adversarial relationship.* **2** (of legal proceedings) in which the parties in a dispute are responsible for finding and presenting evidence: *an adversarial system of justice.* [Say ad vur SAIRY ul]

adversary *noun* (*plural* **adversaries**) **1** an enemy. **2** an opponent in a sport or game. [Say AD vur sairy]

WRITING TIP
adverse, averse

Do not confuse **adverse** with **averse**. **Adverse** means "unfavourable" or "harmful", as in *Adverse weather conditions will make the move difficult*. **Averse** is used of people, nearly always with **to**, and means "having a strong dislike of or opposition to", as in *I am not averse to the idea*.

adverse *adjective* preventing success or development; harmful, unfavourable: *taxes are having an adverse effect on production*. ▶ **adversely** *adverb* **adverseness** *noun*

adversity *noun* (*plural* **adversities**) a difficult or unpleasant situation: *strength in the face of adversity* ◊ *she overcame many adversities*.

advertise *verb* (**advertises**, **advertised**, **advertising**) **1** draw attention to or describe favourably (goods or services) in a public medium to promote sales: *saw it advertised on TV* ◊ *have sold several and I haven't even advertised yet*. **2** make generally or publicly known: *Jo coughed briefly to advertise her presence*. **3** seek to fill a vacancy: *advertised for a new sales rep*.

advertisement *noun* **1** a public announcement advertising goods or services. **2** a person or thing regarded as a means of recommending something: *unhappy clients are not a good advertisement for the company*. [Say ad VUR tiss m'nt or AD vur tize m'nt]

advertiser *noun* a person or company that advertises.

advertorial *noun* an advertisement giving information about a product in the style of an editorial or objective journalistic comment. [Say ad vur TORY ul]

advice *noun* **1** an opinion or recommendation about future action. **2** formal notice of a transaction. ▪ PHRASES **take advice 1** obtain advice, esp. from an expert. **2** act according to advice given.

advisability *noun* the quality of being advisable, sensible, or recommended.

advisable *adjective* recommended, sensible: *it is advisable to wash all fruit before consumption*.

SPELL CHECK
advise, advice

A good suggestion is **advice**.

advise *verb* (**advises**, **advised**, **advising**) **1** give advice to. **2** recommend; offer as advice. **3** (usu. foll. by *of*, or *that* + clause) inform, notify. [Say ad VIZE]

advised *adjective* behaving as someone, esp. the speaker, would recommend; sensible: *you would be advised to check on increases to your pension*.

advisedly *adverb* deliberately and after consideration (used esp. of what might appear a mistake or oversight): *I've used the term "old" advisedly*.

advisement *noun* PHRASES **take under advisement** reserve judgment while considering.

adviser *noun* (also **advisor**) a person who advises, esp. one appointed to do so and regularly consulted.

advisory ▪ *adjective* having the power to advise: *advisory board*. ▪ *noun* (*plural* **advisories**) an advisory statement, esp. about bad weather. [Say ad VISOR ee]

advocacy *noun* **1** (usu. foll. by *of*) public support for or recommendation of a cause, policy, etc. **2** the function of an advocate. [Say ADVA kuh see]

advocate ▪ *noun* **1** (foll. by *of*, *for*) a person who supports or speaks in favour. **2** a person who pleads for another. **3** a lawyer. ▪ *verb* (**advocates**, **advocated**, **advocating**) recommend or support by argument (a cause, policy, etc.): *some advocated an elected Senate*. [Say ADVA k't for the noun, ADVA kate for the verb]

adze *noun* a tool for cutting away the surface of wood,

like an axe with an arched blade at right angles to the handle. [Say ADZ]

Aegean *adjective* of or relating to the Aegean Sea or Islands between Greece and Turkey. [Say a GEE un]

aegis *noun* (*plural* **aegises**) the protection, backing, or support of a particular person or organization: *the talks were held under the aegis of the UN*. [Say EE jiss]

aeon *noun* = EON. [Say EE on]

aerate *verb* (**aerates**, **aerated**, **aerating**) **1** introduce a gas, esp. carbon dioxide, into a liquid, e.g. to make it bubbly. **2** introduce air into (soil etc.). ▶ **aerator** *noun* [Say AIR ate]

aeration *noun* the introduction of air into soil, a liquid, etc.: *the roots require good aeration*. [Say air AY sh'n]

aerial ▪ *adjective* **1** by, from, or involving aircraft: *aerial photography*. **2** existing, moving, etc. in the air. **3** designating events in freestyle skiing in which competitors leap off a ski jump and perform twists and flips in the air before landing. ▪ *noun* **1** = ANTENNA 1. **2** *Football* a pass thrown toward the opponent's end zone. **3** (in *plural*) aerial events in freestyle skiing. [Say AIRY ul]

aerie *noun* **1** a nest of a bird of prey, esp. an eagle, built high up. **2** a high place or position: *from the aerie of their 54th-floor apartment*. [Say AIRY or EERIE]

aero *adjective informal* aerodynamic. [Say AIR oh]

aero- *combining form* **1** relating to air or the atmosphere: *aerodynamics*. **2** relating to aircraft: *aerobatics*. [Say AIR oh]

aerobat *noun* a pilot who performs aerobatics. ▶ **aerobatic** *adjective* [Say AIR oh bat, air oh BAT ick]

aerobatics *plural noun* feats of expert and usu. spectacular flying and manoeuvring of aircraft, e.g. loops, rolls, etc. [Say air oh BAT ics]

aerobe *noun* a micro-organism usu. growing in the presence of air, or needing air for growth. [Say AIR obe]

aerobic *adjective* **1** increasing or pertaining to oxygen consumption by the body: *aerobic exercise*. **2** of or relating to aerobics: *aerobic shoes*. **3** *Biology* of or relating to aerobes. ▶ **aerobically** *adverb* [Say a ROBE ick]

aerobics *plural noun* exercises, esp. those done to music, designed to increase fitness by sustained activity that increases oxygen intake and heart rate. [Say a ROBE icks]

aerodynamic *adjective* **1** of aerodynamics. **2** (of a vehicle etc.) designed to minimize drag. ▶ **aerodynamically** *adverb* [Say air oh die NAM ick]

aerodynamics *plural noun* (usu. treated as *singular*) **1** the interaction between the air and solid bodies moving through it. **2** the study of this. [Say air oh die NAM icks]

aeronautical *adjective* having to do with aeronautics: *an aeronautical engineer*. [Say air oh NOT ick ul]

aeronautics *plural noun* (usu. treated as *singular*) the science or practice of motion or travel in the air. [Say air oh NOT icks]

aerosol *noun* **1 a** a substance packed under pressure with a device for releasing it as a fine spray: *aerosol spray*. **b** the container holding this. **2** a suspension of particles dispersed in air etc. [Say AIR a sol]

aerospace *noun* **1** the earth's atmosphere and outer space. **2** the technology or industry of flight in the atmosphere and in space. [Say AIR oh space]

aesthete *noun* a person who has or professes to have a special appreciation of beauty. [Say ess THEET]

aesthetic ▪ *adjective* **1** concerned with beauty or the appreciation of beauty. **2** having such appreciation; sensitive to beauty. **3** designed to give pleasure through beauty. ▪ *noun* **1** (in *plural*) the philosophy of the beautiful, esp. in art. **2** (in *plural*) aesthetically pleasing elements. **3** a conception of what is beautiful

or artistically valid: *a minimalist aesthetic*. ▶ **aesthetically** *adverb* [Say es THETTIC]

aesthetician *noun* **1** a person versed in or devoted to aesthetics. **2** a beautician. [Say estha TISH un]

aestheticism *noun* the pursuit of beauty, esp. as part of an artistic doctrine that art should be enjoyed for its own sake and not for its moral, political, or religious function. [Say es THETTA sism]

afar *adverb* at or to a distance. PHRASES **from afar** from a distance.

affability *noun* the quality of being affable.

affable *adjective* friendly, good-natured. ▶ **affably** *adverb*

affair *noun* **1** a concern; a matter to be attended to. **2 a** a celebrated or notorious happening or sequence of events. **b** a thing or event of a specified sort: *a black-tie affair*. **3** a romantic or sexual relationship between two people, esp. an adulterous one. **4** (in *plural*) **a** ordinary pursuits of life. **b** business dealings. **c** matters or issues: *current affairs*.

affaire *noun* (usu. **l'affaire**) (followed by a proper name) a controversy or notorious event involving the specified person: *l'affaire Ben Johnson*.

SPELL CHECK
affect, effect ABC✓

Affect is a verb that means "to have an influence on": *Alcohol affects drivers' concentration*. **Effect**, especially in the phrase **have an effect on**, is a noun that means "a result or influence": *Alcohol has a very bad effect on drivers*. **Effect** is also a formal verb meaning "to achieve": *People lack confidence in their ability to effect change in society*.

---

affect[1] *verb* **1 a** produce an effect on; influence. **b** (of a disease etc.) attack. **2** touch the feelings of: *affected me deeply*. ▶ **affecting** *adjective* **affectingly** *adverb*

affect[2] *verb* **1** pretend: *she affected to know what he meant* ◊ *he affected ignorance*. **2** use, wear, or assume something pretentiously or so as to make an impression on others: *an Anglophile who had affected a British accent*.

affectation *noun* **1** behaviour, speech, or writing that is artificial and designed to impress: *she called her room a boudoir, which he thought an affectation ◊ her writing is simple and free of all affectation*. **2** a studied display of real or pretended feeling: *an affectation of calm*.

affected *adjective* **1** influenced or touched by an external factor: *apply the cream to the affected areas*. **2** artificial, pretentious, and designed to impress: *the gesture appeared both affected and stagy ◊ others think his enthusiasm is genuine, but I find him affected*. ▶ **affectedly** *adverb*

affection *noun* a gentle feeling of fondness or liking: *she felt a very deep affection for him ◊ he won a place in her affections*.

affectionate *adjective* loving, fond; showing love or tenderness. ▶ **affectionately** *adverb*

affective *adjective* *Psychology* relating to moods, feelings, and attitudes: *affective disorders*.

affidavit *noun* a written statement confirmed by oath, for use as evidence in court. [Say affa DAY vit]

affiliate • *verb* (**affiliates, affiliated, affiliating**) (foll. by *to*, *with*) **1** attach or connect (to a larger organization); adopt as a member, branch, etc. **2** associate oneself with an organization etc. • *noun* an affiliated person or organization. ▶ **affiliated** *adjective* **affiliation** *noun* [Say a FILLY ate for the verb, a FILLY it for the noun]

affinity *noun* (*plural* **affinities**) **1** (often foll. by *for*, *with*, *between*, or *to*) a spontaneous or natural liking for or

attraction to a person or thing. **2** relationship other than by blood, esp. by marriage or adoption (compare CONSANGUINITY). **3** resemblance in structure between animals, plants, or languages. [Say a FINNA tee]

affirm *verb* **1** assert strongly; state as a fact. **2** *Law* confirm, ratify (a judgment). ▶ **affirmation** *noun*

affirmative • *adjective* **1** agreeing with or consenting to a statement or request: *expected an affirmative answer*. **2** (of a vote) expressing approval. **3** *Grammar* stating that a fact is so; making an assertion: *affirmative sentences*. • *noun* **1** an affirmative statement, reply, or word. **2** (**the affirmative**) a position of agreement or confirmation: *his answer veered toward the affirmative*. • *interjection* yes. PHRASES **in the affirmative** so as to accept or agree to a statement or request; yes: *the answer was in the affirmative*. [Say a FIRMA tiv]

affirmative action *noun* a policy to favour those who often suffer from discrimination, esp. in employment.

affirmatively *adverb* in an affirmative manner; expressing agreement: *Tara nodded her head affirmatively*. [Say a FIRMA tiv lee]

affix • *verb* (**affixes, affixed, affixing**) **1** (usu. foll. by *to*, *on*) attach, fasten. **2** impress (a seal, stamp, etc.). **3** add in writing (a signature or postscript). • *noun* (*plural* **affixes**) a prefix or suffix. ▶ **affixation** *noun* [Say a FIX for the verb, AFF ix for the noun]

afflict *verb* distress with bodily or mental suffering. PHRASES **afflicted with** suffering from.

affliction *noun* **1** physical or mental distress, esp. pain or illness: *poor people in great affliction*. **2** a cause of this: *a crippling affliction of the nervous system*.

affluence *noun* wealth. [Say AFF loo ince]

affluent *adjective* wealthy, rich: *the affluent societies of the western world*. [Say AFF loo int]

afford *verb* **1 a** have enough money, means, time, etc., for; be able to spare: *can afford $50 ◊ could not afford to worry about it*. **b** be in a position to do something (esp. without risk of adverse consequences): *can't afford to let him think so*. **2** provide: *affords a view of the lake*. ▶ **affordability** *noun* **affordable** *adjective*

affront • *noun* an action or remark that causes outrage or offence: *she took their indifference as a personal affront*. • *verb* offend the modesty or self-respect of: *I was affronted when he called my house a shack*. [Say a FRONT]

Afghan • *noun* **1 a** a native or national of Afghanistan, a country in central Asia. **b** a person of Afghan descent. **2** the official language of Afghanistan. **3** (**afghan**) a knitted or crocheted woollen blanket or shawl. **4** (also **Afghan coat**) a kind of sheepskin coat with the skin outside and usu. with a shaggy border. **5** (also **Afghan hound**) a tall hunting dog with long silky hair. • *adjective* of or relating to Afghanistan or its people or language. [Say AF gan]

Afghani • *noun* (*plural* **Afghanis**) = AFGHAN *noun* 1. • *adjective* = AFGHAN *adjective* [Say al GANNY]

aficionado *noun* (*plural* **aficionados**) a person who is very knowledgeable and enthusiastic about an activity, subject, or pastime. [Say a fisha NADDO or a fisha NODDO]

afield *adverb* (in **far afield**) away from home; to or at a distance.

afire *adverb & adjective* **1** on fire. **2** intensely roused or excited: *every Winnipegger is afire with zeal and confidence*. **3** glittering, glowing; coloured like fire.

aflame *adverb & adjective* **1** in flames. **2** = AFIRE 2. **3** red as if on fire: *his cheeks were aflame*.

afloat *adverb & adjective* **1** floating in water or air. **2** on board ship. **3** out of debt or difficulty: *a huge infusion of cash will be needed to keep the company afloat*. **4** in general circulation. **5** full of or covered with a liquid.

afoot *adverb & adjective* **1** in operation; progressing:

plans are afoot for the festival. **2** stirring; on the move. **3 a** on foot: *they arrived afoot.* **b** on one's feet: *slow afoot.*

aforementioned *adjective* denoting a thing or person previously mentioned: *songs from the aforementioned album.*

aforethought *adjective* premeditated: *malice aforethought.*

afoul *adverb* (usu. in **run** or **fall afoul of**) into conflict or difficulty with.

afraid *adjective* **1** alarmed, frightened. **2** unwilling or reluctant for fear of the consequences: *was afraid to go in.* PHRASES **be afraid** admit or declare with (real or politely simulated) regret: *I'm afraid there's none left.*

A-frame *noun* **1** a frame (of a house etc.) having the shape of a capital letter A. **2** an A-frame house. **3** *Forestry* an A-shaped frame supporting running lines in high-lead logging.

afresh *adverb* anew; with a fresh beginning: *we'll have to scrap everything and start afresh.*

African • *noun* **1** a native or inhabitant of Africa. **2** a person of African descent (esp. a dark-skinned person). • *adjective* of or relating to Africa.

African-American *noun* an American citizen of black African origin or descent.

African-Canadian *noun* a Canadian citizen of black African origin or descent.

African elephant *noun* the elephant, *Loxodonta africana*, of Africa, larger than the Indian elephant.

African violet *noun* a plant of the genus *Saintpaulia*, with heart-shaped velvety leaves and blue, purple, pink, or white flowers, grown as a houseplant.

Afrikaans *noun* the language of the Afrikaner people developed from Dutch, an official language of the Republic of South Africa. [Say affra KONCE]

Afrikaner *noun* an Afrikaans-speaking white South African, esp. one of Dutch descent. [Say affra CONNER]

Afro • *adjective* (also **afro**) (of a hairstyle) shaped into a wide curly or frizzy mass. **2** African. • *noun* (*plural* **Afros**) an Afro hairstyle.

Afro- *combining form* African: *Afro-Asian*.

Afro-American • *adjective* of or relating to American blacks or their culture. • *noun* an American black.

Afro-Caribbean • *noun* a person of African descent in or from the Caribbean. • *adjective* of or relating to the Afro-Caribbeans or their culture.

Afrocentric *adjective* centred on Africa or on cultures of African origin, esp. North American black culture.

aft[1] *adverb* at or toward the stern of a ship or tail of an aircraft.

aft[2] *noun* *Cdn informal* afternoon: *I'll see you this aft.*

after • *preposition* **1 a** following in time; later than. **b** past the hour of: *a quarter after eight.* **2** in view of (something that happened shortly before): *after your behaviour tonight what do you expect?* **3** in spite of: *after all my efforts.* **4** behind: *shut the door after you.* **5** in pursuit or quest of: *run after them* ◊ *is after a job.* **6** about, concerning: *asked after her.* **7** in allusion to: *named her Patricia after her mother.* **8** in imitation of (a person, word, etc.): *a painting after Rubens.* **9** next in importance to. • *conjunction* in or at a time later than that when: *left after they arrived.* • *adverb* **1** later in time. **2** behind in place: *look before and after.* • *adjective* **1** later, following: *in after years.* **2** *Nautical* nearer the stern: *after cabins.* PHRASES **after all 1** in spite of all that has happened or has been said etc. **2** in spite of one's exertions, expectations, etc. **after you** a formula used in offering precedence.

afterbirth *noun* the placenta and fetal membranes discharged from the uterus after childbirth.

afterburner *noun* an auxiliary burner in a jet engine to increase thrust.

after-care *noun* care of a patient after a stay in hospital or of a person on release from prison.

afterdeck *noun* the part of a ship's deck nearest the stern.

after-effect *noun* an effect that follows after an interval or after the primary action of something.

afterglow *noun* **1** a light or radiance remaining after its source has disappeared or been removed. **2** a period of happiness, fame, etc. immediately following a successful event.

after-hours *adjective* occurring or operating after the usual or legal operating hours: *an after-hours bar.*

afterlife *noun* **1** life after death. **2** life at a later time.

aftermarket *noun* **1** a market in spare parts and components. **2** *Stock Market* a market in shares after their original issue.

aftermath *noun* **1** the consequences or after-effects of an event, esp. when unpleasant: *the aftermath of the ice storm.* **2** the period immediately following an event.

afternoon *noun* **1** the time from noon to evening. **2** a time compared with this, esp. the later part of something: *the afternoon of life.*

aftershave *noun* a scented astringent lotion for use on the face after shaving.

aftershock *noun* **1** a lesser shock following the main shock of an earthquake. **2** an after-effect.

aftertaste *noun* **1** a taste remaining or recurring after eating or drinking. **2** a persistent feeling etc.

afterthought *noun* an item or thing that is thought of or added later.

SPELL CHECK	ABC✓
afterward, afterword	

The concluding part of a book is the **afterword**.

afterwards *adverb* (also **afterward**) later.

afterword *noun* concluding remarks in a book, either by the author or by someone else.

AG *abbreviation* **1** ATTORNEY GENERAL. **2** *Cdn* AUDITOR GENERAL.

Ag *symbol* the element silver.

ag *abbreviation* *informal* agriculture, agricultural: *ag college.*

again *adverb* **1** another time; once more. **2** as in a previous position or condition: *quite well again.* **3** in addition: *as much again.* **4** besides. **5** on the other hand: *I might, and again I might not.* PHRASES **again and again** repeatedly.

against *preposition* **1** in opposition to: *fight against the invaders* ◊ *am against hanging.* **2** in contact with: *lean against the wall.* **3** to the disadvantage of: *her age is against her.* **4** in contrast to: *against a dark background.* **5** in anticipation of or preparation for: *protected against the cold.* **6** as a compensating factor to: *income against expenditure.* **7** in return for: *issued against payment of the fee.*

Aga Khan *noun* the hereditary spiritual leader of most of the Ismaili Muslims. [Say agga CON]

agape[1] *adverb & adjective* gaping, open-mouthed, esp. with wonder or expectation: *after staring at me agape for several seconds, she fainted.* [Say a GAPE]

agape[2] *noun* **1** a Christian feast in token of fellowship, esp. one held by early Christians in commemoration of the Last Supper. **2** *Theology* Christian fellowship, esp. as distinct from erotic love. [Say AGGA pay]

agar *noun* (also **agar-agar**) a gelatinous substance obtained from any of various kinds of red seaweed, and used as a thickener in food, a culture medium for bacteria, and a laxative. [Say AY gar]

agate *noun* **1** any of several varieties of hard usu.

streaked chalcedony. **2** a coloured toy marble resembling this. [Say AG it]

age • *noun* **1 a** the length of time that a person or thing has existed or is likely to exist: *ten years of age*. **b** a particular point in or part of one's life, often as a qualification: *old age*. **2 a** *informal* (often in *plural*) a long time: *have been waiting for ages*. **b** a distinct period of the past: *Bronze Age ◊ Middle Ages*. **c** a division of geological time, esp. a subdivision of an epoch. **d** a generation. **3** old age: *the wisdom of age*. • *verb* (**ages, aged**; *pres. part.* **aging** or **ageing**) **1** show signs of advancing age. **2** grow old. **3** (esp. of wine or cheese) mature. **4** cause or allow to age. PHRASES **of age** (esp. in law 18 and over, formerly 21 and over): *come of age*.

aged *adjective* **1 a** of the age of: *aged ten*. **b** that has been subjected to aging. **2** having lived long; old. [Say AGE ed for sense 2]

ageing = AGING. [Say AGE ing]

ageism *noun* prejudice or discrimination on the grounds of age. ▶ **ageist** *adjective & noun* [Say AGE ism, AGE ist]

ageless *adjective* **1** never growing or appearing old or outmoded. **2** eternal, timeless.

agency *noun* (*plural* **agencies**) **1 a** an organization or business providing a (usu. specific) service: *advertising agency*. **b** a government office providing a specific service. **2** a person or business operating on behalf of another, esp. at a distance: *our Vancouver agency*. **3 a** the duty or function of an agent. **b** the office or place of business of an agent. **4** action, esp. such as to produce a particular effect: *fertilized by the agency of bees*.

agenda *noun* (*plural* **agendas**) **1** a list of items of business to be considered at a meeting. **2** a series of things to be done: *on the agenda ◊ he vowed to put job creation at the top of his agenda if he is elected*. **3** a plan of action: *she seems to be selflessly interested but I'm sure she has a hidden agenda ◊ everyone on the committee had their own personal agenda*. **4** a book containing a calendar, used to plan one's activities. [Say a JEN duh]

agent *noun* **1** a person who provides a specific service etc.: *insurance agent*. **2** a person who acts for another in business, politics, etc. **3** a person or company that represents an organization, company, or government in a particular territory. **4** a person or thing that exerts power or produces an effect. **5** a spy: *enemy agent*. **6** *Cdn* = INDIAN AGENT.

agent general *noun* (*plural* **agents general**) the chief representative of a Canadian province or Australian state in a foreign country or region.

age of consent *noun* the age at which marriage or consent to sexual intercourse is valid in law.

age of discretion *noun* the esp. legal age at which a person is able to manage his or her own affairs.

Age of Reason *noun* **1** the late 17th and 18th centuries in western Europe and North America, characterized by faith in human reason. **2** (usu. **age of reason**) the age at which a person is considered capable of making rational judgments.

age-old *adjective* having existed for a very long time.

agglomerate • *verb* (**agglomerates, agglomerated, agglomerating**) **1** collect into a mass. **2** accumulate in a disorderly way. • *noun* **1** a mass or collection of things. **2** *Geology* a mass of large volcanic fragments bonded under heat (*compare* CONGLOMERATE *noun* 3). ▶ **agglomeration** *noun* [Say a GLOMMER ate for the verb, a GLOMMER it for the noun]

agglutinate *verb* (**agglutinates, agglutinated, agglutinating**) **1** stick together as with glue: *rhinoceros horns are agglutinated masses of hair*. **2** *Biology* (with reference to bacteria or red blood cells) clump together. ▶ **agglutination** *noun* [Say a GLUE tin ate, a glue tin AY sh'n]

aggrandize *verb* (**aggrandizes, aggrandized, aggrandizing**) **1** increase the power, rank, or wealth of (a person or nation): *an action intended to aggrandize the Frankish dynasty*. **2** cause to appear greater or more important than is the case: *he hoped to aggrandize himself by dying a hero's death*. ▶ **aggrandizement** *noun* [Say a GRAN dize]

WRITING TIP
aggravate

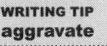

The use of **aggravate** to mean "annoy" is well established, despite being thought wrong by some.

---

aggravate *verb* (**aggravates, aggravated, aggravating**) **1** make a problem, injury, or offence worse or more serious: *military action would only aggravate the situation ◊ his injury was aggravated by overwork*. **2** annoy, exasperate (a person): *tried to appease aggravated travellers who had lost their bags*.

aggravated assault *noun* *Law* assault involving wounding, maiming, disfigurement or endangerment of the life of the victim.

aggravating *adjective* **1** annoying, exasperating: *children can be tedious and aggravating*. **2** that makes worse: *an aggravating factor*. ▶ **aggravatingly** *adverb*

aggravation *noun* **1** an increase in the seriousness of an illness or bad situation: *the drug may cause an aggravation of the condition*. **2 a** annoyance, irritation. **b** nuisance, inconvenience: *by taking the bus, I can avoid the aggravation of city driving*.

aggregate • *noun* **1** a whole formed by combining several (often disparate) elements: *literature as a whole is not an aggregate of exhibits with red and blue ribbons attached to them, like a cat show*. **2** pieces of crushed stone, gravel, etc. used in making concrete. **3 a** *Geology* a mass of minerals formed into solid rock. **b** a mass of particles. • *adjective* formed or calculated by the combination of many separate units or items; total: *the aggregate amount of grants made*. • *verb* (**aggregates, aggregated, aggregating**) collect together; combine into one mass. PHRASES **in the aggregate** as a whole. ▶ **aggregation** *noun* [Say AGRA git for the noun and adjective, AGRA gate for the verb, agra GAY sh'n]

aggression *noun* **1** the act or practice of attacking without provocation. **2** an unprovoked attack. **3** hostile or destructive tendency or behaviour.

aggressive *adjective* **1** of a person: **a** given to aggression; openly hostile. **b** forceful, assertive; energetic, enterprising: *aggressive salespeople*. **2** (of an act) offensive, hostile. **3** suggesting assertiveness or hostility: *aggressive street clothes*. **4** growing or multiplying rapidly: *a very aggressive ivy*. ▶ **aggressively** *adverb* **aggressiveness** *noun*

aggressor *noun* a person or country that attacks without provocation.

aggrieved *adjective* feeling resentment at having been unfairly treated. [Say a GREEVD]

aghast *adjective* filled with horror or shock: *Eric looked at him aghast ◊ he was aghast at the sight of so much blood*. [Say a GAST]

agile *adjective* **1** able to move quickly and gracefully. **2** mentally acute: *her agile mind*. ▶ **agilely** *adverb*

agility *noun* **1** the ability to move quickly and easily: *Gordon had the agility of a man half his age*. **2** the ability to think quickly and in an intelligent way: *mental agility*. [Say a JILLA tee]

aging • *noun* **1** the process of growing old. **2** the act or process of causing to age or mature. *the flavour of*

cheddar becomes more intense with aging. • *adjective* becoming or appearing older.

agism *noun* = AGEISM.

agitate *verb* (**agitates, agitated, agitating**) **1** disturb or excite (a person or feelings). **2** (often foll. by *for, against*) stir up or attempt to stir up public interest or concern. **3** shake or move, esp. briskly. ▶ **agitated** *adjective* **agitatedly** *adverb*

agitation *noun* **1** the action of arousing public concern about an issue and pressing for action on it: *widespread agitation for social reform*. **2** anxiety or nervous excitement: *she was wringing her hands in agitation*. **3** the action of briskly stirring or disturbing something, esp. a liquid.

agitator *noun* **1** a person who agitates for or against a cause etc. **2** an apparatus for shaking or mixing liquid etc., esp. in a washing machine.

agitprop *noun* **1** (**Agitprop**) *hist.* a Soviet agency for the spreading of Communist political propaganda, esp. in literature, film, etc. **2** political and usu. procommunist propaganda. [Say ADGE it prop]

aglow *adjective* glowing.

AGM *abbreviation* ANNUAL GENERAL MEETING.

agnolotti *noun* half-moon-shaped or triangular pasta filled with meat, cheese, etc. [Say anya LOTTY]

agnostic • *noun* a person who believes that nothing is known, or can be known, of the existence or nature of God. • *adjective* of agnostics or agnosticism. ▶ **agnosticism** *noun* [Say ag NOSS tik, ag NOSSTA sism]

Agnus Dei *noun Christianity* **1** a figure of a lamb bearing a cross or flag, as an emblem of Christ. **2** a prayer or hymn beginning with the words "Lamb of God" said or sung before or during Communion in some Christian liturgies. [Say agnes DAY ee or anyooss DAY ee]

> **GRAMMAR CHECK** ⚠️
> **ago**
>
> The correct construction is *It was ten years **ago that** I moved to Vancouver*, not *It is ten years ago since I moved to Vancouver*.

---

ago *adverb* earlier, before the present.

agog *adjective* very eager or curious to hear or see something: *the whole pier was agog when a big boat came into view*.

agonize *verb* (**agonizes, agonized, agonizing**) **1** (often foll. by *over*) undergo (esp. mental) anguish. **2** cause agony to.

agonized *adjective* characterized by or expressing agony: *an agonized look ◊ agonized breathing*.

agonizing *adjective* causing great pain, anxiety, or difficulty: *Tanya faced an agonizing decision.* ▶ **agonizingly** *adverb*

agony *noun* (*plural* **agonies**) **1** extreme mental or physical suffering: *Katherine was in agony when she ripped her calf muscle*. **2** the final stages of a difficult or painful death: *his last agony*.

agora *noun* (in ancient Greece) a public open space used for assemblies and markets. [Say AGGA ruh]

agoraphobia *noun* an abnormal fear of open spaces or public places. ▶ **agoraphobic** *adjective & noun* [Say a gora FOE bee uh, a gora FOE bick]

agrarian *adjective* **1** of or relating to the land or its cultivation: *agrarian economy*. **2** relating to landed property: *agrarian reforms resulted in serfs becoming owners of mid-sized farms*. [Say a GRARE ee un]

agree *verb* (**agrees, agreed, agreeing**) **1** hold a similar opinion. **2** consent: *agreed to go*. **3** (often foll. by *with*) **a** become or be in harmony. **b** suit; be good for: *caviar didn't agree with him*. **c** *Grammar* have the same number, gender, case, or person as. **4** consent to or

approve of (terms, a proposal, etc.). **5** (foll. by *on*) decide by mutual consent: *agreed on a compromise*. PHRASES **agree to differ** leave a difference of opinion etc. unresolved.

agreeable *adjective* **1** pleasant; enjoyable. **2** willing to agree: *was agreeable to going*. **3** (foll. by *to*) acceptable. ▶ **agreeableness** *noun* **agreeably** *adverb*

agreement *noun* **1** the act of agreeing. **2** mutual understanding. **3 a** an arrangement between parties as to a course of action etc. **b** a document outlining such an arrangement. **4** *Grammar* the condition of having the same number, gender, case, or person. **5** a state of being harmonious.

ag rep *noun* (also **ag representative**) *Cdn informal* = AGRICULTURAL REPRESENTATIVE.

> **SPELL CHECK**
> **aggressive**
>
> Warning: **aggressive** is spelled with two g's and two s's.

---

agribusiness *noun* (*plural* **agribusinesses**) **1** agriculture conducted on strictly commercial principles, esp. using advanced technology. **2** an organization engaged in this. **3** the group of industries dealing with the produce of, and services to, farming.

agricultural *adjective* having to do with agriculture.

agriculturalist *noun* an expert in agriculture.

agriculturally *adverb* with regard to agriculture.

agricultural representative *noun Cdn* an employee of an agriculture ministry who advises farmers in a particular region.

agriculture *noun* the science or practice of cultivating the soil for growing crops and rearing animals to provide food, wool, and other products.

agri-food *adjective* esp. *Cdn* (of an industry) concerned with or involved in food production or processing.

agrochemical *noun* a chemical used in agriculture.

agroforestry *noun* agriculture in which there is integrated management of trees or shrubs along with conventional crops or livestock.

agronomic *adjective* having to do with agronomy, the science of soil management and crop production. [Say agra NOM ick]

agronomist *noun* a scientist who studies the relationship between crops and the environment. [Say a GRONNA mist]

agronomy *noun* the science of soil management and crop production. [Say a GRONNA mee]

aground *adjective & adverb* (of a ship) on or onto the bottom of shallow water.

ague *noun* **1** *hist.* a malarial fever, with cold, hot, and sweating stages. **2** a shivering fit. [Say AY gyoo]

AH *abbreviation* used to show the year in the Muslim calendar, calculated from the Hegira in AD 622.

ah *interjection* expressing surprise, pleasure, sudden realization, resignation, etc.

AHA *abbreviation* ALPHA-HYDROXY ACID.

aha *interjection* expressing surprise, triumph, etc.

ahead *adverb* **1** further forward in space or time. **2** in the lead: *ahead 3–1*. **3** in the line of one's forward motion: *construction ahead*. **4** straight forwards. PHRASES **ahead of 1** further forward or advanced than. **2** in the line of the forward motion of.

ahem *interjection* (not usu. clearly articulated) used to attract attention, gain time, or express disapproval.

ahistorical *adjective* unrelated to history; lacking historical context or perspective. [Say ay HISTORICAL]

-aholic *combining form* denoting addiction: *workaholic*.

Ahousat *noun* (also **Ahousaht**) a member of the

principal group of Nuu-chah-nulth, living on the west coast of Vancouver Island. [Say a HOWZ ut]

ahoy *interjection* used to hail a ship or to attract attention.

AI *abbreviation* **1** *Computing* artificial intelligence. **2** artificial insemination.

aid • *noun* **1** help. **2** financial or material help, esp. given by one country to another: *foreign aid*. **3** a material source of help: *teaching aid*. **4** a person or thing that helps. • *verb* **1** help. **2** promote or encourage. PHRASES **in aid of** in support of. **what's this** (or **all this**) **in aid of?** *informal* what is the purpose of this?

aide *noun* **1** an assistant. **2** an aide-de-camp.

aide-de-camp *noun* (*plural* **aides-de-camp**) an officer acting as a confidential assistant to a senior officer. [Say aid duh COMP]

AIDS *noun* (also **Aids**) acquired immune deficiency syndrome, a condition caused by a virus transmitted in the blood, marked by severe loss of resistance to infection and so ultimately fatal.

aikido *noun* a Japanese form of self-defence and martial art, developed from ju-jitsu and involving holds and throws. [Say eye KEE doe or EYE key doe]

ail *verb* trouble or afflict in mind or body: *exercise is good for what ails one*.

ailing *adjective* **1** ill, esp. chronically. **2** in poor condition: *the ailing economy*.

ailment *noun* an illness, esp. a minor one.

aim • *verb* **1** intend or try: *aim at winning ◊ aim to win*. **2** (usu. foll. by *at*) direct or point (a weapon, remark, etc.). **3** take aim. **4** (foll. by *at, for*) seek to attain or achieve. • *noun* **1** a purpose or intention, a desired outcome: *our aim is to reduce poverty*. **2** the directing of a weapon, thing thrown, etc., at an object. PHRASES **take aim** direct a weapon etc. at an object.

aimless *adjective* without direction or purpose: *led an aimless life*. ▶ **aimlessly** *adverb* **aimlessness** *noun*

WRITING TIP
ain't

Ain't is unacceptable in spoken and written English except in intentionally humorous and very informal contexts and phrases, such as *You ain't seen nothing yet!*

---

ain't *contraction non-standard* **1** am not; are not; is not. **2** has not; have not.

Ainu • *noun* (*plural* **Ainu** or **Ainus**) **1** a member of an aboriginal people of northern Japan, physically distinct (with light-coloured skin and round eyes) from the majority population. **2** the language of this people, which is no longer in everyday use. • *adjective* having to do with this people or their language. [Say EYE noo]

SPELL CHECK
air, err

To make a mistake is to **err**.

---

air • *noun* **1** an invisible gaseous substance, a mixture mainly of oxygen and nitrogen. **2 a** the earth's atmosphere. **b** the free or unconfined space in the atmosphere: *in the open air*. **c** the atmosphere as a place where aircraft operate or a medium for transmitting radio waves. **3 a** a distinctive impression or characteristic: *an air of absurdity*. **b** one's manner or bearing, esp. a confident one: *a triumphant air*. **c** (esp. in *plural*) an affected manner; pretentiousness: *gave himself airs*. **4** *Music* a tune or melody. **5** *informal* air conditioning. • *verb* **I** (usu. foll. by *out*) expose (a room etc.) to the open air; ventilate. **2** hang (washed laundry

etc.) to remove dampness. **3** express publicly (an opinion, grievance, etc.). **4** broadcast (a program). PHRASES **by air** by aircraft. **in the air** (of opinions or feelings) prevalent; gaining currency. **on** (or **off**) **the air** in (or not in) the process of broadcasting. **take the air** go out of doors. **up in the air 1** aloft. **2** uncertain, undetermined. **walk on air** feel elated.

air bag *noun* a device that fills with air on impact to protect a vehicle's occupants in a collision.

air ball *noun* *Basketball slang* a shot which results in the ball missing the basket and backboard entirely.

air bladder *noun* **1** a bladder or sac filled with air in fish or some plants (*compare* SWIM BLADDER). **2** any similar bladder or sac made of synthetic material.

airborne *adjective* **1** moving through or carried by the air: *airborne pollutants*. **2** (of aircraft) in the air; in flight. **3** (of military activity) involving paratroops.

air brake *noun* **1** a brake worked by air pressure. **2** a device on an aircraft to reduce its speed.

airbrush • *noun* (*plural* **airbrushes**) a device for spraying colour over a surface by means of compressed air, used by artists and to retouch photographs, esp. to conceal flaws. • *verb* (**airbrushes**, **airbrushed**, **airbrushing**) **1** paint with an airbrush. **2** represent or describe as better or more beautiful than in reality: *an airbrushed vision of the decade*.

air command *noun* **1** a major subdivision of an air force. **2** (**Air Command**) the official name for the Canadian air force.

air-conditioned *adjective* (of a room, building, etc.) equipped with air conditioning.

air conditioning *noun* **1** a system for lowering the temperature and humidity in a building or vehicle. **2** the apparatus for this. ▶ **air conditioner** *noun*

air-cool *verb* cool (an engine etc.) by means of a current of air. ▶ **air-cooled** *adjective*

aircraft *noun* (*plural* **aircraft**) a machine capable of flight, esp. an airplane or helicopter.

aircraft carrier *noun* a warship that carries and serves as a base for airplanes.

aircrew *noun* **1** the crew of an aircraft. **2** (*plural* **aircrew**) a member of such a crew.

airdrop • *verb* (**airdrops**, **airdropped**, **airdropping**) deliver (food, supplies, etc.) by parachute from an aircraft. • *noun* a delivery in this way.

Airedale *noun* a large breed of terrier with a rough coat. [Say AIR dale]

airfare *noun* the price paid by a passenger for transportation by air.

airfield *noun* an area of land where aircraft take off and land, are maintained, etc.

airflow *noun* a current of air, esp. that encountered by a moving aircraft or vehicle.

airfoil *noun* a structure with curved surfaces, e.g. a wing, fin, or tailplane, designed to give lift in flight.

air force *noun* the branch of a nation's armed forces concerned with fighting or defence in the air.

airframe *noun* the body of an aircraft as distinct from its engine(s).

airfreight • *noun* the transport of goods by air. • *verb* transport goods by air.

air gun *noun* a gun using compressed air to propel pellets etc.

airhead *noun* **1** a base for aircraft in enemy territory. **2** *slang* usu. *derogatory* a foolish person.

air hockey *noun* a game in which players use hand-held paddles to direct a plastic disc supported on a cushion of air over an oblong surface, often a large table, into the opponent's goal.

air horn *noun* a horn which produces sound by compressed air.

airily *adverb* in a way that shows a lack of concern: *"There's nothing wrong with him," she said airily.*

airiness *noun* the quality of a room etc. that is spacious and well ventilated.

airing *noun* **1** exposure to fresh air, esp. for exercise or an excursion. **2** exposure (of laundry etc.) to warm air. **3** public expression of an opinion etc.: *the issue deserves a thorough airing*. **4** the action of broadcasting: *the network made money on the first airing of the program*.

airless *adjective* **1** stuffy; not ventilated. **2** without wind or breeze; still. ▶ **airlessness** *noun*

airlift • *noun* the transport of troops and supplies by air. • *verb* transport in this way.

airline *noun* an organization providing a regular public service of air transport on one or more routes.

airliner *noun* a large passenger aircraft.

airlock *noun* **1** a stoppage of the flow in a pump or pipe, caused by an air bubble. **2** a compartment with controlled pressure and parallel sets of doors, to permit movement between areas at different pressures.

airmail • *noun* **1** a system of transporting mail by air. **2** mail carried by air. • *verb* send by airmail.

airman *noun* (*plural* **airmen**) **1** a pilot or member of the crew of an aircraft, esp. in an air force. **2** a member of an air force below commissioned rank.

air mass *noun* (*plural* **air masses**) a very large body of air with a roughly uniform temperature and humidity.

air mattress *noun* (*plural* **air mattresses**) an inflatable mattress for sleeping on or for floating on water.

airplane *noun* a powered heavier-than-air flying vehicle with fixed wings.

airplay *noun* broadcasting (of recorded music).

air pocket *noun* **1** an apparent vacuum in the air causing an aircraft to drop suddenly. **2** (in soil, a pipe, etc.) any bubble of air.

airport *noun* a complex of runways and buildings for the takeoff, landing, and maintenance of civil aircraft, with facilities for passengers.

air power *noun* the ability to defend and attack by means of aircraft, missiles, etc.

air quality index *noun* a numerical indicator of the concentration of pollutants in the air.

air raid *noun* an attack by military aircraft.

air rifle *noun* a rifle using compressed air to propel pellets etc.

airship *noun* a powered balloon that can be steered, esp. one having a rigid elongated structure.

airsick *adjective* affected with nausea due to travel in an aircraft. ▶ **airsickness** *noun*

airspace *noun* **1** the air available to aircraft to fly in, esp. the part subject to the jurisdiction of a particular country. **2** a space filled with (usu. trapped) air, as between two panes of glass etc. **3** *Law* the space above a piece of land or the buildings constructed on it, extending notionally indefinitely upwards.

airspeed *noun* the speed of an aircraft relative to the air through which it is moving (*compare* GROUNDSPEED).

airstream *noun* a current of air; an airflow.

airstrip *noun* a strip of ground suitable for the takeoff and landing of aircraft.

airtight *adjective* **1** not allowing air to pass through. **2** without weakness: *an airtight argument*.

air time *noun* **1** time allotted for a broadcast etc. **2** the starting time for a television or radio program.

air traffic control *noun* an airport department which gives radio instructions to pilots concerning

route, altitude, takeoff, and landing. ▶ **air traffic controller** *noun*

airwaves *plural noun* radio waves used in broadcasting.

airway *noun* **1 a** a recognized route followed by aircraft. **b** (often in *plural*) = AIRLINE. **2 a** the normal passage for air into the lungs. **b** a tubular device for assisting a patient's breathing.

airwoman *noun* (*plural* **airwomen**) a woman pilot or member of the crew of an aircraft, esp. in an air force.

airworthy *adjective* (of an aircraft) fit to fly.

airy *adjective* (**airier, airiest**) **1** (of a room or building) spacious, well lit, and well ventilated. **2** giving an impression of being unconcerned or not serious, typically about something taken seriously by others: *her airy unconcern for economy*. **3 a** delicate, as though filled with or made of air: *airy cream puffs*. **b** giving an impression of light gracefulness and elegance: *her airy presence filled the house*.

airy-fairy *adjective* *informal* impractical, foolishly idealistic: *love might seem an airy-fairy, romantic concept*.

aisle *noun* **1** a passage between rows of seats, rows of shelves in a supermarket, etc. **2** part of a church, esp. one parallel to and divided by pillars from the nave, choir, or transept. [Say ILE]

aitch *noun* the letter H: *drop one's aitches*.

Aivilik *noun* a branch of the Iglulik Inuit of Canada's Arctic. [Say EYE vuh lick]

ajar *adverb & adjective* (of a door) slightly open.

AK-47 *noun* (*plural* **AK-47s**) a Soviet-designed assault rifle, widely used by Communist and guerrilla armies.

a.k.a. *abbreviation* also known as.

akee *noun* = ACKEE. [Say ACKY]

akimbo *adverb* (of the arms) with hands on the hips and elbows turned outwards. [Say a KIM bo]

akin *adjective* of similar character: *something akin to gratitude swept over her*.

Al *symbol* the element aluminum.

Alabaman • *adjective* of or relating to the US state of Alabama. • *noun* a resident or native of Alabama.

alabaster • *noun* a translucent usu. white form of gypsum, often carved into ornaments. • *adjective* **1** of alabaster: *an alabaster vase*. **2** like alabaster in whiteness or smoothness: *her alabaster cheeks flushed with warmth*. [Say ALLA bas ter]

à la carte *adverb & adjective* ordered as separately priced item(s) from a menu, not as part of a set meal. [Say alla CART]

alacrity *noun* speed or willingness: *she accepted his dinner invitation with alacrity*. [Say a LACK ruh tee]

à la mode *adjective* **1** in fashion; fashionable. **2 a** (of desserts) served with ice cream. **b** (of beef) braised in wine and served with vegetables.

alarm • *noun* **1** a warning of danger etc.: *gave the alarm.* **2 a** a sound or device to warn, alert, or signal: *a burglar alarm.* **b** a buzzer etc. on a clock or watch. **c** (also **alarm clock**) a clock with a device that can be made to sound at a certain time, usu. to rouse a person from sleep. **3** frightened expectation of danger or difficulty: *filled with alarm*. • *verb* **1** frighten or disturb. **2** arouse to a sense of danger.

alarming *adjective* frightening. ▶ **alarmingly** *adverb*

alarmism *noun* a tendency to spread unnecessary fear or anxiety.

alarmist • *noun* a person who is considered to be exaggerating a danger and thus causing needless worry or panic. • *adjective* creating needless worry or panic: *alarmist claims about a supposed increase in crime*.

alas *interjection* an expression of regret, sorrow, etc.: *alas, I don't have enough money to go to Europe every month*.

Alaskan • *adjective* of or relating to the US state of Alaska. • *noun* a resident or native of Alaska.

alb *noun* a white vestment reaching to the feet, worn by some Christian clergy.

albacore *noun* **1** a long-finned tuna, *Thunnus alalunga*. **2** any of various other related fish. [Say ALBA core]

Albanian • *noun* **1 a** a native or national of Albania, a republic in SE Europe. **b** a person of Albanian descent. **2** the language of Albania. • *adjective* of or relating to Albania, its people, or its language. [Say al BAINY un]

albatross *noun* (*plural* **albatrosses**) **1** any of several large, long-winged, stout-bodied birds which come ashore only to nest. **2** a source of frustration, difficulty, or guilt that is almost impossible to get rid of: *the national debt is an albatross around the prime minister's neck* ◊ *the party was burdened with the albatross of their original manifesto*. [Say ALBA tross]

albedo *noun* (*plural* **albedos**) the proportion of light or radiation that is reflected by a surface, esp. that of a planet or the moon. [Say al BEE doe]

albeit *conjunction* though: *an improvement, albeit a modest one*. [Say all BE it]

Albertan • *adjective* of or relating to Alberta. • *noun* a resident or native of Alberta.

albino *noun* (*plural* **albinos**) **1** a person or animal born without pigment in the skin and hair (which are white), and the eyes (which are usu. pink). **2** a plant lacking normal colouring. [Say al BINE oh]

album *noun* **1** a blank book for keeping photographs, stamps, etc. in. **2 a** a disc or tape comprising several pieces of music. **b** an integral set of discs or tapes.

albumen *noun* **1** egg white. **2** = ENDOSPERM. [Say al BYOO m'n]

albumin *noun* any of a class of water-soluble proteins found in egg white, milk, blood, etc. [Say al BYOO m'n]

alchemical *adjective* involving, based on, or having to do with alchemy: *alchemical techniques*. [Say al KEM ick ul]

alchemist *noun* a person who studies alchemy. [Say ALKA mist]

alchemy *noun* (*plural* **alchemies**) **1** the medieval forerunner of chemistry, esp. seeking to turn base metals into gold or silver. **2** a process by which paradoxical results are achieved or incompatible elements combined with no obvious rational explanation: *the alchemy of policy-making*. [Say ALKA mee]

alcohol *noun* **1** (also **ethyl alcohol**) a colourless volatile inflammable liquid forming the intoxicating element in spirits etc., also used as a solvent, fuel, etc. **2** any liquor containing this. **3** any of a large class of organic compounds that contain one or more hydroxyl groups attached to carbon atoms.

alcoholic • *adjective* of, containing, or caused by alcohol. • *noun* a person suffering from alcoholism.

Alcoholics Anonymous an organization of alcoholics who attempt to overcome their addiction by counselling and mutual support. Abbreviation: **AA**.

alcoholism *noun* an addiction to the consumption of alcoholic liquor.

alcove *noun* **1** a recess, esp. in the wall of a room: *a dining alcove*. **2** an arbour or shady bower.

aldehyde *noun* any of a class of compounds formed by the oxidation of alcohols. [Say ALDA hide]

al dente *adjective* (of pasta etc.) cooked so as to be still firm when bitten. [Say al DEN tay]

alder *noun* any tree or shrub of the genus *Alnus*, related to the birch, with catkins and toothed leaves.

alderfly *noun* (*plural* **alderflies**) an insect of the genus *Sialis*, found near streams.

alderman *noun* (*plural* **aldermen**) a city councillor. ▶ **aldermanic** *adjective*

alderperson *noun* an alderman or alderwoman.

alderwoman *noun* (*plural* **alderwomen**) a female city councillor.

> **SPELL CHECK** 🗹 ABC
> **ale, ail**
>
> To suffer or be sick is to **ail**.

ale *noun* a beer fermented rapidly at high temperatures.

alert • *adjective* **1** quick to notice any unusual and potentially dangerous or difficult circumstances; vigilant: *an alert police officer discovered a truck full of explosives* ◊ *schools need to be constantly alert to this problem*. **2** able to think clearly; intellectually active: *wasn't feeling very alert at four in the morning*. • *noun* **1** a call or alarm warning of an attack, storm, etc. **2** a period of vigilance in response to such a warning. • *verb* warn someone of a danger, threat, or problem, in the hope that it will be dealt with: *were alerted to the danger* ◊ *alerted the police after the bomb threat*. PHRASES **on** (**the**) **alert** on the lookout against danger or attack. ▶ **alertly** *adverb* **alertness** *noun*

Aleut *noun* (*plural* **Aleut** or **Aleuts**) a member of an Aboriginal people living in the Aleutian Islands and southwestern Alaska. **2** the language of the Aleut. ▶ **Aleutian** *adjective & noun* [Say AL yoot or a LOOT, a LOO sh'n]

alevin *noun* a very young fish, esp. a salmon or trout. [Say ALLA vin]

alewife *noun* (*plural* **alewives**) **1** a fish of the herring family found off the Atlantic coast of North America and in the Great Lakes. **2** any of several related fish.

alfalfa *noun* a leguminous plant with clover-like leaves and flowers, used for fodder.

alfalfa sprouts *plural noun* fine young sprouts of alfalfa, eaten as a salad vegetable or garnish.

alfredo *adjective* (often placed after noun) designating a sauce for pasta made of butter, cream, and Parmesan cheese: *fettuccine alfredo*. [Say al FRAY doe]

alfresco *adverb & adjective* in the open air. [Say al FRESS co]

alga *noun* (*plural* **algae**) (usu. in *plural*) **1** a simple, non-flowering, and typically aquatic plant of a large assemblage that includes the seaweeds and many single-celled forms. Algae contain chlorophyll but lack true stems, roots, leaves, and vascular tissue. **2** (also **blue-green algae**) = CYANOBACTERIA. ▶ **algal** *adjective* [Say AL guh for the singular, AL jee for the plural]

algebra *noun* **1** the branch of mathematics that uses letters and other general symbols to represent numbers and quantities in formulas and equations. **2** a system of this based on given axioms: *linear algebra*.

algebraic *adjective* involving or having to do with algebra. ▶ **algebraically** *adverb* [Say alja BRAY ick]

algicide *noun* a substance that destroys algae. [Say ALJA side]

Algonquian (also **Algonkian**) • *noun* **1** the largest Aboriginal language group in Canada, including Abenaki, Algonquin, Blackfoot, Cree, Maliseet, Mi'kmaq, and Ojibwa. **2** (*plural* **Algonquian** or **Algonquians**) a member of any of the Aboriginal peoples speaking languages of this family, living in the Maritimes, Quebec, Ontario, the Prairies, and the east coast of the US. • *adjective* of the Algonquian peoples or languages. [Say al GON kwee in or al GON kee in]

> **WRITING TIP**
> **Algonquin, Algonquian**
>
> The use of **Algonquin** to refer to the **Algonquian** peoples or their language is widespread but incorrect.

Algonquin • *noun* **1** (also **Algonkin**) (*plural* **Algonquin** or **Algonquins**) a member of an Aboriginal people living along the Ottawa River and its tributaries. **2** (also **Algonkin**) the dialect of Algonquian spoken by the Algonquin. **3** a type of snowshoe with an upturned front and long tapering tail. • *adjective* of the Algonquin or their language. [Say al GON kwin or al GON kin]

algorithm *noun* a process or set of rules used for calculation or problem-solving, esp. with a computer. ▶**algorithmic** *adjective* [Say ALGA rhythm, alga RHYTHMIC]

alias • *adverb* also named or known as. • *noun* (*plural* **aliases**) **1** a false or assumed name. **2** *Computing* a command or address which substitutes for another, more complicated one. • *verb* (**aliases**, **aliased**, **aliasing**) *Computing* assign or use an alias. [Say AILY us]

aliasing *noun* the misidentification of a signal frequency, introducing distortion or error, esp. in a computer image. [Say AILY us ing]

alibi *noun* (*plural* **alibis**) **1** a claim, or the evidence supporting it, that when an alleged act took place one was elsewhere: *she can't have done it, since she has an alibi for all of yesterday evening*. **2** an excuse of any kind; a pretext or justification: *a catch-all alibi for failure and inadequacy*. [Say ALA bye]

alien • *adjective* **1** (often foll. by *to*) unfamiliar; not in accordance or harmony; unacceptable or repugnant: *army discipline was alien to him*. **2** foreign: *alien powers*. **3** of or relating to beings supposedly from other worlds. **4** (of a plant) introduced from elsewhere and naturalized in its new home. • *noun* **1** a person who is not a naturalized citizen of the country where he or she is living. **2** a being from another world. **3** an alien plant.

alienate *verb* (**alienates**, **alienated**, **alienating**) **1 a** cause to become unfriendly or hostile: *the association does not wish to alienate its members*. **b** cause to feel isolated or estranged from (friends, society, etc.): *an urban environment which would alienate its inhabitants*. **2** *Law* transfer ownership of (property) to another person etc.

alienated *adjective* **1** withdrawn in feeling or affection, isolated: *an alienated angst-ridden twenty-year-old*. **2** *Law* transferred to other ownership.

alienation *noun* **1** the state or experience of being isolated from a group or an activity to which one should belong or in which one should be involved: *unemployment may generate a sense of political alienation*. **2** *Psychology* a state of depersonalization or loss of identity in which the self seems unreal, thought to be caused by difficulties in relating to society and the resulting prolonged inhibition of emotion.

alight¹ *verb* (**alights**, **alighted**, **alighting**) **1 a** (often foll. by *from*) descend from a vehicle. **b** dismount from a horse. **2** come to rest or settle; descend to earth from the air. **3** (foll. by *on*) find by chance; notice: *eventually, we alighted on the idea of seeking sponsors* ◊ *her eyes alighted on the item in question*.

alight² *adjective* **1** on fire; burning. **2** lighted up; excited: *eyes alight with expectation*.

align *verb* **1** put in a straight line or bring into line: *the wheels need aligning* ◊ *make sure the shelf is aligned with the top of the cupboard*. **2 align oneself with** give support

to a cause, policy, party, etc.: *by aligning themselves with corporate interests, they could achieve power*. **3** change something slightly so that is in the correct relationship to something else: *domestic prices have been aligned with those in world markets*. ▶**alignment** *noun* [Say a LINE]

alike • *adverb* in a similar way or manner; equally: *all were treated alike*. • *adjective* similar, like one another; indistinguishable: *no two snowflakes are alike*.

alimentary canal *noun* the passage along which food passes from the mouth to the anus. [Say ala MENTA ree]

alimony *noun* money paid to a spouse or former spouse after separation or divorce.

A-line *adjective* (of a garment) having a fitted waist or shoulders and somewhat flared skirt.

aliphatic *adjective* of, denoting, or relating to organic compounds in which carbon atoms form open chains, not aromatic rings. [Say ala FAT ick]

A-list *noun* a list of people or items of the highest importance.

alive *adjective* **1** living, not dead. **2 a** (of a thing) existing; continuing; in operation or action: *kept his interest alive*. **b** under discussion; provoking interest: *the topic is still very much alive*. **3** (of a person or animal) lively, active. **4** charged with an electric current; connected to a source of electricity. **5** aware of; alert or responsive to: *always alive to new ideas*. **6** swarming or teeming with: *in spring those cliffs are alive with auks and gulls*. PHRASES **alive and kicking** *informal* very active; lively. **alive and well** still alive or active (esp. despite contrary assumptions or rumours).

aliyah *noun* the migration of Jews to Israel. [Say olly AW]

alkali *noun* (*plural* **alkalis**) **1 a** any of a class of bases that liberate hydroxide ions in water, usu. form caustic or corrosive solutions, and have a pH of more than 7. **b** any other substance with similar but weaker properties, e.g. sodium carbonate. **2** a soluble salt or mixture of salts existing in excess in soil and damaging crops. [Say ALKA lie]

alkaline *adjective* **1** of, relating to, or having the nature of an alkali; rich in alkali. **2** *Chemistry* having a pH above 7; basic. [Say ALKA line]

alkaline battery *noun* (*plural* **alkaline batteries**) a dry cell with an alkaline electrolyte of potassium hydroxide, with more power and durability than conventional batteries.

alkalinity *noun* the quality of being alkaline: *the alkalinity of the soil*. [Say alka LINNA tee]

alkaloid *noun* any of a series of nitrogenous organic compounds of plant origin, many of which are used as drugs, e.g. morphine, quinine, nicotine. [Say ALKA loyd]

alkane *noun* any of a series of saturated aliphatic hydrocarbons, including methane, ethane, and propane. [Say AL cane]

alkyd *noun* any of the group of synthetic resins derived from various alcohols and acids, commonly used in paints etc. [Say AL kid]

alkyl *noun* (also **alkyl radical**) any radical derived from an alkane by the removal of a hydrogen atom. [Say AL kill]

> **WRITING TIP**
> **all (of)**
>
> All of the following are correct: *all of* the bread, *all* the bread; *all of* our members, *all* our members.

all • *adjective* **1 a** the whole amount, quantity, or extent of. **b** (with *plural*) the entire number of. **2** any whatever: *beyond all doubt*. **3** greatest possible: *with all speed*. • *noun* **1 a** all the persons or things concerned. **b** everything: *that is all*. **2** (foll. by *of*) **a** the whole of.

A

b every one of. **c** as much as: *all of three feet tall*. **d** *informal* affected by; in a state of: *all of a dither*. **3** one's whole strength or resources: *gave her all.* ● *adverb* **1 a** entirely: *dressed all in black* ◊ *all round the room*. **b** as an intensifier: *stop all this grumbling*. **2** *informal* very: *went all shy*. **3** to that extent: *if they go, all the better*. **4** (in games) on both sides: *two all*. ⸢PHRASES⸣ **all along** all the time: *he knew about it all along*. **all but** very nearly: *all but drowned*. **all for** strongly in favour of. **as all get-out** *informal* to a high degree: *stubborn as all get-out*. **all in all** everything considered. **all one** (or **the same**) a matter of indifference: *it's all the same to me*. **all over 1** finished. **2** in or on all parts of (esp. the body). **3** *informal* typically: *that is you all over*. **4** *slang* effusively attentive to (a person). **all the same** nevertheless, in spite of this. **all set** *informal* ready to start. **all that** *informal* particularly; very: *wasn't all that difficult*. **all there** *informal* mentally alert. **all together** all at once; all in one place or in a group: *they came all together* (compare ALTOGETHER). **all very well** an expression used to reject or to imply skepticism about a favourable or consoling remark. **at all** in any way; to any extent: *did not swim at all*. **in all** altogether. **one and all** everyone.

Allah *noun* the name of the Supreme Being in Islam. [Say ALA or OLLA]

all-American ● *adjective* **1** (esp. of an athlete) chosen as one of the best in, or representing the whole of, the US. **2** truly, typically, or exclusively American. ● *noun* an all-American athlete.

all around ● *adjective* **1** (of a person) versatile. **2** comprehensive, affecting everything or everyone. ● *adverb* **1** for each person: *bought drinks all around*. **2** in all respects: *a good performance all around*.

allay *verb* (**allays, allayed, allaying**) **1** diminish (fear, suspicion, etc.): *the report attempts to educate the public and allay fears*. **2** relieve or alleviate (pain, hunger, etc.): *a bowl of cereal partly allayed our hunger*. [Say a LAY]

all-Canadian ● *adjective* **1** (esp. of an athlete) chosen as one of the best in, or representing the whole of, Canada. **2** truly, typically, or exclusively Canadian. ● *noun* an all-Canadian athlete.

all-candidates meeting *noun Cdn* a public meeting held during an election campaign at which all the candidates for an electoral district present their platforms and answer questions from the audience.

all-clear *noun* a signal that danger or difficulty is over.

all-dressed *adjective Cdn* designating an item of food served with all the optional garnishes.

allegation *noun* an assertion or accusation of wrongdoing, esp. an unproven one: *she made allegations of corruption against the administration* ◊ *years of rumour and allegation*. [Say ala GAY sh'n]

allege *verb* (**alleges, alleged, alleging**) declare to be the case, esp. without proof: *the prosecution alleges that she was driving carelessly* ◊ *he is alleged to have mistreated the prisoners*. ▶ **alleged** *adjective* [Say a LEDGE]

allegedly *adverb* as is said to be the case: *crimes allegedly committed during the war*. [Say a LEDGE id lee]

allegiance *noun* **1** loyalty (to a person or cause etc.). **2** the duty of a subject to his or her sovereign or government. [Say a LEE jince]

allegorical *adjective* (also **allegoric**) consisting of or relating to allegory. ▶ **allegorically** *adverb* [Say ala GORE ick ul]

allegorize *verb* (**allegorizes, allegorized, allegorizing**) treat as or by means of an allegory. [Say ALA guh rize]

allegory *noun* (*plural* **allegories**) **1** a story, play, poem, picture, etc., in which each character or event is a symbol representing an idea or a quality, such as truth, evil, death, etc. **2** the use of such symbols. [Say ALA gory]

allegretto *Music* ● *adverb & adjective* in a fairly brisk tempo. ● *noun* (*plural* **allegrettos**) an allegretto passage or movement. [Say ala GRETTO]

allegro *Music* ● *adverb & adjective* in a brisk tempo. ● *noun* (*plural* **allegros**) an allegro passage or movement. [Say a LEG roe]

allele *noun* one of the (usu. two) alternative forms of a gene that occupy the same relative position on a chromosome. ▶ **allelic** *adjective* [Say AL eel, a LEE lick]

alleluia ● *interjection* God be praised (uttered in worship or as an expression of rejoicing). ● *noun* (*plural* **alleluias**) **1** an utterance of the word "alleluia". **2** a piece of music or church liturgy including this. [Say ala LOU yuh or ollay LOU yuh]

all-embracing *adjective* including everything: *an all-embracing theory*.

Allen key *noun* (also **Allen wrench**) an L-shaped tool designed to fit into and turn an Allen screw.

Allen screw *noun* a screw with a hexagonal socket in the head.

allergen *noun* any substance that causes an allergic reaction. ▶ **allergenic** *adjective* [Say ALLER jun, aller JEN ick]

allergic *adjective* **1 a** having an allergy to: *is allergic to nuts*. **b** *informal* having a strong dislike for (a person or thing): *I'm definitely allergic to housework*. **2** caused by or relating to an allergy: *an allergic reaction to penicillin*.

allergist *noun* a physician who specializes in the treatment of allergies. [Say ALLER jist]

allergy *noun* (*plural* **allergies**) **1** a condition of reacting adversely to certain substances, esp. particular foods, pollen, fur, or dust. **2** *informal* a strong dislike.

alleviate *verb* (**alleviates, alleviated, alleviating**) lessen or make less severe (pain, suffering, a problem, etc.): *measures to alleviate unemployment*. ▶ **alleviation** *noun* [Say a LEEVY ate, a leevy AY sh'n]

alley *noun* (*plural* **alleys**) **1 a** a narrow street. **b** a narrow passageway or lane, esp. between or behind buildings. **2** a path or walk in a park or garden. **3** = BOWLING ALLEY. **4** *Baseball* the area between the outfielders in left-centre or right-centre field. **5** *Tennis* either of the two side strips of a doubles court. **6** (usu. **Alley**) an area known for a specified characteristic, esp. a street or lane with a concentration of similar businesses etc.: *Gourmet Alley*. ⸢PHRASES⸣ **up one's alley** *informal* suited to one's tastes, interests, or abilities.

alley cat *noun* a stray cat in an urban area, often mangy or half wild.

alley-oop ● *interjection* encouraging or drawing attention to the performance of some physical, esp. acrobatic, feat. ● *noun* *Basketball* **1** a high lob or pass caught by a leaping teammate. **2** a basket scored by the receiver of such a pass.

alleyway *noun* = ALLEY 1.

All Hallows *noun* = ALL SAINTS' DAY.

alliak *noun* = KOMATIK. [Say ALLEY ack]

alliance *noun* **1** a formal union or agreement to co-operate, esp. among nations with a specific goal. **b** a formal grouping of persons having a common aim. **c** the parties involved. **2** union through marriage. **3** a relationship resulting from an affinity in nature or qualities etc.: *the alliance between Church and State*. **4** (**Alliance**; in full **Christian and Missionary Alliance**) an evangelical Protestant movement founded in New York in the late 19th century.

allied *adjective* **1 a** united or associated in an alliance. **b** (**Allied**) of or relating to the Allies. **2** connected or related: *studied medicine and allied subjects*. [Say AL ide]

Allies *plural noun* **1** the nations allied against the Central Powers in the First World War, primarily the British Empire, France, and the Russian Empire, and

later the US. **2** the nations allied against the Axis powers in the Second World War, primarily the United Kingdom and the Commonwealth, France, and later the Soviet Union, the US, and China.

alligator *noun* **1** a large reptile of South America, China, and the southeastern US, with upper teeth that lie outside the lower teeth and a head broader and shorter than that of the crocodile. **2** any of several large members of the crocodile family. **3** the skin of such an animal or material resembling it.

all-important *adjective* crucial; vitally important.

all-inclusive *adjective* including all or everything.

all-in-one • *adjective* comprising all the necessary features in one indivisible unit. • *noun* a garment combining parts usually worn separately.

alliteration *noun* the occurrence of the same letter or sound at the beginning of adjacent or closely connected words (e.g. *cool*, *calm*, *and collected*). [Say a litter AY sh'n]

alliterative *adjective* having the same letter or sound at the beginning of adjacent or closely connected words: *"sing a song of sixpence" is alliterative*. [Say a LITTER a tiv]

allium *noun* any plant of the genus *Allium*, e.g. onion and garlic. [Say ALLEY um]

all-nighter *noun* *informal* an event or task that continues throughout the night, esp. a study session before an examination.

allocate *verb* (**allocates**, **allocated**, **allocating**) assign, designate, or set aside for a specific purpose.
▶ **allocation** *noun* **allocator** *noun*

allophone *Cdn* (in Quebec) • *noun* an immigrant whose first language is neither French nor English. • *adjective* having a first language other than French, English, or an Aboriginal language. [Say ALA phone]

SPELL CHECK
allot, a lot   ABC✓

A large amount is **a lot**.

---

allot *verb* (**allots**, **allotted**, **allotting**) give or apportion something to someone: *I completed the test in the time allotted* ◊ *how much money has been allotted to us?*

allotment *noun* **1** the action of allotting. **2** a portion allotted. **3** a small piece of land.

all-out • *adjective* total; unrestrained: *all-out war*. • *adverb* (**all out**) with all one's strength; at full speed: *going all out*.

allow *verb* **1** permit (a practice, a person to do something, a thing to happen, etc.). **2** give or provide; permit (a person) to have (a limited quantity or sum). **3** provide or set aside for a purpose; add or deduct in consideration of something: *allow 10% for inflation*. **4 a** admit, agree, concede: *he allowed that it was so*. **b** *informal* state the opinion that. **5 allow oneself** permit oneself, indulge oneself in (conduct): *allowed herself to be persuaded*. **6** (foll. by *for*) take into consideration or account: *allowing for wastage*.
▶ **allowable** *adjective*

allowance *noun* **1 a** an amount or sum given to a person, esp. regularly for a stated purpose. **b** an amount of money given regularly to a child. **2** an amount allowed in reckoning. **3** a deduction or discount: *an allowance for your trade-in*. **4** (foll. by *of*) tolerance of. **5** a portion of something, e.g. land or fabric, allowed for a specified purpose: *road allowance*.
PHRASES **make allowances** **1** take into consideration (mitigating circumstances). **2** look with tolerance upon, make excuses for (a person, bad behaviour, etc.).

alloy • *noun* a metallic substance made by combining

two or more elements at least one of which is a metal, e.g. brass (a mixture of copper and zinc). • *verb* mix (metals). [Say AL oy for the noun, a LOY for the verb]

WRITING TIP
all-points bulletin   ✎

Canadian police forces use the term **general alert** instead of **all-points bulletin**.

---

all-points bulletin *noun* *US* a generally issued alert among police officers, esp. calling for the apprehension of a wanted person. Abbreviation: **APB**.

all-purpose *adjective* suitable for many uses.

all right • *adverb* **1** satisfactorily: *it worked out all right*. **2** as an intensifier: *that's the one all right*. • *adjective* satisfactory; safe and sound. • *interjection* expressing consent or assent to a proposal or order.

All Saints' Day *noun* a Christian festival in honour of the souls in heaven, celebrated on 1 Nov. in Western Churches and on the first Sunday after Pentecost in Eastern Churches.

allsorts *plural noun* an assortment, esp. of licorice candies.

All Souls' Day *noun* 2 Nov., a Catholic holy day with prayers for the souls of the dead in purgatory.

allspice *noun* **1** the aromatic spice obtained from the ground berry of the pimento tree. **2** the berry of this tree. **3** any of various other aromatic shrubs.

all-star • *noun* **1** *Sport* a player chosen as among the finest in his or her league. **2** a superstar. • *adjective* relating to or consisting of all-stars: *an all-star cast*.

all-terrain vehicle *noun* **1** a tank-like military vehicle with treads used to travel over rough terrain. **2** a rugged one-person vehicle with three or four wheels, designed for travel both on and off roads.

all-time *adjective* (of a record etc.) unsurpassed.

all told *adverb* in all; when everything is considered.

allude *verb* (**alludes**, **alluded**, **alluding**) (foll. by *to*) **1** suggest or call attention to indirectly; hint at: *she had a way of alluding to Jean but never saying her name*. **2** mention without discussing at length: *we will allude briefly to the main points*. **3** (of an artist or a work of art) recall (an earlier work or style) in such a way as to suggest a relationship with it: *the photographs allude to Italian Baroque painting*.

allure *noun* attractiveness, personal charm, fascination. ▶ **allurement** *noun*

alluring *adjective* attractive and exciting; fascinating.
▶ **alluringly** *adverb*

SPELL CHECK
allusion, illusion   ABC✓

A false impression or a picture that deceives one's eyes is an **illusion**.

---

allusion *noun* an expression designed to call something to mind without mentioning it explicitly: *an allusion to Shakespeare* ◊ *a classical allusion* ◊ *in the story, the cock crowing three times is an allusion to the Bible story where Peter denies he knows Jesus*.

allusive *adjective* working by, containing, or employing suggestion rather than explicitly mention: *Canadians have shown an inherent attraction to historically allusive "northern" architecture*. ▶ **allusiveness** *noun*

alluvial *adjective* of or relating to alluvium: *rich alluvial soils*. [Say a LOOVY ul]

alluvial fan *noun* a fan-shaped sedimentary deposit formed when a mountain river enters a large valley or plain.

alluvium *noun* (*plural* **alluvia** or **alluviums**) a deposit

of usu. fine fertile soil left during a time of flood, esp. in a river valley or delta. [Say a LOOVY um]

all-weather *adjective* suitable for use whatever the weather.

all-wheel drive *noun* = FOUR-WHEEL DRIVE.

ally • *noun* (*plural* **allies**) **1** a state formally co-operating or united with another for a special purpose, esp. by a treaty. **2** a person or organization that co-operates with or helps another. • *verb* (**allies, allied, allying**) **1** combine or unite a resource or commodity with another for mutual benefit: *he allied his racing experience with his father's business acumen*. **2 ally oneself with** side with or support someone or something: *she allied herself with the forces of change*. [Say AL eye for the noun, AL eye or a LIE for the verb]

alma mater *noun* the university, school, or college which one attended. [Say awl ma MOTTER or al ma MATTER]

almanac *noun* **1** an annual calendar of months and days, usu. with astronomical data and other information. **2** an annual book of general esp. statistical information.

almighty • *adjective* **1** having complete power. **2** (**the Almighty**) God. **3** *informal* very great: *an almighty crash*.

almond *noun* **1** the oval nut-like seed (kernel) of the fruit from the tree *Prunus dulcis*. **2** the tree itself. **3** a very pale beige colour.

almond paste *noun* = MARZIPAN.

almost *adverb* all but; very nearly.

alms *plural noun* charitable donations of money or food given to the poor. [Say OMZ]

almsgiving *noun* the giving of money to the poor as a charitable donation. [Say OMZ giving]

aloe *noun* **1** any plant of the genus *Aloe*, including succulent herbs, shrubs, and trees. **2** (in *plural*) (also **bitter aloes**) a strong laxative obtained from the bitter juice of various species of aloe. **3** (also **American aloe**) = CENTURY PLANT. [Say AL oh]

aloe vera *noun* a plant yielding a juice used in cosmetics and as a treatment for burns. [Say al oh VERRA]

aloft *adjective & adverb* **1** in the air. **2** upwards.

aloha *interjection* (in Hawaii and the S Pacific) a greeting or farewell; hello or goodbye. [Say a LO haw]

alone • *adjective* **1 a** without others present. **b** without others' help. **c** lonely and isolated: *felt alone*. **2** (often foll. by *in*) standing by oneself in an opinion etc.: *was alone in thinking this*. • *adverb* only, exclusively: *you alone can help me*. PHRASES **go it alone** act by oneself without assistance. ▶ **aloneness** *noun*

along • *preposition* **1** from one end to the other end of. **2** on or through any part of the length of. **3** beside or through the length of. **4** during the course of. • *adverb* **1** onward; into a more advanced state: *getting along nicely*. **2** at or to a particular place; arriving: *I'll be along soon*. **3** in company with a person, esp. oneself: *bring a book along*. **4** beside or through part or the whole length of a thing. PHRASES **along with** in addition to; together with.

alongside • *adverb* (sometimes foll. by *of*) at or to the side. • *preposition* **1** close to the side of; next to. **2** in close association with.

aloof *adjective* **1** not friendly or forthcoming; cool and distant: *they were courteous but faintly aloof*. **2** conspicuously uninvolved and uninterested; *typically through distance she stayed aloof from the bickering*. ▶ **aloofly** *adverb* **aloofness** *noun*

aloud *adverb* audibly; not silently or in a whisper.

alpaca *noun* **1** a South American mammal related to the llama, with long shaggy hair. **2** the wool from this animal. **3** fabric made from the wool, with or without other fibres. [Say al PACKA]

alpha *noun* **1** the first letter of the Greek alphabet (A, α). **2** (as an *adjective*) designating the first of a series or set. **3** *Astronomy* the chief star in a constellation. PHRASES **alpha and omega** the beginning and end.

alphabet *noun* the set of letters used in writing a language.

alphabetical *adjective* (also **alphabetic**) **1** of or relating to an alphabet. **2** in the order of the letters of the alphabet. ▶ **alphabetically** *adverb*

alphabetization *noun* the arrangement of a list of words in alphabetical order.

alphabetize *verb* (**alphabetizes, alphabetized, alphabetizing**) arrange (words, names, etc.) in alphabetical order.

alphabet soup *noun* **1** a soup with letter-shaped pieces of pasta. **2** a jumble of words or letters.

alpha-hydroxy acid *noun* any of a class of aliphatic carboxylic acids containing a hydroxyl group, some of which are used in cosmetics for their exfoliating properties. Abbreviation: **AHA**. [Say alfa hy DROXY]

alphanumeric *adjective* (also **alphanumerical**) containing both alphabetical and numerical symbols. [Say alfa new MARE ick]

alpha test • *noun* a preliminary test of computer software etc., usually carried out within the organization developing it (*compare* BETA TEST). • *verb* submit (a product) to an alpha test.

alpine • *adjective* **1 a** of or relating to high mountains. **b** growing or found on high mountains, esp. above the timberline. **2** (**Alpine**) of or relating to the Alps. **3** of or relating to competitive downhill or slalom skiing (*compare* NORDIC *adjective* 3). • *noun* a plant native or suited to mountain districts.

alpine fir *noun* a tall slender fir tree growing at high altitudes in northwestern North America.

already *adverb* **1** before the time in question. **2** as early or as soon as this: *already, at the age of six, he could play the piano*. **3** used as an intensifier to express impatience etc.: *tell the story already!*

alright *disputed* = ALL RIGHT.

ALS *abbreviation* AMYOTROPHIC LATERAL SCLEROSIS.

Alsatian • *adjective* of or relating to Alsace, a region of northeastern France on the border with Germany. • *noun* **1** a native or resident of Alsace. **2** a German dialect spoken in Alsace. [Say al SAY sh'n]

also *adverb* in addition; likewise; besides.

also-ran *noun* **1** a contestant not among the winners in a race, election, etc. **2** an undistinguished person.

Alt *noun* a key on a computer keyboard which alters the function of another key pressed simultaneously.

Alta. *abbreviation* Alberta.

Altaic • *noun* a family of languages including Turkic and Mongolian. • *adjective* denoting or pertaining to this family of languages or its speakers. [Say al TAY ick]

altar *noun* **1** a table or flat-topped block, often of stone, for sacrifice or offering to a deity. **2** *Christianity* a table on which bread and wine are consecrated in the Communion service. **3** *Christianity* the raised area in a church on which the altar, lecterns, pulpit, etc. are found. PHRASES **lead to the altar** marry.

altar boy *noun* a boy who serves as a priest's assistant in a service.

altar call *noun* (esp. in pentecostal Christian worship) an invitation to members of a congregation to gather at the front of the sanctuary, esp. to make a public confession of faith or to request special prayers etc.

altar girl *noun* a girl who serves as a priest's assistant in a service.

aitarpiece *noun* a piece of art, esp. a painting, set above or behind an altar.

altar server *noun* a child or adult who serves as a priest's assistant in a service.

> **SPELL CHECK**   ABC
> **alter, altar**
>
> A table at the front of a church is an **altar**.

alter *verb* **1** make or become different; change. **2** modify the style or size of (clothing). **3** castrate or spay. ▶ **aiterable** *adjective* **alteration** *noun*

altercation *noun* a heated argument or dispute.

alter ego *noun* (*plural* **alter egos**) **1** an intimate and trusted friend. **2** a person's secondary personality.

alternate • *verb* (**alternates**, **alternated**, **alternating**) **1** (often foll. by *with*) (of two things) succeed each other by turns. **2** (foll. by *between*) change repeatedly (between two conditions). **3** (often foll. by *with*) cause (two things) to succeed each other by turns: *we alternated criticism with reassurance*. • *adjective* **1** (with noun in *plural*) every other: *comes on alternate days*. **2** (of things of two kinds) each following and succeeded by one of the other kind: *alternate joy and misery*. **3** (of a sequence etc.) consisting of alternate things. **4** *Botany* (of leaves etc.) placed alternately on the two sides of the stem. **5** = ALTERNATIVE *adjective*. • *noun* a person or thing that substitutes for another.

alternate angles *plural noun* two angles, not adjoining one another, that are formed on opposite sides of a line that intersects two other lines.

alternately *adverb* in alternating order; one after the other in turns: *Gary alternately amused and annoyed his companions ◊ Sonja felt alternately hot and cold with anxiety*.

alternating current *noun* an electric current that reverses its direction at regular intervals (*compare* DIRECT CURRENT). Abbreviation: **AC**.

alternation *noun* the action or result of alternating.

alternative • *adjective* **1** (of one or more things) available or usable instead of another: *an alternative route*. **2** (of two things) mutually exclusive. **3** of or relating to practices that offer a substitute for the conventional ones: *alternative medicine*. • *noun* **1** any of two or more possibilities. **2** the freedom or opportunity to choose between two or more things: *I had no alternative but to go*.

alternative dispute resolution *noun* a method of solving a dispute without resorting to litigation, e.g. mediation, arbitration, etc.

alternatively *adverb* used to introduce a suggestion that is a second choice or possibility: *you are welcome to dine with me; alternatively, you can visit a local restaurant*.

alternator *noun* a generator that produces an alternating current.

although *conjunction* = THOUGH *conjunction* 1-3.

altimeter *noun* an instrument showing height above sea or ground level, esp. in aircraft. [Say al TIMMA tur]

altiplano *noun* the high tableland of central South America. [Say alta PLAN oh]

altitude *noun* **1** the height of an object in relation to a given point, esp. sea level or the horizon. **2** *Astronomy* the angular distance of a celestial body above the horizon. **3** *Geometry* the length of the perpendicular from a vertex to the opposite side of a figure.

altitude sickness *noun* an illness caused by ascent to high altitude, characterized by nausea and exhaustion, resulting from a shortage of oxygen.

alto *noun* (*plural* **altos**) **1** = CONTRALTO. **2 a** the highest adult male singing voice, above tenor. **b** a singer with this voice. **c** a part written for it. **3** the member of a family of instruments pitched second- or third-highest: *alto sax*.

> **SPELL CHECK**   ABC
> **altogether, all together**
>
> **Altogether** does not mean the same as **all together**. **Altogether** means "in total", as in *If Paul comes there will be six of us altogether*, whereas **all together** means "all at once" or "all in one place", as in *Paul and his friends were all together at the show*.

altogether *adverb* **1** totally, completely: *you are altogether wrong*. **2** on the whole: *altogether it had been a good day*. **3** in total: *there are six bedrooms altogether*. PHRASES **in the altogether** *informal* naked.

altruism *noun* the belief in or practice of selfless concern for the well-being of others: *some may choose to work with the disadvantaged out of altruism*. ▶ **altruist** *noun* **altruistic** *adjective* **altruistically** *adverb* [Say AWL true ism or AL true ism, awl true ISS tick or al true ISS tick]

alum¹ *noun* **1** a double sulphate of aluminum and potassium, with astringent properties. **2** any of a group of compounds of double sulphates of a monovalent metal (or group) and a trivalent metal. [Say AL um]

alum² *noun* *informal* an alumnus or alumna. [Say a LUM]

alumina *noun* the compound aluminum oxide occurring naturally as corundum and emery. [Say a LOOMA nuh]

aluminosilicate *noun* a silicate containing aluminum, esp. a rock-forming mineral of this kind, e.g. a feldspar, a clay mineral. [Say a LOOMA no SILLA kut]

aluminum *noun* a silvery light and malleable metallic element resistant to tarnishing by air.

alumna *noun* (*plural* **alumnae**) **1** a female graduate of a specified university or school. **2** a woman who is a former member of a specified group or organization. [Say a LUMNA for the singular, a LUM nee for the plural]

alumnus *noun* (*plural* **alumni**) **1** a graduate of a specified university or other school. **2** a former member of a specified group or organization. [Say a LUM nuss for the singular, a LUM nigh for the plural]

alveolar *adjective* having to do with an alveolus: *the alveolar ridge is the hard part of the roof of the mouth behind the front teeth*. [Say alvy OLE er]

alveolus *noun* (*plural* **alveoli**) **1** any of the many tiny air sacs of the lungs which allow for rapid gaseous exchange. **2** the bony socket for the root of a tooth. [Say alvy OLE us for the singular, alvy OLE ee for the plural]

always *adverb* **1** at all times; on all occasions.

2 whatever the circumstances: *I can always sleep on the floor.*

alyssum *noun* **1** a low-growing widely-cultivated plant having very small white or purple flowers. **2** any plant of the genus *Alyssum*, widely cultivated and usu. having yellow or white flowers. [Say a LISS um]

Alzheimer's disease *noun* (also **Alzheimer's**) a serious disorder of the brain manifesting itself in premature senility. [Say ALTS hymers]

AM *abbreviation* **1** AMPLITUDE MODULATION. **2** the band of radio stations broadcasting with this system.

Am *symbol* americium.

am *1st person singular present of* BE.

a.m. *abbreviation* before noon.

amalgam *noun* **1** a mixture or blend: *a curious amalgam of the traditional and the modern.* **2** an alloy of mercury with one or more other metals, used esp. for dental fillings. [Say a MAL gum]

amalgamate *verb* (**amalgamates, amalgamated, amalgamating**) combine to form one structure, organization, etc.: *she amalgamated her company with another* ◊ *the two airlines have amalgamated.* ▶**amalgamation** *noun* [Say a MALGA mate, a malga MAY sh'n]

amandine *adjective* garnished with (usu. sliced) almonds: *green beans amandine.* [Say AM un deen]

amaranth *noun* a plant of the genus *Amaranthus*, usu. having small green, red, or purple tinted flowers, some species of which are weeds, e.g. pigweed, with other species cultivated as grain crops or ornamentals. [Say AMMA ranth]

amaryllis *noun* (*plural* **amaryllises**) a bulbous plant with showy trumpet-shaped flowers and strap-shaped leaves. [Say amma RILL iss]

amass *verb* (**amasses, amassed, amassing**) gather together or accumulate a large amount or number of valuable material or things over a period of time: *he amassed a fortune estimated at close to five million dollars.*

amateur *noun* **1** a person who engages in a pursuit, e.g. an art or sport, as a pastime rather than for pay: *the actors are amateurs* ◊ *an amateur photographer.* **2** (as an *adjective*) for or done by amateurs: *amateur athletics.* **3** an unskilful or inexperienced person.

amateurish *adjective* characteristic of an amateur, esp. unskilful or inexperienced. ▶**amateurishly** *adverb* **amateurishness** *noun*

amateurism *noun* **1** the characteristic work of an amateur: *their school musical showed very few signs of amateurism.* **2** the status of an amateur, or the belief that participation in an event should be restricted to amateurs: *despite the pretense of amateurism, many of the sport's athletes are highly paid to endorse large corporations.* [Say AMMA chur ism]

amatory *adjective* of or relating to sexual love or desire: *recounted his amatory exploits.* [Say AMMA tory]

amautik *noun* (also **amauti**) *Cdn* (*North*) **1** an Inuit woman's parka with a large hood in which a child may be carried. **2** the large hood of such a parka. [Say am OW tick, am OW tee]

amaze *verb* (**amazes, amazed, amazing**) surprise greatly; overwhelm with wonder. ▶**amazement** *noun*

amazing *adjective* **1** causing great surprise. **2** *informal* exceptional: *an amazing book.* ▶**amazingly** *adverb*

Amazon *noun* **1** a member of a mythical race of female warriors which appears in many Greek legends. **2** (**amazon**) a very tall, strong, or athletic woman. ▶**Amazonian** *adjective* [Say AMMA zon, amma ZONEY un]

ambassador *noun* **1** a diplomat sent by a country on a mission to, or as its permanent representative in, a foreign country. **2** a representative or promoter of a

specified thing: *an ambassador of peace.* ▶**ambassadorial** *adjective* **ambassadorship** *noun*

amber • *noun* **1 a** a yellowish translucent fossilized resin deriving from extinct (esp. coniferous) trees and used in jewellery. **b** the honey-yellow colour of this. **2** a yellow traffic light meaning caution, showing between green for "go" and red for "stop". • *adjective* made of or coloured like amber: *amber beads* ◊ *cats with amber eyes.*

ambergris *noun* a strong-smelling wax-like secretion of the intestine of the sperm whale, found floating in tropical seas and used in perfume manufacture. [Say AMBER griss or AMBER grease]

amberjack *noun* a large brightly-coloured fish found in tropical and subtropical Atlantic waters.

ambidextrous *adjective* **1** (of a person) able to use the right and left hands equally well. **2** (of an object) suited for use with either the right or left hand: *ambidextrous scissors.* [Say amba DEX truss]

ambience *noun* (also **ambiance**) the surroundings or atmosphere of a place: *the relaxed ambience of the cocktail lounge is popular with guests.* [Say AMBY awnce or OMBY awnce or AMBY ince]

ambient *adjective* of or related to the immediate surroundings of something: *the ambient temperature.* [Say AMBY int]

ambiguity *noun* (*plural* **ambiguities**) **1** uncertainty or inexactness of meaning in language: *we can detect no ambiguity in this section of the Act.* **2** a lack of decisiveness or commitment resulting from a failure to make a choice between alternatives: *the film is fraught with moral ambiguity.* [Say am big YOO a tee]

ambiguous *adjective* **1** (of language) open to more than one interpretation; having a double meaning: *the question is rather ambiguous.* **2** unclear or inexact because a choice between alternatives has not been made: *this whole society is morally ambiguous* ◊ *the election results were ambiguous.* ▶**ambiguously** *adverb* **ambiguousness** *noun* [Say am BIG you us]

ambition *noun* the determination to achieve success or distinction, usu. in a chosen field: *my ambition was to become a teacher* ◊ *life offered few opportunities for young people with ambition.*

ambitious *adjective* **1** full of ambition: *his mother was hard-working and ambitious for her four children.* **2** (of a plan or piece of work) intended to satisfy high aspirations and therefore difficult to achieve: *the scope of the book is very ambitious* ◊ *an ambitious enterprise.* ▶**ambitiously** *adverb* **ambitiousness** *noun*

ambivalence *noun* the coexistence in one person of opposing emotions or attitudes towards the same object or situation: *Canadian ambivalence towards the US.* [Say am BIVVA lince]

ambivalent *adjective* having mixed feelings about someone or something: *their ambivalent urge both to embrace and to break with him* ◊ *few were ambivalent about her, either loving or hating her.* ▶**ambivalently** *adverb* [Say am BIVVA l'nt]

amble *verb* (**ambles, ambled, ambling**) **1** walk at an easy pace. **2** (of a horse etc.) move by lifting the two feet on one side together.

ambrosia *noun* **1** (in Greek and Roman mythology) the food of the gods. **2** anything very pleasing to taste or smell. **3** a dessert of sliced oranges and shredded coconut, sometimes also with bananas or pineapple. ▶**ambrosial** *adjective* [Say am BRO zhuh]

ambulance *noun* a vehicle specially equipped for conveying the sick or injured to and from a hospital.

ambulance technician *noun* *Cdn* (*Que.*) = PARAMEDIC.

ambulatory *adjective* **1** (of a patient) able to walk about; not confined to bed. **2** (of treatment) not confining a patient to bed. [Say AM byoo luh tory]

A

ambush • *noun* (*plural* **ambushes**) a surprise attack by persons in a concealed position: *seven members of a patrol were killed in an ambush* ◊ *terrorists waiting in ambush.* • *verb* (**ambushes**, **ambushed**, **ambushing**) **1** attack by means of an ambush: *the guerrillas ambushed them near the bridge.* **2** lie in wait for: *reporters ambushed her every time she went out.*

ameba esp. *US* = AMOEBA. [Say a MEEBA]

ameliorate *verb* (**ameliorates**, **ameliorated**, **ameliorating**) *formal* improve: *the reform did much to ameliorate living standards.* ▶**amelioration** *noun* [Say a MEELYA rate, a meelya RAY sh'n]

amen • *interjection* **1** uttered at the end of a prayer or hymn etc., meaning "so be it". **2** (foll. by *to*) expressing agreement or assent: *amen to that.* • *noun* an utterance of "amen" (sense 1). [Say ah MEN or ay MEN]

amenable *adjective* **1** willing to co-operate; open to suggestion or influence. **2** (foll. by *to*) (of a thing) capable of being acted upon in a particular way: *the patients had cardiac failure not amenable to medical treatment.* [Say a MENNA bull or a MEENA bull]

amend *verb* **1** formally revise or alter (a constitution, legislation, etc.). **2** make minor improvements in (a text or written proposal). **3** correct an error or errors in (a document). **4** improve. ▶**amendable** *adjective*

amending formula *noun* a prescribed method for amending a constitution specifying the proportions of various interested parties that must assent for an amendment to be passed.

amendment *noun* **1** a minor improvement in a document (esp. a legal or statutory one). **2** the formal proposal of changes to a bill being considered by Parliament. **3** an article officially supplementing a constitution. **4** the act or process of improving, esp. one's conduct: *a firm desire of amendment.* **5** something added to soil to improve its texture or fertility: *compost is a natural organic soil amendment.*

amends *noun* PHRASES **make amends** (often foll. by *for*) compensate or make up (for).

amenity *noun* (*plural* **amenities**) (usu. in *plural*) a pleasant or useful feature: *the house is located near to all local amenities.* [Say a MENNA tee]

amenorrhea *noun* (also **amenorrhoea**) an abnormal absence of menstruation. [Say ay menna REE uh]

Amer. *abbreviation* American.

American • *adjective* **1** of, relating to, or characteristic of the US or its inhabitants. **2** (usu. in *combination*) of or relating to the Americas: *Latin American.* **3** designating plants or animals native to the Americas: *American elk.* • *noun* **1** a native or citizen of the US. **2** (usu. in *combination*) a native or inhabitant of the Americas: *North Americans.* **3** the English language as used in the US.

Americana *plural noun* things pertaining to and typical of American culture, e.g. publications, artifacts, cultural activities, etc.

American aloe *noun* = CENTURY PLANT.

American dream *noun* the traditional American belief that in the US success and material prosperity are available to all.

American eagle *noun* = BALD EAGLE.

American elm *noun* an elm, *Ulmus Americana*, native to eastern North America, cultivated as a shade tree, and particularly susceptible to Dutch elm disease.

American football *noun* a form of football played in the US between two teams of 11 players, played on a smaller field than Canadian football, with four downs and slightly different scoring rules.

American Indian *noun* **1** (also **North American Indian**) a member of a group of Aboriginal peoples of the western hemisphere, excluding the Inuit and Aleuts. **2** *Cdn* a member of these peoples who is a citizen or resident of the US.

Americanism *noun* **1 a** a word, sense, or phrase peculiar to or originating from the US. **b** a thing or feature characteristic of or peculiar to the US. **2** attachment to or sympathy for the US.

Americanization *noun* the process of becoming or making something or someone American in character: *the Americanization of immigrants* ◊ *the Americanization of Canadian culture.*

Americanize *verb* (**Americanizes**, **Americanized**, **Americanizing**) **1** make or become American in character. **2** naturalize as an American.

americium *noun* an artificially made radioactive metallic element. [Say amma RISHY um]

Amerindian • *adjective* of or relating to American Indians. • *noun* an American Indian. [Say amma RINDY un]

amethyst *noun* a precious stone of a violet or purple variety of quartz. [Say AMMA thist]

amiability *noun* friendliness: *the owner runs the restaurant with maternal amiability.* [Say aimy a BILLA tee]

amiable *adjective* friendly and pleasant in temperament. ▶**amiably** *adverb* [Say AIMY a bull]

amicable *adjective* showing or done in a friendly spirit: *an amicable meeting.* ▶**amicably** *adverb* [Say AM ick a bull]

amid *preposition* (also **amidst**) **1** in the middle of: *our dream home, set amid magnificent countryside.* **2** in an atmosphere or against a background of: *talks broke down amid recriminations on either side.*

amide *noun* a compound formed from ammonia by replacement of one (or sometimes more than one) hydrogen atom. [Say AM ide or AY mide]

amidships *adverb* (also **amidship**) in or into the middle of a ship.

amigo *noun* (*plural* **amigos**) *informal* (often as a form of address) a friend or comrade. [Say a MEE go]

amine *noun* a compound formed from ammonia by replacement of one or more hydrogen atoms by an organic radical or radicals. [Say AM een or a MEAN]

amino *adjective* of, relating to, or containing the monovalent group -NH$_2$. [Say a MEAN oh]

amino acid *noun* any of a group of organic compounds containing both the carboxyl and amino group, occurring naturally in plant and animal tissues and forming the basic constituents of proteins.

Amish • *noun* (**the Amish**; treated as *plural*) the members of a strict Mennonite group whose communal farms are found in S Ontario and parts of the US, esp. Pennsylvania. • *adjective* of, pertaining to, or characteristic of this group. [Say OMM ish or AY mish]

amiss • *adjective* wrong; out of order; faulty: *knew something was amiss.* • *adverb* wrong; wrongly; inappropriately: *everything went amiss.* PHRASES **take amiss** be offended by: *took my words amiss.*

amity *noun* a friendly relationship: *it did not take long for wartime amity and concord to turn into mistrust, suspicion, and hostility.* [Say AMMA tee]

ammeter *noun* an instrument for measuring electric current in amperes. [Say AMMA tur]

ammo *noun* *informal* ammunition.

ammonia *noun* **1** a colourless strongly alkaline gas with a characteristic pungent smell. **2** a solution of ammonia gas in water.

ammonium *noun* the monovalent ion NH$_4^+$, formed from ammonia. [Say a MOANY um]

ammonium chloride *noun* the salt of ammonia and hydrogen chloride, used as an electrolyte in dry cells and as a constituent of soldering fluxes.

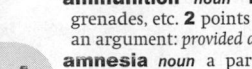

ammunition *noun* **1** a supply of bullets, shells, grenades, etc. **2** points used or usable to advantage in an argument: *provided ammunition for her argument*.

amnesia *noun* a partial or total loss of memory. ▶**amnesiac** *noun & adjective* **amnesic** *adjective & noun* [Say am NEE zhuh, am NEEZY ack, am NEE zick]

amnesty • *noun* (*plural* **amnesties**) **1** a general pardon, esp. for political offences: *an amnesty for draft evaders*. **2** a period during which people may admit an offence without fear of prosecution: *a month-long gun amnesty*. [Say AMNA stee]

amnio *noun informal* = AMNIOCENTESIS. [Say AMNY oh]

amniocentesis *noun* (*plural* **amniocenteses**) the sampling of amniotic fluid by insertion of a hollow needle to determine the condition of an embryo. [Say amny oh sen TEE sis]

amnion *noun* (*plural* **amnia**) the innermost membrane that encloses the embryo of a reptile, bird, or mammal. [Say AMNY un]

amniotic *adjective* having to do with the amnion. [Say amny OT ick]

amniotic fluid *noun* the fluid contained within the amnion, in which the fetus effectively floats.

amoeba *noun* (*plural* **amoebas** or **amoebae**) any usu. aquatic protozoan of the genus *Amoeba*, esp. *A. proteus*, capable of changing shape. ▶**amoebic** *adjective* **amoeboid** *adjective* [Say a MEEBA]

amok *adverb* PHRASES **go** (or **run**) **amok 1** be out of control. **2** run about wildly in an uncontrollable violent rage. [Say a MUCK or a MOCK]

among *preposition* (also **amongst**) **1** surrounded by; in the company of. **2** in the number of: *among us were those who disagreed*. **3** an example of; in the class or category of: *is among the wealthiest people alive*. **4 a** between; shared by: *had $5 among us ◊ divide it among you*. **b** by the joint action or from the joint resources of: *among us we can manage it*. **5** with one another; by the reciprocal action of.

amoral *adjective* lacking a moral sense; unconcerned with the rightness or wrongness of something (*compare* IMMORAL): *an amoral attitude to sex*. ▶**amorality** *noun* [Say ay MORAL, ay more AL it ee]

amorous *adjective* showing, feeling, or relating to sexual desire: *she rejected his amorous advances ◊ felt amorous after two glasses of champagne*. ▶**amorously** *adverb* **amorousness** *noun* [Say AMMER us]

amorphous *adjective* **1** shapeless. **2** vague, ill-organized: *the reform movement was an amorphous grouping of small-l liberals*. **3** *Geology & Chemistry* non-crystalline; having neither definite form nor structure. [Say a MORF us]

amortization *noun* the paying off of a debt by making small regular payments over a period of time.

amortize *verb* (**amortizes**, **amortized**, **amortizing**) **1** gradually pay off (a debt): *a $100,000 mortgage amortized over 20 years*. **2** gradually write off the initial cost of (assets). [Say AMMER tize]

amount • *noun* a quantity, esp. the total of a thing or things in number, size, value, extent, etc. • *verb* (foll. by *to*) be equivalent to in number, size, significance, etc.: *amounted to $100 ◊ amounted to a disaster*. PHRASES **any amount of** a great deal of. **no amount of** not even the greatest possible amount of.

amoxicillin *noun* (also **amoxycillin**) a broad spectrum semi-synthetic penicillin, closely related to ampicillin, used esp. for treating ear and upper respiratory infections. [Say a moxa SILL un]

amp[1] *noun* an ampere.

amp[2] *noun informal* an amplifier.

amp[3] *noun informal* an amputee.

amperage *noun* the strength of an electric current in amperes. [Say AMPA ridge]

ampere *noun* the SI base unit of electric current. Symbol: **A**. [Say AM pair]

ampersand *noun* the sign & (= *and*).

amphetamine *noun* a synthetic drug used esp. as a stimulant. [Say am FETTA mean]

amphibian • *adjective* **1** living both on land and in water. **2** of or relating to the class Amphibia. **3** (of a vehicle or airplane) able to operate on land and water. • *noun* **1** any vertebrate of the class Amphibia, with a life history of an aquatic gill-breathing larval stage followed by a terrestrial lung-breathing adult stage, including frogs, newts, and salamanders. **2** (in general use) a creature living both on land and in water. **3** an amphibian vehicle or airplane. [Say am FIBBY un]

amphibious *adjective* **1** living both on land and in water. **2** of or relating to or suited for both land and water. **3 a** (of a military operation) involving forces landed from the sea. **b** (of forces) trained for such operations. [Say am FIBBY us]

amphitheatre *noun* (also **amphitheater**) **1** an oval or circular building with tiered seats around a central open space. **2** a piece of level ground surrounded naturally by rising slopes. **3** a large lecture theatre with tiered seats. **4** a gallery in a theatre. [Say AMFA theatre]

amphora *noun* (*plural* **amphorae** or **amphoras**) a tall ancient Greek or Roman jar or jug with two handles and a narrow neck. [Say AMFA ruh for the singular, AMFA ree for the plural]

ampicillin *noun* a semi-synthetic penicillin used esp. in treating infections of the urinary and respiratory tracts. [Say ampa SILL un]

> **SPELL CHECK**
> **amphitheatre**   ABC ✓
>
> Warning: **amphitheatre** is spelled with an *h* immediately following the *p*: **amphi-**.

---

ample *adjective* (**ampler**, **amplest**) **1 a** large and accommodating: *leaned back in his ample chair*. **b** (of a person's figure) large: *her ample bosom ◊ had a hard time fitting her ample hips into the tight jeans*. **2** enough or more than enough: *ample time ◊ you have had ample opportunity to write this essay*.

amplification *noun* **1** the action of enlarging or increasing something, esp. the volume or strength of sound, electrical signals, etc. **2** *Genetics* the repeated replication of a gene or sequence of DNA.

amplifier *noun* an electronic device for increasing the strength of electrical signals, esp. for conversion into sound in stereo equipment etc.

amplify *verb* (**amplifies**, **amplified**, **amplifying**) **1** increase the volume or strength of (sound, electrical signals, etc.). **2** cause to become more marked or intense. **3** enlarge upon or expand: *the proposals were amplified into a comprehensive expansion and reform plan*.

amplitude *noun* **1** *Physics* the maximum extent of a vibration or oscillation from the position of equilibrium. **2** *Electricity* the maximum departure of the value of an alternating current or wave from the average value.

amplitude modulation *noun* **1** variation of the amplitude of a radio or other wave as a way of carrying information such as an audio signal (*compare* FREQUENCY MODULATION). **2** the system using such modulation. Abbreviation: **AM**.

amply *adverb* **1** to a satisfactory or adequate degree: *your examples amply demonstrate the point*. **2** to a greater degree than is expected or necessary: *I was amply*

rewarded for the job ◊ the book is amply illustrated with beautiful colour pictures.

amputate *verb* **(amputates, amputated, amputating)** cut off by surgical operation, usu. because of injury or disease. ▶ **amputation** *noun*

amputee *noun* a person who has lost a limb etc. by amputation.

amuck *adverb* = AMOK.

amulet *noun* an ornament or small piece of jewellery worn as a charm against evil. [Say AM yuh lit]

amuse *verb* **(amuses, amused, amusing) 1** cause (a person) to find something funny: *people looked on with amused curiosity.* **2** provide interesting and enjoyable occupation for someone; keep (a person) entertained: *they amused themselves digging through an old encyclopedia ◊ elegant shops that will keep any browser amused for hours.*

amusement *noun* **1** something that amuses, esp. a pleasant diversion, game, or pastime. **2 a** the state of being amused: *we read our horoscopes with amusement.* **b** the act of amusing: *an evening's amusement.* **3** a mechanical device, e.g. a merry-go-round, for entertainment at a fairground etc.

amusement park *noun* a commercially operated fairground with rides, e.g. Ferris wheel, roller coaster, etc., and booths for refreshments and games.

amusing *adjective* causing laughter and providing entertainment: *an amusing incident ◊ I didn't find the joke amusing.* ▶ **amusingly** *adverb*

amyotrophic lateral sclerosis *noun* a progressive degenerative disease of the central nervous system resulting in weakness and wasting of the muscles and ultimately death. [Say ammy a TROFF ick]

an *indefinite article* the form of the indefinite article (see A¹) used before words beginning with a vowel sound: *an egg ◊ an hour ◊ an MP.*

Anabaptism *noun* the doctrine that baptism should only be administered to believing adults. [Say anna BAP tism]

Anabaptist *noun* a member of a Protestant sect believing that baptism should only be administered to believing adults. [Say anna BAP tist]

anabolic steroid *noun* any of a group of synthetic steroid hormones used to increase muscle size. [Say anna BAWL ick]

anachronism *noun* **1** a thing or person belonging or appropriate to a period other than that in which it exists, esp. a thing that is conspicuously old-fashioned: *is the monarchy an anachronism in the 21st century?* **2** something that is placed, for example in a book or play, in the wrong period of history: *having a character consult a wristwatch in a Victorian drama was an anachronism.* ▶ **anachronistic** *adjective* [Say a NACKRA nism, a nackra NISS tick]

anaconda *noun* a South American boa of the genus *Eunectes*, esp. the very large, semiaquatic *E. murinus*, that kills its prey by constriction. [Say anna CONDA]

anaemia *esp. Brit.* = ANEMIA. [Say a NEEMY a]

anaemic *esp. Brit.* = ANEMIC. [Say a NEEM ick]

anaerobic *adjective* **1** growing without air, or requiring oxygen-free conditions to live. **2** (of exercise) in which oxygen is used by the muscles faster than it can be supplied by the bloodstream. [Say anna ROE bick]

anaesthesia *noun* the inability to feel pain, usu. achieved by the administration of gases or the injection of drugs. [Say anniss THEEZ ee uh or anniss THEEZH yuh]

anaesthesiology = ANESTHESIOLOGY.

anaesthetic • *noun* a substance that produces insensitivity to pain etc. • *adjective* producing partial or complete insensitivity to pain etc. [Say anniss THET ick]

anaesthetist *noun* Cdn & Brit. a medical doctor

specializing in the administration of anaesthetics. [Say a NIECE thuh tist or a NESS thuh tist]

anaesthetize *verb* **(anaesthetizes, anaesthetized, anaesthetizing) 1** administer an anaesthetic to. **2** deprive of physical or mental sensation: *an emotional anaesthetizing of the reader takes place.* [Say a NIECE thuh tize or a NESS thuh tize]

anagram *noun* a word or phrase formed by rearranging the letters of another word or phrase: *rasp is an anagram of spar.*

anal *adjective* **1 a** relating to or situated near the anus. **b** (of sexual activity) involving the insertion of one partner's penis into the other's anus. **2** *Psychology* designating or pertaining to a stage of infantile psychosexual development that is thought to involve a preoccupation with the anus and defecation. **3** *informal* = ANAL-RETENTIVE.

analgesia *noun* the absence or relief of pain. [Say annal JEEZ ee uh or annal JEECE ee uh]

analgesic • *adjective* relieving pain. • *noun* a drug that relieves pain. [Say annal JEEZ ick or annal JEECE ick]

analog *adjective* **1** (also **analogue**) (of a watch, clock, etc.) that gives a reading by means of hands or a pointer rather than displayed digits (compare DIGITAL *adjective* 2). **2** (of a computer or electronic process) operating with signals or information represented by a continuously variable quantity, such as spatial position, voltage, etc. (compare DIGITAL *adjective* 3). **3** (of a recording or recording equipment) in which the signal corresponds to a physical variable, such as the groove on a phonograph record or magnetic particles on an audio cassette tape (compare DIGITAL *adjective* 4).

analogical *adjective* involving or expressing analogy.

analogize *verb* **(analogizes, analogized, analogizing)** make a comparison of something with something else to assist understanding. [Say a NALA jize]

analogous *adjective* partially similar: *sleep has often been portrayed as analogous to death.* ▶ **analogously** *adverb* [Say a NALA gus]

analogue *noun* (US **analog**) an analogous or parallel thing. [Say ANNA log]

analogy *noun* (plural **analogies**) **1** a comparison between one thing and another, typically for the purpose of explanation or clarification: *an analogy between the workings of nature and those of human societies ◊ he interprets logical functions by analogy with machines.* **2** *Biology* the resemblance of function between organs essentially different. [Say a NALA jee]

anal-retentive *adjective* (of a person) excessively orderly and fussy.

analysis *noun* (plural **analyses**) **1 a** a detailed examination of the elements or structure of a substance etc. **b** a statement of the result of this. **2** *Chemistry* the determination of the constituent parts of a mixture or compound. **3** psychoanalysis. **4** *Math* the use of algebra and calculus in problem-solving. PHRASES **in the final** (or **last** or **ultimate**) **analysis** after all due consideration; in the end.

analyst *noun* **1** a person engaged or skilled in analysis. **2** a psychoanalyst.

analytic *adjective* = ANALYTICAL.

analytical *adjective* **1** using a logical method of thinking about something in order to understand it, esp. by looking at all the parts separately: *she has a clear analytical mind ◊ an analytical approach to the problem.* **2** using scientific analysis in order to find out about something: *analytical methods of research ◊ analytical chemistry.* ▶ **analytically** *adverb*

analytic geometry *noun* (also **analytical geometry**) geometry involving the use of algebra,

with points represented by a pair of numbers, and lines and curves represented by equations.

analyzable *adjective* (also **analysable**) that may be analyzed.

analyze *verb* (**analyzes, analyzed, analyzing**) (also **analyse; analyses, analysed, analysing**) **1** examine in detail the constitution or structure of. **2** *Chemistry* ascertain the constituents of (a sample of a mixture or compound). **3** examine critically (a book etc.) in order to bring out essential elements or structure. **4** psychoanalyze. ▶**analyzer** *noun* (also **analyser**)

anaphora *noun* **1** the repetition of a word or phrase at the beginning of successive clauses. **2** the use of a word referring to or replacing a word used earlier in a sentence, to avoid repetition, e.g. *do* in I *like it and so do they*. [Say a NAFA ruh]

anaphylactic shock *adjective* an extreme and sometimes fatal allergic reaction to a foreign substance, e.g. a drug or a bee's venom, characterized by a drop in blood pressure and difficulty breathing. [Say anna fuh LACK tick]

anaphylaxis *noun* (*plural* **anaphylaxes**) an extreme allergic reaction to a foreign substance, such as a drug or a bee's venom, to which the body has become hypersensitive following an earlier exposure. [Say anna fuh LAX iss]

anarchic *adjective* with no controlling rules or principles to give order: *an anarchic and bitter civil war*. [Say an ARK ick]

anarchism *noun* the doctrine that all government should be abolished. ▶**anarchist** *noun* **anarchistic** *adjective* [Say ANNER kism, ANNER kist, anner KISS tick]

anarchy *noun* **1** a state of disorder due to absence or non-recognition of authority or other controlling systems: *he must ensure public order in a country threatened with anarchy* ◊ *the country descended into anarchy after the fall of the communists*. **2** absence of government and absolute freedom of the individual, regarded as a political ideal. [Say ANNER kee]

anathema *noun* (*plural* **anathemas**) **1** a detested thing or person: *racial hatred was anathema to her*. **2** a declaration of the Christian Church, excommunicating a person or denouncing a doctrine. [Say a NATHA muh]

anatomical *adjective* (also **anatomic**) of anatomy. ▶**anatomically** *adverb* [Say anna TOM ick ul]

anatomize *verb* (**anatomizes, anatomized, anatomizing**) examine in detail: *band breakups have been anatomized as if they were divorces*. [Say a NATTA mize]

anatomy *noun* (*plural* **anatomies**) **1** the scientific study of the bodily structure of humans, animals, and plants, involving dissection. **2** this structure. **3** *informal* a human body. **4** analysis. [Say a NATTA me]

ancestor *noun* **1** any (esp. remote) person from whom one is descended. **2** an early type of animal or plant from which others have evolved. **3** an early version of a machine, artifact, system, etc. which later became more developed: *the ancestors of today's computers*.

ancestral *adjective* **1** designating or having to do with an ancestor or ancestors: *Joshua is making a family tree to trace his ancestral roots* ◊ *the tribe's ancestral chiefs*. **2** belonging to or inherited from an ancestor or ancestors: *the family's ancestral home*. [Say an SESS trull]

ancestral name *noun* (esp. among the Sne Nay Muxw) the personal name of an ancestor, conferred upon a child as a ceremonial name.

ancestry *noun* (*plural* **ancestries**) **1** lineage or descent. **2** ancestors collectively.

anchor • *noun* **1** a heavy metal weight used to moor a ship to the bottom of a river, lake, sea, etc. or a balloon to the ground. **2** a person or thing that gives stability or security: *she was the anchor of the family*. **3** the main announcer on a news or sports broadcast, who introduces the reports of other broadcasters. **4** a person who plays a crucial part, esp. at the back of a tug-of-war team. **5** a bolt or fitting for attaching something to a wall, floor, etc. **6** a store which is the principal tenant of a shopping centre. • *verb* **1** secure (a ship or balloon) by means of an anchor. **2** fix firmly: *with cords and pitons they anchored him to the rock*. **3** *Broadcasting* act as an anchor: *she anchored the evening news*. **4** base something firmly on something else: *her novels are anchored in everyday experience*. PHRASES **at anchor** moored by means of an anchor.

anchorage *noun* **1** a place where a ship may be anchored. **2** the act of anchoring or lying at anchor. **3** something that provides security for something else: *the plant needs firm anchorage* ◊ *the mother provides emotional anchorage*.

anchorite *noun* a hermit; a religious recluse. [Say ANCHOR ite]

anchorperson *noun* the main announcer on a news or sports broadcast, who introduces the reports of other broadcasters. A female anchorperson may be called an **anchorwoman**; a male anchorperson may be called an **anchorman**.

anchovy *noun* (*plural* **anchovies**) a small Mediterranean fish of the herring family which has a rich flavour and is usu. eaten pickled or in pastes, sauces, etc. [Say ann CHOVE ee or ANCHA vee]

ancien régime *noun* (*plural* **anciens régimes** *pronunc.* same) **1** the political and social system in France before the Revolution of 1789. **2** any superseded regime. [Say awnce YEN ray ZHEEM]

ancient *adjective* **1 a** of long ago. **b** of or pertaining to the world prior to the fall of Rome in 476. **2** having lived or existed long; very old. PHRASES **the ancients 1** the people of ancient times, esp. the Greeks, Romans, Hebrews, and Egyptians. **2** the writers of classical Greece or Rome.

ancient history *noun* **1** the history of the ancient civilizations of the Mediterranean area and the Near East before the fall of the Western Roman Empire in 476. **2** something already long familiar.

ancillary *adjective* **1** (of a person, activity, or service) providing essential support to a central service or industry: *ancillary agencies*. **2** associated, secondary: *relegated women to such ancillary roles as fundraising and Sunday school teaching*. [Say ann SILLA ree]

and *conjunction* **1 a** connecting words, clauses, or sentences that are to be taken jointly. **b** implying progression: *better and better*. **c** implying causation: *do that and I'll hit you*. **d** implying great duration: *he cried and cried*. **e** implying a great number: *miles and miles*. **f** implying addition: *two and two are four*. **g** implying variety: *there are books and books*. **h** implying succession: *walking two and two*. **2** *informal* to: *try and open it*. **3** in relation to: *Canada and NATO*. PHRASES **and/or** either or both of two stated possibilities.

andante *adverb* & *adjective* Music in a moderately slow tempo. [Say an DAWN tay or an DAN tay]

Andean *adjective* of or relating to the region of the Andes, a high mountain range in western South America. [Say an DEE un or ANDY un]

androgen *noun* a male sex hormone or other substance capable of developing and maintaining certain male sexual characteristics. ▶**androgenic** *adjective* [Say ANDRA jen]

androgynous *adjective* **1** having both male and female characteristics. **2** not distinguishably male or female, esp. in appearance. *androgynous teenaged fashion models*. **3** with stamens and pistils in the same flower

or inflorescence. ▶**androgyny** *noun* [Say an DRAW jen iss, an DRAW jen ee]

android *noun* a robot with a human appearance.

androstenedione *noun* a naturally occurring androgenic steroid often taken in concentrated form to raise blood levels of testosterone. [Say andro STEEN die on]

anecdotal *adjective* **1** of, pertaining to, or consisting of anecdotes. **2** based on or consisting of incidental observations or reports rather than systematic research: *anecdotal evidence*. [Say annick DOAT ul]

anecdote *noun* a short account of an entertaining or interesting incident. [Say ANNICK dote]

anemia *noun* a deficiency in the blood, usu. of red cells or their hemoglobin, resulting in pallor and weariness, often caused by a lack of iron in the diet. [Say a NEEMY uh]

anemic *adjective* **1** relating to or suffering from anemia. **2** lacking in colour, spirit, or vitality: *the economic recovery is so anemic as to be barely noticeable*. [Say a NEEM ick]

anemometer *noun* an instrument for measuring the force of the wind. [Say anna MOMMA ter]

anemone *noun* **1** any plant of the genus *Anemone*, related to the buttercup, with flowers of various vivid colours. **2** = PASQUE FLOWER. [Say a NEMMA nee]

aneroid barometer *noun* an instrument that measures air pressure by the action of air on the elastic lid of an evacuated box. [Say ANNA roid]

anesthesia etc. = ANAESTHESIA etc.

anesthesiologist *noun* a doctor specializing in the use of anaesthetics. [Say anniss theezy OLLA jist]

anesthesiology *noun* the science of administering anaesthetics. [Say anniss theezy OLLA jee]

aneurysm *noun* an excessive localized enlargement of a blood vessel. [Say ANYA rism]

anew *adverb* **1** again. **2** in a different way.

angakok *noun* *Cdn* (*North*) an Inuit shaman or healer. [Say ANG guh coke]

angel *noun* **1** a heavenly being serving as a messenger or servant of God, conventionally represented in human form with wings: *guardian angel*. **2 a** a very virtuous person. **b** an obliging person: *be an angel and answer the door*. **3** = SNOW ANGEL.

angel dust *noun* *slang* the hallucinogenic drug phencyclidine hydrochloride.

Angeleno *noun* *esp. US* a native or inhabitant of Los Angeles. [Say anja LEEN oh]

angelfish *noun* (*plural* **angelfish** or **angelfishes**) any of various fish with large fins extending from its back and belly.

angel food cake *noun* (also **angel cake**) a light, usu. tall and ring-shaped cake made of beaten egg whites, sugar, and flour.

angel hair *noun* **1** very fine spaghetti. **2** spun glass with very fine filaments forming a fluffy white material used esp. in Christmas decorations.

angelic *adjective* **1** like or relating to angels. **2** sublimely good, kind, or beautiful. ▶**angelically** *adverb* [Say an JELL ick]

angelus *noun* *Catholicism* **1** a set of prayers commemorating the Incarnation of Jesus and including several repetitions of the Hail Mary, traditionally said at morning, noon, and sunset. **2** a bell announcing this. [Say ANJA luss]

anger • *noun* extreme or passionate displeasure. • *verb* make angry; enrage.

angina *noun* (also **angina pectoris**) a condition marked by severe pain in the chest, often also spreading to the shoulders, arms, and neck, owing to an inadequate blood supply to the heart. [Say an JINE uh (PECKTA riss)]

angiogram *noun* an X-ray made by angiography. [Say AN jee a gram]

angiography *noun* (*plural* **angiographies**) an X-ray of blood and lymph vessels. [Say an jee OGRA fee]

angioplasty *noun* (*plural* **angioplasties**) surgical repair of a damaged blood vessel. [Say AN jee oh plasty]

angiosperm *noun* any plant producing flowers and reproducing by seeds enclosed within a carpel, including herbaceous plants, herbs, shrubs, grasses and most trees (*opp.* GYMNOSPERM). [Say AN jee oh sperm]

angishore *Cdn* (*Nfld & Maritimes*) = HANGASHORE. [Say ANG a shore]

Angle *noun* (usu. in *plural*) a member of a tribe from Schleswig in Northern Europe that settled in eastern Britain in the 5th century, giving their name to England and the English.

angle¹ • *noun* **1 a** the space between two meeting lines or surfaces. **b** the inclination of two lines or surfaces to each other. **2 a** a corner. **b** a sharp projection. **3 a** the direction from which a photograph etc. is taken. **b** the aspect from which a matter is considered. **4** *Cdn* (*Nfld*) a curved inlet in a lake or pond. • *verb* (**angles**, **angled**, **angling**) **1** move or place obliquely. **2** present (information) from a particular point of view: *was angled in favour of the victim*.

angle² *verb* (**angles**, **angled**, **angling**) **1** (often foll. by *for*) fish with hook and line. **2** seek an objective by devious or calculated means: *angled for an invitation*.

angled *adjective* placed or inclined at an angle to something else: *angled windows*.

angler *noun* **1** a person who fishes with a hook and line. **2** (also **anglerfish**) any of various fishes that prey upon small fish, attracting them by filaments arising from the dorsal fin.

Anglian *adjective* having to do with the ancient Angles.

Anglican • *adjective* of or relating to the Church of England or any Church in communion with it, e.g. the Anglican Church of Canada. • *noun* a member of an Anglican Church. ▶**Anglicanism** *noun*

anglicism *noun* **1** an English word, structure, etc. borrowed into another language. **2** a word or custom peculiar to England. [Say ANGLA sism]

anglicize *verb* (**anglicizes**, **anglicized**, **anglicizing**) make English. [Say ANGLA size]

Anglo *noun* (*plural* **Anglos**) **1** *Cdn informal* an anglophone, esp. in Quebec. **2** *US* an English-speaking person of British or northern-European origin (in the US esp. as distinct from Hispanic Americans).

Anglo- *combining form* **1** English. **2** of English origin: *an Anglo-Canadian*. **3** English or British and: *an Anglo-French accord*.

Anglo-American • *adjective* **1** of American and English (or British) descent. **2** English (or British) and American. • *noun* an American of English (or British) descent.

Anglo-Canadian • *adjective* **1** of or pertaining to English-speaking Canadians. **2** English (or British) and Canadian. • *noun* **1** an English-speaking Canadian. **2** a Canadian of English descent.

Anglo-Catholic • *adjective* of a High Church Anglican group which emphasizes its Catholic tradition. • *noun* a member of this group. ▶**Anglo-Catholicism** *noun*

Anglo-French • *adjective* **1** English (or British) and French. **2** of Anglo-French. • *noun* the French language as retained and separately developed in England after the Norman Conquest.

Anglo-Indian • *adjective* **1** of or relating to England and India. **2 a** of British descent or birth but living or having lived long in India. **b** of mixed British and

A

Indian parentage. **3** (of a word) adopted into English from an Indian language. • *noun* an Anglo-Indian person.

Anglo-Irish • *adjective* **1** of English descent living in Ireland. **2** English (or British) and Irish. **3** of the English language as spoken in Ireland. • *noun* **1** the Anglo-Irish language. **2** an Anglo-Irish person.

Anglo-Norman • *adjective* **1** of the Normans in England after the Norman Conquest. **2** of the dialect of French used by them. **3** English and Norman. • *noun* the Anglo-Norman dialect.

anglophile • *noun* a person who is fond of or greatly admires England, the English, or English-speaking culture. • *adjective* being or characteristic of an anglophile. ▶ **anglophilia** *noun* [Say ANGLO file, anglo FILLY uh]

anglophobe *noun* a person who has an intense hatred or fear of anglophones, the English, or England. [Say ANGLA fobe]

anglophobia *noun* intense hatred or fear of anglophones, the English, or England. ▶ **anglophobic** *adjective* [Say angla FOBE ee uh]

anglophone esp. *Cdn* • *adjective* English-speaking. • *noun* an English-speaking person. [Say ANGLA fone]

Anglo-Saxon • *adjective* **1** of the Germanic peoples (Angles, Saxons, and Jutes) who settled in Britain before the Norman Conquest. **2** of English descent. **3** *informal* (of English) plain, esp. crude: *made his feelings known with a few choice Anglo-Saxon words*. • *noun* **1** an Anglo-Saxon person. **2** the Old English language.

Angolan • *noun* a native or inhabitant of Angola, a republic on the west coast of Africa. • *adjective* of or relating to Angola or its people. [Say ang GO lun]

angora *noun* **1** a fabric made from the hair of the angora goat or rabbit. **2** a long-haired variety of cat, goat, or rabbit. [Say ang GORE uh]

angora wool *noun* a mixture of sheep's wool and angora rabbit hair.

angrily *adverb* in an angry manner: *some senators reacted angrily to the prime minister's comment*.

angry *adjective* (**angrier**, **angriest**) **1** feeling or showing anger; extremely displeased or resentful. **2** (of a wound, sore, etc.) inflamed, painful. **3** suggesting or seeming to show anger: *an angry sky*.

angst *noun* **1** a feeling of deep anxiety or dread, typically an unfocused one about the human condition or the state of the world in general: *angst-ridden university students ◊ adolescent angst*. **2** *informal* a feeling of persistent worry about something trivial: *my hair causes me angst*.

angstrom *noun* (also **ångström**) a unit of length equal to 10^{-10} m, used esp. for electromagnetic wavelengths. Symbol: **Å**. [Say ANG strum, ONG strum]

anguish *noun* severe misery or mental suffering.

anguished *adjective* suffering or expressing anguish.

angular *adjective* **1 a** having angles or sharp corners. **b** (of a person) having sharp features: *her angular face*. **2** forming an angle. **3** measured by angle: *angular distance*. ▶ **angularity** *noun*

anhydride *noun* a substance obtained by removing the elements of water from a compound, esp. from an acid. [Say an HIGH dried]

aniline *noun* a colourless oily liquid, used in making dyes, drugs, and plastics. [Say ANNA leen or ANNA lin]

aniline dye *noun* a synthetic dye, esp. one made from aniline.

anima *noun* *Psychology* **1** the part of the psyche which is directed inwards, in touch with the subconscious (opp. PERSONA 1). **2** Jung's term for the feminine part of a man's personality (opp. ANIMUS 3).

animal • *noun* **1** a living organism which feeds on

organic matter, usu. one with specialized sense organs and nervous system, and able to respond rapidly to stimuli. **2** such an organism other than man. **3** a brutish or uncivilized person. **4** *informal* a person or thing of any kind: *there is no such animal ◊ a real party animal*. • *adjective* **1** characteristic of animals. **2** of animals as distinct from vegetables: *animal fat*. **3** characteristic of the instinctive and physical needs of animals; of the flesh rather than the spirit or intellect: *succumbed to his animal lust*.

animal magnetism *noun* power to attract others.

animate • *adjective* **1** having life: *gods in a wide variety of forms, both animate and inanimate*. **2** lively and active: *party photos of animate socialites*. • *verb* (**animates**, **animated**, **animating**) **1** bring to life: *the desert is like a line drawing waiting to be animated with colour*. **2** produce (a film etc.) by animation. **3** give inspiration, encouragement, or renewed vigour to: *she has animated the government with a sense of political direction*. [Say ANNA mitt for the adjective, ANNA mate for the verb]

animated *adjective* **1** full of life and excitement; lively, vigorous: *an animated discussion*. **2** (of a film etc.) using techniques of animation. ▶ **animatedly** *adverb*

animation *noun* **1** vivacity, ardour. **2** the state of being alive. **3** *Film* the technique of filming successive drawings or positions of puppets to create an illusion of movement when the film is shown as a sequence.

animator *noun* a person who makes animated films.

animism *noun* **1** the attribution of a living soul to plants, inanimate objects, and natural phenomena. **2** the belief in a supernatural power that organizes and animates the material universe. ▶ **animist** *noun* **animistic** *adjective* [Say ANNA mism, anna MISS tick]

animosity *noun* (*plural* **animosities**) strong hostility: *an animosity towards women ◊ bitter cultural animosities between French and English*. [Say anna MOSSA tee]

animus *noun* **1** animosity or ill feeling: *a journalistic animus against the medical profession*. **2** motivation to do something: *the reformist animus came from within the party*. **3** *Psychology* Jung's term for the masculine part of a woman's personality (opp. ANIMA 2). [Say ANNA muss]

anion *noun* a negatively charged ion; an ion that is attracted to the anode in electrolysis (opp. CATION). ▶ **anionic** *adjective* [Say AN eye un, an eye ON ick]

anise *noun* **1** an umbel-bearing plant with aromatic seeds. **2** any of several trees and shrubs which bear fruit with the odour of anise. [Say ANNIS]

aniseed *noun* the seed of the anise, used to give a licorice-like flavour. [Say ANNA seed]

Anishinabe (also **Anishnabe**) • *noun* (*plural* **Anishinabe**) **1** the preferred name for the Ojibwa and Cree, part of the Algonquian language group, living in northern Quebec, northern and central Ontario, Manitoba, Saskatchewan, and Alberta. **2** the Algonquian language of this people. • *adjective* of this people or their culture. [Say a nisha NOBBY, a nish NOBBY]

ankh *noun* an ancient Egyptian symbol of life consisting of a looped bar with a shorter crossbar. [Say ANK]

ankle *noun* **1** the joint connecting the foot with the leg. **2** the part of the leg between this and the calf.

anklet *noun* an ornament or fetter worn around the ankle.

annalist *noun* a writer of annals.

annals *plural noun* **1** a narrative of events year by year. **2** historical records. **3** (in proper names) a learned journal.

annatto *noun* **1** a tropical tree, *Bixa orellana*. **2** an orange-red dye obtained from the seed coat of this tree, used esp. as a food colouring. [Say a NAT oh]

anneal *verb* heat (metal or glass) and allow it to cool slowly, esp. to toughen it. [Say a NEAL]

annelid *noun* an animal of the phylum Annelida, members of which, e.g. earthworms, have bodies made up of ring-shaped segments. [Say ANNA lid]

annex • *noun* (*plural* **annexes**) **1** a separate or added building, esp. for extra accommodation. **2** an addition to a document. **3** (now esp. in proper names) an area annexed to a city, usu. for housing development. • *verb* (**annexes**, **annexed**, **annexing**) **1** add or append as a subordinate part. **2** incorporate (territory of another) into one's own. ▶ **annexation** *noun*

annexationism *noun* **1** a policy which favours annexation of territory. **2** *Cdn* any of several historical movements favouring Canadian political union with the US. ▶ **annexationist** *noun*

annihilate *verb* (**annihilates**, **annihilated**, **annihilating**) **1** completely destroy; obliterate: *a bomb of this type could annihilate them all*. **2** defeat utterly; make insignificant or powerless: *their team was annihilated in the playoffs*. ▶ **annihilation** *noun* [Say a NIGH a late, a nigh a LAY sh'n]

anniversary *noun* (*plural* **anniversaries**) **1 a** the yearly return of a date on which an event took place in a previous year. **b** the anniversary of a wedding. **2** the celebration of this.

Anno Domini *adverb* in the year of the Christian era. [Say anno DOMMIN ee]

SPELL CHECK
anoint [ABC ✓]

Warning: When you apply oil to a person's head as part of a religious ceremony you **anoint** them. Do not double the *n* in **anoint**.

---

annotate *verb* (**annotates**, **annotated**, **annotating**) add explanatory notes to (a book, document, etc.). ▶ **annotation** *noun* **annotative** *adjective* **annotator** *noun* [Say ANNO tate, anno TAY sh'n]

announce *verb* (**announces**, **announced**, **announcing**) **1** make publicly known. **2** make known the arrival or imminence of (a guest, dinner, etc.).

announcement *noun* a statement in written or spoken form that makes something known.

announcer *noun* a person who announces speakers, singers, programs, etc., esp. on radio or television.

annoy *verb* cause slight anger or mental distress to: *I was annoyed by the constant chatter*. ▶ **annoyance** *noun* **annoying** *adjective* **annoyingly** *adverb*

annual • *adjective* **1** calculated over or covering a period of a year: *annual income*. **2** occurring every year: *an annual event*. **3** living or lasting for one year. • *noun* **1** a book etc. published once a year under the same title but with different contents. **2** a plant that lives only for a year or less.

annual allowable cut *noun* *Cdn* (*BC*) *Forestry* the volume of wood which may be cut each year in a specified area.

annual general meeting *noun* *Cdn*, *Brit.*, & *Austral.* a yearly meeting of members or shareholders, esp. for holding elections and reporting on the year's events.

annualized *adjective* (of rates of interest, inflation, etc.) calculated on an annual basis, as a projection from figures obtained for a shorter period.

annually *adverb* once every year: *the fair is held annually*.

annual report *noun* a yearly report made by a company's directors, containing the financial statements and a summary of the year's activities.

annuity *noun* (*plural* **annuities**) **1** a fixed sum of money paid to someone each year. **2** an investment of money entitling the investor to a series of equal annual sums. [Say a NEW a tee]

annul *verb* (**annuls**, **annulled**, **annulling**) **1** declare (a marriage etc.) invalid. **2** cancel, abolish. ▶ **annulment** *noun* [Say a NULL]

annulus *noun* (*plural* **annuli**) **1** a ring-shaped part. **2** the area between two concentric circles. [Say ANYA lus]

Annunciation *noun* *Christianity* **1** the occasion on which the angel Gabriel appeared to the Virgin Mary to announce to her that she would give birth to Jesus. **2** the festival commemorating this on 25 March. [Say a nun see AY sh'n]

anode *noun* **1** the positive electrode in an electrolytic cell or electronic valve or tube. **2** the negative terminal of a primary cell such as a battery (*opp.* CATHODE). ▶ **anodic** *adjective* [Say AN ode, a NOD ick]

anodize *verb* (**anodizes**, **anodized**, **anodizing**) coat (a metal, esp. aluminum) with a protective oxide layer by electrolysis. ▶ **anodizer** *noun* [Say ANNA dize]

anodyne • *adjective* not likely to cause offence or disagreement and somewhat dull: *anodyne music*. • *noun* a painkilling drug or medicine. [Say ANNA dine]

anoint *verb* **1** apply oil or ointment to, esp. as a religious ceremony, e.g. at baptism, or the consecration of a priest or king, or in ministering to the sick. **2** choose (a leader, successor, etc.) as though by anointing: *self-anointed authorities love to make declarations about the language*. **3** (usu. foll. by *with*) smear, rub: *roast potatoes anointed with olive oil*.

anointing of the sick *noun* a rite of some Christian denominations (a sacrament in the Catholic Church) in which a gravely ill person is prayed for and anointed with oil as a sign of healing.

anomalous *adjective* deviating from what is standard, normal, or expected: *an anomalous situation* ◊ *sentences which are grammatically anomalous*. ▶ **anomalously** *adverb* [Say a NOMMA lus]

anomaly *noun* (*plural* **anomalies**) something that deviates from what is standard, normal, or expected: *the apparent anomaly that those who produced the wealth were the poorest* ◊ *there are a number of anomalies in the present system*. [Say a NOMMA lee]

anon. *abbreviation* anonymous; an anonymous author.

anonymity *noun* the state of remaining unknown to most other people: *she agreed to the interview on condition of anonymity* ◊ *the anonymity of the big city*. [Say anna NIMMA tee]

anonymous *adjective* **1** not identified by name; of unknown name: *an anonymous phone call* ◊ *the donor wishes to remain anonymous*. **2** of unknown or undeclared source or authorship. **3** having no outstanding, individual, or unusual features; unremarkable or impersonal: *long stretches of dull and anonymous countryside*. **4** (**Anonymous**) (placed after noun) designating a mutual support group in which the members do not have to reveal their names: *Alcoholics Anonymous*. ▶ **anonymously** *adverb*

anorak *noun* **1** a waterproof jacket of cloth or plastic, usu. with a hood and with drawstrings at the waist, cuffs, and hood. **2** a light jacket or cardigan with a drawstring waist. [Say ANNA rack]

anorexia *noun* **1** a lack or loss of appetite for food. **2** (also **anorexia nervosa**) a psychological illness, esp. in young women, characterized by an obsessive desire to lose weight by refusing to eat. [Say anna REXIA (nair VOSA)]

anorexic • *adjective* **1** involving, producing, or characterized by a lack of appetite, esp. in anorexia nervosa. **2** extremely thin. • *noun* a person with anorexia. [Say anna REX ic]

another • *adjective* **1** an additional; one more. **2** a person like or comparable to: *another Gretzky*. **3** a different: *quite another matter*. **4** some or any other: *will not do another man's work*. • *pronoun* **1** an additional one: *have another*. **2** a different one: *take this book and bring me another*. **3** some or any other one: *I love another*.

answer • *noun* **1** something said or done to deal with or in reaction to a question, statement, or circumstance. **2** the solution to a problem. **3** (foll. by *to*) an equivalent or rival: *Quebec's answer to the Champs Élysées*. • *verb* **1** make an answer to: *answer me* ◊ *answer my question*. **2** (often foll. by *to*) make an answer. **3** respond to the summons or signal of: *answer the door*. **4** be satisfactory for (a purpose or need). **5** (foll. by *for*, *to*) be responsible: *you will answer to me for your conduct*. **6** (foll. by *to*) correspond, esp. to a description. PHRASES **answer back** answer a rebuke etc. impudently. **answer to the name of** be called.

answerable *adjective* **1** required to explain or justify one's actions to; responsible or having to report to: *I'm not answerable to you for my every movement*. **2** responsible for: *employers are answerable for the negligence of their employees*. **3** that can be answered.

ant *noun* a widely distributed small insect living in complex social colonies, the males of which have four transparent wings during mating season. PHRASES **have ants in one's pants** fidget, esp. because of nervousness or impatience.

antacid • *noun* a substance that prevents or corrects acidity esp. in the stomach. • *adjective* having these properties.

antagonism *noun* active opposition or hostility: *his antagonism towards the locals* ◊ *the profound antagonism between French and English Canada*. [Say an TAG'n ism]

antagonist *noun* **1** an opponent or adversary. **2** a muscle, organism, or substance that partially or completely opposes the action of another. ▶ **antagonistic** *adjective* [Say an TAG'n ist]

antagonize *verb* (**antagonizes, antagonized, antagonizing**) cause someone to become hostile: *violent protests will antagonize the public*. [Say an TAG'n ize]

Antarctic • *adjective* of the south polar regions. • *noun* these regions. [Say an ARK tic or ant AR tic]

ante • *noun* **1** a stake put up by a player in poker etc. before receiving cards. **2** an amount to be paid in advance. • *verb* (**antes, anted, anteing**) **1** put up as an ante. **2 a** bet, stake. **b** pay: *the report calls on Ottawa to ante up $80 million* ◊ *the owners have to ante up if they want to attract the best talent*. PHRASES **up** (or **raise**) **the ante** increase what is at stake: *the Serb forces tried to up the ante by shooting down our planes*. [Say ANTY]

ante- *prefix* forming nouns and adjectives meaning "before, preceding": *antedate*.

anteater *noun* **1** a toothless mammal with a long snout and sticky tongue, which feeds on ants and termites. **2** any animal resembling this, e.g. an aardvark.

antecedent • *noun* **1** a thing or event that existed before or logically precedes another: *the courtly romance was the antecedent of the modern novel*. **2** *Grammar* a word, phrase, clause, or sentence, to which a following word (esp. a pronoun, usu. following) refers: *in "He grabbed the ball and threw it in the air" "ball" is the antecedent of "it"*. **3** (in *plural*) a person's ancestors or family and social background: *her early life and antecedents have been traced*. • *adjective* preceding in time or order: *the chaos antecedent to creation* ◊ *a patient whose antecedent history is unclear*. [Say anty SEED'nt]

antedate • *verb* (**antedates, antedated, antedating**) **1** exist or occur at a date earlier than.

2 assign an earlier date to (a document, event, etc.), esp. one earlier than its actual date. [Say anty DATE]

antelope *noun* (*plural* **antelope** or **antelopes**) **1** a family of deer-like ruminants abundant in Africa and typically tall, slender, graceful, and swift-moving with smooth hair and upward-pointing horns, including gazelles and gnus. **2** = PRONGHORN.

antenna *noun* **1** (*plural* **antennas**) a metal rod or other structure by which signals are transmitted or received as part of a radio or television transmitting or receiving system. **2** (*plural* **antennae**) one of a pair of mobile appendages on the heads of insects, crustaceans, etc., sensitive to touch and taste. [For *antennae* say an TENNY]

anterior *adjective* nearer the front: *the anterior cruciate ligament is in the knee*. [Say an TEERY er]

anteroom *noun* a small room leading to a main one, esp. one used as a waiting room. [Say ANTY room]

anthem *noun* **1** a solemn song expressing loyalty etc., esp. = NATIONAL ANTHEM. **2** a short choral composition set to a passage of scripture and sung during church services. **3** a song adopted by a group as expressing their feelings, aspirations, etc.

anther *noun* the tip of a stamen containing pollen.

anthill *noun* a mound-like nest built by ants or termites.

anthologist *noun* a person who compiles an anthology. [Say ann THOLLA jist]

anthologize *verb* (**anthologizes, anthologized, anthologizing**) compile or include in an anthology. [Say ann THOLLA jize]

anthology *noun* (*plural* **anthologies**) a published collection of poems, stories, songs, reproductions of paintings, etc. [Say ann THOLLA jee]

anthracite *noun* coal of a hard variety burning with little flame and smoke. [Say AN thruh site]

anthrax *noun* a lethal disease of sheep and cattle caused by bacterial spores and transmissible to humans.

anthropocentric *adjective* regarding human beings as the centre of existence. [Say an thruppa SEN trick]

anthropocentrism *noun* the view of humankind as the central most important element of existence, esp. as opposed to God or animals. [Say an thruppa SEN trism]

anthropoid • *adjective* **1** esp. *Biology* of or relating to the group of higher primates, which includes monkeys, apes, and humans, esp. designating an ape belonging to the family of great apes. **2** resembling a human being in form. • *noun* esp. *Biology* a higher primate, esp. an ape. [Say ANTHRA poid]

anthropological *adjective* referring to or based on the study of human beings. [Say an thruppa LOGICAL]

anthropologist *noun* a person who studies anthropology. [Say anthra POLLA jist]

anthropology *noun* **1** the study of human beings, esp. of their societies and customs. **2** the study of the structure and evolution of human beings as animals. [Say anthra POLLA jee]

anthropomorphic *adjective* **1** of or characterized by anthropomorphism. **2** having or representing a human form. [Say an thruppa MOR fic]

anthropomorphism *noun* the attribution of human characteristics to a god, animal, or thing: *anthropomorphism was common in early treatises on animal behaviour*. [Say an thruppa MORF ism]

anthropomorphize *verb* (**anthropomorphizes, anthropomorphized, anthropomorphizing**) attribute human characteristics or behaviour to a god, animal, or object: *cartoons are full of anthropomorphized cats, mice, and rabbits behaving like humans*. [Say an thruppa MORF ize]

anti • *preposition* opposed to: *is anti everything*. • *noun* (*plural* **antis**) a person opposed to a particular policy etc. [Say AN tee or AN tie]

anti- *prefix* forming nouns and adjectives meaning: **1** opposed to; against: *anticlerical*. **2** preventing: *antifreeze*. **3** designed to destroy or render useless: *anti-aircraft*. **4** the opposite of: *anticlimax*. **5** rival: *antipope*. **6** unlike the conventional form: *anti-hero*. [Say AN tee or AN tie]

antialiasing *noun* the reduction or prevention of aliasing, esp. the smoothing of curved or inclined lines that appear artificially jagged in a computer image. [Say anty AILY us ing]

anti-ballistic missile *noun* a missile designed to intercept and destroy a ballistic missile. Abbreviation: **ABM**. [Say anty buh LISS tick]

antibiotic • *noun* any of various substances, e.g. penicillin, produced by micro-organisms or made synthetically, that can inhibit or destroy susceptible micro-organisms, esp. disease-producing bacteria and fungi. • *adjective* functioning as an antibiotic. [Say anty by OT ic]

antibody *noun* (*plural* **antibodies**) any of various blood proteins produced in response to and then counteracting antigens. Antibodies combine chemically with substances which the body recognizes as alien, such as bacteria, viruses, and foreign substances in the blood.

antic • *noun* **1** (usu. in *plural*) absurd or foolish behaviour. **2** an absurd or silly action. • *adjective* excited, agitated, frenzied.

anti-choice *adjective derogatory* opposed to the principle of allowing women to choose to have an abortion.

Antichrist *noun* **1** an arch-enemy of Christ. **2** a postulated opponent of Christ expected by the early Church to appear before the end of the world.

anticipate *verb* (**anticipates**, **anticipated**, **anticipating**) **1** foresee and deal with ahead of time: *they failed to anticipate a full-scale invasion*. **2** expect; regard as probable: *did not anticipate any difficulty* ◊ *it was anticipated that the rains would slow the military campaign*. **3** look forward to: *her eagerly anticipated holiday*. [Say an TISSA pate]

anticipation *noun* the act or process of anticipating: *her eyes sparkled with anticipation*.

anticipatory *adjective* happening, performed, or felt in anticipation of something: *an anticipatory flash of excitement*. [Say an TISSA puh tory]

anticlerical • *adjective* opposed to the influence of the clergy, esp. in politics. • *noun* an anticlerical person. ▶ **anticlericalism** *noun*

anticlimactic *adjective* serving as a disappointing conclusion to an exciting or impressive series of events: *an anticlimactic ending to an otherwise thrilling movie*.

anticlimax *noun* a trivial conclusion to something significant or impressive, esp. where a climax was expected.

anticoagulant • *noun* any drug or substance that retards or inhibits coagulation, esp. of the blood. • *adjective* retarding or inhibiting coagulation. [Say anty co AG yoo lint]

anticonvulsant • *noun* a drug that prevents or reduces the severity of convulsions, esp. epileptic fits. • *adjective* preventing or reducing convulsions. [Say anty cun VUL sint]

anticyclone *noun* a weather system with high barometric pressure at its centre, usu. associated with calm, dry conditions. [Say anty SIGH clone]

antidepressant • *noun* a drug that alleviates depression. • *adjective* alleviating depression.

antidote *noun* **1** a medicine etc. taken or given to counteract poison. **2** anything that counteracts something unpleasant or harmful: *laughter is a good antidote to stress*.

antifreeze *noun* a substance (usu. ethylene glycol) added to water to lower its freezing point, esp. in the radiator of a motor vehicle.

antigen *noun* a foreign substance, e.g. a toxin, which causes the body to produce antibodies. ▶ **antigenic** *adjective* [Say ANTY jen]

anti-gravity *noun* a hypothetical force opposing gravity.

anti-hero *noun* (*plural* **anti-heroes**) a central character in a story or drama who noticeably lacks conventional heroic attributes.

antihistamine *noun* a substance that counteracts the effects of histamine, used esp. in the treatment of allergies. [Say anty HISTA min or anty HISTA meen]

anti-inflammatory • *adjective* reducing inflammation of body tissues and associated pain, swelling, etc. • *noun* (*plural* **anti-inflammatories**) an anti-inflammatory drug or treatment. [Say anty in FLAMMA tory]

anti-knock *adjective* (of a compound added to motor fuel etc.) preventing premature combustion in an engine.

anti-lock brake *noun* an automobile brake which prevents skidding by alternately locking and freeing the wheels when applied suddenly.

antimatter *noun* *Physics* a hypothetical matter composed solely of antiparticles.

antimony *noun* a brittle silvery-white metallic element used esp. in alloys. [Say ANTA moany]

anti-nuclear *adjective* opposed to the development of nuclear weapons or nuclear power.

antioxidant *noun* **1** a substance (e.g. vitamins C and E) that removes potentially damaging oxidizing substances in a living organism. **2** a substance that inhibits oxidation, esp. used to counteract deterioration of stored food products. [Say anty OXA dint]

antiparticle *noun* *Physics* an elementary particle having the same mass as a given particle but opposite electric or magnetic properties.

antipasto *noun* (*plural* **antipastos** or **antipasti**) **1** a cold appetizer preceding an Italian meal, usu. consisting of meat or fish and vegetables or fruit. **2** a mixture of pickled vegetables served as an appetizer. [Say anty PASS toe for the singular; for *ANTIPASTI* say anty PASS tee]

antipathetic *adjective* having a strong aversion or natural opposition: *it is human nature to be antipathetic to change*. [Say an tippa THETIC]

antipathy *noun* (*plural* **antipathies**) (often foll. by *to*, *for*, *between*) a strong or deep-seated aversion or dislike. [Say an TIPPA thee (with TH as in *THIEF*)]

anti-personnel *adjective* (of a bomb, mine, etc.) designed to kill or injure people rather than to damage buildings or equipment.

antiperspirant • *noun* a substance applied to the skin to prevent or reduce perspiration. • *adjective* that acts as an antiperspirant.

antiphon *noun* **1** a hymn or psalm, the parts of which are sung or recited alternately by two groups. **2** a phrase from this. **3** a Biblical verse sung or recited at a specific moment in a Christian liturgy, e.g. at the

beginning of the Mass or before Communion. [Say ANTA fon]

Antipodean • *adjective* having to do with Australia or New Zealand. • *noun* a person from Australia or New Zealand. [Say an tippa DEE in]

antipodes *plural noun* **1** places on opposite sides of the earth to each other. **2** (**Antipodes**) Australia and New Zealand. [Say an TIPPA deez]

antipope *noun* a person set up as pope in opposition to one (held by others to be) canonically chosen.

antiproton *noun* the negatively charged antiparticle of a proton.

antiquarian • *adjective* **1** of or dealing in antiques or rare books. **2** of the study of antiquities. • *noun* an antiquary. [Say anta KWERRY in]

antiquary *noun* (*plural* **antiquaries**) a person who studies or collects antiques or antiquities. [Say ANTA kwerry]

antiquated *adjective* out of date. [Say ANTA kwated]

antique • *noun* an object of considerable age, esp. an item of furniture or the decorative arts having a high value. • *adjective* **1** of or existing from an early date: *an antique clock*. **2** old-fashioned, archaic: *unions defending antique work practices*. **3** of ancient times: *statues of antique gods*. • *verb* (**antiques, antiqued, antiquing**) **1** give an antique appearance to (furniture etc.) artificially. **2** (usu. as **antiquing** *noun*) shop for antiques.

antiquity *noun* (*plural* **antiquities**) **1** ancient times, esp. the period before the Middle Ages. **2** great age: *a city of great antiquity*. **3** (usu. in *plural*) physical remains or relics from ancient times, esp. buildings and works of art. **4** (in *plural*) customs, events, etc., of ancient times. **5** the people of ancient times regarded collectively. [Say ann TICKWA tee]

anti-Semite *noun* a person hostile to or prejudiced against Jews. [Say anty SEM ite]

anti-Semitic *adjective* hostile to or prejudiced against Jews. [Say anty suh MIT ick]

anti-Semitism *noun* hatred of Jews; unfair treatment of Jews. [Say anty SEMMA tism]

antiseptic • *adjective* **1** counteracting contamination by preventing the growth of disease-causing micro-organisms: *antiseptic mouthwash*. **2** sterile or free from contamination. **3** lacking character or emotion: *their squeaky-clean home epitomizes this antiseptic respectability*. • *noun* an antiseptic substance.

anti-social *adjective* **1** opposed or contrary to normal social instincts or practices. **2** not sociable; unfriendly.

antithesis *noun* (*plural* **antitheses**) **1** a person or thing that is the direct opposite of someone or something else: *love is the antithesis of selfishness*. **2** contrast or opposition between two things: *the antithesis between occult and rational mentalities*. **3** a contrast of ideas expressed by parallelism of strongly contrasted words. [Say an TITH uh sis, an TITH uh seez]

antithetical *adjective* **1** contrasted, opposite: *people whose religious beliefs are antithetical to mine*. **2** connected with, containing, or using the rhetorical device of antithesis. [Say anta THETIC 'll]

antitoxin *noun* an antibody that counteracts a toxin.

antitrust *adjective* US (of a law etc.) opposed to or controlling monopolies (see TRUST *noun* 9).

antivenin *noun* a substance containing antibodies against specific poisons in the venom of esp. snakes, spiders, scorpions, etc. [Say ANTY ven in]

antiviral *adjective* effective against viruses.

antler *noun* **1** each of the branched horns of a (usu. male) deer. **2** a branch of this. ▶ **antlered** *adjective*

antonym *noun* a word opposite in meaning to another, e.g. *bad* and *good*. [Say ANTA nim]

antsy *adjective* (**antsier, antsiest**) *informal* agitated, impatient, or fidgety.

anus *noun* (*plural* **anuses**) the opening at the end of the alimentary canal through which solid waste matter leaves the body.

anvil *noun* **1** a block (usu. of iron) with a flat top, concave sides, and often a pointed end, on which metals are worked in forging. **2** a cloud with a horizontally extended upper part which looks like an anvil: *anvil clouds*.

anxiety *noun* (*plural* **anxieties**) **1** a feeling of worry, nervousness, or unease, typically about an imminent event or something with an uncertain outcome: *he felt a surge of anxiety* ◊ *anxieties about the moral decline of today's youth are unfounded*. **2** desire to do something: *in his anxiety to end the stalemate*. **3** *Psychology* a nervous disorder marked by excessive uneasiness and apprehension, typically with compulsive behaviour or panic attacks. [Say angz EYE a tee]

> **WRITING TIP**
> **anxious**
>
> The use of **anxious** to mean "eager", as in *I'm anxious to meet Marie-Claire*, is well established, despite being considered incorrect by some.

anxious *adjective* **1** worried or troubled: *anxious about our exams*. **2** causing or marked by anxiety: *an anxious moment*. **3** disputed earnestly desiring; eager: *anxious to succeed*. ▶ **anxiously** *adverb* [Say ANK shus]

any • *adjective* **1 a** one, no matter which, of several: *cannot find any answer*. **b** some: *do you have any sugar?* **2 a** minimal amount of: *hardly any difference*. **3** whichever is chosen: *any fool knows that*. **4** an appreciable or significant: *did not stay for any length of time*. • *pronoun* **1** any one: *did not know any of them*. **2** any number: *are any of them yours?* **3** any amount: *is there any left?* • *adverb* at all, in some degree: *is that any good?* ◊ *do not make it any larger*. PHRASES **any time** (or **day** or **minute** etc.) **now** *informal* at any time in the near future.

anybody *noun & pronoun* **1 a** a person, no matter who. **b** a person of any kind. **c** whatever person is chosen. **2** a person of importance: *he isn't anybody*.

anyhow *adverb* **1** anyway. **2** in a disorderly manner or state: *just does his work anyhow*.

> **SPELL CHECK**
> **anymore, any more**
>
> Always spell **any more** as two words when specifying a quantity of something, as in *Surely, Tony, you can't eat any more ice cream!*

anymore *adverb* (also **any more**) **1** any longer; to any further extent: *don't like you anymore*. **2** *informal* nowadays: *almost everyone has a TV anymore*.

> **SPELL CHECK**
> **anyone, any one**
>
> Note the difference between **anyone** and **any one**: *Conrad won't talk to anyone; any one of us could have upset him*.

anyone *pronoun* anybody.

anyplace *adverb informal* anywhere.

anything • *pronoun* **1** a thing, no matter which. **2** a thing of any kind. **3** whatever thing is chosen. • *adverb* (usu. foll. by *like*) in any way whatsoever; at all: *doesn't sound anything like Mozart*. PHRASES **anything but** not at all. *was anything but honest*. **like anything** *informal* with great vigour, intensity, etc.

any time *adverb* at any time.

anyway *adverb* **1** in any way or manner. **2** at any rate. **3** (also *informal* **anyways**) in any case. **4** to resume: *anyway, as I was saying*.

anywhere • *adverb* **1** in or to any place. **2** designating any quantity etc. within a specified range: *anywhere from $10 to $20*. **3** to any extent: *is it anywhere near full?* • *pronoun* any place: *anywhere will do*.

A-OK *abbreviation informal* excellent; in good order.

aorta *noun* (*plural* **aortas**) the main artery, giving rise to the arterial network through which oxygenated blood is supplied to the body from the heart. ▶ **aortic** *adjective* [Say ay ORTA]

A/P *abbreviation* accounts payable.

apace *adverb* swiftly, quickly: *work continues apace*. [Say a PACE]

Apache • *noun* **1** (*plural* **Apache** or **Apaches**) a member of an Aboriginal people of the southwestern US, primarily Arizona and New Mexico. **2** the Athapaskan language of the Apache. • *adjective* of the Apache or their culture or language. [Say a PATCH ee]

apart *adverb* **1** separately; not together. **2** into pieces. **3** to or on one side; aside. **4** to or at a distance. **5** from one another: *can't tell the twins apart*. PHRASES **apart from 1** except for. **2** in addition to: *apart from roses we grow irises*.

apartheid *noun* **1** the former South African policy of segregation and discrimination against non-whites. **2** segregation or discrimination in other contexts: *sexual apartheid*. [Say a PAR tite or a PAR tate or a PAR tate]

apartment *noun* **1 a** one or more rooms rented and used as a residence, esp. in a building with other similar dwellings. **b** a building other than a house divided into several apartments. **2** (usu. in *plural*) a room in a house.

apartment hotel *noun* a hotel with furnished suites of rooms including kitchens, for short-term or long-term rental.

apartness *noun* the quality of being or standing apart; separation.

apathetic *adjective* having or showing no emotion or interest. ▶ **apathetically** *adverb* [Say appa THETIC]

apathy *noun* lack of interest or concern: *widespread apathy amongst voters*. [Say APPA thee (with TH as in THIEF)]

apatite *noun* a naturally occurring crystalline mineral of calcium phosphate and fluoride, used in the manufacture of fertilizers. [Say APPA tite]

APB *abbreviation* US (*plural* **APBs**) ALL-POINTS BULLETIN.

APC *abbreviation* (*plural* **APCs**) ARMOURED PERSONNEL CARRIER.

ape • *noun* **1** any of a family of primates characterized by the absence of a tail, e.g. the gorilla, chimpanzee, or gibbon. **2** (in general use) any monkey. **3** a clumsy or stupid person. • *verb* (**apes**, **aped**, **aping**) imitate, mimic. PHRASES **go ape** *slang* become crazy.

ape man *noun* (*plural* **ape men**) any of various ape-like primates held to be forerunners of present-day humans.

aperitif *noun* an alcoholic drink taken before a meal to stimulate the appetite. [Say a perra TEEF]

aperture *noun* **1** an opening; a gap. **2** a space through which light passes in an optical or photographic instrument. [Say APPER chur]

apex *noun* (*plural* **apexes**) **1** the highest point: *the apex of the roof*. **2** a climax; a high point of achievement etc.: *the apex of his career was when they won the Stanley Cup*. **3** the vertex of a triangle or cone. **4** the highest point in a hierarchy: *at the apex of the financial system are the chartered banks*. **5** (*plural* **apices**) Botany the growing point of a shoot. [Say AY pecks, AY puh seez]

aphid *noun* a small insect with uniformly textured wings, which feeds by sucking sap from leaves, stems, or roots of plants. [Say AY fid or AFF id]

aphis *noun* (*plural* **aphides**) an aphid, esp. of the genus *Aphis*. [Say AY fiss or AFF iss, AYFA deez or AFFA deez]

aphorism *noun* a short pithy saying: *it is a long-standing aphorism in the legal profession that he who acts on his own behalf has a fool for a client*. ▶ **aphoristic** *adjective* [Say AFFER ism]

aphrodisiac • *adjective* that arouses sexual desire. • *noun* an aphrodisiac substance. [Say afro DEEZY ack or afro DIZZY ack]

apiary *noun* (*plural* **apiaries**) a place where bees are kept. [Say APE ee airy]

apices *plural* of APEX 5. [Say AY puh seez]

apiece *adverb* for each one; severally: *ten dollars apiece*.

aplenty *adverb* in great quantity: *bargains aplenty*.

aplomb *noun* assurance or self-confidence, esp. when in a demanding situation: *all the children handle interviews and auditions with aplomb*. [Say a PLOM]

apnea *noun* Medical a temporary cessation of breathing. [Say AP nee ah or ap NEE ah]

apocalypse *noun* **1** catastrophic destruction, esp. the end of the world. **2** an event involving destruction or damage on an awesome or catastrophic scale: *a stock market apocalypse*. **3** (**the Apocalypse**) another name for the biblical book of Revelation, in which the final destruction of the world is described. [Say a POCKA lips]

apocalyptic *adjective* **1** describing or prophesying the complete destruction of the world: *the apocalyptic visions of ecologists*. **2** resembling the end of the world; momentous or catastrophic: *the struggle between the two countries is assuming apocalyptic proportions*. **3** of or resembling the biblical Apocalypse: *apocalyptic imagery*. [Say a pocka LIP tick]

Apocrypha *plural noun* **1** those books of the Septuagint version of the Hebrew Scriptures which were later rejected from the Jewish canon; most are considered canonical by the Catholic and Orthodox Churches, but are not included in the Protestant Bible. **2** (**apocrypha**) writings or reports not considered genuine. [Say a POCKRA fuh]

apocryphal *adjective* **1** of doubtful authenticity. **2** invented, mythical: *an apocryphal story*. **3** of or belonging to the Apocrypha. [Say a POCKRA full]

apogee *noun* **1** the point in a celestial body's orbit where it is furthest from the earth (*opp.* PERIGEE). **2** the highest point in the development of something; the climax or culmination of something: *the Roman Empire, even at its apogee, could not match Europe's current unity* ◊ *baroque music reached its apogee with Bach*. [Say APPA jee]

apolitical *adjective* **1** not interested in or concerned with politics. **2** without political bias. [Say ay POLITICAL]

apologetic • *adjective* regretfully acknowledging or excusing an offence or failure. • *noun* (usu. in *plural*) reasoned arguments or writings in defence of something, esp. of a religion or political theory. ▶ **apologetically** *adverb* [Say a polla JET ick]

apologist *noun* a person who defends something by argument: *apologists for the government*. [Say a POLLA jist]

apologize *verb* (**apologizes**, **apologized**, **apologizing**) make an apology; express regret.

apology *noun* (*plural* **apologies**) **1** a regretful acknowledgement of an offence or failure: *we owe you an apology*. **2** an assurance that no offence was intended. **3** a poor or scanty specimen of: *this apology for a letter*.

apoplectic *adjective* **1** of, causing, suffering, or liable to apoplexy. **2** *informal* enraged. [Say appa PLECK tick]

apoplexy *noun* a sudden loss of consciousness, voluntary movement, and sensation caused by

A

blockage or rupture of a brain artery; a stroke. [Say APPA plexy]

apostasy noun (plural **apostasies**) the abandonment or renunciation of a religious or political belief or principle. [Say a POSSTA see]

apostate • noun a person who renounces a former belief etc.: *sinners and apostates*. • adjective who has renounced a religious or political belief: *an apostate Catholic priest*. [Say a POSS tate]

apostle noun **1** (**Apostle**) **a** any of a group of followers of Christ made up of the twelve disciples and Paul and Barnabas, sent out to preach the gospel after the Resurrection. **b** the first successful Christian missionary in a country or to a people. **2** a leader or outstanding figure, esp. of a reform movement: *apostle of temperance*. **3** a messenger or representative. **4** one of the twelve administrative officials of Mormonism. [Say a POSSLE]

Apostles' Creed noun a Christian creed dating from the 4th century, traditionally ascribed to the Apostles, and now used in many Christian liturgies.

apostolic adjective **1** of or relating to the Apostles: *apostolic writings*. **2** of the Pope regarded as the successor of St. Peter. [Say appa STAW lick]

apostrophe[1] noun a punctuation mark used to indicate: **1** the omission of letters or numbers, e.g. *can't; he's; 1 Jan. '97*. **2** the possessive case (e.g. *Dad's book; boys' coats*). [Say a POSSTRA fee]

apostrophe[2] noun an exclamatory passage in a speech or poem, addressed to a person (often dead or absent) or thing. ▶ **apostrophize** verb (**apostrophizes**, **apostrophized**, **apostrophizing**) [Say a POSSTRA fee, a POSSTRA fize]

apothecary noun (plural **apothecaries**) hist. a person licensed to dispense medicines and drugs. [Say a POTH a carry (POTH rhymes with *BROTH*)]

apotheosis noun (plural **apotheoses**) **1** elevation to divine status: *the apotheosis of the Emperor Augustus*. **2** a glorification of a thing; a sublime example: *apotheosis of the dance ◊ his appearance as Hamlet was the apotheosis of his career*. [Say a pothy OH sis, a pothy OH seez]

app noun Computing informal application.

appal verb = APPALL. [Say a PAUL]

Appalachian • adjective **1** of or relating to the Appalachian Mountains in the eastern US. **2** of or relating to the region or people of Appalachia in eastern North America. • noun a native or inhabitant of Appalachia. [Say appa LAY sh'n]

appall verb (**appalls**, **appalled**, **appalling**) greatly dismay or horrify. [Say a PAUL]

appalling adjective informal shocking, unpleasant; bad. ▶ **appallingly** adverb [Say a PAUL ing]

Appaloosa noun an American breed of horse, having dark spots on a light background. [Say appa LOOSSA]

apparatus noun (plural **apparatuses**) **1** the equipment needed for a particular purpose or function, esp. scientific or technical. **2** complex structure of an organization: *apparatus of government*. **3** the organs used to perform a particular process: *digestive apparatus*. [Say appa RAT us or appa RATE us]

apparel noun clothing, dress. [Say a PAIR'll]

apparent adjective **1** readily perceivable. **2** seeming.

apparently adverb according to what one has heard or read; according to the way something appears: *apparently they're getting back together ◊ I thought she was retiring but apparently she's not*.

apparition noun **1** a sudden or dramatic appearance, esp. of a ghost. **2** a visible ghost. [Say appa RISH'n]

appeal • verb **1** make an earnest or formal request; plead: *appealed for calm*. **2** (usu. foll. by *to*) be attractive or of interest; be pleasing. **3** (foll. by *to*) resort to or cite for support. **4** Law **a** (often foll. by *to*) apply (to a higher court) for a reconsideration of the decision of a lower court. **b** refer to a higher court to review (a case). **c** (foll. by *against*) apply to a higher court to reconsider (a verdict or sentence). **5** request a review of (a decision) by an authority. • noun **1** a serious, urgent, or heartfelt request: *made an appeal for the return of the ring*. **2** an attempt to obtain financial support: *the charity's end-of-year appeal*. **3** Law an application to a higher court for a decision to be reversed: *deciding whether to lodge an appeal ◊ the right of appeal*. **4** attractiveness; appealing quality: *sex appeal*. **5** an address to a principle or quality in anticipation of a favourable response: *an appeal to his better nature*.

appealing adjective attractive, likeable. ▶ **appealingly** adverb

appear verb **1** become or be visible. **2** be evident: *a new problem then appeared*. **3** seem: *appeared healthy*. **4** present oneself publicly or formally, esp. on stage or as the accused or a witness or counsel in a law court: *longed to appear on Broadway ◊ appeared in court for sentencing*. **5** be published: *it appeared in the papers*.

appearance noun **1** an act of performing or participating in a public event: *his guest appearance was sponsored by Laurie, Katherine, and Peng*. **2** the way that someone or something looks: *overly concerned with his appearance ◊ they are similar in appearance*. **3** an impression given by someone or something, although this may be misleading: *gives the appearance of trying hard ◊ read it with every appearance of interest*. **4** an act of becoming visible or noticeable; an arrival: *the sudden appearance of her daughter startled her*. **5** a process of coming into existence or use: *the appearance of the railway*. ▶ PHRASES **keep up appearances** maintain an impression or pretense of affluence, virtue, etc. **make** (or **put in**) **an appearance** be present, esp. briefly. **to all appearances** as far as can be seen.

appearance notice noun Cdn Law a written form given by a police officer to an accused person at the scene of the crime, stating the date, time, and place that the accused must appear in court.

appease verb (**appeases**, **appeased**, **appeasing**) **1** pacify or placate, esp. by making concessions or acceding to demands: *amendments have been added to appease local pressure groups*. **2** satisfy (an appetite, scruples): *a chocolate bar appeased our hunger ◊ we give to charity because it appeases our guilt*. ▶ **appeasement** noun **appeaser** noun

appellant noun Law a person who appeals to a higher court. [Say a PELL'nt]

appellate adjective Law (esp. of a court) concerned with or dealing with appeals. [Say a PELLET]

appellation noun formal a name or title; nomenclature. [Say appa LAY sh'n]

append verb attach, affix, add, esp. to a written document etc.: *the survey results are appended to this chapter ◊ five people had appended their signatures to the petition*.

appendage noun a smaller or less important part of something larger. [Say a PEN didge]

appendectomy noun (plural **appendectomies**) the

surgical removal of the appendix. [Say appen DECKTA mee]

appendicitis noun inflammation of the appendix. [Say a penda SITE iss]

appendix noun (plural **appendices** or **appendixes**) **1** a small outgrowth of tissue forming a tube-shaped sac attached to the lower end of the large intestine. **2** subsidiary matter at the end of a book or document.

appetite noun **1** a desire for food: lost my appetite. **2** a natural desire to satisfy bodily needs, esp. for sexual activity: satisfied his carnal appetites. **3** a strong liking or desire: an insatiable appetite for life.

appetizer noun a small amount of food or drink which stimulates the appetite before a meal.

appetizing adjective pleasing; stimulating an appetite, esp. for food. ▶ **appetizingly** adverb

applaud verb **1** show approval or praise by clapping: the audience applauded vigorously ◊ her speech was applauded enthusiastically. **2** express approval of: the decision was applauded by all the interested parties.

applause noun clapping etc. as an expression of approbation: let's give them a round of applause.

apple noun **1** the round fruit of a tree of the rose family, usu. having thin green or red skin and crisp flesh. **2** (also **apple tree**) the tree bearing this. PHRASES **apples and oranges** irreconcilably different issues etc., esp. when in comparison. **apple of one's eye** a cherished person or thing. **upset the apple cart** spoil careful plans.

apple-cheeked adjective having round, rosy cheeks.

applejack noun a liquor distilled from fermented apple juice.

apple-pie order noun perfect order; extreme neatness: everything was in apple-pie order.

applesauce noun **1** mashed stewed apples, often served with pork or as a dessert. **2** informal nonsense.

appliance noun **1** an electrical or gas-powered device or piece of equipment used for a specific task, esp. for domestic tasks such as washing dishes etc. **2** a prosthetic or orthodontic device.

applicability noun relevance, appropriateness: the applicability of this theory to Canadian reality is doubtful. [Say app lick ABILITY or a plick ABILITY]

applicable adjective relevant or appropriate: applicable taxes extra ◊ the same process will be applicable to all offenders. [Say APP lickable or a PLICKABLE]

applicant noun a person who applies for something.

application noun **1** the action of putting something on a surface: a fresh application of makeup. **2** a formal request, usu. in writing, for employment, membership, etc.: an application for a position ◊ application forms. **3 a** a practical use or relevance: this principle has no application to the present case. **b** the action of putting something into operation: the application of general rules to particular cases ◊ massage has far-reaching medical applications. **4** sustained or concentrated effort; hard work: the job takes a great deal of patience and application. **5** a task that a computer can be programmed to do.

applicator noun **1** a device for applying a substance to a surface. **2** a device to aid insertion of something, e.g. a tampon, into a body orifice. **3** a person who applies something, such as pesticide or paint.

applied adjective (of a subject of study) put to practical use rather than theoretical (compare PURE adjective 8).

appliqué • noun ornamental work in which fabric is cut out and attached, usu. sewn, to the surface of another fabric to form pictures or patterns. • adjective executed in appliqué. • verb (**appliqués**, **appliquéd**, **appliquéing**) decorate with appliqué; make using appliqué technique. [Say APLA kay]

apply verb (**applies**, **applied**, **applying**) **1** make a formal request for something to be done, given, etc.: apply for a job ◊ apply for assistance ◊ applied to be sent overseas. **2** have relevance: does not apply in this case. **3 a** make use of as relevant or suitable; employ: apply the rules. **b** operate: apply the brake. **4 a** put or spread on: applied the ointment to the cut. **b** administer: applied common sense to the problem. **5 apply oneself** devote oneself: applied myself to the task.

appoint verb **1** assign a post or office to: appoint him treasurer. **2** (often foll. by for) fix, decide on (a time, place, etc.). **3** prescribe; ordain: the Bible as appointed to be read in churches.

appointed adjective **1** equipped, furnished: a well-appointed kitchen. **2** (of a time or place) decided on beforehand: she arrived at the appointed time.

appointee noun a person who has been chosen for a job or position of responsibility. [Say a poin TEE]

appointive adjective depending on or filled by appointment: the Canadian Senate is appointive.

appointment noun **1** an arrangement to meet at a specific time and place. **2 a** a post or office available for applicants, or recently filled. **b** a person appointed. **3** (usu. in plural) **a** furniture, fittings. **b** equipment.

apportion verb divide up and share out: courts will apportion damage payments ◊ apportion blame. ▶ **apportionment** noun [Say a PORTION]

apposite adjective apt in the circumstances or in relation to something; well chosen: an apposite quotation ◊ the observations are apposite to the discussion. [Say APPA zit]

apposition noun Grammar the placing of a word next to another, esp. the addition of one noun to another, in order to qualify or explain the first, e.g. William the Conqueror; my friend Sue.

appraisal noun **1** an act of assessing someone or something: Wendy carried out a thorough appraisal ◊ the appraisal value of the house. **2** a formal assessment, typically in an interview, of the performance of an employee over a particular period.

appraise verb (**appraises**, **appraised**, **appraising**) **1** estimate the quality or worth of. **2** evaluate the price of (property, jewellery, etc.). **3** consider (a situation etc.) so as to make a judgment. ▶ **appraisingly** adverb

appraiser noun a person who assesses the worth or value of something, esp. of property, jewellery, etc.

appreciable adjective large enough to be noticed; significant: I don't think it will make any appreciable difference. ▶ **appreciably** adverb [Say a PREESHA bull]

appreciate verb (**appreciates**, **appreciated**, **appreciating**) **1 a** esteem highly; value. **b** be grateful for: we appreciate your sympathy. **c** be sensitive to: appreciate the nuances. **2** understand; recognize: I appreciate that I may be wrong ◊ they failed to appreciate the pressure he was under. **3** (of property etc.) rise in value: their house appreciated in value.

appreciation noun **1** favourable or grateful recognition. **2** an estimation or judgment; sensitive understanding of or reaction to: a quick appreciation of the problem ◊ music appreciation. **3** an increase in value. **4** a (usu. favourable) review of a book, film, etc.

appreciative adjective **1** feeling or showing gratitude for something: the company was appreciative of my efforts. **2** showing pleasure or enjoyment: an appreciative audience. ▶ **appreciatively** adverb

apprehend verb **1** understand: apprehend your meaning. **2** seize, arrest: apprehended the criminal. **3** anticipate with uneasiness or fear: apprehending the results.

apprehension noun **1** uneasiness; dread: felt sick with apprehension ◊ MaryLynne had some apprehensions about

the project. **2** understanding: *his first apprehension of such issues*. **3** arrest: *apprehension of the suspect*.

apprehensive *adjective* uneasily fearful; dreading: *felt apprehensive about the move*. ▶ **apprehensively** *adverb* **apprehensiveness** *noun*

apprentice • *noun* a person who is learning a trade by being employed in it for an agreed period, usu. at lower wages than is normal for that trade. • *verb* (**apprentices**, **apprenticed**, **apprenticing**) **1** engage as an apprentice: *was apprenticed to a builder*. **2** serve as an apprentice. ▶ **apprenticeship** *noun*

apprise *verb* (**apprises**, **apprised**, **apprising**) inform. PHRASES **be apprised of** be aware of.

approach • *verb* (**approaches**, **approached**, **approaching**) **1** come near or nearer to (a place or time). **2** come near or nearer in space or time: *the hour approaches*. **3** make a tentative proposal or suggestion to: *approached me about a loan*. **4 a** be similar in character, quality, etc., to: *doesn't approach her for artistic skill*. **b** approximate to; be slightly less than: *a population approaching 5 million*. **5** set about (a task etc.). **6** (of an aircraft etc.) prepare to land. **7** *Golf* play an approach shot. • *noun* (*plural* **approaches**) **1** an act or means of approaching: *made an approach* ◊ *an approach lined with trees*. **2** an approximation: *an approach to an apology*. **3** a way of dealing with a person or thing: *needs a new approach*. **4** (usu. in *plural*) a sexual advance. **5** the final part of a flight before landing. **6** *Golf* a stroke from the fairway to the green.

approachability *noun* the quality of being friendly and easy to talk to.

approachable *adjective* **1** friendly; easy to talk to. **2** able to be approached.

approbation *noun* approval. [Say appro BAY sh'n]

appropriate • *adjective* suitable or proper. • *verb* (**appropriates**, **appropriated**, **appropriating**) **1** take possession of, esp. without authority. **2** devote (money etc.) to special purposes. ▶ **appropriately** *adverb* **appropriateness** *noun* **appropriation** *noun* [Say a PRO pree it for the adjective, a PRO pree ate for the verb]

approval *noun* **1** the act of approving. **2** a favourable opinion: *looked at him with approval*. PHRASES **on approval** (of goods supplied) to be returned if not satisfactory.

approve *verb* (**approves**, **approved**, **approving**) **1** confirm; declare acceptable. **2** give or have a favourable opinion. PHRASES **approve of 1** pronounce or consider good or satisfactory; commend. **2** agree to. ▶ **approvingly** *adverb*

approx. *abbreviation* **1** approximate. **2** approximately.

approximate • *adjective* fairly accurate: *an approximate guess*. • *verb* (**approximates**, **approximated**, **approximating**) (often foll. by *to*) bring or come near, esp. in quality, number, etc.: *approximates to the truth*. ▶ **approximately** *adverb* [Say a PROXA mit for the adjective, a PROXA mate for the verb]

approximation *noun* an estimate, guess, or result that is approximately correct, or close enough for a particular purpose: *statistics present a crude approximation of reality*.

appurtenance *noun* an accessory or other item associated with a particular activity or style of living: *the appurtenances of consumer culture*. [Say a PERT'n ince]

APR *abbreviation* annual or annualized percentage rate (esp. of interest on loans or credit).

Apr. *abbreviation* April.

après-ski • *noun* the evening, esp. its social activities, following a day's skiing. • *adjective* (of clothes, drinks, etc.) appropriate to social activities following skiing. [Say ap ray SKI]

apricot *noun* **1** a juicy soft fruit, similar to but smaller than a peach, of an orange-yellow colour. **2** the tree bearing this fruit. [Say APRA cot or AYPRA cot]

April *noun* the fourth month of the year.

April Fool *noun* a person tricked on April 1.

April Fool's Day *noun* April 1, traditionally a day on which people play practical jokes on one another.

a priori • *adjective* relating to or denoting reasoning or knowledge which proceeds from theoretical deduction rather than from observation or experience: *a priori assumptions about human nature*. • *adverb* in a way based on theoretical deduction rather than observation: *sexuality may be a factor but it cannot be assumed a priori*. [Say ay pry OR eye]

apron *noun* **1 a** a garment worn to protect the front of a person's clothes from dirt or damage, fastened at the back. **b** a similar garment worn as part of official or ceremonial dress: *Freemason's apron*. **2** the part of a stage in front of the curtain. **3** the hard-surfaced area on an airfield used for manoeuvring or loading aircraft. PHRASES **tied to a person's apron strings** dominated by or dependent on that person (usu. a woman). ▶ **aproned** *adjective*

apropos • *adjective* to the point or purpose; appropriate: *her comment was apropos*. • *preposition informal* (often foll. by *of*) with respect to; concerning: *apropos the meeting* ◊ *apropos of the talk*. • *adverb* **1** appropriately: *spoke apropos*. **2** by the way; incidentally: *apropos, she's not going*. [Say apra POE]

apse *noun* a large semicircular or multi-sided recess, arched or with a domed roof, esp. at the eastern end of a church.

apt *adjective* **1** appropriate, suitable. **2 a** having a tendency, inclined: *apt to lose his temper*. **b** likely: *there is apt to be local interest*. **3** clever; quick to learn: *an apt pupil*.

aptitude *noun* a natural ability or talent: *a remarkable aptitude for languages* ◊ *a high level of technical aptitude*.

aptly *adverb* appropriately, fittingly: *the aptly named Grand Hotel*.

aqua *noun* & *adjective* the colour aquamarine. [Say ACKWA or OCKWA]

aquaculture *noun* the cultivation or rearing of fish or aquatic plants for human consumption. ▶ **aquaculturist** *noun* [Say ACKWA culture]

> **SPELL CHECK** ✓ABC
> **acquaint**
> ··
> Warning: **acquaint** is spelled with a *c*.

aquamarine *noun* **1** a light bluish-green beryl. **2** *noun & adjective* its colour. [Say ackwa MARINE]

Aquarian *Astrology* • *noun* a person born under the sign of Aquarius, between Jan. 22 and Feb. 18. • *adjective* having to do with the sign of Aquarius. [Say a KWERRY un]

aquarium *noun* (*plural* **aquariums** or **aquaria**) **1** a tank of water with transparent sides containing fish or other live aquatic animals and plants. **2** a building in which live aquatic animals are exhibited and studied.

Aquarius *noun* **1** a constellation between Pisces and Capricorn, traditionally regarded as contained in the figure of a water carrier. **2 a** the eleventh sign of the zodiac. **b** a person born when the sun is in this sign, usu. between Jan. 22 and Feb. 18.

aquatic • *adjective* **1** of or relating to water. **2** growing or living in or near water. **3** (of a sport) played in or on water. • *noun* **1** an aquatic plant or animal. **2** (in *plural*) aquatic sports. [Say a KWOT ick]

aqueduct *noun* an artificial channel for conveying

water, esp. in the form of a bridge supported by tall columns across a valley. [Say ACKWA duct]

aqueous *adjective* **1** of, containing, or like water. **2** *Chemistry* dissolved in water: *aqueous formaldehyde*. **3** *Geology* created from sediments laid down in water: *aqueous rocks*. [Say AKE wee us or ACK wee us]

aquifer *noun* a layer of permeable rock able to store significant quantities of water, through which groundwater moves. [Say ACKWA fur]

SPELL CHECK
acquire, acquit   ABC ✓

Note: **acquire** and **acquit** are spelled with a *c*.

Ar *symbol* argon.

A/R *abbreviation* ACCOUNT RECEIVABLE.

Arab • *noun* **1** a member of a Semitic people originally inhabiting Saudi Arabia and surrounding countries, now the Middle East generally. **2** = ARABIAN *noun* 2. • *adjective* of Arabia in the Middle East or the Arabs.

arabesque *noun* **1** *Dance & Figure Skating* **a** a posture with one leg extended straight backwards and usu. raised. **b** a position of the arms in which they are fully extended to the front or side, with palms facing downwards. **2** a design of intertwined leaves etc. [Say air a BESK]

Arabian • *adjective* of or relating to Arabia: *the Arabian desert*. • *noun* **1** a native of Arabia. **2** (also **Arabian horse**) a breed of horse developed in Arabia, renowned for its speed, intelligence, and mild disposition.

Arabian camel *noun* a domesticated camel with one hump, native to the deserts of North Africa and Arabia.

Arabic • *noun* the Semitic language of the Arabs, now spoken in much of northern Africa and the Middle East. • *adjective* of or relating to Arabia (esp. with reference to language or literature).

arabica *noun* **1** coffee or coffee beans from the most widely grown species of coffee plant, *Coffea arabica*. **2** the plant itself. [Say a RABBA kuh]

Arabic numeral *noun* any of the numerals 0, 1, 2, 3, 4, 5, 6, 7, 8, and 9 (compare ROMAN NUMERAL).

arable • *adjective* **1** (of land) plowed, or suitable for plowing and crop production. **2** (of crops) that can be grown on arable land. • *noun* arable land or crops. [Say AIR a bull]

arachnid *noun* any arthropod of the class Arachnida, having four pairs of walking legs and characterized by eyes with only one lens each, e.g. spiders, scorpions, mites, and ticks. [Say a RACK nid]

arak *noun* a Middle Eastern alcoholic spirit, esp. distilled from coco sap or rice. [Say a RACK]

-arama *combining form* = -RAMA.

Aramaic • *noun* a branch of the Semitic family of languages, esp. the language of Syria used as a lingua franca in the Near East from the 6th century BC. • *adjective* of or in Aramaic. [Say air a MAY ic]

Aran *adjective* designating a type of thick knitwear with cables and large diamond designs. [Say AIR in]

Arapaho (also **Arapahoe**) • *noun* **1** (*plural* **Arapaho** or **Arapahos**) a member of an Aboriginal people now living mainly in Wyoming and Oklahoma. **2** the Algonquian language of the Arapaho. • *adjective* of the Arapaho or their language. [Say a RAPPA hoe]

arbiter *noun* **1** = ARBITRATOR. **2** (often foll. by *of*) a judge; an authority: *arbiter of taste*. **3** (often foll. by *of*) a person or organization having entire control of something: *supreme arbiter of academic matters*. [Say ARBA ter]

arbitrage *noun* the buying and selling of stocks or bills of exchange to take advantage of varying prices in different markets. [Say ARBA trizh or ARBA tridge]

arbitrager *noun* = ARBITRAGEUR. [Say ARBA tridger]

arbitrageur *noun* a person who engages in arbitrage. [Say arba truh ZHUR]

arbitrarily *adverb* in a manner that seems to be based on random choice or personal whim, rather than any reason or system: *group leaders were chosen arbitrarily*.

arbitrariness *noun* a manner that seems to be based on random choice or personal whim, rather than any reason or system.

arbitrary *adjective* **1** based on the unrestricted will of a person, not according to a scheme or plan: *his mealtimes were entirely arbitrary*. **2** established at random. **3** (of power or a ruling body) unrestrained and autocratic in the use of authority: *the arbitrary powers of the officials*.

arbitrate *verb* (of an independent person or body) officially settle an argument or a disagreement between two people or groups: *to arbitrate in a dispute* ◊ *a committee was created to arbitrate between management and the unions*.

arbitration *noun* the hearing and resolution of a dispute by a referee, usu. chosen and agreed upon by all parties in the dispute, who has the power to impose a settlement.

arbitrator *noun* a person appointed to settle a dispute, usu. with the power to impose a settlement.

arbor *noun* = ARBOUR.

Arbor Day *noun* (in Canada and other countries) a day dedicated annually to public tree planting.

arboreal *adjective* of, living in, or relating to trees: *squirrels are arboreal mammals*. [Say ar BORRY ul]

arboretum *noun* (*plural* **arboretums** or **arboreta**) a botanical garden devoted to trees. [Say arber EAT'm for the singular; for ARBORETA say arber EETA]

arboricultural *adjective* having to do with the cultivation of trees and shrubs. [Say ar bora CULTURAL]

arboriculture *noun* the cultivation of trees and shrubs. [Say ar BORA culture]

arborio rice *noun* a plump, short-grained rice, sticky when cooked, often used in risotto and other Italian dishes. [Say arb OREO]

Arborite *noun* *Cdn proprietary* a plastic laminate used in countertops, tables, etc. [Say ARBER ite]

arborvitae *noun* any of the evergreen conifers of the genus *Thuja*, including the eastern white cedar and the western red cedar, native to North America and N Asia. [Say arber VEE tie or arber VITE ee]

arbour *noun* a shady garden alcove with the sides and roof formed by trees or climbing plants.

arbutus *noun* (*plural* **arbutuses**) any evergreen tree or shrub of the genus *Arbutus*, having dark green leaves and clusters of small, fragrant, bell-shaped flowers, esp. one native to the Pacific coast of North America, with peeling red bark, the only broadleaf evergreen tree native to Canada. [Say ar BYOO tiss]

SPELL CHECK
arc, ark   ABC ✓

The spelling is **ark** in "Noah's ark", "Holy Ark", and "Ark of the Covenant".

---

arc • *noun* **1** part of the circumference of a circle or any other curve. **2** any curved shape or course. **3** a luminous discharge between two electrodes. • *verb* (**arcs**, **arced**, **arcing**) form an arc.

arcade *noun* **1** a series of arches supporting or set along a wall. **2** a passageway lined with arches. **3** a public place containing coin-operated game machines, esp. video games and pinball machines. ▶ **arcaded** *adjective*

Arcadian • *noun* an idealized peasant or country dweller, esp. in poetry. • *adjective* simple and poetically

rural: *the picturesque, Arcadian, and sublime gardens of the Enlightenment*. [Say ar KAY dee in]

arcane *adjective* mysterious, secret; understood by few: *arcane procedures for electing people*.

arch¹ • *noun* (*plural* **arches**) **1 a** a curved structure spanning an opening, acting as a support for a bridge, roof, floor, etc. **b** an arch used in building as an ornament. **c** a monument whose principal feature is an arch. **2** something shaped like an arch, esp. the curved bony structure on the underside of the foot or the arrangement of teeth in the mouth. • *verb* (**arches**, **arched**, **arching**) **1** form into an arch: *the cat arched its back*. **2** span like an arch. **3** form an arch.

arch² *adjective* self-consciously or affectedly playful or teasing.

arch- *combining form* **1** chief, superior: *archbishop*. **2** pre-eminent of its kind, extreme: *arch-villain*.

archaeological *adjective* having to do with the study of past cultures by examining the remains of buildings and objects found in the ground: *archaeological museum* ◊ *archaeological dig* ◊ *archaeological evidence*. [Say arky a LOGICAL]

archaeologist *noun* a person who studies archaeology. [Say arky OLLA jist]

archaeology *noun* the study of human history and prehistory through the excavation of sites and the analysis of physical remains. [Say arky OLLA jee]

archaeopteryx *noun* the oldest known fossil bird, *Archaeopteryx lithographica*, from the Jurassic period, with teeth, feathers, and a reptilian tail. [Say arky OPTA ricks]

archaic *adjective* **1 a** antiquated: *archaic methods for treatment of criminals*. **b** (of a word etc.) no longer in ordinary use, though retained for special purposes: *"damsel" is an archaic word*. **2** (often **Archaic**) of an early period of art or culture, esp. the 7th and 6th centuries BC in Greece. **3** (**Archaic**) of the period in North American societies between 6000 BC and 500 AD. [Say ar KAY ick]

archaism *noun* **1** the retention or imitation of the old or obsolete, esp. in language or art. **2** an archaic word or expression. [Say AR kay ism]

archangel *noun* **1** an angel of the highest rank. **2** *Christianity* a member of the eighth order of the nine ranks of heavenly beings. [Say ARK angel]

archbishop *noun* the chief bishop of an ecclesiastical province.

archbishopric *noun* the office or diocese of an archbishop.

archdeacon *noun* an Anglican cleric ranking below a bishop, or a member of the clergy of similar rank in other Churches.

archdiocese *noun* the church district for which an archbishop is responsible. [Say arch DIE a siss]

archduchess *noun* (*plural* **archduchesses**) *hist.* the wife or daughter of an Austrian archduke.

archduke *noun hist.* a title of a duke, esp. as the title of a prince of the Austrian Empire.

Archean • *adjective* of or relating to the eon constituting the earlier part of Precambrian time, from about 4 billion to 2.5 billion years ago, in which there was no life on earth. • *noun* this time. [Say ar KEE in]

arched *adjective* **1** having or supported by an arch or arches: *an arched ceiling* ◊ *an arched bridge*. **2** having the curved shape of an arch: *an arched back*.

arch-enemy *noun* (*plural* **arch-enemies**) **1** a chief enemy. **2** Satan.

archeology *noun* = ARCHAEOLOGY. [Say arky OLLA jee]

archeparch *noun* an archbishop in an Eastern-rite church. ▶**archeparchy** *noun* [Say arch EPP ark, arch EPPER kee]

archer *noun* a person who shoots with a bow and arrows.

archery *noun* shooting with a bow and arrows, esp. as a sport.

archetypal *adjective* having all the important qualities and characteristics that make someone or something a typical example of a person or thing: *the Beatles were the archetypal pop group*. [Say arka TYPE 'll]

archetype *noun* **1 a** an original which has been imitated: *the archetype of the Canadian railway hotel was the French château*. **b** a very typical example of a certain person or thing: *with his tall blond good looks and noble bearing, he is the archetype of the ballet prince*. **2** (in Jungian psychology) an inherited primitive mental image, supposed to be present in the collective unconscious. **3** a recurrent symbol or motif in literature, art, etc.: *mythological archetypes of good and evil*. ▶**archetypical** *adjective* [Say ARKA type, arka TYPICAL]

Archimedean *adjective* of or associated with the Greek mathematician Archimedes (d. 212 BC), who established the ratio of the radius of a circle to its circumference and discovered formulas for the surface area and volume of a sphere and of a cylinder. [Say arka MEEDIAN]

Archimedean screw *noun* a device of ancient origin for raising water by means of a rotating spiral tube, or a rotating screw in an inclined cylinder.

Archimedes' principle *noun* the law that a body totally or partially immersed in a fluid is subject to an upward force equal in magnitude to the weight of the fluid it displaces. [Say arka MEE deez]

Archimedes' screw *noun* = ARCHIMEDEAN SCREW.

archipelago *noun* (*plural* **archipelagos**) **1** a group of islands. **2** a sea with many islands. [Say arka PELLA go]

architect *noun* **1** a person who designs buildings and supervises their construction. **2** (foll. by *of*) a person who brings about a specified thing: *architect of economic reform*. **3** = LANDSCAPE ARCHITECT.

architectural *adjective* having to do with architecture: *architectural design* ◊ *architectural history*. ▶**architecturally** *adverb*

architecture *noun* **1** the art or science of designing and constructing buildings. **2** the style of a building as regards design and construction: *Gothic architecture*. **3** buildings or other structures collectively. **4** the structure or design of something: *the architecture of the human body*. **5** the conceptual structure of the various processing elements in a computer or computer system, e.g. memory organization, user interface, etc., and their interconnection.

archival *adjective* having to do with or held in an archive: *archival research* ◊ *archival documents*. [Say ar KIVE 'll]

archive • *noun* **1** (usu. in *plural*) a collection of public, corporate or institutional documents or records. **2** (usu. in *plural*) the place where these are stored. **3** *Computing* a store of (usu. large amounts of) data kept in machine-readable form but not necessarily on a disk. • *verb* (**archives**, **archived**, **archiving**) **1** place or store in an archive. **2** transfer (data) to a store of less frequently used files, e.g. from disk to tape. [Say AR kive]

archivist *noun* a person who maintains and is in charge of archives. [Say ARKA vist]

archly *adverb* in a deliberately or affectedly playful and teasing manner.

archway *noun* a curved structure forming a passage or entrance.

arc lamp *noun* (also **arc light**) a light source using an electric arc between carbon electrodes and producing extremely intense white light.

Arctic • *noun* **1** the area north of the Arctic Circle.

2 an extremely cold, arid, treeless ecological zone including this and, in Canada, the shores of Hudson Bay, Ungava, and the Labrador coast. • *adjective* **1 a** of the Arctic. **b** designating animals and plants of northern species. **2** (**arctic**) designed for use in arctic conditions: *arctic sleeping bag*. **3** (**arctic**) (esp. of weather) very cold. [Say ARK tick or AR tick]

Arctic char *noun* a freshwater fish of the north, with pink flesh similar to salmon.

Arctic Circle *noun* the parallel of latitude 66°33′ north of the equator.

Arctic fox *noun* a small fox, native to the Arctic, whose coat turns white or grey-blue in winter.

Arctic hare *noun* a large hare, whose coat is brown in summer and white in winter, inhabiting the tundra of Canada and Greenland.

Arctic haze *noun* a smog-like form of air pollution found in the Arctic, caused by pollutants originating at northern coal-based industrial centres.

Arctic loon *noun* a loon inhabiting the circumpolar regions, esp. the Pacific coast of North America.

Arctic poppy *noun* (*plural* **Arctic poppies**) any of several golden flowers of the north, including *Papaver radicatum* and *P. macounii*, with four large petals.

Arctic willow *noun* any of several willow-like small shrubs native to the Arctic, also used as ornamentals.

arc welding *noun* a method of welding using an electric arc to melt metal.

ardent *adjective* zealous, eager; fervent, passionate. ▶ **ardently** *adverb*

ardor *noun* = ARDOUR.

ardour *noun* passion: *the rebuff failed to dampen his ardour*.

arduous *adjective* involving or requiring strenuous effort; difficult and tiring: *an arduous journey*. [Say AR joo us or ARD you us]

are[1] *2nd singular present & 1st, 2nd, 3rd plural present of* BE.

are[2] *noun* a metric unit of measure equal to 100 square metres. Abbreviation: **a**. [Say AIR or AR]

area *noun* **1** the extent or measure of a surface: *over a large area* ◊ *3 hectares in area* ◊ *the area of a triangle*. **2** a region or tract: *the southern area*. **3** a space allocated for a specific purpose: *dining area*. **4** a part of something: *an area of the brain*. **5** the scope or range of an activity or study: *very knowledgeable in the area of botany*. **6** a sunken space in front of a building, usu. leading to the basement.

area code *noun* a three-digit prefix to local phone numbers used in making calls from one telephone area to another.

area rug *noun* a rug covering part of a floor only, not extending to the walls.

areaway *noun* = AREA 6.

areca *noun* any tropical palm of the genus *Areca*, native to Asia. [Say AIR icka or a REEKA]

areca nut *noun* the seed of a species of areca, often chewed with betel leaves.

arena *noun* **1** an enclosed building containing an open, usu. oblong central area (esp. an ice surface) for sports, entertainment, or recreation, surrounded by seats for spectators. **2** the central part of an amphitheatre, bullring, stadium, etc., in which the action occurs. **3** a scene of conflict; a sphere of action or discussion: *the political arena*.

aren't *contraction* **1** are not. **2** (in *interrogative*) am not: *Aren't I coming too?*

arête *noun* a sharp narrow mountain ridge formed by the meeting of adjacent glacial valleys. [Say a RET]

Argentine • *adjective* of or relating to Argentina.

• *noun* **1** a native or national of Argentina. **2** a person of Argentine descent. [Say ARJ'n tine]

Argentinian *adjective & noun* = ARGENTINE. [Say arj'n TINNY in]

argh *interjection* expressing usu. feigned pain, disgust, or exasperation.

argillite *noun* a rock of a softness between shale and slate, used in Haida sculpture. [Say ARJA lite]

argon *noun* an inert gaseous element, of the noble gas group, used in arc welding and semiconductor crystals, and to fill light bulbs and vacuum tubes.

argot *noun* the jargon of a group or class, formerly esp. of criminals. [Say ARGO or AR gut]

arguable *adjective* **1** capable of being argued. **2** supportable by argument: *you have an arguable case*. **3** questionable, open to dispute: *a highly arguable assumption*.

arguably *adverb* it may be argued (used to qualify the statement of an opinion or belief: *she is arguably the greatest woman tennis player of all time*.

argue *verb* (**argues**, **argued**, **arguing**) **1** exchange views or opinions, especially heatedly or contentiously; quarrel. **2** indicate; maintain by reasoning. **3** provide reasons supporting or challenging something: *argued against the policy*. **4** challenge, dispute: *argued the referee's call*. **5** treat by reasoning: *argue the point*. **6** suggest, indicate: *a twitch that argued anxiety*. ▶ **arguer** *noun*

argument *noun* **1** an exchange of views, esp. a contentious or prolonged one. **2** (often foll. by *for*, *against*) a reason advanced; a reasoning process: *an argument for conscription*. **3** a summary of the subject matter or line of reasoning of a book. **4** *Math* an independent variable determining the value of a function. **5** *Computing* the part of a command specifying which file etc. the command is to be executed on.

argumentation *noun* **1** methodical reasoning. **2** debate or argument.

argumentative *adjective* **1** fond of arguing. **2** using methodical reasoning. ▶ **argumentatively** *adverb* **argumentativeness** *noun*

argyle (also **argyll**) • *adjective* designating a knitting pattern with diamonds of various colours on a single background colour. • *noun* **1** this pattern. **2** (in *plural*) socks in this pattern. [Say AR gile (with G as in *GIVE*)]

aria *noun* a long, accompanied song for solo voice in an opera, oratorio, etc. [Say ARRY uh or AIRY uh]

arid *adjective* **1 a** (of ground, climate, etc.) extremely dry, parched. **b** too dry to support vegetation; barren. **2** emotionless, uninteresting: *arid writing*. ▶ **aridity** *noun* **aridly** *adverb* [Say AIR id, a RIDDA tee]

Aries *noun* (*plural* **Aries**) **1** a constellation between Pisces and Taurus, traditionally regarded as contained in the figure of a ram. **2 a** the first sign of the zodiac. **b** a person born when the sun is in this sign, usu. between 21 March and 19 April. [Say AIR eez]

aright *adverb* rightly: *I wondered if I'd heard aright*.

arise *verb* (**arises**; *past* **arose**; *past participle* **arisen**; **arising**) **1** begin to exist; originate. **2** result: *accidents can arise from carelessness*. **3** come to one's notice; emerge: *the question of payment arose*. **4** rise, esp. from a seated position or from sleep.

aristocracy *noun* (*plural* **aristocracies**) **1** the highest class in certain societies, typically comprising people of noble birth holding hereditary titles and offices: *the landed aristocracy*. **2 a** government by the nobility. **b** a state governed in this way.

aristocrat *noun* a member of the nobility. [Say uh RISTA crat]

aristocratic *adjective* **1** of or relating to the aristocracy. **2** distinguished in manners or bearing.

Aristotelian • *noun* a disciple or student of the Greek philosopher Aristotle (d. 322 BC), whose thoughts have greatly influenced Western civilization. • *adjective* of Aristotle or his ideas. ▶**Aristotelianism** *noun* [Say erra sta TEELY in or a rista TEELY in]

arithmetic • *noun* **1 a** the science of numbers. **b** one's knowledge of this: *have improved my arithmetic*. **2** the use of numbers; computation: *a problem involving arithmetic*. • *adjective* (also **arithmetical**) of or concerning arithmetic. ▶**arithmetician** *noun*

arithmetic mean *noun* Math **1** the central number in an arithmetic progression. **2** = AVERAGE *noun* 2.

arithmetic progression *noun* Math **1** an increase or decrease by a constant quantity, e.g. 1, 2, 3, 4, etc., 9, 7, 5, 3, etc. **2** (also **arithmetic sequence**) a sequence of numbers showing this.

Arizonan • *adjective* of or relating to Arizona. • *noun* a resident or native of Arizona.

SPELL CHECK	
ark, arc	ABC ✓

A curve is an **arc**. **Arc** is also the spelling in "arc lamp".

ark *noun* **1** = NOAH'S ARK 1. **2** = HOLY ARK. **3** (**Ark**) = ARK OF THE COVENANT. PHRASES **out of the ark** *informal* very antiquated.

Arkansan • *adjective* of or relating to the US state of Arkansas. • *noun* a resident or native of Arkansas. [Say ar CAN s'n]

Ark of the Covenant *noun* (also **Ark of the Testimony**) the wooden chest which in Biblical times contained the tablets of the Law given to Moses by God, the Hebrews' most sacred symbol of God.

Ark of the Law *noun* = HOLY ARK.

arm[1] *noun* **1** each of the two upper limbs of the human body from the shoulder to the hand. **2 a** the forelimb of an animal. **b** the flexible limb of an invertebrate animal, e.g. an octopus. **3** the ability to throw: *that pitcher has an impressive arm*. **4 a** anything resembling an arm in function or in being attached to a larger mass or main stem: *an arm of the sea*. **b** the sleeve of a garment. **c** the side part of a chair etc., used to support a sitter's arm. **d** a large branch of a tree. **e** either of the pieces of an eyeglass frame that extend from the front backwards over the wearer's ears. **5** authority; power: *the long arm of the law*. PHRASES **an arm and a leg** a large sum of money. **arm in arm** (of two or more persons) with arms linked. **as long as your** (or **my**) **arm** *informal* very long. **at arm's length 1** as far as an arm can reach. **2** far enough to avoid undue familiarity or influence. **give one's right arm** sacrifice a great deal. **in arms** (of a baby) too young to walk. **in a person's arms 1** embraced: *held the baby in her arms*. **2** engaged in sexual activity: *the thought of her in the arms of another man drove him crazy*. **on one's arm** supported by one's arm. **under one's arm** between the arm and the body. **within arm's reach** reachable without moving one's position. **with open arms** cordially.

arm[2] • *noun* **1** (usu. in *plural*) **a** a weapon. **b** = FIREARM. **2** (in *plural*) the military profession. **3** a branch of the military, e.g. infantry, cavalry, artillery, etc. **4** a subdivision of an organization, devoted to a specific function or jurisdiction. **5** (in *plural*) heraldic devices: *coat of arms*. • *verb* **1** supply with weapons. **2** supply with tools or other requisites or advantages; equip: *armed with binoculars and a camera*. **3** make (a bomb etc.) able to explode. **4** activate: *armed the burglar alarm*. PHRASES **in arms** armed. **lay down one's arms** cease fighting. **take up arms** begin fighting. **under**

arms ready for war or battle. **up in arms** (usu. foll. by *against, about*) actively rebelling or protesting.

armada *noun* a fleet of warships. [Say ar MODDA]

armadillo *noun* (*plural* **armadillos**) an insect-eating mammal with large claws for digging and a body covered in bony plates, capable of rolling itself into a ball when threatened; armadillos are native to South and Central America and are spreading into the southern US.

Armageddon *noun* **1** New Testament **a** the last battle between good and evil before the Day of Judgment. **b** the place where this will be fought. **2** a vast and deadly armed conflict, esp. one causing the end of the world through nuclear destruction. [Say arma GED'n]

armament *noun* **1** (often in *plural*) military weapons and equipment, esp. guns on a warship or missiles on an airplane. **2** the process of equipping for war.

armature *noun* **1 a** the rotating coil or coils of an electric motor or generator. **b** any moving part of an electrical machine in which a voltage is induced by a magnetic field. **2** a piece of soft iron placed in contact with the poles of a horseshoe magnet to preserve its power. **3** Biology the protective covering of an animal or plant. **4** a metal framework on which a sculpture is moulded with clay etc. [Say ARMA chur]

armchair *noun* **1** a usu. upholstered chair with side supports for the arms. **2** (as an *adjective*) theoretical rather than active or practical: *an armchair quarterback*.

armed *adjective* **1** equipped with or characterized by the use of weapons. **2** (foll. by *with*) equipped, provided or prepared. **3** (of a weapon etc.) activated.

armed forces *plural noun* **1** (**Armed Forces**) the official name of the united military services in Canada. **2** (also **armed services**) the combined military services of a country or group of countries.

Armenian • *noun* **1 a** a native of the region or the republic of Armenia in the Caucasus. **b** a person of Armenian descent. **2** the language of the Armenian people. • *adjective* of Armenia, its language, or the Christian Church established there *c*.300. [Say ar MEENY an]

armful *noun* (*plural* **armfuls**) the amount of something that can be carried in one arm or both arms.

armistice *noun* a cessation of armed conflict by common agreement of the opposing sides. [Say ARMA stiss]

Armistice Day *noun* the anniversary of the armistice of 11 Nov. 1918 ending the First World War (*compare* REMEMBRANCE DAY).

armless *adjective* missing both arms.

armload *noun* the quantity that can be carried in the arms; an armful.

armor *noun* = ARMOUR.

armored *adjective* = ARMOURED.

armory *noun* = ARMOURY.

armour • *noun* **1** protective clothing, made of fabric, metal plates, etc., designed to deflect or absorb the impact of weapons, bullets, etc. **2 a** (also **armourplate**) a protective metal covering for an armed vehicle, ship, etc. **b** armoured fighting vehicles collectively. **3** a protective covering or shell on certain animals and plants. **4** heraldic devices. • *verb* provide with a protective covering.

armoured *adjective* **1** equipped with a protective covering, esp. of metal: *armoured car*. **2** (of an infantry division etc.) equipped with tanks and other armoured vehicles.

armoured personnel carrier *noun* a tank-like vehicle used for transporting troops.

armoury *noun* (*plural* **armouries**) **1** a place where arms are kept; an arsenal. **2** (in *plural*) Cdn a place where

militia units drill and train. **3** an array of weapons, defensive resources, usable material, etc.: *his armoury of comic routines*.

armpit *noun* **1** the hollow under the arm at the shoulder. **2** *slang* a place considered disgusting or contemptible: *the armpit of the world*.

SPELL CHECK
arm's-length, arm's length

Note the difference in spelling between an *arm's-length* relationship and the *refugee board operates at arm's length from the government*. There is no hyphen when the latter kind of structure is used.

---

arm's-length *adjective* **1** without friendliness or intimacy; at a distance. **2** (of institutional or commercial relations) with neither party controlled by the other: *the CBC traditionally has an arm's-length relationship with the government*.

arms race *noun* competition between nations in the development and accumulation of weapons.

arm-twisting *noun* persuasion by the use of moral pressure.

arm wrestling *noun* a trial of strength in which two people, with elbows on a tabletop, grip hands, with each trying to force the other's forearm down onto the table. ▶ **arm wrestle** *verb* (**arm wrestles, arm wrestled, arm wrestling**)

army *noun* (*plural* **armies**) **1** an organized force armed for fighting on land. **2** (usu. as **the Army**) the entire body of land forces of a country. **3** a very large number: *an army of bureaucrats*.

army ant *noun* a blind nomadic tropical ant that forages in large columns, preying chiefly on insects and spiders.

army fatigues *plural noun* loose-fitting clothing, usu. khaki, olive drab, or camouflaged, of a sort worn by soldiers on field duty or when doing manual labour.

army surplus *noun* = SURPLUS *noun* 3.

aroma *noun* a distinctive and pleasing smell, often of food: *the tantalizing aroma of fresh coffee*.

aromatherapist *noun* a person who promotes or practises aromatherapy.

aromatherapy *noun* the use of aromatic plant extracts and essential oils, esp. for relief of stress-related symptoms.

aromatic • *adjective* **1** having a pleasant and distinctive smell: *a massage with aromatic oils*. **2** (of organic compounds) having an unsaturated ring, esp. containing a benzene ring. • *noun* an aromatic substance. ▶ **aromatically** *adverb* [Say erra MAT ick]

arose *past of* ARISE.

around • *adverb* **1** on every side; so as to surround. **2** in various places: *shop around*. **3** *informal* **a** in existence; available: *has been around for weeks*. **b** near at hand: *it's good to have you around*. **4** with circular motion. **5** with return to the starting point or an earlier state. **6 a** with rotation, or change to an opposite position. **b** with change to an opposite opinion etc. **7** to, at, or affecting all or many points of a circumference or an area or the members of a company etc.: *look around*. **8** in every direction from a centre or within a radius. **9** by a circuitous way. **10** to a place. **11** measuring a (specified distance) in girth. • *preposition* **1** on or along the circuit of. **2** on every side of; enveloping. **3** here and there in or near. **4** approximately at; at a time near to. **5** so as to encircle or enclose. **6** at or to points on the circumference of. **7** in various directions from or with regard to: *towns around Calgary*. **8** having as an axis of revolution or as a central point: *turns around its centre of gravity*. **9** so as to double or pass in a curved course: *go

around the corner*. **10** so as to come close from various sides but not into contact. PHRASES **have been around** *informal* be widely experienced, esp. sexually.

arousal *noun* the condition of being aroused or stimulated, esp. sexually.

arouse *verb* (**arouses, aroused, arousing**) **1** evoke or awaken (esp. a feeling, emotion, etc.): *something about the man aroused the guard's suspicions* ◊ *the letter aroused in her a sense of urgency*. **2** awake from sleep: *she had been aroused from a deep slumber*. **3** excite or provoke someone to anger or strong emotions: *an ability to influence the audience and to arouse the masses*. **4** excite sexually.

arpeggio *noun* (*plural* **arpeggios**) the notes of a chord played or sung in succession, either ascending or descending. [Say ar PEDGY o]

arpent *noun* *Cdn hist.* **1** an old French unit of land area equivalent to 3 420 square metres (about 1 acre), the standard measure of land in those areas settled during the French regime, in use until the 1970s. **2** a unit of linear measure equivalent to about 58 metres (190 ft.) used in New France. [Say ARP'nt]

arrack *noun* = ARAK. [Say A rack]

arraign *verb* call on (a person) to answer a criminal charge before a court: *she was arraigned on murder charges*. ▶ **arraignment** *noun* [Say a RAIN]

arrange *verb* (**arranges, arranged, arranging**) **1** put into the required order; classify. **2** plan or provide for; cause to occur: *arranged a meeting*. **3** settle beforehand the order or manner of. **4** take measures; form plans: *arrange to be there at eight*. **5** come to an agreement: *arranged with her to meet later*. **6** *Music* adapt (a composition) for performance with instruments or voices other than those originally specified. **7** settle (a dispute etc.). ▶ **arranger** *noun* (esp. in sense 6).

arranged marriage *noun* a marriage planned and agreed to by the families or guardians of the couple concerned, rather than by the couple themselves.

arrangement *noun* **1** the act or process of arranging or being arranged. **2** the condition of being arranged; the manner in which a thing is arranged. **3** something arranged: *a flower arrangement*. **4** (in *plural*) plans: *make arrangements*. **5** a setting of a piece of music for instruments or voices other than those for which it was first written. **6** settlement of a dispute etc.

arrant *adjective* downright, notorious: *arrant liar*. [Say AIR int]

array • *noun* **1** an imposing or well-ordered series or display: *there is a vast array of literature on the topic* ◊ *a bewildering array of choices*. **2** an ordered arrangement, esp. of troops: *battle array*. **3** attire; an outfit: *in fine array*. **4 a** *Math* an arrangement of quantities or symbols in rows and columns; a matrix. **b** *Computing* an ordered set of related elements. • *verb* **1** dress someone in the clothes specified: *the actors were arrayed in highly individualized costumes evocative of classical Greece*. **2** set in order: *the hostile forces which were arrayed against him*.

arrears *plural noun* an amount still outstanding or uncompleted, esp. a debt unpaid: *she was suing her tenant for the arrears of rent*. PHRASES **in arrears** behind in payments etc.

arrest • *verb* **1** seize (a person) and take into custody, esp. by legal authority. **2** stop or check (esp. a process or moving thing): *the spread of the disease can be arrested*. **3** attract the attention of (a person): *she was arrested by the church's stillness* ◊ *another famous poster arrests your attention*. • *noun* **1** the act of arresting or being arrested, esp. the legal seizure of a person: *the police have yet to make an arrest* ◊ *I am placing you under arrest*. **2** a stoppage of motion: *cardiac arrest*.

arresting *adjective* attracting attention; striking: *at 6 ft 6 he was an arresting figure*.

arrhythmia *noun* deviation from the normal rhythm of the heart. [Say a RITH mee uh]

arrival *noun* **1 a** the act of arriving. **b** an appearance on the scene. **2** a person or thing that has arrived.

arrive *verb* (**arrives, arrived, arriving**) **1** reach a destination; come to the end of a journey or a specified part of a journey. **2** (foll. by *at*) reach (a conclusion, decision, etc.). **3** *informal* establish one's reputation or position. **4** (of a child) be born. **5** (of a thing) be brought. **6** (of a time) come. **7** come on the scene: *CD-ROMs arrived in the late eighties*.

arrogance *noun* the behaviour or attitude of a person who feels superior to or more important than others.

arrogant *adjective* behaving in a proud, unpleasant way because convinced of one's superiority, showing little thought for other people. ▶ **arrogantly** *adverb*

arrow *noun* **1** a sharp pointed wooden or metal stick shot from a bow. **2** a drawn or printed etc. arrow indicating a direction; a pointer.

arrowhead *noun* **1** the pointed end of an arrow. **2** an aquatic or marsh plant of the genus *Sagittaria*, bearing white flowers and arrowhead-shaped leaves. **3** a decorative device resembling an arrowhead.

arrowroot *noun* **1** a Caribbean plant with fleshy tuberous rhizomes. **2** pure edible starch prepared from the tubers of this plant. **3** (also **arrowroot cookie**) a cookie made with arrowroot flour.

arrow sash *noun Cdn hist.* = CEINTURE FLÉCHÉE.

arsenal *noun* **1** a store of weapons. **2** a government establishment for the storage and manufacture of weapons and ammunition. **3** a collection of items, methods, beliefs, etc. available for tackling a problem: *an arsenal of medications*.

arsenic *noun* **1** a non-scientific name for arsenic trioxide, a highly poisonous white powdery substance. **2** a brittle semi-metallic element, used in semiconductors and alloys. [Say ARSA nick]

arson *noun* the act of maliciously setting fire to property. ▶ **arsonist** *noun*

art *noun* **1 a** a human creative skill or its application. **b** work exhibiting this. **2 a** (in *plural*; **the arts**) the various branches of creative activity concerned with the production of imaginative designs, sounds, ideas, etc., e.g. painting, music, writing, etc. considered collectively. **b** any one of these branches. **3** creative activity, esp. painting and drawing, resulting in visual representation: *interested in music but not art*. **4** human skill or workmanship as opposed to the work of nature. **5** (often foll. by *of*) a skill, aptitude, or knack: *keeping people happy is quite an art*. **6** (in *plural*) certain branches of (esp. university) study, esp. the fine arts and humanities, as distinguished from the sciences or technological subjects.

art deco *noun* the predominant decorative art style of the period 1910–30, characterized by precise and boldly delineated geometric motifs, shapes, and strong colours.

art director *noun* **1** the person in charge of the design and production of the costumes and decor for a motion picture. **2** the person in charge of the graphics, layout, etc. of a magazine.

artefact *noun* = ARTIFACT.

artemisia *noun* a bitter aromatic plant of a genus that includes wormwood and sagebrush. Several kinds are used in herbal medicine and many are cultivated for their feathery grey leaves. [Say arta MEEZHA]

arterial *adjective* **1 a** of or relating to an artery: *arterial disease*. **b** (of blood) oxygenated in the lungs and of a bright red colour. **2** (esp. of a road) main, esp. providing direct access to the centre of a city. [Say ar TEERY 'll]

arteriosclerosis *noun* abnormal thickening and hardening of the walls of the arteries. [Say ar teery o skla ROE sis]

artery *noun* (*plural* **arteries**) **1** any of the muscular-walled tubes forming part of the blood circulation system of the body, carrying oxygen-enriched blood from the heart (*compare* VEIN 1). **2** a major road, railway, river, etc.

artesian well *noun* a well bored perpendicularly, esp. through rock, into water-bearing strata lying at an angle, so that natural pressure produces a constant supply of water with little pumping. [Say ar TEE zh'n]

art film *noun* a film aiming for aesthetic effect rather than commercial success.

art form *noun* **1** any medium of artistic expression. **2** an established form of composition, e.g. the novel, sonata, sonnet, etc.

artful *adjective* **1** skilful, clever: *with artful diplomacy that did not disguise his purpose, he thwarted attempts to shut over the meeting*. **2** crafty, deceitful. **3** characterized by skill or art: *an artful photo of a striking woman*. ▶ **artfully** *adverb* **artfulness** *noun*

arthritic *adjective* suffering from or caused by arthritis: *arthritic joints*. [Say arth RIT ick]

arthritis *noun* inflammation of a joint or joints.

arthropod *noun* a large phylum of invertebrate animals that have segmented bodies, external skeletons, and jointed limbs, including insects, spiders, crustaceans, and their relatives. [Say ARTHRA pod]

arthroscopic *adjective* involving arthroscopy: *arthroscopic surgery*. [Say arthra SCOP ic]

arthroscopy *noun* (*plural* **arthroscopies**) examination of, or surgery on, the interior of a joint by the insertion of an instrument called an **arthroscope** through a small incision. [Say ar THROSCA pee]

SPELL CHECK	ABC ✓
Arctic	

Warning: do not forget the *c* before the *t* in **Arctic**.

artichoke *noun* **1** a European plant native to the Mediterranean, cultivated for its large thistle-like flower heads (*see also* JERUSALEM ARTICHOKE). **2** the unopened flower head of this, parts of which are edible.

article • *noun* **1** a particular or separate thing, esp. one of a set: *articles of clothing*. **2** a piece of writing, complete in itself, in a newspaper, magazine, scholarly journal, etc. **3** a separate clause or portion of any document. **4** *Grammar* the definite or indefinite article. **5** (in *plural*) the period of apprenticeship of a law student. • *verb* (**articles, articled, articling**) **1** bind by a written contract, esp. for a period of training. **2** *Cdn* (of a law student) serve one's period of apprenticeship. PHRASES **article of faith 1** a basic point of religious belief. **2** any firmly held belief. **genuine article** something authentic, not imitative.

articulate • *adjective* **1** able to speak fluently and coherently. **2** (of sound or speech) having clearly distinguishable parts. **3** having joints. • *verb* (**articulates, articulated, articulating**) **1** pronounce (words etc.) clearly and distinctly: *he articulated each word with precision ◊ is good for radio because she articulates so well*. **2** express (an idea etc.) coherently: *unable to articulate their emotions*. [Say ar TICK you lit for the adjective, ar TICK you late for the verb]

articulated *adjective* designating a vehicle consisting of two or more sections connected by a flexible joint: *articulated bus*. [Say ar TICK you lated]

articulately *adverb* fluently and coherently: *she argued the point articulately*. [Say ar TICK you lit lee]

articulation *noun* **1** the action of putting into words

an idea or feeling of a specified type: *it would involve the articulation of a theory of a just war*. **2** the formation of clear and distinct sounds in speech: *the articulation of vowels and consonants*. **3** the state of being jointed: *the area of articulation of the lower jaw*. [Say ar tick you LAY sh'n]

artifact *noun* a product of human art and workmanship.

artifice *noun* clever or cunning devices or expedients, esp. used to trick or deceive others: *fashion is an industry dominated by artifice* ◊ *the style is not free from the artifices of the period*. [Say ARTA fiss]

artificial *adjective* **1** produced by human skill or effort rather than originating naturally: *an artificial lake*. **2** formed in imitation of something natural: *artificial flowers*. **3** affected, insincere: *an artificial smile*. **4** designating a device etc. that performs the functions of an organ, limb, etc.: *artificial heart*.

artificial insemination *noun* the injection of semen into the vagina or uterus other than by sexual intercourse. Abbreviation: **AI**.

artificial intelligence *noun* the field of study that deals with the capacity of a machine, esp. a computer, to simulate or surpass intelligent human behaviour. Abbreviation: **AI**.

artificiality *noun* the condition of being artificial or not genuine; an unnatural or insincere quality: *criticized the artificiality of the test situation*. [Say arta fishy ALA tee]

artificial language *noun* **1** a composite language, esp. for international use, made from the words and other elements in several languages, e.g. Esperanto. **2** a language invented for use by computers.

artificial life *noun* computer programs or systems which simulate the behaviour, population dynamics, or other characteristics of living organisms.

artificially *adverb* as a result of human action, intervention, or manipulation, rather than by natural means: *artificially flavoured cakes* ◊ *without competition the company can keep its prices artificially high*.

artificial respiration *noun* the restoration or initiation of breathing by manual or mechanical or mouth-to-mouth methods.

artillery *noun* **1** large-calibre guns used in warfare on land. **2** a branch of the armed forces that uses these.

artisan *noun* a craftsperson specializing in decorative arts, esp. pottery, weaving, etc. ▶ **artisanal** *adjective* [Say ARTA zan or ARTA san]

artist *noun* **1** a person who practises any of the fine arts, esp. painting, sculpting, etc. **2** a person who practises one of the performing arts. **3** a person who shows great skill and inspiration in a particular activity. **4** a habitual performer of a specified (usu. reprehensible) activity: *con artist*.

artistic *adjective* **1** having natural skill in art. **2** made or done with art. **3** of art or artists. ▶ **artistically** *adverb*

artistic director *noun* the director of a performing arts organization in charge of programming and casting decisions etc.

artistry *noun* the skill of an artist: *cosmetic surgery requires artistry as well as medical skill*.

artless *adjective* **1** without guile or deceit: *an artless, naive girl* ◊ *artless sincerity*. **2** without pretentiousness or effort; natural and simple: *an artless literary masterpiece*. **3** clumsy: *awkward, artless prose*. ▶ **artlessly** *adverb*

art nouveau *noun* a European art style of the late 19th century characterized by flowing lines and natural organic forms. [Say art noo VOE]

artsy *adjective* (**artsier**, **artsiest**) *informal* pretentiously or affectedly artistic: *artsy films*.

artsy-craftsy *adjective informal* **1** having a liking for, or

engaged in, handicrafts: *the artsy-craftsy crowd*. **2** characterized by the presence of handicrafts: *artsy-craftsy cutesy gift shops*.

artsy-fartsy *adjective pejorative slang* pretentiously or affectedly artistic.

artwork *noun* **1** a work of art. **2** the illustrations in a printed book. **3** prepared or camera-ready copy.

arty *adjective* (**artier**, **artiest**) = ARTSY.

arugula *noun* a plant with purple-veined pale yellow or white flowers and bitter leaves that are used in salads. [Say a ROOGA la]

arum *noun* **1** any plant of the European genus *Arum*, typically having a white spathe and arrow-shaped leaves. **2** any of various other plants of the family Araceae. [Say AIR um]

Aryan • *noun* **1** (in Nazi and neo-Nazi ideology) a Caucasian not of Jewish descent. **2** a member of a people who invaded northern India in the 2nd millennium BC, displacing the aboriginal inhabitants. • *adjective* having to do with this people or language. [Say AIRY un]

As *symbol* the element arsenic.

as • *adverb & conjunction* ... to the extent to which ... is or does etc.: *I am as tall as he is*. • *conjunction* **1** expressing result or purpose: *came early so as to meet us* ◊ *so good as to exceed all hopes*. **2** having concessive force: *try as he might, he could not do it*. **3 a** in the manner in which: *do as you like*. **b** in the capacity or form of: *I speak as your friend* ◊ *as a matter of fact*. **c** during or at the time that: *came up as I was speaking*. **d** for the reason that; seeing that: *as you are here, we can talk*. **e** for instance: *port cities, as Vancouver*. • *relative pronoun* (with verb of relative clause expressed or implied) **1** that, who, which: *I had the same trouble as you* ◊ *such countries as France*. **2** a fact that: *he lost, as you know*. **PHRASES** **as and when** to the extent and at the time that: *I'll do it as and when I want to*. **as for** with regard to. **as from** on and after (a specified date). **as if!** indicating disbelief or disdain. **as if** (or **though**) as would be the case if: *acts as if he were in charge* ◊ *looks as though we've won*. **as it is** (or **as is**) in the existing circumstances or state. **as it were** in a way; to a certain extent: *she is, as it were, infatuated*. **as of 1** = AS FROM. **2** as at (a specified time). **as to** with respect to; concerning: *said nothing as to money*. **as was** in the previously existing circumstances or state. **as yet** until now or a particular time in the past.

ASA *abbreviation Cdn* ACETYLSALICYLIC ACID.

asana *noun* any of various postures used in yoga. [Say OSSA nuh]

ASAP *abbreviation* as soon as possible.

asbestos *noun* **1** a fibrous silicate mineral that cannot be burned or consumed by fire. **2** this used as a heat-resistant or insulating material. [Say az BEST us]

asbestosis *noun* a lung disease resulting from the inhalation of asbestos particles. [Say az bes TOE sis]

ascend *verb* **1** move upwards; rise. **2** slope or lead up: *the road ascends to the lodge*. **3** climb; go up: *ascended the stairs* ◊ *ascended a trail through the forest* ◊ *the air became colder as we ascended*. **4** rise in rank or status: *some executives ascend to top-level positions* ◊ *the ranks are listed in ascending order, from the lowest to the highest*. **5** (of sound) rise in pitch: *Carolyn's voice had ascended into high-pitched giggles*. **6** go upstream along (a river): *ships could ascend the river only as far as the Lachine Rapids*. **7** go to heaven. **PHRASES** **ascend the throne** become king or queen.

ascendancy *noun* a superior or dominant condition or position: *the NDP reasserted its ascendancy over the splintered Social Credit party* ◊ *the decade saw the ascendancy of a new business class which took over as the province's elite*.

ascendant • *adjective* **1** rising. **2** *Astronomy* rising toward the zenith. **3** *Astrology* just rising above the

A

eastern horizon. **4** predominant. • *noun Astrology* the point of the ecliptic or sign of the zodiac which at a given moment (esp. at a person's birth) is just rising above the eastern horizon. PHRASES **in the ascendant** rising; gaining power or authority: *liberal theories were in the ascendant*.

ascendency *noun* = ASCENDANCY.

ascension *noun* **1** the action of rising to an important position or a higher level: *Nick's ascension to the ranks of pop stardom*. **2** *Christianity* (**Ascension**) **a** the ascent of Christ into heaven on the fortieth day after the Resurrection. **b** (also **Ascension Day**) the day on which Christians annually celebrate the Ascension, either the Thursday forty days after Easter, or the Sunday following this.

> **SPELL CHECK**
> **ascent, assent**
>
> A word for "agreement" is **assent**.

ascent *noun* **1** a climb or walk to the summit of a mountain or hill: *the first ascent of Everest*. **2 a** an upward slope or path that one may walk or climb: *the ascent grew steeper*. **b** a rise to an important position or higher level: *her ascent to power*. **3** an act of rising or moving up through the air: *the first balloon ascent was in 1783*.

ascertain *verb* find out as a definite fact. ▶**ascertainable** *adjective* **ascertainment** *noun* [Say asser TAIN]

ascetic • *noun* a person who practises severe self-discipline and abstains from all forms of pleasure, esp. for religious or spiritual reasons. • *adjective* abstaining from pleasure. ▶**ascetically** *adverb* **asceticism** *noun* [Say a SET ic, a SETTA sism]

ASCII *noun Computing* a standard code for storing and transmitting information. [Say ASKY]

ascorbic acid *noun* a vitamin found in citrus fruits and green vegetables, essential in maintaining healthy connective tissue, a lack of which results in scurvy. *Also called* VITAMIN C. [Say a SCORE bick]

ascot (also **ascot tie**) a broad necktie or scarf covering the area of an open neck or waistcoat. [Say ASS cot]

ascribable *adjective* attributable: *the job losses are ascribable to the company's poor performance this year*.

ascribe *verb* (**ascribes**, **ascribed**, **ascribing**) **1** attribute: *ascribes his well-being to a sound constitution*. **2** regard as belonging: *tough-mindedness is a quality commonly ascribed to top executives* ◊ *ascribed the quotation to Marx*.

aseptic *adjective* **1** free from contamination caused by harmful bacteria, viruses, or other micro-organisms. **2** (of a wound, instrument, or dressing) surgically sterile or sterilized. [Say ay SEPTIC]

asexual *adjective* **1** without sex or sexual organs. **2** (of reproduction) not involving the fusion of gametes. **3** without sexuality. ▶**asexually** *adverb* [Say ay SEXUAL]

ash¹ *noun* (*plural* **ashes**) **1 a** the powdery residue left after the burning of any substance. **b** *Chemistry* such residue used in chemical analysis, e.g. to assess mineral content: *low ash cat food*. **2** (in *plural*) the remains of the human body after cremation or disintegration. **3** ash-like material thrown out by a volcano.

ash² *noun* (*plural* **ashes**) **1** a forest tree with silver-grey bark, compound leaves, and tough, flexible, pale wood. **2** the wood of the ash, used to make hockey sticks and implement handles.

ashamed *adjective* **1** embarrassed or disconcerted by shame: *ashamed of having lied* ◊ *ashamed to be seen with*

him. **2** reluctant (but usu. not actually refusing or declining): *am ashamed to admit that I was wrong*.

ashen *adjective* ash-coloured; deathly pale.

Ashkenazi *noun* (*plural* **Ashkenazim**) a Jew of central, northern, or eastern Europe, or of such ancestry. ▶**Ashkenazic** *adjective* [Say ashka NOZZY, ahska NOZZ im]

ashore *adverb* toward or on the shore or land.

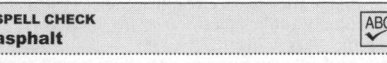

> **SPELL CHECK**
> **asphalt**
>
> Warning: there is no *h* before the *p* in **asphalt**.

ashram *noun* a place of religious retreat for Hindus. [Say ASH rum]

ashtray *noun* a small receptacle for cigarette ash etc.

Ash Wednesday *noun Christianity* the first day of Lent, on which the foreheads of penitents are customarily marked with ashes.

ashy *adjective* **1** very pale. **2** covered with ashes.

Asiago *noun* a hard light yellow cheese made from cow's milk. [Say ozzy OG oh]

Asian • *noun* **1** a native of Asia. **2** a person of Asian descent. • *adjective* of or relating to Asia or its people, customs, or languages.

Asiatic • *noun offensive* an Asian. • *adjective* Asian. [Say ay zhee ATTIC]

aside • *adverb* **1** to or on one side; away. **2** out of consideration: *joking aside*. • *noun* **1** words spoken in a play for the audience to hear, but supposed not to be heard by the other characters. **2** an incidental remark. PHRASES **aside from** apart from. **set aside 1** put to one side. **2** keep for a special purpose or future use. **3** reject or disregard. **4** *Law* annul. **take aside** engage (a person) esp. for a private conversation.

asinine *adjective* stupid. [Say ASSA nine]

ask *verb* **1** call for an answer to or about: *ask him his name* ◊ *ask a question of her*. **2** seek to obtain from another person: *ask a favour of* ◊ *ask to be allowed*. **3** invite; request the company of: *must ask them over* ◊ *asked her to dinner*. **4** (foll. by *for*) seek to obtain, meet, or be directed to: *ask for a donation* ◊ *asking for you*. PHRASES **ask after** inquire about (esp. a person). **ask for it** *slang* invite trouble. **ask me another** *informal* I do not know. **for the asking** (obtainable) for nothing. **I ask you!** an exclamation of disgust, surprise, etc. **if you ask me** *informal* in my opinion.

askance *adverb* with an attitude or look of suspicion or disapproval: *the waiter looked askance at his tattered jeans* ◊ *looked askance at any usage guide that didn't recommend his own particular usage*. [Say a SKANCE]

askew *adverb & adjective* not in a straight or level position: *the door was hanging askew on one twisted hinge* ◊ *her hat was slightly askew*. [Say a SKYOO]

asking price *noun* the price of an object set by the seller.

aslant *adverb* obliquely or at a slant: *the sunlight hits the lake water aslant*. [Say a SLANT]

asleep *adjective & adverb* **1 a** in or into a state of sleep. **b** inactive, inattentive: *the nation is asleep*. **2** (of a limb etc.) numb. **3** *euphemism* dead. PHRASES **asleep at the switch** inattentive.

A/SLt *abbreviation Cdn* ACTING SUB-LIEUTENANT.

asocial *adjective* **1** not social; anti-social. **2** inconsiderate of or hostile to others. [Say ay SOCIAL]

asp *noun* **1** a large nocturnal cobra, native to North Africa and Arabia. **2** either of two small vipers: **a** the **asp viper**, native to southern Europe, resembling a small adder. **b** the **horned asp** with a large head and two small horns above the eyes, found in the deserts of North Africa and southwestern Asia.

asparagus *noun* a plant whose young green or white stems are cooked and eaten as a vegetable.

asparagus fern *noun* a decorative fern-like plant with feathery foliage used in flower arrangements.

aspartame *noun* a very sweet low-calorie sugar substitute derived from amino acids. [Say ASPER tame]

aspect *noun* **1 a** a particular component or feature of a matter: *only one aspect of the problem*. **b** a particular way in which a matter may be considered. **2** a facial expression; an appearance or look (of a person or thing): *a cheerful aspect*. **3** the side of a building or location facing a particular direction: *southern aspect*.

aspen *noun* any of several poplars characterized by leaves which tremble in the slightest wind.

asperity *noun* (*plural* **asperities**) harshness or sharpness of tone or manner: *he pointed this out with some asperity ◊ a certain asperity in his tone*. [Say ass PERRA tee]

aspersion *noun* a disparaging remark attacking the reputation or integrity of someone: *it is not my intention to cast aspersions on the people of this city*. [Say a SPUR zh'n]

asphalt • *noun* **1** a dark bituminous pitch occurring naturally or made from petroleum. **2** a mixture of this with sand, gravel, etc., for surfacing roads etc. • *verb* surface with asphalt. [Say ASH fault or ASS fault]

asphyxia *noun* a lack of oxygen in the blood, causing unconsciousness or death; suffocation. [Say ass FIXIA]

asphyxiate *verb* (**asphyxiates**, **asphyxiated**, **asphyxiating**) suffocate. ▶ **asphyxiation** *noun* [Say ass FIXY ate]

aspic *noun* **1** a clear savoury jelly prepared from meat or fish stock, used as a garnish or glaze or combined with meat, vegetables, etc. in moulded dishes. **2** a dish of jelled tomato juice with vegetables etc. [Say ASS pick]

aspidistra *noun* a bulbous East Asian plant of the lily family, with broad tapering leaves, often grown as a houseplant. [Say aspa DISTRA]

aspirant • *adjective* (of a person) having ambitions to achieve something, typically to follow a particular career: *an aspirant politician*. • *noun* a person who has ambitions to achieve: *an aspirant to the throne*. [Say ASPER int or a SPY rint]

aspirate *Phonetics* • *adjective* **1** pronounced with an exhalation of breath. **2** blended with the sound of *h*. • *noun* **1** a consonant pronounced in this way. **2** the sound of *h*. • *verb* (**aspirates**, **aspirated**, **aspirating**) **1** pronounce with a breath. **2** *Medical* draw (fluid) by suction from a vessel or cavity. [Say ASPER it for the adjective and noun, ASPER ate for the verb]

aspiration *noun* **1** a strong desire to achieve an end; an ambition. **2** the act or process of drawing breath. **3** the action of aspirating. [Say aspa RAY sh'n]

aspire *verb* (**aspires**, **aspired**, **aspiring**) have ambition or strong desire: *aspired to be prime minister ◊ we never thought that we might aspire to those heights*.

Aspirin *noun* (*plural* **Aspirin** or **Aspirins**) *proprietary* **1** a white powder, acetylsalicylic acid, used to relieve pain and reduce fever. **2** a tablet of this.

aspiring *adjective* wishing to attain a specified position, career, etc.: *an aspiring actor*.

ass¹ *noun* (*plural* **asses**) **1 a** either of two kinds of four-legged long-eared animal of the horse family, usu. smaller than a horse and having a braying call. **b** (in general use) a donkey. **2** a stupid person. PHRASES **make an ass of** cause to look absurd or foolish.

ass² *noun* (*plural* **asses**) *coarse slang* **1** the buttocks. **2** the rectum.

assail *verb* **1** make a strong or concerted attack on: *they were assailed by horseflies and mosquitoes*. **2** make a strong or constant verbal attack on: *was assailed with angry questions*. **3** (of an unpleasant feeling or physical sensation) overcome someone suddenly and strongly:

she was assailed by doubts and regrets ◊ stage fright can assail the most stoic performer.

assailant *noun* a person who attacks another, esp. physically.

assassin *noun* a killer, esp. of a political or religious leader.

assassinate *verb* (**assassinates**, **assassinated**, **assassinating**) kill (esp. a political or religious leader) for political or religious motives. ▶ **assassination** *noun*

assault • *noun* **1** a violent physical or verbal attack. **2 a** (in civil law) an act that threatens physical harm to a person. **b** (in criminal law) threatened or actual physical contact without consent. **c** = SEXUAL ASSAULT. **3** (as an *adjective*) relating to or used in a military assault: *assault craft ◊ assault troops*. **4** a final rush on a fortified place, esp. at the end of a prolonged attack. • *verb* **1** make an assault on. **2** sexually assault. PHRASES **assault and battery** *Law* (in civil law) a threatening act that is followed by physical contact without consent, whether or not harm is caused. ▶ **assaultive** *adjective*

assault rifle *noun* a lightweight, automatic or semi-automatic military rifle using high-performance ammunition.

assay • *noun* a test to determine the composition of a substance, esp. the analysis of an ore or metal to determine its purity. • *verb* **1** determine the content or quality of a metal or ore. **2** determine the presence or activity of (a substance) by testing. [Say a SAY or ASS ay]

assemblage *noun* **1 a** a collection of things or gathering of people: *a loose assemblage of diverse groups*. **2 a** the act or an instance of fitting together. **b** an object made of pieces fitted together: *the machine was a vast assemblage of gears and cogs*. **3** a work of art made by grouping found or unrelated objects.

assemble *verb* (**assembles**, **assembled**, **assembling**) **1** gather together; collect. **2** arrange in order. **3** fit together the parts of: *assemble the bicycle*. **4** *Computing* produce (a machine-coded form of a low-level symbolic code).

assembler *noun* **1** a person who assembles a machine or its parts. **2** *Computing* **a** a program for converting instructions written in low-level symbolic code into machine code. **b** the low-level symbolic code itself; an assembly language.

assembly *noun* (*plural* **assemblies**) **1** the action of gathering together as a group for a common purpose: *laws guaranteeing freedom of assembly*. **2 a** a group of persons gathered together for a specific purpose: *an assembly of all the miners in the region*. **b** a general gathering of the members of a school. **3** (also **Assembly**) a legislative council or deliberative body, esp.: **a** = GENERAL ASSEMBLY. **b** = HOUSE OF ASSEMBLY. **c** = LEGISLATIVE ASSEMBLY. **d** = NATIONAL ASSEMBLY. **4** the assembling of a machine or structure or its parts: *a car assembly plant*. **5** a number of component parts fitted together to form a whole: *the aircraft's tail assembly*.

assembly language *noun* *Computing* a low-level language employing mnemonic symbols which correspond exactly to groups of machine instructions.

assembly line *noun* a sequence of machines and workers along which a product moves as it is assembled in stages.

assemblyman *noun* (*plural* **assemblymen**) **1** a member of an (esp. legislative) assembly. **2** *Cdn hist.* (in PEI) one of the two representatives elected to the Legislative Assembly in each riding (*compare* COUNCILLOR).

SPELL CHECK
assent, ascent ABC ✓

A rise is an **ascent**.

---

assent • *verb* **1** consent: *assented to my request.* **2** express agreement: *"That's true," he assented.* • *noun* **1** acceptance or agreement: *a nod of assent.* **2** consent or sanction, esp. official (*see also* ROYAL ASSENT).

assert *verb* **1** declare; state clearly: *assert one's beliefs ◊ assert that it is so.* **2 assert oneself** (of a person) insist on one's rights or opinions; demand recognition: *he was fed up with people ignoring him and decided to assert himself.* **3 assert oneself** (of a prevailing mood, tendency, etc.) become influential: *a sentimentality that asserts itself in his interviews.* **4** make or enforce a claim to: *assert one's rights.* [Say a CERT]

assertion *noun* **1** a confident and forceful statement of fact or belief: *his assertion that his father had deserted his family.* **2** the action of stating something or exercising authority confidently and forcefully: *the assertion of their legal rights.* **3** (also **self-assertion**) insistence on the recognition of one's rights or claims: *don't be a pushover—show some assertion.* [Say a SUR sh'n]

assertive *adjective* having or showing a confident and forceful personality: *the job may call for assertive behaviour.* ▶ **assertively** *adverb* **assertiveness** *noun* [Say a SUR tiv]

assess *verb* (**assesses, assessed, assessing**) **1** determine or estimate the size, quality, or extent of. **2** judge or evaluate. **3 a** estimate the value of (a property) for taxation. **b** fix the amount of (a tax etc.) and impose it on a person or community. **4** penalize or fine a specific amount: *assessed $100 in damages.* ▶ **assessment** *noun*

assessor *noun* **1** a person who makes assessments, esp. one who assesses taxes or estimates the value of property for taxation or insurance purposes. **2** a person called upon to advise a judge, committee of inquiry, etc., on technical questions.

asset *noun* **1 a** a useful or valuable quality. **b** a person or thing possessing such a quality or qualities: *is an asset to the company.* **2** (usu. in *plural*) **a** property and possessions, esp. regarded as having value in meeting debts etc. **b** any possession having value.

assiduous *adjective* showing great care and perseverance: *she was assiduous in pointing out every detail ◊ women were assiduous in performing their religious devotions.* ▶ **assiduously** *adverb* [Say a SID yoo us]

assign • *verb* **1 a** allot as a share, responsibility, task, etc.: *assign homework.* **b** appoint to a position, task, etc. **2** fix (a time, place, etc.) for a specific purpose. **3** ascribe or refer to (a reason, date, etc.): *assigned the manuscript to 1832.* **4** transfer formally (esp. personal property) to. ▶ **assignable** *adjective*

assignation *noun* an appointment to meet someone in secret, typically one made by lovers: *furtive assignations in the shrubbery.* [Say assig NATION]

assignment *noun* **1** a task allotted to a person as part of a job or course of study: *a homework assignment.* **2** the allocation of a job or task to someone or that person being allocated a job or task: *the assignment of tasks is left up to you ◊ I was on assignment for a German magazine.* **3** the allocation or attribution of something as belonging to a person or organization etc.: *the assignment of language rights to the provinces.*

assimilate *verb* (**assimilates, assimilated, assimilating**) **1 a** absorb and digest (food etc.) into the body. **b** absorb (information etc.) into the mind. **2** absorb (people) into a larger group, esp. by causing a minority culture to acquire the characteristics of the

majority culture. **3** be absorbed into the body, mind, or a larger group. **4** make similar to; cause to resemble. ▶ **assimilative** *adjective* [Say a SIMMA late]

assimilation *noun* **1** the process in which the ideas and traditions of one culture or group become integrated with or replaced by those of a larger culture or group: *the assimilation of ethnic minorities into the community.* **2** the absorption of food or nutrients by the body or any biological system. **3** the incorporation of new ideas with previous knowledge. [Say a simma LAY sh'n]

assimilationism *noun* the policy or practice of absorbing minority ethnic groups into a society. ▶ **assimilationist** *noun* & *adjective*

Assiniboine • *noun* **1** (*plural* **Assiniboine** or **Assiniboines**) a member of an Aboriginal people living in S Saskatchewan and NE Montana. **2** the Siouan language of the Assiniboine. • *adjective* of the Assiniboine or their language. [Say a SINNA boin]

assist • *verb* **1** help (a person, process, etc.). **2** act as an assistant: *assisted in the ceremony.* **3** *Hockey* **a** (usu. foll. by on) score an assist. **b** set up (a goal scorer) with an assist. • *noun* **1 a** *Hockey* a point awarded to up to two players who successively touch the puck with their stick immediately before a teammate scores a goal. **b** *Baseball* a fielder's action of helping to put out an opponent. **2** an act of helping. ▶ **assistance** *noun*

assistant *noun* **1** a helper. **2** a person who assists, esp. as a subordinate in a particular role: *assistant coach ◊ the publicist's assistant.*

assisted suicide *noun* suicide effected with the assistance of another person, esp. the taking of lethal drugs, provided by a doctor for the purpose, by a patient considered incurable.

assize *noun* Cdn (usu. in *plural*) **1** a session of a court. **2** a trial or lawsuit held before a travelling judge. [Say a SIZE]

associate • *verb* (**associates, associated, associating**) **1** connect in the mind: *associate red with danger.* **2** join or combine. **3 associate oneself** make oneself a partner; declare oneself in agreement: *did not want to associate myself with the plan.* **4** combine for a common purpose. **5** (usu. foll. by *with*) meet frequently or have dealings. • *noun* **1 a** a business partner or colleague. **2** a friend or companion. **3** a subordinate member of a body, institute, etc. **4** a thing connected with another. • *adjective* **1** joined in companionship, function, or dignity. **2** allied; in the same group or category. **3** of less than full status: *associate member.* [Say a SO see ate or a SO she ate for the verb, a SO see it or a SO she it for the noun or adjective]

association *noun* **1** a group of people or organizations united for a joint purpose: *the Canadian Association of Journalists.* **2** a connection or co-operative link between people or organizations: *Sarah developed a close association with the university ◊ the program was promoted in association with the Department of Music.* **3** the fact of occurring with something else: *cases of cancer found in association with colitis.* **4 a** a mental connection between ideas or things: *the word bureaucracy has unpleasant associations.* **b** the action of making such a connection: *Bathsheba soon made the association between the sound of the can opener and food.* ▶ **associational** *adjective*

associative *adjective* **1** of or involving association: *associative memory.* **2** *Math* & *Computing* involving the condition that a group of quantities connected by operators (*see* OPERATOR 4) gives the same result whatever their grouping, as long as their order remains the same, e.g. $(a \times b) \times c = a \times (b \times c)$. [Say a SO see a tiv or a SO she a tiv]

Assomption sash *noun* (*plural* **Assomption sashes**) *Cdn hist.* = CEINTURE FLÉCHÉE. [Say a SUMP sh'n]

assorted *adjective* **1** of various sorts put together; miscellaneous. **2** sorted into groups. **3** matched: *ill-assorted* ◊ *poorly assorted*.

assortment *noun* a set of various sorts of things or people put together; a mixed collection.

assuage *verb* (**assuages, assuaged, assuaging**) **1** make an unpleasant feeling less intense: *the letter assuaged the fears of most members*. **2** satisfy (an appetite or desire): *an opportunity arose to assuage her desire for knowledge*. [Say a SWAYDGE]

assume *verb* (**assumes, assumed, assuming**) **1** take or accept as being true, without proof, for the purpose of argument or action. **2** simulate or pretend: *assumed an air of indifference*. **3** undertake (an office or duty). **4 a** take on (an aspect, attribute, etc.): *the problem assumed immense proportions*. **b** accept (another's responsibility etc.) as one's own: *assumed the company's debts*. **5** usurp, or seize (power etc.): *assumed the presidency*.

assumption *noun* **1** a thing that is accepted as true or as certain to happen, without proof: *they made certain assumptions about the market* ◊ *we're working on the assumption that the time of death was after midnight*. **2** the action of taking or beginning to take power or responsibility. **3** *Catholicism* (**Assumption**) **a** the reception of the Virgin Mary bodily into heaven. **b** the feast day in honour of this (Aug. 15).

assurance *noun* **1** a positive declaration that a thing is true: *gave an assurance that all damage would be repaired*. **2** confidence or certainty about one's own abilities: *he drove with assurance*.

assure *verb* (**assures, assured, assuring**) **1** (often foll. by *of*) **a** make (a person) sure; convince: *assured him of my sincerity*. **b** tell (a person) confidently: *assured them the bus went to Halifax*. **2** make certain of; ensure the happening etc. of: *will assure her success*.

assured *adjective* **1** certain, guaranteed. **2** self-confident. PHRASES **rest assured** remain confident. ▶ **assuredly** *adverb*

Assyrian • *noun* **1** an inhabitant of Assyria, an ancient country in N Iraq. **2** the Semitic language of Assyria. • *adjective* of or relating to Assyria. [Say a SEERY in]

astatine *noun* a radioactive element which occurs naturally and can be artificially made. [Say ASTA teen]

aster *noun* a plant with bright daisy-like flowers.

asterisk • *noun* a symbol (*) used in printing and writing to mark words etc. for reference, to stand for omitted matter, etc. • *verb* mark with an asterisk.

astern *adverb* *Nautical & Aviation* **1** aft; away to the rear: *both missiles passed astern of the ship*. **2** backwards: *full speed astern*.

asteroid *noun* any of the small planetary bodies revolving around the sun, mainly between the orbits of Mars and Jupiter. ▶ **asteroidal** *adjective*

asteroid belt *noun* the region between the orbits of Mars and Jupiter where most asteroids are found.

asthma *noun* a disorder, often provoked by allergy, causing wheezing and difficulty breathing. [Say AZMA]

asthmatic • *adjective* relating to or suffering from asthma. • *noun* a person suffering from asthma. ▶ **asthmatically** *adverb* [Say azz MAT ic]

astigmatism *noun* a defect in the eye or in a lens resulting in distorted images, as light rays are prevented from meeting at a common focus. [Say a STIGMA tism]

astilbe *noun* a plant with plumelike heads of tiny white, red, orange, or pink flowers. [Say a STILL bee]

astonish *verb* (**astonishes, astonished,**

astonishing) amaze. ▶ **astonishing** *adjective* **astonishingly** *adverb* **astonishment** *noun*

astound *verb* overcome with surprise or shock; amaze. ▶ **astounding** *adjective* **astoundingly** *adverb*

astral *adjective* **1** of or connected with the stars. **2** consisting of stars; starry. **3** relating to or arising from a supposed ethereal existence, esp. of a counterpart of the body, associated with oneself in life and surviving after death. [Say ASS trull]

astray *adverb & adjective* **1** into error or sin or morally corrupt behaviour: *was led astray by her drug-addicted friends*. **2** away from the correct path or direction: *we went astray but a man redirected us*. PHRASES **go astray** be lost or mislaid: *the money had gone astray somehow*.

astride *preposition* **1** with a leg on each side of: *astride the horse*. **2** extending across: *a picturesque village sitting astride the Grand River*.

astringency *noun* a slightly bitter but fresh taste or smell. [Say a STRIN jin see]

astringent • *adjective* **1** causing the contraction of body tissues. **2** checking bleeding. **3 a** severe, austere. **b** harsh and critical: *the astringent reformist tone of his essay*. **4** (of a taste or smell) slightly bitter but fresh: *the astringent taste of lemon juice*. • *noun* an astringent substance or drug. [Say a STRIN jint]

astrolabe *noun* an instrument, usu. consisting of a graduated disc and a pointer, formerly used to make astronomical measurements and as an aid in navigation. [Say ASTRA labe]

astrologer *noun* a person who uses astrology to tell people about their personality, their future, etc.

astrological *adjective* based on or having to do with astrology.

astrology *noun* the study of the movements and relative positions of celestial bodies interpreted as an influence on human affairs.

astronaut *noun* **1** a person who is trained to travel in a spacecraft. **2** *Cdn* (*BC*) a (usu. Asian) immigrant to Canada who commutes back to Hong Kong, Taiwan, etc. frequently to work, while leaving dependants resident in Canada (also as an *adjective*: *astronaut family*).

astronautics *noun* the science of space travel.

astronomer *noun* a person who studies astronomy.

astronomic *adjective* = ASTRONOMICAL.

astronomical *adjective* **1** of or relating to astronomy. **2** extremely large; too large to contemplate: *the costs were astronomical*. ▶ **astronomically** *adverb*

astronomy *noun* the study of the universe and its contents beyond the bounds of the Earth's atmosphere.

astrophysical *adjective* based on or having to do with astrophysics.

astrophysicist *noun* a person who studies astrophysics.

astrophysics *noun* a branch of astronomy concerned with the physics and chemistry of celestial bodies.

Astroturf *noun* *proprietary* a synthetic surface used as a substitute for grass on sports fields etc.

astute *adjective* having or showing an ability to accurately assess situations or people and turn this to one's advantage: *an astute businesswoman*. ▶ **astutely** *adverb* **astuteness** *noun*

asunder *adverb* *literary* apart.

asylum *noun* **1** protection, esp. for those pursued by the law: *seek asylum*. **2** = POLITICAL ASYLUM. [Say a SIGH lum]

asymmetric *adjective* = ASYMMETRICAL. [Say ay slm METRIC]

asymmetrical *adjective* **1** having two sides or parts that are not the same in size or shape: *most people's faces are asymmetrical*. **2** unequal or unbalanced in some

respect: *the asymmetrical relationship between a landlord and a tenant.* ▶ **asymmetrically** *adverb* [Say ay sim METRIC ul]

asymmetry *noun* (*plural* **asymmetries**) lack of symmetry. [Say ay SIMMA tree or ass SIMMA tree]

asymptomatic *adjective* producing or showing no symptoms. [Say ay simpta MAT ic]

asynchronous *adjective* not happening at the same time or at the same rate. ▶ **asynchronously** *adverb* [Say ay SINKRA nus]

At *symbol* astatine.

at *preposition* **1** expressing position, exact or approximate. **2** expressing a point in time: *see you at three.* **3** expressing a point in a scale or range: *at boiling point ◊ at her best.* **4** expressing engagement or concern in a state or activity: *at war.* **5** expressing a value or rate: *sell at $10 each.* **6 a** with or with reference to: *at a disadvantage ◊ annoyed at losing ◊ good at math.* **b** by means of: *drank it at a gulp.* **7** expressing: **a** motion towards: *went at them.* **b** aim towards or pursuit of (physically or conceptually): *aim at the target ◊ laughed at us.* PHRASES **at it 1** engaged in an activity; working hard: *let's get at it.* **2** *informal* repeating a habitual (usu. disapproved of) activity: *found them at it again.* **at that** moreover: *found one, and a good one at that.* **where it's at** *slang* the fashionable scene or activity.

atavism *noun* a reversion to something ancient or ancestral: *the wild land awoke a distant atavism of wandering and adventure.* ▶ **atavistic** *adjective* [Say ATTA vism]

at-bat *noun Baseball* a turn at bat which results in the batter making either a hit or an out.

ATC *abbreviation* AIR TRAFFIC CONTROL.

ate *past of* EAT.

atelier *noun* a workshop or studio, esp. of an artist or designer. [Say attle YAY]

a tempo *adverb Music* in the previous tempo.

Athabascan *noun & adjective* = ATHAPASKAN.

Athabaskan *noun & adjective* = ATHAPASKAN.

Athapascan *noun & adjective* = ATHAPASKAN.

Athapaskan • *noun* **1** an Aboriginal language group of the subarctic regions of the Northwest Territories, the Yukon, northern BC, and the northern Prairie provinces. **2** (*plural* **Athapaskan** or **Athapaskans**) a member of any of the North American peoples speaking languages of this family. • *adjective* of or relating to the Athapaskan peoples or their languages.

Atharva-Veda *noun* an ancient collection of sacred Hindu hymns and incantations, traditionally called the fourth Veda but originating outside Vedic society. [Say a tarva VAYDA or a tarva VEEDA]

atheism *noun* disbelief in the existence of God or gods. ▶ **atheist** *noun* **atheistic** *adjective* [Say AY thee ism]

Athenian • *noun* a native or inhabitant of ancient or modern Athens, a city in Greece. • *adjective* of or relating to ancient or modern Athens. [Say a THEENY un]

atherosclerosis *noun* thickening and hardening of the arteries because of the buildup of fatty deposits. [Say atha roe skla ROE sis]

athlete *noun* **1** a person who trains to compete in sports and other exercises requiring physical skill, strength, and endurance. **2** a person with a natural talent for sports.

athlete's foot *noun* a fungal foot condition causing itching, flaking, and cracking of the skin, esp. between the toes.

athletic *adjective* **1** of or relating to athletes or athletics: *an athletic competition.* **2** muscular or physically fit. **3** active in esp. skilled at, sports. ▶ **athletically** *adverb* **athleticism** *noun*

athletics *plural noun* (usu. treated as *singular*)

competitive activities requiring physical skill and endurance.

athletic supporter *noun* = JOCKSTRAP.

at-home • *noun* a social reception in a person's home. • *adjective* occurring in or remaining in the home.

-athon *combining form* forming nouns denoting: **1** an extended event involving a single activity, usu. to raise money for a charity: *walkathon.* **2** an activity of abnormal length: *talkathon.*

athwart *preposition* from side to side of: *Cree hunting territory lay athwart the route to the Bay.* [Say a THWORT]

Atlantic *adjective* of or adjoining the Atlantic Ocean.

Atlantic Canada *noun* = ATLANTIC PROVINCES.

Atlantic provinces *plural noun* New Brunswick, Nova Scotia, PEI, and Newfoundland (*compare* MARITIMES).

Atlantic salmon *noun* a salmon of the coastal North Atlantic and its freshwater tributaries.

Atlantic Time *noun* the time in a zone including the Maritime provinces, parts of Labrador and eastern Quebec, and eastern Central and South America. **Atlantic Standard Time** is four hours behind GMT; **Atlantic Daylight Time** is three hours behind GMT.

atlas *noun* (*plural* **atlases**) a book of maps or charts.

ATM *abbreviation* (*plural* **ATMs**) AUTOMATED TELLER MACHINE.

atmosphere *noun* **1 a** the envelope of gases surrounding the earth, any other planet, or any substance. **b** the air in any particular place, esp. if unpleasant: *the atmosphere in the bar was unbreathable with cigarette smoke.* **2 a** the pervading tone or mood of a place or situation, esp. with reference to the feelings or emotions evoked: *the hotel has won commendations for its friendly, welcoming atmosphere.* **b** the feelings or emotions evoked by a work of art, a piece of music, etc. **3** *Physics* a unit of pressure equal to mean atmospheric pressure at sea level, 101.325 kilopascals.

atmospheric *adjective* **1** of, relating to, or occurring in the atmosphere: *atmospheric conditions.* **2** possessing or evoking a particular tone, mood, or set of associations: *atmospheric lighting.* [Say atma SFEER ick]

atmospheric pressure *noun* the pressure exerted on the earth's surface by the weight of the air above it.

atmospherics *plural noun* **1** electrical disturbance in the atmosphere, esp. caused by lightning, sometimes resulting in interference with telecommunications. **2** = ATMOSPHERE 2. [Say atma SFEER icks or atma SFAIR icks]

atoll *noun* a ring-shaped coral reef enclosing a lagoon. [Say AT all]

atom *noun* **1 a** the smallest particle of a chemical element that can take part in a chemical reaction. **b** this particle as a source of nuclear energy. **2** *Cdn* a level of children's sports, usu. involving children aged 9–11. **b** a player in this age group. **3** a very small portion of a thing or quality: *not an atom of pity.*

atomic *adjective* **1** concerned with or using atomic energy or atomic bombs. **2** of or relating to an atom or atoms.

atomic age *noun* the current historical period, characterized by the use of atomic energy.

atomic bomb *noun* (also **atom bomb**) a bomb involving the release of energy by nuclear fission.

atomic energy *noun* energy obtained by nuclear fission or fusion.

atomic number *noun* the number of protons in the nucleus of an atom, which is characteristic of a chemical element and determines its place in the periodic table. Symbol: Z.

atomic particle *noun* any one of the particles of which an atom is constituted.

atomic theory *noun Physics* **1** the concept of an atom

as being composed of elementary particles. **2** the theory that all matter is made up of small indivisible particles called atoms, and that the atoms of any one element are identical in all respects but differ from those of other elements and unite to form compounds in fixed proportions.

atomize *verb* (**atomizes, atomized, atomizing**) **1** reduce to very fine particles. **2** break up (a society etc.) into small constituent parts: *considered those living in poverty as an atomized, unorganized mass*.

atomizer *noun* an instrument for emitting liquids as a fine spray.

atonal *adjective* Music not written in any key or mode. ▶ **atonality** *noun* [Say ay TONAL]

atone *verb* (**atones, atoned, atoning**) make amends or reparation: *a sacrifice to atone for the sin*. [Say a TONE]

atonement *noun* **1** reparation for a wrong or injury or sin. **2** (**the Atonement**) Christianity the reconciliation of God and humanity by Jesus Christ.

atop • *preposition* on the top of. • *adverb* on the top.

ATP *abbreviation* adenosine triphosphate, a nucleotide important in living cells which, in breaking down to adenosine diphosphate, provides energy for physiological processes such as muscular contraction.

atrial *adjective* having to do with either or both of the two upper cavities of the heart. [Say AY tree 'll]

atrium *noun* (*plural* **atriums** or **atria**) **1 a** the central court of an ancient Roman house. **b** a central hall or court, often rising through several storeys, with galleries and rooms opening off it. **2 a** cavity in the body, esp. one of two upper cavities of the heart, receiving blood from the veins. [Say AY tree um for the singular; for *ATRIA* say AY tree uh]

atrocious *adjective* **1** very bad or unpleasant: *their manners were atrocious*. **2** extremely savage or wicked: *atrocious cruelty*. ▶ **atrociously** *adverb* [Say a TROE shus]

atrocity *noun* (*plural* **atrocities**) **1** an extremely wicked or cruel act, esp. one involving physical violence or injury: *war atrocities* ◊ *scenes of hardship and atrocity*. **2** a highly unpleasant or distasteful object: *atrocities in cheap red nylon*. [Say a TROSSA tee]

atrophy • *verb* (**atrophies, atrophied, atrophying**) **1** waste away through undernourishment, aging, or lack of use: *the biceps will atrophy* ◊ *atrophied muscles*. **2** gradually decline in effectiveness or vigour due to underuse or neglect: *the imagination can atrophy from lack of use*. • *noun* the process of atrophying. [Say ATRA fee]

Atsina *noun* = GROS VENTRE. [Say at SEENA]

attaboy *interjection* expressing encouragement or admiration.

attach *verb* (**attaches, attached, attaching**) **1** fasten, affix, join. **2** be very fond of or devoted to: *am attached to her*. **3** attribute, assign (some function, quality, or characteristic): *attaches great importance to it*. **4 a** accompany; form part of: *no conditions are attached*. **b** (foll. by *to*) be an attribute or characteristic: *great prestige attaches to the job*. **5 attach oneself to** take part in; join: *attached themselves to the expedition*. ▶ **attachable** *adjective*

attaché *noun* **1** a person appointed to an ambassador's staff, usu. with a special sphere of activity: *cultural attaché*. **2** an attaché case. [Say at ash AY]

attaché case *noun* a small flat rectangular case for carrying documents etc.; a briefcase.

attachment *noun* **1** a thing attached or to be attached, esp. to a machine, device, etc., for a special function. **2** affection, devotion. **3** a means of attaching. **4** the act of attaching or the state of being attached. **5** a file, application, etc. sent as part of an e-mail message.

attack • *verb* **1** act violently against. **2** begin a military offensive against. **3** criticize adversely. **4** act harmfully upon: *a virus attacking the nervous system*. **5** vigorously apply oneself to; begin work on: *attacked his meal with gusto*. **6** make an attack. **7** be in a mode of attack. • *noun* **1** the act or process of attacking. **2** an offensive military operation. **3** Music the action or manner of beginning a piece, passage, etc. **4** gusto, vigour. **5** a sudden occurrence of esp. an illness. **6** Sport **a** offensive action. **b** the players seeking to score goals etc. ▶ **attacker** *noun*

attain *verb* **1** arrive at; reach (a goal etc.). **2** gain, accomplish (an aim, distinction, etc.). **3** (foll. by *to*) arrive at by conscious development or effort. ▶ **attainability** *noun* **attainable** *adjective*

attainment *noun* **1** a thing achieved, esp. a skill or educational achievement: *the earliest cultural attainments of humans*. **2** the action or fact of achieving a goal towards which one has worked: *the attainment of nationhood*.

attempt • *verb* **1** seek to achieve or complete (a task or action): *attempted the exercise* ◊ *attempted to explain*. **2** seek to climb or master (a mountain etc.). • *noun* an act of attempting; an endeavour.

attend *verb* **1 a** be present at: *attended the meeting*. **b** go regularly to: *attend school*. **2 a** be present: *many members failed to attend*. **b** be present in a serving capacity. **3 a** escort, accompany: *she was attended by three bridesmaids*. **b** (foll. by *on*) wait on; serve. **4 a** turn or apply one's mind; focus one's attention: *attend to what I am saying*. **b** (foll. by *to*) deal with: *shall attend to the matter myself*. **5** follow as a result from: *the error was attended by serious consequences*.

attendance *noun* **1** the act of attending or being present. **2** the number of people present.

attendant • *noun* a person employed to wait on others or provide a service: *flight attendant*. • *adjective* **1** accompanying: *attendant circumstances*. **2** waiting on; serving: *ladies attendant on the queen*.

attendee *noun* a person who attends a conference or other gathering.

attender *noun* a person who attends a meeting or other gathering.

attention • *noun* **1** the act or faculty of applying one's mind: *give me your attention*. **2 a** consideration. **b** care: *give special attention to your handwriting*. **3** (in *plural*) **a** ceremonious politeness: *he paid his attentions to her*. **b** wooing, courting: *the subject of his attentions*. **4 a** soldier's drill position, standing upright with feet together and arms stretched downwards: *stand at attention*. • *interjection* **1** calling people to listen to an announcement etc.: *Attention, please!* **2** ordering soldiers to come to attention.

attention deficit disorder *noun* a disorder esp. of children characterized by a short attention span and impulsiveness, often accompanied by hyperactivity.

attentive *adjective* **1** paying attention: *an attentive audience* ◊ *attentive to taxpayers' wishes*. **2** painstakingly polite and concerned about the comfort or well-being of others: *a restaurant with attentive service*. ▶ **attentively** *adverb* **attentiveness** *noun*

attenuate *verb* (**attenuates, attenuated, attenuating**) **1** reduce the force, value, or effect of: *their radical agendas have become somewhat attenuated*. **2** Electricity reduce the amplitude of (a signal or current). ▶ **attenuation** *noun* [Say a TEN you ate]

attenuated *adjective* **1** unnaturally thin: *a look of gaunt, attenuated elegance*. **2** weakened in force or effect: *an attenuated vaccine provokes immunity with less risk of causing the disease*. ▶ **attenuation** *noun*

attest *verb* **1** confirm the validity or truth of. **2** be evidence or proof of. **3** (foll. by *to*) bear witness to.
attestation *noun* **1** the act of attesting. **2** a testimony. [Say a tess TAY sh'n]

A **attic** *noun* **1** the highest storey of a house, usu. immediately under the beams of the roof. **2** a room in the attic area.

Attikamek • *noun* **1** (*plural* **Attikamek** or **Attikameks**) a member of an Aboriginal people living in the upper St. Maurice River valley in Quebec. **2** the Algonquian language of this people. • *adjective* of the Attikamek or their culture or language. [Say a TICKA meck]

attire • *verb* (**attires**, **attired**, **attiring**) dress, esp. in fine clothes or formal wear: *strikingly attired in black silk*. • *noun* clothes, esp. fine or formal.

attitude *noun* **1 a** a settled opinion or way of thinking. **b** behaviour reflecting this: *I don't like his attitude*. **2 a** a bodily posture. **b** a pose adopted in a painting or a play, esp. for dramatic effect: *strike an attitude*. **c** *Dance* a pose with one leg raised and bent in front or behind. **3** *informal* an uncooperative or hostile disposition: *a teenager with attitude*. ▶ **attitudinal** *adjective*

attorney *noun* (*plural* **attorneys**) **1** a person, esp. a lawyer, appointed to act for another in business or legal matters. See also CROWN ATTORNEY, POWER OF ATTORNEY. **2** *US* a lawyer, esp. one representing a client in a law court. [Say a TURN ee]

Attorney General *noun* (*plural* **Attorneys General**) **1** (in Canada) the minister of the Crown (federally and provincially) responsible for the administration of justice and also acting as legal adviser to the government. **2** a similar chief legal officer in other countries.

attract *verb* **1** draw or bring to oneself or itself: *attracts many admirers*. **2** be attractive to; fascinate: *opposites attract*. **3** (of a magnet, gravity, etc.) exert a pull on (an object).

attraction *noun* **1 a** the act or power of attracting: *the attraction of foreign travel*. **b** a person or thing that attracts by arousing interest: *the fair is a big attraction*. **2** *Physics* the force by which bodies attract or approach each other (*opp.* REPULSION).

attractive *adjective* **1** attracting or capable of attracting; interesting: *an attractive proposition*. **2** pleasing or appealing to the senses, esp. to the sight. ▶ **attractively** *adverb* **attractiveness** *noun*
attractor *noun* something that attracts.

attributable *adjective* probably caused by the thing mentioned: *their illness is attributable to a poor diet*.

attribute • *verb* (**attributes**, **attributed**, **attributing**) **1** regard as belonging or appropriate to: *a poem attributed to Shakespeare*. **2** regard as the effect of a stated cause: *delays were attributed to the traffic*. • *noun* **1 a** a quality associated with a person or thing. **b** a characteristic quality. **2** a material object recognized as appropriate to a person, office, or status: *a sceptre is an attribute of majesty*. **3** an attributive adjective or noun. ▶ **attribution** *noun* [Say a TRIBUTE for the verb, ATTRA byoot for the noun]

attributive *adjective* (of an adjective or noun) preceding the word described and expressing an attribute, as *old* in *the old dog* (but not in *the dog is old*) and *expiry* in *expiry date* (*opp.* PREDICATIVE). ▶ **attributively** *adverb* [Say a TRIBUTE iv]

attrition *noun* **1** reduction of a workforce by processes other than firing, as by not replacing employees who retire, die, etc. **2** the action or process of gradually reducing the strength, numbers, or effectiveness of someone or something through sustained attack or

pressure: *many grain elevators have been abandoned or demolished, and the attrition continues at an alarming rate*. See also WAR OF ATTRITION. **3 a** the act or process of gradually wearing out, esp. by friction. **b** abrasion. [Say a TRISH'n]

attune *verb* (**attunes**, **attuned**, **attuning**) make receptive or aware: *a society more attuned to nature* ◊ *listeners must have an opportunity to attune their ears to the sounds created in music since 1910*.

ATV *abbreviation* (*plural* **ATVs**) ALL-TERRAIN VEHICLE.

atypical *adjective* not typical; not conforming to a type. ▶ **atypically** *adverb* [Say ay TYPICAL]

Au *symbol* the element gold.

auburn *adjective* reddish brown (usu. of a person's hair).

auction • *noun* a sale of goods, usu. in public, in which articles are sold to the highest bidder. • *verb* sell by auction. PHRASES **at auction** in an auction sale.
auction block *noun* a place or facility for the auction of goods. PHRASES **on the auction block** available for auction or sale.

auctioneer *noun* a person who conducts auctions professionally, by calling for bids and declaring goods sold. ▶ **auctioneering** *noun*

audacious *adjective* **1** daring, bold: *a series of audacious takeovers*. **2** showing an impudent lack of respect: *an audacious remark*. ▶ **audaciously** *adverb* **audaciousness** *noun* [Say aw DAY shus]

audacity *noun* **1** the willingness to take bold or shocking risks: *the new production of the opera showed imagination and audacity*. **2** behaviour that is shamelessly rude or disrespectful; nerve: *he had the audacity to tell me I was too fat*. [Say aw DASSA tee]

audibility *noun* the ability to be heard.

audible • *adjective* capable of being heard. • *noun* *Football* a play called by the quarterback at the line of scrimmage to replace one previously agreed on. ▶ **audibly** *adverb*

audience *noun* **1 a** the assembled listeners or spectators at an event, esp. a stage performance etc. **b** the people addressed by a film, book, etc. **2** a formal interview with a person in authority: *a private audience with the Pope*.

audio *noun* **1** sound or its (esp. electrical) reproduction. **2** equipment for electrical reproduction of sound, e.g. speakers etc.: *home audio*.

audio- *combining form* hearing or sound.

audiophile *noun* a person who has a particularly strong interest in high-fidelity sound reproduction. [Say AUDIO file]

audio tape • *noun* **1** a magnetic tape on which sound can be recorded. **2** a sound recording on tape. • *verb* (**audiotape**; **audiotapes**, **audiotaped**, **audiotaping**) record (sound, speech, etc.) on tape.

audiovisual *adjective* (esp. of teaching methods) using electrical equipment, e.g. projectors, tape recorders, etc. that are directed at the senses of sight and hearing.

audit • *noun* **1** an official examination and checking of accounts. **2** a detailed examination or analysis, esp. to assess strengths and weaknesses: *environmental audit*. • *verb* (**audits**, **audited**, **auditing**) **1** conduct an audit (of). **2** attend (a class) informally, without working for credits.

audition • *noun* **1** a short performance by a musician, actor, etc. so that their suitability for training or a role may be judged. **2** the power of hearing or listening. • *verb* perform or assess the performance of a candidate at an audition.

auditor *noun* **1** a person who audits accounts. **2** a person who audits a class. **3** a listener.

Auditor General *noun* (*plural* **Auditors General**) *Cdn*

the official responsible for auditing the accounts of a (federal or provincial) government's agencies, departments, and some Crown corporations, and presenting an annual report on government spending to the House of Commons or legislature.

auditorium *noun* (*plural* **auditoriums** or **auditoria**) **1** the part of a theatre etc. in which the audience sits. **2** a building incorporating a large hall for public gatherings, performances, sports events, etc. **3** a large room, esp. in a school, used for assemblies, theatrical performances, etc. and also usu. as a gymnasium.

auditory *adjective* of or relating to the sense of hearing: *the auditory nerves* ◊ *teaching methods using both visual and auditory stimulations.*

Aug. *abbreviation* August.

SPELL CHECK
auger, augur   ABC ✓

When something acts as a sign that things will go well, it is said to **augur** well.

---

auger *noun* **1** a tool resembling a large corkscrew, for boring holes in wood, the ground, ice, etc. **2** a similar device enclosed in a cylinder for moving grain etc. [Say OGGER]

augment *verb* make or become greater; increase or enhance. ▶ **augmentation** *noun*

augur • *verb* be a sign that something will happen in the future as specified: *augurs ill* ◊ *all augured well for our success* ◊ *they feared that these happenings augured a neo-Nazi revival.* • *noun* Roman History a religious official who observed natural signs, interpreting these as an indication of divine approval or disapproval of a proposed action. [Say OGGER]

augury *noun* (*plural* **auguries**) **1** an omen of what will happen in the future: *they heard the sound as an augury of death.* **2** the interpretation of omens. [Say OG yer ee]

August *noun* the eighth month of the year.

august *adjective* inspiring reverence and admiration. ▶ **augustly** *adverb* [Say awe GUST]

Augustan • *adjective* **1** connected with, occurring during, or influenced by the reign of the Roman emperor Augustus (63 BC–AD 14), esp. as an outstanding period of Latin literature. **2** (of a literary period, esp. the 18th century in England) characterized by a refined and classical style. • *noun* a writer of the Augustan age of any literature. [Say a GUST'n]

Augustinian • *adjective* **1** of or relating to St. Augustine of Hippo (354–430), who believed that humans have free will to choose good or evil but, constantly tempted by self-indulgence and the love of momentary pleasure, tend to lapse into sin and can only be freed from it by God's grace. **2** belonging to a religious order observing a rule derived from St. Augustine's writings. • *noun* **1** an adherent of the doctrines of St. Augustine. **2** a member of an Augustinian religious order. [Say ogga STINNY in]

auk *noun* any of a family of marine diving birds with a heavy body, short wings, and black and white plumage, e.g. the guillemot, puffin, and razorbill. [Say OCK]

auklet *noun* any of various small auks, chiefly of the North Pacific.

aunt *noun* **1** the sister of one's father or mother. **2** an uncle's wife.

auntie *noun* (also **aunty**) (*plural* **aunties**) *informal* = AUNT.

au pair *noun* (*plural* **au pairs**) a young person from another country, esp. a woman, helping with housework etc. in exchange for room and board, esp. as a way of learning a language. [Say oh PAIR]

aura *noun* (*plural* **auras**) **1** the distinctive atmosphere that seems to surround and be generated by a person,

place, etc.: *the ceremony retains an aura of mystery.* **2** a supposed emanation surrounding the body of a living creature, allegedly visible to some as a sphere of light, viewed by many spiritualists, mystics, and practitioners of alternative medicine as an essential part of the individual. **3** a warning sensation experienced before an attack of epilepsy or migraine. [Say ORA]

aural *adjective* of or relating to or received by the ear. ▶ **aurally** *adverb* [Say ORAL]

aureole *noun* **1** a halo or circle of light, esp. around the head or body of a portrayed religious figure. **2** a corona around the sun or moon. [Say ORY ole]

aurora *noun* (*plural* **auroras** or **aurorae**) **1** a luminous phenomenon, usu. of shimmering coloured streamers, seen in the upper atmosphere in high latitudes, and caused by the interaction of charged solar particles with atmospheric gases, under the influence of the earth's magnetic field. **2** *literary* the dawn. [Say a RORA for the singular; for *AURORAE* say a RORY]

aurora australis *noun* a southern occurrence of the aurora. [Say a RORA awe STRAL iss]

aurora borealis *noun* a northern occurrence of the aurora. *Also called* NORTHERN LIGHTS. [Say a RORA borry AL iss]

auroral *adjective* having to do with auroras, the northern or southern lights: *auroral display.* [Say a ROAR'll]

auscultation *noun* the act of listening, esp. to sounds from the heart, lungs, etc., as a part of medical diagnosis. ▶ **auscultatory** *adjective* [Say oss cull TAY sh'n, oss CULTA tory]

auspice *noun* (in *plural*) with the help, support, or protection of: *a school that operated under the auspices of the Anglican Church.* [Say OSS piss]

auspicious *adjective* conducive to success; favourable: *it was not the most auspicious time to hold an election.* ▶ **auspiciously** *adverb* **auspiciousness** *noun* [Say oss PISH us]

Aussie *informal* • *noun* **1** an Australian. **2** Australia. • *adjective* Australian. [Say OZZY or OSSY]

austere *adjective* **1** having no comforts or luxuries; harsh: *conditions in the monastery were very austere.* **2** morally strict: *he was an austere man, with a rigidly puritanical outlook.* **3** severely simple; unadorned: *the cathedral is impressive in its austere simplicity.* ▶ **austerely** *adverb* [Say oss TEER]

austerity *noun* (*plural* **austerities**) **1** sternness; moral severity: *he was noted for his austerity and authoritarianism.* **2** frugality or money-saving practices: *a period of financial austerity.* **3** (esp. in *plural*) an austere practice: *the austerities of a monk's life.* [Say oss TERRA tee]

Australian • *noun* **1** a native or national of Australia. **2** a person of Australian descent. • *adjective* of or relating to Australia. ▶ **Australianism** *noun*

Australoid • *adjective* of a race of peoples that diffused from Asia to Australia at a time of lower sea level. • *noun* a person of Australoid ethnological type. [Say OSSTRA loyd]

Australopithecus *noun* any extinct primate of the genus *Australopithecus* having ape-like and human characteristics, or its fossilized remains. [Say osstra lo PITHA cuss]

Austro- *combining form* **1** Austrian; Austrian and: *Austro-Hungarian.* **2** Australian; Australian and.

Austronesian • *noun* a family of languages spoken widely in Malaysia, Indonesia, and other parts of southeast Asia, and in the islands of the central and South Pacific. • *adjective* of or relating to this language family. [Say osstro NEE zh'n]

autarkic *adjective* having to do with autarky. ▶ **autarkical** [Say aw TARK ic]

autarky *noun* (*plural* **autarkies**) **1** self-sufficiency, esp. as an economic system. **2** a state etc. run according to such a system. [Say AW tarky]

auteur *noun* a director who so greatly influences the films directed as to be able to rank as their author. [Say oh TURR]

authentic *adjective* **1 a** of undisputed origin; genuine. **b** reliable or trustworthy. **2** *Music* performed on instruments dating from and with techniques typical of the same period as the piece performed. ▶**authentically** *adverb*

authenticate *verb* (**authenticates, authenticated, authenticating**) **1** establish the truth or genuineness of. **2** validate. ▶**authentication** *noun*

authenticity *noun* the quality of being genuine or true: *the authenticity of the letter is beyond doubt.*

author • *noun* **1** a writer, esp. of books. **2** the originator of an event, a condition, etc.: *the author of all my woes.* • *verb* disputed be the author of.

authorial *adjective* coming from or connected with the author of something. [Say aw THORY ul]

authoritarian • *adjective* **1** favouring, encouraging, or enforcing strict obedience to authority, as opposed to individual freedom: *the transition from an authoritarian to a democratic regime.* **2** tyrannical or domineering: *he had an authoritarian and at times belligerent manner.* • *noun* a person who favours absolute obedience to a constituted authority. ▶**authoritarianism** *noun* [Say a thora TERRY in]

authoritative *adjective* **1** recognized as true or dependable: *clear, authoritative information and advice.* **2** (of a person, behaviour, etc.) commanding or self-confident: *her voice was calm and authoritative.* **3** official: *an authoritative document.* **4** (of a text) considered to be the best of its kind and unlikely to be improved upon: *this is likely to become the authoritative study on the subject.* ▶**authoritatively** *adverb* **authoritativeness** *noun* [Say a THORA tay tiv]

authority *noun* (*plural* **authorities**) **1 a** the power or right to enforce obedience. **b** delegated power: *we have the authority to search this building.* **2** (esp. in *plural*) a person or body having authority, esp. a police or government official. **3 a** an expert in a particular subject. **b** a book etc. that can supply reliable information. **4** considerable force or strength: *spoke with authority.* **5** testimony, evidence: *took it on their authority.* [Say a THORA tee]

authorization *noun* **1** official permission or power to do something; the act of giving permission: *who gave the authorization to release this data?* ◊ *you may not enter without authorization.* **2** a document that gives a person official permission to do something.

authorize *verb* (**authorizes, authorized, authorizing**) give official approval of or permission to an undertaking or agent: *the government authorized the helicopter purchase* ◊ *I authorized her to act for me.*

Authorized Version *noun* = KING JAMES VERSION.

authorship *noun* the origin of a book or other written work: *of unknown authorship.*

autism *noun* a mental condition, usu. present from childhood, characterized by complete self-absorption and a reduced ability to respond to or communicate with the outside world. ▶**autistic** *adjective* [Say OTT ism, ott ISS tick]

auto • *noun* (*plural* **autos**) an automobile: *a new auto* ◊ *auto mechanic.* • *adjective* automatic.

auto- *combining form* **1** originating with, induced by, or pertaining to the self: *autobiography.* **2** operating by itself; automatic: *autofocus.* **3** relating to automobiles or the automobile industry: *automaker.*

autobiographer *noun* a person who writes an autobiography.

autobiographical *adjective* dealing with the writer's own life: *her novels are partly autobiographical.*

autobiography *noun* (*plural* **autobiographies**) **1** a personal account of one's own life, esp. for publication. **2** this as a process or literary form.

autocracy *noun* (*plural* **autocracies**) **1** absolute government by one person. **2** an autocratic country or society. [Say aw TOCKRA see]

autocrat *noun* **1** an absolute ruler. **2** a dictatorial person. ▶**autocratic** *adjective* **autocratically** *adverb* [Say OTTA crat]

autodidact *noun* a self-taught person. ▶**autodidactic** *adjective* [Say otto DIE dact, otto die DACK tick]

autograph • *noun* **1** a signature, esp. that of a celebrity written as a memento for an admirer. **2** a manuscript, musical composition, etc. in an author's or composer's own handwriting: *an autograph copy.* • *verb* sign (a photograph, autograph album, etc.).

autoimmune *adjective* (of a disease) caused by antibodies produced against substances naturally present in the body. ▶**autoimmunity** *noun* [Say otto IMMUNE]

automaker *noun* a company which manufactures automobiles.

automata *plural of* AUTOMATON. [Say a TOMMA tuh]

automate *verb* (**automates, automated, automating**) convert to or operate by automation: *the ticket office has been automated.*

automated teller machine *noun* an electronic machine which allows users to perform banking transactions by inserting an encoded plastic card; a bank machine.

automatic • *adjective* **1** (of a machine, device, etc., or its function) working by itself, without direct human intervention. **2 a** done spontaneously, without conscious thought or intention: *an automatic reaction.* **b** necessary and inevitable: *an automatic penalty.* **3** *Psychology* performed unconsciously or subconsciously. **4 a** (of a firearm) that continues firing until the pressure on the trigger is released or the ammunition is exhausted. **b** (of a pistol) that fires each time the trigger is pulled, without requiring manual reloading. **5** (of a motor vehicle or its transmission) using gears that change automatically according to speed and acceleration. • *noun* **1** an automatic device, esp. a gun or transmission. **2** a vehicle with automatic transmission. ▶**automatically** *adverb*

automatic pilot *noun* **1** a device for keeping an aircraft on a set course. **2** the state of a person doing something by routine or habit, without concentration.

automation *noun* the use or introduction of automatic equipment to save mental and manual labour in a manufacturing or other process or facility.

automatism *noun* **1** *Psychology* **a** the performance of actions unconsciously or subconsciously. **b** such an action. **2** the avoidance of conscious intention in producing works of art, esp. by using mechanical techniques or subconscious associations. [Say a TOMMA tism]

automaton *noun* (*plural* **automata** or **automatons**) **1** a mechanism which operates with concealed motive power, esp. one simulating a living being. **2** a person who behaves without active intelligence or mechanically in a set pattern or routine: *totalitarian states wish to reduce human beings to automatons.* [Say a TOMMA tawn]

automobile *noun* a car.

automotive *adjective* concerned with motor vehicles.

autonomic nervous system *noun* the part of the nervous system responsible for control of the bodily functions not consciously directed, e.g. heartbeat. [Say otta NOM ic]

autonomous *adjective* **1** having self-government: *the federation included sixteen autonomous republics*. **2** acting or existing independently or having the freedom to do so: *autonomous Crown corporations like the CBC*. ▶ **autonomously** *adverb* [Say aw TONNA muss]

autonomy *noun* (*plural* **autonomies**) **1** the right of self-government. **2** personal freedom or independence.

Autopac *noun Cdn* (*Man.*) *proprietary* the vehicle insurance provided by the Manitoba government through Manitoba Public Insurance.

autopilot *noun* = AUTOMATIC PILOT.

autopsy *noun* (*plural* **autopsies**) a post-mortem examination conducted to determine the cause of death. [Say AW topsy]

autoroute *noun* an expressway in Quebec, France, and other French-speaking regions. [Say OTTO root]

auto worker *noun* a labourer employed by an automobile manufacturer.

autumn *noun* **1** the third season of the year, associated with harvests and falling leaves, in the northern hemisphere from September to November and in the southern hemisphere from March to May. **2** *Astronomy* the period from the autumnal equinox to the winter solstice. **3** a time of maturity or imminent decay: *he was in the autumn of his life*.

autumnal *adjective* **1** of, characteristic of, or appropriate to autumn: *autumnal colours*. **2** occurring in autumn: *autumnal equinox*. **3** maturing or blooming in autumn. [Say aw TUM n'll]

autumnal equinox *noun* (*plural* **autumnal equinoxes**) (also **autumn equinox**) the equinox occurring on or about 22 Sept. in the northern hemisphere and on or about 21 March in the southern hemisphere.

auxiliary ● *adjective* **1** (of a person or thing) helpful, giving support. **2** (of services or equipment) subsidiary, additional. **3** (of a sailing vessel) equipped with an engine. ● *noun* (*plural* **auxiliaries**) **1** an auxiliary person or thing. **2** a group of volunteers who assist a church, hospital, etc. with fundraising and other charitable activities. **3** (in *plural*) *Military* foreign or allied troops in a belligerent nation's service. **4** *Grammar* an auxiliary verb. [Say og ZILLYA ree or og ZILLA ree]

auxiliary verb *noun* a verb used in forming tenses, moods, and voices of other verbs, e.g. *will* in *she will go*.

AV *abbreviation* AUDIOVISUAL (teaching aids etc.).

avail ● *verb* **1** help, benefit: *his oxlike physique availed him nothing against the sledgehammer blows of his assailant*. **2** *avail oneself of* take advantage of: *my daughter did not avail herself of my advice*. ● *noun* **1** use: *she tried to get her work recognized but to no avail*. **2** (in *plural*) esp. *Cdn* proceeds or profits, esp. those produced by another person's labour: *living off the avails of prostitution*.

availability *noun* (of a person or thing) the condition of being available: *the availability of computers in schools*.

available *adjective* **1** capable of being used; at one's disposal; obtainable. **2** (of a person) **a** free for consultation or service. **b** not presently involved in a romantic relationship.

avalanche *noun* (*plural* **avalanches**) **1** a mass of snow, ice, rock, etc. tumbling rapidly down a mountainside. **2** a sudden appearance or arrival of anything in large quantities: *faced with an avalanche of work*.

avant-garde ● *noun* pioneers or innovators esp. in art and literature. ● *adjective* (of ideas, works of art, etc.) experimental, progressive. ▶ **avant-gardism** *noun* **avant-gardist** *noun* [Say av ont GARD]

avarice *noun* extreme greed for money or material gain. ▶ **avaricious** *adjective* **avariciously** *adverb* **avariciousness** *noun* [Say AVVA riss, avva RISH iss]

avatar *noun* **1** *Hinduism* the descent of a deity or released soul to earth in bodily form. **2** an incarnation, embodiment, or manifestation of a person or idea: *he set himself up as a new avatar of Arab radicalism*. [Say AVVA tar]

Ave. *abbreviation* Avenue.

avenge *verb* (**avenges**, **avenged**, **avenging**) **1** inflict retribution on behalf of (a person, a violated right, etc.): *swore she would avenge her mother ◊ in his desire to avenge himself on an enemy, he kills his own daughter*. **2** inflict harm in return for an injury or wrong done to oneself or to another: *avenged the murder of his father ◊ they are eager to avenge their defeat.* PHRASES **be avenged** avenge oneself. ▶ **avenger** *noun*

avens *noun* **1** any of various plants of the genus *Geum*. **2** = MOUNTAIN AVENS. [Say AV 'nz]

avenue *noun* **1 a** an urban road or street. **b** (in many North American cities with a grid layout) a road running perpendicular to a street, esp. east–west (*compare* STREET 1d). **2** a road, driveway, or path with trees at regular intervals along its sides. **3** a way of approaching or dealing with something: *explored every avenue to find an answer*.

aver *verb* (**avers**, **averred**, **averring**) *formal* assert or affirm: *the government has averred that unemployment will drop*. [Say a VUR]

average ● *noun* **1 a** the usual amount, extent, or rate. **b** the ordinary standard. **2** the result of adding several amounts together and dividing the total by the number of amounts: *the average of 4, 5, and 9 is 6*. **3** *Baseball* = BATTING AVERAGE. **4** the overall mean of a student's marks, expressed as a percentage, number, or letter grade: *had an 82% average in Grade 12*. ● *adjective* **1** usual, ordinary. **2** estimated or calculated by average. ● *verb* (**averages**, **averaged**, **averaging**) **1** amount on average to: *the sale of the product averaged one hundred a day*. **2** do on average: *averages six hours' work a day*. **3** estimate the average of. PHRASES **average out** result in an average. **law of averages** the principle that if one of two extremes occurs the other will also tend to so as to maintain the normal average. **on average** as an average rate or estimate. ▶ **averagely** *adverb*

WRITING TIP
averse, adverse

Do not confuse **averse** with **adverse**. **Averse** is used of people, nearly always with **to**, and means "having a strong dislike of or opposition to", as in *I am not averse to helping Vince move*. **Adverse** means "unfavourable" or "harmful", as in *Adverse weather conditions will make the move difficult*.

---

averse *adjective* (foll. by *to*) opposed, disinclined: *was not averse to helping me*. [Say a VERSE]

aversion *noun* **1** (usu. foll. by *to*) a dislike or unwillingness: *has an aversion to hard work*. **2** an object of dislike: *my pet aversion is smoking*.

avert *verb* **1** (often foll. by *from*) turn away (one's eyes or thoughts). **2** prevent or ward off (an undesirable occurrence).

Avesta *noun* (usu. as **the Avesta**) the sacred writings of Zoroastrianism. [Say a VESTA]

Avestan ● *adjective* of or relating to the Avesta. ● *noun* the ancient East Iranian language of the Avesta, closely related to Vedic Sanskrit. [Say a VEST'n]

avian *adjective* of or relating to birds. [Say AY vee in]

aviary *noun* (*plural* **aviaries**) a large enclosure or building for keeping birds. [Say AY vee airy]

aviation *noun* **1** the skill or practice of operating aircraft. **2** aircraft manufacture.

aviator *noun* an aircraft pilot.

avid *adjective* **1** eager or enthusiastic: *an avid cyclist*. **2** having a desire for: *she was avid for information about the murder inquiry*. ▶ **avidity** *noun* **avidly** *adverb*

avocado *noun* (*plural* **avocados**) **1 a** (also **avocado pear**) a pear-shaped fruit with rough leathery skin, a smooth oily edible flesh, and a large pit. **b** the tropical evergreen tree bearing this fruit, native to Central America. **2** (also **avocado green**) the light green colour of the flesh of this fruit.

avocation *noun* a secondary activity undertaken in addition to one's main work; a hobby: *music became an avocation, not a profession*. [Say avva KAY sh'n]

avoid *verb* **1** keep away or refrain from (a thing, person, or action). **2** escape. ▶ **avoidable** *adjective* **avoidably** *adverb* **avoidance** *noun* **avoider** *noun*

avoirdupois *noun* **1** (also **avoirdupois weight**) a system of weights based on a pound of 16 ounces or 7,000 grains. **2** *informal* excess body weight. [Say avver da POYZ for the first sense, avwar du PWAH for the second sense]

avow *verb* admit, confess. ▶ **avowal** *noun*

avowed *adjective* admitted: *the avowed author*. ▶ **avowedly** *adverb* [Say a VOWD, a VOW id lee]

avuncular *adjective* **1** (of an older man, esp. in relation to younger people) benevolent and friendly. **2** of or pertaining to an uncle. [Say a VUNK you lur]

aw *interjection* expressing mild protest, entreaty, commiseration, disgust, or disapproval.

AWACS *noun* a long-range radar system for detecting enemy aircraft. [Say AY wax]

await *verb* **1** wait for. **2** (of an event or thing) be in store for: *a surprise awaits you*. **3** wait.

awake • *verb* (**awakes**; *past* **awoke**; *past participle* **awoken**; **awaking**) **1 a** cease to sleep. **b** become active. **2** (foll. by *to*) become aware of: *the authorities finally awoke to the extent of the problem*. **3** rouse from sleep. **4** arouse; provoke: *awoke our interest*. • *adjective* **1** not asleep. **2** aware: *few are awake to the dangers*.

awaken *verb* **1** = AWAKE *verb*. **2** (often foll. by *to*) make aware.

awakening • *noun* an arousal from sleep, inaction, indifference, ignorance, etc.: *a rude awakening*. • *adjective* coming into existence or awareness: *her awakening desire ◊ an awakening consciousness*.

award • *verb* **1** give or order to be given as a prize, payment, or penalty: *awarded them a trophy ◊ was awarded damages*. **2** grant (a contract or commission): *awarded the bridge contract to the lowest bidder*. • *noun* **1** a prize or payment awarded. **2 a** a judicial decision. **b** the penalty awarded by a judicial decision.

aware *adjective* **1** conscious; not ignorant; having knowledge. **2** well-informed. ▶ **awareness** *noun*

awash *adjective* **1** (usu. foll. by *in*, *with*) overrun as if by a flood: *Canada is awash in natural resources*. **2** covered or flooded with water: *the boat rolled violently, its decks awash*.

away • *adverb* **1** to or at a distance from the place, person, or thing in question: *go away ◊ give away*. **2** towards or into non-existence: *sounds die away ◊ explain it away ◊ idled their time away*. **3** constantly, persistently, continuously: *work away*. **4** without delay: *Fire away!* **5** *Baseball* out: *one away*. **6** *Cdn* (*Nfld & Maritimes*) in a place other than the speaker's home province or Atlantic Canada in general: *they're from away*. • *adjective* *Sport* played in an opponent's venue: *away game*. PHRASES **away with** (as *imper.*) let us be rid of.

awe • *noun* a feeling of respect combined with fear or wonder: *stand in awe of*. • *verb* (**awes**, **awed**, **awing**) inspire with awe.

awe-inspiring *adjective* causing awe or wonder; amazing, magnificent.

awesome *adjective* **1** inspiring awe. **2** *slang* excellent. ▶ **awesomely** *adverb* **awesomeness** *noun*

awestruck *adjective* affected or overcome with awe.

awful *adjective* **1 a** unpleasant or horrible: *awful weather*. **b** poor in quality; very bad: *awful handwriting*. **c** *informal* excessive; large: *an awful lot of money*. **2** *literary* inspiring awe: *the awful grandeur of God*.

awfully *adverb* **1** in an unpleasant, bad, or horrible way. **2** *informal* very: *she's awfully young*.

awfulness *noun* an awful quality; extreme unpleasantness: *the memoirs depict the awfulness of war*.

awhile *adverb* for an unspecified length of time: *rest awhile*.

awkward *adjective* **1** difficult to use; unwieldy. **2** clumsy or bungling. **3 a** embarrassed or ill at ease: *felt awkward in such company*. **b** embarrassing: *an awkward silence*. **4** difficult to deal with: *an awkward situation*. ▶ **awkwardly** *adverb* **awkwardness** *noun*

awl *noun* a small pointed tool used for piercing holes, esp. in leather or wood.

awning *noun* a sheet of canvas, plastic, etc. sloping outward from the top of a window, storefront, or doorway or suspended above a ship's deck or other area to provide protection from the sun or rain.

awoke *past of* AWAKE.

awoken *past participle of* AWAKE.

AWOL *abbreviation* *informal* absent without leave. [Say AY woll]

awry • *adverb* **1** crookedly or askew. **2** improperly or amiss. • *adjective* **1** out of the normal or correct position: *he was hatless, his silver hair awry*. **2** amiss or wrong. PHRASES **go awry** go or do wrong: *many youthful romances go awry*. [Say a RYE]

aw-shucks *adjective* *informal* marked by a self-deprecating, self-conscious, or shy manner.

axe • *noun* **1** a chopping tool, usu. of iron with a steel edge and wooden handle. **2** the drastic cutting or elimination of expenditure, staff, etc. **3** dismissal, cancellation, etc.: *he got the axe*. **4** *slang* **a** an electric guitar used in jazz or rock music. **b** a saxophone used in jazz. • *verb* (**axes**, **axed**, **axing**) **1** cut (esp. costs or services) drastically. **2** remove or dismiss. PHRASES **an axe to grind** private ends to serve.

Axel *noun* (also **axel**) *Figure Skating* a one-and-a-half turn jump from the front outside edge of one skate to the back outside edge of the other.

axial *adjective* **1** forming or belonging to an axis. **2** around an axis: *axial rotation*. [Say AXY 'll]

axil *noun* the upper angle between a leaf and the stem it springs from, or between a branch and trunk. [Say AX 'll]

axiom *noun* an established or widely accepted principle. [Say AXY um]

axiomatic *adjective* **1** self-evident: *it is axiomatic that speed and violence are what sells*. **2** relating to or containing axioms. [Say axy uh MAT ic]

axis *noun* (*plural* **axes**) **1 a** an imaginary line about which a body rotates or about which a plane figure is conceived as generating a solid. **b** a line which divides a regular figure symmetrically. **2** *Math* a fixed reference line for the measurement of coordinates etc. **3** *Botany* the central column of an inflorescence or other growth. **4** *Anatomy* the second cervical vertebra. **5** *Physiology* the central part of an organ or organism. **6** an agreement or alliance between two or more countries forming a centre for an eventual larger grouping of nations sharing an ideal or objective.

7 (the Axis) a the alliance of Germany and Italy formed before and during the Second World War, later extended to include Japan and other countries. **b** these countries as a group. [Say AX iss for the singular, AX eez for the plural]

SPELL CHECK **axle, Axel, axil**	

The figure skating jump is an **Axel**; part of a plant is an **axil**.

axle *noun* a rod or spindle (either fixed or rotating) on which a wheel or group of wheels is fixed.

ayatollah *noun* a Shiite religious leader in Iran. [Say eye a TOLA]

aye (also **ay**) • *adverb* **1** *archaic* or *Brit.* yes. **2** (in voting) I assent. **3** (as **aye aye**) *Nautical* a response accepting an order. • *noun* an affirmative answer or assent, esp. in voting. PHRASES **the ayes have it** the affirmative votes are in the majority. [Sounds like *EYE*]

Ayurveda *noun* a form of traditional Hindu medicine using naturally based therapies. ▶**Ayurvedic** *adjective* [Say eye yur VAYDA]

azalea *noun* any of various flowering deciduous shrubs of the genus *Rhododendron*, with pink, purple, white, or yellow flowers. [Say a ZAYLY uh]

Azerbaijani • *noun* **1** (also **Azeri**) a native or inhabitant of Azerbaijan, a country in the Caucasus. **2** the Turkic language of Azerbaijan. • *adjective* of or pertaining to Azerbaijan or its people. [Say azzer by JOHNNY, a ZERRY]

azimuth *noun* **1** the angle between the most northerly point of the horizon and the point directly below a given celestial body, usu. measured clockwise using due north as the zero point. **2** the horizontal angle or direction of a compass bearing. **3** the angle of a recording head on a VCR in relation to the tape. ▶**azimuthal** *adjective* [Say AZZA m'th, azza MOOTH 'll]

Aztec • *noun* **1** a member of the Aboriginal people dominant in central and southern Mexico before the Spanish conquest of 1519. **2** the language of the Aztecs. • *adjective* of the Aztecs or their language. *See also* NAHUATL.

azure *noun & adjective* deep sky-blue. [Say AZH er or AZZ yer]

Bb

B¹ *noun* (also **b**) (*plural* **Bs** or **B's**) **1** the second letter of the alphabet. **2** *Music* the seventh note of the diatonic scale of C major. **3** the second hypothetical person or example. **4** the second highest class or category (of academic marks etc.). **5** *Math* (usu. **b**) the second known quantity. **6** a human blood type of the ABO system. **7** designating the degree of softness of a pencil lead.

B² *symbol* boron.

B³ *abbreviation* (also **B.**) **1** Bachelor. **2** bel(s). **3** billion. **4** bishop. **5** Blessed. **6** bass.

b. *abbreviation* **1** born. **2** billion.

BA *abbreviation* Baseball BATTING AVERAGE.

B.A. *abbreviation* Bachelor of Arts.

Ba *symbol* the element barium.

baa • *verb* (**baas, baaed, baaing**) (esp. of a sheep) bleat. • *noun* (*plural* **baas**) the bleat of a sheep.

baba¹ *noun* a small rich bread-like cake, usu. soaked in rum-flavoured syrup.

baba² *noun* **1** (among people of E European descent) grandmother. **2** *informal* an old woman of E European descent.

baba³ *noun* **1** (among people of Indian descent) father. **2** (also **Baba**) a spiritual leader or holy man in India.

baba ghanouj *noun* a dip, originally Middle Eastern, made from mashed baked eggplant, tahini, garlic and other seasonings. [Say bobba guh NOOSH]

babble • *verb* (**babbles, babbled, babbling**) **1** talk or say in an inarticulate or incoherent manner. **2** chatter excessively or irrelevantly. **3** (of a stream, bird, etc.) produce a succession of indistinct sounds. • *noun* **1 a** incoherent speech. **b** foolish, idle, or childish talk. **2** the murmur of voices, water, etc.

-babble *combining form* forming nouns denoting the jargon of a specified subject or group: *psychobabble*.

babe *noun* **1** a baby. **2** an innocent or helpless person. **3** *slang* sometimes *offensive* a young and attractive person, esp. a woman. PHRASES **babe in arms 1** a small baby, esp. one too young to walk. **2** an innocent or naive person.

babel *noun* **1** a confused noise, esp. of voices. **2** a noisy assembly. **3** a scene of confusion. [Say BAY bull or BABBLE]

babiche *noun* strips of rawhide or sinew used as laces, thread, webbing, etc., e.g. in snowshoes. [Say ba BEESH]

baboon *noun* any of a group of African and Arabian monkeys with a long doglike snout and large teeth.

babushka *noun* **1** a head scarf tied under the chin. **2** an old Slavic woman. [Say ba BOOSH kuh]

baby • *noun* (*plural* **babies**) **1** a very young child, esp. one not yet able to walk. **2** an unduly childish person: *he's such a baby!* **3** the youngest member of a family, team, etc. **4 a** a young or newly born animal. **b** a thing that is small of its kind: *baby corn.* **5** *slang* sometimes *offensive* a young woman; a sweetheart (often as a form of address). **6** *slang* a person or thing regarded with affection or familiarity. **7** one's own responsibility, invention, concern, etc., regarded in a personal way. • *verb* (**babies, babied, babying**) **1** treat like a baby. **2** pamper. PHRASES **throw out the baby with the bathwater** reject the essential with the inessential.

baby blue *noun & adjective* soft, pale blue.

baby blues *plural noun* *informal* attractive blue eyes.

baby bonus *noun* (*plural* **baby bonuses**) *Cdn* family allowance or child tax benefit.

baby boom *noun* a temporary marked increase in the birth rate.

baby boomer *noun* a person born during a baby boom, esp. after 1945.

baby bust *noun* a temporary marked decrease in the birth rate.

baby carriage *noun* (also **baby buggy**; *plural* **baby buggies**) a four-wheeled carriage for a baby.

baby doll *noun* **1** a doll resembling a baby. **2** (in *plural*) (also **baby doll pyjamas**) women's or girls' pyjamas consisting of a hip-length top of a delicate fabric and matching panties.

baby fat *noun* the fatty tissue which gives babies and young children their characteristic plumpness, peaking at nine months of age and diminishing until about the age of seven.

babyhood *noun* the state or period of being a baby: *from babyhood to boardroom, women are now set to out-achieve men.*

babyish *adjective* **1** childish, simple. **2** immature.

Babylonian • *noun* **1** an inhabitant of the ancient city or kingdom of Babylon in Mesopotamia (present-day Iraq), noted for its luxury, its fortifications, and its Hanging Gardens. **2** the language of the Babylonians. • *adjective* of or relating to Babylon. [Say babba LONEY in]

baby's breath *noun* a plant related to pinks and carnations, with tiny usu. white flowers, often used to ornament bouquets of larger flowers.

baby shower *noun* a party given for a pregnant woman at which her female friends and relatives give her presents for the baby.

babysit *verb* (**babysits, babysat, babysitting**) look after a child or children while the parents are out. ► **babysitter** *noun* **babysitting** *noun*

baby tooth *noun* (*plural* **baby teeth**) a tooth belonging to a person's first set of teeth, shed between the ages of five and thirteen.

baccala *noun* cod, esp. dried and salted. [Say backa LAW or bocka LAW]

baccalaureate *noun* **1** a bachelor's degree. **2** an examination intended to qualify successful candidates for higher education. [Say backa LORRY it]

baccarat *noun* a card game like blackjack, in which players take turns betting against the dealer. [Say BACKA raw]

bacchanal *noun* an occasion of wild, drunken revelry. [Say backa NOL or bocka NOL]

bacchanalia *plural noun* a drunken revelry. ► **bacchanalian** *adjective & noun* [Say backa NAILY uh]

bachelor *noun* **1** an unmarried man. **2 a** (also **bachelor's degree**) a degree awarded to someone who has completed undergraduate studies. **b** a person who has been awarded a bachelor's degree. **3** esp. *Cdn* = BACHELOR APARTMENT 1.

bachelor apartment *noun* **1** *Cdn* an apartment consisting of a single large room serving as bedroom and living room, with a separate bathroom. **2** any apartment occupied by a bachelor.

bachelorette *noun* **1** a young unmarried woman. **2** *Cdn* a very small bachelor apartment.

bachelorhood *noun* the period in a man's life when he is a bachelor.

bacilli *noun* (*plural* **bacilli**) **1** any rod-shaped bacterium. **2** (usu. in *plural*) any pathogenic bacterium. [Say ba SILL us, ba SILLY]

bacillus thuringiensis *noun* **1** a bacterium containing a glycoprotein toxic to insects but not to vertebrates. **2** a bacterial pesticide used against spruce budworm, gypsy moth, etc. [Say ba SILL us thuh rin jee EN sis]

back • *noun* **1 a** the rear surface of the human body from the shoulders to the hips. **b** the corresponding upper surface of an animal's body. **c** the spine. **2 a** any surface regarded as corresponding to the human back, e.g. of the head or a chair. **b** the part of a garment that covers the back. **3 a** the less active or visible or important part of something functional, e.g. of a piece of paper. **b** the side or part normally away from the spectator or the direction of motion or attention, e.g. of a car, house, or room: *stood at the back.* **4 a** (in football etc.) a player positioned behind the front line of play. **b** this position. • *adverb* **1** to the rear; away from what is considered to be the front. **2 a** in or into an earlier or normal position or condition: *went back home.* **b** in return: *pay back.* **3** in or into the past: *back in June ◊ three years back.* **4** at a distance: *stand back.* **5** in check: *hold him back.* **6** behind: *five points back.* • *verb* **1 a** help with moral or financial support. **b** bet on the success of. **2** (usu. foll. by *up*) move, or cause (a vehicle etc.) to move, backwards. **3 a** put or serve as a back, background, or support to. **b** *Music* accompany. **4** lie at the back of: *backed by steep cliffs.* **5** (of the wind) move round in a counter-clockwise direction. • *adjective* **1** situated behind, esp. as remote or subsidiary: *back alley.* **2** not current: *back pay.* **3** reversed, backward: *back somersault.* PHRASES **at a person's back** in pursuit or support. **at the back of one's mind** remembered but not consciously thought of. **back and forth** to and fro. **back down** withdraw one's claim or point of view etc.; concede defeat in an argument etc. **(in) back of** behind. **the back of beyond** a very remote or inaccessible place. **back off 1** draw back, retreat. **2** abandon one's intention, stand, etc. **back on to** have its back adjacent to. **back out** (often foll. by *of*) withdraw from a commitment. **back up 1** give (esp. moral) support to. **2** *Computing* make a spare copy of (data, a disk, etc.). **3** (of water) accumulate behind an obstruction. **4** reverse (a vehicle) into a desired position. **5** form a line of vehicles in congested traffic. **get** (or **put**) **a person's back up** annoy or anger a person. **get off a person's back** stop troubling a person. **go back on** fail to honour (a promise etc.). **in back** *informal* in or at the back. **know like the back of one's hand** be entirely familiar with. **(flat) on one's back** injured or ill in bed. **pat** (or **slap** or **clap**) **on the back** a gesture of approval or congratulation. **pat** (or **slap** or **clap**) **a person on the back** congratulate a person. **put one's back into** approach (a task etc.) with vigour. **turn one's back on 1** abandon. **2** ignore. **with one's back to** (or **up against**) **the wall** in a desperate situation; hard-pressed. ▶ **backer** *noun* (in sense 1 of *verb*). **backless** *adjective*

back bacon *noun* *Cdn & Brit.* round, lean bacon cut from the eye of a pork loin.

back bay *noun* *Cdn* a shallow bay off a lake.

backbench *noun* *Cdn, Brit., Austral., & NZ* (*plural* **backbenches**) **1** (often in *plural*) a backbencher's seat. **2** the backbenchers or their seats collectively.

backbencher *noun Cdn, Brit., Austral., & NZ* a member of a legislative assembly who is not a member of the cabinet, an opposition critic, or a party leader.

backbiting *noun* speaking maliciously of an absent person.

backboard *noun* **1** *Basketball* the vertical board to which the basket is attached. **2** (in *plural*) *Hockey* the boards behind the net at each end of the rink. **3** a board placed at or forming the back of anything. **4** a board worn to support or straighten the back.

backbone *noun* **1** the spine. **2** the main support or most important element in a structure, organization, etc. **3** firmness of character.

back-breaker *noun* **1** an extremely arduous task. **2** esp. *Sport* a decisive event or action, esp. one that ensures an opponent's defeat.

back-breaking *adjective* (esp. of manual work) very hard.

back burner *noun* **1** a position receiving little attention or low priority: *the project has been put on the back burner.* **2** a heating element at the rear of a stove.

backcatcher *noun Cdn* = CATCHER 2.

back channel *noun* **1** *Cdn* a backwater or side channel of a river. **2** a person who acts as a secret go-between in diplomatic negotiations. **3** a secretive, covert action.

backcheck *verb* *Hockey* (of a forward) return to the defensive zone and check attacking opponents. ▶ **backchecker** *noun* **backchecking** *noun*

back concession *noun Cdn* (*Ont. & Que.*) **1** a concession at some distance from a more heavily settled road or area. **2** (in *plural*) rural areas.

backcountry *noun* an area away from settled districts.

backcourt *noun* **1** *Tennis* the area between the baseline and the service line. **2** *Basketball* the half of the court which a team defends.

back crawl *noun* = BACKSTROKE 2.

backdate *verb* (**backdates**, **backdated**, **backdating**) **1** put an earlier date to (an agreement etc.) than the actual one. **2** make retroactively valid.

back door • *noun* **1** a door at the back of a house etc. **2** an alternative, usu. indirect or less conspicuous means of gaining an objective. • *adjective* (**backdoor**) **1 a** alternative: *backdoor route.* **b** underhanded: *backdoor deal.* **2** *Basketball* involving a pass from the top of the key to a player who has just run to the side of the basket.

backdraft *noun* **1** a reverse draft of air or other gas. **2** the violent explosion occurring when air suddenly reaches a fire that has consumed all available oxygen, e.g. when a door or window is opened.

backdrop *noun* **1** a painted cloth hung across the back of a stage as the principal part of the scenery. **2** the setting for an event or situation: *the conference took place against a backdrop of increasing diplomatic activity.*

back eddy *noun Cdn* (esp. *BC*) (*plural* **back eddies**) **1** an area of water behind an obstruction in a watercourse in which the current is the reverse of the general direction of flow. **2** = BACKWATER 2.

backfield *noun Football* **1** the area of play behind the line of scrimmage. **2** the players who line up in the backfield collectively, esp. the running backs and quarterback. ▶ **backfielder** *noun*

backfill • *verb* refill an excavated hole with the material dug out of it. • *noun* excavated material used to refill an excavation.

backfire • *verb* (**backfires**, **backfired**, **backfiring**) **1** undergo a mistimed explosion, as in the cylinder or exhaust of an internal combustion engine. **2** (of a plan etc.) have the opposite effect to what was intended. • *noun* **1** a mistimed explosion in the cylinder or exhaust of a vehicle or engine. **2** a fire set deliberately to stop the advance of a forest fire or prairie fire.

backflip *noun* a backwards aerial somersault.

backgammon *noun* **1** a game for two played on a

B

board with pieces moved according to throws of the dice. **2** the most complete form of win in this.

background • *noun* **1** part of a scene, picture, or description, that serves as a setting to the chief figures or objects and foreground. **2** an inconspicuous or obscure position: *kept in the background*. **3** a person's education, knowledge, or social circumstances. **4** explanatory or contributory information or circumstances.

backhand • *noun* **1** any arm motion performed with the arm initially across and in front of the torso, esp.: **a** *Tennis etc.* a stroke made with the back of the hand turned towards the opponent. **b** a blow made with the back of the hand. **2** *Hockey* a shot or pass made by striking the puck with the back of the stick's blade. • *verb* strike with a backhand.

backhanded *adjective* **1** (of an arm motion) performed with the arm initially across the torso, or with the back of the hand: *backhanded catch*. **2** indirect; ambiguous: *a backhanded compliment*.

backhander *noun* a backhand shot, blow, stroke, etc.

backhoe *noun* a digging machine which draws toward itself a bucket attached to a hinged boom.

backing *noun* **1** support. **2** material forming a back or support. **3** musical accompaniment, esp. to a singer.

backlands *plural noun* sparsely settled areas.

backlash *noun* (*plural* **backlashes**) **1** an excessive or marked adverse reaction: *a public backlash against funding cuts*. **2** a sudden recoil or reaction between parts of a mechanism.

backlight • *noun* (also **backlighting**) light illuminating something (esp. a photographic subject or a computer screen) from behind. • *verb* (**backlights**; *past* and *past participle* **backlit** or **backlighted**; **backlighting**) illuminate (esp. a photographic subject, a computer screen, etc.) from behind. ▶ **backlit** *adjective*

backlog • *noun* an accumulation of incomplete work etc. • *verb* (**backlogs, backlogged, backlogging**) **1** overload (a system, process, etc.). **2** amass unfinished tasks or unprocessed material.

back nine *noun* *Golf* the final nine holes on an 18-hole course.

back order *noun* a retailer's order yet to be filled by a supplier. PHRASES **on back order** ordered by a retailer but not yet received from the supplier.

backpack • *noun* a knapsack. • *verb* travel or hike with a backpack. ▶ **backpacker** *noun* **backpacking** *noun*

backpedal *verb* (**backpedals, backpedalled, backpedalling**) **1** pedal backwards on a bicycle etc. **2** reverse one's previous action or opinion. **3** walk or sprint backwards.

backroom *noun* **1** a room at the back of a store, office, etc., usu. off limits to the public. **2** a place where secret plans are made: *a backroom deal*.

back-scratcher *noun* a rod terminating in a clawed hand for scratching one's own back.

back-scratching *noun* the reciprocal provision of help or support, typically underhandedly or illicitly.

back seat *noun* a seat at the back of a vehicle, airplane, etc. PHRASES **take a back seat** occupy a subordinate place.

back-seat driver *noun* **1** a person who rides in the back seat of a car and gives unwanted advice to its driver. **2** a person who criticizes or attempts to control without responsibility.

backside *noun* *informal* the buttocks.

backslapping *adjective* **1** characterized by (excessive) displays of camaraderie. **2** vigorously hearty: *cheerful, backslapping journalists*.

backslash *noun* (*plural* **backslashes**) a diagonal line that slopes backwards (\).

backslide *verb* (**backslides, backslid, backsliding**) relapse into bad ways or error, esp. in ideology. ▶ **backslider** *noun* **backsliding** *noun*

backspace • *verb* (**backspaces, backspaced, backspacing**) move a typewriter carriage, cursor, etc. back one or more spaces. • *noun* the key on a keyboard which performs this function.

backspin *noun* a backward spin imparted to a ball causing it to slow down or roll or bounce back on hitting a surface.

backsplash *noun* (*plural* **backsplashes**) a covering, usu. ceramic, behind a sink, counter, etc., to protect the wall.

backsplit *noun* *Cdn* a house with floors raised half a storey at the rear, having an upper and lower main floor, and an upper and lower basement.

backstabber *noun* a person who betrays a friend or associate. ▶ **backstabbing** *noun & adjective*

backstage • *adverb* *Theatre* out of view of the audience, esp. in the wings or dressing rooms: *went backstage after the performance*. • *adjective* **1** happening or being backstage at a theatre: *a backstage tour*. **2** happening out of the public spotlight: *backstage power struggles in the opera company* ◊ *a backstage deal between politicians*.

backstairs *plural noun* **1** stairs at the back or side of a building. **2** (as an *adjective*) denoting underhand or clandestine activity.

backstop • *noun* **1** a backcatcher. **2** a goaltender. **3** *Sport* a wall, fence, etc. used to keep the ball in the playing area, esp. behind home plate in baseball. • *verb* (**backstops, backstopped, backstopping**) **1** *Sport* serve (a team) as goaltender, catcher, etc. **2** underwrite (a project, loan, company, etc.).

backstreet *noun* **1** a street in a quiet part of a city, away from the main streets. **2** (as an *adjective*) denoting illicit or illegal activity: *a backstreet abortion*.

backstroke *noun* *Swimming* **1** a stroke performed on the back. **2** such a stroke in which the arms are lifted alternately out of the water in a backward circular motion and the legs extended in a kicking action.

backswing *noun* *Sport* the upward or backward motion bringing a bat etc. into position for the swing.

back-to-back • *adjective* (of two events) consecutive: *back-to-back victories*. • *adverb* (**back to back**) **1** with backs adjacent and opposite each other: *we stood back to back*. **2** consecutively: *challenge two opponents back to back*.

back to front • *adverb* with the back at the front. • *adjective* backwards.

back-to-nature *adjective* applied to a movement or enthusiast for a simpler, more natural way of life.

backtrack *verb* **1** retrace one's steps: *Marilyn backtracked and went down into the basement*. **2** reverse one's previous action or opinion: *the government has backtracked on the amendments*. **3** revert to an earlier point in an account: *let me backtrack a moment to when I first started working here*.

backup *noun* **1** moral or technical support: *called for extra backup*. **2 a** something kept in reserve, esp. for emergency replacement. **b** *Sport* an alternate player: *a backup goalie*. **3** *Computing* **a** the procedure for making security copies of data: *backup facilities*. **b** the copy itself: *made a backup*. **4** a line of vehicles in congested traffic. **5** (as an *adjective*) designating a light, beeper, etc. activated when a vehicle is in reverse gear. **6** musical accompaniment: *backup singers*.

backward • *adverb* = BACKWARDS. • *adjective* **1** directed to the rear or starting point: *a backward look*. **2** reversed.

3 mentally retarded or slow. **4** shy, unassertive. **5** unsophisticated, underdeveloped.
▶ **backwardness** noun
backwards adverb **1** away from one's front. **2 a** with the back foremost. **b** in reverse of the usual way. **3 a** into a worse state. **b** into the past. **c** (of a thing's motion) back towards the starting point. PHRASES **backwards and forwards** in both directions alternately; to and fro. **bend** (or **lean**) **over backwards** informal make every effort, esp. to be fair or helpful: *bent over backwards to make me feel comfortable*. **know backwards** be entirely familiar with.
backwash • noun (plural **backwashes**) **1 a** receding waves created by the motion of a ship etc. **b** a backward current of air created by a moving aircraft. **2** water pumped backwards through a swimming pool filter to clean it. **3** slang liquid which flows from the mouth back into the bottle etc. while one is drinking. **4** the motion of a receding wave. • verb (**backwashes**, **backwashed**, **backwashing**) clean (a swimming pool filter) with backwash.
backwater noun **1** stagnant water fed from a stream. **2** a place or condition far from the centre of thought or activity: *the country remained an economic backwater*.
backwoods plural noun **1** remote uncleared land. **2** any remote or sparsely inhabited region.
backyard noun **1** a piece of ground, usu. landscaped, behind a house and belonging to it. **2** a place near at hand: *don't want a garbage dump in my backyard*.
bacon noun cured meat from the back or sides of a pig. PHRASES **bring home the bacon** informal **1** succeed in one's undertaking. **2** supply provision or support: *I have to go to work because it brings home the bacon*.
bacteria plural noun (singular **bacterium**) any of various groups of single-celled micro-organisms lacking organelles and an organized nucleus, some of which can cause disease. ▶ **bacterial** adjective
bacteriology noun the study of bacteria.
Bactrian camel noun a camel with two humps, native to central Asia. [Say BACK tree un]

WRITING TIP
bad, very bad

Instead of saying that something is **bad** or **very bad**, try to use more precise and interesting adjectives to describe things:

her handwriting is **poor/atrocious/appalling/ illegible**

a **foul/disgusting/putrid/fetid** odour

the villain is **evil/wicked/dishonest/corrupt**

a **serious/severe/dreadful** injury

awful/terrible/inclement/nasty weather

an **unfortunate**/an **upsetting**/a **traumatic** experience

a **naughty/disobedient/mischievous/unruly** child

an **awkward/embarrassing/unmanageable** situation

the meal was **poor/unsatisfactory/ unacceptable/unpalatable**

his eyesight is **poor/weak**

the bus service on Don Mills is **execrable/ ludicrously inadequate**

To refer to your health, you can say: I feel **unwell/ sick/terrible**, or: I don't feel (**very**) well. Instead of saying: She feels bad about what she did, you can say: She feels **guilty/regretful/remorseful/ apologetic**.

---

bad • adjective (**worse**; **worst**) **1** inferior, inadequate, defective. **2** unpleasant, unwelcome. **3** harmful. **4** (of food) decayed, putrid. **5** informal ill, injured: *a bad leg*. **6** informal regretful, guilty, ashamed: *feels bad about it*. **7** serious, severe: *a bad headache*. **8 a** morally wicked or offensive: *bad language*. **b** naughty; badly behaved. **9** worthless; not valid: *a bad cheque*. **10** (of a loan, debt, etc.) unlikely to be paid. **11** (**badder**, **baddest**) slang admirable, excellent. • noun **1 a** ill fortune: *take the bad with the good*. **b** ruin: *go to the bad*. **2** the debit side of an account: *$500 to the bad*. PHRASES **from bad to worse** into an even worse state. **in a bad way** ill; in trouble. **not** (or **not so**) **bad** informal fairly good. **too bad** informal (of circumstances etc.) regrettable but now beyond helping.
bad apple noun **1** a rotten apple. **2** a person whose actions disgrace an otherwise admirable group.
bad blood noun ill feeling, animosity.
bad boy noun a man who cultivates an uncooperative or rebellious attitude.
baddy noun (also **baddie**) (plural **baddies**) informal a villain or criminal, esp. in a story, film, etc.
bade see BID. [Say BADE or BAD]
bad faith noun intent to deceive.
bad form noun an offence against social conventions: *it was considered bad form to talk about money*.
badge noun **1** a distinctive emblem worn as a mark of office etc. **2** any feature or sign which reveals a characteristic condition or quality.
badger • noun a heavily built omnivorous nocturnal mammal of the weasel family, usu. having a grey coat with a white stripe flanked by black stripes on its head. • verb pester, harass, tease.
badlands plural noun extensive, barren, strikingly eroded tracts in arid areas, as along the Red Deer River in southern Alberta.
badly adverb (**worse**; **worst**) **1** in a bad manner: *works badly*. **2** informal very much: *wants it badly*. **3** severely: *was badly defeated*.
badminton noun a game in which players use racquets to hit a shuttlecock back and forth across a high net.
bad-mouth verb subject to malicious gossip or criticism.
badness noun the condition of being morally bad.
bad news noun **1** unwelcome information. **2** informal an unpleasant or troublesome person etc.
baffle • verb (**baffles**, **baffled**, **baffling**) confuse or perplex (a person, one's faculties, etc.). • noun **1** (also **baffle plate**) a device used to restrict the flow of fluid, air, etc., through an opening, often found in microphones etc. to regulate the emission of sound. **2** a device used to impede or block access etc.
bafflegab noun official or professional jargon which confuses more than it clarifies.
bafflement noun puzzlement, bewilderment: *his reaction was one of bafflement*.
baffling adjective puzzling, perplexing; difficult to understand or figure out: *a baffling decision ◊ a baffling mystery*. ▶ **bafflingly** adverb
bag • noun **1** a receptacle of flexible material with an opening at the top. **2 a** (usu. in plural) a piece of luggage. **b** a woman's handbag. **3** slang derogatory a woman, esp. regarded as unattractive or unpleasant. **4** an animal's sac containing poison, honey, etc. **5** an amount of game or fish taken by a sportsman. **6** (usu. in plural) baggy folds of skin under the eyes. **7** slang a person's particular interest or preoccupation: *jazz is not my bag*. **8** Baseball first, second, or third base. • verb (**bags**, **bagged**, **bagging**) **1** put in a bag. **2** informal **a** attain, secure: *bagged three awards*. **b** apprehend (a criminal etc.). **c** shoot (game). **d** informal steal. **3** hang loosely;

B

bulge; swell. **PHRASES** **bag and baggage** with all one's belongings. **bag of tricks** *informal* one's (usu. ingenious) resources or techniques: *flattery is in his bag of tricks*. **in the bag** *informal* as good as secured; achieved. **left holding the bag** *informal* abandoned, left to face consequences alone.

bagel *noun* a chewy, ring-shaped bread roll that is simmered before baking.

baggage *noun* **1** suitcases, bags, etc. packed for travelling; luggage. **2** past experiences or long-held ideas and opinions perceived as burdensome: *brought a lot of emotional baggage to the relationship*.

baggataway *noun* a forerunner of lacrosse played by the Aboriginal peoples of eastern North America. [Say buh GATTA way]

Baggie *noun* *proprietary* a small bag made of clear plastic, used for storing sandwiches etc.

bagginess *noun* a baggy quality.

baggy *adjective* (**baggier**, **baggiest**) **1** (of clothes) loosely fitting. **2** puffed out.

bag lady *noun* (*plural* **bag ladies**) a homeless woman who carries her possessions around in shopping bags.

bagman *noun* (*plural* **bagmen**) *Cdn* a political fundraiser.

bagpipe *noun* (usu. in *plural*) a musical instrument consisting of a windbag connected to drone pipes, which produce single sustained notes, and a fingered melody pipe or "chanter". ▶ **bagpiper** *noun*

baguette *noun* a long narrow loaf of French bread. [Say ba GET]

bah *interjection* an expression of contempt or disbelief.

Baha'i *noun* (*plural* **Baha'is**) a member of a monotheistic religion founded in Persia in 1863, emphasizing the unity of all religions and world peace. ▶ **Baha'ism** *noun* [Say buh HI]

Bahamian • *noun* a native or national of the Bahamas in the W Indies. • *adjective* of or relating to the Bahamas. [Say buh HAY mee un]

SPELL CHECK ABC ✓
bail, bale

A bundle of hay is a **bale**.

---

bail[1] • *noun* **1** (also **pretrial release** or **judicial interim release**) the temporary release of an accused person awaiting trial, sometimes on condition that a sum of money is lodged to guarantee their appearance in court: *was released on bail* ◊ *the judge granted bail*. **2** money paid by or for such a person as security. • *verb* **1** release or secure the release of (a prisoner) on payment of bail: *his son called home to get bailed out of jail*. **2** *informal* release from a difficulty; come to the rescue of (esp. financially): *the ministry will always bail out hospitals in financial difficulty*. **PHRASES** **jump** (or **skip** or *formal* **forfeit**) **bail** fail to appear for trial after being released on bail. **stand** (or **post**) **bail** (often foll. by *for*) act as surety (for an accused person).

bail[2] *verb* scoop water out of a boat etc.: *he had to stop rowing to bail water out of the boat* ◊ *the boat will sink unless we bail out*.

bail[3] *verb* **PHRASES** **bail out 1** make an emergency parachute jump from an aircraft. **2** become free of an obligation or commitment; discontinue an activity: *she felt ready to bail out of the corporate rat race*.

bailer *noun* a device used to bail water out of a boat.

bailey *noun* (*plural* **baileys**) **1** the outer wall of a castle. **2** a court enclosed by it.

bailiff *noun* **1** (also **court bailiff**) an officer of the court who serves processes and enforces orders, esp. warrants authorizing the seizure of a debtor's goods. **2** (also **private bailiff**) *Cdn* a person who repossesses

property for private clients. **3** an official in a court of law who keeps order, looks after prisoners, etc.

bailiwick *noun* **1** *Law* the district or jurisdiction of a sheriff or bailiff. **2** a person's sphere of operations or particular area of interest: *she is now directing a major theatre company in her own bailiwick, New Brunswick*.

bailout *noun* a financial rescue.

Bairam *noun* either of two annual Muslim festivals, the **Lesser Bairam**, lasting one day, which follows the fast of Ramadan, and the **Greater Bairam**, lasting three days, seventy days later. [Say by RAM]

bait • *noun* **1** food used to entice prey. **2** a person or thing that is used to catch someone or to attract them: *he had chosen the right bait to persuade her to go* ◊ *the police used him as bait to trap the killers*. • *verb* **1 a** harass or annoy (a person, community, etc.): *red-baiting*. **b** torment (a chained animal): *bear-baiting has been banned*. **2** put bait on (a hook, trap, etc.) to entice a prey.

bait and switch *noun* the practice of luring customers with a limited supply of bargains in order to sell them more expensive items.

SPELL CHECK ABC ✓
baited, bated

To wait anxiously is to wait with **bated** breath.

---

baitfish *noun* (*plural* **baitfish** or **baitfishes**) any small fish eaten by larger fish, often used to lure game fish.

bake • *verb* (**bakes**, **baked**, **baking**) **1 a** cook (food) by dry heat in an oven or on a hot surface, without direct exposure to a flame. **b** undergo the process of being baked. **2** *informal* **a** (usu. as **be baking**) (of weather etc.) be very hot. **b** (of a person) become hot. **3 a** harden (clay etc.) by heat. **b** (of clay etc.) be hardened by heat. • *noun* **1** (esp. in *combination*) baked goods: *bake table*. **2** (in *combination*) a social gathering, esp. a picnic, at which baked food is eaten: *clambake*. **3** a baked dish, esp. a casserole: *sausage and rigatoni bake*.

bakeapple *noun* (also **baked-apple berry**) (esp. Nfld & Maritimes) = CLOUDBERRY.

baked beans *plural noun* dried white beans baked in a tomato sauce.

baker *noun* **1** a person who bakes and sells bread, cakes, etc., esp. professionally. **2** an appliance or dish in which something is baked.

baker's dozen *noun* thirteen.

bakery *noun* (*plural* **bakeries**) a place where bread and cakes are made or sold.

bakeshop *noun* = BAKERY.

bakeware *noun* pans, pie plates, etc., used in baking.

baking powder *noun* a mixture of baking soda and an acid, used to make baked goods rise.

baking soda *noun* sodium bicarbonate used to make baked goods rise, as an antacid, or as a household cleaner and deodorizer.

baklava *noun* a rich sweet dessert of flaky pastry, honey, and nuts. [Say BACKLA vuh or backla VAW]

balaclava *noun* a tight knitted garment covering the whole head and neck with holes for the eyes and mouth. [Say bala CLAVA]

balalaika *noun* a guitar-like musical instrument having a triangular body and 2 to 4 strings, popular in Russia and other Slavic countries. [Say bala LIKE uh]

balance • *noun* **1** an apparatus for weighing, esp. one with a central pivot, beam, and two scales. **2** a counteracting weight or force. **b** (also **balance wheel**) the regulating device in a clock etc. **3 a** an even distribution of weight or amount. **b** stability of body or mind: *regained his balance*. **4** a predominating weight or amount: *the balance of opinion*. **5 a** agreement between or the difference between credits

and debits in an account. **b** the amount of money held in a bank account at a given moment. **c** the difference between an amount due and an amount paid. **d** an amount left over. **6** *Art* harmony of design and proportion. **7 a** the relative volume of various musical parts: *bad balance between violins and trumpets*. **b** the relative volume of two or more stereo speakers. **c** a dial on a stereo for adjusting this. • *verb* (**balances, balanced, balancing**) **1** (foll. by *with*, *against*) offset or compare (one thing) with another. **2** counteract, equal, or neutralize the weight or importance of. **3** bring into, be, or keep in equilibrium. **4** (usu. as **balanced** *adjective*) establish equal or appropriate proportions of elements in: *a balanced diet*. **5** weigh (arguments etc.) against each other. **6 a** compare and esp. equalize debits and credits of (an account): *balance the budget*. **b** (of an account) have credits and debits equal. PHRASES **in the balance** uncertain; at a critical stage. **off balance 1** in danger of falling. **2** unprepared, confused. **on balance** all things considered. **strike a balance** choose a moderate course or compromise.

balance beam *noun* a long narrow wooden beam on which gymnasts perform feats of balance and agility.

balance of payments *noun* the difference in value between payments into and out of a country over a particular period of time.

balance of power *noun* **1** a situation in which political or military strength is divided between two countries or groups of countries: *a commitment to maintaining the balance of power in Europe*. **2** the power held by a small group which can give its support to either of two larger and equally strong groups: *the NDP held the balance of power in the House of Commons*.

balance of trade *noun* the difference in value between imports and exports.

balancer *noun* something that helps to maintain a balance.

balance sheet *noun* **1** a written statement of the assets and liabilities of an organization on a given date. **2** an organization's financial state: *she said her company was working to strengthen its balance sheet*. **3** an accounting of achievements and failures in any field: *a time for looking at the balance sheet of human rights*.

balancing act *noun* the skilful handling of several different tasks simultaneously.

balconied *adjective* (of a building) having a balcony.

balcony *noun* (*plural* **balconies**) **1** a platform enclosed by a wall, railing, etc. on the outside of a building, with access from an upper-floor door. **2** a projecting tier of seats above the main floor in a theatre.

bald *adjective* **1** (of a person) with the scalp wholly or partly lacking hair. **2** (of an animal, plant, etc.) not covered by the usual hair, feathers, leaves, etc. **3** (of a landscape) treeless. **4** with the surface worn away: *a bald tire*. **5** blunt: *a bald statement*. **6** meagre or dull: *a bald style*. **7** marked with white, esp. on the face: *a bald horse*.

bald eagle *noun* a North American eagle with large brown wings and body, a white head, and a yellow bill, the emblem of the US.

balderdash *noun* senseless talk or writing; nonsense.

bald-faced *adjective* shameless: *a bald-faced lie*.

baldheaded *adjective* with little or no hair on the head.

baldie *noun informal* a bald person.

balding *adjective* starting to lose one's hair.

baldly *adverb* in few words with nothing extra or unnecessary; bluntly.

baldness *noun* the condition of being bald.

baldpate *noun* **1** a baldheaded person. **2** a North American duck, the male of which has a white crown.

bale • *noun* **1** a bundle of material tightly wrapped or bound: *a bale of hay*. **2** the quantity in a bale as a unit of measure. • *verb* (**bales, baled, baling**) form into bales.

baleen *noun* whalebone. [Say buh LEEN]

baleen whale *noun* any of various whales of the suborder Mysticeti, having plates of baleen fringed with bristles for straining plankton from the water.

baleful *adjective* **1** (esp. of a manner, look, etc.) gloomy, menacing: *shot a baleful look in his direction*. **2** harmful, destructive: *drug money has had a baleful impact on the country*. ▶ **balefully** *adverb* **balefulness** *noun*

baler *noun* a machine for making bales of hay, straw, etc.

baler twine *noun* = BINDER TWINE.

balk (also esp. *Brit.* **baulk**) • *verb* **1 a** refuse to go on: *terrified of heights, he balked after the first few steps*. **b** hesitate or be unwilling to accept: *balked at paying more for a service they don't even use*. **2** deprive or disappoint: *balked of what they considered to be their rightful inheritance*. **3** *Baseball* commit a balk. • *noun* *Baseball* an illegal motion made by a pitcher which allows the baserunners to advance one base. [Say BOCK]

Balkan *adjective* of or relating to the people or nations of the Balkan Peninsula in SE Europe. [Say BAWL k'n]

balkanization *noun* division of a country etc. into smaller, mutually hostile units. [Say bawl kuh nize AY sh'n]

balkanize *verb* (**balkanizes, balkanized, balkanizing**) divide (a country etc.) into smaller mutually hostile units: *the interprovincial trade situation in Canada is highly balkanized*. [Say bawlka NIZE]

balky *adjective* (also esp. *Brit.* **baulky**) (**balkier, balkiest**) uncooperative: *a balky gearshift*. [Say BOCKY]

ball[1] • *noun* **1** a solid or hollow sphere, esp. for use in a game. **2 a** any roughly spherical object resembling a ball. **b** a rounded part of the body: *ball of the foot*. **3 a** game played with a ball, esp. baseball. **4 a** pitch that is out of the designated strike zone and is not swung at. **b** a ball which has been struck by the batter: *fair ball*. **5** (in *plural*) *coarse slang* **a** the testicles. **b** courage. • *verb* **1** squeeze or wind into a ball. **2** (often foll. by *up*) form or gather into a ball or balls. PHRASES **the ball is in your court** you must be next to act. **on the ball** *informal* alert. **play ball** *informal* co-operate. **start** (or **keep**) **the ball rolling** begin (or maintain the momentum of) an activity.

ball[2] *noun* **1** a formal social gathering for dancing. **2** *informal* an enjoyable time: *have a ball*.

ballad *noun* **1** a poem or song narrating a popular story. **2** a slow sentimental or romantic song.

balladeer *noun* a singer or composer of ballads.

ball and chain *noun* **1** a heavy metal ball secured by a chain to the leg of a prisoner etc. to prevent escape. **2** *informal* **a** a severe hindrance. **b** *derogatory* a wife.

ball-and-socket joint *noun* a joint, e.g. the hip, in which a rounded end lies in a concave cup or socket, allowing considerable freedom of movement.

ballast • *noun* **1** any heavy material carried by a ship etc. to secure stability. **2** coarse stone etc. used to form

B

the bed of a railway track etc. **3** any device used to stabilize the current in a circuit. **4** anything that gives stability or substance: *the film is a light comedy with some serious ideas thrown in for ballast*. • *verb* make a ship stable by putting a heavy substance in its bilge. [Say BAL ist]

ball bearing *noun* **1** a bearing in which the two halves are separated by a ring of small metal balls which reduce friction. **2** one of these balls.

ballboy *noun* (in tennis, baseball, etc.) a boy who retrieves balls that go out of play during a game.

ball club *noun* a baseball team.

ballerina *noun* a female ballet dancer.

ballet *noun* **1 a** a theatrical style of dancing using set steps and techniques and characterized esp. by movement with the legs turned out in the hip sockets and by the women dancing on the tips of their toes. **b** a theatrical work using ballet abstractly or to tell a story. **c** a piece of music composed for a ballet. **d** a performance of ballet. **2** a company performing ballet. ▶ **balletic** *adjective* [Say BAL ay or bal AY, buh LET ick]

ball field *noun* a field on which baseball is played.

ball game *noun* **1** any game played with a ball, esp. a game of baseball. **2** *informal* a particular affair or concern: *a whole new ball game*.

ballgirl *noun* (in tennis, baseball, etc.) a girl who retrieves balls that go out of play during a game.

ball hockey *noun Cdn* **1** a version of hockey played in a gymnasium or in an arena without ice, using a hard plastic ball in place of a puck. **2** a version of hockey, usu. without formal rules, played on a paved surface, using a tennis ball instead of a puck.

ballistic *adjective* **1** of or relating to projectiles. **2** moving under the force of gravity only. PHRASES **go ballistic** *slang* become incensed or act in a hysterical manner. [Say buh LISS tick]

ballistic missile *noun* a missile which is initially powered and guided but falls under gravity on its target.

ballistic nylon *noun* a durable, tightly woven nylon used in bulletproof vests, luggage, etc.

ballistics *plural noun* (usu. treated as *singular*) the science of projectiles and firearms. [Say buh LISS ticks]

balloon • *noun* **1** a small inflatable rubber pouch with a neck, used as a toy or as decoration. **2** a large usu. round bag inflated with hot air or gas to make it rise in the air, often carrying a basket for passengers. **3** an outline enclosing the words or thoughts of characters in a comic strip or cartoon. **4** a tiny inflatable pouch attached to a catheter and used to dilate an artery etc. during angioplasty or other procedures. **5** a large globular drinking glass for brandy or wine. • *verb* **1 a** swell or cause to swell like a balloon. **b** grow or increase dramatically: *the deficit has ballooned*. **2** travel by balloon. ▶ **balloonist** *noun* **ballooning** *noun & adjective*

ballot • *noun* **1** a system of secret voting, usu. by marking a paper with one's choice of candidate etc. **2 a** a single round of voting: *won on the second ballot*. **b** the total number of votes recorded in a ballot. **3** a paper or ticket etc. used in voting. **4** the drawing of lots. • *verb* (**ballots**, **balloted**, **balloting**) **1** (usu. as **balloting** *noun*) **a** vote by ballot. **b** draw lots for precedence etc. **2** solicit votes from: *the union balloted its members*.

ballot box *noun* (*plural* **ballot boxes**) **1** a sealed box into which voters put completed ballots. **2** an election: *lost at the ballot box*.

ballpark *noun* **1** a field or stadium designed for baseball. **2** (as an *adjective*) *informal* (of a price or cost) approximate, rough: *the ballpark figure is $400 to $500*.

PHRASES **in the ballpark** *informal* approximately correct.

ballplayer *noun* a player in a ball game, esp. baseball.

ballpoint *noun* (also **ballpoint pen**) a pen in which the writing point is a tiny rotating ball which rolls ink from an internal cartridge onto the paper.

ballroom *noun* a large room or hall for dancing.

ballroom dancing *noun* formal or recreational social dancing for couples, including the foxtrot, waltz, etc.

ballsy *adjective* (**ballsier**, **ballsiest**) *slang* courageous.

ballyhoo • *noun* extravagant publicity; hype: *all the ballyhoo about the new musical*. • *verb* (**ballyhoos**, **ballyhooed**, **ballyhooing**) publicize or praise extravagantly; hype: *have been ballyhooing echinacea as today's natural miracle*. ▶ **ballyhooed** *adjective*

balm *noun* **1** an aromatic ointment for anointing, soothing, or healing: *lip balm*. **2** a fragrant and medicinal substance which exudes from certain trees and plants. **3** a healing or soothing influence or consolation: *the murmur of the water can provide balm for troubled spirits*. **4** = BALM OF GILEAD 1a. **5** any of various bushy herbs of the mint family, with leaves smelling and tasting of lemon. **6** a pleasant fragrance. [Say BOM]

balm of Gilead *noun* **1 a** any of various evergreen trees native to W Asia and N Africa. **b** a fragrant resin exuded by such a tree. **2** a frequently planted hybrid poplar. **3** a balsam fir. [Say GILLY ad]

balmy *adjective* (**balmier**, **balmiest**) (of weather) warm. [Say BOMMY]

baloney *noun* **1** = BOLOGNA. **2** *informal* nonsense.

balsa *noun* **1** (also **balsa wood**) a tough lightweight wood. **2** the tropical American tree from which this wood is obtained. [Say BAWL suh]

balsam *noun* **1** any of several aromatic resins, such as balm, obtained from various trees and shrubs and used as a base for certain fragrances and medical preparations. **2** an ointment, esp. one composed of a substance dissolved in oil or turpentine. **3** any of various trees or shrubs which yield balsam. **4** any of several flowering plants of the genus *Impatiens*. **5** a healing or soothing agent. [Say BAWL sum]

balsam fir *noun* **1** the North American fir that yields Canada balsam. **2** any of several other firs of northwestern North America, esp. the alpine fir.

balsamic vinegar *noun* an aged sweet red wine vinegar made from white grapes. [Say bawl SAM ick]

Balt *noun* a native or inhabitant of Estonia, Latvia, or Lithuania, countries bordering the Baltic Sea.

Baltic • *adjective* of or relating to the Baltic or the Baltic language group. • *noun* **1 a** (**the Baltic**) an almost landlocked sea of northern Europe. **b** (**the Baltics**) the states bordering this sea. **2** an Indo-European branch of languages including Lithuanian and Latvian.

Baltimore oriole *noun* a bright orange and black North American oriole.

baluster *noun* each of a series of often ornamental short posts supporting a railing etc. [Say BALA stir]

balustrade *noun* a railing supported by balusters, esp. forming an ornamental parapet to a balcony, bridge, or terrace. [Say BALA strade]

bam *interjection* **1** expressing the sound of a hard blow. **2** indicating suddenness.

bamboo *noun* **1** a giant woody grass that grows mainly in the tropics, where it is widely cultivated. **2** its hollow jointed stem, used as building material and to make furniture and tools etc.

bamboo curtain *noun* a political and economic barrier between China and non-Communist countries.

bamboo shoot *noun* a young shoot of bamboo, eaten as a vegetable.

bamboozle *verb* (**bamboozles, bamboozled, bamboozling**) *informal* cheat, swindle: *he bamboozled Canada's largest banks in a massive counterfeit scam*.

ban • *verb* (**bans, banned, banning**) forbid, prohibit, esp. officially or legally: *banned from driving*. • *noun* an official or legal prohibition: *a ban on beer advertising*.

banal *adjective* so lacking in originality as to be obvious and boring: *songs with banal lyrics*. ▶ **banality** *noun* (*plural* **banalities**) **banally** *adverb* [Say buh NAL]

banana *noun* **1** a long curved fruit with soft pulpy flesh and yellow skin when ripe, growing in clusters. **2** (also **banana tree**) any of several tropical and subtropical treelike plants of the genus *Musa* bearing this fruit. *See also* TOP BANANA, SECOND BANANA.

banana belt *noun informal* a region having a relatively warm climate, esp. (for Canadians) the Niagara Peninsula or southern BC.

banana pepper *noun* a small yellow hot pepper.

banana republic *noun* often *derogatory* a small tropical nation, esp. in Central or South America, economically dependent on fruit exports or similar trade.

bananas *adjective informal* **1** crazy or angry. **2** extremely enthusiastic.

banana split *noun* a dessert consisting of a split banana, ice cream, sauce, whipped cream, etc.

band¹ • *noun* **1 a** a flat, thin strip or loop of material, e.g. paper, metal, or cloth, put around something esp. to hold it together or decorate it: *headband*. **b** a strip of material forming part of a garment: *waistband*. **2** a stripe of a different colour or material on an object. **3** any long and narrow strip or grouping: *band of thunderstorms*. **4 a** a range of frequencies or wavelengths in a spectrum (esp. of radio frequencies). **b** a range of values within a series. **5** a ring without a prominent precious stone. **6** a loop of metal or plastic attached to the leg of a bird etc. for identification. **7** a belt connecting wheels or pulleys. • *verb* put a band on, esp. attach an identification band to a bird etc.

band² • *noun* **1** an organized group of people having a common objective: *a band of protesters*. **2** (in Canada) an Indian community officially recognized as an administrative unit by the federal government. **3** *Anthropology* a basic organizational unit in nomadic societies, consisting of several families. **4 a** a group of musicians playing wind and percussion instruments: *brass band*. **b** a group of musicians playing jazz, rock, or pop music. **c** *informal* an orchestra. **5** a herd or flock. • *verb* form into a group for a purpose: *band together*.

bandage • *noun* a strip of material for binding up a wound or protecting an injured part of the body. • *verb* (**bandages, bandaged, bandaging**) bind (a wound etc.) with a bandage.

Band-Aid *noun* **1** *proprietary* an adhesive bandage with a gauze pad for dressing small cuts etc. **2** (also **band-aid**) (often as an *adjective*) a makeshift or temporary solution: *a band-aid solution to a much bigger problem*.

bandana *noun* (also **bandanna**) a coloured handkerchief or head scarf, usu. of cotton, and often having a figured design.

B & B *abbreviation* **1** (*plural* **B & B's**) bed and breakfast. **2** *Cdn* bilingualism and biculturalism.

band council *noun Cdn* a local form of Aboriginal government, consisting of a chief and councillors who are elected for two- or three-year terms to carry on band business. ▶ **band councillor** *noun*

B and E *abbreviation* (*plural* **B and E's**) *slang* BREAKING AND ENTERING.

banded *adjective* **1** marked with bands or stripes: *a banded water snake*. **2** fastened or bound with a band or bands. **3** (of a bird) having a metal ring placed around its leg for identification.

banding *noun* in senses of BAND¹ *verb*, BAND² *verb*.

bandit *noun* **1** a robber, esp. a member of a gang. **2** an outlaw. ▶ **banditry** *noun*

bandleader *noun* the leader of a band of musicians.

bandmaster *noun* the conductor of a band.

bandolier *noun* a belt or strap worn diagonally across the chest with loops or pockets for ammunition. [Say banda LEER]

band saw *noun* an electric saw with a seamless toothed band which rotates clockwise around two wheels.

bandshell *noun* a bandstand in the form of a large concave shell with special acoustic properties.

bandstand *noun* **1** a covered outdoor platform for a band to play on, usu. in a park. **2** any stage or platform for a band.

B & W *abbreviation* (of film etc.) black and white.

bandwagon *noun* (esp. in **jump** (or **climb**) **on the bandwagon**) a party, cause, or group that is fashionable or seems likely to succeed.

bandwidth *noun* the range of frequencies within a given band (*see* BAND¹ *noun* 4a).

bandy • *adjective* (**bandier, bandiest**) **1** (of the legs) curved so as to be wide apart at the knees. **2** (also **bandy-legged**) (of a person) bowlegged. • *verb* (**bandies, bandied, bandying**) **1** (often foll. by *about*) a pass (a story, rumour, etc.) to and fro. **b** throw or pass (a ball etc.) to and fro. **2** (often foll. by *about*) discuss disparagingly: *bandied her name about*. **3** (often foll. by *with*) exchange (blows, insults, etc.): *don't bandy words with me*. • *noun* **1** an early form of hockey played on a field or on ice with a ball and large curved sticks. **2** (*plural* **bandies**) the curved stick used in this sport.

bane *noun* a cause of great distress or annoyance: *the telephone was the bane of my existence*. ▶ **baneful** *adjective*

bang • *noun* **1 a** a loud sudden sound. **b** an explosion. **c** the firing of a gun. **2 a** a sharp blow. **b** the sound of this. **3** *informal* a thrill. **4** (in *plural*) a fringe of hair cut across the forehead. • *verb* **1** strike or shut noisily. **2** make or cause to make the sound of a blow or an explosion. • *adverb* **1** with a bang or sudden impact. **2** *informal* exactly: *bang in the middle*. • *interjection* indicating suddenness or swiftness. PHRASES **bang on** *Cdn & Brit. informal* exactly right. **bang out** *informal* produce (a piece of work etc.) quickly and without attention to detail. **bang up** damage or injure. **bang for one's buck** value for one's money. **with a bang 1** quickly and noisily. **2** with great commotion, publicity, success, etc.

bangbelly *noun* (*plural* **bangbellies**) *Cdn* (*Nfld*) a pudding, cake, or pancake consisting of a dumpling-like mixture fried, baked, or stewed.

banger *noun* **1** a thing that makes a banging noise, e.g. a firecracker or device for scaring away birds etc. **2** (in *combination*) *slang* an engine having a specified number of cylinders: *four-banger*.

Bangladeshi • *noun* (*plural* **Bangladeshi** or **Bangladeshis**) a native or inhabitant of Bangladesh, a country in the Ganges delta. • *adjective* of Bangladesh or its people. [Say bang gla DESHY]

bangle *noun* a rigid bracelet, usu. without a clasp, worn around the arm or ankle.

bang-up *adjective informal* excellent: *a bang-up job*.

banish *verb* (**banishes, banished, banishing**) **1** formally expel (a person), esp. from a country: *banished to Siberia for political crimes*. **2** dismiss from one's presence or mind: *all thoughts of romance were banished from her head*. ▶ **banishment** *noun*

banister *noun* **1** the handrail at the side a staircase. **2** (in *plural*) a handrail and its supporting uprights. **3** (usu. in *plural*) an upright supporting a handrail.

B

B

banjo *noun* (*plural* **banjos** or **banjoes**) a four- or five-stringed musical instrument with a neck and head like a guitar and an open-backed body consisting of parchment stretched over a metal hoop.

bank[1] • *noun* **1** the sloping ground bordering a body of water. **2** the area of ground alongside a river. **3** a slope or raised shelf of ground. **4** an underwater ridge of land: *Grand Banks*. **5** the slope built into a road etc., enabling vehicles to maintain speed around a curve. **6** the tilt of an aircraft etc. to one side during a turn. **7** a mass of cloud, fog, snow, etc. • *verb* **1** (often foll. by *up*) heap or rise into banks. **2 a** (of a vehicle or aircraft) tilt to one side while rounding a curve. **b** cause (a vehicle or aircraft) to do this. **3** contain or confine within a bank or banks. **4** build (a road etc.) higher at the outer edge of a bend to enable fast cornering. **5** heap up (a fire) tightly so that it burns slowly. **6** cause (a puck) to rebound off the boards of a hockey rink.

bank[2] • *noun* **1 a** a financial establishment which uses money deposited by customers for investment, pays it out when required, lends money at interest, etc. **b** a building in which this business takes place. **2 a** an institution which collects a product and stores it for future use: *food bank*. **b** a place where information is stored in a computer: *data bank*. **3 a** the money or tokens held by the banker in some games. **b** the banker or dealer in such games. **4** = PIGGY BANK. • *verb* **1** deposit (money or valuables) in a bank. **2** engage in business as a banker. **3** (often foll. by *at*, *with*) keep money (at a bank). PHRASES **bank on** rely on.

bank[3] *noun* **1** a row of similar objects, esp. of keys, lights, or switches. **2** a tier of oars.

bankable *adjective* **1** reliable: *a bankable reputation*. **2** certain to bring in a profit: *he needed some bankable stars for the film*.

bank barn *noun* (esp. Ont. & US Midlands) a barn built into a hill with an entrance to the top storey on one side and to the lower storey on the other.

bank draft *noun* an order for payment drawn by one bank on another.

banker[1] *noun* **1** a person who manages or owns a bank or group of banks. **2 a** a keeper of the bank in some gambling games. **b** a card game involving gambling.

banker[2] *noun* **1** a fishing boat operating in the waters off Newfoundland, esp. the Grand Banks. **2** a Newfoundland fisherman.

banking[1] *noun* Cdn (Nfld) fishing for cod off the southeast coast of Newfoundland.

banking[2] *noun* the business conducted by or with a bank: *do all my banking by phone*.

bank machine *noun* esp. Cdn = AUTOMATED TELLER MACHINE.

banknote *noun* a piece of paper money issued by a central bank, circulating as a nation's currency.

Bank of Canada *noun* the federally owned central bank which controls Canada's bank rate etc.

bank rate *noun* esp. Cdn the central bank's minimum interest rate on short-term loans to banks etc.

bankroll • *noun* **1** a roll of banknotes. **2** a sum of money; available funds: *the jockey finished the year with a nice bankroll*. • *verb* informal support financially: *the project is being bankrolled by wealthy patrons*.

bankrupt • *adjective* **1 a** legally declared unable to pay debts. **b** undergoing the legal process resulting from this. **2** exhausted or drained (of some quality etc.); deficient, lacking: *the Reform Party is bankrupt of ideas* ◊ *their cause is morally bankrupt*. • *noun* **1** a person who cannot pay his or her debts and whose estate is administered and disposed of for the benefit of the creditors. **2** a person exhausted of or deficient in a

certain attribute: *a moral bankrupt*. • *verb* make bankrupt. ▶ **bankruptcy** *noun* (*plural* **bankruptcies**)

banner • *noun* **1** a large sign or strip of cloth etc. bearing a slogan or design, usu. carried in a procession or hung in a public place. **2** a belief or principle serving as a rallying point: *the government is flying the free trade banner*. **3** (also **banner headline**) a large newspaper headline, esp. one across the top of the front page. **4** a national flag. • *adjective* excellent, outstanding: *a banner year in sales*.

bannister *noun* = BANISTER.

bannock *noun* Cdn a bread similar to tea biscuits, made of flour, water, and fat, sometimes leavened with baking powder, cooked on a griddle or over a fire.

banns *plural noun* an oral or published notice announcing an intended marriage and giving the opportunity for objections.

banquet *noun* **1** an elaborate and extensive feast. **2** a dinner for many people followed by speeches in favour of a cause or in celebration of an event.

banquet hall *noun* **1** a room in which banquets are held. **2** a building containing one or more of these.

banquette *noun* an upholstered bench along a wall, esp. in a restaurant or bar. [Say bang KET]

banshee *noun* (in Gaelic mythology) a female spirit whose wailing warns of death in a family: *the kid dropped her ice cream cone and began to howl like a banshee*.

bantam *noun* **1** any of several small breeds of domestic fowl, of which the rooster is very aggressive. **2** a small but aggressive person. **3** Cdn **a** a level of amateur sport, usu. involving children aged 13–15. **b** a player in this age group.

bantamweight *noun* **1** a weight class in certain sports between flyweight and featherweight, in the professional boxing scale not more than 118 lbs. (53 kg). **2** an athlete of this weight.

banter • *noun* good-humoured teasing. • *verb* talk humorously or teasingly: *the men bantered with the waitresses* ◊ *a good-humoured bantering tone*.

Bantu • *noun* **1** a group of Niger-Congo languages spoken in equatorial and southern Africa, including Swahili, Xhosa, and Zulu. **2** (*plural* **Bantu** or **Bantus**) a member of the peoples speaking these languages. • *adjective* of or relating to these languages or peoples. [Say BAN too]

baptism *noun* **1 a** a religious rite symbolizing admission to the Christian Church, involving sprinkling the forehead with water or total immersion and often accompanied by naming. **b** the act of baptizing or being baptized. **2** any similar rite of initiation, purification, or naming: *this event constituted her baptism as a politician*. ▶ **baptismal** *adjective*

baptism of fire *noun* **1** initiation into battle. **2** a painful new undertaking or experience.

Baptist *noun* a member of a Protestant denomination advocating baptism by total immersion, esp. of adults, as a symbol of membership of and initiation into the Church.

baptistery *noun* (*plural* **baptisteries**) (also **baptistry**; *plural* **baptistries**) **1** the part of a church used for baptism. **2** (in a Baptist church) a tank used for total immersion. [Say BAP tiss tree]

baptize *verb* (**baptizes**, **baptized**, **baptizing**) (also **baptise**; **baptises**, **baptised**, **baptising**) **1** administer baptism to: *she was baptized a Catholic*. **2** give a name or nickname to: *he baptized the science of narratology "narratology"*.

bar[1] • *noun* **1** a long rod or piece of rigid wood, metal, etc., esp. used as an obstruction, fastening, weapon, etc. **2 a** something resembling a bar in being (thought of

as) straight, narrow, and rigid: *chocolate bar*. **b** a band of colour or light, esp. on a flat surface. **c** = CROSSBAR. **d** a metal strip below the clasp of a medal, awarded as an extra distinction. **e** a bank of sand etc. across the mouth of a river or harbour (*compare* SANDBAR). **f** a rail: *towel bar*. **3 a** a barrier of any shape. **b** a restriction: *a bar to promotion*. **c** *Law* a legal obstacle preventing an action or claim. **4 a** a counter in a pub, restaurant, or home across which alcohol or refreshments are served. **b** a room in a restaurant, hotel, etc. in which customers may sit and drink. **c** an establishment serving alcohol. **5** a small shop, stall, department, etc. which specializes in a particular product: *gas bar ◊ snack bar*. **6** any of the sections of usu. equal time value into which a musical composition is divided by vertical lines across the staff. **7 a** a rail in a law court separating the space occupied by the judge, lawyers, and parties to a case from the general public. **b** an enclosure in which an accused person stands before a court of law. **c** a rail marking the end of the chamber in the House of Commons. **8 (the bar)** a lawyers collectively. **b** the profession of lawyer. • *verb* (**bars, barred, barring**) **1 a** fasten (a door, window, etc.) with a bar or bars. **b** (usu. foll. by *in, out*) shut or keep in or out. **2** obstruct, prevent: *bar her progress*. **3** prohibit, exclude: *bar them from attending*. **4** *Law* prevent or delay (an action) by legal obstacle. • *preposition* except: *bar none*. PHRASES **at (the) bar** (of a lawsuit, defendant, etc.) currently before the courts. **be called** (or **admitted**) **to the bar** be formally admitted into the legal profession. **behind bars** in prison.

bar² *noun* a unit of pressure equal to 100 kilopascals.

barachois *noun* (also **barachois pond**) *Cdn* (*Nfld & Maritimes*) a shallow coastal lagoon or pond created by the formation of a sandbar a short distance offshore from a beach. [Say BAR a shwa]

barb *noun* **1** a sharp projection near the end of an arrow, fish hook, etc., which is angled away from the main point to make extraction difficult. **2** a deliberately hurtful remark: *his barb hurt more than she cared to admit*. **3** a beard-like filament at the mouth of some fish, e.g. catfish. **4** any one of the fine hairlike filaments growing from the shaft of a feather, forming the vane.

Barbadian • *noun* **1** a native or national of Barbados, the most easterly of the Caribbean islands. **2** a person of Barbadian descent. • *adjective* of or relating to Barbados or its people. [Say bar BAY dee in]

barbarian • *noun* **1** an uncultured or brutish person. **2** a member of a people regarded as primitive or uncivilized, esp., in ancient times, one not belonging to one of the great civilizations: *Rome was sacked by barbarians*. • *adjective* **1** rough and uncultured. **2** of or pertaining to uncivilized peoples: *the barbarian invasions*. [Say bar BERRY in]

barbaric *adjective* **1** savagely cruel: *he had carried out barbaric acts in the name of war*. **2** rough and uncultured. **3** primitive. ▶ **barbarically** *adverb* [Say bar BEAR ick]

barbarism *noun* **1** the absence of culture and civilized standards: *the collapse of civilization and the return to barbarism*. **2** a word or expression not considered correct. **3** extreme cruelty or brutality: *she called the execution an act of barbarism*. [Say BARBER ism]

barbarity *noun* (*plural* **barbarities**) savage cruelty: *the barbarity displayed by the terrorists ◊ the Nazi barbarities of the last war*. [Say bar BERRA tee]

barbarous *adjective* **1** uncivilized: *a remote and barbarous country*. **2** cruel: *early child-raising practices were*

barbarous *by modern standards*. **3** (esp. of languages) coarse and unrefined. ▶ **barbarously** *adverb* **barbarousness** *noun* [Say BARBER us]

barbecue • *noun* **1 a** a meal, esp. of meat, cooked on an open fire or grill out of doors. **b** a party at which such a meal is cooked and eaten. **2 a** a metal appliance equipped with a grill on which meat etc. is cooked over charcoal or gas flame. **b** a fireplace containing a grill for cooking. • *verb* (**barbecues, barbecued, barbecuing**) cook (esp. meat) on a barbecue.

barbed *adjective* **1** equipped with barbs: *barbed arrows*. **2** (of a remark etc.) deliberately hurtful: *barbed wit*.

barbed wire *noun* wire bearing sharp pointed spikes close together and used in fencing, or in warfare as an obstruction.

barbell *noun* a metal bar with a series of weighted discs at each end, used for weightlifting exercises.

barbeque *noun & verb* (**barbeques, barbequed, barbequing**) = BARBECUE.

barber • *noun* a person who cuts men's hair and shaves or trims beards as an occupation. • *verb* **1** cut the hair or shave or trim the beard of. **2** cut or trim (grass etc.) closely.

barber pole *noun* a pole with spiral red and white stripes, hung outside a barbershop as a business sign.

barbershop *noun* **1** a shop where a barber works. **2** (also **barbershop quartet**) a style of close harmony singing for four male voices.

Barbie *noun* (also **Barbie doll**) **1** *proprietary* a doll representing a slim, fashionably dressed, attractive young woman. **2** a woman with similar characteristics, esp. (*derogatory*) an unintelligent one.

barbital *noun* a long-acting sedative and sleep-inducing drug. [Say BARBA tall]

barbiturate *noun* any derivative of barbituric acid used in the preparation of sedative and sleep-inducing drugs. [Say bar BITCH ur it or bar BITCHA rate]

barbituric acid *noun* an organic acid from which various sedatives and sleep-inducing drugs are derived. [Say barba CHUR ick]

barbotte *noun* (also **barbot**) *Cdn* (*Que. & Ont.*) a large catfish. [Say BAR but]

bar code *noun* a code in the form of a pattern of stripes, used for identification by an optical scanner. ▶ **bar-coded** *adjective* **bar-coding** *noun*

bard *noun* **1** *hist.* a Celtic minstrel. **2** *literary* a poet. PHRASES **the Bard** Shakespeare. ▶ **bardic** *adjective*

SPELL CHECK
bare, bear   ABC ✓

The animal is spelled **bear**. **Bear** is also the spelling for "bring", "endure", and "give birth to".

---

bare • *adjective* **1** unclothed or uncovered: *bare feet*. **2** without appropriate covering or contents: **a** (of a tree) leafless. **b** unfurnished; empty: *bare rooms*. **c** (of a floor) not carpeted. **d** (of ground) without vegetation: *bare rock*. **3** (of a road, surface, etc.) clear of snow and ice. **4 a** undisguised: *the bare truth*. **b** unadorned: *bare facts*. **5 a** scanty: *a bare majority*. **b** mere: *bare necessities*. • *verb* (**bares, bared, baring**) **1** uncover: *bared his teeth*. **2** reveal: *bared her soul*. PHRASES **lay bare** expose, reveal. **with one's bare hands** without using tools or weapons.

bareback *adjective & adverb* on an unsaddled horse etc.

bareboat *noun* a boat, esp. a sailboat, that is rented without a crew: *bareboat charter*.

SPELL CHECK `ABC✓`
bare bones, bare-bones

Note the difference in spelling between the structures *the bare bones of the plot* and *a bare-bones budget of $100,000*.

bare bones *plural noun* essential parts or components: *the bare bones of the plot.* ▶ **bare-bones** *adjective*

barefaced *adjective* shameless and undisguised: *barefaced lie* ◊ *could barefaced patronage be involved?*

barefoot *adjective & adverb* with nothing on the feet.

bare-handed *adjective & adverb* with bare hands.

bare-knuckle *adjective* (also **bare-knuckled**) **1** *Boxing* without gloves; with bare fists. **2** without niceties: *bare-knuckle political campaign.*

barely *adverb* **1** only just; scarcely: *barely escaped.* **2** scantily: *barely furnished.*

bareness *noun* a bare quality or condition.

barf *informal* • *verb* vomit or retch. • *noun* **1** vomited food etc. **2** an attack of vomiting.

bargain • *noun* **1 a** an agreement on the terms of a transaction or sale. **b** this seen from the buyer's viewpoint: *a bad bargain.* **2** something acquired or offered cheaply. • *verb* (often foll. by *with, for*) discuss the terms of a transaction: *bargained for the table.* PHRASES **bargain away** part with for something worthless: *bargained away the farm.* **bargain for** (or **on**) be prepared for; expect: *didn't bargain for bad weather.* **bargain on** rely on. **drive a hard bargain** pursue one's own profit in a transaction keenly. **into** (or **in**) **the bargain** in addition to what was expected. **make** (or **strike**) **a bargain** agree to a transaction.

bargain basement • *noun* a store, or basement of a store, where bargains are available. • *adjective* **1** inexpensive, cheap. **2** of poor quality; inferior.

bargainer *noun* a person who negotiates the terms of a transaction, agreement, etc.

bargaining chip *noun* something which can be used to advantage in negotiations.

bargaining table *noun* a table around which negotiations are conducted.

bargaining unit *noun* a group of workers united for the purpose of collective bargaining.

barge • *noun* **1** a long flat-bottomed boat for carrying freight etc. **2** *Cdn* (*Nfld*) a large boat used to collect, hold, and process cod. **3** a long ornamental boat used for pleasure or ceremony. • *verb* (**barges**, **barged**, **barging**) **1 a** transport (goods) on a barge. **b** travel by barge. **2** (often foll. by *around*) lurch or rush clumsily about. **3** (foll. by *in, into*) **a** intrude or interrupt rudely or awkwardly. **b** collide with: *barged into her.*

barge pole *noun* PHRASES **would not touch with a barge pole** see TOUCH.

bargoon *noun Cdn slang* a bargain.

bar graph *noun* a graph using bars to represent quantity.

bar harbour *noun* a harbour with an entrance that is partially obstructed by a sandbar.

bar-hop *verb* (**bar-hops**, **bar-hopped**, **bar-hopping**) *informal* go from one bar to another, drinking but not staying long in each.

baritone • *noun* **1 a** the second-lowest adult male singing voice. **b** a singer with this voice. **c** a part written for it. **2 a** an instrument that is second-lowest in pitch in its family. **b** its player. • *adjective* of the second-lowest range. [Say BERRA tone]

barium *noun* **1** a white reactive soft metallic element. **2** a mixture of barium sulphate and water which is opaque to X-rays, given to patients requiring

radiological examination of the stomach and intestines: *barium enema.* [Say BERRY um]

bark¹ • *noun* **1** the sharp cry of a dog, fox, etc. **2** a sound resembling this cry. • *verb* **1** (of a dog etc.) give a bark. **2** speak or utter sharply or brusquely. **3** cough fiercely. PHRASES **one's bark is worse than one's bite** one is not as ferocious as one appears. **bark up the wrong tree** be on the wrong track; make an effort in the wrong direction.

bark² • *noun* **1** the tough protective outer sheath of the trunks, branches, and twigs of trees or woody shrubs. **2** this material used for tanning leather or dyeing material. **3** a type of flat usu. chocolate candy containing nuts. • *verb* **1** graze or scrape (one's shin etc.). **2** strip bark from (a tree etc.).

bark³ *noun literary* a ship or boat.

barker *noun* **1** a person who calls out loudly to attract customers to an auction, a stall at a fair, etc. **2** a dog etc. that barks persistently.

barley *noun* any of various hardy cereals with coarse bristles, widely used as food and in making beer and Scotch whisky.

barmaid *noun* a female bartender.

barman *noun* (*plural* **barmen**) a male bartender.

bar mitzvah *noun* **1** the religious initiation ceremony of a Jewish boy who has reached the age of 13. **2** the boy undergoing this ceremony. [Say bar MITSVA]

barn *noun* **1** a large farm building for housing animals, storing grain, etc. **2** *derogatory* a large plain or unattractive building: *that theatre is such a barn.* **3** a large shed for storing road or railway vehicles.

barnacle *noun* a small marine crustacean with an external shell, which, in adult form, attaches itself permanently to a variety of surfaces, including rocks, ships' bottoms, etc., and which is often invoked as the type of something that clings tenaciously. ▶ **barnacled** *adjective* [Say BARNA cull]

barnburner *noun informal* **1** something exciting or successful. **2** a lively or exciting esp. political speech: *delivered a two-hour barnburner.* **3** a game or competition that has a close result.

barn dance *noun* **1** an informal social gathering for dancing, originally in a barn. **2** a dance for a number of couples forming a line or circle.

barn owl *noun* an owl with a heart-shaped usu. white face, black eyes, and relatively long, slender legs, which frequently nests in farm buildings.

barnstorm *verb* **1 a** make a rapid tour holding political meetings. **b** visit (an area) to hold such meetings. **2** give informal flying exhibitions, esp. at country fairs etc.; do stunt flying. **3** tour rural districts giving theatrical performances (formerly often in barns). **4** (of a sports team) tour through an area playing exhibition games. ▶ **barnstormer** *noun*

barn swallow *noun* the common swallow, which builds mud nests on buildings.

barnyard *noun* **1** the usu. fenced area around a barn. **2** (as an *adjective*) earthy, coarse: *barnyard humour.*

barometer *noun* **1** an instrument measuring atmospheric pressure, esp. in forecasting the weather and determining altitude. **2** anything which reflects changes in circumstances, opinions, etc. ▶ **barometric** *adjective* [Say ba ROMMA tur, berra MET rick]

barometric pressure *noun Meteorology* atmospheric pressure • measured using a barometer.

SPELL CHECK `ABC✓`
baron, barren

Land that is unable to produce plants is **barren**.

baron *noun* **1** a member of the lowest order of nobility

in the United Kingdom or other countries. **2** an important businessman or other powerful or influential person: *timber baron*.

baroness *noun* (*plural* **baronesses**) **1** a woman holding the rank of baron either as a life peerage or as a hereditary rank. **2** the wife or widow of a baron.

baronet *noun* a member of the lowest hereditary titled British order, below a baron but above a knight. Baronets are titled "Sir".

baronial *adjective* **1** of or befitting barons. **2** in the turreted style characteristic of Scottish country houses: *the baronial Château Frontenac*. [Say ba ROANY ul]

baroque • *noun* **1** a style of architecture and decorative art of the late 16th to early 18th century, characterized by extensive ornamentation. **2** a style of music from the period 1600–1750, characterized by increasing complexity and emphasis on contrast. • *adjective* **1** of or relating to this period or style: *Handel and Bach were baroque composers*. **2** highly ornate and complex: *a baroque quality in the writing*. [Say ba ROKE]

barque *noun* **1** a sailing ship with the rear mast fore-and-aft-rigged and the remaining (usu. two) masts square-rigged. **2** *literary* any boat. [Say BARK]

barquentine *noun* a sailing ship with the forward mast square-rigged and the remaining (usu. two) masts fore-and-aft-rigged. [Say BARK'n teen]

barracks *plural noun* **1** a building or building complex used to house soldiers. **2** *Cdn* a building housing a local detachment of the RCMP. **3** any building used to accommodate large numbers of people. [Say BARE icks]

barracuda *noun* (*plural* **barracuda** or **barracudas**) a large, voracious, predatory tropical marine fish, with a slender body and large jaws and teeth. [Say berra COODA]

barrage • *noun* **1** a concentrated artillery bombardment over a wide area. **2** a rapid succession of questions or criticisms. **3** an artificial barrier, esp. in a river. **4** a deciding event in fencing, show jumping, etc. • *verb* (**barrages**, **barraged**, **barraging**) subject to a barrage of artillery fire, questions, etc.: *the dictionary department was barraged with plaintive or angry letters*. [Say ba ROZH]

barre *noun* a waist-level horizontal bar on which dancers rest one hand to help keep their balance during some exercises. [Say BAR]

barred *adjective* **1** marked with bars; striped. **2** closed with a bar: *a barred door*.

barred owl *noun* a large owl with large brown vertical streaks on its breast, which inhabits the southern boreal forest of North America.

barrel • *noun* **1** a cylindrical container usu. bulging out in the middle, made of wooden staves with metal hoops around them, or of plastic or metal. **2** the contents of this. **3** a measure of capacity, usu. varying from 30 to 40 imperial gallons (136 to 182 litres). **4** a unit of capacity for oil and petroleum products equal to 35 imperial gallons (about 159 litres). **5** the cylindrical body or trunk of an object, e.g. a pump, pen, etc. **6** the metal tube of a gun, through which the shot is discharged. **7** the fuel outlet from the carburetor on a gasoline engine. • *verb* (**barrels**, **barrelled**, **barrelling**) *informal* move quickly: *barrel along the road*. [PHRASES] **barrel of fun** (or **laughs**) *informal* a great deal of fun. **over a barrel** *informal* in a helpless position.

barrel-chested *adjective* having a large rounded chest.

barrelhead *noun* the flat top of a barrel. [PHRASES] **on the barrelhead** immediately and up front: *paid cash on the barrelhead*.

barrel-jumping *noun* *Cdn* a sport in which a skater jumps over a row of barrels lying on their sides.

barrel organ *noun* a mechanical musical instrument

in which a rotating, pin-studded cylinder acts on a series of pipe valves, strings, or metal tongues.

barrel race *noun* a women's rodeo event in which a mounted rider must navigate a triangular arrangement of three barrels and return to the starting line. ▶ **barrel racer** *noun* **barrel racing** *noun*

barrel roll *noun* an aerobatic manoeuvre in which an aircraft rolls once about its longitudinal axis.

SPELL CHECK   [ABC ✓]
barren, baron

A nobleman or powerful businessperson is a **baron**.

B

barren • *adjective* (**barrener**, **barrenest**) **1 a** unable to bear young. **b** unable to produce fruit or vegetation: *a barren desert*. **2** not producing anything useful or successful: *the team will come through this barren patch and start to win again*. **3** devoid, empty: *England seemed barren of possibilities*. • *noun* **1** (in eastern North America) a tract of elevated flat land that supports shrubs and bushes but no trees. **2** *Cdn* (*NB & NS*) an expanse of marsh or muskeg.

barren ground caribou *noun* (*plural* **barren ground caribou**) a caribou native to the tundra of northern Canada.

barrenness *noun* **1** lack of vegetation: *miles of wilderness and barrenness on the road to Churchill Falls*. **2** infertility.

Barrens, the *plural noun* (also **barrens**, **Barren Grounds**, **Barren Lands**) *Cdn* the treeless, sparsely populated region of N Canada, lying between Hudson Bay and Great Slave and Great Bear lakes.

barrette *noun* a bar-shaped clip or ornament for a woman's or girl's hair.

barricade • *noun* a line of objects placed across a street etc. to prevent passage, often as an act of protest: *a police barricade* ◊ *the demonstrators put up barricades across the highway*. • *verb* (**barricades**, **barricaded**, **barricading**) **1** block with a barricade. **2 barricade oneself in** shut oneself into a place by blocking all the entrances: *terrified children and staff barricaded themselves in classrooms*.

barrier *noun* **1** a fence or other obstacle that bars advance or access. **2** an obstacle or circumstance that keeps people or things apart, or prevents communication: *a language barrier*. **3** anything that prevents progress or success. **4** a gate at a parking garage etc., that controls access. **5** an exposed sandbar that parallels a coast, as on the north shore of PEI: *barrier island*. **6** *informal* = SOUND BARRIER. **7** something that prevents transmission of a substance: *barrier methods of contraception*.

barrier reef *noun* a coral reef separated from the shore by a broad deep channel.

barring *preposition* in the absence of: *barring complications*.

barrio *noun* (*plural* **barrios**) **1** a district of a town in Spain and Spanish-speaking countries. **2** (in the US) the Spanish-speaking quarter of a town or city. [Say BAR ee oh]

barrister *noun* (also **barrister-at-law**; *plural* **barristers-at-law**) a lawyer who pleads cases before the courts. [Say BERRA stir]

barrister and solicitor *noun* *Cdn* a lawyer. All lawyers in Canadian common-law provinces are both barristers and solicitors.

barroom *noun* = BAR[1] 4b.

barrow[1] *noun* **1** = WHEELBARROW. **2** *Cdn* (*Nfld*) a flat, rectangular wooden frame with handles at both ends, used by two people to carry fish etc.

barrow[2] *noun* Archaeology a mound of earth constructed in ancient times to cover one or more burials.

bartender *noun* a person serving drinks at a bar.

▶**bartending** *noun*

barter • *verb* exchange goods or services without using money: *he often bartered a meal for drawings ◊ the company is prepared to barter for Russian oil*. • *noun* **1** trade by exchange of goods. **2** something used to trade in this way: *took some cigarettes to use as barter*.

Bartlett pear *noun* a large, yellow, juicy variety of pear.

basal *adjective* of, at, or forming a base. [Say BASE 'll]

basal metabolism *noun* the chemical processes occurring in an organism at complete rest.

basalt *noun* a dark basic volcanic rock whose strata sometimes form columns. ▶**basaltic** *adjective* [Say BA salt, ba SALT ick]

SPELL CHECK
base, bass

A voice or instrument with a low pitch is a **bass**.

---

base[1] • *noun* **1 a** a part that supports from beneath or serves as a foundation for an object or structure. **b** a notional structure or entity on which something draws or depends: *power base*. **2** a principle or starting point. **3 a** a place from which an operation or activity is directed. **b** Military a military installation from which operations are conducted and where equipment and supporting facilities are concentrated. **4 a** a main or important ingredient of a mixture. **b** a substance, e.g. water, in combination with which pigment forms paint etc. **5** a substance used as a foundation for makeup. **6** Chemistry a substance capable of combining with an acid to form a salt and water and usu. producing hydroxide ions when dissolved in water. **7** Math a number in terms of which other numbers or logarithms are expressed. **8** Architecture the part of a column between the shaft and pedestal or pavement. **9** Geometry a line or surface on which a figure is regarded as standing. **10** Surveying a known line used as a geometrical base for trigonometry. **11** Electronics the middle part of a transistor separating the emitter from the collector. **12** Linguistics a root or stem as the origin of a word or a derivative. **13** Baseball one of the four stations that must be reached in turn when scoring a run. • *verb* (**bases, based, basing**) **1** found or establish: *a theory based on speculation*. **2** station: *troops were based in Cyprus*. PHRASES **cover** (or **touch**) **all the bases** *informal* deal with all the related details. **make it to** (or **reach** etc.) **first base** *informal* achieve the first step of an objective, plan, etc. **off base 1** Baseball not touching a base. **2** *informal* mistaken: *they are totally off base and out of touch*. **b** unprepared, unawares: *the media are constantly trying to catch the government off base*. **touch base** *informal* contact or communicate with someone).

base[2] *adjective* (**baser, basest**) **1** lacking moral worth; ignoble: *the electorate's baser instincts of greed and selfishness*. **2** (of a metal) low in value.

baseball *noun* **1** a game played with teams of nine in which a batter must hit a ball (thrown by the opposing team's pitcher) with a bat, and then complete a diamond-shaped circuit of four bases to score a run. **2** the ball used in this game.

baseboard *noun* a strip of wood along the bottom of a wall in a house.

baseboard heater *noun* a heater attached to a wall near the floor. top. one which provides heat by means of a radiant electric coil.

base hit *noun* Baseball a hit that enables the batter to reach base without a fielder's error and without forcing out a runner already on base.

baseless *adjective* unfounded: *baseless speculation*.

baseline *noun* **1** a line used as a base or starting point. **2** the area on a baseball diamond within which a runner must remain when running between bases. **3** (in tennis, basketball, etc.) the line marking each end of the court. **4** (usu. as an *adjective*) a basic level or standard; something which serves as a basis: *baseline health study*. **5** a line which serves as the basis for subsequent surveying in a town or township.

baseman *noun* (plural **basemen**) Baseball a player whose position is first, second, or third base.

basement *noun* **1** the lowest floor of a building, at least partly below ground level. **2** Sport *informal* the lowest position in the standings.

basepath *noun* Baseball **1** the prescribed path for a baserunner extending between consecutive bases or between first or third base and home plate. **2** (in *plural*) *informal* the aspect of the game concerned with running or stealing bases: *a disaster on the basepaths*.

baserunner *noun* Baseball a member of the batting team who is on base or running between bases.

▶**baserunning** *noun*

bases plural of BASE[1], BASIS.

base unit *noun* a unit (of measurement etc.) that is defined arbitrarily and not by combinations of other units. The base units of the SI system are the metre, kilogram, second, ampere, kelvin, mole, and candela.

bash • *verb* (**bashes, bashed, bashing**) **1 a** strike bluntly or heavily. **b** *informal* attack violently: *bashing the unions*. **c** (often foll. by *in, down*, etc.) damage or break by striking forcibly. **2** (foll. by *into*) collide with. **3** (often as **bashing** *noun*) *informal* deride, criticize: *Toronto-bashing*. • *noun* (plural **bashes**) **1** a heavy blow. **2** *informal* a party or social event. ▶**basher** *noun*

bashful *adjective* reluctant to draw attention to oneself: *a bashful grin*. ▶**bashfully** *adverb* **bashfulness** *noun*

BASIC *noun* a computer programming language using familiar English words, designed for beginners and widely used on microcomputers.

basic • *adjective* **1** forming or serving as a base. **2** fundamental. **3 a** simplest or lowest in level: *basic requirements*. **b** vulgar: *basic humour*. **4** Chemistry having the properties of or containing a base. **5** Geology (of volcanic rocks etc.) having less than 50 percent silica. • *noun* (usu. in *plural*) the fundamental facts or principles. ▶**basically** *adverb*

basic industry *noun* (plural **basic industries**) an industry of fundamental economic importance: *steel mills, auto parts manufacturers, and other basic industries*.

basic training *noun* a period of initial training in the police, armed forces, etc.

basil *noun* an aromatic herb, whose leaves are used as a flavouring in savoury dishes. [Say BAZZLE or BAYZ'll]

basilica *noun* (plural **basilicas**) **1** an ancient Roman public hall with an apse and colonnades, used as a law court and place of assembly. **2** a similar building used as a Christian church. **3** a title of honour awarded to certain Catholic churches by the Pope. [Say ba SILLA ca]

basin *noun* **1 a** a wide shallow open container, esp. one for holding water. **b** a bathroom sink. **2** a hollow rounded depression. **3** any sheltered area of water where boats can moor safely. **4** a round valley. **5** an area drained by rivers and tributaries.

basis *noun* (plural **bases**) **1** the foundation or support of something, esp. an idea or argument. **2** the main or determining principle or ingredient: *on a purely friendly basis*. **3** the starting point for a discussion etc. [Say BAY sis for the singular, BAY seez for the plural]

basis point *noun* one-hundredth of one percent.
bask *verb* **1** sit or lie back lazily in warmth and light: *basking in the sun*. **2** (foll. by *in*) derive great pleasure (from): *basking in glory*.
basket *noun* **1** a container made of interwoven cane etc. **2** a container resembling this. **3** the amount held by a basket. **4** *Basketball* **a** a net fixed on a ring attached to a backboard and raised usu. about 10 feet above the surface of the court. **b** a goal scored through this. **5** a group, category, or range: *a broad basket of goods and services*.
basketball *noun* **1** a game between two teams of five, in which goals are scored by throwing a ball through a basket suspended at either end of a court. **2** the ball used in this game.
basket case *noun informal* a person or thing regarded as useless or unable to cope, esp. as a result of emotional or mental disturbance or bankruptcy: *the world's budgetary basket cases ◊ after 36 hours without sleep, I was a basket case*.
basketful *noun* (*plural* **basketfuls**) **1** the amount of something that can be carried in a basket. **2** a large amount of something.
basketry *noun* **1** the art of making baskets. **2** baskets collectively: *the shop had a display of Mi'kmaq basketry*.
basket sled *noun* (also **basket sleigh**) *Cdn* (*North*) a toboggan with runners and side rails.
basket weave *noun* a weave resembling that of a basket.
basketwork *noun* **1** material woven in the style of a basket. **2** the art of making this.
basmati *noun* (also **basmati rice**) a kind of rice with very long thin grains and a delicate fragrance. [Say bazz MATTY]
Basque • *noun* **1** a member of a people inhabiting the western Pyrenees in northern Spain and southwestern France. **2** the language of this people. • *adjective* of the Basques or their language. [Say BASK or BOSK]
bas-relief *noun* sculpture or carving in which the figures project from the background. [Say baw RELIEF]
bass[1] • *noun* **1 a** the lowest adult male singing voice. **b** a singer with this voice. **c** a part written for it. **2** (also **bass line**) the lowest part in harmonized music. **3 a** an instrument that is the lowest in pitch in its family. **b** its player. **4 a** a bass guitar or double bass. **b** its player. **5** the low-frequency output of a radio etc., corresponding to the bass in music. • *adjective* **1** lowest in musical pitch. **2** having a deep sound. [Sounds like BASE]
bass[2] *noun* (*plural* **bass** or **basses**) any of various edible freshwater and marine fishes of the families Serranidae and Centrarchidae, having spiny fins. [Rhymes with *PASS*]
bass[3] *noun* = BASSWOOD. [Rhymes with *PASS*]
bass clef *noun Music* a sign that indicates that the second highest line of the staff represents the F below middle C.
basset hound *noun* (also **basset**) a breed of hunting dog with a long body, short legs, and droopy ears.
bassinet *noun* a portable basket-like bed for a young baby, often with a hood.
bassist *noun* a bass guitar or double bass player.
bassoon *noun* **1** a bass instrument of the oboe family, with a double reed. **2** its player. ► **bassoonist** *noun*
basso profundo *noun* a bass singer with an exceptionally low range. [Say basso pro FOONDO]
basswood *noun* **1** any of several trees of the linden family, esp. a North American lime tree with large leaves, native to the deciduous forests of eastern North America. **2** the light, soft wood of this tree. [The first part rhymes with *PASS*]

bastard • *noun* **1** a person whose parents are not married to each other. **2** *coarse slang* **a** an unpleasant or despicable person. **b** a person of a specified kind: *lucky bastard*. • *adjective* **1** born of parents not married to each other; illegitimate. **2** (of things) no longer in their pure or original form: *a bastard Darwinism*.
bastardization *noun* corruption, debasement: *complaints about the bastardization of French with English*.
bastardize *verb* (**bastardizes**, **bastardized**, **bastardizing**) copy something but change parts of it so that it is not as good as the original: *a strange bastardized form of French*.
baste[1] *verb* (**bastes**, **basted**, **basting**) moisten (meat) with gravy, melted fat, etc. during cooking.
baste[2] *verb* (**bastes**, **basted**, **basting**) stitch loosely together in preparation for sewing; tack.
baster *noun* a long glass or plastic tube with a rubber bulb at one end, with which liquid can be drawn up and released in order to baste meat. [Say BASTE er]
bastion *noun* **1** a projecting part of a fortification built at an angle to the line of a wall, so as to allow defensive fire in several directions. **2** an institution, place, or person strongly maintaining particular principles, attitudes, or activities: *the last bastion of male chauvinism*. **3** a natural rock formation resembling a bastion. [Say BASS ch'n]
bat[1] • *noun* **1** an implement with a rounded usu. wooden handle and a solid head with a flat or rounded surface, used for hitting a ball in various games, such as baseball. **2** an at-bat. **3** *Cdn* (*Nfld*) a pole 1.5–2.5 m (5–8 ft.) long, having an iron hook and spike on one end, used to kill seals and assist a sealer on the ice. • *verb* (**bats**, **batted**, **batting**) **1** hit with or as with a bat. **2** take a turn at batting. PHRASES **bat around 1** discuss (an idea or proposal). **2** *Baseball* have an inning in which all nine players have an at-bat. **go to bat for** *informal* defend the interests of. **right off the bat** immediately.
bat[2] *noun* a mouselike nocturnal mammal capable of flight by means of membranous wings extending from its forelimbs. PHRASES **have bats in the belfry** be eccentric or crazy. **like a bat out of hell** very fast.
bat[3] *verb* (**bats**, **batted**, **batting**) blink (one's eyelid); flutter (one's eyelashes). PHRASES **bat an eye** (or **eyelash** or **eyelid**) *informal* show reaction or emotion: *she paid the bill without batting an eyelid*.
batch[1] • *noun* (*plural* **batches**) **1** a number of things or persons forming a group or dealt with together. **2** an instalment: *have sent off the latest batch of proofs*. **3** a quantity produced by one operation, or the amount of material necessary for this: *a batch of doughnuts*. **4** (as an adjective) using or dealt with in batches, not as a continuous flow: *batch production*. **5** *Computing* a group of records processed as a single unit. • *verb* (**batches**, **batched**, **batching**) arrange or deal with in batches.
batch[2] *verb* (**batches**, **batched**, **batching**) (esp. in **batch it**) live alone and keep house for oneself, esp. temporarily.
bateau *noun Cdn hist.* (*plural* **bateaux**) a light flat-bottomed boat with pointed bow and stern, propelled by oars, poles, or sails, or drawn by horses. [Say ba TOE for the singular, ba TOE or ba TOES for the plural]
bated *adjective* PHRASES **with bated breath** very anxiously or eagerly.
bath • *noun* (*plural* **baths**) **1** the act or process of immersing the body for washing or therapy: *have a bath*. **2 a** = BATHTUB. **b** this with its contents: *your bath is ready*. **3 a** a vessel containing liquid in which something is immersed, e.g. a film for developing. **b** this with its contents. **4** = BATHROOM. **5** (usu. in *plural*)

B

a building with baths or a swimming pool. • *verb Cdn & Brit.* **1** wash (esp. a person) in a bath. **2** take a bath.

bathe *verb* (**bathes, bathed, bathing**) **1** swim. **2** wash oneself. **3** immerse in or wash or treat with liquid, esp. for cleansing or medicinal purposes: *she bathed and bandaged my knee*. **4** (of sunlight etc.) envelop: *the park lay bathed in sunlight*.

bather *noun* a swimmer. [Say BATHE er]

bathetic *adjective* marked by a sudden unintentional change from a serious tone or mood to a silly or trivial one: *its account of the conscription crisis of 1917 is bathetic rather than moving*. [Say ba THET ick]

bathhouse *noun* **1** a building with baths for public use. **2** a building for changing clothes at a pool etc.

bathing *noun* **1** the activity of washing oneself in a bath. **2** the activity of swimming in the sea or a river etc. [Say BATHE ing]

bathing suit *noun* a garment worn for swimming.

batholith *noun* a dome of igneous rock extending to an unknown depth in the earth's crust. [Say BATH a lith]

bathos *noun* an unintentional lapse in mood from the sublime to the absurd or trivial; a commonplace or ridiculous feature offsetting an otherwise sublime situation: *the word "soap opera" later became synonymous with corniness and bathos*. [Say BAY thoss]

bathrobe *noun* a loose usu. belted robe worn over nightwear, esp. one made of thick terry cloth.

bathroom *noun* **1** a room containing a bath and usu. other washing facilities. **2** a room containing a toilet or toilets. PHRASES **go to the bathroom** *euphemism* urinate or defecate.

bathtub *noun* a tub for bathing in, esp. one that is permanently fixed in a bathroom.

bathtub race *noun Cdn* an event in which bathtubs are motorized and piloted across bodies of water.

bathwater *noun* the water in a bath.

batik • *noun* **1** a method (originally used in Java) of producing coloured designs on textiles by waxing the parts not to be dyed. **2** a piece of cloth treated in this way. • *verb* (usu. as **batiked** *adjective*) produce coloured designs in this way. [Say ba TEEK]

bat mitzvah *noun* **1** a religious initiation ceremony for a Jewish girl aged twelve years and one day, regarded as the age of religious maturity. **2** the girl undergoing this ceremony. [Say bat MITSVA]

baton *noun* **1** a thin stick used by a conductor to direct an orchestra, choir, etc. **2** a short stick or tube carried and passed on by the runners in a relay race. **3** a stick carried and twirled by a drum major or majorette. **4** a staff of office or authority. **5** a police officer's short stout stick; a truncheon. [Say ba TON]

bats *adjective slang* crazy.

batsman *noun* (*plural* **batsmen**) a person who bats or is batting, esp. in cricket.

batt *noun* **1** a sheet of usu. fibreglass insulation sized to fit between studs, joists, or rafters. **2** = BATTING 2.

battalion *noun* **1** a large body of soldiers ready for battle, esp. an infantry unit forming part of a brigade. **2** a large group of people pursuing a common aim or sharing a major undertaking: *a battalion of lawyers and accountants made him ever wealthier*. [Say buh TAL y'n]

batten • *noun* **1** a long flat strip of wood or metal used to hold something in place. **2 a** a thin, narrow strip of wood or plastic inserted in pockets in a sail to maintain its proper shape. **b** a strip of wood or metal for securing a tarpaulin over a ship's hatchway. • *verb* strengthen, fasten, or secure with or as if with battens. PHRASES **batten down the hatches 1** *Nautical* secure a ship's tarpaulins. **2** prepare for a difficulty or crisis.

batter¹ *verb* **1** strike repeatedly with hard blows.

2 (often in *passive*) **a** handle roughly, esp. over a long period. **b** censure or criticize severely.

batter² *noun* **1** a fluid mixture of flour, egg, and a liquid, used for coating food before frying. **2** a mixture of flour and other raw ingredients for a cake etc., more liquid than a dough.

batter³ *noun* a player batting, esp. in baseball.

battered¹ *adjective* (of a person, esp. a woman or child) subjected to repeated violence from a spouse etc.

battered² *adjective* coated in batter and deep-fried.

batterer *noun* a person who batters someone or something.

battering ram *noun hist.* a heavy object swung or rammed against a door to knock it down.

battery *noun* (*plural* **batteries**) **1** a device, consisting of one or more cells, in which chemical energy is converted into electricity. **2** a set of similar units of equipment, esp. connected: *a battery of clocks*. **3** a usu. exhaustive series of tests. **4 a** a fortified emplacement for heavy guns. **b** an artillery unit of guns, personnel, and vehicles. **5** *Law* an act, including touching, inflicting unlawful personal violence on another person, even if no physical harm is done (see ASSAULT 2). **6** *Baseball* the pitcher and the catcher. PHRASES **recharge one's batteries** restore one's strength, enthusiasm, etc.

batting *noun* **1** the action of hitting with a bat. **2** wadding of cotton, polyester, etc. prepared in sheets for use in quilts etc.

batting average *noun Baseball* a statistic indicating a batter's proficiency, calculated by dividing the number of hits by the number of at-bats.

batting cage *noun* a mesh enclosure in which baseball players can practise batting.

batting order *noun* the order in which baseball players take their turn at bat.

battle • *noun* **1 a** a prolonged fight between large organized armed forces. **b** a fight or violent altercation between opposed groups. **2** a contest; a prolonged or difficult struggle: *a battle of wits*. • *verb* (**battles, battled, battling**) **1** struggle; fight persistently: *battled for women's rights*. **2** struggle against: *battled cancer for years*. **3** engage in battle with: *battled the forest fire*. PHRASES **battle it out** fight to a conclusion. **half the battle** the key to the success of an undertaking.

battleaxe *noun* **1** a large axe used in ancient warfare. **2** *informal* a formidable or domineering older woman.

battle cry *noun* (*plural* **battle cries**) **1** a rallying cry used in battle. **2** a rallying cry or slogan of a group of people.

battledress *noun* **1** attire worn for battle. **2** *hist.* a soldier's or airman's everyday khaki uniform.

battlefield *noun* **1** the piece of ground on which a battle is or was fought: *visited Vimy and the other battlefields of Northern France*. **2** = BATTLEGROUND 1.

battleground *noun* **1** a place or situation of strife, conflict, or hostility: *an ideological battleground*. **2** = BATTLEFIELD 1.

battlement *noun* (usu. in *plural*) **1** an alternately high and low parapet along the top of a wall, as part of a fortification. **2** a section of roof enclosed by this. ▶ **battlemented** *adjective*

battler *noun* a person who fights, struggles, or competes persistently.

battle-scarred *adjective* (also **battle-weary**) **1** (of a soldier) scarred or weary from battle. **2** (of a group of people, etc.) exhausted from activity, esp. of a particular kind: *battle-scarred government*. **3** (of a building, city, etc.) **a** damaged by war or violence. **b** *informal* worn out through use.

battleship *noun* a warship of the most heavily armed and armoured class.

battleship grey *noun & adjective* drab, slightly bluish-grey (often used for warships as camouflage).

batty *adjective* (**battier**, **battiest**) *informal* crazy.

bauble *noun* a showy trinket of little value. [Say BOBBLE]

baud *noun* (*plural* **baud** or **bauds**) *Computing etc.* **1** a unit used to express the speed of electronic code signals, corresponding to one information unit per second. **2** (loosely) a unit of data-transmission speed of one bit per second. [Say BOD]

baulk esp. *Brit.* = BALK. [Say BOCK]

baulky esp. *Brit.* = BALKY. [Say BOCKY]

bauxite *noun* a claylike mineral containing varying proportions of alumina, the chief source of aluminum. ▶ **bauxitic** *adjective* [Say BOX ite, box IT ick]

Bavarian • *adjective* of or relating to Bavaria in southwestern Germany, its people, or their dialect. • *noun* **1** a native or inhabitant of Bavaria. **2** the dialect of German used there. [Say buh VERY un]

bawdy • *adjective* (**bawdier**, **bawdiest**) dealing with sexual matters in a comic way; humorously indecent: *an army song with bawdy lyrics*. • *noun* bawdy talk or writing. [Say BODY]

bawdy house *noun* a brothel.

bawl *verb* **1** speak or call out noisily. **2** weep loudly. **3** (of a cow, seal, etc.) cry out, wail. PHRASES **bawl out** *informal* reprimand angrily.

bawn *noun Cdn* (*Nfld*) **1** a meadow near a house etc. **2** a stretch of rocks on which salted cod are spread to dry.

bay[1] *noun* **1** a body of water where the coastline curves inwards. **2** an indentation or recess in a range of hills etc. **3** *Cdn* (*Nfld*) a large indentation on the coast, including several harbours, islands, etc.

bay[2] *noun* **1** (also **bay laurel** or **bay tree**) a Mediterranean laurel, *Laurus nobilis*, having deep green leaves and purple berries. **2** = BAY LEAF.

bay[3] *noun* **1** a space created by a window-line projecting outwards from a wall. **2** a recess; a section of wall between buttresses or columns, esp. in the nave of a church etc. **3** a compartment: *bomb bay*. **4** an area specially allocated or marked off: *loading bay*.

bay[4] • *adjective* (esp. of a horse) dark reddish-brown. • *noun* a bay horse with a black mane and tail.

bay[5] • *verb* **1** (esp. of a large dog) bark or howl loudly and plaintively. **2** (of a group of people) shout loudly, typically to demand something: *the crowd bayed for an encore*. • *noun* the sound of baying, esp. in chorus from hounds in close pursuit. PHRASES **at bay 1** cornered, apparently unable to escape. **2** in a desperate situation. **bring to bay** gain on in pursuit; trap. **hold** (or **keep**) **at bay** hold off (a pursuer). **stand at bay** turn to face one's pursuers.

bayberry *noun* (*plural* **bayberries**) **1** any of various North American shrubs or small trees, having aromatic leaves and bearing berries covered in a wax coating. **2** the fruit of the bay tree. **3** a fragrant, oil-bearing Caribbean tree, *Pimenta acris*.

bay leaf *noun* (*plural* **bay leaves**) the aromatic (usu. dried) leaf of the bay tree, used in cooking (see BAY[2] 1).

bayman *noun* (*plural* **baymen**) **1 a** esp. *US* a person living near a bay. **b** *Cdn* (*Nfld*) an inhabitant of an outport, as opposed to a townsperson. **2** (**Bay man**) *Cdn hist.* an employee of the Hudson's Bay Company.

bayonet • *noun* a stabbing blade attachable to the muzzle of a rifle. • *verb* (**bayonets**, **bayonetted**, **bayonetting**) stab with a bayonet. [Say bay uh NET]

bayou *noun* a marshy offshoot of a river etc. in the southern US, esp. in Louisiana. [Say BY oo]

bay scallop *noun* **1** a scallop of the Atlantic coast of Canada and New England. **2** the edible adductor muscle of this scallop.

bayside • *adjective* situated at or near a (usu. specified) bay. • *noun* (**Bayside**) *Cdn* the area around Hudson Bay: *Bayside post*.

Bay Street *noun Cdn* **1** a street in Toronto where the headquarters of many financial institutions and major law firms are located. **2** the interests of major Canadian corporations and banks: *Bay Street is nervous about the election*.

bay window *noun* a window, usu. with glass on three sides, projecting from an outside wall.

┌───┐
│ **SPELL CHECK**   ABC   │
│ **bazaar, bizarre**   ✓   │
│   │
│ Something very strange is **bizarre**.   │
└───┘

bazaar *noun* **1** (esp. in the Middle East) a marketplace or shopping quarter. **2** a fundraising sale of various articles, esp. for charity. **3** a large store selling miscellaneous items. **4** a place where items of a specified sort are sold: *sex bazaars*.

bazooka *noun* a tubular short-range rocket launcher used against tanks.

BB *noun* (*plural* **BBs**) a small pellet for shooting out of an air rifle or shotgun.

bbl. *abbreviation* barrels (esp. of oil).

BBQ *abbreviation* (*plural* **BBQs**) *informal* barbecue.

BBS *abbreviation* (*plural* **BBS's**) bulletin-board service, a computerized system for the exchange of software and electronic messages.

BC *abbreviation* **1** British Columbia. **2** (**BC**) (of a date) before Christ.

BCD *noun Computing* a code representing decimal numbers as a string of binary digits.

BCE *abbreviation* before the Common Era (used for dates before the Christian era, esp. by non-Christians).

Be *symbol* beryllium.

be (**am**, **are**, **is**; **was**, **were**; **been**; **being**) • *verb* **1** (often preceded by *there*) exist, live: *there is a house on the corner*. **2 a** occur; take place. **b** occupy a position in space. **3** remain, continue. **4** linking subject and predicate, expressing: **a** identity: *she is the person*. **b** condition: *he is ill today*. **c** state or quality: *she is very kind*. **d** opinion: *I am against hanging*. **e** total: *two and two are four*. **f** cost or significance: *it is nothing to me*. • *auxiliary verb* **1** with a past participle to form the passive mood: *it was done ◊ it is said*. **2** with a present participle to form progressive tenses: *we are coming*. **3** with an infinitive to express duty or commitment, intention, possibility, destiny, or hypothesis: *they were never to meet again*. PHRASES **be about** occupy oneself with: *is about her business*. **be at** occupy oneself with: *mice have been at the food*. **be off** *informal* go away; leave.

┌───┐
│ **SPELL CHECK**   ABC   │
│ **beach, beech**   ✓   │
│   │
│ The tree is a **beech**.   │
└───┘

beach • *noun* a pebbly or sandy shore of a body of water, esp. a lake or ocean. • *verb* (**beaches**, **beached**, **beaching**) run or haul up (a boat etc.) on to a beach.

beach ball *noun* a large lightweight inflated ball, esp. for games on the beach.

beachcomb *verb* walk along a beach searching for articles of value.

beachcomber *noun* **1** *Cdn* (*BC*) a person who earns a living by collecting logs that have broken loose from log booms. **2** a person who searches beaches for articles of value. **3** a long wave rolling in from the sea.

B

B

beached *adjective* (of a sea mammal etc.) stranded on the shore, esp. by the action of tides etc.

beachfront • *noun* land that fronts onto a beach. • *adjective* located on or overlooking a beach.

beachhead *noun* **1** a fortified position established on a beach by landing forces. **2** an initial position from which one may advance.

beacon *noun* **1** a fire or light set up in a high or prominent position as a warning etc. **2** a visible warning or guiding point or device, e.g. a lighthouse, navigation buoy, etc. **3** a radio transmitter whose signal helps fix the position of a ship, aircraft, etc.

bead • *noun* **1 a** a small usu. rounded and perforated piece of glass, stone, etc., for threading with others to make jewellery, or sewing on to fabric, etc. **b** (in *plural*) a string of beads. **c** (in *plural*) a rosary. **2** a drop of liquid; a bubble. **3** a small knob in the foresight of a gun. **4** the inner edge of a pneumatic tire that grips the rim of the wheel. • *verb* **1** decorate with beads. **2** string together. **3** cover a surface with drops of moisture: *his face was beaded with perspiration.* **PHRASES** **draw a bead on** take aim at. ▸ **beaded** *adjective*

beadily *adverb* intently and usu. with suspicion: *she stared beadily at us as we passed.*

beading *noun* **1** decoration in the form of or resembling a row of beads, esp. lacelike looped edging. **2** the bead of a tire.

beadle *noun* **1** a ceremonial usher, mace-bearer, etc. in certain universities etc. **2** a Presbyterian church officer attending on the minister. **3** a layperson employed by a church, synagogue, etc., to perform various minor functions. [Say beedle]

beadwork *noun* ornamental work with beads.

beady *adjective* (**beadier**, **beadiest**) (of the eyes) small, round, and bright.

beady-eyed *adjective* **1** with beady eyes. **2** observant.

beagle *noun* a short-legged dog with a short black and white or brown and white coat and floppy ears.

beak *noun* **1 a** a bird's horny projecting jaws; a bill. **b** the similar projecting jaw of other animals, e.g. a turtle. **2** *slang* a hooked nose. ▸ **beaked** *adjective*

beaker *noun* a lipped cylindrical glass vessel for scientific experiments.

beaky *adjective* **1** (of a person's nose) resembling a bird's beak; hooked. **2** (of a person) having such a nose.

be-all and end-all *noun* *informal* a feature of an activity that is more important than anything else, sometimes to the exclusion of everything else: *politics is not the be-all and end-all of human activity.*

beam • *noun* **1** a long sturdy piece of metal or squared timber etc. spanning an opening or room, usu. to support the structure above. **2 a** a ray or shaft of light. **b** a directional flow of particles or radiation. **3** a bright look or smile. **4 a** a series of radio or radar signals as a guide to a ship or aircraft. **b** the course indicated by this: *off beam.* **5** the crossbar of a balance, from which the pans or weights are suspended. **6 a** a ship's breadth at its widest point. **b** *informal* (esp. in **broad in the beam**) the width of a person's hips. **7** (in *plural*) the horizontal cross-timbers of a ship supporting the deck and joining the sides. **8** the side of a ship. **9** = BALANCE BEAM. • *verb* **1** emit or direct (light, radio waves, etc.). **2 a** shine. **b** look or smile radiantly.

beamed *adjective* having a beam or beams: *beamed ceiling.*

bean • *noun* **1 a** any kind of leguminous plant with edible usu. kidney-shaped seeds in long pods. **b** one of these seeds. **2** a similar seed of coffee and other plants. **3** *informal* the head. **4** (in *plural*; with *neg.*) anything at all: *doesn't know beans about it.* • *verb* *informal* hit on the head. **PHRASES** **full of beans** *informal* lively;

in high spirits. **not a hill of beans** *slang* an insignificant amount.

beanbag *noun* **1** a small bag filled with dried beans and used esp. in children's games. **2** a large cushion filled usu. with polystyrene beads and used as a seat.

beanball *noun* *Baseball* a pitch thrown at the batter's head.

bean-counter *noun* *informal derogatory* a person, esp. an accountant or bureaucrat, perceived as placing excessive emphasis on numbers, budgets, etc., esp. to the detriment of creativity. ▸ **bean-counting** *noun*

bean curd *noun* = TOFU.

beanie *noun* a skullcap, esp. of a sort worn formerly by small boys.

bean sprout *noun* (usu. in *plural*) a sprout of a bean seed, esp. of the mung bean, eaten raw or cooked.

beanstalk *noun* the stem of a bean plant.

SPELL CHECK
bear, bare

Something that is uncovered is **bare**. **Bare** also means "the least amount necessary" in phrases like "the bare essentials".

---

bear[1] *verb* (**bears**; *past* **bore**; *past participle* **borne**; **bearing**) **1** carry, bring, or take (esp. visibly): *bear gifts.* **2** show; have as an attribute or characteristic: *bear marks of violence.* **3 a** produce, yield (fruit etc.). **b** give birth to: *she has borne a son.* **4 a** sustain (a weight, responsibility, cost, etc.). **b** stand, endure (an ordeal, difficulty, etc.). **5 a** tolerate: *can't bear her.* **b** admit of; be fit for: *does not bear repeating.* **6** carry in thought or memory: *bear a grudge.* **7** veer in a given direction: *bear left.* **8** bring or provide: *bear him company.* **9 bear oneself** behave (in a certain way). **PHRASES** **bear arms** carry weapons; serve as a soldier. **bear away** (or **off**) win (a prize etc.). **bear down** exert downward pressure. **bear down on** approach rapidly or purposefully. **bear fruit** have results. **bear in mind** take into account having remembered. **bear on** (or **upon**) be relevant to. **bear out** support or confirm (an account or the person giving it). **bear up** raise one's spirits; not despair. **bear with** treat with forbearance; tolerate patiently. **bear witness** testify.

WRITING TIP
borne, born

Borne is the past participle of the verb **bear**, used in all senses listed in this dictionary entry, e.g. *Sara has borne a son*, *The children were borne on his shoulders*, or *Youssef has never borne a grudge.* **Born** is used only in reference to birth, as in *Megan was born in February* or *Jason was born lucky.*

---

bear[2] *noun* **1** any large mammal of the family Ursidae, having thick fur and walking on its soles. **2** a rough, unmannerly, or uncouth person. **3** a person who sells shares hoping to buy them back later at a lower price. **4** (**the Bear**) *informal* Russia.

bearable *adjective* that may be endured or tolerated.

bearberry *noun* (*plural* **bearberries**) **1** a small trailing chiefly North American evergreen shrub with bright red tart berries. **2** the berries of this plant.

beard • *noun* **1** hair growing on the chin and lower cheeks of the face, esp. a man's face. **2** a similar tuft or part on an animal (esp. a goat). • *verb* oppose openly; defy: *I thought I'd have a try at bearding the bully myself.* ▸ **bearded** *adjective*

bearded seal *noun* an Arctic seal with a large mouth surrounded by beardlike bristles.

bearer *noun* **1** a person or thing that bears or carries.

2 a carrier of equipment on an expedition etc. **3** a person who presents a cheque or other order to pay money.

bear hug *noun* a tight embrace.

bearing *noun* **1** a person's bodily attitude or outward behaviour: *a man of military bearing*. **2** relation or relevance to: *the case has no direct bearing on the issues being considered*. **3** endurability: *beyond bearing*. **4** a part of a machine that supports a rotating or other moving part. **5** direction or position relative to a fixed point, measured esp. in degrees. **6** (in *plural*) one's position relative to one's surroundings. **7** = BALL BEARING.

bearish *adjective* **1 a** causing, predicting, or associated with a fall in stock prices. **b** pessimistic. **2** like a bear, esp. in temper; surly. ▶ **bearishly** *adverb*

Bear Lake *noun* = SAHTU DENE *noun*.

bear market *noun* a stock market with falling prices.

bearpaw *noun* **1** the paw of a bear. **2** (also **bearpaw snowshoe**) *Cdn* an almost circular, tailless snowshoe.

bearskin *noun* **1 a** the skin of a bear. **b** a rug etc. made of this. **2** a tall furry hat worn ceremonially by some regiments.

beast *noun* **1** an animal other than a human being, esp. a wild quadruped. **2 a** a brutal person. **b** *informal* an objectionable or unpleasant person or thing. **3** (**the beast**) a human being's brutish or uncivilized characteristics. PHRASES **the nature of the beast** the undesirable but unchangeable essential quality or character of the thing.

beastie *noun jocular* **1** a small animal. **2** a small malevolent creature.

beastly • *adjective* (**beastlier, beastliest**) **1** *informal* objectionable, unpleasant. **2** like a beast; brutal. • *adverb informal* very, extremely.

beast of burden *noun* an animal used for carrying loads.

SPELL CHECK
beat, beet ABC✓

The vegetable is a **beet**.

---

beat • *verb* (**beats**; *past* **beat**; *past participle* **beaten**; **beating**) **1 a** strike (a person or animal) persistently or repeatedly, esp. to harm or punish. **b** strike (a thing) repeatedly, e.g. to sound (a drum etc.). **2** (foll. by *against, at, on*, etc.) **a** pound or knock repeatedly: *waves beat against the shore*. **b** = BEAT DOWN 3. **3 a** overcome; surpass; win a victory over. **b** complete an activity before (another person etc.). **c** be too hard for. **4** mix or stir (ingredients) vigorously so as to incorporate air. **5** (often foll. by *out*) fashion or shape (metal etc.) by blows. **6** (of the heart etc.) pulsate rhythmically. **7** (often foll. by *out*) **a** indicate (a tempo or rhythm) by gestures, tapping, etc. **b** sound (a signal etc.) by striking a drum or other means. **8 a** (of a bird's wings) move up and down. **b** cause (wings) to move in this way. **9** make (a path etc.) by trampling. **10** strike (bushes etc.) to rouse game. **11** *Cdn* (*Nfld*) (of herd animals, esp. seals) migrate. • *noun* **1 a** a main accent or rhythmic unit in music or verse. **b** the indication of rhythm by a conductor's movements: *watch the beat*. **c** (in popular music) a strong rhythm. **d** (as an *adjective*) characterized by a strong rhythm: *beat music*. **2 a** a stroke or blow, e.g. on a drum. **b** a measured sequence of strokes: *the beat of the waves*. **c** a throbbing movement or sound: *the beat of his heart*. **3 a** a route or area allocated to a police officer, reporter, etc. **b** a person's habitual round. **4** *informal* = BEATNIK. • *adjective* **1** *informal* exhausted, tired out: *after four hours of shopping we were all beat*. **2** of the beat generation or its philosophy. PHRASES **beat about** (often foll. by *for*) search (for an excuse etc.). **beat**

around the bush discuss a matter without coming to the point. **to beat the band** in such a way as to defeat all competition. **beat one's breast** strike one's chest in anguish or sorrow. **beat the bushes** search thoroughly: *beating the bushes for work*. **beat the clock** complete a task within a stated time. **beat down 1 a** bargain with (a seller) to lower the price. **b** cause a seller to lower (the price). **2** strike (a resisting object) until it falls. **3** (of the sun, rain, etc.) radiate heat or fall continuously and vigorously. **beat the drum for** publicize, promote. **beaten at the post** defeated at the last moment. **beat in** crush. **beat it** *informal* go away. **beat off** drive back (an attack etc.). **beat a retreat** withdraw. **beat time** indicate or follow a musical tempo with a baton or other means. **beat a person to it** arrive or achieve something before another person. **beat up** give a beating to, esp. with punches and kicks. (**it**) **beats me** I do not understand (it). **two hearts that beat as one** two people who are perfectly united in thought. ▶ **beatable** *adjective*

beaten *adjective* **1** outwitted; defeated. **2** exhausted; dejected. **3** (of gold or any other metal) shaped by a hammer. **4** (of a path etc.) much used. PHRASES **off the beaten track** (or **path**) **1** in or into an isolated place. **2** unusual.

beater *noun* **1** an implement used for beating (e.g. eggs, a drum, etc.). **2** *informal* an old or dilapidated vehicle. **3** a person who beats metal. **4** *Cdn* (*Nfld*) a young harp seal, about three to four weeks old.

beat generation *noun* the members of a movement of young people esp. in the 1950s who rejected conventional society in their dress, habits etc.

beatific *adjective* **1** *informal* blissful: *a beatific smile*. **2** making blessed; imparting supreme happiness. ▶ **beatifically** *adverb* [Say bee a TIFF ick]

beatification *noun* **1** *Catholicism* the act of formally declaring a dead person "blessed", often a step towards being declared a saint and permitting public veneration. **2** the act or fact of making or being blessed. [Say bee atta fuh CAY sh'n]

beatify *verb* (**beatifies, beatified, beatifying**) *Catholicism* announce the beatification of: *Brother André was beatified in 1982*. [Say bee ATTA fie]

beating *noun* **1** a physical punishment or assault. **2** a defeat. PHRASES **take some** (or **a lot of**) **beating** be difficult to surpass.

beatitude *noun* **1** blessedness. **2** (**the Beatitudes**) the blessings listed by Jesus in the Sermon on the Mount, in which the poor in spirit, those who mourn, the meek, those who hunger for righteousness, the merciful, the pure in heart, the peacemakers, and those persecuted for the sake of righteousness are declared blessed. [Say bee ATTITUDE]

beatnik *noun* a member of the beat generation.

beat-up *adjective informal* in a state of disrepair.

beau *noun* (*plural* **beaux** or **beaus**) *dated* or *jocular* an admirer; a boyfriend. [Say BOE for the singular, BOZE or BOE for the plural]

Beaufort scale *noun* a scale of wind speed ranging from 0 (calm) to 12 (hurricane). [Say BOE fort]

Beaujolais *noun* (*plural* **Beaujolais**) a red or white burgundy wine from the Beaujolais district of France. [Say BOE zhuh lay or boe zhuh LAY]

beaut *noun informal* an excellent or beautiful person or thing. [Say BYOOT]

beauteous *adjective literary* beautiful. [Say BYOOTY us]

beautician *noun* **1** a person who gives beauty treatment. **2** a person who runs or owns a beauty salon.

beautification *noun* the process of making improvements to the appearance of something: *fountains, planters, and other urban beautification projects*.

beautiful *adjective* **1** delighting the aesthetic senses: *a beautiful voice*. **2** enjoyable: *had a beautiful time*. **3** excellent: *a beautiful specimen*. ▶ **beautifully** *adverb*

beautify *verb* (**beautifies, beautified, beautifying**) make beautiful; adorn.

beauty • *noun* (*plural* **beauties**) **1 a** a combination of qualities such as shape, colour, etc., that pleases the aesthetic senses, esp. the sight. **b** a combination of qualities that pleases the intellect or moral sense: *the beauty of the argument*. **c** something beautiful. **2 a** an excellent specimen: *what a beauty!* **b** an attractive feature; an advantage: *that's the beauty of the plan!* **3** a beautiful woman. • *interjection* expressing satisfaction etc. PHRASES **beauty is only skin deep** a pleasing appearance is not a guide to character.

beauty contest *noun* (also **beauty pageant**) a competition in which participants, usu. women, are judged on their physical attractiveness.

beauty queen *noun* the woman judged most beautiful in a beauty contest.

beauty salon *noun* (also **beauty parlour**) an establishment in which beauty treatment, esp. hairdressing, is practised professionally.

beauty sleep *noun* sleep as contributing to one's beauty.

beauty spot *noun* **1** a place known for its beauty. **2** (also **beauty mark**) a small natural or artificial mark such as a mole on the face, considered to enhance another feature.

beauty treatment *noun* the use of cosmetics, hairdressing, etc. to enhance personal appearance.

beaux plural of BEAU. [Say BOZE or BOE]

Beaver • *noun* (*plural* **Beaver** or **Beavers**) **1** a member of an Aboriginal people of the Peace River area of Alberta and BC. **2** the Athapaskan language of this people. • *adjective* of or relating to the Beaver or their culture.

beaver • *noun* **1 a** (*plural* **beaver** or **beavers**) any large semiaquatic broad-tailed rodent of the genus *Castor*, native to North America, Europe, and Asia, and able to gnaw down trees and build dams. **b** this as an emblem of Canada. **2 a** the soft, light brown fur of this animal. **b** (also **beaver hat**) *hist.* a hat made from beaver wool. **3** (**Beaver**) a member of the youngest level (ages 5, 6, and 7) in Scouting. **4** *Cdn hist.* **a** = MADE BEAVER. **b** a coin used during the fur trade, having a value equal to one made beaver. • *verb informal* (usu. foll. by *away*) work hard.

beaver dam *noun* a dam of mud and sticks built by beavers across a stream or river.

beaver house *noun* (also **beaver lodge**) a den constructed by beavers from sticks and mud, usu. in a beaver pond.

beaver meadow *noun* a flat, fertile, treeless area created by the silting up of a beaver pond.

beaver pond *noun* a pool of water formed behind a beaver dam.

beaver tail *noun* **1** the broad, flat tail of a beaver. **2** (as an *adjective*) (usu. **beavertail**) having the round, broad shape of a beaver tail: *beavertail snowshoe*. **3** (**Beaver Tail**) *Cdn* (esp. *E. Ont.*) *proprietary* a flat oval of deep-fried dough served esp. with sugar and cinnamon.

beaver wool *noun* the short smooth hair under the thick fur of a beaver pelt.

bebop *noun* a type of jazz originating in the 1940s and characterized by complex harmony and rhythms. ▶ **bebopper** *noun* [Say BEE bop]

becalmed *adjective* (of a sailing ship) deprived of wind and unable to move.

because *conjunction* for the reason that; since. PHRASES **because of** on account of; by reason of.

beck *noun* PHRASES **at a person's beck and call** having constantly to obey a person's orders.

beckon *verb* **1** make a gesture with the hand, arm, or head to encourage or instruct someone to come nearer: *Miranda beckoned to Adam* ◊ *he beckoned Cameron over*. **2** seem to be appealing or inviting: *an academic career beckoned*. ▶ **beckoning** *adjective*

become *verb* (**becomes**; *past* **became**; *past participle* **become**; **becoming**) **1** begin to be. **2 a** look well on; suit: *blue becomes him*. **b** be suitable for: *behaviour that becomes a professional*. PHRASES **become of** happen to: *what will become of me?*

becoming *adjective* **1** flattering the appearance: *what a becoming dress!* **2** suitable; decorous: *a becoming modesty*. ▶ **becomingly** *adverb*

becquerel *noun* *Physics* the SI unit of radioactivity, corresponding to one radioactive decay of a nucleus per second. [Say BECKA rell]

B.Ed. *abbreviation* (*plural* **B.Ed.'s**) Bachelor of Education.

bed • *noun* **1 a** a piece of furniture used for sleeping or resting on. **b** a mattress and covers. **2** any place used by a person or animal for sleep or rest. **3** a bed and associated facilities, esp.: **a** for a patient in a hospital. **b** for a guest in a hotel etc. **4** the act of or usual time for being in bed. **5** the use of a bed: **a** *informal* for sexual intercourse. **b** for rest. **6** a place where something is embedded. **7** a level surface or other base upon which something rests. **8** the body or floor of a truck. **9** a plot of land in which plants are grown. **10** the bottom of a lake, sea, or river. **11** a layer of oysters etc. congregated in a particular spot. • *verb* (**beds, bedded, bedding**) **1** (usu. foll. by *down*) **a** put or go to bed. **b** settle, make oneself comfortable. **2** *informal* have sexual intercourse with. **3** (often foll. by *out*) plant in a garden bed. **4** embed; fix firmly in something. **5 a** arrange as a layer. **b** be or form a layer. PHRASES **bed of roses** a position of ease and luxury. **get up on the wrong side of the bed** be bad-tempered during the day. **go to bed 1** retire for the night. **2** (foll. by *with*) have sexual intercourse. **3** (of a publication) go to press. **be** (or **get**) **in bed with 1** have sexual intercourse with. **2** fraternize or consort with. **make the bed** tidy and arrange the covers of a bed after use. **make one's bed and lie in it** accept the consequences of one's actions. **put to bed 1** cause to go to bed. **2** make (a publication) ready for press.

bed and breakfast *noun* **1** accommodation and breakfast the next morning in a hotel etc. **2** an establishment providing this for one inclusive price.

bedbug *noun* any of several flat, wingless, bloodsucking insects which infest beds and houses.

bedclothes *plural noun* (also **bedcovers**) covers for a bed, such as sheets, blankets, etc.

bedding *noun* **1** the articles which compose a bed, esp. a mattress and bedclothes. **2** a layer of straw etc. on which livestock sleep.

bedding plant *noun* a plant, esp. an annual, suitable for a garden bed.

bedeck *verb* adorn: *she led us into a room bedecked with tinsel*. [Say be DECK]

bedevil *verb* (**bedevils, bedevilled, bedevilling**) **1** (of something bad) cause great and continual trouble to: *the problems that have recently bedevilled the club*. **2** (of a person) torment or harass: *he bedevilled them with petty practical jokes*. [Say be DEVIL]

bedfellow *noun* **1** a person who shares a bed with another. **2** an associate. PHRASES **strange bedfellows** an oddly assorted group of persons, things, etc.

bedlam *noun* a scene of uproar and confusion.

bedlamer *noun Cdn (Nfld)* a young harp seal. [Say BEDLAM er]

bed linen *noun* sheets and pillowcases.

Bedouin • *noun (plural* **Bedouin***)* a member of an Arabic-speaking nomadic people inhabiting the desert regions of the Middle East, traditionally herders of camels, goats, and sheep. • *adjective* of or relating to the Bedouin. [Say BED oo in]

bedpan *noun* a receptacle used by a bedridden patient for urine and feces.

bedraggled *adjective* untidy; the worse for wear: *tired, bedraggled, disgruntled tourists*.[Say be DRAGGLED]

bedrest *noun* confinement of an invalid to bed.

bedridden *adjective* confined to bed by infirmity, esp. permanently.

bedrock *noun* **1** solid rock underlying loose surface material, alluvial deposits, etc. **2** the underlying principles or facts of a theory, character, etc.

bedroll *noun* portable bedding rolled into a bundle.

bedroom *noun* **1** a room for sleeping in. **2** (as an *adjective*) of or referring to sexual suggestiveness: *bedroom eyes*.

bedroom community *noun (plural* **bedroom communities***)* (also **bedroom suburb**) a suburb outside a larger city, inhabited largely by commuters.

bedsheet *noun* = SHEET[1] 1.

bedside *noun* the space beside a bed.

bedside manner *noun* the manner of a doctor when attending a patient.

bedspread *noun* a top cover placed over a bed.

bedspring *noun* **1** a set of springs contained in a mattress or box spring. **2** any of the individual springs.

bedstead *noun* a framework of wood or metal supporting the springs and mattress of a bed.

bedtime *noun* the usual time for going to bed.

bedwetter *noun* a person, esp. a child, who urinates in bed.

bedwetting *noun* urination in bed while asleep.

bee *noun* **1** a stinging four-winged insect which collects nectar and pollen, produces wax and honey, and lives in large communities. **2** a social gathering at which communal work is performed: *quilting bee*. **3** a competition, e.g. in spelling etc., in which competitors take turns answering questions and are eliminated if their answers are wrong. PHRASES **a bee in one's bonnet** an obsession. **the bee's knees** *slang* something outstandingly good: *thinks he's the bee's knees*. **busy bee** a busy person.

SPELL CHECK
beech, beach [ABC ✓]

An expanse of sand or pebbles by a body of water is a **beach**.

---

beech *noun (plural* **beeches***)* **1** any large deciduous tree which grows in temperate regions and has smooth grey bark and glossy leaves. **2** (also **beechwood**) its wood.

beechnut *noun* the small rough-skinned fruit of the beech tree.

beef • *noun* **1** the flesh of a cow, steer, or bull used as food. **2** *(plural* **beeves***)* **a** a cow, steer, or bull raised for its meat. **b** its carcass. **3** *informal* muscle or flesh; strength, size, or power: *needs a little more beef on his bones*. **4** *(plural* **beefs***) slang* a complaint. • *verb slang* complain. PHRASES **beef up** *informal* strengthen, augment.

beefburger *noun* = HAMBURGER 1, 2.

beefcake *noun informal* muscular male physique, esp. when prominently displayed in photographs etc.

beefsteak *noun* a slice of beef, usu. for grilling.

beefsteak tomato *noun (plural* **beefsteak tomatoes***)* any of several large and firm varieties of tomato.

beefy *adjective (***beefier, beefiest***)* **1** like beef: *a beefy red wine*. **2** muscular or robust: *he shrugged his beefy shoulders* ◊ *a beefy linebacker*.

beehive *noun* **1** a structure in which bees are kept, traditionally dome-shaped but now usu. a box with the combs on wooden slides. **2** a busy place: *a beehive of activity*. **3** a woman's high cone-shaped hairstyle. **4** something having a domed shape: *a beehive hut*.

beehive burner *noun Cdn (BC)* a dome-shaped incinerator used to burn waste at a sawmill.

beekeeper *noun* a person who raises honeybees for their honey and beeswax. ▶ **beekeeping** *noun*

beeline *noun* a straight line between two places. PHRASES **make a beeline for** hurry directly to.

been *past participle of* BE.

been there, done that *interjection* indicating that the speaker has already experienced something or is familiar with it, esp. to the point of boredom or complacency.

beep • *noun* **1** a high-pitched noise, esp. one produced electronically. **2** the sound of a car horn. • *verb* **1** emit a beep. **2** cause to beep. **3** summon or alert by means of a beeping device.

beeper *noun* **1** a small device which emits a high-pitched signal when the user is contacted, usu. by telephone. **2** anything that emits a beep.

beer *noun* **1 a** an alcoholic drink made from yeast-fermented malt etc., flavoured with hops. **b** a serving of this. **2** any of several other carbonated drinks flavoured with plant extracts: *ginger beer*.

beer-bellied *adjective* (of a person) having a beer belly.

beer belly *noun (plural* **beer bellies***)* a protruding stomach caused by drinking large quantities of beer.

beer cellar *noun* **1** an underground room for storing beer. **2** a pub located in a basement or cellar.

beer garden *noun* an outdoor garden with tables and chairs where beer is sold and consumed.

beernut *noun* a shelled roasted peanut with a crisp sweet coating.

beer parlour *noun Cdn* a room in a hotel or tavern where beer is served.

beer slinger *noun Cdn informal* a bartender. ▶ **beer slinging** *noun*

beery *adjective (***beerier, beeriest***)* **1** showing the influence of drink in one's appearance or behaviour: *many beery pledges were made*. **2** smelling or tasting of beer: *stale beery breath*.

beeswax *noun* **1** the wax secreted by bees to make honeycombs. **2** this wax refined and used to make candles, ointments, polishes, etc. **3** *informal* business: *mind your own beeswax*.

SPELL CHECK
beet, beat [ABC ✓]

To strike or defeat someone or something is to **beat** them. A rhythm is a **beat**.

---

beet *noun* any plant of the genus *Beta*, esp. *B. vulgaris*, having an edible spherical dark red root used as a vegetable. *See also* SUGAR BEET.

beetle • *noun* an insect with modified front wings forming hard protective cases closing over the back wings. • *verb (***beetles, beetled, beetling***) informal* make one's way hurriedly or with short, quick steps: *beetled off down the street*.

beet red *noun & adjective* an extremely dark shade of red, esp. describing a deep blush.

beeves *plural of* BEEF 2.

B

befall *verb* (**befalls**; *past* **befell**; *past participle* **befallen**; **befalling**) (esp. of something bad) happen to: *a similar fate befell him*.

befit *verb* (**befits**, **befitted**, **befitting**) be appropriate for; suit: *as befits a Quaker, he was a humane man*.

befog *verb* (**befogs**, **befogged**, **befogging**) cause to become confused: *her brain was befogged with lack of sleep*.

before • *conjunction* **1** earlier than the time when. **2** rather than that: *would starve before she stole*. • *preposition* **1 a** in front of. **b** ahead of. **c** under the impulse of: *recoiled before the attack*. **d** awaiting: *the future before them*. **2** earlier than; preceding. **3** rather than: *death before dishonour*. **4 a** in the presence of: *appear before the judge*. **b** for the attention of: *a plan put before the committee*. • *adverb* **1** earlier than the time in question; already. **2** ahead: *go before*. **3** on the front: *hit before and behind*. PHRASES **before God** a solemn oath meaning "as God sees me".

Before Christ *adverb* (of a date) reckoned backwards from the birth of Christ. Abbreviation: **BC**.

beforehand *adverb* in anticipation; in advance; in readiness: *had prepared the meal beforehand*.

befoul *verb* make dirty: *land, air, and water were befouled by industrial waste*.

befriend *verb* be or become friendly with.

befuddle *verb* (**befuddles**, **befuddled**, **befuddling**) cause to become unable to think clearly: *befuddled newspaper readers tried to distinguish the warring factions*. ▶ **befuddlement** *noun*

WRITING TIP
beg the question

The expression **beg the question** can be used to mean "raise the issue" or "invite the obvious question", as in *The rising cost of gasoline prices begs the question, how long can we afford to keep driving our cars?* This is by far the most common use today and widely accepted, despite the fact that some people feel **beg the question** should only be used in its original sense, "assume the truth of an argument without arguing it", as in *By spending so much on education in the fight against drugs we are begging the question of the effectiveness of education*, i.e. we are assuming that through education we can radically reduce drug-taking.

---

beg *verb* (**begs**, **begged**, **begging**) **1** ask for (esp. food, money, etc.): *begged for food* ◊ *a piece of bread which I begged from a farmer*. **2** ask earnestly or humbly: *please, I beg of you* ◊ *I begged her to come with me*. **3** ask formally for: *beg leave*. **4** (of a dog etc.) sit up with the front paws raised expectantly. **5** take or ask leave (to do something): *I beg to differ*. **6** demand: *stories begging to be written*. PHRASES **beg off** decline to take part or attend. **beg a person's pardon** apologize. **beg the question 1** *disputed* pose the question. **2** assume that an argument or proposition is true even though it has not been proved. **3** *informal* evade a difficulty. **go begging** (of a chance or a thing) not be taken.

beget *verb* (**begets**; *past* **begat** or **begot**; *past participle* **begotten**; **begetting**) **1** be the parent, esp. the father of. **2** cause: *violence begets violence*. ▶ **begetter** *noun*

beggar • *noun* **1** a person who begs, esp. one who lives by begging. **2** *informal* a person; a fellow: *poor beggar*. • *verb* **1** reduce to poverty: *why should I beggar myself for you?* **2** exhaust the resources of: *it beggars the imagination to believe that they weren't aware of what was going on*. PHRASES **beggars can't be choosers** those without other resources must take what is offered.

beggary *noun* extreme poverty.

begin *verb* (**begins**; *past* **began**; *past participle* **begun**;

beginning) **1** start; perform the first part of. **2** come into being; arise: **a** in time: *the strike began last week*. **b** in space: *our property begins beyond the river*. **3** start at a certain time: *then began to feel ill*. **4** be begun: *the meeting will begin at 7*. **5 a** start speaking: *"No," she began*. **b** take the first step; be the first to do something: *who wants to begin?* **6** *informal* (usu. with *neg.*) show any attempt or likelihood: *can't begin to compete*. PHRASES **begin at** start from. **begin on** (or **upon**) set to work at. **begin with** take (a subject, task, etc.) first or as a starting point. **to begin with** in the first place.

beginner *noun* a person beginning to learn a skill etc.

beginner's luck *noun* good luck supposed to attend a beginner at games etc.

beginning *noun* **1** the time or place at which anything begins. **2** a source or origin. **3** the first part. PHRASES **the beginning of the end** the first clear sign of the end of something.

begonia *noun* any plant of the genus *Begonia* with brightly coloured sepals and no petals, and often having brilliant glossy foliage. [Say buh GOAN ya]

begot *past of* BEGET.

begotten *past participle of* BEGET.

begrudge *verb* (**begrudges**, **begrudged**, **begrudging**) **1** give reluctantly or resentfully: *people should not begrudge the money that is spent on the arts*. **2** envy (a person) the possession of: *she begrudged Martin his affluence*. ▶ **begrudgingly** *adverb*

beguile *verb* (**beguiles**, **beguiled**, **beguiling**) **1** charm or enchant, often in an underhand or deceptive way: *he beguiled the voters with his good looks*. **2** help time pass pleasantly: *an entertaining story to beguile your idle moments*. **3** trick; cheat: *beguiled him into paying*. ▶ **beguiling** *adjective* **beguilingly** *adverb* [Say be GILE (with G as in *GIVE*)]

beguine *noun* **1** a popular dance of West Indian origin. **2** its rhythm. [Say buh GEEN (with G as in *GEAR*)]

begun *past participle of* BEGIN.

behalf *noun* PHRASES **on behalf of 1** in the interests of (a person, principle, etc.). **2** as representative of: *acting on behalf of my client*.

behave *verb* (**behaves**, **behaved**, **behaving**) **1 a** act or react (in a specified way): *behaved well*. **b** (esp. to or of a child) conduct oneself properly. **c** (of a machine etc.) work well (or in a specified way): *the computer is not behaving today*. **2 behave oneself** show good manners. PHRASES **behave towards** treat (in a specified way).

behaviour *noun* (also **behavior**) **1 a** the way one conducts oneself; manners. **b** the treatment of others; moral conduct. **2** the way in which a vehicle, machine, chemical substance, etc., acts or works. **3** *Psychology* observable pattern of actions (of a person, animal, etc.), esp. in response to a stimulus. PHRASES **be on one's best behaviour** behave well.

behavioural *adjective* (also **behavioral**) of or relating to behaviour.

behavioural science *noun* the scientific study of human behaviour.

behaviourism *noun* (also **behaviorism**) *Psychology* **1** the theory that human and animal behaviour can be explained in terms of conditioning, without appeal to thoughts or feelings, and that psychological disorders are best treated by altering behaviour patterns. **2** such treatment in practice. ▶ **behaviourist** *noun*

behaviour therapy *noun* (*plural* **behaviour therapies**) the treatment of neurotic symptoms by training the patient's responses.

behead *verb* cut off the head of (a person), esp. as a form of execution. ▶ **beheading** *noun*

behemoth *noun* an enormous creature or thing: *their new SUV was a real behemoth*. [Say buh HEE muth]

behest *noun* a command; a request: *they had assembled at his behest*.

behind • *preposition* **1 a** in, towards, or to the rear of. **b** on the farther side of: *behind the bush*. **c** hidden by: *something behind that remark*. **2 a** in the past in relation to: *trouble is behind me now*. **b** late in relation to: *behind schedule*. **3** inferior to: *behind the others in math*. **4 a** in support of: *she's behind the idea*. **b** responsible for; giving rise to: *the reasons behind his resignation*. **5** in the tracks of; following. • *adverb* **1 a** in or to or towards the rear. **b** on the further side. **2** remaining after departure: *stay behind*. **3 a** in arrears: *behind with the rent*. **b** late in accomplishing a task etc.: *working too slowly and getting behind*. **4** in an inferior position: *the team was two points behind*. **5** following: *her dog running behind*. • *noun informal* the buttocks. PHRASES **behind a person's back** without a person's knowledge. **behind the times** antiquated. **come from behind** win after trailing. **fall** (or **lag**) **behind** not keep up; begin to trail. **put behind one 1** refuse to consider. **2** get over (an unhappy experience etc.).

behold *verb* (**beholds, beheld, beholding**) *literary* **1** see or observe (someone or something, esp. of remarkable or impressive nature): *the botanical gardens were a wonder to behold* ◊ *behold your lord and prince!* **2** pay attention.

beholden *adjective* owing gratitude or having a duty to someone in return for help or service: *she didn't like feeling beholden to anyone*.

beholder *noun literary* a person who beholds. PHRASES **in the eye of the beholder** judged differently by different people: *she thinks he's gorgeous but he doesn't do a thing for me; beauty is in the eye of the beholder*.

behoove *verb* (**behooves, behooved, behooving**) (also esp. *Brit.* **behove; behoves, behoved, behoving**) *formal* **1** be a duty or responsibility: *it behooved him to point out that no one in the British press knew much about Canada*. **2** (usu. with *neg.*) be appropriate or suitable: *it ill behooves him to protest*.

beige *noun & adjective* a very pale yellowish brown.

being *noun* **1** existence. **2** the nature or essence (of a person etc.): *his whole being revolted*. **3** a human being. **4** anything that exists or is imagined.

bejesus *noun* (also **bejabbers**) *informal* used as an intensifier: *beat the bejesus out of him*.

bejewelled *adjective* adorned with jewels.

bel *noun* a unit used in the comparison of power levels in electrical communication or intensities of sound, corresponding to an intensity ratio of 10 to 1.

belabour *verb* (also **belabor**) **1** argue or elaborate (a subject) in excessive detail: *there is no need to belabour the point*. **2** attack verbally: *belaboured the candidate*. **3** beat: *Bernard was belabouring Jed with his fists*.

Belarusian • *noun* **1** a native or national of Belarus, a country in Eastern Europe formerly part of the Soviet Union. **2** the Slavic language of Belarus. • *adjective* of Belarus, its people, or language. [Say bella ROOSE yun]

belated *adjective* coming late or too late. ▶ **belatedly** *adverb* **belatedness** *noun*

belay (**belays, belayed, belaying**) • *verb* **1** secure (a rope) around a cleat, pin, rock, etc. **2** *Nautical* stop, halt: *belay there!* • *noun* **1** a spike of rock etc. used for belaying a rope in climbing. **2** an act of belaying. [Say be LAY]

bel canto *noun* a lyrical style of operatic singing using a full rich broad tone and smooth phrasing: *Bellini's bel canto arias*. [Say bell CANTO]

belch • *verb* (**belches, belched, belching**) **1** burp. **2 a** (of a chimney, volcano, etc.) send (smoke etc.) out or up: *factory chimneys belching out smoke*. **b** gush forth: *flames belch from the wreckage*. • *noun* a burp.

beleaguered *adjective* **1** put in a very difficult situation: *the board is supporting the beleaguered director amid calls for his resignation*. **2** besieged: *he is leading a relief force to the aid of the beleaguered city*. [Say be LEE gurd]

belfry *noun* (*plural* **belfries**) a tower or steeple housing bells, esp. forming part of a church. [Say BELL free]

Belgian • *noun* **1** a native or national of Belgium. **2** a person of Belgian descent. **3** (also **Belgian horse**) a draft horse of a large, heavy, and short-legged breed of Flemish origin. • *adjective* of or relating to Belgium.

Belgian endive *noun* the crown of the chicory plant which has been whitened by blanching, used in salads.

belie *verb* (**belies, belied, belying**) **1** (of an appearance) fail to give a true notion or impression of (something): *her lively alert manner belies her age*. **2** fail to fulfill or justify (a claim or expectation): *the quality of the music seems to belie the criticism*. [Say be LIE]

belief *noun* **1 a** a firm opinion or conviction: *my belief is that he did it*. **b** an acceptance (of a thing, fact, statement, etc.): *belief in the afterlife*. **c** a person's religion; religious conviction. **2** (usu. foll. by *in*) trust or confidence. PHRASES **beyond belief** incredible. **to the best of my belief** in my genuine opinion.

believe *verb* (**believes, believed, believing**) **1** accept as true or as conveying the truth. **2** think, suppose: *I believe it's raining*. **3 a** have faith in the existence of: *believes in God*. **b** have confidence in: *believes in alternative medicine*. **c** have trust in the advisability of: *believes in telling the truth*. **4** have (esp. religious) faith. PHRASES **believe one's eyes** (or **ears**) accept that what one apparently sees or hears etc. is true. **believe it or not** *informal* it is true though surprising. **make believe** pretend. ▶ **believability** *noun* **believable** *adjective* **believably** *adverb*

believer *noun* **1** an adherent of a specified religion. **2** a person who believes, esp. in the efficacy of something: *a great believer in exercise*.

belittle *verb* (**belittles, belittled, belittling**) make (a person, action, etc.) seem unimportant or worthless: *I don't wish to belittle your disappointment* ◊ *he was constantly belittling her*. ▶ **belittlement** *noun*

bell¹ • *noun* **1** a hollow usu. metal object in the shape of a deep upturned cup usu. widening at the lip, made to sound a clear musical note when struck. **2 a** a sound or stroke of a bell, esp. as a signal. **b** *Nautical* (preceded by a numeral) the time as indicated every half-hour of a watch by the striking of the ship's bell one to eight times. **3** anything that sounds like or functions as a bell, esp. an electronic device that rings etc. as a signal. **4 a** any bell-shaped object or part, e.g. of a musical instrument. **b** the corolla of a flower when bell-shaped. **5** *Music* (in *plural*) a set of cylindrical metal tubes of different lengths, suspended in a frame and played by being struck with a hammer. **6** *Cdn* the dangling appendage under a moose's neck. • *verb* **1** provide with a bell or bells; attach a bell to. **2** (foll. by *out*) form into the shape of the lip of a bell. PHRASES **bells and whistles** *informal* attractive but non-essential components; gimmicks. **bell the cat** attempt something daring or dangerous. **clear** (or **sound**) **as a bell** perfectly clear or sound. **ring a bell** *informal* revive a distant recollection; sound familiar. **saved by the bell** spared (from an unpleasant occurrence) at the last moment. **with bells on** enthusiastically.

bell² • *noun* the cry of a stag or buck at rutting time. • *verb* make this cry.

Bella Bella *noun* = HEILTSUK *noun*.

Bella Coola *noun* = NUXALK *noun*.

belladonna *noun* **1** a poisonous plant with purple

flowers and purple-black berries. **2** a drug prepared from its root and leaves. [Say bella DONNA]

bell-bottom *noun* **1** a wide flare below the knee of a trouser leg. **2** (in *plural*) trousers with bell-bottoms. ▶ **bell-bottomed** *adjective*

bellboy *noun* = BELLHOP.

bellcast *adjective* designating a style of roof typical of traditional architecture in Quebec, with gables having the shape of a squared-off bell.

belle *noun* **1** a beautiful woman. **2** a woman recognized as the most beautiful: *the belle of the ball*. [Say BELL]

belle époque noun the period of settled comfort and prosperity before the First World War. [Say bell ay POCK]

bellhop *noun* a hotel employee who helps guests with luggage, shows them to rooms, etc.

bellicose *adjective* inclined to war or fighting: *increasingly bellicose statements by both superpowers*. ▶ **bellicosity** *noun* [Say BELLA cose, bella COSSA tee]

bellied *adjective* (in *combination*) having a belly of a specified kind: *pot-bellied*. [Say BELL eed]

belligerence *noun* aggressive or warlike behaviour or attitudes: *the men glared down at us with belligerence ◊ the openly expressed belligerence of Russian leaders showed that defying the US was popular*. [Say buh LIDGER ince]

belligerent • *adjective* **1** engaged in war or conflict as recognized by international law. **2** hostile and aggressive: *the mood at the meeting was belligerent*. • *noun* a nation or person engaged in war or conflict: *chemical weapons which the major belligerents had stockpiled during World War II*. ▶ **belligerently** *adverb* [Say buh LIDGER int]

bellman *noun* (*plural* **bellmen**) = BELLHOP.

bellow • *verb* **1 a** emit a deep loud roar. **b** cry or shout with pain. **2** utter loudly and usu. angrily. • *noun* a bellowing sound. [Say BELLO]

bellows *plural noun* (also treated as *singular*) a device with an air bag that emits a stream of air when squeezed, esp. (also **pair of bellows**) a kind with two handles used for blowing air onto a fire or a kind used in a harmonium or small organ.

bell pepper *noun* see PEPPER *noun* 2.

bell-ringing *noun* **1** the ringing of church bells. **2** *Cdn* the ringing of bells in a legislative assembly to summon members for a vote, esp. when provoked or prolonged as a tactic for stalling debate.

bellwether *noun* **1** an indicator or predictor of something: *this is a bellwether riding; if it votes Conservative, the election is likely to go to the Conservatives*. **2** the leading sheep of a flock, on whose neck a bell is hung.

belly • *noun* (*plural* **bellies**) **1** the part of the human body below the chest, containing the stomach and bowels. **2** the stomach, esp. representing the body's need for food. **3** the front surface of the body from the waist to the groin. **4** the corresponding part or surface of the body of an animal. **5** a cavity or bulging part of anything. • *verb* (**bellies, bellied, bellying**) swell or cause to swell; bulge: *as she leaned forward her sweater bellied out*. PHRASES **belly up** *informal* approach closely: *bellied up to the bar*. **go belly up** *informal* fail; become bankrupt; die.

bellyache *informal* • *noun* a stomach pain. • *verb* (**bellyaches, bellyached, bellyaching**) complain noisily or persistently. ▶ **bellyacher** *noun*

belly button *noun informal* the navel.

belly dance *noun* a solo dance of Middle Eastern origin performed by a woman and involving the rippling of the abdominal muscles. ▶ **belly dancer** *noun* **belly dancing** *noun*

bellyflop *informal* • *noun* a dive in which the body lands

with the belly flat on the water. • *verb* (**bellyflops, bellyflopped, bellyflopping**) perform this dive.

bellyful *noun* (*plural* **bellyfuls**) **1** enough to eat. **2** *informal* enough or more than enough of anything: *she had had her bellyful of hospitals*.

belong *verb* **1** (foll. by *to*) **a** be the property of. **b** be rightly assigned to as a duty, right, part, member, characteristic, etc. **c** be a member of (a club, family, group, etc.). **2** have the right personal or social qualities to be a member of a particular group: *he's nice but just doesn't belong*. **3** (foll. by *in, under*) **a** be rightly placed or classified. **b** fit a particular environment. ▶ **belonging** *noun*

belongings *plural noun* personal possessions.

beloved • *adjective* dearly loved. • *noun* a dearly loved person. [Say LUVD or be LOVE id]

below • *preposition* **1** lower in position. **2** beneath the surface of; at or to a greater depth than: *head below water ◊ below 50 metres*. **3** lower in rank, position, or importance than. • *adverb* **1** at or to a lower point or level. **2 a** on or to a lower floor or deck: *went below*. **b** downstream. **3** further down on a page or later in an article, book, etc. **4** on the lower side: *looks similar above and below*. **5** lower than zero on a temperature scale: *20 below*. **6** *literary* **a** on earth. **b** in hell.

belt • *noun* **1 a** a flat encircling strip of leather, cloth, etc., worn around the waist or from the shoulder to the opposite hip to support clothes, tools, weapons, etc., or as a decorative accessory. **2 a** a belt worn as a sign of rank or achievement. **b** a belt of a specified colour indicating the wearer's level of proficiency in judo, karate, etc. (compare BLACK BELT). **3 a** a circular band of material used as a driving medium in machinery etc. **b** a conveyor belt. **c** a flexible strip for feeding a machine gun with ammunition. **4** a seat belt. **5** a strip of colour or texture etc. differing from that on either side. **6** a zone or region of distinct character or occupancy: *wheat belt ◊ Bible belt*. **7** *informal* a heavy blow or stroke. **8** a strip of reinforcing material (esp. steel) placed beneath the tread of a tire for durability. **9** *informal* a drink. • *verb* **1** put a belt around. **2** fasten with a belt. **3** *informal* hit hard. **4** *informal* rush, hurry: *belted along*. **5** drink quickly. PHRASES **below the belt** unfair or unfairly. **belt out** *informal* sing or utter loudly and forcibly. **belt up** *informal* **1** be quiet. **2** put on a seat belt. **tighten one's belt** curtail expenditure. **under one's belt 1** (of food or drink) consumed. **2** securely acquired: *has a degree under her belt*.

belted *adjective* **1** fastened or ornamented with a belt. **2** (of a tire) having a strip of reinforcing material beneath the tread.

belted kingfisher *noun* = KINGFISHER.

belter *noun* a loud, powerful singer or song.

beltline *noun* **1** the waistline. **2** the area where the hood and doors of an automobile meet the windshield and windows.

beluga *noun* **1** a whale of the Arctic Ocean, found as far south as the St. Lawrence estuary, and white when adult. **2 a** a large kind of sturgeon of the Caspian and Black Seas. **b** caviar obtained from it. [Say buh LOOGA]

belying *pres. part. of* BELIE. [Say be LYING]

bemoan *verb* express discontent or sorrow over: *there's no use bemoaning your lot, just get on with your life*.

bemuse *verb* (**bemuses, bemused, bemusing**) (usu. as **bemused** *adjective*) cause (often somewhat amused) puzzlement. ▶ **bemusedly** *adverb* **bemusement** *noun*

bench • *noun* **1** (*plural* **benches**) a long seat, with or without a back, for several people. **2** a work table used by a carpenter etc., or in a laboratory. **3** (**the bench**) **a** the office or status of a judge. **b** the seat on which

the judge or judges sit in court. **c** a court of law. **d** judges and magistrates collectively. **4** *Sport* **a** a seat used by players when not participating in a game. **b** the substitute players collectively. **5** *Parliament* a seat: *back bench*. **6 a** a bank or shelf of ground. **b** a level ledge in earthwork, masonry, etc. **c** = BENCHLAND. • *verb* (**benches, benched, benching**) *Sport* remove or retire (a player) to the bench esp. for poor performance. PHRASES **behind the bench** *Hockey* serving as a coach. **on the bench** serving as a judge or magistrate.

bench-clearing *adjective* designating an incident in which an entire sports team leaves the players' bench and enters the playing area, usu. to engage in a brawl.

bencher *noun* **1** (*in combination*) *Parliament* an occupant of a specified bench: *backbencher*. **2** *Cdn Law* a member of the regulating body of the law society in all provinces except New Brunswick.

benchland *noun* a relatively narrow, naturally occurring terrace often backed by a steep slope.

benchmark • *noun* **1** a surveyor's mark cut in a wall, post, etc., used as a reference point in measuring comparative elevations. **2** a standard or point of reference: *a benchmark case*. **3** (also **benchmark test**) a way of testing a computer, usu. by a set of programs run on a series of different machines. • *verb* test or check by comparison with a benchmark.

bench penalty *noun* (*plural* **bench penalties**) (also **bench minor**) *Hockey* a minor penalty assessed to a team as a whole and served by a single player.

bench press • *noun* (*plural* **bench presses**) an exercise in which a person lying face upwards on a bench with feet on the floor raises a barbell by extending both arms upward from the chest. • *verb* (**bench presses, bench pressed, bench pressing**) raise (a weight) in a bench press.

benchwarmer *noun* *informal* an athlete who routinely is not selected to play.

bend • *verb* (**bends, bent, bending**) **1 a** force or adapt (esp. something straight) into a curve or angle. **b** (of an object) be altered in this way. **2** move or stretch in a curved course. **3** incline or cause to incline from the vertical. **4** direct or devote (one's attention, energies, etc.): *Eric bent all his efforts to persuading them to donate blankets* ◊ *she bent once more to the task of diverting the wedding guests*. **5** turn (one's steps or eyes) in a new direction. • *noun* **1** a curve in a road or other course. **2** a curved or angled part of anything. **3** (**the bends**) *informal* = DECOMPRESSION SICKNESS. PHRASES **bend one's elbow** drink alcohol. **bend someone's ear** talk to someone, esp. with great eagerness or in order to ask a favour. **bend the rules** interpret or modify rules etc. to suit oneself. **on bended knee** kneeling, esp. in reverence, supplication, or submission. **round the bend** *informal* crazy, insane. ▶ **bendable** *adjective*

bender *noun* **1** *slang* a wild drinking spree. **2** an instrument for bending (pipes etc.).

bendy *adjective* (**bendier, bendiest**) *informal* capable of bending; soft and flexible.

beneath • *preposition* **1** under. **2** unworthy of; too demeaning for: *it was beneath him to reply*. • *adverb* underneath.

Benedictine • *noun* **1** a monk or nun of an order following the description of monastic life set out by St. Benedict (c. 480–c. 550), which prescribed an ordered communal life in which the monks or nuns renounce private property, practise obedience, and devote their time to worship services, prayer, spiritual reading, and work. **2** *proprietary* a liqueur of brandy and herbs, originally made by Benedictines in France. • *adjective* of St. Benedict or the Benedictines. [Say benna DICK teen]

benediction *noun* **1** the utterance of a blessing, esp.

at the end of a religious service. **2** (**Benediction**) a chiefly Catholic service in which the congregation is blessed with the Host, usu. displayed in a monstrance. **3** the state of being blessed. [Say benna DICK sh'n]

benefaction *noun* **1** a donation or gift. **2** an act of giving: *neither private benefaction nor provincial grants met all the costs*. [Say benna FACTION]

benefactor *noun* a person who gives support (esp. financial) to a person or cause. ▶ **benefactress** *noun* [Say BENNA factor]

benefice *noun* **1** a position held by a member of the clergy that ensures an income or a specified property. **2** the income from such a position. [Say BENNA fiss]

beneficence *noun* generosity, kindness: *the arts in Canada have to rely in large part on private beneficence*. [Say buh NEFFA since]

beneficent *adjective* **1** doing good; generous, actively kind: *belief in a beneficent God*. **2** resulting in good: *a beneficent technological discovery such as antibiotics*. ▶ **beneficently** *adverb* [Say buh NEFFA sint]

beneficial *adjective* advantageous; having benefits: *building the opera house had a beneficial effect on the economy* ◊ *the process was beneficial to both the supplier and the customer*. ▶ **beneficially** *adverb*

beneficiary *noun* (*plural* **beneficiaries**) **1** a person who receives or is entitled to receive benefits, esp. under a will or life insurance policy. **2** a person who benefits from a particular event, action, etc. [Say benna FISHY airy or benna FISHERY]

benefit • *noun* **1** a favourable or helpful factor or circumstance; advantage, profit. **2** (often in *plural*) allowance of money etc. to which a person is entitled from a pension plan, government support programs, etc.: *unemployment insurance benefits*. **3** (often in *plural*) an advantage other than salary associated with a job, e.g. dental coverage, life insurance, etc. **4** a public performance, sporting event, etc. held in order to raise money for a particular charity etc. • *verb* (**benefits, benefited, benefiting**) **1** do good to; be of advantage to; improve. **2** (often foll. by *from, by*) receive an advantage or gain. PHRASES **the benefit of the doubt** assumption of a person's innocence, rightness, etc., rather than the contrary in the absence of proof.

benefit of clergy *noun* church sanction or approval: *they lived together without benefit of clergy*.

benevolent *adjective* **1** well meaning and kindly: *a benevolent deity*. **2** charitable: *benevolent fund*. ▶ **benevolence** *noun* **benevolently** *adverb* [Say buh NEVVA l'nt]

Bengali • *noun* **1** a native of Bengal, a region in the northeast of the Indian subcontinent. **2** the language of this people, descended from Sanskrit. • *adjective* of or relating to Bengal or its people or language. [Say ben GALLY or ben GOLLY]

Bengal tiger *noun* a tiger of a variety found in the Indian subcontinent, having unbroken stripes.

benighted *adjective* **1** intellectually or morally ignorant: *they saw themselves as bringers of culture to poor benighted societies*. **2** unfortunate: *the poor benighted souls left under the oppression of the organized state*.

benign *adjective* **1** gentle, kindly: *her benign but firm manner*. **2** (of climate etc.) mild, favourable. **3** (of a disease, tumour, etc.) not malignant. **4** harmless: *benign cleaning products* ◊ *a policy of benign neglect*. ▶ **benignly** *adverb* [Say buh NINE]

bonjamina ficus *noun* (also **Benjamin's fig**) = FICUS BENJAMINA. [Say benja MEENA]

Bennett buggy *noun* (*plural* **Bennett buggies**) *Cdn hist.* a car hitched to horses or oxen, used during the Depression by owners who could not afford gasoline etc.

benny *noun* (*plural* **bennies**) *slang* an amphetamine tablet, esp. as a stimulant.

bent¹ ● *verb past and past participle of* BEND *verb*. ● *adjective* **1** curved or having an angle. **2** determined to do or have: *two couples bent on celebration*. ● *noun* **1** an inclination or bias. **2** (foll. by *for*) a talent for something specified: *a bent for mimicry*. PHRASES **bent out of shape** *informal* upset or annoyed, esp. unreasonably so.

bent² *noun* **1 a** (also **bent grass**) any grass of the genus *Agrostis*, a hardy grass used esp. in golf courses. **b** any of various grasslike reeds, rushes, or sedges. **2 a** stiff stalk of a grass usu. with a flexible base.

bentonite *noun* a highly absorbent clay with many uses, esp. as filler, cat litter, etc. [Say BENTA nite]

benzene *noun* a colourless cancer-causing volatile liquid found in coal tar, petroleum, etc., and used as a solvent and in making plastics etc. [Say BEN zeen]

benzene ring *noun* the hexagonal unsaturated ring of six carbon atoms in the benzene molecule.

benzodiazepine *noun* any of a class of compounds used as tranquilizers, including Valium. [Say benzo die AZZA peen]

benzoic acid *noun* a white crystalline substance used esp. as a food preservative. [Say ben ZO ick]

Beothuk (also **Beothuck**) ● *noun* **1** (*plural* **Beothuk** or **Beothuks**) a member of an Aboriginal people formerly inhabiting Newfoundland but extinct since the early 19th century. **2** the Algonquian language of this people. ● *adjective* of the Beothuk. [Say bee OTH uck]

bequeath *verb* **1** leave (an estate or piece of property) to a person by will: *bequeathed his entire estate to charity*. **2** hand down to posterity: *the historical knowledge bequeathed to them by all the foregoing centuries*. [Say bee QUEETH]

bequest *noun* **1** the action of bequeathing: *this painting was acquired by bequest*. **2** money or property given in a will: *a $1,000 bequest*.

berate *verb* (**berates**, **berated**, **berating**) criticize angrily.

Berber ● *noun* **1** a member of the indigenous mainly Muslim Caucasian peoples of N Africa (now mainly in Morocco and Algeria) speaking related languages. **2** the language or group of languages of these peoples. **3** (**berber**) a type of sturdy carpet having large tightly woven loops, and often having the appearance of tweed. ● *adjective* of the Berbers or their language.

bereaved *adjective* saddened by the death of a loved one. [Say be REEVD]

bereavement *noun* the fact of having lost a relation, friend, etc., by death. [Say be REEV mint]

bereft *adjective* deprived (esp. of a non-material asset): *bereft of hope*. [Say be REFT]

beret *noun* a round brimless cap of felt or cloth that is close-fitting and lies flat on the head. [Say buh RAY]

berg *noun* = ICEBERG.

bergamot *noun* **1** a citrus tree bearing fruit similar to an orange, from the rind of which a fragrant essential oil is extracted. **2** the oil or essence itself, used esp. in perfumes, Earl Grey tea, etc. **3** any of several plants of the mint family smelling like bergamot, esp.: **a** (also **wild bergamot**) a North American plant with purple or pink flowers. **b** a related plant grown for its showy heads of scarlet flowers. **c** a Mediterranean mint grown for its fragrance. [Say BERGA mot]

beriberi *noun* a disease causing inflammation of the nerves due to a lack of vitamin B$_1$ (thiamine), and mainly associated with rice-based diets. [Say berry BERRY]

berkelium *noun* a radioactive metallic element produced by bombardment of americium. [Say ber KEELY um or BERKLY um]

berm *noun* **1 a** a flat strip of land, raised bank, or terrace bordering a river etc. **b** a narrow path or grass strip beside a road. **2 a** narrow ledge, esp. in a fortification between a ditch and a parapet.

Bermuda shorts *plural noun* (also **Bermudas**) knee-length shorts.

berried *adjective* **1** (of a plant) bearing berries: *yellow-berried*. **2** (of a lobster) egg-bearing.

SPELL CHECK

berry, bury

To place something in the ground is to **bury** it.

---

berry *noun* (*plural* **berries**) **1** any small roundish juicy fruit without a stone. **2** *Botany* a fruit with its seeds enclosed in pulp, e.g. the grape, gooseberry, tomato, etc. **3** any of various kernels or seeds, esp. of wheat etc. **4** an egg of a fish or lobster.

berrying *noun* gathering berries.

berserk *adjective* (esp. in **go berserk**) wild, frenzied.

berth ● *noun* **1** a fixed bunk on a ship, train, etc., for sleeping in. **2** a ship's place at a wharf. **3** room for a ship to swing at anchor. **4** sufficient room for a ship to manoeuvre. **5** *Sport* an opportunity for a team or athlete to compete: *a playoff berth*. **6** *Cdn Forestry* a specified area of timberland in which a company or individual is entitled to fell trees. **7** *Cdn* (*Nfld*) a particular area claimed by a boat on fishing grounds. ● *verb* **1** moor (a ship) in its berth. **2** provide a sleeping place for. **3** (of a ship) come to its mooring place. PHRASES **give a wide berth to** avoid: *the first ministers gave a wide berth to the constitutional issue*.

beryl *noun* **1** a kind of transparent precious stone, esp. pale green, blue, or yellow, and consisting of beryllium aluminum silicate. **2** a mineral species which includes this, emerald, and aquamarine. [Sounds like *BARREL*]

beryllium *noun* a hard white metallic element used in making light corrosion-resistant alloys. [Say buh RILLY um]

beseech *verb* (**beseeches**; *past* and *past participle* **beseeched** or **besought**; **beseeching**) ask (someone) for something in an anxious way: *she beseeched him to stop ◊ please, I beseech you!* ▶ **beseeching** *adjective* **beseechingly** *adverb*

beset *verb* (**besets**, **beset**, **besetting**) **1** (of a problem or difficulty) trouble or threaten persistently: *was beset by pain and anxiety after his injury*. **2** surround and attack or harass persistently: *beset by clouds of mosquitoes*. **3** surround or hem in: *the ship was beset by ice and finally sank*.

besetting sin *noun* a fault to which a person or institution is particularly prone: *greed is my besetting sin*.

beside *preposition* **1** at the side of; near. **2** compared with. **3** irrelevant to: *beside the point*. PHRASES **beside oneself** overcome with worry, anger, etc.

besides ● *preposition* **1** in addition to. **2** other than; apart from. ● *adverb* in addition.

besiege *verb* (**besieges**, **besieged**, **besieging**) **1** surround a place with armed forces in order to capture it or force its surrender: *Louisbourg was besieged by the British navy in 1745*. **2** crowd around oppressively: *she spent the whole day besieged by journalists*. **3** harass with requests: *the TV station was besieged with calls*. **4** assail, beset: *besieged by growing crime, violence, and corruption, the city is in decay*. ▶ **besieger** *noun*

besmirch *verb* (**besmirches**, **besmirched**, **besmirching**) **1** make something discoloured or dirty: *besmirched with blood*. **2** dishonour; damage the reputation of: *he had besmirched his family's good name*. [Say be SMIRCH]

besotted *adjective* infatuated: *they were besotted with each other*. [Say be SOTTED]

besought *past and past participle of* BESEECH.

bespeak *verb* (**bespeaks**; *past* **bespoke**; *past participle* **bespoken**; **bespeaking**) suggest; be evidence of: *his gift bespeaks a kind heart*.

bespectacled *adjective* wearing eyeglasses.

bespoke *adjective* **1** (of goods, esp. clothing) made to order. **2** (of a tailor etc.) making goods to order.

best • *adjective* (*superlative of* GOOD) **1** of the most excellent or outstanding or desirable kind. • *adverb* (*superlative of* WELL¹) **1** in the best manner: *does it best*. **2** to the greatest degree: *like it best*. **3** most usefully: *is best ignored*. • *noun* **1** that which is best: *the best is yet to come*. **2** the chief merit or advantage: *brings out the best in him*. **3** a winning majority of (a certain number of games etc. played): *the best of five*. **4** a best performance recorded to date: *her personal best*. • *verb informal* defeat, outwit, outbid, etc. PHRASES **all the best** an expression of goodwill. **as best one can** (or **may**) as effectively as possible under the circumstances. **at best** on the most optimistic view. **at one's best** in peak condition etc. **at the best of times** even in the most favourable circumstances. **be for** (or **all for**) **the best** be desirable in the end. **the best of both worlds** the benefits of two different desirable outcomes, possibilities, etc., without having to choose between them. **the best part of** most of. **do** (or **give it**) **one's best** do all one can. **get the best of** defeat, outwit. **give a person one's best** express one's best wishes to a person. **had best** would find it wisest to. **make the best of** derive what limited advantage one can from (something unsatisfactory or unwelcome); put up with. **to the best of one's ability, knowledge**, etc. as far as one can do, know, etc. **with the best of them** as well as anyone.

best-before date *noun* the date marked on food showing the period after which it will deteriorate.

bestial *adjective* **1** brutish, cruel, savage: *bestial and barbaric behaviour*. **2** sexually depraved; lustful. **3** of or like a beast: *Darwin's revelations about our bestial beginnings*. [Say BEESTY ul or BESTY ul]

bestiality *noun* (*plural* **bestialities**) **1** sexual intercourse between a person and an animal. **2** savagely cruel or depraved behaviour. [Say beesty ALA tee or besty ALA tee]

best man *noun* a bridegroom's chief attendant.

bestow *verb* confer (a gift, right, etc.): *the university bestows this honour on its best student*. ▶ **bestowal** *noun* [Say buh STOE]

bestride *verb* (**bestrides**; *past* **bestrode**; *past participle* **bestridden**; **bestriding**) **1** sit astride on: *she bestrode her horse with an easy grace*. **2** stand astride over. **3** dominate: *he bestrides Alberta politics today*.

bestseller *noun* **1** a book or other item that has sold in large numbers. **2** the author of such a book etc. ▶ **bestselling** *adjective* **bestsellerdom** *noun*

bet • *verb* (**bets**; *past and past participle* **bet** or **betted**; **betting**) **1** risk a sum of money etc. against another's on the basis of the outcome of an unpredictable event (esp. the result of a race, game, etc.): *bet $20 on a horse* ◊ *I bet you ten bucks they lose* ◊ *betting on horses*. **2** *informal* feel sure: *I bet they've forgotten it*. • *noun* **1** the act of betting: *make a bet*. **2** the money etc. staked: *put a bet on*. **3** *informal* an opinion, esp. a spontaneous or quickly formed one: *my bet is that he won't come*. **4** *informal* a choice or course of action: *she's a good bet*. PHRASES **you bet** you can be certain.

beta *noun* **1** the second letter of the Greek alphabet (*B*, *β*). **2** the second of a series or set: *beta carotene*. **3** the second brightest star in a constellation. [Say BAY tuh]

beta blocker *noun* a drug preventing stimulation of beta receptors responsible for increased cardiac action, used to control heart rhythm, treat angina, and reduce high blood pressure, and also sometimes illicitly by athletes such as archers or by musicians to remain calm and reduce trembling.

beta carotene *noun* an isomer of carotene found in carrots etc., and converted in the body to vitamin A.

beta receptor *noun* one of two kinds of receptor in the sympathetic nervous system, which increase the activity of the heart when stimulated.

beta test • *noun* a test of computer hardware or software in the final stages of development, carried out by the users for whom it is intended (*compare* ALPHA TEST). • *verb* submit (a product) to a beta test.

beta version *noun* a version of a computer program or component used in beta testing.

betel *noun* the leaf of an Asian evergreen climbing plant, commonly chewed with parings of the areca nut in Southeast Asia. [Say BEETLE]

betel nut *noun* = ARECA NUT.

bête noire *noun* (*plural* **bêtes noires**) a person etc. one particularly dislikes or fears: *the James Bay project was the crowning success of Hydro-Québec, but also its bête noire*. [Say bet NWAR]

betide *verb* happen to: *woe betide you if you do!*

betoken *verb* **1** be a sign of; indicate: *she wondered if his cold, level gaze betokened indifference or anger*. **2** be a warning or indication of future events: *the falling comet betokened the true end of Merlin's powers*.

betray *verb* **1** place (a person, one's country, etc.) in the hands or power of an enemy. **2** be disloyal to (a person, a person's trust, etc.). **3** reveal involuntarily or treacherously; be evidence of: *his shaking hand betrayed his fear*. ▶ **betrayal** *noun* **betrayer** *noun*

betroth *verb formal* bind with a promise to marry. ▶ **betrothal** *noun* [Say be TROTHE (with TH as in BATHE)]

betrothed *formal* • *noun* the person to whom one is betrothed; one's fiancé or fiancée. • *adjective* engaged to be married. [Rhymes with CLOTHED]

SPELL CHECK
better, bettor ABC✓

A person who bets is a **bettor**.

---

better • *adjective* (*comparative of* GOOD) **1** of a more excellent or outstanding or desirable kind. **2** partly or fully recovered from illness: *feeling better*. • *adverb* (*comparative of* WELL¹) **1** in a better manner: *she sings better*. **2** to a greater degree: *like it better*. **3** more usefully or advantageously: *is better forgotten*. • *noun* **1** that which is better: *the better of the two*. **2** (usu. in plural) one's superior in ability or rank: *take notice of your betters*. • *verb* **1** improve on; surpass: *I can better his offer*. **2** make better; improve. **3 better oneself** improve one's position etc. PHRASES **better off** in a better (esp. financial) position. **better than** more than. **the better part of** most of. **the better to ...** so as to ... better: *the better to see*. **for better or for worse** whatever changes may take place; whatever happens. **get the better of** defeat, outwit; win an advantage over. **go one better 1** outbid etc. by one. **2** outdo another person. **had better** would find it wiser to. **no better than** merely.

better half *noun informal jocular* one's spouse.

betterment *noun* making better; improvement.

betting *noun* gambling by risking money on an unpredictable outcome.

bettor *noun* a person who bets.

B

between • *preposition* **1 a** at or to a point in the area or interval bounded by two or more other points in space, time, etc. **b** along the extent of such an area or interval: *there are five houses between here and the main road* ◊ *works best between five and six*. **2** separating, physically or conceptually: *the distance between here and Regina* ◊ *the difference between right and wrong*. **3 a** by combining the resources of: *great potential between them*. **b** shared by; as the joint resources of: *$5 between them*. **c** by joint or reciprocal action: *an agreement between us*. **4** to and from: *runs between Ottawa and Montreal*. **5** taking one and rejecting the other of: *decide between eating here and going out*. • *adverb* (also **in between**) at a point or in the area bounded by two or more other points in space, time, sequence, etc.: *not fat or thin but in between*. **PHRASES between ourselves** (or **you and me**) in confidence. **between times** (or **whiles**) occasionally.

bevel • *noun* **1** a sloping surface or edge; a slope from the horizontal or vertical in carpentry etc. **2** (also **bevel square**) an adjustable tool for marking angles in carpentry etc. • *verb* (**bevels, bevelled, bevelling**) reduce (a square edge) to a sloping edge: *a bevelled mirror*. [Say BEV'll]

beverage *noun* a drink: *alcoholic beverages*.

beverage room *noun Cdn* a lounge, bar, etc. where alcoholic drinks are sold.

bevy *noun* (plural **bevies**) a group or company of any kind: *he was surrounded by a bevy of beautiful girls*.

bewail *verb* express great regret, disappointment, or bitterness over (something) by complaining about it to others: *we will bewail the loss of our earlier freedoms*.

beware *verb* be cautious, take heed: *beware of the dog* ◊ *beware that you don't fall* ◊ *beware the Ides of March*.

bewilder *verb* utterly perplex or confuse. ▶ **bewildered** *adjective* **bewildering** *adjective* **bewilderingly** *adverb* **bewilderment** *noun*

bewitch *verb* (**bewitches, bewitched, bewitching**) **1** enchant; greatly delight. **2** subject to the influence of magic or witchcraft. ▶ **bewitching** *adjective* **bewitchingly** *adverb*

beyond • *preposition* **1** at or to the further side of: *beyond the river*. **2** outside the scope, range, or understanding of: *beyond repair*. **3** more than. • *adverb* **1** at or to the further side. **2** further on. • *noun* (**the beyond**) the unknown after death.

bezel *noun* **1** the sloped edge of a chisel. **2** the oblique faces of a cut gem. **3 a** a groove holding a watch glass or gem. **b** a rim holding a glass etc. cover, e.g. on a clock, navigational instrument, etc. [Say BEZZLE]

Bhagavad-Gita *noun* a devotional work, the most famous religious text of Hinduism. [Say bogga vod GEETA]

bhangra *noun* a style of popular (esp. dance) music combining Punjabi folk music with rock or disco elements. [Say BANG gra]

BHT *abbreviation* butylated hydroxytoluene, an antioxidant used to retard spoiling in foods containing fats etc.

Bi *symbol* the element bismuth.

bi *noun & adjective* (plural **bis**) *informal* bisexual.

bi- *combining form* forming nouns and adjectives meaning: **1** having two; a thing having two: *bilateral*. **2 a** occurring twice in every one or once in every two: *biweekly*. **b** lasting for two: *biennial*. **3** in two ways: *biconvex*. **4** *Chemistry* a substance having a double proportion of the acid etc. indicated by the simple word: *bicarbonate*.

BIA *abbreviation Cdn* **1** Business Improvement Association, a grouping of businesses which promotes commerce in a designated area and lobbies for the area's interests. **2** Business Improvement Area, the area served by a Business Improvement Association.

biannual *adjective* occurring, appearing, etc., twice a year (compare BIENNIAL). ▶ **biannually** *adverb*

bias • *noun* **1** prejudice in favour of or against one thing, person, or group compared with another, esp. in a way considered to be unfair: *there was evidence of bias against black applicants* ◊ *a bias towards younger people in recruitment* ◊ *a bias in favour of small business*. **2** a systematic distortion of a statistical result due to a factor not allowed for in its derivation. **3** a diagonal line or cut across the weave of a fabric: *a bias-cut skirt* ◊ *bias binding is made from strips of fabric cut on the diagonal*. **4 a** the irregular shape given to a ball in lawn bowling. **b** the oblique course this causes it to run. **5** a steady voltage, magnetic field, etc., applied to an electronic system or device, esp. to minimize distortion in tape recording. • *verb* (**biases, biased, biasing**) influence (usu. unfairly); prejudice: *was effective in biasing the diet preferences of the young*.

biased *adjective* having a bias; prejudiced: *gender-biased language* ◊ *I thought he was the best but I am biased because he is my son*.

bias-ply *adjective* (of a tire) having fabric layers with cords lying crosswise (compare RADIAL *adjective* 4).

biathlete *noun* an athlete competing in a biathlon. [Say by ATHLETE]

biathlon *noun* an athletic contest in cross-country skiing and shooting or cycling and running. [Say by ATH lon]

bib *noun* **1** a piece of cloth or plastic fastened around the neck, esp. of a baby, to keep the clothes clean during a meal. **2** the top front part of an apron, overalls, etc. **3** a coloured patch on the chest of certain dogs, cats, etc. **PHRASES best bib and tucker** best clothes.

bibb *noun* a mild and tender head lettuce with loose, dark green leaves.

Bible *noun* **1 a** the Christian scriptures consisting of the Old and New Testaments. **b** the Jewish scriptures. **c** (also **bible**) any copy of these. **d** a particular edition of the Bible: *New English Bible*. **2** (usu. **bible**) any authoritative book: *the gardener's bible*. **3** the scriptures of any non-Christian religion.

Bible belt *noun* any area known for its fundamentalist Christian beliefs.

Bible school *noun* **1** (also **Bible college**) a post-secondary institution offering courses in theology, esp. for evangelical Protestants. **2** an organized course of study devoted to the Bible.

Biblical *adjective* (also **biblical**) **1** of, concerning, or contained in the Bible: *Biblical prophecies*. **2** resembling the language of the King James Bible; poetic and archaic. **3** very great; on a large scale: *a disaster of almost biblical proportions*. ▶ **biblically** *adverb*

bibliographic *adjective* consisting of or having to do with a list of books: *bibliographic database*. ▶ **bibliographical** *adjective* [Say bib lee oh GRAFF ick]

bibliography *noun* (*plural* **bibliographies**) **1 a** a list of the books referred to in a scholarly work, usu. printed as an appendix. **b** a list of the books of a specific author or publisher, or on a specific subject, etc. **2 a** the history or description of books, including authors, editions, etc. **b** any book containing such information. [Say bib lee OGGRA fee]

bibliophile *noun* a person who collects or is fond of books. [Say BIBBLY oh file]

bicameral *adjective* (esp. of a parliament or legislative body) having two chambers, e.g. a House of Commons and a Senate. [Say by CAMMER ul]

bicarbonate *noun* **1** *Chemistry* any acid salt of carbonic acid. **2** (also **bicarbonate of soda**) = BAKING SODA. [Say by CARBON ate or by CARBON it]

bicentenary • *noun* (*plural* **bicentenaries**) **1** a two-hundredth anniversary. **2** a celebration of this. • *adjective* of a bicentenary. [Say by sen TENNA ree]

bicentennial • *noun* a two-hundredth anniversary. • *adjective* **1** lasting two hundred years or occurring every two hundred years. **2** of or concerning a bicentennial.

bicep *noun informal* a biceps muscle.

WRITING TIP
biceps

Bicep is still considered informal. **Biceps** is the standard form for both the singular and plural.

---

biceps *noun* (*plural* **biceps**) the flexor muscle at the front of the upper arm or at the back of the thigh.

bicker *verb* quarrel pettily; wrangle.

bicolour • *adjective* (also **bicoloured**) having two colours. • *noun* a bicolour blossom or animal.

biconvex *adjective* (esp. of a lens) convex on both sides.

bicultural *adjective* having or involving two cultures, esp. (in Canada) English-Canadian and French-Canadian. ▶ **biculturalism** *noun*

bicuspid • *adjective* having two cusps or points. • *noun* **1** the premolar tooth in humans. **2** a tooth with two cusps. [Say by CUSS pid]

bicycle • *noun* a vehicle with two wheels held in a frame one behind the other, propelled by pedals and steered with handlebars attached to the front wheel. • *verb* (**bicycles**, **bicycled**, **bicycling**) ride a bicycle. ▶ **bicyclist** *noun*

bid • *verb* (**bids**, **bidding**) **1** (*past* and *past participle* **bid**) (often foll. by *for*, *against*) **a** (esp. at an auction) offer (a certain price): *did not bid for the vase* ◊ *bid against the dealer* ◊ *bid $100*. **b** offer to do work etc. for a stated price. **2** (*past* **bade**, **bid**; *past participle* **bidden**, **bid**) utter (greeting or farewell) to: *I bade him welcome*. **3** (*past* and *past participle* **bid**) *Cards* state before play how many tricks one intends to make: *North bids four hearts* ◊ *with this hand, I don't think I should bid*. • *noun* **1 a** (esp. at an auction) an offer (of a price): *a bid of $5*. **b** an offer (to do work, supply goods, etc.) at a stated price; a tender.

2 *Cards* a statement of the number of tricks a player proposes to make. **3** an attempt; an effort: *a bid for power*. PHRASES **bid fair to** seem likely to. (**make a**) **bid for** try to gain: *made a bid for freedom*. [For *bade* say BAYED or BAD]

biddable *adjective* obedient: *today's young women are less biddable than their mothers' generation was*.

bidder *noun* **1** a person or group competing with others to buy something: *the house went to the highest bidder*. **2** a person or group submitting an offer to do work for a particular amount of money, in competition with others: *six bidders competed for the catering contract*.

bidding *noun* **1** the offers made for something being sold: *the bidding soared to $5,000*. **2** *Cards* the act of making a bid or bids. **3** what someone commands or requests: *women came running at his bidding* ◊ *the group effectively coerced him into doing its bidding*.

biddy *noun* (*plural* **biddies**) *slang derogatory* a woman: *old biddy*.

bide *verb* (**bides**, **bided**, **biding**) PHRASES **bide one's time** await one's best opportunity.

bidet *noun* a low oval bathroom fixture used for washing the genital and anal regions. [Say bid AY]

WRITING TIP
biennial, biannual   ✍

Do not confuse **biennial** with **biannual**. Biennial means "occurring one time every two years". **Biannual** means "occurring two times each year".

---

biennial • *adjective* **1** recurring every two years. **2** lasting two years. • *noun* **1** *Botany* a plant that takes two years to grow from seed to fruition and die (*compare* ANNUAL, PERENNIAL). **2** an event celebrated or taking place every two years. ▶ **biennially** *adverb* [Say by ENNY ul]

bier *noun* a movable frame on which a coffin or a corpse is placed or taken to a grave. [sounds like BEER]

biffy *noun* (*plural* **biffies**) (esp. *West*) *informal* **1** an outhouse. **2** a toilet.

bifocal • *adjective* having two focuses, esp. of a lens with a part for distant vision and a part for near vision. • *noun* (in *plural*) bifocal glasses.

bifold • *adjective* designating a two-piece door which moves on tracks and folds along a hinge down the centre. • *noun* a bifold door.

bifurcate *verb* (**bifurcates**, **bifurcated**, **bifurcating**) divide into two branches; fork: *just below Cairo the river bifurcates* ◊ *the trail was bifurcated by a mountain stream*. ▶ **bifurcation** *noun* [Say BY fur kate]

big • *adjective* (**bigger**, **biggest**) **1 a** of considerable size, amount, intensity, etc. **b** of a large or the largest size: *big toe*. **2 a** significant; outstanding: *my big chance*. **b** famous; popular: *a big celebrity*. **3 a** grown up: *a big boy now*. **b** elder: *big sister*. **4** *informal* **a** boastful: *big words*. **b** often ironic generous: *big of him*. **c** ambitious: *big ideas*. **d** (of a game etc.) well-played. **5** advanced in pregnancy: *big with child*. • *adverb informal* in a big manner, esp.: **1** effectively: *went over big*. **2** boastfully: *talk big*. **3** ambitiously: *think big*. **4** to a considerable extent: *win big*. • *noun* (in *plural*) the major baseball leagues. PHRASES **be big on** *informal* be enthusiastic about. **come** (or **go**) **over big** *informal* make a great effect. **come up big** *informal* perform successfully when relied upon to do so. **in a big way 1** on a large scale. **2** *informal* with great enthusiasm, display, etc. **look** (or **talk**) **big** *informal* boast. **make it big** *informal* achieve great success. **too big for one's britches** (or **boots**) *slang* conceited.

bigamy *noun* (*plural* **bigamies**) the crime of marrying

B

when one is lawfully married to another person. ▶**bigamist** noun **bigamous** adjective [Say BIGGA me]

big band noun a large jazz or swing orchestra.

big bang noun **1** Astronomy the violent explosion of all matter from a state of high density and temperature, postulated as the origin of the universe. **2** any sudden or dramatic beginning of drastic change.

Big Blue Machine noun Cdn the Ontario Progressive Conservative Party during the premiership of William Davis (1971–85).

big box noun (plural **big boxes**) a very large, warehouse-style store, often specializing in one kind of merchandise (e.g. books), usu. at lower prices than in other stores.

Big Brother noun **1** an all-powerful dictator or government which keeps the populace under close observation and strict control: *the spectre of a governmental Big Brother looming over the country's broadcasting industry*. **2** an adult who befriends a fatherless child, esp. through an agency.

big business noun large commercial, industrial, or financial companies, esp. when having a significant social, economic, or political influence.

big cat noun any of the larger members of the feline family, e.g. lions, tigers, cougars, etc.

big cheese noun informal a very important person.

Bigfoot noun = SASQUATCH.

big game noun large animals hunted for sport.

biggie noun informal a very important person etc.

biggish adjective somewhat big.

big government noun government characterized by large-scale participation in domestic affairs.

big gun noun informal **1** an important person, company, etc. **2** Sport a high-scoring player.

big head noun informal a conceited person. PHRASES **have a big head** be conceited. ▶**big-headed** adjective

big heart noun a generous nature. ▶**big-hearted** adjective

bighorn noun a North American sheep, *Ovis canadensis*, with large curving horns, esp. native to the Rockies.

big house noun (also **Big House**) **1** slang a prison. **2** a communal dwelling, sometimes up to 18 m (60 ft.) in length, used by West Coast Aboriginal peoples, with a section for each family as well as a central common area. **3** Cdn hist. the residence of the chief trader at a fur trading post.

bight noun **1** a curve or recess in a coastline, river, etc. **2** a loop of rope. [Sounds like *BITE*]

big kahuna noun slang **1** an important person; a big shot. **2** anything very large, esp. a large wave. [Say big kuh HOONA]

big league • noun **1** the highest professional league in a sport, esp. baseball. **2** the highest class in any field: *made it to the big leagues*. • adjective (**big-league**) first-class; worthy of being in the big leagues. ▶**big-leaguer** noun

big lie noun an intentional distortion of facts, esp. by a politician, official body, etc.

big money noun **1** a great deal of money, esp. as pay or profit: *started making big money*. **2** large corporations, the very wealthy, etc.: *the Conservative government seemed dedicated to the interests of big money*.

bigmouth noun a talkative or boastful person.

bigness noun the quality of being big.

big one noun informal **1** a major event. **2** (usu. as **the big one**) an anticipated massive earthquake along the San Andreas Fault in California. **3** a sum of money or a banknote representing it: *fifty big ones*.

bigot noun a person intolerant of another's beliefs,

race, politics, etc. ▶**bigoted** adjective **bigotry** noun (plural **bigotries**) [Say BIG it]

big picture noun (**the big picture**) an issue etc. viewed or understood as a whole.

big screen noun **1** the screen in a movie theatre. **2** (usu. as **the big screen**) movies collectively, esp. as seen in theatres: *appearing on the big screen*.

big shot noun informal an important person, esp. in a corporation etc.

Big Sister noun an adult who befriends a motherless child, esp. through an agency.

big smoke noun informal (**the big smoke**) any large city, esp. (in Canada) Toronto.

big-ticket adjective expensive: *big-ticket items*.

big time informal • noun the highest level of success in a profession, esp. entertainment: *dreams of the big time*. • adverb as an intensifier: *lost big time*. ▶**big-time** adjective **big-timer** noun

big top noun **1** the main tent of a circus. **2** a circus. **3** a tent capable of holding a large gathering.

bigwig noun (also **big wheel**) informal an important person.

bike informal • noun a bicycle or motorcycle. • verb (**bikes**, **biked**, **biking**) ride a bicycle or motorcycle.

biker noun **1** a cyclist, esp. a motorcyclist. **2** a member of a motorcycle gang.

bikeway noun a transportation route reserved for or specially adapted for bicycles.

bikini noun **1** a two-piece bathing suit for women, the bottom half of which consists of skimpy briefs not reaching above the top of the pelvis. **2** a skimpy bathing suit for men, similar to the bottom half of a bikini. **3** = BIKINI BRIEFS. **4** (as an adjective) designating the pubic hairline, esp. of a woman: *bikini line*.

bikini briefs plural noun (also **bikini underwear**) briefs which do not extend above the top of the pelvis.

bilateral adjective **1** having or relating to two sides; affecting both sides: *bilateral hearing*. **2** involving two parties, countries, etc.: *bilateral negotiations*. ▶**bilaterally** adverb [Say by LATERAL]

bilateral symmetry noun a type of body arrangement in which there is only one plane along which an organism can be divided into two symmetrical halves: *the human body is a good example of bilateral symmetry*.

bile noun **1** a bitter greenish-brown alkaline fluid which aids digestion and is secreted by the liver and stored in the gallbladder. **2** bad temper; peevish anger.

bile duct noun the duct which conveys bile from the liver and the gallbladder to the duodenum.

bi-level • adjective **1** having or functioning on two levels. **2** designating a style of two-storey house in which the lower storey is partially sunk below ground level, and the main entrance is between the two storeys. • noun a bi-level house.

bilge noun **1 a** the lowest area inside a ship, where water collects. **b** the area on the outer surface of a ship's hull where the flat bottom meets the vertical side. **2** (also **bilge water**) filthy water that collects inside the bilge. **3** informal nonsense.

bilharzia noun a chronic and debilitating disease of Africa and South America caused by a parasitic flatworm found esp. in standing water, which burrows into a person's body and enters the bloodstream, causing liver and intestinal damage. [Say bill HART see uh]

bilingual • adjective **1** able to speak two languages, esp. fluently (often in Canada understood to mean able to speak English and French). **2** spoken or written in or involving two languages. • noun a bilingual person. ▶**bilingually** adverb [Say by LING gwul or by LING gyoo ul]

bilingualism *noun* **1** the ability to speak two languages, esp. (in Canada) English and French. **2** a policy promoting this among a population. [Say by LING gwul ism or by LING gyoo ul ism]

bilingualize *verb* (**bilingualizes, bilingualized, bilingualizing**) *Cdn* make bilingual. [Say by LING gwul ize or by LING gyoo ul ize]

bilious *adjective* **1** affected by or associated with nausea and vomiting: *a bilious attack ◊ I had eaten too much and felt a little bilious*. **2** bad-tempered: *outbursts of bilious misogyny*. **3** of or like bile; nauseating: *bilious haze*. **4** (of a colour) lurid or sickly: *a bilious olive hue*. [Say BILL yus or BILLY us]

bilk *verb informal* obtain or withhold money from someone by deceit or without justification; cheat or defraud: *government waste has bilked the taxpayers of billions of dollars ◊ fraud masters use computers to bilk the unsuspecting*.

bill¹ • *noun* **1 a** a printed or written statement of charges for goods supplied or services rendered. **b** the amount owed; the cost of something: *ran up a bill of $300*. **2** = BILL OF EXCHANGE. **3** a draft of a proposed law. **4 a** a printed list, esp. a concert or theatre program. **b** the entertainment itself: *double bill*. **5** a banknote: *ten-dollar bill*. **6 a** a poster; a placard. **b** = HANDBILL. • *verb* **1** present publicly: *the trip was billed as a fact-finding tour*. **2** invoice: *bill me for the books*.

bill² *noun* **1** the beak of a bird, esp. when it is slender, flattened, or weak, or belongs to a web-footed bird or a bird of the pigeon family. **2** the muzzle of a platypus. **3** the long, pointed upper jaw of marlins, sailfish, etc. **4** the visor on a baseball cap. PHRASES **bill and coo** behave or talk in a very loving or sentimental manner.

billable *adjective* referring to a period of time for which a customer or client can be charged a fee: *lawyers are always trying to increase their billable hours*.

billboard *noun* a large outdoor board for ads etc.

billed *adjective* (of an animal) having a bill of a particular kind: *duck-billed dinosaur ◊ yellow-billed loon*.

billet¹ • *noun* **1** a place, esp. a private home, where a student, soldier, etc. is provided with accommodation, usu. without charge. **2** a written order requiring a householder to lodge the bearer. • *verb* (**billets, billeted, billeting**) **1** arrange or provide temporary free lodging for: *the young people will be billeted with local Quebec families*. **2** take lodging with a billet: *he's billeted with seven different families in four years*.

billet² *noun* **1** a thick piece of wood, esp. one cut for firewood. **2** a metal bar.

billet-doux *noun* (*plural* **billets-doux**) often *jocular* a love letter. [Say billy DOO for the singular, billy DOOZ for the plural]

billfold *noun* a wallet for keeping paper money.

billiards *noun* **1 a** any of various games played on an oblong cloth-covered table, with a cue used to strike a number of balls. **b** a version of this using three balls, either with pockets around the edge of the table (**English billiards**) or without (**carom**, or **French billiards**). **2** (**billiard**) (in *combination*) used in billiards.

billing *noun* **1** in senses of BILL¹ *verb* **2** placement in a list of performers: *received top billing*.

billion • *noun* **1** a thousand million (1,000,000,000 or 10⁹): *a world population of 5 billion*. **2** (in *plural*) *informal* a very large number: *billions of years*. • *adjective* that amount to a billion. ▶ **billionth** *adjective & noun*

billionaire *noun* a person possessing over a billion dollars, pounds, etc.

bill of exchange *noun* a written order to pay a sum on a given date to the signatory or a named payee.

bill of fare *noun* **1** a menu. **2** an offering of entertainment.

bill of health *noun* **1** *Nautical* a certificate regarding infectious disease on a ship or in a port at the time of sailing. **2** (**clean bill of health**) **a** such a certificate stating that there is no disease. **b** a declaration that a person or thing examined has been found to be free of illness or in good condition.

Bill of Rights *noun* (also **bill of rights**) a statement of the rights of a group of people.

bill of sale *noun* **1** a printed record of a purchase; a receipt. **2** a certificate of transfer of personal property, esp. as a security against debt.

billow • *noun* a large, wavy mass of something, typically cloud, smoke, or steam: *billows of freezing mist*. • *verb* **1** (of smoke, clouds, etc.) move or flow outward with a wavy motion: *smoke was billowing from the chimney ◊ billowing clouds of steam swirled down*. **2** (of fabric) fill with air and swell outwards: *her dress billowed out around her ◊ sails billowing in the wind*. ▶ **billowy** *adjective*

billy *noun* (*plural* **billies**) (also **billycan**) a tin or enamel cooking pot with a lid and wire handle, for outdoor use.

billy club *noun* a police officer's night stick.

billy goat *noun* (also **billy**; *plural* **billies**) a male goat.

bimah *noun* (also **bima**) a raised platform for readers in a synagogue. [Say BEEMA]

bimbo *noun* (*plural* **bimbos**) *slang* usu. *derogatory* (also **bimbette**) a woman, esp. a young, sexually attractive, unintelligent one.

WRITING TIP
bimonthly

The word **bimonthly** is ambiguous, since it can mean either "two times every month" or "one time every two months". Use alternatives like **twice monthly** and **semi-monthly** for the first meaning or **every two months** for the second.

---

bimonthly • *adjective* occurring every two months or twice a month. • *adverb* every two months or twice a month. • *noun* (*plural* **bimonthlies**) a periodical produced bimonthly.

bin • *noun* **1** a large receptacle for storage or for depositing rubbish, recyclables, etc. **2** a partitioned stand for storing bottles of wine. • *verb* (**bins, binned, binning**) *informal* store or put in a bin.

binary • *adjective* **1** related to, composed of, or involving two things: *binary chemical weapons*. **2** of the arithmetical system using 2 as a base. • *noun* (*plural* **binaries**) **1** something having two parts. **2** a binary star. **3** a binary number. [Say BY na ree or BY nairy]

binary code *noun* a coding system using the binary digits 0 and 1 to represent a letter, digit, or other character in a computer (*see* BCD).

binary compound *noun* *Chemistry* a compound having two elements or radicals.

binary number *noun* (also **binary digit**) one of two digits (usu. 0 or 1) in a binary system of notation.

binary system *noun* **1** (also **binary star**) a system of two stars orbiting each other. **2** a system in which information can be expressed by combinations of the digits 0 and 1 (corresponding to "off" and "on").

binational *adjective* involving two nations: *the Canadian political culture is a binational amalgam of British and French elements ◊ a binational panel oversees the free trade agreement between Canada and the US*.

bind • *verb* (**binds, bound, binding**) **1** (often foll. by *to, on, together*) tie or fasten tightly, attach. **2** restrain; put in bonds. **3 a** esp. *Cooking* cause (ingredients) to cohere using another ingredient. **b** hold by chemical bonding; combine with. **4** fasten or hold together as a single mass. **5** compel; impose an obligation or duty on.

6 a edge (fabric etc.) with braid etc. **b** fix together and fasten (the pages of a book) in a cover. **7** constipate. **8** (often foll. by *up*) **a** put a bandage or other covering around. **b** fix together with something put around: *bound her hair.* **9** indenture as an apprentice. **10** (of snow etc.) cohere, stick. **11** be prevented from moving freely. • *noun* **1** a difficult situation; a position that prevents free action. **2** *informal* a nuisance; a restriction. PHRASES **bind over** *Law* order (a person) to do something, esp. keep the peace. **bind up** bandage.

binder *noun* **1** a detachable cover for sheets of paper, magazines, etc. **2** a substance that acts cohesively. **3** *esp. hist.* a machine for binding grain into sheaves. **4** a bookbinder.

binder twine *noun* a coarse twine used esp. to tie bales of hay, straw, etc.

binding • *noun* **1** the strong covering of a book holding the sheets together. **2** the fastening attaching a boot to a ski. **3** a trim for binding raw edges of fabric. • *adjective* **1** legally enforceable: *binding arbitration.* **2** causing or tending to stick together.

bindweed *noun* any of various twining plants of the morning glory family, with funnel-shaped flowers.

Bing cherry *noun* (*plural* **Bing cherries**) a type of large, dark red cherry.

binge • *noun* a period of uncontrolled indulgence in some activity, esp. eating or drinking. • *verb* (**binges, binged, bingeing** or **binging**) eat, drink, shop, etc. in an uncontrolled way. ▶ **binger** *noun*

bingo • *noun* a game for any number of players, each having a card of squares with numbers, which are marked off as numbers are randomly drawn by a caller. • *interjection* indicating a sudden action or event, or satisfaction, etc., as in winning at bingo.

binocular • *adjective* adapted for or using both eyes. • *noun* = BINOCULARS.

binoculars *plural noun* an optical instrument with lenses for each eye, for viewing distant objects.

binomial • *noun* **1** an algebraic expression of the sum or the difference of two terms. **2** a two-part name, esp. the Latin name of a species (consisting of the genus name and the species, e.g. *Homo sapiens*). • *adjective* consisting of two terms: *binomial nomenclature.* ▶ **binomially** *adverb* [Say by NO me ul]

bio *noun* (*plural* **bios**) *informal* **1** a biography. **2** biology.

bio- *combining form* **1** life: *biography.* **2** of living beings: *biochemistry.* **3** biology: *biomedicine.*

bioaccumulate *verb* (**bioaccumulates, bioaccumulated, bioaccumulating**) (of poisons, chemicals, etc.) collect in animal tissue in progressively higher concentrations towards the top of the food chain. ▶ **bioaccumulation** *noun*

biochemistry *noun* the study of the chemical processes of living organisms. ▶ **biochemical** *adjective* **biochemist** *noun*

biocide *noun* **1** a poisonous substance, esp. a pesticide, herbicide, etc. **2** the destruction of life. [Say BY a side]

biodegradability *noun* the ability of a substance to be decomposed.

biodegradable *adjective* (of a substance or object) capable of being decomposed by bacteria or other living organisms and thereby avoiding pollution.

biodegradation *noun* the process of decomposing: *biodegradation of landfill waste.*

biodegrade *verb* (**biodegrades, biodegraded, biodegrading**) decompose through the action of bacteria etc.

biodiversity *noun* the variety of plant and animal life in the world or in a particular habitat. A high level of biodiversity is usu. considered to be important and desirable.

bioengineer *noun* an expert in bioengineering.

bioengineered *adjective* = GENETICALLY ENGINEERED.

bioengineering *noun* **1** = GENETIC ENGINEERING. **2** the use of artificial tissues, organs, or organ components to replace damaged or absent parts of the body, e.g. artificial limbs, pacemakers, etc. **3** the use in engineering or industry of organisms or biological processes.

bioethicist *noun* a person who studies or promotes bioethics.

bioethics *plural noun* (treated as *singular*) the ethics of medical and biological research and practice.

biofeedback *noun* the use of electronic monitoring of a normally automatic bodily function, e.g. temperature, in order to train a person to acquire voluntary control of it.

biogeography *noun* the branch of biology that deals with the geographical distribution of plants and animals.

biographer *noun* a person who writes a biography.

biographical *adjective* based on, recounting, or having to do with the details of a person's life.

biography *noun* (*plural* **biographies**) **1 a** a written account of a person's life, usu. by another. **b** such writing as a branch of literature. **2** the course of a living (usu. human) being's life: *the two men's biographies were quite different.*

biohazard *noun* a risk to human health or the environment arising from biological work, esp. with micro-organisms.

biological • *adjective* **1** (also **biologic**) of or relating to biology or living organisms. **2** (of a parent) involved in the procreation of the child in question, as opposed to its rearing. • *noun* a biological product, esp. one used therapeutically or in biological control.

biological clock *noun* **1** an innate mechanism controlling the rhythmic physiological activities of an organism, e.g. sleep. **2** an innate mechanism regulating the aging process, esp. in relation to the ability to bear children.

biological control *noun* the control of a pest by the introduction of a natural enemy.

biologically *adverb* with respect to biology: *they are biologically normal* ◊ *the area is biologically diverse.*

biological weapon *noun* a weapon which unleashes toxins or harmful micro-organisms.

biologist *noun* a scientist who studies biology.

biology *noun* (*plural* **biologies**) **1** the study of living organisms. **2** the plants and animals of an area.

bioluminescence *noun* the emission of light by living organisms such as the firefly and glow-worm. ▶ **bioluminescent** *adjective* [Say bio looma NESS ince]

biomass *noun* **1** the total quantity or weight of organisms in a given area or of a given species. **2** non-fossilized organic matter (esp. regarded as fuel).

biome *noun* **1** a large, naturally-occurring community of flora and fauna adapted to the conditions in which they occur, e.g. tundra. **2** the geographical region containing such a community. [Say BY ome]

biomechanical *adjective* based on or having to do with biomechanics. ▶ **biomechanically** *adverb*

biomechanics *noun* the study of the mechanical laws relating to the movement or structure of organisms.

biomedical *adjective* having to do with both biology and medicine.

biomedicine *noun* the application of biology to clinical medicine.

bionic *adjective* **1** having artificial body parts or superhuman powers resulting from these. **2** relating to bionics. ▶ **bionically** *adverb* [Say by ON ick]

bionics *plural noun* (treated as *singular*) the study of mechanical systems that function like living organisms or parts of living organisms. [Say by ON icks]

biophysical *adjective* based on or having to do with biophysics.

biophysics *plural noun* (treated as *singular*) the science of the application of the laws of physics to biological phenomena.

biopic *noun informal* a biographical film. [Say BIO pick]

biopsy • *noun* (*plural* **biopsies**) the removal and examination of tissue taken from a living body to discover the presence or extent of a disease. • *verb* (**biopsies**, **biopsied**, **biopsying**) examine (tissue) for diagnostic purposes. [Say BY op see]

bioregion *noun* a region that constitutes a natural ecological community. ▶ **bioregional** *adjective*

biosphere *noun* the regions of the earth's crust and atmosphere occupied by living organisms.

biotech *informal* • *noun* biotechnology. • *adjective* biotechnological.

biotechnological *adjective* having to do with biotechnology.

biotechnology *noun* (*plural* **biotechnologies**) the exploitation of biological processes for industrial and other purposes, esp. genetic manipulation of micro-organisms for the production of antibiotics, hormones, etc.

biotic *adjective* relating to life or living things, esp. in their ecological relations: *biotic diversity*. [Say by OT ick]

biotin *noun* a vitamin of the vitamin B complex, found esp. in egg yolk, liver, and yeast, and involved in the metabolism of carbohydrates, fats, and proteins. [Say BIO tin]

bipartisan *adjective* of or involving two (esp. political) parties: *the reforms received bipartisan approval*. ▶ **bipartisanship** *noun*

bipartite *adjective* **1** shared by or involving two parties: *a bipartite system of public and separate schools*. **2** (of a contract, treaty, etc.) drawn up in two corresponding parts or between two parties. [Say by PAR tite]

biped • *noun* an animal that uses only two legs for walking. • *adjective* two-legged. ▶ **bipedal** *adjective* **bipedalism** *noun* [Say BY ped]

biphenyl *noun* a crystalline hydrocarbon containing two benzene rings. [Say by FENNEL or by FEEN'll]

biplane *noun* an early type of airplane having two sets of wings, one above the other.

bipolar *adjective* **1** having two poles or extremities. **2** characterized by two extremes: *a sharply bipolar division of rich and poor*. **3** (of psychiatric illness) characterized by both manic and depressive episodes: *bipolar disorder*. ▶ **bipolarity** *noun*

birch • *noun* (*plural* **birches**) **1** any tree of the genus *Betula*, having thin peeling bark and slender branches, found predominantly in northern temperate regions. **2** (also **birchwood**) the hard fine-grained pale wood of these trees. **3** (also **birch rod**) a bundle of birch twigs used for flogging. • *verb* beat with a birch (in sense 3). • *adjective* made of or derived from birch.

birchbark *noun* **1** the bark of *Betula papyrifera*, traditionally used by some Algonquian peoples to make canoes etc. **2** such a canoe.

bird *noun* **1** a feathered, warm-blooded vertebrate, having a beak and wings, laying eggs, and usu. able to fly. **2** *informal* a person of a specified type: *a tough old bird*. **3** a shuttlecock. **4** *slang* **a** a booing etc. as an expression of disapproval. **b** a gesture of contempt made by raising the middle finger. PHRASES **a bird in the hand** something secured or certain. **the bird is** (or **has**) **flown** the prisoner etc. has escaped. **the**

birds and the bees *euphemism* sexual activity and reproduction. **birds of a feather** people of like character. **for the birds** *informal* useless, not worth consideration. **have a bird** *slang* become agitated. **eat like a bird** eat very small amounts. **a little bird** *informal* a secret informant.

birdbrain *noun informal* a silly or stupid person. ▶ **birdbrained** *adjective*

bird course *noun Cdn derogatory slang* a university or high-school course requiring little work or ability.

bird dog *noun* **1** a hunting dog trained to retrieve birds. **2** *informal* a scout for a sports team etc.

birder *noun* a birdwatcher.

birdhouse *noun* a box, usu. of wood, designed to attract nesting birds.

birdie • *noun* **1** *informal* a small bird. **2** *Golf* a score of one stroke under par at any hole. **3** a shuttlecock. • *verb* (**birdies**, **birdied**, **birdieing**) *Golf* play (a hole) in one stroke under par.

birding *noun* birdwatching.

birdlife *noun* the birds of a region collectively.

bird of paradise *noun* (*plural* **birds of paradise**) **1** any of various birds found chiefly in New Guinea, the males having brilliantly coloured plumage. **2** a southern African plant with orange and blue flowers, cultivated for flower arrangements.

bird of prey *noun* (*plural* **birds of prey**) a bird which hunts animals for food.

birdseed *noun* a blend of seed used in bird feeders etc.

bird's-eye maple *noun* the wood of the sugar maple used in panelling, cabinetmaking, etc., having a characteristic pattern of round black knots.

bird's-eye view *noun* **1** an overhead view (of a landscape etc.). **2** a general overview (of a subject etc.).

birdsong *noun* the musical call or sound of a bird.

birdwatcher *noun* a person who observes birds in their natural surroundings. ▶ **birdwatching** *noun*

birl *verb* cause (a floating log) to rotate by using one's feet; spin. ▶ **birling** *noun* [Rhymes with *GIRL*]

SPELL CHECK | ABC ✓
birth, berth

Berth is the spelling in "playoff berth". A **berth** is also a bunk on a ship or train.

---

birth • *noun* **1** the emergence of a (usu. fully developed) infant or other young from the body of its mother. **2** the beginning or coming into existence of something: *the birth of socialism*. **3 a** origin, descent, ancestry: *of noble birth*. **b** high or noble birth; inherited position: *she was proud of her beauty and her birth*. **4** (as an *adjective*) designating the parent who gave birth to or fathered a child: *birth mother*. • *verb* give birth to (a baby or other young): *in spring the cows birthed ◊ she had carried him and birthed him*. PHRASES **give birth** bear a child etc. **give birth 1** produce (young) from the womb: *she died giving birth ◊ gave birth to a daughter*. **2** cause to begin, found: *the great struggle for freedom in France gave birth to the French Revolution*.

birth canal *noun* the canal comprising the cervix, vagina, and vulva, through which the fetus passes during delivery.

birth certificate *noun* an official document identifying a person by name and place and date of birth.

birth control *noun* the practice or methods of preventing pregnancy, esp. by contraception.

birth control pill *noun* an oral contraceptive containing progesterone and often estrogen, used to prevent ovulation.

birthdate *noun* one's date of birth.

birthday *noun* **1** the anniversary of a person's birth. **2** the day on which a person etc. was born. **3** the anniversary of the day on which something came into being: *July 1 is Canada's birthday*.

birthday suit *noun jocular* the bare skin; nakedness.

birthing *noun* the act or process of giving birth: *birthing centre*.

birthmark *noun* an unusual brown or red mark on one's body at or from birth.

birthplace *noun* **1** the place where a person was born. **2** a place of origin or commencement: *the birthplace of Confederation*.

birth rate *noun* the number of births per thousand of population per year.

birthright *noun* a right of possession or privilege belonging to one from birth: *privilege is nobody's birthright*. PHRASES **sell one's birthright for a mess of pottage** give up something to which one is entitled in exchange for something of little value (an allusion to the Bible story where Esau sold his birthright of inheriting from his father to his younger twin Jacob for a bean stew).

birthstone *noun* a gemstone popularly associated with the month of one's birth.

biscotti *plural noun* hard, dry, Italian cookies, usu. containing ground nuts. [Say biss COTTY]

biscuit *noun* **1** a dry, hard, flat, baked foodstuff: *dog biscuit*. **2** = TEA BISCUIT. **3** fired pottery that has not been glazed. PHRASES **have had the biscuit** *Cdn slang* be no longer good for anything; be done for.

bisect *verb* **1** divide (a line, angle, or shape) into two exactly equal parts. **2** cut across: *a landscape of wheat fields bisected by long straight roads*. ▶ **bisection** *noun* **bisector** *noun*

bisexual • *adjective* **1** sexually attracted to persons of both sexes. **2** *Biology* having characteristics of both sexes. **3** of or concerning both sexes. • *noun* a bisexual person. ▶ **bisexuality** *noun*

bishop *noun* **1** a member of the highest rank of clerical hierarchy in some Christian denominations, usu. in charge of a diocese, and empowered to confer holy orders. **2** a chess piece which is moved diagonally and has the upper part shaped like a mitre.

bishopric *noun* **1** the office of a bishop. **2** a diocese. [Say BISHOP rick]

bismarck *noun* **1** *Alberta, Sask., & US Midwest* a sugar-coated jam-filled doughnut. **2** *Man.* a cream-filled doughnut, often with a chocolate glaze. [Say BIZ mark]

bismuth *noun* **1** a brittle reddish-white metallic element, occurring naturally and used in alloys. **2** any compound of this used medicinally. [Say BIZ muth]

bison *noun* (*plural* **bison**) either of two heavily built bovines, one native to the North American plains, the other native to Europe, both having a high shoulder hump, shaggy hair, and a large head with short horns. [Say BIZE in or BICE in]

bisque¹ *noun* a rich soup usu. made from shellfish but also from game or vegetables. [Say BISK]

bisque² *noun* a variety of white porcelain that has not been glazed, used for statuettes etc. [Say BISK]

bistro *noun* (*plural* **bistros**) a small restaurant with a somewhat informal atmosphere often serving French food with a prix fixe menu. [Say BEE stroe or BIS troe]

bit¹ *noun* **1** a small piece or quantity. **2 a** a fair amount: *needed a bit of persuading*. **b** *informal* somewhat: *am a bit tired*. **c** (foll. by *of*) *informal* rather: *a bit of an idiot*. **3** a short time or distance: *wait a bit*. **4** a part, esp. of a film etc.: *I liked the bit where they fell in love*. **5** *informal* a unit of 12 ½ cents (used only in even multiples). **6** (as an *adjective*) relating to a minor speaking role in a film etc.: *bit part*. **7** *informal* a characteristic way of behaving: *the* dog did its protective bit. PHRASES **bit by bit** gradually. **bits and pieces** (or **bits and bobs**) an assortment of small items. **do one's bit** *informal* make a useful contribution to an effort or cause. **not a bit** (or **not a bit of it**) not at all. **to bits** into pieces.

bit² *past of* BITE.

bit³ *noun* **1** a metal mouthpiece on a bridle, used to control a horse. **2** a (usu. metal) tool or piece for boring or drilling. **3 a** the cutting or gripping part of a plane etc. **b** the cutting blade or edge of an axe etc. **4** the part of a key that engages with the lock lever. PHRASES **chomp** (or **champ** or **chafe**) **at the bit** be restlessly impatient. **take the bit between** (or **in**) **one's teeth** begin to tackle a task or problem in a determined or independent way.

bit⁴ *noun* *Computing* a unit of information expressed as a choice between two possibilities; a 0 or 1 in binary code.

bitch • *noun* (*plural* **bitches**) **1** a female dog or other canine animal. **2** *offensive slang* a malicious, spiteful, or unpleasant woman. • *verb* (**bitches**, **bitched**, **bitching**) *slang* **1** make spiteful comments: *they were all bitching about their colleagues*. **2** complain.

bitchily *adverb* *slang* in a bitchy, nasty, or spiteful manner: *they gossiped bitchily*.

bitchiness *noun* *slang* spitefulness, nastiness.

bitchy *adjective* (**bitchier**, **bitchiest**) *slang* (of a person or their comments) malicious or spitefully critical; bad-tempered.

SPELL CHECK **bite, byte**	ABC ✓

The computing term is **byte**.

bite • *verb* (**bites**; *past* **bit**; *past participle* **bitten**; **biting**) **1** cut or puncture using the teeth. **2** (foll. by *off, away*, etc.) detach with the teeth. **3** wound with a sting, fangs, etc. **4 a** (of a wheel, screw, etc.) grip, penetrate. **b** *Curling* (of a rock) come to a stop. **5 a** (of fish) accept bait. **b** accept inducement or be taken in by a deception. **6** have a (desired) adverse effect. **7** (in *passive*) **a** take in; swindle. **b** (foll. by *by, with*, etc.) be infected by (enthusiasm etc.). **8** (foll. by *at*) snap at. **9** *slang* be extremely bad or unpleasant: *this movie bites*. • *noun* **1** an act of biting. **2** a wound or sore made by biting. **3 a** a mouthful of food. **b** a snack or light meal. **4** the taking of bait by a fish. **5** pungency (esp. of flavour). **6** incisiveness, sharpness. **7** a pithy quotation or excerpt: *sound bite*. **8** a portion exacted: *the tax bite*. **9** = OCCLUSION 2. PHRASES **bite back** restrain (one's speech etc.). **bite the big one** *slang* **1** die. **2** be very bad or unpleasant. **bite the bullet** *informal* behave bravely or stoically. **bite the dust** *slang* **1** die. **2** fail; break down. **bite the hand that feeds one** hurt or offend a benefactor. **bite a person's head off** *informal* respond fiercely or angrily. **bite one's tongue** refrain from speaking, esp. reluctantly. **bite off more than one can chew** take on a commitment one cannot fulfill. **once bitten twice shy** an unpleasant experience induces caution. **put the bite on** *slang* borrow or extort money from. **take a bite out of** *informal* reduce by a significant amount. **what's biting you?** *slang* what is annoying you? ▶ **biter** *noun*

bite-sized *adjective* (also **bite-size**) **1** small enough to be eaten in one mouthful. **2** very small or short.

biting *adjective* **1** that bites; *biting insects*. **2** stinging, intensely cold. *a biting wind*. **3** sharp: *biting sarcasm*. ▶ **bitingly** *adverb*

bitmap *noun* **1** a representation, e.g. of a computer memory, in which each item is represented by one bit. **2** a graphic display in which characters are formed by

assigning a bit value to each individual pixel.
▶ **bitmapped** *adjective*

bitten *past participle of* BITE.

bitter • *adjective* **1** having a sharp pungent taste. **2 a** caused by or showing mental pain or resentment: *bitter memories.* **b** painful or difficult to accept: *bitter disappointment.* **3 a** virulent: *bitter animosity.* **b** piercingly cold. • *noun* (in *plural*) liquor with a bitter flavour (esp. of wormwood) used as an additive in cocktails. PHRASES **to the bitter end** to the very end in spite of difficulties. ▶ **bitterly** *adverb*

bittern *noun* any of several marsh birds of the heron family, esp. of the genus *Botaurus*, with a booming call.

bitterness *noun* **1** resentment or anger resulting from a sense of unfair treatment: *the wage freeze caused bitterness among the workers.* **2** the pain of an event that is difficult to accept or contemplate: *the bitterness of losing lasted well after the game had ended.* **3** a bitter taste.

bitter pill *noun* something unpleasant that must be accepted or endured.

bittersweet • *adjective* **1** sweet with a bitter aftertaste: *bittersweet chocolate.* **2** arousing pleasure tinged with pain or sorrow: *bittersweet memories of her first love.* • *noun* any of several North American climbing vines of the genus *Celastrus*, esp. *C. scandens*.

bitty *adjective* (**bittier**, **bittiest**) *informal* very small.

bitumen *noun* any of various tarlike mixtures of hydrocarbons derived from petroleum and used for road surfacing and roofing. [Say bit YOU m'n or bit OO m'n]

bituminous *adjective* of or containing bitumen. [Say bit YOU min us or bit OO min us]

bituminous coal *noun* a volatile form of coal burning with a smoky flame.

bivalent • *adjective* **1** having a valence of two. **2** (of homologous chromosomes) associated in pairs. • *noun* any pair of homologous chromosomes. [Say by VAY lint]

bivalve • *noun* an aquatic mollusc which has a compressed body enclosed within two hinged shells, e.g. oysters, mussels, etc. • *adjective* **1** with a hinged double shell: *a bivalve mollusc.* **2** (of a seed capsule) having two valves.

bivouac • *noun* a temporary open encampment e.g. of soldiers or mountaineers. • *verb* (**bivouacs**, **bivouacked**, **bivouacking**) camp in a bivouac, esp. overnight. [Say BIVVA wack]

> **WRITING TIP**
> **biweekly**
>
> The word **biweekly** is ambiguous, since it can mean either "two times every week" or "one time every two weeks". Use alternatives like **twice weekly** and **semi-weekly** for the first meaning or **every two weeks** for the second.

---

biweekly • *adverb* **1** every two weeks. **2** twice a week. • *adjective* produced or occurring biweekly. • *noun* (*plural* **biweeklies**) a biweekly periodical.

biz *noun* *informal* business.

> **SPELL CHECK**
> **bizarre, bazaar**
>
> A large market or store is a **bazaar**.

---

bizarre *adjective* strange in appearance or effect; eccentric. ▶ **bizarrely** *adverb* **bizarreness** *noun*

Bk *symbol* berkelium.

blab *verb* (**blabs**, **blabbed**, **blabbing**) *informal* **1** reveal secrets by indiscreet or foolish talk: *she blabbed to the press* ◊ *there's no need to blab the whole story.* **2** talk foolishly or mindlessly: *they blab on about responsibility.*

blabber *informal* • *noun* (also **blabbermouth**) a person

who blabs. • *verb* (often foll. by *on*) talk foolishly or on trivial matters, esp. for a long time.

black • *adjective* **1** very dark, having no colour from the absorption of all or nearly all incident light. **2** completely dark from the absence of a source of light: *black night.* **3** (also **Black**) **a** belonging or relating to any of various peoples having dark-coloured skin, esp. of African or Australian origin. **b** of or relating to black peoples or their culture: *black studies.* **4** (of the sky, a cloud, etc.) dusky; heavily overcast. **5** angry, threatening: *a black look.* **6** implying disgrace or condemnation: *in his black books.* **7** wicked, sinister: *black-hearted.* **8** gloomy, depressed: *a black mood.* **9** portending trouble or difficulty: *things looked black.* **10** (of hands etc.) dirty, soiled. **11** (of humour or its representation) with sinister as well as comic import: *a black comedy.* **12** (of coffee) without milk. **13** dark in colour as distinguished from a lighter variety: *black bear* ◊ *black pine.* **14** Cards belonging to spades or clubs. • *noun* **1** a black colour or pigment. **2** black clothes or material: *dressed in black.* **3 a** (in a game) a black piece etc. **b** the player using such pieces. **4** the absence of light on a stage or film set: *fade to black.* **5** the credit side of an account: *in the black.* **6** (also **Black**) a black person. • *verb* **1** make black: *blacked his face.* **2** polish with blacking. PHRASES **black out 1** effect a blackout on. **2** undergo a blackout.

black and blue *adjective* discoloured by bruises.

black and white • *noun* writing or printing: *in black and white.* • *adjective* **1** (of film etc.) not in colour. **2** consisting of extremes only, oversimplified: *interpreted the problem in black and white terms.*

black art *noun* = BLACK MAGIC.

black ash *noun* an ash of eastern North America, *Fraxinus nigra*, growing in swampy woodland.

blackball *verb* **1** reject (a candidate) in a vote. **2** exclude.

black bean *noun* **1** any of several leguminous plants of the genus *Phaseolus.* **2** the edible black seed of this plant. **3** a fermented soybean, used as flavouring in oriental cooking.

black bear *noun* either of two bears with black or blue-black fur, one found in North American forests, the other in Asia.

black belt *noun* **1** a black belt worn by a martial arts expert. **2** a person qualified to wear this.

blackberry *noun* (*plural* **blackberries**) **1** a thorny shrub related to the raspberry, bearing white or pink flowers. **2** a black fleshy edible fruit of this plant. **3** *Cdn* (*Nfld*) = CROWBERRY.

blackbird *noun* any of various birds with mainly black plumage, esp. the red-winged blackbird and the grackle.

black blizzard *noun* *Cdn* a dust storm of soil blown by high winds on the prairies.

blackboard *noun* a board with a smooth dark surface used in schools etc. for writing on with chalk.

black box *noun* **1** a flight recorder in an aircraft. **2** any complex piece of equipment, with contents which are mysterious to the user.

black bread *noun* a coarse dark type of rye bread.

black-capped chickadee *noun* see CHICKADEE.

black cherry *noun* (*plural* **black cherries**) **1** a cherry, *Prunus serotina*, of eastern North America, bearing dark, edible fruit. **2** the fruit of this.

blackcurrant *noun* **1** a widely cultivated shrub, *Ribes nigrum*, bearing flowers in racemes. **2** the small dark edible berry of this plant.

Black Death *noun* a pandemic of bubonic and pneumonic plague that killed perhaps one-third of the

B

population of Europe in the mid-14th century and resurfaced throughout the next few centuries.

black diamond noun **1** (in plural) coal. **2** (as an adjective) designating a particularly difficult ski run.

black duck noun a wild duck, Anas rubripes, predominantly dark brown with a purple patch on the wings, found throughout eastern Canada.

blacken verb **1** make or become black or dark. **2** speak evil of, defame: blacken someone's character.

blackened adjective (of food, esp. in Cajun dishes) covered with spices and cooked quickly over high heat.

black English noun the form of English used by some North American blacks, esp. as an urban dialect.

black eye noun bruised or discoloured skin around the eye, esp. resulting from a blow.

black-eyed pea noun **1** a leguminous plant commonly grown for forage in the southern US. **2** the edible seed of this plant.

black-eyed Susan noun any of several daisy-like plants having yellow flowers with dark centres.

black flag noun a pirate's ensign.

blackfly noun (plural **blackflies**) any of various gnatlike flies, esp. of the genus Simulium.

Blackfoot 1 (plural **Blackfoot** or **Blackfeet**) a member of a group of North American Aboriginal peoples comprising the Siksika, Blood, and Peigan, now largely found in S Alberta and Montana. **2** = SIKSIKA noun. **3** the Algonquian language of this people. • adjective of the Blackfoot or their language.

Black Forest cake noun a layered chocolate cake with a filling of cherries and whipped cream.

Black Forest ham noun a variety of sweetened and smoked ham.

black gold noun informal crude oil.

blackguard noun a man who behaves in a dishonourable or contemptible way. [Say BLAG ard or BLAG erd or BLACK guard]

blackhead noun a black-tipped plug of fatty matter in a skin follicle, esp. on the face.

black hole noun **1** a region of space having a gravitational field so intense that no matter and radiation can escape. **2** any inescapable void or place of confinement.

black ice noun thin hard transparent ice, esp. on a road surface or body of water.

blacking noun any black paste or polish, esp. for shoes.

blackish adjective somewhat black.

blackjack • noun **1 a** a card game in which players try to acquire cards with a face value exceeding the dealer's but no more than 21. **b** two cards totalling 21 in this game. **2** a flexible bludgeon of leather-covered lead. **3** a shrubby oak of eastern North America. **4** a pirates' black flag. • verb strike or beat with a blackjack.

blacklist • noun a list of persons under suspicion, in disfavour, etc. • verb put the name of (a person) on a blacklist.

black locust noun a tree native to eastern North America, bearing black pods.

blackly adverb depicting tragic events humorously; grimly, morbidly: a blackly comic view of war.

black magic noun magic involving supposed invocation of evil spirits.

blackmail • noun **1 a** an extortion of payment in return for not disclosing compromising information, a secret, etc.: was subjected to blackmail. **b** any payment extorted in this way: will not pay blackmail **?** the use of threats or the manipulation of someone's feelings to force them to do something: used emotional blackmail to get her way. • verb **1** extort or try to extort money etc.

from (a person) by blackmail. **2** force someone to do something by using threats or manipulating their feelings: blackmailed Jane into being their go-between. ► **blackmailer** noun

black mark noun a record or impression of a person' misdemeanour or discreditable action: the Tiananmen Square massacre was a black mark on human history.

black market noun an illegal trade in officially controlled or scarce items. ► **black marketeer** noun

Black Mass noun (plural **Black Masses**) a travesty of the Mass said to be used in the cult of Satanism.

Black Muslim noun a follower of the Nation of Islam.

black nationalism noun a political and social movement originating in the US in the 1960s, advocating solidarity, pride, and self-government among blacks.

blackness noun **1** the state or quality of being black. **2** the darkness of night, or the nighttime sky: the stars shone against the blackness.

blackout noun **1** a temporary or complete loss of vision, consciousness, or memory. **2** a loss of power, radio reception, etc. **3** a compulsory period of darkness as a precaution against air raids. **4** a temporary suppression of the release of information, esp. from police or government sources. **5** a sudden darkening of a theatre stage. **6** a period in which discounts, esp. on airfare, do not apply.

black pepper noun a spice made from the unripe ground or whole berries of Piper nigrum.

blackpoll noun (also **blackpoll warbler**) a North American warbler, Dendroica striata, the male of which has a black crown in spring.

black powder noun = GUNPOWDER.

black power noun a movement in support of civil rights and political power for blacks.

black raspberry noun (plural **black raspberries**) a North American raspberry, with black berries.

black robe noun Cdn hist. a Christian priest working as a missionary among Aboriginal peoples.

Black Rod noun (also **Usher of the Black Rod** or hist. **Gentleman Usher of the Black Rod**) (in Canada) the principal usher of the Senate, who summons the Commons to the Senate at the opening of Parliament.

black sheep noun informal (plural **black sheep**) an unsatisfactory member of a family, group, etc.; an outcast.

blackshirt noun a member of a militant fascist organization.

blacksmith noun **1** a smith who works in iron. **2** = FARRIER 1. ► **blacksmithing** noun

blacktail noun (also **black-tailed deer**) = MULE DEER.

black tea noun tea fully fermented before drying.

blackthorn noun **1** a North American hawthorn. **2** a thorny European shrub, bearing white-petalled flowers before small blue-black fruits. **3** a walking stick made from the blackthorn.

black tie noun **1** a black bow tie worn with a tuxedo etc. **2** (as an adjective) an occasion requiring that men wear a tuxedo: black-tie dinner (compare WHITE TIE).

blacktop • noun **1** a type of bituminous road-surfacing material; asphalt. **2** a road surfaced with this. • verb (**blacktops**, **blacktopped**, **blacktopping**) surface with blacktop.

black walnut noun **1** a walnut tree, Juglans nigra, of the northeastern US and southern Canada, planted for its edible nut and as an ornamental. **2** the rich, dark brown wood of this tree, much prized in cabinetmaking. **3** the edible nut of this tree.

Black Watch noun **1** the Royal Highland Regiment of

the Canadian Forces. **2** a very dark green and navy blue tartan.

black widow *noun* a venomous black spider, the female of which usu. devours the male after mating.

bladder *noun* **1** any of various sacs in some animals, containing urine, bile, or air, esp. the urinary bladder. **2** an inflated pericarp or vesicle in various plants.

blade • *noun* **1 a** the flat part of a knife, chisel, etc. that forms the cutting edge. **b** a razor blade. **2** the flattened functional part of an oar, skate, hockey stick, etc. **3 a** the flat, narrow, usu. pointed leaf of grass and cereals. **b** the broad thin part of a leaf apart from the petiole. **4 a** a broad flat bone, esp. in the shoulder. **b** a cut of beef from behind the neck and above the shoulder. **5** a dashing, pleasure-seeking young man. • *verb* (**blades, bladed, blading**) = ROLLERBLADE *verb*. ▶ **bladed** *adjective* (also in *combination*). **blader** *noun* **blading** *noun*

blah *informal* • *noun* **1** (also **blah-blah**) pretentious nonsense. **2** (in *plural*) a general feeling of depression. • *adjective* **1** dull, bland, not exciting. **2** lethargic, lacking in enthusiasm. • *interjection* (usu. **blah blah blah**) indicating verbose, tedious speech or writing.

blam • *noun* a loud sharp sound, as of a gunshot or an explosion. • *verb* (**blams, blammed, blamming**) make such a loud sound.

blame • *verb* (**blames, blamed, blaming**) **1** assign fault or responsibility to: *blamed the pilot for the crash*. **2** (foll. by *on*) assign the responsibility for (an error or wrong) to a person etc.: *they blame youth crime on unemployment*. • *noun* **1** responsibility for a bad result. **2** the act of blaming or attributing responsibility: *she got all the blame*. • *adjective* (also **blamed**) *informal* damned, confounded. PHRASES **be to blame** be responsible: *she is not to blame for the accident*. **have only oneself to blame** be solely responsible (for something one suffers). **I don't blame you** etc. I think your etc. action was justifiable. ▶ **blameable** *adjective*

blameless *adjective* innocent; free from blame. ▶ **blamelessly** *adverb* **blamelessness** *noun*

blameworthy *adjective* deserving blame. ▶ **blameworthiness** *noun*

blanch *verb* (**blanches, blanched, blanching**) **1** make white or pale by extracting colour: *the cold light blanched her face*. **2** grow pale from shock, fear, etc.: *she blanched at the suggestion ◊ their faces blanched with fear*. **3 a** peel (almonds etc.) by scalding. **b** immerse (vegetables or meat) briefly in boiling water. **4** whiten (a plant) by depriving it of light: *endives are blanched by covering them with soil*.

bland *adjective* **1** (of food or drink) lacking strong flavour: *bland rice pudding*. **2** lacking strong features or characteristics and therefore uninteresting: *rebelling against the bland uniformity*. **3** (of a person or their behaviour) showing no strong emotion: *his expression was bland and unreadable*.

blandishment *noun* a flattering or pleasing statement or action used to gently persuade someone to do something: *voters will not succumb to the candidates' blandishments*.

blandly *adverb* **1** with little excitement, interest, or emotion: *"No," he answered blandly*. **2** in a plain, ordinary, or uninteresting manner: *the office was blandly decorated*.

blandness *noun* a plain, uninteresting, uninspiring style or condition.

blank • *adjective* **1 a** (of paper) not written or printed on. **b** (of a document) with spaces left for a signature or details. **c** (of a tape, disk, etc.) containing no recorded sound etc. **d** (of a television screen etc.) not displaying any images, characters, etc. **2 a** not filled; empty: *a*

blank space. **b** lacking contrast; sheer: *a blank wall*. **3 a** having or showing no interest or expression: *a blank face*. **b** void of incident or result. **c** puzzled, nonplussed. **d** having (temporarily) no knowledge or understanding: *my mind went blank*. **4** complete, downright: *a blank refusal*. **5** *Curling* (of an end) played without either rink scoring a point. **6** *euphemism* used in place of an adjective regarded as coarse or abusive. • *noun* **1 a** a space left to be filled in a document. **b** a document having blank spaces to be filled. **2** (also **blank cartridge**) a cartridge containing gunpowder but no bullet, used for training etc. **3** an empty space or period of time. **4 a** a coin disc before stamping. **b** a metal or wooden block before final shaping. **5 a** a dash written instead of a word or letter, esp. instead of an obscenity. **b** *euphemism* used in place of a noun regarded as coarse. **6** a blank domino or tile in some games. • *verb* **1** screen, obscure: *clouds blanked out the sun*. **2** *Sport* defeat without allowing to score; shut out. **3** *Curling* play (an end) without either rink scoring a point. PHRASES **draw a blank** provoke no successful response; fail: *the search drew a blank ◊ I started to tell the story then I drew a complete blank*.

blank cheque *noun* **1** a cheque with the amount left for the payee to fill in. **2** *informal* unlimited freedom of action.

blanket • *noun* **1** a large piece of woollen or other material used esp. as a bed cover. **2** a type of woollen cloth similar to a woollen blanket: *blanket coat*. **3** a thick mass or layer that covers something: *blanket of fog*. **4** (often as an *adjective*) traditional Indian life or culture. • *adjective* inclusive: *blanket condemnation*. • *verb* (**blankets, blanketed, blanketing**) **1** cover with or as if with a blanket: *snow blanketed the land*. **2** stifle; keep quiet: *blanketed all discussion*. PHRASES **born on the wrong side of the blanket** illegitimate.

blanket coat *noun* a coat made from a blanket or blanket cloth, esp. (in Canada) = HUDSON'S BAY BLANKET COAT.

blankety *adjective* (also **blankety-blank**) = BLANK *adjective* 6.

blankly *adverb* with no change in facial expression to indicate comprehension, interest, or emotion; vacuously: *when I asked if they spoke English they just looked at me blankly ◊ they spend hours staring blankly at the TV*.

blankness *noun* a plain, bare, or empty quality: *the blankness of the landscape*.

blank verse *noun* verse that does not rhyme, esp. iambic pentameters.

blare • *verb* (**blares, blared, blaring**) make a loud harsh sound: *car horns blared ◊ blaring trumpets*. • *noun* a loud harsh sound.

blarney • *noun* **1** talk which aims to charm, pleasantly flatter, or persuade: *it took all my Irish blarney to keep us out of court*. **2** amusing and harmless nonsense. • *verb* (**blarneys, blarneyed, blarneying**) flatter (a person) with blarney: *blarneyed him into lending her fifty bucks*.

blasé *adjective* unimpressed or indifferent because one has seen or experienced something so often before: *she was becoming quite blasé about the dangers*. [Say blaw ZAY]

blaspheme *verb* (**blasphemes, blasphemed, blaspheming**) swear or curse, making use of religious names etc.; speak irreverently about God or sacred things: *allegations that he had blasphemed against Islam*. ▶ **blasphemer** *noun* [Say blass FEEM]

blasphemous *adjective* sacrilegious against God or sacred things. [Say BLASSFA muss]

blasphemy *noun* (*plural* **blasphemies**) **1** the action or offence of speaking sacrilegiously about God or sacred things: *in the novel, Henry Ford is treated as a god and saying "By Ford!" is blasphemy ◊ shouted incomprehensible*

B

B

blasphemies. **2** something shocking that deeply offends people's idea of what is correct: *in Montreal, criticizing the Canadiens is blasphemy.* [Say BLASSFA me]

blast • *noun* **1** a strong gust of wind. **2 a** an explosion. **b** a destructive wave of highly compressed air spreading outwards from an explosion. **c** the quantity of explosive used in a blasting operation. **3** a single loud note emitted by a brass instrument, whistle, car horn, etc. **4** a gunshot. **5** *informal* a severe reprimand. **6** a strong current of air used in smelting etc. **7** *informal* a good time: *had a blast.* **8** *Sport* a vigorous hit, throw, etc. • *verb* **1** blow up (rocks etc.) with explosives. **2** create out of or from rocks etc. by blasting. **3** make or cause to make a loud or explosive noise: *blasted away on his tuba.* **4 a** *informal* reprimand severely. **b** exclaim vehemently or loudly. **5** *informal* shoot. **6** *Sport* hit or throw forcefully. **7** destroy, ruin: *blasted her hopes.* **8** wither, shrivel, or blight (a plant etc.): *blasted oak.* **9** strike with divine anger; curse. • *interjection* expressing annoyance. PHRASES **full blast** *informal* working at maximum speed etc. **blast from the past** *informal* a forcefully nostalgic event or thing. **blast off** (of a rocket etc.) take off from a launching site.

blasted *adjective* **1** damned; annoying: *that blasted dog!* **2** *informal* drunk.

blaster *noun* a person or thing that blasts.

blast furnace *noun* a smelting furnace into which compressed hot air is driven.

blasthole *noun* a hole containing an explosive charge for blasting.

blast-off *noun* the launching of a rocket etc.

blat • *noun* a loud discordant noise, e.g. the sounding of a horn. • *verb* (**blats, blatted, blatting**) make a loud discordant sound.

blatancy *noun* the flagrant or overt manner in which something considered wicked is done: *I was shocked by the blatancy of their crimes.* [Say BLAIT'n see]

blatant *adjective* **1** flagrant: *blatant attempt to steal.* **2** completely lacking in subtlety: *forcing herself to resist his blatant charm.* ▶**blatantly** *adverb* [Say BLAY t'nt]

blather • *noun* foolish chatter. • *verb* chatter foolishly. ▶**blathering** *noun*

blaze¹ • *noun* **1** a bright flame or fire. **2 a** a bright glaring light: *the sun set in a blaze of orange.* **b** a full light: *a blaze of publicity.* **3** a violent outburst (of passion etc.). **4 a** a glow of colour: *roses were a blaze of scarlet.* **b** a bright display: *a blaze of glory.* • *verb* (**blazes, blazed, blazing**) **1** burn with a bright flame. **2** be brilliantly lighted. **3** be consumed with anger, excitement, etc. **4 a** show bright colours: *blazing with jewels.* **b** emit light: *stars blazing.* **5** *esp. Sport* move quickly. PHRASES **blaze away** (often foll. by *at*) fire continuously with rifles etc. **blaze up** burst into flame. **go to blazes** *informal* go to hell. **like blazes** *informal* **1** with great energy. **2** very fast. **what in blazes** *informal* what on earth.

blaze² • *noun* **1** a white mark on an animal's face. **2** a mark made on a tree by slashing the bark, esp. to mark a route. • *verb* (**blazes, blazed, blazing**) mark (a tree or a path) by chipping bark. PHRASES **blaze a trail** (or **path**) **1** mark out a path or route. **2** be the first to do or study something.

blazer *noun* **1** a jacket of a solid colour, often with a crest and patch pockets, worn as part of a uniform. **2** a plain jacket of a dark solid colour that is not part of a suit.

blazing *adjective* **1** in senses of BLAZE¹ *verb*. **2** very hot: *a blazing hot day.* ▶**blazingly** *adverb*

blazon *verb* display prominently or vividly: *their company name was blazoned all over the media.* [Say BLAYZ'n]

bleach • *verb* (**bleaches, bleached, bleaching**) whiten by a chemical process or by exposure to sunlight. • *noun* (*plural* **bleaches**) **1** a bleaching substance (typically a solution of sodium hypochlorite or hydrogen peroxide), esp. used domestically for whitening laundry and as a disinfectant. **2** the process of bleaching.

bleacher *noun* (usu. in *plural*) **1** uncovered, tiered, inexpensive bench seating at a sports ground, stadium, etc. **2** a similar type of seating in a gymnasium etc.

bleak *adjective* **1** bare, exposed; windswept. **2** unpromising; dreary: *bleak prospects.* **3** cold or harsh: *a bleak wind.* ▶**bleakly** *adverb* **bleakness** *noun*

blearily *adverb* with bleary eyes; in a tired manner: *"I was asleep," she explained blearily.*

bleary *adjective* (**blearier, bleariest**) (of the eyes) looking or feeling dull or unfocussed from sleep or tiredness. **2** *Boris opened a bleary eye* ◊ *bleary-eyed revellers.*

bleat • *verb* **1** (of a sheep, goat, calf, etc.) give its natural tremulous cry. **2** speak or say feebly, foolishly, or plaintively. • *noun* **1** the sound made by a sheep, goat, etc. **2** a weak, plaintive, or foolish exclamation, statement, etc.: *his despairing bleat touched her heart.*

blech *interjection* expressing disgust.

bleed • *verb* (**bleeds, bled, bleeding**) **1** emit blood. **2** draw blood from surgically. **3** extort money from. **4** spend or lose money in large quantities. **5** (of a plant) emit sap. **6 a** (of dye) come out in water. **b** (of colour) run. **7 a** allow (fluid or gas) to escape from a closed system through a valve etc. **b** treat (such a system) in this way. **8** suffer wounds or violent death: *bled for the Revolution.* **9 a** (of a printed area) be cut into when pages are trimmed. **b** cut into the printed area of when trimming. **c** extend (an illustration) to the cut edge of a page. • *noun* **1** a draining of fluid or gas from a closed system. **2** (usu. in *combination*) an act of bleeding: *nosebleed.* PHRASES **bleed dry** (or **white**) drain (a person, country, etc.) of wealth etc. **one's heart bleeds** usu. *ironic* one is very sorrowful.

bleeder *noun* **1** a person or thing that bleeds. **2** *informal* a hemophiliac.

bleeding heart *noun* **1** *informal* a person perceived as overly sentimental, esp. in regard to social problems. **2** any of various plants having heart-shaped pinkish-red flowers hanging from an arched stem.

bleep • *noun* **1** an intermittent high-pitched sound made electronically. **2** this sound or the word itself used as a substitute for an expletive. • *verb* **1** make or cause to make such a sound, esp. as a signal. **2** (often foll. by *out*) substitute a bleep for.

blemish • *noun* (*plural* **blemishes**) **1** a flaw or defect: *a blemish on her character.* **2** a mark on the skin, esp. a pimple, blackhead, scar, etc. • *verb* (**blemishes, blemished, blemishing**) spoil the perfection of.

blend • *verb* **1 a** mix (esp. sorts of coffee, liquor, etc.) together to produce a desired flavour etc. **b** produce by this method: *blended whisky.* **2** form a harmonious compound; become one. **3** mingle or be mingled: *her voice blends in with the others.* **4 a** (often foll. by *in*) mix thoroughly. **b** combine (ingredients) using an electric blender. **5** (esp. of colours) **a** pass imperceptibly into each other. **b** go well together; harmonize. • *noun* **1 a** a mixture, esp. of various sorts of coffee, liquor, etc. **b** a combination (of different abstract or personal qualities). **2** a word blending the sounds and combining the meanings of two others, e.g. *motel.*

blende *noun* any naturally occurring metal sulphide. [Sounds like *BLEND*]

blended family *noun* a family consisting of children from more than one marriage.

blender *noun* **1** an electric kitchen appliance with

rotating blades, used for puréeing, liquefying, or finely chopping. **2** a person or thing that blends.

bless *verb* (**blesses, blessed, blessing**) **1 a** (of a priest etc.) pronounce words, esp. in a religious rite, to confer or invoke divine favour on. **b** bestow divine favour on: *bless this house*. **2 a** consecrate (esp. bread and wine). **b** sanctify. **3** call (God) holy; adore. **4 bless oneself** make the sign of the cross. **5** attribute one's good fortune to (an auspicious time, one's fate, etc.); thank: *bless the day I met her*. **6** make happy or successful: *blessed with children ◊ they were truly blessed*. PHRASES (**God**) **bless me** (or **my soul**) an exclamation of surprise, pleasure, indignation, etc. (**God**) **bless you! 1** an exclamation of endearment, gratitude, etc. **2** an exclamation made to a person who has just sneezed. **I'm blessed** an exclamation of surprise etc. **not have a penny to bless oneself with** be very poor.

blessed *adjective* **1** sanctified, revered. **2** often *ironic* fortunate (in the possession of): *blessed with good health*. **3** *euphemism* cursed; damned: *blessed nuisance!* **4** in paradise. **5** (**Blessed**) *Catholicism* a title given to a beatified person. **6** bringing happiness; blissful: *blessed ignorance*. ▶ **blessedly** *adverb* [Say BLESS id or BLEST (in sense 2 say only BLEST)]

blessedness *noun* **1** happiness. **2** the enjoyment of divine favour. [Say BLESSID nis]

blessing *noun* **1** the act of declaring, seeking, or bestowing (esp. divine) favour: *sought God's blessing ◊ mother gave them her blessing*. **2** grace said before or after a meal. **3** a gift of a deity, nature, etc.; a thing one is glad of. PHRASES **blessing in disguise** an apparent misfortune that eventually has good results.

bleu *noun* *Cdn* esp. *hist.* a Quebec supporter of a Conservative party. [Say BLUH (with *UH* like the *OO* in *BOOK*)]

blew *past of* BLOW[1].

blight ▶ *noun* **1** any plant disease caused by mildews, fungi, insects, etc. **2** any insect or parasite causing such a disease. **3** any obscure force which is harmful or destructive. **4** the act or state of deteriorating or being destroyed: *urban blight*. ▶ *verb* **1** affect a plant with blight: *a peach tree blighted by leaf curl*. **2** spoil, harm, or destroy: *the scandal blighted the careers of several leading politicians ◊ his father's blighted ambitions ◊ developers removed blighted residential slums*.

blimp *noun* **1** a small non-rigid airship. **2** *informal* an obese person.

blind ▶ *adjective* **1** lacking the power of sight. **2 a** without foresight, discernment, or adequate information: *blind effort*. **b** (often foll. by *to*) unwilling or unable to appreciate (a factor, circumstance, etc.): *blind to argument*. **3** not governed by purpose or reason: *blind forces*. **4** reckless: *blind hitting*. **5** concealed, obscured: *blind corner*. **6 a** (of a door, window, etc.) walled up. **b** (of a street etc.) closed at one end. **7** (of flying) without direct observation, using instruments only. **8** (of a wall) having no windows. **9** (of a test or experiment) conducted in a way that does not allow the subject or examiner to prejudice the results. **10** *informal* drunk. ▶ *verb* **1** deprive of sight, permanently or temporarily. **2** rob of judgment; deceive: *blinded them to the danger*. ▶ *noun* **1 a** a screen for a window, esp. on a roller, or with slats. **b** an awning over a store window. **2 a** something designed or used to hide the truth; a pretext. **b** a legitimate business concealing a criminal enterprise. **3** a camouflaged shelter used for observing or hunting wildlife. **4** any obstruction to sight or light. ▶ *adverb* **1** *Aviation* using instruments only: *fly blind*. **2** without guidance: *buy it blind*. **3** to a great extent: *robbed them blind*. PHRASES **blind as a bat** completely

blind. **blind with science** overawe with a display of (often spurious) knowledge. **not a blind bit of** *informal* not the slightest amount of: *didn't do a blind bit of good*. **turn a blind eye to** pretend not to notice.

blind alley *noun* (*plural* **blind alleys**) a course of action leading nowhere.

blind date *noun* **1** a social engagement between two people who have not previously met. **2** either of the two people on a blind date.

blinder *noun* *informal* (usu. in *plural*) = BLINKER *noun* 1.

blindfold ▶ *verb* deprive (a person) of sight by covering the eyes, esp. with a tied cloth. ▶ *noun* a bandage or cloth used to blindfold. ▶ *adjective & adverb* **1** with eyes bandaged. **2** without care or circumspection: *went into it blindfold*.

blinding ▶ *noun* the act of causing blindness. ▶ *adjective* **1** causing temporary or permanent inability to see: *a blinding snowstorm*. **2** dazzlingly bright. **3** extreme; severe: *blinding speed*.

blindingly *adverb* very, extremely: *the reason was blindingly obvious*.

blindly *adverb* **1** without being able to see. **2** without understanding or thought: *plunged in blindly*.

blind man's bluff *noun* (also esp. *Brit.* **blind man's buff**) a game in which a blindfold player tries to catch others while being pushed about by them.

blindness *noun* the condition of being blind.

blind side ▶ *noun* a direction in which one cannot see the approach of danger etc. ▶ *verb* (usu. **blindside, blindsides, blindsided, blindsiding**) **1** attack or strike on the blind side. **2** surprise, take unawares; take advantage of.

blind spot *noun* **1** the point of entry of the optic nerve on the retina, insensitive to light. **2** an area where vision is obscured or hindered, esp. that part of the road which a driver of a motor vehicle cannot see using mirrors. **3** an area in which a person lacks understanding or impartiality: *Ed had a blind spot where these ethical issues were concerned*.

blind trust *noun* **1** a trust independently administering the private business affairs of a person in public office. **2** complete, unthinking faith.

blink ▶ *verb* **1** shut and open the eyes quickly and usu. involuntarily. **2** (often foll. by *at*) look with eyes opening and shutting, esp. in surprise or bewilderment. **3 a** (often foll. by *back*) prevent (tears) by blinking. **b** (often foll. by *away, from*) clear (dust etc.) from the eyes by blinking. **4 a** shine with an unsteady or intermittent light. **b** cause (a light) to flash briefly. **5** back down in a confrontation. ▶ *noun* **1** an act of blinking. **2** a momentary gleam or glimpse. PHRASES **on the blink** *informal* out of order, esp. intermittently. **the blink of an eye** a very short time.

blinker ▶ *noun* **1** (usu. in *plural*) either of a pair of screens attached to a horse's bridle to prevent it from seeing sideways. **2** a device that blinks, esp. a vehicle's turn signal. ▶ *verb* obscure with blinkers.

blinkered *adjective* having narrow, prejudiced views.

blintz *noun* (*plural* **blintzes**) a thin crepe wrapped around a filling, usu. of cream cheese or cottage cheese. [Say BLINTS]

blip ▶ *noun* **1** a quick popping sound; a short bleep. **2** a small image of an object on a radar screen. **3** a temporary movement in statistics. ▶ *verb* (**blips, blipped, blipping**) **1** make a blip. **2** (of figures etc.) rise suddenly and temporarily.

bliss ▶ *noun* **1** perfect joy or happiness: *she gave a sigh of bliss*. **2** a state of spiritual blessedness, typically that reached after death. ▶ *verb* (**blisses, blissed, blissing**) (foll. by *out*) *slang* reach a state of ecstasy.

blissed-out *adjective* *slang* in a state of bliss.

B

blissful *adjective* perfectly happy; joyful. PHRASES **blissful ignorance** fortunate unawareness of something unpleasant. ▶ **blissfully** *adverb*

blister • *noun* **1** a small bubble on the skin filled with serum and caused by friction, burning, etc. **2** a similar swelling on any other surface. • *verb* **1** raise a blister on: *blistered feet*. **2** come up in a blister or blisters.

blistering *adjective* **1** very harsh: *a blistering attack on her character*. **2** very intense: *blistering sun*. **3** very fast: *a blistering shot*. ▶ **blisteringly** *adverb*

blithe *adjective* **1** happy, joyous. **2** careless, casual: *with blithe indifference*. ▶ **blithely** *adverb* **blitheness** *noun* [Rhymes either with *WRITHE* or with the name SMYTH]

blither *verb & noun* = BLATHER. [Rhymes with *DITHER*]

blithering *adjective* *informal* **1** senselessly talkative. **2 a** utter: *blithering idiot*. **b** contemptible. [Rhymes with *DITHERING*]

blitz *informal* • *noun* **1 a** an intensive or sudden (esp. aerial) attack. **b** *informal* any sudden or concentrated effort, esp. on a large scale: *publicity blitz*. **2 (the Blitz)** the intensive German air raids on Britain in 1940. **3** *Football* a play in which one or more defensive backs charge the quarterback of the opposing team. • *verb* **(blitzes, blitzed, blitzing) 1** attack, damage, etc. by a blitz. **2** *Football* charge into the offensive backfield.

blitzed *adjective* *slang* drunk.

blitzkrieg *noun* an intense military campaign intended to bring about a swift victory. [Say BLITS kreeg]

blizzard *noun* **1** a severe snowstorm with high winds. **2** *informal* a large amount: *a blizzard of paperwork*.

bloat • *verb* inflate, swell. • *noun* **1** an accumulation of gas in the stomach or abdomen. **2** the quality of something which has grown beyond manageable size: *administrative bloat*.

bloated *adjective* **1** swollen, puffed. **2** suffering from an excess of gas or water. **3** larger than necessary: *bloated bureaucracy*. **4** excessively wealthy and pampered: *the bloated captains of industry*.

blob *noun* **1** a small roundish mass; a drop of matter. **2** a drop of liquid. **3** a spot of colour. **4** *informal* a large shapeless person. ▶ **blobby** *adjective*

bloc *noun* **1** a combination of nations, parties, groups, or people, formed to promote a particular purpose: *the former Soviet bloc*. **2 (Bloc)** (in Canada) = BLOC QUÉBÉCOIS.

block • *noun* **1** a solid hewn or unhewn piece of hard material, esp. of stone, wood, or ice. **2** a hollow usu. rectangular masonry building unit: *concrete block*. **3** a flat-topped block used as a base for chopping, beheading, hammering on, etc. **4** = AUCTION BLOCK. **5 a** a large building, esp. when subdivided: *East Block of the Parliament Buildings*. **b** = CELLBLOCK. **6 a** an area bounded by (usu. four) streets. **b** the length of one side of this, esp. as a measure of distance: *three blocks away*. **7 a** an obstruction. **b** anything preventing normal progress or operation: *writer's block*. **8** the metal casting containing the cylinders of an internal combustion engine. **9** a pulley or system of pulleys mounted in a case. **10** (in *plural*) = BUILDING BLOCK 3. **11** a piece of wood or metal engraved for printing on paper or fabric. **12** *informal* the head: *knock his block off*. **13** a large quantity or allocation of things treated as a unit, esp. shares, seats in a theatre, etc. **14** a collection of data that can be stored and processed as a single unit. **15** a pad of paper, esp. for drawing. **16** = STARTING BLOCK. **17** *Sport* an obstruction of an opponent or an opponent's play. **18 a** a tract of land offered to an individual settler by a government. **b** a large area of land. **19** a chock for stopping the motion of a wheel etc. • *verb* **1 a** obstruct (a passage etc.). **b** put obstacles in the way of (progress etc.). **2** *Sport* intercept (an opponent or the ball, puck, etc.) with one's body.

• *adjective* treating (many similar things) as one unit: *block booking*. PHRASES **block in 1** sketch roughly; plan. **2** confine. **block out 1 a** shut out (light, noise, etc.). **b** exclude from memory, as being too painful. **2** sketch roughly; plan. **block up 1** confine; shut (a person etc.) in. **2** infill (a window, doorway, etc.) with bricks etc. **on the block** = ON THE AUCTION BLOCK (see AUCTION BLOCK).

blockade • *noun* **1** the surrounding or blocking of access to a place to prevent entry and exit of supplies etc.: *an international economic blockade has created shortages in northern Iraq*. **2** obstruction or prevention of a physiological or mental function. • *verb* **(blockades, blockaded, blockading)** subject to a blockade. PHRASES **run a blockade** enter or leave a blockaded port by evading the blockading force.

blockade-runner *noun* a vessel etc. that attempts to pass through a blockade. ▶ **blockade-running** *noun*

blockage *noun* an obstruction which makes movement or flow difficult or impossible: *a blockage in the pipes* ◊ *the pumps are prone to blockage*.

block and tackle *noun* a system of pulleys and ropes, esp. for lifting.

blockbuster *noun* an extremely popular or financially successful film, book, etc.

block capitals *plural noun* capital block letters.

blocked *adjective* **1** (of a passage) obstructed, clogged, or congested: *a blocked drain*. **2** *Sport* (of a shot or pass etc.) prevented from reaching its target: *a blocked punt*. **3** prevented from happening, succeeding, or progressing: *blocked opportunities* ◊ *a blocked radio transmission*.

blocker *noun* **1** a person or thing that blocks. **2** *Hockey* a glove with a rectangular pad worn by a goalie to protect the hand holding the stick. **3** *Football* a player whose role is to block the opponent's play. **4** a substance which prevents or inhibits a given physiological function.

blockhead *noun* a stupid person. ▶ **blockheaded** *adjective*

block heater *noun* an electric heater used to warm the coolant and hence the engine block of a motor vehicle in winter, allowing for easier starting.

block letters *plural noun* (esp. capital) letters written without serifs and separate from each other.

blocky *adjective* **(blockier, blockiest)** like a block; solid, chunky.

Bloc Québécois *noun* a federal political party advocating Quebec separatism, founded in 1990.

bloke *noun* esp. *Brit. informal* a man, a fellow.

> **WRITING TIP**
> **blond, blonde**
>
> The form **blonde** is more likely to be used of females than of males, e.g. *Rachel's hair is blonde today*. **Blond** can be used of both males and females.

blond (also **blonde**) • *adjective* **1** (of hair or the complexion) light-coloured; fair. **2** (of wood) of a light yellowish colour. • *noun* a person with fair hair and skin. ▶ **blondish** *adjective* **blondness** *noun*

Blood *noun* **1** a member of an Aboriginal people of S Alberta. **2** the Algonquian language of the Blood.

blood • *noun* **1** a usu. red liquid circulating in the arteries and veins of vertebrates that carries oxygen to and carbon dioxide from the tissues of the body. **2** a corresponding fluid in invertebrates. **3** bloodshed, esp. killing. **4** passion, temperament. **5** the blood as the vehicle of hereditary characteristics or relationship; family descent: *musical ability runs in their blood*. **6 a**

relationship; relations: *own flesh and blood*. • *verb* **1** give (a hound) a first taste of blood. **2** initiate (a person) by experience. PHRASES **bad blood** ill feeling. **blood-and-thunder** *informal* sensational, melodramatic. **one's blood is up** one is in a fighting mood. **in one's blood** inherent in one's character. **make one's blood boil** infuriate one. **make one's blood run cold** horrify one. **new** (or **fresh**) **blood** new members admitted to a group, esp. as an invigorating force. **of the blood** royal. **out for a person's blood** set on getting revenge. **taste blood** be stimulated by an early success. **young blood** a younger member or members of a group.

blood bank *noun* **1** a place where supplies of blood or plasma for transfusion are stored. **2** any supply of blood for transfusions.

bloodbath *noun* a massacre.

blood blister *noun* a blister containing blood.

blood brother *noun* a brother by birth or by the ceremonial mingling of blood.

blood-curdling *adjective* horrifying.

blood donor clinic *noun* *Cdn* a usu. temporary location where people can give blood.

blooded *adjective* **1** having blood or a disposition of a specified kind: *cold-blooded*. **2** (of horses etc.) of good pedigree.

blood feud *noun* a feud between families involving killing or injury.

blood group *noun* = BLOOD TYPE.

bloodhound *noun* a large hound of a breed used in tracking, having a very keen sense of smell.

bloodless *adjective* **1** (of the skin or part of the body) drained of colour: *her bloodless lips*. **2** unemotional; cold. **3** without bloodshed: *a bloodless coup*. **4** lacking vitality: *a bloodless chorus*. ▶ **bloodlessly** *adverb*

bloodletting *noun* **1** the removal of some of a person's blood for some purpose, esp. surgically or ritually. **2** bloodshed: *gang members have halted their bloodletting*. **3** *informal* (in a workplace etc.) bitter quarrelling, esp. accompanied by reductions in staff.

bloodline *noun* (usu. in *plural*) **1** (of animals) pedigree. **2** ancestry: *a new set of rights for a small elite, based on bloodlines*.

blood meal *noun* dried blood used for feeding animals and as a fertilizer.

blood money *noun* **1** money paid to the next of kin of a person who has been killed. **2** money paid to a hired murderer. **3** money paid for information about a murder or murderer.

blood poisoning *noun* a diseased state caused by the presence of micro-organisms or toxins in the blood.

blood pressure *noun* the pressure of the blood in the circulatory system, often measured for diagnosis.

blood-red *adjective* red as blood.

blood relative *noun* (also **blood relation**) a relative by birth, not by marriage.

bloodshed *noun* the killing or wounding of people, typically on a large scale during a conflict.

bloodshot *adjective* (of an eyeball) tinged with blood.

blood sport *noun* sport, esp. hunting, involving the wounding or killing of animals.

bloodstain *noun* a discoloration caused by blood.

bloodstained *adjective* **1** stained with blood: *bloodstained clothing*. **2** guilty of bloodshed: *Iran's break with its bloodstained recent past*.

bloodstream *noun* blood in circulation.

bloodsucker *noun* **1** an animal or insect that sucks blood. **2** a person who extorts money or otherwise lives off other people: *"the corporate interests are bloodsuckers*

who siphon any bit of wealth out of Newfoundland," he said*. ▶ **bloodsucking** *adjective*

blood sugar *noun* **1** the amount of glucose in the blood. **2** the glucose itself.

blood test *noun* a scientific examination of a blood sample, esp. for diagnosis, measurement of sugar or alcohol level, etc.

bloodthirsty *adjective* (**bloodthirstier, bloodthirstiest**) **1** having a longing for blood: *bloodthirsty mosquitoes*. **2 a** eager to kill: *bloodthirsty killer*. **b** taking pleasure or showing interest in killing or violence: *bloodthirsty spectators*. **3** (of a film etc.) describing or depicting killing or violence.

blood type *noun* any one of the various types of human blood determining compatibility in transfusion.

blood vessel *noun* a vein, artery, or capillary carrying blood.

blood work *noun* = BLOOD TEST.

bloody • *adjective* (**bloodier, bloodiest**) **1 a** of or like blood. **b** running or smeared with blood. **2 a** involving, loving, or resulting from bloodshed: *bloody battle*. **b** cruel: *bloody murderer*. **3** esp. *Cdn, Brit.*, *Austral.*, & *NZ informal* expressing annoyance or antipathy, or as an intensive: *a bloody shame*. **4** red. • *adverb informal* as an intensive: *you can bloody well do it*. • *verb* (**bloodies, bloodied, bloodying**) make bloody; stain with blood. PHRASES **bloody murder** vociferously: *screaming bloody murder*.

Bloody Caesar *noun* *Cdn* a drink composed of vodka and tomato clam cocktail, garnished with celery.

Bloody Mary *noun* (*plural* **Bloody Marys**) a drink composed of vodka and tomato juice.

bloom • *noun* **1 a** a flower, esp. one cultivated for its beauty. **b** the state of flowering: *the trees were in bloom*. **2** a state of perfection or loveliness; the prime: *a young girl still in the bloom of youth*. **3 a** (of the complexion) a flush; a glow. **b** a delicate powdery surface deposit on plums, grapes, leaves, etc., indicating freshness. **c** a cloudiness on a shiny surface. **4** a scum formed by the rapid proliferation of microscopic algae on water. • *verb* **1** bear flowers; be in flower. **2 a** come into, or remain in, full beauty. **b** flourish; be in a healthy, vigorous state. PHRASES **the bloom is off** the thing in question is no longer new, fresh, or exciting: *the bloom is off Internet stocks*.

bloomer *noun* **1** a plant that blooms (in a specified way): *early autumn bloomer*. **2** a person who develops or matures later (**late bloomer**) or earlier (**early bloomer**) than normal.

bloomers *plural noun* **1** women's loose-fitting knee-length underpants. **2** *informal* any women's underpants.

blooming *adjective* flourishing; healthy.

bloop *Baseball* • *verb* hit (a ball) as a blooper. • *noun* a blooper (also as an *adjective*: *bloop single*).

blooper *noun* *informal* **1** an embarrassing blunder. **2** *Baseball* **a** a fly ball hit just beyond the infield. **b** a ball thrown high by the pitcher.

Bloquiste *noun* *Cdn* a member of the Bloc Québécois. [Say block EEST]

blossom • *noun* **1** a flower or a mass of flowers, esp. of a fruit tree. **2** the stage or time of flowering: *the cherry tree in blossom*. **3** a promising stage: *the blossom of youth*. • *verb* **1** open into flower. **2** reach a promising stage.

blot • *noun* **1** a spot or stain of ink etc. **2** a moral defect in an otherwise good character; a disgraceful act or quality. **3** any disfigurement or blemish. • *verb* (**blots, blotted, blotting**) **1 a** spot or stain with ink; smudge. **b** (of a pen, ink, etc.) make blots. **2 a** use blotting paper or other absorbent material to absorb (liquid), esp. by dabbing or pressing rather than rubbing. **b** (of blotting

paper etc.) soak up (liquid). **3** disgrace: *blotted her reputation.* PHRASES **blot out 1 a** obliterate (writing). **b** obscure (a view, sound, etc.). **2** obliterate (from the memory) as too painful. **3** destroy.

blotch • *noun* (*plural* **blotches**) **1** a discoloured or inflamed patch on the skin. **2** an irregular patch of colour. • *verb* (**blotches, blotched, blotching**) cover with blotches. ▶**blotchy** *adjective* (**blotchier, blotchiest**)

blotter *noun* **1** a sheet or sheets of blotting paper, usu. inserted into a frame. **2** a record of arrests and charges in a police station.

blotting paper *noun* absorbent paper used for soaking up excess ink.

blouse *noun* **1** a woman's or girl's lightweight upper garment, usu. with buttons and a collar. **2** a waist-length belted jacket worn as part of an airman's or soldier's uniform in some military forces. **3** a loose linen or cotton garment, usu. hanging above the knees and belted at the waist. [Rhymes either with *PLOWS* or with *MOUSE*]

blow¹ • *verb* (**blows, blew, blown, blowing**) **1 a** (of the wind or air) move along; act as an air current. **b** be driven by an air current: *papers blew along the sidewalk.* **c** drive with an air current: *blew the sign down.* **2 a** send out (esp. air) by breathing: *blew smoke.* **b** send a directed air current from the mouth. **3** sound or be sounded by blowing. **4 a** direct an air current at: *blew the embers.* **b** (foll. by *off, away,* etc.) clear of by means of an air current: *blew the dust off.* **5** (*past participle* **blowed**) *slang* curse, confound: *blow it!* ◊ *I'll be blowed!* **6 a** clear (the nose) of mucus by blowing. **b** remove contents from (an egg) by blowing through it. **7 a** puff, pant. **b** (esp. in *passive*) exhaust of breath. **8** *slang* a depart suddenly from: *blew the town yesterday.* **b** depart suddenly. **9** explode or cause to explode. **10** melt or cause to melt from overloading: *the fuse has blown.* **11** make or shape (glass or a bubble) by blowing air in. **12** (of a whale) eject air and water through a blowhole. **13** *informal* **a** squander, spend recklessly: *blew $50 on a meal.* **b** spoil, bungle (an opportunity etc.): *he's blown his chance.* **c** waste, esp. by incompetence: *blew a two-goal lead.* • *noun* **1 a** an act of blowing. **b** *informal* a session of jazz playing (on any instrument). **2 a** a gust of wind or air. **b** a storm. PHRASES **blow away** *slang* **1** kill or destroy, esp. with a gun. **2** defeat soundly. **3** impress greatly. **blow a person's cover** reveal a person's secret identity. **blow the doors off something** be outstandingly more successful than something. **blow in** *informal* arrive unexpectedly. **blow a kiss** pretend to place a kiss on one's hand and blow it to a distant person. **blow a person's mind** *slang* **1** impress a person greatly; overwhelm. **2** cause a person to have drug-induced hallucination. **blow off 1** remove or be removed by the force of an air current, esp. the wind. **2** remove by an explosive force, esp. a bomb or bullet. **3** *slang* disregard. **4** *slang* waste (time). **5** *slang* fail to do (work) or attend (classes etc.). **blow out 1** extinguish (esp. a flame) by blowing. **2** send outwards by an explosion. **3** (of a tire) burst. **4** (of a fuse etc.) melt. **5** *slang* defeat convincingly. **b** render useless, break: *he blew out his knee.* **6** cause to lose strength by blowing: *the storm blew itself out.* **blow out of the water** defeat overwhelmingly or completely. **blow over** (of trouble etc.) fade away without serious consequences. **blow one's own horn** etc. praise oneself. **blow one's top** (or **stack**) *informal* explode in rage. **blow up 1** a shatter or destroy by an explosion. **b** explode, erupt. **2** inflate. **3** *informal* a enlarge (a photograph). **b** exaggerate. **4** *informal* come to notice; arise. **5** *informal* lose one's temper.

blow² *noun* **1** a hard stroke with a hand or weapon. **2** a sudden shock or misfortune. PHRASES **come to blows** end up fighting. **in** (or **at**) **one blow** in one operation. **strike a blow for** (or **against**) help (or oppose).

blow-by-blow *adjective* (of a description etc.) giving all the details in sequence.

blowdown *noun* **1** the uprooting of trees by the wind. **2** a tree so felled.

blow-dried *adjective* **1** (of hair) dried with a blow-dryer. **2** (of a person) well-groomed and usu. superficially or pretentiously suave.

blow-dry • *verb* (**blow-dries, blow-dried, blow-drying**) arrange (the hair) while drying it with a hand-held dryer. • *noun* an act of doing this. ▶**blow-dryer** *noun*

blower *noun* **1** *in senses of* BLOW¹ *verb.* **2** a device for creating a current of air. **3** *informal* a telephone.

blowfish *noun* (*plural* **blowfish**) = PUFFERFISH.

blowfly *noun* (*plural* **blowflies**) any of various flies which deposit their eggs on meat and carcasses, e.g. the bluebottle.

blowhard *noun* *informal* a boastful or pompous person.

blowhole *noun* **1** the nostril of a whale, on the top of its head. **2** a hole in ice through which seals or other animals breathe. **3** a vent for air, smoke, etc., in a tunnel etc. **4** a hole in a coastal rock through which jets of water are intermittently forced upward.

blowing snow *noun* snow whipped up by the wind from accumulations on the ground.

blown *past participle of* BLOW¹.

blowout *noun* **1** *informal* a burst tire. **2** *informal* a game, election, etc. with a lopsided result. **3** *informal* an elaborate party or feast; an extravaganza. **4** *informal* a sale in a retail store with drastic price reductions. **5** a rapid uncontrolled upward rush from an oil or gas well.

blowsy *adjective* (**blowsier, blowsiest**) (also **blowzy**; **blowzier, blowziest**) **1** coarse and red-faced. **2** dishevelled, slovenly. [Rhymes with *LOUSY*]

blowtorch *noun* (*plural* **blowtorches**) a portable device which creates a very hot flame, used for welding etc.

blow-up • *noun* (*plural* **blow-ups**) **1** an enlargement (of a photograph etc.). **2** an explosion. **3** *informal* a quarrel. • *adjective* **1** inflatable. **2** enlarged: *a blow-up photograph.*

BLT *noun* (*plural* **BLTs**) a bacon, lettuce, and tomato sandwich.

blubber • *noun* **1** an insulating layer of fat in whales, polar bears and other swimming mammals. **2** body fat. • *verb* weep loudly. ▶**blubbery** *adjective*

bludgeon • *noun* a club with a heavy end. • *verb* **1** beat with a bludgeon. **2** force or bully someone to do something: *she was determined not to be bludgeoned into submission.* [Say BLUDGE in]

blue • *adjective* (**bluer, bluest**) **1** having a colour between green and violet in the spectrum, like that of a clear sky. **2** sad, depressed; (of a state of affairs) gloomy, dismal: *feel blue.* **3** with bluish skin through cold, fear, etc. **4** having blue or a bluish shade as a distinguishing colour: *blue jay.* **5** pornographic: *a blue film.* **6** *Cdn & Brit.* politically conservative. • *noun* **1** a blue colour or pigment. **2** blue clothes or material: *dressed in blue.* **3** (also **Blue**) *Cdn & Brit.* a supporter of a Conservative party **4** any of various small blue-coloured butterflies of the family Lycaenidae. **5** a blue ball, piece, etc. in a game or sport. **6** (**the blue**) the clear sky. PHRASES **until one is blue in the face** repeatedly and at great length until one becomes frustrated, angry, etc. **blue murder** = BLOODY MURDER (*see* BLOODY). **once in a blue**

moon very rarely. **out of the blue** unexpectedly. **talk** etc. **a blue streak** speak etc. in a swift, continuous stream of words.

blueback noun **1** any of several fishes, esp. two species of Pacific coast salmon: **a** Cdn a small or immature coho. **b** = SOCKEYE. **2** Cdn a very young hooded seal.

bluebell noun **1** = HAREBELL. **2** any of several Eurasian plants with clusters of bell-shaped blue flowers on a stem. **3** any of several other plants with blue bell-shaped flowers.

blueberry noun (plural **blueberries**) **1** any of several plants of the genus Vaccinium, cultivated for their edible fruit. **2** the small dark blue fruit of these plants.

blueberry buckle noun Cdn (Maritimes) a cake topped with blueberries and a crumbly topping.

bluebird noun any of various North American songbirds of the thrush family, the males having distinctive blue plumage on the back or head.

blueblood noun **1** a wealthy or socially prominent person. **2** an aristocrat. **3** (**blue blood**) noble birth. ▶ **blue-blooded** adjective

blue book noun **1** (**Blue Book**) Cdn a report of estimated government spending tabled annually in the House of Commons. **2** a book listing the market value of certain consumer items, esp. used cars. **3** a directory listing people considered socially important.

bluebottle noun any of several large blowflies with a metallic-blue body.

blue box noun (plural **blue boxes**) Cdn a blue plastic box for the collection of recyclable materials.

blue cheese noun any of several strong cheeses produced with veins of blue mould, e.g. Roquefort.

blue chip • noun an investment, e.g. in an established, large corporation, considered to be fairly reliable though not entirely without risk. • adjective (usu. **blue-chip**) **1** (of an investment, company, etc.) reliable; consistently giving a good yield: blue-chip stocks ◊ blue-chip clients like American Express, AT&T, and Coca-Cola. **2** of the highest quality.

blue-collar adjective of or relating to manual or industrial labourers, usu. paid hourly wages rather than a salary (compare WHITE-COLLAR 1).

bluefin noun (plural **bluefin** or **bluefins**) (also **bluefin tuna**) the common tuna, Thunnus thynnus.

bluefish noun (plural **bluefish**) **1** a voracious blue-coloured marine food fish, inhabiting warmer waters of the Atlantic and Indian oceans. **2** (also **Boston bluefish**) = POLLOCK.

bluegill noun (plural **bluegill** or **bluegills**) a small colourful North American freshwater sunfish.

blue grama noun a grass of the shortgrass prairie, also grown as an ornamental.

bluegrass noun **1** any of several bluish-green grasses, esp. Kentucky bluegrass, used for fodder and in lawns. **2** a kind of country music characterized by close harmony and virtuosic playing of banjos, guitars, fiddles, etc.

blue-green algae plural noun = CYANOBACTERIA.

blue helmet noun informal a UN peacekeeper.

blue ice noun Cdn a vivid blue ice formed when a large amount of water freezes quickly.

blue jay noun a crested jay of central and eastern North America, Cyanocitta cristata, having a large tail and blue, black, and white plumage.

blue line noun Hockey **1** one of the two lines on the ice surface between the centre and the goal. **2** a team's defencemen collectively.

blue mould noun a bluish fungus of the genus Penicillium growing on food (esp. cheeses) etc.

blueness noun the state or quality of being blue.

Bluenose noun (also **Bluenoser**) Cdn informal a Nova Scotian.

blue pages plural noun the pages of a telephone directory containing listings of government departments and services.

blueprint noun **1** a photographic print of the final stage of engineering or other plans in white on a blue background. **2** a detailed plan, esp. in the early stages of a project or idea.

blue ribbon • noun the highest honour in a competition etc. • adjective (usu. **blue-ribbon**) **1** of the highest quality: a blue-ribbon herd centred on 50 outstanding Hereford cows. **2** (of a committee, jury, etc.) carefully or specially selected for their expertise etc.: a blue-ribbon panel of economists.

blue rinse • noun a preparation for tinting grey hair. • adjective (also **blue-rinse, blue-rinsed**) composed of or relating to esp. conservative elderly women: weekday ballet matinees tend to attract the blue-rinse set.

blues plural noun **1** (**the blues**) a bout of depression: had a fit of the blues. **2** (**the blues**; often treated as singular) a melancholic musical style characterized by frequent blues notes and often in a twelve-bar sequence: Miles Davis brought back lyricism and melody and the blues to jazz ◊ the band played a blues number.

blue spruce noun a North American spruce with bluish-green needles.

bluestem noun any of several tall North American grasses growing in prairie regions.

bluesy adjective (**bluesier, bluesiest**) containing some elements of blues music.

blue water noun open sea.

blue whale noun a baleen whale, Balaenoptera musculus, the largest of all living animals.

bluey adjective = BLUISH.

bluff[1] • verb **1** make a pretense of strength or confidence to gain an advantage: he's been bluffing all along. **2** mislead by bluffing: the object is to bluff your opponent into submission. • noun an attempt to deceive someone into believing that one can or is going to do something. PHRASES **bluff one's way** deal with a difficult situation by using deception: bluffed her way through customs. **call a person's bluff** challenge a person thought to be bluffing.

bluff[2] • noun **1** a steep cliff or bank. **2** Cdn (Prairies) a grove or clump of trees, usu. poplars or willows. • adjective **1** (of a person) good-naturedly blunt, frank: a big, bluff, hearty man. **2** (of a cliff, or a ship's bows) having a vertical or steep broad front.

bluffer noun a person who bluffs.

bluing noun a blue powder or liquid used to prevent white laundry from yellowing.

bluish adjective somewhat blue.

blunder • noun a careless or foolish mistake, esp. an important one. • verb **1** make a blunder; act clumsily or ineptly: one's first blundering attempts. **2** move about clumsily; stumble upon inadvertently: we were blundering about in the darkness ◊ blundered into a tropical rainforest. ▶ **blunderer** noun **blunderingly** adverb

blunt • adjective **1** (of a knife, pencil, etc.) lacking in sharpness; having a worn-down point or edge. **2** (of a person or manner) direct, outspoken. **3** short and with a squared-off end: blunt fingers. • verb **1** make blunt or less sharp. **2** weaken or reduce the sensitivity of (the senses, one's feelings, etc.): their determination had been blunted after several failed attempts. ▶ **bluntly** adverb (in sense 2 of adjective). **bluntness** noun

blur • verb (**blurs, blurred, blurring**) **1** make or become unclear or less distinct. **2** smear; partially efface. **3** make (one's memory etc.) dim or less clear.

B

• *noun* something that appears or sounds indistinct or unclear.

blurb *noun* a promotional (usu. complimentary) description, esp. printed on a book's jacket by its publisher.

blurry *adjective* (**blurrier, blurriest**). without a clear outline; indistinct, not clear: *blurry pictures ◊ their policy is rather blurry*.

blurt *verb* (usu. foll. by *out*) utter abruptly, thoughtlessly, or tactlessly.

blush • *verb* (**blushes, blushed, blushing**) **1 a** develop a pink tinge in the face from embarrassment or shame. **b** (of the face) redden in this way. **2** feel embarrassed or ashamed. **3** be or become red or pink. • *noun* **1** the act of blushing. **2** a pink tinge. **3** (also **blusher**) a cosmetic used to give a pinkish colour to the cheeks. **4** a fairly sweet, pale pink wine. PHRASES **at first blush** on the first glimpse or impression: *the issue of interest rates is more important than might appear at first blush*.

bluster • *verb* **1** talk in a loud, aggressive, or indignant way with little effect: *he threatened and blustered, suggesting she would have to pay for damage to his car though he was at fault ◊ a blustering bully*. **2** (of the wind etc.) blow fiercely: *a blizzard blustered against the sides of the house*. • *noun* loud, aggressive, or indignant talk with little effect: *the bluff and bluster of the negotiation process*. ▶ **blusterer** *noun* **blustery** *adjective*

B movie *noun* a film regarded as second-rate, esp. one which relies on stereotypes and formulas.

BMX *noun* (*plural* **BMXs**) **1** organized bicycle racing on a dirt track, esp. for youngsters. **2** the sturdy, manoeuvrable kind of bicycle used for this.

bn. *abbreviation* billion.

BNA *abbreviation* hist. British North America.

B.O. *abbreviation* **1** *informal* BODY ODOUR. **2** BOX OFFICE.

boa *noun* **1** any of several large snakes found mainly in warm regions, which kill prey by coiling themselves around it and suffocating it. **2** any snake which crushes its prey. **3** a long thin scarf made of feathers or fur.

boa constrictor *noun* a large snake native to tropical America and the West Indies, which crushes its prey.

SPELL CHECK [ABC]
boar, bore

Something dull is a **bore**. **Bore** is also the spelling for "bore a hole", "tidal bore", and "12-bore shotgun".

---

boar *noun* **1** (also **wild boar**) **a** a tusked wild pig of Eurasia and Africa, from which domestic pigs are descended. **b** its flesh. **2** an uncastrated male pig. **3** a male guinea pig etc.

board • *noun* **1 a** a flat thin piece of sawn timber, usu. long and narrow. **b** a material resembling this, made from compressed or synthetic fibres: *cardboard*. **c** a thin slab of wood or a similar substance, often with a covering, used for any of various purposes: *ironing board ◊ notice board*. **d** thick stiff card used in bookbinding. **2** = CIRCUIT BOARD. **3** the provision of regular meals, usu. with accommodation, for payment. **4 a** the directors of a company or other organization. **b** a specially constituted administrative body. **5** (in *plural*) the wooden fencelike structure enclosing the ice surface of a skating rink. **6** (in *plural*) *slang* skis. • *verb* **1 a** go on board (a ship, aircraft, etc.). **b** force one's way on board (a ship etc.) in attack. **c** receive passengers (a plane is now boarding. **d** allow (passengers) on board; load (an airplane). **2 a** receive regular meals, or meals and lodging, for payment. **b** arrange accommodation

away from home for: *boarded the dog*. **c** provide (a lodger etc.) with regular meals. **3** cover with boards; seal or close. **4** *Hockey* bodycheck (an opponent) into the boards with excessive force. PHRASES **across the board** general; generally; applying to all. **go by the board** be neglected, omitted, or discarded: *my education went by the board when my father died*. **on board 1** on or in a ship, train, etc. **2** present and functioning as a member of a team, corporation, etc. **3** *Baseball* on base. **take on board** consider (a new idea etc.).

board and batten *noun* a siding of vertical boards with battens at the joints between the boards.

SPELL CHECK [ABC]
boarder, border

A pattern around the edge of something or the division between two countries is a **border**.

---

boarder *noun* **1** a person who boards, esp. a lodger or a pupil at a boarding school. **2** a person who boards a ship, esp. an enemy.

board foot *noun* a unit of volume for lumber equal to one square foot of one-inch-thick board.

boarding *noun* *Hockey* the infraction of bodychecking an opponent into the boards with excessive force.

boarding house *noun* an establishment providing board and lodging for paying guests.

boarding school *noun* a school at which most or all pupils are resident during the school term.

board of control *noun* *Cdn* (in Ontario) an elected body comprising the mayor of a municipality and controllers elected on a city-wide basis rather than to represent wards.

board of education *noun* (*Ont.* & *US*) **1** a body which administers public schools within a stated jurisdiction. **2** the jurisdiction covered by such a board.

board of trade *noun* = CHAMBER OF COMMERCE.

boardroom *noun* a meeting room in which the directors of a company etc. convene.

boardsailing *noun* = WINDSURFING. ▶ **boardsailor** *noun*

boardwalk *noun* a walkway of crosswise wooden boards, constructed esp. on sand etc.

boast • *verb* **1** declare one's achievements, possessions, or abilities with indulgent pride and satisfaction. **2** own or have as something praiseworthy etc.: *the hotel boasts high standards of comfort*. • *noun* **1** an act of boasting: *I said I would score and it wasn't an idle boast*. **2** something one is proud of: *it was her proud boast that she had never missed a day's work*. ▶ **boaster** *noun*

boastful *adjective* showing excessive pride and self-satisfaction in one's achievements, possessions, or abilities. ▶ **boastfully** *adverb* **boastfulness** *noun*

boat • *noun* **1** a small vessel propelled on water by an engine, oars, or sails. **2** (in general use) a ship of any size. **3** an elongated boat-shaped container for holding gravy, sauce, etc. • *verb* **1** travel or go in a boat, esp. for pleasure. **2** catch (a fish) and bring it into a boat. PHRASES **off the boat** often *offensive* recently arrived from a foreign country. **in the same boat** sharing the same (usu. adverse) circumstances.

boater *noun* **1** a person who boats, esp. as a recreation. **2** a flat-topped hardened straw hat with a brim.

boathouse *noun* a shed at the edge of a river, lake, etc., for housing boats.

boating *noun* the use of boats for recreation etc.

boatload *noun* **1** enough to fill a boat: *denied river passage to the North West Company's boatloads of pemmican*. **2** *informal* a large number: *murres are shot by the boatload on the east coast*.

boatman *noun* (*plural* **boatmen**) a man who hires out boats or provides transport by boat.

boat people *plural noun* refugees who have fled by sea.

boatswain *noun* a ship's officer in charge of equipment and the duties of the crew. [Say BOE z'n]

Bob *noun* PHRASES **Bob's your uncle** *Cdn* & *Brit. slang* an expression of completion or satisfaction.

bob¹ • *verb* (**bobs, bobbed, bobbing**) **1** move quickly up and down, esp. on water. **2** move (the body or part of it) up and down with a slight jerk. • *noun* a jerking or bouncing movement, esp. upward. PHRASES **bob for** try to catch (floating apples etc.) with the mouth, as a game. **bob up** come to the surface or reappear suddenly.

bob² • *noun* **1** a woman's or child's hairstyle cut short and even all around. **2** a weight on a pendulum, plumb line, or kite tail. **3 a** a short runner on a sled etc. **b** = BOBSLED. **4** a horse's docked tail. **5** (also **bobber**) a float used in fishing to suspend a line or net at a fixed depth. • *verb* (**bobs, bobbed, bobbing**) cut (hair) short and even all around.

bobbin *noun* **1** a cylinder or cone holding thread, yarn, wire, etc., used esp. in weaving and machine sewing. **2** a spool or reel.

SPELL CHECK
bobble, bauble   ABC ✓

A small ornament or item of jewellery is a **bauble**.

---

bobble¹ • *verb* (**bobbles, bobbled, bobbling**) **1** move with continual bobbing. **2** mishandle or fumble (a ball). • *noun* a mistake or error, esp. a fumble of a ball.

bobble² *noun* a small woolly or tufted ball as a decoration or trimming.

bobby pin *noun* a flat hairpin of metal bent double.

bobby socks *plural noun* socks reaching just above the ankle, esp. worn by teenage girls in the 1940s.

bobby soxer *noun* an adolescent girl, esp. one of the 1940s, wearing bobby socks.

bobcat *noun* a small North American lynx with a spotted reddish-brown coat and a short tail.

bobolink *noun* a North American songbird the male of which is black with yellow and white markings, and the female yellowish buff. [Say BOBBA link]

bobskate *noun* a child's skate consisting of two parallel blades attached with straps to a shoe etc.

bobsled (also **bobsleigh**) • *noun* a mechanically steered and braked sled for two or four people, used for racing down a steep ice-covered run with many turns. • *verb* (**bobsleds, bobsledded, bobsledding**) race in a bobsled. ▶ **bobsledder** *noun*

bobwhite *noun* a North American quail.

bocce *noun* an Italian form of lawn bowling, usu. played on a narrow dirt-covered court. [Say BOTCHIE]

bocconcini *noun* a mild Italian cheese like mozzarella, in the form of a small ball. [Say bock on CHEENY]

SPELL CHECK
bod, baud   ABC ✓

The computing term is **baud**.

---

bod *noun informal* a body: *has a gorgeous bod*.

bodacious *adjective slang* outstanding, excellent. [Say boe DAY shus]

bode *verb* (**bodes, boded, boding**) suggest a particular outcome: *their argument did not bode well for the future* ◊ *the massacres of 1792 boded ill for the future course of the Revolution*.

Bodhisattva *noun* in Mahayana Buddhism, a person who is able to reach nirvana but delays doing so through compassion for others. [Say boe dee SATVA]

bodice *noun* the part of a woman's dress or blouse (excluding sleeves) above the waist. [Say BOD iss]

bodied *combining form* having a body of the specified shape, colour, character, etc.: *full-bodied*.

bodily • *adjective* of or concerning the body: *bodily functions* ◊ *God is not present in bodily form*. • *adverb* **1** by taking hold of a person's body, esp. with force: *he hauled her bodily from the van*. **2** with one's whole body; with great force: *he launched himself bodily at the door*.

body *noun* (*plural* **bodies**) **1 a** the physical structure of a person or an animal, whether dead or alive. **b** the torso apart from the head and the limbs. **c** a corpse. **2 a** the main or central part of a thing: *the body of the essay*. **b** the bulk or majority; the aggregate: *body of opinion*. **3 a** a group of persons regarded collectively, esp. as having a corporate function: *governing body*. **b** (usu. foll. by *of*) a collection: *body of facts*. **4** a quantity: *body of water*. **5** a piece of matter; a mass: *celestial body*. **6** *informal* a person. **7 a** a full or substantial quality of flavour, tone, etc., e.g. in wine, musical sounds, etc. **b** an appearance of fullness and usu. waviness of the hair. PHRASES **in a body** all together. **keep body and soul together** keep alive, esp. barely. **over my dead body** *informal* entirely without my assent. **take the body** *Hockey* bodycheck.

body bag *noun* a bag for carrying a corpse from the scene of an accident, crime, battle, etc.

bodybuilder *noun* a person who strengthens, shapes, and enlarges their muscles by lifting weights and strenuous exercise. ▶ **bodybuilding** *noun*

bodycheck *Hockey* • *noun* an attempt to obstruct a player by bumping into them, typically with the shoulder or hip. • *verb* hit or obstruct in this way.

body count *noun* a list or total of people killed, esp. in a military operation.

body double *noun* a stand-in for a film actor during stunt or nude scenes.

bodyguard *noun* a person or group of persons escorting and protecting another person.

body language *noun* communication through conscious or unconscious gestures and expressions.

body odour *noun* the smell of the human body, esp. when unpleasant.

body piercing *noun* the piercing of holes in parts of the body other than the earlobes in order to insert rings or other jewellery.

body politic *noun* organized society; a people or nation regarded as a political entity: *the Rowell-Sirois report diagnosed and prescribed treatment for Canada's ailing body politic*.

body search *noun* (*plural* **body searches**) a search of a person's entire body and clothing for a hidden weapon, drugs, etc.

body shop *noun* a shop or garage where repairs to the bodywork of vehicles are carried out.

bodysuit *noun* a close-fitting one-piece stretch garment worn esp. for sporting activities.

bodysurf *verb* ride the crest of a wave without a surfboard. ▶ **bodysurfer** *noun* **bodysurfing** *noun*

bodywork *noun* **1** the structure of a vehicle body. **2** the manufacture or repair of vehicle bodies.

Boer • *noun* a South African of Dutch descent. • *adjective* of or relating to the Boers. [Say BORE]

boffo *adjective slang* (esp. of a film, theatrical performance, etc.) hugely successful; bringing in a great deal of money: *our pre-Broadway tour did boffo business*.

bog • *noun* wet spongy ground too soft to support any heavy body, composed largely of mosses, sedges, rushes, and decomposing plant matter. • *verb* (**bogs,**

B

bogged, bogging) 1 make or become unable to proceed: *was bogged down in paperwork*. **2** sink into mud or wet ground: *the car got bogged down in the lane*.
bogan *noun* (*Maritimes & Maine*) a stagnant backwater adjacent to a river, lake, etc. [Say BOAG'n]
bogey¹ *Golf* • *noun* (*plural* **bogeys**) **1** a score of one stroke over par at any hole. **2** (*formerly*) = PAR 3. • *verb* (**bogeys, bogeyed, bogeying**) play (a hole) in one stroke over par.
bogey² *noun* (*plural* **bogeys**) **1** an evil or mischievous spirit. **2** an awkward or threatening thing or circumstance: *the bogey of economic recession*. **3** *slang* = BOOGER.
bogeyman *noun* (*plural* **bogeymen**) **1** an imaginary evil spirit, esp. invoked to frighten children. **2** a person or thing that is widely regarded as an object of fear: *the violent criminal has replaced the communist as the bogeyman*.
boggle *verb* (**boggles, boggled, boggling**) *informal* be or cause to be startled or baffled: *the mind boggles* ◊ *boggles the mind*.
boggling *adjective* astonishing: *the total was a boggling $10 million* ◊ *mind-boggling*.
boggy *adjective* (**boggier, boggiest**) (of ground) soft, wet, and muddy, like a bog.
bogus *adjective* not genuine or true: *a bogus insurance claim*.
Bohemian • *noun* **1** a native of Bohemia. **2** (also **bohemian**) a socially unconventional person, esp. an artist or writer. • *adjective* **1** of or characteristic of Bohemia, a region of the Czech Republic, or its people. **2** (also **bohemian**) socially unconventional.
▶ **bohemianism** *noun* (in sense 2). [Say boe HEEMY in]
Bohemian waxwing *noun* a waxwing, *Bombycilla garrulus*, which breeds in northwestern North America and northern Eurasia and wanders widely in winter.
boil¹ • *verb* **1 a** (of a liquid) start to bubble up and turn to vapour; reach a temperature at which this happens. **b** (of a vessel) contain boiling liquid: *the kettle is boiling*. **2 a** bring (a liquid or vessel) to a temperature at which it boils. **b** cook by boiling. **c** subject to the heat of boiling water, e.g. to clean. **3 a** (of the sea etc.) churn like boiling water. **b** be greatly agitated, esp. by anger. • *noun* **1** the act or process of boiling; boiling point: *bring to a boil*. **2** a party at which (a usu. specified) food is boiled and eaten: *corn boil*. PHRASES **boil down 1** reduce volume by boiling. **2** reduce to essentials. **3** (*foll. by to*) amount to. **boil over 1** spill over in boiling. **2** lose one's temper; become overexcited.
boil² *noun* an inflamed pus-filled swelling caused by infection of a hair follicle etc.
boiled dinner *noun* a dish of meat and vegetables, esp. beef brisket, potatoes, cabbage, turnip, carrots, etc., stewed together in water.
boiler *noun* **1** a strong vessel for generating steam under pressure. **2** a tank for heating a hot-water supply. **3** a metal tub or other vessel used for boiling.
boilerplate *noun* **1** a piece of rolled steel for making boilers. **2** a standard form, computer subroutine, etc. which can easily be replicated. **3** hackneyed or predictable ideas, language, or writing: *this is no ordinary atlas full of boilerplate information on provincial boundaries, capital cities, and transportation routes*.
boiler room *noun* a room with a boiler and other heating equipment.
boiling *adjective* (also **boiling hot**) *informal* very hot.
boiling point *noun* **1** the temperature at which a liquid starts to boil. **2** a state of high excitement or extreme agitation: *tempers reached the boiling point*.
boing • *noun* a twanging sound, such as that of a compressed spring suddenly released. • *interjection* indicating this sound.

boink *verb & noun* = BONK.
boisterous *adjective* **1** noisy, energetic, and cheerful: *the children's boisterous behaviour*. **2** (of the sea, weather, etc.) stormy, rough. ▶ **boisterously** *adverb* **boisterousness** *noun* [Say BOY stir us]
bok choy *noun* a cabbage-like plant of the mustard family having dark green outer leaves, white stalks, and a yellow centre.
bold • *adjective* **1** confidently assertive; adventurous, courageous. **2** forthright, impudent. **3** vivid, distinct, well-marked: *bold colours*. **4** (also **boldface**) printed in a thick black typeface. • *noun* (also **boldface**) bold type. • *verb* (also **boldface**) set in bold type. PHRASES **as bold as brass** excessively bold or self-assured. **be (or make) so bold as to** presume to; venture to. ▶ **boldly** *adverb* **boldness** *noun*
bole *noun* the stem or trunk of a tree.
bolero *noun* (*plural* **boleros**) **1 a** a Spanish dance in simple triple time. **b** music for or in the time of a bolero. **2** a sleeved or sleeveless open jacket just reaching the waist. [Say buh LAIR oh]
Bolivian • *adjective* of or relating to Bolivia, a country in South America, or its people or culture. • *noun* a native or inhabitant of Bolivia. [Say buh LIVVY un]
boll *noun* a rounded capsule containing seeds, esp. cotton or flax. [Sounds like *BOWL*]
boll weevil *noun* a small weevil of Mexico and the southern US, whose larvae destroy cotton bolls.
bolo *noun* (*plural* **bolos**) **1** a large heavy knife, used esp. in the Philippines. **2** (also **bolo tie**) a necktie of cord or thick string, fastened at the collar with a decorative clasp, typically part of traditional cowboy attire.
bologna *noun* a smoked luncheon meat made from finely minced pork and beef. [Say buh LONEY or buh LONA]
Bolshevik • *noun* **1** *hist.* a member of the radical faction of the Russian socialist party, which became the communist party in 1918. **2** a Russian communist. **3** (in general use) any revolutionary socialist. • *adjective* **1** of the Bolsheviks. **2** communist. ▶ **Bolshevism** *noun* **Bolshevist** *noun* [Say BOWL shuh vick]
bolster • *noun* **1** a long, often cylindrical pillow or cushion. **2** a pad or support, esp. in a machine. • *verb* **1** support, reinforce: *bolstered our morale*. **2** support with a bolster or pillow; prop up. [Say BOWL stir]
bolt • *noun* **1** a sliding bar and socket used to fasten or lock a door, gate, etc. **2** a large usu. metal pin with a head, usu. riveted or used with a nut, to hold things together. **3** a discharge of lightning. **4** the sliding piece of the breech mechanism of a rifle. **5** a sudden escape or dash for freedom. **6** a roll of fabric, paper, etc. • *verb* **1** fasten or lock with a bolt. **2** (*foll. by in, out*) keep (a person etc.) from leaving or entering by bolting a door. **3** fasten together with bolts. **4 a** dash suddenly away, esp. to escape. **b** (of a horse) suddenly gallop out of control. **5** gulp down (food or drink) hurriedly. **6** (of a plant) run to seed. PHRASES **a bolt from** (or **out of**) **the blue** a complete surprise. **bolt upright** rigidly, stiffly.
bomb • *noun* **1 a** a container with explosive, inflammable material, smoke, or gas etc., designed to explode on impact or by means of a time-mechanism or remote-control device. **b** an ordinary object fitted with an explosive device: *letter bomb*. **2** (**the bomb**) the atomic or hydrogen bomb considered as a weapon with supreme destructive power. **3** *informal* a bad failure: *her latest play is a real bomb*. **4** *sport* a long pass, kick, shot or hit. • *verb* **1** attack with bombs; drop bombs on. **2** (*foll. by out*) drive (a person etc.) out of a building or refuge by using bombs. **3** throw or drop bombs. **4** *informal* (often *foll. by out*) fail badly. **5** *informal* move or go very quickly.

bombard verb **1** attack with a number of bombs etc. **2** subject to persistent questioning etc. **3** Physics direct a stream of high-speed particles at (a substance).

Bombardier noun Cdn proprietary an enclosed vehicle which has rear caterpillar treads and front skis so that it can travel over snow and ice. [Say bomba DEER or bom BARD yay]

bombardier noun **1** a member of a bomber crew responsible for sighting and releasing bombs. **2** Cdn & Brit. a non-commissioned officer in the artillery, of a rank equivalent to corporal. [Say bomba DEER]

bombardment noun **1** a continuous attack with bombs, shells, or other missiles. **2** a continuous series of something considered hostile or aggressive: a bombardment of angry letters. **3** Physics a stream of high-speed particles directed at a substance.

bombast noun high-sounding language with little meaning, used to impress people: his speeches are filled with blather and bombast. ▶**bombastic** adjective **bombastically** adverb [Say BOM bast, bom BAST ick]

bombed adjective **1** informal intoxicated. **2** subjected to bombing.

bombed-out adjective **1** (of a person) driven out by bombing. **2** (of a building etc.) rendered uninhabitable by bombing. **3** slang = BOMBED 1.

bomber noun **1** an aircraft equipped to carry and drop bombs. **2** a person using bombs, esp. illegally. **3** Cdn = WATER BOMBER.

bomber jacket noun a short leather or cloth jacket tightly gathered at the waist and cuffs.

bombproof adjective able to resist the effects of blast from a bomb.

bombshell noun **1** an overwhelming surprise or disappointment: the news came as a bombshell ◊ she paused before dropping her bombshell. **2** an artillery bomb. **3** informal a very attractive woman: a blonde bombshell.

bomb shelter noun a room or building built to withstand bombing, used as an air-raid shelter.

bomb squad noun a division of a police force etc. that defuses or safely detonates unexploded bombs.

bona fide • adjective genuine: only bona fide members of the company are allowed to use the logo. • adverb Law in good faith: the court will assume that they have acted bona fide. [Say BONE uh fide or BONNA fide]

bona fides noun **1** honest intentions; sincerity: went to great lengths to establish his liberal bona fides. **2** (as plural) informal documentary evidence showing that a person is what they claim to be: his bona fides are in order. [Say bone a FIE deez]

bonanza noun **1** a source of wealth or good fortune. **2** a large output (esp. of a mine). **3 a** prosperity; good luck. **b** a run of good luck.

bon appétit interjection expressing a wish that someone will enjoy what they are about to eat. [Say bon appa TEE]

bonbon noun a candy, esp. a fancy one.

bond • noun **1 a** a thing that ties another down or together. **b** (usu. in plural) a thing restraining bodily freedom: broke his bonds. **2** (often in plural) **a** a uniting force: sisterly bond. **b** a restraint; a responsibility: bonds of duty. **3** a binding engagement: my word is my bond. **4** a certificate issued by a government or a public company promising to repay borrowed money at a fixed rate of interest at a specified time. **5** adhesiveness. **6** Law a sum of money put up as recognizance, esp. as a guarantee of good conduct: released on $50,000 bond. **7** a strong force of attraction holding atoms together in a molecule or crystal. **8** = BOND PAPER. • verb **1** bind together with an adhesive. **2** adhere; hold together. **3** connect with a bond. **4** place (goods) in bond. **5 a** become emotionally attached. **b** link by an emotional or psychological bond. PHRASES **in bond** (of goods) stored in a bonded warehouse until the importer pays the duty owing.

bondage noun **1** slavery. **2** subjection to constraint, obligation, etc.: young women lost to the bondage of early motherhood. **3** sexual practice that involves the tying up or restraining of one partner.

bonded adjective **1** (of material) reinforced by or cemented to another. **2** (of a person's or company's behaviour or performance) insured by a deposit of money which is paid to the company in the event of the employee's misconduct, theft, etc. **3** emotionally or psychologically linked: a strongly bonded group of females.

bonded warehouse noun a warehouse for the retention of imported goods until duty is paid.

bond paper noun high-quality writing paper, usu. containing cotton fibre.

bond store noun Cdn (Nfld) a liquor store.

bone • noun **1** any of the pieces of hard tissue making up the skeleton in vertebrates. **2** (in plural) **a** the skeleton, esp. as remains after death. **b** the body, esp. as a place of intuitive feeling: felt it in my bones. **3 a** the material of which bones consist. **b** a similar substance such as ivory. **4** (in plural) the essential part of a thing: the bare bones. **5** a strip of stiffening in a corset etc. **6** a pale ivory colour. • verb (**bones, boned, boning**) **1** remove the bones from (meat etc.). **2** stiffen (a garment) with bone etc. PHRASES **bone of contention** a source or ground of dispute. **bone up** (often foll. by on) informal study (a subject) intensively. **close to** (or **near**) **the bone 1** tactless to the point of offensiveness. **2** with little or no money. **have a bone to pick** (usu. foll. by with) have a cause for dispute (with another person). **make no bones about 1** make no attempt to conceal; admit openly. **2** not hesitate: made no bones about revealing her income. **to the bone 1** to the bare minimum: cut expenses to the bone. **2** completely: chilled to the bone. **work one's fingers to the bone** work very hard, esp. thanklessly.

bone-chilling adjective **1** extremely cold. **2** frightening.

bone china noun fine china made of clay mixed with the ash from bones.

boned adjective **1** having bones of a specified sort: fine-boned. **2** (of meat or fish) having the bones removed. **3** (of a corset etc.) having bones as stays.

bonefish noun (plural **bonefish** or **bonefishes**) any of several species of large game fish, esp. Albula vulpes, having many small bones.

bonehead informal • noun a stupid person. • adjective stupid. ▶**boneheaded** adjective

boneless adjective with the bones removed.

bone marrow noun a soft substance in the cavities of bones, of importance in blood cell formation.

bone meal noun crushed or ground bones used esp. as a fertilizer.

boner noun informal a stupid mistake.

boneyard noun informal a cemetery.

bonfire noun a large open-air fire for burning rubbish, as part of a celebration, or as a signal.

Bonfire Night noun Cdn (Nfld) Nov. 5, on which people light very large bonfires of combustible items, e.g. oil barrels and tires, often on prominent heights.

bong noun a low pitched sound as of a bell.

bongo noun (plural **bongos**) either of a pair of small long-bodied drums usu. held between the knees and played with the fingers.

bonhomie noun cheerful outgoing friendliness: he exuded good humour and bonhomie. [Say bon om EE]

bonk • verb hit resoundingly: bonked on the head. • noun

B

an act of knocking or hitting so as to cause a reverberating sound: *my head hit the wall with a bonk*.

bonkers *adjective slang* crazy.

bonnet *noun* **1 a** a woman's or child's hat tied under the chin and usu. with a brim framing the face. **b** *informal* any hat. **2** = WAR BONNET. ▶**bonneted** *adjective*

bonsai *noun* (*plural* **bonsai**) **1** the art of cultivating ornamental artificially dwarfed varieties of trees and shrubs. **2** a tree or shrub grown by this method. [Say BON sigh]

bonspiel *noun* a curling tournament. [Say BON speel]

WRITING TIP
bonus

The phrase **added bonus**, as in *They threw in a key chain as an added bonus*, is redundant and should be avoided in writing. It is better to say *They threw in a key chain as a bonus*.

---

bonus *noun* (*plural* **bonuses**) **1** an unsought or unexpected extra benefit. **2** an amount of money given in addition to normal pay, in recognition of exceptional performance etc.

bonusing *noun Cdn* an act of subsidizing something, esp. to encourage development etc.

bon voyage *interjection & noun* an expression of good wishes to a departing traveller. [Say bon voy OZH]

bony *adjective* (**bonier, boniest**) **1** (of a person) thin with prominent bones. **2** having many bones. **3** of or like bone. **4** (of a fish) having bones rather than cartilage.

boo • *interjection* **1** an expression of disapproval or contempt. **2** a sound intended to surprise. • *noun* an utterance of "boo", esp. as an expression of disapproval or contempt made to a performer etc. • *verb* (**boos, booed, booing**) **1** utter a boo or boos. **2** jeer at (a performer etc.) by booing. **PHRASES** **not say boo to a goose** remain silent, esp. from shyness or timidity.

boob *noun* **1** *slang* a foolish person. **2** *informal* a woman's breast.

booboo *noun informal* a mistake.

boob tube *noun informal* (usu. as **the boob tube**) television; a television set.

booby *noun* (*plural* **boobies**) **1** = BOOB. **2** any of various seabirds of the genus *Sula*, related to the gannet.

booby prize *noun* a prize given to the least successful competitor in a contest.

booby trap • *noun* **1** a trap intended to surprise someone as a practical joke. **2** *Military* an apparently harmless explosive device intended to kill or injure anyone touching it. • *verb* (usu. **booby-trap**) (**booby-traps, booby-trapped, booby-trapping**) place a booby trap or traps in or on.

boodle *noun slang* money, esp. when gained or used dishonestly, e.g. as a bribe.

booger *noun informal* a piece of dried nasal mucus.

boogeyman *noun* (*plural* **boogeymen**) = BOGEYMAN.

boogie • *verb* (**boogies, boogied, boogying**) *informal* **1** dance enthusiastically to rock music. **2** move or go quickly: *let's boogie on out of here*. • *noun* **1** (also **boogie-woogie**) a style of playing blues or jazz on the piano, marked by a persistent bass rhythm. **2** *informal* a dance to rock music. [Say BOOGY (with OO either as in *GOOD* or as in *FOOD*)]

boohoo • *interjection* expressing weeping. • *noun* (*plural* **boohoos**) loud sobbing; bewailing. • *verb* (**boohoos, boohooed, boohooing**) (esp. of a child) weep loudly.

book • *noun* **1 a** a written or printed work consisting of pages glued or sewn together along one side and bound in covers. **b** a literary composition intended for publication. **2** a bound set of blank sheets for writing or keeping records in. **3** a set of tickets, cheques, etc., bound up together. **4** (in *plural*) a set of records or accounts. **5** a main division of a literary work or the Bible. **6** a libretto etc. **7** a telephone directory: *my number's in the book*. **8** a record of bets made and money paid out at a race meeting by a bookmaker. **9** an imaginary record or list: *broke every rule in the book*. • *verb* **1 a** engage (a seat etc.) in advance; make a reservation of. **b** engage (a guest etc.) for some occasion. **2 a** take the personal details of (an offender or rule-breaker). **b** enter in a book or list. **3** issue a railway etc. ticket to. **4** make a reservation: *no need to book*. **PHRASES** **book off** *Cdn* stay home from work, esp. when sick. **booked up** with all places reserved. **bring to book** call to account. **by the book** according to the rules. **close the books** ensure that all pertinent information is entered at the end of an accounting period. **in a person's bad** (or **good**) **books** in disfavour (or favour) with a person. **in my book** in my opinion. **make book 1** give odds, take bets and pay out winnings. **2** bet. **off the books** unofficially, not appearing in payroll reports etc. **on the books 1** (of a rule, law, etc.) publicly recorded. **2** contained in a list of members etc. **throw the book at** *informal* charge or punish to the utmost.

bookbinder *noun* a person who binds books professionally. ▶**bookbinding** *noun*

bookcase *noun* a cabinet containing shelves for books.

bookend • *noun* **1** one of a pair of props used to keep a row of books upright. **2** one of a pair of e.g. television commercials etc. situated at either end of something. **3** *Football* a player positioned at either end of a team's defensive line. • *verb* **1** serve as or provide with something which frames a larger item on either side: *the narrative is bookended by two essays*. **2** (of two people) flank a (third) person.

booker *noun* a person employed to book performers for a concert, theatre engagement, etc.

bookie *noun informal* = BOOKMAKER.

booking *noun* an act of reserving accommodations etc. or of buying a ticket in advance: *the hotel does not handle group bookings* ◊ *early booking is essential*.

bookish *adjective* **1** studious; fond of reading. **2** acquiring knowledge from books rather than practical experience. **3** (of a word, language, etc.) literary; not colloquial. ▶**bookishness** *noun*

bookkeeper *noun* a person who keeps accounts for a business, a public office, etc. ▶**bookkeeping** *noun*

booklet *noun* a small book consisting of a few sheets usu. with paper covers.

bookmaker *noun* a person who takes bets, calculates odds, and pays out winnings. ▶**bookmaking** *noun*

bookmark • *noun* **1** a strip of leather, card, etc., used to mark one's place in a book. **2** a tag or character which can be inserted by a user at a particular point in an electronic text, making it easier to return to that point. **3** an electronic reference to a particular Internet site, which a reader has chosen to store permanently in the browser software, so as to reconnect rapidly with it. • *verb* mark (an Internet site) with a bookmark.

bookseller *noun* a person who sells books, esp. the proprietor of a bookstore.

bookshelf *noun* (*plural* **bookshelves**) **1** a single shelf for books, either attached to a wall or as part of a bookcase. **2** = BOOKCASE. **3** (as an *adjective*) small enough to place on a bookshelf: *bookshelf speakers*.

bookstore *noun* (also **bookshop**) a store where books are sold.

book value *noun* the value of an asset as entered in business or other records (*opp.* MARKET VALUE).

bookworm *noun* **1** *informal* a person who reads a lot. **2** the larva of a moth or beetle which feeds on the paper and glue used in books.

Boolean *adjective* pertaining to a system in which logical propositions are manipulated using the operators "and", "or", and "not". [Say BOOLY in]

boom[1] • *noun* **1** a deep resonant sound, as of a distant explosion or a bass drum. **2** the resonant cry made by some birds and animals, esp. the prairie chicken and bittern. **3** a period of prosperity or sudden activity in commerce. • *verb* **1** make a deep hollow resonant sound. **2** speak or utter with a booming sound. **3** be suddenly prosperous or successful.

boom[2] • *noun* **1 a** a movable arm used for lifting, manoeuvring, etc. **b** a movable arm supporting a camera, microphone, etc. **2 a** a barrier stretched across a river, harbour, etc. to obstruct navigation. **b** a barrier of floating timber used to contain, restrain, or guide floating logs. **c** a similar barrier used to contain oil spills etc. on water. **3** a raft of timber or logs fastened together for transportation on water. **4** a pivoted spar to which the foot of a sail is attached. • *verb* **1** gather or confine (logs) in a boom. **2** move or transport (logs) by forming them into a boom.

boom chain *noun* *Cdn Forestry* a chain linking two boomsticks, used to hold booms of logs together.

boomer *noun* = BABY BOOMER.

boomerang • *noun* a curved flat hardwood projectile used by Australian Aboriginals to kill prey, and often of a kind able to return in flight to the thrower. • *verb* (**boomerangs, boomeranged, boomeranging**) (of a plan etc.) backfire: *misleading consumers will eventually boomerang on a manufacturer*.

booming *adjective* **1** enjoying a period of esp. economic growth or success: *a booming economy*. **2** (of a sound or voice) loud and resonant. **3** forceful, powerful: *a booming slapshot*.

booming ground *noun* **1** *Cdn* a section of a lake, river, etc. where logs are collected into booms. **2** the mating ground of the prairie chicken.

boomlet *noun* a small boom, as in business etc.

boomstick *noun* *Forestry* one of the logs that surrounds a boom and holds it together.

boom town *noun* a town owing its origin, growth, or prosperity to a boom in some commodity or activity.

boomy *adjective* (**boomier, boomiest**) **1** having a loud, deep, resonant sound. **2** of or relating to a boom in business etc.

boon[1] *noun* a thing that is helpful or beneficial: *the book has been a boon to researchers*.

boon[2] *adjective* close, intimate, favourite: *boon companion*.

boondocks *plural noun* (also **boonies**) *informal* rough or isolated country: *the place is out in the boondocks*.

boondoggle *informal* • *noun* **1** work of little or no value done merely to appear busy. **2** a government project with no purpose other than political patronage. • *verb* (**boondoggles, boondoggled, boondoggling**) **1** deceive (a person etc.). **2** do work for the purpose of appearing to be busy.

boor *noun* a rude person. ▶**boorish** *adjective* **boorishly** *adverb* **boorishness** *noun*

boost • *verb* **1** promote or increase the reputation of (a person, scheme, etc.) by praise or advertising. **2** increase or raise: *boost prices*. **3** push from below: *boosted me up the tree*. **4** raise the voltage in (a circuit etc.). **5** recharge (a car battery). **6** *slang* steal. **7** amplify (a radio signal). • *noun* **1** a lift or push from below. **2** an improvement in spirits, confidence, etc. **3** an increase:

a boost in popularity. **4** the action of recharging a car battery.

booster *noun* **1** a device for increasing electrical power or voltage. **2** an auxiliary engine or rocket used to give initial acceleration. **3** a dose of an immunizing agent increasing or renewing the effect of an earlier one: *booster shot*. **4** a keen promoter of a person, organization, or cause: *one of the ballet's biggest boosters*. **5** = BOOSTER SEAT.

booster cable *noun* (usu. in *plural*) = JUMPER CABLE.

boosterism *noun* the tendency to praise, advertise, or promote oneself or one's own (town, country, product, etc.). ▶**boosterish** *adjective*

booster seat *noun* a small seat placed on another seat, e.g. in a car or at a table, to elevate a toddler.

boot[1] • *noun* **1** an outer covering for the foot usu. reaching above the ankle. **2** *informal* a kick. **3** (**the boot**) *informal* dismissal, esp. from employment: *gave them the boot*. • *verb* **1** kick. **2** (often foll. by *out*) dismiss (a person) forcefully. **PHRASES** **die with one's boots on** die in action. **put the boots to** kick brutally. **to boot** as well: *she was a woman of uninspiring appearance and a dreadful bore to boot*. **you bet your boots** *informal* it is quite certain.

boot[2] • *noun* the operation or procedure of booting a computer or an operating system. • *verb* **1** prepare (a computer) for operation by causing an operating system to be loaded into its memory. **2** cause (an operating system) to be loaded in this way. **3** (often. foll. by *up*) load (a routine) into a computer's memory. **4** (of a computer etc.) undergo booting. ▶**bootable** *adjective*

boot camp *noun* *informal* **1** a centre for basic military training. **2** a penal institution in which young, esp. first-time, offenders undergo rigorous exercise and work and military-style discipline.

booted *adjective* having boots on.

booth *noun* (*plural* **booths**) **1** a small temporary structure or stall for the display or sale of goods, e.g. at an exhibition. **2** an enclosure or compartment for various purposes, e.g. voting. **3** a set of a table and benches in a restaurant etc.

bootie *noun* **1** a soft woollen or cloth shoe. **2** a woman's short boot.

bootleg • *adjective* **1** (of alcoholic beverages, drugs, etc.) illicitly produced, transported, or sold. **2** (of a recording) made without authorization, e.g. by illicitly recording a live concert. • *noun* something produced or sold illegally. • *verb* (**bootlegs, bootlegged, bootlegging**) make, distribute, or smuggle illicit goods (esp. alcohol). ▶**bootlegger** *noun*

bootlicker *noun* *informal* a person who behaves obsequiously or servilely.

bootstrap • *noun* a loop at the back of a boot used to pull it on. • *verb* (**bootstraps, bootstrapped, bootstrapping**) make one's way or get oneself into a new state using existing resources; modify or improve by making use of what is already present: *the company is bootstrapping itself out of a marred financial past*. **PHRASES** **pull oneself up by one's bootstraps** better oneself by one's own efforts.

booty *noun* **1** plunder gained by force or violence. **2** something gained or won.

booze *informal* • *noun* **1** alcoholic drink. **2** a drinking bout. • *verb* (**boozes, boozed, boozing**) drink alcoholic liquor, esp. excessively.

booze can *noun* *Cdn* an illegal bar, esp. one operating in a private home.

boozer *noun* *informal* a person who drinks alcohol, esp. to excess.

booze-up *noun* *slang* a drinking bout.

boozy *adjective* (**boozier, booziest**) *informal*

B

B

1 intoxicated. **2** addicted to drink. **3** involving a great deal of alcoholic drink: *a boozy dessert*.

bop¹ *informal* • *noun* = BEBOP. • *verb* (**bops, bopped, bopping**) **1** dance, esp. to pop music. **2** move, go.

bop² *informal* • *verb* (**bops, bopped, bopping**) hit, punch lightly. • *noun* a light blow or hit.

bopper *noun* **1** a young teenager; a teenybopper. **2** a jazz musician; a bebopper.

borage *noun* a plant with hairy leaves and bright blue flowers, sometimes used in salads etc. [Say BORE idge]

borax *noun* **1** a mineral salt occurring in alkaline deposits. **2** the purified form of this salt, used in making glass, as an antiseptic, and as a household cleanser. [Say BORE ax]

Bordeaux *noun* (*plural* **Bordeaux**) any of various red, white, or rosé wines from the district of Bordeaux in southwestern France. [Say bore DOE for the singular, bore DOZE for the plural]

bordello *noun* (*plural* **bordellos**) a brothel. [Say bore DELLO]

SPELL CHECK
border, boarder ☑ABC

Someone who boards or lives at another's house is a **boarder**.

---

border • *noun* **1** the edge or boundary of anything, or the part near it. **2 a** the line separating two areas, esp. countries. **b** the district on each side of this. **3** a distinct edging around anything, esp. for strength or decoration. **4** a long narrow bed of flowers or shrubs in a garden. • *verb* **1** be a border to. **2** provide with a border. **3** (usu. foll. by *on, upon*) **a** adjoin; be situated alongside. **b** come close to being: *this borders on madness*.

border collie *noun* a long-haired usu. black and white dog, often used for herding sheep.

borderline *noun* **1** a marginal position between two categories or qualities: *the borderline between ritual and custom*. **2** a line marking a boundary. • *adjective* verging on each of two categories or conditions without clearly being identifiable as one or the other: *we're not sure what to do because it's a borderline case*.

SPELL CHECK
bore, boar ☑ABC

The wild pig is a **boar**.

---

bore¹ • *verb* (**bores, bored, boring**) **1** make a hole in, esp. with a revolving tool. **2** hollow out (a tube etc.). **3 a** make (a hole) by boring or excavation. **b** make (one's way) through a crowd etc. **4** drill a well (for oil etc.). **5** (of an animal) move by burrowing. • *noun* **1** the hollow of a firearm barrel or of a cylinder in an internal combustion engine. **2** the diameter of this; the calibre. **3** = BOREHOLE.

bore² • *noun* a tiresome or dull person or thing. • *verb* (**bores, bored, boring**) cause to lose all interest by tedious talk or dullness.

bore³ *noun* a high wave caused by rapidly rising tide entering a long shallow narrow inlet.

bore⁴ *past of* BEAR¹.

boreal *adjective* **1** of the North or northern regions. **2** of the north wind. [Say BORRY ul]

boreal forest *noun* the northernmost and coldest forest zone of the northern hemisphere, which forms a belt across North America, Europe, and Asia.

bored *adjective* tired and impatient because one has lost interest or has nothing to do,

boredom *noun* the state of being bored.

borehole *noun* a deep narrow hole, esp. one made in the earth to find water, oil, etc.

borer *noun* **1** any of several worms, molluscs, insects, or insect larvae which bore into wood, other plant material, and rock. **2** a tool for boring.

boric acid *noun* an acid derived from borax, used as a mild antiseptic and in the manufacture of heat-resistant glass and enamels.

boring *adjective* that makes one bored; uninteresting, tedious, dull. ▶ **boringly** *adverb*

WRITING TIP
born, borne 🖉

In the passive, **born** is used only in reference to birth, as in *Megan was born in February* or *Jason was born lucky*. The standard past participle used with all senses of the verb **bear** is **borne**, as in *Sara has borne a son*, *The children were borne on his shoulders*, or *Youssef has never borne a grudge*.

---

born *adjective* **1** existing as a result of birth. **2 a** being such as or likely to become such by natural ability or quality: *a born leader*. **b** having a specified destiny or prospect: *born to shop*. **3** (in *combination*) of a certain status by birth: *Canadian-born* ◊ *well-born*. **4** created or caused: *anger born of frustration*. PHRASES **born and bred** by birth and upbringing. **in all one's born days** *informal* in one's life so far. **not born yesterday** *informal* not stupid; shrewd.

born-again *adjective* **1** of or relating to a Christian who has made a new or renewed commitment to esp. evangelical faith. **2** full of enthusiasm and esp. new-found zeal for a cause: *born-again environmentalists*.

borne 1 *past participle of* BEAR¹. **2** (in *combination*) carried or transported by: *airborne*.

boron *noun* a non-metallic chemical element with semiconductor properties, used in alloy steels and in nuclear control rods. [Say BORE on]

borrow *verb* **1 a** acquire temporarily with the promise or intention of returning. **b** obtain money in this way. **2** use (an idea, invention, etc.) originated by another; plagiarize. **3** (in subtraction) take (one) from a digit of the number being subtracted from, in order to add it as 10 to the digit holding the next lower place. **4** (of a language) adopt (a word form) from another language. PHRASES **borrowed time** an unexpected extension, esp. before an imminent disaster. **borrow trouble** go out of one's way to find trouble. ▶ **borrower** *noun* **borrowing** *noun*

borscht *noun* an originally Eastern European soup with various ingredients including beets and cabbage, and served with sour cream. PHRASES **cheap like borscht** *Cdn informal* extremely cheap. [Say BORSHT]

borzoi *noun* a large Russian wolfhound with a narrow head and silky, usu. white, coat. [Say BORE zoy]

bosom *noun* **1 a** a person's breast or chest, esp. a woman's. **b** *informal* each of a woman's breasts. **c** the enclosure formed by a person's breast and arms. **2** an emotional centre, esp. as the source of an enfolding relationship: *in the bosom of one's family*. [Say BOOZUM (with OO as in BOOK)]

bosom friend *noun* (also **bosom buddy**, *plural* **bosom buddies**) a very close or intimate friend.

bosomy *adjective* (of a woman) having large breasts.

boss¹ • *noun* (*plural* **bosses**) **1** a person who controls or manages an organization, e.g. a political party, union, etc. **3** a person who asserts authority: *let your cats know who's boss*. • *verb* (**bosses, bossed, bossing**) **1** (usu. foll. by *around*) treat in a domineering way; give constant peremptory orders to. **2** be the master or manager of. • *adjective* *slang* first-rate, excellent.

boss² *noun* (*plural* **bosses**) a round knob, stud, etc., esp. on the centre of a shield or in ornamental work.

bossily *adverb* in a bossy manner.

bossiness *noun* bossy behaviour.

bossy *adjective* (**bossier, bossiest**) *informal* domineering; tending to boss.

Boston baked beans *noun* baked beans with salt pork and molasses.

Boston bluefish *noun* (*plural* **Boston bluefish**) Cdn = POLLOCK.

Boston cream pie *noun* a round, vanilla cake with a custard filling and chocolate icing.

Boston fern *noun* an ornamental fern, *Nephrolepis exaltata bostoniensis*.

Bostonian • *noun* a native or inhabitant of Boston, Massachusetts. • *adjective* of or relating to Boston. [Say boss TONY in]

Boston ivy *noun* an ornamental climbing vine, the leaves of which turn a vivid red in autumn.

Boston lettuce *noun* a cultivated salad lettuce having a round head and soft pale leaves.

Boston States *plural noun* Cdn (*Maritimes*) New England.

bosun (also **bo'sun**) = BOATSWAIN. [Say BOE z'n]

botanical • *adjective* (also **botanic**) **1** of or relating to botany. **2** of, relating to, or derived from plants. • *noun* a drug, insecticide, or cosmetic etc. derived from parts of a plant.

botanical garden *noun* (also **botanic garden**) a large garden in which plants are studied and displayed.

botanist *noun* a person who studies plants and their structure.

botany *noun* **1** the study of the physiology, genetics, ecology, and classification of plants. **2** the plant life of a particular area or time.

botch *verb* (**botches, botched, botching**) bungle; do badly: *he botched the job* ◊ *a botched rescue attempt*.

both • *adjective & pronoun* the two, not only one: *both girls* ◊ *the girls are both here*. • *adverb* with equal truth in two cases: *both the boy and his sister are here*. PHRASES **have it both ways** alternate between two incompatible points of view to suit the needs of the moment.

bother • *verb* **1 a** give trouble to; worry, disturb. **b bother oneself with** be anxious about or concerned with. **2 a** go to an effort: *didn't bother to tell me*. **b** (foll. by *with*) be concerned. • *noun* **1 a** a person or thing that bothers or causes worry. **b** a minor nuisance. **2** trouble, worry, fuss. PHRASES **cannot be bothered** will not make the effort needed.

bothersome *adjective* causing bother; troublesome.

bo tree *noun* an Indian fig tree, *Ficus religiosa*, regarded as sacred by Buddhists.

bottle • *noun* **1** a container, usu. of glass or plastic and with a narrow neck, for storing liquid, pills, etc. **2** the amount that will fill a bottle. **3** a bottle with a rubber nipple for feeding babies and small toddlers. **4 a** (**the bottle**) *informal* liquor or other alcoholic drink: *problems drove him to the bottle*. **b** a bottle of an alcoholic drink: *found a bottle in his car*. **5** a metal cylinder for liquefied gas. • *verb* (**bottles, bottled, bottling**) **1** put into bottles or jars. **2** (usu. foll. by *up*) **a** conceal or restrain for a time (esp. a feeling). **b** keep (people) contained or entrapped. PHRASES **hit the bottle** *informal* drink heavily. **on the bottle** *informal* drinking (alcoholic drink) heavily.

bottled *adjective* **1** (of a liquid) contained in a bottle. **2** (of a gas) compressed to a liquid and contained in a tank.

bottle-feed *verb* (**bottle-feeds, bottle-fed, bottle-**

feeding) feed (a baby or young animal) with milk by means of a bottle equipped with a nipple.

bottle green *noun & adjective* dark green.

bottleneck *noun* **1** a point at which the flow of traffic, production, etc., is constricted. **2 a** a smooth cylinder worn on a guitarist's finger used to produce sliding effects on the strings. **b** the guitar style characterized by this.

bottlenose dolphin *noun* (also **bottlenosed dolphin**) any of several dolphins of the genus *Tursiops*, with an elongated beak.

bottler *noun* a person or company which bottles drinks.

bottom • *noun* **1 a** the lowest point or part: *bottom of the stairs*. **b** the part on which a thing rests: *bottom of a saucepan*. **c** the underside. **d** the furthest or inmost part: *bottom of the garden*. **e** (in *plural*) = BOTTOMLAND. **2** *informal* the buttocks. **3** the seat of a chair. **4** the less honourable, important, or successful portion: *at the bottom of his class*. **5** the ground under the water of a lake etc. **6** the basis; the origin: *get to the bottom of the problem*. **7** *Baseball* **a** the second half of an inning, in which the home team bats. **b** the lower third of a batting order. **c** the batters making up this part of the batting order. **8** (in *plural*) the part of a two-piece garment, esp. pyjamas or a bathing suit, worn below the waist. **9** the keel or hull of a ship. • *adjective* **1** lowest. **2** last: *got the bottom score*. PHRASES **at bottom** basically, essentially. **be at the bottom of** be the cause of. **bet one's bottom dollar** *slang* be assured. **bottom falls out** collapse occurs. **bottom out** reach the lowest level. **bottoms up!** a toast made when drinking. **bottom up** upside down. **get to the bottom of** fully investigate and explain.

bottom-feeder *noun* **1** a fish or other organism living and feeding near the bottom of a body of water. **2** *derogatory* a person who exploits or lives parasitically off others. ► **bottom-feeding** *adjective*

bottomland *noun* low-lying, fertile land along a watercourse; a flood plain.

bottomless *adjective* **1** without a bottom. **2** very deep: *a bottomless pit*. **3 a** (of a supply etc.) inexhaustible. **b** (of drinks) refilled at no extra charge. **4** naked below the waist: *bottomless dancers*. **5** featuring bottomless dancers etc.: *a bottomless bar*.

bottom line *noun* **1** the last line of a set of accounts, showing the final profit or loss. **2** net profit or loss. **3** *informal* the deciding or crucial factor.

bottom-up *adjective* **1** proceeding from detail to general theory, or from the bottom upwards. **2** non-hierarchical: *bottom-up decision making*.

botulism *noun* poisoning caused by a toxin produced by the bacillus *Clostridium botulinum* growing in poorly preserved food. [Say BOTCHA lism]

boudoir *noun* a woman's small private room or bedroom. [Say BOO dwar or boo DWAR (with the last syllable rhyming with *FAR*)]

bouffant • *adjective* (of a dress, hair, etc.) puffed out. • *noun* a bouffant hairstyle. [Say boo FONT]

bougainvillea *noun* a tropical plant with large coloured leaves (usu. purple, red, or white). [Say boo gun VILLY uh]

bough *noun* a branch of a tree, esp. a main one. [Rhymes with *HOW*]

bought *past and past participle of* BUY.

boughten *adjective* store-bought; not homemade. [Rhymes with *ROTTEN*]

bouillabaisse *noun* a rich, spicy fish stew, originally from Provence in southern France. [Say BOOYA base]

B

bouillon *noun* a clear broth made by cooking meat or fish in water. [Say BULL y'n or BOOL y'n or BOO yon]

bouillon cube *noun* a cube of concentrated soup stock which dissolves in boiling water to make broth.

boulder *noun* a large stone, esp. one worn smooth.

boulevard *noun* **1** a broad urban road. **2** a broad street, esp. with rows of trees planted along it. **3** (esp. *Cdn*) **a** a strip of grass or other vegetation between a sidewalk and a roadway. **b** a median in the centre of a road, separating opposite directions of traffic. ▶ **boulevarded** *adjective* [Say BULL a vard]

bounce • *verb* (**bounces**, **bounced**, **bouncing**) **1 a** (of a ball etc.) rebound. **b** cause to rebound. **c** bounce repeatedly. **2 a** (of light etc.) reflect. **b** cause (light etc.) to reflect. **3** *informal* **a** (of a cheque) be returned by a bank when there are insufficient funds to meet it. **b** write or present a cheque for which there are insufficient funds. **c** refuse to pay: *the bank bounced my rent cheque*. **4 a** (foll. by *about*, *up*) (of a person, dog, etc.) jump or spring energetically. **b** (foll. by *in*, *out*, etc.) rush noisily, angrily, enthusiastically, etc. **5** *informal* **a** eject forcibly (from a bar etc.). **b** dismiss (from a job). **6** *Baseball* hit a ground ball: *bounced to the shortstop*. **7** (of an e-mail message) be returned to the sender. • *noun* **1 a** a rebound. **b** the power of rebounding: *this ball has good bounce*. **c** a springy quality: *gives your hair bounce*. **2 a** a boost or rise: *a bounce in popularity*. **3** *informal* **a** swagger, self-confidence. **b** liveliness. **4** *slang* an instance of luck: *the bounces went our way*. **5** *slang* an act of ejection or dismissal. PHRASES **bounce back** regain good health, spirits, prosperity, etc. **bounce off the walls** *informal* be extremely excited, agitated, etc.

bouncer *noun* **1** a person employed to eject trouble-makers from a bar etc. **2** *Baseball* a high-bouncing ground ball. **3** a person or thing that bounces.

bounciness *noun* a bouncy or lively quality.

bouncing *adjective* **1** (esp. of a baby) big and healthy. **2** lively and confident: *her usual bouncing, energetic self*.

bouncy *adjective* (**bouncier**, **bounciest**) **1** (of a ball etc.) tending to bounce well. **2** cheerful and lively. **3** resilient, springy.

bound[1] • *verb* **1 a** spring, leap: *bounded out of bed*. **b** walk or run with leaping strides. **2** (of a ball etc.) bounce. • *noun* **1** a springy movement upwards or outwards; a leap. **2** a bounce.

bound[2] • *noun* (usu. in *plural*) a limitation; restriction: *beyond the bounds of possibility* ◊ *enthusiasm to join the union knew no bounds*. • *verb* set bounds to; limit: *views bounded by prejudice*. **2** be the boundary of. PHRASES **in bounds** inside the part of a playing field, court, etc. in which play is conducted. **out of bounds 1** outside the part of a playing field, court, etc. in which play is conducted. **2** outside of the area in which one is allowed to be according to regulations. **3** beyond what is acceptable; forbidden.

bound[3] *adjective* moving in a specified direction or toward a specified goal: *bound for Wawa* ◊ *homeward bound*.

bound[4] • *verb* past and past participle of BIND. • *adjective* **1** tied or secured with rope, cord, etc. **2** certain: *the dictionary's bound to be a hit*. **3** required; obligated: *bound by the law*. **4** (in *combination*) constricted, prevented from advancing: *snowbound*. **5** (of the pages in a book etc.) held together by a binding. PHRASES **bound up with** (or **in**) closely associated with.

boundary *noun* (*plural* **boundaries**) a line marking the limits of an area, territory, etc.

bounden duty *noun* (*plural* **bounden duties**) a solemn responsibility: *it was his bounden duty to keep them on the right path*.

boundless *adjective* unlimited: *boundless enthusiasm*.

bounteous *adjective* *literary* **1** abundant: *the earth yields a bounteous harvest*. **2** freely given: *bounteous affection*. ▶ **bounteously** *adverb*

bountiful *adjective* **1** plentiful: *the ocean provided a bountiful supply of food*. **2** giving generously: *this bountiful God has thought of everything*. ▶ **bountifully** *adverb*

bounty *noun* (*plural* **bounties**) **1** an act of giving in abundance: *for millennia people living along the Nile have depended entirely on its bounty*. **2** a gift or reward, made usu. by a government, esp.: **a** a sum paid for the killing of dangerous or undesirable animals. **b** a sum paid for bringing criminals to justice: *there was a bounty on his head*. **3** an abundance: *the bounties of Nature*.

bounty hunter *noun* a person who pursues criminals or kills animals for a reward. ▶ **bounty hunting** *noun*

bouquet *noun* **1** an arrangement of cut flowers, esp. bound together for carrying. **2** the scent of wine etc. **3** a favourable comment. [Say bo KAY or boo KAY]

bourbon *noun* whisky distilled from corn mash and rye. [Say BUR b'n]

bourgeois often *derogatory* • *adjective* **1** of or characteristic of the middle class, typically with reference to its perceived materialistic values or conventional attitudes: *a rich, bored, bourgeois family* ◊ *these views will shock the bourgeois critics*. **2** upholding the interests of the capitalist class: *bourgeois society took for granted the sanctity of property*. • *noun* (*plural* **bourgeois**) **1** a bourgeois person. **2** *Cdn hist.* = WINTERING PARTNER. [Say boor ZHWAH or BOOR zhwah]

bourgeoisie *noun* **1** the capitalist class who own most of society's wealth and means of production. **2** the middle class, typically with reference to its perceived materialistic values or conventional attitudes. [Say boor zhwah ZEE]

bout *noun* **1 a** a limited period (of intensive work or exercise). **b** a drinking session. **c** a period (of illness): *a bout of the flu*. **2 a** a wrestling or boxing match. **b** a fight. **c** a trial of strength.

boutique • *noun* a small shop or department of a store selling specialized goods or services, esp. fashionable clothes or accessories. • *adjective* designating products, services, etc. produced on a small scale and marketed to a specialized clientele. [Say boo TEEK]

boutonniere *noun* a flower or spray of flowers worn in a buttonhole or on a lapel. [Say boota NEER]

bouzouki *noun* a long-necked Greek form of mandolin. [Say boo ZOOKY]

bovine • *adjective* **1** of or resembling oxen or cattle. **2** stupid, dull. • *noun* a bovine animal. [Say BOE vine]

bovine growth hormone *noun* a growth hormone of cattle, administered in genetically engineered form to dairy cows to increase production.

bow[1] • *noun* **1 a** a knot with a double loop, which can be undone by pulling one end. **b** a ribbon, shoelace, etc., tied with this. **c** a decoration (on a gift, in the hair, etc.) in the form of a bow. **2** a device for shooting arrows with a taut string joining the ends of a curved piece of wood etc. **3** a rod with horsehair stretched along its length, used for playing the violin, cello, etc. **4 a** a shallow curve or bend. **b** a rainbow. **5** the frame or temple of a pair of eyeglasses • *verb* **1** use a bow on (a violin etc.). **2** curve outward like a bow. [Rhymes with SHOW]

bow[2] • *verb* **1 a** incline the head or upper body, esp. in greeting or acknowledgement of applause. **b** incline or

bend downward. **2** submit: *bowed to the inevitable*. **3** cause to incline: *bow your head*. • *noun* an inclining of the head or body in greeting, acknowledgement of applause, etc. PHRASES **bow and scrape** behave in an obsequious way to someone in authority: *waiters bowing and scraping to customers*. **bow down 1** bend or kneel in submission or reverence. **2** crush under the weight of: *was bowed down by the burden*. **bow out 1** make one's exit (esp. formally). **2** retreat, withdraw; retire gracefully. **take a bow** acknowledge applause. [Rhymes with *HOW*]

bow³ *noun* the front end of a boat. PHRASES **shot across the bows** a warning. [Rhymes with *HOW*]

bowdlerize *verb* (**bowdlerizes, bowdlerized, bowdlerizing**) remove or alter material considered improper or offensive in a text or story, esp. making it weaker or less effective: *bowdlerized versions of fairy tales*. [Say BOWD lur ize (with the first syllable rhyming with *LOUD*)]

bowel *noun* **1 a** the part of the alimentary canal below the stomach. **b** (usu. in *plural*) the intestines. **2** (in *plural*) the depths; the innermost parts: *the bowels of the earth*.

bowel movement *noun* **1** discharge from the bowels; defecation. **2** the feces discharged from the body.

bower¹ *noun* **1** a secluded place, esp. in a garden, enclosed by foliage; an arbour. **2** a small hut providing shade in a park or garden. [Rhymes with *FLOWER*]

bower² *noun* either of the two highest cards in euchre, the jack of trumps (**right bower**) and the other jack of the same colour (**left bower**). [Rhymes with *FLOWER*]

bowhead *noun* a large baleen whale, *Balaena mysticetus*, inhabiting Arctic waters. [Say BOE head]

bowhunt *verb* hunt (game) with a bow and arrows. ▶ **bowhunter** *noun* **bowhunting** *noun*

bowing *noun* the manner of playing a violin etc. with a bow.

bowl¹ *noun* **1 a** a usu. round deep basin used for food or liquid. **b** the quantity (of soup etc.) a bowl holds. **c** the contents of a bowl. **2 a** any deep-sided container shaped like a bowl: *toilet bowl*. **b** the bowl-shaped part of a tobacco pipe, spoon, balance, etc. **3 a** a bowl-shaped natural basin. **b** a bowl-shaped structure, esp. an amphitheatre or stadium: *Hollywood Bowl*. **4** (also **bowl game**) *Football* a post-season game or tournament between leading football teams: *Super Bowl*.

bowl² • *verb* **1 a** roll (a ball etc.) along the ground. **b** play a game of bowling. **2** go along rapidly by revolving, esp. on wheels: *the cart bowled along the road*. • *noun* **1** a wooden or hard rubber ball used in lawn bowling. **2** (in *plural*; usu. treated as *singular*) = LAWN BOWLING. PHRASES **bowl over 1** knock down. **2** *informal* **a** impress greatly. **b** overwhelm.

bow legs *plural noun* legs which are curved so as to be wide apart below the knee. ▶ **bowlegged** *adjective* [Rhymes with *SHOW*]

bowler¹ *noun* a person who participates in bowling.

bowler² *noun* (also **bowler hat**) a derby hat.

bowlful *noun* (*plural* **bowlfuls**) the amount of something filling a bowl.

bowling *noun* a game in which players roll a ball toward an arrangement of usu. five or ten pins with the intent of knocking down as many as possible.

bowling alley *noun* (*plural* **bowling alleys**) **1** a long and narrow hardwood lane along which the ball is rolled in the game of bowling. **2** a building containing several of these.

bowsprit *noun* a spar running out from a sailing ship's bow to which the stays supporting the forward mast are fastened. [Say BOE sprit]

bowstring *noun* the string of an archer's bow.

bow tie *noun* **1** a necktie in the form of a bow (BOW¹

noun 1). **2** something in the shape of a bow tie, esp. a form of pasta.

bow-wow • *interjection* an imitation of a dog's bark. • *noun* **1** *informal* a dog. **2** a dog's bark.

box¹ • *noun* (*plural* **boxes**) **1** a container, usu. with flat sides and of firm material such as wood or cardboard. **2** the amount that will fill a box. **3** a separate compartment for any of various purposes, esp.: **a** a private seating area for a small group in a theatre or sports stadium. **b** a stand for a witness or prisoner in a courtroom. **c** a stall for a horse in a stable. **4 a** a rectangular arrangement of people or things, e.g. of four hockey players on a power play. **b** an enclosed area or space. **5** an enclosure or receptacle for holding a specified item or items: *shoe box*. **6 a** a box, either at a post office or at the side of a road, where mail is delivered. **b** a compartment at a newspaper office for receiving replies to a private advertisement. **7** (**the box**) *informal* television. **8 a** any of various electric or electronic devices housed in a box. **b** *slang* a computer. **9** a space or area enclosed by a border on a printed sheet or computer screen. **10** a protective casing for a piece of a machine etc. **11** (**the box**) any of several specially demarcated areas in various sports, esp.: **a** *Hockey* the penalty box. **b** *Baseball* any of the areas designating the positions to be taken by the batter, pitcher, catcher, or coaches. **c** the enclosed area in which box lacrosse is played. • *verb* (**boxes, boxed, boxing**) **1** put in or provide with a box. **2** (foll. by *in, up, out*) surround or confine (a person, vehicle, etc.); restrain from movement.

box² • *verb* (**boxes, boxed, boxing**) **1 a** fight in a boxing match. **b** participate in boxing. **2** slap or punch (esp. a person's ear). • *noun* (*plural* **boxes**) a slap or punch, esp. on the ear.

box³ *noun* = BOXWOOD.

boxboard *noun* a lightweight cardboard used in packaging etc.

box canyon *noun* a narrow canyon with a flat bottom and vertical walls.

boxcar *noun* an enclosed railway freight car, usu. having sliding doors on the sides.

box elder *noun* = MANITOBA MAPLE.

boxer *noun* **1** a person who participates in boxing, esp. for sport. **2** a breed of medium-sized dog with a smooth brown coat and a deeply wrinkled face. **3** (in *plural*) = BOXER SHORTS.

boxer shorts *noun* **1** men's loose-fitting underwear with an elasticized waistband. **2** men's or women's shorts of a similar design.

boxful *noun* (*plural* **boxfuls**) the amount of something filling a box.

boxing *noun* the sport of fighting with the fists, esp. in padded gloves.

Boxing Day *noun* a holiday celebrated on Dec. 26 or the first weekday after Christmas.

boxing glove *noun* each of a pair of heavily padded gloves used in boxing.

Boxing Week *noun* *Cdn* the week between Christmas and New Year's Day.

boxla *noun* = BOX LACROSSE.

box lacrosse *noun* *Cdn* a form of lacrosse played in an enclosed area (usu. a hockey rink without ice) by teams of six players.

boxlike *adjective* resembling a box in shape.

box office *noun* **1** an office for booking seats and buying tickets at a theatre, cinema, stadium, etc. **2** the financial aspect of the arts and entertainment industry: *Swan Lake did well at the box office ◊ the movie was a huge box office hit*.

box score *noun* a table summarizing a baseball game

etc., showing the score, names of players, their statistics, and other information.

box social *noun* a fundraising event at which box lunches are auctioned, often such that the purchaser shares the meal with the person who prepared it.

box spring *noun* a rectangular wooden frame containing vertical springs and used as a support for a mattress.

boxwood *noun* **1** a small slow-growing evergreen tree or shrub with glossy dark green leaves, popular as hedging. **2** the hard wood of this, used for carving, engraving, etc.

boxy *adjective* (**boxier, boxiest**) resembling a box in shape.

boy • *noun* **1** a male child or youth. **2** a young man, esp. regarded as not yet mature. **3** a son. **4** a male belonging to a specified group: *a country boy*. **5** (**the boys**) *informal* a group of men mixing socially. **6** (usu. as a form of address) a male animal: *Down, boy!* • *interjection* expressing pleasure, surprise, etc. PHRASES **boys will be boys** such behaviour from young males is to be expected.

boycott • *verb* **1** combine to coerce or punish (a person, company, etc.) by a systematic refusal of normal commercial or social relations. **2 a** refuse to handle or purchase (goods) to this end. **b** refuse to attend (a meeting etc.) with this aim. • *noun* such a refusal.

boyfriend *noun* **1** a regular male companion or lover. **2** any male friend.

boyhood *noun* the state or time of being a boy.

boyish *adjective* looking or behaving like a boy in a way that is attractive: *boyish enthusiasm*. ▶ **boyishly** *adverb* **boyishness** *noun*

Boy Scout *noun* = SCOUT 4.

boysenberry *noun* (*plural* **boysenberries**) **1** a hybrid of several species of bramble. **2** the large red edible fruit of this plant. [Say BOYS'n berry]

boys in blue *plural noun informal* police officers.

boy toy *noun slang derogatory* **1** an attractive young man who is the lover of an older person. **2** a woman considered to have an overtly sexual image.

boy wonder *noun* a highly talented young man.

bozo *noun* (*plural* **bozos**) *slang* a stupid or annoying person.

BP *abbreviation* **1** boiling point. **2** blood pressure. **3** (**BP**) before the present (era).

BQ *abbreviation* (in Canada) BLOC QUÉBÉCOIS.

Br *symbol* bromine.

Br. *abbreviation* Brother.

bra *noun* (*plural* **bras**) **1** an undergarment worn to support the breasts. **2** a piece of vinyl etc. designed to fit over the front end of a car to protect the finish.

brace • *noun* **1 a** a device that clamps or fastens tightly. **b** a strengthening piece of iron or timber used in building. **2** (in *plural*) *Cdn, Brit., Austral. & NZ* suspenders. **3** (in *plural*) an orthodontic appliance consisting of metal wires and brackets worn on the teeth to straighten them. **4** a device to support an injured joint or other body part: *neck brace*. **5** (*plural* **brace**) a pair, often of birds or mammals killed in hunting: *a brace of quail were cooking in the oven*. **6** a large hand drill consisting of a crank handle and a chuck to hold a bit. **7** a rope attached to the yard of a ship for trimming the sail. **8** a connecting mark { or }. • *verb* (**braces, braced, bracing**) **1** fasten tightly, give firmness to. **2** make steady by supporting. **3** (often **brace oneself**) prepare for a shock etc.: *the CBC was bracing itself for yet more layoffs*.

bracelet *noun* **1** an ornamental band, hoop, or chain worn on the wrist, arm, or ankle. **2** a band or chain

worn around the wrist for identification, esp. for medical purposes. **3** *slang* a handcuff.

bracing • *adjective* invigorating: *the bracing sea air*. • *noun* a system or series of braces.

bracken *noun* **1** a large branching fern with long coarse fronds: *the entrance was overgrown with enormous stands of bracken fern*. **2** a mass of such ferns: *a smoke-blackened remnant of stone and masonry rose through the bracken*.

bracket • *noun* **1** a support attached to and projecting from a vertical surface. **2** a shelf fixed with such a support to a wall. **3** each of a pair of marks () [] {} <> used to enclose words or figures. **4** a group classified as containing similar elements or falling between given limits: *income bracket*. • *verb* (**bracketed, bracketing**) **1 a** link or couple (names, lines, etc.) with a brace. **b** imply a connection or equality between: *he is sometimes bracketed with the "new wave" of movie directors*. **2** *Math* enclose in brackets as having specific relations to what precedes or follows. **3** enclose on either side: *lines of exhaustion bracketed her mouth*.

brackish *adjective* (of water etc.) slightly salty. ▶ **brackishness** *noun*

bract *noun* a modified and often brightly coloured leaf, with a flower or an inflorescence in its axil.

brag • *verb* (**brags, bragged, bragging**) say something in a boastful manner: *loves to brag about her grandchildren* ◊ *he bragged that he was sure of victory*. • *noun* a card game like poker.

braggadocio *noun* boastful speech and behaviour: *Fred, full of braggadocio, had told her about it himself*. [Say bragga DOE chee oh]

braggart *noun* a person who boasts about their achievements or possessions. [Say BRAG ert]

Brahma *noun* (*plural* **Brahmas**) a breed of cattle from India, with a humped shoulder and neck, much used in crossbreeding for its tolerance of heat and drought. [Say BROMMA]

Brahman *noun* (also **brahman**) (*plural* **Brahmans**) **1** a member of the highest Hindu caste, whose members are traditionally eligible for the priesthood. **2** = BRAHMA. ▶ **Brahmanical** *adjective* [Say BRA m'n, bra MAN ick]

Brahmanism *noun* the complex sacrificial pantheistic religion that emerged in post-Vedic India (*c*.900 BC), characterized by the caste system and an early stage in the development of Hinduism. [Say BRA m'n ism]

Brahmin *noun* = BRAHMAN. [Say BRA min]

braid • *noun* **1** a length of hair, straw, etc. in three or more interlaced strands. **2** a woven band of fabric or thread used for edging or trimming. • *verb* plait or intertwine (hair, rope, etc.).

braided *adjective* **1** intertwined in a braid: *a braided loaf of egg bread* ◊ *braided hair*. **2** (of a river) split by deposits into interconnected streams. **3** trimmed or decorated with braid.

braiding • *noun* **1** various types of braid collectively. **2** braided work.

Braille • *noun* a system of writing and printing for the blind, using patterns of raised dots. • *verb* print or transcribe in Braille. [Say BRAIL]

brain • *noun* **1** an organ of soft nervous tissue contained in the skull of vertebrates, functioning as the coordinating centre of sensation, and of intellectual and nervous activity. **2** (in *plural*) the substance of the brain esp. as food. **3 a** a person's intellectual capacity: *has a poor brain*. **b** (often in *plural*) intelligence; high intellectual capacity: *has brains*. **4** *informal* an intelligent person. **5** (**the brains**) *informal* **a** the cleverest person in a group. **b** a person who

originates a complex plan or idea: *the brains behind the robbery.* **6** an electronic device with functions comparable to those of a brain. • *verb* **1** dash out the brains of. **2** strike hard on the head. PHRASES **on the brain** *informal* obsessively in one's thoughts.

brainchild *noun* (*plural* **brainchildren**) *informal* an idea, plan, etc. regarded as the result of a person's mental effort.

brain damage *noun* injury to the brain permanently impairing its functions. ▶ **brain-damaged** *adjective*

brain-dead *adjective* **1** having suffered brain death. **2** *informal derogatory* stupid.

brain death *noun* permanent cessation of the functions of the brain stem that control breathing etc., regarded as indicative of death.

brain drain *noun* *informal* the loss of skilled personnel by emigration.

braininess *noun* intelligence.

brainless *adjective* stupid, foolish.

brainpower *noun* mental ability or intelligence.

brain stem *noun* the central trunk of the brain, upon which the cerebrum and cerebellum are set, and which continues downwards to form the spinal cord.

brainstorm • *noun* **1** a concerted intellectual treatment of a problem by discussing spontaneous ideas about it. **2** = BRAINWAVE 2. **3** a violent or excited outburst often as a result of a sudden mental disturbance. **4** *informal* mental confusion. • *verb* seek solutions to a problem by discussing spontaneous ideas about it: *have the class brainstorm on the topic* ◊ *the group brainstormed ideas.* ▶ **brainstorming** *noun*

brainteaser *noun* *informal* a puzzle or problem.

brain trust *noun* a group of expert advisers.

brainwash *verb* (**brainwashes**, **brainwashed**, **brainwashing**) subject (a person) to a prolonged process by which ideas other than and at variance with those already held are implanted in the mind. ▶ **brainwashing** *noun*

brainwave *noun* **1** (usu. in *plural*) an electrical impulse in the brain. **2** *informal* a sudden bright idea.

brainy *adjective* (**brainier**, **brainiest**) intellectually clever or active.

braise *verb* (**braises**, **braised**, **braising**) fry lightly and then stew slowly with a little liquid in a closed container.

SPELL CHECK
brake, break   ✓ABC

To shatter is to **break**.
---

brake[1] • *noun* **1** (often in *plural*) a device for stopping the motion of a mechanism, esp. a wheel or vehicle, or for keeping it at rest. **2** anything that has the effect of hindering or impeding. • *verb* (**brakes**, **braked**, **braking**) **1 a** apply a brake. **b** slow or come to a stop upon application of a brake. **2** retard or stop with a brake. PHRASES **put on the brakes** slow down.

brake[2] *noun* = BRACKEN.

brake drum *noun* a cylinder attached to a wheel, whose inner surface is gripped by brake shoes when drum brakes are applied.

brakeman *noun* (*plural* **brakemen**) an employee on a train, responsible for maintenance on a journey.

brake shoe *noun* a long curved metal block which presses on the inside of a brake drum when drum brakes are applied.

braless *adjective* not wearing a bra.

bramble *noun* **1** any of various thorny shrubs bearing fleshy red or black berries, esp. the blackberry bush. **2** the edible berry of these shrubs. **3** any of various other shrubs with similar foliage, esp. a wild rose. ▶ **brambly** *adjective*

bran *noun* edible husks of grain separated from flour after grinding.

branch • *noun* **1** (*plural* **branches**) a limb extending from a tree or bough. **2** a lateral extension or subdivision, esp. of a river, road, or railway: *branch line.* **3** a conceptual extension or subdivision, as of a family etc. **4** a local division or office etc. of a large business, bank, library, etc. • *verb* (**branches**, **branched**, **branching**) (often foll. by *off*) **1** diverge from the main part. **2** divide into branches. **3** (of a tree) bear or send out branches. PHRASES **branch out** extend one's field of interest. ▶ **branched** *adjective*

branch plant *noun* *Cdn* a factory etc. owned by a company based in another country (often as an *adjective*: *branch-plant economy*).

brand • *noun* **1 a** a particular make of goods. **b** an identifying trademark, label, etc. **2** (usu. foll. by *of*) a special or characteristic kind: *his particular brand of humour.* **3** an identifying mark burned on livestock or (formerly) prisoners etc. with a hot iron. **4** an iron used for this. **5** a piece of burning, smouldering, or charred wood: *took two burning brands from the fire.* • *verb* **1** mark with a hot iron. **2** mark with disgrace: *was branded a liar* ◊ *the media was intent on branding us as terrorists* ◊ *did not want to get branded with his predecessor's mistakes.* **3** assign a trademark or label to. ▶ **brander** *noun*

brandied *adjective* preserved or flavoured with brandy.

branding iron *noun* an iron for branding cattle etc.

brandish *verb* (**brandishes**, **brandished**, **brandishing**) flourish as a threat or in display: *a man brandishing a knife* ◊ *brandished the trophy above his head.*

brand name *noun* **1** a trade or proprietary name. **2** a product with a brand name.

brand new *adjective* completely or obviously new.

brandy *noun* (*plural* **brandies**) a strong alcoholic liquor distilled from wine or fermented fruit juice.

brant *noun* an Arctic goose, *Branta bernicla*, similar to the Canada goose but smaller and darker.

brash[1] *adjective* **1** self-assertive in a rude, noisy, or overbearing way: *he was brash, cocky, and arrogant.* **2** ostentatious or tasteless; vulgar: *the restaurant was a brash new building.*

brash[2] *noun* loose broken rock or ice.

brashness *noun* a bold, forward, or self-assertive manner.

brass • *noun* (*plural* **brasses**) **1** a yellow alloy of copper and zinc. **2 a** an ornament or other decorated piece of brass. **b** brass objects collectively. **3** *Music* brass wind instruments, e.g. trumpets, trombones, etc. forming a band or a section of an orchestra. **4** (also **top brass**) *informal* persons in authority or of high (esp. military) rank. **5** an inscribed or engraved memorial tablet of brass. **6** *informal* effrontery: *then had the brass to demand money.* • *adjective* made of brass.

brass band *noun* a group of musicians playing brass instruments, sometimes also with percussion.

brasserie *noun* **1** a restaurant, originally one serving beer with food. **2** *Cdn* (*Que.*) a pub. [Say BRASSER ee]

brassica *noun* a plant of the genus *Brassica*, having taproots and erect branched stems, including cabbage, broccoli, and turnip. [Say BRASSA kuh]

brassiere *noun* = BRA 1.

brass knuckles *plural noun* connected metal rings worn on the fingers to make punches more severe.

brass ring *noun* noteworthy success, esp. as seen as a reward for ambition, hard work, etc.: *reach for the brass ring*.

brass tacks *plural noun* *informal* actual details; real business: *get down to brass tacks*.

brassy *adjective* (**brassier, brassiest**) **1** impudent. **2** showy, flamboyant. **3** loud and blaring. **4** of or like brass.

brat *noun* **1** usu. *derogatory* a child, esp. a badly behaved one. **2** a child brought up in a specified milieu: *Forces brat*.

brat pack *noun* *slang* a rowdy, ostentatious group of young celebrities, esp. movie stars. ▶ **brat packer** *noun*

brattiness *noun* bratty behaviour.

brattish *adjective* bratty.

bratty *adjective* selfish, spoiled, and rude; badly behaved.

bratwurst *noun* a type of small German pork sausage.

bravado *noun* a bold manner or a show of boldness intended to impress. [Say bruh VODDO or bruh VADDO]

brave • *adjective* **1** able or ready to face and endure danger, pain, adversity, etc. **2** *literary* splendid: *his medals made a brave show*. • *noun* *hist.* a North American Aboriginal warrior. • *verb* (**braves, braved, braving**) defy; encounter bravely. PHRASES **brave it out** behave defiantly under suspicion or blame. ▶ **bravely** *adverb*

brave new world *noun* usu. *ironic* an era of supposed happiness brought on by technological or social developments.

bravery *noun* **1** brave conduct. **2** a brave nature.

bravo • *interjection* expressing approval of a performer etc. • *noun* (*plural* **bravos**) a cry of bravo.

bravura • *adjective* requiring or displaying brilliant or virtuosic skill: *a bravura performance*. • *noun* brilliant or virtuosic skill, esp. in artistic performance: *executed the solo with effortless bravura*. [Say bra VOORA]

brawl • *noun* a rowdy fight, usu. involving several people: *a drunken brawl*. • *verb* fight or quarrel noisily or roughly. ▶ **brawler** *noun*

brawn *noun* muscular strength in contrast to intelligence: *commando work required as much brain as brawn*.

brawny *adjective* (**brawnier, brawniest**) muscular, strong.

bray • *noun* **1** the cry of a donkey. **2** a sound like this cry, e.g. that of a harshly-played brass instrument, a laugh, etc. • *verb* **1** make a braying sound. **2** utter harshly.

Brayon *Cdn* • *noun* an inhabitant of the Madawaska region of New Brunswick. • *adjective* denoting the Brayons, their mixed Acadian and anglophone culture, etc. [Say bray YON]

brazen • *adjective* **1** bold and shameless: *she asked my boyfriend out, the brazen hussy ◊ the raccoons are so brazen they eat the food right out of the cat's dish*. **2** made of brass. **3** of or like brass, esp. in colour or sound. • *verb* (usu. in phr. **brazen it out**) endure an embarrassing or difficult situation by behaving with apparent confidence and lack of shame. ▶ **brazenly** *adverb* **brazenness** *noun* [Say BRAY z'n]

brazier *noun* **1** a charcoal grill for cooking. **2** a portable heater consisting of a pan or stand for holding lighted coals. [Say BRAZE yer or BRAY zhur]

Brazilian • *adjective* of or relating to Brazil, a country in South America, or its people or culture. • *noun* a native or inhabitant of Brazil.

Brazil nut *noun* the large three-sided nut of the South American tree *Bertholletia excelsa*.

SPELL CHECK [ABC ✓]
breach, breech, breeches

The part of a gun is a **breech**. Short trousers are **breeches**. **Breech** is also the spelling in "breech birth".

breach • *noun* (*plural* **breaches**) **1** the breaking of or failure to observe a law, contract, regulations, etc.: *sued for breach of contract*. **2** a breaking of relations: *a widening breach between government and Church*. **3** a gap, esp. one made by artillery in fortifications. • *verb* (**breaches, breached, breaching**) **1** break through; make a gap in: *the river breached its banks*. **2** break (a law, contract, etc.). **3** (of a whale) leap clear out of the water. PHRASES **step into** (or **fill**) **the breach** give help in a crisis, esp. by replacing someone who has dropped out.

breach of the peace *noun* an infringement or violation of the public peace by any disturbance etc.

bread • *noun* **1** baked food made of flour and a liquid and often raised with yeast. **2** a necessary food: *his day job puts bread on the table*. **b** (also **daily bread**) one's livelihood. **3** *slang* money. • *verb* coat with bread crumbs for cooking. PHRASES **bread and wine** the Eucharist. **break bread** share a meal. **know which side one's bread is buttered (on)** know where one's advantage lies. **take the bread out of a person's mouth** take away a person's living, esp. by competition.

bread and butter • *noun* **1** bread spread with butter. **2** an essential element, esp. that which provides one's livelihood: *their bread and butter is reporting local events*. • *adjective* (usu. **bread-and-butter**) **1** designating something basic and fundamental to one's livelihood: *he worked in such bread-and-butter areas as landlord and tenant foreclosures*. **2** commonplace, humdrum: *bread-and-butter issues like potholes and taxes will be central to the election*. **3** expressing gratitude, esp. for hospitality: *bread-and-butter letter*.

breadbasket *noun* **1** a basket for bread or rolls. **2** a region producing much grain: *the Prairies are Canada's breadbasket*. **3** *slang* the abdomen or stomach.

breadboard *noun* a board for cutting bread on.

breadbox *noun* (*plural* **breadboxes**) a container in which bread is kept.

breadfruit *noun* (*plural* **breadfruit** or **breadfruits**) **1** a tropical evergreen tree, *Artocarpus altilis*, bearing edible usu. seedless fruit. **2** this fruit, which when roasted becomes soft like new bread.

breadknife *noun* (*plural* **breadknives**) a knife with a long saw-like blade, for slicing bread.

breadline *noun* a line of people waiting to receive free food.

breadstick *noun* a long, stick-like piece of crisp bread.

breadth *noun* **1** the distance or measurement from side to side of a thing: *measured 3 metres in breadth ◊ the bank reaches a maximum breadth of about 100 km*. **2** extent, range: *she has the advantage of breadth of experience*. **3** freedom from limitations, esp. in opinion or interests: *the minister is not noted for his breadth of vision*.

breadwinner *noun* a person who earns the money to support a family. ▶ **breadwinning** *noun & adjective*

SPELL CHECK [ABC ✓]
break, brake

A device that stops a car is a **brake**.

break • *verb* (**breaks**; *past* **broke**; *past participle* **broken**; **breaking**) **1 a** separate into pieces under a blow or strain; shatter; fracture. **b** make or become inoperative, esp. from damage. **c** break a bone in or

dislocate (part of the body). **d** break the skin of (the head or crown). **2 a** cause or effect an interruption in: *broke the silence.* **b** have an interval between spells of work: *let's break for coffee.* **3** fail to observe or keep (a law, promise, etc.). **4 a** make or become subdued or weakened: *broke his spirit.* **b** weaken the effect of (a fall, blow, etc.). **c** = BREAK IN 3c. **d** defeat, destroy: *broke the enemy's power.* **e** defeat the object of (a strike, e.g. by employing other personnel). **5** surpass (a record). **6** (foll. by *with*) quarrel or cease association with (another person etc.). **7 a** be no longer subject to (a habit). **b** (foll. by *of*) cause (a person) to be free of a habit: *broke them of their addiction.* **8** reveal or be revealed; (cause to) become known: *the story broke on Friday.* **9 a** (of the weather) change suddenly, esp. after a hot spell. **b** (of waves) curl over and dissolve into foam. **c** (of the day) dawn. **d** (of clouds) move apart. **e** (of a storm) begin violently. **10** *Electricity* disconnect (a circuit). **11 a** (of the voice) change with emotion. **b** (of a boy's voice) change in register etc. at puberty. **12 a** (often foll. by *up*) divide (a set etc.) into parts, e.g. by selling to different buyers. **b** change (a bill, etc.) for coins. **13** ruin (an individual or institution) financially. **14** penetrate, e.g. a safe, by force. **15** decipher (a code). **16** make (a way, path, etc.) by separating obstacles. **17** burst forth: *the sun broke through the clouds.* **18 a** (usu. foll. by *free, loose, out,* etc.) escape from constraint suddenly. **b** escape or emerge from (prison, bounds, cover, etc.). **19** *Baseball* (of a pitch) curve or drop. **20** *Billiards etc.* disperse the balls at the beginning of a game. **21** bring an end to (an undecided condition, state of affairs, etc.): *an effort to break the impasse.* **22** (in golf, bowling, etc.) achieve or surpass (a noteworthy score): *hopes to break 200.* **23** (often foll. by *in*) bring (virgin land) under cultivation. • *noun* **1 a** an act or instance of breaking: *broke his leg, but it was a good clean break.* **b** a point where something is broken; a gap. **2 a** an interval, an interruption; a pause in work. **b** a holiday: *spring break.* **3** a sudden dash (esp. to escape). **4** *informal* an opportunity or chance, esp. one leading to professional success: *lucky break ◊ Selga's big break came when a critic gave her a rave review.* **5** *Sport* = BREAKAWAY 1. **6** *Billiards etc.* **a** a series of points scored during one turn. **b** the opening shot that disperses the balls. **7** *Electricity* a discontinuity in a circuit. PHRASES **break away** make or become free or separate. **break the back of 1** overburden (a person). **2** exert (oneself) greatly. **3** do the hardest or greatest part of (a task). **4** defeat, destroy, crush. **break the bank 1** exhaust all one's financial resources. **2** (in gaming) exhaust the bank's resources; win spectacularly. **break down 1 a** fail in mechanical action; cease to function. **b** (of human relationships etc.) fail, collapse. **c** fail in (esp. mental) health. **d** be overcome by emotion; collapse in tears. **2 a** demolish, destroy. **b** suppress (resistance). **c** force (a person) to yield under pressure. **3** analyze into components. **4** decompose. **break even** emerge from a transaction etc. with neither profit nor loss. **break a game (wide) open** decisively turn a close game in one's favour with dramatic scoring. **break the ice 1** begin to overcome formality or shyness, esp. between strangers. **2** make a start. **break in 1** enter premises by force, esp. with criminal intent. **2** interrupt. **3 a** accustom to a habit etc. **b** wear etc. until comfortable. **c** accustom (a horse) to saddle and bridle etc. **break in on** disturb; interrupt. **break into 1** enter forcibly or violently. **2 a** suddenly begin, burst forth with (a song, laughter, etc.). **b** suddenly change one's pace for (a faster one): *broke into a gallop.* **3** interrupt. **break a leg** (as *interjection*) *Theatre slang* good luck. **break loose 1** escape from constraint or a fixed position suddenly. **2** (of a

condition etc.) develop suddenly: *all hell broke loose.* **break new ground** innovate. **break of day** dawn. **break off 1** detach by breaking. **2** bring to an end. **3** cease talking etc. **break open** open forcibly. **break out 1** escape by force, esp. from prison. **2** begin suddenly; burst forth: *violence broke out.* **3** (usu. foll. by *in*) become covered in (a rash, pimples, etc.). **4** exclaim. **5 a** open up (a receptacle) and remove its contents. **b** remove (articles) from a place of storage. **break step** get out of step. **break (into) a sweat** begin sweating, esp. because of nervousness or physical exertion. **break trail 1** beat a path, e.g. through deep snow or undergrowth. **2** innovate. **break up 1** break into small pieces. **2** disperse; disband. **3 a** terminate a relationship. **b** cause to do this. **4** (of the weather) change suddenly (esp. after a fine spell). **5** (of a frozen body of water) break into blocks of ice at the spring thaw. **6 a** upset or be upset. **b** excite or be excited. **c** convulse or be convulsed. **break wind** release gas from the anus. **give me a break** *informal* expressing skepticism, exasperation, scorn, etc.

breakable • *adjective* that may or is apt to be broken easily. • *noun* (esp. in *plural*) a breakable thing.

breakage *noun* **1 a** a broken thing: *throw everything together, we don't have time to worry about breakages.* **b** damage caused by breaking: *customers must pay for any breakage.* **2** an action of breaking something or the fact of being broken: *look for guarantees against breakage.*

break and enter *noun* = BREAKING AND ENTERING.

breakaway • *noun* **1** (in hockey etc.) a long rush towards the goal or net after having passed all defenders. **2** a divergence or radical change from something established or long standing: *the new party was formed as a breakaway from the Liberals.* • *adjective* **1** broken away or separated from a larger body: *breakaway republic.* **2** designed to break easily to prevent more serious damage: *breakaway mirrors.*

breakdance • *noun* an energetic, acrobatic, solo street dance, usu. involving the moonwalk and spinning on the back or head. • *verb* (**breakdances, breakdanced, breakdancing**) dance a breakdance. ▶ **breakdancer** *noun* **breakdancing** *noun*

breakdown *noun* **1** a mechanical failure. **2** a loss of (esp. mental) health and strength. **3** a collapse or disintegration: *communication breakdown.* **4** chemical or physical decomposition: *the breakdown of ammonia to nitrites.* **5** a detailed analysis: *a detailed cost breakdown.*

breaker *noun* **1** a person or thing that breaks something: *circuit breaker.* **2** a heavy wave that breaks. **3** *Cdn* (*Nfld*) a submerged rock with waves breaking above it. **4** a person who breaks in a horse. **5** a breakdancer. **6** a person who interrupts the conversation of others on a CB radio.

break-even • *adjective* designating the point at which earnings equal expenditures: *current prices are at the break-even or money-losing level.* • *noun* a break-even point.

breakfast • *noun* the first meal of the day. • *verb* have breakfast. PHRASES **eat for breakfast** *slang* destroy (something) or defeat (a person) easily.

break-in *noun* **1** an illegal forced entry into premises, esp. with criminal intent. **2** an illegal accessing of information from a computer.

breaking *adjective* (of news, events, etc.) happening, occurring, esp. at the moment: *late-breaking story.*

breaking and entering *noun* the illegal entering of a building with the intent to commit an indictable offence.

breaking ball *noun* (also **breaking pitch**; *plural* **breaking pitches**) *Baseball* a pitch that drops just before reaching the batter.

breaking-point *noun* the point of greatest strain, at which a thing breaks or a person gives way.

breakneck *adjective* (of speed) dangerously fast.

breakout *noun* **1** (in hockey etc.) a sudden offensive rush. **2** a forcible escape. **3** an outbreak, esp. of pimples etc. **4** the breaking of a gathering into smaller groups for discussion: *breakout groups*.

break point *noun* **1** a place or time at which an interruption or change is made. **2** (usu. **breakpoint**) *Computing* a place in a computer program where the sequence of instructions is interrupted, esp. by another program. **3** *Tennis* **a** a point which would win the game for the player(s) receiving service. **b** the situation at which the receiver(s) may break service by winning such a point. **4** = BREAKING-POINT.

breakthrough *noun* a major advance or discovery.

breakup *noun* **1** disintegration, collapse. **2** the termination of a relationship. **3** *Cdn* (also **spring breakup**) **a** the breaking of a frozen river etc. into blocks of ice at the spring thaw. **b** the time during which this happens.

breakwater *noun* a structure which breaks the force of waves, esp. at the entrance to a harbour.

bream *noun* (*plural* **bream**) **1** a carp-like freshwater fish of Europe, with an arched back. **2** (also **sea bream**) a similarly shaped marine fish. **3** = BLUEGILL.

breast • *noun* **1 a** either of two milk-secreting organs on the upper front of a woman's body. **b** a corresponding organ on females of other mammals, esp. primates. **c** the corresponding usu. rudimentary part of a man's body. **2 a** the upper front part of a human body; the chest. **b** the corresponding part of an animal. **3** a portion of poultry cut from the breast. **4** the part of a garment that covers the breast. **5** the breast as a source of emotion: *wild feelings of frustration were rising up in his breast*. • *verb* **1** face, meet in full opposition: *breast the waves*. **2** reach the top of (a hill). PHRASES **make a clean breast of** confess fully.

breast-beating *noun* an exaggerated display of remorse, sorrow, etc.: *there was much soul-searching and breast-beating over the free trade agreement*.

breastbone *noun* a thin flat vertical bone and cartilage in the chest connecting the ribs.

breasted *combining form* having the sort of breast or breasts described: *red-breasted woodpecker*.

breast-feed *verb* (**breast-feeds**, **breast-fed**, **breast-feeding**) **1** feed (a baby) from the breast. **2** (of a baby) feed from the breast.

breast implant *noun* a small silicone-filled pouch surgically inserted in a breast to enlarge it.

breastplate *noun* a vestment or piece of armour covering the breast.

breaststroke *noun* a stroke performed by a swimmer floating face down, extending the joined hands outward from the chest to above the head and then sweeping them down on either side of the body, while the legs execute a frog kick.

breath *noun* **1 a** the air taken into or expelled from the lungs. **b** one respiration of air. **c** an exhalation of air that can be seen, smelled, or heard: *bad breath*. **2 a** a slight movement of air; a breeze. **b** a whiff of perfume etc. **3** a sign, hint, or suggestion (esp. of a scandalous nature): *he avoided the slightest breath of scandal*. **4** the power of breathing; life. PHRASES **below** (or **under**) **one's breath** in a whisper. **breath of fresh air 1** a small amount of or a brief time in the fresh air. **2** a refreshing change. **catch one's breath 1** cease breathing momentarily or in surprise, suspense, etc. **2** rest after exercise to restore normal breathing. **draw breath** breathe; live. **hold one's breath** cease breathing temporarily. **don't hold your breath** *informal* do not expect something to happen imminently. **in the same breath** (esp. of saying two contradictory things) within a short time. **out of breath** gasping for air, esp. after exercise. **take breath** pause for rest. **take one's breath away** astound; surprise; awe; delight. **waste one's breath** talk or give advice without effect.

breathability *noun* the ability of fabrics to allow air to pass through.

breathable *adjective* **1** (of air) fit to be breathed. **2** (of textiles, clothing, etc.) allowing the passage of air and allowing sweat to evaporate.

Breathalyzer *noun* *proprietary* an instrument for measuring the amount of alcohol in the breath (and hence in the blood) of a driver.

breathe *verb* (**breathes**, **breathed**, **breathing**) **1** take air into and expel it from the lungs. **2** be or seem alive: *is she breathing?* **3 a** utter; say (esp. quietly): *"We're together at last," she breathed*. **b** express; display: *breathed defiance*. **4** take breath, pause. **5 a** send out (as if) with exhaled air: *breathed a sigh of relief*. **b** take in (as if) with breathed air: *breathed the fumes*. **6** (of wine, fabric, etc.) be exposed to fresh air. **7 a** (of textiles, clothing, etc.) allow the passage of air and inhibit condensation. **b** (of the skin) absorb oxygen and get rid of moisture. **8** (of wind) blow softly. PHRASES **breathe easy** (or **freely**) be relieved from tension, suspense, etc. **breathe down a person's neck** be close behind a person, esp. in mistrust or pursuit. **breathe** (**new**) **life into** invigorate; make lively. **breathe one's last** die. **not breathe a word of** keep quite secret.

breather *noun* **1** *informal* a brief pause for rest. **2** a person or animal that breathes, esp. a specified substance or in a specified way: *heavy breathers*.

breathily *adverb* (speak or sing etc.) in a manner that produces a noticeable sound of breathing.

breathiness *noun* a breathy quality or manner.

breathing *noun* the process of taking air into and expelling it from the lungs.

breathing space *noun* (also **breathing room**) **1** a pause or respite; a time to rest, recover, reconsider, etc. **2** a space or area which allows for easy movement, rest, etc.: *our breathing space in the city*.

breathless *adjective* **1** panting, out of breath. **2** holding or as if holding the breath because of excitement, suspense, etc.: *breathless prose*. ▶ **breathlessly** *adverb* **breathlessness** *noun*

breathtaking *adjective* awe-inspiring. ▶ **breathtakingly** *adverb*

breath test *noun* a test of a person's alcohol consumption, using a Breathalyzer.

breathy *adjective* (**breathier**, **breathiest**) (of a singing voice etc.) producing a noticeable sound of breathing, esp. as a result of exertion or strong feelings.

SPELL CHECK
breech, breach [ABC✓]

The breaking of a contract is a **breach**; the spelling is also **breach** in "breach of the peace" and "fill the breach". Whales that jump out of the water are **breaching**.

---

breech *noun* (*plural* **breeches**) **1 a** the part of a cannon behind the bore. **b** the back part of a rifle or gun barrel. **2** (as an *adjective*) designating a birth in which the baby presents in the birth canal with the buttocks or feet foremost.

breeches *plural noun* (also **pair of breeches** *singular*) **1** short trousers, esp. fastened below the knee, now used esp. for riding or in court costume. **2** = BRITCHES.

breech-loader *noun* a gun loaded at the breech, not through the muzzle. ▶ **breech-loading** *adjective*

breed • *verb* (**breeds, bred, breeding**) **1** give birth to (offspring). **2** propagate or cause to propagate; raise (livestock). **3 a** yield; result in: *war breeds famine.* **b** spread: *discontent bred by rumour.* **4** arise: *disease breeds in the tropics.* **5** bring up: *bred to the law.* **6** *Physics* create (fissile material) by nuclear reaction. • *noun* **1** a stock of animals or plants within a species, having a similar appearance, and usu. developed by deliberate selection. **2** a race; a lineage. **3** a sort, a kind. PHRASES **bred and born** = BORN AND BRED (see BORN). **bred in the bone** hereditary. ▶ **breeder** *noun*

breeding *noun* **1** the process of developing or propagating (animals, plants, etc.). **2** child-bearing. **3 a** upbringing or education. **b** behaviour, esp. good manners. **4** wealthy or aristocratic family background.

breeding ground *noun* **1** an area where an animal, esp. a bird, habitually breeds. **2** a thing that favours the development or occurrence of something, esp. something unpleasant: *a breeding ground for political unrest.*

breeze • *noun* **1** a gentle wind. **2** *Meteorology* a wind of 1.6–13.8 m/s (4–31 mph) and between force 2 and force 6 on the Beaufort scale. **3** a wind blowing from land at night or a large body of water during the day. **4** *informal* an easy task. • *verb* (**breezes, breezed, breezing**) **1** (foll. by *in, out, along*, etc.) *informal* come or go in a casual or lighthearted manner. **2** (usu. foll. by *through*) emerge successfully and easily from (a test, competition, etc.).

breezeway *noun* a covered passageway, as between a house and a garage.

breezily *adverb* in a relaxed and cheerily brisk manner: *told breezily to just cut fifty pages.*

breeziness *noun* a relaxed and lively or cheerful manner.

breezy *adjective* (**breezier, breeziest**) **1** pleasantly windy. **2** appearing relaxed, informal, and cheerily brisk: *the text is written in a breezy matter-of-fact manner.*

brekkie *noun Cdn, Brit.,* & *Austral. slang* breakfast.

brethren *plural noun see* BROTHER *noun* 3.

Breton • *noun* **1** a native of Brittany, a region of northwestern France. **2** the Celtic language of Brittany. • *adjective* of Brittany or its people. [Say BRET un]

brevity *noun* **1** concise and exact use of words in writing or speech: *letters may be edited for brevity.* **2** shortness (of time etc.): *the brevity of human life.* [Say BREVVA tee]

brew • *verb* **1 a** make (beer etc.) by infusion, boiling, and fermentation. **b** make (tea, coffee, etc.) by infusion. **2** undergo either of these processes: *the tea is brewing.* **3** (of trouble, a storm, etc.) gather force; threaten: *mischief was brewing.* **4** bring about; concoct: *brewed their fiendish scheme.* • *noun* **1** an amount (of beer etc.) brewed at one time: *this year's brew.* **2** what is brewed (esp. with regard to its quality): *a good strong brew.* **3 a** beer. **b** a serving of beer. **4** the action or process of brewing. **5** a mixture of events, people, or things, which interact to form a more potent whole: *a dangerous brew of political turmoil and violent conflict.*

brewer *noun* a person or company that makes beer.

brewer's yeast *noun* a non-leavening dry yeast of the genus *Saccharomyces*, used in the fermentation of beer and wine, added to some foods as a nutritive agent.

brewery *noun* (*plural* **breweries**) a place where beer etc. is brewed commercially.

brewis *noun Cdn* (*Nfld*) **1** a stew made of hardtack soaked in water and boiled. **2** = FISH AND BREWIS. [Sounds like *BRUISE*]

brewmaster *noun* a master brewer.

brewpub *noun* a bar with on-site brewing facilities.

brewski *noun* (*plural* **brewskis**) *slang* a beer.

briar *noun* = BRIER.

bribe • *noun* a sum of money or other reward offered or demanded in order to procure an (often illegal or dishonest) action or decision in favour of the giver. • *verb* (**bribes, bribed, bribing**) persuade by means of a bribe: *bribed the guard.* ▶ **bribery** *noun*

bric-a-brac *noun* miscellaneous, often old, ornaments, trinkets, furniture, etc., of little value. [Say BRICKA brack]

brick • *noun* **1 a** a small, usu. rectangular, block of fired or sun-dried clay, used in building. **b** the material used to make these. **c** a similar block of concrete etc. **2** a brick-shaped solid object: *a brick of ice cream.* **3** a firm, smooth, white cheese with a brick-like shape, made from cow's milk. • *verb* (foll. by *in, up*) close or block with brickwork. • *adjective* **1** built of brick. **2** = BRICK RED *adjective.* PHRASES **like a ton of bricks** *informal* with crushing weight, force, or authority: *their boss came down on them like a ton of bricks for being so negative about the program.* **run into a brick wall** come up against an insurmountable obstacle: *I wanted him to talk about his feelings, but I just kept running into a brick wall.*

brickbat *noun* **1** a piece of brick, esp. when thrown during a riot etc. **2** an uncomplimentary remark: *the plaudits were beginning to outnumber the brickbats.*

bricklayer *noun* a worker who builds with bricks. ▶ **bricklaying** *noun*

brick red *noun* & *adjective* the dull red colour typical of bricks.

brickwork *noun* **1** construction using brick. **2** a wall, building, etc. made of brick.

SPELL CHECK
bridal, bridle   ABC✔

A horse's headgear is a **bridle**. If you get upset and resentful about something, you **bridle**.

---

bridal *adjective* of or concerning a bride or a wedding.

bride *noun* a woman on her wedding day and for some time before and after it.

bridegroom *noun* a man on his wedding day and for some time before and after it.

bride price *noun* a payment of money or goods made to a bride or her parents by the groom or his parents, esp. in tribal societies.

bridesmaid *noun* **1** a girl or woman attending a bride on her wedding day. **2** a person or group that never quite attains a desired goal: *country music isn't a bridesmaid any more, it's what's happening right now.*

bridge[1] • *noun* **1 a** a structure carrying a road, path, railway, etc., across water, a road, etc. **b** anything providing a connection between different things: *a bridge between cultures.* **2** the superstructure on a ship from which the captain and officers direct operations. **3 a** the upper bony part of the nose. **b** the central part of a pair of eyeglasses, which rests on this and connects the two lenses. **4** an upright piece of wood, metal, etc. on a violin, guitar, etc. over which the strings are stretched. **5** *Music* a transitional piece between main themes. **6** a dental structure used to cover a gap. **7** = LAND BRIDGE. • *verb* (**bridges, bridged, bridging**) **1** be or make a bridge over. **2** span as if with a bridge: *bridged the gap between east and west.* PHRASES **cross that bridge when one comes to it** deal with a problem when and if it arises.

bridge[2] *noun* a card game for four players, in which one player's cards are exposed at a certain point and are then played by his or her partner.

bridge-builder *noun* **1** a person who builds bridges. **2** a person who promotes co-operation between groups.

bridge-building *noun* **1** the activity of building

bridges. **2** the promotion of friendly relations: *for the Sikhs of Abbotsford, the museum's attempt at cross-cultural bridge-building was a step in the right direction.*

bridgehead *noun* **1** a fortified position held on the enemy's side of a river or other obstacle. **2** an initial position established as a basis for advancing further.

bridgework *noun* **1** a dental bridge. **2** the art or process of building bridges.

SPELL CHECK
bridle, bridal ABC ✓

The spelling is **bridal** if you are referring to brides and weddings.

---

bridle • *noun* **1** the headgear used to control a horse, consisting of buckled leather straps, a metal bit, and reins. **2** a restraining thing or influence: *put a bridle on your tongue.* • *verb* (**bridles, bridled, bridling**) **1** put a bridle on (a horse etc.). **2** express offence, resentment, etc.: *she bridled at his tone.*

brie *noun* a kind of ripened soft cheese with a white mould skin. [Say BREE]

brief • *adjective* **1** not lasting long: *a brief visit.* **2** concise in expression; using few words: *a few brief remarks* ◊ *I will be brief.* **3** short; scanty: *a brief halter top.* • *noun* **1** (in *plural*) close-fitting legless underpants. **2** *Law* a written statement of the arguments for a case. **3** instructions given for a task, operation, etc. **4** esp. *Brit.* a set of instructions, e.g. a job description etc. **5** a brief news article or summary. • *verb* instruct (an employee, participant, etc.) in preparation for a task; inform or instruct thoroughly in advance (*compare* DEBRIEF). PHRASES **in brief** in short.

briefcase *noun* a flat rectangular case for carrying documents etc.

briefing *noun* **1** a meeting for giving information or instructions. **2** the information or instructions given. **3** the action of informing or instructing.

briefly *adverb* **1** for a short time: *he had spoken to her only briefly.* **2** in few words: *she explained briefly.*

Brier *noun* the bonspiel for the Canadian men's national curling championship. [Rhymes with *FIRE*]

brier *noun* **1** any prickly bush esp. of a wild rose. **2** a white plant of the heath family, native to southern Europe. **3** a tobacco pipe made from its root. [Rhymes with *FIRE*]

brig *noun* **1** a two-masted square-rigged ship. **2** a prison, esp. on a warship.

brigade *noun* **1** a subdivision of an army. **2** an organized or uniformed band of workers: *fire brigade.* **3** *informal* any group of people with a characteristic in common: *the couldn't-care-less brigade.* **4** *Cdn hist.* a group or fleet of canoes, bateaux, Red River carts, pack horses, etc., travelling together to the same trading post etc.

brigadier *noun* (also **Brigadier**) (in the UK and *hist.* in the Canadian Army) **1** an officer commanding a brigade. **2** a staff officer of similar standing, above a colonel and below a major general. [Say brigga DEER]

brigadier general *noun* (also **Brigadier General**) (in the Canadian Army and Air Force and US Army, Air Force, and Marines) an officer ranking next above colonel.

brigand *noun* a member of a gang that ambushes and robs people or holds them for ransom, esp. in wild or remote areas. ▸ **brigandage** *noun* [Say BRIG und]

brigantine *noun* a two-masted sailing ship with a square-rigged forward mast and a fore-and-aft-rigged mainmast. [Say BRIG un teen]

bright • *adjective* **1** a emitting or reflecting much light, shining. **b** full of light: *a bright apartment.* **2** (of colour) intense, vivid. **3** clever, talented, quick-witted.

4 cheerful, vivacious: *a bright smile* ◊ *was way too bright and perky at breakfast.* **5** full of hope; promising: *a bright future.* • *adverb* esp. *literary* brightly. • *noun* (in *plural*) **1** bright colours. **2** headlights switched to high beam. PHRASES **bright and early** very early in the morning. **bright-eyed and bushy-tailed** *informal* alert and sprightly. **look on the bright side** be optimistic.

brighten *verb* **1** make or become brighter. **2** make or become more cheerful. ▸ **brightener** *noun*

bright lights *plural noun* (**the bright lights**) the glamour and excitement of the city.

brightly *adverb* **1** in a cheerful and lively manner. **2** intensely, vividly: *brightly coloured pyjamas* ◊ *brightly painted toys.* **3** shining or gleaming with light; brilliantly: *fires blazed brightly* ◊ *brightly polished silver.*

brightness *noun* **1** the quality of being intense, vivid, and full of light; brilliance: *I adjusted the brightness of my computer screen.* **2** cheerfulness, liveliness.

brilliance *noun* **1** great brightness. **2** outstanding talent or intelligence.

brilliant *adjective* **1** very bright. **2** outstandingly talented or intelligent. **3** showy. **4** *informal* excellent, superb. ▸ **brilliantly** *adverb*

brim • *noun* **1** the edge or lip of a cup or other vessel, or of a hollow. **2** the projecting edge of a hat. • *verb* (**brims, brimmed, brimming**) fill or be full to the point of overflowing: *large tears brimmed in her eyes* ◊ *a brimming cup.* PHRASES **brim over** overflow; be abundantly provided with: *flowers brimming over with the colours of summer.* **brim with** be full of a particular quality, feeling, etc.: *their lyrics brim with Canadiana in the best tradition of Stompin' Tom Connors.*

brimful *adjective* **1** filled to the brim: *a plate brimful of spaghetti.* **2** abundantly provided with: *brimful of reading matter.*

brimless *adjective* (of a hat) not having a brim.

brimmed *combining form* (esp. of a hat) having the sort of brim described: *he wore a wide-brimmed fedora.*

brimstone *noun archaic* the element sulphur.

brin *noun Cdn* (*Nfld*) burlap: *brin bag.*

brine • *noun* **1** water saturated with or having a high concentration of salt. **2** sea water. • *verb* soak in or saturate with brine: *brined herring.*

bring *verb* (**brings, brought, bringing**) **1** come carrying or leading or accompanying. **2** cause to come or be present. **3** cause or result in: *the pills brought some relief.* **4** be sold for; produce as income. **5** a make (a legal charge). **b** initiate (legal action). **6** cause to become or to reach a particular state: *brought them to their senses.* **7** provide (evidence, an argument, etc.). **8** make (something) move in the direction or way specified. PHRASES **bring about 1** cause to happen. **2** turn (a ship) around. **bring back** call to mind. **bring down 1** cause to fall. **2** lower (a price). **3** *informal* make unhappy or less happy. **4** *informal* damage the reputation of. **5** *Cdn, Austral., & NZ esp. Parliament* present (a budget, law, report, etc.). **bring down the house** get loud applause. **bring forth 1** give birth to. **2** produce, emit, cause. **bring forward 1** move to an earlier date or time. **2** transfer from the previous page or account. **3** draw attention to. **bring home** cause to realize fully. **bring in 1** introduce (legislation, a custom, topic, etc.). **2** yield as income or profit. **bring into play** cause to operate; activate. **bring low** overcome. **bring off 1** cause to happen or appear. **2** accelerate the progress of. **bring out 1** emphasize; make evident. **2** publish. **bring over** convert to one's own side. **bring round** (or **around**) **1** restore to consciousness. **2** persuade. **bring through** aid (a person) through adversity, esp. illness. **bring to bear** exert influence or pressure to achieve a

particular result: *the prisoner was released after pressure had been brought to bear by the aid agencies.* **bring to mind** recall; cause one to remember. **bring to pass** cause to happen. **bring up 1** rear (a child). **2** vomit. **3** call attention to. **4** stop suddenly. **bring on** (or **upon**) **oneself** be responsible for (something one suffers). ▶ **bringer** *noun*

brink *noun* **1** the extreme edge of land before a precipice, river, etc., esp. when a sudden drop follows. **2** the point or state very close to something unknown, dangerous or exciting. PHRASES **on the brink of** about to experience or suffer; in imminent danger of.

brinkmanship *noun* the art or policy of pursuing a dangerous policy to the brink of catastrophe before stopping, typically in politics: *the latest round of constitutional brinkmanship.*

briny • *adjective* (**brinier, briniest**) of brine or the sea; salty. • *noun* (**the briny**) *slang* the sea. [Say BRINE ee]

brio *noun* vigour or vivacity of style or performance: *she told her story with some brio.* [Say BREE oh]

briquette *noun* (also **briquet**) a block of compressed charcoal or coal dust etc. used as fuel. [Say brick ET]

brisk *adjective* **1** active, energetic: *a brisk pace* ◊ *business was brisk.* **2** cold but pleasantly fresh. **3** slightly brusque in manner or nature: *she adopted a brisk, businesslike tone.* ▶ **briskness** *noun*

brisket *noun* **1** the breast of an animal. **2** a cut of beef used esp. to make corned beef.

briskly *adverb* **1** quickly, vigorously. **2** somewhat brusquely.

bristle • *noun* **1** a short stiff hair, esp. one of those on an animal's back or a man's face. **2** a stiff animal hair, or a synthetic substitute, used in clumps to make a brush. • *verb* (**bristles, bristled, bristling**) **1** (of the hair) stand upright, esp. in anger or fear: *the hair on the back of his neck bristled.* **2** show irritation or defensiveness, typically by drawing oneself up: *she bristled at his rudeness* ◊ *the staff are bristling with indignation.* **3** be covered or abundant in: *the roof bristled with TV antennas.*

bristling *adjective* **1** (esp. of hair) close-set, stiff, and spiky: *a bristling beard.* **2** aggressively brisk or tense: *he fills the screen with a restless, bristling energy.*

bristly *adjective* **1** (of hair or foliage) having a stiff and prickly texture. **2** covered with short stiff hairs: *he rubbed his bristly chin.*

bristol board *noun* a kind of fine smooth pasteboard.

Brit *informal* • *noun* a British person. • *adjective* British.

Britannic *adjective* of Britain: *Her Britannic Majesty.*

britches *plural noun informal* any pants, shorts, or underwear. PHRASES **too big for one's britches** more arrogant than one's situation or knowledge allows.

British *adjective* **1** of or relating to Great Britain or the United Kingdom, or to its people or language. **2** of the British Commonwealth or (formerly) the British Empire: *British subject.*

British Columbian • *adjective* of or relating to British Columbia. • *noun* a resident or native of British Columbia.

British connection *noun Cdn hist.* the relationship that existed between Canada and Great Britain.

Britisher *noun* a British subject, esp. of British descent.

Britishness *noun* the condition of being British; a British manner or quality.

British thermal unit *noun* the amount of heat needed to raise 1 lb. of water at maximum density through one degree Fahrenheit. Abbreviation: **BTU.**

Briton *noun* **1** a native or inhabitant of Great Britain or (formerly) the British Empire. **2** one of the people of southern Britain before the Roman conquest.

brittle • *adjective* **1 a** hard but easily broken; fragile. **b** insecure; easily damaged: *brittle nerves.* **2** (of a sound) unpleasantly hard and sharp: *a brittle laugh.* **3** (of a person) lacking in warmth. • *noun* a brittle candy made from nuts and set melted sugar. ▶ **brittleness** *noun*

bro *noun* (*plural* **bros**) *slang* brother; buddy.

SPELL CHECK	ABC
broach, broach	✔

The piece of jewellery is a **brooch**.

broach *verb* (**broaches, broached, broaching**) **1** raise (a sensitive or difficult subject) for discussion. **2** pierce (a cask) to draw liquor. **3** open and start using the contents of (a bottle or other container). **4** (of a fish etc.) break the surface of the water.

broad • *adjective* **1** large in extent from one side to the other. **2** full and clear: *broad daylight.* **3** unmistakable: *broad hint.* **4** general; not taking account of detail: *in the broadest sense* ◊ *the broad facts.* **5** of or including a great variety of people, things, or experiences: *a broad range of options.* **6** tolerant, liberal: *take a broad view.* **7** somewhat coarse: *broad humour.* **8** (of speech) markedly regional: *a broad accent.* • *noun* **1** the broad part of something: *broad of the back.* **2** *slang offensive* a woman.

broadaxe *noun* a large axe with a broad blade, used esp. for shaping or trimming rather than felling.

broadband *noun* a transmission technique utilizing a wide range of frequencies, which enables messages to be communicated simultaneously.

broad-brush *adjective* lacking in detail and finesse: *a broad-brush summary of the topic.*

broadcast • *verb* (**broadcasts, broadcast, broadcasting**) **1 a** transmit (programs or information) by radio or television. **b** spread (information) widely: *we don't want to broadcast our unhappiness to the world.* **2** undertake or take part in a radio or television transmission. **3** scatter (seed etc.) over a large area, esp. by hand. • *noun* a radio or television program or transmission. • *adjective* transmitted by radio or television. • *adverb* over a large area. ▶ **broadcaster** *noun* **broadcasting** *noun*

broadcloth *noun* **1** a closely woven fabric of wool, cotton, silk, or a mixture of the three. **2** a densely woven woollen cloth in a plain or twill weave and having a lustrous finish.

broaden *verb* make or become broader.

broad jump *noun* = LONG JUMP.

broadleaf • *adjective* (also **broad-leaved, broad-leafed**) **1** designating any of a number of weeds, e.g. dandelion, having broad leaves. **2** (of a tree) deciduous and having hard timber. • *noun* (*plural* **broadleaves**) **1** a broadleaf weed. **2** a broadleaf tree.

broadloom *noun* carpet woven in broad widths. ▶ **broadloomed** *adjective*

broadly *adverb* **1** in general and with the exception of minor details: *the climate is broadly similar in the two regions* ◊ *broadly speaking, the risks are as follows.* **2** widely and openly: *he was grinning broadly.*

broadsheet *noun* **1** a sheet of paper printed for posting or distribution, esp. for spreading information. **2** a newspaper with a large format regarded as more serious and less sensationalistic than a tabloid.

broadside • *noun* **1** the firing of all guns from one side of a ship. **2** a strongly worded critical attack: *he launched a broadside against the legalization of marijuana.* **3** the side of a ship above the water between the bow and quarter. **4** = BROADSHEET. • *adverb* with the side turned towards a given object: *the car hit the wall*

B

broadside. • *adjective* sideways. • *verb* run into or collide with on the side: *the truck broadsided the car*.

broad spectrum *adjective* **1** (of a drug) effective against a wide range of pathogens. **2** (of a sunscreen) effective against most wavelengths of sunlight. **3** having a wide range of applications.

brocade • *noun* a rich fabric with a silky finish woven with a raised pattern, and often with gold or silver thread. • *verb* (usu. as **brocaded** *adjective*) weave with this design. [Say bro CADE]

broccoflower *noun* a hybrid of broccoli and cauliflower, resembling a green cauliflower that tastes like broccoli. [Say BROCKA flower]

broccoli *noun* a type of vegetable related to the cauliflower, with a loose cluster of green flower buds.

brochette *noun* a dish consisting of chunks of food, esp. meat, threaded on a skewer and grilled. [Say braw SHET or bruh SHET]

brochure *noun* a pamphlet or leaflet, esp. one giving descriptive information.

brogue¹ *noun* a marked accent, esp. Irish. [Say BROAG]

brogue² *noun* **1** a strong outdoor shoe with ornamental perforated bands. **2** a rough leather shoe. [Say BROAG]

broil *verb* **1** cook by direct exposure to heat; grill. **2** make or become very hot: *the countryside lay broiling in the sun*.

broiler *noun* **1** an appliance or the element in an oven used for broiling. **2** a young chicken raised for broiling or roasting. **3** *informal* a very hot day.

broiling *adjective* very hot: *a broiling summer day*.

broke • *verb* past of BREAK. • *adjective* *informal* having no money; financially ruined. **PHRASES** **go for broke** *slang* risk everything in a strenuous effort.

broken • *verb* past participle of BREAK. • *adjective* **1 a** that has been broken. **b** out of order. **2** reduced to despair; beaten. **3** spoken falteringly and with many mistakes: *broken English*. **4** disturbed, interrupted: *broken time*. **5** uneven: *broken ground*. **6** trained, tamed: *broken to the saddle*. **7** (of a marriage, family, etc.) divided by separation or divorce.

broken-down *adjective* **1** worn out by age, use, or ill-treatment. **2** out of order.

broken-hearted *adjective* overwhelmed with sorrow or grief.▶ **broken-heartedness** *noun*

brokenness *noun* a state of being broken, esp. emotionally.

broker• *noun* **1** an agent who buys and sells or acts for others: *insurance broker* ◊ *mortgage broker*. **2** a member of a stock exchange who deals in stocks and shares. • *verb* negotiate, esp. as an intermediary: *fighting continued despite efforts to broker a ceasefire*.

brokerage *noun* **1** the action or service of a broker. **2** a company providing such a service. **3** a broker's fee.

broking *noun* the action or service of a broker.

brome *noun* (also **brome grass**) an oatlike grass of the temperate zone, sometimes grown for fodder or for ornamental purposes.

bromide *noun* **1** a compound of bromine with a less electronegative element or radical. **2** a preparation of usu. potassium bromide, used as a sedative. **3** a trite and unoriginal idea or remark, esp. one intended to soothe or placate: *feel-good bromides create the illusion of problem-solving*. [Say BRO mide]

bromine *noun* a dark liquid element with a choking irritating smell, used in the manufacture of chemicals for photography and medicine. [Say BRO mean]

bronc *noun informal* = BRONCO.

bronchial *adjective* of or relating to the air passages in

the lungs which diverge from the windpipe: *bronchial pneumonia* ◊ *bronchial tubes*. [Say BRONKY ul]

bronchiole *noun* any of the minute branches into which a bronchus divides. [Say BRONKY ole]

bronchitis *noun* inflammation of the mucous membrane in the bronchial tubes. [Say bron KITE iss]

bronchodilator *noun* a substance which causes widening of the bronchi, used esp. to alleviate asthma. [Say bronco DIE later]

bronchus *noun* (*plural* **bronchi**) any of the major air passages of the lungs, esp. either of the two main divisions of the windpipe. [Say BRON kuss]

bronco *noun* (*plural* **broncos**) a wild or half-tamed horse.

broncobuster *noun informal* a person who breaks in horses.▶ **broncobusting** *noun*

brontosaurus *noun* (*plural* **brontosauruses**) (also **brontosaur**) a large plant-eating dinosaur of the Jurassic and Cretaceous periods, with a long whip-like tail and trunk-like legs.

bronze • *noun* **1** any of a group of alloys of copper and tin. **2** its brownish colour. **3** a thing made of bronze, esp. as a work of art. **4** = BRONZE MEDAL. • *adjective* made of or coloured like bronze. • *verb* (**bronzes**, **bronzed**, **bronzing**) **1** give a bronze-like surface to. **2** make or become brown; tan.

Bronze Age *noun* the period preceding the Iron Age, when weapons and tools were usu. made of bronze.

bronze medal *noun* a medal usu. awarded to a competitor who comes third (esp. in sport).

SPELL CHECK   ABC ✓
brooch, broach

When you raise a subject you **broach** it.

---

brooch *noun* (*plural* **brooches**) an ornament fastened to clothing with a hinged pin. [Sounds like BROACH]

brood • *noun* **1** the young of an animal (esp. a bird) produced at one hatching or birth. **2** *informal* the children in a family. **3** bee or wasp larvae. **4** (as an *adjective*) kept for breeding: *brood mare*. • *verb* **1** (often foll. by *on*, *over*, etc.) worry or ponder (esp. resentfully). **2** (of a bird) sit on eggs to hatch them. **3** (usu. foll. by *over*) (of silence, a storm, etc.) hang or hover closely.

brooder *noun* **1** a heated device or structure for raising chicks etc. **2** a person who broods.

brooding *adjective* **1** (of a person) melancholy, glum. **2** (of a landscape etc.) sombre and giving the impression of hovering over the surroundings. ▶ **broodingly** *adverb*

broody *adjective* (**broodier**, **broodiest**) **1** (of a hen) wanting to brood. **2** sullenly thoughtful or depressed.

brook¹ *noun* a small stream.

brook² *verb* tolerate, allow (typically dissent or opposition): *Jenny would brook no criticism of Matthew*.

brookie *noun informal* = BROOK TROUT.

brook trout *noun* a trout found widely throughout eastern North America.

broom *noun* **1** a brush of bristles, straw, etc. on a long handle, used for sweeping. **2** any of various flowering shrubs with long, thin, green stems and small or few leaves and bearing bright yellow flowers.

broomball *noun* a game like hockey in which players use rubber brooms or broom handles to propel a ball, esp. a volleyball, into the goal. ▶ **broomballer** *noun*

broomstick *noun* the handle of a broom.

Bros. *abbreviation* Brothers (esp. in the name of a company).

broth *noun* **1** a thin soup of meat or fish stock. **2** meat or fish stock that has not been clarified.

brothel *noun* a house etc. where prostitution takes place.

brother • *noun* **1** a man or boy in relation to other sons and daughters of his parents. **2 a** (often as a form of address) a close male friend or associate. **b** a male fellow member of a union etc. **3** (*plural* also **brethren**) **a** a member of a male religious order, esp. a monk. **b** a fellow member of a religion, esp. the Christian Church. **c** an associate in a common cause, association, etc. **4** a fellow human being. • *interjection* expressing mild deprecation or annoyance.

brotherhood *noun* **1 a** the relationship between brothers. **b** brotherly friendliness; companionship. **2 a** an association, society, or community of people linked by a common interest, religion, trade, etc. **b** its members collectively. **3** community of feeling between all human beings.

brother-in-law *noun* (*plural* **brothers-in-law**) **1** the brother of one's wife or husband. **2** the husband of one's sister or sister-in-law.

brotherliness *noun* the sort of mutual kindness and affection typically felt by brothers.

brotherly *adjective & adverb* having or showing the sort of mutual kindness and affection typically felt by brothers: *brotherly love* ◊ *brotherly advice*.

brought *past and past participle of* BRING.

brouhaha (*plural* **brouhahas**) a noisy and overexcited critical response, display of interest, or trail of publicity: *the brouhaha over those infamous commercials* ◊ *all that election brouhaha*. [Say BREW haw haw]

brow *noun* **1** the forehead. **2** (usu. in *plural*) an eyebrow. **3** the summit of a hill or pass. **4** the edge of a cliff, riverbank, etc.

browbeat *verb* (**browbeats**; *past* **browbeat**; *past participle* **browbeaten**; **browbeating**) intimidate someone, typically into doing something, with stern or abusive words: *a witness is being browbeaten under cross-examination* ◊ *he wasn't about to browbeat Peter into anything he didn't want to do*. ▶ **browbeater** *noun*

browed *adjective* having the kind of brow or eyebrows described: *a yellow-browed warbler* ◊ *the bushy-browed professor*.

brown • *adjective* **1** having the colour produced by mixing red, yellow, and black, as of dark wood or rich soil. **2** dark-skinned or suntanned. **3** (of bread) made from a dark flour, e.g. whole wheat. **4** (of species or varieties) distinguished by brown coloration. • *noun* **1 a** brown colour or pigment. **2** brown clothes or material: *dressed in brown*. **3** (in a game or sport) a brown ball, piece, etc. **4** brown bread. • *verb* make or become brown by cooking, sunburn, etc.

brown bear *noun* a large bear of northern North America, Europe, and Asia, including the grizzly bear, kodiak bear, and Siberian brown bear.

brown cow *noun* Cdn a cocktail of coffee liqueur and milk or cream.

browned off *adjective* Brit. & Cdn slang fed up.

brownie *noun* **1** (usu. **Brownie**; in full **Brownie Guide**) a member of the junior branch of the Guides. **2** a small square of rich, usu. chocolate, cake with nuts. **3** a benevolent elf said to haunt houses and do household work secretly.

brownie point *noun informal* a notional credit for something done to please or win favour.

brownish *adjective* somewhat brown.

brown-nose *verb* (**brown-noses**, **brown-nosed**, **brown-nosing**) treat someone in authority with special respect in order to gain their approval. ▶ **brown-noser** *noun* **brown-nosing** *adjective & noun*

brownout *noun* a temporary reduction in electrical power, esp. for conservation.

brown owl *noun* **1** any of various owls, esp. the tawny owl. **2** (**Brown Owl**) Cdn an adult leader of a Brownie pack.

brown rice *noun* unpolished rice with only the husk of the grain removed.

brownshirt *noun* **1** (**Brownshirt**) a member of an early Nazi militia, the Storm Troopers, whose violent intimidation of political opponents played a key role in Hitler's rise to power. **2** a fascist. ▶ **brown-shirted** *adjective*

brown sugar *noun* **1** refined sugar to which molasses has been added. **2** unrefined or partially refined sugar.

browny *adjective* brownish.

browse • *verb* (**browses**, **browsed**, **browsing**) **1** read or survey haphazardly. **2** feed (on leaves, twigs, or scanty vegetation). **3** read or survey (data files etc.), esp. via a network. • *noun* **1** twigs, young shoots, etc., as fodder for cattle etc. **2** an act of browsing.

browser *noun* **1** Computing a program with a graphical user interface for displaying HTML files, used to navigate the World Wide Web. **2** a person or animal that browses.

brr *interjection* expressing cold or shivering.

bruise • *noun* **1** an injury appearing as an area of discoloured skin on a human or animal body, caused by a blow or impact. **2** a similar area of damage on fruit etc. • *verb* (**bruises**, **bruised**, **bruising**) **1 a** inflict a bruise on. **b** hurt mentally: *she tried to bolster her bruised pride* ◊ *an amazing number of easily bruised egos*. **2** be susceptible to bruising: *I bruise very easily*.

bruiser *noun informal* **1** a large tough-looking person. **2** a professional boxer.

bruit *verb* (often foll. by *abroad*, *about*) spread (a report or rumour): *didn't want to have our relationship bruited about the office*. [Say BROOT]

brunch • *noun* a late-morning meal intended to combine breakfast and lunch. • *verb* eat brunch.

brunette • *noun* a woman with dark brown hair. • *adjective* (of a woman) having dark brown hair.

brunt *noun* the worst part or initial impact of a specific action: *education will bear the brunt of the cuts*.

bruschetta *noun* (*plural* **bruschettas**) slices of toasted bread drizzled with olive oil and usu. topped with diced tomatoes, garlic, etc. [Say brew SHETTA or brew SKETTA]

brush • *noun* (*plural* **brushes**) **1** an implement with bristles, wire, etc. set into a block or projecting from the end of a handle, for any of various purposes, esp. cleaning or scrubbing, painting, grooming, etc. **2** the application of a brush; brushing. **3** a short esp. unpleasant encounter. **4** the bushy tail of a fox. **5** either of a pair of thin sticks with long wire bristles for softly playing a drum etc. **6 a** undergrowth; small trees and shrubs. **b** such wood cut and bundled as kindling. **c** land covered with brush. • *verb* (**brushes**, **brushed**, **brushing**) **1 a** sweep or scrub or put in order with a brush. **b** treat (a surface) with a brush so as to change its nature or appearance. **2 a** remove (dust etc.) with a brush. **b** apply (a liquid preparation) to a surface with a brush. **3** graze or touch in passing. PHRASES **brush aside** dismiss or dispose of (a person, idea, etc.) curtly or lightly. **brush off** rebuff; dismiss abruptly. **brush over** paint lightly. **brush up** (usu. foll. by *on*) revive one's former knowledge of (a subject).

brushcut *noun* a very short haircut.

brushcutter *noun* a device with blades for cutting heavy undergrowth.

brushed *adjective* **1** swept or smoothed with a brush. **2** (of metallic surfaces) finished with a non-reflective surface: *brushed aluminum*. **3** (of fabric) brushed so as to raise the nap: *brushed cotton*.

B

brush fire *noun* **1** a fire in brush or scrub. **2** a localized, small-scale flare-up or skirmish.

brushland *noun* = BRUSH 6c.

brushlike *adjective* resembling the bristles of a hairbrush.

brush-off *noun* a rebuff; an abrupt dismissal.

brushwork *noun* the way in which painters use their brush, as evident in their paintings: *canvases characterized by lively, flowing brushwork*.

brushy *adjective* covered with or consisting of small trees and shrubs: *a brushy hill* ◊ *brushy vegetation*.

brusque *adjective* abrupt in manner or speech: *she could be brusque and impatient*. ▶ **brusquely** *adverb* **brusqueness** *noun* [Say BRUSK]

Brussels sprouts *plural noun* **1** a vegetable with small cabbage-like buds close together along a tall single stem. **2** these buds eaten as a vegetable.

brutal *adjective* **1** savagely or coarsely cruel. **2** harsh, merciless: *brutal cold*. **3** *slang* very bad: *a brutal haircut*. ▶ **brutality** *noun* (*plural* **brutalities**)

brutalization *noun* an act of brutalizing someone: *the novel depicts the brutalization of women by macho males*.

brutalize *verb* (**brutalizes, brutalized, brutalizing**) **1** treat someone in a cruel, violent, or inhumane manner: *they brutalize and torture persons in their custody*. **2** desensitize someone to the pain or suffering of others by exposing them to violent behaviour or situations: *he had been brutalized in prison and became cynical*.

brutally *adverb* **1** in a cruel or violent manner: *brutally murdered*. **2** in a harsh or ruthless manner: *brutally cold* ◊ *brutally competitive*. **3** without attempting to spare a person's feelings: *brutally honest*.

brute • *noun* **1 a** a brutal or violent person or animal. **b** *informal* an unpleasant person. **2** an animal as opposed to a human being. **3** a large and very strong person etc. • *adjective* **1** unthinking; entirely physical: *brute strength*. **2** unreasoning and animal-like: *a brute struggle for social superiority* ◊ *a brute beast*.

brutish *adjective* resembling or characteristic of a brute: *brutish behaviour* ◊ *life, said Thomas Hobbes, is nasty, brutish, and short*. ▶ **brutishness** *noun*

B.Sc. *abbreviation* (*plural* **B.Sc.'s**) Bachelor of Science.

B-side *noun* **1** the second side of a recording, esp. the usu. less commercial side of a single. **2** the music on this side.

BST *abbreviation* bovine somatotropin, a growth hormone occurring naturally in cows, sometimes added to cattle feed to boost milk production.

BT *abbreviation* (also **Bt**) BACILLUS THURINGIENSIS.

BTU *abbreviation* (*plural* **BTUs**) BRITISH THERMAL UNIT.

BTW *abbreviation* by the way.

bu. *abbreviation* bushel(s).

bubbe *noun* (*plural* **bubbes**) (also **bubbie**; *plural* **bubbies**) a Jewish grandmother. [Say BUBBA, BUBBY]

bubble • *noun* **1 a** a thin sphere of liquid enclosing air etc. **b** an air-filled cavity in a liquid or a solidified liquid such as glass or amber. **2** a transparent domed cavity. **3** a state or feeling that is unstable and unlikely to last: *many companies enjoyed rapid expansion before the bubble burst*. • *verb* (**bubbles, bubbled, bubbling**) **1 a** rise in or send up bubbles. **b** become manifest; arise as if from a depth: *the fury bubbled up inside her*. **2** make the sound of boiling. **3** be exuberant with laughter, excitement, etc.: *Ellen was bubbling with enthusiasm*.

bubble bath *noun* **1** a preparation for adding to bathwater to make it foam. **2** a bath with this added.

bubble gum *noun* **1** chewing gum that can be blown into bubbles. **2** *slang derogatory* (often as an *adjective*) bland, repetitive pop music intended to appeal esp. to children and young teenagers. **3** (often as an *adjective*) a pink or purple colour like that of bubble gum.

bubbly • *adjective* (**bubblier, bubbliest**) **1** having or resembling bubbles. **2** full of cheerful high spirits. • *noun* (*plural* **bubblies**) *informal* sparkling wine, esp. champagne.

bubonic plague *noun* a highly contagious bacterial disease characterized by fever, delirium, and the formation of swollen inflamed lymph nodes in the armpit or groin known as buboes. Epidemics of the plague occurred in Europe throughout the Middle Ages (notably the Black Death of the 14th century) and as the Great Plague of 1665-6. [Say byoo BON ick or boo BON ick]

buccaneer *noun* **1** a pirate, esp. one who plundered the Spanish colonies of the Caribbean and South American coasts in the late 17th century. **2** a person who acts in a recklessly adventurous and often unscrupulous way, esp. in business. ▶ **buccaneering** *noun* & *adjective* [Say bucka NEAR]

buck¹ • *noun* **1** the male of various animals, esp. the deer. **2** a self-assured young man. • *verb* **1 a** (of a horse) jump upwards with back arched and feet drawn together. **b** (of a vehicle etc.) move jerkily and with a strong up-and-down motion. **2** (usu. foll. by *off*) throw (a rider etc.) in this way. **3 a** oppose, resist: *bucking the trend*. **b** make one's way with difficulty against: *bucking easterly winds*. **4** *Football* charge into (an opponent's line) while carrying the ball. PHRASES **buck for** *informal* strive for (a promotion, advantage, etc.). **buck up** *informal* make or become more cheerful.

buck² *noun* **1** *informal* a dollar. **2** *slang* an object placed as a reminder before a player whose turn it is to deal at poker. PHRASES **buck-naked** *slang* completely naked. **a fast** (or **quick**) **buck** easy money. **pass the buck** *informal* shift responsibility (to another).

buck³ • *verb* cut (a tree) into logs. • *noun* a frame supporting wood for sawing.

buck and doe *noun* *Cdn* (*Ont.*) = STAG AND DOE.

buckbrush *noun* any of various shrubs, esp. potentillas and members of the honeysuckle family, on which wild deer browse.

bucker *noun* **1** a horse or bull that bucks. **2** *Forestry* a person who cuts felled trees into logs for transporting.

bucket • *noun* **1 a** a roughly cylindrical open container of metal, plastic, etc. with a handle, for carrying, drawing, or holding water etc. **b** the amount contained in this. **2** (in *plural*) large quantities of liquid, esp. rain or tears: *wept buckets*. **3** the scoop of a backhoe etc. **4** one of a series of containers on a mechanical conveyor etc. • *verb* (**buckets, bucketed, bucketing**) **1** (often foll. by *along*) move or drive jerkily or bumpily. **2** (often foll. by *down*) (of liquid, esp. rain) pour heavily. ▶ **bucketful** *noun* (*plural* **bucketfuls**)

bucket seat *noun* a seat with a rounded back to fit one person, esp. in a car.

buckeye *noun* **1** any of various trees or shrubs related to the horse chestnut, with large sticky buds and showy red or white flowers. **2** the shiny brown fruit of this plant.

buckle • *noun* **1** a flat often rectangular frame with a hinged pin, for joining the ends of a belt etc. **2** a similarly shaped ornament on a shoe etc. • *verb* (**buckles, buckled, buckling**) **1** (often foll. by *up, on*, etc.) fasten with a buckle. **2** give way or cause to give way under pressure or strain. **3** (often foll. by *under*) submit under pressure. PHRASES **buckle down** make a determined effort. **buckle up** fasten one's seat belt.

bucko *noun* *slang* (*plural* **buckoes**) a young man.

buck-passing *noun* the act of shifting responsibility to another person.

bucksaw noun a woodcutting saw having the blade set within an H-shaped upright frame.

buckshot noun a coarse lead shot used in shotgun shells.

buckskin noun **1 a** the skin of a male deer. **b** a yellowish-tan usu. suede leather made from this or sheepskin. **c** (in plural) clothing made from buckskin, typically fringed jackets and pants worn as traditional cowboy attire. **2** a thick smooth cotton or woollen cloth resembling buckskin.

bucktail noun a fishing lure made of hairs from the tail of a deer etc.

buckthorn noun a thorny shrub or small tree bearing black berries used as a laxative.

bucktooth noun (plural **buckteeth**) an upper front tooth that projects. ▶ **bucktoothed** adjective

buckwheat noun a cereal plant with seeds used for fodder and for flour to make bread and pancakes.

bucolic adjective of or pertaining to an idyllic life in the countryside: the church was lovely for its bucolic setting ◊ suburbanites think of farming and lumbering as bucolic lifestyles close to nature. [Say byoo COL ick]

bud[1] • noun **1** an immature knob-like shoot from which a stem, leaf, or flower develops. **2** a flower or leaf that is not fully open. • verb (**buds, budded, budding**) **1** form a bud or buds. **2** begin to grow or develop: a budding actor. **3** graft a bud (of a plant) on to another plant. PHRASES **in bud** having newly formed buds.

bud[2] noun informal (as a form of address) = BUDDY 2.

Buddhism noun a widespread Asian religion or philosophy, founded by Gautama Buddha in India in the 5th century BC, which teaches that elimination of the self and earthly desires is the highest goal. ▶ **Buddhist** noun & adjective [Say BOOD ism]

buddleia noun (plural **buddleias**) a shrub with fragrant esp. mauve flowers attractive to butterflies. [Say BUD lee uh]

buddy • noun (plural **buddies**) **1** informal a close friend. **2** informal (esp. as a form of address) any male. **3** a person's assigned or chosen companion for some activity, esp. a dangerous one. • verb (**buddies, buddied, buddying**) (often foll. by up) become friendly.

buddy movie noun (also **buddy film**) a film in which camaraderie between two characters of the same sex (usu. men) is a central theme.

budge verb (**budges, budged, budging**) **1 a** make the slightest movement. **b** change one's opinion: he's stubborn, he won't budge. **2** cause or compel to budge: nothing will budge him.

budgerigar noun (also informal **budgie**) a small Australian parakeet, popular as a cage bird, which is green with a yellow head in the wild but is bred in many colours. [Say budge a ree GAR]

budget • noun **1** a periodic (esp. annual) estimate of the revenue and expenditure of a country, organization, etc. **2** a similar estimate for a private individual or family, often over a short period. **3** (as an adjective) inexpensive: a budget bike. **4** the amount of money needed or available (for a specific item etc.): a budget of $200. • verb (**budgets, budgeted, budgeting**) **1** allow or arrange for in a budget: have budgeted for a new car. **2** to plan the expenditure or allotment of (money, time, etc.): we had to budget our time carefully to get the job done. PHRASES **on a budget** with a restricted amount of money. ▶ **budgetary** adjective

budworm noun **1** SPRUCE BUDWORM. **2** a larva destructive to the buds of plants.

buff • adjective of a yellowish beige colour: buff envelope. • noun **1** yellowish beige. **2** informal an enthusiast or expert in a specified subject or activity: film buff. **3** a

thick, dull yellow ox or buffalo leather with a velvety surface: buff gloves. • verb **1** polish (metal, fingernails, etc.). **2** make (leather) velvety like buff, by removing the surface. PHRASES **in the buff** informal naked.

buffalo noun (plural **buffalo** or **buffaloes**) **1** the North American bison. **2** either of two species of ox, the Cape buffalo, native to Africa, or the water buffalo, native to Asia.

buffalo bean noun a plant with yellow flowers and edible pods, native to western North America.

buffalo berry noun (plural **buffalo berries**) **1** a genus of North American shrubs with oblong leaves, including esp.: **a** the **silver buffalo berry**, found from BC to Manitoba. **b** the **Canada buffalo berry**, found in wooded areas across Canada. **2** the edible red or yellow fruit of these plants.

buffalo chip noun a piece of dried buffalo dung, esp. when used as fuel by early settlers on the Prairies.

buffalo grass noun a creeping grass of the North American plains.

buffalo jump noun hist. a cliff over which Plains Aboriginal peoples drove herds of bison to kill them.

buffalo pound noun Cdn hist. a sturdy corral or enclosure into which Plains Aboriginal peoples drove bison in order to kill them.

buffalo robe noun **1** a blanket or rug made of the hairy hide of the North American bison. **2** clothing made from bison skins.

buffalo run noun hist. **1** a buffalo hunt conducted on horseback. **2** a trail made by buffalo.

buffalo stone noun a small fossil found on the prairies, believed by Plains Aboriginal peoples to give their finders great power with the buffalo.

buffer[1] • noun **1** a device that protects against or reduces the effect of an impact. **2** a substance that maintains the hydrogen ion concentration of a solution when an acid or alkali is added. **3 a** a country or area between two potential enemies, regarded as reducing the likelihood of open hostilities: buffer zone. **b** an area, person, thing, etc., that protects from the potentially damaging impact of one person, activity, etc. on another: family and friends can provide a buffer against stress. **4** an intermediate memory for the temporary storage of information during data transfers, e.g. before printing. • verb **1** act as a buffer to. **2** Chemistry treat with a buffer.

buffer[2] noun a device for buffing or polishing.

buffet[1] noun **1 a** a meal consisting of several dishes from which guests serve themselves: buffet lunch. **b** a table or counter from which such meals are served. **c** a restaurant having such a table or counter. **2 a** sideboard or cabinet for china, silverware, etc. [Say buff AY]

buffet[2] verb (**buffets, buffeted, buffeting**) **1 a** strike or knock repeatedly: wind buffeted the trees ◊ 26-foot seas buffeted the craft. **b** strike, esp. repeatedly, with the hand or fist: buffeted from side to side. **2** afflict or harm repeatedly over a long period: a middle class buffeted by the recession. ▶ **buffeting** noun [Say BUFF it]

buffoon noun a ridiculous but amusing person; a clown. ▶ **buffoonery** noun **buffoonish** adjective

bug • noun **1 a** any small insect. **b** Zoology an insect of a large order distinguished by having mouthparts modified for piercing and sucking. **2** informal a micro-organism, esp. a bacterium, or a disease caused by it: a flu bug. **3** a concealed microphone or other device used in electronic surveillance. **4** a mistake or malfunction in a computer program or system etc. **5** informal an obsession, enthusiasm, etc. • verb (**bugs, bugged, bugging**) **1** informal annoy, bother. **2** conceal a microphone in (a room etc.). **3** (often foll. by out) (of the

eyes) bulge. PHRASES **bug off** *informal* go away. **put a bug in a person's ear** suggest something to a person, esp. confidentially.

bugaboo *noun* (*plural* **bugaboos**) **1** a bugbear. **2** an object of fear or anxiety: *bad breath, that bugaboo of romance and social acceptance*. [Say BUGGA boo]

bugbear *noun* **1** a cause of annoyance or anger. **2** an object of baseless fear: *the American bugbear of "national security"*.

bug-eyed *adjective* having bulging eyes.

bugger • *noun* **1** *slang* **a** a person, esp. of a specified kind: *the silly old bugger*. **b** an unpleasant or awkward person or thing: *the bugger won't fit*. **2** a person who commits buggery. • *verb* **1** *slang* as an exclamation of annoyance: *bugger it*. **2** *slang* (often foll. by *up*) ruin; spoil: *really buggered it up*. **3** commit buggery with. • *interjection informal* expressing annoyance. PHRASES **bugger about** (or **around**) (often foll. by *with*) *slang* **1** mess about. **2** mislead; persecute.

buggery *noun* **1** anal intercourse. **2** = BESTIALITY 1.

buggy[1] *noun* (*plural* **buggies**) **1** a light horse-drawn vehicle for one or two people. **2** a small, sturdy, esp. open, automobile: *dune buggy*. **3** = BABY CARRIAGE. **4** a shopping cart.

buggy[2] *adjective* (**buggier, buggiest**) **1** infested with bugs. **2** (of software) having programming errors. **3** *slang* mad or crazy.

bugle • *noun* **1** a brass instrument like a small trumpet, used esp. for military signals. **2** the call of a bull elk at rutting time. • *verb* (**bugles, bugled, bugling**) **1** sound a bugle. **2** sound (a note etc.) on a bugle. **3** (of a bull elk etc.) make a loud bellowing call. ▶ **bugler** *noun* [Say BYOO gull]

build • *verb* (**builds, built, building**) **1 a** construct (a house, vehicle, fire, etc.) by putting parts or material together. **b** commission, finance, and oversee the building of: *built two new hospitals*. **2 a** (often foll. by *up*) establish, develop, or accumulate gradually: *built the business up from nothing*. **b** (often foll. by *on*) base (hopes, theories, etc.). **3** (of sounds etc.) become more intense. • *noun* **1** the proportions of esp. the human body. **2** a style of construction; a make. PHRASES **build in** (or **into**) **1** incorporate as part of a structure. **2** integrate as part of a plan, policy, activity, etc. **build on 1** add (an extension etc.), **2** make further advances after achieving (a success etc.). **build up 1** increase in size or strength. **2** praise; boost. **3** gradually become established. ▶ **builder** *noun* **building** *noun*

building block *noun* **1** a basic component or element: *the building blocks of DNA*. **2** a block of stone or other material used in building. **3** one of a set of wooden or plastic cubes etc. that fit together, as a child's toy.

building code *noun* the body of regulations governing standards of construction.

buildup *noun* **1** a favourable description in advance: *a huge media buildup*. **2** a gradual approach to a climax or maximum: *the buildup to Christmas*. **3** an accumulation or increase: *the buildup of carbon dioxide in the atmosphere*.

built • *verb* past and past participle of BUILD. • *adjective* **1** having a specified build: *sturdily built*. **2** produced by building: *the built environment*. **3** *slang* (of a woman) having large breasts.

built-in • *adjective* **1** forming an integral part of a structure: *a built-in flash*. **2** that is intrinsically part of something: *a built-in bias*. • *noun* a built-in cabinet, appliance, etc.

built-up *adjective* **1** (of a locality) densely covered by houses etc. **2** increased in height etc. by the addition of parts. **3** increased in intensity over a period of time: *built-up frustrations*.

bulb *noun* **1 a** the globular underground organ of an

onion, lily, etc., which contains the following year's bud and scale leaves that serve as food reserves. **b** a plant grown from this, e.g. a daffodil. **2** = LIGHT BULB. **3** any object or part shaped like a bulb.

bulbous *adjective* **1** like a bulb; fat, round, or bulging at one end: *a bulbous nose*. **2** growing from a bulb.

Bulgarian • *noun* **1 a** a native or national of Bulgaria, a country in southeastern Europe. **b** a person of Bulgarian descent. **2** the language of Bulgaria. • *adjective* of or relating to Bulgaria or its people or language.

bulge • *noun* **1 a** a rounded swelling which distorts an otherwise flat or flatter surface. **b** an irregular swelling; a lump. **2** *informal* a temporary increase in quantity or number. • *verb* (**bulges, bulged, bulging**) **1** swell outwards: *the veins in his neck bulged* ◊ *she stared with bulging eyes*. **2** be full of and distended with: *a briefcase bulging with documents*.

bulgur *noun* a cereal food of whole wheat partially boiled then dried. [Say BUL gur]

bulgy *adjective* tending to bulge: *bulgy eyes*.

bulimia *noun* **1** (also **bulimia nervosa**) an emotional disorder in which bouts of extreme overeating are followed by self-induced vomiting, purging, or fasting. **2** insatiable overeating. ▶ **bulimic** *adjective & noun* [Say buh LIMMY uh]

bulk • *noun* **1 a** size; magnitude (esp. large): *the sheer bulk of the barges*. **b** a large mass or shape, esp. of a building or person: *moved quickly in spite of his bulk*. **c** a large quantity. **2** (usu. as **the bulk**; treated as *plural*) the greater part or number. **3** dietary fibre. **4** cargo, esp. unpackaged. • *verb* **1** seem, as regards size or importance: *territorial questions bulked large in diplomatic negotiations*. **2** make (a substance) seem bulkier: *bulked up the book by using thicker paper*. **3** combine (consignments of a commodity) together. • *adjective* pertaining to material bought, sold, handled, etc. in bulk. PHRASES **in bulk 1** loose, not packaged. **2** in large quantities. **bulk up** increase in bulk or mass, esp. build up flesh or muscle.

bulkhead *noun* an upright partition separating the compartments in a ship, aircraft, vehicle, etc.

bulkiness *noun* a bulky quality.

bulky *adjective* (**bulkier, bulkiest**) taking up much space, usu. inconveniently.

bull[1] • *noun* **1 a** an uncastrated male bovine animal. **b** the male of various other large animals, e.g. whale, elephant, moose. **2** a person who buys shares hoping to sell them at a higher price later (*compare* BEAR[2] 3). **3** *slang* nonsensical, foolish, or deceptive talk or writing. **4** *slang* a policeman. • *adjective* **1** like that of a bull: *bull neck*. **2** (in *combination*) Forestry chief or head. PHRASES **bull in a china shop** a reckless or clumsy person. **take the bull by the horns** meet a difficulty boldly. **bull through** force through with great effort: *with brute strength I bulled through my attackers* ◊ *bulled his way through willows and rose bushes*.

bull[2] *noun* a papal edict.

bullcook *noun* a person who performs various chores in a logging camp etc. (e.g. chopping wood, cleaning bunkhouses, etc.).

bulldog *noun* **1** a sturdy, powerful dog with a large head, protruding lower jaw, and smooth hair. **2** a tenacious and courageous person.

bulldogger *noun* *slang* a steer wrestler.

bulldogging *noun* *slang* = STEER WRESTLING.

bulldoze *verb* (**bulldozes, bulldozed, bulldozing**) **1** clear with a bulldozer: *developers are bulldozing the site*. **2** *informal* use force insensitively.

bulldozer *noun* **1** a powerful tractor with a broad

curved vertical blade at the front for clearing ground. **2** a forceful and domineering person.
bullet *noun* **1** a projectile of lead etc. for a rifle, revolver, etc. **2** a small usu. solid circle used to introduce and emphasize an item in a list etc.
bulletin *noun* **1** a short official account, statement, or broadcast report of news. **2** a regular list of information etc. issued by an organization or society.
bulletin board *noun* **1** a board for displaying notices. **2** a system for storing information in a computer so that any authorized user can access and add to it from a remote terminal or personal computer.
bulletproof • *adjective* **1** impenetrable by bullets: *bulletproof vest*. **2** unassailable, safe from criticism etc.: *financially bulletproof*. • *verb* make bulletproof.
bullfight *noun* a sport of baiting and (usu.) killing bulls as a public spectacle, esp. in Spain. ▶ **bullfighter** *noun* **bullfighting** *noun*
bullfrog *noun* any of several frogs with bellowing calls, esp. the largest North American frog, which is often a predator of smaller vertebrates.
bullhead *noun* **1** a North American freshwater catfish that has a large head with several fleshy filaments. **2** any of various northern fishes with large heads bearing spines.
bullheaded *adjective* determined in an obstinate and unthinking way: *a bullheaded belief that she is right*. ▶ **bullheadedly** *adverb* **bullheadedness** *noun*
bullhorn *noun* an electronically amplified megaphone.

SPELL CHECK
bullion, bouillon [ABC ✓]

A type of broth is **bouillon**.

---

bullion *noun* a metal (esp. gold or silver) in bulk before coining, or valued by weight. [Say BULL yun]
bullish *adjective* **1** *Stock Market* causing or associated with a rise in prices. **2** aggressively optimistic. ▶ **bullishly** *adverb* **bullishness** *noun*
bull market *noun* a market with shares rising in price.
bullock *noun* a castrated male of domestic cattle, esp. raised for beef.
bullpen *noun* **1** *Baseball* **a** an area where pitchers, esp. relief pitchers, warm up. **b** the relief pitchers on a team: *the team's bullpen collapsed*. **2** a large cell in which prisoners are held temporarily, in a courthouse, police station, or jail.
bull rider *noun* a participant in the rodeo event of bull riding.
bull riding *noun* a rodeo event in which a rider attempts to remain on a bucking bull for eight seconds while holding onto a rope tied around the animal's middle with one hand.
bullring *noun* an arena for bullfights.
bull's eye *noun* **1 a** the centre of a target. **b** a shot, dart, etc. hitting this. **2** a hemisphere or thick disc of glass in a ship's deck or side to admit light. **3** a small circular window. **4 a** a hemispherical lens. **b** a lantern fitted with this. **5** an accurate guess etc.: *the silence told her she'd scored a bull's eye*.
bull snake *noun* a large yellowish-brown snake found commonly on the plains and prairies of North America.
bull terrier *noun* a stocky, short-haired breed of dog that is a cross between a bulldog and a terrier.
bull trout *noun* a brightly spotted char of western North America, also known as a Dolly Varden.
bullwhip • *noun* a whip with a long heavy lash. • *verb* (**bullwhips**, **bullwhipped**, **bullwhipping**) thrash with such a whip.
bully[1] • *noun* (*plural* **bullies**) a person who uses strength or power to coerce others by fear. • *verb* (**bullies**,

bullied, **bullying**) **1** persecute or oppress by force or threats. **2** pressure or coerce (a person) to do something: *bullied him into agreeing*.
bully[2] *interjection* *slang* expressing admiration or approval: *bully for you!*
bully[3] *noun* (*plural* **bullies**) (also **bully boat**) *Cdn* (*Nfld*) a two-masted decked boat used for fishing on the coasts of northeastern Newfoundland and Labrador.
bulrush *noun* **1** a slender-stemmed marsh or water plant, which is widely used for weaving. **2** a tall water plant with a dark brown velvety cylindrical flower head. **3** *Bible* a papyrus plant.
bulwark *noun* **1** a defensive wall, esp. of earth; a rampart. **2** a person, principle, etc., that acts as a defence: *the security forces are a bulwark against the breakdown of society*. **3** (usu. in *plural*) a ship's side above deck. [Say BULL work]
bum[1] *noun* *Cdn*, *Brit.*, *Austral.*, & *NZ* *informal* the buttocks.
bum[2] *informal* • *noun* **1** a street person or vagrant. **2** a lazy or irresponsible person. **3** an obnoxious person. **4** a person who devotes a lot of time to a specified activity: *beach bum*. • *verb* (**bums**, **bummed**, **bumming**) **1** (often foll. by *around*) loaf or wander around. **2** acquire by begging. **3** (foll. by *out*) disappoint. • *adjective* **1** malfunctioning: *a bum knee*. **2** worthless: *a bum cheque*. **3** unfair, disappointing: *a bum deal*. [PHRASES] **give a person the bum's rush 1** forcibly eject. **2** abruptly dismiss.
bumble *verb* (**bumbles**, **bumbled**, **bumbling**) **1** act ineptly; blunder: *they bumbled around the house*. **2** (foll. by *on*) speak in a rambling incoherent way. **3** make a buzz or hum.
bumblebee *noun* a large hairy bee with a loud buzz, common in temperate regions.
bumbleberry pie *noun* *Cdn* a pie with a filling of mixed berries, e.g. blackberries, raspberries, blueberries, strawberries, etc.
bumbler *noun* a person who acts or speaks in a confused, awkward, or clumsy manner.
bumbling *adjective* inept: *a bumbling idiot*.
bummed *adjective* *informal* (also **bummed out**) disappointed.
bummer *noun* *informal* **1** an annoying or disappointing thing. **2** an idler.
bump • *noun* **1** a dull-sounding blow or collision. **2** a swelling or dent caused by this. **3** an uneven patch on a road, field, etc. • *verb* **1 a** hit or come against with a bump. **b** (of two objects) collide. **2** (foll. by *against*, *into*) hit with a bump; collide with. **3** (often foll. by *against*, *on*) hurt or damage by striking: *bumped my head on the ceiling*. **4** (usu. foll. by *along*) move or travel with much jolting: *bumped along the road*. **5** displace, e.g. from a job (by seniority) or airline reservation. [PHRASES] **bump and grind** move (one's hips etc.) to music, esp. as part of an erotic dance. **bump into** *informal* meet by chance. **like a bump on a log** inertly. **bump off** *slang* murder. **bump up** *informal* increase (prices etc.).
bumper *noun* **1** a horizontal bar or strip fixed across the front or back of a motor vehicle to reduce damage in a collision or as a trim. **2** (usu. as an *adjective*) unusually large or fine: *a bumper crop*. [PHRASES] **bumper to bumper 1** (of traffic) backed up. **2** (of automobile insurance etc.) covering the entire vehicle from one bumper to the other.
bumper car *noun* each of a number of small electric cars in an enclosure at an amusement park etc., driven around and bumped into each other.
bumper sticker *noun* a sticker with a slogan etc. to be displayed on a vehicle's bumper.
bumpily *adverb* in a bumpy manner.

B

bumpiness noun the bumpy nature of something: *the bumpiness of the road*.

bumpkin noun an unsophisticated and socially inept rural person.

bumptious adjective offensively conceited: *Canada is alternately bumptious and diffident about its own achievements*. ▶ **bumptiousness** noun [Say BUMP shuss]

bumpy adjective (**bumpier**, **bumpiest**) **1** having many bumps: *a bumpy road*. **2** affected by bumps: *a bumpy ride*.

bum rap noun informal **1** imprisonment on a false charge. **2** a false accusation: *the team is not a bunch of chokers; it's a bum rap*.

bum steer noun informal false information.

bun noun **1** a small unsweetened bread roll. **2** a small sweetened bread roll or cake, often with dried fruit. **3** (in plural) informal the buttocks. **4** hair worn in a tight coil at the back of the head. PHRASES **have a bun in the oven** slang be pregnant.

bunch • noun **1** a cluster of things growing or fastened together. **2** a collection; a set or lot. **3** informal a group; a gang. **4** informal a large amount; lots: *a bunch of ideas* ◊ *thanks a bunch*. • verb (**bunches**, **bunched**, **bunching**) **1** make into a bunch or bunches; gather into close folds. **2** form into a group or crowd.

bunchberry noun (plural **bunchberries**) a low-growing plant of the dogwood family, which produces white flowers followed by red berries and bright red autumn foliage.

bunch grass noun any of various North American grasses that grow in clumps.

bunchy adjective gathered or arranged in bunches or folds.

bundle • noun **1** a collection of things tied or fastened together. **2** a set of nerve fibres etc. banded together. **3** informal a large amount of money. • verb (**bundles**, **bundled**, **bundling**) **1** (usu. foll. by *up*) tie in or make into a bundle. **2** throw or push, esp. quickly or confusedly: *bundled them into the drawer*. **3** send (esp. a person) away hurriedly or unceremoniously: *bundled them off the premises*. **4** dress: *bundled them into their snowsuits*. **5** sell as a unit: *software bundled with the computer*. PHRASES **be a bundle of nerves** (or **prejudices** etc.) be extremely nervous (or prejudiced etc.). **bundle up** dress warmly or cumbersomely.

bung • noun a stopper for closing a hole in a container, esp. a cask. • verb stop with a bung. PHRASES **bunged up** informal **1** damaged; malfunctioning. **2** closed, blocked. **3** constipated.

bungalow noun **1** a low house having only one storey. **2** Cdn (*Cape Breton*) a summer cottage, esp. a modest one.

bungee cord noun **1** strong elasticized cord or cable. **2** a piece of this, usu. with a hook on each end and used esp. for securing baggage etc. [Say BUN jee]

bungee jump verb jump from a height, as from a bridge or crane, while attached to it by a bungee cord. ▶ **bungee jumper** noun **bungee jumping** noun [Say BUN jee]

bungle • verb (**bungles**, **bungled**, **bungling**) **1** mismanage or fail at (a task). **2** make or tend to make mistakes: *the work of a bungling amateur*. • noun a bungled attempt; bungled work. ▶ **bungler** noun

bunion noun a swelling on the foot, esp. at the first joint of the big toe. [Say BUN yun]

bunk[1] • noun **1** a simple bed, esp. one of two or more arranged on top of one another. **2** a large trough for feeding cattle in a feedlot etc. • verb sleep in or lie on a bunk or improvised bed. PHRASES **bunk down** go to bed.

bunk[2] noun slang nonsense.

bunker noun **1** a large container or compartment for storing fuel. **2** Military a reinforced underground shelter.

3 a sand-filled hollow used as an obstacle in a golf course.

bunkhouse noun **1** a house where workers etc. are lodged. **2** Cdn = BUNKIE.

bunkie noun Cdn a small outbuilding on the property of a summer cottage providing extra sleeping accommodation for guests.

bunny noun (plural **bunnies**) **1** informal a rabbit. **2** derogatory (usu. in combination) a young, attractive woman, esp. one who is sexually available, involved in a particular activity: *ski bunny*. **3** (as an adjective) designating an easy hill for beginner skiers: *bunny hill*.

bunny hug noun Cdn (*Sask.*) a hooded sweatshirt.

Bunsen burner noun a small adjustable gas burner used in scientific work as a source of great heat.

bunt • verb **1** push with the head or horns; butt. **2** Baseball **a** strike or tap (the ball) with the bat without swinging. **b** bunt the ball. • noun **1** an act of bunting. **2** a bunted ball. ▶ **bunter** noun

bunting noun **1 a** flags and other decorations. **b** a loosely woven fabric used for these. **2** (also **bunting bag**) a snug, hooded sleeping bag for infants. **3** any of numerous seed-eating birds related to the finches and sparrows.

buoy • noun an anchored float serving as a navigation mark or to show reefs etc. • verb (usu. foll. by *up*) **a** keep afloat: *I let the water buoy up my weight*. **b** sustain the courage or spirits of (a person etc.); uplift, encourage: *the party was buoyed by an election victory*. **2** mark with a buoy or buoys. [Say BOY or BOOEY]

buoyancy noun **1** the ability or tendency for something to stay afloat in water. **2** a high level of activity in an economy or stock market. **3** cheerfulness. [Say BOYEN see]

buoyant adjective **1 a** able to keep afloat or rise to the top of a liquid or gas. **b** (of a liquid or gas) able to keep something afloat. **2** lighthearted: *the mood at the party was buoyant*. ▶ **buoyantly** adverb [Say BOY ent]

bur noun = BURR noun 1-3.

burb noun informal (usu. in plural) a suburb.

burble • verb (**burbles**, **burbled**, **burbling**) **1** make a murmuring noise: *a burbling brook*. **2** speak ramblingly: *she burbled on but no one was paying attention*. • noun **1** a murmuring noise. **2** rambling speech.

burbot noun a freshwater fish of the cod family, with a broad head and fleshy filaments. [Say BURR bit]

burden • noun **1** a load, esp. a heavy one. **2** an oppressive duty, obligation, expense, emotion, etc. **3** a ship's carrying capacity. **4 a** the refrain or chorus of a song. **b** the chief theme or gist of a speech, book, poem, etc.: *the burden of his speech was that the Liberals had had a glorious past*. • verb **1** load with a burden. **2** cause worry, hardship, or distress to: *burdened with guilt*. PHRASES **burden of proof** the obligation to prove one's case. ▶ **burdensome** adjective

burdock noun a large plant of the daisy family with prickly flowers that become woody burrs after fertilization and cling to animals' coats to aid seed dispersal. [Say BURR dock]

bureau noun (plural **bureaus**) **1 a** Cdn & Brit. a writing desk with drawers and usu. an angled top opening downwards to form a writing surface. **b** a chest of drawers. **2 a** an office or business with a specified function. **b** a government department. [Say BYOOR oh]

bureaucracy noun (plural **bureaucracies**) **1 a** a system of government in which most of the important decisions are made by civil servants rather than by elected representatives. **b** a nation or organization so governed. **2** the officials of such a government, esp. regarded as oppressive and inflexible. **3** excessively complicated administrative procedure, seen as

characteristic of such a system: *a nightmare dealing with the university bureaucracy*. [Say byur OCKRA see]

bureaucrat *noun* an official in a government department, in particular one perceived as being concerned with procedural correctness at the expense of people's needs. [Say BYUR a crat]

bureaucratese *noun* a style of language believed to be characteristic of bureaucrats, marked by jargon, abstractions, circumlocution, etc. [Say byur OCK ra TEEZ]

bureaucratic *adjective* connected with a bureaucracy or bureaucrats and involving complicated official rules that may seem unnecessary: *bureaucratic procedures* ◊ *bureaucratic inefficiency*. [Say byur a CRAT ick]

bureaucratization *noun* the process of making something more bureaucratic. [Say byur ockra tize AY sh'n]

bureaucratize *verb* (**bureaucratizes**, **bureaucratized**, **bureaucratizing**) govern by or transform into a bureaucratic system. [Say byur OCKRA tize]

burg *noun informal* a town or city.

burgeon *verb* begin to grow or increase rapidly: *within a decade after Confederation, Canada's territorial extent had burgeoned*. ▶ **burgeoning** *adjective* [Say BURR jun]

burger *noun* **1** *informal* a hamburger. **2** (*in combination*) a kind of hamburger or variation of it: *cheeseburger* ◊ *fishburger*.

burgher *noun* a middle-class inhabitant of a (usu. specified) city or town. [Sounds like BURGER]

burglar *noun* a person who enters a building illegally in order to steal.

burglary *noun* (*plural* **burglaries**) entry into a building illegally with intent to commit theft, do bodily harm, or do damage; breaking and entering: *a two-year sentence for burglary* ◊ *a series of burglaries*.

burgle *verb* (**burgles**, **burgled**, **burgling**) commit burglary in a house: *our house has been burgled*.

burgundy *noun* (*plural* **burgundies**) **1 a** the wine (usu. red) of Burgundy in east central France. **b** a similar wine from another place. **2** *noun & adjective* the reddish purple colour of burgundy wine.

burial *noun* **1** the burying of a dead body. **2** a funeral. [Say BARE ee ul or BURR ee ul]

burlap *noun* **1** coarse canvas esp. of jute used for sacking etc. **2** a similar lighter material for use in dressmaking or furnishing.

burlesque • *noun* **1 a** comic imitation, esp. in parody of a dramatic or literary work. **b** a performance or work of this kind. **c** humour that depends on comic imitation and exaggeration; absurdity: *the argument descends into burlesque*. **2** a variety show, often including striptease. • *adjective* of or in the nature of burlesque. • *verb* (**burlesques**, **burlesqued**, **burlesquing**) make or give a burlesque of: *a mock heroic novel that burlesques the conventions of medieval romances*. [Say burr LESK]

Burlington bun *noun Cdn* (*NS*) = JELLY DOUGHNUT.

burly *adjective* (**burlier**, **burliest**) big and strong.

Burmese • *noun* (*plural* **Burmese**) **1 a** a native or national of Burma (now Myanmar) in SE Asia. **b** a person of Burmese descent. **2** a member of the largest ethnic group of Burma. **3** the language of this group. • *adjective* of Burma or its people or language. [Say burr MEEZ]

burn • *verb* (**burns**; *past* and *past participle* **burned** or **burnt**; **burning**) **1** be or cause to be consumed or destroyed by fire. **2 a** a blaze or glow with fire. **b** be in the state characteristic of fire. **3** be or cause to be injured or damaged by fire or great heat or by radiation. **4** use or be used as a source of heat, light, or other energy: *the lights burned all night*. **5** char or scorch in cooking. **6** produce (a hole, a mark, etc.) by fire or

heat. **7** colour, tan, or parch with heat or light. **8** put or be put to death by fire. **9 a** brand. **b** (foll. by *in*) imprint by burning. **10** make or be hot, give or feel a sensation or pain of or like heat. **11** make or be passionate; feel or cause to feel great emotion: *burn with shame*. **12** *slang* drive fast. **13** *informal* anger, infuriate. **14** (of acid etc.) gradually penetrate (into) causing disintegration. **15** metabolize in the body: *burn calories*. **16** cause or feel a sharp sensation: *the alcohol burned in her throat*. **17** *informal* swindle or cheat. **18** *Computing* copy data onto (a compact disc). **19** *Curling* touch (a rock in play) with one's foot, broom, etc. **20** *Cdn* (*Nfld*) freeze (a part of the body) in extreme cold; suffer frostbite. • *noun* **1 a** a mark or injury caused by burning. **b** a mark or injury caused by friction or abrasion: *razor burn*. **2 a** an area of forest destroyed by a forest fire. **b** a forest area cleared by intentional burning. PHRASES **burn one's bridges** (or **boats**) do something which makes it impossible to return to an earlier state. **burn the candle at both ends** exhaust one's strength or resources by undertaking too much. **burn down 1 a** destroy (a building) by fire. **b** (of a building) be destroyed by fire. **2** burn less vigorously as fuel fails. **burn one's fingers** or **get one's fingers burned** suffer for meddling or rashness. **burn a hole in one's pocket** (of money) be quickly spent. **burn low** (of fire) be nearly out. **burn the midnight oil** read or work late into the night. **burn off 1** remove by fire. **2** expend: *burn off energy*. **burn out 1** be reduced to nothing by burning. **2** fail or cause to fail by burning. **3** suffer physical or emotional exhaustion. **4** consume the contents of by burning. **burn up 1** get rid of by fire. **2** begin to blaze. **3** *slang* be or make furious. **have money to burn** have more money than one needs.

burner *noun* **1** a person or thing that burns. **2 a** the part of a gas stove etc. that emits and shapes the flame. **b** a heating element on a stovetop. **3** a furnace, esp. of a specified kind: *oil burner*.

burning *adjective* **1** ardent; intense: *burning desire*. **2** hotly discussed, exciting: *burning question*. **3** flagrant: *burning shame*.

burning bush *noun* any of various shrubs with red fruits or red autumn leaves, esp. of the genus *Euonymus*.

burnish • *verb* (**burnishes**, **burnished**, **burnishing**) polish by rubbing. • *noun* the shine on a highly polished surface.

burnout *noun* **1** physical or emotional exhaustion, esp. caused by stress. **2** depression, disillusionment.

burnt • *verb* past and past participle of BURN. • *adjective* **1** marked or affected by burning or as if burning. **2** (of a pigment) made darker by burning.

burnt-out *adjective* **1** physically or emotionally exhausted. **2** destroyed by burning so that only a shell remains.

burp • *verb* **1** belch. **2** make (a baby) belch, usu. by patting its back. • *noun* a belch.

burr • *noun* **1 a** a prickly clinging seed case or flower head. **b** any plant producing these. **2** a rough edge left on cut or punched metal, paper, etc. **3** a surgeon's or dentist's small drill. **4** a whirring sound. **5** a rough sounding of the letter r: *spoke with a Scots burr*. **6** a swirled pattern in the grain of wood: *burr walnut*. • *verb* **1** pronounce with a burr. **2** make a whirring sound. PHRASES **burr under** (or **in**) **one's saddle** a source of irritation, esp. a persistent one.

burrito *noun* (*plural* **burritos**) a tortilla rolled around a spicy filling of meat, beans, etc. [Say buh REE toe]

burro *noun* (*plural* **burros**) esp. *US* a small donkey used as a pack animal. [Say BURR oh]

burrow • *noun* a hole etc. dug by a small animal as a dwelling. • *verb* **1** make or live in a burrow. **2** make (a

hole etc.) by digging. **3** move underneath or press close to something in order to hide oneself or in search of comfort: *the child burrowed deeper into the bed* ◊ *she burrowed her face into the pillow.* **4** investigate: *journalists are burrowing into the premier's business affairs.* ▶ **burrower** *noun*

bursar *noun* a treasurer or other financial officer, esp. of a university or college. [Say BURR sir]

bursary *noun* (*plural* **bursaries**) *Cdn* a financial award to a university student made primarily on the basis of financial need or some other criterion in addition to academic merit. [Say BURSA ree]

burst • *verb* (**bursts, burst, bursting**) **1 a** break suddenly and violently apart by expansion of contents or internal pressure. **b** cause to do this. **c** send (a container etc.) violently apart. **2 a** open forcibly. **b** come open or be opened forcibly. **3 a** (usu. foll. by *in, out*) make one's way suddenly, dramatically, or by force. **b** break away from or through: *the river burst its banks.* **4** (usu. foll. by *with*) have in abundance: *bursting with flavour.* **5** appear or come suddenly: *the sun burst out.* **6** give sudden expression to: *burst into tears.* **7** be as if about to burst because of effort, excitement, etc. **8** suffer bursting of: *burst a blood vessel.* • *noun* **1** an occasion when something bursts; the place where it bursts; *a burst in the water main.* **2** a sudden issuing forth: *burst of flame* ◊ *her breath was coming in short bursts.* **3** a short period of a particular activity or strong emotion that starts suddenly: *burst of applause* ◊ *a burst of activity* ◊ *bursts of gunfire.* PHRASES **bursting at the seams** full to overflowing. **burst out 1** suddenly begin: *burst out laughing.* **2** exclaim.

bury *verb* (**buries, buried, burying**) **1** place (a dead body) in the earth, in a tomb, or in the sea etc. **2** lose by death: *has buried three children.* **3** put under ground: *bury alive.* **b** hide (treasure, a bone, etc.) in the earth. **c** cover up; submerge. **4 a** put out of sight: *buried his face in his hands.* **b** deliberately forget or conceal: *the idea was buried.* **c** put away; forget. **5** involve deeply: *buried herself in her work.* PHRASES **bury the hatchet** cease to quarrel. [Rhymes with *FAIRY* or *FURRY*]

bus • *noun* (*plural* **buses**) **1** a large motor vehicle designed to carry several passengers, esp. one serving the public on a fixed route or as a chartered service. **2** *informal* a car, airplane, etc., functioning like a bus. **3** a defined set of conductors carrying data and control signals within a computer. • *verb* (**buses, bused, busing**) **1** go or transport by bus. **2** carry or remove dishes etc. in a cafeteria: *please bus your own trays.*

busboy *noun* a waiter's assistant who clears tables etc.

bush • *noun* (*plural* **bushes**) **1** a shrub or clump of shrubs with stems of moderate length. **2** a thing resembling this, esp. a clump of hair or fur. **3** *Cdn* a woodlot. **4** (esp. in North and South America, Australia, and Africa) a wild uncultivated district; woodland or forest: *liked camping in the bush* ◊ *the plane went down in bush.* **5** (as an *adjective*) (of a plant) shaped like a bush: *bush beans.* • *verb* (**bushes, bushed, bushing**) (usu. foll. by *out*) branch or spread like a bush.

bush camp *noun* *Cdn* the living quarters, offices, etc., of a mining or lumbering operation in the bush.

bushed *adjective* **1** *informal* tired out. **2** forested; wooded. **3** *Cdn informal* (of a person) **a** living in the bush. **b** crazy; insane (due to isolation).

bushel *noun* **1** (in Canada and other Commonwealth countries) a measure of capacity for grain, fruit, etc., equal to 8 imperial gallons or 36.4 litres. **2** (in the US) a similar unit of measure equal to 64.0 pints or 35.24 litres. ▶ **bushelful** *noun* (*plural* **bushelfuls**)

bush farm *noun* *Cdn hist.* a farm in the bush, esp. one that has not been completely cleared of trees.

bush fever *noun* *Cdn* any of various mental disorders caused by protracted isolation in the bush.

bushland *noun* = BUSH 4.

bush league • *noun* = MINOR LEAGUE *noun* 1. • *adjective* inferior, unsophisticated.

bushman *noun* (*plural* **bushmen**) **1** a person who lives or gains his livelihood in the bush, e.g. a logger. **2** (**Bushman**) **a** a member of an aboriginal people in southern Africa. **b** the language of this people.

bush pilot *noun* a pilot who flies small aircraft into isolated areas.

bush plane *noun* a small plane used for flying into isolated areas, usu. equipped with floats or skis.

bushwhack *verb* **1 a** clear a way through underbrush, dense vegetation, etc.: *it's hard bushwhacking down through the trees to the main trail.* **b** clear land in bush country and establish a settlement. **2** ambush.

bushwhacker *noun* **1** a person who clears land in bush country and settles there. **2** a person who hikes in bush country.

bushwork *noun* the work of a logger in the bush.

bushworker *noun* *Cdn* a logger; a person who works in the bush.

bushy *adjective* (**bushier, bushiest**) **1** growing thickly like a bush: *bushy eyebrows.* **2** having many bushes. **3** covered with bush: *bushy desert areas.*

busily *adverb* in a busy manner: *people run around busily.*

business *noun* **1** one's regular occupation, profession, or trade. **2** a thing that is one's concern: *none of your business.* **3 a** a task or duty. **b** a reason for coming: *what is your business?* **4** serious work or activity: *get down to business.* **5** *derogatory* a matter: *sick of the whole business.* **6** a thing or series of things needing to be dealt with. **7** volume of trade: *did a lot of business.* **8 a** a company etc. **b** commercial enterprises collectively. **9** patronage: *take my business elsewhere.* **10** *euphemism* (esp. of pets) an occurrence of defecation or urination. PHRASES **business as usual** an ongoing, unchanging state of affairs, esp. in adversity. **has no business** has no right. **in business 1** engaged in commercial activity. **2** able to begin operations. **the business end** *informal* the functional part of a tool or device. **in the business of** engaged in. **like nobody's business** *informal* extraordinarily. **make it one's business** to undertake to. **mean business** be in earnest. **mind one's own business** not meddle. **on business** with purpose relating to one's regular occupation. **send a person about his or her business** dismiss a person.

business administration *noun* a program of study at a university or college which trains students for managerial positions in businesses etc.

business class *noun* a more expensive class of airline seating than economy class, typically with roomier seating, better food, and other advantages.

business cycle *noun* recurring periods of increased and decreased economic activity: *the next phase of the business cycle is the inevitable economic slowdown.*

business day *noun* a day on which a business is open to the public.

businesslike *adjective* efficient, systematic, practical.

businessman *noun* (*plural* **businessmen**) a male businessperson.

businessperson *noun* (*plural* **businesspeople**) a person engaged in commerce, esp. at a senior level.

businesswoman *noun* (*plural* **businesswomen**) a female businessperson.

busk *verb* perform (esp. music) for voluntary donations, usu. in the street, at train stations, etc. ▶ **busker** *noun* **busking** *noun*

busload *noun* the number of people travelling in a bus.

buss *informal* • *noun* a kiss. • *verb* (**busses, bussed, bussing**) kiss.

bust¹ *noun* **1 a** the human chest, esp. that of a woman. **b** the circumference of the body at bust level: *a 36-inch bust*. **c** the part of a woman's garment fitting over the bust: *too small in the bust*. **2** a sculpture of a person's head, shoulders, and chest.

bust² *informal* • *verb* (**busts**; *past* and *past participle* **busted** or **bust**; **busting**) **1** burst, break. **2 a** raid, search. **b** arrest. **3** tame (esp. broncos). • *noun* **1** a failure. **2** a sudden economic downturn. **3** a police raid. **4** a punch; a hit. • *adjective* **1** (also **busted**) broken, burst, collapsed. **2** bankrupt. PHRASES **bust a gut 1** become overwrought, upset, etc. **2** exert oneself exceedingly. **bust up 1** bring or come to collapse; explode. **2** (of esp. a married couple) separate. **go bust** become bankrupt.

bustard *noun* a large, heavily built, swift-running bird with long neck, long legs, and stout tapering body.

buster *noun* **1** a person or thing that busts. **2** *informal* fellow (used esp. as a disrespectful form of address). **3** (in *combination*) something that breaks, destroys, or overpowers an undesirable or unpleasant phenomenon: *vitamin C has a reputation as a cold buster*.

bustle • *verb* (**bustles, bustled, bustling**) **1** (often foll. by *about*) **a** work etc. showily, energetically, and officiously. **b** hasten: *bustled about the kitchen*. **2** make (a person) hurry or work hard: *bustled us into the kitchen*. **3** (often foll. by *with*) (of a place) be full of activity: *the small harbour bustled with boats*. • *noun* excited activity.

bustline *noun* **1** the shape or outline of a woman's breasts. **2** the part of a garment covering this.

bust-up *noun* *informal* **1** a quarrel. **2** a marital separation or other breakup. **3** a collapse.

busty *adjective* (**bustier, bustiest**) (of a woman) having a prominent bust.

busy • *adjective* (**busier, busiest**) **1** occupied or engaged in work etc. with the attention concentrated: *was busy packing*. **2** full of activity: *a busy evening*. **3** (of a street etc.) having heavy traffic. **4** (of patterns etc.) overwhelmed by an excess of detail, variety, etc.: *a very busy print*. **5** employed continuously; not resting: *busy as a bee*. **6** (of a telephone line) already in use. • *verb* **busy oneself** (**busies, busied, busying**) keep oneself busy: *busied herself with the accounts*.

busybody *noun* (*plural* **busybodies**) a meddling or prying person.

busyness *noun* a period or state of being busy.

but • *conjunction* **1 a** nevertheless, however. **b** on the other hand. **2** except: *what could we do but run?* **3** without: *it never rains but it pours*. **4** prefixing an interruption: *the weather is ideal - but is that a cloud on the horizon?* • *preposition* except. • *adverb* **1** no more than: *is but a child*. **2** introducing emphatic repetition: *want to see nobody, but nobody*. • *relative pronoun* who not; that not: *there is not a man but feels pity*. • *noun* an objection: *ifs and buts*. PHRASES **but for** without the help or hindrance etc. of: *but for you I'd be rich by now*. **but me no buts** do not attempt to raise objections. **but one** (or **two** etc.) excluding one (or two etc.) from the number: *last but one*.

butane *noun* a hydrocarbon of the alkane series used in liquefied form as fuel. [Say BYOO tane]

butch *slang* • *adjective* masculine; tough-looking. • *noun* **1 a** a mannish woman. **b** a mannish lesbian. **2** a tough, usu. muscular, youth or man.

butcher • *noun* **1 a** a person whose trade is dealing in meat. **b** a person who slaughters animals for food. **2** a person who kills or has killed indiscriminately or brutally. • *verb* **1** slaughter or cut up (an animal) for

food. **2** kill (people) wantonly or cruelly. **3** ruin (a job etc.) through incompetence.

butchery *noun* (*plural* **butcheries**) **1** needless or cruel slaughter (of people). **2** a butcher's trade.

butler *noun* the principal male servant of a household, usu. in charge of serving meals and receiving visitors.

butt¹ • *verb* **1** push or strike with the head or horns. **2** (usu. foll. by *out*) project, jut. **3** (usu. foll. by *against, on*) lie or place with one end flat against; abut. • *noun* **1** a push or blow made with the head or horns. **2** (also **butt joint**) a simple joint in which two pieces of wood etc. are bonded without overlapping. PHRASES **butt in 1** interrupt, meddle. **2** push into (a line of people) out of turn. **butt out** cease to interrupt or meddle.

butt² *noun* **1** (often foll. by *of*) an object of ridicule etc.: *the butt of his jokes*. **2 a** a mound behind a target to stop stray bullets etc. **b** (in *plural*) a shooting range. **c** a target.

butt³ • *noun* **1** (also **butt end**) the thicker end, esp. of a tool or a weapon: *gun butt*. **2 a** cut of pork from the shoulder. **3 a** the stub of a cigar or a cigarette. **b** *slang* a cigarette. **4** *informal* the buttocks. **5** the trunk of a tree, esp. the part just above the ground. • *verb* extinguish (a cigarette) by pressing it into an ashtray etc. PHRASES **butt out 1** extinguish (a cigarette). **2** stop smoking, esp. permanently.

butt⁴ *noun* **1** a large cask for wine or ale. **2** a former unit of measure equal to two hogsheads.

butte *noun* a high isolated hill with steep sides and a flat top, esp. in western North America. [Say BYOOT]

butt-end *verb* *Hockey* jab an opponent with the top end of the shaft of the stick.

butt-ending *noun* *Hockey* the infraction of jabbing an opponent with the top end of the shaft of the stick.

butter • *noun* **1** a pale yellow edible fatty substance made by churning cream and used as a spread or in cooking. **2** a substance of a similar consistency or appearance: *peanut butter*. • *verb* spread, cook, or serve with butter. PHRASES **butter up** *informal* flatter excessively. **look as if butter wouldn't melt in one's mouth** seem demure or innocent, probably deceptively.

butterball *noun* **1** a piece of butter shaped into a ball. **2** *slang* a plump person, animal, etc.

buttercream *noun* a mixture of butter, sugar, etc. used as a filling or icing for a cake.

buttercup *noun* any of various plants of the genus *Ranunculus*, bearing usu. yellow cup-shaped flowers.

buttercup squash *noun* a winter squash with dark green skin and orange flesh.

butterfat *noun* the natural fats derived from milk, consisting mainly of glycerides. Abbreviation: **BF**.

butterfingered *adjective* clumsy, prone to dropping things.

butterfingers *noun* *informal* a clumsy person prone to drop things.

butterflied *adjective* (of shrimp, a steak, etc.) sliced down the centre and spread apart.

butterfly • *noun* (*plural* **butterflies**) **1** an insect with knobbed antennae, a long thin body, and four usu. brightly coloured wings erect when at rest. **2** a showy or frivolous person: *a social butterfly*. **3** (in *plural*) *informal* a nervous sensation felt in the stomach. **4** a swimming stroke in which both arms are lifted out of the water and the legs are kept together while kicking. **5** *Hockey* a kneeling position assumed by a goaltender in which the lower legs are spread apart to cover the bottom part of the goal. **6** *Cdn* a social dance in which trios of people alternate between promenading slowly around the dance floor and whirling each other in circles. • *verb* (**butterflies, butterflied, butterflying**) slice (meat,

B

B

shrimp, etc.) down the centre and spread apart before cooking.

buttermilk *noun* **1** a slightly acid liquid left after churning butter. **2** a dairy product prepared commercially by adding bacterial culture to milk, often used in baking to give a more delicate crumb to cakes, scones, pancakes, etc.

butternut *noun* **1** a deciduous, eastern North American tree of the walnut family, with light grey bark and soft wood. **2** the oily nut of this tree. **3** the soft, light brown wood of this tree.

butternut squash *noun* a pear-shaped variety of winter squash with light yellowish-brown skin and orange flesh.

butterscotch *noun* **1** a brittle candy made from butter, brown sugar, etc. **2** the flavour of this.

butter tart *noun* *Cdn* a tart with a filling of butter, eggs, brown sugar, and usu. raisins.

buttery *adjective* like, containing, or spread with butter.

buttock *noun* (usu. in *plural*) **1** each of two fleshy protuberances on the lower rear part of the human trunk. **2** the corresponding part of an animal.

button • *noun* **1** a small disc or knob sewn on to a garment, either to fasten it by being pushed through a buttonhole, or as an ornament. **2 a** a knob on a piece of mechanical or electronic equipment which performs a particular function when pressed. **b** a small box depicted on a computer screen, representing a function which can be selected by clicking with a mouse. **3** a usu. round badge bearing a slogan etc. fastened to the clothing with a pin. **4** a small round object resembling a button (often as an *adjective*: *button nose*). **5 a** a bud. **b** a button mushroom. **6** *Curling* the circular mark in the centre of the house. **7** *Fencing* a knob covering the point of a foil to make it harmless. • *verb* fasten with buttons. PHRASES **button it** *informal* cease talking. **button one's lip** *informal* remain silent. **button up 1** fasten with buttons. **2** *informal* become silent. **3** *informal* complete (a task etc.) satisfactorily. **on the button** *informal* exactly on target. **push a person's buttons** *informal* exploit a person's fears, emotions, prejudices, etc. **push** (or **press** or **hit**) **the right buttons** play expertly on a person's emotions so as to elicit a desired response. ▶ **buttoned** *adjective*

buttonhole • *noun* a loop or slit made in a garment through which a button may be passed for fastening. • *verb* (**buttonholes, buttonholed, buttonholing**) **1** *informal* attract the attention of and detain (a reluctant listener). **2** make buttonholes in.

button mushroom *noun* a young unopened mushroom.

buttonwood *noun* an eastern North American plane tree with greyish-brown peeling bark, also called a sycamore.

buttress • *noun* **1** a projecting support of stone or brick etc. built against a wall: *flying buttresses are a feature of Gothic cathedrals*. **2** a source of help or support: *there was a demand for a new social order as a buttress against social collapse*. **3** a projecting portion of a hill or mountain. • *verb* **1** support with a buttress. **2** provide with support: *a claim buttressed by facts*. [Say BUTT riss]

buxom *adjective* **1** (of a woman) having large breasts. **2** (of a woman) plump and healthy-looking.

buy • *verb* (**buys, bought, buying**) **1 a** purchase. **b** serve to obtain: *money can't buy happiness*. **2 a** procure (the loyalty etc.) of a person by bribery, promise, etc. **b** win over (a person) in this way. **3** get by sacrifice, great effort, etc.: *his nation was bought with our sweat*. **4** *informal* accept, believe in: *bought my story*. **5** be a buyer for a store etc.: *buys for a furniture chain*. • *noun* *informal* a

purchase: *a good buy*. PHRASES **buy in** buy a stock of. **buy into 1** obtain a share in (an enterprise) by payment. **2** *informal* accept (a line of reasoning etc.). **buy it** (also **buy the farm**) (usu. in *past*) *slang* be killed. **buy off 1** get rid of (a claim, a claimant, a blackmailer) by payment. **2** bribe. **buy oneself out** (or **off**) obtain one's release (esp. from the armed services) by payment. **buy out** pay (a person, company, etc.) to give up an ownership, interest, etc. **buy time** delay an event etc. temporarily. **buy up 1** buy as much as possible of. **2** absorb (another firm etc.) by purchase.

buyer *noun* **1** a purchaser, a customer. **2** a person who selects and purchases stock for a store etc.

buyer's market *noun* an economic position in which goods are plentiful and cheap and buyers have the advantage over sellers.

buyout *noun* the purchase of a controlling share in a company etc.

buzz • *noun* **1** the humming sound of an insect or a machine etc. **2** the sound of a buzzer. **3 a** a confused low sound as of people talking; a murmur. **b** a stir; hurried activity: *a buzz of excitement*. **c** *informal* a rumour. **d** *informal* publicity, esp. created by word of mouth. **4** *slang* a telephone call: *give me a buzz*. **5** *slang* a thrill; a feeling of mild intoxication, esp. from drink or drugs. **6** (also **buzz cut**) *slang* a very short haircut. • *verb* (**buzzes, buzzed, buzzing**) **1** make a humming sound. **2 a** signal or call with a buzzer. **b** *informal* telephone. **3 a** (often foll. by *about*) move or hover busily. **b** (of a place) have an air of excitement or purposeful activity. **4** *informal* throw hard. **5** *Aviation informal* fly fast and very close to (another aircraft, the ground, etc.). PHRASES **buzz off** *slang* go or hurry away.

buzzard *noun* **1** any of a group of birds of prey of the hawk family, with broad wings well adapted for soaring flight. **2** = TURKEY VULTURE. **3** *slang* (*derogatory*) an old person.

buzzer *noun* an electromagnetic device that makes a buzzing noise. PHRASES **at the buzzer** at the end of a game etc.: *scored at the buzzer*.

buzz saw *noun* a circular saw.

buzzword *noun* **1** a fashionable piece of jargon, esp. one that sounds technical. **2** a catchword or slogan, esp. one of little exact meaning.

buzzy *adjective* (**buzzier, buzziest**) **1** lively, energetic, active. **2** making a buzzing sound.

by • *preposition* **1** near. **2** through the agency of. **3** as soon as: *by next week*. **4 a** past, beyond: *drove by the church*. **b** via: *went by Montreal*. **5** in the circumstances of: *by day*. **6** to the extent of: *missed by a foot*. **7** according to. **8** expressing multiplication. • *adverb* past: *they marched by*. • *noun* = BYE[1]. PHRASES **by and by** before long. **by and large** on the whole. **by the by** (or **bye**) incidentally. **by oneself 1 a** unaided. **b** without prompting. **2** alone.

by-boat *noun* (also **bye-boat**) *Cdn hist.* a small fishing boat used by Europeans who travelled to the Maritimes to fish in the summer.

bycatch *noun* fish of species other than that being fished for, caught in fishing nets and usually discarded.

bye[1] *noun* the status of an unpaired competitor in a tournament, who proceeds to the next round as if having won.

bye[2] *interjection* = GOODBYE.

bye-bye • *interjection* *informal* = GOODBYE. • *noun* (also **bye-byes**) (a child's word for) sleep.

by-election *noun* *Cdn, Brit., Austral., & NZ* an election held in a single constituency to fill a vacancy arising during a government's term of office.

bygone • *adjective* past: *bygone years*. • *noun* (in *plural*)

past events, esp. offences. PHRASES **let bygones be bygones** forgive and forget.

bylaw *noun* **1** a rule made by a society etc. for its members. **2** a law made by a body subordinate to a legislature, esp. a municipal government.

byline *noun* **1** a line in a newspaper naming the writer of an article. **2** *Soccer* the goal line or side line.

BYO *abbreviation informal* (also **BYOB**) bring your own (bottle of liquor), e.g. to a social gathering.

bypass • *noun* **1** a road passing around a town or its centre to provide an alternative route for through traffic. **2** a secondary channel or pipe etc. to allow a flow when the main one is closed or blocked. **3** *Medical* **a** an alternative passage for diverting blood or other fluids around an obstruction or away from a particular area during surgery. **b** = CORONARY BYPASS. • *verb* (**bypasses**, **bypassed**, **bypassing**) **1** avoid; go around: *bypass the farm and continue to the road* ◊ *bypassing the standard channels of communication.* **2** provide with a bypass: *the town has been bypassed.*

by-product *noun* **1** an incidental product made in the manufacture of something else: *when burnt, plastic can produce dangerous by-products.* **2** a secondary result: *one of the by-products of unemployment is an increase in crime.*

bystander *noun* a person who is present but does not take part; a spectator or passive witness.

byte *noun* *Computing* a group of usu. eight binary digits, often used to represent one character.

byway *noun* **1** a minor road: *the highways and byways of Ontario.* **2** a minor activity.

byword *noun* **1** a person or thing cited as a notable example: *his name is a byword for luxury.* **2** a familiar saying: *"Small is beautiful," may become the byword of designers this year.*

by-your-leave *noun* a request for permission or an expression of apology for taking a liberty: *took the Aboriginal lands without so much as a by-your-leave.*

Byzantine • *adjective* **1** of or relating to the ancient Greek city of Byzantium (on the site of the modern city of Istanbul in Turkey). **2** (of a system or situation) excessively complicated, and typically involving a great deal of administrative detail: *Byzantine insurance regulations.* **3** carried on by underhand methods; devious: *Byzantine intrigues* ◊ *she has the most Byzantine mind in politics.* **4** (of art etc.) of a highly decorated style developed in the Byzantine Empire. The art is generally rich and stylized (as in religious icons) and the architecture is typified by highly decorated churches with many domes. • *noun* a citizen of Byzantium. [Say BIZZEN teen or BIZZEN tine]

B

Cc

C¹ *noun* (also **c**) (*plural* **Cs** or **C's**) **1** the third letter of the alphabet. **2** *Music* the first note of the diatonic scale of C major (the major scale having no sharps or flats). **3** the third hypothetical person or example. **4** the third highest class or category (of academic marks etc.). **5** *Math* (usu. **c**) the third known quantity. **6** (as a Roman numeral) 100. **7** a size of battery, having a voltage of 1.5 V.

C² *symbol* the element carbon.

C³ *abbreviation* **1** Cape. **2** Conservative. **3** Celsius, Centigrade. **4** coulomb(s). **5** *Cdn* Commons (designating bills introduced in the Commons): *Bill C-54*.

C⁴ *noun* *Computing* a programming language combining the features of high-level and assembly languages.

c. *abbreviation* **1** century; centuries. **2** chapter. **3** cent(s). **4** cold. **5** cubic. **6** cent-. **7** cup(s).

c. *abbreviation* *circa*.

CA *abbreviation* **1** (*plural* **CAs**) (in Canada and Scotland) = CHARTERED ACCOUNTANT. **2** California.

Ca *symbol* the element calcium.

Ca. *abbreviation* California.

ca. *abbreviation* *circa*.

cab¹ • *noun* **1** a taxi. **2** the driver's compartment in a truck, train, tractor, crane, etc. • *verb* (**cabs, cabbed, cabbing**) *informal* travel by taxi.

cab² *noun* a Cabernet wine.

cabal *noun* a secret political clique or faction: *a cabal of dissidents led the revolt*. [Say kuh BAL]

cabana *noun* (*plural* **cabanas**) a cabin or other shelter, esp. at a beach or swimming pool. [Say kuh BAN uh]

cabane à sucre *noun* (*plural* **cabanes à sucre**) *Cdn* (*Que.*) = SUGAR SHACK. [Say ka ban a SOO kruh]

cabaret *noun* **1** a nightclub or restaurant, esp. one in which entertainment is provided while guests eat or drink. **2** the entertainment provided. [Say cabba RAY]

cabbage *noun* a plant with a head of thick green or purple leaves eaten as a vegetable.

cabbage roll *noun* (usu. in *plural*) a boiled cabbage leaf wrapped around a filling of rice and usu. ground meat and baked, usu. with tomato sauce.

cabbie *noun* *informal* a taxi driver.

Cabernet *noun* **1** a variety of black grape (esp. **Cabernet Sauvignon**) used in winemaking. **2** a wine made from these. [Say cabber NAY (so veen YON)]

cabin *noun* **1 a** a small shelter or house, esp. of wood. **b** a summer cottage. **2** a room or compartment in an aircraft or ship for passengers or crew. **3** a driver's cab.

cabin crew *noun* the crew members on an airplane attending to passengers and cargo.

cabinet *noun* **1 a** a cupboard or case with drawers, shelves, etc., for storing or displaying articles. **b** a piece of furniture housing a stereo, television set, etc. **2** (also **Cabinet**) **a** (in Canada, the UK, etc.) a committee of senior ministers responsible for controlling government policy. **b** (in the US) a body of advisers to the President, composed of the heads of the executive departments of the government.

cabinetmaker *noun* a person skilled in making furniture and light woodwork. ▶ **cabinetmaking** *noun*

cabinet order *noun* *Cdn* = ORDER-IN-COUNCIL.

cabinetry *noun* cabinets or fine woodwork.

cabin fever *noun* a condition characterized by lethargy, irritability, anxiety, etc. resulting from long confinement indoors, esp. during the winter.

cable • *noun* **1** a thick rope of wire or hemp. **2** an encased group of insulated wires for transmitting electricity or electrical signals. **3** = CABLE TELEVISION. **4** the chain of an anchor. **b** (also **cable length**) a unit of measure, equal to one-tenth of a nautical mile (185 m) or 100 fathoms in Canadian and British use, and 120 fathoms in the US. **5** (also **cable stitch**) a knitted stitch resembling twisted rope. • *verb* (**cables, cabled, cabling**) **1** transmit a message by cablegram. **2** provide or fasten with a cable or cables.

cable car *noun* a small passenger car (often one of a series) suspended on an endless cable and drawn up and down a mountainside etc. by an engine at one end.

cable television *noun* (also **cablevision**) a broadcasting system with signals transmitted and received by cable (as opposed to antenna), allowing subscribers access to a large number of channels.

cabling *noun* **1** a length or type of cable. **2** the process of installing cable.

caboodle *noun* PHRASES **the whole** (**kit and**) **caboodle** *informal* the whole lot (of persons or things).

caboose *noun* **1** a rail car, usu. at the end of the train, for housing the crew etc. **2** *Cdn* a portable wooden cabin, esp. one on runners which can be pulled over snow.

cacao *noun* (*plural* **cacaos**) **1** a seed pod from which cocoa and chocolate are made. **2** a small evergreen bearing these. [Say kuh KA oh or kuh KAY oh]

cacciatore *adjective* cooked with tomatoes, mushrooms, and herbs: *chicken cacciatore*. [Say catch a TORY]

cache • *noun* **1** a hiding place. **2** *Cdn* (*North*) a place, structure, or device used for storing food, supplies, equipment, etc. **3** the contents of a cache. **4** an auxiliary computer memory from which high-speed retrieval is possible. • *verb* (**caches, cached, caching**) put in a cache. [Say CASH]

cachet *noun* prestige: *cotton flannel has never had the fashion cachet of linen or silk*. [Say ka SHAY or CASH ay]

cackle • *noun* **1** a clucking sound as of a hen or a goose. **2** a loud silly laugh. • *verb* (**cackles, cackled, cackling**) **1** emit a cackle. **2** talk noisily and inconsequentially. **3** utter or express with a cackle.

cacophonous *adjective* **1** causing a harsh, discordant mixture of sounds. **2** clashing, incompatible: *a cacophonous array of colours*. [Say kuh COFFA nus]

cacophony *noun* (*plural* **cacophonies**) **1** a harsh discordant mixture of sound: *a cacophony of alarm bells*. **2** dissonance; discord. [Say kuh COFFA nee]

cactus *noun* (*plural* **cacti** or **cactuses**) **1** a plant found in arid regions, with a thick fleshy stem used for storing water, usu. spines but no leaves, and brilliantly coloured flowers. **2** any of various other succulent or spiny plants.

CAD *abbreviation* **1** computer-aided design. **2** Canadian dollars.

cad *noun* a person who behaves dishonourably.

cadaver *noun* a corpse, esp. for dissection. [Say kuh DAV er]

cadaverous *adjective* resembling a corpse in being very pale, thin, or bony: *looked at the cadaverous mannequins in the shop windows* ◊ *a long, cadaverous face*. [Say kuh DAV er us]

caddis fly *noun* (*plural* **caddis flies**) any of various small nocturnal moth-like insects with hairy wings, living near water.

caddy[1] *noun* (*plural* **caddies**) **1** a small container, sometimes with subdivisions, for holding small items. **2** a small container for tea leaves.

caddy[2] (also **caddie**) • *noun* (*plural* **caddies**) a person who assists a golfer by carrying clubs etc. • *verb* (**caddies, caddied, caddying**) act as a caddy.

cadence *noun* **1** a fall in pitch of the voice, esp. at the end of a phrase or sentence. **2** a modulation or inflection of the voice: *the measured cadences that he used in the Senate*. **3** the resolution at the end of a musical phrase: *the final cadences of the prelude*. **4** rhythm; the measure or beat of sound or movement: *the thumping cadence of the engines*. ▶ **cadenced** *adjective* [Say KAY dinse]

cadenza *noun* (*plural* **cadenzas**) *Music* a virtuosic passage for a solo voice or instrument, usu. near the close of an aria or a concerto movement, sometimes improvised. [Say kuh DEN zuh]

cadet *noun* **1** a member of a corps receiving elementary military or police training, esp. for the rank of an officer. **2** (in Canada) a member of a paramilitary organization for youth aged 12 to 18, run by the reserve forces of the army, navy, or air force.

cadge *verb* (**cadges, cadged, cadging**) get or seek by begging or scrounging: *cadged a fiver off me*. ▶ **cadger** *noun*

cadmium *noun* a soft bluish-white metallic element occurring naturally with zinc ores, and used in making solders and in electroplating. [Say KAD mee um]

cadre *noun* **1** a small, usu. exclusive group with a common objective or specially trained for a particular purpose: *a cadre of professional managers*. **2 a** a group of activists in a communist or revolutionary party. **b** a member of such a group. **3** a permanent establishment of trained soldiers, etc. that can be enlarged when necessary. [Say CAD ruh or CAD ray or COD ray]

Caesar *noun* **1** the title of the Roman emperors, esp. from Augustus to Hadrian. **2** an autocrat. **3** = CAESAR SALAD. **4** *Cdn* = BLOODY CAESAR. [Say SEE zur]

Caesarean (also **Caesarian**) • *adjective* **1** of Julius Caesar or the Caesars. **2** (of a birth) effected by Caesarean section. • *noun* a Caesarean section. [Say suh ZERRY un]

Caesarean section *noun* an operation for delivering a child by cutting through the wall of the abdomen and uterus.

Caesar salad *noun* a salad of romaine lettuce tossed usu. with Parmesan cheese, garlic croutons, bacon bits, and a dressing of oil, lemon juice, raw egg, etc.

CAF *abbreviation* CANADIAN ARMED FORCES.

caf *noun informal Cdn* a cafeteria.

café *noun* **1** a restaurant serving coffee and light meals. **2** a bar or nightclub.

café au lait *noun* **1** strong coffee with a roughly equal portion of hot milk, usu. served in a large mug or bowl. **2** the pale brown colour of this. [Say ka fay oh LAY]

cafeteria *noun* **1** a restaurant where customers collect meals on trays at a counter and usu. pay before sitting down to eat. **2** a lunch room in a school, office, etc.

caffeinated *adjective* containing caffeine. [Say KAF in ate id]

caffeine *noun* a stimulant found in coffee, tea, chocolate, cola, etc. [Say kaf EEN]

caftan *noun* **1** an ankle-length tunic, usu. belted at the waist, worn by men in eastern Europe and the Middle East. **2 a** a woman's long loose dress. **b** a loose shirt or top. [Say KAF tan]

cage • *noun* **1** a structure of bars, wires, wood, etc. used as a place of confinement for birds or animals. **2** any similar framework, esp.: **a** an enclosed platform used as an elevator, esp. in a mine. **b** a protective structure of strong metal bars built into the body of an automobile. **3** a sport of netting or mesh strung around a metal framework, esp.: **a** a hockey net. **b** = BATTING CAGE. **4** a wire face mask attached to a helmet, e.g. of a baseball catcher or hockey goaltender. • *verb* (**cages, caged, caging**) place or keep in a cage.

cagey *adjective* (**cagier, cagiest**) *informal* cautious and uncommunicative; wary: *a spokesman was cagey about the arrangements the company had made*. ▶ **cagily** *adverb*
caginess *noun* (also **cageyness**)

cahoots *plural noun* PHRASES **in cahoots** *slang* colluding or conspiring with: *the area is dominated by guerrillas in cahoots with drug traffickers*. [Say kuh HOOTS]

caiman *noun* a semiaquatic reptile similar to the alligator but with a heavily armoured belly, native to tropical South and Central America. [Say KAY mun]

Cain PHRASES **raise Cain** *informal* make a disturbance; create trouble.

cairn *noun* a mound of rough stones as a monument.

caisse populaire *noun* (*plural* **caisses populaires**) *Cdn* (in Quebec and other francophone communities) a co-operative financial institution similar to a credit union. [Say kess pop yoo LAIR]

cajole *verb* (**cajoles, cajoled, cajoling**) persuade to do something by sustained coaxing or flattery: *cajoled her into selling him her house* ◊ *she pleaded and cajoled as she tried to win his support*. ▶ **cajolery** *noun* [Say kuh JOLE]

Cajun • *noun* **1** a descendant of the French-speaking settlers who were expelled from Acadia in the mid-18th century, living esp. in S Louisiana. **2** the French patois of the Cajuns. • *adjective* **1** of the Cajuns or their language. **2** designating a type of originally Cajun cooking, characterized esp. by the use of strong seasonings. [Say KAY jun]

cake • *noun* **1** a baked sweet food usu. containing flour, eggs, sugar, and often fat and leavening. **2** any of several other foods in a flat round shape: *fish cake*. **3** a flattish compact mass: *a cake of soap*. • *verb* (**cakes, caked, caking**) **1** form into a compact mass. **2** cover (with a hard or sticky mass): *caked with mud*. PHRASES **have one's cake and eat it** (**too**) *informal* enjoy two mutually exclusive alternatives. **a piece of cake** *informal* something easily achieved. **a slice of the cake** a share of assets or benefits.

cakewalk *noun informal* an easy task.

cal (often in *combination*) large calorie(s) (*see* CALORIE 1): *low-cal*.

calabash *noun* **1 a** an evergreen tree, native to tropical America, bearing fruit in the form of large gourds. **b** a gourd from this tree. **2** the shell of this or a similar gourd used as a vessel for water, to make a tobacco pipe, etc. [Say CALA bash]

calabogus *noun Cdn* = CALLIBOGUS. [Say cala BOGUS]

calamari *noun* the flesh of the squid when used as food. [Say cala MAR ee]

calamary *noun* (*plural* **calamaries**) a squid with a long, tapering, horny, internal shell. [Say cala MAR ee]

calamata *noun* = KALAMATA. [Say cala MATTA]

calamine *noun* **1** a pink powder consisting of zinc

carbonate and a small quantity of ferric oxide used as a lotion, e.g. for sunburn, insect bites, or rashes. **2** an ore of zinc, esp. zinc carbonate. [Say CALA mine]

calamitous *adjective* causing great harm or damage; disastrous: *unemployment was reaching calamitous proportions*. ▶ **calamitously** *adverb* [Say kuh LAMMA tiss]

calamity *noun* (*plural* **calamities**) a disaster, a great misfortune. [Say kuh LAMMA tee]

calcareous *adjective* of or containing calcium carbonate; chalky: *calcareous shale*. [Say cal KERRY iss]

calcification *noun Medical* the deposition of calcium salts in tissue. [Say calsa fuh KAY sh'n]

calcify *verb* (**calcifies, calcified**) **1** harden or become hardened by deposition of calcium salts: *the aortic valve may shrink and become calcified*. **2** convert or be converted to calcium carbonate. **3** make or become inflexible or rigid: *feminist theology confronted traditional authority and calcified laws ◊ gradually, her opinions calcified into dogma*. [Say CALSA fie]

calcite *noun* a white or colourless mineral consisting of calcium carbonate. It is a major constituent of limestone, marble, and chalk, and is deposited in caves to form stalactites and stalagmites. [Say CAL site]

calcium *noun* a soft greyish-white metallic element occurring in limestone etc., and in animal bones and teeth, and whose ions and salts are essential to life.

calcium carbonate *noun* a white insoluble solid occurring naturally as chalk, limestone, and marble, used in the manufacture of lime and cement.

calcium phosphate *noun* a white insoluble powder, the main constituent of animal bones and used as a fertilizer and food additive.

calculable *adjective* able to be calculated or estimated: *wind chills that are barely calculable*.

calculate *verb* (**calculates, calculated, calculating**) **1** ascertain or determine by using mathematics or one's judgment. **2** intend or design for a particular purpose: *his speech was calculated to stir up the crowd*. **3** rely or depend on; include as an essential part of one's plans: *I wasn't calculating on your being there*.

calculated *adjective* **1** done with awareness of the likely consequences: *a calculated risk*. **2** designed or suitable: *his remark was calculated to offend*. ▶ **calculatedly** *adverb*

calculating *adjective* (of a person) shrewd, scheming: *he was a coolly calculating, ruthless man*.

calculation *noun* **1** a mathematical determination of the size or number of something: *finding ways of saving money involves complicated calculations*. **2** an assessment of the risks, possibilities, or effects of a situation or course of action: *decisions are shaped by political calculations*.

calculator *noun* a device (esp. a small electronic one) used for making mathematical calculations.

calculus *noun* (*plural* **calculi** or **calculuses**) **1** *Math* **a** a particular method of calculation or reasoning: *calculus of probabilities*. **b** the branch of mathematics that deals with the finding and properties of derivatives and integrals of functions, by methods originally based on the summation of infinitesimal differences (*see* INTEGRAL CALCULUS, DIFFERENTIAL CALCULUS). **2 a** a stone or mass of minerals formed within the body, esp. in the kidney or gallbladder. **b** a hard deposit of saliva, calcium phosphate, etc. that forms on the teeth. [Say CAL cue liss for the singular, CAL cue lie or CAL cue lisses for the plural]

caldera *noun* (*plural* **calderas**) a large volcanic crater, esp. one whose breadth greatly exceeds that of the vent or vents within it, created by a volcanic explosion. [Say cal DARE uh or col DARE uh]

calèche *noun Cdn* a two-wheeled one-horse vehicle with a seat for the driver on the splashboard, commonly used in tourist areas of Quebec. [Say ka LESH]

Caledonian *adjective* of or relating to Scotland. [Say cala DOE nee un]

calendar *noun* **1** a system by which the beginning, length, and subdivisions of the year are fixed. **2** a chart or series of pages showing the days, weeks, and months of a particular year, or giving special seasonal information. **3** a timetable or program of appointments, special events, etc. **4** *Cdn* a book containing a list of courses offered at a university or college, along with general information on registration etc. **5** a list or register, esp. of canonized saints, cases for trial, etc.

SPELL CHECK | ABC ✔
calender, calendar

A chart showing the days, weeks, and months of a year is a **calendar**.

---

calender *noun* a machine in which cloth, paper, etc., is pressed by rollers to glaze or smooth it.

calf¹ *noun* (*plural* **calves**) **1** a young bovine animal. **2** the young of other animals, e.g. elephant, whale, and seal. **3** = CALFSKIN. **4** a floating piece of ice detached from an iceberg. **PHRASES** **in calf** (of a cow) pregnant.

calf² *noun* (*plural* **calves**) the fleshy hind part of the human leg below the knee.

calf roper *noun* a participant in calf roping.

calf roping *noun* a rodeo event in which contestants on horseback chase and lasso a calf before dismounting and tying its legs.

calfskin *noun* the hide of a calf, esp. as leather used in bookbinding and shoemaking.

Calgarian • *noun* a native or inhabitant of Calgary. • *adjective* of or relating to Calgary. [Say cal GARE ee un]

calibrate *verb* (**calibrates, calibrated, calibrating**) **1** mark (a gauge) with a standard scale of readings. **2** correlate the readings of (an instrument) with a standard. **3** determine the calibre of (a gun). **4** determine the correct capacity or value of. [Say CALA brate]

calibration *noun* **1** the act or process of calibrating something: *the measuring devices require calibration*. **2** each of a set of graduations on an instrument etc. [Say cala BRAY sh'n]

calibre *noun* (esp. *US* **caliber**) **1 a** the internal diameter of a gun or tube. **b** the diameter of a bullet or shell. **2** strength or quality of character; ability.

calico • *noun* (*plural* **calicoes** or **calicos**) a cotton fabric with a printed pattern. • *adjective* **1** made of calico. **2 a** (of an animal etc.) having irregular patches of colours, mottled. **b** (of a cat) having a coat with patches of orange tabby, black, and white. [Say CALA co]

Californian • *adjective* of or relating to the US state of California. • *noun* a resident or native of California.

californium *noun* a radioactive metallic element produced artificially from curium. [Say cala FORNY um]

caliper *noun* (usu. in *plural*) **1** an instrument with two pivoting bowed legs for measuring the diameter of convex bodies (**outside calipers**), or with out-turned points for measuring internal dimensions (**inside calipers**). **2** the part of an automobile or bicycle brake assembly which houses the brake pads and grips the disc or wheel: *caliper brakes*.

caliph *noun hist.* the chief Muslim civil and religious ruler, regarded as the successor of Muhammad. [Say KAY lif or CAL if]

caliphate *noun* **1** the position of a caliph. **2** an area of land that is ruled by a caliph. [Say CALA fut]

calisthenics *plural noun* gymnastic exercises to

achieve bodily fitness and grace of movement. [Say cal iss THEN icks]

Cal-Ital *adjective* (of cuisine) combining Californian and Italian elements.

calk esp. *US* = CAULK[1],[2]. [Sounds like *COCK*]

call • *verb* **1 a** cry, shout. **b** (of a bird or animal) emit its characteristic note or cry. **c** attract (a bird etc.) by mimicking its sound. **2** communicate with by telephone or radio. **3** bring to one's presence by calling. **4** pay a brief visit: *call on me.* **5 a** order to take place: *called a meeting.* **b** direct to happen: *called a stop to it.* **6 a** require one's attention: *duty calls.* **b** urge, invite, nominate: *call to the bar.* **7** name; describe as: *call her Liz.* **8** consider: *I call that silly.* **9** rouse from sleep. **10** guess the outcome of tossing a coin etc. **11** (foll. by *for*) require: *called for silence.* **12** read out (a list of names to determine those present). **13** (foll. by *on, upon*) appeal to: *called on us to be quiet.* **14** (of an umpire or referee) **a** assess: *called a penalty.* **b** officiate (a game). **15** *Cards* specify (a suit or contract) in bidding. **16** (foll. by *on*) **a** require (of someone) proof or support for a statement: *they called him on the numbers he presented.* **b** criticize, condemn: *called them on their behaviour.* • *noun* **1** a shout or cry. **2 a** the characteristic cry of a bird or animal. **b** an imitation of this. **c** an instrument for imitating it. **3** a brief visit. **4** an act of telephoning. **5 a** an invitation or summons to be present. **b** an appeal or invitation (from a specific source or discerned by a person's conscience etc.) to follow a certain profession, set of principles, etc. **6 a** duty, need, or occasion: *no call to be rude* ◊ *no call for violence.* **7** a demand: *not much call for it these days.* **8 a** *Sport* a ruling made by an official. **b** a decision: *you make the call.* **9** a signal on a bugle etc.; a signalling whistle. **10** *Stock Market* an option of buying stock at a fixed price at a given date. **11** *Cards* **a** a player's right or turn to make a bid. **b** a bid made. PHRASES **call away** summon elsewhere. **call down 1** invoke. **2** reprimand. **call forth** elicit. **call in 1** withdraw from circulation. **2** seek the advice or services of. **call in** (or **into**) **question** dispute; doubt the validity of. **call into play** make use of. **call off 1** cancel (an arrangement etc.). **2** order (an attacker or pursuer) to desist. **3** chant (the directions) for a square dance etc. **call of nature** a need to urinate or defecate. **call out 1** CALL *verb* 1a. **2** summon (troops etc.) to action. **3** order (workers) to strike. **call the shots** (or **tune**) be in control. **call to mind** recollect; cause one to remember. **call to order 1** request to be orderly. **2** declare (a meeting) open. **call up 1** reach by telephone. **2** imagine, recollect. **3** summon, esp. to serve in the army. **4** promote (a player) to the major leagues. **on** (or **at**) **call 1** (of a doctor etc.) available if required but not formally on duty. **2** (of money lent) repayable on demand.

calla *noun* (*plural* **callas**) a flower of the arum family, with a white spathe and a yellow spadix, esp. the **calla lily** and the **wild calla**, with a cluster of red berries. [Say CALA]

callback *noun* an act of calling back, e.g. by a salesperson or service person, or for a job interview.

caller *noun* **1** a person who calls, esp. one who pays a visit or makes a telephone call. **2** a person who announces something, esp. the directions in a square dance or the numbers in a bingo game.

call girl *noun* a female prostitute who accepts appointments by telephone.

callibogus *noun* *Cdn* (esp. *Nfld*) a mixture of spruce beer and rum with molasses. [Say cala BOGUS]

calligrapher *noun* a person who is skilled in the art of decorative handwriting. [Say kuh LIGRA fur]

calligraphic *adjective* having to do with calligraphy: *a calligraphic pen.* [Say cala GRAPH ick]

calligraphy *noun* **1** handwriting, esp. when fine or pleasing. **2** the art of stylized or beautiful handwriting. [Say kuh LIGRA fee]

calling *noun* **1** a profession or occupation. **2** an inwardly felt call or summons; a vocation.

calling card *noun* **1** a small card with one's name and often address and telephone number, presented when visiting. **2** (**Calling Card**) *proprietary* a credit card issued by a telephone company allowing a customer to charge long-distance calls. **3** a distinctive mark or feature: *mostly I sing Wagner and Strauss; Mozart is not my calling card.*

call letters *plural noun* the letters identifying a radio or television station.

SPELL CHECK   ABC ✓
callous, callus

The usual Canadian spelling for an area of hard skin is **callus**.

callous • *adjective* unfeeling, insensitive: *his callous comments about the murder made me shiver.* • *noun* = CALLUS 1. ▶ **callously** *adverb* **callousness** *noun*

calloused *adjective* (of a part of the body) having an area of hardened skin: *a calloused palm.* [Say CAL oh]

callow *adjective* (esp. of a young person) inexperienced, immature: *earnest and callow undergraduates.* [Say CAL oh]

call sign *noun* **1** a conventional signal identifying a radio transmitter. **2** a name by which a person communicating by radio, esp. an aircraft pilot, is identified.

call to arms *noun* **1** an act of calling up for active military service. **2** an act of inciting or encouraging people to vigorous, usu. defensive action.

call-up *noun* **1** the act or process of calling up, esp. being summoned to the army or promoted to the major leagues. **2** a person who is called up.

SPELL CHECK   ABC ✓
callus, callous

An insensitive person is **callous**.

callus *noun* (*plural* **calluses**) **1** a hard thick area of skin or tissue. **2** a hard tissue formed around bone ends after a fracture. **3** *Botany* a new protective tissue formed over a wound. ▶ **callused** *adjective*

calm • *adjective* **1** tranquil, quiet, windless: *a calm sea.* **2** (of a person or disposition) not agitated: *remained calm throughout the ordeal.* **3** self-assured, confident: *his calm assumption that we would wait.* • *noun* **1** stillness, serenity. **2 a** a period without wind or storm. **b** *Meteorology* absence of wind, force 0 on the Beaufort scale. • *verb* (often foll. by *down*) make or become calm. ▶ **calmly** *adverb* **calmness** *noun*

caloric *adjective* of heat or calories: *a caloric value of 7 calories per gram.* [Say kuh LORE ick]

calorie *noun* a unit of quantity of heat: **1** (also **large calorie**) the amount needed to raise the temperature of 1 kilogram of water through 1°C, often used to measure the energy value of foods. **2** (also **small calorie**) the amount needed to raise the temperature of 1 gram of water by 1°C.

calorific *adjective* pertaining to or high in calories: *the calorific content of foods* ◊ *a calorific dessert.* [Say cala RIF ick]

calumet *noun* a North American Aboriginal tobacco pipe with a clay bowl and long reed stem, smoked esp. as a sign of peace. [Say CAL yuh mit]

calumny *noun* (*plural* **calumnies**) the making of false

and defamatory statements about someone in order to damage their reputation: *he was subjected to the most vicious calumny but never sued*. [Say CAL um nee]

calve *verb* (**calves**, **calved**, **calving**) **1** give birth to a calf. **2** (of an iceberg) break off or shed (a mass of ice).

calves *plural of* CALF[1],[2].

Calvinism *noun* the doctrines of John Calvin (1509–64) or his followers, who promoted democratic church government, the values of thrift, sobriety, and hard work, and the belief that God predestines some people to be damned and others to be saved and that goodness and even material wealth are a sign of God's favour to his chosen ones. ▶**Calvinist** *noun* **Calvinistic** *adjective*

calypso *noun* (*plural* **calypsos**) **1** a kind of West Indian music in syncopated African rhythm, usu. improvised on a topical theme. **2** a song in this style. **3** an orchid with pink, slipper-shaped flowers, found across Canada and parts of the US. [Say kuh LIP so]

calyx *noun* (*plural* **calyces** or **calyxes**) **1** *Botany* the sepals collectively, forming the protective layer of a flower in bud. **2** *Biology* any cup-like cavity or structure. [Say KAY licks or CAL icks for the singular, KAYLA seez or CALA seez for the plural]

cam *noun* a projection on a rotating part in machinery, shaped to impart reciprocal or variable motion to the part in contact with it.

camaraderie *noun* mutual trust and sociability among friends. [Say comma RODDA ree or camma RADDA ree]

camas *noun* (*plural* **camas**) any of several North American plants of the lily family, which are widely cultivated for their starry blue or purple flowers and certain varieties of which bear edible bulbs which were a staple of Aboriginal peoples' diets. [Say CAM iss]

camber • *noun* **1** the slightly convex or arched shape of the surface of a road, ship's deck, aircraft wing, etc. **2** a slight sideways inclination of the wheels of a motor vehicle. • *verb* **1** (of a surface) have a camber. **2** give a camber to; build with a camber.

cambium *noun* (*plural* **cambia** or **cambiums**) a cellular plant tissue responsible for the increase in girth of stems and roots. [Say CAMBY um for the singular, CAMBY uh or CAMBY umz for the plural]

Cambodian • *noun* **1 a** a native or national of Cambodia in SE Asia. **b** a person of Cambodian descent. **2** the Khmer language. • *adjective* of or relating to Cambodia or its people. [Say cam BOADY un]

camboose *noun* Cdn hist. **1** (also **camboose shanty**) a large wooden cabin with a central fireplace, serving as a winter shelter in a logging camp. **2** an open fireplace or cooking stove. [Say cam BOOSE]

Cambrian *adjective* **1** Welsh. **2** of or relating to the first period of the Paleozoic era, lasting from about 590 to 505 million years BP. It was a time of widespread seas and is the earliest period in which fossils, notably trilobites, can be used in geological dating. [Say CAME bree un or CAM bree un]

camcorder *noun* a portable video camera which records picture and sound on a video cassette.

came *past of* COME.

camel *noun* **1** either of two kinds of large long-necked mammals with long slender legs, broad cushioned feet, and either one hump (**Arabian camel**) or two humps (**Bactrian camel**); camels can survive for long periods without food or drink, chiefly by using up the fat reserves in their humps. **2** a fawn colour.

camel hair *noun* **1 a** the hair of a camel. **b** a fabric made of this. **2** a fine soft hair used in artists' brushes.

camellia *noun* an evergreen shrub with shiny leaves and red, pink, or white rose-like flowers. [Say kuh MEALY uh]

Camembert *noun* a kind of soft creamy cheese, usu. with a strong flavour. [Say CAM um bear]

cameo *noun* (*plural* **cameos**) **1** a small piece of hard stone or coral carved so as to stand out slightly from a background of a different colour. **2 a** a small character part in a play or film, usu. brief and played by a distinguished actor or actress: *he played numerous cameo roles*. **b** a short descriptive literary sketch etc.: *cameos of street life*. [Say CAMMY oh]

camera *noun* **1** an apparatus for taking photographs, either for still photographs or for motion-picture film. **2** a piece of equipment which forms an optical image and converts it into electrical impulses for video transmission or storage. ▨PHRASES **in camera** **1** privately: *should city council conduct routine business in camera?* **2** *Law* in a judge's private room: *judges assess the merits of such claims in camera*. **on** (or **off**) **camera** (esp. of an actor or actress) being (or not being) filmed or televised at a particular moment.

cameraman *noun* (*plural* **cameramen**) a camera operator, esp. a male one.

camera operator *noun* (also **cameraperson** *plural* **camerapersons**) a person who operates a film or television camera, esp. professionally.

camera-ready *adjective* Printing (of copy etc.) in a form suitable for immediate photographic reproduction.

camerawoman *noun* (*plural* **camerawomen**) a female camera operator.

camisole *noun* **1** a woman's waist-length sleeveless undergarment with shoulder straps. **2** a similar outer garment. [Say CAMMA sole]

camomile *noun* any of various aromatic plants of the composite family, with daisy-like flowers, used in herbal teas and as a hair lightener. [Say CAMMA mile]

camouflage • *noun* **1 a** the disguising of military vehicles, aircraft, ships, personnel, artillery, and installations by painting or covering them to make them blend with their surroundings. **b** such a disguise or uniform etc. **2** the natural colouring of an animal which enables it to blend in with its surroundings: *the whiteness of polar bears provides camouflage*. **3** actions or devices intended to disguise or mislead: *much of my apparent indifference was merely protective camouflage*. • *verb* (**camouflages**, **camouflaged**, **camouflaging**) **1** hide or disguise by means of camouflage. **2** conceal or disguise (a flaw, emotion, etc.): *grievances should be discussed, not camouflaged*. [Say CAMMA flawzh]

camp[1] • *noun* **1** a temporary overnight lodging in tents etc. in the open. **2** a temporary accommodation of various kinds, usu. consisting of huts or tents, for detainees, homeless persons, etc. **3 a** a complex of buildings for holiday accommodation, usu. with extensive recreational facilities. **b** a summer holiday program for children, offering various recreational or educational activities. **c** a place where such a program is offered. **d** (N Ont., Maritimes, US Northeast & Gulf States) a summer cottage. **4** a place of accommodation for workers at a particular place of employment: *logging camp*. **5** a place where troops are lodged or trained. **6** an ancient fortified site or its remains. **7** the adherents of a particular party or doctrine regarded collectively: *the Conservative camp was crushed*. **8** = TRAINING CAMP. • *verb* **1** set up or spend time in a camp (in senses 1 and 5 of noun). **2** (often foll. by *out*) lodge in temporary quarters or in the open.

camp[2] *informal* • *adjective* **1** (of a man or his manner) ostentatiously and extravagantly effeminate: *a heavily made-up and highly camp actor*. **2** done in an exaggerated

way for esp. humorous effect: *the movie seems more camp than shocking or gruesome.* • **noun** a camp manner or style: *the play is an enjoyable piece of camp.* • **verb** behave or do in a camp way. PHRASES **camp it up** behave affectedly or in an exaggeratedly effeminate way.

campaign • **noun 1** an organized course of action for a particular purpose, esp. to arouse public interest: *a media campaign.* **2** a series of military operations in a definite area or to achieve a particular objective. • **verb** conduct or take part in a campaign: *campaigned against child labour* ◊ *campaigned to reduce alcohol consumption*.
▶ **campaigner** *noun*

campanula *noun* any of various plants with blue, purple, or white bell-shaped flowers, many kinds being cultivated as ornamentals. [Say cam PAN yoo luh]

camper *noun* **1** a person who camps out as a recreation, or lives temporarily at a camp. **2** a vehicle or trailer equipped for camping.

campesino *noun* (*plural* **campesinos**) (in Central or South America) a farmer or peasant. [Say campa SEEN oh]

campfire *noun* an outdoor fire in a camp etc.

camp follower *noun* **1** a civilian, esp. a prostitute, who provides services to personnel in a military camp. **2** a person who is nominally attached to a group but is not fully committed or does not make a substantial contribution to its activities.

campground *noun* an area with facilities for camping.

camphor *noun* a white translucent crystalline volatile substance with an aromatic smell and bitter taste, used to make celluloid and in medicine. [Say CAM fur]

campily *adverb* in an exaggeratedly theatrical or effeminate way.

campiness *noun* the quality of being exaggeratedly theatrical or effeminate.

camping *noun* the act of staying outdoors in a tent.

campion *noun* **1** any plant of the genus *Silene*, with usu. pink or white flowers with notched petals. **2** any of several similar cultivated plants of the genus *Lychnis*. [Say CAM pee un]

camp meeting *noun* an evangelical Christian worship service held outdoors or in a tent, often lasting several days.

camp-out *noun* an occasion on which people camp out.

campsite *noun* any place used for camping.

camp stove *noun* a portable cooking stove used by campers etc., usu. using naphtha as fuel.

campus *noun* (*plural* **campuses**) **1 a** the grounds of a university or college. **b** one of several local branches of a large university. **2** a university or college: *campus newspaper*.

campy *adjective* (**campier, campiest**) **1** deliberately exaggerated and theatrical in style, typically for humorous effect: *those older sitcoms seem so campy today*. **2** ostentatiously and extravagantly effeminate.

campylobacter *noun* a bacterium occurring in unpasteurized dairy products, poultry, and other foods, which can cause food poisoning in humans. [Say campa low BACK tur]

camshaft *noun* a shaft with one or more cams attached.

Can. *abbreviation* Canada; Canadian.

can[1] *auxiliary verb* (*3rd singular present* **can**; *past* **could**) **1 a** be able to; know how to. **b** be potentially capable of. **2** be permitted to.

can[2] • **noun 1** a metal vessel for liquid. **2** a metal container in which food or drink is hermetically sealed to enable storage over long periods. **3** a bin or other similar receptacle: *garbage can*. **4** (**the can**) *slang* **a** prison. **b** a washroom or toilet. **5** *slang* the buttocks.

• **verb** (**canned, canning**) **1** put or preserve in a can or jar. **2** *informal* **a** cease, end. **b** remove. **c** fire, dismiss. **3** record on film or tape for future use. PHRASES **can it** *informal* be quiet. **in the can** *informal* completed, ready (originally of filmed or recorded material).

Canada Day *noun* the annual holiday commemorating the creation of the Dominion of Canada on 1 July 1867 (formerly called DOMINION DAY).

Canada dogwood *noun* a low-growing plant of the dogwood family, which produces white flowers followed by red berries and bright red autumn foliage.

Canada Games *plural noun* a national sports competition, with events divided into summer and winter sports, held in Canada every four years since 1967.

Canada goose *noun* (*plural* **Canada geese**) a wild goose native to North America, with a brownish-grey back, black head and neck, and white cheeks and breast.

Canada jay *noun* = GREY JAY.

Canada lynx *noun* (*plural* **Canada lynx** or **Canada lynxes**) a large lynx of northern North America.

Canadarm *noun* *proprietary* a type of mechanical arm on a space shuttle's cargo bay, used for releasing, retrieving, and repairing satellites etc.

Canada thistle *noun* a perennial thistle with pink or purple flowers, native to Europe and now a flourishing weed in North America.

Canada violet *noun* a violet of eastern North America, bearing flowers with white petals tinged with purple on the back.

Canadian • **noun 1** a native or inhabitant of Canada. **2** (in *plural*) *informal* the Canadian national championships in a given sport. • **adjective** of or relating to Canada or its people.

Canadiana *noun* things pertaining to and typical of Canadian culture, e.g. publications, artifacts, etc.

Canadian Alliance *noun* a right-wing Canadian political party founded in 2000 with the joining of the Reform Party and some members of the Progressive Conservative Party.

Canadian Armed Forces *noun* an unofficial name for the Canadian Forces.

Canadian canoe *noun* a small, lightweight two-person canoe, usu. about 6 m (20 ft.) long.

Canadian English *noun* the English language as it is spoken and written by anglophone Canadians.

Canadian football *noun* a form of football played on a field 110 by 65 yards in which teams of 12 players attempt to throw, carry, or kick an oval ball across their opponents' goal line, and have only three downs in which to progress 10 yards.

Canadian Forces *noun* the official name of the Canadian military, comprised of the former army, navy, and air force.

Canadian French *noun* the French language as it is spoken and written by francophone Canadians.

Canadianism *noun* **1 a** a word or expression originating in Canada. **b** an English or French word or expression used only in Canada. **2** loyalty or devotion to Canada. **3 a** the state of being Canadian. **b** Canadian character or spirit.

Canadianist *noun* a specialist in Canadian studies.

Canadianization *noun* the process of becoming or making something or someone Canadian in character.

Canadianize *verb* (**Canadianizes, Canadianized, Canadianizing**) make or become Canadian in content, ownership, etc.

Canadianness *noun* Canadian qualities or nature.

Canadian whisky *noun* = RYE 2a.

C

C

Canadien *noun* a French Canadian. [Say can ad YEH]

Canadienne *noun* a French-Canadian woman or girl. [Say can ad YEN]

Canajun (also **Canajan**) *Cdn jocular* • *adjective* typically or purely Canadian. • *noun* **1** a Canadian. **2** Canadian English, esp. as allegedly spoken by unsophisticated Canadians. [Say kuh NAY jun]

canal *noun* **1** an artificial waterway for inland navigation or irrigation. **2** any of various ducts or passages in a plant or animal body: *the alimentary canal*.

Can-Am *Cdn* • *adjective* designating an event, esp. a sporting event, for Canadian and American participants. • *noun* a Can-Am event.

canapé *noun* **1** a cracker or small piece of bread with a savoury food on top, often served as an hors d'oeuvre. **2** a sofa. [Say CANNA pay]

canard *noun* an unfounded rumour or story: *the old canard that Ottawa is a dull city*. [Say kuh NARD]

canary • *noun* (*plural* **canaries**) **1** any of various small mostly African finches with yellowish-green plumage and a melodious song, esp. a variety native to the Canary Islands, popular as a cage bird and bred in many colours, esp. bright yellow. **2** (also **canary yellow**) a bright yellow colour. • *adjective* having a bright yellow colour.

cancan *noun* a lively stage dance with high kicking, usu. performed by women holding up the front of their long ruffled skirts.

cancel *verb* (**cancels**, **cancelled**, **cancelling**) **1 a** announce that (something already arranged and decided upon) will not be done or take place; call off. **b** discontinue (an arrangement in progress): *cancel my subscription*. **2** obliterate or delete (writing etc.). **3** mark or pierce (a cheque, stamp, etc.) so that it may not be used again. **4** make void; abolish (a financial obligation): *the debt has been cancelled*. **5** (often foll. by *out*) **a** (of one factor or circumstance) neutralize or counterbalance (another). **b** (of two factors or circumstances) neutralize each other. **6** *Math* strike out (an equal factor) on each side of an equation or from the numerator and denominator of a fraction.

cancellation *noun* **1** the action of cancelling something that has been arranged or planned: *the project was threatened with cancellation*. **2** something that has been cancelled, esp. a booking or reservation: *we will put you on standby in case there are any cancellations*. **3** the marks made by cancelling, esp. a stamp.

cancer *noun* **1 a** any malignant growth or tumour from an abnormal and uncontrolled division of body cells. **b** a disease characterized by this. **2** an evil influence or corruption spreading uncontrollably: *racism is a cancer spreading across Europe*. **3** (**Cancer**) a constellation between Gemini and Leo, regarded as contained in the figure of a crab. **4** (**Cancer**) **a** the fourth sign of the zodiac. **b** a person born when the sun is in this sign, usu. between 21 June and 22 July.

Cancerian *noun* a person born under the astrological sign of Cancer, between 21 June and 22 July. [Say can SERRY in or can SEARY in]

cancerous *adjective* affected by cancer: *cancerous tumours*.

CanCon *noun* *Cdn informal* Canadian content, esp. with reference to quotas in broadcasting.

CanCult *noun* *Cdn informal* Canadian culture.

candela *noun* the SI unit of luminous intensity. [Say can DEELA or can DELLA]

candelabra *noun* (*plural* **candelabras**) (also **candelabrum**, *plural* **candelabra**) a large branched candlestick or lamp for holding several candles or bulbs. [Say canda LABRA or canda LOBRA]

candid • *adjective* **1** straightforward and truthful; not hiding one's thoughts: *a candid discussion*. **2** (of a photograph) taken informally, usu. without the subject's knowledge. • *noun* a candid photograph.

candidacy *noun* the position or status of a candidate in an election: *announced her candidacy*.

candidate *noun* **1** a person who seeks or is nominated for an office, award, etc. **2** a person or thing likely to gain some distinction or position: *she was the perfect candidate for a biography* ◊ *a leading candidate for the title of Winnipeg's ugliest building*. **3** a person entered for an examination: *a doctoral candidate at York University*.

candidly *adverb* in a frank, honest, or open manner.

candied *adjective* **1** (esp. of fruit) preserved with sugar: *candied orange peel*. **2** cooked with a large quantity of sugar: *candied parsnips*.

candle • *noun* a cylinder or block of wax or tallow with a central wick that is burned for light or as a symbol of prayer, commendation to God, etc. • *verb* (**candles**, **candled**, **candling**) **1** test (an egg) for freshness by holding it to the light. **2** esp. *Cdn* (of ice) deteriorate into candle ice. **PHRASES** **cannot hold a candle to** is much inferior to.

candlefish *noun* = EULACHON.

candle ice *noun* (also **candled ice**) esp. *Cdn* ice which has deteriorated into untapered, candle-like icicles before breaking up.

Candlemas *noun* *Christianity* (in some churches) a feast with blessing of candles (2 Feb.), commemorating the Purification of the Virgin Mary and the presentation of Christ in the Temple. [Say CANDLE muss]

candlestick *noun* a holder for one or more candles.

can-do *adjective* *informal* displaying enthusiasm, confidence, and efficiency: *can-do attitude*.

candour *noun* (also **candor**) the quality of being open and honest: *his refreshing candour about the need to raise taxes was his undoing*. [Say CAN dur]

CANDU *noun* (*plural* **CANDUs**) a nuclear reactor using easily replaceable fuel bundles and a heavy water cooling and moderating system.

C. & W. *abbreviation* country and western.

candy *noun* (*plural* **candies**) a very sweet confection, often also including chocolate, nuts, etc.

candy cane *noun* a hard, thin, striped candy with a curved end, often eaten at Christmastime.

candy floss *noun* *Cdn & Brit.* a usu. pale pink fluffy mass of fine threads of sugar wrapped around a stick.

candystripe *noun* a pattern consisting of stripes (usu. red or pink) on a white background.

candystriper *noun* a usu. young volunteer at a hospital.

cane • *noun* **1 a** the hollow jointed stem of giant reeds or grasses, esp. bamboo or sugar cane. **b** the solid stem of slender palms such as rattan. **2** = SUGAR CANE. **3** a raspberry plant. **4** material of cane used in wicker furniture etc. **5 a** a cane used as a walking stick or a support for a plant or an instrument of punishment. **b** any slender walking stick. • *verb* (**canes**, **caned**, **caning**) **1** beat with a cane. **2** weave cane into (a chair etc.).

canine • *adjective* **1** of a dog or dogs. **2** of or belonging to the family Canidae, which includes dogs, wolves, etc. • *noun* **1** a dog. **2** (also **canine tooth**) a pointed tooth between the incisors and premolars. [Say KAY nine]

caning *noun* a beating with a cane as a punishment.

canister *noun* **1** a container, often one of a set, for holding flour, sugar, coffee, tea, etc. **2** a cylinder of shot, tear gas, etc., that explodes on impact. **3** a metallic cylindrical container for storing toxic waste etc.

canker *noun* **1 a** a destructive fungus disease of trees and plants. **b** an open wound in the stem of a tree or

plant. **2** an ulcerous ear disease of animals, esp. cats and dogs. **3** (also **canker sore**) a small sore on the lips or the inside of the mouth. **4** a corrupting influence: *racism remains a canker at the heart of the nation*. ▶ **cankerous** *adjective*

CanLit *abbreviation Cdn informal* Canadian literature.

cannabis *noun* **1** any hemp plant of the genus *Cannabis*, esp. *Cannabis sativa*; marijuana. **2** a preparation of parts of this used as an intoxicant or hallucinogen. [Say CANNA biss]

canned *adjective* **1** supplied in a can: *canned peas*. **2** pre-recorded: *canned laughter ◊ canned music*. **3** *informal* drunk. **4** *informal* (of a speech etc.) prepared in advance to suit many different occasions.

cannelloni *plural noun* tubes or rolls of pasta stuffed with meat or a vegetable mixture. [Say canna LOW nee]

canner *noun* **1** a large cooking vessel in which jars of preserves are immersed in boiling water to be sterilized and vacuum sealed. **2** *Cdn* (*Maritimes*) a lobster designated for canning because it is too small for the market. **3** a person who preserves food by canning: *home canners*.

cannery *noun* (*plural* **canneries**) a factory where food is canned.

cannibal *noun* **1** a person who eats human flesh. **2** an animal that feeds on flesh of its own species. ▶ **cannibalism** *noun* **cannibalistic** *adjective*

cannibalize *verb* (**cannibalizes**, **cannibalized**, **cannibalizing**) use (a machine etc.) as a source of spare parts for others: *cannibalized one of the computers for extra RAM for the server*.

cannily *adverb* in a way that shows shrewdness or good judgment, esp. in business or politics: *one eye cannily focused on audience taste and the other on the company's artistic needs*.

canniness *noun* shrewdness or good judgment, esp. in business or politics.

canning *noun* the process of preserving food in cans or hermetically sealed glass jars.

SPELL CHECK   ABC ✓
cannon, canon

A general rule, a list of works, or a musical composition is a **canon**.

---

cannon • *noun* **1** (*plural* **cannon** or **cannons**) a large gun installed on a carriage or mounting. **2** a similar device for discharging a specific substance: *water cannon*. **3** an automatic aircraft gun firing shells. • *verb* (usu. foll. by *against*, *into*) collide heavily or obliquely.

cannonball *noun* **1** a large usu. metal ball fired by a cannon. **2** *Cdn* (*BC*) a cannonball-like weight tied to commercial fishing lines to control depth and angle. **3** a jump (into a swimming pool etc.) with the knees clasped close to the chest.

cannot *auxiliary verb* can not.

canny *adjective* (**cannier**, **canniest**) having or showing good judgment and shrewdness, esp. in money or business matters: *canny investors will switch banks if they think they are getting a raw deal*.

canoe • *noun* a small narrow boat with pointed ends that curve upwards, usu. propelled by paddling. • *verb* (**canoes**, **canoed**, **canoeing**) travel in a canoe: *canoed down the Ottawa River ◊ canoeing the wilderness rivers of the Yukon*. ▶ **canoeist** *noun* **canoeing** *noun*

canoeman *noun* (*plural* **canoemen**) esp. *Cdn* **1** *hist.* a voyageur. **2** a canoeist.

can of worms *noun informal* a complicated problem: *to question the traditional model opens up too big a can of worms*.

canola *noun* any of various kinds of rapeseed yielding an oil used in cooking: *canola oil*. [Say kuh NO luh]

SPELL CHECK   ABC ✓
canon, cannon

A large gun is a **cannon**.

---

canon *noun* **1 a** a general law, rule, principle, or criterion by which something is judged: *the appointment violated the canons of fair play and equal opportunity*. **b** a church decree or law: *a set of ecclesiastical canons*. **2 a** a member of the clergy who is on the staff of a cathedral. The position is often conferred as an honorary one. **b** a member of certain Roman Catholic orders. **3 a** a collection or list of sacred books etc. accepted as genuine: *the formation of the biblical canon*. **b** the recognized genuine works of a particular author, composer, etc.; a list of these: *the Shakespeare canon*. **c** a collection or list of books generally regarded as most important in a given field: *Gerard Manley Hopkins was firmly established in the canon of English poetry*. **4** *Music* a piece with different parts taking up the same theme successively, either at the same or at a different pitch, like a round: *Pachelbel's canon*.

canonical *adjective* (also **canonic**) **1 a** according to or ordered by canon law: *the canonical rites of the church*. **b** included in the canon of Scripture: *the canonical books of the Bible*. **2** authoritative, standard: *the canonical method of comparative linguistics ◊ canonical writers like Jane Austen*. **3** *Music* in canon form. ▶ **canonically** *adverb* [Say kuh NONNA cull]

canonization *noun* **1** the process of officially declaring someone to be a saint: *the canonization of Marie d'Youville*. **2** the process of exalting someone regarded to be very significant: *the drive for literary canonization*.

canonize *verb* **1 a** declare officially to be a saint, usu. with a ceremony. **b** regard as a saint. **2 a** admit to the canon of Scripture. **b** accept as canonical: *defining and canonizing the true classics of literature*. **3** sanction by Church authority. **4** treat or regard as being above reproach or of great significance: *we have canonized freedom of speech as an absolute value overriding all others*.

canon law *noun* church law.

canopy • *noun* (*plural* **canopies**) **1 a** a covering hung or held up over a throne, bed, person, etc. **b** the sky. **c** an overhanging shelter. **2** *Architecture* a roof-like projection over a niche etc. **3** the uppermost layers of foliage etc. in a forest. **4 a** the expanding part of a parachute. **b** the cover of an aircraft's cockpit. • *verb* (**canopies**, **canopied**, **canopying**) cover with a canopy: *a canopied concert stage*. [Say CANNA pee]

canot du maître *noun* (*plural* **canots du maître**) *Cdn hist.* the largest birchbark canoe of the fur trade, up to 12 m long, used between the St. Lawrence River and Lake Superior. [Say can oh doo METTRA]

canot du nord *noun* (*plural* **canots du nord**) *Cdn hist.* a birchbark canoe of the fur trade, about 9 m long, used on waterways northwest of Lake Superior. [Say can oh doo NOR]

cant[1] *noun* **1** hypocritical and sanctimonious talk, typically of a moral, religious, or political nature: *few took issue with the common cant that Britain was the greatest nation that had ever been*. **2** ephemeral or fashionable catchwords: *"herstories" rather than "histories" as the cant phrase goes*. **3** language peculiar to a class, profession, sect, etc.; jargon: *thieves' cant*.

cant[2] • *noun* **1** a slanting surface: *the outward cant of the curving walls*. **2** a partly trimmed log. • *verb* be or move in a slanting position: *canted his head to one side*.

can't *contraction* can not.

cantaloupe *noun* a small round variety of melon with orange flesh. [Say CANTA lope]

cantankerous *adjective* bad-tempered, quarrelsome. ▶ **cantankerously** *adverb* **cantankerousness** *noun* [Say can TANKA riss]

cantata *noun* (*plural* **cantatas**) a short narrative or descriptive composition with vocal solos and usu. chorus and orchestral accompaniment. [Say can TATTA or can TOTTA]

canteen *noun* **1** a soldier's or camper's water flask. **2 a** a restaurant for employees in an office or factory etc. **b** a shop selling provisions or liquor in a barracks or camp.

canter ● *noun* a gentle gallop. ● *verb* **1** (of a horse or its rider) go at a canter. **2** make (a horse) canter.

cant hook *noun* an iron hook at the end of a long handle, used for rolling logs.

canticle *noun* a song or chant with a Biblical text.

cantilever ● *noun* a long projecting beam or girder fixed at only one end, used chiefly in bridge construction or projecting from a wall to support a balcony etc. ● *verb* support by a cantilever: *one porch is cantilevered out from the wall*.

cantilever bridge *noun* a bridge made of cantilevers projecting from the piers and connected by girders. [Say CANTA lee vur]

canto *noun* (*plural* **cantos**) a division of a long poem.

Cantonese ● *adjective* of Canton (Guangzhou), a city in S China, its inhabitants, their Chinese dialect, or their cuisine. ● *noun* (*plural* same) **1** a native of Canton. **2** the Chinese dialect of SE China and Hong Kong.

cantor *noun* **1** the leader of the singing in church. **2** a person employed to sing the solo prayers in a synagogue. [Say CAN tur]

Canuck *informal* ● *noun* a Canadian. ● *adjective* Canadian.

SPELL CHECK   `ABC ✓`
canvas, canvass

To ask for donations or opinions is to **canvass**.

---

canvas *noun* **1 a** a strong coarse kind of cloth usu. made from cotton or other coarse yarn and used for sails, tents, sturdy bags, etc. and as a surface for oil painting. **b** a piece of this. **2** a painting on canvas, esp. in oils. **3** an open kind of canvas used as a basis for tapestry and embroidery. **PHRASES under canvas 1** in a tent or tents. **2** with sails spread.

canvasback *noun* a wild duck of North America, the male of which has back feathers of a whitish colour like unbleached canvas, and a chestnut head and neck.

SPELL CHECK   `ABC ✓`
canvass, canvas

A kind of cloth is **canvas**.

---

canvass ● *verb* (**canvasses, canvassed, canvassing**) **1 a** solicit votes, charitable donations, support, custom, etc., esp. by going door to door. **b** solicit votes etc. from (people). **c** visit (a building, area, etc.) in order to do this. **2 a** ascertain opinions of. **b** discuss thoroughly: *the issues that were canvassed are still unresolved*. **3** propose (an idea or plan etc.): *early retirement was canvassed as a solution for unemployment*. ● *noun* an act or process of attempting to secure votes or ascertain opinions: *a house-to-house canvass*. ▶ **canvasser** *noun*

canyon *noun* **1** a deep gorge, often with a stream or river. **2** a street hemmed in by tall buildings: *the canyons of downtown Toronto*. ▶ **canyonland** *noun*

cap ● *noun* **1 a** a close-fitting brimless head covering,

often of a soft material and usu. with a visor: *baseball cap*. **b** a head covering worn in a particular profession: *nurse's cap*. **c** an academic mortarboard or soft hat. **2 a** a cover like a cap in shape or position: *kneecap*. **b** a device to seal a bottle or protect the point of a pen etc. **c** the top of a bird's head. **3** = CROWN *noun* 8b. **4** the pileus of a mushroom or toadstool. **5** a small amount of explosive powder contained in metal or paper and exploded by striking, used esp. in toy guns. **6** an upward limit put on something: *salary cap*. ● *verb* (**caps, capped, capping**) **1 a** put a cap on. **b** cover the top or end of. **c** set a limit to: *rate-capping*. **d** seal (a well) to prevent or control the loss of gas or oil. **5** a lie on top of; form the cap of. **b** surpass, excel. **c** serve as a final climax or culmination to; complete: *capped the season with a shutout*. **PHRASES cap in hand** humbly: *we have to go cap in hand begging for funds*. **if the cap fits** = IF THE SHOE FITS (see SHOE). **set one's cap at** try to attract as a suitor.

capability *noun* (*plural* **capabilities**) **1** ability, power; the condition of being capable: *the capability to increase productivity* ◊ *the job is beyond my capabilities*. **2** a facility on a computer for performing a specific task: *a graphics capability*. **3** forces or resources giving a country or state the ability to undertake a particular kind of military action: *their nuclear weapons capability*.

capable *adjective* **1** competent, able, gifted: *she looked enthusiastic and capable*. **2** (foll. by *of*) **a** having the ability or fitness or necessary quality for: *Leigh is quite capable of taking care of herself*. **b** open to or admitting of (explanation or improvement etc.): *the strange events are capable of rational explanation*. ▶ **capably** *adverb*

capacious *adjective* roomy; able to hold much: *she rummaged in her capacious purse*. [Say kuh PAY shuss]

capacitance *noun* the ability of a system to store an electric charge. [Say kuh PASSA tunce]

capacitor *noun* a device of one or more pairs of conductors used to store an electric charge. [Say kuh PASSA tur]

capacity ● *noun* (*plural* **capacities**) **1 a** the ability or power to do, experience, or understand something: *Janet's capacity for hard work* ◊ *Connie's capacity to inspire trust in others* ◊ *Daria's astounding intellectual capacities*. **b** the maximum amount that can be contained or produced etc.: *the stadium's seating capacity* ◊ *the room was filled to capacity* ◊ *the plant is running at full capacity*. **c** the volume, e.g. of the cylinders in an internal combustion engine. **2** a position or function: *in my capacity as a critic*. **3** legal competence. ● *adjective* filling all available space: *capacity crowd*.

cape *noun* **1** a sleeveless cloak. **2** a short sleeveless cloak as a fixed or detachable part of a longer cloak or coat. **3** a headland or promontory.

Cape Ann *noun* Cdn (Nfld) a broad-brimmed rain hat with an extended back flap.

Cape Bretoner *noun* a resident or native of Cape Breton.

Cape Breton pork pie *noun* Cdn a date-filled tart with a rich shortbread-cookie-like pastry.

Cape Cod *noun* a style of rectangular house, usu. one-and-a-half storeys, with a steeply sloping roof.

caped *adjective* wearing a cape.

Cape Island boat *noun* (also **Cape Islander**) Cdn a boat used by inshore fishermen esp. in Nova Scotia, with a high prow and a low stern.

capelin *noun* = CAPLIN. [Say CAP lun or CAPE lun]

caper[1] ● *verb* skip or dance about in a lively or playful manner: *children were capering about the room*. ● *noun* **1** a playful jump or leap: *she did a little caper or dance*. **2 a** an amusing or far-fetched film or TV drama: *a cop caper about intergalactic drug dealers*. **b** *informal* an activity or

escapade, typically one that is illicit or ridiculous: *some sort of organized-crime caper.* PHRASES **cut a caper** (or **capers**) make a playful, skipping movement.

caper² *noun* **1** a bramble-like southern European shrub. **2** (in *plural*) its flower buds cooked and pickled for use as flavouring esp. for a savoury sauce.

capiche *interjection slang* understand? [Say kuh PEESH]

capicollo *noun* (also **capicolla**) spicy Italian cured pork shoulder butt, usu. served in thin slices. [Say cappy CO lo, cappy COLA]

Capilano *noun* a member of a part of the Squamish Aboriginal group, currently residing in the North Vancouver area. [Say cappa LAN oh]

capillarity *noun* = CAPILLARY ACTION. [Say cappa LAIR a tee]

capillary • *noun* (*plural* **capillaries**) **1** of one of the fine branching blood vessels that form a network between arteries and veins. **2** a tube having an internal diameter of hairlike thinness. • *adjective* of or relating to capillaries. [Say kuh PILLA ree]

capillary action *noun* the movement of a liquid up through a narrow tube or opening caused by the surface tension between the liquid and the surrounding material.

SPELL CHECK [ABC ✓]
capital, Capitol

The US legislative building is a **Capitol**.

---

capital • *noun* **1** the city or town in a country, province, etc. at which the principal government institutions (the legislature, judiciary, administrative headquarters) are located. **2** the most noteworthy place for a specified quality: *Canada's sunshine capital*. **3 a** the money or other assets with which a company starts in business. **b** accumulated wealth, esp. as used in further production. **c** money invested or lent at interest. **4** the holders of wealth as a class; capitalists: *a conflict of interest between capital and labour*. **5** a capital letter. **6** the distinct, typically broader section at the head of a pillar or column: *a Corinthian capital*. • *adjective* **1** *informal* excellent, first-rate. **2** involving or punishable by death: *capital punishment* ◊ *a capital offence*. **3** (of letters of the alphabet) large in size and of the form used to begin sentences and names etc. PHRASES **make capital out of** use to one's advantage: *trying to make political capital out of the weaknesses of her opponent*. **with a capital** — emphatically: *art with a capital A*.

capital gain *noun* a profit from the sale of investments or property.

capital goods *plural noun* goods, esp. machinery etc., used or to be used in producing commodities.

capitalism *noun* an economic system in which a country's trade and industry are controlled by private owners for profit, rather than by the state.

capitalist • *noun* **1** a person who uses their wealth to invest in trade and industry for profit in accordance with the principles of capitalism: *the creation of the factory system by nineteenth-century capitalists*. **2** an advocate of capitalism. • *adjective* of or favouring capitalism: *capitalist countries*. ▸ **capitalistic** *adjective*

capitalization *noun* **1 a** the provision of a company or industry with capital. **b** conversion into capital. **2** the use of capital letters in writing, printing, etc.

capitalize *verb* (**capitalizes**, **capitalized**, **capitalizing**) **1 a** provide with capital: *a highly capitalized industry*. **b** calculate or realize the present value of an income; convert into capital. **c** reckon (the value of an asset) by setting future benefits against the cost of maintenance. **2 a** write (a letter of the alphabet) as a capital. **b** begin (a word) with a capital letter. **3** use

to one's advantage; profit from: *an attempt by the opposition to capitalize on the government's embarrassment*.

SPELL CHECK [ABC ✓]
Capitol, capital

The spelling is **capital** for a main city, an upper case letter, money, the top part of a pillar, and in "capital punishment".

Capitol *noun* a building housing a legislature in the US, esp. the federal legislative building in Washington.

Capitol Hill *n.* **1** the hill in Washington, DC, on which the Capitol sits. **2** the US Congress.

capitulate *verb* (**capitulates**, **capitulated**, **capitulating**) cease to resist an opponent or an unwelcome demand; surrender: *they capitulated on one of the union's demands* ◊ *will not capitulate to blackmail* ◊ *Montreal capitulated in 1760.* [Say kuh PITCHA late]

capitulation *noun* the act of capitulating; surrender: *a capitulation to wage demands.* [Say kuh pitcha LAY sh'n]

caplin *noun* a small smelt-like fish of the North Atlantic, used as food and as bait for catching cod etc. [Say CAP lun or CAPE lun]

capon *noun* a young rooster castrated and fattened for eating. [Say KAY pawn]

capote *noun* (also **capot**) *hist.* a long coat with a hood, esp. (in Canada) tied with a colourful sash. [Say kuh POT]

capped *adjective* **1** having the kind of cap described: *snow-capped mountains* ◊ *black-capped chickadee*. **2** sealed with a cap or top. **3** (of a tooth) having a crown.

capper *noun* **1** *informal* an event etc. that surpasses or completes others. **2** a device etc. that applies caps.

cappuccino *noun* (*plural* **cappuccinos**) espresso coffee with milk made frothy with pressurized steam. [Say cappa CHEE no]

capri *noun* (*plural* **capris**) (usu. as an *adjective*) women's close-fitting, tapered pants or leggings extending to just above the ankles: *capri tights.* [Say kuh PREE]

caprice *noun* an unaccountable or whimsical change of mind or conduct: *his caprices had made her life impossible* ◊ *a victim of political caprice.* [Say kuh PREECE]

capricious *adjective* **1** given to sudden and unaccountable changes of mood or behaviour: *a capricious and often brutal administration*. **2** unpredictable: *a capricious climate.* ▸ **capriciously** *adverb* **capriciousness** *noun* [Say kuh PREESH iss or kuh PRISH iss]

Capricorn *noun* **1** a constellation between Sagittarius and Aquarius, regarded as contained in the figure of a goat's horns. **2 a** the tenth sign of the zodiac. **b** a person born when the sun is in this sign, usu. between Dec. 22 and Jan. 19. ▸ **Capricornian** *noun & adjective*

caprock *noun* **1** a hard rock overlying a deposit of oil, gas, coal, etc. **2** a hard rock at the top of a hoodoo, butte, etc.

capsize *verb* (**capsizes**, **capsized**, **capsizing**) overturn: *the boat capsized* ◊ *we capsized the boat*.

capstan *noun* **1** a thick revolving cylinder with a vertical axis, for winding an anchor cable or a halyard etc. **2** a revolving spindle on a tape recorder, that guides the tape past the head. [Say CAP stun]

capstone *noun* **1 a** a stone which caps a structure. **b** = CAPROCK. **2** a culmination or highest point.

capsule *noun* **1 a** small soluble case of gelatin enclosing a dose of medicine and swallowed with it. **2** (also **space capsule**) a detachable compartment of a spacecraft or nose cone of a rocket. **3** a membranous or fibrous envelope around an organ, joint, etc. **4 a** a dry fruit that releases its seeds when ripe. **b** the spore-producing structure of mosses. **5** a concise or highly condensed report: *a capsule review*.

C

captain • *noun* **1 a** a chief or leader. **b** the leader of a team, esp. in sports. **c** a powerful or influential person: *captain of industry*. **2 a** the person in command of a ship. **b** the pilot of a civil aircraft. **3** (also **Captain**) **a** (in Canada, the US, and the UK) an officer in land-based forces ranking below major and above lieutenant. **b** (in Canada and the US) an officer in the air force ranking below major and above lieutenant. **c** (in Canada, the US, and the UK) a naval officer ranking above commander. **d** (in some Canadian police forces) an officer ranking above lieutenant and below inspector. **4 a** a foreman. **b** a supervisor of waiters or bellboys. • *verb* be captain of; lead. ▶ **captaincy** *noun* (*plural* **captaincies**)

caption • *noun* **1** a title or brief explanation appended to an illustration, cartoon, etc. **2** wording appearing on a cinema or television screen as part of a film or broadcast. • *verb* provide with a caption.

captivate *verb* (**captivates**, **captivated**, **captivating**) **1** overwhelm with charm or affection. **2** fascinate. ▶ **captivatingly** *adverb* **captivation** *noun*

captive • *noun* a person or animal that has been taken prisoner or confined. • *adjective* **1** imprisoned or confined: *held them captive in a farmhouse*. **2** in a position of having to comply: *captive audience*. **3** of or like a prisoner: *captive state*. ▶ **captivity** *noun*

captor *noun* a person who takes or holds (a person etc.) captive.

capture • *verb* (**captures**, **captured**, **capturing**) **1 a** take prisoner. **b** seize as a prize. **c** obtain by force or trickery. **2** win control of (something): *captured our imagination*. **3** portray or preserve faithfully, esp. in permanent form: *captured their adventure on film*. **4** *Physics* absorb (a subatomic particle). **5** (in board games) make a move that secures the removal of (an opposing piece) from the board. **6** cause (data) to be stored in a computer. • *noun* **1** the act of capturing. **2** a thing or person captured.

Capuchin *noun* **1** a Franciscan friar of a branch established in 1529 to re-emphasize the ideals of poverty and austerity. **2** (**capuchin**) a South American monkey with cowl-like fur on its head. [Say CAP you chin or CAP oo shin]

car *noun* **1** a road vehicle with an enclosed passenger compartment, powered by an internal combustion engine; an automobile. **2** a wheeled vehicle, esp. of a specified kind: *cable car*. **3** a railway vehicle for carrying passengers or freight. **4** the passenger compartment of an elevator, balloon, etc. **5** = STREETCAR.

carafe *noun* **1** a wide-mouthed glass container for beverages, esp. water or wine. **2** the contents of a carafe. **3** an insulated, decorative jug for serving beverages, esp. coffee. [Say kuh RAF]

caragana *noun* (*plural* **caraganas**) any Asian leguminous shrub of the genus *Caragana*, esp. the Siberian pea, planted as hedging. [Say care a GANNA]

caramel • *noun* **1** sugar or syrup heated until it turns brown, then used as a flavouring, garnish, or colour. **2** a kind of soft candy made with sugar, butter, milk, etc. **3** the light brown colour of caramel. • *adjective* **1** flavoured with caramel. **2** of the light brown colour of caramel. [Say CARE a mel or CARM ul]

caramelize *verb* (**caramelizes**, **caramelized**, **caramelizing**) **1 a** convert (sugar or syrup) into caramel. **b** (of sugar or syrup) be converted into caramel. **2** coat or cook (food) with caramelized sugar or syrup. [Say CARE a muh lize or KARMA lize]

carapace *noun* the hard upper shell of a turtle or a crustacean. [Say CARE a pace]

Caraquet *noun* *Cdn* a small variety of edible oyster found in the waters off New Brunswick. [Say CAR a ket]

carat *noun* **1** a unit of weight for precious stones, equivalent to 200 milligrams. **2** = KARAT.

caravan *noun* **1** a company of people with vehicles or pack animals travelling together, esp. across a desert. **2** a covered motor vehicle with living accommodations. **3** a covered cart or carriage.

caraway *noun* **1** a plant of the parsley family bearing clusters of tiny white flowers. **2** (also **caraway seed**) the fruit of the caraway plant used as flavouring and as a source of oil. [Say CARE a way]

carb *noun* *informal* a carburetor.

carbide *noun* **1** a binary compound of carbon with a lower or comparable electronegativity. **2** a very hard material made of cobalt or nickel and carbides of metals such as tungsten and tantalum, used in the cutting parts of tools.

carbine *noun* a short firearm, usu. a rifle, originally for cavalry use.

carbo *noun* (*plural* **carbos**) *slang* carbohydrate.

carbohydrate *noun* **1** any of a large group of energy-producing organic compounds containing carbon, hydrogen, and oxygen, e.g. starch, glucose, and other sugars. **2** a foodstuff that is high in carbohydrates, e.g. bread, sweets, pasta, etc. [Say carba HI drate]

carbo-load *verb* consume large amounts of carbohydrate, esp. before a sporting event to improve stamina. ▶ **carbo-loading** *noun*

carbon *noun* **1** a non-metallic element occurring naturally as diamond, graphite, and charcoal, and in all organic compounds. **2 a** = CARBON COPY 1. **b** = CARBON PAPER. **3** a rod of carbon in an arc lamp.

carbon-12 *noun* a carbon isotope of mass 12.

carbon-14 *noun* a long-lived radioactive carbon isotope of mass 14, used in carbon dating.

carbonara *adjective* designating a sauce for pasta made of eggs, cream, Parmesan cheese, and pieces of bacon: *linguine carbonara*. [Say carba NAR uh]

carbonate • *noun* a salt of carbonic acid. • *verb* (**carbonates**, **carbonated**, **carbonating**) **1** dissolve carbon dioxide in a liquid to make it bubbly. **2** convert into a carbonate.

carbonated *adjective* (of a beverage) being bubbly due to carbon dioxide.

carbon copy *noun* (*plural* **carbon copies**) **1** a copy made with carbon paper. **2** an exact duplicate: *is a carbon copy of his father*.

carbon cycle *noun* *Biology* the continuous transfer of carbon in various forms from the atmosphere to living organisms by plant photosynthesis, and back to the atmosphere by respiration and decay.

carbon dating *noun* (also **carbon-14 dating**) a method of estimating the age of organic archaeological specimens by determining the ratio of carbon-14 (which decays at a known rate) to another isotope which remains constant.

carbon dioxide *noun* a colourless odourless gas occurring naturally in the atmosphere and formed by respiration.

carbonic acid *noun* a very weak acid formed from carbon dioxide dissolved in water. [Say car BON ick]

Carboniferous • *adjective* of or relating to a period of the Paleozoic era, lasting from about 360 to 286 million years BP, between the Devonian and the Permian. During this time, the first reptiles and seed-bearing

plants appeared, and there were extensive coral reefs and coal-forming swamp forests. • *noun* this geological period. [Say carba NIFFA riss]

carbonize *verb* (**carbonizes**, **carbonized**, **carbonizing**) **1** convert into carbon by heating. **2** reduce to charcoal or coke. **3** coat with carbon.

carbon monoxide *noun* a colourless odourless toxic gas formed by the incomplete burning of carbon.

carbon tetrachloride *noun* a colourless volatile liquid used as a refrigerant and in dry cleaning.

carbonyl *noun* (used as an *adjective*) *Chemistry* the divalent radical CO. [Say CARBON ill]

carboxyl *noun Chemistry* the monovalent acid radical (-COOH), present in most organic acids. ▶**carboxylic** *adjective* [Say car BOX ul, car bock SILL ick]

carburetor *noun* an apparatus for controlling the mixture of gasoline and air in an internal combustion engine. [Say CARBA rate ur]

carcass *noun* (*plural* **carcasses**) **1** the dead body of an animal, esp. one slaughtered for its meat. **2** the bones of a cooked bird. **3** *informal* a human body, living or dead. **4** the skeleton or framework of a building, ship, etc.

carcinogen *noun* any substance that produces cancer. ▶**carcinogenic** *adjective* **carcinogenicity** *noun* [Say car SINNA jin, car sinna JEN ick, car sinna juh NISSA tee]

carcinoma *noun* (*plural* **carcinomas**) a cancer, esp. one arising in epithelial tissue or the lining of the internal organs. [Say karsa NOMA]

card[1] • *noun* **1** thick stiff paper or thin pasteboard. **2 a** a flat piece of this, esp. for writing or printing on. **b** = POSTCARD. **c** a card used to send greetings, issue an invitation, etc.: *birthday card*. **d** = CALLING CARD 1. **e** a card printed with one's name and professional details. **f** a card with a photograph of a sports figure etc., collected as part of a set. **g** a card indicating membership or entitling admission. **3 a** = PLAYING CARD. **b** a similar card in a set designed for a particular game. **c** (in *plural*) card playing; a card game. **d** a specified advantageous usu. political factor: *politicians will play the crime card yet again*. **4 a** a program of events at a race, boxing match, etc. **b** a scorecard. **c** a list of holes on a golf course, on which a player's scores are entered. **5** *informal* an amusing person: *he's a real card!* **6** a printed or written notice or advertisement. **7** a small rectangular piece of plastic issued by a bank or other institution with personal data on it, often machine-readable: *credit card* ◊ *health card*. **8** a circuit board. • *verb* **1** affix to a card. **2** write on a card, esp. for indexing. **3** demand identification from (a person). PHRASES **card up one's sleeve** a plan in reserve. **in the cards** possible or likely. **play one's cards right** (or **well**) act carefully; carry out a scheme successfully. **put** (or **lay**) **one's cards on the table** reveal one's resources, intentions, etc.

card[2] • *noun* **1** a machine through which fibre is fed past a series of wire teeth to align and disentangle the fibre before spinning. **2** a toothed instrument or wire brush for raising the nap on cloth. • *verb* prepare (fibre) with a card.

cardamom *noun* (also **cardamon**) **1** an aromatic plant of the ginger family. **2** the seed capsules of this used as a spice. [Say CARDA mum, CARDA mun]

cardboard • *noun* pasteboard or stiff paper, esp. for making cards or boxes. • *adjective* **1** made of cardboard. **2** lacking depth and realism: *with its superficial, cardboard characters, the novel was typical of her work*.

card-carrying *adjective* **1** registered as a member (e.g. of a union or political party): *a former card-carrying communist*. **2** devoted to a specified pursuit, outlook, or cause: *a card-carrying feminist*.

carded *adjective Cdn* (of an amateur athlete) receiving government funding to pursue training.

cardholder *noun* a person who has a specific card, esp. a credit card.

cardiac • *adjective* of or relating to the heart. • *noun* a person with heart disease. [Say CAR dee ack]

cardiac arrest *noun* a sudden cessation of the heartbeat.

cardigan *noun* a knitted jacket or sweater fastening down the front, usu. with long sleeves.

cardinal • *noun* **1** (as a title **Cardinal**) a leading dignitary of the Catholic Church, one of the college electing the Pope. **2** a North American songbird, the male of which has scarlet plumage. • *adjective* fundamental: *a cardinal rule*.

cardinal humour *noun see* HUMOUR *noun* 5.

cardinal number *noun* a number denoting quantity (one, two, three, etc.), as opposed to an ordinal number (first, second, third, etc.).

cardinal point *noun* one of the four main points of the compass: north, south, east, west.

cardinal sin *noun* **1** = DEADLY SIN. **2** an action perceived as unforgivable: *the cardinal sin is poor taste*.

cardio *noun slang* **1** cardiovascular exercise. **2** cardiovascular fitness.

cardiogram *noun* = ELECTROCARDIOGRAM.

cardiograph *noun* = ELECTROCARDIOGRAPH. ▶**cardiographer** *noun* **cardiography** *noun* [Say CARDY oh graph, cardy OGRA fur, cardy OGRA fee]

cardiologist *noun* a doctor who studies and treats heart diseases. [Say cardy OLLA jist]

cardiology *noun* the branch of medicine concerned with heart diseases and abnormalities. [Say cardy OLLA jee]

cardiopulmonary *adjective* of the heart and lungs. [Say cardy oh PUL muh nerry]

cardiopulmonary resuscitation *noun* a series of emergency techniques used to revive a patient whose heart has stopped, including artificial respiration and heart massage. Abbreviation: **CPR**.

cardiovascular *adjective* of or relating to the heart and blood vessels. [Say cardy oh VASK you lur]

card sharp *noun* (also **card shark**) a person who professionally or habitually cheats at card games.

WRITING TIP
could/couldn't care less

Using *could care less* instead of the more logical *couldn't care less* is perceived by many people as a sign of sloppiness or total disregard for the language. Both of these expressions are informal, so if you are writing or making a formal speech, you would be better off using something else altogether, such as *I am totally indifferent*.

---

care • *noun* **1 a** the process of looking after or providing for someone or something; the provision of what is needed for health or protection: *child care* ◊ *skin care*. **b** *Cdn & Brit.* protective custody or guardianship provided by a child welfare agency for a child whose parents are deemed unable to provide proper care: *was taken into care*. **2** serious attention or thought in doing something properly or avoiding damage to something: *handle with care*. **3** a troubled state of mind arising from worry or anxiety. **4** maintenance: *car care*. **5** a matter of concern; something to be done or seen to. • *verb* (**cares**, **cared**, **caring**) **1 a** feel concern or interest. **b** have an objection; mind. **2** feel liking, affection, regard, or deference: *don't care for jazz*. **3** wish or be willing: *do not care to be seen with him*. **4** in conventional polite offers, esp. of food or drink: *care for a cup of tea?*

C

PHRASES **care for 1** look after, esp. an old or sick person. **2** love or be very fond of. **care of** at the address of: *sent it care of his sister.* **for all one cares** informal denoting a lack of interest or concern: *I could be dying for all you care.* **have a care** take care; be careful. **take care 1** be careful. **2** not fail or neglect: *take care to close the lid tightly.* **3** a conventional expression of good wishes on parting etc. **take care of 1** look after; keep safe. **2** deal with. **3** dispose of.

careen verb rush headlong; hurtle unsteadily: *an electric golf cart careened around the corner.*

career • noun **1 a** one's advancement through life, esp. in a profession. **b** the progress through history of a group or institution. **2** a profession or occupation, esp. as offering advancement. • adjective **1 a** pursuing or wishing to pursue a career: *career woman.* **b** working permanently in a specified profession: *career diplomat.* **2** Sport **a** (of a statistic etc.) accumulated over one's career: *scored 500 career goals.* **b** constituting a high point in one's career: *a career game.* • verb move or swerve about wildly: *the bus careered across the road and went through a hedge.*

careerism noun preoccupation with the goal of personal advancement in one's profession.

careerist noun a person predominantly concerned with personal advancement.

carefree adjective free from anxiety or responsibility.

careful adjective **1** painstaking, thorough. **2** cautious. **3** done with care and attention. **4** showing care or concern for. ▶ **carefully** adverb **carefulness** noun

caregiver noun **1** a parent or guardian who cares for a child. **2** a person who cares for a sick or elderly person. **3** a person employed to look after a child. ▶ **caregiving** noun

careless adjective **1** not taking care or paying attention. **2** insensitive. **3** inaccurate. **4** lighthearted. **5** (foll. by *of*) not concerned about. ▶ **carelessly** adverb **carelessness** noun

care package noun **1** a parcel of food, clothing, or other staple items sent to the needy in a foreign country. **2** a parcel of luxuries (esp. homemade foods) sent to a person who is living away from home.

caress • verb (**caresses, caressed, caressing**) touch or stroke gently or lovingly: *she caressed the girl's forehead* ◊ *the caressing warmth of the sun.* • noun a loving or gentle touch or kiss. ▶ **caressingly** adverb

caretaker noun **1** a custodian or janitor. **2** = CAREGIVER. **3** (as an adjective) exercising temporary authority: *caretaker government.* ▶ **caretaking** noun

careworn adjective showing the effects of prolonged worry.

carful noun (*plural* **carfuls**) the amount of something that can fill a car.

cargo noun (*plural* **cargoes** or **cargos**) goods carried on a ship, aircraft, or other vehicle.

Carib • noun **1** an aboriginal inhabitant of the southern West Indies or the adjacent coasts. **2** the language of this people. • adjective of this people. [Say CARE ib]

Caribbean • noun the part of the Atlantic between the southern W Indies and Central America. • adjective **1** of or relating to this region or its people. **2** of the Caribs or their language. [Say care a BEE in or kuh RIBBY in]

caribou noun (*plural* **caribou**) **1** any of several subspecies of reindeer inhabiting northern Canada and Alaska, esp. the woodland or barren ground caribou. **2** the meat or hide of this animal. **3** Cdn (esp. Que.) a beverage made from red wine and whisky blanc.

Caribou Inuit *plural* noun an inland Inuit people formerly inhabiting the Barrens and relying almost entirely on caribou for food and clothing.

caricature • noun **1** a grotesque usu. comic representation of a person by exaggeration of characteristic traits, in a picture, writing, etc. **2** a ridiculously poor or absurd imitation or version: *a caricature of history.* • verb (**caricatures, caricatured, caricaturing**) make or give a caricature of: *he was cruelly caricatured on the editorial page.* ▶ **caricaturist** noun [Say CARE ick a chur]

caries noun (*plural* **caries**) decay and crumbling of a tooth or bone. [Say CARE eez]

carillon noun **1** a set of bells sounded either from a keyboard or mechanically. **2** a tune played on bells. [Say CARE a lun or CARE a lawn]

caring adjective compassionate or considerate, esp. towards other people. ▶ **caringly** adverb

carjack verb hijack a car or its passengers. ▶ **carjacker** noun **carjacking** noun

carload noun **1** the quantity of freight that can be shipped in a railway car. **2** the number of people that can travel in an automobile.

Carmelite • noun a monk or nun of a Roman Catholic contemplative order. • adjective of or relating to the Carmelites. [Say KARMA lite]

carnage noun the killing of many people, animals, etc., usu. with much bloodshed.

carnal adjective relating to physical, esp. sexual needs and activities: *carnal desire.* ▶ **carnality** noun **carnally** adverb [Say CAR null, car NALA tee]

carnation noun any of certain cultivated varieties of the pink (see PINK[1] 2), with variously coloured, delicately scented showy flowers.

carnival noun **1 a** the festivities usual during the period before Lent in some countries, involving processions, music, dancing, masquerades, etc. **b** any festivities, esp. those occurring during a regular season: *winter carnival.* **2** a travelling fair with exhibits, games, rides, and other amusements. **3** Cdn Figure Skating a non-competitive performance given by the members of a figure skating club. ▶ **carnivalesque** adjective

carnivore noun **1 a** any mammal of the order Carnivora (cats, dogs, bears, seals, etc.) with powerful jaws and teeth adapted for stabbing, tearing, and eating flesh. **b** any other flesh-eating mammal. **2** any insect-eating plant. **3** a person who eats (esp. large amounts of) meat; a person who is not a vegetarian.

carnivorous adjective **1** meat-eating. **2** (of a plant) digesting trapped insects or other animal substances. **3** of or relating to the order Carnivora. **4** (of a person) not vegetarian. [Say car NIV er us]

carob noun **1** (also **carob tree**) an evergreen tree, native to the Mediterranean, bearing edible bean-shaped seed pods. **2** the pod of this tree. **3** the powdered pulp of these pods, used esp. as a substitute for chocolate. [Say CARE ib]

SPELL CHECK	
carol, carrel	ABC ✔

A desk or cubicle in a library is a **carrel**.

carol • noun a joyous song or hymn, esp. one celebrating Christmas. • verb (**carols, carolled, carolling**) **1** sing carols, esp. outdoors at Christmas. **2** sing or say something joyfully: *she was cheerfully carolling the words of the song.*

Carolingian • adjective having to do with the Frankish dynasty, founded by the father of Charlemagne (Pepin III), which ruled in western Europe from 750 to 987. • noun a member of the Carolingian dynasty. [Say care a LIN gee un]

Carolinian • adjective **1** of or relating to a forest region extending from southern Ontario to North and

South Carolina, characterized by broadleaf deciduous trees such as the tulip tree and magnolia. **2** of or relating to the states of South or North Carolina. • *noun* a native or inhabitant of South or North Carolina. [Say care a LINNY in]

caroller *noun* a person who sings esp. Christmas carols.

carom • *noun* *Billiards* a shot in which the cue ball strikes two other balls in succession. • *verb* (**caroms, caromed, caroming**) **1** *Billiards* make a carom. **2** strike and rebound: *the misdirected pass caromed into the net off the defenceman.* [Say CARE um]

carotene *noun* any of several orange-coloured plant pigments found in carrots, tomatoes, etc., acting as a source of vitamin A. [Say CARE a teen]

carotid • *noun* each of the two main arteries carrying blood to the head and neck. • *adjective* of or relating to either of these arteries. [Say kuh ROT id]

carouse • *verb* (**carouses, caroused, carousing**) **1** participate in a noisy or lively drinking party. **2** drink heavily. • *noun* a noisy or lively drinking party. [Say kuh ROUSE (ROUSE rhymes with VOWS]

carousel *noun* **1 a** a large revolving device in a playground, for children to ride on. **b** a merry-go-round. **2** a rotating delivery or conveyor system, esp. for passengers' luggage at an airport. **3** a rotating tray for holding specific objects, esp. on a slide projector or CD player. [Say care a SELL or CARE a sell]

carp[1] *noun* (*plural* **carp**) a freshwater food fish with large scales and fleshy filaments on either side of its mouth.

carp[2] *verb* find fault; complain pettily.

carpaccio *noun* a thin strip of marinated raw meat, esp. beef, as an appetizer. [Say car PATCHY oh]

carpal • *adjective* of the bones in the wrist. • *noun* any of the bones forming the wrist. [Say CARP ul]

carpal tunnel syndrome *noun* a painful disorder of the hand caused by compression of a major nerve in the wrist, often brought about by overexertion.

carpel *noun* the female reproductive organ of a flower, consisting of a stigma, style, and ovary. [Say CARP ul]

carpenter • *noun* a person skilled in woodwork, esp. of a structural kind. • *verb* work or construct as a carpenter: *did some carpentering on the side ◊ the room was carpentered in oak.*

carpentry *noun* **1** the work or occupation of a carpenter. **2** woodwork constructed by a carpenter.

carpet • *noun* **1 a** thick fabric for covering a floor or stairs. **b** a piece of this fabric. **2** an expanse or layer resembling a carpet in being smooth, soft, bright, or thick: *carpet of violets.* • *verb* (**carpets, carpeted, carpeting**) cover with or as with a carpet. PHRASES **call** (or **have up**) **on the carpet** reprimand; reprove. **sweep under the carpet** conceal (a problem or difficulty) in the hope that it will be forgotten.

carpetbagger *noun* **1** a political candidate in an area where the candidate has no local connections. **2** an unscrupulous opportunist: *the Metis feel they were shamelessly exploited by land-grabbing carpetbaggers.*

carpet bowling *noun* *Cdn* an indoor game similar to lawn bowling, played with either round balls or asymmetrical bowls.

carpeting *noun* **1** material for carpets. **2** carpets collectively.

carpool *noun* an arrangement between people to travel together in a single vehicle, usu. with each member taking a turn at driving the others. ▶ **carpool** *verb* **carpooler** *noun* **carpooling** *noun*

carport *noun* a shelter with a roof and open sides for a car, usu. beside a house.

carpus *noun* (*plural* **carpi**) the small bones between the

forelimb and metacarpals in terrestrial vertebrates, forming the wrist in humans. [Say CARP iss for the singular, CARP eye for the plural]

carrageen *noun* an edible purplish-red seaweed of the northern hemisphere. [Say CARE a geen]

carrageenan *noun* (also **carrageenin**) a mixture of polysaccharides extracted from carrageen or similar seaweed and used as a gelling, thickening, and emulsifying agent in food products. [Say care a GEEN in]

SPELL CHECK ABC
carrel, carol

A song is a **carol**.

---

carrel *noun* a small cubicle or desk with high sides in a library, designed for individual study.

carriage *noun* **1** a wheeled passenger vehicle, esp. one with four wheels and pulled by horses. **2** = BABY CARRIAGE. **3 a** the conveying of goods. **b** the cost of this. **4** the part of a machine (e.g. a typewriter) that carries other parts into the required position. **5** (**gun carriage**) a wheeled support for a gun. **6** a person's bearing or deportment: *her carriage was graceful, her movements quick and deft.*

Carrier • *noun* (*plural* **Carrier** or **Carriers**) **1** a member of an Athapaskan people inhabiting the BC interior. **2** the Athapaskan language of this people. • *adjective* of or relating to this people or their language.

carrier *noun* **1** a person or thing that carries or in which something is carried. **2** a person or company undertaking to convey goods or passengers for payment. **3** a part of a bicycle etc. for carrying luggage or a passenger. **4** a person who delivers newspapers, flyers, etc. **5** a person or animal that may transmit a disease or a hereditary characteristic without suffering from or displaying it. **6** = AIRCRAFT CARRIER. **7** a substance used to support or convey a pigment, a catalyst, radioactive material, etc. **8** *Physics* a mobile electron or hole that carries a charge in a semiconductor. **9** (also **carrier wave**) a high-frequency electromagnetic wave modulated in amplitude or frequency to convey a signal.

carrier pigeon *noun* a homing pigeon trained to carry messages tied to its neck or leg.

carriole *noun* **1** a small open carriage for one person. **2** a covered light cart. **3** *Cdn hist.* **a** a horse-drawn sleigh with seats for a driver and often one or more passengers. **b** (*North*) a type of dogsled designed to carry a passenger or load in the front, with a rear platform for the driver to stand on. [Say CARRY ole]

carrion *noun* **1** dead rotting flesh. **2** something vile or filthy.

SPELL CHECK ABC
carrot, karat, carat

The purity of gold is measured in **karats**. Diamonds are measured in **carats**.

---

carrot *noun* **1 a** a cultivated plant of the parsley family, with feathery leaves and a tapering orange-coloured root. **b** this root as a vegetable. **2** a means of enticement or persuasion.

carrot-and-stick *noun* (used as an *adjective*) designating an approach etc. combining rewards for desirable behaviour and punishment for undesirable behaviour: *a carrot-and-stick policy.*

carry • *verb* (**carries, carried, carrying**) **1** support or hold up, esp. while moving. **2** convey with one from one place to another. **3** have on one's person. **4** conduct or transmit: *carries electric current.* **5** take (a process etc.) to a specified point. **6** (foll. by *to*) continue

or prolong. **7** involve, imply; have as a feature or consequence. **8** (in calculations) transfer (a figure) to a column of higher value. **9 a carry oneself** conduct oneself in a specified way, esp. in reference to one's bearing. **b** hold (a part of the body) in a specified way. **10 a** (of a newspaper or magazine) publish; include in its contents, esp. regularly. **b** (of a radio or television station) broadcast, esp. regularly. **11** (of a retailing outlet) keep a regular stock of (particular goods for sale). **12** make regular payments towards (a mortgage, loan, etc.). **13 a** (of sound, esp. a voice) be audible at a distance. **b** (of a missile) travel, penetrate. **14** (of a gun etc.) propel a specified distance. **15 a** win victory or acceptance for (a proposal etc.). **b** win acceptance from: *carried the audience with them*. **c** win, capture (a prize, a fortress, etc.). **d** win (a constituency) in an election. **e** *Golf* cause the ball to pass beyond (a bunker etc.). **16** *Football* attempt to gain yardage by rushing with the ball. **17 a** endure the weight of; support: *columns carry the dome*. **b** be the chief cause of the effectiveness of; be the driving force in. **18** be pregnant with: *is carrying twins*. **19 a** (of a motive, money, etc.) cause or enable (a person) to go to a specified place. **b** (of a journey) bring (a person) to a specified point. **20** sing (a tune) on pitch. • *noun* (*plural* **carries**) **1** an act of carrying. **2** *Golf* the distance a ball travels before reaching the ground. **3** a portage between rivers etc. **4** the range of a gun etc. **5** *Football* an act of rushing with the ball. PHRASES **carry all before one** succeed; overcome all opposition. **carry away 1** remove. **2** inspire; affect emotionally or spiritually. **3** deprive of self-control: *got carried away*. **carry back** take (a person) back in thought to a past time. **carry the can** *Cdn & Brit. informal* bear the responsibility or blame. **carry the day** be victorious or successful. **carry forward** transfer to a new page or account. **carry it off** (or **carry it off well**) do well under difficulties. **carry off 1** take away, esp. by force. **2** win (a prize). **3** (esp. of a disease) kill. **4** render acceptable or passable. **carry on 1** continue: *carry on eating*. **2** engage in (a conversation or a business). **3** *informal* behave strangely or excitedly. **4** (often foll. by *with*) *informal* flirt or have a love affair. **5** advance (a process) by a stage. **carry out 1** put (ideas, instructions, etc.) into practice. **2** perform or conduct (an investigation, test, etc.). **carry over** temporarily suspended and resumed later; postpone. **carry through 1** complete successfully. **2** bring safely out of difficulties. **carry weight** be influential or important. **carry with one** remember; bear in mind. **carryall** *noun* a large bag or case for carrying things. **carrying capacity** *noun* (*plural* **carrying capacities**) **1** the number of people or things that can be carried by a vehicle or on a road. **2** *Ecology* the number of people, animals, or crops that a region can support without environmental damage or degradation: *widespread famine in overpopulated areas where the carrying capacity of the land has been exceeded*. **carrying charge** *noun* **1** the interest on a loan etc. **2** an expense or effective cost arising from unproductive assets such as stored goods or unoccupied premises. **carrying-on** *noun* (also **carryings-on** *plural noun*) **1** a state of excitement or fuss. **2** a questionable piece of behaviour. **3** a flirtation or love affair. **carry-on** • *adjective* (of a suitcase etc.) suitable for carrying onto an airplane, bus, etc., rather than loading as checked baggage. • *noun* a carry-on suitcase. **carry-over** *noun* something transferred or resulting from a previous situation or context: *the slow trading was a carry-over from the big losses of last week*.

cart noun 1 a strong vehicle with two or four wheels

for carrying loads, drawn by a horse, ox, etc. **2** a light vehicle for pushing or pulling by hand: *shopping cart*. **3** a light vehicle with two wheels for driving in, drawn by a single horse. • *verb* **1** convey in or as in a cart. **2** *informal* carry (esp. a cumbersome thing) with difficulty or over a long distance: *carted it home*. PHRASES **cart off** remove, esp. by force or unceremoniously. **put the cart before the horse 1** reverse the proper order or procedure: *it is putting the cart before the horse to reduce taxes before we control the deficit*. **2** take an effect for a cause.

carte blanche *noun* complete freedom to act as one thinks best: *I was given carte blanche as to subject matter for the magazine*. [Say cart BLONSH]

cartel *noun* a group of manufacturers or suppliers with the purpose of maintaining prices at a high level, and controlling production, marketing arrangements, etc.: *the Colombian drug cartels*. [Say car TEL]

Cartesian • *adjective* of or relating to the French philosopher René Descartes (1596–1650), who felt that everything was open to doubt except his own existence, or to his mathematical methods. • *noun* a follower of Descartes. [Say car TEE zhin or car TEEZ yin]

Cartesian coordinates *plural noun* a system for locating a point by reference to its distance from two or three axes intersecting at right angles.

cartful *noun* (*plural* **cartfuls**) the amount of something that can fill a cart.

Carthusian • *noun* a Christian monk or nun of a strictly contemplative order founded in France in 1084, leading a way of life remarkable for its austerity and self-denial. • *adjective* of or relating to the Carthusians. [Say carth YOOZ ee in or carth OO zhin]

cartilage *noun* a firm, elastic, semi-opaque connective tissue of the vertebrate body. [Say CARTA lidge]

cartilaginous *adjective* made of cartilage: *cartilaginous tissue*. [Say carta LADGE uh niss]

cartographer *noun* a person who draws or makes maps. [Say car TOGRA fur]

cartographic *adjective* having to do with the science of drawing maps. ▶ **cartographical** *adjective* [Say carta GRAPH ick]

cartography *noun* the science or practice of map drawing. [Say car TOGRA fee]

carton *noun* **1** a light cardboard or plastic box or container. **2** the contents of a carton.

cartoon • *noun* **1** a humorous drawing in a newspaper, magazine, etc., esp. as a topical comment. **2** = COMIC STRIP. **3** a filmed sequence of drawings using the technique of animation. **4** an artist's full-size preliminary design for a painting, tapestry, mosaic, etc. • *verb* draw cartoons: *political cartooning*.

cartoonish *adjective* like a comic cartoon or its style, esp. by showing simplification or exaggeration of some features. ▶ **cartoonishly** *adverb*

cartoonist *noun* a person who draws cartoons.

cartoon-like *adjective* resembling a cartoon or a character in a cartoon: *cartoon-like features* ◊ *a cartoon-like painting*.

cartoony *adjective* resembling a comic cartoon.

cartridge *noun* **1** a case containing a charge of propelling explosive and a bullet or shot, used in firearms. **2** a spool of film, magnetic tape, etc., in a sealed container ready for insertion into a particular mechanism. **3** a container of ink, toner, etc., for insertion in a pen, printer, photocopier, etc.

cartwheel • *noun* **1** the (usu. spoked) wheel of a cart. **2** a circular sideways handspring with the arms and legs extended. • *verb* **1** perform cartwheels. **2** turn end over end.

carve verb (carves, carved, carving) 1 produce or

shape (a statue etc.) by cutting into a hard material. **2** cut patterns, designs, letters, etc. in (hard material). **3** cut (meat etc.) into slices for eating. **4** cut (a way, passage, etc.). PHRASES **carved in stone** (of a decision etc.) unchangeable. **carve out 1** take from a larger whole. **2** establish (a career etc.) purposefully: *carved out a name for themselves*. **carve (out) a niche** establish oneself in a particular area of a market etc. in order to excel. **carve up 1** divide into several pieces; subdivide (territory etc.). **2** cut (a person) with a knife. ▶ **carver** *noun*

carving *noun* a carved object, esp. as a work of art.

CAS *abbreviation* (in Canada) CHILDREN'S AID SOCIETY.

casaba *noun* (*plural* **casabas**) a melon with a yellow wrinkled skin and whitish flesh. [Say kuh SAW buh]

Casanova *noun* (*plural* **Casanovas**) a man notorious for seducing women. [Say cassa NO vuh]

CASBY *noun* (*plural* **CASBYs**) any of several awards presented annually to Canadian popular music performers, based on voting by the general public. [Say KAZ bee]

cascade • *noun* **1** a small waterfall, esp. forming one in a series or part of a large broken waterfall. **2 a** a succession of electrical devices or stages in a process. **b** a rapid sequence of events: *he envisions a cascade of mass extinctions*. **3** a quantity of material etc. draped in descending folds. **4** a thing that falls or hangs in a way suggestive of a waterfall: *cascades of blond hair*. • *verb* (**cascades**, **cascaded**, **cascading**) fall in or like a cascade.

cascara *noun* (also **cascara sagrada**) the dried bark of the western North American buckthorn, used as a laxative. [Say cass CAR uh (suh GRODDA)]

case¹ *noun* **1** an example of something occurring. **2** a state of affairs, hypothetical or actual. **3** the position or circumstances in which one is. **4 a** an instance of a person receiving professional guidance, e.g. from a doctor or social worker. **b** this person or the circumstances involved. **5** a matter under official investigation, esp. by the police. **6** *Law* **a** a cause or suit for trial. **b** a statement of the facts or evidence for a trial etc. **7** a set of arguments, e.g. in a lawsuit. **8** *Grammar* **a** the relation of a word to other words in a sentence. **b** a form of a noun, adjective, or pronoun expressing this. PHRASES **as the case may be** according to the situation. **get off** (or **on**) **one's case** *informal* stop (or start) harassing one. **in any case** whatever the truth is; whatever may happen. **in case 1** in the event that; if. **2** lest; in provision against a stated or implied possibility: *take an umbrella in case it rains*. **in case of** in the event of. **in the case of** as regards. **in no case** under no circumstances. **in that case** if that is true; should that happen. **is** (or **is not**) **the case** is (or is not) so.

case² • *noun* **1** a container or covering serving to enclose, hold, or contain. **2** a container with its contents. **3** an outer protective covering. **4** an item of luggage, esp. a suitcase. • *verb* (**cases**, **cased**, **casing**) **1** enclose in a case. **2** (foll. by *with*) surround. **3** *slang* reconnoitre (a house etc.) esp. with a view to robbery. PHRASES **have got it cased** *informal* have got everything under control.

case-harden *verb* **1** harden the surface of, esp. give a steel surface to (iron) by carbonizing. **2** make callous: *has our social conscience become toughened, even case-hardened?* ▶ **case-hardened** *adjective*

case history *noun* (*plural* **case histories**) information about a person for use in professional treatment, e.g. by a doctor.

casein *noun* **1** the main protein in milk, esp. in

coagulated form as in cheese. **2** this protein used in making plastics etc. [Say KAY seen or CASEY een]

case law *noun* the law as established by the outcome of former cases (*compare* COMMON LAW, STATUTE LAW).

caseload *noun* the cases with which a doctor etc. is concerned at one time.

casement *noun* a window or part of a window hinged vertically to open like a door.

case study *noun* (*plural* **case studies**) **1** an attempt to understand a person, institution, etc., from collected information. **2** a record of such an attempt. **3** the use of a particular instance of something used or analyzed in order to illustrate a thesis or principle: *Hurricane Andrew would make an excellent case study for understanding tropical cyclones*.

casework *noun* social work concerned with individuals, esp. involving understanding of the client's family and background. ▶ **caseworker** *noun*

SPELL CHECK
cash, cache

A hiding place or a small supply is a **cache**.

---

cash • *noun* **1** money in coins or banknotes, as distinct from cheques, money orders, or payment on credit. **2** (also **cash down**) money given as full payment at the time of purchase, as distinct from credit. **3** *informal* money. **4** *Cdn informal* = CASH REGISTER. • *verb* (**cashes**, **cashed**, **cashing**) give or obtain cash for (a note, cheque, etc.). PHRASES **cash in 1** obtain cash for. **2** *informal* (usu. foll. by *on*) profit (from); take advantage (of). **3** (also **cash in one's chips**) *informal* die. **cash out** count and check cash takings at the end of a day's business.

cash and carry • *adjective* (of a store, sale, etc.) operated on a system of cash payments, with no delivery available. • *noun* a store where this system operates.

cash cow *noun* *informal* a business, product, or operation that provides a steady and abundant cash flow.

cashew *noun* **1** a bushy evergreen tree, native to Central and South America, bearing kidney-shaped nuts attached to fleshy fruits. **2** the edible nut of this tree. [Say CASH oo or ka SHOO]

cash flow *noun* the movement of money as affecting liquidity or as a measure of profitability.

cashier¹ *noun* **1** a person handling customer payments in a store. **2** a person in charge of a bank's or company's cash.

cashier² *verb* dismiss from service, esp. from the armed forces with disgrace.

cashless *adjective* (of a society, economic system, etc.) functioning without cash, all financial transactions being executed electronically or by credit card.

cash machine *noun* = AUTOMATED TELLER MACHINE.

SPELL CHECK
cashmere, Kashmiri

A resident of a region of South Asia is a **Kashmiri**.

---

cashmere *noun* **1** a fine soft wool, esp. that of a Himalayan goat, the Kashmir goat. **2** a luxury material made from this.

cash on delivery *noun* a system of paying the carrier for goods when they are delivered.

cash register *noun* a machine in a store etc. with a drawer for money, recording the amount of each sale, totalling receipts, etc.

cashspiel *noun* *Cdn* a bonspiel in which curlers compete for cash prizes. [Say CASH speel]

cash-strapped *adjective* extremely short of money.

casing *noun* **1** a protective or enclosing cover or shell. **2** the material for this.

casino *noun* (*plural* **casinos**) a room or building for gambling at cards, roulette, slot machines, etc.

cask *noun* **1** a large barrel-like container made of wood, metal, or plastic, esp. one for alcoholic liquor. **2** its contents. **3** its capacity.

casket *noun* **1** a coffin. **2** a small often ornamental box or chest for jewels, letters, etc.

Cassandra *noun* a prophet of disaster, esp. one who is disregarded: *environmentalists are often dismissed as doomsaying Cassandras for their premature predictions of disaster.* [Say kuh SANDRA]

cassava *noun* (*plural* **cassavas**) **1 a** any plant of the genus *Manihot*, esp. the cultivated varieties, **bitter cassava** and **sweet cassava**, having starchy tuberous roots. **b** the roots themselves. **2** a starch or flour obtained from these roots. [Say kuh SAW vuh]

casse-croûte *noun* Cdn (Que.) a snack bar. [Say cass CROOT]

casserole *noun* **1** a covered dish, usu. of earthenware or glass, in which food is cooked, esp. in an oven. **2** food cooked in a casserole, esp. a savoury dish combining meat or fish, vegetables, pasta, sauce, etc.

cassette *noun* a sealed case containing a length of tape, ribbon, etc., ready for insertion in a machine, esp.: **1** a length of magnetic tape wound onto spools, ready for insertion in a tape recorder. **2** a length of photographic film, ready for insertion in a camera.

cassia *noun* (*plural* **cassias**) **1** any of various trees or shrubs of the genus *Cassia*, which yield a variety of products, including esp. senna. **2 a** (also **cassia bark**) the bark of an East Asian tree, which yields an inferior kind of cinnamon that is sometimes used to adulterate true cinnamon. **b** this tree. [Say CASSY uh or CASHA]

cassock *noun* a close-fitting garment with sleeves, fastened at the neck and reaching to the heels, worn under a surplice, alb, etc. by some clerics etc. [Say CASS ick]

cast • *verb* (**casts**, **cast**, **casting**) **1** throw, esp. deliberately or forcefully. **2** (often foll. by *on*, *over*) **a** direct or cause to fall (one's eyes, light, a shadow, a spell, etc.). **b** express (doubts, aspersions, etc.). **3** throw out (a fishing line) into the water. **4** let down (an anchor etc.). **5 a** throw off, get rid of. **b** shed (skin etc.) esp. in the process of growth. **6** record, register, or give (a vote). **7 a** shape (molten metal or plastic material) in a mould. **b** make (a product) in this way. **8** (of dogs etc.) search for a scent. **9** select a performer or performers for the roles in a play, film, etc.: *cast him as Hamlet* ◊ *the film is now being cast.* **10** Cdn (Nfld) catch (caplin) using a cast net. • *noun* **1** an act of throwing something. **b** the distance reached by this. **2** a throw or a number thrown at dice. **3** a throw of a net, fishing line, etc. **4** Fishing **a** that which is cast, esp. the line with hook, fly, etc. **b** a place for casting: *a good cast.* **5 a** an object of metal, clay, etc., made in a mould. **b** a moulded mass of solidified material, esp. plaster protecting a broken limb. **6** the performers taking part in a play, film, etc. **7** form, type, or quality: *cast of mind*. **8** a tinge or shade of colour. **9** a mass of earth excreted by a worm. **PHRASES** **cast about** (or **around** or **round**) make an extensive search (actually or mentally): *cast about for a solution*. **cast adrift** leave to drift. **cast ashore** (of waves etc.) throw to the shore. **cast aside** give up using; abandon. **cast away 1** reject. **2** shipwreck: *he was cast away on a desert island*. **cast in stone** (of a decision etc.) irrevocably set. **cast loose** detach; detach oneself. **cast one's mind back** think back; recall an earlier time. cast a wide net (or a wide net)...

wide) cover a wide field of supply, activity, inquiry, etc. **cast off 1** abandon. **2** Knitting take the stitches off the needle by looping each over the next to finish the edge. **3 a** set a ship free from a quay etc. **b** loosen and throw off (rope etc.). **cast on** Knitting make the first row of loops on the needle. **cast out** expel. **cast up** (of water) deposit (something) on the shore.

castanets *plural noun* a pair of shell-shaped pieces of wood or ivory clicked together with the fingers, esp. as a rhythmic accompaniment to Spanish dance.

castaway • *noun* **1** a shipwrecked person. **2** an outcast; a drifter. **3** a castoff: *the wicker basket was a castaway from the Chinese food store*. • *adjective* **1** shipwrecked. **2** cast aside; rejected.

caste *noun* **1** any of the Hindu hereditary classes whose members have no social contact with other classes, but are socially equal with one another and often follow the same occupations. There are four basic classes in Hindu society: priest, warrior, merchant or farmer, and labourer: *members of the lower castes*. **2** a more or less exclusive social class: *those educated in private schools belong to a privileged caste*. **3** (also **caste system**) a system of such classes. **PHRASES** **lose caste** descend in the social order. ▶ **casteism** *noun* [Say CAST, CAST ism]

caster *noun* **1** a person who casts. **2** a small swivelled wheel (often one of a set) fixed to a leg (or the underside) of a piece of furniture. **3** a small container with holes in the top for sprinkling the contents: *sugar caster*. ▶ **castered** *adjective* (in sense 2).

castigate *verb* (**castigates**, **castigated**, **castigating**) rebuke or punish severely: *political parties alternately woo and castigate the media*.

Castilian • *noun* **1** a native of Castile, a region in central Spain. **2** the language of Castile, standard spoken and literary Spanish. • *adjective* of or relating to Castile. [Say ka STILLY in]

casting *noun* **1** an object made by casting, esp. of molten metal. **2** the action of allocating roles to performers. **3** the list of roles with the performers assigned to them. **4** the action of throwing out a fishing line into the water.

cast iron • *noun* a hard alloy of iron, carbon, and silicon cast in a mould. • *adjective* (also **cast-iron**) **1** made of cast iron. **2** unassailable, unchangeable.

castle • *noun* **1 a** a large fortified building or group of buildings. **b** a formerly fortified mansion. **2** Chess = ROOK. • *verb* (**castles**, **castled**, **castling**) Chess make a special move (once only in a game on each side) in which the king is moved two squares along the back rank and the nearer rook is moved to the square passed over by the king. **PHRASES** **castles in the air** (or **in Spain**) a visionary unattainable scheme; a daydream.

cast net *noun* Fishing a net thrown out and immediately drawn in.

castoff • *adjective* abandoned, discarded. • *noun* a castoff person or thing.

castor[1] *noun* = CASTER 2,3.

castor[2] *noun* (also **castoreum**) a pungent, bitter, reddish-brown substance secreted by beavers, formerly used in medicine and perfumes. [Say cass TORY um]

castor gras *noun* hist. a beaver pelt used as clothing to soften it and to allow the long hairs to fall out, valuable during the fur trade. [Say caster GRAW]

castor oil *noun* a pale yellow oil obtained from the seeds of an African shrub, used as a purgative and lubricant.

castrate *verb* (**castrates**, **castrated**, **castrating**) **1** remove the testicles of. **2** deprive of vigour or power: *when we separate ourselves from nature, something in us is castrated*. ▶ **castration** *noun*

casual • *adjective* **1** accidental; due to chance: *he pretended it was a casual meeting.* **2** not regular or permanent; temporary, occasional: *casual work.* **3 a** unconcerned, uninterested: *was very casual about it.* **b** made or done without great care or thought: *a casual remark.* **c** acting carelessly or unmethodically: *the shockingly casual way in which victims were treated.* **4** (of clothes, social events, etc.) informal, relaxed. **5** (of sexual activity) happening between individuals who are not regular or established sexual partners. • *noun* **1** a casual worker. **2** (usu. in *plural*) casual clothes or shoes. ▶ **casually** *adverb* **casualness** *noun*

casualty *noun* (*plural* **casualties**) **1** a person killed or injured in a war or accident. **2** a thing lost, badly affected, or destroyed: *the champagne flutes were a casualty of the move* ◊ *the building industry was a casualty of the recession.*

casuistry *noun* the use of clever but unsound reasoning, esp. in relation to moral questions.

CAT *abbreviation* Medical COMPUTERIZED AXIAL TOMOGRAPHY.

Cat *noun* proprietary = CATERPILLAR 2b.

cat *noun* **1 a** small soft-furred four-legged domesticated animal. **2** any wild animal of the genus *Felis*, e.g. a lion, tiger, or leopard. **3** a catlike animal of any other species: *civet cat.* **4** *informal* a malicious or spiteful woman. **5** *slang* **a** a person; a fellow: *cool cat.* **b** a jazz enthusiast. **6** = CATFISH. PHRASES **cat got your tongue?** *informal* don't you have anything to say? **cat's whiskers** (or **pyjamas** or **meow** or *Cdn* **ass**) *informal* an excellent person or thing. **first** (or **last**) **kick at the cat** one's first (or last) opportunity to do something. **let the cat out of the bag** reveal a secret, esp. involuntarily. **like a cat on a hot tin roof** (or **on hot bricks**) very agitated or agitatedly. **put** (or **set**) **the cat among the pigeons** cause trouble. **rain cats and dogs** rain very hard.

cataclysm *noun* **1 a** a violent, esp. social or political, upheaval or disaster. **b** a great change. **2** a great flood or deluge. ▶ **cataclysmic** *adjective* **cataclysmically** *adverb* [Say CATTA clism, catta KLIZZ mick]

catacomb *noun* (often in *plural*) an underground cemetery, esp. a Roman subterranean gallery with recesses for tombs. [Say CATTA comb]

Catalan • *noun* **1** a native of the region of Catalonia on the Mediterranean coast of Spain near France, the capital of which is Barcelona. **2** the Romance language of Catalonia, closely related to Castilian Spanish and Provençal. • *adjective* of or relating to Catalonia or its people or language. [Say CATTA lan]

catalepsy *noun* a state of trance or seizure with loss of sensation and consciousness accompanied by rigidity of the body. [Say CATTA lep see]

cataleptic *adjective & noun* suffering from catalepsy. [Say catta LEP tick]

catalogue • *noun* **1** a complete list of items (e.g. articles for sale, books held by a library), usu. in alphabetical or other systematic order and often with a description of each. **2** an extensive list: *a catalogue of crimes.* • *verb* (**catalogues**, **catalogued**, **cataloguing**) **1** make a catalogue of. **2** enter in a catalogue. ▶ **cataloguer** *noun*

catalpa *noun* (*plural* **catalpas**) a tree with heart-shaped leaves, trumpet-shaped flowers, and long pods. [Say kuh TAL puh]

catalyst *noun* **1** Chemistry a substance that, without itself undergoing any permanent chemical change, increases the rate of a reaction. **2** a person or thing that precipitates a change: *global warming may be a catalyst for desirable changes in economic policies.* [Say CATTA list]

catalytic *adjective* Chemistry relating to or involving the acceleration of a reaction by a catalyst. [Say catta LIT ick]

catalytic converter *noun* a device fitted in the exhaust system of some motor vehicles which converts pollutant gases into less harmful ones.

catalyze *verb* (**catalyzes**, **catalyzed**, **catalyzing**) (also **catalyse**; **catalyses**, **catalysed**, **catalysing**) **1** produce (a reaction) by the action of a catalyst. **2** cause an action or process to begin. [Say CATTA lize]

catamaran *noun* **1** a boat with twin hulls in parallel. **2** a raft of yoked logs or boats. **3** *Cdn* (*Nfld*) a heavy sled used for hauling wood. [Say CATTA muh RAN]

cat and mouse *noun* a situation in which two opponents engage in prolonged wary manoeuvres: *a long-term game of cat and mouse between NATO and the Serbs.*

catapult • *noun* **1** *hist.* a military machine worked by a lever and ropes for hurling large stones etc. **2** a mechanical device for launching a glider, an aircraft from the deck of a ship, etc. • *verb* **1** move suddenly and unexpectedly from one state or situation to another: *their debut single catapulted them to the top of the charts.* **2** hurl from or launch with a catapult: *the plane was catapulted back into the air.* **3** leap, hurl, or be hurled forcibly: *the explosion catapulted the car across the road.*

cataract *noun* **1 a** a large waterfall or cascade. **b** a downpour; a rush of water. **2 a** a disease in which the lens of the eye becomes cloudy, causing partial or total blindness. **b** an area clouded in this way.

catarrh *noun* **1** inflammation of the mucous membrane of the nose, air passages, etc. **2** a watery discharge in the nose or throat due to this. ▶ **catarrhal** *adjective* [Say kuh TAR, kuh TAR ul]

catastrophe *noun* a great and usu. sudden disaster. ▶ **catastrophic** *adjective* **catastrophically** *adverb* [Say kuh TASS truh fee, cat iss TROFF ick]

catatonic • *adjective* **1** not able to move or show any reaction to things because of illness, shock, etc.: *certain catatonic manifestations are seen in Parkinsonism.* **2** inert or unemotional: *trying to breathe life into the catatonic film industry.* • *noun* a person in a catatonic state. [Say catta TONIC]

cat burglar *noun* a burglar who enters by climbing to an upper storey.

catcall • *noun* a shrill whistle of disapproval made at sports events, concerts, etc. • *verb* make a catcall.

catch • *verb* (**catches**, **caught**, **catching**) **1 a** lay hold of so as to restrain or prevent from escaping; capture in a trap, in one's hands, etc. **b** (also **catch hold of**) get into one's hands so as to retain, operate, etc. **2** detect or surprise (a person, esp. in a wrongful or embarrassing act). **3** intercept and hold (a moving thing) in the hands etc. **4 a** contract (a disease) by infection or contagion. **b** acquire (a quality or feeling) from another's example. **5 a** reach in time and board (an airplane, bus, etc.). **b** be in time to see etc. (a person or thing about to leave or finish). **6 a** attend. **b** meet with. **7** apprehend: *do you catch my meaning?* **8** (of an artist etc.) reproduce faithfully. **9 a** become fixed or entangled; be checked. **b** cause to do this. **c** hit, deal a blow to: *caught him on the nose.* **10** draw the attention of. **11 a** begin to burn. **b** (of an engine) start. **12** capture and absorb or reflect (light). **13** be the recipient of: *catch hell.* **14** (often foll. by *up*) reach or overtake (a person etc. ahead). **15** check suddenly: *caught her breath.* **16** (foll. by *at*) grasp or try to grasp. **17 catch oneself** stop (oneself) just in time: *caught myself before I said it.* • *noun* (*plural* **catches**) **1 a** an act of catching. **b** *Baseball* a chance or act of catching the ball. **2 a** an amount of a thing caught, esp. of fish. **b** a thing or person caught or worth catching, esp. in marriage. **3** a game in which a ball is thrown back and forth between two or more players. **4 a a** question, trick, etc.,

C

intended to deceive, incriminate, etc. **b** an unexpected or hidden difficulty or disadvantage. **5** a device for fastening a door, window, bag, etc. **6** a check or impediment in the voice, breath, throat, etc. **7** a snag in a sweater etc. **8** a fragment of a song. PHRASES **catch-as-catch-can 1** a style of wrestling with few holds barred. **2** a situation where there are no rules; a free-for-all. **catch it** slang be punished or in trouble. **catch on** informal **1** (of a practice, fashion, etc.) become popular. **2** (of a person) understand what is meant. **catch out 1** detect in a mistake etc. **2** take unawares; cause to be bewildered or confused. **catch up 1 a** (often foll. by with) reach a person etc. ahead. **b** (often foll. by with, on) make up arrears (of work etc.). **2** snatch or pick up hurriedly. **3** (often in passive) **a** involve; entangle. **b** fasten up.

catch-22 noun (plural **catch-22s**) a dilemma or circumstance from which there is no escape because of mutually conflicting or dependent conditions: the catch-22 situation of looking for a job when you have no experience.

catch-all noun a thing designed to be all-inclusive: a catch-all phrase.

catch basin noun **1 a** a storm sewer or artificial pond for catching excess rainwater. **b** a receptacle to trap debris before it enters a storm sewer. **2** an area or organization which attracts people of a specific kind: London had become a catch basin for its landless rural poor.

catcher noun **1** a person or thing that catches. **2** Baseball the fielder positioned behind home plate.

catchiness noun the quality of a song, jingle, etc. that is instantly appealing and memorable.

catching adjective **1** (of a disease) infectious. **2** (of a practice, habit, etc.) likely to be imitated: Jasmine's enthusiasm is catching.

catchment noun **1** the act or process of collecting water. **2** a place where water is collected. **3** (also **catchment area**) **a** the area from which rainfall flows into a river etc. **b** the area served by a school, hospital, etc.

catchphrase noun a phrase or slogan in frequent use.

catch-up noun the act of attempting to reach someone or something which is ahead. PHRASES **play catch-up** attempt to overtake an opponent or competitor.

catchword noun **1** a word or phrase in common (often temporary) use; a topical slogan. **2** a word placed so as to draw attention. **3** Theatre an actor's cue.

catchy adjective (**catchier**, **catchiest**) (of a tune, phrase, etc.) easy to remember.

catechetical adjective (also **catechetic**) **1** of or by oral teaching. **2** according to the catechism of a Christian religion. **3** consisting of or proceeding by question and answer. [Say catta KETTA cull]

catechism noun **1 a** a summary of the principles of a Christian religion in the form of questions and answers. **b** a book containing this. **2 a** a series of questions put to anyone. [Say CATTA kism]

catechist noun a teacher giving oral instruction in Christianity by means of a catechism. [Say CATTA kist]

catechize verb (**catechizes**, **catechized**, **catechizing**) **1** instruct by means of question and answer, esp. from a catechism. **2** put questions to; examine. [Say CATTA kize]

catechumen noun a Christian convert under instruction before baptism. [Say catta CUE min]

categorical adjective unconditional, absolute: a categorical refusal. ▶ **categorically** adverb

categorization noun placement in a particular class or group: the categorization of participants according to age.

categorize verb (**categorizes**, **categorized**, **categorizing**) place in a category or categories.

category noun (plural **categories**) **1** a class or division. **2** Philosophy **a** one of a possibly exhaustive set of classes among which all things might be distributed. **b** any relatively fundamental philosophical concept.

cater verb **1** provide food, drink, etc. for a reception etc.: catered a lunch for 20 people. **2 a** provide for; meet the needs of: the school caters for children with learning disabilities. **b** try to satisfy a particular demand etc.: she catered to his every whim. ▶ **caterer** noun **catering** noun

caterpillar noun **1 a** the larva of a butterfly or moth. **b** (in general use) any similar larva of various insects. **2 a** an endless jointed steel tread passing around the wheels of a tractor etc. for travel on rough ground. **b** (**Caterpillar**) proprietary a vehicle equipped with these treads.

caterwaul • verb make the shrill howl of a cat. • noun a caterwauling noise. [Say CATTER wall]

cat fight noun **1** a dispute in which the participants are spiteful, malicious, and unrestrained. **2** a malicious fight or dispute between women. **3** a fight between cats.

catfish noun (plural same) any of numerous fishes having whisker-like barbels around the mouth.

catgut noun a material made from the twisted intestines of a sheep, horse, or other animal, and used to make the strings of musical instruments, racquets, and surgical sutures.

catharsis noun (plural **catharses**) **1** a release or relieving of emotions, esp. through drama or art: the ancient Greeks believed that seeing strong emotions and horrific events in the theatre provided the audience with catharsis. **2** Psychology the process of freeing and eliminating repressed emotion. [Say kuh THARSE iss for the singular, ku THARSE eez for the plural]

cathartic • adjective **1** providing psychological relief through the open expression of strong emotions: a good cry is very cathartic. **2** strongly laxative. • noun a laxative drug. ▶ **cathartically** adverb [Say ku THART ick]

cathedral noun the principal church of a diocese, containing the bishop's throne.

catheter noun a tube for insertion into a body cavity or blood vessel for introducing or removing fluid etc., esp. one inserted in the bladder to remove urine. [Say CATH a tur]

cathode noun **1** the negative electrode in an electrolytic cell or electronic valve or tube. **2** the positive terminal of a primary cell such as a battery (opp. ANODE). [Say CATH ode]

cathode ray noun a beam of electrons emitted from the cathode of a high-vacuum tube.

cathode ray tube noun a high-vacuum tube in which cathode rays produce a luminous image on a fluorescent screen, used in televisions etc. Abbreviation: **CRT**.

catholic • adjective **1** (**Catholic**) of the Roman Catholic religion. **2** pertaining to the ancient Church before the great schism between East and West, or the Western Church after the schism and before the Reformation, or to any Church standing in historical continuity with it. **3** all-embracing; of wide sympathies or interests: she has catholic tastes; she likes everything. • noun (**Catholic**) a Roman Catholic.

Catholicism noun the faith, practice, and church order of the Roman Catholic Church. [Say kuh THOLLA sism]

Catholic Reformation noun = COUNTER-REFORMATION.

cation noun a positively charged ion; an ion that is attracted to the cathode in electrolysis (opp. ANION). ▶ **cationic** adjective [Say CAT eye in, CAT eye ON ick]

catkin *noun* a spike of usu. downy or silky flowers hanging from a willow, hazel, or other tree.

catlike *adjective* **1** like a cat. **2** stealthy.

cat litter *noun* granular absorbent material, usu. clay, put in a box for a cat to urinate and defecate in indoors.

catnap • *noun* a short sleep. • *verb* (**catnaps, catnapped, catnapping**) have a catnap.

catnip *noun* a white-flowered herb of the mint family, having a smell attractive to cats.

CAT scan *noun* a medical examination using an X-ray apparatus which produces a series of detailed cross-sectional pictures of internal organs, esp. the brain.
▶ **CAT scanner** *noun*

cat's cradle *noun* a child's game in which a loop of string is held between the fingers and patterns are formed.

cattail *noun* = BULRUSH 2.

cattily *adverb* in a catty or deliberately hurtful manner.

cattiness *noun* a catty manner or tone; spitefulness.

cattle *plural noun* large ruminant animals with horns and cloven hoofs, e.g. cows, bison, and buffalo.

cattle guard *noun* a ditch covered by metal bars spaced so as to allow vehicles and pedestrians to pass over but not cattle or other animals.

cattleman *noun* (*plural* **cattlemen**) a person who tends or rears cattle.

cat train *noun* *Cdn* (*North*) a series of linked freight-carrying sleds hauled over snow by a tractor equipped with caterpillar treads.

catty *adjective* (**cattier, cattiest**) **1** sly, spiteful; deliberately hurtful. **2** catlike.

catwalk *noun* **1** a narrow footway along a bridge, above a theatre stage, etc. **2** a narrow platform along which models walk during a fashion show.

Caucasian • *adjective* **1** of or relating to the white or light-skinned race of humans originally inhabiting Europe, N Africa, and the Middle East. **2** of or relating to the Caucasus region between the Black Sea and the Caspian Sea or its people. **3** of or relating to the non-Indo-European languages of this region, e.g. Georgian. • *noun* a Caucasian person. [Say caw KAY zhun]

caucus *noun* (*plural* **caucuses**) **1 a** the members of a legislature belonging to a particular party. **b** a subgroup of these comprising the members from a particular region. **c** a closed-door meeting of either of these groups to discuss policy etc. **2** a group sharing common political goals, esp. a faction within a larger group. **3** a usu. secret meeting of a small group of people to discuss matters concerning a larger group. [Say CAW cuss]

caught *past and past participle of* CATCH.

caul *noun* **1 a** the inner membrane enclosing a fetus. **b** part of this occasionally found on a child's head at birth, thought to bring good luck. **2 a** a fold of tissue connecting the stomach with other organs. **b** this tissue in cattle, pigs, and other animals, used as food. [Sounds like CALL]

cauldron *noun* **1** a large deep bowl-shaped vessel for boiling over an open fire. **2** a situation marked by instability and strong emotions: *a cauldron of repressed anger.*

cauliflower *noun* **1** a variety of cabbage with a large white flower head of immature buds in its centre. **2** the flower head eaten as a vegetable.

caulk¹ • *verb* **1** fill (a seam, crack, etc.) with a watertight or airtight material. **2** make (esp. a boat or window) watertight or airtight by this method. • *noun* (also **caulking**) a substance used to caulk. [Sounds like COCK]

caulk² • *noun* **1** a small spike fitted to the sole of a boot to resist slipping. **2** (also **caulk boot**) a boot equipped with such spikes, used esp. by loggers. • *verb* furnish (a boot) with caulks. [Sounds like COCK or CORK]

causal *adjective* **1** of, forming, or expressing a cause or causes: *the causal factors associated with illness.* **2** relating to, or of the nature of, cause and effect.

causality *noun* **1** the relation of cause and effect. **2** the principle that everything has a cause.

causally *adverb* displaying a relationship of cause and effect: *it is hard to know whether the two phenomena are causally linked.*

causation *noun* **1** the act of causing or producing an effect. **2** = CAUSALITY.

causative *adjective* **1** acting as cause: *a causative factor.* **2** (foll. by *of*) producing; having as effect. **3** *Grammar* expressing cause.

cause • *noun* **1 a** that which produces an effect, or gives rise to an action, phenomenon, or condition. **b** a person or thing that occasions something. **c** a reason or motive; a ground that may be held to justify something: *no cause for complaint.* **2** a reason considered adequate: *he was asked to show cause why he shouldn't be held in contempt of court.* **3** a principle, belief, or purpose which is advocated or supported: *faithful to the cause.* **4 a** a matter to be settled at law. **b** an individual's case offered at law. **5** the side taken by any party in a dispute. • *verb* (**causes, caused, causing**) be the cause of, produce, make happen: *caused a commotion* ◊ *caused me to smile.* PHRASES **cause and effect 1** a cause and the effect it produces; the doctrine of causation. **2** the operation or relation of a cause and its effect. **in the cause of** to maintain, defend, or support: *in the cause of justice.* **make common cause with** join the side of.

cause célèbre *noun* (*plural* **causes célèbres**) a lawsuit or controversial issue that attracts much attention: *female genital mutilation has become an international cause célèbre.* [Say koz suh LEB or koze say LEBRA]

causeway *noun* **1** a raised road or track across low or wet ground or water. **2** a raised path by a road.

caustic • *adjective* **1** capable of burning or corroding organic tissue: *caustic household cleaners.* **2** sarcastic in a scathing and bitter way: *the players were making caustic comments about the refereeing* ◊ *caustic wit.* • *noun* a caustic substance. ▶ **caustically** *adverb* [Say KOSS tick]

caution • *noun* **1** attention to safety; prudence, carefulness. **2** a warning. **3** *Cdn, Brit., & Austral.* a warning to an arrested person that his or her statements may be used as evidence in court. **4** *informal* an amusing or surprising person or thing: *"That Maggie's a caution," said Lloyd. "She means no harm".* • *verb* **1** warn or admonish: *I would caution against making any hasty decisions* ◊ *she cautioned him not to go.* **2** *Cdn, Brit., & Austral. Law* issue a caution to. PHRASES **throw caution to the wind** act imprudently or rashly, esp. intentionally.

cautionary *adjective* giving or serving as a warning.

cautious *adjective* careful. ▶ **cautiously** *adverb* **cautiousness** *noun*

cavalcade *noun* a procession of riders, vehicles, etc.

cavalier • *noun* **1** a gallant or fashionable man, esp. escorting a woman. **2** *hist.* (**Cavalier**) a supporter of Charles I in the English Civil War (1642–9). • *adjective* showing a lack of proper concern: *Anne was irritated by his cavalier attitude.* ▶ **cavalierly** *adverb* [Say cava LEER]

cavalry *noun* (*plural* **cavalries**) (usu. treated as *plural*) **1** soldiers on horseback. **2** soldiers in armoured vehicles. [Say CAV ul ree]

cave • *noun* **1** a large natural underground hollow, esp. with a roughly horizontal opening. **2** a cellar for

storing wine etc. • *verb* (**caves, caved, caving**) explore caves, esp. interconnecting or underground. PHRASES **cave in 1 a** (of a wall, earth over a hollow, etc.) subside, collapse. **b** cause (a wall, earth, etc.) to do this. **2** yield or submit under pressure; give up.

caveat *noun* **1** a warning or proviso of specific stipulations, conditions, or limitations. **2** *Law* a notice entered in a legal registry advising a court official to halt a specific proceeding until the party entering the notice has been contacted. [Say CAV ee at]

caveat emptor *noun* the principle that the buyer alone is responsible if dissatisfied; "buyer beware". [Say cav ee at EMP tore]

cave-in *noun* **1** a collapse of a roof or similar structure, typically underground: *a mine cave-in.* **2** yielding or submitting under pressure: *the government's cave-in to pressure from the airline industry.*

caveman *noun* (*plural* **cavemen**) a prehistoric human, esp. one using a cave as shelter.

cavern *noun* an underground hollow; a vast cave.

cavernous *adjective* of or resembling a cavern in size or appearance: *a cavernous hall.* ▶ **cavernously** *adverb*

caviar *noun* the pickled roe of sturgeon or other large fish, eaten as a delicacy. [Say CAV ee arr]

cavil • *verb* (**cavils, cavilled, cavilling**) make petty or unnecessary objections: *many critics cavilled at the show's lack of scholarly underpinning.* • *noun* a trivial objection. [Say CAV ul]

caving *noun* the exploration of caves as a sport or recreation.

cavity *noun* (*plural* **cavities**) **1** a hollow within a solid body. **2** a decayed part of a tooth.

cavort *verb* **1** jump, dance, or behave excitedly or happily: *the dogs cavorted about the stage with the actors.* **2** apply oneself enthusiastically to sexual or disreputable pursuits: *she was pictured cavorting topless in the south of France with her financial advisor.*

caw • *noun* the harsh cry of a crow, raven, etc. • *verb* utter this cry.

cayenne *noun* (also **cayenne pepper**) a very spicy red powder obtained from ground dried chile peppers. [Say kie YEN or KIE yen or kay EN or KAY en]

Cayuga *noun* (*plural* **Cayuga** or **Cayugas**) **1** a member of an Iroquoian people originally inhabiting central New York State, now living mainly on the Six Nations reserve near Brantford, Ont. **2** the Iroquoian language of this people. ▶ **Cayugan** *adjective* [Say kay OOGA]

CB *abbreviation* (*plural* **CBs**) citizens' band (radio).

CBC *abbreviation* Canadian Broadcasting Corporation.

CBD *abbreviation* (*plural* **CBDs**) CENTRAL BUSINESS DISTRICT.

CC *abbreviation* Companion of the Order of Canada.

cc • *abbreviation* (also **c.c.**) **1** cubic centimetre(s). **2** carbon copy. • *noun* (*plural* **cc's**) a cubic centimetre.

CCD *abbreviation* (*plural* **CCDs**) CHARGE-COUPLED DEVICE.

CCF *abbreviation* Cdn hist. CO-OPERATIVE COMMONWEALTH FEDERATION. ▶ **CCFer** *noun*

CD¹ *abbreviation* **1** Civil Defence. **2** *Corps Diplomatique.*

CD² *noun* (*plural* **CDs**) a compact disc.

Cd *symbol* cadmium.

cd *abbreviation* candela.

Cdn. *abbreviation* Canadian.

CD-ROM *noun* a compact disc with read-only memory (for storage and retrieval of text or data on a computer).

CE *abbreviation* **1** civil engineer. **2** (**CE**) Common Era.

Ce *symbol* cerium.

cease *verb* (**ceases, ceased, ceasing**) stop; bring or come to an end: *ceased to exist.* PHRASES **without cease** continually, unrelentingly.

ceasefire *noun* Military **1** an order to stop firing. **2** a period of truce; a suspension of hostilities

ceaseless *adjective* without end; not ceasing. ▶ **ceaselessly** *adverb*

cecum *noun* (*plural* **ceca**) a pouch-like cavity at the junction of the small and large intestines. [Say SEEK um for the singular, SEEKA for the plural]

cedar *noun* **1** any of various evergreen conifers native to the region from the eastern Mediterranean to central Asia, having tufts of short needles and cones of papery scales. **2** any of various similar conifers yielding timber, including species of arborvitae, cypress, and juniper. **3** (also **cedarwood**) the fragrant durable wood of any cedar tree, often used to line closets, for fencing or siding, etc.

cedar shake *noun* a type of cedar shingle.

cedarstrip *noun* Cdn a technique for making boats, esp. canoes, of long strips of cedar: *cedarstrip canoe.*

cede *verb* (**cedes, ceded, ceding**) **1** give up one's rights to or possession of: *Sioux have never been included in Canada's treaties, as they did not cede lands in this country* ◊ *ceded her place to her colleague.* **2** transfer possession of: *about one-half of Canada's lands have been formally ceded by Aboriginal peoples to the government.*

cedilla *noun* (*plural* **cedillas**) a mark written under the letter *c* in French and Portuguese to show that it sounds like an "s" (as in *façade*). [Say suh DILLA]

CEF *abbreviation* hist. Canadian Expeditionary Force.

CEGEP *abbreviation* (also **Cegep**) (in Quebec) Collège d'enseignement général et professionnel, a post-secondary educational institution offering two-year programs for preparation for university and three-year training programs in professions and trades. [Say SEE jep or SAY zhep]

ceilidh *noun* **1** a party featuring traditional Celtic music, dancing, songs, and stories. **2** a concert at which traditional Scottish music and dancing are performed. [Say KAY lee]

ceiling *noun* **1 a** the upper interior surface of a room or other similar compartment. **b** the material forming this. **2** an upper limit on prices, wages, performance, etc. **3** *Aviation* the maximum altitude a given aircraft can reach. **4** the altitude of the base of a cloud layer. ▶ **ceilinged** *adjective* (in combination).

ceinture fléchée *noun* (*plural* **ceintures fléchées**) Cdn hist. a long, brightly coloured sash woven with an arrow-shaped pattern and worn around the waist, esp. by voyageurs. [Say san tyoor flay SHAY]

cel *noun* a transparent sheet of celluloid etc. which can be drawn on and used in combination with others in the production of animated films.

celeb *noun* informal a celebrity.

celebrant *noun* **1** a person who performs a rite, esp. a priest who officiates at the Eucharist: *the bishop was the principal celebrant.* **2** a person participating in a celebration: *swaying from side to side like celebrants at an Oktoberfest.* **3** a person who celebrates or praises someone or something: *a celebrant of Mediterranean cuisine.* [Say SELLA brunt]

celebrate *verb* (**celebrates, celebrated, celebrating**) **1** mark (a festival or special event) with festivities etc. **2** engage in festivities, usu. after a special event etc. **3** perform publicly and duly (a religious ceremony etc.). **4 a** officiate at (the Eucharist). **b** officiate, esp. at the Eucharist. **5** honour or praise publicly: *a film celebrating the actor's career.*

celebrated *adjective* publicly honoured, widely known.

celebration *noun* the action of marking one's pleasure at an important event or occasion by engaging in enjoyable, usu. social, activity: *a birthday celebration* ◊ *the birth of his son was a cause for celebration.*

celebratory *adjective* celebrating something or marking a special occasion: *a celebratory dinner*.

celebrity *noun* (*plural* **celebrities**) **1** a well-known person. **2** fame: *Natalie's prestige and celebrity grew*. ▶ **celebrityhood** *noun* [Say suh LEB ruh tee]

celery *noun* a plant of the parsley family with closely packed succulent leaf stalks used as a vegetable.

celestial *adjective* **1** heavenly; divinely good or beautiful; sublime. **2 a** of the sky; of the part of the sky commonly observed in astronomy etc. **b** of heavenly bodies. [Say suh LESS chull]

celestial equator *noun* the projection into space of the earth's equator.

celiac *adjective* **1** of or pertaining to the abdominal cavity. **2** afflicted with celiac disease. [Say SEELY ack]

celiac disease *noun* a digestive disorder of the small intestine, causing chronic failure to digest food properly unless gluten is excluded from the diet.

celibacy *noun* a celibate state; abstinence from sex and marriage. [Say SELLA buh see]

celibate ● *adjective* **1** committed to abstinence from sexual relations and from marriage, esp. for religious reasons. **2** abstaining from sex. ● *noun* a celibate person. [Say SELLA bit]

cell *noun* **1** a small room, esp. in a prison or monastery. **2** a compartment, e.g. in a honeycomb. **3** a small group operating as a local branch of a political movement, esp. of a subversive kind. **4** a location or address where a piece of information is stored, esp. in a spreadsheet or database. **5** the local area covered by one of the short-range radio transmitters in a cellular telephone system. **6 a** the basic structural and functional unit of an organism, usu. microscopic, consisting of cytoplasm and a nucleus enclosed in a membrane. **b** an enclosed cavity in an organism etc. **7 a** a battery or other device for generating electricity or producing electrolysis from chemical energy. **b** = SOLAR CELL. **8** an atmospheric mass with roughly uniform properties: *high-pressure cell* ◊ *a storm cell*. **9** a cellular phone.

cellar ● *noun* **1** a room below ground level in a house, often used for storage of food and wine. **2** a stock of wine in a cellar: *has a good cellar*. **3** *Sport informal* = BASEMENT 2. ● *verb* store or put in a cellar.

cellblock *noun* one of several sections of cells into which a large prison is divided.

cellist *noun* a person who plays the cello. [Say CHELL ist]

cello *noun* (*plural* **cellos**) the second-largest instrument of the violin family, held upright on the floor between the knees of the seated player. [Say CHELLO]

Cellophane *noun* *proprietary* a thin transparent packaging material made from viscose. [Say SELLA fane]

cellular ● *adjective* **1** of or having small compartments or cavities. **2** of or consisting of biological cells: *cellular proliferation*. **3** (of a plant) having no distinct stem, leaves, etc. **4** (of a telephone system) using a number of short-range radio transmitters to cover a large area, the signal being switched from one transmitter to the next as the user travels. ● *noun* **1** a cellular telephone. **2** a cellular telephone system. [Say SELL yuh lur]

cellular phone *noun* (also **cellphone**) a portable telephone which operates by means of a cellular network.

cellulite *noun* fatty tissue regarded as causing a dimpled or lumpy texture on the hips and thighs. [Say SELL yuh lite]

celluloid ● *noun* **1** a transparent flammable plastic. **2** motion-picture film: *having made the leap from theatre to celluloid, she can now make more money*. ● *adjective* **1** made of celluloid. **2** relating to film or motion pictures: *producing the season's celluloid froth is a costly business*. [Say SELL yuh loid]

cellulose *noun* **1** a carbohydrate forming the main constituent of the cell walls of plants, used in production of textile fibres. **2** a compound of this in solution, used as a base for paints, lacquers, etc. [Say SELL yuh loase (LOASE rhymes with DOSE or DOZE)]

Celsius *adjective* of or denoting a temperature on the Celsius scale, with 0° as the freezing point of water and 100° as the boiling point: *degrees Celsius*.

Celt *noun* a member of a group of western European peoples, including the pre-Roman inhabitants of Britain and Gaul and their descendants, esp. in Ireland, Wales, Scotland, Cornwall, Brittany, etc. [Say KELT or SELT]

Celtic ● *adjective* of or relating to the Celts. ● *noun* a group of languages spoken by Celtic peoples, including Gaelic, Welsh, and Breton. [Say KELL tick or SELL tick]

cement ● *noun* **1 a** a powdery substance made by subjecting lime and clay to heat, mixed with water to form mortar or used in concrete. **b** concrete. **2** any substance that hardens and fastens on setting. **3** a uniting factor or principle: *suspicion of Central Canada was the cement that bound the Western provinces together*. ● *verb* **1 a** unite with or as with cement. **b** establish or strengthen (a friendship etc.). **2** line or cover with cement.

cemetery *noun* (*plural* **cemeteries**) a burial ground; a graveyard.

cenotaph *noun* a tomb-like monument, esp. a war memorial, to a person or persons whose bodies are interred elsewhere. [Say SENNA taff]

Cenozoic *adjective* of, relating to, or denoting the most recent geological era, following the Mesozoic and lasting from about 65 million years ago to the present day (*compare* MESOZOIC, PALEOZOIC). The Cenozoic has seen the rapid evolution and rise to prominence of mammals, birds, and flowering plants. [Say senna ZO ick or seena ZO ick]

cens *noun* (*plural* **cens**) *Cdn hist.* a token payment made to a seigneur by a habitant, reaffirming the feudal nature of the land tenure. [Say SAWNS]

SPELL CHECK   ABC ✔
censer, censor

To remove something objectionable from a book or movie is to **censor** it.

---

censer *noun* a vessel in which incense is burned, esp. during a religious ceremony etc. [Say SEN sir]

censitaire *noun* *Cdn hist.* a tenant on a seigneury. [Say sawn see TARE]

SPELL CHECK   ABC ✔
censor, sensor, censure

A device that detects light or motion is a **sensor**. To criticize something harshly is to **censure** it.

---

censor ● *noun* an official authorized to examine printed matter, films, news, etc., before public release, and to suppress any parts on the grounds of obscenity, threats to security, etc. ● *verb* **1** act as a censor of. **2** make deletions or changes in. ▶ **censorial** *adjective* [Say SEN sir, sen SORRY ul]

censorious *adjective* severely critical; quick or eager to criticize: *their relationship deteriorated as Thomas became more dictatorial and censorious*. ▶ **censoriousness** *noun* [Say sen SORRY us]

censorship *noun* the practice of officially examining books, movies, etc. and suppressing unacceptable parts.

censure ● *verb* (**censures**, **censured**, **censuring**) express severe disapproval of someone or something,

typically in a formal statement: *the editor was censured for poor taste for running the story.* • *noun* harsh criticism; expression of disapproval: *two MPs were singled out for censure ◊ women gained the confidence to express their views without fear of censure.* [Say SEN shur]

census *noun* (*plural* **censuses**) an official count of a population or of a class of things, often with various statistics noted. [Say SEN suss]

cent *noun* **1 a** a monetary unit in various countries, equal to one-hundredth of a dollar or other decimal currency unit. **b** a coin of this value. **2** *informal* a very small sum of money: *that woman won't get a cent of my money!* **3** *see* PERCENT.

cent. *abbreviation* century.

centaur *noun* Greek Myth a creature with the head, arms, and torso of a man and the body and legs of a horse. [Say SEN tore]

centenary • *noun* (*plural* **centenaries**) **1** a hundredth anniversary. **2** a celebration of this. • *adjective* of or relating to a centenary: *the country's centenary year.* [Say sen TENNER ee or sen TEENER ee]

centennial • *noun* a hundredth anniversary. • *adjective* **1** lasting for a hundred years or occurring every hundred years. **2** of or concerning a centennial; in Canada, esp. that of Confederation, in 1967.

center *etc.* = CENTRE *etc.*

centi- *combining form* **1** one-hundredth, esp. of a unit in the metric system: *centimetre.* **2** hundred. Abbreviation: **c**.

centigrade *adjective* **1** = CELSIUS. **2** having a scale of a hundred degrees.

centigram *noun* a metric unit of mass, equal to one-hundredth of a gram.

centilitre *noun* a metric unit of capacity, equal to one-hundredth of a litre.

centimetre *noun* a metric unit of length, equal to one-hundredth of a metre.

centimetre-gram-second system *noun* the system using the centimetre, gram, and second as basic units of length, mass, and time.

centipede *noun* a predatory invertebrate with a wormlike body of many segments each with two legs.

central • *adjective* **1** of, at, or forming the centre. **2** from the centre. **3** essential, most important. **4** denoting a house's heating, air conditioning, or vacuum system in which the rooms are connected via pipes, ducts, or tubes to a single source of heat, cool air, or suction. • *noun* *informal* a place with a high concentration of a specified thing etc.: *cowboy central.*

central bank *noun* a bank operated by the state, which issues currency etc.

central business district *noun* the area of a town or city where business, shopping, administrative, and entertainment facilities are most densely located.

Central Canada *noun* see CENTRAL PROVINCES.

Central Intelligence Agency *noun* a US federal agency responsible for coordinating government intelligence activities. Abbreviation: **CIA**.

centralism *noun* control of various activities and organizations under a single authority, in Canada esp. that of the federal government. ▶ **centralist** *noun*

centrality *noun* the central position or role of something; prominence, importance: *the centrality of religion in the small community.* [Say sen TRALA tee]

centralization *noun* the concentration of control of an activity or organization under a single authority: *the centralization of political power in the hands of the federal government.*

centralize *verb* (**centralizes**, **centralized**, **centralizing**) **1** bring or come to a centre. **2 a** concentrate (administration) at a single centre:

attempts to centralize power in Ottawa ◊ these changes centralize rather than decentralize. **b** subject to this system: *a highly centralized country.* ▶ **centralizer** *noun*

centrally *adverb* in or from a central position: *the hotel is centrally located.*

central nervous system *noun* the complex of nerve tissues that controls the activities of the body, in vertebrates the brain and spinal cord.

central planning *noun* the complete planning of an economy by a central authority which controls all prices, wages, and production.

central processing unit *noun* (also **central processor**) the part of a computer which controls the system and performs arithmetical and logical operations on data. Abbreviation: **CPU**.

Central provinces *plural noun* Ontario and Quebec (*compare* ATLANTIC PROVINCES, WESTERN PROVINCES).

Central Time *noun* the time in a zone including Saskatchewan, Manitoba, and the central states of the US. **Central Standard Time** is six hours behind GMT; **Central Daylight Time** is 5 hours behind GMT.

centre (also **center**) • *noun* **1** the middle point, equidistant from the ends or from any point on the circumference or surface. **2** a pivot or axis of rotation. **3 a** a place or group of buildings forming a central point in a district, city, etc., or a main area for an activity: *town centre.* **b** a place or group of buildings with a specified function: *detention centre.* **c** (with preceding word) a piece or set of equipment for a number of connected functions: *entertainment centre.* **4** a point of concentration or dispersion. **5** a political party or group holding moderate opinions. **6** the filling in a chocolate etc. **7** *Sport* the middle player in a line or group in some games. **8** a pass from the side to the centre of the playing area, esp. in the offensive zone. **9** (as an *adjective*) of or at the centre: *centre ice.* • *verb* (**centres**, **centred**, **centring**) **1** (foll. by *in*, *on*, *around*) have as its main centre or focus. **2** place in the centre. **3** mark with a centre. **4** (foll. by *in* etc.) concentrate. **5** *Sport* pass (the ball, puck, etc.) from the side to the centre of the playing area, esp. in the offensive zone. **6** *Hockey* be a centreman for (two wingers) or on (a line).

centreboard *noun* a retractable keel on a sailboat.

centred *adjective* **1** having the kind of centre described: *a soft-centred candy.* **2** having the specified subject as the most important or focal element: *career-centred professionals ◊ community-centred policing.* **3** (of a person) well balanced and confident or serene. ▶ **centredness** *noun* (in *combination*)

centre field *noun* Baseball **1** the part of the outfield between left field and right field. **2** the position of the player who covers this area. ▶ **centre fielder** *noun*

centrefold *noun* **1** a centre spread of a magazine, often with a portion that folds out. **2** a usu. naked or scantily clad model pictured on such a spread.

centre ice *noun* the central area of a rink, esp. the spot where faceoffs take place at the start of each period and after every goal.

centreman *noun* (*plural* **centremen**) = CENTRE *noun* 7.

centre of gravity *noun* **1** a point from which the weight of a body or system may be considered to act: *the car's engine is placed so as to provide increased stability from a lower centre of gravity.* **2** the point or object of greatest importance etc.: *Canada's economic centre of gravity is rapidly moving west.*

centrepiece *noun* **1** an ornament for the middle of a table. **2** a principal item.

centre stage • *noun* **1** the central, most prominent area on a theatrical stage. **2** the most prominent position. • *adverb* in or into this position.

centric *adjective* (in *combination*) **1** having a specified centre, focus, or target: *youth-centric advertising*. **2** forming an opinion or evaluation originating from a specified viewpoint: *an Afrocentric perspective*. ▶ **centricity** *noun* [Say SEN trick, sen TRISSA tee]

centrifugal *adjective* moving or tending to move from a centre. [Say sen TRIFFA gull or sentra FEW gull]

centrifugal force *noun* an apparent force that acts outwards on a body moving about a centre.

centrifuge • *noun* a machine with a rapidly rotating device designed to separate liquids from solids or other liquids. • *verb* (**centrifuges, centrifuged, centrifuging**) **1** subject to the action of a centrifuge. **2** separate by centrifuge. [Say SENTRA fuge (FUGE rhymes with HUGE)]

centripetal *adjective* moving or tending to move towards a centre. [Say sen TRIPPA tull]

centripetal force *noun* the force acting on a body in circular motion directing it towards the centre of rotation.

centrism *noun* **1** moderate political views. **2** (in *combination*) beliefs or opinions based on a specified viewpoint: *Eurocentrism*.

centrist *noun* *Politics* a person who holds moderate views.

centurion *noun* the commander of a century in the ancient Roman army. [Say sen CHURRY in]

century *noun* (*plural* **centuries**) **1 a** a period of one hundred years. **b** any of the centuries reckoned from the supposed date of the birth of Christ. **2** *Sport* **a** a score etc. of a hundred, esp. a hundred runs by one batsman in cricket. **b** a group or total of a hundred. **3** a company in the ancient Roman army, originally of 100 men.

century plant *noun* a plant, *Agave americana*, flowering once in many years and yielding sap from which tequila is distilled.

CEO *noun* (*plural* **CEOs**) = CHIEF EXECUTIVE OFFICER.

cephalopod *noun* any mollusc of the class Cephalopoda, having a well-developed head surrounded by tentacles, e.g. octopus, squid, etc. [Say SEFFA luh pod]

cephalosporin *noun* any of a class of semi-synthetic antibiotics derived from a mould of the genus *Cephalosporium*. [Say seffa luh SPORE in]

ceramic • *adjective* **1** designating or pertaining to hard brittle substances produced by the process of strong heating of a non-metallic mineral, esp. clay. **2** of or relating to pottery. • *noun* **1** a ceramic article or product. **2** a substance, esp. clay, used to make ceramic articles.

ceramics *plural noun* **1** ceramic products. **2** (usu. treated as *singular*) the art of making ceramic articles.

SPELL CHECK
cereal, serial

Serial is the spelling in "serial killer", a "TV serial", and for a "serial port" in a computer.

---

cereal • *noun* **1** (usu. in *plural*) **a** any kind of grain used for food. **b** any grass producing this, e.g. wheat, corn, rye, etc. **2** a breakfast food made from a cereal. • *adjective* of edible grain or products of it.

cerebellum *noun* (*plural* **cerebellums** or **cerebella**) the part of the brain at the back of the skull in vertebrates, which controls muscular activity. [Say sare a BELLUM]

cerebral *adjective* **1** of the brain: *a cerebral hemorrhage*. **2** intellectual, not emotional or physical: *Cheryl excelled in cerebral pursuits*. [Say suh REE brull or SARE a brull]

cerebral cortex *noun* the intricately folded outer layer of the cerebrum.

cerebral palsy *noun* a condition marked by weakness and impaired coordination of the limbs, esp. caused by damage to the brain before or at birth.

cerebrospinal fluid *noun* a clear fluid surrounding the brain and spinal cord. Abbreviation: **CSF**. [Say suh ree bro SPINAL]

cerebrum *noun* (*plural* **cerebra**) the principal part of the brain in vertebrates, located in the front area of the skull, which integrates complex sensory and neural functions. [Say su REE brum or SARE a brum]

ceremonial • *adjective* **1** concerning or used in ritual or ceremony: *a ceremonial occasion*. **2** formal: *a ceremonial bow*. • *noun* **1** a system of rites etc. to be used esp. at a formal or religious occasion. **2** one of these rites. ▶ **ceremonially** *adverb*

ceremonious *adjective* behaving or performed in a formal, ritualistic, or elaborate way; relating or appropriate to grand and formal occasions: *he accepted the gifts with ceremonious dignity*. ▶ **ceremoniously** *adverb* **ceremoniousness** *noun* [Say sare a MOANY us]

ceremony *noun* (*plural* **ceremonies**) **1** a formal religious or public rite, observance, or occasion, esp. celebrating a particular event or anniversary. **2** formalities, esp. of an empty or ritualistic kind. PHRASES **stand on ceremony** insist on the observance of formalities. **without ceremony** informally.

cerium *noun* a silvery metallic element occurring naturally in various minerals and used in the manufacture of lighter flints. [Say SEERY um]

cert *noun* *slang* (esp. **dead cert**) an event or result regarded as certain to happen.

certain • *adjective* **1 a** confident, convinced: *certain that I put it here*. **b** indisputable; known for sure: *it is certain that he is guilty*. **2 a** that may be relied on to happen: *it is certain to rain*. **b** destined: *certain to become a star*. **3** definite, unfailing, reliable: *a certain indication of the coming storm*. **4** (of a person, place, etc.) that might be specified, but is not: *a certain lady*. **5** some though not much: *a certain reluctance*. **6** (of a person, place, etc.) existing, though probably unknown to the reader or hearer: *a certain John Smith*. PHRASES **for certain** without doubt. **make certain** = MAKE SURE (see SURE).

certainly *adverb* **1** undoubtedly, definitely. **2** yes.

certainty *noun* (*plural* **certainties**) **1 a** an unquestioned fact. **b** a certain prospect: *his return is a certainty*. **2** an absolute conviction: *has a certainty of his own worth*. **3** a thing or person that may be relied on: *a certainty to win the game*. PHRASES **for a certainty** beyond the possibility of doubt.

certifiable *adjective* **1** able or needing to be certified. **2** *informal* insane. [Say serta FIE a bull]

certificate • *noun* a formal document attesting a fact, esp. birth, marriage, or death, a medical condition, a level of achievement, a fulfillment of requirements, ownership of shares, etc. • *verb* (esp. as **certificated** *adjective*) provide with or license or attest by a certificate. ▶ **certification** *noun*

certified cheque *noun* a cheque the validity of which is guaranteed by a bank.

certify *verb* (**certifies, certified, certifying**) **1** make a formal statement of; attest; attest to. **2 a** declare by certificate that a person is qualified or competent: *certified as a bookkeeper*. **b** declare by certificate that something has met esp. safety standards: *the car has been certified*. **3** officially declare insane: *he should be certified*.

certitude *noun* **1** a feeling of absolute certainty or conviction. **2** a belief held with absolute certainty.

C

cerulean *literary* • *adjective* deep blue like a clear sky. • *noun* this colour. [Say suh RULEY un]

cervical *adjective* **1** of or relating to the neck: *cervical vertebrae*. **2** of or relating to the cervix: *cervical cancer*. [Say SURVA cull]

cervical cap *noun* a contraceptive device consisting of a small cap of a rubber-like plastic placed over the cervix to prevent the passage of sperm.

cervix *noun* (*plural* **cervices**) **1** the narrow lower part of the uterus, extending into the vagina. **2** the neck. [Say SIR vicks for the singular, SURVA sees for the plural]

Cesarean = CAESAREAN. [Say suh ZERRY un]

cesium *noun* a soft silver-white element occurring naturally in a number of minerals, and used in photoelectric cells. [Say SEEZY um]

cessation *noun* a ceasing. [Say suh SAY sh'n]

cession *noun* **1** (often foll. by *of*) the ceding or giving up (of rights, property, and esp. of territory). **2** the territory etc. so ceded. [Sounds like SESSION]

cesspit *noun* **1** a pit for the disposal of refuse. **2** = CESSPOOL.

cesspool *noun* **1** an underground container for the temporary storage of liquid waste or sewage. **2** a centre of corruption, depravity, etc.

cetacean • *noun* any marine mammal of the order Cetacea with a streamlined hairless body and dorsal blowhole for breathing, including whales, dolphins, and porpoises. • *adjective* of cetaceans. [Say suh TAY sh'n]

CF *abbreviation* **1** cystic fibrosis. **2** Canadian Forces.

Cf *symbol* californium.

cf. *abbreviation* compare.

CFA *noun* (*plural* **CFAs**) *Cdn* (*Maritimes* & *Nfld*) = COME FROM AWAY.

CFB *abbreviation* Canadian Forces Base.

CFC *noun* (*plural* **CFCs**) chlorofluorocarbon, any of various usu. gaseous compounds of carbon, hydrogen, chlorine, and fluorine, used in refrigerants etc. and thought to be harmful to the ozone layer.

CFL *abbreviation* Canadian Football League.

CFS *abbreviation* **1** Canadian Forces Station. **2** CHRONIC FATIGUE SYNDROME.

cg *abbreviation* centigram(s).

Chablis *noun* (*plural* **Chablis**) **1** a dry white wine from northeastern France. **2** any dry white wine. [Say sha BLEE for the singular, sha BLEEZ for the plural]

cha-cha (also **cha-cha-cha**) • *noun* (*plural* **cha-chas**) **1** a ballroom dance with a Latin American rhythm. **2** music for or in the rhythm of this. • *verb* (**cha-chas, cha-chaed, cha-chaing**) dance the cha-cha.

chador *noun* a large piece of cloth worn in some countries by Muslim women, wrapped around the body to leave only the face exposed. [Say CHUDDER]

chafe *verb* (**chafes, chafed, chafing**) **1** make or become sore or damaged by rubbing. **2** rub (esp. the skin to restore warmth or sensation). **3** make or become annoyed; fret: *they chafed at the delay*.

chafer *noun* any of various large slow-moving beetles, the adult and larva of which can be very destructive to foliage and plant roots respectively.

chaff • *noun* **1** the husks of grain etc. separated from the seed by winnowing or threshing. **2** chopped hay and straw used as fodder. **3** lighthearted joking; banter. **4** worthless things. • *verb* tease; banter. PHRASES **separate the wheat from the chaff** distinguish valuable people or things from worthless ones: *job interviews help separate the wheat from the chaff*.

chagrin • *noun* acute vexation or mortification. • *verb* affect with chagrin. [Say shuh GRIN]

chain • *noun* **1 a** a connected flexible series of esp. metal links. **b** something resembling this: *a human* chain. **2** (in *plural*) **a** fetters used to confine prisoners. **b** any restraining force. **3** a sequence, series, or set: *chain of events* ◊ *mountain chain*. **4** a group of associated hotels, stores, newspapers, etc., esp. with the same owners or management. **5** a unit of measure of 66 ft. (approx. 20 m) for surveying. **6** *Chemistry* a group of (esp. carbon) atoms bonded in sequence in a molecule. **7** (in *plural*) a set of linked chains fastened around a vehicle's tires to prevent skidding in snow. **8** a chain for fastening a door to its jamb as a security device. • *verb* **1** secure or confine with a chain. **2** confine or restrict (a person): *as a lexicographer, I'm pretty much chained to my desk*. **3** *Computing* link (a file etc.) or be linked with another by the inclusion in each item of an address by which a successor may be located.

chain gang *noun* a team of convicts chained together and forced to work in the open air.

chain letter *noun* one of a sequence of letters the recipient of which is requested to send copies to a specific number of other people.

chain-link *adjective* made of wire in a diamond-shaped mesh: *chain-link fence*.

chain of command *noun* an arrangement in an organization by which orders are carried out.

chain reaction *noun* **1** *Physics* a self-sustaining nuclear reaction, esp. one in which a neutron from a fission reaction initiates a series of these reactions, as in nuclear reactors and bombs. **2** a chemical reaction or other process in which the products themselves promote or spread the reaction, which under certain conditions may accelerate dramatically. **3** a series of events, each caused by the previous one.

chainsaw • *noun* a motor-driven saw with teeth on an endless chain. • *verb* cut with a chainsaw.

chain-smoke *verb* (**chain-smokes, chain-smoked, chain-smoking**) smoke (cigarettes etc.) continually, esp. lighting each from the stub of the last one smoked. ▶ **chain-smoker** *noun* **chain-smoking** *noun*

chair • *noun* **1** a separate seat for one person, of various forms, usu. having a back. **2 a** a professorship. **b** a seat of authority, esp. on a board of directors. **c** a position as a musician in an orchestra. **3 a** a chairperson. **b** the seat or office of a chairperson: *will you take the chair?* • *verb* **1** act as chairperson of or preside over (a meeting). **2** install in a chair, esp. as a position of authority. PHRASES **take a chair** sit down.

chairlift *noun* a series of chairs on an endless cable for carrying passengers up and down a mountain etc.

chairman *noun* (*plural* **chairmen**) **1** a person chosen to preside over a meeting. **2** the permanent president of a committee, a board of directors, a company, etc. **3** (**Chairman**) (since 1949) the leading figure in the Chinese Communist Party. ▶ **chairmanship** *noun*

chairperson *noun* (*plural* **chairpersons** or **chairpeople**) a chairman or chairwoman (used as a neutral alternative).

chairwoman *noun* (*plural* **chairwomen**) a female chairperson.

chaise longue *noun* (*plural* **chaise longues** or **chaises longues**) (also **chaise, chaise lounge**) a chair with an extended seat on which to rest the legs. [Say shays LONZH or shays LONG]

chalcedony *noun* a type of quartz occurring in several different forms, e.g. agate etc. [Say kal SEDDA nee]

Chaldean • *noun* **1 a** a member of an ancient people who lived in Chaldea (in what is now southern Iraq) *c.*800 BC and ruled Babylonia 625–539 BC. They were renowned as astronomers and astrologers. **b** the Semitic language of the Chaldeans. **2** a member of an Eastern Catholic sect in Iran etc. • *adjective* **1** of or

relating to ancient Chaldea or its people or language. **2** of the Chaldean Church. [Say kal DEE un]

chalet *noun* **1** a style of wooden house, typical of the European Alps, having a steeply pitched roof with very deep overhanging eaves. **2** the main building at a ski resort, usu. with rental facilities and a restaurant. **3** *Cdn* (*Que.*) a holiday cottage.

chalice *noun* *Christianity* a wine cup used in the Eucharist. [Say CHAL iss]

SPELL CHECK
chalk, chock

A wooden block is a **chock**. **Chock** is also the spelling in "chock full".

---

chalk • *noun* **1** a white soft earthy limestone (calcium carbonate) formed from the skeletal remains of sea creatures. **2 a** a similar substance (calcium sulphate), sometimes coloured, used for writing or drawing. **b** a piece of this. **3** a series of strata consisting mainly of chalk. **4** *Billiards* a small blue chalk-like cube, rubbed against the tip of a pool cue to reduce slippage. • *verb* rub, mark, draw, or write with chalk. PHRASES **chalk up 1** (foll. by *to*) attribute, charge: *chalk it up to my upbringing.* **2** register (a point scored, a success, etc.).

chalkboard *noun* = BLACKBOARD.

chalkiness *noun* a chalky feel or consistency.

chalky *adjective* (**chalkier**, **chalkiest**) **1** abounding in chalk. **2** white as chalk. **3** having the consistency of chalk.

challah *noun* (*plural* **challahs** or **challoth**) a loaf of white leavened egg bread, often braided, traditionally baked to celebrate the Jewish Sabbath. [Say HALLA for the singular, HALLAS or HALLOT for the plural]

challenge • *noun* **1 a** a summons to take part in a contest or a trial of strength etc. **b** a summons to prove or justify something. **2 a** a demanding or difficult task. **b** a difficult but stimulating task. **3** an objection made to a jury member. **4** a call to respond, esp. a sentry's call for a password etc. **5** an invitation to a sporting contest, esp. one issued to a reigning champion. • *verb* (**challenges**, **challenged**, **challenging**) **1 a** invite to take part in a contest, game, debate, duel, etc.: *challenged her to a game of squash.* **b** invite to prove or justify: *I challenge you to prove that.* **2** dispute: *I challenge that remark.* **3** stretch, stimulate: *challenges him to produce his best.* **4** (of a sentry) call to respond. **5** *Law* object to (a jury member, evidence, etc.).

challenged *adjective* **1** (of a person) disabled: *physically challenged.* **2** *jocular* not having a specified quality, e.g. *vertically challenged* for *short.*

challenger *noun* a person who competes in sports or politics for an important position held by an opponent.

challenging *adjective* stimulatingly difficult.

chamber *noun* **1 a** a hall used by a legislative or judicial body. **b** the body that meets in it. **c** any of the houses of a parliament. **2** (in *plural*) a judge's room used for hearing cases not needing to be taken in court. **3** *Music* (as an *adjective*) of or for a small group of instruments: *chamber music.* **4** an enclosed space in machinery etc. (esp. the part of a gun that contains the cartridge or shell). **5 a** a cavity in a plant or in the body of an animal. **b** a compartment in a structure. **6** a space, cavity, or room constructed for a specific purpose. ▶ **chambered** *adjective*

chamberlain *noun* an officer managing the household of a monarch or great noble. [Say CHAMBER lin]

chambermaid *noun* **1** a housemaid at a hotel etc. **2** a housemaid.

chamber of commerce *noun* an association to promote local commercial interests.

chamber pot *noun* a receptacle for urine etc., used in a bedroom.

chameleon *noun* **1** a small slow-moving lizard with protruding eyes and the ability to change colour according to its surroundings. **2** *derogatory* someone who changes his or her behaviour, opinions, etc. to suit the situation. [Say kuh MEELY un]

chamois *noun* (*plural* **chamois**) **1** soft leather made from the skin of sheep, goats, deer, etc., often used for polishing. **2** an agile goat with short hooked horns living in the mountains of Europe and Asia. [For sense 1 say SHAMMY for the singular, SHAMMIES for the plural; for sense 2 say SHAM wah for the singular, SHAM wahz for the plural]

chamomile *noun* = CAMOMILE.

champ¹ *noun* *informal* a champion.

champ² *verb* & *noun* = CHOMP.

champagne *noun* a bubbly white wine, often used for celebrations. [Say sham PAIN]

champion • *noun* **1** a person, animal, or team etc. that has won a competition: *the provincial tennis champion* ◊ *a champion racehorse.* **2** a person who fights or argues for a cause or on someone's behalf: *a champion of the poor.* • *verb* support the cause of a person, charity, etc.: *for years their organization has championed human rights.*

championship *noun* **1** a competition to decide who is the champion: *won the debating championship* ◊ *the national tennis championships.* **2** the position of a champion: *our team will be playing for the championship.*

chance • *noun* **1 a** a possibility. **b** probability: *chances are that you will be promoted.* **2** a risk: *take a chance.* **3 a** an unplanned occurrence: *just a chance that they met.* **b** the absence of design or discoverable cause: *leave nothing to chance.* **4** an opportunity: *didn't have a chance to speak to him.* **5** the way things happen; fortune; luck: *leave it to chance.* **6** (often **Chance**) the course of events regarded as a power; fate. • *adjective* fortuitous, accidental: *a chance meeting.* • *verb* (**chances**, **chanced**, **chancing**) **1** *informal* risk: *we'll chance it and go.* **2** happen without intention: *I chanced to find it.* PHRASES **by any chance** as it happens; perhaps. **by chance** without design; unintentionally. **chance on** (or **upon**) happen to find, meet, etc. **no chance** there is no possibility of that. **on the chance** (often foll. by *of*, or *that* + clause) in view of the possibility. **stand a chance** have a prospect of success etc. **take a chance** (or **chances**) behave in a risky manner; risk failure. **take a** (or **one's**) **chance on** (or **with**) consent to take the consequences of; trust to luck.

chancel *noun* a part of some churches near the altar, where the priests and the choir sit during services. [Say CHAN sul]

chancellor *noun* **1** the head of government in Germany and Austria. **2** *Cdn & Brit.* the honorary head of a university. [Say CHAN suh lur]

chancery *noun* (*plural* **chanceries**) **1** an office attached to an embassy or consulate. **2** the administrative office of a Catholic diocese. [Say CHAN sur ee]

chancy *adjective* (**chancier**, **chanciest**) risky.

chandelier *noun* an ornamental hanging lamp, often decorated with many small pieces of glass, with branches for several light bulbs or candles. [Say shan duh LEER]

chandler *noun* **1** a person or shop that sells ropes, canvas, and other supplies for ships. **2** a person who makes or sells candles. [Say CHAND lur]

change • *noun* **1 a** an act or process through which something becomes different. **b** an alteration or

modification. **2 a** money given in exchange for money in larger units or a different currency. **b** money returned as the balance of that given in payment. **c** coins. **d** a relatively small amount of something, esp. money: *$10 million and change*. **3** a new experience; variety: *time for a change*. **4 a** the substitution of one thing for another; an exchange: *change of scene*. **b** a set of clothes etc. put on in place of another. **5** (also **change of life**) *informal* menopause. **6** (of the moon) arrival at a fresh phase, esp. at the new moon. • *verb* (**changes, changed, changing**) **1** undergo, show, or subject to change; make or become different. **2 a** take or use another instead of; go from one to another: *changed the tire ◊ changed his doctor ◊ changed trains*. **b** give up or get rid of in exchange: *changed the car for a van*. **3 a** give or get change in smaller denominations for: *can you change a twenty?* **b** exchange (a sum of money) for: *changed our dollars to pounds*. **4** put fresh clothes or coverings on: *change the baby ◊ changed into something more comfortable*. **5** give and receive, exchange: *changed places with her*. **6** change trains etc.: *changed at Montreal*. **7** (of the voice) become deeper in tone. **8** (of the moon) arrive at a fresh phase, esp. become new. **PHRASES** **change of air** a different climate; variety. **change colour** blanch or flush. **change gear** engage a different gear in a vehicle. **change hands 1** pass to a different owner. **2** substitute one hand for another. **change of heart** a conversion to a different view. **change over** change from one system or situation to another. **change the subject** begin talking of something different, esp. to avoid embarrassment. **change one's tune 1** voice a different opinion from that expressed previously. **2** change one's style of language or manner, esp. from an insolent to a respectful tone.

changeable *adjective* **1** tending to change; often changing: *his mood is as changeable as the weather*. **2** able to change or be changed: *a pen with a changeable cartridge*. ▶ **changeableness** *noun*

changeless *adjective* unchanging; eternally: *a changeless universe*. ▶ **changelessly** *adverb*

changeling *noun* in folklore, a child that is secretly left by fairies in exchange for another. [Say CHANGE ling]

SPELL CHECK
changeover, change over ✓

The verb is spelled **change over**: *Our store is going to change over from plastic bags to paper.*

---

changeover *noun* a change from one system or situation to another: *the changeover to the metric system*.

changer *noun* **1** a device for changing something: *channel changer*. **2** a person who changes something: *a money-changer*.

changeup *noun* in baseball, a slow pitch thrown like a fastball to deceive the batter.

Changing of the Guard *noun* **1** a ceremony in which one group of guards is replaced by another, esp. at parliament buildings. **2** (**changing of the guard**) a thorough change in management, approach, etc.

channel • *noun* **1 a** a length of water wider than a strait, joining two larger areas of water. **b** the deeper part of a waterway, which can be navigated by a ship. **c** the bed of a river or stream etc. **2 a** a band of frequencies used for broadcasting a particular set of radio or television programs. **b** a particular television station. **3** a way or system by which news, information, etc. may travel: *your complaint must be made through the proper channels ◊ heard the rumour through the usual channels*. **4** the course in which anything moves; a direction. **5** a tube-like passage for liquid. • *verb* (**channels, channelled, channelling**) **1** guide something in a channel: *rainwater is channelled through the eavestrough*. **2 a** direct something or someone: *officials channelled them through customs*. **b** direct energy, emotions, etc. towards a goal: *channelled all her energy into the project*. **3** form channels in: *deep grooves channelling the soft rock*.

channel cat *noun* (also **channel catfish**) a large edible North American freshwater catfish.

channelling *noun* the practice of acting as a medium for spirits: *her New Age spiritual practices include meditation and channelling*.

channel surfing *noun informal* the act of flipping from one television channel to another using a remote control. ▶ **channel surfer** *noun*

chant • *noun* **1** words sung or shouted repeatedly to the same rhythm: *Fans started the "Go, Leafs, Go!" chant*. **2** a religious song or prayer in which many of the words are sung on the same note. **3** = GREGORIAN CHANT. • *verb* **1** sing or shout something repeatedly, using the same rhythm. **2** sing a religious song or prayer as a chant.

chanteuse *noun* a female singer of popular songs. [Say shon TOOZ (with OO as in TOOK)]

Chanukah *noun* = HANUKKAH.

chaos *noun* **1** complete disorder or confusion: *the burglars left the house in chaos ◊ heavy snow has caused chaos on the roads*. **2** the formless matter believed to have existed before the universe was created. [Say KAY oss]

chaos theory *noun* the theory that provides mathematical methods to explain the chaotic behaviour of systems, such as weather, that seem unpredictable but have an underlying order. Chaos theory shows that tiny changes in the starting conditions of a system can have enormous consequences on the state of the system later on.

chaotic *adjective* in a confused or disorderly state. ▶ **chaotically** *adverb* [Say kay OTT ik, kay OTT ik ly]

chap • *verb* (**chaps, chapped, chapping**) (esp. of the skin) become rough and painful, esp. because of exposure to cold weather or dryness; crack. • *noun informal* **1** a man or boy. **2** the lower part of the jaw or cheek, esp. that of a pig, which may be eaten.

chaparral *noun* dense tangled shrubs and thorny bushes in the southwestern US. [Say shappa RAL]

chapati *noun* (*plural* **chapatis**) a type of thin flat round whole wheat bread from India. [Say chuh POTTY or chuh PATTY]

chapel *noun* **1** *Christianity* a small room or building used for worship, esp. in a school, prison, hospital, etc., or as part of a larger church. **2** a funeral home, or the room in a funeral home in which services are held.

chaperone • *noun* **1** a person who supervises young people on trips etc. **2** a person who ensures that no improper behaviour occurs on a date, at a dance, etc. • *verb* (**chaperones, chaperoned, chaperoning**) act as a chaperone for someone. [Say SHAPPA rone]

chaplain *noun* a member of the clergy whose job is to serve the spiritual needs of people in a school, hospital, prison, the armed forces, etc. [Say CHAP lin]

chapped *adjective* (of the skin) dry and cracking.

chappie *noun informal* = CHAP *noun* 1.

chapping *noun* the state of being chapped: *lip balm prevents chapping*.

chaps *plural noun* **1** protective leather coverings for the legs worn over pants when riding a horse. **2** similar protective leather leggings worn by loggers.

chapter *noun* **1** a main division of a book, usu. with a number or title. **2** a local branch of a club or society. **3** all the priests of a cathedral or the members of another religious community. **4** a period of time in history or a person's life: *a glorious chapter in this*

country's history. PHRASES **chapter and verse** the exact details of something, esp. the exact place where certain information may be found: *the premier, quoting chapter and verse from her campaign promises, maintains her government has honoured its commitments.*

char • *verb* (**chars, charred, charring**) **1** make or become black by burning; scorch. **2** burn or be burned to charcoal. • *noun* (*plural* **char**) **1** a small trout valued as a food and game fish, esp. the Arctic char. **2 a** = DOLLY VARDEN 1. **b** = BROOK TROUT.

character • *noun* **1** all the distinctive qualities, features, etc. of a person or thing: *lying is not in keeping with her character ◊ the two provinces differ in character ◊ the rustic character of this inn.* **2** the ability to handle difficult or dangerous situations; moral strength: *adversity builds character ◊ this game will be a test of the team's character.* **3** reputation: *an attack on his character.* **4** interesting or unusual features: *a house full of character.* **5 a** a person in a novel, play, etc. **b** a part played by a performer. **6** *informal* an unusual person: *your brother is such a character!* **7** a letter or symbol used in a system of printing or writing or on a computer. **8** *Biology* a characteristic that helps identify a species. • *adjective* (of a supporting role or the performer who plays it) portraying a highly individual, esp. eccentric, person: *his portrayal of ruthless villains has gained him fame as an outstanding character actor ◊ Juliet's nurse is a character part.* PHRASES **in character** (or **out of character**) **1** typical (or not typical) of a person's character: *her behaviour was completely out of character.* **2** (of an actor or performer) acting (or not acting) a role: *she would sometimes stay in character even when not on stage.*

character assassination *noun* a malicious attempt to harm or destroy a person's good reputation.

characterful *adjective* interesting, unusual: *characterful homes.*

characteristic • *adjective* typical, distinctive: *she played with characteristic enthusiasm ◊ pollution is characteristic of a big city.* • *noun* a typical or distinctive feature or quality: *what are his good characteristics?* ▶ **characteristically** *adverb*

characterization *noun* **1** a description of the character of someone or something: *wrote a humorous characterization of family life.* **2** the creation of fictitious characters in novels, plays, etc.: *the characterization in his novel is very realistic.*

characterize *verb* (**characterizes, characterized, characterizing**) **1** describe the character of: *historians have characterized the decade as a period of change.* **2** be typical or characteristic of something: *her paintings are characterized by vibrant colours.*

characterless *adjective* **1** lacking interesting features: *a characterless suburb.* **2** lacking moral strength: *a characterless team.*

charade *noun* a situation or event that is clearly false or absurd: *their "happy" marriage is a charade — they really despise one another.* [Say shuh RAID]

charades *noun* a game in which a word, phrase, or title must be guessed from clues acted out silently: *charades is my favourite game.*

charbroil *verb* cook meat etc. on a grill over a charcoal fire etc. ▶ **charbroiled** *adjective*

charcoal • *noun* **1** a porous black substance used esp. as a fuel or for drawing, made by burning wood etc. slowly in an oven with little air. **2** a sketch drawn with charcoal. **3** a dark grey colour. • *adjective* dark grey.

chard *noun* a kind of beet with edible green leaves and white leaf stalks.

Chardonnay *noun* a dry white wine, typically with an oaky flavour. [Say SHARDA nay]

charge • *verb* (**charges, charged, charging**) **1 a** ask (an amount) as a price: *charge $5 a ticket.* **b** ask (a person) for an amount as a price: *you forgot to charge me.* **2 a** debit the cost of to (a person or account): *charge it to my account.* **b** debit (a person or an account): *bought a new car and charged the company.* **3 a** accuse (of an offence): *charged him with theft.* **b** make an accusation that. **4 a** instruct or command: *I charge you to tell the truth.* **b** (of a judge) instruct (a jury). **5** (foll. by *with*) entrust with. **6** make a rushing attack. **7 a** give an electric charge to (a body). **b** store energy in (a battery). **c** (of a battery etc.) receive and store energy. **8** load or fill (a vessel, gun, etc.) to the full or proper extent. **9** (usu. as **charged** *adjective*) **a** saturated with: *air charged with vapour.* **b** pervaded (with strong feelings etc.): *atmosphere charged with emotion.* • *noun* **1 a** a price asked for goods or services. **b** a financial liability or commitment. **2 a** an accusation, esp. against a prisoner brought to trial. **b** a judge's instructions to a jury. **3 a** a task, duty, or commission. **b** care, custody, responsible possession. **c** a person or thing entrusted. **d** the congregation(s) for which a minister is responsible. **4 a** an impetuous rush or attack, esp. in a battle. **b** the signal for this. **5** an amount of explosive needed to fire a gun or cause an explosion. **6 a** the property of matter that is responsible for electricity. If there is an excess of electrons, there is a negative charge; if there is an excess of protons, there is a positive charge. **b** an amount of electricity contained in a substance or stored in a battery etc. **7** *informal* a thrill. **8** a burden or load. PHRASES **charge up 1** recharge (a battery etc.). **2** (usu. as **charged up** *adjective*) excite. **free of charge** at no cost. **in charge** having command. **put a person on a charge** charge a person with a specified offence. **return to the charge** begin again, esp. in argument. **take charge** (often foll. by *of*) assume control or direction. ▶ **chargeable** *adjective*

charge-coupled device *noun* a light-sensitive grid on a silicon microchip that creates digital signals from images, used in video recorders, photocopiers, etc.

charged *adjective* **1** filled or saturated with: *air charged with vapour ◊ the room was charged with excitement.* **2** intense, emotional: *a charged speech.* **3** having a negative or positive electrical charge.

charger *noun* **1** an apparatus for charging a battery. **2** a horse ridden by a soldier in battle.

charging *noun* in hockey, an illegal play in which a player takes more than two steps or strides before bodychecking an opponent.

chariot *noun* an open two-wheeled vehicle drawn by horses, used in ancient warfare and racing.

charioteer *noun* a chariot driver. [Say cherry a TEER]

charisma *noun* great charm or personal power that can attract, influence, and inspire people. [Say kuh RIZ muh]

charismatic • *adjective* **1** having a compelling charm which inspires devotion in others: *a charismatic leader.* **2** (of Christian worship) emphasizing the influence of the Holy Spirit on believers as shown through spontaneous outbursts of praise and the ability to heal the sick and interpret God's will: *the charismatic movement.* • *noun* a person who emphasizes charismatic worship and experiences. ▶ **charismatically** *adverb* [Say care iz MAT ic, care iz MAT ic ly]

charitable *adjective* **1** relating to a charity: *a charitable organization.* **2** generous in giving to those in need. **3** likely to be kind when judging others or their acts or motives: *she was very charitable in her evaluation of our presentation.* ▶ **charitably** *adverb*

charity *noun* (*plural* **charities**) **1** an organization that helps and raises money for those in need. **2 a** the aim

C

of giving money, food, help, etc. to people in need: *he does it out of charity* ◊ *all proceeds of the car wash will go to charity*. **b** the help or money given in this way: *lives on charity*. **3** kindness and sympathy towards others, esp. when judging them. PHRASES **charity begins at home** a person's first duty is to help and care for his or her own family.

charlatan *noun* a person who falsely claims to have a special knowledge or skill. [Say SHARLA tun]

Charleston *noun* a fast dance, popular in the 1920s, in which the knees are turned inwards and the legs are kicked sideways. [Say CHARLES tun]

charley horse *noun* a cramp or soreness in a muscle, esp. in the leg.

charm • *noun* **1 a** the power of pleasing, fascinating, or attracting people: *captivated by her charm*. **b** an attractive feature or quality: *a woman's charms*. **2 a** a small ornament worn on a chain around the wrist. **b** an object worn for good luck or protection from evil: *a lucky charm*. **3** an object or word believed to have magic power; a spell. • *verb* **1** please, attract, or fascinate. **2** control or protect someone with or as if with magic. **3** use charm to convince someone to do or give something: *she was charmed into inviting him to the party*. PHRASES **work like a charm** be immediately and completely successful.

charmed life *noun* a life that has been unusually lucky or happy, as though protected by magic: *she has led a charmed life*.

charmer *noun* **1** a person with an attractive or fascinating personality. **2** a person who uses charm to influence or deceive others.

charming *adjective* delightful, attractive, pleasing. ▶ **charmingly** *adverb*

charmless *adjective* lacking charm; unattractive.

charnel house *noun* a building where bodies are piled in times of mass death, such as a plague. [Say CHAR nul]

chart • *noun* **1** a graph, diagram, or table presenting information, esp. about something that changes over time. **2** a record of medical information concerning a patient. **3** a detailed map used esp. by sailors and pilots. **4** a list, often produced weekly, of the most popular songs or records: *their most recent album went to the top of the charts*. • *verb* **1** make a chart or map of: *they charted the new territory*. **2** plan a route on a chart: *the pilot charted a new course*. **3** follow the path or progress of something as if on a chart: *scientists are charting the progress of the new satellite*.

charter • *noun* **1 a** a written statement by a government granting certain rights to a town, company, university, etc., or allowing a new organization etc. to be founded. **b** a written statement of the main functions and principles of an organization. **2** (**the Charter**) the Canadian Charter of Rights and Freedoms. **3 a** the hiring of a bus, aircraft, etc. for a special purpose. **b** the bus or aircraft etc. chartered. **4** a flight on a charter airline. • *verb* **1** grant a charter to. **2** hire (a bus or aircraft etc.) for a special purpose.

charter airline *noun* an airline that sells discounted blocks of seats to tour operators for resale to individuals. Fares on charter flights tend to cost less than on regularly scheduled flights.

chartered accountant *noun* a person who is fully trained and licensed to practise accounting.

chartered bank *noun* (in Canada) a large, privately owned bank established by government charter and regulated by Parliament.

charter member *noun* an original member.

chartreuse *noun & adjective* pale yellowish green. [Say shar TROOZ (with OO as in ROOK) or shar TRUCE]

chary *adjective* (**charier**, **chariest**) cautiously or suspiciously reluctant to do something; wary: *I am chary of lending him money*. [Sounds like CHERRY]

chase • *verb* (**chases**, **chased**, **chasing**) **1** pursue in order to catch. **2 a** force to leave. **b** dispel: *chase away all fears*. **3 a** hurry in pursuit of (a person). **b** (foll. by *around* etc.) *informal* act or move about hurriedly. **4** (usu. foll. by *up*, *down*) *informal* make efforts to find or obtain quickly. **5** *informal* **a** try to attain. **b** court persistently and openly. • *noun* an act of pursuing someone or something: *caught them after a brief chase*. PHRASES **give chase** pursue a person, animal, etc.; hunt.

chaser *noun* **1** a person or thing that chases. **2** *informal* a drink taken after another of a different kind, e.g. a weaker alcoholic drink after a strong one. **3** a logger who unhooks logs at a landing.

chasm *noun* **1** a deep crack or opening in the ground. **2** a wide difference between people or groups, esp. one that is unlikely to change: *the vast chasm separating rich and poor*. [Say KAZ um]

Chassid *noun* (also **Chasid**) = HASID.

chassis *noun* (*plural* **chassis**) **1** the basic frame of a car, trailer, etc., including the engine, wheels, and other mechanical parts, but not the body. **2** the frame of a stereo, television set, etc. [Say CHASSY or SHASSY for the singular, CHASSIES or SHASSIES for the plural]

chaste *adjective* **1 a** choosing not to have sex with anyone. **b** choosing not to have sex with anyone other than one's spouse. **2** (of behaviour, speech, etc.) not sexual in nature: *a chaste kiss on the cheek*. **3** simple or unadorned in style or design: *chaste architectural style*. ▶ **chastely** *adverb* [Rhymes with WASTE]

chasten *verb* **1** (of a mistake or bad experience) cause someone to be regretful or less confident: *he was chastened by the accident* ◊ *being criticized publicly was a chastening experience for her*. **2** punish: *looked like a chastened schoolboy*. [Say CHASE un]

chastise *verb* criticize, scold: *he chastised his colleagues for their laziness*. [Say CHASS tize]

chastisement *noun* punishment.

chastity *noun* the state or practice of refraining from extramarital sex or esp. all sex. [Say CHASTA tee]

chat • *verb* (**chats**, **chatted**, **chatting**) talk in a friendly, informal way. • *noun* **1** a friendly, informal talk or conversation. **2** any of various small birds with harsh calls. PHRASES **chat up** *informal* chat to or flirt with someone one is attracted to or wants to gain something from.

château *noun* (*plural* **châteaux**) **1** a castle or manor in France. **2** the home of a seigneur or governor in New France. [Say sha TOE or SHA toe for the singular, sha TOZE or SHA toze for the plural]

Château Clique *noun* Cdn *history* a name given to the small group of powerful citizens appointed to important political positions by the governor in Lower Canada prior to 1830. Mostly English-speaking merchants, they tended to promote their own interests instead of addressing the problems of the French-speaking majority. [Say sha toe CLEEK]

Château style *noun* Cdn a style of architecture popular in the early 1900s, in which esp. railway hotels were built with steep copper-covered roofs and round towers in order to look like French châteaux.

chatelaine *noun* the woman in charge of a large house. [Say SHATTA lane]

chat room *noun* (*plural* **chat rooms**) an area on the Internet or another computer network where users can communicate, esp. one dedicated to a particular topic.

chattel *noun* **1** a personal possession. **2** a slave.

PHRASES goods and chattels personal possessions. [Say CHAT ul]

chatter • *verb* **1** talk quickly or non-stop, esp. about trivialities. **2** (of an animal) emit short quick sounds. **3** (of the teeth) click repeatedly together (usu. from cold). • *noun* chattering talk or sounds. ▶**chatterer** *noun*

chatterbox *noun* (plural **chatterboxes**) a talkative person.

chattily *adverb* in a chatty manner.

chattiness *noun* a chatty quality.

chatty *adjective* (**chattier, chattiest**) **1** fond of chatting; talkative. **2** informal and lively: *a chatty letter.*

chauffeur • *noun* a person employed to drive a limousine or other automobile. • *verb* **1** drive a car as a chauffeur. **2** transport by car: *I have to chauffeur my brother to soccer practice.* [Say show FUR, SHOW fur]

chauvinism *noun* excessive or prejudiced loyalty to one's own nationality, race, or sex: *the CIA is one of Washington's great bastions of male chauvinism.* [Say SHOW v'n ism]

chauvinist *noun* a person displaying excessive or prejudiced loyalty to his or her own nationality, race, or sex. ▶**chauvinistic** *adjective* **chauvinistically** *adverb* [Say SHOW v'n ist, show v'n ISS tic]

SPELL CHECK
cheap, cheep   ABC✔

The cry of a bird is a **cheep**.

---

cheap • *adjective* **1** inexpensive; charging low prices. **2** of poor quality: *that radio was so cheap, the tuning dial broke off after two days.* **3** derogatory (of a person) stingy with money. **4** of little worth or deserving contempt: *made us feel cheap* ◊ *a cheap remark* ◊ *a cheap penalty.* • *adverb* inexpensively: *got it cheap* ◊ *doesn't come cheap.* **PHRASES on the cheap** inexpensively. **talk is cheap** actions speak louder than words.

cheapen *verb* make less worthy of respect; degrade: *it was a form of high art that money would only cheapen.*

cheapie *adjective & noun* = CHEAPO.

cheaply *adverb* without spending or costing much money.

cheapness *noun* **1** the quality of something that costs or charges little. **2** stinginess, penny-pinching.

cheapo *informal* • *adjective* inexpensive or of low quality. • *noun* (plural **cheapos**) **1** something inexpensive or of low quality. **2** a stingy person.

cheap shot *noun* **1** a malicious or cruel comment directed at a defenceless person. **2** *Sport* an illegal physical attack against an unsuspecting player.

cheapskate *noun* informal a stingy person; a miser.

cheat • *verb* **1 a** deceive or trick: *cheated him out of his savings.* **b** deprive of: *cheated of a chance to reply.* **2** gain unfair advantage by deception or breaking rules, esp. in a game or examination. **3** avoid (something undesirable) by luck or skill: *cheated fate.* **4** be sexually unfaithful to. • *noun* **1** a person who cheats. **2** a trick, fraud, or deception. **3** an act of cheating. ▶**cheater** *noun*

SPELL CHECK
check, cheque   ABC✔

Cheque is the usual Canadian spelling for the method of payment: *cash a cheque; a paycheque.*

---

check • *verb* **1 a** examine the accuracy, quality, or condition of; inspect. **b** make sure; verify: *checked the train times.* **c** search: *checked the house.* **2** stop or slow the

motion of; curb, restrain: *checked his anger.* **3** *Hockey* **a** physically obstruct the progress of (an opponent). **b** cause (an opponent) to lose possession of the puck. **4** *Chess* move a piece into a position that directly threatens (the opposing king). **5** make a mark next to an item to indicate that it has been dealt with, chosen, or verified. **6** deposit (a coat, luggage, etc.) for temporary storage or dispatch. • *noun* **1** a means or act of testing or ensuring accuracy, quality, satisfactory condition, etc. **2** a measure or policy to ensure against fraud or abuse: *checks and balances.* **3 a** a stopping or slowing of motion; a restraint on action. **b** a person or thing that restrains. **4** *Hockey* an act of checking an opponent. **5** *Chess* the exposure of a king to direct attack from an opposing piece. **6** = CHECK MARK. **7 a** a pattern of small squares or intersecting lines. **b** fabric having this pattern. **8** esp. *US* = CHEQUE etc. **9** a bill in a restaurant. **10** a ticket used to claim an item which has been temporarily stored. • *interjection* expressing assent or agreement. **PHRASES check in 1** arrive or register at a hotel, airport, etc. **2** record the arrival of. **check into 1** register one's arrival at (a hotel etc.). **2** investigate. **check (up) on 1** examine carefully or in detail; ascertain the truth about. **2** keep a watch on (a person, work done, etc.). **check out 1** leave a hotel etc. after paying the appropriate fees. **2 a** investigate; examine for authenticity or suitability. **b** informal look at; give consideration to: *check out that outfit.* **3** (of two or more items, accounts, etc.) agree or correspond when compared. **4** informal die. **check over** examine for errors; verify. **in check** under control, restrained.

checked *adjective* having a checkered pattern.

checker *noun* **1** a person or thing that verifies or examines. **2** *Hockey* **a** a forward whose role is primarily defensive rather than offensive. **b** any player who checks an opponent. **3** a pattern of alternately coloured squares. **4** one of the small round pieces used in the game of checkers.

checkerboard *noun* **1** a board with a pattern of squares of alternating colours, used in the game of checkers. **2** something with a pattern resembling this: *the checkerboard pattern of the prairie farms.*

checkered *adjective* **1** marked with a pattern of small squares of alternating colours. **2** marked by periods of good and bad luck, behaviour, etc.: *a checkered career.*

checkered flag *noun* a flag with a black and white checkered pattern, displayed to drivers or riders at the moment of finishing a race.

checkers *noun* a game for two, played on a checkerboard, in which players attempt to capture all of their opponent's pieces.

SPELL CHECK
check-in, check in   ABC✔

The verb is spelled **check in**: *I'll go check in.*

---

check-in *noun* **1** the act of registering one's arrival at a hotel, airport, etc.: *we arrived an hour early for check-in.* **2** the place where one registers arrival at a hotel etc.

checklist *noun* a list of items to be marked as present or having been dealt with.

check mark *noun* a mark (✓) placed beside an item to indicate that it is correct or has been dealt with, chosen, etc.

checkmate • *noun* *Chess* a situation from which a king cannot escape, indicating that the game is over. • *verb* (**checkmates, checkmated, checkmating**) **1** *Chess* put into checkmate. **2** defeat; thwart: *the city would be checkmated by the provincial government again.*

C

C

checkout *noun* **1** an act of registering one's departure from a hotel etc. **2** a counter at which goods are paid for in a store.

checkpoint *noun* a place, e.g. on a border, where travellers are stopped and their vehicles and documents inspected.

checkroom *noun* a room where coats, luggage, etc. may be temporarily deposited for a fee.

checks and balances *plural noun* (esp. in the US) the constitutional limiting of the power of one branch of government, e.g. the presidency, esp. through the counterbalancing powers of other branches, e.g. the judiciary or legislature.

checkstop *noun* *Cdn* (*West*) a roadside checkpoint where drivers are randomly tested with a Breathalyzer for alcohol consumption.

checkup *noun* a thorough examination, as of a person's general medical condition or dental health.

cheddar *noun* a firm cheese that ranges in colour from white to orange and becomes stronger tasting with age.

cheder *noun* a Jewish school in which Hebrew and religious knowledge are taught. [Say HEY der]

cheek *noun* **1** the side of the face below the eye. **2** *Cdn* the edible tender flesh around the mouth of a fish, esp. cod. **3** impertinence; bold rudeness: *had the cheek to ask*. **4** *slang* either of the buttocks. PHRASES **cheek by jowl** close together; side by side. **turn the other cheek** accept attack etc. meekly; refuse to retaliate.

cheekbone *noun* the bone below the eye that forms the prominent part of the cheek.

cheekily *adverb* in a rude and disrespectful or irreverent manner.

cheekiness *noun* a rude and disrespectful or irreverent manner.

cheeky *adjective* (**cheekier, cheekiest**) showing a lack of respect, esp. boldly or playfully; impertinent.

cheep • *noun* the weak shrill cry of a young bird. • *verb* make such a cry.

cheer • *noun* **1** a shout of encouragement or approval; an organized chant performed by a crowd at a sporting event etc.: *they started that obnoxious school cheer*. **2** cheerfulness: *full of good cheer*. **3** food and drink: *Christmas cheer*. • *verb* **1 a** applaud with shouts; shout for joy. **b** (also **cheer on**) urge or encourage: *the crowd cheered them on through the last stretch of the marathon*. **2** (also **cheer up**) make or become less depressed.

cheerful *adjective* **1** noticeably happy. **2** bright, pleasant: *a cheerful room*. **3** not reluctant: *a cheerful giver*.
▶ **cheerfully** *adverb* **cheerfulness** *noun*

cheerily *adverb* in a cheerful manner.

cheeriness *noun* a cheery quality; cheerfulness.

cheerleader *noun* **1** a person who leads a crowd in formal cheers at a sporting event. **2** a person who rouses his or her colleagues into action.
▶ **cheerleading** *noun*

cheerless *adjective* gloomy, dreary, miserable.
▶ **cheerlessly** *adverb* **cheerlessness** *noun*

cheers *interjection* **1** a drinking toast. **2** goodbye; expressing good wishes (esp. in closing an e-mail).

cheery *adjective* (**cheerier, cheeriest**) **1** lively; in a good mood. **2** that makes people happy.

cheese • *noun* **1** a solid or semi-solid food made from milk, usu. yellow or white. **2** (also **big cheese**) *slang* an important person. • *verb* (**cheeses, cheesed, cheesing**) *slang* exasperate, annoy. PHRASES **say cheese** smile for a photograph.

cheeseburger *noun* a hamburger topped with melted cheese.

cheesecake *noun* **1** a rich sweet cake made with cream cheese or cottage cheese. **2** *informal* the portrayal of women in a sexually provocative manner in photographs.

cheesecloth *noun* thin loosely woven cloth resembling gauze.

cheese cutter *noun* **1** a utensil for slicing cheese. **2** *Cdn* (*Que. & E Ont.*) *slang* = BOBSKATE.

cheesed *adjective* (also **cheesed off**) annoyed.

cheesiness *noun* a cheesy quality.

cheesy *adjective* (**cheesier, cheesiest**) **1** like cheese in taste, smell, appearance, etc. **2** *slang* of poor quality, cheap. **3** *slang* unsophisticated, corny.

cheetah *noun* a large slender spotted cat found in Africa and Asia, the world's fastest-running animal.

chef *noun* a cook, esp. the chief cook in a restaurant. [Say SHEF]

chem *noun* *informal* a chemistry class or course.

chemical • *noun* **1** any of the elements or compounds which constitute all substances. **2** such a substance considered as an artificial component of food etc.: *don't eat that stuff, it's full of chemicals*. • *adjective* of, made by, or employing chemistry or chemicals.

chemical bond *noun* a strong force of attraction holding atoms together in a molecule or crystal.

chemical change *noun* a usu. irreversible change that takes place when the interaction of two or more substances results in the production of a new chemical substance or compound; when sodium and chlorine are brought together, they undergo a chemical change, the product of which is sodium chloride or salt (compare PHYSICAL CHANGE).

chemical dependency *noun* addiction to alcohol or drugs.

chemically *adverb* **1** in terms of chemicals or the chemistry of something: *the two substances are chemically related*. **2** with chemicals; by means of a process involving chemicals: *the sewage is chemically treated*.

chemical reaction *noun* a process in which compounds or elements undergo a change in structure and form new compounds.

chemical warfare *noun* the military use of chemical weapons.

chemical weapon *noun* a weapon that releases a toxic substance, e.g. poison gas.

chemist *noun* a scientist trained in chemistry.

chemistry *noun* (*plural* **chemistries**) **1** the scientific study of the structure of substances, how they react when combined or in contact with one another, and how they behave under different conditions. **2** the chemical constituents or properties of a substance or organism: *studied the chemistry of the local soil*. **3** the interaction, attraction, or rapport existing among two or more people.

chemo *noun* *informal* = CHEMOTHERAPY. [Say KEY moe]

chemotherapy *noun* the treatment of disease, esp. cancer, by use of highly toxic chemical substances

which target rapidly-dividing cells to slow cell division. [Say KEY moe THAIR uh pee]

cheque *noun* a printed form used to order a bank to pay money from the user's account to a specified person.

chequebook *noun* a book of forms for writing cheques and recording the transactions of an account.

chequebook journalism *noun* the payment of large sums by a newspaper etc. for exclusive rights to publish or broadcast stories, esp. personal or scandalous ones.

chequer esp. *Brit.* = CHECKER 3, 4.

chequerboard esp. *Brit.* = CHECKERBOARD.

chequered esp. *Brit.* = CHECKERED.

chequing account *noun* a bank account from which money may be withdrawn with cheques.

cherish *verb* (**cherishes, cherished, cherishing**) **1** love and want to protect: *he cherishes those children* ◊ *they cherish their freedom*. **2** keep a feeling or an idea in one's mind or heart and think of it with pleasure: *cherishing the memories*.

Cherokee • *noun* **1** (*plural* **Cherokee** or **Cherokees**) a member of an Iroquoian people living esp. in Oklahoma and North Carolina. **2** the language of this people. • *adjective* of the Cherokee or their language. [Say CHAIR uh key]

cherry • *noun* (*plural* **cherries**) **1 a** a small soft round fruit, usu. red when ripe, with a single stone in its centre. **b** a tree bearing this fruit or grown for its ornamental flowers. **2** the reddish wood of a cherry tree. • *adjective* of a light red colour.

cherry-pick *verb* selectively choose the most beneficial or profitable items, opportunities, etc. from what is available: *the company should buy the whole airline and not just cherry-pick its best assets*.

cherry-picker *noun* **1** a crane with a hinged arm and a bucket for raising and lowering workers, firefighters, etc. **2** *Cdn* (*BC*) a tractor-like machine with a crane for retrieving logs lost along a road etc.

cherry tomato *noun* (plural **cherry tomatoes**) a small red or yellow tomato.

cherrywood *noun* the reddish wood of a cherry tree.

chert *noun* a form of quartz like flint.

cherub *noun* (*plural* **cherubs**) **1** *Art* a representation of a winged child or the head of a winged child. **2** a beautiful or innocent child. [Say CHAIR ub]

cherubic *adjective* (esp. of a child) with a round and innocent face. [Say chair ROO bic]

cherubim *plural noun* (*singular* **cherub**) **1** *Bible* supernatural beings resembling winged lions with human faces. **2** *Christianity* members of the second order of the nine ranks of heavenly beings. [Say CHAIR oo bim for the plural, CHAIR ub for the singular]

Cheshire cat *noun* PHRASES **grin like a Cheshire cat** smile with a broad, contented grin as if highly amused or knowing a secret. [Say CHESH er]

chess *noun* a game for two, played on a chessboard with 16 pieces each, in which players attempt to place their opponent's king in checkmate.

chessboard *noun* a board with a pattern of squares of alternating colours, used in the game of chess.

chessman *noun* (*plural* **chessmen**) any of the 32 pieces used in the game of chess.

chest *noun* **1** the upper part of the body from the neck to the waist, esp. the front. **2** a large strong box, esp. for storage or transport of items. PHRASES **get a thing off one's chest** *informal* talk about a problem or say something that one has wanted to say for a long time, so that one has a feeling of relief: *you're obviously worried about something; why not get it off your chest?* **play** (or **keep**) **close to one's chest** *informal* be cautious or

secretive: *the press wanted to know the starting lineup, but the coach kept his cards close to his chest*.

chesterfield *noun* *Cdn* a couch.

chestnut • *noun* **1** any of various types of tree producing smooth brown nuts inside prickly cases. **2** the large edible nut of some of these trees. **3** the heavy wood of any of these trees. **4** = HORSE CHESTNUT. **5** a reddish-brown colour. **6** a horse of a reddish-brown or yellowish-brown colour. • *adjective* reddish brown.

chest of drawers *noun* (plural **chests of drawers**) a piece of furniture having a set of drawers in a frame.

chesty *adjective* (**chestier, chestiest**) **1** *informal* having large breasts or a large chest. **2** *slang* arrogant.

chevron *noun* a V-shaped mark or stripe, esp. on the sleeve of military uniform. [Say SHEV run or SHEV ron]

chew • *verb* **1** work (food etc.) between the teeth; crush or indent with the teeth. **2** shred, mangle, mutilate, etc.: *the car chewed up the road*. **3** (foll. by *on* or *over*) think about, discuss. **4** use chewing tobacco, esp. habitually. • *noun* **1** an act of chewing. **2** something intended for chewing, esp. tobacco or candy. PHRASES **chew the cud 1** (of an animal) ruminate. **2** reflect, ponder. **chew the fat** (or **rag**) *slang* chat. **chew out** *informal* reprimand harshly. ▸**chewable** *adjective* **chewer** *noun*

chewiness *noun* a chewy quality.

chewing gum *noun* flavoured and sweetened gum for chewing.

chewing tobacco *noun* flavoured tobacco designed for chewing rather than smoking.

chewy *adjective* (**chewier, chewiest**) requiring much chewing: *chewy bread*.

Cheyenne • *noun* **1** (*plural* **Cheyenne** or **Cheyennes**) a member of an Algonquian people of Oklahoma and Montana. **2** their language. • *adjective* of the Cheyenne or their language. [Say shy ANN or shy ENN]

chez *preposition* at the house or home of: *we spent the afternoon chez Freddie*. [Say SHAY]

ch'i *noun* (also **chi**) the physical life force postulated by certain Chinese philosophers to flow through the body. [Say CHEE]

Chianti *noun* (*plural* **Chiantis**) a dry usu. red Italian wine. [Say key AN tee]

chic • *adjective* (**chicer, chicest**) stylish, elegant (in dress or appearance). • *noun* stylishness, elegance. [Say SHEEK]

Chicana *noun* esp. *US* a female American of Mexican origin. [Say chick ONNA or chick ANNA]

chicanery *noun* (*plural* **chicaneries**) the use of trickery to achieve political, financial, or legal ends: *political chicanery during the leadership race discredited both the party and the province*. [Say shi KAY nuh ree]

Chicano *noun* (*plural* **Chicanos**) esp. *US* a Mexican-American. [Say chick ON oh or chick AN oh]

chi-chi *adjective* attempting stylish elegance but achieving only an over-elaborate pretentiousness: *the tiny chi-chi dining room*. [Say SHEE shee]

chick *noun* **1** a young or newly hatched bird, esp. a chicken. **2** *slang* often *offensive* a young woman.

chickadee *noun* any of various small North American birds, esp. the black-capped chickadee, with a distinctive dark-crowned head.

chicken • *noun* **1** any of several varieties of domestic fowl raised for their flesh or eggs. **2** the flesh of the chicken prepared as food. **3** *informal* a cowardly person. **4** *informal* a contest in which participants attempt to prove their bravery by being the last to yield in a dangerous or reckless race. **5** *informal* involving two cars racing towards each other. • *adjective* *informal* cowardly. • *verb* **chicken out** *informal* withdraw from some activity through fear or lack of nerve. PHRASES **count**

one's chickens (**before they're hatched**) be overconfident in anticipating success or good fortune before it is certain.

chicken-and-egg *adjective* pertaining to the unresolved question as to which of two things caused the other: *his overeating and depression are a chicken-and-egg situation*.

chicken feed *noun* **1** food for domestic fowl. **2** *informal* a small amount of money.

chicken-hearted *adjective* (also **chicken-livered**) easily frightened; lacking nerve or courage.

chicken pox *noun* an infectious disease, esp. of children, with a rash of small blisters.

chicken wire *noun* a light wire netting with a hexagonal mesh.

chickpea *noun* a yellowish-brown pea-shaped seed that can be cooked and eaten.

chickweed *noun* a common weed with slender stems and tiny white flowers.

chicle *noun* the milky juice of the sapodilla tree (a large tropical American evergreen), used in making chewing gum. [Say CHICK ul or CHICK lee]

chicory *noun* a blue-flowered plant grown for its salad leaves and for its root, which can be roasted and ground as a substitute for or an additive to coffee.

chide *verb* (**chides**, **chided**, **chiding**) scold, rebuke: *my friends chided me for not joining them*.

chief • *noun* **1** a leader, esp. of a tribe, clan, or Aboriginal group. **2** the head of a police or fire department etc.; the highest official. • *adjective* **1** first in position, importance, influence, etc.: *chief engineer*. **2** prominent, leading: *our chief concerns*.

chiefdom *noun* the domain of a chief.

chief electoral officer *noun* *Cdn* an official appointed to oversee the conduct of federal, provincial, and territorial elections.

chief executive *noun* **1** = CHIEF EXECUTIVE OFFICER. **2** (**Chief Executive**) the president of the US.

chief executive officer *noun* the highest-ranking executive of a corporation or other institution.

Chief Factor *noun* *Cdn* (in the fur trade) the senior officer overseeing a major trading post and its surrounding district.

chief justice *noun* (in Canada, the US, and several Commonwealth countries) the presiding judge of the Supreme Court or of a court which has several judges.

chiefly *adverb* above all; mainly but not exclusively.

Chief of Defence Staff *noun* the senior military official responsible for the control and administration of the Canadian Forces.

chief of staff *noun* **1** the senior staff officer of a branch of the armed forces. **2** the head of any government staff, esp. the adviser to a prime minister etc.

chieftain *noun* the leader of a tribe or clan; chief.

chiffon *noun* a thin almost transparent fabric made of silk, nylon, etc. [Say shif FON]

chigger *noun* **1** the larva of any of various mites, several of which are parasitic. **2** = CHIGOE.

chigoe *noun* a tropical flea which burrows beneath the skin of humans and animals and causes painful sores. [Say CHIG oh]

chihuahua *noun* a very small dog with smooth hair, large eyes, and prominent ears. [Say chuh WAH wah]

Chilcotin *noun* & *adjective* = TSILHQOT'IN. [Say chill KOTE un]

child *noun* (*plural* **children**) **1** a young human being below the age of puberty. **2** one's son or daughter (at any age). **3** a descendant or product of: *children of Israel* ◊

a child of the TV generation. **4** a childish person. PHRASES **with child** *archaic* pregnant.

child abuse *noun* cruel treatment of a child, esp. by beating, neglect, or sexual molestation.

child-bearing • *noun* the act of giving birth to a child. • *adjective* of, relating to, or suitable for the bearing of a child or children: *women of child-bearing age*.

childbirth *noun* the act of giving birth to a child.

child care *noun* **1** the care and rearing of a child or children. **2** = DAYCARE.

childhood *noun* the state or period of being a child.

childish *adjective* immature, silly. ▶ **childishly** *adverb* **childishness** *noun*

childless *adjective* not having a child or children: *a childless couple*. ▶ **childlessness** *noun*

childlike *adjective* **1** of or resembling a child: *a childlike appearance*. **2** having the qualities of a child, esp. positive ones such as innocence or frankness.

childproof • *adjective* **1** unable to be damaged, operated, or opened by a child: *childproof locks*. **2** designed to be safe for young children: *a childproof kitchen*. • *verb* make childproof: *we've done our best to childproof the kitchen*.

children *plural of* CHILD.

Children's Aid Society *noun* (also **Children's Aid**) (in Canada) an organization to provide assistance or guardianship for homeless or abused children.

child's play *noun* an easy task.

child support *noun* money paid by a parent to his or her divorced spouse for the support of their children.

child tax benefit *noun* (in Canada) a federal government program providing tax-free monthly payments to low- and moderate-income families with children under 18 years of age.

Chilean • *noun* **1** a native or national of Chile, a country on the west coast of South America. **2** a person of Chilean descent. • *adjective* of Chile. [Say CHILLY un or chill AY un]

SPELL CHECK
chili, Chile ☑ ABC

The country in South America is **Chile**.

---

chili *noun* (*plural* **chilies**) **1** the small pod of a type of pepper plant, often dried or made into powder and used to give a hot taste to food. **2 a** a spicy dish of chopped or ground meat, chilies or chili powder, and usu. cooked tomatoes, beans, and onions. **b** a similar dish without meat.

chili con carne *noun* = CHILI 2a. [Say con CAR nee]

chili dog *noun* a hot dog garnished with chili con carne.

chili powder *noun* a hot powder used to spice foods, usu. made with cayenne or dried chilies, garlic, cumin, and other spices.

chili sauce *noun* a spicy sauce made with tomatoes, chilies, and spices.

Chilkat *noun* a member of the Tlingit people inhabiting the Alaskan coast. [Say CHILL cat]

Chilkat blanket *noun* a five-sided ceremonial blanket worn by West Coast Aboriginal peoples, woven from mountain goat hair and shredded cedar bark.

chill • *noun* **1 a** an unpleasant cold sensation; lowered body temperature. **b** a feverish cold: *catch a chill*. **2** unpleasant coldness (of air, water, etc.): *I'll light a fire to take the chill out of the air*. **3 a** a depressing influence: *the news cast a chill over the room*. **4** coldness of manner. • *verb* **1** make or become cold. **2** depress. **3** (*also* **chill out**) *slang* **a** relax, settle down. **b** loiter, hang out.

• *adjective* chilly. PHRASES **take the chill off** warm slightly. ▶ **chiller** *noun*

chilliness *noun* a chilly state or condition.

chilling *adjective* frightening or horrifying, esp. because it is associated with something violent or cruel: *a chilling tale*. ▶ **chillingly** *adverb*

Chilliwack *noun* **1** a member of a Salishan people, a division of the Halkomelem, living in part of the Fraser River valley in BC. **2** the Halkomelem language of this people. [Say CHILL uh wack]

SPELL CHECK   ABC ✓
chilly, chili

The spicy food is **chili**. **Chili** is also the spelling in "chili pepper".

---

chilly *adjective* (**chillier**, **chilliest**) **1** somewhat cold. **2** unfriendly; unemotional.

chime • *noun* **1** a set of tuned bells. **2** the series of sounds given by this. • *verb* (**chimes**, **chimed**, **chiming**) **1 a** (of bells) ring. **b** sound (a bell or chime) by striking. **2** (of a clock or bell) indicate the hour by chiming. PHRASES **chime in** interject a remark: *as usual, Stella chimed in with something irrelevant*.

chimera *noun* **1** *Greek Myth* any mythical beast with parts taken from several animals, esp. a fire-breathing female monster with a lion's head, a goat's body, and a serpent's tail. **2** a thing that is hoped or wished for but is impossible to achieve: *your proposal for economic sovereignty is a chimera*. [Say kye MEER uh or kim EER uh]

chimes *plural noun* **1** a musical instrument comprising a set of tuned bells or bars. **2** a doorbell.

chimichanga *noun* a tortilla wrapped around a filling of esp. meat and deep-fried. [Say chimmy CHAN guh]

chimney *noun* **1** a vertical shaft conducting smoke or steam away from a fire, furnace, etc., often extending above the roof of a house. **2** a glass tube protecting the flame of an oil lamp. **3** a steep narrow crack in a rock face, often used by mountaineers to climb.

chimney sweep *noun* a person whose job is removing soot from inside chimneys.

chimp *noun informal* = CHIMPANZEE.

chimpanzee *noun* an ape with large ears, mainly black coloration, and lighter skin on the face, native to the forests of west and central Africa.

chin *noun* the front of the lower jaw. PHRASES **chin up!** *informal* cheer up! **keep one's chin up** *informal* remain cheerful in difficult circumstances. **take it on the chin** *informal* suffer or endure misfortune, esp. courageously: *investors have been taking it on the chin as stock prices have fallen dramatically*.

china *noun* **1** a kind of fine white ceramic used in making esp. dishes. **2** things made from china, esp. household cups and plates or figurines.

Chinatown *noun* a district of any non-Chinese city in which the population is predominantly Chinese.

chinch bug *noun* a small insect that destroys the shoots of grasses and grains.

chinchilla *noun* **1 a** a small South American rodent with soft grey fur and a long bushy tail. **b** the valuable fur of this animal. **2** a cat or rabbit with silver-grey fur like that of a chinchilla. [Say chin CHILL uh]

Chinese • *adjective* of or relating to China, its people, or its language. • *noun* **1** the language of China, which has several dialects including Mandarin and Cantonese. **2** (*plural* **Chinese**) a person of Chinese nationality or descent.

Chinese checkers *noun* a game for two to six players played with marbles, in which players attempt to move all of their marbles from one point of a star-shaped board to the opposite one.

Chinese New Year *noun* the celebration of the New Year in the Chinese calendar, observed officially for a month starting in late January or early February.

ching *noun* an abrupt ringing sound, esp. one made by a cash register.

chink • *noun* **1** a slight ringing sound, as of glasses or coins striking together. **2** a narrow opening or crack, esp. one that allows light to pass through. • *verb* make a slight ringing sound. PHRASES **a chink in one's armour** a weakness.

chinned *adjective* having a particular kind of chin: *a round-chinned, innocent face*.

Chinook *noun* **1** a member of a Pacific Coast Aboriginal people formerly living along the Columbia River in Oregon and Washington. **2** the language of this people. [Say shin NOOK]

chinook *noun* **1 a** a warm dry wind which blows east of the Rocky Mountains, often causing significant temperature increases in winter. **b** a warm wet southerly wind west of the Rocky Mountains. **2** (also **chinook salmon**) a large silver-coloured salmon with black spots, native to the north Pacific and introduced into the Great Lakes and elsewhere. [Say shin NOOK]

Chinook Jargon *noun* a language consisting of elements of Chinook, Nuu-chah-nulth, English, and French, formerly used by traders in the north Pacific region of North America.

chinos *plural noun* casual pants made from a cotton twill fabric, usu. khaki-coloured. [Say CHEE nose]

chintz *noun* a multicoloured cotton fabric with a glazed finish and often a floral pattern, used esp. for curtains and upholstery. [Say CHINTS]

chintzy *adjective* (**chintzier**, **chintziest**) **1** resembling or decorated with chintz. **2** of poor quality: *chintzy tourist items*. **3** miserly: *a chintzy salary increase*.

chin-up *noun* an exercise in which one raises oneself with one's arms by pulling against a horizontal bar fixed above one's head.

chinwag *informal* • *noun* a talk or chat. • *verb* (**chinwags**, **chinwagged**, **chinwagging**) chat or gossip.

chip • *noun* **1 a** a small piece removed by or in the course of chopping, cutting, or breaking, esp. from hard material such as wood or stone. **b** the place from which such a chip has been removed. **2 a** (also **potato chip**) a wafer-thin slice of potato deep-fried until crisp and eaten as a snack. **b** a similarly thin and crisp food: *nacho chips*. **3** a small piece of chocolate etc. used in baking. **4** *Cdn & Brit.* = FRENCH FRY. **5** a piece of dried bovine dung, esp. when used as fuel. **6** a counter used in some gambling games to represent money. **7** = MICROCHIP *noun*. **8** (also **chip shot**) *Sport* a short shot, kick, or pass with the ball travelling in an arc. • *verb* (**chips**, **chipped**, **chipping**) **1** cut or break (a piece) from a hard material. **2** (often foll. by *at*, *away at*) cut pieces off (a hard material) to alter its shape, break it up, etc. **3** (of stone, china, etc.) be susceptible to being chipped: *will chip easily*. **4** *Sport* strike or kick (the ball) so that it travels in a short arc. PHRASES **chip in** *informal* contribute (money etc.). **a chip off the old block** a child who resembles a parent, esp. in character. **a chip on one's shoulder** a disposition or inclination to feel resentful or aggrieved. **let the chips fall where they may** whatever the consequences. **when the chips are down** when the situation becomes difficult or critical.

chipboard *noun* a rigid sheet made from compressed wood chips, splinters, sawdust, and resin.

C

> **WRITING TIP**
> **Chipewyan, Chippewa**
>
> The Ojibwa living to the east, south, and southwest of the Great Lakes are the **Chippewa**. They should not be confused with the **Chipewyans**, who live in northwestern Canada.

Chipewyan • *noun* (*plural* **Chipewyans**) **1** a member of an Athapaskan people inhabiting much of the northern Prairie provinces and the subarctic NWT. **2** the language of this people. • *adjective* of or relating to this people or their language. [Say chippa WHY un]

chipmunk *noun* a burrowing ground squirrel with alternate light and dark stripes along the back.

chipotle *noun* a hot red pepper, usu. smoked, commonly used in Mexican cooking. [Say chip OAT lay]

chipper • *adjective informal* cheerful and lively. • *noun* a person or tool that chips timber.

> **WRITING TIP**
> **Chippewa, Chipewyan**
>
> **Chippewa** is normally used to refer only to the Ojibwa living to the east, south, and southwest of the Great Lakes. They should not be confused with the **Chipewyans**, an Athapaskan people living in northwestern Canada.

Chippewa *noun & adjective* (*plural* **Chippewa** or **Chippewas**) = OJIBWA. [Say CHIPPA wah]

chippiness *noun* **1** irritability. **2** *Hockey* rough or dirty play.

chippy *adjective* (**chippier, chippiest**) *Cdn informal* **1** short-tempered or irritable. **2** *Hockey* characterized by rough or dirty play.

chip set *noun* a collection of integrated circuits forming the set needed to make an electronic device such as a computer motherboard.

chip shot *noun* a short shot, kick, or pass with the ball travelling in an arc.

chip wagon *noun Cdn* a mobile roadside stand or vehicle selling french fries etc.

chiropodist *noun* esp. *Cdn & Brit.* = PODIATRIST. [Say shuh ROP uh dist or kuh ROP uh dist]

chiropractic *noun* the work of a chiropractor. [Say kye roe PRAK tik]

chiropractor *noun* a person who treats joint disorders, esp. those of the spine, by using his or her hands to press and move the bones. [Say KYE roe prak ter]

chirp • *verb* **1** (of small birds, grasshoppers, etc.) emit a short sharp high-pitched note. **2** speak or say in a lively or cheerful way. • *noun* a chirping sound.

chirpily *adverb* in a chirpy manner.

chirpiness *noun* cheerfulness.

chirpy *adjective* (**chirpier, chirpiest**) *informal* cheerful, lively.

chirrup • *verb* (**chirrups, chirruped, chirruping**) (esp. of small birds) chirp, esp. repeatedly. • *noun* a chirruping sound. ▶ **chirrupy** *adjective* [Say CHUR up]

chisel • *noun* a tool with a sharp flat blade for shaping wood, stone, or metal. • *verb* (**chisels, chiselled, chiselling**) cut or shape with or as if with a chisel: *chiselled the columns out of stone.* ▶ **chiseller** *noun*

chiselled *adjective* (of facial features etc.) strongly and clearly defined: *a finely chiselled jaw.*

chit *noun* a note showing an amount of money owed.

chit-chat *informal* • *noun* light conversation; gossip. • *verb* (**chit-chats, chit-chatted, chit-chatting**) talk informally; gossip.

chitin *noun* a tough semi-transparent substance that is found particularly in the hard shells of crabs, insects, and other arthropods. [Say KITE in]

chitter • *verb* (of a bird, squirrel, etc.) make a chattering or twittering sound. • *noun* a twittering or chattering sound.

chivalric *adjective* of or relating to the historical notion of chivalry.

chivalrous *adjective* (usu. of a man) gallant, honourable, and courteous, esp. towards women. ▶ **chivalrously** *adverb* [Say SHIV 'll rus, SHIV 'll rus lee]

chivalry *noun* **1** courteous behaviour, esp. that of a man towards women. **2 a** (in the Middle Ages) the ideal qualities expected of a knight, such as courage, honour, and concern for weak and helpless people. **b** the religious, moral, and social system of the Middle Ages, based on these qualities: *the age of chivalry.* [Say SHIV 'll ree]

chive *noun* (usu. **chives**) a small plant related to the onion, with dense tufts of long tube-shaped leaves which are used as a flavouring.

chlamydia *noun* **1** (*plural* **chlamydiae**) any of various parasitic bacteria, some of which cause diseases such as trachoma in humans. **2** a urinary or genital infection caused by sexually transmitted chlamydiae. [Say kluh MIDDY uh for the singular, kluh MIDDY ee for the plural]

chloride *noun* any compound of chlorine with another element or group. [Say KLOR ide]

chlorinate *verb* (**chlorinates, chlorinated, chlorinating**) **1** treat (water etc.) with chlorine, esp. to disinfect it. **2** cause to react or combine with chlorine. ▶ **chlorination** *noun* [Say KLOR in ate, klori NAY sh'n]

chlorine *noun* a chemical element, a poisonous pale green gas with a strong smell, used for purifying water, bleaching, etc. Chlorine occurs naturally esp. as sodium chloride in salt and sea water. [Say klor EEN or KLOR een]

chlorofluorocarbon = CFC. [Say kloro FLORO carbon]

chloroform *noun* a colourless sweet-smelling liquid which, when inhaled, makes people unconscious, formerly used as a general anaesthetic. [Say KLOR uh form]

chlorophyll *noun* the green pigment found in most plants, responsible for absorbing light to provide energy for photosynthesis. [Say KLOR a fill]

chock *noun* **1** a block or wedge of wood used to prevent a wheel etc. from moving. **2** a strong metal eye or hook through which a line may be passed or secured.

chockablock *adjective* completely full with people or things: *the street was chockablock with cars.*

chock full *adjective* crammed full of people or things.

chocoholic *noun* (also **chocaholic**) *informal* a person who likes chocolate a great deal.

chocolate • *noun* **1 a** an edible paste or solid made from cacao seeds by roasting, grinding, etc., often combined with flavourings, sugar, cream, etc. **b** a candy made of or coated with this. **c** a drink made by mixing chocolate with (usu. hot) milk or water. **2** (also **chocolate brown**) dark brown. • *adjective* **1** made from or flavoured with chocolate. **2** (also **chocolate brown**) dark brown. ▶ **chocolatey** *adjective*

Choctaw *noun* (*plural* **Choctaw** or **Choctaws**) **1** a member of a Muskogean people originally living in Mississippi and Alabama and later in Oklahoma. **2** the language spoken by this people and the Chickasaw. [Say CHOCK taw]

choice • *noun* **1 a** an act of selecting or making a decision when faced with two or more possibilities: *the choice between good and evil.* **b** a thing or person chosen: *cake is a good choice.* **c** one of two or more possibilities from which one may choose: *these are your choices.* **?** a range from which to choose: *sofas available in a choice of*

40 fabrics. **3** the best or preferred item: *the critics' choice*. **4** the power or opportunity to choose: *what choice do I have?* **5** the right of a woman to choose to have an abortion. • *adjective* (**choicer, choicest**) **1** of superior quality; carefully chosen. **2** designating a grade of canned fruits and vegetables between standard and fancy, where slight variation in size, colour, or maturity is allowed but the produce is almost free from blemishes and other defects. PHRASES **by choice** because one has chosen. **of choice** preferred. **of one's choice** that one has chosen.

choir *noun* **1** an organized group of singers, typically one that takes part in church services or performs regularly in public. **2** the part of some churches between the altar and the nave, used by the choir and clergy. [Say KWIRE]

choke • *verb* (**chokes, choked, choking**) **1** hinder or impede the breathing of, esp. by constricting the windpipe or (of gas, smoke, etc.) by being unbreathable. **2** suffer a hindrance or stoppage of breath: *choked on a piece of food*. **3** (often foll. by *up*) make or become speechless from emotion. **4** retard the growth of or kill (esp. plants) by the deprivation of light, air, nourishment, etc. **5** (often foll. by *back*) suppress (emotions) with difficulty. **6** (often foll. by *up*) block or clog (a passage, tube, etc.). **7** esp. *Sport informal* fail to perform effectively when under pressure. **8** enrich the fuel mixture in (an internal combustion engine) by reducing the intake of air. • *noun* **1** an action or sound of a person or animal having or seeming to have difficulty in breathing: *a little choke of laughter*. **2** the valve in the carburetor of an internal combustion engine that controls the intake of air, esp. to enrich the fuel mixture. PHRASES **choke down** swallow with difficulty. **choke off** impede or stop.

chokeberry *noun* (*plural* **chokeberries**) a North American shrub of the rose family, with white flowers and red autumn foliage and bearing a bitter, scarlet, berry-like fruit.

chokecherry *noun* (*plural* **chokecherries**) a North American cherry tree bearing small bitter cherries suitable for making jellies, wine, etc.

choked *adjective* clogged or plugged: *a snow-choked road*.

choker *noun* **1** a close-fitting necklace or ornamental neckband. **2** a heavy cable with a hook used for gripping and hauling logs. **3** a competitor that fails to perform effectively under pressure.

cholecalciferol *noun* one of the D vitamins, produced by the action of sunlight on a cholesterol derivative widely distributed in the skin. [Say CALL ee cal SIF er all]

cholera *noun* an infectious and often fatal bacterial disease of the small intestine, spread esp. through infected water supplies and causing severe vomiting and diarrhea. [Say CALL er uh]

cholesterol *noun* a substance found throughout the body, especially in fats, blood, and nerve tissue. Cholesterol is an integral part of all cell membranes, but high levels in the blood (mainly derived from animal fats in the diet) are thought to cause damage to the arteries. [Say kuh LESS ter all]

chomp • *verb* munch or chew noisily. • *noun* a chewing noise or motion. PHRASES **chomp at the bit 1** (of a horse etc.) work the bit of a bridle noisily between the teeth. **2** be restlessly impatient to start to do something.

choose *verb* (**chooses**; *past* **chose**; *past participle* **chosen**; **choosing**) **1** select from a number of alternatives. **2** (usu. foll. by *between, from*) take or select one or another. **3** decide, be determined: *chose to stay*

behind. **4** like, prefer: *do as you choose*. PHRASES **cannot choose but** must. **nothing** (or **little**) **to choose between** little or no difference between. ▶ **chooser** *noun*

choosy *adjective* (**choosier, choosiest**) *informal* demanding, fussy: *breeders are choosy about dog food*.

chop • *verb* (**chops, chopped, chopping**) **1 a** cut or fell by a blow, usu. with an axe or other blade. **b** make or prepare by cutting into large pieces: *chop firewood*. **2** cut (esp. meat or vegetables) into small pieces. **3** strike (esp. a ball) with a short downward stroke or blow. **4** *informal* remove; reduce by: *chopped $5,000 from the budget*. • *noun* **1** a cutting blow, esp. with an axe. **2** a thick slice of meat (esp. pork or lamb) usu. including a rib. **3** a short downward stroke or blow in tennis, baseball, boxing, etc. **4** the broken motion of water, usu. owing to the action of the wind against the tide. **5** *Cdn, Brit., & Austral. informal* (**the chop**) *informal* a dismissal from employment. **b** the action of killing or being killed.

chopped liver *noun* **1** a dish of cooked liver, chopped with onions, hard-boiled eggs, and seasonings. **2** *slang* a person or thing regarded as unimportant: *she invited everyone but me; what am I, chopped liver?*

chopper *noun* **1** a person or tool that chops. **2** *informal* a helicopter. **3** *Baseball* a high-bouncing ground ball.

chopping block *noun* a block of wood on which logs etc. are chopped with an axe or on which food is cut with a knife. PHRASES **on the chopping block** likely to be eliminated etc.: *government programs on the chopping block*.

choppy *adjective* (**choppier, choppiest**) **1** (of water) with a rough surface of small, irregular waves. **2** uneven, not smooth: *his writing style is erratic and choppy* ◊ *a choppy stride*.

chops *plural noun* **1** the jaw or mouth. **2** *Music informal* the skill required to play a wind instrument: *I didn't have the chops to play trumpet in the stage band*. PHRASES **bust one's chops** *slang* exert oneself. **bust someone's chops** *slang* nag or criticize.

chopstick *noun* each of a pair of thin sticks of wood or plastic etc., held both in one hand as eating utensils, originally in east Asia.

chop suey *noun* a Chinese-style dish usu. of meat, bean sprouts, bamboo shoots, and onions. [Say chop SOO ee]

SPELL CHECK **choral, coral**	ABC✓
The substance found in the sea is **coral**.	

choral *adjective* of, composed for, or sung by a choir: *a choral concert* ◊ *a choral service*. [Say CORE ul]

SPELL CHECK **chorale, corral**	ABC✓
A pen for horses is a **corral**.	

chorale *noun* **1** a grand but simple hymn tune, or harmonized version of this: *a Bach chorale*. **2** esp. *US* a choir. [Say core AL]

SPELL CHECK **chord, cord**	ABC✓
Parts of the body are the **spinal cord** and **vocal cords**; a type of rope is **cord**.	

chord • *noun* **1** a group of usu. three or more notes sounded together in harmony. **2** *Math* a straight line that joins two points on the edge of a circle or the ends of an arc. • *verb* play a chord, esp. on a guitar. PHRASES **strike** (or **touch**) **a chord** evoke some reaction, esp.

sympathy, in a person or people: *the show on homelessness struck a chord with viewers*.

chordal *adjective* of a musical chord.

chore *noun* **1 a** a routine task, esp. a household one. **b** (**chores**) the routine daily tasks of a farm. **2** any tedious or unpleasant piece of work: *writing all these thank-you cards is such a chore*.

chorea *noun* a medical disorder characterized by jerky involuntary movements affecting esp. the shoulders, hips, and face. [Say kuh REE uh]

choreograph *verb* **1** design and arrange movements for dancers or figure skaters. **2** arrange or direct esp. something involving large numbers of people and complicated interactions: *the ceremony was carefully choreographed*. ▶**choreographer** *noun* [Say COREY a graph, corey OGRA fur]

choreographic *adjective* involving or pertaining to choreography. ▶**choreographically** *adverb* [Say corey a GRAPHIC]

choreography *noun* (*plural* **choreographies**) **1** the art of designing and arranging the movements for a staged dance, figure skating program, etc. **2** the sequence of movements in a dance or figure skating program. [Say corey OGRA fee]

chorion *noun* the outermost membrane surrounding an embryo of a mammal, reptile, or bird. ▶**chorionic** *adjective* [Say COREY un, corey ON ick]

chorister *noun* a person who sings in a choir. [Say CORE ist er]

chortle • *verb* (**chortles**, **chortled**, **chortling**) chuckle gleefully. • *noun* a gleeful chuckle.

chorus • *noun* (*plural* **choruses**) **1** a group (esp. a large one) of singers; a choir. **2** a piece of music composed for a choir. **3** a part of a popular song that is sung after each verse. **4** something said or shouted by many people together: *a chorus of boos*. **5** a group of singers or dancers performing in a musical comedy, opera, etc. **6 a** (in Greek tragedy) a group of performers who comment together on the main action. **b** (in Elizabethan drama) a character who speaks the prologue and other linking parts of the play. **c** the part spoken by the chorus. • *verb* (**choruses**, **chorused**, **chorusing**) (of a group) speak or utter simultaneously: *"Thank you," we chorused*. **PHRASES** **in chorus** all together; in unison: *they responded in chorus*.

chorus line *noun* a group of esp. female singers and dancers performing in a musical comedy, cabaret act, etc., often dancing together in a long line.

chose *past* of CHOOSE.

chosen • *verb past participle* of CHOOSE. • *adjective* **1** selected or preferred: *law was her chosen profession*. **2** destined by God for salvation: *the chosen people*.

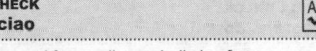

SPELL CHECK
chow, ciao

An Italian word for goodbye or hello is **ciao**.

chow *noun slang* **1** food. **2** (also **chow chow**) a breed of dog developed in China, with a thick coat, compact body, a bluish-black tongue, and a tail curled over the back. **PHRASES** **chow down** eat.

chowder *noun* a thick soup, usu. containing fish, clams, corn, or potatoes.

chow mein *noun* a Chinese-style dish of fried noodles with chopped meat or shrimp etc. and vegetables. [Say chow MAIN]

chrism *noun* a consecrated mixture of oil and balsam used for anointing in rites of the Catholic and Orthodox Churches. [Say KRIZ'm]

Christ *noun* Jesus Christ, the central figure of the Christian religion.

christen *verb* **1** give a person a name at baptism as a sign of admission to the Christian church: *their second child was christened Ruth*. **2** give someone or something a name, esp. one that reflects a notable feature: *because of his exceptional talent he was christened "the Great One"*. **3** *informal* use for the first time: *let's have a drink to christen our new wine glasses*. [Say CRISS'n]

Christendom *noun* the worldwide body of Christians; the Christian world. [Say CRISS'n dum]

christening *noun* a ceremony in which someone is christened; a baptism. [Say CRISS'n ing]

Christian • *adjective* **1** of, based on, or believing in the teachings of Christ. **2** having or showing the qualities associated with Christianity, esp. kindness and fairness: *that's not a very Christian way to behave!* • *noun* a person who has received Christian baptism or is a believer in Christ and his teachings. ▶**Christianization** *noun* **Christianize** *verb* (**Christianizes**, **Christianized**, **Christianizing**)

Christian era *noun* the era reckoned from the traditional date of Christ's birth.

Christianity *noun* the religion based on the teachings of Christ and his disciples, comprising the Catholic, Protestant, and Orthodox faiths.

Christian Reformed *adjective* of or relating to a Calvinist Christian denomination whose followers are mainly of Dutch origin.

Christian Science *noun* the beliefs and practices of the Church of Christ, Scientist, which holds that only God and the mind have ultimate reality, and that sin and illness are illusions that can be overcome by prayer and faith. ▶**Christian Scientist** *noun*

Christie *noun Skiing* a sudden turn in which the skis are kept parallel, used for changing direction or stopping quickly.

Christmas *noun* (*plural* **Christmases**) **1** (also **Christmas Day**) **a** *Christianity* the annual festival of Christ's birth, celebrated by Roman Catholics and Protestants on Dec. 25, and by Ukrainian Catholics and Orthodox Christians on Jan. 7. **b** a national holiday marking this on Dec. 25. **2** the season surrounding this.

Christmas cake *noun Cdn & Brit.* a rich fruitcake eaten at Christmas.

Christmas cracker *noun* a small tube wrapped in decorated paper gathered at both ends, usu. containing a paper hat, small toy, etc., which pops when the ends are pulled to open it, usu. at a Christmas dinner.

Christmas pudding *noun* a rich heavy steamed dessert eaten at Christmas, made with flour, fat, dried fruit, spices, etc.

Christmastime *noun* (also **Christmastide**) the Christmas season.

Christmas tree *noun* **1** an evergreen or artificial tree set up with decorations at Christmas. **2** *Cdn* a Christmas party. **3** a system of pipes and valves which controls the pressure of an oil or natural gas well.

Christmasy *adjective* involved in, enthusiastic about, or characteristic of Christmas celebrations.

chromatic *adjective* **1** *Music* **a** (of a scale) ascending or descending by semitones. **b** (of an instrument) capable of producing all the tones of the chromatic scale: *chromatic harmonica*. **c** having notes not belonging to the prevailing scale: *chromatic chord*. **2** pertaining to colour; brightly coloured. [Say crow MAT ik]

chromatographic *adjective* pertaining to chromatography. [Say CROW muh tuh GRAPH ic]

chromatography *noun* a method of separating or analyzing a mixture of gases, liquids, or dissolved substances by slowly passing it through a material

through which the components of the mixture move at different rates. [Say crow ma TOG ra fee]

chrome *noun* a shiny coating of chromium on the trimmings of a car etc. [Say KROME]

chromed *adjective* plated or trimmed with chromium.

chromium *noun* a hard white metallic element used in alloys and as a shiny silvery decorative coating. [Say CROW me um]

chromosomal *adjective* pertaining to chromosomes. [Say CROW muh SOAM'l]

chromosome *noun* one of the structures within a cell which determine an individual's characteristics, each consisting of a single strand of DNA. A normal human cell contains 46 chromosomes, 23 from each parent. [Say CROW muh soam]

chronic *adjective* **1** persisting for a long time: *a chronic illness* ◊ *chronic unemployment*. **2** having a chronic complaint: *a chronic patient*. **3** *informal* habitual: *a chronic liar*. ▶ **chronically** *adverb*

chronic fatigue syndrome *noun* a disease characterized by extreme fatigue, poor coordination, giddiness, depression, and general malaise, the cause of which is unknown. Abbreviation: **CFS**.

chronicle • *noun* **1** a record of events in the order in which they happened. **2** a narrative, a full account. • *verb* (**chronicles, chronicled, chronicling**) record events in the order of their occurrence. ▶ **chronicler** *noun*

chronograph *noun* **1** a type of very accurate clock. **2** a stopwatch. [Say CRON uh graph or CROW nuh graph]

chronological *adjective* **1** arranged or considered in the order of their occurrence. **2** of or relating to time or chronology. ▶ **chronologically** *adverb* [Say kronna LOGICAL]

chronology *noun* (*plural* **chronologies**) **1** the arrangement of events etc. in the order of their occurrence. **2** a table or document showing this. [Say kruh NOLLA jee]

chronometer *noun* a very accurate clock used esp. in navigation. [Say kruh NOMMA tur]

chrysalis *noun* (*plural* **chrysalises**) **1 a** a butterfly or moth in the dormant stage between larva and adult. **b** the hard outer case enclosing it. **2** a preparatory or transitional state: *he emerged from the chrysalis of adolescence*. [Say KRISS uh liss for the singular, KRISS uh liss ez for the plural]

chrysanthemum *noun* a plant of the daisy family, with brightly coloured flowers. [Say kris SANTH uh mum]

chub *noun* **1** a fish with a short, thick, rounded body and large head, esp. a member of the carp family. **2** a short, fat sausage.

chubbiness *noun* plumpness.

chubby *adjective* (**chubbier, chubbiest**) (esp. of a person etc.) plump and rounded.

chuck • *verb* **1** *informal* **a** fling or throw carelessly or with indifference. **b** (also **chuck out**) throw out. **2** touch playfully, esp. under the chin. • *noun* **1** a playful touch under the chin. **2** a device for holding e.g. a bit in a drill. **3** a cut of beef extending from the neck to the sixth rib. **4** *informal* food, provisions. **5** (*West Coast*) *informal* a large body of water (*compare* SALTCHUCK).

chuckle • *verb* (**chuckles, chuckled, chuckling**) laugh quietly or to oneself. • *noun* a quiet or suppressed laugh.

chuckwagon *noun* **1** a vehicle carrying provisions, cooking utensils, etc., as used on a ranch, originally a wagon covered with a canvas supported by hoops. **2** a small cart resembling this, used in chuckwagon races.

chuckwagon dinner *noun* an informal meal in the style of those served from chuckwagons, usu. consisting of beef, potatoes, baked beans, etc.

chuckwagon race *noun* a rodeo event in which chuckwagons pulled by teams of four horses race on an oval course.

chuff *verb* **1** (of a steam engine etc.) move with a regular sharp puffing sound. **2** make a sound like a puffing steam engine.

chug • *verb* (**chugs, chugged, chugging**) **1** emit a regular muffled explosive sound, as of an engine running slowly. **2** move with this sound: *the boat chugged across the lake*. **3** move slowly but steadily: *Big Biff chugged over the blue line*. **4** *slang* drink in large gulps without pausing. • *noun* a chugging sound.

chugalug *verb* (**chugalugs, chugalugged, chugalugging**) = CHUG 4.

chum • *noun* **1** *informal* a close friend. **2** chopped fish or fish refuse, esp. used as bait. **3** a salmon of the North American Pacific coast. • *verb* (**chums, chummed, chumming**) **1** associate with as a friend: *he chums around with Chantal*. **2** fish using chopped fish as bait.

chumminess *noun* close friendliness.

chummy *adjective* *informal* (**chummier, chummiest**) friendly, sociable.

chump *noun* *informal* a gullible or foolish person.

chunk • *noun* **1 a** a thick solid slice or piece of something firm or hard. **b** a substantial amount or piece. **2** a muffled metallic sound. • *verb* **1** tear or cut into chunks. **2** make a muffled metallic sound.

chunky *adjective* (**chunkier, chunkiest**) **1** containing or consisting of chunks. **2** thick and solid. **3** (of clothes) made of a thick material. **4** (of a person) stocky.

chuppah *noun* (also **chuppa**) a canopy beneath which Jewish marriage ceremonies are performed. [Say HOOP ah (with OO as in BOOK)]

church *noun* (*plural* **churches**) **1** a building for public (usu. Christian) worship. **2** a meeting for public worship in such a building: *met after church*. **3** (also **Church**) the body of all Christians, or a specific organized Christian group of any time, country, or distinct principles of worship: *the medieval Church* ◊ *Church of Scotland*. **4** (also **Church**) institutionalized religion as a political or social force: *Church and State*. PHRASES **poor as a church mouse** very poor.

churchgoer *noun* a person who goes to church, esp. regularly. ▶ **churchgoing** *noun & adjective*

churchman *noun* (*plural* **churchmen**) a male member of the clergy or of a church.

Church of Christ, Scientist *noun* the official name of the Christian Science Church.

Church of England *noun* an English branch of Christianity, which has bishops but rejects the Pope's supremacy; the Anglican Church in England.

Church of Jesus Christ of Latter-day Saints *noun* the official name of the Mormon Church.

Church of Scotland *noun* the official (Presbyterian) Church in Scotland.

churchwarden *noun* *Anglicanism* either of two elected lay representatives of a parish.

churchwoman *noun* (*plural* **churchwomen**) a woman member of the clergy or of a church.

churchy *adjective* **1** excessively pious or intolerantly devoted to the Christian Church. **2** like a church.

churchyard *noun* a yard surrounding a church, esp. a graveyard.

churl *noun* a rude or boorish person.

churlish *adjective* ungrateful or ungracious. ▶ **churlishly** *adverb* **churlishness** *noun*

churn • *noun* a machine for making butter by agitating milk or cream. • *verb* **1** agitate milk or cream in a churn to produce butter. **2** (usu. foll. by *up*) cause

distress to; upset, agitate. **3** (esp. of a liquid) move about violently: *my stomach churned*. **4** (often foll. by *up*) agitate or move (liquid, soil, etc.) vigorously. PHRASES **churn out** produce routinely or mechanically, esp. in large quantities: *churns out a dozen cheap novels a year*.

chute *noun* **1** a sloping or vertical channel, tube, or slide, with or without water, for conveying things to a lower level. **2** a slide into a swimming pool. **3 a** a pen from which an animal is released to begin a race, rodeo event, etc. **b** a narrow passage or enclosure for sheep or cattle. **4** *Cdn* a rapid in a river. **5** *informal* a parachute. [Say SHOOT]

chutney *noun* (plural **chutneys**) a spicy sauce made of fruits or vegetables, vinegar, sugar, etc.

chutzpah *noun* *slang* boldness, esp. if shameless or outrageous: *telling her boss he was wrong took real chutzpah*. [Say HOOTZ puh (with OO as in *HOOK*)]

CI *abbreviation* *Cdn* Collegiate Institute.

Ci *abbreviation* curie.

CIA *abbreviation* CENTRAL INTELLIGENCE AGENCY.

ciao *interjection* *informal* **1** goodbye. **2** hello. [Sounds like *CHOW*]

CIAU *abbreviation* Canadian Inter-university Athletic Union.

cicada *noun* a large transparent-winged insect which makes a loud, shrill, chirping sound, esp. in August. [Say sick AID uh]

CIDA *abbreviation* Canadian International Development Agency. [Say SEE dah]

cider *noun* **1** a thick pure apple juice. **2** (also **hard cider**) an alcoholic drink made from fermented apple juice.

cigar *noun* a cylinder of rolled tobacco leaves for smoking. PHRASES **close but no cigar** *informal* (of an attempt etc.) almost but not quite successful.

cigarette *noun* **1** a thin cylinder of finely-cut tobacco rolled in paper for smoking. **2** a similar cylinder containing a drug or medicated substance.

cilantro *noun* fresh coriander, used as a herb. [Say sill AN tro]

cilia *plural noun* (*singular* **cilium**) **1** tiny hairlike vibrating structures on the surface of some cells, causing currents in the surrounding fluid. **2** eyelashes. [Say SILL ee ah for the plural, SILL ee um for the singular]

ciliary *adjective* pertaining to cilia. [Say SILLY airy]

ciliate • *adjective* (also **ciliated**) having cilia. • *noun* a protozoan with cilia. [Say SILLY ate]

cinch • *noun* **1** *informal* **a** a sure thing; a certainty: *they're a cinch to win*. **b** an easy task: *that last math problem was a cinch*. **2** a firm hold. **3** a girth for a saddle or pack. • *verb* (**cinches, cinched, cinching**) **1** tighten or grip with or as with a cinch: *cinched at the waist with a belt*. **2** *slang* make certain of: *the government denied any evidence to support his claim and thus cinched his conviction*.

cinchona *noun* a South American evergreen tree or shrub with fragrant flowers, whose bark contains quinine. [Say sing CONE uh]

cinder *noun* **1** a small piece of partly-burned coal or wood that has stopped giving off flames but still has combustible matter in it. **2** (in *plural*) ashes: *cleaned the cinders out of the fireplace*.

cinder block • *noun* the standard block used in building warehouses etc., made of cinders mixed with sand and cement. • *adjective* (**cinder-block**) made with cinder blocks: *a cinder-block wall*.

Cinderella *noun* **1** a person or thing whose talents or merits go unrecognized, esp. one that achieves success in the end: *Cinderella team*. **2** a neglected or despised member of a group.

cindery *adjective* covered with, containing, or resembling cinders: *cindery debris was all that remained*.

cinema *noun* movies generally; the production of movies as an art or industry: *a star of the cinema*.

cinematic *adjective* **1** having the qualities characteristic of the cinema: *cinematic techniques*. **2** of or relating to the cinema: *the festival was a cinematic extravaganza*. ▶ **cinematically** *adverb*

cinematographer *noun* the person in charge of lighting and camera operations for a scene being filmed. [Say SIN uh muh TOG ruh fer]

cinematographic *adjective* pertaining to cinematography. [Say SIN uh muh tuh GRAPHIC]

cinematography *noun* the art or technique of shooting motion pictures, involving the choice of film, camera, lens, lighting, camera angle, etc. [Say SIN uh muh TOG ruh fee]

Cineplex *noun* (plural **Cineplexes**) *proprietary* a complex consisting of several separate movie theatres.

cinnamon *noun* **1** a spice from the peeled, dried, and rolled bark of a Southeast Asian tree. **2 a** yellowish-brown. **b** reddish-brown.

cinnamon bun *noun* (also **cinnamon roll**) a baked spiral of dough sprinkled with cinnamon and sugar, often iced and with raisins.

cinquefoil *noun* a plant with leaves consisting of five leaflets. [Say SINK foil]

cipaille *noun* *Cdn* a deep pie with alternating layers of meat and pastry. [Say see PIE]

cipher *noun* **1 a** a secret code or coded message. **b** the key to a secret code. **2** the arithmetical symbol (0) denoting no amount but used to occupy a vacant place in numeration (as in 12.05). **3** a person or thing of no importance: *for years he was all but invisible to the public, a political cipher laughed at in the spiteful way people laugh at the class geek*. [Say SIGH fer]

circa *preposition* (preceding a date) about, approximately: *the play is set in Montreal circa 1860*.

circle • *noun* **1 a** a perfectly round shape; a shape whose boundary is everywhere equally distant from its centre. **b** the line enclosing a circle. **2** a thing or group shaped or arranged roughly in a circle; a ring, circular route, etc. **3** a group of people having similar interests, characteristics, etc.: *circle of friends* ◊ *in scientific circles*. **4** a period or cycle: *the circle of the year*. **5** an action and reaction that intensify each other: *vicious circle*. **6** (among North American Aboriginal peoples) a meeting for prayer, healing, etc. in which the participants gather in a circle. • *verb* (**circles, circled, circling**) move in a circle; form a circle around. PHRASES **circle back** move in a wide loop towards the starting point. **circle the wagons** (of a group) unite in defence of a common interest. **come full circle** return to the starting point. **go round in circles** make no progress despite effort. **run around in circles** *informal* be fussily busy with little result.

circlet *noun* **1** a small circle. **2** a circular band made of precious metal, flowers, etc., worn around the head.

circuit *noun* **1 a** the distance or a course around something: *jogged six circuits of the field*. **b** a racetrack encircling an enclosed area: *the most dangerous corner on the circuit*. **2** a standard series of events or places visited by a group of athletes, a judge, a preacher, etc.: *US tennis circuit* ◊ *circuit court*. **3** *Electricity* **a** the path of a current. **b** the apparatus through which a current passes.

circuit board *noun* a thin rigid board containing an electric circuit.

circuit breaker *noun* an automatic device for stopping the flow of current in an electrical circuit, usu. as a safety measure, e.g. when the circuit is overloaded.

circuit court *noun* (in Canada) a province's superior court travelling to different communities to sit.

circuitous *adjective* **1** (of a route or journey) indirect and usu. long: *a rather circuitous 80-km route through some of the most picturesque areas of lakeland*. **2** (of speech etc.) not direct or straightforward: *the evidence is circumstantial and the argument circuitous*. ▶ **circuitously** *adverb* **circuitousness** *noun* [Say sir CUE it us]

circuit rider *noun* a person, esp. a Methodist preacher, who used to travel from community to community to preach, work, etc.

circuitry *noun* (*plural* **circuitries**) **1** a system of electric circuits. **2** the equipment forming this.

circular • *adjective* **1 a** having the form of a circle. **b** moving or taking place along a circle: *circular tour*. **2** *Logic* (of reasoning) using the point it is trying to prove as evidence for its conclusion: *a circular argument*. **3** (of a letter or advertisement etc.) printed for distribution to a large number of people. • *noun* a leaflet etc. printed for distribution to a large number of people. ▶ **circularity** *noun*

circular saw *noun* a power saw with a rapidly rotating toothed disc.

circulate *verb* (**circulates**, **circulated**, **circulating**) **1** go around from one place or person etc. to the next and so on; be in circulation: *the memo circulated among the staff*. **2** (of blood, sap, etc.) flow through a body, tree, etc. **3** cause to go around: *they circulated the guest book until everyone had signed* ◊ *he has been circulating rumours*. **4** be actively sociable at a party, gathering, etc. ▶ **circulator** *noun*

circulation *noun* **1 a** the movement of blood from and to the heart, or of sap in a tree, etc. **b** the movement of a fluid etc. along a circuit back to its starting point. **2 a** the transmission or distribution (of news or information or books etc.). **b** the number of copies sold, esp. of journals and newspapers: *a daily circulation of 200,000*. **3 a** currency, coin, etc. **b** the movement or exchange of currency in a country etc. PHRASES **in** (or **out of**) **circulation** participating (or not participating) in activities etc.

circulatory *adjective* of or relating to the circulation of blood or sap. [Say SIR cue la tory]

circulatory system *noun* the heart, blood vessels, blood, lymphatic vessels, and lymph, which function together to transport materials such as oxygen, nutrients, water, etc. throughout the body.

circumcise *verb* (**circumcises**, **circumcised**, **circumcising**) **1** cut off the foreskin of for religious or medical reasons. **2** cut off the clitoris (and sometimes the labia) of, usu. as a religious rite. [Say SIR cum size]

circumcision *noun* the act or rite of circumcising or being circumcised. [Say sir cum SIZH un]

circumference *noun* the line enclosing a circle; the length of this: *a circumference of 25,000 miles*.

circumferential *adjective* situated on or having to do with the circumference of something. ▶ **circumferentially** *adverb* [Say sir kum fer EN sh'l]

circumflex *noun* (plural **circumflexes**) (also **circumflex accent**) a mark (ˆ) placed over a vowel in some languages to indicate a contraction, length, or a special quality. [Say SIR cum flex]

circumlocution *noun* the use of many words to say something that could be said in a few words, esp. when one does not wish to speak clearly; evasive talk: *his last published work brings his style of endless circumlocution to its peak* ◊ *In English, euphemisms and circumlocutions abound for the delicate subject of death*. [Say SIR kum luh CUE sh'n]

circumnavigate *verb* (**circumnavigates**, **circumnavigated**, **circumnavigating**) sail or fly around the world. ▶ **circumnavigation** *noun* [Say sir cum NAVIGATE, sir cum NAVIGATION]

circumpolar *adjective* **1** around or near one of the earth's poles: *a circumpolar voyage*. **2** *Astronomy* (of a star or motion etc.) above the horizon at all times in a given latitude. [Say sir cum POLAR]

circumscribe *verb* (**circumscribes**, **circumscribed**, **circumscribing**) **1** (of a line etc.) enclose or outline. **2** set the limits of; confine, restrict: *the new statutes are designed to circumscribe the powers of the Senate*. **3** *Math.* draw a figure around another, touching it at points but not cutting it (*compare* INSCRIBE 3). ▶ **circumscription** *noun* [Say SIR cum scribe, sir cum SCRIP sh'n]

circumspect *adjective* wary, cautious; taking everything into account: *it was suggested that in the future they be a bit more circumspect in the particular words used to convey their message*. [Say SIR cum spect]

circumspection *noun* extreme caution and awareness of risk or danger: *he believed that prohibition had had its day, but he acted with extreme circumspection in making this controversial view known*. [Say sir cum SPEC sh'n]

circumstance *noun* **1** a condition or fact connected with an event or action: *what were the circumstances surrounding her death?* ◊ *a victim of circumstance*. **2** one's state of financial or material welfare: *has had to get used to reduced circumstances*. PHRASES **under the circumstances** since this is the case; since the state of affairs is what it is: *under the circumstances, it wasn't a bad deal at all*. **under** (or **in**) **no circumstances** not at all; never. [Say SIR cum stance]

circumstantial *adjective* **1** (of evidence, a legal case, etc.) consisting of details that strongly suggest something but do not prove it. **2** given in full detail: *a circumstantial account*. [Say sir cum STAN shull]

circumvent *verb* **1** overcome or evade a problem or difficulty, esp. in a clever or sneaky way: *always finds a way of circumventing the rules*. **2** find a way around an obstacle: *she circumvented the media scrum and made for a "No Entry" sign*. [Say sir cum VENT]

circus *noun* (*plural* **circuses**) **1** a travelling show of performing animals, acrobats, clowns, etc.; a performance given by them. **2** *informal* a situation characterized by lively and chaotic activity. **3 a** in ancient Rome, a rounded or oval arena with tiers of seats, for equestrian and other sports and games. **b** a performance given there.

cirque *noun* a half-open steep-sided hollow at the head of a valley or on a mountainside, formed by glacial erosion. [Say SURK]

cirrhosis *noun* a chronic disease of the liver caused esp. by alcoholism or hepatitis. [Say suh ROE sis]

cirrostratus *noun* cloud forming a thin, fairly uniform layer at high altitude. [Say seer oh STRATUS]

cirrus *noun* clouds formed at high altitudes as delicate white wisps. [Say SEER us]

cisco *noun* (*plural* **ciscoes**) any of several North American freshwater whitefishes related to salmon. [Say SIS coe]

Cistercian • *noun* a monk or nun of an order founded in 1098, noted for an austere way of life including a vow of silence. • *adjective* of the Cistercians. [Say sis TUR sh'n]

cistern *noun* a tank or reservoir for storing water. [Say SIS turn]

citadel *noun* a fortress, usu. built on high ground, protecting a city. [Say SITTA del]

citation *noun* **1** a quotation from or reference to a book, paper, or author, esp. in a scholarly work. **2** a summons to appear in court: *a traffic citation*. **3** a mention in an official report of a praiseworthy act or

C

achievement, esp. courage in war: *a citation for bravery*. [Say sigh TAY sh'n]

cite *verb* (**cites**, **cited**, **citing**) **1** quote a book or author as evidence for an argument or statement: *cited a line from Shakespeare* ◊ *cited Shakespeare*. **2** mention as an example or to support an argument: *he cited lower unemployment figures as evidence of the growing economy*. **3** *Military* praise (esp. a member of the armed forces) for a courageous act in an official dispatch. **4** summon to appear in a court of law: *was cited for contempt of court*.

CITES *abbreviation* Convention on International Trade in Endangered Species. [Say SIGH teez]

citified *adjective* usu. *derogatory* characteristic of or adjusted to an urban environment: *citified sons of farmers*. [Say SITTA fide]

citizen *noun* **1** a person who has full rights as a member of a country, either by birth or by being granted such rights. **2** an inhabitant of a city or town. **3** a member of society, esp. as regards one's contribution to it: *the company is a good corporate citizen*.

citizenry *noun* citizens collectively.

citizens' band *noun* a system of local intercommunication by individuals on special radio frequencies. Abbreviation: **CB**.

citizenship *noun* **1** the status of a citizen, along with the rights and duties involved in being a citizen: *was granted Canadian citizenship*. **2** the conduct of a member of society: *an award for good citizenship*.

citrate *noun* a salt or ester of citric acid. [Say SIT rate]

citric acid *noun* a sharp-tasting water-soluble organic acid found in the juice of lemons, oranges, etc.

citron *noun* **1** a shrubby tree bearing large lemon-like fruits with a thick fragrant peel. **2** this fruit. **3** its candied peel, used in baking etc. [Say SIT run]

citronella *noun* **1** a fragrant natural oil used as an insect repellent and in perfume and soap. **2** the south Asian grass from which this oil is obtained. [Say sitra NELLA]

citrus *noun* (*plural* **citrus**) **1** any of a group of related trees and shrubs including lemon, lime, orange, grapefruit, and citron. Citrus trees are widely cultivated in warm regions for their fruit, which has juicy flesh and a pulpy rind. **2** (also **citrus fruit**) fruit from such a tree. ►**citrusy** *adjective*

city *noun* (*plural* **cities**) **1** a large town, esp. a municipality with a large population or area. **2 a** the people of a city: *the whole city celebrated*. **b** the government, administration, or employees of a city: *the city plans to clean up the harbour*. **3** *informal* a situation or place characterized by a specified quality or action: *when the teacher called my name, it was panic city!*

city council *noun* the group of elected councillors governing a city. ►**city councillor** *noun*

city father *noun* any of the prominent citizens or elected officials of a city: *Winnipeg's city fathers saw to it that trees were planted everywhere*.

city hall *noun* **1** the central administrative offices of a municipality: *I designed a city hall and library*. **2** municipal government: *City Hall rejected my application for a building permit*.

city manager *noun* an official directing the administration of a city.

cityscape *noun* a view of a city; a city landscape.

city slicker *noun* usu. *derogatory* a person with the sophisticated tastes and values often associated with city-dwellers, typically regarded as untrustworthy.

city state *noun* (esp. in ancient times) an independent state consisting of a city and its surrounding territory.

city-wide *adjective* open to or occurring throughout an entire city: *city-wide elections*.

civet *noun* **1** (also **civet cat**) a slender nocturnal carnivorous mammal with a barred and spotted coat, native to Africa and Asia. **2** a strong musky perfume obtained from its anal glands. [Say SIV et]

civic *adjective* **1** of a city; municipal: *a civic arena*. **2** of citizens: *civic duty*. [Say SIV ick]

civic centre *noun* **1** a building or building complex containing municipal offices and sometimes other public buildings, such as a library, auditorium, etc. **2** a public building containing an arena, theatre, etc.

civic holiday *noun Cdn* a holiday that is commonly observed but not legislated, esp. the first Monday in August, observed as a holiday in all of Canada except Quebec and PEI.

civics *plural noun* the study of government and the rights and duties of citizenship, esp. as taught in schools.

civil *adjective* **1** of ordinary citizens and their concerns, esp. as distinct from matters concerning the armed forces or the Church: *civil rights* ◊ *civil aviation* ◊ *civil engineer*. **2** occurring between citizens of the same country: *civil unrest*. **3** polite, obliging, not rude. **4** *Law* involving civil law rather than criminal law: *civil trial*. **5** *Cdn* (*Nfld*) (of the weather or sea) calm. [Say SIV ul]

civil code *noun* a body of civil laws, based on Roman and Napoleonic civil law. In Canada, only Quebec has a civil code.

civil defence *noun* the organization and training of civilians for the protection of lives and property during and after attacks in wartime.

civil disobedience *noun* the refusal to comply with certain laws or to pay taxes etc. as a peaceful form of political protest.

civil engineer *noun* an engineer who designs and maintains roads, bridges, dams, etc. ►**civil engineering** *noun*

civilian • *noun* a person not in the armed services or the police force. • *adjective* of or for civilians: *a civilian aircraft* ◊ *a police officer in civilian clothes*.

civility *noun* (*plural* **civilities**) **1** polite behaviour. **2** a polite act or remark: *only had time to exchange civilities*.

civilization *noun* **1 a** an advanced stage of social development and organization. **b** those peoples of the world regarded as having this: *Western civilization*. **2 a** people or nation (esp. of the past) regarded as an element of social evolution: *the civilizations of ancient Egypt and Babylon*. **3** *informal* populated areas, such as cities and towns, esp. compared to uninhabited areas where the comforts of modern life are regarded as being unavailable: *after spending two weeks in a tent up north, it's good to get back to civilization*. **4** the act or process of making or becoming civilized.

civilize *verb* (**civilizes**, **civilized**, **civilizing**) **1** bring a place or people to a stage of social, cultural, and moral development considered to be more advanced. **2** improve the behaviour or manners of: *she has a civilizing influence on him*.

civilized *adjective* **1** having an advanced and organized state of human social development. **2** having high moral standards: *no civilized country should permit such terrible injustice*. **3** having or showing good behaviour or manners: *behave in a civilized way* ◊ *a civilized debate*. **4** having characteristics considered typical of a sophisticated society, esp. comfort, relaxation, lack of aggression, etc.: *afternoon tea is a very civilized custom* ◊ *I like to get up at a civilized hour*.

civil law *noun* **1** law concerning private rights and legal remedies, as opposed to criminal law. **2** a legal system, based on Roman and Napoleonic law, in which laws are set out in a civil code passed by a legislature, as opposed to common law. In Canada, sense 2 applies only in Quebec.

civil libertarian *plural noun* a person who supports the protection or expansion of civil liberties.

civil liberties *noun* fundamental rights, such as freedom of speech, which can be exercised without arbitrary government interference and which are protected, in Canada, by the Charter of Rights and Freedoms.

civil liberty *noun* the freedom to exercise civil liberties.

civil marriage *noun* a marriage that does not involve a religious ceremony but is recognized by law.

civil rights *plural noun* the rights of citizens to political and social freedom and equality.

civil servant *noun* a member of the civil service.

civil service *noun* **1** the permanent branches of public service concerned with government administration, excluding military and judicial branches and elected politicians. **2** the people employed in this.

civil war *noun* a war between citizens of the same country.

Cl *symbol* chlorine.

cl *abbreviation* centilitre(s).

clack • *noun* a sharp sound made by hard objects hitting each other. • *verb* **1** make a clacking sound. **2** chatter, esp. loudly. ▶ **clacker** *noun*

clad *adjective* **1** (of a person) dressed in a particular manner: *leather-clad bikers* ◊ *clad in a T-shirt and jeans*. **2** covered: *an ivy-clad building* ◊ *a house clad in cedar*.

cladding *noun* a protective covering, esp. for the outside walls of a building.

claim • *verb* **1** state that something is the case, esp. without providing evidence. **2** say that one owns or has earned something. **3** submit a request for payment under an insurance policy. **4** (of a disaster) cause the death of. **5** (of a thing) deserve (one's attention etc.). • *noun* **1** an assertion of the truth of something, esp. one that is disputed or in doubt: *claims of innocence*. **2** a demand or request for something considered one's due: *submitted a claim for business expenses*. **3** a right to something: *a claim to the throne*. **4** Mining something that is claimed, esp. a piece of public land granted or taken for mining. PHRASES **claim to fame** a reason for being regarded as unusual or noteworthy: *the town's only claim to fame is that it is the birthplace of Stella Duane*. **lay claim to** declare that one possesses, has achieved, or has a right to something: *the restaurant lays claim to the best burgers in town* ◊ *he laid claim to the inheritance*. **stake a (or one's) claim to** see STAKE[1]. ▶ **claimable** *adjective*

claimant *noun* a person making a claim, esp. in a lawsuit or for a government benefit: *overseas claimants seeking refugee status* ◊ *employment insurance claimants*.

clairvoyance *noun* the power of seeing or knowing things beyond the natural range of the senses, such as being able to see into the future: *before she heard about the accident, she sensed something was wrong, as if by clairvoyance*. [Say clair VOY ance]

clairvoyant • *noun* a person who claims to have a supernatural ability to see things in the future or beyond the natural range of the senses. • *adjective* having clairvoyance. [Say clair VOY ant]

clam • *noun* **1** a usu. edible marine mollusc with two equal shells that can open and close. **2** *informal* a shy or withdrawn person. • *verb* (**clams**, **clammed**, **clamming**) dig for clams. PHRASES **clam up** *informal* refuse to talk: *she clammed up as soon as I mentioned Bob*. **happy as a clam** extremely happy.

clambake *noun* **1** a seaside picnic at which clams etc. are baked and eaten. **2** *informal* any social gathering.

clamber *verb* climb with difficulty or effort using the hands and feet. [Say CLAM bur or CLAMMER]

clam juice *noun* a stock made by boiling clams in water.

clammily *adverb* in a clammy manner: *the fog hangs clammily in the air*.

clamminess *noun* a clammy quality.

clammy *adjective* (**clammier**, **clammiest**) unpleasantly damp or slimy: *I shook his clammy hand* ◊ *the cold, clammy air of the basement*.

clamorous *adjective* **1** noisy: *a clamorous mob*. **2** marked by protest or demand, esp. by many people: *the clamorous call for tax cuts*. ▶ **clamorously** *adverb*

clamour (also **clamor**) • *noun* **1** loud noise, esp. of people shouting: *the clamour of the busy market*. **2** a strongly expressed protest or demand, esp. from a large number of people: *the growing public clamour for his resignation*. • *verb* **1** demand insistently: *clamouring for the cancellation of the program* ◊ *clamouring to have the program cancelled*. **2** make a clamour: *after the referee's controversial call, fans started clamouring*.

clamp • *noun* a device for holding things together tightly. • *verb* **1** fasten together or in place with a clamp. **2** hold something tightly: *she had to clamp a hand over her mouth to keep from laughing*. PHRASES **clamp down** suppress or prevent something, esp. by strictly enforcing a rule etc.: *police are clamping down on drug smugglers*.

clampdown *noun* a severe attempt to restrict or suppress something: *a clampdown on crime*.

clamshell *noun* **1** the shell of a clam. **2** a thing with hinged parts that open and close like the shell of a clam, e.g. a container for takeout food.

clan *noun* **1** the basic social and political organization of many Aboriginal societies, consisting of a number of related groups and families, often sharing a common symbol or totem. **2** a group of families in the Scottish Highlands with a common ancestor. **3** a large, close-knit family: *we had the whole clan over for dinner*. **4** a group with a strong common interest: *a clan of artists*.

clandestine *adjective* kept secret or done secretly: *a clandestine affair with his secretary*. ▶ **clandestinely** *adverb* [Say clan DESS tine or clan DESS tin, clan DESS tin lee]

clang • *noun* a loud ringing sound of metal being struck: *the clang of the bell*. • *verb* make or cause to make a clanging sound: *the puck clanged off the goalpost*.

clangorous *adjective* causing a clangour: *a clangorous fanfare*. ▶ **clangorously** *adverb* [Say KLANG ger us]

clangour *noun* (also **clangor**) a continuous loud ringing noise or commotion: *went deaf because of the clangour of the steam hammers of the mill*. [Say KLANG ger]

clank • *noun* a loud sound made by pieces of metal moving or hitting each other: *the clank of heavy chains*. • *verb* **1** make or cause to make a clanking sound. **2** move with a clanking sound: *the old school bus clanked by*. ▶ **clanky** *adjective*

clannish *adjective* usu. derogatory (of members of a group) tending to associate closely while showing little interest in others outside the group: *the university is very clannish, with almost zero communication off the campus*. ▶ **clannishness** *noun*

clap • *verb* (**claps**, **clapped**, **clapping**) **1** strike the inner surface of one's hands together as a signal or applause. **2** set something in place quickly or with determination: *clapped the handcuffs on her*. **3** slap a person lightly with an open hand, usu. in a friendly way. • *noun* **1** the act of clapping the hands. **2** a sudden loud noise, esp. of thunder. **3** a slap: *a clap on the back*.

clapboard *noun* a type of wooden siding consisting of a series of long boards with overlapping edges: *a cottage covered in clapboard* ◊ *a white clapboard church*. ▶ **clapboarded** *adjective*

C

clapper *noun* a piece of metal fixed loosely inside a bell, which causes the bell to sound by striking its side.

claptrap *noun* absurd or pretentious talk or ideas: *political claptrap*.

claret *noun* a dry red wine, esp. from the Bordeaux region of southwest France. [Say CLAIR it]

clarification *noun* the act or an instance of making something clearer: *this issue needs clarification*.

clarify *verb* (**clarifies, clarified, clarifying**) **1** make a statement or situation clearer and less confusing. **2** remove impurities from; purify: *clarified butter*.

clarinet *noun* **1** a woodwind instrument with a single-reed mouthpiece, a cylindrical tube flared at the end and holes stopped by keys. **2** its player. ▶ **clarinetist** *noun*

clarion call *noun* a strongly expressed request for action: *a clarion call for volunteers*. [Say CLAIR ee un]

clarity *noun* the state or quality of being clear: *a clarity of vision* ◊ *the clarity of her argument*.

clash • *noun* **1** a violent confrontation or disagreement: *clashes broke out between protesters and police*. **2** an incompatibility leading to disagreement: *a clash of cultures* ◊ *a clash between nationalist and regionalist views*. **3** a loud jarring sound of or resembling that of metal objects being struck together: *a clash of cymbals*. • *verb* (**clashes, clashed, clashing**) **1** meet and come into violent conflict or disagreement: *the armies clashed*. **2** fail to match or look good together: *the carpet and wallpaper clash* ◊ *those pants clash with that shirt*. **3** strike together with a loud harsh noise. ▶ **clasher** *noun*

clasp • *noun* **1** a device for fastening things together, e.g. the ends of a belt or necklace. **2** an embrace: *held her in his powerful clasp*. **3** a grip or grasp: *the glass fell from his clasp*. • *verb* **1** hold tightly in the hand or arms: *clasped the microphone in both hands*. **2** place one's hands together, esp. with the fingers interlaced. **3** fasten with a clasp: *clasped the bracelet around her wrist*. PHRASES **clasp hands** shake hands with fervour or affection.

class • *noun* (*plural* **classes**) **1** a set or category of things having some property in common and distinguished from others by type or quality: *trucks and minivans are separate classes of automobiles* ◊ *Mozart is in a different class from other composers*. **2 a** a group of people at the same social or economic level: *the middle class* ◊ *the working class*. **b** a system that divides people into such groups: *the class system*. **3 a** a group of students taught together: *the best mark in the class*. **b** the occasion when they meet: *I have a class at 2:00*. **c** their course of instruction: *science class*. **d** all the students of a school graduating in the same year: *the class of '89*. **4** *informal* sophistication in appearance or behaviour: *she showed a lot of class by thanking her opponent* ◊ *dresses with class*. **5** each of several different levels of comfort etc. available to travellers in a plane, train, etc.: *travelling in first class* ◊ *business class*. **6** *Biology* the second highest group into which animals and plants are divided, below a phylum, and including several orders. • *verb* (**classes, classed, classing**) assign to a class or category: *she is classed as a poet, not a novelist*. • *adjective* showing excellence in style or behaviour: *a class player*. PHRASES **in a class of its own** (also **in a class by oneself**) superior to others of the same kind.

class act *noun* a person or thing showing sophistication in appearance or behaviour: *Rebecca's a well-dressed, polite, considerate woman: a total class act*.

class action *noun* a lawsuit filed by an individual on behalf of a group of people with a common interest or grievance.

class-conscious *adjective* aware of belonging to a particular social class or of the differences between social classes. ▶ **class-consciousness** *noun*

classic • *adjective* **1** judged over time to be of the highest quality and an outstanding example of its kind: *a classic novel*. **2** remarkably and instructively typical: *a classic case of muckraking* ◊ *classic flu symptoms*. **3 a** (of style in art, music, etc.) simple and harmonious; conforming to established standards and methods. **b** = CLASSICAL 1a. **4** (of clothes) made in a simple elegant style not much affected by changes in fashion. • *noun* **1** a writer, artist, or work of art recognized as being of high quality and lasting value: *the film has become a classic*. **2** a thing which is memorable and an outstanding example of its kind: *tonight's game should be a classic*. **3** a garment in classic style. **4** a piece of classical music: *the concert featured light classics*.

classical *adjective* **1 a** of, relating to, or influenced by ancient Greek or Latin literature, art, architecture, or culture. **b** (of language) having the form used by the ancient standard authors: *classical Hebrew*. **2 a** (of music) seen as serious or conventional and following long-established principles, as opposed to folk, rock, pop, jazz, etc. **b** of the period from *c.*1750–1800, when forms such as the symphony, concerto, and sonata were standardized (compare ROMANTIC 4). **3** designating or pertaining to a form or period of an art etc. regarded as representing the height of achievement: *classical ballet*. **4** established and widely accepted; traditional: *the classical view of economic theory*. **5** = CLASSIC *adjective* 3a. ▶ **classically** *adverb*

classical college *noun* *Cdn* (*Que.*) = COLLÈGE CLASSIQUE.

classicism *noun* the following of ancient Greek or Roman principles and style in art and literature, esp. harmony, restraint, and adherence to recognized standards of form and craftsmanship. ▶ **classicist** *noun* [Say CLASSA sism, CLASSA sist]

classics *noun* **1** the works of ancient Greek and Latin writers and philosophers: *she studied the classics at university*. **2** a subject at school or university which involves the study of ancient Greek and Latin literature, philosophy, and history: *a classics student*.

classifiable *adjective* that can be classified: *all elements are classifiable as either metals or non-metals*.

classification *noun* **1 a** the action or process of classifying or being classified: *the classification of disease according to symptoms*. **b** a group or class into which something is put. **2** the arrangement of animals and plants in taxonomic groups according to their structure, origin, etc.

classified • *adjective* **1** arranged in classes or categories. **2** (of information etc.) designated as officially secret. **3** (of newspaper ads) arranged in columns according to various categories. • *noun* a classified ad: *Paul was reading the classifieds*.

classifier *noun* a person or thing that classifies.

classify *verb* (**classifies, classified, classifying**) **1** assign to a category: *books are classified according to subject* ◊ *would you classify this book as a mystery or a thriller?* **2** declare information, documents, etc. as officially secret or available only for certain people.

classiness *noun* classy behaviour or appearance.

classism *noun* prejudice against or in favour of people belonging to a particular social class. ▶ **classist** *adjective & noun*

classless *adjective* making or showing no distinction of classes: *classless society*.

classmate *noun* a fellow member of a class at school

classroom *noun* a room in which a class of students is taught.

class struggle *noun* (also **class war**, **class**

warfare) conflict between social classes, esp. between the wealthy ruling classes and the poorer working classes.

classy *adjective* (**classier, classiest**) **1** stylish, elegant: *classy stationery* ◊ *a classy home*. **2** admirable, esp. by being sophisticated, refined, gracious, etc.: *he delivered a classy tribute to his opponent*.

clastic *adjective* denoting rocks composed of broken pieces of older rocks.

clatter • *noun* **1** a rattling sound like that of hard objects knocking against each other. **2** noisy talk; chatter. • *verb* make or move with a clatter.

clause *noun* **1** a group of words that consists of a subject and predicate and usu. a verb, and which may constitute a sentence or part of a sentence. **2** a paragraph or section in a legal document stating a particular obligation or condition etc.: *a clause forbidding tenants to sublet*.

claustrophobia *noun* an abnormal fear of confined places. [Say klostra PHOBIA]

claustrophobic *adjective* **1** (of a person) suffering from claustrophobia: *crowds make him feel claustrophobic*. **2** (of a place or situation) causing claustrophobia: *a tiny claustrophobic elevator*. ▶ **claustrophobically** *adverb* [Say klostra FOE bick]

clavicle *noun* the collarbone. [Say KLAV ick ul]

claw • *noun* **1 a** a curved pointed horny nail on each digit of an animal's foot. **b** a foot having clawed digits. **2** the pincers of a shellfish. **3** a device resembling a claw, used for grappling, holding, etc. • *verb* **1** scratch, tear, or grab with or as if with the claws or fingernails. **2** proceed by or as if by using one's hands or claws: *she clawed her way to the top of the corporate ladder*. PHRASES **claw back** *Cdn & Brit.* **1** (of a government) recover money paid out in the form of a benefit or allowance, esp. by taxation: *seniors who have hefty RRSPs see their government pension clawed back*. **2** regain something lost with great effort: *managed to claw back some of his dignity*.

clawback *noun* *Cdn & Brit.* a situation in which the government retrieves money paid out, esp. by taxation.

clawed *adjective* having claws or a particular kind of claws: *clawed toes* ◊ *white-clawed crayfish*.

clay *noun* stiff, sticky, fine-grained earth, which can be moulded when wet and is dried and baked to make bricks, pottery, and ceramics. ▶ **clayey** *adjective* **claylike** *adjective*

clay pigeon *noun* a breakable disc thrown up from a trap as a target for shooting.

clean • *adjective* **1** (often foll. by *of*) free from dirt or contaminating matter. **2** clear; unused or unpolluted: *clean air*. **3** free from obscenity or indecency. **4** attentive to personal hygiene and cleanliness. **5** even; straight; free from roughness: *a clean edge*. **6** unobstructed; without difficulty: *a clean getaway*. **7 a** (of a ship, aircraft, or car) streamlined, smooth. **b** well-formed, slender and shapely. **8** skilful: *clean fielding*. **9** legible; having few corrections: *clean copy*. **10** *Sport* fair; played without fouls. **11 a** free from ceremonial defilement or from disease. **b** (of food) not prohibited. **12 a** free from any record of a crime, offence, etc.: *a clean driver's licence*. **b** *informal* above suspicion. **c** *informal* not carrying a weapon or incriminating material. **13** faultless: *a clean triple Axel*. **14** *informal* free from or cured of addiction to drugs. **15** (of a taste etc.) sharp, fresh, distinctive. • *adverb* **1** so as to be free of dirt, garbage, etc.: *sweep the floor clean*. **2** *informal* used to emphasize the completeness of an action, condition, or statement: *I clean forgot to give her the message*. • *verb* **1** (also foll. by *of*) & make or become clean. **2** eat all the food on (one's plate). **3** *Cooking* remove the innards of (fish or fowl). **4** *Weightlifting* raise (a

weight) from the floor to shoulder level in a single movement. • *noun* the act or process of cleaning or being cleaned. PHRASES **clean down** clean by brushing or wiping. **clean one's plate** eat all the food on one's plate. **clean out 1** clean thoroughly. **2** *slang* empty or deprive (esp. of money). **clean up 1 a** clear (a mess) away. **b** put (things) tidy. **c** make (oneself) clean. **2** restore order or morality to. **3** *slang* **a** acquire as gain or profit. **b** make a gain or profit. **clean up one's act** begin to behave responsibly or soberly. **come clean** *informal* own up; confess everything. **clean hands** freedom from guilt. **make a clean job of** *informal* do thoroughly. ▶ **cleanable** *adjective*

clean-cut *adjective* (of a person, esp. a man) having a neat and respectable appearance.

cleaner *noun* a person or thing that cleans something.

cleaners *plural noun* an establishment where clothes are dry cleaned. PHRASES **take to the cleaners** *slang* rob, cheat, or deprive of a great deal of money etc.: *the company was taken to the cleaners in a lawsuit*.

cleanliness *noun* the habit of being clean and neat or keeping things clean and neat. [Say KLEN lee ness]

cleanly¹ *adverb* **1** in a way that produces no dirt, noxious gases, or other pollutants: *fuel that burns cleanly*. **2** without difficulty; smoothly and efficiently: *won the contest cleanly*. [Say CLEAN lee]

cleanly² *adjective* (**cleanlier, cleanliest**) habitually clean or neat. [Say KLEN lee]

clean room *noun* a room that is free from dust and bacteria, used for medical purposes or the assembly of products such as computer parts.

cleanse *verb* (**cleanses, cleansed, cleansing**) **1** make something thoroughly clean: *the nurse cleansed my wound*. **2** rid a place or thing of something seen as unpleasant or unwanted: *cleanse the streets of criminals*. **3** free someone of sin or guilt; purify. [Say KLENZ]

cleanser *noun* a product that cleanses: *a skin cleanser* ◊ *a household cleanser*. [Say KLENZ er]

clean-shaven *adjective* (of a man) without a beard or moustache.

clean slate *noun* **1** an opportunity for a fresh start, forgetting past mistakes: *he starts a new year with a clean slate*. **2** a record of conduct without discredit: *in ten years with the company she has maintained a clean slate*.

cleanup *noun* **1** an act of cleaning up. **2** in baseball, the fourth position in the batting order: *the cleanup hitter* ◊ *he bats cleanup*.

clear • *adjective* **1** free from dirt or contamination. **2** (of weather, the sky, etc.) not dull or cloudy. **3 a** transparent. **b** lustrous, shining; free from obscurity. **4** (of soup) not containing solid ingredients. **5 a** distinct, easily perceived by the senses. **b** unambiguous, easily understood: *make oneself clear*. **c** manifest; not confused or doubtful: *clear evidence*. **6** that discerns or is able to discern readily and accurately: *clear thinking*. **7** confident, certain. **8** (of a conscience) free from guilt. **9** (of a road etc.) unobstructed. **10 a** net, without deduction: *a clear $1000*. **b** complete: *three clear days*. **11** unencumbered by debt, commitments, etc. **12** not obstructed by. **13** (of timber) free from knots: *clear pine*. **14** (of skin) not marked by pimples or other blemishes. • *adverb* **1** clearly: *speak loud and clear*. **2** completely: *got clear away*. **3** apart, out of contact: *stand clear of the doors*. **4** (often foll. by *to*) all the way. • *verb* **1** make or become clear. **2 a** free from prohibition or obstruction. **b** make or become empty or unobstructed. **c** free (land) for cultivation or building by cutting down trees etc. **d** cause people to leave (a room etc.). **3** show or declare (a person) to be innocent. **4** approve (a person) for special duty, access to information, etc. **5** pass over or

C

by safely or without touching. **6** make (an amount of money) as a net gain or to balance expenses. **7** pass (a cheque) through a clearing house. **8** pass through (a customs office etc.). **9** remove (an obstruction, unwanted object, etc.): *clear them out of the way*. **10** *Sport* send (the ball, puck, etc.) out of one's defensive zone. **11** (of physical phenomena) disappear, gradually diminish: *my cold has cleared up*. PHRASES **clear the air 1** make the air less sultry. **2** disperse an atmosphere of suspicion, tension, etc. **clear away 1** remove completely. **2** remove the remains of a meal from the table. **clear the decks** prepare for action, esp. fighting. **clear off 1** get rid of. **2** *informal* go away. **clear out 1** empty. **2** remove. **3** *informal* go away. **clear one's throat** cough slightly to make one's voice clear. **clear up 1** tidy up. **2** solve (a mystery etc.). **3** (of weather) become fine. **clear the way 1** remove obstacles. **2** stand aside. **clear a thing with** get approval or authorization for a thing from (a person). **in the clear** free from suspicion or difficulty. **out of a clear blue sky** as a complete surprise.

clearance *noun* **1** the action or process of removing or getting rid of: *cleaning of the machine should include clearance of blockages*. **2** clear space between two objects or two parts in machinery etc.: *always give cyclists plenty of clearance*. **3** special authorization or permission (esp. for an aircraft to take off or land, or for access to information etc.): *there was a delay in obtaining clearance to overfly Israel ◊ these people don't have security clearance*. **4** (also **clearance sale**) a sale to get rid of stock: *bought her dress on clearance at the Bay*. **5** the removal of buildings, persons, trees, etc., so as to clear land: *forest clearances ◊ slum clearance accelerated during the 1960s*.

clear-cut • *adjective* **1** sharply defined; not vague. **2** of or relating to a method of logging in which all of the trees in an area of forest are harvested at the same time. • *noun* an area of clear-cut forest. • *verb* (**clear-cuts**, **clear-cut**, **clear-cutting**) log an area of forest by cutting down all of the trees. ▶ **clear-cutter** *noun* **clear-cutting** *noun*

clear-eyed *adjective* **1** having clear or bright eyes. **2** able to make good decisions or judgments.

Clear Grit *noun* *Cdn* a member or supporter of the Clear Grit Party, a liberal reform party in Upper Canada during the 1840s and 1850s.

clear-headed *adjective* **1** able to think clearly. **2** (of an idea, argument, etc.) reasoned; well-thought-out: *I was impressed by their clear-headed policy*.

clearing *noun* a treeless area in a forest.

clearing house *noun* **1** a bankers' institution where cheques and bills from member banks are exchanged, so that only the balances need be paid in cash. **2** an organization which collects and distributes information, materials, etc.

clearing pass *noun* *Hockey* a forward pass intended to move the puck out of the defensive zone.

cleat *noun* **1** a metal or wooden fitting with two projecting horns, fastened to a flagpole, boat, etc., around which a rope may be secured. **2** a projecting piece on the bottom or side of a shoe or boot, to improve grip. **3** a projecting piece on a spar, gangway, etc., to improve footing. **4** a piece of metal, wood, etc. attached to something to strengthen or hold it in place.

cleats *plural noun* a pair of shoes with spike-like projections on the sole, esp. for playing field sports.

cleavage *noun* **1** the hollow between a woman's breasts, esp. as exposed by a low-cut garment. **2** a division or splitting. **3** the splitting of rocks, crystals, etc., in a preferred direction. [Say KLEEV idge]

cleave[1] *verb* (**cleaves**; *past* **cleaved** or **clove** or **cleft**; *past participle* **cloven** or **cleft** or **cleaved**;

cleaving) **1 a** chop or break apart, split, esp. along the grain or the line of cleavage: *an old axe used to cleave wood*. **b** come apart in this way: *the slate cleaves into even halves*. **2** make one's way through (air or water).

cleave[2] *verb* (**cleaves**, **cleaved**, **cleaving**) (foll. by *to*) *literary* adhere: *the nation cleaves to its traditions*.

cleaver *noun* a broad-bladed knife used for chopping meat.

clef *noun* *Music* a symbol placed at the beginning of a staff, indicating the pitch of the notes written on it.

cleft • *adjective* split, partly divided: *a cleft chin*. • *noun* a split or fissure: *exposed sloping rock broken by deep clefts*.

cleft palate *noun* a congenital split in the roof of the mouth.

clematis *noun* (*plural* **clematis**) an erect or climbing plant bearing white, pink, or purple flowers and feathery seeds. [Say KLEM uh tis or kluh MAT iss]

clemency *noun* mercy, forgiveness: *they appealed to the judge for clemency*.

clement *adjective* **1** mild, temperate: *clement weather*. **2** merciful: *the courts of a clement country*. [Say KLEM ent]

clementine *noun* a small citrus fruit, thought to be a hybrid between a tangerine and orange. [Say KLEM in tine or KLEM in teen]

clench *verb* (**clenches**, **clenched**, **clenching**) **1** close the teeth or fingers tightly. **2** grasp firmly. **3** = CLINCH *verb* 3.

clerestory *noun* (*plural* **clerestories**) the upper part of a wall in a large church with a row of windows in it, above the lower roofs. [Say CLEAR story]

clergy *plural noun* the people who have been ordained for religious duties, esp. in the Christian church.

clergyman *noun* (*plural* **clergymen**) an esp. male member of the clergy.

clergyperson *noun* (*plural* **clergypersons**) a member of the clergy.

Clergy Reserves *noun* *Cdn* crown lands set aside during the settlement of Upper and Lower Canada, the revenue from which was to be used to support Protestant clergy.

clergywoman *noun* (*plural* **clergywomen**) a female member of the clergy.

cleric *noun* a member of the clergy.

clerical *adjective* **1** of or done by an office clerk or secretary: *I had a clerical job over the summer*. **2** of the clergy. ▶ **clericalism** *noun* **clericalist** *noun*

clerical collar *noun* a stiff upright white collar fastening at the back, worn by the clergy in some Christian denominations.

clerk • *noun* **1** a person employed in an office, bank, store, etc., to keep records, accounts, etc. **2** a salesperson or assistant in a store or hotel. **3** a secretary, agent, or record-keeper of a municipal government: *town clerk*. **4** *Law* **a** an officer of a court who keeps records, issues subpoenas and other court documents, etc. **b** *Cdn* a judge's research assistant. **c** (in full **articled clerk**) a law student who is articling. **5** (in full **clerk of session**) (in Presbyterian and United churches) an elder elected to serve as a congregation's primary officer. **6** a senior official in a legislative assembly. • *verb* work as a clerk.

Clerk of the House *noun* *Cdn & Brit.* the chief administrative officer and procedural adviser of the House of Commons.

Clerk of the Privy Council *noun* *Cdn* the senior public servant in charge of the Privy Council Office.

clever *adjective* (**cleverer**, **cleverest**) **1** quick to understand and learn. **2** skilful: *clever with his hands*. **3** ingenious, cunning: *a clever trick*. **4** witty: *clever dialogue*. ▶ **cleverly** *adverb* **cleverness** *noun*

cliché *noun* a phrase or an idea which is used so often that it is no longer interesting, effective, or relevant: *the interview after the game was filled with clichés about "giving 110%"*. [Say klee SHAY or KLEE shay]
clichéd *adjective* full of clichés. [Say klee SHADE or KLEE shade]
click • *noun* **1** a slight sharp sound as of a switch being operated. **2** a sharp non-vocal suction, used as a speech sound in some languages. **3** *Computing* an act of pressing a button on a mouse. • *verb* **1 a** make a click. **b** cause (one's tongue, heels, etc.) to click. **2** *informal* **a** become clear or understandable: *when I saw them it all clicked*. **b** be successful, secure one's object. **c** (foll. by *with*) become friendly, esp. with a person of the opposite sex. **d** come to an agreement. **3** *Computing* **a** press (one of the buttons on a mouse). **b** select (an item represented on the screen, etc.) by so doing. PHRASES **click in** *informal* (of a system) become active or effective.
clicker *noun* **1** a remote control for a television etc. **2** a person or thing that clicks.
client *noun* **1** a person using the services of a lawyer, architect, social worker, or other professional person; any customer or patron. **2** *Computing* a terminal or workstation that is connected to a server.
clientele *noun* clients collectively; the customers or patrons of a store etc. [Say klye 'n TELL or klee on TELL]
client-server *noun* *Computing* designating a type of system in which a server distributes files and databases to clients: *client-server applications*.
cliff *noun* a hill or other high area with a very steep side.
cliff-hanger *noun* **1** a story etc. with a strong element of suspense; a suspenseful ending to an episode of a serial. **2** a game or situation in which the outcome is uncertain until the very end. ▶ **cliff-hanging** *adjective*
cliffside • *noun* the face of a cliff. • *adjective* situated or occurring beside a cliff: *cliffside restaurant*.
clifftop *noun* the top of a cliff.
climactic *adjective* of or forming a climax.
climate *noun* **1** the regular pattern of weather conditions (temperature, amount of rain, winds, etc.) of a particular place: *they moved to Vancouver for its milder climate*. **2** a region with particular weather conditions: *would rather live in a warmer climate*. **3** the prevailing trend of opinion or public feeling: *the political climate*.
climate control *noun* a system for regulating the humidity and temperature of air through heating and air conditioning. ▶ **climate-controlled** *adjective*

WRITING TIP
climatic, climactic

Do not confuse **climatic** with **climactic**. **Climatic** means "having to do with the weather or climate", as in *Dinosaurs may have become extinct as a result of climatic changes*. **Climactic** means "happening at the most exciting or important moment", as in *The movie ends when the criminals are finally caught in a climactic car chase*.

---

climatic *adjective* of or pertaining to a climate: *harsh climatic conditions*.
climatologist *noun* a scientist who studies climate. [Say clime a TOLLA jist]
climatology *noun* the scientific study of climate. [Say clime a TOLLA jee]
climax • *noun* (plural **climaxes**) **1** the event or point of greatest intensity or interest. **2** *Ecology* a state of equilibrium reached by a plant community. **3** the highest point of sexual pleasure; an orgasm. • *verb* (**climaxes**, **climaxed**, **climaxing**) *informal* bring or come to a climax.

SPELL CHECK
climb, clime   [ABC ✓]

A region considered in terms of its weather is a **clime**.

---

climb • *verb* **1** ascend, mount, go or come up, esp. by using one's hands. **2** (of a plant) grow up a wall, trellis, etc. by clinging with tendrils or by twining. **3** make progress from one's own efforts, esp. in social rank, intellectual or moral strength, etc. **4** (of an aircraft, the sun, etc.) go upwards. **5** slope upwards. **6** (of numbers etc.) increase. • *noun* **1** an ascent by climbing. **2 a** a place, esp. a hill, climbed or to be climbed. **b** a recognized route up a mountain etc. PHRASES **climb down 1** descend with the help of one's hands. **2** withdraw from a stance taken up in argument, negotiation, etc. **climb the walls** *informal* go crazy; become frantic. ▶ **climbable** *adjective*
climber *noun* **1** a mountain climber. **2** a climbing plant.
clime *noun* *literary* **1** a region. **2** a climate.
clinch • *verb* (**clinches**, **clinched**, **clinching**) **1** confirm or settle an argument, deal, etc. conclusively. **2** *Sport* secure a position on a team, in league standings, etc.: *with the win they've clinched a playoff berth*. **3** *informal* embrace. • *noun* **1** a clinching action; a clinched state. **2** *informal* an (esp. loving) embrace.
clincher *noun* *informal* **1** a person or thing that clinches. **2** a remark or argument that settles a matter conclusively: *Perry read out the cost and that was the clincher*. **3** a game or match that clinches a player's or team's position in standings etc.
cline *noun* **1** a continuum with an infinite number of gradations. **2** *Biology* the graded sequence of differences within a species etc.
cling • *verb* (**clings**, **clung**, **clinging**) **1** hold on tightly. **2** become attached to; stick closely to: *the smell clings to one's clothes ◊ static makes the paper bits cling to your hair*. **3** refuse to abandon; remain persistently or stubbornly attached to a belief, power, hope, possessions, etc.: *still clinging to her principles*. **4** be emotionally dependent on a person; stay too close to a person: *clung to me all evening*. **5** stay close to something: *don't cling to the curb*. • *noun* the adhering together of separate objects: *static cling*.
clingy *adjective* (**clingier**, **clingiest**) **1** emotionally dependent: *a clingy child*. **2** (of clothing) sticking to the body and showing its shape.
clinic *noun* **1** a place or occasion for giving medical or dental treatment or advice: *outpatient clinic*. **2** a group of doctors or dentists sharing the same building and working together. **3** a gathering at a hospital bedside for the teaching of medicine or surgery. **4** a conference or short course on a particular subject: *golf clinic*. **5** *see* BLOOD DONOR CLINIC. **6** *see* LEGAL CLINIC.
clinical *adjective* **1 a** of or for the direct examination and treatment of patients and their illnesses: *clinical trials*. **b** based on the observed symptoms. **2** coldly detached: *a clinical interview*. **3** (of a room, building, etc.) bare, merely functional. ▶ **clinically** *adverb*
clinician *noun* a doctor having direct contact with and responsibility for patients, as opposed to one doing research. [Say klin ISH'n]
clink • *noun* **1** a light sharp ringing sound. **2** *slang* prison: *in the clink*. • *verb* **1** make a clink. **2** cause glasses etc. to clink by tapping them together.
clinker *noun* **1** a mass of slag or lava. **2** a stony residue from burnt coal. **3** *informal* a mistake or blunder.
clip[1] • *noun* **1** a device for holding things together or

C

C

for attachment to an object as a marker, esp. a paper clip or a device worked by a spring. **2** a piece of jewellery fastened by a clip. **3** a set of attached cartridges for a firearm. • *verb* (**clips, clipped, clipping**) **1** attach with a clip. **2** grip tightly.

clip² • *verb* (**clips, clipped, clipping**) **1** cut with shears or scissors, esp. cut short or trim (hair, wool, fingernails etc.). **2** trim or remove the hair or wool of (a person or animal). **3** *informal* hit smartly. **4** curtail, diminish, cut short. **5** cut (an article, coupon, etc.) from a newspaper etc. **6** cut the wings of (a bird) so that it is unable to fly. **7** *Football* block (a member of the opposing team) illegally from behind. **8** *slang* swindle, rob. • *noun* **1** an act of clipping, esp. shearing or haircutting. **2** *informal* a smart blow, esp. with the hand. **3** a short sequence from a film, video, etc. **4** *informal* (in phr. **at a fair clip**, etc.) speed, esp. rapid. PHRASES **clip a person's wings** prevent a person from pursuing ambitions or acting effectively.

clip art *noun* artwork, either published in printed form or included as part of computer software, that can be copied into reports, advertisements, etc.

clipboard *noun* **1** a small board with a spring clip for holding papers etc. and providing support for writing. **2** a feature of some computer programs which allows the temporary storage of extracted text, so that it can be edited etc. before being inserted or saved into another file.

clip-clop • *noun* a sound such as the beat of a horse's hooves. • *verb* (**clip-clops, clip-clopped, clip-clopping**) make such a sound.

clip-on • *adjective* attached by a clip: *a clip-on tie*. • *noun* a thing (e.g. a necktie, earring) that attaches by a clip.

clipper *noun* **1** a person or thing that clips. **2** any of various instruments for clipping hair, fingernails, hedges, etc. **3** a fast sailing ship.

clipping *noun* **1** a short piece clipped or cut from a newspaper, magazine, etc. **2** (**clippings**) small pieces of grass etc. produced by clipping or mowing.

clique *noun* a small group of people who associate together and do not readily allow others to join them. ▶ **cliquey** *adjective* **cliquish** *adjective* **cliquishness** *noun* [Say KLEEK, KLEEK ee, KLEEK ish, KLEEK ish ness]

clitoris *noun* a small erectile part of the female genitals at the upper end of the vulva. [Say CLITTER iss]

cloak • *noun* **1** an outdoor garment, usu. sleeveless, hanging loosely from the shoulders. **2** a covering: *cloak of snow*. **3** something which conceals: *a cloak of secrecy*. • *verb* **1** cover with a cloak. **2** cover over: *hills cloaked in trees*. **3** conceal, disguise. PHRASES **under the cloak of** using as a pretext or concealment.

cloak-and-dagger *adjective* involving or characteristic of plotting and intrigue, esp. espionage: *a cloak-and-dagger novel*.

cloakroom *noun* a room where outdoor clothes or luggage may be left by visitors, clients, etc.

clobber *verb* *informal* **1** hit repeatedly; beat up; strike with great force. **2** defeat. **3** criticize severely.

clock • *noun* **1** an instrument for measuring or indicating time by hands on a dial or by displayed numbers. **2** any measuring device resembling a clock, e.g. a speedometer or stopwatch. **3 a** time, when one is trying to do something quickly or under a deadline: *working against the clock* ◊ *rushing to beat the clock*. **b** time, when a runner etc. is trying for a faster time rather than competing against someone else: *running against the clock*. **4** a downy seed head, esp. that of a dandelion. • *verb* **1** attain or register a stated total, number, etc.: *they both clocked 9.8 seconds in the 100 metres* ◊ *my car has clocked up 100,000 km* ◊ *The company just keeps clocking up profit* ◊ *clocking up brownie points*. **2** time a race with a

stopwatch. **3** measure the speed of: *was clocked at 95 mph*. PHRASES **clean someone's clock** *informal* beat someone soundly. **around the clock** all day and (usu.) night: *working around the clock*. **clock in** (or **out**) register one's arrival (or departure) at work, esp. by means of an automatic recording clock. **turn** (or **put**) **the clock back** (or **turn back the clock**) return to an earlier time. **watch the clock** keep a close watch on the passing of time, esp. so as not to exceed minimum working hours. ▶ **clocker** *noun*

clockmaker *noun* a person who makes and repairs clocks and watches. ▶ **clockmaking** *noun*

clock-watcher *noun* a person who keeps a close watch on the passage of time, esp. so as not to exceed minimum working hours. ▶ **clock-watching** *noun*

clockwise *adjective & adverb* moving in a curve in the same direction as the hands of a clock.

clockwork • *noun* a mechanism like that of a mechanical clock, with a spring and gears. • *adjective* **1** driven by clockwork: *a clockwork toy*. **2** regular, mechanical. PHRASES **like clockwork** smoothly, regularly, automatically.

clod *noun* **1** a lump of earth, clay, etc. **2** *informal* a silly or foolish person.

clodhopper *noun* **1** *informal* a large heavy shoe. **2** an unsophisticated person.

clog • *noun* **1** a shoe with a thick wooden sole. **2** a blockage in a drain etc. • *verb* (**clogs, clogged, clogging**) block or become blocked so as to hinder free passage, action, or function: *a clogged drain* ◊ *streetcars clogging the road*.

cloister • *noun* **1** a covered walk, often with a wall on one side and a colonnade open to a quadrangle on the other, esp. in a convent etc. **2 a** a convent or monastery. **b** life in a convent or monastery. • *verb* seclude or shut up in or as if in a convent etc. [Say CLOY ster]

cloistered *adjective* **1** kept away from the outside world; sheltered: *a cloistered upbringing*. **2** living in a convent or monastery, esp. in an order whose members have little or no contact with the outside world.

clomp *verb* walk with heavy steps.

clonal *adjective* pertaining to clones or generated by cloning.

clone • *noun* **1 a** a plant or animal produced artificially from the cells of a single ancestor and therefore exactly the same as it. **b** a group of clones from the same ancestor. **2** a person or thing regarded as identical with another. **3** a microcomputer designed to simulate another, more expensive, model. • *verb* (**clones, cloned, cloning**) produce or copy as a clone.

clonk • *noun* an abrupt heavy sound of impact. • *verb* **1** make such a sound. **2** *informal* hit.

clop • *noun* the sound made by a horse's hooves. • *verb* (**clops, clopped, clopping**) make this sound.

close¹ • *adjective* (**closer, closest**) **1** situated at only a short distance or interval. **2 a** having a strong or immediate relation or connection: *close relatives*. **b** in intimate friendship or association: *we're very close*. **c** corresponding almost exactly: *close resemblance*. **d** fitting tightly. **e** (of hair etc.) short, near the surface. **3** in or almost in contact: *close proximity*. **4** dense, compact, with no or only slight intervals: *close formation*. **5** in which competitors are almost equal: *close contest*. **6** rigorous: *close reasoning*. **7** concentrated, searching: *close attention*. **8** (of air etc.) stuffy or humid. **9** closed, shut. **10 a** hidden, secret, covered. **b** secretive. **11** (of a danger etc.) directly threatening, narrowly avoided. • *adverb* at only a short distance or interval.

close² • *verb* (**closes, closed, closing**) **1 a** shut or

be shut. **b** prevent access to: *closed the border to tourists*. **2 a** bring or come to an end: *closed the debate*. **b** finish speaking: *closed with prayer*. **c** settle or finalize (a deal, offer, etc.). **3 a** (of a business, school, etc.) cease work or business temporarily: *the store closes at six*. **b** temporarily cease work or business at (a business, school, etc.). **4** cease or cause to cease the operation of (an office, business, etc.). **5** withdraw all the money from (a bank account etc.). **6** remove from use or stop using (a room, bed, etc.): *the hospital closed 100 beds*. **7** (of a group of people) come close to or surround someone or something. **8** (of stocks, precious metals, etc.) be at a particular price at the close of a day's trading. **9** make (an electric circuit etc.) continuous. • *noun* a conclusion, an end. PHRASES **close down 1** discontinue (or cause to discontinue) business, esp. permanently. **2** (of a broadcasting station) end transmission esp. until the next day. **close one's eyes to** pay no attention to. **close in 1** come nearer. **2** (of days) get successively shorter with the approach of the winter solstice. **close off** prevent access to by covering or blocking the means of entrance. **close out** discontinue, terminate, dispose of (a business). **close ranks 1** (esp. of soldiers) move closer together. **2** establish or maintain solidarity. **close up 1** shut, esp. temporarily. **2** (of groups of people) move closer. **3** block up. **4** (of an aperture) grow smaller.

close call *noun* a narrow escape.

close-cropped *adjective* (of hair etc.) cut very short.

closed *adjective* **1** not giving access; shut. **2** (of a store etc.) having ceased business temporarily. **3** (of a society, system, etc.) self-contained; not communicating with others. **4** *Cdn* (of a mortgage etc.) that may not be paid off before the stated term without a financial penalty. **5** (of a sport etc.) restricted to specified competitors etc.

closed caption *noun* one of a series of captions along the bottom of a television screen as an aid to the hearing impaired, accessible only through a decoder. ▶ **closed-captioned** *adjective* **closed-captioning** *noun*

closed-circuit *adjective* (of television) transmitted by wires to a restricted set of receivers, as within a building etc.

closed shop *noun* a place of work etc. where all employees must belong to an agreed labour union.

close-fitting *noun* (of a garment) fitting close to the body.

close-knit *adjective* (also **closely-knit**) tightly bound or interlocked; closely united in friendship etc.

closely *adverb* **1** at little distance. **2** intimately. **3** nearly; with close ties or links and little difference: *they are closely related*. **4** accurately, faithfully: *follow the instructions closely*. **5** intently, carefully: *listen closely*.

close-mouthed *adjective* not revealing one's thoughts etc.; tight-lipped.

closeness *noun* **1** a close bond or relationship; intimacy: *there is a closeness between Natalie and her mother*. **2** a close similarity. **3** nearness.

close quarters *plural noun* a cramped place: *live in very close quarters*. PHRASES **at close quarters** very close.

closer *noun* **1** a person or thing that closes. **2** *Baseball* a relief pitcher brought in by a team with a lead to pitch the final innings.

close-set *adjective* set close together.

close shave *noun* *informal* a narrow escape.

closet • *noun* **1** a cupboard or recess, esp. one used for hanging clothes. **2** a small or private room. **3** (as an

adjective) secret, covert: *closet leftist*. • *verb* (**closets, closeted, closeting**) shut away, esp. in private conference or study: *I've been closeted in my room for days, writing this paper*. PHRASES **in the closet 1** keeping one's homosexuality from public knowledge. **2** hidden from public scrutiny. **out of the closet 1** into the open; into public scrutiny. **2** having publicly declared one's homosexuality.

closeted *adjective* secret, covert: *a closeted lesbian*.

close-up *noun* **1** a photograph etc. taken at close range and showing the subject on a large scale. **2** an intimate description.

closing *noun* **1** an act or the process of closing. **2** the end or conclusion, e.g. of a speech. **3** the final phase of a transaction, esp. of buying or selling real estate. **4** something that closes; a fastener.

closure *noun* **1** the act or process of closing. **2** a closed condition. **3** something that closes or seals. **4 a** procedure for ending a debate and taking a vote, esp. in Parliament. **5** conclusion: *catching her murderer will give her family a sense of closure*.

clot • *noun* **1** a lump of solidified liquid, esp. of blood that has been exposed to air. **2** a mass of material stuck together. • *verb* (**clots, clotted, clotting**) form into clots.

cloth *noun* (*plural* **cloths**) **1** woven or felted material; a piece of this. **2** a piece of cloth for a particular purpose; a tablecloth, dishcloth, etc. **3** the clergy: *man of the cloth*.

clothe *verb* (**clothes, clothed** or *formal* **clad, clothing**) **1** put clothes on; provide with clothes. **2** cover as with clothes or a cloth: *hills clothed with grass*.

clothes *plural noun* garments worn to cover the body.

clothes horse *noun* **1** a frame for airing washed clothes. **2** *informal* a person who has many, esp. fashionable, clothes.

clothesline *noun* a rope or wire etc. on which washed clothes are hung to dry.

clothespin *noun* a clip or forked device for attaching clothes to a clothesline.

clothier *noun* a maker or seller of clothes, esp. men's clothes. [Say CLOTHE ee er]

clothing *noun* clothes collectively. [Say CLOTHE ing]

cloud • *noun* **1** a visible mass of condensed watery vapour floating in the atmosphere high above the general level of the ground. **2** a mass of smoke or dust. **3 a** a hazy area in the night sky produced by the light of distant stars. **b** a region of dust, gas, etc., in deep space appearing lighter or darker owing to the reflection, absorption, etc. of light. **4** (foll. by *of*) a great number of insects, birds, etc., moving together. **5 a** a state of gloom, trouble, or suspicion. **b** a frowning or depressed look: *a cloud on his brow*. **6** a local dimness or a vague patch of colour in or on a liquid or a transparent body. • *verb* **1** cover or darken with clouds or gloom or trouble. **2** (often foll. by *over, up*) become overcast or gloomy. **3 a** make unclear: *prejudice clouded the issue*. **b** make unreliable; distort: *alcohol clouded his judgment*. **4** variegate with vague patches of colour. PHRASES **in the clouds 1** unreal, imaginary, mystical. **2** (of a person) abstracted, inattentive. **on cloud nine** *informal* extremely happy. **under a cloud** out of favour, discredited, under suspicion. **with one's head in the clouds** daydreaming, unrealistic.

cloudberry *noun* (*plural* **cloudberries**) a low-growing plant of the raspberry family, with a white flower and an edible amber fruit. *Also called:* BAKEAPPLE.

cloudburst *noun* a sudden violent rainstorm.

cloudiness *noun* a cloudy state.

cloudless *adjective* with no clouds: *a cloudless sky*. ▶ **cloudlessly** *adverb*

cloudy *adjective* (**cloudier, cloudiest**) **1 a** (of the sky) covered with clouds. **b** (of weather) characterized by clouds. **2** not transparent; unclear: *cloudy glass*.

clout • *noun* **1** *informal* influence; power of effective action esp. in politics or business: *doesn't have enough clout to change things*. **2** a heavy blow. • *verb* hit hard.

clove[1] *noun* **1 a** a dried flower bud of a tropical plant, used as a pungent spice. **b** the plant this comes from. **2** any of the small bulbs making up a compound bulb of garlic, shallot, etc.

clove[2] *past of* CLEAVE[1].

cloven *adjective* split, partly divided.

cloven hoof *noun* (also **cloven foot**) the divided hoof of oxen, sheep, goats, etc.

clover *noun* a small plant with usu. three leaves on each stem, and purple, pink or white flowers, growing wild or grown as food for cattle etc. PHRASES **in clover** in ease and luxury.

cloverleaf *noun* (*plural* **cloverleafs**) an intersection of highways with ramps forming the pattern of a four-leaf clover.

clown • *noun* **1** a comic entertainer, esp. in a circus, usu. with a painted face and ridiculous clothing. **2** a silly, foolish, or playful person. • *verb* **1** behave like a clown; act foolishly or playfully: *stop clowning around*. **2** perform a part, an action, etc. like a clown. ▶ **clownish** *adjective* **clownishly** *adverb* **clownishness** *noun*

cloying *adjective* **1** extremely sweet: *it smelled of pine, that cloying scent meant to freshen air*. **2** excessively sentimental: *a romantic, rather cloying story*. ▶ **cloyingly** *adverb*

CLSC *noun Cdn* (in Quebec) a provincially funded community health care clinic.

club • *noun* **1** a heavy stick with a thick end, used as a weapon etc. **2** a stick or bat used in a game to strike a ball, esp. one with a head used in golf. **3 a** a playing card of a suit denoted by a black trefoil. **b** (in *plural*) this suit. **4** an association of persons united by a common interest, usu. meeting periodically for a shared activity: *bridge club*. **5** an organization or premises offering members social amenities, meals, temporary accommodation, etc. **6** an organization or premises having athletic and exercise facilities: *health club*. **7** an organization offering members certain benefits: *book club*. **8** a group of persons, nations, etc., having something in common. **9** a sports team and its administrative staff. **10** a bar or nightclub. • *verb* (**clubs, clubbed, clubbing**) **1** beat with or as with a club. **2** (foll. by *together, with*) combine for joint action, esp. making up a sum of money for a purpose. **3** visit nightclubs etc. PHRASES **join** (or **welcome to**) **the club** you're not the only one to feel that way.

clubber *noun* **1** a member of a club. **2** a person who frequents nightclubs.

clubbiness *noun* a cliquish camaraderie among members of a group or organization.

clubbing *noun* the practice of frequenting nightclubs.

clubby *adjective* (**clubbier, clubbiest**) **1** friendly and sociable with fellow members of a group or organization but not with outsiders. **2** typical of a social club, esp. in sumptuous decor etc.

club foot *noun* (*plural* **club feet**) a congenitally deformed foot, usu. turned downward and inward so that one walks on the outer edge of the foot. ▶ **club-footed** *adjective*

clubhouse *noun* **1** the premises used by a club. **2** the dressing room of a sports team, esp. a baseball team.

club sandwich *noun* (*Cdn* also **clubhouse**

sandwich) a sandwich usu. consisting of two layers of bacon, lettuce, tomato, mayonnaise, and poultry served between three slices of toast or bread.

club soda *noun* water made bubbly by the addition of carbon dioxide under pressure, and used alone or with an alcoholic beverage etc. as a drink.

cluck • *noun* **1** a guttural cry like that of a hen. **2** *slang* a silly or foolish person: *dumb cluck*. • *verb* **1** (of a hen) emit a cluck or clucks. **2** (of a person) make a clucking sound with the tongue. **3** (also **cluck-cluck**) express annoyance, disapproval, etc. by making a similar noise.

clue • *noun* **1** a fact or idea that serves as a guide, or suggests a line of inquiry, in a problem or investigation. **2** a piece of evidence etc. in the detection of a crime. **3** a verbal formula serving as a hint as to what is to be inserted in a crossword. • *verb* (**clues, clued, clueing**) provide a clue to. PHRASES **clue in** *informal* inform. **not have a clue** *informal* be ignorant or incompetent.

clueless *adjective informal* ignorant, stupid. ▶ **cluelessly** *adverb* **cluelessness** *noun*

clump • *noun* **1** (foll. by *of*) a cluster or compact group of things or people, esp. of trees, hair, buildings, etc. **2** an agglutinated mass or lump. **3** a dull thudding sound. • *verb* **1 a** form a clump. **b** heap or plant together. **2** walk with heavy steps. **3** *informal* hit.

clumper *noun Cdn* (Maritimes & Nfld) (also **clumpet**) a large floating chunk of ice.

clumpy *adjective* (**clumpier, clumpiest**) **1** having or forming in clumps: *a lawn of clumpy grass*. **2** awkward, inelegant: *clumpy boots*.

clumsily *adverb* in a clumsy manner.

clumsiness *noun* a clumsy manner.

clumsy *adjective* (**clumsier, clumsiest**) **1** not graceful in movement or shape; awkward. **2** done without skill or ease: *a clumsy forgery*. **3** tactless: *a clumsy apology*. **4** (of tools, furniture, etc.) difficult to use or move; not well designed.

clung *past and past participle of* CLING.

clunk • *noun* a dull sound as of thick pieces of metal striking. • *verb* **1** make such a sound. **2** (often foll. by *along*) move or progress clumsily. **3** hit hard so as to make a clunking sound.

clunker *noun informal* **1** a dilapidated automobile or machine. **2** a failure; flop.

clunking *adjective* = CLUNKY.

clunky *adjective* (**clunkier, clunkiest**) *informal* **1** awkward or clumsy. **2** not sleekly designed: *a clunky station wagon*. **3** tending to make clunking sounds.

cluster • *noun* a close group or bunch of similar things growing or arranged together. • *verb* **1** bring, be, or come into a cluster or clusters. **2** (foll. by *around*) gather.

cluster bomb *noun* an anti-personnel bomb spraying smaller bombs or shrapnel when detonated.

clutch[1] • *verb* (**clutches, clutched, clutching**) **1 a** seize eagerly. **b** grasp tightly. **2** (foll. by *at*) snatch suddenly. • *noun* (*plural* **clutches**) **1** a tight grasp. **2** (in *plural*) power or control: *in his clutches*. **3 a** (in a motor vehicle) a device for connecting and disconnecting the engine to the transmission. **b** the pedal operating this. **c** an arrangement for connecting or disconnecting working parts of a machine. **4** a decisive or crucial situation: *came through in the clutch*. **5** = CLUTCH BAG. • *adjective Sport slang* **1** occurring at a decisive time: *a clutch home run*. **2** (of a person) performing well at crucial times.

clutch[2] *noun* (*plural* **clutches**) **1 a** a set of eggs to be hatched at one time. **b** the brood resulting from this. **2** a group of people or of similar items.

clutch bag *noun* (also **clutch purse**) a handbag without a handle or strap.

clutter • *noun* **1** a crowded and untidy collection of

things. **2** an untidy state. • *verb* (often foll. by *up*, *with*) crowd untidily, fill with clutter.

cluttered *adjective* crowded so as to cause confusion, esp. with many small objects.

Clydesdale *noun* a draft horse of a heavy powerful breed, usu. dark-coloured with thick white hair on the lower legs. [Say CLIDE'S dale]

CM *abbreviation* Member of the Order of Canada.

Cm *symbol* curium.

cm *abbreviation* centimetre(s).

C-note *noun* slang a one-hundred-dollar bill.

Co *symbol* cobalt.

Co. *abbreviation* **1** company. **2** county. PHRASES **and Co.** *informal* and the rest of them; and similar things.

c/o *abbreviation* care of.

co- *prefix* added to: **1** nouns, with the sense "joint, mutual, common": *co-pilot*. **2** adjectives and adverbs, with the sense "jointly, mutually": *co-dependent*. **3** verbs, with the sense "together with another or others": *co-operate*.

coach • *noun* (*plural* **coaches**) **1** a bus which is comfortably equipped for longer journeys. **2 a** a person who trains or instructs a sports team or athlete. **b** a private tutor. **c** a person who teaches an actor, singer, etc. in specific aspects of their art. **3** economy class seating in an aircraft, train, etc. **4** a four-wheeled carriage, usu. closed and drawn by one or more horses. • *adverb* in economy class seating. • *verb* (**coaches, coached, coaching**) **1** train or instruct (a student, sports team, etc.) as a coach. **2** work as a coach. **3** give hints to; prime with facts. ▶ **coachable** *adjective*

coach house *noun* a building designed to hold horse-drawn coaches or carriages.

coaching *noun* the process or job of training an athlete, team, performer, etc.

coachman *noun* (*plural* **coachmen**) the driver of a horse-drawn carriage.

coady *noun* Cdn (Nfld) a thick sweetened sauce, usu. made from boiled molasses. [Say CO dee]

coagulate *verb* (**coagulates, coagulated, coagulating**) (of a fluid, esp. blood) change or be changed from a liquid to a solid or semi-solid state: *blood had coagulated around the edges of the gash* ◊ *these infectious bacteria can coagulate plasma*. ▶ **coagulation** *noun* [Say co AG yuh late]

coal *noun* **1 a** a hard black or blackish rock, mainly carbonized plant matter, found in underground seams and used esp. as a fuel. **b** a piece or pieces of this for burning. **2** (in *plural*) burning or charred pieces of coal, wood, etc. in a fire. **3** = CHARCOAL 1. PHRASES **coals to Newcastle** something brought or sent to a place where it is already plentiful. **rake** (or **haul**) **over the coals** reprimand severely.

coalesce *verb* (**coalesces, coalesced, coalescing**) **1** come together and form one whole: *the puddles had coalesced into a shallow stream* ◊ *the separate details coalesce to form a single body of scientific thought*. **2** combine elements in a mass or whole: *the problem of coalescing disparate information sources into a practical form*. ▶ **coalescence** *noun* **coalescent** *adjective* [Say co a LESS, co a LESS unce, co a LESS unt]

coalfield *noun* an extensive area with strata containing coal.

coalition *noun* a temporary alliance for combined action, esp. of distinct political parties forming a government. [Say co a LISH'n]

coal oil *noun* dated kerosene or petroleum.

coal tar *noun* a thick black sticky liquid distilled from coal and used as a source of benzene and many other organic chemicals.

SPELL CHECK ABC
coarse, course

A track, a series of classes, or a part of a meal is a **course**.

---

coarse *adjective* (**coarser, coarsest**) **1 a** rough or loose in texture or grain; made of large particles. **b** (of a person's features) rough or large. **2** lacking refinement or delicacy; crude, obscene: *coarse humour*. ▶ **coarsely** *adverb* **coarseness** *noun*

coarsen *verb* make or become coarse.

coast • *noun* **1 a** the border of the land near the sea; the seashore. **b** (**the Coast**) the Pacific coast of North America. **2** a run, usu. downhill, in or on a vehicle without the use of power. • *verb* **1** ride or move, usu. downhill, without use of power. **2** make progress without much effort. PHRASES **the coast is clear** there is no danger of being observed or caught. ▶ **coastal** *adjective*

coastal boat *noun* Cdn (Nfld) a boat carrying supplies, mail, and some passengers to outports.

coaster *noun* **1** a small tray or mat for a bottle or glass. **2 a** a sled or toboggan. **b** a roller coaster. **3** a ship that travels along the coast from port to port.

coast guard *noun* **1** (also **Coast Guard**) **a** (in Canada) an organization whose responsibilities include rescue at sea or on major lakes, icebreaking, maintaining aids to navigation, and resupply of remote northern settlements. **b** a similar organization in another country. **2** a member of a coast guard.

coastline *noun* the line of the seashore, esp. with regard to its shape: *a rugged coastline*.

Coast Salish *noun* (*plural* **Coast Salish**) = SNE NAY MUXW.

coast-to-coast *adjective* & *adverb* **1** across a continent or island. **2** *Basketball* from one end of the court to the other while in possession of the ball.

Coast Tsimshian *noun* (*plural* **Coast Tsimshian**) **1** a member of a part of the Tsimshian linguistic group living on the northwest coast of BC. **2** the language of these people.

coat • *noun* **1** an outer garment with sleeves and often extending below the hips. **2 a** an animal's fur, hair, etc. **b** *Physiology* a structure, esp. a membrane, enclosing or lining an organ. **c** a skin, rind, or husk. **d** *Botany* a layer of a bulb etc. **3 a** a layer or covering. **b** a covering of paint etc. laid on a surface at one time. • *verb* **1** apply a coat of paint etc. to; provide with a layer or covering. **2** (of paint etc.) form a covering over.

coat check *noun* a place at a theatre, restaurant, etc. where coats, bags, etc. may be left with an attendant.

coated *adjective* **1** covered with a coat of some substance. **2** having a coat of a specified sort. **3** (of paper) treated with a coating of clay to provide a glazed surface.

coat hanger *noun* = HANGER 2.

coating *noun* **1** a thin layer or covering. **2** a substance used for covering in a thin layer.

coat of arms *noun* (*plural* **coats of arms**) a shield or other arrangement of the heraldic bearings of a person, family, government, etc.

coattail *noun* each of the flaps extending below the waist from the back of a tailcoat. PHRASES **(riding) on the coattails of** undeservedly benefiting from (another's success).

co-author • *noun* an author who collaborates with another on a book or article. • *verb* be a co-author of.

coax[1] *verb* (**coaxes, coaxed, coaxing**) **1** persuade gradually by flattery or by continued patient trial: *coaxed her to join the team* ◊ *try coaxing him into going*.

2 (foll. by *out of*) obtain by coaxing. **3** manipulate (a thing) carefully or slowly. [Say COKES]

coax² • *adjective=* COAXIAL. • *noun* coaxial cable. [Say CO ax]

coaxial *adjective* **1** having a common axis. **2** *Electricity* (of a cable or line) transmitting (telephone, telegraph, television, or radio signals) by means of two concentric conductors separated by an insulator. [Say co AX ee ul]

coaxing *noun* gentle attempts to persuade someone to do something or to get a machine to start.

cob *noun* **1** the cylindrical centre of an ear of corn, to which the rows of kernels are attached. **2** a sturdy horse with short legs. **3** a male swan.

cobalt *noun* a silvery-white magnetic metallic element, used in many alloys. [Say CO bawlt]

cobalt-60 *noun* a long-lived radioisotope of cobalt, used as a radioactive tracer and in cancer therapy.

cobalt blue *noun* **1** a pigment containing a cobalt salt. **2** *noun & adjective* the deep blue colour of this.

cobalt bomb *noun* **1** a container of cobalt-60 or other radioisotope used in cancer treatment. **2** a hydrogen bomb designed to disperse radioactive cobalt.

cobble¹ • *noun* a small stone, larger than a pebble, rounded by the action of water. • *verb* (**cobbles, cobbled, cobbling**) (esp. as **cobbled** *adjective*) pave with cobblestones.

cobble² *verb* (**cobbles, cobbled, cobbling**) **1** mend or patch up (esp. shoes). **2** join or assemble roughly.

cobbler *noun* **1** a person who mends shoes, esp. professionally. **2** a baked dessert of fruit topped with a tea-biscuit crust.

cobblestone *noun* a small rounded stone used for paving.

COBOL *noun Computing* a programming language designed for use in commerce. [Say CO bawl]

cobra *noun* any of a number of venomous Asian and African snakes which can dilate their necks to form a hood when disturbed. [Say CO bra]

cobweb *noun* **1 a** a fine network of threads spun by a spider from a liquid secreted by it, used to trap insects etc. **b** the thread of this. **2** anything compared with a cobweb, esp. in flimsy texture. **3** (in *plural*) a state of mental inertia: *a walk will clear the cobwebs*. ▶ **cobwebbed** *adjective* **cobwebby** *adjective*

coca *noun* a South American shrub, the dried leaves of which yield cocaine. [Say CO kuh]

cocaine *noun* a white crystalline alkaloid derived from coca leaves, used as a local anaesthetic or in various forms as a narcotic with euphoric effects.

co-chair • *noun* a person who chairs a committee jointly with another or others. • *verb* act as a co-chair for (a committee etc.).

cochlea *noun* (*plural* **cochleae**) the spiral cavity of the internal ear, in which the sensory reception of sound occurs. ▶ **cochlear** *adjective* [Say COCKLY uh for the singular, COCKLY ee for the plural]

cock • *noun* **1 a** a male bird, esp. of a domestic fowl; a rooster. **b** the male of certain sea creatures, e.g. the lobster or clam. **2** = WOODCOCK. **3 a** a firing lever in a gun which can be raised to be released by the trigger. **b** the cocked position of this: *at full cock*. **4** *Curling* the position at the end of the rink at which rocks are aimed. **5** a tap or valve controlling flow. **6** *Brit.* & *Cdn* (*Nfld*) *slang* (usu. **old cock** as a form of address) a friend; a fellow. • *verb* **1** raise or make upright or erect. **2** turn or move (the eye or ear) attentively or knowingly. **3** set aslant, or turn up the brim of (a hat). **4** raise the cock of (a gun). PHRASES **at half cock** only partly ready.

cockade *noun* a rosette etc. worn in a hat as a badge of office etc. or as part of a uniform ▶ **cockaded** *adjective*

cock-a-doodle-doo *noun* a rooster's crow.

cockatiel *noun* (also **cockateel**) a small delicately coloured crested Australian parrot. [Say cocka TEEL]

cockatoo *noun* an Australian parrot, with a large crest of feathers standing up on its head.

cockerel *noun* a young rooster. [Say COCKER ul]

cocker spaniel *noun* a small breed of spaniel with a silky coat and long drooping ears.

cockeyed *adjective informal* **1** crooked, askew, not level. **2** (of a scheme etc.) absurd, not practical. **3** drunk. **4** squinting. [Say COCK eyed]

cockfight *noun* a fight between pitted cocks, often fitted with metal spurs, usu. with spectators betting on the outcome. ▶ **cockfighting** *noun*

cockiness *noun* arrogance; bold confidence.

cockle *noun* **1** an edible mollusc with a chubby ribbed bivalve shell. **2** its shell. PHRASES **warm the cockles of one's heart** make one contented; be satisfying.

cockney • *noun* (*plural* **cockneys**) **1** a native of the East End of London, England. **2** the dialect or accent typical of this area. • *adjective* of or characteristic of cockneys or their dialect or accent. [Say COCK nee]

cockpit *noun* **1 a** a compartment for the pilot (or the pilot and crew) of an aircraft or spacecraft. **b** a similar compartment for the driver in an automobile. **c** a space for the helmsman in some small yachts. **d** the space for the paddler in a kayak. **2** an arena of war or other conflict. **3** a place where cockfights are held.

cockroach *noun* (*plural* **cockroaches**) any of various flat brown insects, typically a stout-bodied scavenger resembling a beetle, with hardened forewings; esp. the large dark brown *Blatta orientalis* and *Periplaneta americana*, which infest households, warehouses, etc.

cocksure *adjective* presumptuously or arrogantly confident.

cocktail *noun* **1** a usu. alcoholic drink made by mixing various spirits, fruit juices, etc. **2** (as an *adjective*) **a** denoting a small item of food served as an hors d'oeuvre etc.: *cocktail wiener*. **b** denoting a place or occasion where drinks are served: *cocktail party*. **3** a dish of mixed ingredients: *fruit cocktail*. **4** a mixture of substances or factors, esp. when dangerous or unpleasant in its effects: *financial pressure plus isolation can be a deadly cocktail for some people*. **5** a number of different drugs used together to treat a condition: *a new cocktail of drugs has made life better for many AIDS patients*.

cocky *adjective* (**cockier, cockiest**) **1** conceited, arrogantly confident. **2** saucy, impudent.

coco *noun* (*plural* **cocos**) (also **coconut palm**) a tall tropical palm tree bearing coconuts.

cocoa *noun* **1** a powder made from crushed cacao seeds, often with other ingredients. **2** a drink made from this powder and hot water or milk. [Say COCO]

cocoa bean *noun* a cacao seed.

cocoa butter *noun* a fatty substance obtained from cocoa beans and used in confectionery, cosmetics, etc.

coconut *noun* **1** a large oval brown seed of the coco, with a hard shell and edible white fleshy lining enclosing a milky juice. **2** (also **coconut palm**) = COCO. **3** the edible white fleshy lining of a coconut.

coconut milk *noun* **1** the white milky liquid found inside the coconut. **2** a coconut-flavoured liquid obtained by soaking grated coconut in water.

cocoon • *noun* **1 a** a silky case spun by many insect larvae for protection as pupae. **b** a similar structure made by other animals. **2** anything which encloses or protects like a cocoon: *wrapped in a cocoon of bedding* ◊ *a warm cocoon of love*. **3** a protective covering sprayed on metal equipment to prevent corrosion. • *verb* **1** wrap in or form a cocoon. **2** spray with a protective coating.

cocooner *noun* a person who spends his or her leisure time at home instead of going out.

cocooning *noun* the practice of spending one's leisure time at home instead of going out.

COD *abbreviation* **1** collect on delivery. **2** cash on delivery.

cod *noun* (*plural* **cod**) any large marine food fish of the family Gadidae, esp. *Gadus morhua*.

coda *noun* **1** *Music* the concluding passage of a piece or movement, usu. forming an addition to the basic structure. **2** the concluding section of a dance, drama, or literary work. **3** a concluding event or series of events: *his new novel is a kind of coda to his previous work*. [Say CO duh]

coddle *verb* (**coddles, coddled, coddling**) **1** treat indulgently or over-attentively: *as a child, she was coddled and sheltered*. **2** cook (an egg) in water below boiling point.

code • *noun* **1 a** a pre-arranged system of words, letters, numbers, signals, or symbols, used to represent others for brevity or to ensure secrecy. **b** any similar system used for conveying specific information with arbitrarily assigned symbols: *postal code*. **c** = GENETIC CODE. **2 a** a set of instructions written in a programming language. **b** the language itself. **c** = BAR CODE. **3 a** a systematic collection of statutes. **b** a set of rules on any subject: *dress code*. **4 a** the prevailing morality of a society or class: *code of honour*. **b** a person's standard of moral behaviour. • *verb* (**codes, coded, coding**) **1** put (a message, program, etc.) into code. **2** (foll. by *for*) *Biochemistry* be the genetic code for (an amino acid etc.). PHRASES **bring up to code** renovate an older building to make it conform to revised, more stringent building code regulations.

codec *noun* a device that converts an analog signal into an encoded digital form, and decodes digital signals into analog form, used in telephone systems and in video systems for computers. [Say CO deck]

codeine *noun* an alkaloid derived from morphine and used to relieve pain. [Say CO deen]

codependency *noun* excessive emotional or psychological dependence on supporting or caring for a partner, esp. one with an illness or addiction.

codependent • *adjective* emotionally or psychologically dependent on supporting or caring for another person, esp. a person with an addiction or illness. • *noun* a codependent person.

coder *noun* a person or device that converts letters, symbols, or signals into code.

code-share *verb* (**code-shares, code-shared, code-sharing**) (of two or more airlines) list certain flights in a reservation system under each other's names. ▶ **code-sharing** *noun*

codfish *noun* (*plural* **codfish**) = COD.

codger *noun* (usu. in **old codger**) *informal* a person, esp. an old or strange one. [Rhymes with *ROGER*]

codicil *noun* an addition explaining, modifying, or revoking a will or part of one. [Say CO duh sill]

codification *noun* the arrangement of laws etc. into a systematic code. [Say CO duh fuh CAY sh'n]

codify *verb* (**codifies, codified, codifying**) arrange (laws etc.) systematically into a code. [Say CO duh fie]

cod-liver oil *noun* an oil pressed from the fresh liver of cod or related fishes, rich in vitamins D and A.

coed *informal* • *adjective* **1** coeducational. **2** open to both males and females. • *noun dated* a female student at a coeducational institution. [Say CO ed]

coeducation *noun* the education of male and female students together. ▶ **coeducational** *adjective*

coefficient *noun* **1** *Math* a quantity placed before and multiplying an algebraic expression (e.g. 4 in $4x^y$).

2 *Physics* a multiplier or factor that measures some property: *coefficient of expansion*. [Say co EFFICIENT]

coerce *verb* (**coerces, coerced, coercing**) (often foll. by *into*) persuade or restrain (a person) by force: *coerced me into signing*. [Say co URSS]

coercion *noun* the act or process of coercing: *coercion is unlikely to prompt people to join such groups*. ▶ **coercive** *adjective* **coercively** *adverb* **coerciveness** *noun* [Say co UR sh'n, co UR siv]

coeval • *adjective* having the same age or date of origin: *these lavas were coeval with the volcanic activity*. • *noun* a person of roughly the same age as oneself; a contemporary: *Orwell and his coevals*. [Say co EVIL]

coexist *verb* (often foll. by *with*) **1** exist together (in time or place). **2** (esp. of nations) exist in mutual tolerance though professing different ideologies etc. ▶ **coexistence** *noun* **coexistent** *adjective*

co-extensive *adjective* extending over the same space, time, or limits.

coffee • *noun* **1 a** a drink made from the roasted and ground beanlike seeds of a tropical shrub of the genus *Coffea*. **b** a cup of this. **2 a** the shrub yielding these seeds, one or more of which are contained in each berry. **b** these seeds raw, or roasted and ground. **3** the pale brown colour of coffee mixed with milk. • *adjective* **1** of the colour of coffee mixed with milk. **2** flavoured with coffee. PHRASES **wake up and smell the coffee** become aware of (usu. unpleasant) realities.

coffee cake *noun* a type of cake or sweet bread topped or filled with cinnamon sugar, often containing nuts or raisins.

coffee house *noun* **1** a place serving coffee and other refreshments. **2** a form of entertainment, usu. jazz or folk music or poetry readings etc., performed cabaret-style.

coffee klatch *noun* (*plural* **coffee klatches**) an informal gathering for conversation at which coffee is served, esp. one involving women.

coffee shop *noun* a small informal restaurant, esp. in an office building, serving simple meals and beverages.

coffee table *noun* a small low oblong table.

coffee-table book *noun* a large lavishly illustrated book suitable for prominent display.

coffer *noun* **1** a box, esp. a large strongbox for valuables. **2** (in *plural*) a treasury or store of funds: *this tax provides $18 billion to the public coffers every year*. **3** *Architecture* a sunken panel in a ceiling, soffit, etc.

coffered *adjective* (of a ceiling etc.) having sunken panels.

coffin *noun* a long narrow usu. wooden box in which a corpse is buried or cremated.

cog *noun* **1 a** each of a series of teeth on the edge of a wheel or shaft transferring motion by engaging with another series. **b** (also **cogwheel**) a wheel or shaft furnished with these. **2** a person who plays a minor or routine role in an organization.

cogency *noun* the soundness and persuasiveness of an argument etc.: *the book first appeared in 1990, but its thirteen essays have greater cogency now*. [Say CO jin see]

cogeneration *noun* the utilization of otherwise wasted energy for heating or for generating electricity. [Say co GENERATION]

cogent *adjective* (of arguments etc.) clear, logical, and convincing: *she put forward some cogent reasons for abandoning the plan*. ▶ **cogently** *adverb* [Say CO jint]

cogged *adjective* having cogs or teeth: *a cogged wheel*.

cogitate *verb* (**cogitates, cogitated, cogitating**) ponder, meditate: *went down to the study to cogitate*. ▶ **cogitation** *noun* [Say CODGE a tate, codge a TAY sh'n]

cognac *noun* a high-quality brandy, properly that

distilled in Cognac in western France. [Say CON yack or CONE yack]

cognate • adjective **1** (of a word) having the same linguistic family or derivation (as another); representing the same original word or root (e.g. English *father*, German *Vater*, Latin *pater*). **2** related; connected: *cognate subjects such as physics and chemistry*. • noun a cognate word. [Say COG nate]

cognition noun the mental action or process of acquiring knowledge and understanding through thought, experience, and the senses: *child studies centring on theories of cognition*. [Say cog NISH'n]

cognitive adjective connected with mental processes of understanding: *a child's cognitive abilities* ◊ *cognitive psychology*. ▶ **cognitively** adverb [Say COG nuh tiv]

cognizance noun **1** knowledge, awareness, or notice: *he was instructed to bring the affair to the cognizance of the court*. **2** Law the right of a court to deal with a matter: *the court has cognizance over cases of this kind*. PHRASES **take cognizance of** notice or take account of, esp. officially. [Say COG nizz ince]

cognizant adjective (foll. by *of*) having knowledge or being aware of: *statesmen must be cognizant of the political boundaries within which they work*. [Say COG nizz'nt]

cognoscenti plural noun connoisseurs; discerning experts: *it was hailed by the cognoscenti as one of the best golf courses in the world*. [Say cog nuh SENTY or cog nuh SHENTY]

cogwheel noun = COG 1b.

cohabit verb (**cohabits, cohabited, cohabiting**) **1** exist together in a peaceful or harmonious way: *the album showed how the saxophone could cohabit with heavy metal guitar*. **2** live together in a sexual and romantic relationship without marriage. ▶ **cohabitation** noun

cohere verb (**coheres, cohered, cohering**) **1** (of parts or a whole) stick together, remain united: *she made the series of fictions cohere into a convincing sequence*. **2** (of reasoning etc.) be logical or consistent: *this view does not cohere with their other beliefs*.

coherence noun the situation in which all parts of an argument etc. fit together well: *your arguments are good, but the essay lacks coherence*.

coherent adjective **1** (of a person) able to speak intelligibly and articulately. **2** (of speech, an argument, etc.) logical and consistent; easily followed. **3** united as or forming a whole: *divided into a number of geographically coherent kingdoms*. **4** Physics (of electromagnetic waves) having a constant phase relationship. Lasers, for example, produce coherent light. ▶ **coherently** adverb [Say co HERE int]

cohesion noun **1** the action or fact of forming a united whole: *the work at present lacks cohesion*. **2** Physics the sticking together of particles of the same substance. ▶ **cohesive** adjective **cohesively** adverb **cohesiveness** noun [Say co HEE zh'n]

coho noun (plural **coho** or **cohos**) a silver salmon of the north Pacific.

cohort noun **1** a companion or colleague: *a few of his cohorts remembered seeing him the night before he disappeared*. **2 a** a group of persons with a common demographic or statistical characteristic: *delays in the onset of chronic disease among the current elderly cohort*. **b** persons banded or grouped together, esp. in a common cause: *a cohort of civil servants drafting and rewriting legislation*. **3** a band of warriors.

coif[1] noun a close-fitting cap, esp. as worn by nuns under a veil. [Say COYF]

coif[2] • noun a hairstyle. • verb (**coifs, coiffed, coiffing**) (usu. as **coiffed** adjective) arrange or style (hair). [Say KWOFF]

coiffure • noun a hairstyle. • verb (**coiffures,**

coiffured, coiffuring) style (hair), often in a specified way. ▶ **coiffured** adjective [Say kwoff YOOR]

coil • noun **1** anything arranged in a joined sequence of concentric circles. **2** a length of rope, a spring, etc., arranged in this way. **3** a single turn of something coiled. **4** a lock of hair twisted and coiled. **5** a contraceptive device in the form of a coil inserted in the uterus. **6 a** (in full **induction coil**) a coil for generating intermittent high voltage from a direct current. **b** any helix of wire through which electric current passes, as in a transformer or electromagnet. **7** a length of wire, piping, etc., wound in circles or spirals. • verb **1** arrange in a series of concentric loops or rings. **2** twist or be twisted into a circular or spiral shape. **3** move in a smooth, flowing way.

coin • noun **1** a piece of flat usu. round metal stamped and issued by a government as money. **2** metal money collectively. **3** slang money, wealth: *they've got coin*. • verb **1** invent or devise (esp. a new word or phrase). **2** make (metal) into coins. **3** make (coins) by stamping. PHRASES **coin money** informal make a large amount of money quickly. **the other side of the coin 1** the opposite view of the matter. **2** an apparently contrasting aspect of a situation. **to coin a phrase** ironic introducing a banal remark or cliché.

coinage noun **1** the act or process of coining. **2 a** coins collectively. **b** a system or type of coins in use. **3 a** an invention, esp. of a new word or phrase. **b** a newly invented word or phrase.

coincide verb (**coincides, coincided, coinciding**) **1** occur at or during the same time. **2** occupy the same portion of space. **3** be in agreement. [Say co in SIDE]

coincidence noun a remarkable concurrence of events or circumstances without apparent causal connection.

coincident adjective occurring together in space or time.

coincidental adjective **1** in the nature of or resulting from a coincidence. **2** happening or existing at the same time. ▶ **coincidentally** adverb

coin-op noun **1** a coin-operated machine, esp. a computer video game. **2** a laundromat.

coin-operated adjective (of a machine) automatically activated when the user inserts a coin or coins.

coital adjective having to do with sexual intercourse. [Say COY tul or CO it ul]

coitus noun sexual intercourse. [Say COY tiss or CO it iss]

coitus interruptus noun intercourse in which the penis is withdrawn before ejaculation. [Say inter RUP tiss]

coke[1] • noun **1** a solid substance left after the gases have been extracted from coal, used as fuel and in metallurgy. **2** a residue left after the incomplete combustion of petroleum. • verb (**cokes, coked, coking**) convert (coal) into coke.

coke[2] slang • noun cocaine. • verb (**cokes, coked, coking**) drug (esp. oneself) with cocaine.

cokehead noun slang a person addicted to or habitually using cocaine.

cola noun **1** a small tree native to west Africa, bearing seeds containing caffeine. **2** a sweet carbonated drink usu. flavoured with cola seeds.

colander noun a metal or plastic container with holes in it, used to strain off liquids. [Say COLL 'n der]

colby noun a mild, soft-textured cheese resembling cheddar.

cold • adjective **1** of or at a low or relatively low temperature. **2** not heated; cooled after being heated. **3** (of a person) feeling cold. **4** lacking ardour, friendliness, or affection **5** depressing, uninteresting: *cold facts*. **6 a** dead. **b** informal unconscious. **7** informal at one's mercy: *had me cold*. **8** sexually frigid. **9** Sport not

performing well. **10** (of a scent in hunting) having become weak. • *noun* **1 a** the prevalence of a low temperature, esp. in the atmosphere. **b** cold weather; a cold environment: *went out into the cold*. **2** an infection in which the mucous membrane of the nose and throat becomes inflamed, causing runny nose, sneezing, sore throat, coughing, etc. • *adverb* **1** completely, entirely: *cold sober*. **2** unrehearsed, without preparation. PHRASES **cold (hard) cash** cash, esp. in large quantities and as opposed to credit. **in cold blood** without feeling or passion; deliberately, ruthlessly. **out in the cold** ignored, neglected. **throw** (or **pour**) **cold water on** be discouraging or disparaging about.

cold-blooded *adjective* **1** having a body temperature varying with that of the environment (e.g. of fish). **2** callous; deliberately cruel. ▶**cold-bloodedly** *adverb* **cold-bloodedness** *noun*

cold call *noun* an unsolicited sales call to a prospective customer by phone or in person. ▶**cold-call** *verb*

cold-cock *verb slang* punch or strike (a person) in the head, esp. to render unconscious.

cold cuts *plural noun* slices of cold cooked meats.

cold deck *noun Forestry* a pile of logs intended to be moved or processed at a later time.

cold draw *noun Curling* a shot in which a rock is curled into the house without touching another rock.

cold feet *plural noun informal* loss of nerve or confidence.

cold fish *noun* a person, little moved by emotions, regarded as hard and unfeeling.

cold frame *noun* a box-shaped frame with a glass top, placed over plants to protect them from the weather.

cold front *noun* the forward edge of an advancing mass of cold air.

cold-hearted *adjective* lacking affection or warmth. ▶**cold-heartedly** *adverb* **cold-heartedness** *noun*

coldly *adverb* without any emotion or warm feelings; in an unfriendly way: *she stared at him coldly*.

coldness *noun* **1** a lack of warm feelings; unfriendly behaviour. **2** the state of being cold.

cold shoulder • *noun* a show of intentional unfriendliness. • *verb* (**cold-shoulder**) be deliberately unfriendly to.

cold sore *noun* inflammation and blisters in and around the mouth, caused by a virus infection.

cold storage *noun* **1** storage in a refrigerator or other cold place for preservation. **2** a state in which something (esp. an idea) is put aside temporarily.

cold sweat *noun* a state of sweating due to fear or illness.

cold turkey *informal* • *noun* **1** abrupt withdrawal from addictive drugs. **2** the symptoms of this. • *adverb* abruptly. PHRASES **go cold turkey** cease (esp. an addictive habit) completely and abruptly.

cold war *noun* **1** a state of prolonged hostility between nations short of armed conflict, often consisting of threats, violent propaganda, and subversive political activities. **2** (**Cold War**) relations of this nature between the Soviet Union and the US and their respective allies in the decades following the Second World War. ▶**Cold Warrior** *noun*

cole *noun* any of various brassicas, esp. cabbage or rape.

Coleman stove *noun proprietary* a camp stove.

coleslaw *noun* a salad of shredded raw cabbage with a dressing and often other vegetables. [Say COLE slaw]

colic *noun* **1** severe spasmodic abdominal pain. **2** a condition in young babies characterized by long, loud crying. ▶**colicky** *adjective* [Say COLLICK]

coliform • *adjective* of or pertaining to a group of bacteria typified by *Escherichia coli*, which inhabit the

large intestine of humans and animals and when present in water indicate fecal contamination. • *noun* a bacillus of this group. [Say COLLA form]

SPELL CHECK   [ABC✓]
coliseum, Colosseum

The large amphitheatre in Rome is the **Colosseum**.

---

coliseum *noun* a large amphitheatre, stadium, arena, etc.

colitis *noun* inflammation of the colon lining. [Say kuh LITE iss]

collaborate *verb* (**collaborates, collaborated, collaborating**) (often foll. by *with*) **1** work jointly, esp. in a literary or artistic production. **2** co-operate traitorously with an enemy. ▶**collaboration** *noun* **collaborationist** *noun* & *adjective* **collaborative** *adjective* **collaboratively** *adverb* **collaborator** *noun*

collage • *noun* **1 a** a form of art in which various materials (e.g. photographs) are arranged and assembled or glued to a backing. **b** a work of art done in this way. **2** a literary, musical, or cinematic work involving several genres or elements. **3** a collection of unrelated things. • *verb* (**collages, collaged, collaging**) arrange in a collage. [Say kuh LOZH]

collagen *noun* a protein found in animal connective tissue, yielding gelatin on boiling. [Say COLLA jin]

collapse • *noun* **1** the tumbling down or falling in of a structure or hollow body. **2 a** sudden failure or breakdown of a plan, undertaking, organization, etc. **3** a physical or mental breakdown. • *verb* (**collapses, collapsed, collapsing**) **1 a** undergo or experience a collapse. **b** cause to collapse. **2** *informal* sit or lie down and relax, esp. after prolonged effort: *collapsed into a chair*. **3 a** (of furniture etc.) be foldable and capable of storage in a small space. **b** fold (furniture) in this way. ▶**collapsible** *adjective*

collar • *noun* **1** the part of a shirt, dress, coat, etc., that goes around the neck, either upright or folded over. **2 a** a band of linen, lace, or other material encircling the neck or forming the upper part of a garment. **b** = CLERICAL COLLAR. **c** a band worn around the neck for a specific purpose: *cervical collar*. **3** a band put around the neck of a dog or other animal, esp. in order to control or identify it. **4** a band or ring fastened over a pipe, rod, etc. in order to restrain or connect. **5** a coloured marking resembling a collar around the neck of a bird or animal. **6** *Cdn* (*Nfld*) a rope or chain with a looped end used to moor a boat. • *verb* **1** seize (a person) by the collar or neck. **2** capture, arrest. **3** *informal* accost and detain (a reluctant listener etc.).

collarbone *noun* either of the two curved bones joining the breastbone and the shoulder blade.

collard *noun* (also **collards, collard greens**) a variety of cabbage without a distinct heart.

collared *adjective* having a collar or the kind of collar described: *a collared dove* ◊ *wide-collared shirts*.

collarless *adjective* not having a collar.

collate *verb* (**collates, collated, collating**) **1** sort or arrange (pages) in the correct order. **2** analyze and compare (texts, statements, etc.) to identify points of agreement and difference. **3** assemble from different sources. [Say CO late or kuh LATE]

collateral • *noun* security pledged as a guarantee for repayment of a loan. • *adjective* **1** side by side: *collateral veins*. **2** additional but subordinate; secondary: *was not acting for any collateral purpose*. [Say kuh LATTER ul]

collateral damage *noun* destruction or injury to civilians as the unintended or unexpected result of a military attack.

collation *noun* **1** the action of collating something:

data management and collation. **2** a light informal meal. [Say co LAY sh'n or coll AY sh'n]

colleague *noun* a person with whom one works, esp. in a profession or business.

collect¹ • *verb* **1** bring or come together; assemble, accumulate. **2** systematically seek and acquire (e.g. books, stamps) as a continuing hobby. **3 a** demand or obtain (taxes, contributions, payment due, etc.) from a person or persons. **b** (often foll. by *on*) receive a payment. **4** come for and take away: *garbage is collected once a week.* **5 a collect oneself** regain control of oneself esp. after a shock. **b** concentrate (one's energies, thoughts, etc.). **6** receive (an award, prize, etc.). • *adjective & adverb* (of a telephone call, parcel, etc.) to be paid for by the recipient.

collect² *noun* a short prayer of the Anglican and Roman Catholic Churches, esp. one assigned to a particular day or season. [Say COLL ect]

collected *adjective* **1** calm and cool; not perturbed or distracted. **2** (esp. of literary works) gathered together in one place or publication.

collectible • *adjective* **1** worth collecting. **2** able to be collected. • *noun* an item sought by collectors.

collection *noun* **1** the act or process of collecting or being collected. **2** any group of things systematically assembled, esp.: **a** specimens or collectibles acquired by a specialist or hobbyist: *Ray showed us his mineral collection.* **b** the holdings of a museum, library, etc. **c** a book of short stories, poems, or essays, or a recording including several songs or compositions. **d** a line of fashionable clothes, cosmetics, furniture etc. offered by a designer or retail store. **3** an accumulation. **4 a** the collecting of money, esp. in church or for a charitable cause. **b** the amount collected. **5** the regular removal of mail, garbage, etc. for dispatch or disposal.

collective • *adjective* **1** formed by or constituting a collection. **2** taken as a whole: *our collective opinion.* **3** of or from several or many individuals: *collective memory.* • *noun* **1 a** a co-operative enterprise. **b** its members. **c** (also **collective farm**) (in communist countries) the state-owned holdings of several farmers run as a joint enterprise. **2** (also **collective noun**) a noun that is grammatically singular and denotes a collection or number of individuals (e.g. *assembly, family, troop*). ▸ **collectively** *adverb*

collective agreement *noun* an agreement between a union and an employer arrived at through collective bargaining.

collective bargaining *noun* the process by which wages etc. for all members of a bargaining unit are negotiated between the union and an employer.

collective memory *noun* (plural **collective memories**) the memory of a group of people, often passed from one generation to the next.

collective ownership *noun* the ownership of land and means of production by a number of people for their common benefit.

collective unconscious *noun* (in Jungian theory) the part of the unconscious mind derived from ancestral memory and experience common to all.

collectivism *noun* the theory and practice of the collective ownership of land and the means of production. ▸ **collectivist** *noun*

collectivity *noun* (plural **collectivities**) **1** a group or community of people bound together by common beliefs or interests: *a French collectivity within North America.* **2** the quality of having common beliefs or interests: *a sense of collectivity among prairie farmers.* [Say coll eck TIVVA tee]

collectivization *noun* organization on the basis of collective ownership. [Say kuh leck tiv ize AY sh'n]

collectivize *verb* (**collectivizes**, **collectivized**, **collectivizing**) organize something on the basis of ownership by the people or the state, abolishing private ownership or involvement: *collectivized agriculture was a hallmark of the Communist system.* [Say kuh LECK tiv ize]

collector *noun* **1** a person who collects, esp. things of interest as a hobby. **2** a person who collects due payments etc.: *tax collector.* **3** a thing that collects, esp. solar energy or heat. **4** *Cdn* a lane running parallel to the express lanes of a freeway affording access between it and other roads. **5** *Cdn* (*Nfld*) (also **collector boat**) a boat which gathers catches of cod from several locations and transports them to a single location for processing.

collector's item *noun* a valuable object, esp. one of interest to collectors.

college *noun* **1** an establishment for further or higher education: **a** an institution within a university, usu. with residence facilities and freedom to establish a course of study but without degree-granting privileges. **b** a faculty within a university. **c** a school for specialized professional education: *business college.* **d** = COMMUNITY COLLEGE. **e** *Cdn* = CEGEP. **f** post-secondary education in general. **2** the buildings or premises of a college. **3** the students and teachers in a college. **4** an organized body of persons with shared functions and privileges: *College of Physicians.* PHRASES **give a thing the** (**old**) **college try** put forth one's best effort despite the unlikelihood of success.

collège classique *noun* (plural **collèges classiques**) *Cdn hist.* (in Quebec) a private school offering a four-year secondary education and a four-year post-secondary program leading to a BA, with the curriculum emphasizing classics, literature, philosophy, and religion. [Say kaw lezh cla SEEK]

collegial *adjective* **1** characterized by collaboration among colleagues. **2** pertaining to or involving a body of colleagues. **3** of or pertaining to a college. ▸ **collegiality** *noun* **collegially** *adverb* [Say kuh LEE jul or kuh LEE jee ul, kuh lee jee ALA tee]

collegiate • *adjective* **1** of or pertaining to colleges or universities: *collegiate sports.* **2** constituted of or belonging to colleges. • *noun Cdn* (also **collegiate institute**) (in some provinces) a public secondary school, originally one having specialist teachers and a prescribed classical curriculum. [Say kuh LEE jit]

collide *verb* (**collides**, **collided**, **colliding**) (often foll. by *with*) **1** strike together with an abrupt or violent impact. **2** be in conflict.

collie *noun* a sheepdog of a breed originating in Scotland, with a long pointed nose and long hair.

collier *noun* **1** a coal miner. **2 a** a ship transporting coal. **b** a member of its crew. [Say COLLY er]

colliery *noun* (plural **collieries**) a coal mine. [Say COLL yuh ree]

collision *noun* **1** a violent impact of a moving body, esp. a vehicle, with another or with a fixed object. **2** the clashing of opposed interests or considerations. **3** *Physics* the action of particles striking or coming together.

colloquial *adjective* belonging to or proper to ordinary or familiar conversation. [Say kuh LOKE wee ul]

colloquialism *noun* **1** a colloquial word or phrase. **2** the use of colloquialisms. [Say kuh LOKE wee ul ism]

colloquially *adverb* in ordinary or familiar conversation; informally: *the Niagara Peninsula is known colloquially as "the Banana Belt".* [Say kuh LO kwee ul ee]

colloquium *noun* (plural **colloquia**) an academic conference focused on a specific topic. [Say kuh LOKE wee um]

collude *verb* (**colludes**, **colluded**, **colluding**)

conspire together for a fraudulent or underhanded purpose: *OPEC colluded with the major oil companies to create an oil shortage that raised prices*. [Say kuh LOOD]

collusion *noun* a secret agreement, esp. for a fraudulent purpose: *the extent of the government's cover-up and collusion became clear*. [Say kuh LOO zh'n]

cologne *noun* a dilute solution of alcohol and a concentrate of perfume. [Say kuh LONE]

colon[1] *noun* a punctuation mark (:) with several uses: **1** to introduce a quotation or a list of items. **2** to separate clauses when the second expands or illustrates the first. **3** between numbers in a statement of proportion: *10:1*. **4** to separate hour from minutes in rendering the time: *9:30*. **5** in Biblical references to separate chapter and verse: *John 3:16*. [Say CO lun]

colon[2] *noun* the lower part of the large intestine, from the cecum to the rectum. [Say CO lun]

colonel *noun* (also **Colonel**) **1** (in Canada and the US) an officer in the armed forces ranking above a lieutenant colonel and below a brigadier general. Abbreviation: **Col** *Cdn* or **Col.** **2** a lieutenant colonel. [Say KER nul]

colonial • *adjective* **1 a** of or relating to a colony or colonies. **b** (of mentalities, attitudes, etc.) typical of people living in a colony or former colony, esp. in their dependence on and admiration for the mother country or other dominant culture. **2** of or relating to the period of a nation's history during which it was under the rule of a mother country. **3** (of architecture or furniture) built, designed in, or in a style characteristic of a colonial period. **4** (of plants or animals) living in colonies. • *noun* **1** a person inhabiting a colony. **2** a house built in colonial style.

colonialism *noun* **1** a policy of acquiring or maintaining colonies. **2** the exploitation or subjugation of a people by a larger or wealthier power. ▶ **colonialist** *noun & adjective*

colonic *adjective* having to do with the colon. [Say kuh LONNICK]

colonist *noun* a settler in or inhabitant of a colony.

colonist car *noun* *Cdn hist.* a railway car furnished with slatted wooden platforms for sitting or sleeping and equipped with a small stove.

colonization *noun* **1 a** the process of sending settlers to live in an area in order to establish political control over the area or the people already living there: *European colonization of North America*. **b** the process of settling in an area. **2** the establishment or proliferation of a type of plant or animal in an area.

colonize *verb* (**colonizes, colonized, colonizing**) **1 a** establish a colony or colonies in (a country or area). **b** settle as colonists. **2** establish or join a colony. **3** (of one country, society, etc.) impose its culture on (another). **4** (of plants, animals, and micro-organisms) become established (in an area). ▶ **colonizer** *noun*

colonnade *noun* a row of columns, esp. supporting a roof etc. ▶ **colonnaded** *adjective* [Say colla NADE]

colonoscopy *noun* (*plural* **colonoscopies**) a procedure in which an illuminated fibre optic tube is introduced through the anus to examine the colon, remove polyps, or obtain tissue specimens. [Say co luh NOSCA pee]

colony *noun* (*plural* **colonies**) **1 a** a group of people who settle in a new territory (whether or not already inhabited) and form a community connected with a mother country. **b** the territory of such settlers. **2** any country or area subject to the colonial rule of another. **3** a group of people of common nationality, religion, or (esp. artistic) occupation inhabiting a particular area in a city. **4 a** a group which is segregated from a larger population, either freely or through expulsion: *nudist*

colony. **b** the territory occupied by such a group. **5** a community of Hutterites. **6** a collection of plants or animals connected, in contact, or living close together.

color etc. = COLOUR etc.

Colorado potato beetle *noun* a yellow and black striped beetle, the larva of which is highly destructive to the potato plant.

Colorado spruce *noun* = BLUE SPRUCE.

coloration *noun* (also **colouration**) **1** colouring; a scheme or method of applying colour. **2** the natural (esp. variegated) colour of living things or animals. [Say colour AY sh'n]

coloratura *noun* **1** elaborate ornamentation of a vocal melody with runs and trills. **2** a singer (esp. a soprano) skilled in this method of singing. [Say colour a TURA]

colossal *adjective* of immense size, scope, extent, or amount. ▶ **colossally** *adverb* [Say kuh LOSS ul]

SPELL CHECK
Colosseum, coliseum   ABC ✓

A large theatre or stadium is a **coliseum**.

Colosseum *noun* a large amphitheatre in Rome, begun by the emperor Vespasian *c.*75 AD. [Say colla SEE um]

colossus *noun* (*plural* **colossi**) **1** a gigantic person, building, etc. **2** a statue much bigger than life-size. **3** an extremely powerful person etc. [Say kuh LOSS iss for the singular, kuh LOSS eye for the plural]

colostomy *noun* (*plural* **colostomies**) an operation on the colon to make an opening in the abdominal wall to provide an artificial anus. [Say kuh LOSS tuh mee]

colour (also **color**) • *noun* **1 a** the sensation produced on the eye by rays of light when resolved as by a prism etc. into different wavelengths. **b** the perception of colour by the eye; a system of colours. **2** one, or any mixture, of the constituents into which light can be separated as in a spectrum or rainbow, sometimes including (loosely) black and white. **3** a colouring substance, e.g. a paint or pigment. **4** the use of all colours, not only black and white, in photography, television, etc. **5** analysis, trivia, statistics, etc. provided by a sports broadcaster as a supplement to the play-by-play (also as an *adjective*: *colour commentary*). **6 a** a pigmentation of the skin, esp. as determined by race or ethnicity. **b** a skin colour or race other than white: *people of colour*. **7** ruddiness of complexion: *a healthy colour*. **8** quality, mood, or variety in music, literature, speech, etc.; distinctive character or timbre. **9** (in *plural*) **a** a coloured ribbon or uniform etc. worn to signify membership in a particular school, club, team, or group. **b** the flag of a regiment or ship. **c** a national flag. **10** coloured clothing: *wash the colours separately*. • *verb* **1** apply colour to. **2** influence: *coloured by experience*. **3** misrepresent, esp. with spurious detail: *a highly coloured account*. **4** take on colour; blush. **PHRASES** **show one's true colours** reveal one's true character or intentions. **under false colours** falsely, deceitfully.

colouration *noun* = COLORATION.

colour-blind *adjective* **1** unable to distinguish certain colours. **2** (of a company, project, etc.) showing no racial bias. ▶ **colour-blindness** *noun*

coloured (also **colored**) • *adjective* **1** having colour(s). **2** (also **Coloured**) *offensive* **a** wholly or partly of non-white descent. **b** of or relating to coloured people. • *noun* **1** (also **Coloured**) *offensive* a coloured person. **2** (in *plural*) = COLOUR noun 10.

colourfast *adjective* (also **colorfast**) dyed in colours that will not fade or be washed out.

colourful *adjective* (also **colorful**) **1** having much or

varied colour; bright. **2** full of interest; vivid, lively. ▶**colourfully** adverb **colourfulness** noun

colouring noun (also **coloring**) **1** the act or process of using colour(s). **2** the style in which a thing (e.g. a painting) is coloured. **3 a** facial complexion. **b** natural colour (e.g. of a bird). **4** an artificial colouring agent.

colourize verb (**colourizes, colourized, colourizing**) (also **colorize, colorizes, colorized, colorizing**) colour (a black and white film etc.) by means of a computer.

colourless adjective (also **colorless**) **1** without colour. **2** lacking character or interest. **3** dull or pale in hue. ▶**colourlessly** adverb

colour of right noun Cdn the right of ownership of a thing: to commit theft one must take something fraudulently and without colour of right.

colt noun **1** a young uncastrated male horse, usu. less than four years old. **2** a young or inexperienced person. ▶**coltish** adjective

columbine noun a garden plant with delicate leaves and pointed blue, pink, or yellow flowers that hang down. [Say CAWL um bine]

column noun **1** an upright cylindrical pillar often slightly tapering and usu. supporting an entablature or arch, or standing alone as a monument. **2** a structure or part shaped like a column. **3** a vertical cylindrical mass of liquid or vapour. **4 a** a vertical division of a page, chart, etc., containing a sequence of figures or words. **b** the figures or words themselves. **5** a part of a newspaper regularly devoted to a particular subject. **6** an arrangement of troops in successive lines, with a narrow front. ▶**columnar** adjective **columned** adjective [Say CAWL um, cawl UM ner]

columnist noun a journalist contributing a regular column to a newspaper etc. [Say COLL um nist]

SPELL CHECK	ABC ✓
coma, comma	

The punctuation mark is a **comma**.

coma noun (plural **comas**) a prolonged deep unconsciousness, caused esp. by severe injury or excessive use of drugs.

comatose adjective **1** in a coma. **2** drowsy, sleepy, lethargic. [Say CO muh toce]

comb • noun **1** a toothed strip of rigid material for tidying and arranging the hair, or for keeping it in place. **2** a device or part of a machine having a similar design or purpose. **3 a** the red fleshy crest of a fowl, esp. a rooster. **b** a similar growth in other birds. **4** a honeycomb. • verb **1** arrange or tidy (the hair) by drawing a comb through. **2** search (a place) thoroughly. PHRASES **comb out 1** tidy and arrange (hair) with a comb. **2** remove with a comb.

combat • noun **1** a fight, struggle, or contest. **2** an armed encounter with enemy forces (also as an adjective: combat zone). • verb (**combats, combatted, combatting**) fight.

combatant • noun a person engaged in fighting. • adjective **1** fighting. **2** for fighting. [Say com BAT'nt]

combative adjective ready or eager to fight. ▶**combativeness** noun [Say k'm BAT iv]

combination noun **1** the act of joining or mixing two or more things to form a single unit: the combination of recession and falling property values proved fatal. **2** a combined state: these four factors work together in combination. **3** a combined set of things or people: his treatment was a combination of surgery, radiation, and drugs ◊ this colour combination is stunningly effective. **4** a sequence of numbers or letters used to open a lock. **5** a selection of a given number of elements from a larger number of elements, without regard to the order of the elements chosen (compare PERMUTATION).

combine • verb (**combines, combined, combining**) **1** join together; unite for a common purpose. **2** possess (qualities usually distinct) together: combines charm and authority. **3 a** coalesce in one substance. **b** cause to do this. **c** form a chemical compound. **4** co-operate. **5** harvest (crops etc.) by means of a combine. • noun **1** a combination of esp. commercial interests to control prices etc. **2** a self-propelled machine that reaps and threshes in one operation.

combined adjective **1** united; joined together: combined choirs. **2** (of an action, etc.) performed by a group acting together: combined effort.

combining form noun Grammar a linguistic element used in combination with another element to form a word, e.g. bio- = life, -graphy = writing.

combo noun (plural **combos**) informal **1** a small jazz or dance band. **2** any combination: seafood combo.

combust verb **1** consume or destroy by fire. **2** be consumed or destroyed by fire. [Say kum BUST]

combustible • adjective capable of or used for burning. • noun a combustible substance. [Say kum BUST a bull]

combustion noun **1** burning; consumption by fire. **2** the development of light and heat from the chemical combination of a substance with oxygen. [Say kum BUS ch'n]

come verb (**comes**; past **came**; past participle **come**; **coming**) **1** move, be brought towards, or reach a place thought of as near or familiar to the speaker or hearer. **2** reach or be brought to a specified situation or result: came into prominence. **3** reach or extend to a specified point: comes within a mile of us. **4** traverse or accomplish: have come a long way. **5** occur, happen: how did you come to break it? **6** take or occupy a specified position in space or time. **7** become perceptible or known. **8** be available. **9** become. **10** (foll. by of) **a** be descended from. **b** be the result of. **11 a** originate in; have as its source. **b** have as one's home. **12** informal play the part of: don't come the bully with me. **13** informal when a specified time is reached: come the revolution. **14** (as interjection) expressing caution or reserve: come, it can't be that bad. PHRASES **come about** happen; take place. **come across 1** be effective or understood. **2** slang (foll. by with) hand over what is wanted. **3** meet or find by chance. **come again** informal **1** make a further effort. **2** (as imper.) what did you say? **come along 1** arrive, appear. **2** make progress; move forward. **3** (as imper.) hurry up. **come away 1** become detached or broken off: came away in my hands. **2** (foll. by with) be left with a feeling, impression, etc.: came away with many misgivings. **come back 1** return. **2** recur to one's memory. **3** become fashionable or popular again. **4** reply, retort. **come before 1** be dealt with by (a judge etc.). **2** have greater importance than. **come between 1** interfere with the relationship of. **2** prevent contact between. **come by 1** pass; go past. **2** call on a visit: why not come by tomorrow? **3** acquire, obtain: came by a new bicycle. **come down 1** come to a place or position regarded as lower. **2** lose position or wealth: has come down in the world. **3** be handed down by tradition or inheritance. **4** show a downward trend. **5** reach a decision or recommendation. **6** be dependent on (a factor): it comes down to cost. **7** criticize harshly; rebuke, punish. **8** begin to suffer from (a disease). **9** (of rain) fall heavily. **10** (of a decision, budget, etc.) be announced or delivered. **come for** come to collect or receive, **come forward 1** advance. **2** offer one's help, services, etc. **come in 1** enter a house or room. **2** take a specified position in a race etc.:

came in third. **3** become fashionable or seasonable. **4 a** have a useful role or function. **b** prove to be: *came in handy.* **c** have a part to play: *where do I come in?* **5** be received: *more news has just come in.* **6** begin speaking, esp. in radio transmission. **7** be elected; come to power. **8** (foll. by *for*) receive (usu. something unwelcome). **come into** receive, esp. as heir. **come off 1** *informal* (of an action) succeed. **2** turn out: *came off badly.* **3** be detached or detachable (from). **4** fall (from). **come off it** *informal* an expression of disbelief or refusal to accept another's opinion, behaviour, etc. **come on 1** continue to come. **2** advance, esp. to attack. **3** make progress. **4** begin: *I've got a cold coming on.* **5** appear on the stage, field of play, etc. **6** be heard or seen on television, on the telephone, etc. **7** expressing encouragement. **8** = COME UPON. **9** (foll. by *to*) make sexual advances to. **10** (of a light, appliance, etc.) start functioning. **come out 1** become known. **2** appear or be published. **3 a** declare oneself; make a decision: *came out in favour of joining.* **b** openly declare one's homosexuality. **4 a** be satisfactorily visible in a photograph etc., or present in a specified way: *the dog didn't come out.* **b** (of a photograph) be produced satisfactorily or in a specified way: *they all came out well.* **5** (of a stain etc.) be removed. **6** make one's debut on stage or in society. **7** (foll. by *in*) be covered with: *came out in a rash.* **8** (of a problem) be solved. **9** (foll. by *with*) declare openly. **come over 1** come from some distance or nearer to the speaker: *come over here.* **2** change sides or one's opinion. **3 a** (of a feeling etc.) overtake or affect. **b** *informal* feel suddenly: *came over faint.* **4** appear or sound in a specified way. **5** affect or influence. **come round 1** pay an informal visit. **2** recover consciousness. **3** be converted to another person's opinion. **4** (of a date or regular occurrence) recur. **come through 1** be successful; survive. **2** survive or overcome (a difficulty). **3** provide support, assistance, etc. when needed. **come to 1** recover consciousness. **2** reach in total; amount to. **3** reach a particular (usu. bad) situation or state of affairs: *what is the world coming to?* **come to hand** become available; be recovered. **come to nothing** have no useful result in the end; fail. **come to pass** happen, occur. **come to rest** cease moving. **come to that** *informal* in fact; if that is the case. **come under 1** be classified as or among. **2** be subject to (influence or authority). **come up 1** come to a place or position regarded as higher. **2** attain wealth or position: *come up in the world.* **3 a** (of an issue, problem, etc.) arise. **b** (of an event etc.) occur, happen: *coming up next.* **4 a** approach a person, esp. to talk. **b** approach or draw near to a specified time, event, etc. **5** match (a standard etc.). **6** (foll. by *with*) produce (an idea etc.), esp. in response to a challenge. **come up against** be faced with or opposed by. **come upon 1** meet or find by chance. **2** attack by surprise. **come what may** no matter what happens. **have it coming to one** *informal* be about to get what one deserves. **how come?** *informal* why? **if it comes to that** in that case. **not know if one is coming or going** be confused from being very busy. **to come** future; in the future: *the year to come ◊ still to come.* **where a person is coming from** a person's meaning, intention, or personality.

comeback *noun* **1** a return to a previous (esp. successful) state. **2** *informal* a retaliation or retort.

comedian *noun* **1** a humorous entertainer on stage, television, etc. **2** an actor in comedy. **3** a person who behaves comically.

comedic *adjective* involving or having to do with comedy. [Say kuh MEE dick]

comedienne *noun* a female comedian. [Say kuh meedy EN]

comedown *noun* **1** a loss of status; decline or degradation. **2** a disappointment.

comedy *noun* (*plural* **comedies**) **1 a** a play, film, etc., of an amusing or satirical character, usu. with a happy ending. **b** the dramatic genre consisting of works of this kind. **2** an amusing incident or series of incidents in everyday life. **3** humour, esp. in a work of art etc.

comedy of errors *noun* **1** a comedy in which the humour derives from mistaken identities, misunderstandings, etc. **2** any event made laughable by an accumulation of mistakes.

come from away *noun* Cdn (*Maritimes & Nfld*) a person who is not from the Atlantic region generally.

come-hither *adjective* *informal* enticing, flirtatious.

comeliness *noun* attractiveness. [Say KUM lee niss]

comely *adjective* (**comelier, comeliest**) (esp. of a woman) pleasant to look at. [Say KUM lee]

come-on *noun* *informal* **1** a gesture, remark, description, etc. intended to attract or persuade. **2** a remark or behaviour intended to allure someone sexually.

comer *noun* **1** a person who comes, esp. as an applicant, participant, etc. **2** *informal* a person likely to be a success. ▪ PHRASES **all comers** any applicants (with reference to a position etc. that is unrestricted in entry). [Say KUMMER]

comet *noun* a hazy object usu. with a nucleus of ice and dust surrounded by gas and with a tail pointing away from the sun, moving about the sun in an eccentric orbit. ▸ **cometary** *adjective*

comeuppance *noun* *informal* one's deserved fate or punishment: *got his comeuppance.* [Say come UP ince]

comfort ▪ *noun* **1** consolation; relief in affliction. **2 a** a state of physical well-being; being comfortable. **b** (usu. in *plural*) things that make life easy or pleasant. **3** a cause of satisfaction. **4** a person who consoles or helps one. ▪ *verb* soothe in grief; console. ▸ **comforting** *adjective* **comfortingly** *adverb*

comfortable *adjective* **1** giving ease: *comfortable shoes.* **2** free from discomfort. **3** *informal* having an adequate standard of living. **4** having no qualms: *did not feel comfortable about refusing.* **5** with a wide margin: *a comfortable win.* ▸ **comfortableness** *noun* **comfortably** *adverb*

comforter *noun* **1 a** a person who comforts. **b** (**Comforter**) *Christianity* the Holy Spirit. **2** a warm quilt.

comfort food *noun* food, esp. rich in carbohydrates, which provides psychological comfort as well as nourishment.

comfortless *adjective* **1** dreary, cheerless. **2** without comfort.

comfort zone *noun* **1** the range of temperature and relative humidity within which people, animals, etc. feel comfortable. **2** the immediate area around a person where encroachment is considered threatening or uncomfortable. **3** a range of action etc. with which a person feels comfortable, often complacently so.

comfrey *noun* (*plural* **comfreys**) a herb with large hairy leaves and clusters of usu. white or purple bell-shaped flowers. [Say KUM free]

comfy *adjective* (**comfier, comfiest**) *informal* comfortable. [Say KUM fee]

comic ▪ *adjective* **1** of, or in the style of, comedy: *a comic actor.* **2** causing or meant to cause laughter. ▪ *noun* **1** a professional comedian. **2 a** (**comics**) a section of a newspaper containing comic strips. **b** = COMIC BOOK.

comical *adjective* causing laughter. ▶**comically** *adverb*

comic book *noun* a book or magazine containing a single narrative told through comic strips.

comic opera *noun* (*plural* **comic operas**) **1** an opera with much dialogue, usu. with humorous treatment. **2** this genre.

comic relief *noun* **1** comic episodes in a play etc. intended to offset more serious portions. **2** the relaxation of tension etc. provided by such episodes.

comic strip *noun* a horizontal series of drawings in a comic book, newspaper, etc., usu. telling a story.

coming • *adjective* **1** approaching, next: *this coming Sunday*. **2** of potential importance: *a coming entrepreneur*. • *noun* arrival; approach. PHRASES **coming and going** (or **comings and goings**) activity, esp. intense.

> **SPELL CHECK**
> **committee**
>
> Warning: **committee** is spelled with two *m*'s, two *t*'s, and two *e*'s.

comma *noun* **1** a punctuation mark (,) indicating a pause between parts of a sentence, or dividing items in a list, a string of figures, etc. **2** (also **comma butterfly**, *plural* **comma butterflies**) a butterfly with a white comma-shaped mark on the underside of the rear wings.

command • *verb* **1** give formal order or instructions to. **2** have authority or control over. **3 a** restrain, master. **b** have at one's disposal or within reach (skill, resources, etc.): *commands an extensive knowledge of history*. **4** deserve and get (sympathy, respect, etc.). **5** dominate (a strategic position) from a superior height; look down over. • *noun* **1** an authoritative order. **2** mastery, control: *good command of languages*. **3** the exercise or tenure of authority, esp. naval or military: *has command of this ship*. **4** *Military* **a** *Cdn* one of the three divisions of the Canadian Forces: *Air Command*. **b** a body of troops etc.: *Bomber Command*. **c** a district under a commander: *Western Command*. **5 a** an instruction causing a computer to perform one of its basic functions. **b** a signal initiating such an operation. PHRASES **in command of** commanding; having under control. **under command of** commanded by.

commandant *noun* a commanding officer, esp. of a particular force etc. [Say COMMON dont or common DANT]

command economy *noun* (*plural* **command economies**) an economy, e.g. that of Cuba, which relies on the direction of a central governing body.

commandeer *verb* **1** seize (men or goods) for military purposes. **2** take possession of without authority.

commander *noun* a person who commands, esp. (also **Commander**) a naval officer next in rank below captain. Abbreviation: **Cdr**.

commander-in-chief *noun* (*plural* **commanders-in-chief**) the supreme commander, esp. of a nation's forces.

commanding *adjective* **1** dignified, exalted, impressive. **2** (of a hill or other high point) giving a wide view. **3** (of an advantage, a position, etc.) controlling; superior: *a commanding lead*. ▶**commandingly** *adverb*

commanding officer *noun* (also **Commanding Officer**) the officer in command of a military unit, formation, or force. Abbreviation: **CO**.

commandment *noun* a command from God.

commando *noun* (*plural* **commandos**) **1** a group of soldiers specially trained for carrying out quick attacks in enemy areas. **2** a member of such a group.

commemorate *verb* (**commemorates**, **commemorated**, **commemorating**) **1** preserve in memory by some celebration. **2** (of a stone, plaque, etc.) be a memorial of. [Say kuh MEMMA rate]

commemoration *noun* **1** an act of commemorating. **2** a service or part of a service in memory of a person, an event, etc. [Say kuh memma RAY sh'n]

commemorative *adjective* intended to help people remember and respect an important person or event in the past: *a commemorative plaque*. [Say kuh MEMMA ruh tiv]

commence *verb* (**commences**, **commenced**, **commencing**) *formal* begin.

commencement *noun* *formal* **1** a beginning. **2** a ceremony for the conferral of diplomas.

commend *verb* **1** entrust: *commends his soul to God*. **2** praise. **3** recommend. **4 commend itself** find favour with: *this approach commended itself to the politicians*.

commendable *adjective* praiseworthy. ▶**commendably** *adverb*

commendation *noun* **1** praise: *the film deserved the highest commendation*. **2** an award or official statement giving public praise: *a commendation for bravery*. [Say com en DAY sh'n]

commensurate *adjective* corresponding in size or degree; in proportion: *salary will be commensurate with experience* ◊ *such heavy responsibility must receive commensurate reward*. ▶**commensurately** *adverb* [Say kuh MEN sur it]

comment • *noun* a remark etc. conveying an opinion, explanation, or criticism. • *verb* make (esp. critical) remarks. PHRASES **no comment** I decline to answer your question.

commentary *noun* (*plural* **commentaries**) **1** a set of explanatory or critical notes on a text etc. **2** a descriptive spoken account (esp. on radio or television) of an event or a performance as it happens. **3** something that serves to illustrate or exemplify something: *homelessness is a sad commentary on our society*.

commentator *noun* **1** a person who provides a commentary on an event etc. **2** the writer of a commentary. **3** a person who writes or speaks on current events.

commerce *noun* financial transactions, esp. the buying and selling of merchandise, on a large scale.

commercial • *adjective* **1** of, engaged in, or concerned with, commerce. **2** of or relating to the production of esp. foodstuffs on an industrial scale. **3** (of radio or television) funded by the revenue from broadcast advertising. **4** (of an airline, aircraft, vehicle, etc.) engaged in, used by, or suitable for business or commerce; not private or governmental: *commercial flight*. **5** of, relating to, or suitable for office buildings etc.: *commercial land*. **6** usu. *derogatory* having profit as a primary aim rather than artistic etc. value. • *noun* a television or radio advertisement.

commercialism *noun* **1** the principles and practice of commerce. **2** (esp. excessive) emphasis on financial profit as a measure of worth.

commercialization *noun* the process of becoming commercialized or of commercializing something. [Say commercial ize AY sh'n]

commercialize *verb* (**commercializes**, **commercialized**, **commercializing**) **1** manage an organization or activity in a way designed to make a profit: *commercialized agriculture*. **2** exploit or spoil for the purpose of gaining profit. ▶**commercialized** *adjective* [Say COMMERCIAL ize]

commercially *adverb* in terms of commerce; in a

manner associated with the buying and selling of goods and services. [Say COMMERCIAL ee]

commie *slang derogatory* communist.

commingle *verb* (**commingles, commingled, commingling**) mingle together. [Say kuh MINGLE]

commiserate *verb* (**commiserates, commiserated, commiserating**) (usu. foll. by *with*) express or feel pity. ▶**commiseration** *noun* [Say kuh MIZZER ate]

commish *noun* (*plural* **commishes**) *informal* a commissioner, esp. a commissioner of a professional sports league. [Say kuh MISH]

commissary *noun* (*plural* **commissaries**) **1** a deputy or delegate. **2** a store for the sale of food and other goods, esp. to soldiers etc. [Say COMMA serry]

commission • *noun* **1 a** the authority to perform a task or certain duties. **b** a person or group entrusted esp. by a government with such authority. **c** an instruction, command, or duty given to such a group or person. **2** an order for something, esp. a work of art, to be produced specially. **3** *Military* **a** a warrant conferring the rank of officer to ranks of second lieutenant or sub-lieutenant and higher. **b** the rank so conferred. **4 a** the authority to act as agent for a company etc. in trade. **b** a percentage paid to the agent or sales representative from the profits of goods etc. sold, or business obtained. **c** the pay of a commissioned agent. **5** the act of committing (a crime, sin, etc.). **6** the office or department of a commissioner. **7** *hist.* the government of Newfoundland, consisting of a governor and six commissioners, appointed by the Crown between 1934 and 1949. • *verb* **1** authorize or empower by a commission. **2** give an artist etc. a commission for a piece of work. **3 a** *Military* appoint (an officer) by means of a commission. **b** prepare (a ship) for active service. **4** bring (a machine, equipment, etc.) into operation. PHRASES **in commission** (of a warship etc.) manned, armed, and ready for service. **out of commission** not in service, not in working order.

commissioner *noun* **1** a person appointed, esp. by a commission, to perform a specific task. **2** a person appointed as a member of a commission. **3** a representative of the supreme authority in a district, department, etc. **4** (in the OPP and RCMP) the highest ranking officer. **5** a person appointed by an athletic league etc. to perform various administrative and judicial functions: *baseball commissioner*.

Commissioner for Oaths *noun* a person, e.g. a lawyer, MP, MLA or MPP, etc., authorized to administer oaths and take affidavits.

commit *verb* (**commits, committed, committing**) **1** entrust for: **a** safekeeping. **b** treatment, usu. destruction: *committed the book to the flames*. **2** perpetrate (esp. a crime or blunder): *commit murder*. **3** pledge (esp. oneself) to a certain course or policy: *does not like committing herself*. **4** pledge or engage oneself firmly: *we expect you to commit to the project*. **5** consign (a person) to a mental hospital, prison, etc., by or as if by legal authority. **6** *Politics* refer (a bill etc.) to a committee. PHRASES **commit to memory** memorize.

commitment *noun* **1** a promise to do something or to behave in a particular way: *the company's commitment to quality ◊ she doesn't want to make a big emotional commitment to him at the moment*. **2** an engagement or (esp. financial) obligation that restricts freedom of action: *I have business commitments and can't come ◊ buying a house is a big financial commitment*. **3** the willingness to work hard and devote one's energy and time to a job, activity, or relationship: *a career as a dancer requires total commitment ◊ are men in their twenties really afraid of*

commitment? **4** an act of pledging or setting aside something: *a major commitment of money and time*.

committal *noun* **1** the act of committing a person to an institution, esp. prison or a mental hospital. **2** the burial of a dead body.

committed *adjective* **1** having a strong dedication to a cause or belief. **2** obliged (to take a certain action).

committee *noun* **1** a body of persons elected or appointed for a specific function by, and usu. out of, a larger body. **2** (also **parliamentary committee**) (in the Commonwealth) such a body drawn from the upper or lower houses of a legislature, appointed to consider the details of a proposed bill after its second reading. **3** = COMMITTEE OF THE WHOLE.

committee of the whole *noun* **1** a committee comprising all the members of a legislative body or other organization. **2** (also **Committee of the Whole House**) the entire House of Commons when sitting as a committee to discuss the details of a proposed bill.

commode *noun* **1** a chest of drawers. **2 a** a bedside table with a cupboard containing a chamber pot. **b** a chamber pot concealed in a chair with a hinged cover. **3** *informal* a toilet or bathroom. [Say kuh MODE]

commodification *noun* the action of turning something into or treating something as a (mere) commodity: *the commodification of art extends today to all the agencies who expect to make greater profits from it*. ▶**commodify** *verb* (**commodifies, commodified, commodifying**) [Say kuh modda fuh KAY sh'n, kuh MODDA fie]

commodious *adjective* roomy and comfortable: *the indoor mall is bright and the new grocery store is attractive and commodious*. [Say kuh MOADY us]

commodity *noun* (*plural* **commodities**) **1** an article that can be bought and sold, esp. a product as opposed to a service. **2** any of several raw or partially processed materials, e.g. grain or metals. **3** a useful thing: *water is a precious commodity that we often take for granted*. [Say kuh MODDA tee]

commodore *noun* **1** (also **Commodore**) (in Canada and the UK, and formerly also in the US) a naval officer ranking above captain and below rear admiral. **2** the commander of a squadron or other group of vessels smaller than a fleet. [Say COMMA dore]

common • *adjective* (**commoner, commonest**) **1 a** occurring often: *a common mistake*. **b** ordinary or ordinary qualities; without special rank or position: *the common people*. **2 a** shared by, coming from, or done by, more than one: *common knowledge*. **b** belonging to, open to, or affecting, the whole community or the public: *common land*. **3** *derogatory* low-class; vulgar. **4** of the most familiar type: *common loon*. **5** *Math* belonging to two or more quantities: *common denominator*. • *noun* **1** (**the Commons**) = HOUSE OF COMMONS. **2** a piece of land set aside for public use, esp. as a park or recreation area in a city or town. **3** (in *plural*) **a** the common people as opposed to those in authority. **b** the common people viewed as forming part of a political system, esp. as opposed to those of aristocratic status. PHRASES **common or garden** *informal* ordinary. **in common 1** in joint use; shared. **2** of joint interest: *have little in common*. **in common with** in the same way as. **short commons** insufficient food.

commonality *noun* (*plural* **commonalities**) **1** the sharing of an attribute: *the explanations show a high degree of commonality in their reasoning*. **2** a shared feature or attribute: *beyond these commonalities, however, Prairie women were divided by large gulfs of class and ethnicity*. [Say common ALA tee]

common carrier *noun* **1** a person or company undertaking to transport any goods or person in a

specified category. **2** a company providing public telecommunications services.

common denominator *noun* **1** Math a common multiple of the denominators of several fractions. **2** a common feature of members of a group.

commoner *noun* one of the common people, as opposed to the aristocracy.

Common Era *noun* the era reckoned from the traditional date of Christ's birth.

common ground *noun* a point or argument accepted by both sides in a dispute.

common law *noun* **1** law derived from custom and judicial precedent rather than statutes (*compare* CASE LAW, STATUTE LAW). **2** (usu. as an *adjective*) denoting a relationship between cohabiting partners, recognized as a marriage in some common law jurisdictions but not brought about by a civil or ecclesiastical ceremony.

commonly *adverb* usually; very often; by many people.

common market *noun* **1** a group of countries imposing few or no duties on trade with one another and a common tariff on trade with other countries. **2** (**Common Market**) the European Economic Community.

common noun *noun* (also **common name**) *Grammar* a name denoting a class of objects or a concept as opposed to a particular individual, e.g. *boy*, *beauty*.

commonplace • *adjective* lacking originality; trite. • *noun* **1 a** an everyday saying. **b** an ordinary topic of conversation. **2** anything usual or trite.

common sense • *noun* sound practical sense, esp. in everyday matters. • *adjective* = COMMONSENSICAL.

commonsensical *adjective* possessing or marked by common sense. [Say common SENSE ick ul]

common share *noun* (also **common stock**) an ordinary capital share in a company, yielding a flexible dividend (*compare* PREFERRED SHARE).

commonwealth *noun* **1** a community of people viewed as a political entity in which everyone has an interest. **2** (**Commonwealth**) **a** (also **the Commonwealth of Nations**) an international association comprising members of the former British Empire. **b** *hist.* the republican period of government in Britain 1649–60.

commotion *noun* **1** a confused and noisy disturbance or outburst. **2** loud and confusing noise.

communal *adjective* **1** relating or belonging to a community; for common use: *communal bathroom*. **2** of or relating to a commune. **3** of or relating to ethnic or religious groups within a larger community: *communal violence*. ▶ **communally** *adverb* [Say kuh MYOON ul]

commune[1] *noun* a group of people who live together and share responsibilities, possessions, etc.: *a 1970s hippie commune*. [Say COM yoon]

commune[2] *verb* (**communes**, **communed**, **communing**) **1** speak confidentially and intimately: *I was communing with colleagues all around the world*. **2** feel in close touch: *he spent an hour communing with nature on the bank of a stream*. [Say kuh MYOON]

communicable *adjective* (esp. of a disease) able to be passed on. [Say kuh MYOON ick a bull]

communicate *verb* (**communicates**, **communicated**, **communicating**) **1 a** transmit or pass on (information) by speaking, writing, or other means. **b** transmit (heat, motion, etc.). **c** pass on (an infectious illness). **2** succeed in conveying information, evoking understanding etc.: *she communicates well*. **3** (often foll. by *with*) share a feeling or understanding; relate socially. **4** (often foll. by *with*) (of a room etc.) have a common connecting door. **5** *Christianity* **a** administer Holy Communion to. **b** receive Holy Communion.

communication *noun* **1 a** the imparting or exchanging of information: *direct communication between the two countries will provide greater understanding*. **b** a letter or message containing such information or news: *have received a communication from our head office*. **c** the means of sending or receiving information, such as telephone lines or computers: *satellite communications* ◊ *a communications network*. **2** a means of travelling or of transporting goods, such as roads and railways: *a city providing excellent road and rail communications*. **3** (in *plural*) **a** the science and practice of transmitting information esp. by electronic or mechanical means. **b** a field of study encompassing writing and broadcasting skills as they apply to media and business. **c** the function of communicating information to the public by a company, organization, etc. (also as an *adjective*: *communications officer*).

communicative *adjective* **1** talkative, informative. **2** ready to communicate. **3** designating styles of teaching, esp. of a second language, that emphasize the communication of meaning in real-life situations.

communicator *noun* a person who is able to explain his or her ideas and feelings clearly to others.

communion *noun* **1** the sharing or exchanging of intimate thoughts and feelings, esp. when the exchange is on a mental or spiritual level: *living in communion with nature*. **2** the common participation in a mental or spiritual experience. **3** (also **Communion**) **a** (also **Holy Communion**) the service of Christian worship at which bread and wine are consecrated and shared. **b** participation in the Communion service. **4** a relationship of recognition and acceptance between Christian denominations (signified by a willingness to give or receive the Eucharist): *the Orthodox Churches are not in communion with Rome*. **5** a group of Christian communities or churches which recognize one another's ministries or that of a central authority: *the Anglican communion*.

communiqué *noun* an official communication, esp. a news report. [Say kuh MYOON a kay]

communism *noun* **1** a system of society with the state controlling the means of producing everything and each member working for the common benefit according to his or her capacity and receiving according to his or her needs. **2** (usu. **Communism**) **a** the movement or political party advocating such a system, esp. as derived from Marxism and seeking the overthrow of capitalism by a proletarian revolution. **b** the communistic form of society established in the 20th century in the former USSR and elsewhere.

communist • *noun* **1** a person advocating or practising communism. **2** (**Communist**) a member of a Communist Party. • *adjective* **1** of or relating to communism: *a communist play*. **2** (**Communist**) of or relating to Communism. ▶ **communistic** *adjective*

community *noun* (*plural* **communities**) **1 a** all the people living in a specific locality. **b** a specific locality, including its inhabitants. **c** Cdn (Nfld & PEI) a small incorporated municipality. **2** a body of people having a religion, profession, etc., in common: *the immigrant community*. **3** fellowship of interests etc.; similarity: *community of intellect*. **4** joint ownership or liability: *community of goods*. **5** (**the community**) the public. **6** Ecology a group of animals or plants living or growing together in the same area. **7** (as an *adjective*) = COMMUNITY ACCESS: *community channel*.

community access *noun* Cdn a type of television programming that is made available to community groups or members of the public.

community care *noun* public health care

emphasizing the treatment of long-term patients in their communities rather than in hospitals etc.

community centre *noun* a place providing social and recreational facilities for a neighbourhood.

community college *noun* a post-secondary educational institution offering training esp. in specific employment fields.

community hall *noun Cdn* a hall maintained by a community for holding suppers, dances, wedding receptions, etc.

community service *noun* work, esp. voluntary and unpaid, or stipulated by a community service order, in the community.

community service order *noun* an order for a convicted offender to perform a period of unpaid work in the community.

commutable *adjective* **1** convertible into money. **2** *Law* (of a punishment) able to be commuted. **3** within commuting distance. [Say kuh MUTE a bull]

commute • *verb* (**commutes**, **commuted**, **commuting**) **1** travel to and from one's daily work, esp. from suburbs to the centre of a city by car or public transit. **2** *Law* change (a judicial sentence etc.) to another less severe: *the death sentence was commuted to a prison term*. **3** (often foll. by *into, for*) change (one kind of payment) for another: *tithes were commuted into an annual sum varying with the price of corn*. • *noun* **1** an act of commuting. **2** a distance travelled by a commuter. [Say kuh MUTE]

commuter • *noun* a person who travels some distance to work, esp. from suburbs to the centre of a city by car or public transit. • *adjective* **1** relating to or for the use of commuters. **2** of or relating to a flight, aircraft, or airline that flies comparatively short distances, usu. between small communities. [Say kuh MUTE er]

Comox *noun* (*plural* **Comox** or **Comoxes**) **1** a member of an Aboriginal group, part of the Salishan linguistic group, living on Vancouver Island. **2** the language of this people. [Say CO mox]

comp *noun informal* **1** a competition. **2** a complimentary ticket, pass, etc. **3** a comprehensive examination. **4** composition. **5** compensation: *workers' comp*.

compact[1] • *adjective* **1** closely or neatly packed together. **2** (of a piece of equipment, a room, etc.) well-fitted and practical though small. **3** (of style etc.) condensed; brief. **4** (esp. of the human body) small but well-proportioned. **5** designating a car larger than a subcompact and smaller than a mid-size. • *verb* join or press firmly together. • *noun* **1** a small, flat case for face powder, a mirror, pills, etc. **2** a compact car.

compact[2] *noun* an agreement or contract between two or more parties.

compact disc *noun* a disc on which information or sound is recorded digitally and reproduced by reflection of laser light.

compaction *noun* the action or process of compacting something or becoming compacted: *soil compaction*.

compactly *adverb* so as to be or become compact.

compactness *noun* the quality of being compact.

compactor *noun* a device used to compact something: *trash compactor*.

companion *noun* **1 a** (often foll. by *in, of*) a person who accompanies, associates with, or shares with, another. **b** a person employed to live with and assist another. **2** a handbook or reference book on a particular subject. **3** a thing that matches another. **4** (**Companion**) a member of the highest grade of the Order of Canada.

companionable *adjective* agreeable as a companion.

companionship *noun* good fellowship; friendship.

company *noun* (*plural* **companies**) **1 a** a number of people assembled; a crowd; an audience. **b** guests or a guest. **2** companionship, esp. of a specific kind: *do not care for their company*. **3 a** a commercial business. **b** (usu. **Company**) the partner or partners not named in the title of a firm: *Smith and Company*. Abbreviation: **Co. 4 a** a group of performers. **b** the organization to which they belong, including administrators, fundraisers, etc. **5** a subdivision of an infantry battalion usu. commanded by a major or a captain. **6** a group of Guides. PHRASES **be in good company** discover that one's companions, or better people, have done the same as oneself. **in company** not alone. **in company with** together with. **keep company** (often foll. by *with*) associate habitually. **keep a person company** accompany a person. **part company 1** separate: *parted company until the weekend*. **2** (often foll. by *with*) **a** cease to associate. **b** differ, disagree.

company town *noun* a town, esp. in an isolated area, that is dependent upon one company, e.g. a mine, for all or almost all of its employment etc.

comparable *adjective* (often foll. by *to, with*) **1** fit to be compared; worth comparing. **2** able to be compared. **3** similar. ▶ **comparably** *adverb* [Say COMP er a bull or COMPARE a bull]

GRAMMAR CHECK
comparative   ⚠

When singling out which of two items is better, larger, etc., use the comparative form. Say it is **the better of the two**, not **the best of the two**.

---

comparative • *adjective* **1** perceptible by comparison; relative: *in comparative comfort*. **2** estimated by comparison: *the comparative merits of the two ideas*. **3** (esp. of sciences etc.) of or involving comparison: *comparative anatomy*. **4** *Grammar* (of an adjective or adverb) expressing a higher degree of a quality, but not the highest possible (e.g. *braver*, *more fiercely*). • *noun Grammar* **1** the comparative expression or form of an adjective or adverb. **2** a word in the comparative. ▶ **comparatively** *adverb* [Say COMPARE a tiv]

compare • *verb* (**compares**, **compared**, **comparing**) **1** (usu. foll. by *to*) express similarities in; liken: *compared the landscape to a painting*. **2** (often foll. by *to, with*) estimate the degree of sameness or difference of: *compared radio with television* ◊ *that lacks quality compared to this*. **3** (often foll. by *with*) bear comparison: *compares favourably with the rest*. **4** (often foll. by *with*) be equal or equivalent to. • *noun literary* comparison: *beyond compare*. PHRASES **compare notes** exchange ideas or opinions.

comparison *noun* **1** a consideration or estimate of the similarities or dissimilarities between two things or people: *they drew a comparison between Gandhi's teaching and that of other teachers* ◊ *the two books invite comparison*. **2** an analogy: *perhaps the best comparison is seasickness*. **3** the quality of being similar or equivalent: *there's no comparison with tubing: disking requires strength, balance, and agility*. **4** *Grammar* the formation of the comparative and superlative forms of adjectives and adverbs. PHRASES **bear** (or **stand**) **comparison** (often foll. by *with*) be able to be compared favourably. **beyond comparison 1** totally different in quality. **2** greatly superior; excellent. **in comparison with** compared to.

compartment *noun* a space within a larger space, separated from the rest by partitions, e.g. in a ship, wallet, desk, etc.

compartmental *adjective* consisting of or relating to compartments or a compartment.

compartmentalize *verb* (**compartmentalizes**,

compartmentalized, **compartmentalizing**) divide into compartments or categories.

compass noun (plural **compasses**) **1** (also **magnetic compass**) an instrument showing the direction of magnetic north and bearings from it. **2** (often in plural) an instrument for taking measurements and describing circles, with two legs connected at one end by a movable joint. **3** area, extent; scope (e.g. of knowledge or experience): the event had political repercussions which are beyond the compass of this book. **4** the range of tones of a voice or a musical instrument.

compassion noun sympathetic pity and concern for the sufferings or misfortunes of others.

compassionate adjective feeling or showing sympathy and concern for others. ▶**compassionately** adverb

compatibility noun **1** the ability of people or things to exist together without problems or conflict. **2** the ability of machines, esp. computers and computer programs, to be used together.

compatible • adjective **1 a** able to coexist; well-suited: a compatible couple. **b** consistent: their views are not compatible with their actions. **2** (of equipment etc.) capable of being used in combination. • noun (usu. in combination) Computing a piece of equipment that can use software etc. designed for another brand of the same equipment.

compatriot noun a native or inhabitant of one's own country or region. [Say kum PAY tree it]

compel verb (**compels**, **compelled**, **compelling**) **1** force, constrain: compelled them to admit it. **2** bring about (an action) by force: compel submission.

compelling adjective arousing strong interest, conviction, or admiration. ▶**compellingly** adverb

compendium noun (plural **compendiums** or **compendia**) a collection of detailed items of information, esp. in a book. [Say kum PENDY um]

compensate verb (**compensates**, **compensated**, **compensating**) (often foll. by for) **1** provide something good to balance or reduce the bad effects of damage, loss, etc.; make up for: nothing can compensate for the loss of a loved one. **2** pay somebody money because they have suffered some damage, loss, injury, etc.: her lawyers say she should be compensated both for her injuries and for the suffering she had been caused. **3** act so as to neutralize or correct a deficiency or abnormality: the output voltage rises, compensating for the original fall. **4** Psychology offset a disability or frustration by development in another direction: they identified with radical movements to compensate for their inability to relate to individual human beings.

compensation noun **1 a** the act of compensating. **b** the process of being compensated. **2** something, esp. money, given as a recompense. **3** a salary or wages. **4** Psychology the result of compensating.

compensatory adjective **1** providing, effecting, or aiming at compensation. **2** (of a payment) intended to compensate someone who has experienced loss, suffering, or injury: $50 million in compensatory damages. **3** reducing or offsetting unpleasant or unwelcome effects: the government is taking compensatory actions to keep interest rates down. [Say kum PENSA tory]

compete verb (**competes**, **competed**, **competing**) **1** strive for superiority or supremacy. **2** take part (in a contest etc.).

competence noun (also **competency** plural **competencies**) **1 a** ability; the state of being competent: he does not have the competence to cope with this situation. **b** an area in which a person is competent; a skill: literature and the visual arts simply happen to be my major interests and, in varying degrees, my competences.

2 Law the legal capacity (of a court, a magistrate, etc.) to deal with a matter. [Say COMPA tince]

competent adjective **1 a** adequately qualified or capable: not competent to drive. **b** effective: a competent swimmer. **2** Law (of a judge, court, or witness) legally qualified or qualifying. ▶**competently** adverb [Say COMPA tint]

competition noun **1** the activity of competing or contending with others (for supremacy, a position, a prize, etc.): there is fierce competition between the banks ◊ was banned from competition for doping abuses. **2** an event or contest in which people compete. **3** the person, people, or products over whom or which one is attempting to establish one's supremacy or superiority, esp. in business or sports: the dictionary outsold the competition. **4** Biology interaction between organisms etc. that share a limited environmental resource.

competitive adjective **1** involving, offered for, or by competition. **2** (of prices etc.) low enough to compare well with those of rival products etc. **3** (of a person) having a strong urge to win; keen to compete. ▶**competitively** adverb **competitiveness** noun

competitor noun **1** a person who competes. **2** a rival, esp. in business or commerce.

compilation noun **1 a** the act of compiling. **b** the process of being compiled. **2** something compiled, esp. a book etc. composed of separate articles etc. [Say compa LAY sh'n]

compile verb (**compiles**, **compiled**, **compiling**) **1 a** collect (material) into a list, volume, etc. **b** make up (a volume etc.) from such material. **2** Computing produce (a machine-coded form of a high-level program). **3** Sport accumulate (a large number of): compiled a score of 160.

compiler noun **1** Computing a program for translating a high-level programming language into machine code. **2** a person who compiles.

complacency noun (also **complacence**) a feeling of satisfaction with oneself or with a situation, so that one does not think any change is necessary: his early success led to complacency and arrogance ◊ despite signs of an improvement in the economy, there is no room for complacency. [Say kum PLAY sun see]

complacent adjective smugly self-satisfied. ▶**complacently** adverb [Say kum PLAY sint]

complain verb **1** express dissatisfaction: is always complaining. **2** (foll. by of) announce that one is suffering from (an ailment): complained of a headache.

complainant noun Law a plaintiff in certain lawsuits.

complainer noun a person who complains, esp. habitually.

complaint noun **1** an act of complaining. **2** a grievance. **3** an ailment or illness. **4** Law the plaintiff's case in a civil action.

SPELL CHECK
complement, compliment

When you praise someone, you **compliment** them or pay them a **compliment**.

---

complement • noun **1 a** a thing that contributes extra or contrasting features to something else in such a way as to improve or emphasize its quality: wood is a perfect complement to any decor. **b** one of a pair, or one of two things that go together: the other can be present not as an opponent or a threat but as a complement. **2** (often **full complement**) the number required to make a group complete: the college opened with a full complement of five professors in arts and theology. **3** Grammar a word or phrase added to a verb to complete the predicate of a sentence, e.g. angry in He became angry. **4** Geometry the amount by

which an angle is less than 90°. • **verb 1** complete. **2** form a complement to: *the antique furniture complements the rustic features of the house.*

complementarity *noun* (*plural* **complementarities**) a complementary relationship or situation: *a culture based on the complementarity of men and women.* [Say compla men TARE a tee]

SPELL CHECK
complementary, complimentary

Someone who praises you is **complimentary**.
Something given free of charge is **complimentary**.

---

complementary *adjective* (of two or more different things) combining in such a way as to form a complete whole or to enhance or emphasize each other's qualities: *distinguished collections of dinnerware and complementary accessories.*

complementary angle *noun* either of two angles making up 90°.

complementary colours *plural noun* **1** two colours of light that, when combined, produce white light, e.g. yellow and blue. **2** two colours that are the opposite of one another, e.g. a primary colour and the secondary colour formed by the mixture of the other two primary colours (for instance red and green).

complete • *adjective* **1** having all its parts: *the set is complete.* **2** finished: *my task is complete.* **3** of the maximum extent or degree: *a complete surprise.* **4** Football (of a forward pass) caught by the receiver. • *verb* (**completes, completed, completing**) **1** finish. **2 a** make whole or perfect. **b** make up the amount of: *completes the quota.* **3** fill in the answers to (a questionnaire etc.). **4** Football make or execute (a forward pass) successfully. PHRASES **complete with** having (as an important accessory): *comes complete with instructions.* ▶**completed** *adjective* **completely** *adverb* **completeness** *noun* **completion** *noun*

complex • *noun* (*plural* **complexes**) **1** a building, network, etc. made up of related parts: *arts complex.* **2** a related group of usu. repressed feelings or thoughts which cause abnormal behaviour or mental states: *inferiority complex.* **3** (in general use) a preoccupation or obsession: *has a complex about punctuality.* **4** a set of symptoms occurring at the same time. **5** a compound in which molecules or ions form coordinate bonds to a metal atom or ion. • *adjective* **1** consisting of related parts: *a complex network of water channels.* **2** complicated: *a complex problem.*

complexion *noun* **1** the natural colour, texture, and appearance of the skin, esp. of the face. **2** an aspect; a character: *puts a different complexion on the matter.* ▶**complexioned** *adjective* (also in *combination*)

complexity *noun* (*plural* **complexities**) **1** the state of being complicated or difficult to understand: *an issue of great complexity.* **2** a feature of a complicated process or situation: *the complexities of family life.*

complexly *adverb* in a complex or complicated manner.

complex sentence *noun* a sentence containing a subordinate clause or clauses, e.g. *I couldn't go because I was sick ◊ she was aware that they weren't pleased* (compare COMPOUND SENTENCE, SIMPLE SENTENCE).

compliance *noun* the action or practice of obeying rules or requests, esp. those made by an authority: *repairs were carried out in compliance with the building code ◊ tax reform would encourage increased compliance by small business.* [Say kum PLY unce]

compliant *adjective* **1** ready to agree with others or obey rules, esp. to an excessive degree: *a compliant labour*

force. **2** meeting or in accordance with rules or standards: *spent a lot of money to ensure the computers were year 2000 compliant.* ▶**compliantly** *adverb* [Say kum PLY unt]

complicate *verb* (**complicates, complicated, complicating**) make or become difficult, confused, or complex.

complicated *adjective* complex; intricate.

complication *noun* **1 a** an involved or confused condition or state. **b** a difficulty. **2** a secondary disease or condition aggravating a previous one.

complicit *adjective* involved with others in an illegal activity. [Say kum PLISS it]

complicity *noun* partnership in a crime or wrongdoing: *they were accused of complicity in the attempt to overthrow the government.* [Say kum PLISS it ee]

SPELL CHECK
compliment, complement

Something added to enhance or improve something else is a **complement**. A burgundy necktie may **complement** a blue suit.

---

compliment • *noun* **1 a** a spoken or written expression of praise. **b** an act or circumstance implying praise: *their success was a compliment to their efforts.* **2** (in *plural*) **a** formal greetings, esp. as a written accompaniment to a gift etc.: *with the compliments of the management.* **b** praise: *my compliments to the cook.* • *verb* (often foll. by *on*) congratulate; praise. PHRASES **compliments of 1** given free of charge: *won a book, compliments of Oxford.* **2** usu. *ironic* thanks to: *a 75-cent surcharge, compliments of the Minister of Finance.* **pay a compliment to** praise. **return the compliment 1** give a compliment in return for another. **2** retaliate or recompense in kind.

SPELL CHECK
complimentary, complementary

Something that enhances or improves something else is **complementary**.

---

complimentary *adjective* **1** expressing a compliment; praising: *Jenny was very complimentary about Leslie's riding ◊ complimentary remarks.* **2** (of a service, goods, theatre ticket, etc.) provided free of charge: *a complimentary bottle of wine.*

comply *verb* (**complies, complied, complying**) (often foll. by *with*) act in accordance (with a wish, command, regulation, etc.).

component • *noun* a part of a larger whole or system. • *adjective* being part of a larger whole: *component parts.* ▶**componentry** *noun*

comport *verb formal* conduct oneself; behave: *articulate students who comported themselves well in television interviews.* [Say kum PORT]

comportment *noun* behaviour: *we will be judged on our comportment in our daily lives.* [Say kum PORT m'nt]

compose *verb* (**composes, composed, composing**) **1 a** construct or create (a work of art, esp. literature or music). **b** compose music. **2** (often in *passive*) constitute; make up: *the committee is composed of workers and managers.* **3** put together to form a whole, esp. artistically; order; arrange: *composed the group for the photographer.* **4 compose oneself** calm; settle: *she paused for a minute to compose herself and then continued.* **5** *Printing* **a** set up (type) to form words and blocks of words. **b** set up (a manuscript etc.) in type.

composed *adjective* calm; having one's feelings under control.

composer *noun* a person who composes (esp. music).

C

composite • *adjective* **1** made up of various parts; blended. **2** (esp. of a synthetic building material) made up of recognizable constituents: *creating high-strength composite materials by mixing ceramics with aluminum.* **3** relating to or denoting plants of the daisy family. • *noun* **1** a thing made up of several parts or elements: *the character was based on a composite of the mothers of two of my friends.* **2** a synthetic building material. **3** any plant of the daisy family, having a head of many small flowers forming one bloom. [Say COMPA zit]

composite high school *noun* Cdn (*Alberta*) (also **composite school**) a secondary school offering both vocational and academic courses.

composite index *noun* a stock market index based on the performance of a selection of stocks.

composition *noun* **1 a** the act of putting together; formation or construction. **b** something so composed; a mixture. **c** the constitution of such a mixture; the nature of its ingredients: *the powers and composition of the Senate.* **2 a** a literary or musical work. **b** the act or art of producing such a work. **c** a piece of writing assigned as an exercise. **d** the craft of writing: *taught grammar and composition.* **e** an artistic arrangement (of parts of a picture, subjects for a photograph, etc.). **3** a compound artificial substance, esp. one serving the purpose of a natural one. **4** the preparing of text for printing. ▶ **compositional** *adjective* **compositionally** *adverb*

compost • *noun* a mixture of decomposing vegetable matter, table scraps, manure, etc., used to fertilize soil. • *verb* **1** treat (soil) with compost. **2** make (manure, vegetable matter, etc.) into compost. **3** degrade into compost. ▶ **compostable** *adjective*

composter *noun* (also **compost bin**) a container for table scraps etc. used to create compost.

composure *noun* calmness; self-control: *she was struggling to regain her composure.* [Say kum POE zhur]

compote *noun* fruit preserved or cooked in syrup. [Say COM pote or COM pot]

compound • *noun* **1** a mixture of two or more things, qualities, etc. **2** (also **compound word**) a word made up of two or more existing words. **3** Chemistry a substance formed from two or more elements chemically united in fixed proportions. **4** an enclosed area, as for a prison etc. • *adjective* **1 a** made up of several ingredients. **b** consisting of several parts. **2** combined; collective. **3** Zoology consisting of individual organisms. **4** Biology consisting of several or many parts. **5 a** (of a noun) that is a compound. **b** (of a verb tense) formed using an auxiliary verb. • *verb* **1** mix or combine (ingredients, ideas, motives, etc.): *grief compounded with fear.* **2** increase or complicate (difficulties etc.): *their isolation only compounds their problems.* **3** make up (a composite whole). **4** combine (words or elements) into a word. **5** increase by compound interest.

compound eye *noun* an eye consisting of numerous visual units, as found in insects and crustaceans.

compound fracture *noun* a fracture involving the exposure of the bone through a skin wound.

compound interest *noun* interest payable on capital and its accumulated interest.

compound leaf *noun* a leaf consisting of several or many leaflets.

compound lens *noun* = LENS 2.

compound sentence *noun* a sentence with more than one independent clause, joined by a coordinating conjunction, and having no subordinate clauses, e.g. *I went up the stairs and she came down* (compare COMPLEX SENTENCE, SIMPLE SENTENCE).

comprehend *verb* **1** grasp mentally; understand (a person or a thing). He couldn't comprehend her reasons for marrying the other guy. **2** include; encompass: *family study cannot comprehend all things.*

comprehensible *adjective* that can be understood: *comprehensible English.* ▶ **comprehensibly** *adverb*

comprehension *noun* the act or capability of understanding, esp. writing or speech: *comprehension of spoken French ◊ why he would do it is beyond comprehension.*

comprehensive • *adjective* **1** complete; including all or nearly all elements, aspects, etc.: *a comprehensive collection of photographs.* **2** (of motor vehicle insurance) providing complete protection. • *noun* (also **comprehensive examination**) a test of one's learning or proficiency in all aspects, elements, etc. of a subject.

comprehensive high school *noun* Cdn a secondary school offering both vocational and academic courses.

comprehensive land claim *noun* Cdn a land claim made on a usu. large area of land which was never ceded or surrendered by treaty or purchase.

comprehensively *adverb* in a comprehensive or thorough manner: *the matter has been comprehensively discussed.*

comprehensiveness *noun* the quality of being comprehensive, thorough, or complete.

compress • *verb* (**compresses**, **compressed**, **compressing**) **1** squeeze together. **2** bring into a smaller space or shorter extent. **3** Computing condense (data etc.) for easier handling, storage, etc. • *noun* a cloth or ice pack etc. pressed onto part of the body to relieve inflammation, stop bleeding, etc.

compressed air *noun* air at more than atmospheric pressure.

compressible *adjective* capable of being compressed.

compression *noun* **1** the act of compressing or being compressed. **2** the reduction in volume (causing an increase in pressure) of the fuel mixture in an internal combustion engine before ignition.

compressor *noun* an instrument or device for compressing, esp. a machine used for increasing the pressure of air or other gases.

WRITING TIP
comprise

Such uses as *The team is comprised of six players* and *Women comprise a large proportion of the class* are strongly opposed by some, who prefer *The team is composed* (or *made up*) *of six players* and *Women constitute* (or *make up*) *a large proportion of the class.* The disputed uses are very common, however, and considered acceptable by many.

---

comprise *verb* (**comprises**, **comprised**, **comprising**) **1** consist of, be composed of: *the book comprises 350 pages.* **2** make up, compose: *the essays comprise his total work.*

compromise • *noun* **1** the settlement of a dispute by each side making concessions: *reached a compromise.* **2** an intermediate state between conflicting opinions, actions, etc., reached by mutual concession or modification: *a compromise between ideals and practicality.* **3** the acceptance, for convenience, of standards that are lower than desirable: *she would accept no compromise on quality.* • *verb* (**compromises**, **compromised**, **compromising**) **1** settle a dispute by mutual concession: *in the end we compromised.* **2** bring into disrepute or danger esp. by indiscreet, foolish, or reckless behaviour: *compromised our relationship ◊ situations in which the troops could be compromised.* **3** do something that is against one's principles or fails to meet the standards one has set: *we will not compromise on*

safety ◊ *I refuse to compromise my principles.*
▶**compromiser** *noun*
comptroller *noun* (also **controller**) an official or executive in charge of financial affairs. [Sounds like CONTROLLER or like komp TROLL ur]
compulsion *noun* **1** the action of compelling; an obligation: *she was not warned that she was under no compulsion to accompany the police officers.* **2** an irresistible urge to a form of behaviour, esp. against one's conscious wishes: *he felt a compulsion to babble on about his experience.*
compulsive *adjective* resulting from or relating to or acting from, or as if from, an irresistible urge, esp. against one's conscious wishes: *a compulsive gambler* ◊ *compulsive eating.* ▶**compulsively** *adverb* **compulsiveness** *noun*
compulsory • *adjective* required by law or a rule: *compulsory courses.* • *noun* (*plural* **compulsories**) (also **compulsory figure**) one of a number of specified figures that must be performed as a component of a competition, e.g. in figure skating or synchronized swimming.
compunction *noun* a feeling of guilt or moral scruple that prevents or follows the doing of something bad: *he had no compunction about manipulating the facts to his advantage* ◊ *got rid of them without the slightest compunction.* [Say kum PUNK sh'n]
computable *adjective* able to be calculated or computed.
computation *noun* **1** the process of mathematical calculation: *statistical computations.* **2** the use of computers, esp. as a subject of research or study.
computational *adjective* **1** of or pertaining to computing. **2** using computers to assist in analysis: *computational linguistics.*
compute *verb* (**computes, computed, computing**) **1** reckon or calculate (a number, an amount, etc.). **2** *informal* make sense: *their explanation doesn't compute.*
computer *noun* an electronic device for storing and processing data (usu. in binary form), according to instructions given to it in a variable program.
computer graphics *noun* **1** visual images produced or modified by means of a computer. **2** the use of a computer to generate and manipulate these.
computerization *noun* **1** conversion to a system that is operated or controlled by computers. **2** the conversion of information to a form that is stored or processed by a computer.
computerize *verb* (**computerizes, computerized, computerizing**) organize with or convert to a system using computers: *computerized her recipes* ◊ *the Wheat Pool computerized its facilities.* ▶**computerized** *adjective*
computerized axial tomography *noun* tomography in which the X-ray scanner makes many sweeps of the body and the results are processed by computer to give a cross-sectional image. Abbreviation: **CAT**.
computer language *noun* any of numerous systems of rules, words, and symbols for writing computer programs or representing instructions etc.
computer literacy *noun* the knowledge and skill to be able to use a computer; familiarity with the operation of computers.
computer-literate *adjective* familiar with the operation of computers.
computer science *noun* the study of the principles and use of computers.
computer virus *noun* a hidden code within a computer program intended to corrupt a system or destroy data stored in it.
computing *noun* the use or operation of computers.

comrade *noun* **1 a** a workmate, friend, or companion. **b** (also **comrade-in-arms**) a fellow soldier etc. **2** a fellow socialist or communist (often as a form of address). ▶**comradely** *adjective* **comradeship** *noun*
con[1] *informal* • *noun* (*plural* **cons**) **1** a swindle in which the swindler first gains the victim's confidence (also as an *adjective*: *con man*). **2** a deceiving comment, action, etc. • *verb* (**cons, conned, conning**) **1** swindle: *conned them out of their money.* **2** deceive: *you can't con me: you're not really sick!* **3** persuade after dishonestly gaining trust: *readers are conned into buying trash.*
con[2] *noun* (*plural* **cons**) (usu. in *plural*) a reason against: *weighed the pros and cons.*
con[3] *noun* (*plural* **cons**) *slang* a convict.
con artist *noun* **1** a swindler: *a group of female con artists nicknamed the "sob-and-rob" gang.* **2** a person skilled at deception: *two weeks after their wedding she learned he was a con artist who was already married.*
concatenate *verb* (**concatenates, concatenated, concatenating**) link together (a chain of events, things, etc.): *concatenate all the files into one big one.* [Say k'n CATTA nate]
concatenation *noun* a series of interconnected things or events: *a concatenation of circumstances which had finally led to the murder.* [Say k'n catta NATION]
concave *adjective* having an outline or surface curved like the interior of a circle or sphere (compare CONVEX). ▶**concavity** *noun* (*plural* **concavities**) [Say CON cave, k'n CAVITY]
conceal *verb* **1** keep secret: *concealed her motive from him.* **2** not allow to be seen; hide: *concealed the letter.*
concealer *noun* **1** a cosmetic which covers blemishes and dark spots on the skin, esp. the circles under the eyes. **2** a person or thing that conceals.
concealment *noun* the act of concealing something; the state of being hidden: *the concealment of evidence.*
concede *verb* (**concedes, conceded, conceding**) **1 a** admit to be true: *conceded that his work was poor* ◊ *know when to argue and when to concede a point.* **b** admit defeat in a match or contest: *he conceded defeat.* **2** grant, yield, or surrender (a right, a privilege, points or a start in a game, etc.): *the right of women to university education was conceded only after some years of struggle.* **3** *Sport* allow an opponent to score (a goal) or to win (a match), etc.
conceit *noun* **1** excessive pride in oneself or one's powers, abilities, etc. **2 a** a far-fetched comparison, esp. as a stylistic affectation; a convoluted or unlikely metaphor: *the idea of the wind singing is a prime romantic conceit.* **b** an artistic device: *the director's brilliant conceit was to film this tale in black and white.*
conceited *adjective* full of conceit; vain. ▶**conceitedly** *adverb* **conceitedness** *noun*
conceivable *adjective* capable of being imagined. ▶**conceivably** *adverb*
conceive *verb* (**conceives, conceived, conceiving**) **1** become pregnant: *couples struggling with failure to conceive.* **2** cause an embryo to come into being: *his mother was 44 when he was conceived.* **3 a** devise, compose, formulate (a plan etc.): *the dam project was originally conceived in 1977* ◊ *a brilliantly conceived and executed robbery.* **b** apprehend, understand, perceive: *we cannot conceive of such things happening to us.* **4** develop (an emotion, feeling, etc.): *I had conceived a passion for another.*
concentrate • *verb* (**concentrates, concentrated, concentrating**) **1** focus all one's

attention or mental ability. **2 a** bring toward or collect at a centre: *industry is concentrated in the east*. **b** cause to converge or be focused on: *such things concentrate the mind*. **3** increase the strength of (a liquid etc.) by removing water or any other diluting agent. **4** bring (ore etc.) to a state of greater purity by mechanical means. • *noun* **1** a concentrated substance. **2** a concentrated form of esp. food.

concentrated *adjective* **1** (of an emotion etc.) intense, strong. **2** increased in strength or value by concentrating: *concentrated orange juice*. **3** wholly directed toward one thing: *a concentrated effort*.

concentration *noun* **1 a** the act or power of focusing one's attention or mental effort: *needs to develop concentration*. **b** dealing with one particular thing above all others: *concentration on the needs of the young can mean that the elderly are forgotten*. **2 a** a close gathering of people or things: *a concentration of resources* ◊ *the island has the greatest concentration of seabirds in the Atlantic Provinces*. **b** the action of gathering together closely: *the next century saw the concentration of power in the hands of the nobles*. **3** the weight of substance in a given weight or volume of material: *the gas can collect in dangerous concentrations*.

concentration camp *noun* a camp for the detention or extermination of political prisoners, internees, etc., esp. one run by Nazi Germany.

concentrator *noun* **1** a device used to concentrate something. **2** an industrial facility where mineral ores are purified by being separated from other rock.

concentric *adjective* (esp. of circles) having a common centre. ▶ **concentrically** *adverb*

concept *noun* **1** a general notion; an abstract idea. **2 a** an idea, theme or design, esp. as the basis for development or execution. **b** the product of this: *a new concept in swimwear*. **3** an idea or mental picture of a group or class of objects formed by combining all their aspects.

conception *noun* **1** the action of conceiving a child or of one being conceived: *an unfertilized egg before conception* ◊ *a rise in premarital conceptions*. **2** an idea or plan, esp. as being new or daring: *the time between a product's conception and its launch*. **3** an understanding: *his conception of God was simplistic*. **4** a general notion; an abstract idea: *the conception of a balance of power*. PHRASES **no conception of** an inability to imagine: *the administration had no conception of women's problems*.

conceptual *adjective* of mental conceptions or concepts: *philosophy deals with conceptual difficulties*.

conceptualization *noun* an idea, view, or generalization of something: *the conceptualization of life as a series of chapters in a book*.

conceptualize *verb* (**conceptualizes**, **conceptualized**, **conceptualizing**) form a concept or idea of.

conceptually *adverb* in terms of a concept or abstract idea: *a conceptually simple task*.

concern • *verb* **1 a** be relevant or important to: *this concerns you*. **b** relate to; be about. **2 concern oneself** interest or involve oneself: *don't concern yourself with my problems*. **3** worry, affect: *it concerns me that he is always late*. • *noun* **1 a** anxiety, worry. **b** solicitude, interest in others' well-being: *known for his warmth and concern*. **2 a** a matter of interest or importance to one, esp. causing anxiety. **b** (usu. in *plural*) affairs, private business: *meddling in my concerns*. **3** a business: *quite a prosperous concern*. PHRASES **have a concern in** have an interest or share in. **have no concern with** have nothing to do with. **to whom it may concern** to those who have a proper interest in the matter (as an address to the reader of a reference etc.).

concerned *adjective* **1** involved, interested: *the people concerned*. **2** troubled, anxious: *concerned about him*. PHRASES **as** (or **so**) **far as I am concerned** as regards my interests.

concerning *preposition* about, regarding.

concert *noun* **1** a musical performance of usu. several separate compositions. **2 a** public performance of a variety of entertainments, e.g. music, dancing, comedy skits, etc. **3** (as an *adjective*) performing in concerts, esp. as a professional soloist: *concert pianist*. PHRASES **in concert 1** (often foll. by *with*) acting jointly and accordantly. **2** (of a musician) in a performance.

concerted *adjective* **1** combined together; jointly arranged or planned. **2** serious: *a concerted effort*.

concertina *noun* (*plural* **concertinas**) a musical instrument held in the hands and stretched and squeezed like bellows, having reeds and a set of buttons at each end to control the valves. [Say con ser TINA]

concertmaster *noun* the principal first-violin player in an orchestra.

concerto *noun* (*plural* **concertos** or **concerti**) a composition for a solo instrument or instruments accompanied by an orchestra. [Say k'n CHAIR toe for the singular; for *CONCERTI* say k'n CHAIR tee]

concession *noun* **1 a** the action of conceding, granting, or yielding something: *in Manitoba, by contrast, the Metis resistance had won the grudging concession of provincehood*. **b** a thing that is granted, esp. in response to demands; a thing conceded: *the government was unwilling to make any further concessions*. **c** a gesture, esp. a token one, made in recognition of a demand or prevailing standard: *her only concession to fashion was her ornate silver ring*. **2 a** a preferential allowance or rate given by an organization, government, etc.: *tax concessions*. **b** the right to use land or other property, granted esp. by a government or local authority, esp. for a specific use. **c** the right, given by a company, to sell goods, esp. in a particular territory. **d** the land or property used or given. **3** a booth or stand in a stadium, theatre, etc., where esp. refreshments and souvenirs are sold. **4** *Cdn* **a** (*Ont.* & *Que.*) a tract of surveyed farmland, itself further divided into lots. **b** esp. *Ont.* a rural road separating concessions.

concession line *noun Cdn* (*Ont.*) **1** a surveying line separating concessions. **2** (also **concession road**) = CONCESSION 4b.

concessive *adjective* **1** of or tending to concession: *we must look for a more concessive approach*. **2 a** (of a preposition or conjunction) introducing a phrase or clause which might be expected to preclude the action of the main clause, but does not (e.g. *in spite of*, *although*). **b** (of a phrase or clause) introduced by a concessive preposition or conjunction. [Say kun SESS iv]

conch *noun* (*plural* **conches** or **conchs**) **1** a thick heavy spiral shell, occasionally bearing long projections, of various marine gastropod molluscs of the family Strombidae. **2** any of these gastropods. [Say KONTCH or KONK]

concierge *noun* **1** (esp. in France) a person in charge of the entrance of a building, often also serving as a caretaker. **2** a hotel employee responsible for attending to special needs of guests, making taxi reservations, etc. [Say kon see AIRZH]

conciliate *verb* (**conciliates**, **conciliated**, **conciliating**) **1** attempt to settle an esp. labour dispute by hearing all disputing parties and recommending solutions. **2** stop someone being angry or discontented; placate: *concessions were made to conciliate the peasantry*. [Say kun SILLY ate]

conciliation *noun* **1** *Law* the hearing and attempted

resolution of a dispute by an appointed conciliator. **2** the use of conciliating measures: *what is important now is not finger pointing but conciliation, a desire for peace and a resolution of this conflict.* [Say kun silly AY sh'n]

conciliator *noun* a person or organization that tries to make angry people calm so they can discuss or solve their problems successfully. [Say kun SILLY ay tur]

conciliatory *adjective* having the intention or effect of making angry people calm: *a conciliatory approach.* [Say kun SILLY a tory]

concise *adjective* giving a lot of information clearly and in a few words: *a concise account of the country's history.* ▶ **concisely** *adverb* **conciseness** *noun*

conclave *noun* **1** a private meeting. **2** *Catholicism* **a** the assembly of cardinals for the election of a pope. **b** the meeting place for a conclave. [Say CON clave]

conclude *verb* (**concludes, concluded, concluding**) **1** bring or come to an end. **2** infer (from given premises): *concluded that he was wrong.* **3** settle, arrange (a treaty etc.). **4** state in conclusion.

conclusion *noun* **1** a final result; a termination. **2** a judgment reached by reasoning. **3** the summing-up of an argument, book, etc. **4** the settling or arrangement of a treaty or agreement: *the conclusion of a free trade accord.* **5** *Logic* a proposition that is reached from given premises; the last part of a syllogism. PHRASES **in conclusion** to conclude.

conclusive *adjective* **1** (of evidence or argument) having or likely to have the effect of proving a case; decisive, convincing: *conclusive evidence ◊ the findings were by no means conclusive.* **2** (of a victory) achieved easily or by a large margin. ▶ **conclusively** *adverb*

concoct *verb* **1** make by combining elements not usually mixed together, esp. from what is available. **2** invent (a story, a lie, etc.). ▶ **concoction** *noun*

concomitant • *adjective* naturally accompanying or associated: *she loved travel, even with all its concomitant worries ◊ alliances and treaties are concomitant with trade and war.* • *noun* a phenomenon that naturally accompanies or follows something: *saloons, brothels, tawdry hotels, and overcrowded shacks were concomitants of the gold rush.* ▶ **concomitantly** *adverb* [Say k'n COMMA tint]

concord *noun* **1** agreement or harmony between people or things: *it did not take long for concord to turn into mistrust, suspicion, and hostility.* **2** a treaty.

concordance • *noun* **1** a book containing an alphabetical list of the important words used in a book or by an author, usu. with citations of the passages concerned. **2** an alphabetized list of all the words in a text or group of texts, usu. with some accompanying text. • *verb* make a concordance to (a book etc.). ▶ **concordancing** *noun* [Say kun CORE dince]

Concord grape *noun* a variety of dark purple grape of the northeastern US and southern Ontario, used esp. for making juice, jelly, etc.

concourse *noun* **1** an open central area in a large public building, airport, etc. **2** an indoor shopping area, often on the lowest (usu. underground) level of an office building or office complex. **3** *formal* a crowd: *a vast concourse of onlookers.*

concrete • *adjective* **1 a** existing in a material form; real. **b** specific, definite: *a concrete proposal.* **2** *Grammar* (of a noun) denoting a material object as opposed to an abstract quality, state, or action. • *noun* a durable building material made from a mixture of gravel, sand, cement, and water, which forms a stonelike mass on hardening. • *verb* (**concretes, concreted, concreting**) **1** cover with concrete. **2** embed in concrete. ▶ **concretely** *adverb* **concreteness** *noun*

concubine *noun* (among polygamous peoples) a woman who lives with a man but has lower status than his wife or wives. [Say CON cue bine]

concur *verb* (**concurs, concurred, concurring**) agree: *the authors concurred with the majority ◊ we strongly concur with this recommendation ◊ the police concurred that liquor was a problem.*

concurrence *noun* **1** agreement: *nothing can be done without the concurrence of the senior official.* **2** an example of two or more things happening at the same time: *an unfortunate concurrence of events.* [Say kun CUR ince]

concurrent *adjective* **1** existing or in operation at the same time: *concurrent sentencing means that sentences for several offences are served at the same time rather than consecutively.* **2** *Math* (of three or more lines) meeting at or tending toward one point. ▶ **concurrently** *adverb* [Say cun CUR int]

concussed *adjective* temporarily unconscious or confused because of a blow to the head, sometimes with associated bruising to the brain: *wasn't concussed because she was wearing her bicycle helmet.* [Say k'n CUSS]

concussion *noun* **1** *Medical* a period of unconsciousness caused by a blow to the head, sometimes accompanied by bruising to the brain and after-effects such as confusion or temporary incapacity. **2** a violent shock or shaking as from a heavy blow: *the concussion of a nearby explosion.*

condemn *verb* **1** express utter disapproval of: *the plan was condemned by campaigners.* **2** sentence someone to a particular punishment, esp. death: *the rebels had been condemned to death ◊ the haunted eyes of the condemned man.* **3** show or suggest one's guilt: *his looks condemn him.* **4** pronounce (a building etc.) unfit to use or live in. **5** doom or assign (to something unwelcome or painful): *condemned to spending hours ironing.* ▶ **condemnation** *noun* **condemnatory** *adjective*

condensation *noun* **1** the act of condensing. **2** any condensed material (esp. water on a cold surface). **3** a concise summarized version of something: *read the Reader's Digest condensation instead of the whole novel.* **4** *Chemistry* a reaction in which two molecules combine to form a larger molecule, producing a small molecule such as water as a by-product.

condensation trail *noun* = CONTRAIL.

condense *verb* (**condenses, condensed, condensing**) **1** make denser or more concentrated. **2** express in fewer words; make concise. **3** reduce or be reduced from a gas or solid to a liquid.

condensed milk *noun* milk thickened by evaporation and sweetened, usu. tinned.

condenser *noun* **1** an apparatus or vessel for condensing vapour. **2** a person or thing that condenses.

condescend *verb* **1** usu. *ironic* be gracious enough (to do a thing) esp. while showing one's sense of dignity or superiority: *condescended to attend the meeting.* **2** (foll. by *to*) derogatory behave as if one is on equal terms with (an inferior), usu. while maintaining an attitude of superiority. ▶ **condescending** *adjective* **condescendingly** *adverb*

condescension *noun* a condescending attitude: *her smile was a mixture of pity and condescension.*

condiment *noun* a spice or foodstuff used in small quantities to enhance the flavour of other foods, e.g. salt and pepper, vinegar, etc.

condition • *noun* **1** something upon the fulfillment of which something else depends. **2 a** the state of being or fitness of a person or thing: *in good condition.* **b** an ailment or abnormality: *a heart condition.* **3** (in *plural*) circumstances, esp. those affecting the functioning or existence of something: *working conditions.* • *verb* **1 a** bring into a good or desired state or condition.

b make fit. **2** teach or accustom to adopt certain habits etc.: *conditioned by society*. **3** govern, determine: *his behaviour was conditioned by his drunkenness*. **4 a** impose conditions on. **b** be essential to: *the two things condition each other*. **5** apply conditioner to (hair, the skin, etc.). PHRASES **in** (or **out of**) **condition** in good (or bad) condition. **in no condition to** certainly not fit to. **on condition that** with the stipulation that.

conditional • *adjective* **1** dependent; not absolute; containing a condition or stipulation: *a conditional offer* ◊ *the settlement is conditional on her not making any public statements on the matter*. **2** (of a clause, sentence, mood, proposition etc.) expressing a condition on which something depends, e.g. the first clause in *if she wins, we will be rich*. • *noun* **1** esp. *Grammar & Logic* a word, clause, proposition, etc., expressing or including a condition. **2** *Grammar* the conditional mood.

conditional discharge *noun* an order made by a criminal court whereby an offender will not be sentenced for an offence unless a further offence is committed within a stated period.

conditionally *adverb* with a condition or set of conditions: *the offer was made conditionally* ◊ *the sale was conditionally approved*.

conditioned *adjective* (of behaviour) brought on unconsciously as an automatic response to a stimulus that has a learned association with something else.

conditioned reflex *noun* (also **conditioned response**) a reflex response to a non-natural stimulus, established by training: *the cat's fear of men is a conditioned response, resulting from abuse by a male owner*.

conditioner *noun* a substance or device that improves the condition of something, esp. the hair.

conditioning • *noun* **1** the act of bringing a person, animal, or thing into good condition. **2** degree of fitness, esp. aerobic capacity. **3** the training or accustoming of a person or animal to give conditioned responses. • *adjective* that conditions.

condo *noun* (*plural* **condos**) = CONDOMINIUM 1.

condolence *noun* (often in *plural*) an expression of sympathy: *my condolences on your loss*. [Say k'n DOLE ince]

condom *noun* **1** a rubber sheath worn on the penis during sexual intercourse as a contraceptive or to prevent infection. **2** (also **female condom**) a plastic sheath inserted into the vagina prior to intercourse to prevent pregnancy or infection.

condominium *noun* **1 a** an apartment building, office building, or townhouse complex in which units are individually owned and the shared parts of the property are owned in common. **b** a unit in such a building or complex. **2** the joint control of a country's affairs by other countries.

condone *verb* (**condones**, **condoned**, **condoning**) accept or allow to continue behaviour that is considered morally wrong or offensive: *the college cannot condone any behaviour that involves illicit drugs*.

condor *noun* **1** (also **Andean condor**) a large vulture of South America, having black plumage with a white neck ruff and a fleshy wattle on the forehead. **2** (also **California condor**) a small vulture of California.

conducive *adjective* contributing or helping (toward something): *not conducive to negotiation*. [Say k'n DOO siv or k'n DYOO sive]

conduct • *noun* **1** behaviour; way of acting. **2** the action or manner of directing or managing (business, war, etc.). • *verb* **1** direct or manage (business etc.). **2** carry out or administer: *conduct an investigation*. **3 a** be the conductor of (an orchestra, choir, etc.). **b** direct the performance (of a piece of music) **4** *Physics* transmit (heat, electricity, etc.) by conduction. **5 conduct oneself** behave in a specified way:

conducted *themselves with poise and dignity*. **6** lead or guide (a person or persons).

conductance *noun Physics* the power of a specified material to conduct electricity. Symbol: **G**.

conduction *noun* **1 a** the transmission of heat through a substance from a region of higher temperature to a region of lower temperature. **b** the transmission of electricity through a substance by the application of an electric field. **2** the conducting of liquid through a pipe etc.

conductive *adjective* having the property of conducting (esp. heat, electricity, etc.).

conductivity *noun* the conducting power of a specified material.

conductor *noun* **1 a** a person who directs the performance of an orchestra or choir etc. **2** *Physics* **a** a thing that conducts or transmits heat or electricity. **b** = LIGHTNING ROD. **3 a** a person who collects fares in a bus etc. **b** a person in charge of a train.

conduit *noun* **1** a channel or pipe for conveying liquids. **2** a person, organization, etc. through which anything is conveyed: *a conduit for information*. **3 a** a tube or trough for protecting insulated electric wires. **b** a length or stretch of this. [Say CON do it or CON dyoo it]

cone *noun* **1** a solid figure with a circular (or other curved) plane base, tapering to a point. **2** a thing of a similar shape, solid or hollow. **3** the reproductive structure of conifers and related plants, often woody and cone-shaped. **4 a** a conical wafer for holding ice cream. **b** such a cone filled with ice cream. **5** a light-sensitive cell of one of the two types present in large numbers in the retina of the eye, responding mainly to bright light and responsible for sharpness of vision and colour perception.

coneflower *noun* any of several North American daisy-like plants having flowers with conelike centres.

confab *noun informal* a conversation. [Say CON fab]

confection *noun* **1** a sweet dessert or candy. **2** an elaborate or highly contrived thing: *Margery was magnificent in a swirling confection of crimson*.

confectioner *noun* a maker or retailer of confectionery.

confectionery *noun* (*plural* **confectioneries**) **1 a** candy and other sweets. **b** a candy factory or store. **c** a corner store. **2** the art or business of making candy or sweets.

confederacy *noun* (*plural* **confederacies**) **1** a league or alliance of persons, states, etc. **2** (usu. **Confederacy**) **a** a league or alliance of Aboriginal peoples: *the Iroquois Confederacy*. **b** the Confederate states in the US Civil War. [Say k'n FEDDER uh see]

confederate • *adjective* **1** esp. *Politics* allied; joined by an agreement or treaty. **2** (**Confederate**) being or relating to the eleven southern states (Alabama, Arkansas, Florida, Georgia, Louisiana, Mississippi, North Carolina, South Carolina, Tennessee, Texas, and Virginia) which seceded from the US in 1860–61 and formed a confederacy of their own, thus precipitating the Civil War: *the Confederate states* ◊ *the Confederate flag*. **3** *Cdn* (*Nfld*) of or relating to the political movement which supported the union of Newfoundland and Canada. • *noun* **1** (**Confederate**) a supporter of the Confederate states in the US Civil War. **2** *Cdn* (*Nfld*) (**Confederate**) a supporter of the political union of Newfoundland and Canada. **3** an accomplice, esp. in criminal activity. ▶**confederated** *adjective* [Say k'n FEDDER it, k'n FEDDER ate id]

confederation *noun* **1** a union or alliance of peoples,

countries, unions, etc. **2 (Confederation) a** (in Canada) the federal union of provinces and territories forming Canada, originally including Ontario, Quebec, New Brunswick, and Nova Scotia and subsequently expanded: *Manitoba joined Confederation in 1870*. **b** (in Newfoundland) the political union of Newfoundland and Canada. **c** (also **Confederation Day**) (in Canada) the date of the creation of the Dominion of Canada, 1 July 1867: *this union has seen some rough times since Confederation*. **d** (in Newfoundland) the date of the political union of Newfoundland and Canada, 31 March 1949. **3** the action of joining by an agreement or treaty.

confederationist *Cdn esp. hist.* • *noun* a supporter of Confederation. • *adjective* of or relating to a political movement supporting Confederation.

confer *verb* (**confers**, **conferred**, **conferring**) **1** (often foll. by *on*, *upon*) grant or bestow (a title, degree, favour, etc.). **2** (often foll. by *with*) converse, consult.

conference • *noun* **1** a meeting for discussion or presentation of information, esp. a regular one held by an association or organization. **2** the linking of several telephones, computer terminals, etc., so that each user may communicate with the others simultaneously (also as an *adjective*: *conference call*). **3** a division within a sports league. **4 a** an assembly which discusses church issues, formulates policy, etc. **b** a group of churches whose representatives meet regularly in such an assembly. **5** an association of nations etc. for a specified purpose. • *verb* (**conferences**, **conferenced**, **conferencing**) (usu. as **conferencing** *noun*) take part in a conference or conference call. PHRASES **in conference** engaged in discussion.

conferral *noun* the action of granting a diploma, benefit, authority, etc.: *the conferral of this power upon judges*. [Say k'n FUR ul]

confess *verb* (**confesses**, **confessed**, **confessing**) **1** acknowledge or admit (a fault, wrongdoing, etc.). **2** admit reluctantly; concede: *I confess I have my doubts*. **3 a** declare (one's sins) to a priest. **b** (of a priest) hear the confession of.

confession *noun* **1 a** a formal statement admitting that one is guilty of a crime: *the police managed to extract a confession*. **b** an admission or acknowledgement that one has done something about which one is ashamed or embarrassed: *by his own confession, he had strayed perilously close to alcoholism*. **c** (in *plural*) intimate revelations about a person's private life or occupation, esp. as presented in a sensationalized form in a book, newspaper, or film: *confessions of a mobster*. **2 a** a formal admission of one's sins with repentance and desire of absolution, esp. privately to a priest as a religious duty: *she still had not been to confession*. **b** that part of the public litany in some Christian churches in which a general acknowledgement of sinfulness is made. **3** (also **confession of faith**) **a** a formal declaration of one's religious beliefs. **b** a statement of one's principles: *his words are a political confession of faith*.

confessional • *noun* an enclosed stall in a church in which a priest hears confessions. • *adjective* **1** of or relating to confession: *his confessional outpourings*. **2** denominational: *confessional schools*.

confessor *noun* **1** a priest who hears confessions and gives counsel. **2** a person who makes a confession.

confetti *noun* small bits of paper, usu. coloured, thrown on festive occasions, esp. at the bride and groom at weddings.

confidant *noun* a person to whom secrets, problems, etc. are confided. [Say CONFA dawnt]

confidante *noun* a woman to whom secrets, problems, etc. are confided.

confide *verb* (**confides**, **confided**, **confiding**) **1** tell someone secrets and personal information trusting they will not divulge it: *confided his fears to his mother* ◊ *you can always confide in your friends*. **2** *literary* (foll. by *to*) entrust (an object of care, a task, etc.) to.

confidence *noun* **1** firm trust; faith. **2 a** belief in own's own abilities. **b** assurance or certainty. **3 a** something told confidentially. **b** the telling of private matters with mutual trust. **4** *Parliament* majority support for a government, policy, etc. expressed by a legislature. PHRASES **in confidence** as a secret. **take into one's confidence** confide in.

confidence game *noun* a swindle in which the victim is persuaded to trust the swindler in some way.

confident *adjective* **1** feeling or showing confidence; self-assured; bold: *spoke with a confident air*. **2** assured, trusting: *confident that he will come*.

confidential *adjective* **1** spoken, written or kept in confidence. **2** indicating private intimacy: *a confidential tone*. **3** entrusted with secrets: *confidential secretary*. ▶**confidentiality** *noun* **confidentially** *adverb*

confidently *adverb* in a confident or self-assured manner.

configurable *adjective* (esp. of computer equipment) that can be arranged in a particular way for a specific task.

configuration *noun* **1 a** an arrangement of parts or elements in a particular form or figure. **b** the form, shape, or figure resulting from such an arrangement. **2** *Computing* the interrelating or interconnecting of a computer system or elements of it so that it will accommodate a particular specification.

configure *verb* (**configures**, **configured**, **configuring**) **1** put together in a certain configuration. **2** interconnect or interrelate (a computer system or elements of it) so as to fit it for a designated task.

confine • *verb* (**confines**, **confined**, **confining**) (often foll. by *to*) **1** (also **confine oneself**) keep or restrict (within certain limits etc.): *confine your remarks to ten minutes*. **2** hold captive; imprison. **3** oblige (a person) to remain indoors, in bed, etc., through illness, bad weather, etc. • *noun* (usu. in *plural*) a limit or boundary: *within the confines of the town*.

confinement *noun* **1** the state of being forced to stay in a closed space, prison, etc. **2** *dated* the time of a woman's giving birth.

confirm *verb* **1** provide support for the truth or correctness of; make definitely valid. **2** establish more firmly (power, possession, etc.). **3** (foll. by *in*) encourage (a person) in (an opinion etc.): *he was confirmed in his belief in free speech*. **4** ratify (a treaty, possession, title, etc.). **5** administer the religious rite of confirmation to.

confirmation *noun* **1** a statement, letter, etc. that shows that something is true, correct, or definite: *I'm still waiting for confirmation of the test results*. **2 a** a

religious rite confirming a baptized person as a full member of the Christian Church. **b** a ceremony in which a young person is formally confirmed as an adult member of the Jewish faith.

confirmatory *adjective* that does or is intended to confirm or prove something: *confirmatory evidence* ◊ *a confirmatory test*.

confirmed *adjective* **1** firmly settled in some habit or condition: *a confirmed bachelor*. **2** valid: *confirmed reservations*.

confiscate *verb* (**confiscates, confiscated, confiscating**) **1** take or seize by authority. **2** appropriate to the public treasury (by way of a penalty). ▶ **confiscation** *noun*

conflagration *noun* **1** a great and destructive fire. **2** something destructive on a large scale: *the Balkans were once again the spark plug for a global conflagration*. [Say confla GRAY sh'n]

conflate *verb* (**conflates, conflated, conflating**) blend or fuse together: *the issues of race and class are separate and should not be conflated*. ▶ **conflation** *noun*

conflict • *noun* **1** a situation involving serious disagreement or argument: *she found herself in conflict with her parents over her future career* ◊ *the government has done nothing to resolve the conflict over nurses' pay*. **2** a violent situation or period of fighting: *the situation deteriorated into armed conflict*. **3** a situation in which there are opposing ideas, opinions, feelings, or wishes; a situation in which it is difficult to choose: *the story tells of a classic conflict between love and duty* ◊ *there was a conflict between her business and her domestic life*. **4** a difficulty caused by the occurrence of two events at the same time: *I can't go to the game; I have a conflict*. **5** a state of mind in which a person experiences a clash of opposing wishes or needs: *bewildered by her own inner conflict, she could only stand there feeling vulnerable*. • *verb* **1** clash; be incompatible. **2** (often foll. by *with*) struggle or contend.

conflicting *adjective* not compatible; contradictory: *conflicting opinions*.

conflict of interest *noun* (*plural* **conflicts of interest**) the situation of a politician, corporate officer, etc., whose private interests might benefit from his or her public actions or influence.

confluence *noun* **1** the place where two rivers etc. meet. **2** a coming together: *a confluence of ideas*. [Say CON floo ince]

conform *verb* **1** behave, dress, etc., according to socially acceptable conventions or standards: *adolescents are under a lot of pressure to conform* ◊ *the Metis were expected to change their way of life to conform with that of the dominant society*. **2** be in accordance with; comply with: *conform to safety standards* ◊ *the new building will need to conform with the bylaws*.

conformance *noun* = CONFORMITY 1, 2.

conformation *noun* the shape or structure of something, esp. an animal.

conformism *noun* a tendency to conform to accepted behaviour or established practices.

conformist • *noun* **1** a person who conforms to an established practice; a conventional person. **2** a person who conforms to the practices of an established church, esp. the Church of England. • *adjective* (of a person) conforming to established practices.

conformity *noun* (*plural* **conformities**) **1** behaviour in accordance with socially accepted conventions or standards: *loyalty to one's party need not imply unquestioning conformity*. **2** compliance with standards, rules, or laws: *conformity to regulation*. **3** compliance with the practices of an established church, esp. the Church of England.

confound *verb* **1** throw into perplexity or confusion: *his behaviour confounded me*. **2** mix up; confuse (in one's mind): *she confounded fact with fiction*. **3** damn (used in mild curses): *confound it!*

confounded *adjective* *informal* used for emphasis, usu. to express annoyance: *he was a confounded nuisance*.

confront *verb* **1 a** face in hostility or defiance. **b** face up to and deal with (a problem, difficulty, etc.). **2** (of a difficulty etc.) present itself to: *countless obstacles confronted us*. **3** (foll. by *with*) bring (a person) face to face with (a circumstance), esp. by way of accusation: *confronted them with the evidence*. **4** meet or stand facing. ▶ **confrontation** *noun* **confrontational** *adjective*

Confucian • *adjective* having to do with Confucianism or its founder, Confucius. • *noun* an adherent of Confucianism. [Say k'n FYOO sh'n]

Confucianism *noun* a system of philosophical and ethical teachings founded by Confucius in China in the 6th century BC, emphasizing respectful relationships with other people, including respect for ancestors. ▶ **Confucianist** *noun & adjective* [Say k'n FYOO sh'n ism]

confuse *verb* (**confuses, confused, confusing**) **1** disconcert, perplex, bewilder. **2** mix up in the mind; mistake (one for another). **3** make indistinct: *confuses the issue*. **4** throw into disorder.

confused *adjective* **1** perplexed. **2** unclear: *confused thinking*. **3** (esp. of an elderly person) mentally infirm. **4** disorderly: *a confused jumble of clothes*. ▶ **confusedly** *adverb*

confusing *adjective* difficult to understand; not clear.

confusingly *adverb* in a way that is confusing: *confusingly contradictory*.

confusion *noun* **1 a** uncertainty about what is happening, intended, or required: *there seems to be some confusion about which procedures to follow* ◊ *she cleared up the confusion over the party's policy*. **b** the state of being bewildered or unclear in one's mind about something: *he looked about him in confusion*. **2 a** a confused state; disorder: *trampled in the confusion of battle* ◊ *the bond market was thrown into confusion*. **b** (foll. by *of*) a disorderly jumble: *a confusion of brown cardboard boxes*. **3** a riot or similar disturbance: *confusion broke out at the announcement*.

conga *noun* (*plural* **congas**) **1** a Latin American dance of African origin, usu. performed by people in a single line, one behind another, who take three steps forward and then kick. **2** (also **conga drum**) a tall, narrow, low-toned drum beaten with the hands.

congeal *verb* **1** make or become semi-solid by cooling. **2** (of blood etc.) coagulate. **3** (of ideas etc.) take shape or become fixed, esp. to form a whole: *our social structure never congealed into the rigid hierarchy of Victorian England*. ▶ **congealed** *adjective* [Say k'n JEEL]

congenial *adjective* **1** (of a person, character, etc.) pleasant because like oneself in temperament or interests: *his need for congenial company*. **2** (of a place, activity, etc.) suited or agreeable: *wide-open spaces seem especially congenial to UFO sightings*. ▶ **congeniality** *noun* [Say k'n JEENY ul]

congenital *adjective* **1** (esp. of a disease, defect, etc.) existing from birth. **2** having a specified nature deeply ingrained as if from birth: *a congenital liar*. ▶ **congenitally** *adverb*

congested *adjective* **1** (of a part of the body) abnormally full of blood: *congested lungs*. **2** so crowded with traffic or people as to hinder movement: *congested streets* ◊ *the country is congested with tourists*. **3** (of the respiratory tract) blocked with mucus so as to hinder breathing: *my chest feels very congested*.

congestion *noun* **1** abnormal accumulation of blood

or mucus in a part of the body. **2** crowding or obstruction, esp. of traffic.

congestive *adjective* involving or produced by congestion of a part of the body: *congestive heart failure*.

conglomerate *noun* **1** a number of things or parts forming a whole but remaining distinct entities: *the Earth is a specialized conglomerate of organisms*. **2** a group or corporation formed by the merging of separate and diverse firms: *a media conglomerate*. **3** a rock made up of small stones held together. ▶ **conglomeration** *noun* [Say k'n GLOMMER it]

Congolese • *adjective* of or relating to Congo (formerly Zaire), the Republic of the Congo, or the region surrounding the Congo River in central Africa. • *noun* **1** (*plural* **Congolese**) a native or resident of any of these regions. **2** any of the Bantu languages spoken by the Congolese people. [Say konga LEEZ]

congrats *interjection informal* congratulations.

congratulate *verb* (**congratulates**, **congratulated**, **congratulating**) **1** express pleasure at the happiness or good fortune or excellence of (a person): *congratulated him on his marriage* ◊ *the staff are to be congratulated for their excellent service*. **2 congratulate oneself** feel pride or satisfaction: *she congratulated herself on her powers of deduction* ◊ *the Director was congratulating himself that nothing could go wrong*.

congratulation *noun* **1** the expression of praise and good wishes: *a letter of congratulation*. **2** (also as *interjection*; usu. in *plural*) words expressing one's praise for an achievement or good wishes on a special occasion: *congratulations on winning!* ◊ *Robyn deserved special congratulations for a job well done*.

congratulatory *adjective* expressing congratulations: *a congratulatory handshake*. [Say k'n GRATCH'll a tory or k'n GRADGE'll a tory]

congregate *verb* (**congregates**, **congregated**, **congregating**) collect or gather into a crowd: *some 4000 demonstrators had congregated at a border point*.

congregation *noun* **1 a** a group of people assembled for religious worship. **b** a group of people regularly attending a particular church etc. **2** the process of congregating; collection into a crowd or mass. **3** a crowd gathered together: *large congregations of birds may cause public harm*. **4** Catholicism a group of people obeying a common religious rule but under less solemn vows than members of the older religious orders: *Sisters of the Congregation of Notre-Dame*.

congregational *adjective* **1** of a congregation. **2** (**Congregational**) of Congregationalism.

Congregationalism *noun* a system of ecclesiastical organization whereby individual churches are largely self-governing. ▶ **Congregationalist** *noun*

congress *noun* **1** (**Congress**) **a** the national legislative body of the US, comprising the House of Representatives and the Senate. **b** this body during any two-year term. **2** the national legislative body in some other countries. **3** a formal meeting of delegates for discussion. **4** a society or organization. ▶ **congressional** *adjective*

congressman *noun* (*plural* **congressmen**) a member of the US Congress, esp. of the House of Representatives.

congressperson *noun* (*plural* **congresspersons** or **congresspoople**) a member of the US Congress, esp. of the House of Representatives.

congresswoman *noun* (*plural* **congresswomen**) a female member of the US Congress, esp. of the House of Representatives.

congruence *noun* **1** agreement, consistency: *there was no congruence between merit and reward in the old system*.

2 Math the state of being congruent. [Say CON groo ince or con GROO ince]

congruent *adjective* **1** in agreement or harmony: *the rules may not be congruent with the requirements of the law*. **2** Math coinciding exactly when superimposed. ▶ **congruently** *adverb* [Say CON groo int or con GROO int]

conic *adjective* of, pertaining to, or resembling a cone.

conical *adjective* cone-shaped.

conifer *noun* any evergreen tree of a group usu. bearing cones, including pines, yews, cedars, and redwoods. [Say CONNA fur]

coniferous *adjective* belonging to a group of evergreen trees and shrubs bearing cones, including pines, yews, cedars, and redwoods. [Say kuh NIFFER us]

conjectural *adjective* based on, involving, or given to conjecture: *the evidence was deemed too conjectural*. [Say k'n JECK chur ul]

conjecture • *noun* an opinion based on incomplete information; guessing: *conjectures about the newcomer were many and varied* ◊ *I demand facts, not conjecture*. • *verb* (**conjectures**, **conjectured**, **conjecturing**) form an opinion on incomplete information: *Isbister conjectured that the south end of Boothia Peninsula was pierced by a strait* ◊ *the word has been conjectured to be of Arabic origin*. [Say k'n JECK chur]

conjoin *verb* join, combine: *the catkins and the palm leaf were conjoined as symbols of Easter*.

conjoined twins *plural noun* twins joined at any part of the body and sometimes sharing organs etc.

conjugal *adjective* of marriage or the relation between husband and wife: *conjugal visits for prisoners*. [Say CONJA gull]

conjugate • *verb* (**conjugates**, **conjugated**, **conjugating**) **1** Grammar inflect (a verb) in its various forms of voice, mood, tense, number or person. **2** Biology **a** unite sexually. **b** (of gametes) become fused. • *adjective* joined together, esp. as a pair. [Say CONJA gate for the verb, CONJA gut for the adjective]

conjugation *noun* Grammar the variation of the form of a verb to show its voice, mood, tense, number, and person. [Say conja GAY shun]

conjunction *noun* **1** a word used to connect clauses or sentences or words in the same clause (e.g. *and*, *but*, *if*). **2** a combination (of events or circumstances): *a conjunction of favourable political and economic circumstances*. **3** the alignment of two bodies in the solar system so that they have the same longitude as seen from the earth. PHRASES **in conjunction with** together with.

conjunctiva *noun* (*plural* **conjunctivas** or **conjunctivae**) the mucous membrane that covers the front of the eye and lines the inside of the eyelids. ▶ **conjunctival** *adjective* [Say con junk TIVE uh]

conjunctivitis *noun* inflammation of the conjunctiva; pink eye. [Say conjunctive ITE iss]

conjuncture *noun* a combination of events; a state of affairs: *it was due to the happy conjuncture of two facts* ◊ *the wider political conjuncture*.

conjure *verb* (**conjures**, **conjured**, **conjuring**) **1** cause to appear or disappear as if by magic. **2** perform tricks which are seemingly magical. **3** call upon (a demon, spirit, etc.) to appear. **4** evoke. PHRASES **conjure up 1** bring into existence or cause to appear as if by magic. **2** cause to appear to the eye or mind; evoke. [Say CON jur]

conjuring *noun* the performance of seemingly magical tricks, esp. by rapid movements of the hands. [Say CON juring]

conjuror *noun* (also **conjurer**) a performer of conjuring tricks. [Say CON jur er]

conk[1] *verb informal* PHRASES **conk out 1** (of a machine

etc.) break down. **2** (of a person) become exhausted and give up. **3** (of a person) fall asleep.

conk² *slang* • *noun* **1** the head. **2** a blow, esp. on the nose or head. • *verb* hit, esp. on the head.

con man *noun* (*plural* **con men**) a man who cheats or tricks someone, esp. out of money, by first gaining their trust.

connect *verb* **1** join or be joined. **2** associate mentally or practically: *never connected her with the theatre*. **3** (of an airplane etc.) be synchronized at its destination with another airplane etc., so that passengers can transfer. **4** put into communication by telephone. **5** establish contact: *let's try to connect next week*. **6 a** join (a house etc.) to a source of electricity, gas, water, etc. **b** hook up (a phone, television, etc.) to a telecommunications system. **7 a** unite or associate with others in relationships etc.: *he is connected with the mayor's office*. **b** establish a rapport based on common interests, opinions etc. **8** form a logical sequence; be meaningful: *the two ideas do not connect*. **9** *informal* hit or strike effectively: *connect with the ball*.

connected *adjective* **1** joined in sequence. **2** (of ideas etc.) coherent. **3** related or associated. ▶**connectedness** *noun*

connecting rod *noun* the rod between the piston and the crankshaft etc. in an internal combustion engine or between the wheels of a locomotive.

connection *noun* **1** the action of linking one thing to another: *connection to the gas supply was delayed for three days*. **2** the point at which two things are connected: *a faulty electrical connection caused the machine to stop*. **3 a** a relationship in which a person, thing, or idea is linked or associated with something else: *cannot see the connection between the two ideas ◊ sufferers deny that their problems have any connection with drugs*. **b** a telephone or computer link: *got a bad connection ◊ a connection to the Internet*. **4** arrangement or opportunity for catching a connecting airplane etc.; the airplane etc. itself: *missed the connection*. **5 a** the linking up of an electric current by contact. **b** a device for effecting this. **6** a relative or associate, esp. one with influence: *has connections at city hall ◊ a business connection*.

connective *adjective* serving or tending to connect: *connective tissue*. ▶**connectivity** *noun*

connector *noun* a device used to keep two or more things together.

conner *noun* (also **connor**) *Cdn* (*Nfld*) a saltwater bottom-feeding fish, *Tautogolabrus adspersus*, found commonly around rocks and wharves.

connivance *noun* help in doing something wrong; the failure to stop something wrong from happening: *the crime was committed with the connivance of a police officer*. [Say kuh NIVE 'nce]

connive *verb* (**connives, connived, conniving**) **1** conspire to do something immoral, illegal, or harmful: *the government had connived with security forces in permitting murder*. **2** disregard or tacitly consent to (a wrongdoing): *have modern art and big business connived in marginalizing certain racial groups?* ▶**conniver** *noun* **conniving** *adjective* & *noun* [Say kuh NIVE]

connoisseur *noun* an expert judge in matters of taste: *a connoisseur of fine wine*. ▶**connoisseurship** *noun* [Say conna SIR or conna SOOR]

connotation *noun* **1** an idea or feeling which a word evokes for a person in addition to its literal or primary meaning: *the word "discipline" has unhappy connotations of punishment and repression*. Compare DENOTATION. **2** the implying of such ideas and feelings: *the work functions both by analogy and by connotation*. [Say conna TAY sh'n]

connote *verb* (**connotes, connoted, connoting**) **1** (of a word etc.) imply or suggest an idea or feeling in

addition to the literal meaning: *pointed windows have come to connote church architecture*. Compare DENOTE. **2** (of a fact) imply as a consequence or condition: *a housing co-operative usually connotes a high degree of commitment to a community project*. [Say kuh NOTE]

conquer *verb* **1 a** overcome and control (an enemy or territory) by military force. **b** be victorious. **2** overcome by effort: *conquered his fear*. **3** climb (a mountain) successfully. **4** gain the admiration, love, etc. of. ▶**conquerable** *adjective* **conqueror** *noun*

conquest *noun* **1** the act of taking control of a country, city, etc. by military force: *the conquest of the Aztecs by the Spanish*. **2 a** conquered territory: *colonial conquests around the globe*. **b** the act of gaining control over something that is difficult or dangerous: *the conquest of the Prairies*. **3** a person that someone has persuaded to love or have sex with them: *I'm just one of his many conquests*. **4** (**the Conquest**) the British conquest of French North America in 1763. **5** (**the Conquest, the Norman Conquest**) the conquest of England by the Norman French in 1066.

conquistador *noun* (*plural* **conquistadores** or **conquistadors**) a conqueror, esp. one of the 16th-century Spanish conquerors of Mexico and Peru. [Say con QUISTA dor; for the plurals say con quista DOR ez, con QUISTA dors]

consanguinity *noun* relationship by descent from a common ancestor; blood relationship. [Say con san GWINNA tee]

conscience *noun* **1** a moral sense of right and wrong esp. as felt by a person and affecting behaviour. **2** an inner feeling as to the goodness or otherwise of one's behaviour: *my conscience is clear*. **PHRASES in all** (or **good** or **all good**) **conscience** in such a way that one's conscience is clear. **on one's conscience** causing one feelings of guilt. [Say CON shince]

conscientious *adjective* **1** (of a person or conduct) wishing or showing the wish to do what is right, esp. to do one's work or duty well and thoroughly. **2** relating to a person's conscience: *I oppose the death penalty on conscientious grounds*. ▶**conscientiously** *adverb* **conscientiousness** *noun* [Say conshy EN chuss]

conscientious objector *noun* a person who for reasons of conscience objects to conforming to a requirement, esp. that of military service.

conscious • *adjective* **1** awake and aware of one's surroundings and identity. **2** aware, knowing: *conscious of his inferiority*. **3** (of actions, emotions, etc.) realized or recognized by the doer; intentional: *made a conscious effort not to laugh*. **4** (in combination) aware of; concerned with: *appearance-conscious*. • *noun* (**the conscious**) the conscious mind. ▶**consciously** *adverb*

consciousness *noun* **1** the state of being conscious: *lost consciousness*. **2** awareness of one's existence. **3 a** awareness, perception: *had no consciousness of being ridiculed*. **b** (in combination) awareness of, concern with: *class-consciousness*. **4** the totality of the thoughts and feelings of a person or group, esp. relating to a particular sphere: *moral consciousness*.

consciousness-raising *noun* the activity of increasing esp. social or political awareness.

conscript • *verb* enlist by conscription. • *noun* a person enlisted by conscription. [Say k'n SCRIPT for the verb, CON script for the noun]

conscription *noun* compulsory enlistment for military service. [Say k'n SCRIP sh'n]

consecrate *verb* (**consecrates, consecrated, consecrating**) **1** make or declare sacred; dedicate formally to a religious purpose. **2** (in Christian belief) make (bread and wine) into the body and blood of Christ. **3** devote (one's life etc.) to (a purpose). **4** ordain

(esp. a bishop) to a sacred office. ▶**consecrated** *adjective* **consecration** *noun* [Say CONSA crate]

consecutive *adjective* **1** following continuously, in uninterrupted sequence. **2** in unbroken or logical order. ▶**consecutively** *adverb*

consensual *adjective* of or by consent or consensus: *consensual sex*. [Say k'n SENSUAL]

consensus *noun* (*plural* **consensuses**) **1** general agreement (of opinion etc.): *a consensus of opinion* ◊ *an attempt to reach a consensus on the issue of security*. **2** (as an *adjective*) based on the majority view: *consensus politics*.

consent • *verb* (often foll. by *to*) express willingness, give permission, agree. • *noun* voluntary agreement, permission, compliance.

consenting adult *noun* an adult who consents to something, esp. a sexual act.

consequence *noun* **1** the result or effect of an action or condition. **2 a** importance: *it is of no consequence*. **b** social distinction: *persons of consequence*. PHRASES **in consequence** as a result. **face** (or **take**) **the consequences** accept the results of one's choice or action.

consequent *adjective* **1** following as a result or consequence. **2** logically consistent.

consequential *adjective* **1** following as a result or consequence: *a loss of confidence and a consequential withdrawal of funds*. **2** resulting from an act, but indirectly: *consequential damages*. **3** (of a person) important: *the new congress lacked consequential leaders*. ▶**consequentially** *adverb*

consequently *adverb & conjunction* as a result.

conservancy *noun* (*plural* **conservancies**) **1** a body concerned with the preservation of natural resources. **2** conservation; official preservation (of forests etc.).

conservation *noun* preservation, esp. of the natural environment.

conservationist *noun* a supporter or advocate of environmental conservation.

conservatism *noun* **1** any of several political philosophies, esp. one opposing radical reform, placing value in established institutions, and subjugating individual freedom to order, rank, security, and the good of the community, or one promoting individualism and non-intervention by the state. **2** opposition to change.

conservative • *adjective* **1 a** opposed to rapid change or innovation and holding to traditional attitudes. **b** (of taste etc.) sober and conventional: *wore a conservative suit*. **2** (of an estimate etc.) purposely low; moderate, cautious. **3 a** (**Conservative**) of or characteristic of a Conservative party. **b** espousing the tenets of political conservatism. **4** tending to conserve. • *noun* **1** a conservative person. **2** (**Conservative**) a supporter or member of a Conservative party.

Conservative Judaism *noun* a branch of Judaism allowing only minor changes in traditional ritual etc.

conservatively *adverb* in a cautious, conventional, or conservative manner.

Conservative Party *noun* **1** a Canadian political party, officially named the Progressive Conservative Party. **2** a similar party elsewhere.

conservatory *noun* (*plural* **conservatories**) **1** a school of esp. classical music or other arts. **2** a greenhouse. **3** a glassed-in sunroom attached to a house.

conserve • *verb* (**conserves**, **conserved**, **conserving**) **1** store up; keep from harm, damage, or depletion, esp. for later use. **2** preserve (food, esp. fruit), usu. with sugar. • *noun* a jam-like mixture, often of several fruits.

consider *verb* **1** contemplate mentally, esp. in order to

reach a conclusion. **2** examine the merits of (a course of action, a candidate, claim, etc.). **3** give attention to. **4** take into account. **5** have the opinion. **6** believe; regard as: *consider it settled*. **7** show thoughtfulness for: *consider his feelings*. **8** look at. PHRASES **all things considered** taking everything into account.

considerable *adjective* **1** enough in amount or extent to need consideration. **2** much: *considerable pain*. **3** notable, important. ▶**considerably** *adverb*

considerate *adjective* thoughtful toward other people. ▶**considerately** *adverb*

consideration *noun* **1** careful thought. **2** thoughtfulness for others: *companies should show more consideration for their employees*. **3** a fact or a thing taken into account in deciding or judging something: *the idea was motivated by political considerations*. **4** compensation; a payment or reward: *you can buy the books for a small consideration*. **5** *Law* (in a contractual agreement) anything given or promised or forborne by one party in exchange for the promise or undertaking of another. PHRASES **in consideration of** in return for; on account of. **take into consideration** include as a factor, reason, etc.; make allowance for. **under consideration** being considered.

considered *adjective* formed after careful thought: *a considered opinion*.

considering *preposition* **1** in view of; taking into consideration: *considering their youth* ◊ *considering that he was the youngest player, he played well*. **2** *informal* all in all: *not so bad, considering*.

consign *verb* **1** commit decisively or permanently: *consigned to years of misery* ◊ *she consigned his letter to the recycling box*. **2** deliver something to a person's custody, typically in order for it to be sold: *consigned three paintings to the auctioneers*. [Say k'n SIGN]

consignment *noun* **1** a batch of goods destined for or delivered to someone: *a consignment of carpets*. **2** (as an *adjective*) designating a store selling goods on consignment. PHRASES **on consignment** (of goods) delivered to a shop etc. to be sold, with the original seller reimbursed only on sale of the goods.

consist *verb* **1** (foll. by *of*) be composed; have specified ingredients or elements. **2** (foll. by *in*, *of*) have its essential features as specified: *its beauty consists in the use of colour*.

consistency *noun* (*plural* **consistencies**) **1** the degree of firmness or viscosity, esp. of thick liquids: *the sauce has the consistency of whipped butter*. **2** the state of being consistent; conformity with other or earlier attitudes, practice, etc.: *the board ensures consistency and fairness in regulations*.

consistent *adjective* (usu. foll. by *with*) **1** compatible or in harmony; not contradictory: *the injuries are consistent with falling from a great height*. **2** (of a person, behaviour, or process) unchanging in achievement or effect over a period of time. **3** not containing any logical contradictions: *but your argument is not consistent*. ▶**consistently** *adverb*

consolation *noun* **1** the comfort received by a person after a loss or disappointment: *there was some consolation in knowing that others were worse off*. **2** a consoling thing, person, or circumstance: *the children were a great consolation to him after his wife died*.

consolation prize *noun* a prize given to a competitor who just fails to win a main prize.

consolatory *adjective* intended to comfort a person after a loss or disappointment: *a consolatory hug*. [Say k'n SOLLA tory]

console[1] *verb* (**consoles**, **consoled**, **consoling**) comfort, esp. in grief or disappointment. [Say k'n SOLE]

console[2] *noun* **1** a panel or unit accommodating a set

of switches, controls, etc. **2** a cabinet for television or radio equipment etc. **3** *Music* a cabinet with the keyboards, stops, pedals, etc., of an organ. [Say CON sole]

consolidate *verb* (**consolidates, consolidated, consolidating**) **1** make or become strong or solid. **2** reinforce or strengthen (one's position, power, etc.). **3** combine (territories, companies, debts, etc.) into one whole. ▶ **consolidated** *adjective*

consolidated school *noun Cdn* a school replacing several smaller schools in a district.

consolidation *noun* combination of several elements into a stronger, more effective, or more coherent whole: *land consolidation* ◊ *the consolidation of power*.

consolidator *noun* a person or company that consolidates.

consommé *noun* a clear soup made with meat stock. [Say CONSA may]

consonant • *noun* **1** a speech sound in which the breath is at least partly obstructed, and which to form a syllable must be combined with a vowel. **2** a letter or letters representing this. • *adjective* in agreement or harmony: *the findings are consonant with other research*.

consort[1] • *noun* **1 a** a wife or husband, esp. of royalty: *prince consort*. **b** a partner, companion, associate, etc. **2** a ship sailing with another. • *verb* habitually associate with someone, typically with the disapproval of others: *you chose to consort with the enemy*.

consort[2] *noun* a group of musicians, esp. playing early music: *recorder consort*.

consortium *noun* (*plural* **consortia** or **consortiums**) an association, esp. several large companies in a joint venture. [Say k'n SORE tee um or k'n SORE sh'm for the singular, k'n SORE tee uh or k'n SORE shuh for the plural]

conspicuous *adjective* **1** clearly visible; striking to the eye; attracting notice: *he was very thin, with a conspicuous Adam's apple*. **2** remarkable of its kind: *she showed conspicuous bravery*. [Say k'n SPICK you us]

conspicuous consumption *noun* the buying of expensive goods, palatial homes, etc. in order to impress people with one's wealth.

conspicuously *adverb* in a plain or clearly visible manner: *they sat conspicuously in the front row*. [Say k'n SPICK you us lee]

conspiracy *noun* (*plural* **conspiracies**) **1** a secret plan to commit a crime or do harm. **2** the act of conspiring. [Say k'n SPEAR a see]

conspiracy theory *noun* (*plural* **conspiracy theories**) a belief that some covert but influential agency or organization is responsible for an unexplained event.

conspirator *noun* a person who takes part in a conspiracy. [Say k'n SPEAR a tor]

conspiratorial *adjective* **1** pertaining to or characteristic of a conspirator or conspiracy. **2** suggestive of a conspirator: *conspiratorial whispers*. ▶ **conspiratorially** *adverb* [Say k'n speera TORY ul]

conspire *verb* (**conspires, conspired, conspiring**) **1** combine secretly to plan and prepare an unlawful or harmful act. **2** (of events or circumstances) seem to be working together, esp. disadvantageously: *circumstances had conspired against them* ◊ *everything conspired to make her life miserable*.

Const. *abbreviation* constable.

constable *noun* **1** (in Canada, the UK, Australia, NZ, etc.) a police officer of the lowest rank. **2** an officer of the peace, as a bailiff etc., with minor judicial duties.

constabulary *noun* (*plural* **constabularies**) a police force: *Royal Newfoundland Constabulary*. [Say k'n STAB you lerry]

constancy *noun* **1** the quality of being unchanging and dependable, faithfulness: *dogs are islands of*

constancy and strength. **2** the quality of being enduring and unchanging: *the constancy of the tradition*.

constant • *adjective* **1** continuous: *needs constant attention*. **2** occurring frequently: *constant complaints*. **3** unchanging: *speed remained constant*. **4** faithful, dependable. • *noun* **1** anything that does not vary. **2** *Math* a component of a relationship between variables that does not change its value. **3** *Physics* **a** a number expressing a relation, property, etc., and remaining the same in all circumstances. **b** such a number that remains the same for a substance in the same conditions. ▶ **constantly** *adverb*

constellation *noun* **1 a** a group of stars whose outline is traditionally regarded as forming a particular figure. **b** one of eighty-eight sections based on these into which the sky has been divided. **2** a group of associated persons, ideas, etc.: *a remarkable constellation of talent and dedication*.

consternation *noun* anxiety or dismay causing mental confusion: *to his consternation his car wouldn't start*.

constipate *verb* (usu. in *passive*) (**constipates, constipated, constipating**) **1** cause constipation in. **2** obstruct abnormally: *emotionally constipated*. ▶ **constipated** *adjective*

constipation *noun* a condition in which there is difficulty in emptying the bowels, usu. associated with hardened feces.

constituency *noun* (*plural* **constituencies**) **1** a body of voters in a specified area who elect a representative member to a legislative body. **2** the area represented in this way. **3** a body of customers, supporters, etc.: *the magazine hoped to enlarge its constituency*. [Say k'n STITCH oo in see]

constituent • *adjective* **1** composing or helping to make up a whole. **2** able to make or change a (political etc.) constitution: *constituent assembly*. **3** appointing or electing. • *noun* **1** a member of a constituency (esp. political). **2** a component part: *the essential constituents of the human diet*. [Say k'n STITCH oo int]

constitute *verb* (**constitutes, constituted, constituting**) **1** be the components or essence of; make up, form. **2 a** amount to: *constitutes an official warning*. **b** formally establish: *does not constitute a precedent*. **3** establish by law: *the legally constituted government of a sovereign country*.

constitution *noun* **1** the act or method of constituting; the composition (of something). **2 a** the body of fundamental principles or established precedents according to which a state or other organization is acknowledged to be governed. **b** a (usu. written) record of this. **3** a person's physical state as regards vitality, health, strength, etc. **4** a person's mental or psychological makeup.

constitutional • *adjective* **1** of, consistent with, authorized by, or limited by a political constitution: *constitutional monarchy*. **2** inherent in, stemming from, or affecting the physical or mental constitution. • *noun* a walk taken regularly to maintain or restore good health.

constitutionalism *noun* **1** a constitutional system of government. **2** the adherence to or advocacy of such a system.

constitutionalist • *noun* **1** a proponent of constitutional government. **2** an expert in constitutional matters. • *adjective* of or pertaining to a constitution.

constitutionality *noun* acceptability according to a constitution: *they questioned the constitutionality of the law*.

constitutionally *adverb* according to a constitution.

constitutional monarchy *noun* a nation whose official head of state is a king or queen with powers that are limited by the nation's constitution; Canada is a constitutional monarchy.

constitutive *adjective* **1** forming a part or constituent of something; component: *memory is one of the constitutive elements of Mavis Gallant's fiction*. **2** forming an essential element of something: *language is constitutive of thought*. **3** having the power to establish or give organized existence to something. [Say k'n STITCH you tiv]

constrain *verb* **1** restrict severely: *agricultural activity is considerably constrained by climate*. **2** compel toward a particular course of action: *most individuals feel legally and morally constrained to deal honestly with their insurers*.

constrained *adjective* **1** in senses of CONSTRAIN *verb*. **2** forced; not natural: *a constrained manner*.

constraint *noun* **1** the act or result of constraining or being constrained. **2** a limitation on motion or action. **3** the restraint of natural feelings or their expression; a constrained manner.

constrict *verb* **1** make or become narrow or tight, esp. by encircling pressure: *chemicals that constrict the blood vessels ◊ he felt his throat constrict*. **2** restrict, obstruct: *the fear and reality of crime constrict many people's lives*. ▶ **constriction** *noun* **constrictive** *adjective*

constrictor *noun* any snake (esp. a boa) that kills by coiling around its prey and compressing it.

construct • *verb* **1** make by fitting parts together; build, form (something physical or abstract). **2** *Math* draw or delineate, esp. accurately to given conditions: *construct a triangle*. • *noun* a thing constructed, esp. by the mind.

construction *noun* **1** the act or a mode of constructing. **2 a** a thing constructed. **b** repair or building work on a stretch of road. **3** the building industry. **4** an interpretation or explanation: *put a strict construction on the law*. **5** the manner in which something is arranged; structure. **6** *Grammar* an arrangement of words according to syntactical rules. ▶ **constructional** *adjective*

constructive *adjective* helpful, useful: *constructive criticism*. ▶ **constructively** *adverb*

constructivism *noun* an originally Russian artistic movement in which assorted (usu. mechanical or industrial) objects are combined into non-representational and mobile structural forms. ▶ **constructivist** *noun*

constructor *noun* a person or company that builds things, esp. cars or aircraft.

construe *verb* (**construes, construed, construing**) **1** interpret (words or actions): *his words could hardly be construed as an apology*. **2** combine (words) grammatically: *"rely" is construed with "on"*.

consul *noun* **1** an official appointed by a nation to live in a foreign city and protect the interests of the nation's citizens in the region and promote trade. **2** *hist.* either of two annually elected chief magistrates in ancient Rome. ▶ **consular** *adjective*

consulate *noun* the building officially used by a consul. [Say CONSA lit]

consult *verb* **1** seek information or advice from. **2** have discussions or confer with someone, typically before undertaking a course of action: *they knocked down my fence and I wasn't even consulted ◊ the government must consult with interested parties*.

consultancy *noun* (plural **consultancies**) the professional practice or position of a consultant.

consultant *noun* a person who gives professional advice or services in a specialized field, esp. on a freelance basis.

consultation *noun* **1** a meeting arranged to consult (esp. with a physician). **2** the act or process of formally consulting or discussing: *they improved standards in consultation with consumer groups*.

consultative *adjective* giving advice or making decisions; advisory: *a consultative committee*.

consulting *adjective* giving professional advice to others working in the same field: *consulting physician*.

consumable • *adjective* that can be consumed; intended for consumption. • *noun* a commodity that is eventually used up, worn out, or eaten.

consume *verb* (**consumes, consumed, consuming**) **1** eat or drink. **2** use up (time, energy, resources, etc.). **3** completely destroy; reduce to nothing or to tiny particles: *fire consumed the building*. **4** engage the full attention of: *consumed with rage*.

consumer • *noun* **1** a person who consumes, esp. one who uses a product. **2** a purchaser of goods or services. • *adjective* intended for use by consumers, esp. domestically, rather than in business or manufacturing: *consumer goods*.

consumerism *noun* **1** the protection or promotion of consumers' interests. **2** preoccupation with consumer goods and their acquisition. **3** the promoting of consumer spending for the economic benefit of society. ▶ **consumerist** *adjective* & *noun*

consumer price index *noun* an index of price changes for standard consumer goods and services, expressed as a percentage of the prices in a base year.

consumer society *noun* (also **consumer culture**) a society in which the marketing and consumption of goods and services is an important social and economic activity.

consummate • *verb* (**consummates, consummated, consummating**) **1 a** make (a marriage) legally complete by having sex: *his first wife refused to consummate their marriage ◊ got an annulment because the marriage had never been consummated*. **b** give sexual expression to (love, a non-marital union, etc.). **2** complete: *the sale of the property has been consummated*. • *adjective* **1** complete, perfect, of the highest level: *consummate artistry*. **2** perfectly skilled: *a consummate general*. ▶ **consummately** *adverb* **consummation** *noun* [Say CONSA mate for the verb, CONSA mit for the adjective]

consumption *noun* **1** the using up of a resource: *we should reduce our energy consumption*. **2** *hist.* any disease causing wasting of tissues, esp. tuberculosis. **3** an amount consumed: *a daily consumption of 5 cups of coffee*. **4** the purchase and use of goods and services by the public: *consumption rather than thrift is the catchword of the decade*. **5** the eating, drinking, or ingesting of something: *liquor is sold for consumption off the premises ◊ food unfit for human consumption*. **6** the reception of information or entertainment, esp. by a mass audience: *offered a quite different policy for public consumption*.

consumptive *adjective* *hist.* affected with a wasting disease, esp. pulmonary tuberculosis: *from birth he was sickly and consumptive*.

contact • *noun* **1 a** the state or condition of touching, meeting, or communicating. **b** the first interaction between Europeans and Aboriginal peoples in parts of the world colonized by Europeans. **2** a person who is or may be communicated with for information, supplies, assistance, etc. **3** *Electricity* **a** a connection for the passage of a current. **b** a device for providing this. **4** a person likely to carry a contagious disease through being associated with an infected person. **5** (usu. in plural) *informal* a contact lens. • *adjective* caused by touching: *contact dermatitis*. • *verb* **1** get into

C

communication with (a person). **2** begin correspondence or personal dealings with.

contact cement *noun* an instantly-bonding adhesive applied to both surfaces to be bonded.

contact lens *noun* a small glass or plastic lens placed directly on the eyeball to correct vision.

contact sport *noun* a sport in which participants come into bodily contact with one another.

contagion *noun* **1 a** the communication of disease from one person to another by bodily contact. **b** a contagious disease: *Todd's rapid response saved most of the Plains Cree from infection and prevented the contagion from spreading.* **2** the spreading of a harmful idea or theory: *the contagion of disgrace.* [Say k'n TAY jin]

contagious *adjective* **1 a** (of a person) likely to transmit disease by contact. **b** (of a disease) transmitted in this way. **2** (of emotions, reactions, etc.) likely to affect others: *contagious enthusiasm.* ▶**contagiously** *adverb*

contain *verb* **1** hold or be capable of holding within itself; include, comprise. **2** (of measures) consist of or be equal to: *a metre contains 100 centimetres.* **3** prevent (an enemy, costs, etc.) from moving, spreading, or increasing. **4** restrain (oneself, one's feelings, etc.).

contained *adjective* **1** included, enclosed. **2** restrained: *immense but contained power and passion.*

container *noun* **1** a vessel, box, etc., for holding particular things. **2** a large boxlike receptacle of standard design for the transport of goods, esp. one readily transferable between forms of transport.

containment *noun* **1** *in senses of* CONTAIN *verb.* **2** the action or policy of preventing the expansion of a hostile country or influence.

contaminant *noun* something which contaminates.

contaminate *verb* (**contaminates**, **contaminated**, **contaminating**) **1** make impure by contact or mixture; pollute. **2** infect. **3** introduce radioactivity into (a substance where it is harmful or undesirable). ▶**contamination** *noun*

contemplate *verb* (**contemplates**, **contemplated**, **contemplating**) **1** look at or consider in a calm, reflective manner. **2** regard (an event) as possible. **3** intend. **4** meditate. ▶**contemplation** *noun*

contemplative • *adjective* of or given to (esp. religious) contemplation. • *noun* a person whose life is devoted to contemplation, esp. a monk or nun of a cloistered order devoted to prayer. ▶**contemplatively** *adverb* [Say CON tum play tiv for the adjective, k'n TEMPLA tiv for the noun]

contemporaneous *adjective* existing or occurring at the same time: *Pythagoras was contemporaneous with Buddha* ◊ *Toronto's City Hall and the contemporaneous Toronto-Dominion Centre.* ▶**contemporaneously** *adverb* [Say k'n tempa RAINY us]

contemporary • *adjective* **1** living or occurring at the same time: *the event was recorded by a contemporary historian.* **2** approximately equal in age: *this series of paintings is contemporary with other works in an earlier style.* **3** (of styles etc.) following the latest ideas or fashion: *contemporary art.* **4** living or existing at the present: *the tension and complexities of our contemporary society.* • *noun* (*plural* **contemporaries**) **1** a person or thing living or existing at the same time as another: *he was a contemporary of Darwin.* **2** a person of roughly the same age as another: *my contemporaries at school.*

contempt *noun* **1** a feeling that a person or a thing is beneath consideration or worthless, or deserving scorn or extreme reproach: *he showed his contempt for his job by doing it very badly.* **2** disregard for something that should be taken into account: *an arrogant contempt for the wishes of the majority.* **3** (also **contempt of court**)

disobedience to or disrespect for a court of law and its officers: *he was held to be in contempt and was fined.* PHRASES **beneath contempt** utterly worthless or despicable. **hold in contempt** despise.

contemptible *adjective* deserving contempt; despicable: *a display of contemptible cowardice.*

contemptuous *adjective* showing contempt: *she was intolerant and contemptuous of the majority of the human race.* ▶**contemptuously** *adverb*

contend *verb* **1** struggle to surmount a difficulty or danger: *she had to contend with his uncertain temper.* **2** engage in a struggle or campaign to achieve something: *factions within the party were contending for the succession to the presidency* ◊ *contending emotions* ◊ *disputes continued between the contending parties.* **3** assert: *she contends that the judge was wrong.*

contender *noun* an esp. serious challenger or competitor.

content[1] • *adjective* **1** (often foll. by *with*) satisfied; adequately happy. **2** willing: *I am content to sit here for the rest of the day.* • *verb* make content; satisfy: *we will have to content ourselves with that.* • *noun* a contented state. PHRASES **to one's heart's content** to the full extent of one's desires.

content[2] *noun* **1** what is contained in something. **2 a** the amount of a substance contained: *sodium content.* **b** the proportion of a specified feature present: *Canadian content.* **3** the substance or material dealt with (in a speech, work of art, etc.) as distinct from its form or style. **4** the capacity or volume of a thing. **5** (in *plural*) (also **table of contents**) a list of the titles of chapters etc. given at the front of a book, periodical, etc.

contented *adjective* happy, satisfied. ▶**contentedly** *adverb* **contentedness** *noun*

contention *noun* **1** a point maintained in an argument: *her major contention is that the theatre should be engaging, provocative, and always entertaining.* **2** a dispute or argument: *the captured territory was one of the main areas of contention between the two countries.* PHRASES **in contention** competing, esp. with a good chance of success. **out of contention** having lost any chance of succeeding.

contentious *adjective* **1** involving heated argument: *a contentious debate.* **2** controversial: *a contentious issue.* **3** fond of arguing; likely to argue: *the students were contentious and belligerent.* ▶**contentiously** *adverb* **contentiousness** *noun* [Say k'n TEN shus]

contentment *noun* satisfied, tranquil happiness.

contest • *noun* **1 a** a competition, raffle, draw, etc. **b** a competition for a political position: *the leadership contest.* **2 a** dispute; a controversy: *a contest between liberal and traditional views.* • *verb* **1** challenge or dispute: *the former chairman contests his dismissal.* **2** debate: *the issues have been hotly contested.* **3** contend or compete for (a prize, parliamentary seat, etc.): *she declared her intention to contest the election.* PHRASES **no contest** indicating a clearly undisputed winner in some supposed competition. ▶**contestable** *adjective*

contestant *noun* a person who takes part in a contest or competition.

contestation *noun* **1** the action or process of disputing or arguing: *resistance and contestation make for exciting art.* **2** an assertion contended for: *he would not agree with my contestation.* [Say con tess TAY shun]

contested *adjective* **1** that is the subject of argument or debate: *a hotly contested issue.* **2** that is the subject or object of battle or competition: *a bitterly contested election* ◊ *the contested territory along the border.*

▶**context** *noun* **1** the parts of something written or spoken that immediately precede and follow a word or

passage and clarify its meaning. **2** the circumstances relevant to something under consideration. PHRASES **in** (or **out of**) **context** with (or without) the surrounding words or circumstances: *must be seen in context*.

contextual *adjective* connected with a particular context: *contextual factors*. ▶ **contextualization** *noun* **contextualize** *verb* **contextually** *adverb*

contiguity *noun* the state of bordering or being in direct contact with something: *Canada and the US are nations bound by geographical contiguity*. [Say conta GYOO uh tee]

contiguous *adjective* (usu. foll. by *with*, *to*) **1** touching, adjoining, in contact. **2** neighbouring, in close proximity. **3** esp. *US* used in reference to the continental US, excluding Alaska and Hawaii. ▶ **contiguously** *adverb* [Say kun TIG you us]

continence *noun* **1** the ability to control one's bladder and bowels. **2** the ability to exercise self-restraint, esp. sexually.

continent[1] *noun* **1** any of the main continuous expanses of land (Europe, Asia, Africa, North and South America, Australia, Antarctica). **2** (**the Continent**) the mainland of Europe as distinct from the British Isles.

continent[2] *adjective* **1** able to control movements of the bowels and bladder. **2** exercising self-restraint, esp. sexually.

continental • *adjective* **1** of or characteristic of a continent. **2 a** (**Continental**) of or relating to mainland Europe. **b** (of cooking etc.) reflecting the traditions of various European countries. • *noun* an inhabitant of mainland Europe.

continental breakfast *noun* a light breakfast of coffee, rolls, etc.

continental divide *noun* the boundary between separate drainage basins on a continent, esp. (**Continental Divide**) the North American watershed formed by the Rocky Mountains.

continental drift *noun* the slow movement of the continents relative to each other over the surface of the earth.

continental glacier *noun* a permanent layer of ice covering an extensive part of a continent.

continentalism *noun* the belief that Canada and the US should pursue greater economic, political, and cultural co-operation, esp. in contrast to nationalistic policies. ▶ **continentalist** *noun* & *adjective*

continental shelf *noun* (plural **continental shelves**) the area of seabed around a large land mass where the sea is relatively shallow compared with the open ocean.

contingency *noun* (plural **contingencies**) **1** a future event or circumstance which is possible but cannot be predicted with certainty: *a detailed contract which attempts to provide for all possible contingencies ◊ a contingency plan*. **2** a provision for such an event or circumstance: *supplies were kept as a contingency against a blockade*. **3** an incidental expense: *allow an extra fifteen percent on the budget for contingencies*. **4** the absence of certainty in events. [Say k'n TINGE 'n see]

contingent • *noun* **1** a group with common origins, interests, etc. representing a larger body: *the Canadian contingent was out in full force for the world figure skating championships*. **2** a force contributed to form part of an army or navy. • *adjective* **1** (usu. foll. by *on*, *upon*) conditional, dependent (on an uncertain event or circumstance): *resolution of the conflict was contingent on the signing of a ceasefire agreement*. **2** subject to chance: *the contingent nature of the job*. [Say k'n TINGE 'nt]

WRITING TIP
continual, continuous

Note the difference between **continual** and **continuous**: **continual** refers to something happening frequently, with intervals, as in *I couldn't work because of the continual interruptions*; **continuous** refers to something that is non-stop, as in *I couldn't sleep because of the continuous pounding of rain on the roof*. Only **continuous** can refer to something uninterrupted over a distance, as in *a continuous row of houses* or *a continuous stretch of road*.

---

continual *adjective* **1** constantly or frequently recurring. **2** always happening. ▶ **continually** *adverb*

continuance *noun* **1** a state of remaining or continuing in existence or operation: *his interests encouraged him to favour the continuance of the war ◊ the party leaders use their power to ensure their continuance in office*. **2** the duration of an event or action: *the trademarks shall be used only during the continuance of this agreement*. **3** *Law* an adjournment or postponement of proceedings to a future date.

continuation *noun* **1** the action of carrying something on over a period of time or the state of being carried on: *the continuation of discussions about a permanent peace*. **2** a part that is attached to and an extension of something else: *once a separate town, it is now a continuation of the suburbs*.

continue *verb* (**continues**, **continued**, **continuing**) **1** persist in, maintain, not stop (an action etc.). **2 a** resume or prolong (a narrative, journey, etc.). **b** recommence after a pause: *we'll continue shortly*. **3** be a sequel to. **4** remain: *the weather will continue cold*. **5** *Law* adjourn (proceedings) until some future date.

continuing education *noun* **1** instruction intended esp. for adult, part-time students. **2** courses given to update participants in a particular field of study.

continuity *noun* (plural **continuities**) **1 a** the state of being continuous. **b** an unbroken succession. **c** a logical sequence. **2 a** the detailed and self-consistent scenario of a film or broadcast. **b** the maintenance of consistency or of a continuous flow of action in a film sequence. [Say conta NEW it ee]

continuous *adjective* **1** unbroken, uninterrupted. **2** (often foll. by *with*) connected throughout in time or space. **3** *Grammar* = PROGRESSIVE *adjective* 6. **4** (of paper etc.) designating a folded stack or roll perforated to form separate sheets. ▶ **continuously** *adverb* **continuousness** *noun*

continuum *noun* (plural **continua**) a series of similar items in which each is almost the same as the ones next to it but the last is very different from the first: *a continuum of oppression ranging from a sexist joke to brutal murder*. [Say kun TIN you um, kun TIN you uh]

contort *verb* twist or be twisted out of normal shape: *a spasm of pain contorted his features ◊ her face contorted with anger*. ▶ **contorted** *adjective*

contortion *noun* **1** the act or process of twisting. **2** a twisted state, esp. of the face or body. **3** a thing or idea distorted by a twisting of character, meaning, context, etc.: *the verbal contortions of the politician*.

contortionist *noun* a person who twists and bends their body into strange and unnatural positions to entertain, e.g. in a circus.

contour *noun* **1** an outline, esp. representing or bounding the shape of something with a curving form. **2** the outline of a natural feature, e.g. a coast or mountain mass. **3** = CONTOUR LINE 1. **4** the defining

traits of a person's character, a society, etc., perceived as a linkage of common and delimiting characteristics.

contoured *adjective* **1** designed or shaped to fit a specific form: *contoured seats*. **2** having contour lines.

contour line *noun* **1** a line on a map joining points of equal altitude. **2** a line in a painting etc. joining points or enclosing an area of similar colour etc.

contour map *noun* a map marked with contour lines to depict the differing elevations of the land.

contra- *combining form* against, opposite: *contradict*.

contraband • *noun* **1** anything that has been smuggled, imported, or exported illegally. **2** prohibited trade; smuggling. **3** (also **contraband of war**) goods forbidden to be supplied by neutrals to belligerents. • *adjective* **1** forbidden to be imported or exported (at all or without payment of duty). **2** concerning traffic in contraband: *contraband trade*.

contraception *noun* the use of contraceptives.

contraceptive • *adjective* preventing pregnancy. • *noun* a device, drug, etc. preventing pregnancy.

contract • *noun* **1** a written or spoken agreement between two or more parties, intended to be enforceable by law. **2** a document recording this. **3** marriage regarded as a legal arrangement. **4** *Bridge etc.* a commitment to win the number of tricks bid. **5** *informal* a criminal arrangement for someone to be killed in exchange for money. • *verb* **1 a** make or become smaller. **b** draw together (muscles, the brow, etc.) or be drawn together. **2 a** (usu. foll. by *with*) make a contract. **b** enter formally into a business or legal arrangement: *The player is contracted to play until June ◊ contracted for the delivery of gravel to the site.* **c** (often foll. by *out*) arrange (work) to be done by contract. **d** place under a contract. **3** catch or develop (a disease). **4** form or develop (a friendship, habit, etc.). **5** enter into (marriage). **6** incur (a debt etc.).

contract bridge *noun* the most common form of bridge, in which only tricks bid and won count.

contraction *noun* **1** the process of becoming smaller: *expansion and contraction of metal ◊ the sudden contraction of the markets left them with a lot of unwanted stock.* **2 a** a shortening or tensing of a muscle in response to a nerve impulse. **b** the tensing of the muscles in the uterus esp. during labour: *the contractions were coming every five minutes.* **3 a** a shortening of a word. **b** a contracted word or group of words: *"can't" is a contraction.*

contractor *noun* a person who undertakes a contract, esp. to provide materials, do building, etc

contractual *adjective* of, in the nature of, or secured by a contract. ▶ **contractually** *adverb*

contradict *verb* **1** affirm the contrary of (a statement etc.). **2 a** deny or express the opposite of a statement made by (a person). **b** make a contradictory statement. **3** be in opposition to or in conflict with: *evidence contradicted our theory.*

contradiction *noun* **1** the statement of a position opposite to one already made: *the second sentence appears to be in flat contradiction of the first ◊ the experiment provides a contradiction of the hypothesis ◊ I think I can say, without fear of contradiction, that this is the best thing we have seen.* **2** a combination of statements, ideas, or features of a situation which are opposed to one another: *the proposed new system suffers from a set of internal contradictions.* PHRASES **contradiction in terms** a statement containing two words that contradict each other's meaning: *safe disposal of uranium tailings is a contradiction in terms.*

contradictory *adjective* **1** expressing a denial or opposite statement. **2** (of statements etc.) mutually opposed or inconsistent. **3** (of a person) inclined to contradict.

contradistinction *noun* difference made apparent by contrast: *in contradistinction to their earlier show, which was loud and brash, they are now being more poetic.*

contrail *noun* a visible stream of water droplets or ice crystals in the exhaust of an aircraft. [Say CON trail]

contraindicate *verb* (**contraindicates**, **contraindicated**, **contraindicating**) cause (a medication, course of treatment, etc.) to be inappropriate: *many drugs and medical procedures are contraindicated during pregnancy.* ▶ **contraindication** *noun* [Say contra INDICATE]

contralto *noun* (*plural* **contraltos**) **1 a** the lowest female singing voice. **b** a singer with this voice. **2** a part written for contralto. [Say kun TRAWL toe or kun TRAL toe]

contraption *noun* often *derogatory* or *jocular* a machine, esp. a strange, improvised, or particularly intricate one.

contrapuntal *adjective* having two or more tunes played together to form a whole; using counterpoint: *baroque music is contrapuntal.* [Say contra PUNT ul]

contrarian • *noun* a person who opposes majority opinions, attitudes, etc., esp. in economic matters. • *adjective* going against popular opinion or current practice. ▶ **contrarianism** *noun* [Say con TRERRY un]

contrary • *adjective* **1** opposite in nature, direction or meaning: *he ignored contrary advice and agreed on the deal.* **2** mutually opposed: *his mother had given him contrary messages.* **3** (of a wind) unfavourable, blowing in an opposite direction to one's course. **4** *informal* perversely inclined to disagree or to do the opposite of what is expected or desired: *she is sulky and contrary where her work is concerned.* • *noun* (*plural* **contraries**) (usu. as **the contrary**) the opposite. • *adverb* (foll. by *to*) in opposition or contrast: *contrary to popular belief, chocolate does not cause acne.* PHRASES **on the contrary** intensifying a denial of what has just been implied or stated. **to the contrary** to the opposite effect: *he continued to drink despite medical advice to the contrary.* [Say CON trary except for sense 4, which is pronounced kun TRERRY]

contrast • *noun* **1 a** a juxtaposition or comparison showing striking differences. **b** a difference so revealed. **2** (often foll. by *to*) a thing or person having qualities noticeably different from another. **3** the degree of difference between tones in a television picture or a photograph. • *verb* (often foll. by *with*) **1** compare or set together so as to reveal a difference: *people contrasted her with her sister ◊ compare and contrast ancient Greek and Roman civilization.* **2** differ strikingly: *his friend's success contrasted with his own failure.* ▶ **contrasting** *adjective* **contrastingly** *adverb*

contravene *verb* (**contravenes**, **contravened**, **contravening**) **1** infringe, violate (a law, standards, guidelines, etc.): *he contravened the Official Secrets Act.* **2** (of things) conflict with: *an act may be considered a crime if it seriously contravenes values fundamental to our society.* [Say contra VEEN]

contravention *noun* an action which offends against a law, treaty, or other ruling: *contravention of the Act is punishable by imprisonment ◊ the date of the alleged contravention.* PHRASES **in contravention of** infringing, violating (a law etc.). [Say contra VEN sh'n]

contribute *verb* (**contributes**, **contributed**, **contributing**) **1** give (money, an idea, help, etc.) toward a common purpose. **2** help to bring about a result etc.: *contributed to their downfall.* **3** supply (an article etc.) for publication with others in a journal etc. ▶ **contributing** *adjective* [Say kun TRIB yoot]

contribution *noun* **1** the act of giving or contributing. **2** something given, esp. money. **3** an article etc. provided for a publication.

contributor *noun* **1** a person who contributes articles for a magazine or newspaper, or reports for a radio or television program. **2** a person who donates money to a cause. **3** a causal factor in the occurrence of something: *sulphur dioxide is a major contributor to acid rain*.

contributory *adjective* **1** contributing to a result; partly responsible for. **2** operated by means of contributions: *contributory pension scheme*.

contributory negligence *noun* failure on the part of an injured party to take adequate precautions to prevent accident or injury.

contrite *adjective* feeling or expressing remorse at the recognition that one has done wrong: *a contrite tone ◊ suddenly contrite, Tremblay hangs his head*. ▶ **contritely** *adverb* [Say CON trite or kun TRITE]

contrition *noun* the condition of being distressed in mind for some fault or injury done, usu. with resolution to make amends.

contrivance *noun* **1 a** a device made for a particular purpose: *an assortment of electronic equipment and mechanical contrivances*. **b** an obviously artificial construction or presentation of parts or details: *the story is told with an absence of contrivance or literary device*. **2** an elaborate act or plan, esp. a deceitful one. [Say kun TRIVE unce]

contrive *verb* (**contrives, contrived, contriving**) **1** create or bring about by deliberate use of skill and artifice: *his opponents contrived a cabinet crisis ◊ she contrived to be alone with him despite the supervision*. **2 a** manage: *contrived to make matters worse*. **b** plot or scheme.

contrived *adjective* so obviously planned as to seem unnatural or forced: *the plot seemed contrived*.

control • *noun* **1** the power of directing; command. **2** the power of restraining, esp. self-restraint. **3 a** a means of restraint. **b** prevention of the spread or proliferation of something: *disease control*. **4** (usu. in *plural*) a means of regulating prices etc. **5 a** a device or switch used to control something: *control panel*. **b** (usu. in *plural*) the switches etc. by which an aircraft or car is controlled. **6** (also **control key**) *Computing* a key which is held down while another key is depressed, altering the function of the latter. **7** a person or group that checks, monitors, or controls something. **8 a** a standard of comparison for checking the results of a survey or experiment. **b** a person or thing acting as such a standard. • *verb* (**controls, controlled, controlling**) **1** dominate or have command of. **2** regulate or exert control over. **3** curb, restrain, or hold in check: *control yourself*. **4** serve as a standard of comparison for a test, study, etc. **5** check, verify. PHRASES **in control** (often foll. by *of*) directing an activity. **out of control** no longer subject to containment, restraint, or guidance. **under control** being controlled; in order.

control freak *noun informal* a person with a near obsessive desire for order and control of self, others, surroundings, etc.

control group *noun* a group forming the standard of comparison in an experiment.

controllability *noun* the ability to be controlled.

controllable *adjective* that can be controlled.

controlled experiment *noun* an experiment designed with strictly controlled variables so that the effects of any one factor may be precisely observed.

controlled substance *noun* (also **controlled drug**) any addictive or behaviour-altering substance the possession of which is restricted by law, e.g. cocaine.

controller *noun* **1** a person or device that regulates,

directs, or controls. **2** = COMPTROLLER. **3** *Cdn* (in Ontario) a member of a board of control.

controlling interest *noun* ownership of sufficient stock in a company to enable a shareholder to exert control over policy, management, etc.

controlling shareholder *noun* an individual who owns a sufficient number of shares in a company to have a controlling interest in it.

control tower *noun* a tall structure at an airport etc. from which air traffic is controlled.

controversial *adjective* causing or subject to dispute. ▶ **controversialist** *noun* **controversially** *adverb*

controversy *noun* (*plural* **controversies**) a prolonged argument or dispute, esp. when conducted publicly and over a matter of opinion. [Say CONTRA versey]

controvert *verb* **1** deny the truth of something: *subsequent work from the same laboratory controverted these results*. **2** argue about: *the views in the article have been controverted*. ▶ **controverted** *adjective*

contusion *noun* a region of injured tissue or skin in which blood capillaries have been ruptured; a bruise: *escaped the accident with scrapes and contusions*. [Say kun TYOO zhun]

conundrum *noun* **1** a riddle, esp. one with a pun in its answer. **2** a hard or puzzling question or issue: *one of the most difficult conundrums for experts*. [Say kuh NUN drum]

conurbation *noun* an extended urban area, usu. consisting of several towns merging with the suburbs of a city. [Say conner BAY sh'n]

convalesce *verb* (**convalesces, convalesced, convalescing**) recover one's health after illness or medical treatment. [Say conva LESS]

convalescence *noun* a time spent recovering from an illness etc. [Say conva LESS ince]

convalescent • *adjective* **1** recovering from an illness. **2** pertaining to convalescents: *convalescent home*. • *noun* a person recovering from an illness or injury. [Say conva LESS int]

convection *noun* **1** the movement caused within a fluid by the tendency of hotter and therefore less dense material to rise, and colder, denser material to sink under the influence of gravity, resulting in the transference of heat. **2** the atmospheric process of air transfer, esp. of hot air upward.

convection current *noun* a stream of fluid or air that results from heating.

convective *adjective* involving or having to do with the circulation in a liquid or gas of rising, warmer regions and cooler, sinking ones.

convene *verb* (**convenes, convened, convening**) **1 a** call or arrange (a meeting etc.). **b** call together (people) for a meeting. **2** assemble or meet together, esp. for a common purpose. **3** summon (a person) before a tribunal.

convener *noun* = CONVENOR.

convenience *noun* **1** the quality of being convenient. **2** freedom from difficulty or trouble. **3** an advantage: *your help was a great convenience*. **4** any thing, esp. an installation or device, that saves or simplifies effort. PHRASES **at your convenience** at a time or place that suits you. **at your earliest convenience** as soon as you can.

convenience store *noun* a small, conveniently located store with extended opening hours.

convenient *adjective* **1** (often foll. by *for, to*) **a** serving one's comfort, interests, or needs. **b** easily accessible. **c** suitable. **d** free of trouble or difficulty. **2** available or occurring at a suitable time or place: *will try to find a convenient moment*. **3** well situated for some purpose. ▶ **conveniently** *adverb*

convenor *noun* a person who arranges meetings of groups or committees.

convent • *noun* **1** a religious community, esp. of nuns, under vows. **2** the premises occupied by this. **3** (also **convent school**) a school attached to and run by a convent. • *adjective* of or associated with a convent.

convention *noun* **1 a** general agreement, esp. on social behaviour etc. by implicit consent of the majority: *he was an upholder of convention and correct form* ◊ *social conventions for meeting and greeting people.* **b** a custom or customary practice, esp. an artificial or formal one: *the pictorial conventions of mass-media imagery.* **2 a** a formal assembly or conference for a common purpose. **b** an assembly of the delegates of a political party to select candidates for office. **3 a** a formal agreement. **b** an agreement between nations, somewhat less formal than a treaty: *the Geneva Convention governs the status and treatment of captured and wounded military personnel and civilians in wartime.*

conventional *adjective* **1** depending on or according with convention. **2** (of a person) conforming to social conventions. **3 a** usual: *conventional office attire.* **b** traditional, normal (in opposition to recent inventions etc.): *conventional or microwave ovens.* **4** not spontaneous, sincere, or original. **5** (of weapons or power) non-nuclear. **6** *Art* following accepted models, traditions, etc. instead of directly imitating nature or working out original ideas. ▶ **conventionality** *noun* **conventionally** *adverb*

conventional wisdom *noun* a common body of accumulated opinion etc. on a certain subject.

conventioneer *noun* a person attending a convention.

converge *verb* (**converges**, **converged**, **converging**) **1 a** come together from several diverse points toward a common point: *three major expressways converge in metropolitan Halifax* ◊ *two people whose lives converge briefly from time to time.* **b** (of ideas, policies, aims, etc.) move toward a common conclusion, opinion, etc.; become more similar **2** (of lines) tend to meet at a point: *lines of longitude converge toward the poles.* **3** approach from different directions: *half a million sports fans will converge on the city.*

convergence *noun* the action, fact, or property of converging: *the convergence of lines in the distance* ◊ *a curious convergence between feminist and anti-feminist organizations on the topic of unequal pay.*

convergent *adjective* **1** coming closer together, esp. in characteristics or ideas: *convergent opinions.* **2** having to do with the tendency of unrelated animals and plants to evolve superficially similar characteristics under similar environmental conditions: *convergent evolution.*

conversant *adjective* well experienced or acquainted with a subject etc. [Say k'n VERSE int]

conversation *noun* the informal exchange of ideas by spoken word.

conversational *adjective* **1** consisting of or relating to conversation: *conversational skills.* **2** appropriate to an informal conversation: *her tone was casual and conversational.*

conversationalist *noun* a person who is fond of or excels at conversing.

converse¹ *verb* (**converses**, **conversed**, **conversing**) engage in conversation. [Say kun VERSE]

converse² • *adjective* having characteristics which are the reverse of something else already mentioned: *the converse argument should also be stressed.* • *noun* something that is opposite or contrary. *If you look at English recipes before 1603, little cream is used, whereas the converse is true in Scotland.* ▶ **conversely** *adverb* [Say CON verse, kun VERSE lee]

conversion *noun* **1 a** the act or an instance of changing one's beliefs, opinions, etc. **b** *Christianity* repentance and change to a Godly life. **2** an adaptation of a building for new purposes. **3 a** the changing of funds from one currency to another. **b** the changing of units, measurements, etc. from one system or expression to another: *conversion of miles to kilometres.* **4** alteration to a car, rifle, etc. to enhance its performance. **5 a** the physical transformation of something from one substance, state, etc. to another: *conversion of food into energy.* **b** the transformation of fertile into fissile material in a nuclear reactor. **6** *Sport* the scoring of additional points in certain sports, e.g. by a successful kick in football. **7** *Computing* **a** the adaptation of software designed for one system to another system. **b** the transfer or copying of data from one storage medium to another.

convert • *verb* **1** (usu. foll. by *into*) change in form, character, or function. **2** change or cause to change beliefs, opinions, etc. **3** change (stocks, units in which a quantity is expressed, etc.) into others of a different kind. **4** make structural alterations in (a building) so as to serve a new purpose. **5** *Football* complete (a touchdown) by kicking a goal or crossing the goal line. **6** be converted or convertible: *the sofa converts into a bed.* **7 a** adapt (software) from one system to another. **b** transfer or copy (data) from one storage medium to another. • *noun* **1** (often foll. by *to*) a person who has been converted to a different belief, opinion, etc. **2** *Cdn Football* the scoring of points after a touchdown by kicking the ball between the uprights (for one point) or by carrying or passing the ball over the defending team's goal line (for two points).

converter *noun* **1** a person or thing that converts. **2 a** an electrical apparatus for the conversion of alternating current into direct current or vice versa. **b** an apparatus for converting a signal from one frequency to another. **c** an auxiliary apparatus that allows a television or radio to pick up channels for which it was not originally designed. **3** = CATALYTIC CONVERTER.

convertibility *noun* **1** the ability to be changed into a different form. **2** the ability of currency to be converted into other forms, esp. into gold or US dollars.

convertible • *adjective* **1** that may be converted. **2** (of currency, bonds, etc.) that may be converted into other forms, esp. into gold or US dollars. **3** (of a car) having a folding or detachable roof. **4** *Cdn* designating a mortgage which may not be paid off before the stated term without a financial penalty, but which may be converted to a longer term without penalty. • *noun* **1** a car with a folding or detachable roof. **2** bonds or securities which can be readily changed to common stock.

convex *adjective* having an outline or surface curved like the exterior of a circle or sphere (compare CONCAVE). ▶ **convexly** *adverb*

convey *verb* **1** communicate (an idea, meaning, etc.). **2** transport or carry (goods, passengers, etc.). **3** *Law* transfer the title to (property).

conveyance *noun* **1 a** the act or process of carrying. **b** the communication (of ideas etc.). **c** transmission. **2** a means of transport; a vehicle. **3** *Law* **a** the transfer of property from one owner to another. **b** a document effecting this.

conveyor *noun* **1** a person or thing that conveys. **2** (also **conveyor belt**) a flexible, endless belt moving on rollers used to convey articles or materials.

convict • *verb* (often foll. by *of*) declare guilty, esp. by

the verdict of a jury or the decision of a judge. • *noun* **1** a person found guilty of a criminal offence. **2** a person serving a prison sentence.

conviction *noun* **1** a formal declaration by the verdict of a jury or the decision of a judge in a court of law that someone is guilty of a criminal offence: *has two previous convictions* ◊ *the dangerous offender provisions should be more easily usable by prosecutors at the time of conviction*. **2** a firm belief or opinion: *strong political convictions* ◊ *his conviction that it was not an accident became stronger* ◊ *his voice lacked conviction*.

convince *verb* (**convinces, convinced, convincing**) persuade (a person) to believe, realize, or agree.

convinced *adjective* firmly persuaded: *a convinced pacifist*.

convincing *adjective* **1** persuading by argument or evidence: *a convincing case*. **2 a** plausible or seeming worthy of belief: *a convincing message*. **b** leaving no margin of doubt, substantial: *a convincing victory*. ▶ **convincingly** *adverb*

convivial *adjective* **1 a** (of a person) friendly, fond of good company. **b** sociable and lively: *convivial banter*. **2** festive: *a convivial atmosphere*. ▶ **conviviality** *noun* **convivially** *adverb* [Say kun VIVVY ul, kun vivvy ALA tee]

convocation *noun* **1** a formal assembly at a university or college for graduation ceremonies. **2** a large, formal gathering of people. **3** *Cdn Law* a meeting of the elected governing officials of a provincial law society.

convoke *verb* (**convokes, convoked, convoking**) *formal* call (people) together to a meeting etc.; summon to assemble.

convoluted *adjective* **1** (of style, meaning, etc.) complicated, difficult to comprehend: *a convoluted plot*. **2** intricately folded, coiled, or twisted: *walnuts come in hard, convoluted shells*. [Say CONVA loot id]

convolution *noun* **1** a complex or confused condition or issue: *the convolutions of farm policy*. **2** a coil or twist: *adorned with elaborate convolutions*. [Say conva LOO sh'n]

convoy • *noun* a group of ships or vehicles travelling together, typically one accompanied by armed troops, warships, or other vehicles for protection. • *verb* **1** (of a warship) escort (a merchant or passenger vessel). **2** escort, esp. with armed force. PHRASES **in convoy** under escort with others; as a group.

convulse *verb* (**convulses, convulsed, convulsing**) **1** suffer violent involuntary contraction of the muscles, producing contortion of the body or limbs: *she convulsed, collapsing to the floor in pain*. **2** laugh or cause to laugh uproariously. **3** throw a country into violent social or political upheaval: *a wave of mass strikes convulsed the Ruhr, Berlin, and central Germany*.

convulsion *noun* **1** (usu. in *plural*) violent irregular motion of a limb or limbs or the body caused by involuntary contraction of muscles. **2** a violent natural disturbance, esp. an earthquake. **3** violent social or political agitation: *the convulsions of 1939–45*. **4** (in *plural*) uncontrollable laughter.

convulsive *adjective* producing or consisting of sudden, violent, and uncontrollable body movements: *a convulsive disease* ◊ *she gave a convulsive sob*. ▶ **convulsively** *adverb*

SPELL CHECK	
COO, COUP	✓ABC

A sudden overthrow of government or a successful event is a **coup**.

coo • *noun* a soft murmuring sound like that of a dove. • *verb* (**coos, cooed, cooing**) **1** make the sound of a coo. **2** talk or say in a soft or amorous voice.

cook • *verb* **1** prepare food for consumption, esp. by heating. **2** (of food) undergo cooking. **3** *informal* falsify or alter (accounts etc.): *cooked the books*. **4** *informal* **a** perform music with excitement or inspiration. **b** perform or proceed well: *things are really cooking here tonight*. **5** (as **be cooking**) *informal* be happening or about to happen: *what's cooking?* • *noun* a person who cooks, esp. professionally or in a specified way: *a good cook*. PHRASES **cook a person's goose** ruin a person's chances. **cook up** *informal* invent or concoct (a story, excuse, etc.).

cookbook *noun* a book containing recipes and other information about cooking.

cooker *noun* a container or device for cooking food.

cookery *noun* the art or practice of cooking.

cookhouse *noun* **1** a building used for cooking, esp. on a ranch, logging camp, etc. **2** a ship's galley.

cookie[1] *noun* **1** a small sweet biscuit. **2** *slang* a person: *one tough cookie*. PHRASES **toss** (or **lose**) **one's cookies** *slang* vomit. **the way the cookie crumbles** *informal* how things turn out.

cookie[2] *noun* **1** a cook, esp. in a work camp or in the military. **2** a cook's assistant in a work camp.

cookie cutter *noun* **1** a stamp for cutting cookie dough into a particular shape. **2** (as an *adjective*) denoting something mass-produced or lacking any distinguishing characteristics: *a cookie cutter mentality that eliminated individuality from domestic architecture*.

cookie jar *noun* **1** a container for cookies. **2** a reserve of good things, usu. off-limits: *caught with their hands in the cookie jar*.

cooking *noun* **1** the art or process by which food is prepared for consumption. **2** (as an *adjective*) suitable for or used in cooking: *cooking apple* ◊ *cooking utensils*.

cook-off *noun* a cooking competition in which competitors assemble to prepare their entries.

cookout *noun* a gathering with an open-air cooked meal.

cookstove *noun* an esp. wood-burning stove used for cooking.

cooktop *noun* a cooking unit consisting of burners or elements, esp. built into a countertop.

cookware *noun* utensils for cooking, esp. pans etc.

cool • *adjective* **1** of or at a fairly low temperature, moderately cold: *a cool day*. **2** suggesting or achieving coolness: *cool clothes*. **3** calm, unexcited. **4** lacking zeal or enthusiasm. **5** unfriendly. **6** *informal* **a** excellent, esp. appealing to youth. **b** (of a person, style, etc.) following the latest fashions; hip. **c** considered socially acceptable by a group (esp. youth). **7** calmly audacious: *a cool customer*. **8** (preceded by a) *informal* at least: *cost me a cool thousand*. • *noun* **1** coolness. **2** cool air; a cool place. **3** *slang* calmness, composure: *lose one's cool*. • *verb* (often foll. by *down, off*) make or become cool. PHRASES **cool as a cucumber** completely unruffled. **cool it** *informal* relax, calm down. **cool out** *informal* relax, calm down.

coolant *noun* a cooling agent, esp. fluid, to remove heat from an engine etc.

cooler *noun* **1** an insulated, usu. portable container for keeping drinks etc. cool. **2** a vessel in which a thing is cooled. **3** a mixture of wine or spirits and soda water, often with a fruit flavour. **4** *slang* prison or a prison cell.

cool-headed *adjective* not easily excited.

coolie *noun* an unskilled, low paid labourer in or from India, China, or other Asian countries.

cooling-off period *noun* an interval to allow for a change of mind before commitment to action.

coolish *adjective* somewhat cool.

coolly *adverb* **1** in a way that is not friendly, interested, or enthusiastic: *he received my suggestion coolly*. **2** in a calm manner: *she coolly sank the ten-foot putt*.

coolness *noun* the quality of being cool.

coon *noun* a raccoon.

coonskin *noun* **1** the skin of a raccoon. **2** a cap etc. made of this.

SPELL CHECK
coop, coupe ✅

A kind of car is a **coupe**.

---

coop ● *noun* **1** a cage or pen for confining poultry. **2** a small place of confinement, esp. a prison. ● *verb* **1** put or keep (a fowl) in a coop. **2** (often foll. by *up*) confine (a person) in a small space. PHRASES **fly the coop** *informal* leave abruptly.

co-op *noun informal* **1** a co-operative business or store. **2** a co-operative housing complex.

co-operate *verb* (**co-operates, co-operated, co-operating**) **1** work or act together, esp. agreeably, towards the same end. **2** assist someone or comply with their requests: *refused to co-operate with the police*.

co-operation *noun* **1** working together to the same end. **2** the formation and operation of co-operatives.

co-operative ● *adjective* **1** characterized by co-operation, esp. rather than competition: *a co-operative venture*. **2** willing to co-operate. **3** (of a farm, store, or other business, or a society owning such businesses) owned and run jointly by its members, with profits shared among them. **4** designating a type of non-profit housing where the housing complex is jointly owned by the occupants, who pay rent on their individual unit to cover costs but cannot sell their unit. ● *noun* a co-operative institution.

Co-operative Commonwealth Federation *noun hist.* (in Canada) a progressive labour party formed in 1932, refounded as the NDP in 1961.

co-operatively *adverb* in a co-operative manner.

co-operator *noun* a person who co-operates.

co-opt *verb* **1 a** absorb into a larger (esp. political) group. **b** take over, adopt: *the green parties have had most of their ideas co-opted by bigger parties*. **2** appoint to membership of a body by invitation of the existing members. ▶ **co-optation** *noun*

coordinate ● *verb* (**coordinates, coordinated, coordinating**) **1** bring (various parts, movements, activities, etc.) into a proper or required relation to ensure harmony or effective operation etc. **2** work or act together effectively. ● *adjective* **1** equal in rank or importance. **2** in which the parts are coordinated; involving coordination. **3** *Grammar* (of parts of a compound sentence) equal in rank and fulfilling identical functions. ● *noun* **1** *Math* each of a set of magnitudes used to fix the position of a point, line, or plane. **2** (often in *plural*) each of a combination of numbers or letters indicating the location of a place on a map. **3** a person or thing equal in rank or importance. **4** (in *plural*) matching items of clothing.

coordinated *adjective* **1** put together so as to ensure efficient functioning. **2** matching: *colour-coordinated*. **3** able to move various parts of the body in harmony: *Katherine's not very coordinated*.

coordinate geometry *noun* = ANALYTIC GEOMETRY.

coordinating conjunction *noun* any of a number of conjunctions (*and*, *or*, *but*, *yet*, *for*, *so*, *whereas*) which can join independent clauses.

coordination *noun* **1** the harmonious or effective working together of different parts. **2** the organization of the different elements of a complex body or activity so as to enable them to work together effectively: *both countries agreed to intensify efforts at economic policy coordination*. **3** the ability to control one's movements

properly or effectively, esp. of one part of the body in conjunction with another: *hand-eye coordination*.

coordinator *noun* a person responsible for bringing together the different elements of a complex activity or organization in a manner that will ensure efficiency or harmony: *the candidate's campaign coordinator*.

coot *noun* **1** a dark grey or black marsh bird, with the upper mandible extended backwards to form a white plate on the forehead. **2** a scoter. **3** *informal derogatory* a stupid person, esp. an elderly person.

cootie *noun slang* a body louse.

cop *informal* ● *noun* a police officer. ● *verb* (**cops, copped, copping**) **1** catch or arrest (an offender). **2** receive or attain: *she copped an award for her role in the film*. PHRASES **cop out 1** withdraw; give up an attempt. **2** go back on a promise. **cop an attitude** assume an esp. arrogant posture, attitude, etc. **cop a plea** plea bargain.

copayment *noun* a payment made by a beneficiary (esp. for health services) in addition to that made by an insurer.

cope[1] *verb* (**copes, coped, coping**) deal effectively or contend successfully with a person, task, or situation.

cope[2] *noun* a long cloaklike vestment worn by a priest or bishop in ceremonies and processions.

Copernican system *noun* (also **Copernican theory**) the theory that the planets (including the earth) move around the sun. [Say kuh PURNA kin]

copier *noun* a machine or person that copies (esp. documents).

co-pilot *noun* a second pilot in an aircraft.

coping *noun* the action of dealing with difficult circumstances: *coping mechanisms*.

copious *adjective* abundant, plentiful: *she took copious notes*. ▶ **copiously** *adverb* **copiousness** *noun* [Say COPE ee us]

copolymer *noun* a polymer with units of more than one kind. ▶ **copolymerize** *verb* [Say CO polla mer]

cop-out *noun* an act of avoiding a responsibility or commitment.

copper[1] ● *noun* **1** a malleable red-brown natural metallic element, used esp. as an electrical conductor and in alloys. **2** a copper or bronze coin, esp. a penny. ● *adjective* made of or coloured like copper.

copper[2] *noun slang* a police officer.

copperhead *noun* a venomous but rarely fatal viper, *Agkistrodon contortrix*, native to North America.

Copper Inuit *plural noun* an Inuit people living along the Coppermine River in the NWT.

coppery *adjective* of or like copper, esp. in colour.

co-produce *verb* (**co-produces, co-produced, co-producing**) produce (a play, film, broadcast, etc.) jointly with another producer. ▶ **co-producer** *noun* **co-production** *noun*

cops and robbers *noun* a children's game in which the participants stalk, chase, and pretend to shoot each other as police officers and criminals.

copse *noun* a small group of trees. [Say COPS]

Copt *noun* **1** a native Egyptian in the Hellenistic and Roman periods (from 323 BC to the 4th century AD). **2** a Christian of the Coptic Church.

copter *noun informal* a helicopter.

Coptic ● *noun* the language of the Copts, now used only in the Coptic Church. ● *adjective* of the Copts.

Coptic Church *noun* the native Christian Church of Egypt.

copulate *verb* (**copulates, copulated, copulating**) have sexual intercourse. [Say COP you late]

copulation *noun* sexual intercourse. [Say cop you LAY sh'n]

copulative *adjective* **1** *Grammar* (of a word) that connects words or clauses linked in sense: *copulative verbs like "be" and "become".* **2** relating to sexual intercourse. [Say COP you la tiv]

copy • *noun* (*plural* **copies**) **1** a thing made to imitate or be identical to another. **2** a single specimen of a publication or issue. **3 a** matter to be printed. **b** material for a newspaper or magazine article: *scandals make good copy.* **c** the text of an advertisement. **4** a model to be copied. • *verb* (**copies, copied, copying**) **1** make a copy of. **2** (foll. by *to*) send a copy of (a letter) to a third party. **3** do the same as; imitate.

copycat *noun informal* a person who copies another, esp. slavishly: *copycat remark.*

copy-edit *verb* (**copy-edits, copy-edited, copy-editing**) edit (copy) for printing.

copy editor *noun* a person who edits copy, esp. to correct grammatical, stylistic, or punctuation errors.

copyist *noun* **1** a person who makes (esp. written) copies. **2** an imitator.

copyright • *noun* the exclusive legal right granted for a specified period to an author, designer, etc., or another appointed person, to print, publish, perform, film, or record original literary, artistic, or musical material. • *adjective* (of such material) protected by copyright. • *verb* secure copyright for (material).

copywriter *noun* a person who writes or prepares copy (esp. of advertising material) for publication. ▶**copywriting** *noun*

coquette *noun* a woman who flirts. ▶**coquettish** *adjective* **coquettishly** *adverb* [Say co KET]

coral • *noun* **1 a** a hard stony substance secreted by various marine creatures as an external skeleton, typically forming large reefs in warm seas. **b** any of these usu. colonial organisms. **2** a reddish-pink colour. **3** the unfertilized roe of a lobster or scallop, which is used as food and becomes reddish when cooked. • *adjective* **1** of a reddish-pink colour. **2** made of coral.

SPELL CHECK
cord, chord   ABC ✓

Chord is the spelling for notes played or sung together or for a line joining two points of a circle.

---

cord • *noun* **1** long thin flexible material made from several twisted strands, esp. thicker than string and finer than rope. **2** a structure in the body resembling a cord: *spinal cord.* **3 a** a ribbed fabric, esp. corduroy. **b** (in *plural*) corduroy pants. **c** a cord-like rib on fabric. **4** an insulated electric cable bringing power to appliances etc. **5** a measure of cut wood (usu. 128 cu. ft., 3.6 cubic metres). • *verb* fasten or bind with cord.

corded *adjective* **1** (of cloth) ribbed. **2** provided with cords. **3** (of muscles) standing out like taut cords.

cordgrass *noun* a grass growing in wet and marshy ground.

cordial • *adjective* **1** heartfelt. **2** friendly. • *noun* **1** a fruit-flavoured drink. **2** a comforting or pleasant-tasting medicine. ▶**cordiality** *noun* **cordially** *adverb* [Say CORE jul or CORDY ul, cordy ALA tee]

cordillera *noun* a system or group of usu. parallel mountain ranges together with intervening plateaux etc., esp. as a major continental feature. ▶**cordilleran** *adjective* [Say kor DILL ER uh or cordil YAIR uh]

cordless *adjective* (of an electrical appliance, telephone, etc.) working from an internal source of energy etc. (esp. a rechargeable battery).

cordon • *noun* **1** a line or circle of police, soldiers, guards, etc., esp. preventing access to or from an area. **2** an ornamental cord or braid. • *verb* (often foll. by *off*) enclose or separate with a rope, police, etc.

cordon bleu *Cooking* • *adjective* **1** of the highest class: *a cordon bleu chef.* **2** designating a type of chicken or veal dish consisting of a cutlet of meat stuffed with ham and Swiss cheese, breaded and shallow fried. • *noun* a cordon bleu cook. [Say cor don BLOO (with OO as in *LOOK*)]

corduroy *noun* **1** a thick cotton fabric with velvety ribs. **2** (in *plural*) corduroy pants.

corduroy road *noun* esp. *hist.* a road made of tree trunks laid across muddy or swampy ground.

cordwood *noun* wood that is or can be measured in cords.

SPELL CHECK
core, corps   ABC ✓

A group of people is a **corps**: *army corps; press corps; danced in the corps.*

---

core • *noun* **1** the hard central part of various fruits, containing the seeds. **2** the central or most important part of anything: *core curriculum.* **3** the central part of the earth, esp. that within the mantle, with a radius of 3 500 km (2,200 miles). **4** (also **core lanes**) *Cdn* the express lanes on a highway, usu. separated from the collector lanes. **5** the central part of a nuclear reactor, containing the fissile material. **6** the inner strand of an electric cable, rope, etc. **7** a piece of soft iron forming the centre of an electromagnet etc. **8** an internal mould filling a space to be left hollow in a casting. **9** the central part cut out (esp. of rock etc. in boring). • *verb* (**cores, cored, coring**) remove the core from.

coreopsis *noun* (*plural* **coreopsis**) a plant of the daisy family having rayed usu. yellow flowers. [Say cory OP sis]

corer *noun* a device used to remove a core from an apple, a rock, the sea floor, etc.

corgi *noun* (*plural* **corgis**) (also **Welsh corgi**) a short-legged dog with a foxlike head. [Say COR ghee]

coriander *noun* **1** a plant, *Coriandrum sativum*, with leaves used for flavouring and small round aromatic fruits. **2** (also **coriander seed**) the dried fruit used for flavouring curries etc. [Say CORY ander]

Corinthian • *adjective* **1** of ancient Corinth in S Greece. **2** *Architecture* of an order characterized by ornate decoration and flared capitals with rows of spiny leaves. • *noun* a native of Corinth. [Say kuh RINTH ee in]

Coriolis effect *noun* a hypothetical force used to explain rotating systems, such that the movement of air or water over the surface of the rotating earth is directed clockwise in the northern hemisphere and counter-clockwise in the southern hemisphere. [Say korry OH liss]

cork • *noun* **1** the buoyant light brown bark of the cork oak. **2** a bottle stopper of cork or other material. **3** a float of cork used in fishing etc. **4** *Botany* a protective layer of dead cells immediately below the bark of woody plants. **5** (as an *adjective*) made of cork. • *verb* **1** close with a cork. **2** *Baseball* hollow out and fill (a bat) with cork illicitly to make it lighter. **3** blacken with burnt cork. PHRASES **put a cork in it** *slang* be quiet.

corkboard *noun* **1** board made of compressed cork. **2** a piece of this for posting bulletins etc.

cork boot *noun Cdn* (*BC*) a logger's boot with spiked soles.

corked *adjective* **1** stopped with a cork. **2** (of wine) spoiled by a decayed cork. **3** blackened with burnt cork.

corker *noun informal* **1** an excellent or astonishing person or thing. **2** something that puts an end to a discussion etc.

corking *adjective informal* strikingly impressive or excellent.

corkscrew • *noun* **1** a spirally twisted steel device for extracting corks from bottles. **2** a thing with a spiral

shape: *corkscrew curls*. • *verb* move or twist in a spiral motion: *the plane was corkscrewing out of control*.

corky *adjective* (**corkier, corkiest**) **1** resembling cork. **2** (of wine) spoiled by a decayed cork.

corm *noun* an underground swollen stem base of some plants, e.g. gladiolus and iris.

cormorant *noun* a diving, fish-eating water bird with shiny black plumage. [Say CORMER unt]

corn[1] *noun* **1 a** a cereal plant yielding large, edible, usu. yellow grains set in rows on a cob. **b** the cob or grains of this. **2 a** any cereal before or after harvesting, esp. the chief crop of a region. **b** a grain or seed of a cereal plant. **3** *informal* something corny or trite.

corn[2] *noun* a small painful area of thickened skin on the foot, esp. on the toes, caused by pressure.

cornball *adjective* = CORNY 1.

cornbread *noun* bread, esp. a quick bread, made from cornmeal.

corncob *noun* the cylindrical centre of an ear of corn, to which rows of grains are attached.

cornea *noun* (*plural* **corneas**) the transparent circular part of the front of the eyeball. ▸ **corneal** *adjective* [Say CORNY uh]

corn earworm *noun* **1** a moth, *Heliothis armigera* or *H. zea*, whose larvae are a pest of cultivated plants, esp. of corn in North America. **2** a larva of this moth.

corned beef *noun* **1** beef brisket cured in brine and boiled. **2** low quality beef preserved in brine and saltpetre, chopped and pressed and packaged in tins.

corner • *noun* **1** a place where converging sides or edges meet. **2** a projecting angle, esp. where two streets meet. **3** the internal space or recess formed by the meeting of two sides, esp. of a room. **4** a difficult position, esp. one from which there is no escape: *driven into a corner*. **5** a secluded or remote place. **6** a region or quarter, esp. a remote one: *from the four corners of the earth*. **7** the action or result of buying or controlling the whole available stock of a commodity, thereby dominating the market. **8** *Boxing & Wrestling* **a** an angle of the ring, esp. one where a contestant rests between rounds. **b** a contestant's supporters offering assistance at the corner between rounds. • *verb* **1** force (a person or animal) into a difficult or inescapable position. **2 a** establish a corner in (a commodity). **b** dominate (dealers or the market) in this way. **3** (esp. of or in a vehicle) go around a corner. ▸PHRASES◂ **in a person's corner** supporting a person. **just around the corner** *informal* very near, imminent. **turn a** (or **the**) **corner** pass from one situation to another, particularly making a decisive change for the better.

cornerback *noun* *Football* a defensive player or position covering the sideline behind the line of scrimmage.

cornerstone *noun* **1 a** a stone that forms the base of a corner of a building, joining two walls. **b** a foundation stone. **2** an important quality or feature on which a particular thing depends or is based: *habitat protection must be the cornerstone of any endangered species legislation*.

SPELL CHECK　　　　　　　　　ABC ✔
cornet, coronet

A small crown is a **coronet**.

---

cornet *noun* **1** a brass instrument resembling a trumpet but shorter and wider. **2** its player. ▸ **cornetist** *noun*

cornflower *noun* a plant with daisy-like deep-blue flowers: *he has cornflower blue eyes*.

cornice *noun* **1** a moulding around the wall of a room

---

just below the ceiling. **2** a horizontal moulded projection crowning a building or structure. [Say COR niss]

corniness *noun* the quality of something that is unoriginal, trite, dated, or mawkishly sentimental.

Cornish • *adjective* of or relating to Cornwall in southwestern England. • *noun* the ancient Celtic language of Cornwall.

Cornish hen *noun* a compact, meaty chicken slaughtered at six weeks to provide a single-serving sized bird, usu. roasted.

cornmeal *noun* a coarse powder made by grinding corn: *cornmeal muffins*.

corn on the cob *noun* corn cooked and eaten from the corncob.

corn roast *noun* a party at which corn on the cob is cooked and eaten.

cornrow *noun* (usu. in *plural*) each of a series of small tight braids made close to the head.

cornsilk *noun* the threadlike styles on an ear of corn.

cornstalk *noun* the stalk of a corn plant.

cornstarch *noun* purified starch from corn, used as a thickener and as an absorbent powder.

corn syrup *noun* glucose syrup, esp. when made from corn flour.

cornucopia *noun* (*plural* **cornucopias**) **1 a** a symbol of plenty consisting of a goat's horn overflowing with flowers, fruit, and grain. **b** an ornamental vessel shaped like this. **2** an abundant supply: *in the post-war years a cornucopia of benefits was showered on the public*. [Say corn yuh COPEY uh]

corny *adjective* (**cornier, corniest**) **1** *informal* **a** trite. **b** feebly humorous. **c** sentimental. **d** old-fashioned; out of date. **2** of or abounding in corn.

corolla *noun* (*plural* **corollas**) the petals of a flower, typically forming a whorl within the sepals and enclosing the reproductive organs. [Say kuh RAWL uh or kuh ROLE uh]

corollary *noun* (*plural* **corollaries**) a situation, an argument, or a fact that is the natural and direct result of another: *the huge increases in unemployment were the corollary of budget cuts*. [Say kuh RAWL uh ree]

corona *noun* (*plural* **coronae** or **coronas**) **1 a** a small circle of light round the sun or moon. **b** the rarefied gaseous envelope of the sun, seen as an irregularly shaped area of light around the moon's disc during a total solar eclipse. **2** *Botany* a crownlike outgrowth from the inner side of a corolla. [Say kuh ROE nuh for the singular; for CORONAE say kuh ROE nee]

coronary • *adjective* of or relating to the heart or coronary arteries. • *noun* (*plural* **coronaries**) (also **coronary thrombosis**, *plural* **coronary thromboses**) a blockage of blood flow to the heart caused by a blood clot in a coronary artery. [Say CORA nerry]

coronary artery *noun* (*plural* **coronary arteries**) either of two arteries supplying blood to the heart.

coronary bypass *noun* (*plural* **coronary bypasses**) a surgical procedure to relieve obstruction of the coronary arteries by creating an additional channel connecting the aorta to a point beyond the obstruction.

coronation *noun* the act or ceremony of crowning a sovereign or a sovereign's consort.

coroner *noun* a public official responsible for investigating violent, suspicious, or accidental deaths, and certifying deaths occurring outside hospital

---

SPELL CHECK　　　　　　　　　ABC ✔
cornet, cornet

The instrument like a trumpet is a **cornet**.

---

coronet *noun* **1** a small crown (esp. as worn, or used as

a heraldic device, by a peer or peeress). **2** a circlet of precious materials, esp. as a woman's headdress or part of one. ▶ **coroneted** *adjective*

Corp. *abbreviation* **1** Corporation. **2** Corporal.

corporal¹ *noun* **1 a** (in the Canadian army and air force) a non-commissioned officer ranking above private and below master corporal. **b** (in the UK and *hist.* in Canada) a non-commissioned army or air force officer ranking next below sergeant. **2** (in some police forces) a police officer ranking below sergeant.

corporal² *adjective* of or relating to the human body.

corporal punishment *noun* punishment inflicted on the body, esp. by beating.

corporate *adjective* **1** of or relating to business corporations: *the company is working on a new corporate identity ◊ corporate sponsorship of the arts.* **2** (of a large company or group) authorized to act as a single entity and recognized as such in law: *corporate body.* **3** of or shared by all the members of a group: *the service emphasizes the corporate responsibility of the congregation.* ▶ **corporately** *adverb*

corporate raider *noun* a person who mounts an unwelcome takeover bid by buying up a company's shares on the stock market, esp. one who makes a practice of doing so.

corporation *noun* **1** a group of people authorized to act as an individual and recognized in law as a single entity, esp. in business. **2** the legal entity which carries on the business of a municipality.

corporatism *noun* a political ideology or system, esp. associated with fascist states, in which business, industry, labour, etc. are organized as corporate entities. ▶ **corporatist** *adjective*

SPELL CHECK   ⌨ABC
corps, corpse

A dead body is a **corpse**.
---

corps *noun* (*plural* **corps**) **1** *Military* **a** a body of troops with special duties: *intelligence corps.* **b** a main subdivision of an army in the field, consisting of two or more divisions. **2** a body of people engaged in a special activity: *press corps.* **3** = CORPS DE BALLET. [The singular sounds like *CORE*; for the plural say *CORZ*]

corps de ballet *noun* the group of dancers of the lowest rank in a ballet company. [Say cor duh bal LAY]

corpse *noun* a dead (usu. human) body.

corpulence *noun* the quality of being fat; obesity. [Say CORP you lince]

corpulent *adjective* fat. [Say CORP you lint]

Corpus Christi *noun* *Christianity* a feast commemorating the Eucharist, observed the second Thursday after Pentecost, or on the following Sunday. [Say corp us KRISS tee]

corpuscle *noun* a minute body or cell in an organism, esp. (in *plural*) the red or white cells in the blood of vertebrates. ▶ **corpuscular** *adjective* [Say CORE pussle, cor PUS kyoo lur]

SPELL CHECK   ⌨ABC
corral, chorale

A stately and simple hymn tune is a **chorale**.
---

corral • *noun* **1** a pen for horses etc. **2** a trap for capturing wild animals or fish. • *verb* (**corrals, corralled, corralling**) **1** drive or keep in or as in a corral: *he corralled us into the living room.* **2** *informal* capture; get: *corralled some new members for the team.* [Say kuh RAL]

correct • *adjective* **1** true, right, accurate. **2** (of conduct etc.) proper, right. **3** in accordance with good

standards of taste etc. • *verb* **1** set right; amend (an error, omission, etc., or the person responsible for it). **2** mark the errors in (written or printed work etc.). **3** substitute the right thing for (the wrong one). **4 a** admonish or rebuke (a person). **b** punish (a person or fault). **5** counteract (a harmful quality, ailment, etc.). **6** adjust (an instrument etc.) to function accurately or accord with a standard. **7** (of stock prices) stabilize, esp. after a sharp decline or increase. PHRASES **correct for** adjust or recalculate (statistical data etc.) to compensate for a deviant factor. ▶ **correctable** *adjective*

correction *noun* **1** the act or process of correcting: *send it back for correction.* **2** a change that rectifies an error or inaccuracy: *I've made a few small corrections ◊ the paper got the thief's name wrong and published a correction.* **3** (usu. **corrections**) **a** the treatment of convicted offenders through incarceration, parole, etc. **b** the administrative system which oversees such treatment.

correctional *adjective* **1** of or pertaining to the corrections system: *correctional facility.* **2** of or pertaining to correction.

correction line *noun* *Cdn* (*Prairies*) *Surveying* **1** one of a set of parallel lines of latitude 24 miles apart along which correction is made for the discrepancy between straight surveying lines and northward-converging meridians. **2** a jog in a road where it intersects one of these lines.

corrective • *adjective* serving or tending to correct or counteract something undesired or harmful: *the manager was informed so that corrective action could be taken.* • *noun* (usu. foll. by *to*) something, e.g. a theory or a practice, that corrects or counteracts a tendency viewed as harmful: *the move might be a useful corrective to some inefficient practices within hospitals.*

correctly *adverb* in the most accurate or appropriate manner.

correctness *noun* **1** the quality of being appropriate, proper, or in accordance with accepted rules or standards: *moral correctness ◊ political correctness.* **2** the quality of being right or accurate.

corrector *noun* a device used to correct something.

correlate • *verb* (**correlates, correlated, correlating**) **1** have a mutual relationship or connection, in which one thing affects or depends on another: *the study found that success in the educational system correlates highly with socio-economic background.* **2** (usu. foll. by *with*) bring into a mutual relation; establish the likely relation between: *we should correlate general trends in public opinion with trends in the content of TV news.* • *noun* each of two related or complementary things (esp. so related that one implies the other): *social segregation is one of the most reliable correlates of suicide.* [Say CORA late for the verb, CORA lit for the noun]

correlation *noun* **1** a mutual relation between two or more things: *a correlation between smoking and cancer.* **2** the act or process of correlating. **3** *Statistics* **a** interdependence of variable quantities. **b** a quantity measuring the extent of this.

correlative • *adjective* **1** (often foll. by *with, to*) having a mutual relation; corresponding. **2** *Grammar* (of words) corresponding to each other and regularly used together: *"neither" and "nor", "either" and "or" are correlative conjunctions.* • *noun* a correlative word or thing. [Say kuh RELATIVE]

correspond *verb* **1 a** be analogous or similar. **b** match; agree in amount, position, etc.: *my tally corresponds with yours.* **c** be in harmony or agreement. **2** communicate by interchange of letters.

correspondence *noun* **1** similarity or harmony.

2 a communication by letters. **b** letters sent or received.

correspondence course *noun* a course of study conducted by mail.

correspondent *noun* **1** a person employed to contribute material for publication in a periodical or for broadcasting: *a CBC correspondent*. **2** a person who writes letters to a person or newspaper, esp. regularly. **3** a person or firm having regular business relations with another, esp. in another country.

corresponding *adjective* **1** identical; equivalent: *of corresponding height*. **2** analogous in position, purpose, etc. **3** belonging together as a unit: *a skirt with its corresponding jacket*. **4** handling correspondence: *corresponding secretary*. ▶ **correspondingly** *adverb*

corridor *noun* **1** a passage from which doors lead into rooms. **2** a passage in a railway car from which doors lead into compartments. **3** a densely populated belt of land with major overland and air transportation routes: *the Quebec-Windsor corridor*. **4 a** a strip of territory that runs through that of another state and secures access to the sea or some desired part. **b** a right-of-way reserved for utilities: *hydro corridor*. **5** a route to which aircraft are restricted, esp. over a foreign country. **6** an extent of land characterized by a specific activity, e.g. wildlife migration.

corridors of power *plural noun* the upper echelons of government, business, etc., where power and influence are considered to reside.

corroborate *verb* (**corroborates, corroborated, corroborating**) confirm or give support to (a statement or belief, or the person holding it), esp. in relation to witnesses in a law court. ▶ **corroboration** *noun* **corroborative** *adjective* [Say kuh ROBBA rate]

corrode *verb* (**corrodes, corroded, corroding**) **1 a** wear away, esp. by chemical action. **b** be worn away; decay. **2** destroy gradually: *corroded his self-esteem*. ▶ **corroded** *adjective*

corrosion *noun* **1** the process of corroding, esp. of a rusting metal. **2** damage caused by corroding.

corrosive • *adjective* **1** tending to corrode or consume. **2** destructive; wearing: *the corrosive effects of famine*. • *noun* a corrosive substance. ▶ **corrosively** *adverb* **corrosiveness** *noun*

corrugated *adjective* formed into alternate ridges and grooves, esp. to strengthen: *corrugated cardboard*. [Say CORA gated]

corrupt • *adjective* **1** influenced by or using bribery or fraudulent activity. **2** morally depraved; wicked. **3** (of a text, language, etc.) harmed (esp. made suspect or unreliable) by errors or alterations. **4** (of a computer disk or program) contaminated with errors; not usable. • *verb* **1** make or become corrupt or depraved. **2** affect or harm by errors or alterations. ▶ **corrupter** *noun* **corruptible** *adjective*

corruption *noun* **1** use of corrupt practices, esp. bribery or fraud. **2** moral deterioration, esp. widespread. **3 a** irregular alteration (of a text, language, etc.) from its original state. **b** an irregularly altered form of a word. **4** decomposition.

corruptly *adverb* in a dishonest or immoral manner.

corsage *noun* an arrangement of flowers worn by a woman at the front of a dress below the shoulder, or at the waist or wrist. [Say core SAWZH]

corset *noun* **1** a closely-fitting undergarment worn by women to shape and support the torso. **2** a similar garment worn by men and women because of injury, weakness, or deformity. ▶ **corseted** *adjective*

Corsican • *adjective* of or relating to Corsica, an island off the west coast of Italy, forming an administrative

region of France. • *noun* **1** a native of Corsica. **2** the Italian dialect of Corsica.

cortège *noun* **1** a procession, esp. for a funeral. **2** a person's entourage. [Say core TEZH]

cortex *noun* (*plural* **cortices**) **1** the outer part of an organ, esp. of the brain (**cerebral cortex**) or kidneys (**renal cortex**). **2** *Botany* **a** an outer layer of tissue immediately below the epidermis. **b** bark. ▶ **cortical** *adjective* [Say CORE tex, CORTA seez, CORE tickle]

corticosteroid *noun* (also **corticoid**) **1** any of a group of steroid hormones produced in the adrenal cortex and concerned with regulation of salts and carbohydrates, inflammation, and sexual physiology. **2** an analogous synthetic steroid. [Say corta co STEROID]

cortisone *noun* a steroid hormone produced by the adrenal cortex or synthetically, used medicinally esp. against inflammation and allergy. [Say CORTA zone]

Cortland *noun* a red variety of apple.

corundum *noun* extremely hard crystallized alumina, used esp. as an abrasive, and varieties of which, e.g. ruby, are gemstones. [Say kuh RUN dum]

corvée *noun* *hist.* **1** a day's work of unpaid labour due to a feudal lord from a vassal. **2** labour enforced by statute, esp. on road maintenance etc. [Say CORE vay]

corvette *noun* a small naval escort vessel.

Cosa Nostra *noun* a US criminal organization resembling and related to the Mafia. [Say cozza NOSTRA]

co-sign *verb* sign (a document, esp. a cheque, lease, etc.) jointly with another. ▶ **co-signer** *noun*

cosine *noun* *Math* the ratio of the side adjacent to an acute angle (in a right-angled triangle) to the hypotenuse. [Say CO sine]

cosmetic • *adjective* **1** intended to adorn or beautify the body, esp. the face. **2** intended to improve only appearances: *a cosmetic change*. **3** (of surgery) aimed at improving, restoring, or modifying the appearance. • *noun* (often in *plural*) a cosmetic preparation, esp. for the face. ▶ **cosmetically** *adverb*

cosmic *adjective* **1** of or connected with the whole universe or cosmos, esp. as distinct from the earth. **2** of or for space travel. **3** immeasurably vast: *this was disaster on a cosmic scale*. ▶ **cosmically** *adverb*

cosmic dust *noun* small particles of matter distributed throughout space.

cosmic rays *plural noun* (also **cosmic radiation** *noun*) radiation from outer space that reaches the earth from all directions, usu. with high energy and penetrative power.

cosmogony *noun* (*plural* **cosmogonies**) **1** a theory or account of the origin of the universe: *in their cosmogony, the world was thought to be a square, flat surface*. **2** the branch of science that deals with the origin of the universe. [Say koz MOGGA nee]

cosmological *adjective* based on or having to do with the scientific study of the origin and development of the universe. [Say cosma LOGICAL]

cosmologist *noun* a scientist who studies cosmology. [Say coz MOLLA jist]

cosmology *noun* (*plural* **cosmologies**) **1** the study of the origin and development of the universe. **2** an account or theory of the origin of the universe. [Say koz MOLLA jee]

cosmonaut *noun* a Russian or *hist.* Soviet astronaut.

cosmopolitan • *adjective* **1 a** familiar with and at ease in many different countries and cultures: *her knowledge of languages made her very cosmopolitan*. **b** consisting of people from many or all parts: *Toronto is a very cosmopolitan city*. **2 a** free from national limitations or prejudices. **b** sophisticated; worldly. **c** having an exciting and glamorous character associated with travel and a mixture of cultures: *their*

designs became a byword for cosmopolitan chic. **3** Ecology (of a plant, animal, etc.) widely distributed. • *noun* a cosmopolitan person. ▶**cosmopolitanism** noun [Say cozma POLLA tin]

cosmos[1] *noun* (plural **cosmoses**) **1** the universe, esp. as a well-ordered whole: *humanity's place in the cosmos*. **2** an ordered system of ideas etc.: *the new gender-free intellectual cosmos*.

cosmos[2] *noun* (plural **cosmos**) a plant bearing single daisy-like blossoms of various colours, esp. pale and deep pink and white, frequently grown in gardens.

Cossack • *noun* **1** a member of a people living on the northern shores of the Black and Caspian seas, originally famous for their military skill. **2** a member of a Cossack military unit. • *adjective* of, relating to, or characteristic of the Cossacks.

cosset *verb* (**cossets, cosseted, cosseting**) care for and protect in an overindulgent way: *they are members of a cosseted, privileged class*. [Say KOSS it]

cost • *verb* (**costs, cost, costing**) **1** have as a price. **2 a** involve as a loss or sacrifice: *it cost him his life*. **b** necessitate or involve the expenditure of (time, trouble, etc.). **3** (past and past participle **costed**) fix or estimate the cost or price of. **4** informal be costly: *that ring will cost you*. • *noun* **1** what a thing costs. **2** a loss or sacrifice; an expenditure of time, effort, etc. **3** (in plural) **a** expenses for running a home or business: *cutting costs*. **b** legal expenses, esp. those allowed in favour of the winning party or against the losing party in a suit. PHRASES **at all costs** (or **at any cost**) no matter what the cost or risk may be. **at cost** at the initial cost; at cost price. **at the cost of** at the expense of losing or sacrificing. **cost a person dear** (or **dearly**) involve a person in a high cost or a heavy penalty. **to a person's cost** with loss or disadvantage to a person.

co-star • *noun* **1** a film, television, or stage star appearing with another or other stars of equal importance. **2** a film, television, or stage star whose status in a production is slightly below that of a star. • *verb* (**co-stars, co-starred, co-starring**) **1** take part as a co-star. **2** (of a production) include as a co-star.

Costa Rican • *adjective* of or relating to Costa Rica, a republic in Central America, or its people. • *noun* a native or inhabitant of Costa Rica. [Say costa REEK'n]

cost-benefit *adjective* assessing the relation between the cost of an operation and the value of the resulting benefits: *cost-benefit analysis*.

cost-effective *adjective* effective or productive in relation to its cost. ▶**cost-effectively** *adverb* **cost-effectiveness** *noun*

costing *noun* (often in plural) **1** the determination of the cost of producing or undertaking something. **2** the cost so arrived at.

costliness *noun* the quality of something that is costly or expensive.

costly *adjective* (**costlier, costliest**) **1** costing much; expensive. **2** involving great loss or sacrifice: *a costly mistake*. **3** of great value.

cost of living *noun* the level of prices esp. of the basic necessities of life.

cost price *noun* the price paid for a thing by a person who later sells it.

costume • *noun* **1** a style or fashion of dress, esp. that of a particular place, time, nationality, or class. **2** an ensemble of unusual or period clothes worn at Halloween etc. **3** clothing for a particular activity: *riding costume*. **4** a theatrical performer's clothes for a part. • *verb* (**costumes, costumed, costuming**) provide with a costume. ▶**costuming** *noun*

costume jewellery *noun* relatively inexpensive jewellery made of metal, wood, plastic, etc., often set with artificial or semi-precious stones.

cosy *adjective* = COZY.

cot *noun* a small folding or portable bed.

cotangent *noun* Math the ratio of the side adjacent to an acute angle (in a right-angled triangle) to the opposite side. [Say CO tangent]

coterie *noun* a group of people who associate closely: *he was followed around by a coterie of fans*. [Say CO tur ee]

cotoneaster *noun* any shrub of the genus *Cotoneaster*, bearing usu. bright red berries. [Say kuh tony ASTER]

cottage • *noun* **1** a dwelling used for vacation purposes, usu. located in a rural area near a lake or river. **2** Cdn (Que.) a small, two-storey house in the city. **3** a small simple house, typically one in the country or used by workers on a farm. • *verb* (**cottages, cottaged, cottaging**) vacation at a cottage.

cottage cheese *noun* soft white cheese made from skimmed milk curds.

cottage hospital *noun* Cdn (Nfld) a small hospital with non-specialist medical services.

cottage industry *noun* (plural **cottage industries**) a business activity partly or wholly carried on at home.

cottager *noun* a person vacationing at or living in a cottage.

cottage roll *noun* Cdn a pickled, boneless, prepared ham from the pork butt.

cottaging *noun* the spending of time at a cottage.

cotter *noun* **1** a bolt or wedge for securing parts of machinery etc. **2** (also **cotter pin**) a split pin that opens after passing through a hole.

cotton • *noun* **1** a soft white fibrous substance covering the seeds of certain plants. **2 a** (also **cotton plant**) such a plant. **b** cotton plants cultivated as a crop. **3** thread or cloth made from the fibre. • *verb* informal take a liking to (a person): *Maritimers have never exactly cottoned to people from away*. PHRASES **cotton on** (often foll. by to) informal begin to understand.

cotton batting *noun* (Cdn also **cotton batten**) fluffy cotton wadding used for crafts, first aid, etc.

cotton candy *noun* candy floss.

cotton gin *noun* a machine for separating cotton from its seeds.

cotton grass *noun* a sedge of the genus *Eriophorum*, with fruiting heads of long white cottony hairs.

cotton-pickin' *adjective* (also **cotton-picking**) esp. US slang damned: *get your cotton-pickin' hands off me!*

cottontail *noun* a rabbit of the North American genus *Sylvilagus*, most species of which have a white fluffy underside to the tail.

cottonwood *noun* any of several poplars, native to North America, having seeds covered in white cottony hairs.

cottony *adjective* resembling cotton in feel or appearance: *cottony clouds ◊ cottony softness*.

cotyledon *noun* an embryonic leaf in seed-bearing plants. [Say cotta LEED'n]

couch[1] • *noun* (plural **couches**) **1** an upholstered piece of furniture for several people; a sofa. **2** a long padded seat with a headrest at one end, esp. one on which a psychiatrist's or doctor's patient reclines during examination. • *verb* (**couches, couched, couching**) **1** express in words of a specified kind: *couched in simple language*. **2** cause (an animal) to lie down.

couch[2] *noun* (also **couch grass**) any of several grasses having long creeping roots.

couch potato *noun* (plural **couch potatoes**) slang a person who spends much time watching television.

cougar *noun* a moderately large wild cat with a golden

or greyish coat and long black-tipped tail, found in parts of North and South America.

cough • *verb* **1** expel air from the lungs with a sudden sharp sound produced by abrupt opening of the glottis, to remove an obstruction or congestion. **2** (of an engine, gun, etc.) make a similar sound. • *noun* **1** an act of coughing. **2** a condition of the respiratory organs causing coughing. **3** a tendency to cough. PHRASES **cough up** (also **cough out**) **1** eject by coughing. **2** *slang* bring out or hand over (money or information) reluctantly. **3** *slang* yield or eject: *cough up the puck*. ▶ **cougher** *noun*

could *auxiliary verb* (3rd. singular **could**) *past of* CAN[1], used esp.: **1 a** in reported speech: *she said she could come*. **b** to express the conditional mood: *he could have been on time if he had left earlier*. **2** to express a question or polite request: *could you please come?* **3** to express probability: *that could be right*. **4** to ask permission: *could I leave?* **5** to offer a suggestion, advice, etc.: *you could try looking it up*. **6** to express habitual action: *when I was a child, I could not play hockey*.

couldn't *contraction* could not.

coulee *noun* a deep ravine with steep sides, formed by heavy rain or melting snow. [Say COOLY]

coulis *noun* (*plural* **coulis**) a purée of fruit, tomatoes, etc., thin enough to pour. [Say COOLY]

coulomb *noun* the SI unit of electric charge, equal to the quantity of electricity conveyed in one second by a current of one ampere. Symbol: **C**. [Say COO lom]

---

council *noun* **1 a** an advisory, deliberative, or administrative body of people formally constituted and meeting regularly. **b** a meeting of such a body. **2** the elected administrative body of a municipality. **3** a body of persons chosen as advisers: *Privy Council*. **4** an ecclesiastical assembly.

---

councillor *noun* **1** esp. *Cdn & Brit.* an elected member of a municipal council. **2** a member of a council. **3** *Cdn hist.* (in PEI) one of the two representatives elected to the Legislative Assembly in each riding (*compare* ASSEMBLYMAN 2). ▶ **councillorship** *noun*

---

counsel • *noun* **1** advice, esp. formally given. **2** consultation, esp. to seek or give advice. **3** (*plural* **counsel**) a lawyer; a body of these advising in a case. **4** a plan of action. • *verb* (**counsels, counselled, counselling**) **1** advise (a person): *I counselled her to go*. **2 a** give advice to (a person) on social or personal problems, esp. professionally. **b** assist or guide (a person) in resolving personal difficulties. PHRASES **keep one's own counsel** not confide in others.

counselling *noun* **1** the act or process of giving counsel. **2** the process of assisting and guiding clients, esp. by a trained person on a professional basis, to resolve esp. personal, social, or psychological problems and difficulties (*compare* COUNSEL *verb* 2a).

---

counsellor *noun* (also **counselor**) **1** a person who gives counsel; an adviser. **2** a person trained to give guidance on personal, social, or psychological problems: *marriage counsellor*. **3** any of the supervisors of a children's camp.

count[1] • *verb* **1** determine the total number or amount of. **2** repeat numbers in ascending order; conduct a reckoning. **3** include or be included: *you can count me in*. **4** consider (a person or thing) to be (lucky etc.): *count yourself lucky*. **5** have value; matter: *that try doesn't count*. **6** depend or rely on: *I'm counting on you*. • *noun* **1 a** the act of counting; a reckoning: *after a count of fifty*. **b** the sum total of a reckoning: *pollen count*. **2** *Law* each charge in an indictment: *guilty on ten counts*. **3** a count of up to ten seconds by a referee when a boxer is knocked down. **4** the act of counting the votes after an election. **5** one of several points under discussion: *you're wrong on three counts*. **6** *Baseball* the number of balls and strikes called against a batter during a single at-bat. PHRASES **count against** be reckoned to the disadvantage of. **count one's blessings** be grateful for what one has. **count one's chickens (before they're hatched)** be over-optimistic or hasty in anticipating good fortune. **count the cost 1** consider the risks before taking action. **2** suffer the consequences of a careless or foolish action. **count the days** (or **hours** etc.) be impatient. **count down** recite numbers backwards to zero, esp. as part of a rocket-launching procedure. **count on** (or **upon**) **1** depend on, rely on; expect confidently. **2** make allowance for. **count on (the fingers of) one hand** reckon as no more than five. **count out 1** count while taking from a stock. **2** complete a count of ten seconds over (a fallen boxer etc.), indicating defeat. **3** (in children's games) select (a player) for dismissal or a special role by use of a counting rhyme etc. **4** *informal* exclude from a plan or reckoning: *count me out*. **count sheep** imagine sheep jumping over a fence and count them, to combat insomnia. **count up** find the sum of. **down** (or **out**) **for the count 1** *Boxing* defeated by being unable to rise within ten seconds. **2** *informal* **a** defeated or demoralized. **b** soundly asleep. **keep count** take note of how many there have been etc. **lose count** fail to take note of the number etc. **not counting** excluding from the reckoning. **stand up and be counted** state publicly one's support.

count[2] *noun* (in some countries) a noble corresponding in rank to an English earl.

countable *adjective* **1** that can be counted. **2** *Grammar* (of a noun) that can form a plural or be used with the indefinite article.

countdown *noun* **1 a** the act of counting down, esp. at the launching of a rocket etc. **b** the procedures carried out during this time. **2** the final moments before any significant event.

countenance • *noun* **1 a** the face. **b** the facial expression: *her smiling countenance*. **2** composure: *we kept our countenance with difficulty*. **3** favour; moral support. • *verb* (**countenances, countenanced, countenancing**) give approval to (an act etc.): *cannot countenance the use of force*. [Say COUNTA nince]

counter[1] *noun* **1** a long flat-topped fixture in a store, bank, cafeteria, bar, kitchen, etc., at a height suitable for working or serving standing up. **2 a** a small disc or other object used for keeping score etc., esp. in some board games. **b** a token representing a coin. **3** an

apparatus used for counting. **4** *Physics* an apparatus used for counting individual ionizing particles etc. **5** a person or thing that counts. PHRASES **over the counter** by ordinary retail purchase, without a prescription or permit etc. **under the counter** (esp. of the sale of scarce goods) surreptitiously, esp. illegally.

counter² • *verb* **1** speak or act in opposition to: *countered our proposal with their own*. **2** respond to hostile speech or action: *"What would you like me to do about it?" she countered*. **3** give a return blow while parrying: *he countered with a left hook*. • *adverb* in the opposite direction to or in conflict with: *some actions by the authorities ran counter to the call for leniency*. • *adjective* responding to something of the same kind, esp. in opposition: *years of argument and counter argument*. • *noun* **1** a thing which opposes or prevents something else: *I am writing to offer a counter to the letter to the editor that appeared last week* ◊ *an effective counter to the threat from the north has been massive deployment of troops*. **2** *Boxing* a counterpunch.

counter- *combining form* denoting: **1** retaliation, opposition: *counter-threat*. **2** opposite direction: *counter-current*. **3** correspondence, duplication, or substitution: *counterpart* ◊ *countersign*.

counteract *verb* act against something in order to reduce its force or neutralize it: *how can we counteract global warming?* ◊ *caffeine helped counteract the effects of the pill*. ▶ **counteraction** *noun*

counter-argument *noun* an argument in reply or opposition to another.

counterattack • *noun* an attack in reply to an attack by an enemy or opponent. • *verb* attack in reply.

counterbalance • *noun* **1** a weight balancing another. **2** an argument, force, etc., having the opposite effect to that of another and so preventing it from exercising a disproportionate influence: *the film was a counterbalance to the Hollywood image of Indians*. • *verb* (**counterbalances**, **counterbalanced**, **counterbalancing**) act as a counterbalance to.

counterclaim • *noun* **1** a claim made against another claim. **2** *Law* a claim made by a defendant in a suit against the plaintiff. • *verb* make a counterclaim (for).

counter-clockwise • *adverb* in a curve opposite in direction to the movement of the hands of a clock. • *adjective* moving counter-clockwise.

countercultural *adjective* having to do with or belonging to a counterculture.

counterculture *noun* a culture having values or lifestyles that are in opposition to those of the current accepted culture.

counterfeit • *adjective* (of money etc.) not genuine; forged. • *noun* a forgery; an imitation. • *verb* **1** imitate fraudulently (money, documents, etc.); forge. **2** pretend (feelings etc.): *counterfeited interest*. ▶ **counterfeiter** *noun* **counterfeiting** *noun* [Say COUNTER fit]

counter-insurgency *noun* action against insurrection: *counter-insurgency operations*.

counter-intelligence *noun* action taken to prevent or thwart spying by an enemy.

counterintuitive *adjective* contrary to intuition. [Say counter INTUITIVE]

counterman *noun* (*plural* **countermen**) a person who works behind a counter, e.g. in a cafeteria or diner.

countermeasure *noun* an action taken to counteract a danger, threat, etc.

countermove • *noun* a move or action in opposition to another. • *verb* make a countermove.

counteroffensive *noun* **1** *Military* an attack made against an attacking force. **2** any attack made from a

defensive position: *the group of professors has launched a counteroffensive against the attack on political correctness*.

counterpart *noun* **1** a person or thing holding a position or performing a function that corresponds to that of another person or thing in a different area: *the minister held talks with her French counterpart*. **2** one of two copies of a legal document.

counterpoint • *noun* **1 a** the art or technique of setting, writing, or playing a melody or melodies in conjunction with another, according to fixed rules. **b** a melody played in conjunction with another. **2** a contrasting element, theme, etc.: *I have used my interviews with parents as a counterpoint to a professional judgment*. **3** contrast. • *verb* **1** *Music* add counterpoint to. **2** set (an argument, theme, etc.) in contrast to (a main element): *the war footage is counterpointed with jolly popular songs of the time*.

counterpoise • *noun* **1** a force, factor, or influence that balances or neutralizes another: *an unfortunate but necessary counterpoise to Communism*. **2** a counterbalancing weight. • *verb* (**counterpoises**, **counterpoised**, **counterpoising**) **1** have an opposing and balancing effect. **2** bring into contrast: *the novel counterpoised the rural and urban milieux*.

counterproductive *adjective* having the opposite of the desired effect.

counterpunch • *noun* (*plural* **counterpunches**) a punch or attack given in return. • *verb* (**counterpunches**, **counterpunched**, **counterpunching**) make a counterpunch or counterpunches.

Counter-Reformation *noun* *hist.* the reform of the Catholic Church in the 16th and 17th centuries in response to the Protestant Reformation; it was marked by a return to piety, discipline, and order, esp. amongst newly formed religious orders such as the Jesuits, asserted the significance of Rome as the centre of the Church, encouraged popular devotions, esp. to the Eucharist, the Blessed Virgin, and the Saints, reasserted certain Catholic doctrines such as the need for good works as well as faith, and saw a flourishing of highly ornamented religious art and architecture.

counter-revolution *noun* a revolution opposing a former one or reversing its results. ▶ **counter-revolutionary** *adjective* & *noun* (*plural* **counter-revolutionaries**)

countersign *verb* add a signature to (a document previously signed by oneself or another).

countersink • *verb* (**countersinks**, **countersunk**, **countersinking**) **1** enlarge and bevel (the rim of a hole) so that a screw or bolt can be inserted flush with the surface. **2** sink (a screw etc.) in such a hole. • *noun* a tool used to countersink a hole.

counter-tenor *noun* **1 a** an adult male alto singing voice. **b** a singer with this voice. **2** a part written for counter-tenor.

counterterrorism *noun* measures to combat terrorism.

countertop *noun* the flat working surface of a counter, esp. in a kitchen.

countervail • *verb* oppose forcefully and usu. successfully: *a countervailing influence*. • *noun* *Cdn* a countervailing duty.

countervailing duty *noun* a tax put on imports to offset a subsidy in the exporting country or a tax on similar goods not from abroad.

counterweight *noun* a counterbalancing weight.

countess *noun* **1** the wife or widow of a count or an earl. **2** a woman holding the rank of count or earl.

countless *adjective* too many to be counted.

C

countrified *adjective* often *derogatory* (of manners, appearance, etc.) rural or rustic. [Say CUN truh fied]

country *noun* (*plural* **countries**) **1** the territory of a nation with its own government; a nation. **2 a** rural districts as opposed to cities or towns: *lives in the country.* **b** styles of clothing, fabric, furnishing, etc. supposed to be typically rural, usu. inspired by historical fashions. **3** the land of a person's birth or citizenship. **4** a territory marked by some particular characteristic: *maple country.* **5** an area of interest or knowledge. **6** a region associated with a particular person, esp. a writer or painter: *Leacock country.* **7** a national population, esp. as voters. **8** = COUNTRY AND WESTERN. PHRASES **across country** not keeping to roads. **by a country mile** *informal* by a great extent. **go** (or **appeal**) **to the country** *Cdn & Brit.* test public opinion by dissolving Parliament and holding a general election.

country and western *noun* a style of music combining elements of British folk music as preserved in the rural or southern areas of North America, cowboy songs, and other styles of popular music, often dealing with themes of lost love.

country club *noun* a suburban sport and social club, with facilities for golf and usu. tennis etc.

country elevator *noun Cdn* (*Prairies*) a grain elevator equipped to unload grain from trucks, store it, and load it into rail cars.

country food *noun Cdn hist.* game, fish, or other foods that can be obtained while in the bush.

country house *noun* **1** a usu. large house in the country, esp. the residence of a wealthy person. **2** *Cdn* (*Que.*) a summer cottage.

countryman *noun* (*plural* **countrymen**) **1** a person living in a rural area. **2 a** (also **fellow-countryman**) a person of one's own country or region. **b** (often in *combination*) a person from a specified country or region.

country marriage *noun Cdn hist.* a common-law marriage between a fur trader of European descent and an Aboriginal or Metis woman.

country music *noun* = COUNTRY AND WESTERN.

countryside *noun* **1 a** a rural area. **b** rural areas in general. **2** the inhabitants of a rural area.

countrywide *adjective* throughout a nation.

country wife *noun Cdn hist.* the Aboriginal or Metis common-law wife of a fur trader.

countrywoman *noun* (*plural* **countrywomen**) **1** a woman living in a rural area. **2 a** a person of one's own country or region. **b** (often in *combination*) a person from a specified country or region.

county *noun* (*plural* **counties**) any of the territorial divisions of some countries or provinces, for electoral, judicial, or local government purposes.

county council *noun* the elected governing body of an administrative county. ▶ **county councillor** *noun*

county seat *noun* (also **county town**) the administrative capital of a county.

> **SPELL CHECK** ABC✓
> **coup, coupe**
>
> A kind of car is a **coupe**.

coup *noun* **1** a notable or successful stroke or move: *it was a major coup getting such a prestigious contract.* **2** a violent or illegal seizure of power from a government: *a military coup.* **3** (among Plains Aboriginal peoples) the act of touching an enemy in battle and escaping, considered a heroic act. PHRASES **count coup** (among Plains Aboriginal peoples) perform a coup or tell of having done so. [Say COO]

coup de grâce *noun* (*plural* **coups de grâce**) **1** a final stroke, esp. to kill a wounded animal or person.

2 something that puts a definitive end to something: *the coup de grâce for ranching was the severe winter of 1906.* [Say coo duh GRASS or coo duh GRAWSS]

coup d'état *noun* (*plural* **coups d'état**) a violent or illegal seizure of power from a government. [Say coo day TAW]

> **SPELL CHECK** ABC✓
> **coupe, coup**
>
> A sudden overthrow of government or a successful event is a **coup**.

coupe *noun* a two-door car with a hard roof, esp. one seating only two persons. [Say COOP]

> **GRAMMAR CHECK** ⚠
> **a couple (of)**
>
> The use of **couple** without a following **of**, as in *They each had a couple beers*, is highly informal and should be avoided in writing.

couple • *noun* **1 a** two: *a couple of girls.* **b** about two: *a couple of hours.* **2** (often treated as *singular*) **a** two people who are romantically involved. **b** a pair of partners in dancing, figure skating, etc. • *verb* (**couples, coupled, coupling**) **1** fasten or link together; connect (esp. railway cars etc.). **2** associate in thought or speech: *high unemployment coupled with inflation.* **3** bring or come together as companions or partners. **4** copulate.

coupler *noun* **1** a person or thing that couples or links things together. **2** = COUPLING 1. **3** a transformer used for connecting electric circuits.

couplet *noun* two successive lines of verse, usu. rhyming and of the same length.

coupling *noun* **1 a** a link connecting railway cars etc. **b** a device for connecting parts of machinery. **2** a thing that couples or links things together. **3** the act of a person that couples.

coupon *noun* **1** a certificate entitling the bearer to a discount on a purchase etc. **2** a form in a newspaper, magazine, etc., which may be filled in and sent as an application for a purchase, information, etc. **3** a voucher given with a retail purchase, a certain number of which entitle the holder to a discount, premium, etc. **4** a detachable portion of a bond etc. which is given up in return for a payment of interest. **5** a detachable ticket entitling the holder to a ration of food etc., esp. in wartime. [Say COO pon or CYOO pon]

courage *noun* the ability to disregard fear; bravery. PHRASES **courage of one's convictions** the courage to act on one's beliefs.

courageous *adjective* brave, fearless. ▶ **courageously** *adverb* **courageousness** *noun*

coureur de bois *noun Cdn hist.* (*plural* **coureurs de bois**) a French or Metis fur trader, esp. one employed by the Hudson's Bay or North West Companies. [Say coo RUR duh BWAH]

courier • *noun* **1** a person or company hired to convey documents, packages etc. from sender to recipient. **2** a person who transports drugs, arms, etc. illegally, esp. from one country to another. **3** a special messenger. • *verb* ship (a package etc.) by courier.

> **SPELL CHECK** ABC✓
> **course, coarse**
>
> Something that is rough is **coarse**.

course • *noun* **1** a continuous onward movement or progression. **2** a line along which a person or thing moves; a direction taken: *the course of the river.* **3** the ground on which a race, golf game, etc. takes place.

4 a a series of lectures, lessons, etc., in a particular subject. **b** a book for such a course: *A Modern French Course.* **5** any of the successive parts of a meal. **6 a** sequence of medical treatment etc.: *a course of antibiotics.* **7** a line of conduct. **8** a continuous horizontal layer of brick, stone, shingles, etc., in a building. **9** a channel in which water flows. • *verb* (**courses, coursed, coursing**) (esp. of liquid) run, esp. fast: *blood coursed through her veins.* PHRASES **the course of nature** ordinary events or procedure. **in the course of** during. **in the course of time** as time goes by; eventually. **of course** as is or was to be expected. **on** (or **off**) **course** following (or deviating from) the desired direction or goal. **run** (or **take**) **its course** (esp. of an illness) complete its natural development.

coursebook *noun* a book designed for use on a particular course of study.

courseware *noun* material (esp. computer programs) designed for use in an educational or training course.

coursework *noun* the work done during a course of study, esp. when counting towards a student's grade.

court • *noun* **1** (also **court of law**) **a** an assembly of a judge or judges and other persons acting as a tribunal in civil and criminal cases. **b** a regular session of a court. **c** a courtroom or courthouse. **2 a** a demarcated quadrangular area for playing certain games: *tennis court.* **b** a subdivision of this area. **3** = ATRIUM 1b. **4 a** the establishment, retinue, and courtiers of a sovereign. **b** a sovereign and his or her councillors, constituting a ruling power. **c** a sovereign's residence. **d** an assembly held by a sovereign. **5** attention paid to a person whose favour, love, or interest is sought: *paid court to her.* **6** (in Presbyterian and United churches) any of several governing bodies made up of clergy and elders, e.g. sessions etc. • *verb* **1 a** try to win the affection or favour of (a person). **b** pay amorous attention to: *courting couples.* **2** seek to win (applause, fame, etc.). **3** invite (misfortune) by one's actions: *courting disaster.* PHRASES **go to court** take legal action. **hold court** preside (esp. pompously) over a group of attendants, admirers, etc. **in court** appearing as a party or an advocate in a court of law. **out of court** **1** (of a plaintiff) not entitled to be heard. **2** (of a settlement) arranged before a hearing or judgment can take place.

courteous *adjective* polite, kind, or considerate in manner. ▶**courteously** *adverb* **courteousness** *noun* [Say KER tee us]

courtesan *noun hist.* **1** a prostitute, esp. one with wealthy or upper-class clients. **2** the mistress of a wealthy man. [Say CORTA zan]

courtesy *noun* (*plural* **courtesies**) **1** courteous behaviour; good manners. **2** a courteous act. PHRASES **by courtesy** by favour, not by right. **by courtesy of** with the formal permission of (a person etc.). **courtesy of** thanks to. [Say KER tuh see]

courthouse *noun* a building in which a judicial court is held.

courtier *noun* a person who attends or frequents a sovereign's court. [Say CORE tee ur]

courtliness *noun* a polite and refined manner.

courtly *adjective* (**courtlier, courtliest**) polished or refined in manners, as befitting a royal court.

courtly love *noun* a highly conventionalized medieval tradition of love between a knight and a married noblewoman, first developed by the troubadours of southern France and extensively employed in European literature of the time. The love of the knight for his lady, characterized by devoted service to her, was regarded as an ennobling passion and the relationship was typically unconsummated.

court martial • *noun* (*plural* **courts martial**) a judicial court for trying members of the armed services. • *verb* (**court-martial**) (**court-martials, court-martialled, court-martialling**) try by a court martial.

Court of Appeal *noun* a court of law hearing appeals against judgments in lower courts, esp. (in Canada) the highest appeal court in a province or territory.

court of first instance *noun* a court of primary jurisdiction.

court order *noun* a direction issued by a court or a judge, usu. requiring a person to do or not do something.

court reporter *noun* **1** an official stenographer in a law court. **2** a journalist who reports on trials, etc.

courtroom *noun* the place or room in which a court of law meets.

courtship *noun* **1 a** courting, esp. with intent to marry. **b** the behaviour of male and female animals, birds, etc. prior to and during mating. **c** a period of courtship. **2** an attempt, often protracted, to gain advantage by flattery, attention, etc.: *the country's courtship of foreign investors.*

courtyard *noun* an area enclosed by walls or buildings, often opening off a street.

couscous *noun* **1** a type of N African pasta in granules made from crushed durum wheat. **2** a dish of this, often with meat or fruit added. [Say COOSE coose (rhymes with *GOOSE*)]

cousin *noun* **1 a** (also **first cousin**) the child of one's uncle or aunt. **b** any other relative with whom one shares a common ancestor; a second cousin, etc. **c** a person who is married to one's cousin. **2** a person or thing related to another by common features etc.: *the new motorbikes are not proving as popular as their four-wheeled cousins.* **3** (usu. in *plural*) applied to the people of kindred races or nations: *our American cousins.*

couth *jocular* • *adjective* cultured; well-mannered: *it is more couth to hold your shrimp genteelly by the tail when eating.* • *noun* good manners; cultured behaviour: *casual Fridays had made official the tendency to move away from unwritten rules of corporate couth.* [Rhymes with *YOUTH*]

couture • *noun* **1** the design and manufacture of fashionable clothes. **2** high fashion. • *adjective* (of clothing) highly fashionable. [Say coo CHOOR]

couturier *noun* a person who designs and oversees the making of high-fashion clothes. [Say coo TOORY ay]

covalence *noun* **1** the linking of atoms by a covalent bond. **2** the number of pairs of electrons an atom can share with another. [Say co VAY lince]

covalent *adjective* **1** relating to, designating, or characterized by chemical bonds. **2** formed by sharing of electrons usu. in pairs by two atoms in a molecule: *covalent bond.* ▶**covalently** *adverb* [Say co VAY lint]

cove *noun* a small, esp. sheltered, bay in the shoreline of an ocean, lake, river, etc.

covenant • *noun* **1** an agreement; a contract. **2** *Law* **a** a contract drawn up under a seal. **b** a clause of a covenant. **3** (**Covenant**) *Bible* an agreement between God and a person, nation, etc. *See also* ARK OF THE COVENANT. • *verb* agree, esp. by legal covenant: *the landlord covenants to repair property.* [Say CUVVA nint]

cover • *verb* **1** protect or conceal by means of a cloth, lid, etc. **2** extend over; occupy the whole surface of: *covered in dirt.* **3** protect; clothe. **4** include; deal with: *the talk covered recent discoveries.* **5** travel (a specified distance). **6 a** report (events, a meeting, etc.). **b** investigate as a reporter. **7** be enough to defray

(expenses, a bill, etc.): *$20 should cover it*. **8 cover oneself** take precautionary measures so as to protect oneself: *had covered myself by saying I might be late*. **9** (foll. by *for*) deputize or stand in for (a colleague etc.): *will you cover for me?* **10** *Military* **a** aim a gun etc. at. **b** (of a fortress, guns, etc.) command (a territory). **c** stand behind (a person in the front rank). **d** protect (an exposed person etc.) by being able to return fire. **11** *Sport* **a** esp. *Baseball* stand behind (another player) to stop any missed balls. **b** (in hockey, football, etc.) keep close to so as to prevent the free movement of (a player of the other side). **c** defend (an area of a field or court, a base, etc.). **12** perform or record a cover (of a song etc.). • *noun* **1** something that covers or protects, esp.: **a** a lid. **b** the binding of a book, magazine, etc. **c** either board or sheet of this. **d** an envelope or the wrapper of a parcel: *under separate cover*. **e** a stamped envelope of interest to stamp collectors. **f** (in *plural*) bedclothes. **2** a hiding place; a shelter. **3** woods or undergrowth sheltering game or covering the ground. **4 a** a pretense; a screen: *under cover of humility*. **b** a spy's pretended identity or activity, intended as concealment. **c** *Military* a supporting force protecting an advance party from attack. **5 a** funds, esp. obtained by insurance, to meet a liability or secure against a contingent loss. **b** the state of being protected: *third party cover*. **6** = COVER CHARGE. **7** a recording or performance of a previously recorded song etc., made esp. to take advantage of the original's success (also as an *adjective*: *cover version*). **PHRASES break cover** (of an animal, esp. game, or a hunted person) leave a place of shelter, esp. vegetation. **cover one's tracks** conceal evidence of what one has done. **cover up 1** completely cover or conceal. **2** conceal (circumstances etc., esp. illicitly). **3** assist in a deception: *refused to cover up for them*. **from cover to cover** from beginning to end of a book etc. **take cover** use a natural or prepared shelter against an attack.

coverage *noun* **1** an area or an amount covered. **2** the amount of press etc. publicity received by a particular story, person, etc. **3** a risk covered by an insurance policy. **4** an area reached by a particular broadcasting station or advertising medium.

coverall *noun* (usu. in *plural*) a one-piece garment worn over other clothing to protect it.

cover charge *noun* an extra charge levied per head in a restaurant, nightclub, etc.

covered *adjective* **1** provided with a lid. **2** provided with a covering. **3 a** enclosed: *covered bridge*. **b** (of a ship) decked. **4** thickly laid over or enveloped: *snow-covered hills*. **5** insured. **6** wearing a hat, veil, etc.

covered wagon *noun* a large wagon with an arched canvas roof, used by pioneers for travel westward across the prairies.

cover girl *noun* a female model whose picture appears on magazine covers etc.

covering *noun* anything that covers something else for protection, concealment, etc.

covering letter *noun* (also **cover letter**) a letter which accompanies a resumé, package, etc.

coverlet *noun* a bedspread.

cover-point *noun* **1** *Hockey hist.* a player who stands just in front of point to prevent the puck from coming near the goal. **2** *Lacrosse* a player positioned just in front of point.

cover story *noun* **1** a story in a magazine that is illustrated or advertised on the front cover. **2** an invented story intended to mislead or to conceal one's true actions, motives, etc.

covert • *adjective* secret or disguised: *covert operations*. • *noun* a shelter, esp. a thicket or wooded area which

hides game. ▶ **covertly** *adverb* [Say CO vert, co VERT or CUV ert for the adjective, CO vert or CUV ert for the noun]

cover-up *noun* **1** an act of concealing circumstances, esp. illicitly. **2** any loose outer garment worn over a bathing suit, exercise clothes, etc.

cover version *noun* = COVER *noun* 7.

covet *verb* (**covets**, **coveted**, **coveting**) **1** desire wrongfully or inordinately, esp. something belonging to another person. **2** long for or desire greatly, but not inappropriately: *she's been coveting that spiffy bike helmet for months*. ▶ **coveted** *adjective*

covetous *adjective* **1** wrongfully eager to possess something. **2** greatly desirous (of something). ▶ **covetously** *adverb* **covetousness** *noun* [Say CUVVET us]

covey *noun* (*plural* **coveys**) **1** a brood of game birds, as partridges, ptarmigan, etc. **2** a small party or group of people or things. [Say CUVVY]

cow[1] *noun* **1 a** a fully grown female of any bovine animal, esp. of the genus *Bos*, used as a source of milk and beef. **b** a domestic bovine animal (regardless of sex or age). **c** a female domestic bovine animal which has borne a calf (compare HEIFER). **2** the female of other large animals, esp. the moose, elephant, whale, and seal. **PHRASES have a cow** *slang* become angry, hysterical, excited, etc. **till the cows come home** *informal* an indefinitely long time.

cow[2] *verb* (usu. in *passive*) intimidate, frighten, or browbeat into submission: *cowed by the threats*.

coward *noun* a person with little courage who shows shameful fear in the face of danger, pain, etc.

cowardice *noun* lack of courage.

cowardly *adjective* **1** of or like a coward; lacking courage. **2** (of an action) done against a person who cannot retaliate: *a cowardly attack on a helpless victim*.

cowbell *noun* **1** a bell worn round a cow's neck for easy location of the animal. **2** a similar bell used as a percussion instrument.

cowberry *noun* (*plural* **cowberries**) **1** an evergreen shrub, *Vaccinium vitis-idaea*, bearing red berries. **2** this berry.

cowbird *noun* any of several North American orioles, esp. the brown-plumaged *Molothrus ater*, which lays its eggs in other birds' nests.

cowboy *noun* **1** a person who herds and tends cattle, esp. in western North America. **2** *informal* **a** a person who acts outside of established rules, conventions, etc. **b** an unscrupulous or reckless person, esp. an unqualified one.

cowboy boot *noun* a square-heeled boot with a pointed toe, extending to mid-calf and usu. with decorative tooling or stitching.

cowboy hat *noun* a hat, usu. of felt, with a high crown and broad brim.

cowboys and Indians *noun* a children's game in which the participants imitate the supposed actions of cowboys and Indians in conflict.

cowcatcher *noun* a metal frame at the front of a locomotive for pushing aside obstacles on the line.

cower *verb* crouch or shrink back, esp. in fear. [Rhymes with FLOWER]

cowgirl *noun* a woman who herds and tends cattle.

cowhand *noun* a person who tends cattle.

cowhide *noun* **1 a** a cow's hide. **b** leather made from this. **2** a leather whip made from cowhide.

Cowichan • *noun* (*plural* **Cowichan**) **1** a member of an Aboriginal people living on SE Vancouver Island. **2** the language of this people, a dialect of Halkomelem. • *adjective* of or relating to this people. [Say COW itch un]

Cowichan sweater *noun* *Cdn* a hand-spun, heavy-knit pullover sweater made by the Cowichan.

cowl *noun* **1 a** the hood of a monk's habit. **b** a loose hood. **c** a monk's hooded habit. **2** the hood-shaped covering of a chimney or ventilating shaft. **3** (also **cowling**) the removable cover of a vehicle or aircraft engine. ▶**cowled** *adjective* [Rhymes with *OWL*]

cowlick *noun* a projecting lock of hair, esp. at the crown or forehead.

co-worker *noun* a person who works with another.

cowpie *noun* (also **cow patty, cow pat**) a flat, round piece of cow dung.

cowpoke *noun* (also **cowpuncher**) = COWBOY 1.

cowpox *noun* a contagious disease of cows, of which the virus was formerly used in smallpox vaccines.

co-write *verb* (**co-writes**; *past* **co-wrote**; *past participle* **co-written**; **co-writing**) write (something) together with another person. ▶**co-writer** *noun*

cowslip *noun* **1** a primula with fragrant yellow flowers, growing in pastures. **2** = SHOOTING STAR 2.

cowtown *noun* a town or city in a cattle area of western North America, esp. one involved in the cattle industry.

cox • *noun* (*plural* **coxes**) a coxswain, esp. of a racing boat. • *verb* (**coxes, coxed, coxing**) act as a cox. ▶**coxless** *adjective*

coxcomb *noun* *archaic* a vain and conceited man.

coxswain *noun* **1** a person who steers, esp. in a rowboat. **2** the senior petty officer in a small ship. [Say COX'n or COX swain]

coy *adjective* (**coyer, coyest**) **1** (esp. of a woman) making a pretence of shyness or modesty which is intended to be alluring but is often regarded as irritating: *she treated him to a coy smile of invitation.* **2** irritatingly reticent: *always coy about his age.* ▶**coyly** *adverb* **coyness** *noun*

coyote *noun* **1** a wolflike wild dog native to North America, noted for its cunning. **2** a hero and trickster figure in North American Aboriginal folklore. [Say kye OH tee or KYE ote]

cozily *adverb* in a cozy or comfortable manner.

coziness *noun* a cozy, comfortable, or friendly quality.

cozy • *adjective* (**cozier, coziest**) **1** comfortable, warm, or snug. **2** intimate and friendly: *a cozy restaurant.* **3** (of a transaction or arrangement) working to the mutual advantage of those involved (used to convey a suspicion of corruption): *a cozy contract.* **4** *derogatory* avoiding or not offering challenge or difficulty; complacent: *a rather cozy assumption among audit firms that they would never actually go bust.* • *noun* (*plural* **cozies**) a cover to keep something hot, esp. a teapot. PHRASES **cozy up to** (**cozies, cozied, cozying**) *informal* **1** ingratiate oneself with: *she decided to resign rather than cozy up to hardliners in the party.* **2** snuggle up to.

CP *abbreviation* **1** Canadian Pacific (Railway etc.). **2** Canadian Press. **3** cerebral palsy.

CPI *abbreviation* CONSUMER PRICE INDEX.

Cpl *abbreviation* CORPORAL[1].

CPP *abbreviation* Canada Pension Plan.

CPR *abbreviation* **1** CARDIOPULMONARY RESUSCITATION. **2** Canadian Pacific Railway.

cps *abbreviation* **1** *Computing* characters per second. **2** cycles per second.

CPU *noun* (*plural* **CPUs**) CENTRAL PROCESSING UNIT.

Cr *symbol* chromium.

crab[1] • *noun* **1 a** any of numerous ten-footed crustaceans having the first pair of legs modified as pincers. **b** the flesh of a crab as food. **2** (also **crab louse**) (often in *plural*) a parasitic louse infesting hairy parts of the body and causing extreme irritation. • *verb* (**crabs, crabbed, crabbing**) fish for crabs.

crab[2] *noun* (also **crabapple**) **1** a small, sour apple. **2** any of several trees bearing this fruit.

crab[3] *informal* • *verb* (**crabs, crabbed, crabbing**) find fault, criticize; grumble. • *noun* a bad-tempered person.

crabbed *adjective* **1** (of handwriting) cramped and hard to decipher. **2** = CRABBY. **3** difficult to understand: *crabbed legal language.*

crabber *noun* **1** a person who fishes for crabs. **2** a boat used in crab fishing.

crabbily *adverb* in a crabby or ill-tempered manner.

crabbiness *noun* a crabby or ill-tempered manner.

crabby *adjective* (**crabbier, crabbiest**) surly, irritable, or morose.

crabgrass *noun* any of several creeping grasses infesting lawns, esp. of the genus *Digitaria*.

crack • *noun* **1 a** a sudden sharp or explosive noise: *the crack of a whip.* **b** (in a voice) a sudden harshness or change in pitch. **2** a sharp blow. **3 a** a narrow opening formed by a break. **b** a partial fracture, with the parts still joined. **c** a chink. **4** *informal* a joke or gibe; a witty or cutting remark. **5** *informal* **a** an attempt: *I'll have a crack at it.* **b** an opportunity: *a crack at the job.* **6** (also **crack cocaine**) *slang* a potent, highly addictive hard crystalline form of cocaine broken into small pieces and inhaled or smoked for its stimulating effect. **7** the exact moment: *the crack of dawn.* • *verb* **1** break without a complete separation of the parts. **2** make or cause to make a sudden sharp or explosive sound. **3** break or cause to break with a sudden sharp sound. **4** break down, esp. under severe pressures, e.g. torture. **5** (of the voice, esp. of an adolescent boy or a person under strain) change tone, break, become harsh. **6 a** decipher, find a solution to (a problem, code, etc.). **b** break into or force open: *cracked the safe.* **7** tell (a joke etc.) in a jocular way. **8** *informal* hit sharply or hard: *cracked her head on the ceiling.* **9** gain access to: *crack the job market.* **10 a** open (a bottle): *crack a beer.* **b** open slightly: *crack open the window.* • *adjective* *informal* excellent; first-rate: *a crack shot.* PHRASES **crack a book** *informal* study or research. **crack down on** *informal* take severe measures against. **crack a smile** *informal* begin to smile. **crack the whip** *informal* exercise authority. **crack up** *informal* **1** suffer a mental or emotional breakdown. **2** burst into laughter suddenly. **3** cause to break into laughter: *he cracked me up.* **crack wise** *informal* to make wisecracks. **get cracking** *informal* begin promptly and vigorously. **have a crack at** *informal* attempt. **not all it's cracked up to be** *informal* not all a thing seems to be.

crackdown *noun* enforcement of severe or repressive measures (esp. against law-breakers, activists, etc.).

cracked *adjective* **1** having cracks. **2** *informal* eccentric, mad, or crazy. **3** damaged, injured, or impaired: *cracked hands.* **4** varying or broken in tone, e.g. voice or sounds: *a cracked voice.*

cracked wheat *noun* wheat that has been crushed into small pieces.

cracker *noun* **1 a** a thin, dry biscuit often eaten with cheese. **b** a cookie: *a graham cracker.* **2** a paper cylinder both ends of which are pulled, esp. at Christmas, making a sharp noise and releasing a small toy etc. **3** a firework exploding with a sharp noise.

crackerjack *slang* • *adjective* exceptionally fine or expert. • *noun* an exceptionally fine thing etc.

crackers *adjective* *slang* **1** crazy. **2** wildly enthusiastic.

crackhead *noun* *slang* a habitual user of crack cocaine.

crack house *noun* a gathering place where crack cocaine is bought, sold, or used.

crackie *noun* *Cdn* (*Nfld*) a small, yappy mongrel dog.

C

crackle • *verb* (**crackles, crackled, crackling**) make short, sharp cracking sounds like something burning on a fire: *the radio crackled*. • *noun* such a sound.

crackling *noun* the crisp skin of roast pork.

crackly *adjective* having or making a crackling sound: *a crackly phone line*.

crackpot *slang* • *noun* an eccentric or impractical person. • *adjective* crazy, unworkable: *a crackpot scheme*.

crack-up *noun informal* **1** a mental breakdown. **2** a car crash. **3** a collapse or disintegration.

cradle • *noun* **1 a** a baby's bed with high sides, esp. one mounted on rockers. **b** a place in which a thing begins, esp. a civilization etc., or is nurtured in its infancy. **2** a framework resembling a cradle, esp.: **a** one on which a ship etc. rests during construction or repairs. **b** one on which a worker is suspended to work on a ceiling, a ship, the vertical side of a building, etc. **c** the part of a telephone on which the receiver rests when not in use. • *verb* (**cradles, cradled, cradling**) **1 a** hold, contain, or shelter as if in a cradle: *cradled his head in her arms*. **b** support, rock, or move gently as though in a cradle: *cradled on the waves*. **2** *Lacrosse* carry (the ball) in the stick's net, esp. when running with it. PHRASES **from the cradle** from infancy: *a socialist from the cradle*. **from (the) cradle to (the) grave** from infancy till death. **rob the cradle** become romantically involved with someone much younger.

cradleboard *noun* (among some North American Aboriginal peoples) a board to which an infant is strapped.

cradle-to-grave *adjective* from birth to death.

craft • *noun* **1 a** (esp. in *combination*) a trade or an art: *statecraft* ◊ *the craft of pottery*. **b** (usu. in *plural*) the product of such skill. **2** skill, esp. in practical arts. **3** the activity of producing handiwork. **4** (*plural* **craft**) a boat, aircraft, or spacecraft. **5** cunning or deceit. • *verb* make, fashion, or hone in a skilful way: *crafted a poem*.

crafter *noun* = CRAFTSPERSON.

craftily *adverb* in a clever or cunning manner.

craftiness *noun* a clever or cunning quality.

craft shop *noun* **1** a small store in which handicrafts, usu. made locally, are sold. **2** (also **craft store**) a store in which craft supplies are sold.

craftsman *noun* (*plural* **craftsmen**) **1** a skilled worker who has usu. completed a period of apprenticeship or training. **2** a person who practises a handicraft.

craftsmanship *noun* **1** the quality of execution in a thing made. **2** skilled workmanship.

craftsperson *noun* (*plural* **craftspeople**) a person who practises a handicraft, esp. a highly skilled artisan.

craftswoman *noun* (*plural* **craftswomen**) **1** a skilled female worker who has usu. completed a period of apprenticeship or training. **2** a woman who practises a handicraft.

crafty *adjective* (**craftier, craftiest**) cunning, wily.

crag *noun* a steep or rugged rock.

craggy *adjective* (**craggier, craggiest**) **1** (of a landscape) having crags. **2** (esp. of a person's face) rugged; angular, with sharply defined features, e.g. jutting cheekbones etc.

cram *verb* (**crams, crammed, cramming**) **1 a** fill to bursting; stuff: *the room was crammed*. **b** force (a thing) into: *cram the books into the bag*. **2** prepare for a test by intensive study. **3** *informal* eat greedily. PHRASES **cram in** push in to bursting point: *crammed in another five people*.

cramp • *noun* **1** a painful involuntary contraction of a muscle or muscles from the cold, exertion, etc. **2** = WRITER'S CRAMP. **3** (usu. in *plural*) a painful muscle contraction in the abdomen, uterus, etc., esp. preceding or accompanying menstruation. • *verb*

1 affect with a cramp or cramps. **2** confine, restrict, or hamper (energies etc.). **3** become stiff or incapacitated because of a cramp. PHRASES **cramp a person's style** prevent a person from acting freely or naturally.

cramped *adjective* **1** (of handwriting) small, tightly packed, and difficult to read. **2** uncomfortably limited or restricted in space: *cramped quarters*.

crampon *noun* a spiked iron plate fixed to a boot for walking on ice, climbing, etc. [Say CRAMP on]

cranberry *noun* (*plural* **cranberries**) **1** an evergreen shrub grown commercially for its red acid fruit. **2** a berry from this used for a sauce, in cooking, and for juice.

crane • *noun* **1** a machine for moving heavy objects, usu. by suspending them from a projecting beam. **2 a** a tall wading bird with long legs, a long neck, and a straight bill. **b** = GREAT BLUE HERON. **3** a trolley with a long boom supporting a platform on which a camera can be mounted. • *verb* (**cranes, craned, craning**) stretch out (one's neck) in order to see.

cranesbill *noun* any of various herbaceous plants of the genus *Geranium*, having beaked fruits.

cranial *adjective* of or relating to the skull. [Say CRAY nee ul]

cranial nerve *noun* each of twelve pairs of nerves which originate directly in the brain, not from the spinal cord, and which reach the external surface of the body through natural skull apertures.

cranium *noun* (*plural* **craniums** or **crania**) the part of the skeleton that encloses the brain; the skull. [Say CRAY nee um for the singular; for *CRANIA* say CRAY nee uh]

crank¹ • *noun* part of an axle or shaft bent at right angles for converting reciprocal into circular motion and vice versa. • *verb* **1** cause to move by means of a crank. **2** start (an engine etc.), esp. by turning a crank. PHRASES **crank out** *informal* produce quickly in a mechanical or mass-produced fashion: *cranks out pulp novels*. **crank up 1** start, turn on, or power up (a machine, appliance, etc.): *crank up the engine*. **2** *informal* increase (speed, sound, etc.): *crank up the volume*. **3** stimulate, stir up, or produce: *crank up enthusiasm*. **turn one's crank** *slang* please, appeal to, or excite one's interest.

crank² • *noun* **1** an eccentric person, esp. one obsessed by a particular theory. **2** a bad-tempered person. • *adjective* of, by, or pertaining to an eccentric or unbalanced person: *crank theories*.

crank call *noun* a harassing telephone call usu. made by young people as a prank.

crankcase *noun* a metal covering enclosing an engine's crankshaft, connecting rods, etc.

crankily *adverb* in a cranky or ill-tempered manner.

crankiness *noun* a cranky or ill-tempered manner.

crankshaft *noun* a shaft driven by one or more cranks.

cranky *adjective* (**crankier, crankiest**) **1** bad-tempered. **2** working badly: *a cranky old plane*.

cranny *noun* (*plural* **crannies**) a small narrow opening or hole; a chink, crevice, or crack: *nooks and crannies*.

crap¹ *slang* • *noun* **1 a** feces. **b** an act of defecation. **2** nonsense or falsehood: *he talks crap*. **3** something valueless: *the poetry was crap*. **4** garbage: *pick up that crap*. • *verb* (**craps, crapped, crapping**) defecate. PHRASES **cut the crap** *slang* get to the point; stop evading the issue.

crap² *noun* **1** (in *plural*) a gambling game in which two dice are thrown with the aim of scoring 7 or 11 on a first throw or any score but 7 on a second throw. **2 a** losing score of 2, 3, or 12 on a first throw in craps. PHRASES **crap out 1** make a losing throw while shooting craps. **2** *informal* **a** fail. **b** withdraw from a game etc. **shoot craps** play craps.

crape *noun* **1** CREPE. **2** a fabric, usu. of black silk or imitation silk, formerly used for mourning clothes.

crappie *noun* a North American freshwater sunfish.

crappy *adjective* (**crappier**, **crappiest**) *slang* **1** markedly inferior. **2** disgusting, unfair, nasty: *a crappy comment*. **3** unwell: *I feel crappy*.

crapshoot *noun slang* a gamble, risk, or highly uncertain venture. ▶ **crapshooter** *noun*

crash • *verb* (**crashes**, **crashed**, **crashing**) **1** make or cause to make a loud smashing noise. **2** throw, move, drop, or fall with a loud smashing noise. **3 a** collide or cause (a vehicle) to collide violently with another vehicle, obstacle, etc. **b** overturn or cause to overturn (a vehicle) at high speed. **4** fall or cause (an aircraft) to fall violently to the land or water. **5** (usu. foll. by *into*) collide violently: *crashed into the window*. **6** undergo financial ruin: *the market crashed*. **7** *informal* enter without permission: *crashed the party*. **8** *informal* be heavily defeated: *crashed to a 4–0 defeat*. **9** *Computing* (of a machine or system) fail suddenly. **10** *informal* pass (a red traffic light etc.). **11** (often foll. by *out*) *slang* **a** sleep, esp. in an improvised setting. **b** stay somewhere temporarily. **12** *slang* experience depression, exhaustion, etc. as the effects of cocaine etc. wear off. • *noun* (*plural* **crashes**) **1** a loud and sudden smashing noise. **2 a** a violent collision, esp. of one vehicle with another or with an object. **b** the violent fall of an aircraft to the land or water. **3** a sudden collapse of the stock market etc. **4** *Computing* a sudden failure which puts a system out of action. **5** (as an *adjective*) marked by an urgent and concentrated effort, esp. for immediate results etc.: *a crash course*. **6** a dramatic decrease in numbers. PHRASES **crash and burn** *informal* collapse or fail utterly.

crashing *adjective informal* overwhelming: *a crashing bore*.

crash-land *verb* **1** (of an aircraft or pilot) make an emergency landing, usu. with damage to the craft. **2** cause to crash-land. ▶ **crash landing** *noun*

crash test • *verb* assess (a product, usu. a vehicle) for safety and reliability under severe conditions often including collisions etc. • *noun* such a test.

crass *adjective* (**crasser**, **crassest**) **1** unsubtle: *crass materialism*. **2** insensitive, rude: *a crass remark*. **3** extreme: *crass stupidity*. ▶ **crassly** *adverb* **crassness** *noun*

crate • *noun* **1** a case or box, often of slatted wood, for storing esp. fragile goods for transportation. **2** *slang* an old airplane or other vehicle. • *verb* (**crates**, **crated**, **crating**) pack in a crate.

crater • *noun* **1** the mouth of a volcano. **2** a bowl-shaped cavity, esp. that made by the explosion of a bomb. **3** a hollow with a raised rim on the surface of a planet or moon, caused by the impact of a meteorite. • *verb* make a crater or craters in. ▶ **cratered** *adjective*

cravat *noun* a scarf worn inside an open-necked shirt, esp. by men. [Say kruh VAT]

crave *verb* (**craves**, **craved**, **craving**) **1** feel a powerful desire or need for something: *if only she had shown her daughter the love she craved ◊ craves carbohydrates all winter long*. **2** *dated* ask for: *I must crave your indulgence*. ▶ **craver** *noun*

craven • *adjective* contemptibly lacking in courage; cowardly: *a craven abdication of his duty*. • *noun* a cowardly person. ▶ **cravenly** *adverb*

craving *noun* a strong desire or longing.

craw *noun* the crop of a bird or insect. PHRASES **stick in one's craw** *informal* be difficult to accept.

crawfish *noun* (*plural* **crawfish**) a large marine spiny lobster.

crawl • *verb* **1** move slowly, esp. on hands and knees. **2** (of an insect, snake, etc.) move slowly with the body close to the ground etc. **3** move or progress slowly. **4** (often foll. by *to*) *informal* behave obsequiously or ingratiatingly: *they'll come crawling to me when they realize they can't do it on their own*. **5** (often foll. by *with*) be or seem to be covered or filled with crawling or moving things, people etc.: *crawling with shoppers*. **6** (esp. of the skin) feel a creepy sensation. **7** swim with a crawl stroke. • *noun* **1** an act of crawling. **2** a slow rate of movement. **3** a high-speed swimming stroke with alternate overarm movements and rapid straight-legged kicks. **4 a** (usu. in *combination*) *informal* a leisurely journey between places of interest: *culture-crawl*. **b** = PUB-CRAWL.

crawler *noun* **1** a person or thing that crawls, esp. a baby or an insect. **2** (also **night crawler**) *informal* an earthworm.

crawl space *noun* a low, constricted space, usu. in a house, for storage or to gain access to wiring etc.

crayfish *noun* (*plural* **crayfish**) **1** a small lobster-like freshwater crustacean. **2** a crawfish.

crayon • *noun* a stick or pencil of coloured wax etc. used for drawing. • *verb* (**crayons**, **crayoned**, **crayoning**) draw or colour with crayons: *her daughter just crayoned a picture on the wall ◊ children love to crayon*.

craze • *verb* (**crazes**, **crazed**, **crazing**) (usu. in *passive*) make insane: *crazed with grief*. • *noun* **1** a usu. temporary enthusiasm: *a craze for hula hoops*. **2** the object of this: *dinosaurs are the latest craze*.

crazed *adjective* **1** mentally impaired, insane. **2** manic, wildly enthusiastic: *dance-crazed teens*.

crazily *adverb* in a wild or crazy manner.

craziness *noun* a crazy quality or state.

crazy • *adjective* (**crazier**, **craziest**) **1** *informal* **a** mentally unstable, insane. **b** foolish, impractical. **2** *informal* extremely enthusiastic. **3** *slang* **a** exciting, wild: *a crazy party*. **b** excellent. • *noun* (*plural* **crazies**) *slang* (usu. in *plural*) a person who is wild, eccentric, unbalanced, etc.

crazy eights *noun* (treated as *singular*) a card game, usu. played by children, in which a player plays a card of the same suit or denomination as the preceding one, with eight being a wild card.

crazy quilt *noun* **1** a patchwork quilt made of material of various shapes, sizes, and colours. **2** an apparently random collection (e.g. of laws, districts, etc.): *a crazy quilt of cities, towns, townships, and counties*.

> **SPELL CHECK**
> **creak, creek** ABC
>
> A stream or brook is a **creek**.

creak • *noun* a harsh scraping or squeaking sound. • *verb* **1** make a creak. **2 a** move with a creaking noise. **b** move slowly or stiffly.

creakily *adverb* in a way that makes a creaking noise.

creaky *adjective* (**creakier**, **creakiest**) **1** creaking or liable to creak. **2 a** stiff or frail: *creaky joints*. **b** (of a practice, institution, etc.) outmoded.

cream • *noun* **1 a** the fatty content of milk which gathers at the top and can be made into butter by churning. **b** this eaten (often whipped) with a dessert, as a cake filling, etc. **2** (usu. as **the cream**) the best or choicest part of something, esp. an elite group of people. **3** a creamlike preparation, esp. a cosmetic: *hand cream*. **4** a very pale yellow or off-white colour. **5 a** a filling, dessert, etc. with a creamy consistency.

b a soup or sauce containing milk or cream. **c** a full-bodied mellow sweet sherry. **d** a sandwich cookie with a cream filling. **e** a chocolate-covered, usu. fruit-flavoured, fondant. • *verb* **1 a** take the cream from (milk). **b** (usu. foll. by *off*) take the best or a specified part from. **2** work (butter, esp. with sugar etc.) to a creamy consistency. **3** *informal* defeat decisively (esp. in a game etc.). **4** *slang* **a** a hit: *creamed him with my purse.* **b** beat thoroughly. • *adjective* pale yellow; off-white.

cream cheese *noun* a soft, rich, spreadable, and unripened cheese made from milk or cream.

creamed *adjective* **1** prepared in a cream sauce. **2** (of honey) whipped or churned. **3** (of cottage cheese) having the curds combined with milk.

creamer *noun* **1** a jug or container for cream. **2 a** a non-dairy product used as a substitute for cream or milk in coffee or tea. **b** a small, single-serving container of this or of cream.

creamery *noun* (*plural* **creameries**) a factory producing butter or cheese.

creaminess *noun* a creamy taste, colour, or consistency.

cream pie *noun* a pie with a custard-like filling, often with a whipped cream topping.

cream puff *noun* **1** a ball-shaped pastry shell filled with whipped cream etc. **2** *informal* a weak, ineffectual person.

cream sauce *noun* **1** a sauce containing a high proportion of cream. **2** a white sauce made from milk and thickened with butter and flour.

cream soda *noun* a vanilla-flavoured soft drink.

creamy *adjective* (**creamier, creamiest**) like cream in taste, colour, or consistency.

crease • *noun* **1 a** a line in paper etc. caused by folding etc. **b** a vertical line pressed into trousers with an iron. **c** a fold or wrinkle. **2** a marked area in front of the goal in hockey or lacrosse into which the puck or the ball must precede the players. • *verb* (**creases, creased, creasing**) **1** make creases in (material). **2** become creased.

create *verb* (**creates, created, creating**) **1** cause to exist; make (something) new or original. **2** have as a result; produce (a feeling etc.).

creation *noun* **1 a** the action or process of bringing something into existence: *creation of a coalition government* ◊ *job creation.* **b** a thing which has been made or invented, esp. something showing artistic talent: *she treats fictional creations as if they were real people.* **2 a** (usu. **the Creation**) the creating of the universe regarded as an act of God. **b** (usu. **Creation**) everything so created; the universe.

creationism *noun* a theory attributing all matter, biological species, etc., to separate acts of creation, esp. according to a literal interpretation of the Biblical book of Genesis, rather than to evolution. ▶ **creationist** *noun & adjective*

creation myth *noun* (also **creation story**, *plural* **creation stories**) an account of the origins of the universe and humankind in which the planets and all living things are attributed to specific acts of divine creation rather than to natural processes postulated in scientific theories such as the big bang theory and the theory of evolution.

creative *adjective* **1** of or involving the skilful and imaginative use of something to produce e.g. a work of art: *creative energies.* **2** able to create things, usu. in an imaginative way: *the wardrobe staff are such creative*

people. **3** inventive; having a good imagination and original ideas. ▶ **creatively** *adverb*

creative writing *noun* the writing of fiction, plays, etc.

creativity *noun* the imagination required to conceive and produce original ideas or a work of art; the ability to be creative.

creator *noun* **1** a person who creates. **2** (**the Creator**) God.

creature *noun* **1 a** an animal, as distinct from a human being. **b** any living being: *we are all God's creatures.* **2** a person of a specified kind: *you heartless creature!* **3** a person or organization considered to be completely under the control of another: *the village teacher was expected to be the creature of his employer.* **4** a person whose character is defined by a specified influence: *creatures of our culture.* PHRASES **creature of habit** a person set in an unvarying routine.

creature comforts *plural noun* material comforts such as good food, warmth, etc.

crèche *noun* = NATIVITY SCENE. [Say CRESH or CRAYSH]

cred *noun informal* credibility: *street cred.*

credence *noun* **1** belief in or acceptance of something as true: *psychoanalysis finds little credence among laymen.* **2** believability. PHRASES **give credence to 1** believe. **2** (also **lend credence to**) (of a fact etc.) support or reinforce the believability of. [Say CREE dince]

credential *noun* (usu. in *plural*) evidence of a person's achievements or trustworthiness, usu. in the form of references etc.: *recruitment is based on academic credentials.* ▶ **credentialed** *adjective*

credibility *noun* **1** the condition of being trusted or believed in: *the government's loss of credibility.* **2** the quality of being convincing or believable: *the book's anecdotes have scant regard for credibility.*

credible *adjective* **1** (of a person or statement) believable or worthy of belief: *few people found his story credible* ◊ *a credible witness.* **2** (of a threat etc.) convincing. ▶ **credibly** *adverb*

credit • *noun* **1** a source of honour, pride, etc.: *she is a credit to the school.* **2** the acknowledgement of merit. **3** a good reputation. **4 a** acknowledgement of competence: *give me some credit!* **b** something believable or trustworthy: *that statement has credit.* **5 a** a person's financial standing; the sum of money at a person's disposal in a bank etc. **b** the power to obtain goods etc. before payment. **6** (usu. in *plural*) **a** an acknowledgement of a contributor's services to a film, television program, etc., usually listed at the beginning or end. **b** a film or television program etc. in which a person has participated. **7** a reputation for solvency and honesty in business. **8 a** (in bookkeeping) the acknowledgement of being paid. **b** the sum entered. **c** = TAX CREDIT. **9 a** official recognition that a student has completed a course meeting the requirements of a diploma or degree. **b** a value ascribed to a course: *needed three credits.* • *verb* (**credits, credited, crediting**) **1** ascribe (often without certainty) an accomplishment to: *was credited with the discovery.* **2** believe: *cannot credit it.* **3** (usu. foll. by *to, with*) enter in an account as being paid. PHRASES **do credit to** (or **do a person credit**) enhance the reputation of. **get credit for** be given credit for. **give a person credit for 1** enter (a sum) to a person's credit. **2** ascribe (a good quality) to a person. **give credit to** believe. **on credit** with an arrangement to pay later. **take credit (for)** accept praise or commendation, esp. for something one is not responsible for. **to one's credit** in one's praise, commendation, or defence.

WRITING TIP
creditable, credible

Do not confuse **creditable** with **credible**. **Creditable** means "worthy of praise but not outstanding", as in *Jenny and Clive turned in a creditable performance in the three-legged race, finishing fifth*. **Credible** means "believable", as in *The lawyers tried to show that the witness was not credible*.

---

creditable *adjective* **1** (of a performance, effort, or action) deserving public acknowledgement and praise but not necessarily outstanding or successful: *in spite of its faults, the building is a creditable piece of work*. **2** that can be credited: *tax-creditable*. ▶ **creditably** *adverb*

credit card *noun* a card issued by a bank or business authorizing the obtaining of goods on credit.

Créditiste *noun Cdn* a member or supporter of the Quebec Social Credit Party. [Say creddy TEEST]

credit line *noun* = LINE OF CREDIT.

creditor *noun* a person to whom a debt is owing.

credit rating *noun* an estimate of one's suitability to receive credit.

credit union *noun* a banking co-operative offering financial services to members.

creditworthiness *noun* the extent to which a person or company is considered suitable to receive credit.

creditworthy *adjective* (of a person or company) considered suitable to receive credit, esp. because of being reliable in paying money back in the past.

credo *noun* (*plural* **credos**) **1** a set of principles held by a specified group, esp. as a philosophy: *he announced his credo in his first editorial*. **2** (**Credo**) a prayer summarizing Christian belief, esp. the Apostles' or Nicene creed. [Say CREE doe or CRAY doe]

credulity *noun* the ability or a willingness to believe that something is true or real: *the movie's plot stretches credulity to the limit*. [Say kruh DYOOLA tee]

credulous *adjective* having or showing too great a readiness to believe things: *contempt for her credulous countrymen who took gossip as gospel*. ▶ **credulously** *adverb* **credulousness** *noun* [Say CRED you lus]

Cree • *noun* (*plural* **Cree** or **Crees**) **1** a member of a part of the Algonquian linguistic family, living from the east coast to the Rocky Mountains, and forming the largest Aboriginal group in Canada. **2** the language of this people. • *adjective* of the Cree or their language.

creed *noun* **1** a set of principles or opinions, esp. as a philosophy of life: *liberalism was more than a political creed*. **2** (often **the Creed**) a prayer summarizing Christian beliefs. **3** a system of religious belief: *people of many creeds and cultures*.

Creek • *noun* **1** a member of a North American Aboriginal confederacy of the Muskogee and some other peoples. **2** the Muskogean language of the Muskogee. • *adjective* of or relating to this people or their culture or language.

SPELL CHECK
creek, creak

A harsh scraping or squeaking sound is a **creak**.

---

creek *noun* a tributary of a river; a stream or brook. **PHRASES** **up the creek** *slang* **1** in difficulties or trouble. **2** crazy. [Rhymes either with SEEK or with SICK]

creel *noun* **1** a large wicker basket for fish. **2** an angler's fishing basket.

creep • *verb* (**creeps, crept, creeping**) **1** move with the body prone and close to the ground; crawl. **2** move

slowly and stealthily or timidly. **3** enter slowly (into a person's affections, life, awareness, etc.): *a feeling crept over her*. **4** (of a plant) grow along the ground or up a wall by means of tendrils etc. **5** (as **creeping** *adjective*) developing slowly and steadily: *creeping inflation*. **6** (of the flesh) feel as if insects etc. were creeping over it, as a result of fear, horror, etc. • *noun* **1 a** the act of creeping. **b** slow movement, esp. at a steady but almost imperceptible pace: *an attempt to prevent the slow creep of costs*. **2** (in *plural*; **the creeps**) *informal* a nervous feeling of revulsion or fear. **3** *informal* an unpleasant or obnoxious person. **PHRASES** **creep up on** approach (a person) stealthily or unnoticed.

creeper *noun* **1** any climbing or creeping plant. **2** any bird that climbs. **3** *slang* a soft-soled shoe.

creepily *adverb* in a way that causes an unpleasant feeling of fear or unease: *the street was creepily deserted*.

creepiness *noun* a quality that causes an unpleasant feeling of fear or unease: *the creepiness of the old house*.

creepy *adjective* (**creepier, creepiest**) *informal* causing an unpleasant feeling of fear or unease.

creepy-crawly *informal* • *noun* (*plural* **creepy-crawlies**) an insect, worm, etc. • *adjective* creeping and crawling.

cremate *verb* (**cremates, cremated, cremating**) burn (a corpse etc.) to ashes, esp. ceremonially. ▶ **cremation** *noun* [Say CREAM ate or cream ATE]

crematorium *noun* (*plural* **crematoria** or **crematoriums**) a building in which corpses are cremated. [Say creama TORY um]

creme *noun* **1** a creamy substance used as a filling etc., not containing real cream: *creme-filled cookies*. **2** a toiletry, cosmetic, or ointment having the consistency of cream.

crème brûlée *noun* (*plural* **crèmes brûlées**) a baked custard topped with caramelized sugar. [Say crem broo LAY]

crème caramel *noun* (*plural* **crème caramels**) a baked custard cooked in a caramel-coated dish, usu. inverted so that the caramel forms a sauce over the custard. [Say crem cara MEL]

crème de la crème *noun* the best part; the elite. [Say crem duh luh CREM]

Creole • *noun* **1 a** a descendant of European (esp. Spanish) settlers in the W Indies or Central or South America. **b** a white descendant of French settlers in the southern US. **c** a person of mixed European and black descent. **2 a** a language formed from the contact of a European language (esp. English, French, or Portuguese) with another (esp. African) language. **b** (usu. **creole**) a former pidgin language that has become the sole or native language of a community, as in Haiti. • *adjective* **1** of a Creole or Creoles. **2** (usu. **creole**) of Creole origin or production. [Say CREE ole]

creosote • *noun* **1** (also **creosote oil**) a dark brown oil distilled from coal tar, used as a wood preservative. **2** a colourless fluid distilled from wood tar, used as an antiseptic. • *verb* treat with creosote. [Say CREE uh sote]

crepe *noun* **1** a woven or knitted fabric with a wrinkled surface. **2** a thin pancake, usu. with a savoury or sweet filling. **3** (also **crepe rubber**) a very hard-wearing wrinkled sheet rubber used for the soles of shoes etc. **4** (also **crepe paper**) thin crinkled paper. [Say CRAPE or CREP]

crept *past and past participle of* CREEP.

crescendo • *noun* (*plural* **crescendos**) **1** *Music* a passage gradually increasing in loudness. **2 a** a progress towards a climax: *a crescendo of emotions*. **b** a climax: *reached a crescendo then died away*. • *verb* (**crescendoes, crescendoed, crescendoing**) increase gradually in loudness or intensity. [Say kruh SHENDO]

C

crescent • *noun* **1** the curved sickle shape of the waxing or waning moon. **2** anything of this shape. **3** a curving street. **4** a crescent-shaped item of food, esp. a bread roll or cookie. **5 a** the crescent-shaped emblem of Islam or Turkey. **b** (**the Crescent**) the world or power of Islam. • *adjective* crescent-shaped.

cress *noun* (*plural* **cresses**) a plant of the cabbage family, usu. with pungent edible leaves, e.g. watercress.

crest • *noun* **1 a** a comb or tuft of feathers, fur, etc. on a bird's or animal's head. **b** something resembling this, esp. a plume of feathers on a helmet. **c** a helmet; the top of a helmet. **2** the top of something, esp. of a wave etc. **3** a shield or coat of arms: *our school crest*. **4 a** a line along the top of the neck of some animals. **b** the hair growing from this; a mane. **5** the highest level reached by a river in flood. • *verb* **1** reach the crest of (a hill, wave, etc.). **2 a** provide with a crest. **b** serve as a crest to. **3** (of a wave) form into a crest. **4** (of a river in flood) reach its highest level. ▸ PHRASES **the crest of a wave** the most favourable moment in one's progress. ▸ **crested** *adjective* (also in *combination*).

crestfallen *adjective* sad and disappointed: *came back empty-handed and crestfallen*.

Cretaceous • *adjective* **1** (**cretaceous**) of the nature of chalk. **2** of or relating to the last period of the Mesozoic era, lasting from about 144 to 65 million years BP, between the Jurassic and Tertiary periods. The period was marked by a warm climate and higher sea level; the first flowering plants emerged and the domination of the dinosaurs continued, although they died out quite abruptly towards the end of it. • *noun* this geological era or system. [Say kruh TAY shuss]

Cretan • *noun* a native of Crete, an island SE of the Greek mainland where a Minoan civilization flourished in the 2nd millennium BC. • *adjective* of or relating to Crete or the Cretans. [Say CREET'n]

cretin *noun* **1** a person who is deformed and mentally retarded as the result of a thyroid deficiency. **2** *informal derogatory* a stupid person. ▸ **cretinism** *noun* **cretinous** *adjective* [Say CRET'n or CREET'n]

cretons *plural noun Cdn* (*Que.*) a spread of shredded pork cooked with onions in pork fat. [Say kruh TON]

crevasse *noun* a deep open crack, esp. in a glacier. [Say kruh VASS]

crevice *noun* a narrow opening or fissure, esp. in a rock or building etc.

crew[1] • *noun* (*often treated as plural*) **1 a** a group of people operating a ship, aircraft, train, etc. **b** such a group as distinguished from the captain or officers. **c** a body of people working together; a team. **2** *informal* a company of people: *a crew of disenchanted idealists*. • *verb* supply or act as a crew or member of a crew (for).

crew[2] *past of* CROW[2].

crewcut *noun* a very short haircut; a brushcut.

crewman *noun* (*plural* **crewmen**) a member of a crew.

crewneck *noun* **1** a close-fitting round neckline, esp. on a sweater. **2** a sweater etc. with a crewneck.

crib • *noun* **1** a bed for a baby or young child, having barred sides. **2** a barred container or rack for animal fodder. **3** *informal* **a** a sheet of notes, answers to questions, etc. used surreptitiously by students as an aid in an exam etc. **b** plagiarized work etc. **4** (also **cribbing**) heavy crossed timbers used in foundations in loose soil, to support a pier, to form a dam, etc. **5 a** *informal* cribbage. **b** (in cribbage) a set of cards discarded by the players and used by the dealer. • *verb* (**cribs**, **cribbed**, **cribbing**) *informal* copy (another person's work) unfairly or without acknowledgement: *he often cribbed from other researchers*.

cribbage *noun* a card game in which the dealer may

score from the cards in the crib (*see* CRIB *noun* **5b**), esp. using pegs in a board for keeping score.

crib death *noun* = SUDDEN INFANT DEATH SYNDROME.

crick • *noun* a sudden painful stiffness in the neck or the back etc. • *verb* produce a crick in (the neck etc.).

cricket[1] *noun* any of various grasshopper-like insects of the family Gryllidae, the males of which produce a characteristic chirping sound.

cricket[2] • *noun* a game played on a field with two teams of 11 players taking turns to bowl at a wicket defended by a batting player of the other team. • *verb* (**crickets**, **cricketed**, **cricketing**) play cricket. ▸ **cricketer** *noun*

cried *past and past participle of* CRY.

crier *noun* **1** a person who cries. **2** an officer who makes public announcements in a public place etc.

crime *noun* **1 a** an offence punishable by law. **b** illegal acts as a whole: *resorted to crime*. **2** an action considered to be evil, shameful or wrong, though not illegal: *they condemned apartheid as a crime against humanity*. **3** a shameful act: *a crime to waste it*.

criminal • *noun* a person who has committed a crime or crimes. • *adjective* **1** of, involving, or concerning crime: *criminal records*. **2** having committed (and usu. been convicted of) a crime. **3** relating to or expert in criminal law rather than civil or political matters: *criminal lawyer*. **4** deplorable and shocking: *many children never fulfill their potential, and that is a criminal waste*.

Criminal Code *noun* a federal statute embodying most of Canada's criminal law and specifying criminal procedures and sentencing options.

criminal harassment *noun Cdn* the criminal offence of stalking.

criminality *noun* the fact of people being involved in crime; criminal acts or behaviour: *the underlying causes of criminality*. [Say crimmin ALA tee]

criminalization *noun* the act or process of criminalizing an activity or those involved in it.

criminalize *verb* (**criminalizes**, **criminalized**, **criminalizing**) **1** turn (an activity) into a criminal offence by making it illegal: *the law criminalizes assisted suicide*. **2** turn (a person) into a criminal, esp. by making his or her activities illegal.

criminal law *noun* law concerned with the prosecution of crime (*opp.* CIVIL LAW 1).

criminally *adverb* in a criminal manner; according to the laws that deal with crime: *criminally negligent*.

criminal negligence *noun Cdn Law* an offence involving a wanton or reckless disregard for the lives or safety of others.

criminologist *noun* a person who studies crime.

criminology *noun* the scientific study of crime.

crimp • *verb* **1** compress into small folds or ridges: *crimp the edges of the pie*. **2** make narrow wrinkles or flutings in. **3** make waves in (the hair) with a hot iron. • *noun* a crimped thing or form. ▸ PHRASES **put a crimp in** *informal* thwart; interfere with.

crimson • *adjective* of a rich deep purplish red. • *noun* this colour. • *verb* make or become crimson.

cringe *verb* (**cringes**, **cringed**, **cringing**) **1** bend one's head and body in fear, apprehension, or disgust. **2** feel excessively embarrassed: *I cringed at his tactlessness*. **3** behave obsequiously: *we are surrounded by cringing yes-men*.

crinkle • *noun* **1** a wrinkle or crease in paper, cloth, etc. **2** fabric with a wrinkled surface: *crinkle cotton*. • *verb* (**crinkles**, **crinkled**, **crinkling**) form crinkles.

crinkle-cut *adjective* (of vegetables) cut with wavy edges.

crinkly *adjective* having small creases, wrinkles, or kinks: *a crinkly dress* ◊ *crinkly hair*.

crinoline *noun* a stiffened or hooped petticoat worn to make a skirt stand out. [Say KRINNA lin]

cripes *interjection slang* expressing surprise, anger, etc.

cripple • *noun* a person who is permanently impaired in movement, esp. one unable to walk normally. • *verb* (**cripples, crippled, crippling**) **1** cause someone to become unable to walk or move properly: *a young boy was crippled for life*. **2** cause severe and disabling damage to a machine etc.: *the pilot managed to land the crippled plane*. **3** weaken or damage (an institution, enterprise, etc.) seriously: *crippled by lack of funding*. ▶**crippled** *adjective* **crippling** *adjective* **cripplingly** *adverb*

crisis *noun* (*plural* **crises**) **1** a time of danger or great difficulty: *the current economic crisis* ◊ *the monarchy was in crisis*. **2** the turning point, esp. of a disease. **3** a decisive moment. [Say CRY seez for the plural]

crisis centre *noun* a place offering immediate counselling, treatment, etc. to people who are victims of sexual assault, physical abuse, etc.

crisis management *noun* **1** the practice of taking managerial action only when a crisis has developed. **2** the management of a crisis situation.

crisp • *adjective* **1** hard but brittle. **2** (of air or weather) dry and cold. **3** (of a style or manner) brisk and decisive, esp. dismissive. **4** (of pictures etc.) clear and distinct. **5** (of cloth etc.) slightly stiff. **6** (of hair) closely curling. **7** (of fruit or vegetables) firm and fresh. **8** invigorating to the sense of smell or taste. • *noun* **1** a baked dessert made of fruit topped with a crumbly mixture of flour, oats, butter, and sugar. **2** a thing overdone in roasting etc.: *burned to a crisp*. **3** a crisp cookie. • *verb* **1** make or become crisp. **2** curl in short stiff folds or waves.

crispbread *noun* **1** a thin crisp biscuit of crushed rye etc. **2** these collectively.

crisper *noun* a compartment in a refrigerator for storing fruit and vegetables.

crispiness *noun* a crispy quality.

crisply *adverb* **1** in a clear, sharp, or clean manner: *crisply drawn images* ◊ *crisply ironed shirts*. **2** until crisp or crispy: *crisply fried potatoes*. **3** in an abrupt or decisive manner, without hesitation: *"Time to go," he said crisply*.

crispness *noun* a crispy quality.

crispy *adjective* (**crispier, crispiest**) having a pleasingly firm, dry, and brittle surface or texture: *crispy bits of salt pork*.

criss-cross • *verb* (**criss-crosses, criss-crossed, criss-crossing**) **1** a cross or intersect repeatedly. **b** move crosswise. **2** mark or make with a criss-cross pattern. • *noun* (*plural* **criss-crosses**) **1** a pattern of crossing lines. **2** the crossing of lines or currents etc. • *adjective* crossing; in cross lines: *criss-cross marking*. • *adverb* crosswise.

crit *noun informal* **1** = CRITICISM 2. **2** = CRITIQUE *noun*.

criterion *noun* (*plural* **criteria**) a principle or standard that a thing is judged by. [Say cry TEERY in for the singular, cry TEERY uh for the plural]

critic *noun* **1** a person who expresses an unfavourable opinion: *critics of the new legislation say it is too broad*. **2 a** a person who reviews, analyzes, or judges the merits of literary, artistic, theatrical, or musical works etc., esp. regularly or professionally. **b** a person who writes or broadcasts reviews of restaurants, wine, etc. **3** a person engaged in the study of the content and message of writings. **4** *Cdn* a member of an opposition party monitoring and criticizing a specific government ministry: *finance critic*.

critical *adjective* **1 a** making or involving adverse or disapproving comments or judgments: *I was critical of the previous administration* ◊ *a critical review*. **b** expressing or involving criticism: *she won great critical acclaim*. **c** involving judgment or discernment: *use your critical sense*. **2** skilful at or engaged in criticism. **3** providing commentary or analysis: *a critical edition of Milton*. **4 a** of or at a crisis; involving risk or suspense: *in critical condition*. **b** decisive, crucial: *of critical importance* ◊ *at the critical moment*. **5 a** *Math & Physics* marking transition from one state etc. to another: *critical angle*. **b** (of a nuclear reactor) maintaining a self-sustaining chain reaction. ▶**criticality** *noun* (in sense 5). **critically** *adverb*

critical mass *noun* **1** the amount of fissile material needed to maintain a nuclear chain reaction. **2** the amount of anything required to achieve a desired effect: *a critical mass of volunteers*.

criticism *noun* **1** fault-finding; disapproval: *can't stand criticism* ◊ *listed several criticisms*. **2 a** the work of a critic. **b** an article, essay, etc., expressing or containing an analytical evaluation of something.

criticize *verb* (**criticizes, criticized, criticizing**) **1** find fault with; censure. **2** discuss critically.

critique • *noun* a detailed analysis and assessment of something, esp. a literary, philosophical, or political theory. • *verb* (**critiques, critiqued, critiquing**) discuss critically. [Say crit EEK]

critter *noun informal* an animal, insect, etc.

croak • *noun* **1** a deep hoarse sound as of a frog or a raven. **2** a sound resembling this. • *verb* **1** utter a croak. **2** *slang* **a** die. **b** kill.

croaky *adjective* (**croakier, croakiest**) (of a voice) croaking; hoarse.

Croat *noun & adjective* = CROATIAN. [Say CROW at]

Croatian • *noun* **1 a** a native or inhabitant of Croatia, a country in SE Europe. **b** a person of Croatian descent. **2** the language of the Croatians, a form of Serbo-Croat written in the Roman alphabet. • *adjective* of Croatia, the Croatians, or their language. [Say crow AY sh'n]

croc *noun informal* a crocodile.

crochet • *noun* **1** a handicraft in which yarn is made up into a patterned fabric by means of a small slender hooked rod: *crochet hook*. **2** work made in this way. • *verb* (**crochets, crocheted, crocheting**) make in such a way: *crocheted an afghan* ◊ *I wish I'd learned how to crochet*. [Say crow SHAY]

crock *noun* **1** an earthenware pot or jar. **2** *informal* something untrue, deceitful, etc.: *their story was just a crock*.

crocked *adjective slang* drunk.

crockery *noun* earthenware or china dishes, plates, etc.

crocodile *noun* **1** any of a group of large tropical and subtropical amphibious reptiles with thick scaly skin, long tail, and long jaws, related to alligators. **2** leather from its skin, used to make bags, shoes, etc.

crocodile tears *noun* **1** insincere grief. **2** tears shed without feeling any real sorrow, pain, etc.

crocus *noun* (*plural* **crocuses**) **1** a spring-flowering plant, growing from a corm and having white, yellow, or purple flowers. **2** *see* PRAIRIE CROCUS.

Crohn's disease *noun* a chronic inflammatory disease of the intestines, esp. the colon and ileum, causing ulcers and fistulae. [Rhymes with *BONES*]

croissant *noun* a rich, flaky, crescent-shaped bread roll. [Say crwah SONN]

crokinole *noun* esp. *Cdn* a game in which wooden discs are flicked across a round wooden board towards its centre. [Say CROKA nole]

Cro-Magnon • *adjective* of a tall broad-faced European race, the earliest form of modern human in Europe, who appeared *c*.35,000 years ago. • *noun* a Cro-Magnon person. [Say crow MAG non]

crone *noun* an old woman who is thin and ugly.

crony *noun* (*plural* **cronies**) often *derogatory* a close friend or companion. [Say CROW nee]

cronyism *noun* the appointment of friends to political posts without due regard to their qualifications; patronage. [Say CROW nee ism]

crook • *noun* 1 *informal* **a** a criminal. **b** a swindler. 2 the hooked staff of a shepherd or bishop. 3 **a** a bend, curve, or hook. **b** anything hooked or curved. • *verb* bend, curve. • *adjective* crooked.

crooked *adjective* (**crookeder, crookedest**) 1 **a** not straight or level; bent, curved, twisted. **b** deformed, bent with age. 2 *informal* dishonest. ▶**crookedly** *adverb* **crookedness** *noun*

croon • *verb* hum or sing in a low subdued voice, esp. sentimentally. • *noun* such singing. ▶**crooner** *noun*

crop • *noun* 1 **a** the produce of cultivated plants, esp. cereals. **b** the season's total yield of this: *a good crop*. 2 **a** group or an amount produced or appearing at one time: *this year's crop of students*. 3 the stock or handle of a whip. 4 **a** a style of hair cut very short. **b** the cropping of hair. 5 **a** the pouch in a bird's gullet where food is prepared for digestion. **b** a similar organ in other animals. • *verb* (**crops, cropped, cropping**) 1 **a** cut off. **b** (of animals) bite off (the tops of plants). 2 **a** cut (hair, edges of a book, a dog's ears, etc.) short. **b** trim (a photograph) to fit a space. 3 gather or reap (produce). 4 (foll. by *with*) sow or plant (land) with a crop. 5 (of land) bear a crop. PHRASES **crop out** *Geology* appear at the surface. **crop up** 1 appear or come to one's notice unexpectedly. 2 *Geology* = CROP OUT.

crop-duster *noun* 1 a small plane used for crop-dusting. 2 the pilot of such a plane.

crop-dusting *noun* the sprinkling of powdered insecticide or fertilizer on crops, esp. from the air.

cropper *noun* PHRASES **come a cropper** *slang* 1 fail badly. 2 fall heavily.

croquet *noun* a game played on a lawn, in which mallets are used to drive wooden balls through a series of hoops. [Say crow KAY or CROW kay]

cross • *noun* (*plural* **crosses**) 1 an upright post with a transverse bar, as used in antiquity for crucifixion. 2 **a** (**the Cross**) in Christianity, the cross on which Christ was crucified. **b** a representation of this as an emblem of Christianity. **c** = SIGN OF THE CROSS. 3 a staff surmounted by a cross. 4 **a** a thing or mark shaped like a cross, esp. a figure made by two short intersecting lines (+ or x). **b** a monument in the form of a cross, esp. on a tomb. 5 **a** cross-shaped decoration awarded for personal valour. 6 **a** an intermixture of animal breeds or plant varieties. **b** an animal or plant resulting from this. 7 a mixture or compromise of two things: *a cross between jazz and blues*. 8 *Boxing* a blow with a crosswise movement of the fist. 9 a trial or affliction; something to be endured. • *verb* (**crosses, crossed, crossing**) 1 go across or to the other side of (a road, river, sea, etc.). 2 place or be across one another: *the roads cross near the bridge* ◊ *cross one's legs*. 3 draw a line or lines across: *cross your t's*. 4 (foll. by *off, out*) cancel or obliterate or remove from a list with lines drawn across. 5 **cross oneself** make the sign of the cross. 6 **a** pass in opposite or different directions. **b** (of letters between

two correspondents) each be dispatched before receipt of the other. 7 **a** cause to interbreed. **b** cross-fertilize (plants). 8 *slang* cheat; double-cross. • *adjective* 1 angry. 2 reaching from side to side. 3 intersecting. 4 opposed. PHRASES **at cross-purposes** misunderstanding or conflicting with one another. **bear one's cross** accept trials and misfortunes stoically. **cross one's fingers** (or **keep one's fingers crossed**) 1 put one finger across another as a sign of hoping for good luck. 2 trust in good luck. **cross the floor** *Cdn & Brit.* join the opposing side in a legislature, leadership convention, etc. **cross one's heart** make a solemn pledge, esp. by crossing one's front. **cross one's mind** (of a thought etc.) occur to one, esp. transiently. **cross over** 1 pass over (a street, boundary, etc.). 2 move from one culture or artistic style to another. **cross paths** (or **cross one's path**) encounter or meet. **cross swords** (often foll. by *with*) encounter in opposition; have an argument or dispute. **cross wires** (or **get one's wires crossed**) have a misunderstanding.

crossbar *noun* a horizontal bar between two upright bars, e.g. on a bicycle or hockey net.

crossbeam *noun* a transverse beam in a structure.

crossbill *noun* a stout finch having a bill with crossed mandibles for opening pine cones.

crossbones *noun* a representation of two crossed thigh bones, usu. under the figure of a skull, as an emblem of piracy or death.

crossbow *noun* a bow fixed across a wooden stock, with a groove for an arrow and a mechanism for drawing and releasing the string.

crossbreed • *noun* 1 a breed of animals or plants produced by crossing different breeds. 2 an individual animal or plant of a crossbreed. • *verb* (**crossbreeds, crossbred, crossbreeding**) produce or modify by crossing different breeds.

cross-check • *verb* 1 check by a second or alternative method, or by several methods. 2 (in hockey and lacrosse) obstruct (an opponent) by holding one's stick horizontally in both hands and thrusting it at the opponent's body. • *noun* an instance of cross-checking.

cross-country • *adjective & adverb* 1 across fields or open country: *cross-country running*. 2 across a country: *a cross-country train trip*. • *adjective* of or designating the sport of skiing across the countryside using long, narrow skis. • *noun* (*plural* **cross-countries**) a cross-country sport or race.

cross-cultural *adjective* of or relating to different cultures or comparison between them. ▶**cross-culturally** *adverb*

cross-current *noun* 1 a current in a body of water flowing across the main current. 2 a conflicting tendency or movement: *strong cross-currents of debate*.

crosscut • *verb* (**crosscuts, crosscut, crosscutting**) 1 cut across (a piece of wood etc.). 2 switch back and forth between two or more sequences or shots in a film so they appear to be taking place at the same time. • *adjective* cut across the main grain or axis. • *noun* a diagonal cut, path, etc.

cross-dress *verb* wear clothes usu. worn by a person of the opposite sex, esp. for sexual pleasure. ▶**cross-dresser** *noun*

cross-dressing *noun* the practice of wearing clothes usu. worn by a person of the opposite sex, esp. for sexual pleasure.

crosse *noun* (in women's field lacrosse) the stick. [Sounds like CROSS]

cross-examination *noun* 1 the questioning of a witness called by the other party in a court of law to

check testimony already given. **2** any aggressive interrogation.

cross-examine *verb* (**cross-examines**, **cross-examined**, **cross-examining**) **1** examine (a witness in a law court) esp. to check, extend or discredit testimony already given. **2** interrogate with minute and persistent questioning. ▶ **cross-examiner** *noun*

cross-eyed *adjective* (as a disorder) having one or both eyes turned permanently inwards towards the nose.

cross-fertilization *noun* **1** fertilization from one of a different species. **2** fruitful interchange of ideas etc. ▶ **cross-fertilize** *verb* (**cross-fertilizes**, **cross-fertilized**, **cross-fertilizing**)

crossfire *noun* **1** lines of gunfire crossing one another simultaneously from different positions. **2** used to refer to a situation in which two or more groups are attacking or arguing with each other: *the sponsors are caught in the crossfire of the battle between the world champion and his team boss.*

cross fox *noun* a yellowish North American variety of the red fox with a cross-shaped patch across the shoulders.

cross-grained *adjective* **1** (of timber) having a grain that runs across the regular grain. **2** stubbornly contrary or bad-tempered: *Bruce was a cross-grained and boastful individual.*

crosshairs *noun* a pair of fine wires crossing at right angles at the focus of an optical instrument or gun sight, for use in positioning, aiming, or measuring.

cross-hatch *verb* (**cross-hatches**, **cross-hatched**, **cross-hatching**) shade with intersecting sets of parallel lines. ▶ **cross-hatching** *noun*

crossing *noun* **1** a place where things (esp. roads) cross. **2** a place at which one may cross a street, railway tracks, etc. **3** a journey across water. **4** *Biology* mating.

cross-legged *adjective* with one leg crossed over the other.

crossly *adverb* in a cross or angry manner.

Cross of Valour *noun* Canada's highest award for bravery, given to civilians and military personnel who perform selfless acts of courage in the face of extreme danger. Abbreviation: **CV**.

crossover • *noun* **1** a point or place of crossing from one side to the other. **2** the process of crossing over, esp. from one style or genre of music etc. to another. • *adjective* **1** having a part that crosses over. **2** that crosses over, esp. from one style or genre to another.

crosspiece *noun* a transverse beam or other component of a structure etc.

cross-pollinate *verb* (**cross-pollinates**, **cross-pollinated**, **cross-pollinating**) **1** pollinate (a plant) from another: *plants can be cross-pollinated by hand or by bees.* **2** blend together (styles of music, ideas, etc.). ▶ **cross-pollination** *noun*

cross-reference • *noun* a reference from one part of a book, article, etc., to another. • *verb* provide with cross-references.

cross rib *noun* a cut of beef from the front part of the ribs, below the blade.

crossroad *noun* **1** a road that crosses a main road or connects two main roads. **2** = CROSSROADS.

crossroads *noun* **1** an intersection of two or more roads. **2** a critical turning point: *we are at a crossroads.*

cross-section *noun* **1 a** a cutting of a solid at right angles to an axis. **b** a plane surface produced in this way. **c** a representation of this. **2** a representative sample, esp. of people. **3** *Physics* a quantity expressing the probability of interaction between particles. ▶ **cross-sectional** *adjective*

cross-stitch • *noun* **1** a stitch formed of two stitches crossing each other. **2** needlework done using this stitch. • *verb* (**cross-stitches**, **cross-stitched**, **cross-stitching**) sew or embroider with cross-stitches.

crosstown • *adjective* **1** extending across or following a route across a town or city. **2** coming from the other side of a town or city, esp. in reference to two competing sports teams in the same town: *crosstown rivals.* • *adverb* **1** across a town or city. **2** to a rival team in the same city: *was traded crosstown.*

cross-train *verb* **1** train in two or more sports to improve performance, esp. in one's main sport. **2** train (an employee etc.) in more than one skill. ▶ **cross-trainer** *noun* **cross-training** *noun*

crosswalk *noun* a pedestrian crossing.

crossways *adverb* = CROSSWISE *adverb*.

crosswind *noun* a wind blowing across one's direction of travel.

crosswise *adjective & adverb* **1** across; transverse or transversely. **2** in the form of a cross; intersecting.

crossword *noun* (also **crossword puzzle**) a puzzle of a grid of squares and blanks into which words crossing vertically and horizontally have to be filled from clues.

crostini *plural noun* small pieces of toasted bread topped with vegetables etc., served as an appetizer. [Say cross TEENY]

crotch *noun* (*plural* **crotches**) **1** the place where legs join the trunk of the human body. **2** the part of a pair of pants, underwear, etc. where the two legs or panels join. **3** a fork of a tree or branch.

crotcheriness *noun* a peevish or crotchety manner.

crotchety *adjective* peevish, irritable.

crouch • *verb* (**crouches**, **crouched**, **crouching**) stoop low with the legs bent close to the body, esp. for concealment, or (of an animal) before pouncing; be in this position. • *noun* (*plural* **crouches**) an act of crouching; a crouching position.

croup[1] *noun* an inflammation of the larynx and trachea in children, with a hard cough and difficulty in breathing. [Say CROOP]

croup[2] *noun* the rump or hindquarters esp. of a horse. [Say CROOP]

croupier *noun* the person in charge of a gaming table, raking in and paying out money etc. [Say CROOPY ur or CROOPY ay]

crouton *noun* a small cube of fried or toasted bread used as a garnish for soups, salads, etc. [Say CROO tawn]

Crow • *noun* (*plural* **Crow** or **Crows**) **1** a member of an Aboriginal people living in southern Montana. **2** the Siouan language of this people. • *adjective* of or relating to this people or their culture or language.

crow[1] *noun* **1** any large black bird of the genus *Corvus*, having a powerful black beak, e.g. the omnivorous common crow of North America, *C. brachyrhynchos.* **2** any similar bird of the family Corvidae, e.g. the raven or magpie. **3** *slang* derogatory a woman, esp. an old or ugly one. PHRASES **as the crow flies** in a straight line. **eat crow** *informal* be forced to admit a mistake.

crow[2] • *verb* **1** (**crows**, *past* **crowed** or **crew**, **crowing**) (of a rooster) utter its characteristic loud cry. **2** make a sound expressing a feeling of happiness or triumph: *Ruby crowed with delight.* **3** say something in a tone of gloating satisfaction: *avoid crowing about your success.* • *noun* **1** a rooster's cry. **2** a happy or triumphant cry made by a person: *she gave a little crow of triumph.*

crowbar *noun* an iron bar with a flattened end, used as a lever.

crowberry *noun* (*plural* **crowberries**) **1** a heathlike evergreen shrub bearing black berries. **2** the flavourless edible berry of this plant.

crowd • *noun* **1** a large number of people gathered

together, usu. without orderly arrangement. **2** a mass of spectators; an audience. **3** *informal* a particular company or set of people: *the crowd from marketing*. **4 (the crowd)** the mass or multitude of people: *go along with the crowd*. **5** a large number (of things). • *verb* **1 a** come together in a crowd. **b** force one's way: *we crowded into the bar*. **2 a** force or compress into a confined space: *crowded the children into the gym*. **b** fill or make abundant with: *was crowded with tourists*. **3 a** (of a number of people) come aggressively close to. **b** *informal* harass or pressure (a person). **4** *informal* approach (a specified age, time, etc.) closely: *must be crowding fifty*. PHRASES **crowd out** exclude by crowding. ▶ **crowded** *adjective*

crowfoot *noun* **1** = BUTTERCUP. **2** a grass widely naturalized in North America.

crown • *noun* **1** a monarch's ornamental and usu. jewelled headdress. **2 (the Crown)** **a** the monarch, esp. as head of state. **b** the power or authority residing in the monarchy. **3 a** a wreath of leaves or flowers etc. worn on the head, esp. as an emblem of victory. **b** an award or distinction gained by a victory or achievement, esp. in sport. **4** a crown-shaped thing, esp. a device or ornament. **5** the top part of a thing, esp. of the head or a hat. **6 a** the highest or central part of an arched or curved thing: *crown of the road*. **b** a thing that completes or forms the summit. **7 a** the part of a plant just above and below the ground. **b** the leaves and upper branches of a tree. **8 a** the part of a tooth projecting from the gum. **b** an artificial replacement or covering for this. **9** = CROWN ATTORNEY. • *verb* **1** put a crown on. **2** give a person royal authority. **3** encircle or rest on the top of: *the hill was crowned with an oak tree*. **4 a** (often as **crowning** *adjective*) be or cause to be the finishing touch to: *the crowning glory*. **b** bring (efforts) to a happy issue. **5** fit a crown to (a tooth). **6** *slang* hit on the head. **7** promote (a piece in checkers) to king.

Crown attorney *noun* (*plural* **Crown attorneys**) (also **Crown counsel**, **Crown prosecutor**) *Cdn* a lawyer who conducts prosecutions of indictable offences on behalf of the Crown.

crown colony *noun* (*plural* **crown colonies**) a colony controlled by a foreign monarchy.

Crown corporation *noun* *Cdn* a corporation owned by the federal or provincial governments.

crown jewel *noun* **1** (in *plural*) the regalia and other jewellery worn by a sovereign on certain state occasions. **2** the most valuable or most beautiful possession, feature, etc.: *the crown jewel of my record collection*.

crown land *noun* (in Canada and other Commonwealth nations) land owned by federal or provincial or state governments.

crown of thorns *noun* **1** a starfish which has spines on its upper surface and feeds on coral polyps. **2** a plant with very thorny stems and small flowers surrounded by showy bracts, often grown as a houseplant.

crown prince *noun* a male heir to a sovereign throne.

crown princess *noun* (*plural* **crown princesses**) **1** the wife of a crown prince. **2** a female heir to a sovereign throne.

Crown reserve *noun* *Cdn hist.* a portion of land reserved for the Crown as a source of revenue free from the control of the colonial legislature.

Crown witness *noun* (*plural* **Crown witnesses**) *Cdn* a witness called to testify by the Crown.

Crow rate *noun* *Cdn hist.* a reduced rate for shipping grain or flour by rail from Western to Eastern Canada.

crow's feet *plural noun* wrinkles at the outer corner of a person's eye.

crow's nest *noun* a barrel etc. fixed at the masthead of a sailing vessel as a shelter for a lookout man.

crozier *noun* **1** a hooked staff carried by a bishop as a symbol of pastoral office. **2** the curled tip of a young plant, esp. a fern. [Say CROW zhur or CROW zee ur]

CRT *abbreviation* cathode ray tube.

CRTC *abbreviation* Canadian Radio-television and Telecommunications Commission.

crucial *adjective* **1** decisive, critical: *negotiations were at a crucial stage*. **2** very important: *this game is crucial to our survival*. ▶ **crucially** *adverb*

crucible *noun* **1** a container in which metals etc. are heated. **2** a severe test or trial: *tested in the crucible of combat*. **3 a** place or situation in which different elements interact to produce something new: *country music was rooted in the traditions of the Old World but formed in the crucible of the New World*. [Say CROO suh bull]

crucifer *noun* **1** a cruciferous plant, with four petals arranged in a cross. **2** a person carrying a processional cross or crucifix. [Say CROO suh fur]

cruciferous *adjective* of, relating to, or denoting plants of the cabbage family. [Say croo SIFFER us]

crucifix *noun* (*plural* **crucifixes**) a model or image of a cross with a figure of Christ on it. [Say CROO suh fix]

crucifixion *noun* **1** the execution of a person by nailing or binding them to a cross. **2 (Crucifixion)** the crucifixion of Christ. [Say croo suh FICK shun]

cruciform *adjective* cross-shaped (esp. of a church with transepts). [Say CROO suh form]

crucify *verb* (**crucifies**, **crucified**, **crucifying**) **1** put to death by fastening to a cross. **2 a** cause extreme pain to. **b** persecute; torment. **c** criticize or punish harshly: *our fans would crucify us if we lost*. **3** defeat thoroughly in an argument, game, etc. [Say CROO suh fie]

crud *noun* *slang* **1** a deposit of dirt, grease, encrusted food, etc. **2** an unpleasant person. **3** something of little value: *who wrote this crud?* ▶ **cruddy** *adjective*

crude • *adjective* (**cruder**, **crudest**) **1 a** in the natural or raw state; not refined: *crude oil*. **b** rough, unpolished; lacking finish. **2 a** offensive, indecent: *a crude gesture*. **b** (of an action or statement or manners) rude, blunt. **3 a** *Statistics* (of figures) not adjusted or corrected. **b** rough: *a crude estimate*. • *noun* unrefined petroleum. ▶ **crudely** *adverb* **crudeness** *noun*

crudités *plural noun* an hors d'oeuvre of mixed raw vegetables often served with a sauce into which they are dipped. [Say croo dee TAY]

crudity *noun* (*plural* **crudities**) an unrefined, unsophisticated, rough, or vulgar quality or element: *the crudity of their methods and equipment* ◊ *the novel's structural crudities* ◊ *the crudity of his language*.

cruel *adjective* (**crueller**, **cruellest**) **1** causing pain or suffering, esp. deliberately: *a cruel remark*. **2** indifferent to or gratified by another's suffering: *her eyes were cruel and hard*. **3** merciless; harsh; unrelentingly severe: *cruel fate*. ▶ **cruelly** *adverb*

cruelty *noun* (*plural* **cruelties**) **1** a cruel act or attitude; indifference to another's suffering: *we can't stand cruelty to animals* ◊ *the barbarous cruelties to which a runaway slave was subject*. **2** a succession of cruel acts; a continued cruel attitude: *he has treated her with extreme cruelty*. **3** *Law* physical or mental harm inflicted (whether or not intentional), esp. as a ground for divorce.

cruise • *verb* (**cruises**, **cruised**, **cruising**) **1** make a journey aboard ship calling at a series of ports usu. according to a predetermined plan, esp. for pleasure. **2** sail about without a precise destination. **3 a** (of a motor vehicle or aircraft) travel at a moderate or economical speed. **b** (of a vehicle or its driver) travel without a specific destination: *cruising the streets*. **c** *slang*

walk or drive about (the streets etc.) in search of a sexual (esp. homosexual) partner. **4** achieve an objective, win a race etc., with ease. **5** inspect an area of forest to estimate the volume of timber on it. • *noun* **1** a cruising voyage on board a ship, esp. as a holiday (also as an *adjective*: *cruise ship*). **2** the act or an instance of cruising. **3** a survey or estimate of the volume of timber in an area.

cruise control *noun* a device on some motor vehicles that can be set to maintain a predetermined constant speed without use of the accelerator pedal.

cruise missile *noun* a missile able to fly at a low altitude and guide itself by reference to the features of the region it crosses.

cruiser *noun* **1** a warship of high speed and medium armament. **2** a police patrol car. **3** a person who estimates the volume of timber in an area of forest.

cruller *noun* a small, sweet cake made of a rich dough twisted and deep-fried. [Can be said to rhyme with *DULLER, RULER,* or *FULLER*]

crumb • *noun* **1 a** a small fragment, esp. of bread. **b** a small particle; bit: *a crumb of sympathy*. **2** the soft inner part of a loaf of bread or a cake. • *verb* **1** cover with bread crumbs. **2** break into crumbs.

crumble • *verb* (**crumbles, crumbled, crumbling**) **1** break or fall into crumbs or fragments. **2** (of power, a reputation, etc.) gradually disintegrate. • *noun* **1** = CRISP *noun* 1. **2** a crumbly or crumbled substance.

crumbly *adjective* (**crumblier, crumbliest**) consisting of, or apt to fall into, crumbs or fragments.

crumby *adjective* (**crumbier, crumbiest**) like or covered in crumbs.

crummy • *adjective* (**crummier, crummiest**) *informal* **1** dirty, squalid: *a crummy apartment*. **2** inferior, worthless. **3** sick or depressed: *I feel crummy*. • *noun* (*plural* **crummies**) an old or converted vehicle for transporting loggers from their camp to work.

crumpet *noun* a small, round, spongelike yeast cake resembling an English muffin, eaten toasted.

crumple • *verb* (**crumples, crumpled, crumpling**) **1** crush or become crushed into a compact mass or irregular creases. **2** collapse, give way: *she crumpled to the floor*. • *noun* a crease or wrinkle.

crumple zone *noun* a part of a motor vehicle, esp. the extreme front and rear, designed to crumple easily in a crash and absorb impact.

crumply *adjective* crumpled.

crunch • *verb* (**crunches, crunched, crunching**) **1 a** crush noisily with the teeth. **b** grind (gravel, dry snow, etc.) under foot, wheels, etc. **2** (often foll. by *along*, *through*) make a crunching sound in walking, moving, etc. **3** *informal* process (large amounts of numbers or data) esp. by computer. • *noun* (*plural* **crunches**) **1** crunching; a crunching sound. **2** crunchiness: *nuts add crunch to a salad*. **3** *informal* a shortage or reduction: *housing crunch*. **4** *informal* a decisive event or moment. **5** (often in *plural*) a half sit-up, in which a person raises the upper body a few centimetres off the ground rather than sitting up fully. ▶ **cruncher** *noun*

crunchiness *noun* a crunchy quality.

crunchy • *adjective* (**crunchier, crunchiest**) hard and crispy. • *noun* (*plural* **crunchies**) something that crunches when eaten: *the cats don't like the new crunchies*.

crusade • *noun* **1** (usu. **Crusade**) any of several medieval military expeditions made by Europeans to recover the Holy Land from the Muslims. **2** a vigorous campaign in favour of a cause. • *verb* (**crusades, crusaded, crusading**) engage in a crusade. ▶ **crusader** *noun*

crush • *verb* (**crushes, crushed, crushing**) **1** compress with force or violence, so as to break,

bruise, etc. **2** reduce to powder by pressure. **3** crease or crumple by rough handling. **4** defeat or subdue completely. **5** (usu. in *passive*) humiliate; disappoint; upset: *I was crushed by his comment*. **6** advance in large numbers: *the crowd crushed into the stadium*. • *noun* (*plural* **crushes**) **1** an act of crushing. **2** a crowded mass of people. **3** *informal* **a** (usu. foll. by *on*) a (usu. passing) infatuation. **b** the object of an infatuation. ▶ **crushable** *adjective* **crusher** *noun* **crushing** *adjective* (esp. in sense 4 of *verb*) **crushingly** *adverb*

crust • *noun* **1 a** the hard outer part of a loaf of bread. **b** a slice of bread from the end of the loaf. **c** a hard dry scrap of bread. **2 a** the pastry covering of a pie, tart, etc. **b** the bottom, usu. of pastry, of a pie, tart, pizza, etc. **3** a hard casing of a softer thing, e.g. a harder layer over soft snow. **4** *Geology* the outer portion of the earth. **5 a** a coating or deposit on the surface of anything. **b** a hard dry formation on the skin, a scab. • *verb* **1** cover or become covered with a crust. **2** form into a crust.

crustacean • *noun* a usu. aquatic, hard-shelled arthropod, e.g. the crab, lobster, and shrimp. • *adjective* of or relating to crustaceans. [Say kruh STATION]

crusted *adjective* having a crust.

crustiness *noun* **1** the quality of something having a crisp crust. **2** a gruff or crabby manner; grouchiness.

crusty *adjective* (**crustier, crustiest**) **1** having a crisp crust: *a crusty loaf*. **2** irritable. **3** hard, crust-like.

crutch *noun* (*plural* **crutches**) **1** a support for a lame person, usu. with a crosspiece at the top fitting under the armpit. **2** any support or prop: *alcohol is a crutch for many people*.

crux *noun* (*plural* **cruxes**) **1** the decisive point at issue: *the crux of the matter is that attitudes have changed*. **2** a difficult matter; a puzzle: *the most famous textual crux in the Old Testament*.

cry • *verb* (**cries, cried, crying**) **1** (often foll. by *out*) make a loud or shrill sound, esp. to express pain, grief, etc., or to appeal for help. **2** shed tears. **3** (often foll. by *out*) say or exclaim loudly or excitedly. **4** (of an animal, esp. a bird) make a loud call. • *noun* (*plural* **cries**) **1** a loud inarticulate utterance of grief, pain, fear, joy, etc. **2** a loud excited utterance of words. **3** an urgent appeal or entreaty. **4** a period of weeping. **5 a** public demand; a strong movement of opinion. **b** a watchword or rallying call. **6** the natural utterance of an animal, esp. of birds. **7** the call of a street vendor etc. PHRASES **cry one's eyes** (or **heart**) **out** weep bitterly. **cry from the heart** a passionate appeal or protest. **cry off** *informal* withdraw from a promise or undertaking. **cry out for** demand as a self-evident requirement or solution. **cry up** praise, extol. **a far cry 1** a long way. **2** a very different thing. **for crying out loud** *informal* an exclamation of surprise or annoyance. **in full cry** (esp. of hounds) in keen pursuit.

crybaby *noun* (*plural* **crybabies**) **1** a person, esp. a child, who sheds tears frequently. **2** a whiny or self-pitying person.

crying *adjective* (of an injustice or other evil) flagrant, demanding redress: *a crying shame*.

cryogenic *adjective* used in or having to do with the scientific study of the production and effects of very low temperatures: *thousands of doses of semen await a purchaser in the big chill of a liquid nitrogen cryogenic tank*. ▶ **cryogenically** *adverb* [Say cry oh JEN ick]

cryogenics *noun* **1** the branch of physics dealing with the production and effects of very low temperatures. **2** = CRYONICS. [Say cry oh JEN icks]

cryonic *adjective* used in or having to do with the practice of deep-freezing human corpses for possible revival in the future. [Say cry ON ick]

cryonics *noun* the practice of deep-freezing the bodies

of those who have died of an incurable disease, in the hope of a future cure. [Say cry ON icks]

crypt noun an underground room or vault, esp. one beneath a church, used usu. for burial. [Say CRIPT]

cryptic adjective **1 a** obscure in meaning: *he found his boss's utterances too cryptic*. **b** (of a crossword clue etc.) indirect; indicating the solution in a way that is not obvious. **c** mysterious, enigmatic. **2** (of coloration etc.) serving to camouflage an animal in its natural environment. ▶**cryptically** adverb [Say CRIP tic]

cryptographer noun a person who writes or solves codes. [Say crip TOGRA fur]

cryptographic adjective having to do with cryptography. ▶**cryptographically** adverb [Say cripta GRAPHIC]

cryptography noun the art of writing or solving codes and ciphers. [Say crip TOGRA fee]

crystal • noun **1 a** a clear transparent mineral, esp. quartz. **b** a piece of this. **2 a** highly transparent glass, usu. containing lead oxide. **b** articles made of this, such as glassware and ornaments. **3** the glass over a watch face. **4** *Electronics* a crystalline piece of semiconductor. **5** *Chemistry* **a** an aggregation of molecules with a definite internal structure and the external form of a solid enclosed by symmetrically arranged plane faces. **b** a solid whose constituent particles are symmetrically arranged. • adjective made of, like, or clear as crystal. PHRASES **crystal clear 1** unclouded, transparent. **2** readily understood.

crystal ball noun a glass globe used in crystal gazing.

crystal gazing noun the process of concentrating one's gaze on a crystal ball supposedly in order to obtain a picture of future events etc.

crystalline adjective **1** of, like, or clear as crystal: *the air continued crystalline and as clear as ever*. **2** *Chemistry & Geology* having the structure and form of a crystal: *the Precambrian crystalline rock that makes up the Canadian Shield*. [Say CRISTA line or CRISTA leen]

crystalline lens noun a transparent lens enclosed in a membranous capsule behind the iris of the eye.

crystallization noun the process of forming crystals.

crystallize verb (**crystallizes**, **crystallized**, **crystallizing**) **1** form or cause to form crystals: *when most liquids freeze they crystallize*. **2** make or become definite and clear: *vague feelings of unrest crystallized into something more concrete* ◊ *writing can help to crystallize your thoughts*. **3** coat or impregnate or become coated or impregnated with sugar: *crystallized fruit*.

crystallographer noun a scientist who studies crystals. [Say crystal OGGRA fur]

crystallography noun the science of crystal structure and properties. [Say crystal OGGRA fee]

Cs symbol cesium.

c/s abbreviation cycles per second.

CSA abbreviation Canadian Standards Association.

CSB noun (plural **CSBs**) Canada Savings Bond.

C-section noun = CAESAREAN SECTION.

CSIS abbreviation Canadian Security Intelligence Service. [Say SEE sis]

CSR noun (plural **CSRs**) customer service representative.

CST abbreviation Central Standard Time.

Cst. abbreviation Cdn Constable.

CT abbreviation **1** Connecticut (in official postal use). **2** *Medical* computerized tomography. **3** CENTRAL TIME.

ct. abbreviation carat.

Ctrl. abbreviation Computing Control key.

CT scan noun = CAT SCAN.

Cu symbol the element copper.

cu. abbreviation cubic.

cub • noun **1** the young of a fox, bear, lion, etc. **2** (**Cub**)

a member of the junior level (ages 8, 9, and 10) in Scouting. **3** (also **cub reporter**) *informal* a young or inexperienced newspaper reporter. • verb (**cubs**, **cubbed**, **cubbing**) give birth to (cubs).

Cuban • adjective of or relating to Cuba or its people. • noun a native or national of Cuba.

cubbyhole noun **1** a very small room. **2** a small compartment.

cube • noun **1** a solid contained by six equal squares. **2** a cube-shaped block. **3** the product of a number multiplied by its square. • verb (**cubes**, **cubed**, **cubing**) **1** find the cube of (a number). **2** cut (food etc.) into small cubes.

cube van noun (also **cube truck**) *Cdn* a truck resembling a van at the front, with a taller and wider cube-like storage compartment behind.

cubic adjective **1** cube-shaped. **2** of three dimensions. **3** involving the cube (and no higher power) of a number: *cubic equation*. **4** designating a volume equal to that of a cube whose side is one of the linear unit specified: *cubic yard*.

cubicle noun a small partitioned space, esp. screened for privacy.

cubism noun a style and movement in art, esp. painting, in which objects are represented as an assemblage of geometrical forms. Pablo Picasso was a strong proponent of cubism in the years 1908–14. ▶**cubist** noun & adjective **cubistic** adjective

cuckold • noun a man whose wife is unfaithful. • verb make a cuckold of. [Say CUCK old]

cuckoo • noun **1** any of various birds, e.g. the black-billed cuckoo or yellow-billed cuckoo of North America, with brown backs and white underparts, or a Eurasian grey or brown speckled bird which leaves its eggs in the nests of small birds and has a distinctive two-note call. **2** *informal* a crazy or foolish person. • adjective *informal* crazy, foolish.

cuckoo clock noun a clock that strikes the hour with a sound like a cuckoo's call, usu. with the emergence on each note of a mechanical cuckoo.

cucumber noun **1** a long green fleshy fruit eaten esp. as a salad vegetable or pickled. **2** the climbing plant, *Cucumis sativus*, yielding this fruit.

cud noun **1** half-digested food returned from the first stomach of ruminants (e.g. cows) to the mouth for further chewing. **2** any substance, e.g. tobacco, used by a person to keep in the mouth and chew. PHRASES **chew the cud** think or talk reflectively: *we chewed the cud and drank a few beers*.

cuddle • verb (**cuddles**, **cuddled**, **cuddling**) **1** hold in an affectionate embrace, hug. **2** nestle together, lie close and snug. • noun the action of holding someone close in the arms to show love or affection: *the cats like a cuddle in the morning*. ▶**cuddler** noun

cuddly adjective (**cuddlier**, **cuddliest**) **1** pleasant to cuddle. **2** (of a person) plump.

cudgel • noun a short thick stick used as a weapon. • verb (**cudgels**, **cudgelled**, **cudgelling**) beat with a cudgel. PHRASES **cudgel one's brains** think hard about a problem. **take up the cudgels** make a vigorous defence: *he did not feel fit to take up the cudgels in his party's defence*. [Say CUDGE ul]

SPELL CHECK	
cue, queue	ABC ✓

A lineup or a sequence of computer tasks is a **queue**.

cue[1] • noun **1** something said or done on stage which serves as a signal for another performer or technician to speak, enter, or execute an action: *Arleane stood in the*

wings and waited for her cue. **2 a a** stimulus to perception, understanding, etc. **b** a signal for action: *Miriam's arrival was the cue for more champagne.* **c** a hint on how to behave in particular circumstances: *if you're not sure which fork to use just follow my cue.* **3** a facility for playing through an audio or video recording very rapidly until a desired starting point is reached. • *verb* (**cues**, **cued**, **cueing**) **1** give a cue to. **2** put (a piece of audio equipment, esp. a record player or tape recorder) in readiness to play a particular part of the recorded material. **PHRASES** **on cue** at the correct moment. **take one's cue from** follow the example or advice of.

cue² *Billiards etc.* • *noun* a long straight tapering rod for striking the ball. • *verb* (**cues**, **cued**, **cueing**) **1** strike (a ball) with a cue. **2** use a cue.

cue ball *noun Billiards etc.* the usu. white ball that is to be struck with the cue.

cue card *noun* a small card from which a person giving a speech, a television presenter, etc. reads lines.

cuff¹ • *noun* **1 a** the end part of a sleeve. **b** the part of a glove covering the wrist. **2** the lower turned up end of a pant leg. **3** (in *plural*) *informal* handcuffs. **4** the inflatable band wound around a limb when blood pressure is measured. **5** a muscle ringing a joint: *rotator cuff.* • *verb informal* put handcuffs on. **PHRASES** **off-the-cuff** *informal* without preparation, improvised: *an off-the-cuff spoof.*

cuff² • *verb* strike with an open hand. • *noun* such a blow.

cuffed *adjective* **1** handcuffed. **2** having a cuff or cuffs, esp. the kind described: *a cuffed blouse ◊ high-cuffed pants.*

cufflink *noun* a device of two joined studs etc. to fasten the sides of a cuff together.

cuisine *noun* a style or method of cooking, esp. of a particular country or establishment. [Say quiz EEN]

cuke *noun informal* a cucumber.

cul-de-sac *noun* (*plural* **cul-de-sacs**) **1** a street or passage closed at one end. **2** a route or course leading nowhere; a position from which one cannot escape: *was the new position a career cul-de-sac?* [Say CULL duh sack or KOOL duh sack (KOOL rhymes with WOOL)]

culinary *adjective* of or for cooking: *savour the region's culinary delights.* [Say CULLA nare ee or KYOOLA nare ee]

cull • *verb* **1** select, choose, or gather from a large quantity or amount: *knowledge culled from books.* **2** pick or gather (flowers, fruit, etc.). **3** select (animals), esp. poor or surplus specimens for killing. **4** remove (timber) as being inferior. • *adjective* rejected as being surplus or inferior: *cull apples.* • *noun* **1** an act of culling. **2** an animal or animals culled. **3** an item picked out as being surplus or inferior. ▶ **culler** *noun*

culminate *verb* (**culminates**, **culminated**, **culminating**) **1** (usu. foll. by *in*) reach its highest or final point: *the antagonism culminated in war.* **2** bring to its highest or final point: *her arrest culminated a countrywide search for the baby.* **3** (of a celestial object) reach its greatest altitude, be on the meridian. ▶ **culmination** *noun* [Say CULMA nate, culma NATION]

culottes *plural noun* a woman's garment that hangs like a skirt but has separate legs, like trousers. [Say coo LOTS or COO lots]

culpability *noun* responsibility for a crime or wrongdoing; guilt. [Say kulpa BILLA tee]

culpable *adjective* deserving blame: *manslaughter is culpable homicide, but lacking the intention to kill that is an ingredient in murder ◊ cabinet ministers may be held politically culpable for their own actions and those of their officials.* ▶ **culpably** *adverb* [Say KULPA bull]

culprit *noun* **1** a person accused of or guilty of an offence. **2** a person or thing held responsible for something: *smoking is often the culprit in heart disease.*

cult *noun* **1 a** a system of religious veneration and

devotion directed towards a particular figure or object: *the cult of the Virgin.* **b** a relatively small group of people having religious beliefs or practices regarded by others as strange or sinister: *a network of Satan-worshipping cults.* **c** the members of such a sect. **2 a** a misplaced or excessive admiration for a particular person or thing: *the cult of success.* **b** a popular fashion esp. followed by a specific section of society. **3** (as an *adjective*) denoting a person or thing popularized in this way: *cult film.* ▶ **cultic** *adjective* **cultish** *adjective* **cultishness** *noun* **cultism** *noun* **cultist** *noun*

cultivar *noun* a plant variety produced in cultivation by selective breeding: *two very popular cultivars of leaf lettuce are Grand Rapids and Black-seeded Simpson.*

cultivate *verb* (**cultivates**, **cultivated**, **cultivating**) **1 a** prepare and use (soil etc.) for crops or gardening. **b** break up (the ground) with a cultivator. **c** remove weeds using a cultivator or hoe. **2 a** raise or produce (crops). **b** culture (bacteria etc.). **c** raise or produce (mussels, pearls, etc.). **3 a** make (the mind, feelings, etc.) more educated and sensitive. **b** pay attention to or nurture (a person or a person's friendship). **4** try to acquire or develop (a talent, attitude, manner, etc.).

cultivated *adjective* **1** (of a person, manners, etc.) having or showing education and good taste; refined. **2 a** (of land) used for growing crops. **b** (of plants) grown on farms etc. **3** (of mussels, pearls, etc.) grown in farms.

cultivation *noun* **1** the preparation and use of land for growing plants or crops: *fertile land that is under cultivation.* **2** the deliberate development of a particular relationship, quality, or skill.

cultivator *noun* **1 a** a mechanical implement for breaking up the ground and uprooting weeds. **b** a two- or three-pronged hand tool used for weeding and loosening soil. **2** a person or thing that cultivates: *they were herders of cattle and cultivators of corn.*

cult of personality *noun* = PERSONALITY CULT.

cultural *adjective* **1** of or relating to artistic or intellectual activity seen as cultivating the mind: *music, art, and other cultural activities.* **2** of or pertaining to the ideas, customs, and social behaviour in a society or civilization: *Canada's cultural diversity.*

cultural imperialism *noun* the increasing influence in one country of the culture of another.

culturally *adverb* in terms of culture: *a culturally diverse community.*

cultural sovereignty *noun* *Cdn* the power of a country to maintain independence in its cultural activities from another, culturally dominant, nation.

culture • *noun* **1 a** the arts and other manifestations of human intellectual achievement regarded collectively: *a city lacking in culture.* **b** a refined understanding of this; intellectual development: *a person of culture.* **2 a** the customs, civilization, and achievements of a particular time or people: *studied Mi'kmaq culture.* **b** the mode of behaviour within a particular group: *corporate culture.* **3 a** the cultivation of plants; the rearing of bees, silkworms, etc. **b** the cultivation of the soil. **4** a quantity of micro-organisms and the nutrient material supporting their growth. • *verb* (**cultures**, **cultured**, **culturing**) maintain (bacteria etc.) in conditions suitable for growth.

cultured *adjective* **1** having refined taste and manners and a good education. **2** caused to develop by artificial means or in an artificial nutrient medium.

cultured pearl *noun* a pearl formed by an oyster after the insertion of a foreign body into its shell.

culture shock *noun* the feeling of disorientation experienced by a person suddenly subjected to an unfamiliar culture or way of life.

C

culvert *noun* **1** an underground channel carrying water across a road etc. **2** a channel for an electric cable.

cum *preposition* (usu. in *combination*) with, combined with, also used as: *a farmhouse-cum-museum*.

cumbersome *adjective* inconvenient in size, weight, or shape; unwieldy. ▶ **cumbersomely** *adverb*

cumin *noun* **1** a plant, *Cuminum cyminum*, bearing aromatic seeds. **2** these seeds used as flavouring, esp. in curry powder. [Say CUM in or CUE min]

cummerbund *noun* a wide, often horizontally pleated sash worn around the waist, esp. with a tuxedo.

cumulative *adjective* **1** increasing or increased in amount, force, etc., by successive additions: *cumulative evidence*. **2** formed by successive additions: *learning is a cumulative process*. ▶ **cumulatively** *adverb* **cumulativeness** *noun* [Say CUE myoo luh tiv]

cumulonimbus *noun* a cumulus cloud developed to a great height and producing rain or hail; a thundercloud. [Say cue myoo lo NIMBUS]

cumulus *noun* **1** clouds formed in rounded masses heaped on each other above a flat base. **2** a cloud of this type. [Say CUE myuh luss]

cuneiform • *adjective* **1** wedge-shaped. **2** of, relating to, or using the wedge-shaped writing impressed usu. in clay in ancient Babylonian etc. inscriptions. • *noun* cuneiform writing. [Say cue NAY uh form or cue NEE uh form]

cunnilingus *noun* stimulation of the female genitals using the tongue or lips. [Say cunna LING gus]

cunning • *adjective* (**more cunning, cunningest**) **1** having or showing skill in achieving one's ends by deceit or evasion: *a cunning liar*. **2** ingenious: *a cunning plan*. **3** attractive, quaint. • *noun* craftiness; skill in deceit: *a statesman to whom cunning had come as second nature*. **2** skill, ingenuity: *what resources of energy and cunning it took just to survive*. ▶ **cunningly** *adverb*

cup • *noun* **1** a small bowl-shaped container, often with a handle, for drinking from. **2 a** its contents: *a cup of tea*. **b** a measure of capacity esp. in cooking, equal to eight fluid ounces (237 ml). **3** a cup-shaped thing, esp. the calyx of a flower or the socket of a bone. **4** an ornamental cup-shaped trophy as a prize for victory or prowess, esp. in a sports contest. **5** one's fate or fortune: *a bitter cup*. **6** either of the two cup-shaped parts of a bra. **7** the chalice used or the wine taken at the Eucharist. **8** *Golf* the hole on a putting green or the metal container in it. **9** the hard protective triangular shell in a jockstrap. **10** a shallow bowl-shaped cooking utensil: *muffin cups*. • *verb* (**cups, cupped, cupping**) **1** form (esp. one's hands) into the shape of a cup. **2** take or hold as in a cup. PHRASES **one's cup of tea** *informal* what interests or suits one. **in one's cups** drunk.

cupboard *noun* a recess or piece of furniture with a door and (usu.) shelves, in which things are stored.

cupcake *noun* **1** a small cake baked in a cup-shaped mould. **2** a term of endearment.

cupful *noun* (*plural* **cupfuls**) the amount of something that would fill a cup.

cupidity *noun* greed for money or possessions: *if the gold found on Baffin Island by Frobisher had been real, it would have attracted the cupidity of the English*. [Say cue PIDDA tee]

cupola *noun* **1** a rounded dome forming or adorning a roof or ceiling. **2** a revolving dome protecting mounted guns in a fort or on a warship etc. [Say CUE puh luh]

cur *noun* **1** a worthless or snappy dog. **2** a contemptible person.

curable *adjective* that can be cured.

curaçao *noun* (*plural* **curaçaos**) a liqueur of spirits flavoured with the peel of bitter oranges. [Say cura a SO]

curare *noun* a resinous bitter substance prepared from plants, which causes paralysis, formerly used to poison arrows by Aboriginals of South America, and as a muscle relaxant in surgery. [Say kyuh RAR ee or kuh RAR ee]

curate[1] *noun* **1** *Catholicism* the priest of a parish in continental Europe. **2** a member of the clergy assisting a parish priest. PHRASES **curate's egg** a thing that is partly good and partly bad. [Say CURE it]

curate[2] *verb* (**curates, curated, curating**) **1** act as curator of (a museum, exhibits, etc.); look after and preserve. **2** select, organize, and present items for (an exhibition, film festival, etc.). **3** perform the duties of a curator. [Say CURE ate]

curative *adjective* tending or able to cure (esp. disease): *the water was believed to have curative powers*.

curator *noun* **1** an employee of a museum etc. responsible for the collections. **2** a person who curates an exhibition. **3** *Cdn* (*Que.*) = PUBLIC CURATOR. ▶ **curatorial** *adjective* **curatorship** *noun* [Say CURE ate ur, cure a TORY ul]

curb • *noun* **1** the raised, usu. concrete border along the side of a street etc. **2** a check or restraint. **3** a strap etc. fastened to the bit and passing under a horse's lower jaw, used as a check. **4** an enclosing border or edging such as the frame round the top of a well or a fender round a hearth. • *verb* **1** restrain. **2** have (one's dog) defecate by the curb rather than on the sidewalk. **3** put a curb on (a horse).

curbside *noun* **1** the area adjacent to a curb (often as an *adjective*: *curbside recycling*). **2** (as an *adjective*) denoting a transaction conducted outside an office or usual place of business.

curd *noun* (often in *plural*) a coagulated substance formed by the action of acids on milk, which may be made into cheese or eaten as food.

curdle *verb* (**curdles, curdled, curdling**) make into or become curds. PHRASES **make one's blood curdle** fill one with horror.

cure • *verb* (**cures, cured, curing**) **1** restore (a person or animal) to health. **2** eliminate (a disease, evil, etc.). **3** preserve (meat, fruit, tobacco, or skins) by salting, drying, etc. **4 a** vulcanize (rubber). **b** harden (concrete or plastic). **c** (of glue, caulking, etc.) set, harden. **5** undergo a process of curing. • *noun* **1** restoration to health. **2** a means of curing a disease. **3** a course of medical or healing treatment. **4 a** the office or function of a curate. **b** a parish or other sphere of spiritual ministration. **5 a** the process of curing rubber or plastic. **b** (with qualifying adjective) the degree of this. **6** the process of curing meat, fruit, etc.

curé *noun* a parish priest in Quebec, France, etc. [Say cure AY]

cure-all *noun* a panacea; a universal remedy.

curettage *noun* the use of or an operation involving the use of a curette. [Say cure ET idge or cure a TAWZH]

curette • *noun* a surgeon's small scraping instrument. • *verb* (**curettes, curetted, curetting**) clean or scrape with a curette. [Say cure ET]

curfew *noun* **1 a** a regulation restricting or forbidding the public circulation of people, esp. requiring people to remain indoors between specified hours, usu. at night. **b** a requirement that one be home etc. by a certain time. **2** the hour designated as the beginning of such a restriction. **3** a daily signal indicating this. **4** the ringing of a bell at a fixed evening hour. PHRASES **break curfew** fail to observe a curfew.

Curia *noun* the papal court at the Vatican, by which the Roman Catholic Church is governed. [Say CURE ee uh]

curie *noun* **1** a unit of radioactivity, corresponding to 3.7×10^{10} disintegrations per second. Abbreviation: **Ci.**

2 a quantity of radioactive substance having this activity. [Say CURE ee]
curio *noun* (*plural* **curios**) a rare or unusual object: *traditional artifacts and curios were on display.* [Say CURE ee oh]
curiosity *noun* (*plural* **curiosities**) **1** an eager desire to know; inquisitiveness. **2** a strange, rare, or interesting object or thing: *he showed them some of the curiosities of the house.*
curious *adjective* **1** eager to learn or know. **2** strange: *a curious sensation overwhelmed her.* ▶ **curiously** *adverb*
curium *noun* an artificially made radioactive metallic element. [Say CURE ee um]
curl • *verb* **1 a** bend or coil into a spiral. **b** form or make something form into a curved shape, esp. so that the edges are rolled up. **2** move in a spiral form: *smoke curling upwards.* **3 a** (of the upper lip) be raised slightly on one side as an expression of contempt or disapproval. **b** cause (the lip) to do this. **4 a** play curling. **b** play (a game of curling). • *noun* **1** a lock of curled hair. **2** anything spiral or curved inwards. **3 a** a curling movement or act. **b** the state of being curled. **4** an exercise in which part of the body (e.g. the arms, legs, or abdomen) is curled and then released. PHRASES **curl up 1** lie or sit with the knees drawn up. **2** *informal* writhe with embarrassment or horror. **make a person's hair curl** *informal* shock or horrify a person.
curler *noun* **1** a pin or roller etc. for curling the hair. **2** a player in the game of curling.
curlew *noun* (*plural* **curlew** or **curlews**) a bird with a usu. long slender down-curved bill.
curlicue *noun* a decorative curl or twist.
curliness *noun* a curly quality: *the curliness of her hair.*
curling *noun* **1** in senses of CURL *verb.* **2** a game played on ice, in which large round stones are slid across the surface towards a mark.
curly *adjective* (**curlier**, **curliest**) **1** having or arranged in curls. **2** not straight or flat: *curly lettuce.*
curmudgeon *noun* a bad-tempered person. ▶ **curmudgeonly** *adjective* [Say cur MUDGE in]

SPELL CHECK
currant, current ABC ✓

Current is the spelling for a stream of air or water or a modern trend. **Current** is also the spelling in "current events".

currant *noun* **1** a dried fruit of a small seedless variety of grape, much used in cooking. **2 a** any of various shrubs of the genus *Ribes* producing red, white, or black berries. **b** a berry of these shrubs.
currency *noun* (*plural* **currencies**) **1 a** the money in general use in a country: *the American dollar is a very strong currency.* **b** anything seen as a medium through which transactions are completed: *technical knowledge is the currency of power.* **2** the condition of being current; prevalence, e.g. of words or ideas: *since the Gulf War, the term has gained new currency.*

SPELL CHECK
current, currant ABC ✓

The fruit is a **currant**.

current • *adjective* **1** belonging to the present time; happening now: *current events.* **2** (of money, opinion, a rumour, a word, etc.) in general circulation or use. • *noun* **1** a body of water, air, etc., moving in a definite direction, esp. through a stiller surrounding body. **2 a** an ordered movement of electrically charged particles. **b** a quantity representing the intensity of such movement. **3** a general tendency or course (of

events, opinions, etc.): *Quebec's language legislation runs against the current of bilingualism in the rest of Canada.*
current account *noun* **1** the part of a country's balance of payments account that records non-capital transactions. **2** a bank account from which money may be drawn without notice.
current affairs *plural noun* esp. *Cdn & Brit.* (also **current events**) events of political or social interest and importance happening in the world at the present time: *current affairs programming at the CBC.*
currently *adverb* at the present time; now.
curricular *adjective* having to do with the prescribed course of study at a school. [Say kuh RICK yoo lur]
curriculum *noun* (*plural* **curricula**) **1** the subjects that are studied or prescribed for study. **2** any program of activities. [Say kuh RICK yoo lum for the singular, kuh RICK yoo luh for the plural]
curriculum vitae *noun* (*plural* **curricula vitae** or **curricula vitarum**) a brief account of one's education, qualifications, and previous occupations. Abbreviation: **c.v.** [Say kuh rick yoo lum VEE tie]
curry[1] • *noun* (*plural* **curries**) a dish of meat, vegetables, etc., cooked in a highly spiced sauce, usu. served with rice. • *verb* (**curries**, **curried**, **currying**) prepare or flavour with hot-tasting spices: *curried beef.*
curry[2] *verb* (**curries**, **curried**, **currying**) groom (a horse) with a curry comb. PHRASES **curry favour** attempt to gain someone's favour by acting obsequiously: *a wimpish attempt to curry favour with the new boss.*
curry comb *noun* a hand-held metal serrated device for grooming horses.
curry powder *noun* a preparation of turmeric, cumin, and other spices for making curry.
curse • *noun* **1** a solemn utterance intended to invoke a supernatural power to inflict destruction or punishment on a person or thing. **2** the evil supposedly resulting from a curse. **3** a violent exclamation of anger; a profane oath. **4** a thing that causes evil or harm. **5** (**the curse**) *slang* menstruation; a menstrual period. • *verb* (**curses**, **cursed**, **cursing**) **1 a** utter a curse against. **b** (in *imper.*) may God curse. **2** (usu. in *passive*; foll. by *with*) afflict with: *cursed with blindness.* **3 a** utter expletive curses; swear. **b** feel or express negative thoughts about: *cursed my luck.*
cursed *adjective* damnable, abominable. [Say CURSE id or CURST]
curses *interjection* expressing annoyance.
cursive • *adjective* (of writing) done with joined characters. • *noun* cursive writing.
cursor *noun* a movable indicator on a computer screen identifying a particular position in the display, esp. the position that the program will operate on with the next keystroke.
cursorily *adverb* in a hurried manner, esp. insufficient attention to details: *I glanced cursorily the contract.* [Say CURSOR uh lee]
cursory *adjective* hasty, hurried; superficial: *examination.* [Say CURSOR ee]
curt *adjective* noticeably or rudely brief.
curtail *verb* cut short; reduce: *curtail* ▶ **curtailment** *noun* [Say cur TAIL]
curtain • *noun* **1** a piece of cloth etc. screen, usu. movable sideways or upward window or between the stage and theatre. **2** *Theatre* the rise or fall of the beginning or end of an act or sce the end. **4** any concentration of s barrier: *a curtain of fog.* • *verb* (foll. curtain or curtains.

C

curtain call *noun* an appearance by a performer or performers to take a bow at the end of a performance.
curtained *adverb* having a curtain or curtains: *curtained windows*.
curtly *adverb* in a rudely brief or abrupt manner.
curtsy (also **curtsey**) • *noun* (*plural* **curtsies** or **curtseys**) a woman's or girl's formal greeting or salutation made by bending the knees and lowering the body. • *verb* (**curtsies, curtsied, curtsying** or **curtseys, curtseyed, curtseying**) make a curtsy.
curvaceous *adjective* *informal* having a shapely figure with voluptuous breasts and hips. [Say cur VAY shuss]
curvature *noun* **1** the fact of being curved or the degree to which something is curved: *spinal curvature ◊ the curvature of the earth.* **2** *Math* **a** the deviation of a curve from a straight line, or of a curved surface from a plane. **b** the quantity expressing this. [Say CURVA chur]
curve • *noun* **1** a line or surface having along its length a regular deviation from being straight or flat, as exemplified by the surface of a sphere or lens. **2** a curved form or thing. **3** a curved line on a graph. **4** (also **curveball**) **a** *Baseball* a ball pitched so that it curves away from the side from which it was thrown. **b** something unexpected or unsettling. **5 a** a curved line on a graph illustrating a tendency. **b** a tendency which could be plotted on a graph as a curve. • *verb* (**curves, curved, curving**) **1** bend or shape so as to form a curve. **2** move or send along a curved path.
▶ **curved** *adjective*
curvy *adjective* (**curvier, curviest**) **1** having many curves. **2** (of a woman's figure) shapely.
cushion • *noun* **1** a pad or bag of cloth etc. stuffed with a mass of soft material and used as a soft support for sitting etc. **2** a means of protection against shock, jarring, etc. **3** a buffer of savings, time, etc. or (in sports) a comfortable lead in score meant to mitigate the effects of difficulty, possible future distress, etc.: *the surplus will be used to create a cushion against economic downturns in the future.* **4** a body of air supporting a hovercraft etc. • *verb* **1** provide or protect with a cushion or cushions. **2** provide with a defence; protect. **3** mitigate the adverse effects of: *cushioned the blow.*
▶ **cushioned** *adjective* **cushioning** *noun* **cushiony** *adjective*
cushy *adjective* (**cushier, cushiest**) *informal* **1** (of a job tc.) easy and pleasant. **2** (of a seat, surroundings, etc.) comfortable.
oun **1** an apex or peak. **2** the horn of a crescent
3 *Math* the point at which two arcs meet from direction terminating with a pointed end, esp. of a leaf. **5** a cone-
ce on the surface of a tooth esp. a
a pocket or fold in a valve of the
cusp at a point marking a
: *on the cusp of burnout.*
es) **1** an obscene or
tory a strange and
cious cuss. • *verb*
foul language.
stubborn.
USS id]
dish
rd
ured
starch.
custody or
ertaining to the
or pertaining to

imprisonment or forcible institutionalization: *a custodial sentence.*
custodian *noun* **1** a person responsible for maintaining a building etc.; a caretaker or janitor. **2** a person who has custody of and responsibility for another person, a thing, etc.
custody *noun* **1 a** legal guardianship, esp. of a minor: *the judge awarded custody to the mother.* **b** safekeeping, protective care: *the property was placed in the custody of a trustee.* **2** (often preceded by *in* or *into*) the charge or keeping of the police; imprisonment: *remains in custody.*
PHRASES **take into custody** arrest.
custom • *noun* **1 a** a traditional and widely accepted way of behaving or doing something that is specific to a particular society, place, or time: *the Canadian custom of planting the garden on the Victoria Day weekend.* **b** a thing that one does habitually: *it's our custom to go to the cottage every weekend.* **2** *Law* established usage having the force of law. **3 a** a habitual business patronage: *if you don't provide better service, we'll take our custom elsewhere.* **b** regular dealings or customers. **4** (in *plural*; also treated as *singular*) **a** a duty levied on certain imported and exported goods. **b** the official department that administers this. **c** the area at an airport, border, etc. where customs officials deal with incoming goods, baggage, etc. • *adjective* CUSTOM-MADE.
customarily *adverb* according to the usual custom or practice: *passengers customarily tip the cab driver.*
customary *adjective* **1** usual, commonly done: *it is customary to mark an occasion like this with a toast.* **2** *Law* in accordance with custom rather than common law or statute.
customer *noun* **1** a person who buys goods or services from a store or business. **2** a person one has to deal with: *one tough customer.*
customizable *adjective* (esp. of computer equipment) able to be modified to suit the particular individual or task.
customization *noun* the process of modifying something to suit the particular individual or task.
customize *verb* (**customizes, customized, customizing**) make to order or modify according to individual requirements. ▶ **customized** *adjective*
custom-made *adjective* (also **custom-built** etc.) made to an individual customer's order or specifications.
cut • *verb* (**cuts, cut, cutting**) **1** penetrate or wound with a sharp-edged instrument. **2** divide, trim, or be divided with a knife etc. **3** (foll. by *loose, open*, etc.) make loose, open, etc. by cutting. **4** (esp. as **cutting** *adjective*) cause sharp physical or mental pain to: *a cutting remark ◊ a cutting wind.* **5** reduce (wages, time, services, etc.). **6 a** shape (a gem, key, etc.) by cutting. **b** make (a path, tunnel, etc.) by removing material. **7** perform: *cut a caper.* **8** cross: *the line cuts the circle at two points.* **9** pass, esp. in a hurry or as a shorter way: *cut across the grass.* **10** renounce (a connection). **11** deliberately fail to attend (a class etc.). **12** *Cards* **a** divide (a pack) into two parts. **b** select a dealer etc. by dividing the pack. **13** *Film* **a** edit (a film or tape). **b** stop filming or recording. **c** (foll. by *to*) go quickly to (another shot). **14** switch off (an engine etc.). **15** dilute. **16** remove (lines etc.) from a text. **17** dissolve, clean away: *cut the grease.* **18** swerve sharply; make a sudden turn or change in direction: *cut left.* • *adjective* **1** divided or separated into pieces. **2** made by cutting, grinding, etc.: *cut glass.* **3** lowered or reduced: *cut-price competitors.* • *noun* **1** an act of cutting. **2** a division or wound made by cutting. **3** a stroke with a knife, sword, whip, etc. **4 a** a reduction (in prices, wages, etc.). **b** a cessation (of a power supply etc.). **5 a** an abrupt transition between film shots,

achieved by splicing two distinct shots together. **b** a single song, piece, etc. on an album, CD, etc. **6** a wounding remark or act. **7** the way or style in which a garment, the hair, etc., is cut. **8** a piece of meat cut from a carcass. **9** *informal* a share of profits. **10** *Sport* an exclusion from a team, tournament, etc.: *the final cuts will be made Friday*. **11 a** a railway cutting. **b** a passage cut through rock or gravel in building a road, canal, etc. **12** a quantity of a crop, esp. timber, cut in a season. PHRASES **a cut above** *informal* noticeably superior to. **be cut out** be suited: *was not cut out to be a teacher*. **cut across** transcend or take no account of (normal limitations etc.): *their concerns cut across normal rivalries*. **cut and dried 1** completely decided; pre-arranged; inflexible. **2** (of opinions etc.) ready-made, lacking freshness. **cut and thrust** a lively interchange of argument etc. **cut back 1** reduce (expenditure etc.). **2** prune (a tree etc.). **cut both ways 1** serve both sides of an argument etc. **2** (of an action) have both good and bad effects. **cut a corner** go across and not around a corner. **cut corners** do a task etc. perfunctorily or incompletely, esp. to save time or money. **cut down 1 a** bring or throw down by cutting. **b** kill, disable; defeat, ruin: *cut down in battle*. **2** reduce the length of. **3** reduce one's consumption: *try to cut down on beer*. **cut a person down to size** *informal* ruthlessly expose the limitations of a person's importance, ability, etc. **cut one's eye teeth** attain experience and some sophistication. **cut from the same cloth** of the same nature; alike. **cut in 1** interrupt. **2** pull in too closely in front of another vehicle (esp. having passed it). **3** give a share of profits etc. to (a person). **4** connect (a source of electricity, etc.). **5** join in a card game by taking the place of a player who cuts out. **6** interrupt a dancing couple to take over from one partner. **cut into 1 a** make a cut in. **b** divide. **2** interfere with and reduce: *cuts into my free time*. **cut it** *informal* function or perform adequately: *couldn't cut it in the big leagues*. **cut it out** (usu. in *imper.*) *informal* stop doing something. **cut loose** begin to act freely. **cut one's losses** (or **a loss**) abandon an unprofitable enterprise before losses become too great. **cut the mustard** *slang* reach the required standard. **cut no ice** *slang* **1** have no influence or importance. **2** achieve little or nothing. **cut off 1** remove (an appendage) by cutting. **2 a** bring to an abrupt end or (esp. early) death. **b** prevent from continuing: *cut off supplies*. **c** interfere with the progress of, esp. by abruptly pulling one's vehicle into another's lane of traffic. **d** disconnect (esp. a person engaged in a telephone conversation). **3 a** prevent from travelling or venturing out: *was cut off by the snow*. **b** (as **cut off** *adjective*) isolated, remote. **4** disinherit. **cut out 1** remove from the inside by cutting. **2** make by cutting from a larger whole. **3** omit; leave out: *cut him out of our loop*. **4** *informal* stop doing or using (something): *cut out chocolate ◊ let's cut out the arguing*. **5** cease or cause to cease functioning: *the engine cut out*. **cut short 1** interrupt; terminate prematurely: *cut short his visit*. **2** make shorter or more concise. **cut a** (or **the**) **rug** *slang* dance. **cut (a person) some slack** *slang* allow an individual some leeway in conduct, performance, etc. **cut one's teeth on** acquire initial practice or experience from (something). **cut a tooth** have it appear through the gum. **cut to the bone 1** reduce (expenditures) to a minimum. **2** chill thoroughly. **cut to the chase** *informal* get to the point. **cut up 1** cut into pieces. **2** slash, wound, etc.: *we were all cut up and bruised*. **3** (usu. in *passive*) distress greatly: *was very cut up about it*. **4** criticize severely. **5** behave in a comical or unruly manner. **make the cut** *informal* **1** be

selected for a team, short list, etc. **2** achieve a specified status, condition, etc.

cut-and-paste *noun* the process of assembling text by adding or combining sections from other texts.

cutaneous *adjective* of the skin: *cutaneous pigmentation*. [Say cue TAINY us]

cutaway *adjective* **1** (of a diagram etc.) with some parts left out to reveal the interior. **2** (of a coat) with the front below the waist cut away.

cutback *noun* a reduction in something, esp. expenditure: *cutbacks in defence spending*.

cutbank *noun* a steep cliff or riverbank resulting from erosion.

cute *adjective* (**cuter**, **cutest**) *informal* **1** attractive. **2** quaintly or affectedly attractive. **3** endearing, charming: *a cute picture of little Eriq in a washtub*. ▶ **cutely** *adverb* **cuteness** *noun*

cutesy *adjective* (**cutesier**, **cutesiest**) dainty or quaint to an affected degree.

cuticle *noun* **1** the dead skin at the base of a fingernail or toenail. **2** the outer cellular layer of a hair. **3** the epidermis. **4** the outer layer of an organism, esp. a protective often waxy layer covering the epidermis of a plant or invertebrate. [Say CUE tuh cull]

cutie *noun slang* an attractive person, esp. a woman.

cutie-pie *noun informal* **1** darling, sweetheart. **2** an attractive person, animal, etc.

cutlass *noun* (*plural* **cutlasses**) a short sword with a slightly curved blade, esp. of the type formerly used by sailors. [Say CUT luss]

cutlery *noun* knives, forks, and spoons for use at table.

cutlet *noun* **1** a small, thin piece of boneless veal etc. usu. served fried. **2** a flat patty of ground meat or nuts and bread crumbs etc.

cutline *noun* **1** a caption to an illustration. **2** a line marked on wood etc. that indicates where a cut should be made. **3** *Cdn* a line cut through the bush, e.g. as a survey line, etc.

cut-off *noun* **1** the point at which something is cut off. **2** a device for stopping a flow. **3** (in *plural*) shorts, esp. made from cut-down jeans. **4** a time after which some action is no longer possible, effective, etc.: *cut-off date*. **5** *Baseball* the interception by an infielder of a ball thrown from outfield, e.g. to relay the ball to home plate. **6** a road to a specific town etc. which turns off a larger thoroughfare.

cut-out ● *noun* **1 a** a figure cut out of paper etc. **b** a person perceived as characterless or lacking in individuality: *the characters in these ballets are just cardboard cut-outs*. **2 a** device for automatic disconnection, the release of exhaust gases, etc. ● *adjective* of or like a cut-out (in sense 1).

cutover ● *adjective* (of timberland etc.) having had the saleable timber felled and removed. ● *noun* cutover land.

cut-rate *adjective* (also **cut-price**) selling or sold at a reduced price.

cutter *noun* **1** a person or thing that cuts, esp. a person who takes measurements and cuts cloth, as a tailor etc. **2 a** a small, fast sailing ship. **b** a small, lightly armed government boat: *a Coast Guard cutter*. **3** a light horse-drawn sleigh.

cutthroat ● *noun* **1** a murderer. **2** (also **cutthroat trout**) a species of trout, *Salmo clarki*, with an orange or red mark under the jaw. ● *adjective* (of competition) ruthless and intense.

cutting ● *noun* **1** a piece or section cut from something. **2** a piece cut from a plant for propagation. **3** an excavated channel through high ground for a railway or road. **4** *Forestry* **a** a stand of timber. **b** the site

C

of a logging operation. • *adjective* causing sharp physical or mental pain: *a cutting remark*.

cutting edge • *noun* **1** an edge that cuts. **2** the forefront of a movement etc. • *adjective* (**cutting-edge**) pioneering, innovative.

cuttlefish *noun* (*plural* **cuttlefish** or **cuttlefishes**) (also **cuttle**) a swimming marine mollusc that resembles a broad-bodied squid, having eight arms and two long tentacles that are used for grabbing prey. It has the habit of ejecting a black fluid when alarmed.

cutworm *noun* any of various caterpillars that eat through young plants level with the ground.

CV *abbreviation* (in Canada) CROSS OF VALOUR.

c.v. *abbreviation* (*plural* **c.v.'s**) CURRICULUM VITAE.

CVS *abbreviation* chorionic villus sampling, a procedure for obtaining information about a fetus in which a sample of tissue is taken from hairlike projections in the mucous membrane of the chorion.

cyanide *noun* a highly poisonous chemical compound. [Say SIGH a nide]

cyanobacteria *plural noun* (*singular* **cyanobacterium**) single-celled organisms found in many environments and capable of photosynthesizing. [Say sigh a no BACTERIA for the plural, sigh a no BACTERIUM for the singular]

cyber- *combining form* of computers, esp. pertaining to artificial intelligence or virtual reality.

cybernetic *adjective* used in or having to do with the science of communications and automatic control systems in both machines and living things.

cybernetics *plural noun* (usu. treated as *singular*) the scientific study of communication and control, esp. concerned with comparing human and animal brains with machines and electronic devices.

cyberpunk *noun* **1** a style of science fiction featuring urban counterculture in a world of high technology and virtual reality. **2** *Computing slang* a highly proficient hacker.

cyberspace *noun* **1** the forum in which the global electronic communications network operates. **2** the electronic realm in which virtual reality is experienced.

cybersquatter *noun* a person who registers well-known company or brand names as Internet domain names, in the hope of later selling them back to the brand owner at a profit. ▶ **cybersquatting** *noun*

cyborg *noun* a person whose physical abilities are extended beyond normal human limitations by machine technology (as yet undeveloped).

cycad *noun* a palmlike plant of tropical and subtropical regions, often growing to a great height. [Say SIGH cad]

cyclamen *noun* a plant, having pink, red, or white flowers with petals folded backwards, often grown as a houseplant. [Say SICK luh min]

cycle • *noun* **1 a** a recurrent series or period (of events, phenomena, etc.). **b** the time needed for one such series or period. **2 a** *Physics etc.* a recurrent series of operations or states. **b** *Electricity* = HERTZ. **3** a series of songs, poems, etc., usu. on a single theme. **4** a bicycle, tricycle, or similar machine. **5** *Computing* **a** (also **cycle time**) the time required for one cycle of the memory system. **b** a set of operations which is repeated regularly and in the same sequence. • *verb* (**cycles, cycled, cycling**) **1** ride a bicycle etc. **2** move in cycles.

cyclic *adjective* **1 a** recurring or revolving in cycles; regularly repeated: *there are many cyclic processes in nature*. **b** belonging to a chronological cycle. **c** of, pertaining to, or characterized by cycles. **2** with constituent atoms forming a ring. **3** of a cycle of songs etc. **4** (of a flower) with its parts arranged in whorls

5 *Math* of a circle or other closed curve. [Say SIKE lick or SICK lick]

cyclical • *adjective* = CYCLIC 1. • *noun* (usu. in *plural*) industries, companies, etc. that are heavily dependent on global economic circumstances for their success. ▶ **cyclically** *adverb* [Say SIKE lick ul or SICK lick ul]

cycling *noun* **1** travelling or touring on a bicycle etc. **2** bicycle racing, usu. on a lightweight bicycle with low handlebars. **3** the act of moving in cycles.

cyclist *noun* a rider of a bicycle.

cyclone *noun* **1 a** a system of winds rotating inwards to an area of low barometric pressure. **b** a tornado. **2 a** a wind system of this kind formed in localized areas over tropical oceans, sometimes developing into a hurricane or typhoon. **b** such a wind system having hurricane-force winds, originating in the Indian Ocean. **3** a centrifugal machine for separating solids. ▶ **cyclonic** *adjective* [Say SIGH clone, sigh CLON ick]

Cyclops *noun* (*plural* **Cyclops**) (in Greek mythology) a member of a race of one-eyed giants. [Say SIGH clops]

cyclosporin *noun* a drug used to prevent the rejection of grafts and transplants. [Say sike luh SPORE in]

cygnet *noun* a young swan. [Say SIG nit]

cylinder *noun* **1 a** a uniform solid or hollow body with straight sides and a circular section. **b** a thing of this shape, e.g. a container for liquefied gas. **2** a cylinder-shaped part of various machines, esp. a piston chamber in an engine. **3** the rotating part of a revolver which houses the cartridge chambers. PHRASES **firing** (or **hitting** etc.) **on all cylinders** working at peak efficiency and capacity.

cylinder head *noun* the end cover of a cylinder in an internal combustion engine, against which the piston compresses the cylinder contents.

cylindrical *adjective* shaped like a cylinder: *huge cylindrical gas tanks*.

cymbal *noun* a musical instrument consisting of a concave brass or bronze plate, struck with another or with a stick etc. to make a ringing sound.

cynic *noun* **1** a person with little faith in human goodness who sarcastically doubts or despises sincerity and merit. **2** (**Cynic**) one of a school of ancient Greek philosophers, marked by a belief in self-control as the essence of virtue and an ostentatious contempt for ease and pleasure.

cynical *adjective* **1** believing that people are motivated by self-interest; distrustful of human sincerity or integrity. **2** doubtful as to whether something will happen or whether it is worthwhile: *most residents are cynical about plans to clean up the city's beaches*. **3** concerned only with one's own interests and typically disregarding accepted or appropriate standards in order to achieve them. **4** sneering, mocking, sarcastic: *a cynical laugh*. ▶ **cynically** *adverb*

cynicism *noun* **1** belief that people do things only to help themselves and not for good or honest reasons. **2** pessimism about whether something will happen or succeed or whether it is worthwhile: *cynicism about the chances of bringing peace to the war-torn region*. **3** lack of concern that something beneficial or advantageous to oneself might hurt others. **4** sneering or sarcastic speech or attitude. [Say SINNA sism]

cypress *noun* (*plural* **cypresses**) **1** a coniferous tree with hard wood and dark foliage. **2** the wood of this tree. [Say SIGH priss]

Cypriot • *noun* a native or national of Cyprus, an island in the E Mediterranean south of Turkey. • *adjective* of Cyprus. [Say SIP ree ut]

Cyrillic • *adjective* denoting the alphabet derived from Greek, adapted by the Slavic peoples, and now used for

Russian, Ukrainian, etc. • *noun* this alphabet. [Say suh RILL ick]

cyst *noun* **1** *Medical* an abnormal sac containing fluid, pus, etc. **2** *Biology* **a** a hollow organ, bladder, etc., in an animal or plant, containing a liquid secretion. **b** a cell or cavity enclosing reproductive bodies, an embryo, parasite, micro-organism, etc. [Say SIST]

cystic *adjective* **1** characterized by, of the nature of, or having a cyst. **2** of the urinary bladder or gallbladder. [Say SIS tick]

cystic fibrosis *noun* a hereditary disease characterized by abnormal mucus production which affects esp. the lungs, pancreas, and gastrointestinal tract. Abbreviation: **CF**.

cytological *adjective* having to do with the scientific study of the structure and function of plant and animal cells. [Say sigh toe LOGICAL]

cytologist *noun* a person who studies the structure and function of plant and animal cells, esp. to detect and identify disease. [Say sigh TOLLA jist]

cytology *noun* the microscopic study of cells, esp. to detect and identify disease. [Say sigh TOLLA jee]

cytoplasm *noun* the material or protoplasm within a living cell, apart from its nucleus. ▶ **cytoplasmic** *adjective* [Say SIGH toe plasm, sigh toe PLASMIC]

czar *noun* **1** *hist.* the title of the emperor of Russia before 1917. **2** a person with great authority or power: *some large-scale farmers did seem like cereal czars*. [Say ZAR]

czarina *noun* *hist.* the title of the empress of Russia before 1917. [Say zar EENA]

czarist *noun* of or pertaining to Russia under the rule of the czars, before 1917: *the czarist pogroms of the 1880s*. [Say ZAR ist]

Czech • *noun* **1** a native or national of the Czech Republic or *hist.* Czechoslovakia. **2** the Slavic language spoken in the Czech Republic or *hist.* Czechoslovakia. • *adjective* **1** of or relating to the Czech Republic or *hist.* Czechoslovakia. **2** of or relating to the Czech language. [Say CHECK]

Czechoslovak (also **Czechoslovakian**) • *noun* a native or national of Czechoslovakia, a former state in central Europe. • *adjective* of or relating to Czechoslovaks or the former state of Czechoslovakia. [Say checko SLOW vack]

C

Dd

D¹ *noun* (also **d**) (*plural* **Ds** or **D's**) **1** the fourth letter of the alphabet. **2** *Music* the second note of the diatonic scale of C major. **3** the fourth hypothetical person or example in a series etc. **4** the fourth class or category (of academic marks etc.) denoting a barely acceptable quality. **5** *Math* the fourth known quantity, group, section, etc. **6** (as a Roman numeral) 500. **7** a size of battery, having a voltage of 1.5 V.

D² *symbol* **1** deuterium. **2** *Physics* density.

D³ *abbreviation* (also **D.**) **1** a government department. **2** dimension: *3-D*. **3** digital (recording).

d. *symbol* deci-.

'd *verb* (usu. after pronouns) had, would: *I'd ◊ he'd*.

DA *abbreviation* (*plural* **DAs**) *US* district attorney.

D/A *abbreviation* Computing digital to analog.

da *abbreviation* deca-.

dab • *verb* (**dabs**, **dabbed**, **dabbing**) **1** press a surface briefly with a cloth etc., without rubbing, esp. in cleaning or to apply a substance. **2** (foll. by *on*) apply (a substance) by dabbing a surface. **3** (usu. foll. by *at*) pat; tap. • *noun* **1** a brief application of a cloth, sponge, etc. to a surface without rubbing. **2** a small amount of something: *a dab of paint*. PHRASES **smack dab** *adverb* informal exactly, directly. ▶ **dabber** *noun*

dabble *verb* (**dabbles**, **dabbled**, **dabbling**) **1** (usu. foll. by *in*, *at*) take a casual or superficial interest or part (in a subject or activity). **2** splash, play, move the feet, hands, etc. about in (usu. a small amount of) liquid. **3** (of a duck) feed in shallow water with splashing and quick bill movements. ▶ **dabbler** *noun*

dachshund *noun* a breed of dog with short legs and a long body. [Say DACKS hund or DOCKS hund]

Dacron *noun* proprietary a polyester used as fabric.

dad *noun* informal father.

dada *noun* informal father. [Say DAD uh]

Dada *noun* an early 20th-century movement in art, literature, music, and film, rejecting and mocking artistic and social conventions and emphasizing the illogical and the absurd. ▶ **Dadaism** *noun & adjective*

daddy *noun* (*plural* **daddies**) informal **1** father. **2** the oldest or supreme example: *had a daddy of a headache*.

daddy-long-legs *noun* (*plural* **daddy-long-legs**) any of various arachnids of the family Opilionidae, with very long thin legs, found in humus and on tree trunks.

daemon *noun* **1** = DEMON 5. **2** *Computing* in some operating systems, an unseen program that controls a peripheral device. [Sounds like DEMON]

daffodil *noun* **1 a** a bulbous plant with a yellow or white trumpet-shaped crown. **b** a flower of any of these plants. **2** a pale-yellow colour.

daffy *adjective* (**daffier**, **daffiest**) slang silly, foolish.

dagger *noun* **1** a short stabbing weapon with a pointed and edged blade. **2** a symbol (†) used as a reference mark in printed matter or to indicate that a person is deceased. PHRASES **look daggers at** glare angrily at.

dahlia *noun* a plant of the daisy family, of Mexican origin, cultivated for its multi-coloured single or double flowers. [Say DAILY uh]

daikon *noun* a long, thin, white oriental radish. [Say DIE con]

dailiness *noun* the quality of something that happens daily.

daily • *adjective* **1** done, produced, or occurring every day or every weekday. **2** constant, regular. **3** calculated, measured, etc. by the day: *a daily quota*. • *adverb* **1** every day; from day to day. **2** constantly. • *noun* (*plural* **dailies**) informal a daily newspaper.

daintily *adverb* in a dainty or delicate manner: *Dana nibbled daintily on the asparagus*.

daintiness *noun* a dainty quality or manner.

dainty • *adjective* (**daintier**, **daintiest**) **1** delicately pretty: *a dainty lace handkerchief*. **2** delicate and graceful in build or movement. **3** (of food) delicious or pleasing to the palate: *a dainty morsel*. • *noun* (*plural* **dainties**) **1** a choice morsel. **2** *Cdn* (*Prairies & Northwestern Ont.*) (in *plural*) fancy cookies, cakes, etc. served at social gatherings.

daiquiri *noun* (*plural* **daiquiris**) a cocktail of rum, sugar, and usu. lime juice, sometimes also with puréed strawberries or bananas etc. [Say DACKA ree]

dairy *noun* (*plural* **dairies**) **1** a building or room for the storage, processing, and distribution of milk and its products. **2** a store where dairy products are sold. **3** milk and milk products. **4** (as an *adjective*) of, containing, or concerning milk and its products. **5** *Cdn* (*Cape Breton*) a convenience store.

dairying *noun* the business of producing, storing, and distributing milk and its products.

dais *noun* (*plural* **daises**) a low platform, usu. at the end of a room and used to support a table, throne, etc. [Say DIE iss or DAY iss]

daisy *noun* (*plural* **daisies**) **1** a small plant, *Bellis perennis*, bearing flowers each with a yellow disc and white rays. **2** any other plant with daisy-like flowers, esp. the larger ox-eye daisy. PHRASES **pushing up the daisies** slang dead and buried.

daisy chain • *noun* **1** a string of daisies threaded together. **2** a group of several connected things, events, etc. • *verb* (**daisy-chain**) esp. *Computing* link (several pieces of hardware, etc.) together in succession. ▶ **daisy-chained** *adjective*

Dakota • *noun* (*plural* **Dakota** or **Dakotas**) **1** a member of a North American Aboriginal people inhabiting the upper Mississippi and Missouri river valleys. **2** the Siouan language of this people. • *adjective* of or relating to the Dakota. [Say duh CO tuh]

dal *noun* **1** a kind of lentil or split pea, a common foodstuff in India. **2** a dish made with this. [Sounds like DOLL]

dale *noun* a valley, esp. in Northern England.

dalliance *noun* **1** brief or casual involvement with something: *McGill was my last dalliance with the education system*. **2** a casual love affair. [Say DALLY ince]

Dall sheep *noun* (also **Dall's sheep**) a white thinhorn sheep, *Ovis dalli dalli*, of the mountains of northwestern Canada and Alaska. [Sounds like DOLL]

dally¹ *verb* (**dallies**, **dallied**, **dallying**) **1** waste time, esp. frivolously. **2** have a casual sexual or romantic relationship with: *he should stop dallying with movie stars*. **3** show a casual interest in something, without committing oneself seriously: *the company has been dallying with the idea of opening a new office*.

dally² (*West*) • *noun* (*plural* **dallies**) a loop of rope wound around a saddle horn etc. to act as a brake. • *verb* (**dallies, dallied, dallying**) loop (a rope) around a saddle horn etc.

Dalmatian *noun* a large dog having white, short hair with dark spots. [Say dal MAY sh'n]

dam • *noun* **1** a barrier constructed to hold back water and raise its level, forming a reservoir or preventing flooding. **2** = BEAVER DAM. **3** anything functioning as a dam does. • *verb* (**dams, dammed, damming**) **1** provide or confine with a dam. **2** (often foll. by *up*) block up; hold back; obstruct.

damage • *noun* **1** harm or injury impairing the value or usefulness of something, or the health or normal function of a person. **2** (in *plural*) *Law* a sum of money claimed or awarded in compensation for a loss or an injury: *she was awarded $248,000 in damages after the car accident*. **3** (**the damage**) *informal* cost: *what's the damage?* • *verb* (**damages, damaged, damaging**) **1** inflict damage on. **2** (esp. as **damaging** *adjective*) detract from the reputation of: *a damaging admission*.

damage control *noun* action taken to lessen the effects of damage after an accident, bad publicity, etc.

damaged *adjective* that has been physically harmed and is, as a result, less valuable, useful, or functional.

damage deposit *noun* a sum of money given as a deposit against possible future damage to something rented or leased.

damaging *adjective* causing damage; having a harmful effect: *these damaging lies ruined his reputation* ◊ *damaging ultraviolet rays*.

damask *noun* a woven fabric (esp. silk or linen) with a pattern visible on both sides, used esp. for table linens. [Say DAM isk]

dame *noun* slang offensive a woman.

damn • *verb* **1** curse (a person or thing). **2** doom to hell; cause the damnation of. **3** condemn, censure: *a review damning the performance*. **4 a** (often as **damning** *adjective*) (of a circumstance, piece of evidence, etc.) show or prove to be guilty; bring condemnation upon. **b** be the ruin of. **5** used when swearing at a person or thing: *damn you!* • *noun* slang a negligible amount: *not worth a damn*. • *interjection* informal expressing emphatic annoyance, frustration, approval, etc. • *adjective & adverb* informal = DAMNED. PHRASES **damn fool** *informal* foolish, stupid: *that's a damn fool idea*. **damn near** (also **damned near**) *informal* almost: *damn near died*. **damn well** *informal* (as an emphatic) simply: *damn well do as I say*. **damn with faint praise** praise so unenthusiastically as to imply disapproval: *to say that gluten-free bread is better than no bread at all may be damning with faint praise, but it's true*. **I'll be** (or **I'm**) **damned if** I certainly do not, will not, etc. **not give a damn** *informal* not care at all. **well I'll be** (or **I'm**) **damned** *informal* exclamation of surprise, dismay, etc.

damnable *adjective* very bad or unpleasant: *leave this damnable place behind*. [Say DAM nuh bull]

damnation • *noun* condemnation to eternal punishment, esp. in hell. • *interjection* informal expressing anger or annoyance. [Say dam NATION]

damned *informal* • *noun* (in Christian belief) those condemned by God to suffer eternal punishment in hell: *the souls of the damned*. • *adjective* informal used for emphasis, esp. to express anger or frustration: *none of your damned business*. • *adverb* informal extremely: *damned hot*. PHRASES **damned if you do and damned if you don't** unable to win approval no matter what one does.

damnedest *adjective* informal most surprising or extraordinary: *the damnedest thing you ever saw*. PHRASES **do one's damnedest** do one's utmost.

damp • *adjective* slightly wet; moist. • *noun* diffused moisture in the air, on a surface, or in a solid, esp. as a cause of inconvenience or danger. • *verb* **1** make damp; moisten. **2** (often foll. by *down*) **a** take the force or vigour out of: *damp one's enthusiasm*. **b** make (a fire) burn less strongly by reducing the flow of air to it. **3** reduce or stop the vibration of (esp. the strings of a musical instrument). PHRASES **damp off** (of a plant) die from a fungus attack in damp conditions.

dampen *verb* **1** make or become damp. **2** make less strong or intense: *nothing could dampen her enthusiasm*.

damper *noun* **1** a person or thing that discourages, or reduces enthusiasm: *the remoteness of the area put a damper on development enthusiasm*. **2** a device that reduces shock or noise. **3** a movable metal plate in a flue to control the draft, and so the rate of combustion. **4** a pad silencing a piano string except when removed by means of a pedal or by the note's being struck.

dampness *noun* the state of being slightly wet.

damsel *noun* archaic or jocular a young unmarried woman.

damselfly *noun* (*plural* **damselflies**) any of various insects of the order Odonata, like a dragonfly but with its wings folded over the body when resting.

dance • *verb* (**dances, danced, dancing**) **1** move about rhythmically alone or with a partner or in a group, usu. in fixed steps or sequences to music, for pleasure, as entertainment, or as a ritual. **2** move in a lively way; skip or jump about. **3 a** perform (a specified dance or form of dancing). **b** perform (a specified role) in a ballet etc. **4** move up and down (on water, in the field of vision, etc.). **5** move (esp. a child) up and down. • *noun* **1** a sequence of steps or bodily motions etc., usu. performed to music. **2** a set of lively movements resembling a dance: *he gesticulated comically and did a little dance in the hallway*. **3** a social gathering for dancing. **4** the art of dancing: *a dance critic*. **5** a piece of music having a rhythm or style that is suitable for a particular dance. **6** a dancing or lively motion. **7** a formal or stylized pattern of movements etc. performed by an animal or bird. **8** = ICE DANCING. PHRASES **dance attendance on** do one's utmost to please someone by attending to all their needs or requests. ▶ **danceable** *adjective*

dance hall *noun* **1** a public establishment for dancing. **2** an uptempo usu. electronic style of popular music, originating in the dance halls of Jamaica, derived from reggae and elements of rap and ragga.

dancer *noun* **1** a person who performs a dance. **2** a person whose profession is dancing.

dancey *adjective* **1** (of music) suitable for dancing to. **2** involving a great deal of dancing.

dancing girl *noun* a girl or woman who performs esp. erotic or music hall dances.

D. and C. *noun* (*plural* **D. and C.'s**) an operation in which the cervix is dilated and the uterine lining scraped off with a curette.

dandelion *noun* a plant with jagged leaves and a large bright yellow flower on a hollow stalk, followed by a globular head of seeds with downy tufts.

dander¹ *noun* PHRASES **get one's dander up** *informal* lose one's temper; become angry.

dander² *noun* dandruff, esp. in the hair of animals.

dandle *verb* (**dandles, dandled, dandling**) move a baby or young child up and down on one's knees or in one's arms.

dandruff *noun* dead skin in small scales in the hair.

dandy • *noun* (*plural* **dandies**) **1** a man unduly devoted to style and fashion in dress and appearance. **2** *informal* an excellent thing. • *adjective* (**dandier, dandiest**) *informal* very good of its kind; splendid, first-rate. ▶ **dandyish** *adjective* **dandyism** *noun*

D

D

Dane noun **1** a native or national of Denmark. **2** hist. a Viking invader of England in the 9th–11th centuries.

dang adjective & interjection informal = DAMN.

danger noun **1** liability or exposure to harm. **2** a thing that causes or is likely to cause harm. **3** an unwelcome possibility: the danger that people will do nothing. PHRASES **in danger of** likely to incur or to suffer from.

dangerous adjective involving or causing danger. ▶ **dangerously** adverb **dangerousness** noun

dangle verb (**dangles**, **dangled**, **dangling**) **1** be loosely suspended, so as to be able to sway to and fro. **2** hold or carry loosely suspended. **3** hold out (a hope, temptation, etc.) enticingly: early retirement is a carrot that many companies dangle before older employees.

dangling adjective **1** (of a participle in an absolute clause or phrase) having no expressed subject, but having an implicit subject that is different than the subject of the clause modified, e.g. talking in while talking on the cellphone, the car ran into the ditch. **2** hanging loosely: she swung from the dangling rope.

dangly adjective tending to dangle: dangly earrings.

Danish • adjective of or relating to Denmark or the Danes. • noun **1** the Danish language. **2** (**the Danish**; treated as plural) the Danish people. **3** (plural **Danishes**) (also **Danish pastry**, plural **Danish pastries**) a sweet, flaky roll topped with icing, fruit, etc.

dank adjective disagreeably damp and cold. ▶ **dankly** adverb **dankness** noun

dapper adjective neat and trim, esp. in dress, appearance, or bearing.

dapple verb (**dapples**, **dappled**, **dappling**) mark with spots or rounded patches of colour or shade: the floor was dappled with moonlight. ▶ **dappled** adjective

dapple grey • adjective (of an animal's coat) grey or white with darker spots. • noun a dapple grey horse.

dare • verb (**dares**, **dared**, **daring**) **1** (3rd singular present **dares** or sometimes **dare**) venture (to); have the courage or impudence (to): if they dare to come ◊ how dare you? **2** defy or challenge (a person): I dare you to own up. • noun **1** an act of daring. **2** a challenge, esp. to prove courage. PHRASES **I dare say 1** it is probable. **2** probably; I grant that much: I dare say, but you are still wrong.

daredevil • noun a recklessly daring person. • adjective recklessly daring. ▶ **daredevilry** noun

daring • noun adventurous courage. • adjective prepared to take risks. ▶ **daringly** adverb

dark • adjective **1** with little or no light. **2** of a deep or sombre colour. **3** (of a person) with deep brown or black hair, complexion, or skin. **4** gloomy, dismal: dark thoughts. **5** evil, sinister: dark deeds. **6** sullen, angry: a dark mood. **7** remote, mysterious, little-known: the dark and distant past. • noun **1** absence of light. **2** nightfall: after dark. **3** a dark area or colour, esp. in painting. PHRASES **in the dark 1** with little or no light. **2** lacking information.

Dark Ages plural noun **1 a** the period of western European history between the fall of the Roman Empire and the high Middle Ages, c.500–1100, during which Germanic tribes swept through Europe, often attacking and destroying towns and settlements. It was judged to have been a time of relative lack of learning, though scholarship was kept alive in the monasteries and learning was encouraged at the courts of Charlemagne in Europe and Alfred the Great in England. **b** a similar period in the history of Greece and other Aegean countries from the end of the Bronze Age until the beginning of the historical period. **2 dark ages** any period of supposed lack of enlightenment: this judge is living in the dark ages.

darken verb make or become dark or darker. PHRASES **darken a door** appear at a place: I'll never darken this door again! ▶ **darkener** noun

dark horse noun a little-known person etc. who is unexpectedly successful or prominent: the Korean movie was the dark horse of the film festival.

darkish adjective somewhat dark.

darkly adverb **1 a** in a threatening, mysterious, or ominous way: Dirk hinted darkly that all was not well. **b** in a depressing or pessimistic way: I wondered darkly if I was wasting my time. **2** showing a dark colour: a darkly silhouetted figure.

darkness noun **1 a** the partial or total absence of light: the office was in darkness. **b** night: we pulled into town as darkness fell. **2** the quality of being dark in colour. **3** wickedness, evil, or mystery: the forces of darkness.

darkroom noun a room for developing photographic work, with normal light excluded.

darling • noun **1** a beloved or lovable person or thing. **2** a favourite. **3** informal a pretty or endearing person or thing. • adjective **1** beloved, lovable. **2** favourite. **3** informal charming or pretty.

darn¹ • verb mend (esp. knitted material, or a hole in it) by interweaving yarn across the hole with a needle. • noun a darned area in material.

darn² verb, interjection, adjective, & adverb informal a milder form of DAMN.

darndest adjective (also **darnedest**) a milder form of DAMNEDEST.

darned adjective & adverb informal a milder form of DAMNED.

darnel noun any of several grasses of the genus Lolium, native to Europe and N Africa and naturalized in North America, planted as pasture grasses or to stabilize soil.

darning noun **1** the action of a person who darns. **2** things to be darned.

darning needle noun **1** a long needle with a large eye, used in darning. **2** a dragonfly.

darn tootin' informal • interjection indicating fervent agreement. • adverb & adjective used as an intensifier: darn tootin' I mind! PHRASES **you're darn tootin'** you're darn right.

dart • noun **1** a small pointed object thrown or fired as

a weapon. **2 a** a small pointed object with feathers or plastic fins, used in the game of darts. **b** (in *plural*) an indoor game in which such darts are thrown at a circular target to score points: *darts is very popular in England*. **3** a sudden rapid movement. **4** a stitched tapered tuck for shaping a garment. • *verb* **1** move or go suddenly or rapidly. **2** direct suddenly (a glance etc.).

dartboard *noun* a circular board marked with numbered segments, used as a target in darts.

darter *noun* **1** a large water bird with a narrow head and long thin neck. **2** any of various small quick-moving freshwater fish of North America.

Darwinian • *adjective* **1** of or relating to Charles Darwin's (1809–92) theory of the evolution of species by natural selection. **2** characterized by ruthless competition for survival: *sees the Palestinian-Israeli conflict as part of an inevitably cruel Darwinian struggle between Israelis and Arabs that can only be resolved by superior might*. • *noun* an adherent of Darwin's theory. ▶ **Darwinism** *noun* **Darwinist** *noun* [Say dar WINNY un, DARWIN ism]

dash • *verb* (**dashes**, **dashed**, **dashing**) **1** rush hastily or forcefully. **2** strike or fling with great force, esp. so as to shatter. **3** frustrate, daunt, discourage: *dashed their hopes*. **4** *informal* (esp. **dash it** or **dash it all**) = DAMN *verb* 1. **5** splash or splatter. • *noun* **1** a rushing movement; a sudden advance. **2** a horizontal stroke in writing or printing to mark a pause or break in sense or to represent omitted letters or words. **3** a small amount of something: *a dash of salt*. **4** impetuous vigour and confidence. **5** a short race; a sprint. **6** the longer signal of the two used in Morse code (*compare* DOT *noun* 3). **7** = DASHBOARD. PHRASES **dash off** write or finish hurriedly.

dashboard *noun* the surface below the windshield of a motor vehicle or aircraft, containing instruments and controls.

dasher *noun* (also **dasher board**) one of the boards surrounding a hockey rink.

dashing *adjective* **1** attractive and fashionable: *a dashing red waistcoat*. **2** attractive in a romantic, adventurous way: *a dashing figure with flowing hair and an elegant tweed jacket*. ▶ **dashingly** *adverb*

dastardly *adjective* wicked and cruel: *pirates and their dastardly deeds*. [Say DASS turd lee]

> **WRITING TIP**
> **data, datum**
>
> In specialized scientific fields, **data** is treated as the plural of **datum**, taking a plural verb, as in *The data were collected and classified*. However, in modern non-scientific use, it is often treated similarly to a word like **information**, which takes a singular verb. Sentences like *The data was collected over a number of years* are now widely accepted in standard English.

---

data *noun* **1** quantities or characters operated on by a computer. **2** (treated as *singular*) a body or series of facts; information. **3** (treated as *plural*) facts, statistics. **4** *plural* of DATUM. [Say DAT uh or DATE uh]

database *noun* (also **data bank**) an organized store of data, esp. one that may be accessed by a computer.

datable *adjective* that can be dated (to a particular time).

data glove *noun* a device worn like a glove and containing sensors linked to a representation of a hand in a computer display, allowing the manual manipulation of images in virtual reality.

data processing *noun* a series of operations on data,

esp. by a computer, to retrieve or classify etc. information. ▶ **data processor** *noun*

date¹ • *noun* **1** a day of the month, esp. specified by a number. **2** a particular day or year, esp. when a given event occurred. **3** a statement (usu. giving the day, month, and year) in a document or inscription etc., of the time of composition or publication. **4 a** a social engagement, often of a romantic nature, with one other person. **b** a person with whom one has a social engagement: *my date is picking me up*. **5** the period to which a work of art etc. belongs. **6** the time when an event happens or is to happen. **7** (in *plural*) the dates of a person's birth and death, usu. in years: *Laurier's dates are 1841–1919*. • *verb* (**dates**, **dated**, **dating**) **1** mark with a date. **2 a** assign a date to (an object, event, etc.). **b** (foll. by *to*) assign to a particular time, period, etc. **3** make or go out on a date with a person: *they are now dating regularly*. **4** (often foll. by *from*, *back to*, etc.) have its origins at a particular time. **5** become evidently out of date: *a design that does not date*. **6** indicate or expose as being out of date: *that hat really dates you*. PHRASES **to date** until now. **up to date** meeting or according to the latest requirements, knowledge, or fashion.

date² *noun* **1** a dark oval single-stoned fruit. **2** (also **date palm**) the tall tree *Phoenix dactylifera*, native to W Asia and North Africa, bearing this fruit.

datebook *noun* an appointment diary.

dated *adjective* **1** old-fashioned. **2** marked with a date.

dateline • *noun* **1** (**Date Line**) the line from north to south partly along the meridian 180° from Greenwich, to the east of which the date is a day earlier than it is to the west. **2** a line at the head of a dispatch or special article in a newspaper showing the date and place of writing. • *verb* (**datelines**, **datelined**, **datelining**) provide (a newspaper story) with a dateline.

date rape *noun* the rape of a girl or woman by a person with whom she is on a date.

date square *noun* *Cdn* a dessert consisting of date filling spread on an oatmeal base and covered with a crumble topping, served cut into squares.

dating *noun* **1** the activity of going out on a date or dates. **2** the process or technique of establishing the date of an object or event.

dative *Grammar* • *noun* the case of nouns and pronouns (and words in agreement with them) indicating an indirect object or recipient. • *adjective* of or in the dative. [Say DAY tiv]

datum *noun* (*plural* **data**) **1** a piece of information. **2** a thing known or granted; an assumption or premise from which inferences may be drawn. **3** a fixed starting point of a scale etc.: *datum line*. **4** *see also* DATA. [Say DAT um or DATE um]

daub • *verb* **1** spread (paint, plaster, or some other thick substance) crudely or roughly on a surface. **2** coat or smear (a surface) with paint etc. **3 a** paint crudely or unskilfully. **b** lay (colours) on crudely and clumsily. • *noun* **1** paint or other substance daubed on a surface: *daubs of paint*. **2** plaster, clay, etc., for coating a surface, esp. mixed with straw and applied to laths or wattles to form a wall. **3** a painting executed without much skill.

daughter *noun* **1** a girl or woman in relation to either or both of her parents. **2** a female descendant. **3** (foll. by *of*) a female member of a family, nation, etc. **4** (foll. by *of*) a woman who is regarded as the spiritual descendant of a person or thing. **5** a cell etc. formed by the division etc. of another. ▶ **daughterly** *adjective*

daughter-in-law *noun* (*plural* **daughters-in-law**) the wife of one's son.

daunt *verb* discourage, intimidate. ▶ **daunting** *adjective*

dauntless *adjective* intrepid, persevering.

davit *noun* a small crane on a ship, esp. one of a pair for suspending or lowering a lifeboat. [Say DAV it or DAVE it]

dawdle *verb* (**dawdles, dawdled, dawdling**) **1** walk or move slowly. **2** be slow; waste time: *Euan dawdled over the last of his toast.* ▶**dawdler** *noun*

dawn • *noun* **1** the first light of day; daybreak. **2** the beginning of a phenomenon or period of time, esp. one perceived as favourable: *the dawn of civilization.* • *verb* **1** (of a day) begin; grow light. **2** begin to appear or develop; become visible. **3** (often foll. by *on, upon*) begin to become evident or understood (by a person).

dawning *noun* **1** daybreak. **2** the beginning of something.

day *noun* **1** the time between sunrise and sunset. **2 a** a period of 24 hours as a unit of time, esp. from midnight to midnight, corresponding to a complete revolution of the earth on its axis. **b** a corresponding period on other planets. **3** the time in a day during which work or another activity is engaged in: *an eight-hour day.* **4** daylight: *clear as day.* **5 a** (also in *plural*) a period of the past or present: *the modern day ◊ the old days ◊ in my day things were different.* **b** (**the day**) the present time: *the issues of the day.* **6** a point of time: *will do it one day.* **7 a** the date of a specific festival. **b** a day associated with a particular event or purpose: *payday ◊ Christmas day.* **8** a particular date; a date agreed on. PHRASES **all in a** (or **the**) **day's work** part of normal routine. **any day** at any time; under any conditions: *my dog Sleuth can beat yours any day!* **any day now** in the immediate future: *could happen any day now.* **at the end of the day** in the final reckoning, when all is said and done. **call it a day** end a period of activity, esp. content that enough has been done. **day after day** without respite. **day and night** all the time. **day by day** gradually. **day in, day out** routinely, constantly. **from day one** from the beginning. **if one is a day** adding emphasis to an estimate of a person's age: *he must be sixty if he's a day.* **not one's day** a day of successive misfortunes for a person. **one of these days** before very long. **one of those days** a day when things go badly. **that will be the day** *informal* that will never happen. **win the day** be successful.

daybook *noun* an appointment diary.

daybreak *noun* the first appearance of light in the morning.

day camp *noun* a camp which children attend during the day, usu. only on summer weekdays.

daycare *noun* **1** the supervision of children during the workday by people other than their parents. **2** the care provided by a daycare centre. **3** (also **daycare centre**) a place where daycare is provided.

daydream • *noun* a pleasant fantasy or reverie. • *verb* (**daydreams, daydreamed, daydreaming**) indulge in this. ▶**daydreamer** *noun* **daydreaming** *noun &* *adjective*

Day-Glo • *noun* proprietary a make of fluorescent paint or other colouring. • *adjective* coloured with or like this.

day job *noun* a job with regular daytime hours, esp. as opposed to artistic pursuits: *don't quit your day job.*

daylight *noun* **1** the light of day. **2** dawn: *before daylight.* **3** a visible gap or interval: *I see daylight around the door frame.*

daylights *plural noun informal* senses or wits: *scared the daylights out of me ◊ beat the living daylights out of him.*

daylight saving *noun* (also **daylight savings**) the achieving of longer evening daylight, esp. in summer, by setting the time an hour ahead.

daylight time *noun* (also **daylight saving time**) time as adjusted for daylight saving.

day lily *noun* (*plural* **day lilies**) any plant of the genus *Hemerocallis*, whose flowers last only a day.

daylong *adjective* lasting for a day.

Day of Atonement *noun* = YOM KIPPUR.

Day of Judgment *noun* = JUDGMENT DAY.

day of reckoning *noun* the time when something must be atoned for or revenged: *there will be a day of reckoning for the arrogance of the Tories and their inability to hear the concerns of Ontarians.*

day pack *noun* a small backpack for use on one-day hikes or for carrying books etc.

day pass *noun* (*plural* **day passes**) **1** a certificate etc. entitling a person to unlimited use of a transit system, amusement park, etc. throughout a day. **2** a permit allowing a jailed offender to leave prison for a day.

day release *noun Cdn* release of a jailed offender during the day or for a short period of time, e.g. to attend school or for employment.

day school *noun* a school not providing boarding for students.

daytime *noun* the part of the day when there is natural light.

Daytimer *noun* proprietary an appointment diary.

day-to-day *adjective* **1** involving daily routine. **2** planning for only one day at a time.

day trader *noun* a person who tries to make quick profits by buying extremely volatile stocks and holding them for a very short time, usu. less than a full day. ▶**day trading** *noun*

daze • *verb* (**dazes, dazed, dazing**) stupefy, bewilder. • *noun* a state of confusion or bewilderment. ▶**dazed** *adjective* **dazedly** *adverb*

dazzle • *verb* (**dazzles, dazzled, dazzling**) **1** blind temporarily or confuse the sight of by an excess of light. **2** impress or overpower (a person) with knowledge, ability, or any brilliant display or prospect. • *noun* bright confusing light. ▶**dazzled** *adjective* **dazzlement** *noun* **dazzler** *noun* **dazzling** *adjective* **dazzlingly** *adverb*

dB *abbreviation* decibel(s).

DC *abbreviation* **1** (also **d.c.**) direct current. **2** District of Columbia.

D-Day *noun* **1** the day (6 June 1944) on which Allied forces invaded northern France to begin the liberation of western Europe. **2** the day on which an important operation is to begin or a change to take effect.

DDT *abbreviation* dichlorodiphenyltrichloroethane, a colourless chlorinated hydrocarbon used as an insecticide, now banned in many countries.

de- *prefix* added to verbs and their derivatives to form verbs and nouns implying removal or reversal: *decentralize ◊ de-ice ◊ demoralization.*

deacon • *noun* **1** (in churches with a hierarchy) a minister of the third order, below bishop and priest. **2** (in some Protestant Churches) a layperson elected or appointed to assist the minister, manage the congregation's secular affairs, etc. • *verb* appoint or ordain as a deacon. [Say DEE kun]

deaconess *noun* (*plural* **deaconesses**) **1** a laywoman with functions similar to a deacon's. **2** = DIACONAL MINISTER. [Say dee kun ESS]

deactivate *verb* (**deactivates, deactivated, deactivating**) make inactive or less reactive. ▶**deactivation** *noun*

dead • *adjective* **1** no longer alive. **2** *informal* extremely tired or unwell. **3** affected by loss of sensation; numb: *my fingers are dead.* **4** (foll. by *to*) unconscious of; insensitive to. **5 a** no longer effective or in use; obsolete, extinct. **b** no longer functioning. **6** (of a fire etc.) no longer burning. **7** inanimate. **8 a** lacking force or vigour; dull, lustreless, muffled. **b** (of sound) not

resonant. **9 a** quiet; lacking activity. **b** motionless, idle. **10 a** (of a microphone, telephone, etc.) not transmitting any sound, esp. because of a fault. **b** (of a circuit, conductor, etc.) carrying or transmitting no current: *a dead battery*. **11 a** (of the ball etc. in a game) out of play. **b** (of play) suspended. **12** abrupt, complete, exact, unqualified, unrelieved: *in dead silence* ◊ *a dead certainty*. **13** without spiritual life or energy. • *adverb* **1** absolutely, exactly, completely: *dead on target* ◊ *dead ahead* ◊ *dead last*. **2** *informal* very, extremely: *dead broke*. • *noun* (**the dead**) **1** (treated as *plural*) those who have died. **2** a time of silence or inactivity: *the dead of night*. PHRASES **dead drunk** so drunk as to be immobile or insensible. **dead from the neck up** *informal* stupid. **dead in the water 1** (of a ship etc.) motionless, esp. as a result of damage, malfunction, etc. **2** not progressing or functioning: *the economy is dead in the water*. **dead to the world** *informal* fast asleep; unconscious. **play dead** pretend to be dead by lying still. **stop dead in one's tracks** stop abruptly and decisively. **wouldn't be caught** (or **seen**) **dead in** (or **with**) *informal* shall have nothing to do with; shall refuse to wear etc.

dead air *noun* **1** a pause in a radio etc. transmission during which the speakers are silent etc. **2** air trapped for insulating purposes, as in layers of clothing.

deadbeat *noun* **1 a** someone who avoids paying debts. **b** (also **deadbeat dad** or **deadbeat father**) a man who avoids paying child support. **2** a worthless sponging idler.

deadbolt *noun* a bolt engaged by turning a knob or key, rather than by spring action.

dead duck *noun slang* **1** a person in a hopeless position. **2** an unsuccessful or useless person or thing.

deaden *verb* **1** deprive of or lose vitality, force, brightness, sound, feeling, etc. **2** (foll. by *to*) make insensitive.

dead end • *noun* **1 a** a closed end of a road, passage, etc. **b** a street or road with a dead end. **2** a situation offering no prospects of progress or advancement. • *verb* (**dead-end**) (of a road or one's progress, development, etc.) come to an end.

deadfall *noun* **1** a trap in which a raised weight is made to fall on and kill esp. large game. **2** a tangled mass of fallen trees, branches, etc. **3** a dead tree that has fallen to the ground.

deadhead • *noun* **1** a faded flower head. **2** a useless or unenterprising person. **3** a sunken or submerged log, esp. one that is a hazard to boats. • *verb* remove deadheads from (a plant).

dead heat *noun* **1** a race in which two or more competitors finish at exactly the same time. **2** a situation in which all participants, competitors, etc. receive the same number of votes etc.

dead horse *noun* PHRASES **flog** (or **beat**) **a dead horse** waste effort by trying to do something that is no longer possible.

dead language *noun* a language no longer commonly spoken, e.g. Latin.

dead letter *noun* **1** a law or practice no longer observed or recognized. **2** an undeliverable piece of mail.

deadline *noun* a time limit for the completion of an activity etc.

deadliness *noun* the deadly quality or nature of something: *did not realize the virus's potential deadliness*.

deadlock • *noun* **1** a situation, esp. one involving opposing parties, in which no progress can be made. **2** a type of lock requiring a key to open or close it. • *verb* bring or come to a standstill because of fundamental disagreement: *the meeting is deadlocked*. ▶ **deadlocked** *adjective*

deadly • *adjective* (**deadlier, deadliest**) **1** a causing

or able to cause fatal injury or serious damage. **b** poisonous. **2** intense, extreme: *deadly dullness*. **3** (of an aim etc.) extremely accurate or effective. **4** deathlike: *deadly gloom*. **5** *informal* dreary, dull. • *adverb* **1** like death; as if dead: *her skin was deadly pale*. **2** extremely, intensely: *deadly serious*.

deadly nightshade *noun* a poisonous plant with purple flowers and purple-black berries.

deadly sin *noun* a sin regarded as leading to damnation, esp. pride, covetousness (greed for material things), lust, gluttony (excessive indulgence in food and drink), envy, anger, or sloth (laziness).

dead march *noun* (*plural* **dead marches**) a funeral march.

dead meat *noun informal* a person or thing that is doomed or finished: *if they don't come, we're dead meat*.

dead-on *adjective* **1** exactly right. **2** perfectly on target.

deadpan • *adjective & adverb* with a face or manner lacking all expression or emotion. • *verb* (**deadpans, deadpanned, deadpanning**) say in a deadpan manner: *"I'm an undercover dentist," he deadpanned*.

dead set *adjective* (foll. by *against*) fiercely opposed.

dead weight *noun* **1** an inert mass. **2** a heavy weight or burden.

deadwood *noun informal* one or more useless or unprofitable people or things: *in writing, unnecessary words are deadwood*.

deaf *adjective* **1** wholly or partly without hearing. **2** refusing to listen or comply: *deaf to all entreaties*. **3** insensitive to harmony, rhythm, etc.: *tone-deaf*. PHRASES **deaf as a post** completely deaf. **fall on deaf ears** be ignored. **turn a deaf ear** ignore or refuse to listen to.

deafen *verb* **1** (often as **deafening** *adjective*) overpower with sound. **2** deprive of hearing by noise, esp. temporarily. ▶ **deafeningly** *adverb*

deafness *noun* the inability to hear; partial or total hearing impairment.

deal • *verb* (**deals, dealt, dealing**) **1** (foll. by *with*) **a** take measures concerning (a problem, person, etc.), esp. in order to put something right. **b** do business with; associate with. **c** discuss or treat (a subject). **2** (foll. by *in*) sell or be concerned with commercially: *deals in insurance*. **3** distribute or apportion to several people etc. **4** distribute (cards) to players for a game or round. **5** cause to be received; administer: *deal a heavy blow*. **6** *informal* include (a person) in an activity: *deal me in*. • *noun* **1** (usu. **a good** (or **great**) **deal**) *informal* **a** a large amount: *a great deal of trouble*. **b** to a considerable extent: *is a good deal better*. **2** an agreement, esp. in business on certain terms for buying or doing something. **3** a specified form of treatment given or received: *got a fair deal*. **4 a** the distribution of cards by dealing. **b** a player's turn to do this: *it's my deal*. **c** the round of play following this. **d** a set of hands dealt to players. PHRASES **it's a deal** *informal* expressing assent to an agreement.

de-alcoholized *adjective* (of an alcoholic drink) having had all or almost all alcohol removed.

dealer *noun* **1** a person etc. dealing in (esp. retail) goods: *car dealer*. **2** the player dealing at cards. **3** a person who deals in illegal drugs. ▶ **dealership** *noun* (in sense 1).

dealings *plural noun* contacts or transactions.

dealt *past and past participle of* DEAL.

dean *noun* **1 a** the head of a university faculty or department. **b** a college or university official with disciplinary and advisory functions. **2** the head of the chapter of a cathedral. **3** the most senior or most

prominent of a particular category or body of people: *the dean of Canadian literature*.

dear • *adjective* **1 a** beloved or much esteemed. **b** used as a merely polite or ironic form: *my dear man*. **2** used as a formula of address, esp. at the beginning of letters. **3** precious. **4** earnest, deeply felt: *my dearest wish*. **5 a** expensive. **b** (of money) available as a loan only at a high rate of interest. • *noun* (esp. as a form of address) a dear person. • *adverb* at a high price or great cost: *will cost you dear*. • *interjection* expressing surprise, dismay, pity, etc.

dearie *noun* usu. *jocular or ironic* (esp. as a form of address) *my dear*. PHRASES **dearie me!** *interjection* expressing surprise, dismay, etc.

dearly *adverb* **1** affectionately, fondly: *love her dearly*. **2 a** earnestly; keenly. **b** very much, greatly: *would dearly love to go*. **3** at a high price or great cost.

dearth *noun* a scarcity or lack. [Rhymes with EARTH]

death *noun* **1** the ending of life. **2** the event that terminates life. **3 a** the fact or process of being killed or killing: *stone to death*. **b** the fact or state of being dead: *eyes closed in death*. **4 a** the destruction or permanent cessation of something: *was the death of our hopes*. **b** *informal* something terrible or appalling. **5** (usu. **Death**) a personification of death, esp. as a destructive power, usu. represented by a skeleton. PHRASES **at death's door** close to death. **be the death of 1** cause the death of. **2** be very harmful to. **catch one's death** *informal* catch a serious chill etc. **do to death 1** kill. **2** overdo. **fate worse than death** *informal* a disastrous misfortune or experience. **like death warmed over** *slang* very tired or ill. **put to death** kill or cause to be killed. **to death** to the utmost: *bored to death*.

deathbed *noun* a bed as the place where a person is dying or has died (also as an *adjective*: *deathbed conversion*). PHRASES **on one's deathbed** near death.

death camp *noun* a prison camp in which many people die or are put to death.

death certificate *noun* an official statement of the cause and date and place of a person's death.

death knell *noun* **1** the tolling of a bell to mark a person's death. **2** an event that heralds the end or destruction of something: *the bill sounded the death knell of the official policy of assimilation*.

deathless *adjective* often ironic unforgettable: *another fine example of Ms. Wade's deathless prose*.

deathlike *adjective* typical of death: *nothing could rouse Stephen from his deathlike slumber*.

deathly • *adjective* (**deathlier, deathliest**) suggestive of death: *deathly silence*. • *adverb* **1** in a deathly way: *deathly pale*. **2** extremely: *deathly ill*.

death metal *noun* a form of heavy metal music whose lyrics deal esp. with death, violence, and Satanism.

death penalty *noun* punishment by being put to death.

death rate *noun* the number of deaths per thousand of population per year.

death row *noun* a prison block or section for prisoners sentenced to death, esp. in the US.

death sentence *noun* **1** a judicial sentence of punishment by death. **2** a situation implying imminent or premature death: *a cancer diagnosis is not a death sentence*.

death squad *noun* an armed paramilitary group formed to kill political enemies etc.

death trap *noun* *informal* a dangerous or unhealthy building, vehicle, etc.

death wish *noun* (*plural* **death wishes**) a desire (usu. unconscious) for the death of oneself or another: *cyclists who don't wear helmets must have a death wish*.

debacle *noun* **1** an utter failure or disaster, esp. a sudden one: *last year's playoff debacle of losing in the first round to Seattle*. **2 a** a breakup of ice in a river, with resultant flooding. **b** a sudden rush of water carrying stone and other debris. [Say duh BOCK ul or duh BACK ul]

debark[1] *verb* = DISEMBARK. [Say dee BARK or duh BARK]

debark[2] *verb* remove the bark from (a tree, log, etc.).

debase *verb* (**debases, debased, debasing**) **1** lower in quality, value, or character: *the love episodes debase the dignity of the drama ◊ the debased traditions of sportsmanship ◊ war debases people*. **2** *hist.* lower the value of (coin) by reducing the content of precious metal. ▶**debasement** *noun*

debatable *adjective* **1** questionable; subject to dispute: *it is debatable whether standards in education have slipped ◊ a public-works project with debatable military value*. **2** capable of being debated: *a debatable issue*. ▶**debatably** *adverb*

debate • *verb* (**debates, debated, debating**) **1** discuss or dispute about (an issue, proposal, etc.) esp. formally in a legislative assembly, public meeting, etc. **2** consider different sides of a question; ponder (a matter): *am debating the pros and cons of gas versus electric stoves ◊ I haven't made up my mind; I'm still debating*. **3** engage in a debate with (someone). • *noun* **1** a formal discussion on a particular matter, esp. in a legislative assembly etc. **2** argument, discussion: *open to debate*. **3** a contest in which the affirmative and negative sides of a question are presented by opposing speakers. ▶**debater** *noun*

debauch • *verb* (**debauches, debauched, debauching**) **1** corrupt morally: *an electorate debauched by state handouts*. **2** cause to indulge in immoral or excessive sexual activity or excessive drinking. **3** seduce (a woman). • *noun* (*plural* **debauches**) a bout of excessive indulgence in such activities: *looked utterly unaffected by the previous night's debauch*. ▶**debauched** *adjective* [Say duh BOTCH]

debauchery *noun* (*plural* **debaucheries**) excessive indulgence in pleasures of the flesh, esp. sex, alcohol, or drugs. [Say duh BOTCHA ree]

debenture *noun* an unsecured loan certificate issued by a company. [Say duh BEN chur]

debilitate *verb* (**debilitates, debilitated, debilitating**) **1** make someone very weak and infirm: *this sickness kills at least 600 horses a year and debilitates many more*. **2** hinder, delay, or weaken: *the measure would debilitate public schools*. ▶**debilitating** *adjective* **debilitation** *noun* [Say duh BILLA tate, duh billa TAY sh'n]

debility *noun* (*plural* **debilities**) **1** feebleness, esp. of health: *physical debility often robs us of dignity*. **2** a disability or handicap. [Say duh BILLA tee]

debit • *noun* **1** an entry in an account recording a sum owed or paid out. **2** the sum recorded. **3** the total of such sums. **4** the debit side of an account. • *verb* (**debits, debited, debiting**) (of a bank or other financial organization) remove an amount of money from a customer's account, typically as payment for services or goods: *$10,000 was debited from their account ◊ your bank account will be automatically debited for the amount of your gas bill*.

debit card *noun* a card enabling the holder to pay for purchases electronically by transferring funds from a bank account.

debonair *adjective* confident, stylish, and charming:

Trudeau's reputation as a wealthy debonair bachelor had preceded him to Washington. [Say debba NAIR]

debone *verb* (**debones**, **deboned**, **deboning**) remove the bones from (poultry etc.).

debrief *verb* discuss a completed mission, undertaking, or event with. ▶ **debriefing** *noun*

debris *noun* **1** scattered fragments, esp. of something wrecked or destroyed. **2** an accumulation of loose material, e.g. from rocks or plants. [Say duh BREE or deb REE]

debt *noun* **1** a sum of money owed. **2** a state of obligation to pay something owed: *winning the lottery allowed them finally to get out of debt.* **3** gratitude for kindness, help, influence, etc. PHRASES **in a person's debt** under an obligation to a person. [Say DET]

debtor *noun* a person, country, etc. that owes a debt.

debug *verb* (**debugs**, **debugged**, **debugging**) **1** identify and remove defects from (a machine, computer program, etc.). **2** trace and remove concealed listening devices.

debugger *noun* a program for debugging.

debugging *noun* **1** the identification and removal of errors from computer hardware or software. **2** the detection and removal of concealed listening devices from an area.

debunk *verb* *informal* **1** show the good reputation or aspirations of (a person, institution, etc.) to be false: *comedy takes delight in debunking heroes.* **2** expose the false nature of: *she debunks all the myths about the glamorous life of an actress.* ▶ **debunker** *noun*

debut • *noun* **1** the first public appearance of a person in a specified role, esp. a performer. **2** the first appearance of a young woman of marriageable age in fashionable society. • *adjective* first; inaugural: *their debut album.* • *verb* (**debuts**, **debuted**, **debuting**) make a debut. [Say day BYOO or DAY byoo]

debutante *noun* a (usu. wealthy) young woman making her social debut. [Say DEB you tont]

Dec. *abbreviation* December.

deca- *combining form* (also **dec-** before a vowel) **1** having ten. **2** tenfold. **3** ten, esp. of a metric unit: *decagram.*

decade *noun* **1** ten years. **2** a set, series, or group of ten. **3** a set of ten Hail Marys as part of the rosary. [Say DECK ade except for sense 3, for which say DECK id]

decadence *noun* **1** moral or cultural deterioration, esp. after a peak or culmination of achievement: *he denounced Western decadence.* **2** decadent behaviour; luxurious self-indulgence: *triple chocolate fudge cake — pure decadence.* [Say DEKKA dince]

decadent • *adjective* **1 a** in a state of moral or cultural deterioration: *a decadent Hollywood lifestyle.* **b** of a period of decadence. **2** self-indulgent: *a decadent soak in the tub.* **3** (of food, esp. dessert) very rich or sweet. • *noun* a decadent person. ▶ **decadently** *adverb* [Say DEKKA dint]

decaf *informal* • *noun* decaffeinated coffee. • *adjective* decaffeinated.

decaffeinate *verb* (**decaffeinates**, **decaffeinated**, **decaffeinating**) **1** remove the caffeine from. **2** reduce the quantity of caffeine in (usu. coffee). ▶ **decaffeinated** *adjective* **decaffeination** *noun*

decal *noun* a picture or design transferred from specially prepared paper to the surface of glass, plastic, etc. [Say DEE cal or DECK ul]

decamp *verb* **1** depart suddenly, esp. to relocate one's business or household to another area: *now they have decamped to the south of France.* **2** leave hurriedly to avoid prosecution or detection: *embezzled some money and decamped with the proceeds.*

decant *verb* gradually pour off (liquid, esp. wine or a solution) from one container to another, esp. without disturbing the sediment. [Say duh CANT]

decanter *noun* a stoppered glass container into which wine or liquor is decanted. [Say duh CANT er]

decapitate *verb* (**decapitates**, **decapitated**, **decapitating**) cut off the head of. ▶ **decapitation** *noun* [Say dee CAPPA tate]

decathlete *noun* an athlete who participates in a decathlon. [Say duh KATH leet]

decathlon *noun* an athletic contest in which each competitor takes part in ten events. [Say duh KATH lon]

decay • *verb* **1 a** rot, decompose. **b** cause to rot or decompose. **2** decline or cause to decline in quality, power, energy, beauty, etc. **3** *Physics* **a** (of a substance etc.) undergo change by radioactivity. **b** undergo a gradual decrease in magnitude of a physical quantity. • *noun* **1** a rotten or ruinous state; a process of wasting away. **2** decline in health, quality, etc. **3** *Physics* **a** change into another substance etc. by radioactivity. **b** a decrease in the magnitude of a physical quantity, esp. the intensity of radiation.

SPELL CHECK ABC
decease, disease

An illness is a **disease**.

---

decease *noun* *formal* esp. *Law* death.

deceased • *adjective* dead. • *noun* (usu. as **the deceased**) a person who has died, esp. recently.

deceit *noun* **1** the act or process of deceiving, esp. by concealing the truth. **2** a dishonest trick or stratagem. **3** willingness to deceive.

deceitful *adjective* **1** (of a person) using deceit, esp. habitually. **2** (of an act, practice, etc.) intended to deceive. ▶ **deceitfully** *adverb* **deceitfulness** *noun*

deceive *verb* (**deceives**, **deceived**, **deceiving**) **1** make (a person) believe what is false; mislead purposely. **2** be unfaithful to, esp. sexually. PHRASES **be deceived** be mistaken or deluded: *the area may seem to offer nothing of interest, but don't be deceived.* **deceive oneself** persist in a mistaken belief; fail to admit to oneself that something is true: *if she thinks he'll marry her, she's deceiving herself.* ▶ **deceiver** *noun*

decelerate *verb* (**decelerates**, **decelerated**, **decelerating**) move or cause to move more slowly; slow down. ▶ **deceleration** *noun* **decelerator** *noun* [Say duh SELLA rate, duh seller AY sh'n]

December *noun* the twelfth month of the year.

decency *noun* (*plural* **decencies**) **1** behaviour that conforms to acceptable standards of morality or respectability: *she had the decency to come and confess.* **2** avoidance of being shocking or obscene: *a loose dress, rather too low-cut for decency.* **3** (in *plural*) the requirements of correct behaviour.

SPELL CHECK ABC
decent, descent

A downward movement or slope is a **descent**.

---

decent *adjective* **1** conforming with current standards of behaviour or propriety. **2** respectable. **3** satisfying a fair standard; acceptable. **4** kind, obliging: *was decent enough to apologize.* **5** *informal* sufficiently clothed to see visitors: *are you decent?* ▶ **decently** *adverb*

decentralization *noun* **1** the transfer of power from central to local government. **2** the reorganization of a centralized institution, organization, etc. on the basis of greater local or regional autonomy.

decentralize *verb* (**decentralizes**, **decentralized**, **decentralizing**) **1** transfer (powers, functions, etc.) from a central to a local or regional government,

authority, etc. **2** move departments of a large organization away from a single administrative centre to other locations, usu. granting them some degree of autonomy. ▶ **decentralized** *adjective*

deception *noun* **1** the act of deliberately making someone believe something untrue: *a drama full of lies and deception*. **2** a thing that deceives: *the deliberate distortions and deceptions of the racist group*.

deceptive *adjective* giving an appearance or impression different from the true one; misleading: *he put the question with deceptive casualness*. ▶ **deceptively** *adverb* **deceptiveness** *noun*

deci- *combining form* one-tenth, esp. of a unit in the metric system: *decimetre*.

decibel *noun* **1** a unit (one-tenth of a bel) used in the comparison of two power levels relating to electrical signals or sound intensities, one of the pair usually being taken as a standard. Abbreviation: **dB**. **2** *informal* a degree of noise: *his voice went up several decibels*. [Say DESSA bull or DESSA bell]

decide *verb* (**decides**, **decided**, **deciding**) **1 a** (often foll. by *on*, *about*) come to a resolution as a result of consideration. **b** have or reach as one's resolution about something: *decided to stay*. **2 a** resolve or settle (a question, dispute, etc.). **b** cause (a person) to reach a resolution: *was unsure about going but the weather decided me*. **3** (usu. foll. by *between*, *for*, *against*, *in favour of*, or *that* + clause) give a judgment concerning a matter.

decided *adjective* **1** definite, unquestionable: *a decided difference*. **2** (of a person, esp. as a characteristic) having clear opinions; resolute.

decidedly *adverb* undoubtedly, undeniably.

decider *noun* **1** a game, race, etc., to decide between competitors finishing equal in a previous contest. **2** any person or thing that decides.

deciduous *adjective* **1** (of a tree) shedding its leaves annually. **2** (of leaves, horns, teeth, etc.) shed periodically. [Say duh SIDGE yoo us or duh SID yoo us]

decigram *noun* a metric unit of mass, equal to 0.1 gram. [Say DESSA gram]

decilitre *noun* a metric unit of capacity, equal to 0.1 litre. [Say DESSA litre]

decimal • *adjective* **1** (of a system of numbers, measures, etc.) based on the number ten, in which the smaller units are related to the principal units as powers of ten (units, tens, hundreds, thousands, etc.). **2** of tenths or ten; reckoning or proceeding by tens. • *noun* (also **decimal fraction**) a fraction whose denominator is a power of ten, esp. when expressed positionally by units to the right of a decimal point. ▶ **decimally** *adverb*

decimal place *noun* the position of a digit to the right of a decimal point.

decimal point *noun* a period placed before a numerator in a decimal fraction.

WRITING TIP
decimate

Historically, the meaning of **decimate** is "kill one in every ten". Although this sense has been almost completely superseded by the more general sense, "kill or destroy a large proportion of", it is important to recognize that a sentence like *The epidemic decimated the tiny town of 400 people* could be interpreted to mean that only ten percent of the town's residents died rather than a much greater number. For this reason, it may be better to use a word like **devastate**, **annihilate**, **obliterate**, or **destroy**.

---

decimate *verb* (**decimates**, **decimated**,

decimating) **1** destroy a large proportion of. **2** kill or remove one in every ten of. ▶ **decimation** *noun* [Say DESSA mate]

decimetre *noun* a metric unit of length, equal to 0.1 metre. [Say DESSA metre]

decipher *verb* **1** succeed in understanding (anything obscure or unclear): *cannot decipher his handwriting*. **2** convert (a text written in cipher) into an intelligible script or language. ▶ **decipherable** *adjective* [Say duh SIGH fur]

decision *noun* **1** the act or process of deciding. **2** a conclusion or resolution reached, esp. as to future action, after consideration. **3** *Baseball* a win or loss credited to a pitcher. **4** *Boxing* a victory determined by points. **5 a** the settlement of a question. **b** a formal judgment.

decisive *adjective* **1** that decides an issue; conclusive. **2** able to decide quickly and effectively. ▶ **decisively** *adverb* **decisiveness** *noun*

deck • *noun* **1 a** a platform in a ship covering all or part of the hull's area at any level and serving as a floor. **b** the accommodation on a particular deck of a ship. **2** anything compared to a ship's deck. **3** a component that carries a particular recording medium (such as a disc or tape) in sound-reproduction equipment. **4** a pack of cards. **5** a level unroofed area, usu. of wooden planks, adjoining a house. **6** the flat, usu. concrete area surrounding a swimming pool. **7** a pile of logs ready for hauling, milling, etc. • *verb* **1** (often foll. by *out*) decorate, adorn. **2** furnish with or cover as a deck. **3** *slang* knock (a person) to the ground. PHRASES **below deck** (or **decks**) in or into the space below a ship's main deck. **on deck 1** in the open air on a ship's main deck. **2** (esp. of a batter in baseball) next in line.

deck chair *noun* a folding chair of wood and canvas, of a kind used on deck on passenger ships.

-decker *combining form* having a specified number of decks or layers: *double-decker*.

deck shoe *noun* a shoe resembling a moccasin with rubber soles, leather uppers, and laces, usu. having a second lace looped around the heel.

declaim *verb* utter or deliver words or a speech in a rhetorical or impassioned way, as if to an audience: *I declaimed my opening line*.

declamation *noun* **1** the act or art of declaiming. **2** a rhetorical exercise or set speech. **3** an impassioned speech. [Say deckla MAY sh'n]

declamatory *adjective* expressing feelings or opinions in a strong, confident, or dramatic way in writing or speech: *a fervent and declamatory speech on behalf of the workers*. [Say duh CLAMMA tory]

declaration *noun* **1** the act or process of declaring. **2 a** a formal, emphatic, or deliberate statement or announcement. **b** a statement asserting or protecting a legal right. **3** a written public announcement of intentions, terms of an agreement, etc. **4** *Law* **a** a plaintiff's statement of claim. **b** an affirmation made instead of taking an oath.

declarative • *adjective* **1** of the nature of, or making, a declaration: *declarative statements*. **2** *Grammar* (of a sentence) that takes the form of a simple statement. • *noun* a declarative sentence. [Say duh CLAIRA tiv]

declare *verb* (**declares**, **declared**, **declaring**) **1** announce openly or formally: *declare war*. **2** pronounce (a person or thing) to be something: *declared him to be an imposter*. **3** (often foll. by *that* + clause) assert emphatically. **4** acknowledge possession of (dutiable goods, taxable income, etc.). **5** *Cards* **a** name (the trump suit etc.). **b** reveal that one holds (certain combinations of cards etc.) for scoring. **6** (of things) make evident, prove. **7** (often foll. by *for*, *against*)

take the side of one party or another. **8** announce oneself to be a candidate (for some electoral race). PHRASES **declare oneself** reveal one's intentions or identity. **well, I declare** (or **I do declare**) an exclamation of incredulity, surprise, or vexation.

declared *adjective* **1** that has been declared or made known: *the government's declared intention to reduce crime*. **2** (of a person) admitted: *a declared enemy of the system*.

declaw *verb* **1** remove the claws from (a cat). **2** remove the force, vigour, or influence from: *the environmental movement was declawed during the eighties*.

declension *noun* **1** *Grammar* the variation of the form of a noun, pronoun, or adjective, by which its grammatical case, number, and gender are identified. **2** the class in which a noun etc. is put according to the exact form of this variation. **3** the entire set of inflected forms of a word setting out in order the different forms of a noun etc. [Say deckla KLEN sh'n]

declination *noun* **1** the angular distance of a star etc. north or south of the celestial equator. **2** *Physics* the angular deviation of a compass needle from true north. [Say deckla NAY sh'n]

decline • *verb* (**declines, declined, declining**) **1** deteriorate; lose strength or vigour. **2 a** reply with formal courtesy that one will not accept (an invitation, honour, etc.). **b** refuse, esp. formally and courteously. **c** turn away from (a challenge, battle, discussion, etc.). **d** give or send a refusal. **3 a** slope downwards or bend down. **b** bend (something) down. **4** *Grammar* state the forms of (a noun, pronoun, or adjective) corresponding to cases, number, and gender. **5 a** diminish in numbers or size. **b** decrease in price etc. • *noun* **1 a** a decrease in numbers, rates, etc. **b** gradual loss of vigour or excellence. **2** decay, deterioration. **3** a fall in price or value. PHRASES **on the decline** in a declining state; falling off. ▸ **decliner** *noun*

Deco *noun* (also **deco**) = ART DECO (often as an *adjective*: *Deco apartments*). [Say DECK oh]

decode *verb* (**decodes, decoded, decoding**) **1** convert (a coded message) into intelligible language. **2** analyze and interpret (written or spoken communication etc.) (*compare* ENCODE 2): *dictionaries are a very useful tool to help people decode what they read*. **3** *Electronics* convert or unscramble (a coded signal) into an accessible format.

decoder *noun* **1** a person or thing that decodes (texts etc.). **2** an electronic device for analyzing stereophonic signals and feeding separate amplifier channels. **3** an electronic device connected to a television to unscramble encoded transmissions, esp. cable programs.

decolonization *noun* the withdrawal of a state from a colony, resulting in the colony's independence.

decolonize *verb* (**decolonizes, decolonized, decolonizing**) (of a state) withdraw from (a colony), leaving it independent.

decommission *verb* **1** close down (a nuclear reactor etc.). **2** take (a ship or aircraft) out of service.

decomposable *adjective* that can be decomposed.

decompose *verb* (**decomposes, decomposed, decomposing**) **1** destroy or be destroyed gradually by natural chemical processes: *a decomposing corpse* ◊ *as the waste materials decompose, they produce methane gas*. **2** separate (a substance, light, etc.) into its elements or simpler constituents. **3** disintegrate; break up.

decomposer *noun* an organism, esp. a soil bacterium, fungus, or invertebrate, that decomposes organic material.

decomposition *noun* **1** the gradual destruction or decay of organic matter by natural chemical processes.

2 the separation of a chemical compound into its component elements or simpler constituents.

decompress *verb* (**decompresses, decompressed, decompressing**) **1 a** subject to decompression. **b** relieve or reduce the compression on. **2** restore (computer files compacted for storage or distribution) to normal size. **3** *informal* calm down, relax.

decompression *noun* **1** the process of relieving or reducing pressure. **2** a gradual reduction of air pressure on a person who has been subjected to high pressure (esp. underwater). **3** a sudden reduction of air pressure in an aircraft etc. to the surrounding external pressure. **4** the act or process of restoring compacted computer files to their normal size.

decompression chamber *noun* a chamber in which atmospheric pressure can be raised or lowered, e.g. for subjecting a person to decompression.

decompression sickness *noun* a disorder, esp. of deep-sea divers, caused by nitrogen bubbles forming in the tissues from a too rapid decompression and characterized by pain, paralysis, etc.

decongestant • *adjective* that relieves (esp. nasal) congestion. • *noun* a medication that relieves nasal congestion. [Say dee cun JEST int]

deconstruct *verb* **1** (in literature and philosophy) analyze a text in order to show that there is no fixed meaning within the text but that the meaning is created each time in the act of reading. **2** undo the construction of, take to pieces: *social forms which will have to be deconstructed before socialism can be developed*.

deconstruction *noun* (in literature and philosophy) a theory that states that it is impossible for a text to have one fixed meaning, and emphasizes the reader's role in producing meaning. ▸ **deconstructionism** *noun* **deconstructionist** *adjective & noun*

deconstructive *adjective* based on or having to do with the principles of deconstruction.

decontaminate *verb* (**decontaminates, decontaminated, decontaminating**) remove contamination or the risk of it from (an area, person, etc.) affected by radioactivity, infectious disease, harmful chemicals, etc. ▸ **decontamination** *noun*

decor *noun* **1** the overall effect, style, etc. of the decorations and furnishings of a room etc. **2** the furnishing and decoration of a room etc. [Say day CORE or duh CORE or DAY core]

decorate *verb* (**decorates, decorated, decorating**) (often foll. by *with*) **1** make (something) more attractive by adding colour, adornments, etc. **2** provide (a room or building) with new paint, wallpaper, etc. **3** award (a person) a medal, military decoration, etc. ▸ **decorated** *adjective*

decoration *noun* **1** the process or art of decorating. **2** a thing that decorates or serves as an ornament. **3** a medal etc. conferred and worn as an honour.

decorative *adjective* **1** serving to decorate: *the decorative touches have made this house a warm and welcoming home*. **2** ornamental rather than operational: *purely decorative arches*. [Say DECK ruh tiv]

decorative arts *plural noun* the arts that produce high-quality objects which are both useful and beautiful, e.g. ceramics, furniture making, etc.

decoratively *adverb* in a decorative manner.

decorator *noun* **1** an interior decorator. **2** a person who decorates (a cake etc.). **3** (as an *adjective*) chosen or fashioned to contribute to a plan of interior design: *decorator fabrics*.

decorous *adjective* polite and appropriate in a particular social situation; not shocking: *a decorous kiss*. ▸ **decorously** *adverb* [Say DECKER us]

decorum *noun* behaviour required by politeness or

D

decency: *a breach of decorum in the House of Commons*. [Say duh CORE um]

decoy • *noun* **1 a** a person or thing used to mislead or to lure an animal or person into a trap or danger. **b** a bait or enticement. **2** a bird or animal, or an imitation of one, used to attract others. **3** *Military* an aircraft, missile, etc. used to distract the enemy, mislead radar, etc. • *verb* allure or entice, esp. by means of a decoy.

decrease • *verb* (**decreases, decreased, decreasing**) make or become smaller, fewer, weaker, less, etc. • *noun* the process of reducing something or the amount by which something is reduced: *a decrease in births*. ▶ **decreasingly** *adverb*

decree • *noun* **1** an official order issued by a legal authority. **2** a judgment or decision of certain law courts. • *verb* (**decrees, decreed, decreeing**) order by or as if by decree.

decrepit *adjective* **1** weakened or worn out by age and infirmity: *a decrepit old man*. **2** worn out by long use; dilapidated: *a row of decrepit houses*. ▶ **decrepitude** *noun* [Say duh CREP it, duh CREPPA tude]

decriminalization *noun* the process of legalizing an activity or possession considered criminal: *lobbying for the decriminalization of marijuana*.

decriminalize *verb* (**decriminalizes, decriminalized, decriminalizing**) make or treat (an action etc.) as no longer criminal; legalize (esp. a drug, its possession, or use).

decry *verb* (**decries, decried, decrying**) strongly criticize, esp. publicly: *the measures were decried as useless*. [Say duh CRY]

decrypt *verb* decipher or decode: *the computer can be used to decrypt and encrypt sensitive transmissions*. ▶ **decryption** *noun*

dedicate *verb* (**dedicates, dedicated, dedicating**) **1** (foll. by *to*) **a** devote (esp. oneself) to a noble task or purpose. **b** commit, contribute, or set apart resources etc. for a particular cause or effort. **2** (foll. by *to*) **a** inscribe or address (one's own book, music, etc.) to a patron or friend as a compliment, mark of respect, etc. **b** request (a song or video) to be played on the radio or television as a greeting or token of affection for a friend. **3** (often foll. by *to*) consecrate with solemn rites (a building etc.) to a god, saint, sacred purpose, etc. **4 a** formally open (a building etc.) to the public. **b** devote (a monument etc.) to the memory of someone deceased etc.

dedicated *adjective* **1** (of a person) devoted to an aim or vocation; having single-minded loyalty or integrity. **2** (of equipment etc.) designed, manufactured, or installed so as to be available only for a particular purpose or a particular category of user. **3** solemnly or formally set apart for a specific use or purpose.

dedication *noun* **1** the quality of being dedicated or committed to a task or purpose: *Cathy's dedication to her duties was exemplary* ◊ *Joseph was a model of hard work and dedication*. **2** the words with which a book etc. is dedicated. **3** a formal ceremony commemorating a public opening of a building, monument, etc.

deduce *verb* (**deduces, deduced, deducing**) (often foll. by *from*) infer; draw as a logical conclusion.

deduct *verb* (often foll. by *from*) subtract, take away, withhold (an amount, portion, etc.).

deductible • *adjective* that may be deducted, esp. from tax to be paid or taxable income. • *noun* a sum payable by an insured party in the event of a claim, the insurer paying the amount by which the claim exceeds this sum.

deduction *noun* **1 a** the act or process of deducting. **b** an amount deducted, c an allowable amount, expense, etc. deducted from taxable income. **2** the

process of using information already acquired in order to understand a particular situation or to find the answer to a problem (*compare* INDUCTION 3a): *Doug arrived at the solution by a simple process of deduction* ◊ *we can examine the bones of dinosaurs and make deductions about how they lived*.

deductive *adjective* using knowledge about things that are generally true in order to think about and understand particular situations or problems: *deductive reasoning*. ▶ **deductively** *adverb*

deed • *noun* **1** an action that is performed intentionally or consciously, esp. a brave, skilful, or conspicuous one: *a tale of heroic deeds* ◊ *I've done my good deed for the day*. **2** actual fact or performance, often as contrasted with words: *had erred in word and deed*. **3** a written or printed document under seal often used for a legal transfer of ownership. • *verb* convey or transfer by legal deed.

deejay *noun* *informal* a disc jockey.

deem *verb* regard, consider, judge.

de-emphasis *noun* a reduced emphasis.

de-emphasize *verb* (**de-emphasizes, de-emphasized, de-emphasizing**) reduce the importance or prominence given to something.

deep • *adjective* **1** extending far down from the top or far in from the surface or edge. **2 a** extending to or lying at a specified depth: *water 6 feet deep* ◊ *ankle-deep*. **b** in a specified number of ranks one behind another: *six deep*. **3** situated far down, back, or in: *a cabin deep in the bush*. **4** coming or brought from far down or in: *deep breath*. **5** low-pitched: *deep voice*. **6 a** intense, profound, extreme: *deep sleep*. **b** (of a colour) vivid, darkly hued: *a deep red*. **c** mysterious or obscure: *a deep secret*. **7** heartfelt, absorbing: *deep affection*. **8** fully absorbed or overwhelmed: *deep in debt*. **9** profound: *deep thinker*. **10** *Baseball* relatively far in or into the outfield: *deep right field*. **11** *Sport* far into usu. the opposing team's territory. **12** (of prices, discounts, etc.) significantly larger than customary or expected. **13** cunning or secretive: *that Clyde is a deep one*. • *noun* **1** (**the deep**) *literary* the sea. **2** *Nautical* a deep part of the sea, esp. below 3000 fathoms or approx. 6000 metres. **3** the most intense part (of the night, the winter). • *adverb* **1** deeply: *dig deep*. **2** far down, in, on, or back: *lived deep in the bush*. **3** for an extended period, long (into): *read deep into the night*. **4 a** *Baseball* far into usu. the outfield: *play deep*. **b** *Sport* far into usu. the other team's territory: *deep in the end zone*. PHRASES **go off the deep end** *informal* **1** go crazy. **2** lose control and give way to anger or emotion. **3** act without due regard to common sense, moderation, etc. **in deep** inextricably involved in or committed (usu. to something complicated or unpleasant). **jump** (or **be thrown**) **in at the deep end** face (or be made to face) a difficult problem, undertaking, etc., with little experience of it.

deep-dish • *noun* (usu. as an *adjective*) **1** a baking pan or dish with high sides and a flat bottom: *deep-dish pizza*. **2** something shaped like this: *a deep-dish satellite*. • *adjective* **1** (of a pie) not having a bottom crust. **2** serious, staunch, ardent: *a deep-dish conservative*.

deep ecology *noun* an approach to environmentalism that considers humanity and the natural world to be inextricably interconnected.

deepen *verb* **1** make or become deep or deeper. **2** make or become more serious, intense, or severe.

deep-freeze • *noun* **1** a refrigerator in which food can be quickly frozen and kept for long periods at a very low temperature. **2** a suspension of activity. **3** a period of very cold weather. • *verb* (**deep-freezes, deep-froze,**

deep-frozen, deep-freezing) freeze or store (food) in a deep-freeze.

deep-fried *adjective* (of food) fried in hot oil or fat.

deep-fry *verb* (**deep-fries, deep-fried, deep-frying**) fry (food) in hot oil or fat deep enough to cover it.

deep fryer *noun* (also **deep fat fryer**) a deep, heavy pan or appliance capable of holding 3-4 cm of hot fat in which food is immersed for frying.

deeply *adverb* **1** far down or in: *she breathed deeply*. **2** intensely, thoroughly, very much: *we are deeply concerned* ◊ *he sleeps deeply*.

deep pocket *noun informal* (usu. in *plural*) substantial financial resources: *we need backers with deep pockets*. ▶ **deep-pocketed** *adjective*

deep-rooted *adjective* **1** (esp. of convictions) firmly established. **2** having long roots: *deep-rooted grasses*.

deep sea *noun* the deeper parts of the ocean.

deep-seated *adjective* (of emotion, disease, etc.) firmly established, profound.

deep-set *adjective* **1** (of the eyes) set deeply in the sockets. **2** firmly fixed or established.

deep-six *verb* (**deep-sixes, deep-sixed, deep-sixing**) *slang* **1** defeat thoroughly, destroy completely: *deep-sixed her opponent*. **2** abandon, dispose of, discard: *deep-sixed the proposal*.

deep space *noun* the regions beyond the solar system or the earth's atmosphere.

deepwater *noun* water of great depth (often as an *adjective*: *deepwater diving*).

SPELL CHECK
deer, dear   ABC

Something cherished or loved is **dear**.

---

deer *noun* (*plural* **deer**) any four-hoofed grazing animal of the family Cervidae, the males of which usu. have deciduous branching antlers, or of the related families Tragulidae and Moschidae (lacking horns).

deer fly *noun* (*plural* **deer flies**) a bloodsucking fly.

deer mouse *noun* (*plural* **deer mice**) any mouse of the genus *Peromyscus*, common throughout North America.

deerskin • *noun* leather from a deer's skin. • *adjective* made from a deer's skin.

DEET *noun* N,N-diethyl-meta-toluamide, the active ingredient in many insect repellents.

def *adjective slang* excellent.

deface *verb* (**defaces, defaced, defacing**) **1** spoil the appearance of something, esp. by drawing or writing on it: *charged with defacing public property* ◊ *defacing library books is disgraceful*. **2** make illegible.

de facto • *adjective* that exists or is such in fact, whether legally acknowledged or not: *a de facto ruler* ◊ *the military took de facto control of the country*. • *adverb* in fact, whether by right or not (*compare* DE JURE): *he continued to rule the country de facto*.

defamation *noun* the act of causing harm to someone by saying or writing critical or false things about them: *she sued the magazine for defamation of character*. [Say deffa MAY sh'n]

defamatory *adjective* intended to harm a person's reputation with false claims; slanderous or libellous: *the restaurant's owners claimed the reviewer's negative comments were defamatory*. [Say duh FAMMA tory]

defame *verb* (**defames, defamed, defaming**) attack the good reputation of; speak ill of: *the newspaper denies any intention to defame the senator's reputation*.

defang *verb* **1** extract the fangs of. **2** render harmless: *Iraq's neighbours want Baghdad defanged*.

default • *noun* **1 a** failure to fulfill an obligation, esp. to appear, pay, or act in some way. **b** *Sport* failure to compete in or finish a game, contest, etc. **2** a pre-

selected option adopted by a computer program when no alternative is specified by the user. • *verb* **1** fail to fulfill an obligation, esp. to pay money or to appear in a law court: *the bank sold off their house because they defaulted on their mortgage*. **2** *Sport* fail to appear for or complete a game, contest, etc. **3** lose by default. **4** *Computing* revert automatically to a pre-selected option when no other choice or change is selected: *when you start a new letter the system will default to its own style*. PHRASES **by default 1** because of absence or failure to act. **2** because of a lack of opposition. **in default 1** having failed to carry out the terms of a contract, esp. a financial obligation: *the shipper was in default* ◊ *the buyers were in default in payment*. **2** (of a loan) not repaid according to the terms of the lender: *the mortgage is in default*. **in default of** because of the absence of: *accepted what he had said in default of any evidence to disprove it*. **win by default** win because an opponent fails to be present. ▶ **defaulted** *adjective*

defaulter *noun* [Say DEE fault, duh FAULT]

defeat • *verb* **1** overcome in a battle or other contest. **2** frustrate, thwart: *the last steep hill defeated her* ◊ *this line of reasoning defeats me*. **3** reject (a motion etc.) by voting. • *noun* **1** failure to win or be successful at something: *the party faces defeat in the election* ◊ *Claire will never admit defeat*. **2** the act of winning a victory over something: *the defeat of fascism*.

defeatism *noun* excessive readiness to accept defeat. ▶ **defeatist** *noun & adjective*

defecate *verb* (**defecates, defecated, defecating**) discharge feces from the body. ▶ **defecation** *noun* [Say DEFFA kate, deffa KAY sh'n]

defect • *noun* a shortcoming, failing, or imperfection. • *verb* abandon one's country or cause in favour of another: *a number of writers and musicians defected from the Soviet Union to the West in the 1960s* ◊ *she defected from the party just days before the election*. ▶ **defection** *noun*

defective *adjective* having a fault or faults; not perfect or complete: *a defective gene*.

defector *noun* a person who defects to another country, political party, organization, etc.

defence *noun* (also **defense**) **1** the act of defending from or resisting attack: *soldiers who died in defence of their country* ◊ *when her brother was criticized she leapt to his defence*. **2** something that provides protection against attack from enemies, the weather, illness, etc.: *humour is a more effective defence than violence* ◊ *the harbour's defences*. **3** the military resources of a country. **4 a** justification, vindication. **b** a speech or piece of writing used to this end. **c** the act of defending a thesis or dissertation. **5 a** the defendant's case in a lawsuit. **b** the counsel for the defendant. **6** *Sport* **a** the role of defending one's goal etc. against attack. **b** the plays, moves, or tactics aimed at such resistance. **c** the players in a team who perform this role. **7** = DEFENCE MECHANISM.

defenceless *adjective* vulnerable; unable to protect or defend oneself due to lack of strength or resources: *defenceless animals* ◊ *the village is defenceless against attack*. ▶ **defencelessness** *noun*

defenceman *noun* (*plural* **defencemen**) a player in a defensive position in hockey or lacrosse.

defence mechanism *noun* **1** a usu. unconscious mental process to avoid conscious conflict or anxiety. **2** the body's reaction against disease organisms.

defend *verb* **1** (often foll. by *against, from*) resist an attack made on; protect (a person or thing) from harm or danger. **2 a** speak or write in favour of. **b** present (a thesis or dissertation) orally to examiners and answer questions, challenges etc. **3** conduct the case for (a defendant in a lawsuit). **4** *Sport* **a** protect (a goal etc.);

D

D

resist an attack on (the goal etc.). **b** compete to retain (a title) in a contest. ▶ **defendable** adjective

defendant noun a person etc. sued or accused in court.

defender noun **1** a person who defends and believes in protecting something: a passionate defender of human rights. **2** Sport a player in a defensive position.

defense noun = DEFENCE.

defensible adjective **1** able to be supported by reasons or arguments that show that it is right or should be allowed; justifiable: is abortion morally defensible? **2** that can be easily defended from attack.

defensive adjective **1** done or intended for defence or to defend: troops are taking up a defensive position around the town. **2** (of a person or attitude) very anxious to challenge or avoid criticism: don't ask him about his plans — he just gets defensive. **3** Sport (of players) primarily concerned with preventing the other team from scoring. PHRASES **on the defensive 1** expecting criticism. **2** in an attitude or position of defence.

defensive back noun Football **1** a player in charge of covering esp. the receivers in the defensive backfield, usu. a cornerback or safety. **2** this position.

defensively adverb **1** in a way that shows one is anxious to avoid or challenge criticism. **2** Sport in terms of defence: the team has improved defensively.

defensiveness noun a defensive manner or behaviour.

defensive zone noun Sport the end of the field, court, or rink in which one's goal etc. is to be defended.

defer verb (**defers, deferred, deferring**) **1** put off to a later time: the department deferred the decision for six months. **2** (foll. by to) yield or make concessions in opinion or action: Josh deferred to Cheryl's superior judgment. [Say duh FUR]

deference noun courteous regard, respect: he addressed her with the deference due to age. PHRASES **in** (or **out of**) **deference to** out of respect for: the women wore veils in deference to the customs of the country ◊ the flags were lowered out of deference to the bereaved family. ▶ **deferential** adjective **deferentially** adverb [Say DEF rinse, deffer EN sh'll]

deferral noun the act of postponing or delaying something until a later time: the government is offering a one-year deferral on tax payments. [Say duh FUR ul]

defiance noun open disobedience, bold resistance: nuclear testing was resumed in defiance of an international ban ◊ a conscious act of defiance.

defiant adjective showing defiance; openly disobedient: a defiant teenager ◊ a defiant message. ▶ **defiantly** adverb

defibrillation noun the application of an electric shock to the heart to stop fibrillation and encourage the resumption of coordinated contractions. ▶ **defibrillator** noun [Say dee fib ruh LAY sh'n, dee FIB ruh lay tur]

deficiency noun (plural **deficiencies**) **1** the state of not having, or not having enough of, something that is essential: iron deficiency can cause anemia. **2** a fault or a weakness in something or someone that makes it or them less successful: deficiencies in the computer system. **3** the amount by which a thing, esp. revenue, falls short. [Say duh FISHIN see]

deficient adjective **1** (usu. foll. by in) not having enough of a specified quality or ingredient: a diet that is deficient in vitamin A. **2** insufficient in quantity, force, etc.: the documentary evidence is deficient. [Say duh FISH int]

deficit noun **1** the amount by which a thing (esp. a sum of money) is too small: there's a deficit of $3 million in the total needed to complete the project ◊ the team had to come back from a 2-0 deficit in the first period. **2** an excess of liabilities or expenditures over assets or income in a

given period, esp. a fiscal year: the annual operating deficit. **3** a shortage: sleep deficit. [Say DEFFA sit]

deficit financing noun financing of (esp. government) spending by borrowing.

deficit spending noun spending, esp. by the government, financed by borrowing.

defile • verb (**defiles, defiled, defiling**) **1** make dirty or no longer pure. **2** corrupt morally. **3** make unfit for ritual or ceremonial use: you've defiled sacred grounds. • noun a gorge or narrow passage. [Say duh FILE]

defilement noun an act of spoiling, violating, or desecrating something.

definable adjective that can be defined; capable of being set out, described, or outlined.

define verb (**defines, defined, defining**) **1** give the exact meaning of (a word etc.). **2** describe or explain the scope, essential qualities, etc. of (something): define one's position. **3** make clear, esp. in outline: well-defined image. **4** determine or indicate the boundary or extent of (something).

defined adjective **1** having a definite or specified outline or form. **2** clearly marked; definite: clearly defined boundaries.

definite adjective **1** having exact and discernible limits. **2** clearly defined. **3** certain, sure.

definite article noun Grammar the word (the in English) preceding a noun and implying a specific or known instance e.g. the book on the table.

definitely • adverb **1** in a definite manner. **2** certainly; without doubt: they were definitely there. • interjection informal yes, certainly.

definition noun **1 a** the act or process of defining. **b** a statement of the meaning of a word or the nature of a thing. **2 a** the degree of distinctness in outline of an object or image (esp. of an image produced by a lens or shown in a photograph or on a film or television screen). **b** the distinctness of the outline of a muscle. PHRASES **by definition** by its very nature: a bestseller is not by definition a bad book.

> **WRITING TIP**
> **definitive, definite**
>
> **Definitive** should not be used as a synonym for **definite**. **Definitive** means authoritative, unconditional, and final, as in The prime minister issued a definitive statement outlining her economic policy. **Definite** means clear, unambiguous, and without doubt, as in The demonstrators were making a definite statement of their concerns about the prime minister's economic policy.

definitive adjective **1** (of an answer, verdict, etc.) conclusive, final. **2** (of an edition etc.) most complete and authoritative. ▶ **definitively** adverb

deflate verb (**deflates, deflated, deflating**) **1 a** let air or gas out of (a tire, balloon, etc.). **b** be emptied of air or gas. **2** lose or cause to lose confidence or conceit: all the criticism had left her feeling totally deflated. **3** Economics reduce the amount of money being used in a country so that prices fall or stay steady. **4** reduce the level of (an emotion or feeling): her anger was deflated. ▶ **deflated** adjective

deflation noun **1** the action of air being removed from something. **2** a reduction in the amount of money in a country's economy so that prices fall or remain the same. ▶ **deflationary** adjective

deflect verb **1** bend or turn aside from a straight course or intended purpose: the puck deflected off Reid's body into the goal ◊ he raised his arm to try to deflect the blow. **2** redirect (criticism etc.) from the intended target: all attempts to deflect attention from his private life

have failed. **3** prevent someone from doing something that they are determined to do: *the government will not be deflected from its commitments.*

deflection *noun* **1 a** the action of turning, or the state of being turned, from a straight line or course. **b** the amount of such deviation. **2** *Physics* the displacement of a pointer on an instrument from its zero position.

deflector *noun* a device used to deflect something, e.g. a plate used to deflect a flow of air, water, or heat.

deflower *verb* have sex with a virgin.

defogger *noun* a device in vehicles for clearing condensation, frost, and ice from windshields etc.

defoliant *noun* a chemical that strips leaves from trees etc., often used in warfare. [Say dee FOLEY int]

defoliate *verb* (**defoliates, defoliated, defoliating**) remove leaves from trees etc., esp. as a military tactic. ▶ **defoliation** *noun* [Say dee FOLEY ate, dee foley AY sh'n]

deforest *verb* clear land of forests or trees. ▶ **deforestation** *noun* **deforested** *adjective*

deform *verb* change or spoil the usual or natural shape of.

deformation *noun* **1** the process or result of changing and spoiling the normal shape of something: *the deformation of the human body in much Cubist art.* **2** a change in the normal shape of something as a result of injury or illness. [Say def or MAY shun]

deformed *adjective* having an abnormal shape or form; misshapen: *he was born with deformed hands.*

deformity *noun* (*plural* **deformities**) **1** the state of being deformed or misshapen. **2** a malformation, esp. of body or limb.

defraud *verb* illegally obtain money from (a person) by deception or trickery: *they were accused of defrauding the company of $14,000* ◊ *all three men were charged with conspiracy to defraud.* ▶ **defrauder** *noun*

defray *verb* provide money to pay (a cost or expense): *the raffle proceeds will help to defray the cost of the evening.*

defrost • *verb* **1 a** free (the interior of a refrigerator) of excess frost. **b** remove frost or ice from (esp. the windshield of a motor vehicle). **2** thaw (frozen food). **3** become unfrozen. • *noun* **1** a device for defrosting, esp. one that stops ice forming on a windshield. **2** the setting on an appliance which causes defrosting. ▶ **defroster** *noun* **defrosting** *noun*

deft *adjective* **1** (of a person's movements) skilful and quick: *deft footwork* ◊ *she finished off the painting with a few deft strokes of the brush.* **2** demonstrating skill and cleverness: *their deft avoidance of the topic.* ▶ **deftly** *adverb* **deftness** *noun*

defunct *adjective* **1** no longer existing: *the defunct federal Social Credit Party.* **2** no longer used or in fashion: *a largely defunct railway network.* [Say duh FUNCT]

SPELL CHECK
defuse, diffuse

To spread or disperse in all directions or to mix with something is to **diffuse**. Something spread out is **diffuse**.

---

defuse *verb* (**defuses, defused, defusing**) **1** remove the fuse from (a bomb) so that it cannot explode. **2** reduce the tension or potential danger in (a crisis, difficulty, etc.): *sometimes humour can defuse a situation.*

defy *verb* (**defies, defied, defying**) **1** resist (an authority etc.) openly; refuse to obey. **2** (of a thing) resist completely: *defies solution.* **3** challenge (a person) to do or prove something: *I defy you to try it.* **4** challenge the power of (esp. something immutable): *defying the laws of gravity.* [Say duh FIE]

deg. *abbreviation* degree.

degeneracy *noun* a degenerate quality or state: *scenes of crime and degeneracy.* [Say duh JENNER a see]

degenerate • *adjective* **1** having moral standards that have fallen to a level that is very low and unacceptable to most people: *a degenerate popular culture.* **2** *Biology* having changed to a lower type. • *noun* an immoral or corrupt person, esp. a sexual deviant. • *verb* (**degenerates, degenerated, degenerating**) (often foll. by *into*) **1** lose, or become deficient in, the qualities proper to one's kind. **2** deteriorate physically, mentally, or morally. **3 a** revert to a lower type; gradually change into something inferior. **b** (of an organ or tissue) deteriorate to a simpler structure or less active form. [Say duh JENNER it for the noun and adjective, duh JENNER ate for the verb]

degeneration *noun* **1** the process of becoming worse or less acceptable in quality or condition: *intensive farming has caused severe degeneration of the land.* **2** deterioration and loss of function in the cells of a tissue or organ: *degeneration of the muscle fibres.* [Say duh jenner AY sh'n]

degenerative *adjective* **1** of or tending to decline and deteriorate: *the young generation had fallen into a degenerative backslide.* **2** characterized by progressive, often irreversible deterioration: *degenerative diseases like multiple sclerosis.* [Say duh JENNER a tiv]

degradable *adjective* capable of being decomposed or broken down into a simpler chemical form: *degradable plastics.* [Say duh GRADE a bull]

degradation *noun* **1** a situation in which a person has lost all self-respect and the respect of other people: *a trail of human misery and degradation.* **2** the process of something being damaged or made worse: *environmental degradation.* [Say deggra DAY sh'n]

degrade *verb* (**degrades, degraded, degrading**) **1** show or treat a person in a way that makes them seem not worth any respect or not worth taking seriously: *this poster is offensive and degrades women.* **2** lower in character or quality: *vast areas of natural habitat have been degraded.* **3** break down or deteriorate chemically: *when exposed to light the materials will degrade* ◊ *the bacteria will degrade hydrocarbons.*

degraded *adjective* **1 a** lowered in rank, position, reputation, etc. **b** diminished in quality or value. **2** (of soil etc.) differing from its natural or primary state as a result of cultivation, erosion, etc.

degrading *adjective* humiliating. ▶ **degradingly** *adverb*

degree *noun* **1** a stage in an ascending or descending scale, series, or process. **2** a stage in intensity or amount: *to a high degree.* **3** an academic rank conferred by a college or university after completion of a course or as an honour. **4** *Math* a unit of measurement of angles, one-ninetieth of a right angle. Symbol: ° (as in 45°). **5** a unit of latitude or longitude used to define points on the earth's surface. Symbol: °. **6** *Physics* a unit in a scale of temperature, hardness, etc. Symbol: °. **7** *Medical* any of three grades (first, second, third) used to categorize burns according to their severity. **8** a grade of crime or criminality: *first-degree murder.* **9** a step in direct genealogical descent. **10** *Grammar* any of three stages (positive, comparative, superlative) in the comparison of an adjective or adverb. **11** *Music* the classification of a note by its position in the scale. **12** *Math* the highest power of unknowns or variables in an equation etc.: *equation of the third degree.* **13** a unit of measurement of alcohol content. Symbol: °. PHRASES **by degrees** gradually. **to a degree** somewhat.

degree day *noun* a unit used to determine the heating requirements for buildings, representing a fall

of one degree below a specified average outdoor temperature, usu. 18°C, for one day.

dehumanization *noun* the process of depriving a person of their positive human qualities, such as kindness, pity, etc.

dehumanize *verb* (**dehumanizes, dehumanized, dehumanizing**) **1** cause someone to lose their human qualities, such as kindness, pity, etc.: *the dehumanizing effects of poverty and squalor.* **2** make impersonal or machine-like.

dehumidifier *noun* a machine used to remove moisture from the air.

dehumidify *verb* (**dehumidifies, dehumidified, dehumidifying**) remove moisture from (esp. air).

dehydrate *verb* (**dehydrates, dehydrated, dehydrating**) **1 a** remove water from (esp. foods for preservation). **b** make dry, esp. make (the body) deficient in water. **2** lose water. ▶**dehydrated** *adjective* **dehydration** *noun* **dehydrator** *noun*

de-ice *verb* (**de-ices, de-iced, de-icing**) **1** remove ice from (esp. aircraft wings, where ice formation reduces lift). **2** prevent the formation of ice on.

de-icer *noun* a device or substance for removing ice from a windshield, aircraft, etc.

deification *noun* the worship or treatment of someone or something as a god: *the deification of medieval kings* ◊ *the deification of technology.* [Say dee if a KAY sh'n or day if a KAY sh'n]

deify *verb* (**deifies, deified, deifying**) **1** make a god of: *she was deified by the early Romans as a fertility goddess.* **2** regard or worship as a god: *a culture that deifies the almighty dollar.* [Say DEE a fie or DAY a fie]

deign *verb* do something in a way that shows one thinks one is too important to do it; condescend: *she deigned to grace us with her presence.* [Say DANE]

de-index *verb* (**de-indexes, de-indexed, de-indexing**) cancel the indexation to inflation of (pensions or other benefits). ▶**de-indexation** *noun*

deindustrialization *noun* the shift from industry to other forms of activity.

deindustrialize *verb* (**deindustrializes, deindustrialized, deindustrializing**) make less or no longer industrial. ▶**deindustrialized** *adjective*

deinstitutionalization *noun* the release of a long-term inmate from an institution such as a mental hospital or a prison.

deinstitutionalize *verb* (**deinstitutionalizes, deinstitutionalized, deinstitutionalizing**) remove from an institution or from the effects of institutional life: *the changes aim to deinstitutionalize mentally ill people.* ▶**deinstitutionalized** *adjective*

deism *noun* belief in the existence of a supreme being, specifically of a creator who does not intervene in the universe. The term is used chiefly of an intellectual movement of the 17th and 18th centuries which accepted the existence of a creator on the basis of reason, but rejected belief in a supernatural deity who interacts with humankind (*compare* THEISM). ▶**deist** *noun* **deistic** *adjective* [Say DEE ism]

deity *noun* (*plural* **deities**) **1** a god or goddess: *Hindu deities.* **2** (**the Deity**) the Creator, God. [Say DEE a tee or DAY a tee]

déjà vu *noun* a feeling of having already experienced a present situation: *I have a sense of déjà vu, that I have done all this before.* [Say day zhah VOO]

dejected *adjective* sad and disappointed: *he sat dejected and alone in the jail cell.* ▶**dejectedly** *adverb* **dejection** *noun*

de jure *adjective & adverb* according to a rightful entitlement or claim; by right (compare DE FACTO): *he had been de jure king since his father's death* ◊ *Nova Scotia was*

transformed from a British colony de jure to a British colony de facto. [Say duh JURY or day JURAY]

deke *esp. Hockey slang* ● *noun* a fake shot or movement done to draw a defensive player out of position and thus create a better opportunity to score. ● *verb* (**dekes, deked, deking**) **1** deceive (a defensive player) with a fake shot or movement. **2** avoid (an obstacle) or evade (an issue): *ran across the road, deking around the cars.* **3** move or go quickly: *deked into the store to pick up a newspaper* ◊ *deked in and out of the crowd.*

Delaware ● *noun* (*plural* **Delaware** or **Delawares**) **1** a member of an Aboriginal people formerly inhabiting the Delaware River basin in the northeastern US, some of whom moved north and now live near London, Ont. **2** the Algonquian language of this people. ● *adjective* of or relating to this people.

delay ● *verb* **1** postpone; defer: *they may decide to delay the next round of tax cuts.* **2** make late: *was delayed at the doctor's office.* **3** loiter; procrastinate: *don't delay!* ● *noun* **1** the act of delaying: *report it to the police without delay.* **2** a period of time by which something is late or postponed: *a two-hour delay.*

delayed penalty *noun* (*plural* **delayed penalties**) *Hockey* **1** a penalty which the referee has signalled, but for which play has not yet been stopped. **2** the interval between the signalling of the penalty and the stopping of play.

delectable ● *adjective* **1** (of food) delicious: *the delectable smell of freshly baked bread* ◊ *delectable chocolate truffles.* **2** *jocular* (of a person) very attractive: *his delectable body* ◊ *Steve's latest girlfriend, the delectable Tara.* ● *noun* (in *plural*) delicious food or dishes, esp. desserts: *the menu may include such delectables as marinated loin of lamb.* ▶**delectably** *adverb* [Say LECTA bull]

delegate ● *noun* **1** a person chosen or elected to represent others at a conference, convention, etc. **2** a member of a committee. ● *verb* (**delegates, delegated, delegating**) **1** (often foll. by *to*) **a** commit (authority, power, etc.) to another person, typically one less senior: *the power delegated to him must never be misused.* **b** entrust a task to another person: *if I'm ever going to get any sleep I'm going to have to learn to delegate.* **2** send, choose, or authorize (a person) to do something as a representative: *I've been delegated to organize the Christmas party.*

delegate-general *noun* (*plural* **delegates-general**) *Cdn* (*Que.*) the chief representative of the province of Quebec in a foreign country or region.

delegation *noun* **1** a group of delegates. **2** the act or process of delegating or being delegated.

delete ● *verb* (**deletes, deleted, deleting**) **1** remove or obliterate (written or printed matter). **2** remove (an item) from a catalogue, so that it is no longer offered for sale. ● *noun* (also **delete key**) *Computing* a key which is held down in order to remove characters from a document, screen display, etc.

deleterious *adjective* harmful and damaging (to the mind or body): *the deleterious effect of stress on health.* ▶**deleteriously** *adverb* [Say della TEERY us]

deletion *noun* the action of striking out, erasing, or deleting written or printed matter; something deleted.

deli *noun* (*plural* **delis**) *informal* a delicatessen.

deliberate ● *adjective* **1 a** done on purpose: *a deliberate act of vandalism* ◊ *the speech was a deliberate attempt to embarrass the government.* **b** fully considered; not impulsive. **2** done or acting in a careful or unhurried way; *he spoke in a slow and deliberate way.* ● *verb* (**deliberates, deliberated, deliberating**) think or discuss carefully: *the jury deliberated for an hour* ◊ *deliberated the question.* ▶**deliberately** *adverb*

deliberateness *noun* [Say duh LIBBER it for the adjective, duh LIBBER ate for the noun]

deliberation *noun* **1** careful consideration. **2** (often in *plural*) formal debate or discussion, as of a committee, jury, etc. **3** slow and careful movement or thought: *uttering each syllable with care and deliberation*.

deliberative *adjective* relating to or intended for consideration or discussion: *a deliberative assembly*. [Say duh LIBBER a tiv]

delicacy *noun* (*plural* **delicacies**) **1** (esp. in craftsmanship or artistic or natural beauty) fineness or intricacy of structure or texture: *miniature pearls of exquisite delicacy*. **2** a special or expensive food. **3** the quality of requiring discretion or sensitivity: *a situation of some delicacy*. **4** consideration for the feelings of others: *she handled the situation with great sensitivity and delicacy*. **5** (esp. in a person, a sense, or an instrument) accuracy of perception. [Say DELLA kuh see]

delicate *adjective* **1 a** fine in texture or structure: *his delicate hands*. **b** of exquisite quality or workmanship. **c** (of a colour) subtle or subdued. **d** (of a flavour or scent) subtle; faint. **2 a** not robust; easily damaged: *delicate china teacups* ◊ *the delicate ecological balance of the rainforest*. **b** (of a person) susceptible to illness. **3 a** requiring or showing careful handling: *a delicate situation* ◊ *displayed the most delicate tact in dealing with the problem*. **b** (of an instrument) highly sensitive. **4** deft: *a delicate touch*. **5** (of colours, flavours, and smells) light and pleasant: *a delicate fragrance*. ▶ **delicately** *adverb*

delicatessen *noun* **1** a place selling cooked meats, cheeses, and unusual or foreign prepared foods. **2** such foods collectively. [Say della kuh TESS in]

delicious • *adjective* **1** highly delightful and enjoyable to the taste or sense of smell. **2** entertaining; very enjoyable: *delicious gossip*. • *noun* (**Delicious**, *plural* **Delicious**) a slightly elongated, sweet, red or yellow variety of eating apple. ▶ **deliciously** *adverb* **deliciousness** *noun*

delight • *noun* **1** great pleasure. **2** something giving pleasure. • *verb* **1** (often foll. by *with*) please greatly: *delighted with the result*. **2** take great pleasure; be highly pleased: *they delight in humiliating us*. ▶ **delighted** *adjective* **delightedly** *adverb*

delightful *adjective* causing great delight. ▶ **delightfully** *adverb* **delightfulness** *noun*

delimit *verb* (**delimits**, **delimited**, **delimiting**) determine the limits of: *agreements delimiting fishing boundaries*. ▶ **delimitation** *noun*

delineate *verb* (**delineates**, **delineated**, **delineating**) describe, draw, or explain something in detail: *our objectives need to be precisely delineated* ◊ *the ship's route is clearly delineated on the map*. ▶ **delineation** *noun* [Say duh LINNY ate, duh linny AY sh'n]

delinquency *noun* (*plural* **delinquencies**) **1** minor crime such as vandalism, esp. when committed by young people: *juvenile delinquency*. **2** neglect of one's duty: *he implied grave delinquency on his host's part*. **3** failure to pay an outstanding debt: *credit card delinquency*. [Say duh LING kwun see]

delinquent • *noun* an offender: *juvenile delinquent*. • *adjective* **1** guilty of a minor crime or a misdeed. **2** failing in one's duty, esp. to pay money owed: *a delinquent borrower*. **3** (of a sum of money) not having been paid in time: *a delinquent loan*. [Say duh LING kwunt]

deliquesce *verb* (**deliquesces**, **deliquesced**, **deliquescing**) **1** (of organic matter) become liquid, typically during decomposition. **2** *Chemistry* (of a solid) become liquid by absorbing moisture from the air. ▶ **deliquescent** *adjective* [Say della KWESS in]

delirious *adjective* **1** affected with delirium; temporarily or apparently mad; raving. **2** wildly excited, ecstatic. **3** (of behaviour) betraying delirium or ecstasy. ▶ **deliriously** *adverb* [Say duh LEERY us]

delirium *noun* **1** an acutely disordered state of mind involving incoherent speech, hallucinations, and frenzied excitement, occurring in intoxication, fever, etc. **2** great excitement, ecstasy. [Say duh LEERY um]

delirium tremens *noun* a psychotic condition typical of withdrawal in chronic alcoholics, involving tremors, hallucinations, anxiety, and disorientation. [Say duh leery um TREM enz]

deliver *verb* **1 a** distribute (letters, parcels, ordered goods, etc.) to the addressee or the purchaser. **b** (often foll. by *to*) hand over: *delivered the boy safely to his teacher*. **2** utter or recite (an opinion, verdict, speech, etc.): *delivered a speech* ◊ *delivered himself of a sermon*. **3** give forth or produce: *this printer delivers high-quality printouts*. **4 a** give birth to: *delivered a girl*. **b** assist at a birth: *delivered six babies* ◊ *delivered the patient successfully*. **5** launch or aim (a blow, ball, or attack). **6** save, rescue, or set free: *delivered from his enemies*. **7** hand over: *delivered his soul up to God*. **8** *informal* (often foll. by *on*) provide what is expected or what one has promised. **9** cause (a substance, data, etc.) to be conveyed: *deliver the medication intravenously*. **10** present or render (an account). **11** *Law* hand over formally (esp. a sealed deed to a grantee). PHRASES **deliver the goods** *informal* carry out one's part of an agreement. ▶ **deliverable** *adjective*

deliverance *noun* the state of being rescued from danger, evil, or pain: *promised deliverance from hunger, disease, and illiteracy*.

deliverer *noun* a person who delivers something, esp. one who saves, rescues, or frees someone: *hailed him as a deliverer who would rescue them from foreign domination*.

delivery *noun* (*plural* **deliveries**) **1 a** the delivering of letters, goods, etc. **b** a regular distribution of letters, goods, etc. **c** something delivered. **2 a** the process of childbirth. **b** an act of this. **3 a** the uttering of a speech etc. **b** the manner or style of such a speech: *a measured delivery*. **4 a** an act of throwing, esp. of a baseball. **b** the style of such an act: *a good delivery*. **5** provision, esp. of services: *health care delivery systems*. **6** the act of giving or surrendering. PHRASES **take delivery of** receive (something purchased).

dell *noun* a small usu. wooded hollow or valley.

delphinium *noun* a plant of the buttercup family, with tall spikes of usu. blue flowers. [Say del FINNY um]

delt *noun* *slang* a deltoid muscle.

delta *noun* **1** a triangular tract of deposited earth, alluvium, etc., at the mouth of a river, formed by its diverging outlets. **2** the fourth letter of the Greek alphabet (Δ, δ). **3** (as an *adjective*) designating the fourth of a series or set. **4** *Astronomy* the fourth brightest star in a constellation. ▶ **deltaic** *adjective* [Say del TAY ick]

deltoid *noun* (also **deltoid muscle**) a thick muscle covering the shoulder joint and used for raising the arm away from the body. [Say DEL toid]

delude *verb* (**deludes**, **deluded**, **deluding**) deceive or mislead: *is deluding himself if he thinks he can win*.

deluge • *noun* **1** a great flood. **2** a great outpouring (of words, paper, etc.). **3** a heavy fall of rain. **4** (**the Deluge**) the Flood recorded in the Bible which took place during the time of Noah and submerged the whole world. • *verb* (**deluges**, **deluged**, **deluging**) **1** overwhelm with a great number or amount: *deluged with complaints* ◊ *deluged by calls*. **2** flood: *a thunderstorm deluged the tent*. [Say DEL yonzh or DEL yooge]

delusion *noun* **1** a false belief or impression: *he was suffering from paranoid delusions and hallucination* ◊ *love can be nothing but a delusion*. **2** the act of believing or

D

making someone believe something untrue: *what a capacity television has for delusion*. ▶ **delusional** *adjective*

delusions of grandeur *plural noun* a false idea of oneself as being important, noble, famous, etc.

deluxe *adjective* **1** of a superior kind. **2** luxurious.

delve *verb* (**delves, delved, delving**) **1** (often foll. by *in, into*) **a** make a laborious search in documents etc.; research. **b** search energetically. **2** *literary* dig.

demagogic *adjective* (of a political leader or political tactics) attempting to win support by using arguments based on emotion rather than reason: *a demagogic politician ◊ demagogic rhetoric*. [Say demma GODGE ick]

demagogue *noun* **1** a leader or orator who tries to win support by inflaming people's emotions and prejudices. **2** *hist.* a leader of the people, esp. in ancient times. ▶ **demagoguery** *noun* **demagogy** *noun* [Say DEMMA gog, demma GOGGA ree, DEMMA godge ee]

demand • *noun* **1** an insistent and peremptory request. **2** the desire of purchasers or consumers for a commodity: *demand for CD players has increased*. **3** an urgent claim or requirement. • *verb* **1** ask for (something) insistently and urgently. **2** require or need: *a task demanding skill*. **3** insist on being told. **PHRASES** **in demand** sought after. **on demand** as soon as a demand is made: *a cheque payable on demand*.

demanding *adjective* **1** requiring skill, effort, etc. **2** hard to satisfy; exacting. ▶ **demandingly** *adverb*

demarcate *verb* (**demarcates, demarcated, demarcating**) mark or establish the boundaries or limits of something: *plots of land have been demarcated by barbed wire*. [Say DEE mar kate]

demarcation *noun* a border or line that separates two things, such as groups of people or areas of land: *it was hard to draw clear lines of demarcation between work and leisure ◊ social demarcations*. [Say dee mar KAY sh'n]

demean *verb* lower the dignity of; debase: *his behaviour demeaned the profession*.

demeaning *adjective* putting someone in a position that does not give them the respect they deserve: *she found it demeaning to work for her former employee*.

demeanour *noun* (also **demeanor**) outward behaviour or bearing: *she maintained a professional demeanour throughout*. [Say duh MEANER]

demented *adjective* **1** *informal* driven to behave irrationally due to anger, distress, or excitement. **2** suffering from dementia. ▶ **dementedly** *adverb*

dementia *noun* a chronic or persistent disorder of the mental processes marked by memory disorders, personality changes, impaired reasoning, etc., due to brain disease or injury. [Say duh MENSHA]

demerit *noun* **1** a fault or disadvantage: *the merits and demerits of the scheme*. **2** a mark given to an offender, esp. in a school or the armed forces or for traffic offences.

Demerol *noun* *proprietary* a brand of narcotic pain reliever. [Say DEMMER awl]

demigod *noun* **1 a** a partly divine being. **b** the offspring of a god or goddess and a mortal. **2** *informal* a person of compelling beauty, powers, or personality.

demilitarization *noun* the removal of all military forces from an area.

demilitarize *verb* (**demilitarizes, demilitarized, demilitarizing**) remove a military organization or forces from (an area etc.): *a demilitarized zone*.

demineralization *noun* the removal of minerals from water.

demineralize *verb* (**demineralizes, demineralized, demineralizing**) remove minerals from (water etc.). ▶ **demineralized** *adjective*

demise *noun* **1** death: *left a will on her demise*. **2** termination or failure: *the demise of the business*. [Say duh MIZE]

demo *noun* (*plural* **demos**) *informal* **1** = DEMONSTRATION 1, 2. **2** (often as an *adjective*) demonstrating the capabilities of a group of musicians, computer software, etc.: *demo disc*. [Say DEM oh]

demobilization *noun* the release of troops from active military service, esp. at the end of a war.

demobilize *verb* (**demobilizes, demobilized, demobilizing**) release someone from military service, esp. at the end of a war: *the army has demobilized 200 000 soldiers in the last two years*.

democracy *noun* (*plural* **democracies**) **1 a** a form of government in which the power resides in the people and is exercised by them either directly or by means of elected representatives. **b** a state so governed. **2** any organization governed on democratic principles. **3** a classless and tolerant form of society.

democrat *noun* **1** an advocate of democracy. **2** (**Democrat**) (in the US) a member or supporter of the Democratic Party. **3** (also **democrat wagon**) *hist.* a light wagon seating two or more people and usu. drawn by two horses.

democratic *adjective* **1** (of a country, state, system, etc.) controlled by representatives who are elected by the people of a country; connected with this system. **2** favouring social equality: *a very democratic activity which all can enjoy*. **3** (**Democratic**) (in the US) of the Democratic Party. ▶ **democratically** *adverb*

Democratic Party *noun* one of the two main US political parties, considered to support social reform and international commitment.

democratization *noun* the process of making a country or institution more democratic. [Say dim ockra tize AY sh'n]

democratize *verb* (**democratizes, democratized, democratizing**) make (a state, institution, etc.) democratic. [Say dim OCKRA tize]

demodulate *verb* (**demodulates, demodulated, demodulating**) *Physics* extract (a modulating signal) from its carrier.

demographer *noun* a person who studies the statistics of births, deaths, disease, etc. [Say dem OGRA fur]

demographic • *adjective* having to do with the structure of populations or population statistics, esp. those showing average age, income, marital status, etc.: *the demographic trend is towards an older population*. • *noun* a demographic category: *networks are competing for the young female demographic*. ▶ **demographically** *adverb* [Say demma GRAPHIC]

demographics *plural noun* population statistics, esp. those showing average age, income, marital status, etc.: *Japan has the most potential because of its demographics: a growing population with large disposable incomes*. [Say demma GRAPHICS]

demographic transition *noun* the cycle of changing birth and death rates in a population, in which a decline in the number of deaths typically precedes a decline in the number of births, resulting in rapid population growth in the intervening period.

demography *noun* the study of statistics such as births, deaths, income, or the incidence of disease, which illustrate the changing structure of human populations. [Say dem OGRA fee]

demolish *verb* (**demolishes, demolished, demolishing**) **1 a** pull down (a building). **b** completely destroy or break. **2** refute (an argument, theory, etc.). **3** overthrow (an institution). **4** *jocular* eat up completely and quickly.

demolition *noun* the action or process of demolishing or being demolished: *the building was saved from demolition*.

demolition derby *noun* (*plural* **demolition derbies**) a competition in which drivers crash old cars into each other, the winner being the last vehicle still running.
demon *noun* **1** an evil spirit, esp. one thought to possess a person. **2** (often as an *adjective*) a forceful, fierce, or skilful performer of a specified activity: *a demon lover* ◊ *in doubles I was a demon at the net.* **3** an evil passion or habit: *the demon drink.* **4** a cruel or destructive person: *those kids can be little demons sometimes!* **5** an inner or attendant spirit: *the demon of creativity.* PHRASES **a demon for work** *informal* a person who works strenuously.
demonic *adjective* **1** of or like demons: *a demonic appearance.* **2 a** supposedly possessed by an evil spirit. **b** of or concerning such possession: *demonic powers.* ▶**demonically** *adverb*
demonization *noun* the portrayal of someone or something as wicked and threatening: *the demonization of political opponents.*
demonize *verb* (**demonizes**, **demonized**, **demonizing**) portray as wicked and threatening: *a common human tendency to demonize our enemies.*
demonology *noun* (*plural* **demonologies**) **1** the study of demons. **2** belief in demons. **3** the depiction of a group of persons or things as evil. [Say demon OLLA jee]
demonstrable *adjective* capable of being shown or logically proven: *a demonstrable need* ◊ *there is no demonstrable link between the two events.* ▶**demonstrably** *adverb* [Say duh MON struh bull]
demonstrate *verb* (**demonstrates**, **demonstrated**, **demonstrating**) **1** describe and explain (a scientific theory, machine, etc.) with the help of examples, experiments, practical use, etc. **2 a** logically prove the truth of: *our findings demonstrate a link between diet and cancer.* **b** be proof of the existence of. **3** make known by outward indications; show evidence of (feelings etc.). **4** take part in or organize a public demonstration. **5** act as a demonstrator.
demonstration *noun* **1 a** a practical exhibition or explanation of something by experiment or example in order to teach or inform: *a cooking demonstration.* **b** a practical display of a piece of equipment etc. to show how it works and its capacity. **2** a public meeting, march, etc., for a political or moral purpose. **3** proof provided by logic, argument, etc.: *it is not capable of mathematical demonstration.* **4** the outward showing of feeling etc.: *physical demonstrations of affection like kissing.* **5** a show of military force.
demonstrative • *adjective* **1** showing feelings openly, esp. of affection: *a very demonstrative person.* **2** logically conclusive; giving proof: *the work is demonstrative of their skill.* **3** serving to point out or exhibit; illustrative. **4** *Grammar* (of an adjective or pronoun) indicating the person or thing referred to, e.g. *this, that, those.* • *noun* a demonstrative adjective or pronoun. ▶**demonstratively** *adverb* **demonstrativeness** *noun* [Say duh MON struh tiv]
demonstrator *noun* **1** a person who takes part in a political demonstration etc. **2 a** a person who demonstrates esp. machines, equipment, etc. to prospective customers. **b** a machine, etc., esp. a car, used for such demonstrations.
demoralization *noun* loss of confidence or hope; discouragement.
demoralize *verb* (**demoralizes**, **demoralized**, **demoralizing**) destroy (a person's) morale. ▶**demoralizing** *adjective* **demoralizingly** *adverb*
demote *verb* (**demotes**, **demoted**, **demoting**) move someone to a lower position or rank, often as a punishment: *formerly minister of immigration, she was demoted to junior health minister.* ▶**demotion** *noun*

demur • *verb* (**demurs**, **demurred**, **demurring**) raise doubts or objections or show reluctance: *at first she demurred, but then finally agreed.* • *noun* (also **demurral**) the act or process of objecting or hesitating over something: *agreed without demur.* [Say duh MUR]
demure *adjective* (**demurer**, **demurest**) **1** quiet and reserved. **2** affectedly shy and quiet; coy. **3** (of attire) modest. ▶**demurely** *adverb* **demureness** *noun* [Say dem YOOR (YOOR rhymes with POOR)]
demystification *noun* the clarification or simplification of a complicated or obscure subject.
demystify *verb* (**demystifies**, **demystified**, **demystifying**) make something easier to understand and less complicated by explaining it in a clear and simple way: *this book attempts to demystify technology.*
demythologize *verb* (**demythologizes**, **demythologized**, **demythologizing**) **1** remove mythical elements from (a legend, famous person's life, etc.): *this biographer undertakes to demythologize C.S. Lewis.* **2** reinterpret what some consider to be the mythological elements in (the Bible): *we refuse to demythologize the teaching of Jesus and his apostles about demons.* [Say dee myth OLLA jize]
den • *noun* **1** a wild animal's lair. **2** a room in a home serving as an informal place for reading, pursuing a hobby, etc. **3** a place of crime or vice: *opium den.* • *verb* (**dens, denned, denning**) live in or as if in a den.
denationalize *verb* (**denationalizes**, **denationalized**, **denationalizing**) transfer (a nationalized industry etc.) from ownership by the government to private ownership; privatize: *the government decided to denationalize Air Canada.*
denature *verb* (**denatures**, **denatured**, **denaturing**) **1** change the properties of (a protein etc.) by heat, acidity, etc. **2** make (alcohol) unfit for drinking, esp. by the addition of a toxic or foul-tasting substance. **3** change the essential nature of (a person, a literary work, etc.): *they have denatured their theology into schemes for personal growth.* ▶**denatured** *adjective*
dendrite *noun* **1 a** a stone or mineral with natural treelike markings. **b** such marks on stones or minerals. **2** a branching process of a nerve cell conducting signals to a cell body. [Say DEN drite]
Dene *noun* (*plural* **Dene**) a member of a group of Aboriginal peoples of the Athapaskan linguistic family, living esp. in the Canadian north. [Say DEN ay]
dengue *noun* a tropical viral disease causing fever and acute pains in the joints. [Say DENG ghee]
deniability *noun* the ability of something to be denied.
deniable *adjective* that may be denied.
denial *noun* **1** the action of declaring something to be untrue: *Sandy shook his head in denial.* **2** a refusal of a request or wish: *a denial of insurance to people with certain medical conditions.* **3** a statement that a thing is not true: *official denials of involvement* ◊ *his denial that he was having an affair.* **4** *Psychology* the usu. subconscious suppression of an unacceptable truth or emotion. PHRASES **in denial** in a state in which one suppresses (usu. unconsciously) a painful or unacceptable wish or experience etc.
denier[1] *noun* a person who denies something: *a genocide denier.* [Say DENY ur]
denier[2] *noun* a unit of weight by which the fineness of silk, rayon, or nylon yarn is measured. [Say DEN yur]
denigrate *verb* (**denigrates**, **denigrated**, **denigrating**) criticize unfairly; treat as having no value or importance: *a culture that denigrates the value of husbands and fathers both at home and at work* ◊ *I do not wish to denigrate her achievements.* ▶**denigration** *noun*
denigrator *noun* [Say DENNA grate, denna GRAY sh'n]

D

D

denim *noun* **1** a usu. blue hard-wearing cotton twill fabric used for jeans, overalls, etc. **2** (in *plural*) *informal* jeans, overalls, etc. made of this.

denizen *noun* an inhabitant, occupant, or frequent visitor of a place: *polar bears, denizens of the frozen north* ◊ *the denizens of the local pub.* [Say DENNA zin]

denomination *noun* **1** a branch of the Christian Church: *Christians of all denominations attended the conference.* **2** a unit of value, esp. of money: *coins and banknotes of various denominations.* **3** the rank of a playing card within a suit, or of a suit relative to others.

denominational *adjective* **1** of or relating to a particular denomination. **2** (of education) according to the principles of a religious denomination.
▶ **denominationalism** *noun*

denominator *noun* Math the number below the line in a fraction; a divisor.

denotation *noun* the meaning or signification of a term, as distinct from its implications or connotations.

denote *verb* (**denotes, denoted, denoting**) **1** be a sign of; indicate: *a very high temperature often denotes a serious illness.* **2** mean, convey: *culture is the all-encompassing term which has been used to denote the totality of uniquely human creations.* **3** stand as a name or symbol for; signify: *the red triangle denotes danger.*

denouement *noun* **1** the final unravelling of a plot or complicated situation. **2** the final scene in a play etc., in which the plot is resolved. [Say day noo MON]

denounce *verb* (**denounces, denounced, denouncing**) **1** accuse publicly; condemn. **2** inform against. ▶ **denouncer** *noun*

dense *adjective* (**denser, densest**) **1** closely compacted in substance; thick: *dense fog.* **2** crowded together. **3** *informal* stupid. ▶ **densely** *adverb*

density *noun* (*plural* **densities**) **1** the degree of compactness of a substance: *a reduction in bone density.* **2** Physics degree of consistency measured by the quantity of mass per unit volume. **3** the quantity of people or things in a given area or space: *areas of low population density* ◊ *a density of 5,000 per square kilometre.* **4** *informal* stupidity.

dent • *noun* **1** a slight mark or hollow in a surface made by, or as if by, a blow with a hammer etc. **2** a noticeable effect: *lunch made a dent in our funds.* • *verb* **1** mark with a dent. **2** have (esp. an adverse) effect on: *this neither deterred him nor dented his enthusiasm.*

dental *adjective* **1** of or relating to the teeth. **2** of or relating to dentistry.

dental floss *noun* a strong, soft thread used to clean between the teeth.

denticare *noun* Cdn a plan for providing dental care funded by some provincial governments.

dentine *noun* a hard dense bony tissue forming the bulk of a tooth. [Say DEN teen]

dentist *noun* a person who is qualified to treat the diseases and conditions that affect the mouth, jaws, teeth, etc., esp. to repair and extract teeth and to insert artificial ones. ▶ **dentistry** *noun*

denture *noun* an artificial replacement for one or more teeth attached to a removable plate or frame.

denude *verb* (**denudes, denuded, denuding**) strip something bare of its covering, possessions, or assets: *the site had been denuded of grass by all the activity* ◊ *since there is no limit on clear-cutting, hundreds of square miles have been completely denuded.* [Say duh NUDE]

denunciation *noun* a public condemnation of someone or something: *an angry denunciation of the government's policies* ◊ *all parties joined in bitter denunciation of the terrorists.* ▶ **denunciatory** *adjective* [Say duh nun see AY sh'n, duh NUN see a tory]

Denver *noun* (also **Denver sandwich**, *plural* **Denver sandwiches**) a sandwich containing an omelette made with ham, onions, and sometimes green pepper.

deny *verb* (**denies, denied, denying**) **1** declare untrue or non-existent: *denied the charge* ◊ *denied that it is so.* **2** repudiate or disclaim: *denied his faith.* **3** refuse (a person or thing, or something to a person): *denied her the satisfaction of seeing him cry.* **PHRASES deny oneself** go without: *it's hard to deny yourself chocolate.*

deodorant *noun* a substance sprayed or rubbed on to the body or sprayed into the air to remove or conceal unpleasant smells.

deodorize *verb* (**deodorizes, deodorized, deodorizing**) remove or destroy the smell of. ▶ **deodorizer** *noun*

deoxygenate *verb* (**deoxygenates, deoxygenated, deoxygenating**) remove oxygen from. ▶ **deoxygenated** *adjective* [Say dee OXYGEN ate]

deoxyribonucleic acid *noun* see DNA. [Say dee OXY rye bo new CLAY ick]

dep *noun* Cdn (Que.) = DEPANNEUR.

depanneur *noun* Cdn (Que.) a convenience store. [Say deppa NUR]

depart *verb* **1** a (usu. foll. by *from*) go away; leave: *the train departs from this platform.* **b** (usu. foll. by *for*) start; set out: *buses depart for Hamilton every hour.* **2** (usu. foll. by *from*) diverge; deviate: *departs from standard practice.* **3** leave by death: *departed this life.*

departed • *adjective* bygone. • *noun* (**the departed**) *euphemism* a particular dead person or dead people.

department *noun* **1** a separate part of a complex whole, esp.: **a** a branch of municipal, provincial, or federal administration: *fire department.* **b** a branch of study and its administration at a university, school, etc.: *the physics department.* **c** a specialized section of a large store: *hardware department.* **d** a subdivision of a company or organization: *marketing department.* **2** *informal* an area of special expertise: *don't ask me about baking — that's not my department.*

departmental *adjective* of or belonging to a department.

department store *noun* a large store stocking many varieties of goods in different departments.

departure *noun* **1** the action of leaving, typically to start a journey. **2** a deviation from an accepted, prescribed, or traditional course of action or thought: *a departure from their usual style* ◊ *their latest CD represents a new departure.*

depend *verb* (usu. foll. by *on, upon*) **1** be controlled or determined by. **2** a be unable to do without: *depends on her mother.* **b** rely on: *I'm depending on you to come.* **3** be grammatically dependent on. **PHRASES depending on** according to. **depend on it!** you may be sure! **it** (or **it all** or **that**) **depends** expressing uncertainty or qualification in answering a question.

dependability *noun* reliability.

dependable *adjective* trustworthy and reliable. ▶ **dependably** *adverb*

SPELL CHECK	
dependant, dependent	ABC ✓

The usual Canadian spelling for "determined by" or "unable to do without" is **dependent**: *Caspar is dependent upon his uncle.*

dependant *noun* a person who relies on another esp. for financial support.

dependence *noun* **1** the state of being dependent, esp. on financial or other support. **2** the state of being dependent on a drug, physically or psychologically.

dependency *noun* (*plural* **dependencies**) **1** a country or province controlled by another. **2** the fact or

condition of being dependent on another for financial or emotional support. **3** the state of being dependent on drugs.

> **SPELL CHECK**
> **dependent, dependant**
>
> A person who relies on another is a **dependant**.

dependent • *adjective* **1** conditional: *the various benefits will be dependent on length of service.* **2** unable to do without (esp. a drug). **3** requiring someone or something for financial, emotional, or other support: *an economy heavily dependent on oil imports ◊ households with dependent children.* **4** *Math* (of a variable) having a value determined by that of another variable. **5** *Grammar* (of a clause, phrase, or word) subordinate to a sentence or word. • *noun* = DEPENDANT. ▶ **dependently** *adverb*

depersonalization *noun* esp. *Psychology* the loss of one's sense of identity.

depersonalize *verb* (**depersonalizes, depersonalized, depersonalizing**) **1** make impersonal. **2** deprive of personality.

depict *verb* **1** represent in a drawing or painting etc. **2** portray in words; describe. ▶ **depiction** *noun*

depilatory • *adjective* that removes unwanted hair. • *noun* (*plural* **depilatories**) a depilatory substance. [Say duh PILLA tory]

deplane *verb* (**deplanes, deplaned, deplaning**) disembark or remove from an airplane.

deplete *verb* (**depletes, depleted, depleting**) **1** reduce or be reduced in numbers or quantity: *fish stocks are severely depleted ◊ the depleting ozone layer.* **2** exhaust: *their energies were depleted.* ▶ **depleter** *noun* **depletion** *noun*

deplorable *adjective* **1** exceedingly bad: *a deplorable meal.* **2** deserving strong condemnation: *the deplorable conditions in which most prisoners are held.* ▶ **deplorably** *adverb* [Say duh PLORE a bull]

deplore *verb* (**deplores, deplored, deploring**) feel or express strong disapproval of something: *we deplore all violence.* [Say duh PLORE]

deploy *verb* **1** bring or send (armaments, armed forces, etc.) into position for action. **2** *Military* **a** cause (troops) to spread out from a column into a line. **b** (of troops) spread out in this way. **3** move into a position for effective action: *the air bags deploy automatically.* **4** use (talents, arguments, stylistic devices, etc.) effectively. ▶ **deployment** *noun*

depolarization *noun* a reduction or loss of polarization.

depolarize *verb* (**depolarizes, depolarized, depolarizing**) reduce or remove the polarization of.

depoliticize *verb* (**depoliticizes, depoliticized, depoliticizing**) **1** make (a person, an organization, etc.) non-political. **2** remove from political activity or influence: *the goal was to depoliticize broadcasting and free it of government control.* [Say dee puh LITTA size]

depopulate *verb* (**depopulates, depopulated, depopulating**) reduce the population of: *some regions have been depopulated by famine.* ▶ **depopulation** *noun*

deport *verb* expel (an immigrant or foreigner) from a country, e.g. for criminal activity. ▶ **deportation** *noun*

deportee *noun* a person who has been or is being deported.

deportment *noun* **1** a person's behaviour or manners: *advisers on correct dress and deportment.* **2** the way in which a person stands and moves: *the tenor playing Siegfried had a perfect physical appearance, but his stage deportment was completely unheroic.*

depose *verb* (**deposes, deposed, deposing**) remove (esp. a ruler) from power suddenly and forcefully: *he president was deposed in a military coup.*

deposit • *noun* **1 a** a sum of money placed or kept in an account in a bank. **b** anything stored or entrusted for safekeeping, usu. in a bank. **2 a** a sum payable as a first instalment on an item bought, or as a pledge for a contract. **b** a returnable sum payable on the short-term rental of a car, boat, etc. **c** a sum payable for a refillable bottle or other container, refunded when the empty container is returned. **d** = DAMAGE DEPOSIT. **3** *Cdn & Brit.* a sum of money deposited by an election candidate and forfeited if he or she fails to receive a certain proportion of the votes. **4 a** a natural layer or accumulation of sand, rock, minerals, etc. **b** a layer of precipitated matter on a surface, e.g. scale in a kettle. • *verb* (**deposits, deposited, depositing**) **1 a** put or lay down in a (usu. specified) place. **b** (of water, wind, etc.) leave (matter etc.) lying in a displaced position. **2 a** store or entrust for keeping. **b** pay (a sum of money) into a bank account. **3** pay (a sum) as a first instalment or as a pledge for a contract. **4** insert (coins) in a vending machine etc. ▶ **PHRASES** **on deposit** (of money) placed in a bank account.

deposition *noun* **1** the action of depositing something: *pebbles formed by the deposition of calcium in solution.* **2** *Law* **a** the process of giving sworn evidence: *the deposition of four expert witnesses.* **b** a formal, usu. written, statement to be used as evidence. **3** the action of removing someone from power, esp. a monarch. [Say deppa ZISH un or deepa ZISH un]

depositor *noun* a person who deposits money etc.

depot *noun* **1** a storehouse. **2 a** a bus station. **b** a building for the servicing, parking, etc. of esp. buses, trains, or trucks. **3** *Military* **a** a storehouse for equipment etc. **b** a military establishment at which recruits or other troops are assembled.

depraved *adjective* corrupt, esp. morally: *this is the work of a depraved mind.*

depravity *noun* moral corruption; wickedness: *many novels deal with depravity, few with goodness.* [Say duh PRAVA tee]

deprecate *verb* (**deprecates, deprecated, deprecating**) **1** express disapproval of or a wish against (a plan, proceeding, purpose, etc.); plead earnestly against: *deprecate hasty action.* **2 a** express disapproval of a person: *he sniffed in a deprecating way.* **b** (usu. in *combination*) disparage, belittle: *self-deprecating.* ▶ **deprecatingly** *adverb* **deprecation** *noun* **deprecatory** *adjective* [Say DEPRA kate, depra KAY sh'n, DEPRA kuh tory]

depreciable *adjective* **1** capable of depreciating. **2** able to be depreciated for tax purposes: *non-depreciable assets like land.* [Say duh PREESHA bull]

depreciate *verb* (**depreciates, depreciated, depreciating**) **1** diminish in value: *the car has depreciated.* **2** make something seem unimportant or of no value: *are we conditioned through years of schooling to depreciate things Canadian?* **3** reduce the value, as stated in the company's accounts, of a particular asset over a particular period of time: *the company depreciates computer purchases over three years.* [Say duh PREESHY ate]

depreciation *noun* **1** a reduction in the value of an asset with the passage of time, due in particular to wear and tear. **2** *Economics* a decrease in the value of a currency. [Say duh preeshy AY sh'n]

depredation *noun* (usu. in *plural*) an act of attacking, damaging, or plundering: *protecting grain from the depredations of rats and mice.* [Say depra DAY sh'n]

depress *verb* (**depresses, depressed, depressing**) **1** push or pull down; lower. **2** make dispirited or dejected. **3** *Economics* reduce the activity of (esp. trade).

D

depressant • *adjective* (of a drug) reducing functional or nervous activity. • *noun* a depressant drug or substance: *alcohol is a depressant*.

depressed *adjective* **1** dispirited or miserable. **2** *Psychology* suffering from depression. **3** suffering from economic hardship. **4** pressed down; having a flattened or hollowed surface. **5** (of the price of a commodity etc.) persistently lower than normal.

depressing *adjective* causing or resulting in a feeling of miserable dejection. ▶ **depressingly** *adverb*

depression *noun* **1 a** *Psychology* a state of extreme sadness; a mood of hopelessness and feelings of inadequacy, often with physical symptoms such as loss of appetite, insomnia, etc.: *post-natal depression*. **b** a reduction in vitality, vigour, or spirits: *there was a general feeling of depression amongst the staff after Kip left*. **2 a** a long period of financial and industrial decline; a severe recession, with high unemployment and widespread poverty. **b** (**the** (**Great**) **Depression**) the depression which began in 1929 and lasted throughout most of the 1930s. **3** *Meteorology* a lowering of atmospheric pressure, esp. the centre of a region of minimum pressure or the system of winds around it. **4** a sunken place or hollow on a surface: *the original shallow depressions slowly became ponds*. **5** the action of pressing down on something: *depression of the plunger delivers two units of insulin*.

depressive • *adjective* **1** tending to depress: *the mood was bleak and depressive*. **2** *Psychology* involving or characterized by depression: *takes Prozac to combat depressive tendencies*. • *noun* *Psychology* a person suffering or with a tendency to suffer from depression.

depressor *noun* **1 a** a muscle that causes the lowering of some part of the body. **b** a nerve that lowers blood pressure. **2** *Medical* an instrument for pressing down an organ etc.: *tongue depressor*.

depressurize *verb* (**depressurizes, depressurized, depressurizing**) **1** cause a drop in the pressure of the gas inside (a container). **2** lose air pressure.

deprivation *noun* **1** the damaging lack of material benefits considered to be basic necessities in a society: *neglected children suffering from social deprivation*. **2** the lack or denial of something considered to be a necessity: *sleep deprivation*. [Say depra VAY sh'n]

deprive *verb* (**deprives, deprived, depriving**) (usu. foll. by *of*) dispossess; stop from enjoying.

deprived *adjective* **1** (of a child etc.) suffering from the effects of a poor or loveless home. **2** (of an area) having inadequate housing, facilities, employment, etc. **3** suffering a lack of a benefit that is considered important: *the men felt sexually deprived*.

Dept. *abbreviation* Department.

depth *noun* **1 a** the distance from the top or surface to the bottom of something. **b** the distance from the nearest to the farthest point of something or from the front to the back. **2** extensive and detailed study or knowledge: *third-year courses go into more depth*. **3 a** complexity and profundity of thought: *the book has unexpected depth*. **b** intensity of emotion etc.: *a man of compassion and depth of feeling*. **4** an intensity of colour, darkness, etc. **5** (in *plural*) **a** deep water, a deep place. **b** a low, depressed state. **c** the lowest or inmost part. **6** the middle: *in the depth of winter*. PHRASES **in depth** comprehensively, thoroughly, or profoundly. **out of one's depth 1** in water over one's head. **2** engaged in a task or on a subject too difficult for one.

depth charge *noun* an explosive device that detonates under water, esp. for dropping on a submarine etc.

depth finder *noun* an instrument used for measuring the depth of water by radar, ultrasound, etc.

depth sounder *noun* an instrument used for measuring the depth under a ship by ultrasound.

deputation *noun* a group of people appointed to represent others; a delegation. [Say dep yoo TAY sh'n]

depute *verb* (**deputes, deputed, deputing**) appoint or instruct someone to perform a task for which one is responsible: *she was deputed to put our views to the committee*. [Say duh PYOOT]

deputize *verb* (**deputizes, deputized, deputizing**) **1** appoint (a person) to perform a task: *we have been deputized to sit on a new technology and communications task force*. **2** temporarily act or speak on behalf of someone else: *Brenda got a job deputizing for a lecturer on maternity leave*. [Say DEP yoo tize]

deputy *noun* (*plural* **deputies**) a person appointed or delegated to act for another or others (also as an *adjective*: *deputy manager*).

deputy minister *noun* Cdn the senior civil servant in a government department or ministry.

derail *verb* **1** cause (a train etc.) to leave the rails. **2** (of a train) leave the rails. **3** obstruct the progress of (a person, plan, etc.): *this latest incident could derail the peace process*.

derailleur *noun* a bicycle gear in which the ratio is changed by switching the line of the chain while pedalling so that it jumps to a different sprocket. [Say dee RAILER]

derailment *noun* an accident in which a train leaves the track.

derange *verb* (**deranges, deranged, deranging**) throw into confusion; disorganize; cause to act irregularly: *stress deranges the immune system*.

deranged *adjective* unable to behave and think normally, esp. because of mental illness; insane: *a deranged mind*.

derangement *noun* the inability to behave and think normally, esp. because of mental illness; insanity: *he seemed to be on the verge of total derangement*.

Derby *noun* (*plural* **Derbies**) **1 a** an annual horse race run at Epsom Downs, near London, England. **b** any of several other important annual horse races. **2** (**derby**) a sporting contest or race open to all who wish to participate. **3** (**derby**) a man's hard felt hat with a round dome-shaped crown. [Sense 1a rhymes with *BARBIE*]

deregulate *verb* (**deregulates, deregulated, deregulating**) remove regulations or restrictions from. ▶ **deregulation** *noun* **deregulator** *noun*

derelict • *adjective* **1** (esp. of property) ruined; dilapidated. **2** negligent (of duty etc.): *they would have been derelict in their duty if they had not investigated the charges*. • *noun* a social outcast; a person without a home, job, or property: *derelicts who could fit all their possessions in a paper bag*. [Say DERRA likt]

dereliction *noun* **1** the shameful failure to carry out one's obligations: *dereliction of duty*. **2** the state of having been abandoned and become dilapidated: *an image of inner-city derelictions*. [Say derra LICK sh'n]

deride *verb* (**derides, derided, deriding**) be scornful of; ridicule: *his views were derided as old-fashioned*.

de rigueur *adjective* required by custom or etiquette: *evening dress is de rigueur*. [Say duh rig UR]

derision *noun* ridicule; mockery: *her speech was greeted with howls of derision*. [Say duh RIZH un]

derisive *adjective* expressing contempt or ridicule: *a short, derisive laugh*. ▶ **derisively** *adverb* [Say duh RISE iv]

derisory *adjective* **1** scornful: *his derisory gaze swept over her*. **2** so small or unimportant as to be ridiculous: *they were given a derisory pay raise*. [Say duh RICE a ree]

derivation *noun* **1** the obtaining or developing of something from a source or origin: *the derivation of scientific laws from observation*. **2** the formation of a word from another word or from a root in the same or another language: *bicycle is a word of Greek derivation*. **3** *Math* a sequence of statements showing that a formula, theorem, etc., is a consequence of previously accepted statements. [Say derra VAY sh'n]

derivative • *adjective* (typically of an artist or work of art) imitative of the work of another person, and usu. disapproved of for that reason: *some people say he is derivative, that all he does is sing like Sinatra and play like Monk*. • *noun* **1** something derived from another source: *the aircraft is a derivative of the Falcon 20G*. **2** a word derived from another or from a root in the same or another language: *"ubiquitous" is a derivative of the Latin word for "where"* ◊ *"quickly" is a derivative of "quick"*. **3** a chemical compound that is derived from another: *crack is a highly addictive cocaine derivative*. **4** *Math* a quantity measuring the rate of change of another. **5** *Finance* an arrangement or instrument (such as a future, option, or warrant) whose value derives from and is dependent upon the value of an underlying variable asset, such as a commodity, currency, or security. [Say duh RIVVA tiv]

derive *verb* (**derives, derived, deriving**) **1 a** get: *she derived great pleasure from painting*. **b** obtain a substance from something: *the new drug is derived from fish oil*. **2** come or develop from a source: *the word "gym" is derived from the Greek word for "naked"* ◊ *words whose spelling derives from Samuel Johnson's incorrect etymology* ◊ *Marx derived his philosophy of history from Hegel*. **3** *Math* obtain (a function or equation) from another by a sequence of logical steps, for example by differentiation. [Say duh RIVE]

dermal *adjective* having to do with the dermis or skin.

dermatitis *noun* a condition of the skin in which it becomes red, swollen, sore, and usu. itchy, sometimes with small blisters, resulting from direct irritation of the skin by something external or an allergic reaction; eczema. [Say durma TITE iss]

dermatological *adjective* having to do with the diagnosis and treatment of skin disorders. ▶ **dermatologically** *adverb* [Say durma tuh LOGICAL]

dermatologist *noun* a doctor who studies and treats skin disorders. [Say durma TOLLA jist]

dermatology *noun* the study of the diagnosis and treatment of skin disorders. [Say durma TOLLA jee]

dermis *noun* **1** (in general use) the skin. **2** the thick layer of living tissue below the epidermis that forms the true skin, containing blood capillaries, nerve endings, sweat glands, hair follicles, etc.

derogatory *adjective* showing a negative or disrespectful attitude; disparaging: *made a derogatory remark*. [Say duh ROGGA tory]

derrick *noun* **1** a kind of crane for moving or lifting heavy weights, having a movable pivoted arm. **2** the framework over an oil well or similar excavation, holding the drilling machinery.

derrière *noun informal* the buttocks. [Say derry AIR]

derring-do *noun* heroic courage or action, esp. as in adventure stories: *tales of derring-do*. [Say derring DOO]

dervish *noun* (*plural* **dervishes**) a member of any of several Muslim fraternities vowed to poverty and austerity.

DES *abbreviation* Computing Data Encryption Standard.

descant *noun* an independent soprano melody usu. sung or played above a basic melody, esp. of a hymn tune. [Say DESS cant]

descend *verb* **1** go or come down. **2** (usu. foll. by *on*) **a** make a sudden attack. **b** *informal* make an unexpected and usu. unwelcome visit. **3** (usu. foll. by *from, to*) **a** (often in *passive*) originate with or derive from (a progenitor or predecessor). **b** (of property, qualities, rights, etc.) be passed by inheritance. **4** (foll. by *to*) stoop to something unworthy: *descend to violence*. **5** move downstream along (a river etc.) to the sea etc.

descendant *noun* (often foll. by *of*) **1** a person or animal descended from another. **2** something deriving from or following after the form, function, or style of another, earlier instance, model, etc.: *fundamentalism was a descendant of these revivalist movements*.

SPELL CHECK	
descent, dissent	

Difference of opinion or sentiment is **dissent**.

descent *noun* **1** an action of moving downwards, dropping, or falling: *the plane had gone into a steep descent*. **2** a downward slope, esp. a path or track: *a steep, badly eroded descent to the shore*. **3 a** lineage, family origin: *is of Scottish descent*. **b** the transmission of qualities, property, privileges, etc. by inheritance. **4** a fall or decline to a lower state or condition: *the country's swift descent into anarchy*. **5** a sudden violent attack: *mustered his troops for a descent on the camp*.

descramble *verb* (**descrambles, descrambled, descrambling**) convert or restore (an electronic signal) to intelligible form, esp. through an electronic device. ▶ **descrambler** *noun*

describe *verb* (**describes, described, describing**) **1 a** portray in words; give a detailed or graphic account of. **b** (foll. by *as*) assert to be; call: *described him as an agitator*. **2 a** mark out or draw (esp. a geometrical figure): *described a triangle*. **b** move in (a specified way, esp. a curve): *described a parabola*.

description *noun* **1 a** a spoken or written representation (of a person, object, or event): *bystanders were able to give a description of the thief*. **b** the action of giving such a representation: *the novelist's powers of description* ◊ *the horrors to which they were subjected defy description*. **2** a sort, kind, or class: *no food of any description*. PHRASES **answers** (or **fits**) **the description** has the qualities specified.

descriptive *adjective* **1** serving or seeking to describe. **2** describing or classifying without expressing feelings or judging: *a purely descriptive account*. **3** *Linguistics* describing a language without comparing, endorsing, or condemning particular usage, vocabulary, etc. **4** *Grammar* (of an adjective) describing a quality of the noun, rather than its relation, position, etc., e.g. *blue* as distinct from *few*. ▶ **descriptively** *adverb*

desecrate *verb* (**desecrates, desecrated, desecrating**) treat (a sacred place or thing) with violent disrespect; violate: *desecrated graves*. ▶ **desecration** *noun* [Say DESSA crate, dessa CRAY sh'n]

desegregate *verb* (**desegregates, desegregated, desegregating**) abolish racial segregation in (schools etc.) or of (people etc.). ▶ **desegregation** *noun* [Say dee SEGRA gate, dee segra GAY sh'n]

desensitization *noun* a reduction in sensitivity to something. [Say dee sensa tize AY sh'n]

desensitize *verb* (**desensitizes, desensitized, desensitizing**) **1** reduce or destroy the sensitivity of (photographic materials, an allergic person, etc.). **2** reduce or eliminate emotional responses to, esp. through repeated exposure: *desensitized to violence*. [Say dee SENSA tize]

desert¹ *verb* **1** abandon, give up; leave without intention of returning. **2** forsake or abandon (a cause, person, etc., esp. one having a claim on a person): *deserted his wife and children*. **3** (of a power or faculty) fail (someone): *his presence of mind deserted him*. **4** *Military* run away from or forsake (one's duty etc.). ▶**deserter** *noun* **desertion** *noun* [Say duh ZURT]

desert² • *noun* **1** a dry, barren area of land, often sand-covered, with few inhabitants, little fresh water, and scanty vegetation: *there is a small desert near Shilo in southern Manitoba ◊ Victoria Island has such scant rain and snowfall that it is described as an arctic desert*. **2** an uninteresting or intellectually barren place, subject, etc.: *a cultural desert*. • *adjective* of or like a desert: *overgrazing has created desert conditions*. [Say DEZ urt]

desert³ *noun* (usu. in *plural*) **1** acts or qualities deserving reward or punishment. **2** just reward or punishment: *just deserts*. [Say duh ZURT]

deserted *adjective* empty, abandoned: *a deserted house*.

desertification *noun* the transformation of fertile land into a desert or arid waste. [Say duh zurt iffa KAY sh'n]

desert island *noun* a remote (usu. tropical) island presumed to be uninhabited.

deserve *verb* (**deserves**, **deserved**, **deserving**) be entitled to or worthy of (a reward, punishment, etc.): *deserves to be imprisoned ◊ deserved a prize*. ▶**deserved** *adjective*

deservedly *adjective* with good reason: *the restaurant is deservedly popular ◊ Diane was chosen for the job, and deservedly so*. [Say duh ZUR vid lee]

deserving *adjective* worthy; that deserves help, praise, a reward, etc.: *a deserving cause*.

desiccate *verb* (**desiccates**, **desiccated**, **desiccating**) **1** remove the moisture from, dry (esp. food for preservation). **2** deprive (land, plants, etc.) thoroughly of moisture: *the soil is exposed to the desiccating rays of the sun*. [Say DESSA kate]

desiccated *adjective* **1 a** deprived or freed of moisture. **b** (of food) dried for preservation· *desiccated coconut*. **2** (of a person, text, etc.) deprived of energy or feeling· *the book presents more than a desiccated history of ideas*. [Say DESSA kate id]

desiccation *noun* the process of becoming completely dry. [Say dessa KAY sh'n]

desideratum *noun* (*plural* **desiderata**) something lacking but needed and desired: *to the Indians, civilization was not a universal desideratum*. [Say duh zidda RAT um for the singular, duh zidda RATTA for the plural]

design • *noun* **1** a preliminary plan or sketch for the making or production of a building, machine, garment, etc. **2 a** the art of planning and creating something in accordance with appropriate functional and aesthetic criteria. **b** the selection and arrangement of artistic or functional elements making up a work of art, machine, etc. **c** = INTERIOR DESIGN. **3 a** the general arrangement or layout of a product. **b** an example or a completed version of a sketch, concept, or pattern. **c** an established version of a product: *one of our most popular designs*. **4** a motif or pattern of lines, shapes, etc. **5 a** a plan, purpose, or intention. **b** a plot, scheme, or intrigue. • *verb* **1 a** make drawings and plans for the construction or production of (a building, machine, garment, etc.). **b** plan and execute (a structure, work of art, etc.) skilfully or artistically. **2 a** intend (something)

for a specific purpose. **b** form a plan or scheme of; contrive: *designed an attack*. **3** be a designer of works of art, buildings, garments, etc. PHRASES **by design** on purpose. **have designs on 1** have one's sights set on. **2** hope to establish a romantic or sexual relationship with. **3** plan to attack or appropriate.

designate • *verb* (**designates**, **designated**, **designating**) **1** appoint to an office or function. **2** mark or point out clearly: *designate the boundaries*. **3** give a name or title to: *was designated Athlete of the Year*. **4** serve as the name or distinctive mark of. • *adjective* (placed after noun) appointed to a position but not yet officially occupying it: *bishop designate*. ▶**designated** *adjective* [Say DEZ ig nate for the verb, DEZ ig nit for the adjective]

designated driver *noun* a person who abstains from alcohol at a social gathering so as to be fit to drive others home.

designated hitter *noun* *Baseball* a non-fielding player named before the start of a game to bat for the pitcher anywhere in the batting order. Abbreviation: **DH**.

designation *noun* **1** a name, description, or title: *her official designation is Financial Controller*. **2** the act or process of designating: *the legislation should allow for the designation of dangerous offenders prior to and following sentencing*. **3** the appointment or nomination of a (person, city, etc.) to (a particular office, status, etc.): *the fort is being considered for designation as a heritage site*.

designed *adjective* **1** planned, intended. **2** outlined, formed, or framed according to some design.

designer *noun* **1 a** a person who designs things, e.g. clothing, machines, theatre sets, books, etc. **b** an interior designer. **2** (as an *adjective*) **a** (of clothing etc.) bearing the name or label of a famous designer and so considered prestigious: *designer jeans*. **b** (of ideas, objects, etc.) being or seeming fashionable or trendy: *designer beers*. **c** (of chemicals etc.) designed for a specific purpose or function: *designer herbicides*.

designer drug *noun* **1** a drug synthesized to mimic a legally restricted or prohibited drug without being subject to such restriction. **2** a specially formulated drug designed to be highly effective against a precisely targeted disease, chemical process, etc.

designing *adjective* acting in a calculating, deceitful way: *we have too long been the dupes of designing politicians*.

desirability *noun* **1** the quality of being desirable as an attractive, useful, or necessary course of action: *I question the desirability of selling the house*. **2** the quality of being sexually attractive.

desirable *adjective* **1 a** worth having or doing: *desirable accommodations*. **b** advisable: *a desirable law*. **2** arousing sexual desire; very attractive. ▶**desirably** *adverb*

desire • *noun* **1** an unsatisfied longing or craving. **2** sexual appetite. **3** something desired: *finally obtained her heart's desire*. • *verb* (**desires**, **desired**, **desiring**) **1 a** strongly wish for or want: *she never achieved the status she so desired ◊ failed to achieve the desired effect*. **b** feel sexual desire for. **2** request: *desires a cup of tea*. PHRASES **leave something to be desired** be bad or unacceptable: *the service in the restaurant left a lot to be desired*.

desirous *adjective* (usu. foll. by *of*) having desire; wishful, wanting: *desirous of doing well*. [Say duh ZYE russ]

desist *verb* cease: *the defendant was ordered to desist from committing further breaches of the injunction*.

desk *noun* **1** a piece of furniture with a writing surface, often having drawers or compartments. **2** a service counter in a library, hotel, etc. at which a specific function is performed: *information desk*. **3** a section of an office, e.g. of a newspaper, that handles a

particular matter, topic, etc.: *the sports desk*. **4** a music stand, esp. shared by two orchestra members. **5** (as an *adjective*) **a** designating an item for use at a desk: *a desk dictionary*. **b** designating something done or someone working at a desk: *a desk job*.

desktop *noun* **1** the working surface of a desk. **2** (as an *adjective*) of a size and nature suitable for use on a desk, esp. designating or pertaining to a microcomputer. **3** a desktop computer.

desktop publishing *noun* the design and production of high-quality printed matter using a desktop computer and a laser printer.

desolate • *adjective* **1** (of a person) forlorn, wretched, and usu. solitary: *was left desolate and weeping*. **2 a** (of a building or place) uninhabited, ruined, neglected, barren: *desolate Arctic wastes*. **b** dismal, depressing: *desolate prospects*. • *verb* (**desolates, desolated, desolating**) depopulate or devastate, lay waste to: *the droughts desolated the already dry plains*. [Say DESSA lit for the adjective, DESSA late for the verb]

desolated *adjective* **1** made wretched or forlorn: *desolated by grief*. **2** made barren or uninhabitable: *a grey, awful, desolated world*. [Say DESSA late id]

desolation *noun* **1** loneliness, grief, or wretchedness, esp. caused by desertion: *her death left him with a terrible sense of desolation*. **2** the state of a place that is ruined or destroyed and offers no joy or hope to people: *a scene of utter desolation*. [Say dessa LAY sh'n]

despair • *noun* the complete loss or absence of hope. • *verb* (often foll. by *of*) lose or be without hope: *despaired of ever seeing her again*. PHRASES **be the despair of** be the cause of despair by badness or unapproachable excellence: *he's the despair of his parents*. ▶ **despairing** *adjective* **despairingly** *adverb*

despatch (**despatches, despatched, despatching**) esp. *Brit.* = DISPATCH.

desperado *noun* (*plural* **desperadoes** or **desperados**) esp. *hist.* a desperate or reckless person, esp. a person ready for any deed of lawlessness or violence. [Say despa RODDO or despa RADDO]

desperate *adjective* **1** reckless from despair, esp. to the point of violence or lawlessness. **2 a** extremely grave, critical, or serious: *a desperate situation*. **b** undertaken as a last resort, esp. as staking all on a small chance: *a desperate remedy*. **3** extreme, excessive: *desperate poverty*. **4** (usu. foll. by *for*) needing or desiring very much. ▶ **desperately** *adverb*

desperation *noun* a state of despair, typically one which results in rash or extreme behaviour: *in desperation, she called Louise and asked for her help*.

despicable *adjective* deserving hatred or contempt; very unpleasant or evil: *a despicable crime*. ▶ **despicably** *adverb* [Say duh SPICKA bull]

despise *verb* (**despises, despised, despising**) look down on (someone etc.) as inferior, worthless, or contemptible. ▶ **despised** *adjective*

despite *preposition* notwithstanding; in spite of.

despoil *verb* **1** spoil, destroy, make useless: *abandoned buildings and despoiled countrysides*. **2** *literary* rob, deprive by force or violence: *despoiled her of her inheritance*.

despondency *noun* a state of low spirits caused by loss of hope or courage. [Say duh SPON din see]

despondent *adjective* characterized by loss of courage or enthusiasm; dejected. ▶ **despondently** *adverb* [Say duh SPON dint]

despot *noun* **1** an absolute ruler: *Catherine the Great was considered an enlightened despot*. **2** a cruel, tyrannical, and oppressive ruler. **3** any person in authority who acts like a tyrant. ▶ **despotic** *adjective* **despotically** *adverb* [Say DESS pot, dess POT ick lee]

despotism *noun* the exercise of absolute political

power or rule, esp. cruelly and tyrannically. [Say DESPA tism]

SPELL CHECK
dessert, desert

A dry, sandy region is a **desert**. To abandon someone is to **desert** them. Someone who gets what they deserve gets their *just deserts*.

dessert *noun* a sweet food eaten at the end of a meal. [Say duh ZURT]

destabilization *noun* the process of upsetting the stability of something, esp. a country or government by foreign interference.

destabilize *verb* (**destabilizes, destabilized, destabilizing**) **1** upset the stability of: *the heat created by the flowing gas would destabilize the permafrost*. **2** undermine (a government, economy, etc.), so as to make it politically unstable.

destination *noun* a place to which a person or thing is going or being sent.

destined *adjective* **1** having a future decided or planned beforehand, esp. by fate or as if by fate: *she is destined for greatness*. **2** (foll. by *for*) bound (for a certain place): *destined for PEI*. [Say DESS tinned]

destiny *noun* (*plural* **destinies**) **1 a** fate or the predetermined course of events. **b** (often **Destiny**) the power or agency that supposedly predetermines events etc. **2** what is destined to happen to a particular person etc.: *it was their destiny to be rejected*.

destitute *adjective* completely impoverished; without food, shelter, etc. ▶ **destitution** *noun* [Say DESTA toot or DESTA tyoot, desta TOO sh'n or desta TYOO sh'n]

destroy *verb* **1** demolish, pull or break down; shatter, smash to pieces. **2** put an end to or do away with: *destroyed his confidence*. **3** kill (esp. a sick or savage animal). **4** make useless, spoil utterly. **5** utterly discredit or ruin financially, professionally, or in reputation. **6** defeat, annihilate: *destroyed the enemy*.

destroyer *noun* **1** a person or thing that destroys. **2** a small, lightly armoured and heavily armed warship.

destruct • *verb* destroy (one's own rocket etc.) deliberately, esp. for safety reasons. • *noun* **1** an act of destructing. **2** (as an *adjective*) designating something capable of causing the destruction of itself, some other object, etc.: *destruct mechanism*.

destructible *adjective* able or liable to be destroyed.

destruction *noun* **1** the action or process of causing so much damage to something that it no longer exists or cannot be repaired: *the destruction of the rainforests* ◊ *the avalanche left a trail of destruction*. **2** the action or process of killing or being killed: *weapons of mass destruction*. **3** a cause of someone's ruin: *gambling was his destruction*. **4** the ruination or ending of a system or state of affairs: *the destruction of a traditional way of life*.

destructive *adjective* **1** (often foll. by *to, of*) destroying or tending to destroy: *destructive behaviour*. **2** negative in attitude or criticism; refuting without suggesting, helping, amending, etc.: *destructive criticism*. ▶ **destructively** *adverb* **destructiveness** *noun*

desultorily *adverb* in a desultory manner; in a random, wandering, or half-hearted manner: *we chatted desultorily about this and that*. [Say DESSLE torra lee]

desultory *adjective* **1** going constantly from one subject to another in a half-hearted way; unfocused: *the desultory conversation faded*. **2** lacking a plan, purpose, or enthusiasm: *a few people were left, dancing in a desultory fashion*. [Say DESSLE tory]

detach *verb* (**detaches, detached, detaching**) **1** unfasten and remove; disconnect or disengage. **2** *Military* separate and send off (a part from a main body,

e.g. a ship, regiment, officer, etc.) for a particular purpose. ▶ **detachable** *adjective*

detached *adjective* **1** impartial, unemotional: *a detached viewpoint.* **2** esp. *Cdn & Brit.* (esp. of a house) separate, not joined to another or others.

detachment *noun* **1 a** a state of aloofness from or indifference to other people, public opinion, etc.: *felt a sense of detachment from what was going on.* **b** the state of not being influenced by others or one's own feelings: *in judging these issues a degree of critical detachment is required.* **2** the act or process of detaching or being detached: *structural problems resulted in cracking and detachment of the wall.* **3** *Military* **a** the action of separating a number of troops etc. from a main military body for a particular purpose. **b** a separate group or unit of an army etc. used for such a purpose. **4** *Cdn* the office or headquarters of a police district patrolled by the RCMP, OPP, etc.

detail • *noun* **1** a small or subordinate particular. **2** small items or particulars (esp. in an artistic work) regarded collectively: *has an eye for detail.* **3 a** a minor decoration on a building, in a picture, etc. **b** a small part of a picture etc. shown alone or considered in isolation. **4** *Military* **a** a small detachment of soldiers etc. for special duty. **b** this special duty: *kitchen detail.* • *verb* **1** relate or describe minutely, give particulars of: *detailed the plans.* **2** *Military* assign for special duty. **3** decorate (a carving, car, etc.) with intricate drawings or designs.

detailed *adjective* **1** (of a picture, story, etc.) having many details. **2** itemized: *a detailed list.* **3** thorough in handling details.

detailing *noun* the treatment of detail in a work of art, building, design, etc.

detain *verb* **1** keep in confinement or under restraint as a prisoner, esp. without charge. **2** delay or keep (someone) waiting.

detainee *noun* a person detained in custody, esp. for political reasons.

detect *verb* **1** discover or perceive the existence or presence of: *the tests are designed to detect the disease early* ◊ *an instrument that can detect small amounts of radiation* ◊ *do I detect a note of criticism?* **2** discover or investigate (crime etc.). ▶ **detectable** *adjective*

detection *noun* **1** the action or process of identifying the presence of something concealed: *the early detection of cancer* ◊ *many problems escape detection.* **2** the work of a detective: *an expert from the RCMP Crime Detection Lab.*

detective *noun* **1** a person, esp. a member of a police force, employed to investigate crime: *police detective* ◊ *detective agency.* **2** (in Canadian police forces with a detective branch) an officer ranking above constable. **3** (as an *adjective*) designating a type of fiction describing crime and the detection of criminals: *detective novel.*

detector *noun* a device which detects something liable to escape observation or indicates something out of the ordinary: *smoke detector* ◊ *lie detector.*

détente *noun* an easing of hostility or strained relations, esp. between nations: *a new international climate of détente.* [Say day TONT]

detention *noun* **1** the state of imprisonment or confinement, esp. of a criminal or political offender: *he committed suicide while in police detention* ◊ *detention centre.* **2** the punishment of being kept in school after hours: *was given a detention for swearing at the teacher.*

detention centre *noun* **1** an institution for the short-term detention of criminals, esp. young offenders. **2** a camp or centre, esp. one established during or after a war, to house refugees, prisoners of war, etc.

deter *verb* (**deters**, **deterred**, **deterring**) **1** prevent or discourage (a person) through fear or dislike of the consequences: *only a health problem would deter her from seeking re-election.* **2** prevent the occurrence of: *strategists think about how to deter war.* [Say duh TUR]

detergent *noun* **1** a water-soluble cleansing agent which combines with impurities and dirt to make them more soluble, and differs from soap in not forming a scum with the salts in hard water. **2** any additive with a similar action, e.g. holding dirt in suspension in lubricating oil.

deteriorate *verb* (**deteriorates**, **deteriorated**, **deteriorating**) make or become worse or lower in quality, character, etc.

deterioration *noun* the process of becoming progressively worse: *the gradual deterioration in her health* ◊ *environmental deterioration.*

determinant • *noun* a factor which decisively affects the nature or outcome of something: *the single most important determinant of church membership was gender.* • *adjective* serving to determine or decide something: *a determinant factor.*

determinate *adjective* having exact and discernible limits or form. [Say duh TURMA nit]

determination *noun* **1** firmness of purpose. **2 a** the process of deciding, determining, or calculating. **b** the result of such consideration. **3 a** the conclusion of a dispute by the decision of a judge or an arbitrator. **b** the decision so reached.

determine *verb* (**determines**, **determined**, **determining**) **1** find out or establish precisely. **2** decide or settle: *determined who should go.* **3** be a decisive factor in regard to: *demand determines supply.* **4** make or cause (a person) to make a decision: *we determined to go at once.* **5** fix or define the position of.

determined *adjective* showing determination. ▶ **determinedly** *adverb* [Say duh TERM ind lee]

determinism *noun* *Philosophy* the doctrine that all events, including human action, are determined by causes regarded as external to the will. ▶ **determinist** *noun* **deterministic** *adjective*

deterrence *noun* **1** the use of deterrents to discourage or prevent someone from doing something: *deterrence is an important part of crime prevention.* **2** the threat of the use of vast military power intended to prevent an enemy from attacking: *nuclear deterrence.* [Say duh TUR ince]

deterrent • *noun* **1** a thing that discourages or is intended to discourage someone from doing something. **2** military strength or combat capability, esp. nuclear, intended to deter an enemy from attack. • *adjective* able or intended to deter: *the deterrent effect of heavy prison sentences.* [Say duh TUR int]

detest *verb* hate, loathe.

detestable *adjective* deserving to be detested; intensely hateful. ▶ **detestably** *adverb*

detonate *verb* (**detonates**, **detonated**, **detonating**) **1** set off (an explosive charge). **2** (of an explosive charge) be set off, explode. ▶ **detonator** *noun* [Say DET'n ate]

detonation *noun* **1** the act or process of detonating. **2** a violent explosion. [Say det'n AY sh'n]

detour • *noun* a divergence from a direct or intended route, esp. one that avoids a blocked road etc. • *verb* make or cause to make a detour.

detox *informal* • *noun* (plural **detoxes**) **1** = DETOXIFICATION. **2 a** a detoxification clinic, program, etc. **b** = DRUNK TANK. • *verb* (**detoxes**, **detoxed**, **detoxing**) **1** subject (an alcoholic or drug addict) to detoxification. **2 a** (of a person) subject oneself to

D

detoxification. **b** recover temporarily from the effects of alcohol or drugs.

detoxification noun **1** the process of removing toxic substances or qualities. **2** medical treatment of an alcoholic or drug addict involving abstention from drink or drugs until the bloodstream is free of toxins. [Say dee toxa fuh KAY sh'n]

detoxify verb (**detoxifies**, **detoxified**, **detoxifying**) **1** subject (an alcoholic or drug addict) to detoxification. **2** remove toxic substances or qualities from (something): *the process uses chemical reagents to detoxify the oil ◊ the liver naturally detoxifies many foreign chemicals that enter the body*. [Say dee TOXA fie]

detract verb take something away from; diminish or belittle: *the poor service at the restaurant detracted from my enjoyment of the meal ◊ no amount of criticism can detract from her achievements*. ▶ **detraction** noun

detractor noun a person who disparages or belittles another's achievements, merits, etc.: *health-care reform will not be without its detractors*.

detriment noun **1** harm, damage, disadvantage: *this tax cannot be introduced without detriment to people's living standards*. **2** something causing this: *such tests are a detriment to good education*. PHRASES **to the detriment of** to the disadvantage of: *he is engrossed in his job to the detriment of his health*. [Say DETRA mint]

detrimental adjective harmful, damaging, or causing loss. ▶ **detrimentally** adverb [Say detra MENTAL]

detritus noun **1** matter produced by erosion, such as gravel, silt, etc.: *the stones are water-smoothed cobbles, detritus of the most recent Ice Age*. **2 a** debris of any kind: *found it amid the detritus of white wine and croissant sandwiches*. **b** something abandoned or left behind: *the detritus of failed good ideas*. **3** the organic litter produced by decomposing leaves etc. [Say duh TRITE us]

deuce¹ noun **1** the two in dice or playing cards. **2 a** Sport two points, goals, runs, etc. **b** Tennis the score of 40 all, at which two consecutive points are needed to win. **3** informal the number two as an identifying feature for various items. [Say DOOCE or DYOOCE]

deuce² noun informal the Devil, used esp. as an exclamation of surprise or annoyance: *who the deuce are you?* PHRASES **a** (or **the**) **deuce of** a very bad or remarkable: *a deuce of a problem*. **the deuce to pay** trouble to be expected. [Say DOOCE or DYOOCE]

deuterium noun a stable isotope of hydrogen with a mass about double that of the usual isotope. [Say due TEERY um]

Deutschmark noun (also **Deutsche Mark**) the chief monetary unit of Germany. [Say DOITCH mark]

devaluation noun **1** an act of reducing or underestimating the worth or importance of something: *he knows what it is to suffer absolute emotional and intellectual devaluation*. **2** a reduction in the official value of a currency in relation to other currencies: *repeated devaluations of the peso*.

devalue verb (**devalues**, **devalued**, **devaluing**) **1** reduce or underestimate the worth or value of: *I resent the way people seem to devalue my achievement*. **2** reduce the value of (a currency) in relation to other currencies or to gold (opp. REVALUE 2): *the dinar was devalued by twenty percent*.

devastate verb (**devastates**, **devastated**, **devastating**) **1** destroy or ruin something: *the city was devastated by a huge earthquake ◊ bad weather has devastated the tourist industry*. **2** overwhelm with shock or grief; upset deeply: *devastated by the news*.

devastating adjective crushingly effective; overwhelming. ▶ **devastatingly** adverb

devastation noun **1** great destruction or damage, esp. over a wide area: *the earthquake caused widespread*

devastation. **2** overwhelming shock or grief: *words could not convey my devastation at the news that he was leaving*.

develop verb (**develops**, **developed**, **developing**) **1 a** make or become bigger or fuller. **b** bring or come into existence or to an active or visible state: *symptoms developed rapidly*. **2 a** elaborate more fully and systematically the details of (a thought, argument, plot, etc.). **b** (of a thought, argument, plot, etc.) unfold in this way. **3 a** grow or cause to grow to maturity or to a more advanced state: *some teens develop early*. **b** (of organisms) evolve or progress from a simpler or lower to a higher or more complex type. **4** begin to exhibit or suffer from: *developed an infection*. **5 a** make (a tract of land) suitable for new purposes, esp. residential, industrial, etc. **b** realize the resource potential of (a site or property) by mining etc. **6** create or design (a program, product, etc.). **7** treat (photographic film etc.) chemically to make the latent image visible. ▶ **developable** adjective

developed country noun an industrialized country that is economically and socially advanced with a high standard of living.

developer noun **1** a person or company that develops land, esp. a builder. **2** a chemical agent for developing photographs. **3** a person or thing which develops (a product etc.).

developing country noun (plural **developing countries**) a country that is becoming economically more advanced and more industrialized.

development noun **1 a** the gradual growth of something so that it becomes stronger, more advanced, etc.: *the baby's development in the womb ◊ traces the development of the novel as a genre*. **b** the process of working up (an idea, product, etc.) for marketing etc.: *the development of a new vaccine ◊ developments in aviation technology*. **2 a** a stage of growth or advancement. **b** a full-grown state. **3** a significant change in a course of action, events, circumstances, etc.: *the latest developments in the ongoing saga*. **4** the process of developing a photograph. **5 a** a developed tract of land, esp. a new housing area. **b** the process of converting land to a new purpose by constructing buildings or making use of its resources: *opposed to development on the moraine*. **6** industrialization or economic advancement of a country or area.

developmental adjective **1** pertaining to the process of achieving physical, mental, or social maturity: *developmental delays*. **2** of or pertaining to development. ▶ **developmentally** adverb

development bank noun a bank set up by a government or group of governments designed to contribute to the economic development and social progress of a particular area.

deviance noun difference from usual or accepted standards, esp. in social or sexual behaviour: *a study of social deviance and crime*. [Say DEE vee ince]

deviant • adjective different from what most people consider to be normal and acceptable: *deviant behaviour*. • noun a person who or thing which deviates from the normal, esp. from normal social or sexual practices. [Say DEE vee int]

deviate verb (**deviates**, **deviated**, **deviating**) turn aside or diverge (from a course of action, rule, truth, accepted standards, etc.): *the bus had to deviate from its usual route because of a road closure ◊ she never deviated from her original plan*. [Say DEE vee ate]

deviation noun **1** the action of diverging from an established course or accepted standard: *studies of social deviation ◊ deviations from Standard English*. **2** Statistics the amount by which a single measurement differs from the mean. **3** the deflection of a compass needle caused

D

by local deposits of iron, regional magnetic disturbances, etc. [Say dee vee AY sh'n]

device *noun* **1 a** a thing made or adapted for a particular purpose, esp. something mechanical. **b** an explosive contrivance, esp. a nuclear bomb. **2** a method of doing something that produces a particular result or effect: *sending advertising by mail is very successful as a marketing device.* **3 a** an emblematic or heraldic design. **b** an artistic drawing, design, pattern, etc. **4** any literary technique deliberately employed to achieve a specific effect, e.g. figures of speech etc.: *parallel structure is an effective rhetorical device.* PHRASES **leave a person to his (or her) own devices** leave a person to do as he or she wishes.

devil *noun* **1** (usu. **the Devil**) (in Christian and Jewish belief) the supreme spirit of evil; Satan. **2** an evil spirit; a superhuman malignant being. **3 a** a wicked or cruel person. **b** a mischievously energetic, clever, or self-willed person. **4** *informal* a person or animal: *lucky devil*. **5** fighting spirit, mischievousness: *the devil is in him tonight*. **6** *informal* something difficult or awkward: *this door is a devil to open*. **7** (**the devil, the Devil**) *informal* used as an exclamation of surprise or annoyance: *who the devil are you?* PHRASES **between the devil and the deep blue sea** in a dilemma. **a devil of** *informal* a considerable, difficult, or remarkable. **the devil to pay** trouble to be expected. **go to the devil 1** be damned. **2** (in *imper.*) used to express anger or annoyance. **like the devil** with great energy. **speak of the devil** said when a person appears just after being mentioned.

devilled *adjective* (of eggs, ham, etc.) prepared with spicy seasonings.

devil-may-care *adjective* cheerful and reckless: *a devil-may-care manner*.

devil's advocate *noun* **1** a person who supports an opposing or unpopular view in order to provoke argument or discussion: *if I may play devil's advocate for a moment, what will happen if you don't get the money?* **2** *Catholicism* the official whose function is to argue the case against beatification or canonization of a candidate.

devil's food cake *noun* a chocolate cake with a reddish tinge.

devious *adjective* (of a person, plan etc.) not straightforward or sincere; underhand. ► **deviously** *adverb* **deviousness** *noun* [Say DEE vee us]

SPELL CHECK
devise, device   ABC ✓

A gadget or tool is a **device**.

---

devise *verb* (**devises, devised, devising**) **1** plan or invent by careful thought. **2** *Law* leave (real estate) by the terms of a will. ► **deviser** *noun* [Say duh VIZE]

devitalize *verb* (**devitalizes, devitalized, devitalizing**) take away strength and vigour from. [Say dee VITALIZE]

devoid *adjective* totally lacking: *her letter was devoid of warmth and feeling*. [Say duh VOID]

devolution *noun* **1** the delegation of power, esp. by central government to local or regional administration. **2 a** descent or passing on through a series of stages. **b** descent by natural or due succession from one to another of property or qualities. **3** the transfer of a right that has not been exercised to an ultimate owner. **4** *Biology* degeneration. [Say devva LOO sh'n or deeva LOO sh'n]

devolve *verb* (**devolves, devolved, devolving**) **1 a** transfer or delegate (duties, responsibility, power, etc.) to another person or organization at a lower level:

the federal government has shown an alarming tendency to devolve its responsibilities onto the provinces. **b** (of work or duties) pass to (a deputy etc.): *his duties devolved on a comrade.* **2** *Law* (of property etc.) be transferred from one owner to another, esp. by inheritance.

Devonian • *adjective* of or relating to the fourth period of the Paleozoic era, from about 408 to 360 million years BP, between the Silurian and Carboniferous periods. During this period, fish became abundant, the first amphibians evolved, and the first forests appeared. • *noun* the Devonian period or the system of rocks dating from this time. [Say duh VOE nee un]

devote *verb* (**devotes, devoted, devoting**) apply or give over (resources etc. or oneself) to (a particular activity or purpose or person): *devoted my time to reading.*

devoted *adjective* very loving or loyal: *a devoted husband.* ► **devotedly** *adverb* **devotedness** *noun*

devotee *noun* **1** a zealous enthusiast or supporter: *a devotee of science fiction.* **2** a strong believer in a particular religion: *devotees of Krishna.* [Say dev oh TEE]

devotion *noun* **1** enthusiastic attachment or loyalty (esp. to a person or cause): *Eleanor's devotion to her husband* ◊ *devotion to duty.* **2 a** religious worship: *the monks led a life of devotion.* **b** (in *plural*) prayers: *a book of devotions.*

devotional *adjective* of, pertaining to, or characterized by (esp. religious) devotion. ► **devotionalism** *noun*

devour *verb* **1** eat hungrily or greedily. **2** consume destructively; waste; destroy: *devouring the world's resources.* **3** take in greedily with the eyes or ears: *devoured book after book.* **4** (usu. in *passive*) absorb the attention of: *devoured by anxiety.* ► **devourer** *noun*

devout *adjective* **1** believing strongly in a particular religion and obeying its laws and practices: *devout Christians and Muslims.* **2** earnestly sincere: *devout hope.* ► **devoutly** *adverb*

dew *noun* **1** atmospheric vapour condensing in small drops on cool surfaces at night. **2** beaded or glistening moisture resembling this: *a fine dew of perspiration.*

dewberry *noun* (*plural* **dewberries**) **1** a bluish fruit like the blackberry. **2** any of various shrubs of the genus *Rubus* bearing this.

dewdrop *noun* a drop of dew.

Dewey Decimal Classification *noun* (also *informal* **Dewey decimal system**) a decimal system of library classification.

dewlap *noun* **1** a loose fold of skin hanging from the throat of cattle, dogs, etc. **2** similar loose skin round the throat of an elderly person.

DEW Line *noun* a network of radar stations stretching along the Arctic coast from Alaska to Baffin Island, built in the 1950s to provide advance warning of an aircraft or missile attack.

deworm *verb* rid (a dog, cat, etc.) of worms. ► **dewormer** *noun* [Say dee WURM]

dew point *noun* the temperature at which dew forms.

dew worm *noun* = EARTHWORM.

dewy *adjective* (**dewier, dewiest**) **1 a** wet with dew. **b** moist as if with dew: *a dewy complexion.* **2** = DEWY-EYED. **3** of or like dew.

dewy-eyed *adjective* innocently trusting; naive.

dexterity *noun* **1** skill in performing tasks, esp. with the hands: *Peng's dexterity with chopsticks.* **2** the ability to do something skilfully; cleverness: *verbal dexterity* ◊ *the disaster was handled with dexterity.* [Say deck STAIR a tee]

dexterous *adjective* (also **dextrous**) **1** demonstrating neat skill, esp. with the hands. **2** clever, esp. in dealing with difficult situations: *some dexterous financing* ◊ *dexterous politician that he was, the PM managed to resolve the crisis with a typically Canadian compromise.*

▶**dexterously** *adverb* **dexterousness** *noun* [Say DECKS truss]

dextromethorphan *noun* a cough suppressant acting by making the cough centre in the brain less sensitive to incoming stimuli. [Say DECK stro muth ORF in]

dextrose *noun* a form of glucose. [Say DECK strose (STROSE rhymes with *DOSE* or *DOZE*)]

DH • *noun* (*plural* **DHs**) DESIGNATED HITTER. • *verb* (**DH's**, **DH'd**, **DH'ing**) **1** act as a designated hitter. **2** use (a player) as a designated hitter: *the Jays DH'ed him last night*. • *abbreviation* Skiing DOWNHILL.

dhal *noun* = DAL. [Sounds like *DOLL*]

dharma *noun* **1** (in Hinduism) the eternal law of the cosmos, inherent in the nature of things, upheld (but not created or controlled) by the gods; in the context of individual action, it denotes the social rules codified in the law books. **2** (in Buddhism) the true doctrine as preached by the Buddha. [Say DARR muh]

dhoti *noun* (*plural* **dhotis**) the loincloth worn by male Hindus. [Say DOE tee]

dhow *noun* a ship used on the E African, Arabian, and Indian coasts, with a triangular sail on a long yard at an angle of 45° to the mast. [Say DOW, rhymes with *HOW*]

DHS *abbreviation* Cdn District High School.

dia. *abbreviation* diameter.

diabetes *noun* (also **diabetes mellitus**) a metabolic disorder caused by a deficiency of the pancreatic hormone insulin, in which sugar and starch are not properly absorbed from the blood, characterized by thirst, emaciation, and excessive excretion of urine with glucose. [Say die a BEE teez or die a BEE tiss]

diabetic • *adjective* **1** of or relating to or having diabetes. **2** for use by diabetics. • *noun* a person suffering from diabetes. [Say die a BET ick]

diabolical *adjective* (also **diabolic**) **1** of the Devil. **2** devilish; inhumanly cruel or wicked. **3** fiendishly clever or cunning or annoying. ▶**diabolically** *adverb* [Say die a BOLLA cull]

diaconal *adjective* **1** of a deacon or deaconess. **2** of a diaconal minister. [Say die ACKA null or dee ACKA null]

diaconal minister *noun* Cdn (in Presbyterian and United churches) a person who has completed a designated course of study at a theological college and is employed by a congregation etc. to provide religious education, pastoral visits, etc., esp. for children, youth, the elderly, etc.

diadem *noun* a crown or headband worn as a sign of sovereignty. [Say DIE a dem]

diagnose *verb* (**diagnoses**, **diagnosed**, **diagnosing**) make a diagnosis of (a disease, a mechanical fault, etc.) from its symptoms: *the test can diagnose a variety of malfunctions* ◊ *the illness was diagnosed as cancer* ◊ *he has recently been diagnosed with angina* ◊ *she was diagnosed as a diabetic*. [Say die ug NOCE]

diagnosis *noun* (*plural* **diagnoses**) **1** the identification of an illness or disease by means of a patient's symptoms: *early diagnosis is essential* ◊ *a diagnosis of Crohn's disease was made*. **2** a conclusion reached from analysis of a problem or situation: *it's hardly a hasty diagnosis to say the Blue Jays choked*. [Say die ig NO sis for the singular, die ig NO seez for the plural]

diagnostic *adjective* of or assisting diagnosis. ▶**diagnostically** *adverb* **diagnostician** *noun* [Say die ig NOSS tick, die ig noss TISH un]

diagnostics *noun* **1** (treated as *plural*) Computing programs and other mechanisms used to detect and identify faults in hardware or software. **2** (treated as *singular*) the science or study of diagnosing disease. [Say die ig NOSS ticks]

diagonal • *adjective* **1** crossing a straight-sided figure from corner to corner. **2** oblique. • *noun* a line joining two non-adjacent corners. ▶**diagonally** *adverb*

diagram • *noun* **1** a drawing showing the general scheme or outline of an object and its parts. **2** a graphic representation of the course or results of an action or process. **3** Math a figure made of lines used in proving a theorem etc. • *verb* (**diagrams**, **diagrammed**, **diagramming**) represent by means of a diagram.

diagrammatic *adjective* in the form of a diagram. [Say die a gruh MAT ick]

dial • *noun* **1** the face of a clock or watch, marked to show the hours etc. **2** a similar flat plate marked with a scale for measuring weight, volume, pressure, consumption, etc., indicated by a pointer. **3** a movable disc on a telephone which is rotated for each digit of a number being called. **4 a** a rotating knob or button on a radio or television set for selecting wavelength or channel. **b** a similar selecting device on other equipment, e.g. a washing machine. **5** television or radio broadcasting: *a new program on the dial*. • *verb* (**dials**, **dialed** or **dialled**, **dialing** or **dialling**) **1** make a telephone call to: *dialed 911*. **2** (often foll. by *up*) (of a modem) connect with (another modem).

dialect *noun* **1** a form of speech peculiar to a particular region. **2** a subordinate variety of a language with non-standard vocabulary, pronunciation, or grammar. ▶**dialectal** *adjective*

dialectic *noun* **1** Philosophy a method of discovering the truth of ideas by discussion and logical argument and by considering ideas that are opposed to each other. **2** the existence or action of opposing forces or tendencies in society etc.

dialectical *adjective* **1** relating to the logical discussion of ideas and opinions: *dialectical ingenuity*. **2** concerned with or acting through opposing forces: *a dialectical opposition between social convention and individual liberties*. ▶**dialectically** *adverb*

dialectical materialism *noun* the Marxist theory (adopted as the official philosophy of the Soviet communists) that political and historical events result from a conflict of social forces and are interpretable as a series of contradictions and their solutions. The conflict is seen as caused by material needs.

dialectics *noun* (treated as *singular* or *plural*) = DIALECTIC 1.

dialectologist *noun* a linguist who studies dialects. [Say die a leck TOLLA jist]

dialectology *noun* the study of dialects. [Say die a leck TOLLA jee]

dialer *noun* (also **dialler**) **1** an electronic device which dials phone numbers automatically. **2** a person who dials a telephone.

dialogue • *noun* **1 a** a conversation between two or more people. **b** conversation in written form, esp. between characters in a novel, play etc. **2 a** discussion or diplomatic contact between representatives of different nations, blocs, etc. **b** the exchange of proposals, valuable or constructive communication, etc. between different groups. **3** a conversation; a talk. • *verb* (**dialogues**, **dialogued**, **dialoguing**) take part in a dialogue; converse.

dial tone *noun* an uninterrupted telephone tone indicating that a caller may start to dial.

dial-up *adjective* pertaining to or designating a data transmission link that uses the telephone system.

dialysis *noun* (*plural* **dialyses**) **1** the separation of particles in a liquid by differences in their ability to pass through a membrane into another liquid. **2** the purification of blood, e.g. of a person with inadequately functioning kidneys, by this technique. [Say die ALA sis for the singular, die ALA seez for the plural]

D

diameter *noun* **1** a straight line passing from side to side through the centre of a circle or sphere. **2** the length of this line. [Say die AMMA tur]

diametrical *adjective* **1** of or along a diameter. **2** (of difference etc.) complete, like that between opposite ends of a diameter: *he's the diametrical opposite of Gabriel*. ▶ **diametrically** *adverb* [Say die a METRICAL]

diamond • *noun* **1 a** a usu. colourless or lightly tinted precious stone of great brilliance and hardness, used in jewellery and for cutting and abrading. **b** a piece of jewellery set with one or more diamonds. **2** a rhombus placed with its diagonals horizontal and vertical. **3** *Baseball* **a** the space delimited by the bases. **b** the entire field. **4 a** a playing card of a suit denoted by a red rhombus. **b** (in *plural*) this suit. • *adjective* **1** made of or set with diamonds or a diamond. **2** rhombus-shaped.

diamond anniversary *noun* (*plural* **diamond anniversaries**) the 60th (or 75th) anniversary of a wedding, graduation, etc.

diamondback *noun* **1** an edible freshwater turtle native to North America, with lozenge-shaped markings on its shell. **2** a North American rattlesnake with diamond-shaped markings.

diamond in the rough *noun* a person, place, or thing having many good qualities though lacking refinement, manners, or style.

diamond willow *noun* **1** a willow found across Canada, with a diamond pattern, caused by fungi, on the bark and wood. **2** the timber from such a willow.

diaper • *noun* a piece of folded cloth or disposable absorbent material wrapped around a baby's bottom to absorb and retain urine and feces. • *verb* put a diaper on (a baby).

diaper rash *noun* (*plural* **diaper rashes**) redness and irritation of a baby's skin around the genitals or buttocks, caused by contact with wet diapers.

diaphanous *adjective* (of fabric etc.) light and delicate, and almost transparent: *was wearing a diaphanous nightgown*. [Say die AFFA nuss]

diaphragm *noun* **1** a muscular, dome-shaped partition which separates the thorax from the abdomen, and whose contraction leads to expansion of the lungs in respiration. **2** a thin, dome-shaped device of rubber placed over the cervix before intercourse to prevent conception. **3** a vibrating disc or cone producing sound waves, e.g. in telephone receivers, loudspeakers, etc. **4** a thin sheet of material used as a partition, esp. in a tube or pipe. **5** a device for varying the effective aperture of the lens in a camera etc. **6** a partition in animal and plant tissues. [Say DIE a fram]

diarist *noun* a person who keeps a diary. [Say DIE a rist]

diarrhea *noun* (also esp. *Brit.* **diarrhoea**) **1** a condition of excessively frequent and loose bowel movements. **2** watery or semi-liquid feces characteristic of this condition. ▶ **diarrheal** *adjective* [Say die a REE uh]

diary *noun* (*plural* **diaries**) **1** a daily written record of events, feelings, or thoughts. **2** a book for this or for noting future engagements, usu. printed and with a calendar and other information.

Diaspora *noun* **1** (**the Diaspora**) **a** the dispersion of the Jews among the Gentiles, mainly in the 8th–6th centuries BC. **b** Jews dispersed in this way. **c** Jews or Jewish communities outside the state of Israel. **2** (also **diaspora**, *plural* **diasporas**) **a** any group of people similarly dispersed: *one should not treat the people of China and the Chinese diaspora as one cultural entity*. **b** their dispersion: *the names on the headstones bear silent witness to the diaspora of the Red River Metis*. [Say ASPER uh]

diatom *noun* a microscopic single-celled alga which has a cell wall of silica. [Say DIE a tum]

diatomaceous earth *noun* a soft, fine-grained deposit composed of fossil diatoms, used as a filter, filler, etc., in various manufacturing processes, and as an insecticide in gardening. [Say die a tuh MAY shuss]

diatonic *adjective* *Music* **1** (of a scale, interval, etc.) involving only notes proper to the prevailing key without chromatic alteration. **2** (of a melody or harmony) constructed from such a scale. [Say die a TONIC]

diatribe *noun* a forceful and bitter verbal attack against something: *she storms out with a diatribe against male chauvinism*.

diazepam *noun* a tranquilizing muscle-relaxant drug with anticonvulsant properties used to relieve anxiety, tension, etc. Also called VALIUM. [Say die AZZA pam]

diazinon *noun* an insecticide derived from pyrimidine. [Say die AZZA non]

dibber *noun* (also **dibble**) a hand-held tool with a pointed end, used for making holes in the ground for seeds or young plants.

dibs *plural noun slang* a first claim or option to use or have something: *I have first dibs on that book*.

WRITING TIP
dice, die

Although historically **dice** is the plural of **die**, in modern standard English **dice** is both the singular and the plural, so that *Throw the dice* could refer to either one **die** or more than one **dice**.

---

dice • *plural noun* **1 a** small cubes usu. made of plastic or wood, marked on each side with 1–6 spots, used in games and gambling. **b** (treated as *singular*) one of these cubes (see DIE²). **2** a game played with one or more such cubes. **3** food cut into small cubes for cooking. • *verb* (**dices**, **diced**, **dicing**) **1** cut (food) into small cubes. **2 a** play or gamble with dice. **b** take great risks, gamble: *dicing with death*. PHRASES **no dice** *slang* no success or luck.

dicer *noun* **1** an appliance for dicing vegetables etc. **2** a person who plays or gambles with dice.

dicey *adjective* (**dicier**, **diciest**) *slang* risky; uncertain.

dichotomous *adjective* exhibiting or characterized by a division or contrast between two things that are or are represented as being opposed or entirely different: *the city of Victoria has a dichotomous character, a mixture of the genteel and the great outdoors*. [Say die COTTA miss]

dichotomy *noun* (*plural* **dichotomies**) **1** a division or contrast between two things that are or are represented as being opposed or entirely different: *a dichotomy between rich and poor*. **2** *Botany* repeated branching into two equal parts. [Say die COTTA me]

dick *noun slang* a detective.

dickens *noun informal* (esp. in exclamations) the Devil: *what the dickens are you doing here?*

Dickensian *adjective* **1** of or relating to the English novelist Charles Dickens (1812–70) or his work. **2** resembling or reminiscent of the situations, poor social conditions, or comically repulsive characters described in Dickens's work: *the couple grew up in Dickensian circumstances in London's east end*. [Say duh KENZY un]

dicker *verb* bargain; haggle.

dicot *noun* = DICOTYLEDON. [Say DIE cot]

dicotyledon *noun* any flowering plant having two cotyledons (seed leaves). Dicotyledons constitute the larger of the two great divisions of flowering plants, and typically have broad stalked leaves with net-like veins (e.g. daisies, oaks). ▶ **dicotyledonous** *adjective* [Say die cotta LEE din, die cotta LEE din us]

dicta *plural* of DICTUM.

Dictaphone *noun* proprietary a machine for recording and playing back dictated words.

dictate • *verb* (**dictates, dictated, dictating**) **1** say or read aloud (words to be written down or recorded). **2** tell someone what to do, esp. with no consideration for their wishes: *the czar's attempts to dictate policy* ◊ *they are in no position to dictate terms* ◊ *what right do they have to dictate how we live our lives?* ◊ *I will not be dictated to.* **3** control or influence how something happens: *when we take our vacations is very much dictated by Greg's work schedule* ◊ *it's generally your job that dictates where you live now* ◊ *we can make changes as circumstances dictate.* • *noun* (usu. in *plural*) an order, rule, or command that must be obeyed: *the dictates of conscience* ◊ *the dictates of fashion.*

dictation *noun* **1 a** the saying of words to be written down or recorded: *does your secretary take dictation?* **b** the activity of taking down a passage that is read aloud by a teacher as a test of spelling, writing, or language skills: *always hated French dictations.* **c** the material that is dictated. **2** the action of giving orders authoritatively or categorically.

dictator *noun* **1** a ruler with unrestricted authority, esp. one who suppresses or succeeds a democratic government. **2** a domineering person: *her father was a dictator and the whole family was afraid of him.*

dictatorial *adjective* **1** of or typical of a ruler with total power: *a dictatorial regime.* **2** tending to tell people what to do in an autocratic way: *his dictatorial manner.* ▶ **dictatorially** *adverb* [Say dicta TORY ul]

dictatorship *noun* **1** a state ruled by a dictator. **2 a** the position, rule, or period of rule of a dictator. **b** rule by a dictator. [Say dick TATER ship]

diction *noun* **1** the manner of clearly pronouncing vowels and consonants in speaking etc.: *John was constantly trying to improve his singers' diction.* **2** the choice of words or phrases in speech etc.: *Wordsworth rejected poetic diction in favour of ordinary language.*

dictionary *noun* (*plural* **dictionaries**) **1** a book that lists (usu. in alphabetical order) and explains the words of a language or gives equivalent words in another language. **2** a reference book on any subject, the items of which are arranged in alphabetical order.

dictum *noun* (*plural* **dicta** or **dictums**) **1** a formal pronouncement from an authoritative source. **2** a saying or maxim: *the old dictum, "Might is right".*

did *past of* DO[1].

didactic *adjective* **1** intended to teach, particularly in having moral instruction as an ulterior motive: *a didactic novel that set out to expose social injustice* ◊ *didactic poetry.* **2** in the manner of a teacher, particularly so as to treat someone in a patronizing way: *the immediate emotional and intellectual impact of visual images is lost in his didactic prose style.* ▶ **didactically** *adverb* **didacticism** *noun* [Say die DACK tick, die DACTA sism]

diddle *verb* (**diddles, diddled, diddling**) *informal* **1** cheat, swindle. **2** (often foll. by *with*) adjust; toy with: *diddled with the controls.* **3** waste time. ▶ **diddler** *noun*

diddly *noun* (also **diddley**) *slang* = DIDDLY-SQUAT.

diddly-squat *noun* (also **diddley-squat**) *slang* **1** (with *neg.*) anything, the least bit: *doesn't mean diddly-squat to me.* **2** nothing at all.

didn't *contraction* did not.

---

die[1] *verb* (**dies, died, dying**) **1** cease to live: *died of hunger.* **2 a** come to an end: *the project died within six months.* **b** break down: *the engine died.* **c** (of a flame) go out. **3** be exhausted or tormented: *nearly died of*

boredom. **4** *informal* be overcome with embarrassment, laughter, etc.: *nearly died when she said that.* **5** suffer (a specified death): *died a natural death.* PHRASES **be dying** wish for longingly or intently: *am dying to see you.* **die away** become weaker or fainter to the point of extinction. **die back** (of a plant) decay from the tip towards the root. **died and gone to heaven** *informal* having reached a state of supreme bliss. **die down** become less loud or strong. **die hard** die reluctantly, not without a struggle: *old habits die hard.* **die off 1** die one after another until few or none are left. **2** fade away gradually. **die out** become extinct, cease to exist. **never say die** keep up courage, not give in. **to die for** *informal* extremely good or desirable: *chocolate to die for.*

WRITING TIP ✎
die, dice

Although historically **die** is the singular of **dice**, in modern standard English **dice** is both the singular and the plural, so that *Throw the dice* could refer to either one **die** or more than one **dice**.

---

die[2] *noun* **1** singular of DICE *noun* 1a. **2** (*plural* **dies**) **a** an engraved device for stamping a design on coins, medals, etc. **b** a device for stamping, cutting, or moulding material into a particular shape. **c** an internally threaded hollow tool for cutting a screw thread. PHRASES **as straight** (or **true**) **as a die 1** quite straight. **2** entirely honest or loyal. **the die is cast** an irrevocable step has been taken.

dieback *noun* the progressive dying back of a shrub or tree shoot owing to disease or unfavourable conditions.

die-cast *adjective* formed by pouring molten metal into a reusable mold: *die-cast model cars.*

die-casting *noun* the process or product of casting from metal moulds.

dieffenbachia *noun* a tropical American evergreen plant of the arum family, often grown as a houseplant and having poisonous sap which can cause loss of the power of speech or death. [Say dee fin BACKY uh]

diehard • *noun* a conservative or stubborn person. • *adjective* **1** resolutely opposing change. **2** staunchly loyal: *a diehard fan.*

die-off *noun* a sharp decline in a natural population, due to some factor other than human intervention.

diesel *noun* **1** (also **diesel engine**) an internal combustion engine in which the heat produced by the compression of air in the cylinder ignites the fuel. **2** a vehicle driven by a diesel engine. **3** (also **diesel fuel**) a petroleum product used as fuel in diesel engines. [Say DEEZ ul]

diet[1] • *noun* **1** the kinds of food that a person or animal habitually eats. **2** a special course of food to which a person is restricted, esp. for medical reasons or to control weight. **3** a regular occupation or series of activities to which one is restricted or which form one's main concern, usu. for a purpose: *a diet of light reading and fresh air.* • *verb* (**diets, dieted, dieting**) restrict oneself to small amounts or special kinds of food, esp. to control one's weight. • *adjective* suitable for consumption by someone on a special (esp. calorie-reduced) diet: *diet pop.*

diet[2] *noun* a legislative assembly in certain countries, e.g. Japan.

dietary *adjective* of, relating to, or provided by diet. [Say DIE a terry]

dietary fibre *noun* the part of a foodstuff that cannot be digested or absorbed; roughage.

dieter *noun* a person who is trying to lose weight on a diet.

dietetic *adjective* **1** of or relating to diet: *dietetic advice.*

2 (of foodstuffs, etc.) suitable for a specific (esp. calorie-reduced) diet: *dietetic candies*. [Say die a TET ick]

dietetics *plural noun* (usu. treated as *singular*) the scientific study of diet and nutrition. [Say die a TET icks]

dietitian *noun* (also **dietician**) an expert in dietetics. [Say die a TISH in]

diff *noun informal* difference: *what's the diff?*

SPELL CHECK
differ, defer

To put something off is to **defer** it.

---

differ *verb* **1** (often foll. by *from*) be unlike or distinguishable. **2** disagree: *I have to differ with you on that* ◊ *medical opinion differs as to how to treat the disease.*

SPELL CHECK ABC
difference, deference

Respect or consideration is **deference**: *In deference to one of the guests, who was a vegetarian, we did not serve meat.*

---

difference *noun* **1** the state or condition of being different or unlike. **2** a point in which things differ; a distinction. **3** a degree of unlikeness. **4 a** the quantity by which amounts differ: *make up the difference*. **b** the remainder left after subtraction. **5 a** a disagreement, quarrel, or dispute. **b** the grounds of disagreement: *put aside their differences.* PHRASES **make a** (or **all the** etc.) **difference** (often foll. by *to*) have a significant effect or influence (on a person, situation, etc.). **make no difference** (often foll. by *to*) have no effect (on a person, situation, etc.). **with a difference** having a new or unusual feature.

WRITING TIP
different, very different

Instead of saying that something is **different** or **very different**, try to use more precise and interesting adjectives to describe things:

diverse/dissimilar/varying tastes
contrasting/inconsistent/incompatible styles
opposing/differing/disparate views
a **changed/altered/modified** form
three **separate/distinct/discrete** categories
a collection of **assorted/miscellaneous/various/sundry** items
her music is **unusual/distinctive/unconventional**

---

different *adjective* **1** (often foll. by *from*, *than*) unlike, distinguishable in nature, form, or quality (from another). **2** distinct, separate; not the same one. **3** *informal* unusual: *wanted to do something different*.

GRAMMAR CHECK ⚠
different from/than

Although **different from** is often considered the most acceptable construction in sentences like *Cars are different from boats*, it is both common and acceptable to use **different than**, as in *Cars are different than boats*. **Different than** is even more widely accepted in comparisons where a clause rather than a noun follows **than**, as in *Donna is a different person than she was a year ago*, which is shorter than the alternative, *Donna is a different person from the one she was a year ago*.

---

differential *adjective* of, exhibiting, or depending on

a difference: *the differential treatment of prisoners based on sex and social class* ◊ *differential rates of pay*. • *noun* **1** difference in the amount, value or size of something, especially the difference in rates of pay for people doing different work in the same industry or profession: *other statistics suggest that regional policies are no longer able to cope with highly resistant unemployment or income differentials*. **2** *Math* an infinitesimal difference between successive values of a variable. **3** (also **differential gear**) a gear allowing power to be divided between two axles in line with one another and able to rotate at different speeds, e.g. when a vehicle corners. ▶ **differentially** *adverb* [Say diffa REN shull]

differential calculus *noun* a branch of mathematics concerned with the determination, properties, and application of derivatives and differentials (*compare* INTEGRAL CALCULUS).

differential equation *noun* an equation involving derivatives of a function or functions.

differentiate *verb* (**differentiates**, **differentiated**, **differentiating**) **1** be the particular thing that shows that things or people are not the same: *the male's yellow beak differentiates it from the female* ◊ *little now differentiates the firm's products from its rivals*. **2** find differences: *it's difficult to differentiate between the two varieties* ◊ *I can't differentiate one variety from another*. **3** make or become different in the process of growth or development: *the receptors are developed and differentiated into sense organs*. **4** *Math* transform (a function) into its derivative. ▶ **differentiated** *adjective* **differentiation** *noun* [Say diffa REN shee ate]

differently *adverb* in a different way or in different ways.

differing *adjective* that are not the same; varying, inconsistent, different: *differing accounts of the incident*.

difficult *adjective* **1 a** needing much effort or skill. **b** troublesome, perplexing. **2 a** not easy to please or satisfy. **b** uncooperative. **3** characterized by hardships or problems: *a difficult period in her life*.

difficulty *noun* (*plural* **difficulties**) **1** the state or condition of being difficult. **2 a** a difficult thing. **b** (often in *plural*) a cause of distress or hardship: *financial difficulties*. PHRASES **make difficulties** be uncooperative. **with difficulty** not easily.

diffidence *noun* modesty or lack of self-confidence; a shy or reserved manner: *she overcame her natural diffidence and addressed the crowd*. [Say DIFFA dince]

diffident *adjective* modest, shy, or reserved because of a lack of self-confidence: *he was at first somewhat diffident about expressing his views* ◊ *a diffident, maidenly woman who spoke little and listened attentively*. ▶ **diffidently** *adverb* [Say DIFFA dint]

diffract *verb Physics* (of the edge of an opaque body, a narrow slit, etc.) break up (a beam of light) into a series of dark or light bands or coloured spectra. ▶ **diffraction** *noun* [Say duh FRACT]

SPELL CHECK ABC
diffuse, defuse

If you make a bomb harmless, you **defuse** it

---

diffuse • *adjective* spread out over a wide area, not concentrated: *these fixtures provide a perfect balance of direct and diffuse light* ◊ *diffuse pain*. • *verb* (**diffuses**, **diffused**, **diffusing**) **1** spread or be spread widely; reach a large area: *the problem is how to diffuse power without creating anarchy* ◊ *technologies diffuse rapidly*. **2** *Physics* become or cause (a fluid, gas, individual atom, etc.) to become intermingled with a substance by movement, typically in a specified direction or at a specified speed: *oxygen molecules diffuse across the*

D

membrane ◊ *gas is diffused into the bladder.* **3** make light shine less brightly by spreading it in many directions: *the moon was fuller than the night before, but the light was diffused by cloud.* ▶**diffused** *adjective* **diffusely** *adverb* [Say dif FYOOSS for the adjective, duh FYOOZ for the verb] **diffuser** *noun* **1** a person or thing that diffuses, esp. a device for diffusing light. **2** a duct for broadening an airflow and reducing its speed. [Say dif FYOOZ ur]

diffusion *noun* **1** the spreading of something more widely: *the diffusion of Marxist ideas.* **2** *Physics & Chemistry* the intermingling of substances by the natural movement of their particles: *the rate of diffusion of a gas.* **3** the spread of elements of culture etc. to another region or people: *the diffusion of immigrants' building traditions in the Canadian Prairies provides a fascinating picture of cultural and architectural assimilation.* **4** the action of spreading light evenly so as to reduce glare and harsh shadows. [Say dif FYOO zhun]

dig • *verb* (**digs, dug, digging**) **1** break up and remove or turn over soil, ground, etc., with a tool, one's hands, (of an animal) claws, etc. **2 a** break up and displace (the ground etc.) in this way. **b** (foll. by *up*) break up the soil of (a piece of land): *dug up the lawn and planted flowers.* **3** make (a hole, grave, tunnel, etc.) by digging. **4** (often foll. by *up*, *out*) **a** obtain or remove by digging or by an action similar to digging: *dug the puck out of the corner.* **b** find or discover after searching. **5** excavate (an archaeological site). **6** *dated slang* like, appreciate, or understand. **7** (often foll. by *in*, *into*) thrust or poke into or down into: *dug its teeth into my leg.* **8** make one's way by digging: *dug through the mountainside.* • *noun* **1** a thrust or poke: *a dig in the ribs.* **2** *informal* a pointed or critical remark: *could not resist a dig at their hometown.* **3** an archaeological excavation. **4** (in *plural*) *informal* lodgings. PHRASES **dig deep 1** draw on one's innermost resources: *dug deep to finish the race.* **2** give generously from one's financial resources: *dug deep to help the flood victims.* **dig in one's heels** be obstinate. **dig in** *informal* begin eating. **dig in** (**oneself**) **in 1** prepare a defensive trench or pit. **2** establish one's position. **dig one's own grave** do something which causes one's own failure or ruin.

Digby chicken *noun* (also **Digby chick**) *Cdn (Maritimes)* a dried or cured herring.

digest • *verb* **1** assimilate (food) in the stomach and bowels. **2** (of food) undergo digestion. **3** understand and assimilate mentally. • *noun* **1** a regular or occasional summary of current literature or news. **2** a methodical summary esp. of a body of laws. ▶**digester** *noun* **digestibility** *noun* **digestible** *adjective*

digestion *noun* **1** the process of digesting. **2** the capacity to digest food: *has weak digestion.*

digestive • *adjective* **1** of or relating to digestion. **2** aiding or promoting digestion. • *noun* **1** a substance that aids digestion. **2** (also **digestive cookie** or **digestive biscuit**) *Cdn & Brit.* a usu. round semi-sweet whole wheat cookie.

digger *noun* **1** a person who digs. **2** a tool or machine for digging. **3** a miner. **4** *informal* a person who works diligently, esp. a hockey player etc.

digit *noun* **1** any numeral from 0 to 9, esp. when forming part of a number. **2** each of a series of these representing increasingly higher powers of ten in a decimal-based numeral: *a six-digit income.* **3** a finger, thumb, or toe.

digital • *adjective* **1** of or relating to a numerical digit or digits. **2** (of a clock, watch, etc.) that gives a reading by means of displayed digits instead of hands. **3 a** (of a computer) operating on data represented as a series of usu. binary digits or in similar discrete form. **b** of or

relating to computers: *the digital age.* **4 a** (of a recording) with sound information represented in digits for more reliable transmission. **b** (of a recording medium) using this process. **5** of or relating to a finger or fingers. • *noun* a digital device, esp. a watch or clock.

digitalis *noun* a drug prepared from the dried leaves of foxgloves and containing substances that stimulate the heart muscle. [Say didge a TALLIS]

digitalize *verb* (**digitalizes, digitalized, digitalizing**) = DIGITIZE.

digitally *adverb* in digital form; in a manner that uses signals or information represented by discrete values of a physical quantity such as voltage or magnetic polarization: *digitally remastered tapes.*

digitization *noun* the conversion of data etc. into digital form.

digitize *verb* (**digitizes, digitized, digitizing**) convert (data etc.) into digital form. ▶**digitizer** *noun*

dignified *adjective* **1** having or expressing dignity. **2** noble or stately in appearance or manner.

dignify *verb* (**dignifies, dignified, dignifying**) **1** give dignity or distinction to. **2** give a pretentious name to (something unworthy or unimportant): *it is a misnomer to dignify such works with the term Art.* **3** represent or treat as worthy: *will not dignify you with an answer.*

dignitary *noun* (*plural* **dignitaries**) a person holding high rank or office.

dignity *noun* (*plural* **dignities**) **1** a composed and serious manner or style. **2** the state of being worthy of honour or respect. **3** worthiness, excellence. **4** a high or honourable rank or position. **5** high regard or estimation. PHRASES **beneath one's dignity** not considered worthy enough for one to do. **stand on one's dignity** insist (esp. by one's manner) on being treated with due respect.

digress *verb* (**digresses, digressed, digressing**) depart from the main subject temporarily in speech or writing. ▶**digression** *noun* **digressive** *adjective* [Say die GRESS]

digs *plural noun see* DIG *noun* 4.

Dijon mustard *noun* a mild mustard paste using brown and black varieties of seed blended with white wine. [Say dee ZHON or DEE zhon]

dike • *noun* **1** a long wall etc. built to prevent flooding. **2** a ditch or artificial watercourse. **3** a barrier or obstacle; a defence. • *verb* (**dikes, diked, diking**) provide or defend with a dike or dikes.

dilapidated *adjective* in a state of disrepair or ruin as a result of age or neglect: *dilapidated shacks.* [Say duh LAPPA dated]

dilapidation *noun* a state of disrepair or ruin: *was distressed at the dilapidation of their ancestral home.* [Say duh lappa DAY sh'n]

dilatation *noun* **1** the widening or expansion of a hollow organ or cavity. **2** the process of dilating. [Say die luh TAY sh'n]

dilatation and curettage *noun* = D. AND C.

dilate *verb* (**dilates, dilated, dilating**) **1** make or become wider or larger (esp. of an opening in the body): *dilated pupils* ◊ *her eyes dilated with fear* ◊ *red wine can help to dilate blood vessels.* **2** speak or write at length: *fortunate indeed are those who do not have to listen to some boomer gasbag dilate on the excellences of their generation.* ▶**dilation** *noun* [Say DIE late or die LATE, die LAY sh'n]

dilatory *adjective* slow to act or causing delay: *the tenant was somewhat dilatory in making his monthly payments* ◊ *an incompetent and dilatory leadership* ◊ *dilatory procedural tactics in the legislature.* [Say DILLA tory]

dilemma *noun* **1** a situation in which a choice has to be made between two or more equally undesirable alternatives. **2** a difficult situation.

D

dilettante *noun* a person who cultivates an area of interest, such as the arts, superficially, without real commitment or knowledge: *I cringed at the likelihood that since I was not paid, men would see me as a dilettante ◊ a dilettante architect.* ▶ **dilettantism** *noun* [Say DILLA tont]

diligence *noun* careful and persistent work or effort: *she shows great diligence in her school work ◊ the captain exercised all reasonable diligence to prevent the ship from sinking.* [Say DILLA jince]

diligent *adjective* having or showing care and conscientiousness in one's work or duties: *after diligent searching, he found the parcel ◊ a diligent student.* ▶ **diligently** *adverb* [Say DILLA jint]

dill *noun* **1** a herb with yellow flowers and aromatic seeds. **2** the leaves or seeds of this plant used for flavouring etc.

dillweed *noun* the leaves of the dill plant used as a seasoning.

dilly *noun* (*plural* **dillies**) *informal* a remarkable or excellent person or thing.

dilly-dally *verb* (**dilly-dallies**, **dilly-dallied**, **dilly-dallying**) *informal* waste time through aimless wandering or indecision: *don't dilly-dally for too long*.

dilute • *verb* (**dilutes**, **diluted**, **diluting**) **1** reduce the strength of (a fluid) by adding water or another solvent. **2** make something weaker or less effective: *large classes dilute the quality of education that children receive.* • *adjective* **1** (esp. of a fluid) diluted, weakened. **2** (of a colour) washed out; low in saturation. **3** *Chemistry* (of a substance) in solution: *dilute sulphuric acid.* ▶ **diluted** *adjective* **dilution** *noun*

dim • *adjective* (**dimmer**, **dimmest**) **1 a** only faintly luminous or visible; not bright. **b** obscure; ill-defined. **2** not clearly perceived or remembered. **3** *informal* stupid; slow to understand. **4** (of the eyes) not seeing clearly. **5** not likely to succeed or happen: *a dim chance.* • *verb* (**dims**, **dimmed**, **dimming**) **1** make or become dim or less bright. **2** lower the beam of (a vehicle's headlights) to reduce dazzle. PHRASES **take a dim view of** *informal* **1** disapprove of. **2** feel gloomy about.

dime *noun* **1** a ten-cent coin. **2** a small amount of money. PHRASES **a dime a dozen** very cheap or commonplace. **on a dime** *informal* **1** within a small area or short distance. **2** quickly, instantly.

dimension • *noun* **1** a measurable extent of any kind, as length, breadth, depth, area, and volume. **2** (in *plural*) size, scope, extent. **3** an aspect or facet of a situation, problem, etc. **4** *Algebra* one of a number of unknown or variable quantities contained as factors in a product: x^3, x^2y, xyz, are all of three dimensions. ▶ **dimensional** *adjective* (also *in combination*) **dimensionality** *noun* **dimensionless** *adverb* **dimensionless** *adjective*

dimer *noun* *Chemistry* a compound consisting of two identical molecules linked together. [Say DIE mur]

dime store *noun* **1** = FIVE-AND-DIME STORE. **2** (**dime-store**) (as an *adjective*) **a** bought at a dime store. **b** cheap, of poor quality: *dime-store psychology*.

diminish *verb* (**diminishes**, **diminished**, **diminishing**) **1** make or become smaller or less. **2** make someone or something seem less impressive or valuable: *I don't wish to diminish the importance of their contribution.* PHRASES **law of diminishing returns** the fact that an increase in expenditure, investment, taxation, etc., beyond a certain point ceases to produce a proportionate yield.

diminished *adjective* reduced; made smaller or less.

diminishment *noun* decrease in size, extent, or influence.

diminuendo *noun* *Music* (*plural* **diminuendos**) **1** a gradual decrease in loudness. **2** a passage to be performed with such a decrease. [Say dim in yoo EN doe]

diminution *noun* a reduction in the size, extent, or importance of something: *a diminution in value ◊ with wisdom comes a diminution of passion.* [Say dim in YOO sh'n]

diminutive • *adjective* **1** very small: *a diminutive figure dressed in black.* **2** (of a word or suffix) implying smallness, either actual or suggesting affection, scorn, etc.: *-ette is a diminutive ending.* • *noun* **1** a word or suffix indicating that something is small. **2** a short informal form of a word, especially a name: *"Kate" is a common diminutive of "Katherine".* [Say duh MIN you tiv]

dimly *adverb* **1** with little light or brightness; faintly: *a dimly lit room.* **2** with little clarity; vaguely: *I was dimly aware of her situation.*

dimmer *noun* (also **dimmer switch**, *plural* **dimmer switches**) a device for varying the brightness of an electric light.

dimness *noun* lack of light or brightness.

dimple • *noun* **1** a small hollow or dent in the flesh, esp. in the cheeks or chin. **2** a round depression, e.g. in a golf ball. • *verb* (**dimples**, **dimpled**, **dimpling**) **1** produce or show dimples. **2** produce dimples in (a cheek etc.). **3** make a dent or depression in (a piece of sheet metal, the surface of a body of water, etc.). ▶ **dimpled** *adjective* **dimply** *adjective*

dim sum *noun* an assortment of small Chinese dumplings with various savoury fillings.

dim-wit *noun* *informal* a stupid person. ▶ **dim-witted** *adjective*

din • *noun* a prolonged loud and distracting noise. • *verb* (**dins**, **dinned**, **dinning**) **1** (foll. by *into*) instill (something) by constant repetition: *a runner-up, he dinned into them, was a loser.* **2** make a din: *the sound dinning in my ears was the telephone ringing.*

dine *verb* (**dines**, **dined**, **dining**) **1** eat dinner. **2** give dinner to. PHRASES **dine out 1** have dinner away from home. **2** (foll. by *on*) be entertained to dinner etc. because of (one's ability to relate an interesting event, story, etc.).

diner *noun* **1** a person who dines. **2** a small restaurant, esp. serving short-order food. **3** a railway carriage equipped as a restaurant.

dinette *noun* **1** a small room or part of a room used for eating meals. **2** a table and chairs for this. [Say die NET]

ding[1] • *verb* make a ringing sound. • *noun* a ringing sound, as of a bell.

ding[2] *informal* • *noun* a dent: *has a ding in the fender.* • *verb* **1** make a dent in: *dinged my car.* **2** hit: *dinged myself on the hip.* **3** make to pay (esp. an excessive or unjustified amount): *travellers are now being dinged with a fuel surtax.*

ding-a-ling • *noun* **1** the sound of a bell or bells. **2** *informal* a crazy or stupid person: *he's a real ding-a-ling.* • *adjective* crazy, eccentric: *what a ding-a-ling idea.*

dingbat *noun* *informal* a stupid or eccentric person.

ding-dong • *noun* **1** the sound of alternate chimes, as of two bells. **2** a crazy or stupid person. • *adjective* crazy: *a ding-dong idea.*

dinghy *noun* (*plural* **dinghies**) any of various small boats, esp. an inflatable boat for emergency use. [Say DING ee]

dingo *noun* (*plural* **dingoes**) a wild or half-domesticated Australian dog, *Canis dingo*.

SPELL CHECK	ABC ✓
dingy, dinghy	
A small boat is a **dinghy**.	

dingy *adjective* (**dingier**, **dingiest**) **1** dirty-looking. **2** drab. **3** lacking light. [Say DIN jee]

dining *noun* the action of eating dinner.

dining room *noun* a room in which meals are eaten.

dink[1] *noun* *slang* **1** the penis. **2** a foolish, stupid, or obnoxious person.

dink² *noun slang* **1** a well-off young working couple with no children. **2** either partner of this.

dinky *adjective* (**dinkier, dinkiest**) *informal* trifling, insignificant.

dinner *noun* **1** the main meal of the day. **2** a formal meal, often in honour of a person or event. PHRASES **done like dinner** *Cdn & Austral. informal* utterly defeated.

dinner theatre *noun* **1** a theatre in which dinner, included in the price of the ticket, is served usu. before the performance. **2** the type of theatre performed in such a place.

dinnertime *noun* the time at which dinner is customarily eaten.

dino *noun* (*plural* **dinos**) *informal* a dinosaur: *dino tracks*.

dinosaur *noun* **1** an extinct reptile of the Mesozoic era, often of enormous size. **2** a person or thing that has not adapted to new conditions: *sees the US as a social and political dinosaur ◊ many of the dinosaur backbench Tory MPs will vote against the bill.* PHRASES **go the way of the dinosaur** become obsolete or extinct.

dint • *noun* a dent. • *verb* mark with dints. PHRASES **by dint of** by force or means of: *she succeeded by dint of hard work.*

diocesan • *adjective* of or concerning a diocese. • *noun* the bishop of a diocese. [Say die OSSA sin or die OSSA zin]

diocese *noun* a district under the pastoral care of a bishop. [Say DIE a seez or DIE a sis]

diode *noun* *Electronics* a semiconductor allowing the flow of current in one direction only and having two terminals. [Say DIE ode]

diorama *noun* **1** a scenic painting in which changes in colour and direction of illumination simulate a sunrise etc. **2** a representation of a scene with three-dimensional figures, often against a painted background. **3** a small-scale model or film set. [Say die a RAMA]

dioxide *noun* an oxide containing two atoms of oxygen which are not linked together. [Say die OXIDE]

dioxin *noun* any of a class of cyclic compounds produced as chemical by-products, esp. the highly toxic tetrachlorodibenzoparadioxin (TCDD). [Say die OXIN]

dip • *verb* (**dips, dipped, dipping**) **1** put or let down briefly into liquid etc.; immerse. **2 a** go below a surface or level. **b** (of a level of income, activity, etc.) decline slightly, esp. briefly. **3** take or have a downward slope: *the road dips.* **4** go under water and emerge quickly. **5** (foll. by *into*) **a** read briefly from (a book etc.). **b** take a cursory interest in (a subject). **6** (foll. by *into*) **a** put a hand, ladle, etc., into a container to take something out. **b** spend from or make use of one's resources: *dipped into our savings.* **7** lower or be lowered, esp. in salute. **8** (often foll. by *up, out of*) remove or scoop up (liquid, grain, etc., or something from liquid). • *noun* **1** an act of dipping or being dipped. **2** a liquid into which something is dipped. **3** a brief swim. **4** a brief downward slope, followed by an upward one, in a road etc. **5** a usu. thick sauce into which food is dipped before eating. **6** an item of food, esp. a sandwich, served with a dipping sauce: *beef dip.* **7** an ice cream cone dipped in melted chocolate etc. **8** a depression or hollow. **9** *Astronomy & Surveying* the apparent depression of the horizon from the line of observation, due to the curvature of the earth. **10 a** the angle made with the horizontal at any point by the earth's magnetic field. **b** the downward inclination of the needle in a magnetic compass etc. **11** *slang* a foolish or bumbling person.

diphtheria *noun* an acute infectious bacterial disease with inflammation of a mucous membrane esp. of the throat, resulting in the formation of a false membrane causing difficulty in breathing and swallowing. [Say dif THEERY uh or dip THEERY uh]

diphthong *noun* **1** a speech sound in one syllable in which the articulation begins as for one vowel and moves as for another (as in *coin, loud,* and *side*). **2** a pair of vowels representing the sound of a diphthong or single vowel (as in *feat*). [Say DIF thong or DIP thong]

diploid *Biology* • *adjective* (of an organism or cell) having two complete sets of chromosomes per cell. • *noun* a diploid cell or organism. [Say DIP loyd]

diploma *noun* **1** a certificate awarded for passing an examination, completing a course of study, etc. **2** the qualification conferred with a diploma.

diplomacy *noun* **1 a** the management of international relations by negotiation. **b** expertise in this. **2** skill or tact in dealing with people etc.

diplomat *noun* **1** a person engaged by a government to conduct official negotiations with other countries; a member of a diplomatic service. **2** a tactful person.

diplomatic *adjective* **1 a** of or involved in diplomacy. **b** skilled in diplomacy. **2** tactful; skilful in personal relations. ▶ **diplomatically** *adverb*

diplomatic immunity *noun* the exemption of diplomatic staff abroad from arrest, taxation, etc.

dipolar *adjective* consisting of two equal and oppositely charged or magnetized poles separated by a distance. [Say die POLAR]

dipole *noun* **1** *Physics* two equal and oppositely charged or magnetized poles separated by a distance. **2** *Chemistry* a molecule in which a concentration of positive charges is separated from a concentration of negative charges. **3** (also **dipole antenna**) an antenna composed of two equal straight rods mounted in line with one another and having an electrical connection in the centre. [Say DIE pole]

dipper *noun* **1** any of several stocky short-tailed songbirds which habitually bob up and down, are commonly found in fast-flowing streams, and swim and walk under water to feed. **2** a ladle. **3** an item of food suitable for dipping, e.g. a potato chip, a raw vegetable, etc. **4** *Cdn* (*Nfld & PEI*) a small, lidless saucepan with a long handle.

dippy *adjective* (**dippier, dippiest**) *informal* foolish or unintelligent.

dipstick *noun* **1** a graduated rod for measuring the depth of a liquid, esp. in a vehicle's engine. **2** a chemically sensitive stick or strip of paper etc. dipped into a liquid (esp. a urine sample) for diagnostic purposes. **3** *slang* a foolish or inept person; an idiot.

dipsy-doodle esp. *Cdn slang* • *verb* (**dipsy-doodles, dipsy-doodled, dipsy-doodling**) esp. *Hockey* evade the defending team by using feints, dekes, swerving motions, and finesse in stickhandling etc. • *noun* **1** an evasive movement of this type. **2** a tactic designed to confuse, evade, or outwit opponents or competitors.

dipterous *adjective* **1** of or relating to the insect order Diptera, whose members have two membranous wings, e.g. houseflies, mosquitoes, etc. **2** *Botany* having two wing-like appendages. [Say DIPTER us]

dire *adjective* (**direr, direst**) **1 a** calamitous, dreadful: *dire straits.* **b** ominous: *dire warnings.* **2** urgent: *in dire need.*

direct • *adjective* **1 a** extending or moving in a straight line or by the shortest route. **b** (of a journey) not involving any changes of airplane, train, etc. **2 a** straightforward. **b** frank. **3** without intermediaries or the intervention of other factors: *the direct result ◊ direct sunlight.* **4** (of descent) lineal, not collateral. **5** exact, complete, greatest possible (esp. where contrast is implied): *the direct opposite.* **6** (of a quotation, translation, etc.) literal; word for word.

• *adverb* **1** in a direct way or manner; without an intermediary or intervening factor: *buy direct from the manufacturer.* **2** by a direct route: *send it direct to head office.* • *verb* **1** guide, esp. with advice. **2** control the movement of: *directing traffic.* **3** administer, oversee. **4** give a formal order or command to: *directed her to leave immediately.* **5 a** address or give indications for the delivery of (a letter etc.). **b** tell or show (a person) the way to a destination. **6 a** point, aim, or cause (a blow or missile) to move in a certain direction. **b** aim or address (one's attention, energies, communication, etc.). **7 a** supervise the performing, staging, etc., of (a film, play, etc.). **b** supervise the performance of (an actor etc.). **8** conduct (a group of musicians).

direct access *noun* = RANDOM ACCESS.

direct current *noun* an electric current flowing in one direction only. Abbreviation: **DC, d.c.**

direct debit *noun Cdn & Brit.* **1** an arrangement, authorized by the holder of an account in a bank etc., for the regular debiting of the account at the request of the payee. **2** payment by means of a debit card, in which funds are transferred electronically from the cardholder's bank account to the account of a merchant etc.

direct deposit *noun* the electronic transfer of money from one bank account to another.

direct-dial • *verb* (**direct-dials, direct-dialed** or **direct-dialled, direct-dialing** or **direct-dialling**) dial a long-distance telephone number without making use of the operator. • *adjective* (of a telephone) capable of direct dialing. ▶ **direct dialing** *noun*

direction *noun* **1** the act or process of directing. **2** (usu. in *plural*) an order or instruction, esp. each of a set guiding use of equipment etc. **3 a** the course or line along which a person or thing moves or looks, or which must be taken to reach a destination. **b** (in *plural*) guidance on how to reach a destination. **c** the point to or from which a person or thing moves or looks. **4** the tendency taken by events, research, etc. PHRASES **sense of direction** the ability to know without guidance the direction in which one is or should be moving.

directional *adjective* **1** of or indicating direction. **2** *Electronics* **a** concerned with the transmission of radio or sound waves in a particular direction. **b** (of equipment) designed to receive radio or sound waves most effectively from a particular direction or directions and not others. ▶ **directionally** *adverb*

direction finder *noun* a device for determining the source of radio waves, esp. as an aid in navigation.

directionless *adjective* without direction, aim, or purpose.

directive • *noun* a general instruction from an authority: *the government has issued a new set of directives on pollution.* • *adjective* serving to direct: *the agency is seeking a central, directive role in national energy policy.*

directly *adverb* **1 a** without delay. **b** presently, shortly. **2** exactly: *directly opposite.* **3** in a direct manner.

direct mail *noun* advertising material sent unsolicited through the mail to usu. large numbers of prospective customers or donors. ▶ **direct mailing** *noun*

direct marketer *noun* a person who sells directly to consumers rather than through retailers.

direct marketing *noun* selling by dealing directly with consumers rather than through retailers.

directness *noun* the quality of being simple and clear, so that it is impossible not to understand.

direct object *noun* a noun, noun phrase or pronoun that refers to a person or thing that is directly affected by the action of a verb: *in "I met him downtown", the word "him" is the direct object.*

director *noun* **1** a person who directs, controls, or manages something, esp. an institution or a major division of a company. **2** a member of the board which governs the affairs of a company etc. **3** a person who directs a film etc., esp. professionally. **4** a conductor, esp. of a choir or band etc. of which the director is a performing instrumentalist. **5** (in Quebec municipal police forces) the highest ranking officer.

directorate *noun* **1 a** a government agency or subdivision of a ministry with a specific responsibility. **2** a board of directors. **3** the office of director.

director general *noun* (*plural* **directors general**) **1** the chief executive of an organization, especially a public one. **2** *Cdn* **a** a rank in the civil service immediately below assistant deputy minister. **b** a person holding this rank. **3** (in the SQ) the highest ranking officer.

directorial *adjective* having to do with a director; in one's capacity as director: *directorial techniques* ◊ *in this film she makes her directorial debut.* [Say duh reck TORY ul]

directorship *noun* the position of a member of a board of directors.

directory *noun* (*plural* **directories**) **1 a** a book listing alphabetically or thematically a particular group of individuals (e.g. telephone subscribers) or organizations with various details. **b** a large board listing names of departments, individuals, etc. and giving their location, esp. in a building. **2** a computer file listing other files or programs etc.

direct payment *noun* payment by means of a debit card, in which funds are transferred electronically from the cardholder's bank account to the account of a merchant etc.

direct proportion *noun* a relation between quantities whose ratio is constant: *sensors emit an electronic signal in direct proportion to the amount of light detected.*

direct speech *noun* the reporting of speech by repeating the actual words of a speaker, for example: *"I'm going," she said.* In contrast, *She said that she was going* is REPORTED SPEECH.

direct tax *noun* (*plural* **direct taxes**) a tax paid directly to the government, e.g. income tax or property tax.

dirge *noun* **1** a lament for the dead, esp. as part of a funeral service. **2** any song or piece of music that is too slow and mournful. [Rhymes with URGE]

dirigible *noun* an airship; a blimp. [Say DEER idge uh bull]

dirt *noun* **1** unclean matter that soils. **2 a** earth, soil. **b** earth, gravel, etc., used to make a surface for a road etc. (usu. as an *adjective*: *dirt road*). **3 a** obscene or foul language. **b** information, especially of a scandalous nature; gossip. **4** excrement: *dog dirt.* **5** a person or thing considered worthless. PHRASES **do a person dirt** *slang* harm or injure a person's reputation maliciously. **eat dirt** suffer insults, humiliation, etc. without retaliating. **hit the dirt 1** drop to the floor, ground, etc. **2** *Baseball slang* slide into base. **treat like dirt** treat (a person) contemptuously; abuse.

dirt bike *noun* a motorcycle designed for use on dirt roads and in cross-country racing.

dirt cheap *adjective & adverb informal* extremely cheap.

dirtiness *noun* the quality of being dirty.

dirt poor *adjective* very poor.

dirty • *adjective* (**dirtier, dirtiest**) **1** unclean. **2** causing one to become dirty: *a dirty job.* **3** pertaining to or obsessed with sexual activity: *dirty joke* ◊ *dirty mind.* **4** unpleasant, nasty. **5** dishonest, unfair: *dirty play.* **6** (of weather) rough, squally. **7** (of a colour) not pure or clear. • *adverb informal* in a malicious, unfair, or underhanded manner: *fight dirty.* • *verb* (**dirties,**

dirtied, dirtying) make or become dirty. PHRASES **dirty one's hands** (or **get one's hands dirty**) *informal* acquire practical experience, esp. as opposed to theoretical knowledge. **do the dirty on** *informal* play a mean trick on. **talk dirty** *informal* use obscene language.

dirty laundry *noun* (also **dirty linen**) intimate secrets, esp. of a scandalous nature. PHRASES **wash** (or **air**) **one's dirty laundry** (or **linen**) **in public** be indiscreet about one's domestic quarrels etc.

dirty look *noun informal* a look of disapproval or disgust etc.

dirty thirties *noun* esp. *Cdn informal* **1** the Great Depression of the 1930s. **2** the years of drought coinciding with this on the Prairies.

dirty trick *noun* **1** a spiteful and underhanded act. **2** (in *plural*) dishonest, secret and often illegal activity by a political group or other organization, that is intended to harm the reputation or success of an opponent: *a dirty tricks campaign*.

dirty word *noun* **1** an offensive or indecent word. **2** a thing regarded with dislike or approval: *profit is not a dirty word*.

dirty work *noun* unpleasant, difficult, or illegal activity.

dis *slang* • *verb* (**disses, dissed, dissing**) put (a person etc.) down; bad-mouth. • *noun* (*plural* **disses**) a disrespectful comment or attitude.

disability *noun* (*plural* **disabilities**) **1 a** a physical or mental handicap, either congenital or caused by injury, disease, etc. **b** the condition of having such a handicap. **2** a lack of some asset, quality, or attribute, that prevents one's doing something. **3** incapacity created or recognized by the law.

disable *verb* (**disables, disabled, disabling**) **1** make unable to function: *the burglars gained entry to the building after disabling the alarm*. **2** (of a disease, injury, or accident) limit someone in their movements, senses, or activities: *it's an injury that could disable someone for life* ◊ *a progressively disabling disease*.

disabled *adjective* **1** having reduced physical or mental abilities, esp. through injury or disease. **2** for the use of people with physical disabilities: *disabled parking space*. **3** made incapable of action or use.

disabled list *noun Baseball* a list of injured players who are unable to play, usu. for a specified length of time.

disablement *noun* the state of being disabled or the process of becoming disabled: *the insurance policy covers sudden death or disablement*.

disabuse *verb* (**disabuses, disabused, disabusing**) persuade someone that a belief or idea is mistaken: *let me disabuse you of the notion that you can succeed without hard work*.

disaccharide *noun* a sugar whose molecule contains two linked monosaccharides. [Say die SACKA ride]

disadvantage • *noun* an unfavourable circumstance or condition that reduces the chance of success or effectiveness. • *verb* cause disadvantage to: *some pension plans may disadvantage women*. PHRASES **at a disadvantage** in an unfavourable position relative to someone or something else: *I was at a disadvantage compared to the younger members of the team* ◊ *the fact that he didn't speak a foreign language put him at a distinct disadvantage*. **to one's disadvantage** so as to cause harm to one's interests or standing: *I hope my lack of experience won't be to my disadvantage*.

disadvantaged *adjective* suffering from social or economic deprivation or discrimination.

disadvantageous *adjective* causing someone to be in a worse situation compared to other people: *the deal will not be disadvantageous to your company*.

disaffected *adjective* dissatisfied with one's situation, organization, belief, etc. and therefore not loyal to it: *some disaffected members left to form a new party*.

disaffection *noun* discontentedness, esp. with political or social structures: *growing disaffection amongst voters* ◊ *student disaffection*.

disaggregate *verb* (**disaggregates, disaggregated, disaggregating**) separate into component parts: *a method for disaggregating cells*. ▶ **disaggregation** *noun* [Say dis AGGRA gate]

disagree *verb* (**disagrees, disagreed, disagreeing**) (often foll. by *with*) **1** hold a different opinion. **2** quarrel. **3** (of factors or circumstances) not correspond. **4** have an adverse effect upon (a person's health, digestion, etc.).

disagreeable *adjective* **1** unpleasant, not to one's liking. **2** quarrelsome. ▶ **disagreeably** *adverb*

disagreement *noun* **1** a lack of consensus or approval, often resulting in debate or argument: *there has been some disagreement about the details*. **2** lack of consistency or correspondence: *disagreement between the results of the two assessments*.

disallow *verb* **1** refuse to allow or accept as valid; prohibit. **2** annul (a statute) passed by a lower legislative body. ▶ **disallowance** *noun*

disappear *verb* **1** cease to be visible; pass from sight. **2** cease to exist or be in circulation or use. **3** (of a person or thing) go missing. ▶ **disappearance** *noun*

disappoint *verb* **1** fail to fulfill a desire or expectation of (a person). **2** frustrate (hopes etc.).

disappointed *adjective* frustrated or saddened by not having one's expectation etc. fulfilled in some regard: *disappointed with you*. ▶ **disappointedly** *adverb*

disappointing *adjective* failing to fulfill one's hopes or expectations. ▶ **disappointingly** *adverb*

disappointment *noun* **1** an event, thing, or person that disappoints. **2** a feeling of distress, vexation, etc., resulting from this.

disapproval *noun* possession or expression of an unfavourable or critical opinion: *he voiced his disapproval of drinking and driving*.

disapprove *verb* (**disapproves, disapproved, disapproving**) have or express an unfavourable opinion: *she wants to be an actress but her parents disapprove* ◊ *he strongly disapproved of the changes*. ▶ **disapproving** *adjective* **disapprovingly** *adverb*

disarm *verb* **1** deprive of a weapon or weapons. **2 a** (of a nation) reduce the size, armament, etc. of one's armed forces. **b** cause (a nation) to do this. **3** remove the fuse from (a bomb etc.). **4** deprive of the power to injure. **5** cause to feel less angry, critical, or hostile: *he disarmed her immediately by apologizing profusely* ◊ *the best way to disarm your critics is to make them laugh*. **6** deactivate (an alarm system etc.).

disarmament *noun* the reduction by a nation of its military forces and weapons.

disarming *adjective* reducing suspicion, anger, hostility, distrust, etc.: *a disarming smile*. ▶ **disarmingly** *adverb*

disarrange *verb* (**disarranges, disarranged, disarranging**) bring into disorder.

disarray *noun* disorder, confusion: *the peace talks broke up in disarray* ◊ *our plans were thrown into disarray by her arrival* ◊ *we're decorating, so everything's in complete disarray at home*.

disassemble *verb* (**disassembles, disassembled, disassembling**) take (a machine etc.) to pieces. ▶ **disassembly** *noun*

D

disassociate *verb* **(disassociates, disassociated, disassociating)** = DISSOCIATE. ▶**disassociation** *noun*

disaster *noun* **1** a great or sudden misfortune. **2 a** a complete failure. **b** a person or enterprise ending in failure.

disaster area *noun* **1 a** an area affected by a natural disaster, e.g. flooding etc. **b** *US* such an area that is officially declared eligible for emergency relief funds and services from the government. **2** a place characterized by extreme disorderliness or misfortune.

disastrous *adjective* **1** causing great damage: *a disastrous fire*. **2** highly unsuccessful: *the team is off to a disastrous start*. ▶**disastrously** *adverb*

disavow *verb* disclaim knowledge of, responsibility or support for, or belief in: *disavowed their pledge to halt cross-border raids* ◊ *disavowed their leader's racist statement*. ▶**disavowal** *noun* [Say dissa VOW]

disband *verb* **1** break up the organization of (a group etc.). **2** (of an organization) cease to work or act together.

disbar *verb* **(disbars, disbarred, disbarring)** deprive (a lawyer) of the right to practise. ▶**disbarment** *noun*

disbelief *noun* **1** lack of belief. **2** astonishment.

disbelieve *verb* **(disbelieves, disbelieved, disbelieving)** be unable or unwilling to believe (a person or statement). ▶**disbeliever** *noun* **disbelieving** *adjective* **disbelievingly** *adverb*

disburse *verb* **(disburses, disbursed, disbursing)** pay out money from a fund that has been collected for a specific purpose: *our goal has been to disburse the funds in a manner which the donors themselves would have wanted*. ▶**disbursement** *noun* [Say diss BURSE]

SPELL CHECK
disc, disk ABC ☑

Disk is the usual Canadian spelling for computer storage devices other than "compact disc": *floppy disk; hard disk; optical disk; magnetic disk; disk drive*.

---

disc *noun* (also **disk**) **1 a** a flat thin circular object. **b** a round, flat or apparently flat surface. **2** (also **intervertebral disc**) a layer of cartilage between vertebrae. **3** a sound or video recording in the form of a disc. **4** the close-packed cluster of tubular florets in the centre of a composite flower. **5** = DISK *noun*.

discard • *verb* **1** reject or get rid of as unwanted or superfluous. **2 a** remove or put aside (a playing card) from one's hand. **b** play (a card) from a remaining suit when not following suit or trumping. • *noun* **1** a rejected or abandoned item or person. **2** a discarded playing card.

disc brake *noun* a brake employing the friction of pads against a disc which is attached to the wheel.

discern *verb* **1** perceive through the senses, esp. by sight: *we could just discern the house in the distance*. **2** recognize or detect: *failed to discern her potential*. ▶**discernible** *adjective* **discernibly** *adverb* [Say dis SERN]

discerning *adjective* having or showing good judgment, taste, or insight: *the discerning customer will recognize this as a high quality product*. ▶**discerningly** *adverb* [Say dis SERN ing]

discernment *noun* the ability to judge well: *he shows great discernment in his choice of friends* ◊ *she is a woman of the highest taste and discernment*. [Say dis SERN mint]

discharge • *verb* **(discharges, discharged, discharging) 1 a** let go, release, esp. from a duty, commitment, or period of confinement. **b** relieve (a bankrupt) of residual liability. **2** dismiss from office, employment, etc. **3 a** fire (a gun etc.). **b** (of a gun etc.) fire (a bullet etc.). **4 a** pour out or cause to pour out; emit (pus, liquid, etc.). **b** (foll. by *into*) (of a river etc.) flow into (esp. a large body of water). **5 a** carry out, perform (a duty or obligation). **b** relieve oneself of (a financial commitment). **6** release an electrical charge from. **7** remove cargo from (a ship etc.). • *noun* **1** the action of discharging someone from a hospital or from a post: *referrals can be discussed before discharge from hospital* ◊ *offending policemen receive a dishonourable discharge*. **2** an action of releasing someone from the custody or restraint of the law: *the defendant was given an absolute discharge*. **3** an act of firing a gun etc. **4** the action of allowing a liquid, gas, or other substance to flow out from where it is confined; the liquid or matter so discharged: *industrial discharge has turned the river into an open sewer* ◊ *a greenish nasal discharge*. **5 a** the payment (of a debt). **b** the performance (of a duty etc.): *directors must exercise skill in the discharge of their duties*. **6** *Physics* **a** the release of a quantity of electric charge from an object. **b** a flow of electricity through the air or other gas esp. when accompanied by the emission of light. **c** the conversion of chemical energy in a cell into electrical energy.

disciple *noun* **1 a** a follower or pupil of a leader, philosophy, etc.: *a disciple of the economist John Maynard Keynes*. **2 a** one of the followers of Jesus during his lifetime, esp. one of the Apostles. **b** a professed Christian. ▶**discipleship** *noun* [Say dis SIPE ul]

disciplinarian *noun* a person who practises or upholds firm discipline: *a strict disciplinarian*. [Say dissa plin AIRY in]

disciplinary *adjective* relating to the punishment of those who break rules: *a disciplinary hearing* ◊ *the firm took disciplinary action against him*. [Say DISSA plin airy]

discipline • *noun* **1 a** training, esp. of the mind and character, aimed at producing self-control, obedience, orderly conduct, etc.: *lack of discipline at home meant that many pupils found it difficult to settle in to the ordered environment of the school*. **b** the controlled behaviour resulting from such training: *poor discipline in the ranks* ◊ *her determination and discipline in going to German class every Tuesday night were admirable*. **2 a** method of training the mind or body or of controlling behaviour; an area of activity where this is necessary: *spiritual discipline*. **3** a branch of instruction or learning: *the scientific disciplines*. • *verb* **(disciplines, disciplined, disciplining) 1** punish, reprimand: *the officers were disciplined for using racist language*. **2** train to be obedient, self-controlled, skilful, etc. **3 discipline oneself** train oneself to do something one thinks is beneficial, esp. in spite of reluctance: *she disciplined herself to exercise at least three times a week* ◊ *dieting is a matter of disciplining yourself*.

disciplined *adjective* showing a controlled form of behaviour or way of working: *a disciplined approach to management* ◊ *I know he'll do his exercises every day because he's very disciplined*. [Say DISSA plinned]

disc jockey *noun* (plural **disc jockeys**) a person who introduces and plays recorded music on a radio program, at a dance, etc.

disclaim *verb* deny or disown: *disclaim responsibility*.

disclaimer *noun* **1** a statement that denies something, esp. knowledge or responsibility: *the novel*

carries the usual disclaimer about the characters bearing no relation to living persons. **2** Law a statement in which a person says officially that they do not claim the right to do something.

disclose verb (**discloses, disclosed, disclosing**) **1** make known; reveal: disclosed the truth ◊ no details were disclosed. **2** expose to view: the door swung open, disclosing a long dark passage.

disclosure noun **1** the action of making new or secret information known: disclosure of all campaign donations is required. **2** a revelation: a spate of new disclosures point to their involvement.

disc number noun Cdn hist. a number used in an identification system introduced in 1940 by the federal government in order to identify individual Inuit.

disco noun informal (plural **discos**) **1** a place or event at which recorded popular music is played for dancing, often with elaborate lighting and other special effects. **2** = DISCO MUSIC.

discoloration noun an unattractive change in the colour of something, such as through staining, fading, or tarnishing: a yellowish discoloration of the book's pages.

discolour verb (also **discolor**) spoil or cause to spoil the colour of something.

discolouration noun = DISCOLORATION.

discombobulate verb (**discombobulates, discombobulated, discombobulating**) jocular disturb; disconcert. ▶ **discombobulation** noun

discomfit verb (**discomfits, discomfited, discomfiting**) make someone feel confused, uneasy, or embarrassed: she was not noticeably discomfited by the request ◊ discomfiting questions. ▶ **discomfiture** noun [Say dis KUM fit]

discomfort • noun **1 a** slight pain. **b** mental uneasiness: she felt some discomfort about taking drugs. **2** a lack of physical comfort. • verb make uneasy, disturb: women are most discomforted by the gap between who they are and what they are supposed to be.

disco music noun a style of dance music with a strong, repetitive rhythm, and the use of electronic instrumentation, popular esp. in the 1970s.

disconcert verb make someone feel anxious, confused or embarrassed: his answer rather disconcerted her. ▶ **disconcerted** adjective **disconcerting** adjective **disconcertingly** adverb [Say dis kun SERT]

disconnect verb **1 a** detach or separate something connected: disconnected my phone ◊ disconnect the hose. **b** become detached. **2** detach (a customer) from a network of services, e.g. telephone, cable television, electricity, etc. **3** interrupt (a telephone connection): I was on hold for five minutes and then I was disconnected. **4** break a connection between (people, actions, etc.): take all violence out of television drama and you disconnect it from reality.

disconnected adjective **1** (of speech, writing, etc.) incoherent and illogical. **2** not connected.

disconnection noun **1** separation, detachment, or isolation from people or things, esp. those with which one was formerly associated: after losing his job he felt a profound sense of loss and disconnection. **2** the action of disconnecting parts.

disconsolate adjective very unhappy and unable to be comforted: disconsolate because they could find no work. ▶ **disconsolately** adverb [Say dis CONSA lit]

discontent noun lack of contentment, dissatisfaction.

discontented adjective dissatisfied. ▶ **discontentedly** adverb

discontinuation noun the action of ceasing to do, provide, or use something: the discontinuation of therapy.

discontinue verb (**discontinues, discontinued, discontinuing**) **1** cease or cause to cease to exist or be made: that model has been discontinued. **2** give up: the doctor recommended discontinuing antidepressants. **3** cease subscribing to or paying for (a newspaper, service, etc.).

discontinuity noun (plural **discontinuities**) a distinct break or change in a process, or sharp difference of characteristics between parts of something: changes in government have led to discontinuities in policy.

discontinuous adjective not continuous; stopping and starting again: women typically have discontinuous patterns of employment.

discord noun **1** disagreement; quarrelling: a prosperous family who showed no signs of discord. **2** lack of agreement or harmony between things: the discord between indigenous and Western cultures. **3** a combination of musical notes that sound harsh together.

discordance noun lack of harmony or agreement; conflict: many of the tensions in the world result from a discordance between cultural and political organization. [Say dis CORE dince]

discordant adjective **1** not in agreement; combining with other things in a way that is strange or unpleasant: discordant views ◊ the functional modernity of the computer struck a discordant note amid the elegant eighteenth-century furniture. **2** (of sounds) not in harmony; dissonant: modern music is often discordant. ▶ **discordantly** adverb [Say dis CORE dint]

discotheque noun = DISCO 1. [Say DISCO teck]

discount • noun **1** a deduction from a bill or amount due given esp. for prompt or advance payment or to a special category of buyers. **2** a deduction from the face value of a bond, treasury bill, promissory note, or other bill of exchange when it is purchased before its maturity date. • verb **1** disregard as being unreliable or unimportant: discounted his story. **2 a** detract from; lessen; deduct (esp. an amount from a bill etc.). **b** reduce in price. **3** buy or sell (a bill of exchange before its maturity date) at a price less than its face value. • adjective **1** selling goods at less than the normal retail price: discount store. **2** sold at less than the normal retail price: discount fares. PHRASES **at a discount** below the nominal or usual price (compare PREMIUM). ▶ **discounter** noun

discourage verb (**discourages, discouraged, discouraging**) **1** deprive of courage, confidence, or enthusiasm. **2** (usu. foll. by from) dissuade: discouraged him from going. **3** oppose or deter: the police presence is designed to discourage drug use. ▶ **discouragement** noun **discouraging** adjective **discouragingly** adverb

discourse • noun **1** communication in speech or writing: an imagined discourse between two people travelling in France. **2** a long and serious discussion of a subject in speech or writing: a discourse on issues of gender and sexuality ◊ she was hoping for some lively political discourse at the meeting. **3** the body of statements, analysis, etc., both written and spoken, concerning a specific subject, esp. as typified by recurring terms and concepts: the language of feminist discourse. • verb (**discourses, discoursed, discoursing**) **1** talk; converse. **2** speak or write learnedly or at length (on a subject): he discoursed for hours on the problems of the education system.

discourteous adjective impolite; rude. ▶ **discourteously** adverb **discourteousness** noun [Say dis COURTEOUS]

discourtesy noun (plural **discourtesies**) **1** bad manners; rudeness. **2** an impolite act or remark.

discover *verb* **1 a** find out or become aware of, whether by research or searching or by chance: *discovered a new entrance*. **b** be the first to find or find out: *discovered insulin*. **2** (in show business) find and promote as a new singer, actor, etc. ▶ **discoverable** *adjective* **discoverer** *noun*

> **WRITING TIP**
> **discover, discovery**
>
> The use of the words **discover** and **discovery** in reference to European exploration of other continents is widely considered to be offensive to Aboriginal peoples. Rather than saying *The Vikings may have discovered Canada*, it would be better to say *The Vikings may have been the first Europeans to reach Canada*.

discovery *noun* (*plural* **discoveries**) **1** the act or process of discovering or being discovered. **2** a person or thing discovered. **3** *Law* the compulsory disclosure, by a party to an action, of facts etc. on which the other party wishes to rely.

Discovery Day *noun* (in the Yukon) a statutory holiday observed on the third Monday in August, commemorating the discovery of gold in the Klondike on August 17, 1896.

discovery well *noun* the first productive well drilled in an oil exploration area.

discredit • *noun* **1** harm to reputation: *brought discredit on the enterprise ◊ Canada, to its discredit, did not speak out against these atrocities*. **2** a person or thing causing such harm: *he is a discredit to his family*. • *verb* (**discredits, discredited, discrediting**) **1** harm the good reputation of. **2** take away the credibility of or destroy confidence in (an effort, a person, etc.).

discreditable *adjective* tending to bring harm to a reputation: *the internment of Japanese Canadians was a discreditable incident in our history*.

discredited *adjective* **1** (of a person or thing) having a tarnished reputation; no longer trusted or respected: *a discredited politician*. **2** having been shown to be false or unreliable: *discredited evidence*.

> **SPELL CHECK**
> **discreet, discrete** ABC
>
> Things that are separate or distinct are **discrete**.

discreet *adjective* careful not to reveal much or draw attention to oneself in speech or action, esp. to avoid social embarrassment, avoid giving offence, or gain an advantage: *he was always very discreet about his love affairs ◊ you ought to make a few discreet enquiries before you sign anything ◊ a discreet glance at the clock told me the interview had lasted an hour*. ▶ **discreetly** *adverb*

discrepancy *noun* (*plural* **discrepancies**) an illogical or surprising lack of compatibility or similarity between two or more facts: *there's a discrepancy between Mary's account and Bernard's ◊ pointed out the discrepancies in the minister's statement*. [Say dis CREP'n see]

> **SPELL CHECK**
> **discrete, discreet** ABC
>
> Someone who can keep a secret is **discreet**.

discrete *adjective* **1** consisting of distinct or individual parts; independent of other things of the same type: *the organisms can be divided into discrete categories*. **2** *Math* specified only for a distinct set of points: *discrete variables*. ▶ **discretely** *adverb* **discreteness** *noun*

discretion *noun* **1** the quality of behaving or speaking

in such a way as to avoid causing offence or revealing private information: *this is confidential, but I know that I can rely on your discretion ◊ Jane is the soul of discretion ◊ use the utmost discretion when you talk to her*. **2** the freedom or power to decide what should be done in a particular situation: *how much to tell terminally ill patients is left to the discretion of the doctor ◊ honorary fellowships may be awarded at the discretion of the council*. See also AGE OF DISCRETION. PHRASES **at one's discretion** as one pleases: *tipping is at your discretion*. **discretion is the better part of valour** it's better to avoid danger than to confront it. **use one's discretion** act according to one's own judgment. [Say dis CRESH'n]

discretionary *adjective* used, adopted, etc. when considered necessary: *discretionary powers*. [Say dis CRESH'n airy]

discriminate *verb* (**discriminates, discriminated, discriminating**) **1** (often foll. by *between*) make or see a distinction; differentiate: *when do babies learn to discriminate sounds? ◊ a number of features discriminate this species from others*. **2** (usu. foll. by *against*) make an unjust or prejudiced distinction in the treatment of different categories of people or things, esp. unjustly and on the basis of race, age, sex, etc.: *practices that discriminate against women ◊ it is illegal to discriminate on grounds of race, sex, or religion*.

discriminating *adjective* **1** able to judge the good quality of something: *a discriminating audience*. **2** practising or showing racial, sexual, etc. discrimination: *discriminating remarks*. ▶ **discriminatingly** *adverb*

discrimination *noun* **1** an act, instance, policy, etc. of unfavourable treatment based on prejudice, esp. regarding race, age, or sex: *victims of racial discrimination ◊ discrimination against gay people must stop*. **2** good taste or judgment; the ability to discern what is of high quality: *those who could afford to buy showed little taste or discrimination*. **3** recognition and understanding of the difference between one thing and another: *discrimination between right and wrong ◊ young children lack the ability to make subtle discriminations*.

discriminatory *adjective* making or showing an unfair or prejudicial distinction between different groups of people, esp. on the basis of race, age, or sex: *discriminatory hiring*. [Say dis CRIMMIN a tory]

discursive *adjective* **1** rambling, digressing from subject to subject: *students often write dull, second-hand, discursive prose*. **2** (of a style of speech or writing) fluent and expansive rather than formulaic or abbreviated: *the short story is concentrated, whereas the novel is discursive ◊ the definitions in this dictionary are more discursive than in others*. ▶ **discursively** *adverb* [Say dis CURSE iv]

> **SPELL CHECK**
> **discus, discuss** ABC
>
> To talk over an issue is to **discuss** it.

discus *noun* (*plural* **discuses**) **1** a heavy thick-centred disc thrown in ancient Greek games. **2** a similar disc thrown in modern sporting events. **3** the sport of discus throwing. [Say DISK iss]

discuss *verb* (**discusses, discussed, discussing**) **1** hold a conversation about. **2** debate or examine by argument.

discussion *noun* **1** a conversation or exchange of views, esp. on specific subjects; informal debate. **2** a speech or a piece of writing that discusses many different aspects of a subject: *this book is a detailed discussion of the issue of genetically modified foods*.

disdain • *noun* a feeling or attitude of scorn or contempt: *treated me with disdain ◊ a disdain for the law ◊*

he turned his head away in disdain. • **verb 1** consider to be unworthy of one's consideration: *immigrants accept the jobs disdained by the local workforce ◊ the aristocrats disdained the new rich.* **2** refuse to do something out of feelings of pride or superiority: *the Globe disdained to publish my letter.* ▶ **disdainful** *adjective* **disdainfully** *adverb*

disease *noun* **1** an unhealthy condition of the body or mind; illness, sickness. **2** a corresponding physical condition of plants. **3** something that is very wrong with people's attitudes or way of life or with society: *greed is a disease of modern society ◊ suffering from the peculiarly Canadian disease of self-deprecation.*

diseased *adjective* **1** affected with disease. **2** abnormal, disordered: *a diseased view of humanity.*

SPELL CHECK
dissect ABC ✓

Warning: **dissect** is spelled with two *s*'s.

---

disembark *verb* leave or remove from a ship, aircraft, train, etc. ▶ **disembarkation** *noun*

disembodied *adjective* **1** coming from a person or place that cannot be seen or identified: *disembodied voices.* **2** separated from the body or a concrete form: *disembodied spirits.* ▶ **disembodiment** *noun*

disembowel *verb* (**disembowels, disembowelled, disembowelling**) remove the bowels or entrails of. ▶ **disembowelled** *adjective* **disembowelment** *noun* [Say dissem BOWEL]

disempower *verb* make (a person, group, etc.) less powerful or confident: *hospitals can disempower people.* ▶ **disempowered** *adjective* **disempowerment** *noun*

disenchanted *adjective* no longer feeling enthusiasm for someone or something; not believing something is good or worth doing: *she was becoming disenchanted with her job as a lawyer.* ▶ **disenchantment** *noun*

disenfranchise *verb* (**disenfranchises, disenfranchised, disenfranchising**) **1** deprive (a person) of the right to vote: *the law disenfranchised some 3,000 voters on the basis of a residence qualification.* **2** prevent from having a say in or control over matters that affect one: *they claimed that business had received preferential treatment at the policy formulation stage, disenfranchising concerned elements of the public.* ▶ **disenfranchised** *adjective* **disenfranchisement** *noun* [Say dis in FRAN chize]

disengage *verb* (**disengages, disengaged, disengaging**) **1 a** detach, free, loosen, or separate (parts etc.): *disengaged the clutch ◊ I disengaged his hand from mine.* **b** disengage oneself detach oneself; get loose: *they clung together for a moment and then she disengaged herself.* **c** become detached: *the booster rockets disengaged and fell to the sea.* **2** Military remove (troops) from a battle or a battle area: *the ceasefire gave the commanders a chance to disengage their forces ◊ the only means by which the Americans could disengage from Korea.*

disengaged *adjective* uncommitted, emotionally detached: *the students were oddly disengaged, as if they didn't believe they could control their lives.*

disengagement *noun* **1** the action or process of withdrawing from involvement in a particular activity, situation, or group: *the process of disengagement from such a massive project inevitably caused friction.* **2** emotional detachment; objectivity: *authorial detachment and disengagement do not always suit first-person narrators.* **3** the withdrawal of military forces or the renunciation of military or political influence in a particular area. **4** the process of separating or releasing something or of becoming separated or released: *the mechanism prevents accidental disengagement.*

disentangle *verb* (**disentangles, disentangled, disentangling**) **1 a** separate different arguments, ideas, etc. that have become confused: *it's not easy to disentangle the truth from the official statistics.* **b** free someone or something from something that has become wrapped or twisted around it or them: *"I must go," she said, disentangling her fingers from Gabriel's.* **c** disentangle oneself remove oneself from a situation seen as constricting and complicated: *she has just disentangled herself from a painful relationship.* **2** get rid of the twists and knots in something: *he was disentangling a coil of rope.* ▶ **disentanglement** *noun*

disequilibrium *noun* (*plural* **disequilibria**) a lack or loss of equilibrium, stability; an imbalance: *a state of emotional disequilibrium.* [Say dis equal LIB ree um]

disestablish *verb* (**disestablishes, disestablished, disestablishing**) end the official status of a national Church: *a campaign to disestablish the Church of England.* ▶ **disestablishment** *noun*

disfavour (also **disfavor**) • *noun* **1** disapproval or dislike. **2** the state of being disliked: *fell into disfavour.* • *verb* regard or treat with disfavour.

disfigure *verb* (**disfigures, disfigured, disfiguring**) spoil the appearance or beauty of; deface, deform. ▶ **disfigured** *adjective* **disfigurement** *noun*

disfranchise *verb* (**disfranchises, disfranchised, disfranchising**) = DISENFRANCHISE.

disgorge *verb* (**disgorges, disgorged, disgorging**) **1** vomit or eject (matter) from the throat or stomach. **2** discharge the contents of; empty: *the boat disgorged passengers onto the pier.* **3** cause to pour out: *the pipe disgorges sewage into the lake.* **4** give up (funds, esp. those that have been wrongfully acquired): *he was compelled to disgorge any secret profits he made on the transaction.*

disgrace • *noun* **1** the loss of reputation; shame. **2** a person or thing that brings dishonour or shame: *the bus service is a disgrace.* • *verb* (**disgraces, disgraced, disgracing**) **1** bring shame or discredit on or be a disgrace to. **2** degrade from a position of honour; dismiss from favour. **PHRASES** **in disgrace** having lost respect or reputation; out of favour. ▶ **disgraceful** *adjective* **disgracefully** *adverb*

disgruntled *adjective* discontented; irritated, annoyed. ▶ **disgruntlement** *noun*

disguise • *verb* (**disguises, disguised, disguising**) **1 a** (often foll. by *as*) alter the appearance, dress, mannerisms, etc. of (a person) so as to conceal true identity. **b** alter so as to make unrecognizable: *disguised his voice.* **2** misrepresent or cover up: *disguised their intentions.* • *noun* **1** a garment, style, manner, etc. assumed as a means of concealment or deception: *wore a false nose as a disguise.* **2** the act of altering one's appearance in order to conceal one's identity: *Wendy is a master of disguise.* **PHRASES** **in disguise 1** wearing a concealing costume etc. **2** appearing to be the opposite: *his injury turned out to be a blessing in disguise since the hours of physio made him much stronger.* ▶ **disguised** *adjective*

disgust • *noun* (usu. foll. by *at, for*) **1** repugnance; strong and instinctive aversion to something that is physically loathsome, morally offensive, etc. **2** a strong distaste for a food, drink, medicine, etc.; nausea. • *verb* **1** offend the sensibilities or principles of: *their behaviour disgusts me.* **2** excite physical nausea and loathing in. **PHRASES** **in disgust** as a result of disgust: *left in disgust.* ▶ **disgustedly** *adverb*

disgusting *adjective* arousing disgust; sickening, repulsive. ▶ **disgustingly** *adverb*

dish • *noun* (*plural* **dishes**) **1 a** a shallow, usu. flat-bottomed container made of glass, ceramic, metal, etc., used for holding or serving food. **b** the food served in a

D

dish. **c** food prepared in a particular way: *an Italian dish*. **2** (in *plural*) dirty plates, cutlery, pots, etc. after a meal. **3 a** a dish-shaped receptacle, object, or cavity. **b** = SATELLITE DISH. • *verb* (**dishes, dished, dishing**) **1** put (food) into a dish for serving. **2** make concave or dish-shaped. **3** *informal* gossip about (someone). **PHRASES** **dish it out** *informal* deal out punishment, criticism, etc. **dish out** *informal* deal out, distribute, esp. roughly or indiscriminately. **dish up 1** serve or prepare to serve (food). **2** *informal* seek to present (facts, argument, etc.) attractively. **dish the dirt** (often foll. by *on*) *informal* spread scandal or gossip.

disharmony *noun* (*plural* **disharmonies**) a lack of agreement leading to tension between people: *marital disharmony*.

dishearten *verb* cause to lose courage, confidence, hope, etc. ▶**disheartening** *adjective* **dishearteningly** *adverb*

dishevelled *adjective* (of the hair, clothes, appearance, etc.) disordered, unkempt, untidy. [Say dih SHEV'ld]

dishonest *adjective* (of a person, act, or statement) fraudulent or insincere. ▶**dishonestly** *adverb*

dishonesty *noun* (*plural* **dishonesties**) **1** a lack of honesty, esp. a willingness to cheat, steal, lie, or act fraudulently. **2** a dishonest or fraudulent act.

dishonour (also **dishonor**) • *noun* **1** a state of shame or disgrace. **2** something that causes shame or disgrace: *a dishonour to his profession*. • *verb* **1** disgrace: *dishonoured his name*. **2** treat without honour or respect.

dishonourable *adjective* (also **dishonorable**) **1** causing disgrace. **2** (of a person) unprincipled; having no sense of honour. ▶**dishonourably** *adverb*

dishwasher *noun* **1** a machine for washing dishes. **2** a person who washes dishes. ▶**dishwashing** *noun*

dishwater *noun* **1** water in which dishes have been washed. **2** *informal* (often as an *adjective*) something weak, diluted, or resembling dishwater.

disillusion • *noun* disappointment resulting from the discovery that something is not as good as one believed it to be. • *verb* cause someone to realize that a belief they hold is false: *I hate to disillusion you, but not everyone is as honest as you*. ▶**disillusionment** *noun*

disincentive • *noun* something that tends to discourage a particular action etc.: *a sudden fall in profits provided a further disincentive to new investors*. • *adjective* tending to discourage: *higher taxes have major disincentive effects on work effort*.

disinclination *noun* unwillingness or reluctance: *a disinclination for work* ◊ *disinclination to go*.

disincline *verb* (**disinclines, disinclined, disinclining**) make unwilling or reluctant: *he was strongly disinclined to believe anything that she said*. ▶**disinclined** *adjective*

disinfect *verb* cleanse (a wound, room, etc.) of infection by destroying germs, esp. with a disinfectant.

disinfectant • *noun* a usu. commercially produced chemical liquid or spray that destroys germs etc. • *adjective* of disinfectants or causing disinfection.

disinfection *noun* the action of cleaning something with a disinfectant in order to destroy germs etc.

disinformation *noun* deliberately false information, esp. as supplied by governments, the military, etc.

disingenuous *adjective* not candid or sincere, typically by pretending that one knows less about something than one really does: *disingenuous professions of loyalty to the free market by those who profit from wage discrimination*. ▶**disingenuously** *adverb* **disingenuousness** *noun* [Say dis in JEN you us]

disinherit *verb* (**disinherits, disinherited, disinheriting**) reject as one's heir; deprive of the right of inheritance: *the owner, an elderly widower, had disinherited his children*. [Say dis in HAIR it]

disintegrate *verb* (**disintegrates, disintegrated, disintegrating**) **1** break up into small parts, typically as the result of impact or decay: *when the missile struck, the car disintegrated in a sheet of searing flame*. **2** *Physics* **a** (of a nucleus, particle, or radioactive substance) undergo disintegration. **b** cause (a substance, atom, or nucleus) to undergo disintegration. **3** *informal* deteriorate mentally or physically. **4** become much less strong or united and be gradually destroyed: *the government's authority was rapidly disintegrating*.

disintegration *noun* **1** the process of losing cohesion: *the twin problems of economic failure and social disintegration*. **2** the process of coming to pieces: *the disintegration of infected cells*. **3** breakdown of the personality: *loss of self-esteem leads to the disintegration of a proud man*. **4** *Physics* a process in which a nucleus or other subatomic particle emits a smaller particle or divides into smaller particles.

disinter *verb* (**disinters, disinterred, disinterring**) **1** remove or dig up from the ground. **2** discover something that has been hidden or lost for a long time: *he has disinterred a Bach cantata*. [Say dis in TUR]

> **WRITING TIP**
> **disinterest**
>
> The use of **disinterest** to mean "lack of interest" is sometimes criticized, though it is more commonly used in this sense than in the sense "impartiality". The phrase *lack of interest* avoids ambiguity and accusations of incorrect usage.

disinterest *noun* **1** impartiality: *the narrator of the story is bound by apparent laws of detachment and disinterest*. **2** *disputed* lack of interest: *his total disinterest in money puzzled his family*.

> **WRITING TIP**
> **disinterested**
>
> In informal writing and speech, **disinterested** should not be used to mean "not interested, bored, uninterested". The most common sense of **disinterested** is "unbiased, impartial", as in *The case should be heard by a disinterested judge and jury*. Those who use **disinterested** to mean **uninterested** risk being misunderstood.

disinterested *adjective* **1** unbiased; not influenced by one's own advantage: *a disinterested critic*. **2** *disputed* uninterested. ▶**disinterestedly** *adverb* **disinterestedness** *noun*

disjointed *adjective* (of speech, writing, etc.) incoherent, rambling; not properly connected. ▶**disjointedly** *adverb* **disjointedness** *noun*

> **SPELL CHECK**
> **disk, disc**
>
> **Disc** is the usual Canadian spelling for a flat circular object ("disc-shaped", "disc brake"), the part of the spine ("slipped disc"), and for audio and video recording terms ("compact disc", "Mini Disc", "laser disc", "disc jockey"). However, **disk** is the usual spelling in "floppy disk", "hard disk", "optical disk", "magnetic disk", and "disk drive".

disk • *noun* (also **disc**) **1 a** (also **magnetic disk**) a computer storage device consisting of a rotatable disc or discs with a magnetic coating. **b** (also **optical disk**) a smooth non-magnetic disc with large storage capacity for data recorded and read by laser, esp. a CD-ROM. **2** =

DISC. **3 a** = DISKER. **b** a circular steel blade on a disker. • *verb* till (soil) with a disker.

disk drive *noun* Computing a device that can store and retrieve data from rotating magnetic or optical disks.

disker *noun* (also **disk harrow**) a farm implement using sharp, curved disks to till land, remove weeds, etc.

diskette *noun* = FLOPPY *noun*.

diskless *adjective* Computing (of a workstation etc.) not containing a disk drive.

dislikable *adjective* that arouses dislike; unpleasant, objectionable: *one of the movie's dislikable characters*.

dislike • *verb* (**dislikes, disliked, disliking**) have an aversion or objection to; not like. • *noun* **1** a feeling that something is distasteful, unpleasant, objectionable, etc. **2** an object of dislike.

dislikeable *adjective* = DISLIKABLE.

dislocate *verb* (**dislocates, dislocated, dislocating**) **1** disturb the normal connection of (esp. a joint in the body): *dislocated his shoulder*. **2** disorder or disrupt: *trade was dislocated by the famine*. **3** displace or put out of a former or proper position: *many Aboriginal peoples had been dislocated by war*.

dislocation *noun* **1** the act or result of dislocating, esp. the displacement of a bone from its natural position. **2** disturbance from a proper, original, or usual place or state: *these policies could cause severe economic and social dislocation*.

dislodge *verb* (**dislodges, dislodged, dislodging**) remove from an established or fixed position: *the wind dislodged one or two tiles from the roof* ◊ *the rebels have so far failed to dislodge the President*.

disloyal *adjective* not loyal to a person, country, or group to which one has obligations: *he was accused of being disloyal to the government* ◊ *a disloyal remark* ◊ *it was very disloyal of you to repeat what I'd said to Peter*. ▶ **disloyalty** *noun*

dismal *adjective* **1** causing or showing gloom; cheerless, miserable. **2** dreary or sombre: *dismal brown walls*. **3** *informal* feeble or inept: *a dismal performance*. ▶ **dismally** *adverb* **dismalness** *noun*

dismantle *verb* (**dismantles, dismantled, dismantling**) **1** take apart: *dismantle a faulty motor*. **2** end (a system, organization, etc.) in a gradual and planned way: *dismantled apartheid*. ▶ **dismantler** *noun*

dismay • *noun* consternation or anxiety distress, typically that caused by something unexpected: *she could not hide her dismay at the result* ◊ *he looked at her in dismay* ◊ *to her dismay, her name was not on the list* ◊ *the news has been greeted with dismay*. • *verb* fill with consternation or anxiety: *he was dismayed at the change in his old friend*. ▶ **dismaying** *adjective* **dismayingly** *adverb*

dismember *verb* **1** tear or cut the limbs from. **2** divide up (a country etc.). ▶ **dismemberment** *noun*

dismiss *verb* (**dismisses, dismissed, dismissing**) **1 a** send away; cause (a person) to leave one's presence. **b** disband (an assembly or army). **c** (of an assembly etc.) disperse; break ranks. **2** discharge from employment, office, etc., esp. dishonourably. **3** banish (a thought, feeling, etc.) from the mind; treat as unworthy of consideration. **4** treat (a subject) summarily: *dismissed his application*. **5** *Law* refuse further hearing to (a case). ▶ **dismissal** *noun* **dismissible** *adjective*

dismissive *adjective* showing that one does not believe a person or thing to be important or worth consideration: *she was always dismissive of other women*. ▶ **dismissively** *adverb* **dismissiveness** *noun*

dismount • *verb* get off a horse, bicycle, etc. • *noun* an act or method of dismounting (from a horse, parallel bars, etc.).

disobedience *noun* failure or refusal to obey the rules or someone in authority. [Say dis oh BEEDY ince]

disobedient *adjective* disobeying; rule-breaking. ▶ **disobediently** *adverb* [Say dis oh BEEDY int]

disobey *verb* **1** fail or refuse to obey (orders, rules, a person, etc.); disregard. **2** be disobedient or show disobedience. [Say dis oh BAY]

disorder • *noun* **1** confusion, disarray; lack of order or regular arrangement. **2** a disturbance or commotion, esp. a breach of public order. **3** *Medical* an ailment or disturbance of the normal state of body or mind. • *verb* **1** disarrange; throw (a situation etc.) into confusion. **2** *Medical* upset the health or proper function of the body or mind. ▶ **disordered** *adjective*

disorderliness *noun* a disorderly state or disorderly conduct.

disorderly *adjective* **1** involving or contributing to a breakdown of peaceful and law-abiding behaviour: *disorderly conduct* ◊ *they were arrested for being drunk and disorderly*. **2** lacking organization; untidy: *newspapers in a disorderly pile by the door*.

disorganization *noun* a confused or disorganized condition.

disorganize *verb* (**disorganizes, disorganized, disorganizing**) destroy the system, order, or organization of; throw into confusion. ▶ **disorganized** *adjective*

disorient *verb* **1** confuse (a person) as to his or her whereabouts or bearings. **2** confuse (a person) as to what is true, correct, etc.: *disoriented by grief and exhaustion*. ▶ **disorientation** *noun*

disown *verb* **1** refuse to acknowledge (a person) as one's own or as connected with oneself. **2** disclaim (an idea, intention, result, etc.).

disparage *verb* (**disparages, disparaged, disparaging**) regard or represent as being of little worth: *I don't mean to disparage your achievements*. ▶ **disparagement** *noun* **disparaging** *adjective* **disparagingly** *adverb* [Say dis PAIR idge]

disparate *adjective* **1** (of two or more things) so different from each other that they cannot be compared or cannot work together: *a critical study that aims to cover such disparate forms as Anglo-Saxon poetry and the modern novel*. **2** made up of parts or people that are very different from each other: *a disparate group of individuals*. ▶ **disparately** *adverb* [Say DISPA rit]

disparity *noun* a great difference or gap, esp. one regarded as unfair: *economic disparities between the East and West*. [Say dis PAIRA tee]

dispassion *noun* a calm, rational, or impartial manner.

dispassionate *adjective* calm, impartial; free from the influence or effect of strong emotion: *she dealt with life's disasters in a calm, dispassionate way*. ▶ **dispassionately** *adverb*

dispatch • *verb* (**dispatches, dispatched, dispatching**) **1** send off to a destination or for a purpose. **2** kill, execute. **3** perform (business, a task, etc.) promptly; finish off. **4** *informal* eat (food, a meal, etc.) quickly. • *noun* **1** the sending of someone or something to a destination or for a purpose: *a resolution authorizing the dispatch of a peacekeeping force*. **2** the killing of someone or something: *the legendary dispatch of villains by heroes of Greek myth*. **3 a** an official written message on state or esp. military affairs: *a confidential dispatch from Ottawa to the premiers*. **b** a report sent in by a newspaper's correspondent, usu. from a foreign country. **c** any written message requiring fast delivery. **4** promptness, efficiency: *the situation might change, so he should proceed with dispatch*.

dispatcher *noun* a person who coordinates the departure of taxis, buses, trains, etc.

dispel *verb* (**dispels, dispelled, dispelling**) make something, esp. a feeling or belief, go away or disappear: *his speech dispelled any fears about his health*.

dispensable *adjective* able to be replaced or done without: *they considered music and art lessons dispensable*.

dispensary *noun* (plural **dispensaries**) **1** a place in a clinic, pharmacy, etc. where medicines are dispensed. **2** a public or charitable institution offering medical advice and the dispensing of medicines. [Say dis PENSA ree]

dispensation *noun* **1** the action of distributing or supplying something: *the flagrant dispensation of federal goodies by John A. Macdonald*. **2** an exemption from a religious or legal observance, penalty, etc.: *he received papal dispensation* ◊ *the pope granted Henry a dispensation to marry Elizabeth of York*. **3** exemption from a rule or usual requirement: *as long as a pregnant pilot is in good health, she can fly without special dispensation*. **4** (in Christian theology) a divinely ordained order prevailing at a particular period of history: *the Mosaic dispensation*. [Say dis pen SAY sh'n]

dispense *verb* (**dispenses, dispensed, dispensing**) **1** distribute or deal out as a share from a common stock. **2** administer (a sacrament, justice, etc.). **3** make up and give out (medicine etc.) according to a doctor's prescription. **4** (usu. foll. by *from*) grant (a person) a dispensation from an esp. religious obligation. **5 a** do without; render needless: *dispense with formalities*. **b** give exemption from (a rule).

dispenser *noun* **1** an automatic machine that dispenses an item or a specific amount of something, e.g. soap etc. **2** a person who dispenses something.

dispersal *noun* the action of distributing, spreading, or sending things or people in different directions over a wide area: *the dispersal of seeds* ◊ *crowd dispersal*.

SPELL CHECK
disperse, disburse ABC ✓

If you distribute money you **disburse** it.

---

disperse *verb* (**disperses, dispersed, dispersing**) **1 a** drive, throw, send, or scatter in different directions. **b** become scattered, dispelled, or dissipated: *the clouds dispersed*. **2 a** (of people in a crowd etc.) separate and go different ways. **b** cause to do this. **3** (usu. in *passive*) place or station at widely separated points. **4** distribute or put (books, currency, etc.) into circulation, esp. from a main source or centre. **5** *Chemistry* distribute (small particles) uniformly in a medium. **6** *Physics* separate (white light) into its coloured constituents. ▶ **disperser** *noun*

dispersion *noun* **1** the action or process of distributing or spreading things or people over a wide area: *some seeds rely on birds for dispersion*. **2** the state of being dispersed over a wide area: *geographical dispersion along the St. Lawrence made it difficult for people to go to church*. [Say dis PUR zh'n]

dispirited *adjective* having lost enthusiasm or hope: *a dispirited party was recovering from a humbling electoral setback*. ▶ **dispiritedly** *adverb*

dispiriting *verb* discouraging. ▶ **dispiritingly** *adverb*

displace *verb* (**displaces, displaced, displacing**) **1 a** replace (a thing) with another. **b** supplant or take the place of (a person), esp. in some official capacity: *moderates have displaced the extremists on the committee*. **2** move or shift from its accustomed place. **3** force (a person) to leave his or her home, country, etc., esp. because of military or political pressures.

displaced person *noun* esp. *hist.* a refugee or person forced to leave his or her home country because of war, persecution, etc. Abbreviation: **DP**.

displacement *noun* **1** the moving of something from its place or position: *a displacement of the vertebra*. **2** the removal of someone or something by someone or something else which takes their place: *the party's somewhat precarious displacement of the Conservatives as the official opposition*. **3** the enforced departure of people from their homes, typically because of war, persecution, or natural disaster: *the building of hydro dams and resultant flooding often results in the displacement of people*. **4** *Physics* the amount by which anything is displaced, esp. the amount of a fluid displaced by a solid floating or immersed in it. **5** *Psychology* the unconscious transfer of strong unacceptable emotions from one object to another: *this phobia was linked with the displacement of fear of his father*. **6** *Geology* the relative movement on either side of a fault plane: *the largest fault has an estimated displacement of 15 m*.

display • *verb* show. • *noun* **1** a notable or conspicuous demonstration of a particular type of behaviour, emotion, or skill: *a hint of malice underlying her display of concern*. **2 a** a performance, show, or event intended for public entertainment: *a display of fireworks* ◊ *an aerobatics display team*. **b** a collection of objects arranged for public viewing: *the museum houses an informative display of rocks* ◊ *the plans for the new opera house have recently gone on display to the public*. **c** a presentation (of merchandise etc.) designed to show the product to advantage: *conference delegates are invited to visit our book display*. **3** the conspicuous exhibition of one's wealth. **4** the distinct behaviour of some birds and fish, used esp. to attract a mate. **5 a** the presentation of data, images, etc. on a computer screen etc. **b** the information so presented.

displease *verb* (**displeases, displeased, displeasing**) make indignant or angry; offend. PHRASES **be displeased** (often foll. by *at*, *with*) be indignant or dissatisfied. ▶ **displeasing** *adjective*

displeasure *noun* disapproval; dissatisfaction; anger.

disposable • *adjective* **1** intended to be used once and then thrown away: *disposable diapers*. **2** that can be thrown away or disposed of safely: *disposable alkaline batteries*. **3** (esp. of financial assets) available for use. • *noun* a thing designed to be thrown away after one use.

disposable income *noun* **1** income available after taxes, expenses, etc. for spending, saving, or investment. **2** the total amount of money at the disposal of consumers in a country, community, etc.

disposal *noun* **1** the action or process of throwing away or getting rid of something: *the disposal of radioactive waste*. **2** the sale of shares, property, or other assets: *the disposal of her shares in the company*. **3** (esp. as **waste disposal**) the disposing of garbage. PHRASES **at one's disposal 1** available for one's use: *put a helicopter at their disposal*. **2** subject to one's orders or decisions: *I am at your disposal till Sunday*.

dispose *verb* (**disposes, disposed, disposing**) **1** make willing. **2** place suitably or in order: *disposed the pictures in sequence*. **3** determine the course of events. PHRASES **dispose of 1 a** settle or deal conclusively with (an issue, opponent, etc.). **b** get rid of. **c** finish (a task etc.). **d** kill. **2** sell. **3** prove (a claim, an argument, an opponent, etc.) to be incorrect. **4** *informal* consume (food).

disposed *adjective* **1** inclined, prepared, or in the mood (to do something etc.): *was disposed to release them*. **2** having a specified mental inclination (usu. in *combination*): *ill disposed*. **3** subject, liable, or having a physical inclination to.

disposer *noun* a device used for disposal, esp. of garbage: *waste disposer*.

disposition *noun* **1 a** temperament or character, esp. as displayed in dealings with others: *a gentle disposition*. **b** (often foll. by *to*) a natural tendency or inclination: *a disposition to overeat*. **2** the way something is placed or arranged, esp. in relation to other things: *the plan need not be accurate so long as it shows the disposition of the rooms*. **3** (usu. in *plural*) **a** *Military* the stationing of troops ready for attack or defence. **b** the action of arranging or ordering people or things in a particular way: *the state is given widespread powers regarding the disposition and control of the armed forces*. **4 a** the action of distributing or transferring property or money to someone, in particular in a will: *this is a tax which affects the disposition of assets on death*. **b** the power to deal with something as one pleases: *if Napoleon had had railways at his disposition, he would have been invincible*.

dispossess *verb* (**dispossesses, dispossessed, dispossessing**) deprive someone of something that they own, typically land or property: *some historians argue that the Metis were swindled out of their land in Manitoba by a deliberate government conspiracy to dispossess them* ◊ *people dispossessed of their cultural identity*. ▶ **dispossessed** *adjective* **dispossession** *noun*

disproportion *noun* the state of being out of proportion with something else: *indignation at the disproportion between the company's profits and the wretchedness of their employees*.

disproportionate *adjective* too large or small in comparison with something else: *poorer people spend a disproportionate amount of their income on housing*. ▶ **disproportionately** *adverb*

disprove *verb* (**disproves, disproved, disproving**) prove false; refute.

disputable *adjective* open to question; contentious.

disputation *noun* debate or argument: *promoting consensus rather than disputation*.

disputatious *adjective* **1** (of a person) fond of having heated arguments: *disputatious academics*. **2** (of an argument or situation) motivated by or causing strong opinions. ▶ **disputatiously** *adverb* **disputatiousness** *noun* [Say dis pyoo TAY shuss]

dispute ● *verb* (**disputes, disputed, disputing**) **1** argue about something; discuss heatedly: *the point has been much disputed*. **2** question the truth, correctness, or validity of: *the accusations are not disputed*. **3** compete for; strive to win: *the two drivers crashed while disputing the lead*. ● *noun* **1** a controversy; a debate. **2** a quarrel. **3** a disagreement between management and employees, esp. one leading to industrial action. PHRASES **beyond** (or **without**) **dispute** certainly; indisputably. **in dispute** being argued about. **open to dispute** not yet decided definitely: *such estimates are always open to dispute*. ▶ **disputed** *adjective*

disqualification *noun* **1 a** the act or an instance of disqualifying. **b** the state of being disqualified. **2** a fact or condition that disqualifies someone from a position or activity: *being female is no longer a disqualification for a military career*.

disqualify *verb* (**disqualifies, disqualified, disqualifying**) **1** (often foll. by *from*) bar from a competition or pronounce ineligible as a winner because of an infringement of the rules etc. **2** (often foll. by *for, from*) make or pronounce ineligible or not suitable: *his age disqualifies him for the job*. **3** (often foll. by *from*) deprive of legal capacity, power, or right: *disqualified from practising as a doctor*.

disquiet ● *verb* worry; make anxious: *she felt disquieted at the lack of interest the girl had shown*. ● *noun* anxiety:

public disquiet about the safety of the new trains. ▶ **disquieting** *adjective*

disquisition *noun* a long or elaborate treatise or discourse on a subject. [Say dis quiz ISH'n]

disregard ● *verb* pay no attention to: *the board disregarded my recommendations* ◊ *safety rules were disregarded*. ● *noun* (often foll. by *of, for*) lack of regard or respect: *a total disregard for other people's feelings*.

disrepair *noun* the state of being in poor condition, esp. due to neglect: *in disrepair*.

disreputable *adjective* **1** of bad reputation: *she spent the evening with her disreputable brother Stefan*. **2** not respectable in appearance; shabby; untidy: *he was heavy, grubby, and vaguely disreputable*. ▶ **disreputableness** *noun* **disreputably** *adverb* [Say dis REP you tuh bull]

disrepute *noun* a lack of good reputation or respectability: *fall into disrepute*. [Say dis ree PYOOT]

disrespect ● *noun* a lack of respect or courtesy. ● *verb* *informal* have or show no respect or reverence for. ▶ **disrespectful** *adjective* **disrespectfully** *adverb*

disrobe *verb* (**disrobes, disrobed, disrobing**) undress, esp. remove the clothes worn for an official ceremony: *she began to disrobe* ◊ *she remembers being disrobed*.

disrupt *verb* make it difficult for something to continue in the normal way; bring disorder to: *demonstrators disrupted the meeting* ◊ *bus services will be disrupted tomorrow because of the bridge closure*. ▶ **disruption** *noun* **disruptive** *adjective* **disruptively** *adverb*

diss *verb* = DIS *verb*.

dissatisfaction *noun* a lack of satisfaction; disappointment, frustration, unhappiness: *tenants have expressed their dissatisfaction with the apartment*.

dissatisfy *verb* (**dissatisfies, dissatisfied, dissatisfying**) make discontented; fail to satisfy.

dissect *verb* **1** cut into pieces. **2** cut up (a plant or animal) to examine its parts, structure, etc., or (a corpse) for a post mortem. **3** analyze; criticize or examine in detail: *her latest novel was dissected by the critics*. ▶ **dissection** *noun* [Say dis SECT or dis SECT]

dissemble *verb* (**dissembles, dissembled, dissembling**) **1** conceal one's motives; talk or act hypocritically: *he was a very honest person who was incapable of dissembling*. **2** disguise or conceal (a feeling or intention): *she smiled, dissembling her true emotion*. ▶ **dissembler** *noun* [Say dis SEM bull]

disseminate *verb* (**disseminates, disseminated, disseminating**) spread (esp. ideas) widely: *their findings have been widely disseminated*. ▶ **dissemination** *noun* **disseminator** *noun* [Say dis EMMA nate]

dissension *noun* disagreement giving rise to quarrelling or conflict: *the party was ripped apart by dissension over his leadership*.

SPELL CHECK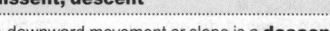

dissent, descent
....
A downward movement or slope is a **descent**.

---

dissent ● *verb* **1** think differently; disagree: *two ministers dissented from the official view*. **2** differ in religious opinion, esp. from the doctrine of an established or orthodox church. ● *noun* **1** a difference of opinion or an expression of this: *political dissent* ◊ *voices of dissent began to rise against the established authority* ◊ *stability only exists in the country because dissent has been suppressed*. **2** the refusal to accept the doctrines of an established or orthodox church.

dissenter *noun* a person who dissents.

dissenting *adjective* expressing disagreement or a difference of opinion: *Norton cast the dissenting vote*.

dissertation *noun* a detailed discourse on a subject, esp. one submitted in partial fulfilment of the requirements of a doctorate. [Say disser TAY sh'n]

disservice *noun* an unhelpful or hurtful action: *you have done us a disservice by ignoring this fact.* [Say dis SERVICE]

dissidence *noun* protest against an official policy. [Say DIS id ince]

dissident • *adjective* disagreeing, esp. with an established government, system, etc.: *fears retribution for her dissident stand.* • *noun* a person who opposes official policy, esp. that of an authoritarian regime: *the government has released imprisoned dissidents.* [Say DIS id int]

dissimilar *adjective* unlike, not similar: *the two languages are completely dissimilar from each other.* ► **dissimilarity** *noun* (*plural* **dissimilarities**)

dissipate *verb* (**dissipates, dissipated, dissipating**) **1 a** cause (a cloud, vapour, fear, darkness, etc.) to disappear or disperse: *her laughter soon dissipated the tension in the air.* **b** disperse, scatter, disappear: *eventually, his anger dissipated.* **2** break up; bring or come to nothing: *what started as an effort to outline specific needs soon dissipated into a vague discussion of generalities.* **3** squander or fritter away (money, energy, etc.): *our energies were too often dissipated in supporting lost causes.*

dissipated *adjective* enjoying activities that are harmful such as drinking too much alcohol: *he plays a dissipated American writer living in Europe.*

dissipation *noun* **1** living a life of harmful but enjoyable activities; debauched living: *a life of drunkenness and dissipation.* **2** wasteful expenditure: *concerns about the dissipation of the country's wealth.* **3** scattering, dispersion, or disintegration: *even Liberal strategists concede they may lose several seats with the dissipation of Trudeaumania.*

dissociate *verb* (**dissociates, dissociated, dissociating**) **1** disconnect or become disconnected; separate: *she tried to dissociate the two events in her mind.* **2** *Chemistry* decompose, esp. reversibly. **3** *Psychology* cause (a person's mind) to develop more than one centre of consciousness. PHRASES **dissociate oneself from 1** declare oneself unconnected with. **2** decline to support or agree with (a proposal etc.): *he dissociated himself from the party's more extreme views.*

dissociation *noun* **1** the disconnection or separation of something from something else or the state of being disconnected: *the dissociation of political and moral ideas.* **2** *Psychology* separation of normally related mental processes, resulting in one group functioning independently from the rest, leading in extreme cases to disorders such as multiple personality.

dissolute *adjective* enjoying immoral activities and not caring about behaving in a morally acceptable way: *the drunken, dissolute, but noble-hearted lawyer Sydney Carton.* [Say DISSA lute]

dissolution *noun* **1** disintegration; decomposition: *dissolution of bare limestone is relatively slow.* **2** the act of officially ending a marriage, business partnership, or political alliance: *the dissolution of the Soviet Union.* **3** the dismissal or dispersal of an assembly, esp. of a parliament at the end of its term. **4** bringing or coming to an end: *the dissolution of barriers of class and race.* **5** immoral living: *Jagger and Richards had taken two different paths to dissolution: the jet set and heroin.* [Say dissa LOO sh'n]

dissolve • *verb* (**dissolves, dissolved, dissolving**) **1** make or become liquid, esp. by immersion or dispersion in a liquid. **2** disappear or cause to disappear gradually. **3 a** dismiss or disperse (an assembly, esp. parliament). **b** (of an assembly) be dissolved. **4** annul or put an end to (a partnership, marriage, etc.). **5** (of a person) become enfeebled or emotionally overcome. **6** change gradually (from one film or video image into another). • *noun* the act or process of dissolving a film or video image.

dissonance *noun* **1** lack of harmony among musical notes. **2** a tension or clash resulting from the combination of two conflicting elements. [Say DISSA nince]

dissonant *adjective* **1** *Music* lacking harmony: *dissonant chords.* **2** unsuitable or unusual in combination; clashing: *Jackson uses both harmonious and dissonant colour choices.* [Say DISSA nint]

dissuade *verb* (often foll. by *from*) discourage (a person); persuade against: *dissuaded him from continuing.* ► **dissuasion** *noun* **dissuasive** *adjective* [Say dis SWADE]

dissymmetry *noun* (*plural* **dissymmetries**) **1** lack of symmetry: *dance uses both symmetry and dissymmetry to create beautiful images.* **2** symmetry as of mirror images or the left and right hands (esp. of crystals with two corresponding forms). [Say dis SYMMETRY]

distance • *noun* **1** the condition of being far off; remoteness. **2 a** a space or interval between two things. **b** the length of this: *a distance of 20 km.* **3** a distant point or place: *came from a distance.* **4** the avoidance of familiarity; aloofness. **5** a remoter field of vision: *saw him in the distance.* **6** an interval of time: *can't remember what happened at this distance.* **7 a** the full length of a race etc. **b** *Boxing* the scheduled length of a fight. • *verb* (**distances, distanced, distancing**) place far off: *distanced herself from them* ◊ *distanced himself from their philosophy.* PHRASES **at a distance** far off. **go the distance 1** *Boxing* complete a fight without being knocked out. **2** complete, esp. a hard task; endure an ordeal. **keep one's distance** maintain one's reserve. **within hailing distance** not far; close enough to be called to. **within walking distance** near enough to walk to.

distant *adjective* **1 a** far away in space or time. **b** at a specified distance: *three miles distant from them.* **2** remote or far apart in position, time, resemblance, etc.: *a distant relative.* **3** not intimate; reserved; cool. **4** remote; abstracted: *a distant stare.* **5** faint, vague: *a distant memory.* ► **distantly** *adverb*

distant early warning *noun* see DEW LINE.

distaste *noun* (usu. foll. by *for*) dislike; aversion.

distasteful *adjective* unpleasant or offensive: *the bad language in the film was distasteful and unnecessary.* ► **distastefulness** *noun*

distemper[1] • *noun* **1** a type of paint that is mixed with water and used on walls. **2** a method of painting using this. • *verb* paint (walls etc.) with distemper.

distemper[2] *noun* **1 a** (also **canine distemper**) a disease of dogs, causing fever, coughing, and catarrh. **b** (also **feline distemper**) a usu. fatal viral disease of cats, causing fever, vomiting, and diarrhea. **c** a disease of various other animals. **2** uneasiness: *the modern world's distemper with religious teachings.*

distempered *adjective* disordered, disturbed; uneasy: *in that distempered summer I was sure the whole world was against me.*

distend *verb* swell out by pressure from within: *distended stomach.* ► **distension** *noun* [Say dis TEND]

distill *verb* (**distills, distilled, distilling**) **1** purify (a liquid) by vaporizing it with heat, then condensing it with cold and collecting the result. **2 a** extract the essence of (a plant etc.) usu. by heating it in a solvent. **b** extract the essential meaning or implications of (an

idea etc.): *the notes I made on my travels were distilled into a book*. **3** make (esp. liquor) by distilling raw materials.

distillate *noun* a product of distillation: *a petroleum distillate*. [Say DISTA lit or DISTA late]

distillation *noun* **1 a** an act of distilling a liquid or liquor. **b** the act of extracting the essential meaning or implications of an idea etc.: *her style is the distillation of a lifetime of reading and listening*. **2** something distilled: *the movie is a perfect distillation of adolescence*.

distiller *noun* a person who distills, esp. a manufacturer of alcoholic liquor.

distillery *noun* (*plural* **distilleries**) a place where liquor is distilled. [Say dis TILLA ree]

WRITING TIP
distinct, distinctive

Do not confuse **distinct** and **distinctive**. **Distinct** refers to something that stands out as being different from its surroundings, while **distinctive** refers to a quality that distinguishes one thing from another. *Distinct red spots on the back of the beetle* tells you that the red spots stood out clearly or were easily distinguished, while *distinctive red spots on the back of the beetle* indicates that the red spots are what sets this beetle apart from other beetles.

---

distinct *adjective* **1 a** not identical; separate; individual: *the results of the survey fell into two distinct groups*. **b** different in kind or quality; unlike: *the existence of a Canadian literature distinct from European and American literature*. **2 a** clearly perceptible: *here was a distinct smell of gas*. **b** clearly understandable; definite. **3** unmistakable, decided: *a distinct impression*.

distinction *noun* **1** a difference or contrast between similar things or people: *completely unaware of class distinctions ◊ philosophers didn't use to make a distinction between arts and science*. **2** the separation of things or people into different groups according to their attributes or characteristics: *the provisions of the law are applicable without distinction to everyone*. **3** a decoration or honour awarded to someone: *Virginia gained the highest distinction awarded for excellence in teaching*. **4** excellence that sets someone or something apart from others: *a film of distinction*. **5** a grade in an examination etc. denoting great excellence: *passed with distinction*. **6** the quality of being somehow special or set apart from others: *Holy Trinity Church has the distinction of being the oldest-known church in Saskatchewan ◊ the dubious distinction of finishing dead last*.

distinctive *adjective* having a quality or characteristic that makes something different and easily noticed: *clothes with a distinctive style ◊ the male bird has distinctive black and white markings on its head*. ▶ **distinctively** *adverb* **distinctiveness** *noun*

distinctly *adverb* **1** clearly, unmistakably, plainly: *I distinctly remember telling him*. **2** characteristically, quintessentially: *chicken fricot is a distinctly Acadian dish*.

distinctness *noun* the quality of being distinct.

distinguish *verb* (**distinguishes**, **distinguished**, **distinguishing**) **1 a** see or point out the difference of; draw distinctions: *cannot distinguish one from the other*. **b** constitute such a difference: *this distinguishes us from the competition*. **2** be a mark or property of; characterize. **3** discover by listening, looking, etc.: *could distinguish two voices*. **4** make prominent or noteworthy: *distinguished herself by winning*. **5** (foll. by *between*) make or point out a difference between. ▶ **distinguishable** *adjective*

distinguished *adjective* **1 a** of high standing: *a distinguished career in medicine*. **b** eminent; famous.

2 having a distinguished air, features, manner, etc.: *I think grey hair makes you look very distinguished*.

distort *verb* **1 a** put out of shape; make or become crooked or unshapely. **b** distort the appearance of, esp. by curved mirrors, imperfect lenses, etc. **2** misrepresent (motives, facts, statements, etc.). **3** *Electronics* change the form of (a signal) during transmission or amplification. ▶ **distorted** *adjective*

distortion *noun* **1 a** the action of giving a misleading or false account or impression of: *a distortion of the facts*. **b** the action of twisting out of shape: *these bugs suck the sap of plants, causing weakening and distortion*. **2** *Electronics* a change in the form of a signal during transmission etc. usu. with some impairment of quality. **3** the characteristic fuzzy sound of electric guitars in some forms of popular music, e.g. heavy metal.

distract *verb* draw away the attention of: *you're distracting me from my work ◊ I find the noise distracting*.

distracted *adjective* unable to concentrate because one's mind is preoccupied by something worrying or unpleasant. ▶ **distractedly** *adverb*

distraction *noun* **1 a** the act of distracting, esp. the mind. **b** something that distracts; an interruption. **2** a relaxation from work; an amusement. **3** a lack of concentration. **4** perplexity. **5** frenzy; madness. **PHRASES** **to distraction** almost to a state of madness.

distraught *adjective* very worried, upset, etc.: *he's still too distraught to speak about the tragedy*. [Say dis TROT]

distress • *noun* (*plural* **distresses**) **1** severe trouble, anxiety, sorrow, etc. **2** *Medical* the state of an organ etc. that is not functioning normally or adequately. • *verb* (**distresses**, **distressed**, **distressing**) **1** subject to distress; exhaust; afflict. **2** cause anxiety to; make unhappy; vex. **3** scratch or mark (clothing, furniture, etc.) to simulate the effects of age and wear. **PHRASES** **in distress 1** suffering or in danger. **2** (of a ship, aircraft, etc.) in danger or damaged.

distressed *adjective* **1** suffering from distress. **2** impoverished: *living in distressed circumstances*. **3** (of furniture, leather, etc.) having simulated marks of age and wear.

distressing *adjective* causing extreme sorrow or worry: *a particularly distressing news item*.

distressingly *adverb* in a manner that causes distress: *incidents of this kind are distressingly common*.

distribute *verb* (**distributes**, **distributed**, **distributing**) **1** give shares of. **2** spread throughout a region; scatter. **3** divide into parts; arrange; classify. **4** supply (goods etc.) to customers.

distributed computing *noun* computing using a client-server system.

distribution *noun* **1** the action of sharing something out among a number of recipients: *an annual sum for distribution among researchers*. **2** the way in which something is shared out among a group or spread over an area: *changes to the environment have affected distribution of wildlife in the area ◊ the unfair distribution of wealth in society*. **3** the action or process of supplying goods to stores and other businesses that sell to consumers: *director of distribution ◊ has the Canadian distribution rights for the CD*. **4** *Statistics* the way in which a characteristic is spread over members of a class. ▶ **distributional** *adjective*

distributive • *adjective* **1 a** concerned with the supply of goods to shops and other businesses that sell to consumers: *transport and distributive industries*. **b** concerned with the way in which things are shared between people· *the distributive effects of public spending*. **2** *Math* governed by or stating the condition that when an operation is performed on two or more quantities already combined by a second operation, the result is

the same as when it is performed on each quantity individually and the products then combined. [Say dis TRIBUTE iv]

distributor *noun* **1** a person or company that supplies goods to stores etc. **2** *Electricity* a device in an internal combustion engine for passing the current to each spark plug in turn. [Say dis TRIBUTE ur]

district *noun* **1** a territory marked off for special administrative purposes. **2** an area which has common characteristics: *the wine-growing district.*

district attorney *noun* (in the US) the prosecuting law officer of a district. Abbreviation: **DA**.

distrust • *noun* a lack of trust. • *verb* have no trust or confidence in; doubt. ▶ **distrustful** *adjective*

disturb *verb* **1** break the rest, calm, order, or quiet of; interrupt. **2** agitate; worry, unsettle: *your story disturbs me.* **3** move from a settled position, disarrange: *the papers had been disturbed.*

disturbance *noun* **1** the interruption of a settled and peaceful condition: *helicopters can cause disturbance to residents.* **2** a breakdown of peaceful and law-abiding behaviour; a riot: *serious disturbances in the streets* ◊ *was charged with causing a disturbance in a public place.* **3** the disruption of healthy function: *suffered from a severe mental disturbance.* **4** *Meteorology* a low-pressure feature.

disturbed *adjective* **1** in senses of DISTURB. **2** emotionally or mentally unstable or abnormal.

disturbing *adjective* causing anxiety or shock; upsetting. ▶ **disturbingly** *adverb*

disulphide *noun* (also **disulfide**) a chemical with two atoms of sulphur in each molecule. [Say die SULFIDE]

disuse *noun* a disused state: *rusty because of disuse.* PHRASES **fall into disuse** cease to be used: *carolling seems to have fallen into disuse.*

disused *adjective* no longer used: *came across a disused hunting camp.*

ditch • *noun* (*plural* **ditches**) **1** a long narrow excavated channel esp. for drainage. **2** a watercourse, stream, etc. • *verb* (**ditches, ditched, ditching**) **1** make or repair ditches. **2** *informal* **a** get rid of. **b** cease consorting with (esp. a lover etc.). **c** abandon. **3 a** bring (an aircraft) down on water in an emergency. **b** drive (a vehicle) into a ditch. **4** (of an aircraft) make a forced landing on water. ▶ **ditcher** *noun*

dither • *verb* hesitate; be indecisive. • *noun* *informal* **1** a state of agitation or apprehension. **2** a state of hesitation; indecisiveness. ▶ **ditherer** *noun*

dithered *adjective* (of a computer image) shaded by dithering.

dithering *noun* **1** in senses of DITHER *verb*. **2** *Computing* a method of creating apparently smooth gradations of shade or continuous tones by gradually spacing single-tone pixels (*compare* GREY-SCALE).

dithery *adjective* tending to dither or be indecisive.

Ditidaht *noun* (*plural* **Ditidaht** or **Ditidahts**) = NITINAT. [Say DITTY dot]

ditto *noun* (*plural* **dittos**) **1** (in accounts, inventories, lists, etc.) the aforesaid, the same. **2** *informal* (replacing a word or phrase to avoid repetition) the same: *came in late last night and ditto the night before.*

ditty *noun* (*plural* **ditties**) a short simple song.

ditz *noun* (*plural* **ditzes**) a ditzy person.

ditzy *adjective* (**ditzier, ditziest**) (also **ditsy, ditsier, ditsiest**) *informal* (usu. of a woman) silly or foolish.

diuretic • *adjective* causing increased output of urine. • *noun* a diuretic drug or substance. [Say die a RET ick]

diurnal *adjective* **1** of or during the day. **2** daily; of each day. **3** *Astronomy* occupying one day: *the diurnal rotation of the earth.* **4** (of animals) active in the daytime: *unlike most other bats, this species is diurnal.* **5** (of plants)

open only during the day. ▶ **diurnally** *adverb* [Say die UR n'll]

diva *noun* (*plural* **divas**) a great or famous woman singer; a prima donna. [Say DEEVA]

divalent *adjective* *Chemistry* having a valence of two; bivalent. [Say die VAY lint]

divan *noun* **1** a backless sofa. **2** a bed consisting of a base and mattress, usu. with no board at either end. [Say dih VAN]

dive • *verb* (**dives**; *past* **dived** or **dove**; *past participle* **dived; diving**) **1** plunge headfirst and with arms outstretched into water. **2** go to a deeper level in water. **3** swim under water using breathing equipment. **4** plunge steeply downwards through the air. **5** move quickly or suddenly in a downward direction or under cover. **6** (in hockey etc.) fall deliberately in an attempt to draw a penalty on one's opponent. • *noun* **1** an act or instance of diving. **2** *informal* a seedy, rundown nightclub, bar, etc. **3** (in hockey, soccer, etc.) a deliberate fall in an attempt to draw a penalty on one's opponent. PHRASES **dive in** *informal* help oneself (to food).

dive-bomb *verb* **1** (of an aircraft) bomb (a target) while diving towards it. **2** (of a bird, insect, etc.) descend rapidly from a height to attack something. ▶ **dive-bomber** *noun*

diver *noun* **1** a person who dives. **2** any of various diving birds, esp. of the family Gaviidae; a loon.

diverge *verb* (**diverges, diverged, diverging**) **1 a** proceed in a different direction or in different directions from a point: *the coastal road diverges from the freeway just north of the next town.* **b** take a different course or different courses: *their interests diverged.* **2** (often foll. by *from*) depart from a set course: *diverged from his parents' wishes.*

divergence *noun* **1** a tendency to be different or to develop in different directions: *the divergence of the two dialects* ◊ *a divergence from his normal behaviour.* **2** a difference or conflict in opinions, interests, wishes, tendencies, etc.: *divergences of attitude.*

divergent *adjective* **1** tending to be different or develop in different directions: *divergent interpretations.* **2** *Psychology* (of thought) tending to reach a variety of possible solutions when analyzing a problem.

diverse *adjective* unlike in nature or qualities; varied: *people from diverse cultures* ◊ *my interests are very diverse.* ▶ **diversely** *adverb* [Say die VERSE]

diversification *noun* **1** the process of varying or diversifying something: *the diversification of the high school curriculum.* **2** the process of spreading investments over several enterprises to reduce the risk of loss. **3** the process of expanding or varying the range of products or services handled by a company. [Say die verse iffa CAY sh'n]

diversify *verb* (**diversifies, diversified, diversifying**) **1** change or make something change so that there is greater variety: *patterns of family life are diversifying and changing.* **2** spread (investment, efforts, etc.) over several enterprises or products, esp. to reduce the risk of loss: *farmers are being encouraged to diversify into new crops.* **3** (of a company etc.) expand the range of products handled: *the company is diversifying into food, beverages, and hotels.* [Say die VERSE if eye]

diversion *noun* **1** the action of turning something aside from its course: *a river diversion project* ◊ *the diversion of his energies into other channels.* **2** something intended to distract someone's attention from something more important: *a smoke bomb created a diversion while the robbery took place.* **3** an activity that is done for pleasure, esp. for taking one's mind away from tedious or serious concerns: *our chief diversion was*

reading. **4** an artificial watercourse created to divert the flow of water from one body to another or to provide drainage. ▶ **diversionary** *adjective*

diversity *noun* (*plural* **diversities**) **1** the condition or quality of being diverse; variety: *the biological diversity of the rainforests* ◊ *a rich diversity of opinion*. **2** a variety: *there is a need for greater diversity and choice in education*. [Say die VERSA tee or div VERSA tee]

divert *verb* **1 a** turn aside from a direction or course: *northbound traffic will have to be diverted onto minor roads* ◊ *the course of the stream has now been diverted*. **b** draw the attention of; distract. **2** (often as **diverting** *adjective*) entertain; amuse: *the play was a clever, diverting whodunit*. ▶ **divertingly** *adverb* [Say die VERT or div VERT]

divest *verb* **1** sell off (a subsidiary company, investments, etc.). **2** unclothe; strip: *divested himself of his jacket*. **3** deprive; free, rid: *must divest ourselves of such prejudices*. [Say die VEST]

divestiture *noun* = DIVESTMENT. [Say die VESTA chur]

divestment *noun* the action or process of selling off subsidiary business interests or investments.

divide • *verb* (**divides, divided, dividing**) **1** separate into parts. **2** distribute or share out. **3** disagree or cause to disagree. **4** form a boundary between. **5** *Math* **a** find how many times (a number) contains another number. **b** (of a number) be susceptible of division without a remainder. **6** (of a legislative assembly) separate or be separated into two groups for voting. • *noun* **1 a** a dividing or boundary line; a gulf: *the divide between rich and poor*. **b** a separation: *the cultural divide*. **2** a line of high land that separates two river systems; a watershed: *settlers crossing the great divide*. PHRASES **divided against itself** consisting of opposing factions: *a party divided against itself can never hope to attract new members*.

dividend *noun* **1 a** a sum of money to be divided among a number of persons, e.g. to shareholders, members of a co-operative, creditors of an insolvent estate, etc. **b** an individual's share of a dividend. **2** *Math* a number to be divided by a divisor. **3** a benefit from any action: *their long training paid dividends*. [Say DIVVA dend]

divider *noun* anything which divides a whole into sections, esp. an insert in a binder, notebook, etc., or a screen etc., dividing a room into two parts.

dividing line *noun* a real or notional line between sharply contrasted things, characteristics, etc.

divination *noun* the act of finding out and saying what will happen in the future, esp. as supposedly gained by supernatural means: *astrology, palmistry, and other forms of divination*. [Say divva NATION]

divine • *adjective* (**diviner, divinest**) **1 a** of, from, or like God or a god. **b** devoted to God; sacred: *divine service*. **2 a** more than humanly excellent, gifted, or beautiful. **b** *informal* excellent; delightful. • *verb* (**divines, divined, divining**) **1** discover by guessing, intuition, inspiration, or magic. **2** foresee, predict: *his brother usually divined his ulterior motives*. **3** practise divination. **4** discover water by dowsing. • *noun* **1** a cleric, usu. an expert in theology. **2** (**the Divine**) providence or God. ▶ **divinely** *adverb* **diviner** *noun*

diving *noun* **1** *in senses of* DIVE. **2** the sport of performing dives, esp. with elaborate twists etc. of the body.

diving board *noun* an elevated board projecting over water, used for diving from.

divinity *noun* (*plural* **divinities**) **1** the state or quality of being a god. **2 a** a god. **b** (**the Divinity**) God. **3** the study of religion; theology. **4** a type of fudge made with beaten egg whites and nuts.

divisible *adjective* **1** capable of being divided, physically or mentally: *the area is divisible into two zones*.

2 (foll. by *by*) *Math* containing (a number) a number of times without a remainder. [Say dih VIZZA bull]

division *noun* **1** the action of separating something into parts or the process of being separated: *cell division*. **2** *Math* the process of dividing one number by another. **3** disagreement or discord: *a country with ethnic and cultural divisions*. **4** *Parliament* the separation of members of a legislative body into two sets for counting votes for and against. **5** one of two or more parts into which a thing is divided. **6** a major unit of administration or organization, esp.: **a** a group of army brigades or regiments. **b** *Cdn* an administrative unit of a police force. **c** *Sport* a grouping of teams or athletes within a league etc. **d** = SCHOOL DIVISION. **7** a district defined for administrative purposes.

divisional *adjective* based on or having to do with an organizational or administrative division: *divisional manager* ◊ *divisional playoff*.

Divisional Court *noun* *Cdn* (in Ontario) a court consisting of tribunals of three judges, which hears appeals from lower provincial courts and provincial administrative tribunals.

division of labour *noun* the specialization of workers in the process of production or any other economic, domestic, etc. activity.

division of powers *noun* (in Canada) the separation of governmental responsibilities and privileges into federal and provincial jurisdictions.

division sign *noun* the sign (÷), placed between two numbers to indicate that the one preceding the sign is to be divided by the one following it.

divisive *adjective* causing disagreement: *the divisive issue of abortion*. ▶ **divisively** *adverb* **divisiveness** *noun* [Say dih VISS iv or dih VICE iv or dih VIZZ iv]

divisor *noun* **1** a number by which another is to be divided. **2** a number that divides another without a remainder: *3 is a divisor of 21*. [Say dih VIZE ur]

divorce • *noun* **1 a** the legal dissolution of a marriage. **b** a legal decree of this. **2** a severance or separation: *a divorce between thought and feeling*. • *verb* (**divorces, divorced, divorcing**) **1** separate (from) by divorce: *they divorced last year* ◊ *a divorced couple* ◊ *divorced him for neglect*. **2** detach, separate: *divorced from reality*.

divorcee *noun* a divorced person, esp. a divorced woman. [Say dih vor SAY or dih vor SEE]

divulge *verb* (**divulges, divulged, divulging**) disclose; reveal (a secret etc.): *the police refused to divulge the identity of the suspect*. [Say dih VULGE or dih VULGE]

divvy *verb* *informal* (**divvies, divvied, divvying**) (often foll. by *up*) share out; divide.

Diwali *noun* a major Hindu festival held in October or November honouring the goddess of prosperity, during which gifts are exchanged and lamps lit. [Say dee WOLLY]

Dixieland *noun* a kind of jazz with a strong two-beat rhythm and collective improvisation.

DIY *abbreviation* do-it-yourself. ▶ **DIYer** *noun*

dizzily *adverb* in a dizzy or confused way.

dizziness *noun* a dizzy or confused state.

dizzy • *adjective* (**dizzier, dizziest**) **1 a** giddy, unsteady. **b** feeling confused. **c** *informal* scatterbrained. **2** causing giddiness: *dizzy heights*. • *verb* (**dizzies, dizzied, dizzying**) **1** make dizzy. **2** bewilder: *dizzied by all the choices*. ▶ **dizzying** *adjective* **dizzyingly** *adverb*

DJ • *noun* (*plural* **DJs**) a disc jockey. • *verb* (**DJs, DJed, DJing**) act as a disc jockey.

DL *abbreviation* Baseball DISABLED LIST.

dl *abbreviation* decilitre(s).

DM *abbreviation* **1** *Cdn* Deputy Minister. **2** (also **D-mark**) Deutschmark. **3** dextromethorphan.

dm *abbreviation* decimetre(s).

DNA *abbreviation* (*plural* **DNAs**) deoxyribonucleic acid, the self-replicating material which is present in nearly all living organisms, esp. as a constituent of chromosomes, and is the carrier of genetic information. Each molecule of DNA consists of two strands coiled around each other in a structure like a spiral ladder. Each rung of the ladder consists of a pair of chemical groups called bases (of which there are four types), which combine in specific pairs so that the sequence on one strand of the spiral is complementary to that on the other; it is the specific sequence of the bases which constitutes the genetic information.

DNA fingerprinting *noun* = GENETIC FINGERPRINTING.

DND *abbreviation* (in Canada) Department of National Defence.

do¹ • *verb* (**does**; *past* **did**; *past participle* **done**; **doing**) **1** perform, carry out. **2** produce, make: *she was doing a painting*. **3** bestow, grant; have a specified effect on: *a walk would do you good* ◊ *do me a favour*. **4** act: *do as I do*. **5** work at: *what does your mother do?* ◊ *we're doing Chaucer*. **6** suffice: *a sandwich will do*. **7** deal with: *I must do my hair before we go*. **8 a** traverse (a certain distance): *we did fifty miles today*. **b** travel at a specified speed: *he was doing about eighty*. **9** *informal* act or behave like: *did a Houdini*. **10** *informal* finish: *I'm done in the bathroom*. **11** cook: *the potatoes aren't done yet*. **12** be in progress: *what's doing?* **13** *informal* visit: *we did all the art galleries*. **14** *informal* **a** (often as **done** *adjective*) exhaust; tire out: *the climb has completely done me*. **b** beat up, defeat, kill. **c** ruin: *now you've done it*. **15** *slang* take (a drug). • *auxiliary verb* **1 a** (except with *be*, *can*, *may*, *ought*, *shall*, *will*) in questions and negative statements: *do you understand?* **b** (except with *can*, *may*, *ought*, *shall*, *will*) in negative commands: *don't be silly*. **2** *ellipt.* or in place of verb or verb and object: *you know her better than I do*. **3** forming emphatic present and past tenses: *I do want to* ◊ *they did go*. **4** in inversion for emphasis: *did she but know it*. • *noun* (*plural* **dos** or **do's**) **1** *informal* an elaborate event, party, or operation. **2** *informal* a hairdo. PHRASES **do away with** *informal* **1** abolish. **2** kill. **do in 1** *slang* **a** kill. **b** ruin, do injury to. **2** *informal* exhaust, tire out. **do or die** persist regardless of danger. **do a person out of** *informal* unjustly deprive a person of; swindle out of. **do up 1** fasten, secure. **2** *informal* **a** refurbish, renovate. **b** adorn, dress up.

do² *noun* (*plural* **dos**) *Music* **1** (in tonic sol-fa) the first and eighth note of a major scale. **2** the note C in the fixed-do system. [Rhymes with GO]

DOA *abbreviation* dead on arrival (at hospital etc.).

doable *adjective* able to be done; practical. [Say DOO a bull]

D.O.B. *abbreviation* date of birth.

Doberman *noun* (also **Doberman pinscher**) a breed of large dog with a smooth coat, frequently used as a guard dog. [Say DOBER m'n (PIN sher)]

doc *noun informal* **1** doctor. **2** buddy, fellow: *what's up, doc?* **3** documentary. **4** *Computing* document.

docile *adjective* quiet and easy to control: *a docile child*. ▶**docilely** *adverb* **docility** *noun* [Say DOSS ile, or DOE sile, doss ILLA tee]

dock¹ • *noun* **1 a** a structure extending out from shore into a lake etc., either floating or on piles, to which boats are tied when not in use. **b** a ship's berth, a wharf. **2** an artificially enclosed body of water for the loading, unloading, and repair of ships. **3** (in *plural*) a range of docks with wharves and offices; a dockyard. **4** = LOADING DOCK. **5** = DRY DOCK. • *verb* **1** bring or come into a dock. **2 a** join (spacecraft) together in space. **b** (of spacecraft) be joined.

dock² *noun* the enclosure for the accused in a criminal court. PHRASES **in the dock** on trial.

dock³ *noun* any of various plants of the genus *Rumex*, with a spike of many small, green flowers.

dock⁴ • *verb* **1** cut short an animal's tail. **2** deduct a part from wages, supplies, etc.: *the government docks 10% off the top for taxes*. • *noun* the solid bony part of an animal's tail.

docket *noun* **1** a list of causes for trial or persons having causes pending. **2** *Business* a document or label that shows what is in a package, which goods have been delivered, which jobs have been done, etc.

dockside *noun* (often as an *adjective*) the area immediately adjacent to a dock.

dockyard *noun* an area with docks and equipment for building and repairing ships.

doctor • *noun* **1 a** a qualified practitioner of medicine; a physician or surgeon. **b** (esp. as an honorific) a qualified dentist, veterinarian, optometrist, or chiropractor. **2** a person who holds a doctorate. **3** *informal* a person who carries out repairs. • *verb informal* **1 a** treat medically. **b** (esp. as **doctoring** *noun*) practise as a physician. **2** castrate or spay. **3** mend. **4** adulterate: *the wine had been doctored*. **5** tamper with: *they were suspended for doctoring the results of the test*. PHRASES **what the doctor ordered** *informal* something beneficial or desirable: *the festival was just what the doctor ordered to banish the mid-winter blahs*.

doctoral *adjective* of or relating to a doctorate.

doctorate *noun* the highest university degree in any faculty.

Doctor of Philosophy *noun* **1** a doctorate awarded in the humanities, social sciences, pure sciences, etc. **2** a person holding such a degree. Abbreviation: **Ph.D.**

doctrinaire • *adjective* seeking to apply a theory or doctrine in all circumstances without regard to practical considerations; theoretical and impractical: *a doctrinaire communist*. [Say dock trin AIR]

doctrinal *adjective* of, relating to, or concerned with a doctrine or doctrines: *the doctrinal position of the church* ◊ *a rigidly doctrinal approach*. ▶**doctrinally** *adverb* [Say dock TRINE ul or DOCK trin'll]

doctrine *noun* **1** a principle of religious or political etc. belief. **2** a set of such principles. [Say DOCK trin]

docudrama *noun* a dramatized television film based on real events. [Say DOCK you drama]

document • *noun* **1** a piece of written or printed matter that provides a record or evidence of events, an agreement, ownership, identification, etc. **2** *Computing* a file, esp. a text file. • *verb* **1** prove by or provide with documents or evidence: *our findings have been well-documented*. **2** record in a document: *the results are documented in Chapter 3*. **3** provide with citations or references to support statements made: *a well-documented essay*.

documentarian *noun* **1** (also **documentarist**) a director or producer of documentaries. **2** a photographer specializing in producing a factual record.

documentary • *noun* (*plural* **documentaries**) a film or broadcast program based on real events, places, or circumstances and usu. intended primarily to record or inform. • *adjective* **1** consisting of documents: *documentary evidence*. **2** providing a factual record or report.

documentation *noun* **1** the provision of documents. **2** the preparation or use of documentary evidence or authorities. **3** documents produced as evidence or proof of something. **4** a collection of documents relating to a process or event, esp. the written specification and instructions accompanying a computer program.

dodder *verb* tremble or totter, esp. from age.

▶**dodderer** *noun* **doddering** *adjective* **doddery** *adjective*

dodge • *verb* (**dodges, dodged, dodging**) **1** (often foll. by *about, around*) move quickly to one side or quickly change position, to elude a pursuer, blow, etc. **2 a** evade by cunning or trickery: *dodged paying the fare*. **b** elude (a pursuer, opponent, blow, etc.) by a sideways movement etc. • *noun* **1** a quick movement to avoid or evade something. **2** a clever trick or expedient.

dodger *noun* **1** a person who dishonestly avoids doing something: *tax dodgers*. **2** a screen on a ship's bridge etc. as protection from spray etc.

dodo *noun* (*plural* **dodos** or **dodoes**) **1** an extinct large flightless bird native to Mauritius. **2** a stupid person: *what a dodo*. PHRASES **as dead as the** (or **a**) **dodo 1** completely or unmistakably dead. **2** entirely obsolete. [Say DOE doe]

doe *noun* a female deer, reindeer, hare, or rabbit.

doe-eyed *adjective* (esp. of a woman) having large gentle dark eyes.

doer *noun* **1** a person who does something. **2** a person who acts rather than merely talking etc. [Say DOO ur]

does 3rd *singular present of* DO[1].

doesn't *contraction* does not.

doff *verb literary* take off (one's hat, clothing).

dog • *noun* **1** any four-legged flesh-eating animal of the genus *Canis*, of many breeds domesticated and wild. **2** the male of any of these animals. **3** *informal* **a** a despicable person. **b** a person of a specified kind: *a lucky dog*. **c** *slang* an unattractive person, esp. a woman. **4** a mechanical device for gripping. **5** *slang* something of poor quality, e.g. an ill-performing stock, a bad movie, etc. **6** = HOT DOG *noun* 1. • *verb* (**dogs, dogged, dogging**) follow closely and persistently; pursue, track. PHRASES **die like a dog** die miserably or shamefully. **dog in the manger** a person who prevents others from using something, although that person has no use for it. **dog's age** *informal* a long time. **dog's breakfast** *informal* a mess. **a dog's life** a miserable or wretched existence. **go to the dogs** *informal* deteriorate, be ruined. **put on the dog** *informal* behave pretentiously. **sick as a dog** very ill. **work like a dog** work very hard.

dog collar *noun* **1** a collar for a dog. **2 a** *informal* a stiff upright white collar fastening at the back, worn by the clergy in some Christian denominations. **b** a straight high collar. **3** a jewelled band worn around the neck.

dog days *plural noun* **1** the hottest period of the year. **2** *informal* a period of inactivity, lethargy, etc.: *the housing market goes into its dog days in winter*.

dog-eared *adjective* (of a book etc.) with the corners worn or battered with use.

dog-eat-dog *adjective informal* ruthlessly competitive: *the dog-eat-dog world of business*.

dogfight *noun* **1** a fight between dogs. **2** a close combat between fighter aircraft. **3** a violent and confused fight.

dogfish *noun* (*plural* **dogfish** or **dogfishes**) any of various small sharks.

dogged *adjective* not giving up easily: *dogged persistence* ◊ *their dogged defence of the city*. ▶**doggedly** *adverb* **doggedness** *noun* [Say DOG id]

doggerel *noun* poetry that is badly written or ridiculous, sometimes because the writer has not intended it to be serious: *scribbling doggerel for the local paper*. [Say DOGGER ul]

doggone *adjective & adverb slang* damned.

doggy • *adjective* **1** of or like a dog. **2** devoted to dogs. • *noun* (also **doggie**) (*plural* **doggies**) a little dog; a pet name for a dog.

doggy bag *noun* a bag given to a customer in a restaurant or a guest at a party etc. for putting leftovers in to take home.

doghouse *noun* a shelter for a dog. PHRASES **in the doghouse** *informal* in disgrace or disfavour.

dogie *noun* (*West*) a motherless or neglected calf. [Say DOE ghee]

dogleg • *noun* a sharp bend like that in a dog's hind leg. • *adjective* (also **doglegged**) bent sharply. • *verb* (**doglegs, doglegged, doglegging**) bend sharply.

doglike *adjective* resembling a dog in appearance or behaviour.

dogma *noun* a belief or set of beliefs held by an authority or group, which others are expected to accept without argument.

dogmatic *adjective* **1** being certain that one's beliefs are right and that others should accept them, without paying attention to evidence or other opinions: *a dogmatic statement* ◊ *there is a danger of becoming too dogmatic about teaching methods*. **2** of or in the nature of dogma; doctrinal: *his morality was always that of dogmatic Christianity*. ▶**dogmatically** *adverb* [Say dog MAT ick]

dogmatism *noun* a tendency to be dogmatic. ▶**dogmatist** *noun* [Say DOGMA tism]

dog meat *noun* **1** the flesh of a dog. **2** meat to be used as food for dogs. **3** *informal* a person who is defeated etc.: *touch that and you're dog meat!*

do-good *adjective* actively trying to help others.

do-gooder *noun* a person who actively tries to help others, esp. one considered unrealistic or officious. ▶**do-goodery** *noun* **do-gooding** *noun & adjective*

dog-paddle • *noun* an elementary swimming stroke with short quick movements of the arms and legs beneath the body. • *verb* (**dog-paddles, dog-paddled, dog-paddling**) swim using this stroke.

Dogrib • *noun* (*plural* **Dogrib** or **Dogribs**) **1** a member of a Dene Aboriginal people living along the north shore of Great Slave Lake. **2** the Athapaskan language of this people. • *adjective* of this people or their language.

dog salmon *noun* a salmon of the North American Pacific coast; a chum salmon.

dogsled • *noun* a sled designed to be pulled by dogs. • *verb* (**dogsleds, dogsledded, dogsledding**) travel by dogsled. ▶**dogsledding** *noun*

dog's tooth *noun* (*plural* **dog's tooths** or **dog's teeth**) (also **dog's tooth violet**) any plant of the genus *Erythronium*, often with speckled leaves, e.g. *E. americanum* of eastern North America and *E. grandiflorum* of western North America.

dog tag *noun* **1** a tag attached to a dog's collar, giving an identification number, the dog's name, the owner's phone number, or vaccination information. **2** *slang* a soldier's metal identity tag.

dog-tired *adjective* utterly exhausted.

dogwood *noun* **1** any of various shrubs or small trees, including the flowering dogwoods and the low-growing bunchberry. **2** any of various similar trees. **3** the wood of the dogwood.

doh *noun* = DO[2].

DOHC *abbreviation* (of an automobile engine etc.) double overhead camshaft.

doily *noun* (*plural* **doilies**) a small ornamental mat of paper, lace, etc., e.g. on a table, or on a plate for cookies, sandwiches, etc.

doing *noun* **1** an action; the performance of a deed: *it was my doing*. **2** activity, effort: *it takes a lot of doing*.

do-it-yourself • *adjective* of work, esp. building, decorating, etc.) done or to be done by an amateur at home. • *noun* such work. ▶**do-it-yourselfer** *noun*

dojo *noun* (*plural* **dojos**) **1** a room or hall in which judo

D

and other martial arts are practised. **2** a mat on which judo etc. is practised. [Say DOE joe]

doldrums *plural noun* (usu. as **the doldrums**) **1** boredom or depression: *he's been in the doldrums ever since she left him.* **2** a period of inactivity or state of stagnation or sluggishness: *despite these measures, the economy remains in the doldrums.* [Say DOLE drums or DOLL drums]

dole • *noun* (usu. as **the dole**) *informal* benefit claimable by the unemployed from the government. • *verb* (**doles, doled, doling**) (usu. foll. by *out*) deal out, distribute: *the government doled out millions for community projects.* PHRASES **on the dole** *informal* receiving government unemployment benefits.

doleful *adjective* **1** mournful, sad: *a doleful expression.* **2** dreary, dismal: *a doleful landscape.* ▶ **dolefully** *adverb* **dolefulness** *noun*

doll • *noun* **1** a usu. small model of a human figure, usu. a child or woman, esp. for use as a toy. **2** *informal* **a** an attractive person. **b** a helpful or kind person. **c** an affectionate or familiar form of address. • *verb* (foll. by *up*) dress up smartly.

dollar *noun* **1** the chief monetary unit of Canada, the US, Australia, and certain other countries. **2** money available to be spent: *the spectator dollar.* PHRASES **bet dollars to doughnuts** maintain as a certainty.

dollar store *noun* a store selling low-priced, often discontinued or remaindered items.

dollhouse *noun* (also **doll's house**) **1** a miniature toy house for dolls. **2** a very small house.

doll-like *adjective* resembling a doll, esp. in prettiness or daintiness.

dollop • *noun* **1** a shapeless lump of something soft, esp. food. **2** something added as if in dollops: *they could use a dollop of common sense.* • *verb* (**dollops, dolloped, dolloping**) serve out in large shapeless quantities: *the physio dolloped cold jelly onto my wrist.*

dolly *noun* (*plural* **dollies**) **1** a child's name for a doll. **2** a small four-wheeled cart for moving appliances, boxes, etc. **3** a movable platform for a movie or video camera.

Dolly Varden *noun* (*plural* **Dolly Varden** or **Dolly Vardens**) **1** a brightly spotted char, *Salvelinus malma*, of western North America. **2** a woman's large hat with one side drooping and with a floral trimming.

dolomite *noun* a mineral or rock of calcium magnesium carbonate. ▶ **dolomitic** *adjective* [Say DOLLA mite or DOLA mite, dolla MIT ick or dola MIT ick]

dolphin *noun* any of various porpoise-like sea mammals having a slender beak-like snout.

dolt *noun* a stupid person. ▶ **doltish** *adjective*

-dom *suffix* forming nouns denoting a class of people (or the attitudes etc. associated with them) regarded collectively: *officialdom.*

domain *noun* **1** an area under one rule: *the Spice Islands were within the Spanish domains.* **2** a sphere of control or influence: *economic activities were the exclusive domain of the Europeans.* **3** *Math* the set of possible values of an independent variable. **4** (also **domain name**) the parts of an e-mail address following the @ symbol.

dome • *noun* **1** a rounded vault as a roof. **2** a stadium with a domed roof. **3 a** a natural vault or canopy (of the sky, trees, etc.). **b** the rounded summit of a hill etc. **4** a dome-shaped landform or underground structure. **5** a raised, glassed-in area of the roof of a railway car, allowing passengers a full view of surrounding scenery. **6** *slang* the head. • *verb* (**domes, domed, doming**) (usu. as **domed** *adjective*) cover with or shape as a dome.

domestic • *adjective* **1** of the home, household, or family affairs. domestic appliances. **2** of or within one's

own country, not foreign or international: *domestic affairs* ◊ *domestic flights.* **3** (of an animal) kept by or living with human beings. **4** fond of home life. • *noun* a household servant.

domestically *adverb* **1** within one's own country: *domestically produced goods.* **2** in a way suggesting fondness for home life: *I'm not very domestically inclined.*

domesticate *verb* (**domesticates, domesticated, domesticating**) **1** tame (an animal) to live with humans. **2** naturalize (a plant etc.).

domesticated *adjective* **1** (of an animal or plant) kept by humans for work, food, or companionship; not wild. **2** (of a person) skilled at and fond of household tasks such as cooking, cleaning, sewing, etc.

domestication *noun* **1** the process of taming an animal to live with humans. **2** the process of growing a plant to be used as food.

domesticity *noun* home or family life: *an atmosphere of happy domesticity* ◊ *a life of domesticity and parenthood.* [Say doe mess TISSA tee or domma STISSA tee]

domestic violence *noun* violent acts occurring within a household.

domicile *formal* • *noun* a dwelling place; one's home: *the suspect proceeded to his domicile at a high rate of speed.* • *verb* (**domiciles, domiciled, domiciling**) (usu. as **domiciled** *adjective*) establish or settle in a place: *she's not domiciled in Canada and so can't vote.* [Say DOMMA sile]

dominance *noun* **1** power, influence, or predominance over others; superiority: *the worldwide dominance of Hollywood.* **2** *Genetics* the phenomenon whereby, in an individual containing two allelic forms of a gene, one is expressed to the exclusion of the other.

dominant • *adjective* **1** most important, powerful, or influential: *they are now in an even more dominant position in the market.* **2 a** (of an allele) expressed even when inherited from only one parent. **b** (of an inherited characteristic) appearing in an individual even when its allelic counterpart is also inherited (*compare* RECESSIVE *adjective* 1). **3 a** designating the predominant species in a plant or animal community. **b** (of an animal) allowed priority in access to food, mates, etc. by others of its species because of success in previous aggressive encounters: *the wolf pack is led by the dominant male.* **4** *Music* based on or pertaining to the fifth note of the diatonic scale of any key. • *noun* **1** a dominant trait or gene. **2** a dominant species in a plant or animal community. **3** *Music* the fifth note of the diatonic scale of any key. ▶ **dominantly** *adverb*

dominate *verb* (**dominates, dominated, dominating**) **1** have a commanding influence on; exercise control over: *as a child he was dominated by his father* ◊ *she says a lot in meetings, but doesn't dominate.* **2** (of a person, sound, event, etc.) be the most influential or noticeable factor in: *the French horns dominate this movement of the symphony.* **3** (of a building etc.) have a commanding position over: *the grain elevators dominate the harbour.* ▶ **dominating** *adjective*

domination *noun* the exercise of control or influence, or the state of being so controlled: *US cultural and economic domination of Canada.*

dominator *noun* a person who dominates.

domineering *adjective* trying to control other people without considering their wishes, opinions or feelings: *he was brought up by a cold and domineering father* ◊ *a domineering personality.*

Dominican[1] • *adjective* **1** of or relating to the Order of Friars Preaching, devoted to preaching and the study of theology. **2** of or relating to either of the two female religious orders founded on Dominican principles. • *noun* a Dominican friar, nun, or sister. [Say duh MINNA k'n]

Dominican² • *noun* **1** a native or an inhabitant of the island of Dominica in the W Indies. **2** a native or an inhabitant of the Dominican Republic, a country in the Caribbean, on the island of Hispaniola. • *adjective* **1** of or pertaining to Dominica. **2** of or pertaining to the Dominican Republic. [Say duh MINNA k'n]

dominion *noun* **1** sovereign authority; control: *soon the country was under her sole dominion*. **2** the territory of a sovereign or government: *the vast dominions of the Empire*. **3** the title of each of the self-governing territories of the Commonwealth. **4** *hist.* **a** (**the Dominion**) *informal* Canada. **b** *Cdn* (*Nfld*) Newfoundland as a self-governing part of the Commonwealth prior to 1949.

Dominion Day *noun hist.* = CANADA DAY.

domino *noun* (*plural* **dominoes**) **1** any of 28 small oblong tiles, marked with 0–6 dots on each half. **2** (in *plural*, usu. treated as *singular*) a game played with these.

domino effect *noun* the effect of one event triggering a succession of other events, like a falling domino at the beginning of a line of upended dominoes: *the plunge in stock prices in Tokyo set off a domino effect in the global markets*.

SPELL CHECK
don, dawn   ABC✓

The first light of morning is **dawn**.

---

don¹ *noun* **1** (**Don**) **a** a Spanish title prefixed to a man's first name. **b** a Spanish gentleman; a Spaniard. **2** an Italian title of respectful address, esp. to a priest. **3** *Cdn* a senior person in a university residence, usu. responsible for the students and community life. **4** a high-ranking member of the Mafia.

don² *verb* (**dons, donned, donning**) put on (clothing).

donair *noun* spiced lamb cooked on a spit, served in slices, and usu. rolled in pita bread. [Say doe NAIR]

donate *verb* (**donates, donated, donating**) **1** give or contribute (money etc.), esp. voluntarily, to a fund or institution. **2** allow doctors to remove blood or a body organ in order to help somebody who needs it.

donation *noun* **1** the act or an instance of donating: *sign your organ donation card*. **2** something, esp. an amount of money, donated.

done • *verb past participle of* DO¹. • *adjective* **1** finished, completed. **2** *informal* socially acceptable: *the done thing*. **3 a** (often with *in*) *informal* tired out. **b** (often with *up*) fixed up or made more attractive: *the motel was newly done up*. **4** (of food) cooked sufficiently. PHRASES **done for** *informal* **1** in serious trouble. **2** finished, destroyed. **have done with** be rid of or have finished dealing with.

doneness *noun* the degree to which food is cooked.

Don Juan *noun* a man with a reputation for seducing women. [Say don WON rhymes with *DON*)]

donkey *noun* (*plural* **donkeys**) **1** a domesticated hoofed mammal of the horse family with long ears and a braying call, used as a beast of burden. **2** *informal* a stupid or foolish person. **3** (also **donkey engine**) a small auxiliary engine.

donnybrook *noun* a scene of uproar; a brawl: *the political donnybrook of prairie elections*.

donor *noun* **1** a person who gives or donates something, e.g. to a charity. **2** a person who provides blood for a transfusion, an organ or tissue for transplant, etc.

don't • *contraction* do not. • *noun* a prohibition; an injunction not to do something: *dos and don'ts*.

donut *noun* = DOUGHNUT.

doodad *noun* something not readily nameable, esp. a gadget or ornament of an unnecessary kind.

doodle • *verb* (**doodles, doodled, doodling**) **1** scribble or draw, esp. absent-mindedly. **2** play idly on an instrument. **3** waste time. • *noun* a figure drawn absent-mindedly. ▶ **doodler** *noun* **doodling** *adjective*

doo-doo *noun slang* **1** excrement. **2** serious trouble: *we're in deep doo-doo*.

doofus *noun* (*plural* **doofuses**) a stupid or inept person.

doohickey *noun* (*plural* **doohickeys**) *informal* an unspecified object or small device, esp. a mechanical one.

doom • *noun* **1** a grim fate or destiny. **2** impending death, disaster, or ruin. • *verb* (usu. foll. by *to*) condemn or destine to some fate: *doomed to destruction*.

doom and gloom *noun* a general feeling of despair and pessimism.

doomed *adjective* certain to fail, suffer, die, etc.: *a doomed marriage*.

doomsayer *noun* a person who predicts esp. political or economic disaster: *the doomsayers said that the company would never recover*. ▶ **doomsaying** *noun*

doomsday *noun* **1** (in some beliefs) the day at the end of the world on which the judgment of humankind is expected to take place, when each person is rewarded or punished according to his or her merits. **2** any day of decisive judgment or final dissolution. **3** (also as an *adjective*) a projected time of destruction of the world, esp. by nuclear means: *doomsday weapons*. PHRASES **till doomsday** forever.

doomsday clock *noun* **1** a symbolic clock created to measure the world's proximity to the final midnight of nuclear destruction. **2** this image applied to an approaching crisis.

doomsday cult *noun* a cult which believes that the end of the world is at hand, esp. one whose members commit mass suicide on a chosen date.

doomy *adjective* **1** portending, suggesting, or predicting doom. **2** ominous, gloomy: *doomy music*.

door *noun* **1 a** a barrier for closing and opening an entrance. **b** this as representing a house etc.: *lives two doors away*. **2 a** an entrance or an exit; a doorway. **b** a means of access or approach. **c** (**the door**) the entrance to a theatre, club, etc. at which admission must be paid or tickets shown. **3** something resembling a door in its movement or function, e.g. a lid, valve, or cover. PHRASES **close** (or **shut**) **the door to** (or **on**) exclude the opportunity for. **lay something at a person's door** regard someone as responsible for something: *the failure is laid at the government's door*. **leave the door open** ensure that an option remains available. **lie at a person's door** be the fault or responsibility of a person. **open the door to** create an opportunity for. **out of doors** outside the house, esp. in or into the open air.

do-or-die *adjective* denoting a determination not to be deterred by any danger or difficulty, esp. in a desperate situation or circumstance.

doorknob *noun* **1** a usu. round handle on a door which is turned to open or close the door. **2** *slang* an idiot; a stupid person.

doorless *adjective* without doors.

doorman *noun* (*plural* **doormen**) an attendant at the entrance to a hotel etc.

doormat *noun* **1** a mat at an entrance to a building for wiping mud etc. from the shoes. **2** a passive, submissive person.

doornail *noun* PHRASES **dead as a doornail** completely or unmistakably dead.

doorpost *noun* (also **door jamb**) each of the uprights of a door frame.

door prize *noun* something awarded as a prize at a gathering, usu. through a draw.

doorstep *noun* a step leading up to the outer door of a house etc. PHRASES **on one's doorstep** very close.

doorstop *noun* **1** a weight or wedge placed under a door to keep it open. **2** a device fixed to the ground or wall to prevent a door from opening too widely.

door-to-door • *adjective* **1** (of selling or a salesperson) covering each house on a street, in an area, etc. **2** (of journeys, deliveries, etc.) direct. • *adverb* (**door to door**) calling at each house in turn: *travelled door to door*.

doorway *noun* **1** an opening into a building or a room, esp. one closed or opened by a door. **2** a means or medium of approach or access: *a doorway to freedom*.

doozy *noun* (*plural* **doozies**) (also **doozer**) *slang* something amazing, remarkable, or incredible.

dope • *noun* **1 a** *slang* a narcotic drug. **b** a drug taken by an athlete or given to a horse etc. to affect performance. **2** *slang* a silly or stupid person. **3** *slang* essential facts, details, or information about a subject, esp. of a kind not generally divulged: *the inside dope*. **4** a thick liquid, cream, or gel used as a lubricant, repellent, etc.: *bug dope*. **5** a substance added to gasoline etc. to increase its effectiveness. • *verb* (**dopes, doped, doping**) **1 a** administer stimulating or stupefying drugs to (an athlete, horse, etc.). **b** *informal* take addictive drugs. **2** *informal* treat (food or drink) with drugs: *maybe they doped her glass of pop*. **3** *informal* (foll. by *out*) work out, infer, or find out by calculation or surmise: *doped out the plans*. PHRASES **doped up** *slang* heavily under the influence of drugs. ▶ **doper** *noun*

dopey *adjective* (**dopier, dopiest**) *informal* **1** stupid, silly. **2 a** half asleep. **b** stupefied by or as if by a drug.

doping *noun* the use of any substance, foreign or natural to the body, to artificially enhance performance in sporting competition.

Doppler effect *noun* an increase (or decrease) in the frequency of sound, light, or other waves as the source and observer move toward (or away from) each other.

doré *noun* (*plural* **doré** or **dorés**) *Cdn* the walleye. [Say dor AY]

dork *noun* *slang* a socially awkward, often stupid person. ▶ **dorky** *adjective* (**dorkier, dorkiest**)

dorm *noun* *informal* dormitory.

dormancy *noun* **1** a period of inactivity or sleep. **2** a period in which a plant is alive but not growing.

dormant *adjective* **1 a** lying inactive as in sleep; sleeping: *dormant butterflies*. **b** *Biology* alive but with development suspended: *dormant fruit trees*. **2** (of a volcano etc.) temporarily inactive. **3** (of potential faculties etc.) latent or not in current operation: *dormant talent*.

dormer *noun* **1** (also **dormer window**) a projecting upright window in a sloping roof. **2** the projecting construction which supports the window.

dormitory *noun* (*plural* **dormitories**) **1** a university or college residence. **2** a large room containing beds, esp. in a school or other institution. **3** a small town or suburb from which people travel to work in a city etc. (also as an *adjective*: *dormitory suburb*). [Say DORMA tory]

dormouse *noun* (*plural* **dormice**) a small mouselike hibernating rodent with a long bushy tail.

dorsal *adjective* *Anatomy, Zoology, & Botany* of, on, or near the back: *dorsal fin*. ▶ **dorsally** *adverb* [Say DOR s'll]

Dorset *noun* a prehistoric culture which flourished in the eastern Arctic *c.*1000 BC–AD 1000, before being displaced by that of the Inuit. [Say DOR sit]

dory[1] *noun* (*plural* **dories**) any of various marine fish having a compressed body and flat head, used as food.

dory[2] *noun* (*plural* **dories**) a small flat-bottomed fishing boat with high sides.

doryman *noun* (*plural* **dorymen**) *Cdn* a person who fishes from a dory.

dosage *noun* the size or frequency of a dose of medicine etc.

dose • *noun* **1** an amount of a medicine or drug taken or to be taken at one time. **2** a quantity of something administered or allocated, e.g. work, praise, etc. **3** the amount of ionizing radiation to which a person or thing is exposed. • *verb* (**doses, dosed, dosing**) **1** treat (a person or animal) with doses of medicine. **2** divide into, or administer in, doses.

dossier *noun* a set of documents, esp. a collection of information about a person, event, or subject: *we have a dossier on her* ◊ *a dossier of complaints*. [Say DOSSY ay]

dot • *noun* **1 a** a small spot. **b** such a mark written or printed as part of an *i* or *j*, as a period, as one of a series of marks to signify omission, etc. **c** a decimal point. **d** a period used in an electronic mail address or file name. **2** *Music* **a** a point placed after a note or rest to lengthen it by half as much again. **b** a point placed over a note to indicate that it is to be performed staccato. **3** the shorter signal of the two used in Morse code (compare DASH *noun* 6). **4** a tiny or apparently tiny object: *a dot on the horizon*. **5** a small amount: *a dot of icing*. • *verb* (**dots, dotted, dotting**) **1 a** mark with a dot or dots. **b** place a dot over (a letter). **2** *Music* mark (a note or rest) to show that the time value is increased by half. **3** occur singly throughout (an area) or over (a surface). PHRASES **dot the i's and cross the t's** *informal* **1** emphasize details. **2** add the final touches to a task, exercise, etc. **on the dot** exactly on time.

dote *verb* (**dotes, doted, doting**) (foll. by *on, upon*) be foolishly or excessively fond of. ▶ **doting** *adjective* **dotingly** *adverb*

dotted line *noun* a line of dots or dashes on a document, esp. to indicate the space left for a signature. PHRASES **sign on the dotted line** agree fully or formally.

dottiness *noun* a silly or confused nature.

dotty *adjective* (**dottier, dottiest**) *informal* **1** silly or confused, esp. due to old age. **2** eccentric. **3** absurd. **4** (foll. by *about, over*) infatuated with.

double • *adjective* **1 a** consisting of two usu. equal parts or things. **b** consisting of two identical parts. **2** twice as much or many: *double the number* ◊ *double thickness*. **3** having twice the usual size, quantity, strength, value, etc.: *double whisky*. **4 a** designed or suitable for two people: *double bed*. **b** (of bedding) suitable for a double bed. **5 a** having some essential part double: *double room*. **b** (of a flower) having more than one circle of petals. **6 a** having two different roles, interpretations, applications, etc.: *double meaning*. **b** characterized by deceitfulness: *leads a double life*. **7** *Music* lower in pitch by an octave: *double bassoon*. **8** *Figure Skating & Dance* (of a jump, pirouette, etc.) involving two revolutions. • *adverb* **1** at or to twice the amount, extent, etc.: *counts double*. **2** two at once or two together: *sleep double*. • *noun* **1 a** a double quantity or thing; twice as much or many. **b** *informal* an alcoholic drink with a double measure of liquor. **2 a** a counterpart of a person or thing. **b** a person who looks exactly like another. **3** (in *plural*) *Sport* (in tennis, badminton, etc.) a game between two pairs of players. **4** *Baseball* a successful hit which allows a player to get to second base safely. **5** *Figure Skating & Dance* a double jump, pirouette, etc. **6** = BODY DOUBLE. **7** a double room in a hotel, residence, etc. **8** *Bowling* two strikes in a row. • *verb* (**doubles, doubled, doubling**) **1** make, become, or amount to twice as much or many. **2 a** fold (paper, cloth, etc.) over on itself so as to bring the two parts into contact. **b** become folded. **3** (usu.

foll. by *as*) perform or function in an additional capacity. **4** turn sharply in flight or pursuit; take a tortuous course. **5** *Music* (often foll. by *on*) play two or more musical instruments: *the clarinetist doubles on tenor sax*. **6** *Baseball* **a** make a double. **b** cause (a baserunner) to advance through a double. **c** (usu. foll. by *in*) cause (a run) to score by hitting a double. **d** tag out (a baserunner) as the second action of a double play. **7** (foll. by *up*) **a** bend or curl up. **b** cause to do this, esp. by a blow. **c** be overcome with pain or laughter. **d** share or assign to a room, quarters, etc., with another or others. PHRASES **on** (or **at**) **the double** hurrying. **bent double** folded, stooping. **double back** take a new direction opposite to the previous one. **double or nothing** a gamble in which the player either gains twice the bet or loses everything. **see double** perceive or seem to perceive two images of one object.

Double-A = AA 1, 2, 3.

double-action *adjective* **1** (of a firearm) needing only a single pull of the trigger to cock and fire the weapon. **2** (of a fishing reel) having a spool that turns twice for every turn of the handle.

double agent *noun* a person who pretends to spy for one country or organization while actually working for a hostile or rival one.

double-barrelled *adjective* **1** (of a gun) having two barrels. **2** having two parts or aspects: *a double-barrelled argument*.

double bass *noun* (*plural* **double basses**) **1** the largest and lowest-pitched instrument of the violin family. **2** a player of this instrument.

double bill *noun* two films, plays, etc. presented to an audience one after the other in the same program.

double bind *noun* a situation in which a person is confronted with two irreconcilable demands or a choice between two undesirable courses of action.

double-blind • *adjective* designating a test or experiment in which neither the tester nor the subject has knowledge of identities or other factors that might lead to bias. • *noun* such a test or experiment.

double-bogey *Golf* • *noun* (*plural* **double-bogeys**) a score of two strokes over par on a hole. • *verb* (**double-bogeys, double-bogeyed, double-bogeying**) complete (a hole) in two strokes over par.

double boiler *noun* a saucepan with an upper pot heated by boiling water in a lower one.

double bond *noun* a pair of bonds between two atoms in a molecule.

double-book *verb* accept two reservations simultaneously for (the same seat, room, etc.), esp. to ensure that at least one will be used.

double-breasted *adjective* (of a coat etc.) having a large overlap of material at the front which is usu. fastened with two rows of buttons.

double-check *verb* verify twice or in two ways.

double-click *verb* *Computing* **1** press and release the button of a mouse twice in quick succession to activate a program etc. **2** click on (an icon etc.) in this way.

double-cross • *verb* (**double-crosses, double-crossed, double-crossing**) deceive or betray (a person one is supposedly helping). • *noun* (*plural* **double-crosses**) an act of doing this.

double date • *noun* a date on which two couples go together. • *verb* (**double dates, double dated, double dating**) go on a double date.

double-dealing • *noun* deceit, esp. in business. • *adjective* deceitful or practising deceit.

double-decker *noun* **1** a bus having an upper and lower deck. **2** *informal* anything consisting of two layers, e.g. a sandwich.

double-digit *adjective* equal in quantity, rate, etc. to a number, esp. a percentage, between 10 and 99.

double-dipping *noun* **1** the practice of converting an occupational pension to a lump sum and then drawing a government pension that would not otherwise be due. **2** the practice of receiving an income from two jobs, esp. a pension from a former job and a salary from a current one.

double-edged *adjective* **1** having two contradictory aspects or possible outcomes: *the consequences can be double-edged* ◊ *experienced first-hand the double-edged quality of life in a small town — security and boredom*. **2** (of a knife etc.) having two cutting edges. PHRASES **a double-edged sword** a situation or course of action having both positive and negative effects.

double entendre *noun* **1** a word or phrase open to two interpretations, one usu. indecent. **2** humour using such words or phrases. [Say double on TONDRA]

double exposure *noun* *Photography* the action or result of exposing the same frame, plate, etc. on two separate occasions, either accidentally or deliberately.

double figures *plural noun* the numbers from 10 to 99.

doubleheader *noun* **1** two games etc. in succession between the same or different opponents, esp. on the same day. **2** two events, occurrences, etc. happening one after the other.

double helix *noun* (*plural* **double helices**) a pair of parallel helices with a common axis, esp. in the structure of DNA.

double minor *noun* *Hockey* two minor penalties, imposed for a single offence considered to be severe but accidental, served sequentially.

GRAMMAR CHECK
double negatives   ⚠

Sentences such as *I didn't do nothing* meaning *I didn't do anything* are ungrammatical. Sentences in which two negative elements are used to create a positive statement, as in *It was a slow but not unpleasant drive*, suggesting the drive was somewhat pleasant, are standard and acceptable.

---

double negative *noun* a negative statement containing two negative elements, e.g. *didn't say nothing*.

doubleness *noun* the quality of something that consists of two equal, identical, or similar parts, interpretations, etc.

double-park *verb* park (a vehicle) alongside one that is already parked parallel to a curb etc.

double play *noun* *Baseball* a play in which two runners are put out.

double-quick *adjective & adverb* very quick or quickly.

doublespeak *noun* = DOUBLE-TALK *noun*.

double standard *noun* a rule etc. applied more strictly to some people than to others (or to oneself).

double star *noun* two stars actually or apparently very close together.

doublet *noun* **1** *hist.* a man's short close-fitting jacket, with or without sleeves. **2** either of a pair of similar things, esp. two words that are derived from the same root word but have different meanings, such as *hotel* and *hospital*, or *fashion* and *faction*. [Say DUB lit]

double take *noun* a delayed reaction to something unexpected, immediately after one's first reaction: *Tony glanced at her, then did a double take*.

double takeout *noun* *Curling* a shot which hits and knocks out of the house two of an opponent's rocks.

double-talk • *noun* **1** language or talk that is usu. deliberately ambiguous or misleading. **2** meaningless

D

gibberish. • *verb* **1** persuade (a person) through double-talk. **2** engage in double-talk. ▶ **double-talking** *adjective*

double-team *verb Basketball etc.* block (an opposing player) with two players. ▶ **double-teaming** *noun*

doublethink *noun* **1** the mental capacity to accept as equally valid two entirely contradictory opinions or beliefs, esp. as a result of political indoctrination. **2** the practice of doing this.

double time *noun* **1** a rate of pay equal to twice the standard rate, usu. given for working on holidays etc. **2** *Military* a marching pace in which approximately twice as many steps per minute are made as in slow time.

double vision *noun* the simultaneous perception of two images of one object.

double whammy *noun* (*plural* **double whammies**) *informal* a twofold blow or setback.

doubly *adverb* **1** more than usual: *I made doubly sure the doors were locked.* **2** in two ways or for two reasons: *this snake is doubly dangerous because it can bite or crush its prey.*

doubt • *noun* **1** a feeling of uncertainty; an undecided state of mind. **2** an inclination to disbelieve. **3** an uncertain state of affairs. **4** a lack of full proof or clear indication: *benefit of the doubt.* • *verb* **1** feel uncertain or undecided about. **2** hesitate to believe or trust (a person, claim, etc.). **3** have doubts or be undecided in opinion or belief. **PHRASES** **beyond (a) doubt** certainly. **beyond a shadow of a doubt** definitely, absolutely. **give (a person) the benefit of the doubt 1** assume innocence rather than guilt, esp. when the evidence is conflicting: *Maggie says she didn't do it, and I think we should give her the benefit of the doubt.* **2** incline to a more favourable or kindly decision, estimate, etc.: *let's give them the benefit of the doubt and say $30.* **in doubt 1** (of a person) in a state of mental uncertainty or indecision. **2** (of an issue etc.) open to question, not certainly known or decided. **no doubt** in all likelihood or certainly. **without (a) doubt** unquestionably. ▶ **doubter** *noun*

doubtful *adjective* **1** feeling doubt, uncertainty, or misgivings; unsure or guarded in one's opinion. **2** causing doubt; ambiguous; uncertain in meaning etc. **3** (of a person) unreliable, of dubious character: *a doubtful ally.* ▶ **doubtfully** *adverb* **doubtfulness** *noun*

doubtless *adverb* (often qualifying a sentence) **1** certainly. **2** probably, in all likelihood.

douche • *noun* **1 a** a jet of liquid applied to part of the body, esp. the vagina, for cleansing or medicinal purposes. **b** the application of this. **2 a** a device for producing such a jet. • *verb* (**douches**, **douched**, **douching**) **1** treat with a douche. **2** use a douche. ▶ **douching** *noun* [Say DOOSH]

dough *noun* **1 a** a thick mixture of flour, water, etc. for baking into bread, pastry, etc. **b** any soft, pasty mass. **2** *slang* money.

doughnut *noun* **1** a small spongy cake of sweetened and deep-fried dough, usu. ring-shaped, or spherical with a jam or cream filling. **2** any of various circular objects with a hole in the middle. **PHRASES** **do doughnuts** *slang* (of a driver) cause a car to spin in wide circles by slamming on the brakes, esp. for fun.

doughty *adjective* (**doughtier**, **doughtiest**) fearless, valiant: *a doughty fighter for freedom of speech* ◊ *the doughty colonists settled near the river.* [Say DOUTY]

doughy *adjective* (**doughier**, **doughiest**) **1** having the form or consistency of dough. **2** pale and sickly in colour. [Say DOE ee]

Douglas fir *noun* (also **Douglas pine** or **Douglas spruce**) **1** any large conifer of the genus *Pseudotsuga*, of western North America. **2** the wood of this tree.

Doukhobor *noun* a member of an originally Russian

Christian sect whose beliefs include pacifism, reverence for their chosen religious leaders, and the rejection of church liturgy and secular governments. [Say DOOKA bore]

dour *adjective* severe, stern, or sullenly obstinate in manner or appearance: *a hard, dour, humourless fanatic.* ▶ **dourly** *adverb* **dourness** *noun* [Can be rhymed either with *POWER* or with *POOR*]

SPELL CHECK	ABC ✓
douse, dowse	

To search for water with a Y-shaped stick is to **dowse**.

douse *verb* (**douses**, **doused**, **dousing**) **1** soak a person or thing in or with water or another liquid: *douse him with perfume* ◊ *French toast doused in maple syrup.* **2** extinguish (a light, fire, etc.): *douse the campfire and let's go to bed.* [Rhymes with *MOUSE*]

dove[1] *noun* **1** any bird of the family Columbidae, with short legs, small head, and large breast. **2** a gentle or innocent person. **3 a** a person who believes in a policy of negotiation and conciliation rather than warfare or confrontation (*compare* HAWK[1] 2). **b** a symbol of innocence, harmlessness, or peace. **4** (**Dove**) *Christianity* a representation of the Holy Spirit. **5** a soft grey colour.

dove[2] *past and past participle of* DIVE.

dovetail • *noun* **1** a joint formed by one or more tenons in the shape of a dove's spread tail, fitting into the mortises of corresponding shape, used esp. in making furniture etc. **2** a tenon or mortise of such a joint. • *verb* **1** join together by means of a dovetail. **2** fit together or become adjusted perfectly, so as to form a compact or harmonious whole: *enable parents to dovetail their career and family life* ◊ *wants flights that dovetail with the working day.*

dowager *noun* **1** a widow with a title or property derived from her late husband: *Queen dowager.* **2** *informal* a dignified elderly woman. [Say DOW a jer]

dowdiness *noun* a dowdy or unfashionable quality. [Say DOW dee niss]

dowdy *adjective* (**dowdier**, **dowdiest**) **1** (of clothes) unfashionable; unattractively dull. **2** (of a person, esp. a woman) frumpy; unattractively dressed.

dowel • *noun* a headless peg of wood, metal, or plastic for holding together components of a structure. • *verb* (**dowels**, **dowelled**, **dowelling**) fasten with a dowel or dowels. ▶ **dowelled** *adjective* [Rhymes with *TOWEL*]

dowelling *noun* cylindrical rods for cutting into dowels. [Rhymes with *TOWELLING*]

Dow–Jones Average *noun proprietary* an index of the average level of share prices on the New York Stock Exchange at any time, based on the daily price of a selection of representative stocks.

dowitcher *noun* a North American wading bird related to sandpipers and having a long, straight bill. [Say DOW itch ur]

down[1] • *adverb* **1** in, into, or toward a lower place: *fall down.* **2** to or in a more southerly place: *drove down from Ottawa to Toronto.* **3 a** in or into a low or weaker position or condition: *down with a cold.* **b** in a position of lagging or loss: *we were down by three.* **c** (of a computer system) out of action or unavailable for use (esp. temporarily). **4** from an earlier to a later time: *customs handed down.* **5** to a finer or thinner consistency or a smaller amount or size: *grind down* ◊ *water down.* **6** lower in price or value: *gas is down.* **7** into a more settled state: *calm down.* **8** in writing: *copy it down.* **9** (of part of a larger whole) paid; dealt with: *no money down* ◊ *three down, six to go.* **10** *Football* (of the ball) not in play. • *preposition* **1** downwards along, through, or into.

2 from top to bottom of. **3** along: *walk down the road.* **4** at or in a lower part of. • *adjective* **1** directed downwards. **2** depressed; in low spirits. • *verb informal* **1** knock, shoot or bring down: *downed the plane.* **2** defeat (a team, player, etc.): *the Leafs downed the Canadiens.* **3** swallow (a drink), esp. quickly. • *noun* **1** *Football* any of a fixed number of attempts (3 in Canadian football, 4 in American football) to advance the ball a total of 10 yards. **2** an act of putting down (esp. an opponent in wrestling). **3** a reverse of fortune: *ups and downs.* PHRASES **be down on** *informal* disapprove of; show animosity toward. **be down to 1** be attributable to. **2** be the responsibility of. **3** have used up everything except: *down to their last nickel.* **down for the count 1** (of a boxer) knocked unconscious. **2** completely defeated. **down in the dumps** depressed; in low spirits. **down on one's luck** *informal* **1** temporarily unfortunate. **2** dispirited by misfortune. **down the road** (or **line**) *informal* in the future; later on. **down tools** *informal* cease work, esp. to go on strike. **down to the wire** *informal* right up to the very last minute or the very end. **down with** *interjection* expressing strong disapproval or rejection of a specified person or thing. **when you get** (or **come**) (**right**) **down to it** in the final analysis.

down² *noun* **1 a** small soft feathers that cover and insulate the entire body of a young bird. **b** small soft feathers that lie between and beneath the surface feathers of an adult bird. **c** such feathers, usu. from ducks and geese, used to fill pillows etc. **2** fine soft hair esp. on the face. **3** short soft hairs on some leaves, fruit, etc. **4** a fluffy substance, e.g. thistledown.

down³ *noun* **1** (usu. in *plural*) an area of open rolling land. **2** (usu. **the Downs**) undulating chalk and limestone uplands esp. in S England. **3** (in *plural*) often used in the names of racetracks: *Assiniboia Downs.*

down-and-dirty *adjective informal* highly competitive or unprincipled: *few election campaigns have been rougher than the down-and-dirty Senate struggle in Virginia.*

down-and-out • *adjective* **1** penniless. **2 a** *Boxing* unable to resume the fight. **b** (of a team, business etc.) out of the running; no longer successful. • *noun* (also **down-and-outer**) a destitute and often homeless person.

down-at-the-heels *adjective* **1 a** (of a person) shabby; slovenly. **b** (of a neighbourhood, building, etc.) rundown; dilapidated. **2** (**down-at-heel**) (of shoes) with the heels worn down.

downbeat • *noun Music* **1** an accented beat, usu. the first of the bar. **2** a downward movement of a conductor's stick or hand indicating such a beat. • *adjective* pessimistic; gloomy.

downcast *adjective* **1** (of eyes) looking downwards. **2** (of a person) dejected.

downdraft *noun* a downward current of air.

downer *noun slang* **1** a depressant or tranquilizing drug, esp. a barbiturate. **2 a** a depressing person or experience. **b** a depressed mood or state.

downfall *noun* **1 a** a fall from prosperity or power. **b** the cause of this. **2** a sudden heavy fall of rain etc.

downfield *adverb* in or to a position nearer to the opponents' end of a football, soccer, etc. field.

downgrade • *verb* (**downgrades, downgraded, downgrading**) **1** make lower in rank or status: *downgraded the company's credit rating.* **2** make something or someone seem less important or valuable: *most Japanese histories ignore or downgrade Japanese Christian history.* • *noun* **1** an instance of reducing someone or something's rank, status, or level of importance: *a downgrade in the company's credit rating.*

2 a downward gradient, esp. on a railway or road. PHRASES **on the downgrade** in decline.

downhearted *adjective* dejected; in low spirits.

downhill • *adverb* in a descending direction, esp. toward the bottom of an incline. • *adjective* **1** sloping down. **2** deteriorating. **3 a** designating skiing performed on a mountain or steep slope. **b** of or pertaining to downhill racing: *downhill champion.* • *noun Skiing* a downhill race on a steep track marked by poles set at least 8 m apart, through which the skier has to pass. PHRASES **go downhill** *informal* decline, deteriorate (in health, state of repair, etc.). ▶ **downhiller** *noun*

down-home *adjective* unpretentious; unaffected: *down-home hospitality.*

down in the mouth *adjective informal* unhappy.

down-island *Cdn* (*BC*) • *adverb* to or in a more southerly part of Vancouver Island. • *adjective* directed southwards on Vancouver Island: *a down-island tour.*

downlink • *noun* a communications link for signals coming from a satellite to earth. • *verb* provide with or send by a downlink.

download • *verb* **1** copy or transfer (software or data) from one storage device or computer to another (esp. a smaller remote one). **2** *Cdn* shift or relegate responsibilities or costs for (a program) from one level of government to a lower one. • *noun* a transfer of data. ▶ **downloadable** *adjective*

down-market *adjective & adverb informal* relating to or directed toward the less affluent sector of the market.

down payment *noun* a partial payment made at the time of purchase.

downplay *verb* minimize the importance of.

downpour *noun* a heavy fall of rain.

downrigger *noun* a trolling rig consisting of a cable attached underneath a boat to a fishing line, used to troll live bait at or near the bottom of a body of water.

downright • *adverb* thoroughly: *downright rude.* • *adjective* **1** utter; complete: *a downright lie.* **2** (of a person's speech or behaviour) straightforward; blunt.

downriver *adverb & adjective* at or towards a point nearer the mouth of a river.

downscale • *adjective* at the lower end of a scale, esp. a social or economic scale: *a downscale neighbourhood.* • *verb* (**downscales, downscaled, downscaling**) reduce or restrict in size or scale: *they are currently downscaling the show, and will go on tour to smaller venues.*

downshift • *verb* **1** change to a lower gear in a motor vehicle. **2** slow down; become less busy. • *noun* a change to a lower gear.

downside *noun informal* the negative aspect of something; a disadvantage or drawback.

downsize *verb* (**downsizes, downsized, downsizing**) **1** reduce in size: *downsize the deficit.* **2** (often euphemistic) lay off or fire (workers). ▶ **downsizing** *noun*

downspout *noun* a pipe to carry rainwater from an eavestrough to a drain or to ground level.

Down's syndrome *noun* (also **Down syndrome**) a congenital form of mental retardation due to a chromosome defect, in which the affected individual has a flattened facial profile, weak muscles, etc.

downstage *adjective & adverb* at or to the front of the stage.

downstairs • *adverb* **1** down a flight of stairs. **2** to or on a lower floor. • *adjective* situated downstairs. • *noun* the main floor or basement of a house etc.

downstream • *adverb* in the direction of the flow of a stream etc. • *adjective* situated or occurring downstream.

D

downstroke *noun* a downward stroke, esp. of a machine part or a pen on paper.

downswing *noun* **1** a downward trend, esp. in economic conditions. **2** the downward movement of a golf club etc. when a player is about to hit the ball.

downtime *noun* **1** time during which a machine, esp. a computer, is unavailable for use, usu. as a result of malfunction or regular preventive maintenance. **2** time not spent working; leisure or recovery time.

down-to-earth *adjective* practical; realistic.

downtown • *adjective* being or located in the central part of a town or city, esp. the business district: *downtown Victoria*. • *noun* a downtown area. • *adverb* in or into a downtown area. ▶ **downtowner** *noun*

downtrodden *adjective* oppressed; badly treated: *a downtrodden nation during centuries of colonization*.

downturn *noun* a decline, esp. in economic or business activity.

down under (also **Down Under**) *informal* • *adverb* in or to Australia or New Zealand. • *noun* Australia or New Zealand.

downward • *adverb* (also **downwards**) **1** toward a lower place or position. **2** toward something which is lower in order, inferior, or less important. **3** onward from an earlier to a later time. • *adjective* directed, moving, extending, pointing, or leading downward. ▶ **downwardly** *adverb*

downwind • *adverb* in the direction toward which the wind is blowing. • *adjective* occurring or situated downwind.

downy *adjective* (**downier, downiest**) **1** of, like, or covered with down. **2** soft and fluffy.

dowry *noun* (*plural* **dowries**) property or money brought by a bride to her husband at marriage. [Say DOW ree]

SPELL CHECK	ABC
dowse, douse	✓

Douse is the usual Canadian spelling for "drench or soak".

dowse¹ *verb* (**dowses, dowsed, dowsing**) search for underground water or minerals by holding a Y-shaped stick or rod which dips abruptly when over the right spot. [Rhymes with *PLOWS*]

dowse² *verb* (**dowses, dowsed, dowsing**) = DOUSE. [Rhymes with *HOUSE*]

dowser *noun* a person who searches for underground water or minerals with a special stick or rod etc. [Say DOW zer]

doyen *noun* the most senior or prominent male member of a body of people: *he became the doyen of Canadian physicists*. [Say DOY en or doy EN]

doyenne *noun* the most senior or prominent female member of a body of people: *the doyenne of food writers*. [Say doy EN]

doz. *abbreviation* dozen.

doze • *verb* (**dozes, dozed, dozing**) sleep lightly; be half asleep. • *noun* a short light sleep. PHRASES **doze off** fall lightly asleep.

dozen *noun* (*plural* **dozen** or **dozens**) **1** twelve: *a dozen eggs*. **2** *informal* about twelve; a fairly large indefinite number: *several dozen people*. **3** (*in plural*) *informal* very many: *dozens of mistakes*. PHRASES **by the dozen** in large quantities. ▶ **dozenth** *adjective*

dozy *adjective* (**dozier, doziest**) **1** drowsy; tending to doze. **2** *Brit.* & *Cdn informal* slow-witted or lazy.

DP *abbreviation* (*plural* **DPs**) **1** DATA PROCESSING. **2** *hist.* DISPLACED PERSON. **3** *Baseball* double play.

dpi *abbreviation* *Computing* dots per inch.

Dr. *abbreviation* **1** Doctor. **2** Drive.

drab • *adjective* (**drabber, drabbest**) **1** of a dull brownish colour. **2** lacking brightness or colour; dreary. **3** dull; uninteresting: *a drab novel*. • *noun* fabric of a dull brownish colour: *troops dressed in olive drab*. ▶ **drably** *adverb* **drabness** *noun*

drachma *noun* (*plural* **drachmas** or **drachmae**) **1** the chief monetary unit of Greece. **2** a silver coin of ancient Greece. [Say DRACKMA; for *DRACHMAE* say DRACKMY]

draconian *adjective* very harsh or severe (esp. of laws). [Say druh CONEY in]

draft • *noun* **1 a** a preliminary written version of a speech, document, book, etc. (also as an *adjective*: *draft statement*). **b** a sketch or drawing of something to be constructed. **2** a current of air in a confined space, e.g. a room or chimney. **3** a system of selection by which sports teams acquire the rights to esp. unsigned players (also as an *adjective*: *draft pick*). **4** esp. *US* compulsory military service. **5** = DRAFT BEER. **6 a** a single act of drinking. **b** the amount drunk in this. **c** a dose of liquid medicine. **7 a** a written order for payment of money by a bank. **b** the drawing of money by means of this. **8** the depth of water needed to float a ship. **9 a** the drawing in of a fishing net. **b** the fish taken at one drawing. • *verb* **1** prepare a draft of (a speech, document, etc.). **2 a** acquire the rights to esp. unsigned sports players. **b** esp. *US* conscript for military service. **3** select for any special duty or purpose. • *adjective* (of an animal) used for pulling a cart, plow, etc.: *draft horses*. PHRASES **on draft** (of beer etc.) ready to be drawn from a keg; not bottled or canned.

draft beer *noun* beer drawn from a keg, not in a bottle or can.

draft dodger *noun* a person who evades compulsory military service, esp. in the US. ▶ **draft dodging** *noun*

draftee *noun* a person drafted for military service or by a sports team. [Say draf TEE]

drafter *noun* **1** a person who prepares a rough version of an official or legal document. **2** a person who makes drawings, plans, or sketches; a draftsman.

draftsman *noun* (*plural* **draftsmen**) **1 a** a person who makes detailed technical plans or drawings. **b** an artist skilled in drawing. **2** a person who drafts documents, esp. legal or parliamentary ones.

drafty *adjective* (**draftier, draftiest**) (of a room etc.) letting in sharp currents of air.

drag • *verb* (**drags, dragged, dragging**) **1** pull along with effort or difficulty. **2 a** allow (one's feet etc.) to trail along the ground. **b** trail along the ground: *your coat is dragging*. **c** (of time etc.) go or pass slowly or tediously. **3** use grapnels, nets, or drags to search the bottom of a river etc. for a drowned person or lost object. **4** *informal* persuade (a person) to come or go somewhere unwillingly. **5** continue at tedious length. **6** *Computing* move (a window, icon, etc.) from one place to another on a screen, esp. by using a mouse. **7** draw on (a cigarette etc.). • *noun* **1** *Physics* the force resisting the motion of a body through a liquid or gas. **2** *informal* a boring or dreary person, duty, performance, etc. **3** *slang* clothes usually worn by the opposite sex, esp. women's clothes worn by a man: *a fashion show, complete with men in drag*. **4** *slang* a draw on a cigarette etc. **5** *slang* influence, pull. **6** an obstruction to progress: *high UI premiums have been a drag on small businesses' ability to create jobs*. **7** an apparatus for dredging or recovering drowned persons etc. from under water. **8** = DRAGNET 1. PHRASES **drag one's feet** (or **heels**) be deliberately slow or reluctant to act. **drag in** introduce (a subject) irrelevantly. **drag out** make something last an unnecessarily long time. **drag up** *informal* deliberately mention (an unwelcome subject).

drag and drop *noun* a software technique for moving objects on the screen using a mouse.

dragger *noun* a trawler. ▶**draggerman** *noun* (*plural* **draggermen**)

dragnet *noun* **1** a net drawn through water or across ground to trap fish or game. **2** a systematic hunt for criminals etc.

dragon *noun* **1** a mythical monster like a reptile, usu. able to breathe out fire. **2** a fierce person, esp. a woman. **3** (also **flying dragon**) a lizard, *Draco volans*, with a long tail and membranous wing-like structures. **4** an esp. newly industrialized Asian country with a powerful economy.

dragon boat *noun* a long wooden boat with a carved dragon's head on its prow and a carved dragon's tail at its stern, propelled by 22 paddlers and used in races.

dragonfly *noun* (*plural* **dragonflies**) any of various insects having a long body and two unequal pairs of large wings usu. spread while resting.

dragoon • *noun* **1** *hist.* a mounted infantryman armed with a carbine. **2** (often **Dragoon**) a member of any of several cavalry (now armoured) regiments: *Royal Canadian Dragoons*. • *verb* force or persuade someone to do something that they do not want to do: *she had been dragooned into doing the housework*. [Say druh GOON]

drag queen *noun* *slang* a male homosexual transvestite.

drag race *noun* a race between cars starting from a standstill. ▶**drag racer** *noun* **drag racing** *noun*

dragster *noun* a car built or modified for drag races.

drag strip *noun* a straight stretch of road built or used for drag races.

drain • *verb* **1** draw off liquid from. **2** (often foll. by *away*, *off*, *through*) flow or trickle away. **3** (of dishes, cutlery, etc.) become dry as liquid flows away. **4** (often foll. by *of*) exhaust or deprive (a person or thing) of strength, resources, property, etc. **5** gradually disappear or fade: *my hope drained away*. **6 a** drink (liquid) to the dregs. **b** empty (a glass etc.) by drinking. • *noun* **1 a** a channel, conduit, or pipe carrying off liquid, esp. an artificial conduit for water or sewage. **b** a tube for drawing off the discharge from an abscess etc. **2** a constant outflow or expenditure: *a drain on my resources*. PHRASES **down the drain** *informal* lost, wasted.

drainage *noun* the process by which water or liquid waste is drained from an area: *the land has poor drainage*.

drainage basin *noun* the area of land drained by a river and its tributaries.

drainer *noun* a device for draining; anything on which things are put to drain.

drainpipe *noun* a pipe for carrying off water, sewage, etc., from a building.

drake *noun* a male duck.

drama *noun* **1** a play for acting or broadcasting. **2 a** plays as a branch of literature and a performing art. **b** the art of acting. **3** an exciting or emotional event, set of circumstances, etc. **4** dramatic quality: *the drama of the situation*. [Say DRAMMA or DROMMA]

dramatic *adjective* **1 a** of drama or the study of drama. **b** of acting. **2** (of an event, circumstance, etc.) sudden and exciting or unexpected. **3** vividly striking. **4** (of a gesture etc.) theatrical; overdone; absurd. ▶**dramatically** *adverb* [Say druh MAT ick]

dramatics *plural noun* (often treated as *singular*) **1** the production and performance of plays. **2** exaggerated or showy behaviour. [Say druh MAT icks]

dramatist *noun* a writer of dramas.

dramatization *noun* the adaptation of a novel or presentation of an incident as a play or film.

dramatize *verb* (**dramatizes**, **dramatized**, **dramatizing**) **1** adapt (a novel, incident, etc.) to form a dramatic work, esp. a play or film. **2** express or react to (something) in a dramatic way: *don't worry too much about what she said — she tends to dramatize things*.

drank *past of* DRINK.

drape • *verb* (**drapes**, **draped**, **draping**) **1** hang, cover loosely, or adorn with cloth etc. **2** arrange (clothes or hangings) carefully in folds. **3** place or hang loosely or casually. • *noun* **1** a curtain or drapery. **2** a piece of drapery. **3** the way in which a garment or fabric hangs.

drapery *noun* (*plural* **draperies**) **1** clothing or hangings arranged in folds. **2** (often in *plural*) a curtain or hanging. **3** the arrangement of clothing in sculpture or painting.

drastic *adjective* having a strong or far-reaching effect; severe. ▶**drastically** *adverb*

drat *informal* • *verb* (**drats**, **dratted**, **dratting**) curse: *drat the thing!* • *interjection* expressing anger or annoyance. ▶**dratted** *adjective*

draught *esp. Brit.* = DRAFT *noun* 2, 5, 6, 8, 9, & *adjective*. [Sounds like DRAFT]

draughtsman *noun* (*plural* **draughtsmen**) *esp. Brit.* = DRAFTSMAN. [Sounds like DRAFTSMAN]

draughty *adjective* (**draughtier**, **draughtiest**) *esp. Brit.* = DRAFTY. [Sounds like DRAFTY]

draw • *verb* (**draws**; *past* **drew**; *past participle* **drawn**; **drawing**) **1** pull or cause to move toward or after one. **2** pull (a thing) up, over, or across. **3** pull (curtains etc.) open or shut. **4** take (a person) aside, esp. to talk to. **5** attract; bring to oneself or to something; take in: *drew a deep breath ◊ drew large crowds*. **6** trace (a line, mark, or figure). **7** produce a picture by tracing lines and marks. **8** make a drawing. **8** make one's or its way, proceed, move, come: *drew near the bridge ◊ draw to a close*. **9** (foll. by *at*, *on*) inhale smoke from (a cigarette, pipe, etc.). **10** take out; remove (a gun from a holster, etc.). **11** obtain or take from a source: *draw a salary ◊ draw inspiration*. **12** deduce (a conclusion). **13 a** elicit, evoke. **b** bring about, entail: *draw criticism ◊ drew a penalty*. **14** haul up (water) from a well. **15** cause (blood) to flow. **16** obtain (beer etc.) from a keg. **17** obtain by lot: *drew the winner*. **18** (foll. by *on*) make a demand on a person, a person's skill, memory, imagination, etc. **19** (of a ship) require (a specified depth of water) to float in. **20** *Curling* slide (a rock) so that it stops in the target area without striking another rock. • *noun* **1** an act of drawing. **2 a** a person or thing that draws customers, attention, etc. **b** the power to attract attention. **3** the drawing of lots, esp. a raffle or lottery. **4** a tied game. **5** a suck on a cigarette etc. **6** the act of removing a gun from its holster in order to shoot. **7** *Football* a play in which the quarterback hands the ball off to a running back who is running toward the line of scrimmage. **8** *Curling* a shot in which the rock stops within the target area without striking another rock. **9** (*West*) a shallow valley; ravine. PHRASES **draw back** withdraw from an undertaking. **draw fire** (also **draw heat**) attract hostility, criticism, etc. **draw in 1 a** (of successive days) become shorter because of the changing seasons. **b** (of a day) approach its end. **c** (of successive evenings or nights) start earlier because of the changing seasons. **2** persuade to join, entice. **3** (of a train, bus, etc.) arrive at a station. **draw the line** set a limit (of tolerance etc.). **draw off 1** drain away (liquid). **2** withdraw (troops). **draw on 1** utilize. **2** put (gloves, boots, etc.) on. **draw out 1** remove; pull out: *drew out a gun*. **2** prolong. **3** elicit. **4** induce to talk. **5** (of successive days) become longer because of the changing seasons. **6** (of a train, bus, etc.) leave a station etc. **draw up 1** compose or draft (a document etc.).

2 (of a vehicle) come to a halt. **3** make (oneself) stand straight. **4** (foll. by *with*, *to*) gain on or overtake. **quick on the draw** quick to act or react.

drawback *noun* a disadvantage.

drawbridge *noun* a bridge hinged at one end so as to be raised to prevent passage or to allow ships etc. to pass.

drawdown *noun* **1** a lowering of the water level in a lake, pond, etc. **2** a withdrawal of oil from a reservoir. **3** an act of raising money through loans; borrowing. **4** a reduction or withdrawal, esp. of troops.

drawer *noun* **1** a boxlike storage compartment without a lid, sliding in and out of a frame, table, etc.: *chest of drawers*. **2** (in *plural*) **a** *hist.* or *jocular* underpants. **b** *slang* pants or trousers. **3** a person or thing that draws, esp.: **a** a person who draws a cheque etc. **b** a person who draws pictures.

drawing *noun* **1 a** the art of representing objects by line, using pencil, pen, etc., rather than paint. **b** a picture produced in this way. **2** a sketch, diagram, etc.

drawing board *noun* a large flat board on which paper is placed for drawing plans etc. PHRASES **back to the drawing board** back to begin afresh: *they rejected our proposal, so it's back to the drawing board*.

drawing card *noun* a performer, show, attraction, etc. that draws a large audience.

drawing-room *noun* a room, esp. in a large private house, in which people relax and guests are received and entertained.

drawl • *verb* speak with drawn-out vowel sounds. • *noun* a drawling utterance or way of speaking.

drawn • *verb* past participle of DRAW. • *adjective* looking strained from fear, anxiety, or pain.

drawn-out *adjective* lasting a very long time, often too long.

draw play *noun Football* a play in which the quarterback hands the ball off to a running back who is running toward the line of scrimmage.

drawstring *noun* a string that can be pulled to tighten the mouth of a bag, the waist of a garment, etc.

dread • *verb* fear greatly: *I dread going to the dentist* ◊ *I dread to think what Russell will say*. • *noun* **1 a** great fear or apprehension. **b** an object of fear or apprehension: *my greatest dread is that my parents will find out*. **2 a** slang a person with dreadlocks. **b** (in *plural*) = DREADLOCKS. • *adjective* dreaded: *he was stricken with the dread disease and died*.

dreaded *adjective* **1** regarded with apprehension: *the dreaded news came that Joe had been wounded*. **2** *informal* regarded with mock fear: *did I hear the dreaded word "homework"?*

dreadful *adjective* **1** terrible; causing great fear or suffering. **2** troublesome, disagreeable; very bad. ▶ **dreadfully** *adverb* **dreadfulness** *noun*

dreadlocked *adjective* having one's hair twisted into tight braids or ringlets hanging down on all sides.

dreadlocks *plural noun* a hairstyle in which the hair is washed but not combed and twisted while wet into tight braids or ringlets hanging down on all sides.

dream • *noun* **1 a** a series of pictures or events occurring in the mind during sleep. **b** (also **waking dream**) a similar experience of one awake. **2** a daydream or fantasy. **3** an ideal, aspiration, or ambition. **4** a beautiful or ideal person or thing. **5** a state of mind out of touch with reality: *lives in a dream*. • *verb* (**dreams**; *past* and *past participle* **dreamt** or **dreamed**; **dreaming**) **1** experience a dream. **2** imagine in or as if in a dream. **3 a** contemplate the possibility of, have any conception or intention of: *would not dream of upsetting them*. **b** think of as a possibility: *never dreamt that he would come*. **4** be

unrealistic or not practical. **5** fall into a reverie. • *adjective* ideal: *dream home*. PHRASES **a dream come true** an ideal or desired situation or thing. **dream in colour** (or **Technicolour**) *Cdn* be wildly unrealistic. **dream up** imagine, invent. **like a dream** *informal* easily, effortlessly.

dreamboat *noun informal* a very attractive or ideal person, esp. of the opposite sex.

dream catcher *noun* a webbed hoop believed by some woodland Aboriginal groups to protect a person from bad dreams.

dreamer *noun* **1** a person who has ideas or plans that are not practical or realistic. **2** a person who does not pay attention to what is happening around them, but thinks about other things instead. **3** a person who dreams or is dreaming.

dreamily *adverb* **1** in a manner that suggests one is preoccupied with or distracted by pleasant thoughts: *Monica gazed dreamily out the window*. **2** in a pleasant, gentle, and relaxing manner: *the melodies develop dreamily*. **3** in a way that resembles a dream more than real life: *the images appear dreamily on the screen*.

dreamland *noun* **1** an ideal or imaginary land. **2** sleep.

dreamless *adjective* without dreams: *a dreamless sleep*. ▶ **dreamlessly** *adverb*

dreamlike *adjective* as if existing or happening in a dream rather than in real life.

dreamscape *noun* a dreamed or dreamlike scene: *a TV-shaped dreamscape of suburban patios and family dens*.

dream team *noun slang* **1** a team, real or hypothetical, composed of the top players in a given sport. **2** a group of people considered to be the stars of their field, discipline, etc.

dreamy *adjective* (**dreamier**, **dreamiest**) **1** looking as though one is preoccupied with pleasant thoughts and distracted from one's present surroundings: *a dreamy smile*. **2** (of a person or idea) imaginative, but not realistic: *George was dreamy, but not very practical*. **3** dreamlike; vague; misty. **4** *informal* very attractive or ideal, esp. to the opposite sex. **5** *informal* delightful; marvellous: *a dreamy house*.

drearily *adverb* in a dreary or gloomy manner: *the rain fell drearily*.

dreariness *noun* a dull or gloomy quality.

dreary *adjective* (**drearier**, **dreariest**) dismal, dull, gloomy.

dreck *noun slang* **1** garbage; worthless junk. **2** a person or thing having no redeeming qualities.

dredge[1] • *verb* (**dredges**, **dredged**, **dredging**) **1 a** mention something that has been forgotten, esp. something unpleasant or embarrassing: *the papers keep trying to dredge up details of his love life*. **b** manage to remember something, esp. something that happened a long time ago: *she was dredging up memories from the depths of her mind*. **2** bring up or clear mud etc. from a river, harbour, etc. to make it deeper or to search for something: *waste dredged up from the sea bed* ◊ *they're dredging the harbour* ◊ *they dredge the lake for gravel*. • *noun* an apparatus used to scoop up objects or to clear mud etc. from a river or sea floor.

dredge[2] *verb* (**dredges**, **dredged**, **dredging**) coat (food) with flour, sugar, etc.

dredger *noun* a boat designed for dredging harbours or other bodies of water.

dregs *plural noun* **1 a** the last drops of a liquid, mixed with little pieces of solid material left in the bottom of a container: *he threw the coffee dregs down the sink*. **b** the worst and most useless parts: *the dregs of humanity*. **2 a** small remnant; the last parts of something: *the last*

dregs of daylight. PHRASES **drink to the dregs** consume leaving nothing: *drank life to the dregs*.

dreidel *noun* a small four-sided spinning top with a Hebrew letter on each side, used in a gambling game played during Hanukkah. [Say DRAY dill]

drench *verb* (**drenches, drenched, drenching**) **1** wet thoroughly. **2** saturate; soak (in liquid). **3** cover thoroughly all over: *sunlight drenched the garden*.

dress • *verb* (**dresses, dressed, dressing**) **1 a** clothe. **b** wear clothes of a specified kind or in a specified way: *dresses well*. **2 a** put on clothes. **b** put on formal or evening clothes, esp. for dinner. **3** decorate or adorn. **4 a** treat (a wound) with ointment etc. **b** apply a dressing to (a wound). **5 a** add a dressing to (a salad etc.). **b** clean and prepare (poultry etc.) for cooking or eating. • *noun* (*plural* **dresses**) **1** a one-piece woman's garment consisting of a bodice and skirt. **2** clothing, esp. a whole outfit etc.: *fussy about his dress*. **3** formal or ceremonial costume: *the men were all in evening dress*. **4** an external covering: *birds in their winter dress*. PHRASES **dress down** *informal* **1** dress informally. **2** reprimand or scold. **dress for success** wear expensive, tailored clothes in the workplace in order to cultivate a professional image. **dress up 1** dress (oneself or another) in good clothes, esp. for a special occasion. **2** (esp. of a child) dress in a costume or in special clothes for entertainment. **3** decorate; make more attractive. **4** present something in such a way that it appears better than it really is: *the company dressed up the sales figures a little*.

dressage *noun* **1** the training of a horse in obedience and deportment, esp. for competition. **2** the execution by a horse of precise movements in response to its rider. [Say druh SAWZH]

dress code *noun* a set of rules specifying the required manner of dress at a school, office, club, etc.

dresser *noun* **1** a chest of drawers. **2** a sideboard with shelves above for displaying plates etc. **3** a person who helps theatrical performers to put on and remove costumes. **4** a person who dresses in a specified way: *a snappy dresser*.

dressing *noun* **1** *in senses of* DRESS *verb*. **2 a** a sauce for salads, esp. a mixture of oil, vinegar etc.: *French dressing*. **b** = STUFFING 2. **3 a** a bandage for a wound. **b** ointment etc. used to dress a wound. **4** compost etc. spread over land: *cover the seed bed with a light top dressing of topsoil*.

dressing-down *noun informal* a severe reprimand.

dressing gown *noun* a loose usu. belted robe worn over nightwear or while resting.

dressing room *noun* a room in a sports stadium, theatre, etc. where athletes or performers change into their uniforms or stage clothes.

dressing table *noun* a piece of furniture with a flat top, an upright mirror, and usu. drawers underneath, for use while applying makeup etc.

dressmaker *noun* a person who makes clothes professionally. ▸ **dressmaking** *noun*

dress rehearsal *noun* the final rehearsal of a play etc., with the performers in costume.

dress shirt *noun* **1** a man's long-sleeved shirt, usu. worn with a tie. **2** a man's usu. starched white shirt worn with evening dress.

dress uniform *noun* formal military dress worn on ceremonial occasions.

dress-up *noun* the action of dressing up in costume.

dressy *adjective* (**dressier, dressiest**) **1** (of clothes etc.) suitable for a formal occasion. **2** (of an occasion or place) requiring formal dress or one's best clothes: *a dressy restaurant*. **3** stylish; elegant: *the dressy, well-fed, first-night audience*.

drew *past of* DRAW.

dribble • *verb* (**dribbles, dribbled, dribbling**) **1** allow saliva to flow from the mouth. **2** flow or allow to flow in drops or a trickling stream. **3 a** (in basketball) bounce (the ball), either to move forward or to prepare for a pass. **b** (esp. in soccer and field hockey) advance (the ball) with slight touches of the feet or stick. **4** move with little momentum: *the puck dribbled into the net*. • *noun* **1** the act of dribbling: *shot from the dribble*. **2** a small trickling stream. **3** a small amount: *a tiny dribble of hope*. ▸ **dribbler** *noun* **dribbly** *adjective*

dribs and drabs *plural noun informal* small scattered amounts: *did the work in dribs and drabs*.

dried *past and past participle of* DRY.

drier¹ *comparative of* DRY.

drier² = DRYER.

driest *superlative of* DRY.

drift • *noun* **1 a** slow movement or variation. **b** such movement caused by a slow current. **2** the intention of what is said etc. **3** a large mass of snow, sand, etc., accumulated by the wind. **4** the deviation of a vessel, aircraft, or projectile from its intended or expected course as the result of currents or winds. **5** = CONTINENTAL DRIFT. • *verb* **1** be carried by or as if by a current of air or water. **2** move or progress passively, casually, or aimlessly: *friends drifted apart*. **3 a** pile or be piled by the wind into drifts. **b** cover (a field, a road, etc.) with drifts. **4** (of a current) carry. PHRASES **drift off** fall asleep, esp. gradually.

drifter *noun* **1** an aimless or rootless person. **2** a boat used for drift net fishing.

drift net *noun* a large net for herrings etc., kept upright by weights and floats, and allowed to drift with the tide. ▸ **drift netter** *noun* **drift netting** *noun*

driftwood *noun* wood floating on, or driven ashore by, water.

drill • *noun* **1 a** a tool or machine with a usu. detachable revolving pointed end, used for boring cylindrical holes, sinking wells, etc. **b** a dentist's rotary tool for cutting away part of a tooth etc. **2 a** instruction or training in military exercises. **b** rigorous discipline or methodical instruction, esp. when learning or performing tasks. **c** a rehearsal of the routine procedure to be followed in an emergency: *fire drill*. **d** a routine or exercise. **3** *informal* a recognized procedure: *you know the drill*. **4** a machine used for making furrows, sowing, and covering seed. **5** a small furrow for sowing seed in. **6** a strong cotton or linen fabric. • *verb* **1** make a hole with a drill through or into (wood, metal, etc.). **2** esp. *Military* subject to or undergo discipline by drill. **3** impart (knowledge etc.) by a strict method or by repetition, etc. **4** *slang* **a** shoot with a gun. **b** punch or hit (a person) sharply: *drilled me one in the stomach*. **c** cause (a ball etc.) to move rapidly: *drilled the puck down the ice*.

driller *noun* a person who drills, esp. a worker on a drilling rig who drills for oil etc.

drilling platform *noun* = PLATFORM 3.

drilling rig *noun* a structure with equipment for drilling an oil well etc.

drily *adverb* = DRYLY.

drink • *verb* (**drinks**; *past* **drank**; *past participle* **drunk**; **drinking**) **1** swallow a liquid. **2** take alcohol, esp. to excess: *I don't drink* ◊ *drank himself to death*. **3** (of a plant, porous material, etc.) absorb (moisture). **4** wish (a person's good health, luck, etc.) by drinking: *drank his*

D

health. • *noun* **1 a** a liquid for drinking. **b** an amount of this: *a drink of milk.* **2 a** alcoholic liquor. **b** a portion, glass, etc. of this. **c** excessive indulgence in alcohol: *drink is his vice.* **3 (the drink)** *informal* a body of water. PHRASES **drink deep** take a large draft or drafts. **drink in** listen to or watch closely or eagerly: *drank in every word.* **drink off** drink the whole (contents) of at once. **drink to** toast; wish success to. **drink a person under the table** *informal* remain sober longer than one's drinking companion. **drink up** drink the whole of. ▶ **drinkability** *noun* **drinkable** *adjective*

drinker *noun* **1** a person who drinks (something). **2** a person who drinks alcohol, esp. to excess.

drinking box *noun* (*plural* **drinking boxes**) *Cdn* a small plasticized cardboard carton of juice etc. packaged with a straw.

drinking water *noun* water pure enough for drinking.

drip • *verb* (**drips, dripped, dripping**) **1** fall or let fall in drops. **2** be so wet as to shed drops: *dripped with blood.* • *noun* **1 a** the action or sound of liquid falling steadily in small drops: *the drip, drip, drip of the leaky roof.* **b** a drop of liquid. **2** *informal* a stupid, dull, or ineffective person. **3** *Medical* = DRIP-FEED *noun.* **4** (as an *adjective*) pertaining to coffee made by pouring boiling water through ground coffee in a paper filter: *drip coffee.* PHRASES **dripping wet** very wet. **dripping with** full of or covered with.

drip-dry • *verb* (**drip-dries, drip-dried, drip-drying**) **1** (of fabric etc.) dry crease-free when hung up to drip. **2** leave (a garment etc.) hanging up to dry. • *adjective* able to be drip-dried.

drip-feed • *verb* (**drip-feeds, drip-fed, drip-feeding**) supply a patient with fluid, nutrients, or drugs by an apparatus that passes them drop by drop into the veins. • *noun* **1** the continuous intravenous introduction of fluid into the body. **2** the fluid so introduced. **3** the apparatus used to do this.

dripping *noun* (often in *plural*) **1** fat melted from roasted meat and used for cooking. **2** water, oil, wax, etc., dripping from anything.

drippy *adjective* (**drippier, drippiest**) **1** tending to drip. **2** *informal* (of a song etc.) sloppily sentimental. **3** *informal* (of a person) ineffectual; lacking character.

drive • *verb* (**drives**; *past* **drove**; *past participle* **driven**; **driving**) **1** urge in some direction, esp. forcibly: *drove back the wolves.* **2** force: *was driven to complain ◊ drove him mad ◊ drives herself too hard.* **3** operate; be competent to operate, or travel in a motor vehicle. **4** (of wind, water, etc.) carry along, propel, send, or cause to go in some direction. **5** force (a stake, nail, etc.) into place by blows. **6** effect or conclude forcibly: *drove a hard bargain.* **7** (of steam or other power) set or keep (machinery) going. **8** *Sport* hit or kick (the ball, puck, etc.) forcefully. **9** *Baseball* (often foll. by *in*) **a** cause the advance of (a baserunner) by a base hit or sacrifice fly. **b** cause (a run) to be scored by a base hit or sacrifice fly. **10** *Golf* strike (a ball) with a driver from the tee. **11** float (timber) down a river etc. • *noun* **1** an act of driving in a motor vehicle. **2 a** the capacity for achievement; motivation and energy. **b** an inner urge to attain a goal or satisfy a need: *sex drive.* **3 a** a street or road, esp. a curving one. **b** = DRIVEWAY. **4** *Military* a forceful advance or attack. **5** an organized effort to achieve a usu. charitable purpose: *a famine-relief drive.* **6 a** the act or an instance of driving a puck, ball, etc. **b** the flight of the puck or ball etc. so driven. **c** *Football* a series of plays that advances the ball towards the opposing end of the field. **d** *Golf* a shot, made esp. from the tee with a driver, intended to travel a great distance. **7 a** the transmission of power to machinery the wheels of a motor vehicle, etc.: *front-wheel drive.* **b** the position of a

steering wheel in a motor vehicle: *left-hand drive.* **c** the gear position or function in an automatic transmission which imparts forward motion. **8** *Computing* a device that can store and retrieve data on disks or tape. **9** an act of impelling along (cattle, game, etc.): *cattle drive.* **10** *Cdn* = LOG DRIVE. PHRASES **drive at** seek, intend, or mean: *what is she driving at?* **drive out** take the place of; oust; exorcise, cast out (evil spirits etc.). ▶ **driveable** *adjective* (also **drivable**)

drive-by • *adjective* (of a crime etc.) carried out from a moving vehicle. • *noun* (*plural* **drive-bys**) a drive-by shooting.

drive-in • *adjective* (of a movie theatre, restaurant, etc.) that can be visited without getting out of one's car. • *noun* such a movie theatre, restaurant, etc.

drivel • *noun* silly nonsense. • *verb* (**drivels, drivelled, drivelling**) talk foolishly: *he was drivelling on about the glory days.* [Say DRIV'll]

drivelling *adjective* prone to incoherent or nonsensical speech: *a drivelling idiot.* [Say DRIV ling]

driven • *verb* past participle of DRIVE. • *adjective* **1** (of snow) piled into drifts or made smooth by the wind. **2** urged onward, impelled, forced. **3** (of a person) showing intensity or compulsion in behaviour. **4** motivated or determined by a specified factor or feeling: *our prices are market-driven.* **5** controlled by the means specified: *menu-driven.* PHRASES **white** (or **pure**) **as driven snow** immaculately white or pure.

driver *noun* **1** a person who drives a vehicle. **2** *Golf* a club with a flat face and wooden head, used for driving from the tee. **3** *Computing* a program that controls the operation of a device. **4** a person who herds or drives a usu. specified type of animal. PHRASES **in the driver's seat** in charge. ▶ **driverless** *adjective*

driver's licence a licence permitting a person to drive a motor vehicle.

driveshaft *noun* a rotating shaft that transmits power esp. to the differential in a motor vehicle.

drive shed *noun* *Cdn* (esp. *Ont.*) a large shed used for storing farm machinery, vehicles, etc.

drive-through • *adjective* designating a restaurant etc. at which customers are served without leaving their cars: *a drive-through car wash ◊ order your burger at our drive-through window.* • *noun* a place where drive-through service is offered.

drivetrain *noun* the system in a motor vehicle which connects the transmission to the drive axles.

driveway *noun* **1** a paved or gravelled parking area leading to a garage or house. **2** a private road or lane leading to a house, barn, etc.

driving *adjective* **1** moving rapidly, esp. before the wind: *a driving rain.* **2** energetic: *a driving rhythm.* **3** used when driving a motor vehicle: *driving gloves.*

driving range *noun* *Golf* an area for practising drives.

driving shed *noun* *Cdn* (esp. *Ont.*) = DRIVE SHED.

drizzle • *noun* **1** very fine rain. **2** esp. *Cooking* a fine trickle. • *verb* (**drizzles, drizzled, drizzling**) **1** (esp. of rain) fall in very fine drops: *it's drizzling again.* **2** esp. *Cooking* sprinkle in fine drops or a thin trickle: *drizzle melted chocolate over the raspberry glaze.* ▶ **drizzly** *adjective*

droll *adjective* curious or unusual in a way that provokes dry amusement: *her unique brand of droll self-mockery.* [Rhymes with ROLL]

drone • *noun* **1** a non-working male honeybee, whose sole function is to mate with fertile females. **2** a person who does no useful work and lives off others: *the drones of officialdom who constitute the civic bureaucracy.* **3** a continuous low noise he spoke in a low drone ◊ the distant drone of traffic.* **4 a** a pipe, esp. of a bagpipe, sounding a continuous note of fixed low pitch. **b** the note emitted

by this. **5** a remote-controlled pilotless aircraft or missile. • *verb* (**drones, droned, droning**) **1** make a deep humming sound. **2** speak or utter in a boring tone for a long time: *he reached for another beer while Jim droned on*.

drool • *verb* **1** have saliva coming out of the mouth; slobber. **2** (often foll. by *over*) show much pleasure or infatuation. • *noun* saliva.

droop • *verb* **1** hang or allow to hang down; decline or sag, esp. from weariness. **2 a** (of the eyes) look downwards. **b** (of the sun) sink. **3** lose heart; be dejected; flag. • *noun* an act of drooping: *the exhausted droop of her shoulders*.

drooping *adjective* hanging or sagging, esp. due to fatigue or dejection: *the drooping branches of a willow tree* ◊ *he stood with drooping shoulders and sad eyes*.

droopy *adjective* (**droopier, droopiest**) **1** drooping: *a droopy moustache*. **2** lacking strength or spirit: *a typical fashion model, willowy, mellow, slightly droopy*.

drop • *verb* (**drops, dropped, dropping**) **1** fall or cause to fall. **2** sink to the ground. **3** make or become lower, weaker, or less. **4** abandon or discontinue. **5** place or leave (something) without ceremony. **6** *informal* collapse from exhaustion. **7** lose (a point, game, etc.). **8** mention casually. • *noun* **1** a small round or pear-shaped portion of liquid. **2** an instance of falling or dropping. **3** a small drink, esp. of alcohol. **4** an abrupt fall or slope. **5** *informal* a delivery. **6** a candy or lozenge. PHRASES **at the drop of a hat** given the slightest excuse. **drop anchor** anchor ship. **drop back** (or **behind** or **to the rear**) fall back; get left behind. **drop back into** return to (a habit etc.). **drop the ball** make a mess of something; fumble. **drop a brick** *informal* make an indiscreet or embarrassing remark. **drop dead 1** die suddenly, usu. from a heart attack or stroke. **2** *slang* an exclamation of intense scorn. **drop in** (or **by**) *informal* call casually as a visitor. **a drop in the ocean** (or **a bucket**) a very small amount, esp. compared with what is needed or expected. **drop into** *informal* **1** call casually at (a place). **2** fall into (a habit etc.). **drop it!** *slang* stop that! **drop names** casually mention the names of famous people one knows or pretends to know in order to impress others. **drop off 1** decline gradually. **2** *informal* fall asleep. **3** = sense 5 of *verb*. **4** leave or deposit (something) at an assigned place. **drop out** *informal* cease to participate, esp. in a race, a course of study, or in conventional society. **fit** (or **ready**) **to drop** extremely tired. **have the drop on** *informal* have the advantage over. **one's jaw drops** one shows sudden surprise, dismay, or disappointment.

drop cloth *noun* a sheet of cloth or plastic used to protect furniture, floors, etc. when painting.

drop-dead *slang* • *adverb* stunningly: *drop-dead gorgeous*. • *adjective* stunningly beautiful: *drop-dead looks*.

drop-down *adjective* designating a computer menu or list that appears below a heading when the heading is selected with a mouse.

drop-in • *adjective* **1** (of a place or function) at which one can turn up without prior appointment or referral: *drop-in centre*. **2** designed to drop into position. • *noun informal* **1** a place or function at which one can turn up informally, without prior appointment or referral. **2** an unexpected visitor or visit.

drop kick • *noun* **1** *Football etc.* a kick made by dropping the ball and kicking it on the bounce **2** a movement in which a wrestler jumps into the air and kicks his or her opponent with both feet simultaneously, then drops onto one side. • *verb* **1** kick (a ball, a field goal, etc.) by means of a drop kick. **2** make a drop kick.

droplet *noun* a tiny drop of liquid.

drop-off *noun* **1 a** an act of dropping off or delivering something or someone. **b** a place where this can be done. **2** a decline, a decrease: *a drop-off in sales*. **3** a sheer downward slope.

dropout *noun* **1** *informal* a person who has dropped out of society. **2** a person who leaves school before completing the program.

drop pass *noun* (*plural* **drop passes**) a backwards pass of a ball or puck, often executed without turning or looking around.

dropped *adjective* in a lower position than usual: *dropped waist*.

dropper *noun* **1** a device for administering liquid, esp. medicine, in drops. **2** a person or thing that drops.

droppings *plural noun* **1** the dung of animals or birds. **2** something that falls or has fallen in drops.

dropsy *noun* (*plural* **dropsies**) a condition characterized by an excess of watery fluid collecting in the cavities or tissues of the body.

dross *noun* **1** something regarded as worthless; rubbish. **2** foreign matter, dregs, or mineral waste, esp. the scum separated from metals in melting. [Rhymes with CROSS]

drought *noun* **1** the continuous absence of rain; dry weather. **2** the prolonged lack of something: *ended a 15-game scoring drought*. [Rhymes with SHOUT]

drove¹ *past of* DRIVE.

drove² *noun* **1** a large number (of people etc.) doing the same thing: *people arrived in droves*. **2** a herd or flock being driven or moving together: *a drove of cattle*.

drover *noun* a person who drives herds to market.

drown *verb* **1** kill or be killed by submersion in liquid. **2** submerge; flood; drench: *drowned the fields in six feet of water*. **3** deaden (grief etc.) with drink: *drowned his sorrows*. **4** (often foll. by *out*) make (a sound) inaudible by means of a louder sound. **b** overcome by superior strength: *their complaints were drowned out by a chorus of approval from environmental activists*. PHRASES **like a drowned rat** *informal* extremely wet and bedraggled.

drowse *verb* (**drowses, drowsed, drowsing**) be dull and sleepy or half asleep. [Rhymes with PLOWS]

drowsily *adverb* in a drowsy or sleepy manner.

drowsiness *noun* a tired or sleepy feeling; fatigue: *these allergy drugs cause drowsiness*.

drowsy *adjective* (**drowsier, drowsiest**) **1** half asleep; dozing. **2** making one feel sleepy. **3** very peaceful and quiet: *a drowsy small town*.

drub *verb* (**drubs, drubbed, drubbing**) **1** hit or beat someone repeatedly. **2** defeat thoroughly. **3** criticize or reprimand harshly. ▶ **drubbing** *noun*

drudge *noun* a person who does hard, dull, or menial work: *she was little more than a drudge around the house*. ▶ **drudgery** *noun*

drug • *noun* **1** a medicinal substance. **2** a narcotic, hallucinogen, or stimulant, esp. one causing addiction. • *verb* (**drugs, drugged, drugging**) **1** add a drug to (food or drink). **2 a** administer a drug to. **b** stupefy with a drug.

druggie *noun informal* a drug addict.

druggist *noun* a pharmacist.

druggy *adjective* (**druggier, druggiest**) *informal* of or associated with narcotic drugs.

drugstore *noun* a pharmacy that also sells cosmetics, household items, drinks, snacks, etc.

Druid *noun* **1** a priest, magician, or soothsayer in the ancient Celtic religion of Gaul (France), Britain, or Ireland. **2** a member of a present-day group claiming to represent or be derived from this religion. ▶ **Druidic**

D

adjective **Druidical** adjective **Druidism** noun [Say DROO id, droo ID ick, droo ID ick'll, DROO id ism]

drum • noun **1 a** a percussion instrument made of a hollow cylinder or hemisphere covered at one or both ends and sounded by striking. **b** (often in plural) a drummer or a percussion section: the drums are playing too loud. **c** a sound made by or resembling that of a drum. **2** something resembling a drum in shape, esp.: **a** a cylindrical container or receptacle for oil, etc. **b** a cylinder or barrel in machinery on which something is wound etc. **3** the membrane of the middle ear; the eardrum. **4** (also **drum fish**) a marine fish with a swim bladder that produces a drumming sound. • verb (**drums, drummed, drumming**) **1** play on a drum. **2** beat, tap, or thump (knuckles, feet, etc.) continuously (on something). **3** (of a bird or an insect) make a loud, hollow noise with quivering wings. PHRASES **drum into** drive (a lesson) into (a person) by persistence. **drum up** summon, gather, or call up: drum up some support.

drum brake noun a brake in which shoes on a vehicle press against the drum on a wheel.

drum dance noun a dance, accompanied by drumming, combining traditional Inuit dancing with Scottish and French-Canadian jigs and reels.

drumlin noun a long low oval mound or small hill, usu. one of a group, consisting of compacted boulder clay moulded by the action of glaciers.

drum machine noun an electronic device that imitates the sound of percussion instruments.

drum major noun the leader of a marching band.

drum majorette noun a member of a female baton-twirling parading group.

drummer noun **1** a person who plays a drum or drums. **2** informal a sales representative.

drum roll noun a rapid succession of notes on a drum.

drumstick noun **1** a stick used for beating a drum. **2** the lower joint of the leg of a cooked chicken etc.

drunk • adjective **1** rendered incapable by alcohol. **2** (often foll. by with) overcome or elated with joy, success, power, etc. • noun **1** a habitually drunk person. **2** slang a drinking bout; a period of drunkenness.

drunkard noun a person who is drunk, esp. habitually. [Say DRUNK erd]

drunken adjective **1** rendered incapable by alcohol. **2** caused by or exhibiting drunkenness: a drunken brawl. **3** fond of drinking esp. to excess. ▶ **drunkenly** adverb **drunkenness** noun

drunk tank noun slang a prison cell where persons arrested for drunkenness are detained, esp. overnight.

drupe noun any fleshy or pulpy fruit enclosing a stone containing one or a few seeds, e.g. a plum.

drupelet noun a small drupe usu. in an aggregate fruit, e.g. a raspberry. [Say DROOP lit]

druthers noun informal preference, choice; one's way: if I had my druthers. [Rhymes with OTHERS]

Druze noun a member of a political or religious sect of Islamic origin but regarded as heretical by the Muslim community at large, living chiefly in Lebanon and Syria: Druze militia.

dry • adjective (**drier; driest**) **1** lacking moisture. **2** (of wine etc.) not sweet: dry sherry. **3 a** meagre, plain: dry facts. **b** uninteresting: dry as dust. **4** (of a joke etc.) subtle, ironic, and quietly expressed. **5 a** prohibiting the sale of alcoholic drink. **b** abstaining from alcohol or drugs. **6 a** (of toast, bread, etc.) without butter, margarine, etc. **b** (of bread, rolls, etc.) stale. **7** (of provisions, groceries, etc.) solid, not liquid. **8** (of a person etc.) unsympathetic. **9** (of a cow etc.) not yielding milk. **10** informal a thirsty: feel dry. **b** causing thirst: this is dry work. **11** (of beer) having little or no

aftertaste, due to longer brewing. • verb (**dries, dried, drying**) **1** make or become dry by wiping, evaporation, draining, etc. **2** (usu. as **dried** adjective) preserve (food etc.) by removing the moisture: dried fruit. **3** (often foll. by up) Theatre informal forget one's lines. • noun (plural **dries**) dry ginger ale: rye and dry. PHRASES **come up dry** be unsuccessful. **dry out 1** become fully dry. **2** (of a drug addict, alcoholic, etc.) undergo treatment to cure addiction. **dry up 1** make utterly dry. **2** (of moisture) disappear utterly. **3** (of a well etc.) cease to yield water. **4** informal (esp. in imper.) cease talking. **5** disappear or cease: the market dried up. **go dry** enact legislation for the prohibition of alcohol.

dry battery noun (plural **dry batteries**) a battery consisting of dry cells.

dry cell noun an electric cell in which the electrolyte is absorbed in a solid to form a paste, preventing spillage.

dry clean verb clean (clothes etc.), or be cleanable, with organic solvents without using water. ▶ **dry cleaner** noun **dry cleaning** noun

dry cough noun a cough not producing phlegm.

dry-cure verb (**dry-cures, dry-cured, dry-curing**) cure (meat etc.) without pickling in liquid. ▶ **dry-cured** adjective

dry dock noun an enclosure for the building or repairing of ships, from which water can be removed.

SPELL CHECK ABC✓
dryer, drier

Something that is "more dry" is **drier**.

---

dryer noun a machine or apparatus for drying the hair, laundry, etc.

dry fly noun (plural **dry flies**) an artificial fishing fly which is made to float lightly on the water.

dry goods plural noun **1** fabrics, clothing, etc. **2** Cdn & Brit. solid as opposed to liquid foodstuffs.

dry ice noun **1** solid carbon dioxide, which passes directly from solid to vapour at $-78.5°C$ and is used as a refrigerant and to create theatrical effects of fog. **2** the fog produced in this way.

dryland noun **1** (**dry land**) land as opposed to the sea, a river, etc.: it was a great relief to be back on dry land after such a rough crossing. **2** an area or land where rainfall is low (also as an adjective: dryland farming). **3** a surface not covered by snow or ice as used for training by skiers, skaters, etc. (also as an adjective: dryland training).

dryly adverb **1** in an understatedly humorous, somewhat mocking manner: "Well, at least it's not purple," she commented dryly. **2** in a way indicating absence of moisture.

dry measure noun a measure of capacity for dry products such as grains etc.

dryness noun a dry quality: crops are suffering due to the heat and dryness ◊ dryness of the hands and lips.

dry rot noun **1** a decayed state of wood in poorly ventilated conditions, caused by certain fungi. **2** these fungi.

dry run noun informal a rehearsal of a performance or procedure before the real one: couples often consider living together as a dry run for marriage.

dry spell noun **1** a period of dry weather. **2** a period of unproductiveness: a creative dry spell coincided with his personal problems.

dry suit noun a waterproof rubber suit worn for water sports and diving, under which warm clothes can be worn.

drywall • noun prefabricated sheets of plaster sandwiched between heavy paper, used for interior walls. • verb install drywall (on a wall etc.). ▶ **drywaller** noun **drywalling** noun

dry well *noun* **1** a well, drilled for oil, water, gas, etc., that is unproductive. **2** a shaft or chamber constructed in the ground in order to aid drainage, sometimes containing pumping equipment.

DSC *abbreviation* (*plural* **DSCs**) Distinguished Service Cross.

DSM *abbreviation* (*plural* **DSMs**) Distinguished Service Medal.

DT *abbreviation* (also **DT's**) DELIRIUM TREMENS.

SPELL CHECK
dual, duel `ABC✓`

A conflict involving two parties is a **duel**.

---

dual *adjective* **1** having two parts or aspects: *her dual role as composer and conductor*. **2** divided in two; double: *dual ownership*. [Say DUE ul]

dual citizenship *noun* the status of a person who is a citizen of more than one country concurrently.

dualism *noun* **1** the division of something conceptually into two opposed or contrasted aspects, or the state of being so divided: *a dualism between man and nature*. **2** *Philosophy* the theory that in any domain of reality there are two independent underlying principles, e.g. mind and matter, form and content. **3** *Theology* **a** the theory that the forces of good and evil are equally balanced in the universe. **b** the theory of the dual (human and divine) personality of Christ. ▶**dualist** *noun* **dualistic** *adjective* **dualistically** *adverb* [Say DUE ul ism]

duality *noun* (*plural* **dualities**) the state of having two parts or aspects, esp. contrasting or opposite ones: *Canada's linguistic duality*. [Say due ALA tee]

dual-purpose *adjective* **1** (of a vehicle) usable for passengers or goods. **2** (of a farm animal) able to be used for two purposes, e.g. (of a cow) providing both meat and milk.

dub¹ *verb* (**dubs, dubbed, dubbing**) **1** confer an order of knighthood upon (a person) by the ritual touching of the shoulder with a sword. **2** give (a person or thing) a name, nickname, or title.

dub² • *verb* (**dubs, dubbed, dubbing**) **1** provide (a film etc.) with an alternative soundtrack, esp. in a different language. **2** add (sound effects or music) to a film or a broadcast. **3** combine (soundtracks) into one. **4** transfer or make a copy of (a tape or disc). • *noun* a dubbed tape etc.

dub³ *noun* **1** (also **dub music**) a remixed version of a piece of recorded (esp. reggae) music, usu. with the melodic line removed and special effects added. **2** (also **dub poetry**) a kind of performance poetry in Jamaican (or black English) vernacular.

dubbing *noun* an alternative soundtrack to a film etc.

dubious *adjective* **1** hesitating or doubting: *dubious about going*. **2** of questionable value or truth: *a dubious claim*. **3** unreliable; suspicious: *dubious company*. **4** of doubtful result: *a dubious undertaking*. ▶**dubiously** *adverb* **dubiousness** *noun* [Say DUE bee us]

ducal *adjective* of or pertaining to a duke: *the ducal palace*. [Say DUKE'll]

ducat *noun* **1** any of various gold or silver coins, formerly current in most European countries. **2** *informal* a ticket, esp. for admission, a train, etc. [Say DUCK it]

duchess *noun* (*plural* **duchesses**) (as a title usu. **Duchess**) **1** a duke's wife or widow. **2** a woman holding the rank of duke in her own right. [Say DUTCH iss]

duchy *noun* (*plural* **duchies**) the territory of a duke or duchess: *the Duchy of Cornwall*. [Say DUTCHIE]

duck¹ *noun* **1 a** any of various swimming birds, esp. the domesticated form of the mallard or wild duck. **b** the female of this (*opp.* DRAKE). **c** the flesh of a duck as

food. **2** a fellow, individual, etc., esp. a somewhat eccentric one: *he's an odd duck*. PHRASES **like a duck to water** adapting very readily. **like water off a duck's back** *informal* (of complaints etc.) producing no effect.

duck² • *verb* **1** plunge, dive, or dip under water and emerge: *ducked him in the pond*. **2 a** stoop suddenly or move quickly, esp. as an evasive measure: *ducked out of sight*. **b** lower (esp. the head) momentarily. **3** *informal* (often foll. by *out*) avoid or dodge; withdraw (from): *ducked out of the engagement*. • *noun* **1** a quick swim or plunge into water etc. **2** a quick lowering of the head, rapid evasive movement, etc.

duck³ *noun* **1** a strong linen or cotton fabric used for the outer clothing of sailors, small sails, etc. **2** (in *plural*) trousers made of this: *white ducks*.

duckbill • *noun* **1** (also **duck-billed platypus**, *plural* **duck-billed platypuses**) = PLATYPUS. **2** (also **duck-billed dinosaur**) = HADROSAUR. • *adjective* (also **duck-billed**) having the shape of a duck's bill.

duckling *noun* **1** a young duck. **2** its flesh as food.

duckweed *noun* any of various plants, esp. of the genus *Lemna*, growing on the surface of still water.

ducky • *noun* (also **rubber ducky**) (*plural* **duckies**) a toy duck made of plastic, rubber, etc. • *adjective* *ironic* fine, splendid.

duct *noun* **1** a channel or tube for conveying air, fluid, cable, etc. **2 a** a tube or passage in the body conveying fluids or secretions such as tears, lymph, etc. **b** *Botany* any of the vessels of the vascular tissue of plants, containing air, water, etc. ▶**ducted** *adjective*

ductile *adjective* **1** (of a substance) able to be deformed without losing toughness; pliable, not brittle. **2** (of a metal) able to be drawn out into a thin wire: *gold is a ductile metal*. [Say DUCK tile]

ducting *noun* **1** a system of ducts. **2** material, esp. tubing or piping, in the form of a duct or ducts.

ductless *adjective* lacking or not using a duct or ducts, esp. of a gland secreting directly into the bloodstream.

duct tape *noun* tape of plastic-backed webbed cloth, used for household repairs. ▶**duct-tape** *verb* (**duct-tapes, duct-taped, duct-taping**)

ductwork *noun* a system of ducts.

dud *noun* *slang* **1** a useless, unsuccessful, ineffectual, or unsatisfactory person or thing: *a box office dud* ◊ *dud materials*. **2** a shell etc. that fails to explode. **3** a dishonoured cheque. **4** (in *plural*) clothes.

dude *slang* • *noun* **1** a fellow or person. **2** a person, usu. male, fastidiously concerned with clothes, appearance, etc. **3** a city dweller, esp. one vacationing on a ranch in western Canada or the US. • *verb* (**dudes, duded, duding**) dress or fix up, esp. in a showy way.

dude ranch *noun* (*plural* **dude ranches**) a cattle ranch converted to a vacation resort for tourists, featuring riding, camping, barbecues, etc.

due • *adjective* **1** owing as a debt or an obligation: *our thanks are due to him* ◊ *$500 was due*. **2** belonging to or incumbent upon (a person) by right, by duty, or as a necessity: *his due reward*. **3** proper, sufficient: *due consideration*. **4** attributable to: *death was due to cardiac arrest*. **5** expected or intended to arrive or appear at a certain time: *a train is due at 7:30*. **6** scheduled to do something: *due to speak tonight*. • *noun* **1** a thing which is owed to a person legally or morally: *a fair hearing is my due*. **2** (in *plural*) **a** what a person owes, esp. obligations, responsibilities, etc. **b** a payment, esp. the membership fees for a club etc.: *union dues*. • *adverb* (of a point of the compass) exactly, directly: *went due east*. PHRASES **due to** because of, owing to: *was late due to an accident*. **fall** (or **become**) **due** (of a bill etc.) be immediately payable. **in due course** (or **time**) **1** at about the appropriate time. **2** in the natural order. **pay one's**

dues 1 fulfill one's obligations. **2** undergo hardships to succeed or gain experience.

due date *noun* **1** the date on which payment of a bill etc. falls due. **2** the date, in a pregnancy, on which a child is predicted to be born. **3** the date on which a library book, rented item, etc. must be returned.

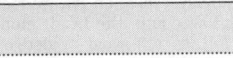

SPELL CHECK
duel, dual

Something with two parts or aspects is **dual**: *dual citizenship*.

---

duel • *noun* **1** a private fight between two people, pre-arranged and fought with deadly weapons, usu. to settle a quarrel over a matter of honour. **2** any contest between two people, causes, animals, etc.: *a duel of wits*. • *verb* (**duels, duelled, duelling**) fight a duel or duels. ▶ **dueller** *noun* **duellist** *noun* [Say DUE ul]

SPELL CHECK
due, duly

Warning: **duly** is spelled without an *e*.

---

due process *noun* (also **due process of the law**) the administration of justice through the courts in accordance with established rules and principles: *due process means that people have the right to give their side of the story* ◊ *the government has been accused of bypassing due process in the name of political expediency*.

duet • *noun* a performance by, or a composition written to be performed by, two voices, instrumentalists, etc. ▶ **duettist** *noun* [Say due ET]

duff *noun* **1** a boiled pudding. **2** the decaying vegetable matter which covers the forest ground. **3** *informal* buttocks: *get off your duff*.

duffer *noun* *slang* **1** a person, often elderly, without practical ability. **2** a person who is incapable, inefficient, or useless in his or her business, occupation, or sport: *plainly this is a book by a duffer*.

duffle *noun* (also **duffel**) **1** a coarse, closely woven, woollen cloth with a thick nap. **2** a sportsman's or camper's equipment, food, clothing, etc. **3** (also **duffle bag**) a large, cylindrical canvas bag closed by a drawstring and carried over the shoulder.

dug *past and past participle of* DIG.

dugout *noun* **1 a** *Sport* a low shelter at the side of a baseball diamond etc. with seating for the team manager, trainer, players, etc. **b** a roofed shelter, esp. for troops in trenches. **2 a** a rough shelter hollowed out in a bank or hillside, usu. roofed with turf, canvas, etc. **b** *Cdn* (*Prairies*) a large hole in the ground used to catch and hold rain, spring runoff, etc. **3** a canoe made from a hollowed out tree trunk.

duh *interjection* indicating stupidity or scorn for the expression of something self-evident.

du jour *adjective* (placed after noun) of the day; trendy or fashionable: *did not exactly follow the technique du jour*. See also SOUP DU JOUR. [Say doo ZHOOR]

duke • *noun* **1** (as a title usu. **Duke**) **a** a person holding the highest hereditary title of the nobility and ranking next below a prince, esp. in Britain. **b** a sovereign prince ruling a duchy or small nation, esp. in certain European countries. **2** *slang* the hand or fist: *put up your dukes!* • *verb* (**dukes, duked, duking**) *slang* fight, esp. with the fists: *they decided to duke it out*.

dukedom *noun* **1** a duchy or the territory ruled by a duke. **2** the rank of duke.

dulcimer *noun* **1** a musical instrument with strings stretched over a trapezoidal sounding board or box, played by being struck with hammers. **2** a zither-like

folk instrument with three or four strings, played by plucking or strumming. [Say DULLSA mer]

dull • *adjective* **1** uninteresting. **2** (of the weather) cloudy. **3 a** (esp. of a knife edge etc.) blunt. **b** (of colour, light, or taste) not bright or keen. **4** (of a pain etc.) usu. prolonged and indistinct, not acute: *a dull ache*. **5** slow to understand. **6** (of sound) indistinct, muffled, not clear or loud: *a dull thud*. • *verb* make or become dull. **PHRASES** **dull the edge of** blunt or make less sensitive, interesting, effective, amusing, etc.: *the passage of time has dulled the edge of her grief*. ▶ **dulled** *adjective* **dullish** *adjective* **dullness** *noun*

dully *adverb* **1** in an indistinct manner: *the door thudded dully behind her*. **2** in a dim manner: *dully gleaming coins*. **3** in a depressed, uninterested, or uninspired manner: *the old men chatted dully*. [Say DULL lee]

dulse *noun* an edible seaweed with red wedge-shaped fronds. [Rhymes with PULSE]

duly *adverb* **1** in due manner, order, form, or time: *arrived duly at 9:30*. **2** correctly, properly, or sufficiently: *the document was duly signed and authorized by the inspector*. [Say DUE lee]

dumb • *adjective* **1 a** (of a person) unable to speak, usu. because of a congenital defect or deafness; mute. **b** (of an animal) naturally unable to speak: *our dumb friends*. **2** temporarily silenced by surprise, shyness, grief, etc.: *struck dumb by this revelation*. **3** (of an action, expression, etc.) performed or made without speech. **4** *informal* stupid. **5** (of a computer terminal etc.) not programmable, able only to transmit data to or receive data from a computer (*opp.* INTELLIGENT 2b). **6** (of missiles etc.) firing in a straight line until hitting something (*opp.* SMART 7b). • *verb* *slang* (usu. foll. by *down*) reduce or adapt (a text etc.) to a lower level of understanding.

dumbbell *noun* **1** a short bar with a weight at each end, used for exercise, muscle building, etc. **2** *slang* a stupid person or a fool.

dumbfound *verb* greatly astonish or amaze: *she was dumbfounded at the sight that met her eyes*.

dumbly *adverb* **1** without speaking: *she nodded dumbly in response*. **2** in a way suggesting mental inactivity: *I sat dumbly in front of the TV*. **3** without understanding: *"Huh?" he said, looking at me dumbly*.

dumbo *noun* (*plural* **dumbos**) *slang* a stupid person.

dumbstruck *adjective* greatly shocked or surprised and so lost for words.

dummy • *noun* (*plural* **dummies**) **1** a model of a human being, esp.: **a** a ventriloquist's doll. **b** a figure used to model clothes in a store window etc. **c** a target used for firearms practice. **d** a mannequin used in crash tests for vehicles etc. **2** (often as an *adjective*) an imitation of an object used to replace or resemble a real or normal one, as in a display etc. **3** *informal* a stupid person. **4 a** a figurehead present only for appearances or a person taking no significant part in an activity. **b** a person who is merely a tool for another, buying etc. on another's behalf. **5** *Cdn & Brit.* a baby's soother. **6** *Bridge* **a** the partner of the declarer, whose cards are exposed after the first lead. **b** this player's hand. **7** *Military* a blank round of ammunition. • *adjective* sham, fictitious: *a dummy corporation*. **PHRASES** **dummy up** *slang* refuse to talk.

dump • *noun* **1** a site for depositing garbage or waste. **2** a heap of garbage left at a dump. **3** *informal* an unpleasant or dreary place. **4** *Military* a temporary store of weapons or provisions. **5** *Computing* an act of dumping stored data. **6** (also **log dump**) a place where logs are piled such as on a riverbank, near a road or railway etc., in preparation for being moved to the mill. • *verb* **1** deposit or dispose of (garbage or something unwanted). **2** put down (something) firmly and

carelessly. **3** abandon (someone). **4** *Computing* copy (stored data) to a different location. **5** send (goods) to a foreign market for sale at a low price. PHRASES **dump on** *slang* **1** criticize severely, treat with scorn or contempt, or defeat heavily. **2** thwart: *fate dumped on my plans*.

dump-and-chase *adjective* Cdn Hockey designating a strategy of play in which a player shoots the puck far down the ice and then chases after it.

dumper *noun* **1** a large metal bin for garbage. **2 a** a person or company that dumps garbage etc., esp. one that disposes of toxic waste covertly or illegally. **b** a thing that dumps or disposes of garbage etc. PHRASES **into the dumper** *informal* into a dire state or condition: *the market went into the dumper*.

dumping *noun* **1** the practice of discarding garbage, hazardous waste, etc., esp. covertly or illegally. **2** the practice of putting goods on the market at low prices, either in large quantities or in a foreign market.

dumping ground *noun* **1** = DUMP 1a. **2** a catch-all category, institution, etc. used for something unclassified or as a place of last resort for those considered undesirable: *a dumping ground for criminals*.

dumpling *noun* **1 a** a small piece of dough, sometimes with a filling, boiled in water or in stew. **b** a dessert consisting of apple or other fruit enclosed in dough and baked. **2** *informal* a small fat person.

dumps *plural noun informal* PHRASES **down in the dumps** (of a person) depressed or unhappy.

Dumpster *noun proprietary* a very large garbage container, usu. emptied by being mechanically lifted onto a truck.

dump truck *noun* a usu. open topped truck with a body that tilts or opens at the back for unloading.

dumpy *adjective* (**dumpier, dumpiest**) short, rounded, and stout.

dun *verb* (**duns, dunned, dunning**) make persistent demands on (someone), esp. for repayment of a debt.

dunce *noun* a person slow at learning.

dune *noun* a ridge of loose sand etc. formed by the wind, esp. beside the sea or in a desert.

dune buggy *noun* (*plural* **dune buggies**) a low, lightweight motor vehicle with wide tires for recreational driving on sand.

dung *noun* the excrement of animals; manure.

dungaree *noun* **1** a coarse, hard-wearing cotton fabric, often blue. **2** (in *plural*) trousers, esp. jeans, made of dungaree or similar material. **3** (in *plural*) trousers with a bib, esp. as worn by children; bib overalls. [Say dun ga REE]

dung beetle *noun* any of various beetles which lay their eggs in dung or roll up balls of dung for their larvae to feed on.

dungeon *noun* a strong underground cell for prisoners. [Say DUN jin]

dunk • *verb* **1** dip (bread, a biscuit, etc.) into soup, coffee, etc. while eating. **2 a** immerse, dip: *was dunked in the river*. **b** *slang* baptize. **3** *Basketball* shoot (the ball) down through the hoop by jumping so that the hands are above the ring. • *noun* **1** (also **dunk shot** or **slam dunk**) *Basketball* a shot made by jumping and pushing the ball down through the basket from above. **2** an act of immersing oneself in a lake etc. ▶ **dunker** *noun*

dunlin *noun* a long-billed sandpiper of Arctic and temperate regions, the male of which has a reddish back and a black patch on the front. [Say DUN lin]

Dunne-Za *noun* = BEAVER. [Say dunna ZAW]

duo *noun* (*plural* **duos**) **1** a pair of actors, entertainers, etc.: *a comedy duo*. **2** *Music* a duet.

duodenum *noun* the first part of the small intestine

immediately below the stomach. [Say due oh DEE num or due ODDA num]

duopoly *noun* (*plural* **duopolies**) *Economics* a condition in which two suppliers dominate the market for a commodity or service. [Say due OPPA lee]

Duo-Tang *noun* Cdn proprietary a report folder of cardboard, having three flexible metal fasteners to insert through the holes of looseleaf paper.

dupe¹ • *noun* a person who is deluded or deceived by another. • *verb* (**dupes, duped, duping**) deceive: *Canadians have been duped into believing otherwise*.

dupe² *slang* • *noun* a duplicate, esp. a duplicate negative made from a positive print. • *adjective* duplicate: *dupe transparencies*.

duplex • *noun* (*plural* **duplexes**) **1 a** = SEMI-DETACHED. **b** a residential building divided into two apartments, esp. a two-storey dwelling with a separate apartment on each floor. **2** the capacity of a computer etc. to send and receive data simultaneously along a communications link such as a telephone etc. • *adjective Computing* (of a circuit) allowing the transmission or reception of signals in opposite directions simultaneously over a single channel etc. (opp. SIMPLEX 2). • *verb* (**duplexes, duplexed, duplexing**) make (a cable, system, etc.) capable of transmitting in two directions simultaneously. ▶ **duplexed** *adjective* **duplexing** *noun* [Say DUE plex]

duplicate • *adjective* **1** copied or exactly like something already existing (in any number of copies): *a duplicate licence is issued to replace a lost one*. **2 a** having two corresponding parts etc.: *a duplicate application form*. **b** doubled or consisting of twice the number or quantity: *duplicate computer facilities*. • *noun* **1** one of two or more things exactly alike, so that each is a double of some original: *Liz and I are getting rid of any of our books that are duplicates*. **2** (also **duplicate bridge** or **whist**) a form of bridge or whist in which the same hands are played successively by different players. • *verb* (**duplicates, duplicated, duplicating**) **1** multiply by two. **2 a** make or be an exact copy of. **b** make or supply copies of: *duplicated the leaflet for distribution*. **3** repeat (an action etc.), esp. unnecessarily: *felt that she was duplicating work that had already been done*. PHRASES **in duplicate** consisting of two exact copies. ▶ **duplication** *noun* [Say DUE plick it for the adjective and noun, DUE plick ate for the verb]

duplicator *noun* a thing that duplicates, esp. a machine for making copies.

duplicitous *adjective* dishonest, deceitful: *treacherous, duplicitous behaviour*. [Say due PLISS it us]

duplicity *noun* (*plural* **duplicities**) the quality or practice of being two-faced, deceitful in manner or conduct, or double-dealing: *accused the government of hypocrisy and duplicity*. [Say due PLISS it ee]

durability *noun* the ability to withstand damage, decay, or wear: *we painted the deck to improve its durability*.

durable • *adjective* capable of lasting or able to withstand change, decay, or wear: *made from durable, ripstop nylon*. • *noun* (in *plural*; also **durable goods**) goods which remain useful over time, such as cars, machinery, etc., as opposed to those produced for immediate consumption: *consumer durables*.

duration *noun* the time during which something lasts or continues. PHRASES **for the duration 1** for a very long time: *don't worry about me — I'm here for the duration*. **2** until the end of a particular activity: *outlawed the sale of liquor for the duration of the war*.

duress *noun* compulsion, esp. imprisonment, threats, or violence: *that contract was signed under duress, and so it is invalid* ◊ *the criminals resorted to duress and fraud to get their way*. [Say dur ESS or dyur ESS]

D

during *preposition* **1** throughout the duration of: *read during the meal*. **2** at some point in the duration of.

durum *noun* a kind of wheat having hard seeds and yielding a flour used in the manufacture of pasta: *durum semolina*. [Say DUR um or DYUR um]

dusk *noun* **1** the darker stage of twilight in the evening. **2** = NIGHTFALL.

dusky *adjective* (**duskier, duskiest**) **1** shady, shadowy, dim. **2** somewhat dark in colour. **3** (of a complexion) swarthy, dark hued.

dust • *noun* **1 a** finely powdered earth, dirt, etc., lying on the ground or on surfaces and blown about by the wind. **b** fine powder of any material: *sawdust*. **c** any substance pulverized. **d** a cloud of finely powdered earth or of other fine particles floating in the air. **2** that to which anything is reduced by disintegration or decay, esp. a dead person's remains. **3** an act of dusting: *give the table a dust*. • *verb* **1** clear (furniture etc.) of dust. **2** sprinkle with powder, dust, sugar, etc. **3** apply a dustlike chemical to an object, esp. as a means of discovering fingerprints. PHRASES **dust off 1** remove the dust from. **2** use, apply, or enjoy again after a long period of neglect. **eat (a person's) dust** *slang* **1** fall far behind. **2** an expression of contempt or dismissal: *Eat my dust!* **in the dust** *informal* **1** humiliated. **2** far behind or much inferior. **not see a person for dust** *informal* find that a person has made a hasty departure: *when the police start looking around this place, you won't see me for dust!* **shake the dust off** (or **from**) **one's feet** depart indignantly or disdainfully. **throw dust in a person's eyes** mislead a person by misrepresentation or by diverting attention from a point. **when the dust settles** when things quieten down or clear.

dustball *noun* *informal* a clump of dust, lint, etc. found indoors, esp. in corners, under furniture, etc.

dust bowl *noun* an unproductive dry region where vegetation has been lost and soil reduced to dust, esp. an area of the North American prairies where drought, overgrazing, and poor land management in the 1930s resulted in much of the topsoil blowing away, causing great hardship as thousands were forced to leave.

dust bunny *noun* (*plural* **dust bunnies**) *informal* = DUSTBALL.

dust devil *noun* a small whirlwind common in dry regions which becomes visible as it whips up dust, debris, leaves, etc.

duster *noun* **1 a** a cloth, brush, etc. for dusting surfaces. **b** a person who dusts. **c** a device for sifting or applying dust. **2** a short, light, usu. cotton bathrobe or item of clothing worn to bed, esp. for women. **3** *Baseball* a pitch thrown at the batter's head.

dusting *noun* **1** the action of removing dust. **2** the action of sprinkling with dust, powder, etc.: *crop-dusting*. **3** a thin layer of dust, powder, snow, etc.

dust jacket *noun* a removable, usu. decorated paper cover used to protect a book from dirt etc.

dustpan *noun* a small pan into which dust etc. is brushed from the floor.

dust-up *noun* *informal* a fight, quarrel, or disturbance.

dusty *adjective* (**dustier, dustiest**) **1 a** full of or covered with dust. **b** of the nature of or resembling dust. **2** (of a topic etc.) uninteresting, unsatisfactory. **3** (of a colour) dull or muted: *dusty rose*.

Dutch • *adjective* of, relating to, or associated with the Netherlands. • *noun* **1** the language of the Netherlands. **2** (**the Dutch**; treated as *plural*) the people of the Netherlands or their descendants. PHRASES **go Dutch** share expenses equally.

Dutch elm disease *noun* a fungal disease of elms.

Dutchie *noun* a usu. square, raised, glazed doughnut containing raisins.

Dutchman *noun* (*plural* **Dutchmen**) **1 a** a native or national of the Netherlands. **b** a person of Dutch descent. **2** a Dutch ship. **3** *slang* a German.

Dutch oven *noun* a large covered container, casserole, or cooking pot for braising etc.

Dutch Reformed Church *noun* a Christian denomination based on the teachings of Dutch Calvinists.

Dutchwoman *noun* (*plural* **Dutchwomen**) **1** a woman who is a native or national of the Netherlands. **2** a woman of Dutch descent.

dutiable *adjective* liable to customs taxes or other duties. [Say DUTY a bull]

dutiful *adjective* **1** doing or observant of one's duty: *a very dutiful son*. **2** (of a response, action, etc.) characteristic of, resulting from, or expressing a sense of duty: *fulfills her tasks in a dutiful manner*. ▸ **dutifully** *adverb* **dutifulness** *noun*

duty *noun* (*plural* **duties**) **1** a moral or legal obligation or responsibility: *his duty to report it*. **2** payment due to the government on the import, export, manufacture, or sale of goods or on the transfer of property etc.: *probate duty*. **3** an action required by a person's business, occupation, or function: *his duties as caretaker*. **4** (as an *adjective*) **a** (of a person) having specific duties or being on duty: *duty officer*. **b** (of an accessory, post, etc.) for use by an individual while on duty: *duty station*. **c** (of a visit, call, or other undertaking) done as a duty rather than as a pleasure. PHRASES (**above and**) **beyond the call of duty** much more than expected by obligation. **do duty for** serve as or pass for (something else): *the bass section does duty for the accompaniment*. **on** (or **off**) **duty** engaged (or not engaged) in one's work.

duty-free (of goods etc.) exempt from payment of customs and excise duties, esp. as a small personal allowance on entering or re-entering a country.

duvet *noun* a quilt, filled with down or a fluffy synthetic fibre, used instead of an upper sheet and blankets. [Say doo VAY or DOO vay]

DVD *noun* (*plural* **DVDs**) *proprietary* a digital recording medium similar in appearance to a CD but with much increased storage capacity, capable of storing a full-length feature film; a digital video disc.

dwarf • *noun* (*plural* **dwarfs** or **dwarves**) **1 a** a person of abnormally small stature, esp. one with a normal-sized head and body but short limbs. **b** (also as an *adjective*) an animal or plant much below the ordinary size for the species. **2** any of a mythological race of diminutive beings, figuring esp. in Scandinavian folklore, who are typically skilled in mining and metalworking and often possess magical powers. **3** (also **dwarf star**) a small, dense star with low to average luminosity. • *verb* (**dwarfs, dwarfed, dwarfing**) **1** stunt or restrict the growth or development of. **2** cause (something similar or comparable) to seem small or insignificant: *the tall office buildings surround and dwarf the church*. ▸ **dwarfed** *adjective*

dwarfish *adjective* resembling a dwarf, esp. in size; abnormally small.

dwarfism *noun* (in medical or technical contexts) unusually or abnormally low stature or small size.

dweeb *noun* *slang* a nerd, esp. a studious or boring

person. ▶**dweebish** *adjective* **dweeby** *adjective* (**dweebier, dweebiest**)

dwell *verb* (**dwells, dwelt** or **dwelled, dwelling**) *literary* reside: *dwelt near a waterfall ◊ for the last few years he has been dwelling in a ruined farmhouse*. PHRASES **dwell on** (or **upon**) spend time on; write, brood, or speak at length on: *always dwells on his grievances*. ▶**dweller** *noun*

dwelling *noun* (also **dwelling place**) a house or place of residence.

dwindle *verb* (**dwindles, dwindled, dwindling**) become gradually reduced in size, quantity, quality, value, or importance. ▶**dwindling** *adjective*

Dy *symbol* dysprosium.

dye • *noun* **1** a substance used to change the colour of hair, fabric, wood, etc. **2** (also **dyestuff**) a substance yielding a dye, esp. for colouring materials in solution. • *verb* (**dyes, dyed, dyeing**) change the colour of something, esp. by using a special liquid or substance.

dyed-in-the-wool *adjective* **1** having strong beliefs or opinions that are never going to change: *a dyed-in-the-wool Liberal*. **2** (of a fabric) made of yarn dyed in its raw state.

dyer *noun* a person who dyes cloth etc.

> **SPELL CHECK**
> **dying, dyeing**   ABC✓
>
> The process of colouring a fabric etc. is **dyeing**.

dying • *adjective* **1** connected with, or at the time of, death: *her dying words*. **2** about to die: *a dying art*. **3** coming to an end: *the dying days of the age of sail*. • *noun* the act of ceasing to live, function, etc. PHRASES **to one's dying day** for the rest of one's life.

dyke *noun* = DIKE.

dynamic • *adjective* **1** (of a person) forceful, and having a lot of energy: *a dynamic personality*. **2** (of a process) always changing and making progress: *a dynamic economy*. **3** (also **dynamical**) *Physics* of or relating to forces producing motion. **4** (also **dynamical**) of or concerning dynamics. **5** *Music* relating to the volume of sound. **6** *Computing* (of memory etc.) depending on an applied voltage to refresh it periodically. • *noun* a force that stimulates change or progress within a system or process: *once a congregation built a large church, it put into play a dynamic with far-reaching consequences*. ▶**dynamically** *adverb*

dynamics *plural noun* **1** (usu. treated as *singular*) **a** *Mechanics* the branch of mechanics concerned with the motion of bodies under the action of forces. **b** the branch of any science in which forces or changes are considered: *aerodynamics ◊ population dynamics*. **2** the motive forces, physical or moral, affecting behaviour and change in any sphere: *the family dynamics of western society*. **3** the varying degree of volume of sound in musical performance: *they sing with a scrupulous regard for the tempos and dynamics*.

dynamism *noun* energizing or dynamic action or power: *the dynamism of the city*. [Say DIE nuh mism]

dynamite • *noun* **1** a high explosive consisting of nitroglycerine mixed with an absorbent. **2** a potentially dangerous person etc. **3** *informal* a powerful or impressive person or thing. • *verb* (**dynamites, dynamited, dynamiting**) charge or shatter with dynamite. • *adjective informal* excellent or powerful. ▶**dynamiter** *noun*

dynamo *noun* (*plural* **dynamos**) **1** a machine converting mechanical into electrical energy, esp. by rotating coils of copper wire in a magnetic field. **2** *informal* an energetic person. [Say DIE nuh moe]

dynastic *adjective* having to do with a dynasty. [Say die NASS tick]

dynasty *noun* (*plural* **dynasties**) **1** a line of hereditary rulers: *the Qing dynasty ruled China from 1644 to 1912*. **2** a succession of leaders in any field: *rebuilding the Montreal Canadiens dynasty*. [Say DIE nuh stee]

dysentery *noun* a disease with inflammation of the intestines, causing severe diarrhea with blood and mucus. [Say DISSIN terry or DISSIN tree]

dysfunction *noun* an abnormality or impairment of function: *liver dysfunction*. [Say dis FUNCTION]

dysfunctional *adjective* not working in a satisfactory or successful way: *children from dysfunctional families*.

dyslexia *noun* disorders that involve difficulty in learning to read but that do not affect general intelligence. ▶**dyslexic** *adjective & noun* [Say dis LEXIA]

dyspepsia *noun* indigestion. [Say dis PEPSI uh]

dyspeptic *adjective* **1** of or relating to indigestion. **2** ill-tempered: *in a dyspeptic letter he described his countrymen as "diseased"*. [Say dis PEP tick]

dysprosium *noun* a naturally occurring soft metallic element, used as a component in certain magnetic alloys. [Say dis PROZY um]

dystrophy *noun* a disorder in which an organ or tissue of the body wastes away. *See also* MUSCULAR DYSTROPHY. [Say DISTRA fee]

D

Ee

E¹ *noun* (also **e**) (*plural* **Es** or **E's**) **1** the fifth letter of the alphabet. **2** the third note of the scale of C major.

E² *abbreviation* (also **E.**) **1** East, Eastern. **2** (also **e**) *slang* **a** the drug ecstasy. **b** a tablet of this. **3** emissivity.

E³ *symbol* Physics energy: $E = mc^2$.

e *symbol* Math the base of natural logarithms, equal to approx. 2.71828.

e- *combining form* electronic: *e-file*.

each • *adjective* every one of two or more persons or things, regarded separately. • *pronoun* each person or thing. PHRASES **each and every** every single.

each other *pronoun* one another.

eager *adjective* full of keen desire: *eager to learn*.

eager beaver *noun informal* a very diligent person.

eagerly *adverb* in a keen or enthusiastic manner: *the eagerly awaited release of the band's new CD*.

eagerness *noun* an eager attitude; enthusiasm.

eagle • *noun* **1 a** any of various large birds of prey with keen vision and powerful flight. **b** a figure of an eagle, esp. as a symbol of the US, or formerly as a Roman or French ensign. **2** Golf a score of two strokes under par at any hole. • *verb* (**eagles, eagled, eagling**) Golf play (a hole) in two strokes less than par.

eagle eye *noun* keen sight. ▶ **eagle-eyed** *adjective*

eaglet *noun* a young eagle. [Say EE glit]

ear¹ *noun* **1 a** the organ of hearing and balance in humans and vertebrates, esp. the external part of this. **b** an organ sensitive to sound in other animals. **2** the faculty for discriminating sounds: *an ear for music* ◊ *plays by ear*. **3** an ear-shaped thing, esp. the handle of a jug. PHRASES **all ears** listening attentively. **bring about one's ears** bring down upon oneself. **give ear to** listen to. **have a person's ear** receive a favourable hearing. **have** (or **keep**) **an ear to the ground** be alert to rumours or the trend of opinion. **in one ear and out the other** heard but disregarded or quickly forgotten. **out on one's ear** dismissed ignominiously. **up to one's ears** *informal* deeply involved or occupied.

ear² *noun* the seed-bearing head of a cereal plant.

earache *noun* a (usu. prolonged) pain in the ear.

eardrum *noun* the membrane separating the outer ear and middle ear and transmitting vibrations resulting from sound waves to the inner ear.

eared *adjective* (in *combination*) having the kind of ears described: *a floppy-eared dog* ◊ *the short-eared owl*.

earflap *noun* a flap attached to the side of a hat or cap, used for covering the ear in cold weather.

earful *noun* (*plural* **earfuls**) *informal* **1** a lot of talking: *if you stay for coffee with her you'll get an earful*. **2** a strong reprimand: *I got an earful from the coach after the game*.

earl *noun* a British nobleman ranking between a marquess and a viscount. ▶ **earldom** *noun*

Earl Grey *noun* a type of tea flavoured with bergamot.

earliness *noun* the fact or habit of being early: *the earliness of the hour*.

earlobe *noun* the lower soft external part of the ear.

early *adjective & adverb* (**earlier, earliest**) **1** before the usual or expected time. **2** of or at the beginning of a particular time, period, or sequence. PHRASES **at the earliest** not before. *Monday at the earliest*. **early days**

yet (or **still early days**) early in time for something to happen: *should save for retirement, but it's early days yet*.

early bird *noun informal* a person who arrives, gets up, etc. early or earlier than others. PHRASES **the early bird gets the worm** *informal* the person who seizes the earliest opportunity will be successful.

early music *noun* medieval, Renaissance, and baroque music, esp. as played on period instruments.

early warning *noun* advance warning of an imminent (esp. nuclear) attack.

earmark • *noun* an identifying mark or distinguishing characteristic: *their latest album exhibits all the earmarks of their earlier successes*. • *verb* set aside for a special purpose: *the money was earmarked for arts funding*.

earmuff *noun* (usu. in *plural*) either of a pair of ear coverings connected by a band across the top of the head, and worn to protect the ears from the cold.

SPELL CHECK
earn, urn

A decorative container or vase is an **urn**.

earn *verb* **1 a** obtain (income) in return for labour or services. **b** (of capital invested) bring in as interest or profit. **2 a** deserve; be entitled to; obtain as the reward for hard work or merit. **b** incur (a reproach, reputation, etc.). **3** Baseball score (a run) without any error on the fielding side. ▶ **earned** *adjective*

earned run *noun* Baseball a run that is not the result of an error or passed ball.

earned run average *noun* Baseball the average number of earned runs scored against a pitcher in every nine innings pitched.

earner *noun* **1** a person who earns money, usu. of a specified kind or level, in return for labour or services: *a wage earner* ◊ *high-income earners*. **2** a company, stock, product, etc. that brings in income of a specified kind or level: *her new business has turned out to be a big earner*.

earnest • *adjective* very serious and sincere: *an earnest young man* ◊ *despite her earnest efforts, she could not find a job* ◊ *when I looked over, he was in earnest conversation with his father*. • *noun* a token or foretaste: *success in Normandy was an earnest of total victory*. PHRASES **in earnest** serious(ly), not joking(ly); with determination. ▶ **earnestly** *adverb* **earnestness** *noun*

earnings *plural noun* money earned.

EARP *abbreviation* (in Canada) Environmental Assessment and Review Process.

earphone *noun* **1** each of a pair of receivers attached to each other so that they fit over or inside the ears, used for listening to a radio, stereo, etc. **2** a similar device with a receiver that fits inside one ear.

earpiece *noun* **1** the part of a telephone etc. held to the ear during use. **2** the part of a pair of glasses, a helmet, etc., that fits over the wearer's ear.

ear-piercing • *adjective* loud and shrill. • *noun* the piercing of the ears to allow the wearing of earrings.

earplug *noun* either of two pieces of soft material placed in the ears to keep out cold air, water or noise.

earring *noun* a piece of jewellery worn in or on (esp. the lobe of) the ear.

earshot *noun* the distance over which something can be heard: *within earshot* ◊ *out of earshot*.

ear-splitting *adjective* excessively loud.

earth *noun* **1** (also **Earth**) the planet on which we live. **2** the inhabitants of this planet. **3 a** dry land; the ground: *fell to earth*. **b** the material that makes up the earth's surface; dirt, soil. **4** the present abode of mankind, as distinct from heaven or hell. **5** the hole of a badger, fox, etc. **6** (**the earth**) *informal* a huge amount: *cost the earth*. **7** any of several metallic oxides that are stable, dry, and lacking in taste and odour, e.g. alumina, zirconia, etc. PHRASES **come back** (or **down**) **to earth** return to realities. **gone to earth** in hiding. **on earth** *informal* **1** existing anywhere: *the happiest person on earth*. **2** as an intensifier: *what on earth?*

earthbound *adjective* **1** attached to the earth: *only one face of the moon is visible to earthbound observers*. **2** moving toward the earth: *on the lookout for earthbound asteroids*.

earthen *adjective* **1** made of earth: *an earthen floor*. **2** made of baked clay: *an earthen jar*.

earthenware *noun* pottery made of clay fired to a porous state which can be made watertight by the use of a glaze.

earthiness *noun* **1** an odour, taste, texture, etc. resembling or suggestive of earth or soil, esp. in wine. **2** an uninhibited or coarse attitude, esp. about sex or bodily functions.

earthling *noun* an inhabitant of the earth, esp. as regarded in fiction by outsiders.

earthly *adjective* **1** of the earth or human life on earth. **2** *informal* remotely possible: *is no earthly use*.

earth mother *noun* **1** a spirit or god symbolizing the earth. **2** a woman who seems very suited to being a mother.

earthmover *noun* a vehicle or machine for moving earth. ▶ **earthmoving** *noun*

earthquake *noun* **1** a convulsion of the superficial parts of the earth due to the release of accumulated stress as a result of faults in strata or volcanic action. **2** a severe disturbance, disruption, or upheaval.

earth science *noun* any of various sciences concerned with the earth or part of it, or its atmosphere (e.g. geology, meteorology). ▶ **earth scientist** *noun*

earth-shattering *adjective* (also **earth-shaking**) having a traumatic effect. ▶ **earth-shatteringly** *adverb*

earthward • *adverb* (also **earthwards**) toward the earth. • *adjective* moving or directed toward the earth.

earthwork *noun* an artificial bank of earth in fortification or road building etc.

earthworm *noun* any of various worms living and burrowing in the ground, with bodies made up of ring-shaped segments.

earthy *adjective* (**earthier**, **earthiest**) **1** of or like earth or soil. **2** somewhat coarse or crude; unrefined: *earthy humour*.

earwax *noun* a waxy secretion produced by the ear.

earwig *noun* a small brown insect with a long body and two curved pointed parts called pincers that stick out at the back end of its body.

ease • *noun* **1** absence of difficulty; effortlessness. **2** freedom or relief from pain, anxiety, trouble, embarrassment, constraint, etc. **3** freedom from toil; leisure: *a life of ease*. • *verb* (**eases, eased, easing**) **1** relieve from pain or anxiety etc.: *eased my mind*. **2** (often foll. by *off, up*) **a** become less painful or burdensome. **b** relax; begin to take it easy. **c** slow down; moderate one's behaviour, habits, etc. **3** *Meteorology* become less severe: *the wind will ease*

tonight. **4 a** relax; slacken; make a less tight fit. **b** move or be moved carefully into place: *eased it into the hole*. PHRASES **at ease 1** free from anxiety or constraint. **2** *Military* **a** in a relaxed attitude, with the feet apart. **b** the order to stand in this way. **at one's ease** free from embarrassment, awkwardness, or undue formality.

easel *noun* a standing frame, usu. of wood, for supporting an artist's work, a blackboard, etc.

easement *noun Law* a right-of-way or a similar right over another's land.

easily *adverb* **1** without difficulty. **2** by far: *easily the best*. **3** very probably: *it could easily snow*.

east • *noun* **1 a** the point of the horizon where the sun rises at the equinoxes (cardinal point 90° to the right of north). **b** the compass point corresponding to this. **c** the direction in which this lies. **2** (usu. **the East**) **a** the regions or countries lying to the east of Europe. **b** *hist.* the former Communist States of E Europe. **3** the eastern part of a country, town, etc. • *adjective* **1** toward, at, near, or facing east. **2** coming from the east: *east wind*. • *adverb* **1** toward, at, or near the east. **2** (foll. by *of*) further east than.

eastbound *adjective & adverb* travelling or leading eastwards.

Easter *noun* **1** (also **Easter Day** or **Easter Sunday**) a Christian festival (held on a variable Sunday in March or April) commemorating Christ's resurrection. **2** the season in which this occurs, esp. the weekend from Good Friday to Easter Monday.

Easter lily *noun* **1** a white-flowered lily native to Japan, traditionally displayed at Easter. **2** any of various spring-flowering lilies or similar plants, esp. species of the dog's tooth violet.

easterly • *adjective & adverb* **1** in an eastern position or direction. **2** (of a wind) blowing from the east. • *noun* (*plural* **easterlies**) a wind blowing from the east.

eastern *adjective* **1** of or in the east; inhabiting the east. **2** lying or directed toward the east. **3** (**Eastern**) of or in the Far East or Middle East.

Eastern Church *noun* the branch of the Christian Church which developed in the territories formerly part of the Eastern Roman Empire, e.g. Greece and other lands surrounding the eastern Mediterranean, and spread to Russia, Ukraine, etc., including the Orthodox Churches and those churches with a similar liturgical rite but in communion with the Roman Catholic Church.

easterner *noun* a native or inhabitant of the east.

eastern hemisphere *noun* the half of the earth east of the prime meridian, containing Europe, Asia, Africa, and Australia.

easternmost *adjective* furthest to the east.

Eastern rite *noun* a Christian Church observing a liturgical rite based on the Eastern tradition, esp. one in communion with the Catholic Church.

Eastern Time *noun* the time in a zone including most of Ontario and Quebec as well as the eastern US. **Eastern Standard Time** is five hours behind GMT; **Eastern Daylight Time** is four hours behind GMT.

WRITING TIP
East Indian

The term **South Asian** is now often preferred to **East Indian** as a general term designating the Indian subcontinent and its people.

East Indian • *adjective* of or pertaining to the Indian subcontinent or its indigenous peoples or their descendants. • *noun* a person descended from the indigenous peoples of the Indian subcontinent.

E

Eastmain Cree *noun* (*plural* **Eastmain Cree** or **Eastmain Crees**) a member of a Cree people living at the mouth of the Eastmain River on the shore of James Bay. [Say EAST main]

east-northeast *noun* the direction or compass point midway between east and northeast.

east-southeast *noun* the direction or compass point midway between east and southeast.

eastward • *adjective* & *adverb* (also **eastwards**) toward the east. • *noun* an eastward direction or region.
▶ **eastwardly** *adjective* & *adverb*

WRITING TIP
easy, easily

The use of **easy** as an adverb is usually restricted to phrases such as *Easy does it*, *Take it easy*, and *Go easy on the whipped cream*. Outside of such expressions, the adverb **easily** is more standard: write *we beat them* **easily**, not *we beat them* **easy**.

---

easy • *adjective* (**easier**, **easiest**) **1** not difficult. **2 a** free from discomfort. **b** comfortably off: *easy circumstances*. **3** free from embarrassment, awkwardness, constraint, etc.; relaxed and pleasant: *an easy manner*. **4** easily persuaded: *easy prey*. **5** (of a person) sexually available. **6** moderate: *an easy pace*. **7** (of a slope) gentle, gradual. **8** loosely fitting. **9** *Stock Market* (of goods, money on loan, etc.) not much in demand. **10** (of credit) obtainable without stringent requirements of the borrower. • *interjection* go carefully; move gently. PHRASES **easy come easy go** *informal* what is easily got is soon lost or spent. **easy does it** *informal* go carefully. **easy on the eye** (or **ear** etc.) *informal* pleasant to look at (or listen to etc.). **go easy** (foll. by *with*, *on*) be sparing or cautious. **I'm easy** *informal* I have no preference. **stand easy!** *Cdn* & *Brit.* Military permission to a squad standing at ease to relax their attitude further. **take it easy 1** proceed gently or carefully. **2** relax; avoid overwork. **3** (often as *interjection*) calm down.

easy chair *noun* a large comfortable chair, usu. an armchair.

easygoing *adjective* relaxed in manner.

easy listening *noun* music that appeals to conventional tastes and is not loud, raucous, etc.

easy money *noun* money got without effort.

eat *verb* (**eats**; *past* **ate**; *past participle* **eaten**; **eating**) **1** consume as food. **2 a** destroy gradually, esp. by corrosion, erosion, disease, etc. **b** begin to consume or diminish (resources etc.). **3** *informal* trouble, vex: *what's eating you?* **4** *informal* (of a machine etc.) cause (something) to disappear or be destroyed by absorbing it into its workings: *the bank machine ate my card*. PHRASES **eat one's hat** *informal* admit one's surprise in being wrong (only as a proposition unlikely to be fulfilled): *I'll eat my hat if that's true*. **eat one's heart out** suffer from excessive longing or envy. **eat out** have a meal away from home, esp. in a restaurant. **eat out of a person's hand** be entirely submissive to a person. **eat up 1** eat or consume completely. **2** use or deal with rapidly or wastefully: *eats up gasoline* ◊ *eats up the miles*. **3** encroach upon or annex: *eating up the neighbouring municipalities*. **4** absorb, preoccupy: *eaten up with pride*. **5** *informal* receive with vigorous enjoyment. **6** consume; use up: *this project is eating up a lot of my time*. **eat one's words** admit that one was wrong.

eatable • *adjective* that is in a condition to be eaten (*compare* EDIBLE). • *noun* (usu. in *plural*) food.

eater *noun* a person or animal that eats a particular thing or in a particular way: *she's not really a meat eater* ◊ *he's a fussy eater*.

eatery *noun* (*plural* **eateries**) *informal* a restaurant.

eating *adjective* **1** suitable for eating: *eating apple*. **2** used for eating: *eating place*. **3** of or relating to the process of eating: *eating disorders*.

eats *plural noun* *informal* food.

eau de cologne *noun* a dilute fragrance made from alcohol and concentrated perfume. [Say oh duh kuh LONE]

eau de toilette *noun* (*plural* **eaux de toilette**) a dilute form of perfume that is somewhat stronger than eau de cologne. [Say oh duh twah LET]

eaves *plural noun* the underside of a projecting roof.

eavesdrop *verb* (**eavesdrops**, **eavesdropped**, **eavesdropping**) listen secretly to a conversation.
▶ **eavesdropper** *noun*

eavestrough *noun* (also **eavestroughing**) (esp. *Cdn*) a shallow trough attached to the eaves of a building to collect runoff from the roof. [Say EAVES troff]

ebb • *noun* **1** the movement of the tide out to sea (also as an *adjective*: *ebb tide*) (opp. FLOOD *noun* 3). **2** a flowing away; decline or decay: *another sign of the ebb of the old leader's influence*. • *verb* (often foll. by *away*) **1** (of tidewater) flow out to sea. **2** decline; run low: *his life was ebbing away*. PHRASES **at a low ebb** in a poor condition or state of decline: *the annual hunt was declining and the fisheries were at a low ebb*. **ebb and flow** a continuing process of decline and upturn in circumstances. **on the ebb** in decline.

Ebola *noun* a tropical African virus that causes a severe, infectious, generally fatal disease characterized by fever and severe internal bleeding. [Say i BOLA]

ebony • *noun* (*plural* **ebonies**) **1** a heavy hard dark wood used for furniture. **2** any of various trees producing this. • *adjective* **1** made of ebony. **2** black like ebony. [Say EBBA nee]

ebullience *noun* lively enthusiasm; cheerful excitement and energy: *his infectious ebullience energized the whole room*. [Say i BULLY ince (with BULLY rhyming either with SULLY or with WOOLLY)]

ebullient *adjective* (of a person) enthusiastic and lively; full of cheerful excitement; bubbly: *after having lunch with the man of her dreams, she sounded downright ebullient*.
▶ **ebulliently** *adverb* [Say i BULLY int (with BULLY rhyming either with SULLY or with WOOLLY)]

eccentric • *adjective* **1** odd or capricious in behaviour or appearance: *an eccentric guy, but very intelligent*. **2 a** not placed or not having its axis etc. placed centrally (*compare* CONCENTRIC). **b** (often foll. by *to*) (of a circle) not concentric (to another). **c** (of an orbit) not circular. • *noun* an eccentric person. ▶ **eccentrically** *adverb* **eccentricity** *noun* (*plural* **eccentricities**) [Say eck SEN trick, eck sen TRISSA tee]

ecclesiastic • *noun* a member of the Christian clergy. • *adjective* = ECCLESIASTICAL. [Say i cleezy ASTICK]

ecclesiastical *adjective* of or relating to the Christian Church or the clergy. ▶ **ecclesiastically** *adverb* [Say i cleezy ASTICK'll]

ECE *abbreviation* **1** early childhood education. **2** early childhood educator.

ECG *abbreviation* (*plural* **ECGs**) **1** electrocardiogram. **2** electrocardiograph.

echelon *noun* (often in *plural*) a level or rank in an organization, in society, etc.; those occupying it: *the highest echelons of the organization*. [Say ESHA lon]

echinacea *noun* **1** a plant of the genus *Echinacea*, of eastern North America, esp. the purple coneflower, *E. purpurea*. **2** a preparation made from the roots of an echinacea plant used as a herbal remedy esp. for its wound-healing properties and to boost the immune system. [Say ecka NAYSHA]

echo • *noun* (*plural* **echoes**) **1 a** the repetition of a sound by the reflection of sound waves. **b** the secondary sound produced. **2** a reflected radio or radar beam. **3** a repetition of an idea, feeling, etc.: *his love for her found an echo in her own feelings.* **4** (often in *plural*) circumstances or events reminiscent of or remotely connected with earlier ones: *a romantic thriller with echoes of James Bond.* • *verb* (**echoes, echoed, echoing**) **1 a** (of a place) resound with an echo. **b** (of a sound) be repeated; resound. **2** repeat (a sound) by an echo. **3** repeat or imitate the words, opinions, or actions of (a person).

echo sounder *noun* a sounding apparatus for determining the depth of water beneath a ship by measuring the time taken for an echo to be received.

eclair *noun* an elongated cream puff filled with cream or custard, esp. with chocolate icing. [Say ay CLAIR or i CLAIR]

eclectic • *adjective* not following one style or set of ideas but choosing from or using a wide variety: *she has very eclectic tastes in literature* ◊ *his house is an eclectic mixture of the antique and the modern.* • *noun* an eclectic person. ▶ **eclectically** *adverb* **eclecticism** *noun* [Say i CLECK tick, i CLECK tuh sism]

eclipse • *noun* **1** the obscuring of the reflected light from one celestial body by the passage of another between it and the eye or between it and its source of illumination. **2** a deprivation of light or the period of this. **3** a rapid or sudden loss of importance or prominence, esp. in relation to another or a newly-arrived person or thing: *her election as leader marked the eclipse of the party's old guard.* • *verb* (**eclipses, eclipsed, eclipsing**) **1** (of a celestial body) obscure the light from or to (another). **2** deprive of prominence or importance; outshine, surpass. PHRASES **in eclipse** surpassed; in decline: *the humanities are in eclipse in university life.* [Say i CLIPS]

ecliptic *noun* the sun's apparent path among the stars during the year. [Say i CLIP tick]

eco *noun informal* ecology (also as an *adjective*: *eco freak*). [Say ECKO or EEKO]

eco- *combining form* ecology, ecological.

E. coli *noun* (in full **Escherichia coli**) a species of bacillus which normally inhabits the large intestine and, under certain conditions, can cause disease, esp. when transferred to other sites such as the urinary tract. [Say ee CO lye]

ecological *adjective* having to do with the relation of plants and living creatures to each other and to their environment: *the area's ecological balance.* ▶ **ecologically** *adverb* [Say eeka LOGICAL or ecka LOGICAL]

ecologist *noun* **1** a scientist who studies ecology. **2** a person who is interested in ecology and the protection of the environment. [Say i COLLA jist]

ecology *noun* (*plural* **ecologies**) **1** the branch of biology dealing with the relations of organisms to one another and to their physical surroundings. **2** (also **human ecology**) the study of the interaction of people with their environment. [Say i COLLA jee]

e-commerce *noun* financial transactions conducted over the Internet.

econometric *adjective* based on or having to do with the branch of economics that deals with the application of mathematics, esp. statistics, to economic data: *econometric analysis.* [Say i conna METRIC]

econometrics *plural noun* (usu. treated as *singular*) the branch of economics that deals with the use of mathematical methods, esp. statistics, in describing economic systems. [Say i conna METRICS]

economic *adjective* **1** of, pertaining to, or concerned with economics or the economy. **2** justified in terms of profitability: *many organizations must become larger if they are to remain economic.* **3** (of a subject etc.) considered in relation to trade, industry, and the creation of wealth: *economic geography.* **4** = ECONOMICAL.

economical *adjective* **1** thrifty, careful in the use of resources. **2** inexpensive. **3** = ECONOMIC. PHRASES **economical with the truth** used euphemistically to describe a person or statement that lies or deliberately withholds information. ▶ **economically** *adverb*

economic growth *noun* the rate of expansion of the national income, esp. the growth of output of goods and services per head of the population over a stated period of time.

economic indicator *noun* a statistical measure indicating the relative strength or weakness of selected economic variables such as output, inflation, debt burden, foreign investment, etc.

economics *plural noun* (treated as *singular*) **1** the social science of the production and distribution of wealth in theory and practice. **2** the financial considerations attaching to a particular activity, commodity, etc.: *the economics of publishing.*

economist *noun* an expert in or student of economics.

economize *verb* (**economizes, economized, economizing**) reduce expenses, make savings: *I have to economize where I can* ◊ *people on low incomes may try to economize on food.* ▶ **economizer** *noun* **economizing** *noun*

economy *noun* (*plural* **economies**) **1 a** the wealth and resources of a community, esp. in terms of the production and consumption of goods and services. **b** a particular kind of this: *a capitalist economy.* **c** the administration or condition of an economy. **2 a** frugality or the careful management of resources: *small cars offer better fuel economy.* **b** (often in *plural*) financial saving: *there were many economies to be made by moving out of Toronto.* **3** sparing or careful use of resources etc.: *economy of language.* **4** the cheapest class of some service or product, esp. of air travel. **5** (as an *adjective*) (of a product) offering the customer the best value for money spent, esp. a large quantity for a proportionally lower cost: *economy size.*

economy class *noun* the cheapest class of air travel, hotel accommodation, etc.

economy of scale *noun* (*plural* **economies of scale**) (usu. in *plural*) proportionate savings gained by using larger quantities.

ecosphere *noun* **1** the earth's biosphere, esp. when the interaction between the living and non-living components is emphasized. **2** the region of space around the sun or a star where conditions are such that planets are theoretically capable of sustaining life. [Say EEKO sphere]

ecosystem *noun* a biological community of interacting organisms and their physical environment.

eco-terrorism *noun* **1** violence carried out to further environmentalist ends. **2** politically motivated damage to the natural environment. ▶ **eco-terrorist** *noun*

ecotourism *noun* tourism to exotic or wilderness, often threatened, natural environments, esp. intended to support conservation efforts. ▶ **ecotourist** *noun*

ecstasy *noun* (*plural* **ecstasies**) **1** an overwhelming feeling of joy or rapture. **2** a sort of trance or rapture such as is supposed to accompany religious, prophetic, or mystical inspiration. **3** *slang* a powerful stimulant and hallucinogenic drug (see MDMA). PHRASES **in ecstasies** filled with pleasure. [Say ECK sta see]

ecstatic *adjective* **1** very happy or excited: *ecstatic about her new job.* **2** involving a mystical experience in which one feels that one is taken out of oneself: *an*

E

ecstatic vision of God. ▶**ecstatically** *adverb* [Say ick STATIC]

ECT *abbreviation* ELECTROCONVULSIVE THERAPY.

ectoderm *noun* the outermost layer of an embryo in early development, giving rise to epidermis and neural tissue. ▶**ectodermal** *adjective* [Say ECTO derm, ecto DERM'll]

ectopic pregnancy *noun* (*plural* **ectopic pregnancies**) a pregnancy in which the fertilized ovum is implanted somewhere other than in the uterus, e.g. in a Fallopian tube.

ectoplasm *noun* the dense, clear, outer layer of the cytoplasm in some cells (*compare* ENDOPLASM). ▶**ectoplasmic** *adjective* [Say ECTO plasm]

ecumenical *adjective* **1 a** of or representing the whole Christian world. **b** of or representing Christians of several denominations. **2** seeking or promoting worldwide Christian unity that transcends doctrinal differences. [Say eck you MENNA cul or eek you MENNA cul]

ecumenical council *noun* any of the various general councils of the early church or of the modern Catholic Church, whose decisions are considered authoritative.

ecumenism *noun* the principle or aim of promoting unity among the world's Christian Churches. [Say eck YOU m'n ism or ECK you m'n ism]

eczema *noun* superficial skin inflammation, usu. with itching and discharge from blisters. [Say eck ZEE muh]

ed *noun informal* education: *driver ed*.

ed. *abbreviation* **1** edited by. **2** (*plural* **eds.**) edition. **3** (*plural* **eds.**) editor. **4** education: *B.Ed*. **5** educated.

Edam *noun* a mild, round, pressed Dutch cheese, usu. pale yellow with a red rind. [Say EE d'm or EE dam]

eddy • *noun* (*plural* **eddies**) **1** a circular or contrary movement of water causing a small whirlpool. **2** a movement of wind, fog, or smoke resembling this. • *verb* (**eddies, eddied, eddying**) whirl around in an eddy or eddies: *waves swirled and eddied around the rocks*.

edelweiss *noun* (*plural* **edelweiss**) an alpine plant with woolly white bracts around the flower heads, growing in rocky places. [Say AID'll vice]

edema *noun* a condition characterized by an excess of watery fluid collecting in the cavities or tissues of the body. *Also called* DROPSY. [Say i DEEMA]

Eden *noun* (also **Garden of Eden**) **1** an unspoiled paradise: *Sherbrooke was his boyhood home and it acquires the glow of a lost Eden as he reminisces*. **2** the abode of Adam and Eve in the Biblical account of the Creation, from which they were expelled for disobediently eating the fruit of the tree of knowledge. ▶**Edenic** *adjective* [Say EE d'n, i DEN ick]

edge • *noun* **1** the outside limit of an object, area, or surface. **2** a line along which two surfaces of a solid intersect. **3** the sharpened side of a blade. **4 a** (as a personal attribute) incisiveness, excitement. **b** an advantage, superiority. • *verb* (**edges, edged, edging**) **1** move gradually or furtively towards an objective. **2** provide with an edge or border. **3** defeat by a small margin. **4** *Sport* tilt or incline (a ski or skate) sideways to make one edge dig into the snow or ice. PHRASES **on edge 1** tense and restless or irritable. **2** eager, excited. **set a person's teeth on edge** (esp. of a taste or sound) cause a person acute irritation or discomfort, as if eating sour fruit. **take the edge off** dull, weaken; make less effective or intense.

edged *adjective* **1** (usu. in *combination*) having an edge or border, esp. of a specified kind. **2** having a cutting edge.

edger *noun* a tool for making, trimming, or finishing an edge, e.g. of a flower bed.

edgewise *adverb* (also esp. *Brit.* **edgeways**) **1** with the edge forward, uppermost, or towards the viewer. **2 a** sideways. **b** edge to edge. PHRASES **get a word in edgewise** contribute to a conversation when the dominant speaker pauses briefly.

edginess *noun* **1** nervousness or irritability. **2** an intensity or sharp quality in music or writing.

edging *noun* **1** something forming an edge. **2** the process of making an edge. **3** *Skiing* the tilting or angling of a ski so that it cuts into the snow.

edgy *adjective* (**edgier, edgiest**) **1** irritable, nervously anxious. **2 a** sharp-edged, not smooth. **b** (of humour, writing, etc.) characterized by sharp observation or wit. **3** slightly unconventional; innovative and typical of something at the forefront of a movement: *new television shows love to describe themselves as edgy*.

EDI *abbreviation* ELECTRONIC DATA INTERCHANGE.

edible • *adjective* fit or suitable to be eaten (often used to contrast with unpalatable or poisonous examples): *nasturtium seeds are edible*. • *noun* (in *plural*) things that may be eaten, food.

edict *noun* an order proclaimed by authority, esp. a proclamation having the force of law. [Say EE dict]

edification *noun* the improvement of the mind or character: *the books were intended for the edification of the masses*. [Say edda fih CAY sh'n]

edifice *noun* **1** a building, esp. a large, imposing, or stately one. **2** a complex organizational or conceptual structure. [Say EDD i fiss]

edify *verb* (**edifies, edified, edifying**) (of a circumstance etc.) instruct and improve morally or intellectually. ▶**edifying** *adjective* [Say EDDA fie]

edit • *verb* (**edits, edited, editing**) **1** assemble, prepare, or modify (written material) esp. for publication. **2** be in overall charge of the content and arrangement of (a newspaper etc.). **3** prepare (a film, tape, etc.) by rearrangement, cutting, or collation of recorded material to form a unified sequence. **4** (foll. by *out*) remove (a part) from a text etc. • *noun* **1 a** the action or process of editing. **b** a change or correction made as a result of editing. **2** an edited item. ▶**editable** *adjective*

edition *noun* **1** a form or version of a book etc. at its first publication and after each revision or change of format: *that book is now available in a paperback edition*. **2** a whole number of similar copies of a book, newspaper, artwork, etc. issued at one time. **3** a particular version or instance of a broadcast, esp. of a regular program or feature. **4** a person or thing that is compared to another as a copy to an original: *the building was a simpler edition of its namesake*.

editor *noun* **1** a person who edits material for publication or broadcasting. **2** a person who selects or commissions material for publication. **3** a person in charge of the running and contents of a newspaper, periodical, etc., or of one particular section of it. **4** a person who cuts and edits film, videotape, soundtracks, etc. **5** a computer program enabling the user to write or alter programs, text, or other information. **6** a machine used to edit film, videotape, etc.

editorial • *adjective* **1 a** of or concerned with editing or editors: *the editorial team*. **b** of or pertaining to an editorial. **2** written or approved by an editor. **3** distinguished from news and advertising matter: *editorial content*. • *noun* a newspaper article or a radio or TV broadcast giving the opinion of an editor, station owner, etc. on a topical issue. ▶**editorialist** *noun*

editorialize *verb* (**editorializes, editorialized, editorializing**) (of a newspaper, editor, or broadcaster) make comments or express opinions rather than just

report the news: *a Halifax newspaper editorialized that radical reforms were needed*.

editorially *adverb* **1** having to do with editing or an editor: *the magazine is editorially strong*. **2** in or by means of an editorial column or statement: *the newspaper has criticized the government editorially*.

editor-in-chief *noun* (*plural* **editors-in-chief**) the chief editor of a publication, magazine, etc.

editorship *noun* the position of an editor or the period during which this is held.

Edmontonian • *noun* a native or inhabitant of Edmonton. • *adjective* of or relating to Edmonton. [Say ed m'n TONY in]

EDT *abbreviation* Eastern Daylight Time.

educate *verb* (**educates**, **educated**, **educating**) **1** give intellectual, moral, and social instruction to. **2** train or instruct for a particular purpose: *was educated in construction and engineering*.

educated *adjective* **1** having had an education, esp. to a higher level than average. **2** characterized by or displaying cultivated taste, learning, culture, etc. **3** based on experience or study: *an educated guess*.

education *noun* **1** the process of educating or being educated. **2** the theory and practice of teaching: *a master's degree in education*.

educational *adjective* **1** concerned with education. **2** having the power to educate. ▶**educationally** *adverb*

educative *adjective* having to do with education or teaching something: *educative films* ◊ *the educative role of the community*. [Say EDGE oo kuh tiv or ED you kuh tiv]

educator *noun* **1** a person who teaches, educates, or is in the business of education, e.g. a principal etc. **2** an educational specialist.

edutainment *noun* entertainment with an educational aspect. [Say edge oo TAIN m'nt or ed you TAIN m'nt]

Edwardian • *adjective* of, characteristic of, or associated with the reign of Edward VII of England (1901–10). • *noun* a person belonging to this period. [Say ed war WAR dee un (with WAR rhyming either with *FAR* or with *FOR*)]

-ee *suffix* forming nouns denoting: **1** the person affected directly or indirectly by the verbal action: *addressee* ◊ *employee*. **2** a person concerned with or described as: *absentee*.

EEC *abbreviation* European Economic Community.

EEG *abbreviation* (*plural* **EEGs**) **1** ELECTROENCEPHALOGRAM. **2** ELECTROENCEPHALOGRAPH(Y).

SPELL CHECK 🔤
eek, eke
....
Eke is the spelling in "eke out".

---

eek *interjection* expressing surprise, mild alarm, etc.

eel *noun* a snakelike fish which spends most of its life in fresh water but breeds in warm deep oceans.

eelgrass *noun* (*plural* **eelgrasses**) **1** a marine plant with long ribbon-like leaves. **2** any submerged freshwater plant of the genus *Vallisneria*.

eensy *adjective* (also **eensy-weensy**) *informal* tiny.

eerie *adjective* (**eerier**, **eeriest**) inspiring unease or fear. ▶**eerily** *adverb* **eeriness** *noun*

efface *verb* (**effaces**, **effaced**, **effacing**) **1** rub or wipe out (a mark etc.): *with time, the words are effaced by rain*. **2** obliterate or wipe out (a memory, mental impression, etc.): *his performance was so brilliant that it effaced all memories of any others*. [Say i FACE]

SPELL CHECK 🔤
effect, affect
....
Sometimes people confuse the words **affect** and **effect**. **Effect**, especially in the phrase **have an effect on**, is a noun that means "a result or influence": *Alcohol has a very bad effect on drivers*. **Effect** is also a formal verb meaning "to achieve": *People lack confidence in their ability to effect change in society*. **Affect** is a verb that means "to have an influence on": *Alcohol affects drivers' concentration*.

---

effect • *noun* **1** the result or consequence of an action etc. **2** efficacy: *the drug had little effect*. **3** an impression produced on a spectator, hearer, etc.: *my words had no effect*. **4** (in *plural*) (also **personal effects**) property, luggage, etc. **5** (in *plural*) (also **special effects**) the lighting, sound, etc. used to enhance a play, film, broadcast, etc. **6** a scientific phenomenon: *greenhouse effect*. **7** the state of being operative: *came into effect last year*. • *verb* **1** bring about (an event or result) or accomplish (an intention or desire). **2** cause to exist or occur. **PHRASES** **bring into effect** accomplish, realize. **for effect** for the sake of making an impression. **give effect to** make operative or put into force: *the purpose of the act is to give effect to the principle of equal opportunity for all*. **in effect** used to convey that something is in practice the case, even if it is not formally acknowledged to be so: *the minister's powers allow her, in effect, to ban programs*. **take effect** prove successful, come into force, or become operative. **to the effect that** the general substance or gist being. **to that effect** having that result or implication.

effective *adjective* **1 a** having a definite or desired effect: *drugs that are effective against cancer*. **b** efficient: *effective use of space*. **2** impressively powerful in effect: *a very effective staging of the play*. **3** actual, existing in fact rather than officially or theoretically: *took effective control in their absence*. **4** coming into operation: *effective May 1st*. ▶**effectively** *adverb* **effectiveness** *noun*

effectual *adjective* **1** effective, efficacious, or capable of producing the intended result or effect. **2** (of a legal document) valid, binding. ▶**effectually** *adverb*

effeminacy *noun* typically feminine characteristics or behaviour in a man or boy. [Say if FEMMA nuh see]

effeminate *adjective* **1** (of a man) feminine in appearance or manner; unmasculine. **2** characterized by or proceeding from weakness, delicacy, etc. ▶**effeminately** *adverb* [Say if FEMMA nit]

effervesce *verb* (**effervesces**, **effervesced**, **effervescing**) bubble or give off bubbles of gas, e.g. as a result of chemical reaction. [Say effer VESS]

effervescence *noun* **1** a fizzy quality, esp. in sparkling wine. **2** a vivacious and enthusiastic manner: *Kristi's effervescence is contagious*. [Say effer VESS ince]

effervescent *adjective* **1** bubbly, fizzy. **2** (of a person) showing great enthusiasm, excitement, etc.; lively, energetic, and vivacious. [Say effer VESS int]

effete *adjective* **1** affected: *effete trendies from art college*. **2** no longer capable of effective action, esp. as a result of having overly refined tastes or manners or being self-indulgent: *the authority of an effete aristocracy began to dwindle*. [Say if FEET]

efficacious *adjective* (of a thing) producing or sure to produce the desired effect; effective: *the most cost-effective and efficacious method of eliminating gypsy moths*. ▶**efficaciously** *adverb* [Say effa KAY shuss]

efficacy *noun* the ability of something, esp. a drug or medical treatment, to produce the desired result: *to evaluate the efficacy and safety of the treatment*. [Say EFFA kuh see]

E

efficiency *noun* (*plural* **efficiencies**) **1 a** the state or quality of being efficient. **b** effectiveness, competence, or the ability to accomplish or fulfill what is intended. **c** an action aimed at achieving greater efficiency: *administrative efficiencies*. **2** *Mechanics & Physics* the ratio of useful work performed to the total energy expended or heat taken in. **3** (also **efficiency unit**) *Cdn* a hotel room etc. with limited washing and cooking facilities. [Say i FISHN see]

efficient *adjective* **1** productive with minimum waste or effort. **2** (of a person) capable, acting effectively. **3** characterized by high or specified efficiency: *energy-efficient*. ▶ **efficiently** *adverb* [Say i FISH int]

effigy *noun* (*plural* **effigies**) **1** a representation of a person in the form of a sculptured figure, dummy, etc. **2** a crude representation of a person, esp. for ridicule, scorn, derision, etc. PHRASES **burn in effigy** subject a usu. crude image of a person to a punishment desired for the person represented, e.g. burning. [Say EFFA jee]

effluent *noun* sewage or industrial waste discharged into a body of water. [Say EFF loo int]

effluvium *noun* (*plural* **effluvia**) **1** (usu. in *plural*) waste material or refuse, esp. when transported by water. **2** an unpleasant or noxious odour or exhaled substance. [Say if LOOVY um, if LOOVY ah]

effort *noun* **1** strenuous physical or mental exertion. **2** a vigorous or determined attempt. **3** *Mechanics* a force applied to a thing in motion along the direction of motion. **4** an achievement, accomplishment, or result of any concentrated or special activity: *not bad for a first effort*. **5** an undertaking engaged in by a group to support some specific action: *the war effort*.

effortful *adjective* involving a great deal of effort: *charm can't be seen to be effortful*.

effortless *adjective* **1** requiring no physical or mental exertion. **2** achieved with admirable ease; not showing signs of effort: *admired the ballet dancer's effortless grace*. ▶ **effortlessly** *adverb* **effortlessness** *noun*

effrontery *noun* (*plural* **effronteries**) behaviour that is shamelessly confident and very rude: *he had the effrontery to accuse me of lying*. [Say i FRONTER ee]

effusion *noun* **1** an instance of giving off something such as a liquid, light, or smell: *a massive effusion of poisonous gas*. **2** usu. *derogatory* an unrestrained flow of speech or writing, esp. regarded as an excessive outpouring of emotion etc.: *this very escapism lends a poetic dimension to the novel when Paul takes off on fanciful lyrical effusions*. **3** an escape of blood, pus, etc. into a body cavity. [Say e FYOO zh'n]

effusive *adjective* showing or expressing feelings of gratitude, pleasure, or approval in an unrestrained and heartfelt manner: *effusive praise*. ▶ **effusively** *adverb* **effusiveness** *noun* [Say e FYOO siv]

e.g. *abbreviation* for example.

egalitarian • *adjective* **1** of or relating to the principle of equal rights and opportunities for all: *a fairer, more egalitarian society*. **2** advocating this principle. • *noun* a person who advocates or supports egalitarian principles. ▶ **egalitarianism** *noun* [Say i gal a TERRY in]

egg¹ *noun* **1 a** the more or less spheroidal reproductive body produced by females of animals such as birds, reptiles, fish, etc. and enclosed in a protective layer, shell, or firm membrane. **b** the egg of a domestic fowl, esp. of a hen, used for food. **2** (also **egg cell**) *Biology* an ovum, female gamete, or reproductive cell in animals and plants. **3** *informal* a person, usu. of a specified character: *a bad egg*. **4** anything resembling or imitating an egg, esp. in shape or appearance. PHRASES **have** (or **put**) **all one's eggs in one basket** *informal* risk everything on a single venture. **lay an egg** (of a performer, performance, etc.) fail badly. **teach one's**

grandmother to suck eggs (usu. in *neg.*) presume to instruct a person in something already known. **walk on eggs** or **eggshells** see EGGSHELL. **with egg on one's face** *informal* in a condition of looking foolish or being embarrassed or humiliated by the turn of events.

egg² *verb* (foll. by *on*) urge, incite, provoke, or tempt.

egg beater *noun* **1** a small, hand-operated, rotary beater, used for beating eggs, whipping cream, etc. **2** *slang* a helicopter.

egghead *noun informal* a person regarded as intellectual.

eggnog *noun* a thick drink, served hot or cold, consisting of beaten eggs, milk or cream, sugar, flavourings, and usu. rum or brandy.

eggplant *noun* a white or purple egg-shaped fruit eaten as a vegetable.

egg roll *noun* a deep-fried appetizer consisting of a thin shell of egg dough filled with a mixture of bean sprouts, minced meat, bamboo shoots, etc.

eggs Benedict *noun* a dish consisting of poached eggs on a slice of ham on toast with hollandaise sauce.

eggshell • *noun* **1** the thin shell or external covering of a bird's egg. **2** anything very fragile: *the truck would crush his car like an eggshell*. • *adjective* **1** (of china) of extreme thinness, fragility, and delicacy. **2** (of paint or finish) having the slight sheen or pale colour of a bird's egg. PHRASES **walk on eggshells** walk warily or proceed cautiously: *the divorce has the estranged couple's friends walking on eggshells*.

egg white *noun* albumen or the translucent fluid surrounding the yolk of an egg.

eggy *adjective* (**eggier**, **eggiest**) (of food) having eggs as a prominent ingredient: *a particularly eggy batter*.

egg yolk *noun* the yellow, internal part of a bird's egg which is rich in protein and fat to nourish the embryo.

ego *noun* (*plural* **egos**) **1** a person's sense of self-esteem and self-importance: *winning the prize was a real boost to her ego* ◊ *he has the biggest ego of anyone I've ever met*. **2** *Psychology* that part of the mind which mediates between the conscious and the unconscious and is responsible for reality testing and a sense of personal identity. [Say EE go]

egocentric • *adjective* self-centred. • *noun* an egocentric person. ▶ **egocentricity** *noun* [Say ee go SEN trick, ee go sen TRISSA tee]

egoism *noun* **1** an ethical theory that regards self-interest as the foundation of morality. **2** systematic self-centredness. **3** = EGOTISM. ▶ **egoist** *noun* **egoistic** *adjective* [Say EE go ism]

egomania *noun* obsessive self-love or self-centredness. ▶ **egomaniac** *noun* **egomaniacal** *adjective* [Say ee go MANIA]

egotism *noun* **1** the practice of continually talking about oneself. **2** an exaggerated opinion of oneself. **3** extreme selfishness. ▶ **egotist** *noun* **egotistic** *adjective* **egotistical** *adjective* **egotistically** *adverb* [Say EE go tism]

ego trip *informal* • *noun* an action or activity performed or indulged in to draw attention to one's abilities, for vanity's sake, etc. • *verb* (**ego-trip, ego-trips, ego-tripped, ego-tripping**) indulge in an ego trip. ▶ **ego-tripper** *noun*

egregious *adjective* flagrant, shocking, or outstandingly bad: *an egregious error*. ▶ **egregiously** *adverb* **egregiousness** *noun* [Say i GREEDGE iss]

egret *noun* any of various herons usu. having white feathers in the breeding season. [Say EE grit]

Egyptian • *adjective* of or relating to ancient or modern Egypt or its language or people. • *noun* **1** a native of ancient or modern Egypt or a national of the

Arab Republic of Egypt. **2** the Hamitic language used in Egypt until the 3rd c. AD. [Say i JIP shun]

Egyptologist *noun* a person who studies the language, history, and culture of ancient Egypt.

Egyptology *noun* the study of the language, history, and culture of ancient Egypt. [Say egypt OLLA jee]

eh *interjection informal* **1** inviting assent: *nice day, eh?* **2** *Cdn* ascertaining the comprehension, continued interest, agreement, etc. of the person or persons addressed: *it's way out in the suburbs, eh, so I can't get there by bike.* **3** expressing inquiry or surprise. **4** asking for something to be repeated or explained.

EI *abbreviation Cdn* employment insurance.

Eid *noun* **1** (also **Eid ul-Fitr**) a Muslim festival at the end of Ramadan. **2** (also **Eid ul-Adha**) a Muslim festival marking the culmination of the annual pilgrimage to Mecca. [Say EED, eed ul FITRA, eed ul ODDA]

eider *noun* (also **eider duck**) a large northern sea duck, esp. the common eider, the male of which is largely black and white and the female dull brown, or the king eider. [Rhymes with *RIDER*]

eight *cardinal number* one more than seven, or two less than ten.

eight ball *noun* **1** a variety of pool in which the winner is the first side to sink all seven of its own balls (either the striped ones or those in solid colours) and then sink the eight ball. **2** the black ball, numbered eight, in this. PHRASES **behind the eight ball 1** in a difficult situation, at a disadvantage. **2** baffled, stymied.

eighteen *cardinal number* one more than seventeen, or eight more than ten. ▶ **eighteenth** *ordinal number*

eighteen-wheeler *noun informal* a large transport truck having eighteen wheels.

eighth *ordinal number* constituting number eight in a sequence. ▶ **eighthly** *adverb*

eighth note *noun Music* a note having the time value of an eighth of a whole note and represented by a large dot with a hooked stem.

eighth rest *noun Music* a rest having the time value of an eighth note.

800 number *noun* a toll-free telephone number, with 800 in place of an area code, used esp. for business etc. to encourage customers at a distance to call or order.

eightieth *adjective, noun, & adverb* the ordinal number corresponding to eighty.

eighty *cardinal number* (*plural* **eighties**) ten less than ninety. PHRASES **eighty-first, -second**, etc. the ordinal numbers between eightieth and ninetieth. **eighty-one, -two**, etc. the cardinal numbers between eighty and ninety.

eighty-six *verb* (**eighty-sixes**, **eighty-sixed**, **eighty-sixing**) *slang* reject, discard, dismiss or destroy (a thing, person, idea, etc.).

einsteinium *noun* a radioactive metallic element produced artificially from plutonium. [Say ine STINEY um]

either • *adjective & pronoun* **1** one or the other of two: *either book.* **2** each of two: *on either side of the road.* • *adverb & conjunction* **1** as one possibility: *is either black or white.* **2** as one choice or alternative: *either come in or go out.* **3 a** any more than the other: *I didn't like it either.* **b** moreover: *there is no time to lose, either.* PHRASES **either way** in either case or event. [Say EYE ther or EE ther]

either-or • *noun* an unavoidable choice between alternatives. • *adjective* involving such a choice.

ejaculate • *verb* (**ejaculates**, **ejaculated**, **ejaculating**) **1** forcefully eject semen on achieving orgasm. **2** suddenly eject (any matter) from the human, animal, or plant body. **3** utter (words) suddenly. • *noun* semen that has been ejaculated from the body.

▶ **ejaculation** *noun* **ejaculator** *noun* **ejaculatory** *adjective* [Say i JACK you late for the verb, i JACK you lit for the noun, i jack you LAY sh'n, i JACK you luh tory]

eject • *verb* **1** send or drive out or away by force. **2** propel or be propelled from an aircraft or spacecraft in an ejection seat. **3** cause to be removed or drop out, e.g. a disk or tape from a machine, a spent cartridge from a gun. • *noun* a device, computer command, etc. which causes something to be ejected: *eject button.* ▶ **ejectable** *adjective*

ejection *noun* **1** the action of ejecting or the process of being ejected: *his ejection from the game for fighting.* **2** an emergency procedure in which a pilot is catapulted out of and away from an aircraft: *the ejection seat rocketed O'Grady into the air.*

eke *verb* (**ekes**, **eked**, **eking**) PHRASES **eke out 1** manage to live with very little money: *eking out the final days of each month with borrowed funds* ◊ *many petty traders barely eked out a living.* **2** make a small supply of something such as food or money last longer by using only small amounts of it: *she managed to eke out her student loan till the end of the year.* [Say EEK]

EKG *abbreviation* (*plural* **EKGs**) **1** electrocardiogram. **2** electrocardiograph.

elaborate • *adjective* **1** detailed and complicated in design and planning: *elaborate security precautions* ◊ *elaborate wrought-iron gates.* **2** (of an action) lengthy and exaggerated: *he made an elaborate pretence of yawning.* • *verb* work out or explain in detail: *the key idea of the book is expressed in the title and elaborated in the text.* ▶ **elaborately** *adverb* **elaborateness** *noun* **elaboration** *noun* [Say i LABBA rut for the adjective, i LABBA rate for the verb]

élan *noun* style, vivacity, energy arising from enthusiasm: *she performed with skill and élan.* [Say ay LON]

elapse *verb* (**elapses**, **elapsed**, **elapsing**) (of time) pass by. [Say i LAPS]

elastic • *adjective* **1** able to resume its normal bulk or shape spontaneously after being stretched or squeezed. **2** flexible; adaptable: *elastic rules.* **3** springy. **4** (of a person or feelings) not permanently or easily depressed. • *noun* **1** elastic cord or fabric, usu. woven with strips of rubber. **2** (also **elastic band**) = RUBBER BAND. ▶ **elasticity** *noun* [Say il LASTIC, il lass TISS ity]

elasticized *adjective* **1** (of a fabric) made elastic by weaving with rubber thread. **2** (of part of a garment, esp. a waistline, neckline, or cuff) made stretchy by the insertion of elastic in a casing. [Say il LASTA sized]

elated *adjective* extremely happy; filled with joy: *she was elated when she saw her marks* ◊ *I was elated to hear the news.* [Say il LATE id]

elation *noun* great happiness and excitement: *he felt elation at the prospect of the new job.*

elbow • *noun* **1 a** the joint between the forearm and the upper arm. **b** the part of the sleeve of a garment covering the elbow. **2** an elbow-shaped bend, corner, or pipe. **3** a push with an elbow. • *verb* (foll. by *aside, out,* etc.) **1** thrust or jostle (a person or oneself). **2** make (one's way) by thrusting or jostling. PHRASES **at one's elbow** close at hand. **give a person the elbow** *informal* dismiss or reject a person. **out at (the) elbows 1** (of a coat etc.) worn out; shabby. **2** (of a person) ragged, poor. **up to the elbows** *informal* busily engaged (in).

elbow grease *noun informal* hard manual work, esp. vigorous polishing or cleaning.

elbowing *noun Hockey* the illegal action of fouling an opponent with an elbow.

elbow room *noun* **1** adequate space to move or work in. **2** freedom from restriction; opportunity.

elder[1] • *adjective* (of two indicated persons, esp. when

related) senior; of a greater age: *elder brother*. • *noun* (often as **the elder**) **1 a** the older or more senior of two indicated (esp. related) persons: *is my elder by ten years*. **b** (**Elder**) a title to distinguish between related persons of renown: *Pliny the Elder*. **2** (in *plural*) **a** persons of greater age or seniority: *respect your elders*. **b** persons venerable because of age and wisdom: *the village elders*. **3** an official in the Presbyterian, United, or Mormon Churches who assists in the administration and government of the Church.

elder[2] *noun* a shrub or tree with white flowers and usu. blue-black or red berries.

elderberry *noun* (*plural* **elderberries**) the edible berry of the elder.

elderly *adjective* (of a person) past middle age.

elder statesman *noun* an older experienced person, esp. a politician, whose advice is often sought.

eldest • *adjective* first-born or oldest surviving (member of a family, son, daughter, etc.). • *noun* (often as **the eldest**) the eldest of three or more indicated.

El Dorado *noun* (*plural* **El Dorados**) **1** a fabled city or country abounding in gold, formerly believed to exist upon the Amazon. **2** (usu. **Eldorado**) a place of great abundance or opportunity: *the Klondike gold rush caught the imagination of the world and gave credence to the myth of a northern Eldorado*. [Say el duh ROD oh]

elect • *verb* **1** choose (a person) by vote. **2** choose (a thing, a course of action, etc.) in preference to an alternative: *the principles they elected to follow*. **3** *Theology* (of God) choose (persons) in preference to others for salvation. • *adjective* **1** *Theology* chosen by God. **2** (in *combination*, after a noun designating office) chosen but not yet in office: *president-elect*. • *noun* (**the elect**; treated as *plural*) **1** a specially chosen group of people; an elite. **2** *Theology* those chosen by God for salvation. ▶ **electability** *noun* **electable** *adjective*

election *noun* **1** selection by vote of candidates for a position: *Pam has agreed to stand for election* ◊ *the choice of when to hold an election lies with the prime minister*. **2** *Theology* the doctrine of Calvin (see CALVINISM) that God chooses some people for salvation without relation to their faith or good works.

electioneer *verb* **1** take part in an election campaign. **2** seek election by currying favour with voters. ▶ **electioneering** *noun*

elective • *adjective* **1** (of an office or its holder) filled or appointed by election. **2** (of a body of people) having the power to elect: *an elective assembly*. **3** (of a surgical operation etc.) optional; not urgently necessary. **4** (of a course of study etc.) chosen by the student; optional. • *noun* an elective course of study.

elector *noun* a person who has the right to vote.

electoral *adjective* relating to electors or elections. ▶ **electorally** *adverb* [Say il LECTER ul or il leck TORE ul]

electorate *noun* the body of persons entitled to vote in a country or constituency. [Say il LECTER it]

electric • *adjective* **1** of, worked by, or charged with electricity. **2** producing or capable of generating electricity. **3** (of a musical instrument) amplified electronically. **4** causing or charged with sudden and dramatic excitement: *the atmosphere was electric*. • *noun* **1** an electric car, train, etc. **2** (in *plural*) electrical appliances or circuitry.

electrical *adjective* **1** of or concerned with or of the nature of electricity. **2** operating by electricity. ▶ **electrically** *adverb*

electrical storm *noun* a thunderstorm.

electric chair *noun* a chair used for capital punishment by electrocution.

electric eel *noun* an eel-like freshwater fish native to

South America, which possesses electric organs and can give a severe electric shock.

electric fence *noun* (also **electric fencing**) a fence (often consisting of a single strand of wire) which gives a mild electric shock to an animal touching it.

electric field *noun* a region in which an electric charge experiences a force, usu. because of a distribution of other charges.

electric guitar *noun* a guitar in which the vibrations of the strings are converted by a pickup into electrical signals and amplified.

electrician *noun* a person who installs or maintains electrical equipment.

electricity *noun* **1** a form of energy resulting from the existence of charged particles (electrons, protons, etc.), either statically as an accumulation of charge or dynamically as a current. **2** a supply of electric current for heating, lighting, etc. **3** excitement, tension.

electric ray *noun* a sluggish bottom-dwelling marine ray that typically lives in shallow water and can produce an electric shock for the capture of prey and for defence.

electric shock *noun* **1** the effect of a sudden discharge of electricity on a person or animal, usually with stimulation of the nerves and contraction of the muscles. **2** = SHOCK TREATMENT 1.

electrification *noun* the process of charging or supplying something with electricity: *the electrification of the streetcar system* ◊ *a rural electrification program brought TVs and fridges to the villages*.

electrify *verb* (**electrifies**, **electrified**, **electrifying**) **1** charge with electricity; pass an electric current through. **2** convert (machinery or the place or system employing it) to the use of electric power: *the railway line was electrified in the 1950s*. **3** excite: *her performance electrified the audience*.

electro *noun* (*plural* **electros**) **1** = ELECTROPLATE *noun*. **2** (also as an *adjective*) a style of dance music with a fast electronic beat backed by a synthesizer.

electro- *combining form* of, relating to, or caused by electricity: *electromagnet*.

electrocardiogram *noun* a chart or record produced by an electrocardiograph, used in the diagnosis of heart disease. Abbreviation: **ECG**, **EKG**. [Say electro CARDIO gram]

electrocardiograph *noun* an instrument that records or displays the electric activity of the heart by means of electrodes attached to the skin. Abbreviation: **ECG**, **EKG**. ▶ **electrocardiography** *noun* [Say electro CARDIO graph, electro cardy OGGRA fee]

electroconvulsive therapy *noun* a method of treating certain mental illnesses in which an electric current is passed through the brain so as to produce a convulsion. Abbreviation: **ECT**. [Say electro CONVULSIVE]

electrocute *verb* (**electrocutes**, **electrocuted**, **electrocuting**) injure or kill by electric shock: *her father was electrocuted by power cables brought down in a storm*. ▶ **electrocution** *noun*

electrode *noun* a conductor through which electricity enters or leaves an electrolyte etc.

electroencephalogram *noun* a chart or record produced by an electroencephalograph. Abbreviation: **EEG**. [Say electro en SEFFA luh gram]

electroencephalograph *noun* an instrument that records or displays the electrical activity of the brain, using electrodes attached to the scalp. Abbreviation: **EEG**. ▶ **electroencephalography** *noun* [Say electro en SEFFA luh graph, electro en seffle OGGRA fee]

electrologist *noun* a person who removes excess body or facial hair using electrolysis. [Say il leck TRAWLA jist]

electrolysis *noun* **1** the separation of a liquid (or

electrolyte) into its chemical parts by passing an electric current through it. **2** the removal of excess hair by passing an electric current through the root. [Say il leck TRAWLA sis or ee leck TRAWLA sis]

electrolyte *noun* **1** a liquid, esp. that present in a battery, which contains ions and can be decomposed by electrolysis. **2** (usu. in *plural*) the ionized or ionizable constituents of a living cell, blood, etc. ▶ **electrolytic** *adjective* [Say ELECTRA lite, electra LIT ick]

electromagnet *noun* a piece of soft iron that becomes magnetic when an electric current is passed through the coil surrounding it.

electromagnetic *adjective* having both an electrical and a magnetic character or properties.

electromagnetic field *noun* a field of force created by changing electric and magnetic fields.

electromagnetic radiation *noun* a kind of radiation including visible light, radio waves, gamma rays, X-rays, etc., in which electric and magnetic fields vary simultaneously.

electromagnetism *noun* the magnetic forces produced by electricity.

electromechanical *adjective* of a mechanical device which is electrically operated.

electromotive force *noun* a difference in potential that tends to give rise to an electric current. Abbreviation: **emf**, **EMF**. [Say electro MOE tiv]

electron *noun* a stable subatomic particle with a charge of negative electricity, found in all atoms and acting as the primary carrier of electricity in solids.

electronegative *adjective* (of an element) tending to acquire electrons in chemical reactions. ▶ **electronegativity** *noun*

electronic *adjective* **1** relating to electrons or electronics. **2** (of a device) using electronic components. **3** using the electronic transmission or storage of information, as by computer: *electronic text*. **4** (of music or musical instruments) produced by or producing sounds by electronic means. ▶ **electronically** *adverb*

electronic bulletin board *noun* = BBS.

electronic data interchange *noun* a computer protocol for the exchange of electronic information, used by banks, businesses, etc. for invoicing, ordering, etc. Abbreviation: **EDI**.

electronic publishing *noun* the publishing of books etc. in machine-readable form rather than on paper.

electronics *plural noun* **1** (treated as *singular*) a branch of physics and technology concerned with the behaviour and movement of electrons in a vacuum, gas, semiconductor, etc. **2** the circuits used in this. **3** (treated as *plural*) electronic devices.

electron lens *noun* a device for focusing a stream of electrons by means of electric or magnetic fields.

electron microscope *noun* a microscope with high magnification and resolution, employing electron beams in place of light and using electron lenses.

electron volt *noun* a unit of energy equal to the work done on an electron in moving it through a potential difference of one volt. Abbreviation: **eV**.

electroplate • *verb* (**electroplates**, **electroplated**, **electroplating**) coat (a utensil etc.) with a thin layer of chromium, silver, etc., using electrolysis. • *noun* electroplated articles.

electropositive *adjective* **1** electrically positive. **2** (of an element) tending to lose electrons in chemical reactions.

electroshock • *noun* = ELECTROCONVULSIVE THERAPY. • *adjective* (of medical treatment) by means of electric shocks. • *verb* **1** treat (a patient) with electroconvulsive therapy. **2** kill (an animal) with an electric current.

electrostatic *adjective* of or relating to stationary electric charges or electrostatics. ▶ **electrostatically** *adverb* [Say electro STATIC]

electrostatics *plural noun* (treated as *singular*) the study of stationary electric charges or fields as opposed to electric currents.

elegance *noun* **1** refined style, simplicity, and good taste in manner or appearance: *Amanda dresses with casual elegance ◊ his writing combines elegance and wit*. **2** gracefulness or finesse in one's actions: *she handled the situation with elegance*. **3** luxury.

elegant *adjective* **1** tasteful, stylish, and refined in appearance. **2** showing refined grace in movement: *an elegant dancer*. **3** (of a mode of living etc.) of refined luxury. **4** ingeniously simple and satisfying: *an elegant solution*. ▶ **elegantly** *adverb*

elegiac *adjective* (esp. of a work of art) having a pleasing quality of gentle and wistful mournfulness: *the same elegiac and lonely tone continues to haunt the later poetry*. ▶ **elegiacally** *adverb* [Say ella JYE ick]

elegy *noun* (plural **elegies**) (in modern literature) a poem of serious reflection, typically a lament for the dead: *Gray's Elegy in a Country Churchyard*. [Say ELLA jee]

element *noun* **1** a component part or group; a contributing factor or thing. **2** *Chemistry & Physics* any of the hundred or so substances that cannot be resolved by chemical means into simpler substances, each consisting of atoms with the same atomic number. **3** a resistance wire that heats up in an electric heater, stove, kettle, etc. **4** (in *plural*) weather, esp. wind and storm: *offered no protection against the elements*. **5** (in *plural*) the rudiments of learning or of a branch of knowledge: *the elements of style*. **6** (in *plural*) the bread and wine of the Eucharist. **7** *Math & Logic* an entity that is a single member of a set. **PHRASES** **in** (or **out of**) **one's element** in (or out of) one's accustomed or preferred surroundings. **reduced to its elements** analyzed.

elemental *adjective* **1** essential; basic: *elemental truths*. **2** of the forces of nature, esp. seen as powerful and uncontrolled. **3** pertaining to chemical elements. **4** (of a chemical element) not chemically combined with another. **5** of the four elements.

elementary *adjective* **1 a** dealing with or arising from the simplest facts of a subject; rudimentary, introductory. **b** simple. **2** of or pertaining to elementary school. **3** *Chemistry* not decomposable.

elementary particle *noun* a subatomic particle, esp. one not known to be decomposable into simpler particles.

elementary school *noun* a school offering primary education, usu. for the first six or eight grades and also usu. including kindergarten.

elephant *noun* (plural **elephants** or **elephant**) the largest living land animal, of which two species survive, the larger African elephant and the smaller Indian elephant, both with a trunk and long tusks.

elephant seal *noun* either of two very large seals, of which the males have inflatable snouts.

elevate *verb* (**elevates**, **elevated**, **elevating**) raise: *elevate your heart rate with exercise ◊ elevate the level of discussion*.

elevated *adjective* **1** high in rank: *an elevated status*. **2** having a high moral or intellectual level: *elevated language ◊ elevated sentiments*. **3** higher than the area around; above the level of the ground: *the house is in an elevated position, overlooking the town ◊ an elevated highway*. **4** higher than normal: *elevated blood pressure*.

elevation *noun* **1** the process, state, or fact of elevating or being elevated. **2** the height above a given level, esp. sea level. **3** a high place or position. **4 a** a drawing made by projection on a vertical plane. **b** an

E

E

exterior face of a building or structure. **5 a** the capacity of a dancer to attain height in jumps. **b** the height attained in a jump. **6** the angle with the horizontal, esp. of a gun or of the direction of a celestial object.

elevator *noun* **1** a platform or compartment housed in a shaft for raising and lowering persons or things to different floors of a building etc. **2** (also **grain elevator**) a tall building, typically one having several cylindrical concrete silos or (on the prairies) a box-shaped wooden construction with a pitched roof, incorporating an elevating device which conveys grain from an unloading platform to bins where it is sorted, stored and cleaned before onward shipment. **3** the movable part of a tailplane for changing the pitch of an aircraft. **4** a device for hoisting or raising something. **5** something which elevates, esp. a muscle that raises a limb.

eleven *cardinal number* one more than ten.

eleventh *ordinal number* constituting number eleven in a sequence. PHRASES **the eleventh hour** the last possible moment.

elf *noun* (*plural* **elves**) **1** a mythological being, esp. one that is small and mischievous. **2** a small person.

elfin *adjective* **1** of elves; of or like an elf. **2** (of a person or their features) small and delicate, typically with an attractively mischievous or strange charm.

SPELL CHECK
elicit, illicit

Something secret or illegal is **illicit**.

---

elicit *verb* (**elicits, elicited, eliciting**) draw out or evoke (an answer, response, etc.) from someone in reaction to one's own actions or questions: *my cats are beautiful and clever and elicit admiring comments wherever they go ◊ sexist jokes would elicit laughter from men and groans from women.* [Say il LISS it]

elide *verb* (**elides, elided, eliding**) omit (a vowel, consonant, or syllable) when speaking: *the "t" in "often" may be elided.* [Say il LIDE]

eligibility *noun* the right to have or do something, based on having the right qualifications: *once a skater turns pro, she loses her eligibility to compete in amateur events ◊ a life sentence with no eligibility for parole.* [Say ella juh BILLA tee]

eligible *adjective* **1** (often foll. by *for*) fit or entitled to be chosen for a position, award, etc. **2** meeting specified preconditions: *eligible to receive EI benefits.* **3** desirable or suitable, esp. as a partner in marriage. ▶ **eligibly** *adverb* [Say ELLA juh bull]

eliminate *verb* (**eliminates, eliminated, eliminating**) **1** remove, get rid of: *credit cards eliminate the need to carry a lot of cash ◊ this diet claims to eliminate toxins from the body.* **2** exclude from consideration; ignore as irrelevant: *the police have eliminated two suspects from their investigation.* **3** exclude from further participation in a competition etc. by defeat. **4** murder (a rival or political opponent: *most of the regime's left-wing opponents were eliminated.* **5** discharge (waste matter) from the body. ▶ **elimination** *noun* **eliminator** *noun*

elision *noun* the omission of a vowel, consonant, or syllable in pronouncing (as in *I'm, let's*). [Say il LIZH un or ee LIZH un]

elite ● *noun* **1** (**the elite**) the best or choice part of a larger body or group. **2** a class or group of persons possessing wealth, power, prestige, etc.: *the ruling elite.* ● *adjective* of or belonging to an elite. [Say il LEET]

elitism *noun* **1** a way of organizing a system, society, etc. so that only a few people, esp. the wealthy, have power or influence or access to it: *many people believe that private education encourages elitism ◊ the performing arts are unjustly accused of elitism.* **2** the feeling of being better than other people that being part of an elite encourages. ▶ **elitist** *noun & adjective* [Say il LEET ism]

elixir *noun* **1 a** a preparation supposedly able to change metals into gold. **b** (also **elixir of life**) a magic liquid supposedly able to prolong life indefinitely. **c** a magical or medicinal potion: *an elixir guaranteed to induce love.* **2** a supposed remedy for all ills. [Say il LIX ur or ee LIX ur]

Elizabethan ● *adjective* of the period of Elizabeth I of England (reigned 1558–1603). ● *noun* a person, esp. a poet or dramatist, of the time of Elizabeth I, e.g. Shakespeare, Marlowe, and Spenser. [Say il lizza BEETH un]

elk *noun* (*plural* **elk** or **elks**) **1** a wapiti. **2** (**Elk**) a member of the Benevolent and Protective Order of Elks, a social and charitable organization.

elkhound *noun* a large Scandinavian hunting dog with a shaggy coat.

ellipse *noun* a regular oval, traced by a point moving in a plane so that the sum of its distances from two other points is constant, or resulting when a cone is cut by an oblique plane which does not intersect the base (*compare* HYPERBOLA). [Say il LIPS]

ellipsis *noun* (*plural* **ellipses**) **1** the omission from a sentence of words not needed to complete the construction or sense. **2** a set of three dots etc. indicating an omission. [Say il LIP sis for the singular, il LIP seez for the plural]

ellipsoid ● *noun* a solid or surface of which at least one set of parallel cross-sections are ellipses and the rest circles. ● *adjective* (also **ellipsoidal**) having the shape of an ellipsoid. [Say il LIP soid]

elliptic *adjective* (also **elliptical**) **1** of, relating to, or having the form of an ellipse. **2** (of writing or speech) very concise, often so as to be obscure or cryptic: *the witches' elliptical prophecies to Macbeth.* ▶ **elliptically** *adverb* [Say il LIP tick]

elm *noun* **1** a shade tree with asymmetrical toothed leaves. **2** (also **elmwood**) the wood of the elm.

El Niño *noun* (*plural* **El Niños**) an irregularly occurring southward current in the equatorial Pacific Ocean, associated with weather changes and ecological damage. [Say el NEEN yo]

elocution *noun* **1** the art of clear and expressive speech, esp. of distinct pronunciation and articulation. **2** a particular style of speaking. ▶ **elocutionist** *noun* [Say ella CUE sh'n]

elongate ● *verb* (**elongates, elongated, elongating**) **1** lengthen, prolong. **2** *Botany* grow, become longer; have a slender or tapering form. ● *adjective* *Botany & Zoology* long in proportion to width. ▶ **elongated** *adjective* [Say ee LONG gate or EE long gate]

elongation *noun* **1** the act or process of lengthening or being lengthened. **2** a part of a line etc. formed by lengthening. [Say ee long GAY sh'n]

elope *verb* (**elopes, eloped, eloping**) run away secretly with a lover, esp. to get married. ▶ **elopement** *noun* **eloper** *noun*

eloquence *noun* fluent and persuasive speaking or writing: *it required all of Laurier's eloquence to get the members to vote for the bill.* [Say ELLA quince]

eloquent *adjective* **1** fluent or persuasive in speaking or writing: *an eloquent speech.* **2** clearly expressive or indicative: *an eloquent performance.* ▶ **eloquently** *adverb* [Say ELLA quint]

else *adverb* **1** besides: *nowhere else ◊ who else.* **2** instead: *what else could I say? ◊ someone else.* PHRASES **or else** **1** otherwise: *run, or else you will be late.* **2** *informal* a warning or threat of the consequences should a

previously expressed order, expectation, etc. not be carried out or realized: *clean up your room, or else!*

elsewhere *adverb* in or to some other place.

elucidate *verb* (**elucidates**, **elucidated**, **elucidating**) explain, clarify: *the aim of the report is to elucidate the main points of the new regulations ◊ I will try to elucidate what I think the problems are ◊ let me elucidate.* ▶ **elucidation** *noun* [Say il LUCE a date, il luce a DAY sh'n]

SPELL CHECK
elude, allude

When you refer to something you **allude** to it.

---

elude *verb* (**eludes**, **eluded**, **eluding**) **1** escape cleverly from (a danger, difficulty, pursuer, etc.): *he managed to elude his pursuers by escaping into the forest ◊ the drug dealer eluded prosecution.* **2** fail to be grasped or remembered by (someone): *the logic of this eluded most people ◊ the cause of the disease has eluded researchers.* **3** (of an achievement, or something desired or pursued) fail to be attained by someone: *sleep still eluded her ◊ recognition has eluded him since the 70s.*

elusive *adjective* difficult to find, catch, achieve, or pin down: *success continued to be elusive ◊ the elusive Canadian identity.* ▶ **elusively** *adverb* **elusiveness** *noun* [Say il LOO sive or ee LOO sive]

elves plural of ELF.

'em *pronoun* informal them: *let 'em all come.*

emaciate *verb* (esp. as **emaciated** *adjective*) (**emaciates**, **emaciated**, **emaciating**) make abnormally thin or feeble. ▶ **emaciation** *noun* [Say im MAY see ate, im may see AY sh'n]

e-mail • *noun* **1** messages distributed by electronic means esp. from one computer system to one or more recipients. **2** a message sent by e-mail: *received 5 e-mails.* **3** the e-mail system. • *verb* send e-mail.

emanate *verb* (**emanates**, **emanated**, **emanating**) **1** come (from a source): *the sound of loud music emanated from the building ◊ the proposal originally emanated from the UN.* **2** emit (something abstract but perceptible): *she emanates strength and confidence.* [Say EMMA nate]

emanation *noun* something given off by something: *lightning was thought to be an emanation from the earth ◊ the noxious emanations from the corpses.* [Say emma NATION]

emancipate *verb* (**emancipates**, **emancipated**, **emancipating**) **1** set free, esp. from legal, social, or political restrictions: *swimming without a suit has got to be one of the most emancipating feelings I know ◊ Figaro emancipates himself from the very tradition of comedy.* **2** free from slavery: *Abraham Lincoln emancipated American slaves.* [Say im MAN suh pate]

emancipated *adjective* **1** not restricted by law or by moral or social conventions: *emancipated women.* **2** liberated, as from slavery. [Say im MAN suh pate id]

emancipation *noun* **1** the process of becoming or setting free, esp. from legal, social, or political restrictions: *the period is marked by Canada's growing independence and emancipation from British political control ◊ the granting of full political and civil liberties to Roman Catholics in Britain and Ireland was effected by the Catholic Emancipation Act of 1829.* **2** the process of setting someone free from slavery: *the emancipation of all slaves in the US was proclaimed in 1862.* [Say im man suh PAY sh'n]

emasculate *verb* (**emasculates**, **emasculated**, **emasculating**) **1** make (a person, idea, or piece of legislation) weaker or less effective: *the government has starved the Canada Council, crippled the CBC, and emasculated the National Film Board.* **2** castrate: *I regularly emasculated our young goats.* **3** deprive (a man) of his male role or identity: *because I was a successful businesswoman, my husband said I was emasculating him.* ▶ **emasculation** *noun* [Say im MASS cue late]

embalm *verb* **1** preserve (a corpse) from decay by means of injection of a preservative, e.g. formaldehyde, into the arteries. **2** preserve someone or something in an unaltered state: *Shakespeare's plays are too often embalmed by tradition.* ▶ **embalmer** *noun* [Say em BOM]

embankment *noun* an earth or stone bank for keeping back water, or for carrying a road or railway.

SPELL CHECK
embarrass

Warning: in the word **embarrass** you double the *r* and double the *s*.

---

embargo • *noun* (*plural* **embargoes**) **1** an order prohibiting ships from entering or leaving a country's ports, usu. issued in anticipation of war. **2** an official, usu. temporary, suspension of commerce or other activity. **3** a prohibition: *an embargo on discussion.* • *verb* (**embargoes**, **embargoed**, **embargoing**) **1** place (ships, trade, etc.) under embargo. **2** seize (a ship, goods) for state service. [Say em BAR go]

embark *verb* **1** put or go on board a ship or aircraft. **2** (foll. by *on, upon*) engage in an activity or undertaking. ▶ **embarkation** *noun* (in sense 1).

embarrass *verb* (**embarrasses**, **embarrassed**, **embarrassing**) cause (a person) to feel awkward or self-conscious or ashamed. ▶ **embarrassingly** *adverb*

embarrassed *adjective* **1** feeling awkward or self-conscious or ashamed. **2** having or showing financial difficulties: *living in embarrassed circumstances.* ▶ **embarrassedly** *adverb*

embarrassment *noun* **1 a** a feeling of awkward confusion, shame, or self-consciousness. **b** a cause of this: *their behaviour is an embarrassment.* **2** a state of financial difficulty; shortage of money: *he asked her to buy lunch, pleading his temporary financial embarrassment.*

embassy *noun* (*plural* **embassies**) **1 a** the residence or offices of an ambassador. **b** the ambassador and staff attached to an embassy. **2** a deputation or mission to a foreign country. [Say EMBA see]

embattled *adjective* **1** (of a person) beset by problems or difficulties: *the worst may not be over for the embattled prime minister.* **2** (of a place or people) involved in or prepared for war: *the embattled Yugoslavian republics.*

embed *verb* (**embeds**, **embedded**, **embedding**) **1** fix firmly in a surrounding mass: *embedded in concrete.* **2** fix (an idea, attitude, etc.) firmly within a structure: *the Victorian values embedded in Tennyson's poetry.*

embellish *verb* (**embellishes**, **embellished**, **embellishing**) **1** beautify, adorn: *blue silk embellished with gold embroidery.* **2** add interest to (a narrative) with fictitious additions: *Josie embellished her account of the accident to make it more interesting.* ▶ **embellisher** *noun* **embellishment** *noun* [Say em BELL ish]

ember *noun* (usu. in *plural*) a small piece of glowing coal or wood in a dying fire.

embezzle *verb* (**embezzles**, **embezzled**, **embezzling**) divert (money etc.) fraudulently to one's own use in violation of trust. ▶ **embezzlement** *noun* **embezzler** *noun*

embittered *adjective* very hostile or discontented.

emblazon *verb* inscribe a conspicuous design, logo, slogan, etc. on a surface: *baseball caps emblazoned with the team's logo ◊ the royal coat of arms was emblazoned on the door.* [Say em BLAZE un]

emblem *noun* **1** a symbol or representation typifying or identifying an institution, quality, etc. **2** a heraldic

E

device or symbolic object as a distinctive badge. [Say EM blum]

emblematic *adjective* **1** that represents or is a symbol of something. **2** that is considered typical of a situation, an area of work, etc.: *the violence is emblematic of what is happening in our inner cities.* [Say embla MAT ick]

embodiment *noun* a person or thing that represents or is a typical example of an idea or a quality: *Gil is the embodiment of the successful businessman.* [Say em BODY mint]

embody *verb* (**embodies, embodied, embodying**) **1** be an expression of or give a tangible or visible form to (an idea, quality, or feeling): *a national rowing team that embodies competitive spirit and skill.* **2** include or contain (something) as a constituent part: *the changes in law embodied in the Young Offenders Act.*

embolden *verb* (usu. in *passive*) make bold; encourage. [Say em BOWL din]

emboss *verb* (**embosses, embossed, embossing**) (usu. as **embossed** *adjective*) carve or mould a design on (a surface) so that it stands out in relief: *an embossed brass dish.* ▶ **embosser** *noun* **embossing** *noun*

embrace • *verb* (**embraces, embraced, embracing**) **1** hold (a person) closely in the arms, esp. as a sign of affection. **2** accept eagerly (an offer, opportunity, etc.): *eagerly embraced the chance to work on such an important project.* **3** adopt (a course of action, doctrine, cause, etc.): *much of the population quickly embraced Islam.* **4** include, comprise: *his career embraces a number of activities — writing, acting, and directing.* • *noun* **1** an act of embracing. **2** the act of holding someone in one's arms.

embroider *verb* **1** decorate cloth etc. with needlework. **2** embellish (a narrative etc.) with fictitious additions. [Say em BROY dur]

embroidery *noun* (*plural* **embroideries**) **1** the art of embroidering. **2** embroidered work; a piece of this. **3** fictitious additions to (a story etc.): *fanciful embroidery of the facts.* [Say em BROY dur ee]

embroil *verb* involve (a person, company, etc.) in an argument, conflict, or difficult situation: *the region was embroiled in civil war* ◊ *the legislature is embroiled in a debate over school funding.*

embryo *noun* (*plural* **embryos**) **1 a** an unborn or unhatched offspring. **b** a human offspring in the first eight or twelve weeks from conception. **2 a** rudimentary plant contained in a seed. **3** a thing in a rudimentary stage: *the embryo of an idea* ◊ *an embryo politician.* PHRASES **in embryo** undeveloped: *this essay contains in embryo all of the themes of her later novels.* ▶ **embryonic** *adjective* [Say EM bree oh, em bree ON ick]

embryo transfer *noun* **1** the removal of an embryo from a superior cow, sow, etc. and its replacement inside an inferior one, performed to increase the potential number of offspring from superior livestock. **2** the transfer of a human embryo from one female, or from storage, to another for gestation.

emcee *informal* • *noun* (*plural* **emcees**) a master of ceremonies. • *verb* (**emcees, emceed, emceeing**) act as master of ceremonies.

emerald • *noun* **1** a bright green precious stone, a variety of beryl. **2** (also **emerald green**) the colour of this. • *adjective* (also **emerald green**) bright green.

emerge¹ *verb* (**emerges, emerged, emerging**) **1** come up or out into view, esp. when formerly concealed. **2** (of facts, circumstances, etc.) come to light, become known, esp. as a result of inquiry etc. **3** become recognized or prominent: *emerged as a contender.* **4** (of a question, difficulty, etc.) become apparent. **5** survive an ordeal etc. with a specified result: *emerged unscathed.*

emerge² *noun Cdn slang* = EMERGENCY 4.

emergence *noun* **1** the process of beginning to exist or becoming known or important: *the emergence of new technology is changing the way people do business* ◊ *the emergence of the candidate as a bona fide contender has been a surprise.* **2** the process of coming up or out into view.

emergency *noun* (*plural* **emergencies**) **1** a sudden state of danger, conflict, etc., requiring immediate action. **2 a** a medical condition requiring immediate treatment. **b** a patient with such a condition. **3** (as an *adjective*) characterized by or for use in an emergency: *emergency telephone.* **4** a part of a hospital for handling emergencies (often as an *adjective*: *emergency ward*).

emergency brake *noun* a brake on a car etc., usually operated by hand, used to stop it if the main brakes fail, and to prevent it from rolling while parked.

emergency locator transmitter *noun* a radio transmitter on an aircraft activated automatically by the inertia of impact and serving as a homing beacon for searching aircraft. Abbreviation: **ELT.**

emergency room *noun* = EMERGENCY 4.

emergent *adjective* **1** becoming apparent: *emergent vegetation.* **2** (of a nation) newly formed or made independent: *the emergent democracies of eastern Europe.*

emeritus *adjective* retired and retaining one's title as an honour: *professor emeritus.* [Say im MERIT us]

emery *noun* a coarse form of corundum used in powdered form as an abrasive.

emery board *noun* a strip of thin wood or board coated with emery or another abrasive, used as a nail file.

emery cloth *noun* (also **emery paper**) cloth or paper covered with emery, used for polishing or cleaning metals etc.

emetic • *adjective* that causes vomiting. • *noun* an emetic medicine. [Say im MET ick]

emigrant • *noun* a person who emigrates. • *adjective* emigrating.

emigrate *verb* (**emigrates, emigrated, emigrating**) leave one's own country to settle in another. ▶ **emigration** *noun*

émigré *noun* an emigrant, esp. an exile: *the daughter of Russian émigrés.* [Say EMMA gray]

eminence *noun* **1** distinction; recognized superiority: *her eminence in cinematography.* **2** (**Eminence**) a title used in addressing or referring to a cardinal: *His Eminence.* [Say EMMA nince]

eminent *adjective* **1** distinguished, notable: *one of the world's most eminent musicians.* **2** used to emphasize the presence of a positive quality: *the organ's eminent suitability for church music.* ▶ **eminently** *adverb* [Say EMMA nint]

emir *noun* a title of various Muslim rulers, esp. in the Middle East. [Say em MEER]

emirate *noun* the rank, domain, or reign of an emir. [Say EMMA rit or EMMA rate]

emissary *noun* (*plural* **emissaries**) a person sent on a special (usu. diplomatic) mission. [Say EM iss airy]

emission *noun* **1** the process or an act of emitting. **2** a thing emitted, as exhaust, radiation, fluid, etc.

emissive *adjective* having the power to radiate light, heat, etc. ▶ **emissivity** *noun* [Say im MISS iv, im miss IV a tee]

emit *verb* (**emits, emitted, emitting**) **1 a** send out (heat, light, exhaust, etc.). **b** discharge from the body. **2** give forth (a sound). [Say im MIT]

emitter *noun* something which emits, esp. a region in a transistor producing carriers of current. [Say im MIT ur]

Emmenthal *noun* a kind of hard yellow Swiss cheese with many large holes in it. [Say EM in tawl]

Emmy *noun* (*plural* **Emmys**) (in the US) a statuette awarded annually to an outstanding television program or performer.

emollient • *adjective* that softens or soothes the skin: *an emollient cream.* • *noun* an emollient cream etc. [Say im MOLLY int]

emote *verb* (**emotes, emoted, emoting**) *informal* show excessive emotion. [Say im MOTE or ee MOTE]

emoticon *noun* a (usu. sideways) representation of a facial expression constructed out of keyboard characters, added to an esp. e-mail message to help establish the tone, e.g. :-(representing a sad face. [Say im MOTE a con or ee MOTE a con]

emotion *noun* **1** a strong mental or instinctive feeling such as love, sorrow, or fear. **2** emotional intensity or sensibility: *he spoke with emotion.*

emotional *adjective* **1** of or relating to the emotions. **2 a** (of a person) liable to excessive emotion. **b** showing strong emotion, esp. by weeping. **3** expressing or based on emotion. **4** likely to excite emotion. ▶ **emotionalism** *noun* **emotionality** *noun* **emotionally** *adverb*

emotionless *adjective* not showing any emotion: *an emotionless voice.*

emotive *adjective* **1** of or characterized by emotion: *the comparisons tend to be emotive rather than analytic.* **2** tending to excite emotion: *abortion is an emotive issue.* **3** arousing feeling; not purely descriptive: *the paper ran an emotive article on the terrorist attack.*

empathetic *adjective* having the ability to understand and share another person's feelings. ▶ **empathetically** *adverb* [Say em PATHETIC]

empathize *verb* (**empathizes, empathized, empathizing**) understand and share another person's feelings and experiences, esp. because one has been in a similar situation: *counsellors should be able to empathize with the people they're trying to help.* [Say EMPA thize]

empathy *noun* the ability to understand and share another person's feelings and experiences. [Say EM puth ee]

emperor *noun* **1** the male sovereign of an empire. **2** a male sovereign of higher rank than a king.

emphasis *noun* (*plural* **emphases**) **1** special importance or prominence attached to a thing, fact, idea, etc.: *emphasis on economy.* **2** stress laid on a word or words to indicate special meaning or importance. **3** vigour or intensity of expression: *Lionel spoke with emphasis and with complete conviction.* [Say EMFA sis for the singular, EMFA seez for the plural]

emphasize *verb* (**emphasizes, emphasized, emphasizing**) **1** bring (a thing, fact, etc.) into special prominence; put emphasis or stress on. **2** lay stress on (a word in speaking).

emphatic *adjective* **1** (of language, tone, or gesture) forcibly expressive: *the minister made an emphatic speech expressing support for the legislation.* **2** (of words) used to give emphasis. **3** expressing oneself with emphasis: *the children were emphatic that they wanted to go.* **4** (of an action or event or its result) definite and clear: *an emphatic playoff win.* ▶ **emphatically** *adverb*

emphysema *noun* enlargement of the air sacs of the lungs causing breathlessness. [Say emfa ZEEM uh]

empire *noun* **1** an extensive group of states or countries under a single supreme authority, esp. an emperor. **2** a large commercial organization etc. owned or directed by one person or group. **3** (**the Empire**) **a** the British Empire. **b** the Holy Roman Empire. **4** a type or period of government in which the sovereign is called emperor: *the French Second Empire lasted from 1852–1870.* **5** (as an *adjective*) denoting a style of dress with a waistline under the bust and often a low

neckline, originally popular during the first French Empire (1804–14): *empire waist.* **6** (**Empire**) a red, sweet and tart eating apple, with characteristics of both McIntosh and Delicious apples.

empire builder *noun* a person who deliberately acquires extra territory, authority, etc. esp. unnecessarily. ▶ **empire building** *noun*

empirical *adjective* (also **empiric**) based on, concerned with, or verifiable by observation or experience rather than theory or pure logic: *they provided considerable empirical evidence to support their argument.* ▶ **empirically** *adverb* [Say em PEERA cull]

empiricism *noun* Philosophy the theory that all knowledge is derived from sense-experience rather than being based on reason. ▶ **empiricist** *noun* & *adjective* [Say em PEERA sism]

emplacement *noun* a platform or defended position where a gun is placed for firing.

employ • *verb* **1** use the services of (a person) in return for payment. **2** use (a thing, time, energy, strategy, etc.) esp. to good effect. **3** (often foll. by *in*) keep (a person) occupied. • *noun* the state of being employed, esp. for wages. PHRASES **in the employ of** employed by.

employability *noun* the suitability of a person for employment, based on their skills and qualifications.

employable *adjective* **1** qualified for employment and available for work. **2** usable.

employee *noun* a person employed for wages or salary.

employer *noun* a person or organization that pays people to work for them.

employment *noun* **1** the act of employing or the state of being employed. **2** the prevalence or proportion of this in a given area: *politicians promising increased employment.* **3** a person's regular trade or profession.

employment insurance *noun* Cdn a federal government program providing payments to eligible unemployed people, funded by tax revenues and contributions by employers and workers.

emporium *noun* (*plural* **emporia** or **emporiums**) **1** a specialized retail store etc.: *perfume emporium.* **2** a large retail store selling a wide variety of goods. **3** a centre of commerce, a market. [Say em PORE ee um for the singular, em PORE ee uh for the plural]

empower *verb* **1** authorize, license. **2** give power to: *the courts were empowered to give harsher sentences to repeat offenders.* **3** provide with the means, opportunity, etc. necessary for independence, self-assertion, etc.: *the movement empowered women and gave them confidence in themselves.* ▶ **empowerment** *noun*

empress *noun* (*plural* **empresses**) **1** the wife or widow of an emperor. **2** a female sovereign of an empire. **3** a female sovereign of higher rank than a queen.

emptiness *noun* **1 a** sadness, loneliness, or unfulfillment resulting from a loss or from a sense that something has lost its value or purpose: *her departure left him with a feeling of emptiness.* **b** the quality of something that has no value, purpose, or likelihood of fulfillment: *nothing could fill the emptiness of their marriage.* **2** the fact that there is nothing or nobody in a place: *the silence and emptiness of the house did not scare her.* **3** a place that is empty: *he stared out at the vast emptiness that was the sea.*

empty • *adjective* (**emptier, emptiest**) **1** containing nothing. **2** meaningless: *empty threats* ◊ *an empty existence.* **3** Math (of a class or set) containing no members or elements. • *verb* (**empties, emptied, emptying**) **1** make empty; remove all or some of the contents of. **2** (often foll. by *into*) transfer (the contents of a container). **3** become empty. **4** (usu. foll. by *into*) (of a river) discharge itself (into the sea etc.). • *noun* (*plural* **empties**) *informal* a container (esp. a bottle) left empty

E

of its contents. PHRASES **run on empty** continue to function though having exhausted all one's resources, sustenance, etc.

empty-handed *adjective* **1** bringing or taking nothing. **2** having achieved or obtained nothing. ▶ **empty-handedly** *adverb*

empty nest *noun* a household where the parents alone remain after the children have grown up and left.

empty nester *noun* either of a couple whose children have grown up and left home.

emu *noun* (*plural* **emus**) a large shaggy flightless Australian bird related to the ostrich and capable of running at high speed. [Say EE myoo or EE moo]

emulate *verb* (**emulates, emulated, emulating**) **1** match or surpass (a person or achievement), esp. by imitation: *lesser men trying to emulate his greatness*. **2** imitate: *hers is not a hairstyle I wish to emulate*. **3** *Computing* reproduce the function or action of (a different computer or software system). ▶ **emulation** *noun* **emulator** *noun* [Say EM yoo late, em yoo LAY sh'n]

emulsifier *noun* **1** any substance that stabilizes a dispersion of one liquid in another, esp. a food additive used to stabilize processed foods. **2** an apparatus used for dispersing one liquid in another by shaking or stirring a substance. [Say im MULL suh fire]

emulsify *verb* (**emulsifies, emulsified, emulsifying**) make into or become an emulsion: *mustard helps to emulsify a vinaigrette*. [Say im MULL suh fie]

emulsion *noun* **1** a fine dispersion of one liquid in another, esp. as paint, medicine, etc. **2** a mixture of a silver compound suspended in gelatin etc. for coating plates or films. [Say im MULL shun]

enable *verb* (**enables, enabled, enabling**) **1** give (a person etc.) the means or authority to do something: *the software enables you to access the Internet in seconds*. **2** make possible. **3** esp. *Computing* make (a device) operational.

enabler *noun* a person or thing which enables, esp. a person who helps others to achieve their potential or develop skills.

enabling *adjective* (of legislation) empowering a person or body to take certain action.

enact *verb* **1 a** establish (a law, legal penalty, etc.). **b** make (a bill etc.) law: *this legislation was enacted in 1998*. **2** play (a part or scene on stage or in life): *prepare a script for practice, and then enact the scene*.

enactment *noun* **1** a law enacted. **2** the process of enacting.

enamel • *noun* **1** a glasslike opaque or semi-transparent coating on metallic or other hard surfaces for ornament or as a preservative lining. **2 a** a smooth hard coating. **b** (also **enamel paint**) a paint that dries to give a smooth hard coat. **3** the hard glossy natural coating over the crown of a tooth. **4** painting done in enamel. • *verb* (**enamels, enamelled, enamelling**) coat (a metal etc.) with enamel.

enamour *verb* (also **enamor**) **1** inspire with love or liking: *it is not difficult to see why Edward is enamoured of her*. **2** charm, delight: *she was truly enamoured of Montreal*. [Say in AMMER]

encamp *verb* **1** settle in a military camp. **2** lodge in the open in tents.

encampment *noun* **1** a place where troops etc. are encamped. **2** the process of setting up a camp.

encapsulate *verb* (**encapsulates, encapsulated, encapsulating**) **1** enclose in or as in a capsule. **2** summarize; express the essential features of. ▶ **encapsulation** *noun*

encase *verb* (**encases, encased, encasing**) **1** put into a case. **2** surround as with a case.

encephalitis *noun* inflammation of the brain. [Say en seffa LITE is]

enchant *verb* (usu. in *passive*) **1** delight. **2** bewitch. ▶ **enchanted** *adjective* **enchantedly** *adverb*

enchanter *noun* a person who enchants, esp. by supposed use of magic.

enchanting *adjective* delightfully charming or attractive: *an enchanting view*. ▶ **enchantingly** *adverb*

enchantment *noun* **1** a captivating charm or beauty: *the castle's Gothic architecture creates an air of enchantment*. **2** a feeling of delight or captivation; an enraptured condition: *his enchantment with her work is evident*.

enchilada *noun* (*plural* **enchiladas**) a tortilla with chili sauce and usu. a filling, esp. meat. PHRASES **the whole enchilada** a thing in its entirety. [Say encha LADA]

encircle *verb* (**encircles, encircled, encircling**) **1** surround, encompass. **2** form a circle around.

enclave *noun* **1** a portion of territory of one state surrounded by territory of another or others, as viewed by the surrounding territory. **2** a group of people who are culturally, intellectually, or socially distinct from those surrounding them: *Serbian enclaves in Bosnia-Herzegovina* ◊ *grew up in an English enclave in Montreal*. [Say ON clave or EN clave]

enclose *verb* (**encloses, enclosed, enclosing**) **1** (often foll. by *with, in*) **a** surround with a wall, fence, etc. **b** shut in on all sides. **2** fence in (common land) so as to make it private property. **3** put in a receptacle (esp. in an envelope together with a letter). **4** esp. *Math* bound on all sides; contain. **5** hem in on all sides.

enclosure *noun* **1** the act of enclosing, esp. of fencing in common land so as to make it private property. **2** an enclosed space or area. **3** a thing enclosed with a letter. **4** an enclosing fence etc.

encode *verb* (**encodes, encoded, encoding**) **1** put (a message etc.) into code or cipher. **2** *Linguistics* convert ideas into linguistic expression (*compare* DECODE 2). **3** (of a gene or stretch of nucleic acid) specify the genetic code for (a protein or peptide). ▶ **encoder** *noun*

encomium *noun* (*plural* **encomiums** or **encomia**) a formal or high-flown expression of praise: *an encomium to present progress*. [Say en CO me um]

encompass *verb* (**encompasses, encompassed, encompassing**) **1** surround or form a circle about: *the fog soon encompassed the whole river valley*. **2** contain, include comprehensively: *no studies encompass all sectors of medical care*.

encore • *noun* **1** a call by an audience or spectators for the repetition of an item, or for a further item. **2** such an item. **3** a repetition of an event. • *interjection* again.

encounter • *verb* **1** meet, come across, esp. by chance or unexpectedly. **2** meet as an opponent: *the police encountered a crowd of demonstrators*. • *noun* **1** a meeting by chance. **2** a meeting in conflict: *had a close encounter with death*. **3** an act of sexual intercourse: *her first sexual encounter*. **4** an exposure to something, esp. for the first time: *it was their first encounter with French literature*.

encourage *verb* (**encourages, encouraged, encouraging**) **1** give courage, confidence, or hope to. **2** urge, advise: *I encouraged her to go to the police*. **3** stimulate by help, reward, etc. **4** promote or assist (an enterprise, opinion, etc.). ▶ **encouragement** *noun* **encourager** *noun* **encouraging** *adjective* **encouragingly** *adverb*

encroach *verb* (**encroaches, encroached, encroaching**) **1** (foll. by *on, upon*) intrude, esp. on another's territory or rights. **2** advance gradually beyond due limits. ▶ **encroachment** *noun*

encrust *verb* **1** cover with a crust. **2** overlay with an

ornamental crust of precious material: *encrusted with jewels*.

encrypt *verb* convert (data) into code, esp. to prevent unauthorized access. ▶ **encryption** *noun*

encumber *verb* restrict or burden (someone or something) in such a way that free action or movement is difficult: *she was encumbered by her heavy skirt* ◊ *they had arrived encumbered with families*.

encumbrance *noun* **1** a burden or impediment: *she was happy to spend the weekend free of all the encumbrances of her job and family*. **2** a mortgage or other charge on property or assets: *the spouse will have to consent to the encumbrance of the land*.

encyclical • *noun* a papal letter addressed to bishops and all members of the Catholic Church. • *adjective* (of a letter) for wide circulation. [Say en SICK lick ul]

encyclopedia *noun* (*plural* **encyclopedias**) a book or set of books, usu. arranged alphabetically, giving information on many subjects or on many aspects of one subject. [Say en sike luh PEEDY uh]

encyclopedic *adjective* **1** of or resembling an encyclopedia, esp. in embracing all branches of learning. **2** (of knowledge etc.) comprehensive. [Say en sike luh PEED ick]

end • *noun* **1** the extreme limit or the point beyond which a thing does not continue. **2** death, destruction, downfall: *met an untimely end*. **3** an aim, goal, or purpose: *will do anything to achieve his ends*. **4** a piece left over. **5** (**the end**) *informal* the limit of endurability. **6** the part or share, esp. of an enterprise or activity, with which a person is concerned: *no problem at my end*. **7** one half or side of a rink, court, or playing field. **8** *Curling* one of the frames of a game during which each player on both teams delivers two rocks. **9** *Football* **a** the lineman positioned furthest from centre. **b** the position occupied by this player. • *verb* **1** bring or come to an end. **2** (foll. by *in*) lead to, have as a result or conclusion: *will end in tears*. **3** (foll. by *by* or *up*) do, achieve, or come eventually to, esp. some specified state: *ended up making a fortune*. ▣ PHRASES **at an end** exhausted or completed. **at the end of one's rope** (or **tether**) having reached the limits of one's patience, resources, abilities, etc. **come to a bad end** meet with ruin or disgrace. **end it** (**all**) *informal* commit suicide. **end of the road 1** the terminus of a road, path, etc. **2** the point at which a hope or endeavour has been abandoned. **end of the world 1** a calamitous matter or situation. **2** the cessation of life on earth. **end-on** with the end facing one, or with the end adjoining the end of the next object. **end to end 1** lengthwise, with the ends in contact. **2** from one end to another. **from end to end** from one end to the other or throughout the length of something. **in the end** finally, ultimately, in the long run. **keep one's end up** do one's part, hold one's own, or sustain one's part in an undertaking or performance, esp. despite difficulties. **make ends meet** live within one's income. **no end** *informal* to a great extent, very much. **no end of** *informal* much or many of: *no end of trouble*. **on end 1** in an upright position. **2** consecutively or continuously: *for three weeks on end*.

endanger *verb* **1** place in danger. **2** jeopardize the continuance of (a species etc.).

endangered species *noun* **1** a species of plant, animal, etc. in danger of extinction, esp. when formally designated as such by a government, environmental protection agency, etc. **2** a category of person, phenomenon, etc., which is in danger of disappearing.

endangerment *noun* **1** the act of exposing a person to risk, harm, or danger. **2** the condition of a plant or animal species in danger of extinction.

endear *verb* (usu. foll. by *to*) make dear to or beloved by.

endearing *adjective* inspiring love or affection: *an endearing smile*. ▶ **endearingly** *adverb*

endearment *noun* **1** an expression of love, affection, or fondness such as a pet name, caress, etc.: *they were whispering endearments to each other*. **2** fondness, affection: *"my dear" is a term of endearment*.

endeavour (also **endeavor**) • *verb* try earnestly: *I will endeavour to do my best*. • *noun* an attempt to do something, esp. something new or difficult: *please make every endeavour to arrive on time*. [Say en DEV ur]

endemic • *adjective* **1** (of a disease, condition, etc.) regularly found in a particular place or among a particular group of people and difficult to get rid of, esp. as a result of permanent local factors: *malaria is endemic in many hot countries* ◊ *complacency is endemic in industry today*. **2** (of a plant or animal) native and usu. restricted to a certain country or area: *species endemic to Madagascar*. • *noun* an endemic disease, plant, or animal. ▶ **endemically** *adverb* [Say en DEM ick]

ending *noun* **1** a termination, conclusion, or completion: *the ending of the cold war*. **2** an end or final part, esp. of a literary work, metrical line, or piece of music. **3** an inflected final part of a word. **4** the furthest part or point of something: *a nerve ending*.

endive *noun* **1** (also called **Belgian endive**) the crown of the chicory plant which has been whitened by blanching, used in salads. **2** a curly-leaved plant, *Cichorium endivia*, used in salads. [Say EN dive]

endless *adjective* **1** infinite, without end, eternal. **2** continual, incessant. **3** *informal* (of a number, quality, etc.) innumerable, unlimited: *drank endless cups of coffee*. **4** (of a belt, chain, etc.) made in the form of a loop, having the ends joined, for continuous action over wheels etc. ▶ **endlessly** *adverb* **endlessness** *noun*

end line *noun* **1** *Sport* a boundary line marking the end of the field, court, etc. **2** a line forming a conclusion.

endnote *noun* a note, similar to a footnote, printed at the end of a book, chapter, article, etc.

endocrine • *adjective* **1** (of a gland) secreting directly into the blood. **2** of or pertaining to such glands or their secretions. • *noun* an endocrine gland, e.g. the thyroid, adrenal, or pituitary gland. [Say ENDO crine]

endocrinologist *noun* a specialist in the structure and physiology of endocrine glands and hormones. [Say endo crin OLLA jist]

endocrinology *noun* the branch of medicine that deals with the structure and physiology of endocrine glands and hormones. [Say endo crin OLLA jee]

end of steel *noun* (also **end of the steel**) a terminus or the limit to which a railway (completed or under construction) extends.

endometrial *adjective* having to do with the mucous membrane lining the uterus: *endometrial cancer*. [Say endo MEE tree ul]

endometriosis *noun* a condition in which endometrial tissue grows in the pelvic cavity, resulting in pelvic pain and the formation of cysts. [Say endo mee tree OH sis]

endometrium *noun* (*plural* **endometria**) the mucous membrane lining the uterus. [Say endo MEE tree um]

endoplasm *noun* the inner, usu. granular, fluid of the cytoplasm of some cells, e.g. amoebae (*compare* ECTOPLASM). ▶ **endoplasmic** *adjective* [Say ENDO plasm]

endorphin *noun* any of a group of peptide neurotransmitters occurring naturally in the brain and having pain-relieving properties. [Say en DOR fin]

endorsation *noun* see ENDORSEMENT.

endorse *verb* (**endorses**, **endorsed**, **endorsing**) **1 a** declare one's approval of (a candidate etc.). **b** confirm (a statement or opinion). **2 a** sign on the

E

back of (a cheque) either as payee or to make (it) payable to someone other than the stated payee. **b** sign (a bill) to accept responsibility for paying it.

endorsement noun **1** (Cdn also **endorsation**) an act of giving one's public approval or support to someone or something: *the election victory is a clear endorsement of their policies*. **2** (also **product endorsement**) a recommendation of a product or service, esp. in exchange for remuneration, which can be cited in advertising material: *celebrity endorsement*. **3** something with which a document etc. is endorsed, esp. a signature or comment: *there is a spot for the endorsement on the back of the cheque*.

endoscope noun a flexible medical instrument, consisting of illuminated optical tubes, designed for viewing the internal cavities or hollow organs of the body. ▶ **endoscopic** adjective **endoscopy** noun (plural **endoscopies**) [Say ENDO scope, endo SKOP ick, en DOSS kuh pee]

endoskeleton noun an internal skeleton as found in vertebrates. [Say ENDO skeleton]

endosperm noun nutritive material surrounding the germ in some plant seeds. [Say ENDO sperm]

endothermic adjective **1** (of a chemical reaction or process) accompanied by or requiring the absorption of heat. **2** (of an animal) dependent on or capable of internal generation of heat. [Say endo THERMIC]

endotoxin noun a toxin in a bacterial cell which is released when the cell disintegrates. [Say ENDO toxin]

endow verb **1 a** bequeath or give a permanent income to (a person, institution, etc.). **b** establish (an academic chair, annual prize, etc.) by providing the funds needed to maintain it. **2** (usu. foll. by *with*) enrich or provide with (a quality, ability, talent, etc.). ▶ **endowed** adjective

endowment noun **1** the action of endowing someone or something: *raised a lot of money for the endowment of the university*. **2** assets, esp. property or income, with which a person or organization is endowed, esp. a fund the capital of which is never used but which generates interest to cover operating expenses: *the ballet's endowment is currently at $5 million*. **3** a quality or ability: *the island's rich natural endowments* ◊ *Sherry is not boastful about her many endowments*.

endpaper noun a usu. blank leaf of paper at the beginning and end of a book, fixed to the inside cover.

end product noun the final product, esp. of a manufacturing process, radioactive decay series, etc.

end run noun **1** Football an attempt by a player to run with the ball round the flank of his own team. **2** a tactic or manoeuvre used to achieve one's ends by indirect means, esp. to outwit someone else: *every broadcast bureaucrat is doing an end run around the CRTC and knocking on the federal communications minister's door*.

endurable adjective able to be tolerated or endured.

endurance noun **1** the fact, habit, or power of enduring something unpleasant: *beyond endurance*. **2 a** the ability of a person or thing to last, hold out, or withstand prolonged strain: *endurance test*. **b** the ability of a metal or other substance to withstand the repeated applications of stress.

endure verb (**endures, endured, enduring**) **1 a** (of a person) undergo (a difficulty, hardship, etc.), esp. without giving way. **b** (of a thing) withstand (strain, pressure, etc.) without being damaged, compromised, etc. **2 a** tolerate (a person): *cannot endure him*. **b** bear: *cannot endure to see her treated like that*. **3** remain in existence, last, persist. **4** submit to, experience without resisting. ▶ **enduring** adjective **enduringly** adverb

end-user noun **1** the person who is the intended ultimate recipient of user of a product. **2** Computing the

final destination of information transferred within a system, e.g. an operator, program, etc.

endways adverb (also **endwise**) **1** with its end uppermost, foremost, or towards the viewer. **2** end to end. **3** lengthwise.

end zone noun Football the rectangular area between the goal line and the end line, into which the ball must be carried or passed to score a touchdown.

ENE abbreviation east-northeast.

enema noun (plural **enemas**) **1** the injection of liquid or gas into the rectum or colon, esp. to expel the contents. **2** a fluid so injected. **3** a syringe or other appliance used for this purpose. [Say ENNA muh]

enemy noun (plural **enemies**) **1 a** a person or group actively nursing hatred for or seeking to harm another person, group, or cause. **b** (usu. foll. by *of*, *to*) an adversary or opponent. **2 a** an armed foe, esp. another nation. **b** the hostile army or military force of a nation opposing or at war with one's own. **c** a member of such a force. **d** a hostile ship, aircraft, etc. **3** a thing that harms, injures, or is prejudicial to another: *poverty and ignorance are the enemies of progress*. PHRASES **be one's own worst enemy** have the habit of bringing trouble upon oneself by one's own actions or behaviour.

energetic adjective showing or involving great activity or vitality. ▶ **energetically** adverb

energize verb (**energizes, energized, energizing**) **1** infuse energy or vigour into (a person, work, movement, etc.). **2** provide energy for the operation of (a device), esp. by means of an electrical current. ▶ **energized** adjective **energizer** noun

energy noun (plural **energies**) **1** a person's force, vigour, or capacity for and tendency to strenuous activity. **2** (in plural) individual powers in use: *devote your energies to this*. **3** Physics **a** the quantity of work a system is capable of doing, usu. measured in joules. **b** this ability provided in a readily utilized form, such as an electric current or piped gas. **c** resources that can be drawn on for this purpose.

enervate verb (**enervates, enervated, enervating**) cause someone to feel drained of energy or vitality: *the climb up the stairs had enervated him*. ▶ **enervating** adjective **enervation** noun [Say ENNER vate, enner VAY sh'n]

enfant terrible noun (plural **enfants terribles**) a person whose behaviour, ideas, etc. annoy, shock, or embarrass those with more conventional attitudes or opinions. [Say on fon tare EEB luh]

enfeeble verb (**enfeebles, enfeebled, enfeebling**) weaken, make feeble. ▶ **enfeebled** adjective

enfold verb **1** surround or cover completely: *he shut off the engine and silence enfolded them*. **2** hold or clasp someone lovingly in one's arms: *they greeted me like an old friend, enfolded me in warm embraces*.

enforce verb (**enforces, enforced, enforcing**) **1** compel performance or observance of (a law etc.). **2** cause something to happen by necessity or force: *you can't enforce co-operation between the players* ◊ *a period of enforced absence*. ▶ **enforceability** noun **enforceable** adjective **enforcement** noun

enforcer noun **1** a person, organization, etc. that enforces something. **2** Hockey a highly aggressive player whose fighting and intimidation skills serve to protect other players on his team. **3** slang a person who imposes his will on others by violence and intimidation, esp. as a member of a criminal group.

enfranchise verb (**enfranchises, enfranchised, enfranchising**) **1** grant (a person) the rights of a citizen, esp. the right to vote. **2** Cdn give up one's status as an Indian. ▶ **enfranchisement** noun

engage verb (**engages, engaged, engaging**)

1 arrange to employ or hire (a person). **2 a** attract and hold fast (a person's attention, interest, etc.). **b** draw (a person) into a conversation. **3** reserve for one's own use. **4 a** bring (a component) into operation: *engage the clutch*. **b** (usu. foll. by *with*) (of parts of a machine etc.) interlock or fit together to prevent or transmit movement. **c** cause (gears, cogs, etc.) to do this. **5 a** enter into combat with or attack (an enemy etc.). **b** bring (forces) into battle. **6** take part in or be occupied by (a thing).

engagé • *adjective* (of a writer, artist, etc.) showing social, moral, or political commitment. • *noun Cdn hist.* a boatman, originally usu. French-Canadian, hired by a trader, explorer, or fur company to work the inland trade. [Say ong ga ZHAY]

engaged *adjective* **1** under a promise to marry. **2** (of a person) occupied, busy. **3** concerned, committed, actively participating in issues etc.: *an engaged, professional historian.* **4** (of gears etc.) in operation. **5** (of a baby's head) descended into the mother's pelvic area in the final weeks of pregnancy.

engagement *noun* **1** the act or state of engaging or being engaged. **2** an appointment with another person. **3** a betrothal. **4** an encounter between hostile forces. **5** a moral commitment or obligation. **6** a period or position of employment, esp. for a set term. **7** the period during which a theatrical performance is being produced at a given location.

engaging *adjective* pleasing, attractive, charming. ▶ **engagingly** *adverb* **engagingness** *noun*

Engelmann spruce *noun* a spruce of the Rocky Mountains, *Picea engelmannii*. [Say ENG gull m'n]

engender *verb* give rise to; bring about (a feeling etc.): *the issue engendered controversy ◊ problems engendered by the restructuring of the company.* [Say en GENDER]

engine *noun* **1** a machine for producing energy of motion from some other form of energy, esp. heat that the machine itself generates. **2 a** a railway locomotive. **b** = FIRE ENGINE. **c** a stationary steam engine. **3** (foll. by *of*) a thing that achieves or causes a specified goal: *exports used to be the engine of growth*.

engine block *noun* the metal casting housing the cylinders etc. of an internal combustion engine.

engined *combining form* having the kind of engine described: *a twin-engined helicopter ◊ a rear-engined car*.

engineer • *noun* **1** a person qualified in any branch of engineering, esp. as a qualified professional. **2** = CIVIL ENGINEER. **3 a** a person who designs or makes engines. **b** a person who is in charge of or maintains an engine or other machine. **4** a person who drives an engine, esp. a railway locomotive. **5** a soldier in a division of an army that specializes in engineering and the design as well as construction of military works. • *verb* **1** arrange for something to happen or take place, esp. when this is done secretly in order to gain an advantage: *she engineered a further meeting with him.* **2** design, make: *the car is beautifully engineered and a pleasure to drive.* **3** deliberately alter or modify some specific aspect of a particular model, substance, etc., e.g. genes.

engineering *noun* **1** the application of science for directly useful purposes, as construction, propulsion, communication, or manufacture. **2** the work done by or the occupation of an engineer. **3** the action of working artfully to bring something about. **4** a field of study or activity concerned with deliberate alteration or modification in some particular area: *genetic engineering*.

English • *adjective* **1** of or relating to England, its language, its people, or their descendants. **2** *Cdn* of or relating to English-speaking Canadians. • *noun* **1** the language descended from that of the Germanic invaders of England in the 5th century and now used in many varieties in the British Isles, Canada and other Commonwealth countries, the US, and often internationally. **2 (the English) a** the people of England. **b** English-speaking people. **3** English language or literature as a subject of study.

English Canadian • *noun* **1** an English-speaking Canadian. **2** a Canadian of English descent. • *adjective* **(English-Canadian)** of, by, or pertaining to English Canada or English Canadians.

English cucumber *noun* a long, thin-skinned, seedless variety of cucumber.

English ivy *noun* an ivy with many varieties grown as houseplants and as climbers and ground cover.

Englishman *noun* (*plural* **Englishmen**) a man who is English by birth, descent, or naturalization.

English muffin *noun* a small, round, flat, yeast bread, usu. served split and toasted.

Englishwoman *noun* (*plural* **Englishwomen**) a woman who is English by birth, descent, or naturalization.

engorge *verb* (**engorges**, **engorged**, **engorging**) cause to swell with blood, water, or another fluid: *the veins in his neck were engorged.* ▶ **engorged** *adjective*

engrave *verb* (**engraves**, **engraved**, **engraving**) **1** cut words or designs on wood, stone, metal, etc.: *the silver cup was engraved with her name ◊ her name was engraved on the silver cup.* **2** cut or produce (a design) for printing by removing parts of the surface of a plate or block. **3** impress deeply or indelibly on a person's memory etc.: *the date of the accident remains engraved on my mind.* ▶ **engraved** *adjective* **engraver** *noun*

engraving *noun* **1** a print made from an engraved plate. **2** the process or art of cutting a design etc. on metal, stone, etc. **3** an engraved design or inscription.

engross *verb* (**engrosses**, **engrossed**, **engrossing**) absorb the whole attention of (a person): *as the business grew, it totally engrossed her.* ▶ **engrossing** *adjective*

engulf *verb* **1** surround or cover completely: *she was engulfed by a crowd of reporters ◊ the vehicle was engulfed in flames.* **2** swallow up: *Europe might be engulfed by war.* **3** affect strongly: *fear engulfed him.* ▶ **engulfment** *noun*

enhance *verb* (**enhances**, **enhanced**, **enhancing**) **1 a** increase or further improve the good quality, value or status of: *this is an opportunity to enhance the reputation of the company ◊ the skilled use of makeup to enhance your best features.* **b** exaggerate or make (a colour etc.) appear greater or brighter, esp. by contrast. **2 a** improve (a thing), esp. in quality or usefulness. **b** add on to or provide (a computer etc.) with more advanced or sophisticated features. ▶ **enhancement** *noun* **enhancer** *noun*

enigma *noun* a puzzling, perplexing, or unexplained person or thing: *even after years of living together he still remains an enigma to me.* [Say en NIGMA]

enigmatic *adjective* mysterious and difficult to understand: *an enigmatic smile.* ▶ **enigmatically** *adverb* [Say en ig MAT ick]

enjoin *verb* **1** order or strongly advise someone to do something; say that a particular action or quality is necessary: *enjoined by his lawyers to drop his lawsuit altogether.* **2** *Law* prohibit or restrain (a person) by an injunction: *the father had been enjoined from entering the marital home based on the wife's allegations of physical abuse.*

enjoy *verb* **1** take delight or pleasure in. **2** have the use or benefit of (something pleasant or advantageous). **3** experience: *enjoy good health.* **4** have an enjoyable experience. ▪ PHRASES **enjoy oneself** experience

pleasure. ▶ **enjoyable** *adjective* **enjoyableness** *noun* **enjoyably** *adverb* **enjoyment** *noun*

enlarge *verb* (**enlarges, enlarged, enlarging**) **1 a** make or become larger or wider. **b** make more comprehensive or increase in range or scope. **2 a** describe in greater detail. **b** (usu. foll. by *upon*) write or speak at great length or in detail. **3** produce an enlargement of (a photograph). ▶ **enlarged** *adjective*

enlargement *noun* **1** the process or result of something becoming or being made larger: *the enlargement of the company's overseas business activities.* **2** *Photography* a print that is larger than the negative from which it is produced.

enlarger *noun* an apparatus for producing photographic enlargements.

enlighten *verb* **1** give someone greater knowledge and understanding about a subject or situation: *she didn't enlighten him about her background.* **2** give spiritual knowledge or insight to (a person). ▶ **enlightening** *adjective*

enlightened *adjective* having or showing an understanding of people's needs, a situation, etc. that is not based on old-fashioned attitudes and prejudice: *enlightened opinions ◊ an enlightened approach to teaching ◊ even without being altruistic, intelligent people often act out of enlightened self-interest; for instance, an employer who improves working conditions may improve profits.*

enlightenment *noun* **1** knowledge about and understanding of something; the process of understanding something or making someone understand it: *the papers provided little enlightenment about the cause of the accident ◊ cultural enlightenment.* **2** (**the Enlightenment**) the 18th-century philosophical movement in Europe in which reason and individualism were emphasized at the expense of tradition. **3** *Buddhism* a state of pure and unqualified knowledge and intuitive insight.

enlist *verb* **1** enrol in the armed forces. **2** engage or secure (a person etc.) as a means of help or support: *enlisted the help of the public in solving the crime.* ▶ **enlistment** *noun*

enliven *verb* **1** make something more interesting or more fun; liven up: *the wartime routine was enlivened by a series of concerts.* **2** make someone more cheerful or animated: *he is used to backing unpopular causes, and the unpopularity of the UN enlivens rather than dispirits him.* ▶ **enlivening** *adjective* [Say en LIE v'n]

en masse *adverb* all together or as a group. [Say on MASS]

enmesh *verb* (**enmeshes, enmeshed, enmeshing**) **1** catch or entangle in a net. **2** involve in an esp. undesirable situation that it is not easy to escape from: *West Germany became enmeshed in the unexpectedly expensive and troublesome unification with East Germany.*

enmity *noun* (*plural* **enmities**) feelings of hatred or opposition towards someone: *enmity between ethnic groups ◊ personal enmities and political conflicts ◊ her action earned her the enmity of her colleagues.* [Say ENMA tee]

ennoble *verb* (**ennobles, ennobled, ennobling**) **1** lend greater dignity or nobility of character to: *she seemed ennobled by her grief.* **2** give the rank of noble to (a person). ▶ **ennoblement** *noun* **ennobling** *adjective* [Say en NOBLE]

ennui *noun* boredom or mental weariness from lack of occupation or interest: *the older player needs a young player to excite him and motivate him through his late-career ennui.* [Say on WEE]

enormity *noun* (*plural* **enormities**) **1** monstrous wickedness: *recognized the enormity of his crime.* **2** an act of extreme wickedness: *the enormities of the Hitler regime.* **3** the large size or scale of something: *was not daunted*

by the enormity of the task ◊ *people are still coming to terms with the enormity of the disaster.* [Say en NORMA tee]

enormous *adjective* excessive in size or intensity. ▶ **enormously** *adverb* **enormousness** *noun*

enough • *adjective* as much or as many as required: *enough sugar ◊ enough money to buy a house.* • *noun* as much as is needed. • *adverb* **1** sufficiently: *are you warm enough?* **2** passably: *she sings well enough.* **3** very: *oddly enough.* • *interjection* that is enough. PHRASES **enough is enough** stop, no more. **enough said** no more need be said. **have enough to do** (**to achieve something**) have no easy task. **have had enough** be satiated with, tired of, or want no more of.

enquire *verb* = INQUIRE.

enquiry *verb* = INQUIRY. [Say en QUIRE ee]

enrage *verb* (**enrages, enraged, enraging**) make furious or very angry. ▶ **enraged** *adjective*

enrapture *verb* (**enraptures, enraptured, enrapturing**) give someone great pleasure or joy: *the audience will be enraptured by this moving family saga.*

enrich *verb* (**enriches, enriched, enriching**) **1 a** make wealthy or wealthier: *top party members had enriched themselves.* **b** endow with mental or spiritual wealth: *science has enriched all our lives.* **2 a** enhance, heighten or make (a thing) richer in quality, colour, flavour, etc. **b** fertilize or make (soil or land) more productive. **c** improve the nutritive quality of (food) by adding vitamins etc. **3** add something valuable or worthwhile to the contents of (a collection, book, etc.). **4** make (a course or program of study) more challenging, esp. by adding coursework etc. which is not part of the standard curriculum. **5** increase the proportion of a particular constituent in (a substance), esp. enrich uranium with isotope U-235. ▶ **enriched** *adjective* **enriching** *adjective* **enrichment** *noun*

enrol *verb* (also **enroll**) (**enrols** or **enrolls, enrolled, enrolling**) **1 a** enter one's name on a list, esp. as a commitment to membership of a society, class, etc. **b** join, esp. as a member, student, etc. **2 a** write the name of (a person) on a list for membership etc. **b** (usu. foll. by *in*) incorporate (a person) as a member of a society etc.

enrollee *noun* a person who has officially joined or enrolled in a course, school, etc. [Say en roll EE]

enrolment *noun* (also **enrollment**) **1** the action of enrolling or being enrolled: *enrolment is the first week in September ◊ school enrolments have been dropping.* **2** the number of persons enrolled: *what is the current enrolment at the University of Ottawa?*

en route *adverb* on or along the way: *we stopped for a picnic en route ◊ the bus broke down en route from Boston to Halifax.* [Say on ROOT]

ensconce *verb* (**ensconces, ensconced, ensconcing**) establish or settle comfortably or safely: *comfortably ensconced in a red leather armchair ◊ once she was ensconced as leader, she found it was sometimes difficult to get men to do what she wanted.* [Say en SCONCE]

ensemble *noun* **1 a** a thing viewed as the sum of its parts. **b** the general effect of this. **2** an outfit or a set of clothes that harmonizes and is worn together. **3** a group of actors, dancers, musicians, etc. who perform together in a production, esp. the supporting members as opposed to the stars or principals. **4** *Music* **a** a group of singers or musicians, esp. a small group of soloists, who perform together. **b** a piece of music sung or played by the whole group of musicians rather than by soloists. **c** the manner in which this is performed: *good ensemble.* [Say on SOM bull]

enshrine *verb* (**enshrines, enshrined, enshrining**) **1** integrate (a right, principle, etc.) into a law, constitution, etc. so as to preserve it perpetually: *these*

rights are enshrined in the country's constitution. **2** contain in a way that preserves or cherishes: *an old locomotive is enshrined at the museum.* ▶ **enshrinement** *noun*

ensign *noun* **1** a military or naval standard, esp. a flag flown at the stern of a vessel to show its nationality. **2** each of three such standards with the union flag in the corner (*see also* RED ENSIGN). **3** the lowest rank of commissioned officer in the US navy and coast guard. [Say EN sign or EN sin]

enslave *verb* (**enslaves, enslaved, enslaving**) **1** make (a person) completely subject to or dominated by habit, superstition, passion, etc. **2** reduce (a person) to slavery or deprive (a person) of political freedom. ▶ **enslavement** *noun*

ensnare *verb* (**ensnares, ensnared, ensnaring**) entrap, entangle in difficulties, or catch in or as in a snare.

ensue *verb* (**ensues, ensued, ensuing**) happen afterwards or as a result: *an argument ensued.* ▶ **ensuing** *adjective* [Say en SUE]

ensuite *Cdn & Brit.* • *adverb* forming a single unit, with one room leading into another. • *adjective* (of a room) adjoining or forming part of the same set. • *noun* an ensuite room, esp. a bathroom. [Say on SWEET]

ensure *verb* (**ensures, ensured, ensuring**) **1** make certain the occurrence of (an event, situation, outcome, etc.). **2** secure (a thing for a person etc.). **3** (usu. foll. by *against*) make safe from a risk etc.

ENT *abbreviation Medical* ear, nose, and throat.

entail *verb* **1** necessitate as a consequence, have as an inevitable accompaniment, or involve unavoidably: *entails much effort.* **2** *Law* bequeath (property etc.) so that it remains within a family. ▶ **entailment** *noun*

entangle *verb* (**entangles, entangled, entangling**) **1** cause to get caught in something that is tangled or that impedes movement or extrication. **2** interlace or cause to become tangled so that separation is difficult. **3 a** involve (a person) in difficulties, doubtful undertakings, etc. **b** involve (a person) in a compromising relationship etc. **4** make (a thing) tangled, complicated, or intricate.

entanglement *noun* **1** the act or condition of entangling or being entangled. **2 a** a thing that entangles. **b** a complication or embarrassment. **3** a compromising, esp. amorous, relationship.

entente *noun* **1** = ENTENTE CORDIALE. **2** a group of nations in such a relation. **3** an agreement to co-operate between esp. opposing parties. [Say on TONT]

entente cordiale *noun* (*plural* **ententes cordiales**) a friendly understanding or informal alliance between nations. [Say on tont cordy AL]

enter • *verb* **1** go or come in. **2** penetrate. **3 a** write or record (particulars) in a list, register, account book, etc. **b** input (data) into a computer or issue (a command) to a computer program. **4** register as a competitor. **5** enrol as or become a member of (a society, school, etc.). **6** introduce, make known, or present (a matter etc.) for consideration: *entered a protest.* **7** put into an official record, esp. record in due form in a court of law, deliberative body, etc. **8** (foll. by *into*) **a** engage in (conversation, relations, an undertaking, etc.). **b** subscribe to or bind oneself by (an agreement etc.). **c** form part of (one's calculations, plans, etc.). **9** (foll. by *on, upon*) **a** begin, undertake, or begin to deal with (a subject). **b** assume the functions of (an office). • *noun* the key on a computer keyboard or button on a computer window which when pressed or clicked instructs the computer to execute a command or enters a blank line into a text.

enterprise *noun* **1** an undertaking, esp. a bold or difficult one: *the music festival is a new enterprise which we*

hope will become an annual event. **2** (as a personal attribute) readiness to engage in such undertakings: *discouraged individual enterprise.* **3** a business; an activity undertaken for money: *state-owned enterprises.* **4** businesses collectively: *grants to encourage enterprise in the region.* ▶ **enterpriser** *noun*

enterprising *adjective* **1** ready to engage in enterprises: *one enterprising farmer opened up his field as a parking lot and charged people $10 to park there.* **2** imaginative, energetic: *many enterprising residents took matters into their own hands and "liberated" quantities of useful goods for themselves.* ▶ **enterprisingly** *adverb*

entertain *verb* **1** amuse; occupy agreeably. **2 a** receive or treat as a guest. **b** receive guests: *they entertain a great deal.* **3** give attention or consideration to (an idea, feeling, or proposal).

entertainer *noun* a person who entertains, esp. professionally on stage etc.

entertaining *adjective* amusing. ▶ **entertainingly** *adverb*

entertainment *noun* **1** the action of providing or being provided with amusement or enjoyment: *everyone just sits in front of the box for entertainment.* **2** a public performance or show: *a theatrical entertainment.* **3** amusement: *much to my entertainment.* **4** the action of receiving a guest or guests and providing them with food and drink: *my entertainment budget doesn't stretch to fancy restaurants.*

enthrall *verb* (**enthralls, enthralled, enthralling**) captivate: *the child watched, enthralled by the bright moving images* ◊ *this book will enthrall readers of all ages.* ▶ **enthralling** *adjective* [Say en THRAWL]

enthrone *verb* (**enthrones, enthroned, enthroning**) (usu. in *passive*) install (a king, bishop, etc.) on a throne, esp. ceremonially. ▶ **enthronement** *noun*

enthuse *verb* (**enthuses, enthused, enthusing**) *informal* **1** be or make enthusiastic. **2** (often foll. by *about*) speak enthusiastically.

enthusiasm *noun* **1** strong interest or admiration. **2** great eagerness. ▶ **enthusiast** *noun* **enthusiastic** *adjective* **enthusiastically** *adverb*

entice *verb* (**entices, enticed, enticing**) attract by the offer of pleasure or reward: *the prices are expected to entice customers away from other stores* ◊ *try and entice the child to eat.* ▶ **enticement** *noun* **enticing** *adjective* **enticingly** *adverb* [Say en TICE]

entire *adjective* **1** whole, complete. **2** not broken or decayed. **3** unqualified, absolute: *an entire success.* **4** in one piece; continuous.

entirely *adverb* **1** wholly: *their input is entirely absent from the final report.* **2** solely: *entirely for my benefit.*

entirety *noun* (*plural* **entireties**) (usu. foll. by *of*) the sum total. PHRASES **in its entirety** in its complete form; completely. [Say en TIRE tee or en TIE ruh tee]

entitle *verb* (**entitles, entitled, entitling**) **1** to give somebody the right to have or to do something: *you will be entitled to your pension when you reach 65* ◊ *everyone's entitled to their own opinion* ◊ *this ticket does not entitle you to travel first class.* **2** give (a book etc.) the title of.

entitlement *noun* **1** something to which a person is entitled, esp. a social benefit: *demanding the same rights and entitlements enjoyed by citizens.* **2** the fact of being entitled or qualified: *threatened our entitlement to benefits.*

entity *noun* (*plural* **entities**) a thing with distinct existence, as opposed to a quality or relation: *she had a gift for bringing an audience into focus so that they became one single entity.* [Say ENTA tee]

entomb *verb* place in or as in a tomb: *pharaohs entombed in the pyramids of Egypt* ◊ *as many as 1 000 people were dead, entombed in collapsed buildings.* ▶ **entombment** *noun*

entomological *adjective* having to do with the study of insects. [Say enta muh LOGICAL]

entomologist *noun* a scientist who studies insects. [Say enta MOLLA jist]

> **WRITING TIP**
> **entomology, etymology**
>
> The study of word histories is **etymology**.

entomology *noun* the study of the forms and behaviour of insects. [Say enta MOLLA jee]

entourage *noun* people attending an esp. important person: *the prime minister and members of his immediate entourage* ◊ *an entourage of adoring fans.* [Say onta RAWZH]

entrails *plural noun* **1** the internal bodily organs, esp. the intestines. **2** the innermost parts: *sorting through the entrails of the affair.* [Say EN trails]

entrance¹ *noun* **1** the act of entering a room, building, or place, esp. in a way that attracts attention: *John's sudden entrance took everyone by surprise.* **2 a** a door, passage, etc., by which one enters. **b** a point of entering something: *the entrance to the harbour.* **3** the right or privilege of admission (also as an *adjective*: *university entrance exam*). **4** the moment, or point in the script, when an actor, dancer, etc. comes on stage.

entrance² *verb* (**entrances**, **entranced**, **entrancing**) fill someone with wonder and delight, holding their entire attention: *I was entranced by a cluster of trees which lit up by glow-worms.* ▶ **entrancing** *adjective* **entrancingly** *adverb* [Say en TRANCE]

entrant *noun* **1** a person who enters a competition; a candidate in an examination etc. **2** a person who enters a school, profession, etc. or becomes a member of an organization etc. **3** a company, product, etc. which enters a new market, field, etc. [Say EN trint]

entrap *verb* (**entraps**, **entrapped**, **entrapping**) **1** catch in or as in a trap. **2** beguile or trick (a person).

entrapment *noun* **1** the act of entrapping; the process of being entrapped: *the spider's prey is forever improving ways to avoid entrapment.* **2** the act of tricking someone into committing a crime so that they can be arrested for it.

entreat *verb* ask earnestly: *she entreated him not to go.*

entreaty *noun* (*plural* **entreaties**) an earnest request: *despite her entreaties, he left.*

entree *noun* **1** the main dish of a meal. **2** the right or privilege of admission, esp. to an exclusive group: *sees European trade fairs as a useful entree into new markets.* [Say ON tray]

entrench *verb* (**entrenches**, **entrenched**, **entrenching**) **1** to establish something very firmly so that it is very difficult to change: *consumerism is deeply entrenched in our society* ◊ *this idea had firmly entrenched itself in his consciousness.* **2** establish (a military force) in trenches or other fortified positions. **3** safeguard (rights etc.) by constitutional provision: *freedom of speech is entrenched in Canada's Charter of Rights and Freedoms.* PHRASES **entrench oneself** adopt a well-defended position.

entrenched *adjective* (of an attitude etc.) not easily modified: *a deeply entrenched male-female power relationship.*

entrenchment *noun* **1** the state of being firmly established: *the growing entrenchment of Marxist academics.* **2** the process of applying extra legal safeguards to a right by constitutional provision: *the entrenchment of individual rights in the Charter of Rights and Freedoms.* **3** a system of trenches.

entrepreneur *noun* a person who starts or organizes a commercial business, esp. one involving financial risk. ▶ **entrepreneurial** *adjective* **entrepreneurialism**

noun (also **entrepreneurism**). **entrepreneurship** *noun* [Say ontra pruh NUR, ontra pruh NURRY ul]

entropic *adjective* characterized by randomness, unpredictability, or a gradual decline into disorder: *the entropic tendencies of the marketplace.* [Say en TROPIC]

entropy *noun* **1** *Physics* a thermodynamic quantity representing the unavailability of a system's thermal energy for conversion into mechanical work, often interpreted as the degree of disorder or randomness in the universe. Symbol: **S**. **2** lack of order or predictability; gradual decline into disorder: *entropy reigns in the marketplace.* **3** a measure of the rate of transfer of information in a message etc. [Say ENTRA pee]

entrust *verb* make someone responsible for doing something or taking care of someone: *she entrusted the task to her nephew* ◊ *she entrusted her nephew with the task* ◊ *the rebuilding of London's churches was entrusted to the brilliant young architect, Christopher Wren.*

entry *noun* (*plural* **entries**) **1** an act of coming or going in: *the door was locked, but they forced an entry.* **2** a place of entrance; a door, gate, etc. **3 a** the right, means, or opportunity to enter a place or be a member of something: *refugees seeking entry to the country.* **b** the action of undertaking something or becoming a member of something: *Newfoundland's entry into Confederation.* **4** an actor's entrance on stage. **5** an item entered in a diary, list, account book, etc. **6 a** a word, phrase, abbreviation, etc. entered in a dictionary, encyclopedia, etc. **b** this and its accompanying definition or explanation. **7** a person or thing competing in a race, contest, etc.: *from the thousands of entries we received, four winners were selected.* **8** the start or resumption of a performer's part in a musical composition. **9** the act of entering (data etc.) into a file, database, etc.: *data entry.*

entry-level *adjective* **1** (of employment) suitable for inexperienced applicants. **2** relatively unsophisticated and low in cost: *entry-level computers.*

entwine *verb* (**entwines**, **entwined**, **entwining**) **1** to twist or wind something around something else: *they strolled along with arms entwined* ◊ *the balcony was entwined with roses.* **2** to be very closely involved or connected with something: *their lives are entwined.*

enumerate *verb* (**enumerates**, **enumerated**, **enumerating**) **1** specify (items); mention one by one: *let me enumerate the benefits for you.* **2** *Cdn* **a** enter (a person's name) on a list of voters for an election: *Aboriginal voters would be enumerated in the national enumeration.* **b** prepare the voters list for an area, usu. by conducting a house-to-house survey: *I wasn't home when they enumerated my neighbourhood.* **3** count; establish the number of. ▶ **enumeration** *noun* [Say in NEW mur ate, in new mur AY sh'n, in NEW mur a tiv]

enumerator *noun* **1** a person who enumerates. **2** a person employed in census taking. **3** *Cdn* a person employed to conduct a survey to register voters. [Say in NEW mur ate ur]

enunciate *verb* (**enunciates**, **enunciated**, **enunciating**) **1** pronounce (words) clearly. **2** to express an idea clearly and in definite terms: *she enunciated their vision of the future.* ▶ **enunciation** *noun* [Say in NUN see ate, in nun see AY sh'n]

envelop *verb* (**envelops**, **enveloped**, **enveloping**) wrap someone or something up or cover them or it completely: *she was enveloped in a huge white towel* ◊ *clouds enveloped the mountain tops* ◊ *darkness fell and enveloped the town* ◊ *a feeling of despair enveloped him.* [Say en VELL up]

envelope *noun* **1** a folded paper container, usu. with a sealable flap, for a letter etc. **2** the structure within a balloon or airship containing the gas. **3** *Botany* any

enveloping structure esp. the calyx or corolla (or both). **PHRASES** **push** (or **push the edge of**) **the envelope** go to the greatest length that an activity allows. [Say ENVA lope or ONVA lope]

enviable *adjective* (of a person or thing) exciting or likely to excite envy. ▶ **enviably** *adverb* [Say ENVY a bull]

envious *adjective* (often foll. by *of*) feeling or showing envy. ▶ **enviously** *adverb* [Say ENVY us]

environment *noun* **1** the physical surroundings, conditions, etc., in which a person lives, works, etc.: *a smoke-free work environment.* **2** the area surrounding a place. **3 a** external conditions as affecting plant and animal life. **b** (usu. **the environment**) the totality of the physical conditions on the earth or a part of it, esp. as affected by human activity. **4** *Computing* the overall structure within which a user, computer, or program operates. **5** a large artistic creation intended to be experienced with several senses while one is surrounded by it. ▶ **environmental** *adjective*

environmentalism *noun* **1** concern with or advocacy of the protection of the environment. **2** a belief that environment has the primary influence on the development of a person or group.

environmentalist *noun* a person who is concerned with or advocates the protection of the environment.

environmentally *adverb* in terms of the environment: *environmentally responsible homeowners ◊ environmentally harmful waste.*

environmentally friendly *adjective* (also **environment-friendly**) not harmful to the environment.

environs *plural noun* a surrounding district, esp. around an urban area: *the easiest way to see old Yarmouth and its environs is by bike.* [Say en VIRE enz]

envisage *verb* (**envisages**, **envisaged**, **envisaging**) **1** have a mental picture of a thing or conditions not yet existing: *she envisages more co-operation between schools and social service agencies in the months ahead.* **2** contemplate or conceive: *they envisage society as a group of risk-sharing citizens.* [Say en VIZ idge]

envision *verb* envisage, visualize. [Say en VISION]

envoy *noun* a messenger or representative, esp. on a diplomatic mission. [Say ON voy or EN voy]

envy • *noun* (*plural* **envies**) **1** a feeling of discontented or resentful longing aroused by another's better fortune etc. **2** the object or ground of this feeling: *their house is the envy of the neighbourhood.* • *verb* (**envies**, **envied**, **envying**) feel envy of.

enzymatic *adjective* **1** having to do with enzymes. **2** using or requiring enzymes to act as a catalyst in a biochemical process, such as digestion. [Say enza MAT ick]

enzyme *noun* a protein produced by living cells and functioning as a catalyst in a specific biochemical reaction. [Say EN zime]

Eocene • *adjective* of or denoting the second epoch of the Tertiary period, between the Paleocene and the Oligocene, lasting from about 54.9 to 38 million years BP. It was a time of rising temperatures, and there was an abundance of mammals, including the first horses, bats, and whales. • *noun* this epoch. [Say EE oh seen]

eon *noun* **1** a very long or indefinite period: *eons ago, when I was still in high school.* **2** *Astronomy* a billion years. **3** the largest division of geological time, composed of two or more eras. [Say EE on]

EP *abbreviation* extended play, allowing six hours of material to be recorded on a standard video tape.

eparch *noun* the chief bishop of an eparchy. [Say EPP ark]

eparchy *noun* (*plural* **eparchies**) a diocese in an Eastern-Rite church. [Say EPP arr key]

epaulette *noun* (also **epaulet**) a decoration on the shoulder of a coat etc., esp. on a uniform. [Say eppa LET]

épée *noun* *Fencing* a sharp-pointed duelling sword, often used with the end blunted. [Say ay PAY]

ephedra *noun* (*plural* **ephedras**) an evergreen shrub with trailing stems and scale-like leaves. [Say ef FEDRA]

ephedrine *noun* an alkaloid drug found in some ephedras, causing constriction of the blood vessels and widening of the bronchial passages, used to relieve asthma, hayfever, colds, etc. [Say EFFA drin]

ephemera *plural noun* things that are important or used for only a short period of time: *a collection of postcards, tickets and other ephemera.* [Say FEM er uh]

ephemeral *adjective* lasting or of use for only a short time; transitory: *Diefenbaker's national charisma proved ephemeral, and he was out of power in five years.* [Say ef FEM er ul or ef FEEM er ul]

epic • *noun* **1** a long poem narrating the adventures or deeds of heroic or legendary figures or the past history of a nation. **2** a long film, book, or other work portraying heroic deeds and adventures or covering an extended period of time: *a Hollywood biblical epic.* • *adjective* **1** having the features of an epic: *an epic poem.* **2** grand or heroic in scale or character: *his epic journey around the world ◊ a tragedy of epic proportions.* ▶ **epically** *adverb*

epicentre *noun* **1** the point at which an earthquake reaches the earth's surface. **2** the centre or heart of something: *Los Angeles was the epicentre of popular culture in the '80s.* [Say EPPA centre]

epicure *noun* a person with refined tastes, esp. in food and drink: *they fancy themselves as epicures in avoiding no-name brands.* [Say EPPA cure]

epicurean • *noun* **1** = EPICURE. **2** (**Epicurean**) a disciple or student of the Greek philosopher Epicurus (341–270 BC), who held pleasure, esp. mental pleasure and freedom from anxiety, to be the highest good. • *adjective* **1** characteristic of an epicure. **2** (**Epicurean**) of or concerning Epicurus or his ideas. ▶ **Epicureanism** *noun* [Say eppa CURE ee un]

epidemic • *noun* **1** a widespread occurrence of a disease in a community at a particular time. **2** a wide prevalence of something usu. undesirable: *an epidemic of fear, blame, and denial.* • *adjective* of, relating to, or of the nature of an epidemic; widespread (*compare* ENDEMIC): *typhus was raging in epidemic proportions at the front ◊ college alcohol abuse is epidemic.*

epidemiologic *adjective* = EPIDEMIOLOGICAL.

epidemiological *adjective* having to do with the incidence, distribution, and possible control of diseases and other factors relating to health. ▶ **epidemiologically** *adverb* [Say eppa deemy a LOGIC]

epidemiologist *noun* a person who studies the incidence, distribution, and possible control of diseases and other factors relating to health. [Say eppa deemy OLLA jist]

epidemiology *noun* the branch of medicine that deals with the incidence, distribution, and possible control of diseases and other factors relating to health. [Say eppa deemy OLLA jee]

epidermal *adjective* having to do with the outer layer of cells covering an organism, such as the outer layer of an animal's skin or the outer layer of tissue in a plant. [Say eppa DERMAL]

epidermis *noun* **1** the outer cellular layer of the skin. **2** *Botany* the outer layer of cells of leaves, stems, roots, etc. [Say eppa DERMIS]

epidural • *adjective* **1** on or around the tough outermost membrane enveloping the brain and spinal cord. **2** (of an anaesthetic) introduced into the space around this membrane of the spinal cord. • *noun* an

E

epidural anaesthetic, used esp. in childbirth to produce loss of sensation below the waist. [Say eppa DUR ul]

epiglottis noun (plural **epiglottises**) a flap of cartilage at the root of the tongue, which is depressed during swallowing to cover the windpipe. [Say eppa GLOTTIS]

epigram noun **1** a short witty poem. **2 a** a saying or maxim, esp. a proverbial one: *the epigram that it is impossible to fool all the people all the time is only marginally consoling.* **b** a pointed remark or expression, esp. a witty one. ►**epigrammatic** adjective [Say EPPA gram, eppa gruh MAT ick]

epigraph noun **1** a quotation at the beginning of a chapter, book, etc. **2** an inscription on a statue, building, tomb, coin, etc. [Say EPPA graph]

epilepsy noun a condition in which a person has attacks of disordered brain function, usu. causing loss of awareness or consciousness and sometimes convulsions. [Say EPPA lep see]

epileptic • adjective of or relating to epilepsy. • noun a person with epilepsy. [Say eppa LEP tick]

epilogue noun **1** the concluding part of a literary work. **2** a speech or short poem addressed to the audience by an actor at the end of a play. [Say EPPA log]

epinephrine noun = ADRENALIN. [Say eppa NEFF rin]

epiphany noun (plural **epiphanies**) **1 (Epiphany)** a Christian festival observed on Jan. 6 or the following Sunday, in the Orthodox Church commemorating the baptism of Jesus and in the Western Church the manifestation of Jesus to the three wise men. **2** a manifestation of a god or demigod. **3** a sudden and important manifestation or realization: *Why did they change their minds? What caused the epiphany?* [Say ep PIFFA nee]

epiphyte noun a plant growing but not parasitic on another, e.g. a moss. ►**epiphytic** adjective [Say EPPA fite, eppa FIT ick]

episcopacy noun (plural **episcopacies**) **1** government of a Church by bishops. **2** = EPISCOPATE. [Say ep PISKA puh see]

episcopal adjective **1** of a bishop or bishops. **2** (of a Church) constituted on the principle of government by bishops. **3 (Episcopal)** of or relating to the Episcopal Church. [Say ep PISKA pull]

Episcopal Church noun the Anglican Church in the US and Scotland.

episcopalian • adjective **1** of or advocating government of a Church by bishops. **2** of or belonging to an episcopal Church or **(Episcopalian)** the Episcopal Church. • noun **(Episcopalian)** a member of the Episcopal Church. ►**episcopalianism** noun [Say ep piska PAILY un]

episcopate noun **1** the office or tenure of a bishop. **2 (the episcopate)** the bishops collectively. [Say ep PISKA pit]

episiotomy noun (plural **episiotomies**) a surgical cut made at the opening of the vagina during childbirth, to aid delivery. [Say ep peezy OTTA me or ep pizzy OTTA me]

episode noun **1** one event or a group of events as part of a sequence. **2** each of the parts of a serial story or broadcast. **3** an incident or set of incidents in a narrative. **4** an incident that is distinct but contributes to a whole: *a romantic episode in her life.*

episodic adjective **1** containing or consisting of a series of separate parts or events: *an episodic narrative.* **2** occurring at irregular intervals: *episodic storm surges in the Beaufort Sea are a hazard to coastal structures.* **3** (of a novel etc.) made up of unconnected episodes: *the film is an episodic account of the effect of the war on a small community.* ►**episodically** adverb [Say eppa SOD ick]

epistemological adjective having to do with the

theory of knowledge, esp. with regard to its methods and validation. [Say ep pista muh LOGICAL]

epistemology noun the theory of knowledge, esp. with regard to its methods and validation. Epistemology is the investigation of what distinguishes justified belief from opinion. [Say ep pista MOLLA jee]

epistle noun **1** formal or jocular a letter, esp. a long one on a serious subject. **2 (Epistle) a** any of the letters of the apostles in the New Testament. **b** an extract from an Epistle read in a church service. [Say ep PISSLE]

epitaph noun words written in memory of a person who has died, esp. as a tomb inscription. [Say EPPA taff]

epithelial adjective having to do with the thin tissue forming the outer layer of a body's surface and lining many hollow structures. [Say eppa THEELY ul]

epithelium noun (plural **epitheliums** or **epithelia**) the thin tissue forming the outer layer of a body's surface and lining many hollow structures. [Say eppa THEELY um]

epithet noun **1** a descriptive word expressing a quality or attribute, esp. used with or as a name: *the campaign against alcoholism earned the city the epithet "Toronto the Good".* **2** such a word as a term of abuse: *racial epithets were scrawled on the walls.* [Say EP ith et]

epitome noun a perfect example of something: *the room is the epitome of Swiss luxury.* [Say ep PITTA me]

epitomize verb (**epitomizes**, **epitomized**, **epitomizing**) to be a perfect example of something: *the fighting qualities of the team are epitomized by the captain* ◊ *these movies seem to epitomize the 1950s.* [Say ep PITTA mize]

epoch noun **1** a period of time in history, especially one during which important events or changes happen: *the emperor's death marked the end of an epoch in the country's history.* **2** a division of geological time that is a subdivision of a period and is itself subdivided into ages: *the Pliocene epoch.* **3** Astronomy the point in time at which a particular phenomenon takes place, esp. an arbitrarily fixed date relative to which planetary or stellar measurements are expressed. ►**epochal** adjective [Say EP ock or EE pock]

eponymous adjective **1** (of a person, character, etc.) giving their name to something they are a part of: *the dog was a collie, just like the eponymous heroine of Lassie.* **2** (of a thing) named after a particular person: *she opened her eponymous restaurant, Chez Charmaine, last winter.* **3** (of a word) derived from the name of a person: *"cardigan" is an eponymous word named after the 7th Earl of Cardigan.*

epoxide noun a compound containing an oxygen atom bonded in a triangular arrangement to two carbon atoms. [Say ep OXIDE]

epoxy • adjective relating to or derived from an epoxide, esp. designating epoxy resins and the substances made from them. • noun (plural **epoxies**) (also **epoxy resin**) a synthetic resin which sets permanently when heated, containing epoxy groups or a substance made from them and used as a coating, adhesive, etc. • verb (**epoxies**, **epoxied**, **epoxying**) secure with epoxy glue etc. [Say ep POXY]

Epsom salts noun (as singular or plural) a preparation of hydrated magnesium sulphate used medicinally as an anti-inflammatory, purgative, etc.

equable adjective **1** not easily disturbed or angered: *an equable temperament* ◊ *he was in a remarkably equable mood when he spoke to reporters last night.* **2** (of motion, temperature, etc.) uniform, moderate, free from fluctuation or variation: *an equable climate.* ►**equably** adverb [Say EKWA bull]

equal • adjective **1** (often foll. by to, with) **a** identical in amount, size, value, intensity, etc. **b** on the same level in rank, power, excellence, etc. **2** evenly

proportioned or balanced: *an equal contest*. **3** having the same rights or status: *human beings are essentially equal*. **4** applicable to all in the same way: *equal rights*. • *noun* a person or thing equal to another, esp. in rank, status, or characteristic quality. • *verb* (**equals, equalled, equalling**) **1** be equal to in number, quality, etc. **2** match, rival, or achieve something that is equal to (an achievement) or to the achievement of (a person). PHRASES **be equal to** have the ability or resources for.

equality *noun* (*plural* **equalities**) **1** the condition of being equal in quantity, magnitude, etc. **2** the condition of having equal rank, power, excellence, etc. with others. **3** *Math* an equation or symbolic expression of the fact that two quantities are equal.

equality rights *plural noun Cdn Politics* the rights guaranteed in section 15 of the Canadian Charter of Rights and Freedoms to equal treatment for all before and under the law regardless of race, national or ethnic origin, colour, religion, sex, age, or disability.

equalization *noun* the act or an instance of equalizing: *the equalization of pay rates by gender*.

equalization payment *noun* (also **equalization grant**) *Cdn* an unconditional transfer by the federal government of funds from general revenues to a poorer province to ensure that all provinces provide comparable levels of service and taxation.

equalize *verb* (**equalizes, equalized, equalizing**) **1** make things equal in size, quantity, value, etc. in the whole of a place or group: *a policy to equalize the distribution of resources throughout the country* ◊ *we need to equalize the workload among the teaching staff*. **2** score a goal or point that ties a match: *Owen equalized early in the second half*. **3** *Electricity* **a** correct or modify (a signal) with an equalizer. **b** compensate for (an imbalance) by means of an equalizer.

equalizer *noun* **1** a thing that makes inequalities equal. **2** *Electricity* a network designed to modify a frequency response, esp. so as to compensate for distortion. **3** a goal etc. that ties the score in a game. **4** *slang* a weapon, esp. a gun.

GRAMMAR CHECK
equally   ⚠

The phrase **equally as** is redundant and should not be used to make a comparison, as in I *enjoy books, but I find movies equally as interesting*. It is correct to say either I *enjoy books, but I find movies equally interesting* or I *find movies as interesting as books*.

---

equally *adverb* **1** in an equal manner: *treated them all equally*. **2** to an equal degree: *is equally important*. **3** in equal shares or amounts.

equal opportunity *noun* **1** the opportunity or right to be considered for employment or promotion without discrimination on the grounds of race, gender, disability, etc. **2** the practice or policy of not discriminating in this way (often as an *adjective*: *an equal opportunity employer*).

equal pay *noun* the policy of giving the same rate of pay for a particular job, similar work, or work of equal value, regardless of the gender of the person doing it.

equal sign *noun* (also **equals sign**) the symbol =, used to indicate mathematical or other equality.

equanimity *noun* mental composure, evenness of temper, esp. in misfortune: *the losers accepted the judge's decision with equanimity*. [Say ekwa NIMMA tee]

equate *verb* (**equates, equated, equating**) **1** think that something is the same as something else or is as important: *some parents equate education with exam success* ◊ *I don't see how you can equate the two things*. **2** be equal or

equivalent to: *a $5 000 raise equates to 25%*. **3** esp. *Math* state the equality of (a thing) with or to another.

equation *noun* **1** the act of making something equal or considering something as equal: *the equation of wealth with happiness can be dangerous*. **2 a** a statement that two mathematical expressions are equal (indicated by the sign =). **b** the relationship between factors to be taken into account when considering a matter: *there are a host of other environmental variables, such as soil conditions, annual rainfall, temperature, that have to be put into the equation*. **3** a formula indicating a chemical reaction by means of the symbols for the elements or compounds involved in it.

equator *noun* **1 a** an imaginary line around the earth or other body, equidistant from the poles and marking the division between the northern and southern hemispheres. **b** the irregular line, passing around the earth near the geographical equator, on which the earth's magnetic field is horizontal. **2** *Astronomy* = CELESTIAL EQUATOR. **3** a circle on any spherical body that divides it into two equal parts, esp. one equidistant from the two poles of rotation.

equatorial *adjective* **1 a** of an equator, esp. that of the earth. **b** situated on, occurring near, or being characteristic of the earth's equator or equatorial regions. **2** (of the orbit of a satellite) lying in the plane of the equator. [Say ekwa TORY ul or eekwa TORY ul]

equestrian • *adjective* **1 a** of or relating to horses and horseback riding. **b** (of a person etc.) skilled in horseback riding. **2** (of a portrait or statue) representing a person on horseback. • *noun* a person who is skilled at horseback riding. [Say i KWESTRY in]

equidistant *adjective* separated by an equal distance or equal distances: *the farm was equidistant from Montreal and Toronto*. [Say ekwa DISTANT or EEKWA distant]

equilateral *adjective* having all its sides equal in length: *an equilateral triangle*. [Say ekwa LATERAL or EEKWA lateral]

equilibrium *noun* (*plural* **equilibria** or **equilibriums**) **1** a state of balance, especially between opposing forces or influences: *the delicate equilibrium between energy entering the atmosphere and energy leaving it is upset* ◊ *a state of equilibrium between French and English influences*. **2** a state of mental or emotional calm: *he sat down to try and recover his equilibrium*. **3** *Economics* a situation in which supply and demand are matched and prices stable. [Say eekwa LIB ree um or ekwa LIB ree um for the singular, eekwa LIB ree uh or ekwa LIB ree uh for the plural]

equine *adjective* of, like, or affecting a horse or horses. [Say ECK wine or EEK wine]

equinox *noun* (*plural* **equinoxes**) either of the two occasions in the year, the vernal equinox in spring and the autumnal equinox in the fall, when the sun crosses the celestial equator and day and night are of equal length everywhere. [Say EKWA nox or EEKWA nox]

equip *verb* (**equips, equipped, equipping**) **1** supply, fit out, or provide with what is needed. **2** (usu. in *passive*) provide with the mental, emotional, or physical abilities or resources needed for a task etc.

equipment *noun* **1** tools, articles, clothing, etc. used or required for a particular purpose. **2** intellectual or physical resources. **3** the process of equipping or being equipped.

equitable *adjective* characterized by fairness or equity: *an equitable distribution of resources*. ▶ **equitably** *adverb* [Say EKWA tuh bull]

equity *noun* (*plural* **equities**) **1** fairness, impartiality, even-handedness. **2** a system of natural justice allowing a fair judgement in a situation where the existing laws are not satisfactory. **3 a** (also **equity capital**) the value of a company's shares. **b** (**equities**)

E

shares in a company which pay relatively low, profit-related dividends rather than fixed interest. **4** the value of a property after all charges and debts have been paid. **5 (Equity)** (also **Actors' Equity Association**) a union for actors, dancers, and other performers. [Say EKWA tee]

equivalence *noun* the fact or condition of being equal in value, amount, meaning, importance, etc.: *there is no straightforward equivalence between economic progress and social well-being*.

equivalency *noun* (*plural* **equivalencies**) = EQUIVALENCE.

equivalent • *adjective* equal in value, amount, meaning, importance, etc.: *eight kilometres is roughly equivalent to five miles ◊ 250 grams or an equivalent amount in ounces ◊ the new regulation was seen as equivalent to censorship*. ▶ **equivalently** *adverb*

equivocal *adjective* **1** (of words etc.) vague or capable of more than one interpretation: *she gave an equivocal answer, typical of a politician*. **2** (of evidence, signs, etc.) of uncertain significance: *the experiments produced equivocal results*. **3** (of a person) vague: *men tended to be more equivocal in answering that question*. ▶ **equivocally** *adverb* [Say i KWIV uh cull]

equivocate *verb* (**equivocates, equivocated, equivocating**) use ambiguous language so as to conceal the truth or avoid committing oneself: *when pressed for clear answers, she merely equivocated*. ▶ **equivocation** *noun* [Say i KWIVVA kate]

ER *noun* (*plural* **ERs**) EMERGENCY ROOM (*see* EMERGENCY 4).

Er *symbol* erbium.

er *interjection* expressing the inarticulate sound made by a speaker who hesitates or is uncertain what to say.

-er¹ *suffix* forming nouns from nouns, adjectives, and many verbs, denoting: **1 a** a person involved with or in something, esp. as an occupation or profession: *teacher*. **b** an animal or thing that does a specified action or activity: *computer ◊ eye-opener*. **2 a** a person who or thing which has or is, esp. a specified attribute, form, or nature: *foreigner ◊ four-wheeler*. **b** a thing suitable for a specified function: *broiler*. **3 a** person or thing belonging to or connected with: *airliner ◊ old-timer ◊ whaler*. **4** a person belonging to, originating from, or resident in a specified place or group: *Newfoundlander*.

-er² *suffix* forming the comparative of adjectives: *wider ◊ hotter* and adverbs: *faster*.

ERA *abbreviation* **1** (also **era**) *Baseball* EARNED RUN AVERAGE. **2** *US* Equal Rights Amendment, a proposed constitutional amendment prohibiting discrimination on the basis of gender.

era *noun* **1** a period of years numbered from a particular, noteworthy event: *the Christian era*. **2 a** a usu. lengthy period of history characterized by a particular state of affairs, series of events, etc.: *the pre-Roman era*. **b** a date or period to which an event, item, etc. is assigned. **3** a major division of geological time that is a subdivision of an eon and is itself subdivided into periods: *the Mesozoic era*.

eradicate *verb* (**eradicates, eradicated, eradicating**) **1** get rid of, remove or destroy completely: *the government attempted to eradicate all opposition*. **2** uproot, root out, or pull out by the roots. ▶ **eradication** *noun* [Say i RADDA kate, i radda KAY sh'n]

erasable *adjective* that can be erased: *data is stored temporarily on an erasable optical disk*.

erase *verb* (**erases, erased, erasing**) **1** rub out or obliterate (something written, typed, drawn, etc.). **2** remove all traces of, esp. from one's memory or mind. **3** remove recorded material from (a magnetic tape or medium).

eraser *noun* a thing that erases, esp. a piece of rubber or plastic used for removing pencil and ink marks.

erasure *noun* **1** an act or instance of erasing: *the accidental erasure of all data on your hard drive*. **2** a word etc. that has been erased; a place or mark left by this: *the essay was full of erasures*. [Say i RAY shur]

erbium *noun* a soft, silvery metallic element occurring naturally and used in special alloys. [Say URBY um]

ere *preposition* & *conjunction* *literary* or *archaic* before (of time): *ere noon ◊ ere they come*. [Sounds like *AIR*]

erect • *adjective* **1 a** upright, vertical, not bending or stooping. **b** (of an optical image) having the same orientation as the subject, not inverted. **2** (of the penis, clitoris, or nipples) enlarged and firm, esp. in sexual excitement. **3 a** (of hair) bristling, standing up from the skin. **b** (of an animal's tail or ears) standing out stiffly from the body. • *verb* **1** raise or set in an upright position. **2** build, construct, set up. **3** create, establish, devise, or form: *to erect trade barriers*.

erectile *adjective* **1** that can be erected or become erect. **2** (of tissue or an organ) able to become erect when suitably stimulated. [Say i RECK tile]

erection *noun* **1** the action of erecting a structure or monument: *the erection of barricades at strategic places*. **2** an enlarged and rigid state of the penis, typically in sexual excitement.

ergonomic *adjective* **1** having to do with the study of the relationship between people and their working environment, esp. as it affects efficiency and safety. **2** designed to improve people's working conditions and to help them work more efficiently: *the new chairs feature an ergonomic design that is better for the back*. ▶ **ergonomically** *adverb* [Say urga NOM ick]

ergonomics *noun* (treated as *singular* or *plural*) the field of study that deals with the relationship between people and their working environment, esp. as it affects efficiency and safety. [Say urga NOM icks]

Erie *noun* (*plural* **Erie** or **Eries**) **1** a member of an Aboriginal people that lived along the south shore of Lake Erie, but were dispersed after 1650 and absorbed into the Iroquois. **2** their Algonquian language.

ermine *noun* (*plural* **ermine** or **ermines**) **1** a weasel that has brown fur in the summer turning mainly white in the winter, with the tail remaining black-tipped. **2** the white fur of an ermine used in clothing, often with the black tails displayed for the sake of effect. [Say UR min]

erode *verb* (**erodes, eroded, eroding**) **1** wear away (esp. soil or rock), destroy or be destroyed gradually: *the cliff face has been steadily eroded by the sea ◊ the rocks have eroded away over time*. **2** make or become gradually diminished in value etc.: *her confidence has been slowly eroded by repeated failures*. ▶ **eroded** *adjective*

erogenous *adjective* (esp. of a part of the body) sensitive to sexual stimulation: *erogenous zone*. [Say i RODGE uh nus]

eros *noun* romantic or sexual love or desire: *a story full of heartache and eros*. [Say AIR oss or EAR ose (with OSE as in *DOSE*)]

erosion *noun* **1** the wearing away of the earth's surface by wind, water, or glacial action: *soil erosion*. **2** the gradual destruction or diminution of something: *the erosion of support for the party*.

erosional *adjective* caused by or resulting from erosion: *erosional cliffs*.

erotic *adjective* of, relating to, or tending to arouse sexual desire or excitement. [Say i ROT ick]

erotica *noun* intentionally erotic literature or art. [Say i ROT ick uh]

erotically *adverb* in an erotic or sexually arousing manner. [Say i ROT ick lee]

eroticism noun **1** erotic nature or character. **2** the use of or response to erotic images or stimulation. [Say i ROTTA sism]

eroticize verb make erotic or endow with an erotic quality: *adolescents are being conditioned to eroticize violence when they watch mainstream Hollywood videos.* ► **eroticized** adjective [Say i ROTTA size]

err verb **1** be mistaken or incorrect: *past forecasts have often erred seriously.* **2** do wrong: *if you find that your puppy has erred in your absence, it's best to overlook the transgression and clean it up.* PHRASES **err on the side of** show too much rather than risk showing too little of a specified quality: *errs on the side of generosity.* [Sounds like *AIR*]

errand noun a short trip, often on another's behalf, to buy or deliver something, take a message, etc. PHRASES **errand of mercy** a journey to give help, relieve suffering etc.

errant adjective **1 a** erring, doing wrong, deviating from an accepted standard: *measures to discipline errant members of the community.* **b** erratic or breaking with the dominant pattern, movement, etc.: *soaked by an errant wave.* **2** *literary* or *archaic* travelling in search of adventure: *knight errant.* [Say AIR int]

errata plural noun (*singular* **erratum**) errors in a printed text, noted and corrected in a list. [Say i RATTA for the plural, i RAT um for the singular]

erratic • adjective **1** inconsistently variable in conduct, movement, etc.; unpredictable: *she had learned to live with his sudden changes of mood and erratic behaviour* ◊ *Mary is a gifted but erratic player.* **2** (of a boulder etc.) differing from surrounding rock and believed to have been brought from a distance by glacial action. • noun a large block of rock carried by a glacier and deposited some distance from where it was formed. ► **erratically** adverb [Say i RAT ick]

erroneous adjective incorrect: *numerous inflammatory statements and erroneous statistics.* ► **erroneously** adverb [Say i RONEY us]

error noun **1** a mistake. **2** the condition of being wrong in conduct or judgment: *led into error.* **3** a wrong opinion or judgment. **4** the amount by which something is incorrect or inaccurate in a calculation or measurement. **5** *Baseball* a fielder's misplay, such as a fumble or wild throw, allowing a batter to reach base, a runner to advance, etc. ► **errorless** adjective

ersatz adjective imitation (esp. of inferior quality): *sports cars parked in front of that ersatz Toronto castle, Casa Loma.* [Say AIR zats or UR zats]

erstwhile adjective former, previous: *what will reconcile us with our erstwhile friends?* [Say URST while]

erudite adjective having or showing great knowledge that is gained from academic study: *she could turn any conversation into an erudite discussion.* ► **eruditely** adverb **erudition** noun [Say AIR oo dite or AIR you dite, air oo DISH in or air you DISH in]

erupt verb **1** break out or burst forth suddenly or dramatically: *a number of colonies erupted in violence.* **2** (of a volcano) become active and eject lava etc. **3 a** (of a rash, boil, etc.) appear on the skin. **b** (of the skin) produce a rash, pimples, etc. **4** (of the teeth) break through the gums in normal development. ► **eruption** noun

erythrocyte noun one of the principal cells in the blood of vertebrates, containing the pigment hemoglobin and transporting oxygen and carbon dioxide to and from the tissues. [Say i RITH roe site]

erythromycin noun an antibiotic similar in its effects to penicillin. [Say i rith roe MICE in]

Es symbol einsteinium.

Esc abbreviation *Computing* escape (key).

escalate verb (**escalates, escalated, escalating**) to become or make something greater, worse, more serious, etc.: *the fighting escalated into a full-scale war* ◊ *the costs of health care are escalating.* ► **escalating** adjective

escalation noun

escalator noun a moving staircase consisting of an endless chain of steps on a circulating belt.

escapade noun a daring, reckless, or adventurous act. [Say ESKA paid]

escape • verb (**escapes, escaped, escaping**) **1** break free or free oneself by fleeing or struggling. **2** (of a gas, liquid, etc.) leak or seep out from a container or pipe etc. **3** get off safely or succeed in avoiding danger, punishment, etc. **4** avoid or elude (a commitment, danger, etc.). **5** elude the notice or memory of: *nothing escapes you.* **6** (of words etc.) be uttered inadvertently by. • noun **1** an act of escaping or avoiding danger, injury, etc.: *made their escape from prison* ◊ *no hope of escape from her disastrous marriage.* **2** (often as an adjective) a possibility or means of escaping: *escape route.* **3** a leakage of gas etc. **4** a temporary relief from reality or worry: *romantic novels provided an escape from their humdrum existence.* **5** (also **escape key**) *Computing* a key which either ends the current operation or changes the function of other keys pressed subsequently.

escapee noun a person, esp. a prisoner, who has escaped. [Say i SCAPE ee or ess kay PEE]

escaper noun a person who escapes.

escapism noun the tendency to seek distraction and relief from reality, esp. in the arts or through fantasy: *the pure escapism of adventure movies.* ► **escapist** noun & adjective

escargot noun (*plural* **escargots** pronunc. same) a snail as an item of food. [Say es car GO]

escarpment noun a long, steep-sided ridge, esp. one at the edge of a plateau or separating areas of land at different heights.

Escherichia coli noun (also ***E. coli***) a species of bacillus which normally inhabits the large intestine and, under certain conditions, can cause disease, esp. when transferred to other sites such as the urinary tract. [Say esha ricky uh CO lie]

eschew verb *literary* carefully or deliberately avoid, abstain from, or shun: *he had eschewed politics in favour of a life practising law.* [Say es CHEW]

escort • noun **1** one or more persons, vehicles, ships, etc. accompanying another, esp. for protection, security, or as a mark of rank or status. **2** a person accompanying a person of the opposite sex socially. **3 a** a usu. young, attractive person legitimately employed to provide another with entertainment etc. **b** *euphemism* a prostitute. • verb accompany for protection, guidance, courtesy, etc.

ESE abbreviation east-southeast.

esker noun a long, narrow ridge, usu. of sand and gravel, deposited in a river valley by a stream flowing under a former glacier or ice sheet.

WRITING TIP
Eskimo

The word *Eskimo* is no longer used for the Aboriginal people inhabiting northern Canada or their language. The people are now referred to as *Inuit* and their language is *Inuktitut.*

Eskimo • noun (*plural* same or **Eskimos**) **1** (in former use) a member of an Aboriginal people inhabiting northern Canada, Alaska, Greenland, and eastern Siberia. **2** the language of this people. • adjective of or relating to the Eskimos or their language.

E

ESL *abbreviation* English as a second language.

esophagus *noun* (*plural* **esophagi** or **esophaguses**) the part of the alimentary canal from the mouth to the stomach. [Say i SOFFA gus for the singular, i SOFFA jie for the plural]

esoteric *adjective* intended only for, or intelligible only to, the initiated or those with special knowledge: *he tries to impress people with his esoteric tastes.* [Say esso TARE ick or ee so TARE ick]

ESP *abbreviation* extrasensory perception.

especially *adverb* **1** chiefly, pre-eminently. **2** particularly or much more than in other cases.

Esperanto *noun* an artificial language invented in 1887 and based on roots common to the chief European languages with endings standardized. [Say espa RAN toe]

espionage *noun* the practice of spying or of using spies. [Say ESS pee a nozh]

esplanade *noun* a level, open space along a waterfront, where people may walk or drive. [Say espla NADE or ESPLA nod]

espousal *noun* (foll. by *of*) the action or an act of adopting or supporting a cause: *his espousal of utopian socialism.* [Say es POW zull]

espouse *verb* (**espouses, espoused, espousing**) adopt or support (a cause etc.): *they espoused the notion of equal opportunity for all in education.* [Say es POWZ]

espresso *noun* (*plural* **espressos**) strong, concentrated, black coffee made by forcing steam through ground coffee beans. [Say es PRESSO]

esprit de corps *noun* loyalty and devotion to, as well as regard for the honour and interests of, a group to which one belongs: *the ministry had been permeated from top to bottom with an esprit de corps, a desire to contribute to Canada's stature in the world.* [Say es pree duh CORE]

Esquimalt *noun* (*plural* **Esquimalt** or **Esquimalts**) a member of a Salishan Aboriginal group living near Esquimalt, BC. [Say esk WYE malt]

WRITING TIP
-ess

Gender-neutral words like *actor*, *heir*, *server*, and *flight attendant* are often preferred to "female" words ending in **-ess** (*actress*, *heiress*, *waitress*, *stewardess*), which, though still common, are often seen as old-fashioned and patronizing. Some nouns using **-ess** are still acceptable, however (*abbess*, *goddess*, and *princess*, for instance).

-ess *suffix* forming nouns denoting females: *actress*.

essay • *noun* **1 a** a written composition, usu. short and in prose, on any subject. **b** a short, coherent composition in any medium: *photo essay.* **2** *formal* an attempt: *his first essay in politics was a complete disaster.* • *verb* *formal* attempt, try: *the first time the artist has essayed the use of colour on this scale.* [Say ESS ay for the noun, ess SAY for the verb]

essayist *noun* a person who writes essays to be published. [Say ESS ay ist]

essence *noun* **1 a** the indispensable quality or element identifying a thing or determining its character. **b** the intrinsic nature or quality of something. **2 a** an extract of a plant, drug, etc. usu. obtained by distillation and containing all the source's important qualities in concentrated form. **b** a perfume or scent, esp. as an alcoholic solution of volatile substances. PHRASES **in essence** fundamentally, essentially. **of the essence** very important.

essential • *adjective* **1** absolutely necessary; indispensable. **2** fundamental, basic: *essential principles*. **3** (of an amino acid or a fatty acid) required by a living organism for normal growth, but not produced by the

organism and therefore required in the diet. • *noun* (esp. in *plural*) a basic or indispensable element or thing.

essential element *noun* any of various chemical elements, such as calcium, magnesium, etc., required by living organisms for normal growth.

essentially *adverb* considering only the most basic or important aspects of a person or thing: *the two plans differ slightly but are essentially the same* ◊ *the article focuses essentially on Stella Duane's career before the accident.*

essential oil *noun* an oil taken from a plant, used in perfume and in aromatherapy.

EST *abbreviation* **1** Eastern Standard Time. **2** electroshock treatment.

-est *suffix* forming the superlative of adjectives: *nicest* ◊ *happiest* and adverbs: *soonest*.

establish *verb* (**establishes, established, establishing**) **1** found or consolidate (a business, system, etc.) on a permanent basis. **2** (foll. by *in*) settle (a person or oneself) in some capacity: *we are now established in our new house.* **3** (esp. as **established** *adjective*) achieve permanent acceptance for (a custom, belief, practice, institution, etc.). **4 a** validate; place beyond dispute (a fact etc.). **b** find out; ascertain. **5** (of a person) gain recognition and acceptance: *established herself as an expert.* **6** bring about; achieve: *establish contact.* **7** enact; decree in law. **8** (in a novel, film, etc.) make a (character, setting, etc.) plausible and convincing: *the first soliloquy establishes him as an evil character.* ▶ **established** *adjective*

established church *noun* a religious denomination recognized by a national government as its nation's official church.

establishment *noun* **1** the action of establishing something or being established: *the establishment of a Palestinian state.* **2 a** a business, public institution, or household: *hotels or catering establishments.* **b** the premises or staff of such an organization: *she entered this establishment as our housemaid.* **3 a** (also **Establishment**) the group in a society exercising authority or influence, and seen as resisting change. **b** any influential or controlling group: *rumblings of discontent among the medical establishment.*

estate *noun* **1** a property consisting of an extensive area of land usu. with a large house. **2** *Law* all of a person's assets and liabilities, esp. at death. **3** a property where grapes, rubber, tea, etc., are cultivated. **4** (also **estate of the realm**) esp. *hist.* an order or class forming (or regarded as) a part of the body politic, consisting of the first estate (the clergy), the second estate (the aristocracy), and the third estate (the commons).

esteem • *verb* **1** (usu. in *passive*) have a high regard for; greatly respect: *his work was esteemed by artists attending the auction.* **2** *formal* consider, deem: *esteemed it an honour.* • *noun* high regard; respect. ▶ **esteemed** *adjective*

ester *noun* any of a class of organic compounds produced by replacing the hydrogen of an acid by an alkyl, etc. group, many of which occur naturally as oils and fats.

esthete etc. = AESTHETE etc. [Say ess THEET]

estimable *adjective* worthy of esteem: *people of estimable skill and pride.* [Say ESS timma bull]

estimate • *noun* **1** a judgment or calculation of the approximate cost, value, size, etc. of something. **2** an appraisal of the character or qualities of a person or thing. **3** a price specified as that likely to be charged for work to be undertaken. • *verb* (**estimates, estimated, estimating**) **1** form an approximate idea of or rough calculation of (a number, size, etc.). **2** fix (a price etc.) by estimate. ▶ **estimated** *adjective*

estimation *noun* **1** the process or result of estimating. **2** judgment or opinion of worth: *in my estimation*.

estimator *noun* a person who calculates the approximate cost, value, size, etc. of something.

Estonian • *noun* **1 a** a native of Estonia, a country in the Baltics. **b** a person of Estonian descent. **2** the language of Estonia, related to Hungarian and Finnish. • *adjective* of or relating to Estonia or its people or language. [Say ess TONY un]

estranged *adjective* **1** (of a person) no longer close, on friendly terms, or in communication with someone: *Harriet felt more estranged from her daughter than ever* ◊ *estranged brothers*. **2** (of a husband or wife) no longer living with his or her spouse.

estrangement *noun* a period or state in which one is no longer close, on friendly terms, or in communication with someone: *it may be difficult for couples to become reconciled after estrangement* ◊ *Henry felt a growing sense of estrangement from his community*.

estrogen *noun* **1** any of various steroid hormones developing and maintaining female characteristics of the body. **2** this produced artificially for use in oral contraceptives etc. [Say ESTRA jen]

estuarine *adjective* having to do with the mouth of a large river, where the tide flows in. [Say ESS choo a rine]

estuary *noun* (*plural* **estuaries**) the tidal mouth of a large river, where the tide flows in. [Say ESS choo airy]

ET *abbreviation* **1** EASTERN TIME. **2** extraterrestrial.

ETA *abbreviation* estimated time of arrival.

et al. *abbreviation* and others.

etc. *abbreviation* = ET CETERA.

et cetera *adverb* **1 a** and the rest; and similar things or people. **b** or similar things or people. **2** and so on. [Say et SETTER uh]

etch *verb* (**etches, etched, etching**) **1 a** engrave (metal, glass, or stone) by coating it with a protective layer, drawing on this with a needle, and then covering with acid or other corrosive that attacks the parts the needle has exposed. **b** engrave (a plate) in this way in order to print from it. **2** engrave by any method: *we looked at the outline that Dave had etched with an awl in the hard clay*. **3** (foll. by *on, upon*) impress deeply (esp. on the mind): *the image is etched indelibly in my memory*.

etching *noun* **1** a print made from an etched plate. **2** the art of producing these plates.

eternal *adjective* **1** without an end or beginning in time. **2** essentially unchanging: *eternal truths*. **3** *informal* seeming not to cease: *your eternal nagging*. PHRASES **the Eternal** God. ▶ **eternally** *adverb*

eternity *noun* (*plural* **eternities**) **1** infinite or unending (esp. future) time. **2** *Theology* the condition into which the soul enters at death; the afterlife. **3** the quality, condition, or fact of being eternal. **4** (often preceded by *an*) a very long time.

ethane *noun* a colourless odourless gaseous hydrocarbon of the alkane series, occurring in natural gas. [Say ETH ane or EETH ane]

ethanol *noun* *Chemistry* = ALCOHOL 1. [Say ETHA nawl]

ether *noun* **1 a** a colourless volatile organic liquid used as an anaesthetic or solvent. **b** any of a class of organic compounds with a similar structure to this, having an oxygen joined to two alkyl etc. groups. **2** *hist.* a medium formerly assumed to permeate space and fill the gaps between particles of matter. [Say EETH ur]

ethereal *adjective* extremely delicate and light; seeming to belong to another, more spiritual, world: *ethereal music* ◊ *her ethereal beauty* ◊ *in a translucent sky, the domes and spires of the city looked almost ethereal*. ▶ **ethereally** *adverb* [Say i THEERY ul, i theery ALA tee]

ethic • *noun* a set of moral principles, esp. those of a specified religion, school of thought, etc.: *the Puritan ethic*. • *adjective* = ETHICAL.

ethical *adjective* **1** connected with beliefs and principles about what is right and wrong: *ethical issues*. **2** morally correct; honourable: *while it's not illegal, what they do certainly isn't ethical*. ▶ **ethically** *adverb*

ethicist *noun* a person who studies ethics and makes recommendations about ethical dilemmas. [Say ETHA sist]

ethics *plural noun* **1** (usu. treated as *singular*) the science of morals in human conduct. **2** (treated as *plural*) moral principles; rules of conduct: *medical ethics*. **3** (treated as *plural*) moral correctness: *Canadians began to take the ethics of their coaches and athletes for granted*.

Ethiopian • *noun* **1** a native or national of Ethiopia, a country in NE Africa. **2** a person of Ethiopian descent. • *adjective* **1** of or relating to Ethiopia. **2** of or designating a biogeographical region comprising Africa south of the Sahara. [Say eethy OPE ee un]

ethnic • *adjective* **1** (of a population group) sharing a distinctive cultural and historical tradition, often associated with race, nationality, or religion. **2** relating to race or culture: *ethnic group*. **3** (of clothes, music, etc.) characteristic of or influenced by the traditions of a particular people or culture, esp. a minority within another culture or one regarded as exotic. **4** denoting origin by birth or descent rather than nationality: *ethnic Turks living in Germany*. • *noun* a member of an (esp. minority) ethnic group. ▶ **ethnically** *adverb* (*plural* **ethnicities**)

ethnic cleansing *noun* *euphemism* the mass expulsion or extermination of people from opposing ethnic or religious groups within a certain area.

ethnicity *noun* (*plural* **ethnicities**) the fact or state of belonging to a social group that has a common national or cultural tradition: *we welcome all candidates regardless of age, gender, or ethnicity* ◊ *the diverse experience of women of different ethnicities*. [Say eth NISSA tee]

ethnic minority *noun* (*plural* **ethnic minorities**) a (usu. identifiable) group different from the main population of a community by race or cultural background.

ethnobotany *noun* **1** the traditional knowledge of a people concerning plants and their uses. **2** the study of such knowledge. [Say ethno BOTANY]

ethnocentric *adjective* evaluating other peoples and cultures (esp. negatively) according to the assumptions or preconceptions of one's own people or culture: *a white, ethnocentric school curriculum*. ▶ **ethnocentricity** *noun*

ethnocentrism *noun* [Say ethno SEN trick, ethno sen TRISSA tee]

ethnocultural *adjective* pertaining to or having ethnic groups: *Montreal's ethnocultural pluralism will continue to survive*. [Say ethno CULTURAL]

ethnographer *noun* a person who studies different peoples and cultures. [Say eth NOGGRA fur]

ethnographic *adjective* having to do with the scientific description of peoples and cultures with their customs, habits, and mutual differences. ▶ **ethnographically** *adverb* [Say ethno GRAPHIC]

ethnography *noun* the scientific description of peoples and cultures with their customs, habits, and mutual differences. [Say eth NOGGRA fee]

ethnohistorical *adjective* having to do with the history of races and cultures, esp. non-Western ones.

ethnohistory *noun* the study of the history of races and cultures, esp. non-Western ones.

ethnological *adjective* having to do with the study of the characteristics of different peoples and the differences and relationships between them.

ethnologist *noun* a person who studies the

characteristics of different peoples and the differences and relationships between them. [Say eth NOLLA jist]

ethnology *noun* the branch of knowledge that deals with the characteristics of different peoples and the differences and relationships between them. [Say eth NOLLA jee]

ethological *adjective* having to do with the study of human or animal behaviour. [Say eetho LOGICAL]

ethologist *noun* a person who studies human or animal behaviour. [Say eeth OLLA jist]

ethology *noun* **1** the science of animal behaviour. **2** the science of character formation in human behaviour. [Say eeth OLLA jee]

ethos *noun* the characteristic spirit or attitudes of a community, people, or system, or of a literary work etc.: *the ethos of consumerism ran directly counter to Victorian respectability.* [Say EETH oss]

ethyl *noun* the monovalent radical derived from ethane by removal of a hydrogen atom. [Say ETHEL]

ethylene *noun* a gaseous hydrocarbon occurring in natural gas and crude oil, and used in the manufacture of polyethylene. [Say ETHA leen]

ethylene glycol *noun* a colourless viscous liquid used as an antifreeze and in the manufacture of polyesters.

etiological *adjective* **1** having to do with the scientific study of the causes of disease. **2** based on or having to do with an investigation or explanation of the cause or reason for something: *an etiological tale of how the elephant got its trunk.* [Say eaty oh LOGICAL]

etiology *noun* the scientific study of the causes of disease. [Say eaty OLLA jee]

etiquette *noun* **1** the conventional rules of social or official behaviour. **2 a** the customary behaviour of members of a profession, sports team, etc. towards each other. **b** the unwritten code governing this: *medical etiquette.* [Say ETTA kit]

Etruscan • *adjective* of ancient Etruria in W Italy, esp. its pre-Roman civilization. • *noun* **1** a native of Etruria. **2** the language of Etruria. [Say i TRUSS kin]

-ette *suffix* forming nouns meaning: **1** small: *kitchenette.* **2** imitation or substitute: *leatherette.* **3** female: *usherette* ◊ *majorette.*

etymological *adjective* having to do with the study of the origin of words and how their meanings have changed throughout history. ▶ **etymologically** *adverb* [Say etta muh LOGICAL]

etymology *noun* (*plural* **etymologies**) **1** the study of the origin of words and how their meanings have changed throughout history. **2** the origin of a word and the historical development of its meaning. [Say etta MOLLA jee]

Eu *symbol* europium.

eucalyptus *noun* (*plural* **eucalyptuses** or **eucalypti**) **1** a tree native to Australasia, cultivated for its timber and for the oil from its leaves. **2** (also **eucalyptus oil**) the essential oil from eucalyptus leaves, used esp. in medicinal preparations, perfumes, etc. [Say yuke a LIP tuss for the singular, yuke a LIP tie for the plural]

Eucharist *noun* **1** (in the Catholic, Anglican and Orthodox churches) the sacrament commemorating the Last Supper, in which bread and wine are consecrated and consumed. **2** the consecrated elements, esp. the bread: *receive the Eucharist.* ▶ **Eucharistic** *adjective* **Eucharistical** *adjective* [Say YUKE a rist, yuke a RISS tick]

euchre • *noun* **1** a card game for two to four players in which the highest cards are the joker (if used), the jack of trumps, and the other jack of the same colour in a pack with the lower cards removed, the aim being to win at least three of the five tricks played. **2** an act of euchring or being euchred. • *verb* (**euchres**, **euchred**,

euchring) **1** (in euchre) prevent (a bidder) from winning three or more tricks, thereby scoring points oneself. **2** *slang* deceive, outwit. **3** *Cdn, Austral., & NZ slang* ruin: *if we miss the bus, we're euchred!* [Say YOO cur]

Euclidean *adjective* of the Greek mathematician Euclid (*c.*300 BC), esp. the system of geometry based on his principles. [Say yoo KLIDDY un]

eugenic *adjective* having to do with the science of improving a population by controlled breeding for desirable inherited characteristics. [Say you GENIC]

eugenicist *noun* a person who studies the science of improving a population by controlled breeding for desirable inherited characteristics. [Say you JENNA sist]

eugenics *plural noun* (treated as *singular*) the science of improving a population by controlled breeding for desirable inherited characteristics. [Say you GENICS]

eukaryote *noun* an organism consisting of a cell or cells in which the genetic material is DNA in the form of chromosomes contained within a distinct nucleus. ▶ **eukaryotic** *adjective* [Say you CARRY oat, yoo carry OTT ick]

eulachon *noun* (*plural* **eulachon** or **eulachons**) a small oily food fish of the Pacific coast of North America, belonging to the smelt family. Aboriginal peoples used eulachon as candles by inserting a cloth wick into them. [Say YOOLA con]

eulogize *verb* (**eulogizes**, **eulogized**, **eulogizing**) **1** praise highly in speech or writing: *overly sentimental eulogizing of female empowerment.* **2** compose or deliver a funeral oration in praise of a person: *when he died he was eulogized as having been "sweet and affable".* [Say YOOLA jize]

eulogy *noun* (*plural* **eulogies**) **1** a speech or piece of writing in praise of a person who has just died. **2** an expression of praise: *a ten-minute eulogy of their newest appointee.* [Say YOOLA jee]

eunuch *noun* **1** a castrated man, esp. (*hist.*) one employed at an oriental harem or court. **2** a person lacking effectiveness: *Clinton was a eunuch president after the Republican landslide in 1994.* [Say YOO nick]

euonymus *noun* (*plural* **euonymus**) any tree or shrub of the genus *Euonymus*, e.g. the burning bush. [Say yoo ONNA muss]

euphemism *noun* **1** a mild or vague expression substituted for one thought to be too harsh or direct, e.g. *pass away* for *die.* **2** the use of such expressions. ▶ **euphemistic** *adjective* **euphemistically** *adverb* [Say YOOFA mism, yoofa MISS tick, YOOFA mize]

euphony *noun* (*plural* **euphonies**) pleasantness of sound, esp. of a word or phrase; harmony: *attracted by the euphony and rhythm of the poem.* [Say YOOFA nee]

euphoria *noun* an extremely strong feeling of happiness and excitement that usually lasts only a short time: *I was in a state of euphoria all day* ◊ *euphoria soon gave way to despair.* ▶ **euphoric** *adjective* **euphorically** *adverb* [Say yoo FOREY uh]

Eurasian • *adjective* **1** of mixed European and Asian parentage. **2** of Europe and Asia. • *noun* a Eurasian person. [Say yoor ASIAN]

eureka *interjection* I have found it! (announcing a discovery etc.). [Say yoo REEKA]

Euro *noun* (*plural* **Euros**) the European currency unit adopted by the European Union.

Euro- *combining form* Europe, European.

Eurocentric *adjective* **1** having or regarding Europe as its centre. **2** presupposing the supremacy of Europe and Europeans. ▶ **Eurocentricity** *noun* **Eurocentrism** *noun* [Say yoor oh SEN trick, yoor oh SEN trism]

European • *adjective* **1** of or in Europe. **2 a** descended from natives of Europe. **b** originating in or

characteristic of Europe. **3 a** happening in or extending over Europe. **b** concerning Europe as a whole rather than its individual countries. **4** of or relating to the European Union. • *noun* **1** a native or inhabitant of Europe. **2** a person descended from natives of Europe. **3** a white person, esp. in a country with a predominantly non-white population. ▶ **Europeanization** *noun* **Europeanize** *verb*

European plan *noun* a system of charging for a hotel room only without meals. Abbreviation: **EP**.

europium *noun* a soft silvery metallic element. [Say yoo ROPE ee um]

eurythmic *adjective* **1** of or in harmonious proportion (esp. of architecture). **2** involving harmonious bodily movement, esp. as developed with music into a system of education: *eurythmic dancing*. [Say yuh RHYTHMIC]

euthanasia *noun* an act of painlessly killing a person or animal suffering from an incurable condition. ▶ **euthanize** *verb* (**euthanizes, euthanized, euthanizing**) [Say yootha NAY zhuh, YOOTHA nize]

eutrophic *adjective* (of a lake etc.) rich in nutrients and therefore supporting a dense plant population, which kills animal life by depriving it of oxygen. ▶ **eutrophication** *noun* [Say yoo TROFF ick or yoo TROFE ick, yoo troffa KAY sh'n or you trofe a KAY sh'n]

eV *abbreviation* electron volt.

evacuate *verb* (**evacuates, evacuated, evacuating**) **1** move people from a place of danger to a safer place: *police evacuated nearby buildings ◊ children were evacuated from London to escape the bombing ◊ families were evacuated to safer parts of the city*. **2** move out of a place because of danger, and leave the place empty: *employees were urged to evacuate their offices immediately ◊ locals were told to evacuate*. **3** produce a vacuum in (a vessel etc.). **4 a** empty (the bowels or other bodily organ). **b** discharge (feces etc.). ▶ **evacuation** *noun*

evacuee *noun* a person evacuated from a place of danger. [Say vac you EE]

evade *verb* (**evades, evaded, evading**) **1 a** escape from, avoid (pursuers, arrest, etc.) esp. by guile or trickery. **b** avoid doing (one's duty etc.). **c** avoid giving a direct answer to (a question, questioner, etc.). **2** fail to pay (tax due). ▶ **evader** *noun*

evaluate *verb* (**evaluates, evaluated, evaluating**) **1** assess, appraise: *evaluate the situation*. **2** find or state the number or amount of. ▶ **evaluation** *noun* **evaluative** *adjective* **evaluator** *noun* [Say i VALUE a tiv]

evanescent *adjective* (of an impression or appearance etc.) quickly fading; having no permanence: *as evanescent as champagne bubbles*. [Say evva NESS int]

evangelical • *adjective* (also **evangelic**) **1** of or according to the teaching of the gospel or the Christian religion. **2** of or denoting a branch of Protestant Christianity emphasizing the authority of Scripture, personal conversion, and the doctrine of salvation by faith in the reconciliation of God and mankind through Jesus Christ. **3** wanting very much to persuade people to accept one's views and opinions: *she delivered her speech with evangelical fervour*. • *noun* a person who believes in evangelical doctrines or belongs to an evangelical church. ▶ **evangelicalism** *noun* **evangelically** *adverb* [Say ee van JELL ick ul or evan JELL ick ul]

evangelism *noun* **1** the preaching or spreading of the Christian gospel. **2** zealous advocacy of a cause or doctrine. [Say i VAN juh lism or ee VAN juh lism]

evangelist *noun* **1** a preacher of the Christian gospel. **2** a person, esp. a layperson, engaged in travelling Christian missionary work. **3** a zealous advocate or promoter of a cause or doctrine. **4** (**Evangelist**) any of the writers of the four Gospels (Matthew, Mark, Luke, and John). [Say i VAN juh list or ee VAN juh list]

evangelistic *adjective* **1** of evangelists or evangelism: *an evangelistic crusade*. **2** of or relating to the four Evangelists. [Say i van juh LISS tick or ee van juh LISS tick]

evangelization *noun* the activity of preaching the gospel and trying to convert someone to Christianity. [Say i van juh lize AY sh'n or ee van juh lize AY sh'n]

evangelize *verb* (**evangelizes, evangelized, evangelizing**) **1** preach the Christian gospel to. **2** convert (a person) to Christianity. **3** try to win support for a cause: *evangelize about forest conservation*. ▶ **evangelizer** *noun* [Say i VAN juh lize or ee VAN juh lize]

evaporate *verb* (**evaporates, evaporated, evaporating**) **1** turn from solid or liquid into vapour: *all the water in the bowl evaporated*. **2** lose or cause to lose moisture by evaporation: *the sun is constantly evaporating the earth's moisture*. **3** disappear, especially by gradually becoming less and less: *her confidence had now completely evaporated ◊ their lead in the polls evaporated overnight*.

evaporated milk *noun* thick unsweetened milk, usu. bought in tins, which has had some of its liquid removed by evaporation.

evaporation *noun* **1** the process of a liquid changing into a vapour. **2** a gradual process of disappearing or ceasing to exist: *he has noticed an evaporation of his savings since he stopped working*.

evaporator *noun* something that causes evaporation.

evasion *noun* **1** the act or a means of evading a duty, question, etc. **2** a statement made to avoid dealing with something or talking about something honestly and directly: *his speech was full of evasions and half-truths*.

evasive *adjective* **1** not willing to give clear answers to a question: *evasive answers ◊ Tessa was evasive about why she had not been at home that night ◊ John, normally so honest, was now being evasive in the extreme*. **2** enabling evasion or escape: *the plane took evasive action to avoid being hit by the missile*. ▶ **evasively** *adverb* **evasiveness** *noun* [Say i VAY siv]

eve *noun* **1** the evening or day before a church festival or any date or event: *Christmas Eve*. **2** the time just before anything: *the eve of the election*.

even[1] • *adjective* (**evener, evenest**) **1** level. **2 a** (of an action, movement, etc.) uniform: *an even pace*. **b** equal in number, amount, value, score, etc. **c** equally balanced. **3** (usu. foll. by *with*) in the same plane or line. **4** (of a person's temper etc.) calm. **5 a** (of a number such as 4, 6) divisible by two without a remainder. **b** bearing such a number: *no parking on even dates*. **c** not involving fractions; exact: *in even dozens*. **6** neither owed nor owing money; square: *give me $10 and we're even*. **7** (of a chance, bet, etc.) as likely to succeed as not. • *adverb* used for emphasis: *never even opened the letter*. • *verb* make or become even. ▸PHRASES◂ **even so** nevertheless. **even though** despite the fact that. **get (or be) even with** have one's revenge on.

even[2] *noun archaic* or *literary* evening.

even-handed *adjective* impartial, fair: *he had an even-handed approach to the negotiations*. ▶ **even-handedly** *adverb* **even-handedness** *noun*

evening • *noun* **1** the end part of the day, esp. from about 6 p.m., or sunset if earlier, to bedtime: *this evening ◊ evening meal*. **2** an outing or party of a specified type, happening in the evening: *a theatre evening*. **3** *literary* a time compared with this, esp. the last part of a person's life. • *interjection* good evening.

evening dress *noun* **1** (also **evening clothes, evening wear**) clothes worn for formal occasions in the evening. **2** = EVENING GOWN.

evening gown *noun* a woman's long formal dress.

E

evening primrose *noun* a plant with yellow flowers, from whose seeds an oil is extracted for medicinal use.

evenly *adverb* **1** in a smooth, regular, or equal manner. **2** calmly.

evenness *noun* **1** a smooth, regular, or even quality. **2** a calm manner: *a man of uncommon evenness of temper.*

evensong *noun* a service of evening prayer, esp. that of Anglican churches.

even-steven *adjective* (also **even-Steven**) *informal* **1** having no balance of debt on either side. **2** (of a game etc.) equal; tied.

even strength *noun* Hockey a situation where both teams have the same number of players on the ice.

event *noun* **1** a thing that happens or takes place, esp. one of importance. **2** a planned public or social occasion: *a number of events to raise money for charity.* **3** an item in a sports program, or the program as a whole: *the giant slalom event.* PHRASES **in any event** (or **at all events**) whatever happens. **in the event** as it turns (or turned) out. **in the event of** if (a specified thing) happens. **in the event that** if it happens that.

eventful *adjective* marked by many events or incidents, esp. noteworthy ones: *an eventful career.* ▶ **eventfully** *adverb* **eventfulness** *noun*

eventual *adjective* occurring or existing in due course or at last; ultimate.

eventuality *noun* (*plural* **eventualities**) a possible event or outcome: *you must be prepared for all eventualities.*

eventually *adverb* in the end, esp. after a long delay, dispute, or series of problems: *our flight eventually left, five hours late.*

ever *adverb* **1** at all times; always: *ever hopeful* ◊ *ever after.* **2** at any time: *have you ever been to Paris?* ◊ *as good as ever.* **3** as an emphatic word: **a** in any way; at all: *how ever did you do it?* ◊ *when will they ever learn?* **b** (preceded by *as*) in any manner possible: *be as quick as ever you can.* **c** *informal* really: *did she ever feel like an idiot.* **4** (in combination) constantly: *ever-present.* **5** (foll. by *so, such*) very; very much: *thanks ever so much.* **6** (foll. by comparative) constantly, increasingly: *grew ever larger.* PHRASES **did you ever?** *informal* did you ever hear or see the like? **ever since** throughout the period since.

evergreen ● *adjective* **1** (of a plant) retaining green leaves or needles throughout the year (compare DECIDUOUS 1). **2** having an enduring freshness, success, or popularity: *this symphony is an evergreen favourite.* ● *noun* an evergreen plant.

everlasting ● *adjective* **1** lasting forever. **2** lasting for a long time, esp. so as to become unwelcome: *I get so tired of my mother's everlasting tuna noodle casserole!* **3** (of flowers) keeping their shape and colour when dried. ● *noun* **1** any of various plants, chiefly of the composite family, with flowers of papery texture that retain their shape and colour after being dried, esp. a helichrysum. **2** (also **everlasting pea**) a plant with large flowers, naturalized in North America. ▶ **everlastingly** *adverb*

evermore *adverb* forever; always.

every *adjective* **1** each single: *heard every word.* **2** each at a specified interval in a series: *take every third one* ◊ *every four days.* **3** all possible; the utmost degree of: *has every prospect of success.* PHRASES **every bit as** *informal* (in comparisons) quite as: *every bit as good.* **every now and again** (or **now and then**) from time to time. **every other** each second in a series: *every other day.* **every so often** at intervals; occasionally. **every time** *informal* **1** without exception. **2** without hesitation. **every which way** *informal* **1** in all directions. **2** in a disorderly manner.

everybody *pronoun* every person.

everyday *adjective* **1** occurring every day. **2** suitable for or used on ordinary days: *everyday dishes.* **3** commonplace, usual: *everyday life.*

Everyman *noun* the ordinary man or human being: *it is Everyman's dream car.*

everyone *pronoun* every person; everybody. PHRASES **everyone who is anyone** (also **everybody who is anybody**) every person who is important etc.

everything *pronoun* **1** all things; all the things of a group or class. **2** a great deal: *he owes her everything.* **3** the essential consideration: *speed is everything.* PHRASES **have everything** *informal* possess every attraction, advantage, etc.

everywhere *adverb* (also *informal* **everyplace**) in every place.

Everywoman *noun* the ordinary or typical woman.

evict *verb* expel (a tenant) from a property by legal process. ▶ **eviction** *noun*

evidence ● *noun* **1** the available facts, circumstances, etc. supporting or otherwise a belief, proposition, etc., or indicating whether or not a thing is true or valid. **2** Law information used to establish facts in a legal investigation or admissible as testimony in a law court. **3** a sign or indication: *evidence of hard work.* ● *verb* be evidence of; demonstrate: *is very popular, as evidenced by the large turnout.* PHRASES **call in evidence** Law summon (a person) as a witness. **in evidence** noticeable, conspicuous: *when we arrived at the park not a single person was in evidence.*

evident *adjective* plain or obvious (visually or intellectually).

evidently *adverb* **1** plainly, obviously. **2** (qualifying a whole sentence) it is plain that; it would seem that: *evidently, we're too late.* **3** (said in reply) so it appears.

evil ● *adjective* **1** morally bad. **2** harmful or tending to harm, esp. intentionally or characteristically: *the evil effects of high taxes.* **3** disagreeable or unpleasant: *an evil smell.* **4** unlucky; causing misfortune: *evil days.* ● *noun* **1** a moral force regarded as the source of harm or human wickedness, esp. as opposed to goodness: *the world is stalked by relentless evil* ◊ *good and evil in eternal opposition.* **2** a manifestation of this, esp. in people's actions; wickedness: *we will never forget the evil that took place last Thursday.* **3** something that is morally wrong, harmful, or undesirable: *sexism, racism, and other social evils.* PHRASES **speak evil of** slander: *you shouldn't speak evil of the dead.*

evildoer *noun* a person who does evil. ▶ **evildoing** *noun*

evil eye *noun* a gaze or stare superstitiously believed to be able to cause harm.

evilly *adverb* in a wicked or evil manner.

evil one *noun* the embodiment of evil in certain religious beliefs, esp. (in Christianity) Satan.

evince *verb* (**evinces, evinced, evincing**) **1** indicate or make evident: *man's inhumanity to man as evinced in the use of torture.* **2** show that one has (a quality): *her letters evince the excitement she felt.* [Say i VINCE]

eviscerate *verb* formal **1** remove the inner organs of a body: *the goat had been skinned and neatly eviscerated.* **2** remove an important or significant part of something: *the government is proposing a budget which would eviscerate medicare.* ▶ **evisceration** *noun* [Say i VISSER ate, i visser AY sh'n]

evocation *noun* an act of evoking: *a brilliant evocation of childhood in the 1960s*. [Say ee voe KAY sh'n]

evocative *adjective* tending to evoke (esp. feelings or memories): *powerfully evocative lyrics ◊ the building's cramped interiors are highly evocative of past centuries*. ▶**evocatively** *adverb* **evocativeness** *noun* [Say i VOCKA tiv]

evoke *verb* (**evokes, evoked, evoking**) inspire or draw forth (memories, a response, etc.): *the music evoked memories of her youth ◊ his case is unlikely to evoke public sympathy*.

evolution *noun* **1** gradual development, esp. from a simple to a more complex form. **2 a** the development of an animal or plant, or part of one, from a rudimentary to a mature state. **b** a process by which different kinds of organism come into being by the differentiation and genetic mutation of earlier forms over successive generations, viewed as an explanation of their origins. **3** the appearance or presentation of events etc. in due succession: *the evolution of the plot*. ▶**evolutionary** *adjective* [Say evva LOO sh'n]

evolutionism *noun* belief in the theories of evolution and natural selection.

evolutionist *noun* a person who believes in evolution as explaining the origin of species.

evolve *verb* (**evolves, evolved, evolving**) **1** develop or come forth gradually. **2** (of an organism, part or feature) come into being through evolutionary development. **3** (usu. in *passive*) produce or develop in the course of evolution.

ewe *noun* a female sheep. [Say YOO]

ewer *noun* a large pitcher or water jug with a wide mouth. [Say YOO ur]

ex¹ *noun* (*plural* **exes**) *informal* a former spouse, lover, etc.

ex² *abbreviation* example.

ex³ *noun* (*plural* **exes**) *Cdn* exhibition.

ex- *prefix* forming nouns from titles of office, status, etc., meaning "formerly": *ex-convict ◊ ex-wife*.

exacerbate *verb* (**exacerbates, exacerbated, exacerbating**) make (a problem, bad situation, or negative feeling) worse: *these problems were exacerbated by the policies of the provincial government*. ▶**exacerbation** *noun* [Say ex ASSER bate, ex asser BAY sh'n]

exact • *adjective* **1** correct in all details. **2** precise. **3** strict. **4** (of a scientific method, instrument, etc.) not allowing vagueness or uncertainty. • *verb* **1** demand and get something from someone: *she was determined to exact a promise from him*. **2** make something bad happen to someone: *stress can exact a high price from workers ◊ he exacted a terrible revenge for their treatment of him*.

exacting *adjective* **1** making great demands. **2** calling for much effort. ▶**exactingly** *adverb*

exaction *noun* **1** the action of demanding and obtaining something from someone, esp. a payment or service: *he supervised the exaction of tolls at various ports*. **2** a sum of money demanded: *the exactions of the Treasury Board*.

exactitude *noun* the quality of being very accurate and exact: *scientific exactitude*.

exactly *adverb* **1** accurately, precisely; in an exact manner: *worked it out exactly*. **2** in exact terms: *exactly when did it happen?* **3** (said in reply) quite so; I agree completely. PHRASES **not exactly** *informal* by no means.

exactness *noun* the quality of being precise or exact.

exactor *noun* *Cdn* a bet on the first- and second-place finishers in a race, specifying their order of finish.

exactor box *noun* *Cdn* a bet on three or more horses in one race, specifying the first- and second-place finishers, not specifying their order of finish.

SPELL CHECK
exaggerate   [ABC ✓]

Warning: in the word **exaggerate** you double the g but not the r.

exaggerate *verb* (**exaggerates, exaggerated, exaggerating**) **1** give an impression of (a thing), esp. in speech or writing, that makes it seem larger or greater etc. than it really is. **2** enlarge or alter beyond normal or due proportions: *with exaggerated politeness*. ▶**exaggerated** *adjective* **exaggeratedly** *adverb* **exaggeration** *noun* **exaggerator** *noun*

SPELL CHECK
exalt, exult   [ABC ✓]

To feel joy as a result of triumph or success is to **exult**.

---

exalt *verb* **1** raise in rank or power etc.: *the party will continue to exalt its hero*. **2** praise highly. **3** (usu. as **exalted** *adjective*) make lofty or noble: *an exalted style*. [Say ex AWLT]

exaltation *noun* **1** a feeling or state of extreme happiness: *she was in a frenzy of exaltation*. **2** the action of elevating someone in rank, power, or character: *the eighteenth-century exaltation of the individual*. **3** the action of praising someone or something highly: *you'd have to be a baseball junkie to sit through this endless exaltation of Babe Ruth*. [Say ex awl TAY sh'n]

exam *noun* = EXAMINATION 2, 3.

examination *noun* **1** the action or process of conducting an inspection or investigation: *the role of the bureaucracy has come under increasing examination*. **2** a detailed inspection or investigation: *a thorough medical examination*. **3** a test of the proficiency or knowledge of students or other candidates for a qualification by oral or written questions. **4** the formal questioning of the accused or of a witness in court.

examination for discovery *noun* (*plural* **examinations for discovery**) *Cdn Law* a pretrial meeting to disclose the evidence that will be presented at a civil trial.

examination-in-chief *noun* (*plural* **examinations-in-chief**) *Cdn & Brit. Law* an examination in a court made by the party that called the person to give evidence.

examine *verb* (**examines, examined, examining**) **1** inquire into the nature or condition etc. of. **2** look closely or analytically at. **3** test the proficiency of, esp. by examination (see EXAMINATION 3). **4** check the health of (a patient) by inspection or experiment. **5** *Law* formally question (the accused or a witness) in court.

examiner *noun* **1** a person whose official duty is to check that things are being done correctly and according to the rules of an organization. **2** a person who marks or writes the questions for a test or exam. **3** = MEDICAL EXAMINER.

example *noun* **1** a thing characteristic of its kind or illustrating a general rule. **2** a person, thing, or piece of conduct, regarded in terms of its fitness to be imitated: *you are a bad example*. **3** a circumstance or treatment seen as a warning to others; a person so treated: *shall make an example of you*. PHRASES **for example** by way of illustration.

exasperate *verb* (**exasperates, exasperated, exasperating**) irritate intensely. [Say ex ASPER ate]

exasperated *adjective* extremely annoyed, esp. if one can do nothing to improve the situation: *she was becoming exasperated with all the questions they were asking*. ▶**exasperatedly** *adverb* [Say ex ASPER ate ed]

exasperating *adjective* extremely annoying: *he's the*

E

most difficult and exasperating man I know. ▶ **exasperatingly** *adverb* [Say ex ASPER ate ing]

exasperation *noun* extreme or intense irritation or annoyance: *he shook his head in exasperation ◊ a sigh of exasperation.* [Say as asper AY sh'n]

excavate *verb* (**excavates, excavated, excavating**) **1 a** make (a hole or channel) by digging. **b** dig out material from (the ground). **2** reveal or extract by digging. **3** *Archaeology* dig systematically into the ground to explore (a site). ▶ **excavation** *noun* **excavator** *noun*

> **SPELL CHECK**
> **exceed, accede**
>
> To agree to something or to take office is to **accede**.

exceed *verb* **1** be greater or more numerous than: *the price must not exceed $20.* **2** go beyond what is allowed, necessary, or advisable: *exceeded the speed limit.* **3** surpass, excel (a person or achievement).

exceeding *adjective* surpassing in amount or degree. **exceedingly** *adverb* extremely.

excel *verb* (**excels, excelled, excelling**) (often foll. by *in, at*) **1** be pre-eminent or the most outstanding: *excels at sports.* **2 excel oneself** perform exceptionally well: *Rick's cooking was always good but this time he really excelled himself.*

> **SPELL CHECK**
> **accelerate**
>
> To speed up is to **accelerate**.

excellence *noun* the quality of being excellent; great merit.

Excellency *noun* (*plural* **Excellencies**) (usu. preceded by *Your, His, Her, Their*) a title used in addressing or referring to certain high officials, e.g. governors general, ambassadors, and (in some countries) senior Church dignitaries.

excellent *adjective* extremely good; pre-eminent. ▶ **excellently** *adverb*

> **SPELL CHECK**
> **except, accept**
>
> When you receive something willingly you **accept** it.

except ● *verb* (often as **excepted** *adjective* placed after object) exclude from a general statement, condition, etc.: *excepted her from the amnesty.* ● *preposition* (also **excepting**) (often foll. by *for*) not including; other than: *all here except for Liz.* ● *conjunction* (usu. foll. by *that*) with the exception; only.

exception *noun* a person or thing that is excluded from a general statement or does not follow a rule: *nobody had much money and I was no exception ◊ we have decided to make an exception in your case.* PHRASES **take exception** (often foll. by *to*) **1** object; make objections to. **2** be offended (by); be resentful (about). **with the exception of** except; not including.

exceptional *adjective* **1** forming an exception. **2** not typical: *exceptional circumstances.* **3** unusually good. **4** (of a schoolchild) having mental or physical disabilities. ▶ **exceptionally** *adverb*

> **SPELL CHECK**
> **exercise**
>
> Warning: there is no *c* at the beginning of the second syllable of **exercise**.

excerpt ● *noun* a short extract from a book, film, piece

of music, etc. ● *verb* take an excerpt or excerpts from a book etc.

excess ● *noun* (*plural* **excesses**) **1** an amount of something that is more than necessary, permitted, or desirable: *are you suffering from an excess of stress in your life? ◊ he started drinking to excess after losing his job.* **2** the amount by which one quantity or number exceeds another: *the excess of expenditure over revenue.* **3** extreme behaviour that is unacceptable, illegal, or immoral: *bouts of alcoholic excess ◊ the inevitable tabloid excesses.* ● *adjective* exceeding a set or limited amount or number; extra: *excess weight.* PHRASES **in** (or **to**) **excess** exceeding the proper amount or degree. **in excess of** more than; exceeding.

excess baggage *noun* **1** baggage exceeding a weight allowance and liable to an extra charge. **2** something perceived as superfluous and burdensome: *was carrying some excess baggage around the hips and middle, so began to diet ◊ the justice and legal system sees victims as excess baggage.*

excessive *adjective* **1** too much or too great. **2** more than what is normal or necessary. ▶ **excessively** *adverb* **excessiveness** *noun*

exchange ● *noun* **1** an act of giving one thing and receiving another (esp. of the same type or value) in its place: *an exchange of prisoners of war ◊ the exchange of information.* **2 a** the giving of money for its equivalent in the money of the same or another country. **b** the fee or percentage charged for this. **3** a place where telephone calls are connected between different lines. **4** a place where commodities, securities, etc. are bought and sold: *grain exchange.* **5** a place where an item may be exchanged for another similar item: *needle exchange.* **6 a** a short conversation, esp. a disagreement or quarrel: *there was a heated exchange.* **b** a sequence of letters between correspondents. **7** a reciprocal visit between two people or groups from different regions or countries (also as an *adjective*: *exchange student*). ● *verb* (**exchanges, exchanged, exchanging**) **1** (often foll. by *for*) give or receive (one thing) in place of another. **2** give and receive as equivalents (e.g. things or people, blows, information, etc.); give one and receive another of. **3** substitute an equivalent item for (one purchased and returned). **4** (often foll. by *with*) make an exchange. PHRASES **in exchange** (often foll. by *for*) as a thing exchanged (for). ▶ **exchangeable** *adjective* **exchanger** *noun*

exchange rate *noun* the value of one currency in terms of another.

excise¹ ● *noun* a duty or tax levied on goods and commodities produced or sold within the country of origin: *motorists want the excise tax on gasoline lowered or removed.* ● *verb* (**excises, excised, excising**) charge excise on (goods). [Say EK size]

excise² *verb* (**excises, excised, excising**) **1** remove (a passage of a book etc.): *the clauses were excised from the treaty.* **2** cut out (an organ etc.) by surgery: *the precision with which surgeons can excise brain tumours.* ▶ **excision** *noun* [Say ek SIZE, ek SIZH un]

excitable *adjective* **1** (esp. of a person) easily excited. **2** (of an organism, tissue, etc.) responding to a stimulus. ▶ **excitably** *adverb*

excitation *noun* **1** the action or state of exciting or being excited; excitement. **2 a** the application of energy to a particle, object, or physical system. **b** the state of enhanced activity in a cell, organism, or tissue as a result of stimulation.

excite *verb* (**excites, excited, exciting**) **1 a** rouse a person's feelings or emotions. **b** arouse sexually. **2** bring about or give rise to (a feeling or action): *the ability to excite interest in others.* **3** promote the activity of

(an organism, tissue, etc.) by stimulus. **4** *Electricity* **a** cause (a current) to flow in the winding of an electromagnet. **b** supply a signal. **5** *Physics* **a** cause the emission of (a spectrum). **b** cause (a substance) to emit radiation. **c** put (an atom etc.) into a state of higher energy. ▶ **excitedly** *adverb* **excitement** *noun* **exciter** *noun* (esp. in senses 4, 5). **exciting** *adjective* **excitingly** *adverb*

exclaim *verb* cry out suddenly, esp. in anger, surprise, pain, etc.

exclamation *noun* a sudden cry or remark, esp. expressing surprise, anger, or pain.

exclamatory *adjective* of or serving as an exclamation. [Say ex KLAMMA tory]

exclude *verb* (**excludes, excluded, excluding**) **1** deliberately not include something in what one is doing or considering: *the cost of borrowing has been excluded from the inflation figures* ◊ *try excluding sugar and fat from your diet* ◊ *buses run every hour, Sundays excluded*. **2** prevent someone or something from entering a place or taking part in something: *women are still excluded from some country clubs* ◊ *she felt excluded by the other girls.* **3** decide that something is not possible: *we should not exclude the possibility of negotiation* ◊ *the police have excluded theft as a motive for the murder*.

exclusion *noun* **1** the process or state of excluding or being excluded: *exclusion of air creates a vacuum* ◊ *the exclusion of robbery as a motive.* **2** an item or eventuality specifically not covered by a contract or insurance policy: *some policies have a long list of exclusions limiting coverage.* PHRASES **to the exclusion of** so as to exclude: *don't discuss a few topics to the exclusion of all others.* ▶ **exclusionary** *adjective*

exclusion order *noun* **1** *Cdn & Brit.* an official order preventing a person (esp. a criminal) from entering a country. **2** *Cdn* an order made by a judge to clear spectators, reporters, etc. from a courtroom.

exclusive • *adjective* **1** excluding other things. **2** (foll. by *of*) not including; except for: *earned $100 a night, exclusive of tips.* **3** tending to exclude others, esp. socially. **4** catering for few or select customers; high-class. **5 a** (foll. by *to*) (of a commodity) not obtainable elsewhere. **b** (of a newspaper article) not published elsewhere. **6** restricted or limited to; existing or available only in: *a fish exclusive to the Richelieu River.* **7** employed or followed or held to the exclusion of all else: *exclusive rights.* • *noun* an article or story published by only one newspaper or periodical. ▶ **exclusively** *adverb* **exclusiveness** *noun* **exclusivity** *noun* [Say ex clue SIVVA tee]

excommunicate *verb* *Christianity* (**excommunicates, excommunicated, excommunicating**) officially exclude from participation in the sacraments, or from formal communion with the Church. ▶ **excommunication** *noun*

ex-con *noun informal* a former inmate of a prison.

excoriate *verb* (**excoriates, excoriated, excoriating**) **1** criticize severely: *the papers which had been excoriating him were now praising him.* **2** damage or remove part of the surface of (the skin). ▶ **excoriation** *noun* [Say ex COREY ate, ex corey AY sh'n]

excrement *noun* waste matter discharged from the bowels; feces. [Say EX kruh mint]

excrescence *noun* **1** a distinct outgrowth on a human or animal body or on a plant, esp. one that is the result of disease or abnormality. **2** an unattractive or superfluous addition or feature: *removing the excrescences of later renovations.* [Say ex CRESS ince]

excrete *verb* (**excretes, excreted, excreting**) (of a living organism or cell) separate and expel as waste (a

substance, esp. a product of metabolism): *excess bicarbonate is excreted by the kidney* ◊ *the butterfly pupa neither feeds nor excretes.* ▶ **excretion** *noun* **excretory** *adjective* [Say ex CREET, ex CREE sh'n, EXCRA tory]

excruciating *adjective* (of physical or mental pain) intense, acute. ▶ **excruciatingly** *adverb* [Say ex KROOSHY ate ing]

exculpate *verb* (**exculpates, exculpated, exculpating**) *formal* show or declare that (someone) is not guilty of wrongdoing: *the article exculpated the mayor.* ▶ **exculpation** *noun* **exculpatory** *adjective* [Say EX cull pate, ex cull PAY sh'n, ex CULPA tory]

excursion *noun* **1** a short journey, esp. one made by a group of people together for pleasure. **2** a group of people making such a trip. **3** a trip at a reduced rate, e.g. on a train, ship, etc. (also as an *adjective*: *excursion fare*). ▶ **excursionist** *noun* [Say ex CUR zh'n]

excuse • *verb* (**excuses, excused, excusing**) **1** attempt to lessen the blame attaching to (a person, act, or fault). **2** (of a fact or circumstance) serve in mitigation of (a person or act). **3** obtain exemption for (a person or oneself). **4 a** (foll. by *from*) release (a person) from a duty etc. **b** allow (a person) to leave. **5** overlook or forgive (a fault or offence). **6** (foll. by *for*) forgive (a person) for a fault. **7** not insist upon (what is due). **8 excuse oneself** apologize for leaving. • *noun* **1** a reason put forward to mitigate or justify an offence, fault, etc. **2** an apology: *made my excuses.* **3** *informal* a poor or inadequate example of: *a poor excuse for a novel.* PHRASES **excuse me** a polite apology.

exec *informal* • *noun* an executive. • *adjective* executive.

execrable *adjective* **1** of very poor quality: *the bus service on Don Mills Road is execrable* ◊ *execrable taste.* **2** worthy of condemnation: *ethically execrable behaviour.* [Say EX uh cribble]

execrate *verb* express or feel great loathing for: *he was a strong nationalist and as such was reviled and execrated outside of Quebec.* [Say EX uh crate]

executable *Computing* • *adjective* (of a file) that can be loaded and run as a program on a computer. • *noun* an executable file.

execute *verb* (**executes, executed, executing**) **1 a** carry out a sentence of death on (a condemned person). **b** kill as a political act. **2** carry into effect, perform (a plan, duty, command, operation, etc.). **3 a** carry out a design for (a product of art or skill). **b** perform (a musical composition, dance, etc.). **4** make (a legal instrument) valid by signing, sealing, etc. **5** put into effect (a judicial sentence, the terms of a will, etc.). **6** *Computing* run or process (a command, program, etc.).

execution *noun* **1** the act of killing someone, esp. as a legal punishment: *mass arrests and executions* ◊ *in a gangland-style execution, the biker boss was shot to death in a restaurant.* **2** the carrying out or putting into effect of a plan, order, or course of action: *the idea was good, but the execution was poor.* **3** technique or style of performance in the arts, esp. music: *the music is varied in tempo and brilliant in execution.* **4** the putting into effect of a legal instrument or order: *the executor who does not benefit from the will may serve as a witness to its execution.*

executioner *noun* an official who carries out a sentence of death.

executive • *noun* **1** a person or body with managerial or administrative responsibility in a business organization etc. **2** the branch of a government concerned with putting laws into effect. In Canada, the executive of the federal government consists of the prime minister and cabinet. **3** the person or persons in whom is vested the supreme executive authority of a country or state. • *adjective* **1 a** designating the branch of government that deals with putting into effect laws

E

E

and judicial sentences. **b** of or pertaining to the executive of a government. **2 a** concerned with administration or management. **b** relating to, designed for, or used by executives: *executive suite*. **3** *informal* exclusive; of the finest quality: *executive homes*.

executive council *noun* *Cdn* **1** a provincial or territorial cabinet. **2** *hist.* (in colonial government) a body of advisers appointed by the governor.

executive director *noun* a person employed by a non-profit organization to oversee operations and management and implement the policy decisions of the board of directors.

executive federalism *noun* *Cdn* the practice of establishing Canadian constitutional, social, and economic policy at meetings of First Ministers and cabinet ministers, esp. behind closed doors.

executor *noun* a person appointed in a will to carry out its instructions. [Say eg ZECK yoo tur]

executrix *noun* (*plural* **executrixes**) a woman appointed in a will to carry out its instructions. [Say eg ZECK yoo trix]

exegesis *noun* (*plural* **exegeses**) critical explanation of a text, esp. of Scripture. ▶ **exegetic** *adjective* **exegetical** *adjective* [Say exa JEE sis for the singular, exa JEE seez for the plural, exa JET ick]

exemplar *noun* a person or thing serving as a typical example or appropriate model. [Say ex EM plur]

exemplary *adjective* **1** fit to be imitated; outstandingly good: *exemplary behaviour*. **2 a** serving as a warning: *exemplary sentencing may discourage the ultra-violent minority*. **b** *Law* (of damages) exceeding the amount needed for simple compensation. [Say ex EMPLA ree]

exemplification *noun* the illustration of a point, principle, etc. by means of an example: *this county is a living exemplification of agriculture and the natural heritage working together*. [Say ex empla fuh KAY sh'n]

exemplify *verb* (**exemplifies**, **exemplified**, **exemplifying**) **1** illustrate by example; give an example of. **2** be an example of: *an RCMP operation which exemplifies current trends*. [Say ex EMPLA fie]

exempt • *adjective* **1** free from an obligation or liability etc. imposed on others. **2** (foll. by *from*) not liable to. • *verb* (foll. by *from*) free from an obligation, esp. one imposed on others. ▶ **exemption** *noun*

SPELL CHECK   ABC ✓
exercise, exorcise

To drive out an evil spirit with prayers or magic is to **exorcise** it.

---

exercise • *noun* **1** activity requiring physical effort, done esp. as training or to sustain or improve health. **2** mental or spiritual activity, esp. as practice to develop a skill. **3** (often in *plural*) a particular task or set of tasks devised as exercise, practice in a technique, etc. **4 a** the use or application of a mental faculty, right, etc. **b** practice of an ability, quality, etc. **5** (often in *plural*) military drill or manoeuvres. **6** (foll. by *in*) a process directed at or concerned with something specified: *was an exercise in public relations*. **7** (usu. in *plural*) a formal or traditional routine or ceremony: *opening exercises*. • *verb* (**exercises**, **exercised**, **exercising**) **1** use or apply (a faculty, right, influence, restraint, etc.): *all citizens should exercise their right to vote in elections*. **2** perform (a function). **3 a** take (esp. physical) exercise. **b** provide (an animal) with exercise. **4** occupy the thoughts of; perplex, worry: *the knowledge that a better solution was possible still exercised her*. PHRASES **exercise in futility** an activity which proves to be absolutely futile. **the object** (or **point**) **of the**

exercise the essential purpose of an action or procedure. ▶ **exerciser** *noun*

exert *verb* **1** bring to bear (a quality, force, influence, etc.): *the moon exerts a force on the earth* ◊ *is trying to exert an influence over the next generation*. **2 exert oneself** use one's efforts or endeavours; strive.

exertion *noun* **1** physical or mental effort: *she was panting with the exertion* ◊ *a well-earned rest after their mental exertions*. **2** the application of a force, influence, or quality: *the exertion of authority*.

exfoliate *verb* (**exfoliates**, **exfoliated**, **exfoliating**) **1** (of bone, the skin, a mineral, etc.) come off in scales or layers. **2 a** shed (material) in scales or layers. **b** cause (the skin etc.) to shed flakes or scales: *exfoliate your legs to get rid of dead skin*. **3** (of a tree) throw off layers of bark: *the bark exfoliates in papery flakes*. ▶ **exfoliation** *noun* [Say ex FOLEY ate, ex foley AY sh'n]

exhalation *noun* **1** an expiration of air from the lungs: *she let her breath out in a long exhalation of relief*. **2** an amount of vapour or fumes given off. [Say ex huh LAY sh'n]

exhale *verb* (**exhales**, **exhaled**, **exhaling**) **1** breathe out (esp. air or smoke) from the lungs: *she sat back and exhaled deeply* ◊ *he exhaled the smoke toward the ceiling*. **2** give off or be given off in vapour: *the jungle exhaled mists of early morning*.

exhaust • *verb* **1** consume or use up the whole of: *within three days they had exhausted their supply of food* ◊ *we have exhausted all the possibilities*. **2 a** (often as **exhausted** *adjective* or **exhausting** *adjective*) use up the strength or energy of; tire out. **b** drain (soil) of nutritive ingredients. **3** talk about or study a subject until there is nothing else to say about it: *I think we've exhausted that particular topic*. **4** draw out (a gas etc.). • *noun* **1** expelled waste air or other gases etc., esp. those produced by an engine after combustion. **2** (also **exhaust pipe**) the pipe or system by which these are expelled. **3** the process of expulsion of these gases. ▶ **exhaustible** *adjective* **exhaustingly** *adverb*

exhaustion *noun* **1** the action or state of using something up or of being used up completely: *the rapid exhaustion of fossil fuel reserves*. **2** a state of extreme mental or physical fatigue: *Rod was pale with exhaustion*.

exhaustive *adjective* thorough; examining, including, or considering all elements or aspects: *she has undergone exhaustive tests but they still don't know what's wrong with her*. ▶ **exhaustively** *adverb*

exhibit • *verb* (**exhibits**, **exhibited**, **exhibiting**) **1** show something in a public place for people to enjoy or to give them information: *they will be exhibiting their new designs at the trade fairs this spring* ◊ *only one painting was exhibited in the artist's lifetime* ◊ *she exhibits regularly in several local art galleries*. **2** show clearly (a quality, feeling, or ability): *the patient exhibited signs of fatigue and memory loss*. • *noun* **1** a thing or collection of things forming part or all of an exhibition. **2** a document or other item produced in a law court as evidence.

exhibition *noun* **1** a display (esp. public) of works of art, industrial products, etc.: *an exhibition of Group of Seven paintings*. **2** *Cdn* a large regional fair, esp. with amusements, agricultural exhibits, and craft displays, usu. lasting for an extended period. **3** a world's fair. **4** a display or demonstration of a particular skill, feeling, or kind of behaviour: *a fine exhibition of basket-weaving* ◊ *an appalling exhibition of bad manners*. **5** (as an *adjective*) denoting games whose outcomes do not affect the teams' standings, esp. those played before the start of a regular season: *exhibition games*. PHRASES **make an exhibition of oneself** behave so as to appear ridiculous.

exhibitionism *noun* **1** extravagant behaviour that is

intended to attract attention or admiration. **2** a mental condition characterized by the compulsion to display one's genitals indecently in public.

exhibitionist *noun* **1** a person who likes to attract attention by behaving publicly in an extravagant or outrageous manner. **2** a person who displays their genitals in public. ▶ **exhibitionistic** *adjective*

exhibitor *noun* a person who provides an item or items for an exhibition.

exhilarate *verb* (often as **exhilarating** *adjective* or **exhilarated** *adjective*) (**exhilarates, exhilarated, exhilarating**) affect with great liveliness or joy; raise the spirits of. ▶ **exhilaratingly** *adverb* **exhilaration** *noun* [Say ex ILLA rate, ex illa RAY sh'n]

exhort *verb* urge or advise strongly or earnestly: *the party leader exhorted her members to start preparing for the election*. ▶ **exhortation** *noun* [Say ex ORT, ex or TAY sh'n]

exhumation *noun* the act of digging up a buried corpse. [Say ex oo MAY sh'n or ex yoo MAY sh'n]

exhume *verb* (**exhumes, exhumed, exhuming**) **1** dig out, unearth (esp. a buried corpse). **2** revive, bring to light (esp. something lost): *what on earth could have led the theatre's director to exhume this dreary museum piece of a play?* [Say ex OOM or ex YOOM]

exigency *noun* (*plural* **exigencies**) (usu. in *plural*) an urgent need or demand: *foreign issues are too apt to be dominated by the immediate exigencies of party politics*. [Say EX idge in see or ex IDGE in see]

SPELL CHECK
exhilarate   ABC ✓

Warning: **exhilarate** is spelled with an *h*: **exhil-**.

---

exile • *noun* **1** expulsion, or the state of being expelled, from one's native land or home, esp. for political reasons. **2 a** long absence from home, esp. as constrained by circumstances. **b** exclusion from a group, accustomed place, etc. **3** a person expelled or long absent from his or her native country, home, etc. **4** (also **Babylonian exile, Exile**) the captivity of the Jews in Babylon in the 6th century BC. • *verb* (**exiles, exiled, exiling**) (foll. by *from*) **1** officially expel (a person) from his or her native country or town etc. **2** exclude (a person or thing) from a group etc.

exist *verb* **1** have being. **2** (of circumstances etc.) occur; be found. **3** live with no pleasure under adverse conditions: *felt he was merely existing*. **4** maintain life: *can hardly exist on this salary*.

existence *noun* **1** the fact or condition of being or existing. **2** the manner of one's existing or living, esp. under adverse conditions. **3** all that exists.

existent *adjective* existing, actual, current.

existential *adjective* **1** of or relating to existence. **2** concerned with existence, esp. with human existence as viewed by existentialism. [Say exa STEN shull]

existentialism *noun* a theory emphasizing the existence of the individual person as a free and responsible agent determining their own development in a meaningless world through acts of the will. Existentialism tends to be atheistic, to belittle scientific knowledge, and to deny the existence of objective values, stressing instead the reality and significance of human freedom and experience. ▶ **existentialist** *noun & adjective* [Say exa STEN shull ism]

existing *adjective* in use, operation, or existence at the time being discussed.

exit • *noun* **1** a passage or door by which to leave a room, building, etc. **2** the act of going out. **3** the act of departing from or ceasing to participate or engage in: *he made a hasty exit from the room* ◊ *the team's early exit*

from the playoffs. **4** a place where vehicles can leave a highway or major road. • *verb* (**exits, exited, exiting**) **1** go out of a room, building, etc. **2** (of a vehicle) leave (a highway or major road). **3** terminate (a computer session, program, etc.).

exit poll *noun* an unofficial poll in which voters leaving a polling station are asked how they voted.

exodus *noun* (*plural* **exoduses**) **1** a mass departure of people: *the mass exodus from the city to the lake in the summer* ◊ *the play was so awful that there was a general exodus from the theatre at the intermission*. **2** (**Exodus**) *Bible* the departure of the Israelites from slavery in Egypt and their journey across the Red Sea and through the wilderness led by Moses. [Say EXA dus]

exonerate *verb* (**exonerates, exonerated, exonerating**) officially state that someone is not responsible for something that they have been blamed for: *the police report exonerated Lewis from all charges of corruption*. ▶ **exoneration** *noun* [Say ex ONNA rate, ex onna RAY sh'n]

exorbitance *noun* the unreasonably high price etc. of something. [Say ex ORBA tince]

exorbitant *adjective* (of a price etc.) grossly excessive. ▶ **exorbitantly** *adverb* [Say ex ORBA tint]

exorcise *verb* (**exorcises, exorcised, exorcising**) (also **exorcize, exorcizes, exorcized, exorcizing**) **1 a** endeavour to expel (a supposed evil spirit) by religious ceremonies, prayers, etc. **b** free (a person or place) of a supposed evil spirit. **2 a** remove (an evil influence): *inflation has been exorcised*. **b** free (a person or place) of an evil influence. ▶ **exorcism** *noun* **exorcist** *noun*

exoskeleton *noun* a rigid external covering for the body in certain animals, esp. arthropods, providing support and protection. [Say EXO skeleton]

exotic • *adjective* **1** introduced from or originating in or existing in a foreign or distant place: *exotic birds*. **2** attractively or remarkably strange or unusual; bizarre: *she was wearing a very exotic outfit*. • *noun* an exotic person or thing.

exotica *plural noun* remarkably strange or rare things. [Say ex OTT ick uh]

exotically *adverb* in a manner that is unusual and characteristic of a foreign or distant place: *he grows all kinds of exotically named plants in his garden*.

exotic dancer *noun* = STRIPPER 1.

exoticism *noun* a foreign or unusual character or nature: *New Zealanders use the name Aotearoa to lend a bit of Polynesian exoticism to the land*. [Say ex OTTA sism]

expand *verb* **1** increase in size, scope, or importance. **2** (often foll. by *on*) give a fuller description or account. **3 a** set or write out in full (something condensed or abbreviated). **b** *Math* rewrite (a product, power, or function) as a sum. **4** spread out flat. ▶ **expandable** *adjective* **expander** *noun* **expanding** *adjective*

expanse *noun* **1** a wide continuous area or extent of land, space, etc. **2** an amount of expansion.

expansion *noun* **1** the action of becoming larger or more extensive: *the rapid expansion of the cities*. **2** enlargement of the scale or scope of (esp. commercial) operations: *our business has been undergoing expansion since we adopted e-commerce*. **3** increase in the amount of a state's territory or area of control: *German expansion in the 1930s*. **4** an increase in the volume of fuel etc. when combustion occurs in the cylinder of an engine. **5** a thing formed by the enlargement, broadening, or development of something: *the book is an expansion of a lecture Martha gave last year*. **6** *Sport* the addition of new teams to a league (often as an *adjective*: *expansion team*).

expansionary *adjective* (of a policy or action)

E

intended to result in economic or political expansion: *an expansionary phase of the business cycle*.

expansionism *noun* a policy or theory advocating esp. territorial expansion. ▶ **expansionist** *noun*

expansive *adjective* **1** covering a large amount of space: *Canada's expansive and difficult terrain*. **2** covering a large subject area, rather than trying to be exact and use few words: *we need to look at a more expansive definition of the term* ◊ *the piece is written in his usual expansive style*. **3** friendly and willing to talk a lot: *she was clearly relaxed and in an expansive mood*. **4** (especially of a period of time) encouraging economic expansion: *in the expansive 1960s bright university graduates could advance rapidly*. ▶ **expansively** *adverb* **expansiveness** *noun*

expat *noun & adjective informal* = EXPATRIATE. [Say EX pat]

expatriate • *adjective* **1** living abroad, esp. for a long period. **2** expelled from one's country, home, etc.; exiled. • *noun* an expatriate person. [Say ex PAY tree it]

expect *verb* **1 a** regard as likely; assume as a future event or occurrence: *I expect that you will behave* ◊ *I expect you to behave*. **b** look for as appropriate or one's due (from a person): *I expect co-operation*. **c** foresee or look forward to the arrival of: *expecting guests*. **2** *informal* think, suppose. **3** be pregnant with: *expecting twins*. PHRASES **be expecting** *informal* be pregnant. ▶ **expectable** *adjective*

expectancy *noun* (*plural* **expectancies**) **1** a state of expectation. **2** what can reasonably be expected: *life expectancy*.

expectant *adjective* **1** revealing expectation: *an expectant look*. **2** (of a mother or father) expecting the birth of a child. ▶ **expectantly** *adverb*

expectation *noun* **1** a strong belief that something will happen or be the case in the future: *really had not lived up to expectations* ◊ *an expectation that the government will provide for us in our old age* ◊ *stocked up on sandbags in expectation of a flood*. **2** a hope that something good will happen: *there was an air of expectation and curiosity*.

expectorant • *adjective* causing the coughing out of phlegm etc. • *noun* an expectorant medicine. [Say ex PECTA rint]

expedience *noun* = EXPEDIENCY. [Say ex PEEDY ince]

expediency *noun* (*plural* **expediencies**) **1** the use of methods to achieve the most immediate and beneficial results, based on convenience and practicality rather than moral concerns: *the government has been accused of bypassing due process in the name of political expediency*. **2** the convenience or suitability of an action or type of behaviour in a certain situation: *early settlers built their homes for expediency and not for show*. [Say PEEDY in see]

expedient • *adjective* **1** useful or necessary for a particular purpose, but not always fair or right: *the government has clearly decided that a cut in interest rates would be politically expedient*. **2** suitable, appropriate: *holding a public enquiry into the scheme was not expedient*. • *noun* a means of attaining an end: *the disease was controlled by the simple expedient of not allowing anyone to leave the city*. [Say PEEDY int]

expedite *verb* (**expedites**, **expedited**, **expediting**) make a process happen more quickly: *we have developed rapid order processing to expedite deliveries to customers* ◊ *she promised to expedite economic reforms*. [Say EXPA dite]

expedition *noun* **1** a journey or voyage for a particular purpose, esp. tourism, exploration, or scientific research. **2** the personnel or ships etc. undertaking this. **3** promptness, speed: *the landlord shall remedy the defects with all possible expedition*.

expeditionary *adjective* of or used in an expedition, esp. a military expedition to a foreign country: *one of the*

founding officers of the 22nd Battalion of the Canadian Expeditionary Force lost a leg at Vimy. [Say expa DISH'n airy]

expeditious *adjective* acting or done with speed and efficiency: *the need for expeditious settlement of land claims*. ▶ **expeditiously** *adverb* [Say expa DISH us]

expel *verb* (**expels**, **expelled**, **expelling**) (often foll. by *from*) **1** compel the departure of (a person) from a school etc. **2** force out or eject (a substance from a body etc.). **3** order or force to leave a building etc.

expend *verb* spend or use up (money, energy, etc.).

expendable *adjective* of little significance when compared to an overall purpose, and therefore able to be abandoned or allowed to be killed or destroyed: *it was outrageous that the lives of Iraqi citizens were considered expendable in order to save the lives of American troops*.

expenditure *noun* **1** the action of spending funds: *an increase in expenditure on health care*. **2** a thing (esp. a sum of money) expended: *our expenditures have, alas, exceeded our income*.

expense *noun* **1** cost incurred; payment of money. **2** (usu. in *plural*) **a** costs incurred in doing a particular job etc.: *will pay your expenses*. **b** an amount paid to reimburse this: *offered me $120 per day expenses*. **3** a thing that is a cause of much expense: *the house is a real expense*. PHRASES **at the expense of** so as to cause loss or damage or discredit to (something). **at a person's expense 1** causing a person to suffer injury, ridicule, etc. **2** with costs paid by a person.

expense account *noun* a list of an employee's expenses to be reimbursed by the employer.

expensive *adjective* **1** costing much. **2** charging high prices. **3** causing much expense: *has expensive tastes*. ▶ **expensively** *adverb* **expensiveness** *noun*

experience • *noun* **1** actual observation of or practical acquaintance with facts or events. **2** knowledge or skill resulting from this. **3 a** an event regarded as affecting one: *an unpleasant experience*. **b** the fact or process of being so affected: *learned by experience*. **4** the events that have taken place within the knowledge of an individual, a community, etc.: *the Canadian experience*. • *verb* (**experiences**, **experienced**, **experiencing**) **1** have experience of; undergo. **2** feel or be affected by (an emotion etc.).

experienced *adjective* **1** having had much experience. **2** skilled from experience: *an experienced driver*.

experiential *adjective* involving or based on experience. *experiential knowledge* ◊ *experiential learning methods*. ▶ **experientially** *adverb* [Say ex peery EN shull]

experiment • *noun* **1** a procedure undertaken to make a discovery, test a hypothesis etc., or demonstrate a known fact. **2** a procedure or course of action tentatively adopted without being sure that it will achieve its purpose. • *verb* make an experiment.

experimental *adjective* **1** based on or making use of experiment: *experimental psychology*. **2 a** used in experiments: *experimental animal*. **b** based on untested ideas or techniques and not yet established: *an experimental drug*. **3** (of an artistic work or technique) involving a radically new style: *experimental music*.

experimental farm *noun* (also **experimental station**) *Cdn* an agricultural research centre, esp. one established through Agriculture Canada.

experimentalism *noun* the use of experiment or innovation in the arts. ▶ **experimentalist** *noun*

experimentally *adverb* in or by means of an experiment or series of experiments: *the theory was confirmed experimentally*.

experimentation *noun* the activity or process of experimenting: *experimentation with new teaching methods*.

experimenter *noun* **1** a person who conducts an experiment. **2** a person who uses new or experimental techniques; an innovator.

expert • *adjective* **1** having special knowledge or skill in a subject. **2** involving or resulting from this: *expert advice*. • *noun* a person having special knowledge or skill. ▶ **expertly** *adverb* **expertness** *noun*

expertise *noun* expert skill, knowledge, etc. [Say ex pur TEEZ]

expert system *noun* a computer program into which has been incorporated the knowledge of experts on a particular subject so that non-experts can use it for making decisions, evaluations, or inferences.

expiate *verb* (**expiates**, **expiated**, **expiating**) accept punishment or make amends for (wrongdoing): *we find it just that the offender should expiate his crime through suffering*. ▶ **expiation** *noun* [Say EX pee ate, ex pee AY sh'n]

expiration *noun* **1** expiry. **2** breathing out.

expire *verb* (**expires**, **expired**, **expiring**) **1** (of a period of time, validity, etc.) come to an end. **2** (of a document, authorization, etc.) cease to be valid; become void. **3** (of a person) die. **4** exhale (air etc.) from the lungs.

expiry *noun* (*plural* **expiries**) **1** the end of the validity or duration of something. **2** death.

explain *verb* **1** make (something) clear or intelligible with detailed information etc. **2** account for (one's conduct, a phenomenon, etc.): *that doesn't explain why you didn't phone*. PHRASES **explain away** minimize the significance of (a difficulty or mistake) by providing reasons for it. **explain oneself 1** make one's meaning clear. **2** give an account of one's motives or conduct. ▶ **explainable** *adjective* **explainer** *noun*

explanation *noun* **1** a statement or account that makes something clear: *the birth rate is central to any explanation of population trends*. **2** a reason or justification given for an action or belief: *Freud tried to make sex the explanation for everything ◊ my application was rejected without explanation*.

explanatory *adjective* serving to explain. [Say ex PLANNA tory]

expletive *noun* an oath or swear word: *he dropped the book on his foot and muttered several expletives under his breath*. [Say EXPLA tiv or ex PLEE tiv]

explicable *adjective* that can be explained: *his behaviour is only explicable in terms of his recent illness*. [Say ex PLICKA bull or EX plicka bull]

explicate *verb* (**explicates**, **explicated**, **explicating**) **1** make clear, explain. **2** analyze and develop (an idea, principle, etc.) in detail: *attempting to explicate the relationship between crime and economic forces*. ▶ **explication** *noun* [Say EXPLA kate, expla KAY sh'n]

explicit *adjective* **1** expressly stated or conveyed, leaving nothing merely implied; stated in detail: *gave me very explicit directions on how to get there*. **2** expressing views bluntly and openly: *she was quite explicit about why she had left*. **3** describing or representing nudity or intimate sexual activity. ▶ **explicitly** *adverb* **explicitness** *noun* [Say ex PLISS it]

explode *verb* (**explodes**, **exploded**, **exploding**) **1 a** (of gas, gunpowder, a bomb, etc.) expand suddenly, burst, or fly into pieces with a loud noise owing to a release of internal energy. **b** cause (a bomb etc.) to explode. **2** give vent suddenly to emotion, esp. anger. **3** increase suddenly or rapidly, esp. in size, numbers, amount, etc. **4** appear suddenly and with great impact. **5** show (a theory etc.) to be false or baseless.

exploit • *noun* a bold or daring feat. • *verb* **1** make use of (a resource etc.); derive benefit from. **2** usu. *derogatory* utilize or take advantage of (esp. a person) for one's own ends. ▶ **exploitability** *noun* **exploitable** *adjective* **exploitation** *noun* **exploitative** *adjective* **exploiter** *noun* **exploitive** *adjective*

exploration *noun* **1** the action of travelling in or through an unfamiliar area in order to learn about it or find something in it: *space exploration ◊ a profitable Alberta oil and gas exploration company*. **2** a thorough analysis of a subject or theme: *her latest book is an exploration of female relationships*.

exploratory *adjective* **1** (of discussion etc.) preliminary, serving to establish procedure etc. **2** involving exploration or investigation: *exploratory surgery*.

explore *verb* (**explores**, **explored**, **exploring**) **1** travel extensively (through a country etc.) in order to learn or discover about it. **2 a** inquire (into); investigate thoroughly. **b** experiment, try something new (in music etc.). **3** *Surgery* examine (a part of the body) in detail. **4** search for new deposits of minerals, oil, etc. ▶ **explorer** *noun*

explosion *noun* **1** a violent and destructive shattering or blowing apart of something, as is caused by a bomb. **2** a violent expansion in which energy is transmitted outwards as a shock wave. **3 a** a sudden outburst of noise. **b** a sudden outbreak of feeling, esp. anger. **4** a rapid or sudden increase in numbers, size, or amount: *the population explosion ◊ there has been an explosion of interest in the subject*.

explosive • *adjective* **1** able or tending or likely to explode. **2 a** highly controversial. **b** (of a situation etc.) dangerously tense. **3** rapid, sudden; violent: *explosive growth*. **4** (of an athlete) characterized by bursts of energy. • *noun* an explosive substance. ▶ **explosively** *adverb* **explosiveness** *noun*

Expo *noun* (also **expo**) (*plural* **Expos**) **1** a large international exhibition. **2** an exhibition for a specific industry or with a specific theme: *bridal expo*.

exponent *noun* **1** a person who supports an idea, theory, etc. and persuades others that it is good: *she was a leading exponent of free trade ◊ Huxley was an exponent of Darwin's theory of evolution*. **2** a person who is able to perform a particular activity with skill: *the most famous exponent of the art of mime*. **3** a raised symbol or expression beside a numeral indicating how many times it is to be multiplied by itself, e.g. $2^3 = 2 \times 2 \times 2$. [Say ex POE nint]

exponential • *adjective* **1** *Math* of or indicated by a mathematical exponent. **2** (of an increase etc.) more and more rapid. • *noun* *Math* an exponential quantity. [Say expa NEN chull]

exponential growth *noun* the growth of something by greater and greater amounts, experienced when a fixed rate of growth or interest is applied over a period of time to a continuously growing total, e.g. a population or bank account.

exponentially *adverb* more and more rapidly: *the sport's popularity has grown exponentially since the Olympics*. [Say expa NEN chuh lee]

export • *verb* **1** send out (goods, services, etc.) to another country, esp. for sale. **2** spread or introduce (a trend, ideology, etc.) into another country: *American pop music has been exported around the world*. **3** *Computing* transmit (data) from a system for use elsewhere. • *noun* **1** the process of exporting. **2 a** an exported article or service. **b** (in *plural*) an amount exported: *exports exceeded $50m*. ▶ **exportable** *adjective* **exporter** *noun*

expose *verb* (**exposes**, **exposed**, **exposing**) **1** remove the covering from or leave uncovered or unprotected. **2** (foll. by *to*) **a** cause to be liable to or in danger of: *was exposed to great danger*. **b** introduce, or lay open to (an influence etc.). **3** *Photography* subject (a

film) to light, esp. by operation of a camera. **4** reveal the identity or fact of (esp. a person or thing disapproved of or guilty of crime etc.). **5** disclose; make public: *my job as a journalist is to expose the truth* ◊ *he did not want to expose his fears and insecurity to anyone*. **6** leave (a person) in the open to die. PHRASES **expose oneself** display one's genitals publicly and indecently.

exposé *noun* a report of the facts about something, esp. a report in the media that reveals something discreditable: *an exposé of political influence on the RCMP*. [Say expo ZAY]

exposed *adjective* **1** open to: *exposed to the east*. **2** vulnerable: *Miranda felt exposed and lonely*.

exposition *noun* **1** a comprehensive description and explanation of an idea or theory: *an exposition and defence of Marx's writings*. **2** *Music* the part of a movement in which the principal themes are first presented. **3** a large public exhibition of art or trade goods.

expositor *noun* a person or thing that explains complicated ideas or theories: *a lucid expositor of difficult ideas*. [Say ex POZZA tur, ex POZZA tory]

expository *adjective* intended to explain or describe something: *the essay is an exercise in expository prose* ◊ *an important expository scene between the two characters in the play*. [Say ex POZZA tur, ex POZZA tory]

exposure *noun* **1 a** the act or condition of exposing or being exposed (to cold, danger, radiation, an influence, etc.). **b** the duration or extent of this condition. **2** the physical condition resulting from being exposed to the elements, esp. in severe conditions: *died from exposure*. **3** the revelation of an identity or fact, esp. when concealed or likely to find disapproval. **4 a** the action of exposing a film etc. to the light. **b** the duration of this action. **c** the extent to which the film is exposed (dependent on shutter speed and aperture). **d** an area of film etc. so exposed. **5** the way in which something is situated in relation to compass direction, wind, sunshine, etc. **6** publicity; presence in the public eye.

expound *verb* set out in detail (a doctrine, theory, etc.): *he expounded his views on the subject to me at length* ◊ *the theory of language expounded by Chomsky* ◊ *she expounded on the government's policies*. ▶**expounder** *noun*

express[1] *verb* (**expresses**, **expressed**, **expressing**) **1** represent or make known (thought, feelings, etc.) in words or by gestures, conduct, etc. **2 express oneself** say what one thinks or means. **3** esp. *Math* represent by symbols. **4** squeeze out (liquid or air).

express[2] • *adjective* **1 a** operating at high speed. **b** (of a train, bus, elevator, etc.) making relatively few stops before reaching its destination. **c** (of a road, lane, etc.) designed for express traffic. **2** definitely stated, not merely implied: *her express intention was that the money should be given to the performing arts*. **3** done, made, or sent for a special purpose: *the schools were founded for the express purpose of teaching deaf children*. **4** (of messages or goods) delivered immediately or rapidly. • *adverb* by express courier or train. • *noun* (*plural* **expresses**) **1** an express train, bus, etc. **2** (in company names) a courier. • *verb* (**expresses**, **expressed**, **expressing**) send by express courier or delivery.

expressible *adjective* that can be expressed.

expression *noun* **1** the process of making known one's thoughts or feelings: *she accepted his expressions of sympathy* ◊ *these tastes found expression in Liana's painting* ◊ *freedom of expression is a basic human right*. **2** a word or phrase, esp. a common saying or figure of speech: *he's a pain in the butt, if you'll pardon the expression*. **3** *Math* a collection of symbols expressing a quantity. **4** a person's facial appearance, esp. as indicating feeling: *a sad expression*. **5** a strong show of feeling when

performing: *danced well but lacked expression*. **6** the appearance in a phenotype of a character or effect attributed to a particular gene.

expressionism *noun* (also **Expressionism**) a style of painting, music, drama, etc., in which an artist or writer seeks to express emotional experience rather than impressions of the external world. Expressionists typically reject traditional ideas of beauty or harmony and use distortion, exaggeration, and other non-naturalistic devices to emphasize and express the inner world of emotion, often incorporating violence and the grotesque. ▶**expressionist** *noun & adjective* **expressionistic** *adjective*

expressionless *adjective* not showing feelings or thoughts etc.: *an expressionless face*.

expressive *adjective* **1** full of expression: *an expressive look*. **2** (foll. by *of*) serving to express: *the spires are expressive of religious aspiration*. ▶**expressively** *adverb* **expressiveness** *noun* **expressivity** *noun*

expressly *adverb* **1** clearly, definitely: *he was expressly forbidden to touch my things*. **2** for a special and deliberate purpose: *the hall was expressly designed for wedding receptions*.

expresso *noun* = ESPRESSO.

expressway *noun* a highway for fast-moving traffic, esp. in urban areas, with limited access and a median dividing opposing traffic.

expropriate *verb* (**expropriates**, **expropriated**, **expropriating**) (esp. of a government) take away property from its owner: *the city stepped in to expropriate the land for a park*. ▶**expropriation** *noun* [Say ex PRO pree ate, ex pro pree AY sh'n]

expulsion *noun* **1** the action of depriving someone of membership in an organization: *expulsion from the union*. **2 a** the process of forcing someone to leave a place, esp. a country: *the espionage allegations led to the expulsion of senior diplomats from the country*. **b** (**the Expulsion**) *Cdn Hist.* the eviction of francophones from Acadia in 1755. **3** the act of dismissing a student permanently from a school: *the girls were threatened with expulsion*. **4** the process of forcing something out of somewhere. ▶**expulsive** *adjective* [Say ex PUL shun, ex PULSE iv]

expunge *verb* (**expunges**, **expunged**, **expunging**) **1** erase, remove (esp. a passage from a book or a name from a list): *details of his criminal activities were expunged from the file*. **2** wipe out, destroy: *what happened just before the accident was expunged from her memory*. [Say ex PUNGE]

expurgate *verb* (**expurgates**, **expurgated**, **expurgating**) remove matter thought to be objectionable from a book, a conversation, etc.: *she gave an expurgated account of what had happened* ◊ *an expurgated version of Gulliver's Travels*. [Say EX pur gate]

exquisite *adjective* **1** extremely beautiful or pleasing: *exquisite craftsmanship* ◊ *her wedding dress was exquisite*. **2** keenly felt: *exquisite pleasure*. **3** highly sensitive or discriminating: *exquisite taste*. ▶**exquisitely** *adverb* **exquisiteness** *noun* [Say ex QUIZ it or EX quiz it]

extant *adjective* (esp. of a document, species, etc.) still existing, surviving: *extant remains of the ancient wall* ◊ *a limited number of documents from the period are still extant*. [Say EX t'nt or ex TANT]

SPELL CHECK ABC✔
ecstasy

Warning: there is no *x* in **ecstasy**.

---

extempore *adjective & adverb* without preparation: *an extempore speech*. [Say ex TEMPA ree]

extemporize *verb* (**extemporizes**, **extemporized**,

E

extemporizing) compose or produce (music, a speech, etc.) without preparation. ► **extemporization** *noun* [Say ex TEMPA rize, ex tempa rize AY sh'n]

extend *verb* **1** lengthen or make larger in space or time. **2** stretch or lay out at full length. **3** reach or be or make continuous over a certain area. **4 a** have a certain scope: *the permit does not extend to camping.* **b** increase the scope or range of application of: *extend their control over the region.* **5 a** offer (an invitation, hospitality, kindness, etc.). **b** accord, grant (financial credit). **6** tax the powers of (an athlete, student, performer, etc.) to the utmost. ► **extendable** *adjective*

extended family *noun* (*plural* **extended families**) **1** one's family including or esp. one's grandparents, aunts, uncles, cousins, etc. **2** such a group living in the same household or near each other.

extender *noun* **1** a person or thing that extends. **2** a substance added to paint, ink, glue, etc., to dilute its colour or increase its bulk.

extensible *adjective* **1** capable of extending or being extended. **2** *Computing* denoting or having to do with a metalanguage that allows users to define their own customized markup languages, esp. in order to display documents on the World Wide Web. [Say ex TENSA bull]

extension *noun* **1** the action or process of making something larger: *the extension of the President's powers.* **2** a part that is added to something to enlarge or prolong it: *the railway's southern extension.* **3** a part enlarging or added on to a building. **4** an application of an existing system or activity to a new area: *direct marketing is an extension of telephone sales.* **5 a** a subsidiary telephone on the same line as the main one. **b** its number. **6** an additional period of time, esp. extending allowance for a project etc. **7** extramural instruction by a university or college: *extension course.* **8** an extension cord. **9** a string of letters after a period in the name of a computer file, often identifying the file as belonging to a certain category. PHRASES **by extension** taking the same line of argument further: *the study shows how television, and by extension, the media, alter political relationships.*

extension cord *noun* an electrical cable attached to the cord of an appliance etc., so that it can be plugged into a distant outlet.

extensive *adjective* **1** covering a large area in space or time. **2** having a wide scope; far-reaching, comprehensive: *extensive knowledge.* **3** *Agriculture* involving cultivation from a large area, with a minimum of special resources (*compare* INTENSIVE *adjective* 2). ► **extensively** *adverb* **extensiveness** *noun*

extensor *noun* (also **extensor muscle**) a muscle that extends or straightens out part of the body.

extent *noun* **1** the space over which a thing extends. **2** the width or limits of application; scope: *to the full extent of their power.* **3** the whole of a space or area of a specified kind: *the extent of the ocean.*

extenuating *adjective* showing reasons why a wrong or illegal act, or a bad situation, should be judged less seriously or excused: *there were extenuating circumstances and the defendant did not receive a prison sentence ◊ illness and other extenuating circumstances that may have affected a student's performance will be considered.* [Say ex TEN yoo ate]

exterior • *adjective* **1 a** of or on the outer side (*opp.* INTERIOR). **b** (foll. by *to*) situated on the outside of (a building etc.). **c** coming from without. **d** intended for the outside or outer surfaces. **2** *Film* outdoor. • *noun* **1** the outward aspect or surface of a building etc. **2** the outward or apparent behaviour or demeanour of a person. **3** *Film* an outdoor scene.

exterminate *verb* (**exterminates**, **exterminated**, **exterminating**) **1** destroy utterly (esp. something

living). **2** get rid of; eliminate (a pest, disease, etc.). ► **extermination** *noun* **exterminator** *noun*

external • *adjective* **1 a** of or situated on the outside or visible part (*opp.* INTERNAL). **b** coming or derived from the outside or an outside source. **2** relating to a country's foreign affairs. **3** outside the conscious subject: *the external world.* **4** (of medicine etc.) for use on the outside of the body. **5** pertaining to or consisting of outward acts or observances. **6** pertaining to a device that is subsidiary or peripheral to a computer system: *external modem.* • *noun* (in *plural*) **1** the outward features or aspect: *instruction in theology there paid too much attention to externals, such as the administration of the sacraments, and too little to intellectual development.* **2** external circumstances. **3** inessentials.

external affairs *plural noun* **1** a country's relations with other countries. **2** (treated as *singular*) the government department concerned with these.

externalize *verb* (**externalizes**, **externalized**, **externalizing**) **1** treat (a fact, responsibility, etc.) as existing or occurring outside of oneself or in the external world. **2** *Psychology* attribute (one's own feelings etc.) to others, the external environment, etc. **3** show what one is thinking and feeling by what one says or does: *the rejected child may externalize pain through aggressive or disruptive behaviour.*

externally *adverb* **1** on, from, or in terms of the outside of something: *externally the house is similar to the others.* **2** from a source outside the subject affected: *the team is supported externally by corporate sponsors.*

external relations *plural noun* **1** = EXTERNAL AFFAIRS. **2** = PUBLIC RELATIONS.

extinct *adjective* **1 a** (of a species, language, etc.) no longer surviving in the world at large or in a specific locale. **b** (of a family) having no living descendant. **2** (of a volcano) no longer active. **3** (of life, hope, etc.) terminated, quenched. **4** (of a type of person, job or way of life) no longer in existence in society: *servants are now almost extinct in modern society.*

extinction *noun* a situation in which a plant, an animal, a way of life etc. stops existing: *a tribe threatened with extinction ◊ the whooping crane was in danger of extinction ◊ a campaign to save wild koalas from extinction.*

extinguish *verb* (**extinguishes**, **extinguished**, **extinguishing**) **1** quench, put out, or cause (a flame, light, etc.) to die out. **2** destroy, put an end to, or obscure utterly (a feeling, quality, etc.): *news of the bombing extinguished all hope of peace.* **3 a** abolish or wipe out (a debt), esp. by full payment. **b** *Law* nullify or render void (a right, claim, etc.). [Say ex TING gwish]

extinguisher *noun* a device used for extinguishing, esp. a fire extinguisher. [Say ex TING gwish er]

extirpate *verb* (**extirpates**, **extirpated**, **extirpating**) **1** kill all the members of (a race, nation, etc.) or make (a species) extinct locally, but not globally. **2** do away with: *to extirpate traditional political and religious practices, laws required that chiefs be elected, and forbade religious ceremonies like the Sun Dance.* ► **extirpation** *noun* [Say EX tur pate, ex tur PAY sh'n]

extol *verb* (**extols**, **extolled**, **extolling**) praise enthusiastically: *doctors often extol the virtues of eating less fat.* [Say ex TOLL]

extort *verb* obtain (esp. money) by force, threats, persistent demands, etc. ► **extortion** *noun*

extortionate *adjective* **1** (of a price etc.) exorbitant or grossly excessive: *loans at extortionate rates of interest.* **2** using or given to extortion: *no one can escape the parking authority's extortionate grasp.* ► **extortionately** *adverb* [Say ex TORE shun it]

extortionist *noun* a person who obtains esp. money by force or threats. [Say ex TORE shun ist]

extra • *adjective* additional; more than is usual or necessary or expected. • *adverb* **1** more than the usual, specified, or expected amount. **2** additionally. • *noun* **1** an extra or additional thing. **2** a thing for which an extra charge is made. **3** a person engaged temporarily to fill out a scene in a film or play, esp. as one of a crowd. **4** a special issue of a newspaper etc.

extra- *combining form* **1** outside, beyond. **2** beyond the scope of.

extra-base hit *noun Baseball* a base hit that allows a batter safely to reach more than one base.

extra-billing *noun Cdn* the practice of a doctor charging patients fees in excess of what provincial health insurance will pay.

extracellular *adjective* situated or taking place outside a cell or cells. [Say extra SELL yuh lur]

extract • *verb* **1** remove or take out (a tooth etc.) from a containing body or cavity, usu. with some degree of effort, force, dexterity, etc. **2** obtain (money, information, etc.) with difficulty or against a person's will. **3** obtain (a natural resource) from the earth. **4** take (a part) from a whole, esp. select or reproduce (a passage of writing, music, etc.) for quotation or performance. **5** obtain (constituent elements, juices, etc.) from a thing or substance by chemical or physical means such as pressure, distillation, etc. **6** derive (happiness, pleasure, amusement, etc.) from a specified source or situation. **7** draw out (the sense of something), deduce (a principle) etc. • *noun* **1** an excerpt or short passage taken from a book, piece of music, etc. **2** a preparation containing the active principle of a substance in concentrated form: *vanilla extract.*

extraction *noun* **1** the action of taking out something, esp. using effort or force: *the extraction and processing of primary resources* ◊ *floss your teeth to avoid extractions.* **2** the ethnic origin of someone's family: *of Scottish extraction.*

extractive *adjective* of, involving, or concerned with the extraction of natural resources or products, esp. non-renewable ones.

extractor *noun* **1** a machine that extracts one thing from another, e.g. juice from fruit, water from wet laundry, etc. **2** the part of a breech-loading firearm which removes the cartridge. **3** a tool or instrument for loosening or removing tight-fitting parts etc.

extracurricular *adjective* **1** (of an activity or subject of study) not included in the normal curriculum. **2** outside the normal routine, job expectations, etc. **3** *informal* extramarital. [Say extra kuh RICK you lur]

extradite *verb* (**extradites**, **extradited**, **extraditing**) **1** hand over (a person accused or convicted of a crime) to the foreign country etc. in which the crime was committed. **2** obtain the extradition of (a person) from another country. [Say EXTRA dite]

extradition *noun* the surrender or delivery of a person into the jurisdiction of another country in order that he or she may be tried by that country for crimes committed there. [Say extra DISH un]

extramarital *adjective* involving a usu. sexual relationship between a married person and someone other than his or her spouse. [Say extra MARITAL]

extramural *adjective* designating educational activity conducted off the premises of a university, college, or school. [Say extra MURAL]

extraneous *adjective* **1** not directly connected with the particular situation one is in or the subject one is dealing with: *one is obliged to wade through many pages of extraneous material.* **2** of external origin: *coughs and extraneous noises can be edited out of the recording.*
▶ **extraneously** *adverb* [Say ex TRAINY us]

extraordinaire *adjective* (placed after noun) remarkable or outstanding in a particular capacity: *Houdini, escape artist extraordinaire.* [Say ex TRORE din air]

extraordinarily *adverb* to a remarkable degree: *she is extraordinarily talented.*

extraordinary *adjective* **1** unusual, remarkable, or out of the regular course of order. **2** exceeding what is usual in amount, degree, extent, or size, esp. to the point of provoking astonishment, admiration, or disapproval. **3** (of an official etc.) additional to regular staff or specially employed: *ambassador extraordinary.* [Say ex TRORE din airy or extra ORDINARY]

extrapolate *verb* (**extrapolates**, **extrapolated**, **extrapolating**) **1** estimate something or form an opinion about something, using the facts that one has now and that are valid for one situation and supposing that they will be valid for the new one: *the figures were obtained by extrapolating from past trends* ◊ *we have extrapolated these results from research done elsewhere* ◊ *the results cannot be extrapolated to other patient groups.* **2** *Math* extend (a range of values, a curve, etc.) on the assumption that the trend exhibited inside the given part is maintained outside of it (*compare* INTERPOLATE 3).
▶ **extrapolation** *noun* [Say ex TRAPPA late, ex trappa LAY sh'n]

extrasensory *adjective* regarded as derived by means other than the known senses, e.g. by telepathy, clairvoyance, etc. [Say extra SENSA ree]

extrasensory perception *noun* the supposed ability to perceive outside, past, or future events without the use of known senses. Abbreviation: **ESP**.

extraterrestrial • *adjective* **1** existing or occurring beyond the earth or its atmosphere. **2** (in science fiction) from outer space. • *noun* (in science fiction) a being, esp. an intelligent one, from outer space. [Say extra tuh RESS tree ul]

extraterritorial *adjective* situated or (of laws etc.) valid outside a country's territory: *extraterritorial fishing zones.* [Say extra TERRITORIAL]

extravagance *noun* **1 a** wastefulness or excessive spending or use of resources. **b** a purchase or payment difficult to justify except as a whim or indulgence. **2** lack of moderation; excessive elaborateness in style, speech, or action: *the extravagance of the decor.* [Say ex TRAVVA gince]

extravagant *adjective* **1** immoderate, excessive, or wasteful in use of resources, esp. money. **2** exorbitant or costing much. **3 a** (of ideas, speech, or behaviour) going beyond what is reasonable, usual, or justifiable: *extravagant claims.* **b** astonishingly elaborate or showy: *this variety of rose produces extravagant blooms.*
▶ **extravagantly** *adverb* [Say ex TRAVVA gint]

extravaganza *noun* an event featuring elaborate and colourful spectacle, massive participation, lavish expenditure, etc. [Say ex travva GANZA]

extra-virgin *adjective* (of olive oil) made from the first pressing, cold pressed, and thus of high quality.

extreme • *adjective* **1 a** reaching a high or the highest degree or being exceedingly great or intense: *in extreme danger.* **b** (of a case, circumstance, etc.) having some feature or characteristic in the utmost degree. **2 a** severe, stringent, lacking restraint or moderation: *extreme measures.* **b** (of a person, opinion, etc.) going to great lengths, advocating severe and drastic measures, or being immoderate in opinion. **3 a** outermost, furthest from the centre: *the extreme edge.* **b** situated at either end. **c** last, utmost, very far advanced in any direction. **4** *Politics* radical or being on the far left or right of a party. **5** designating sports performed in a hazardous environment, involving a high physical risk: *extreme skiing.* • *noun* **1** (often in *plural*) one or other of

two things as remote or as different as possible in position, nature, or condition. **2** a thing at either end of anything. **3** the highest degree, the greatest length, or the most extreme measure of anything. PHRASES **go to extremes** take an extreme course of action. **go to the other extreme** take a diametrically opposite course of action. **in the extreme** to an extreme degree. ▶ **extremely** adverb

extreme unction noun the former name for the Roman Catholic sacrament of anointing the sick, esp. those thought to be near death.

extremism noun extreme or fanatical political or religious views, and belief in the use of extreme measures to promote these.

extremist • noun **1** a person who holds extreme or fanatical political or religious views, esp. one who resorts to or advocates extreme measures to promote these. **2** a person who tends to go to extremes. • adjective of or pertaining to extremists or extremism.

extremity noun (plural **extremities**) **1** the furthest point, end or limit of something: the lake is situated at the eastern extremity of the mountain range. **2** (in plural) the outermost parts of the body, esp. the hands and feet. **3** the degree to which a situation, a feeling, an action, etc. is extreme, difficult or unusual: those who had views on the other side seem to have been excluded, whatever the moderation or extremity of the views. [Say ex TREMMA tee]

extricate verb free or disentangle (esp. a person) from a constraint or difficulty: he knew how to extricate himself from difficulties with truly exasperating dexterity ◊ they managed to bend the window frame and extricate the dazed driver. ▶ **extrication** noun [Say EXTRA kate, extra KAY sh'n]

extrovert • noun **1** Psychology a person whose thoughts and interests are predominantly concerned with things outside the self. **2** an outgoing or sociable person (compare INTROVERT). • adjective typical or characteristic of an extrovert. ▶ **extroverted** adjective [Say EXTRA vert]

extrude verb (**extrudes, extruded, extruding**) **1** (foll. by from) thrust, force out, or expel. **2** shape (metal, plastics, etc.) by forcing through a die. ▶ **extruded** adjective **extruder** noun [Say ex TRUDE]

extrusion noun **1** the process of forcing or being forced through or out of something. **2** a a method of forming a material such as metal or plastic by forcing it through a specially shaped nozzle. **b** something made by means of this process. [Say ex TRUE zhun]

exuberance noun **1** lively energy and excitement: he approaches everything with a youthful exuberance. **2** a vigorous and imaginative artistic style: her paintings are characterized by exuberance. **3** a healthy, luxuriant condition of plants etc.: we admired the garden for its lush exuberance. [Say ex OO bur ince or ex YOO bur ince]

exuberant adjective **1** (of people or their actions) lively, high-spirited, effusive in display of feelings: an exuberant performance. **2** characterized by a vigorously imaginative artistic style: exuberant, over-the-top sculptures. **3** (of a plant etc.) growing luxuriously or profusely: exuberant foliage. ▶ **exuberantly** adverb [Say ex OO bur int or ex YOO bur int]

exude verb (**exudes, exuded, exuding**) **1** come out or cause to come out slowly; ooze: the plant exudes a sticky fluid ◊ slime exudes from the fungus. **2 a** (of a person) display (a quality, emotion etc.) abundantly and openly: exuded charm and confidence. **b** (of a place) have a strong atmosphere of: the building exudes an air of tranquility. [Say ex OOD or ex YOOD]

exult verb show or feel great joy and excitement, esp. as the result of a success: exulting in her escape, Leonora closed the door behind her ◊ "We won!" she exulted ◊ Christiane was exulting over the newly recovered closeness and affection with her daughters. ▶ **exultation** noun **exultant** adjective **exultantly** adverb **exultingly** adverb [Say ex ULT, ex ul TAY sh'n]

exurb noun a town or community beyond the suburbs of a large city. ▶ **exurban** adjective

eye • noun **1** the organ of sight in humans and animals. **2** (in singular or plural) **a** sight or the faculty of sight. **b** perception: see it through a woman's eyes ◊ in the eyes of the law. **3 a** a mark or spot resembling an eye, occurring on eggs, insect wings, etc. **b** the leaf bud of a potato. **4** the relatively calm region at the centre of a storm or hurricane. **5** the hole in a needle through which thread is passed. **6** a ring or loop for a bolt or hook etc. to pass through. **7** the main mass of lean meat in a cut of meat, esp. beef: eye of round. • verb (**eyes, eyed, eyeing**) **1** watch or observe closely, esp. admiringly or with curiosity or suspicion. **2** ogle or look at (a person) amorously or with sexual interest. PHRASES **all eyes 1** watching intently. **2** general attention: all eyes were on us. **close one's eyes to** ignore, refuse to recognize or consider. **an eye for an eye** retaliation in kind. **have an eye for** be capable of perceiving or appreciating. **have one's eye on** wish or plan to procure. **have eyes bigger than one's stomach** wish or expect to eat more than one can. **have eyes for** be interested in: had eyes for no other. **have an eye to** have as one's objective or prudently consider. **hit a person (right) between the eyes** informal be very obvious or impressive. **keep an eye on** keep under careful observation. **keep an eye open** (or **out**) (often foll. by for) watch carefully. **keep one's eyes open** (or **peeled** or **skinned**) watch out or be on the alert. **make eyes** (or **sheep's eyes**) (foll. by at) look amorously or flirtatiously at. **my eye** slang nonsense. **one in the eye** (foll. by for) a disappointment or setback, esp. for someone regarded as deserving it. **open a person's eyes** be enlightening or revealing to a person. **see eye to eye** (often foll. by with) be in full agreement. **up to the** (or **one's**) **eyes in 1** inundated with or deeply engaged or involved in (a thing): up to the eyes in work. **2** up to the utmost limit: mortgaged up to the eyes. **with one's eyes open** deliberately or with full awareness. **with one's eyes shut** (or **closed**) **1** easily or with little effort. **2** unobservant or without awareness: goes around with his eyes shut. **with an eye to** with a view to or prudently considering.

eyeball • noun the firm white sphere of the eye within the eyelids and socket. • verb slang look or stare at. PHRASES **eyeball-to-eyeball** informal confronting or encountering closely. **to** (or **up to**) **the eyeballs** informal to a great extent.

eyebrow noun the line of hair growing along the ridge above each eye socket. PHRASES **raise eyebrows** cause surprise, disbelief, or disapproval. **raise one's eyebrows** (or **an eyebrow**) show surprise, disbelief, or mild disapproval.

eye-catcher noun a person or thing which catches the eye, through attractiveness, uniqueness, etc. ▶ **eye-catching** adjective

E

eyed *adjective* having eyes or circular markings of the kind described: *a one-eyed giant* ◊ *eagle-eyed sleuths* ◊ *black-eyed peas*.

eye doctor *noun* **1** an ophthalmologist. **2** an optometrist.

eyedropper *noun* = DROPPER 1.

eyeful *noun* (*plural* **eyefuls**) *informal* **1** a complete view or a good look at something. **2** a visually striking scene or thing, esp. an attractive person. PHRASES **get an eyeful** take a good, long look.

eyeglass *noun* **1** (in *plural*) a pair of lenses, in a frame resting on the nose and ears, used to correct defective eyesight or protect the eyes. **2** a lens for correcting or assisting defective sight.

eyelash *noun* a hair, or one of the rows of hairs, growing on the edge of the eyelid.

eyeless *adjective* without eyes.

eyelet *noun* **1** a small hole in paper, leather, cloth, etc., for string or rope etc. to pass through. **2** a metal ring reinforcement for this. **3** a small eye, esp. a small mark on a butterfly's wing (*compare* EYE *noun* 3a). **4 a** a form of decoration in embroidery, composed of usu. round eyelets finished along the edge, which produces an open work effect. **b** a lightweight fabric having many small embroidered holes in a decorative pattern.

eyelid *noun* either of the upper or lower folds of skin that meet when the eye is closed.

eyeliner *noun* a cosmetic applied as a line around the eye, usu. next to the lashes, to accentuate the eyes.

eye-opener *noun* *informal* a thing or experience that enlightens, surprises, etc. ▶ **eye-opening** *adjective*

eyepiece *noun* the lens or lenses at the end of telescope etc. to which the eye is applied and through which an image is viewed or magnified.

eye-popping *adjective* surprising, astonishing, esp. visually spectacular.

eyeshadow *noun* a coloured cosmetic applied to the eyelids, around the eyes, etc. to enhance the eyes.

eyesight *noun* the faculty or power of seeing.

eyesore *noun* a very ugly thing, esp. a building.

eye tooth *noun* a canine tooth, esp. in the upper jaw. PHRASES **would give one's eye teeth for** would make any sacrifice to obtain.

eyewitness • *noun* a person who has personally seen a thing done or happen and can testify to it. • *verb* (**eyewitnesses, eyewitnessed, eyewitnessing**) be an eyewitness to (an event).

e-zine *noun* a magazine or fanzine published in electronic format.

Ff

F¹ *noun* (also **f**) (*plural* **Fs** or **F's**) **1** the sixth letter of the alphabet. **2** *Music* the fourth note of the diatonic scale of C major. **3** the lowest category of academic mark, denoting a failing grade.

F² *abbreviation* (also **F.**) **1** Fahrenheit. **2** female. **3** a fine, moderately soft pencil lead, between B and H. **4** *Physics* force. **5** (in Ontario) FAMILY 8.

F³ *symbol* fluorine.

f *abbreviation* (also **f.**) **1** female. **2** *Grammar* feminine. **3** (*plural* **ff.**) following page etc. **4** *Music* forte. **5** (*plural* **ff.**) folio. **6** frequency. **7** *Math* function. **8** from.

fa *noun* Music **1** (in tonic sol-fa) the fourth note of a major scale. **2** the note F in the fixed-do system.

fab *adjective informal* fabulous, marvellous.

Fabian • *noun* a member or supporter of the Fabian Society, a socialist organization founded in England in 1884 to promote cautious and gradual political change. • *adjective* relating to or characteristic of the Fabians. ▶ **Fabianism** *noun* [Say FAY bee un]

fable *noun* **1** a tale, esp. with animals as characters, conveying a moral. **2** myths and legendary tales collectively: *a land rich in fable*. **3** a false statement or lie: *the fables that she had woven for the policeman*. **4** a thing falsely claimed to exist or having no existence outside popular legend etc.: *the towering example of pseudo-history is the fable that Canada was intended to be "two nations"*.

fabled *adjective* **1** famous. **2** celebrated in fable.

fabric *noun* **1** a woven, knitted, or felted material; a textile. **2** a structure or framework, esp. the walls, floor, and roof of a building. **3** the essential structure or essence of a thing: *the fabric of society*.

fabricate *verb* (**fabricates**, **fabricated**, **fabricating**) **1** construct or manufacture, esp. from prepared components: *you will have to fabricate an exhaust system*. **2** invent or concoct (a story, evidence, etc.): *the prisoner claimed the police had fabricated his confession*. **3** forge (a document). ▶ **fabrication** *noun* **fabricator** *noun*

fabulous *adjective* **1** extraordinary, esp. extraordinarily large: *fabulous wealth*. **2** excellent, marvellous, terrific: *a fabulous dancer*. **3** having no basis in reality; legendary, mythical: *fabulous creatures*. ▶ **fabulously** *adverb* **fabulousness** *noun*

FAC *abbreviation* Cdn Firearms Acquisition Certificate.

facade *noun* **1** the face of a building, esp. its principal front. **2** an outward appearance, esp. a deceptive one: *they seem happy together, but it's all a facade* ◊ *squalor and poverty lay behind the city's glittering facade*. [Say fuh SOD]

face • *noun* **1** the front of the head from the forehead to the chin. **2** the expression of the facial features: *had a happy face*. **3** a distorted look, grimace, etc. intended to express a usu. negative emotion: *don't make a face!* **4** the surface of a thing, esp. as regarded or approached. **5 a** the working surface of an implement etc. **b** the marked or picture side of a playing card. **c** either side of a coin, but esp. the side bearing the effigy. **6** = TYPEFACE. **7 a** the outward appearance of an immaterial thing: *the unacceptable face of capitalism*. **b** outward show: *put a good face on the matter*. **8 a** person, esp. conveying some quality or association: *some younger faces*. **9** respectable reputation: *a loss of face*. **10** makeup: *I have to put on my face*. **11** the

inscribed side of a document etc. • *verb* (**faces**, **faced**, **facing**) **1** look or be positioned towards or in a certain direction. **2** (of an illustration etc.) stand on the opposite page to: *facing page 20*. **3** confront, meet boldly: *face one's critics*. **4** confront, present itself to (a person etc.): *the problem that faces us*. **5** *Lacrosse* **a** start or restart play by placing the ball between the sticks of the two opposing players. **b** place (the ball) in this way to start or restart play. PHRASES **face a charge** (or **charges**) be forced to appear in court accused of something. **face off 1** *Hockey & Lacrosse* start or restart play by a faceoff. **2** assume a confrontational attitude; contend or compete against. **face up to** confront, accept bravely, or stand up to. **in one's** (or **the**) **face 1** directly at or straight against one. **2** confronting or irritatingly present. **in face** (or **the face**) **of 1** despite. **2** when confronted by. **3** in the presence of. **let's face it** *informal* we must be honest or realistic about it. **on the face of it** apparently, superficially, or obviously. **the face of the earth 1** the surface of the earth. **2** anywhere. **to a person's face** openly in a person's presence.

face card *noun* the king, queen, or jack in playing cards.

face cloth *noun* Cdn & Brit. a small cloth, usu. of terry, for washing one's face, hands, etc.

faced *adjective* (also in *combination*) **1** having a face or expression of a specified kind. **2** having a surface of a specified kind: *marble-faced houses*.

faceless *adjective* without an individual identity, lacking an individualized character; remote and impersonal: *faceless bureaucrats*.

facelift *noun* **1** cosmetic surgery to remove wrinkles etc. by tightening the skin of the face. **2** a procedure to improve the appearance of a thing, esp. the repairing of the facing on a building etc.

face mask *noun* **1** any covering or device to shield or protect the face, usu. covering the whole face, nose and mouth, or nose and eyes. **2** (also **facial mask**) a preparation beneficial to the complexion, spread over the face and removed when dry.

faceoff *noun* **1** *Hockey & Lacrosse* the action of starting or restarting play by dropping or placing the puck or ball between two opposing players' sticks. **2** a direct confrontation.

facet *noun* **1** a particular aspect of a thing: *the report examines every facet of the prison system*. **2 a** one side of a many sided body, esp. when flat and smooth. **b** any of the cut and polished faces of a cut gem. **3** one segment of a compound eye of an insect or crustacean. ▶ **faceted** *adjective* (also in *combination*) [Say FASS it]

facetious *adjective* **1** not intended seriously or literally: *don't take me seriously; I was just being facetious*. **2** trying to appear amusing and witty at a time when other people think it inappropriate, and when it would be better to be serious: *compounded the offence by making facetious remarks about this grave and potentially dangerous issue*. ▶ **facetiously** *adverb* [Say fuh SEE shuss]

face to face • *adverb* closely or directly viewing, confronting, etc. • *adjective* (**face-to-face**) with the people involved facing each other or in each other's presence: *face-to-face discussions*.

face value *noun* the value printed or stamped on money or postage stamps. PHRASES **take** (or **accept**) **at face value** assume (a thing, person, etc.) is genuinely what it, he, she, etc. appears to be.

facial • *adjective* of or for the face. • *noun* a beauty treatment for the face. ▶ **facially** *adverb* [Say FAY shull]

facile *adjective* **1** usu. *derogatory* **a** easily obtained or achieved and so not highly valued: *a facile victory*. **b** (esp. of theory or argument) appearing neat and comprehensive only by ignoring the true complexities of an issue: *a facile generalization*. **2** (of a person) having a superficial or simplistic knowledge or approach: *a man of facile and shallow intellect*. [Say FASS ile or FASS eel]

facilitate *verb* (**facilitates**, **facilitated**, **facilitating**) make (an action, result, etc.) easier or more easily achieved. ▶ **facilitation** *noun* **facilitative** *adjective* [Say fuh SILLA tate, fuh silla TAY sh'n, fuh SILLA tuh tiv]

facilitator *noun* **1** a person or thing that facilitates. **2** a person who, as part of a group, encourages discussion and other activity without directing it or controlling it actively. [Say fuh SILLA tay tur]

facility *noun* (*plural* **facilities**) **1** a natural ability to learn or do something easily: *she has a great facility for languages* ◊ *he plays the piano with surprising facility*. **2** a building, service, equipment, etc. that is provided for a particular purpose: *leisure facilities* ◊ *a new health care facility*. **3** *euphemism* (in *plural*) a toilet or washroom. [Say fuh SILLA tee]

facing *noun* **1** an esp. interior layer of material covering part of a garment etc. for contrast or strength. **2** a layer of brick etc. which forms the face of a building, wall, etc.

facsimile *noun* **1** (often as an *adjective*) an exact copy, esp. of writing, printing, a picture, etc.: *facsimile edition*. **2 a** (often as an *adjective*) production of an exact copy of a document etc. by electronic scanning and transmission of the resulting data (*see also* FAX). **b** a copy produced in this way. **3** something that resembles something else strongly. PHRASES **in facsimile** as an exact copy. [Say fack SIMMA lee]

fact *noun* **1** a thing that is known to have occurred, exist, or be true. **2** a thing that is believed or claimed to be true. PHRASES **before** (or **after**) **the fact** before (or after) the occurrence of a pertinent event. **facts and figures** precise information, details, etc. **hard fact** (or **facts**) **1** inescapable truth (or truths). **2** concrete evidence. **in** (or **in point of**) **fact 1** in reality. **2** (in summarizing) in short. **the fact of the matter** the truth.

fact-finding • *noun* the discovery and establishment of the facts of an issue. • *adjective* **1** engaged in the finding out of facts. **2** (of a committee etc.) set up to discover and establish the facts of an issue.

faction *noun* **1** a small, organized, and self-interested or dissenting group or class of people within a larger one, esp. in politics: *rival factions within the administration*. **2** a state of dissension within an organization: *a party divided by faction and intrigue*.

factional *adjective* connected with the factions of an organization or political party: *factional conflict*. ▶ **factionalism** *noun*

fact of life *noun* **1** something, esp. unpleasant, that cannot be ignored and must be accepted. **2** (**the facts of life**) information about sexual functions and practices, esp. as given to children and teenagers.

factoid • *noun* **1** an assumption or speculation that is reported and repeated so often that it becomes accepted as fact. **2** a brief or trivial item of news or information. • *adjective* being or having the character of a factoid; containing factoids.

factor • *noun* **1** a circumstance, fact, or influence contributing to a result. **2** *Math* a whole number etc. that when multiplied with another produces a given number or expression. **3** *Biology* a gene etc. determining hereditary character. **4** (foll. by identifying number) any of several substances in the blood, identified by numerals, which contribute to coagulation: *factor VIII*. **5** *Cdn hist.* an employee of the Hudson's Bay Company, ranking higher than a chief trader, in charge of a trading post. • *verb Math* resolve into factors or express as a product of factors. PHRASES **factor in** introduce as a factor. **factor out** exclude from an assessment.

factory *noun* (*plural* **factories**) **1** a building or buildings containing equipment for manufacturing or processing. **2** *Cdn hist.* a main trading post, esp. a large centre for the transshipment of furs: *York Factory*.

factory outlet *noun* a store in which factory-made goods, often surplus stock, are sold directly by the manufacturer to consumers at discount prices.

factory ship *noun* a fishing ship with facilities for immediate processing of the catch.

factual *adjective* **1** based on, concerned with, or of the nature of fact or facts. **2** actual, true. ▶ **factuality** *noun* **factually** *adverb* [Say FACK choo ul, fack choo ALA tee]

faculty *noun* (*plural* **faculties**) **1** an aptitude or ability for a particular activity: *the faculty of understanding complex issues* ◊ *a faculty for seeing his own mistakes*. **2** any of the physical or mental abilities that a person is born with: *the faculty of sight* ◊ *she retained her mental faculties until the day she died* ◊ *in full possession of one's faculties*. **3 a** a group of university departments concerned with a major division of knowledge: *faculty of arts*. **b** the teaching staff of a university or college.

fad *noun* a craze or something briefly but enthusiastically taken up, esp. by a group. ▶ **faddish** *adjective* **faddishly** *adverb* **faddishness** *noun* **faddism** *noun* **faddist** *noun*

fade • *verb* (**fades, faded, fading**) **1** lose or cause to lose colour. **2** lose freshness or strength. **3 a** (of colour, light, etc.) disappear gradually; grow pale or dim. **b** (of sound) grow faint. **4** (of a feeling etc.) diminish. **5** (foll. by *away, out*) (of a person etc.) disappear or depart gradually. **6** (foll. by *in, out*) *Film & Broadcasting* **a** cause (a picture) to come gradually in or out of view on a screen, or to merge into another shot. **b** make (the sound) more or less audible. • *noun* an act of causing a film or television picture to darken and disappear gradually: *a fade to black would bring the sequence to a close*. PHRASES **fade away** *informal* languish, grow thin.

fadeaway *noun* **1** *Baseball* = SCREWBALL 1. **2** *Basketball* a shot made while the shooter jumps or falls away from the basket.

fade-in *noun* a filmmaking and broadcasting technique whereby an image is made to appear gradually or the volume of sound is gradually increased from zero.

fade-out *noun* **1** a filmmaking and broadcasting technique whereby an image is made to disappear gradually or the volume of sound is gradually decreased to zero. **2** *informal* a gradual reduction, disappearance, etc.

Fahrenheit *adjective* of or measured on a scale of temperature on which water freezes at 32° and boils at 212° under standard conditions. [Say FAIR in hite]

fail • *verb* **1** be or declare to be unsuccessful. **2** disappoint; let down; not serve when needed. **3** (of supplies, crops, etc.) be or become lacking or insufficient. **4** become weaker; cease functioning; break down: *her health is failing*. • *noun* a failure in an examination or test. PHRASES **without fail** for certain, whatever happens.

failed *adjective* **1** unsuccessful; not good enough: *a failed actor*. **2** deficient; broken down: *a failed battery*.

failing • *noun* a fault or shortcoming; a weakness, esp. in character. • *preposition* in default of; in the absence of: *failing a reconciliation, they will divorce*.

fail-safe *adjective* **1** reverting to a safe condition in the event of a breakdown etc. **2** totally reliable or safe.

failure *noun* **1** lack of success. **2** an unsuccessful person, thing, or attempt. **3** non-performance, non-occurrence. **4** breaking down or ceasing to function: *heart failure*. **5** a cessation in the existence or availability of something. **6** bankruptcy, collapse.

SPELL CHECK
faint, feint

A move made to deceive an opponent is a **feint**.

---

faint • *adjective* **1 a** indistinct, pale, dim. **b** (of a sound) not clearly perceived. **2** (of a person) weak or giddy; inclined to faint. **3** slight, remote, inadequate: *a faint chance*. **4** feeble, half-hearted: *faint praise*. **5** timid: *a faint heart*. • *verb* **1** lose consciousness. **2** become faint. • *noun* a sudden loss of consciousness. PHRASES **not have the faintest** *informal* have no idea.

faint-hearted *adjective* cowardly, timid.

faintly *adverb* **1** in a barely visible, audible, or perceptible manner: *I could hear him crying faintly* ◊ *a faintly bitter smell*. **2** slightly, remotely: *the tune is faintly reminiscent of the theme from "Star Trek"*. **3** in a feeble or half-hearted manner: *I smiled faintly at the suggestion*. **4** in a weak or barely conscious manner.

faintness *noun* **1** a weak or feeble quality: *one of the symptoms is faintness*. **2** a dim, quiet, or barely perceptible quality.

SPELL CHECK
fair, fare   ABC

The money charged for a bus or cab ride is a **fare**. Food or other things offered for consumption can also be called **fare**. Something that does not succeed is said to "**fare** badly".

---

fair¹ • *adjective* **1** just; in accordance with the rules. **2** blond; light or pale in colour or complexion. **3** of (only) moderate quality or amount; average. **4 a** (of weather) fine and dry. **b** (of the wind) favourable. **c** (of the sky) cloudless. **5** clean: *fair copy*. **6** beautiful, attractive. **7** *Baseball* (of a batted ball) that lands or is caught within the legal area of play. • *adverb* **1** in a fair manner. **2** exactly, completely: *was hit fair on the jaw*. PHRASES **fair and square 1** exactly. **2** honest, above-board. **a fair deal** equitable treatment. **fair enough** *informal* that is reasonable or acceptable. **fair name** a good reputation. **the fair sex** *dated* or *jocular* women. **fair's fair** *informal* all involved should act fairly. **fair shake** (also **fair crack**) *informal* a fair opportunity; an equal chance. **in a fair way** likely to. **no fair** *informal* (that is) unfair.

fair² *noun* **1** a usu. annual exhibition of produce, livestock, crafts, etc., held esp. in rural areas in conjunction with a travelling midway: *fall fair*. **2** an exhibition, esp. to promote particular products: *trade fair*. **3** a periodical gathering for the sale of goods, often with entertainments.

fair game *noun* a thing or person one may legitimately pursue, exploit, etc.

fairground *noun* (usu. in *plural*) a place where a fair is held.

fair-haired *adjective* **1** having fair hair. **2** favoured; favourite: *he's her fair-haired boy now*.

fairing *noun* a streamlining structure added to a ship, aircraft, vehicle, etc.

fairly *adverb* **1** in a fair manner; justly. **2** moderately, acceptably: *fairly good*. **3** to a noticeable degree: *fairly narrow*. **4** used as an intensifier: *fairly glowed*. PHRASES **fairly and squarely** = FAIR AND SQUARE (*see* FAIR¹).

fairness *noun* **1** the quality of treating people equally or in a way that is reasonable: *we have a responsibility to uphold fairness and justice*. **2** (of skin or hair) a pale colour. PHRASES **in (all) fairness (to someone)** used to introduce a statement that defends someone who has just been criticized, or that explains another statement that may seem unreasonable: *in fairness to Todd, he wasn't feeling very well the day of the game*.

fair play *noun* reasonable treatment or behaviour.

fairway *noun* **1** the part of a golf course between a tee and its green, kept free of rough grass. **2** a navigable channel; a regular course or track of a ship.

fair-weather *adjective* (of a person) tending to be unreliable in times of difficulty: *fair-weather friend*.

SPELL CHECK
fairy, ferry   ABC

A passenger boat is a **ferry**.

F

fairy • *noun* (*plural* **fairies**) a small imaginary being with magical powers. • *adjective* **1** of or relating to fairies. **2** like a fairy; delicate, small.

fairy godmother *noun* a person who provides unexpected help.

fairyland *noun* **1** the imaginary home of fairies. **2** an enchanted region.

fairy tale • *noun* (also **fairy story**) **1** a tale about fairies. **2** an unbelievable story. • *adjective* (**fairy-tale**) **1** of or relating to fairy tales. **2** resembling a fairy tale. **3** highly unlikely.

fait accompli *noun* (*plural* **faits accomplis**) a thing that has been done and is past arguing or altering: *the results were presented to the shareholders as a fait accompli*. [Say fett a com PLEE]

faith *noun* **1** complete trust or confidence. **2** strong religious belief: *unquestioning faith* ◊ *has lost her faith*. **3** a particular religion: *the Christian faith* ◊ *the children are learning to understand people of different faiths*. **4** duty or commitment to fulfill a trust, promise, etc.: *keep faith*. **5** (as an *adjective*) concerned with a supposed ability to cure by faith rather than treatment: *faith healing*.

faithful *adjective* **1** showing faith. **2** loyal, trustworthy, constant. **3** remaining sexually loyal to one's spouse, lover, etc. **4** true to fact: *a faithful account*. **5 a** (**the Faithful**) the believers in a religion, esp. Muslims and Christians. **b** (**the faithful**) the loyal adherents of a political party. ▶ **faithfully** *adverb* **faithfulness** *noun*

faithless *adjective* **1** disloyal. **2** without religious faith. ▶ **faithlessness** *noun*

fajita *noun* (*plural* **fajitas**) (usu. in *plural*) a dish consisting of small strips of grilled spiced beef or chicken rolled in a tortilla and garnished with fried chopped vegetables, grated cheese, and usu. guacamole, salsa, and sour cream. [Say fuh HEAT uh]

fake • *noun* **1** a thing or person that is not genuine. **2** a trick. **3** *Sport* a movement intended to deceive an opponent. • *adjective* counterfeit; not genuine. • *verb* (**fakes, faked, faking**) **1** make (a false thing) appear genuine. **2** make a pretense of having (a feeling, illness, etc.). **3** pretend; fake something. **4** *Sport* deceive (an opponent) by a misleading movement. PHRASES **fake out** *slang* deceive or trick (a person etc.). ▶ **faker** *noun*

fakery *noun* (*plural* **fakeries**)

fakir *noun* a Muslim (or, sometimes, a Hindu) holy man

without possessions who lives by asking other people for money or food. [Say FAY keer or fuh KEER]

falafel *noun* **1** a spicy fried patty of ground chickpeas or beans. **2** these served in a pita. [Say fuh LAWFUL]

falcon *noun* a bird of prey that is active during the day, having long pointed wings, sometimes trained to hunt small game for sport. [Say FAWL kun or FAL kun]

falconer *noun* **1** a keeper and trainer of hawks. **2** a person who hunts with hawks. [Say FAWL kun ur or FAL kun ur]

falconry *noun* the breeding and training of hawks; the sport of hawking. [Say FAWL kun ree or FAL kun ree]

fall • *verb* (**falls**; *past* **fell**; *past participle* **fallen**; **falling**) **1** descend rapidly from a higher to a lower level. **2** collapse forwards or downwards. **3** become detached and descend or disappear. **4** hang down. **5** (of a sound) become lower or quieter. **6** occur: *darkness fell*. **7** decline, diminish: *standards have fallen*. **8** cut down (a tree etc.). **9 a** (of the face) show dismay or disappointment. **b** (of the eyes or a glance) look downwards. **10** lose power or status: *the government will fall*. **11** pass into a specified condition: *fell ill*. **12** be defeated. **13** die: *fall in battle*. **14** (foll. by *on*, *upon*) **a** attack. **b** meet with. **c** embrace or embark on avidly. **15** (foll. by *to* + verbal noun) begin: *fell to wondering*. • *noun* **1** an act of falling; a sudden rapid descent. **2** (also **Fall**) autumn. **3** that which falls or has fallen, e.g. snow, rocks, etc. **4** overthrow, downfall: *the fall of Rome*. **5 a** succumbing to temptation. **b** (**the Fall**) in Christian and Jewish theology, the lapse into a sinful state and the origin of the human condition (of suffering, toil, death, and sinfulness) resulting from the first act of disobedience by Adam and Eve. **6** (esp. in *plural*) a waterfall, cataract, or cascade. PHRASES **fall apart** (or **to pieces**) **1** break into pieces. **2** (of a situation etc.) disintegrate; be reduced to chaos. **3** lose one's capacity to cope. **fall away 1** (of a surface) incline abruptly. **2** gradually vanish. **fall back** retreat. **fall back on** have recourse to in difficulty. **fall behind 1** be outstripped by one's competitors etc.; lag. **2** be in arrears. **fall for** *informal* **1** be captivated or deceived by. **2** admire; yield to the charms or merits of. **fall afoul** (or **foul**) **of** come into conflict with; quarrel with. **fall in 1** take one's place in military formation. **2** collapse inwards. **fall into line 1** take one's place in the ranks. **2** conform or collaborate with others. **fall into place** begin to make sense or cohere. **fall in with 1** meet by chance. **2** agree with; accede to; humour. **3** coincide with. **fall off 1** (of demand etc.) decrease, deteriorate. **2** withdraw. **fall out 1** quarrel. **2** (of the hair, teeth, etc.) become detached. **3** *Military* come out of formation. **4** result; come to pass; occur. **fall out of** gradually discontinue (a habit etc.). **fall over oneself** *informal* **1** be eager or competitive. **2** be awkward, stumble through haste, confusion, etc. **fall short 1** be or become deficient or inadequate. **2** (of a missile etc.) not reach its target. **fall short of** fail to reach or obtain. **fall through** fail; come to nothing. **fall to** begin an activity, e.g. eating or working. **take the fall** *informal* receive blame or punishment, esp. in the place of someone else.

fallacious *adjective* wrong; based on a mistaken belief: *a fallacious argument*. [Say fuh LAY shuss]

fallacy *noun* (*plural* **fallacies**) **1** a mistaken belief, esp. based on unsound argument. **2** faulty reasoning; misleading or unsound argument. [Say FAL a see]

fallback • *noun* **1** a reserve; something that may be used in an emergency. **2** a falling back or reduction. • *adjective* reserve, emergency: *fallback plan*.

fallen • *verb past participle of* FALL. • *adjective* **1** having

fallen or dropped from a higher place, value, etc.: *fallen leaves*. **2** killed in war.

fallen woman *noun dated* a way of describing a woman in the past who had a sexual relationship with someone who was not her husband.

faller *noun* **1** a person, animal, or thing that falls. **2** a logger who cuts down trees.

fall guy *noun slang* **1** an easy victim. **2** a person who is blamed or punished for something wrong that someone else has done.

fallibility *noun* the ability to be wrong or to make mistakes: *human fallibility*. [Say fal a BILLA tee]

fallible *adjective* capable of making mistakes: *even experts can be fallible*. ▶ **fallibly** *adverb* [Say FAL a bull]

falling *noun* the felling of trees for timber.

falling-out *noun* (*plural* **fallings-out**) a quarrel.

fall-off *noun* a decrease, deterioration, withdrawal, etc.

Fallopian tube *noun* either of two tubes in female mammals along which ova travel from the ovaries to the uterus. [Say fuh LOPEY in]

fallout *noun* **1** radioactive debris caused by a nuclear explosion or accident. **2** the adverse side effects of a situation etc.

fallow • *adjective* **1 a** (of land) plowed and harrowed but left unsown for a year. **b** uncultivated. **2** inactive: *the huge dance floor seldom lies fallow* ◊ *long fallow periods when nothing seems to happen*. • *noun* fallow or uncultivated land. [Say FAL oh]

fall supper *noun Cdn* = FOWL SUPPER.

false • *adjective* **1** not according with fact. **2 a** sham, artificial: *false teeth* ◊ *false modesty*. **b** appearing to be such, esp. deceptively: *a false lining*. **3** not actually so: *buying a cheap computer is a false economy, because you will need to replace or upgrade it sooner*. **4** improperly so called: *false acacia*. **5** deceptive: *false advertising*. **6** (foll. by *to*) deceitful, treacherous, or unfaithful. **7** fictitious or assumed: *a false name*. **8** unlawful: *false imprisonment*. • *adverb* in a false manner: *play someone false*.

false alarm *noun* **1** an alarm given needlessly, either intentionally or in error. **2** a situation in which danger threatens but never materializes.

falsehood *noun* **1** the state of being false or untrue. **2** a false or untrue thing. **3** the act of lying.

falsely *adverb* **1** based on faulty reasoning or wrong information; incorrectly, unjustly: *she was falsely accused of the crime*. **2** in a misleading, deceptive, or dishonest way: *he was falsely claiming to be a doctor* ◊ *many products are falsely labelled "natural"*. **3** in an unnatural or artificial manner: *falsely inflated house prices*.

false memory syndrome *noun* apparent memory of an event, esp. childhood sexual abuse, that did not occur, created by psychological techniques such as hypnosis, dream interpretation, etc.

false pretenses *plural noun* misrepresentations made with intent to deceive: *sold under false pretenses*.

false start *noun* **1** an invalid or disallowed start in a race. **2** an unsuccessful attempt to begin something.

falsetto *noun* (*plural* **falsettos**) **1** a method of voice production used by male singers, esp. tenors, to sing notes higher than their normal range. **2** a singer using this method. [Say fawl SET oh]

falsification *noun* the act of altering information or evidence in order to mislead. [Say false a fuh KAY sh'n]

falsify *verb* (**falsifies**, **falsified**, **falsifying**) **1** fraudulently alter or make false (a document, evidence, etc.). **2** show to be false: *the hypothesis is falsified by the evidence*. [Say FALSE a fie]

falsity *noun* the state of not being true or genuine: *a case where truth or falsity is irrelevant*. [Say FALSE a tee]

falter *verb* **1** stumble, stagger; go unsteadily. **2** waver;

lose courage. **3** stammer; speak hesitatingly. **4** show loss of momentum, energy, or functioning: *the economy was faltering.* ▶ **falteringly** *adverb* [Say FAWL tur]

fame *noun* renown; the state of being famous.

famed *adjective* famous; much spoken of: *famed for its good food.*

familial *adjective* of, occurring in, or characteristic of a family or its members. [Say fuh MILLY ul]

familiar • *adjective* **1 a** (often foll. by *to*) well known; no longer novel. **b** common, usual; often encountered or experienced. **2** (foll. by *with*) knowing a thing well or in detail: *am familiar with all the problems.* **3** (often foll. by *with*) well acquainted (with a person); in close friendship. **4** excessively informal; impertinent: *after a few drinks his boss started getting too familiar for his liking.* **5** unceremonious, informal: *you seem to be on very familiar terms with your instructor.* • *noun* **1** a close friend or associate. **2** (also **familiar spirit**) a demon supposedly attending and obeying a witch etc.

familiarity *noun* (*plural* **familiarities**) **1** the state of being well known. **2** close acquaintance, knowledge. **3** a close relationship. **4** familiar or informal behaviour, esp. excessively so: *she addressed me with an easy familiarity that made me feel at home ◊ was shocked by his familiarity.*

familiarization *noun* the process of becoming familiar or well acquainted with something: *there is a one-year familiarization program for new employees.*

familiarize *verb* (**familiarizes**, **familiarized**, **familiarizing**) **1** (foll. by *with*) make (a person) conversant or well acquainted. **2** make (a thing) well known or more easily understood: *these exercises will help to familiarize the terms used in this textbook.*

familiarly *adverb* **1** in the way that is well known to people: *meteors are familiarly known as "shooting stars".* **2** in a friendly and informal manner, sometimes in a way that is too informal to be pleasant: *the stranger rushed up and embraced him familiarly.*

family *noun* (*plural* **families**) **1** a group of people related by blood, legal or common-law marriage, or adoption. **2 a** the members of a household, esp. parents and their children. **b** a person's children. **c** a person's spouse and children. **d** (as an *adjective*) serving the needs of families: *family doctor.* **3 a** all the descendants of a common ancestor. **b** a race or group of peoples from a common stock. **4** all the languages ultimately derived from a particular early language, regarded as a group. **5** a brotherhood of persons or nations united by political or religious ties. **6** a group of objects distinguished by common features. **7** *Biology* a group of related genera of organisms within an order in taxonomic classification. **8** *Cdn* (*Ont.*) a classification code indicating that a film is considered appropriate for viewing by people of all ages. Abbreviation: **F.** PHRASES **in the family way** *informal* pregnant.

family allowance *noun Cdn hist.* a universal monthly payment made by the federal government to mothers of children under 18.

Family Compact *noun Cdn* **1** a name given to the ruling class in Upper Canada in the early 19th century, esp. to the members of the legislative and executive councils. This governing Tory elite was held together by ties of family, patronage, and social and political beliefs, and promoted British institutions such as a social hierarchy and an established Church. **2** any influential clique or faction.

family law *noun* the part of the legal system that deals with matters affecting families, e.g. divorce etc.

family man *noun* (*plural* **family men**) a man having a wife and children, esp. one fond of family life.

family planning *noun* the planning of the number of children in a family by using birth control.

family room *noun* a room in a house used by family members for relaxation etc.

family therapy *noun* a form of psychotherapy aimed at improving communication and relationships within a family. ▶ **family therapist** *noun*

family tree *noun* a chart showing relationships and lines of descent.

famine *noun* **1** extreme scarcity of food. **2** a shortage of something specified: *a labour famine.*

famished *adjective* very hungry, starving.

famous *adjective* **1** (often foll. by *for*) celebrated; well known. **2** *informal* excellent. **3** notorious. PHRASES **famous last words** (an ironic comment on or rejoinder to) an overconfident or boastful assumption that may well be proved wrong by events.

famously *adverb* **1** *informal* excellently: *he wasn't difficult at all — we got along famously.* **2** notably: *they have famously reclusive lifestyles.*

fan¹ • *noun* **1** an apparatus, usu. with rotating blades, giving a current of air for ventilation etc. **2** a device, usu. folding and forming a semicircle when spread out, for agitating the air to cool oneself. **3** anything spread out like a fan, e.g. a bird's tail or kind of ornamental vaulting. **4** = ALLUVIAL FAN. • *verb* (**fans**, **fanned**, **fanning**) **1 a** blow a current of air on, with or as with a fan. **b** agitate (the air) with a fan. **2** (of a breeze) blow gently on; cool. **3** sweep away by or as by the wind from a fan. **4** (usu. foll. by *out*) spread out in the shape of a fan. **5** (often foll. by *on*) *Hockey* miss or make only partial contact with the puck while attempting to pass or shoot etc. **6** *Baseball* **a** (of a pitcher) strike out (a batter). **b** (of a batter) strike out. **7** make more ardent: *fanned her desire.* PHRASES **fan the flames of** increase the intensity of: *fanned the flames of nationalism.*

fan² *noun* a devotee or admirer of a particular activity, performer, etc.: *hockey fan.*

fanatic • *noun* **1** a person filled with excessive and often misguided enthusiasm for something. **2** *informal* a person who is devoted to a hobby, pastime, sport, etc.: *curling fanatic.* • *adjective* excessively enthusiastic.

fanatical *adjective* **1** filled with excessive and often misguided enthusiasm for or devotion to a cause etc.: *a powerful cult leader with a fanatical group of followers.* **2** having an obsessive interest, enthusiasm, or concern: *a fanatical Habs supporter ◊ he was fanatical about keeping the house tidy.* ▶ **fanatically** *adverb* [Say fuh NAT ick ul]

fanaticism *noun* extreme beliefs or behaviour, esp. in connection with religion or politics. [Say fuh NATTA sism]

fan belt *noun* a belt that drives a fan to cool the radiator in a motor vehicle.

fancier *noun* **1** a connoisseur or follower of some activity or thing. **2** a breeder of a certain type of animal or plant.

fanciful *adjective* **1** existing only in the imagination or fancy: *the Man in the Moon is one of a number of fanciful lunar inhabitants.* **2** (of a person or their thoughts or ideas) over-imaginative and unrealistic: *a fanciful story about a pot of gold.* **3** (of things) designed or decorated in an odd but creative manner: *a fanciful hat.* ▶ **fancifully** *adverb* **fancifulness** *noun*

fancy • *noun* (*plural* **fancies**) **1** an individual taste or inclination. **2** a caprice or whim. **3** a thing favoured, e.g. a horse to win a race. **4** an arbitrary supposition. **5 a** the faculty of using imagination or of inventing imagery. **b** a mental image. **6** delusion; unfounded belief. • *adjective* (**fancier**, **fanciest**) **1 a** elaborate; not plain. **b** of high quality or very expensive. **2 a** (of foods etc.) of fine quality. **b** designating a grade of canned fruits and vegetables that are of the highest

quality, as nearly perfect as possible, and uniform in colour and size. • **verb** (**fancies, fancied, fancying**) **1** be inclined to suppose. **2** *informal* have an unduly high opinion of (oneself, one's ability, etc.). **3** select (a horse, team, etc.) as the likely winner. **4** (in *imperative*) an exclamation of surprise: *fancy their doing that!* **5** picture to oneself; conceive, imagine. PHRASES **catch** (or **take**) **the fancy of** please; appeal to. **fancy up** *informal* make more fancy, elegant, etc. **take a fancy to** become (esp. inexplicably) fond of. ▶ **fancily** *adverb*

fancy footwork *noun* **1** skilful or agile use of the feet, esp. in sports, dancing, etc. **2** agility in negotiation, evasion, etc.

fancy-free *adjective* (often in phr. **footloose and fancy-free**) without (esp. emotional) commitments.

fancy-pants *adjective informal* hotshot.

fandom *noun* the world of fans, esp. of fans of science fiction magazines and conventions. [Say FAN dum]

fanfare *noun* **1** a short showy or ceremonious sounding of trumpets, bugles, etc. **2** an elaborate display; a burst of publicity.

fang *noun* **1** a sharply pointed canine tooth, e.g. of a dog or wolf. **2 a** the tooth of a venomous snake, by which poison is injected. **b** the biting mouthpart of a spider. PHRASES **bare one's fangs** show oneself ready for confrontation. ▶ **fanged** *adjective* (also in *combination*). **fangless** *adjective*

fanny *noun* (*plural* **fannies**) *slang* the buttocks.

fanny pack *noun* a small pouch for money or other valuables, worn on a belt around the waist etc.

fantail *noun* **1** a pigeon with a broad fan-shaped tail. **2** a fan-shaped tail or end. ▶ **fantailed** *adjective*

fantasia *noun* a musical or other composition free in form and often in improvisatory style, or which is based on several familiar tunes. [Say fan TAY zhuh]

fantasize *verb* (**fantasizes, fantasized, fantasizing**) **1 a** daydream about something one wishes to happen. **b** indulge in a sexual fantasy. **2** imagine; create a fantasy about.

fantastic *adjective* (also **fantastical**) **1** *informal* excellent, extraordinary. **2** *informal* very large; lavish: *a fantastic increase in salary.* **3** grotesque or quaint in design etc.: *a fantastic costume ornamented with feathers, paint, and other decorations.* **4** existing only in the imagination; unreal or impossible: *had a vision of a fantastic, maze-like building.* ▶ **fantastically** *adverb*

fantasy *noun* (*plural* **fantasies**) **1** the faculty of inventing images, esp. extravagant or visionary ones. **2** a sequence of mental images developed in the imagination and arising from conscious or unconscious wishes or attitudes, esp. involving sexual relations. **3** a whimsical speculation: *the notion of being independent is a child's ultimate fantasy.* **4** a musical composition, free in form, esp. involving variation on an existing work or the imaginative representation of a situation or story. **5** a genre of imaginative fiction involving fantastic stories, often in a magical pseudo-historical setting.

fantasyland *noun* an imaginary world where all fantasies are fulfilled.

fanzine *noun* a magazine for fans, esp. those of science fiction, sport, or popular music. [Say FAN zeen]

FAO *abbreviation* Food and Agriculture Organization (of the United Nations).

FAQ *noun* a text file containing a list of "frequently asked questions" and answers relating to a particular subject, esp. one giving basic information on a topic to users of an Internet newsgroup.

far *adverb & adjective* (**further, furthest** or **farther, farthest**) at or to or by a great distance or degree. PHRASES **as far as 1** to the distance of (a place). **2** to the extent that: *as far as I'm concerned.* **by far** by a great amount. **far and away** by a very large amount. **far and near** everywhere. **far and wide** over a large area. **far be it from me** I am reluctant to (esp. express criticism etc.): *far be it from me to complain, but this meat is still raw.* **far from** very different from being; tending to the opposite of: *the problem is far from being solved.* **go far 1** achieve much. **2** contribute greatly. **3** be adequate. **go too far** go beyond the limits of what is reasonable, polite, etc. **how far** to what extent. **so far 1** to such an extent or distance; to this point. **2** until now. **so** (or **in so**) **far as** (or **that**) to the extent that. **so far so good** progress has been satisfactory up to now.

faraway *adjective* **1** remote; long-past. **2** (of a look) dreamy. **3** (of a voice) sounding as if from a distance.

farce *noun* **1** a coarsely comic dramatic work based on ludicrously improbable events. **2** absurdly futile proceedings: *the debate turned into a drunken farce.*

farcical *adjective* ridiculous and not worth taking seriously: *it was a farcical trial* ◊ *a situation verging on the farcical.* [Say FARSA cul]

SPELL CHECK
fare, fair   ABC✓

Something done according to the rules is **fair**. **Fair** is also used for blond hair or a clear sky. An exhibition is a **fair**.

---

fare • *noun* **1 a** the price a passenger has to pay to be conveyed by bus, airplane, etc. **b** a passenger paying to travel in a public vehicle, esp. a taxi. **2** a range of food provided by a restaurant etc. **3** something presented to the public, esp. for entertainment: *typical Hollywood fare.* • *verb* (**fares, fared, faring**) **1** progress; get on: *how did you fare?* **2** happen; turn out.

Far East *noun* China, Japan, and other countries of eastern Asia. ▶ **Far Eastern** *adjective*

farewell • *interjection* goodbye. • *noun* **1** leave-taking (also as an *adjective*: *farewell party*). **2** parting good wishes.

far-fetched *adjective* (of an idea, explanation, etc.) strained, unconvincing, improbable.

far-flung *adjective* **1** extending far; widely distributed. **2** remote; isolated: *far-flung northern communities.*

far gone *adjective* **1** *informal* in an advanced state of drunkenness, illness, etc. **2** past: *those days are far gone.*

farm • *noun* **1** an area of land, and the buildings on it, used for growing crops, rearing animals, etc. **2** a place or establishment for breeding a particular type of animal, growing fruit, etc.: *fish farm.* **3** a place for the storage of oil or oil products. • *verb* **1** use land for growing crops, rearing animals, etc. **2** breed (fish etc.) commercially. **3** (often foll. by *out*) delegate or subcontract (work) to others. ▶ **farmer** *noun*

farmhand *noun* **1** a worker on a farm. **2** *informal* a player on a farm team, esp. one who has just been called up to the major leagues.

farmhouse *noun* a dwelling (esp. the main one) attached to a farm.

farming *noun* the activity or business of growing crops and/or raising livestock.

farmland *noun* land used or suitable for farming.

farmstead *noun* a farm and its buildings as a unit. [Say FARM sted]

farm team *noun* (also **farm club**) a minor-league sports team affiliated with and serving as a source of players for a major-league team.

farmyard *noun* a yard or enclosure attached to a farmhouse.

Far North *noun* (in Canada) the Arctic and sub-Arctic regions of the country.

far-off *adjective* remote; distant: *a far-off battlefield*.

far-out *adjective slang* **1** unconventional; avant-garde. **2** excellent.

far-reaching *adjective* **1** extending widely. **2** having important consequences or implications.

farrier *noun* **1** a smith who shoes horses. **2** a person who treats the disease and injuries of horses. [Say FERRY ur]

farrow • *noun* a litter of pigs. • *verb* (of a sow) give birth to (pigs). ▶ **farrowing** *noun*

Farsi *noun* the modern Persian language. [Say FAR see]

far-sighted *adjective* **1** having foresight. **2** able to see distant things more clearly than those close by. ▶ **far-sightedly** *adverb* **far-sightedness** *noun*

fart *coarse slang* • *verb* **1** emit intestinal gas from the anus. **2** (foll. by *about*, *around*) behave foolishly; waste time. • *noun* **1** an emission of intestinal gas from the anus. **2** an annoying or unpleasant person.

WRITING TIP
farther, further

Farther and **further** can both be used to describe physical distance: *We walked farther* (or *further*) *than I had expected*; *Lethbridge is farther* (or *further*) *than I thought*. Of the two, **further** is more likely to be used to mean "to a greater extent" (*Nothing could be further from the truth*). Only **further** is used to mean "in addition" (*We must decide when and, further, where to hold the meeting*), "additional" (*Please reply without further delay*), and "promote" (*He used them to further his own career*). Similarly, **farthest** and **furthest** are both used to describe physical distance (*She walked farthest* (or *furthest*); *She walked to the farthest* (or *furthest*) *point*), but **furthest** is more likely to be used to mean "to the greatest extent or degree" (*These are the people furthest removed from the political process*).

---

farther = FURTHER *adverb* 1, *adjective* 1.

farthest = FURTHEST.

farthing *noun hist.* (in the UK) a coin and monetary unit worth a quarter of an old penny.

Far West *noun* (in Canada) **1** *hist.* the regions west of Ontario, sequentially Manitoba, Saskatchewan, Alberta, and British Columbia, as settlement advanced westward. **2** the area west of the Prairies.

fascia *noun* (*plural* **fascias** or **fasciae**) **1** a flat horizontal band of wood, aluminum, etc. around the edge of a roof, to which eavestroughs are attached. **2** *Anatomy* a thin sheath of fibrous tissue. **3** *Zoology & Botany* a stripe or band of colour. [Say FAY shuh or FASHY uh; for sense 3 say FASHY uh]

fascinate *verb* (**fascinates**, **fascinated**, **fascinating**) capture the interest of. ▶ **fascinated** *adjective* **fascinating** *adjective* **fascinatingly** *adverb* **fascination** *noun* [Say FASSA nate]

Fascism *noun* **1** *hist.* the totalitarian principles and organization of the extreme right-wing nationalist movement in Italy (1922–43). **2** (also **fascism**) **a** any similar nationalist and authoritarian movement, esp. German National Socialism. **b** *derogatory* any system of extreme right-wing or authoritarian views. ▶ **Fascist** *noun & adjective* (also **fascist**). **Fascistic** *adjective* (also **fascistic**). [Say FASH ism]

fashion • *noun* **1** the current popular custom or style, esp. in dress or social conduct (also as an *adjective*: *fashion designer*). **2** a manner or style of doing something: *in a peculiar fashion*. **3** appearance; characteristic form. **4** fashionable society: *a woman of fashion*. • *verb* make into a particular or the required form: *the scientist fashioned a technique for catching loons to study them*.

PHRASES **after** (or **in**) **a fashion** as well as is practically possible, though not satisfactorily. **in** (or **out of**) **fashion** fashionable (or not fashionable) at the time in question.

fashionable *adjective* **1** following, suited to, or influenced by the current fashion. **2** characteristic of or favoured by those who are leaders of social fashion: *a fashionable resort*. ▶ **fashionableness** *noun* **fashionably** *adverb*

fashion plate *noun* a person who consistently dresses in the current fashion.

fast[1] • *adjective* **1** moving or capable of moving at high speed. **2** (of a clock etc.) showing a time ahead of the correct time. **3 a** (of a photographic film) needing only a short exposure. **b** (of a lens) having a large aperture. **4 a** firmly fixed or attached. **b** secure; firmly established: *Matthew and Zoe are fast friends*. **5** (of a colour) not fading in light or when washed. **6** involving exciting or shocking activities. • *adverb* **1** quickly. **2** firmly: *stand fast*. **3** completely: *fast asleep*. **PHRASES** **pull a fast one** *informal* try to deceive or gain an unfair advantage.

fast[2] • *verb* abstain from all or some kinds of food or drink, esp. as a religious observance or in preparation for medical procedures. • *noun* an act or period of fasting.

fast and furious • *adverb* **1** rapidly. **2** eagerly, uproariously. • *adjective* **1** rapid, fast-paced: *a fast and furious game*. **2** (of a party, music, etc.) lively, energetic.

fastball *noun* **1** a baseball pitch thrown at or near a pitcher's maximum speed. **2** *Cdn* = FAST PITCH.

fast break *noun* (in basketball, football, etc.) a swift attack from a defensive position.

fast-breeder *noun* (also **fast-breeder reactor**) a reactor using fast neutrons to produce the same fissile material as it uses.

fasten *verb* **1** make or become fixed or secure. **2** lock securely; shut in. **3** direct (a look, thoughts, etc.) fixedly or intently. **4 a** take hold of: *fasten on an idea*. **b** single out: *looking for someone to blame, he fastened on me*. **5** become closed or attached: *this dress fastens in the back*. ▶ **fastener** *noun*

fastening *noun* a fastener.

fast food *noun* food prepared for quick sale or serving, esp. in a snack bar or restaurant.

fast-forward • *noun* **1** a control on a tape or video player for advancing the tape rapidly. **2** a facility for playing through a tape etc. very rapidly until a desired starting point is reached. • *adjective* designating such a control. • *verb* advance (a tape) rapidly, sometimes while simultaneously playing it at high speed.

fastidious *adjective* **1** overly scrupulous in matters of taste, cleanliness, propriety, etc.; fussy. **2** easily disgusted; squeamish. ▶ **fastidiously** *adverb* **fastidiousness** *noun* [Say fas TIDDY us]

fast lane *noun* **1** a traffic lane on a highway etc. used by high-speed vehicles as a driving lane and by other vehicles as a passing lane. **2** a means or route of rapid progress. **3** a hectic, highly pressured lifestyle.

fastness *noun* **1** a stronghold. **2** the capacity of a dye not to fade or wash out.

fast neutron *noun* a neutron with high kinetic energy, esp. one released in nuclear fission and not slowed by a moderator etc.

fast pitch *noun* a variety of the game of softball, featuring fast underhand pitching.

fast-talk *informal* • *verb* persuade by rapid or deceitful talk. • *noun* (**fast talk**) such talk. ▶ **fast talker** *noun* **fast-talking** *adjective*

fast track • *noun* a route, course, method, etc., which provides for more rapid results than usual. • *verb* (**fast-**

F

F

track) **1** give priority to; treat as urgent: *fast-track the proposal*. **2** advance quickly: *fast-track through the ranks*. ▶**fast-tracker** *noun*

fat • *noun* **1 a** any of a group of natural esters of glycerol and various fatty acids found in the adipose tissue of animals and in some plants. **b** animal or vegetable tissue containing this. **c** fat from animals or plants, purified and used for cooking. **2** excessive presence of fat in a person or animal. **3** excess; surplus: *trim the fat in the budget*. • *adjective* (**fatter, fattest**) **1** (of a person or animal) having excessive fat. **2** (of an animal) plump; well fed. **3** containing much fat. **4** greasy, oily. **5** (of land or resources) fertile, rich; yielding abundantly. **6 a** thick: *a fat book*. **b** substantial as an asset or opportunity: *a fat cheque*. **7** *informal ironic* very little; not much: *fat chance*. • *verb* (**fats, fatted, fatting**) make or become fat. PHRASES **the fat is in the fire** trouble is imminent. **kill the fatted calf** celebrate, esp. at a prodigal's return. **live off** (or **on**) **the fat of the land** have the best of everything.

fatal *adjective* **1** causing or ending in death: *a fatal accident*. **2** (often foll. by *to*) destructive; ruinous; ending in disaster: *made a fatal mistake*.

fatalism *noun* **1** the belief that all events are predetermined and therefore inevitable. **2** a submissive attitude to events as being inevitable. ▶**fatalist** *noun* **fatalistic** *adjective* **fatalistically** *adverb* [Say FATAL ism]

fatality *noun* (*plural* **fatalities**) **1** a death that is caused in an accident or a war or by some other act of violence: *several people were injured, but there were no fatalities*. **2** deadliness: *the fatality of certain diseases*. **3** the belief or feeling that one has no control over one's fate: *a sense of fatality gripped her*. [Say fay TALLA tee or fuh TALLA tee]

fatally *adverb* **1** in a way that causes or ends in death: *she was fatally injured*. **2** in a way that is destructive or ruinous: *the plan was fatally flawed from the start*.

fat cat *noun slang derogatory* a wealthy person, esp. a complacent one who lives off the proceeds of other people's labour.

fate *noun* **1** the things, especially bad things, that will happen or have happened to someone or something: *the fate of the three men is unknown* ◊ *the court will decide our fate* ◊ *each of the managers suffered the same fate* ◊ *the government had abandoned the refugees to their fate*. **2** the power that is believed to control everything that happens and that cannot be stopped or changed: *fate was kind to me that day* ◊ *by a strange twist of fate, Andy and I were on the same plane*.

fated *adjective* determined or controlled by fate.

fateful *adjective* important, decisive; having far-reaching usu. bad consequences: *she looked back now to that fateful day in December* ◊ *will always be remembered for making that fateful decision*.

fathead *noun informal* a stupid person. ▶**fatheaded** *adjective*

father • *noun* **1 a** a man in relation to a child or children born from his fertilization of an ovum. **b** a man who has care of a child, esp. by adoption or remarriage. **2** any male animal in relation to its offspring. **3** (usu. in *plural*) a progenitor or forefather. **4** (also **Father**) an originator, designer, or early leader. **5** (**Fathers**) (also **Fathers of the Church**) early Christian theologians whose writings are regarded as especially authoritative. **6** (also **Father**) (often as a title or form of address) a priest. **7** (**the Father**) (in Christian belief) the first person of the Trinity. **8** (**Father**) a venerable person, esp. as a title in personifications: *Father Time*. **9** (usu. in *plural*) the leading men or elders in a city or state: *city fathers*. • *verb* **1** beget; be the father of. **2** behave as a father

towards. **3** bring (a scheme etc.) into existence. ▶**fatherhood** *noun*

father-in-law *noun* (*plural* **fathers-in-law**) the father of one's husband or wife.

fatherland *noun* one's native country.

fatherless *adjective* without a father, either because he has died or because he does not live with his children: *fatherless children*.

fatherly *adjective* **1** like or characteristic of a father in affection, care, etc.: *fatherly concern*. **2** of a father.

Father of Confederation *noun Cdn* any of the delegates who represented colonies of British North America at the three conferences which led to Confederation in 1867.

Father's Day *noun* a day (usu. the third Sunday in June) established for a special tribute to fathers.

Father Time *noun* the personification of time as an old man with a scythe and hourglass.

fathom • *noun* (*plural* often **fathom** when preceded by a number) a measure of six feet (1.8 m), esp. used in taking depth soundings. • *verb* **1** grasp or comprehend (a problem). **2** measure the depth (of water) with a long line weighted at the end. ▶**fathomless** *adjective* [Say FA thum (with TH as in *THEM*)]

fatigue • *noun* **1 a** extreme tiredness after physical or mental exertion. **b** a state of indifference brought about by excessive appeals to one's generosity, compassion, etc.: *donor fatigue*. **2** weakness in materials, esp. metal, caused by repeated variations of stress. **3** a reduction in the efficiency of a muscle, organ, etc., after prolonged activity. **4 a** a non-military duty in the army, often as a punishment. **b** (in *plural*) clothing worn for such a duty; army fatigues. • *verb* (**fatigues, fatigued, fatiguing**) tire, exhaust.

fats *noun slang offensive* a fat person.

fatso *noun* (*plural* **fatsos**) *slang offensive* a fat person.

fatten *verb* **1** make fat (esp. animals for slaughter). **2** grow or become fat.

fattening *adjective* (of foods) high in calories.

fatty • *adjective* (**fattier, fattiest**) **1** consisting of or containing fat. **2** marked by abnormal deposition of fat. **3** like fat; oily, greasy. • *noun* (*plural* **fatties**) *slang offensive* a fat person (esp. as a nickname).

fatty acid *noun* any of a class of organic compounds consisting of a hydrocarbon chain and a terminal carboxyl group, esp. those occurring as constituents of lipids.

fatuous *adjective* very silly and showing a lack of intelligence; purposeless, idiotic: *a fatuous comment* ◊ *a fatuous grin*. ▶**fatuously** *adverb* **fatuousness** *noun* [Say FATCH oo us]

fatwa *noun* (*plural* **fatwas**) (in Islamic countries) a ruling on a religious matter given by a mufti. [Say FAT wuh]

faucet *noun* = TAP[1] 1. [Say FOSSET]

fault • *noun* **1** a defect or imperfection. **2** a thing wrongly done. **3** responsibility for wrongdoing, error, etc.: *it's your own fault*. **4** a break or other defect in an electric circuit. **5** *Geology* an extended break in the continuity of strata or a vein. **6** *Tennis etc.* a service of the ball not in accordance with the rules, esp. one which falls outside prescribed limits. • *verb* **1** find fault with; blame. **2** *Geology* break the continuity of (strata or a vein). **3** commit a fault. PHRASES **at fault** guilty; to blame. **find fault** (often foll. by *with*) make an adverse criticism; complain. **to a fault** (usu. of a commendable quality etc.) excessively: *generous to a fault*.

faultless *adjective* without fault; free from defect or error. ▶**faultlessly** *adverb* **faultlessness** *noun*

fault line *noun Geology* the line of intersection of a fault with the earth's surface or with a horizontal plane.

fault plane *noun Geology* the surface of a fault fracture along which the rock masses on either side have been displaced.

faulty *adjective* (**faultier, faultiest**) having faults.

SPELL CHECK   ABC ✓
faun, fawn

A young deer is a **fawn**. A light brown colour is **fawn**. If you behave obsequiously to someone, you **fawn** over them.

faun *noun* a minor Roman god with a human face and torso and a goat's horns, legs, and tail.

fauna *noun* the animal life of a particular region, geological period, or environment. ▶**faunal** *adjective*

faux *adjective* false, imitation: *faux fur*. [Say FOE]

faux pas *noun* (*plural* **faux pas**) an embarrassing or tactless act or remark in a social situation: *realizing his faux pas, Bert slunk to the back of the line*. [Say foe PAW for the singular, foe PAWS for the plural]

fave *noun & adjective slang* = FAVOURITE.

favela *noun* a Brazilian shack, slum, or shantytown. [Say fuh VELLA]

favour (also **favor**) • *noun* **1** an act of kindness beyond what is due or usual. **2** approval, goodwill; friendly regard: *look with favour on*. **3** partiality; too lenient or generous treatment: *as an examiner she showed no favour to any candidate*. **4** a small gift, such as a noisemaker or paper hat, often given to guests at a party. **5** a thing given or worn as a mark of favour or support, e.g. a badge or a knot of ribbons. **6** (usu. in *plural*) sexual relations, esp. as offered by a woman. • *verb* **1** regard or treat with favour or partiality. **2** give support or approval to. **3** facilitate, help (a process etc.): *the wind favoured their sailing*. **4** tend to confirm (an idea or theory). **5** (foll. by *with*) oblige: *favour me with a reply*. **6** avoid putting too much strain on (an injured limb etc.). **7** resemble in features: *she favours her mother*. PHRASES **find favour** be liked; prove acceptable. **in favour 1** meeting with approval. **2** (foll. by *of*) **a** in support of. **b** to the advantage of. **in one's favour** to a person's advantage. **out of favour** lacking approval.

favourable *adjective* (also **favorable**) **1** approving. **2** giving consent: *a favourable answer*. **3** (often foll. by *to*) helpful, suitable: *legislation favourable to our interests*. ▶**favourableness** *noun* **favourably** *adverb*

favoured *adjective* (also **favored**) **1** treated with preference or partiality: *the favoured daughter*. **2** having special advantages: *the favoured caste*.

favourite (also **favorite**) • *adjective* preferred to all others: *my favourite book*. • *noun* **1** a specially favoured person or thing. **2** *Sport* a competitor thought most likely to win.

favouritism *noun* (also **favoritism**) the unfair favouring of one person or group at the expense of another.

SPELL CHECK   ABC ✓
fawn, faun

A mythical creature that is half goat and half man is a **faun**.

fawn[1] *noun* **1** a young deer in its first year. **2** *noun & adjective* a light yellowish brown.

fawn[2] *verb* (of a person) behave in an obsequious manner; praise or admire excessively: *real reporters don't fawn over their famous subjects*. ▶**fawning** *adjective* **fawningly** *adverb*

fax • *noun* (*plural* **faxes**) **1** facsimile transmission (see FACSIMILE *noun* 2). **2 a** a copy produced or message sent by this. **b** a machine for transmitting and receiving these. • *verb* (**faxes, faxed, faxing**) transmit (a document) in this way.

SPELL CHECK   ABC ✓
faze, phase

Each stage of a process is a **phase**. To introduce something gradually is to "**phase** it in".

faze *verb* (**fazes, fazed, fazing**) (often as **fazed** *adjective*) *informal* disconcert, perturb: *doesn't faze me*.

FBI *abbreviation* (in the US) Federal Bureau of Investigation.

FD *abbreviation Cdn* forest district.

FDA *abbreviation* (in the US) Food and Drug Administration.

Fe *symbol* the element iron.

fealty *noun* (*plural* **fealties**) **1** *hist.* a feudal tenant's or vassal's fidelity to a lord. **2** allegiance: *they refused to swear fealty to their country*. [Say FEEL tee]

fear • *noun* **1** an unpleasant emotion caused by exposure to danger, expectation of pain, etc. **2** a cause of fear. **3** anxiety for the safety of: *in fear of their lives*. **4** danger; likelihood (of something unwelcome): *there is little fear of failure*. • *verb* **1** be frightened of: *all his employees fear him* ◊ *fear persecution* ◊ *don't worry, you have nothing to fear from us* ◊ *she feared to tell him the truth*. **2** feel that something bad might have happened or might happen in the future: *he has been missing for three days now and police are beginning to fear the worst* ◊ *hundreds of people are feared dead*. **3** know or understand with fear or regret: *I fear you haven't been chosen*. PHRASES **for fear of** (or **that**) to avoid the risk of (or that). **never fear** there is no danger of that.

fearful *adjective* **1** afraid. **2** terrible: *we heard a fearful noise*. **3** *informal* extremely unwelcome or unpleasant: *we made a fearful mess of the room*. ▶**fearfully** *adverb* **fearfulness** *noun*

fearless *adjective* without fear; courageous, brave. ▶**fearlessly** *adverb* **fearlessness** *noun*

fearsome *adjective* **1** frightening, dreadful: *a giant of a monster, more fearsome than any creature she had ever encountered*. **2** inspiring awe or admiration: *fearsome dedication*. ▶**fearsomely** *adverb*

feasibility *noun* the state or degree of being easily or conveniently done: *the feasibility of screening athletes for cardiac disease*.

feasible *adjective* **1** easily or conveniently done. **2** likely, probable: *a feasible explanation*. ▶**feasibly** *adverb*

feast • *noun* **1 a** a large or sumptuous meal. **b** a banquet for many guests, often with entertainment. **2** a gratification to the senses or mind. **3 a** an annual religious celebration. **b** a day dedicated to a particular saint. • *verb* **1** partake of a feast; eat and drink sumptuously. **2** enjoy; take pleasure in: *feast on movies*. PHRASES **feast one's eyes** take pleasure in beholding. **feast or famine** either too much or too little.

feat *noun* a noteworthy act or achievement.

feather • *noun* **1** any of the appendages growing from a bird's skin, consisting of a partly hollow horny stem fringed with fine strands. **2** one or more of these as decoration etc. **3** a piece or pieces of feather attached to the base of an arrow to direct its flight. **4** something resembling a feather, as a tuft of hair standing upright on a person's head. • *verb* **1** cover or line with feathers. **2** *Rowing* turn (an oar) so that it passes through the air edgewise. **3** *Aviation & Nautical* cause (propeller blades) to rotate in such a way as to lessen the air or water resistance. **4** float, move, or wave like feathers. **5** (of ink, lipstick, etc.) break into tiny feather-like lines

F

when applied to a surface. **6** execute (a pass) or pass (a puck, ball, etc.) lightly or gracefully. **PHRASES a feather in one's cap** an achievement to be proud of. **feather one's nest** make oneself richer, more comfortable, etc. usu. at someone else's expense. **in fine** (or **high**) **feather** *informal* in good spirits. **ruffle** (a person's) **feathers** disturb or annoy (a person).

featherbed • *noun* **1** a bed with a mattress stuffed with feathers. **2** something (esp. a job, situation, etc.) comfortable or easy. • *verb* (**featherbeds**, **featherbedded**, **featherbedding**) provide a worker or business with advantageous working conditions at the expense of production and efficiency: *featherbedding seemed to be the rule: there was barely enough work in the office for one clerk, let alone three* ◊ *an inefficient, featherbedded assembly line*.

feathered *adjective* (also in *combination*). **1** (of a bird) covered with feathers: *black-feathered ostriches*. **2** decorated with feathers: *a feathered hat*.

featherless *adjective* not having feathers.

featherweight *noun* **1 a** a weight in certain sports intermediate between bantamweight and lightweight, in the amateur boxing scale 54–57 kg, but differing for professionals and wrestlers (also as an *adjective*: *featherweight championship*). **b** a boxer etc. of this weight. **2** a very light person or thing. **3** (as an *adjective*) trifling or unimportant.

feathery *adjective* light and soft; like a feather: *feathery leaves* ◊ *feathery snowflakes*.

feature • *noun* **1** a distinctive or characteristic part of a thing. **2** a distinctive part of the face, esp. with regard to shape and visual effect. **3** something offered for sale as a special. **4** a distinctive or regular article in a newspaper or magazine. **5 a** (also **feature film**) a full-length film intended as the main item in a movie theatre program. **b** a broadcast or part of a broadcast devoted to a particular topic. • *verb* (**features, featured, featuring**) **1 a** make a special display or attraction of; give special prominence to. **b** include as a characteristic part. **2** have as or be an important actor, participant, or topic in a film, broadcast, etc. **3** be a feature or special attraction. ▶ **featured** *adjective* (also in *combination*).

feature-length *adjective* of the length of a typical feature film or program, usu. at least an hour long.

featureless *adjective* without any qualities or noticeable characteristics: *the countryside is flat and featureless*.

Feb. *abbreviation* February.

febrile *adjective* of or relating to fever. [Say FEE brile or FEB rile]

February *noun* (*plural* **Februaries**) the second month of the year. [Say FEB roo airy or FEB yoo airy]

fecal *adjective* of waste matter discharged from the bowels: *fecal matter*. [Say FEEK'll]

feces *noun* waste matter discharged from the bowels. [Say FEE seez]

feckless *adjective* **1** feeble, ineffective: *her husband was a charming, but lazy and feckless man*. **2** unthinking, irresponsible: *the feckless exploitation of the world's natural resources*. ▶ **fecklessly** *adverb* **fecklessness** *noun*

fecund *adjective* **1** fertile; highly productive of offspring, fruit, etc.: *the fecund countryside south of Turin*. **2** intellectually prolific or creative: *a fecund imagination*. ▶ **fecundity** *noun* [Say FEEK'nd or FECK'nd, fi CUNDA tee]

fed[1] *past and past participle* of FEED.

fed[2] *noun slang* **1** Cdn (in *plural*) the federal government. **2** US (also **Fed**) a federal official, esp. a member of the FBI.

federal *adjective* **1** of a system of government in which

power is divided between a central government and several regional ones. **2** relating to or affecting such a federation. **3** of or relating to the central government as distinguished from the separate units constituting a federation: *federal laws*. ▶ **federally** *adverb*

Federal Court of Canada *noun* Cdn a court with jurisdiction to hear civil and criminal cases referred by federal boards, or tribunals, and to rule on constitutional questions referred by the Attorney General.

federalism *noun* **1** a federal system of government. **2** advocacy of a federal system of government; in Canada esp. support of Confederation in opposition to Quebec separatism. ▶ **federalist** *noun & adjective*

federate • *verb* (**federates, federated, federating**) (esp. as **federated**) organize or be organized on a federal basis. • *adjective* having a federal organization.

federation *noun* **1** a group of provinces, states, etc. forming a single centralized unit, within which each keeps some internal autonomy. **2** an organization or group within which smaller divisions have some degree of internal autonomy: *the Canadian Federation of Independent Business*. **3** the action of forming political units or organizations into a single group with centralized control.

fedora *noun* a low soft felt hat with a crown creased lengthwise. [Say fuh DORA]

fed up *adjective informal* discontented or bored, esp. from a surfeit of something.

fee *noun* **1** a payment made to a professional person or to a professional or public body in exchange for advice or services. **2** money paid as part of a special transaction, for a privilege, admission to a society, etc.: *enrolment fee*. **3** (in *plural*) money paid (esp. to a school or university) for tuition.

feeble *adjective* (**feebler, feeblest**) **1** weak. **2** lacking energy, force, or effectiveness: *a feeble argument*. **3** dim. **4** lacking in character or intelligence.

feeble-minded *adjective* **1** unintelligent. **2** mentally deficient. ▶ **feeble-mindedness** *noun*

feebleness *noun* the condition of being feeble: *was surprised by the feebleness of his argument*.

feebly *adverb* in a feeble manner: *Jennifer smiled feebly*.

feed • *verb* (**feeds, fed, feeding**) **1** supply with food. **2** (usu. foll. by *on*) eat. **3** nourish; make grow. **4 a** maintain a supply of raw material, fuel, etc., to (a fire, machine, etc.). **b** (foll. by *into*) supply (material) to a machine. **c** (often foll. by *into*) (of a river, road etc.) flow or merge into another. **d** insert further coins into (a meter) to continue its function, validity, etc. **5** (foll. by *on*) **a** be nourished by. **b** derive benefit from. **6** relay or supply electrical signals or power to, esp. as part of a larger network or system. **7** Sport send a pass to (a player). **8** seek to satisfy (an appetite, passion, etc.). **9** (of plants) take nutrients from the soil. • *noun* **1** food, esp. for farm animals. **2** an act of giving food, esp. to animals or a baby, or of having food given to one: *when is the baby's next feed?* **3** *informal* a meal. **4** a locally broadcast radio or television program transmitted by satellite or network to a larger audience. **PHRASES off one's feed** *slang* having no appetite.

feedback *noun* **1** information about the result of an experiment, performance, etc. **2** Electronics **a** the return of a fraction of the output signal from one stage of a circuit, amplifier, etc., to the input of the same or a preceding stage. **b** a signal so returned.

feeder *noun* **1** a person who supplies food for another person, an animal, etc. **2** a person, plant, or animal that feeds in a specified manner: *the baby is a good feeder*. **3** a receptacle from which animals may feed. **4** an animal being fattened for market (usu. as an *adjective*:

feeder steers). **5** a tributary stream. **6** a branch road, bus route, airline, etc., linking outlying districts with a main transportation system. **7** a school, sports team, etc. which supplies students, players, etc. to a larger or more senior school or team. **8 a** a main carrying electricity to a distribution point. **b** an electrical connection between an antenna and a transmitter or receiver of electromagnetic waves. **9** a person or apparatus which supplies material to a machine: *an automatic paper feeder*.

feeding frenzy *noun* **1** an instance of ravenous eating by a group of animals. **2** *informal* competitive, unscrupulous behaviour, esp. as exhibited by journalists covering a sensational story.

feedlot *noun* a farming operation where livestock are fed or fattened.

feedstock *noun* raw material to supply a machine or industrial process.

feel • *verb* (**feels, felt, feeling**) **1** perceive, examine, or search by touch. **2** experience (an emotion, sensation, etc.). **3** be emotionally affected by: *felt the rebuke deeply*. **4** have a belief, attitude, or impression. **5** give an impression of being: *the air feels chilly*. **6** (foll. by *for*) have pity or compassion for. • *noun* **1** an act of touching something to examine it. **2** a physical or mental sensation produced by an object, situation, etc.: *nylon with a cotton feel* ◊ *she loved the feel of the sun on her skin* ◊ *the restaurant has a modern bistro feel*. **3 a** a sensitive appreciation or an easy understanding of something: *a feel for languages*. **b** a sense of familiarity, competence, or comfort with something: *haven't got the feel of this car yet*. PHRASES **feel free** not be reluctant or hesitant: *feel free to help yourself to another cookie*. **feel like 1** feel as though or similar to. **2** desire (a thing) or have an inclination towards (doing a thing). **feel no pain** *slang* be very drunk. **feel out** investigate cautiously. **feel up to** feel capable or be ready to face or deal with. **feel one's way** proceed carefully or act cautiously. **make one's influence** (or **presence** etc.) **felt** have a noticeable effect.

feeler *noun* **1** an organ in certain animals for testing things by touch or for searching for food. **2** a tentative proposal or suggestion, esp. to elicit a response or test opinion: *put out feelers*. **3** a person or thing that feels, tries, or tests.

feel-good *adjective* *informal* caused, causing, or characterized by positive feelings.

feeling • *noun* **1 a** a sense of touch or the capacity to feel. **b** a physical sensation. **2** a particular emotional reaction: *a feeling of despair* ◊ *hurt my feelings* ◊ *had strong feelings about it*. **3** a particular and usu. intuitive sensitivity, aptitude, or appreciation: *had a feeling for literature*. **4** an opinion, notion, or belief not based solely on reason. **5** the capacity or readiness to feel, esp. sympathy or compassion. **6 a** the general emotional effect produced on a hearer, spectator, etc. by a work of art, piece of music, etc. **b** emotional sensibility in artistic execution: *played with feeling*. • *adjective* **1** sensitive, sympathetic. **2** showing emotion. **3** sentient or capable of sensation. ▶ **feelingly** *adverb*

feet *plural of* FOOT.

feign *verb* simulate or pretend to be affected by: *feigned indifference*. ▶ **feigned** *adjective* [Say FANE]

feint • *noun* a sham move, attack, blow, etc. to divert attention or fool an opponent or enemy. • *verb* make a feint. [Sounds like *FAINT*]

feisty *adjective* (**feistier, feistiest**) *informal* **1** spirited, energetic, forceful, or exuberant, esp. when faced with opposition. **2** touchy, irritable, quarrelsome. ▶ **feistily** *adverb* **feistiness** *noun* [Say FICE tee]

felafel *noun* = FALAFEL. [Say fuh LAWFUL]

feldspar *noun* any of a group of aluminum silicates of potassium, sodium, or calcium, which are the most abundant minerals in the earth's crust.

felicitous *adjective* **1** (of a name, expression, etc.) strikingly suitable: *a felicitous turn of phrase* ◊ *the Guelph mayor with the felicitous name of John Counsell*. **2** pleasing, delightful: *the view was the room's only felicitous feature*. ▶ **felicitously** *adverb* [Say fuh LISSA tus]

felicity *noun* (*plural* **felicities**) **1** intense happiness: *their marriage was a model of domestic felicity*. **2 a** the quality of being well chosen or suitable: *the story is told with great felicity of style*. **b** a well-chosen or successful feature, esp. in a speech or piece of writing: *her book displays many subtle linguistic felicities*. [Say fuh LISSA tee]

feline • *adjective* **1** of or relating to the cat family Felidae. **2** catlike, esp. in beauty or slyness. • *noun* any member of the cat family. [Say FEE line]

fell[1] *past of* FALL *verb*

fell[2] • *verb* **1** cut down (esp. a tree). **2** strike or knock down (a person or animal). • *noun* an amount of timber cut in one season.

fell[3] *adjective* *literary* of terrible evil or ferocity; deadly: *sorcerers use spells to achieve their fell ends*. PHRASES **at** (or **in**) **one fell swoop** in a single action or effort.

fella *noun* (also **fellah**) *informal* = FELLOW 1.

fellate *verb* (**fellates, fellated, fellating**) perform fellatio on (a man).

fellatio *noun* stimulation of the penis using the mouth. [Say fuh LAY show]

feller[1] *noun* = FELLOW 1.

feller[2] *noun* a person or thing that fells something, esp. trees as timber.

feller-buncher *noun* a large machine used to shear trees just above ground level and pile them.

fellow *noun* **1** *informal* a man or boy. **2** a person in the same position, involved in the same activity, or otherwise associated with another: *she has a very good reputation among her fellows* ◊ *many caged birds live longer than their fellows in the wild*. **3** a thing of the same kind as or otherwise associated with another: *the page has been torn away from its fellows*. **4 a** a graduate student receiving a stipend for a period of research. **b** a member of the governing body in some universities. **5** a member of a learned society. **6** (as an *adjective*) belonging to the same class or activity: *fellow Canadian*.

fellowship *noun* **1** companionship or friendly association with others. **2 a** a group of people or a society sharing a common interest or aim, e.g. a religious group, fraternity, or guild. **b** membership in such a group or society. **3 a** an award of money to a graduate student in return for some research, teaching, etc. **b** a post as a fellow in a college etc.

fellow-traveller *noun* **1** a person who travels with another. **2** a person who sympathizes with, but is not a member of, a particular party or movement, esp. the Communist party.

felon *noun* a criminal. [Say FELL'n]

WRITING TIP
felony

The term **felony** is no longer used in Canadian law. Crimes in Canada are classified as **indictable offences** or **summary conviction offences**. **Felony** can still be used in a figurative sense, as in *some reporters commit journalistic felony by unscrupulous reporting*.

felony *noun* (*plural* **felonies**) **1** a (usu. violent) crime. **2** (in the US) a violent crime classified as graver than a misdemeanour, usu. punishable by a prison term of more than a year: *he was deported to California, where he faces 25 felony charges, including 12 of murder*. [Say FELLA nee]

felquiste *noun Cdn hist.* a member of the FLQ. [Say fell KEEST]

felt[1] • *noun* **1** a fabric made of wool, fur, or other fibrous material consolidated by heat and mechanical action so that the fibres are matted together. **2 a** a piece of felt. **b** something made of felt. **3** a heavy layer of material, usu. matted and fibrous, used in construction for roofing, insulation, etc. • *verb* make into felt; mat or press together: *the beaver's woolly fur was felted for cloth or hats*.

felt[2] *past and past participle of* FEEL.

felted *adjective* covered with felt: *a felted roof*.

felt pen *noun* a pen with a writing tip made of felt etc.

felt tip *noun* **1** the writing point of a felt pen. **2** a felt pen. ▶ **felt-tipped** *adjective*

fem. *abbreviation* feminine.

female • *adjective* **1** of the sex that can bear offspring or produce eggs. **2** (of a plant, flower, etc.) bearing fruit or having pistils, but lacking stamen. **3** of or consisting of women, girls, or female animals. **4** (of a screw, socket, etc.) manufactured hollow or moulded to receive a corresponding, inserted, male part. • *noun* a female person, animal, or plant.

female condom *noun* = CONDOM 2.

femaleness *noun* the quality of being female: *has rejected traditional femaleness*.

feminine • *adjective* **1** of or characteristic of women. **2** having qualities traditionally associated with women, esp. delicacy and prettiness: *a feminine frilled blouse*. **3** *Grammar* of or denoting the gender to which belong words classified as female on the basis of sex or some arbitrary distinction, such as form. • *noun* **1** *Grammar* a feminine gender or word. **2** feminine qualities collectively. ▶ **femininity** *noun*

feminism *noun* **1** the advocacy of equality of the sexes, esp. through the establishment of the political, social, and economic rights of women. **2** the movement associated with this. ▶ **feminist** *noun & adjective*

feminization *noun* the action or process of feminizing or becoming feminized: *the feminization of poverty*.

feminize *verb* (**feminizes, feminized, feminizing**) **1** make characteristic of or associated with women: *as office roles changed, clerical work was increasingly feminized*. **2** induce female physiological characteristics in. ▶ **feminized** *adjective*

femme fatale *noun* (*plural* **femmes fatales**) a woman to whom a person feels irresistibly attracted, usu. with dangerous or unhappy results. [Say fem fuh TAL]

femoral *adjective* of or relating to the femur or thigh: *femoral artery*. [Say FEMMER ul]

femur *noun* (*plural* **femurs** or **femora**) **1** the thigh bone in vertebrates, the thick bone between the hip and the knee. **2** the third articulated segment of the leg in insects and some other arthropods. [Say FEE mur for the singular, FEMMER uh for the plural]

fen *noun* **1** a tract of low land covered wholly or partially with shallow water or subject to frequent flooding. **2** wet land with alkaline, neutral, or only slightly acid peaty soil.

fence • *noun* **1** a barrier enclosing an area of ground. **2** a large, upright obstacle for a horse to jump over. **3** a person or establishment that deals in stolen goods. • *verb* (**fences, fenced, fencing**) **1 a** surround, divide, etc. (a thing) with a fence. **b** build a fence or fences. **2 a** (foll. by *in*) surround or enclose (a person, thing, etc.) with a fence. **b** (foll. by *off*) separate (one area from another): *fenced off one end of the garden*. **3** (foll. by *out*) keep out or exclude with or as with a fence. **4** deal in (stolen goods). **5** practise the art or sport of fencing. **6** engage in skilful argument: *lawyers can go for the jugular when fencing with an ornery opponent*. PHRASES (**sit**) **on the fence** (remain) neutral or undecided in a dispute etc; (be) uncommitted.

fenceline *noun* **1** the continuous extent of fence encompassing a piece of land, esp. on a farm or ranch. **2** the line or boundary marked by a fence.

fence-mending *noun* making peace with an opponent; reconciliation: *in the aftermath of this nasty lawsuit, there was a lot of fence-mending to be done*.

fencer *noun* a person who takes part in the sport of fencing.

fence-sitter *noun* a person who remains neutral or uncommitted on an issue. ▶ **fence-sitting** *noun & adjective*

fencing *noun* **1** a set or extent of fences. **2** material for making fences. **3** the action of putting up a fence. **4** the practice or sport of engaging in combat with swords, esp. according to a set of rules.

fend *verb* **1** (foll. by *for*) support or look after (esp. oneself). **2** (usu. foll. by *off*) ward off (an attack), keep (a thing) away, or defend from (a threat etc.).

fender *noun* **1 a** the mudguard or area around the wheel well of a motor vehicle. **b** *disputed* the bumper of a motor vehicle. **c** the mudguard of a bicycle etc. **2** *Nautical* a piece of rubber etc. hung over a ship's side to protect it against chafing or impact. **3** a low frame bordering a fireplace to keep in falling coals etc. **4** any thing used to keep something off, prevent a collision, etc.

fender-bender *noun slang* a usu. minor collision between vehicles.

feng shui *noun* (in Chinese thought) a system of good and evil influences in the natural surroundings, considered when siting or designing buildings etc. [Say feng SHOOEY or fung SHWAY]

Fenian • *noun* a member of the Irish Republican Brotherhood, a militant 19th-c. nationalist organization founded among the Irish in the US, whose members encouraged revolutionary activity and aimed to overthrow the British government in Ireland. The Fenians staged an unsuccessful revolt in Ireland in 1867 and were responsible for isolated revolutionary acts against the British, including raids from the US into Canada in the 1860s and the assassination of the Canadian politician D'Arcy McGee in 1868. The Fenian raids helped to unite Canadians in favour of Confederation. • *adjective* of or relating to the Fenians. [Say FEENY in]

fennel *noun* **1** a yellow-flowered plant with fragrant seeds and fine leaves with a mild licorice flavour used as flavouring. **2** the seeds of this. **3** (also **sweet fennel**) a variety of this with swollen leaf bases eaten as a vegetable.

feral *adjective* **1** (of animals) belonging to or forming a wild population ultimately descended from individuals which escaped from captivity or domestication: *feral*

cats. **2** resembling a wild animal: *with feral deftness, Joe slipped among the crowds.* [Say FEAR ul or FAIR ul]

ferment • *noun* social, political, etc. excitement, agitation, or unrest: *Germany at this time was in a state of religious ferment.* • *verb* experience or cause to undergo a chemical change because of the action of yeast or bacteria, often changing sugar to alcohol: *fruit juices ferment if kept too long.* ▶ **fermented** *adjective*

fermentation *noun* the chemical breakdown of a substance by micro-organisms such as yeasts and bacteria, esp. of sugar to ethyl alcohol in making beers, wines, and liquors.

fermenter *noun* **1** a container in which fermentation takes place. **2** an organism which causes fermentation.

fermium *noun* a radioactive metallic element produced artificially. [Say FURMY um]

fern *noun* a flowerless plant reproducing by spores and usu. having feathery fronds. ▶ **ferny** *adjective*

ferocious *adjective* **1** savagely fierce, cruel, or violent: *a ferocious beast.* **2** *informal* (as an intensifier) very great, extreme: *a ferocious headache* ◊ *ferocious determination.* **3** characterized by or involving aggression, bitterness, and determination: *a ferocious debate over Canada's joining the US.* ▶ **ferociously** *adverb*

ferocity *noun* the quality or state of being ferocious: *the police were shocked by the ferocity of the attack* ◊ *she hated him with a ferocity that astonished him.* [Say fur OSSA tee]

ferret • *noun* a small half-domesticated animal of the weasel family kept as a pet or (in Europe) used to catch rabbits, rats, etc. • *verb* (**ferrets, ferreted, ferreting**) **1** (foll. by *out*) search out (secrets, criminals, etc.): *determined to ferret out the truth about what happened.* **2** search or rummage about: *she opened the drawer and ferreted around for her keys.* [Say FAIR it]

ferric *adjective* **1** of or containing iron. **2** of or containing iron in a trivalent form (compare FERROUS). [Say FAIR ick]

Ferris wheel *noun* a large, upright wheel revolving on a fixed axle, with seats suspended from its rims.

ferrous *adjective* **1** (of an alloy etc.) containing iron in significant quantities. **2** of or containing iron in a divalent form (compare FERRIC). [Say FAIR us]

ferrule *noun* **1** a usu. metal ring or cap strengthening the end of a stick or tube. **2** a band strengthening or forming a joint. [Say FAIR ool]

> **SPELL CHECK**
> **ferry, fairy**
>
> The small imaginary being is a **fairy**.

ferry • *noun* (*plural* **ferries**) **1** (also **ferry boat**) a boat which conveys passengers, vehicles, etc. across water as a regular service. **2** the service itself or the place where it operates. • *verb* (**ferries, ferried, ferrying**) **1** convey or go in a boat etc. across water. **2** transport from one place to another, esp. as a regular service.

fertile *adjective* **1** (of soil) fruitful or rich in the materials needed to produce and support vegetation. **2 a** (of a human being, animal, or plant) able to produce offspring. **b** producing many offspring. **c** (of a seed, egg, etc.) capable of becoming a new individual. **3 a** (of the mind) inventive, full of or able to produce new ideas: *she has a very fertile imagination.* **b** conducive to creativity, productivity, etc.: *a fertile field for research.* **4** (of nuclear material) able to become fissile by the capture of neutrons. [Say FUR tile or FURTLE]

fertility *noun* **1** the quality of being fertile. **2** the actual number of births: *countries that actively encourage limits to fertility.*

fertility rate *noun* the average number of births per year for each woman of child-bearing age, usu. between the ages of 15 and 45.

fertilization *noun* **1** *Biology* the fusion of male and female gametes during sexual reproduction to form a zygote. **2** the application of fertilizer to soil.

fertilize *verb* (**fertilizes, fertilized, fertilizing**) **1 a** make fertile or productive. **b** enrich (soil, plants, etc.), esp. with minerals, nutrients, etc. **2** cause to develop a new individual by introducing male reproductive material.

fertilizer *noun* a chemical or natural substance added to soil to make it more fertile.

fervency *noun* intensity of feeling; ardour; zeal.

fervent *adjective* ardent, impassioned, intense: *fervent love.* ▶ **fervently** *adverb*

fervid *adjective* intensely enthusiastic or passionate, esp. to an excessive degree: *she had a fervid interest in sex.* ▶ **fervidly** *adverb*

fervour *noun* (also **fervor**) passion, zeal. [Say FUR vur]

fescue *noun* any grass of the genus *Festuca*, valuable for lawns, pasture, and fodder. [Say FESS cue]

fess *verb* (**fesses, fessed, fessing**) (usu. foll. by *up*) *informal* confess.

fest *noun* **1** a festival or special occasion: *the country music fest.* **2** (in *combination*) an activity of a specified type engaged in by a group of people: *gabfest.*

fester *verb* **1** make or become infected and filled with pus. **2** (of feelings, thoughts, etc.) become more bitter and angry.

festival • *noun* **1** a day or period of celebration, religious or secular. **2** a series of performances of music, drama, films, etc.: *film festival.* • *adjective* of or concerning a festival.

festival of lights *noun* **1** = HANUKKAH. **2** = DIWALI.

festive *adjective* **1** of or characteristic of a feast or festival. **2** joyous, cheerful. **3** designating the time around Christmas and Hanukkah: *the festive season.* ▶ **festively** *adverb* **festiveness** *noun*

festivity *noun* (*plural* **festivities**) **1** (often in *plural*) a celebration. **2** rejoicing, merriment.

festoon • *noun* **1** a garland of flowers, leaves, ribbons, etc. hung in a curve. **2** something hanging in a downward curve: *festoons of grey cobwebs hung from the ceiling.* • *verb* **1** adorn elaborately with chains, garlands, and other decorations. **2** cover abundantly: *the border was festooned with signs.* [Say fess TOON]

feta *noun* a very soft, white cheese of Greek origin, made from ewe's milk or goat's milk. [Say FETTA]

fetal *adjective* **1** of or pertaining to a fetus. **2** being a fetus: *fetal lambs.* [Say FEET'll]

fetal alcohol syndrome *noun* a syndrome of birth defects caused by alcohol consumption during pregnancy, including facial abnormalities, impaired mental and physical development, etc.

fetal position *noun* a curled position of the body, with the head and legs pulled in towards the torso, resembling that of a fetus in the uterus.

fetch • *verb* (**fetches, fetched, fetching**) **1 a** go for and bring back (a person or thing): *fetch a doctor.* **b** cause to come: *the concert fetched a crowd of 15,000.* **2** sell for (a price); realize (a profit): *fetched $10.* **3** *informal* give (a blow, slap, etc.): *fetched him a slap on the face.* • *noun* (*plural* **fetches**) **1** an act of fetching, retrieving, bringing from a distance, etc. **2** a game, usu. played with a dog, in which a person throws a ball, stick, etc. and the dog retrieves it. ▮PHRASES▮ **fetch and carry** run backwards and forwards with things or be a mere servant. **fetch up** *informal* arrive, come to rest.

fetching *adjective* attractive. ▶ **fetchingly** *adverb*

fete • *noun* a festival, fair, or great entertainment.

• *verb* (**fetes, feted, feting**) honour or entertain (a person) lavishly and in a special way. [Say FATE]

Fête nationale *noun* (also **Fête nationale du Québec**) (in Quebec) the official name for the holiday celebrated on June 24, formerly (and commonly still) called St. Jean Baptiste Day. [Say fet nass yuh NAL]

fetid *adjective* foul smelling. [Say FET id or FEET id]

fetish *noun* (*plural* **fetishes**) **1** *Psychology* a part of the body, object, action, etc. acting as a focus for sexual desire: *Victorian men developed fetishes focusing on feet, shoes, and boots.* **2** an inanimate object worshipped as having inherent magical powers or as being inhabited by a spirit. **3** an object, principle, etc. evoking irrational, even obsessive, devotion or respect: *she has a fetish about cleanliness* ◊ *he makes a fetish of his work* ◊ *has a fetish for fedoras.* ▶**fetishism** *noun* **fetishist** *noun* **fetishistic** *adjective* [Say FETTISH]

fetishization *noun* **1** the process of making a fetish of something or someone: *white men's fetishization of Asian women.* **2** the process of overvaluing or paying undue respect to something or someone: *the Russians seem to have entered the Western world by consuming French culture to the point of fetishization.* [Say fettish ize AY sh'n]

fetishize *verb* (**fetishizes, fetishized, fetishizing**) **1** make a fetish of. **2** overvalue or pay undue respect to. [Say FETTISH ize]

fetlock *noun* the part of a horse's leg forming a projection above and behind the hoof where a tuft of hair often grows.

fetter • *noun* **1** a shackle or chains put on a prisoner's or slave's feet to limit movement. **2** something that confines, impedes, etc.: *this vote is a chance for the Liberal members to throw off the fetters of party discipline.* • *verb* **1** bind with fetters etc. **2** restrict, impede, or hinder in any way.

fettle *noun* condition: *in fine fettle.*

fettuccine *noun* (also **fettucini**) pasta made in ribbons. [Say fet oo CHEENY]

fetus *noun* (*plural* **fetuses**) the unborn offspring of a mammal from the time when the main features of an adult can be recognized. [Say FEET us]

feud • *noun* **1** a prolonged mutual hostility, esp. between two families, tribes, etc., with murderous assaults in revenge for a previous injury: *a family feud.* **2** a prolonged or bitter quarrel or dispute. • *verb* conduct or participate in a feud.

feudal *adjective* of, according to, or resembling feudalism.

feudalism *noun* (also **the feudal system**) the dominant social system in medieval Europe in which the nobility held lands from the Crown in exchange for military service, and vassals were in turn tenants of the nobility, while the peasants (villeins or serfs) were obliged to live on their lord's land and give him homage, labour, and a share of the produce, notionally in exchange for military protection.

fever *noun* **1 a** an abnormally high body temperature, often as a sign of illness. **b** any of various diseases characterized by this: *scarlet fever.* **2** intense excitement or agitation: *Stanley Cup fever has gripped the country.*

fevered *adjective* **1** affected by or suffering from a fever. **2** highly excited: *a fevered imagination.*

feverfew *noun* a plant with feathery leaves and white daisy-like flowers, formerly used to reduce fever.

feverish *adjective* **1 a** having symptoms resembling those of a fever. **b** of the nature or indicative of a fever. **2** excited, hectic, or restless. ▶**feverishly** *adverb* **feverishness** *noun*

fever pitch *noun* a state of extreme excitement.

fèves au lard *noun* Cdn (Que.) baked beans with pork. [Say FEV oh lar]

few • *adjective* not many. • *pronoun* (as *plural*) **1** (preceded by *a*) some, but not many: *a few of his friends.* **2** a small number, not many: *few are chosen.* **3** (**the few**) **a** the minority. **b** the elect. PHRASES **every few** once in every small group of: *every few days.* **few and far between** neither numerous nor frequent. **have a few** *informal* take several alcoholic drinks. **no fewer than** as many as (a specified number). **quite** (or **not**) **a few** a considerable number.

fey *adjective* **1** having a strange, almost otherworldly, whimsical charm. **2** usu. *ironic* or *derogatory* (of a person, behaviour, etc.) affected. [Say FAY]

fez *noun* (*plural* **fezzes**) a red brimless felt cap with a flat top and tassel, worn by men in some Muslim countries.

ff *abbreviation Music* fortissimo.

ff. *abbreviation* and the following (pages, lines, etc.).

fiancé *noun* (*plural* **fiancés**) a man to whom one is engaged to be married. [Say fee ON say or fee on SAY]

fiancée *noun* (*plural* **fiancées**) a woman to whom one is engaged to be married. [Say fee ON say or fee on SAY]

fiasco *noun* (*plural* **fiascos**) a complete and ridiculous failure. [Say fee ASS co]

fiat *noun* **1** a formal authorization: *prices have been fixed by government fiat.* **2** a declaration by someone in power. [Say FEE ut]

fib • *noun* a trivial lie, esp. about something unimportant. • *verb* (**fibs, fibbed, fibbing**) tell a fib. ▶**fibber** *noun*

fibre *noun* (also esp. *US* **fiber**) **1 a** a threadlike element in plant tissue, esp. an elongated cell with thick walls and no protoplasm. **b** any threadlike structure forming part of the muscular, nervous, connective, or other tissue in an animal body. **2 a** a thread or filament forming part of a textile. **b** any material consisting of animal, vegetable, or synthetic fibres, esp. a substance that can be spun, woven, or felted. **3** a thread formed from glass, metal, etc. **4 a** the texture or structure of a thing. **b** the essence of a person's character: *lacks moral fibre.* **5** = DIETARY FIBRE. ▶**fibred** *adjective* (also in combination). **fibreless** *adjective*

fibreboard *noun* (also esp. *US* **fiberboard**) a building material made of wood or other plant fibres compressed into boards.

fibreglass *noun* (also esp. *US* **fiberglass**) any material consisting of glass filaments woven into a textile or paper, or embedded in plastic etc., for use as a construction or insulation material.

fibre optic *adjective* relating to or used in fibre optics: *fibre optic cables.*

fibre optics *plural noun* **1** transmission of information, by means of infrared light signals, along a thin glass fibre. **2** (treated as *plural*) the fibres etc. so used.

fibril *noun* **1** a small or delicate fibre, esp. a constituent strand of an animal, vegetable, or synthetic fibre. **2** the ultimate subdivision of a fibre. [Say FIE brill]

fibrillate *verb* (**fibrillates, fibrillated, fibrillating**) (of a muscle, esp. in the heart) undergo a quivering movement or contract irregularly fibril by fibril. ▶**fibrillation** *noun* [Say FIB ruh late]

fibromyalgia *noun* an inflammation of fibrous connective tissue, usu. rheumatic and painful. [Say fie bro my AL juh]

fibrosis *noun* (*plural* **fibroses**) a thickening and scarring of connective tissue, usu. as a result of injury. [Say fie BROE sis]

fibrous *adjective* consisting of or like fibres. [Say FIE brus]

fibula *noun* (*plural* **fibulae** or **fibulas**) the smaller outer bone of the two bones in the lower part of the leg between the knee and the ankle. ▶ **fibular** *adjective* [Say FIB you luh for the singular, FIB you lee for the plural]

fickle *adjective* inconstant, changeable, esp. in loyalty. ▶ **fickleness** *noun*

fiction *noun* **1** an invented idea or statement or narrative; an imaginary thing. **2** literature, esp. novels, describing imaginary events and people. **3** a belief or statement which is false, but is often held to be true because it is useful to do so: *she claims that overpopulation is a convenient fiction that has legitimized an unwarranted intrusion into the lives of poor people*. ▶ **fictional** *adjective* **fictionally** *adverb* **fictionalization** *noun* **fictionalize** *verb* (**fictionalizes**, **fictionalized**, **fictionalizing**)

fictitious *adjective* invented by someone rather than true: *all the places and characters in my novel are fictitious* ◊ *the account he gives of his childhood is fictitious*. ▶ **fictitiously** *adverb* [Say fick TISH us]

fictive *adjective* created by imagination; not real.

ficus *noun* (*plural* **ficus**) a tree or shrub of the mulberry family, including the fig and the rubber plant. [Say FEE kus or FIKE us]

Ficus benjamina *noun* (*plural* **Ficus benjamina**) a tropical tree with drooping branches, frequently grown as a houseplant. [Say FEE kus (or FIKE us) benja MEENA]

fiddle • *noun* **1** a stringed instrument played with a bow, esp. a violin. **2** *informal* an act of cheating or fraud. • *verb* (**fiddles**, **fiddled**, **fiddling**) **1 a** (often foll. by *with*) play restlessly. **b** (often foll. by *around*) move aimlessly. **c** act idly or frivolously. **d** (usu. foll. by *with* or *around with*) tinker; make minor adjustments (esp. in an attempt to make improvements). **2** *slang* cheat; falsify: *fiddled the figures to get the results they wanted*. **3 a** play the fiddle. **b** play (a tune etc.) on the fiddle. PHRASES **as fit as a fiddle** in very good health. **play second fiddle** take a subordinate role.

fiddlehead *noun* the young, curled, edible frond of certain ferns.

fiddlehead green *noun* *Cdn* (usu. in *plural*) = FIDDLEHEAD.

fiddler *noun* **1** a person who plays a fiddle. **2** a North American crab, the male of which has one of its claws held in a position like a violinist's arm.

fiddlesticks *interjection* expressing scorn etc.

fiddling *noun* **1** the action of playing a fiddle, esp. in folk music. **2** the action of tinkering or playing with something.

fiddly *adjective* (**fiddlier**, **fiddliest**) *informal* intricate, awkward, or tiresome to do or use.

fidelity *noun* **1** (often foll. by *to*) faithfulness, loyalty. **2** sexual faithfulness to one's spouse, lover, etc. **3** exact correspondence to the original: *the fidelity of the translation to the original text*. **4** precision in reproduction of sound: *high fidelity*. [Say fuh DELLA tee]

fidget • *verb* (**fidgets**, **fidgeted**, **fidgeting**) move or act restlessly or nervously, usu. while maintaining basically the same posture. • *noun* **1** a person who fidgets. **2** (usu. in *plural*) a bodily uneasiness seeking relief in spasmodic movements; such movements. **b** a restless mood. ▶ **fidgety** *adjective*

fiduciary *adjective* involving trust, esp. with regard to the relationship between a trustee and a beneficiary: *alleging they broke fiduciary and contractual obligations*. [Say fuh DOOSHY airy or fuh DYOOSHY airy]

fief *noun* a piece of land held under the feudal system. [Say FEEF]

fiefdom *noun* **1** a fief. **2** a person's sphere of operation or control, esp. when there is seemingly no check on it from the outside: *layers of bureaucracy manned by officials who guard their fiefdoms with jealous zeal*. [Say FEEF dum]

field • *noun* **1** an area of open land, esp. one used for pasture or crops. **b** (as an *adjective*) grown in a field, as opposed to in a greenhouse etc.: *field tomatoes*. **2** a piece of land for a specified purpose, esp. an area marked out for games: *football field*. **3** the participants in a contest or sport. **4** an area rich in some natural product: *gas field*. **5** an expanse of ice, snow, sea, sky, etc. **6 a** a battlefield. **b** the scene of a campaign. **c** (as an *adjective*) (of artillery etc.) light and mobile for use on campaign. **7** an area of operation or activity; a subject of study: *outstanding in her field*. **8 a** the region in which a force is effective: *magnetic field*. **b** the force exerted in such an area. **9** a range of perception: *field of vision*. **10** *Math* a system subject to two operations analogous to those for the multiplication and addition of real numbers. **11** (as an *adjective*) **a** (of an animal or plant) found in the countryside, wild: *field mouse*. **b** carried out or working in the natural environment, not in a laboratory etc.: *field test*. **12** the background of a picture, coin, flag, etc. **13** *Computing* a part of a record, representing an item of data. • *verb* **1** *Baseball* **a** act as a fielder. **b** stop (and return) (the ball). **2 a** select (a team or individual) to play in a game. **b** deploy (an army). **c** propose (a candidate). **3** deal with (a succession of questions etc.). PHRASES **in the field 1** on a military campaign. **2** working etc. away from one's laboratory, headquarters, etc. **play the field** *informal* avoid exclusive attachment to one person or activity etc. **take the field 1** begin a campaign. **2** (of a sports team) go on to a playing field to begin a game.

field day *noun* **1** wide scope for action or success; a time occupied with exciting events: *anglers are having a field day*. **2** *Military* an exercise, esp. in manoeuvring. **3** a day spent in exploration, scientific investigation, etc., in the natural environment. **4** a day at which an entire school competes in outdoor track and field events.

fielder *noun* *Baseball etc.* **1** a player who fields the ball. **2** a member (other than the pitcher) of the side that is fielding, esp. an outfielder.

field goal *noun* **1** *Football* a goal scored by a drop kick or place kick from the field. **2** *Basketball* a two- or three-point basket; any basket other than a free throw.

field guide *noun* a book for the identification of birds, flowers, etc., in the field.

field hockey *noun* a game played between two teams on a field with curved sticks and a small hard ball.

field lacrosse *noun* a type of lacrosse played on an open field with teams of ten men or twelve women.

field of vision *noun* all that comes into view when the eyes are turned in some direction.

field party *noun* (*plural* **field parties**) *Cdn* a large outdoor party held in an open field.

fieldstone *noun* unfinished stone, esp. when used as a building material.

field test • *verb* test (a device) in the environment in which it is to be used. • *noun* a test of a device etc. in the environment in which it is to be used.

field trial *noun* **1** a test or competition between gun dogs to determine their ability to perform in actual hunting conditions. **2** = FIELD TEST *noun*.

field trip *noun* **1** a school trip, e.g. to a museum, a

park, etc., to gain knowledge or experience away from the classroom. **2** a research trip to study something at first hand.

fieldwork *noun* the practical work of a surveyor, collector of scientific data, sociologist, etc., conducted in the natural environment rather than a laboratory, office, etc. ▶ **fieldworker** *noun*

fiend *noun* **1 a** an evil spirit, a demon. **b (the fiend)** the Devil. **2 a** a very wicked or cruel person. **b** a person causing mischief or annoyance. **3** (with a qualifying word) *informal* **a** a devotee: *fitness fiend*. **b** an addict: *dope fiend*. [Say FEEND]

fiendish *adjective* **1** like a fiend; extremely cruel or unpleasant. **2** extremely difficult. ▶ **fiendishly** *adverb* **fiendishness** *noun* [Say FEEND ish]

fierce *adjective* (**fiercer, fiercest**) **1** angry and aggressive in a way that is frightening: *a fierce dog*. **2** (of a feeling, emotion, or action) showing a heartfelt and powerful intensity: *a fierce passion* ◊ *the bill was passed despite fierce opposition*. **3** unpleasantly strong or intense; uncontrolled: *fierce heat*. PHRASES **something fierce** *slang* to a great degree: *I miss him something fierce*. ▶ **fiercely** *adverb* **fierceness** *noun*

fiery *adjective* (**fierier, fieriest**) **1** consisting of or flaming with fire. **2** like fire in appearance, bright red. **3 a** hot as fire. **b** acting like fire; producing a burning sensation. **4 a** flashing, ardent: *fiery eyes*. **b** showing strong emotions, especially anger: *fiery temper* ◊ *a fiery passion*. [Say FIRE ee]

fiesta *noun* (*plural* **fiestas**) **1** a holiday or festivity. **2** a religious festival in Spanish-speaking countries. [Say fee ESTA]

fife *noun* a kind of small shrill flute used with the drum in military music.

fifteen *cardinal number* one more than fourteen. ▶ **fifteenth** *ordinal number*

fifth *ordinal number* **1** constituting the number 5 in a sequence. **2** *Music* **a** an interval or chord spanning five consecutive notes in the diatonic scale (e.g. C to G). **b** a note separated from another by this interval. PHRASES **take the Fifth** (in the US) exercise the right guaranteed by the Fifth Amendment.

Fifth Amendment *noun* an amendment to the US constitution which states that no person may be compelled to give testimony that might incriminate himself or herself.

fifth column *noun* a group working for an enemy within a country at war etc. ▶ **fifth columnist** *noun*

fifth wheel *noun* **1** an extra wheel for a four-wheeled vehicle. **2** an extra or unnecessary person or thing. **3** a coupling between a vehicle used for towing and a trailer. **4** (also **fifth wheel trailer**) a camper-trailer.

fiftieth *ordinal number* corresponding to fifty.

fifty *cardinal number* (*plural* **fifties**) the product of five and ten. PHRASES **fifty-first, -second**, etc. the ordinal numbers between fiftieth and sixtieth. **fifty-one, -two,** etc. the cardinal numbers between fifty and sixty.

fifty-fifty • *adjective* equal, with equal shares or chances: *on a fifty-fifty basis*. • *adverb* equally, half and half: *go fifty-fifty*.

fig *noun* **1** a soft pear-shaped fruit with many seeds, eaten fresh or dried. **2** (also **fig tree**) a broad-leaved deciduous tree bearing figs. PHRASES **not care** (or **give**) **a fig** not care at all.

fig. *abbreviation* **1** figure. **2** figurative. **3** figuratively.

figgy duff *noun* *Cdn* (*Nfld*) a type of boiled pudding containing raisins.

fight • *verb* (**fights, fought, fighting**) **1** contend, struggle, or quarrel with an opponent or enemy in a war, battle, conflict, etc. **2 a** contend about (an issue, election, etc.). **b** maintain (a lawsuit, cause, etc.) against an opponent. **3** campaign or strive determinedly to achieve something. **4** strive to overcome (disease, fire, fear, etc.). • *noun* **1 a** a combat between two or more persons, animals, or parties. **b** a boxing match. **c** a battle. **d** an argument. **2** a conflict or struggle; a vigorous effort in the face of difficulty. **3** power or inclination to fight: *has no fight left*. PHRASES **fight back 1** counterattack. **2** (also **fight down**) suppress (one's feelings, tears, etc.). **fight for 1** fight on behalf of. **2** fight to secure (a thing). **fight off** repel with effort. **fight out** (usu. **fight it out**) settle (a dispute etc.) by fighting. **make a fight of it** (or **put up a fight**) offer resistance.

fighter *noun* **1** a person or animal that fights. **2** a fast military aircraft designed for attacking other aircraft. **3** a person with great determination etc.

fighter bomber *noun* an aircraft serving as both fighter and bomber.

fighting chance *noun* an opportunity of succeeding by great effort: *if we stay healthy I think we'll have a fighting chance of making the playoffs*.

fighting words *plural noun* *informal* words likely to provoke a fight or indicating a willingness to fight.

figment *noun* a thing existing only in the imagination: *these symptoms are just a figment of your imagination*.

Fig Newton *noun* *proprietary* a small rectangular plain cookie with a filling of mashed figs, raisins, etc.

figuration *noun* **1** ornamentation by means of figures or designs. **2** *Music* ornamental patterns of scales, arpeggios, etc.: *the figuration of the accompaniment comes out too strongly*.

figurative *adjective* **1** (of language) used in a way that is different from the usual literal meaning, in order to create a particular mental image. For example, "she exploded with rage" shows a figurative use of the verb *explode*. **2** (of art) showing people, animals and objects as they really look: *a figurative artist*. ▶ **figuratively** *adverb* [Say FIGURE a tiv]

figure • *noun* **1 a** the external form or shape of a thing. **b** bodily shape, esp. of a woman: *has a very nice figure*. **2** a person as seen in outline but not identified. **3** a character or personage, esp. an important or well-known one; *a public figure*. **4** an artistic representation of the human form. **5 a** a numerical symbol, esp. any of the ten in Arabic notation. **b** an amount of money, a value: *cannot put a figure on it*. **6** *Geometry* a two-dimensional space enclosed by a line or lines, or a three-dimensional space enclosed by a surface or surfaces. **7** a diagram or illustrative drawing. **8** (in skating) a prescribed pattern of movements from a stationary position. **9** (also **figure of speech**) a word or phrase used in a non-literal sense to add rhetorical force or interest to a spoken or written passage. • *verb* (**figures, figured, figuring**) **1** appear or be mentioned, esp. prominently: *figures significantly in the book*. **2** represent in a diagram or picture. **3** imagine; picture mentally. **4** embellish with a pattern: *figured satin*. **5 a** calculate. **b** do arithmetic. **6 a** understand, think, consider, expect to be the case: *she figured there wasn't any point arguing with them so she let the matter go*. **b** *informal* be likely or understandable: *that figures*. PHRASES **figure on** count on, expect. **figure out 1** work out by arithmetic or logic. **2** understand. **go figure** *informal* it escapes explanation.

figure eight *noun* **1** the shape of the number eight. **2** something with this shape.

figurehead *noun* **1** a person who is in a high position in a country or an organization but who has no real power or authority: *the president of the club is not just a figurehead*. **2** a carving at a ship's prow.

figure skate *noun* a type of skate having a fairly long, narrow blade with toe picks, used in figure skating.

figure skater *noun* a person who performs a type of ice skating in which the skater combines a number of movements including steps, jumps, turns, etc.

figure skating *noun* a type of ice skating in which the skater combines a number of movements including steps, jumps, turns, etc.

figurine *noun* a small esp. ornamental statue or figure.

Fijian • *adjective* of or relating to Fiji, a country in the S Pacific, its people, or language. • *noun* **1** a native or national of Fiji. **2** the Austronesian language of this people. [Say fee JEE In]

filament *noun* **1** a slender threadlike body or fibre (esp. in animal or vegetable structures). **2** a conducting wire or thread with a high melting point in a light bulb etc., heated or made incandescent by an electric current. **3** *Botany* the part of the stamen that supports the anther. ▶ **filamentous** *adjective* [Say FILLA mint]

filbert *noun* a hazelnut.

filch *verb* (**filches, filched, filching**) *informal* pilfer, steal. ▶ **filcher** *noun*

file[1] • *noun* **1** a folder, box, etc., for holding loose papers, esp. arranged for reference. **2** a set of papers kept in this. **3** a collection of (usu. related) data stored under one name. **4** *Cdn* issues and responsibilities in a specified area, considered collectively: *the unity file*. • *verb* (**files, filed, filing**) **1** place (papers) in a file or among (esp. public) records. **2** submit (a petition for divorce, an application for a patent, etc.). **3** (of a reporter) send (a story, information, etc.) to a newspaper. PHRASES **file away** place in a file, or make a mental note of, for future reference. **on file** in a file or filing system. ▶ **filer** *noun*

file[2] • *noun* a line of persons or things one behind another. • *verb* (**files, filed, filing**) walk in a file.

file[3] • *noun* a tool with a roughened surface or surfaces, usu. of steel, for smoothing or shaping wood, fingernails, etc. • *verb* (**files, filed, filing**) smooth or shape with a file. PHRASES **file away** remove (roughness etc.) with a file. ▶ **filer** *noun*

file server *noun Computing* a device which manages shared access to centralized files in a network.

filet *noun* **1** a kind of net or lace with a square mesh. **2** a fillet of meat or fish. [Say fuh LAY or FILL it]

filet mignon *noun* a small tender piece of beef from the end of the tenderloin. [Say fuh LAY mee NYON]

filial *adjective* having to do with the feelings or behaviour of a child towards its parent: *filial affection*. [Say FILLY ul]

filibuster • *noun* a long speech made in a parliament in order to delay a vote: *Liberal senators agreed to end their latest filibuster of the upper chamber*. • *verb* deliver a filibuster: *opposition parties filibustered debate for approximately 26 hours*. ▶ **filibusterer** *noun* [Say FILLA huster]

filigree *noun* **1** ornamental work of fine wire formed into delicate tracery; fine metal openwork: *a new owner installed distinctive wrought iron filigree outside the inn*. **2** anything delicate resembling this: *Chantelle wore cowgirl boots, tall brown leather with a floral filigree*. ▶ **filigreed** *adjective* [Say FILLA gree]

filing[1] *noun* (usu. in *plural*) a particle rubbed off by a file.

filing[2] *noun* **1** the act of placing something in a file. **2** the act of submitting a petition, application, etc.

filing cabinet *noun* (also **file cabinet**) a piece of furniture with drawers for storing documents.

Filipina • *noun* a woman or girl who is a native or national of the Philippines. • *adjective* who is a Filipina. [Say filla PEENA]

Filipino • *noun* (*plural* **Filipinos**) a native or national of the Philippines, a country in SE Asia. • *adjective* of or relating to the Philippines or the Filipinos. [Say filla PEENO]

fill • *verb* **1** make or become full. **2** block up (a cavity or hole in a tooth). **3** appoint a person to hold (a vacant post). **4** hold (a position). **5** supply (a prescription, order for goods, etc.). **6** occupy (vacant time). **7** satisfy, fulfill (a need or requirement). • *noun* **1** as much as one wants or can bear: *eat your fill*. **2** material used for filling something, esp. earth etc. used to fill a hole or raise the level of the ground. PHRASES **fill the bill** be suitable or adequate. **fill in 1** add information to complete (a form etc.). **2 a** complete (a drawing etc.) within an outline. **b** fill (an outline) in this way. **3** fill (a hole etc.) completely. **4** act as a substitute. **5** occupy oneself during (time between other activities). **6** *informal* inform (a person) more fully. **fill out 1** enlarge to the required size. **2** become enlarged or plump. **3** fill in (a document etc.). **fill up 1** make or become completely full. **2** fill the fuel tank of (a car etc.). **3** provide what is needed to occupy vacant parts or places or deal with deficiencies in.

filler *noun* **1** a substance used to fill holes or cracks or to increase the bulk of something. **2** an item filling space in a newspaper etc.

filles du roi *plural noun Cdn hist.* women of marriageable age sent from France to New France under royal direction between 1663–73 to be married to the men then living in the colony. [Say fee doo RWAH]

fillet • *noun* **1 a** a fleshy boneless piece of meat from near the loins or the ribs. **b** (also **fillet steak**) the undercut of a sirloin. **c** a boned longitudinal section of a fish. **2** a headband, ribbon, string, or narrow band, for binding the hair or worn round the head. • *verb* (**fillets, filleted, filleting**) **1** remove bones from (fish or meat). **2** divide (fish or meat) into fillets. [Say FILL it; for the food senses you can also say fuh LAY]

fill-in *noun* a person or thing put in as a substitute or to fill a vacancy.

filling *noun* any material that fills or is used to fill, esp.: **1** a piece of material used to fill a cavity in a tooth. **2** the edible substance between the slices of bread in a sandwich or enclosed by pastry in a pie etc.

filling station *noun* a gas station.

fillip *noun* something that adds interest or excitement or gives something a boost: *the support of such a celebrity was an encouraging fillip to her election campaign*.

fill-up *noun* **1** a thing that fills something up. **2** the act of filling up a fuel tank etc.

filly *noun* (*plural* **fillies**) **1** a young female horse, usu. before it is four years old. **2** *informal offensive* a girl or young woman.

film • *noun* **1** a thin coating or covering layer. **2** a strip or sheet of plastic or other flexible base coated with light-sensitive emulsion for exposure in a camera. **3 a** a story or event recorded by a camera. **b** (in *plural*) the cinema industry. **4** a slight veil or haze etc. • *verb* **1 a** make a photographic film of (a scene, person, etc.). **b** make a cinema or television film of (a book etc.). **c** be (well or ill) suited for reproduction on film. **2** cover or become covered with or as with a film.

filmgoer *noun* a person who frequents the cinema.

filmic *adjective* of or relating to films.

filmmaker *noun* a director or producer of films. ▶ **filmmaking** *noun*

filmography *noun* (*plural* **filmographies**) a list of films by one director etc. or on one subject.

filmy *adjective* (**filmier**, **filmiest**) **1** thin and translucent. **2** covered with or as with a film.

filo *noun* = PHYLLO. [Say FIE lo]

Filofax *noun* (*plural* **Filofaxes**) *proprietary* a portable looseleaf datebook including pages for addresses, notes, etc. [Say FIE lo fax]

filter • *noun* **1** a porous device for removing impurities or solid particles from a liquid or gas passed through it. **2** = FILTER TIP. **3** a screen or attachment for absorbing or modifying light, X-rays, etc. **4** a device for suppressing electrical or sound waves of frequencies not required. • *verb* **1** pass or cause to pass through a filter. **2** (foll. by *through*, *into*, etc.) make way gradually. **3** (foll. by *out*) leak or cause to leak. PHRASES **filter out** remove (impurities etc.) by means of a filter.

filter feeder *noun* Zoology an animal that feeds by filtering out plankton or nutrients suspended in water.

filter tip *noun* **1** a filter attached to a cigarette for removing impurities from the inhaled smoke. **2** a cigarette with this. ▶ **filter-tipped** *adjective*

filth *noun* **1** any very dirty and unpleasant substance: *stagnant pools of filth*. **2** foul or obscene language, printed material, etc. **3** corruption.

filthily *adverb* in a dirty, disgusting, or obscene manner.

filthiness *noun* the condition or quality of being dirty, disgusting, or obscene: *the filthiness of her hands*.

filthy • *adjective* (**filthier**, **filthiest**) **1** extremely or disgustingly dirty. **2** obscene. • *adverb* **1** filthily: *filthy dirty*. **2** *informal* extremely: *filthy rich*.

filtrate *noun* filtered liquid.

filtration *noun* the process of filtering something.

SPELL CHECK
fin, Finn
A person from Finland is a **Finn**.

fin *noun* **1** an organ on various parts of the body of many aquatic vertebrates and some invertebrates, including fish and cetaceans, for propelling, steering, and balancing: *dorsal fin*. **2** a small projecting surface or attachment on an aircraft, rocket, or car for ensuring aerodynamic stability. **3** an underwater swimmer's flipper. **4** a fin-like projection on the keel of a boat etc., used to increase stability. **5** a fin-like projection on any device, for improving heat transfer etc.

finagle *verb* (**finagles**, **finagled**, **finagling**) *informal* act or obtain dishonestly: *mysterious financial finagling*. ▶ **finagler** *noun* [Say fuh NAY gull]

final • *adjective* **1** situated at the end, coming last. **2** conclusive, decisive, not alterable, putting an end to doubt. **3** reached as the outcome of a process: *the final costs*. • *noun* **1** (usu. in *plural*) the last or deciding heat or game in sports or in a competition. **2** the edition of a

newspaper published latest in the day. **3** (usu. in *plural*) the last examination in an academic course.

finale *noun* **1 a** the last movement of an instrumental composition. **b** a piece of music closing an act in an opera. **2** the close of a drama etc. **3** a conclusion: *a dramatic finale to the day's events*. [Say fuh NALLY]

finalist *noun* a competitor in the final of a competition etc.

finality *noun* (*plural* **finalities**) the quality of being final and impossible to change: *the finality of death* ◊ *there was a note of finality in his voice* ◊ *"No," she said with finality*.

finalize *verb* (**finalizes**, **finalized**, **finalizing**) **1** put into final form. **2** complete; bring to an end. **3** approve the final form or details of. ▶ **finalization** *noun*

finally *adverb* **1** after a long time. **2** as the last in a series of related events or objects. **3** used to introduce a final point or reason: *finally, it is common knowledge that travel broadens the horizons*. **4** in such a way as to put an end to doubt and dispute: *the matter was not finally settled until much later*.

final solution *noun* the policy under the German Nazi regime of exterminating European Jews.

finance • *noun* **1** the management of money. **2** monetary support for an enterprise. **3** (in *plural*) the money resources of a country, company, or person. • *verb* (**finances**, **financed**, **financing**) provide capital for (a person, purchase, or enterprise), esp. as a loan. [Say FIE nance or fuh NANCE]

finance company *noun* (*plural* **finance companies**) a company that provides money to consumers for purchasing goods on credit.

financial *adjective* of or pertaining to revenue or money matters.

financial institution *noun* an organization, e.g. a bank or finance company, that collects funds from individuals etc. and invests these funds or lends them to borrowers.

financially *adverb* in terms of revenue or money matters: *the company is not financially stable*.

financial year *noun* Cdn & Brit. = FISCAL YEAR.

financier *noun* a person who is concerned with or skilled in finance, esp. on a large scale. [Say fie nan SEER or fin an SEER]

financing *noun* an act, instance, or the process of obtaining or providing funds, capital, etc. for an investment, purchase, etc., esp. by borrowing: *low 2% financing on new cars*.

finback *noun* (also **finback whale**) a large baleen whale which has a prominent dorsal fin.

finch *noun* (*plural* **finches**) a small seed-eating songbird that typically has a stout bill and colourful plumage.

find • *verb* (**finds**, **found**, **finding**) **1 a** discover, obtain, or attain by or as if by search or effort. **b** become aware of. **c** gain or recover the use of: *I found my tongue*. **2 a** perceive or experience: *find no sense in it*. **b** (often in *passive*) discover to be present: *the word is not found in Shakespeare*. **c** learn or prove (a thing) to be through experience, trial, etc.: *finds it too cold*. **3** (of a jury, judge, etc.) authoritatively decide and declare (a person) to be innocent, guilty, etc., or (an issue, offence, etc.) to be that specified: *found him guilty*. **4** reach by a natural or normal process: *water finds its own level*. • *noun* **1** a discovery of treasure, minerals, etc. **2** a thing or person discovered, esp. when of value. PHRASES **find against** Law decide against (a person), judge to be guilty. **find for** Law decide in favour of (a person), judge to be innocent. **find God** experience religious conversion. **find one's feet 1** become able to walk or get the use of one's feet. **2** grow in ability or confidence, develop one's powers, acquire knowledge or capability in a new job, etc. **find it in one's heart**

prevail upon oneself, be willing: *can you find it in your heart to forgive me?* **find oneself 1** discover that one is: *found herself agreeing.* **2** discover and attain one's special place, power, or vocation. **find out 1** discover or detect (a wrongdoer etc.). **2** get information: *find out about airfares.* **3** discover: *find out where we are.* **4** discover the truth, a fact, etc. **find one's way 1** (often foll. by *to*) manage to reach a place. **2** (often foll. by *into*) be brought or get.

finder *noun* **1 a** a person who finds. **b** a device which finds something, esp. an instrument for determining or discerning something: *fish finder.* **2** the viewfinder of a camera. PHRASES **finders keepers** *informal* whoever finds a thing is entitled to keep it.

fin de siècle • *noun* the end of a century or the moods, attitudes, etc. characteristic of such a time. • *adjective* **1** characteristic of the end of the 19th century, esp. in world-weariness, decadence, or sophistication: *fin de siècle art.* **2** decadent: *there was a fin de siècle atmosphere in the club.* **3** designating or characteristic of the end of a century. [Say fan duh SYECK luh]

finding *noun* **1** (often in *plural*) a result or conclusion of an official inquiry. **2** a verdict of a court or jury.

fine¹ • *adjective* **1** of superior quality. **2** excellent, admirable, or of striking merit: *a fine painting.* **3 a** clear, pure, refined, or free from dross or impurity. **b** (of gold or silver) containing a high, usu. specified proportion of pure metal. **4 a** handsome, beautiful. **b** imposing, dignified: *a fine figure of a man.* **c** large, of a good size: *fine buildings.* **5** well, in good health or spirits: *I'm fine, thank you.* **6** (of weather, a day, etc.) free from rain or fog, esp. bright and clear with sunshine. **7 a** extremely thin or slender: *a fine thread.* **b** (of a weapon, tool, etc.) having a sharp point or edge: *a fine blade.* **c** in small particles. **d** worked in thin, delicate thread. **e** (esp. of print) small. **f** (of a pen) having a narrow point or tip. **8** (of speech, writing, etc.) elegant, ornate, or affected. **9 a** capable of delicate perception or discrimination: *a fine eye for detail.* **b** subtle or perceptible only with difficulty: *a fine distinction.* **10 a** delicately beautiful or exquisitely fashioned: *fine crystal.* **b** (of feelings) refined. **11** *ironic* difficult, inopportune, etc.: *another fine mess.* • *adverb informal* very well: *suits me fine.* PHRASES **cut** (or **run**) **it fine** allow very little margin of time, room for error, etc. **fine and dandy** *informal* **1** great, first-rate. **2** (of a person) very well. **not to put too fine a point on it** to speak bluntly.

fine² • *noun* a sum of money exacted as a penalty for an offence. • *verb* (**fines, fined, fining**) impose a fine upon or punish (a person) by a fine: *fined him $50.*

fine art *noun* **1** (in *plural*) those arts appealing to the intellect or the sense of beauty, as literature, music, and esp. painting, sculpture, and architecture. **2** a high accomplishment or a thing requiring a high degree of skill: *the fine art of collecting ◊ the fine art of enjoying life ◊ has getting out of work down to a fine art.*

fine-grained *adjective* **1** having a fine grain. **2** consisting of very small particles.

finely *adverb* **1** into very small grains or pieces: *finely chopped herbs.* **2** in a beautiful or impressive way: *a finely furnished room ◊ finely dressed dancers.* **3** in a very delicate or exact way: *a finely tuned engine.*

fineness *noun* **1** the quality of being made of thin threads or lines close together: *fineness of detail.* **2** the quality of something: *the fineness of the gold.*

fine print *noun* the information in legal documents etc. which is often printed in small type and contains important details that are easy to overlook.

finer points *plural noun* details or aspects recognized

and appreciated only by those who are very familiar with a thing, field, etc.: *by this time the four of us had figured out the game's finer points.*

finery *noun* showy or elegant dress or decoration.

finesse • *noun* **1** skill in dealing with people or situations cleverly or tactfully. **2** delicacy, refinement, or discrimination. **3** subtle or delicate manipulation: *a certain amount of finesse is required to fine-tune the heat output.* • *verb* (**finesses, finessed, finessing**) **1** do (something) in a subtle and delicate manner: *his third shot, which he attempted to finesse, missed by a fraction.* **2** evade or trick by finesse.

finest • *adjective* superlative of FINE¹ *adjective.* • *noun* the police of a specified city: *Ottawa's finest.*

fine-tooth comb *noun* (also **fine-toothed comb**) a comb with narrow, close-set teeth, e.g. one used to comb lice or fleas out of hair, fur, etc. PHRASES **go over with a fine-tooth comb** check or search thoroughly.

fine-tune *verb* (**fine-tunes, fine-tuned, fine-tuning**) make small adjustments to (a mechanism etc.) in order to obtain the best possible results. ▸ **fine tuning** *noun*

finger • *noun* **1** any of the terminal members of the hand, including or excluding the thumb. **2** the part of a glove etc. intended to cover a finger. **3** an object, structure, item of food, etc. shaped like a finger. **4** the breadth or length of a finger as a rough unit of measurement. • *verb* **1** touch, feel, or turn about with the fingers. **2** *Music* play with the fingers. **3** *informal* indicate (a person or thing) for a specific purpose etc. **4** *slang* **a** inform on or identify (a criminal) to the police. **b** indicate (a victim) to criminals. PHRASES **give (a person) the finger** *slang* make an obscene gesture with the middle finger raised as a sign of contempt. **have a finger in the pie** be concerned, esp. officiously, in a matter. **lay a finger on** touch however slightly. **point a** (or **the**) **finger at (someone)** accuse or identify as responsible. **put one's finger on** point to or identify with precision (a cause of trouble etc.). **put the finger on** *slang* inform against (a person), identify (an intended victim), etc. **twist** (or **wrap**) **around one's finger** (or **little finger**) **1** persuade (a person) without difficulty. **2** dominate (a person) completely.

fingerboard *noun* a piece of wood on a guitar, violin, etc. where the strings are pressed against the neck of the instrument with the fingers to vary the tone.

fingered *adjective* (usu. in *combination*) having fingers of a specified kind or number.

finger food *noun* food so served that it can be eaten conveniently without cutlery.

fingering *noun* a manner or technique of using the fingers in playing a musical instrument etc.

fingerling *noun* a parr or any very young fish.

fingernail *noun* the nail at the tip of each finger.

fingerpaint • *noun* a thick, jellylike paint that can be applied with the fingers, esp. for use by children. • *verb* apply such paint. ▸ **fingerpainting** *noun*

finger pointing *noun* an act of accusing or blaming.

fingerprint • *noun* **1** an impression made on a surface by the fingertips, esp. as used for identifying individuals. **2** any distinctive characteristic, sign, pattern etc. definitively identifying a particular person, substance, action, etc.: *the faint chemical fingerprint of plastic explosives.* • *verb* record the fingerprints, DNA pattern, etc. of (a person).

fingertip • *noun* the tip of a finger. • *adjective* (of controls etc.) that can be controlled by a light movement of the fingers. PHRASES **at one's fingertips** readily accessible. **by one's fingertips** barely: *the premier clung on to power by his fingertips.*

F

finial *noun* **1** an ornament finishing off the highest point of a roof etc. **2** an ornamental knob on the top of a piece of furniture, stairpost, etc. [Say FINNY ul]

finicky *adjective* **1** fussy. **2** needing much attention to detail.

SPELL CHECK
finish, Finnish ABC ✓

Someone from Finland is **Finnish**.

---

finish • *verb* (**finishes, finished, finishing**) **1** (often foll. by *off*) complete, come or bring to an end. **2 a** (usu. foll. by *off*) *informal* kill, destroy, or reduce to utter exhaustion or helplessness. **b** (often foll. by *off, up*) consume or go through the whole or the remainder of (food, drink, paint, etc.). **3 a** complete the manufacture of (cloth, woodwork, etc.) by surface treatment. **b** apply varnish, paint, etc. to (wood). **c** put the final touches to. **4** complete the fattening of (cattle etc.) for sale or slaughter. **5** (foll. by *with*) have no more to do with. • *noun* **1 a** the end, last part, or last stage of a thing. **b** the point at which a race, hunt, or other contest or event ends. **c** a conclusive defeat of one person or party by another: *fight to the finish.* **2 a** method, material, or texture used for surface treatment of wood, cloth, etc. **3** a thing which finishes or gives completeness or perfection to something.

finished *adjective* **1 a** ended, completed, or brought to a conclusion. **b** having passed through the final stage of manufacture or elaboration: *the finished product.* **2** ruined, doomed, or no longer effective: *finished as a politician.* **3** accomplished or highly proficient. **4** (of cattle) appropriately fattened for market or slaughter. **5** (of part of a building, esp. a basement) having the walls and ceiling covered with drywall, panelling, etc.

finisher *noun* **1** a person who finishes something, esp. a race, contest, or similar event. **2** a worker or machine performing the final operation in a process.

finishing touch *noun* (*plural* **finishing touches**) a last action, added effect, or final detail completing and enhancing a piece of work, production, etc.

finish line *noun* a line which indicates the end of a race.

finite *adjective* **1** having limits or bounds: *every computer has a finite amount of memory.* **2** not infinitely small: *one's chance of winning may be small but it is finite.* **3** *Grammar* (of a verb form) having a specific tense, number, and person. ▶ **finitely** *adverb* [Say FIE nite]

fink *slang* • *noun* **1** an unpleasant person. **2** an informer. • *verb* **1** (foll. by *on*) inform on. **2** back out of something or let a person down: *the administration finked out and did not follow through.*

Finn *noun* **1** a native or national of Finland, a country on the Baltic Sea. **2** a person of Finnish descent.

finned *adjective* (also in *combination*) having a fin or fins (of a specified kind): *a long-finned pilot whale.*

Finnic *adjective* of or pertaining to the Finns, or the group of people ethnically allied to the Finns.

SPELL CHECK
Finnish, finish ABC ✓

To complete something is to **finish** it.

Finnish • *adjective* of, pertaining to, or characteristic of Finland, the Finns, or their language. • *noun* the language of the Finns.

fiord *noun* = FJORD. [Say FYORD or FEE ord]

fir *noun* **1** (also **fir tree**) an evergreen coniferous tree with needles borne singly on the stems. **2** its wood.

fire • *noun* **1 a** the state of process of combustion, in which substances combine chemically with oxygen, manifested as a hot, bright, shifting body of gas or as incandescence. **b** the flame or incandescence so produced. **2** a conflagration or destructive burning, esp. of a large area or mass: *forest fire.* **3** fuel in a state of combustion or a mass of burning material in a grate, furnace, etc. **4** the action of firing guns etc. **5 a** zeal, fervour, enthusiasm. **b** liveliness of imagination or poetic inspiration. **c** a vehement or burning passion or emotion. **6** burning heat, fever. **7** luminosity or a glowing or flashing appearance resembling that of fire. • *verb* (**fires, fired, firing**) **1** discharge a gun etc. **2** light (gunpowder), let off (a firework), or explode (a mine). **3** (often foll. by *off*) deliver or utter (a speech, questions, etc.) in rapid succession or in a sharp, explosive manner: *fired insults at us.* **4** dismiss (an employee) from a job. **5** set fire to with the intention of damaging or destroying. **6** (of an explosive etc.) catch fire or be ignited. **7** (of an internal combustion engine, or a cylinder in one) undergo ignition of its fuel. **8** supply (a furnace, engine, boiler, or power station) with fuel. **9 a** inspire, inflame, or stimulate (the imagination). **b** fill (a person) with enthusiasm. **10 a** subject to the action or effect of fire. **b** bake or dry (pottery, bricks, etc.). ▸ PHRASES **catch fire 1** begin to burn. **2 a** (of an idea, trend, etc.) become popular. **b** (of an individual) become motivated, enthusiastic. **fight fire with fire** use similar strategies, methods, etc. as one's opponent does. **fire and brimstone 1** the torments of hell. **2** preaching etc. emphasizing eternal damnation. **fire away** *informal* begin or go ahead. **fire up 1** *informal* **a** stimulate, fill with enthusiasm, or excite. **b** start up (an engine etc.). **2** show sudden anger. **fired-up 1** (of an engine etc.) started. **2** (of a person) highly motivated or enthused. **light a fire under** cause to work faster, decide rapidly, etc. **on fire 1** burning. **2** excited. **set fire to** (or **set on fire**) ignite, kindle, cause to burn. **set the world on fire** do something remarkable or sensational. **take fire 1** catch fire. **2** become enthused, dynamic, energetic, etc. **under fire 1** being shot at. **2** being rigorously criticized or questioned.

firearm *noun* (usu. in *plural*) a portable gun of any sort, e.g. a pistol, rifle, etc.

fireball *noun* **1** a large, bright meteor. **2 a** a ball of flame or fire. **b** a ball of flame resulting from a nuclear explosion. **3 a** a very energetic person. **b** a person with a fiery temper. **4** lightning appearing as a glowing ball.

firebomb • *noun* a bomb that makes a fire start burning after it explodes, esp. a Molotov cocktail. • *verb* attack or destroy with a firebomb.

firebox *noun* (*plural* **fireboxes**) **1** an enclosed space in which a fire is made in a fireplace, stove, etc. **2** the fuel chamber of a steam engine or boiler.

firebrand *noun* **1** a person who or a thing which creates strife, inflames passion, causes trouble, etc.: *Claudia was a firebrand, speaking, organizing, teaching, and taking part in everything.* **2** a piece of burning wood: *firebrands were being thrown from the castle walls.*

firebreak *noun* an obstacle, usu. a strip of land cleared or plowed, designed to stop fire from spreading in a forest, on grasslands, etc.

fire-breathing *adjective* **1** (of a person) having an aggressive manner. **2** (of a dragon etc.) capable of breathing fire.

fire brigade *noun* esp. *Brit.* an organized body of firefighters.

firecracker *noun* a small firework that explodes with a cracking noise.

fire drill *noun* a rehearsal of the procedures to be used in case of fire.

fire engine noun a heavy vehicle carrying equipment for fighting fires.

fire-engine red • adjective of a deep vibrant red. • noun this colour.

fire escape noun an emergency staircase etc., esp. on the outside of a building, for use during a fire.

fire extinguisher noun a portable apparatus for discharging chemicals, water, etc. to put out a fire.

firefight noun a skirmish or battle involving the exchange of gunfire.

firefighter noun a person whose job is to extinguish fires, esp. a member of a fire department. ▶ **firefighting** noun & adjective

firefly noun (plural **fireflies**) a soft-bodied beetle related to the glow-worm, the winged male and flightless female of which both have organs that are capable of producing light.

fire hall noun Cdn a fire station; a building where fire trucks and firefighters are housed.

fire hydrant noun a pipe, usu. on the side of the street, with a valve for drawing water from a main to which a hose can be attached for extinguishing fires.

firelight noun light from a fire or fires.

fireman noun (plural **firemen**) **1** a firefighter. **2** a stoker or person who tends a furnace or the fire of a steam engine, steamship, etc.

firepit noun a pit dug into the ground or made from stones etc. in which a fire is made and maintained.

fireplace noun **1** a place for a domestic fire, esp. a partially enclosed place at the base of a chimney. **2** a structure surrounding this or the area in front of it.

firepower noun **1** the destructive capacity of guns, missiles, a military force, etc.: the new tanks were superior in design and firepower. **2** financial, intellectual, physical, or emotional strength: with a $4.5 billion company behind him, he has the firepower he needs to succeed.

fireproof • adjective able to resist fire or great heat. • verb make fireproof. ▶ **fireproofing** noun

fire-resistance noun the state or quality of being fire-resistant.

fire-resistant adjective **1** almost completely non-flammable. **2** = FIRE-RETARDANT.

fire-retardant adjective capable of slowing or stopping the spread of fire.

fire sale noun **1** a sale, usu. at low prices, of goods remaining after a fire. **2** a sale of anything at a remarkably low price.

fireside • noun the area around a fireplace (used esp. with reference to a person's home or family life). • adjective **1** situated beside or pertaining to a domestic fire or fireplace. **2** intimate or relaxed, esp. designating an informal political talk broadcast to the nation: fireside chat.

firestorm noun **1** a very intense and destructive fire (typically one caused by bombing) in which strong currents of air are drawn into the blaze from the surrounding area making it burn more fiercely: firestorms after a nuclear exchange. **2** an intense and forceful response: the changes to the Education Act set off a political firestorm.

fire-wagon adjective slang (in hockey) designating a dramatic manner of play which emphasizes offensive teamwork, heavy checking, hard passing, and speed.

firewall noun **1** a fireproof wall to prevent the spread of fire. **2** Computing a system designed to control the passage of information between networks.

firewater noun informal strong alcoholic liquor.

fireweed noun any of several plants that spring up on burnt land, esp. the willow herb, a plant with narrow leaves and pink or purple flowers.

firewood noun wood used or to be used as fuel.

firework noun **1** a device containing chemicals that burn or explode spectacularly. **2** (in plural) **a** an outburst of passion, esp. anger: there were fireworks at the meeting as the directors were questioned by disgruntled shareholders. **b** an impressive display of wit, brilliance, or skill.

SPELL CHECK $\boxed{\text{ABC} \checkmark}$
fiery

Warning: **fiery** is spelled with the e before the r.

---

firing noun **1** the discharge of guns etc. **2** the action of subjecting something to heat or fire, esp. the process which hardens clay into pottery etc. **3** the action of being discharged from one's employment: there have been a lot of firings here at the office lately!

firing line noun **1** the front line in a battle, nearest the enemy. **2** the forefront of or leading part in an activity, controversy, etc. PHRASES **on the firing line** subject to challenge, criticism, blame, etc. because of one's responsibilities or position.

firing range noun = RANGE noun 8.

firing squad noun a group of soldiers detailed to shoot a condemned person.

firm¹ • adjective **1 a** hard, resistant to pressure or impact, or of solid or compact structure. **b** securely fixed, stable; not easily moved. **c** steady or controlled, not shaking or wavering: a firm voice. **2** (of a person, opinion, etc.) resolute, determined, not easily swayed or shaken: firm belief. **3** (of an offer etc.) not liable to cancellation after acceptance. • adverb firmly: stand firm. • verb make or become firm, secure, compact, or solid. PHRASES **a firm hand** strong discipline or control. **firm up 1** work to tone and improve the condition of the muscles, voice, etc. **2** put (a thing) in final, fixed form, tidying up details etc. **3** strengthen, reinforce (standing, credibility, etc.). **4** become firm.

firm² noun a partnership or company for carrying on a business.

firmament noun literary the arch or vault of the skies.

firmly adverb in a strong or definite way.

firmness noun the quality or condition of being strong, hard, or definite: firmness of purpose.

firmware noun a permanent kind of software programmed into the read-only memory in certain types of computers.

firn noun crystalline or granular snow, esp. on the upper part of a glacier, where it has not yet been compressed into ice.

first • adjective **1 a** earliest or preceding all others in time, order, or experience. **b** coming next after a specified or implied time: shall take the first bus. **2** foremost in position, rank, or importance: first mate. **3** Music denoting one of two or more parts for the same instrument or voice, often the highest or more prominent of the two. **4** most willing or likely: should be the first to admit it. **5** basic or evident: first principles. • noun **1** the first part, the beginning, or the person or thing first mentioned or occurring. **2** the first occurrence of something notable. **3** the first day of a month. **4** first gear. **5 a** first place in a race. **b** the winner of this. **c** Football = FIRST DOWN. **d** Baseball the first inning. **e** Baseball = FIRST BASE. • adverb **1** before any other person or thing in time, rank, serial order, etc.: first of all. **2** before another specified or implied thing, time, event, etc.: do this first. **3** for the first time. **4** rather or in preference to something else: I'd die first. PHRASES **at first** at the beginning. **at first hand** gained or coming directly from the original source. **first off** informal at first, first of all. **first things first**

the most important things before any others. **from the first** from the beginning. **from first to last** throughout. **in the first place** as the first consideration.

first aid noun help given to a sick or injured person until proper medical treatment is available.

first base noun Baseball **1** the first of the bases that must be touched to score a run. **2** the position of the player covering this base and the area of the infield surrounding it. PHRASES **get to first base** informal make a successful start; achieve the first step of an undertaking. ▶ **first baseman** noun

first-born • adjective eldest. • noun the eldest child of a person.

first class • noun **1** a set of persons grouped together as the best. **2** the most comfortable and costly seating in an airplane, train, etc. **3** the class of mail given priority in handling. • adjective **1** belonging to, achieving, or travelling by, etc. the first class. **2** very good; of the best quality. • adverb by the best or quickest form of transport or mail: send it first class.

first-come, first-served noun a system of providing service to people strictly in the order in which they arrive, apply, etc.

first contact noun the first interaction between colonizers and an Aboriginal people.

first cousin noun the child of one's uncle or aunt.

first-degree adjective **1 a** designating the most serious category of crime. **b** (of murder) premeditated and without circumstances that would justify a lesser charge or sentence. **2** denoting the least serious category of burn, those that affect only the surface of the skin, causing reddening.

first down noun Football **1** the first of three attempts (four attempts in American football) to advance the ball ten yards. **2** the achievement of an advance of ten or more yards, by which the offensive team is entitled to a new series of downs.

first gear noun the lowest gear on a car, bicycle, etc.

first generation adjective **1 a** designating the offspring born to immigrants once they have settled in their adopted country: my mother's parents were both born in Scotland — she's a first generation Canadian. **b** designating the immigrants themselves: a first generation Canadian, she arrived from Vietnam in 1982. **2** of or belonging to an initial model, program, period, etc.: the first generation computers had little processing power.

first-hand adjective & adverb direct, from the original source or personal experience: first-hand accounts of activities behind enemy lines ◊ data which is obtained first-hand from customers.

first lady noun **1** (plural **first ladies**) the leading woman in some specified activity or profession: the first lady of Canadian theatre. **2** (**First Lady** (plural **First Ladies**)) (in the US) the wife of the President.

first line noun **1** the preliminary effort, resources, etc. ready for immediate use or action: first line of defence. **2** (often as an adjective) the thing, treatment, group of people, etc., which is most advanced or of the highest quality: a first line National Hockey League rookie.

firstly adverb (in enumerating topics, arguments, etc.) in the first place, first (compare FIRST adverb).

first mate noun (on a merchant ship) the officer second-in-command to the master.

First Meridian noun Cdn the north-south line, 97 degrees 27 minutes west, from which land in the prairies is surveyed.

First Minister noun Cdn **1** the prime minister of Canada. **2** the premier of a province.

First Nation noun Cdn an Indian band, or an Indian

community functioning as a band but not having official band status.

first officer noun **1** the mate on a merchant ship. **2** the second-in-command to the captain on an aircraft.

first past the post adjective Cdn & Brit. **1** winning a race etc. by being the first to reach the finish line. **2** (of an electoral system) in which only the person or party who gets the most votes is elected.

WRITING TIP
First Peoples, First Nations

In Canada, the term **First Peoples** includes Indians, Inuit, and Metis. The term **First Nations** refers only to Indian bands and does not include the Inuit or Metis.

First Peoples plural noun the Aboriginal peoples of a particular country or region etc.

first person noun Grammar **1** a set of pronouns and verb forms used by a speaker to refer to himself or herself, or to a group including himself or herself: "I am" is the first person singular of the present tense of the verb "to be" ◊ "I", "me", "we" and "us" are first person pronouns. **2** a way of writing a novel, etc. as if one of the characters is telling the story using the word "I": a novel written in the first person.

first principles plural noun the fundamental concepts or assumptions on which a theory, system, or method is based: we must start again and go right back to first principles.

first-rate adjective **1** of the highest class, excellent. **2** informal very well: feeling first-rate.

first reading noun the first of three successive occasions on which a bill must have been presented to a legislature before it becomes law.

first refusal noun the right or privilege of deciding to take or leave a thing before it is offered to others: should tenants have first refusal if the landlord decides to sell?

first-run adjective designating the initial period in which a film, movie, etc. is first shown publicly.

first-string • noun the primary and usu. starting line of a team, with the best players. • adjective of or like the best of a series, team, etc. ▶ **first-stringer** noun

first team noun a lineup of first-string players.

first thing informal • noun (usu. as **the first thing**) the most elementary thing, aspect, etc. of something: doesn't know the first thing about it. • adverb **1** before anything else: we must establish a budget first thing. **2** very early in the morning: first thing tomorrow.

first-timer noun a person who does or is something for the first time.

First World noun the industrialized capitalist countries of western Europe, North America, Japan, Australia, and New Zealand.

firth noun an estuary or narrow inlet of the sea.

SPELL CHECK
fiery ABC

Warning: **fiery** is spelled with an e before the r.

---

fiscal adjective **1** of or related to public revenue, usu. taxes: Liberal monetary and fiscal policy. **2** pertaining to financial matters: the domestic fiscal crisis. **3** designating a fiscal year: the budget for fiscal 2002. ▶ **fiscally** adverb

fiscal year noun a period of twelve months over which annual accounts and taxes are calculated.

fish • noun (plural **fish** or **fishes**) **1** a vertebrate cold-blooded animal with gills and fins living wholly in water. **2** any animal living wholly in water, e.g. cuttlefish, shellfish, jellyfish. **3** the flesh of fish as food. **4** Cdn (Nfld) cod. • verb (**fishes**, **fished**, **fishing**)

1 a try to catch fish, esp. with a line or net. **b** *Cdn* (*Nfld*) engage in sea fishery, esp. for cod, as opposed to freshwater angling. **2** fish for (a certain kind of fish) or in (a certain stretch of water). **3** (foll. by *for*) **a** search, grope, or feel for in water or a concealed place. **b** try to obtain or elicit by indirect means or artifice: *fishing for compliments*. **4** retrieve with careful or awkward searching: *fished some gum out of her purse*. PHRASES **a big fish in a small** (or **little**) **pond** a comparatively significant figure in a small group, community, etc. **drink like a fish** drink excessively. **fish or cut bait** act on or disengage from a matter, an issue, etc. **fish out** depopulate (a lake, area of ocean, etc.) through excessive fishing. **fish out of water** a person in an unfamiliar, unsuitable, or unwelcome environment or situation. **other** (or **plenty more** etc.) **fish in the sea** other people or things as good as the one that has failed or been lost. **other fish to fry** other matters to attend to.

fishable *adjective* **1** (of water) able to be fished in; suitable for fishing in: *twenty fishable kilometres of open river*. **2** (of fish) able to be caught: *Canada's fishable stock of haddock*.

fish and brewis *noun Cdn* (*Nfld*) a dish of salt cod and hardtack soaked in water and then fried and garnished with fried salt pork.

fishboat *noun Cdn* (esp. *BC*) a fishing boat.

fishbowl *noun* **1** a usu. round glass bowl for keeping pet fish in. **2** a place, situation, etc. in which one's life and activities are carefully and usu. publicly observed, commented upon, etc.: *I work in a fishbowl — there is no privacy in this office at all!* ◊ *a huge fishbowl studio*.

fish cake *noun* a small patty of flaked or minced fish and mashed potato, usu. coated in batter or bread crumbs and fried.

fish camp *noun* (esp. *North*) a camp used as a base by a group engaged in fishing, sometimes run as a business with rudimentary lodging, supplies, etc.

fisher *noun* **1 a** a large North American forest-dwelling weasel, valued for its fur. **b** its pelt. **2** a fisherman, either professional or recreational.

fisherman *noun* (*plural* **fishermen**) a person who catches fish as a livelihood or for sport.

fishery *noun* (*plural* **fisheries**) **1 a** a fish hatchery or place where fish are reared. **b** a fishing ground or area where fish are caught. **2** the occupation or industry of catching or rearing fish.

fish eye *noun* **1** (also **fish-eye lens**) a very wide-angle lens with a field of vision covering up to 180°, the scale being reduced towards the edges. **2** an eye of or like that of a fish.

fish farm *noun* a place where fish are bred for food. ▶ **fish farmer** *noun* **fish farming** *noun*

fish finder *noun* a device equipped with sonar to locate schools of fish in a body of water.

fish flake *noun Cdn* (*Nfld*) a rack on which to dry fish, usu. consisting of a framework of poles covered with spruce boughs to allow free air circulation.

fish fry *noun* (*plural* **fish fries**) a usu. outdoor social gathering at which fish are cooked and eaten.

fish hook *noun* a barbed hook for catching fish.

fish hut *noun Cdn* a small, portable shack placed over a hole in the ice of a lake to protect a person ice fishing.

fishing *noun* the catching of fish as food or as a job, sport, or hobby.

fishing boat *noun* any watercraft used for fishing.

fishing camp *noun* **1** an establishment, usu. by a lake, providing accommodation, equipment, etc. for sport fishermen. **2** = FISH CAMP.

fishing derby *noun* (*plural* **fishing derbies**) a fishing

competition in which participants try for the largest catch in a variety of fish categories.

fishing hole *noun* **1** a favoured spot in a lake, on a river, etc. for catching fish. **2** an opening cut in lake or river ice for ice fishing.

fishing line *noun* a long thread of nylon etc. to which a baited hook, sinker, float, etc., are attached, used with a fishing rod for catching fish.

fishing rod *noun* (also **fishing pole**) a long, tapering, usu. jointed rod to which a fishing line and usu. a reel are attached.

fishing stage *noun Cdn* (esp. *Nfld*) a shed near the shoreline for gutting, heading, salting, etc. fish before they are dried on flakes.

fishing station *noun Cdn* a small sheltered cove from which fishing is undertaken on a seasonal basis, esp. in Newfoundland.

fish ladder *noun* a series of pools built like steps to enable fish to ascend a fall or dam to reach their spawning grounds.

fishlike *adjective* resembling or like a fish.

fishmonger *noun* a person who sells fish. [Say FISH mong gur or FISH mung gur]

fishnet *noun* **1** (often as an *adjective*) an open, meshed fabric or a garment made of it: *fishnet stockings*. **2** a net for catching fish.

fish pond *noun* **1** a pond or pool in which fish are kept. **2** an attraction at a fair etc. where contestants use a rod and line to attempt to extract a prize etc. from a pool, enclosure, etc.

fish sauce *noun* a spicy condiment made from fermented anchovies, used in oriental cuisine.

fish stick *noun* a small, oblong piece of flaked or minced fish coated in batter etc. and fried.

fish store *noun* **1** a store selling fish. **2** *Cdn* (*Nfld & Maritimes*) a building where offshore fisherman store dried cod ready for collection or export.

fishtail • *verb* move the rear of a vehicle from side to side, or (of the rear of a vehicle) move from side to side. • *noun* something shaped like a fish's tail: *a sequined fishtail dress*.

fishway *noun Cdn* a lock built to aid fish in passing a waterfall etc. on their way upstream to spawn.

fishy *adjective* (**fishier**, **fishiest**) **1 a** of or like fish, esp. in smell or taste. **b** (of an eye) dull, vacant looking: *she had great, round, fishy eyes*. **c** consisting of fish: *a fishy meal*. **2** *slang* of dubious character, suspect.

fissile *adjective* **1** capable of undergoing nuclear fission. **2** (esp. of rock) easily split. [Say FISS ile or FISSLE]

fission *noun* **1** *Physics* the spontaneous or impact-induced splitting of a heavy atomic nucleus, accompanied by a release of energy. **2** the division of a cell or organism into new cells or organisms as a mode of reproduction. **3** the action of splitting or dividing into pieces: *every part of the former Yugoslavia is far worse off now than when the fission began*. ▶ **fissionable** *adjective* [Rhymes either with MISSION or with VISION]

fission bomb *noun* an atomic bomb.

fissure • *noun* **1** an opening, usu. long and narrow, made by cracking, splitting, or separation of esp. rock or ice: *the Great Rift Valley is a fissure in the earth's crust so large that it can be seen from space*. **2** a division or split: *the referendum may deepen the fissures in Quebec society*. • *verb* (**fissures**, **fissured**, **fissuring**) split or crack. [Say FISHER or FIZHER]

fist *noun* a tightly closed hand. ▶ **fisted** *adjective*

fist fight *noun* a fight with bare fists. ▶ **fist fighting** *noun*

fistful *noun* (*plural* **fistfuls**) **1** a quantity held in a fist. **2** a large quantity.

F

fistula *noun* (*plural* **fistulas** or **fistulae**) an abnormal or surgically made passage between a hollow organ and the body surface or between two hollow organs. [Say FIST you luh for the singular; for *FISTULAE* say FIST you lee]

fit[1] • *adjective* (**fitter, fittest**) **1** suitable: *my car is not fit to be driven on such rough roads* ◊ *you are not fit to be my assistant* ◊ *is fit for use* ◊ *this food is not fit for human consumption.* **2** in good health or athletic condition, esp. having excellent cardiovascular function. **3** proper, becoming, right: *it is fit that.* • *verb* (**fits, fitted** or (esp. in senses 1, 4, 6, and 7) **fit, fitting**) **1 a** be of the right shape and size for: *my shoes don't fit.* **b** adjust (an object) to the contours of its receptacle or counterpart: *fitted shelves into the alcove.* **c** (often foll. by *in, into*) (of a component) be correctly positioned: *that piece fits here.* **d** find room for: *can't fit another person.* **2 a** make suitable; adapt. **b** make ready or competent: *her education fitted her for the diplomatic service.* **3** (usu. foll. by *with*) supply, furnish: *fitted the boat with a new rudder.* **4** fix in place: *fit a lock on the door.* **5** try clothing on (a person) in order to adjust it to the right size and shape: *fitted me for a new suit.* **6** be in harmony with, befit, become: *the punishment fits the crime.* **7** be suitable for: *this fits our needs.* • *noun* **1** the way in which a garment, component, etc., fits: *a tight fit.* **2** suitability, compatibility: *a perfect fit between the employee and the job.* • *adverb informal* in a suitable manner, appropriately: *was laughing fit to bust.* PHRASES **fit the bill** be suitable or adequate. **fit in 1** be (esp. socially) compatible or accommodating: *doesn't fit in with the group.* **2** find space or time for (an object, engagement, etc.): *fitted me in at the last minute.* **fit out** (or **up**) (often foll. by *with*) equip. **see** (or **think**) **fit** decide or choose (a specified course of action): *she saw fit to go to the party with him.*

fit[2] *noun* **1** a sudden seizure of epilepsy, hysteria, apoplexy, fainting, or paralysis. **2** a sudden brief attack of an illness or of symptoms: *fit of coughing.* **3** a sudden short bout or burst: *fit of giggles.* **4** an attack of strong feeling: *fit of rage.* **5** a capricious impulse: *a fit of generosity.* PHRASES **by** (or **in**) **fits and starts** spasmodically. **give a person a fit** *informal* surprise or outrage him or her. **have** (or **throw**) **a fit** *informal* be greatly surprised or outraged.

fitful *adjective* active or occurring irregularly or intermittently: *a fitful night's sleep.* ▶ **fitfully** *adverb*

fitness *noun* **1** the quality or state of being physically fit (also as an *adjective*: *fitness program*). **2** the quality of being suitable, qualified, or morally fit for something.

fitted *adjective* made or shaped to fill a space or cover something closely or exactly: *fitted sheet.*

fitter *noun* **1** a person who supervises the cutting, fitting, altering, etc. of garments or shoes. **2** a person who fits together and adjusts machine etc. parts.

fitting • *noun* **1** the process or an act of having a garment etc. fitted: *she's coming tomorrow for a fitting.* **2** (usu. in *plural*) decorative metal handles, corners, etc., on furniture, bathtubs, etc. **3** a small standard part or component. • *adjective* suitable or appropriate: *the award was a fitting tribute to her years of devoted work* ◊ *it is fitting that the new centre for European studies should be in a university that teaches every European language.* ▶ **fittingly** *adverb*

fitting room *noun* a room in a store or in a dressmaker's premises etc. where garments are tried on.

five *cardinal number* one more than four.

five-and-a-half *noun* (*plural* **five-and-a-halfs**) *Cdn* (*Que.*) an apartment having three bedrooms, a kitchen, a living room, and a bath.

five-and-dime store *noun* (also **five-and-dime, five-and-ten**) **1** *hist.* a store where all the articles were

originally priced at five or ten cents. **2** a store selling a wide variety of cheap household and personal goods.

five-a-side • *adverb Hockey* with each team playing at full strength, i.e. with five skaters and a goalie. • *adjective* designating soccer played with five players on each team. • *noun* a game of five-a-side soccer.

fivefold *adjective & adverb* **1** five times as much or as many: *a fivefold increase in funding* ◊ *the subscription rate rose fivefold.* **2** consisting of five parts.

Five Nations *plural noun hist.* the Seneca, Cayuga, Onondaga, Oneida, and Mohawk, who formed the League of the Iroquois in the 16th century.

five-pin bowling *noun Cdn* a variety of bowling in which players have three chances to knock down five pins, each of different scoring value, using a smaller ball than in 10-pin bowling.

fiver *noun informal* a five-dollar bill.

five senses *plural noun* (**the five senses**) sight, hearing, smell, taste, and touch.

five-star *adjective* (of a hotel, restaurant, etc.) given five stars in a grading, esp. where this indicates the highest quality.

fix • *verb* (**fixes, fixed, fixing**) **1** repair. **2** put in order, adjust: *fix your tie.* **3** make firm or stable; fasten, secure. **4** decide, settle, specify (a price, date, etc.). **5** implant (an idea or memory) in the mind. **6 a** (foll. by *on, upon*) direct steadily, set (one's eyes, gaze, attention, or affection). **b** attract and hold (a person's attention, eyes, etc.). **c** (foll. by *with*) single out with one's eyes etc. **7** place definitely or permanently; establish. **8** determine the exact nature, position, etc., of; refer (a thing or person) to a definite place or time. **9 a** make (eyes, features, etc.) rigid. **b** (of eyes, features, etc.) become rigid. **10** *informal* prepare (food or drink). **11 a** deprive of fluidity or volatility. **b** lose fluidity or volatility. **12** *informal* punish or deal with (a person). **13** *informal* arrange the result of (a race, match, etc.) fraudulently: *the competition was fixed.* **14** make (a pigment, photographic image, etc.) fast or permanent. **15** (of a plant or micro-organism) assimilate (nitrogen or carbon dioxide) by forming a non-gaseous compound. **16** castrate or spay (an animal). **17** allocate or determine the incidence of (a responsibility, liability etc.). **18** prepare; plan: *we're fixing to leave at 10:00.* • *noun* (*plural* **fixes**) **1** *informal* a position hard to escape from; a dilemma or predicament. **2** *informal* a repair, esp. to a computer program. **3 a** the act of finding one's position by bearings or astronomical observations. **b** a position found in this way. **4** *slang* **a** a dose of a narcotic drug to which one is addicted. **b** a dose of or indulgence in anything which one craves and enjoys immensely: *sugar fix* ◊ *needs a ballet fix at least once a month.* **5** *informal* a clear understanding: *get a fix on her mood.* PHRASES **be fixed** (usu. foll. by *for*) be disposed or affected (regarding): *how is he fixed for money?* **fix up 1** arrange, organize, prepare. **2** upgrade, improve. **3** (often foll. by *with*) provide (a person): *fixed me up with a job.* ▶ **fixable** *adjective*

fixate *verb* (**fixates, fixated, fixating**) be or become obsessed with: *Canadian economists fixated on free trade.*

fixation *noun* **1** an obsessive interest in or feeling about someone or something: *our fixation with diet and fitness* ◊ *a fixation on the past.* **2** the action of making something firm or stable: *sand dune fixation.* **3** the process by which some plants and micro-organisms combine chemically with gaseous nitrogen or carbon dioxide to form non-gaseous compounds.

fixative *noun* a substance used to set or fix colours, hair, specimens, etc. [Say FIXA tiv]

fixed-do *adjective* applied to a system of reading music in which C is called "do", D is called "re", etc.,

irrespective of the key in which they occur. [DO sounds like *DOE*]

fixed income *noun* income from a pension, investment, etc. that is set at a particular figure and does not rise with the rate of inflation.

fixed link *noun* *Cdn & Brit.* a permanent means of transit (e.g. a bridge or tunnel) between two geographical areas separated by water.

fixedly *adverb* continually, without looking away, but often with no real interest: *he stared fixedly at the letter.* [Say FIX id lee]

fixed-wing *adjective* designating aircraft of the conventional type, as opposed to helicopters etc.

fixer *noun* **1** a person or thing that fixes. **2** a substance used for fixing a photographic image etc. **3** *informal* a person who makes arrangements, esp. of an illicit kind: *a renegade establishment of developers, bankers, and political fixers.*

fixings *plural noun* **1** the necessary ingredients for a dish, meal, etc.: *have all the salad fixings ready before you make the dressing.* **2** appropriate trimmings etc. for a dish: *Thanksgiving turkey with all the fixings.*

fix-it *noun* the action or an act of fixing something (usu. as an *adjective*: *fix-it project*).

fixity *noun* (*plural* **fixities**) the quality of being firm and not changing: *she has great fixity of purpose.*

fixture *noun* **1** something fixed or fastened in position: *a light fixture.* **b** *informal* a person or thing confined to or established in one place: *he's a permanent fixture at this restaurant.* **2** (in *plural*) *Law* articles attached to a house or land and regarded as legally part of it.

fizz • *verb* (**fizzes, fizzed, fizzing**) **1** make a hissing or spluttering sound. **2** (of a drink) make bubbles and a hissing sound. • *noun* (*plural* **fizzes**) **1** a hissing or spluttering sound. **2** bubbles: *the champagne has lost its fizz.* **3** *informal* excitement, energy: *the band lacks fizz.*

fizziness *noun* the state or quality of being bubbly.

fizzle • *verb* (**fizzles, fizzled, fizzling**) **1** make a feeble hissing or spluttering sound. **2** (often foll. by *out*) end feebly. • *noun* **1** a feeble hissing or spluttering sound. **2** a failure, a fiasco.

fizzy *adjective* (**fizzier, fizziest**) bubbly; effervescent.

fjord *noun* a long, narrow, and deep inlet of sea between high cliffs. [Say FYORD or FEE ord]

fl. *abbreviation* fluid.

Fla. *abbreviation* Florida.

flab *noun* *informal* fat; flabbiness.

flabbergast *verb* (esp. as **flabbergasted** *adjective*) overwhelm with astonishment. [Say FLABBER gast]

flabbiness *noun* **1** the condition or quality of having soft, loose, fatty flesh or of being overweight: *the flabbiness around his waist.* **2** the condition or quality of lacking vigour or of being feeble: *the moral flabbiness of modern scholarship.*

flabby *adjective* (**flabbier, flabbiest**) **1** (of flesh etc.) hanging down. **2** (of a person) having soft, loose, fatty flesh; overweight. **3** (of character etc.) feeble; lacking vigour.

flaccid *adjective* **1** (of flesh etc.) lacking stiffness; hanging or lying loose; limp: *she took his flaccid hand in hers.* **2** lacking vigour; feeble: *the flaccid leadership campaign was causing concern.* [Say FLASS id or FLACK sid]

flack[1] *slang* • *noun* a publicist. • *verb* **1** act as a publicist. **2** promote (a product, event, etc.).

flack[2] *noun* = FLAK.

flag[1] • *noun* **1** a piece of cloth, usu. oblong or square, attachable by one edge to a pole or rope and used as a country's emblem or as a standard, signal, etc. **2** the tail of an animal, esp. a deer or setter. • *verb* (**flags, flagged, flagging**) **1 a** grow tired; lose vigour. **b** droop; become limp. **2 a** place a flag on or over. **b** mark out with or as if with a flag or flags. PHRASES **flag down** signal to (a vehicle or driver) to stop. **keep the flag flying** continue the fight. **wave the flag 1** make a display of one's patriotism. **2** (foll. by *for*) assert one's allegiance to (a cause etc.). **wrap oneself in the flag** assert one's allegiance to one's country.

flag[2] • *noun* a flat usu. rectangular stone slab used for paving; a flagstone. • *verb* (**flags, flagged, flagging**) pave with flagstones.

flag[3] *noun* **1** any plant with a bladed leaf (esp. several irises) growing on moist ground. **2** the long slender leaf of such a plant.

flagellate[1] *verb* (**flagellates, flagellated, flagellating**) **1** flog (someone), either as a religious discipline or for sexual pleasure: *he flagellated himself with branches.* **2 flagellate oneself** criticize oneself harshly and publicly: *journalists are now flagellating themselves for their sensationalistic coverage of the event.* ▶ **flagellation** *noun* [Say FLADGE uh late]

flagellate[2] • *adjective* (also **flagellated**) having flagella. • *noun* a protozoan having one or more flagella. [Say FLADGE uh lit]

flagellum *noun* (*plural* **flagella**) **1** a long lash-like appendage found esp. on microscopic organisms. **2** *Botany* a runner; a creeping shoot. [Say fluh JELLUM for the singular, fluh JELLA for the plural]

flagger *noun* a person who waves or uses a flag, esp. to stop traffic in a construction zone.

flagging[1] *adjective* losing vigour, vitality, etc.

flagging[2] *noun* paving of flagstones.

flagon *noun* **1** a large bottle in which wine etc. is sold. **2** a large vessel usu. with a handle, spout, and lid, to hold wine etc. [Rhymes with *WAGON*]

flagpole *noun* a pole on which a flag may be hoisted. PHRASES **run something up the flagpole** test (an idea etc.).

flagrant *adjective* (of an action) shocking because it is done in a very obvious way and shows no respect for people, laws, etc.: *a flagrant abuse of human rights.* ▶ **flagrantly** *adverb* [Say FLAY grint]

flagship *noun* **1** a ship, esp. in a fleet or squadron, having an admiral on board. **2** something considered a leader or superior example of its kind: *this dictionary is the flagship of Oxford's language arts publishing program.*

flagstone *noun* a flat usu. rectangular stone slab used for paving. ▶ **flagstoned** *adjective*

flag-waver *noun* a person who makes an excessive display of patriotism.

flag-waving • *noun* an excessive display of patriotism. • *adjective* behaving in this manner.

flail • *noun* a tool consisting of a wooden staff with a short heavy stick swinging from it, used for beating wheat etc. to separate the grain from the husk and straw. • *verb* **1** beat (grain) with a flail. **2** wave or swing wildly or erratically: *with arms flailing.* **3** (often foll. by *about, around*) **a** move with one's limbs swinging wildly, usu. in desperation. **b** attempt desperately but unsuccessfully to find a direction to follow.

> **SPELL CHECK**
> **flair, flare** ✓ABC
>
> **Flare** is the spelling for a bright flame or the widening part of a skirt or pant leg. Something that suddenly becomes active or intense is said to "**flare up**".

flair *noun* **1** special talent, aptitude, or ability: *a flair for languages.* **2** an instinct for selecting or performing

what is excellent, useful, etc. **3** originality; stylishness of dress, manner, etc.

flak noun **1** anti-aircraft fire. **2** adverse criticism; hostile reaction: *he's taken a lot of flak for his left-wing views ◊ she came in for a lot of flak from the press.*

flake¹ • noun **1 a** a small thin light piece of snow. **b** a similar piece of another material, esp. one that has peeled or split off a surface or object: *paint flakes*. **2** (in *plural*) any of various kinds of flaked breakfast cereal, esp. cornflakes. **3** a natural division of the flesh of some fish. **4** *slang* a crazy or eccentric person. • verb (**flakes, flaked, flaking**) take off, shed, come away, or separate in flakes. **PHRASES** **flake out** *informal* fall asleep or drop from exhaustion.

flake² noun a stage for drying fish etc.

flakiness noun **1** the quality of being flaky. **2** *informal* craziness or eccentricity.

flaky adjective (**flakier, flakiest**) **1** of or like flakes; separating easily into flakes. **2** *slang* crazy, eccentric.

flambé • adjective (of food) covered with alcohol and set alight briefly: *the shrimps flambé are exquisite*. • verb (**flambés, flambéed, flambéing**) cover (food) with alcohol and set alight briefly: *fill the crepes with strawberries and flambé with your favourite liqueur.* [Say flom BAY or flam BAY]

flamboyance noun the quality of being exuberant, confident, and stylish in a way that attracts attention: *he lacked the flamboyance of other members of the band.*

flamboyant adjective **1** (of people or their behaviour) different, confident, and exciting in a way that attracts attention: *a flamboyant gesture ◊ he was flamboyant and temperamental on and off the stage.* **2** bright, colourful, and noticeable: *flamboyant clothes.* ▶ **flamboyantly** adverb

flame • noun **1** ignited gas: *the fire burned with a steady flame*. **2 a** a bright light; brilliant colouring. **b** a brilliant orange-red colour. **3 a** strong passion, esp. love: *fan the flame*. **b** *informal* a boyfriend or girlfriend. **4** *slang* an angry message of censure or disparagement sent by one user of a computer network to another. • verb (**flames, flamed, flaming**) **1** emit or cause to emit flames. **2** (of an emotion) appear suddenly and fiercely: *hope flamed in her*. **3** shine or glow like flame: *leaves flamed in the autumn sun.* **4** send someone an abusive or very angry message on the Internet. **5** (of a person's face) suddenly become red with anger or embarrassment: *Jess's cheeks flamed.* **PHRASES** **go up in flames** be consumed by fire. ▶ **flameless** adjective **flamelike** adjective

flamenco noun (*plural* **flamencos**) **1** a style of Spanish music played esp. on the guitar and accompanied by singing and dancing. **2** a strongly rhythmical dance performed to this music. [Say fluh MENG co]

flame-proof adjective **1** (esp. of a fabric) treated so as to be non-flammable. **2** (of cookware) that can be used in the oven or on a cooking element.

flame-thrower noun a weapon that projects a stream of burning fuel.

flaming adjective **1** burning and covered in flames. **2** *informal* full of anger: *a flaming argument.* **3** bright red or orange in colour: *the flaming autumn leaves of the St. Lawrence valley.*

flamingo noun (*plural* **flamingos** or **flamingoes**) a tall long-necked web-footed wading bird with a crooked bill and pink, scarlet, and black plumage.

flammability noun the quality or condition of being easily set on fire or highly combustible.

flammable adjective easily set on fire.

flan noun an open pastry or sponge pie case containing a fruit, jam, or savoury filling.

flange • noun a projecting flat rim, collar, or rib, used for strengthening or attachment, or (on a wheel) maintaining position on a rail. • verb (**flanges, flanging**) (esp. as **flanged**) provide with a flange. ▶ **flangeless** noun [Say FLANDGE]

flank • noun **1 a** the fleshy or muscular part of the side of a person or animal between the ribs and the hip. **b** a cut of meat, esp. beef, from the underside of an animal between the ribs and the hind legs: *flank steak.* **2** the side of a mountain, building, etc. **3** the right or left side of an army or other body of persons. • verb **1** be situated at both sides of: *she left the courtroom flanked by armed guards ◊ they drove through the flat wheat fields that flanked Highway 1.* **2** *Military* attack down or from the sides, or rake with gunfire from the sides.

flanker noun (in football) an offensive player who lines up to the outside of an end.

flannel noun **1** any of various loose-textured soft woollen or synthetic fabrics of plain or twilled weave and slightly napped on one side. **2** = FLANNELETTE. **3** (in *plural*) flannel garments, esp. trousers.

flannelette noun a napped cotton fabric imitating the texture of flannel, used for sheets, pyjamas, etc.

flap • verb (**flaps, flapped, flapping**) **1** move wings, the arms, etc. up and down when flying, or as if flying. **2 a** (esp. of curtains, loose cloth, etc.) swing or sway about; flutter, esp. with accompanying noise. **b** cause to sway or sway about, flutter or flop, esp. with accompanying noise. • noun **1** a piece of cloth, wood, paper, etc. hinged or attached by one side only and often used to cover a gap, e.g. the folded part of an envelope or book jacket, the cover of a pocket, etc. **2** one up-and-down motion of a wing, an arm, etc. **3** *informal* **a** a state of agitation; panic: *don't get into a flap.* **b** trouble, confrontation. **4** a hinged or sliding section of an aircraft wing used to control lift. **5** a light blow with something broad.

flapjack noun a pancake.

flapper noun (in the 1920s) a fashionable young woman intent on enjoying herself and flouting conventional standards of behaviour.

flare • verb (**flares, flared, flaring**) **1** burn or cause to burn suddenly with a bright unsteady flame. **2** burst into anger etc.; burst forth. **3** widen or cause to widen gradually towards the top or bottom: *flared trousers*. • noun **1** a dazzling irregular flame or light, esp. in the open air. **b** a sudden outburst of flame. **2 a** a bright flame used as a signal of distress etc. **b** a device that produces such a flame. **c** a flame dropped from an aircraft to illuminate a target etc. **3** *Astronomy* a sudden burst of radiation from a star. **4** a sudden outburst of emotion etc. **5 a** a gradual widening, esp. of a skirt or trousers. **b** (in *plural*) wide-bottomed pants, originally popular during the late 1960s and 1970s. **PHRASES**

F

flare up 1 burst into a sudden blaze. **2** become suddenly angry or active.

flare-up *noun* an outburst of flame, anger, activity, a disease, etc.

flash • *verb* (**flashes, flashed, flashing**) **1** emit or reflect or cause to emit or reflect light briefly, suddenly, or intermittently. **2** break suddenly into flame; give out flame or sparks. **3** send or reflect like a sudden flame or blaze: *his eyes flashed fire*. **4 a** burst suddenly into view or perception: *flashed into my mind*. **b** move swiftly. **5 a** send (news etc.) by radio, television, etc. **b** (of a message, image, etc.) show or be shown briefly on a television or movie screen. **c** signal to (a person) by shining lights or headlights briefly. **6** *informal* **a** show or display briefly: *flashed an identification card*. **b** show or display ostentatiously: *flashed her engagement ring*. **7** *slang* (esp. of a man) expose one's genitals briefly and indecently. • *noun* (*plural* **flashes**) **1** a sudden bright light or flame, e.g. of lightning. **2** a very brief time; an instant: *in a flash*. **3 a** a brief, sudden burst of feeling: *a flash of hope*. **b** a sudden display (of wit, understanding, etc.). **4** = NEWS FLASH. **5** *Photography* a device producing a flash of intense light, used for photographing by night, indoors, etc. **6** *Cdn & Brit.* a coloured patch of cloth on a uniform etc. as a distinguishing emblem. **7** vulgar display, ostentation. **8** a bright patch of colour. **9** = HOT FLASH. • *adjective informal* gaudy; vulgar: *a flash car*. ᴾᴴᴿᴬˢᴱˢ **flash in the pan** a promising start followed by failure.

flashback *noun* **1** a scene in a film, novel, etc. set in a time earlier than the main action. **2** a vivid, often recurrent remembrance of a usu. distressing event from the past.

flashbulb *noun* a bulb producing a flash of light used for photography under conditions of low light.

flasher *noun* **1** *slang* a man who indecently exposes his genitals in public. **2 a** an automatic device for switching lights rapidly on and off. **b** a sign or signal, e.g. hazard lights on a vehicle, using this device.

flash flood *noun* a sudden local flood due to heavy rain etc.

flashily *adverb* in a showy or gaudy way.

flashiness *noun* the quality or condition of being showy or gaudy.

flashing *noun* a usu. metallic strip preventing water penetration at the junction of a roof with a wall etc.

flashlight *noun* a portable, battery-powered light.

flash memory *noun* *Computing* a type of memory that retains data in the absence of a power supply.

flashpoint *noun* **1** the temperature at which vapour from oil etc. will ignite in air. **2** the point at which anger, indignation, etc. becomes uncontrollable. **3** a place or situation which has the potential to explode into sudden violence or controversy.

flashy *adjective* (**flashier, flashiest**) showy; gaudy.

flask *noun* **1 a** a narrow-necked bulbous bottle used in chemistry. **b** a similarly shaped bottle used for storing oil, wine, etc. **2** = HIP FLASK. **3** = THERMOS.

flat¹ • *adjective* (**flatter, flattest**) **1 a** horizontally level: *a flat roof*. **b** even: *a flat stomach*. **c** with a level surface and little depth; shallow: *a flat heel*. **d** spread out on a single plane; extending at full length. **2** unqualified: *a flat refusal*. **3 a** dull: *spoke in a flat tone*. **b** without energy; dejected. **c** (of a joke etc.) trite; not funny. **4** (of a drink etc.) lacking in flavour; stale; esp. having lost effervescence. **5** (of a tire) deflated. **6** *Music* **a** below true or normal pitch. **b** (of a key) having a flat or flats in the signature. **c** (as **B flat** etc.) a semitone lower than B etc. **7** not proportional or variable: *flat fee*. **8** (of a painting, photograph, etc.) **a** lacking contrast. **b** lacking perspective. **9** (of paint etc.) not glossy;

matte. **10** (of a market, prices, etc.) inactive. • *adverb* **1** spread out, esp. on another surface: *lay flat on the floor*. **2** *informal* **a** completely, absolutely: *flat broke*. **b** exactly: *in five minutes flat*. **3** *Music* below the true or normal pitch. • *noun* **1** the flat part of anything; something flat. **2** (usu. in *plural*) **a** level ground, esp. a plain or swamp. **b** nearly level ground over which the tide flows or which is covered by shallow water: *mud flats*. **3** *Music* **a** a note lowered a semitone below natural pitch. **b** the sign (♭) indicating this. **4** *informal* a flat tire. **5** a woman's shoe with a low heel or no heel. **6** a shallow box or container for growing seedlings or shipping produce etc. **7** *Theatre* a flat section of scenery mounted on a frame. ᴾᴴᴿᴬˢᴱˢ **fall flat** not win approval; fail to live up to expectations: *my joke fell flat*. **flat out 1** at top speed. **2** using all one's strength, energy, or resources. **3** directly, bluntly: *told me flat out*.

flat² *noun* one or more rooms, usu. on one floor, rented and used as a residence.

flatbed *noun* (also **flatbed trailer** or **flatbed truck**) a trailer or truck, the body of which is an open platform without raised sides or ends.

flatbread *noun* any of various flat, thin breads, often not raised with yeast, e.g. pita.

flatcar *noun* a railway car without a roof or raised sides, used for carrying freight.

flatfish *noun* (*plural* **flatfish** or **flatfishes**) a marine fish having an asymmetric appearance with both eyes on one side of a flattened body.

flat foot *noun* (*plural* **flat feet**) (usu. in *plural*) a foot with a less than normal arch.

flat-footed *adjective* **1** having flat feet. **2** *informal* awkward: *flat-footed prose*. **3** *informal* unprepared: *was caught flat-footed*.

flatland *noun* (often in *plural*) a region of flat land. ▶**flatlander** *noun*

flatly *adverb* **1** showing little interest or emotion: *"You'd better go," she said flatly*. **2** in a firm and unambiguous manner; absolutely: *they flatly refused to pay* ◊ *his view seems to me flatly contrary to our evidence*.

flatness *noun* **1** the quality or condition of being flat or level: *the incredible flatness of the prairies*. **2** lack of sharpness and clarity in a sound; deadness of tone, voice, etc. **3** lack of depth; superficiality: *there is a certain flatness to the characters*. **4** the quality in speech or writing of lacking animation, brilliance, or pointedness.

flatten *verb* **1** make or become flat. **2** *informal* knock down. ᴾᴴᴿᴬˢᴱˢ **flatten out** bring an aircraft parallel to the ground.

flatter *verb* **1** compliment unduly; overpraise, esp. for gain or advantage. **2 flatter oneself** please, congratulate, or delude oneself: *I flatter myself that I can sing*. **3 a** make (a person) appear to the best advantage: *that blouse flatters you*. **b** (esp. of a portrait, a painter, etc.) represent too favourably. **4** gratify the vanity of; make (a person) feel honoured. **5** use flattery. ▶**flatterer** *noun* **flattering** *adjective* **flatteringly** *adverb*

flattery *noun* exaggerated or insincere praise, esp. that given to further one's own interests: *flattery will get you nowhere*.

flattish *adjective* somewhat flat in physical appearance, tone, energy, etc.

flatulence *noun* an uncomfortable feeling caused by having too much gas in the stomach. [Say FLATCH oo lince]

flatulent *adjective* **1 a** causing formation of gas in the alimentary canal. **b** caused by or suffering from this. **2** (of speech etc.) inflated, pretentious: *a never-ending sequence of clichés and flatulent jargon*. [Say FLATCH oo lint]

flatware *noun* domestic cutlery.

flatwater *noun* slowly moving water, as in a river etc.

flatworm *noun* a worm with a flattened body and no body cavity or blood vessels, including tapeworms, flukes, etc.

WRITING TIP
flaunt, flout

Do not confuse **flaunt** with **flout**. To **flaunt** something is to show off or display it arrogantly, as in *Angus is always flaunting his wealth*. To **flout** something means to "disregard something openly", as in *Angus parks his car wherever he likes, flouting all parking regulations*.

---

flaunt *verb* display ostentatiously (oneself or one's finery); show off: *flaunted his gold cufflinks*. PHRASES **if you've got it, flaunt it** *informal* one should make a conspicuous or confident show of one's wealth or attributes rather than be modest. [Say FLONT]

WRITING TIP
flautist, flutist

Some people believe that **flautist** is the only correct word for a person who plays the flute. In fact, **flutist** is perfectly acceptable and more common than **flautist** in North American English.

---

flautist *noun* a flute player. [Say FLOT ist or FLOUT ist]

flavour (also **flavor**) • *noun* **1** a distinctive or characteristic taste. **2** an indefinable characteristic quality: *a romantic flavour*. **3** a distinctive quality of something, esp. one recalling something else: *the distinctive flavour of South Florida* ◊ *the film retains much of the book's exotic flavour*. **4** an indication of the essential character of something: *I have tried to convey something of the flavour of the argument*. **5** = FLAVOURING. • *verb* give flavour to. PHRASES **flavour of the month** (or **week**) a temporary trend or fashion. ▶ **flavourful** *adjective*

flavouring *noun* (also **flavoring**) a substance used to flavour food or drink.

flavourless *adjective* having no flavour: *the meat was tough and flavourless*.

flaw • *noun* **1** a fault or weakness in a person's character: *we all have our flaws, no one's perfect*. **2** a crack or chip in china, weaving defect in cloth, etc. **3** a mistake or shortcoming in a plan, theory, or legal document which causes it to fail or reduces its effectiveness: *the argument is full of fundamental flaws* ◊ *the report reveals fatal flaws in security at the airport*. • *verb* (of an imperfection) mar, weaken, or invalidate (something): *the computer game was flawed by poor programming*. ▶ **flawed** *adjective* **flawless** *adjective* **flawlessly** *adverb* **flawlessness** *noun*

flax *noun* (plural **flaxes**) **1** a blue-flowered plant cultivated for the textile fibre made from its stalks (linen) and for its seeds. **2** this textile fibre.

flaxen *adjective* **1** of flax. **2** (of hair) pale yellow.

flay *verb* **1** strip the skin or hide off, esp. by beating. **2** criticize severely. **3** peel off (skin, bark, peel, etc.).

SPELL CHECK
flea, flee

To run away is to **flee**.

---

flea *noun* a small wingless jumping insect which feeds on human and other blood.

fleabane *noun* a plant of the daisy family supposed to drive away fleas.

flea-bitten *adjective* **1** bitten by or infested with fleas. **2** shabby.

flea collar *noun* an insecticidal collar for pets.

flea market *noun* a usu. outdoor market with individual vendors selling second-hand goods, antiques, discontinued merchandise, produce, etc.

fleck • *noun* **1** a small patch of colour or light. **2** a small particle or speck. • *verb* cover or mark something with small areas of a particular colour or with small pieces of something: *the fabric was red, flecked with gold*.

fledge *verb* (**fledges, fledged, fledging**) **1** (of a bird) grow feathers. **2** bring up (a young bird) until it can fly.

fledged *adjective* (of a young bird) having wing feathers that are large enough for flight; able to fly.

fledgling • *noun* a young bird. • *adjective* young or new; inexperienced: *a fledgling democracy*.

SPELL CHECK
flee, flea ABC

The insect is a **flea**.

---

flee *verb* (**flees, fled, fleeing**) **1** run or hurry away; escape (esp. from danger, threat, etc.). **2** run away from; leave abruptly; shun: *fled the room* ◊ *fled her advances*. **3** vanish; pass away: *all hope had fled*.

fleece • *noun* **1 a** the woolly covering of a sheep or similar animal. **b** the amount of wool sheared from a sheep at one time. **2** a soft warm fabric with a pile, used in nightwear and athletic wear and for lining coats etc. • *verb* (**fleeces, fleeced, fleecing**) **1** (often foll. by *of*) strip (a person) of money, valuables, etc.; swindle. **2** remove the fleece from (a sheep etc.); shear. ▶ **fleeced** *adjective* (also in *combination*).

fleecy *adjective* (**fleecier, fleeciest**) of or like a fleece.

fleet[1] *noun* **1 a** a number of warships under one commander-in-chief. **b** (**the fleet**) all the warships and merchant ships of a nation. **2** a number of ships, aircraft, buses, trucks, taxis, etc. operating together or owned by one proprietor.

fleet[2] *adjective* *literary* swift; nimble: *fleet of foot*.

fleeting *adjective* lasting only a short time: *a fleeting glimpse*. ▶ **fleetingly** *adverb*

Fleming *noun* **1** a native of medieval Flanders, a region in the southwestern part of the Low Countries. **2** a member of a Flemish-speaking people inhabiting northern and western Belgium. [Say FLEM ing]

Flemish • *adjective* of or relating to Flanders, a region in the southwestern part of the Low Countries. • *noun* **1** the West Germanic language of Flanders, comprising a group of Dutch dialects, now one of the two official languages of Belgium. **2** (**the Flemish**) the people of Flanders; Flemish-speaking people. [Say FLEM ish]

flense *verb* (**flenses, flensed, flensing**) **1** remove the blubber or skin from (a whale or seal). **2** strip off (skin). ▶ **flenser** *noun* [Rhymes with FENCE]

flesh *noun* **1 a** the soft, esp. muscular, substance between the skin and bones of an animal or a human. **b** plumpness; fat: *has put on flesh*. **2** the body as opposed to the mind or the soul, esp. considered as sinful. **3** the pulpy substance of a fruit or a plant. **4 a** the visible surface of the human body with reference to its colour or appearance. **b** = FLESH COLOUR. PHRASES **flesh out** make or become substantial. **go the way of all flesh** die or come to an end: *our business went the way of all flesh*. **in the flesh** in bodily form, in person. **make a person's flesh creep** frighten or horrify a person, esp. with tales of the supernatural etc. **sins of the flesh** sins related to physical indulgence, esp. sexual gratification.

flesh and blood • *noun* **1** the body or its substance. **2** humankind. **3** human nature, esp. as being fallible. • *adjective* actually living, not imaginary or supernatu-

ral. PHRASES **one's own flesh and blood** near relatives.

flesh colour *noun* a light brownish pink. ▶**flesh-coloured** *adjective*

flesh-eating disease *noun* a disease in which bodily tissue is rapidly destroyed by streptococcal bacteria.

fleshed *adjective* (usu. in *combination*) having flesh of a usu. specified kind: *an orange-fleshed melon*.

fleshly *adjective* of or relating to human desire or bodily appetite: *fleshly pleasures*.

fleshy *adjective* (**fleshier, fleshiest**) **1** plump, fat. **2** (of plant or fruit tissue) pulpy. **3** like flesh in appearance or texture.

fleur-de-lys *noun* (also **fleur-de-lis**) (*plural* **fleurs-de-lys** or **fleurs-de-lis**) **1** a figure of a lily composed of three petals bound together near their bases, used as a symbol of Quebec and in the former royal arms of France. **2** the flag of the province of Quebec. [Say *flur duh LEE* or *flur duh LEECE* for either the singular or the plural]

SPELL CHECK [ABC✓]
flew, flu, flue

The illness is the **flu**. The part of a chimney is a **flue**.

---

flew *past of* FLY¹.

flex *verb* (**flexes, flexed, flexing**) **1** bend (a joint, limb, etc.) or be bent. **2** move (a muscle) or (of a muscle) be moved to bend a joint. PHRASES **flex one's muscle(s)** assert one's strength or power.

flexibility *noun* **1** ability to be bent. **2** readiness to yield to influence or persuasion. **3** the quality or condition of being adaptable or versatile: *computers offer a much greater degree of flexibility in the way work is organized*. **4** the quality or condition of being able to bend, twist, and contort the limbs and torso easily and to a greater degree than average: *exercises to develop the flexibility of the dancers*.

flexible *adjective* **1** able to bend without breaking; pliable; pliant. **2** willing or disposed to yield to influence or persuasion or to adapt to circumstances; not rigid. **3** adaptable; versatile; variable: *flexible hours*. **4** (of a person) able to bend, twist, and contort the limbs and torso easily and to a greater degree than average. ▶**flexibly** *adverb*

flexor *noun* (also **flexor muscle**) a muscle that bends part of the body (*compare* EXTENSOR).

flex-time *noun* **1** a system of working a set number of hours with the starting and finishing times chosen within agreed limits by the employee. **2** the hours worked in this way.

flick • *noun* **1 a** a light, sharp, quickly retracted blow with a whip etc. **b** the sudden release of a bent finger or thumb, esp. to propel a small object. **2 a** a sudden movement or jerk. **3 a** a quick turn of the wrist in playing games, esp. in throwing or striking a ball. **4 a** slight, sharp sound. **5** *informal* a movie. • *verb* **1** strike, move, or remove with a rapid action of the fingers: *flicked away the dust*. **2 a** give a flick with (a whip, towel, etc.). **3** activate (a light, electrical appliance, etc.) by flicking a switch: *flicked on the lights*. **4** move rapidly, esp. back and forth. PHRASES **flick through 1** turn over (cards, pages, etc.). **2 a** turn over the pages etc. of, by a rapid movement of the fingers. **b** look cursorily through (a book etc.).

flicker • *verb* **1** (of light) shine unsteadily or fitfully. **2** (of a flame) burn unsteadily. **3** (of an eyelid, a video image, etc.) quiver; vibrate. **b** (of the wind) blow lightly and unsteadily. **4** (of hope etc.) increase and decrease unsteadily and intermittently. • *noun* **1** a flickering movement or light. **2 a** brief period of hope,

recognition, etc. **3** a North American woodpecker that often feeds on ants on the ground. PHRASES **flicker out** die away after a final flicker.

flickery *adjective* that flickers; flickering.

flier *noun* = FLYER.

flight¹ *noun* **1 a** the act or manner of flying through the air. **b** the swift movement or passage of a projectile etc. through the air. **2 a** a journey made through the air or in space. **b** a unit of two or more military aircraft. **3** a flock or large body of birds, insects, etc., esp. when migrating. **4** (usu. foll. by *of*) a series, esp. of stairs between floors, or of hurdles across a race track. **5** an extravagant soaring: *a flight of fancy*. **6** the trajectory and pace of a ball in games. **7** the distance that a bird, aircraft, or missile can fly. PHRASES **take flight** fly.

flight² *noun* **1 a** the act or manner of fleeing. **b** a hasty retreat. **2** *Economics* the selling of currency, investments, etc. in anticipation of a fall in value: *capital flight*. PHRASES **put to flight** cause to flee. **take** (or **take to**) **flight** flee.

flight attendant *noun* an airline employee who serves meals etc. during a flight.

flight crew *noun* a team of people who ensure the effective operation and safety of an aircraft flight.

flight deck *noun* **1** the deck of an aircraft carrier used for takeoff and landing. **2** the part of an aircraft where the pilot, navigator, etc. perform their duties.

flightiness *noun* the condition or quality of being frivolous, fickle, or changeable.

flightless *adjective* (of a bird etc.) naturally unable to fly.

flight recorder *noun* a device in an aircraft to record technical details during a flight, which may be used in the event of an accident to discover its cause.

flighty *adjective* (**flightier, flightiest**) **1** frivolous, fickle, changeable. **2** crazy.

flim-flam *noun* **1** nonsense. **2** a deception or swindle. ▶**flim-flammer** *noun*

flimsily *adverb* **1** constructed etc. in a way that is lightly or carelessly assembled or easily damaged. **2** in an unconvincing manner: *a flimsily based legal challenge*.

flimsy *adjective* (**flimsier, flimsiest**) **1** lightly or carelessly assembled; easily damaged: *a flimsy structure*. **2** (of an excuse etc.) unconvincing: *a flimsy pretext*. **3** (of clothing) thin: *a flimsy blouse*.

flinch *verb* (**flinches, flinched, flinching**) **1** draw back in pain or expectation of a blow etc.; wince. **2** avoid thinking about or doing something unpleasant: *she never flinched from facing up to trouble*.

fling • *verb* (**flings, flung, flinging**) **1** throw or hurl (an object) forcefully. **2 fling oneself** rush headlong (into a person's arms etc.). **3** utter (words) forcefully. **4** suddenly spread (the arms). **5** put on or take off (clothes) carelessly or rapidly. **6** go angrily or violently; rush: *flung out of the room*. **7** put or send suddenly or violently: *was flung into jail*. **8** discard or put aside thoughtlessly or rashly. • *noun* **1** a period of indulgence or wild behaviour: *one final fling before a tranquil retirement*. **2** a short, spontaneous, sexual relationship: *had a fling with him when she was in college*. **3** any of various energetic, whirling, Scottish dances, esp. the Highland fling. **4** an attempt or trial: *have a fling at writing a novel*.

flint *noun* **1 a** a hard grey stone of nearly pure silica occurring naturally as nodules or bands in chalk. **b** a piece of this. esp. as flaked or ground to form a primitive tool or weapon. **2** a piece of hard alloy of rare-earth metals used to give an igniting spark in a lighter etc. **3** a piece of flint used with steel to produce fire. **4** used in comparisons to anything hard and

F

F

unyielding: *mean faces with eyes like flints.* ▶ **flinty** adjective **(flintier, flintiest)**

flip • verb **(flips, flipped, flipping) 1 a** flick or toss (a coin etc.) with a quick movement so that it spins in the air. **b** decide or settle a question, tie, etc. by flipping a coin. **2** turn over. **3** cause (something) to move with a flick of the fingers. **4 a** turn (a page in a book) with a flick of the fingers. **b** move through a book etc. by flipping. **c** (of pages) flip over: *pages flipping in the breeze*. **d** open (a book, box, etc.) with a brisk movement of the fingers. **5** change or switch (the channel on a television etc.), esp. by using a remote control. **6 a** move (a switch etc.) with a flick of the fingers. **b** (usu. foll. by *on*, *off*) turn (a light, an appliance, etc.) on or off by flipping a switch: *flip on the TV*. **7** resell (real estate, stocks, etc.), esp. to make a large profit. **8** *slang* **a** become suddenly excited or enthusiastic. **b** = FLIP OUT. **9** move about with sudden jerks. • noun **1** an act of flipping over. **2 a** a light blow; a flick. **b** an act of activating a switch etc. with a flip. **3** a somersault. **4** *Figure Skating* a jump in which the skater takes off from the back inside edge of one skate, using the toe of the second foot to provide momentum, goes through one or more counter-clockwise rotations, and lands on the second foot. **5** an act of flipping real estate, stocks, etc. **6** = FLIP SIDE. **7** (as an *adjective*) *Hockey* designating a type of pass or shot in which the puck is propelled a few inches above the surface of the ice so as to be above the blade of an opponent's stick: *flip shot*. • adjective informal glib; flippant. PHRASES **flip one's lid** (also **wig**) *slang* = FLIP OUT. **flip out 1** lose self-control; become enraged. **2** become insane.

flip-flop • noun **1** an abrupt reversal of policy. **2** a usu. rubber sandal with a thong between the big and second toe. **3** a backward somersault. **4** a repeated flapping sound. • verb **(flip-flops, flip-flopped, flip-flopping)** make a flip-flop. • adverb in a flapping manner.

flippancy noun the quality or an example of being flippant. [Say FLIP'n see]

flippant adjective treating serious things lightly: *sorry, I didn't mean to sound flippant.* ▶ **flippantly** adverb [Say FLIP'nt]

flipper noun **1** a broadened limb of a seal, penguin, etc., used in swimming. **2** a flat rubber attachment worn on the foot for underwater swimming. **3** a person or thing that flips. **4** = SPATULA 1c. **5** a remote control for a television etc.

flipper pie noun *Cdn* (*Nfld*) a pie with a filling of seal flippers.

flip side noun informal **1** = B-SIDE. **2** the reverse or opposite of a person or thing.

flirt • verb **1** show sexual interest in (a person) without any serious intent. **2 a** superficially interest oneself (with an idea etc.). **b** come close to; have a brush with (danger etc.): *flirting with disaster.* • noun a person who habitually flirts. ▶ **flirtation** noun

flirtatious adjective behaving in a way that shows a sexual attraction to someone that is not serious: *a flirtatious giggle*. ▶ **flirtatiously** adverb **flirtatiousness** noun [Say flur TAY shus]

flirty adjective **(flirtier, flirtiest)**. = FLIRTATIOUS.

flit • verb **(flits, flitted, flitting) 1** move lightly, softly, or rapidly. **2** fly lightly; make short flights: *flitted from branch to branch*. • noun an act of flitting. ▶ **flitter** noun

flitter verb flit about; flutter.

float • verb **1** rest or move, or cause (a buoyant object) to rest or move, on the surface of a liquid without sinking. **2** move with a liquid or current of air; drift: *the clouds floated high up*. **3** *informal* **a** move in a leisurely or casual way. **b** (often foll. by *before*) hover before the eye or mind: *the prospect of lunch floated before them*. **4** move

or be suspended freely in a liquid or a gas. **5** be free from attachment, commitment, etc. **6 a** bring (a company, scheme, etc.) into being; launch. **b** offer (stock, shares, etc.) on the stock market. **7 a** (of currency) be allowed to have a fluctuating exchange rate. **b** cause (currency) to float. **c** (of an interest rate) fluctuate or be allowed to fluctuate according to market conditions. **8** arrange a loan for someone. **9** (of water etc.) support; bear along (a buoyant object). **10** put forward (an idea, proposal, etc.); circulate. **11** waft (a buoyant object) through the air. • noun **1** a thing that floats, esp.: **a** a raft. **b** a buoyant piece of cork or plastic attached to a fishing line as an indicator of a fish biting. **c** a buoyant object supporting the edge of a fishing net. **d** the hollow or inflated part or organ supporting a fish etc. in the water; an air bladder. **e** a hollow structure fixed underneath an aircraft enabling it to float on water. **f** a floating device on the surface of water, fuel, etc., controlling the flow. **g** a floating platform attached to a bank, dock, etc., and used as a landing for boats or float planes. **2** a vehicle carrying a display in a parade etc. **3 a** *Cdn* & *Brit.* a sum of money used to provide change at the beginning of a period of selling in a store etc. **b** a small sum of money for minor expenditure; petty cash. **4** a soft drink with a scoop of ice cream floating in it. **5** a tool used for smoothing plaster etc.

floatation noun = FLOTATION.

float base noun *Cdn* a place on a river, lake, etc. where float planes dock.

float camp noun *Cdn* (*BC*) a log raft supporting the living quarters etc. of a coastal logging crew.

floater noun **1** a person or thing that floats. **2** a voter who is undecided or may change allegiance from one party to another. **3** a person who frequently changes occupation etc.

floathouse noun (*BC*, *US Northwest*, & *Alaska*) a house constructed on a log raft, usu. built so that it can be towed from one mooring to another.

floating adjective **1 a** supported on water. **b** in or on a ship or boat: *a floating disco*. **2 a** not settled in a definite place. **b** fluctuating; variable: *floating interest rates*. **3** (of an internal organ) not in its proper position: *floating kidney*.

floating point noun *Computing* a decimal etc. point that does not occupy a fixed position in the numbers processed.

float plane noun an airplane equipped with floats instead of wheels, so that it can land on water.

flock[1] • noun **1 a** a number of animals of one kind, esp. birds, feeding or travelling together. **b** a number of domestic animals, esp. sheep, goats, or geese, kept together. **2** a large crowd of people. **3 a** a Christian congregation or body of believers, esp. in relation to one priest or minister. **b** a family of children, a number of pupils, etc. • verb **1** congregate. **2** move in great numbers; troop: *people flocked to the beach*.

flock[2] noun **1** a lock or tuft of wool, cotton, etc. **2 a** (also in *plural*) material for quilting and stuffing made of wool refuse or torn-up cloth: *a flock mattress*. **b** powdered wool or cloth, applied to wallpaper, fabrics, etc. to form a raised velvetlike pattern. ▶ **flocked** adjective **flocking** noun

floe noun a sheet of floating ice. [Sounds like FLOW]

flog verb **(flogs, flogged, flogging) 1 a** beat with a whip, stick, etc. (as a punishment or to urge on). **b** make work through violent effort: *flogged the engine*. **2** *slang* **a** sell, esp. by aggressive effort. **b** publicize; promote. PHRASES **flog to death** *informal* talk about at tedious length. ▶ **flogger** noun **flogging** noun

flood • noun **1 a** an overflowing or influx of water

beyond its normal confines, esp. over land; an inundation. **b** the water that overflows. **2 a** an outpouring of water; a torrent: *a flood of rain.* **b** something resembling a torrent: *a flood of memories.* **3** the inflow of the tide (also as an *adjective*: *flood tide*) (*opp.* EBB noun 1). **4** *informal* a floodlight. **5 (the Flood)** any universal flood as described by various ancient religious traditions, esp. the one recorded in the Bible as occurring in the time of Noah. • *verb* **1 a** cover with or overflow in a flood: *flooded the basement.* **b** overflow as if with a flood: *the market was flooded with foreign goods.* **2** irrigate: *flooded the paddy fields.* **3** deluge (a burning house, a mine, etc.) with water. **4** (often foll. by *in*, *through*) arrive in great quantities: *complaints flooded in.* **5** become inundated: *the bathroom flooded.* **6** overfill (a carburetor) with fuel. **7** (of rain etc.) fill (a river) to overflowing. **8** build up (the surface of a skating rink etc.) by covering it with water and allowing it to freeze.

floodgate *noun* **1** a gate opened or closed to admit or exclude water, esp. the lower gate of a lock. **2** (usu. in *plural*) a restraint or check holding back tears, rain, etc.

flooding *noun* the action or process of covering an area of land that is usually dry with water after a heavy rain or after a river etc. overflows, or of being covered in this way: *there will be heavy rain with flooding in some areas.*

floodlight • *noun* **1** a large powerful light (usu. one of several) to illuminate a building, playing field, stage, etc. **2** the illumination so provided. • *verb* **(floodlights, floodlit, floodlighting)** illuminate with floodlights.

flood plain *noun* a relatively flat plain along the bank of a river etc. that is naturally subject to flooding.

flood water *noun* the water left by flooding.

floodway *noun* a channel for diverting flood waters away from a city etc.

floor • *noun* **1** the lower surface of a room. **2 a** the bottom of the sea, a lake, a cave, a cavity, etc. **b** any level area. **3** all the rooms etc. on the same level of a building: *the sixth floor.* **4 a** (in a legislative assembly) the part of the house in which members sit and from which they speak. **b** the right to speak next in debate: *gave her the floor.* **5** Stock Market the large central hall where trading takes place. **6** the minimum of prices, wages, etc. • *verb* **1** furnish with a floor. **2** bring to the ground; knock (a person) down. **3** *informal* confound, baffle: *was floored by the puzzle.* **4** *informal* get the better of; overcome. **5** push (the accelerator pedal of a motor vehicle) all the way to floor, to gain maximum power or speed. [PHRASES] **from the floor** (of a speech etc.) given by a member of the audience, not by those on the platform etc. **take the floor 1** begin to dance on a dance floor etc. **2** speak in a debate.

floorboard *noun* **1** (usu. in *plural*) a long wooden board used for flooring. **2** the floor of a car etc.

floor hockey *noun* a form of hockey played on an indoor floor, usu. using plastic sticks and a plastic puck or ball.

flooring *noun* the materials with which a floor is made or covered.

floor-length *adjective* reaching to the floor.

floor plan *noun* **1** a diagram of the rooms etc. on one storey of a building. **2** the arrangement of rooms in a house, apartment, etc.

floozie *noun* (also **floozy**) (*plural* **floozies**) *informal* a promiscuous girl or a woman.

flop • *verb* **(flops, flopped, flopping) 1** sway about heavily or loosely: *hair flopped over her face.* **2** move in an ungainly way. **3** sit, kneel, lie, or fall awkwardly or suddenly: *flopped down on to the bench.* **4** *slang* (esp. of a play, film, book, etc.) fail; collapse: *flopped on Broadway.* **5** make a dull sound as of a soft body landing, or of a

flat thing slapping water. • *noun* **1 a** a flopping movement. **b** the sound made by it. **2** *informal* a failure.

-flop *combining form* Computing floating-point operations per second: *megaflop.*

flophouse *noun* *informal* a cheap boarding house, esp. one used by vagrants, transients, etc.

floppiness *noun* the quality or condition of tending to flop or of not being firm or rigid.

floppy • *adjective* **(floppier, floppiest)** tending to flop; not firm or rigid. • *noun* (*plural* **floppies**) (also **floppy disk**) Computing a flexible removable magnetic disk for the storage of data.

flora *noun* (*plural* **floras**) **1** the plants of a particular region, geological period, or environment. **2** a catalogue of the plants of a defined area, with descriptions of them, comments on the more unusual species, etc. **3** (also **intestinal flora**) the beneficial bacteria normally present in the intestines.

floral • *adjective* **1** of, made of, or pertaining to flowers: *floral arrangement.* **2** decorated with or depicting flowers: *floral print.* • *noun* **1** something with a floral design. **2** a perfume scent of or like that of flowers.

Florentine • *adjective* **1 a** of or relating to Florence in Italy. **b** denoting the art, styles, etc. developed in Renaissance Florence. **2 (florentine)** (of a dish) served on a bed of spinach. • *noun* **1** a native or inhabitant of Florence. **2** a thin cookie containing nuts and candied fruit and coated on one side with chocolate. [Say FLOR un teen]

floret *noun* **1** each of the small flowers making up a composite flower head. **2** any of the segments into which a head of broccoli etc. may be divided. **3** a tiny blossom or flowering plant. [Say FLOR it for senses 1 and 3; say flor ET for sense 2]

florid *adjective* **1** (of a person's complexion) ruddy or flushed. **2** (of a book, a picture, music, architecture, etc.) elaborately ornate, ostentatious, or showy: *the florid prose of the nineteenth century.* [Say FLOR id]

florist *noun* a person who retails flowers and ornamental plants.

floss • *noun* (*plural* **flosses**) **1 a** the rough silk enveloping a silkworm's cocoon. **b** the silk down in corn and certain other plants. **2** untwisted silk or fine cotton thread used in embroidery. **3** = DENTAL FLOSS. • *verb* **(flosses, flossed, flossing)** clean between (the teeth) with dental floss. ▶ **flossing** *noun*

flotation *noun* **1** the process of launching or financing a commercial enterprise, esp. by selling shares. **2 a** the action or process of floating in a liquid etc. **b** buoyancy: *this wetsuit gives good flotation.*

flotilla *noun* **1** a fleet of boats or small ships. **2** a small fleet of warships. [Say flo TILLA]

flotsam *noun* **1** wreckage of a ship or its cargo found floating on the water. **2** (also **flotsam and jetsam**) **a** odds and ends, bits and pieces, various unimportant items: *the room was cleared of boxes and other flotsam.* **b** people who have been rejected by society: *the human flotsam of the inner city.* [Say FLOT sum]

flounce[1] • *verb* **(flounces, flounced, flouncing)** go or move in an exaggeratedly impatient or angry manner: *he stood up in a fury and flounced out.* • *noun* a sudden movement of the body, usu. as an expression of annoyance, impatience, or disdain: *she left the room with a flounce.*

flounce[2] • *noun* a frill or wide ornamental strip of material gathered and sewn to a skirt, dress, etc., so that its lower edge hangs full and free. • *verb* **(flounces, flounced, flouncing)** adorn or trim with a flounce or flounces. ▶ **flouncy** *adjective*

flounder[1] *verb* **1** struggle or show confusion in thoughts, words, or actions. **2** manage something

badly or with difficulty. **3** move or struggle clumsily or with difficulty through mud, snow, etc. ▶**floundering** *noun*

flounder² *noun* (*plural* **flounder** or **flounders**) a flatfish used for food.

flour • *noun* **1** a fine powder obtained by grinding grain, esp. wheat, used for making bread, cakes, etc. **2** a fine powder made from other foodstuffs, e.g. potatoes, nuts, etc. • *verb* sprinkle or cover with flour. ▶**floured** *adjective*

SPELL CHECK
fluorescent, fluoride

Warning: words like **fluorescent** and **fluoride** etc. are spelled with the *u* before the *o*.

---

flourish • *verb* (**flourishes, flourished, flourishing**) **1 a** (of a plant) grow vigorously. **b** prosper, be successful. **c** be in one's prime or at the height of one's fame or excellence. **d** be in good health. **2** spend one's life or be active during a specified period: *the English poet Geoffrey Chaucer flourished in the 14th century.* **3** show ostentatiously: *flourished his cheque book.* **4** wave (a weapon, one's limbs, etc.) vigorously. • *noun* (*plural* **flourishes**) **1** an ostentatious gesture with a weapon, a hand, etc.: *removed his hat with a flourish.* **2** an ornamental curving decoration of handwriting. **3** an elaborate rhetorical or literary expression. **4** a fanfare played by brass instruments. ▶**flourishing** *adjective* [Say FLUR ish]

floury *adjective* (**flourier, flouriest**) **1** covered with flour: *Katherine wiped her hands on her floury apron.* **2** of or resembling flour: *floury white makeup.*

WRITING TIP
flout, flaunt

Do not confuse **flout** with **flaunt**. To **flout** something is to disregard it openly, as in *Angus parks his car wherever he likes, flouting all parking regulations.* To **flaunt** something is to show off or display it arrogantly, as in *Angus is always flaunting his wealth.*

---

flout *verb* express contempt or disrespect for (the law, rules, etc.) by openly refusing to heed or obey: *flouted convention by shaving her head.*

SPELL CHECK
flow, floe

A sheet of floating ice is a **floe**.

---

flow • *verb* **1** glide along as a stream: *the Red River flows through Winnipeg.* **2 a** (of a liquid, esp. water) spring or well up, gush out. **b** (of blood, tears, etc.) be spilled. **3** (of blood, money, electric current, etc.) circulate. **4** (of people or things) move freely and continuously: *traffic flowed down the hill.* **5** (of talk, literary style, etc.) proceed easily and smoothly. **6** (of a garment, hair, etc.) hang easily or gracefully, or lie in undulating folds. **7** (often foll. by *from*) result from or be caused by: *his failure flows from his shyness.* **8** (esp. of the tide) come in, rise and advance. **9** (of wine etc.) be poured out abundantly. • *noun* **1 a** a flowing movement in a stream. **b** the quantity that flows; the rate of flowing: *a sluggish flow.* **c** a flowing liquid: *couldn't stop the flow.* **d** the act or fact of flowing. **2** any continuous movement, outpouring, etc. that resembles the flow of a river and denotes a copious supply: *a continuous flow of complaints.* **3** the incoming or rise of a tide or a tidal river. PHRASES **go with the flow** *informal* be relaxed and not resist the tide of events.

flow chart *noun* (also **flow diagram**) **1** a diagram showing the movement, development, or action of things or persons through the different stages or processes of a series. **2** a graphic representation of a computer program in relation to its sequence of functions (as distinct from the data it processes).

SPELL CHECK
flower, flour

When you bake a cake or bread you use **flour**.

---

flower • *noun* **1** the part of a plant from which the fruit or seed is developed, esp. the reproductive organ containing one or more pistils or stamens or both, and usu. a corolla and calyx. **2** a blossom and usu. its stem considered independently of the growing plant. **3** a flowering plant, esp. one cultivated for its flowers. **4 a** the prime or most active or vigorous period in a person's life: *a young woman in the flower of youth.* **b** the finest embodiment of a quality etc. **c** the pick or choicest person, thing, etc. of a number of persons, things, etc.: *the flower of the golden age of Great Lakes transport, the likes of which we'll never see on the inland seas again.* **5** (of a plant) the state of being in bloom: *the milkweed was in flower.* • *verb* **1** (of a plant) produce flowers. **2 a** develop into. **b** reach a peak, be in or attain one's fullest perfection, highest stage of development, etc.

flowerbearer *noun* Cdn a person, often a child, who follows the pallbearers in a funeral procession, carrying wreaths of flowers.

flower box *noun* (*plural* **flower boxes**) a rectangular container filled with soil in which flowers, herbs, etc. are grown, usu. on a balcony or windowsill.

flower child *noun* a hippie, esp. in the late 1960s, who advocated a simple idealistic lifestyle based on love and peace.

flowered *adjective* **1** having flowers of a specified quality. **2** decorated with flowers or a flower pattern.

flower girl *noun* a child bridesmaid.

flowering *adjective* **1** (of a plant) capable of producing flowers, esp. having showy flowers in contrast to a similar plant with the flowers inconspicuous or absent: *flowering dogwood.* **2** (of a plant) in bloom.

flowerpot *noun* **1** a container made of clay or plastic for growing plants in. **2** Cdn a tall column or island of rock formed by water erosion, often with vegetation on top, found esp. in the Bay of Fundy and Georgian Bay.

flower power *noun* the ideas of the flower children regarded as an instrument for changing the world.

flowery *adjective* **1** decorated with flowers or floral designs. **2** (of literary style, manner of speech, etc.) high-flown, ornate. **3** full of flowers: *a flowery meadow.* **4** of, like, or reminiscent of flowers: *a flowery scent.*

flowing *adjective* **1** (of language, style, etc.) fluent, coming easily and smoothly. **2** (of a line, a curve, or a contour) smoothly continuous. **3** (of hair, a garment, a sail, etc.) unconfined, streaming, hanging loosely, easily, and gracefully. **4 a** gliding or running along. **b** brimming, abundant, or copious.

flown *past participle of* FLY¹.

fl. oz. *abbreviation* fluid ounce.

FLQ *abbreviation* (in Canada) FRONT DE LIBÉRATION DU QUÉBEC.

FLQ crisis *noun* = OCTOBER CRISIS.

SPELL CHECK
flu, flue

The part of a chimney is a **flue**.

---

flu *noun* (*plural* **flus**) influenza.

flub *informal* • *verb* (**flubs, flubbed, flubbing**) botch, bungle, or perform badly. • *noun* a thing badly or clumsily done; a blunder.

fluctuate *verb* (**fluctuates, fluctuated, fluctuating**) change frequently in size, amount, quality, etc., esp. from one extreme to another: *oil prices fluctuated between $20 and $40 a barrel* ◊ *temperatures can fluctuate by as much as 10 degrees* ◊ *the documentary follows the fluctuating fortunes of one marketing company* ◊ *my mood seems to fluctuate from day to day*. ▸ **fluctuation** *noun* [Say FLUCK choo ate]

SPELL CHECK
flue, flu   [ABC ✓]

The illness is the **flu**.

---

flue *noun* **1** a duct for the passage of smoke, waste gases, etc. in a chimney. **2** a channel for conveying heat, esp. a hot-air passage in a wall.

fluency *noun* (*plural* **fluencies**) **1** a ready command of words or of a specified foreign language: *fluency in French and Spanish is required for this job*. **2** a smooth, easy flow of words, wit, etc., esp. in speech or writing. [Say FLOO in see]

fluent *adjective* **1 a** (of speech or literary style) flowing naturally and readily. **b** able to speak a language easily and without hesitation: *is fluent in German*. **c** articulate, able to speak quickly and easily. **2** (of movement etc.) easy and graceful. ▸ **fluently** *adverb* [Say FLOO int]

fluff • *noun* **1** soft, light, feathery material coming off blankets etc. **2** a piece of downy material, esp. a soft mass of fur or feathers. **3** *informal* a mistake or error made in speaking, delivering theatrical lines, playing a game, etc. **4** something unimportant, insubstantial, or insignificant. • *verb* **1** (often foll. by *up*) make or become fluffy; shake into or become a soft, fluffy mass. **2** *informal* blunder or make a mistake, esp. in a game or performance: *fluffed his opening line*.

fluffiness *noun* **1** the quality or condition of being like or covered in fluff. **2** the quality or condition of being light and airy. **3** the quality or condition of lacking depth, seriousness, or substance.

fluffy *adjective* (**fluffier, fluffiest**) **1** of or like fluff. **2** covered in fluff; downy. **3** light and airy: *fluffy mashed potatoes*. **4** lacking depth, seriousness, or substance.

flugelhorn *noun* a valved brass wind instrument with a cup-shaped mouthpiece and a conical bore, like a cornet but with a broader tone. [Say FLOOG'll horn]

fluid • *noun* a substance, esp. a gas or liquid, lacking definite shape and capable of flowing and yielding to the slightest pressure. • *adjective* **1** able to flow and alter shape freely. **2** changing readily, not settled or stable: *the situation is fluid*. **3** (of speech etc.) fluent. **4** (of movement) smoothly flowing. ▸ **fluidity** *noun* **fluidly** *adverb*

fluid ounce *noun* a unit of capacity equal to one-twentieth of an imperial pint (approx. 28.4 ml), or (in the US) equal to one-sixteenth of a pint (approx. 29.6 ml). Abbreviation: **fl. oz.**

fluke¹ *noun* a piece of luck, an unexpected success, or an unlikely but usu. fortunate chance occurrence.

fluke² *noun* **1** a parasitic flatworm which typically has suckers and hooks for attachment to the host. **2** a flatfish, esp. a flounder.

fluke³ *noun* **1** a broad triangular plate on the arm of an anchor. **2** the barbed head of a lance, harpoon, etc. **3** either of the two lobes of a whale's tail.

flu-like *adjective* resembling the flu.

flume *noun* **1** an artificial channel conveying water etc. for industrial use, esp. for the transport of logs or timber. **2** a deep, narrow channel or ravine with a stream running through it. **3** a water chute or waterslide at an amusement park or swimming pool.

flummox *verb* (**flummoxes, flummoxed, flummoxing**) *informal* bewilder, disconcert. [Say FLUM ix]

flung *past and past participle of* FLING.

flunk *verb* *informal* **1 a** (of a student) fail (an examination, course, etc.). **b** (of a teacher) fail (a student etc.). **2** (often foll. by *out*) fail utterly and quit or be dismissed from school etc.

flunky *noun* (*plural* **flunkies**) (also **flunkey**, *plural* **flunkeys**) usu. *derogatory* a person who performs relatively menial tasks for someone else.

fluorescence *noun* **1** the visible or invisible radiation produced from certain substances as a result of incident radiation of a shorter wavelength as X-rays, ultraviolet light, etc. **2** the property of absorbing light of short (invisible) wavelength and emitting light of longer (visible) wavelength. [Say flor ESSENCE]

fluorescent • *adjective* **1** (of a substance) of, having, or showing fluorescence. **2** (of colours) very bright and glowing, similar to colours produced by fluorescence. • *noun* (also **fluorescent light, fluorescent bulb**, etc.) a light or bulb radiating largely by fluorescence, esp. a tubular lamp in which phosphor on the inside surface of the tube is made to light up by ultraviolet radiation from mercury vapour. [Say flor ESS'nt]

fluoridate *verb* (**fluoridates, fluoridated, fluoridating**) add traces of fluoride to (drinking water etc.) to reduce or prevent tooth decay. ▸ **fluoridated** *adjective* **fluoridation** *noun* [Say FLORA date]

fluoride *noun* a binary compound of fluorine, esp. as used to prevent tooth decay. [Say FLOR ide]

fluorine *noun* a naturally occurring, poisonous, pale yellow gaseous element. [Say FLOR een]

fluoxetine *noun* an organic compound used (orally, as the hydrochloride) as an antidepressant (compare PROZAC). [Say flu OXA teen]

flurry • *noun* (*plural* **flurries**) **1** a short, usu. localized shower of snow. **2** a sudden burst of intense activity. **3** a number of things happening or arriving at once: *a flurry of penalties*. • *verb* (**flurries, flurried, flurrying**) **1** agitate or confuse by haste or noise. **2** (of a person) move quickly in a busy or agitated way: *the waiter flurried between them*.

flush¹ • *verb* (**flushes, flushed, flushing**) **1 a** (of the face) redden because of a rush of blood to the skin: *he flushed with embarrassment*. **b** glow with a warm colour, light, etc.: *sky flushed pink*. **2 a** cleanse (a toilet, drain, etc.) by a rushing flow of water. **b** (often foll. by *away, down*) dispose of (an object) in this way. **c** (often foll. by *out*) remove by a sudden rush of water or other liquid. **3** *Computing* cleanse, dump, or erase (a buffer etc.). • *noun* (*plural* **flushes**) **1 a** a flow of blood to the face, neck, etc. that causes red colouring. **b** a glow of light or colour. **2 a** a sudden rush of water, esp. as caused for a specific purpose. **b** the cleansing of a toilet, drain, etc. by flushing. **3** a rush of emotion, elation, etc., esp. as produced by a victory, success, etc.: *the flush of triumph*. **4** the freshness and vigour of youth or a beginning, or the best and most fully developed stage: *in the full flush of success*. **5** facial redness, esp. caused by fever, alcohol, etc.

flush² *adjective* **1** (often foll. by *with*) completely level, even, or continuous with another surface: *the sink is flush with the counter*. **2** *informal* having plenty of something, esp. money: *flush with cash*. **3** (of text) even or level with the margin, neither indented nor protruding.

flush³ *noun* (*plural* **flushes**) a hand of cards all of one suit, esp. in poker.

flush⁴ *verb* (**flushes, flushed, flushing**) **1** cause (esp.

a game bird) to fly up suddenly, esp. from undergrowth. **2** (of a bird) fly up and away, esp. from undergrowth. PHRASES **flush out** force or drive (a person) out of a hiding place etc.

flushable *adjective* able to be disposed of by flushing down a toilet: *this product is flushable and biodegradable.*

flushed *adjective* (often foll. by *with*) glowing or blushing, esp. with emotion, excitement, etc.

fluster • *verb* make or become nervous, confused, agitated, etc. • *noun* a nervous or agitated state: *the main thing is not to get all in a fluster.* ▶ **flustered** *adjective*

flute • *noun* **1 a** a high-pitched woodwind instrument of metal or wood, having holes along it, stopped by the fingers or keys. **b** a flute player. **2 a** *Architecture* an ornamental vertical groove in a column. **b** a narrow, furrow-like frill on a dress etc. **c** any similar cylindrical groove. **3 a** tall narrow wineglass, used esp. for sparkling wine. • *verb* (**flutes, fluted, fluting**) make, shape, or carve flutes or grooves in a thing as decoration. ▶ **fluted** *adjective* **fluting** *noun*

WRITING TIP
flutist, flautist

Some people believe that **flautist** is the only correct word for "a flute player". In fact, **flutist** is perfectly acceptable and more common than **flautist** in North American English.

---

flutist *noun* a flute player.

flutter • *verb* **1** flap the wings lightly and quickly in flying or trying to fly. **2** fall with a quivering motion: *leaves fluttered to the ground.* **3** move or cause to move in a quick, irregular way: *the wind fluttered the flag.* **4** hover or move about aimlessly and restlessly. **5** (of a pulse or heartbeat) beat feebly or irregularly, esp. because of nervous excitement. **6** tremble with excitement or agitation. • *noun* **1** an act of fluttering: *there was a flutter of wings at the window.* **2** tremulous excitement or agitation: *was in a flutter.* **3** an abnormally rapid but regular heartbeat. **4** a rapid variation in the pitch or loudness of a sound, not audible as such, but heard as distortion, esp. in a recording. **5** a vibration. PHRASES **flutter one's eyelashes** open and close one's eyes rapidly in a coyly flirtatious manner. ▶ **fluttering** *adjective & noun* **fluttery** *adjective*

flux *noun* (*plural* **fluxes**) **1 a** a process of flowing or flowing out: *the flux of men and women moving back and forth.* **b** the flowing in of the tide: *flux and reflux.* **2** a stream or flood, esp. of people, talk, etc. **3** continuous change: *in a state of flux.* **4 a** *Metallurgy* a substance mixed with a metal etc. to promote fusion. **b** a substance used to make colour fusible in enamelling, pottery, etc. **5** *Physics* **a** the rate of flow of any fluid across a given area. **b** the amount of fluid crossing an area in a given time. **6** *Physics* the amount of radiation or particles incident on an area in a given time. **7** *Electricity* the total electric or magnetic field passing through a surface.

fly[1] • *verb* (**flies**; *past* **flew**; *past participle* **flown**; **flying**) **1** move through the air with wings. **2** (of an aircraft or its occupants) **a** travel through the air or through space. **b** traverse (a region or distance) by flying: *flew the Vancouver–Victoria route.* **3 a** control or pilot the flight of (esp. an aircraft). **b** transport in an aircraft. **4 a** cause to fly or remain aloft: *build and fly a kite.* **b** (of a flag, hair, etc.) wave or flutter. **c** set or keep (a flag) flying. **5** pass or rise quickly over or up an obstacle. **6 a** go, move, or travel quickly. **b** (of time) pass swiftly, rush by. **7 a** flee. **b** *informal* depart hastily. **8 a** be forced or driven off or away suddenly and quickly: *sent me flying.* **b** (of a door, window, etc.) be thrown suddenly (open, up, etc.): *the door flew open.*

9 (foll. by *at*) **a** hasten or spring violently. **b** attack or criticize fiercely. **10** flee from, escape in haste. **11** *Baseball* (*past & past participle* **flied**) hit a fly ball. **12** *informal* meet with approval, acceptance, success, etc.: *the plan will fly.* **13** (of snow) fall, esp. for the first time in the winter: *before the snow flies.* • *noun* (*plural* **flies**) **1 a** a zippered or buttoned opening, esp. from the waist to the crotch at the front of a pair of trousers. **b** a flap on a garment, esp. trousers, to contain or cover such a fastening. **2 a** a flap of material at the entrance of a tent. **b** an extra layer of fabric placed on top of a tent to repel moisture. **3** (in *plural*) the space above a theatre stage which is behind the proscenium, into which scenery is raised. **4** *Baseball* a fly ball. **5 a** the breadth of a flag from the staff to the end (compare HOIST *noun* 3a). **b** the part of the flag which is furthest from the staff (compare HOIST *noun* 3b). PHRASES **fly high 1** be happy, enthusiastic, etc. **2** excel, prosper. **3** pursue a high ambition. **fly in the face of** disregard, defy, or oppose rashly something that is generally accepted, e.g. an opinion, decision, facts, etc. **fly into a rage** (temper etc.) become suddenly or violently angry. **fly off the handle** *informal* lose one's temper suddenly and unexpectedly. **fly the coop** *informal* escape or leave without warning, esp. a domestic or work situation, one's responsibilities or obligations, etc. **on the fly 1** quickly, esp. while on the go or in the midst of doing something else. **2** (of something hit or thrown) while still flying through the air, before touching the ground: *caught it on the fly.*

fly[2] *noun* (*plural* **flies**) **1** any flying insect of a large order characterized by a single pair of transparent wings and sucking (and often also piercing) mouthparts. **2** (usu. in *combination*) used in names of flying insects of other orders: *firefly ◊ mayfly.* **3** a natural fly or an imitation of this consisting of a hook with silk and feathers etc., used as bait in fishing. PHRASES **catch flies** *informal* have one's mouth open for a prolonged time for no reason; breathe with one's mouth open. **fly in the ointment** a minor irritation that spoils an otherwise satisfactory situation or occasion. **fly on the wall** an unnoticed observer. **like flies** in large numbers or quantities. **no flies on** *informal* nothing to diminish (a person's) astuteness. **not hurt a fly** be kind, gentle, and unwilling to injure, offend, or cause unhappiness.

fly-away *adjective* **1** (of hair, a garment, etc.) loose, streaming, or tending to fly out or up. **2** (of a person, action, etc.) sudden, impulsive, or flighty.

fly ball *noun Baseball* a ball hit up into the air with the result that it is easily caught.

flyby *noun* (*plural* **flybys**) **1** a flight past a position, esp. the approach of a spacecraft to a planet etc. for observation. **2** an often low-level, ceremonial procession, usu. in formation, of aircraft.

fly-by-night • *adjective* **1** unreliable or dishonest. **2** short-lived. • *noun* (also **fly-by-nighter**) an untrustworthy, dishonest, or unreliable person, esp. one who shirks debts.

fly cast *verb* (**fly casts, fly cast, fly casting**) fish with a rod and artificial flies rather than live bait, using a whip-like motion to cast the line. ▶ **fly caster** *noun* **fly casting** *noun*

flycatcher *noun* any of various birds catching flying insects esp. in short flights from a perch.

flyer *noun informal* **1 a** a pilot or aviator. **b** a person who flies in an aircraft as a passenger, esp. on a commercial carrier: *frequent flyer.* **2** a small advertising leaflet that is widely distributed. **3** a thing, creature, etc. that flies or is carried through the air. **4** a risky, esp. a speculative investment. **5** a fast-moving animal or vehicle. **6** an ambitious or outstanding person: *high flyer.*

fly fish verb (**fly fishes**, **fly fished**, **fly fishing**) fish with an artificial fly as bait. ▶ **fly fisher** noun **fly fisherman** noun (plural **fly fishermen**) **fly fishing** noun

fly-in • noun (plural **fly-ins**) 1 the action or an act of travelling or delivering goods etc. by air to a specific and usu. remote place. 2 a service etc. provided for people who arrive by air. • adjective 1 of or for people arriving by air, esp. in a remote region: *fly-in canoe trips*. 2 accessible only by plane, helicopter, etc.: *fly-in lodge*.

flying • adjective 1 that flies or flies about: *flying saucer*. 2 fluttering, waving, or hanging loose in the air etc. 3 hasty, brief: *a flying visit*. 4 designed for rapid movement. 5 passing or travelling swiftly: *a flying puck*. 6 (of an animal) able to make very long leaps by using wing-like membranes etc.: *flying squirrel*. 7 *Figure Skating* designating a spin which the skater commences with a vigorous leap through the air. • noun the action of piloting or travelling in an aircraft or spacecraft. PHRASES **with flying colours** with distinction.

flying buttress noun (plural **flying buttresses**) a buttress, usu. on an arch, which slants upwards to a wall from a pier or other support.

flying fish noun (plural **flying fish** or **flying fishes**) any of various tropical fishes capable of gliding above the water by means of wing-like fins.

flying saucer noun any unidentified, esp. circular, flying object, popularly supposed to have come from outer space.

flyline noun 1 a type of line used in fly fishing. 2 *Cdn* a point or height above which flies do not normally fly.

fly-out adjective indicating services etc. that require flying out of a relatively easily accessible area into a remote region: *fly-out Arctic char fishing*.

flyover noun 1 a flight of aircraft, usu. at low level, for observation, as part of a military display, etc. 2 (also **flypast**) a ceremonial flight of aircraft past a person or a place.

fly rod noun a very light, flexible rod designed for use in fly casting. ▶ **fly rodding** noun

flytrap noun 1 any of various plants that catch flies, esp. the Venus flytrap. 2 a trap in which to catch flies.

flyway noun 1 the regular line of flight followed by a migrating bird. 2 a vast area occupied by bird populations containing both winter and breeding grounds linked by migratory routes.

flyweight noun 1 a weight in certain sports below bantamweight, in the amateur boxing scale 48-51 kg but differing for professionals and wrestlers. 2 an athlete of this weight.

flywheel noun a heavy wheel on a revolving shaft used to regulate machinery or accumulate power.

FM abbreviation 1 FREQUENCY MODULATION. 2 radio stations broadcast using this.

Fm symbol fermium.

f-number noun *Photography* the ratio of the focal length to the effective diameter of a lens, e.g. *f5*, indicating that the focal length is five times the diameter.

foal • noun the young of a horse or related animal. • verb (of a mare etc.) give birth to a foal. ▶ **foaling** noun [Rhymes with *POLE*]

foam • noun 1 a mass of small bubbles formed on or in liquid by agitation, fermentation, etc. 2 a froth of saliva or sweat. 3 rubber (also **foam rubber**) or plastic (also **foam plastic**) solidified in a lightweight cellular mass with many small gas bubbles. 4 any of various chemical substances forming a thick mass of bubbles and used for various purposes: *shaving foam*. • verb emit foam; froth. PHRASES **foam at the mouth** be very angry. ▶ **foaming** adjective **foam-like** adjective **foamy** adjective (**foamier**, **foamiest**)

fob¹ noun 1 (also **fob chain**) a chain attached to a watch for carrying in a waistcoat or waistband pocket. 2 a tab or ornament on a key ring.

fob² verb (**fobs**, **fobbed**, **fobbing**) PHRASES **fob off** 1 (often foll. by *with* a thing) deceive into accepting something inferior. 2 (often foll. by *on* to a person) palm or pass off (an inferior thing).

focaccia noun (plural **focaccias**) a type of flat Italian bread usu. topped with herbs etc. [Say fuh CATCH uh]

focal adjective of, at, or in terms of a focus.

focal length noun 1 the distance between the centre of a mirror or lens and its focus. 2 the equivalent distance in a compound lens or telescope.

focal point noun = FOCUS noun 1a, 3.

fo'c'sle noun = FORECASTLE. [Say FOKE s'll]

focus • noun (plural **focuses** or **foci**) 1 *Physics* **a** the point at which rays or waves (of light, heat, sound, etc.) meet after reflection or refraction, or from which divergent rays or waves appear to proceed. **b** the distance from a lens etc. to this point (compare FOCAL LENGTH). 2 **a** *Optics* the point at which an object must be situated for an image of it given by a lens or mirror to be well defined: *bring into focus*. **b** the adjustment of the eye or a lens necessary to produce a clear image: *the binoculars were not in focus*. **c** a state of clear definition: *the photograph was out of focus*. 3 the centre of interest, activity, or greatest energy: *focus of attention*. 4 *Math* one of a number of points from which the distances to any point of a given curve or solid obey a simple arithmetic relation. 5 the primary or principal site of an infection, malignant growth, or other disease. 6 *Geology* the place of origin of an earthquake, storm, volcanic eruption, etc. • verb (**focuses**, **focused**, **focusing**) 1 bring into focus etc. 2 adjust the focus of a lens, the eye, etc. 3 (often foll. by *on*) concentrate or be concentrated on. 4 converge or make converge to a focus. [For the plural say FOCUS iz or either FOE kye or FOE sigh]

focus group noun a representative selection of people surveyed for their opinions.

fodder noun 1 dried hay or straw etc. for cattle etc.: *a barn full of winter fodder* ◊ *fodder crops*. 2 **a** something that feeds or stimulates (creativity etc.): *the story was wonderful fodder for the newspapers*. **b** people viewed as dispensable commodities: *the soldiers were seen as nothing but cannon fodder*.

foe noun an enemy or opponent.

foetus noun (plural **foetuses**) esp. *Brit.* = FETUS. [Say FEET us]

fog • noun 1 **a** a thick cloud of water droplets or smoke suspended in the atmosphere at or near the earth's surface, restricting or obscuring visibility. **b** any abnormal darkened state or obscurity in the atmosphere. **c** an opaque mass of smoke etc.: *insecticide fog*. 2 *Photography* cloudiness on a developed negative etc. obscuring the image. 3 a state of confusion, uncertainty, perplexity, etc. • verb (**fogs**, **fogged**, **fogging**) 1 **a** envelop or cover with fog or condensed vapour. **b** bewilder (a person), confuse (an idea), etc. 2 become covered with fog or condensed vapour. 3 *Photography* cause cloudiness on (a negative etc.). 4 treat with something in the form of a spray, esp. insecticide. PHRASES **in a fog** puzzled; at a loss.

fogey noun (plural **fogeys**) (also **fogy**, plural **fogies**) a person with old-fashioned ideas: *old fogey*. ▶ **fogeyish** adjective [Say FOE ghee]

fogger noun a device that produces an opaque mass of pesticide etc.: *an insecticide fogger*.

fogging noun the action or process of enveloping or covering something with fog or condensed vapour.

foggy adjective (**foggier**, **foggiest**) 1 (of the atmosphere) thick or obscured with fog. 2 vague,

confused, unclear. **3** (of a photograph) cloudy, obscured by a deposit of silver etc. PHRASES **not have the foggiest** *informal* have no idea at all.

foghorn *noun* a deep sounding instrument for warning ships in fog.

fog lamp *noun* a headlight for improving visibility in fog.

fogy *noun* (*plural* **fogies**) = FOGEY. [Say FOE ghee]

foible *noun* a minor weakness or idiosyncrasy: *I admit I have some foibles, but really I'm a very stable guy ◊ the foibles of this word processing program.* [Say FOY bull]

foie gras *noun* the liver of fattened geese or ducks eaten as a delicacy, esp. in the form of a pâté. [Say fwah GRAH]

foil¹ *verb* stop something from happening, esp. something illegal; prevent somebody from doing something; thwart: *customs officials foiled an attempt to smuggle priceless paintings out of the country ◊ the smugglers were foiled.*

foil² *noun* **1 a** metal hammered or rolled into a thin sheet. **b** aluminum foil: *cover with foil.* **2 a** a person or thing that enhances the qualities of another by contrast: *the gritty textures of shingles and stone are a good foil for the precise and elegant woodwork.* **b** a character in a story whose qualities or actions serve to emphasize those of another character by providing a strong contrast with them: *the passively obedient Helen Burns serves as a foil to the rebellious Jane Eyre.*

foil³ *noun* a light blunt-edged sword with a button on its point, used in fencing.

foist *verb* (foll. by (*off*) *on*, (*off*) *upon*) impose (an unwelcome person or thing) on.

folate *noun* a salt or ester of folic acid. [Say FOE late]

fold¹ ● *verb* **1** bend or close (a flexible thing) over. **2** become or be able to be folded. **3** (foll. by *away*, *up*) make compact by folding. **4 a** bring together and cross or intertwine (the arms, legs, etc.). **b** (of a bird, insect, etc.) bring (the wings) together from an extended position. **5** *informal* (often foll. by *up*) **a** collapse, disintegrate. **b** (of an enterprise) fail; go bankrupt. **c** close. **6** lay (one's cards) face down on the table etc., so as to withdraw from play. **7** (foll. by *in*) mix (an ingredient with others) using a gentle cutting and turning motion. **8** *literary* embrace: *folded him to her breast.* **9** clasp (the arms). **10** wrap, envelop. ● *noun* **1** a form or shape produced by the gentle draping of a loose, full garment or piece of cloth: *the fabric fell in soft folds.* **2** a line or crease produced in paper or cloth as a result of folding it. **3** an area of skin that sags or hangs loosely. **4** a hollow among hills. **5** *Geology* a curvature of strata.

fold² *noun* **1** an enclosure for sheep. **2** a body of believers or members of a Church. **3** a community or group of people sharing a way of life, values, etc.: *welcomed her back into the fold.*

-fold *suffix* forming adjectives and adverbs from cardinal numbers, meaning: **1** in an amount multiplied by: *repaid tenfold.* **2** consisting of so many parts: *threefold blessing.*

foldable *adjective* able to be folded, or designed to be folded.

foldaway *adjective* adapted or designed to be folded away.

fold-down *adjective* designed to be folded down for use.

folder *noun* **1** a folding cover or holder for loose papers. **2** a folded leaflet. **3** *Computing* a directory in a computer system in which files may be accumulated.

folding *adjective* **1** that can be folded, so that it can be carried or stored in a small place: *a folding chair.* **2** (of a door) having vertically jointed sections that can be folded together to one side to allow access.

fold-out ● *noun* an oversize page in a book etc. to be unfolded by the reader. ● *adjective* designed to be unfolded for use: *a fold-out bed.*

foley *adjective* designating sound effects in a motion picture etc. recorded separately from the shooting of the image and subsequently matched with it on the soundtrack: *foley artist.* [Rhymes with GOALIE]

foliage *noun* leaves: *a drive in the country to view the glorious fall foliage.* [Say FOLEY idge]

foliate *adjective* decorated with leaves or leaflike patterns: *complex floral and foliate carvings.* [Say FOLEY it]

foliated *adjective* **1** decorated with leaves or leaflike patterns. **2** *Geology* consisting of thin sheets. [Say FOLEY ated]

folic acid *noun* a B vitamin, found in leafy green vegetables and liver, deficiency of which causes a defective formation of red blood cells. [Say FOLLIC or FOE lick]

folio *noun* (*plural* **folios**) **1** a leaf of paper etc., esp. one numbered only on the front. **2** a sheet of paper folded once making two leaves of a book. **3** a book made of such sheets.

folk *noun* (*plural* **folk** or **folks**) **1** (treated as *plural*) people in general or of a specified class: *townsfolk ◊ just regular folks.* **2** (usu. as **folks**) one's parents or relatives. **3** (treated as *singular*) a people. **4** (treated as *singular*) *informal* = FOLK MUSIC. **5** (as an *adjective*) originating from the beliefs or customs of ordinary people; traditional: *folk art ◊ folk dance ◊ folk tale ◊ folk medicine.*

folkie *informal* ● *noun* a devotee of folk music; a folksinger. ● *adjective* of or relating to folk music.

folkish *adjective* of the common people; unsophisticated.

folklore *noun* **1** the traditional beliefs, stories, customs, etc. of a people: *a story from Irish folklore.* **2** popular myth relating to a particular group: *Hollywood folklore.* ▶ **folkloric** *adjective* **folklorist** *noun*

folk medicine *noun* medicine of a traditional kind, employing herbal remedies etc.

folk music *noun* **1** traditional music as made by the common people of a region etc. and transmitted orally. **2** contemporary music composed in this style.

folk-rock *noun* folk music incorporating the stronger beat of rock music and using electric instruments. ▶ **folk-rocker** *noun*

folksiness *noun* **1** the quality or condition of being friendly or sociable. **2** the quality or condition of having the characteristics of folk art or culture, esp. in being artificially folkish.

folksinger *noun* a singer of folk songs.

folk song *noun* **1** a song having a tune and lyrics that have been handed down esp. orally from one generation to the next in a particular region. **2** a song written in this style.

folksy *adjective* (**folksier**, **folksiest**) **1** friendly, informal. **2** having the characteristics of folk art etc.; artificially folkish.

folkways *plural noun* the traditional behaviour of a people.

folky *adjective* (**folkier**, **folkiest**) **1** = FOLKSY 2. **2** = FOLKISH.

follicle *noun* **1** a small cavity, sac, or gland, esp. (also **hair follicle**) the gland or cavity at the root of a hair. **2** a dry fruit that is derived from a single carpel and opens on one side only to release its seeds. [Say FOLLA cull]

follow *verb* **1** go or come after. **2** go along (a route, path, etc.). **3** take as a guide or leader. **4** conform to: *follow your example.* **5** practise (a trade or profession). **6** undertake (a course of study etc.). **7** understand. **8** maintain awareness of the current state or progress

of (events etc. in a particular sphere). **9** provide with a sequel or successor. **10 a** be necessarily true as a result of something else. **b** be a result of. **11** strive after; pursue: *followed fame and fortune.* PHRASES **follow one's nose** trust to instinct. **follow on** continue. **follow out** carry out; adhere precisely to (instructions etc.). **follow suit 1** *Cards* play a card of the suit led. **2** conform to another person's actions. **follow through 1** continue (an action etc.) to its conclusion. **2** *Sport* continue the movement of a stroke after the ball etc. has been struck or thrown. **follow up 1** pursue, develop, supplement. **2** make further investigation of.

follower *noun* **1** an adherent or devotee. **2** a person or thing that follows. **3** a mechanical part whose motion or action is derived from that of another part to which force is applied.

following • *preposition* coming after in time; as a sequel to. • *noun* **1** a body of adherents or devotees. **2** that which follows: *see the following.* • *adjective* that follows or comes after.

follow-on *adjective* following or coming after as the next step in a progression.

follow-the-leader *noun* a game in which players must do as the leader does.

follow-through *noun* **1** the continuing of an action or task to its conclusion: *we assure follow-through on all aspects of the contract.* **2** a continuation of the movement of a bat etc. after a ball etc. has been struck.

follow-up *noun* a subsequent or continued action, measure, experience, etc.

folly *noun* (*plural* **follies**) **1** foolishness; lack of good sense. **2** a foolish act, idea, etc. **3** an ornamental building, usu. a tower or mock Gothic ruin.

foment *verb* stir up or worsen trouble, agitation, etc.: *the policy fomented discontent in the Prairies.* [Say foe MENT]

fond *adjective* **1** (foll. by *of*) having affection or a liking for. **2** affectionate: *a fond farewell.* **3** doting: *a fond parent.* **4** (of hopes, dreams, etc.) cherished but not likely to be realized: *has fond hopes of becoming prime minister.*

fondant *noun* **1** a creamy, thick paste made of sugar and water, used as an icing or filling. **2** a candy made of or filled with this paste. [Say FOND'nt]

fondle *verb* (**fondles, fondled, fondling**) **1** touch or stroke lovingly; caress. **2** sexually molest (a person) by touching etc.

fondly *adverb* **1** in a way that shows great affection: *he looked at her fondly.* **2** in a hopeful way that is silly or unreasonable: *I fondly imagined that you cared for me.*

fondness *noun* **1** affection or tenderness. **2** an inclination for: *a fondness for chocolate.*

fondue *noun* **1** a dish of flavoured melted cheese into which cubes of bread are dipped. **2** any other dish in which pieces of food are dipped into hot oil or sauce. [Say fon DOO]

font[1] *noun* **1** a receptacle in a church for baptismal water. **2** the reservoir for oil in a lamp.

font[2] *noun* **1** a selection of type of one face and size. **2** a set of letters, numbers, and symbols of a unified design and given size that may be displayed on a computer screen or printed out.

fontina *noun* a mild, semi-soft to firm, pale yellow cow's milk cheese. [Say fon TEENA]

food *noun* **1** any substance that can be taken into the body to maintain life and growth; nourishment (also as an *adjective*: *food grain* ◊ *food fish*). **2** solid nourishment, as opposed to drink. **3** a nutritive substance absorbed by a plant from the earth or air. **4** ideas as a resource for or stimulus to mental work: *food for thought.*

food bank *noun* a charitable institution which provides food to the needy.

food chain *noun* a hierarchy of organisms in which each feeds on those below and is the source of food for those above.

food court *noun* an area, esp. in a shopping mall, with a variety of fast-food stalls surrounding a shared area with tables and chairs.

foodie *noun* *informal* a person who is interested in esp. exotic or trendy food; a gourmet.

foodland *noun* *Cdn* farmland; land that is or may be used for the production of food.

food poisoning *noun* illness due to bacteria or other toxins in food.

food processor *noun* a domestic kitchen appliance for chopping, grating, slicing, blending, or mixing.

foodstuff *noun* any substance suitable as food.

food web *noun* the system of interdependent food chains in a community.

fool • *noun* a person who acts unwisely or imprudently; a stupid person. • *verb* **1** deceive so as to cause to appear foolish. **2** trick; cause to do something foolish. **3** act in a joking, frivolous, or teasing way. • *adjective informal* foolish, silly. PHRASES **act** (or **play**) **the fool** behave in a silly way. **fool around 1** behave in a playful or silly way. **2 a** engage in sexual activity. **b** engage in adulterous sexual activity. **3** waste time. **fool with** handle idly; play with carelessly. **make a fool of** make (a person or oneself) look foolish; trick or deceive. **no** (or **nobody's**) **fool** a shrewd or prudent person.

foolhardiness *noun* the condition or quality of being rashly or foolishly bold; recklessness.

foolhardy *adjective* (**foolhardier, foolhardiest**) rashly or foolishly bold; reckless.

foolish *adjective* (of a person, action, etc.) lacking good sense or judgment; unwise. ▶**foolishly** *adverb* **foolishness** *noun*

foolproof *adjective* so straightforward or simple as to be incapable of misuse or mistake.

foolscap *noun* a type of usu. lined writing paper measuring $8\frac{1}{2}$ by 14 inches (22 by 35.5 cm). [Say FULL scap or FOOLS cap]

fool's gold *noun* iron pyrites.

foot • *noun* (*plural* **feet**) **1 a** the lower extremity of the leg below the ankle. **b** the part of a sock etc. covering the foot. **2 a** the lower or lowest part of anything, e.g. a mountain, a page, stairs, etc. **b** the lower end of a table. **c** the end of a bed where the user's feet normally rest. **d** a part of a chair, appliance, etc. on which it rests. **3** the base, often projecting, of anything extending vertically. **4** a step, pace, or tread; a manner of walking: *fleet of foot.* **5** (*plural* **feet** or **foot**) a unit of linear measure equal to 12 inches (30.48 cm). **6** (in poetry) a group of syllables (one usu. stressed) constituting a metrical unit. **7** the part of the body of an invertebrate by which it moves or sticks to things. **8** the part by which a petal is attached. • *verb* **1** (usu. as **foot it**) **a** traverse (esp. a long distance) by foot. **b** dance. **2** pay (a bill). PHRASES **feet of clay** a fundamental weakness in a person otherwise revered. **get off on the wrong** (or **right**) **foot** make a bad (or good) start. **get one's feet wet** begin to participate. **have one's** (or **both**) **feet on the ground** be practical. **have a foot in the door** have a prospect of success. **have one foot in the grave** be near death or very old. **my foot!** *interjection* expressing strong contradiction. **not put a foot wrong** make no mistakes. **off one's feet** so as to be unable to stand, or in a state compared with this: *was rushed off my feet.* **on foot** walking, not driving or riding etc. **on one's feet 1** standing. **2** completely recovered from an illness or time of trouble. **3** in motion: *fast on one's feet.* **put one's best foot forward** make every effort; proceed with determination. **put one's feet up**

informal take a rest. **put one's foot down** *informal* **1** be firmly insistent or repressive. **2** accelerate a motor vehicle. **put one's foot in one's mouth** (also **put one's foot in it**) *informal* commit a blunder or indiscretion. **set foot in** (or **on**) enter; go into. **think on one's feet** think or react rapidly under stress etc. **under foot 1** on the ground. **2** in the way.

footage *noun* **1** length or distance in feet. **2** an amount of film made for showing, broadcasting, etc.

foot-and-mouth disease *noun* a contagious viral disease of cattle etc., characterized by ulceration of the hoofs and around the mouth.

football *noun* **1** a game in which each of two teams attempts to move a ball across the other's goal line, esp.: **a** *Cdn* = CANADIAN FOOTBALL. **b** *US* = AMERICAN FOOTBALL. **2** a large inflated ball of a kind used in these. **3** a topical issue or problem that is the subject of continued argument or controversy: *the funding issue became a political football during the election.* ▶ **footballer** *noun*

footboard *noun* **1** a board to support the feet or a foot. **2** an upright board at the foot of a bed.

footbridge *noun* a bridge for use by pedestrians.

foot-dragger *noun* a person who shows deliberate slowness or reluctance to act or proceed.

foot-dragging *noun* deliberate slowness or reluctance to act or proceed.

footed *adjective* (also in *combination*) having feet, esp. of a specified kind or number: *four-footed* ◊ *web-footed*.

footer *noun* **1** (in *combination*) a person or thing of so many feet in length or height: *six-footer*. **2** a line or block of text appearing at the foot of each page of a document etc.

footfall *noun* the sound of a footstep.

foothill *noun* (often in *plural*) any of the low hills at the base of a mountain or mountain range.

foothold *noun* **1** a place, esp. in climbing, where a foot can be supported securely. **2** a secure initial position.

footing *noun* **1** a foothold; a secure position: *lost her footing*. **2** the basis on which an enterprise is established or operates; the position or status of a person in relation to others: *on an equal footing*. **3** (usu. in *plural*) the part of a foundation resting directly on the earth.

footlights *plural noun* a row of lights along the front of a stage at the level of the performers' feet.

footloose *adjective* (often in phr. **footloose and fancy-free**) free to go where or act as one pleases.

footman *noun* (*plural* **footmen**) a male servant in a house in the past, who opened the door to visitors, served food at table, etc.

footnote • *noun* **1** a note printed at the foot of a page referring to a marked part of the text on the page. **2** an event, comment, etc. that is added or subordinated to something more central or important: *a footnote to history*. • *verb* (**footnotes**, **footnoted**, **footnoting**) supply with a footnote or footnotes.

footpad *noun* **1** *hist.* a highway robber on foot rather than mounted on a horse. **2** one of the pads on the sole of an animal's foot.

footpath *noun* a path for walking along.

footprint *noun* **1** the impression left by a foot or shoe. **2** the area over which an aircraft is audible, a broadcast can be received, etc. **3** the surface area taken up by something, such as a computer etc.

foot race *noun* a running race.

footrest *noun* a support for the feet or a foot.

footsie *noun informal* PHRASES **play footsie with a person** touch or caress a person's feet lightly with one's own feet, usu. under a table, as a playful expression of affection or sexual interest.

foot soldier *noun* **1** a soldier who fights on foot; an infantry soldier. **2** a person who works for a cause at the basic level rather than in the leadership.

footstep *noun* **1** a step taken in walking. **2** the sound of this. **3** a footprint. PHRASES **follow** (or **tread**) **in a person's footsteps** do as another person did.

footstool *noun* a stool for resting the feet on.

footwear *noun* anything worn on the feet.

footwork *noun* the use of the feet, esp. skilfully, in sports, dancing, etc.

foo yong *noun* a Chinese dish or sauce made with eggs mixed and cooked with other ingredients. [Say foo YONG]

fop *noun* an affectedly elegant or fashionable man; a dandy. ▶ **foppish** *adjective*

for • *preposition* **1** in the interest or to the benefit of; intended to go to: *these flowers are for you* ◊ *wish to see it for myself*. **2** in defence, support, or favour of: *fight for one's rights*. **3** suitable or appropriate to: *a dance for beginners*. **4** with reference to; regarding; so far as concerns: *don't care for him* ◊ *MP for Winnipeg North*. **5** representing or in place of: *here for my uncle*. **6** in exchange against: *swapped it for a bigger one*. **7 a** as the price of: *give me $5 for it*. **b** at the price of: *bought it for $20*. **c** to the amount of: *a bill for $100*. **8** as the penalty of: *fined heavily for it*. **9** in requital of: *that's for upsetting my sister*. **10** as a reward for: *here's $10 for your trouble*. **11 a** with a view to; in the hope or quest of; in order to get: *go for a walk* ◊ *run for a doctor*. **b** on account of: *could not speak for laughing*. **12** corresponding to: *word for word*. **13** to reach; in the direction of; towards: *left for Fredericton*. **14** conducive to; in order to achieve: *take the pills for a sound night's sleep*. **15** so as to start promptly at: *the meeting is at seven-thirty for eight*. **16** through or over (a distance or period); during: *sang for two hours*. **17** in the character of; as being: *knew it for a lie* ◊ *I for one refuse*. **18** because of; on account of: *could not speak for tears*. **19** in spite of; notwithstanding: *for all your fine words*. **20** considering or making due allowance with regard to: *good for a beginner*. • *conjunction* because, since.

forage • *noun* **1** food for cattle etc., esp. hay or grass. **2** a wide search over an area to obtain something, esp. food or provisions. • *verb* (**forages**, **foraged**, **foraging**) go searching; rummage (esp. for food). ▶ **forager** *noun* [Say FOR idge]

foray *noun* **1** a sudden attack; a raid. **2** a brief, vigorous attempt to be involved in a different activity, profession, etc.: *a brief foray into computer science*. [Say FOR ay]

forb *noun* any herbaceous plant other than a grass.

forbear[1] *verb* (**forbears**; *past* **forbore**; *past participle* **forborne**; **forbearing**) *literary* stop oneself from saying or doing something that one could or would like to say or do: *could not forbear from speaking out* ◊ *she forbore to ask any further questions*. [Say for BARE]

> **SPELL CHECK**
> **forbear, forebear**
>
> The usual Canadian spelling for an ancestor is **forebear**.

forbear[2] *noun* = FOREBEAR. [Say FOR bare]

forbearance *noun* patient self-control; tolerance: *her screaming nieces severely tested her forbearance*.

forbid *verb* (**forbids**; *past* **forbade** or **forbad**; *past participle* **forbidden**; **forbidding**) **1** order not: *I forbid you to go*. **2** refuse to allow (a thing, or a person to have a thing): *I forbid it*. **3** refuse a person entry to: *the gardens are forbidden to children*. PHRASES **God** (or **heaven**) **forbid** may it not happen! ▶ **forbidden** *adjective* [For *forbade* say either for BADE or for BAD]

forbidding *adjective* seeming unfriendly and frightening: *the house looked dark and forbidding.*

force • *noun* **1** power; exerted strength. **2** coercion or compulsion, esp. with the use or threat of violence. **3 a** military strength. **b** (in *plural*) troops; fighting resources. **c** (**Forces**) = CANADIAN FORCES. **d** an organized body of people, esp. soldiers, police, or workers. **4** binding power; validity. **5** effect; precise significance: *the force of their words.* **6** mental or moral strength; influence: *force of habit.* **7** *Physics* **a** an influence tending to cause the motion of a body. **b** the intensity of this equal to the mass of the body and its acceleration. **8** a person or thing regarded as exerting influence: *a force for good.* **9** *Baseball* = FORCEOUT. • *verb* (**forces**, **forced**, **forcing**) **1** constrain (a person) by force or against his or her will. **2** make a way through or into by force; break open by force. **3** drive or propel violently or against resistance. **4** impose or press (on a person): *forced their views on us.* **5 a** cause or produce by effort: *forced a smile.* **b** attain by strength or effort: *forced an entry.* **c** make (a way) by force. **6** strain or increase to the utmost. **7** artificially hasten the development or maturity of (a plant). **8** seek or demand quick results from; accelerate the process of: *force the pace.* **9 force oneself on** rape: *forced himself on her.* **10** *Baseball* **a** cause (a runner) to be put out in a forceout. **b** cause (a runner or run) to score or be scored, esp. by walking a batter with the bases full. PHRASES **by force of** by means of. **force a person's hand** make a person act prematurely or unwillingly. **force the issue** render an immediate decision necessary. **in force 1** valid, effective. **2** in great strength or numbers. **join forces** combine efforts.

forced *adjective* **1** compelled, imposed, or obtained by force; compulsory: *forced labour.* **2** produced or maintained with effort; strained, unnatural: *a forced smile.* **3** required by emergency or necessity: *a forced landing.* **4** produced or supplied by artificial means: *forced air.* **5** (of a plant, crop, etc.) made to bear, or produced, out of the proper season.

force-feed *verb* (**force-feeds**, **force-fed**, **force-feeding**) **1** force (a person or animal) to take food. **2** compel (a person) to absorb or assimilate propaganda, opinions, etc.

force field *noun* (in science fiction) an invisible barrier of force.

forceful *adjective* **1** vigorous, powerful. **2** (of speech) compelling. ▶ **forcefully** *adverb* **forcefulness** *noun*

forceout *noun* *Baseball* (also **force play**) a play in which a runner is put out after being forced (by another runner) to advance when he or she is unable to do so safely.

forceps *noun* (*plural* **forceps**) a surgical tool for grasping and holding, resembling scissors but with blunt grasping ends instead of blades.

forcible *adjective* done by or involving force: *forcible confinement.* ▶ **forcibly** *adverb*

ford • *noun* a shallow place where a river or stream may be crossed by wading or in a vehicle. • *verb* cross (water) at a ford.

fore • *adjective* situated in front. • *noun* the front part, esp. of a ship; the bow. • *interjection* *Golf* a warning to a person in the path of a ball. PHRASES **to the fore** in front; conspicuous.

fore and aft • *adverb* at both front and rear; going from front to rear. • *adjective* (**fore-and-aft**) **1** (of a sail or rigging) set lengthwise, not on the yards. **2** backwards and forwards. **3** (*BC* & *US Northwest*) designating a logging road constructed of logs laid end to end.

forearm *noun* **1** the part of the arm from the elbow to the wrist or the fingertips. **2** the corresponding part in a foreleg or wing.

forebear *noun* (also **forbear**) (usu. in *plural*) an ancestor. [Say FOR bare]

foreboding • *noun* an expectation of trouble or evil; an omen: *the sound of her voice made my entire body tense with foreboding.* • *adjective* threatening, esp. evil: *the castle looked dark and foreboding.* ▶ **forebodingly** *adverb*

forecast • *verb* (**forecasts**; *past* and *past participle* **forecast** or **forecasted**; **forecasting**) predict; estimate or calculate beforehand. • *noun* a calculation or estimate of something future, esp. coming weather. ▶ **forecaster** *noun* **forecasting** *noun*

forecastle *noun* (also **fo'c'sle**) the forward part of a ship where the crew has its lodgings. [Say FOKE s'll]

forecheck *verb* *Hockey* (of a player or team) play an aggressive style of defence, checking opposing players before they can organize an attack. ▶ **forechecker** *noun* **forechecking** *noun*

foreclose *verb* (**forecloses**, **foreclosed**, **foreclosing**) **1** (esp. of a bank) take control of someone's property because they have not paid their mortgage: *the bank foreclosed on Jake's ranch and broke it up into smaller parcels.* **2** reject something as a possibility; exclude: *the judge's words effectively foreclosed any possibility of an early release.* ▶ **foreclosure** *noun*

foredeck *noun* **1** the deck at the forward part of a ship. **2** the forward part of the deck.

forefather *noun* (usu. in *plural*) **1** an ancestor. **2** a member of a past generation of a family or people.

forefinger *noun* the finger next to the thumb.

forefoot *noun* (*plural* **forefeet**) **1** either of the front feet of an animal. **2** the front part of the human foot.

forefront *noun* **1** the foremost part. **2** the leading position.

foregoing *adjective* preceding; previously mentioned.

foregone conclusion *noun* an easily foreseen or predictable result.

foreground • *noun* **1** the part of a view, esp. in a picture, that is nearest the observer. **2** the most conspicuous position. • *verb* place in the foreground; make prominent.

forehand *noun* **1** *Tennis etc.* a stroke played with the palm of the hand facing the opponent. **2** the part of a horse in front of the seated rider.

forehead *noun* the part of the face above the eyebrows.

foreign *adjective* **1** of or from or situated in or characteristic of a country or a language other than one's own. **2** dealing with other countries: *foreign service.* **3** of another district, society, etc. **4** (often foll. by *to*) unfamiliar, strange, uncharacteristic: *her*

F

behaviour is foreign to me. **5** coming from outside: *removed a foreign body from her eye*.

foreign affairs *plural noun* the activities and interests of a nation that involve its relations with other nations.

foreign aid *noun* money, food, etc. given or lent by one country to another.

foreigner *noun* **1** a person born in or coming from a country other than one's own. **2** *informal* a person not belonging to a particular place or group; a stranger or outsider: *I am still regarded as a foreigner by the locals*.

foreign exchange *noun* **1** the currency of other countries. **2** dealings in these.

foreign legion *noun* a body of foreign volunteers in a modern, esp. the French, army.

foreign minister *noun* (also **foreign secretary**) esp. *Brit.* a government minister in charge of his or her country's relations with other countries.

foreignness *noun* the condition or quality of being of or from or situated in or characteristic of a country or a language other than one's own.

foreign service *noun* the branch of a national government concerned with the official representation of a country abroad by diplomats etc.

foreknow *verb* (**foreknows**; *past* **foreknew**; *past participle* **foreknown**; **foreknowing**) know beforehand.

foreknowledge *noun* knowledge of something before it happens: *did anyone have foreknowledge of the attack on Pearl Harbour?*

foreleg *noun* each of the front legs of a quadruped.

forelimb *noun* any of the front limbs of an animal.

forelock *noun* a lock of hair growing just above the forehead. PHRASES **touch** (or **tug** etc.) **one's forelock** defer to a person of higher social rank.

foreman *noun* (*plural* **foremen**) **1** a worker with supervisory responsibilities. **2** the member of a jury who presides over its deliberations and speaks for it.

foremost ● adjective the most notable; first in status or position: *the world's foremost authority on the subject*. **● adverb** in the first place: *first and foremost*.

foremother *noun* (usu. in *plural*) a female ancestor or predecessor.

forensic ● adjective 1 of or used in connection with courts of law, esp. in relation to crime detection: *forensic evidence*. **2** of or employing forensic science. **● noun** (usu. in *plural*) **1** forensic science. **2** a forensic science department, esp. as part of a police force. [Say fuh REN zick]

forensic accountant *noun* an accountant who investigates matters of fraud, embezzlement, etc. and prepares an analysis of financial information suitable for use in court.

forensic accounting *noun* the use of accounting skills to investigate matters of fraud, embezzlement, etc. and to prepare an analysis of financial information suitable for use in court.

forensic science *noun* the application of scientific knowledge to the investigation of crime, e.g. the analysis of tissue samples found at the scene of a crime.

forepart *noun* the foremost part; the front.

foreperson *noun* (*plural* **forepersons** or **forepeople**) **1** a worker with supervisory responsibilities. **2** the member of a jury who presides over its deliberations and speaks on its behalf.

foreplay *noun* stimulation preceding sexual intercourse.

forerunner *noun* a person or thing that came before and influenced someone or something else that is similar; a sign of what is going to happen: *country music was undoubtedly one of the forerunners of rock and roll.*

foresee *verb* (**foresees**; *past* **foresaw**; *past participle*

foreseen; **foreseeing**) see or be aware of beforehand. **▶ foreseeability** *noun* **foreseeable** *adjective*

foreshadow *verb* **1** be a sign or warning of something that will happen in the future: *the loss in the by-election foreshadowed defeat in the next general election*. **2** (of an event in a novel etc.) be an indication or sign of later events: *the shattering of the family portrait rather clumsily foreshadowed the breakup of the family itself through the course of the novel*. **▶ foreshadowing** *noun*

foreshore *noun* the part of the shore between high- and low-water marks, or between the water and cultivated or developed land.

foreshorten *verb* show or portray (an object) with the apparent shortening due to visual perspective. **▶ foreshortening** *noun*

foresight *noun* the ability to predict what is likely to happen and to use this to prepare for the future: *she had had the foresight to prepare herself financially in case of an accident*.

foreskin *noun* the fold of skin covering the end of the penis.

forest *noun* **1** a large area covered chiefly with trees and undergrowth. **2** a large number or dense mass of vertical objects: *a forest of tall buildings*. PHRASES **not see the forest for the trees** be unable to perceive or understand the overall situation because one is preoccupied with details.

forestall *verb* **1** act in advance of (someone) in order to prevent them from doing something: *she made to rise but Erika forestalled her and greeted him first*. **2** prevent or obstruct (an anticipated event or action) by taking action ahead of time: *they will present their resignations to forestall a vote of no confidence*. [Say for STALL]

forestation *noun* the establishing of a forest.

forested *adjective* covered in forest: *thickly forested hills*.

forester *noun* **1** a person in charge of a forest or skilled in forestry. **2** (**Forester**) a member of the Independent Order of Foresters, an organization of men devoted to charitable activities.

forest fire *noun* an uncontrolled fire in a forest.

forest floor *noun* the ground in a forest, specifically the layer of more or less decayed organic debris forming the upper soil of a forest.

forest green *noun & adjective* a dark green colour.

forestland *noun* land that is covered with forest.

forest ranger *noun* an official who patrols, manages, and protects a public forest.

forestry *noun* the science and practice of planting, caring for, and managing forests.

foretaste *noun* a small experience of something before it actually happens; a sample in anticipation.

foretell *verb* (**foretells**; **foretold**; **foretelling**) tell of or presage (an event etc.) before it takes place.

forethought *noun* careful thought to make sure that things are successful in the future: *he had had the forethought to book in advance*.

forever ● adverb 1 for all future time; in perpetuity. **2** continually, persistently: *is forever complaining*. **3** *informal* for an extremely long time: *talked on the phone forever*. **● noun** *informal* an extremely long time.

forevermore *adverb* an emphatic form of FOREVER *adverb* 1.

forewarn *verb* warn beforehand. PHRASES **forewarned is forearmed** knowing about problems, dangers, etc. before they happen makes one better prepared for them.

forewing *noun* either of the two front wings of a four-winged insect.

forewoman *noun* (*plural* **forewomen**) **1** a female worker with supervisory responsibilities. **2** a woman who presides over a jury and speaks on its behalf.

> **SPELL CHECK**
> **foreword, forward**
>
> The opposite of *backward* is **forward**.

foreword *noun* introductory remarks at the beginning of a book, often by a person other than the author.

forfeit • *noun* **1** a fine or penalty for wrongdoing or for a breach of rules in clubs etc. or in games. **2** (in *plural*) a game in which forfeits are exacted. **3** something surrendered as a penalty. **4** the process of forfeiting. • *adjective* lost or surrendered as a penalty: *the lands which he had acquired were automatically forfeit*. • *verb* (**forfeits, forfeited, forfeiting**) lose the right to, be deprived of, or have to pay as a penalty: *forfeited their deposit ◊ had to forfeit the game*. [Say FOR fit]

forfeiture *noun* Law the act of forfeiting something: *the forfeiture of property*. [Say FOR fit chur]

forgave *past of* FORGIVE.

forge¹ • *verb* (**forges, forged, forging**) **1** write (a document or signature) in order to pass it off as written by another. **2** create or devise (an alliance, bond, etc.). **3** shape (esp. metal) by heating in a fire and hammering. • *noun* **1** a blacksmith's workshop. **2** a furnace or hearth for melting or refining metal.

forge² *verb* (**forges, forged, forging**) move forward gradually or steadily. PHRASES **forge ahead 1** take the lead in a race. **2** move forward or make progress rapidly.

forger *noun* a person who makes illegal copies of money, documents, etc. in order to deceive people.

forgery *noun* (*plural* **forgeries**) **1** the action of forging, counterfeiting, or falsifying a document etc. **2** a forged or spurious thing, esp. a document, signature, banknote, or work of art.

> **WRITING TIP**
> **forget, forgotten**
>
> Some people say *I haven't forgot about our meeting*, but it is better to say *I haven't forgotten about our meeting*.

forget *verb* (**forgets**; *past* **forgot**; *past participle* **forgotten** or **forgot**; **forgetting**) **1** not remember: *forgot to come ◊ forgot how to do it*. **2** inadvertently omit to bring or mention or attend to. **3** put out of mind; cease to think of: *forgive and forget*. PHRASES **forget (about) it!** *informal* take no more notice of it; there is no need for apology or thanks. **forget oneself 1** neglect one's own interests. **2** act unbecomingly or unworthily. ▶ **forgettable** *adjective*

forgetful *adjective* apt to forget; absent-minded. ▶ **forgetfully** *adjective* **forgetfulness** *noun*

forget-me-not *noun* **1** a low-growing plant with small yellow-eyed bright blue flowers. **2** any of several Rocky Mountain plants of the borage family.

forging *noun* **1** an act of creating a copy of something for the purposes of deception. **2** the process of shaping metal by heating in a fire and hammering.

forgivable *adjective* that can be understood and forgiven: *his rudeness was forgivable in the circumstances*.

forgive *verb* (**forgives**; *past* **forgave**; *past participle* **forgiven**; **forgiving**) **1** cease to feel angry or resentful towards; pardon (an offender or offence). **2** remit or let off (a debt or debtor). ▶ **forgiveness** *noun*

forgiving *adjective* **1** inclined readily to forgive. **2** tolerant; accepting of differences in ability etc.: *is forgiving of beginners*. ▶ **forgivingly** *adverb*

> **SPELL CHECK**
> **forgo, foregoing, foregone**
>
> A predictable result is a "**foregone** conclusion". In written passages, something just mentioned may be referred to as "the **foregoing**".

forgo *verb* (**forgoes**; *past* **forwent**; *past participle* **forgone**; **forgoing**) omit or decline to take or use (a pleasure, advantage, etc.); go without: *no one was prepared to forgo their lunch hour to attend the meeting*.

forgot *past of* FORGET.

forgotten *past participle of* FORGET.

fork • *noun* **1** an implement with two or more prongs used for holding food. **2** a similar much larger instrument used for digging, lifting, etc. **3** any pronged device or component: *tuning fork*. **4** a forked support for a bicycle wheel. **5 a** a divergence of anything, e.g. a stick, road, or river, into two parts. **b** the place where this occurs. **c** either of the two parts: *take the left fork*. **d** a major tributary of a river. **e** (in *plural*) the confluence of two rivers and the surrounding area: *the forks of the Red and the Assiniboine*. **6** a flash of forked lightning. • *verb* **1** form a fork or branch by separating into two parts. **2** take one or the other road etc. at a fork. **3** dig or lift etc. with a fork. PHRASES **fork out** (or **up**) *informal* hand over or pay, usu. reluctantly. **fork over 1** *informal* = FORK OUT. **2** turn over (soil etc.) with a fork.

forkball *noun* Baseball a pitch in which the ball is held with the thumb, index finger, and middle finger spread.

forked *adjective* (also in *combination*) having a divided or pronged end or branches: *a deeply forked tail*.

forked lightning *noun* a lightning flash in the form of a zigzag or branching line.

forkful *noun* (*plural* **forkfuls**) the amount that a fork holds: *scooped up a forkful of mashed potato*.

forklift *noun* (also **forklift truck**) a vehicle with a horizontal fork in front for lifting and carrying loads.

forlorn *adjective* **1** sad and abandoned or lonely. **2** pitiful state; of wretched appearance. **3** hopeless, forsaken. ▶ **forlornly** *adverb* [Say for LORN]

form • *noun* **1** shape. **2** the mode in which a thing exists or manifests itself: *detergent in liquid form*. **3 a** a kind: *different forms of government*. **b** an artistic or literary genre: *sonnet form*. **4** a printed document with blank spaces for information to be inserted. **5** what is usually done: *common form*. **6** a set order of words; a formula. **7** behaviour according to a rule or custom. **8** (**the form**) correct procedure: *knows the form*. **9** (of an athlete, horse, etc.) condition of health and training: *is in top form*. **10** general state or disposition: *was in great form*. **11** formality or mere ceremony. **12** Grammar **a** one of the ways in which a word may be spelled or pronounced or inflected. **b** the external characteristics of words apart from their meaning. **13 a** arrangement and expression of ideas esp. in the arts. **b** style in literary or musical composition. **14** a mould, frame, or block in or on which something is shaped. • *verb* **1** make into or take a certain shape. **2** be the material of; make up or constitute: *forms part of the structure*. **3** train or instruct. **4** develop or establish as a concept, institution, or practice: *form an idea ◊ formed an alliance*. **5** (foll. by *into*) embody, organize. **6** come or bring into existence; take shape or develop. ▶ **formable** *adjective*

formal • *adjective* **1** used or done or held in accordance with rules, convention, or ceremony: *a formal occasion*. **2** ceremonial; required by convention: *a formal call*. **3** precise or symmetrical: *a formal garden*. **4** prim or stiff in manner. **5** perfunctory, having the form without the spirit. **6** valid or correctly so called

F

because of its form; explicit and definite: *a formal agreement*. **7** in accordance with recognized forms or rules. **8** (of education) officially given at a school, university, etc. **9** of or concerned with (outward) form or appearance, esp. as distinct from content or matter. • *noun* **1** a dance etc. to which evening dress is worn. **2** an evening gown. ▶ **formally** *adverb*

formaldehyde *noun* a colourless, pungent, toxic gas used as a disinfectant and preservative and in the manufacture of resins. [Say for MALDA hide]

formalism *noun* a style or method in art, music, literature, science, religion, etc. that pays more attention to the rules and the correct arrangement and appearance of things than to inner meaning and feelings: *the defence of formalism is always that it serves to control an excess of feeling*. ▶ **formalist** *noun*

formality *noun* (*plural* **formalities**) **1 a** a formal or ceremonial act, requirement of etiquette, regulation, or custom (often with an implied lack of real significance). **b** a thing done simply to comply with a rule. **2** the rigid observance of rules or convention. **3** ceremony; elaborate procedure. **4** being formal; precision of manners.

formalization *noun* the process of giving definite shape or legal formality to something.

formalize *verb* (**formalizes**, **formalized**, **formalizing**) **1** give legal or formal status to: *we would like to have a contract so that we can formalize our arrangement*. **2** give something a definite structure or shape: *we tried to formalize our thoughts*.

formal wear *noun* clothes customarily worn on formal occasions, e.g. tuxedos or evening dresses.

format • *noun* **1** the shape and size of a book, periodical, etc. **2** the style or manner of an arrangement, design or procedure. **3** *Computing* a defined structure for holding data etc. in a record for processing or storage. • *verb* (**formats**, **formatted**, **formatting**) **1** arrange or put into a format. **2** *Computing* prepare (a storage medium) to receive data.

formation *noun* **1** the action of forming; the process of being formed: *the formation of the Great Lakes*. **2** a structure or arrangement of parts: *a cloud formation*. **3** a particular arrangement, e.g. of troops, aircraft in flight, etc.: *battle formation* ◊ *flew in formation*. **4** an assemblage of rocks or series of strata having some common characteristic.

formative *adjective* having an important and lasting influence upon (a person's character etc.): *a child's formative years*.

former • *adjective* **1** of or occurring in the past or an earlier period: *in former times*. **2** having been previously: *her former husband*. • *noun* (**the former**) the first or first mentioned of two (*opp.* LATTER *noun*).

formerly *adverb* in the past; in former times.

form-fitting *adjective* = CLOSE-FITTING.

Formica *noun* proprietary a hard durable plastic laminate used for working surfaces etc. [Say for MIKE uh]

formidable *adjective* inspiring fear or respect through being impressively large, powerful, intense, or capable: *in debate she was a formidable opponent* ◊ *the two players together make a formidable combination* ◊ *had to overcome formidable obstacles*. ▶ **formidably** *adverb* [Say for MIDDA bull or FOR midda bull]

formless *adjective* shapeless; without determinate or regular form. ▶ **formlessness** *noun*

form letter *noun* a standardized letter to deal with frequently occurring matters.

formula *noun* (*plural* **formulas** or (esp. in senses 1, 2) **formulae**) **1** a set of chemical symbols showing the constituents of a substance and their relative proportions. **2** a series of letters, numbers, or symbols that represent a mathematical rule or law: *the formula πr^2 is used to calculate the area of a circle*. **3 a** a fixed form of words, esp. one used on social or ceremonial occasions: *a legal formula*. **b** a rule unintelligently or slavishly followed; an established or conventional usage (also as an *adjective*: *formula fiction*). **c** a statement, procedure, or method for achieving something, esp. reconciling different aims or opinions: *they're trying to work out a peace formula acceptable to both sides in the dispute* ◊ *there's no magic formula for a perfect marriage*. **4 a** a list of ingredients or a preparation made according to such a list: *the secret formula for the blending of the whisky* ◊ *an original coal tar formula that prevents dandruff*. **b** an infant's liquid food preparation, given as a substitute for breast milk. **5** a classification of race car, esp. by the engine capacity. [For *formulae* say FOR mew lee]

formulaic *adjective* **1** being or containing a verbal formula or set form of words: *a formulaic greeting*. **2** produced in accordance with a slavishly followed rule or style; predictable: *much romantic fiction is stylized, formulaic, and unrealistic*. [Say for mew LAY ick]

formulate *verb* (**formulates**, **formulated**, **formulating**) **1** make according to a formula: *this new kitchen cleaner is formulated to cut through grease and dirt*. **2** express clearly and precisely: *she has lots of good ideas, but she has difficulty formulating them*. **3** devise, create: *formulate a plan*. ▶ **formulation** *noun*

fornicate *verb* (**fornicates**, **fornicated**, **fornicating**) (of people not married or not married to each other) have sexual intercourse. ▶ **fornication** *noun* **fornicator** *noun*

for-profit *adjective* designating an institution run with the aim of making a profit, esp. one providing public service: *for-profit child care*.

forsake *verb* (**forsakes**; *past* **forsook**; *past participle* **forsaken**; **forsaking**) **1** give up; renounce: *she forsook the glamour of the city and went to live in northern Manitoba*. **2** withdraw one's help, friendship, or companionship from: *he swore he would never forsake her*.

SPELL CHECK   ⬛ABC✓
foresee

Warning: do not forget the *e* before the *s* in **foresee**.

---

forsythia *noun* an ornamental shrub bearing yellow flowers in early spring. [Say for SITH ee uh]

fort *noun* **1** a fortified building or position. **2** *hist.* a trading post, originally fortified.

forte[1] *noun* a person's strong point; a thing in which a person excels: *languages were never my forte*. [Say FOR tay]

forte[2] • *adjective* performed loudly. • *adverb* loudly. [Say FOR tay]

fortepiano *noun* (*plural* **fortepianos**) *Music* a piano made in the 18th or early 19th century. [Say fortay PIANO]

SPELL CHECK   ⬛ABC✓
forth, fourth

After *third* comes **fourth**.

---

forth *adverb* (only in set phrases and after certain verbs, esp. *bring*, *come*, *go*, and *set*) **1** forward; into view. **2** onward in time: *from this time forth* ◊ *henceforth*. **3** forwards. **4** out from a starting point: *set forth*. ▪ PHRASES **and so forth** and so on; and the like.

forthcoming *adjective* **1** about or likely to appear or happen: *the forthcoming elections* ◊ *a list of forthcoming books*. **2** produced when wanted: *no reply was forthcoming*. **3** (of a person) informative, responsive: *wasn't very forthcoming when asked about my boyfriend*.

forthright *adjective* direct and outspoken;

straightforward: *a woman of forthright views*.
▶**forthrightly** *adverb* **forthrightness** *noun*
forthwith *adverb* (esp. in official use) immediately: *the agreement between us is terminated forthwith*.
fortieth *ordinal number* corresponding to forty.
fortification *noun* **1** the action of fortifying; the process of being fortified: *the fortification of the frontiers*. **2** (usu. in *plural*) a defensive wall or other reinforcement built to strengthen a place against attack.
fortify *verb* (**fortifies, fortified, fortifying**) **1** provide or equip with defensive works so as to strengthen against attack: *a fortified town*. **2** strengthen or invigorate mentally or morally; encourage: *he fortified himself against the cold with a stiff brandy* ◊ *although fortified by its election success, the government remains cautious in its policies*. **3** strengthen the structure of. **4** strengthen (wine) with alcohol: *sherry and vermouth are fortified wines*. **5** increase the nutritive value of (food, esp. with vitamins).
fortissimo *Music* • *adjective* performed very loudly. • *adverb* very loudly. [Say for TISSA moe]
fortitude *noun* moral strength or courage, esp. in the endurance of pain or adversity.
fortnight *noun* a period of two weeks.
fortnightly *esp. Brit.* • *adjective* done, produced, or occurring once a fortnight. • *adverb* every fortnight.
Fortran *noun* (also **FORTRAN**) a high-level programming language used esp. for scientific calculations.
fortress *noun* (*plural* **fortresses**) **1** a military stronghold, esp. a strongly fortified town fit for a large garrison. **2** any place or source of refuge, security, or protection: *the western and rural base could no longer be counted on to remain the NDP fortress it had been in the past*.
fortuitous *adjective* due to or characterized by chance, esp. lucky chance: *the similarity between the paintings may not be simply fortuitous* ◊ *from a cash standpoint, the company's timing is fortuitous*. ▶**fortuitously** *adverb* [Say for TOO it us or for TYOO it us]
fortunate *adjective* **1** favoured by fortune; lucky: *I have been fortunate enough to visit many parts of the world as a lecturer*. **2** materially well off: *remember those less fortunate than yourselves*.
fortunately *adverb* **1** luckily, successfully. **2** (qualifying a whole sentence) it is fortunate that.
fortune *noun* **1 a** chance or luck as a force in human affairs. **b** a person's destiny or future; fate. **2** (**Fortune**) this force personified, often as a deity. **3** (in *singular* or *plural*) luck (esp. favourable) that befalls a person or enterprise. **4** good luck. **5** prosperity. **6** great wealth; a huge sum of money. [PHRASES] **tell a person's fortune** make predictions about a person's future.
fortune cookie *noun* a small cookie containing a slip of paper printed with a prediction, joke, etc., served esp. in Chinese restaurants.
fortune teller *noun* a person who claims to predict future events in a person's life. ▶**fortune telling** *noun*
forty *cardinal number* (*plural* **forties**) the product of four and ten. [PHRASES] **forty-first, -second**, etc. the ordinal numbers between fortieth and fiftieth. **forty-one, -two**, etc. the cardinal numbers between forty and fifty.
forty-five *noun* **1** a small phonograph record played at 45 rpm. **2** a .45 calibre revolver. **3** (*Maritimes & New England*) a card game for two to six players in which the player or side first reaching forty-five points wins.
fortyish *adjective* about forty (in age, measurements, etc.).
forty-ninth parallel *noun* the parallel of latitude 49° north of the equator, esp. as forming the boundary between Canada and the US west of Lake of the Woods.

forty-ouncer *noun* (also *Cdn slang* **forty-pounder**) a forty-ounce bottle of liquor.
forum *noun* (*plural* **forums**) **1** a place of or meeting for public discussion: *an international forum on drug abuse* ◊ *television is now an important forum for political debate*. **2** a periodical, television program, etc. giving an opportunity for discussion. **3** a court or tribunal. **4** *hist.* a public square or marketplace in an ancient Roman city used for judicial and other business.

SPELL CHECK
forward, foreword

The introduction to a book is a **foreword**.

---

forward • *adjective* **1** directed or moving towards a point in advance: *a forward movement*. **2 a** situated in front; near or at the front. **b** *Nautical* belonging to the forepart of a ship. **3** bold in manner; presumptuous. **4** *Business* **a** relating to future produce, delivery, etc.: *forward contract*. **b** prospective; advanced; with a view to the future: *forward planning*. **5** advanced; progressing towards or approaching maturity or completion. • *noun* an attacking player positioned near the front of a team in hockey, soccer, etc. • *adverb* **1 a** to the front; into prominence: *come forward*. **b** into a position for consideration or discussion: *bring forward a proposal*. **2** in advance; ahead: *sent them forward*. **3** onward so as to make progress: *not getting any further forward*. **4** towards the future; continuously onward: *from this time forward*. **5** (also **forwards**) **a** towards the front in the direction one is facing. **b** in the normal direction of motion or of placement. **c** with continuous forward motion: *backwards and forwards*. **6** *Nautical & Aviation* in, near, or towards the bow or nose. • *verb* **1** send (a letter etc.) on to a further destination. **2** help to advance; promote. **3** advance (a videotape etc.) forward.
forwarder *noun* a person or organization that dispatches or delivers goods.
forward-looking *adjective* (also **forward-thinking**) progressive; favouring change.
forwardness *noun* behaviour that is too confident or too informal.
forwent *past of* FORGO.
fossil • *noun* **1** the remains or impression of a prehistoric plant or animal, usu. petrified while embedded in rock, amber, etc. (often as an *adjective*: *fossil bones*). **2** *informal* an antiquated or unchanging person or thing: *he can be a cantankerous old fossil at times*. • *adjective* of or like a fossil: *fossil remains*.
fossil fuel *noun* a natural fuel such as coal or gas formed in the geological past from the remains of living organisms.
fossilization *noun* the process or action of becoming a fossil or of preserving (an animal or plant) so that it becomes a fossil.
fossilize *verb* (**fossilizes, fossilized, fossilizing**) **1** preserve (an animal or plant) so that it becomes a fossil: *the hard parts of the body are readily fossilized* ◊ *the fossilized remains of a dinosaur*. **2** become a fossil: *flowers do not readily fossilize*.
foster • *verb* **1 a** promote the growth or development of. **b** encourage or harbour (a feeling). **2** bring up (a child that is not one's own by birth). **3** cherish; have affectionate regard for (an idea, scheme, etc.). • *adjective* **1** having a family connection by fostering and not by birth: *foster child*. **2** involving or concerned with fostering a child: *foster home*.
fought *past and past participle of* FIGHT.

F

SPELL CHECK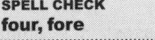
foul, fowl

A turkey is a type of **fowl**.

---

foul • *adjective* **1** offensive to the senses, esp. through having a disgusting smell or taste or being unpleasantly soiled: *his foul breath*. **2** angry or disagreeable: *in a foul mood*. **3 a** containing or charged with noxious matter: *foul air*. **b** clogged, choked. **4** morally offensive: *foul language*. **5 a** unfair; against the rules of a game etc.: *by fair means or foul*. **b** *Baseball* of or relating to a foul ball or foul line. **6** (of the weather) wet, rough, stormy. • *noun* **1** *Sport* a violation of the rules. **2** a collision or entanglement, esp. in riding, rowing, or running. • *adverb* **1** unfairly; contrary to the rules. **2** *Baseball* outside the foul lines: *hit the ball foul*. • *verb* **1** make or become foul or dirty. **2** (of an animal) make dirty with excrement. **3** *Baseball* hit a foul ball. **4** *Sport* commit a foul against a player. **5** (often foll. by *up*) become or cause (an anchor, cable, etc.) to become entangled or muddled. **6** be or become jammed or clogged. **7** (usu. foll. by *up*) *informal* spoil or bungle. PHRASES **cry foul** protest. **foul out 1** *Baseball* (of a batter) be made out by hitting a foul ball which is caught on the fly by a member of the opposing team. **2** *Basketball* be put out of the game for exceeding the permitted number of fouls.

foul ball *noun* *Baseball* a ball struck so that it falls outside the foul lines.

foul line *noun* **1** *Baseball* either of the straight lines extending from home plate and marking the limit of the playing area within which a ball is deemed to be fair. **2** *Basketball* a line on the court 15 ft. (4.6 m) from the backboard, from which free throws are made.

foul-mouthed *adjective* using obscene and offensive language.

foulness *noun* **1** a foul quality or state. **2** a foul substance or deposit.

foul play *noun* **1** *Sport* unfair play. **2** treacherous or violent activity, esp. murder.

foul-up *noun* a muddled or bungled situation.

found[1] *past and past participle of* FIND.

found[2] *verb* **1 a** establish (esp. with an endowment). **b** originate or initiate (an institution, society, etc.). **2** be the original builder or begin the building of (a town etc.). **3** lay the base of (a building etc.). **4** (foll. by *on, upon*) **a** construct or base (a story, theory, rule, etc.) according to a specified principle or ground. **b** have a basis in.

found[3] *verb* melt and mould metal or glass.

foundation *noun* **1** the solid base on which a building rests. **2** a body or ground on which other parts are overlaid. **3** a basis or underlying principle. **4 a** the act of establishing or constituting (esp. an endowed institution) on a permanent basis. **b** an institution, e.g. a monastery, college, or hospital, maintained by an endowment. **c** an organization with a permanent fund devoted to financing research, the arts, and other charitable causes. **d** a fund devoted to the permanent maintenance of an institution or organization; an endowment. **5** (also **foundation garment**) a woman's supporting undergarment, e.g. a bra, girdle, etc. **6** a cosmetic in liquid or powdered form applied to the face as a base for other makeup and to even out skin tone.
▶ **foundational** *adjective*

foundation stone *noun* **1** a stone laid with ceremony to celebrate the founding of a building. **2** the main ground or basis of something.

founder[1] *noun* a person who founds an institution etc.

founder[2] *verb* **1** (of a ship) fill with water and sink.

2 (of a plan etc.) fail. **3** (of earth, a building, etc.) fall down or in, give way. **4** (of a horse or its rider) fall to the ground, fall from lameness, stick fast in mud etc.

founder[3] *noun* a person who manufactures articles of cast metal; the owner or operator of a foundry.

found-in *noun* *Cdn* a person arrested for being discovered in a brothel, an illegal bar, etc.

founding father *noun* a person associated with the founding of something.

foundling *noun* an abandoned infant of unknown parentage.

found object *noun* an object found or picked up at random and presented as a rarity or a work of art.

foundry *noun* (*plural* **foundries**) a factory where metal is melted and moulded into various objects.

fount *noun* a source of a desirable quality or commodity: *our guide was a fount of knowledge*.

fountain *noun* **1 a** a spray or sprays of water made to spout for ornamental purposes. **b** a structure built for this to rise and fall in. **2** a structure for the public supply of drinking water. **3** a source (in physical or abstract senses): *the pills seemed like a virtual fountain of youth in tablet form*. **4** = SODA FOUNTAIN.

fountainhead *noun* a source or origin: *the fountainhead of power*.

fountain pen *noun* a pen with a reservoir or cartridge holding ink.

SPELL CHECK
four, fore

The front part of something is the **fore**. Something that gains a prominent position "comes to the **fore**". **Fore!** is what golfers shout to clear a fairway.

---

four *cardinal number* one more than three. **3** a size etc. denoted by four. PHRASES **on all fours** on hands and knees.

four-and-a-half *noun* (*plural* **four-and-a-halfs**) *Cdn* (*Que.*) an apartment having two bedrooms, a kitchen, a living room, and a bath.

four-by-four *noun* (also **4 × 4** *plural* **4 × 4s**) **1** a four-wheeled automotive vehicle, esp. a truck, with four-wheel drive. **2** a piece of wood measuring four inches by four in cross-section.

four-colour *adjective* (of a printing or photographic process) involving the principle in which three primary colours and black are used in combination to produce almost any other colour.

fourfold *adjective* & *adverb* **1** four times as much or as many. **2** consisting of four parts. **3** amounting to four.

4-H club *noun* a club for the instruction of young people in citizenry and agriculture.

four-leaf clover *noun* a clover leaf with four leaflets, thought to bring good luck.

four-letter word *noun* any of several short words referring to sexual or excretory functions, regarded as coarse or offensive.

four-part *adjective* arranged for four voices to sing or instruments to play.

fourplex *noun* (*plural* **fourplexes**) a residential building divided into four self-contained apartments.

four-poster *noun* (also **four-poster bed**) a bed with a post at each corner supporting a canopy.

foursome *noun* **1** a group of four persons. **2** a golf match between two pairs with partners playing the same ball.

four-square • *adjective* **1** (of a building etc.) square in shape, solid, and strong: *the four-square clarity of the International Style as exemplified in so many office towers*. **2** (of a person) firm, steady, and determined; forthright. • *adverb* resolutely; with determination: *the*

government ministers have all said they stand four-square behind seniors.

four-star *adjective* (of a hotel, restaurant, etc.) given four stars in a grading in which this denotes the highest standard or the next standard to the highest.

four-stroke • *adjective* **1** (of an internal combustion engine) having a cycle of four strokes (intake, compression, combustion, and exhaust). **2** (of a vehicle) having a four-stroke engine. • *noun* a four-stroke engine or vehicle.

fourteen *cardinal number* one more than thirteen. ▶**fourteenth** *ordinal number*

fourth *ordinal number* **1** corresponding to that of the number 4 in the sequence 1–4. **2** a quarter. **3** *Music* **a** an interval or chord spanning four consecutive notes in the diatonic scale, e.g. C to F. **b** a note separated from another by this interval.

fourth estate *noun* (also **Fourth Estate**) the press; journalists or the profession of journalism.

fourth-generation *adjective* (of a computer) distinguished by large-scale integrated-circuit technology and very large rapid-access memory and belonging essentially to the post-1970 period.

fourthly *adverb* used to introduce the fourth of a list of points in a speech or piece of writing.

Fourth World *noun* the poorest nations in the least developed parts of the world, esp. in Africa and Asia.

four-wheel *adjective* **1** having four wheels. **2** acting on all four wheels of a vehicle.

four-wheel drive *noun* a system in a motor vehicle which supplies power to all wheels in order to improve traction, cornering, etc.

four-wheeler *noun* *slang* **1** a four-wheeled all-terrain vehicle. **2** = FOUR-BY-FOUR 1.

fowl (*plural* **fowl** or **fowls**) • *noun* **1** any domestic cock or hen of various birds kept for eggs and meat. **2** the flesh of birds, esp. a domestic cock or hen, as food. **3** a bird or birds collectively: *guinea fowl* ◊ *wildfowl*. • *verb* catch or hunt wildfowl.

fowl supper *noun* (also **fall supper**) *Cdn* a fundraising dinner at which turkey or other poultry is served, held in the autumn by a church or community group.

fox • *noun* (*plural* **foxes**) **1 a** any of various wild flesh-eating mammals of the dog family, with a sharp snout, bushy tail, and usu. red or grey fur. **b** the fur of a fox. **2** a cunning or sly person. **3** *slang* an attractive young woman: *Sandra's a real fox.* • *verb* (**foxes, foxed, foxing**) deceive, baffle, trick.

foxglove *noun* a tall plant with erect spikes of purple or white flowers like the fingers of a glove.

foxhole *noun* a hole in the ground used as a shelter against enemy fire.

foxhound *noun* a kind of hound bred and trained to hunt foxes.

foxiness *noun* **1** the condition or quality of resembling a fox. **2** craftiness or cunning. **3** the condition or quality of being sexually attractive.

foxlike *adjective* **1** resembling a fox: *a foxlike head.* **2** crafty, cunning.

fox terrier *noun* a short-haired breed of terrier originally used for unearthing foxes.

foxtrot • *noun* **1** a ballroom dance characterized by varied combinations of slow and quick steps. **2** the music for this. • *verb* (**foxtrots, foxtrotted, foxtrotting**) perform this dance.

foxy *adjective* (**foxier, foxiest**) **1** of or like a fox. **2** sly or cunning. **3** reddish brown. **4** *slang* (of a woman) sexually attractive.

foyer *noun* an entrance hall or other large area in a hotel, theatre, apartment building, etc. [Say FOY ay]

FR *abbreviation Cdn* Forest Region.

Fr *symbol* francium.

Fr. *abbreviation* **1** Father. **2** French.

fr. *abbreviation* **1** franc(s). **2** from.

fracas *noun* (*plural* **fracases**) a noisy disturbance or quarrel: *the fracas in the Senate over the GST.* [Say FRACK us]

fractal *Math* • *noun* a curve or geometrical figure, each part of which has the same statistical character as the whole. • *adjective* of or relating to a fractal. [Say FRACK t'll]

fraction *noun* **1** a numerical quantity that is not a whole number (e.g. $1/2$, 0.5). **2** a small, esp. very small, part, piece, or amount. **3** a part or subdivision of a whole: *a fraction of the population.* **4** a portion of a mixture separated by distillation etc.

fractional *adjective* **1** of or relating to or being a fraction. **2** very slight: *we outbid the others by a fractional amount.* **3** *Chemistry* relating to the separation of parts of a mixture by making use of their different physical properties: *fractional distillation.* ▶**fractionalize** *verb* (**fractionalizes, fractionalized, fractionalizing**) **fractionally** *adverb* (esp. in sense 2).

fractious *adjective* **1** irritable, bad-tempered: *they fight and squabble like fractious children.* **2** (of an organization) unruly; difficult to control: *the king struggled to unite his fractious kingdom.* ▶**fractiously** *adverb* **fractiousness** *noun* [Say FRACK shuss]

fracture • *noun* **1** breakage or breaking, esp. of a bone or cartilage; a crack or split. **2** the surface appearance of a freshly broken rock or mineral. • *verb* (**fractures, fractured, fracturing**) **1** undergo or cause to undergo a fracture. **2** break or cause to break: *the stones in the wall fractured.* **3** (of a society, organization, etc.) split into several parts so that it no longer functions or exists: *her support was fractured by the scandal.*

fragile *adjective* **1** easily broken. **2** of delicate frame or constitution; not strong. **3** vulnerable, easily destroyed: *fragile ecosystem.* ▶**fragility** *noun*

fragment • *noun* **1** a part broken off; a detached piece. **2** an isolated or incomplete part. **3** the remains of an otherwise lost or destroyed whole, esp. the extant remains or unfinished portion of a book or work of art. • *verb* break or separate into fragments: *pop music has fragmented into a multitude of different styles.*

fragmentary *adjective* **1** consisting of small parts that are disconnected or incomplete: *excavations have revealed fragmentary remains of masonry* ◊ *fragmentary evidence.* **2** *Geology* composed of fragments of previously existing rocks.

fragmentation *noun* **1** the process of breaking into fragments: *the fragmentation of society into small interest groups.* **2** (as an *adjective*) designating a weapon that is designed to break up into small rapidly-moving fragments: *fragmentation grenade.*

fragrance *noun* **1** a sweet scent. **2** something scented, esp. a perfume, eau de cologne, etc. ▶**fragranced** *adjective* [Say FRAY grince]

fragrant *adjective* pleasant smelling. ▶**fragrantly** *adverb* [Say FRAY grint]

frail *adjective* **1** (of a person) physically weak or delicate. **2** easily damaged or broken. **3** morally weak; unable to resist temptation.

F

frailty *noun* (*plural* **frailties**) **1** the condition of being frail. **2** weakness in a person's character or morals: *human frailty* ◊ *the frailties of human nature*.

frame • *noun* **1** a case or border enclosing a picture, window, etc. **2** the basic rigid supporting structure of anything, e.g. of a building or vehicle. **3** (in *plural*) a structure of metal, plastic, etc. holding the lenses of a pair of eyeglasses. **4** a human or animal body, esp. with reference to its size or structure: *her frame shook with laughter*. **5** the general ideas or structure that form the background to something: *in this course we hope to look at literature in the frame of its social and historical context*. **6** a temporary state (esp. in **frame of mind**). **7 a** a single complete image or picture on a cinema film or transmitted in a series of lines by television. **b** one of the separate drawings of a comic strip. **8** *Sport informal* an inning, period, etc. **9** *Bowling* **a** any of the ten divisions of a bowling game. **b** one of the compartments on a scorecard where the score from a single frame is recorded. **10** a boxlike structure of glass etc. for protecting plants. • *verb* (**frames, framed, framing**) **1 a** set in or provide with a frame. **b** serve as a frame for. **2** construct by a combination of parts or in accordance with a design or plan. **3** formulate or devise the essentials of (a complex thing, idea, theory, etc.). **4** *informal* concoct a false charge or evidence against; devise a plot with regard to. **5** articulate (words). • *adjective* (of a building) made of a wooden frame covered with boards, siding, etc.: *frame house*. ▶ **framer** *noun*

frame of reference *noun* a set of standards or principles governing behaviour, opinions, judgments, etc.: *whether you consider them "great" writers depends on your frame of reference*.

framework *noun* **1** an essential supporting structure. **2** a basic system.

framing *noun* **1** a framework; a system of frames. **2** the act or process of framing or constructing something.

franc *noun* the chief monetary unit of France, Belgium, Switzerland, and several other countries.

franchise • *noun* **1** the right to vote in elections. **2 a** authorization granted to an individual or group by a company to sell its goods or services. **b** the store, restaurant, etc., granted such authorization. **3 a** authorization granted to an individual or group by a professional sports league to own and operate a team as a member of the league. **b** the team granted such authorization. **4** a right or privilege granted to a person or corporation. • *verb* (**franchises, franchised, franchising**) grant a franchise to. ▶ **franchisee** *noun* **franchisor** *noun* (also **franchiser**)

Franciscan • *noun* a monk or nun of an order founded in 1209 by St. Francis of Assisi (*c.* 1181–1226), an Italian who renounced his family's wealth to live a life of poverty and charity. • *adjective* of St. Francis or his order. [Say fran SIS k'n]

francium *noun* a radioactive metallic element occurring naturally in uranium and thorium ores. [Say FRAN see um]

francization *noun* (also **francisation**) *Cdn* (*Que.*) the establishment or adoption of French as the official or working language of business, education, etc. [Say fran size AY sh'n]

francize *verb* (**francizes, francized, francizing**) *Cdn* (*Que.*) cause (a person, business, etc.) to adopt French as an official or working language. [Say FRAN size]

Franco *noun* (*plural* **Francos**) *Cdn* a francophone.

Franco- *combining form* **1** French; French and: *Franco-German.* **2** (**franco-**) regarding France, the French, or French-speakers: *francophile*.

Franco-Albertan *Cdn* • *noun* a francophone Albertan. • *adjective* of or relating to Franco-Albertans.

Franco-Canadian *Cdn* • *noun* a Canadian whose principal language is French. • *adjective* **1** of or relating to French-speaking Canadians. **2** of or relating to Canada and France.

Franco-Columbian *Cdn* • *noun* a francophone British Columbian. • *adjective* of or relating to Franco-Columbians.

Franco-Manitoban *Cdn* • *noun* a francophone Manitoban. • *adjective* of or relating to Franco-Manitobans.

Franco-Ontarian *Cdn* • *noun* a francophone Ontarian. • *adjective* of or relating to Franco-Ontarians.

francophile *noun* a person who admires French or francophone culture. ▶ **francophilia** *noun* [Say FRANCO file, franco FILLY uh]

francophone esp. *Cdn* • *noun* a French-speaking person. • *adjective* French-speaking.

Francophonie *noun Cdn* **1** (also **la Francophonie, the Francophonie**) a loosely united group of nations in which French is a first, official, or culturally significant language. **2** (also **francophonie**) francophones within Canada. [Say frank oh foe NEE]

franglais *noun often derogatory* **1** those elements of the French language that have been recently borrowed from English. **2** broken French as spoken by anglophones. [Say frong GLAY]

Frank *noun* a member of a Germanic nation that conquered Gaul in the 6th century and controlled much of western Europe for several centuries afterwards.

SPELL CHECK	ABC ✔
frank, franc	
The French unit of money is the **franc**.	

frank[1] • *adjective* **1** candid, outspoken: *a frank opinion*. **2** undisguised: *frank admiration*. • *verb* stamp (a letter) with an official mark (esp. other than a normal postage stamp) to record the payment of postage.

frank[2] *noun* = FRANKFURTER.

Frankenstein *noun* a thing that becomes terrifying to its maker.

frankfurter *noun* a seasoned smoked sausage made of beef and pork.

frankincense *noun* an aromatic substance obtained from trees, used as incense. [Say FRANK in sense]

Frankish • *adjective* of or relating to the Franks or their language. • *noun* any of the West Germanic dialects spoken by the Franks.

Franklin stove *noun* a cast iron wood stove of the same general shape as a fireplace, usu. having doors on the front.

frankly *adverb* **1** in a frank manner. **2** (qualifying a whole sentence) to be frank.

frankness *noun* openness; outspokenness.

frankum *noun Cdn* (*Nfld*) the hardened resin of a spruce tree, often used as chewing gum. [Say FRANK um]

Fransaskois *noun* (*plural* **Fransaskois**) *Cdn* a francophone resident of Saskatchewan. [Say fran sas KWAH]

frantic *adjective* **1** wildly excited; frenzied. **2** characterized by great hurry or anxiety; desperate. ▶ **frantically** *adverb*

frappé • *adjective* (esp. of wine) iced, cooled. • *noun* (*plural* **frappés**) **1** an iced drink. **2** a soft sherbet. [Say frap AY]

frat *noun informal* a fraternity.

fraternal *adjective* **1** of a brother or brothers. **2** suitable to a brother. **3** (of twins) developed from

separate ova and not necessarily closely similar. **4** of or concerning a fraternity or other male society or lodge. ▶ **fraternalism** *noun* **fraternally** *adverb*

fraternity *noun* (*plural* **fraternities**) **1** a male students' society in a university or college. **2** a religious brotherhood. **3** a group or company with common interests, or of the same professional class: *the banking fraternity*.

fraternization *noun* **1** the action or process of associating, making friends, or behaving as intimates. **2** the action or process of entering into friendly relations with enemy troops or the inhabitants of an occupied country. [Say fratter nize AY sh'n]

fraternize *verb* (**fraternizes**, **fraternized**, **fraternizing**) behave in a friendly manner, especially towards someone that one is not supposed to be friendly with: *she was accused of fraternizing with the enemy*. [Say FRATTER nize]

frat house *noun* a house where members of a fraternity live or hold meetings or parties etc.

fratricidal *adjective* of or relating to the killing of one's brother or sister: *a fratricidal struggle*. [Say fratra SIDE ul]

fratricide *noun* **1** the killing of one's brother or sister. **2** a person who does this. [Say FRATRA side]

fraud *noun* **1** wrongful or criminal deception intended to result in financial or personal gain: *he was convicted of fraud* ◊ *welfare frauds*. **2** a person or thing that is not what it is claimed or expected to be: *they're liars and frauds, all of them*. **3** a dishonest trick or stratagem: *we could easily see though their fraud*. [Say FROD]

fraudulence *noun* the quality or fact of being fraudulent; deceit. [Say FROD you lince]

fraudulent *adjective* intended to deceive someone, usually in order to make money illegally: *fraudulent advertising* ◊ *fraudulent insurance claims*. ▶ **fraudulently** *adverb* [Say FROD you lint]

fraught *adjective* **1** (foll. by *with*) filled or attended with: *fraught with danger*. **2** *informal* causing or affected by great anxiety or distress: *there was a fraught silence* ◊ *he sounded a bit fraught*. [Say FROT]

fray¹ *verb* **1** wear through or become worn, esp. (of fabric, rope, etc.) become unwoven as a result of frequent use or abrasion. **2** (of nerves, temper, etc.) become strained; deteriorate.

fray² *noun* **1** conflict, fighting. **2** a noisy quarrel or brawl.

frazil *noun* (also **frazil ice**) slush consisting of small ice crystals formed in water too turbulent to freeze over. [Say FRAZZLE]

frazzle *verb* (**frazzles**, **frazzled**, **frazzling**) (usu. as **frazzled** *adjective*) *informal* **1** wear out; exhaust, esp. from stress. **2** char; shrivel up with burning. PHRASES **to a frazzle** completely; absolutely: *worn to a frazzle*.

freak • *noun* **1** (also **freak of nature**) a monstrosity; an abnormally developed individual or thing. **2** (often as an *adjective*) an abnormal or bizarre occurrence: *a freak storm*. **3** *informal* **a** an unconventional person. **b** a person with a specified enthusiasm or interest: *health freak*. **c** a person who undergoes hallucinations; a drug addict. • *verb* (often foll. by *out*) *informal* **1** become or make very angry, frightened, excited, etc. **2** undergo or cause to undergo hallucinations or a strong emotional experience, esp. from use of narcotics.

freaking *adjective* *euphemism* expressing annoyance, or as an intensifier: *going out of his freaking mind*.

freakish *adjective* very strange, unusual or unexpected: *freakish weather*. ▶ **freakishly** *adverb* **freakishness** *noun*

freak-out *noun* *informal* an act of freaking out; a hallucinatory experience.

freak show *noun* a sideshow at a fair, featuring people or animals with abnormal physical features.

freaky *adjective* (**freakier**, **freakiest**) very odd, strange, or eccentric.

freckle • *noun* (often in *plural*) any of a number of light brown spots on the skin, often caused by exposure to the sun. • *verb* (**freckles**, **freckled**, **freckling**) **1** (usu. as **freckled** *adjective*) spot with freckles. **2** be spotted with freckles. ▶ **freckly** *adjective*

free • *adjective* (**freer**; **freest**) **1** not in bondage to or under the control of another; having personal rights and social and political liberty. **2** (of a nation, or its citizens or institutions) subject neither to foreign domination nor to despotic government; having national and civil liberty: *a free society*. **3 a** unrestricted, unimpeded; not restrained or fixed. **b** at liberty; not confined or imprisoned. **c** released from ties or duties; unimpeded. **d** unrestrained as to action; independent: *set free*. **4 a** not subject to; exempt from: *free of tax*. **b** not containing or subject to a specified (usu. undesirable) thing: *free from disease*. **5** able or permitted to take a specified action: *you are free to choose*. **6** unconstrained: *free gestures*. **7 a** available without charge. **b** not subject to tax, duty, trade restraint, or fees. **8 a** clear of engagements or obligations: *are you free tomorrow?* **b** not occupied or in use: *the bathroom is free now*. **c** clear of obstructions. **9** open to all comers. **10** lavish, profuse; using or used without restraint: *very free with their money*. **11** (of a literary style) not observing the strict laws of form. **12** (of a translation) conveying the broad sense; not literal. **13** impudent. **14** (of movement) under no force other than that of gravity or inertia: *free flight*. **15** *Physics* **a** not modified by an external force. **b** not bound in an atom or molecule. **16** *Chemistry* not combined: *free oxygen*. • *adverb* **1** away from or out of a position in which someone or something is stuck or trapped: *the wagon broke free from the train*. **2** without cost or payment. • *verb* (**frees**, **freed**, **freeing**) **1** make free; set at liberty. **2** (foll. by *of, from*) relieve from (something undesirable). **3** disengage, disentangle. PHRASES **for free** *informal* free of charge, gratis. **free and easy** *informal*, unceremonious. **free on board** (or **rail**) without charge for delivery to a ship or railway car. **free up** *informal* **1** make available. **2** make less restricted. **it's a free country** *informal* the action proposed is not illegal or forbidden. **make free with 1** take liberties with. **2** use as one's own.

-free *combining form* free of or from: *duty-free* ◊ *cruelty-free*.

free agency *noun* the state or fact of not being under contract, and so able to sell one's services to any team.

free agent *noun* **1** a person with freedom of action: *the Nuremberg trials laid down the principle that man remains a free agent even in the worst of tyrannies*. **2** a professional athlete who is not under contract, and may sell his or her services to any team. ▶ **free agentry** *noun* (in sense 2).

free association *noun* **1** a method of investigating a person's unconscious by eliciting from him or her spontaneous associations with ideas proposed by the examiner. **2** any process in which one thought, word, image, etc. suggests the next without following a logical or conscious direction.

freebase *slang* • *noun* cocaine that has been purified by heating with ether, and is taken by inhaling the fumes or smoking the residue. • *verb* (**freebases**, **freebased**, **freebasing**) **1** purify (cocaine) for smoking or inhaling. **2** smoke or inhale (freebased cocaine). ▶ **freebaser** *noun*

F

F

freebie *informal* • *noun* a thing provided free of charge. • *adjective* free; provided without charge: *a freebie trip*.

freeboard *noun* the part of a ship's side between the waterline and the deck.

Free Church *noun* (*plural* **Free Churches**) a Church dissenting or seceding from an established church.

freedom *noun* **1** the condition of being free or unrestricted. **2 a** personal or civic liberty. **b** absence of slave status. **3** the power of self-determination; independence of fate or necessity. **4** the state of being free to act: *we have the freedom to leave*. **5** the esp. political right to act, speak, etc. as one pleases without interference: *freedom of speech* ◊ *freedom of religion*. **6** (foll. by *from*) the condition of being exempt from or not subject to (a defect, burden, etc.). **7** (foll. by *of*) **a** full or honorary participation in (membership, privileges, etc.). **b** unrestricted use of (facilities etc.). **8** facility or ease in action. **9** boldness of conception.

freedom fighter *noun* a person who takes part in violent resistance to a political system etc.

free enterprise *noun* a system in which private business operates in competition and largely free of governmental control. ▶ **free enterpriser** *noun*

free fall • *noun* **1** movement under the force of gravity only, esp.: **a** the part of a parachute descent before the parachute opens. **b** the movement of a spacecraft in space without thrust from the engines. **2** any state of falling rapidly: *prices were in free fall*. • *verb* (**free-fall, free-falls, free-fell, free-falling**) (esp. as **free-falling** *adjective & noun*) move in a free fall.

free-floating *adjective* **1** (of an emotion) having no particular focus or cause: *free-floating anxiety*. **2** (of people) not attached or committed to any particular cause, party, etc. **3** able to move relatively freely.

free-for-all *noun* (*plural* **free-for-alls**) a fight, competition, or argument in which many people take part, usu. having no rules.

free-form *adjective* of an irregular shape or structure; not constrained by conventional rules etc.

freehand • *adjective* (of a drawing or plan etc.) done by hand without special instruments or guides. • *adverb* in a freehand manner.

free hand *noun* freedom to act at one's own discretion: *the provinces gave the companies virtually a free hand to develop and apply their own management plans*.

freehold • *noun* **1** permanent and absolute tenure of land or property with freedom to dispose of it at will. **2** land or property or an office held by such tenure. • *adjective* held by or having the status of freehold: *freehold townhouses for sale*. ▶ **freeholder** *noun*

free kick *noun* Soccer a set kick allowed to be taken by one side without interference from the other.

freelance • *noun* (also **freelancer**) a person offering services on a temporary basis, esp. to several businesses etc. for particular assignments. • *verb* (**freelances, freelanced, freelancing**) act as a freelance. • *adverb* as a freelance: *has been working freelance*.

free-living *adjective* Biology living freely and independently.

freeload *verb* behave as a freeloader or sponger.

freeloader *noun* slang a person who eats or drinks at others' expense; a sponger. ▶ **freeloading** *noun*

free love *noun* sexual relations according to choice and unrestricted by marriage.

free lunch *noun* (*plural* **free lunches**) a lunch provided free of charge. ▐PHRASES▌ **there's no (such thing as a) free lunch** nothing is without cost.

freely *adverb* **1** not under the control of another; as one wishes: *I roamed freely*. **2 a** without restriction or interference: *air can freely circulate*. **b** in copious or generous amounts: *the wine flowed freely*. **3** openly and

honestly: *you may speak freely*. **4** willingly and readily; without compulsion: *I freely confess to this failing*.

freeman *noun* (*plural* **freemen**) a person who is not a slave or serf.

free market *noun* a market in which prices are determined by unrestricted competition.

free marketeer *noun* a supporter or advocate of free-market economics.

Freemason *noun* a member of an international fraternity for mutual help and fellowship (the *Free and Accepted Masons*), with elaborate secret rituals. ▶ **Freemasonry** *noun* [Say FREE may sun]

freer *comparative of* FREE.

free radical *noun* an uncharged atom or group of atoms with one or more unpaired electrons.

free-range *adjective* **1** (of hens etc.) kept in natural conditions with freedom of movement. **2** (of eggs) produced by such birds.

free ride *noun* something obtained at no cost or with no effort. ▶ **free rider** *noun*

free safety *noun* (*plural* **free safeties**) Football a secondary defensive player who has no assigned position at the snap of the ball but may roam the field behind the line of scrimmage.

freesia *noun* a bulbous plant native to Africa, with fragrant coloured flowers. [Say FREE zhuh or FREEZY uh]

free skate *noun* (also **free skating program**) a part of a figure skating competition consisting of a program for which the music and the number and type of jumps and other elements are chosen freely by the skater.

free speech *noun* the right to express opinions freely.

free spirit *noun* an independent or uninhibited person. ▶ **free-spirited** *adjective*

freest *superlative of* FREE.

free-standing *adjective* **1** not supported by another structure. **2** autonomous: *a free-standing clinic*.

freestone *noun* a peach or other fruit having a stone to which the flesh does not cling when the fruit is ripe.

freestyle • *adjective* of a race or contest) in which all styles are allowed, esp.: **1** Swimming in which any stroke may be used. **2** Wrestling with few restrictions on the holds permitted. • *noun* **1** freestyle swimming or wrestling. **2** the front crawl. ▶ **freestyler** *noun*

free-swimming *adjective* (of an aquatic organism) capable of swimming around freely; not fixed in one position or attached to any object.

freethinker *noun* a person who rejects dogma or authority, esp. in religious belief. ▶ **freethinking** *noun & adjective*

free throw *noun* Sport **1** an unimpeded throw awarded to a player following a foul etc. **2** Basketball such a throw allowing a shot at the basket, taken from behind a marked line.

free trade *noun* international trade free from protectionist tariffs, quotas, export subsidies, and other government intervention.

free trader *noun* **1** an advocate of free trade. **2** Cdn hist. a fur trader who was not affiliated with any of the large fur trading companies.

free verse *noun* poetry which doesn't rhyme and whose lines don't flow with a regular rhythm.

free vote *noun* a parliamentary vote in which MPs are not constrained to vote along party lines.

freeware *noun* software available without charge.

freeway *noun* **1** = EXPRESSWAY. **2** a toll-free highway.

free weight *noun* a barbell, dumbbell, or other weight not attached to a machine, used in weightlifting exercises.

freewheeling *adjective* not hampered by rules,

responsibilities, or conventions; allowed to run or operate freely: *the freewheeling '60s* ◊ *a freewheeling debate*.

free will • *noun* **1** the power to make one's own decisions without being controlled by fate. **2** the ability to act at one's own discretion, esp. regarding good and evil: *I did it of my own free will*. • *adjective* (usu. **free-will**) (of a donation etc.) voluntary.

SPELL CHECK
freeze, frieze   ABC ✓

A broad sculpted or painted decoration on a wall is a **frieze**.

---

freeze • *verb* (**freezes**; *past* **froze**; *past participle* **frozen**; **freezing**) **1** turn or be turned into ice or another solid by cold. **2** be or feel very cold. **3** cover or become covered with ice. **4** (foll. by *to, together*) adhere or be fastened by frost: *the curtains froze to the window*. **5** be or become obstructed or closed by the formation of ice: *the pipes froze*. **6** preserve (food) by refrigeration below freezing point. **7 a** make or become motionless or powerless through fear, surprise, etc., or when ordered to do so. **b** react or cause to react with sudden aloofness or detachment. **8** stiffen or harden, injure or kill, by chilling: *frozen to death*. **9** *informal* make (part of the body) insensitive to pain, esp. by injection of a local anaesthetic. **10** prevent (credits, assets, etc.) temporarily or permanently from being converted into money. **11** fix or stabilize (prices, wages, etc.) at a certain level. **12** arrest (an action) at a certain stage of development. **13** = FREEZE-FRAME *verb*. **14** *Computing* (of a computer screen) cease to respond to input from the keyboard or mouse. **15** *Curling* draw a rock up against a stationary rock without causing the second rock to move. **16** *Sport* keep possession of (the ball, puck, etc.) for an extended period of time, esp. without attempting to score. • *noun* **1** a state of frost; a period or the coming of frost or very cold weather. **2** the fixing or stabilization of prices, wages, etc. **3** = FREEZE-FRAME *noun*. **4** a decision by one or more nations to stop or limit the manufacture or development of (esp. nuclear) weapons. PHRASES **freeze out** *informal* exclude from business, society, etc. by competition or boycott etc. **freeze up** obstruct or be obstructed by the formation of ice.

freeze-dry *verb* (**freeze-dries**, **freeze-dried**, **freeze-drying**) preserve (esp. food) by freezing it and then drying it very quickly.

freeze-frame • *noun* (also as an *adjective*) the facility of stopping a film or videotape in order to view a motionless image. • *verb* (**freeze-frames**, **freeze-framed**, **freeze-framing**) use freeze-frame on (an image, recording, etc.).

freezer *noun* a refrigerated cabinet or room for preserving food at very low temperatures.

freeze-thaw *adjective* denoting a cycle of alternate freezing and thawing and the weathering effect that is produced when meltwater seeps into cracks in rock etc. and expands as it freezes, causing the cracks to broaden and rock etc. to break.

freeze-up *noun* esp. *Cdn* the freezing up of a river, lake, etc., esp. in the fall.

freezing *adjective* **1** (of temperatures) at or near the freezing point. **2** *informal* (also **freezing cold**) very cold.

freezing point *noun* **1** the temperature at which a liquid freezes. **2** the freezing point of water, 0°C (32°F): *temperatures will drop below the freezing point*.

freezing rain *noun* rain that freezes on impact with the ground or other solid objects.

freight • *noun* **1** goods transported by water, air, or land. **2** the transportation of such goods. **3** a charge for transportation of goods. **4** a freight train. • *verb* **1** transport (goods) as freight. **2** fill something with esp. too much of a particular mood or tone: *a speech freighted with sentiment*. [Say FRATE]

freight canoe *noun* (also **freighter canoe**) *Cdn hist.* a large canoe used for transporting freight.

freight car *noun* a railway car for carrying freight.

freighter *noun* a ship or aircraft designed to carry freight. [Say FRATE er]

freight train *noun* a train transporting freight.

French • *adjective* **1** of or relating to France or its people or language. **2** of or relating to French Canada or French Canadians. **3** having the characteristics attributed to the French people. • *noun* **1** the Romance language of France, also used in Canada, Belgium, Switzerland, and elsewhere. **2** (**the French**) (treated as *plural*) **a** the people of France. **b** the people of French Canada. PHRASES **pardon** (or **excuse**) **my French** *informal* excuse my use of coarse language.

French bread *noun* white, yeast-raised bread, usu. in a long loaf with a crisp crust.

French Canadian • *noun* a Canadian whose principal language is French. • *adjective* (**French-Canadian**) of or relating to French-speaking Canadians.

French door *noun* a long glass door, often one of a pair, and usu. opening onto a patio or balcony.

French dressing *noun* **1** a creamy, sweet salad dressing, usu. orange in colour. **2** a salad dressing of vinegar and oil, usu. seasoned.

French fact *noun Cdn* (**the French fact**) francophone culture as a distinct component of Canadian society.

French French *Cdn* • *noun* the French language as spoken in France, esp. as opposed to that spoken in Quebec. • *adjective* (**French-French**) of or relating to the French people or language of France, esp. as opposed to those of Quebec.

french-fried *adjective* (of a food, esp. potato) that has been deep-fried.

french fry *noun* (*plural* **french fries**) a strip of potato which has been deep-fried.

French horn *noun* a valved brass wind instrument with a long, coiled tube and a wide bell, played with one hand placed in the bell to soften the tone.

Frenchify *verb* (**Frenchifies**, **Frenchified**, **Frenchifying**) (usu. as **Frenchified** *adjective*) make French in form, character, or manners.

French immersion *noun Cdn* an educational program in which anglophone students are taught entirely in French.

French kiss *noun* (*plural* **French kisses**) a kiss with one partner's tongue inserted in the other's mouth. ▶**French kiss** *verb* (**French kisses**, **French kissed**, **French kissing**)

Frenchman *noun* (*plural* **Frenchmen**) **1** a native or national of France. **2** a francophone.

Frenchness *noun* the quality or condition of being French: *recognized the building's Frenchness and its expression of Canadian nationalism*.

French regime *noun* the period of French rule in Canadian history, until 1763.

French toast *noun* bread dipped in egg and milk and fried.

French window *noun* = FRENCH DOOR.

Frenchwoman *noun* (*plural* **Frenchwomen**) **1** a female native or national of France. **2** a francophone woman.

frenetic *adjective* frantic, frenzied: *a scene of frenetic activity*. ▶**frenetically** *adverb* [Say fruh NET ick]

frenzied *adjective* wildly excited or uncontrolled: *a frenzied attack* ◊ *frenzied fans*.

frenzy *noun* (*plural* **frenzies**) a state or period of uncontrolled excitement or wild behaviour: *a frenzy of activity* ◊ *the speaker worked the crowd up into a frenzy* ◊ *an outbreak of patriotic frenzy* ◊ *a killing frenzy*.

Freon *noun* *proprietary* any of a group of hydrocarbons containing fluorine, chlorine, and sometimes bromine, used in aerosols, refrigerants, etc. [Say FREE on]

frequency *noun* (*plural* **frequencies**) **1** the rate at which something happens or is repeated. **2 a** the state of being frequent; frequent occurrence. **b** the process of being repeated at short intervals. **3 a** *Physics* the rate of recurrence of a vibration, oscillation, cycle, etc.; the number of repetitions in a given time, esp. per second. Abbreviation: **f**. **b** the number of cycles per second of a carrier wave used for radio transmission. **c** a waveband; a channel. **4** *Statistics* the ratio of the number of actual to possible occurrences of an event.

frequency band *noun* *Electronics* = BAND¹ 4a.

frequency modulation *noun* **1** variation of the frequency of a radio or other wave as a way of carrying information such as an audio signal. **2** the system using such modulation. Abbreviation: **FM**.

frequency response *noun* *Electronics* the way in which the output–input ratio of an amplifier or other device depends on the signal frequency.

frequent • *adjective* **1** occurring often or in close succession. **2** habitual, constant: *a frequent caller*. • *verb* attend or go to habitually. [Say FREE quint; for the verb you can also say free QUENT]

frequent flyer *noun* **1** a person who travels by air frequently. **2** (as an *adjective*) designating programs of rewards offered by airlines to their passengers, or the points accumulated for the rewards.

frequently *adverb* often.

fresco *noun* (*plural* **frescoes**) **1** a painting done in watercolour on a wall or ceiling while the plaster is still wet. **2** this method of painting. ▶**frescoed** *adjective*

fresh • *adjective* **1 a** newly made or obtained: *fresh sandwiches*. **b** (of snow) newly fallen. **2 a** other, different; not previously used or used: *start a fresh page* ◊ *fresh ideas*. **b** additional: *fresh supplies*. **3** (foll. by *from*) lately arrived from (a specified place or situation). **4** not stale or musty or faded: *fresh eggs* ◊ *fresh memories*. **5 a** (of food) not preserved by drying, salting, canning, freezing, etc. **b** (of fruit) not cooked. **6** not salty: *fresh water*. **7 a** pure, untainted, refreshing, invigorating: *fresh air*. **b** bright and pure in colour: *a fresh complexion*. **8** (of the wind) brisk; of fair strength. **9** *informal* **a** cheeky, presumptuous. **b** showing esp. disrespectful or presumptuous sexual or romantic interest: *I couldn't believe it when he started getting fresh with me*. • *adverb* newly, recently (esp. in combination: *fresh-baked*). PHRASES **fresh out of** **1** recently out of: *fresh out of school*. **2** having just run out of: *fresh out of bread*.

freshen *verb* **1** make something fresh or fresher; revive something. **2** (esp. of a cow) begin to yield new milk after giving birth. **3** add fresh wine, spirits, etc., to (a drink which has been standing for some time). PHRASES **freshen up** refresh oneself by washing, changing one's clothes, etc. ▶**freshener** *noun*

freshet *noun* **1** a rush of fresh water flowing into the sea. **2** the flood of a river from heavy rain or melted snow. [Say FRESH it]

fresh-faced *adjective* having a clear and young-looking complexion.

freshly *adverb* newly; recently: *freshly ground coffee*.

freshman • *noun* (*plural* **freshmen**) **1** a first-year student at university or college. **2** a first-year student

in high school or junior high school. • *adjective* **1** of or relating to a freshman. **2** (of a course, etc.) requisite or suitable for first-year students: *freshman biology*. **3** inexperienced; doing something for the first time: *a freshman MP*. **4** first: *her freshman year with the force*. **5** (of a level of school sports competition for younger, less experienced players.

freshness *noun* the quality or condition of being fresh: *we guarantee the freshness of all our produce* ◊ *the cool freshness of the water*.

freshwater *adjective* of or found in fresh water, not the sea.

fret¹ *verb* (**frets**, **fretted**, **fretting**) **1 a** feel or express anxiety, worry, unhappiness, etc. **b** (of a baby) express unhappiness, discomfort, etc., esp. by intermittent whimpering. **2** cause anxiety or distress to .

fret² *noun* each of a sequence of bars or ridges on the fingerboard of some stringed musical instruments (esp. the guitar) for fixing the positions of the fingers to produce the desired notes.

fretboard *noun* a fretted fingerboard on a guitar etc.

fretful *adjective* anxious, distressed, or irritated. ▶**fretfully** *adverb* **fretfulness** *noun*

fretted *adjective* (of a stringed instrument, e.g. a guitar) having bars or ridges on which the fingers are placed to produced the right notes.

fretwork *noun* patterns cut into wood, metal, etc. to decorate it.

Freudian • *adjective* **1** of or relating to Sigmund Freud (1856–1939), his theories, or his methods of psychoanalysis, esp. with reference to the importance of sexuality in human behaviour. **2** (of a person's speech or behaviour) possibly revealing one's subconscious thoughts or feelings. • *noun* a follower of Freud or his methods. ▶**Freudianism** *noun* [Say FROY dee un]

Freudian slip *noun* an unintentional, esp. spoken error that seems to reveal subconscious feelings.

Fri. *abbreviation* Friday.

friable *adjective* able to be easily crumbled or reduced to powder: *the soil was very friable*. [Say FRY a bull]

friar *noun* a member of any of certain religious orders of men, esp. the Augustinians, Carmelites, Dominicans, and Franciscans.

fricassee • *noun* a dish of white meat such as chicken, veal, or rabbit, cut up, stewed in stock, and served in a thick white sauce. • *verb* (**fricassees**, **fricasseed**, **fricasseeing**) make a fricassee of. [Say FRICKA see]

fricot *noun* *Cdn* (*Maritimes*) a hearty Acadian stew containing potatoes and meat, fish, or seafood. [Say frick OH]

friction *noun* **1** the action of one surface or object rubbing against another. **2** the resistance an object or surface encounters in moving over another. **3** a clash of wills, temperaments, or opinions; mutual animosity arising from disagreement. ▶**frictional** *adjective* **frictionless** *adjective*

Friday • *noun* the sixth day of the week, following Thursday. • *adverb* **1** on Friday. **2** (**Fridays**) each Friday.

fridge *noun* *informal* = REFRIGERATOR 1.

fried • *adjective* **1** cooked by frying. **2** *informal* thoroughly worn out, exhausted, etc. **3** *slang* intoxicated. • *verb* past and past participle of FRY¹.

friend *noun* **1** a person with whom one enjoys mutual affection and regard (usu. rather than family bonds). **2** a sympathizer: *a friend of order*. **3 a** a person who is an ally, on the same side, or not an enemy: *friend or foe?* **b** (usu. in *plural*) a patron or supporter of a cause etc.: *Friends of the Library*. **4** a romantic or sexual partner. **5 a** a person already mentioned or under

discussion: *my friend at the next table then left the room*. **b** an acquaintance, associate, or person known casually. **c** used as a polite or ironic form of address. **6 (Friend)** a member of the Society of Friends; a Quaker. PHRASES **be friends (with)** be on good or intimate terms (with). **friends in high places** highly placed people able or ready to use their influence on one's behalf. **make friends (with)** get on good or intimate terms (with). **my honourable friend** *Cdn* & *Brit.* used in the House of Commons to refer to another member of one's own party. **my learned friend** used by a lawyer in court to refer to another lawyer. ▶ **friendless** *adjective*

friendly *adjective* (**friendlier, friendliest**) **1** acting as or like a friend, kindly. **2 a** (often foll. by *with*) on amicable terms. **b** not hostile or in opposition. **c** not seriously competitive: *a friendly rivalry*. **3** characteristic of friends, showing or prompted by kindness. **4** favourably disposed, inclined to approve or help. **5 a** (of a thing) serviceable, convenient, opportune. **b** = USER-FRIENDLY. **6** (esp. in *combination*) not harming; helping: *ozone-friendly*. ▶ **friendliness** *noun*

friendship *noun* **1 a** the feeling or relationship that friends have. **b** a relationship between friends: *our friendship is very important to me* ◊ *she formed close friendships with women*. **2** a state of mutual trust and support: *a conference to promote international friendship*.

friendship centre *noun* *Cdn* an institution established in a predominantly non-Aboriginal community to provide counselling and social services etc. to Aboriginal people.

Friesian *adjective & noun* = FRISIAN. [Say FREE zhun or FREEZY un]

frieze *noun* **1** any broad, horizontal band of sculpted, painted, or other decoration, esp. along a wall near the ceiling. **2** (in classical architecture) a band of stone, often sculpted, above the beam supported by the columns and below the roof. **3** a horizontal band of sculpture filling this. [Sounds like FREEZE]

frigate *noun* **1** *Cdn* & *Brit.* a naval escort vessel between a corvette and a destroyer in size. **2** *US* a similar ship between a destroyer and a cruiser in size. [Say FRIG it]

fright *noun* **1 a** sudden or extreme fear. **b** an experience that makes one feel fear: *gave me a fright* ◊ *I got the fright of my life*. **2** a person or thing looking grotesque or ridiculous. PHRASES **take fright** become frightened.

frighten *verb* **1** scare, terrify, or fill with fright. **2** drive or force by fright: *frightened them into submission*. **3** become scared: *doesn't frighten easily*. ▶ **frightening** *adjective* **frighteningly** *adverb*

frightful *adjective* **1 a** dreadful, shocking, revolting. **b** ugly, hideous. **2** *informal* extremely bad: *a frightful idea*. **3** *informal* very great, extreme. ▶ **frightfully** *adverb* **frightfulness** *noun*

frigid *adjective* **1** extremely cold: *frigid temperatures*. **2** (of a woman) **a** unable to achieve orgasm or experience sexual excitement during intercourse. **b** not showing any sexual desire or responsiveness. **3** lacking friendliness or enthusiasm: *Henrietta looked back with a frigid calm*. ▶ **frigidity** *noun* **frigidly** *adverb* [Say FRIDGE id, frih JIDDA tee]

frill *noun* **1 a** an ornamental edging of material, having one side gathered or pleated and the other left loose so as to have a fluted or wavy appearance. **b** a natural fringe of hair, feathers, etc. resembling this on an animal, esp. a bird. **2** an optional or additional extra that is not necessary or essential, but serves for embellishment, decoration, etc. ▶ **frilled** *adjective*

frilly • *adjective* (**frillier, frilliest**) **1** having a frill or frills. **2** resembling a frill. • *noun* (*plural* **frillies**) (in *plural*) *informal* women's underwear.

fringe *noun* **1** an ornamental bordering of threads left loose or formed into tassels or twists. **2** a natural border of hair etc. in an animal or plant. **3 a** the outer edge or margin of an area etc.: *in the northern fringes of Saskatchewan*. **b** (also as an *adjective*) an unofficial, unconventional, and often extreme approach, opinion, etc.; something non-mainstream: *fringe theatre*. **4** a thing, part, or area of secondary or minor importance.

fringe benefit *noun* an extra benefit given to an employee in addition to salary or wages, e.g. health insurance, a company car, etc.

fringed *adjective* **1** having a fringe: *a fringed jacket* ◊ *a rich robe of gold, fringed with black velvet*. **2** (of a plant or animal) having a natural border of hair or fibre: *slightly fringed leaves*. **3** having a border of a specified sort: *the school is set amid parkland and fringed by marinas*.

fringing reef *noun* a coral reef forming a ring around an island close to the shore.

frippery *noun* (*plural* **fripperies**) **1** unnecessary items of ornament or decoration, e.g. in clothing. **2** something that is superficial and mindless: *a travel writer contributed a piece of frippery about Ottawa*.

Frisbee *noun* *proprietary* a concave plastic disc for skimming through the air as an outdoor game.

Frisian • *adjective* of Friesland (a province of the Netherlands), the Frisians, or the Frisian language. • *noun* **1** a native or inhabitant of Friesland. **2** the West Germanic language of Friesland, the closest relative of English. [Say FREE zhun or FRIZZY un]

frisk • *verb* **1** search (a person) by feeling quickly over the body in search of a concealed weapon etc. **2** leap, skip, or frolic playfully. • *noun* the act of frisking a person.

frisky *adjective* (**friskier, friskiest**) **1** lively, playful. **2** *informal* amorous, sexually excited.

frisson *noun* an emotional thrill, esp. a shiver of excitement: *a frisson of alarm ran down my spine*. [Say FREE sawn]

frittata *noun* (*plural* **frittatas**) a type of omelette in which chopped vegetables, meat, etc. are added to the beaten eggs before they are fried. [Say fruh TATTA]

fritter¹ *verb* (usu. foll. by *away*) waste (money, time, energy, etc.) triflingly, indiscriminately, etc.

fritter² *noun* a piece of fruit, meat, etc., coated in batter and deep-fried: *apple fritter*.

fritz *noun* PHRASES **on the fritz** *slang* broken, defective.

frivolity *noun* (*plural* **frivolities**) behaviour that is silly or amusing, esp. when this is not suitable: *it was just a piece of harmless frivolity* ◊ *I can't waste time on such frivolities*. [Say friv VOLLA tee]

frivolous *adjective* **1 a** (of activities) silly or wasteful: *it is outrageous that the government considers music teaching to be frivolous*. **b** (of a claim, charge, etc.) having no reasonable grounds: *rules to stop frivolous lawsuits*. **2** (of people) foolish, lighthearted, not sensible or serious. ▶ **frivolously** *adverb* [Say FRIVVA luss]

frizz • *verb* (**frizzes, frizzed, frizzing**) **1** form (hair) into tight curls. **2** (of hair etc.) curl tightly, esp. so as to be difficult to style. • *noun* frizzy hair.

frizzle • *verb* (**frizzles, frizzled, frizzling**) **1 a** fry, toast, or grill, with a sputtering noise. **b** burn or shrivel. **2 a** form (hair) into tight curls. **b** (of hair etc.) curl tightly. • *noun* frizzled hair.

frizzy *adjective* (**frizzier, frizziest**) formed of a mass of small, tight curls: *frizzy red hair*.

frock *noun* **1** a monk's or priest's long gown with loose sleeves. **2** *Brit.* a girl's or woman's dress.

frock coat *noun* a usu. double-breasted coat with

skirts extending almost to the knees and not cut away, but of the same length in front as behind.

frog *noun* any of various small amphibians with a tailless smooth-skinned body with legs developed for jumping, esp. (as distinct from toads) any of those which have a smooth skin and leap rather than walk. **PHRASES** **frog in the** (or **one's**) **throat** *informal* hoarseness.

froggy *adjective* **1** of or like a frog or frogs. **2** abounding in frogs.

frog kick *noun* Swimming a type of kick in which the legs are pulled towards the body, then thrust outward, before being brought together again quickly.

frogman *noun* (*plural* **frogmen**) a scuba diver engaged in police or military operations.

frolic • *verb* (**frolics, frolicked, frolicking**) play about cheerfully. • *noun* **1** a lively and enjoyable activity. **2** fun, gaiety, or merriment.

from *preposition* expressing separation or origin. **PHRASES** **from day to day** (or **hour to hour** etc.) daily (or hourly etc.); as the days (or hours etc.) pass. **from time to time** occasionally or intermittently.

frond *noun* the leaf or leaflike part of a palm, fern, or similar plant: *birds twittered in the palm fronds*.

front • *noun* **1 a** the side or part of a thing normally nearer or towards the spectator. **b** the side or part of a thing facing forward. **c** a position or place situated directly before or ahead of a thing, observer, etc.: *the front of the mouth*. **2** any face of a building, esp. that of the main entrance. **3** an area where fighting takes place during a war: *more Canadian troops were sent to the front*. **4 a** a sector of activity regarded as resembling a military front: *there was some good news on the jobs front*. **b** a political group organized to pursue a particular objective or set of objectives. **5 a** the most forward or conspicuous position: *come to the front*. **b** a leading position in a race or contest. **6 a** an outward appearance or show, esp. used as a cover for another trait, motive, etc.: *put up a brave front*. **b** a pretext, premise, etc.: *the arguments are false on several fronts*. **7** a person or organization serving as a cover for subversive or illegal activities: *front man*. **8** (**the front**) frontage or the land facing a road or alongside a body of water. **9** Meteorology the forward edge of an advancing mass of cold or warm air. **10** the part of a garment, esp. of a dress or shirt, which covers the upper part of the front of the body. • *adjective* **1** of or pertaining to the front. **2** situated in front. • *verb* **1** have the front facing or directed in a specific direction. **2** (foll. by *for*) *slang* act as a front or cover for. **3** furnish with a specific front, material, etc.: *fronted with stone*. **4** lead or be the most prominent member of (a band, organization, etc.). **5 a** stand opposite to, have the front towards. **b** (of a building) have its front on the side of (a street etc.). **6** Broadcasting act as presenter, promoter, or host of (a television program etc.). **PHRASES** **in front 1** in the lead or in an advanced position. **2** in a position exactly ahead, facing the spectator. **in front of 1** ahead of, in advance of. **2** in the presence of, confronting. **out front** in front of a building etc.

frontage *noun* **1 a** the front of a building or lot. **b** the extent of this. **2 a** land abutting on a street or on water: *river frontage farms*. **b** the land between the front of a building and the road.

frontal *adjective* **1 a** of, at, or on the front: *a frontal attack*. **b** of the front as seen by an onlooker: *a frontal view*. **2** of the forehead or front part of the skull. ▶ **frontally** *adverb*

frontal lobe *noun* each of the paired lobes of the brain lying immediately behind the forehead, including

areas concerned with behaviour, learning, and voluntary movement.

front bench *noun* the foremost seats in Parliament, occupied by the leading members of the government and opposition. ▶ **front-bencher** *noun*

front burner *noun* **1** a position receiving much attention or high priority: *has been brought to the front burner*. **2** a heating element at the front of a stove.

frontcourt *noun* Sport **1** the part of the court closest to the front wall in games such as squash, racquetball, etc. **2** Basketball **a** the offensive half of a court for a given team. **b** the centre and two forwards who play offensively in that half of the court.

Front de Libération du Québec *noun* (in Canada) a Quebec separatist terrorist organization esp. active in the 1960s and early 1970s. Abbreviation: **FLQ**. [Say FRON duh lee bay rass YON doo kay BECK]

front end *noun* **1** the forward part of a motor vehicle, train, etc. **2** (**front-end**) that part of a computer system that a user deals with directly, esp. a device providing input or access to a central computer or other parts of a network. **3** (**front-end**) designating money paid or charged at the beginning of a transaction: *front-end commission*.

front-end loader *noun* **1** a machine with a scoop or bucket on an articulated arm at the front for digging and loading dirt etc. **2** a hydraulic bucket or scoop that fits onto the front of a tractor.

frontier • *noun* **1 a** the border between two countries. **b** the district on each side of this. **2** the limits of attainment or knowledge in a subject. **3** the part of a country held to form the furthest limit of its settled or inhabited regions. • *adjective* **1** of, belonging to, or situated on the frontier. **2** characteristic of life on a frontier, esp. being remote from the comforts of civilization. [Say frun TEER or frawn TEER]

frontiersman *noun* (*plural* **frontiersmen**) a man living on a frontier, or on or beyond the borders of civilization. [Say frun TEERS mun or frawn TEERS mun]

frontispiece *noun* an illustration facing the title page of a book or of one of its divisions. [Say FRUN tiss piece]

front line *noun* **1 a** Military the line of fighting closest to the enemy. **b** a role or position of immediate involvement with crises, social problems, etc.: *working on the front lines against AIDS*. **2** the most important, advanced, or responsible position: *on the front line of interactive television*. **3** the players in a jazz band other than the rhythm section.

front office *noun* a main executive or administrative office of a business, organization, etc.

front page *noun* the first page of a newspaper, esp. as containing important or remarkable news.

front-runner *noun* **1** the candidate, contestant, etc. most likely to succeed. **2** an athlete or horse running best when in the lead. ▶ **front-running** *adjective*

front-wheel drive *noun* a drive system in a car etc. in which power operates through the front wheels.

frosh *noun* (*plural* **frosh**) *slang* = FRESHMAN *noun*

frost • *noun* **1 a** dew or water vapour frozen into tiny white crystals that cover the ground etc. when the temperature falls below the freezing point. **b** a consistent temperature below freezing point causing frost to form: *a frost warning*. **2** (of colours of lipstick, eyeshadow, etc.) a silvery, iridescent shade. • *verb* **1** (usu. foll. by *over, up*) become covered with frost. **2** cover with or as if with frost, powder, etc. **b** freeze and usu. kill or injure (a plant etc.) with frost. **3 a** cover or decorate (a cake etc.) with icing. **b** coat with sugar. **4** *informal* annoy or anger. **5** chemically treat selected strands of hair to produce highlights etc.

frostbite *noun* injury to body tissues, esp. the nose,

ears, fingers, or toes, caused by intense cold, in extreme cases resulting in gangrene.

frostbitten *adjective* (of body tissues) injured by exposure to intense cold.

frosted *adjective* **1** covered with frost: *tramping down the frosted roads of Saskatchewan*. **2** (of glass or a window) having a translucent textured surface so that it is difficult to see through. **3** (of food) decorated or dusted with icing or sugar.

frost-free *adjective* **1** (of a region, period, etc.) experiencing no frost. **2** (of a freezer etc.) able to defrost automatically.

frost heave *noun* the uplift of soil or other surface deposits, esp. on a road, due to expansion of groundwater on freezing.

frostily *adverb* in an unfriendly way; coldly: *"No thank you," she said frostily*.

frosting *noun* **1** icing for a cake etc. **2** a rough surface on glass etc. **3** a process of treating hair to produce highlights chemically.

frost line *noun* **1** the maximum ground depth below which frost does not penetrate. **2** the lower limit of permafrost.

frosty *adjective* (**frostier, frostiest**) **1** very cold, esp. cold with frost. **2** covered with or as with hoarfrost. **3** cold and unfriendly in manner: *a frosty look*.

froth • *noun* **1 a** a collection of small bubbles in liquid, caused by shaking, fermenting, etc.; foam. **b** impure matter on liquid; scum. **c** something that looks like a mass of small bubbles on liquid: *a froth of black lace*. **2** worthless or unsubstantial talk, ideas, or activities: *producing the season's celluloid froth is a costly business*. **3** foaming saliva, esp. as in rabies etc. • *verb* **1 a** emit froth: *frothing at the mouth*. **b** (of liquid) gather froth or run foaming over etc. **2** cause (beer etc.) to foam.

frothing *adjective* = FROTHY 1: *frothing water surges up with the pounding waves*.

frothy *adjective* (**frothier, frothiest**) **1** full of or covered with a mass of small bubbles: *steaming mugs of frothy coffee*. **2** light and entertaining but of little substance: *lots of frothy interviews*.

frown • *verb* **1 a** contract the eyebrows and wrinkle the forehead, esp. in anger, worry, or deep thought. **b** make a glum expression, esp. with the corners of the mouth turned down. **2** express disapproval: *promiscuity was frowned upon*. • *noun* a look expressing severity, disapproval, or deep thought.

froze *past of* FREEZE.

frozen • *verb* *past participle of* FREEZE. • *adjective* **1 a** exposed or subject to extreme cold. **b** solidified by exposure to cold. **2** (of food) preserved by refrigeration to below freezing point. **3** emotionally frigid, unfriendly, or unresponsive. **4** (of a mechanism etc.) fixed, immobile, e.g. with rust, cold, etc. **b** (of a joint etc.) stiffened or immobile from an injury etc. **5** (of a credit or asset) that cannot be converted into cash at maturity or some other given time.

fructose *noun* a simple sugar found in honey and fruits. [Say FROOK tose or FRUK tose (FROOK rhymes with BOOK; TOSE rhymes with DOSE)]

frugal *adjective* **1** using only as much money or food as is necessary; thrifty: *if you want to save for a trip to Europe, you'll have to be frugal*. **2** (of things, esp. food) plain, simple, or provided in small quantity and with avoidance of excess: *a frugal lunch of soup and crackers*. ▶ **frugality** *noun* **frugally** *adverb* [Say FROO gull, froo GALA tee]

fruit • *noun* **1 a** the usu. sweet and fleshy edible product of a plant or tree, containing seed. **b** (in *singular*) these in quantity: *eats fruit*. **2** the seed-bearing structure of a plant or tree, as a means

of reproduction, e.g. an acorn, pea pod, cherry, etc. **3** (usu. in *plural*) any plant product used as food, e.g. vegetables, grains, etc.: *fruits of the earth*. **4** (usu. in *plural*) a product, outcome, or anything, concrete or abstract, produced by an activity, process, etc.: *fruits of his labours*. • *verb* bear or cause to bear fruit.

fruit bat *noun* a bat with a large snout and large eyes that feeds chiefly on fruit.

fruitcake *noun* **1** a cake containing a high proportion of mixed dried fruit and often nuts. **2** *slang* an eccentric or mad person.

fruit cocktail *noun* = FRUIT SALAD.

fruit fly *noun* (*plural* **fruit flies**) any of various small flies that feed on rotting or fermenting fruit, much used in genetic research because of their large chromosomes, numerous varieties, and rapid rate of reproduction.

fruitful *adjective* **1 a** (of a tree etc.) producing much fruit. **b** (of soil etc.) fertile, inducing fertility in plants etc. **2 a** producing good results: *a fruitful collaboration*. **b** abundantly productive of ideas or some other immaterial thing: *a fruitful source of information*. **3** producing offspring, esp. prolifically. ▶ **fruitfully** *adverb* **fruitfulness** *noun*

fruitiness *noun* the quality or condition of resembling, tasting like, or smelling like fruit.

fruiting *adjective* (of a tree or other plant) bearing fruit, esp. at a specified time or of a specified kind: *planted a fruiting rose*.

fruition *noun* the realization or successful outcome of aims, hopes, plans, etc.: *after months of hard work, our plans finally came to fruition* ◊ *his extravagant ideas were never brought to fruition*. [Say froo ISH un]

fruitless *adjective* **1** useless, unsuccessful: *his fruitless attempts to publish poetry*. **2** not bearing fruit. ▶ **fruitlessly** *adverb*

fruit salad *noun* various fruits cut up and served in syrup, juice, etc.

fruity *adjective* (**fruitier, fruitiest**) **1 a** of, relating to, or resembling fruit, esp. in taste or smell. **b** (of wine) tasting of the grape. **2** (of a voice etc.) mellow, deep, or of a full rich quality.

frump *noun* a dowdy, unattractive woman. ▶ **frumpily** *adverb* **frumpiness** *noun* **frumpy** *adjective* (**frumpier, frumpiest**)

frustrate *verb* (**frustrates, frustrated, frustrating**) **1** upset or discourage (a person). **2** make (efforts) ineffective: *parliament frustrated his reforms*. **3** prevent (a person) from achieving a purpose. **4** disappoint (a hope).

frustrated *adjective* **1** discontented because unable to achieve one's desire. **2** sexually unfulfilled.

frustrating *adjective* causing one to feel annoyed and impatient because one cannot do or achieve what one wants. ▶ **frustratingly** *adverb*

frustration *noun* **1** the feeling of being upset or annoyed, esp. because of inability to change or achieve something: *I sometimes feel like screaming with frustration*. **2** an event or circumstance that causes one to have such a feeling: *the inherent frustrations of my job*. **3** the prevention of the progress, success, or fulfillment of something: *the frustration of their wishes*.

fry[1] • *verb* (**fries, fried, frying**) **1** cook or be cooked in hot fat. **2** *informal* overload, burn out, etc. (electronic components etc.). **3** *slang* electrocute or be electrocuted. **4** *informal* **a** burn or overheat, esp. with effects analogous to those of frying food. **b** (of the sun) scorch (a person etc.). **5** *slang* **a** destroy: *drugs fry the brain*. **b** upset or annoy intensely. • *noun* (*plural* **fries**) **1** (in *plural*) = FRENCH FRY. **2** a dish of fried food, esp. meat.

fry² *plural noun* **1** young or newly hatched fish. **2** the young of other creatures produced in large numbers, e.g. bees or frogs.

> **SPELL CHECK**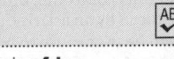
> **fryer, friar**
>
> A member of a religious order is a **friar**.

fryer *noun* **1** a pot etc. for frying food, esp. in deep fat. **2** a person who fries. **3** a chicken suitable for frying.

frying pan *noun* (also **fry pan**) a flat, shallow pan with a long handle, used for frying food. PHRASES **out of the frying pan into the fire** from a bad situation to a worse one.

f-stop *noun* an f-number setting on a camera.

Ft. *abbreviation* **1** Fort. **2** (**ft.**) foot, feet.

FTA *abbreviation* Free Trade Agreement.

FTP *Computing* • *abbreviation* file transfer protocol. • *verb* (**FTP's, FTP'd, FTPing**) implement this protocol on (a data item etc.).

fuchsia *noun* **1** a shrub with drooping red or purple or white flowers. **2** a bright purple-pink shade of red. [Say FEW shuh]

fuddle *verb* (**fuddles, fuddled, fuddling**) confuse or stupefy, esp. with alcoholic liquor.

fuddy-duddy *slang* • *noun* (*plural* **fuddy-duddies**) an old-fashioned or quaintly fussy person. • *adjective* old-fashioned; quaintly fussy.

fudge • *noun* **1** a soft crumbly or chewy kind of candy made with milk, sugar, butter, etc. **2** designating rich chocolate cakes, cookies, sauces, etc.: *a fudge sundae*. **3** *informal* nonsense. **4** *informal* a piece of dishonesty or faking. • *verb* (**fudges, fudged, fudging**) **1** put together in a makeshift or dishonest way; fake: *fudged the budget figures*. **2** deal with vaguely or inadequately, usu. deliberately, so as to mislead or avoid making a definite choice: *the minister tried to fudge the issue by saying she did not want to specify periods*. **3** practise such methods: *fudged on the issue of pay raises*. • *interjection* expressing disbelief or annoyance.

fuehrer *noun* = FÜHRER. [Say FYUR er]

fuel • *noun* **1** material, esp. oil, gas, wood, coal, etc., burned or used as a source of heat or power. **2** food as a source of energy. **3** material used as a source of nuclear energy. **4** anything that sustains or inflames emotion or passion: *the premier's comments added fuel to the debate over taxes*. • *verb* (**fuels, fuelled, fuelling**) **1** supply with fuel. **2** sustain or inflame (an argument, feeling, etc.): *drink fuelled his anger*. **3** take in or get fuel.

fuel cell *noun* a cell producing an electric current direct from a chemical reaction.

fuel efficiency *noun* the efficient use of fuel in an engine or other system. ▶ **fuel-efficient** *adjective*

fuel-injected *adjective* (of an internal combustion engine) powered by the direct introduction of fuel under pressure into the combustion chamber.

fuel injection *noun* the direct introduction of fuel under pressure into the combustion chamber of an internal combustion engine.

fuel rod *noun* a rod-shaped can of nuclear fuel, esp. one used in a nuclear reactor.

fugitive • *noun* a person who flees, esp. from justice, an enemy, danger, or a master. • *adjective* **1** fleeing; that runs or has run away: *a fugitive criminal*. **2** quick to disappear, fleeting; of short duration: *he entertained a fugitive idea that Bella needed him*.

fugue *noun* **1** *Music* a composition in which a short melody or phrase is introduced by one part and successively taken up by others and developed by interweaving the parts. **2** *Psychology* (also **fugue state**)

loss of awareness of one's identity, often coupled with flight from one's usual environment. [Say FYOOG]

führer *noun* a tyrannical leader (esp. as a title of Adolf Hitler). [Say FYUR er]

fulcrum *noun* (*plural* **fulcrums** or **fulcra**) **1** the point against which a lever is placed to get a purchase or on which it turns or is supported. **2** the means by which influence etc. is brought to bear: *the church was another fulcrum of family life*. [Say FULL crum (FULL rhymes with PULL or HULL)]

fulfill *verb* (**fulfills, fulfilled, fulfilling**) **1** bring to completion or reality; achieve or realize (something desired, promised, or predicted): *he won't be able to fulfill his ambition to visit Dublin*. **2** carry out (a task, duty, or role) as required, pledged, or expected: *demanded that the government fulfill the commitments it made during the last election campaign*. **3** satisfy or meet (a requirement, condition, or need): *have fulfilled all the requirements for graduation*. PHRASES **fulfill oneself** develop one's gifts and character to the full.

fulfilled *adjective* completely happy; satisfied.

fulfilling *adjective* deeply satisfying.

fulfillment *noun* **1** satisfaction or happiness as a result of fully developing one's abilities or character: *she did not believe that marriage was the key to happiness and fulfillment*. **2** the achievement of something desired, promised, or predicted: *winning the championship was the fulfillment of a childhood dream*. **3** the meeting of a requirement, condition, or need: *the fulfillment of the requirements for graduation*.

full¹ • *adjective* **1** holding all its limits will allow: *the bucket is full*. **2** having eaten to one's limits or satisfaction. **3** abundant, satisfying: *led a full life* ◊ *full details*. **4** having or holding an abundance of: *full of interest* ◊ *full of mistakes*. **5** (foll. by *of*) **a** engrossed in thinking about: *full of his work*. **b** unable to refrain from talking about: *full of the news*. **6** reaching the specified or usual or utmost limit: *full membership* ◊ *waited a full hour*. **7 a** (of tone or colour) deep and rich; intense. **b** (of light) intense. **c** (of motion etc.) vigorous: *at full gallop*. **d** (of sound) strong, resonant. **e** (of wine etc.) rich in quality or tone. **8** plump; *a full figure*. **9** (of clothes) amply cut; made of much material arranged in folds or gathers. **10** (of the heart etc.) overcharged with emotion. **11** having all the qualifications or privileges of a designation; of the highest rank: *full professor*. • *adverb* **1** very: *you know full well*. **2** exactly: *hit him full on the nose*. PHRASES **full of oneself** selfish, conceited. **full nine yards** *slang* everything. **full speed** (or **steam**) **ahead!** an order to proceed at maximum speed or to pursue a course of action energetically. **full up** completely full. **in full 1** without abridgement. **2** to or for the full amount: *paid in full*. **in full swing** at the height of activity. **in full view** entirely visible. **to the full** to the utmost extent.

full² *verb* cleanse and thicken (cloth).

fullback *noun* **1** *Football* a running back who lines up behind the rest of his team at the scrimmage. **2** *Soccer etc.* a defensive player, or a position near the goal.

full blood *noun* **1** pure descent; unmixed ancestry. **2** a person or animal of unmixed ancestry.

full-blooded *adjective* **1** of unmixed race: *a full-blooded Cree*. **2** vigorous, enthusiastic, and without compromise: *his belief in full-blooded socialism*.

full-blown *adjective* **1** fully developed, complete: *full-blown AIDS*. **2** (of flowers) very open.

full-bodied *adjective* rich in quality, tone, flavour, etc.

full bore *informal* • *adverb* at maximum power, speed, etc.: *ran full bore down the street.* • *adjective* complete: *a full bore socialist* ◊ *a full bore survey of natural history.*

full-court press *noun* **1** *Basketball* an aggressive defence tactic in which the team without the ball harasses the opposing team the whole length of the court. **2** an attack; an offensive campaign: *a full-court press of opposition, including tactical delays and parliamentary manoeuvres, to stop the appointment.*

full deck *noun* a complete set of playing cards. **PHRASES** **not playing with a full deck** *slang* not of normal intelligence or sanity.

full dress • *noun* clothes worn on ceremonial or formal occasions. • *adjective* (**full-dress**) thorough, complete: *a full-dress debate in the media.*

full-face *adverb & adjective* with all the face visible to the observer: *a full-face portrait.*

full-featured *adjective* (of computers, electronic equipment, etc.) having many features; up-to-date.

full-figure *adjective* **1** (of a painting, statue, etc. of a person) representing the entire body. **2 a** plump. **b** (also **full-figured**) oversize: *ladies' full-figure blouses.*

full-flavoured *adjective* (of food, wine, etc.) strong and distinct in taste.

full-fledged *adjective* of full rank or status: *a full-fledged political party.*

full-grown *adjective* having reached maturity.

full house *noun* **1** a maximum or large attendance at a theatre, stadium, etc. **2** *Cards* a poker hand with three of a kind and a pair.

full-length *adjective* **1** of normal, standard, or maximum length. **2** (of a mirror, portrait, etc.) showing the whole height of the human figure.

full moon *noun* **1** the moon in its fullest phase, with its whole disc illuminated. **2** the time when this occurs.

fullness *noun* **1** the state of being full. **2** (of sound, colour, etc.) richness, volume, body. **PHRASES** **in the fullness of time** after a due length of time has gone by; eventually: *he'll tell us in the fullness of time.*

full out • *adverb* at full power, speed, etc. • *adjective* (**full-out**) complete: *full-out drunkenness.*

full-scale *adjective* **1** not reduced in size; having the same size as the original. **2** utilizing all available resources; all-out: *a full-scale investigation.*

full-service *adjective* **1** designating a gas station, restaurant, etc. where service is provided entirely by staff (*compare* SELF-SERVE 1). **2** providing a wide range of products or services: *a full-service gym.*

full-size • *adjective* (also **full-sized**) **1** of the standard size of its kind: *a full-size washing machine.* **2** (of a car) of the largest size, usu. having a wheelbase over 105 inches and a 4 litre engine. • *noun* a full-size car.

full term *noun* the completion of a normal pregnancy.

full-time • *adjective* occupying or using the whole of the available working time: *a full-time job.* • *adverb* on a full-time basis: *works full-time.* • *noun* (**full time**) the total normal duration of work etc.

full-timer *noun* a person who works a full-time job.

fully *adverb* **1** completely, entirely: *I fully understand the fears of the workers* ◊ *this issue is discussed more fully in chapter 7.* **2** no less or fewer than: *fully 60 people attended.*

fully-fledged *adjective* = FULL-FLEDGED.

fulmar *noun* a medium-sized seabird with a stout body, robust bill, and rounded tail. [Say FULL mur]

fulminate *verb* (**fulminates**, **fulminated**, **fulminating**) express criticism loudly and forcefully: *fulminating against the GST.* ▶ **fulmination** *noun* [Say FULL min ate, full min AY sh'n (*FULL* rhymes with *HULL* or *PULL*)]

WRITING TIP
fulsome ✏️

Because **fulsome** can mean either "excessively flattering" or "abundant", a sentence like *Desmond showered the president with fulsome praise* can be ambiguous: is Desmond's praise abundant but genuine, or insincere? Avoid using **fulsome** unless it is obvious from the context which sense is intended, as in *Desmond, sincerely moved by the president's presentation, showered her with fulsome praise* or *Desmond, who had a reputation for obsequiousness, showered the president with fulsome praise.*

---

fulsome *adjective* **1** (of praise etc.) excessively complimentary or flattering; effusive, overdone. **2** abundant. ▶ **fulsomely** *adverb*

fumble • *verb* (**fumbles**, **fumbled**, **fumbling**) **1** use the hands awkwardly, grope about: *fumbled in her pockets for change.* **2** handle or deal with clumsily or nervously. **3** *Football etc.* fail to keep hold of a ball after having touched it or transported it. **4** make one's way clumsily: *fumbled his way across the garden.* • *noun* an act of fumbling. ▶ **fumblingly** *adverb*

fume • *noun* (usu. in *plural*) exuded gas or smoke or vapour, esp. when harmful or unpleasant. • *verb* (**fumes**, **fumed**, **fuming**) **1** emit fumes. **2** feel (esp. suppressed) anger: *was fuming at their ineptitude.*

fumigate *verb* (**fumigates**, **fumigated**, **fumigating**) disinfect (something contaminated or infested) with the fumes of certain chemicals. ▶ **fumigation** *noun* **fumigator** *noun* [Say FUME a gate]

fun • *noun* **1** amusement, esp. lively or playful. **2** a source of this. **3** playfulness; good humour: *she's full of fun.* **4** (also **fun and games**) lighthearted or amusing activities. • *adjective* *informal* amusing, entertaining, enjoyable: *a fun thing to do.* • *verb* (**funs**, **funned**, **funning**) *informal* have fun; fool, joke. **PHRASES** **for fun** (or **for the fun of it**) not for a serious purpose. **in fun** as a joke, not seriously. **make fun of** (or **poke fun at**) mock; ridicule.

function • *noun* **1** an activity or purpose natural to or intended for a person or thing: *bridges perform the function of providing access across water* ◊ *I was losing control of my bodily functions* ◊ *the auditor's function is to review the company's accounts and report to the shareholders.* **2** a large or formal social event or ceremony. **3** *Math* a variable quantity regarded in relation to another or others in terms of which it may be expressed or on which its value depends: *x is a function of y and z.* **4** something dependent on another factor or factors: *university attendance as a function of family income.* **5** *Computing* a part of a program that corresponds to a single value. • *verb* **1** fulfill a function. **2** operate; be in working order.

functional *adjective* **1** of or having a special activity, purpose, or task; relating to the way in which something works or operates: *there are important functional differences between left and right brain.* **2** functioning; able to work: *is this machine functional?* **3** (esp. of buildings) designed or intended to be practical rather than attractive. **4** *Math* of a function.

functional illiteracy *noun* the state or condition of being unable to read or write well enough to complete everyday tasks, such as reading a menu etc.

functional illiterate *noun* a person who cannot read or write well enough to complete everyday tasks, such as reading a menu etc.

functionalism *noun* **1** (in the arts) the doctrine that the design of an object should be determined solely by its function, rather than by aesthetic considerations. **2** (in the social sciences) the theory that all aspects of a society serve a function and are necessary for the survival of that society. **3** belief in or stress on the practical application of a thing. ► **functionalist** *noun & adjective*

functionality *noun* **1** the quality of being suited to serve a purpose well; practicality: *I like the feel and functionality of this bakeware*. **2** the purpose that something is designed or expected to fulfill: *manufacturing processes may be affected by the functionality of the product*. **3** the range of operations that can be run on a computer or other electronic system: *new software with additional functionality*.

functionally *adverb* **1** in terms of the particular function, operation, or purpose of a thing: *the systems differ functionally*. **2** in a way that meets (or fails to meet) a person's everyday needs: *we want the students to become functionally bilingual*.

functionally illiterate *adjective* (of a person) unable to read or write well enough to complete everyday tasks, such as reading a menu etc.

functionary *noun* (*plural* **functionaries**) a person who performs official functions or duties; an official.

function key *noun* *Computing* a key which is used to generate instructions.

fund • *noun* **1** a permanent stock of something ready to be drawn upon: *a fund of knowledge*. **2** a reserve of money or investments, esp. one set apart for a purpose. **3** (in *plural*) money resources. • *verb* provide with money. ► **funded** *adjective* **funder** *noun*

fundamental • *adjective* of, affecting, or serving as a base or foundation; essential, primary, original. • *noun* **1** (usu. in *plural*) a fundamental rule, principle, or article. **2** *Music* the lowest note of a chord.

fundamentalism *noun* **1** a form of Protestant Christianity which upholds belief in the strict and literal interpretation of the Bible, including its narratives, doctrines, prophecies, and moral laws. **2** strict maintenance of ancient or fundamental doctrines of any religion, esp. Islam. ► **fundamentalist** *noun & adjective*

fundamentally *adverb* **1** in central or primary respects: *two fundamentally different concepts of democracy*. **2** (qualifying a whole sentence) used to make an emphatic statement about the basic truth of something: *fundamentally, this is a matter for doctors*.

funding *noun* **1** money provided, esp. by an organization or government, for a particular purpose. **2** the action or practice of providing such money.

fundraiser *noun* **1** a person who seeks financial support for a cause, enterprise, etc. **2** a social function, sale, etc. held to raise money for a cause, enterprise, etc. ► **fundraising** *noun*

funeral • *noun* **1 a** a ceremony or service held shortly after a person's death, usu. including the person's burial or cremation. **b** a burial or cremation procession. **2** *informal* one's (usu. unpleasant) concern: *that's your funeral*. • *adjective* of or used etc. at a funeral: *funeral oration*.

funeral director *noun* an undertaker.

funeral home *noun* (also **funeral parlour, funeral chapel**) an establishment where the dead are prepared for burial or cremation.

funerary *adjective* of or used at a funeral or funerals: *both of these cultures practised elaborate funerary ceremonies*. [Say FEW nur airy]

funereal *adjective* having the mournful, sombre character appropriate to a funeral: *funereal wreaths* ◊ *his funereal gloominess was legendary*. [Say few NEERY ul]

fungal *adjective* of or caused by a fungus or fungi: *fungal diseases*. [Say FUN gull]

fungicidal *adjective* of the nature of, acting as, or characteristic of a fungus-destroying substance. [Say funga SIDE ul or funja SIDE ul]

fungicide *noun* a fungus-destroying substance. [Say FUNGA side or FUNJA side]

fungo *noun* *Baseball* (*plural* **fungoes**) **1** a fly ball hit in the air for practice. **2** (also **fungo bat**) a lightweight practice bat. [Say FUN go]

fungus *noun* (*plural* **fungi** or **funguses**) **1** any plant without leaves, flowers, or green colouring, usu. growing on other plants or on decaying matter, including moulds, yeasts, mushrooms, and toadstools. **2** a covering of mould or a similar fungus, e.g. on a plant or wall. **3** used to describe something that has appeared or grown rapidly and is considered unpleasant or unattractive: *there was a fungus of outbuildings behind the house*. [Say FUN guy or FUN jye for the plural]

funhouse *noun* (in an amusement park) a building with trick mirrors, shifting floors, etc., designed to scare or amuse patrons as they walk through.

funk *noun* *informal* **1** fear, panic. **2** a dejected state of mind: *in a funk*. **3** a style of popular music of US black origin. **4** a strong, unpleasant smell.

funky *adjective* (**funkier, funkiest**) **1** (esp. of jazz or rock music) earthy, bluesy, with a heavy rhythmical beat. **2** *informal* **a** fashionable, trendy. **b** unconventional, striking. **3** having a strong, unpleasant smell. ► **funkily** *adverb* **funkiness** *noun*

funnel • *noun* **1** a narrow tube or pipe widening at the top, for pouring liquid, powder, etc., into a small opening. **2** a metal chimney on a steam engine or ship. • *verb* (**funnels, funnelled, funnelling**) **1** guide or move through or as through a funnel: *the wind funnelled down through the valley*. **2** direct, channel: *funnel money to local charities*.

funnel cloud *noun* a funnel-shaped cloud produced in a low-pressure vortex in the centre of a spiral storm, e.g. a tornado or waterspout.

funnily *adverb* in a strange or amusing way: *you do think funnily*. PHRASES **funnily enough** used to admit that a situation or fact is surprising or curious: *funnily enough, I was starting to like the idea*.

funny • *adjective* (**funnier, funniest**) **1** amusing. **2** strange, perplexing. **3** *informal* slightly unwell. **4** eccentric: *a funny old man*. **5** underhand, deceitful. • *noun* (*plural* **funnies**) (usu. in *plural*) *informal* **1** a comic strip in a newspaper. **2** a joke.

funny bone *noun* **1** the part of the elbow over which the ulnar nerve passes, which, when struck, causes a tingling sensation in the arm and hand. **2** a sense of humour: *he knows where Canada's funny bone is, and he knows how to tickle it*.

funny farm *noun* *slang* a psychiatric hospital.

funny money *noun* *informal* **1** inflated or counterfeit currency. **2** *Cdn hist.* twenty-five-dollar certificates issued to Albertans in 1937 by the Social Credit government of William Aberhart.

SPELL CHECK
fur, fir ✓ABC

The evergreen tree is a **fir**.

fur *noun* **1 a** the fine, soft, thick hair of certain animals. **b** the skin of such an animal with the fur on it; a pelt. **2 a** the coat of certain animals, or fabric resembling these, as material for making, trimming, or lining clothes. **b** a garment made of or trimmed or lined with fur. PHRASES **the fur is flying** *informal* there is trouble or a disturbance.

furball *noun* **1** an accumulation of fur ingested by a cat etc. during self-grooming and then spit up. **2** *jocular* a small furry animal, esp. a pet.

fur-bearer *noun* a furred animal, esp. one whose fur is of value in the marketplace. ▶ **fur-bearing** *adjective*

furbish *verb* give a fresh look to (something old or shabby); renovate: *the newly furbished church*. ▶ **furbisher** *noun*

fur brigade *noun* Cdn hist. a convoy of Red River carts, York boats, canoes, etc. which transported furs etc. to and from isolated trading posts.

furious *adjective* **1** extremely angry. **2** raging, violent, intense. **3** rapid, requiring intense energy: *a furious schedule*. ▶ **furiously** *adverb* **furiousness** *noun*

furl *verb* **1** roll up and secure (a sail, umbrella, flag, etc.). **2** become furled.

furlong *noun* an eighth of a mile (201.168 metres).

furlough *noun* leave of absence, esp. granted to a soldier or missionary. [Say FUR lo]

furnace *noun* **1** an appliance fired by gas or oil in which air or water is heated to be circulated throughout a building to heat it. **2** an enclosed structure for intense heating by fire, esp. of metals or water. **3** a very hot place.

furnish *verb* (**furnishes, furnished, furnishing**) **1** provide (a house, room, etc.) with all necessary contents, esp. movable furniture. **2** supply someone with (something); give (something) to someone: *she was able to furnish me with details of the incident*. **3** be a source of; provide: *fish furnish an important source of protein*.

furnished *adjective* (of a house, apartment, etc.) rented with furniture.

furnishings *plural noun* the furniture, carpets, draperies, etc. in a house, room, etc.

furniture *noun* **1** the movable equipment of a house, room, etc., e.g. tables, chairs, and beds. **2** accessories, e.g. the handles and lock of a door. PHRASES **part of the furniture** *informal* a person or thing taken for granted.

furor *noun* great anger or excitement shown by a number of people, usually caused by a public event: *his novel about Jesus caused a furor among Christians* ◊ *the recent furor over the tax increases*.

furred *adjective* **1** (of a garment) lined or trimmed with fur. **2** (of an animal) with fur.

furrier *noun* **1** a person who makes, cleans, and repairs fur garments. **2** a person who buys and sells furs.

furrow • *noun* **1** a narrow trench made in the ground by a plow. **2** a rut, groove, or deep wrinkle. • *verb* **1** plow. **2 a** make furrows, grooves, etc. in. **b** mark with wrinkles. **3** (esp. of the brow) become furrowed.

furrowed *adjective* (of the forehead or face) marked with lines or wrinkles caused by frowning, anxiety, or concentration: *she stroked her furrowed brow*.

furry *adjective* (**furrier, furriest**) **1** of or like fur. **2** covered with or wearing fur.

fur seal *noun* any of several eared seals with thick fur on the underside used commercially as sealskin.

WRITING TIP
further, farther

Further and **farther** can both be used to describe physical distance: *We walked further* (or *farther*) *than I had expected*; *Lethbridge is further* (or *farther*) *than I thought*. Of the two, **further** is more likely to be used to mean "to a greater extent" (*Nothing could be further from the truth*). Only **further** is used to mean "in addition" (*We must decide when and, further, where to hold the meeting*), "additional" (*Please reply without further delay*), and "promote" (*He used them to further his own career*).

further • *adverb* **1 a** to or at a more advanced point in space or time: *it's not safe to proceed further*. **b** at a greater distance: *nothing was further from his thoughts*. **2** to a greater extent, more: *will inquire further*. **3** in addition; furthermore: *I may add further*. • *adjective* **1** more distant or advanced: *on the further side*. **2** more, additional, going beyond what exists or has been dealt with: *threats of further punishment*. • *verb* promote, favour, help on (a scheme, undertaking, movement, or cause). PHRASES **further to** *formal* following on from (esp. an earlier letter etc.). **till further notice** to continue until explicitly changed.

furthermore *adverb* in addition, besides (esp. introducing a fresh consideration in an argument).

furthermost *adjective* (of an edge or extreme) at the greatest distance from a central point or implicit standpoint: *the furthermost end of the street*.

WRITING TIP
furthest, farthest

The form **farthest** is used esp. with reference to physical distance, although **furthest** is preferred by many even in this sense.

furthest • *adjective* **1** most distant in space, direction, or time; most remote. **2** longest; most extended in space. • *adverb* **1** to or at the greatest distance in space or time; most remote. **2** to the highest degree or extent; most: *she is the furthest advanced of all my students*.

furtive *adjective* **1** attempting to avoid notice or attention, typically because of guilt or a belief that discovery would lead to trouble: *they spent a furtive day together* ◊ *he stole a furtive glance at her*. **2** suggestive of guilty nervousness: *the look in his eyes became furtive*. ▶ **furtively** *adverb* **furtiveness** *noun*

fur trade *noun* the business of trapping, transporting, and selling furs, esp. as carried on between European traders and Aboriginal peoples in North America from the 17th to the 19th century. ▶ **fur trader** *noun* **fur trading** *adjective*

fury *noun* (*plural* **furies**) **1** wild and passionate anger, rage. **2** violence of a storm, disease, etc. **3** (**Fury**) (usu. in *plural*) (in Greek mythology) a spirit of punishment, often represented as one of three goddesses who executed the curses pronounced upon criminals, tortured the guilty with stings of conscience, and inflicted famines. **4** an angry, malignant, or abusively domineering woman. PHRASES **like fury** *informal* with great force or effect.

fuse[1] • *verb* (**fuses, fused, fusing**) **1** melt with intense heat; liquefy. **2** blend or amalgamate into one whole by or as by melting. **3** provide (a circuit, plug, etc.) with a fuse. **4** (of anatomical structures, groups of atoms, etc.) coalesce, join. • *noun* a device or component for protecting an electric circuit, containing a strip of wire of easily melted metal and placed in the circuit so as to break it by melting when

an excessive current passes through. PHRASES **blow a fuse** *informal* **1** cause a fuse to melt by passing excessive current through it. **2** lose one's temper.

fuse² • *noun* **1** a device for igniting a bomb or explosive charge, consisting of a tube or cord etc. filled or saturated with combustible matter. **2** a component in a shell, mine, etc., designed to detonate an explosive charge on impact, after an interval, or when subjected to a magnetic or vibratory stimulation. • *verb* (**fuses, fused, fusing**) fit a fuse to. PHRASES **have a short fuse** anger easily.

fuse box *noun* a box housing the fuses for circuits in a building.

fuselage *noun* the body of an airplane, to which the wings and tail are fitted. [Say FYOOZ a lazh or FYOOZ uh lozh]

fusible *adjective* that can be easily fused or melted. [Say FEW zuh bull]

fusilier *noun* **1** a member of any of several regiments formerly armed with light muskets called fusils. **2** *hist.* a soldier armed with a fusil. [Say few zuh LEER]

fusillade • *noun* **1** a continuous discharge of firearms. **2** a sustained outburst of criticism etc.: *faced with such a fusillade of accusations, Ronny found himself with no choice but to recount the whole embarrassing incident.* • *verb* **1** assault (a place) by a fusillade. **2** shoot down (persons) with a fusillade. [Say few zuh LAID or few zuh LOD]

fusilli *plural noun* pasta in the form of short spirals. [Say foo ZILLY or few ZILLY]

fusion *noun* **1** the process or result of joining two or more things together to form one: *the fusion of copper and zinc to produce brass* ◊ *the movie displayed a perfect fusion of image and sound.* **2** a coalition. **3** = NUCLEAR FUSION. **4** a kind of music in which elements of more than one popular style are combined, esp. jazz and rock.

fusion bomb *noun* a bomb deriving its energy from nuclear fusion, esp. a hydrogen bomb.

fuss • *noun* **1** nervous excitement or activity, esp. of an unnecessary kind. **2** a display of excitement, worry, or enthusiasm, esp. over something unimportant. **3** a sustained protest or dispute. • *verb* (**fusses, fussed, fussing**) **1 a** make a fuss. **b** busy oneself restlessly with trivial things. **c** (often foll. by *about*) move fussily. **d** (of a baby) express discomfort or unhappiness by whimpering etc. **2** agitate, worry. PHRASES **make a fuss** complain vigorously. **make a fuss over** treat (a person or animal) with great or excessive attention.

fuss-budget *noun* *informal* (also **fusspot**) a person given to fussing.

fussily *adverb* in a manner that is full of unnecessary details or difficult to please: *fussily detailed sets.*

fussiness *noun* the quality of being inclined to fuss, full of unnecessary details, or difficult to please.

fussy *adjective* (**fussier, fussiest**) **1** inclined to fuss. **2** full of unnecessary detail or decoration. **3** difficult to please. PHRASES **be not fussy about 1** be indifferent about. **2** not like particularly.

fustiness *noun* **1** the quality or condition of being stale-smelling, musty, or stuffy. **2** the quality or condition of being antiquated or old-fashioned.

fusty *adjective* (**fustier, fustiest**) **1** stale-smelling, musty: *a dark fusty room* ◊ *wearing fusty old clothes.* **2** antiquated, old-fashioned: *fusty ideas* ◊ *a fusty old professor.*

futile *adjective* useless. ▶ **futilely** *adverb* **futility** *noun* [Say FEW tile or FEW tul, few TILLA tee]

futon *noun* **1** a Japanese quilted mattress rolled out on the floor for use as a bed. **2** a type of low wooden sofa bed having such a mattress. [Say FOO tawn]

future • *adjective* **1** going or expected to happen or be or become. **2** *Grammar* (of a tense or participle) describing an event yet to happen. • *noun* **1** time to come: *past, present, and future.* **2** what will happen in the future: *the future is uncertain.* **3** the future condition of a person, country, etc. **4** a prospect of success etc.: *there's no future in it.* **5** *Grammar* the future tense. **6** (in *plural*) *Stock Market* **a** goods and stocks sold for future delivery. **b** contracts for these. PHRASES **in future** from now onward.

future perfect *noun* *Grammar* a tense giving the sense *will have done.*

future shock *noun* a state of distress or disorientation due to rapid social or technological change.

futurism *noun* (also **Futurism**) an early 20th-century movement in art, literature, music, etc., concerned with celebrating and incorporating into art the energy and dynamism of modern technology.

futurist *noun* **1** (also **Futurist**) a supporter or follower of futurism. **2** a person who is concerned with or studies the future.

futuristic *adjective* **1** suitable for the future; ultra-modern: *futuristic design.* **2** (also **Futuristic**) of futurism. **3** relating to the future. ▶ **futuristically** *adverb*

fuzz • *noun* **1** a mass of soft light particles; fluff. **2** fluffy or frizzled hair. **3** *slang* **a** the police. **b** a police officer. **4** an indistinct sound, image, etc. • *verb* (**fuzzes, fuzzed, fuzzing**) make or become fluffy or blurred.

fuzzily *adverb* in a way that is blurred, indistinct, or imprecise: *a fuzzily conceived project.*

fuzziness *noun* **1** the quality or condition of having or being like fuzz: *fuzziness and ridges on the tongue.* **2** the quality or condition of being blurred, indistinct, or imprecise: *I woke up early, with none of the fuzziness I had other days.* **3** the quality or condition of not being crisp or distinct: *there's a great deal of fuzziness in this recording.*

fuzzy *adjective* (**fuzzier, fuzziest**) **1 a** like fuzz. **b** frizzy. **2 a** blurred, indistinct, esp. in shape or outline. **b** imprecise, vague: *fuzzy thinking.* **c** (of a guitar sound etc.) buzzing, not crisp or distinct.

fwd *abbreviation* forward.

f.w.d. *abbreviation* **1** four-wheel drive. **2** front-wheel drive.

FX *abbreviation* = SPECIAL EFFECTS.

FYI *abbreviation* for your information.

Gg

G¹ *noun* (also **g**) (*plural* **Gs** or **G's**) **1** the seventh letter of the alphabet. **2** *Music* the fifth note in the diatonic scale of C major.

G² *abbreviation* (also **G.**) **1** *informal* = GRAND *noun* 2. **2** good. **3** Gulf. **4** (in Manitoba) = GENERAL *adjective* 4.

G³ *symbol* **1** gauss. **2** giga-. **3** conductance. **4** guanine.

g¹ *abbreviation* (also **g.**) **1** gelding. **2** gas. **3** gauge.

g² *symbol* **1** gram(s). **2 a** gravity. **b** acceleration due to gravity.

GA *abbreviation* Georgia (US) (in official postal use).

Ga *symbol* gallium.

GAA *abbreviation* = GOALS-AGAINST AVERAGE.

gab *informal* • *noun* talk; chatter. • *verb* (**gabs**, **gabbed**, **gabbing**) talk, chatter. PHRASES **gift of the gab** the facility of speaking eloquently or profusely.

gabardine *noun* (also **gaberdine**) **1** a smooth durable twill-woven cloth esp. of worsted or cotton. **2** a garment made of this, esp. a raincoat. [Say GABBER deen]

gabble • *verb* (**gabbles**, **gabbled**, **gabbling**) **1** speak incoherently or inarticulately. **2** (of geese, chickens, etc.) gaggle, cackle, etc. • *noun* **1** voluble confused unintelligible talk. **2** the inarticulate noises made by some animals.

gabby *adjective* (**gabbier**, **gabbiest**) *informal* excessively or annoyingly talkative.

gabfest *noun* *informal* **1** a gathering in which there is much talking. **2** a prolonged conversation.

gable *noun* **1 a** the triangular upper part of a wall enclosed by the two sloping planes of a ridged roof. **b** (also **gable end**) a gable-topped wall. **2** a gable-shaped canopy over a window or door. ▶ **gabled** *adjective*

gad¹ *verb* (**gads**, **gadded**, **gadding**) (foll. by *about*, *around*) go about idly or in search of pleasure.

gad² *interjection* (also **Gad**) an expression of surprise or emphatic assertion.

gadfly *noun* (*plural* **gadflies**) **1** a cattle-biting fly, esp. a horsefly. **2** a person who repeatedly criticizes or harasses others, esp. those in authority: *considered a troublemaker and gadfly by the ruling establishment of Upper Canada, Mackenzie was popular with ordinary people.*

gadget *noun* an ingenious mechanical or electronic device or tool, esp. a non-essential one designed for a specific purpose.

gadgetry *noun* gadgets collectively.

gadolinium *noun* a soft silvery metallic element occurring naturally. [Say gadda LINNY um]

Gael *noun* a Gaelic Celt, formerly esp. a Scottish Celt. [Say GALE]

Gaelic • *noun* any of the Celtic languages spoken in Ireland and Scotland. • *adjective* of or relating to the Celts of Ireland or Scotland, or their languages. [Say GAY lick]

gaff • *noun* **1 a** a stick with an iron hook for landing large fish, seals, etc. **b** a barbed fishing spear. **2** a spar to which the head of a fore-and-aft sail is bent. • *verb* seize (a fish etc.) with a gaff.

gaffe *noun* an indiscreet act or remark. [Say GAFF]

gaffer *noun* **1** the chief electrician in a film or television production unit. **2** an old man. **3** *Cdn* (*Nfld*) a boy or youth at work with adults.

gag • *noun* **1** a piece of cloth etc. thrust into or held over the mouth to prevent speaking or crying out. **2** a thing or circumstance restricting free speech. **3** *Parliament* a closure of a debate in a legislative assembly. **4** a joke or comic scene in a play, film, etc., or as part of a comedian's act. **5** an actor's interpolation in a dramatic dialogue. **6 a** a joke or hoax. **b** a humorous action or situation. • *verb* (**gags**, **gagged**, **gagging**) **1** apply a gag to. **2** silence; deprive of free speech: *the new laws are seen as an attempt to gag the press.* **3 a** choke or retch. **b** cause to do this.

gaga *adjective* *slang* **1** senile. **2** slightly crazy. **3** exceedingly enthusiastic or infatuated: *went gaga over him.*

SPELL CHECK   ABC ✓

gage, gauge

Gauge is the usual Canadian spelling for "gauge a reaction", "temperature gauge", and "12-gauge shotgun".

---

gage *esp. US* = GAUGE.

gaggle • *noun* **1** a flock of geese. **2** *informal* a disorderly, noisy group of people or things. • *verb* (**gaggles**, **gaggled**, **gaggling**) (of geese) cackle.

gag order *noun* *informal* **1** a court order banning the publication of information disclosed at a trial etc. **2** (also **gag rule**) any order, law, etc. banning the disclosure of information.

Gaia 1 *Ecology* the earth perceived as a vast self-regulating organism, its living and non-living systems forming an indivisible whole that is kept alive by all living organisms themselves. **2** (in Greek mythology) the earth personified as a goddess. ▶ **Gaian** *adjective* & *noun* [Say GUY uh, GUY un]

gaiety *noun* **1** the state of being lighthearted or merry; mirth. **2** merrymaking, amusement. **3** a bright appearance. [Say GAY a tee]

gaily *adverb* **1** in a gay or lighthearted manner. **2** with a bright or colourful appearance.

gain • *verb* **1** obtain or secure (usu. something desired or favourable): *gain recognition.* **2** acquire (a sum) as profits or as a result of changed conditions; earn. **3** obtain as an increment or addition: *gain momentum.* **4** win (a victory). **5** (foll. by *in*) make a specified advance or improvement: *gained in stature.* **6** (of a clock etc.) have the fault of becoming fast. **7** (often foll. by *on*, *upon*) come closer to a person or thing pursued. **8** *formal* reach a place, usually after a lot of effort: *at last she gained the shelter of the forest.* • *noun* **1** something gained, achieved, etc. **2** an increase of possessions etc.; a profit, advance, or improvement. **3** the acquisition of wealth. **4** (in *plural*) sums of money acquired. **5** an increase in amount, weight, etc. PHRASES **gain time** improve one's chances by causing or exploiting a delay. ▶ **gainer** *noun*

gainful *adjective* (of employment) paid. ▶ **gainfully** *adverb*

gainsay *verb* (**gainsays**, **gainsaid**, **gainsaying**) deny, contradict: *there is no gainsaying the improvement in working conditions that unions have secured.* ▶ **gainsayer** *noun* [Say GAIN say]

A barrier that can be opened is a **gate**. An obstacle on a slalom course is a **gate**.

gait *noun* **1** a manner of walking. **2** the manner of forward motion of esp. a horse, e.g. walk, gallop, trot.

gaiter *noun* a covering of cloth, leather, etc. for the ankle, or ankle and lower leg, and often extending to the instep, worn over the shoe.

gal *noun* *slang* a girl or woman.

gal. *abbreviation* gallon(s).

gala *noun* (*plural* **galas**) a festive or special occasion: *a gala performance*. [Say GAL uh or GALE uh]

galactic *adjective* of or relating to a galaxy or galaxies, esp. the Milky Way.

galaxy *noun* (*plural* **galaxies**) **1** any of many independent systems of stars, gas, dust, etc., held together by gravitational attraction. **2** (**Galaxy**) = MILKY WAY. **3** (foll. by *of*) a brilliant company or gathering: *a galaxy of film greats were present at the gala*.

gale *noun* **1 a** a very strong wind. **b** *Meteorology* a wind of force 8 on the Beaufort scale, or 34–40 knots. **2** *Nautical* a storm. **3** an outburst, esp. of laughter.

galena *noun* lead sulphide, the principal ore of lead. [Say guh LEENA]

Galician¹ *hist.* • *noun* **1** a late 19th-century or early 20th-century Slavic immigrant to western Canada, esp. a Ukrainian. **2** the language of Galicians. • *adjective* of or pertaining to Galicians. [Say guh LISH un]

Galician² • *noun* **1** a native or inhabitant of Galicia, a medieval Castilian kingdom, later a Spanish province. **2** the language of Galicia, closely related to Portuguese. • *adjective* of or pertaining to Galicia or its inhabitants. [Say guh LISH un]

gall • *noun* **1** rude behaviour showing a lack of respect that is surprising because the person doing it is not embarrassed: *then they had the gall to complain!* ◊ *I almost admired the utter gall of the man*. **2** *formal* a bitter feeling full of hatred; resentment: *words full of venom and gall*. **3** a swelling on plants and trees caused by insects, disease, etc. **4** the bile of animals. • *verb* make someone feel upset and angry, esp. because something is unfair: *it galls me to have to apologize to her*.

gall. *abbreviation* gallon(s).

gallant • *adjective* **1** brave, noble. **2** markedly attentive or polite, esp. to women. **3** (of a ship, horse, etc.) grand, fine, stately. • *noun* a ladies' man; a lover. ▶ **gallantly** *adverb* [Say GAL'nt]

gallantry *noun* (*plural* **gallantries**) **1** bravery; dashing courage. **2** polite attention or respect, esp. given by men to women. [Say GAL un tree]

gallbladder *noun* the vessel storing bile after its secretion by the liver and before release into the intestine.

galleon *noun* *hist.* a square-rigged ship with three or more decks and masts, having a high forecastle and poop, used chiefly by Spain from the 15th to the 18th century, originally as a warship. [Say GALLEY un]

galleria *noun* (*plural* **gallerias**) a collection of stores under one often high glass roof. [Say gal a REE uh]

gallery *noun* (*plural* **galleries**) **1** a room or building for showing works of art. **2** a balcony, esp. a platform projecting from the inner wall of a church, hall, etc., providing extra room for spectators etc. or reserved for musicians, the press, etc. **3 a** the highest balcony in a theatre, usu. with the cheapest seats. **b** its occupants. **4** a covered space for walking in, partly open at the side. **5** (esp. *Que.*, *Nfld.*, & *Gulf States*) a veranda, esp. one surrounding a building on all sides. **6** a long narrow room, passage, or corridor. **7** *Military* & *Mining* a horizontal underground passage. **8** a collection or assembly, esp. on display: *a gallery of celebrities*. PHRASES **play to the gallery** seek to win approval by appealing to popular taste.

galley *noun* (*plural* **galleys**) **1** *hist.* **a** a low flat single-decked vessel using sails and oars, and usu. rowed by slaves or criminals. **b** an ancient Greek or Roman warship with one or more banks of oars. **c** a large open rowboat, e.g. that used by the captain of a man-of-war. **2** the kitchen in a ship, aircraft, camper, etc. **3** (also **galley proof**) a proof in the form of long single-column strips, not in sheets or pages.

Gallic *adjective* **1** French or typically French. **2** of the Gauls. [Say GAL ick]

Gallicism *noun* a French word or usage, esp. one adopted in another language. [Say GAL a sism]

galling *adjective* causing anger, bitterness, or resentment. ▶ **gallingly** *adverb* [Rhymes with *FALLING*]

gallium *noun* a soft bluish-white metallic element which melts just above room temperature, used in high-temperature thermometers etc. [Say GALLEY um]

gallivant *verb* **1** (often foll. by *around*) idly search for pleasure; gad about. **2** flirt. [Say GAL a vant]

gallon *noun* **1 a** (also **imperial gallon**) (in Britain and other Commonwealth countries and formerly in Canada) a measure of capacity equal to eight pints and equivalent to 4.55 litres, used esp. for liquids. **b** (also **US gallon**) (in the US) a measure of capacity equivalent to 3.79 litres, used for liquids. **2** (usu. in *plural*) *informal* a large amount.

The poll is a **Gallup** poll.

gallop • *noun* **1** the fastest pace of a horse or other quadruped, with all the feet off the ground together in each stride. **2** a ride at this pace. • *verb* (**gallops**, **galloped**, **galloping**) **1 a** (of a horse etc. or its rider) go at the pace of a gallop. **b** make (a horse etc.) gallop. **2 a** run with leaping strides, as in a gallop. **b** move or progress rapidly: *galloping inflation*. PHRASES **at a gallop** at the pace of a gallop.

gallows *plural noun* (usu. treated as *singular*) **1** a structure, usu. of two uprights and a crosspiece, for the hanging of criminals. **2** (**the gallows**) execution by hanging. [Say GAL oze]

gallstone *noun* a small hard mass forming in the gallbladder or bile ducts from bile pigments, cholesterol, and calcium salts.

A horse's pace is a **gallop**.

Gallup poll *noun* an assessment of public opinion by questioning a representative sample.

galoot *noun* *informal* a person, esp. a strange or clumsy one.

galore *adverb* in abundance: *flowers galore*.

galosh *noun* (*plural* **galoshes**) (usu. in *plural*) a waterproof overshoe, usu. of rubber.

galumph *verb* *informal* move noisily or clumsily.

galvanic *adjective* **1** of or producing an electric current by chemical action. **2** making people react in a sudden and dramatic way: *a galvanic cry*. ▶ **galvanically** *adverb* [Say gal VAN ick]

galvanize *verb* (**galvanizes**, **galvanized**, **galvanizing**) **1** rouse forcefully, esp. by shock or

excitement: *was galvanized into action.* **2** coat (metal, esp. iron or steel) with zinc (usu. without the use of electricity) as a protection against rust. ▶ **galvanizer** *noun* [Say GALVA nize]

gam *noun* informal (usu in *plural*) a leg, esp. a woman's attractive leg.

gambit *noun* **1** a chess opening in which a player sacrifices a piece or pawn to secure an advantage. **2** an opening move in a discussion etc. **3** a trick, esp. to secure an advantage: *her scare tactics were a desperate last gambit in the final week of a campaign she was clearly losing.*

gamble • *verb* (**gambles, gambled, gambling**) **1** play games of chance for money, esp. for high stakes. **2 a** bet (a sum of money) in gambling. **b** (often foll. by *away*) lose (assets) by gambling. **3** take great risks in the hope of substantial gain. **4** (foll. by *on*) act in the hope or expectation of: *gambled on fine weather.* • *noun* **1** a risky undertaking or attempt, esp. in the hope of substantial gain. **2** an act of gambling. ▶ **gambler** *noun*

gambol • *verb* (**gambols, gambolled, gambolling**) frolic playfully. • *noun* a playful frolic. [Sounds like *GAMBLE*]

game¹ • *noun* **1 a** an amusement, diversion, pastime, etc. **b** a form of contest played according to rules and decided by skill, strength, or luck. **2** a single portion of play forming a scoring unit in some contests, e.g. tennis. **3** (in *plural*) a meeting for athletic etc. contests: *Olympic Games.* **4** a winning score in a game; the state of the score in a game: *the game is two all.* **5** the apparatus necessary to play a game, esp. a board or computer game. **6** one's level of achievement in, or style of playing a game: *improving their game.* **7 a** a piece of fun; a jest: *was only playing a game with you.* **b** (in *plural*) tricks: *none of your games!* **8** a scheme or undertaking etc. regarded as a game: *so that's your game.* **9 a** a policy or plan of action. **b** = GAME PLAN. **10 a** wild animals or birds hunted for sport or food. **b** the flesh of these. **11** a hunted animal; a quarry or object of pursuit or attack. • *adjective* **1** spirited; eager and willing. **2** having the spirit or energy; eagerly prepared: *she's game for anything* ◊ *I'm game to go.* • *verb* (**games, gamed, gaming**) **1** play at games of chance for money; gamble. **2** = WAR GAME. PHRASES **the game is up** the scheme is revealed or foiled. **give the game away** reveal something one would rather keep hidden, esp. inadvertently. **game over** esp. *Cdn slang* all is lost; there is no more hope. **off** (or **on**) **one's game** playing badly (or well). **play the game** behave fairly or according to the rules.

game² *adjective* (of a leg, arm, etc.) lame, crippled.

game bird *noun* **1** a bird shot for sport or food. **2** a bird of a large group that includes pheasants, grouse, quails, guinea fowl, etc.

game fish *noun* (*plural* **game fish** or **game fishes**) a kind of fish caught for sport.

gamekeeper *noun* a person employed to breed and protect game.

gamelan *noun* **1** an Indonesian orchestra with a wide range of metal percussion instruments. **2** a kind of xylophone used in this. [Say GAMMA lan]

gamely *adverb* in a way that seems brave, although a lot of effort is required: *Patti tried gamely to finish the match even though her back was out.*

game misconduct *noun* Hockey a penalty banishing a player for the rest of the current game.

gameness *noun* the quality of being spirited, eager, or willing: *he soon established a reputation for gameness.*

game plan *noun* **1** a winning strategy worked out in advance for a particular match. **2** a plan of campaign, esp. in politics.

gamer *noun* **1** *informal* an athlete known for consistently making a strong effort. **2** a person who plays a game or games.

game show *noun* a television program in which people compete in a game or quiz, usu. for prizes.

gamesmanship *noun* the art or practice of defeating an opponent by psychological or other questionable (but not strictly illegal) means.

games room *noun* (also **game room**) a room, esp. in a hotel, student residence, etc., equipped for playing games, e.g. table tennis, billiards, darts, etc.

gamete *noun* a mature haploid reproductive cell (male or female) which unites with another of the opposite sex in sexual reproduction to form a zygote. [Say GAM eet]

game warden *noun* an official locally supervising game, hunting and fishing, etc.

game-winner *noun* the goal, run, etc. that puts one team ahead of the other by the end of the game.

gamey *adjective* = GAMY.

gamine • *noun* **1** a girl with mischievous or boyish charm. **2** a girl street urchin. • *adjective* of or like a gamine: *a short, gamine haircut.* [Say GAM een]

gaminess *noun* the quality or condition of having the strong flavour or scent of game kept until it is well aged: *the slight gaminess of duck.*

gaming table *noun* a table used for gambling.

gamma *noun* **1** the third letter of the Greek alphabet (Γ, γ). **2** *Astronomy* the third brightest star in a constellation. **3** designating high-energy electromagnetic radiation of wavelengths shorter than those of X-rays: *gamma rays.*

gamma globulin *noun* a mixture of blood plasma proteins, mainly immunoglobulins, often given to boost immunity.

gamut *noun* the whole series or range or scope of anything: *the whole gamut of crime.* PHRASES **run the gamut** experience, include, or perform the complete range. [Say GAM ut]

gamy *adjective* (**gamier, gamiest**) having the strong flavour or scent of game kept until it is well aged.

gander *noun* **1** a male goose. **2** *informal* a look, a glance.

gang *noun* **1 a** an organized group of criminals. **b** *informal* a group of people who regularly associate together. **c** an organized territorial group of esp. urban youth demanding loyalty from members, engaging in various criminal activities, and often violently rivalling other groups. **2** a set of workers, slaves, or prisoners. PHRASES **gang up** *informal* **1** (foll. by *on*) combine against. **2** (often foll. by *with*) act in concert.

gangbuster *informal* • *noun* a person who takes part in the aggressive breakup of criminal gangs. • *adjective* (often as **gangbusters**) outstandingly successful. PHRASES **go gangbusters** be vigorously successful. **like gangbusters** energetically, vigorously.

gangland *noun* the world of organized crime: *a gangland killing.*

gangling *adjective* (of a person) loosely built; lanky.

ganglion *noun* (*plural* **ganglia**) **1 a** an enlargement or knot on a nerve etc. containing an assemblage of nerve cells. **b** a mass of grey matter in the central nervous system forming a nerve nucleus. **2** a cyst, esp. on a tendon sheath. [Say GANGLY un]

gangly *adjective* (**ganglier, gangliest**) = GANGLING.

gangplank *noun* a plank usu. with cleats nailed on it for boarding or disembarking from a ship etc.

gangrene *noun* death and decomposition of a part of the body tissue, usu. resulting from obstructed circulation or bacterial infection. [Say GANG green]

gangsta *noun* **1** *slang* = GANGSTER. **2** (also **gangsta**

G

rap) a style of rap music, chiefly from the Los Angeles area, the lyrics of which centre on the violence of gang culture, racism, police brutality, etc.
gangster *noun* a member of a gang of violent criminals. ▶ **gangsterish** *adjective* **gangsterism** *noun*
gangway • *noun* **1 a** an opening in the bulwarks by which a ship is entered or left. **b** a bridge laid from ship to shore or to another ship. **c** a passage on a ship, esp. a platform connecting the quarterdeck and forecastle. **2 a** temporary arrangement of planks for crossing muddy or difficult ground on a construction site etc. • *interjection* make way!
ganja *noun* a potent form of marijuana for smoking. [Say GAN juh or GON juh]
gannet *noun* a large seabird with mainly white plumage, which catches fish by plunging headfirst into the water and nests in large colonies on ledges of coastal islands. [Say GAN it]
gantlet *noun* = GAUNTLET². [Say GANT lit]
gantry *noun* (*plural* **gantries**) **1** a bridge-like overhead structure whose span supports railway or road signals etc. **2** a structure supporting a rocket prior to launching. [Say GAN tree]
gaol *noun* esp. *Brit.* = JAIL. ▶ **gaoler** *noun* [Sounds like JAIL]
gap *noun* **1** an empty space or interval. **2** a wide (usu. undesirable) divergence in views, sympathies, development, etc.: *generation gap*. **3** a gorge or pass. PHRASES **fill** (or **close** etc.) **the gap** make up a deficiency.
gape • *verb* (**gapes, gaped, gaping**) **1** be or become open: *this blouse gapes over the bustline*. **2** stare with one's mouth wide open, in amazement or wonder. • *noun* a wide-open expanse. ▶ **gaper** *noun* **gaping** *adjective*
gap-toothed *adjective* having gaps between the teeth.
garage *noun* **1** a building or shed for the storage of a motor vehicle or vehicles. **2 a** an establishment that sells gasoline, repairs motor vehicles, etc. **b** the area at such an establishment where vehicles are serviced. **3** denoting raw, unpolished, usu. energetic guitar-based rock music, esp. as played by amateurs in suburban garages or basements: *garage rock*. [Say guh ROZH or guh RODGE or guh RADGE or guh RAZH]
garage sale *noun* a sale of used household goods, clothes, books, etc. held in the garage or on the lawn of a private house.
garb • *noun* clothing, esp. of a distinctive kind: *prison garb*. • *verb* dress in distinctive clothes: *garbed in loud-checked suits and a beret* ◊ *a black-garbed figure*.
garbage *noun* **1 a** refuse. **b** household waste. **2** anything worthless. **3** nonsense. **4** *Computing* incorrect or useless data: *garbage in, garbage out*.
garbage disposal *noun* (also **garbage disposer**) a system installed in a kitchen sink, with blades in the drain to mulch refuse.
garbageman *noun* a person employed to remove garbage and transport it to a dump.
garbanzo *noun* (*plural* **garbanzos**) = CHICKPEA. [Say gar BON zo]
garble • *verb* (**garbles, garbled, garbling**) reproduce (a message, sound, or transmission) in a confused and distorted way: *the diction was sometimes so garbled it sounded like Frisian rather than English*. • *noun* garbled speech or sounds.
garburator *noun* *Cdn* a garbage disposal. [Say GARBA rater]
garçon *noun* (*plural* **garçons**) a waiter in a French restaurant, hotel, etc. [Say gar SON (with ON as in French)]
garden • *noun* **1 a** a piece of ground adjoining a private house, used for growing flowers, vegetables,

etc. **b** a backyard or front yard adjoining a private house, usu. including a lawn and vegetable or flower garden. **2** ornamental grounds laid out for public enjoyment: *botanical gardens*. **3** an especially fertile region: *the Garden of the Gulf*. **4** (often in *plural*) a large hall or sports arena: *Maple Leaf Gardens*. • *verb* cultivate or work in a garden. ▶ **gardened** *adjective* **gardening** *noun*
gardener *noun* a person who gardens or is employed to tend a garden.
gardenia *noun* **1** a tree or shrub of warm climates with large fragrant white or yellow flowers. **2** its flower. [Say gar DEEN yuh]
garden path *noun* a path through a garden. PHRASES **lead a person down** (or **up**) **the garden path** mislead a person into error, folly, etc.
garden salad *noun* a salad made with common garden vegetables, e.g. lettuce, tomatoes, cucumbers.
garden-variety *adjective* commonplace: *most restaurants were the garden-variety Cantonese*.
gargantuan *adjective* enormous, gigantic: *an Atlantic salmon of gargantuan proportions*. [Say gar GAN choo un]
gargle • *verb* (**gargles, gargled, gargling**) **1** wash one's mouth and throat, esp. for medicinal purposes, with a liquid kept in motion by a stream of air which is breathed out. **2** make a sound as when doing this. • *noun* **1** a liquid for gargling. **2** the sound of gargling.
gargoyle *noun* **1** a grotesque carved human or animal face or figure projecting from the gutter of a (esp. a Gothic) building usu. as a spout to carry water clear of a wall. **2** any grotesque figure of a human or animal. ▶ **gargoylish** *adjective*
garish *adjective* overly bright or decorated: *the garish neon of the tourist strip in Niagara Falls*. ▶ **garishly** *adverb* **garishness** *noun* [Say GARE ish]
garland *noun* a wreath of flowers, leaves, etc., worn on the head or around the neck, or hung as a decoration. ▶ **garlanded** *adjective* decorated with a garland: *a maypole garlanded with flowers*.
garlic *noun* **1** a strong-smelling pungent-tasting bulb, divided into cloves, used as a flavouring in cooking and in herbal medicine. **2** the central Asian plant, closely related to the onion, that produces this bulb. ▶ **garlicky** *adjective*
garment *noun* an article of clothing.
garner *verb* **1** obtain or gather (information etc.): *the police struggled to garner sufficient evidence*. **2** earn, get: *garnered 40 percent of the vote*.
garnet *noun* **1** a precious stone consisting of a deep red glassy silicate mineral. **2** *noun & adjective* deep red.
garnish • *verb* (**garnishes, garnished, garnishing**) **1** decorate or embellish (esp. food). **2** *Law* serve notice on (a person) for the purpose of legally seizing money belonging to a debtor or defendant. • *noun* a decoration or embellishment, esp. to food.
garnishee *Law* • *noun* a third party required to surrender money belonging to a debtor or defendant in compliance with a court order obtained by the creditor or plaintiff: *a creditor may also obtain a garnishee order against a debtor's wages*. • *verb* (**garnishees, garnisheed, garnisheeing**) recover a debt from (a person, his or her wages) by garnishee order: *if he defaults on child support, we will try to garnishee his wages*. [Say garnish EE]
garret *noun* a top-floor or attic room, esp. a dismal one (in popular mythology one inhabited by an impoverished artist). [Say GARE it]
garrison • *noun* **1** the troops stationed in a fortress, town, etc., to defend it. **2** the building occupied by them. • *verb* **1** provide (a place) with or occupy as a garrison. **2** place on garrison duty. [Say GARE iss un]

garrotte • *noun* **1** a wire or cord, esp. one with handles attached at each end, used for strangling a person. **2** a method of execution by strangulation in which an iron or wire collar is tightened around the neck. **3** the apparatus used for this. • *verb* (**garrottes, garrotted, garrotting**) strangle or throttle by means of a wire, cord, etc. [Say guh ROT]

garrulous *adjective* talkative, esp. on trivial matters: *she became positively garrulous after a few glasses of wine*. ▶ **garrulously** *adverb* **garrulousness** *noun* [Say GARE uh lus]

garter *noun* **1 a** a band worn to keep a sock or stocking up. **b** a similar band for keeping a shirt sleeve up. **2** a suspender for a sock or stocking, attached to a garter belt.

garter belt *noun* an undergarment with suspenders for holding up socks or stockings.

garter snake *noun* a common, harmless North American snake that has well-defined lengthwise stripes on the back and favours damp habitats.

gas • *noun* (*plural* **gases**) **1** any airlike substance which moves freely to fill any space available, irrespective of its quantity, esp. one that does not become liquid or solid at ordinary temperatures. **2** such a substance (esp. found naturally or extracted from coal) used as a domestic or industrial fuel, e.g. natural gas, propane: *gas stove*. **3 a** gasoline. **b** the gas pedal. **4** nitrous oxide or another gas used as an anaesthetic (esp. in dentistry). **5** a gas or vapour used as a poisonous agent to disable an enemy in warfare. **6** *informal* pointless idle talk; boasting. **7** *slang* an enjoyable, attractive, or amusing thing or person: *the party was a gas*. **8** intestinal gas. • *verb* (**gases, gassed, gassing**) **1** expose to gas, esp. to kill or make unconscious. **2** (usu. foll. by *up*) *informal* fill (the tank of a motor vehicle) with gasoline. **3** give off gas. **4** *informal* talk idly or boastfully. PHRASES **run out of gas** lose one's impetus or energy.

gasbag *noun* **1** a container of gas, esp. for holding the gas for a balloon or airship. **2** *slang* an idle talker.

gas bar *noun* *Cdn* a gas station, esp. one without a garage, consisting of a kiosk and pumps only.

gas chamber *noun* an airtight chamber that can be filled with poisonous gas to kill people or animals.

gaseous *adjective* of or like gas: *gaseous emissions from motor vehicles*. [Say GASSY us or GASH us]

gas-fired *adjective* using natural gas as the fuel.

gash • *noun* (*plural* **gashes**) **1** a long and deep slash, cut, or wound: *a nasty gash in his arm*. **2** a cleft such as might be made by a slashing cut: *the explosion left a wide gash in the rock*. • *verb* (**gashes, gashed, gashing**) make a gash in; cut.

gasket *noun* a sheet or ring of rubber etc., shaped to seal the junction of metal surfaces. PHRASES **blow a gasket** *slang* lose one's temper.

gaslight *noun* **1** a jet of burning gas, usu. heating a mantle, to provide light. **2** light emanating from this. ▶ **gaslit** *adjective*

gasohol *noun* a mixture of gasoline and ethyl alcohol used as fuel. [Say GAS a hall]

gasoline *noun* a volatile inflammable liquid obtained from petroleum and used as fuel in motor vehicles etc.

gasp • *verb* **1** catch one's breath with an open mouth as in exhaustion or astonishment. **2** strain to obtain by gasping: *gasped for air*. **3** utter with gasps. • *noun* a convulsive catching of breath.

gas pedal *noun* the accelerator pedal on a motor vehicle.

gaspereau *noun* (*plural* **gaspereaux**) *Cdn* = ALEWIFE 1. [Say GASPER oh]

Gaspesian *Cdn* • *noun* a native or resident of the Gaspé Peninsula. • *adjective* of or pertaining to the Gaspé Peninsula. [Say gas PAY zhun]

gassed *adjective* **1** *in senses of* GAS *verb*. **2** *informal* drunk.

gassy *adjective* (**gassier, gassiest**) **1 a** of or like gas. **b** full of gas. **2** *informal* (of talk etc.) pointless, verbose: *the gassy jargon of bureaucracy*.

gastric *adjective* of the stomach: *gastric acid*.

gastritis *noun* inflammation of the lining of the stomach. [Say gas TRITE us]

gastro- *combining form* (also **gastr-** before a vowel) stomach.

gastroenteritis *noun* inflammation of the stomach and intestines, usu. caused by bacterial toxins or viral infections and causing vomiting and diarrhea. [Say gastro enta RITE us]

gastrointestinal *adjective* of or relating to the stomach and the intestines. [Say gastro INTESTINAL]

gastronomic *adjective* connected with cooking and eating good food: *a gastronomic delight*. ▶ **gastronomical** *adjective* [Say gastra NOM ick]

gastronomy *noun* **1** the practice, study, or art of eating and drinking well. **2** the cuisine of an area: *traditional American gastronomy*. [Say guh STRONNA mee]

gastropod *noun* any of a large class of molluscs that move along by means of a large muscular foot, e.g. a snail, slug, etc. [Say GASTRA pod]

> **SPELL CHECK**
> **gate, gait**
>
> The way a person walks is their **gait**.

gate¹ • *noun* **1** a barrier, usu. hinged, used to close an opening made for entrance and exit through a wall, fence, etc. **2 a** such an opening, esp. in the wall of a city, enclosure, or large building. **b** a monument resembling a gate or gateway, esp. adorning the entrance to a park etc. **3** a means of entrance or exit. **4** a numbered place of access to aircraft at an airport or trains at a train station. **5 a** an electrical signal that causes or controls the passage of other signals. **b** an electrical circuit with an output which depends on the combination of several inputs. **6** a device regulating the passage of water in a lock etc. **7 a** the number of people entering by payment at the gates of a sporting event etc. **b** (also **gate money**) the proceeds taken for admission. **8** *slang* dismissal. **9** = STARTING GATE. **10** a barrier at a level crossing or at a toll booth. **11** *Skiing* an arrangement of two flexible poles implanted in the snow of a slalom course between which a skier must pass. • *verb* (**gates, gated, gating**) **1** *Electricity* subject (a signal) to the action of a gate. **2** *Cdn* retain (an inmate, esp. a dangerous offender) in prison for the full length of a sentence, by arresting the inmate as soon as he or she is released under mandatory supervision. PHRASES **get** (or **be given**) **the gate** *slang* be dismissed.

gate² *noun* **1** (preceded by or prefixed by a name) a street: *Westgate*. **2** *Cdn* (*PEI*) a lane or driveway.

-gate *combining form* forming nouns denoting an actual or alleged scandal (and usu. an attempted cover-up): *Irangate*.

gatecrash *verb* (**gatecrashes, gatecrashed, gatecrashing**) go to a party or social event without being invited.

gatecrasher *noun* an uninvited guest at a party etc.

gated *adjective* **1** (of a road, fence, etc.) having a gate or gates to control the movement of traffic or animals. **2** (of a subdivision etc.) enclosed by walls etc. with access controlled by security guards.

gatehouse *noun* a house standing by a gateway, esp. to a large house or park.

gatekeeper *noun* **1** an attendant at a gate, controlling entrance and exit. **2** a thing or person that controls access to or availability of information etc.

gatepost *noun* a post on which a gate is hung or against which it shuts. PHRASES **between you and me and the gatepost** *informal* in strict confidence.

gateway *noun* **1** an entrance with or opening for a gate. **2** a frame or structure built over a gate. **3** a means of access or entry: *Winnipeg is the gateway to the Prairies*. **4** a device or software used to connect two networks.

gather • *verb* **1** bring or come together. **2** a draw together: *gathered her scarf around her*. **b** take (a person) into one's embrace: *gathered him into her arms*. **3** a pick a quantity of (flowers etc.). **b** collect (grain etc.) as a harvest. **4** infer or understand. **5** be subjected to or affected by the accumulation or increase of: *gathering dust* ◊ *gather speed*. **6** (often foll. by *up*) summon up (one's thoughts, energy, etc.) for a purpose. **7** a draw (material) together in folds or wrinkles. **b** pucker or draw together (part of a dress) by running a thread through. • *noun* (in *plural*) a part of a garment that is gathered or drawn in. ▶ **gatherer** *noun*

gathering • *noun* **1** an assembly or meeting. **2** the gathers formed by drawing up a fabric. • *adjective* increasing in intensity etc.

gator *noun informal* an alligator.

GATT *abbreviation* General Agreement on Tariffs and Trade.

gauche *adjective* **1** socially awkward: *I felt awkward and gauche, an outclassed country bumpkin.* **2** tactless. [Say GOASH]

gaucho *noun* (*plural* **gauchos**) **1** a cowboy from the South American pampas. **2** (in *plural*) (also **gaucho pants**) wide, calf-length pants. [Say GOW cho (*GOW* rhymes with HOW*)]

gaudily *adverb* in a way that is tastelessly or extravagantly bright or showy.

gaudiness *noun* the quality or condition of being tastelessly or extravagantly bright or showy.

gaudy *adjective* (**gaudier**, **gaudiest**) tastelessly or extravagantly bright or showy.

gauge • *noun* **1** a standard measure to which certain things must conform, esp.: **a** the measure of the inner diameter of an esp. shotgun barrel, representing the number of lead balls of that diameter required to make one pound. **b** the fineness of a textile. **c** the thickness of sheet metal, wire, or other usu. thin materials or objects. **2** any of various instruments for measuring or determining this, or for measuring length, thickness, or other dimensions or properties. **3** the distance between a pair of rails or the wheels on one axle. **4** a means of estimating; a criterion or test: *property is the best gauge of wealth*. **5** a graduated instrument measuring the force or quantity of rainfall, pressure, fuel, wind, etc. • *verb* (**gauges**, **gauged**, **gauging**) **1** measure exactly (esp. objects of standard size). **2** determine the capacity of. **3** estimate or form a judgment of (a person, temperament, situation, etc.).

Gaul *noun* a native or inhabitant of ancient Gaul, a region of Europe corresponding to France, Belgium, the southern Netherlands, southwestern Germany, and northern Italy.

gaunch *noun* *Cdn* (esp. *BC & Alberta*) *slang* underwear.

gaunt *adjective* **1** (of a person) very thin, usually because of illness, hunger or worry: *she looked gaunt and exhausted*. **2** grim or desolate in appearance: *the trees stood gaunt and broken against the heavy sky.* [Say GONT]

gauntlet[1] *noun* **1** a sturdy glove long enough to cover the wrist and part of the forearm. **2** *hist.* an armoured glove. PHRASES **take** (or **pick**) **up the gauntlet**

accept a challenge. **throw down the gauntlet** issue a challenge.

gauntlet[2] *noun* **1** a former esp. military punishment in which the offender was required to pass between two rows of people and receive blows from them. **2** an ordeal or series of ordeals: *the gauntlet of entrance exams.* PHRASES **run the gauntlet** be subjected to harsh criticism.

SPELL CHECK ⟨ABC⟩
guarantee

Warning: *a* follows *u* in **guarantee**.

---

gauss *noun* (*plural* **gauss** or **gausses**) a unit of magnetic induction, equal to one ten-thousandth of a tesla. Abbreviation: **G**. [Rhymes with MOUSE]

gauze *noun* **1** a thin transparent fabric of silk, cotton, etc. **2** *Medical* thin loosely woven material used for dressings and swabs. **3** a fine mesh of wire etc.

gauzy *adjective* (**gauzier**, **gauziest**) like gauze; thin and translucent: *a gauzy dress*.

gave *past of* GIVE.

gavel *noun* a small hammer used by an auctioneer, or for calling a meeting to order, or by judges in the US. [Say GAV ul]

Gawd *interjection* *slang* an exclamation of surprise, anger, etc.

gawk *verb* *informal* stare stupidly. ▶ **gawker** *noun*

gawkiness *noun* the quality or condition of being awkward or ungainly.

gawky *adjective* (**gawkier**, **gawkiest**) awkward or ungainly.

gay • *adjective* **1 a** homosexual. **b** of or pertaining to homosexuals: *a gay bar*. **2 a** lighthearted and carefree; mirthful. **b** characterized by cheerfulness or pleasure: *a gay life*. **c** brightly coloured; showy, brilliant: *a gay scarf*. • *noun* a homosexual, esp. male. ▶ **gayness** *noun*

gay bashing *noun informal* the unprovoked attacking of a homosexual or homosexuals.

gaze • *verb* (**gazes**, **gazed**, **gazing**) look fixedly. • *noun* a fixed or intent look.

gazebo *noun* (*plural* **gazebos** or **gazeboes**) a small structure in a garden, park etc., usu. open or with screens on all sides to give a wide view. [Say guh ZEE bo]

gazelle *noun* a small slender antelope with curved horns and a fawn coloured coat with white underparts, found in open country in Africa and Asia. [Say guh ZEL]

gazer *noun* a person who looks at or studies something: *she is a crystal ball gazer*.

gazette *noun* **1** a newspaper (used esp. in names). **2** (in Canada and other Commonwealth countries) an official journal with a list of government appointments, bankruptcies, and other public notices. [Say guh ZET]

gazetteer *noun* a geographical index or dictionary. [Say gazza TEER]

gazillion *noun informal* **1** an exaggeratedly large number: *gazillions of dictionaries*. **2** (in *plural*) an exaggeratedly large amount of money: *made gazillions*.

gazpacho *noun* (*plural* **gazpachos**) a Spanish soup made from tomatoes, peppers, cucumbers, garlic, etc., and served cold. [Say guh SPATCH oh]

GB *abbreviation* Great Britain.

Gbyte *abbreviation* gigabyte.

Gd *symbol* gadolinium.

GDP *abbreviation* GROSS DOMESTIC PRODUCT.

GDR *abbreviation* *hist.* German Democratic Republic.

Ge *symbol* germanium.

gear • *noun* **1** (often in *plural*) **a** a set of toothed wheels that work together to receive and transmit force and motion. **b** a mechanism using gears to transmit and

control motion, esp. to the road wheels of a vehicle. **2** a particular state of adjustment of engaged gears: *second gear*. **3** a state of speed or activity: *the campaign moved into top gear*. **4** a mechanism of wheels, levers, etc., usu. for a special purpose: *winding gear*. **5** (also **landing gear**) the undercarriage of an aircraft. **6** equipment or tackle for a special purpose: *fishing gear*. **7** clothing, equipment, and accessories, esp. for a specified purpose or of a specified type: *police in riot gear*. **8** an indeterminate quantity of belongings and objects, esp. if perceived as burdensome: *clear all of your old gear out of the attic*. • *verb* **1** adjust or adapt to suit a specified purpose, need, or recipient. **2** (often foll. by *up*) equip with gears. **3** (usu. foll. by *up*) **a** make ready or prepared. **b** prepare, get ready. PHRASES **be geared** (or **all geared**) **up** *informal* be ready or enthusiastic. **gear down** engage a lower gear in a vehicle. **gear up 1** (of groups of people, cities, corporate bodies, etc.) prepare or equip, esp. over a period of time in anticipation of some intense activity. **2** speed up or intensify: *gear up production*. **3** engage a higher gear in a vehicle. **gear oneself up** provide oneself with progressively more supplies, courage, etc. in order to face a daunting prospect. **give a person the gears** *Cdn* pester, hassle. **in gear 1** with a gear engaged. **2** operating properly or efficiently. **in high gear** operating at maximum efficiency. **out of gear 1** with no gear engaged. **2** out of order. **shift** (or **change** etc.) **gears** change one's pace, direction, strategy, etc., esp. in progress.

gearbox *noun* **1** the casing that encloses a set of gears. **2** a set of gears with its casing, esp. in a motor vehicle; transmission.

gearing *noun* a set or arrangement of gears in a machine.

gearshift *noun* a lever used to engage or change gear, esp. in a motor vehicle.

gearwheel *noun* a toothed wheel in a set of gears.

gecko *noun* (*plural* **geckos** or **geckoes**) any of various house lizards found in warm climates, with adhesive feet for climbing vertical surfaces.

gee *interjection informal* a mild expression of surprise, discovery, dismay, etc.

geek *noun informal* **1** an uninteresting, ineffectual, socially inept person; a nerd. **2** a person thoroughly devoted to one usu. technical interest, study, etc., often at the expense of social interaction: *computer geek*. ▶ **geeky** *adjective*

geese plural of GOOSE.

gee whiz *informal* • *interjection* = GEE. • *adjective* (usu. as **gee-whiz**) characterized by (often naive) astonishment or wonder, usu. at new technologies: *gee-whiz journalism*.

geez *interjection* expressing exasperation etc.

geezer *noun slang* a person, esp. an old man.

Geiger counter *noun* a device which detects and counts ionizing particles to measure radioactivity. [Say GUY gur]

geisha *noun* (*plural* **geisha** or **geishas**) **1** a Japanese hostess trained in entertaining men with dance and song. **2** a Japanese prostitute. [Say GAY shuh]

SPELL CHECK   ABC ✓
gel, jell

The usual Canadian spelling is **jell** in "Our ideas are beginning to jell", "This team is really starting to jell", and "The liquid will jell overnight in the fridge."

---

gel • *noun* **1** a semi-solid suspension of a solid dispersed in a liquid. **2** a jellylike substance used for setting hair.

• *verb* (**gels**, **gelled**, **gelling**) **1** = JELL. **2** apply gel to (hair etc.).

gelatin *noun* (also **gelatine**) a virtually colourless tasteless transparent water-soluble protein derived from collagen and obtained by prolonged boiling of animal skin, tendons, ligaments, etc., used in food preparation, photography, glue, etc.

gelatinous *adjective* **1** of or like gelatin. **2** of a jellylike consistency. [Say jel LATIN us]

gelato *noun* (*plural* **gelati**) an Italian sherbet-like ice cream made with milk or cream and relatively low in butterfat. [Say jel LATTO or jel LOTTO for the singular, jel LATTY or jel LOTTY for the plural]

geld *verb* **1** castrate (a male animal). **2** deprive of some essential part; weaken.

gelding *noun* a gelded animal, esp. a male horse.

gelignite *noun* a high explosive made from a gel of nitroglycerine in a base of wood pulp and sodium or potassium nitrate, much used in rock blasting. [Say JELL ignite]

gem *noun* **1** a precious stone, esp. when cut and polished or engraved. **2** an object, person, event, etc. of great beauty, worth, or excellence.

Gemara *noun Judaism* the later of the two parts of the Talmud, consisting of a rabbinical commentary on the first part (the Mishnah). [Say guh MAR uh]

Gemini *noun* (*plural* **Geminis**) **1** a constellation between Taurus and Cancer, traditionally regarded as contained in the figures of twins. **2 a** the third sign of the zodiac. **b** a person born when the sun is in this sign, usu. between May 21 and June 20. **3** *Cdn* any of several awards presented by the Academy of Canadian Cinema and Television for excellence in Canadian English-language television. ▶ **Geminian** *noun & adjective* [Say JEM in eye or JEM in ee, jemmin EYE un or jemmin EE un]

gemstone *noun* a precious stone used as a gem.

Gen. *abbreviation* General.

gendarme *noun* a soldier employed in specific public police duties, esp. in some French-speaking countries. [Say zhon DARM]

gender *noun* **1** (in some languages) each of the classes (masculine, feminine and sometimes neuter) into which nouns, pronouns and adjectives are divided. Different genders may have different endings, etc. **2** (in some languages) the division of nouns, pronouns and adjectives into different genders: *in French the adjective must agree with the noun in number and gender*. **3 a** a person's sex; either of the sexes: *differences between the genders are encouraged from an early age*. **b** one's characteristics or traits determined socially, rather than biologically, as a result of one's sex: *traditional concepts of gender*.

gender-bender *noun* a person who or thing which adopts or portrays non-traditional gender roles. ▶ **gender-bending** *noun & adjective*

gendered *adjective* of, relating to, or determined by one's sex as expressed by social or cultural distinctions.

gender gap *noun* the discrepancy in opportunities, status, attitudes, etc. between men and women.

genderless *adjective* without distinction of gender: *a genderless pronoun* ◊ *a genderless society*.

gender-neutral *adjective* **1** denoting a word which cannot be taken to refer to one sex only, e.g. *firefighter* as opposed to *fireman*. **2** (of language etc.) using gender-neutral words whenever appropriate.

gender role *noun* one's behaviour, lifestyle, etc. regarded in light of one's sex.

gender-specific *adjective* characteristic of, pertaining to, or referring to one sex only.

gene *noun* a unit of heredity composed of DNA or RNA

and forming part of a chromosome etc., that determines a particular characteristic of an individual.

genealogical adjective of or relating to the study or tracing of lines of family history: genealogical research. ▶**genealogically** adverb [Say jeany a LOGICAL]

genealogist noun a person who studies family history. [Say jeany OLLA jist or jeany ALA jist]

genealogy noun (plural **genealogies**) **1 a** a line of descent traced continuously from an ancestor. **b** an account of this. **2** the study and investigation of lines of descent. **3** a plant's or animal's line of development from earlier forms. [Say jeany OLLA jee or jeany ALA jee]

gene map noun Biology a diagram showing the arrangement of genes on a chromosome.

gene mapping noun the determination of a gene's location on a chromosome.

gene pool noun the whole stock of different genes in an interbreeding population.

genera plural of GENUS. [Say JENNER uh]

general • adjective **1** affecting or concerning all or most people or things; not specialized or limited. **2** involving only the main features or elements and disregarding exceptions. **3** chief or principal: general manager ◊ Secretary-General. **4** (in Alta., BC, Man., & Sask.) designating a film deemed suitable for all audiences. Abbreviation: **G**. • noun **1** (also **General**; abbreviation: **Gen** Cdn or **Gen.**) **a** (in the Canadian Army or Air Force) an officer of the highest rank. **b** a similar officer in other military forces. **c** a lieutenant general, major general, or brigadier general. **2** a commander of an army. **3** a tactician or strategist of specified merit: a great general. PHRASES **as a general rule** in most cases. **in general 1** as a normal rule; usually. **2** for the most part.

general admission noun **1** admission to unreserved seating at a concert, sports event, etc. **2** the section of a theatre etc. with unreserved seats: sat in general admission. **3** the admission fee to an event etc. charged to those who are not eligible for a discounted rate.

general anaesthetic noun an anaesthetic that affects the whole body, usu. with loss of consciousness.

General Assembly noun **1** the main deliberative body of the UN, with a delegate from each member country. **2** (in Presbyterian churches) an annual national meeting of representative clergy and elders, constituting the highest court of the church.

general election noun the election of representatives to a legislature from all constituencies of a country, province, etc.

generalist noun a person competent or knowledgeable in several different fields or activities (opp. SPECIALIST).

generality noun (plural **generalities**) **1** a statement that discusses general principles or issues rather than details or particular examples: spoke in broad generalities ◊ he confined his comments to generalities. **2** the quality of being general rather than detailed or exact: an account of such generality is of little value. **3** most of a group of people or things: this view is held by the generality of leading scholars.

generalization noun **1** a general statement or concept obtained by inference from specific cases: he was making sweeping generalizations. **2** the action of generalizing: such anecdotes cannot be a basis for generalization.

generalize verb (**generalizes**, **generalized**, **generalizing**) **1** use a particular set of facts or ideas in order to form an opinion that is considered valid for a different situation: it would be foolish to generalize from a single example. **2** make a general statement about something and not look at the details: it is dangerous to

generalize about women. **3** apply a theory, idea, etc. to a wider group or situation than the original one: these conclusions cannot be generalized to the whole country ◊ we are now in a position to generalize the lessons we have learnt. **4** (of a disease) spread to other parts of the body.

generally adverb **1** usually; in most cases. **2** in a general sense; without regard to particulars or exceptions: generally speaking. **3** for the most part; extensively: generally known. **4** in most respects: are generally well-behaved.

general practice noun **1** the work of a doctor who treats people in the community rather than at a hospital and who is not a specialist in one particular area of medicine: he is in general practice. **2** a place where a doctor like this works: she runs a general practice.

general practitioner noun a doctor working in the community and treating cases of all kinds in the first instance, as distinct from a consultant or specialist.

general public noun the people of a community collectively, esp. those not enjoying special privileges.

general-purpose adjective having a range of potential uses or functions; not specialized in design.

general relativity noun see RELATIVITY 2b.

general staff noun the staff assisting a military commander in planning and administration.

general strike noun a strike of workers in all or most occupations.

generate verb (**generates**, **generated**, **generating**) **1** bring into existence; produce: the proposal has generated a lot of interest ◊ the sale will generate some income. **2** produce (electricity).

generation noun **1** all the people born at a particular time, regarded collectively: my generation. **2** a single step in descent or pedigree: a second-generation Canadian. **3** a stage in (esp. technological) development: fourth-generation computers. **4** members of a specific group or category who became prominent at the same time: the new generation of rock guitarists. **5** the average time in which children are ready to take the place of their parents (usu. reckoned at about 30 years). **6** production by natural or artificial process, esp. the production of electricity or heat. **7** procreation; the propagation of species. ▶**generational** adjective

generation gap noun differences of outlook or opinion between those of different generations.

Generation X noun the generation born after that of the baby boomers (roughly from the early 1960s to mid-1970s). ▶**Generation Xer** noun

generative adjective **1** of or concerning procreation: the generative systems of mature female mammals. **2** able to produce, productive. [Say JENNER a tiv]

generator noun **1** a machine for converting mechanical into electrical energy; a dynamo. **2** an apparatus for producing gas, steam, etc. **3** a person or thing that generates something.

generic • adjective **1** characteristic of or relating to an entire class; general: sexual assault is a generic term used for all sexual crimes. **2** Biology characteristic of or belonging to a genus. **3** designating a word that can apply or refer to both men and women. **4** (of goods, esp. a drug) having no brand name. • noun a generic product, esp. a drug. ▶**generically** adverb [Say jen AIR ick]

generosity noun **1** the quality of being kind and generous. **2** the quality or fact of being plentiful or large: diners certainly cannot complain about the generosity of the portions.

generous adjective **1** (of a person or an institution) giving willingly more of something, esp. money, than is strictly necessary or expected. **2** (of help) given abundantly and willingly. **3** consisting of or

representing a large amount of money, esp. when considered excessive or undeserved. **4** (of a person or an action) manifesting an inclination to recognize the positive aspects of someone or something, often disinterestedly. **5** (of something offered) favouring the recipient's interests rather than the giver's: *we offered them generous terms*. **6** leaning towards the positive: *a generous estimate*. **7 a** ample, abundant, copious: *a generous portion*. **b** (of wine) rich and full. **8** (of rooms etc.) spacious; (of clothing) ample. ▶ **generously** *adverb*

genesis *noun* (*plural* **geneses**) the origin, or mode of formation, of a thing: *this tale had its genesis in fireside stories*. [Say JENNA sis for the singular, JENNA seez for the plural]

gene-splicing *noun* the process of removing a chosen gene or sequence of genes from one organism and causing it to be integrated into the genetic material of another, usu. a bacterium, in order that it may produce the protein for which the gene codes.

gene therapy *noun* the introduction of normal genes into cells in place of missing or defective ones in order to correct genetic disorders.

genetic *adjective* **1** of heredity or genes: *genetic and environmental factors*. **2** of genetics: *an attempt to control mosquitoes by genetic techniques*. ▶ **genetically** *adverb*

genetically engineered *adjective* **1** (of an organism) having a genome that has been artificially altered by genetic engineering. **2** (of a protein, chemical, etc.) produced by a genetically engineered organism.

genetic code *noun* the means by which genetic information is stored as sequences of nucleotide bases in the chromosomal DNA.

genetic engineering *noun* the deliberate modification of the characters of an organism by the manipulation of the genetic material.

genetic fingerprint *noun* any set of genetic characteristics derived from an individual's tissues or secretions, esp. when used for identification in a similar way to conventional fingerprints.

genetic fingerprinting *noun* (also **genetic profiling**) the analysis of characteristic patterns in DNA as a way of identifying individuals.

geneticist *noun* a specialist in genetics. [Say jen NETTA sist]

genetic map *noun* a representation of a chromosome including the positions of its genes. ▶ **genetic mapping** *noun*

genetics *plural noun* **1** (treated as *singular*) the study of heredity and the variation of inherited characteristics. **2** (treated as *singular* or *plural*) the genetic properties or features of an organism, characteristic, etc.: *the genetics of disease resistance*.

genial *adjective* **1** friendly and cheerful: *the meeting proved surprisingly genial*. **2** (of the climate) mild and warm. ▶ **geniality** *noun* **genially** *adverb* [Say JEANY ul, jeany ALA tee]

genie *noun* **1** (*plural* **genies** or **genii**) **a** = JINNI. **b** a spirit of Arabian folklore, esp. one contained within a bottle, lamp, etc., and capable of granting wishes. **2** (**Genie**) *Cdn* any of several awards presented by the Academy of Canadian Cinema and Television for excellence in filmmaking. [Say JEANY for the singular, JEANIES or JEANY eye for the plural]

genital • *adjective* of the reproductive organs. • *noun* (in *plural*) the external reproductive organs.

genital herpes *noun* a disease characterized by genital blisters, caused by a variety of the herpes simplex virus.

genitalia *plural noun* the genitals. [Say jenna TAIL yuh]

genitive *Grammar* • *noun* the case of nouns and pronouns (and words in grammatical agreement with them) corresponding to *of*, *from*, and other prepositions and indicating possession or close association. • *adjective* of or in the genitive. [Say JENNA tiv]

genius *noun* (*plural* **geniuses**) **1** (*plural* **geniuses**) **a** an exceptional intellectual or creative power or other natural ability or tendency. **b** a person having this. **c** this ability as manifest in a work of art etc.: *the genius of her painting*. **2** the spirit watching over or protecting a person, place, institution, etc. **3** a person or spirit regarded as powerfully influencing a person for good or evil: *he sees Adams as the man's evil genius*. **4** the prevalent feeling or associations etc. of a nation, age, etc.: *Boucher's paintings did not suit the austere genius of neoclassicism*.

genocidal *adjective* of or relating to the mass extermination of human beings, esp. of a particular race or nation: *a new global court to prosecute genocidal killers*. [Say jenna SIDE ul]

genocide *noun* the mass extermination of human beings, esp. of a particular race or nation. [Say JENNA side]

genome *noun* **1** the haploid set of chromosomes of an organism. **2** the genetic material of an organism. ▶ **genomic** *adjective* [Say JEE nome, jee NOM ick]

genotype *noun* the genetic constitution of an individual (*compare* PHENOTYPE). [Say JEAN oh type or JEN oh type]

genre • *noun* **1** a kind or style, esp. of art or literature, e.g. novel, satire, science fiction. **2** (also **genre painting**) the painting of scenes from ordinary life. • *adjective* denoting a film etc. following the conventions of a recognizable genre. [Say ZHON ruh]

gent *noun informal* (often *jocular*) a gentleman.

genteel *adjective* **1** affectedly or ostentatiously refined, stylish, or polite: *afternoon tea is a very genteel institution*. **2** often *ironic* of or appropriate to the upper classes. ▶ **genteelly** *adverb*

gentian *noun* a plant found esp. in mountainous regions, usu. having violet or vivid blue trumpet-shaped flowers. [Say JEN sh'n]

SPELL CHECK	
Gentile, genteel	ABC ✓

Someone who is polite or refined is **genteel**.

Gentile • *adjective* not Jewish. • *noun* a person who is not Jewish. [Say JEN tile]

gentility *noun* **1** refined manners and habits, esp. as associated with wealthy and well-bred people. **2** affected or pretentious refinement or politeness. **3** people of noble birth. [Say jen TILLA tee]

gentle • *adjective* (**gentler**, **gentlest**) **1** not rough; mild or kind. **2 a** modest; not severe or drastic: *a gentle rebuke* ◊ *a gentle breeze*. **b** gradual: *gentle slope*. **c** not harsh: *gentle shampoo*. **3** (of birth, pursuits, etc.) of or fit for people of elevated social position. **4** (of an animal) docile. • *verb* (**gentles**, **gentled**, **gentling**) make or become gentle or docile.

gentleman *noun* (*plural* **gentlemen**) **1** a man (in polite or formal use). **2 a** a courteous and honourable man: *he behaved throughout like a perfect gentleman*. **3** a man of good social position or of wealth and leisure. **4** (in *plural* as a form of address) a male audience or the male part of an audience.

gentlemanly *adjective* like a gentleman in looks or behaviour; befitting a gentleman.

gentleman's agreement *noun* an agreement which is based upon the trust and honour of all parties but not legally enforceable.

Gentleman Usher of the Black Rod *noun* see BLACK ROD.

gentrification *noun* the conversion of a working-class or inner-city neighbourhood etc. into an area of middle-class residence. [Say jentra fuh KAY sh'n]

gentrifier *noun* a person who converts or supports the conversion of a working-class or inner-city neighbourhood etc. into an area of middle-class residence. [Say JENTRA fie er]

gentrify *verb* (**gentrifies**, **gentrified**, **gentrifying**) convert (a working-class or inner-city neighbourhood etc.) into an area of middle-class residence. [Say JENTRA fie]

gentry *plural noun* **1** people of high social standing. **2** (in the UK) the class of people next below the nobility in social standing: *a member of the landed gentry.*

genuflect *verb* **1** bend the knee to the ground, esp. in worship or as a sign of respect: *she genuflected in front of the crucifix.* **2** display excessive respect for: *many academics were genuflecting before the altar of Quebec separatism.* ▶ **genuflection** *noun* [Say JEN you fleckt]

genuine *adjective* **1** really coming from its stated, advertised, or reputed source. **2** properly so called; not sham. **3** (of an opinion etc.) sincere. **4** (of a person) free from affectation or hypocrisy. ▶ **genuinely** *adverb* **genuineness** *noun* [Say JEN you in or JEN you ine]

genus *noun* (*plural* **genera**) *Biology* a taxonomic grouping of organisms having common characteristics distinct from those of other genera, usu. containing several or many species and being one of a series constituting a taxonomic family. [Say JEE nus or JEN us for the singular, JENNER uh for the plural]

Gen X *noun slang* = GENERATION X. ▶ **Gen-Xer** *noun*

geo- *combining form* **1** earth: *geology.* **2** global: *geopolitics.*

geocentric *adjective* **1** having or representing the earth as the centre: *the medieval view of the universe was geocentric rather than heliocentric.* **2** measured from or considered in relation to the centre of the earth.

geochemical *adjective* based on or having to do with geochemistry.

geochemist *noun* a person who studies the chemistry of the earth and its rocks, minerals, etc.

geochemistry *noun* the chemistry of the earth and its rocks, minerals, etc.

geode *noun* **1** a small cavity lined with crystals or other mineral matter. **2** a rock containing such a cavity. [Say JEE ode]

geodesic • *adjective* **1** of or relating to the branch of mathematics dealing with the shape and area of the earth or large portions of it. **2** of, involving, or consisting of a geodesic line. • *noun* (also **geodesic line**) the shortest possible line between two points on a surface. [Say geo DEE sick or geo DESS ick]

geodesic dome *noun* a dome constructed of short struts along geodesic lines, forming a light open framework of triangles or polygons, combining the structural advantages of the sphere and the tetrahedron.

geoduck *noun* a giant mud-burrowing bivalve mollusc occurring on the west coast of North America, where it is collected for food. [Say GOOEY duck]

geographer *noun* a person who studies the earth's physical features, resources, and climate, and the physical aspects of its population.

geographical *adjective* (also **geographic**) of or relating to geography. ▶ **geographically** *adverb*

geographic information system *noun* a computer system which allows the user to analyze, display and manipulate spatial data (e.g. data from remote sensing). Abbreviation: **GIS**.

geography *noun* **1** the study of the earth's physical features, resources, and climate, and of human activity as it affects and is affected by these, including the distribution of populations and resources and political and economic activities. **2** the way in which the physical features of a place are arranged: *the geography of New York City* ◊ *Kim knew the geography of the building.*

geological *adjective* (also **geologic**) relating to the science of the earth, including the composition, structure, and origin of rocks. ▶ **geologically** *adverb*

geological time *noun* **1** the time which has elapsed since the earth's formation (up to the beginning of the historical period). **2** time measured with reference to geological events.

geologist *noun* a person who studies the science of the earth, including the composition, structure, and origin of its rocks.

geology *noun* **1** the science of the earth, including the composition, structure, and origin of its rocks. **2** this science applied to any other planet or celestial body. **3** the geological features of a district.

geometer *noun* **1** a person skilled in geometry. **2** a moth of a large family distinguished by having twig-like caterpillars that move by alternately hunching and stretching the body. [Say jee OMMA tur]

geometric • *adjective* (also **geometrical**) **1** of, according to, or like geometry. **2** (of a design, architectural feature, etc.) characterized by or decorated with regular lines and shapes. • *noun* a print, pattern, fabric, etc. with a geometric design. ▶ **geometrically** *adverb*

geometric mean *noun* the central number in a geometric progression, also calculable as the nth root of a product of n numbers (as 9 from 3 and 27).

geometric progression *noun* a progression of numbers with a constant ratio between each number and the one before (as 1, 3, 9, 27).

geometry *noun* (*plural* **geometries**) **1 a** the branch of mathematics concerned with the properties and relations of points, lines, surfaces, and solids. **b** particular system describing these properties etc.: *Euclidean geometry.* **2** the relative arrangement of objects or parts: *the geometry of spiders' webs.*

geomorphic *adjective* of or relating to the form of the landscape and other natural features of the earth's surface. [Say geo MORF ick]

geomorphological *adjective* of or relating to the study of the physical features of the surface of the earth and their relation to its geological structures. [Say geo morfa LOGICAL]

geomorphology *noun* the study of the physical features of the surface of the earth and their relation to its geological structures. [Say geo morf OLLA jee]

geophysical *adjective* of or relating to geophysics.

geophysicist *noun* a person who studies geophysics.

geophysics *noun* the science concerned with all aspects of the physical properties and processes of the earth and planetary bodies, including seismology, gravity, magnetism, etc.

geopolitical *adjective* of or relating to geopolitics. ▶ **geopolitically** *adverb*

geopolitics *noun* **1 a** the politics of a country as determined by its geographical features. **b** the study of this. **2** politics on a global scale.

Georgian¹ *adjective* **1 a** of or characteristic of the time of Kings George I–IV of England (1714–1830). **b** designating or resembling the style of architecture of this period, typified in domestic architecture by red-brick houses with regularly spaced sash windows, white paintwork, and doorways with pediments. **2** of or characteristic of the time of Kings George V and VI of

England (1910–52), esp. of the literature of 1910–20. [Say JORE jin]

Georgian² • *adjective* of or relating to the US state of Georgia. • *noun* a native or resident of Georgia. [Say JORE jin]

Georgian³ • *adjective* of or relating to Georgia, a country in SE Europe. • *noun* **1** a native of Georgia; a person of Georgian descent. **2** the language of Georgia. [Say JORE jin]

geoscience *noun* earth sciences, e.g. geology, geophysics. ▶ **geoscientist** *noun* [Say geo SCIENCE]

geotechnical *adjective* of or pertaining to practical applications of geological science in building, etc.

geothermal *adjective* relating to, originating from, or produced by the internal heat of the earth.

geranium *noun* **1** a plant that is widely cultivated for its red, pink, or white flowers and fragrant leaves; a pelargonium. **2** a herb or shrub that bears long narrow fruit shaped like the bill of a crane. [Say jur RAINY um]

gerbil *noun* a mouselike desert rodent with long hind legs found in Africa and Asia, commonly kept as a pet. [Say JUR bull]

geriatric • *adjective* of or relating to old age or old people. • *noun* an old person, esp. one receiving special care. [Say jerry AT rick]

geriatrics *plural noun* (usu. treated as *singular*) a branch of medicine or social science dealing with the health and care of old people. [Say jerry AT rick]

germ *noun* **1** a micro-organism, esp. one which causes disease. **2 a** a portion of an organism capable of developing into a new one; the rudiment of an animal or plant. **b** an embryo of a seed: *wheat germ*. **3** an original idea etc. from which something may develop; an elementary principle: *the germ of a solution*.

German • *noun* **1** a native or national of Germany. **2** a person of German descent. **3** the language of Germany, also used in Austria and Switzerland. • *adjective* of or relating to Germany or its people or language.

germane *adjective* relevant (to a subject under consideration): *remarks that are germane to the discussion*. [Say jur MANE]

Germanic • *adjective* **1** of the language group including English, German, Dutch, and the Scandinavian languages. **2** of the Scandinavians, Anglo-Saxons, or Germans. **3** having characteristics considered typically German. • *noun* **1** the Germanic family of languages. **2** the (unrecorded) early language from which other Germanic languages developed. [Say jur MANIC]

germanium *noun* a lustrous brittle semi-metallic element occurring naturally in sulphide ores and used in semiconductors. [Say jur MAINY um]

German measles *noun* a contagious disease, rubella, that resembles a mild form of measles but can cause fetal malformations if caught early in pregnancy.

German shepherd *noun* a large, strong, black and tan dog with a shaggy tail, used as a guard dog and in police work.

germ cell *noun* **1** a cell containing half the number of chromosomes of a somatic cell and able to unite with one from the opposite sex to form a new individual; a gamete. **2** any embryonic cell with the potential of developing into a gamete.

germicidal *adjective* relating to or being a substance destroying germs, esp. those causing disease. [Say jerma SIDE ul]

germicide *noun* a substance destroying germs, esp. those causing disease. [Say JERMA side]

germinate *verb* (**germinates**, **germinated**, **germinating**) **1 a** sprout, bud, or put forth shoots. **b** cause to sprout or shoot. **2** come into existence: *an*

idea for a novel began to germinate in her mind. ▶ **germination** *noun*

germ warfare *noun* the systematic spreading of micro-organisms to cause disease in an enemy population.

gerontologist *noun* a person who studies gerontology. [Say jare un TOLLA jist]

gerontology *noun* the scientific study of old age, the process of aging, and the special problems of old people. [Say jare un TOLLA jee]

gerrymander • *verb* **1** manipulate the boundaries of (a constituency etc.) so as to favour some party or class: *the city had been gerrymandered so that the Protestant minority retained control*. **2** manipulate (a situation etc.) to gain advantage. • *noun* this practice. ▶ **gerrymandering** *noun*

gerund *noun* Grammar a noun formed from a verb, in English ending in -*ing*, and designating an action or state, e.g. *smoking is bad for you*. [Say JARE ind]

gesso *noun* (*plural* **gessoes**) plaster of Paris as used in painting as a ground or in sculpture. [Say JESSO]

gestalt *noun* Psychology an organized whole that is perceived as more than the sum of its parts. [Say guh STAWLT]

Gestapo *noun* the German secret police under Nazi rule. It ruthlessly suppressed opposition to the Nazis in Germany and occupied Europe, and sent Jews and others to concentration camps. [Say guh STOPPO]

gestate *verb* (**gestates**, **gestated**, **gestating**) **1** carry (a fetus) in gestation: *rabbits gestate for approximately 28 days*. **2** develop (an idea etc.): *a research trip she made while gestating her new book*. [Say JES tate]

gestation *noun* **1 a** the process of carrying or being carried in the womb between conception and birth. **b** this period. **2** the private development of a plan, idea, etc.: *various ideas are in the process of gestation*. ▶ **gestational** *adjective* [Say jes TAY sh'n]

gesticulate *verb* (**gesticulates**, **gesticulated**, **gesticulating**) use esp. lively gestures instead of or in addition to speech. ▶ **gesticulation** *noun* [Say jes TICK yoo late, jes tick yoo LAY sh'n]

gesture • *noun* **1** a movement of the hand or head to express thought or feeling: *Alex made a gesture of apology ◊ so much is conveyed by gesture*. **2** an action to evoke a response or convey intention, usu. friendly: *we do not accept responsibility but we will refund the money as a gesture of goodwill*. • *verb* make a gesture. ▶ **gestural** *adjective* **gesturally** *adverb*

gesundheit *interjection* expressing a wish of good health, esp. to a person who has sneezed. [Say guh ZUN tite]

get *verb* (**gets**; *past* **got**; *past participle* **got** or **gotten**; **getting**) **1** come to have. **2** go to reach or catch (a bus, train, etc.). **3** prepare (a meal etc.). **4** become or cause to become. **5** obtain as a result of calculation. **6** establish or be in communication with via telephone or radio; receive (a radio signal, television channel, etc.). **7** experience or suffer; have inflicted on one. **8 a** succeed in bringing, placing, etc. **b** succeed or cause to succeed in coming or going. **9** (preceded by *have*) **a** possess. **b** be bound or obliged. **10** induce; prevail upon. **11** *informal* understand (a person or an argument). **12** *informal* inflict punishment or retribution on, esp. in retaliation. **13** *informal* **a** annoy. **b** move; affect emotionally. **c** attract, obsess. **d** amuse. **14** develop an inclination as specified. **15** begin. **16** catch in an argument; corner, puzzle. **17** establish (an idea etc.) in one's mind. **18** answer (a telephone, doorbell, etc.). **PHRASES** **be getting on for** be approaching (a specified time, age, etc.). **get across 1** manage to communicate (an idea etc.). **2** (of an idea

G

etc.) be communicated successfully. **get ahead** be or become successful. **get along** (or **on**) **1** live harmoniously. **2** (as *imperative*) nonsense! **get around 1** (also **get about**) **a** travel extensively or fast; go from place to place. **b** manage to walk, move about, etc. (esp. after illness). **c** (of news) be circulated, esp. orally. **2 a** evade (a law etc.). **b** successfully coax or cajole (a person) esp. to secure a favour. **get around to** deal with (a task etc.) in due course. **get at 1** reach; get hold of. **2** *informal* imply. **3** *informal* nag, criticize, bully. **get away 1** escape. **2** (foll. by *with*) escape blame or punishment for. **get back 1** move back or away. **2** return, arrive home. **3** recover (something lost). **4** (usu. foll. by *to*) contact later. **get back at** *informal* retaliate against. **get by** *informal* **1** just manage, even with difficulty. **2** be acceptable. **get down 1** alight, descend (from a vehicle, ladder, etc.). **2** record in writing. **3** manage to swallow. **4** lower oneself closer to the floor or ground. **5** *slang* be uninhibited or unrestrained, esp. in dancing or socializing. **get a person down** depress or deject a person. **get down to** begin working on or discussing. **get even** (often foll. by *with*) **1** achieve revenge; act in retaliation. **2** equalize the score. **get his** (or **hers** etc.) *slang* **1** be killed. **2** suffer retribution. **get hold of 1** grasp (physically). **2** understand. **3** make contact with (a person). **4** acquire. **get in 1** enter; gain entrance. **2** arrive. **3** be elected. **get into** become interested or involved in. **get it** *slang* be punished or in trouble. **get it into one's head** firmly believe or maintain. **get nowhere** fail despite one's efforts. **get off 1** *informal* be acquitted; escape with little or no punishment. **2** start. **3** alight; alight from (a bus etc.). **get (a crop** etc.) **off** harvest. **get a person off** *informal* cause a person to be acquitted. **get off on** *slang* be excited or aroused by; enjoy greatly. **get on 1** make progress; manage. **2** enter (a bus etc.). **3** = GET ALONG 1. **4** (usu. as **getting on**) *informal* grow old. **get on to** *informal* **1** make contact with. **2** understand; become aware of. **get out 1** leave or escape. **2** manage to go outdoors. **3** alight from a vehicle. **4** transpire; become known. **5** succeed in uttering, publishing, etc. **6** (as *interjection*) (also **get out of here!**, **get out of town!**) expressing disbelief. **get a person out** help a person to leave or escape. **get out of 1** avoid or escape (a duty etc.). **2** abandon (a habit) gradually. **get a thing out of** manage to obtain it from (a person) esp. with difficulty. **get over 1** recover from (an illness, upset, etc.). **2** overcome (a difficulty). **3** manage to communicate (an idea etc.). **4** overcome one's disbelief about. **get a thing over** (or **over with**) complete (a tedious task) promptly. **get one's own back** *informal* have one's revenge. **get somewhere** make progress; be initially successful. **get through 1** pass or assist in passing (an examination, an ordeal, etc.). **2** finish or use up (esp. resources). **3** make contact by telephone. **4** (foll. by *to*) succeed in making (a person) listen or understand. **get a thing through** cause it to overcome obstacles, difficulties, etc. **get to 1** reach. **2** annoy. **3** = GET DOWN TO. **get together 1** gather, assemble. **2** put (something) in order so as to perform effectively: *it's about time you got your act together*. **get up 1** rise or cause to rise from sitting etc., or from bed after sleeping or an illness. **2** ascend or mount, e.g. on a bicycle. **3** (of fire, wind, or the sea) begin to be strong or agitated. **4** prepare or organize. **5** enhance or refine one's knowledge of (a subject). **6** work up (a feeling, e.g. anger). **7** produce or stimulate: *get up speed*. **8** dress or arrange elaborately; make presentable; arrange the appearance of. **9** (foll. by *to*) *informal* indulge or be involved in: *getting up to mischief*. **have got it bad** (or **badly**) *slang* be obsessed or affected emotionally.

get-at-able *adjective informal* accessible.

getaway *noun* **1** an escape, esp. after committing a crime: *made a clean getaway ◊ a getaway car*. **2 a** a place far from work or home, visited for relaxation, e.g. a cottage, resort, etc. **b** a relaxing holiday, esp. far from one's work or home.

get-go *noun informal* the very beginning (of a project etc.): *knew from the get-go that it was futile*.

get-out *noun* PHRASES **as all get-out** *informal* to a high degree: *stubborn as all get-out*.

get-rich-quick *adjective* designed to make a lot of money fast: *a get-rich-quick scheme*.

getter *noun* a person or thing that gets a specified desirable thing: *an attention-getter ◊ a vote-getter*.

get-together *noun informal* a social gathering.

getup *noun informal* a style or arrangement of dress etc., esp. an elaborate one.

get-up-and-go *noun informal* energy, enthusiasm.

gewgaw *noun* a gaudy ornament or trinket.

geyser *noun* an intermittently gushing hot spring that throws up a tall column of water. [Say GUY zur]

GFI *abbreviation* (also **GFCI**) ground-fault (circuit) interrupter, a circuit breaker integrated into an outlet, esp. for use in bathrooms or outdoors.

GG *abbreviation* **1** Governor General. **2** *Cdn* = GOVERNOR GENERAL'S AWARD.

Ghanaian • *adjective* of or relating to Ghana, a country in W Africa. • *noun* a native or national of Ghana; a person of Ghanaian descent. [Say guh NAY un]

ghastly • *adjective* (**ghastlier**, **ghastliest**) **1** horrible, frightful. **2** *informal* objectionable, very unpleasant. **3** deathlike, pallid. • *adverb* in a ghastly or sickly way: *ghastly pale*.

ghee *noun* clarified butter as used in Indian cuisine, esp. from the milk of a buffalo or cow. [Say GEE (with G as in GEESE)]

gherkin *noun* **1** a small variety of cucumber, or a young green cucumber, used for pickling. **2 a** a trailing plant with small cucumber-like fruits used for pickling. **b** this fruit. [Say GUR kin]

ghetto *noun* (*plural* **ghettos** or **ghettoes**) **1** a part of a city, esp. a slum area, occupied by a minority group or groups. **2** *hist.* an area of a city in which Jews were required to live. **3** a situation in which a group is segregated because of discrimination or its own preference: *the women in the company were in a female ghetto with only eight salary levels through which to advance*.

ghettoize *verb* (**ghettoizes**, **ghettoized**, **ghettoizing**) restrict to a certain category by prejudice: *Canadian authors were invisible to the general public, ghettoized in the Canadiana section by booksellers, along with 101 Things to do with Maple Sugar cookbooks*.

ghost • *noun* **1** the supposed apparition of a dead person or animal; a disembodied spirit. **2** a shadow or mere semblance: *not a ghost of a chance*. **3** a secondary or duplicated image produced by defective television reception or by a telescope. • *verb* write a book, article, etc. for another person, under whose name it is then published: *a journalist claimed to have ghosted the book from tapes*. PHRASES **give up the ghost** *informal* die.

ghosting *noun* **1** in senses of GHOST *verb*. **2** the appearance of a "ghost" (*see* GHOST *noun* 3) in a television picture.

ghostlike *adjective* resembling a ghost or a place haunted by ghosts.

ghostly *adjective* (**ghostlier**, **ghostliest**) like a ghost.

ghost town *noun* a deserted town with few or no remaining inhabitants.

ghost write *verb* (**ghost writes, ghost wrote, ghost writing**) write a book, article, etc. for another person, under whose name it is then published.

ghost writer *noun* a person who writes on behalf of the credited author of a work.

ghoul *noun* **1** an evil spirit or phantom. **2** a person morbidly interested in death, disaster, etc. **3** a spirit in Arabic folklore preying on corpses. ▶ **ghoulish** *adjective* **ghoulishly** *adverb* **ghoulishness** *noun* [Say GOOL]

GHz *abbreviation* gigahertz.

GI *noun* (*plural* **GIs**) a private soldier in the US Army.

giant • *noun* **1** an imaginary or mythical being of human form but superhuman size. **2** an abnormally tall or large person, animal, plant, or thing. **3** a person, company, etc. of exceptional ability, prominence, importance, etc. **4 a** a star of relatively great size and luminosity. **b** any of the enormous gaseous planets Jupiter, Saturn, Uranus, and Neptune. • *adjective* **1** of extraordinary size or force, gigantic. **2** of exceptional importance, ability, or prominence: *a giant leap in science*. **3** (of a plant or animal) of a very large kind. ▶ **giantism** *noun* **giant-like** *adjective*

giant slalom *noun Skiing* a downhill event with a longer course and wider turns than standard slalom.

giardia *noun* a microscopic organism, *Giardia lamblia*. [Say jee ARDY uh]

giardiasis *noun* infection of the intestines with giardia, often from drinking untreated lake water, causing diarrhea etc. [Say jee arr DIE a sis]

gibber *verb* speak fast and inarticulately; chatter incoherently. ▶ **gibbering** *noun & adjective* [Say JIBBER]

gibberish *noun* unintelligible or meaningless speech or writing; nonsense. [Say JIBBER ish]

gibbon *noun* a small, slender, tree-dwelling ape, with powerful arms and loud hooting calls, native to the forests of Southeast Asia. [Say GIB un]

gibe *noun & verb* = JIBE¹. [Say JIBE]

giblets *plural noun* the liver, gizzard, heart, neck, etc., of a fowl, usu. removed and kept separate when the bird is prepared for cooking. [Say JIB lits]

GIC *noun* (*plural* **GICs**) *Cdn* = GUARANTEED INVESTMENT CERTIFICATE.

giddily *adverb* in a giddy manner.

giddiness *noun* the state or condition of being giddy.

giddy *adjective* (**giddier, giddiest**) **1** having a sensation of whirling and a tendency to fall, stagger, or spin around; dizzy. **2 a** overexcited as a result of success, pleasurable emotion, etc. **b** (of a person) not serious; interested only in having fun: *Isabel's giddy young sister* ◊ *the giddy 1920s*. **3** tending to make one giddy: *the giddy rise and ebb of adolescent emotion*.

giddying *adjective* tending to make one giddy: *the giddying speed of the revolving doors*.

giddy-up *interjection* (also **giddyap**) commanding a horse to go or go faster.

GIFT *noun* gamete intrafallopian transfer, a technique for assisting conception by introducing mixed ova and sperm into a Fallopian tube.

gift • *noun* **1 a** a thing given freely; a present. **b** denoting a usu. decorated container or wrapping for gifts, given along with the presents: *gift bag*. **2 a** natural ability or talent. **3** the power to give: *this is an award totally in the personal gift of the adjudicator*. **4** an act of giving something as a present: *his mother's gift of a pen*. • *verb* endow with: *human beings are gifted with a moral sense*. PHRASES **look a gift horse in the mouth** find fault with what has been given.

gifted *adjective* **1** exceptionally talented or intelligent. **2** designating programs of study for children of above average intelligence or artistic talent. ▶ **giftedness** *noun*

giftware *noun* goods sold as being suitable as gifts.

giftwrap • *verb* (**giftwraps, giftwrapped, giftwrapping**) wrap attractively as a gift. • *noun* decorative paper etc. for wrapping gifts.

gig *informal* • *noun* **1** a live performance by or engagement for a musician or group of musicians. **2** a job or employment, esp. likely to be temporary, for example as an actor. **3** *hist.* a small light carriage with two wheels, pulled by one horse. **4** a gigabyte. • *verb* (**gigs, gigged, gigging**) perform in gigs or a gig.

giga- *combining form* **1** denoting a factor of 10^9 (i.e. one billion): *gigawatt*. **2** *Computing* (in the binary system) denoting a factor of 2^{30} (i.e. 1 073 741 824): *gigabyte*.

gigabyte *noun Computing* 1 073 741 824 (i.e. 2^{30}) bytes as a measure of data capacity, or loosely 1 000 000 000. [Say GIGGA byte or JIGGA byte]

gigantic *adjective* very large; enormous. ▶ **gigantically** *adverb*

gigantism *noun* **1** abnormal largeness. **2** *Medical* excessive growth due to hormonal imbalance. [Say JYE gan tism or jye GAN tism]

giggle • *verb* laugh in half-suppressed, high-pitched spasms, esp. in a silly manner or out of nervousness. • *noun* **1** such a laugh. **2** (**the giggles**) a fit of giggling. **3** *informal* an amusing person or thing. ▶ **giggler** *noun*

giggly *adjective* (**gigglier, giggliest**) laughing a lot in a silly, nervous way.

GIGO *abbreviation Computing* garbage in, garbage out. [Say GUY go]

gigolo *noun* (*plural* **gigolos**) **1** a young man paid by an older woman to be her escort or lover. **2** a professional male dancing partner or escort. [Say JIGGA lo]

Gila monster *noun* a large carnivorous venomous lizard of Mexico and the southwestern US, black with orange or pink markings. [Say HEE luh]

SPELL CHECK
gild, guild   ABC✓

The usual Canadian spelling for an association of people with related jobs or interests is **guild**.

---

gild *verb* (**gilds, gilded, gilding**) **1** cover thinly with gold or a substance resembling gold: *the wooden base is first coated in plaster, then gilded*. **2** tinge with a golden colour or light: *the sun of late evening is gilding the feathery grass*. PHRASES **gild the lily** try to improve what is already beautiful or excellent: *some people add a little brandy to the recipe but I feel this is gilding the lily*.

gilded *adjective* **1** covered with a thin layer of gold or gold paint: *a gilded picture frame*. **2** wealthy and privileged: *Ivy League colleges are for the nation's gilded youth*.

gilded cage *noun* a luxurious but restrictive environment.

gilding *noun* **1** the act or art of covering thinly with gold or a substance resembling gold. **2** such a covering.

gill • *noun* (usu. in *plural*) **1** the respiratory organ in fishes and other aquatic animals. **2** the vertical radial plates on the underside of mushrooms and other fungi. **3** the flesh below a person's jaws and ears: *green at the gills*. • *verb* **1** gut or clean (a fish). **2** catch in a gill net. PHRASES **to the gills** completely, thoroughly, fully: *fed to the gills*. ▶ **gilled** *adjective* (also in *combination*)

gill net *noun* a net suspended vertically to entangle fish by the gills.

gillnetter *noun* **1** a person who fishes using gill nets. **2** a ship or boat designed for fishing with gill nets.

G

gilt • *adjective* covered thinly with gold or a gold-like substance. • *noun* gold or a gold-like substance applied in a thin layer to a surface.

gilt-edged *adjective* **1** (of a page, book, etc.) having a gilded edge. **2** of the highest quality; first-rate. **3** (of securities, stocks, etc.) having a high degree of reliability as an investment.

gimcrack *adjective* showy but flimsy and worthless: *gimcrack souvenirs*. ▶ **gimcrackery** *noun* [Say JIM crack]

gimme *informal* • *contraction* give me. • *interjection* give it to me. • *noun* (*plural* **gimmes**) **1** a task, e.g. kicking a short field goal, regarded as too easy to bungle. **2** *Golf* (in informal games) a short easy putt one is not required to attempt. • *adjective* designating an item given away, esp. for promotional purposes: *gimme cap*.

gimmick *noun* *informal* a trick or device, often underhanded, esp. for attracting attention, publicity, or trade. ▶ **gimmickry** *noun* **gimmicky** *adjective*

gimp¹ *noun* a twist of silk etc. with cord or wire running through it, used esp. as a trimming on upholstery.

gimp² *slang* • *noun* **1** a lame person or leg. **2** a stupid or contemptible person. • *verb* limp, hobble. ▶ **gimpy** *adjective*

gin¹ *noun* **1** a hard liquor distilled from grain or malt and flavoured esp. with juniper berries. **2** = GIN RUMMY.

gin² • *noun* **1** a snare or trap. **2** a machine for separating cotton from its seeds. • *verb* (**gins, ginned, ginning**) treat (cotton) in a gin.

ginger • *noun* **1 a** a hot spicy root usu. powdered for use in cooking, or preserved in syrup, or candied. **b** the Southeast Asian plant from which this root is taken. **2** ginger ale. • *adjective* of a light reddish-yellow colour: *ginger cat*. • *verb* **1** flavour with ginger: *gingered pear pumpkin pie*. **2** *informal* rouse or enliven: *they were getting desperate, and decided to ginger things up with an explosion*.

ginger ale *noun* a carbonated clear amber drink flavoured with ginger extract.

ginger beer *noun* **1** an effervescent, cloudy soft drink strongly flavoured with ginger. **2** an effervescent mildly alcoholic cloudy drink, made by fermenting a mixture of ginger and syrup.

gingerbread *noun* **1** a cake or cookie made with molasses and flavoured with ginger. **2** elaborate carving or other trim on buildings, usu. along the eaves or on porches etc.: *gingerbread trim*.

gingerly *adverb* carefully, cautiously: *made his way gingerly down icy Yonge Street*.

gingersnap *noun* a brittle, ginger-flavoured cookie.

gingery *adjective* like ginger in colour or flavour.

gingham *noun* a plain-woven cotton cloth of dyed yarn, esp. striped or checked. [Say GING um]

gingiva *noun* the firm area of flesh around the roots of the teeth; the gum. ▶ **gingival** *adjective* [Say JIN jiv uh or jin JIVE uh, jin JIVE ul]

gingivitis *noun* inflammation of the gums. [Say jin juh VITE is]

ginkgo *noun* (also **gingko**) (*plural* **ginkgos** or **ginkgoes**) **1** an originally Chinese and Japanese tree with fan-shaped leaves and yellow flowers. **2** a herbal remedy derived from the leaves of this, used to improve mental function and circulation.

ginormous *adjective* *Cdn & Brit. slang* very large; enormous. [Say jye NOR mus]

gin rummy *noun* a form of rummy in which a player holding cards totalling ten or less may terminate play.

ginseng *noun* **1** any of several plants with roots used for medicinal purposes, found in East Asia and North America. **2** the root of this plant. [Say JIN seng]

gipsy *noun* = GYPSY.

giraffe *noun* a large African mammal, the tallest living animal, with a long neck and forelegs and a skin of dark patches separated by lighter lines.

gird *verb* (**girds, girded, girding**) *literary* **1** encircle, attach, or secure with a belt or band. **2** enclose or encircle: *Ireland is girded by a coastline of unparalleled beauty*. **3** (foll. by *for*) prepare for action, a conflict, etc.: *candidates from all parties girded themselves for the election*. **PHRASES** **gird** (or **gird up**) **one's loins** prepare for action.

girder *noun* a large iron or steel beam or compound structure for bearing loads, esp. in bridge-building.

girdle • *noun* **1** a woman's corset extending from waist to thigh. **2** a belt or cord worn around the waist. **3** a thing that surrounds like a belt: *a communications girdle around the world*. **4** the bony support for a limb: *pelvic girdle*. • *verb* (**girdles, girdled, girdling**) **1** surround with or as with a girdle: *midriff-girdling stretch belts* ◊ *globe-girdling Canadian wheelchair athlete Rick Hansen*. **2** remove a ring of bark from a branch or tree to kill it: *the farmer clears a plot of land in the jungle by girdling trees and letting them die*.

girl *noun* **1** a female child or youth. **2** *informal* a young (esp. unmarried) woman. **3** *informal* a daughter. **4** *informal* a girlfriend or sweetheart. **5** often *offensive* a female servant. **6** often *offensive* a grown woman. **7** a woman belonging to a specified group: *a country girl*. **8** (**the girls**) *informal* a group of women mixing socially.

girlfriend *noun* **1** a regular female companion or lover. **2** a female friend.

Girl Guide *noun* *Cdn, Brit., Austral.,* & *NZ* a member of a girls' organization promoting outdoor activity, leadership, and community service.

girlhood *noun* the state or time of being a girl: *they had been friends since girlhood*.

girlie (also **girly**) *informal* • *adjective* **1** (of a magazine etc.) depicting nude or partially nude young women in erotic poses. **2** like, characteristic of, or appropriate for a girl or young woman: *the hotel also has some girlie pink paper*. • *noun* (*plural* **girlies**) *offensive* a young woman.

girlish *adjective* of or like a young girl. ▶ **girlishly** *adverb* **girlishness** *noun*

girth *noun* **1 a** the distance around a thing: *a tree one metre in girth*. **b** size, esp. of an overweight person: *alcohol adds girth to the abdominal area*. **2** a band around the body of a horse to secure the saddle etc.

GIS *abbreviation* **1** *Cdn* Guaranteed Income Supplement, a federally-supported supplement to the monthly pension payments of those with little income other than that derived from Old Age Security. **2** GEOGRAPHIC INFORMATION SYSTEM.

gist *noun* the substance or essence of a matter: *the gist of my theory*. [Say JIST]

git *interjection* *informal* get going; get along.

gitch *noun* *Cdn slang* underwear.

Gitksan *noun* (*plural* **Gitksan** or **Gitksans**) **1** an Aboriginal group living along the Skeena River in north central BC. **2** the Tsimshian language of this group. [Say git K'SAWN]

give • *verb* (**gives, gave, given**) **1** transfer the possession of freely; cause to receive or have. **2** be inclined to or fond of: *is given to speculation*. **3** yield as a product or result: *the field gives fodder for twenty years*. **4** yield to pressure. **5** devote: *gave his life to table tennis*. **6** present; offer; show; hold out: *gave her his arm*. **7** *Theatre* read, recite, perform, act, etc. **8** impart; be a source of: *gave him my sore throat* ◊ *gave its name to the*

battle. **9** allow (esp. a fixed amount of time): *can give you five minutes*. **10** value: *gives nothing for their opinions*. **11** concede: *I give you the victory*. **12** deliver (a judgment etc.) authoritatively: *gave his verdict*. **13** provide (a party, meal, etc.) as host: *gave a banquet*. • *noun* **1** capacity to yield or bend under pressure; elasticity. **2** ability to adapt or comply: *no give in his attitudes*. PHRASES **give and take** exchange (concessions, words, or blows). **give as good as one gets** retort adequately in words or blows. **give away 1** transfer as a gift. **2** hand over (a bride) ceremonially to a bridegroom. **3** betray or expose to ridicule or detection. **4** esp. *Sport* give inadvertently to the opposition. **give away** a penalty. **give back** return (something) to its previous owner or in exchange. **give forth** emit; publish; report. **give the game** (or **show**) **away** reveal a secret or intention. **give a person** (or **the devil**) **his or her due** acknowledge, esp. grudgingly, a person's rights, abilities, etc. **give in 1** cease fighting or arguing; yield. **2** hand in (a document etc.) to an official etc. **give it to a person** *informal* scold or punish. **give me** I prefer or admire: *give me Lake Huron*. **give off** emit (vapour etc.). **give oneself airs** act pretentiously or snobbishly. **give oneself up** surrender to one's pursuers. **give oneself up to 1** abandon oneself to an emotion, esp. despair. **2** addict oneself to. **give on to** (or **into**) (of a window, corridor, etc.) overlook or lead into. **give or take** *informal* add or subtract (a specified amount or number) in estimating. **give out 1** announce; emit; distribute. **2** cease or break down from exhaustion etc. **3** run short. **give over 1** *informal* cease from doing; abandon (a habit etc.); desist: *give over sniffing*. **2** hand over. **3** devote. **give rise to** cause, induce, suggest. **give a person to understand** inform authoritatively. **give up 1** resign; surrender. **2** part with. **3** deliver (a wanted person etc.). **4** pronounce incurable or insoluble; renounce hope of. **5** renounce or cease (an activity). **give a person what for** *informal* punish or scold severely. **give one's word** (or **word of honour**) promise solemnly. **what gives?** *informal* what is the news?; what's happening?; what's the problem? **would give the world** (or **one's right arm** etc.) **for** covet or wish for desperately.

give-and-take *noun* an exchange of words, concessions, etc.; a compromise.

giveaway *noun informal* **1** an inadvertent betrayal or revelation. **2** an act of giving away. **3 a** something given away free. **b** something sold at a low price. **4** *Sport* the inadvertent turning over of the puck, ball, etc. to an opponent.

giveback *noun* a union's agreement to reduce wages in exchange for benefits.

given • *adjective* **1** as previously stated or assumed; granted: *given that he is a liar, we cannot trust him* ◊ *given her interest in children, teaching seems the right job for her*. **2** *Law* (of a document) signed and dated: *given this day the 30th June*. • *noun* a known fact or situation: *in Canada, wide open spaces are a given*.

given name *noun* a name given to a child at or shortly after birth, distinguished from the surname.

giver *noun* a person or organization that gives: *they are enormous givers to charity*.

gizmo *noun* (plural **gizmos**) *informal* a gadget.

gizzard *noun* **1** the second part of a bird's stomach, for grinding food usu. with grit. **2** a muscular stomach of some fish, insects, molluscs, etc. **3** *informal* the throat. PHRASES **stick in one's gizzard** *informal* be distasteful.

glacial *adjective* **1** of or resembling ice: *glacial temperatures* ◊ *glacial blue eyes*. **2** of, pertaining to, characterized or produced by the presence or action of glaciers: *a glacial lake*. **3** (of movement or progress) resembling that of a glacier; extremely slow: *the population increased at the glacial rate of one-tenth of one percent*. ▶ **glacially** *adverb* [Say GLAY shull]

glaciated *adjective* covered or having been covered by glaciers or ice sheets: *glaciated hills*. ▶ **glaciation** *noun* [Say GLAY see ate id]

glacier *noun* a slowly-moving mass or river of ice formed by the accumulation and compaction of snow on mountains or in areas of prolonged cold climate. [Say GLAY shur or GLAY she ur]

glad[1] *adjective* (**gladder**, **gladdest**) **1 a** pleased; delighted. **b** relieved: *glad about the way it turned out*. **c** (usu. foll. by *of*) grateful: *glad of a chance to talk about it*. **d** willing and eager: *shall be glad to come*. **2 a** (of news, events, etc.) giving joy: *glad tidings*. **b** expressing joy: *a glad expression*. PHRASES **give a person the glad eye** *informal* cast an amorous glance at a person.

glad[2] *noun informal* a gladiolus.

gladden *verb* make glad.

glade *noun* an open space in a wood or forest.

glad hand • *noun* a warm, often superficial, greeting or welcome. • *verb* (**glad-hand**) (esp. of a politician, celebrity, etc.) greet or welcome warmly, often superficially. ▶ **glad-hander** *noun*

gladiator *noun* **1** *hist.* a man trained to fight with a sword or other weapons at ancient Roman shows. **2** a person defending or opposing a cause: *unions and businesses have been the chief gladiators for labour and capital*. ▶ **gladiatorial** *adjective*

gladiolus *noun* (plural **gladioli** or **gladioluses**) (also *informal* **gladiola**) a plant of the iris family, with sword-shaped leaves and usu. brightly coloured flower spikes. [Say gladdy OH lus for the singular, gladdy OH lie or gladdy OH lus is for the plural]

gladly *adverb* **1** willingly: *Katherine would gladly pay extra for a good seat*. **2** happily; with thanks: *when I offered her my coat, she accepted it gladly*.

gladness *noun* joy; happiness.

glam *informal* • *adjective* **1** glamorous. **2** designating a kind of pop music characterized by the extravagant dress, makeup, etc. of its performers, originally popular in the early 1970s: *glam rock*. • *noun* glamour.

glamorize *verb* (**glamorizes**, **glamorized**, **glamorizing**) make glamorous or attractive: *television glamorizes violence*.

glamorous *adjective* having glamour: *one of the world's most glamorous women*. ▶ **glamorously** *adverb*

glamour *noun* (also **glamor**) **1** physical attractiveness, esp. when achieved by makeup, elegant clothing, etc. **2** an attractive or exciting quality, esp. one which is inaccessible to the average person: *hopeful young actors and actresses dazzled by the glamour of Hollywood*.

glance • *verb* (**glances**, **glanced**, **glancing**) **1** cast a momentary look. **2 a** (esp. of a bullet, ball, etc.) bounce (off an object) obliquely. **b** (esp. of a weapon etc.) strike (an object) obliquely. **3** pass quickly over a subject or subjects: *glances over a number of difficult topics*. **4** (of a bright object or light) flash, dart, or gleam; reflect: *the sun glanced off the knife*. • *noun* **1** a brief look: *took a glance at the paper*. **2** a flash or gleam: *a glance of sunlight*. PHRASES **at a glance 1** immediately upon looking. **2** presented in a manageable format: *carpentry at a glance*. **at first glance** on the first impression; initially. ▶ **glancing** *adjective* **glancingly** *adverb*

gland *noun* **1 a** an organ in an animal body secreting substances for use in the body or for ejection. **b** a structure resembling this, such as a lymph gland. **2** *Botany* a secreting cell or group of cells on the surface of a plant structure.

glandular *adjective* of or relating to a gland or glands. [Say GLAND you lur]

G

glandular fever noun infectious mononucleosis.

glans noun (plural **glandes**) the rounded part forming the head of the penis or clitoris. [Say GLANZ for the singular, GLAN deez for the plural]

glare¹ • verb (**glares, glared, glaring**) 1 look fiercely or fixedly. 2 shine or reflect light dazzlingly or disagreeably. • noun 1 a strong fierce (often reflected) light, esp. sunshine. b oppressive public attention: *the glare of fame.* 2 a fierce or fixed look: *a glare of defiance.*

glare² adjective (esp. of ice) smooth and glassy.

glaring adjective 1 obvious, conspicuous: *a glaring error.* 2 shining or reflecting light oppressively or harshly. 3 staring fiercely. ▶ **glaringly** adverb

glasnost noun hist. (in the former Soviet Union) the policy or practice of more open government and wider dissemination of information. [Say GLAZ nost]

glass noun 1 a a hard, brittle, usu. transparent, translucent, or shiny substance, made by fusing sand with soda and lime and sometimes other ingredients. b = PLEXIGLAS. 2 (often collect.) an object or objects made from, or partly from, glass, esp.: a a drinking vessel. b a mirror. c a window. d a greenhouse: *rows of lettuce under glass.* e a magnifying lens. 3 (in plural) a eyeglasses. b binoculars; opera glasses. 4 the amount of liquid contained in a glass.

glass-blower noun a person who blows and shapes semi-molten glass to make glassware.

glass-blowing noun the blowing of semi-molten glass to make glassware.

glass ceiling noun an unacknowledged barrier to advancement into the higher positions in a profession or company, esp. affecting women and members of minorities: *it wasn't so much that women had problems getting hired, but that they couldn't crash through the glass ceiling into management.*

glassed-in adjective surrounded by or enclosed in glass: *a glassed-in sundeck.*

glassful noun (plural **glassfuls**) the amount that a drinking glass will hold.

glasshouse noun Cdn & Brit. a greenhouse.

glass-making noun the manufacture of glass.

glassware noun articles made from glass, esp. drinking glasses, tableware, etc.

glassy adjective (**glassier, glassiest**) 1 of or resembling glass, esp. in smoothness. 2 (of the eye, expression, etc.) abstracted; dull; fixed: *fixed her with a glassy stare.*

glatt kosher adjective strictly kosher.

glaucoma noun a condition of the eye with increased pressure within the eyeball, causing gradual loss of sight. [Say glaw COMA]

glaze • noun 1 a vitreous substance, usu. a special glass, used to give a hard shiny surface to pottery. 2 a a smooth shiny coating of sugar etc., on food. b a semi-liquid icing, often with a glossy sheen. 3 a thin topcoat of transparent paint used to modify the tone of the underlying colour. 4 a smooth surface formed by glazing. 5 a thin coating of ice. • verb (**glazes, glazed, glazing**) 1 a fit (a window, picture, etc.) with glass. b provide (a building) with glass windows. 2 a cover (pottery, food, etc.) with a glaze. b fix (paint) on pottery with a glaze. 3 (often foll. by over) (of the eyes) become fixed or glassy. 4 coat with a thin layer of ice.

glazing noun 1 the action of installing windows. 2 windows. 3 material used to produce a glaze.

gleam • noun 1 a reflected, brief, or faint light. 2 a faint, sudden, intermittent, or temporary show or expression: *a gleam of hope ◊ a gleam in her eye.* • verb 1 emit gleams. 2 shine with a reflected, intermittent, or faint brightness. 3 (of a quality) be indicated: *fear gleamed in his eyes.*

glean verb 1 collect or scrape together (news, facts, gossip, etc.) in small quantities: *we look to past decisions to glean principles and to make new laws.* 2 a gather (ears of grain etc.) after the harvest. b strip (a field etc.) after a harvest: *root crops are harvested throughout autumn, until winter finally extends its snowy mantle over our gleaned plots.* ▶ **gleaner** noun

gleanings plural noun things gleaned, esp. facts: *gleanings from the press and the Internet.*

glee noun delight, esp. triumphant.

glee club noun a choir, esp. at a school.

gleeful adjective exuberantly or triumphantly joyful: *a gleeful chuckle.* ▶ **gleefully** adverb **gleefulness** noun

glen noun a narrow valley.

glib adjective (**glibber, glibbest**) 1 (of speakers and speech) using words that are clever, but are not sincere, and do not show much thought: *a glib salesman ◊ glib answers.* 2 Cdn (esp. PEI) slippery, smooth: *glib ice.* ▶ **glibly** adverb **glibness** noun

glide • verb (**glides, glided, gliding**) 1 (of a bird, boat, skater, stream, snake, etc.) move with a smooth continuous motion. 2 a (of an aircraft, esp. a glider) fly without engine power. b (of a pilot) fly a glider. 3 of time etc.: a pass gently and imperceptibly. b (often foll. by into) pass and change gradually and imperceptibly: *night glided into day.* 4 move quietly or stealthily. • noun 1 a smooth continuous movement. 2 a gliding dance or dance step. 3 a flight in a glider. 4 a device affixed to the bottom of chair or table legs so that they can be slid across a floor more easily.

glider noun 1 a an aircraft that flies without an engine. b a glider pilot. 2 a person or thing that glides.

glimmer • verb shine faintly or intermittently. • noun 1 a feeble or wavering light. 2 (usu. foll. by of) a faint gleam (of hope etc.). 3 a glimpse.

glimmering • noun = GLIMMER noun. • adjective that glimmers. ▶ **glimmeringly** adverb

glimpse • noun (often foll. by of) 1 a momentary or partial view: *caught a glimpse of her.* 2 a faint and transient appearance: *glimpses of the truth.* • verb (**glimpses, glimpsed, glimpsing**) 1 see faintly or partly: *glimpsed his face in the crowd.* 2 (often foll. by at) cast a passing glance.

glint • verb flash or cause to flash; glitter; sparkle; reflect. • noun a brief flash of light; a sparkle.

glissando noun Music a continuous rapid slide of adjacent notes upwards or downwards. [Say glis SAN doe]

glisten verb shine, esp. like a wet object, snow, etc.; glitter.

glitch noun a sudden irregularity or malfunction (of equipment, a plan, etc.).

glitter • verb 1 shine, esp. with a bright reflected light; sparkle. 2 be showy or splendid: *glittered with diamonds.* • noun 1 a gleam. 2 showiness; splendour. 3 tiny pieces of sparkling material. 4 Cdn (Nfld) a freezing rain: *glitter storm.* b the coating of ice deposited by this.

glitterati plural noun informal jocular fashionable, wealthy literary or show-business people. [Say glitta ROTTY]

glittery adjective shining brightly with many small flashes of light: *a glittery suit.*

glitz noun informal extravagant but superficial display.

glitzy adjective (**glitzier, glitziest**) informal extravagantly showy; gaudy (often used to suggest superficial glamour): *a glitzy bar on Ste-Catherine.*

gloat verb (often foll. by on, upon, over) show that one is happy about one's own success or someone else's failure, in an unpleasant way: *she was still gloating over her rival's disappointment ◊ having lost a large percentage of the vote, they were in no position to gloat.* ▶ **gloater** noun **gloatingly** adverb

glob noun a lump of semi-liquid substance, e.g. mud.

The language of literary criticism

Figurative language

Imagery is language that produces pictures in the mind. The term can be used to discuss the various stylistic devices listed below, especially **figures of speech** (ways of using language to convey or suggest a meaning beyond the literal meaning of the words).

Metaphor is the imaginative use of a word or phrase to describe something else, to show that the two have the same qualities:

All the world's a stage
And all the men and women merely
players.

(William Shakespeare, *As You Like It*)

In **simile** the comparison between the two things is made explicit by the use of the words "as" or "like":

I wandered lonely as a cloud

(William Wordsworth, *Daffodils*)

Like as the waves make towards the pebbled
shore,
So do our minutes hasten to their end.

(Shakespeare, Sonnet 60)

Metonymy is the fact of referring to something by the name of something else closely connected with it, used especially as a form of shorthand for something familiar or obvious, as in "I've been reading Shakespeare" instead of "I've been reading the plays of Shakespeare".

Allegory is a style of writing in which each character or event is a symbol representing a particular quality. In John Bunyan's *Pilgrim's Progress* Christian escapes from the City of Destruction, travels though the Slough of Despond, visits Vanity Fair and finally arrives at the Celestial City. He meets characters such as the Giant Despair and Mr. Worldly Wiseman and is accompanied by Faithful and Hopeful.

Personification is the act of representing objects or qualities as human beings:

Love bade me welcome: yet my soul drew back,
Guilty of dust and sin.

(George Herbert, *Love*)

Pathetic fallacy is the effect produced when animals and things are shown as having human feelings. For example, in John Milton's poem, *Lycidas*, the flowers are shown as weeping for the dead shepherd, Lycidas.

Patterns of sound

Alliteration is the use of the same letter or sound at the beginning of words that are close together. It was used systematically in Old English poetry but in modern English poetry is generally used only for a particular effect:

On the bald street breaks the blank day.

(Alfred, Lord Tennyson, *In Memoriam*)

Assonance is the effect created when two syllables in words that are close together have the same vowel sound but different consonants, or the same consonants but different vowels:

It seemed that out of the battle I escaped
Down some profound dull tunnel long since
scooped...

(Wilfred Owen, *Strange Meeting*)

Onomatopoeia is the effect produced when the words used contain similar sounds to the noises they describe:

murmuring of innumerable bees

(Tennyson, *The Princess*)

Other stylistic effects

Irony is the use of words that say the opposite of what you really mean, often in order to make a critical comment.

Hyperbole is the use of exaggeration:

An hundred years should go to praise
Thine eyes and on thy forehead gaze

(Andrew Marvell, *To His Coy Mistress*)

An **oxymoron** is a phrase that combines two words that seem to be the opposite of each other:

Parting is such sweet sorrow

(Shakespeare, *Romeo and Juliet*)

A **paradox** is a statement that contains two opposite ideas or seems to be impossible:

The Child is father of the Man.

(Wordsworth, "My heart leaps up...")

Poetry

Lyric poetry is usually fairly short and expresses thoughts and feelings. Examples are Wordsworth's *Daffodils* and Dylan Thomas's *Fern Hill*.

Epic poetry can be much longer and deals with the actions of great men and women or the history of nations. Examples are Homer's *Iliad* and Virgil's *Aeneid*.

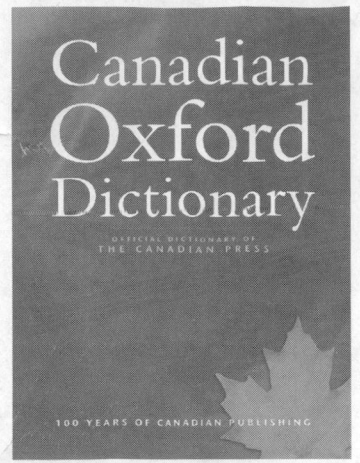

Canadian
Oxford
Dictionary
OFFICIAL DICTIONARY OF
THE CANADIAN PRESS

100 YEARS OF CANADIAN PUBLISHING

"The best Canuck wordbook yet, eh?"

The Globe and Mail

Now available in a major new edition, the *Canadian Oxford Dictionary* continues to set a new authoritative standard for Canadian dictionaries. The first edition spent over a year on *The Globe and Mail* bestseller list and won the Canadian Booksellers Association's Libris Award for Non-Fiction Book of the Year and Specialty Book of the Year.

The official dictionary of The Canadian Press

~

300,000 words, phrases, and definitions

~

Over 2,200 uniquely Canadian words and senses

~

Now includes recommended word breaks

~

Extensive encyclopedic entries covering people, places, mythological figures, and historical events

~

Over 850 Canadian biographies, 100 new to this edition

global *adjective* **1** worldwide: *global marketplace*. **2 a** relating to or embracing a group of items etc.; total. **b** *Computing* operating or applying through the whole of a file, program, etc.

global economy *noun* **1** the economic trends and conditions of the world's countries, seen as interrelated and regarded as a whole: *a recent slump in the global economy*. **2** the system of international trade, esp. featuring fewer trade barriers and increasing economic links between countries.

globalization *noun* the action or an act of making or becoming global.

globalize *verb* (**globalizes**, **globalized**, **globalizing**) make or become global.

globally *adverb* **1** in a global manner; throughout the world: *there are over 300 species globally*. **2 a** in a way that relates to or embraces a group of items etc. **b** *Computing* in a way that operates or applies through the whole of a file, program, etc.: *make the changes to the file globally*.

Global Positioning System *noun* a system of satellites and portable receivers able to pinpoint each receiver's location anywhere on the earth's surface, used in navigating and in surveying.

global village *noun* the world as one interdependent community linked by telecommunications.

global warming *noun* the increase in temperature of the earth's atmosphere supposedly caused by the greenhouse effect.

globe *noun* **1 a** (**the globe**) the planet earth. **b** a planet, star, or sun. **c** any spherical body; a ball. **2** a spherical representation of the earth or of the constellations with a map on the surface. **3** a golden sphere as an emblem of sovereignty; an orb. **4** any spherical glass vessel, esp. a fishbowl, a lamp, etc.

globetrotter *noun* *Informal* a person who travels frequently and extensively.

globetrotting • *noun* frequent and extensive travelling. • *adjective* engaging in frequent and extensive travelling: *a globetrotting executive*.

globular *adjective* spherical; shaped like a globule or composed of globules: *the plant has distinctive globular flowers*. [Say GLOB yoo lur, glob yoo LARA tee]

globule *noun* a small globe or round particle; a drop. [Say GLOB yool]

globulin *noun* any of a group of single proteins which dissolve only in salt solutions, esp. those forming a large fraction of blood serum protein. [Say GLOB yoo lin]

glockenspiel *noun* a musical instrument consisting of a series of bells or metal bars or tubes suspended or mounted in a frame and struck by hammers. [Say GLOCK un speel]

gloom *noun* **1** darkness; obscurity. **2** sadness.

gloom and doom *noun* = DOOM AND GLOOM.

gloomily *adverb* in a depressed or depressing manner: *she sighed gloomily*.

gloomy *adjective* (**gloomier**, **gloomiest**) **1** dark; unlighted. **2** depressed; sullen. **3** dismal; depressing.

gloop *noun* *informal* semi-liquid or sticky material.

glop *slang* • *noun* a liquid or sticky mess. • *verb* (**glops**, **glopped**, **glopping**) **1** scoop, drop, or toss (a semi-liquid substance). ▶ **2** (of a semi-liquid substance) drop, collect, ooze, or splat. ▶ **gloppy** *adjective*

Gloria *noun* **1** any of various Christian prayers or hymns beginning with the word *Gloria*. **2** a musical setting of this.

glorification *noun* the act or process of glorifying or being glorified: *the glorification of war*.

glorified *adjective* made out to be more splendid or important than in reality: *just a glorified office boy*.

glorify *verb* (**glorifies**, **glorified**, **glorifying**) **1** exalt to heavenly glory; make glorious. **2** praise.

glorious *adjective* **1** possessing glory; illustrious. **2** conferring glory; honourable: *a glorious sacrifice*. **3** splendid: *a glorious day*. **4** *ironic* intense: *a glorious muddle*. ▶ **gloriously** *adverb* **gloriousness** *noun*

glory • *noun* (*plural* **glories**) **1** high renown or fame; honour. **2** praise and thanksgiving: *Glory to the Lord*. **3** resplendent majesty or magnificence: *the glory of Versailles*. **4** a thing that brings renown or praise; a distinction. **5** the bliss and splendour of heaven. **6** *informal* a state of exaltation, prosperity, happiness, etc.: *is in his glory playing with his trains*. • *verb* pride oneself; exult: *glory in their skill*. PHRASES **go to glory** *slang* die; be destroyed.

gloss¹ *noun* **1 a** a surface shine or lustre. **b** a smooth finish. **2 a** deceptively attractive appearance. **b** a way of explaining something to make it seem more attractive or acceptable: *the director put a Hollywood gloss on the war*. **3** (also **gloss paint**) paint formulated to give a hard glossy finish. **4** a cosmetic applied to add lustre to skin: *lip gloss*. PHRASES **gloss over 1** seek to conceal beneath a false appearance. **2** conceal or evade by mentioning briefly or misleadingly.

gloss² • *noun* an explanatory word or phrase inserted between the lines or in the margin of a text; a comment, interpretation, or paraphrase. • *verb* (**glosses**, **glossed**, **glossing**) **1** add a gloss or glosses to (a text, word, etc.). **2** write or introduce glosses.

glossary *noun* (*plural* **glossaries**) an alphabetical list of terms or words found in or relating to a specific subject or text, with explanations; a brief dictionary.

glossiness *noun* shininess; smoothness.

glossy • *adjective* (**glossier**, **glossiest**) **1** having a shine; smooth. **2** (of paper etc.) smooth and shiny. **3** (of a magazine etc.) printed on such paper. **4** having a deceptively smooth and attractive appearance: *glossy TV newsmagazines*. • *noun* (*plural* **glossies**) *informal* **1** a glossy magazine. **2** a photograph with a glossy surface.

glottis *noun* (*plural* **glottises**) the space at the upper end of the windpipe and between the vocal cords, affecting voice modulation through expansion or contraction.

glove • *noun* **1** a covering for the hand, having separate fingers. **2** a padded protective glove worn by a goalie, boxer, baseball player, etc. • *verb* (**gloves**, **gloved**, **gloving**) **1** (usu. as **gloved** *adjective*) cover or provide with a glove or gloves. **2** catch (a ball, puck, etc.) in a glove. PHRASES **drop the** (or **one's**) **gloves 1** (in hockey) remove one's gloves to indicate willingness to fight. **2** *Cdn* engage in or indicate willingness to engage in a debate, confrontation, etc.: *halfway through the interview, he dropped the gloves*. **fit like a glove** fit exactly. **take off the gloves** *Cdn* ready oneself or indicate readiness for a confrontation. **with the gloves off** mercilessly; unfairly.

glovebox *noun* **1** = GLOVE COMPARTMENT. **2** a closed chamber with sealed-in gloves for handling infants, radioactive material, etc.

glove compartment *noun* a recess for small articles in the dashboard of a motor vehicle.

glow • *verb* **1 a** throw out light and heat. **b** shine with a steady light like something heated in this way. **2** (of the cheeks) redden, esp. from cold or exercise. **3** (often foll. by *with*) **a** (of the body) be heated, esp. from exertion; sweat. **b** express or experience strong emotion, esp. joy: *glowed with pride*. **4** show a warm colour: *the painting glows with warmth*. • *noun* **1** a glowing state. **2** a bright warm colour, esp. the red of cheeks. **3** ardour; passion. **4** a feeling induced by good health, exercise, etc.; well-being.

G

glower • *verb* stare or scowl angrily. • *noun* a glowering look. ▶ **gloweringly** *adverb* [Rhymes with *FLOWER*]

glowing *adjective* **1** shining; giving light and heat: *glowing coals*. **2** expressing pride or praise: *a glowing report*. ▶ **glowingly** *adverb*

glow-worm *noun* a soft-bodied beetle with luminescent organs in the abdomen, esp. the wingless female, which emits light to attract the flying male.

glucose *noun* **1** a simple sugar containing six carbon atoms, which is an important energy source in living organisms and obtainable from some carbohydrates by hydrolysis. **2** a syrup containing glucose sugars from the incomplete hydrolysis of starch. [Say GLUE kose (KOSE rhymes with *GROSS* or *GROWS*)]

glue • *noun* an adhesive substance used for sticking objects or materials together. • *verb* (**glues**, **glued**, **gluing** or **glueing**) **1** fasten or join with glue. **2** keep or put very close. **3** set fixedly: *eyes glued to the TV*.

glue gun *noun* an electric tool like a handgun, for melting and applying glue stored as hard sticks.

gluey *adjective* (**gluier**, **gluiest**) resembling or of the nature of glue; sticky.

glug • *verb* (**glugs**, **glugged**, **glugging**) **1** make a hollow, usu. repetitive gurgling sound, as of liquid being poured from a bottle. **2** pour or drink (a liquid) with such a sound. • *noun* such a sound.

glum *adjective* (**glummer**, **glummest**) looking or feeling dejected; sullen, morose. ▶ **glumly** *adverb* **glumness** *noun*

glut • *noun* **1** *Economics* supply exceeding demand; a surfeit: *a glut in the market*. **2** an excessive quantity: *the information glut*. • *verb* (**gluts**, **glutted**, **glutting**) **1** *Economics* overstock (a market) with goods. **2** fill to excess; choke up. **3** feed (a person, one's stomach, etc.) or indulge (an appetite, a desire, etc.) to the full; satiate.

glutamate *noun* see MONOSODIUM GLUTAMATE. [Say GLOOTA mate]

glute *noun* *slang* (usu. in *plural*) a gluteus muscle.

gluten *noun* a mixture of proteins present in cereal grains, responsible for the elasticity of dough. [Say GLUE tin]

gluteus *noun* (*plural* **glutei**) any of the three muscles in each buttock. [Say GLUE tee us for the singular, GLUE tee eye for the plural]

gluteus maximus *noun* (*plural* **glutei maximi**) **1** the largest and outermost muscle of each buttock. **2** *slang* the buttocks. [For the plural, say GLUE tee eye MAXA mye]

glutinous *adjective* sticky; like glue. [Say GLUE tin us]

glutton *noun* **1** an excessively greedy eater. **2** (often foll. by *for*) *informal* a person insatiably eager: *a glutton for work*. PHRASES **a glutton for punishment** a person eager to take on hard or unpleasant tasks. ▶ **gluttonous** *adjective* **gluttonously** *adverb*

gluttony *noun* habitual greed or excess in eating.

glyceride *noun* any fatty-acid ester of glycerol. [Say GLISSA ride]

glycerine *noun* (esp. *US* **glycerin**) = GLYCEROL. [Say GLISSA rin]

glycerol *noun* a colourless sweet viscous liquid, a by-product of soap manufacture, used as an emollient and laxative, in explosives, etc. [Say GLISSA rawl]

glycogen *noun* a polysaccharide serving as a store of carbohydrates, esp. in animal tissues, and yielding glucose on hydrolysis. [Say GLYE kuh jen]

glycol *noun* any alcohol containing two hydroxyl groups in each molecule, esp. ethylene glycol. [Say GLYE call]

glycolysis *noun* the breakdown of glucose by enzymes in most living organisms to release energy. [Say glye CALL a sis]

G

glycoprotein *noun* any of a group of compounds consisting of a protein combined with a carbohydrate. [Say glyco PROTEIN]

glyph *noun* **1** a sculptured character or symbol. **2** a symbol or pictorial representation, as in computing or on a sign. ▶ **glyphic** *adjective* [Say GLIFF]

GM *abbreviation* (*plural* **GMs**) general manager.

gm *abbreviation* gram(s).

GMT *abbreviation* Greenwich Mean Time.

gnarled *adjective* (of a tree, hands, etc.) knobbly, twisted, rugged. [Say NARLD]

gnarly *adjective* **1** = GNARLED. **2** *slang* excitingly rough or dangerous. [Say NARLY]

gnash *verb* (**gnashes**, **gnashed**, **gnashing**) **1** grind (the teeth), esp. in anger or exasperation. **2** (of the teeth) grind. [Say NASH]

gnat *noun* any small two-winged biting fly, e.g. a midge or blackfly. [Say NAT]

gnaw *verb* **1 a** wear away by biting. **b** bite, nibble. **2** corrode, consume, torture, etc. with pain, fear, etc.: *was gnawed by doubt*. [Say NAW]

gnawing *adjective* persistent; worrying. ▶ **gnawingly** *adverb* [Say NAWING]

gneiss *noun* a usu. coarse-grained metamorphic rock foliated by mineral layers, principally of feldspar, quartz, and mica. [Sounds like *NICE*]

gnocchi *plural noun* an Italian dish of small dumplings usu. made from potato, flour, etc. [Say NYOCKY]

gnome *noun* **1 a** a dwarfish legendary creature supposed to guard the earth's treasures underground; a goblin. **b** a figure of a gnome, esp. as a garden ornament. **2** (esp. in *plural*) *informal* a person with sinister influence, esp. financial: *gnomes of Zurich*. [Say NOME]

gnomon *noun* the rod or pin etc. on a sundial that shows the time by its shadow. [Say NO mon]

gnostic • *adjective* **1** relating to knowledge, esp. esoteric mystical knowledge. **2** (**Gnostic**) of or concerning Gnosticism or the Gnostics. • *noun* (**Gnostic**) (usu. in *plural*) an adherent of Gnosticism. [Say NOSS tick]

Gnosticism *noun* a heretical movement prominent in the Christian Church in the 2nd century, emphasizing the redeeming power of special knowledge understood by only a few. [Say NOSSTA sism]

GNP *abbreviation* gross national product.

gnu *noun* a large antelope native to southern Africa, with a large erect head and brown stripes on the neck and shoulders. [Sounds like *NEW*]

GNWT *abbreviation* *Cdn* Government of the Northwest Territories.

GRAMMAR CHECK
went, gone ⚠

Never say *I should have went*. The correct form is *I should have gone*.

---

go • *verb* (**goes**; *past* **went**; *past participle* **gone**; **going**) **1 a** start moving or be moving from one place or point in time to another; travel, proceed. **b** proceed in order to: *went to find him* ◊ *go and buy some bread*. **c** *informal* expressing annoyance: *they've gone and broken it*. **2** make a special trip for; participate in; proceed to do: *went shopping* ◊ *often goes running*. **3** lie or extend in a certain direction: *the road goes to Antigonish*. **4** leave; depart: *they had to go*. **5** move, act, work, etc.: *the clock doesn't go*. **6 a** make a specified movement: *go like this with your foot*. **b** make a sound (often of a specified kind): *the gun went bang* ◊ *the doorbell went*. **c** *informal* say: *so he goes, "Why not?"*. **d** (of an animal) make (its characteristic cry): *the cow went "moo"*. **7** be in a specified state: *go hungry*. **8 a** pass into a specified condition: *gone bad* ◊ *went to sleep*. **b** *informal* die. **c** proceed or escape in a

specified condition: *the crime went unnoticed*. **9** (of time or distance) pass, elapse; be traversed: *ten days to go ◊ the last mile went quickly*. **10 a** (of a document, verse, song, etc.) have a specified content or wording; run: *the tune goes like this*. **b** be current or accepted: *so the story goes*. **c** be suitable; fit; match: *the shoes don't go with the hat*. **d** be regularly kept or put: *the forks go here*. **e** find room; fit: *this won't go into the cupboard*. **11 a** turn out, proceed: *things went well ◊ Montreal went Liberal*. **b** be successful: *make the party go*. **c** progress: *we've still a long way to go*. **12 a** be sold: *went for $50*. **b** (of money) be spent: *$200 went on a new jacket*. **13 a** be relinquished, dismissed, or abolished: *the car will have to go*. **b** fail, decline; give way, collapse: *his sight is going*. **14** be acceptable or permitted; be accepted without question: *anything goes ◊ what Susan says goes*. **15** (often foll. by *by*, *with*, *on*, *upon*) be guided by; judge or act on or in harmony with: *a good rule to go by*. **16** attend or visit or travel to regularly: *goes to church ◊ this train goes to Edmonton*. **17** *informal* proceed (often foolishly) to do: *don't go making him angry*. **18** act or proceed to a certain point: *will go so far and no further*. **19** (of a number) be capable of being contained in another: *6 goes twice into 12*. **20** (usu. foll. by *to*) be allotted or awarded: *the job went to his rival*. **21** (foll. by *to*, *towards*) amount to; contribute to: *this will go towards your holiday*. **22** (in *imper.*) begin motion (a starter's order in a race): *ready, set, go!* **23** (usu. foll. by *to*) refer or appeal: *go to him for help*. **24** (often foll. by *on*) take up a specified profession: *went on the stage ◊ went to sea*. **25** (usu. foll. by *by*, *under*) be known or called: *goes by the name of Droopy*. **26** (in *imper.*) *informal* proceed to: *go jump in the lake*. **27** (foll. by *for*) apply to; have relevance for: *that goes for me too*. **28** urinate or defecate: *went on the carpet*. • *noun* (*plural* **goes**) **1** vigour: *she has a lot of go in her*. **2** vigorous activity: *it's all go*. **3** *informal* a success: *made a go of it*. **4** *informal* a turn; an attempt: *I'll have a go ◊ it's my go*. **5** a project, undertaking, etc. which has been given the go-ahead: *the new subway line is a go*. **6** an experience: *had a rough go of it*. • *adjective* *informal* functioning properly: *all systems are go*. **PHRASES as** (or **so**) **far as it goes** an expression of caution against taking a statement too positively: *the work is good as far as it goes*. **as (a person or thing) goes** as the average is: *a good actor as actors go*. **from the word go** *informal* from the very beginning. **give it a go** *informal* make an effort to succeed. **go about 1** busy oneself with; set to work at. **2** = GO AROUND 2. **go against 1** be contrary to: *goes against my principles*. **2** have an unfavourable result for: *decision went against them*. **go ahead** proceed without hesitation. **go along with** agree to; take the same view as. **go around 1** (foll. by *with*) be regularly in the company of. **2** (foll. by pres. part.) make a habit of doing: *goes around telling lies*. **go at** take in hand energetically; attack. **go away** depart, esp. from home for a holiday etc. **go back 1** return (to). **2 a** extend backwards in space or time: *goes back to the 18th century*. **b** (also **go way back**) (of two or more people or things) have known one another for a very long time: *Marty and I go way back*. **3** (of the hour, a clock, etc.) be set to an earlier standard time: *the clocks go back in the autumn*. **go back on** fail to keep (one's word, promise, etc.). **go by 1** pass. **2** be dependent on; be guided by. **go down 1 a** (of an amount) become less. **b** subside; abate: *the flood went down*. **c** decrease in price; lose value. **2 a** (of a ship) sink. **b** (of an aircraft) crash. **c** (of the sun) set. **3** (usu. foll. by *to*) be continued to a specified point. **4** deteriorate; fail; (of a computer network etc.) cease to function. **5 a** be recorded in writing. **b** be remembered: *this will go down as their greatest triumph*. **6** be swallowed. **7** (often foll. by *with*) find acceptance.

8 (often foll. by *before*) fall (before a conqueror). **9** *slang* happen. **go far** be very successful. **go for 1** go to fetch. **2** be accounted as or achieve: *went for nothing*. **3** prefer; choose: *that's the one I go for*. **4** *informal* strive to attain: *go for it!* **5** *informal* attack: *the dog went for him*. **go forward 1** proceed, progress. **2** (of the hour, a clock, etc.) be set to a later time, esp. daylight time. **go halves** (or **shares**) (often foll. by *with*) share equally. **go in 1** enter a room, house, etc. **2** (of the sun etc.) become obscured by cloud. **go in for** take as one's object, style, pursuit, principle, etc. **going!**, **gone!** an auctioneer's announcement that bidding is closing or closed. **go into 1** enter (a profession, Parliament, etc.). **2** take part in; be a part of. **3** investigate. **4** elaborate on: *went into the family's history*. **go a long way 1** (often foll. by *towards*) have a great effect. **2** (of food, money, etc.) last a long time, buy much. **3** = GO FAR. **go off 1** explode. **2** leave the stage. **3** gradually cease to be felt. **4** (esp. of foodstuffs) deteriorate; decompose. **5** go to sleep; become unconscious. **6** begin. **7** (of an alarm) begin to sound. **8** *informal* lose one's taste or enthusiasm for: *I've gone off sweet things*. **go off well** (or **badly** etc.) (of an enterprise etc.) be received or accomplished well (or badly etc.). **go on 1** continue, persevere: *decided to go on with it ◊ went on trying ◊ unable to go on*. **2** *informal* **a** talk at great length. **b** (foll. by *at*) admonish: *went on and on at him*. **3** proceed: *went on to become a star*. **4** happen: *what's going on?* **5** conduct oneself: *shameful, the way they went on*. **6** appear on stage. **7** (of a garment) be large enough for its wearer. **8** take one's turn to do something. **9** *informal* use as evidence: *police don't have anything to go on*. **go on!** *informal* an expression of encouragement or disbelief. **go out 1** leave a room, house, etc. **2 a** be broadcast. **b** be distributed. **3** be extinguished. **4** (often foll. by *with*) be dating. **5** leave one's home for recreation, esp. to visit a restaurant, friends, etc. **6** (of a government) leave office. **7** cease to be fashionable. **8** *informal* lose consciousness. **9** (of workers) strike. **10** (usu. foll. by *to*) (of the heart etc.) expand with sympathy etc. towards: *my heart goes out to them*. **11** *Golf* play the first nine holes in a round. **12** *Cards* be the first to dispose of one's hand. **13** (of a tide) turn to low tide. **14** *Cdn* (of winter ice on a lake, river, etc.) break up in the spring. **go over 1** inspect the details of; rehearse; retouch. **2** (often foll. by *to*) change one's allegiance or religion. **3** (of a play, joke, etc.) be successful: *went over well in Vancouver*. **go round 1** spin, revolve. **2** be long enough to encompass. **3** (of food etc.) suffice for everybody. **4** (usu. foll. by *to*) visit informally. **5** = GO AROUND. **go through 1** be dealt with or completed. **2** discuss in detail; scrutinize in sequence. **3** perform (a ceremony, a recitation, etc.). **4** undergo. **5** *informal* use up; spend (money etc.). **6** make holes in. **7** (of a book) be successively published (in so many editions). **go through with** not leave unfinished; complete. **go to hell** (or **blazes** etc.) *slang* an exclamation of dismissal, contempt, etc. **go together 1** match; fit. **2** be dating. **go to it!** *informal* begin work! **go to show** (or **prove**) serve to demonstrate (or prove). **go under** sink; fail; succumb. **go up 1** increase in price. **2** be consumed (in flames etc.); explode. **3** (of a building) be under construction. **go well** (or **ill** etc.) (often foll. by *with*) turn out well, (or ill etc.). **go with 1** be harmonious with; match. **2** agree to; take the same view as. **3 a** be a pair with. **b** be dating. **4** follow the drift of. **go without** manage without; forgo. **have a go at 1** attempt, try. **2** esp. *Brit.* attack, criticize. **on the go** *informal* **1** in constant motion. **2** constantly working. **3** in progress; happening. **to go 1** still to be dealt with. **2** (of fast food etc.) to be consumed off the premises. **who goes there?** a sentry's challenge.

G

goad • *noun* **1** an implement, such as a pointed or electrified rod, used for herding cattle etc. **2** anything that torments, incites, or stimulates: *in some farming societies, drought can be the goad for change.* • *verb* **1** urge on with a goad. **2** (usu. foll. by *on*, *into*) irritate; stimulate: *goaded him into retaliating.*

go-ahead • *noun* permission to proceed. • *adjective* **1** enterprising: *a go-ahead business.* **2** *Sport* designating a goal, run, etc. which puts the scoring team ahead of its opponent: *scored the go-ahead goal.*

goal *noun* **1** the object of an ambition or effort; a destination; an aim: *Fredericton was our goal.* **2 a** (in hockey etc.) a pair of posts with a crossbar between which the puck or ball has to be sent to score. **b** a cage or basket used similarly in other sports. **c** a successful attempt to score: *it's a goal!* **d** a point won: *scored 3 goals.* **3** a point marking the end of a race. **4** the position of goalkeeper.

goalie *noun* = GOALKEEPER.

goalkeeper *noun* a player stationed to protect the goal in various sports. ▶ **goalkeeping** *noun*

goalless *adjective* without either team scoring a goal: *the second period was goalless* ◊ *a goalless home tie.*

goalmouth *noun* (in hockey, soccer, etc.) the space between or directly in front of the goalposts.

goalpost *noun* either of the two upright posts of a goal.

goals-against average *noun* *Hockey* the average number of goals scored per game against a specified goaltender. Abbreviation: **GAA**.

goaltender *noun* (esp. in hockey) a goalkeeper.

goaltending *noun* **1** (esp. in hockey) the action of defending a goal. **2** (in basketball) the illegal blocking or deflecting of an attempted basket while the ball is descending or on the rim.

goat *noun* **1 a** a hardy, short-haired, domesticated mammal with backward curving horns and (in the male) a beard. It is kept for its milk and meat, and is noted for its lively and frisky behaviour. **b** a wild mammal related to this. **2** *informal* a foolish person. **3** a lecherous man. PHRASES **get a person's goat** *informal* irritate a person.

goat-antelope *noun* any antelope-like member of the goat family, including the mountain goat.

goatee *noun* a small beard on the point of the chin, like that of a goat. ▶ **goateed** *adjective* [Say go TEE]

goatherd *noun* a person who tends goats.

goatskin *noun* **1** the skin of a goat. **2** a garment or bottle made out of goatskin.

gob *slang* • *noun* **1** a clot or lump of esp. slimy or soft matter. **2** *slang* a Cdn spittle. **b** a globule of spittle. **3** (in *plural*; foll. by *of*) lots of. • *verb* (**gobs**, **gobbed**, **gobbing**) Cdn & Brit. spit.

gobble • *verb* (**gobbles**, **gobbled**, **gobbling**) **1** eat hurriedly and noisily; devour. **2** (often foll. by *up*) **a** seize avidly, grab, snatch. **b** consume, use up. **3 a** (of a male turkey) make a characteristic swallowing sound in the throat. **b** make such a sound when speaking, esp. when excited, angry, etc. • *noun* a gobbling sound.

gobbledegook *noun* (also **gobbledygook**) *informal* unintelligible jargon.

gobbler *noun* *informal* a male turkey.

go-between *noun* an intermediary; a negotiator.

goblet *noun* a drinking vessel with a foot and a stem, usu. of glass.

goblin *noun* a mischievous ugly dwarf-like creature of folklore.

goby *noun* (*plural* **gobies**) a small marine fish whose belly fins are joined to form a sucker or disc. [Say GO bee]

go-cart *noun* **1** = GO-KART. **2** an unpowered small esp. homemade riding cart, either sent down a slope or pushed.

god *noun* **1 a** (in many religions) a superhuman being or spirit worshipped as having power over nature, human fortunes, etc. a deity. **b** an image, idol, animal, or other object worshipped as divine or symbolizing a god. **2** (**God**) (in monotheistic religions) the creator and ruler of the universe. **3 a** an adored, admired, or influential person. **b** something worshipped like a god: *makes a god of success.* **4** (**God!**) an exclamation of surprise, anger, etc. PHRASES **by God!** an exclamation of surprise etc. **God bless** an expression of good wishes on parting. **God damn** (**you, him,** etc.) may (you etc.) be damned. **God forbid** used to express a wish that something will not happen: *God forbid that this should happen to anyone ever again* ◊ *if you were, God forbid, in a serious car accident, would you want your organs donated to help someone else?* **God the Father, Son, and Holy Ghost** *Christianity* the Persons of the Trinity. **God grant** (foll. by *that* + clause) may it happen. **God help** (**you, him,** etc.) an expression of concern for or sympathy with a person. **God knows 1** it is beyond all knowledge: *God knows what will become of him.* **2** I call God to witness that: *God knows we tried hard enough.* **God willing** if Providence allows. **in God's name** an appeal for help. **my** (or **oh**) **God!** an exclamation of surprise, anger, etc. **play God** attempt to control people or events, esp. in matters traditionally outside the realm of human influence. **with God** dead and in Heaven.

godawful *adjective* *slang* very unpleasant, inferior, etc.

godchild *noun* (*plural* **godchildren**) a person in relation to a godparent.

goddaughter *noun* a female godchild.

goddess *noun* (*plural* **goddesses**) **1** a female deity. **2** a woman who is adored, esp. for her beauty.

godfather *noun* **1** a male godparent. **2** a person directing an illegal organization, esp. the Mafia. **3** the most experienced or influential member of an organization etc., treated with deference and respect.

God-fearing *adjective* **1** having a deep respect for God and leading a virtuous life. **2** earnestly religious.

godforsaken *adjective* **1** (of a place) dismal; lacking in comfort. **2** remote; isolated.

godhead *noun* **1 a** the state of being God or a god: *he is a human being aspiring to godhead.* **b** divine nature. **2** an adored, admired, or influential person; an idol: *America's current talk show godhead.* **3** (**the Godhead**) God: *both masculine and feminine aspects of the Godhead.*

godless *adjective* **1** wicked. **2** without a god. **3** not recognizing God. ▶ **godlessness** *noun*

godlike *adjective* **1** resembling God or a god in some quality, esp. in great or absolute power or influence. **2** befitting or appropriate to God or a god.

godliness *noun* the state or quality of being religious.

godly *adjective* religious.

godmother *noun* a female godparent.

godparent *noun* a person who presents a child at baptism, answering questions on the child's behalf and promising to take responsibility for their religious education.

godsend *noun* an unexpected but welcome event, thing, or person.

godson *noun* a male godchild.

Godspeed *noun* (as an expression of good wishes to a person starting a journey etc.) good fortune.

goer *noun* **1** (often in *combination*) a person who attends, esp. regularly: *churchgoer* ◊ *concert-goer.* **2** a person or thing that goes: *a slow goer.*

goes *3rd singular present of* GO.

G

gofer *noun informal* a person who runs errands, esp. in an office.

go-getter *noun informal* an aggressively enterprising person, esp. in business. ▶ **go-getting** *adjective*

goggle • *noun* (in *plural*) **1** eyeglasses for protecting the eyes from glare, dust, water, etc. **2** *informal* eyeglasses. • *verb* (**goggles**, **goggled**, **goggling**) **1** (often foll. by *at*) stare with wide, round eyes, esp. in surprise or wonder. **2** (of the eyes) be rolled about; protrude.

goggle-eyed *adjective* having staring or bulging eyes.

go-go *adjective* **1 a** (of a dancer) performing at a nightclub or disco, esp. in scanty clothing. **b** (of a nightclub etc.) featuring go-go dancers. **2** *informal* unrestrained; energetic: *spent the go-go 1980s getting rich in the life insurance business*. **3** *informal* (of investment) speculative: *invested in go-go technology stocks*.

going • *noun* **1 a** the act or process of going. **b** a departure. **2 a** the condition of the ground for walking, riding, etc. **b** progress affected by this: *found the going very laborious*. **c** progress affected by all circumstances: *it'll be tough going for the party this election*. • *adjective* **1** in or into action: *set the clock going*. **2** existing, available; to be had: *one of the best going*. **3** current, prevalent: *the going rate*. PHRASES **get going** start steadily talking, working, etc.: *can't stop them when they get going*. **going for one** *informal* acting in one's favour: *he's got a lot going for him*. **going on fifteen** etc. approaching one's fifteenth etc. birthday. **going on for** approaching (a time, an age, etc.): *must be going on for 6 years*. **going to** intending or intended to; about to; likely to: *it's going to sink!* **to be going on with** to start with; for the time being. **while the going is good** while conditions are favourable.

going concern *noun* a thriving business.

going-over *noun* (*plural* **goings-over**) *informal* **1** an inspection or overhaul. **2** a thrashing. **3** a scolding.

goings-on *plural noun* unusual, surprising, or morally undesirable happenings or events.

goitre *noun* a swelling of the neck caused by enlargement of the thyroid. [Say GOY tur]

go-kart *noun* a miniature race car with a skeleton body.

gold • *noun* **1** a yellow metallic element occurring naturally in quartz veins and gravel, and precious as a monetary medium, in jewellery, etc. **2** the colour of gold. **3** a coins or articles made of gold. **b** money in large sums, wealth. **4** something precious, beautiful, or brilliant: *all that glitters is not gold*. **5** (in full **gold medal**) a medal of gold awarded to the winner of a competition. • *adjective* **1** made wholly or chiefly of gold. **2** coloured like gold. **3** (of an album, CD, etc.) having sold a specified high number of copies.

gold card *noun* a credit card issued only to people with a high credit rating and giving benefits not available to holders of the standard card.

gold dust *noun* gold in fine particles as often found naturally.

golden *adjective* **1 a** made or consisting of gold. **b** yielding gold. **2** coloured or shining like gold: *golden hair*. **3** precious; excellent: *a golden opportunity*. **4** (esp. in nicknames for places) wealthy: *Golden Horseshoe*.

golden age *noun* **1** a supposed past age when people were happy and innocent. **2** the period of greatest esp. artistic achievement: *the golden age of comics*. **3** old age, esp. after retirement.

golden ager *noun* an old person, esp. a retired person over 65.

golden boy *noun informal* a popular or successful man or boy.

Golden Delicious *noun see* DELICIOUS *noun*

goldeneye *noun* a migratory duck, the male of which has a large dark head with a white cheek patch and bright yellow eyes.

golden handshake *noun informal* a payment given as compensation for dismissal or compulsory retirement.

golden jubilee *noun* **1** the fiftieth anniversary of a sovereign's accession. **2** any other fiftieth anniversary.

golden parachute *noun informal* financial compensation guaranteed to company executives dismissed as a result of a merger or takeover.

golden retriever *noun* a retriever with a thick coat ranging in colour from pale yellow to golden-orange (feathery on the neck, legs, and tail).

goldenrod *noun* a plant of the daisy family, which bears tall spikes of small bright yellow flowers.

golden rule *noun* **1** a basic principle of action: *as far as equipment goes, the golden rule has to be not to take too much*. **2** the principle "do unto others as you would have them do unto you".

golden wedding *noun* the fiftieth anniversary of a wedding.

goldeye *noun* a silvery freshwater fish with a golden iris, of central North America, much favoured as a delicacy in Manitoba, esp. when smoked, when it becomes a reddish-gold colour.

goldfield *noun* a district in which gold is found.

goldfinch *noun* (*plural* **goldfinches**) a brightly coloured songbird with predominantly yellow plumage.

goldfish *noun* (*plural* **goldfish**) a small reddish-golden Chinese carp kept for ornament or as a pet.

goldfish bowl *noun* **1** a globular glass container for goldfish. **2** a situation lacking privacy: *was living in a goldfish bowl of publicity*.

gold leaf *noun* gold beaten into a very thin sheet, used for decorating objects made out of other materials.

gold mine *noun* **1** a place where gold is mined. **2** *informal* a source of wealth. **3** *informal* a source of valuable information or resources: *this book is a gold mine of information*. ▶ **gold miner** *noun* **gold mining** *noun*

gold plate • *noun* **1** vessels made of gold. **2** material plated with gold. • *verb* (**gold-plate**, **gold-plates**, **gold-plated**, **gold-plating**) plate with gold.

gold-plated *adjective* **1** plated with gold. **2** wealthy or luxurious, esp. excessively so: *a gold-plated pension plan*.

gold rush *noun* a rush to a newly discovered goldfield.

goldsmith *noun* a person who makes gold articles.

gold standard *noun* a system in which the value of a currency is defined in terms of gold, for which the currency may be exchanged.

golf • *noun* a game played on a park-like course, in which a small hard ball is driven with clubs into a series of 18 or 9 holes with the fewest possible strokes. • *verb* play golf.

golf club *noun* **1** a long thin club with a metal or wooden head used in golf. **2 a** an association for playing golf. **b** the premises used by a golf club.

golfer *noun* a person who plays golf.

golly *interjection* expressing mild surprise.

gonad *noun* an animal organ producing gametes, e.g. the testis or ovary. [Say GO nad]

gonadotropin *noun* (also **gonadotrophin**) *Biochemistry* any of various hormones stimulating the

activity of the gonads. [Say go nadda TROE pin, go nadda TROE fin]

gondola *noun* (*plural* **gondolas**) **1** a light flat-bottomed boat used on Venetian canals, with a central cabin and a high point at each end, worked by one oar at the stern. **2** an enclosed compartment suspended from an airship or balloon. **3** an enclosed cabin suspended from a cable, as in a ski lift. [Say GONDA luh]

gondolier *noun* the oarsman on a gondola. [Say gonda LEER]

gone • *verb* past participle of GO. • *adjective* **1 a** lost; hopeless. **b** dead. **2** used up. **3** *informal* pregnant for a specified time: *three months gone*. **4** *slang* completely enthralled or entranced, esp. by rhythmic music, drugs, etc. PHRASES **gone on** *slang* infatuated with.

goner *noun slang* a person or thing that is doomed, ended, etc.; a person beyond hope or help.

gong *noun* **1** a metal disc with a turned rim, giving a resonant note when struck. **2** the resonant sound of a struck gong.

gonna *contraction informal* going to: *we're gonna win!*

gonorrhea *noun* (also esp. *Brit.* **gonorrhoea**) a venereal disease with inflammatory discharge from the urethra or vagina. ▶ **gonorrheal** *adjective* [Say gon uh REE uh]

gonzo *adjective* **1** *informal* bizarre; crazy. **2** of or associated with journalistic writing of an exaggerated, subjective, and fictionalized style.

goo *noun informal* a sticky or slimy substance.

goober *noun* (also **goober pea**) a peanut or peanut plant.

WRITING TIP
good, very good

Instead of saying that something is **good** or **very good**, try to use more precise and interesting adjectives to describe things:

a **talented/skilful/superb** athlete

a **masterful/proficient/distinguished/ brilliant** musician

an **enjoyable/entertaining/exciting/ engrossing** movie

the food here is **delicious/appetizing/tasty**

a **suitable/fitting/appropriate** response

his excuse was **valid/legitimate/acceptable**

an **honest/honourable/admirable** woman

a **generous/benevolent/gracious/obliging** host

a **well-behaved/polite/well-mannered** child

a **reliable/dependable/trustworthy** employee

a **hard-working/keen/conscientious/ diligent** student

our **close/intimate/dear/valued** friends

When referring to pleasant weather, you can use words like: **fair**, **mild**, **clear**, **calm**, or **tranquil**.

---

good • *adjective* (**better**, **best**) **1** to be desired or approved of. **2** having the required qualities; of a high standard. **3** morally right; virtuous. **4** well behaved. **5** enjoyable or satisfying. **6** appropriate. **7** thorough. **8** at least. • *noun* **1** that which is morally right or beneficial. **2** merchandise or possessions. PHRASES **good as** practically: *he as good as told me*. **be (a certain amount) to the good** have as net profit or advantage. **for good (and all)** finally, permanently. **good and** *informal* used as an intensifier before an adjective or adverb: *raining good and hard*. **good for 1** beneficial to; having a good effect on. **2** able to perform; inclined for: *good for a ten-mile walk*. **3** able to be trusted to pay: *is good*

for $100. **good for you!** (or **him!**, **her!**, etc.) exclamation of approval towards a person. **have** (or **get**) **the goods on a person** *slang* have (or acquire) advantageous information about a person. **in good time 1** with no risk of being late. **2** (also **all in good time**) in due course but without haste. **make good 1** make up for, compensate for, pay (an expense). **2** fulfil (a promise); effect (a purpose or an intended action). **3** demonstrate the truth of (a statement); substantiate (a charge). **4** gain and hold (a position). **5** replace or restore (a thing lost or damaged). **6** accomplish what one intended. **no good** useless: *it is no good arguing* ◊ *my idea was no good*. **to the good** having as profit or benefit. **up to no good** making mischief.

Good Book *noun* (**the Good Book**) the Bible.

goodbye • *interjection* expressing good wishes on parting, ending a telephone conversation, etc., or said with reference to a thing got rid of or irrevocably lost. • *noun* (*plural* **goodbyes**) a parting; a farewell.

good cholesterol *noun* high-density lipoprotein.

good cop/bad cop *adjective informal* designating a procedure or routine used in interrogating, negotiating, or in public relations, in which one of two partners assumes a harsh, uncompromising attitude and the other a more lenient or mild one.

good faith *noun* honesty or sincerity of intention.

good form *noun* what complies with current social conventions. PHRASES **in good form** in a state of good health or training.

good-for-nothing • *adjective* worthless. • *noun* a worthless person.

Good Friday *noun* the Friday before Easter Sunday, commemorating the Crucifixion of Christ.

good guy *noun informal* a hero; a person viewed favourably in a conflict.

good-hearted *adjective* kindly, well-meaning.

good-humoured *adjective* genial, cheerful, amiable. ▶ **good-humouredly** *adverb*

goodie *noun* = GOODY *noun*

goodie bag *noun* a bag of treats, goodies, or promotional items, given as a gift or prize.

good-looking *adjective* handsome; attractive.

good luck • *noun* **1** good fortune. **2** an omen of this. • *interjection* an exclamation of well-wishing.

goodly *adjective* (**goodlier**, **goodliest**) **1** good-looking, handsome. **2** of imposing size etc.

good-natured *adjective* kind, patient; easygoing. ▶ **good-naturedly** *adverb*

goodness • *noun* **1** virtue; excellence, esp. moral. **2** kindness, generosity: *had the goodness to wait*. **3** what is good or beneficial in a thing. • *interjection* (as a substitution for "God"): *goodness knows*.

good offices *plural noun* influence, esp. as used to others' benefit; connections: *the trip was arranged through the good offices of my MP*.

good riddance *interjection* expressing welcome relief from an unwanted person or thing.

goods and services tax *noun* Cdn & NZ a value-added tax levied on a broad range of consumer goods and services. Abbreviation: **GST**.

good-tempered *adjective* having a good temper; not easily annoyed. ▶ **good-temperedly** *adverb*

good-time *adjective* recklessly pursuing pleasure.

goodwill *noun* **1** kindly feeling. **2** the established reputation of a business etc. as enhancing its value. **3** cheerful consent or acquiescence; readiness, zeal.

good word *noun* (often in phr. **put in a good word for**) words in recommendation or defence of a person.

good works *plural noun* charitable acts.

goody • *noun* (*plural* **goodies**) **1** (usu. in *plural*) something good or attractive, esp. to eat, often given as a treat or reward. **2** = GOODY-GOODY *noun*. **3** *informal* a good or favoured person, esp. a hero in a story, film, etc. • *interjection* expressing childish delight.

goody-goody *informal* • *noun* (*plural* **goody-goodies**) a smug or obtrusively virtuous person. • *adjective* obtrusively or smugly virtuous.

goody two-shoes *noun* = GOODY-GOODY.

gooey *adjective* (**gooier**, **gooiest**) *slang* **1** viscous, sticky. **2** sickly, sentimental. ▶ **gooeyness** *noun*

goof *informal* • *noun* **1** a foolish or stupid person. **2** a mistake, a blunder. • *verb* **1** (foll. by *up*) bungle, mess up. **2** (often foll. by *up*) blunder, make a mistake. **3** (often foll. by *off*) idle. **4** (foll. by *around*, *about*) fool around, mess about.

goofball *informal* • *noun* **1** a blundering or eccentric person. **2** a pill containing a narcotic drug, esp. a barbiturate. • *adjective* eccentric or silly.

goofily *adverb* in a silly, ridiculous, or odd manner.

goofiness *noun* silliness; ridiculousness.

goof-up *noun informal* a mistake, a blunder.

goofy *adjective* (**goofier**, **goofiest**) silly, ridiculous, odd.

googlie-eyed *adjective* (also **googly-eyed**) = GOGGLE-EYED.

goo-goo *adjective* **1** designating the behaviour etc. of a baby; infantile: *goo-goo sounds*. **2** indicating excessive or foolish infatuation: *making goo-goo eyes*.

gook *noun slang* a slimy or sticky substance. [Rhymes with *KOOK* or *COOK*]

goon *noun slang* **1** a person employed to terrorize esp. political or industrial opponents. **2** *informal* a hockey player who intimidates opponents by rough play and fighting. **3** a stupid person. ▶ **goony** *adjective*

goop *noun* = GLOOP. ▶ **goopy** *adjective* (**goopier**, **goopiest**)

goose • *noun* (*plural* **geese**) **1 a** a large water bird with short legs, webbed feet, and a broad bill. **b** the female of this (*opp.* GANDER). **2** *informal* a silly person. • *verb* (**gooses**, **goosed**, **goosing**) **1** *slang* poke (a person) in the buttocks. **2** esp. *US informal* (often foll. by *up*) energize, strengthen, invigorate, or increase. PHRASES **what's good** (or **sauce**) **for the goose is good** (or **sauce**) **for the gander** what is appropriate in one case is appropriate in others.

gooseberry *noun* (*plural* **gooseberries**) **1** a round edible yellowish-green berry with a thin usu. translucent skin enclosing seeds in a juicy flesh. **2** any of various thorny shrubs bearing this fruit.

goosebumps *plural noun* (also **goose pimples**, **gooseflesh** *noun*) the small pimple-like bumps appearing on the skin because of cold, fright, etc.

goose egg *noun informal* **1** a zero score in a game or examination. **2** a lump appearing after hitting one's head etc. or being hit.

goosefoot *noun* (*plural* **goosefoots**) a plant of temperate regions, with leaves shaped like the foot of a goose. Some are edible, and many are common weeds.

gooseneck *noun* a long thin flexible metal tube resembling the neck of a goose: *gooseneck lamp*.

goose step • *noun* a marching step in which the knees are kept locked and the legs are lifted high, usu. associated with militaristic regimes. • *verb* (**goose-step**: **goose-steps**, **goose-stepped**, **goose-stepping**) march in this way.

gopher *noun* **1** a buff-coloured ground squirrel of the prairies of western North America; a Richardson's ground squirrel. **2** (also **pocket gopher**) a burrowing rodent native to Central and North America, having external cheek pouches and sharp front teeth.

3 *Computing* a computer program designed to help users reach and search other sites on the Internet. **4** = GOFER.

Gordian knot *noun* an extremely difficult or involved problem: *clouds are the Gordian knot in the whole climate change problem*. PHRASES **cut the Gordian knot** solve a problem by force or by evasion: *an attempt to cut the Gordian knot of Irish politics*.

gore • *noun* **1** blood that has been shed, esp. as a result of violence. **2** *informal* bloodshed, carnage. • *verb* (**gores**, **gored**, **goring**) pierce with a horn, tusk, etc.

Gore-Tex *noun* proprietary a breathable laminated waterproof fabric.

gorge • *noun* **1** a narrow opening between hills or a rocky ravine, often with a stream running through it. **2** an act of gorging; a feast. • *verb* (**gorges**, **gorged**, **gorging**) **1** (usu. foll. by *on*) feed greedily. **2 gorge oneself** eat a lot in a greedy way, esp. to excess. PHRASES **one's gorge rises** one is sickened: *looking at it, Wendy felt her gorge begin to rise*.

gorgeous *adjective* **1** strikingly beautiful. **2** very pleasant: *gorgeous weather*. **3** richly coloured, sumptuous, magnificent. ▶ **gorgeously** *adverb* **gorgeousness** *noun*

Gorgonzola *noun* a type of rich cheese with bluish-green veins. [Say gorgun ZOLA]

SPELL CHECK
gorilla, guerrilla
A member of a small, independent army is a **guerrilla**.

gorilla *noun* (*plural* **gorillas**) **1** the largest anthropoid ape, native to Central Africa, having a large head, short neck, and prominent mouth. **2** *informal* a heavily built man of aggressive demeanour.

go-round *noun* each of several recurring turns, opportunities, or chances: *do better on the next go-round*.

gorp *noun* = TRAIL MIX.

gorse *noun* a spiny yellow-flowered shrub found growing on European wastelands.

gory *adjective* (**gorier**, **goriest**) **1** involving or depicting bloodshed; bloodthirsty: *a gory film*. **2** covered in gore. **3** resembling gore: *a gory red*. PHRASES **gory details** *jocular* explicit details.

gosh *interjection* expressing mild surprise.

goshawk *noun* a large short-winged hawk, resembling a large sparrow hawk. [Say GOSS hawk]

gosling *noun* a young goose. [Say GOZZ ling]

gospel *noun* **1** the teaching or revelation of Christ. **2** (**Gospel**) **a** the record of Christ's life and teaching in the first four books of the New Testament. **b** each of these books. **c** a portion from one of them read at a service. **3** (also **gospel truth**) a thing regarded as absolutely true: *take my word as gospel*. **4** a principle one acts on or advocates. **5** (also **gospel music**) a fervent, spirited style of evangelical religious music, esp. as originally sung by US Blacks.

gospeller *noun* a person who preaches or promotes the Gospel or a gospel.

gossamer • *noun* **1** a filmy substance of small spiders' webs. **2** delicate filmy material. **3** a thread of gossamer. • *adjective* light and flimsy: *a gossamer curtain of rain*. [Say GOSSA mur]

gossip • *noun* **1 a** easy talk or writing esp. about persons or social incidents. **b** idle talk; groundless rumour. **c** denoting a tabloid or section of a newspaper etc. devoted to news or rumours about celebrities: *gossip columnist*. **2** a person who indulges in gossip. • *verb* (**gossips**, **gossiped**, **gossiping**) talk or write gossip. ▶ **gossiper** *noun* **gossipy** *adjective*

got *past and past participle of* GET.

gotch *noun* (also **gotchies** *plural noun*) *Cdn slang* underpants.

gotcha *interjection* informal expressing satisfaction at having exploited another's gullibility or weakness, uncovered another's faults, etc.

Goth *noun* **1** a member of a Germanic tribe that invaded the Roman Empire in the 3rd–5th centuries. **2** an uncivilized or ignorant person. **3** (**goth**) **a** a style of rock music derived from punk, often with apocalyptic or mystical lyrics. **b** a member of a subculture favouring black clothing, white and black makeup, metal jewellery, and goth music.

Gothic • *adjective* **1** of the Goths or their language. **2** in the style of architecture prevalent in western Europe in the 12th–16th centuries, characterized by pointed arches, flying buttresses, and ribbed vaults. **3** (of a novel etc.) in a style popular in the 18th–19th centuries, with supernatural or horrifying events. • *noun* **1** the Gothic language. **2** Gothic architecture. ▶ **Gothicism** *noun*

go-to guy *noun* (also **go-to person** etc.) *slang* (esp. in sports) the person on a team most often relied on to accomplish a task.

gotten *past participle of* GET.

gouache *noun* **1** a method of painting in opaque pigments ground in water and thickened with a glue-like substance. **2** these pigments. **3** a picture painted in this way. [Say goo AWSH or GWASH]

Gouda *noun* a flat round usu. Dutch cheese with a yellow rind. [Say GOO duh]

gouge • *noun* **1** a chisel with a concave blade, used in carpentry, sculpture, and surgery. **2** a groove or mark made by gouging. **3** an act of gouging. • *verb* (**gouges**, **gouged**, **gouging**) **1** cut with or as with a gouge. **2** force out esp. an eye with the thumb with or as with a gouge. **3** *informal* take an unjustly large sum of money from (someone); swindle. ▶ **gouger** *noun*

goulash *noun* (*plural* **goulashes**) a Hungarian soup or stew of meat and vegetables, usu. highly seasoned with paprika. [Say GOO lash]

gourd *noun* **1** **a** any of various fleshy usu. large fruits with a hard skin, often used as containers, ornaments, etc. **b** any of various climbing or trailing plants bearing this fruit. **2** the hollow hard skin of the gourd fruit, dried and used as a drinking vessel, water container, etc. **PHRASES** **out of one's gourd** *slang* crazy. [Rhymes with *TOURED*]

gourmand *noun* **1** a glutton: *gourmands will be pleased to know that ulcers are not caused by overeating.* **2** a gourmet: *this bakery is a must stop for pastry gourmands.* [Say goor MOND (goor rhymes with *TOUR*)]

gourmet • *noun* a connoisseur of good food, having a discerning palate. • *adjective* **1** (of food) of very high quality, suitable to refined tastes. **2** of or suitable for a gourmet. [Say GOOR may or GORE may]

gout *noun* **1** a disease with inflammation of the smaller joints, esp. the toe, as a result of excess uric acid salts in the blood. **2 a** a drop, esp. of blood. **b** a splash or spot. ▶ **gouty** *adjective*

Gov. *abbreviation* **1** Governor. **2** Government.

govern *verb* **1 a** rule or control (a state, subject, etc.) with authority; conduct the policy and affairs of (an organization etc.). **b** be in government. **2 a** control or influence (a person, a function, the course of events, etc.). **b** be the predominating influence. **3** be a standard or principle for; constitute a law for; serve to decide (a case). **4** check or control (esp. passions). **5** be in military command of (a fort, town). ▶ **governability** *noun* **governable** *adjective*

governance *noun* the action or manner of governing: *a more responsible system of governance will be required.*

governess *noun* (*plural* **governesses**) a woman employed to teach children in a private household.

government *noun* **1 a** the governing body of a state: *government controls.* **b** a particular administration in office: *the government's economic record will undoubtedly cost the Tories the election.* **2** the system by which a state or community is governed: *recent cutbacks in government are making subsidies less available.* **3** the action or manner of controlling or regulating a state, organization, or people: *rules for the government of the hospital.* ▶ **governmental** *adjective* **governmentally** *adverb*

Government House *noun* the official residence of the representative of the Crown, e.g. a Lieutenant-Governor.

Government Leader *noun* (in Canada) the leader of any of the Territorial governments.

governor *noun* **1** a person who governs; a ruler. **2 a** (also **governor-in-chief**) an official governing a province, town, etc. **b** a representative of the Crown in a colony. **3** the executive head of each state or territory of the US. **4** an officer commanding a fortress or garrison. **5** the head or a member of a governing body of an institution. **6** *Cdn hist.* **a** the officer in charge of a fort or factory of the Hudson's Bay Company. **b** (also **governor-in-chief**) the Hudson's Bay Company's chief officer in Canada.

Governor General *noun* (*plural* **Governors General**) the representative of the Crown in a Commonwealth country that regards the Queen as head of state.

Governor General's Award *noun* (also **Governor General's Literary Award**) *Cdn* an award presented annually by the Governor General in each of several categories of Canadian literature.

Gov. Gen. *abbreviation* Governor General.

Govt. *abbreviation* (also **govt.**, **gov't.**) government.

gown • *noun* **1** a loose flowing garment, esp. a long dress worn by a woman. **2** the official robe of a judge, cleric, member of a university, etc. **3** a protective garment worn in a hospital etc. by a staff member during surgery or by a patient. • *verb* (usu. as **gowned** *adjective*) attire in a gown.

goy *noun* (*plural* **goyim** or **goys**) *slang* a non-Jew. ▶ **goyish** *adjective* (also **goyishe**) [For *goyim* say GOY im; for *goyishe* say GOY ish uh]

GP *abbreviation* **1** general practitioner. **2** Grand Prix.

GPA *abbreviation* GRADE POINT AVERAGE.

GPS *abbreviation* GLOBAL POSITIONING SYSTEM.

gr *abbreviation* (also **gr.**) **1** gram(s). **2** grains. **3** gross.

grab • *verb* (**grabs**, **grabbed**, **grabbing**) **1 a** seize suddenly, roughly, or firmly. **b** capture, arrest. **2** take greedily or unfairly. **3** *slang* attract the attention of, impress. **4** (foll. by *at*) make a sudden snatch at. **5** purchase, obtain, or consume (esp. food) hastily: *grabbed a pizza.* **6** (of the brakes of a motor vehicle) act harshly or jerkily. • *noun* **1** a sudden clutch or attempt to seize. **2** a mechanical device for clutching. **3** the practice of grabbing; rapacious proceedings esp. in politics and commerce: *tax grab.* **PHRASES** **up for grabs** *slang* easily obtainable.

grab bag *noun* **1** a bag concealing various prizes, treats, etc., from which one draws blindly. **2** an assortment of small items in a sealed bag which one buys or is given without knowing what the contents are. **3** a miscellaneous assortment.

grabber *noun* a person or thing that grabs (an object, a person's attention, etc.).

grabby *adjective* informal **1** tending to grab; greedy, grasping. **2** attracting attention; arousing people's interest: *a grabby title.*

grab rail *noun* (also **grab handle** etc.) a handle or rail

etc. by grabbing which one may maintain one's balance, steady oneself, etc.
grace • *noun* **1** attractiveness, esp. in elegance of proportion or manner or movement; gracefulness. **2** courteous good will: *had the grace to apologize.* **3** an attractive feature; an accomplishment: *social graces.* **4** (in Christian belief) the favour of God; a divine saving and strengthening influence. **5** goodwill, favour: *fall from grace.* **6** delay granted as a favour: *a five-day grace period.* **7** a short thanksgiving before or after a meal. **8** (**Grace**) (in Greek mythology) each of three beautiful sister goddesses, who bestowed beauty and charm. **9** (**Grace**) (preceded by *His, Her, Your*) forms of description or address for a duke, duchess, or archbishop. • *verb* (**graces, graced, gracing**) (often foll. by *with*) confer honour or dignity on: *graced us with his presence.* PHRASES **days of grace** the time allowed by law for payment of a sum due. **in a person's good** (or **bad**) **graces** regarded by a person with favour (or disfavour). **with good** (or **bad**) **grace** as if willingly (or reluctantly).
graceful *adjective* having or showing grace or elegance. ▶ **gracefully** *adverb* **gracefulness** *noun*
graceless *adjective* lacking grace or elegance or charm. ▶ **gracelessly** *adverb* **gracelessness** *noun*
gracious • *adjective* **1** kindly, courteous. **2** (of God) merciful, benign. **3** characterized by elegance and usu. wealth: *gracious living.* • *interjection* expressing surprise. ▶ **graciously** *adverb* **graciousness** *noun*
grackle *noun* a songbird of the North American blackbird family, the male of which has shiny black plumage with a blue-green sheen. *Also called* BLACKBIRD.
grad *noun* *informal* **1** a university or high school graduate. **2** *Cdn* a graduation ceremony. **3** *Cdn* a dinner followed by a dance to celebrate graduation; a prom.
gradation *noun* (usu. in *plural*) **1** a scale or series of successive changes, stages, or degrees: *the Act fails to provide a clear gradation of offences.* **2** a stage or change in such a scale or series: *minute gradations of distance.* **3** a minute change from one shade, tone, or colour to another: *subtle gradations of green and blue.* [Say gray DAY sh'n or gruh DAY sh'n]
grade • *noun* **1 a** a certain degree in rank, merit, proficiency, quality, etc. **b** a class of persons or things of the same grade. **2** a step or stage in a process. **3** a mark indicating the quality of a student's work. **4 a** a class in school, concerned with a particular year's work and usu. numbered from one upwards. **b** (in *combination*) *Cdn* a pupil of a specified grade in a school: *the grade threes are visiting the museum on Thursday.* **5 a** a gradient or slope. **b** the rate of ascent or descent. **c** the level at which the ground meets the foundation of a building. • *verb* (**grades, graded, grading**) **1** arrange in or allocate to grades; sort. **2** (foll. by *up, down, off, into,* etc.) pass gradually between grades, or into a grade. **3** give a grade to (a student or academic work). **4** reduce (a road etc.) to easy gradients or to a level. PHRASES **at grade** on the same level. **make the grade** *informal* reach the desired standard.
grade point *noun* (esp. in post-secondary education) a numerical value assigned to a grade received in a course, multiplied by the number of credits awarded for the course.
grade point average *noun* (esp. in post-secondary education) an indication of a student's academic achievement, being the total number of grade points received divided by the number of credits awarded.
grader *noun* **1** a person or thing that grades. **2** (in *combination*) a pupil of a specified grade in a school. **3** (in full **road grader**) a vehicle with a heavy blade, used in road construction for levelling the ground.

grade school *noun* elementary school.
gradient *noun* **1 a** a stretch of road, railway, etc., that slopes from the horizontal. **b** the amount of such a slope. **2** the rate of rise or fall of temperature, pressure, etc., in passing from one region to another. [Say GRAY dee int]
gradual • *adjective* **1** taking place or progressing slowly or by degrees. **2** not rapid or steep or abrupt. • *noun Christianity* a Biblical text, usu. a Psalm, sung or recited between the Epistle and Gospel in the Mass.
gradualism *noun* **1** a policy of gradual reform rather than sudden change or revolution: *our organization has a long history of gradualism rather than abrupt or drastic action.* **2** the theory of gradual evolutionary change. ▶ **gradualist** *noun*
gradually *adverb* slowly over a long period of time.
graduate • *noun* **1 a** a person who has been awarded an academic degree. **b** designating or involved in education undertaken beyond the first or bachelor's degree: *graduate student.* **2** a person who has completed a course of study. • *verb* (**graduates, graduated, graduating**) **1 a** receive an academic degree or a high school diploma. **b** (foll. by *from*) complete a course of study at a specified place or level. **2** confer a degree, diploma, etc. upon. **3 a** (foll. by *to*) move up to (a higher grade of activity etc.). **b** (foll. by *as, in*) gain specified qualifications.
graduated *adjective* **1** arranged in grades or gradations; advancing or proceeding by degrees. **2** marked with lines to indicate degrees, grades, or quantities. **3** (of tax) apportioned according to a scale.
graduated licensing *noun* a gradual process of awarding driving privileges to new drivers, in which novices are allowed to drive only under certain conditions for a specified period and must pass a road test before advancing to the next level.
graduate school *noun* **1** a department of a university for advanced work by graduates. **2** study undertaken at a university by graduates.
graduation *noun* **1** the receiving or conferring of an academic degree or diploma. **2** a ceremony at which degrees are conferred. **3** each or all of the marks on a vessel or instrument indicating degrees of quantity etc.
Graeco-Roman *adjective* = GRECO-ROMAN.
graffiti *plural noun* (often treated as *singular*) (*singular* **graffito**) inscriptions or drawings scribbled, scratched, or sprayed on a surface. [Say gruh FEETY for the plural, gruh FEET oh for the singular]
graffitied *adjective* **1** (of a surface) covered with graffiti: *graffitied walls.* **2** written as graffiti: *graffitied initials.*
graft¹ • *noun* **1** *Botany* **a** a shoot inserted into a slit of stock, from which it receives sap. **b** the place where a graft is inserted. **c** the process or result of inserting a shoot of a plant. **2 a** a piece of living tissue, organ, etc., transplanted surgically. **b** the process or result of doing this. • *verb* **1** cut a piece from a living plant and attach it to another plant. **2** insert a graft. **3** transplant (living tissue): *they can graft a new hand on to the nerve ends.* **4** insert or fix (a thing) permanently to another: *western-style government could not easily be grafted on to a profoundly different country.*
graft² *informal* • *noun* **1** practices, esp. bribery, used to secure illicit gains in politics or business. **2** such gains. • *verb* seek or make such gains.
grafter *noun* a person who makes gains by shady or dishonest means, esp. a politician who abuses his or her position to make such gains.
graham *adjective* designating coarse-grained whole wheat flour, or crackers etc. made from this. [Say GRAY um or GRAM]

G

Grail *noun* (also **grail**) **1** (in medieval legend) the cup or platter used by Christ at the Last Supper, and in which Joseph of Arimathea received Christ's blood at the Cross. **2** any object of a quest: *profit has become the grail for this company*.

grain • *noun* **1 a** wheat or any other cereal plant used as food. **b** their fruit. **c** any particular species of cereal plant. **2** a fruit or seed of a cereal. **3 a** a small hard particle of salt, sand, etc. **b** a discrete particle or crystal, usu. small, in a rock or metal. **4** the smallest unit of weight in the troy and avoirdupois systems (approx. 0.0648 grams), equivalent to $^1/_{5760}$ of a pound troy and $^1/_{7000}$ of a pound avoirdupois. **5** the smallest possible quantity: *not a grain of truth in it.* **6 a** roughness of surface. **b** *Photography* each of the tiny light-sensitive particles in a photograph or negative. **7** the texture of skin, wood, stone, etc.; the arrangement and size of constituent particles. **8 a** a pattern of lines of fibre in meat, wood, fabric, or paper. **b** lamination or planes of cleavage in stone, coal, etc. • *verb* paint in imitation of the grain of wood or marble. PHRASES **against the grain** contrary to one's natural inclination or feeling. ▶ **grained** *adjective*

grain elevator *noun* = ELEVATOR 2.

graininess *noun* the quality of being grainy or granular: *there was a slight graininess to the pictures.*

grainy *adjective* (**grainier, grainiest**) **1** granular: *a juicy, grainy texture.* **2** *Photography* showing visible grains of emulsion, as characteristic of old photographs or modern high-speed film. **3** (of sound, esp. recorded music) having a rough or gravelly quality: *the grainy sound of pirated cassettes.*

gram *noun* a metric unit of mass equal to one-thousandth of a kilogram.

-gram *combining form* forming nouns denoting a thing written or recorded or expressed (often in a certain way): *epigram ◊ monogram ◊ telegram ◊ kiss-o-gram.*

grama *noun* (*plural* **gramas**) (also **grama grass**) any of various chiefly North American pasture and ornamental grasses. [Say GRAM uh]

gramma *noun* (*plural* **grammas**) *informal* = GRANDMA.

grammar *noun* **1** the rules in a language for changing the form of words, depending on their position and role in relation to other words, and joining them into sentences: *the basic rules of grammar ◊ English grammar.* **2** a person's manner of using grammatical forms; speech or writing judged as good or bad according to its conformity to rules of grammar: *his grammar is appalling.* **3** a book on grammar.

grammarian *noun* an expert in grammar. [Say gruh MARY un]

grammatical *adjective* **1** of or relating to grammar. **2** conforming to the rules of grammar. ▶ **grammaticality** *noun* **grammatically** *adverb* [Say gruh MATTA cull, gruh matta CAL a tee]

Grammy *noun* (*plural* **Grammys**) *proprietary* (in the US) any of several annual awards given by the American National Academy of Recording Arts and Sciences for outstanding achievements in the record industry.

gramophone *noun* an instrument reproducing recorded sound by a stylus resting on a rotating grooved disc. [Say GRAMMA phone]

grampa *noun* (also **gramps**) *informal* = GRANDPA.

gran *noun* *informal* grandmother.

granary *noun* (*plural* **granaries**) a building where grain is stored. [Say GRAIN a ree or GRAN a ree]

grand • *adjective* **1 a** splendid, magnificent. **b** solemn or lofty in conception, execution, or expression. **c** showy, ostentatious. **2** chief; of chief importance: *grand staircase.* **3** (also **Grand**) of the highest rank; surpassing all others: *grand champion.* **4** *informal*

excellent, enjoyable: *had a grand time ◊ in grand condition.* **5** belonging to high society: *a grand affair.* **6** in names of family relationships, denoting the second degree of ascent or descent: *grand-aunt.* **7** great: *Grand Hotel.* **8** comprehensive, final: *grand total.* **9** *Law* serious, important: *grand larceny* (compare PETTY 4). • *noun* **1** = GRAND PIANO. **2** (*plural* **grand**) (usu. in *plural*) *slang* a thousand dollars or pounds.

grand chief *noun* the chief of a grand council or national or regional Aboriginal organization.

grandchild *noun* (*plural* **grandchildren**) a child of one's son or daughter.

grand council *noun* a group of chiefs representing several different First Nations, organized as a council.

granddad *noun* (also **grandad**) *informal* **1** grandfather. **2** an elderly man.

granddaddy *noun* (*plural* **granddaddies**) *informal* **1** = GRANDDAD. **2** the greatest or most notable example or instance of something: *the granddaddy of all winter storms.*

granddaughter *noun* a female grandchild.

grande dame *noun* (*plural* **grandes dames**) **1** a dignified woman of high rank or eminence: *the grande dame of the British stage flew in from London.* **2** a venerable institution, esp. an old and impressive hotel, theatre, etc.: *the grande dame of Montreal hotels, the Ritz has been dispensing Old World hospitality since 1912.* [Say grand DOM]

grandee *noun* a person of high rank or eminence: *craning his neck to catch a glimpse of the TV and media grandees on their way into the hotel.* [Say gran DEE]

grandeur *noun* **1** splendor and impressiveness, esp. of appearance or style: *the austere grandeur of mountain scenery.* **2** high rank or social importance: *Emile has unfulfilled dreams of grandeur ◊ she has a sense of grandeur about her.* [Say GRAND ur or GRAND yur]

grandfather • *noun* a male grandparent. • *verb* exempt a pre-existing class of people or things from the requirements of a new regulation: *the existing coal-burning power plants were grandfathered, and need not comply with the emissions laws.*

grandfather clock *noun* a clock in a tall wooden case, driven by weights and a pendulum.

grandfatherly *adjective* of or resembling a grandfather: *a warm, grandfatherly man.*

grand finale *noun* **1** the usu. elaborate final scene of a theatrical performance, often involving the whole cast. **2** an elaborate or impressive conclusion to anything: *the grand finale was a chocolate torte.*

grandiloquence *noun* the use of pompous or boastful language. [Say gran DILLA quince]

grandiloquent *adjective* pompous or extravagant in language, style, or manner, esp. in a way that is intended to impress: *a grandiloquent celebration of American patriotism.* ▶ **grandiloquently** *adverb* [Say gran DILLA quint]

grandiose *adjective* **1** producing or meant to produce an imposing effect. **2** planned on an ambitious or magnificent scale. **3** (of speech, writing, etc.) pompous or arrogant. ▶ **grandiosity** *noun* [Say grandy OSE or GRANDY ose (with OSE as in *GROSS*), grandy OSSA tee]

grandkid *noun* *informal* = GRANDCHILD.

grandly *adverb* in a grand manner.

grandma *noun* *informal* grandmother.

grandmaster *noun* **1** a chess player of the highest class. **2** (**Grand Master**) the head of a military order of knighthood, of Freemasons, etc.

grandmother *noun* a female grandparent. PHRASES **teach one's grandmother to suck eggs** presume to advise a more experienced person. ▶ **grandmotherly** *adjective*

grandness *noun* the condition or quality of being grand: *the grandness of the house impressed him*.

grandpa *noun* (*plural* **grandpas**) *informal* grandfather.

grandparent *noun* a parent of one's father or mother.

grand piano *noun* (*plural* **grand pianos**) a large full-toned piano standing on three legs, with the body, strings, and soundboard arranged horizontally and in line with the keys.

Grand Prix *noun* (*plural* **Grands Prix**) any of several important international sporting events, esp. in auto racing. [Say gron PREE for the singular and plural]

grand prize *noun* the most valuable prize in a raffle etc. for which many prizes are given.

grand slam *noun* **1** *Bridge* the winning of 13 tricks. **2** the winning of all of the most important championships or matches in a sport, esp. tennis. **3** *Baseball* a home run hit when all three bases are occupied by a runner, thus scoring four runs.

grandson *noun* a male grandchild.

grandstand • *noun* the main stand, usu. roofed, for spectators at a racetrack etc. • *verb* seek to impress others, esp. by acting showily or pretentiously: *this issue deserves a debate based on substance, not political game playing and grandstanding*. ▶ **grandstander** *noun*

granite *noun* **1** a granular crystalline igneous rock of quartz, mica, feldspar, etc., used for building. **2** curling rocks. ▶ **granitic** *adjective* [Say GRAN it, gruh NIT ick]

granny *noun* (also **grannie**) (*plural* **grannies**) *informal* grandmother.

granny flat *noun* part of a house made into self-contained accommodation, as for an elderly relative.

granny glasses *plural noun* round wire-rimmed eyeglasses.

Granny Smith *noun* an originally Australian variety of bright green apple.

granola • *noun* a mixture of rolled oats, nuts, raisins, brown sugar, etc. eaten as a breakfast cereal or pressed into bars. • *adjective* *jocular* designating persons with liberal politics, esp. concerned with environmental protection, and typified as leading an unconventional or hippie life including the eating of health foods.

grant • *verb* **1 a** consent to fulfill (a request, wish, etc.): *granted all they asked*. **b** allow (a person) to have (a thing): *granted me my freedom*. **2** give (rights, property, etc.) formally; transfer legally. **3** admit as true; concede, esp. as a basis for argument: *I grant that her heart is in the right place, but she should take a closer look at the facts*. • *noun* **1** the process of granting or a thing granted. **2 a** a sum of money given by the state for any of various purposes, e.g. to finance education. **b** a tract of land given by the state to private interests. **3** *Law* the documented transfer of the ownership of property from one person to another. PHRASES **take for granted 1** assume something to be true or valid. **2** cease to appreciate through familiarity.

grantee *noun* esp. *Law* a person to whom a grant or conveyance is made. [Say gran TEE]

grantor *noun* esp. *Law* a person or institution that makes a grant or conveyance. [Say gran TORE]

granular *adjective* **1** of or like grains or granules. **2** having a granulated surface or structure; grainy: *the surface of the rock was granular*.

granulate *verb* (**granulates**, **granulated**, **granulating**) form into grains: *granulated sugar*.

granulation *noun* the action or process of forming into granules or grains.

granule *noun* a small grain. [Say GRAN yule]

grape *noun* **1** a berry (usu. purple, black, or green) growing in clusters on a vine, eaten fresh or dried and used in making wine. **2** (**the grape**) *informal* wine.

grapefruit *noun* (*plural* **grapefruit**) **1** a large round yellow citrus fruit with an acid juicy yellow or pink pulp. **2** the tree bearing this fruit.

grape hyacinth *noun* a small plant of the lily family, bearing clusters of usu. blue flowers.

grapevine *noun* **1** any of various vines of North America and Eurasia, esp. one bearing grapes used as food or for winemaking. **2** *informal* the means of transmission of unofficial information or rumour: *heard it through the grapevine*.

graph • *noun* **1** a diagram showing the relation between variable quantities, usu. of two variables, each measured along one of a pair of axes at right angles. **2** *Math* a collection of points whose coordinates satisfy a given relation. • *verb* plot on a graph.

graphic • *adjective* **1** of or relating to the visual or descriptive arts, esp. writing and drawing. **2** vividly descriptive; conveying all (esp. unwelcome or unpleasant) details. • *noun* a visual image (*compare* GRAPHICS).

graphical *adjective* **1** of or in the form of graphs. **2** graphic.

graphically *adverb* **1** in the form of drawings or diagrams: *this data is shown graphically on the opposite page*. **2** very clearly and in great detail: *the murders are graphically described in this article*.

graphical user interface *noun* (also **graphical interface**) software which provides a computer user with icons or other simple graphic representations of a program's available commands or options, which can be manipulated directly, e.g. with a mouse.

graphic artist *noun* a person trained in or working in the graphic arts.

graphic arts *plural noun* the visual and technical arts involving design, writing, drawing, printing, etc.

graphics *plural noun* (usu. treated as *singular*) **1** the products of the graphic arts, esp. commercial design or illustration. **2** the use of diagrams in calculation and design. **3** (also **computer graphics**) *Computing* **a** the use of computers linked to monitors to generate and manipulate visual images. **b** visual images produced by computer processing.

graphics card *noun* (also **graphics board**) a circuit board which when connected to a computer increases the computer's ability to produce, display, or manipulate graphics.

graphite *noun* a crystalline form of carbon used as a solid lubricant, in pencils, and as a moderator in nuclear reactors etc. [Say GRAF ite]

graph paper *noun* paper with intersecting lines forming small squares of equal size, used for graphs.

grapnel *noun* **1** a device with iron claws, attached to a rope and used for dragging or grasping. **2** a small anchor with several flukes.

grappa *noun* a brandy distilled from the fermented residue of grapes after pressing in winemaking.

grapple • *verb* (**grapples**, **grappled**, **grappling**) **1** fight at close quarters or in close combat. **2** (foll. by *with*) try to manage or overcome a difficult problem etc. **3 a** grip with the hands; come to close quarters with. **b** seize with or as with a grapnel; grasp. • *noun* **1 a** a hold or grip in or as in wrestling. **b** a contest at close quarters. **2** a grapnel. ▶ **grappler** *noun*

grapple yarder *noun* (also **grapple skidder**) a powerful tractor-like vehicle with a large set of claws, used to haul logs to an assembly area.

grappling hook *noun* (also **grappling iron**) = GRAPNEL 1.

grasp • *verb* **1 a** clutch at; seize greedily. **b** hold firmly; grip. **2** (foll. by *at*) try to capture; accept avidly. **3** understand or realize (a fact or meaning). • *noun* **1** a firm hold; a grip. **2** (foll. by *of*) **a** mastery or control: *a*

G

grasp of the situation. **b** a mental hold or understanding: *a grasp of the facts*. PHRASES **within one's grasp** capable of being grasped, achieved, or comprehended by one. ▶ **graspable** *adjective*

grasping *adjective* always trying to get money, possessions, power, etc. for oneself; greedy.

grass • *noun* (*plural* **grasses**) **1 a** vegetation belonging to a group of small plants with green blades that are eaten by cattle, horses, sheep, etc. **b** any species of this. **c** any plant of this family, which includes cereals, reeds, and bamboos. **2** pasture land. **3** lawn. **4** *slang* marijuana. • *verb* (**grasses**, **grassed**, **grassing**) cover with turf. PHRASES **not let the grass grow under one's feet** be quick to act or to seize an opportunity. **out to grass 1** out to graze. **2** in retirement.

grass dance *noun* a competitive North American Aboriginal men's dance, originating on the Plains, noted for its fluid movements and sliding steps.

grasshopper *noun* **1** a plant-eating insect with legs adapted for jumping and a flat-sided head with large compound eyes and antennae. **2** a cocktail usu. consisting of cream, chocolate liqueur, and mint liqueur in equal portions.

grassland *noun* a large open area covered with grass, e.g. a prairie.

grassroots *plural noun* **1** a fundamental level or source: *improving the game at the grassroots level*. **2** ordinary people, esp. as voters; the rank and file of an organization, esp. a political party: *a grassroots movement of popular participation revitalized the program*.

grassy *adjective* (**grassier**, **grassiest**) **1** covered with or abounding in grass. **2** resembling grass.

grate¹ *verb* (**grates**, **grated**, **grating**) **1** reduce to small shreds by rubbing on a serrated surface. **2** (often foll. by *against*, *on*) rub with a harsh scraping sound. **3** (often foll. by *on*) **a** sound harshly or discordantly. **b** have an irritating effect. **4** (of a hinge etc.) creak.

grate² *noun* **1** = GRATING. **2** a frame of metal bars for holding the fuel in the recess of a fireplace etc. **3** the recess of a fireplace or furnace.

grateful *adjective* thankful; feeling or showing gratitude. ▶ **gratefully** *adverb*

grater *noun* a device for reducing cheese or other food to small shreds.

gratification *noun* the state of feeling pleasure when something goes well or when one's desires are satisfied: *instant gratification*. [Say grat if a KAY sh'n]

gratify *verb* (**gratifies**, **gratified**, **gratifying**) **1** please, satisfy: *we were gratified by the response from our readers ◊ as they will not be content with mere words, it is with deeds that you must gratify them*. **2** indulge in or yield to (a feeling or desire): *resisted calling for the death penalty merely to gratify their desire for vengeance*. ▶ **gratifying** *adjective* **gratifyingly** *adverb*

gratin *noun* **1** a crisp brown crust usu. of bread crumbs or melted cheese. **2** a dish cooked with this. [Say gra TAN]

gratiné (also **gratinée**) • *adjective* cooked with a crisp brown crust usu. of bread crumbs or melted cheese. • *noun* = GRATIN. [Say gra tee NAY]

grating • *adjective* **1** sounding harsh: *a grating laugh*. **2** having an irritating effect. • *noun* a framework of parallel or crossed metal bars.

gratingly *adverb* **1** in an irritating manner. **2** with a harsh sound.

gratis *adverb & adjective* free; without charge. [Say GRAT iss]

gratitude *noun* the feeling of being grateful or the desire to express one's thanks.

gratuitous *adjective* uncalled for: *gratuitous depictions*

of violence. ▶ **gratuitously** *adverb* **gratuitousness** *noun* [Say gruh TOO it us or gruh TYOO it us]

gratuity *noun* (*plural* **gratuities**) money given in recognition of services; a tip. [Say gruh TOO it ee or gruh TYOO it ee]

grave¹ *noun* **1** a hole or trench dug in the ground where a dead body is buried. **2** (**the grave**) death, esp. as indicating mortal finality. **3** something compared to or regarded as a grave. PHRASES **turn** (or **roll**) **over in one's grave** (of a dead person) react with imagined disgust or repugnance at the actions of those still living.

grave² • *adjective* **1 a** serious: *a grave matter*. **b** dignified, solemn: *a grave look*. **2** extremely serious or threatening: *grave danger*. • *noun* a mark (`) placed over a vowel in some languages to denote pronunciation, length, etc. [Say GROV for the noun]

gravedigger *noun* a person who digs graves.

gravel • *noun* a mixture of coarse sand and small water-worn or pounded stones, used for paths and roads and as an aggregate. • *verb* (**gravels**, **gravelled**, **gravelling**) lay or strew with gravel.

gravelly *adjective* **1** of or like gravel. **2** having or containing gravel. **3** (of a voice) deep and rough-sounding.

gravely *adverb* seriously: *nodded gravely ◊ gravely ill*.

graven *adjective* engraved, carved: *graven image*. [Say GRAVE un]

graveside *noun* the ground at the edge of a grave.

gravesite *noun* the location of a grave.

gravestone *noun* = TOMBSTONE.

graveyard *noun* **1** a cemetery, esp. one located near a church. **2** *informal* = GRAVEYARD SHIFT. **3** a place in which obsolete or derelict objects are stored: *an appliance graveyard*.

graveyard shift *noun* **1** a work shift beginning around midnight and lasting until morning. **2** the workers on duty during this period.

gravitas *noun* seriousness: *he was considered not to have sufficient authority or the necessary gravitas to play Shakespeare's tragic hero*. [Say GRAVVY tass or GRAVVY toss]

gravitate *verb* (**gravitates**, **gravitated**, **gravitating**) **1** (foll. by *to*, *toward*) move or be attracted to some source of influence: *young people gravitating to the cities in search of work*. **2** move or tend by force of gravity toward. [Say GRAVVA tate]

gravitation *noun* **1** a force of attraction between any particle of matter in the universe and any other. **2** the effect of this, esp. the falling of bodies to the earth. **3** a natural tendency or movement toward a person etc. ▶ **gravitational** *adjective* [Say gravva TAY sh'n]

gravitational field *noun* the region of space surrounding a body in which another body experiences a force of attraction.

gravity *noun* **1 a** the force that attracts a body toward the centre of the earth or toward any other physical body having mass. **b** the degree of intensity of this measured by acceleration. **2** importance, seriousness; the quality of being grave: *the gravity of the crime*.

gravity-fed *adjective* supplied with material by its fall under gravity: *a gravity-fed shower*.

gravity feed *noun* the supply of material by its fall under gravity.

gravlax *noun* a Scandinavian dish of dry-cured salmon marinated in salt, sugar, dill, etc.

Gravol *noun* *Cdn proprietary* a medication used to counter nausea and vomiting and prevent motion sickness.

gravy *noun* (*plural* **gravies**) **1** the juices and fat from cooked meat, usu. thickened and used as a sauce. **2** *slang* **a** money easily acquired. **b** an unexpected bonus.

G

gravy train *noun slang* a source of easy financial benefit.

gray *adjective, noun, & verb* = GREY.

grayling *noun* a silver-grey freshwater fish with a long high dorsal fin.

graze[1] *verb* (**grazes**, **grazed**, **grazing**) **1** (of cattle, sheep, etc.) eat growing grass. **2** feed (cattle etc.) on growing grass. **3** *informal* **a** eat snacks or small meals throughout the day. **b** casually sample something, esp. food on a store shelf. **c** flick rapidly between television channels.

graze[2] • *verb* (**grazes**, **grazed**, **grazing**) **1** rub or scrape (a part of the body, esp. the skin) so as to break the surface without causing bleeding. **2** touch lightly in passing. • *noun* a superficial wound; a scrape.

grazer *noun* an animal that eats growing grass.

grazing *noun* **1** *in senses of* GRAZE[1],[2]. **2** grassland suitable for pasture.

grease • *noun* **1** oily or fatty matter esp. in a semi-solid state and as a lubricant in engines etc. **2** the melted fat of a dead animal. **3** oily matter in wool that has not been processed. • *verb* (**greases**, **greased**, **greasing**) **1** smear or lubricate with grease. **2** smear (a cookie sheet, baking pan, etc.) with fat before using. PHRASES **grease the palm** *of informal* bribe. **like greased lightning** *informal* very fast.

greasepaint *noun* a waxy composition used as makeup for theatrical performers.

greaser *noun slang* a tough youth, esp. male, with the greased hair characteristic of members of motorcycle gangs of the 1950s.

grease trail *noun Cdn* any of the forest paths used for centuries as trade routes connecting the Pacific coast with the interior, named after the eulachon oil which was one of the most important items traded.

greasewood *noun* a resinous dwarf shrub of the goosefoot family, which grows in dry valleys in western North America.

greasiness *noun* **1** the quality or condition of being of or like grease. **2** the quality or condition of being covered with grease or containing too much grease.

greasy *adjective* (**greasier**, **greasiest**) **1 a** of or like grease. **b** smeared or covered with grease: *greasy dishes*. **c** containing or having too much grease: *greasy chicken*. **2 a** slippery. **b** (of a person or manner) friendly in a way that does not seem sincere; smarmy: *a greasy smile* ◊ *he told me how well I'd done in that greasy way of his*.

greasy spoon *noun informal* a cheap diner serving greasy food.

SPELL CHECK
great, grate

To shred, rub, or scrape something is to **grate** it. The metal rack for holding logs in a fireplace is a **grate**.

---

great • *adjective* **1** of an amount, extent, or intensity considerably above average. **2** important, pre-eminent: *the great thing is not to get caught.* **3** grand, imposing: *the great hall.* **4 a** (esp. of a public or historic figure) distinguished; prominent. **b** (**the Great**) as a title denoting the most important of the name: *Alexander the Great.* **5 a** (of a person) remarkable in ability, character, achievement, etc.: *a great thinker.* **b** (of a thing) outstanding of its kind: *the Great Lakes.* **6** competent, skilled. **7** fully deserving the name of; doing a thing habitually or extensively: *a great believer in tolerance.* **8** (also **greater**) the larger of the name, species, etc.: *great horned owl.* **9** (**Greater**) (of a city etc.) including adjacent urban areas: *Greater Toronto.* **10** *informal* very enjoyable or satisfactory; attractive, fine: *had a great time* ◊ *it would be great if we won.* **11** (in names of family

relationships) denoting one degree further removed upwards or downwards: *great-uncle.* • *noun* a great or outstanding person or thing. • *adverb informal* excellently, well, successfully. • *interjection* **1** used to express admiration, approval, appreciation, etc.: *Great! Thanks for coming!* **2** *ironic* used to express dismay, disappointment, etc.: *Great! The tire's flat again!* PHRASES **great and small** all classes or types. (**the**) **great and** (**the**) **good** often *ironic* distinguished and worthy people. **to a great extent** largely.

great blue heron *noun* a predominantly greyish blue heron widespread throughout North America.

great circle *noun* a circle on the surface of a sphere whose plane passes through the sphere's centre. The shortest surface route between any two points on the earth is the one that travels along the great circle which includes them both.

greatcoat *noun* a long heavy overcoat.

Great Dane *noun* a breed of very large, powerful, short-haired dog.

great deal *noun see* DEAL *noun* 1.

Great Divide *noun* (**the Great Divide**) **1** the boundary between life and death. **2** (usu. **great divide**) *jocular* or *literary* the boundary between two contrasting conditions, cultures, etc.

great grey owl *noun* a very large grey hornless owl of northern coniferous forests, having a large facial disc, yellow eyes, and long tail.

great horned owl *noun* a large powerful North American owl with prominent ear tufts.

greatly *adverb* by a considerable amount; much: *greatly admired* ◊ *greatly superior*.

greatness *noun* the quality of being great, esp. distinguished or eminent: *Bach's greatness as a composer*.

great unwashed *noun informal* (**the great unwashed**) the lower classes.

Great War *noun* (**the Great War**) the First World War.

Great White North *noun Cdn jocular* (**the Great White North**) Canada.

great white shark *noun* a large and dangerous greyish shark, found in the temperate and tropical regions of all oceans.

grebe *noun* a diving water bird with a long neck, lobed toes, and almost no tail.

Grecian *adjective* (of architecture or beauty) following Greek models or ideals. [Say GREE sh'n]

Greco-Roman *adjective* **1** of or relating to the Greeks and Romans. **2** *Wrestling* denoting a style attacking only the upper body. [Say grecko ROMAN]

greed *noun* an excessive desire, esp. for wealth or food.

greedily *adverb* **1** hungrily: *devoured the cookies greedily*. **2** covetously: *protects her own solitude greedily*. **3** keenly, eagerly: *she stared at him greedily*.

greediness *noun* **1** excessive longing for wealth or gain. **2** eagerness, keenness. **3** excessive indulgence in food or drink; gluttony.

greedy *adjective* (**greedier**, **greediest**) **1** wanting wealth to excess. **2** having or showing an excessive appetite for food or drink. **3** very keen or eager; needing intensely: *greedy for affection*.

Greek • *noun* **1 a** a native or national of modern Greece; a person of Greek descent. **b** a citizen or citizen of any of the ancient states of Greece; a member of the Greek people. **2** the Indo-European language of Greece. • *adjective* of Greece or its people or language; Hellenic. PHRASES **Greek to me** *informal* incomprehensible to me.

Greek Orthodox Church *noun* (also **Greek Church**) the national Church of Greece.

Greek salad *noun* a salad of lettuce, tomatoes, cucumbers, olives, feta, and olive oil vinaigrette.

green • *adjective* **1** of the colour between blue and yellow in the spectrum; coloured like grass, emeralds, etc. **2 a** covered with leaves or grass. **b** mild and without snow: *a green Christmas*. **3** (of fruit etc. or wood) unripe or unseasoned. **4** not dried, smoked, or tanned. **5** inexperienced, naive. **6 a** (of the complexion) pale, sickly-hued. **b** jealous, envious **7** young, flourishing. **8** not withered or worn out: *a green old age*. **9** vegetable: *green salad*. **10 a** (also **Green**) concerned with or supporting protection of the environment as a political principle. **b** (of a consumer product) not harmful to the environment in its manufacture or use. • *noun* **1** a green colour or pigment. **2** green clothes or material: *dressed in green*. **3 a** a piece of public or common grassy land: *village green*. **b** a grassy area used for a special purpose: *putting green*. **c** *Golf* a putting green. **4** (in *plural*) green vegetables. **5** a green light. **6** a green ball, piece, etc., in a game or sport. **7** (also **Green**) a member or supporter of an environmentalist group or party. **8** *slang* money. **9** green foliage or growing plants. • *verb* make or become green. PHRASES **green up** (of vegetation or a landscape etc.) become green, as in the spring.

greenback *noun* **1 a** a US legal tender note. **b** the US dollar. **2** any of various green-backed animals.

green bean *noun* **1** any bean plant, esp. the French bean, grown for its edible young pods rather than for its seeds. **2** this pod.

greenbelt *noun* an area of open land around a city, the development of which is restricted.

Green Beret *noun* *informal* an American or British commando.

green card *noun* *US* a permit allowing a foreign national to live and work permanently in the US.

greenchain *noun* an endless conveyor taking trimmed lumber from the saws to a sorting area.

greenery *noun* green foliage or growing plants.

green-eyed *adjective* **1** having green eyes. **2** jealous.

green fee *noun* a charge for playing one round of golf.

greengrocer *noun* a retailer of fruit and vegetables.

greenhorn *noun* an inexperienced or foolish person.

greenhouse *noun* a transparent glass or plastic building for rearing or hastening the growth of plants.

greenhouse effect *noun* the heating of the earth's surface and lower atmosphere attributed to an increase in carbon dioxide and other gases, which are more transparent to incoming solar radiation than to reflected radiation from the earth.

greenhouse gas *noun* any of various gases that contribute to the greenhouse effect.

greenie *noun* *informal* a person concerned about environmental issues.

greening *noun* **1** the process or result of making something green, or becoming green. **2** the planting of trees etc. in urban or desert areas. **3** the process of becoming or making aware of or sensitive to ecological issues. **4** a variety of apple that is green when ripe.

greenish *adjective* fairly green in colour: *was wearing a greenish overcoat*.

greenkeeper *noun* = GREENSKEEPER.

Greenlander *noun* a native or inhabitant of Greenland.

green light • *noun* **1** a signal to proceed on a road, railway, etc. **2** *informal* permission to go ahead with a project. • *verb* (**green-light**) give permission or approval for a project to go ahead.

green manure *noun* growing plants plowed into the soil as fertilizer.

greenness *noun* **1** green colour. **2** green vegetation.

3 awareness of ecological issues; commitment to environmental conservation.

green onion *noun* an onion taken from the ground before the bulb has formed, with slender green hollow leaves.

Green Paper *noun* *Cdn & Brit.* a preliminary report of Government proposals, for discussion.

green pepper *noun* the unripe fruit of a sweet pepper, which is mild in flavour and widely used in cooking.

green revolution *noun* **1** an increase in crop production, esp. in developing countries, achieved by using artificial fertilizers, pesticides, and high-yield crop varieties. **2** a rise of environmental concern in industrialized countries.

green room *noun* a room in a theatre, studio, etc. in which performers may relax when they are not on stage, on the air, etc.

greens fee *noun* = GREEN FEE.

greenskeeper *noun* the keeper of a golf course.

greensward *noun* **1** grassy turf. **2** an expanse of this. [Say GREENS ward]

green tea *noun* tea made from steam-dried, not fermented, leaves.

green thumb *noun* *informal* a talent for gardening. ▶ **green-thumbed** *adjective*

greenway *noun* an undeveloped strip of land in an urban area, usu. including a trail and following a natural feature such as a river or ridge.

Greenwich Mean Time *noun* the local time on the 0° meridian, used as an international basis of time reckoning. Abbreviation: **GMT**. [Say GREN itch]

green-winged teal *noun* see TEAL *noun* 1.

greeny *adjective* greenish: *greeny yellow*.

greet *verb* **1** welcome or address politely on meeting or arrival. **2** receive or acknowledge in a specified way: *was greeted with derision*. **3** (of a sight, sound, etc.) become apparent to or noticed by. ▶ **greeter** *noun*

greeting *noun* **1** a polite word or sign of welcome or recognition: *Mandy shouted a greeting*. **2** the action of giving such a sign: *she raised her hand in greeting*. **3** (often in *plural*) an expression of goodwill.

greeting card *noun* a decorative card sent to convey greetings.

gregarious *adjective* **1** fond of company; sociable: *she's very outgoing and gregarious*. **2 a** (of animals or birds) living in groups. **b** (of plants) growing in clusters. ▶ **gregariously** *adverb* **gregariousness** *noun* [Say gruh GARRY us]

Gregorian calendar *noun* the general calendar in use today, introduced in 1582 as a correction of the Julian calendar, with 365 days in standard years and 366 days in all years exactly divisible by four except century years, which must be exactly divisible by 400 to have 366 days. [Say gruh GORY un]

Gregorian chant *noun* very old church music of western Europe, sung in unison without instrumental accompaniment. [Say gruh GORY un]

gremlin *noun* *informal* **1** an imaginary mischievous sprite regarded as responsible for mechanical faults. **2** any similar cause of trouble.

grenade *noun* **1** a small bomb thrown by hand (**hand grenade**) or launched mechanically. **2** a similar missile containing chemicals which disperse on impact, used for extinguishing fires etc.

grenadier *noun* *hist.* **1** a soldier armed with grenades. **2** a soldier selected for height and strength to be part of an elite unit. [Say grenna DEER]

grenadine *noun* a sweet red syrup flavoured with pomegranates. [Say GRENNA dean]

grew *past of* GROW.

G

grey • *adjective* **1** of a colour intermediate between black and white, as of ashes or lead. **2 a** (of the weather etc.) dull, dismal; heavily overcast. **b** bleak, depressing. **3 a** (of hair) turning white with age etc. **b** (of a person) having grey hair. **4** nondescript, unable to be identified. • *noun* **1 a** a grey colour or pigment. **b** grey clothes or material: *dressed in grey.* **2** a grey or white horse. • *verb* **1** make or become grey. **2** *informal* age.

grey area *noun* an ill-defined situation etc., not readily categorized or conforming to an existing set of rules.

greybeard *noun* often *derogatory* an old man.

Grey Cup *noun Cdn* **1** the trophy presented each year to the team winning the Canadian Football League championship. **2** the game deciding this championship.

greyhound *noun* a breed of tall slender dog having keen sight and capable of high speed, used in racing.

greyish *adjective* somewhat grey.

grey jay *noun* a common North American jay, having grey, black, and white plumage, notorious for its boldness in scavenging from backwoods camps and picnic grounds.

grey market *noun* the unofficial but not illegal buying and selling of goods, esp. bypassing standard distribution channels. ▶ **grey marketer** *noun*

grey matter *noun* **1** the darker tissues of the brain and spinal cord consisting of nerve cell bodies and branching dendrites. **2** *informal* intelligence.

Grey Nun *noun* a member of any of five Roman Catholic women's communities, each with a history traceable to the Sisters of Charity of the Hôpital Général, in Montreal.

grey-scale *Computing* • *adjective* designating the production of black and white images by the assigning of one of several shades of grey to each pixel (*compare* DITHERING 2). • *noun* a grey-scale image.

grey squirrel *noun* a common grey or black squirrel of eastern North America.

greystone *noun Cdn* **1** grey stones used in building walls, houses, etc. **2** a house etc. made of greystone.

grey water *noun* mildly contaminated household waste water from sinks, washing machines, etc.

grey whale *noun* a large mottled grey baleen whale of north Pacific waters.

grid *noun* **1 a** a framework of spaced parallel bars. **b** a network of lines, esp. of two series of regularly spaced lines crossing one another at right angles. **c** a set of points arranged so that lines passing through them would form a grid. **2** a system of numbered squares printed on a map and forming the basis of map references. **3 a** a network of water mains, gas lines, etc. **b** = POWER GRID. **4** a pattern of lines marking the starting places on a motor racing track. **5** an arrangement of town or city streets in a rectangular pattern. ▶ **gridded** *adjective*

griddle *noun* a flat pan with little or no rim, used esp. for frying.

gridiron *noun* **1** a cooking utensil of metal bars for broiling or grilling. **2 a** a football field (with parallel lines marking out the area of play). **b** *informal* the game of football: *the gridiron season.* **3** = GRID 5. [Say GRID iron]

gridlock *noun* **1** a traffic jam affecting a whole network of intersecting streets. **2** = DEADLOCK *noun* 1: *Congress shares top billing with the presidency in a gridlock that makes a mockery of Washington.* ▶ **gridlocked** *adjective*

grid road *noun Cdn* **1** a road following the surveyed divisions of a township, municipality, etc. **2** (*Sask.*) a road forming part of a provincial grid system

constructed in the 1950s, with north-south roads one mile apart, and east-west roads two miles apart.

grief *noun* **1** deep or intense sorrow or mourning. **2** the cause of this. **3** *informal* trouble; annoyance. PHRASES **come to grief** meet with disaster; fail. **good grief!** an exclamation of surprise, alarm, etc.

grievance *noun* **1** a real or fancied cause for complaint. **2** an official allegation that something is unjust, inequitable, or illegal: *the union has filed a grievance.*

grieve *verb* (**grieves, grieved, grieving**) **1** suffer grief, esp. at another's death. **2** cause grief or great distress to. **3** file a grievance against (a person or thing): *an employee grieved the awarding of the position to a junior person.* ▶ **griever** *noun*

grievous *adjective* very serious and often causing great pain or suffering: *the victim of grievous injustice.* ▶ **grievously** *adverb* **grievousness** *noun*

griffin *noun* a mythical creature with an eagle's head and wings and a lion's body.

griffon *noun* **1** a small terrier-like dog with coarse or smooth hair. **2** (also **griffon vulture**) a large vulture with predominantly pale brown plumage. [Sounds like GRIFFIN]

grift *noun & verb* esp. *US slang* = GRAFT². ▶ **grifter** *noun*

grill • *noun* **1 a** a cooking apparatus consisting of a series of metal bars over a heat source. **b** this series of metal bars, on which food is directly placed for cooking. **2** a dish of food cooked on a grill. **3** (also **grill room**) a restaurant serving grilled food. • *verb* **1** cook or be cooked on a grill or griddle. **2** subject or be subjected to extreme heat, esp. from the sun. **3** subject to severe questioning or interrogation.

grille *noun* (also **grill**) **1** a grating or latticed screen, used as a partition or to allow discreet vision. **2** a metal grid protecting the radiator of a vehicle. [Say GRILL]

grilling *noun* an intense interrogation or period of questioning: *Gordon faced a grilling over the missing cash.*

grilse *noun* (*plural* **grilse**) a young salmon that has returned to fresh water for the first time.

grim *adjective* (**grimmer, grimmest**) **1** having a stern or forbidding appearance. **2** harsh. **3** joyless: *a grim truth.* **4** unpleasant. **5** ominous. PHRASES **like grim death** with great determination.

grimace • *noun* a distortion of the face made in disgust, pain, etc. or to amuse. • *verb* (**grimaces, grimaced, grimacing**) make a grimace. [Say GRIM iss]

grime *noun* dirt, esp. ingrained in a surface.

grimed *adjective* blackened with grime.

grimly *adverb* **1** in a serious or joyless manner: *they talked grimly about their war experiences.* **2** in a depressing manner: *the movie is grimly realistic.* **3** in an ominous or sinister manner.

Grim Reaper *noun* a personification of death, esp. as a skeletal or faceless hooded figure with a scythe.

grimy *adjective* (**grimier, grimiest**) covered with grime; dirty.

grin • *verb* (**grins, grinned, grinning**) **1** smile broadly, showing the teeth. **2** make a forced, unrestrained, or stupid smile. • *noun* the act or action of grinning. PHRASES **grin and bear it** take pain or misfortune stoically.

grinch *noun* (*plural* **grinches**) a person that seeks to deprive others of joy or happiness.

grind • *verb* (**grinds, ground, grinding**) **1** reduce to small particles or powder by crushing, esp. by passing through a mill. **2 a** reduce, sharpen, or smooth by friction. **b** rub or rub together gratingly: *grind one's teeth.* **3** (often foll. by *down*) oppress: *grinding poverty.* **4 a** work or study hard. **b** (foll. by *out*) produce with effort: *grinding out verses.* **c** (foll. by *on*) (of a sound)

G

continue gratingly or monotonously. **5** *slang* rotate the hips or pelvis in a suggestive manner, esp. in a dance. • *noun* **1** a crushing or grating sound or motion: *the crunch and grind of bulldozers.* **2** *informal* hard dull work: *the daily grind.* **3** the fineness of something that has been ground: *a very coarse grind.* **4** *slang* the action of rotating the hips or pelvis in a dance etc. PHRASES **grind to a halt** stop laboriously.

grinder *noun* **1** a person or thing that grinds (often in *combination*: *coffee grinder*). **2** *slang* an athlete known more for consistently working hard than for remarkable skill. **3** a molar tooth.

grindingly *adverb* in an oppressive, tedious, or seemingly endless manner.

grindstone *noun* a revolving disc used for grinding, sharpening, and polishing. PHRASES **keep one's nose to the grindstone** work hard and continuously.

gringo *noun* (*plural* **gringos**) often *derogatory* a foreigner, esp. a North American or British person, in a Latin American country.

grip • *verb* (**grips, gripped, gripping**) **1** take a firm hold of. **2** (of a feeling or emotion) deeply affect (a person): *was gripped by fear.* **3** compel the attention or interest of. • *noun* **1 a** a firm hold; a tight grasp or clasp. **b** a manner of grasping or holding. **2** the power of holding attention. **3 a** mental or intellectual understanding or mastery. **b** effective control of a situation or one's behaviour etc.: *lose one's grip.* **4 a** a part of a machine that grips or holds something. **b** a part or attachment by which a tool, implement, weapon, etc., is held in the hand. **5 a** a member of a camera crew responsible for moving and setting up equipment. **b** a stagehand. **6** a travelling bag. PHRASES **come to grips with** approach purposefully; begin to deal with. **get a grip** gain or regain composure or control. **in the grip of** dominated or affected by (esp. an adverse circumstance or unpleasant sensation).

gripe • *verb* (**gripes, griped, griping**) *informal* complain, esp. peevishly. • *noun* **1** *informal* **a** a complaint. **b** the act of griping. **2** (usu. in *plural*) gastric or intestinal pain; colic. ▶ **griper** *noun*

gripper *noun* any of various devices used to grip.

gripping *adjective* exciting or interesting in a way that holds one's attention; compelling: *a gripping drama.*

grisly *adjective* (**grislier, grisliest**) causing horror, disgust, or fear: *grisly photographs from the trenches of the First World War.* [Sounds like GRIZZLY]

grist *noun* **1** grain that is to be or has been ground. **2** malt crushed for brewing. **3** (also **grist for the** (or **one's**) **mill**) a subject to be used, discussed, processed, etc., esp. for profit or advantage: *the former MP supplied grist for Ottawa's perpetually churning rumour mill.*

gristle *noun* tough cartilaginous tissue, esp. as occurring in meat. ▶ **gristly** *adjective* [Say GRISSLE]

gristmill *noun* a mill for grinding grain.

grit • *noun* **1** small particles of stone or sand. **2** coarse sandstone. **3** the texture or coarseness of sandpaper, stone, etc. **4** (**Grit**) *Cdn* a supporter or member of the Liberal Party. **5** *hist.* = CLEAR GRIT. **5** *informal* pluck, endurance; strength of character. • *verb* (**grits, gritted, gritting**) clench (the teeth). ▶ **grittily** *adverb* **grittiness** *noun* **gritty** *adjective* (**grittier, grittiest**)

grits *plural noun* **1** (treated as *singular* or *plural*) esp. *US* **a** coarsely ground grain, esp. corn. **b** = HOMINY. **2** oats that have been husked but not ground.

grizzled *adjective* having, or streaked with, grey hair.

grizzly • *adjective* (**grizzlier, grizzliest**) grizzled. • *noun* (*plural* **grizzlies**) (also **grizzly bear**) a large variety of brown bear found in North America and northern Russia.

groan • *verb* **1 a** make a deep sound expressing pain, grief, disapproval, or pleasure. **b** utter with groans. **2** complain inarticulately. **3** (usu. foll. by *under, beneath, with*) be loaded or oppressed. • *noun* the sound made in groaning.

groaner *noun* **1** a person who groans or complains. **2** a bad joke or pun.

groats *plural noun* hulled or crushed grain, esp. oats.

grocer *noun* a person who owns or operates a grocery store.

grocery *noun* (*plural* **groceries**) **1** (in *plural*) food and other general household supplies. **2** (also **grocery store**) a store where groceries are sold.

grog *noun* **1** a drink of liquor (originally rum) and water. **2** *informal* any alcoholic drink.

groggily *adverb* in a dazed, dopey, or unsteady manner: *I got up groggily and turned on the light.*

groggy *adjective* (**groggier, groggiest**) dazed or unsteady, as from a hangover, blows, lack of sleep, etc.

groin *noun* **1** the part of the body where the thighs meet the abdomen. **2 a** the lower abdomen. **b** the esp. male genitals. **3** *Architecture* **a** an edge formed by intersecting vaults. **b** an arch supporting a vault.

grommet *noun* a metal, plastic, or rubber eyelet, esp. placed in a hole to protect or insulate a rope or cable etc. passed through it. [Say GROM it]

groom • *noun* **1** = BRIDEGROOM. **2** a person employed to take care of horses. • *verb* **1 a** tend to, esp. brush the coat of (a horse, dog, etc.). **b** (of an animal) clean the fur of (itself or another animal). **2 a** give a neat or tidy appearance to (a person etc.). **b** carefully attend to (a lawn). **c** keep (cross-country ski trails etc.) open. **3** prepare or train (a person) for a particular purpose or activity. ▶ **groomer** *noun*

groomsman *noun* (*plural* **groomsmen**) = BEST MAN.

groove • *noun* **1 a** a channel or hollow, esp. one made to guide motion or receive a corresponding ridge. **b** a spiral track cut in a phonograph record. **2** an established routine or habit. **3** *Music slang* an established rhythmic pattern: *got a groove going.* • *verb* (**grooves, grooved, grooving**) **1** make a groove or grooves in. **2** *slang* **a** play music (esp. jazz or dance music) rhythmically. **b** dance or move rhythmically to music. **c** enjoy oneself. PHRASES **in the groove** *slang* **1** doing or performing well. **2** fashionable.

groovy *adjective* (**groovier, grooviest**) **1** *slang* (*dated* or *jocular*) fashionable and exciting; enjoyable, excellent. **2** of or like a groove.

grope • *verb* (**gropes, groped, groping**) **1** feel about or search blindly or uncertainly with the hands. **2** search mentally: *groping for the answer.* **3** feel (one's way) towards something. **4** *slang* fondle clumsily for sexual pleasure. • *noun* an act of groping someone. ▶ **groper** *noun*

grosbeak *noun* any of various finch-like birds with heavy bills and usu. brightly coloured plumage. [Say GROSS beak]

gross • *adjective* **1** bloated; repulsively fat. **2** (of a person, manners, or morals) coarse, unrefined, or indecent. **3** *slang* repulsive, disgusting. **4** flagrant;

conspicuously wrong: *gross negligence*. **5** total; not net: *gross income*. • *verb* (**grosses, grossed, grossing**) produce or earn as gross profit or income. • *noun* (*plural* **gross**) **1** gross income, receipts, etc. **2** an amount equal to twelve dozen. PHRASES **gross out** *slang* disgust, esp. by repulsive or obscene behaviour.

gross domestic product *noun* the annual total value of goods produced and services provided in a country excluding transactions with other countries.

grossly *adverb* (used for emphasis in describing something one disapproves of) extremely: *the system is grossly unfair* ◊ *these news stories are grossly exaggerated*.

gross national product *noun* the annual total value of goods produced and services provided in a country.

grossness *noun* a rude, disgusting, or indecent quality.

gross-out *noun* *slang* something that is repulsive or disgusting: *a gross-out horror flick*.

gross ton *noun* see TON 5a.

Gros Ventre *noun* (*plural* **Gros Ventre** or **Gros Ventres**) **1** a member of an Aboriginal people living in Montana and (formerly) in southern Saskatchewan. **2** their Algonquian language. [Say GROW vont]

grotesque • *adjective* **1** comically or repulsively distorted; monstrous, unnatural. **2** incongruous, absurd. • *noun* **1** a decorative form interweaving human and animal features. **2** a comically distorted figure or design.▶ **grotesquely** *adverb* [Say grow TESK]

grotesquerie *noun* (also **grotesquery**) **1** a grotesque quality or grotesque things collectively: *her cartoons combine caricature with grotesquerie*. **2** a grotesque element: *she describes, in great detail, each of the character's grotesqueries*. [Say grow TESKER ee]

grotto *noun* (*plural* **grottoes** or **grottos**) **1** a small picturesque cave. **2** an artificial ornamental cave, e.g. in a park.

grotty *adjective* (**grottier, grottiest**) *slang* unpleasant, dirty, shabby, unattractive.

grouch *informal* • *noun* (*plural* **grouches**) a discontented person. • *verb* (**grouches, grouched, grouching**) grumble.

grouchily *adverb* in a grumpy or grouchy manner.

grouchiness *noun* a grumpy or grouchy nature or behaviour.

grouchy *adjective* (**grouchier, grouchiest**) *informal* discontented, grumpy.

ground[1] • *noun* **1 a** the surface of the earth, esp. as contrasted with the air around it. **b** a part of this specified in some way: *low ground*. **2** soil, earth: *stony ground*. **3 a** a position, area, or distance on the earth's surface. **b** the extent of activity etc. achieved or of a subject dealt with: *the book covers a lot of ground*. **4** (often in *plural*) a foundation, motive, or reason: *excused on the grounds of poor health*. **5** an area of a special kind or designated for special use (often in *combination*: *fishing grounds*. **6** (in *plural*) an area of usu. enclosed land attached to a building. **7** an area or basis for consideration, agreement, etc.: *common ground*. **8 a** (in painting) the prepared surface giving the predominant colour or tone. **b** (in embroidery, ceramics, etc.) the undecorated surface. **9** (in *plural*) solid particles, esp. of coffee, forming a residue. **10** *Electricity* a connection between an electrical circuit and the earth, conducting electricity harmlessly to the ground in case of a fault. **11** the bottom of (used of the sea or a large body of water: *the ship touched ground*. • *verb* **1 a** refuse authority for (a pilot or an aircraft) to fly. **b** *informal* temporarily restrict the esp. social activities of (esp. a child or teenager), usu. as a punishment. **2 a** run (a ship) aground. **b** (of a ship) run aground. **3** (foll. by *in*) instruct thoroughly (in a subject). **4** (often as **grounded** *adjective*) (foll. by *on*)

base (a principle, conclusion, etc.) on. **5** (often as **grounded** *adjective*) connect (an electrical circuit) to the ground, directly or indirectly, so that the electricity is conducted harmlessly to the earth in case of a fault. **6** alight on the ground. **7** *Baseball* hit the ball along the ground, esp. for an easy out: *grounded to second*. PHRASES **break ground 1** begin the excavation for a new construction project. **2** (also **break new ground**) introduce or discover a new method, system, etc. **cut the ground from under a person's feet** anticipate and pre-empt a person's arguments, plans, etc. **fall to the ground** (of a plan etc.) fail. **from the ground up 1** completely, thoroughly. **2** from the most basic stage to the most complex: *redesigned from the ground up*. **gain** (or **make**) **ground 1** advance steadily; make progress. **2** (foll. by *on*) get closer to (a person or thing pursued). **get off the ground** *informal* make a successful start. **ground out** *Baseball* hit the ball along the ground to an infielder and be put out at first base. **hold** (or **stand**) **one's ground** not retreat or give way. **lose ground 1** retreat, decline. **2** lose the advantage or one's position in an argument, contest, etc. **on the ground** at the point of production or operation; in practical conditions. **on one's own ground** on one's own territory or subject; on one's own terms. **thin on the ground** not numerous. **work** (or **run** etc.) **oneself into the ground** *informal* work etc. to the point of exhaustion.

ground[2] *past and past participle of* GRIND.

groundbreaking • *adjective* **1** innovative, pioneering. **2** of or relating to a groundbreaking. • *noun* the act or ceremony of breaking ground for a new construction project.

ground cover *noun* **1** a plant covering the surface of the earth, esp. a low-growing spreading plant that inhibits the growth of weeds. **2** such plants collectively.

grounder *noun* (also **ground ball**) (esp. in baseball) a ball that is hit or passed along the ground.

ground-fault interrupter *noun* see GFI.

groundfish *noun* (*plural* **groundfish** or **groundfishes**) any fish living on or near the bottom of the sea, including halibut, sole, cod, etc.

ground glass *noun* glass made non-transparent by grinding etc.

groundhog *noun* a woodchuck.

Groundhog Day *noun* Feb. 2, when the groundhog is said to come out of hibernation; according to folklore, if it sees its shadow on that day, six more weeks of winter may be expected.

grounding *noun* basic training or instruction in a subject.

groundless *adjective* without motive or justification.

ground level *noun* **1** the level of the ground. **2** the ground floor.

groundout *noun* *Baseball* a play in which the batter hits a ball along the ground to an infielder and is put out at first base.

ground plan *noun* **1** the plan of a building at ground level. **2** the general outline of a scheme.

groundsheet *noun* a waterproof sheet spread on the ground to give protection from moisture, esp. in a tent.

groundskeeper *noun* a person who maintains a playing field or court etc.

groundspeed *noun* an aircraft's speed relative to the ground (*compare* AIRSPEED).

ground squirrel *noun* **1** a squirrel-like rodent, e.g. a chipmunk, gopher, etc. **2** any squirrel of the genus *Spermophilus* living in burrows.

groundstroke *noun* *Tennis* a stroke played after the ball has bounced.

groundswell *noun* **1** a large or extensive swell of the

G

sea caused by a distant or past storm or an earthquake. **2** an increasingly forceful presence (esp. of public opinion): *sensing a groundswell of public outrage, they decided to drop the ad*.

groundwater *noun* water held in soil or rock, esp. that below the water table.

groundwood *noun* designating low-grade newsprint, pulp, etc. that has not been treated or coated: *groundwood paper*.

groundwork *noun* work that is done as preparation for other work that will be done later: *officials are laying the groundwork for a summit conference of world leaders*.

ground zero *noun* **1** the point on the ground or on the surface of the water directly under or above an exploding (usu. nuclear) bomb. **2** *informal* the very beginning or starting point: *if you're at ground zero in terms of knowledge, go to the library*.

group • *noun* **1** a number of persons or things located close together, or considered or classed together. **2** a small band, esp. one that plays popular music. **3** *Chemistry* **a** a set of ions or radicals giving a characteristic qualitative reaction. **b** a set of elements occupying a column in the periodic table and having broadly similar properties. **c** a combination of atoms having a recognizable identity in a number of compounds. • *verb* **1** form or be formed into a group. **2** (often foll. by *with*) place in a group or groups. **3** form (colours, figures, etc.) into a well-arranged and harmonious whole. **4** classify.

grouper *noun* a large fish of the sea bass family, with a heavy body, big head, and wide mouth.

group home *noun* a home where several unrelated people live together under supervision or care.

groupie *noun slang* **1** an ardent follower of touring pop groups, esp. a young woman seeking sexual relations with them. **2** a fan, enthusiast, or follower.

grouping *noun* **1** a process of allocation to groups. **2** a formation or arrangement in a group or groups.

groupthink *noun* the practice of thinking or making decisions as a group, often resulting in poor quality decision-making.

groupware *noun* software designed to facilitate collective working by a number of different users.

grouse • *noun* (*plural* **grouse**) **1** a game bird with a plump body and feathered legs. **2** the flesh of a grouse used as food. **3** a complaint. • *verb* (**grouses, groused, grousing**) *informal* grumble or complain pettily. [Rhymes with *MOUSE*]

grout • *noun* a thin mortar for filling gaps in tiling etc. • *verb* provide or fill with grout.

grove *noun* **1** a small wood or group of trees, esp. one with little or no undergrowth. **2** an orchard planted for the cultivation of citrus fruit, olives, etc.

grovel *verb* (**grovels, grovelled, grovelling**) behave obsequiously in seeking favour or forgiveness. ▶**groveller** *noun* **grovelling** *adjective* **grovellingly** *adverb* [Say GROV'll]

grow *verb* (**grows**; *past* **grew**; *past participle* **grown**; **growing**) **1** increase in size, degree, or in any way regarded as measurable, e.g. authority or reputation: *grew in stature*. **2 a** develop or exist as a living plant or natural product. **b** develop in a specific way or direction: *growing sideways*. **c** germinate, sprout; spring up. **3** be produced; come naturally into existence; arise. **4 a** become gradually: *grow rich*. **b** come by degrees: *grew to like it*. **5** (foll. by *into*) **a** become, having grown or developed: *will grow into a fine athlete*. **b** become large enough for or suited to: *will grow into the coat* ◊ *grew into her new job*. **6** (foll. by *on*) become gradually more favoured by. **7 a** produce (plants, fruit, etc.) by cultivation. **b** bring forth. **c** allow (a beard etc.) to

develop or increase in length. **8** (in *passive*; foll. by *over, up*) be covered with a growth. **9** cause (the economy, a corporation, etc.) to grow or increase in size, value, etc.: *a plan designed to grow the company's market share*. PHRASES **grow out of 1** become too large to wear (a garment). **2** become too mature to retain (a childish habit etc.). **3** be the result or development of. **grow together** coalesce. **grow up 1 a** advance to maturity. **b** (esp. in *imperative*) begin to behave sensibly. **2** (of a custom) arise, become common.

grower *noun* **1** a person growing produce: *fruit grower*. **2** a plant that grows in a specified way: *a fast grower*.

growing pains *plural noun* **1** early difficulties in the development of an enterprise etc. **2** neuralgic pain in children's legs due to fatigue etc.

growing season *noun* the time of year when rainfall and temperature allow plants to grow.

growl • *verb* **1 a** (often foll. by *at*) (esp. of a dog) make a low guttural sound, usu. of anger. **b** murmur angrily. **2** utter with a growl. • *noun* **1** a growling sound, esp. made by a dog. **2** an angry murmur; a complaint.

growler *noun* **1** a person or thing that growls. **2** a small iceberg.

grown • *verb past participle* of GROW. • *adjective* adult.

grown-up • *adjective* **1** adult. **2** suitable for or characteristic of an adult. • *noun* an adult person.

growth *noun* **1** the act or process of growing. **2** an increase in size or value. **3** something that has grown or is growing. **4** an abnormal formation, esp. a tumour.

growth hormone *noun* a substance which stimulates the growth of a plant or animal.

growth ring *noun* a concentric layer of wood, shell, etc., developed during an annual or other regular period of growth.

grub • *noun* **1** the larva of an insect, esp. a beetle. **2** *informal* food. • *verb* (**grubs, grubbed, grubbing**) **1** dig superficially. **2 a** clear (the ground) of roots and stumps. **b** clear away (roots etc.). **3** (foll. by *up, out*) get by digging: *grubbing up weeds*.

grubber *noun* **1** (usu. in *combination*) *derogatory* a person devoted to amassing something: *vote-grubber* ◊ *money-grubber*. **2** an implement for digging up weeds etc. **3** a person who or animal which grubs.

grubbiness *noun* a dirty quality.

grub box *noun* (*plural* **grub boxes**) *Cdn* a box or other container for carrying and storing food on an expedition etc.

grubby *adjective* (**grubbier, grubbiest**) **1** dirty, grimy. **2** of or infested with grubs.

grubstake *informal* • *noun* material or provisions supplied to an enterprise in return for a share in the resulting profits (originally in prospecting). • *verb* (**grubstakes, grubstaked, grubstaking**) provide with a grubstake: *grubstake me, and I'll make you a rich man*. ▶**grubstaker** *noun*

grudge • *noun* a persistent feeling of ill will or resentment, esp. one due to an insult or injury: *bears a grudge against me*. • *verb* (**grudges, grudged, grudging**) **1** be resentfully reluctant to give, grant, or allow (a thing): *surely you don't grudge her her success?* **2** be reluctant to do (a thing): *grudged paying so much*.

grudge match *noun* (*plural* **grudge matches**) a contest or competition involving personal antipathy between competitors.

grudging *adjective* reluctant; not willing. ▶**grudgingly** *adverb* **grudgingness** *noun*

gruel *noun* a liquid food of oatmeal etc. boiled in milk or water.

gruelling *adjective* (also **grueling**) extremely demanding, severe, or tiring. ▶**gruellingly** *adverb*

G

gruesome *adjective* horrible, grisly, disgusting. ▶ **gruesomely** *adverb* **gruesomeness** *noun*

gruff *adjective* **1 a** (of a voice) low and harsh. **b** (of a person) having a gruff voice. **2** surly, terse, rough-mannered. ▶ **gruffly** *adverb* **gruffness** *noun*

grumble • *verb* (**grumbles, grumbled, grumbling**) **1 a** complain peevishly. **b** be discontented. **2** rumble. • *noun* **1** a complaint. **2** a rumble. ▶ **grumbler** *noun* **grumbling** *adjective* & *noun* **grumblingly** *adverb*

grump *informal* • *noun* **1** a grumpy person. **2** (in *plural*) a fit of sulks. • *verb* **1** be grumpy. **2** utter grumpily.

grumpily *adverb* in a grouchy or grumpy manner.

grumpiness *noun* a grouchy or grumpy nature or behaviour.

grumpy *adjective* (**grumpier, grumpiest**) morosely irritable; surly.

grunge *noun* **1** grime, dirt. **2** (also **grunge rock**) an aggressive style of rock music characterized by a raucous guitar sound and lazy delivery: *grunge band.* **3** a style of dress associated with this music, characterized by loose-fitting, often second-hand clothes. ▶ **grunginess** *noun* **grungy** *adjective* (**grungier, grungiest**)

grunt • *noun* **1** a low guttural sound made by a pig. **2** a sound resembling this. **3** *slang* a low-ranking labourer: *grunt work.* **4** *slang* an infantry soldier. **5** any of numerous tropical marine fishes that produce a grunting sound. **6** a dessert of berries (esp. blueberries) baked with a doughy topping. • *verb* **1** (of a pig) make a grunt or grunts. **2** (of a person) make a low inarticulate sound resembling this, esp. to express fatigue etc. **3** utter with a grunt.

grunter *noun* **1** a person or animal that grunts, esp. a pig. **2** a grunting fish, esp. = GRUNT *noun* 5.

Gruyère *noun* a firm pale yellow cheese made from cow's milk. [Say groo YAIR]

gryphon *noun* = GRIFFIN. [Say GRIFFIN]

GST *abbreviation* Cdn & NZ GOODS AND SERVICES TAX.

G-string *noun* **1** a narrow strip of cloth etc. covering only the genitals and attached to a string around the waist, as worn esp. by strippers. **2** (usu. **G string**) *Music* a string, e.g. on a violin, sounding the note G.

G-suit *noun* a garment with inflatable pressurized pouches, worn by pilots and astronauts to enable them to withstand high acceleration.

GT *noun* (*plural* **GTs**) a fast high-performance luxury touring sedan.

Gt. *abbreviation* Great.

GTA *abbreviation* Greater Toronto Area.

GTi *adjective* designating a high-performance car with a fuel-injected engine.

guacamole *noun* a dip or spread made from mashed avocados mixed with chopped onion, tomatoes, chili peppers, and seasoning. [Say gwocka MOLEY]

SPELL CHECK	
gauge	ABC ✓

Warning: *u* follows *a* in **gauge**.

guanine *noun* a compound that occurs in guano and fish scales, and is one of the four constituent bases of amino acids. [Say GWON een]

guano *noun* (*plural* **guanos**) **1** the excrement of seabirds, esp. that found in the islands off Peru and used as manure. **2** an artificial manure, esp. that made from fish. [Say GWONNO]

guar *noun* a drought-resistant leguminous plant grown esp. in the Indian subcontinent as a vegetable and fodder crop and as a source of guar gum. [Say GWAR (rhymes with *FAR*)]

guarantee • *noun* **1 a** a formal promise or assurance, esp. that an obligation will be fulfilled or that something is of a specified quality and durability. **b** a document giving such an undertaking. **2** = GUARANTY. **3** a person making a guaranty or giving a security. **4** a thing that makes something certain to happen or be the case: *there's no guarantee that she will come.* • *verb* (**guarantees, guaranteed, guaranteeing**) **1 a** give or serve as a guarantee for; answer for the due fulfillment of (a contract etc.) or the genuineness of (an article). **b** assure the permanence etc. of. **c** provide with a guarantee. **2** give a promise or assurance: *I guarantee to look after him* ◊ *we guarantee that you will have a good time.*

guaranteed investment certificate *noun* Cdn a certificate guaranteeing a fixed interest rate on a sum of money deposited for a fixed term, usu. between one and seven years, which may not be withdrawn before term. Abbreviation: **GIC**.

guarantor *noun* a person who gives a guarantee or guaranty. [Say GAIR un tor or GAIR un ter]

guaranty *noun* (*plural* **guaranties**) **1** a written or other undertaking to answer for the payment of a debt or for the performance of an obligation by another person liable in the first instance. **2** a thing serving as security for a guaranty. [Say GAIR un tee]

guard • *verb* **1** (often foll. by *from, against*) watch over and defend or protect from harm. **2** keep watch by (a door etc.) so as to control entry or exit. **3** supervise (prisoners etc.) and prevent from escaping. **4** (foll. by *against*) take precautions. **5** (in various games) protect (a piece, card, etc.) with set moves. • *noun* **1** a state of vigilance or watchfulness. **2** a person who keeps watch at a prison etc., or who protects. **3** a body of soldiers etc. serving to protect a place or person. **4** a part of an army detached for some purpose: *advance guard.* **5** (in *plural*) (usu. **Guards**) any of various bodies of troops nominally employed to guard a ruler. **6 a** a thing that protects or defends. **b** a piece of protective equipment designed to prevent injury to a usu. specified part of the body: *mouth guard.* **7** (often in *combination*) a device fitted to a machine, weapon, etc., to prevent injury or accident to the user. **8** a protective or defensive player, esp.: **a** (in football) the player on either side of the centre on the offensive line. **b** (in basketball) either of the two players positioned in the backcourt. **9** (in curling) a rock positioned in front of the house to protect those behind it. PHRASES **be on** (or **keep** or **stand**) **guard** (of a sentry etc.) keep watch. **lower one's guard** (also **let one's guard down**) reduce vigilance against attack. **off** (or **off one's**) **guard** unprepared for some surprise or difficulty. **on** (or **on one's**) **guard** prepared for all contingencies; vigilant. **raise one's guard** become vigilant against attack.

guarded *adjective* **1** (of a remark etc.) cautious, avoiding commitment. **2** defended, protected; kept under guard. ▶ **guardedly** *adverb* **guardedness** *noun*

guardian *noun* **1** a defender, protector, or keeper. **2** a person having legal custody of another person and his or her property when that person is incapable of managing his or her own affairs.

guardian angel *noun* a spirit conceived as watching over a specific person or place.

guardianship *noun* the state or position of being responsible for someone or something: *they applied for guardianship of the children* ◊ *the land is under the guardianship of the people who use it.*

guardrail *noun* a rail fitted as a support or to prevent an accident, e.g. along the edge of a highway or balcony.

guardsman *noun* (*plural* **guardsmen**) a soldier belonging to a body of guards.

G

guar gum *noun* a fine powder obtained by grinding the endosperm of seeds of guar, used in the food, paper, and other industries.

Guatemalan • *noun* a native or inhabitant of Guatemala, a country in Central America. • *adjective* of or relating to Guatemala. [Say gwotta MOLL un]

guava *noun* (*plural* **guavas**) **1** a small tropical American tree bearing an edible pale yellow fruit with pink juicy flesh. **2** this fruit. [Say GWOVVA]

gubernatorial *adjective* esp. *US* of or relating to a governor. [Say goober nuh TORY ul]

guck *noun* slang a sticky or slimy substance.

Guernsey *noun* (*plural* **Guernseys**) a light brown and white dairy cow of a breed originally from Guernsey in the Channel Islands. [Say GURN zee]

guerrilla *noun* **1** a person taking part in an irregular war waged by small bands operating independently, often against a stronger, more organized force, with surprise attacks etc.: *guerrilla warfare*. **2** *informal* an activist using controversial or sensational means to support a cause. [Say gur ILLA]

guess • *verb* (**guesses, guessed, guessing**) **1** estimate without calculation or measurement, or on the basis of inadequate data. **2** form a hypothesis or opinion about; conjecture; think likely: *I guess it to be around noon*. **3** conjecture or estimate correctly by guessing: *you have to guess the weight*. **4** (foll. by *at*) make a conjecture about. **5** *informal* suppose: *I guess you're right*. • *noun* (*plural* **guesses**) an estimate or conjecture: *my guess is that within a year we will have a referendum*. PHRASES **anybody's** (or **anyone's**) **guess** something very vague or difficult to determine. **I guess** *informal* I think it likely; I suppose. **keep a person guessing** *informal* withhold information. ▶**guesser** *noun*

guesstimate *informal* • *noun* an estimate based more on guesswork than calculation. • *verb* (**guesstimates, guesstimated, guesstimating**) form a guesstimate of. [Say GUESS tuh mit for the noun, GUESS ti mate for the verb]

guesswork *noun* the process of or results obtained by guessing.

guest • *noun* **1** a person (usu. invited) visiting another's house or invited to have a meal etc. at the expense of the inviter. **2** a person lodging at a hotel, boarding house, etc. **3** **a** a visiting performer invited to take part with a regular body of performers: *guest artist*. **b** a person who takes part by invitation in a radio or television program: *guest star*. **4** a person attending a social gathering at the request of or accompanying someone invited specifically. • *verb* be a guest on a radio or television show or in a theatrical performance etc. PHRASES **be my guest** *informal* make what use you wish of the available facilities.

guff *noun* slang **1** nonsense; foolish talk. **2** insolent talk. PHRASES **no guff** *Cdn* **1** a declaration of truthfulness. **2** an expression of mock surprise at a statement.

guffaw • *noun* a coarse or boisterous laugh. • *verb* **1** utter a guffaw. **2** say with a guffaw. [Say guh FAW]

GUI *noun* (*plural* **GUIs**) *Computing* a graphical user interface. [Say GOOEY]

guidance *noun* **1** advice or information aimed at resolving a problem, difficulty, etc. **2** the process of guiding or being guided. **3** the control of a missile or spacecraft in its course.

guidance counsellor *noun* a person, esp. at a school, who counsels others regarding career decisions etc.

guide • *noun* **1** a person who leads or shows the way, or directs the movements of a person or group. **2 a** a person who conducts travellers on tours etc. **b** a professional mountain climber in charge of a group.

c someone hired to lead a hunting or fishing expedition. **3** an adviser. **4** a directing principle or standard: *let your conscience be your guide*. **5** a book with essential information on a subject, esp. = GUIDEBOOK 1. **6** a thing marking a position or guiding the eye. **7** a soldier, vehicle, or ship whose position determines the movements of others. **8** *Mechanics* **a** a bar, rod, etc., directing the motion of something. **b** a gauge etc. controlling a tool. **9** (**Guide**) *Cdn, Brit., Austral.*, & *NZ* = GIRL GUIDE. • *verb* (**guides, guided, guiding**) **1** act as guide to; lead or direct. **2** arrange the course of (events). **2** be the principle, motive, or ground of (an action, judgment, etc.). **3** direct the affairs of (a nation etc.).

guidebook *noun* **1** a book of information about a place for visitors, tourists, etc. **2** a manual or handbook.

guide dog *noun* a dog trained to guide a blind person.

guideline *noun* (often in *plural*) a principle or criterion guiding or directing action.

Guiding *noun* the Girl Guide movement.

> **SPELL CHECK**
> **guild, gild**
>
> To cover something with gold is to **gild** it.

guild *noun* **1** an association of people for mutual aid or the pursuit of a common goal: *the Screen Actors' Guild*. **2** a medieval association of craftsmen or merchants: *the guild of clockmakers*. [Rhymes with *BUILD*]

guile *noun* clever and esp. deceitful behaviour: *a young man without experience, without guile or deceitfulness*. ▶**guileful** *adjective* **guileless** *adjective* **guilelessly** *adverb* [Say GILE (with a hard *G* as in *GIVE*)]

guillemot *noun* any of several diving seabirds of the auk family, with black (or brown) and white plumage and pointed bills, found in the northern latitudes. [Say GILLA mot (with a hard *G* as in *GIVE*)]

guillotine • *noun* **1** *hist.* a machine with a heavy knife blade sliding vertically in grooves, used for beheading. **2** a device for cutting paper, metal, etc. **3** *Parliament* a method of preventing delay in the discussion of a legislative bill by fixing times at which various parts of it must be voted on. • *verb* (**guillotines, guillotined, guillotining**) **1** use a guillotine on. **2** *Parliament* end discussion of (a bill) by applying a guillotine. [Say GILLA teen or GHEE uh teen (with a hard *G* as in *GIVE*)]

> **SPELL CHECK**
> **guilt, gilt**
>
> Something covered with gold is **gilt**.

guilt *noun* **1** the fact of having committed a specified or implied offence. **2 a** culpability. **b** the feeling of this. PHRASES **guilt by association** guilt ascribed to a person not because of any evidence but because of his or her association with an offender.

guiltily *adverb* in a way that shows one feels guilty: *she looked down guiltily and said she was sorry*.

guiltiness *noun* = GUILT.

guiltless *adjective* innocent; not blameworthy. ▶**guiltlessly** *adverb*

guilt trip • *noun* **1** an intense feeling of guilt, esp. induced by others pointing out offences. **2** an attempt to make another feel guilty by pointing out (supposed) offences. • *verb* (**guilt-trip**) (**guilt-trips, guilt-tripped, guilt-tripping**) attempt to induce a feeling of guilt in (someone), esp. by pointing out (supposed) offences.

guilty *adjective* (**guiltier, guiltiest**) **1** culpable of or responsible for a wrong. **2** conscious of or affected by

guilt: *a guilty conscience*. **3** concerning guilt: *a guilty secret*. **4 a** (often foll. by *of*) having committed a (specified) offence. **b** *Law* judged to have committed a specified offence.

guinea fowl *noun* (*plural* **guinea fowl** or **guinea fowls**) a large African game bird with slate-coloured white-spotted plumage, raised for food. [Say GINNY fowl (with a hard *G* as in *GIVE*)]

guinea pig *noun* **1** a tailless domesticated South American rodent, originally raised for food, now usu. kept as a pet or for research. **2** a person or thing used as a subject for experiment: *students in fifty schools are to act as guinea pigs for these new teaching methods*.

guise *noun* an external form, appearance, or manner of presentation often concealing the true nature of something: *his speech presented racist ideas under the guise of nationalism* ◊ *the story appears in different guises in different cultures*. [Sounds like GUYS]

guitar *noun* a usu. six-stringed musical instrument with a fretted fingerboard, played by plucking or strumming. ▶ **guitarist** *noun*

gulag *noun* **1** (also **Gulag**) *hist.* the system of forced-labour camps in the Soviet Union, esp. in the period 1930–55. **2** a camp or prison within this system, or any political labour camp. [Say GOO lag]

gulch *noun* (*plural* **gulches**) **1** a ravine, esp. one in which a stream flows. **2** a steep, narrow ravine or cove cutting inland from a shoreline cliff.

gulf *noun* **1** a stretch of sea consisting of a deep inlet with a narrow mouth. **2** (**the Gulf**) **a** the Gulf of Mexico. **b** the Persian Gulf. **c** the Gulf of St. Lawrence. **3** a deep crack in the ground. **4** a large difference between two people or groups in the way that they think, live or feel: *the gulf between rich and poor is enormous*.

gull¹ *noun* any of various kinds of long-winged web-footed birds, usu. having white and black or grey plumage and a bright bill.

gull² *verb* dupe, fool: *they are distrustful and disrespectful of the average person while being easily gulled by those with money, influence, or fame*.

gullet *noun* **1** the food passage extending from the mouth to the stomach; the esophagus. **2** the throat.

gullibility *noun* the ability to be easily persuaded or deceived: *Ralph's gullibility made him an easy target for practical jokes*.

gullible *adjective* easily persuaded or deceived; credulous. ▶ **gullibly** *adverb* [Say GULLA bull]

gullied *adjective* (of land) having gullies: *today all that is left are deeply gullied badlands*.

gull-wing *adjective* **1** (of a car door) hinged along the top and opening outwards and upwards. **2** (of a car) having gull-wing doors.

gully *noun* (*plural* **gullies**) (also **gulley**, *plural* **gulleys**) a small ravine, esp. formed by water after heavy rain.

gulp • *verb* **1** (often foll. by *down*) swallow hastily, greedily, or with effort. **2** swallow gaspingly or with difficulty; choke. **3** (foll. by *down*, *back*) stifle, suppress (esp. tears). • *noun* **1** an act of gulping: *drained it in one gulp*. **2** an effort to swallow. **3** a large mouthful of a drink. ▶ **gulper** *noun* **gulpy** *adjective*

gum¹ • *noun* **1 a** a sticky secretion of some trees and shrubs that hardens on drying but is soluble in water (*compare* RESIN 1). **b** an adhesive substance made from this. **2 a** = CHEWING GUM. **b** = BUBBLE GUM. **3** (in full **gum arabic**) a gum exuded by some acacias, used as a glue and as an emulsifier. **4** = GUM TREE. • *verb* (**gums, gummed, gumming**) **1** smear or cover with gum: *gummed reinforcements*. **2** fasten with gum: *the receipts are gummed into a book*. **3** make (a birchbark canoe) watertight by sealing its seams with melted pine gum.

PHRASES **gum up 1** (of a mechanism etc.) become clogged or obstructed with stickiness. **2** *informal* interfere with the smooth running of: *gum up the works*.

gum² • *noun* (usu. in *plural*) the firm flesh around the roots of the teeth. • *verb* (**gums, gummed, gumming**) (of someone without teeth) chew with the gums as though with teeth.

gumbo *noun* (*plural* **gumbos**) **1 a** okra. **b** a spicy chicken or seafood soup thickened with okra, rice, etc. **2** a heavy clayey soil that is sticky and non-porous when wet; thick clinging mud.

gumboot *noun* a rubber boot usu. reaching the knee.

gumdrop *noun* a soft coloured candy, often made with gelatin.

gum line *noun* the point where the tooth protrudes from the gum.

gummi *noun* a rubbery coloured and flavoured candy, often in the shape of animals, insects, etc.: *gummi spiders*.

gummy¹ *adjective* (**gummier, gummiest**) **1** viscous, sticky. **2** covered with or producing a sticky substance: *his eyes are all gummy*.

gummy² *adjective* (**gummier, gummiest**) toothless: *a delightful toddler with a gummy grin*.

gumption *noun* *informal* commonsensical or spirited initiative and resourcefulness: *Dan's new wife had the gumption to put her foot down and head Dan off from those crazy schemes*.

gumshoe *noun* **1** a galosh. **2** *informal* a detective.

gum tree *noun* a tree exuding gum, esp. a eucalyptus.

gun • *noun* **1** a kind of weapon (of any size from a hand-held pistol to a mounted piece of artillery), consisting of a metal tube from which bullets or other projectiles are propelled with great force, esp. by a contained explosion. **2** any device imitative of this. **3** a device for discharging something under pressure (often in combination: *grease gun*). **4** a gunman. **5** the firing of a gun. **6** *Sport informal* (esp. in hockey) a prolific scorer. • *verb* (**guns, gunned, gunning**) **1 a** (often foll. by *down*) shoot (a person) with a gun. **b** shoot at with a gun. **2** *informal* accelerate (an engine or vehicle). **3** *informal* (foll. by *for*) **a** seek out determinedly to attack or rebuke. **b** go determinedly or energetically after. **PHRASES** **go great guns** *informal* proceed forcefully or vigorously or successfully. **jump the gun** *informal* start before a signal is given, or before an agreed time. **stick to one's guns** *informal* maintain one's position under attack. **under the gun** *informal* under pressure: *we're under the gun to get this done*.

gunboat *noun* a small vessel of shallow draft and having relatively heavy guns.

gunboat diplomacy *noun* political negotiation supported by the use or threat of military force.

gun dog *noun* a dog bred or trained to assist hunters, e.g. by pointing, retrieving, flushing, etc.

gunfight *noun* a fight with firearms. ▶ **gunfighter** *noun*

gunfire *noun* **1** the firing of a gun or guns, esp. repeatedly. **2** the noise from this.

gunge *informal* • *noun* = GUNK *noun*. • *verb* (**gunges, gunged, gunging**) (usu. foll. by *up*) clog or obstruct with gunge.

gung-ho *adjective* enthusiastic, eager.

gungy *adjective* (**gungier, gungiest**) clogged or covered with gunk or gunge. [Say GUN jee]

gunk *slang* • *noun* sticky or viscous matter, esp. when messy. • *verb* (often foll. by *up*) soil or clog with gunk. ▶ **gunky** *adjective* (**gunkier, gunkiest**)

gunman *noun* (*plural* **gunmen**) a person armed with a gun, esp. in committing a crime.

gunmetal • *noun* **1** (also **gunmetal grey**, **gunmetal**

G

blue) a dull bluish-grey colour. **2** an alloy of copper and tin or zinc, formerly used for guns. • *adjective* dull bluish grey.

gunnel *noun* = GUNWALE.

gunner *noun* **1 a** (also **Gunner**) a private in the artillery. Abbreviation: **Gnr. b** any member of the artillery. **2** a person who operates a gun, esp. on an aircraft or ship.

gunnery *noun* **1** the design and operation of esp. large guns. **2** the firing of guns.

gunny *noun* (*plural* **gunnies**) **1** coarse sacking, usu. of jute; burlap. **2** (also **gunny sack**) a sack made of this.

gunplay *noun* the use of guns.

gunpoint *noun* PHRASES **at gunpoint** threatened with a gun or an ultimatum etc.

gunpowder *noun* an explosive powder made of potassium nitrate, sulphur, and charcoal, used for fuses, fireworks, and blasting.

gunrunner *noun* a person engaged in the illegal sale or importing of firearms etc. ▶ **gunrunning** *noun*

gunship *noun* a heavily-armed helicopter etc.

gunshot *noun* **1** a shot fired from a gun. **2** the sound of this. **3** the range of a gun: *within gunshot*.

gun-shy *adjective* **1** (esp. of a hunting dog) afraid of a gun or the sound that it makes. **2** hesitant or nervous, esp. because of a previous unpleasant experience: *people today are gun-shy because they don't want those terrible reviews in the Times and the show to close overnight*.

gunsight *noun* a sight on a gun (see SIGHT *noun* 6).

gunslinger *noun* esp. *US slang* a gunfighter. ▶ **gunslinging** *noun & adjective*

gunsmith *noun* a person who makes, sells, and repairs firearms. ▶ **gunsmithing** *noun*

gunstock *noun* the esp. wooden mounting for the barrel and firing mechanism of a rifle etc.

gunwale *noun* the upper edge of the side of a boat or ship. [Say GUN ul]

guppy *noun* (*plural* **guppies**) a small freshwater fish of the West Indies and South America, frequently kept in aquariums, and giving birth to live young.

gurdwara *noun* a Sikh temple. [Say gurd WAR uh (WAR rhymes with *FAR*)]

gurdy *noun* (*plural* **gurdies**) *Cdn* a winch on a fishing boat used to haul in a line, net, etc.

gurgle • *verb* (**gurgles, gurgled, gurgling**) **1** make a bubbling sound like water from a bottle or flowing over stones. **2** (of liquid) flow with such a sound. **3** (of a baby) make a guttural noise indicating happiness: *the baby gurgled happily*. • *noun* a gurgling sound. ▶ **gurgly** *adjective*

Gurkha *noun* **1** a member of the principal Hindu race in Nepal. **2** a Nepalese soldier serving in the British army. [Say GURKA]

gurney *noun* a wheeled stretcher used to transport patients in a hospital etc. [Say GURNY]

gurry *noun* fish entrails or offal as refuse from cleaning fish. [Rhymes with *HURRY*]

guru *noun* (*plural* **gurus**) **1** a Hindu spiritual teacher or head of a religious sect. **2** an influential teacher or popular expert: *a management guru*. **3** each of the ten first leaders of the Sikh religion.

gush • *verb* (**gushes, gushed, gushing**) **1** emit or flow in a sudden and copious stream. **2** speak or behave with effusiveness or sentimental affectation: *Robert is not one to gush*. • *noun* (*plural* **gushes**) **1** a sudden or abundant stream. **2** exaggerated effusiveness or enthusiasm: *romantic gush and twaddle*.

gusher *noun* an oil well from which oil flows without being pumped.

gushing *adjective* **1** expressing so much enthusiasm,

praise, or emotion that it does not seem sincere: *the dust jacket is covered with gushing comments about the author and her previous work*. **2** from which something flows abundantly: *gushing fountains*.

gushy *adjective* (**gushier, gushiest**) excessively effusive or sentimental.

gusset *noun* **1** a piece of material let into a garment etc. to strengthen or enlarge a part. **2** a bracket strengthening an angle of a structure.

gussy *verb* (**gussies, gussied, gussying**) *Informal* **1** dress up, esp. for a special occasion: *you don't have to get all gussied up to go to these restaurants*. **2** make more attractive or showy: *for a photography competition, don't mat your prints or gussy them up in any way*.

gust • *noun* **1** a sudden strong rush of wind. **2** a burst of rain, fire, smoke, or sound. **3** a passionate or emotional outburst: *gusts of laughter*. • *verb* blow in gusts.

gustatory *adjective* concerned with tasting or the sense of taste. [Say GUSTA tory]

gusto *noun* enthusiasm or vigour.

gusty *adjective* (**gustier, gustiest**) characterized by or blowing in strong winds.

gut • *noun* **1 a** the lower alimentary canal or a part of this; the intestine. **b** *informal* the abdomen or belly: *punched in the gut*. **2** (in *plural*) the bowel or entrails, esp. of animals. **3** (in *plural*) *informal* personal courage and determination; vigorous application and perseverance. **4** (in *plural*) *informal* the belly as the source of appetite: *greedy guts*. **5** (in *plural*) **a** the contents of anything, esp. representing substantiality. **b** the essence of a thing, e.g. of an issue or problem. **6** material for violin or racquet strings or surgical use made from the intestines of animals. **7 a** a sound or strait. **b** a defile or narrow passage. **8** (as an *adjective*) **a** instinctive: *a gut reaction*. **b** fundamental: *a gut issue*. • *verb* (**guts, gutted, gutting**) **1** (often in *passive*) remove or destroy (esp. by fire) the internal fittings of (a house etc.). **2** take out the guts of (a fish). **3** remove the essential components of. **4** extract the essence of (a book etc.).

PHRASES **hate a person's guts** *informal* dislike a person intensely. **have someone's guts for garters** *Cdn & Brit.* be extremely angry at someone. **sweat** (or **work** etc.) **one's guts out** *informal* work etc. extremely hard or energetically.

gutbucket *adjective* designating a very spirited, robust, or raw style of music, esp. jazz.

gutless *adjective* *informal* lacking courage or determination. ▶ **gutlessly** *adverb* **gutlessness** *noun*

gut-level *adjective* instinctive; heartfelt.

gutsiness *noun* *informal* courage, toughness.

gutsy *adjective* (**gutsier, gutsiest**) *informal* courageous; tough.

gutted *adjective* in senses of GUT *verb*.

gutter • *noun* **1 a** a channel at the side of a street to carry away runoff. **b** esp. *US & Brit.* = EAVESTROUGH. **2** (**the gutter**) **a** a poor or degraded background or environment: *worked their way out of the gutter*. **b** a sordid or vulgar situation: *get your mind out of the gutter*. **3** an open conduit or channel along which liquid etc. flows out. **4** a groove. **5** a track made by the flow of water. **6** the channel running along each side of a bowling lane. **7** the space between open pages of a book, magazine, etc. • *verb* **1** (of a candle) melt away as the wax forms channels down the side. **2** (of a candle flame) flicker before being extinguished, esp. as the last wax melts away.

gutter press *noun* sensational journalism concerned esp. with the private lives of public figures.

guttersnipe *noun* **1** a street urchin. **2** an ill-mannered street person or vagrant.

guttural *adjective* **1** (of a sound) produced at the back of the throat. **2** (of speech) characterized by guttural sounds. ▶ **gutturally** *adverb* [Say GUTTER ul]

guy¹ *noun* **1** *informal* a man; a fellow. **2** (in *plural*) *informal* a person of either sex.

guy² • *noun* a rope or line fixed to the ground to secure a tent or other structure: *guy wires ◊ guy ropes.* • *verb* secure with a guy or guys.

Guyanese • *noun* a native or inhabitant of Guyana, a country in South America. • *adjective* of or relating to Guyana. [Say guy uh NEEZ]

guzzle *verb* (**guzzles, guzzled, guzzling**) eat, drink, or consume excessively or greedily. ▶ **guzzler** *noun*

Gwich'in • *noun* (*plural* **Gwich'in**) **1** a member of an Aboriginal people living in Alaska, the Yukon, and the NWT. **2** the Athapaskan language of the Gwich'in. • *adjective* of or relating to this people. [Say GWITCHEN]

gybe • *verb* (**gybes, gybed, gybing**) **1** (of a fore-and-aft sail or boom) swing across in wearing or running before the wind. **2** cause (a sail) to do this. **3** (of a ship or its crew) change course so that this happens. • *noun* a change of course causing gybing. [Say JIBE]

gym *noun* *informal* **1** a gymnasium. **2** physical education. **3** gymnastics.

gymnasium *noun* (*plural* **gymnasiums**) a room or building equipped for gymnastics, indoor sports, physical training, etc.

gymnast *noun* an expert in gymnastics.

gymnastic *adjective* of or involving gymnastics. ▶ **gymnastically** *adverb*

gymnastics *plural noun* (also treated as *singular*) **1** exercises developing or displaying physical agility and coordination, usu. in competition. **2** other forms of physical or mental agility: *verbal gymnastics.*

gymnosperm *noun* any of various plants having seeds unprotected by an ovary, including conifers, cycads, and ginkgos. [Say JIM no sperm]

gym shoe *noun* = RUNNING SHOE.

gynecological *adjective* having to do with the physiological functions and diseases of women and girls, esp. those affecting the reproductive system: *gynecological exam.* [Say guy nuh cuh LOGICAL]

gynecologist *noun* (also **gynaecologist**) a medical specialist who deals with the functions and diseases of women and girls, esp. those affecting the reproductive system. [Say guy nuh COLLA jist]

gynecology *noun* (also **gynaecology**) the branch of physiology and medicine that deals with the functions

and diseases of women and girls, esp. those affecting the reproductive system. [Say guy nuh COLLA jee]

> **WRITING TIP**
> **gyp**
>
> Some people object to **gyp** because they feel it is related to the word *gypsy*, although this has not been proven. For this reason and because it is considered slang, it should be avoided in writing and speech. You can use words like **cheat, swindle, shortchange**, or **fleece** instead.

---

gyp *slang* • *verb* (**gyps, gypped, gypping**) cheat, swindle. • *noun* an act of cheating; a swindle. [Say JIP]

gyppo *noun* (also **gypo**) a minor or small-time logging operator or contractor. [Say JIPPO]

gyproc *noun* (also **gyprock**) = DRYWALL *noun.* [Say JIP rock]

gypsum *noun* a hydrated form of calcium sulphate occurring naturally and used in the building industry and to make plaster of Paris. [Say JIP sum]

gypsumboard *noun* = DRYWALL. [Say JIP sum board]

gypsy *noun* (*plural* **gypsies**) (also **Gypsy**) a member of a travelling people of Europe and North America, of Hindu origin, speaking a language (Romany) related to Hindi, and traditionally living by seasonal work, itinerant trade, and fortune telling.

gypsy moth *noun* a kind of moth the caterpillars of which are very destructive to foliage.

gyrate *verb* (**gyrates, gyrated, gyrating**) **1** revolve around a fixed point or axis; go in a circle or spiral. **2** move one's hips rhythmically in a circular pattern, esp. in a sexually suggestive way. ▶ **gyration** *noun*

gyre *esp. literary* • *verb* (**gyres, gyred, gyring**) whirl, gyrate. • *noun* **1** a whirling, a vortex; a gyration. **2** a circulatory ocean current. [Say JIRE (rhymes with FIRE)]

gyrfalcon *noun* the largest falcon, found in Arctic regions and occurring in several colours. [Say JUR falcon]

gyro¹ *noun* (*plural* **gyros**) *informal* **1** = GYROSCOPE. **2** = GYROCOMPASS. [Say JYE roe]

gyro² *noun* (*plural* **gyros**) a sandwich of pita bread filled with slices of spiced meat cooked on a spit, tomatoes, onions, etc. [Say YEE roe]

gyrocompass *noun* (*plural* **gyrocompasses**) a non-magnetic compass giving true north and bearings from it by means of a gyroscope. [Say JYE ro compass]

gyroscope *noun* a wheel or disc mounted so as to spin rapidly about an axis whose orientation is not fixed but is unperturbed by tilting of the mount, esp. used in stabilizers, gyrocompasses, navigation systems, etc. ▶ **gyroscopic** *adjective* [Say JYE ruh scope]

G

Hh

H¹ *noun* (also **h**) (*plural* **Hs** or **H's**) **1** the eighth letter of the alphabet. **2** anything having the form of an H (esp. in *combination*: *H-girder*).

H² *abbreviation* (also **H.**) **1** hardness. **2** (of a pencil lead) hard. **3** *slang* heroin.

H³ *symbol* hydrogen.

h¹ *abbreviation* (also **h.**) **1** height. **2** hot. **3** hour(s). **4** husband. **5** *Baseball* hit. **6** hundred.

h² *symbol* hecto-.

Ha *symbol* hahnium.

ha¹ *interjection* expressing surprise, suspicion, triumph, etc.

ha² *abbreviation* hectare(s).

habeas corpus *noun* **1** a writ requiring a person to be brought before a judge or into court, esp. to investigate the lawfulness of his or her detention. **2** the right to such a writ as protection against unlawful detention. [Say HAY be us CORP us]

haberdasher *noun* a dealer in men's clothing and accessories. [Say HABBER dasher]

haberdashery *noun* (*plural* **haberdasheries**) **1** men's clothing and accessories. **2** a shop or establishment dealing in these, esp. as a department in a store. [Say HABBER dasher ee]

habit *noun* **1** a customary practice or way of acting: *has a habit of ignoring me*. **2** a practice that a person does often and almost without thinking, esp. one that is hard to give up. **3** *informal* a craving for or dependency on an addictive drug or drugs. **4 a** the dress of a particular religious order. **b** (also **riding habit**) an outfit designed to be worn by a rider on horseback. **5** *Biology & Mineralogy* the characteristic mode of growth and general external form of a plant or mineral: *a tree with neat conical habit and level twisting branches*. PHRASES **make a habit of** do regularly.

habitability *noun* the suitability of a place for living.

habitable *adjective* fit or suitable for habitation; that can be inhabited.

habitant *noun hist.* (in Canada) a French settler in rural Quebec, esp. a farmer. [Say abbey TON (with TON as in French)]

habitat *noun* the natural environment characteristically occupied by an organism or distinguished by the set of organisms which occupy it: *a wetland habitat*.

habitation *noun* **1** the action of dwelling in or inhabiting; occupancy by inhabitants: *not fit for human habitation*. **2** a house or home.

habit-forming *adjective* causing addiction.

habitual *adjective* **1** done constantly or as a habit. **2** usual: *he trudged along his habitual route*. **3** having a specified habit: *a habitual smoker*. ▶ **habitually** *adverb*

habituate *verb* (**habituates**, **habituated**, **habituating**) (often foll. by *to*) make used to something; accustom: *she had habituated the chimps to humans*. ▶ **habituation** *noun* [Say huh BICH oo ate]

habitué *noun* a habitual visitor to a place: *they were habitués of the Pen and Pencil Club*. [Say huh BICH oo AY]

hacienda *noun* (in Spanish-speaking countries) **1** an estate or plantation, esp. one used for farming or ranching. **2** the house on such an estate. [Say hassy ENDA]

hack¹ • *verb* **1** cut or chop with heavy blows, esp. in a rough or random fashion. **2** (often foll. by *at*) deliver cutting blows. **3** (of an editor etc.) shorten (a piece of writing, film footage, etc.), esp. detrimentally. **4** *informal* (usu. foll. by *into*) use a computer to gain unauthorized access to data in a system. **5** *slang* cope with, tolerate. **6** cough repeatedly with a short, dry cough. • *noun* **1** an act of hacking or chopping, esp. a hacking blow. **2** a short, dry, hard cough. **3** *Curling* a rubber, metal, or wooden insert in the ice, used as a starting block to steady the foot when delivering a stone. **4** *informal* an attempt to break into a computer system. PHRASES **hack around** *informal* **1** idly pass the time or wander aimlessly. **2** pass the time by computer hacking.

hack² • *noun* **1 a** a writer of mediocre literary or journalistic work. **b** *informal* usu. *derogatory* a journalist. **2** a person who does the hard and often boring work for an organization, esp. a politician: *a party hack*. **3 a** a taxi. **b** a taxi driver. **4** a horse for ordinary riding. • *adjective* **1** typical of a hack; commonplace: *hack work*. **2** used as a hack: *a hack horse*.

hackberry *noun* (*plural* **hackberries**) **1** a tree of the elm family, native to North America, bearing purple edible berries. **2** the berry of this tree.

hacker *noun* **1** a person or thing that hacks. **2** *informal* **a** a computer user who attempts to gain unauthorized access to computer systems. **b** a computer user who is expert in programming. ▶ **hackery** *noun*

hacking *adjective* (of a cough) short, dry, and frequently repeated.

hackle *noun* **1** a long feather or series of feathers on the neck or saddle of certain birds, e.g. the domestic rooster. **2** (in *plural*) the hairs along the back of a dog, which rise when it is angry or alarmed. PHRASES **make a person's hackles rise** or **raise some** (or a **person's**) **hackles** anger or annoy a person.

hackney *noun* (*plural* **hackneys**) **1 a** a light harness horse with a compact body and a characteristic high-stepping trot. **b** a horse of average size and quality for ordinary riding. **2** *hist.* designating any of various vehicles kept for hire: *hackney carriage*.

hackneyed *adjective* (of a phrase etc.) made commonplace or trite by overuse. [Say HACK need]

hacksaw *noun* a saw with a narrow blade set in a frame, for cutting metal.

had past and past participle of HAVE.

haddock *noun* (*plural* **haddock**) a marine fish of the North Atlantic, related to the cod, which is popular as a food fish and has great commercial value. [Say HAD ick]

hadj *noun* = HAJJ. [Say HADGE]

hadji *noun* = HAJJI. [Say HADGEY]

hadn't *contraction* had not.

hadrosaur *noun* a large dinosaur of the late Cretaceous period, with jaws flattened like the bill of a duck. [Say HADRO sore]

haem *noun* esp. *Brit.* = HEME. [Say HEEM]

haemato- etc. esp. *Brit.* = HEMATO- etc. [Say HEEMA toe]

haemo- etc. esp. *Brit.* = HEMO- etc. [Say HEEMO]

hafnium *noun* a silvery lustrous metallic element occurring naturally with zirconium, used in tungsten alloys for filaments and electrodes. [Say HAFNY um]

haft *noun* the handle of a dagger or knife etc.

hag *noun* an ugly old woman.

Haggadah *noun* (*plural* **Haggadahs, Haggadoth**) **1** the non-legal element of the Talmud, consisting esp. of illustrative legends or parables (*compare* HALACHA). **2** a book containing the text recited at the Seder, on the first two nights of Passover. [Say ha ga DUH for the singular, ha ga DUH or ha ga DOH for the plural]

haggard *adjective* looking exhausted and distraught, esp. from fatigue, worry, deprivation, etc. [Say HAG'rd]

haggis *noun* (*plural* **haggises**) a Scottish dish consisting of a sheep's or calf's offal mixed with suet, oatmeal, etc., and boiled in a bag made from the animal's stomach or in an artificial bag.

haggle *verb* (**haggles, haggled, haggling**) (often foll. by *about, over*) dispute or wrangle over a price, deal, etc. ▶ **haggler** *noun* **haggling** *noun*

hagiographer *noun* a writer of the lives of saints. [Say haggy OGGRA fur]

hagiographic *adjective* (of a biography) written in an overly praising or idealized way; offering more praise than the subject deserves: *his magnificent, if somewhat hagiographic, biography of Freud*. ▶ **hagiographical** *adjective* [Say haggy uh GRAPHIC]

hagiography *noun* (*plural* **hagiographies**) **1** the writing of the lives of saints. **2** an idealized biography of any person. [Say haggy OGGRA fee]

hah *interjection* = HA[1].

hahnium *noun* an artificially produced radioactive element. [Say HONNY um]

Haida • *noun* **1** (*plural* **Haida** or **Haidas**) a member of an Aboriginal people living on the west coast of Canada. **2** the language of this people. • *adjective* of this people or their language or culture. [Say HI duh]

haiku *noun* (*plural* **haiku**) **1** a type of very short Japanese poem, having three parts, usu. 17 syllables, and often about a subject in nature. **2** an imitation of this in another language. [Say HI koo]

hail[1] • *noun* **1** pellets of frozen rain falling in showers. **2** (foll. by *of*) a barrage or onslaught (of bullets, curses, questions, etc.). • *verb* hail falls: *it is hailing*.

hail[2] • *verb* **1** (often foll. by *as*) acclaim, commend, or endorse vigorously: *hailed as a success*. **2** signal to or attract the attention of: *hailed a taxi*. **3** (foll. by *from*) (of a person) have one's home or origins in (a place): *hails from Windsor*. **4** greet enthusiastically. • *interjection* expressing greeting. ▶ **hailer** *noun*

Hail Mary *noun* (*plural* **Hail Marys**) **1** a prayer asking the Virgin Mary to pray for the world, beginning with the salutation used by the angel Gabriel when he told her that she was pregnant with Jesus. **2** *Football* a very long forward pass made in the final seconds of a half or game, esp. as a desperate effort to score when completion is unlikely: *won on a Hail Mary play*.

hailstone *noun* a pellet of hail.

hailstorm *noun* a period of heavy hail.

SPELL CHECK
hair, hare

The animal resembling a large rabbit is a **hare**. A rash or foolish idea is **hare-brained**.

hair *noun* **1 a** any of the fine threadlike strands growing from the skin of mammals, esp. from the human head. **b** these collectively: *has red hair*. **2** anything resembling a hair. **3** a fine, elongated plant structure, esp. an outgrowth from the epidermis of a plant, e.g. a root hair. **4** a very small degree, quantity, or extent. PHRASES **get in a person's hair** *informal* persistently irritate or annoy a person. **hair of the dog (that bit you)** an alcoholic drink taken to cure a

hangover. **let one's hair down** *informal* abandon restraint, behave freely or wildly. **make one's hair stand on end** alarm or horrify one. **not turn a hair** remain apparently unmoved or unaffected.

hairball *noun* a ball of hair which collects in the stomach of a cat etc. as a result of the animal licking its coat.

hairbrush *noun* (*plural* **hairbrushes**) a brush for arranging or smoothing the hair.

haircut *noun* **1** an act of cutting the hair. **2** the style in which the hair is cut. ▶ **haircutter** *noun* **haircutting** *noun*

hairdo *noun* (*plural* **hairdos**) the particular way in which esp. a woman's hair is styled.

hairdresser *noun* **1** a person who cuts and styles hair, esp. professionally. **2** the business or establishment of a hairdresser. ▶ **hairdressing** *noun*

haired *combining form* having the colour or kind of hair described: *a grey-haired gentleman* ◊ *a long-haired cat*.

hairiness *noun* the quality of a person or thing that is covered with lots of hair.

hairless *adjective* not having hair.

hairlike *adjective* slender and fine, like hair.

hairline *noun* **1** the natural line on the head at which a person's hair stops growing, esp. on the forehead. **2** a very thin line or crack etc.: *hairline fracture*.

hairnet *noun* a fine, light net worn on the head to keep the hair in place.

hairpiece *noun* a piece of false hair augmenting a person's natural hair or covering a bald spot.

halrpin *noun* **1** a U-shaped pin for fastening the hair. **2** a sharp curve: *a hairpin turn*.

hair-raising *adjective* extremely alarming; terrifying.

hair shirt *noun* **1** a shirt made of a very rough cloth woven from hair, worn as a form of self-discipline or to make up for one's sins. **2** (**hair-shirt**) (as an *adjective*) austere, harsh, self-sacrificing: *hair-shirt determination*.

hairsplitting *adjective & noun* making excessively fine distinctions; quibbling.

hairspray *noun* a fixative solution sprayed onto the hair to keep it in place.

hairstyle *noun* a particular way of arranging the hair. ▶ **hairstyling** *noun* **hairstylist** *noun*

hair-trigger *noun* **1** a trigger of a firearm set for release at the slightest pressure. **2** (as an *adjective*) quickly and easily provoked: *has a hair-trigger temper*.

SPELL CHECK
hairy, harry

To harass or annoy someone is to **harry** them.

hairy *adjective* (**hairier, hairiest**) **1** made of or covered with hair. **2** having the feel or appearance of hair. **3** *slang* difficult, frightening, or problematic.

Haisla • *noun* (*plural* **Haisla** or **Haislas**) **1** a member of a major language group of northern Wakashan, of which the Kitamaat in BC are the only survivors. **2** the language of the Haisla. • *adjective* of or relating to this people or their culture or language. [Say HICE luh]

Haitian • *noun* **1** a native or inhabitant of Haiti, a country in the Caribbean. **2** (also **Haitian Creole**) the French-based Creole language spoken in Haiti. • *adjective* of the Haitians or their language. [Say HAY sh'n]

hajj *noun* the pilgrimage to Mecca undertaken in the twelfth month of the Muslim year, constituting one of the religious duties of Islam. [Say HADGE]

hajji *noun* (*plural* **hajjis**) a Muslim who has been to Mecca as a pilgrim: also (**Hajji**) used as a title. [Say HADGEY]

hake *noun* **1** any of various blue-grey and silver fishes

H

related to the cod, found in shallow temperate seas. **2** either of two reddish-brown food fishes of the northwest Atlantic, related to the cod.

Halacha noun (plural **Halachahs**, **Halachoth**) **1** Jewish law and jurisprudence, based on the Talmud, esp. the Mishna, and subsequent rabbinical rulings (compare HAGGADAH 1). **2** a law, tradition, or legal ruling included as a binding part of this law. ▶ **Halachic** adjective [Say huh LAW huh for the singular, huh I AW huhs or huh LAW hot for the plural]

Halakah noun plural **Halakahs** or **Halakoth**) = HALACHA.

halal • adjective denoting or relating to meat prepared as prescribed by Muslim law: *halal butchers*. • noun meat prepared in this way. [Say hal AL]

halcyon • adjective **1** calm, peaceful: *halcyon days*. **2** (of a period) happy, prosperous. • noun a kingfisher native to Europe, Africa, and Australasia, which has brightly coloured plumage. [Say HAL see un]

SPELL CHECK
hale, hail

Frozen rain falling in pellets is **hail**. When you wave to a cab driver or a friend, or when you commend someone, you **hail** them.

H

hale adjective (esp. of an old person) strong and healthy (esp. in **hale and hearty**).

half • noun (plural **halves**) **1** either of two equal or corresponding parts, groups, etc. into which a thing is or might be divided. **2** either of two equal periods of play in sports. **3** esp. Soccer & Rugby informal = HALFBACK. • adjective **1** of an amount or quantity equal to a half. **2** partial, incomplete, imperfect, or falling short of a full or perfect amount, degree, type, etc.: *half measures*. • adverb **1** partly, nearly, or to the extent of half: *only half cooked* ◊ *half-laughing*. **2** to a certain extent, somewhat: *half-dead* ◊ *am half inclined to agree*. **3** (in reckoning time) by the amount of half (an hour etc.): *half past two*. PHRASES **by half** excessively: *too clever by half*. **by halves** imperfectly or incompletely: *never does things by halves*. **go halves** (or **half and half**) share equally in something with another person. **half a chance** informal the slightest opportunity: *given half a chance*. **the half of it** informal the rest or more important part of something: *you don't know the half of it*. **half past** (of time) thirty minutes past the hour. **not half 1** not nearly: *not half long enough*. **2** informal not at all: *not half bad*.

half a dozen noun six.

half-and-half • adverb in equal parts. • adjective that is half one thing and half another. • noun a mixture of milk and cream having 10% milk fat.

halfback noun **1** Football a back lined up on one or the other side of the fullback. **2** Soccer a player positioned behind the forwards and in front of the fullbacks. **3** Rugby a forward playing primarily in an offensive capacity.

half-baked adjective incompletely considered, planned, or developed: *half-baked ideas* ◊ *half-baked poets*.

half-breed noun offensive a person of mixed race.

half-brother noun a male related to one or more other persons, male or female, by having one biological parent in common.

half court noun **1** the section of a court in basketball, tennis, etc. which is the domain of one opposing team, player, etc. **2** (**half-court**) esp. Basketball designating an offensive or defensive game plan devised to be used within one half of the court.

half-cut adjective Cdn & Brit. slang fairly drunk.

half-dead adjective **1** in a state in which death seems

as likely as recovery. **2** in a state of extreme exhaustion or weakness.

half-dozen noun six or about six.

half-hear verb (**half-hears**, **half-heard**, **half-hearing**) hear (a thing) incompletely.

half-hearted adjective lacking courage, enthusiasm, or determination. ▶ **half-heartedly** adverb

half hitch noun (plural **half hitches**) a noose or knot formed by passing the end of a rope around its standing part and then through the loop.

half-hour noun **1** (also **half an hour**) a period of 30 minutes. **2** a point of time 30 minutes after any hour o'clock. ▶ **half-hourly** adjective & adverb

half-life noun (plural **half-lives**) **1** the time taken for half of a sample of a particular radioactive isotope to decay into other materials. **2** the time taken for half of a dose of a drug etc. to disappear in the body after administration.

half-light noun a dim, imperfect light, esp. that at dusk or dawn.

half-mast noun **1** the position of a flag halfway down the mast, as a mark of respect for a person who has died. **2** informal the position of a garment halfway to that normal: *trousers at half-mast*.

half moon noun **1** the moon when only half its illuminated surface is visible from earth. **2** the time when this occurs. **3** a semicircular object.

half nelson noun Wrestling see NELSON.

half note noun Music a note having the time value of two quarter notes or half a whole note and represented by a hollow ring with a stem.

half-pint noun **1** an amount of liquid equal to half a pint. **2** slang a short person.

half-pipe noun a snow tunnel or U-shaped cut in the snow, similar to the stunt ramps used by skateboarders, but used by snowboarders.

half rest noun Music a rest having the time value of a half note.

half section noun (West) a half of a square mile of esp. agricultural land, 320 acres (approx. 130 hectares).

half shell noun half of the shell of an oyster etc., esp. as used for serving food: *oysters on the half shell*.

half-sister noun a female related to one or more other persons, male or female, by having one biological parent in common.

half-slip noun an article of lingerie resembling a skirt, worn underneath dresses and skirts.

half-staff noun = HALF-MAST.

half-starved adjective poorly fed; suffering from malnourishment; having insufficient food.

half-step noun **1** Music a semitone. **2** a small or partial step in a specific direction.

half-timbered adjective Architecture having walls with a timber frame and a brick or plaster filling, typical in Tudor houses. ▶ **half-timbering** noun

halftime noun **1** the time at which half of a game or contest is completed. **2** a short interval occurring at this time.

half-ton noun a pickup truck with a carrying capacity of approximately half a ton.

halftone noun **1 a** an image, produced by photographic or electronic means, in which an effect of continuous tone is simulated by dots of various sizes or lines of various thicknesses. **b** the process which produces such an image. **2** Music a semitone. **3** an intermediate tone between the extreme lights and extreme shades.

half-track noun a military or other vehicle with wheels at the front and caterpillar tracks at the rear.

half-truth *noun* a statement that conveys only part of the truth, esp. deliberately.

halfway • *adverb* **1** at or to a point equidistant between two others: *halfway to Regina*. **2** to some extent, more or less: *is halfway decent*. • *adjective* midway or equidistant between two points: *reached a halfway point*.

halfway house *noun* **1** a residence where ex-prisoners, mental patients, etc. live and receive treatment to help prepare them for their return to society. **2** the halfway point in a progression.

halfwit *noun informal* an extremely foolish or stupid person. ▶ **halfwitted** *adjective*

halibut *noun* (*plural* **halibut**) any of several very large flatfishes fished intensively for food. [Say HALA b't]

halide *noun* a binary compound of a halogen with another group or element. [Say HAL ide or HAIL ide]

Haligonian • *noun* a native or resident of Halifax, Nova Scotia. • *adjective* of or pertaining to Halifax or Haligonians. [Say hala GO nee un]

Halkomelem • *noun* (*plural* **Halkomelem**) **1** a member of an Aboriginal people living in southwestern BC. **2** the Salishan language of the Halkomelem. • *adjective* of or relating to this people or their culture or language. [Say hall kuh MAY lum]

SPELL CHECK
hall, haul

To drag something is to **haul** it. A long distance is a "long **haul**".

---

hall *noun* **1 a** a corridor or passage in a building. **b** a space or passage into which the front entrance of a house etc. opens. **2** a large room or building for meetings, meals, concerts, etc. **3** a building containing lecture rooms etc. that is part of a university. **4** (in a college etc.) a common dining room, esp. for members of the institution. **5** the building of a union, fraternity, guild, etc.

hallal *adjective & noun* = HALAL. [Say hal AL]

hallelujah *interjection & noun* = ALLELUIA.

hallmark *noun* **1** a mark used for indicating a standard of gold, silver, and platinum. **2** any distinctive feature: *declining property values, rising crime, and other hallmarks of urban decay*.

Hall of Fame *noun* (*plural* **Halls of Fame**) **1** a building with memorials of people who have excelled in a specific activity, esp. in a particular sport. **2** (usu. **hall of fame**) a group famous in a particular sphere: *it's a candidate for the salsa hall of fame*. ▶ **Hall of Famer** *noun*

halloo (also **hallo**) • *interjection* calling attention to or expressing surprise. • *noun* the cry "halloo". • *verb* (**halloos**, **halloos**, **hallooed**) cry "halloo". [Say huh LOO]

hallowed *adjective* **1** (especially of old things) respected and important: *one of the theatre's most hallowed traditions*. **2** that has been made holy: *be buried in hallowed ground*.

Halloween *noun* (also **Hallowe'en**) the eve of All Saints' Day, 31 October.

Halloween apples *interjection Cdn* (*Prairies*) uttered by children going door to door on Halloween to collect candies etc.

hallucinate *verb* (**hallucinates**, **hallucinated**, **hallucinating**) experience hallucinations. [Say huh LOO sin ate]

hallucination *noun* the apparent or alleged perception of an object not actually present. [Say huh loo sin AY shun]

hallucinatory *adjective* causing or having to do with hallucinations: *hallucinatory drugs ◊ hallucinatory visions*. [Say huh LOO sin a tory]

hallucinogen *noun* a drug causing hallucinations. ▶ **hallucinogenic** *adjective* [Say huh LOO sinna jen, huh loo sinna JEN ick]

hallway *noun* an entrance hall or corridor.

halo *noun* (*plural* **halos** or **haloes**) **1** a disc or circle of light shown surrounding the head of a sacred person. **2** a circle of white or coloured light around a luminous body, esp. the sun or moon. [Say HAY low]

haloed *adjective* surrounded by a halo. [Say HAY lode]

halogen *noun* **1** any of the group of non-metallic elements (fluorine, chlorine, bromine, iodine, and astatine) which form halides (e.g. sodium chloride) by simple union with a metal. **2** designating lamps etc. using a filament surrounded by a halogen, usu. iodine vapour. ▶ **halogenic** *adjective* [Say HALA jen]

halt • *noun* **1** a usu. temporary stop; an interruption of progress: *come to a halt*. **2** a temporary stoppage on a march or journey. • *verb* stop; come or bring to a halt. **PHRASES** **call a halt** (**to**) decide to stop.

halter • *noun* **1** a rope or strap with a noose for horses or cattle. **2** (also **halter top**) a style of woman's top fastened behind the neck and across the back, leaving the arms, shoulders, upper back, and often the midriff bare. **3** a rope with a noose for hanging a person. • *verb* put a halter on (a horse etc.).

halting *adjective* (esp. of speech or movement) stopping and starting often, esp. because one is uncertain or not very confident: *a halting conversation ◊ a toddler's first few halting steps*. ▶ **haltingly** *adverb*

halvah *noun* (also **halva**) a sweet confection of sesame flour and honey. [Say HAL vuh]

halve *verb* (**halves**, **halved**, **halving**) **1** divide into two halves or parts. **2** reduce by half. **3** share equally (with another person etc.).

halves *plural of* HALF.

halyard *noun Nautical* a rope or tackle for raising or lowering a sail or yard etc. [Say HAL y'rd]

ham *noun* **1 a** the upper part of a pig's leg salted and dried or smoked for food. **b** the meat from this. **2** the back of the thigh; the thigh and buttock. **3** *slang* an inexpert or unsubtle actor or piece of acting. **4** *informal* the operator of an amateur radio station: *ham radio*. **PHRASES** **ham it up** overact.

hamatsa *noun* **1** a dance among the Kwagiulth in which the main dancer is inspired by the spirit of a man-eating monster hungering for human flesh. **2** a dancer embodying the monster. [Say huh MATSA]

hamburger *noun* (also **hamburg**) **1** a patty of ground beef, seasonings, etc. **2** this fried or grilled and eaten in a soft bread roll. **3** ground beef.

ham-fisted *adjective informal* = HAM-HANDED. ▶ **ham-fistedly** *adverb* **ham-fistedness** *noun*

ham-handed *adjective informal* clumsy, heavy-handed, bungling. ▶ **ham-handedness** *noun*

Hamiltonian • *noun* a native or inhabitant of Hamilton, Ontario. • *adjective* of or relating to Hamilton. [Say ham'll TONY un]

Hamite *noun* a member of a group of north African peoples, including the ancient Egyptians and Berbers. [Say HAM ite]

Hamitic • *noun* a group of African languages including ancient Egyptian and Berber. • *adjective* **1** of or relating to this group of languages. **2** of or relating to the Hamites. [Say huh MIT ick]

hamlet *noun* a small village, esp. one that is unincorporated.

hammer • *noun* **1 a** a tool with a heavy metal head at right angles to the handle, used for breaking, driving nails, etc. **b** a similar contrivance, as for exploding the charge in a gun, striking the strings of a piano, etc. **2** an auctioneer's mallet, indicating by a rap that an article

H

is sold. **3 a** a metal ball of about 7 kg, attached to a wire for throwing in an athletic contest. **b** the sport of throwing the hammer. **4** *Curling* the last rock of an end. • *verb* **1 a** hit or beat with or as with a hammer. **b** strike loudly; knock violently (esp. on a door). **2 a** drive in (nails) with a hammer. **b** fasten or secure by hammering: *hammered the lid down.* **3** (often foll. by *in*) inculcate (ideas, knowledge, etc.) forcefully or repeatedly. **4** *informal* utterly defeat; inflict heavy damage on. **5** (foll. by *at, away at*) work hard or persistently at. PHRASES **under the hammer** to be sold at an auction. **hammer out 1** make flat or smooth by hammering. **2** work out the details of (a plan, agreement, etc.) laboriously. **3** play (a tune, esp. on the piano) loudly or clumsily.

hammer and sickle *noun* the symbols of the industrial worker and the peasant used as the emblem of the former USSR and of communism.

hammer and tongs *adverb informal* with great vigour and commotion: *they went at it hammer and tongs, neither giving way.*

hammered *adjective* **1** (of metal, etc.) shaped or formed with a hammer. **2** *informal* drunk.

hammerhead *noun* a shark of tropical and temperate oceans that has a flattened, laterally elongated head bearing the eyes and nostrils at the extremities.

hammering *noun* the sound or action of hitting something with a hammer or fists: *there was a hammering at the door.*

hammerlock *noun* **1** a hold in which an opponent's arm is twisted and bent behind the back. **2** a strong hold: *a cheerleader placed a hammerlock on my heart.*

hammock *noun* a bed of canvas or rope network, suspended by cords at the ends. [Say HAM ick]

hammy *adjective* (**hammier, hammiest**) **1** of or like ham. **2** *informal* (of an actor or acting) over-theatrical.

hamper[1] *noun* **1** a large basket usu. with a hinged lid and containing food: *picnic hamper.* **2** a package of food or other essentials for a needy person: *distributing Christmas hampers.* **3** a usu. covered basket or other receptacle for dirty laundry.

hamper[2] *verb* **1** prevent the free movement or activity of. **2** impede, hinder.

hamster *noun* a burrowing rodent with a short tail and large cheek pouches for storing food, kept as a pet or laboratory animal.

hamstring • *noun* **1** each of five tendons at the back of the knee in humans. **2** the great tendon at the back of the hock in quadrupeds. • *verb* (**hamstrings, hamstrung, hamstringing**) **1** cripple by cutting the hamstrings of (a person or animal). **2** prevent the activity or efficiency of (a person or enterprise): *all countries, Canada included, are hamstrung by their current economic situation.*

Han • *noun* (*plural* **Han**) **1** a member of a small Aboriginal group living along the Yukon River. **2** the Athapaskan language of this people. • *adjective* of or relating to this people or their culture or language. [Say HON]

hand • *noun* **1 a** the end part of the human arm beyond the wrist, including the fingers and thumb. **b** in other primates, the end part of a forelimb, also used as a foot. **2 a** (often in *plural*) control, management: *in good hands.* **b** agency or influence: *suffered at their hands.* **c** a share in an action; active support. **3** help: *Katie gave me a hand.* **4** a thing compared with a hand or its functions, esp. the pointer of a clock or watch. **5** the right or left side or direction relative to a person or thing. **6 a** a skill, esp. in something practical: *a hand for making pastry.* **b** a person skilful in some respect. **7** a person who does or

makes something, esp. distinctively: *a picture by the same hand.* **8** an individual's writing or the style of this; a signature: *in one's own hand.* **9** a person etc. as the source of information etc.: *at first hand.* **10** a pledge of marriage. **11** a person as a source of manual labour esp. in a factory, on a farm, or on board ship. **12 a** the playing cards dealt to a player. **b** the player holding these. **c** a round of play. **13** *informal* applause: *got a big hand.* **14** the unit of measure of a horse's height, equal to 4 inches (10.16 cm). • *verb* **1** (foll. by *in, to, over,* etc.) deliver; transfer by hand or otherwise. **2** convey verbally: *handed me a lot of abuse.* **3** *informal* give away too readily: *handed them the advantage.* PHRASES **all hands 1** the entire crew of a ship. **2** the entire workforce. **at hand 1** close by. **2** about to happen. **by hand 1** by a person and not a machine. **2** delivered privately, rather than by the post office. **(from) hand to mouth** satisfying only one's immediate needs. **get** (or **have** or **keep**) **one's hand in** become (or be or remain) practised in something. **hand and foot** completely: *waited on them hand and foot.* **hand down 1 a** pass the ownership or use of to another. **b** transmit (a custom etc.) from one generation to the next. **2 a** transmit (a decision) from a higher court etc. **b** express (an opinion or verdict). **hand in glove** in collusion or association. **hand in hand 1** holding hands. **2** in close association. **hand it to** *informal* acknowledge the merit of (a person). **hand off 1** *Football* hand (the ball) to another player, rather than passing or throwing it. **2** give or hand (a thing) to another person. **hand on** pass (a thing) to the next in a series or succession. **hand out 1** serve, distribute. **2** award, allocate: *the judge handed out stiff sentences.* **hand over** deliver; surrender possession of. **hand over fist** *informal* with rapid progress. **hands down** (esp. of winning) with no difficulty. **hands off 1** a warning not to touch or interfere with something. **2** *Computing* not requiring manual use of controls. **hands on 1** *Computing* of or requiring personal operation at a keyboard. **2** involving or offering active participation rather than theory. **hands up!** an instruction to raise one's hands in surrender or to signify assent or participation. **hand-to-hand** (of fighting) at close quarters. **have** (or **take**) **a hand in** share or take part in. **have one's hand in the till** steal from one's employer; embezzle; take bribes. **have one's hands full** be fully occupied. **have one's hands tied** *informal* be unable to act. **in hand 1** receiving attention. **2** in reserve; at one's disposal. **3** under one's control. **lay** (or **put**) **one's hands on** *see* LAY[1]. **off one's hands** no longer one's responsibility. **on every hand** (or **all hands**) to or from all directions. **on hand 1** available. **2** present, in attendance. **on one's hands** resting on one as a responsibility. **on** (**one's**) **hands and knees** crouching down with the palms and the knees touching the ground. **on the one** (or **the other**) **hand** from one (or another) point of view. **out of hand 1** out of control. **2** peremptorily: *refused out of hand.* **put** (or **set**) **one's hand to** start work on; engage in. **to hand 1** within easy reach. **2** (of a letter) received. **turn one's hand to** undertake (as a new activity).

handbag *noun* a woman's purse.

handball *noun* **1 a** a game in which a ball is hit with the hand in a walled court. **b** the small, hard ball used in this game. **2** *Soccer* intentional touching of the ball with the hand or arm by a player other than the goalkeeper in the goal area, constituting a foul.

hand barrow *noun Cdn (Nfld)* = BARROW[1] 2.

handbasket *noun* a small basket. PHRASES **go to hell in a handbasket** degenerate, esp. rapidly.

handbill *noun* a printed notice distributed by hand.

handbook *noun* a short manual or guidebook.

handbrake *noun* a brake operated by hand.

handcart *noun* a small cart pushed or drawn by hand. PHRASES **go to hell in a handcart** degenerate, esp. rapidly.

handcraft • *noun* = HANDICRAFT. • *verb* make by handicraft. ▸ **handcrafted** *adjective*

handcuff • *noun* (in *plural*) a pair of lockable linked metal rings for securing a person's wrists. • *verb* **1** put handcuffs on. **2** prevent (a person) from acting freely or effectively.

-handed *adjective* (in *combination*) **1** for or involving a specified number of hands (in various senses): *two-handed*. **2** using chiefly the hand specified: *left-handed*. ▸ **-handedly** *adverb* **-handedness** *noun* (both in sense 2)

handful *noun* (*plural* **handfuls**) **1** a quantity that fills the hand. **2** a small number or amount. **3** *informal* a troublesome person or task.

hand grenade *noun* see GRENADE 1.

handgrip *noun* **1** a grasp with the hand. **2** a handle designed for easy holding.

handgun *noun* a small firearm held in and fired with one hand.

hand-held • *adjective* designed to be held in the hand. • *noun* a small hand-held computer.

handhold *noun* something for the hands to grip on (in climbing, sailing, etc.).

handicap • *noun* **1 a** a disadvantage imposed on a superior competitor in order to make the chances more equal. **b** a race or contest in which this is imposed. **2** the number of strokes by which a golfer normally exceeds par for the course. **3** a thing that makes progress or success difficult. **4** a physical or mental disability. • *verb* (**handicaps**, **handicapped**, **handicapping**) **1** impose a handicap on. **2** place (a person) at a disadvantage.

handicapped *adjective* suffering from a physical or mental disability.

handicapper *noun* **1 a** a person appointed to fix or assess a competitor's handicap, esp. in horse racing or golf. **b** a person who predicts the outcome of an event or competition. **2** (in *combination*) a person or horse having a specified handicap: *a high handicapper*.

handicraft *noun* **1** an art, skill, or trade that requires both manual and artistic ability. **2** work produced by such a skill or art.

handily *adverb* **1** in a handy manner. **2** easily: *won the contest handily*. **3** conveniently.

handiwork *noun* work done or a thing made by hand, or by a particular person: *painters come from all over the province to display their handiwork* ◊ *this looks like the handiwork of an arsonist*.

handkerchief *noun* (*plural* **handkerchiefs** or **handkerchieves**) a square of cotton, linen, silk, etc., usu. carried in the pocket for wiping one's nose, etc.

handle • *noun* **1** the part by which a thing is held, carried, or controlled. **2** a fact that may be taken advantage of: *gave a handle to his critics*. **3** *informal* a personal name or title. **4** the feel of goods, esp. textiles, when handled. • *verb* (**handles**, **handled**, **handling**) **1** touch, feel, operate, or move with the hands. **2** manage or deal with; treat in a particular or correct way: *unable to handle the situation*. **3** deal in (goods). **4** (of a vehicle, machine, tool, etc.) react or behave in a specified way in response to use, operation, or direction. **5 handle oneself** behave, esp. under pressure. PHRASES **get a handle on** *informal* understand the basis of or reason for a situation, circumstance, etc. ▸ **handleable** *adjective*

handlebar *noun* (often in *plural*) the steering bar of a bicycle etc., with a handgrip at each end.

handlebar moustache *noun* a thick moustache with ends curving upwards.

handled *combining form* having the kind of handle or handles described: *long-handled shears* ◊ *bone-handled knives*.

handler *noun* **1** a person or thing that handles something. **2** a person who handles or deals in certain commodities. **3** a person who trains and looks after an animal (esp. a police dog). **4** a person who looks after or represents a public figure, esp. a politician.

handline *noun* a fishing line worked or drawn by hand. ▸ **handliner** *noun*

handling *noun* **1** the action of touching, feeling, or holding something in one's hands: *toys that can stand up to rough handling*. **2** treatment or manner of dealing with something. **3** the process of packing, transporting, and delivering goods etc.: *handling charges*. **4** the way in which a vehicle handles.

handlogger *noun* a person who logs by hand, using tools such as an axe or saw rather than a feller-buncher etc. ▸ **handlogging** *noun*

handmade *adjective* made by hand and not by machine, esp. as designating superior quality.

handmaid *noun* (also **handmaiden**) *archaic* a female servant or helper.

hand-me-down *noun* an article of clothing etc. passed on from another person.

handoff *noun* the act of handing something off to another person.

handout *noun* **1** something given free to a needy person. **2** a statement given to the press etc. **3** a fact sheet, graph, summary of a speech, etc. distributed to a class or audience. **4** anything given away free, e.g. a sample of a product. **5** a payment made by esp. a government to a person, agency, etc. perceived as providing nothing in return.

handover *noun* **1** the act of moving power or responsibility from one person or group to another; the period during which this is done: *the smooth handover of power from a military to a civilian government*. **2** the act of giving a person or thing to someone in authority: *the handover of the hostages*.

hand-pick *verb* **1** pick (fruit etc.) by hand. **2** choose carefully or personally. ▸ **hand-picked** *adjective*

handprint *noun* the print or mark of a hand.

handrail *noun* a narrow rail for holding as a support on stairs etc.

handsaw *noun* a saw worked by one hand.

handset *noun* a telephone mouthpiece and earpiece forming one unit.

hands-free *adjective* (of a telephone etc.) designed to be operated without the use of the hands.

handshake *noun* the shaking of a person's hand with one's own as a greeting etc.

hand signal *noun* a manual indication by a cyclist or driver of his or her intention to stop, turn, etc.

hands-off *adjective* **1** (of a policy, attitude, etc.) characterized by the lack of intervention: *a hands-off approach to the problem*. **2** (of flying, driving, etc.) without the use of the hands: *hands-off piloting*.

handsome *adjective* (**handsomer**, **handsomest**) **1** (of a person) good-looking. **2** (of a building etc.) imposing, attractive. **3 a** generous: *a handsome present*. **b** (of a price, fortune, etc.) considerable.

handsomely *adverb* **1** generously. **2** finely.

handsomeness *noun* the quality of being handsome.

hands-on *adjective* characterized by active

H

participation or involvement: *hands-on computer experience*.

handspring *noun* a somersault in which one lands first on the hands and then on the feet.

handstand *noun* an act of balancing on one's hands while putting one's legs straight up in the air.

hand tool *noun* a tool operated by hand, without electricity.

handwashing *noun* **1** washing of the hands. **2** washing by hand.

handwoven *adjective* (of cloth) woven by hand, as opposed to by a machine.

hand-wringing • *noun* exaggerated lamentation or anguish: *except for crocodile tears and hand-wringing, there has been little reaction from Ottawa*. • *adjective* characterized by hand-wringing.

handwriting *noun* **1** writing with a pen, pencil, etc. **2** a person's particular style of writing. PHRASES **handwriting on the wall** clear signs of approaching failure or disaster. ▶ **handwritten** *adjective*

handy *adjective* (**handier**, **handiest**) **1** convenient to handle or use; useful. **2** ready to hand; placed or occurring conveniently. **3** clever with the hands.

> **SPELL CHECK**
> **handicraft, handiwork**
>
> Warning: the words **handicraft** and **handiwork** are spelled with an *i*, not with a *y*.

handyman *noun* (*plural* **handymen**) a person able or employed to do occasional domestic repairs and minor renovations.

handyperson *noun* (*plural* **handypersons**) a person able or employed to do occasional domestic repairs and minor renovations.

> **WRITING TIP**
> **hung, hanged**
>
> Note that while the past of *most* senses of **hang** is **hung**, the past for the sense "suspend from a rope by the neck until dead" is **hanged**: *the leader of the rebellion was hanged in a public execution; when they hanged the notorious Captain Kidd, the rope broke*.

hang • *verb* (**hangs**; *past* and *past participle* **hung** except in sense 7; **hanging**) **1** secure or cause to be supported from above, esp. with the lower part free. **2** set up (a door, gate, etc.) on its hinges so that it moves freely. **3** place (a picture) on a wall or in an exhibition. **4** attach (wallpaper) in vertical strips to a wall. **5** *informal* attach the blame for (a thing) to (a person): *you can't hang that on me*. **6** decorate by hanging pictures or decorations etc. **7** (*past* and *past participle* **hanged**) **a** suspend or be suspended by the neck with a noosed rope until dead, esp. as a form of capital punishment. **b** as a mild oath: *hang the expense*. **8** let droop: *hung her head*. **9** remain static in the air. **10** be present or imminent, esp. oppressively or threateningly: *a hush hung over the room*. **11 a** depend on: *everything hangs on the discussions*. **b** listen closely to: *hangs on their every word*. **12** prevent (a jury) from reaching a verdict. **13** (of a computer or computer system) cease to respond to input from the keyboard or mouse. **14** *slang* (usu. foll. by *with*) associate with (a person). • *noun* **1** the way a thing hangs or falls. **2** a downward droop or bend. PHRASES **get the hang of** *informal* understand the technique or meaning of. **hang a left** (or **right**) *informal* make a left (or right) turn. **hang around 1 a** loiter or dally; not move away. **b** linger near (a person or place). **c** wait. **2** (often foll. by *with*) associate with (a person etc.). **hang back 1** show reluctance to

act or move. **2** remain behind. **hang fire** be slow in taking action or in progressing. **hang heavily** (or **heavy**) (of time) pass slowly. **hang in** *informal* **1** persist, persevere. **2** linger. **hang loose** *informal* be casual or unconcerned. **hang on** *informal* **1** continue or persevere, esp. with difficulty. **2** (often foll. by *to*) continue to hold or grasp. **3** (foll. by *to*) retain; fail to give back. **4** wait for a short time. **hang one's hat** be resident. **hang out 1** hang from a window, clothesline, etc. **2** protrude or cause to protrude downwards. **3** (foll. by *of*) lean out of (a window etc.). **4** *slang* reside or be often present. **5** = HANG AROUND 2. **hang a person out to dry** abandon a person to a usu. unpleasant fate. **hang together 1** make sense. **2** remain associated. **hang tough** *informal* be or remain inflexible. **hang up 1** hang from a hook, peg, hanger, etc. **2** (often foll. by *on*) end a telephone conversation, esp. abruptly. **3** cause delay or difficulty to: *is really hung up on her father*. **5** = HANG *verb* 13. **hang up one's skates** *Cdn* give up; quit or retire: *the premier will hang up his skates next spring*. **let it all hang out** *slang* be uninhibited or relaxed. **might as well be hanged for a sheep as a lamb** if the penalty for a more serious crime, offence, act of foolishness, etc. is no greater than for a less serious one, then one might as well continue in one's criminal, foolish, etc. behaviour. **not care** (or **give**) **a hang** *informal* not care at all.

hangar *noun* a building with extensive floor area, for housing aircraft etc. [Say HANG er]

hangashore *noun* *Cdn* (*Nfld & Maritimes*) **1** a weak or sickly person. **2** an idle or lazy person. [Say HANG a shore]

hangdog *adjective* having a dejected or guilty appearance.

> **SPELL CHECK**
> **hanger, hangar**
>
> A building that houses airplanes is a **hangar**.

hanger *noun* **1** a person or thing that hangs. **2** a shaped piece of wood or plastic etc. from which clothes may be hung.

hanger-on *noun* (*plural* **hangers-on**) a follower or dependant, esp. an unwelcome one.

hang-glider *noun* **1** a frame with a fabric airfoil stretched over it, from which the operator is suspended and controls flight by body movement. **2** a person who practises hang-gliding. ▶ **hang-gliding** *noun*

hanging • *noun* **1** the act or practice of executing a person by hanging. **2** a tapestry hung on a wall etc. • *adjective* **1** that hangs or is hung; suspended. **2** (of a crime) punishable by hanging: *a hanging offence*. **3** (of a judge, jury, etc.) inclined towards giving a death sentence: *a hanging judge*.

hangman *noun* (*plural* **hangmen**) **1** an executioner who hangs condemned persons. **2** a word game for two players, in which the tally of failed guesses is kept by drawing a representation of a body on a gallows.

hangnail *noun* a piece of torn skin at the root of a fingernail, causing soreness.

hangout *noun* *informal* a place one frequently visits, esp. to relax or socialize etc.

hangover *noun* **1** a severe headache and other after-effects caused by drinking an excess of alcohol. **2** a feeling, custom, habit, etc. that remains from the past, although it is no longer practical or suitable: *the insecure feeling that was a hangover from her childhood*.

hangup *noun* *slang* an emotional problem or inhibition.

hanker *verb* long for; crave: *he had hankered for fame all his life* ◊ *she hankered to go back to Fiji.* ▶ **hankering** *noun*

hanky *noun* (also **hankie**) (*plural* **hankies**) *informal* a handkerchief.

hanky-panky *noun slang* **1** naughtiness, esp. sexual misbehaviour. **2** dishonest dealing; trickery.

Hansard *noun* the official verbatim record of debates in parliaments in Canada, the UK, and many other parliaments throughout the Commonwealth. [Say HAN serd]

hantavirus *noun* (*plural* **hantaviruses**) any of various viruses spread esp. by rodents and causing acute respiratory disease, kidney failure, etc. [Say HANTA virus]

Hanukkah *noun* the eight-day Jewish festival of lights, usu. in December, commemorating the purification of the Temple in 165 BC. [Say HONNA kuh]

haphazard *adjective* with no particular order or plan; not organized well; random: *the books had been piled on the shelves in a haphazard fashion* ◊ *the government's approach to the problem was haphazard.* ▶ **haphazardly** *adverb* **haphazardness** *noun*

hapless *adjective* unlucky: *defeated the hapless visitors 8-0.* ▶ **haplessly** *adverb* **haplessness** *noun*

haploid ● *adjective* (of an organism or cell) with a single set of chromosomes. ● *noun* a haploid organism or cell.

happen *verb* **1** occur. **2** have the (good or bad) fortune to: *I happened to meet her.* **3** be the (esp. unwelcome) fate or experience of: *what happened to you?* **4** (foll. by *on*) encounter or discover by chance. **5** (foll. by *along, by,* etc.) come or turn up in a place casually or as if by chance. PHRASES **as it happens** in fact; in reality: *as it happens, it turned out well.*

happening ● *noun* **1** an event or occurrence. **2** an improvised or spontaneous theatrical etc. performance. ● *adjective slang* exciting, trendy.

happenstance *noun* a thing that happens by chance: *I wanted to meet people by happenstance, not make appointments with them.*

happily *adverb* **1** in a cheerful way; with feelings of pleasure or satisfaction: *children playing happily on the beach* ◊ *Emma and I are happily married.* **2** by good luck; fortunately: *happily for him, the death penalty has been abolished.* **3** willingly: *she happily gives to charity.* **4** in a way that is suitable or appropriate: *the two styles fit together happily.*

happiness *noun* a feeling of pleasure or satisfaction; a happy state.

happy *adjective* (**happier, happiest**) **1** feeling or showing pleasure or contentment. **2 a** fortunate; characterized by happiness. **b** (of words, behaviour, etc.) appropriate, pleasing: *that wasn't the happiest choice of words.* **3** *informal* slightly drunk. **4** (in *combination*) *informal* inclined to use excessively or at random: *trigger-happy.*

happy-go-lucky *adjective* cheerfully casual.

happy hour *noun* a period of the day when drinks are sold at reduced prices in bars, hotels, etc.

happy hunting ground *noun* a place where success or enjoyment is obtained.

happy medium *noun* a compromise; the avoidance of extremes.

hara-kiri *noun* **1** ritual suicide by disembowelment with a sword, formerly practised by Samurai to avoid dishonour. **2** a self-destructive action or course: *political hara-kiri.* [Say haira KEERY]

harangue ● *noun* **1** a lengthy and earnest speech. **2** a passionate verbal attack or reprimand. ● *verb* (**harangues, harangued, haranguing**) lecture or make a harangue (to). [Say huh RANG]

SAY IT RIGHT
harass

Harass can be pronounced with the stress on the first or second syllable. The pronunciation with the stress on the second syllable, huh RASS, is the more common one and is perfectly acceptable, despite being considered incorrect by some people.

harass *verb* (**harasses, harassed, harassing**) **1** trouble and annoy continually or repeatedly. **2** make repeated attacks on (an enemy or opponent). ▶ **harasser** *noun* **harassing** *noun & adjective* **harassingly** *adverb* [Say huh RASS or HAIR us]

harassment *noun* aggressive pressure or intimidation. [Say huh RASS m'nt or HAIR us m'nt]

harbinger *noun* a person or thing that signals the approach of another; a forerunner: *the flowers were a beautiful harbinger of spring.* [Say HAR binge er]

harbour (also **harbor**) ● *noun* a place of shelter for ships. ● *verb* **1** give shelter to (esp. a criminal or wanted person). **2** keep in one's mind, esp. resentfully: *harbour a grudge.* **3** come to anchor in a harbour.

harbourfront ● *noun* land adjacent to a harbour. ● *adjective* situated or occurring beside a harbour.

harbourmaster *noun* an official in charge of a harbour.

harbour seal *noun* a small seal of coastal marine waters and estuaries.

hard ● *adjective* **1** (of a substance, material, etc.) firm and solid; not easily cut. **2** difficult. **3** difficult to bear; entailing suffering: *hard luck.* **4** (of a person) unfeeling; severely critical. **5** (of a season or the weather) severe, harsh: *a hard winter* ◊ *a hard frost.* **6** harsh or unpleasant to the senses: *a hard voice.* **7 a** strenuous, enthusiastic, intense: *a hard worker* ◊ *a hard fight.* **b** severe, uncompromising: *a hard bargain* ◊ *hard words.* **c** (of a turn) sharp, extreme: *make a hard left at the corner.* **d** *Politics* extreme; most radical: *the hard right.* **8 a** (of liquor) strongly alcoholic; designating spirits rather than wine or beer. **b** (of a beverage) containing alcohol; fermented: *hard cider.* **9** (of drugs) potent and addictive. **10** (of pornography) highly suggestive and explicit. **11** (of water) containing mineral salts that make lathering difficult. **12** established; not disputable; reliable: *hard facts* ◊ *hard data.* **13** (of wheat) containing a hard kernel rich in gluten, used to make bread flour (*compare* SOFT *adjective* 12). **14** (of money) **a** in coins as opposed to paper currency. **b** in currency as opposed to cheques etc. **15** (of a consonant) guttural (as *c* in *cat, g* in *go*). ● *adverb* **1** intensely: *is raining hard* ◊ *hard-working.* **2** with difficulty or effort: *hard-earned.* **3** so as to be hard or firm: *frozen hard.* **4** in close proximity: *following hard on their heels.* **5** with great force or genuine sorrow: *she took his death very hard.* PHRASES **be hard on 1** be difficult for. **2** be severe in one's treatment or criticism of. **3** be unpleasant to (the senses). **be hard put** find it difficult: *I'd be hard put to think of a better candidate than you.* **go hard with** turn out to (a person's) disadvantage. **hard at it** *informal* busily working or occupied. **hard by** near; close by. **a hard case 1** *informal* an intractable person. **2** a case of hardship. **a hard** (or **tough**) **nut to crack** *informal* **1** a difficult problem. **2** a person or thing not easily understood or influenced. **hard on** (or **upon**) close to in pursuit etc. **take a hard line** be unyielding or determined in asserting one's position; be strict.

hard and fast *adjective* (of a rule or a distinction made) definite, unchangeable, strict.

hardback *noun* = HARDCOVER.

hardball ● *noun* **1** = BASEBALL. **2** *slang* uncompromising

methods or dealings, esp. in politics: *the opposition decided to play hardball on this issue*. • *adjective* tough; uncompromising: *hardball tactics* ◊ *hardball politics*.

hardboard *noun* stiff board made of compressed and treated wood pulp.

hard-boiled *adjective* **1** (also **hard-cooked**) (of an egg) cooked in water in the shell until the white and the yolk are solid. **2** (of a person) tough, shrewd.

hard bread *noun* Cdn (Nfld) a thick, oval biscuit baked without salt and dried in a kiln.

hard candy *noun* (plural **hard candies**) a candy made of corn syrup and boiled sugar, usu. coloured and flavoured.

hard copy *noun* (plural **hard copies**) printed material produced by computer, usu. on paper.

hard core • *noun* **1** the small central group in an organization, or in a particular group of people, who are the most active or who will not change their beliefs or behaviour: *it's really only the hard core that bothers to go to meetings*. **2** a type of punk rock music characterized by a fast tempo and more emphasis on rhythm than melody. • *adjective* (usu. **hard-core**) **1** designating the most uncompromising members of a group: *hard-core Marxists*. **2** (of pornography) explicit, obscene.

hardcover *adjective & noun* • *adjective* (of a book) bound in stiff covers. • *noun* a hardcover book.

hard disk *noun* Computing a large-capacity rigid usu. magnetic storage disk.

hard done by *adjective* Cdn & Brit. harshly or unfairly treated.

hard-earned *adjective* that has taken a great deal of effort to earn or acquire.

harden *verb* **1** make or become hard or harder. **2** become, or make (one's attitude etc.), uncompromising or less sympathetic. **3** (of prices etc.) cease to fall or fluctuate. PHRASES **harden off** make (a plant) less sensitive to cold by gradually increasing its exposure. ▶ **hardener** *noun*

hardening *noun* (also **hardening of the arteries**) = ARTERIOSCLEROSIS.

hard hat *noun* **1** protective headgear worn on construction sites etc. **2** informal a construction worker.

hard-headed *adjective* **1** practical, realistic; not sentimental. **2** stubborn. ▶ **hard-headedly** *adverb* **hard-headedness** *noun*

hard-hearted *adjective* unfeeling, unsympathetic. ▶ **hard-heartedly** *adverb* **hard-heartedness** *noun*

hard-hitting *adjective* forceful, tough; not sparing the feelings: *a hard-hitting report*.

hardiness *noun* **1** the ability to endure harsh or difficult conditions. **2** the ability of plants to survive outdoors in winter.

hard labour *noun* heavy manual work as a punishment, esp. in a prison.

hardline *adjective* unyielding, firm. ▶ **hardliner** *noun*

hard luck *noun* worse fortune than one deserves.

GRAMMAR CHECK
hardly ⚠

Words like **hardly**, **scarcely**, and **barely** should not be used with negative constructions, as in *I can't hardly wait for the weekend*. It is correct to say *I can hardly wait for the weekend*, *I can scarcely believe my eyes*, or *I can barely see*.

---

hardly *adverb* **1** scarcely; only just: *we hardly knew them*. **2** only with difficulty: *could hardly speak*. **3** probably not or almost certainly not: *she will hardly come now*. PHRASES **hardly any** almost no; almost none. **hardly ever** very rarely.

hard maple *noun* = SUGAR MAPLE.

hardness *noun* **1** the quality of being firm and solid. **2** an unfeeling or severely critical manner: *there was a hardness in his voice*. **3** a quality of water that contains mineral salts and does not lather easily.

hard news *noun* news that is of immediate interest to a broad audience, usu. dealing with serious issues such as politics, wars, disasters, etc. (compare SOFT NEWS).

hard-nosed *adjective* informal not affected by feelings when trying to get something; tough-minded, determined: *a hard-nosed journalist*.

hard of hearing *adjective* somewhat deaf.

hardpack *noun* snow with a very dense, tightly packed surface.

hard palate *noun* the front part of the palate.

hardpan *noun* a hardened layer of clay occurring in or below the soil profile.

hard-pressed *adjective* **1** closely pursued. **2** burdened or oppressed (with work, etc.). **3** in (esp. financial) difficulty: *hard-pressed taxpayers*. **4** unable or barely able: *she'll be hard-pressed to finish in time*.

hard return *noun* a line break inserted by the operator of a word processor, e.g. at the end of a paragraph (compare SOFT RETURN).

hard rock *noun* rock music with a heavy beat, distorted amplified guitar-playing, and loud vocals.

hardrock miner *noun* a miner who works in large, underground formations of esp. igneous or metamorphic rock.

hardrock mining *noun* mining underground in large formations of esp. igneous or metamorphic rock, e.g. the Canadian Shield.

hardscrabble *adjective* providing or yielding a meagre output and requiring much effort: *earned a hardscrabble living*.

hard sell *noun* aggressive salesmanship or advertising.

hard-shell *adjective* (also **hard-shelled**) having a hard shell.

hardship *noun* **1** severe suffering or lack of comforts or necessities: *the economic hardship facing most regions of the country*. **2** the circumstance causing this.

hard stuff *noun* slang hard drugs or strong liquor.

hardtack *noun* = SHIP'S BISCUIT.

hardtop *noun* **1 a** a road paved with a hard surface, esp. tar and gravel. **b** the material used for such a road. **2** a car with a rigid (sometimes detachable) roof.

hard up *adjective* **1** short of money. **2** (foll. by *for*) at a loss for; lacking.

hardware *noun* **1** tools, building materials, and household articles. **2** heavy machinery or armaments. **3** the mechanical and electronic components of a computer etc. (compare SOFTWARE 1).

hard-wearing *adjective* able to stand much wear.

hard-wired *adjective* **1** involving or achieved by permanently connected circuits designed to perform a specific function. **2** furnished or equipped with a natural ability to do something, as if programmed: *from the beginning, he seemed hard-wired for math*. **3** (of an ability) innate and difficult to modify: *fear is hard-wired into our brains*.

hardwood • *noun* **1** the wood from a deciduous broadleaf tree, as distinguished from that of conifers. **2** a tree producing such wood. • *adjective* **1** made of hardwood. **2** containing hardwoods: *hardwood forest*.

hard-working *adjective* diligent.

hardy *adjective* (**hardier**, **hardiest**) **1** robust; capable of enduring difficult conditions. **2** (of a plant) able to withstand winter in the open air.

Hare *noun* (plural **Hare** or **Hares**) **1** a member of a Dene Aboriginal group living along the north Mackenzie River. **2** the Athapaskan language of this people.

H

hare *noun* a fast-running, long-eared mammal resembling a large rabbit, with a short tail, tawny fur, and hind legs longer than forelegs. PHRASES **run with the hare and hunt with the hounds** try to remain on good terms with both sides.

harebell *noun* a plant with slender stems and pale-blue bell-shaped flowers.

hare-brained *adjective* crazy and unlikely to succeed: *a hare-brained idea.*

Hare Krishna *noun* **1** a sect devoted to the worship of the Hindu deity Krishna. **2** (*plural* **Hare Krishnas**) a member of this sect. [Say har ee KRISHNA]

harelip *noun* often *offensive* a congenital split in the upper lip. ▶ **harelipped** *adjective*

harem *noun* **1** (*hist.* or in conservative Muslim communities) **a** the women of a Muslim household, esp. the wives and concubines, living in a separate part of the house. **b** separate women's quarters designed for privacy and seclusion in a Muslim household. **2** a group of female animals sharing a mate. [Say HAIR um]

har har *interjection* expressing (esp. mirthless or disparaging) laughter.

hark *verb* (usu. in *imper.*) listen attentively. PHRASES **hark back** mention again or remember an earlier subject, event, etc.

harken *verb* listen: *the premier has harkened to cries that the GTA is in trouble.* PHRASES **harken back** mention again or remember an earlier subject, event, etc.

harlequin • *noun* (also **harlequin duck**) a small duck of northern coasts and rivers, the male having deep grey-blue plumage with chestnut and white markings. • *adjective* in varied colours; variegated. [Say HARLA quin]

harlot *noun* a prostitute or promiscuous woman. ▶ **harlotry** *noun* [Say HAR lut]

harm • *noun* **1** physical injury, esp. that which is inflicted on purpose. **2** material damage: *it's unlikely to do much harm to the engine.* **3** actual or potential ill effect or danger: *I can't see any harm in it.* • *verb* cause harm to. PHRASES **do more harm than good** make matters worse (despite good intentions). **out of harm's way** in safety.

harmattan *noun* a very dry, dusty wind on the West African coast, occurring from December to February. [Say har MAT un]

harmful *adjective* causing or likely to cause harm. ▶ **harmfully** *adverb* **harmfulness** *noun*

harmless *adjective* **1** not able or likely to cause harm. **2** inoffensive. ▶ **harmlessly** *adverb* **harmlessness** *noun*

harmonic • *adjective* of, relating to, or characterized by musical harmony: *a basic four-chord harmonic sequence*. • *noun Music* a higher and quieter note produced when another note is sung or played. [Say har MONN ick]

harmonica *noun* a small rectangular wind instrument with a row of metal reeds along its length, held against the lips and moved from side to side to produce different notes by blowing or sucking. [Say har MONICA]

harmonically *adverb* in terms of harmony: *the music is harmonically rich and diverse.* [Say har MONN ick lee]

harmonious *adjective* **1** sweet-sounding, tuneful. **2** forming a pleasing or consistent whole: *the decor is a harmonious blend of traditional and modern.* **3** free from disagreement or dissent: *Marcie wanted to build a harmonious relationship with her father.* ▶ **harmoniously** *adverb* [Say har MOANY us]

harmonium *noun* a keyboard instrument in which the notes are produced by air driven through metal reeds by bellows operated by the feet. [Say har MOANY um]

harmonization *noun* **1 a** the process of making things coordinated or consistent: *harmonization of rules*

among *the city's minor hockey leagues.* **b** the process of combining taxes, esp. (in Canada) the GST and the provincial sales tax in Nova Scotia, New Brunswick, and Newfoundland and Labrador. **2** *Music* the addition of notes to a melody to produce harmony.

harmonize *verb* (**harmonizes**, **harmonized**, **harmonizing**) **1** add notes to (a melody) to produce harmony. **2** (often foll. by *with*) bring into or be in harmony. **3** sing or play in harmony. **4** make or form a pleasing or consistent whole. **5** coordinate or make consistent.

harmonized sales tax *noun Cdn* a value-added tax on goods and services combining the GST and the provincial sales tax in Nova Scotia, New Brunswick, and Newfoundland and Labrador. Abbreviation: **HST**.

harmony *noun* (*plural* **harmonies**) **1 a** a combination of simultaneously sounded musical notes to produce chords and chord progressions, esp. as having a pleasing effect. **b** the study of this. **c** the parts of a harmonized piece of music other than the melody. **2** the quality of forming a pleasing or consistent whole: *delightful cities where new and old blend in harmony.* **3** agreement: *man and machine in perfect harmony.* PHRASES **in harmony 1** (of singing etc.) producing chords; not discordant. **2** (often foll. by *with*) in agreement.

harness • *noun* (*plural* **harnesses**) **1** the equipment of straps and fittings by which a horse or other draft animal is fastened to a cart etc. and controlled. **2** a similar arrangement for fastening a thing to a person's body, for restraining a young child, etc. • *verb* (**harnesses**, **harnessed**, **harnessing**) **1 a** put a harness on (esp. a horse). **b** (foll. by *to*) attach by a harness. **2** make use of (natural resources, esp. to produce energy. • *adjective* of or relating to harness racing: *harness driver*. PHRASES **in harness** in the routine of daily work.

harness race *noun* a type of horse race in which a horse pulls a two-wheeled vehicle and its driver with a trotting or pacing gait.

harness racing *noun* a form of racing in which a horse pulls a two-wheeled vehicle and its driver with a trotting or pacing gait.

harp • *noun* **1** a large upright roughly triangular musical instrument consisting of a frame housing a graduated series of vertical strings, played by plucking with the fingers. **2** (also **mouth harp**) *informal* a harmonica. • *verb* (foll. by *on*, *on about*) talk repeatedly and tediously about. ▶ **harpist** *noun*

harpoon • *noun* a barbed spearlike weapon with a rope attached, for hunting seals, whales etc. • *verb* spear with or as with a harpoon. ▶ **harpooner** *noun*

harp seal *noun* a seal with a harp-shaped dark mark on its back, of the northwest Atlantic and the Barents and White Seas.

harpsichord *noun* a keyboard instrument with horizontal strings which are plucked mechanically. ▶ **harpsichordist** *noun* [Say HARPSA cord]

harpy *noun* (*plural* **harpies**) **1** (in Greek and Roman mythology) a monster with a woman's head and body and bird's wings and claws. **2** a nagging unpleasant woman.

SPELL CHECK	
harass	ABC ✓
Warning: **harass** is spelled with only one *r*.	

harridan *noun* a bad-tempered woman. [Say HAIRA d'n]

harrier *noun* **1** a hound used for hunting hares. **2** a bird of prey with long wings for swooping over the ground.

H

harrow • *noun* a heavy frame with iron teeth dragged over plowed land to break up clods, remove weeds, cover seed, etc. • *verb* pull a harrow over (land). [Say HAIR oh]

harrowing *adjective* very shocking or frightening and disturbing: *a harrowing experience ◊ a harrowing film ◊ the book makes harrowing reading.* ▶ **harrowingly** *adverb*

harrumph (also **harumph**) • *verb* **1** clear the throat or make a similar sound, esp. in an ostentatious manner. **2** say gutturally, esp. expressing disapproval. • *interjection* expressing disapproval. • *noun* a guttural sound made by clearing the throat, expressing disapproval. [Say huh RUMF]

harry *verb* (**harries**, **harried**, **harrying**) **1** persistently carry out attacks on (an enemy or an enemy's territory): *they harried the retreating army.* **2** harass; annoy with repeated requests, questions, etc.: *the government is being mercilessly harried by the environmental lobby.*

harsh *adjective* **1** unpleasantly rough, sharp, or irritating, esp. to the senses. **2** severe, cruel. **3** physically disagreeable; bleak, stark: *harsh terrain.* ▶ **harshly** *adverb* **harshness** *noun*

hart *noun* the male of the European red deer, usu. over five years old.

harum-scarum *informal* • *adjective* wild and reckless: *a wild, harum-scarum youth.* • *adverb* in a wild and reckless manner: *Bjorn hurtled harum-scarum toward the finish line.* [Say hair um SCARE um]

harvest • *noun* **1 a** the process of gathering in crops etc. **b** the season when this takes place. **2** the season's yield or crop. • *verb* **1** gather (crops, timber, etc.) as a harvest. **2** kill or remove (wild animals) for food, sport, or population control: *harvest lobsters.* **3** remove (cells, tissues, organs) from a person or animal for transplants, experiments, or other purposes. ▶ **harvestable** *adjective* **harvester** *noun*

harvest excursion *noun* *Cdn hist.* a low-priced train trip for workers travelling to the West to harvest crops.

harvest moon *noun* the full moon nearest to the autumnal equinox.

harvest table *noun* a large rectangular wooden dining table.

has 3rd singular present of HAVE.

has-been *noun* *informal* a person or thing that has lost a former importance or usefulness.

hash¹ • *noun* (*plural* **hashes**) **1** a dish of cooked meat cut into small pieces and recooked, usu. with vegetables. **2 a** mixture; a jumble. **b** a mess. • *verb* (**hashes**, **hashed**, **hashing**) **1** cut (meat etc.) into small pieces; make into a hash. **2** (often foll. by *out, over*) *informal* talk over, discuss exhaustively. PHRASES **make a hash of** *informal* make a mess of; bungle. **settle a person's hash** *informal* deal with and subdue a person: *if he comes back here again I'll soon settle his hash!*

hash² *noun informal* hashish.

hash browns *plural noun* chopped boiled potatoes, often with onions, fried until brown.

hashish *noun* a resinous product of the top leaves and tender parts of hemp, smoked or chewed for its narcotic effects. [Say ha SHEESH or HASH eesh]

hash mark *noun* **1** the symbol #. **2** *Football* a short cross stripe on each five-yard line, 24 yards in from and parallel to each sideline, enclosing a central zone within which all plays must start. **3** *Hockey* one of four short lines on the edges of each faceoff circle.

Hasid *noun* (*plural* **Hasidim**) (also **Hassid**, *plural* **Hassidim**) a member of any of several mystical Jewish sects, esp. one founded in the 18th century. ▶ **Hasidic** *adjective* **Hasidism** *noun* [Say HASS id for the singular, HASS id im for the plural; huh SID ick, HASS id ism]

hasn't *contraction* has not.

hasp *noun* a hinged metal clasp that fits over a staple and can be secured by a padlock.

hassle *informal* • *noun* **1** a prolonged trouble or inconvenience. **2** an argument or involved struggle. • *verb* (**hassles**, **hassled**, **hassling**) **1** harass, annoy; cause trouble to. **2** argue, quarrel.

hast *archaic* 2nd singular present of HAVE.

haste *noun* **1** quickness or speed of motion or action, esp. as prompted by urgency or pressure. **2** quickness of action without due consideration; rashness. PHRASES **in haste** quickly, hurriedly. **make haste** hurry.

hasten *verb* **1** make haste; hurry: *she saw his frown and hastened to explain.* **2** cause to occur or be ready or be done sooner: *increasing contact with tourists threatens to hasten the erosion of the traditional Sami culture.*

hastily *adverb* in a rash or hurried manner: *Barb made her decision hastily, and now she regrets it.*

hasty *adjective* (**hastier**, **hastiest**) **1** hurried; acting quickly or hurriedly. **2** said, made, or done too quickly or too soon.

hat *noun* **1** a covering for the head, often with a brim and worn out of doors. **2** *informal* a person's occupation or capacity, esp. one of several: *wearing his managerial hat.* PHRASES **hat in hand** in a supplicating manner; obsequiously. **hats off** (as *interjection*; foll. by *to*) expressing admiration or appreciation. **keep it under one's hat** *informal* keep it secret. **out of a hat** by random selection. **pass the hat** collect contributions of money. **take off one's hat to** *informal* acknowledge admiration for. **throw** (**or toss**) **one's hat in the ring** take up a challenge.

hatband *noun* a band of ribbon etc. around a hat above the brim.

hatch¹ *noun* (*plural* **hatches**) **1 a** an opening in a door, floor, or ceiling of a building. **b** an opening in a wall between two rooms, esp. a kitchen and a dining area, through which dishes etc. are passed. **2** an opening or door in an aircraft, spacecraft, etc. **3 a** an opening in a ship's deck for lowering cargo into the hold. **b** a trap door or cover for this: *batten the hatches.* **4** the rear hinged door of a hatchback. PHRASES **down the hatch** *slang* (as a drinking toast) drink up, cheers!

hatch² • *verb* (**hatches**, **hatched**, **hatching**) **1 a** (of a young bird or fish etc.) emerge from the egg. **b** (of an egg) produce a young animal. **2** incubate (an egg). **3** devise (a plot etc.). • *noun* (*plural* **hatches**) a newly hatched brood.

hatch³ *verb* (**hatches**, **hatched**, **hatching**) mark (a surface, e.g. a map or drawing) with close parallel lines.

hatchback *noun* **1** a car with a sloping back hinged at the top to form a door. **2** such a hinged door.

hatchery *noun* (*plural* **hatcheries**) a place for hatching eggs, esp. of fish or poultry.

hatchet *noun* **1** a light short-handled axe. **2** a tomahawk.

hatchet job *noun* *informal* a fierce verbal attack on a person, esp. in print.

hatchetman *noun* (*plural* **hatchetmen**) *informal* **1** a hired killer. **2** a harsh or vindictive critic. **3** a person employed to carry out unpleasant tasks, e.g. reducing staff etc.

hatching *noun* close parallel lines forming shading esp. on a map or an architectural drawing.

hatchling *noun* a bird or fish that has just hatched.

hatchway *noun* = HATCH¹ 3a.

hate • *verb* (**hates**, **hated**, **hating**) **1** feel hatred or intense dislike toward. **2** *informal* **a** dislike. **b** be reluctant (to do something): *I hate to disturb you.* • *noun* **1** hatred; intense dislike. **2** *informal* a hated person or

thing. **3** (as an *adjective*) motivated by sexual, racial, or other forms of intolerance: *hate literature*.

hateful *adjective* **1** arousing hatred. **2** full of hatred: *a hateful diatribe*. ▶ **hatefulness** *noun*

hate mail *noun* letters sent (usu. anonymously) in which the sender expresses hostility toward the recipient.

hate-monger *noun* a person who promotes hatred and intolerance against an identifiable group. ▶ **hate-mongering** *noun*

hater *noun* (often in *combination*) a person who hates esp. the sort of person or thing described.

hatful *noun* (*plural* **hatfuls**) **1** a considerable amount: *Steffi had a hatful of stories to tell us about her trip.* **2** the amount of something that can fill a hat.

hath *archaic 3rd singular present of* HAVE.

hatless *adjective* not wearing a hat.

hatpin *noun* a long pin, often decorative, for securing a hat to the head.

hatred *noun* intense dislike or ill will.

hatted *adjective* (usu. in *combination*) wearing a hat, esp. the kind or colour of hat described.

hatter *noun* a maker or seller of hats. PHRASES **mad as a hatter** wildly eccentric.

hat trick *noun* **1** the scoring of three goals, points etc. by one person during a game. **2** three successes.

Haudenausanee *noun & adjective* (*plural* **Haudenausanee** or **Haudenausanees**) = IROQUOIS. [Say hodda nuh SAWN ee]

haughtily *adverb* in an arrogant or superior manner. [Say HOTTA lee]

haughtiness *noun* arrogance and disdain. [Say HOT ee niss]

haughty *adjective* (**haughtier**, **haughtiest**) arrogantly self-admiring and disdainful. [Say HOTTY]

haul • *verb* **1** pull or drag forcibly. **2** transport by truck, cart, etc. **3 a** draw (a net) through water to catch fish. **b** lift (fish) in a net or on a line to the surface. **4** (usu. foll. by *into*, *up*) *informal* bring for reprimand or trial. • *noun* **1 a** an amount gained or acquired. **b** the quantity of fish caught in one draft of the net. **2** a distance to be traversed: *a short haul*. PHRASES **haul off** *informal* **1** withdraw a little in preparation: *he hauled off and hit me*. **2** leave, depart. **haul out 1** take or drag out. **2** (of seals and walruses) come out of the water to rest on the rocky slopes of the shore.

haulage *noun* **1** the commercial transport of goods. **2** a charge for this. [Say HAUL idge]

haulback *noun* Forestry a lighter line for drawing a cable back to its original position after it has been used to move a log away.

hauler *noun* **1** a person or thing that hauls. **2** a person or firm engaged in the transport of goods.

hauling *noun* the process of transporting logs from the cutting area to the mill or shipping point.

haulout *noun* **1** the action of hauling a boat out of water. **2** a place along the shore where marine mammals haul out.

haunch *noun* (*plural* **haunches**) **1** (often in *plural*) fleshy part of the buttock with the thigh. **2** the leg and loin of a deer etc. as food.

haunt • *verb* **1** (of a ghost) visit (a place) regularly, usu. reputedly giving signs of its presence. **2** (of a person or animal) frequent or be persistently in (a place). **3** (of a memory etc.) return repeatedly to the mind of, esp. in a distressing manner. **4** (of an action, a phenomenon, etc.) cause difficulty or problems to (a person, organization, etc.), usu. long after the fact: *that letter will come back to haunt you.* • *noun* **1** (often in *plural*) a

place frequented by a person. **2** a place frequented by animals, esp. for food and drink.

haunted *adjective* **1** frequented by a ghost: *a haunted house.* **2** troubled, world-weary: *a haunted face.*

haunting • *adjective* (of a memory, melody, etc.) poignant, wistful, evocative. • *noun* a visitation by a ghost. ▶ **hauntingly** *adverb*

Hausa • *noun* (*plural* **Hausa** or **Hausas**) **1 a** a people of West Africa and the Sudan. **b** a member of this people. **2** the Hamitic language of this people, widely used in West Africa. • *adjective* of or relating to this people or language. [Say HOW suh or HOW zuh]

haute *adjective* upper-class, elegant, prestigious: *haute cuisine*. [Say OAT or HOAT]

hauteur *noun* haughtiness of manner: *there's no celebrity hauteur about him.* [Say owe TUR]

Havana *noun* (also **Havana cigar**) a cigar made at Havana or elsewhere in Cuba. [Say huh VANNA]

havarti *noun* a mild, semi-soft Danish cheese with small irregular holes. [Say huh VARTY]

GRAMMAR CHECK
could/should/would have

Use **have**, not **of**, in expressions like **might have**, **could have**, **would have**, and **should have**: *I should have been more careful* (not *I should of been more careful*).

---

have • *verb* (**has**, **had**, **having**) • *verb* **1** possess, own, or hold. **2** experience; undergo: *have difficulty.* **3** be able to make use of. **4** perform the action indicated by the noun specified: *he had a look around.* **5** demonstrate (a personal attribute). **6** suffer from (an illness or disability). **7** cause to be in a particular state. **8** cause to be done for one by someone else. **9** place, hold, or keep in a particular position. **10** be the recipient or host of. **11** eat or drink. **12** tolerate. • *auxiliary verb* used with a past participle to form the perfect, pluperfect, and future perfect tenses, and the conditional mood. • *noun* (in *plural*) *informal* people with plenty of money etc.: *the haves and the have nots.* PHRASES **be had** *informal* be cheated or deceived. **had better** would find it prudent to. **have got to** *informal* = HAVE TO. **have had it** *informal* **1** have missed one's chance. **2** be no longer useful or appropriate: *these old boots have had it.* **3** have been killed, defeated, etc. **4** be tired or fed up with: *I've had it with your excuses!* **have it 1** (foll. by *that* + clause) express the view that. **2** win a decision in a vote etc. **3** *informal* have found the answer etc. **have it coming** can expect unpleasant consequences to follow. **have it in for** *informal* be hostile or ill-disposed toward. **have it out** (often foll. by *with*) *informal* attempt to settle a dispute by discussion or argument. **have on 1** be wearing (clothes). **2** be committed to (an engagement). **3** *informal* tease, play a trick on. **have out** get (a tooth etc.) extracted: *had her tonsils out.* **have something (or nothing) on a person 1** know something (or nothing) discreditable or incriminating about a person. **2** have an (or no) advantage or superiority over a person. **have to** be obliged to, must. **have up** *informal* bring (a person) before a court of justice, interviewer, etc.

haven *noun* **1** a harbour or port. **2** a place of refuge: *the hotel is a haven of peace and tranquility* ◊ *the river banks are a haven for wildlife* ◊ *the camp offers a haven to refugees.* [Say HAY v'n]

have-not *noun* (usu. in *plural*) *informal* a person etc. lacking wealth or resources.

have-not province *noun* Cdn a province whose per capita tax revenue falls below a certain average level

and which is therefore entitled to receive equalization payments from the federal government.

haven't *contraction* have not.

have province *noun Cdn* a province whose per capita tax revenue exceeds a certain average level and which does not therefore receive equalization payments from the federal government.

havoc *noun* widespread destruction; great confusion or disorder. PHRASES **play havoc with** *informal* cause great confusion or difficulty to. **wreak havoc** devastate, cause damage to. [Say HAVE ick]

haw¹ *noun* the hawthorn or its fruit.

haw² *noun* a transparent eyelid of horses, dogs, etc., esp. when inflamed.

haw³ • *interjection* expressing hesitation. PHRASES **hum and haw** hesitate, esp. in speaking.

Hawaiian • *noun* **1 a** a native of Hawaii, a group of 20 islands in the N Pacific. **b** a person of Hawaiian descent. **2** the Malayo-Polynesian language of Hawaii. • *adjective* **1** of or relating to Hawaii or its people or language. **2** (of pizza) garnished with ham and pineapple. [Say huh WHY in]

Hawaiian guitar *noun* a steel-stringed instrument, usu. held horizontally, in which a characteristic glissando effect is produced by sliding a metal bar along the strings as they are plucked.

Hawaiian shirt *noun* a brightly coloured and gaily patterned shirt.

haw haw *interjection* used to represent the sound of a loud or boisterous laugh.

SPELL CHECK
hawk, hock

To deposit an item with a pawnbroker is to **hock** it. The joint of an animal's hind leg is the **hock**.

hawk¹ • *noun* **1** a bird of prey with a characteristic curved beak, broad rounded wings, and a long tail. **2** *Politics* a person who advocates an aggressive or warlike policy, esp. in foreign affairs. • *verb* hunt game with a hawk. PHRASES **watch like a hawk** watch intently and unceasingly.

hawk² *verb* carry about or offer around (goods) for sale.

hawk³ *verb* **1** clear the throat noisily. **2** (foll. by *up*) bring (phlegm etc.) up from the throat.

hawker *noun* a person who travels about selling goods.

hawkish *adjective Politics* preferring aggressive policies or the use of military action rather than peaceful means in order to resolve a dispute. ►**hawkishly** *adverb* **hawkishness** *noun*

hawk moth *noun* a darting and hovering moth with narrow forewings and a stout body.

hawkweed *noun* a plant of the daisy family, which typically has yellow or orange dandelion-like flowers and often grows as a weed.

hawse *noun* **1** the part of a ship's bows containing holes through which a cable or anchor rope passes. **2** the space between the head of an anchored vessel and the anchors. [Say HOZZ]

hawser *noun* a thick rope or cable for mooring or towing a ship. [Say HOZZER]

hawthorn *noun* a thorny shrub or tree of the rose family, with white, red, or pink blossoms and small dark red fruit.

hay • *noun* grass, clover, alfalfa, etc., cut and dried for animal fodder. • *verb* make hay. PHRASES **hit the hay** *informal* go to bed. **make hay** (**while the sun shines**) seize opportunities for profit or enjoyment.

SPELL CHECK
heyday

Warning: the first part of *heyday* is spelled with an *e*.

hayfever *noun* an allergic reaction to the airborne pollen of grasses or other plants, manifested in summer and causing sneezing, nasal congestion, watery eyes, and in some cases asthmatic symptoms.

hayfield *noun* a field where hay is being or is to be made.

haying *noun* the activity of making grass etc. into hay: *haying equipment* ◊ *haying season.*

haylage *noun* animal feed made from grass etc. which has been partially dried and then preserved in a silo. [Say HAY lidge]

hayloft *noun* = LOFT *noun* 2.

haymaker *noun* **1** a person who tosses and spreads hay to dry after mowing. **2** an apparatus for shaking and drying hay. **3** *slang* a forceful blow or punch. ►**haymaking** *noun*

haymow *noun* **1** hay stored in a stack or barn. **2** the part of a barn for the storage of hay. [Say HAY mow (with mow rhyming either with *WOW* or with *BLOW*)]

hay privilege *noun Cdn* (*Man.*) *hist.* **1** the right of Red River settlers to cut hay on the uncultivated land lying behind each river lot. **2** the land to which this right pertained.

hayride *noun* a pleasure ride in an open wagon etc. filled with hay or straw.

hayseed *noun* **1** grass seed obtained from hay. **2** *informal* a rustic or yokel.

haystack *noun* a packed pile of hay with a pointed or ridged top.

haywire *noun* wire for binding bales of hay, straw, etc. PHRASES **go haywire** go wrong; become confused or crazy.

hazard • *noun* **1** a danger or risk. **2** a source of this. **3** *Golf* an obstruction in playing a shot, e.g. a bunker, water, etc. **4** (in *plural*) (also **hazard lights**) flashing lights on a vehicle (usu. the turn signals operating simultaneously) warning that the vehicle is stationary or slowing or reversing unexpectedly. • *verb* **1** venture on; suggest tentatively: *hazard a guess.* **2** run the risk of. **3** expose to danger; risk.

hazardous *adjective* risky, dangerous. ►**hazardously** *adverb* **hazardousness** *noun*

hazardous waste *noun* toxic or radioactive waste materials that could be harmful to the environment, created as by-products of industrial manufacturing or the generation of nuclear power.

haze¹ *noun* **1** obscuration of the atmosphere near the earth by fine particles of water, smoke, or dust. **2** mental obscurity or confusion.

haze² *verb* (**hazes**, **hazed**, **hazing**) subject (new students etc.) to abuse and ridicule as an initiation.

hazel • *noun* **1** a shrub or small tree with broad leaves, bearing round brown edible nuts. **2** wood from the hazel. **3** a golden-brown or greenish-brown colour (esp. of the eyes). • *adjective* (esp. of the eyes) of a golden-brown or greenish-brown colour.

hazelnut *noun* the fruit of the hazel.

hazily *adverb* **1** in a vague or indistinct manner: *the issue is hazily defined.* **2** in a confused or uncertain manner: *he stared hazily at the horse in his swimming pool.*

haziness *noun* a vague or uncertain quality.

hazy *adjective* (**hazier**, **haziest**) **1** misty. **2** vague, indistinct. **3** confused, uncertain.

HB *abbreviation* hard black (pencil lead).

Hb *symbol* hemoglobin.

HBC *abbreviation Cdn* Hudson's Bay Company.

H-bomb *noun* = HYDROGEN BOMB.

HC *abbreviation* House of Commons.

HCFC *abbreviation* (*plural* **HCFCs**) hydrochlorofluorocarbon (similar to CFC but thought to be less harmful to the ozone layer).

HDL *abbreviation* (*plural* **HDLs**) HIGH-DENSITY LIPOPROTEIN.

HDTV *abbreviation* high-definition television.

He *symbol* helium.

WRITING TIP

he

The use of **he** to refer to a person of unspecified sex, as in *Every child needs to know that he is loved*, is often criticized as sexist. Suitable alternatives include *Every child needs to know that he or she is loved* and *All children need to know that they are loved*. In sentences in which **he** appears after **everyone**, **anyone**, or **someone**, as in *Everyone can do whatever he likes*, **he** can again be replaced by **he or she**, *Everyone can do whatever he or she likes*, although this option sometimes results in sentences that are long or awkward. Another possibility is to use **they**: *Everyone can do whatever they like*. This use of **they** may be considered incorrect by some, however; see usage note at THEY.

---

he • *pronoun* **1** the man or boy or male animal previously named or in question. **2** a person etc. of unspecified sex, esp. referring to one already named or identified: *if anyone comes he will have to wait*. • *noun* **1** a male; a man. **2** (in *combination*) male: *he-goat*.

head • *noun* **1** the part of a human's or an animal's body, containing the brain, mouth, and sense organs. **2** the head regarded as the seat of intellect or repository of information. **3** *informal* a headache, esp. resulting from a blow or from intoxication. **4** a thing like a head in form or position, esp.: **a** the part of a tool, weapon, golf club, etc. used to strike with **b** the flattened top of a nail. **c** the ornamented top of a pillar. **d** a mass of leaves or flowers at the top of a stem. **e** the flat end of a drum. **f** the foam on top of a glass of beer etc. **g** the upper horizontal part of a window frame, door frame, etc. **h** = SHOWER HEAD. **5** life when regarded as vulnerable: *it cost him his head*. **6 a** a person in charge; a director or leader. **b** a position of leadership or command. **7** the front or forward part of something, e.g. a procession. **8** the upper end of something, e.g. a table or bed. **9** the top or highest part of something, e.g. a page, stairs, etc. **10** a person or individual regarded as a numerical unit: *$10 per head*. **11** (*plural* **head**) **a** an individual animal as a unit. **b** (as *plural*) a number of cattle or game as specified: *20 head*. **12 a** the side of a coin bearing the image of a head. **b** (usu. in *plural*) this side as a choice when tossing a coin. **13 a** the source of a river, stream etc. **b** the end of a lake, bay, etc. at which a river enters it. **14** the height or length of a head as a measure: *his horse won by a head*. **15** the component of a machine that is in contact with or very close to what is being processed or worked on, esp.: **a** the component on a tape recorder that touches the moving tape in play and converts the signals. **b** = PRINTHEAD. **16 a** a confined body of water or steam in an engine etc. **b** the pressure exerted by this. **17** a promontory (esp. in place names). **18** a culmination, climax, or crisis. **19** the fully developed top of a boil etc. • *adjective* chief or principal: *head office*. • *verb* **1** be at the head or front of. **2** (often foll. by *up*) be in charge of. **3 a** provide with a head or heading. **b** (of an inscription, title, etc.) be at the top of, serve as a heading for. **4 a** (often foll. by *for*) face or move in a specified direction or toward a specified result: *is*

heading for trouble. **b** direct in a specified direction. **5** *Soccer* strike (the ball) with the head. PHRASES **above** (**or over**) **one's head** beyond one's ability to understand. **bang one's head against a wall** *informal* be frustrated in an attempt to do something. **come to a head 1** (of a boil etc.) suppurate. **2** reach a crisis or climax. **give a person his or her head** allow a person to act freely. **go to one's head 1** (of liquor) make one dizzy or slightly drunk. **2** (of success) make one conceited. **have one's head (screwed) on straight** be sensible. **head and shoulders** *informal* by a considerable amount. **head back** return home etc. **head in the sand** refusal to acknowledge an obvious danger or difficulty. **head off 1** get ahead of so as to intercept and turn aside. **2** forestall. **head over heels 1** turning over completely in forward motion as in a somersault etc. **2** topsy-turvy. **3** utterly, completely. **heads will roll** *informal* people will be disgraced or dismissed. **head to head** in direct competition or conflict. **hold up one's head** be confident or unashamed. **in one's head 1** in one's thoughts or imagination. **2** by mental process without use of physical aids. **keep one's head** remain calm. **keep one's head above water** *informal* **1** keep out of debt. **2** avoid succumbing to difficulties. **keep one's head down** *informal* remain inconspicuous in difficult or dangerous times. **lose one's head** lose self-control; panic. **make head(s) or tail(s) of** (usu. with *neg.* or *interrog.*) understand at all. **off one's head** *slang* crazy. **off the top of one's head** *informal* impromptu; without careful thought or investigation. **one's head off** noisily or excessively: *laughed his head off*. **on one's** (or **one's own**) **head** as one's sole responsibility. **out of one's head 1** *slang* crazy or delirious. **2** from one's imagination or memory. **over one's head 1** beyond one's ability to understand. **2** without one's knowledge or involvement, esp. when one has a right to this. **3** with disregard for one's own (stronger) claim: *was promoted over their heads*. **put heads together** consult together. **put into a person's head** suggest to a person. **turn a person's head** make a person conceited. **turn heads** cause people to notice.

headache *noun* **1** a continuous pain in the head. **2** *informal* **a** a worrying problem. **b** a troublesome person. ▶ **headachy** *adjective*

headband *noun* a band worn around the head as decoration or to keep the hair off the face.

headbanger *noun* *slang* a fan of heavy metal music.

headbanging *noun* vigorous head-shaking in time to heavy metal music.

headboard *noun* an upright panel forming or placed behind the head of a bed etc.

head-butt • *noun* a forceful thrust with the top of the head into the chin or body of another person. • *verb* attack (another person) with a head-butt.

head case *noun* *informal* a mentally ill or unstable person.

headcheese *noun* a jellied preparation from chopped meat from a boiled pig's head.

headdress *noun* (*plural* **headdresses**) an ornamental covering or band for the head.

headed *combining form* having the kind of head described: *a fuzzy-headed baby* ◊ *a flat-headed nail*.

header *noun* **1** *Soccer* a shot or pass made with the head. **2** *informal* a headlong fall or dive. **3** a line or block of text appearing at the top of each page of a document etc. (compare FOOTER 2). **4** a brick or stone laid at right angles to the face of a wall (compare STRETCHER 2). **5** a beam crossing and supporting the ends of joists, studs, or rafters.

headfirst • *adverb* **1** with the head foremost.

2 without thinking carefully before acting: *rushed headfirst into marriage*. • *adjective* with the head foremost.

headgear *noun* **1 a** something worn on the head, as a hat, cap, or headdress. **b** a protective covering for the head, as a helmet. **2** machinery etc. at the top of a mine shaft. **3** the parts of a harness around a horse's head. **4** orthodontic equipment worn on the head and attached to braces on the teeth.

headhunt *verb* find and recruit skilled personnel to work for a company, esp. by enticing them to leave their present jobs with promises of better salaries or benefits and higher status in the company.

headhunter *noun* **1** an agency or agent specializing in recruiting skilled staff for an organization etc. **2** a member of a tribe that collects the heads of dead enemies as trophies. ▶ **headhunting** *noun*

heading *noun* **1 a** a title at the head of a page or section of a book etc. **b** a division or section of a subject of discourse etc. **2** the extension of the top of a curtain above the tape that carries the hooks or the pocket for a wire. **3** the course of an aircraft, ship, etc.

headlamp *noun* **1** = HEADLIGHT. **2** a small lamp attached to a hat or worn strapped to the forehead.

headland *noun* a promontory.

headless *adjective* without a head.

head lettuce *noun* lettuce having tightly clustered, usu. pale leaves forming a round compact head.

headlight *noun* **1** a strong light at the front of a motor vehicle or railway engine. **2** the beam from this.

headline • *noun* **1** a heading at the top of an article or page, esp. in a newspaper. **2** (in *plural*) the most important items of news in a newspaper or broadcast news bulletin. • *verb* (**headlines**, **headlined**, **headlining**) **1** give a headline to. **2** appear as the chief performer (at). PHRASES **hit** (or **make**) **the headlines** *informal* be given prominent attention as news.

headliner *noun* a headlining performer; a star.

headlock *noun* a hold with an arm around the opponent's head.

headlong *adverb & adjective* **1** with the head foremost. **2** in a rush.

headman • *noun* (*plural* **headmen**) the chief man of a village, tribe etc. • *verb* (**headmans**, **headmanned**, **headmanning**) *Hockey* pass (the puck) to a team member who is closer to the opposing team's net.

headmaster *noun* the principal in charge of a school.

headmistress *noun* (*plural* **headmistresses**) a woman principal in charge of a school.

head of hair *noun* the hair on a person's head, esp. as a distinctive feature.

head of state *noun* (*plural* **heads of state**) the title of the head of a state, usu. the leader of the ruling party or a monarch.

head-on *adjective & adverb* **1** with the front foremost: *a head-on crash* ◊ *hit us head-on*. **2** in direct confrontation.

headphone *noun* (usu. in *plural*) a pair of earphones joined by a band placed over the head, for listening to audio equipment etc.

headpiece *noun* any covering for the head, esp. a decorative one worn by a bride.

headpond *noun* *Cdn* (*Maritimes*) a pond created behind a dam.

headquarter *verb* provide with headquarters (at a specific location): *a consulting firm headquartered in Waterloo*.

headquarters *noun* (as *singular* or *plural*) **1** the administrative centre of an organization. **2** the

premises occupied by a military commander and the commander's staff.

headrest *noun* a support for the head attached to a dentist's chair, the seat of a motor vehicle, etc.

headroom *noun* **1** the space above a driver's or passenger's head in a vehicle, between a person's head and a doorway, ceiling, etc. **2** the space or clearance between the top of a vehicle and the underside of a bridge etc. which it passes under.

head scarf *noun* (*plural* **head scarves**) a scarf worn around the head and tied under the chin.

headset *noun* a set of headphones, often with a microphone attached, used esp. in telephone and radio communication.

headship *noun* the position of chief or leader: *preached about male headship being God's will*.

head shop *noun* *slang* a store selling drug paraphernalia.

headspace *noun* **1** space left in the top of a jar, bottle, etc. to allow room for expansion of contents. **2** *slang* mindset, attitude: *when I'm here, I'm in a totally different headspace from the modern world*.

headstand *noun* a movement in which one balances on one's head and puts one's legs straight up in the air.

head start *noun* an advantage granted or gained at an early stage.

headstone *noun* a (usu. inscribed) stone set up at the head of a grave.

headstrong *adjective* self-willed and obstinate.

heads-up *informal* • *noun* a warning: *gave them a heads-up*. • *adjective* alert, perceptive: *a heads-up baseball player*. • *interjection* (**heads up**) look out!

head table *noun* a table at a wedding, conference, etc. where the guests of honour sit.

head tax *noun* (*plural* **head taxes**) a tax levied esp. on new immigrants to a country.

head-to-head • *adjective* involving two parties confronting each other. • *adverb* confronting another party.

head waiter *noun* a waiter who supervises other waiters, busboys, etc.

headwater *noun* (in *singular* or *plural*) streams flowing from the sources of a river.

headway *noun* **1** progress. **2** the rate of progress of a ship. **3** = HEADROOM.

headwind *noun* a wind blowing from directly in front.

headword *noun* a word forming a heading, e.g. of an entry in a dictionary.

heady *adjective* (**headier**, **headiest**) **1** (of liquor) potent, intoxicating. **2** affecting the senses strongly: *a heady aroma*. **3** exhilarating: *the heady days of youth*.

SPELL CHECK
heal, heel

Part of the foot is the **heel**. Dogs are taught to **heel**. A leaning boat is said to **heel**. Someone who behaves inconsiderately is a **heel**.

---

heal *verb* **1** (of a wound or injury) become sound or healthy again. **2** cause (a wound, disease, or person) to heal or be cured, or be made sound again. **3** repair, correct (an undesirable condition, esp. a breach of relations); put right (differences etc.). **4** alleviate (sorrow etc.). **5** recover from mental trauma.

healer *noun* **1** a person who heals others, esp. a faith healer. **2** a thing which heals or assists in healing.

healing • *noun* **1** the process of becoming or making someone healthy again. **2** the process of recovering from an emotional shock. • *adjective* that helps something or someone to heal: *a healing ointment* ◊ *the healing forces of nature*.

health *noun* **1** the state of being well in body or mind: *he was restored to health.* **2** a person's mental or physical condition: *retired because of bad health.* **3** soundness, esp. financial or moral. **4** a toast drunk in someone's honour.

health card *noun* *Cdn* a card identifying a person as eligible to receive medical treatment paid for by a public insurance plan.

health care *noun* the maintenance and improvement of health, esp. as administered by organized medical services and facilities.

health food *noun* natural food eaten for its health-giving qualities.

healthful *adjective* conducive to good health; beneficial. ▸ **healthfulness** *noun*

healthily *adverb* in a way that promotes or demonstrates good health: *I'm trying to eat healthily.*

healthiness *noun* **1** a state of good health. **2** the quality of being good for one's health.

health plan *noun* a medical insurance plan, either one provided by a government or one offered as an employment benefit.

healthy *adjective* (**healthier, healthiest**) **1** having, showing, or promoting good health. **2** beneficial, helpful: *a healthy respect for experience.* **3** ample, considerable: *a healthy portion.* **4** (of a business etc.) sound, functioning well.

heap • *noun* **1 a** a collection of things lying haphazardly one on another. **b** a mass of something in an untidy pile: *she collapsed in a heap on the floor.* **2** (esp. in *plural*) *informal* a large number or amount: *there's heaps of time.* **3** *slang* an old or dilapidated thing, esp. a motor vehicle or building. • *verb* **1** collect or be collected in a heap. **2** load copiously or to excess. **3** accord or offer copiously to: *heaped insults on them.*

heaping *adjective* (of a spoonful etc.) with the contents piled above the brim.

hear *verb* (**hears, heard, hearing**) **1** perceive (sound etc.) with the ear. **2** listen to: *heard them on the radio.* **3** listen judicially to and judge (a case, plaintiff, etc.). **4** be told or informed. **5** (foll. by *from*) be contacted by, esp. by letter or telephone. **6** be ready to obey (an order): *you're not going out — do you hear me?* **7** grant (a prayer). PHRASES **be unable to hear oneself think** be unable to think clearly because of the noise. **have heard of** be aware of. **hear a pin drop** hear the slightest noise. **hear! hear!** *interjection* expressing agreement (esp. with something said in a speech). **hear a person out** listen to all that a person says. **hear tell** be informed. **will not hear of** will not allow or agree to. ▸ **hearable** *adjective* **hearer** *noun*

hearing *noun* **1** the faculty of perceiving sounds. **2** the range within which sounds may be heard; earshot: *within hearing.* **3** the action or an act of listening. **4** an opportunity to state one's case: *give them a fair hearing.* **5** the listening to evidence and pleadings in a law court or other officially constituted body.

hearing aid *noun* a small device to amplify sound, worn by a partially deaf person in or behind the ear.

hearing ear dog *noun* (also **hearing dog**) a dog trained to guide a deaf person.

hearken *verb* = HARKEN. [Say HARK'n]

hearsay *noun* rumour, gossip.

hearse *noun* a vehicle for conveying the coffin at a funeral. [Rhymes with *PURSE*]

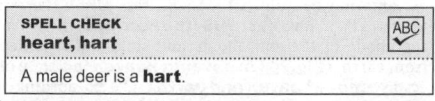

SPELL CHECK ABC

heart, hart

A male deer is a **hart**.

heart *noun* **1** a hollow muscular organ maintaining the circulation of blood by rhythmic contraction and dilation. **2** the region of the heart; the breast. **3** the heart regarded as the centre of thought, feeling, and emotion (esp. love). **4 a** courage or enthusiasm: *lose heart.* **b** one's mood or feeling: *change of heart.* **5 a** the central or innermost part of something. **b** the vital part or essence: *the heart of the matter.* **6** the close compact head of a cabbage, lettuce, etc. **7 a** a heart-shaped thing. **b** a conventional representation of a heart with two equal curves meeting at a point at the bottom and a cusp at the top. **8 a** a playing card of a suit denoted by a red figure of a heart. **b** (in *plural*) this suit. **c** (in *plural*) a card game in which players avoid taking tricks containing a card of this suit. **9** a beloved person: *dear heart.* PHRASES **after one's own heart** such as one likes or desires. **at heart 1** in one's innermost feelings. **2** basically, essentially. **break a person's heart** overwhelm a person with sorrow, esp. by ending a romantic relationship. **by heart** in or from memory. **close** (or **near**) **to one's heart 1** dear to one. **2** affecting one deeply. **from the heart** (or **the bottom of one's heart**) sincerely, profoundly. **give** (or **lose**) **one's heart** fall in love (with). **have a heart** be merciful. **have the heart** be insensitive or hard-hearted enough: *didn't have the heart to ask him.* **have** (or **put**) **one's heart in** be keenly involved in or committed to (an enterprise etc.). **have one's heart in one's mouth** be greatly alarmed or apprehensive. **have one's heart in the right place** be sincere or well-intentioned. **heart and soul** (with) all one's energies and affections. **heart of gold** a generous nature. **heart of stone** a stern or cruel nature. **hearts and minds** emotional and intellectual support. **heart to heart** candidly, intimately. **in one's heart of hearts** in one's innermost feelings. **sing** (or **play** etc.) **one's heart out** sing or play etc. to the fullest extent of one's ability. **take to heart** be much affected or distressed by. **wear one's heart on one's sleeve** make one's feelings apparent. **with all one's heart** sincerely; with all goodwill. **with one's whole heart** without doubts or reservations.

heartache *noun* mental anguish or grief.

heart attack *noun* a sudden occurrence of coronary thrombosis usu. resulting in the death of part of a heart muscle.

heartbeat *noun* **1** a pulsation of the heart. **2** the central or most important part or place: *the heartbeat of the nation.* PHRASES **in a heartbeat** in a very brief space of time.

heartbreak *noun* overwhelming sorrow or distress. ▸ **heartbreaker** *noun* **heartbreaking** *adjective* **heartbreakingly** *adverb* **heartbroken** *adjective*

heartburn *noun* a burning sensation in the chest resulting from indigestion.

-hearted *combining form* **1** having or showing the kind of feelings or character described, esp. in terms of one's ability to feel compassion for others: *kind-hearted gentleman ◊ a cold-hearted criminal.* **2** having or showing the attitude described, esp. in terms of courage or seriousness: *a light-hearted joke ◊ this movie is not for the faint-hearted.*

hearten *verb* make or become more cheerful. ▸ **heartening** *adjective* **hearteningly** *adverb*

heart failure *noun* a severe failure of the heart to function properly, esp. as a cause of death.

heartfelt *adjective* sincere; deeply felt.

hearth *noun* **1 a** the floor of a fireplace. **b** the area in front of a fireplace. **2** this symbolizing the home. **3** the bottom of a blast furnace where molten metal collects. PHRASES **hearth and home** the home and its comforts. [Say HARTH]

H

heartily *adverb* **1** in a hearty manner; with goodwill, appetite, or courage. **2** very; to a great degree (esp. with reference to personal feelings): *am heartily sick of it*.

heartiness *noun* **1** strength, vigour, spirit: *hymns sung with great heartiness*. **2** the large size of a meal or one's appetite. **3** warmth and sincerity of feelings.

heartland *noun* the central or most important part of an area.

heartless *adjective* unfeeling, pitiless. ▶ **heartlessly** *adverb* **heartlessness** *noun*

heart-lung machine *noun* a machine that temporarily takes over the functions of the heart and lungs, esp. in surgery.

heart rate *noun* the pulse, calculated by counting the number of beats of the heart per unit of time.

heart-rending *adjective* causing great sorrow or distress. ▶ **heart-rendingly** *adverb*

heart-searching *noun* the thorough examination of one's own feelings and motives.

heartsick *adjective* very sad.

heart-stopper *noun* a book or movie etc. that is very suspenseful or thrilling.

heart-stopping *adjective* very suspenseful or thrilling.

heartstrings *plural noun* one's deepest feelings or emotions.

heartthrob *noun* **1** *informal* an extremely attractive (usu. male) person, esp. an actor or other celebrity. **2** beating of the heart.

heart-to-heart • *adjective* (of a conversation etc.) candid, intimate. • *noun* a candid or personal conversation.

heartwarming *adjective* emotionally rewarding or uplifting. ▶ **heartwarmingly** *adverb*

heartwood *noun* the dense inner part of a tree trunk yielding the hardest timber.

heartworm *noun* **1** a parasitic nematode worm which infests the hearts of dogs. **2** the disease due to infestation by heartworm.

hearty • *adjective* (**heartier**, **heartiest**) **1** loudly vigorous and cheerful: *her laugh was far too hearty to be genuine*. **2** (of a meal or appetite) large. **3** warm, friendly: *a hearty welcome*. **4** heartfelt, genuine, sincere: *hearty congratulations to everyone involved* ◊ *a hearty dislike of office politics*. • *noun* (*plural* **hearties**) (usu. in *plural*) (as a form of address) fellows, esp. fellow sailors.

heat • *noun* **1 a** the condition of being hot. **b** the sensation or perception of this. **c** high temperature of the body. **2** *Physics* **a** a form of energy arising from the random motion of the molecules of bodies, which may be transferred by conduction, convection, or radiation. **b** the amount of this needed to cause a specific process, or given off in a process. **3** hot weather: *succumbed to the heat*. **4 a** warmth of feeling. **b** anger or excitement: *the heat of the argument*. **5** (foll. by *of*) the most intense part or period of an activity: *in the heat of the battle*. **6** a (usu. preliminary or trial) round in a race or contest. **7** the receptive period of the sexual cycle, esp. in female mammals: *in heat*. **8** spiciness. **9** *slang* intensive pursuit, e.g. by the police. **10** *slang* adverse criticism; blame. • *verb* (often foll. by *up*) **1** make or become hot or warm. **2** inflame; excite or intensify. PHRASES **in the heat of the moment** during or resulting from intense activity, without pause for thought. **turn the heat on** *informal* concentrate an attack or criticism on (a person).

heated *adjective* **1** (of a person, discussions, etc.) angry; inflamed with passion or excitement. **2** made hot. ▶ **heatedly** *adverb*

heater *noun* **1** a device for warming the air in a room,

car, etc. **2** a container with an element etc. for heating the contents: *water heater*. **3** *slang* a gun.

heat exchanger *noun* a device for the transfer of heat from one medium to another.

heath *noun* **1** an area of flattish uncultivated land with low shrubs. **2** any plant growing on a heath, e.g. heather.

heathen • *noun* **1** *derogatory* a person who does not belong to a widely held religion (esp. who is not Christian, Jewish, or Muslim) as regarded by those that do. **2** an unenlightened person; a person regarded as lacking culture or moral principles. **3** (**the heathen**) heathen people collectively. • *adjective* **1** of or relating to heathens; pagan. **2** having no religion. ▶ **heathenism** *noun* [Say HEE then]

heather *noun* **1** an evergreen shrub with purple bell-shaped flowers. **2** any of various shrubs growing esp. on moors or in mountainous regions. [Rhymes with WEATHER]

heathland *noun* an extensive area of heath.

heating *noun* **1** the imparting or generation of heat. **2** equipment or devices used to provide heat, esp. to a building.

heat lamp *noun* a lamp used for its heat as well as its light.

heatproof *adjective* (also **heat-resistant**) able to resist great heat.

heat pump *noun* a device for the transfer of heat from a colder area to a hotter area by using mechanical energy.

heat rash *noun* an itchy rash of small raised red spots caused by inflammation of the sweat glands.

heat-seeking *adjective* (of a missile etc.) able to detect infrared radiation to guide it to its target.

heat sink *noun* a device or substance for absorbing excessive or unwanted heat.

heatstroke *noun* a feverish condition caused by excessive exposure to high temperature.

heat-treat *verb* subject metal to heat to modify its properties. ▶ **heat-treated** *adjective*

heat treatment *noun* the use of heat for medical purposes or to modify the properties of a metal etc.

heave • *verb* (**heaves**; *past* and *past participle* **heaved** or esp. *Nautical* **hove**; **heaving**) **1** lift or haul (a heavy thing) with great effort. **2** utter with effort or resignation: *heaved a sigh*. **3** throw. **4** rise and fall rhythmically or spasmodically. **5** *Nautical* haul by rope. **6** retch or vomit. **7** rise up above the general surface; expand, shift: *the floor heaved during the winter*. • *noun* **1 a** an act of heaving, esp. a strong pull. **b** an uneven area of road etc. caused by heaving due to frost. **2** *Geology* a sideways displacement in a fault. **3** (**the heaves**) *slang* a bout of retching or vomiting. PHRASES **heave in sight** (or **into view**) come into view. **heave to** esp. *Nautical* bring or be brought to a standstill. ▶ **heaver** *noun*

heave-ho • *noun* (**the** (**old**) **heave-ho**) *slang* rejection or dismissal: *the bank gave him the heave-ho*. • *interjection* a sailors' cry, esp. on raising the anchor.

heaven *noun* **1** (also **Heaven**) a place regarded in some religions as the abode of God and the angels, and of the good after death, often characterized as above the sky. **2** a place or state of supreme bliss. **3** *informal* something delightful. **4** God, Providence (often as an exclamation or mild oath: *for heaven's sake* ◊ *heavens*). *what will they think of next?*). **5** (**the heavens**) the sky as the abode of the sun, moon, and stars and regarded from earth. PHRASES **in seventh heaven** in a state of ecstasy. **move heaven and earth** make extraordinary efforts: *I will move heaven and earth to help you*.

H

heavenly *adjective* **1** of heaven; divine. **2** of the heavens or sky. **3** *informal* very pleasing; wonderful.

heavenly body *noun* a natural object in outer space, e.g. the sun, a star, a planet, etc.

heavenly hash *noun* a flavour of ice cream combining chocolate ice cream, marshmallow, chocolate chunks, and chocolate-coated almonds.

heavenly host *noun* the angels.

heaven-sent *adjective* wonderfully opportune.

heavenward *adverb* (also **heavenwards**) up into the sky or toward the heavens.

heavier-than-air *adjective* (of an aircraft) weighing more than the air it displaces.

heavily *adverb* **1** with great weight or force: *the van was heavily loaded* ◊ *he fell heavily to the ice* ◊ *it rained heavily last night*. **2** to a great extent or degree: *she drinks heavily* ◊ *the play was heavily criticized*. **3** in or by a large number of esp. people: *heavily populated areas* ◊ *a heavily travelled route* ◊ *our proposal is heavily backed*. **4** deeply: *I slept heavily* ◊ *she sighed heavily*. **5** slowly and with difficulty: *he grabbed his cane and walked heavily to the door*. **6** in a serious or sombre manner: *he speaks heavily of death*.

heaviness *noun* **1** great physical weight. **2** intense grief: *heaviness of heart*. **3** the quality of a book or movie etc. that is difficult to follow or understand because of its seriousness, complexity, or slow pace.

heavy • *adjective* (**heavier, heaviest**) **1 a** of great or exceptionally high weight. **b** (of a person) overweight. **2 a** of great density. **b** *Physics* having a greater than the usual mass (esp. of isotopes and compounds containing them). **3** abundant: *a heavy crop* ◊ *heavy fighting* ◊ *a heavy drinker*. **4 a** striking or falling with force: *heavy blows* ◊ *heavy rain*. **b** (of a body of water) having large powerful waves. **5** (of rock music etc.) highly amplified with a strong beat. **6** (of machinery, artillery, etc.) very large of its kind; large in calibre etc. **7** causing a strong impact: *heavy drugs*. **8** needing much physical effort: *heavy work*. **9** (foll. by *with*) laden. **10 a** (of a speech, writing, etc.) serious or sombre in tone or attitude; dull, tedious. **b** (of an issue etc.) grave; important, weighty. **11 a** (of food) hard to digest. **b** (of a literary work etc.) hard to read or understand. **12** (of ground) difficult to traverse or work. **13 a** oppressive; hard to endure: *heavy demands*. **b** (of the atmosphere, weather, etc.) oppressive, sultry. **14 a** coarse, ungraceful: *heavy features*. **b** unwieldy. **15** sad, dejected: *a heavy heart*. **16** loud and deep in sound: *a heavy thud*. • *noun* (plural **heavies**) **1** *informal* a large violent person; a thug. **2** a villainous or tragic role or actor in a play etc. (usu. in *plural*). **3** anything large or heavy of its kind, e.g. a piece of artillery. • *adverb* heavily (esp. in *combination*: *heavy-laden*). PHRASES **heavy on** using a lot of: *heavy on gas*.

heavy cream *noun* = WHIPPING CREAM.

heavy-duty *adjective* **1** intended to withstand hard use. **2** *informal* significant in size, amount, etc.

heavy-handed *adjective* **1** not showing a sympathetic understanding of the feelings of other people: *a heavy-handed approach*. **2** using unnecessary force: *heavy-handed police methods*. **3** (of a person) using too much of something in a way that can cause damage: *don't be heavy-handed with the salt*. ▶ **heavy-handedly** *adverb* **heavy-handedness** *noun*

heavy hitter *noun informal* an important or powerful person.

heavy hydrogen *noun* = DEUTERIUM.

heavy industry *noun* (plural **heavy industries**) industry producing metal, machinery, etc.

heavy metal *noun* **1** a type of highly amplified, loud, vigorous rock music with a strong, usu. fast beat and often theatrical performance. **2** metal of high density.

heavy-set *adjective* (of a person) stocky, burly.

heavy water *noun* water in which the hydrogen in the molecules is partly or wholly replaced by the isotope deuterium, which has a mass approximately twice that of the normal isotope. Heavy water is used in nuclear reactors to retard neutrons and control the rate of fission.

heavyweight *noun* **1 a** a weight in certain sports, in the amateur boxing scale over 81 kg but differing for professional boxers and wrestlers. **b** a sportsman of this weight. **2 a** person, animal, or thing of above average weight. **3** *informal* a person of influence or importance.

Hebraic *adjective* having to do with the Hebrew language or people: *Hebraic poetry*. [Say he BRAY ick]

Hebrew • *noun* **1** a member of a Semitic people originally centred in ancient Palestine and having a descent traditionally traced from Abraham, Isaac, and Jacob. **2 a** the language of this people. **b** a modern form of this used esp. in Israel. • *adjective* **1** of or in Hebrew. **2** of the Hebrews or the Jews.

Hebrew Bible *noun* the sacred writings of Judaism, called by Christians the Old Testament, consisting of the Torah (the Law or Pentateuch), the Prophets, and the Hagiographa or Writings.

heck *informal* • *interjection* a mild exclamation of surprise or dismay. • *adverb* as an intensifier: *a heck of a job*. PHRASES **what the heck** expressing indifference, dismissal of a difficulty, etc.

heckle • *verb* (**heckles, heckled, heckling**) interrupt and harass (a public speaker). • *noun* an act of heckling. ▶ **heckler** *noun*

heckuva *adjective & adverb informal* = HELLUVA.

hectare *noun* a metric unit of land measure, equal to 100 ares (2.471 acres or 10,000 square metres). Abbreviation: **ha**. [Say HECK tair or HECK tar]

hectic *adjective* busy and confused; characterized by feverish excitement or haste. ▶ **hectically** *adverb*

hecto- *combining form* a hundred, esp. of a unit in the metric system. Abbreviation: **h**.

hectogram *noun* a metric unit of mass, equal to one hundred grams.

hectolitre *noun* a metric unit of capacity, equal to one hundred litres.

hectometre *noun* a metric unit of length, equal to one hundred metres.

hector *verb* bully, intimidate. ▶ **hectoring** *adjective*

he'd *contraction* **1** he had. **2** he would.

heder *noun* = CHEDER. [Say HAY der]

hedge • *noun* **1** a fence or boundary formed by closely growing bushes or shrubs. **2** a protection against possible loss or diminution: *buy gold as a hedge against inflation*. **3 a** statement made to avoid firm commitment. • *verb* (**hedges, hedged, hedging**) **1** surround or bound with or as with a hedge. **2** (foll. by *in*) enclose. **3 a** reduce one's risk of loss on (a bet or speculation) by compensating transactions on the other side. **b** avoid a definite decision or commitment. **4** make or trim hedges. PHRASES **hedge one's bets** protect oneself against loss or error by supporting more than one side in a contest, an argument, etc.

hedgehog *noun* **1** a small nocturnal insect-eating mammal with a pig-like snout and a coat of spines, and rolling itself up into a ball for defence. **2** a porcupine or other animal similarly covered with spines.

hedgerow *noun* a row of bushes etc. forming a hedge.

hedonism *noun* **1** belief in pleasure as the highest good and mankind's proper aim. **2** behaviour based on this; devotion to or pursuit of pleasure. ▶ **hedonist** *noun* **hedonistic** *adjective* [Say HEED'n ism or HED'n ism]

heebie-jeebies *plural noun slang* a state of nervous depression or anxiety.

H

heed • *verb* attend to; take notice of. • *noun* careful attention.

heedful *adjective* (often foll. by *of*) mindful, attentive; careful, cautious. ▶**heedfully** *adverb*

heedless *adjective* inattentive, regardless; careless: *went out, heedless of the rain.* ▶**heedlessly** *adverb* **heedlessness** *noun*

hee-haw • *noun* the bray of a donkey. • *verb* emit a braying sound.

hee hee *interjection* representing laughter, esp. in amusement, derision, triumph, etc.

SPELL CHECK
heel, heal

When someone recovers they **heal**.

---

heel[1] • *noun* **1** the back part of the foot below the ankle. **2** the corresponding part in vertebrate animals. **3 a** the part of a sock etc. covering the heel. **b** the part of a shoe or boot supporting the heel. **c** (in *plural*) high-heeled shoes. **4** a thing like a heel in form or position, e.g. the part of the palm next to the wrist, or the part of a golf club near where the head joins the shaft. **5** *informal* a person regarded with contempt or disapproval. **6** (as *interjection*) a command to a dog to walk close to a person's heels. • *verb* **1** fit or renew a heel on (a shoe or boot). **2** (of a dog) follow obediently at a person's heels. PHRASES **at** (or **on**) **the heels of** following closely after (a person or event). **cool one's heels** be kept waiting. **take to one's heels** run away. **turn on one's heel** turn sharply round.

heel[2] • *verb* (of a ship etc.) lean over owing to the pressure of wind or an uneven load (*compare* LIST[2]). • *noun* the act or amount of heeling.

heelless *adjective* (of footwear) not having a raised heel.

heft • *verb* lift (something heavy), esp. to judge its weight. • *noun informal* weight, heaviness.

hefty *adjective* (**heftier, heftiest**) **1** (of a person) big and strong. **2** (of a thing) large, heavy, powerful. **3** substantial, considerable: *a hefty fee increase.*

hegemonic *adjective* ruling or dominant in a political or social context: *Japan is using its surplus to establish a hegemonic position in world markets.* [Say hedge uh MON ick]

hegemony *noun* (*plural* **hegemonies**) control by one country, organization, etc. over other countries, etc. within a particular group: *the country's continuing desire for political and military hegemony.* [Say huh JEMMA nee]

hegira *noun* **1** (**Hegira**) **a** Muhammad's departure from Mecca to Medina in AD 622. **b** the Muslim era reckoned from this date. **2** a general exodus or departure: *the hegira of East Berliners to Hungary.* [Say huh JYE ruh or HEDGE i ruh]

heh heh *interjection* expressing chuckling.

heifer *noun* a cow that has not borne a calf, or has borne only one calf. [Say HEFFER]

height *noun* **1** the measurement from base to top or (of a standing person) from head to foot. **2** the elevation above ground or a recognized level (usu. sea level). **3** any considerable elevation. **4** (often in *plural*) **a** a high place or area. **b** rising ground. **c** the state of being high above the ground: *afraid of heights.* **5** the top of something. **6 a** the most intense part or period of anything: *the battle was at its height.* **b** an extreme instance or example: *the height of fashion.*

heighten *verb* make or become higher or more intense. ▶**heightened** *adjective*

height of land *noun* esp. *Cdn* a watershed.

Heiltsuk • *noun* (*plural* **Heiltsuk** or **Heiltsuks**) **1** a member of an Aboriginal group living on the coast of BC. **2** the Wakashan language of this people. • *adjective* of the Heiltsuk or their culture or language. [Say HAILT sook]

Heimlich manoeuvre *noun* a first-aid procedure to dislodge a foreign object from a choking person's windpipe by applying a sudden upward thrust of the fist to the victim's upper abdomen. [Say HIME lick]

heinous *adjective* utterly wicked: *the heinous crime of first-degree murder.* ▶**heinously** *adverb* [Say HAY niss]

heir *noun* **1** a person entitled to property or rank as the legal successor of its former owner: *heir to the throne.* **2** a person deriving or morally entitled to some thing, quality, etc., from a predecessor: *they saw themselves as the true heirs of the Enlightenment.* [Sounds like *AIR*]

heir apparent *noun* (*plural* **heirs apparent**) **1** an heir whose claim cannot be set aside by the birth of another heir. **2** a person considered likely to succeed to another, e.g. as head of political party or corporation.

heiress *noun* (*plural* **heiresses**) a woman who will inherit or has inherited great wealth: *a wealthy London banking heiress.* [Say AIR iss]

heirloom • *noun* **1** a piece of personal property that has been in a family for several generations. **2** a piece of property received as part of an inheritance. • *adjective* of or designating seeds that have been passed down from one generation to another, or the fruits or vegetables grown with them. [Say AIR loom]

heir presumptive *noun* (*plural* **heirs presumptive**) an heir whose claim may be set aside by the birth of another heir.

heist *slang* • *noun* a robbery. • *verb* rob. [Say HICED (rhymes with *PRICED*)]

hejira *noun* = HEGIRA. [Say huh JYE ruh or HEDGE i ruh]

held *past and past participle of* HOLD[1].

helianthus *noun* (*plural* **helianthus**) any of various plants of the daisy family, esp. the sunflower. [Say heely ANTH us]

helical *adjective* having the form of a helix; spiral: *the two helical DNA strands.* [Say HELL ick ul or HEEL ick ul]

helices *plural of* HELIX. [Say HEEL uh seez or HELL uh seez]

helichrysum *noun* any of various plants of the daisy family, some of which retain their shape and colour when dried. [Say hella CRY z'm]

helicopter • *noun* a type of aircraft without wings, obtaining lift and propulsion from horizontally revolving overhead blades or rotors, and capable of moving vertically and horizontally. • *verb* transport or fly by helicopter.

heli-logging *noun* the removal of felled timber by helicopter. ▶**heli-log** *verb* (**heli-logs, heli-logged, heli-logging**) **heli-logger** *noun*

heliocentric *adjective* **1** having, representing, or regarding the sun as centre: *the medieval view of the universe was geocentric rather than heliocentric.* **2** measured from or considered in relation to the centre of the sun: *heliocentric distance.* [Say heely uh SEN trick]

helium *noun* a colourless, light, inert, gaseous element occurring in deposits of natural gas, used in airships and as a refrigerant.

helix *noun* (*plural* **helices**) **1** an object of coiled form, either a spiral curve around an axis like a corkscrew or a coiled curve in one plane. **2** *Math* a three-dimensional curve on a conical or cylindrical surface which becomes a straight line when the surface is unrolled into a plane. [Say HEE licks for the singular, HEEL uh seez or HELL uh seez for the plural]

hell • *noun* **1 a** the abode of the dead; in Christian, Jewish, and Islamic belief, the place of punishment or torment where the souls of the damned are confined after death. **b** the kingdom, power, inhabitants, or forces of hell collectively. **2 a** a place or state of suffering, misery, or wickedness. **b** extreme chaos,

turmoil, etc.: *all hell broke loose*. **3** criticism, punishment, or difficulty. • *interjection informal* used as an exclamation of surprise, annoyance, etc. PHRASES **as hell** *informal* as an intensifier: *sure as hell*. **beat** (or **scare**, etc.) **the hell out of** *informal* beat, scare, etc. excessively, severely, or beyond all measure. **(come) hell or high water** *informal* (through) great difficulties, (despite) any obstacles or problems. **for the hell of it** *informal* for fun; on impulse. **from hell** *slang* indicating the worst possible example, instance, etc.: *the date from hell*. **the hell** (usu. preceded by *what, where, who, etc.*) *slang* expressing anger, disbelief, etc. or merely emphatic: *who the hell are you?* **hell** (or **hell-bent**) **for leather** *informal* at full speed. **hell of a** (or **helluva**) *slang* exceedingly bad, good, remarkable, etc.: *one hell of an athlete*. **hell on wheels** *slang* a wild or terrible person or thing, esp. one of great speed or ferocity. **hell's bells** *slang* expressing anger or annoyance. **hell's half acre** *slang* a great distance. **hell to pay** *informal* great trouble, discord, pandemonium, etc., esp. as a result of previous action. **in hell** *slang* as an intensifier: *what in hell have you done?* **like hell** *informal* **1** recklessly, desperately, exceedingly. **2** *ironic* not at all, on the contrary. **not a hope in hell** *informal* no chance at all. **play hell** (or **merry hell**) **with** *informal* **1** be upsetting or disruptive to. **2** damage. **raise hell** *informal* cause trouble, create chaos. **till** (or **until** or **when**) **hell freezes over** *informal* never or to (or at) some date in the impossibly distant future. **to hell** *slang* as an intensifier: *shot to hell*. **to hell and gone** *slang* **1** a great distance. **2** endlessly, forever. **to hell with** *slang* **1** expressing exasperated dismissal of (a person, thing, etc.). **2** endlessly, forever. **what the hell** *informal* expressing dismissal of a difficulty etc., i.e. it is of no importance.

he'll *contraction* he will; he shall.

hell-bent *adjective informal* recklessly determined.

hellebore *noun* **1** a poisonous evergreen plant with large white, green, or purplish flowers. **2** a plant of the lily family, with pleated leaves and a tall dense spike of small flowers. [Say HELLA bore]

Hellenic *adjective* having to do with ancient or modern Greece. [Say hell EN ick or hell EEN ick]

Hellenism *noun* **1** Greek character or culture (esp. of ancient Greece). **2** the study or imitation of Greek culture. [Say HELLEN ism]

Hellenistic *adjective* of or relating to the period of Greek history 323 BC–31 BC, during which Greek culture spread through the Mediterranean and into the Near East and Asia. [Say hellen ISS tick]

hellfire *noun* **1** the fire or fires of hell. **2 a** the punishments and torments of hell. **b** (as an *adjective*) (esp. of preaching) emphasizing the damnation of unsaved souls and the eternal punishments of hell.

hellhole *noun* an unbearable place.

hellion *noun informal* **1** a rowdy, troublemaking, disreputable person. **2 a** rowdy, mischievous, or difficult child. [Say HELL yun]

hellish *adjective* **1** of or like hell. **2** *informal* extremely difficult or unpleasant. ▶**hellishly** *adverb*

hello • *interjection* **1 a** an expression of informal greeting, or of surprise. **b** used to begin a telephone conversation. **2** used to call attention. **3** used to reproach ignorance or inattention. • *noun* (*plural* **hellos**) an utterance of "hello"; a greeting.

hellraiser *noun* a person who causes trouble or creates chaos, esp. habitually. ▶**hellraising** *adjective & noun*

helm • *noun* **1** a tiller or wheel by which a ship's rudder is controlled. **2** the amount by which this is turned: *more helm needed*. **3** a position of leadership or government: *had the helm of CBC Radio in Montreal*. • *verb* **1** steer

or guide with a helm: *the first boat was helmed by a local sailor*. **2** lead; control: *the director who helmed this coming-of-age tale set in 1955 Ontario*. PHRASES **at the helm** in control; at the head (of an organization etc.).

helmet *noun* **1** any of various protective head coverings worn by soldiers, miners, athletes, motorcyclists, etc. **2** a device fitting over the head and including a screen on which virtual reality images are displayed. ▶**helmeted** *adjective* **helmetless** *adjective*

helmsman *noun* (*plural* **helmsmen**) a person who steers a ship.

help • *verb* **1** aid, assist. **2** improve (a situation or problem. **3** (usu. with *neg.*) **a** a refrain from: *could not help laughing*. **b** be unavoidable: *can't help it*. **c help oneself** make an effort on one's own behalf, extricate oneself from a difficulty: *couldn't help himself*. • *noun* **1** assistance or a source of assistance. **2** an employee or domestic servant, or several collectively. PHRASES **can't** (or **cannot**) **help but** be obliged to or unable to do other: *can't help but share his worry*. **help oneself** (often foll. by *to*) **1** serve oneself (with food). **2** take without seeking help or permission. **help a person out** give a person help, esp. in difficulty. **not if I can help it** not if I can prevent it. **so help me** (or **help me God**) (as an invocation or oath) as I keep my word, as I speak the truth, etc.

helpdesk *noun* a service which helps users who have problems with esp. computers.

helper *noun* someone or something that helps or assists a person, process, etc.

helpful *adjective* giving or productive of help; useful. ▶**helpfully** *adverb* **helpfulness** *noun*

helping *noun* **1** a portion of food. **2** a portion of something offered: *generous helpings of propaganda*.

helpless *adjective* **1** unable to function independently or act without help. **2** lacking help or protection; defenceless. **3** unable to help. ▶**helplessly** *adverb* **helplessness** *noun*

helpline *noun* a telephone service providing help and advice, either for personal problems or for an item one has bought.

helpmate *noun* a helpful companion or partner, usu. a husband or wife.

help-wanted index *noun* Cdn a rough, seasonally adjusted measure of the job market calculated from help-wanted advertisements in newspapers.

helter-skelter • *adverb & adjective* in disorderly haste, random order, or confusion. • *noun* disorder or confusion.

hem[1] • *noun* **1** the border of a piece of cloth, esp. a cut edge turned under and sewn down. **2** HEMLINE. • *verb* (**hems, hemmed, hemming**) turn under and sew in the edge of (a piece of cloth etc.). PHRASES **hem in** confine; restrict the movement of.

hem[2] • *interjection* calling attention or expressing hesitation by a slight cough or clearing of the throat. • *noun* an utterance of this. • *verb* (**hems, hemmed, hemming**) hesitate in speech. PHRASES **hem and haw** hesitate in speaking, esp. through indecision, disagreement, etc.

he-man *noun* (*plural* **he-men**) *informal* often *ironic* a particularly strong, masterful, or virile man.

hematite *noun* ferric oxide occurring as a dark red mineral which is an important ore of iron. [Say HEEMA tite]

hemato- *combining form* = HEMO-. [Say HEEMA toe]

hematology *noun* the branch of medicine that deals with the blood, esp. in. disorders. [Say heema TOLLA jee]

hematoma *noun* Medical a solid swelling of clotted blood within the tissues. [Say heema TOE muh]

heme *noun* a non-protein compound containing iron,

H

responsible for the red colour of hemoglobin. [Say HEEM]

hemi- *combining form* half.

hemipterous *adjective* belonging to or having to do with the order of insects that includes bugs, aphids, cicadas, and many others with piercing or sucking mouthparts. [Say hem IP tuh rus]

hemisphere *noun* **1** a half of the earth, esp. as divided by the equator (into *northern* and *southern hemisphere*) or by an imaginary line passing through the poles (into *eastern* and *western hemisphere*). **2** (also **cerebral hemisphere**) each of the halves of the cerebrum. **3** half of a sphere. ▶**hemispheric** *adjective* **hemispherical** *adjective* [Say HEM iss fear]

hemline *noun* the line or level of the lower edge of a skirt, dress, or coat.

hemlock *noun* **1 a** a plant of the parsley family, with a purple-spotted stem, fern-like leaves, and small white flowers. **b** a poisonous potion obtained from this. **2** (also **hemlock fir** or **hemlock spruce**) **a** a coniferous tree which has foliage that smells like hemlock when crushed. **b** the timber or pitch of these trees.

hemo- *combining form* blood. [Say HEEMO]

hemodialysis *noun* = DIALYSIS 2. [Say heemo die ALA sis]

hemoglobin *noun* a red, oxygen-carrying substance containing iron, present in the red blood cells of vertebrates. [Say HEEMA globe in]

hemophilia *noun* a usu. hereditary disorder with a tendency to bleed severely from even a slight injury, through the failure of the blood to clot normally. [Say heema FEELY uh]

hemophiliac *noun* a person with hemophilia. [Say heema FEELY ack]

hemorrhage • *noun* **1** an escape of blood from a ruptured blood vessel, esp. when profuse. **2** a damaging or uncontrolled outflow of something, esp. of people or assets from a country, organization, etc.: *the massive hemorrhage of American technology to the former Soviet Union*. • *verb* (**hemorrhages, hemorrhaged, hemorrhaging**) **1** undergo a hemorrhage; bleed heavily. **2** expend (money etc.) in large amounts; lose or dissipate, esp. wastefully: *the company has been hemorrhaging jobs since the recession*. [Say HEM er idge]

hemorrhoid *noun* (usu. in *plural*) swollen veins at or near the anus. [Say HEMMA roid]

hemp *noun* **1** (also **Indian hemp**) the cannabis plant, esp. when grown for its fibre. **2** its fibre extracted from the stem and used to make rope and stout fabrics. **3** any of several narcotic drugs made from the hemp plant (*compare* CANNABIS, MARIJUANA). **4** any of several other plants yielding fibre, e.g. manila hemp.

hen *noun* **1 a** a female bird, esp. of a domestic fowl. **b** (in *plural*) domestic fowls of either sex. **2** a female lobster or crab or salmon. PHRASES **rare as hen's teeth** exceedingly rare.

hence *adverb* **1** from this time: *two years hence*. **2 a** for this reason; as a result of inference: *hence we seem to be wrong*. **b** from this source, fact, or circumstance.

henceforth *adverb* (also **henceforward**) from this time onward.

henchman *noun* (*plural* **henchmen**) usu. *derogatory* **1** a trusted supporter or faithful follower who always obeys the orders of his or her leader. **2** an often unscrupulous, self-serving, and ambitious subordinate or lackey.

henge *noun* a prehistoric monument consisting of a circle of stone or wooden uprights, such as Stonehenge in southern England, which was built in several phases from *c.* 2950 BC.

henhouse *noun* a building in which poultry roost.

henna *noun* **1** a tropical shrub with small pink, red, or white flowers. **2** the reddish dye from its shoots and leaves esp. used to colour hair.

hennaed *adjective* dyed with henna.

henpeck *verb* (of a woman) constantly harass, nag, or domineer over (a man, esp. her husband). ▶**henpecked** *adjective*

henry *noun* (*plural* **henries** or **henrys**) the SI unit of inductance.

hep[1] *adjective & verb* = HIP[3].

hep[2] *noun* *informal* hepatitis.

heparin *noun* a compound occurring in the liver and other tissues which inhibits blood coagulation. [Say HEPPA rin]

hepatic *adjective* of or relating to the liver. [Say hep ATTIC]

hepatitis *noun* inflammation of the liver. [Say heppa TITE iss]

hepatitis A *noun* a form of viral hepatitis transmitted in food, causing fever and jaundice.

hepatitis B *noun* a severe form of viral hepatitis transmitted in infected blood and other body fluids, causing fever, debility, and jaundice.

hepatitis C *noun* a very serious form of hepatitis, transmitted through untreated blood and blood products and often resulting in chronic disease.

hepcat *noun* *slang* **1** a jazz musician. **2** a hip person.

heptagon *noun* a plane figure with seven sides and angles. ▶**heptagonal** *adjective* [Say HEPTA gon, hep TAGGA nul]

heptahedron *noun* (*plural* **heptahedrons** or **heptahedra**) a solid figure with seven faces. [Say hepta HEE drun]

GRAMMAR CHECK
her, she ⚠️

The use of **her** instead of **she** after the verb "to be", as in *It's her on the phone*, is now considered acceptable in writing as well as speech. In sentences like *It is she who keeps calling*, however, **she** must be used instead of **her**. To avoid sounding excessively formal, such a sentence could be reworded *She's the one who keeps calling*, which is much more natural. *See also* usage note at THAN.

---

her • *pronoun* **1** objective case of SHE: *I like her*. **2** *informal* she: *it's her all right* ◊ *am older than her*. • *possessive adjective* **1** of or belonging to her or herself: *her house*. **2** (**Her**) (in titles) that she is: *Her Majesty*.

herald • *noun* **1** an official messenger bringing news. **2** a forerunner: *spring is the herald of summer*. • *verb* **1** proclaim the approach of: *her arrival heralds a new era*. **2** acclaim: *heralded as the year's biggest success*. [Say HAIR uld]

heraldic *adjective* of or concerning heraldry. [Say hair AL dick]

heraldry *noun* **1** the study of the coats of arms and the history of old families. **2** colourful ceremony: *the pomp and heraldry of the changing of the guard*. [Say HAIR uld ree]

herb *noun* **1** any non-woody seed-bearing plant which dies down to the ground after flowering. **2** any plant with leaves, seeds, or flowers used for flavouring, food, medicine, scent, etc. [Say HERB or ERB]

herbaceous *adjective* **1** of or like herbs (*see* HERB 1). **2** (of a plant) not woody or not having a woody stem. [Say her BAY shiss]

herbal • *adjective* pertaining to or containing herbs, esp. in therapeutic and culinary use. • *noun* a book with descriptions and accounts of the properties of these. [Say HERB'll or ERB'll]

herbalism *noun* the study or practice of the medicinal

and therapeutic use of plants, now especially as a form or alternative medicine. [Say HERB'll ism or ERB'll ism]

herbalist *noun* **1 a** a person who practises or advocates the use of herbs to treat disease. **b** a dealer in medicinal herbs. **2** a person skilled in herbs, esp. an early botanical writer. [Say HERB'll ist or ERB'll ist]

herbal tea *noun* (also **herb tea**) an infusion of dried herbs, usu. non-caffeinated.

herbarium *noun* (*plural* **herbaria**) **1** a systematically arranged collection of dried plants. **2** a book, room, or building for these. [Say her BERRY um]

herbed *adjective* flavoured with herbs. [Say HERB'd or ERB'd]

herbicide *noun* a substance toxic to plants and used to destroy unwanted vegetation. [Say HER buh side]

herbivore *noun* an animal that feeds on plants. ▶ **herbivorous** *adjective* [Say HERB uh vore, her BIV er us]

herby *adjective* abounding in herbs. [Say HERBY or ERBY]

Herculean *adjective* **1** having or requiring great strength or effort: *getting this house cleaned was a Herculean task*. **2** of, like, or pertaining to Hercules, a hero in Greek and Roman mythology who possessed superhuman strength and courage: *he has a Herculean physique*. [Say her cue LEE in]

SPELL CHECK · ABC✓
herd, heard

The past tense of *hear* is **heard**.

---

herd • *noun* **1** a large number of animals, esp. cattle, feeding, travelling, or kept together. **2** *derogatory* **a** a large number of people. **b** (**the herd**) the majority viewed as mindless followers: *prefers not to follow the herd*. • *verb* **1** go, drive, or cause to go together in or as in a herd: *herded together for warmth*. **2** tend (sheep, cattle, etc.). **3** drive (an animal or person) in a particular direction: *herded a cow off the road*. PHRASES **ride herd on** keep watch on or control over, esp. by close supervision: *rode herd on the contractors to keep the project on time and on budget*. ▶ **herder** *noun* **herding** *noun*

herdsman *noun* (*plural* **herdsmen**) the owner or keeper of herds (of domestic animals).

SPELL CHECK · ABC✓
here, hear

To detect sound is to **hear**.

---

here • *adverb* **1** in or at or to this place or position. **2** indicating a person's presence or a thing offered: *here is your coat*. **3** at this point in the argument, situation, etc.: *here I have a question*. • *noun* this place. • *interjection* **1** calling attention: *here, where are you going with that?* **2** indicating one's presence in a roll call. PHRASES **here and now 1** at this very moment; immediately. **2** (**the here and now**) the present reality. **here and there** in various places. **here goes!** *informal* an expression indicating the start of a bold act. **here's to** I drink to the health, success, etc. of. **here we are** *informal* **1** said as acknowledgement of a given state: *here we are, broke again*. **2** said on arrival at one's destination. **here we go again** *informal* the same, usu. undesirable, events are recurring. **here you are 1** said on handing something to somebody. **2** said in acknowledgement of an individual's presence, condition, or achievement: *and here you are, a doctor*. **neither here nor there** of no importance or relevance.

hereabouts *adverb* about or near this place.

hereafter • *adverb* **1 a** from now on; in the future.

b *formal* HEREINAFTER. **2** in the world to come (after death). • *noun* **1** the future. **2** life after death.

hereby *adverb* as a result of this. [Say HERE by]

hereditary *adjective* **1** (of a characteristic, disease, etc.) able to be passed down from one generation to another. **2 a** descending by inheritance. **b** holding a position by inheritance. **3** the same as or resembling what one's parents had: *a hereditary hatred*. **4** of or relating to inheritance. [Say huh REDDA terry]

heredity *noun* **1 a** the passing on of physical or mental characteristics genetically from one generation to another. **b** these characteristics in a particular individual. **2** the genetic constitution of an individual. [Say huh REDDA tee]

Hereford *noun* a breed of red and white beef cattle. [Say HER ferd or HERRA ferd]

herein *adverb* *formal* **1** in this document, book, etc. **2** in this matter, particular, case, etc. [Say here IN]

hereinafter *adverb* esp. *Law formal* **1** from this point on. **2** in a later part of this document etc. [Say here in AFTER]

heresy *noun* (*plural* **heresies**) **1** a belief or an opinion that is against the principles of a particular religion; the fact of holding such beliefs: *he was burned at the stake for heresy* ◊ *the heresies of the early Protestants*. **2** a belief or opinion that disagrees strongly with what most believe: *the idea is heresy to most employees of the company*. [Say HERRA see]

heretic *noun* **1** the holder of an unorthodox opinion in a subject, field, etc.: *his belief in strong government spending makes him a heretic in today's economic climate*. **2** *esp. hist.* a person believing in or practising religious heresy. ▶ **heretical** *adjective* **heretically** *adverb* [Say HERRA tick, huh RET ick ul]

hereto *adverb* *formal* with regard to this point or to this matter, subject, etc.

heretofore *adverb* *formal* formerly, before this time.

herewith *adverb* **1** with this (esp. of an enclosure in a letter etc.). **2** hereby.

heritability *noun* the ability of characteristics to be transmitted from parent to offspring. [Say herra tuh BILLA tee]

heritable *adjective* (of a characteristic) transmissible from parent to offspring. [Say HERRA tuh bull]

heritage *noun* **1 a** things such as works of art, cultural achievements and folklore that have been passed on from earlier generations. **b** a nation's buildings, monuments, countryside, etc., esp. when regarded as worthy of preservation. **c** esp. *Cdn* designating a building, site, river, etc. significant for its historic, architectural, or environmental value and which is protected from alteration, development, etc. by the government: *a heritage building*. **2** inherited circumstances, benefits, etc.: *a heritage of violence*.

Heritage Day *noun* *Cdn* **1** the third Monday in February, marked unofficially as a celebration of Canada's history and heritage. **2** (in the Yukon) the fourth Friday in February, observed as a holiday in the public service and some other workplaces. **3** a day designated by a particular region, ethnic group, etc. as a time to celebrate a shared history and culture.

heritage fund *noun* esp. *Cdn* (often **Heritage Fund**) a fund established by a province, region, city, etc. from supplementary revenue either as a hedge against difficult economic times or as a resource for future social and cultural development.

heritage language *noun* *Cdn* a language, other than English or French, which is a person's mother tongue or that of his or her ethnocultural group.

herky-jerky *adjective* *slang* (of a movement) spasmodic or occurring at an irregular rate.

hermaphrodite • *noun* **1 a** an animal normally

having both male and female sexual organs, e.g. many snails and earthworms. **b** a plant having stamens and pistils in the same flower. **2** a human being in whom both male and female sex organs are present, or in which the sex organs contain both ovarian and testicular tissue. • *adjective* combining the characteristics of or consisting of both sexes. ▶**hermaphroditic** *adjective* **hermaphroditism** *noun* [Say her MAFFRA dite, her maffra DIT ick, her MAFFRA dite ism]

hermetic *adjective* (also **hermetical**) **1** completely airtight. **2** protected from outside influences: *the sterile and hermetic offices of officialdom*. **3 a** intended only for, or intelligible only to, those with special knowledge: *a logically reasoned but hermetic document*. **b** of alchemy or other occult sciences: *hermetic art*. ▶**hermetically** *adverb* [Say her MET ick]

hermit *noun* **1** a person who, from religious motives, has retired into the solitary life, esp. a Christian who lives in a remote place to study the Bible or pray. **2** any person living in solitude or shunning human society. **3** a soft spicy cookie, usu. containing raisins and nuts.

hermitage *noun* a hermit's dwelling, esp. when small and remote.

hermit crab *noun* a type of crab that lives in a cast-off mollusc shell for protection.

hernia *noun* (*plural* **hernias**) a rupture or the abnormal displacement and protrusion of part of an organ through the wall of the cavity containing it, esp. of the abdomen. ▶**herniated** *adjective* [Say HER nee uh, HER nee ate id]

herniated disc *noun* a disc between vertebrae that has become displaced, causing pain because of pressure on the nerves of the spine.

hero *noun* (*plural* **heroes**) **1** a person distinguished by courage, noble deeds, outstanding achievements, etc. **2** the chief, esp. male, character in a poem, play, story, etc. **3** *Greek History* a man of superhuman strength, courage, or qualities, favoured by the gods. **PHRASES** **hero's welcome** a rapturous welcome, like that given to a successful warrior.

heroic • *adjective* **1 a** (of an act or a quality) bold, daring, or characteristic of or fit for a hero. **b** (of an effort etc.) great or courageous, but also desperate. **c** (of a person) like a hero. **2** (of poetry etc.) dealing with heroes and their deeds, esp. those of ancient Greece. • *noun* (in *plural*) heroic behaviour, esp. if unduly, extravagantly, or recklessly bold. ▶**heroically** *adverb*

heroin *noun* a highly addictive drug derived from morphine, often used as a narcotic.

heroine *noun* **1** a woman noted or admired for nobility, courage, outstanding achievements, etc. **2** the chief female character in a poem, play, story, etc.

heroism *noun* heroic conduct or qualities.

heron *noun* a large fish-eating wading bird with long legs, a long S-shaped neck, and a long pointed bill.

hero-worship • *noun* idealization of an admired person. • *verb* (**hero-worships**, **hero-worshipped**, **hero-worshipping**) idolize or be excessively devoted to (a person). ▶**hero-worshipper** *noun*

herpes *noun* (*plural* **herpes**) any of several infectious diseases caused by a herpesvirus and characterized by outbreaks of blisters on the skin etc., e.g. genital herpes. [Say HER peez]

herpes simplex *noun* a viral infection producing usu. localized inflammation, as blisters, cold sores, conjunctivitis, oral and vaginal inflammation, etc.

herpesvirus *noun* any of a group of related viruses that includes those causing shingles, chicken pox, and herpes simplex. [Say HER peez virus]

herring *noun* (*plural* **herring** or **herrings**) a fairly small silvery fish that is abundant in coastal waters and is of great commercial importance as a food fish in many parts of the world.

herringbone *noun* **1** any zigzag pattern or arrangement resembling the pattern of a herring's bones, as of stones, bricks, tiles, etc. **2** a stitch with a similar zigzag pattern. **3** this pattern, or cloth woven in it. **4** *Skiing* a method of ascending a slope with the skis pointing outwards.

herring choker *noun* *Cdn* esp. (*Maritimes*) *informal* a Maritimer, esp. a New Brunswicker.

herring gull *noun* a large gull with dark wing tips, which scavenges from fishing boats, garbage dumps, canneries, etc.

herring scull *noun* (also **herring school**) *Cdn* (*Nfld*) a school of herring appearing in inshore waters.

SPELL CHECK	
hers	ABC

Warning: **hers** is not spelled with an apostrophe.

hers *possessive pronoun* the one or ones belonging to or associated with her: *it is hers* ◊ *hers are over there*. **PHRASES** **of hers** of or belonging to her: *a friend of hers*.

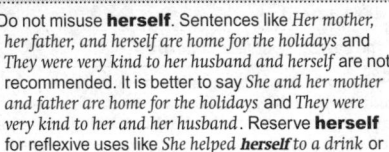

GRAMMAR CHECK	
herself	⚠

Do not misuse **herself**. Sentences like *Her mother, her father, and herself are home for the holidays* and *They were very kind to her husband and herself* are not recommended. It is better to say *She and her mother and father are home for the holidays* and *They were very kind to her and her husband*. Reserve **herself** for reflexive uses like *She helped **herself** to a drink* or emphatic ones like *She **herself** was once an artist like you*.

herself *pronoun* **1 a** *emphatic form* of SHE or HER: *she herself will do it*. **b** *reflexive form* of HER: *she has hurt herself*. **2** in her normal state of body or mind: *does not feel quite herself today*. **PHRASES** **be herself** act in her normal unconstrained manner.

hertz *noun* (*plural* **hertz**) the SI unit of frequency, equal to one cycle per second. Abbreviation: **Hz**. [Sounds like HURTS]

he's *contraction* **1** he is. **2** he has.

he/she *pronoun* a written representation of "he or she" used to indicate both sexes.

hesitancy *noun* the quality of being tentative, slow, or uncertain in doing or saying something: *there was a hesitancy in his voice*. [Say HEZZA tince]

hesitant *adjective* tending to be slow in speaking or acting because of uncertainty or unwillingness. ▶**hesitantly** *adverb* [Say HEZZA tint]

hesitate *verb* (**hesitates**, **hesitated**, **hesitating**) **1** show or feel indecision or uncertainty; pause in doubt: *hesitated over her choice*. **2** be deterred by scruples; be reluctant: *I hesitate to inform against him*. **3** stammer, falter, or pause momentarily in speech. ▶**hesitatingly** *adverb* **hesitation** *noun*

Hesquiaht • *noun* (*plural* **Hesquiaht** or **Hesquiahts**) **1** a member of a Nuu-chah-nulth Aboriginal group living on the west coast of Vancouver Island. **2** the Wakashan language of the Hesquiaht. • *adjective* of this people or their culture or language. [Say HESS kwee ot]

Hessian • *noun* a native of Hesse in western Germany. • *adjective* of or concerning Hesse. [Say HESH'n]

hetero *informal* • *noun* (*plural* **heteros**) a heterosexual. • *adjective* heterosexual. [Say HETTER oh]

hetero- *combining form* other, different.

heterodox *adjective* (of a person, opinion, etc.) not

conforming with accepted or orthodox standards or beliefs. ▶ **heterodoxy** noun [Say HETTER uh dox]

heterogeneity noun the quality of something that consists of many different kinds of people or things: *Ari's paper is on the ethnic heterogeneity of Montreal.* [Say hetter uh juh NAY uh tee]

heterogeneous adjective diverse in character or content: *not all of the suburbs became ethnically heterogeneous.* ▶ **heterogeneously** adverb [Say hetter uh GENIUS]

heterosexism noun discrimination or prejudice by heterosexuals against or towards homosexuals. ▶ **heterosexist** adjective & noun [Say hetter oh SEXISM]

heterosexual • adjective **1** feeling or involving sexual attraction to persons of the opposite sex. **2** concerning heterosexual relations or people. • noun a heterosexual person. ▶ **heterosexuality** noun [Say hetter oh SEXUAL]

het up adjective informal excited, overwrought.

heuristic • adjective **1** designating a book or method that allows one to discover things for oneself. **2** Computing proceeding to a solution by trial and error. • noun **1** a heuristic process or method. **2** (in plural, usu. treated as singular) Computing the study and use of heuristic techniques in data processing. [Say hure ISS tick]

SPELL CHECK
hew, hue   ABC ✓

A colour or shade is a **hue**. **Hue** is also the spelling in "hue and cry".

---

hew verb (**hews**; past **hewed**; past participle **hewn** or **hewed**; **hewing**) **1 a** (often foll. by *down, away, off*) chop or cut (a thing) with an axe, a sword, etc. **b** cut (a block of wood etc.) into shape. **2** (usu. foll. by *to*) conform: *there are still those who hew to the old ways.*

hewer noun **1** a person who hews. **2** a person who cuts coal from a seam. PHRASES **hewers of wood and drawers of water** menial drudges; labourers.

hex[1] • verb (**hexes, hexed, hexing**) bewitch. • noun (plural **hexes**) a magic spell.

hex[2] adjective hexagonal: *hex nut.*

hexa- combining form (also **hex-** esp. before a vowel) six.

hexagon noun a plane figure with six sides and angles. ▶ **hexagonal** adjective [Say HEXA gon, hex AGGA nul]

hexahedron noun (plural **hexahedrons** or **hexahedra**) a solid figure with six faces. [Say hexa HEE drun]

hexavalent adjective having a valence of six. [Say hexa VAY lint]

hey interjection calling attention or expressing joy, surprise, inquiry, enthusiasm, greeting, etc. PHRASES **what the hey** expressing dismissal of a difficulty.

heyday noun the flush or full bloom of youth, vigour, prosperity, etc.

HF abbreviation HIGH FREQUENCY.

Hf symbol hafnium.

Hg symbol the element mercury.

hg abbreviation hectogram(s).

HGH abbreviation HUMAN GROWTH HORMONE.

hi interjection as a greeting or calling attention.

hiatus noun (plural **hiatuses**) **1** a pause in activity: *after a five-month hiatus, the talks resumed.* **2** a space, especially in a piece of writing or in a speech, where something is missing. [Say hi AY tiss]

hiatus hernia noun the protrusion of an organ, esp. the stomach, through the diaphragm.

Hib noun a bacterium, *Haemophilus influenzae* type B, causing infant meningitis: *Hib vaccine.*

Hibachi noun (plural **Hibachis**) proprietary a small, portable charcoal brazier with a grill. [Say huh BOTCH ee]

hibernate verb (**hibernates, hibernated, hibernating**) **1** (of some animals) spend the winter in a dormant state. **2** (of human beings) escape or withdraw from a harsh winter. ▶ **hibernation** noun

Hibernian • adjective of or concerning Ireland. • noun a native of Ireland. [Say hi BERN ee un]

hibiscus noun (plural **hibiscuses**) a plant of the mallow family, cultivated for its large bright-coloured flowers. [Say hib ISS cuss or high BISS cuss]

hic interjection expressing the sound of a hiccup, esp. a drunken hiccup.

hiccup • noun **1** an involuntary spasm of the diaphragm and respiratory organs, with sudden closure of the glottis and characteristic coughlike sound. **2** a temporary or minor stoppage or difficulty. • verb (**hiccups, hiccuped, hiccuping**) make a hiccup or series of hiccups.

hick informal derogatory • noun a country dweller. • adjective rural or unsophisticated.

hickey noun (plural **hickeys**) informal **1** a red mark on the skin, caused by biting or sucking during sexual play. **2** a gadget (compare DOOHICKEY).

hickory noun (plural **hickories**) **1** a North American tree of the walnut family, which yields tough heavy timber and bears sometimes edible nuts (see PECAN). **2** the wood of these trees. **3** a flavour given to food by smoking it over burning hickory wood.

hicksville noun derogatory a non-urban area.

hidden past participle of HIDE[1].

hidden agenda noun a secret or ulterior motive behind an action, statement, etc.

hidden tax noun (plural **hidden taxes**) a tax paid by a manufacturer, distributor, or retailer, that is included in the price charged to the consumer.

hide[1] verb (**hides**; past **hid**; past participle **hidden** or archaic **hid; hiding**) **1** put or keep out of sight: *hid it under the cushion.* **2** conceal oneself. **3** (usu. foll. by *from*) keep (a fact) secret. **4** conceal (a thing) from sight intentionally or not: *trees hid the house.* PHRASES **hide one's light under a bushel** conceal one's merits. **hide out** (or **up**) remain in concealment.

hide[2] • noun **1** the skin of an animal, esp. when tanned or dressed. **2** informal the human skin: *saved her own hide.* • verb (**hides, hided, hiding**) informal flog. PHRASES **neither hide nor hair** not the slightest trace.

Hide-A-Bed noun proprietary a sofa bed.

hide-and-seek noun **1** (also **hide-and-go-seek**) a children's game in which one or more players seek a person who is hiding. **2** a process of attempting to find an evasive person or thing.

hideaway • noun a hiding place or place of retreat. • adjective hidden or concealed, esp. when not in use: *hideaway bed.*

hidebound adjective unwilling or unable to change because of tradition or convention: *their followers were seen as hidebound and unthinking.*

hideous adjective **1** frightful, repulsive, or revolting, to the senses or the mind. **2** informal unpleasant. ▶ **hideously** adverb **hideousness** noun

hideout noun informal a hiding place.

hidey-hole noun informal a hiding place.

hiding[1] noun **1** the action of concealing. **2** the state of remaining hidden: *go into hiding.*

hiding[2] noun informal a thrashing.

hierarchical adjective based on or having to do with a hierarchy; arranged in order of rank: *the company is based on a hierarchical system in which the president has the most authority.* [Say hire ARK ick ul]

H

hierarchy *noun* (*plural* **hierarchies**) **1** a system, especially in a society or an organization, in which people are organized into different levels of importance from highest to lowest: *the social hierarchy ◊ she's high up in the management hierarchy.* **2** the group of people in control of a large organization or institution. **3** a system that ideas or beliefs can be arranged into: *a hierarchy of needs.* [Say HIRE arky]

hieratic *adjective* **1** of or concerning priests: *literacy was restricted to a hieratic elite.* **2** of the ancient Egyptian writing of abridged hieroglyphics as used by priests. **3** of or concerning Egyptian or Greek traditional styles of art. [Say hire ATTIC]

hieroglyph *noun* a picture of an object representing a word, syllable, or sound, as used in ancient Egyptian and other writing. [Say HI ruh glif]

hieroglyphic • *adjective* of or written in hieroglyphs. • *noun* (**hieroglyphics**) **1** hieroglyphs. **2** handwriting that is difficult to read. [Say hi ruh GLIF ick]

hi-fi *informal* • *adjective* of or relating to high fidelity. • *noun* (*plural* **hi-fis**) a set of equipment for high-fidelity sound reproduction.

higgledy-piggledy *adverb & adjective* in confusion or disorder.

high • *adjective* **1 a** of great vertical extent. **b** of a specified height. **2** far above ground or sea level etc.: *a high altitude.* **3** extending above the normal or average level. **4** of exalted, esp. spiritual, quality. **5** great in rank or status **6** great in amount, value, size, or intensity. **7** *Christianity* tending towards or involving an elaborate or formal style of worship: *high Anglican.* **8** *informal* **a** (often foll. by *on*) intoxicated by alcohol or esp. drugs. **b** exhilarated; ecstatic. **9** (of a sound or note) of high frequency; at the top end of the scale or of a singer's register etc. **10** (of a period, an age, a time, etc.) at its peak: *high noon ◊ High Renaissance.* **11** *Geography* (of latitude) near the North or South Pole. **12** (of a gear) having an output speed relatively close to that of the input speed. **13** (foll. by *in*) having an elevated proportion of: *high in fibre.* • *noun* **1** a high, or the highest, level or figure. **2** an area of high barometric pressure. **3** *informal* **a** a euphoric drug-induced state. **b** a state of excitement. • *adverb* **1** far up; aloft. **2** in or to a high degree. **3** at a high price. **4** (of a sound) at or to a high pitch: *sang high.* PHRASES **from on high** from heaven or a high place. **high on the agenda** (or **list**) considered a priority for discussion or action. **high opinion of** a favourable opinion of. **on high** in or to heaven or a high place. **on one's high horse** *informal* behaving superciliously or arrogantly. **run high 1** (of the sea) have a strong current with high tide. **2** (of feelings) be strong. **to high heaven** to a high degree: *stank to high heaven.*

high altar *noun* the chief altar of a church.

high and dry *adverb* (usu. in phr. **leave high and dry**) **1** stranded without resources. **2** (of a ship) out of the water, esp. stranded.

high and low *adverb* everywhere.

high and mighty *adjective informal* arrogant.

High Arctic *noun* the part of the Canadian Arctic that lies within the Arctic Circle.

highball • *noun* a drink of liquor diluted with a soft drink etc., served with ice in a tall glass. • *verb informal* (of a train, truck, etc.) move at full speed.

high beam *noun* (usu. in *plural*) a bright headlight beam, used for long-range illumination.

highboy *noun* a tall chest of drawers on legs.

highbrow *informal* • *adjective* intellectual; cultural. • *noun* an intellectual or cultured person.

highbush *adjective* designating varieties of

cranberries or blueberries growing on a relatively tall bush.

high chair *noun* an infant's chair with long legs and a tray, for use at meals.

High Church • *noun* a tradition within the Anglican Church emphasizing ritual, priestly authority, sacraments, and historical continuity with Catholic Christianity. • *adjective* of or relating to this tradition.

high-class *adjective* of high quality.

high command *noun* **1** the leaders of a military force and associated staff. **2** the chief headquarters of a military force.

High Commission 1 an embassy from one Commonwealth country to another. **2** an international commission, such as one under the auspices of the UN. ▶ **High Commissioner** *noun*

high-concept *noun* designating films etc. based on an uncomplicated and easily promoted central theme: *another high-concept blockbuster.*

High Court *noun* a supreme court of justice for civil cases.

high-cut *adjective* (of shorts, underpants, bodysuits, etc.) having the leg holes cut high up on the side.

high-definition *adjective* designating or providing a relatively clear or distinct image: *high-definition TV.*

high-density lipoprotein *noun* the form of lipoprotein involved in the transport of cholesterol and associated with lower risk of arteriosclerosis and heart attack.

high-end *adjective* of or associated with the most expensive section of the market: *a high-end stereo.*

higher education *noun* post-secondary education at university, college, etc.

higher-up *noun* (*plural* **higher-ups**) *informal* a person of higher rank; a superior.

highest common factor *noun* the highest number that can be divided exactly into each of two or more numbers.

high explosive *noun* an extremely explosive substance used in shells, bombs, blasting, etc.

highfalutin *adjective informal* absurdly pretentious.

high fashion *noun* the leading fashion houses or their products.

high fidelity *noun* the reproduction of sound with little distortion, giving a result very similar to the original: *high-fidelity sound.*

high-five *slang* • *noun* a gesture of celebration or greeting in which two people slap each other's palms with their arms outstretched over their heads. • *verb* (**high-fives**, **high-fived**, **high-fiving**) **1** greet with a high-five. **2** make a high-five. ▶ **high-fiving** *noun*

high-flown *adjective* (of language etc.) extravagant and grand-sounding: *if your writing sounds stiff or pompous, you may be using too many high-flown phrases.*

high flyer *noun* **1** an ambitious person. **2** a person or thing with great potential for achievement.

high-flying *adjective* **1** (of a person) ambitious. **2** (of stocks, securities, etc.) having great value or perceived value. **3** (of an airplane, ball, etc.) flying high in the air.

high frequency *noun* (*plural* **high frequencies**) a frequency, esp. in radio, of 3 to 30 megahertz. Abbreviation: **HF.** ▶ **high-frequency** *adjective*

High German *noun* standard written and spoken German.

high-grade • *adjective* **1** of high quality. **2** (of ore) rich in metal value and commercially profitable. • *verb* (**high-grades**, **high-graded**, **high-grading**) **1** steal (high-grade ore) from a mine. **2** cut down (the best trees) from a forest. ▶ **high-grading** *noun*

high ground *noun* **1** ground that is naturally elevated

and therefore strategically advantageous. **2** the position of esp. moral superiority in a debate etc.: *can we afford to maintain the moral high ground but lose votes?*

high-handed *adjective* disregarding others' feelings. ▶ **high-handedly** *adverb* **high-handedness** *noun*

high hat *noun* **1** a top hat. **2** = HI-HAT.

high-heeled *adjective* (of footwear) having high heels. **high heels** *plural noun* women's shoes with high heels.

High Holidays *plural noun* the Jewish festivals of Rosh Hashanah and Yom Kippur.

high-impact *adjective* **1** (of plastics etc.) able to withstand great impact without breaking. **2** designating esp. aerobic exercises that place a great deal of potentially harmful stress on the body. **3** having a great effect or lasting impression: *a high-impact movie*.

highjinks *plural noun* = HIJINKS.

high jump *noun* an athletic event consisting of jumping as high as possible over a bar of adjustable height. ▶ **high jumper** *noun* **high jumping** *noun*

high kick *noun* **1** a kick high in the air, esp. in dancing. **2** a traditional Inuit game in which participants try to kick an object suspended above them and land on the foot used to kick. ▶ **high-kicking** *adjective*

highland • *noun* (usu. in *plural*) **1** an area of high land. **2** (**the Highlands**) **a** the mountainous part of Scotland. **b** any similar area of hilly plateau: *Cape Breton Highlands*. • *adjective* of or in a highland or the Highlands.

Highland cattle *noun* a breed of shaggy-haired cattle with long, curved, widely-spaced horns.

highlander *noun* a person who lives in an area of high land, esp. (**Highlander**) one who lives in the Scottish Highlands.

Highland games *plural noun* a sports meeting and cultural festival, typically consisting of Scottish athletic events and other activities such as dancing etc.

high lead *noun* *Cdn Forestry* the high cable or line attached to a spar tree, from which logs are suspended to move them from the cutting area.

high-level *adjective* **1** (of negotiations etc.) conducted by high-ranking people. **2** (of a programming language) not machine-dependent and usu. at a level of abstraction close to a standard spoken language.

high life *noun* **1** (also **high living**) a luxurious existence. **2** (usu. **highlife**) a West African style of dance music characterized by traditional drumming and syncopated melodies.

highlight • *noun* **1** (in a painting etc.) a light area, or one seeming to reflect light. **2** a moment or detail of vivid interest; an outstanding feature. **3** (usu. in *plural*) a bright tint in the hair, e.g. as produced by bleaching. • *verb* **1** draw attention to. **2** mark with a highlighter. **3** create highlights in (the hair).

highlighter *noun* a marker pen which overlays colour on a printed word etc., leaving it emphasized.

highly *adverb* **1** in a high degree: *highly amusing*. **2** favourably: *think highly of her*.

high maintenance *adjective* requiring much or frequent maintenance, attention, etc.

High Mass *noun* a Mass in which the prayers are sung rather than spoken.

high-minded *adjective* having high moral principles. ▶ **high-mindedly** *adverb* **high-mindedness** *noun*

high muckamuck *noun* = MUCKY-MUCK.

highness *noun* (*plural* **highnesses**) **1** the state of being high. **2** (**Highness**) a title used in addressing and referring to a prince or princess: *Her Royal Highness*.

high-octane *adjective* **1** (of fuel used in internal combustion engines) of very good quality and very efficient. **2** high-powered; potent: *a high-octane dessert*.

high-pitched *adjective* **1** (of a sound) high. **2** (of a roof) steep.

high-powered *adjective* (also **high-power**) **1** having great power or energy. **2** important or influential.

high pressure • *noun* **1** a high degree of activity or exertion. **2** a condition of the atmosphere with the pressure above 101.3 kilopascals. • *adjective* (usu. **high-pressure**) **1** having or involving a pressure that is above the ordinary: *high-pressure propane*. **2** (of a job, etc.) demanding; having a high level of stress. **3** (of a sales technique, etc.) forceful, persistent.

high priest *noun* **1** a chief priest in some non-Christian religions. **2** a chief exponent of a political or cultural movement, esp. one who promotes the cause with dogmatism and fervour: *the self-appointed high priest of Canadian liberalism*.

high priestess *noun* (*plural* **high priestesses**) **1** a chief priestess in some non-Christian religions. **2** a woman who is the chief exponent of a political or cultural movement, esp. one who promotes the cause with dogmatism and fervour: *the high priestess of the conservation movement*.

high profile *noun* exposure to attention or publicity. ▶ **high-profile** *adjective*

high-quality *adjective* of high quality.

high-ranking *adjective* of high rank, senior.

high relief *noun* see RELIEF 7.

high rigger *noun* the logger responsible for climbing, topping, and rigging the spar tree.

high-rise • *adjective* (of a building) having many storeys. • *noun* such a building.

high-risk *adjective* involving or exposed to danger.

high road *noun* a direct route: *on the high road to success*.

high roller *noun* *slang* a person who gambles large sums or spends freely.

high school *noun* a secondary school. ▶ **high-school** *adjective*

high sea *noun* (also **high seas**) open seas not within any country's jurisdiction.

high season *noun* the period during which the most people travel, book accommodation, etc.

high-security *adjective* **1** (of a prison, lock, etc.) extremely secure. **2** (of a prisoner) kept in a high-security prison.

high sign *noun* *informal* a surreptitious gesture indicating that all is well or that the coast is clear.

high-speed *adjective* **1** operating at great speed. **2** (of steel) suitable for tools, cutting so rapidly as to become red-hot.

high-spirited *adjective* vivacious; cheerful.

high spirits *plural noun* vivacity; energy; cheerfulness.

high-stakes *adjective* **1** designating a gambling game where the stakes are high. **2** (of an activity) highly risky; dangerous.

high-step *verb* (**high-steps**, **high-stepped**, **high-stepping**) (esp. as **high-stepping** *adjective*) walk or move lifting one's feet high off the ground.

high-stick *verb* (**high-sticks**, **high-sticked**, **high-sticking**) *Hockey* illegally strike another player, deliberately or accidentally, with the stick held above shoulder level.

high-sticking *noun* (in ice and field hockey) an illegal raising of the blade of the stick above shoulder level.

high-strung *adjective* very sensitive or nervous.

hightail *verb* *informal* PHRASES **hightail it** hurry.

high-tech • *adjective* **1** (of interior design etc.) imitating styles more usual in industry etc., esp. using steel, glass, or plastic in a functional way. **2** employing, requiring, or involved in high technology. • *noun* (**high tech**) = HIGH TECHNOLOGY.

high technology *noun* advanced technological development, esp. in electronics.

high-tensile *adjective* (of metal) very strong under tension.

high tension *noun* = HIGH VOLTAGE.

high tide *noun* **1** the tide at its fullest. **2** the time of this.

high time *noun* a time that is late or overdue: *it is high time they arrived*.

high-toned *adjective* stylish or superior: *an oasis of high-toned culture*.

high-top • *adjective* designating shoes, esp. athletic shoes, whose uppers come above the ankle bone. • *noun* (in *plural*) high-top shoes.

high treason *noun see* TREASON 1.

high voltage • *noun* electrical potential large enough to cause injury or damage if diverted. • *adjective* (also **high-voltage**) **1** involving high electrical voltage. **2** displaying a great deal of energy: *a high-voltage performance*.

high water *noun* = HIGH TIDE.

high-water mark *noun* **1** the level reached at high water. **2** the maximum recorded value or highest point of excellence: *a high-water mark in post-war jazz*.

highway *noun* **1 a** a main road, esp. one between towns or cities. **b** a public road. **c** a much-travelled route leading directly to a place: *the Mackenzie River: history's highway to the Arctic Ocean*. **2** a direct course of action: *on the highway to success*.

highwayman *noun* (*plural* **highwaymen**) *hist.* a man, usu. mounted and armed with a gun, who robbed travellers on public roads.

highway robbery *noun informal* a price or charge that is unreasonably or exorbitantly high.

high wire *noun* a high tightrope.

hi-hat *noun* a pair of cymbals mounted one above the other on an upright rod, with a sprung pedal at the base to move the upper cymbal down onto the other.

hijab *noun* a veil worn by some Muslim women to cover the hair, forehead, etc. [Say HIDGE ob]

hijack • *verb* **1** seize control of (an aircraft in flight etc.), esp. to force it to a different destination. **2** take over (an organization etc.) by force or deceit in order to redirect it: *demonstrators fear that the rally could be hijacked by extremists*. • *noun* an occurrence of hijacking. ▶ **hijacker** *noun*

hijinks *plural noun informal* boisterous joking or merrymaking. [Say HI jinks]

hijra *noun* = HEGIRA. [Say HIDGE ruh]

hike • *noun* **1** a long walk, esp. in the country, taken for pleasure or exercise. **2** an increase (of prices etc.). • *verb* (**hikes, hiked, hiking**) **1** go for a long walk, esp. across country. **2** (usu. foll. by *up*) **a** hitch up (clothing etc.). **b** work upwards out of place, become hitched up. **3** increase (prices etc.). PHRASES **take a hike** *slang* go away: *told him to take a hike*. ▶ **hiker** *noun*

hiking boot *noun* a moderately low-cut leather boot with a heavy tread, worn esp. when hiking.

hilarious *adjective* exceedingly funny. ▶ **hilariously** *adverb* **hilarity** *noun*

hill *noun* **1** a naturally raised area of land, not as high as a mountain. **2** (often in *combination*) a heap; a mound: *anthill*. **3** a sloping piece of road. **4** (**the Hill**) **a** (in Canada) = PARLIAMENT HILL. **b** (in the US) = CAPITOL HILL. **5 a** a heap formed around a plant by banking up soil. **b** a cluster of plants in such a hill or on level ground. PHRASES **old as the hills** very ancient. **over the hill** *informal* **1** past the prime of life; declining. **2** past the crisis.

hillbilly *esp. US* • *noun* (*plural* **hillbillies**) **1** *informal*,

often *derogatory* a person from a remote or mountainous area, esp. in the Appalachians. **2** country music of or like that of the southern US. • *adjective* of, like, or relating to hillbillies.

hillock *noun* a small hill or mound. [Say HILL uck]

hillside • *noun* the sloping side of a hill. • *adjective* located on the side of a hill.

hilltop *noun* the summit of a hill.

hilly *adjective* (**hillier, hilliest**) having many hills.

hilt *noun* **1** the handle of a sword, dagger, etc. **2** the handle of a tool. PHRASES **to the hilt** completely.

him *pronoun* **1** *objective case of* HE: *I saw him*. **2** *informal* he: *it's him ◊ is taller than him*.

Himalayan *adjective* relating to the Himalayas, a vast mountain system in southern Asia which includes Mount Everest, the highest mountain in the world. [Say himma LAY in]

himself *pronoun* **1 a** *emphatic form of* HE or HIM: *he himself will do it*. **b** *reflexive form of* HIM: *he has hurt himself*. **2** in his normal state of body or mind: *does not feel quite himself today*.

hind[1] *adjective* (esp. of parts of the body) situated behind or at the back, posterior: *hind leg*.

hind[2] *noun* a female deer (esp. a red deer), esp. in and after the third year.

hinder[1] *verb* impede, delay. [Say HIN der]

hinder[2] *adjective* rear, hind: *the hinder part*. [Say HIND er]

Hindi • *noun* **1** a group of spoken dialects of northern India. **2** a literary form of Hindustani with a Sanskrit-based vocabulary, an official language of India. • *adjective* of or concerning Hindi. [Say HIN dee]

hindmost *adjective* furthest behind; most remote.

hindquarters *plural noun* the hind legs and adjoining parts of a quadruped.

hindrance *noun* **1** a person or thing that makes it more difficult for someone to do something or for something to happen: *the high price is a hindrance for buyers ◊ to be honest, she was more of a hindrance than a help*. **2** the act of making it more difficult for someone to do something or for something to happen: *completed their journey without further hindrance*. [Say HIN drince]

hindsight *noun* wisdom after the event: *realized with hindsight that they were wrong ◊ in hindsight, the price looks even worse*.

Hindu • *noun* (*plural* **Hindus**) a follower of Hinduism. • *adjective* of or concerning Hindus or Hinduism.

Hinduism *noun* the main religious and social system

of India, including a belief in reincarnation, the worship of several gods, and an ordained caste system as the basis of society.
Hindustani • *noun* *hist.* the Delhi dialect of Hindi, widely used throughout India as a lingua franca. • *adjective* of or relating to northwestern India or its people, or Hindustani. [Say hindu STANNY]
hinge • *noun* **1** a movable joint on which something swings open or is closed. **2** a central point or principle on which everything depends: *his illness is the hinge on which this story hangs.* • *verb* (**hinges**, **hinged**, **hinging**) **1** (foll. by *on*) **a** depend (on a principle, an event, etc.): *everything hinges on his acceptance.* **b** (of a door etc.) hang and turn (on a post etc.). **2** attach with or as if with a hinge. ▶ **hinged** *adjective*
hint • *noun* **1** a slight or indirect indication or suggestion. **2** a small piece of practical information; a tip. **3** a very small trace, a slight indication: *a hint of perfume.* • *verb* suggest slightly or indirectly: *hinted that they were wrong.* PHRASES **hint at** give a hint of or refer indirectly to. **take a** (or **the**) **hint** understand what is meant or stated indirectly and act accordingly.
hinterland *noun* **1** a remote or fringe area; backcountry. **2** the area around or beyond a major town, coastal stretch, or river: *a market town serving its rich agricultural hinterland.*
hip[1] *noun* **1** a projection of the pelvis and upper thigh bone on each side of the body in human beings and quadrupeds. **2** the part on each side of the human body between the top of the legs and the waist.
hip[2] *noun* the fruit of a rose, esp. a wild kind.
hip[3] *adjective* (**hipper**, **hippest**) *slang* **1** following the latest fashion in esp. music, clothes, etc.; stylish. **2** (often foll. by *to*) understanding, aware.
hip[4] *interjection* introducing a united cheer: *hip, hip, hooray.*
hip bone *noun* a bone forming the hip, esp. the ilium.
hip check *Hockey* • *noun* a type of bodycheck in which a player suddenly thrusts his or her hips to the side to obstruct or hit an opponent who is attempting to skate past. • *verb* (**hip-check**) hit or obstruct in this way.
hip dysplasia *noun* an abnormal development of the hip joint in some mid- to large-sized dogs.
hip flask *noun* a small metal bottle for liquor etc., carried in a hip pocket.
hip hop *noun* **1** a style of popular music of US black origin, featuring frequently politically inspired raps delivered above spare, electronic backing. **2** the subculture associated with this, including graffiti art, breakdancing, etc. ▶ **hip-hopper** *noun*
hipped roof *noun* = HIP ROOF.
hippie *noun* *informal* **1** (esp. in the 1960s) a young person who rejected traditional societal values, advocated free love, peace, etc., and adopted an unconventional appearance, typically with long hair, jeans, beads, etc. **2** a person resembling a hippie in dress, beliefs, etc. ▶ **hippiedom** *noun*
hippo *noun* (*plural* **hippos**) *informal* a hippopotamus.
hippocampus *noun* (*plural* **hippocampi**) **1** a sea horse. **2** the elongated ridges on the floor of each lateral ventricle of the brain, thought to be the centre of emotion and the autonomic nervous system. [Say hippa CAMPUS for the singular, hippa CAM pee for the plural]
hippopotamus *noun* (*plural* **hippopotamuses** or **hippopotami**) **1** a large, thick-skinned, four-legged mammal native to Africa, inhabiting rivers, lakes, etc. **2** (also **pygmy hippopotamus**) a smaller related African mammal inhabiting forests and swamps.
hippy[1] *noun* (*plural* **hippies**) = HIPPIE.
hippy[2] *adjective* (**hippier**, **hippiest**) having large hips.

hip roof *noun* a roof with both the sides and the ends inclined.
hipster *noun* *slang* a person who is hip.
hip waders *plural noun* waders that come up to the hips.
hire • *verb* (**hires**, **hired**, **hiring**) **1** employ (a person) for wages or a fee. **2** procure the temporary use of (a thing) for an agreed payment. • *noun* **1** the action of hiring someone or something. **2** a recently hired employee. PHRASES **for** (or **on**) **hire** ready to be hired. **hire out 1** grant the temporary use of (a thing) for an agreed payment. **2 hire oneself out** make oneself available for employment.

> **SPELL CHECK**
> **hierarchy, hieroglyph**
>
> Warning: **hierarchy** and **hieroglyph** are spelled *hier-*.

hired gun *noun* *informal* **1 a** an expert brought in to resolve complex esp. legal or financial problems, disputes, etc. **b** a person, e.g. a lobbyist, able to attain power or influence for others quickly and efficiently. **2 a** a bodyguard or other person hired to protect or fight for another. **b** a person contracted to kill another, e.g. a hit man or gunfighter.
hired hand *noun* a person employed to do usu. manual work on a farm, ranch, etc.
hireling *noun* usu. *derogatory* a person who works primarily for monetary gain, esp. without other motives such as job satisfaction etc.
hirsute *adjective* **1** hairy, shaggy. **2** covered with long soft or moderately stiff hairs. [Say her SUIT]

> **WRITING TIP**
> **his**
>
> The use of **his** to refer to a person of unspecified sex, as in *Every student must do his homework*, is often criticized as sexist. Suitable alternatives include *Every student must do his or her homework* and *All students must do their homework*, or simply *All students must do homework*. The use of the plural pronoun **their** following a singular noun, as in *Every student must do their homework*, is considered incorrect by some, but is becoming more and more accepted in writing and speech. *See usage note at* THEIR.

his *possessive adjective* of or belonging to him or himself. PHRASES **his and hers** (of matching items) for husband and wife, or men and women. **of his** of or belonging to him: *a friend of his.*
Hispanic • *adjective* **1** of or relating to Spain or to Spanish-speaking countries. **2** of or relating to Hispanics. • *noun* a Spanish-speaking person living in the US or Canada, esp. one of Latin American descent. [Say hiss PANIC]
hiss • *verb* (**hisses**, **hissed**, **hissing**) **1 a** make a sharp sibilant sound: *the goose hissed angrily.* **b** make this sound to show disapproval or derision: *the audience booed and hissed.* **2** whisper (a threat etc.) urgently or angrily. • *noun* (*plural* **hisses**) **1** a sharp sibilant sound as of the letter *s*. **2** *Electronics* audible interference. ▶ **hissy** *adjective*
hissy fit *noun* *informal* a temper tantrum; an angry outburst.
histamine *noun* an amine causing contraction of smooth muscle and dilation of capillaries, released by most cells in response to injury and in allergic and inflammatory reactions. [Say HISTA min or HISTA mean]
histology *noun* (*plural* **histologies**) **1** the study of the

H

microscopic structure of tissues. **2** the microscopic structure of tissues. [Say hiss TOLLA jee]

historian *noun* **1** a writer of history, esp. a critical analyst, rather than a compiler. **2** a person learned in history, esp. one professionally engaged in teaching and researching history: *a Canadian historian*.

historic *adjective* famous or important in history or potentially so: *a historic moment*.

historical *adjective* **1** of or concerning history: *historical evidence*. **2** belonging to history, not to prehistory or legend: *scholars occupied with the search for the historical Jesus*. **3** (of the study of a subject) based on an analysis of its development over a period: *historical lexicography*. **4** belonging to the past, not the present: *she writes biographies of famous historical figures*. **5** (of a novel, a film, etc.) dealing or professing to deal with historical events: *I've been reading a historical novel set in the 1830s*. **6** in connection with history, from the historian's point of view: *of purely historical interest*.
▶ **historically** *adverb*

historicism *noun* **1 a** the theory that social and cultural phenomena are determined by history. **b** the belief that historical events are governed by laws. **2** the tendency to regard historical development as the most basic aspect of human existence. **3** an excessive regard for past styles etc.: *an obsession with historicism on the part of performers and the public*. [Say hiss TORRA cism]

historiographer *noun* **1** an expert in or student of historiography. **2** a writer of history, esp. an official historian. [Say hiss tory OGGRA fer]

historiography *noun* **1** the writing of history. **2** the study of history-writing. [Say hiss tory OGGRA fee]

history *noun* (*plural* **histories**) **1** a continuous, usu. chronological, record of important or public events. **2 a** the study of past events, esp. human affairs. **b** the total accumulation of past events, esp. relating to human affairs or to the accumulation of developments connected with a particular nation, person, thing, etc.: *the history of Canada ◊ has a history of illness*. **3** an eventful past: *this house has a history*. **4 a** a systematic or critical account of or research into a past event, development, movement, etc.: *the history of broadcasting*. **b** a similar record or account of natural phenomena. **5** a historical play. PHRASES **be history** *informal* be no longer existing, relevant, or important: *one more mistake and I'll be history*. **go down in history** be remembered or recorded in history. **make history 1** do or take part in something important enough to be recorded in the world's or one's country's history. **2** do something unusual or important, esp. something never before done in an art, science, profession, sport, etc. **the rest is history** a concluding statement suggesting that the events succeeding those already related are so familiar as to need no repetition.

histrionic ● *adjective* (of behaviour) theatrical; dramatically exaggerated: *a histrionic outburst*. ● *noun* (in *plural*) insincere and dramatic behaviour designed to impress: *she was used to her mother's histrionics*.
▶ **histrionically** *adverb* [Say histry ON ick]

hit ● *verb* (**hits**, **hit**, **hitting**) **1** strike. **2** affect the feelings, conscience, etc. of a person, esp. deeply or painfully: *the loss hit him hard*. **3** *informal* **a** encounter: *hit a snag*. **b** arrive at: *hit an all-time low*. **4** *slang* kill, attack, or rob. **5** occur forcefully to: *the seriousness of the situation hit him later*. **6** *informal* give (a person) a playing card, alcoholic drink, etc. **7** *slang* (also foll. by *up*) request, ask, or beg (a person), esp. for money. **8** represent or imitate exactly: *hit the exact colour*. ● *noun* **1 a** a blow; a stroke. **b** a collision. **2** a shot etc. that hits its target. **3** a popular success, esp. in entertainment. **4** *slang* **a** a violent crime, esp. a contract killing. **b** a dose of

something, esp. an illegal drug. **5** *Baseball* = BASE HIT. **6** *Computing* a successful attempt, esp. an instance of identifying an item of data which matches the requirements of a search etc. **7** a connection made to a Web site; an instance of a Web site being accessed by a user. PHRASES **hit back** retaliate. **hit below the belt 1** esp. *Boxing* hit an opponent below the waist, esp. in the genitals. **2** treat or behave unfairly. **hit the books** study, esp. intensely or diligently. **hit the bottle** (or **booze** etc.) *informal* drink too much habitually or over a period of time. **hit the bricks** *slang* go on strike. **hit the deck** *informal* fall to the floor, ground, etc. **hit the ground running** *informal* **1** begin a task, endeavour, etc. with the basic preparation already completed. **2** proceed with enthusiasm and dynamism. **hit home 1** become fully and often painfully clear. **2** (of remarks etc.) have the intended, often painful, effect. **hit it** *Music* begin playing. **hit it off** *informal* get on well or have a good and harmonious relationship (with a person). **hit the nail on the head** guess correctly or express the truth precisely. **hit on 1** (also **hit upon**) find (what is sought), esp. by chance. **2** *slang* make sexual overtures toward (a person). **hit out** deal vigorous physical or verbal blows: *hit out at her enemies*. **hit the road** (also **trail**) *slang* depart. **hit the sack** (or **hay**) *informal* go to bed. **make** (or **be**) **a hit** be successful or popular.

hit-and-miss *adjective* (also **hit-or-miss**) aimed or done carelessly, at random, or haphazardly.

hit and roll *noun Curling* (*plural* **hit and rolls**) a play in which a rock strikes and glances off a stationary rock, sliding into a better position and usu. knocking the other rock into a less advantageous position.

hit and run ● *noun* (*plural* **hit and runs**) **1 a** a motor vehicle accident in which the driver who caused the accident flees the scene. **b** a military etc. attack using swift actions followed by immediate withdrawals. **2** *Baseball* the departure of a runner from his or her base as soon as the pitcher begins to throw to the batter. ● *adjective* (**hit-and-run**) relating to or (of a person) committing a hit and run: *hit-and-run fatalities*.

hit and stay *noun* (also **hit and stick**) *Curling* (*plural* **hit and stays** or **hit and sticks**) a play in which a rock strikes an opponent's rock directly, knocking it into a less advantageous position and, at the same time, assumes the position of the previously stationary rock.

hitch ● *verb* (**hitches**, **hitched**, **hitching**) **1** fasten with a loop, hook, etc. **2** move with a jerk: *hitched the pillow to a comfortable position*. **3** *informal* = HITCHHIKE. **4** catch, snag, or become caught on something. ● *noun* (*plural* **hitches**) **1** an impediment; a temporary obstacle: *the unit ran without a hitch*. **2** an abrupt pull or push; a jerk. **3** any of various kinds of noose or knot used to fasten one thing temporarily to another. **4** a contrivance for fastening one thing to another: *trailer hitch*. PHRASES **get hitched** *informal* marry. **hitch up 1** lift (esp. clothing) with a jerk. **2** meet, join, or become associated with. **hitch one's wagon to a star** associate oneself with a person more prominent than oneself; make use of powers or opportunities greater than one's own.

hitchhike *verb* (**hitchhikes**, **hitchhiked**, **hitchhiking**) travel by seeking free lifts in passing vehicles. ▶ **hitchhiker** *noun* **hitchhiking** *noun*

hi-tech *adjective* = HIGH-TECH.

hither *adverb* to or towards this place.

hither and thither *adverb* (also **hither and yon**) here and there, in various directions, to and fro.

hitherto *adverb* until this time, up to now.

hitless *adjective Baseball* without a hit.

hit list *noun slang* **1** a list of prospective victims esp. of

assassination. **2** a list of people, programs, etc. against whom some action is being planned.

hitmaker *noun informal* an entertainer, esp. a musician, who consistently produces a number of bestselling records etc.

hit man *noun* (*plural* **hit men**) *slang* a hired assassin.

hit-or-miss *adjective* = HIT-AND-MISS.

hit parade *noun informal* **1** a list of the current bestselling records of popular music. **2** any listing of popular people, things, etc. in a specified field.

hitter *noun Baseball* **1** a player who hits or who is at bat: *Patti is one of our best hitters*. **2** (*in combination*) a game in which the pitcher allows the number of hits indicated: *Chris pitched a three-hitter last game*.

Hittite • *noun* **1** a member of an ancient, non-Semitic people of Asia Minor and Syria. **2** the Indo-European language of the Hittites, written in cuneiform and deciphered in the early 20th century. • *adjective* of or relating to the Hittites or their language. [Say HIT ite]

HIV *abbreviation* human immunodeficiency virus, a retrovirus which causes AIDS.

hive • *noun* **1 a** a beehive. **b** the bees in a hive. **2** a place in which people are busily occupied: *the kitchen became a hive of activity*. • *verb* (**hives**, **hived**, **hiving**) **1** place (bees) in a hive. **2** (of bees) enter a hive. PHRASES **hive off 1** separate from a larger group. **2** form into or assign (work) to a subsidiary department or company.

hives *plural noun* any of various skin conditions characterized by itchy red welts caused by allergic reaction, emotional stress, etc.

hiya *interjection informal* a word used in greeting.

hl *abbreviation* hectolitre(s).

hm *abbreviation* hectometre(s).

HMCS *abbreviation* Her (or His) Majesty's Canadian Ship (as a designation for a Canadian naval vessel).

hmm *interjection* expressing hesitation, reflection, etc.

HMS *abbreviation* Her (or His) Majesty's Ship (as a designation for a British naval vessel).

Ho *symbol* holmium.

ho *interjection* **1** (also *in combination*) an expression of admiration or (often repeated as **ho! ho!**), derision, surprise, or triumph. **2** a call for attention. **3** (*in combination*) an addition to the name of a destination etc.: *westward ho*.

hoar *noun* (also **hoarfrost**) frozen water vapour deposited in clear still weather on vegetation etc.

> SPELL CHECK
> **hoard, horde** ABC ✓
>
> A crowd of people is a **horde**.

hoard • *noun* **1** a stock or store (esp. of money) put away: *he came back to rescue his little hoard of gold*. **2** an amassed store of facts etc.: *a hoard of secret information about his work*. • *verb* **1** (often foll. by *up*) amass (money etc.) and put away; store: *thousands of antiques hoarded by a compulsive collector*. **2** accumulate more than one's current requirements of food etc. in a time of scarcity: *many of the refugees had hoarded rations*. ▶ **hoarder** *noun*

hoarding *noun* a temporary board fence erected around a construction site etc.

> SPELL CHECK
> **hoarse, horse** ABC ✓
>
> The animal is a **horse**.

hoarse *adjective* (**hoarser**, **hoarsest**) **1** (of the voice) husky; croaking. **2** having such a voice, due to illness, shouting, etc. ▶ **hoarsely** *adverb* **hoarseness** *noun*

hoary *adjective* (**hoarier**, **hoariest**) **1 a** (of hair) grey

or white with age. **b** (of a person) having such hair; aged. **2** old and trite: *a hoary joke*. **3** *Botany & Zoology* covered with short white hairs.

hoax • *noun* (*plural* **hoaxes**) a humorous or malicious deception; a practical joke. • *verb* (**hoaxes**, **hoaxed**, **hoaxing**) deceive with a hoax. ▶ **hoaxer** *noun*

hob[1] *noun* a flat metal shelf at the side of a fireplace, having its surface level with the top of the grate, used esp. for heating a pan etc.

hob[2] *noun* PHRASES **play** (or **raise**) **hob** cause mischief or act disruptively: *the rain played hob with the summer theatre performances*.

hobble • *verb* (**hobbles**, **hobbled**, **hobbling**) **1 a** walk lamely; limp. **b** proceed haltingly in action or speech: *hobbled lamely to his conclusion*. **2** tie together the legs of a horse etc. to prevent it from straying. **3 a** cause (a person etc.) to limp. **b** hinder or interfere with (a person, plan, etc.). • *noun* **1** an uneven or infirm gait: *he finished the game reduced to a hobble*. **2** a rope, clog, etc. used for hobbling a horse etc.

hobby *noun* (*plural* **hobbies**) a favourite leisure-time activity or occupation.

hobby horse *noun* **1** a child's toy consisting of a long stick with a figure of a horse's head on one end. **2** a favourite topic of conversation. **3** a rocking horse.

hobbyist *noun* a person who pursues a particular hobby: *the hockey memorabilia interest hobbyists*.

hobgoblin *noun* **1** a mischievous imp or sprite. **2** something to be feared superstitiously; a bugbear: *her particular hobgoblin is sloppy spelling*.

hobnail *noun* a heavy-headed nail formerly used for boot soles. ▶ **hobnailed** *adjective*

hobnob *verb* (**hobnobs**, **hobnobbed**, **hobnobbing**) (usu. foll. by *with*) mix socially or informally.

hobo *noun* (*plural* **hoboes** or **hobos**) a vagrant.

> SPELL CHECK
> **hock, hawk**
>
> The bird of prey is a **hawk**. **Hawk** also means "clear the throat" or "go around offering goods for sale".

hock[1] *noun* **1** the joint of a quadruped's hind leg between the knee and the fetlock. **2** a knuckle of pork; the lower joint of a ham.

hock[2] *verb informal* pawn. PHRASES **in hock 1** in debt. **2** in pawn.

hockey *noun* **1** a game played on ice between two teams of six players each, in which players try to shoot a puck into the opposing team's net with sticks. **2** any of a number of variations of this, such as street hockey. *See also* FIELD HOCKEY.

hockey bag *noun* a large esp. nylon bag for carrying hockey equipment, usu. with pockets for skates.

hockey cushion *noun Cdn* a skating rink with hockey boards, esp. an outdoor rink of natural ice.

hockey jacket *noun Cdn* an outer jacket, usu. of nylon with a quilted lining, with a hockey team's crest on the chest and the owner's name, position, number, etc. embroidered on the arm.

hockey mom *noun* (also **hockey mother**) a mother deeply committed to a child's hockey practice, career, etc.

hockey pants *plural noun* knee-length, high-waisted padded pants worn by hockey players to protect their thighs, hips, and kidneys.

hockey puck *noun* **1** = PUCK 1. **2** an object the size or shape of a hockey puck.

hockey socks *plural noun* long woollen leggings extending from thigh to ankle, held up by a garter belt and with stirrups for the feet, worn by hockey players.

hockey stick *noun* a stick with a flat, slightly curved blade at the lower end, used to control, pass, and shoot the puck in hockey.

hockey tape *noun* an adhesive tape used esp. on the blade of a hockey stick to strengthen it or on the handle to improve the grip.

hocus-pocus *noun* **1** meaningless talk or activity, often designed to draw attention away from and disguise what is actually happening: *some people still view psychology as a lot of hocus-pocus*. **2** a form of words often used by a person performing conjuring tricks. [Say hoke us POKE us]

hod *noun* a V-shaped open trough on a pole used for carrying bricks, mortar, etc.

hodgepodge *noun* a mixture of heterogeneous things, a jumble.

Hodgkin's disease *noun* a malignant but often curable disease of the lymphatic system usu. characterized by enlargement of the lymph nodes, liver, and spleen. [Say HODGE kins]

hoe • *noun* a long-handled tool with a thin metal blade, used for weeding etc. • *verb* (**hoes, hoed, hoeing**) weed (crops); loosen (earth); dig up or cut down with a hoe.

hoedown *noun* **1** a lively party with square dancing, country music, etc. **2** the music played at such a party.

hog • *noun* **1 a** a domesticated pig, esp. a castrated male reared for slaughter. **b** a wild animal of the pig family, e.g. a warthog. **2** *informal* **a** a greedy person. **b** a person who hoards selfishly or monopolizes something: *a puck hog*. **3** *slang* a large, heavy motorcycle. • *verb* (**hogs, hogged, hogging**) *informal* take greedily; hoard selfishly; monopolize. PHRASES **go (the) whole hog** *informal* do something completely or thoroughly. **live high on** (or **off**) **the hog** *informal* live luxuriously.

hogback *noun* (also **hog's back**) a ridge of land sloping steeply on each side.

hog line *noun* Curling either of two lines drawn across each end of a rink at one-sixth of the rink's length from the tee, which a rock must cross to count in the game.

hognose snake *noun* any of several harmless North American snakes which have an upturned snout.

hogshead *noun* **1** a large cask. **2** a liquid or dry measure, varying according to the commodity, but usu. about 220 to 245 litres. [Say HOGS head]

hog-tie *verb* (**hog-ties, hog-tied, hog-tying**) **1** secure by fastening the hands and feet or all four feet together. **2** restrain, impede: *the Conservatives had the House of Commons hog-tied by procedural snares*.

hogwash *noun* *informal* nonsense, rubbish.

hog-wild *adjective* *informal* exceedingly excited or enthusiastic.

ho ho *interjection* **1** representing deep jolly laughter. **2** expressing surprise, triumph, or derision.

ho-hum • *adjective* dull, routine, boring. • *interjection* expressing boredom.

hoick *verb* *informal* (often foll. by *out*) lift or pull, esp. with a jerk.

hoi polloi *noun* the masses; the common people: *she always tried to avoid mixing with the hoi polloi*. [Say hoy puh LOY]

hoisin sauce *noun* a sweet, spicy, dark red sauce made from soybeans, vinegar, sugar, garlic, and spices, widely used in southern Chinese cooking. [Say HOY zin]

hoist • *verb* **1** raise or haul up. **2** raise by means of ropes and pulleys etc. • *noun* **1** an apparatus for hoisting. **2** an act of hoisting, a lift. **3 a** the perpendicular height of a flag or sail (*compare* FLY¹ *noun* 5a). **b** the part of a flag nearest the staff (*compare* FLY¹ *noun* 5b). **c** a group of flags raised as a signal.

hoity-toity *adjective* haughty, snobbish, pretentious.

Hokan • *noun* a group of languages spoken by certain Aboriginal peoples of California, the US southwest, and Mexico. • *adjective* designating or pertaining to such languages. [Say HOE k'n]

hokey *adjective* (**hokier, hokiest**) *slang* sentimental, contrived. ▶ **hokeyness** *noun*

hokum *noun* *slang* **1** sentimental, popular, sensational, or unreal situations, dialogue, etc., in a film or play etc.: *classic B-movie hokum*. **2** nonsense: *he dismissed the president's speech as corporate hokum*. [Say HOE k'm]

hold¹ • *verb* (**holds, held, holding**) **1** grasp, carry, or support. **2** keep or detain. **3** have in one's possession. **4** contain or be capable of containing. **5** have or occupy a job or position. **6** have a belief or opinion. **7** stay or cause to stay at a certain value or level. **8** adhere or cause to adhere to a commitment. **9** continue to follow a course. **10** arrange and take part in a meeting or conversation. **11** regard someone or something with a specified feeling. **12** refrain from adding or using. • *noun* **1** an act or manner of grasping someone or something. **2** a handhold. **3** a degree of power or control. **4** a tentative reservation. PHRASES **get (a) hold of** **1** acquire, obtain, etc. **2** contact or communicate with, esp. by telephone. **hold (a thing) against (a person)** resent or regard (a thing) as discreditable to (a person). **hold back 1** impede the progress of; restrain. **2** keep (a thing) to or for oneself. **3** (often foll. by *from*) hesitate; refrain. **hold by** (or **to**) adhere to (a choice, purpose, etc.). **hold court** preside over one's admirers etc., like a sovereign. **hold down 1** repress. **2** *informal* be competent enough to keep (one's job etc.). **3** secure, restrain, or limit. **hold everything!** cease action or movement. **hold the fort 1** act as a temporary substitute. **2** cope in an emergency. **hold forth 1** offer (an inducement etc.). **2** usu. *derogatory* speak at length or tediously. **hold a person's hand** give a person guidance or moral support. **hold hands** grasp one another by the hand as a sign of affection or for support or guidance. **hold one's head high** behave proudly and confidently. **hold one's horses** *informal* stop; slow down. **hold in** keep in check, confine. **hold it!** stop; cease and desist. **hold the line 1** not yield. **2** maintain a telephone connection. **hold one's nose** compress the nostrils to avoid a bad smell. **hold off 1** delay; not begin. **2** keep one's distance. **hold on 1** keep one's grasp on something. **2** wait a moment. **3** (when telephoning) not hang up. **hold out 1** stretch forth (a hand etc.). **2** offer (an inducement etc.). **3** maintain resistance. **4** persist or last. **hold out for** continue to demand. **hold out on** *informal* refuse something to (a person). **hold over 1** postpone, keep for future consideration. **2** retain for an additional period: *the movie was held over for another week*. **hold something over** threaten (a person) constantly with something. **hold together 1** cohere. **2** cause to cohere. **3** retain one's composure, esp. in difficult circumstances. **hold one's tongue** *informal* be silent. **hold to ransom 1** keep (a person) prisoner until a ransom is paid. **2** demand concessions from by threats of damaging action. **hold true** (or **good**) be valid; apply. **hold up 1 a** support; sustain. **b** maintain (the head etc.) erect. **2** exhibit; display. **3** arrest the progress of; obstruct. **4** stop and rob by violence or threats. **hold water** (of reasoning) be sound; bear examination. **hold with** (usu. with *neg.*) *informal* approve of: *don't hold with motorbikes*. **left holding the bag** left with unwelcome responsibility. **on hold 1** (when telephoning) holding the line. **2** reserved: *the book is on hold*. **3** (esp. in phr. **put on hold**) temporarily inactive or receiving little attention. **take hold** (of a custom or

habit) become established. **there is no holding him** (or **her** etc.) used to say that someone is particularly determined or cannot be prevented from doing something: *once she gets onto the subject of politics there's no holding her.* **with no holds barred** with no restrictions, all methods being permitted.

hold[2] *noun* a cavity in the lower part of a ship or aircraft in which the cargo is stowed.

holder *noun* **1** (often in *combination*) a device or implement for holding something. **2** the possessor of a title, record, office, bank account, etc.

holding *noun* **1 a** land held by lease. **b** the tenure of land. **2** (usu. in *plural*) stocks, property, etc. held. **3** *Sport* the action of illegally restraining or obstructing one's opponent. **4** the collection of books etc. in a library.

holding company *noun* (*plural* **holding companies**) a company created to hold the shares of other companies, which it then controls.

holding pattern *noun* **1** the (usu. circular) flight path maintained by an aircraft awaiting permission to land. **2** a state or period of no progress or change.

holding tank *noun* a tank for short-term storage.

holdout *noun* **1** an act of resisting something or refusing to accept what is offered: *a defiant holdout against a commercial culture.* **2** a person or organization acting in such a way.

hold-over *noun* **1** a person or thing left over from the past; a relic. **2** a person who remains in office, on a team, etc. beyond the regular term etc.

holdup *noun* **1** a stoppage or delay by traffic, inclement weather, etc. **2** a robbery, esp. by the use of threats or violence.

> **SPELL CHECK**
> **hole, whole**
>
> Something complete is **whole**.

hole • *noun* **1** an empty space in a solid body. **2** an animal's burrow. **3** a cavity or receptacle into which the ball must be propelled in various sports or games, e.g. golf. **4** *informal* a small, mean, or dingy abode. **5** a dungeon or prison cell, esp. a cell used for solitary confinement. **6** *informal* an awkward or embarrassing situation. **7** a deep place in a river, stream, etc.: *swimming hole.* **8** *Golf* **a** a point scored by a player who gets the ball from tee to hole with the fewest strokes. **b** the terrain or distance from tee to hole. **9** an opening or vacancy: *the hiring filled a hole in our department.* • *verb* (**holes**, **holed**, **holing**) **1** make a hole or holes in. **2** put into a hole. **3** (often foll. by *out*) send (a golf ball) into a hole. PHRASES **dig a hole for oneself** create a difficult situation for oneself, from which escape is difficult. **hole up** *informal* **1** hide oneself. **2** take shelter (for the night, the winter, etc.). **in the hole** *informal* in debt. **make a hole in** use a large amount of.

hole-in-one *noun* (*plural* **holes-in-one**) *Golf* a shot that enters the hole from the tee.

hole in the wall *noun* a small dingy place (esp. of business).

> **SPELL CHECK**
> **holey, holy**
>
> Something associated with God or religion is **holy**.

holey *adjective* having many holes.

holiday • *noun* **1 a** a day on which most work, school, and business ceases, esp. in honour of a person or event. **b** a religious festival. **2** esp. *Cdn, Brit., Austral. & NZ* (often in *plural*) a period of rest from work, school, etc., usu. for a certain number of weeks per year. **3** (in *plural*) (also **holiday season**) the festive period surrounding Christmas, Hanukkah, and New Year's. **4** (as an *adjective*) festive: *holiday colours.* • *verb* spend a holiday. PHRASES **take a holiday** have a break from work.

holier-than-thou *adjective* *informal* self-righteous.

holiness *noun* **1** sanctity; the state of being holy. **2** (**Holiness**) a title used when referring to or addressing the Pope.

holism *noun* *Medical* the treating of the whole person including mental and social factors rather than just the symptoms of a disease. ▶**holistic** *adjective* **holistically** *adverb* [Say HOLE ism]

hollandaise sauce *noun* a creamy sauce of melted butter, egg yolks, lemon juice, etc. [Say HOLLAN days]

holler *informal* • *verb* shout. • *noun* a loud cry, noise, or shout.

hollow • *adjective* **1 a** having a hole or cavity inside; not solid throughout. **b** having a depression; sunken: *hollow cheeks.* **2** (of a sound) echoing, as though made in or on a hollow container. **3** without significance; meaningless: *a hollow triumph.* **4** insincere; cynical; false: *a hollow laugh* ◊ *hollow promises.* • *noun* **1** a hollow place; a hole. **2** a valley; a basin. **3** (also **hollow of the hand**) the enclosed space formed by the palm of the hand with the fingers curled inwards. • *verb* (often foll. by *out*) make hollow; excavate. ▶**hollowly** *adverb* **hollowness** *noun*

hollow-point • *adjective* (of ammunition) made with a hollow point, so as to shatter on impact. • *noun* a hollow-point bullet.

holly *noun* (*plural* **hollies**) **1** an evergreen shrub, typically having dark green leaves, small white flowers, and red berries. **2** its branches and foliage used as decorations at Christmas.

hollyhock *noun* a tall plant of the mallow family, with large showy flowers of various colours.

Hollywood *noun* the American motion picture industry or its products.

holmium *noun* a soft silvery metallic element occurring naturally in apatite. [Say HOLE mee um]

holocaust *noun* **1** a case of large-scale destruction, esp. by fire or nuclear war. **2** (**the Holocaust**) the mass murder esp. of Jews under the Nazi regime 1941–5. **3** a sacrifice consumed by fire. [Say HOLLA cost]

Holocene • *adjective* of or relating to the second epoch of the Quaternary period, following the Pleistocene and lasting from about 10,000 years ago to the present, coinciding with the development of human agricultural settlement and civilization. • *noun* this geological period or system. [Say HOLLA seen]

hologram *noun* **1** a three-dimensional image formed by the interference of light beams from a laser or other coherent light source. **2** a photograph of the interference pattern, which when suitably illuminated produces a three-dimensional image. [Say HOLLA gram]

holograph • *adjective* wholly written by hand by the person named as the author. • *noun* a holograph document. [Say HOLLA graph]

holographic *adjective* having to do with the use or production of holograms. [Say holla GRAPHIC]

holography *noun* the study or production of holograms. [Say huh LOGGRA fee]

Holstein *noun* (also **Holstein-Friesian**) a large black and white breed of dairy cattle, noted for high milk production. [Say HOLE steen or HOLE stine]

holster *noun* a leather case for a pistol or revolver, worn on a belt or under an arm or fixed to a saddle.

holubtsi *plural noun* *Cdn* (esp. *West*) cabbage rolls. [Say HAUL up chee]

H

holy (**holier, holiest**) • adjective **1** morally and spiritually excellent or perfect, and to be revered. **2** belonging to, devoted to, or empowered by God. **3** consecrated, sacred. **4** used in exclamations: holy cow! • interjection expressing amazement etc.

Holy Ark noun a chest or cabinet containing the Torah scrolls in a synagogue.

Holy Bible noun = BIBLE 1a.

Holy Communion noun see COMMUNION 3a.

holy day noun a religious festival.

Holy Father noun the Pope.

Holy Ghost noun see HOLY SPIRIT.

Holy Grail noun = GRAIL.

Holy Innocents plural noun **1** the children massacred by King Herod in his attempt to kill the child Jesus. **2** (also **Feast of the Holy Innocents**) a feast day commemorating this, celebrated in some Western Christian churches on Dec. 28 and in Eastern churches on Dec. 29.

holy jumpin' interjection Cdn slang expressing surprise, disbelief, etc.

holy moly interjection slang (also **holy moley**) expressing great surprise, admiration, etc.

holy of holies noun **1** the inner chamber of the sanctuary in the Jewish temple, separated by a veil from the outer chamber. **2** jocular a special room or building that can only be visited by important people: the hearing room, the holy of holies, was a surprising mix of ritual and informality. **3** a thing regarded as most sacred: he plans his assault on motoring's holy of holies — the toughest endurance race in the world.

holy orders plural noun the status of a member of the clergy, esp. the grades of bishop, priest, and deacon.

holy roller noun slang derogatory **1** a member of a Pentecostal or other charismatic group characterized by religious excitement. **2** a highly vocal devout person.

Holy Saturday noun the day before Easter Sunday.

Holy Scripture noun the Bible.

Holy See noun the papacy or the papal court.

Holy Spirit noun (in Christian theology) one of the persons of the Trinity, considered as God acting in the world as a spirit.

Holy Thursday noun the Thursday before Easter.

Holy Trinity noun see TRINITY 1.

holy war noun a war waged in support of a religious cause.

holy water noun water dedicated to holy uses, or blessed by a priest.

Holy Week noun the week before Easter.

homage noun **1** special honour or respect shown publicly: world leaders paid homage to the man who inspired India ◊ they stood in silent homage around the grave. **2** hist. formal public acknowledgement of feudal allegiance, by which a man declared himself bound to the service of the lord from whom he held land. [Say HOM idge]

homburg noun a man's felt hat with a narrow curled brim and a lengthwise dent in the crown. [Say HOM burg]

home • noun **1** the place where one lives. **2** one's family background: comes from a good home. **3** an institution for persons needing professional care. **4** the place where a thing originates. **5 a** Baseball = HOME PLATE. **b** the finishing point in a race. **c** (in games) the place where one is free from attack. **d** (in some sports) the goal. **e** Lacrosse a player in an attacking position near the opponents' goal. • adjective **1 a** of or

H

connected with one's home. **b** carried on, done, or made at home: home movies. **c** proceeding from home. **2** carried on or produced in one's own country: the home market. **3** Sport played on one's own ground etc.: home game ◊ home win. **4** in the neighbourhood of home. • adverb **1** to or at one's home. **2 a** to the point aimed at: the thrust went home. **b** as far as possible: drove the nail home. • verb (**homes, homed, homing**) **1** (esp. of a trained pigeon) return home. **2** (often foll. by on, in on) (of a vessel, missile, etc.) be guided towards a destination or target by a landmark, radio beam, etc. PHRASES **at home 1** in one's own house or native land. **2** at ease as if in one's own home: make yourself at home. **3** (usu. foll. by in, on, with) familiar or well informed. **4** available to callers. **come home to** become fully realized by. **heading home** Curling in or during the final end of a game. **home free** assured of success or safety: if we make it to the border we're home free.

home and school noun (also **home and school association**) esp. Cdn a local organization of parents and teachers to promote better communication and improve educational facilities.

home-baked adjective baked at home or at the restaurant etc. where it is served. ► **home baking** noun

home base noun **1** headquarters: our home base is in Brampton. **2** Baseball = HOME PLATE.

homebody noun (plural **homebodies**) a person who likes to stay at home.

homeboy noun esp. US slang **1** a person from one's own town or neighbourhood. **2** a close friend, esp. a member of one's gang.

homebrew noun **1** beer or other alcoholic drink brewed at home. **2** Cdn a person, esp. an athlete, who is a native of the country or locality where competition is held. ► **home-brewed** adverb

homebuilt adjective built in an individual's home.

homebuyer noun a person who buys a house, condominium, etc.

home care noun care, esp. medical care, given or received at home: home care nurse.

home child noun Cdn (usu. in plural) one of a number of orphaned or destitute children sent from Britain to Canada from about 1850 to the early 1900s to serve as farm or domestic help.

homecoming noun **1** arrival at home. **2** a reunion, esp. of former students.

home ec noun home economics.

home economics plural noun (often treated as singular) the study of household management, usu. including cooking, nutrition, sewing, child-raising, budgeting, etc. ► **home economist** noun

home fires plural noun PHRASES **keep the home fires burning** maintain a family home, esp. while one of its members is away for a prolonged period.

home fry noun (plural **home fries**) (usu. in plural) a slice of usu. boiled potato that has been fried in a frying pan, as opposed to being deep-fried.

homegirl noun esp. US slang **1** a girl from one's own town or neighbourhood. **2** a close friend, esp. a member of one's gang.

homegrown adjective **1** raised or cultivated on one's own land. **2** native to or produced in one's own country, locality, etc.

home ice noun the rink where a hockey team or curling rink normally plays its home games.

home invasion noun a robbery usu. perpetrated by a group while the occupants are present.

homeland noun **1** one's native land. **2** hist. a partially self-governing area in South Africa set aside for a particular indigenous African people or peoples under

apartheid; the homelands were abolished in 1994. **3** any similar semi-autonomous area: *their political aim is a separate Tamil homeland*.

homeless *adjective* lacking a home. ▶**homelessness** *noun*

homely *adjective* (**homelier, homeliest**) **1** (esp. of people or their features) unattractive. **2** simple, plain, unpretentious: *a modest manual with homely advice*. **3** comfortable in the manner of a home, cozy.

homemade *adjective* made at home.

homemaker *noun* **1** a person who runs a household for their family, esp. as a primary occupation. **2** a person who cooks meals, cleans house, etc. for an elderly, sick, or disabled person. ▶**homemaking** *adjective & noun*

home movie *noun* (also **home video**) a film (or video) made at home or of one's own activities.

homeopath *noun* a person who practises homeopathy. [Say HOME ee oh path]

homeopathic *adjective* having to do with the treatment of disease by minute doses of drugs that in a healthy person would produce symptoms of the disease: *homeopathic medicine*. ▶**homeopathically** *adverb* [Say home ee oh PATH ick]

homeopathy *noun* the treatment of disease by minute doses of drugs that in a healthy person would produce symptoms of the disease. [Say home ee OPP uth ee]

home opener *noun* a sports team's first home game of a new season.

homeostasis *noun* the tendency towards a relatively stable equilibrium between interdependent elements, esp. as maintained by physiological processes. ▶**homeostatic** *adjective* [Say home ee oh STAY sis, home ee oh STATIC]

homeowner *noun* a person who owns his or her own home. ▶**home ownership** *noun*

home page *noun* a computer screen that serves as an introduction to a network site, from which a number of options may be selected.

home plate *noun* Baseball a base beside which the batter stands and which a runner must reach to score a run.

homer Baseball • *noun* a home run. • *verb* hit a homer.

Homeric *adjective* **1** of, or in the style of, the Greek epic poet Homer (c. 700 BC) or the epic poems ascribed to him, the *Iliad*, recounting Achilles' role in the final stages of the Trojan War, and the *Odyssey*, telling of the voyage home of Odysseus (Ulysses) after the war. **2** of Greece in the era described in these poems (12th–13th centuries BC), known as the Bronze Age because of the use of bronze in making tools and weapons. **3** epic, large-scale: *a Homeric effort*. [Say hoe MAIR ick]

homeroom *noun* **1** a classroom in which a group of students assembles daily with the same teacher for announcements, opening exercises, etc. before dispersing to other classes. **2** the period during which students assemble in a homeroom. **3** the group of students who assemble for a given homeroom.

home rule *noun* (also **Home Rule**) a movement for the government of a colony, dependent country, etc. by its own citizens, esp. the movement advocating devolved government for Ireland, 1870–1914.

home run *noun* Baseball a hit that allows the batter to make a complete circuit of the bases.

home-school *verb* teach one's child in one's own home rather than send him or her to school. ▶**home-schooler** *noun* **home-schooling** *noun*

home shopping *noun* shopping carried out from home using catalogues, satellite TV channels, etc.

homesick *adjective* depressed by longing for one's home during absence from it. ▶**homesickness** *noun*

homesite *noun* a lot or piece of land suitable for building a house on.

homespun • *adjective* **1 a** (of cloth) made of yarn spun at home. **b** (of yarn) spun at home. **2** plain, simple, unsophisticated: *a Hamilton crown attorney, folksy and homespun, prosecuted the case*. • *noun* homespun cloth.

homestand *noun* a series of games played at a team's own venue.

homestead • *noun* **1** an area of public land (usu. a quarter section) granted to a settler in exchange for a small fee, and on certain conditions, usu. that the settler establish a dwelling and cultivate a certain area of land within a specified time. **2** a house, esp. a farmhouse, and outbuildings. • *verb* settle on land as a homestead: *he homesteaded in Alberta* ◊ *they homesteaded the prairies with straightforward courage, honesty, and conviction*. ▶**homesteader** *noun*

home stretch *noun* (plural **home stretches**) **1** the straight section of a racetrack leading to the finish line. **2** the final stage or phase of anything.

homestyle *adjective* (esp. of food) of a kind made or done at home.

home theatre *noun* a home audio-video system designed to simulate as closely as possible the viewing conditions in a movie theatre.

hometown *noun* the town of one's birth or early life or present fixed residence.

home truth *noun* basic but unwelcome information concerning oneself.

home turf *noun* one's own territory.

homeward • *adverb* (also **homewards**) towards home. • *adjective* going or leading towards home.

homeward-bound *adjective* on the way home.

homework *noun* **1** work to be done at home, esp. by a school pupil. **2** preparatory work or study: *when you're buying a house, you have to do your homework*.

homeworker *noun* a person who works from home, esp. doing low-paid piecework.

homey *adjective* (**homier, homiest**) suggesting home; cozy. ▶**homeyness** *noun*

homicidal *adjective* **1** likely to kill or murder: *a homicidal madman*. **2** causing or having to do with a person's tendency to want to kill or murder: *homicidal dreams* ◊ *homicidal behaviour*. [Say homma SIDE ul]

homicide *noun* the intentional killing of a human being by another. [Say HOMMA side]

homiletic • *adjective* (also **homiletical**) of homilies. • *noun* (usu. in plural) the art of preaching. [Say homma LET ick]

homily *noun* (plural **homilies**) **1** a sermon. **2** a tedious moralizing discourse. [Say HOMMA lee]

homing *adjective* **1** (of a pigeon) trained to fly home, bred for long-distance racing, carrying messages, etc. **2** (of a device) for guiding (something) to a target etc.

hominid • *noun* a primate of the family Hominidae, which includes humans (*Homo sapiens*) and their fossil ancestors. • *adjective* of this family. [Say HOM in id]

hominoid • *adjective* of hominids or of chimpanzees and related apes (e.g. gorillas and orangutans). • *noun* an animal resembling a human. [Say HOM in oid]

hominy *noun* esp. US coarsely ground kernels of corn esp. boiled with water or milk. [Say HOM in ee]

homme du nord *noun* (plural **hommes du nord**) Cdn hist. a voyageur who spent winters in the interior. [Say om due NOR]

Homo *noun* **1** any primate of the genus of *Homo*, including modern humans and various extinct species.

H

2 *jocular* (with Latin or mock-Latin adjectives in imitation of zoological nomenclature) in names intended to personify some aspects of human life or behaviour: *Homo economicus*.

homo *noun* *Cdn* homogenized milk typically having a butterfat content of 3.25 percent.

homoerotic *adjective* **1** homosexual. **2** arousing sexual desire in a person of the same sex. ▶ **homoeroticism** *noun* [Say homo EROTIC]

homogeneity *noun* the quality of something that consists of parts or of people that are all the same or of the same type: *the neighbourhood has shed its ethnic homogeneity and is now one of the most culturally diverse communities in the city.* [Say home uh juh NAY uh tee]

homogeneous *adjective* **1** consisting of things or people that are all the same or all of the same type: *ethnically homogeneous areas of New Brunswick.* **2** *Math* containing terms all of the same degree. ▶ **homogeneously** *adverb* [Say home uh GENIOUS]

homogenization *noun* the process of becoming or making something homogeneous. [Say huh modge uh nize AY sh'n]

homogenize *verb* (**homogenizes**, **homogenized**, **homogenizing**) **1** make or become homogeneous: *an ongoing process that is effectively homogenizing world culture by minimizing regional variations.* **2** treat (milk) so that the fat droplets are emulsified and the cream does not separate. [Say huh MODGE uh nize]

homogenized *adjective* **1** homogeneous. **2** (of milk) having the fat droplets emulsified, esp. (in Canada) designating homogenized milk with a butterfat content of 3.25 percent. [Say huh MODGE uh nized]

> **WRITING TIP**
> **homogenous, homogeneous**
>
> The use of **homogenous** to mean "all of the same kind" or "uniform" is considered incorrect by many people and is best avoided. The correct word is **homogeneous**.

homogenous *adjective* *disputed* = HOMOGENEOUS. [Say huh MODGE un us]

homograph *noun* a word spelled like another but of different meaning or origin, e.g. "palm" (a tree) and "palm" (of the hand). [Say HOMMA graf]

homologous *adjective* *Biology* **1** (of organs etc.) similar in position and structure but not necessarily in function. **2** (of chromosomes) pairing at meiosis and having the same structural features and pattern of genes. [Say huh MOLLA gus]

homonym *noun* a word of the same spelling (also called **homograph**) or sound (also called **homophone**) as another but of different meaning, e.g. "palm" (a tree) and "palm" (of the hand), or "deer" and "dear", or "sow" (plant seeds) and "sow" (female pig). [Say HOMMA nim]

homophobe *noun* a person who has an extreme aversion to homosexuals and homosexuality. [Say HOME uh fobe]

homophobia *noun* a hatred or fear of homosexuals or homosexuality. ▶ **homophobic** *adjective* [Say home uh PHOBIA]

homophone *noun* a word having the same sound as another but of different spelling and meaning (e.g. *pair*, *pear*). [Say HOMMA phone]

Homo sapiens *noun* modern humans regarded as a species. [Say SAY pee enz]

homosexual • *adjective* **1** feeling or involving sexual attraction to persons of the same sex. **2** concerning homosexual relations or people. • *noun* a homosexual person. ▶ **homosexuality** *noun*

homy *adjective* (**homier**, **homiest**) = HOMEY.

Hon. *abbreviation* **1** Honourable. **2** Honorary.

hon *noun* *informal* honey (as a term of endearment).

honcho *noun* *slang* (*plural* **honchos**) a leader or manager; the person in charge.

hone • *verb* (**hones**, **honed**, **honing**) **1** sharpen a blade by grinding it using a stone. **2** make more effective or focused: *honing her skills as a performer.* • *noun* a stone used to sharpen blades.

honest • *adjective* **1** fair and just in character or behaviour, not cheating or stealing. **2** free of deceit and untruthfulness. **3** fairly earned: *an honest day's work.* **4** (of an act or feeling) showing fairness. **5** (of a thing) unsophisticated. • *adverb* *informal* genuinely, really: *I didn't take it, honest!* PHRASES **do one's honest best** do the best that one can. **make an honest woman of** *informal* marry (esp. a pregnant woman).

honestly • *adverb* **1** in an honest way. **2** really: *I don't honestly know.* • *interjection* expressing exasperation, dismay, etc.: *Honestly! You're always complaining!*

honest-to-God *adjective* (also **honest-to-goodness**) *informal* genuine, real.

honesty *noun* **1** the quality of being honest. **2** truthfulness. **3** (*plural* **honesties**) a plant with purple or white flowers and flat, round, semi-transparent seed pods.

honey *noun* (*plural* **honeys**) **1** a sweet sticky yellowish fluid made by bees from nectar collected from flowers. **2** the colour of this. **3** a person or thing excellent of its kind: *a honey of a movie.* **4** darling. **5** (as an *adjective*) designating something that is used to hold or carry sewage, manure, etc.: *honey bucket.*

honey bag *noun* *Cdn* (*North*) *informal* a plastic bag used as a receptacle for human waste.

honeybee *noun* the common bee, domesticated for its honey and typically kept in a hive.

honeybun *noun* (also **honeybunch**, *plural* **honeybunches**) (esp. as a form of address) darling.

honeycomb • *noun* **1** a structure of hexagonal cells of wax, made by bees to store honey and eggs. **2 a** pattern arranged hexagonally. **b** fabric made with a pattern of raised hexagons etc. **3** tripe from the second stomach of a ruminant. • *verb* **1** fill with cavities or tunnels, undermine. **2** mark with a honeycomb pattern. ▶ **honeycombed** *adjective*

honeydew *noun* **1** a sweet sticky substance found on leaves and stems, excreted by aphids. **2** a variety of melon with smooth pale skin and sweet green flesh.

honeyed *adjective* **1** of or containing honey. **2** (of words) intending to please or flatter: *honeyed compliments.*

honeymoon • *noun* **1** a holiday spent together by a newly married couple. **2** an initial period of enthusiasm or goodwill. • *verb* spend a honeymoon. ▶ **honeymooner** *noun*

honeysuckle *noun* a shrub with fragrant yellow, orange, white or pink flowers.

honk • *noun* **1** the cry of a goose. **2** the harsh sound of a car horn. **3** a sound similar to either of these, e.g. of a person blowing their nose. • *verb* **1** emit or give a honk. **2** cause to do this.

honker *noun* **1** *informal* a goose, esp. a wild goose. **2** a person or thing that honks.

honking *adjective* (also **honkin'**) *slang* very large.

honky-tonk *noun* *informal* **1** ragtime piano music. **2** a cheap or disreputable nightclub, dance hall, etc.

honorarium *noun* (*plural* **honorariums** or **honoraria**) a fee, esp. a voluntary payment for professional services rendered without the normal fee. [Say onna RERRY um]

honorary *adjective* (also **honourary**) **1 a** conferred as an honour, without the usual requirements, functions, etc.: *honorary degree*. **b** holding such a title or position: *honorary colonel*. **2** (of an office or its holder) unpaid: *honorary treasurer*. **3** (of an obligation) depending on honour, not legally enforceable.

honorific • *adjective* (of a title etc.) showing respect for a person. • *noun* an honorific: *"Mr." is an honorific*. ▶ **honorifically** *adverb* [Say onna RIFF ick]

honour (also **honor**) • *noun* **1** high respect; glory; reputation. **2** adherence to what is right or to a conventional standard of conduct. **3** nobleness of mind. **4** a thing conferred as a distinction, esp. an official award for bravery or achievement. **5** privilege: *had the honour of being invited*. **6 a** an exalted position. **b** (**Honour**) (preceded by *your*, *his*, *her*, etc.) a title of respect given to a lower court judge etc. **7** a person or thing that brings honour: *she is an honour to her profession*. **8** (in *plural*) **a** special distinction for proficiency in an examination. **b** a course of degree studies more specialized than for a general degree. • *verb* **1** respect highly. **2** confer honour on. **3** accept or pay (a bill or cheque) when due. **4** acknowledge. ▓PHRASES▓ **do the honours** perform the duties of a host to guests etc. **in honour of** as a celebration of. **on** (or **upon**) **my honour** an expression of sincerity.

honourable *adjective* (also **honorable**) **1 a** deserving respect and admiration: *a long and honourable career in government*. **b** showing high moral standards: *an honourable man*. **c** allowing someone to keep their good name and the respect of others: *they urged her to do the honourable thing and resign* ◊ *he received an honourable discharge from the army*. **2** (**Honourable**) a title indicating eminence or distinction, given esp. to an MP, an upper court judge, a Lieutenant-Governor, etc.

honourable mention *noun* a citation given to a contestant, entry, etc. which has considerable merit but has not been awarded a prize.

honouree *noun* (also **honoree**) a person who is honoured, esp. by receiving an award or special presentation.

honour roll *noun* **1** a list of students who have achieved grades above a certain average during a term or school year. **2** a list of the local citizens etc. who died or served in the armed forces.

honours student *noun* **1** (also **honour student**) a student who has high grades. **2** a student in an honours program at university.

honour system *noun* a system of conduct which relies on the honour of those concerned to adhere to certain standards, unenforced by supervision etc.

hoo *interjection* expressing surprise or apprehension, or requesting attention: *hoo boy!*

hooch *noun informal* alcoholic liquor, esp. if illicit.

hood¹ • *noun* **1 a** a covering for the head and neck, whether part of a coat etc. or separate. **b** a separate garment like a hood worn over a university gown or a surplice to indicate the wearer's degree. **2** a hinged cover over the engine of a motor vehicle. **3** a canopy to protect users of machinery or incorporating a fan to remove fumes, cooking odours, etc. **4** the hood-like structure or marking on the head or neck of a cobra, seal, etc. • *verb* cover with a hood.

hood² *noun slang* a gangster or gunman.

'hood *noun* esp. *US slang* a neighbourhood, esp. one in the inner city.

-hood *suffix* forming nouns: **1** of condition or state: *childhood* ◊ *falsehood*. **2** indicating a collection or group: *sisterhood*.

hooded *adjective* **1** having a hood; covered with or as with a hood. **2** wearing a hood. **3** (of eyes) having large, partly closed eyelids.

hooded seal *noun* a seal with a grey and white blotched coat found in the Arctic and North Atlantic Oceans. The male has a nasal sac that is inflated into a hood in display.

hoodless *adjective* (of clothing) not having a hood.

hoodlum *noun* **1** a street hooligan, a young thug. **2** a gangster. [HOOD rhymes with GOOD or FOOD]

hoodoo *noun* (*plural* **hoodoos**) a column or pinnacle of weathered rock. [Say HOO doo]

hoodwink *verb* deceive, delude.

hooey *noun & interjection slang* nonsense, humbug.

hoof • *noun* (*plural* **hoofs** or **hooves**) **1** the horny part of the foot of a horse, antelope, and other ungulates. **2** *jocular* the human foot. • *verb* (**hoofs**, **hoofed**, **hoofing**) *slang* kick or shove. ▓PHRASES▓ **hoof it** *slang* **1** go on foot. **2** dance. **on the hoof** (of cattle) not yet slaughtered. ▶ **hoofed** *adjective* (also in *combination*). [With OO as in HOOD or HOOP]

hoofer *noun informal* a professional dancer, esp. a tap or jazz dancer. [With OO as in HOOD or HOOP]

hoofprint *noun* the impression in the ground made by an animal's hoof.

hoo-ha *noun slang* (*plural* **hoo-has**) a commotion, a row; uproar, trouble.

hook • *noun* **1 a** a piece of metal or other material bent back at an angle or with a round bend, for catching hold or for hanging things on. **b** (also **fish hook**) a bent piece of wire, usu. barbed and baited, for catching fish. **2** a curved cutting instrument: *pruning hook*. **3** *Hockey* an act or the process of illegally hindering the advancement of the person with the puck by jabbing at his or her body from the side or rear with the blade of one's stick. **4** *Golf, Baseball, etc.* **a** ball or bowl's deviation from a straight line. **b** the action or an act of hooking a ball. **c** = HOOK SHOT. **5** *Boxing* a short swinging blow with the elbow bent and rigid. **6 a** something that captures attention or entices: *a marketing hook*. **b** an item or theme around which a news story, radio segment, etc. can be developed. **7** (in *plural*) *slang* hands or fingers. • *verb* **1** grasp, secure, catch, attach, or be attached with a hook. **2** (foll. by *up*) **a** connect or set up (stereo components, a VCR, etc.). **b** attach (a house, vehicle, etc.) to a central source of electricity, water, etc. **c** *informal* meet or become involved with: *got hooked up with a guy from Amsterdam*. **3** *slang* steal. **4** *slang* work as a prostitute. **5** *Hockey* illegally hinder the advancement of the person with the puck by jabbing at his or her body from the side or rear with the blade of one's stick. ▓PHRASES▓ **by hook or by crook** by one means or another; by fair means or foul. **get one's hooks on** (or

into) get hold of. **hook, line, and sinker** entirely. **off the hook 1** *informal* no longer in difficulty or trouble. **2** (of a telephone receiver) not on its rest, and so preventing incoming calls. **on the hook** *informal* responsible for: *on the hook for a bad loan*.

hookah *noun* an oriental tobacco pipe with a long tube passing through water for cooling the smoke as it is drawn through. [Say HOOK uh]

hook and eye *noun* **1** a small metal hook and loop as a fastener on a garment. **2** a similar device consisting of a hook and screw eye used to fasten esp. a door.

hooked *adjective* **1** hook-shaped: *hooked nose*. **2** furnished with a hook or hooks. **3** *in senses of* HOOK *verb*. **4** (of a rug or mat) made by pulling woollen yarn through canvas with a hook. **5** *informal* (often foll. by *on*) addicted to or captivated by.

hooker *noun* **1** *slang* a prostitute. **2** = HOOKTENDER.

hooking *noun* *Hockey* an illegal check in which a player attempts to hinder or pull down an opponent by tugging with the blade of the stick, usu. from behind.

hook shot *noun* *Basketball* a one-handed shot in which the player lobs the ball over the head with a sweeping movement of the arm.

hooktender *noun* a person in charge of the chokermen on a logging crew.

hookup *noun* **1** a connection, esp. an interconnection of broadcasting equipment for special transmissions. **2** a link to a source of electricity, water, etc. in a campground etc.

hookworm *noun* **1** a parasitic nematode worm that inhabits the intestines of humans and other animals, having a hooklike mouthpart with which it attaches itself to the wall of the gut, puncturing the blood vessels and feeding on the blood. **2** a disease caused by one of these, often resulting in severe anemia.

hooky[1] *noun* PHRASES **play hooky** *slang* play truant.

hooky[2] *adjective* (of a song) catchy.

hooligan *noun* a noisy and violent person. ▶ **hooliganism** *noun*

hoop • *noun* **1** a circular band of metal, wood, etc., esp. for binding the staves of casks etc. or for forming part of a framework. **2** a ring of wood, plastic, or metal rolled along as a toy or used in various exercises, esp. by children. **3** *Basketball* **a** the round metal frame of the basket. **b** (also **hoops**) the game of basketball. **4** a circle of flexible material for expanding a woman's petticoat or skirt. **5 a** a circular earring. **b** the circular band of a finger ring. **6** an arch of iron etc. through which the balls are hit in croquet. • *verb* bind or encircle with hoops. PHRASES **jump through hoops** do something difficult or complicated in order to achieve something.

hoop dance *noun* a dance among certain North American Aboriginal peoples in which the dancer suspends many, often multicoloured hoops with the arms, legs, and body, to create patterns. ▶ **hoop dancer** *noun*

hoopla *noun* *informal* **1** extravagant publicity; hype. **2** commotion; excitement; lively activity.

hoopster *noun* *slang* a basketball player.

hooray *interjection* = HURRAH.

hoosegow *noun* *slang* a prison.

hoot • *noun* **1** an owl's cry. **2** the sound made by a train whistle etc. **3** a shout expressing scorn or disapproval; an inarticulate shout. **4** *informal* **a** a shout of laughter. **b** a cause of laughter or merriment. **5** (also **two hoots**) *slang* anything at all: *don't give a hoot* ◊ *doesn't matter two hoots*. • *verb* **1 a** (of an owl) utter its cry. **b** (of a train whistle etc.) make a hoot. **c** (often foll. by *at*) make loud sounds, esp. of scorn or disapproval or

merriment: *hooted with laughter*. **2** assail with scornful shouts.

hootch *noun* = HOOCH.

hooter *noun* **1** *slang* a nose. **2** a person or animal that hoots. **3** (usu. in *plural*) *slang* a woman's breast.

hooves *plural of* HOOF. [With OO as in HOOD or HOOP]

hop[1] • *verb* (**hops, hopped, hopping**) **1** (of a bird, frog, etc.) spring with two or all feet at once. **2** (of a person) **a** a jump on one foot. **b** make small jumps up and down on both feet. **3** move or go quickly: *hopped out of his chair*. **4** cross (a ditch etc.) by hopping. **5** *informal* **a** make a quick trip. **b** make a quick change of position or location: *bar-hop*. **6** *informal* jump into or board (a vehicle, plane, etc.). **7** (usu. as **hopping** *noun*) (esp. of aircraft) pass quickly from one (place of a specified type) to another. • *noun* **1** a hopping movement. **2** *informal* an informal gathering for dancing. **3** a short trip, esp. in an aircraft; a stage of a flight or journey. **4** a bounce of a ball etc. PHRASES **hop in** (or **out**) *informal* get into (or out of) a car etc.

hop[2] *noun* **1** a climbing plant cultivated for the cones borne by the female. **2** (in *plural*) **a** the ripe cones of this, used to give a bitter flavour to beer. **b** *informal* beer.

hope • *noun* **1** expectation and desire combined, e.g. for a certain thing to occur: *has high hopes of getting the job*. **2 a** a person, thing, or circumstance that gives cause for hope. **b** grounds for hope, promise. **3** what is hoped for. • *verb* (**hopes, hoped, hoping**) **1** (often foll. by *for*) feel hope. **2** expect and desire: *I hope you can leave early*. **3** feel fairly confident. PHRASES **hope against hope** continue to hope for something even though it is very unlikely. **not a hope** *informal* no chance at all.

hope chest *noun* a chest containing linen, clothing, china, etc. stored by a woman in preparation for her marriage.

hopeful • *adjective* **1** feeling hope. **2** causing or inspiring hope. **3** likely to succeed, promising. • *noun* a person likely to succeed.

> **WRITING TIP**
> **hopefully**
>
> **Hopefully** is used much more commonly in written and spoken English to mean "it is to be hoped that", as in *Hopefully Sujit will invite us to dinner*, than to mean "in a hopeful manner", as in *We waited hopefully for Sujit to invite us to dinner*. Nevertheless, there are those who object very strongly to the first use. The case against it is weak, but it may be safer not to use a sentence like *Hopefully Sujit will invite us to dinner* in formal writing to avoid fierce criticism. An acceptable alternative is *I* (or *we*) *hope that Sujit will invite us to dinner*.

hopefully *adverb* **1** in a hopeful manner. **2** (qualifying a whole sentence) it is to be hoped: *hopefully, the car will be ready by then*.

hopefulness *noun* the condition or quality of having hope.

hopeless *adjective* **1** having or feeling no hope; despairing. **2** admitting no hope: *a hopeless case*. **3** inadequate: *am hopeless at tennis*. **4** without hope of success; futile. ▶ **hopelessly** *adverb* **hopelessness** *noun*

Hopi • *noun* (*plural* **Hopi** or **Hopis**) **1** a member of a North American Aboriginal people living chiefly in northeastern Arizona. **2** the language of this people. • *adjective* of or pertaining to the Hopi. [Say HOE pee]

hopped up *adjective* *slang* **1** intoxicated; stimulated with or as with a drug. **2** excited, enthusiastic. **3** (of a motor vehicle) having had its engine altered to give improved performance; souped-up.

H

hopper *noun* **1** a person who hops. **2** a grasshopper or other hopping insect. **3** a container tapering downward, esp. one through which grain passes into a mill. **4** (also **hopper car**) a railway car able to discharge grain etc. through openings in its floor.

hopping *adjective* **1** in senses of HOP[1]. **2** *informal* very active, lively: *a hopping party.*

hopping mad *adjective informal* very angry.

hopscotch • *noun* a children's game of hopping on one foot into and over squares or oblongs marked on the ground in order to retrieve a stone etc. thrown into one of them. • *verb* (**hopscotches**, **hopscotched**, **hopscotching**) **1** play hopscotch. **2** jump, as if playing hopscotch. **3** travel from place to place.

hop, skip, and a jump *noun* (also **hop, skip, and jump**) a short distance.

horde *noun* **1** usu. *derogatory* a large group, a gang. **2** a moving swarm or pack (of insects, wolves, etc.).

horehound *noun* **1** a plant with a white cottony covering on its stem and leaves. **2** its bitter aromatic juice used against coughs etc.

horizon *noun* **1** the line at which the earth and sky appear to meet: *the sun rose above the horizon.* **2** range or limit of mental perception, experience, interest, etc.: *she wanted to leave home and broaden her horizons.* **3** a geological stratum or set of strata, or layer of soil, with particular characteristics. PHRASES **on the horizon** (of an event) just imminent or becoming apparent.

horizontal • *adjective* **1 a** parallel to the plane of the horizon, at right angles to the vertical. **b** (of machinery etc.) having its parts working in a horizontal direction. **2** a involving or combining companies engaged in the same stage or type of production: *horizontal integration.* **b** of or concerned with the same work, status, etc.: *my new job is more of a horizontal move than a promotion.* • *noun* a horizontal line, plane, etc. ▶ **horizontally** *adverb*

hork *slang* • *verb* spit. • *noun* the act of spitting.

hormonal *adjective* of, involving, acting as, or caused by a hormone or hormones: *hormonal changes during pregnancy.* ▶ **hormonally** *adverb*

hormone *noun* **1** a regulatory substance produced in an organism and transported in tissue fluids such as blood or sap to stimulate cells or tissues into action. **2** a synthetic substance with a similar effect. **3** (in *plural*) *informal* the hormones regulating the sex drive: *young men with highly active hormones.*

hormone replacement therapy *noun* treatment with estrogens to alleviate menopausal symptoms.

horn *noun* **1 a** a hard permanent outgrowth, often curved and pointed, on the head of cattle and other esp. hoofed mammals, found singly, in pairs, or one in front of another. **b** the hard substance of which animal horns are made. **2** each of two deciduous branched appendages on the head of (esp. male) deer. **3** a hornlike projection on the head of other animals, e.g. a snail's tentacle etc. **4** the substance of which horns are composed. **5** anything resembling or compared to a horn in shape. **6 a** = FRENCH HORN. **b** a wind instrument played by lip vibration, originally made of horn, now usu. of brass. **c** a horn player. **7** an instrument sounding a warning or other signal: *car horn* ◊ *foghorn.* **8** a receptacle or instrument made of horn, e.g. a drinking vessel. **9** a horn-shaped projection, e.g. on a saddle. **10** *informal* a telephone.

11 a representation of an animal's horn as appearing on the head of a supernatural (esp. evil) being or as a symbol of a cuckold. PHRASES **horn in** *slang* **1** (usu. foll. by *on*) intrude. **2** interfere. **horn of plenty** cornucopia. **on the horns of a dilemma** faced with a decision involving equally unfavourable alternatives. **pull** (or **draw**) **in one's horns** become less assertive or ambitious; draw back.

hornbeam *noun* a tree with a smooth bark and a hard tough wood.

hornbill *noun* a tropical bird with a large bony growth on its curved bill.

hornblende *noun* a dark brown, black, or green mineral composed of calcium, magnesium, and iron silicates.

horned *adjective* having a horn or horns.

horned lark *noun* a brown and white lark which has two black tufts on the head.

horned owl *noun* = GREAT HORNED OWL.

hornet *noun* any of various large social wasps with a severe sting.

hornet's nest *noun* a state of trouble, outrage, opposition, etc.: *his letter to the papers stirred up a real hornet's nest.*

hornless *adjective* not having a horn or horns: *hornless cattle.*

hornpipe *noun* **1** a lively dance, usu. for one person, originally to the accompaniment of a wind instrument, and esp. associated with the merrymaking of sailors. **2** the music for this.

horn-rimmed *adjective* (esp. of eyeglasses) having rims made of horn or a substance resembling it. ▶ **horn-rims** *plural noun*

hornworm *noun* any of several moth larvae having a hornlike spike on the tail, some of which are pests to vegetables.

horny *adjective* (**hornier**, **horniest**) **1** of or like horn. **2** hard like horn, callous: *horny-handed.* **3** wearing or having a horn or horns. **4** *slang* **a** sexually excited. **b** lecherous.

horoscope *noun* **1** a forecast of a person's future purportedly based on a diagram showing the relative positions of the stars and planets at a particular time, e.g. the time of that person's birth. **2** such a diagram.

horrendous *adjective* horrifying; awful. ▶ **horrendously** *adverb*

horrible *adjective* **1** causing or likely to cause horror; hideous, shocking. **2** unpleasant, excessive: *horrible weather.* ▶ **horribly** *adverb*

horrid *adjective* **1** horrible, revolting. **2** unpleasant, disagreeable: *horrid children.* ▶ **horridly** *adverb* **horridness** *noun*

horrific *adjective* horrifying: *suffered horrific injuries in the accident.* ▶ **horrifically** *adverb*

horrify *verb* (**horrifies**, **horrified**, **horrifying**) arouse horror in; shock, scandalize. ▶ **horrifying** *adjective* **horrifyingly** *adverb*

horror *noun* **1** an intense feeling of loathing and fear. **2 a** intense dislike. **b** intense dismay. **3 a** a person or thing causing horror: *the horrors of war.* **b** *informal* a bad or mischievous person etc. **c** *informal* something considered ugly or tacky: *this chesterfield is a horror!* **4** (**the horrors**) *informal* a fit of horror, depression, or nervousness, esp. as in delirium tremens. **5** a genre of literature, film, etc. designed to excite pleasurable feelings of horror by depiction of the supernatural, violence, etc.

horrors *interjection* an exclamation of (esp. mock) dismay.

horror-stricken *adjective* (also **horror-struck**) horrified, shocked.

H

hors d'oeuvre *noun* (*plural* **hors d'oeuvre** or **hors d'oeuvres**) a small item of food served as an appetizer or at a reception etc. [Say or DERV]

> **SPELL CHECK**
> **horse, hoarse**
>
> Someone with a sore throat and a raspy voice is **hoarse**.

horse • *noun* **1** a solid-hoofed plant-eating quadruped with flowing mane and tail, used for riding and to carry and pull loads. **2** a padded wooden block used for vaulting over by gymnasts and athletes. **3 a** a frame or structure on which something is mounted or supported. **b** = SAWHORSE. **c** = CLOTHES HORSE 1. **4** *slang* heroin. **5** *informal* a unit of horsepower. • *verb* (**horses, horsed, horsing**) *informal* (foll. by *around*) fool around. PHRASES **change horses in midstream** change one's ideas, plans, etc. in the middle of a project or process. **from the horse's mouth** (of information etc.) from the person directly concerned or another authoritative source. **horse of a different** (or **another**) **colour** a thing significantly different.

horse-and-buggy *adjective* old-fashioned, bygone: *outdated, horse-and-buggy technology*.

horseback • *noun* the back of a horse, esp. as sat on in riding. • *adverb* on horseback.

horse bun *noun* *Cdn* *slang* a piece of horse manure.

horse chestnut *noun* **1** a large ornamental tree, with upright conical clusters of white or pink or red flowers. **2** the dark brown fruit of this (like an edible chestnut, but with a coarse bitter taste).

horse-drawn *adjective* pulled by a horse or horses.

horsefly *noun* (*plural* **horseflies**) a fly, the female of which inflicts a painful bite on horses and other large mammals, including humans, to suck blood.

horsehair *noun* hair from the mane or tail of a horse, used for padding etc.: *horsehair sofa*.

horsehide *noun* **1** the hide of a horse. **2** leather made from the hide of a horse. **3** *informal* a baseball.

horseman *noun* (*plural* **horsemen**) **1** a rider on horseback. **2** a skilled rider. **3** *Cdn* *slang* a member of the RCMP.

horsemanship *noun* the art of riding on horseback; skill in doing this.

horseplay *noun* boisterous play.

horseplayer *noun* a person who gambles on horse races.

horsepower *noun* (*plural* **horsepower**) **1** an imperial unit for measuring the power of an engine etc., equal to about 750 watts. Abbreviation: **hp. 2** the power of an engine etc. measured in terms of this.

horse race *noun* **1** a race between horses with riders. **2** any close competition, e.g. an election etc. ▶ **horse racing** *noun*

horseradish *noun* **1** a plant of the cabbage family, with long lobed leaves. **2** the pungent root of this scraped or grated as a condiment.

horse sense *noun* *informal* plain common sense.

horseshoe *noun* **1** an iron shoe for a horse shaped like the outline of the hard part of the hoof. **2** a representation of this as a good luck charm. **3** an object shaped like C or U (e.g. a magnet). **4** (in *plural*) a game in which horseshoes are tossed at an iron stake.

horseshoe crab *noun* a large marine invertebrate with a horseshoe-shaped shell, a long tail spine, and ten legs.

horsetail *noun* **1** the tail of a horse. **2** a plant with a hollow jointed stem and scale-like leaves.

horse trade *verb* (**horse trades, horse traded,**

horse trading) **1** deal in horses. **2** engage in shrewd bargaining. ▶ **horse trader** *noun*

horse trading *noun* **1** dealing in horses. **2** shrewd bargaining: *the horse trading on constitutional issues is about to begin*.

horsewhip • *noun* a whip for driving horses. • *verb* (**horsewhips, horsewhipped, horsewhipping**) beat with a horsewhip.

horsewoman *noun* (*plural* **horsewomen**) **1** a woman who rides on horseback. **2** a skilled woman rider.

horsey *adjective* (also **horsy**) (**horsier, horsiest**) **1** of, pertaining to, or resembling a horse or horses. **2** concerned with or devoted to horses or horse racing: *the horsey set*.

horticultural *adjective* of or relating to the art or science of garden cultivation: *the horticultural society's annual plant sale*. ▶ **horticulturally** *adverb*

horticulture *noun* the art or science of gardening. ▶ **horticulturist** *noun* (also **horticulturalist**).

hosanna *noun & interjection* (*plural* **hosannas**) (esp. in Jewish and Christian worship) a shout of adoration used in praise of God or Christ. [Say hoe ZANNA]

hose • *noun* **1** a flexible tube conveying water for watering plants, putting out fires, etc. **2 a** (as *plural*) stockings and socks. **b** *hist.* tights: *doublet and hose*. • *verb* (**hoses, hosed, hosing**) **1** water or spray or drench with a hose. **2** *slang* deceive, swindle.

hoser *noun* *Cdn* *slang* **1** an idiot. **2** an uncultivated person, esp. an unintelligent, inarticulate, beer-drinking lout.

hosiery *noun* stockings and socks. [Say HOE zuh ree]

hospice *noun* a home for people who are ill (esp. terminally). [Say HOSS piss]

hospitable *adjective* **1** pleased to welcome guests; generous and friendly to visitors: *the local people are very hospitable to strangers*. **2** having good conditions that allow things to grow; having a pleasant environment: *a hospitable climate* ◊ *the countryside in the north is less hospitable*. ▶ **hospitably** *adverb* [Say hoss PITTA bull]

hospital *noun* **1** an institution providing medical and surgical treatment and nursing care for ill or injured people. **2** an establishment for the treatment of sick or injured animals.

hospitality *noun* the friendly and generous reception and entertainment of guests or strangers.

hospitality suite *noun* (also **hospitality room**) a suite or room in a hotel etc. set aside for the entertainment of guests.

hospitalization *noun* the act or process of sending or admitting a patient to hospital.

hospitalize *verb* (**hospitalizes, hospitalized, hospitalizing**) send or admit (a patient) to hospital.

Host *noun* the bread that is used in the Christian service of Communion, after it has been blessed.

host[1] *noun* **1** a large number of people or things. **2** (also **heavenly host, host of heaven**) the angels.

host[2] • *noun* **1** a person who receives or entertains another as a guest. **2** an emcee or interviewer, esp. on a television or radio program. **3** an animal or plant having a parasite. **4** an animal or person that has received a transplanted organ etc. • *verb* act as host to (a person) or at (an event).

hosta *noun* a shade-loving perennial garden plant with green or variegated leaves and loose clusters of tubular mauve or white flowers. [Say HOSS tuh]

hostage *noun* a person seized or held as security for the fulfillment of a condition.

hostel *noun* **1** a place providing temporary accommodation for the homeless etc. **2** = YOUTH HOSTEL. **3** a house or residence or lodging for students, nurses, etc.

hosteller *noun* a person who stays in youth hostels, esp. while travelling.

hostelling *noun* the practice of staying in youth hostels, esp. while travelling.

hostelry *noun* (*plural* **hostelries**) an inn.

hostess *noun* (*plural* **hostesses**) **1** a woman who receives or entertains a guest. **2 a** a woman employed to welcome and seat customers of a restaurant etc. **b** a woman employed to greet and entertain esp. male customers of a nightclub etc. **3** a woman employed as an emcee or interviewer, esp. on a television or radio program. **4** a woman employed to tend to passengers on an aircraft, train, etc.: *air hostess*.

hostile *adjective* **1** of an enemy. **2 a** (often foll. by *to*) aggressively opposed; showing strong rejection. **b** showing strong dislike. **3** (of a takeover bid) liable to be opposed by the management of the target company. ▶ **hostilely** *adverb* [Say HOSS tile or HOSS tull]

hostility *noun* (*plural* **hostilities**) **1** hostile behaviour; unfriendliness or opposition: *their hostility to all outsiders*. **2** (in *plural*) acts of warfare: *he called for an immediate end to hostilities*.

hot • *adjective* (**hotter**, **hottest**) **1** having a high temperature. **2** feeling or producing an uncomfortable sensation of heat. **3** feeling or showing intense excitement, anger, lust, or other emotion. **4** currently popular, fashionable, or interesting. **5** *informal* (of goods) stolen and difficult to dispose of because easily identifiable. **6** (often **hot on**) *informal* very knowledgeable or skilful. **7** (**hot on**) *informal* strict about. • *verb* (**hots**, **hotted**, **hotting**) (usu. foll. by *up*) *informal* **1** make or become hot. **2** make or become active, lively, exciting, or dangerous. PHRASES **blow** (or **run**) **hot and cold** *informal* vacillate; be alternately enthusiastic and indifferent. **have the hots for** *slang* be sexually attracted to. **hot and bothered** in a state of exasperated agitation. **hot and heavy** intense. **hot off the press** very recently published. **hot on the heels of** in close pursuit of. **hot under the collar** feeling anger, resentment, or embarrassment. **not so hot** *informal* only mediocre.

hot air *noun informal* empty, boastful, or excited talk.

hot-air balloon *noun* a balloon consisting of a bag in which air is heated by burners located below it, causing it to rise, often carrying a basket for passengers. ▶ **hot-air ballooning** *noun*

hot and sour soup *noun* an Oriental soup having a spicy and slightly acidic broth.

hotbed *noun* **1** a bed of earth heated by fermenting manure, for raising or forcing plants. **2** (foll. by *of*) an environment promoting the growth of something, esp. something unwelcome: *hotbed of vice*.

hot-blooded *adjective* ardent, passionate.

hot button *noun informal* an emotionally or politically sensitive topic or issue: *environmental concerns are still the hot buttons of global debate*.

hotcake *noun* US a pancake. PHRASES **sell like hotcakes** sell rapidly and in great numbers.

hot chocolate *noun* a drink made from cocoa, sugar, and hot water or milk.

hot cross bun *noun* a sweet bun, usu. containing raisins and dried fruit peel, marked with a cross, traditionally eaten on Good Friday.

hot dog • *noun* **1 a** a hot wiener sandwiched in an elongated soft roll. **b** a wiener. **2** *slang* a person who performs stunts, esp. when skiing or surfing. • *interjection slang* expressing approval. • *verb* (**hot-dog**; **hot-dogs, hot-dogged, hot-dogging**) *slang* perform stunts. ▶ **hot-dogger** *noun*

hotel *noun* **1** an establishment providing meals and lodging for payment. **2** *Austral.*, *NZ*, & *Cdn* a tavern.

Hotel-Dieu *noun* a name given to a hospital in French-speaking areas or to one established by a French-speaking order of nuns. [Say HOTEL dyoo (with OO as in FOOT)]

hotelier *noun* a person who owns or manages a hotel. [Say HOTEL ee er]

hot flash *noun* (*plural* **hot flashes**) a sudden feeling of heat during menopause.

hotfoot • *adverb* in eager haste: *he rushed hotfoot to the teacher to object.* • *verb* (**hotfoots, hotfooted, hotfooting**) hurry eagerly: *hotfoot it.*

hothead *noun* an impetuous, fiery, quick-tempered person. ▶ **hotheaded** *adjective* **hotheadedly** *adverb* **hotheadedness** *noun*

hothouse • *noun* **1** a heated building, usu. largely of glass, for rearing plants out of season or in a climate colder than is natural for them: *hothouse flowers*. **2** an environment that encourages the rapid growth or development of something: *Canada will not replace the US as a hothouse for new technology*. • *adjective* characteristic of something reared in a hothouse; sheltered, sensitive: *the tariff wall encouraged the hothouse growth of foreign branch plants in this country*.

hot key *Computing* • *noun* a key or combination of keys that has been programmed to cause an immediate change in the operating environment, such as the execution of a program. • *verb* use such a key or keys.

hotline *noun* **1** a direct exclusive communication link between heads of government etc., esp. for emergencies. **2** a telephone link that is specially arranged and used for a particular purpose: *a hotline for reporting stolen cards*. **3** *Cdn* a radio phone-in show.

hotliner *noun* *Cdn* **1** the host of a radio phone-in show. **2** a person who calls a radio phone-in show.

hotlink *noun* & *verb* = HYPERLINK.

hotly *adverb* **1** eagerly: *hotly anticipated*. **2** passionately: *hotly debated*. **3** angrily.

hot pants *plural noun* very brief, tight shorts for women.

hot pepper *noun* any of various very spicy fruits of tropical plants of the nightshade family.

hot pink *noun* & *adjective* a bright, deep pink colour.

hot plate *noun* an electrical appliance with a flat metal surface, used for cooking or keeping food hot.

hot potato *noun* (*plural* **hot potatoes**) *informal* a controversial or awkward matter or situation.

hot rod • *noun* a motor vehicle modified to have extra power and speed. • *verb* (**hot-rod, hot-rods, hot-rodded, hot-rodding**) **1** soup up (a vehicle, amplifier, etc.). **2** drive a hot rod. ▶ **hot rodder** *noun*

hot seat *noun* *slang* **1** a position of difficult responsibility. **2** the electric chair.

hotshot *informal* • *noun* **1** an important or exceptionally able person. **2** a skilful player of football, basketball, etc., esp. one who is showy. • *adjective* **1** important, able, expert: *a hotshot lawyer*. **2** displaying skills in a flamboyant manner: *a hotshot ballplayer*.

H

hot spot *noun* **1** a small region that is relatively hot. **2** a lively or dangerous place.

hot spring *noun* a spring of naturally hot water.

hot stuff *noun* *informal* **1** an important, impressive, or popular person or thing. **2** a sexually attractive person.

hot-tempered *adjective* impulsively angry.

Hottentot often *offensive* • *noun* = NAMA *noun* 1, 2. • *adjective* = NAMA *adjective*. [Say HOT un tot]

hot tub *noun* a large tub filled with hot aerated water and used by one or several people for recreation or physiotherapy. ▶ **hot tubber** *noun* **hot tubbing** *noun*

SPELL CHECK
haughty

Warning: **haughty** is not spelled like *hot*.

---

hot water bottle *noun* a container, usu. made of rubber, filled with hot water, esp. to warm a bed.

hot-wire *verb* (**hot-wires, hot-wired, hot-wiring**) *slang* start the engine of (a car etc.) by bypassing the ignition system.

Houdini *noun* a person skilled at escaping. [Say hoo DEENY]

hound • *noun* **1 a** a dog used for hunting, esp. one able to track by scent. **b** *informal* any dog. **2** (usu. in *combination*) a person keen in pursuit of something: *newshound*. • *verb* **1** harass or pursue relentlessly. **2** urge on or nag (a person). ▶ **hounder** *noun*

houndstooth *noun* a check pattern with notched corners suggestive of a canine tooth.

hour *noun* **1** a twenty-fourth part of a day and night, 60 minutes. **2** a definite time of day, a specific point in time: *a late hour*. **3** (in *plural*, with preceding numerals in form 08:00, 20:30, etc.) this number of hours and minutes past midnight on the 24-hour clock: *will assemble at 20:00 hours*. **4 a** a period set aside for some purpose: *lunch hour*. **b** (in *plural*) a fixed period of time for work, use of a building, etc.: *office hours*. **c** (in *plural*) one's habitual time of getting up or esp. going to bed: *keeps late hours*. **5** a short indefinite period of time: *an idle hour*. **6** the present time: *question of the hour*. **7 a** a time for action etc.: *the hour has come*. **b** the moment of one's death: *your hour has come*. **8** the distance travelled in one hour: *we are an hour from Fredericton*. **9** (**the hour**) the point of time at which each of the twelve or twenty-four hours measured by a timepiece ends and the next begins: *buses leave on the hour*. PHRASES **after hours** after the normally permitted business hours. **at all hours** at any hour of the day, no matter how early or late. **till** (or **until**) **all hours** till very late. **the wee (small) hours** the hours after midnight, usu. 1 to 4 o'clock.

hourglass *noun* (*plural* **hourglasses**) **1** a reversible device with two connected glass bulbs containing sand that takes an hour to pass from the upper to the lower bulb. **2** (as an *adjective*) narrow in the middle and curving strongly outward above and below: *hourglass figure*.

hour hand *noun* the short hand on a clock or watch which indicates the hours.

hourly • *adjective* **1** done or occurring every hour. **2 a** reckoned hour by hour: *hourly wage*. **b** (of a worker etc.) hired or paid by the hour. • *adverb* every hour: *reapply sunscreen hourly and after swimming*.

house • *noun* **1** a building for human habitation. **2** a building for a special purpose: *opera house*. **3** a building for keeping animals etc. **4 a** a religious community. **b** the buildings occupied by it. **5** a family, esp. a royal family: *House of Windsor*. **6** a firm or institution, esp. a printing or publishing firm, or a couture establishment. **7 a** a legislative or deliberative assembly. **b** the building where it meets. **8** (**the House**) **a** (in Canada) the House of Commons. **b** (in the US) the House of Representatives. **9 a** an audience in a theatre etc. **b** a theatre. **10** *Astrology* any of the signs of the zodiac considered as the seat of the greatest influence of a particular planet. **11** *Curling* the space within the outermost circle drawn around either tee. **12** = HOUSE MUSIC. **13** a casino or other establishment for gambling. **14** *Cdn hist.* a trading post, esp. inland, for the fur trade: *Norway House*. • *verb* (**houses, housed, housing**) **1** provide (a person, a population, etc.) with a house or houses or other accommodation. **2** store (goods etc.). **3** enclose or encase (a part or fitting). **4** fix (a piece of wood etc.) in a socket, joint, mortise, etc. PHRASES **bring the house down** make the audience laugh or applaud loudly. **clean house 1** do housework. **2** wipe out corruption, inefficiency, etc. **a house divided** a home, organization, party, etc. with dissension in its ranks. **keep house** provide for, maintain, or manage a household. **like a house on fire 1** vigorously, fast. **2** successfully, excellently. **on the house** at the management's expense; free. **put** (or **get, set,** etc.) **one's house in order** organize one's own affairs efficiently, esp. before telling others how to organize their affairs. **set up house** begin to live in a separate dwelling.

house arrest *noun* detention in one's own house etc.

house band *noun* a band that regularly performs at a certain club.

houseboat *noun* a boat equipped for living in, usu. on inland waters. ▶ **houseboating** *noun*

housebound *adjective* unable to leave one's house through illness etc.

house brand *noun* a food item or household product that bears the name of the store which sells it and usu. costs less than its brand name equivalent.

housebreak *verb* (**housebreaks, housebroke, housebroken, housebreaking**) train (a pet) to urinate and defecate outside or in a litter box.

housebreaker *noun* a person who breaks into a house or building intending to steal. ▶ **housebreaking** *noun*

housebroken *adjective* (of a pet) having been trained to urinate and defecate outside or in a litter box.

house call *noun* a visit made to a patient in his or her own home by a doctor etc.

houseclean *verb* clean the interior of a house or apartment.

housecleaning *noun* **1** the cleaning of the interior of a house or apartment. **2** the revamping of a company, department, etc. by eliminating personnel, reorganizing systems, etc.: *a report by the auditor general brought a brisk housecleaning and a reduction in staff*.

housecoat *noun* a dressing gown.

housedress *noun* (*plural* **housedresses**) a plain dress usu. of light cotton, for wearing around the house while doing housework etc.

house finch *noun* (*plural* **house finches**) a red-breasted North American finch.

housefly *noun* (*plural* **houseflies**) a small common fly occurring worldwide around human habitation, which lays its eggs in decaying organic matter, posing a health risk due to its contamination of food.

houseful *noun* (*plural* **housefuls**) a large number of people in a house: *he grew up in a houseful of women*.

house guest *noun* a guest staying for some days in a private house.

H

household *noun* **1** the occupants of a house regarded as a unit. **2** a house and its affairs. **3** (as an *adjective*) of or for use in a house: *household appliances*.

household effects *plural noun* the movable contents of a house, e.g. furniture, appliances, etc.

householder *noun* **1** a person who owns or rents a house. **2** the head of a household.

household name *noun* (also **household word**) **1** a familiar name or saying. **2** a familiar person or thing.

househusband *noun* a husband who works full-time in the home, taking care of the children, managing the household, etc., while his wife goes out to work.

housekeeper *noun* **1** a person employed to manage a household. **2** a person employed to manage the cleaning staff in a hotel, hospital, etc.

housekeeping *noun* **1 a** the maintenance of a household, including esp. the domestic chores of cleaning etc. **b** operations of maintenance, record-keeping, etc. in an organization. **2** (as an *adjective*) (of rental cottages, etc.) having a stove, refrigerator, and other basic facilities: *housekeeping cottages*. **3** the general maintenance operations enhancing, but not directly affecting, a computer system's performance, e.g. elimination of obsolete files etc. **4** money allowed or set aside for the management of household affairs etc.

house leader *noun* **1** (also **House Leader**) (in Canada) an MP chosen by his or her party to coordinate the party's strategy in the House of Commons, supervise the party whip, schedule speakers during question period, etc. **2** (in the US) a politician holding a position of prominence in the House of Representatives.

house league *noun Cdn* a sports league in which the players on all teams are members of the same school, organization, etc.

housemaid *noun* a female servant in a house, esp. one who cleans rooms etc.

housemate *noun* a fellow occupant of a house, apartment, etc.

house music *noun* a form of popular dance music characterized by the extensive use of drum machines and sampling, and having a fast beat and heavy synthesized bass lines.

House of Assembly *noun* **1** *Cdn* (in Newfoundland and Nova Scotia) the provincial legislature. **2** *Cdn hist.* the legislature in a province of British North America, usu. the lower, elected house. **3** the legislature in certain Commonwealth nations.

house of cards *noun* **1** an insecure scheme etc.: *he claims he never knew the bank was a house of cards built on fake deposits and phony loans*. **2** a tower-like structure built by balancing playing cards against and on top of each other.

House of Commons *noun* (in Canada and the UK) **1** the lower house of Parliament, composed of elected members. **2** the building in which this meets.

house of God *noun* (also **house of worship**) a place of worship, e.g. a church, chapel, temple, etc.

House of Lords *noun* (in the UK) the chamber of Parliament composed of peers and bishops.

House of Representatives *noun* the lower house of the US Congress and other legislatures.

houseplant *noun* a plant suitable for growing indoors.

houseroom *noun* space or accommodation in one's house. PHRASES **not give houseroom to** not have in any circumstances.

house-sit *verb* (**house-sits, house-sat, house-sitting**) live in and look after a house while its owner is away. ▶ **house-sitter** *noun* **house-sitting** *noun*

Houses of Parliament *plural noun* (in Canada and the UK) the central legislative body, composed of a lower elected chamber and an upper appointed chamber.

house sparrow *noun* a common brown and grey sparrow that nests in the eaves and roofs of houses.

house style *noun* a particular printer's or publisher's etc. preferred way of presenting text, including rules for spelling, punctuation, etc.

house-to-house *adjective & adverb* calling at each house in turn.

house trailer *noun* **1** a trailer, such as that used in camping, that can be pulled by a car or truck and is equipped with beds, sinks, etc. **2** = MOBILE HOME.

house-train *verb* esp. *Brit.* = HOUSEBREAK. ▶ **house-trained** *adjective*

housewares *plural noun* utilitarian household items, esp. kitchen utensils.

housewarming *noun* a party celebrating a move to a new home.

housewife *noun* (*plural* **housewives**) a woman (usu. married) managing a household, esp. as her primary occupation. ▶ **housewifely** *adjective*

housework *noun* regular work done in housekeeping, esp. cleaning, laundry, etc.

housing *noun* **1 a** houses, apartments, etc. collectively. **b** the provision of these. **2** a rigid casing, esp. for moving or sensitive parts of a machine.

housing development *noun* **1** = DEVELOPMENT 5. **2** the planning and building of a large group of homes.

housing project *noun* a government-subsidized housing development with relatively low rents

HOV *abbreviation* (*plural* **HOVs**) high-occupancy vehicle: *HOV lane*.

hove *past of* HEAVE.

hovel *noun* a small miserable dwelling. [Say HUV'll or HOV'll]

hover • *verb* **1** (of a bird, insect, helicopter, etc.) maintain a stationary position in the air. **2** (often foll. by *about, around*) wait close at hand, linger. **3** be in an indeterminate or irresolute state, waver: *the dollar hovered around 65 cents American*. • *noun* an act or state of hovering.

hovercraft *noun* (*plural* **hovercraft**) a vehicle that travels over land or water supported on a cushion of air produced by jet engines.

how[1] *interrogative adverb* **1** in what way or by what means. **2** in what condition or health. **3** to what extent or degree. **4** the way in which. PHRASES **and how!** *slang* very much so (chiefly used ironically or intensively). **how about 1** would you like: *how about a drink?* **2** what is to be done about. **3** what is the news about. **how many** what number. **how much** what amount or price. **how so?** how can you show that that is so? **how's that?** what is your opinion or explanation of that? **how's that for …?** isn't that a remarkable instance of …?: *how's that for irony?*

how[2] *interjection* a greeting attributed to North American Indians.

how do you do (also *informal* **how-de-do**) • *interjection* (also *informal* **howdy**) a greeting on first being introduced. • *noun* (*plural* **-dos**) **1** an inquiry of "how do you do?". **2** (**how-do-you-do**) an awkward or embarrassing situation: *what a fine how-do-you-do that would be*.

H

however *adverb* **1** nevertheless; yet. **2 a** in whatever way: *do it however you want.* **b** to whatever extent, no matter how: *must go however inconvenient.* **3** *informal* in what way, by what means: *however did that happen?*

howitzer *noun* a short, relatively light gun for high-angle firing of shells at low speeds. [Say HOW itz er]

howl • *noun* **1** a long loud doleful cry uttered by a dog, wolf, etc. **2** a prolonged wailing noise, e.g. as made by a strong wind. **3** a loud cry of pain, rage, anguish, etc. **4** a yell of derision or merriment. **5** *informal* a cause of laughter or merriment. • *verb* **1 a** (of a dog, wolf, etc.) emit a long, loud, doleful cry. **b** (of a person) utter a long, loud cry of pain, derision, laughter, etc. **2** (esp. of a child) weep loudly. **3** utter (words) with a howl. **4** (of an inanimate object, esp. the wind etc.) make a prolonged wailing noise. **5** move very quickly with or as with a howling noise: *squalls of wet, sticky snow howled up the river valley.* PHRASES **howl down** prevent (a speaker) from being heard by howls of derision.

howler *noun* **1** (also **howler monkey**) a fruit-eating monkey with a loud howling call, native to the forests of South America. **2** *informal* a glaring and usu. amusing mistake, esp. in the use of words. **3** a person or animal that howls.

howling *adjective* **1** that howls. **2** *slang* extreme: *a howling shame.*

how-to • *adjective* instructive: *how-to book.* • *noun* (plural **how-tos**) the instructions for doing something: *the how-tos of plumbing.*

hoya *noun* a climbing shrub with pink, white, or yellow waxy flowers. [Say HOY uh]

h.p. *abbreviation* (also **HP**) **1** horsepower. **2** high pressure.

HQ *abbreviation* headquarters.

HR *abbreviation* *Baseball* home run.

hr. *abbreviation* (plural **hrs.**) hour.

HRH *abbreviation* Her or His Royal Highness.

HRT *abbreviation* = HORMONE REPLACEMENT THERAPY.

HST *abbreviation* *Cdn* HARMONIZED SALES TAX.

HT *abbreviation* *Physics* high tension.

HTLV *abbreviation* human T-cell lymphotrophic virus, a small family of retroviruses causing diseases of the immune system, such as certain leukemias.

HTML *abbreviation* HYPERTEXT MARKUP LANGUAGE.

http *abbreviation* *Computing* hypertext transfer protocol, a protocol that supports the retrieval of data on the Internet, esp. of hypertext on the World Wide Web.

hub *noun* **1** the central part of a wheel, rotating on or with the axle, and from which the spokes radiate. **2** a central point of interest, importance, activity, etc. **3** a large airport serving as a transfer point between flights.

hub and spoke *adjective* of or designating an air transportation system in which local flights take passengers to a large regional airport, where they transfer to other flights to their final destinations.

Hubbard squash *noun* (plural **Hubbard squash** or **Hubbard squashes**) a variety of winter squash, usu. oval with pointed ends, with green skin and orange flesh.

hubbub *noun* **1** a confused din, esp. from a crowd of people. **2** a disturbance or uproar.

hubby *noun* (plural **hubbies**) *informal* a husband.

hubcap *noun* a cover for the hub of a vehicle's wheel.

hubris *noun* **1** excessive pride or self-confidence: *the corporate takeover that symbolized Wall Street's hubris and arrogance in the 1980s.* **2** (in Greek tragedy) the protagonist's excessively high opinion of himself or herself leading to defiance of moral laws or the prohibitions of the gods. This leads eventually to the protagonist's downfall through divine retribution, known as nemesis, the vengeance of the gods. [Say HEW briss]

huck *verb* *Cdn* (*West*) *informal* throw: *hucked a rock at it.*

huckleberry *noun* (plural **huckleberries**) **1** any of various low-growing North American shrubs of the heather family. **2** the soft blue or black fruit of this plant.

huckster *noun* **1** a mercenary person ready to make a profit out of anything. **2** a person who uses aggressive methods to sell things, esp. one working in advertising. ▶ **hucksterism** *noun*

huddle • *verb* (**huddles, huddled, huddling**) **1** (often foll. by *up*) crowd together; nestle closely. **2** (often foll. by *up*) coil one's body into a small space. **3** confer, discuss. • *noun* **1** (in team sports, esp. football) a brief gathering of players during a game to receive instructions on the next play. **2** *informal* a close or secret conference: *go into a huddle.* **3** a confused or crowded mass of people or things.

Hudson's Bay blanket *noun* *Cdn* (also **Hudson's Bay point blanket**) a durable woollen blanket woven in a variety of patterns, including cream with wide stripes of green, red, yellow, and indigo.

Hudson's Bay blanket coat *noun* (also **Hudson's Bay coat**) a warm, heavy, woollen winter coat or parka, made of Hudson's Bay blanket cloth.

hue *noun* **1** a colour; a particular shade of a colour: *his face took on an unhealthy whitish hue.* **2** a type of belief or opinion: *supporters of every political hue.*

hue and cry *noun* a loud clamour or outcry.

hued *adjective* (usu. in *combination*) coloured: *rainbow-hued* ◊ *bronze-hued.*

huff • *verb* **1** give out loud puffs of air, steam, etc. **2** say in an offended or irritated tone: *"well, nobody asked you," she huffed irritably.* • *noun* a fit of petty annoyance. PHRASES **in a huff** annoyed and offended.

huffily *adverb* in an offended or annoyed manner.

huffy *adjective* (**huffier, huffiest**) **1** apt to take offence. **2** offended.

hug • *verb* (**hugs, hugged, hugging**) **1** squeeze tightly in one's arms, esp. with affection. **2 a** keep close to (the shore, curb, etc.). **b** fit tightly around. **3** cherish or

H

cling to (beliefs, prejudices etc.). • *noun* a strong esp. affectionate clasp with the arms.

huge *adjective* (**huger**, **hugest**) **1** extremely large. **2** (of immaterial things) very great: *a huge success*.

hugely *adverb* **1** enormously: *hugely successful*. **2** very much: *enjoyed it hugely*.

huggable *adjective* cuddly; that invites hugging: *a huggable plush toy*.

hugger *noun* **1** a person or thing that hugs. **2** usu. *derogatory* a person who is fond of or tries to protect (something specified): *tree huggers*.

Huguenot *noun hist.* a French Protestant in the 16th or 17th century, esp. one persecuted for his or her beliefs or involved in civil war. [Say HEW guh not or HEW guh no]

huh *interjection* **1** expressing disgust, surprise, inquiry, etc. **2** inviting assent: *busy, huh?*

hula *noun* (*plural* **hulas**) (also **hula-hula** *plural* **hula-hulas**) a Hawaiian dance with flowing arm movements symbolizing or imitating natural phenomena, historical events, etc.

Hula Hoop *noun proprietary* a large, usu. plastic hoop for spinning around the body by hula-like movements of the waist and hips.

hula skirt *noun* a long grass skirt as worn by a hula dancer.

hulk • *noun* **1** the body of a dismantled ship. **2** *informal* a large unwieldy person or thing: *a great hulk of a man*. **3** the shell of something abandoned or destroyed: *the empty hulk of the burned out mill*. • *verb* **1** move in a clumsy way: *I saw figures hulking towards us in the night*. **2** be bulky or massive; rise like a hulk: *two concrete viaducts hulking in the dim yellow light*.

hulking *adjective informal* bulky; large and clumsy.

hull • *noun* **1** the body or frame of a ship, airship, etc. **2** the outer covering of a fruit, esp. the pod of peas and beans, the husk of grain, or the green calyx of a strawberry. • *verb* remove the hulls from (fruit etc.).

hullabaloo *noun* (*plural* **hullabaloos**) *informal* an uproar or clamour. [Say HULL a buh LOO]

hum • *verb* (**hums**, **hummed**, **humming**) **1** make a low steady continuous sound like that of a bee. **2** sing (a wordless tune) with closed lips. **3** *informal* be in an active state: *really made things hum*. **4** *Brit. & Cdn informal* smell unpleasantly. • *noun* **1** a humming sound. **2** an unwanted low-frequency noise in an amplifier etc., caused by variation of electric current. PHRASES **hum and haw** hesitate, esp. in speaking.

human • *adjective* **1** of, belonging to, or characteristic of people or humankind. **2** consisting of human beings: *the human race*. **3** of or characteristic of humankind as opposed to God, animals, or machines, esp. susceptible to the weaknesses of humankind: *is only human*. **4** showing (esp. the better) qualities of humankind, e.g. kindness, compassion, etc.: *proved to be very human*. • *noun* a human being, esp. as distinguished from an animal.

human being *noun* any man, woman, or child of the species *Homo sapiens*.

human capital *noun* the training, skills, etc. of an individual or group of individuals collectively, viewed as a resource contributing to economic growth.

humane *adjective* **1** benevolent, compassionate. **2** inflicting the minimum of pain: *humane trap*.

human ecology *noun see* ECOLOGY 2.

humanely *adverb* **1** in a benevolent or compassionate manner: *treats her employees humanely*. **2** in a way that inflicts minimum pain or discomfort: *the animals were killed humanely*.

humaneness *noun* benevolence, compassion.

humane society *noun* an organization concerned with the protection and humane treatment of animals, which usu. operates shelters for stray, sick, or abused animals.

human geography *noun* the branch of geography dealing with how human activity affects or is influenced by the earth's surface.

human growth hormone *noun* a hormone secreted by the pituitary gland which stimulates the growth of bone and body tissue and affects the metabolism of proteins, carbohydrates, and lipids.

human immunodeficiency virus *noun* = HIV.

human interest *noun* (in a newspaper etc.) reference to personal experience and emotions etc.

humanism *noun* **1** an outlook or system of thought attaching prime importance to human rather than divine or supernatural matters. **2** a belief or outlook emphasizing common human needs, seeking solely rational ways of solving human problems, and being concerned with humanity as responsible and progressive intellectual beings. **3** (often **Humanism**) a Renaissance cultural movement which turned away from the medieval educational tradition (which aimed esp. at a better understanding of Christianity) and revived interest in ancient Greek and Roman thought and literature.

humanist *noun* **1** an adherent of humanism. **2** a humanitarian. **3** *hist.* a scholar (esp. in the 14th–16th centuries) of Roman and Greek literature and antiquities. ▶ **humanistic** *adjective*

humanitarian • *noun* a person who seeks to reduce human suffering and improve life for human beings: *Walter, a true humanitarian, supports the arts and established a fund for the homeless*. • *adjective* concerned with improving the lives of humanity and reducing suffering, esp. by social reform, aid, etc.: *they are calling for the release of the hostages on humanitarian grounds*. ▶ **humanitarianism** *noun*

humanity *noun* **1 a** people in general: *crimes against humanity*. **b** the state of being a person rather than a god, an animal or a machine: *the story was used to emphasize the humanity of Jesus* ◊ *united by their common humanity*. **2** humaneness, kindness: *the judge was praised for her courage and humanity*. **3** (**humanities**) learning concerned with human culture, esp. the study of literature, art, history, philosophy, etc.

humanization *noun* **1** the act or process of making human, or of giving a human character to. **2** the act or process of making more humane: *the reform and humanization of the capitalist system*.

humanize *verb* (**humanizes**, **humanized**, **humanizing**) **1** make human; give a human character to: *her paintings of humanized dolls*. **2** make more humane or civilized; make more pleasant for humans: *these measures are intended to humanize the prison system*.

humankind *noun* human beings collectively.

humanly *adverb* **1** by human means: *what you have asked me to do is not humanly possible*. **2** in a human manner: *a humanly flawed institution*. **3** from a human point of view: *God is more than we humanly can see*.

human nature *noun* the general characteristics and feelings shared by humankind.

humanness *noun* the quality, condition, or fact of being human: *trying to preserve our humanness*.

humanoid • *adjective* having an appearance or

character resembling a human: *the life form they were searching for was of humanoid appearance.* • *noun* (esp. in science fiction) a machine or creature that looks and behaves like a human being: *claimed she'd been abducted by humanoids in a UFO near Langley.*

human race *noun* the division of living creatures to which people belong; humankind.

human relations *plural noun* the study of relations with or between people or individuals usu. to enhance performance, esp. in a work environment.

human resources *plural noun* **1** people, esp. personnel or workers, as a significant asset of a business, organization, etc. **2** the department in a business, organization, etc. which deals with the hiring, training, management, etc. of employees.

human rights *plural noun* basic rights held to belong to every living person, e.g. the right to freedom etc.

humble • *adjective* (**humbler, humblest**) **1 a** (of a person) not proud; having or showing a low or modest estimate of one's own importance. **b** offered with or affected by such an estimate: *if you want my humble opinion.* **2** of low social or political rank: *humble origins.* **3** (of a thing) of modest pretensions, dimensions, etc. • *verb* (**humbles, humbled, humbling**) **1** make humble. **2** lower the rank or status of. PHRASES **eat humble pie** make a humble apology; accept humiliation. ▶ **humbleness** *noun* **humbly** *adverb*

humbug • *noun* **1** deceptive or false talk or behaviour. **2** an imposter. **3** *Brit.* & *Cdn* a hard candy usu. flavoured with peppermint. **4** nonsense, rubbish. • *verb* (**humbugs, humbugged, humbugging**) *informal* deceive, hoax: *he realized he had been humbugged.*

humdinger *noun* *slang* an excellent or remarkable person or thing.

humdrum *adjective* boring and always the same: *humdrum routine work.*

> **SPELL CHECK**   [ABC ✓]
> **humerus, humorous**
>
> Something funny is **humorous**.

humerus *noun* (*plural* **humeri**) **1** the bone of the upper arm in humans. **2** the corresponding bone in other vertebrates. [Sounds like HUMOROUS; for *humeri* say HUMOUR eye]

humid *adjective* (of the air or climate) warm and damp.

humidex *noun* *Cdn* a scale indicating the personal discomfort level resulting from combined heat and humidity.

humidifier *noun* a device for keeping the atmosphere moist in a room etc.

humidify *verb* (**humidifies, humidified, humidifying**) make (air etc.) humid or damp.

humidity *noun* (*plural* **humidities**) **1** a quantity representing the amount of water vapour in the atmosphere or a gas: *the temperature is 20, with humidity at 65%.* **2** conditions in which the air is very warm and damp: *these plants need heat and humidity* ◊ *couldn't stand the summers in Toronto because of the humidity.*

humiliate *verb* (**humiliates, humiliated, humiliating**) make humble; injure the dignity or self-respect of. ▶ **humiliating** *adjective* **humiliatingly** *adverb* **humiliation** *noun* **humiliator** *noun*

humility *noun* humbleness; a modest view of one's importance: *admitted with sincere humility that she was surprised to win the award.*

hummable *adjective* (of a song or tune) catchy; easy to remember or hum: *the song had a hummable melody.*

hummer *noun* *informal* a hummingbird.

hummingbird *noun* a very small North American bird with a long, thin bill and iridescent plumage, which feeds from flowers while hovering and makes a characteristic humming sound when in flight, caused by the rapid vibration of its wings.

hummock *noun* **1** a hillock or knoll. **2** a piece of forested ground rising above a marsh. **3** a hump or ridge in an ice field. ▶ **hummocky** *adjective* [Say HUM uck]

hummus *noun* a thick sauce or spread made from ground chickpeas and sesame oil flavoured with lemon and garlic. [Say HUM us]

humongous *adjective* *slang* huge, enormous.

humorist *noun* a person who is known for his or her humorous writing or talking.

> **SPELL CHECK**   [ABC ✓]
> **humorist, humorous**
>
> Unlike the word **humour**, the words **humorist** and **humorous** are rarely spelled with a *u* before the *r*. In fact, only in Canada are they *ever* spelled with a *u*: everyone in the rest of the world (including Britain) always spells them as **humorist** and **humorous**.

humorous *adjective* **1** showing humour or a sense of humour: *a humorous person.* **2** comic, funny. ▶ **humorously** *adverb* **humorousness** *noun*

> **SPELL CHECK**   [ABC ✓]
> **humorous, humerus**
>
> The bone in the arm is the **humerus**.

humour (also **humor**) • *noun* **1** the condition of being amusing or comic. **2** (also **sense of humour**) the ability to perceive or express humour or take a joke. **3** a mood or state of mind: *bad humour.* **4** an inclination or whim. **5** (also **cardinal humour**) each of the four chief fluids of the body (blood, phlegm, yellow bile (choler) and black bile (melancholy)) that were thought in the Middle Ages and into early modern times to determine a person's physical and mental qualities by the relative proportions in which they were present. Blood as the dominant humour made a person cheerful; phlegm, calm; yellow bile, quick-tempered; black bile, sad. • *verb* agree with someone's wishes, even if they seem unreasonable, in order to keep the person happy: *she thought it best to humour him rather than get into an argument.* PHRASES **out of humour** displeased. ▶ **-humoured** *adjective* **-humouredly** *adverb* **humourless** *adjective* **humourlessly** *adverb* **humourlessness** *noun*

hump • *noun* **1** a rounded protuberance on the back of a camel etc., or as an abnormality on a person's back. **2 a** a rounded, raised mound of earth etc. **b** a mountain or mountain range. **3** *Cdn* (*BC*) a humpback salmon. • *verb* **1** *informal* lift or carry (heavy objects etc.) with difficulty. **2 a** make humped or hump-shaped. **b** rise in a hump-like shape. **3** *slang* hurry, move, or act, esp. with effort. PHRASES **over the hump** over the worst.

humpback *noun* **1** (also **humpback whale**) a large black baleen whale with white markings on its flippers and a dorsal fin forming a hump, noted for its lengthy vocalizations or "songs". **2** (also **humpback salmon**) = PINK SALMON. **3** = HUNCHBACK. ▶ **humpbacked** *adjective*

humped *adjective* having a hump or humps; shaped like a hump: *a humped back.*

humph • *interjection* an inarticulate sound expressing doubt or dissatisfaction. • *verb* utter "humph". • *noun* an utterance of "humph".

humungous *adjective* = HUMONGOUS.

SPELL CHECK
humus, hummus

The spicy chickpea paste eaten as a dip is
hummus.

humus noun the organic constituent of soil, usu.
formed by the decomposition of plants and leaves by
soil bacteria. [Say HEW muss]
Hun noun **1** a member of a warlike Asiatic nomadic
people who invaded and ravaged Europe in the 4th–5th
centuries. **2** a reckless or uncivilized destroyer of
something.
hunch • verb (**hunches, hunched, hunching**) **1** raise
one's shoulders and bend the top of one's body
forward: *he hunched over his glass ◊ he thrust his hands in
his pockets, hunching his shoulders*. **2** (often foll. by *up*) sit
with the body hunched. • noun (plural **hunches**) **1** an
intuitive feeling or conjecture. **2** a hump.
hunchback noun **1** a person having a deformed,
hunched, or protruding back. **2** such a back.
▶ **hunchbacked** adjective
hundred cardinal number **1** ten more than ninety.
2 used to express whole hours in the 24-hour system:
thirteen hundred hours. PHRASES **a** (or **one**) **hundred
percent 1** entire(ly), complete(ly). **2** (usu. with neg.)
fully recovered. ▶ **hundredfold** adjective & adverb
hundredth ordinal number
hundredweight noun (plural **hundredweight** or
hundredweights) **1** (also **metric hundredweight**)
a unit of weight equal to 50 kg. **2** US a unit of weight
equal to 100 lb. (about 45.4 kg). Abbreviation: **cwt**.

WRITING TIP
hung, hanged

Note that while the past of *most* senses of **hang** is
hung, the past for the sense "suspend from a rope
by the neck until dead" is **hanged**: *the leader of the
rebellion was hanged in a public execution; when they
hanged the notorious Captain Kidd, the rope broke*.

hung • verb past and past participle of HANG. • adjective
1 (of a jury) unable to agree on a verdict. **2** (of an
elected body) in which no political party has a clear
majority. **3** slang (of a male) having large sexual organs.
Hungarian • noun **1 a** a native or national of
Hungary, a country in central Europe. **b** a person of
Hungarian descent. **2** the language of Hungary, related
to Finnish and Estonian. • adjective of or relating to
Hungary or its people or language. [Say hung GARY un]
hunger • noun **1 a** a feeling of pain, weakness, or
discomfort, caused by lack of food. **b** lack of food;
famine: *alleviate world hunger*. **2** (often foll. by *for, after*) a
strong desire. • verb **1** (often foll. by *for, after*) have a
craving or strong desire. **2** feel hunger.
hunger strike noun the refusal of food as a form of
protest, esp. by prisoners. ▶ **hunger striker** noun
hungover adjective informal suffering from a hangover.
hungrily adverb **1** in a hungry manner; with hunger:
wolfed the food down hungrily. **2** longingly.
hungry adjective (**hungrier, hungriest**) **1** feeling or
showing hunger; needing food. **2** (also in *combination*)
eager, greedy, craving, esp. for money, power, etc. **3** (of a
period, place, etc.) marked by a scarcity of food.
hunk noun **1 a** a large piece cut off: *a hunk of bread*. **b** a
thick or clumsy piece. **2** informal a sexually attractive,
well built and ruggedly handsome man.
hunker verb (often foll. by *down*) **1** squat or crouch with
the haunches nearly touching the heels, esp. for shelter
or concealment. **2** hide or take shelter: *hunkered down
for the winter*. PHRASES **hunker down** apply oneself.

hunky adjective (**hunkier, hunkiest**) informal (of a man)
well built and sexually attractive.
hunky-dory adjective informal excellent.
hunt • verb **1 a** pursue and kill (wild animals or game)
for sport or food. **b** (of an animal) chase (its prey).
2 (foll. by *after, for*) seek, search: *hunting for a job*.
3 pursue with hostility. **4** scour (a district) in pursuit of
game. • noun **1** an act of looking for something; a
search. **2** an act of hunting wild animals: *the seal hunt*.
PHRASES **hunt down** pursue and capture. **hunt out**
find by searching; track down.
hunted adjective (of a look etc.) expressing alarm or
terror as of one being hunted.
hunter noun **1 a** a person or animal that hunts. **b** a
horse used in hunting. **2** a person who seeks
something.
hunter-gatherer noun a member of a people whose
mode of subsistence is based on hunting animals and
gathering plants etc.
hunter green noun & adjective a dark, slightly
yellowish green.
hunting noun the practice of pursuing and killing wild
animals.
hunting dog noun = GUN DOG.
Huntington's chorea noun (also **Huntington's
disease**) a hereditary disease marked by degeneration
of the brain cells and causing jerky involuntary
movements and progressive mental impairment.
huntsman noun (plural **huntsmen**) **1** a hunter. **2** a
hunt official in charge of hounds.

SPELL CHECK
hurdle, hurtle

To move wildly at a dangerous speed is to **hurtle**.

hurdle • noun **1** each of a series of light frames to be
cleared by athletes in a race. **2** an obstacle or difficulty.
• verb (**hurdles, hurdled, hurdling**) **1 a** run in a
hurdle race. **b** clear (a hurdle). **2** overcome (a
difficulty). ▶ **hurdler** noun
hurdy-gurdy noun (plural **hurdy-gurdies**) **1** a musical
instrument with a droning sound, played by turning a
handle, esp. one with a rosined wheel turned by the
right hand to sound the drone strings, and keys played
by the left hand. **2** informal a barrel organ.
hurl • verb **1** throw with great force. **2** utter (abuse etc.)
vehemently. **3** slang vomit. **4** Baseball slang pitch. • noun
1 a forceful throw. **2** the act of hurling.
hurler noun **1** a person or thing that hurls. **2** Baseball a
pitcher.
hurley noun **1** (also **hurling**) an Irish game somewhat
resembling field hockey, played with broad sticks. **2** a
stick used in this.
hurly-burly noun boisterous activity; commotion.
Huron • noun **1** (plural **Huron** or **Hurons**) a member of
an Aboriginal group formerly living around Lake
Simcoe, with present-day populations living north of
Quebec City and in Oklahoma. **2** the Iroquoian
language of this people. • adjective of or relating to the
Huron or their language or culture.
hurrah (also **hurray**) • interjection & noun an
exclamation of joy or approval. • verb (**hurrahs,
hurrahed, hurrahing**) cry or shout "hurrah" or
"hurray".
hurricane noun **1** a tropical cyclone with winds
greater than 65 knots (125 kph) accompanied by heavy
rain, esp. one originating in the western North
Atlantic. **2** a wind of 65 knots (125 kph) or more, force
12 on the Beaufort scale.
hurried adjective **1** hasty; done rapidly owing to lack of

time: *had a hurried supper.* **2** pressed for time: *hurried waiters.* ▶**hurriedly** *adverb* **hurriedness** *noun*

hurry • *noun* (*plural* **hurries**). • *verb* (**hurries, hurried, hurrying**) move or act or cause to move or act with great or undue haste. PHRASES **hurry up** (or **along**) make or cause to make haste. **in a hurry 1** hurrying, rushed; in a rushed manner. **2** *informal* easily or readily: *you won't beat that in a hurry.*

hurt • *verb* (**hurts, hurt, hurting**) **1** cause pain or injury to. **2** cause mental pain or distress to (a person, feelings, etc.). **3** suffer physical pain or mental anguish: *my arm hurts* ◊ *she's really hurting.* **4** (foll. by *for*) have a pressing need for. **5** *informal* experience harm or misfortune: *sales have been hurting.* **6** influence adversely: *the recession has hurt ticket sales.* • *noun* **1** bodily or material injury. **2** harm, wrong. • *adjective* **1** physically injured: *a hurt knee.* **2** emotionally wounded: *hurt pride.* **3** (of a facial expression, etc.) suggesting that one has been emotionally injured or offended: *a hurt look.*

hurtful *adjective* causing (esp. mental) hurt. ▶**hurtfully** *adverb* **hurtfulness** *noun*

hurting *adjective* **1** suffering, esp. mentally. **2** (of music, esp. country and western songs) lamenting one's misfortunes. **3** *slang* pitiful, contemptible.

SPELL CHECK
hurtle, hurdle   ABC ✓

An obstacle is a **hurdle**.

---

hurtle *verb* (**hurtles, hurtled, hurtling**) move or hurl rapidly or with a clattering sound.

husband • *noun* a married man esp. in relation to his wife. • *verb* manage carefully with a view to not wasting; use (resources) economically: *she waited, husbanding her strength for her next visitors.*

husbandry *noun* **1** the cultivation of plants and animals; farming. **2** the application of science to farming, esp. to raising livestock: *he came from Finland to teach people in the North the skill of reindeer husbandry.*

hush • *verb* (**hushes, hushed, hushing**) make or become silent or quiet. • *interjection* calling for silence. • *noun* (*plural* **hushes**) an expectant stillness or silence. PHRASES **hush up 1** be quiet. **2** suppress public mention of (an affair).

hush-hush *adjective informal* (esp. of an official plan or enterprise etc.) highly secret or confidential.

hush money *noun* money paid to prevent the disclosure of a discreditable matter.

hush puppy *noun* (*plural* **hush puppies**) US (*South*) a deep-fried ball of cornmeal batter.

husk • *noun* **1** the dry outer covering of some fruits or seeds, esp. of a nut or grain. **2** the coarse leaves enclosing an ear of corn. **3** the worthless outside part of a thing: *he had sapped her strength and left her a used-up husk.* • *verb* remove a husk or husks from.

huskily *adverb* with a hoarse or rough voice.

husky¹ *adjective* (**huskier, huskiest**) **1** (of a person or voice) sounding rough as if dry in the throat, often because of emotion; hoarse. **2** big and strong.

husky² *noun* (*plural* **huskies**) a breed of dog used in the Arctic for pulling sleds.

hussar *noun* a soldier of a light cavalry regiment. [Say hoo ZARR (with HOO as in *HOOK*)]

hussy *noun* (*plural* **hussies**) *derogatory* a wanton or impudent girl or woman.

hustings *noun* the political campaigning leading up to an election, e.g. canvassing and making speeches: *party leaders may be more frank on the hustings than within parliament.*

hustle • *verb* (**hustles, hustled, hustling**) **1** push or move (someone) in a specified direction in a hurried, esp. rough and aggressive way: *was hustled into a waiting car.* **2** move quickly. **3 a** work hard: *if you want it, you'll have to hustle for it.* **b** obtain by hard work and persistence. **4** sell or obtain (illegal or stolen goods) using aggressive tactics: *they survive by hustling on the streets.* **5** market or sell aggressively. **6 a** *slang* engage in prostitution. **b** (esp. of a prostitute) solicit (a sexual partner). • *noun* **1** (also **hustle and bustle**) busy movement or activity, esp. of many people. **2** the quality or an instance of working hard or aggressively. **3** an act or instance of hustling. **4** *informal* a fraud or swindle. **5** a fast, vigorous dance popular particularly during the disco craze of the 1970s, set to a strong beat and incorporating Latin American, swing, and rock elements. PHRASES **hustle one's buns** (or **butt**) *slang* get a move on; move or act quickly.

hustler *noun* *slang* **1** an active, enterprising, or unscrupulous individual. **2** a prostitute.

hut *noun* a small simple or crude house or shelter.

hutch *noun* (*plural* **hutches**) **1** a box or cage, usu. with a wire mesh front, for keeping small animals, esp. rabbits. **2 a** a usu. open shelving unit placed on top of a sideboard, desk, etc. **b** a piece of furniture incorporating this.

Hutterite • *noun* a member of an Anabaptist sect living esp. in rural communal settlements and holding all property in common. • *adjective* of or relating to the Hutterites or their beliefs. [Say HUTTER ite]

Hutu • *noun* (*plural* **Hutu** or **Hutus**) a member of a Bantu-speaking people forming the majority population in Rwanda and Burundi. • *adjective* of or relating to the Hutu people. [Say HOO too]

HVAC *abbreviation* heating, ventilating, and air conditioning.

hwy. *abbreviation* highway.

hyacinth *noun* **1** a bulbous plant with racemes of usu. purplish-blue, pink, or white bell-shaped fragrant flowers. **2** any of various plants of the lily family resembling this. **3** = GRAPE HYACINTH. **4** the purplish-blue colour of the hyacinth flower. [Say HI a synth]

hyaluronic acid *noun* a viscous fluid carbohydrate found in the fluid lubricating joints and tendon sheaths etc. [Say HI ul yoo RON ick]

hybrid • *noun* **1** the offspring of two plants or animals of different species or varieties. **2** *offensive* a person of mixed racial or cultural origin. **3** a thing composed of mixed or incongruous elements: *a hybrid of western pop and traditional folk song.* **4** *Linguistics* a word with parts taken from different languages. • *adjective* **1** bred as a hybrid from different species or varieties. **2** formed from mixed, esp. incongruous elements: *Mexico's hybrid post-Conquest culture.* [Say HI brid]

hybridization *noun* **1** the production of hybrids by crossbreeding or cross-fertilization. **2** the action or result of hybridizing something: *the dance performance was an example of transcultural hybridization and the mixing of sacred and profane expressions of Gitksan and European peoples.* [Say hi brid ize AY sh'n]

hybridize *verb* (**hybridizes, hybridized, hybridizing**) **1** subject (a species etc.) to crossbreeding. **2 a** produce hybrids. **b** (of an animal or plant) interbreed. [Say HI brid ize]

hybrid offence *noun* *Cdn* a crime which may be treated as either a summary conviction offence or an indictable offence, at the discretion of the Crown.

hydra *noun* (*plural* **hydras**) **1** a freshwater polyp with a tubular body and tentacles around the mouth. **2** something which is hard to destroy or overcome because of its pervasive or enduring quality or its many

aspects: *his battle with the hydra of bureaucracy.* [Say HI druh]

hydrangea *noun* (*plural* **hydrangeas**) a shrub with rounded or flat flowering heads of small white, pink, or blue florets, native to North America and Asia. [Say hi DRAIN juh or hi DRAIN jee uh]

hydrant *noun* = FIRE HYDRANT.

hydrate • *noun* *Chemistry* a compound of water combined with another compound or with an element. • *verb* (**hydrates, hydrated, hydrating**) **1** combine chemically with water. **2** cause to absorb water. ▶ **hydrated** *adjective* **hydration** *noun* [Say HI drate, hi DRAY sh'n]

hydraulic *adjective* **1** (of water, oil, etc.) conveyed through pipes or channels usu. by pressure. **2** (of a mechanism etc.) operated by liquid moving in this manner: *hydraulic lift.* **3** of or concerned with hydraulics: *hydraulic engineer.* **4** hardening under water: *hydraulic cement.* ▶ **hydraulically** *adverb* [Say hi DRAWL ick]

hydraulics *plural noun* **1** (usu. treated as *singular*) the science of the conveyance of liquids through pipes etc. esp. as motive power. **2** hydraulically operated devices. [Say hi DRAWL icks]

hydro • *noun* (*plural* **hydros**) **1** *Cdn* electricity. **2** hydroelectricity. **3** a hydroelectric power plant. **4** (**Hydro**) *Cdn* an electric utility. • *adjective* **1** *Cdn* of or relating to electricity: *hydro bill.* **2** of or relating to hydroelectricity: *hydro dam.*

hydrocarbon *noun* *Chemistry* a compound of hydrogen and carbon.

hydrocephalic • *adjective* suffering from hydrocephalus, an accumulation of fluid in the brain which makes the head enlarge and can cause mental handicap. • *noun* a person with hydrocephalus. [Say hydro suh FAL ick]

hydrocephalus *noun* an accumulation of fluid in the brain, esp. in young children, which makes the head enlarge and can cause mental handicap. [Say hydro SEFFA luss]

hydrochloric acid *noun* a solution of the colourless gas hydrogen chloride in water.

hydrochloride *noun* a compound of an organic base with hydrochloric acid.

hydro corridor *noun* *Cdn* a right-of-way for a hydro line.

hydrocortisone *noun* a steroid hormone produced by the adrenal cortex, used medicinally to treat inflammation and rheumatism. [Say hydro CORTA zone]

hydrodynamic *adjective* of or relating to the science of forces acting on or exerted by fluids.

hydrodynamics *noun* the science of forces acting on or exerted by fluids.

hydroelectric *adjective* **1** generating electricity by utilization of water power. **2** (of electricity) generated in this way. ▶ **hydroelectricity** *noun*

hydrofoil *noun* **1** a boat equipped with a device consisting of planes for lifting its hull out of the water to increase its speed. **2** this device.

hydrogen *noun* a colourless gaseous element, without taste or odour, the lightest of the elements and occurring in water and all organic compounds. [Say HI druh jun]

hydrogenate *verb* (**hydrogenates, hydrogenated, hydrogenating**) **1** charge with or cause to combine with hydrogen. **2** (often as **hydrogenated** *adjective*) add hydrogen to (an edible oil) to convert it into a saturated fat, usu. solid at room temperature. ▶ **hydrogenation** *noun* [Say hi DRAW jin ate, hydrogen AY sh'n]

hydrogen bomb *noun* an immensely powerful bomb utilizing the explosive fusion of hydrogen nuclei.

hydrogen peroxide *noun* **1** a colourless viscous unstable liquid with strong oxidizing properties. **2** an aqueous solution of this used esp. as a disinfectant or bleach.

hydrogen sulphide *noun* a poisonous gas with a disagreeable smell, formed by rotting animal matter.

hydrogeological *adjective* of or relating to the branch of geology dealing with underground and surface water. [Say hydro geo LOGICAL]

hydrogeologist *noun* a person who studies the branch of geology dealing with underground and surface water. [Say hydro GEOLOGIST]

hydrogeology *noun* the branch of geology dealing with underground and surface water. [Say hydro GEOLOGY]

hydrographer *noun* a scientist who surveys and charts seas, lakes, rivers, etc. [Say hi DRAW gruh fur]

hydrographic *adjective* of or relating to the science of surveying and charting seas, lakes, rivers, etc. [Say hydro GRAPHIC]

hydrography *noun* the science of surveying and charting seas, lakes, rivers, etc. [Say hi DRAW gruh fee]

hydro line *noun* *Cdn* an elevated or buried wire for the transmission of electricity.

hydrologic *adjective* of or relating to the properties of the earth's water, esp. of its movement in relation to land: *the hydrologic history of the region.* ▶ **hydrological** *adjective* [Say hydro LOGIC]

hydrological cycle *noun* the circulation of water between the atmosphere and the earth's surface through precipitation and evaporation.

hydrologist *noun* a scientist who studies the properties of the earth's water, esp. of its movement in relation to land. [Say hi DRAWL a jist]

hydrology *noun* the science of the properties of the earth's water, esp. of its movement in relation to land. [Say hi DRAWL a jee]

hydrolysis *noun* the chemical reaction of a substance with water, usu. resulting in decomposition. ▶ **hydrolytic** *adjective* [Say hi DRAWL a sis, hydro LIT ick]

hydrolyze *verb* (**hydrolyzes, hydrolyzed, hydrolyzing**) (also **hydrolyse, hydrolyses, hydrolysed, hydrolysing**) subject to or undergo the chemical action of water. [Say HYDRO lize]

hydrolyzed vegetable protein *noun* (also **hydrolyzed plant protein**) a flavour-enhancing food additive made from plant protein that has been broken down into amino acids.

hydrophobia *noun* **1** a morbid aversion to water, esp. as a symptom of rabies in humans. **2** rabies, esp. in humans. [Say hydro FOE be uh]

hydrophobic *adjective* **1** of or suffering from hydrophobia. **2** tending to repel or fail to mix with water: *hydrophobic leather.* [Say hydro FOE bick]

hydrophone *noun* an instrument for the detection of sound waves in water.

hydroplane • *noun* **1** a light fast motorboat designed to skim over the surface of water. **2** a fin-like attachment which enables a submarine to rise and fall in water. • *verb* (**hydroplanes, hydroplaned, hydroplaning**) **1** (of a vehicle) glide uncontrollably on the wet surface of a road. **2** (of a boat) skim over the surface of water with its hull lifted.

hydro pole *noun* *Cdn* a vertical pole supporting a hydro line.

hydroponic *adjective* of, relating to, or grown by hydroponics: *hydroponic vegetables* ◊ *grown in hydroponic trays.* ▶ **hydroponically** *adverb* [Say hydro PAWN ick]

hydroponics *noun* the process of growing plants in

H

sand, gravel, or liquid, without soil and with added nutrients. [Say hydro PAWN icks]

hydro power *noun* hydroelectricity.

hydrosphere *noun* the waters of the earth's surface, such as lakes and seas, and sometimes including water over the earth's surface, such as clouds.

hydrostatic *adjective* of the equilibrium of liquids and the pressure exerted by liquid at rest. [Say hydro STATIC]

hydro station *noun* Cdn **1** a hydroelectric generating station. **2** a station reducing the high voltage of electric power transmission to that suitable for supply to customers; a substation.

hydrotherapy *noun* the use of water in the treatment of disorders, usu. exercises in swimming pools for arthritic or partially paralyzed patients.

hydro tower *noun* Cdn a tall metal structure erected as a support for high-voltage electrical lines.

hydrous *adjective* containing water. [Say HI druss]

hydroxide *noun* a metallic compound containing oxygen and hydrogen either in the form of the hydroxide ion (OH-) or the hydroxyl group (-OH). [Say hi DROX ide]

hydroxyl *noun* Chemistry the monovalent group containing hydrogen and oxygen, as -OH. [Say hi DROX'll]

hyena *noun* any of several carnivorous scavenging animals somewhat resembling a dog, but with the hind limbs shorter than the forelimbs. [Say hi EE nuh]

hygiene *noun* **1** the branch of knowledge that deals with the maintenance of health, esp. the conditions and practices conducive to it. **2** conditions or practices conducive to maintaining health. **3** cleanliness. [Say HI jean]

hygienic *adjective* conducive to health; clean and sanitary. ▶ **hygienically** *adverb* [Say hi JEN ick or hi JEAN ick]

hygienist *noun* a specialist in the promotion and practice of cleanliness for the preservation of health. [Say hi JEN ist or hi JEAN ist]

hymen *noun* a membrane which partially closes the opening of the vagina and is usu. broken at the first occurrence of sexual intercourse. [Say HI mun]

hymn • *noun* **1** a song of praise, esp. to God in Christian worship, usu. a metrical composition sung in a religious service. **2** a song of praise in honour of a god or other exalted being or thing. • *verb* praise or celebrate in hymns. [Say HIM]

hymnal *noun* a book of hymns. [Say HIM nul]

hype *slang* • *noun* extravagant or intensive publicity promotion: *don't believe all the hype — the book isn't that good*. • *verb* (**hypes, hyped, hyping**) promote with extravagant publicity: *his much hyped new movie*.

hyped up *adjective* informal very worried or excited.

hyper *adjective* slang hyperactive, high-strung.

hyperactive *adjective* **1** (of a person, esp. a child) showing constantly active and sometimes disruptive behaviour. **2** abnormally active: *a hyperactive pituitary gland*. ▶ **hyperactivity** *adverb* **hyperactivity** *noun*

hyperbola *noun* (*plural* **hyperbolas** or **hyperbolae**) Geometry the curve produced when a cone is cut by a plane that makes a larger angle with the base than the side of the cone does. [Say hi PERBA luh for the singular, hi PERBA lee for the plural]

hyperbole *noun* (*plural* **hyperboles**) **1** an exaggerated statement not meant to be taken literally, used for emphasis, e.g. "I'm starving to death" said by someone who is merely very hungry. **2** extravagant exaggeration: *the film is being promoted with all the usual hyperbole*. [Say hi PERBA lee]

hyperbolic *adjective* **1** of or relating to a hyperbola. **2** of the nature of or using hyperbole; exaggerated:

relatively free of the hyperbolic excesses typically found in his books. [Say hyper BAWL ick]

hyperextend *verb* extend or stretch (a limb, digit, etc.) so much that it bends the opposite way from normal. ▶ **hyperextension** *noun*

hypericum *noun* a shrub with five-petalled yellow flowers. [Say hi PARE e kum]

hyperinflation *noun* monetary inflation at a very high rate.

hyperkinetic *adjective* **1** characterized by excessive or spasmodic movement. **2** highly energetic: *hyperkinetic ads for beer and cars*. **3** (of children) hyperactive. [Say hyper kin ETT ick]

hyperlink • *noun* a software link in a hypertext system connecting cross-referenced items. • *verb* connect by means of a hyperlink.

hypermedia *noun* = MULTIMEDIA *noun*.

hyperplasia *noun* the enlargement of an organ etc. [Say hyper PLAZE ee uh]

hyperreal *adjective* (esp. of an artificial environment or an artistic creation) created or represented with such attention to detail as to appear more real than reality. ▶ **hyperrealism** *noun* **hyperrealistic** *adjective* **hyperreality** *noun* [Say hyper REAL]

hypersensitive *adjective* **1** abnormally or excessively sensitive. **2** (of an individual) having an adverse bodily reaction to a particular substance in doses that do not affect most individuals. ▶ **hypersensitivity** *noun*

hypersonic *adjective* relating to speeds of more than five times the speed of sound (Mach 5).

hyperspace *noun* space of more than three dimensions, esp. (in science fiction) a notional space-time continuum in which motion and communication at speeds greater than that of light are supposedly possible.

hypertension *noun* abnormally high blood pressure.

hypertext *noun* a software system allowing extensive cross-referencing between related sections of text and associated graphic material.

Hypertext Markup Language *noun* the system of tagging used in hypertext to indicate how any downloaded text should be formatted.

WRITING TIP
hyperthermia, hypothermia

Do not confuse **hyperthermia** and **hypothermia**. **Hyperthermia** is a condition in which a person's body temperature is above normal. **Hypothermia** is a condition in which a person's body temperature is below normal.

---

hyperthermia *noun* the condition of having a body temperature greatly above normal. [Say hyper THURR me uh]

hyperventilate *verb* (**hyperventilates, hyperventilated, hyperventilating**) breathe at an abnormally rapid rate, resulting in an increased loss of carbon dioxide, and often accompanied by dizziness.

hyperventilation *noun* breathing at an abnormally rapid rate, resulting in an increased loss of carbon dioxide, and often accompanied by dizziness.

hypha *noun* (*plural* **hyphae**) a microscopic threadlike structure in the vegetative part of a fungus. [Say HI fuh for the singular, HI fee for the plural]

hyphen • *noun* the sign (-) used to join words semantically or syntactically (as in *pick-me-up*, *rock-forming*), to indicate the division of a word at the end of a line, or to indicate a missing or implied element (as in *man- and womankind*). • *verb* = HYPHENATE *verb*.

hyphenate *verb* (**hyphenates, hyphenated,**

hyphenating) 1 write (a compound word) with a hyphen. **2** join (words) with a hyphen.

hyphenated *adjective* **1** (of a word) spelled with a hyphen. **2** (of a person) having dual nationality or mixed background or ancestry: *Scottish-Canadians, Ukrainian-Canadians and other hyphenated Canadians*.

hyphenation *noun* **1** the use of a hyphen to join words or divide a word. **2** (in printing etc.) the division of words at the end of lines, marked with hyphens.

hypnosis *noun* a state like sleep in which the subject acts only on external suggestion. [Say hip NOCE iss (NOCE rhymes with *GROSS*)]

hypnotherapist *noun* a person who practises psychotherapy involving hypnotism. [Say hip no THERAPIST]

hypnotherapy *noun* psychotherapy involving hypnotism. [Say hip no THERAPY]

hypnotic • adjective 1 of or producing hypnotism. **2** (of a drug) sleep-inducing. **3** (of a person's gaze, musical rhythms, etc.) producing a trancelike state or fascination. **• noun 1** a thing, esp. a drug, that produces sleep. **2** a person under or open to the influence of hypnotism. ▶ **hypnotically** *adverb* [Say hip NOT ick]

hypnotism *noun* the study or practice of hypnosis. ▶ **hypnotist** *noun* [Say HIP no tism]

hypnotize *verb* (**hypnotizes, hypnotized, hypnotizing**) **1** produce hypnosis in. **2** fascinate; capture the mind of (a person). [Say HIP no tize]

hypo *noun* (*plural* **hypos**) *informal* = HYPODERMIC *noun*.

hypoallergenic *adjective* having little tendency, or a reduced tendency, to cause an allergic reaction. [Say hypo al er JEN ick]

hypochondria *noun* abnormal and unnecessary anxiety about one's health. [Say hypo CON dree uh]

hypochondriac • noun a person suffering from hypochondria. **• adjective** (also **hypochondriacal**) of or affected by hypochondria. [Say hypo CON dree ack, hypo con DRY a cull]

hypocrisy *noun* (*plural* **hypocrisies**) behaviour in which someone pretends to have moral standards or opinions that they do not actually have: *he condemned the hypocrisy of those politicians who do one thing and say another*. [Say hip OCKRA see]

hypocrite *noun* a person who pretends to have moral standards or opinions that they do not actually have. ▶ **hypocritical** *adjective* **hypocritically** *adverb* [Say HIPPO crit, hippo CRITICAL]

hypodermic • adjective 1 of or relating to the area beneath the skin. **2 a** (of a drug etc. or its application) injected beneath the skin. **b** (of a needle, syringe, etc.) used to do this. **• noun** a hypodermic injection or syringe. ▶ **hypodermically** *adverb* [Say hypo DERMIC]

hypoglycemia *noun* (also **hypoglycaemia**) a deficiency of glucose in the bloodstream. ▶ **hypoglycemic** *adjective* [Say hypo glye SEAMY uh]

hypotenuse *noun* the side opposite the right angle of a right-angled triangle. [Say hi POTTA noose or hi POTTA nooz or hi POTTA nyooz]

hypothalamus *noun* (*plural* **hypothalami**) the region of the brain which controls body temperature, thirst, hunger, etc. [Say hypo THALLA muss for the singular, hypo THALLA my for the plural]

hypothermia *noun* the condition of having an abnormally low body temperature. ▶ **hypothermic** *adjective* [Say hypo THURR me uh, hypo THURR mick]

hypothesis *noun* (*plural* **hypotheses**) **1** an idea or explanation of something that is based on a few known facts but that has not yet been proved to be true or correct: *there is little evidence to support this hypothesis*. **2** guesses and ideas that are not based on certain knowledge; speculation: *it would be pointless to engage in hypothesis before we have the facts*. [Say hi PAW thuh sis for the singular, hi PAW thuh seez for the plural]

hypothesize *verb* (**hypothesizes, hypothesized, hypothesizing**) assume as a hypothesis: *she hypothesized that the comets condensed from the outer portion of the original nebula from which the sun and planets were born*. [Say hi PAW thuh size]

hypothetical *adjective* **1** based on situations or ideas which are possible and imagined but not necessarily real or true: *a hypothetical situation* ◊ *let's take the hypothetical case of Sheila, a mother of two …* ◊ *I wasn't asking about anybody in particular — it was a purely hypothetical question*. **2** of or based on or serving as a hypothesis. ▶ **hypothetically** *adverb* [Say hi puh THET ick'll]

hypoxia *noun* *Medical* a deficiency of oxygen reaching the tissues. ▶ **hypoxic** *adjective* [Say hi POXY uh, hi POX ick]

hyrax *noun* (*plural* **hyraxes**) a small plant-eating mammal with a compact body, a very short tail, and feet with nails like hoofs, found in Africa and the Middle East. [Say HI rax]

hyssop *noun* **1** a small, bushy, aromatic herb of the mint family, the leaves of which are used in cooking and herbal medicine. **2** *Bible* **a** a plant whose twigs were used for sprinkling in Jewish rites. **b** a bunch of this used in purification. **3** (also **giant hyssop**) any of various tall plants with structures resembling lips. [Say HISSUP]

hysterectomy *noun* (*plural* **hysterectomies**) the surgical removal of the uterus. [Say hista RECTA me]

hysteria *noun* **1** an emotional state, caused by grief or fear etc., accompanied by uncontrollable laughter, weeping, etc. **2** a functional disturbance of the nervous system. **3** an excited and exaggerated reaction to an event: *public hysteria about AIDS*. [Say hiss TERRY uh]

hysteric *noun* **1** (in *plural*) **a** a fit of hysteria. **b** *informal* overwhelming mirth or laughter: *we were in hysterics*. **2** a hysterical person. [Say hiss TARE ick]

hysterical *adjective* **1** of or affected with hysteria. **2** *informal* extremely funny or amusing. ▶ **hysterically** *adverb* [Say hiss TARE ick'll]

Hz *abbreviation* hertz.

H

Ii

I¹ *noun* (also **i**) (*plural* **Is** or **I's**) **1** the ninth letter of the alphabet. **2** (as a Roman numeral) 1.

I² *pronoun* used by a speaker or writer to refer to himself or herself.

I³ *symbol* **1** the element iodine. **2** electric current.

I⁴ *abbreviation* (also **I.**) **1** Island(s). **2** Isle(s). **3** (in the US) (used in designating highways) interstate: *I-95*. **4** institute.

iamb *noun* (in poetry) a metrical foot consisting of one short (or unstressed) followed by one long (or stressed) syllable; a group of two syllables with the rhythm of *tah-DAH*. [Say EYE am]

iambic • *adjective* of or using iambs. • *noun* (usu. in *plural*) iambic verse. [Say eye AM bick]

iambus *noun* (*plural* **iambuses** or **iambi**) = IAMB. [Say eye AM bus for the singular, eye AM bye for the plural]

IBC *abbreviation* Inuit Broadcasting Corporation.

IBD *abbreviation* INFLAMMATORY BOWEL DISEASE.

I-beam *noun* a girder with a cross-section shaped like an I.

Iberian • *adjective* of ancient Iberia, the peninsula now comprising Spain and Portugal; of Spain and Portugal. • *noun* **1** a native of ancient Iberia. **2** any of the languages of ancient Iberia. [Say eye BEERY un]

ibex *noun* (*plural* **ibexes**) a wild goat-antelope with a chin beard and thick curved ridged horns, esp. of mountainous areas of Europe, northern Africa, and Asia. [Say EYE bex]

ibid. *abbreviation* in the same book or passage etc.

ibis *noun* (*plural* **ibises**) a wading bird with a curved bill, long neck, and long legs, which nests in colonies. [Say EYE biss]

Ibo • *noun* **1** (*plural* **Ibo** or **Ibos**) a member of a people of southeast Nigeria. **2** the language of this people, related to Yoruba. • *adjective* of this people. [Say EE bo]

ibuprofen *noun* an analgesic and anti-inflammatory drug used esp. as a stronger alternative to ASA. [Say eye byoo PRO fin]

IC *abbreviation* integrated circuit.

i/c *abbreviation* in charge.

ICBM *abbreviation* (*plural* **ICBMs**) INTERCONTINENTAL BALLISTIC MISSILE.

ice • *noun* **1 a** frozen water. **b** a sheet of ice used as a playing surface for hockey, curling, broomball, etc. **2** a frozen mixture of fruit juice or flavoured water and sugar. **3** *slang* diamonds. **4** *slang* a crystalline form of the drug methamphetamine, inhaled or smoked (illegally) as a stimulant. • *verb* (**ices**, **iced**, **icing**) **1** mix with or cool in ice: *iced drinks*. **2** (often foll. by *over, up*) **a** cover or become covered with ice. **b** freeze. **3** spread or cover (a cake etc.) with icing. **4** *Hockey* shoot (the puck) from one's own half of the rink to the far end of the other half. **5** *Cdn* select (a team or individual) to play in a hockey game. **6** *informal* clinch (a victory, deal, etc.). PHRASES **on ice 1** (of an entertainment etc.) performed by skaters. **2** *informal* held in reserve; awaiting further attention. **on thin ice** in a risky situation.

ice age *noun* a period when ice sheets were particularly extensive, esp. in the Pleistocene epoch (from about 2,000,000 to 10,000 years ago).

iceberg *noun* a large floating mass of ice detached from a glacier or ice sheet and carried out to sea. PHRASES **the tip of the iceberg** a small perceptible part of something (esp. a difficulty) the greater part of which is hidden.

iceberg lettuce *noun* any of various crisp lettuces with pale, compact leaves.

ice-blue *noun* & *adjective* a clear, piercing blue, like that seen in a block of ice.

iceboat *noun* **1** a lightly built boat with runners and a sail for travelling at speed over ice, esp. as a sport. **2** a fishing vessel with facilities for the refrigeration of fish. ▶ **iceboater** *noun* **iceboating** *noun*

icebound *adjective* **1** (of a ship) confined by ice. **2** (of a harbour, coast, etc.) obstructed or sealed off by ice.

icebox *noun* (*plural* **iceboxes**) **1** an insulated chest, cabinet, etc. for storing food, cooled by means of a block of ice. **2** esp. *US* a refrigerator.

icebreaker *noun* **1** a ship specially built or adapted for breaking a channel through ice. **2** something that serves to relieve inhibitions, start a conversation, etc. ▶ **icebreaking** *noun* & *adjective*

ice bridge *noun* *Cdn* a formation of ice across a river solid enough to support traffic.

ice cap *noun* a permanent covering of ice e.g. in polar regions. ▶ **ice-capped** *adjective*

ice-cold *adjective* as cold as ice.

ice cream *noun* a frozen dessert made of cream or milk, sugar, flavourings or fruit, etc.

ice cube *noun* a small block of ice made in a refrigerator.

ice dancer *noun* a figure skater who engages in a form of esp. competitive figure skating based on ballroom dancing and performed by couples.

ice dancing *noun* (also **ice dance**) a form of esp. competitive figure skating based on ballroom dancing and performed by couples.

iced tea *noun* a cold drink of sweetened tea, often flavoured with lemon etc.

icefall *noun* a steep part of a glacier like a frozen waterfall.

icefield *noun* **1** an expanse of ice, esp. in polar regions. **2** a large flat area of floating ice.

ice-fish *verb* (**ice-fishes**, **ice-fished**, **ice-fishing**) fish through holes cut in the ice on a lake etc.

ice fisherman *noun* (*plural* **ice fishermen**) a person who fishes through holes cut in the ice on the surface of a lake etc., esp. as a form of recreation.

ice fishing *noun* the act or an instance of fishing through holes cut in the ice on the surface of a lake etc.

ice floe *noun* = FLOE.

ice fog *noun* fog made up of minute ice crystals suspended in the air.

ice-free *adjective* (of a harbour, river, etc.) free from ice.

ice hockey *noun* = HOCKEY 1.

ice hole *noun* Cdn a hole cut through the ice on the surface of a lake etc., used for ice fishing.

ice house *noun* a building often partly or wholly underground for storing ice.

ice hut *noun* Cdn = FISH HUT.

ice jam *noun* an obstruction in a river etc. caused by broken ice.

Icelander *noun* **1** a native or national of Iceland. **2** a person of Icelandic descent.

Icelandic • *adjective* of or relating to Iceland. • *noun* the Scandinavian language of Iceland. [Say ice LAND ick]

icemaker *noun* **1** an appliance for making ice cubes etc. **2** the person who maintains the ice at a rink.

ice margin *noun* **1** the edge of a glacier. **2** the edge of an ice floe.

ice milk *noun* a sweet frozen food similar to ice cream but containing less butterfat.

ice-out *noun* the time of year at which a body of water becomes free of ice.

ice pack *noun* **1** = PACK ICE. **2** a waterproof package containing ice or another frozen substance, used to cool an injured or inflamed part of the body or to keep food cold.

ice pad *noun* Cdn = RINK 1.

ice palace *noun* **1** Cdn informal a hockey arena. **2** a large building made or carved from ice.

ice pan *noun* a slab of floating ice.

ice pick *noun* a pointed implement for breaking up pieces of ice.

ice plant *noun* **1** a South African plant that has leaves covered with glistening fluid-filled hairs that resemble ice crystals. **2** Cdn a machine or factory for making ice, e.g. at a skating rink.

ice rink *noun* = RINK noun 1.

ice road *noun* Cdn a winter road built across frozen lakes, rivers, muskeg, etc.

icescape *noun* a landscape covered with ice.

ice sculpture *noun* **1** the art of carving forms in blocks of ice. **2** a sculpture carved in ice.

ice sheet *noun* a permanent layer of ice covering an extensive tract of land.

ice shelf *noun* (plural **ice shelves**) a floating sheet of ice permanently attached to a land mass.

ice skate • *noun* = SKATE¹ noun 1. • *verb* (**ice-skate, ice-skates, ice-skated, ice-skating**) skate on ice. ▶**ice-skater** *noun* **ice-skating** *noun*

ice storm *noun* a storm of freezing rain, that leaves a deposit of ice.

ice tea *noun* = ICED TEA.

ice time *noun* esp. Hockey **1** time spent by a hockey etc. player engaged in play: *got a lot of ice time in the playoffs.* **2** the time during which a team, league, etc. may use an ice rink: *could only get ice time at midnight.*

ice water *noun* water from, or cooled by, ice.

Icewine *noun* **1** esp. Cdn proprietary a very sweet wine made from ripe grapes left to freeze on the vine before being picked, and still frozen when they go into the press. **2** (**icewine**) a similar wine made in California from artificially frozen grapes.

ichthyologist *noun* a scientist who studies fish. [Say ick thee OLLA jist (with TH as in THIN)]

ichthyology *noun* the study of fish. [Say ick thee OLLA jee (with TH as in THIN)]

ichthyosaur *noun* (also **ichthyosaurus**) an extinct marine reptile with a long head, tapering body, four flippers, and usu. a large tail. [Say ICK thee a sore (with TH as in THIN)]

icicle *noun* **1** a hanging tapering piece of ice, formed by the freezing of dripping water. **2** a thin strip of foil or silver Mylar used as a Christmas tree decoration.

icily *adverb* in a very cold way.

icing *noun* **1** a sweet mixture of sugar with butter or egg whites and flavouring etc., used as a coating or filling for cakes etc. **2** the formation of ice on a ship or aircraft. **3** Hockey **a** the act of icing the puck (see ICE verb 4). **b** the penalty for this. PHRASES **icing on the cake** an attractive though inessential addition or enhancement.

icing sugar *noun* finely powdered sugar, usu. combined with a little cornstarch, for making icing for cakes etc.

ICJ *abbreviation* INTERNATIONAL COURT OF JUSTICE.

ick *interjection* informal an expression of distaste or revulsion.

icky *adjective* (**ickier, ickiest**) informal **1** sweet, sticky, sickly. **2** (as a general term of disapproval) nasty, repulsive.

icon *noun* **1** a devotional painting or carving, usu. on wood, of Christ or another holy figure, esp. in the Eastern Church. **2** an image or statue. **3** a symbol or small graphic representation, e.g. on a computer screen of a program, option, or window, esp. one of several for selection. **4** an object of particular admiration, esp. as a representative symbol of something: *a cultural icon of the 1960s.*

iconic *adjective* **1** constituting a cultural icon: *the iconic cowboy of the US western myth.* **2** of or pertaining to a computer icon.

iconoclasm *noun* **1** the breaking of images. **2** the assailing of cherished beliefs or conventions: *the iconoclasm of the 1960s.* [Say eye CONNA klaz um]

iconoclast *noun* **1** a person who attacks cherished beliefs or conventions: *the stigma that any taint of creationism can bring to a scientific reputation has kept all but the boldest iconoclasts from doubting Darwinian theory in public.* **2** a person who destroys images used in religious worship, esp. hist. during the 8th–9th centuries in the Churches of the East, or as a Puritan of the 16th–17th centuries. ▶**iconoclastic** *adjective* [Say eye CONNA klast, eye conna KLAST ick]

iconographic *adjective* using or having to do with images or symbols that will be understood or interpreted with particular significance by the viewer or audience: *their paintings captured the iconographic essence of Canada—a bleak landscape of jack pines, rock outcroppings, and storm-driven lakes.* [Say eye conna GRAPHIC]

iconography *noun* (plural **iconographies**) **1** the visual images and symbols typical of an art form, an artistic movement, an artist, a culture, etc.: *the elements of her style are drawn from the movies, the media, and pop iconography.* **2** the illustration of a subject by drawings or figures. [Say ike un OGRA fee]

ICU *abbreviation* intensive care unit.

icy *adjective* (**icier, iciest**) **1** very cold. **2** covered with or abounding in ice. **3** (of a tone or manner) unfriendly, hostile: *an icy stare.* **4** like ice: *icy blue eyes.*

ID *abbreviation* identification, identity: *ID card.*

I.D. *abbreviation* Cdn (Alberta) IMPROVEMENT DISTRICT.

Id *noun* = EID.

I'd *contraction* **1** I had. **2** I would.

id. *abbreviation* idem (in the same place).

Ida Red *noun* (also **Idared**) a large, tart, red apple with greenish-yellow patches.

idea *noun* **1** a conception or plan formed by mental effort. **2 a** a mental impression or notion; a concept.

b a vague belief or fancy: *had an idea you were married.* **3** an intention, purpose, or essential feature: *the idea is to make money*. PHRASES **get** (or **have**) **ideas** *informal* be ambitious, rebellious, etc. **give a person ideas** give a person expectations or hopes that may not be realized. **have no idea** *informal* not know at all. **not one's idea of** *informal* not what one regards as: *not my idea of a pleasant evening*. **put ideas into a person's head** suggest ambitions etc. he or she would not otherwise have had. **that's an idea** *informal* that proposal etc. is worth considering. **that's the idea!** that's the correct way to proceed etc. **the (very) ideal** *informal* an exclamation of disapproval or disagreement. **what's the big idea?** expressing disapproval of effrontery, stupidity, etc.

ideal • *adjective* **1** most suitable: *this beach is ideal for children* ◊ *she's the ideal candidate for the job* ◊ *the trip to Paris will be an ideal opportunity to practise my French* ◊ *it was not the ideal solution to the problem.* **2** impossibly perfect; existing only in the imagination or as an idea: *the search for ideal love* ◊ *in an ideal world there would be no poverty and disease.* **3** embodying an idea. **4** relating to or consisting of ideas; dependent on the mind. • *noun* **1** a perfect type, or a conception of this. **2** an actual thing as a standard for imitation. **3** (usu. in *plural*) an esp. moral standard of perfection.

idealism *noun* **1** the practice of forming or following after ideals, esp. unrealistically (*compare* REALISM). **2** the representation of things in ideal or idealized form. **3** any of various systems of thought in which the objects of knowledge are held to be in some way dependent on the activity of mind (*compare* REALISM). ▶ **idealist** *noun* **idealistic** *adjective* **idealistically** *adverb*

idealization *noun* the act or process of considering or representing a person or thing as perfect or ideal.

idealize *verb* (**idealizes**, **idealized**, **idealizing**) consider or represent as perfect or ideal.

ideally *adverb* **1** perfectly; in accordance with an ideal. **2** in theory or principle. **3** in thought or the imagination.

identical *adjective* **1** (often foll. by *with*) (of different things) exactly the same in every detail. **2** (of one thing viewed at different times) one and the same. **3** (of twins) developed from a single fertilized ovum, therefore of the same sex and usu. very similar in appearance. ▶ **identically** *adverb*

identifiable *adjective* that can be recognized: *identifiable groups* ◊ *the house is easily identifiable by the large apple tree outside.* ▶ **identifiably** *adverb*

identification *noun* **1** the action or process of identifying someone or something or the fact of being identified. **2** something that identifies a person: *they asked to see my identification* ◊ *identification card*.

identifier *noun* **1** a person or thing that identifies. **2** *Computing* a sequence of characters used to identify or refer to a set of data.

identify *verb* (**identifies**, **identified**, **identifying**) **1** establish the identity of; recognize. **2** establish or select by consideration or analysis of the circumstances: *identify the best method.* **3** associate (a person or oneself) inseparably or very closely (with a party, policy, etc.): *the Liberals became identified with the Quiet Revolution.* **4** (often foll. by *with*) treat (a thing) as identical: *Venus, the Roman goddess of love, was identified with the Greek goddess, Aphrodite.* **5** (foll. by *with*) regard oneself as sharing characteristics of (another person). PHRASES **identify oneself** state or show who one is.

identity *noun* (*plural* **identities**) **1 a** the quality or condition of being a specified person or thing. **b** individuality, personality: *lost her identity.*

2 identification or the result of it: *mistaken identity* ◊ *identity card*. **3** the state of being the same in substance, nature, qualities, etc.; absolute sameness: *no identity of interests between them.* **4** *Algebra* **a** the equality of two expressions for all values of the quantities expressed by letters. **b** an equation expressing this, e.g. $(x + 1)^2 = x^2 + 2x + 1$. **5** *Math* **a** (also **identity element**) an element in a set, left unchanged by any operation to it. **b** a transformation that leaves an object unchanged.

identity crisis *noun* (*plural* **identity crises**) a period of emotional disturbance in which a person has difficulty in determining his or her identity and role in relation to society.

ideological *adjective* of caused by belief in a system of ideas or way of thinking: *ideological differences.* ▶ **ideologically** *adverb* [Say eye dee a LOGICAL]

ideologist *noun* a person whose actions are influenced by belief in a system of ideas or way of thinking. [Say eye dee OLLA jist]

ideologue *noun* a person whose actions are influenced by a strong belief in a set of strict principles: *the former chief Communist ideologue was accused of inviting the Soviets to invade Czechoslovakia in 1968.* [Say EYE dee a log or IDEA log]

ideology *noun* (*plural* **ideologies**) a system of ideas or way of thinking, usu. relating to politics or society, or to the conduct of a class or group, and regarded as justifying actions, esp. one that is held implicitly or adopted as a whole and maintained regardless of the course of events. [Say eye dee OLLA jee]

ides *plural noun* the eighth day after the nones in the ancient Roman calendar (the 15th day of March, May, July, October, the 13th of other months). [Rhymes with HIDES]

idiocy *noun* (*plural* **idiocies**) utter foolishness; idiotic behaviour or an idiotic action. [Say IDDY a see]

idiom *noun* **1** a group of words established by usage and having a meaning not deducible from those of the individual words, e.g. *down in the dumps*. **2** a form of expression peculiar to a language, person, or group of people. **3 a** the language of a people or country. **b** the specific character of this. **4** a characteristic mode of expression in music, art, etc. [Say IDDY um]

idiomatic *adjective* **1** relating to or conforming to idiom. **2** characteristic of a particular language. [Say iddy a MAT ick]

idiosyncrasy *noun* (*plural* **idiosyncrasies**) **1** a person's particular way of thinking, behaving, etc. that is clearly different from that of others: *wearing a raincoat, even on a hot day, is one of her idiosyncrasies.* **2** anything highly individualized or eccentric. ▶ **idiosyncratic** *adjective* **idiosyncratically** *adverb* [Say iddy oh SINK ruh see, iddy oh sin KRAT ick]

idiot *noun* a stupid person; an utter fool.

idiot box *noun* (*plural* **idiot boxes**) *informal* **1** television. **2** a television set.

idiotic *adjective* very stupid: *an idiotic question.* ▶ **idiotically** *adverb*

idiot-proof *adjective* = FOOLPROOF.

idiot savant *noun* (*plural* **idiot savants**) a person considered mentally retarded but who displays brilliance in a specific area esp. related to memory skills. [Say idiot sa VONT]

idiot string *noun* (also **idiot strings**) *Cdn* a string attached to each of two mittens or gloves and strung through the sleeves and across the inside back of a child's coat, to prevent the mittens etc. from being lost.

idle • *adjective* (**idler, idlest**) **1 a** (of a person) not working, doing nothing. **b** lazy. **2** (of a thing) inactive, not in use. **3** (of time etc.) unoccupied. **4 a** (of a thought, speculation, etc.) having no particular purpose: *idle curiosity*. **b** (of an action, word, etc.) trifling, ineffective, or worthless. • *verb* (**idles, idled, idling**) **1 a** (of an engine) run slowly without doing any work. **b** cause (an engine) to idle. **2 a** be idle, pass the time in idleness. **b** cause to be idle: *the closure idled 750 workers*. **3** (foll. by *away*) pass (time etc.) in idleness. • *noun* idling or idling speed of an engine. ▶ **idleness** *noun*

idler *noun* **1** a person who idles or is idle. **2** a habitually lazy person. [Say IDE lur]

idly *adverb* **1** with no particular reason, purpose, or motivation. **2** in an inactive or lazy way. [Say IDE lee]

idol *noun* **1** an image of a deity etc. used as an object of worship. **2** *Bible* a false god. **3** a person or thing that is the object of excessive or supreme adulation.

idolater *noun* a worshipper of idols. [Say eye DOLL a tur]

idolatrous *adjective* treating someone or something as an idol: *our idolatrous worship of the automobile*.

idolatry *noun* (*plural* **idolatries**) **1** the worship of idols. **2** excessive devotion to or veneration for a person or thing: *their support for the team borders on idolatry*. [Say eye DOLL a tree]

idolize *verb* (**idolizes, idolized, idolizing**) venerate or love extremely or excessively.

idyll *noun* **1** a short poem or other piece of writing that describes a peaceful and happy scene, esp. in rustic life. **2** a happy and peaceful place, event or experience, especially one connected with the countryside: *a two-week idyll of uninterrupted bliss*. [Say ID'll]

idyllic *adjective* peaceful and beautiful; perfect, without problems: *a house set in idyllic surroundings ◊ leading an idyllic existence ◊ the cottage sounds idyllic*. ▶ **idyllically** *adverb* [Say i DILL ick]

i.e. *abbreviation* that is to say.

if • *conjunction* **1** introducing a conditional clause; on the condition or supposition that. **2** even though: *I'll finish it, if it takes me all day*. **3** whether: *see if you can find it*. **4** expressing wish or surprise: *if I could just try! ◊ if it isn't my old hat!* **5** with implied reservation, and perhaps not: *very rarely if at all ◊ took little if any*. **6** despite being: *a useful if cumbersome device*. • *noun* **1** a condition or supposition: *too many ifs about it*. **2** an uncertainty: *if he wins — and it's a big if — he'll be the first Canadian to do so*. PHRASES **if anything** if any degree, perhaps even: *if anything, it's too large*. **if only 1** even if for no other reason than: *I'll come if only to see her*. **2** (often *ellipt.*) an expression of regret: *if only I could swim!* **3** an expression of a wish with reference to present or future time. **ifs, ands, or buts** (usu. in *neg.*) reservations, arguments against.

iffy *adjective* (**iffier, iffiest**) *informal* **1** uncertain, doubtful. **2** of questionable quality.

Ig *abbreviation* immunoglobulin.

Igbo (*plural* **Igbo** or **Igbos**) = IBO. [Say IG bo]

igloo *noun* (also **iglu**) **1** a dome-shaped Inuit dwelling built of snow. **2** any other dome-shaped Inuit dwelling.

Iglulik *noun* (*plural* **Iglulik**) (also **Igloolik**, *plural* **Igloolik**) **1** a member of an Inuit people inhabiting the eastern Arctic, esp. living on Baffin Island and the Melville Peninsula. **2** their language. [Say ig LOO lick]

igneous *adjective* (esp. of rocks) produced by volcanic or magmatic action. [Say IG nee us]

ignite *verb* (**ignites, ignited, igniting**) **1** set fire to; cause to burn. **2** catch fire. **3** *Chemistry* heat to the point of combustion or chemical change. **4** provoke or excite (feelings etc.).

igniter *noun* a person who or device which ignites something, esp. a device to set fire to an explosive or combustible.

ignition *noun* **1 a** the action of igniting the fuel in the cylinder of an internal combustion engine. **b** the mechanism for starting this process. **2** the action of setting something on fire or starting to burn.

ignoble *adjective* (**ignobler, ignoblest**) dishonourable. ▶ **ignobly** *adverb* [Say ig NOBLE]

ignominious *adjective* shameful, disgraceful, humiliating: *an ignominious defeat ◊ she made one mistake and her career came to an ignominious end*. ▶ **ignominiously** *adverb* [Say igna MINI us]

ignominy *noun* (*plural* **ignominies**) public shame and loss of honour; disgrace: *they suffered the ignominy of defeat*. [Say ig NOMMA nee or IGNA mini]

ignorable *adjective* capable of being ignored or disregarded: *an easily ignorable branch of pop culture*.

ignoramus *noun* (*plural* **ignoramuses**) an extremely ignorant person. [Say igna RAY muss or igna RAM us]

ignorance *noun* (often foll. by *of*) lack of knowledge.

ignorant *adjective* **1 a** lacking knowledge or experience. **b** (foll. by *of, in*) uninformed (about a fact or subject). **2** *informal* ill-mannered, uncouth. ▶ **ignorantly** *adverb*

ignore *verb* (**ignores, ignored, ignoring**) refuse to take notice of or accept; intentionally disregard.

iguana *noun* any of various large lizards having a spiny crest along the back and throat appendages, occasionally kept as a pet. [Say ig WONNA]

IHS *abbreviation* Jesus.

ikebana *noun* the Japanese art of flower arrangement, with formal display according to strict rules. [Say icka BONNA]

ikon *noun* = ICON 1, 2.

IL *abbreviation* **1** Illinois (in official postal use). **2** = INTERLEUKIN.

ileitis *noun* **1** inflammation of the ileum. **2** = CROHN'S DISEASE. [Say illy ITE iss]

ileum *noun* (*plural* **ilea**) the third and last portion of the small intestine. [Say ILLY um]

ilium *noun* (*plural* **ilia**) **1** the bone forming the upper part of each half of the human pelvis. **2** the corresponding bone in animals. [Say ILLY um]

ilk *noun informal* usu. derogatory a family, class, or set.

I'll *contraction* I will; I shall.

ill • *adjective* **1** out of health; sick: *is ill ◊ was taken ill with pneumonia*. **2** (of health) unsound. **3** (of an omen, condition, etc.) unlucky, unfavourable, disastrous: *ill fortune*. **4** harmful, disagreeable, objectionable: *ill effects*. **5** hostile, unkind: *ill feeling*. **6** immoral, wicked: *house of ill repute*. • *adverb* **1** badly, wrongly, unskilfully, or inefficiently: *ill-matched*. **2 a** imperfectly: *ill-provided*. **b** scarcely: *can ill afford to do it*. **3** unfavourably or unhappily: *it would have gone ill with them*. • *noun* **1** injury, harm. **2** evil; the opposite of good. **3** something unfriendly, unfavourable, or injurious.

PHRASES **ill at ease** embarrassed, uneasy. **speak ill of** say something unfavourable about.
ill-advised *adjective* **1** acting foolishly or imprudently. **2** (of a plan etc.) not well formed or considered. ▶ **ill-advisedly** *adverb*
ill-bred *adjective* badly brought up, badly behaved.
ill-conceived *adjective* badly planned or conceived.
ill-considered *adjective* = ILL-ADVISED 2.
ill-defined *adjective* not accurately analyzed or described: *an ill-defined role*.
ill-disposed *adjective* (often foll. by *towards*) not friendly or pleasant; unfavourably disposed.
ill effect *noun* (usu. in *plural*) a harmful or unpleasant consequence, result, effect, etc.
illegal • *adjective* **1** not legal. **2** contrary to law. **3** *Sport* against or prohibited by the rules or regulations. • *noun* an illegal immigrant. ▶ **illegality** *noun* (*plural* **illegalities**) **illegally** *adverb*
illegibility *noun* the state or condition of being difficult or impossible to read. [Say ill ledge a BILLA tee]
illegible *adjective* difficult or impossible to read; not legible. ▶ **illegibly** *adverb* [Say ill LEDGE a bull]
illegitimacy *noun* the state or condition of being illegitimate. [Say illa JITTA muh see]
illegitimate *adjective* **1** (of a child) born of parents not married to each other. **2** not allowed by a particular set of rules or by law: *illegitimate use of company property*. ▶ **illegitimately** *adverb* [Say illa JITTA mutt]
ill-equipped *adjective* not adequately equipped, qualified, or prepared: *was ill-equipped for such a job* ◊ *we are ill-equipped to deal with such a large number of inquiries*.
ill-fated *adjective* unlucky, doomed; bringing or having bad fortune: *an ill-fated voyage*.
ill feeling *noun* bad feeling; animosity.
ill-fitting *adjective* fitting badly: *an ill-fitting suit*.
ill-founded *adjective* (of an idea etc.) groundless.
ill-gotten *adjective* gained by dishonest or unlawful means.
illiberal *adjective* intolerant, narrow-minded: *the most illiberal, anti-enlightenment notions*. [Say ill LIBERAL]

SPELL CHECK
illicit, elicit

To evoke a response or obtain an answer is to **elicit** them.

illicit *adjective* **1** unlawful, forbidden: *illicit dealings*. **2** secret: *an illicit affair*. ▶ **illicitly** *adverb* [Say ill LISS it]
ill-informed *adjective* inadequately or wrongly informed.
illiteracy *noun* the quality or condition of being unable to read or write. [Say ill LITTER a see]
illiterate • *adjective* **1** unable to read or write. **2 a** having or showing little or no education. **b** ignorant in a particular field: *culturally illiterate*. • *noun* an illiterate person. [Say ill LITTER it]
ill-mannered *adjective* having bad manners; rude.
ill-matched *adjective* badly matched; unsuited.
ill-natured *adjective* churlish, unkind.
illness *noun* **1** an ailment. **2** the state of being ill.
illogic *noun* reasoning or thought which is not considered logical.
illogical *adjective* devoid of or contrary to logic. ▶ **illogicality** *noun* (*plural* **illogicalities**) **illogically** *adverb*
ill-prepared *adjective* badly or inadequately prepared.
ill-suited *adjective* **1** not suited to doing something; unsuitable. **2** inappropriate.
ill temper *noun* irritability. ▶ **ill-tempered** *adjective*
ill-timed *adjective* done or occurring at an inappropriate or unsuitable time.

ill-treat *verb* treat badly or cruelly; abuse. ▶ **ill-treatment** *noun*
illuminate *verb* (**illuminates**, **illuminated**, **illuminating**) **1** light up; make bright. **2** help to explain (a subject etc.). **3** decorate (an initial letter etc.) with elaborate designs in gold, silver, or brilliant colours. **4** decorate (buildings etc.) with lights as a sign of festivity. [Say ill LOO min ate]
illuminating *adjective* helping to clarify or explain: *an illuminating discussion*. [Say ill LOO min ate ing]
illumination *noun* **1** lighting or light: *higher levels of illumination are needed for reading*. **2** spiritual or intellectual enlightenment: *for parents genuinely looking for illumination, this book might as well have been written in Serbo-Croatian*. **3 a** the decoration of a medieval manuscript with elaborate tracery or designs in gold, silver, bright colours, etc. **b** a design or illustration used in such decoration. [Say ill loo min AY sh'n]
illumine *verb* (**illumines**, **illumined**, **illumining**) *literary* **1** light up; make bright: *the sky was weakly illumined by a crescent moon*. **2** enlighten spiritually. [Say ill LOO min]
illus. *abbreviation* **1** illustration. **2** illustrated.
ill-use • *verb* (**ill-uses**, **ill-used**, **ill-using**) treat unkindly or badly. • *noun* ill-treatment. ▶ **ill-used** *adjective*

SPELL CHECK
illusion, allusion

When you make an indirect or passing reference to something you are making an **allusion**.

illusion *noun* **1** a false idea or belief, especially about someone or about a situation: *I have no illusions about her feelings for me*. **2** something that seems to exist, but in fact does not: *mirrors in a room often give an illusion of space* ◊ *the idea of absolute personal freedom is an illusion*. **3** a figment of the imagination. **4** = OPTICAL ILLUSION. **5** a thin and transparent kind of fine net fabric. **PHRASES** **be under no illusions** have no esp. positive expectations. **be under the illusion** believe mistakenly.
illusionist *noun* a person who produces illusions, esp. a conjuror. ▶ **illusionistic** *adjective*

SPELL CHECK
illusive, elusive

Don't confuse **illusive** with **elusive**. Something hard to catch, obtain, or achieve is **elusive**: *we hoped to catch the elusive brook trout*; something unreal like an illusion is **illusive**: *the tragedy behind our neighbours' illusive happiness*.

illusive *adjective* deceptive; illusory. [Say ill OO siv]
illusory *adjective* based on illusion; not real: *an illusory sense of freedom*. [Say ill LOOZA ree or ill LOOSE a ree]
illustrate *verb* (**illustrates**, **illustrated**, **illustrating**) **1 a** provide (a book etc.) with pictures. **b** elucidate (a description etc.) by drawings or pictures. **2** serve as an example of. **3** explain or make clear, esp. by examples.
illustration *noun* **1** a drawing or picture illustrating a book, magazine article, etc. **2** an example serving to elucidate. **3** the action or fact of illustrating something, either pictorially or by exemplification: *by way of illustration, I refer to the following case*.
illustrative *adjective* (often foll. by *of*) serving as an explanation or example. [Say ILL us tray tiv]
illustrator *noun* a person who draws or creates pictures for magazines, books, advertising, etc.

illustrious *adjective* distinguished, renowned. ▶**illustriousness** *noun* [Say ill LUSS tree us]

ill will *noun* bad feeling; animosity.

ill wind *noun* an unfavourable circumstance.

I'm *contraction* I am.

image • *noun* **1** a representation of a person or thing in sculpture, painting, photography, etc. **2** the character or reputation of a person, organization, product, etc. as generally perceived by the public, esp. a cultivated favourable reputation. **3** an optical appearance or counterpart produced by light or other radiation from an object reflected in a mirror, refracted through a lens, etc. **4** semblance, likeness: *God created man in His own image*. **5** a person or thing that closely resembles another: *is the image of his father*. **6** a typical example: *the very image of a southern gentleman*. **7** a word or phrase that describes something in an imaginative way: *poetic images of the countryside*. **8** an idea or mental representation. • *verb* (**images, imaged, imaging**) **1 a** make an image of; portray. **b** imagine or form a mental picture of. **2** obtain a representation of by radar, x-rays, etc.

image maker *noun* **1** a person employed to create a public image for a politician, product, etc. **2** a carver, sculptor, etc. of images. ▶**image making** *noun*

image processing *noun* (also **image manipulation**) the analysis and manipulation of a usu. digitized image, esp. to improve its quality. ▶**image processor** *noun*

imagery *noun* (*plural* **imageries**) **1** language that produces pictures in the minds of people reading or listening: *poetic imagery*. **2** pictures, photographs: *satellite imagery*. **3** visual images collectively: *the impact of computer-generated imagery on contemporary art*.

imaginable *adjective* that can be conceived or imagined: *the greatest difficulty imaginable*.

imaginary *adjective* existing only in the imagination.

imagination *noun* **1 a** a mental faculty forming images or concepts of external objects not present to the senses. **b** the action or process of imagining or forming such images. **2** the ability of the mind to be creative or resourceful.

imaginative *adjective* having or showing imagination or new and exciting ideas; inventive: *an imaginative child* ◊ *recipes that make imaginative use of tofu*. ▶**imaginatively** *adverb*

imagine *verb* (**imagines, imagined, imagining**) **1 a** form a mental image or concept of. **b** picture to oneself (something non-existent or not present to the senses). **2** think or conceive: *imagined them to be red*. **3** guess: *cannot imagine what they are doing*. **4** suppose, be of the opinion. **5** as an exclamation of surprise: *just imagine!*

imaging *noun* **1** the creation of images of internal organs etc. through tomography etc., used as a diagnostic tool. **2** the practice of formulating and using mental pictures to control pain etc.

imaginings *plural noun* things imagined; fantasies.

imagism *noun* a movement in early 20th-century poetry which, in revolt against Romanticism, sought clarity of expression through the use of precise images and free verse. ▶**imagist** *noun & adjective* **imagistic** *adjective* [Say IMAGE ism, image ISS tick]

imam *noun* **1** a leader of prayers in a mosque. **2** a title of various Muslim leaders, esp. of one succeeding Muhammad as leader of Shiite Islam. [Say im MAM]

IMAX *noun* *proprietary* a technique of wide-screen cinematography in which 70 mm film is shot and projected in such a way as to produce a celluloid image approximately ten times larger than that normally obtained from standard 35 mm film.

imbalance *noun* **1** lack of balance. **2** a lack of proportion or relation between corresponding things.

imbecile • *noun* **1** *informal* a stupid person. **2** a person of abnormally weak intellect, esp. an adult with the mental development of a five-year-old. • *adjective* mentally weak; stupid, idiotic. ▶**imbecilic** *adjective* **imbecility** *noun* (*plural* **imbecilities**) [Say IMBA sill or IMBA sile, imba SILL ick, imba SILLA tee]

imbed *verb* = EMBED.

imbibe *verb* (**imbibes, imbibed, imbibing**) **1** drink (esp. alcoholic liquor). **2** absorb or assimilate (ideas etc.). **b** absorb (moisture, heat, etc.). ▶**imbiber** *noun*

imbroglio *noun* (*plural* **imbroglios**) a complicated, confused, or embarrassing situation, esp. a political or interpersonal one: *finding a solution to the garbage imbroglio*. [Say im BRO lee oh]

imbue *verb* (**imbues, imbued, imbuing**) inspire or permeate (with feelings, opinions, or qualities): *her voice was imbued with an unusual seriousness*. [Say im BYOO]

IMF *abbreviation* International Monetary Fund, an organization established in 1945 to promote international trade and monetary co-operation and the stabilization of exchange rates.

imitate *verb* (**imitates, imitated, imitating**) **1** follow the example of; copy the action(s) of. **2** mimic. **3** be, become, or make oneself like, intentionally or unintentionally.

imitation • *noun* **1** an act of imitating a person's speech or mannerisms, esp. for comic effect: *does a good imitation of Elvis*. **2** a copy. **3** a counterfeit; something made to look like something else. • *adjective* made in imitation of something genuine: *imitation leather*.

imitative *adjective* imitating; following a model or example: *the style is imitative of Basque architecture*.

imitator *noun* a person or thing that copies someone or something else: *we have countless imitators*.

immaculate *adjective* **1** pure, spotless; perfectly clean and tidy. **2** perfectly or extremely well executed: *an immaculate performance*. **3** free from moral stain or fault. ▶**immaculately** *adverb* [Say im MACK yoo lit]

Immaculate Conception *noun* *Catholicism* **1** the doctrine that God preserved the Virgin Mary from the taint of original sin from the moment she was conceived. **2** Dec. 8, the feast of the Immaculate Conception.

SPELL CHECK
immanent, imminent

Something about to happen is **imminent**.

---

immanent *adjective* present as a natural part of something; present everywhere: *the immanent presence of the divine in the world* (*opp.* TRANSCENDENT 3). [Say IMMA nint]

immaterial *adjective* **1** of no essential consequence; unimportant, irrelevant: *it was immaterial to her where the jacket was stored as long as it was properly looked after*. **2** not material; without physical form or substance: *immaterial thoughts*. [Say im MATERIAL]

immature *adjective* **1 a** (of cells, animals, etc.) not mature or fully developed. **b** (of plants, fruit, etc.) unripe. **2** lacking emotional or intellectual development. ▶**immaturity** *noun*

immeasurable *adjective* not measurable; immense. ▶**immeasurably** *adverb*

immediacy *noun* (*plural* **immediacies**) the quality of bringing one into direct and instant involvement with something, giving rise to a sense of urgency or excitement: *e-mail has the immediacy of a scribbled note*. [Say im MEEDY a see]

immediate *adjective* **1** occurring or done at once or without delay: *an immediate reply*. **2 a** nearest in time

or space: *the immediate future*. **b** (of family) designating those of closest relation, usu. parents, children, spouses, and siblings. **3** most pressing or urgent; of current concern: *our immediate concern*. **4** (of a thing or action in relation to another) having direct effect; not separated by something intervening: *the immediate cause of death*.

immediately *adverb* **1** instantly, without pause or delay: *answered the phone immediately*. **2** without intermediary; in direct connection or relation: *who is immediately responsible?* **3** with no object, distance, time, etc. intervening: *immediately in front of you*.

immemorial *adjective* **1** ancient beyond memory or record: *since time immemorial*. **2** very old or long established: *an immemorial custom*. [Say im MEMORIAL]

immense *adjective* **1** immeasurably large or great. **2** considerable: *made an immense difference*.

immensely *adverb* very much: *enjoyed myself immensely*.

immensity *noun* (*plural* **immensities**) the large size of something: *the immensity of the universe* ◊ *we were overwhelmed by the sheer immensity of the task*.

immerse *verb* (**immerses**, **immersed**, **immersing**) **1** dip, plunge, or submerge in a liquid. **2** absorb or involve deeply in a particular activity or condition: *immersed herself in her studies*.

immersion *noun* **1 a** a method of teaching a foreign language by the exclusive use of that language, usu. at a special school, in a special class, etc.: *immersion program*. **b** a class, course, or system of study based on the immersion method. **2** the action of immersing someone or something in a liquid: *immersion in cold water resulted in rapid loss of heat*. **3** baptism by immersing the whole person in water. **4** mental absorption in an activity etc. [Say im MUR zh'n]

immigrant • *noun* **1** a person who immigrates. **2 a** an animal or plant that has migrated into a given area, esp. one now living there. **b** an animal (esp. a bird) that regularly or occasionally migrates into a given area. • *adjective* of, pertaining to, or concerning immigrants or immigration.

immigrate *verb* (**immigrates**, **immigrated**, **immigrating**) **1** come as a permanent resident to a country other than one's native land. **2** (of an animal or plant) migrate to a different geographical region, esp. when this leads to continuous occupation of the area by the species.

immigration *noun* **1 a** the process of coming to live in another country permanently. **b** the number of people who do this: *a rise in immigration*. **2** the process of authorizing or monitoring immigration: *immigration officer*. **3** (**Immigration**) the government ministry in charge of regulating immigration. **4** a control point at an airport, border, etc. where the documentation of people wanting to enter a country is checked.

immigration building *noun* (also **immigration hall**, **immigration shed**) *Cdn hist.* a building used to shelter immigrants until they found their own homes.

imminence *noun* the quality or fact of being about to happen: *the imminence of death*. [Say IM in ince]

imminent *adjective* (of an event, esp. danger) about to happen. ▶**imminently** *adverb* [Say IM in int]

immobile *adjective* **1** not moving. **2** not able to move or be moved. ▶**immobility** *noun* [Say im MOE bile or im MOE bull, immo BILLA tee]

immobilize *verb* (**immobilizes**, **immobilized**, **immobilizing**) **1** make or keep immobile. **2** make (esp. a vehicle or troops) incapable of being moved. **3** keep (a limb or patient) restricted in movement for healing purposes. ▶**immobilization** *noun* [Say im MOE bull ize]

immoderate *adjective* excessive; lacking moderation:

trying to curb his *immoderate use of alcohol*. ▶**immoderately** *adverb* [Say im MODERATE]

immodest *adjective* **1** lacking modesty. **2** lacking due decency: *immodest dress*. ▶**immodestly** *adverb* **immodesty** *noun* [Say im MODEST]

immolate *verb* (**immolates**, **immolated**, **immolating**) kill or offer as a sacrifice, esp. by burning. ▶**immolation** *noun* [Say IMMA late, imma LAY sh'n]

immoral *adjective* **1** not conforming to accepted standards of morality (compare AMORAL). **2** morally wrong, esp. in sexual matters. **3** depraved, dissolute. ▶**immorality** *noun* **immorally** *adverb*

immortal • *adjective* **1 a** living forever; not mortal. **b** divine. **2** worthy or worthy to be famous for all time: *Churchill's immortal words, "This was their finest hour"*. • *noun* **1 a** an immortal being. **b** (in *plural*) an esp. ancient Greek god or other being who is believed to live for ever. **2** a person (esp. an author) of enduring fame. ▶**immortality** *noun* **immortalize** *verb* (**immortalizes**, **immortalized**, **immortalizing**)

immovable *adjective* **1** unable to be moved. **2** steadfast, unyielding. ▶**immovably** *adverb*

immune *adjective* **1 a** resistant to a particular infection, toxin, etc., owing to the presence of specific antibodies or sensitized white blood cells: *adults are often immune to German measles*. **b** of, pertaining to, or producing immunity: *immune mechanism*. **2** free or exempt from or not subject to (some undesirable factor or circumstance): *immune from prosecution*.

immune system *noun* those structures and functions of an organism responsible for maintaining immunity.

immunity *noun* (*plural* **immunities**) **1** the ability of an organism to resist a specific infection, toxin, etc. **2** freedom or exemption from an obligation, penalty, or unfavourable circumstance: *the rebels were given immunity from prosecution*. **3** ability to be unaffected by something: *exercises designed to build an immunity to fatigue*.

immunization *noun* the act or process of making a person or animal immune, esp. to infection, usu. by inoculation. [Say im yoo nize AY sh'n]

immunize *verb* (**immunizes**, **immunized**, **immunizing**) make immune, esp. to infection, usu. by inoculation. [Say IM yoo nize]

immunodeficiency *noun* a reduction in a person's normal immune defences. ▶**immunodeficient** *adjective* [Say im yoo no duh FISHIN see, im yoo no duh FISH int]

immunoglobulin *noun* any of a group of structurally related proteins which function as antibodies. Abbreviation: **Ig**. [Say im yoo no GLOB yoo lin]

immunological *adjective* **1** of or relating to the scientific study of resistance to infection in humans and animals. **2** of or relating to immunity or the immune system: *immunological disorders*. [Say im yoo nuh LOGICAL]

immunologist *noun* a scientist who studies resistance to infection in humans and animals. [Say im yoo NOLLA jist]

immunology *noun* the scientific study of resistance to infection in humans and animals. [Say im yoo NOLLA jee]

immunotherapy *noun* (*plural* **immunotherapies**) the prevention or treatment of disease with substances that stimulate the body's production of antibodies. [Say im yoo no THERAPY]

immutability *noun* the quality or condition of being unchangeable, invariable, or unalterable: *cartoons possess an almost ageless immutability*. [Say im mute a BILLA tee]

immutable *adjective* that cannot be changed; that will

never change; unchangeable: *an immutable fact* ◊ *this decision should not be seen as immutable*. ▶ **immutably** *adverb* [Say im MUTE a bull]

imp *noun* **1** a mischievous child. **2** a small mischievous devil or sprite.

WRITING TIP

impact

Impact is often used as a verb to mean "affect or influence", as in *The weather will impact on how long it takes to drive to the cottage* and *How are the cuts to welfare impacting low-income families?* Such uses sound jargony and can often be replaced to advantage with **affect**, as in *How are the cuts to welfare affecting low-income families?*

---

impact • *noun* **1** the action of one body coming forcibly into contact with another. **2** an effect or influence, esp. when strong. • *verb* **1** have an impact on. **2** come forcibly into contact with a usu. larger body or surface: *the helicopter exploded on impacting the ground*.

impacted *adjective* **1 a** (of a tooth) wedged between another tooth and the jaw. **b** (of a fractured bone) with the parts crushed together. **c** (of feces) lodged in the intestine. **2** (of an area) overcrowded, esp. so as to put severe pressures on public services, etc.

impact statement *noun* a formal written account of how a person, place, etc. has been or will be affected by a specific incident, process, etc.

impair *verb* damage or weaken (esp. an ability): *ozone is a noxious form of oxygen which impairs vision and breathing*.

impaired *adjective* **1** *Cdn* (of driving or the driver of a car, boat, snowmobile, etc.) adversely affected by alcohol or narcotics, specifically, for legal purposes, having a blood alcohol level greater than .08 (i.e. having more than 80 mg of alcohol in 100 ml of blood). **2** (usu. in *combination*) disabled, handicapped: *hearing impaired*. **3** that has been impaired: *impaired hearing*.

impairment *noun* the state or fact of being impaired, esp. in a specified faculty: *a degree of mental or physical impairment* ◊ *a speech impairment*.

impala *noun* (*plural* **impala**) a medium-sized reddish-brown grazing antelope of southern and eastern African savannah. [Say im PALA]

impale *verb* (**impales**, **impaled**, **impaling**) transfix or pierce with a sharp instrument: *the collector was ready to impale the netted insect with a pin*.

impart *verb* (often foll. by *to*) **1** communicate (news, information, etc.): *the teachers imparted a great deal of knowledge to their students*. **2** give a particular quality to something: *the spice imparts an Eastern flavour to the dish*.

impartial *adjective* treating all sides in a dispute etc. equally; unprejudiced, fair. ▶ **impartiality** *noun* **impartially** *adverb* [Say im PAR shull, im parshy ALA tee]

impassable *adjective* (of a road, an area, etc.) impossible to travel on or through, especially because it is in bad condition or it has been blocked by something: *the roads are totally impassable to cars in winter* ◊ *the river formed an impassable barrier for migrating animals*.

impasse *noun* a position from which progress is impossible; deadlock: *she is attempting to end the impasse* ◊ *negotiations have reached an impasse*. [Say IM pass]

impassioned *adjective* ardent: *an impassioned plea*.

impassive *adjective* not showing any feeling or emotion: *her impassive expression* ◊ *the two men remained impassive throughout the trial*. ▶ **impassively** *adverb*

impasto *noun* *Art* **1 a** the process of laying on paint thickly. **b** the paint so applied. **2** this technique of painting. [Say im PASTO]

impatience *noun* **1** intolerance of delay; restless longing or eagerness: *in his impatience to be off* ◊ *has a*

great deal of impatience. **2** failure to bear suffering, annoyance, etc. calmly or serenely.

impatiens *noun* (*plural* **impatiens**) any of several colourful flowering plants of the balsam family, popular as houseplants and garden plants. [Sounds like *IMPATIENCE*]

impatient *adjective* **1 a** (often foll. by *at*, *with*) lacking patience or tolerance. **b** (of an action) showing a lack of patience. **2** restlessly eager: *was impatient to begin*. ▶ **impatiently** *adverb*

impeach *verb* (**impeaches**, **impeached**, **impeaching**) **1** esp. *US* charge (the holder of a public office) with misconduct. **2** raise doubts about something; question: *impeached Mary's motives* ◊ *the judge impeached his testimony*. ▶ **impeachment** *noun*

impeccable *adjective* **1** (of behaviour, performance, etc.) faultless, exemplary. **2** (of clothing, accommodations, etc.) flawlessly clean and tidy. ▶ **impeccably** *adverb* [Say im PECK a bull]

impecunious *adjective* having little or no money: *he came from an impecunious family*. [Say im puh CUE nee us]

impedance *noun* **1** *Electricity* the total effective resistance of an electric circuit etc. to alternating current, arising from ohmic resistance and reactance. **2** an analogous mechanical property. [Say im PEE dince]

impede *verb* (**impedes**, **impeded**, **impeding**) delay or stop the progress of something; hinder, hamper: *work on the building was impeded by severe weather*.

impediment *noun* **1** a hindrance or obstruction in doing something: *a serious impediment to scientific progress*. **2** a defect in speech, e.g. a lisp or stammer. [Say im PEDDA m'nt]

impel *verb* (**impels**, **impelled**, **impelling**) **1** drive, force, or urge into action: *financial difficulties impelled her to desperate measures*. **2** drive forward; propel: *did not know what hidden force impelled him to the kitchen*.

impending *adjective* (usu. of an unpleasant event) that is going to happen very soon: *an impending disaster* ◊ *his impending death*.

impenetrability *noun* the quality or condition of being impenetrable: *the impenetrability of government trade regulations*. [Say im penna truh BILLA tee]

impenetrable *adjective* **1** that cannot be entered, passed through or seen through: *an impenetrable jungle* ◊ *impenetrable darkness* ◊ *the Japanese market used to be more or less impenetrable*. **2** impossible to understand: *an impenetrable mystery* ◊ *their jargon is impenetrable to an outsider* ◊ *her expression was impenetrable*. ▶ **impenetrably** *adverb* [Say im PENNA truh bull]

imperative • *adjective* **1** of vital importance; crucial: *immediate action was imperative* ◊ *it is imperative that educational standards are maintained*. **2** commanding: *an imperative tone of voice*. **3** *Grammar* (of a mood) expressing a command (e.g. *wait!*). • *noun* **1** *Grammar* **a** the imperative mood. **b** a word, form, etc. in the imperative mood. **2** a command. **3** an essential or urgent thing: *the university has a moral imperative to address the needs of racial and ethnic minorities*. ▶ **imperatively** *adverb* [Say im PAIR a tiv]

imperceptible *adjective* **1** that cannot be perceived. **2** very slight, gradual, or subtle. ▶ **imperceptibly** *adverb* [Say im pur SEPTA bull]

imperfect • *adjective* **1** not fully formed or done; faulty, incomplete. **2** (of a tense) denoting a (usu. past) action in progress but not completed at the time in question (e.g. *they were singing*). • *noun* **1** the imperfect tense. **2** a word, form, etc. in the imperfect. ▶ **imperfectly** *adverb*

imperfection *noun* **1** incompleteness. **2 a** faultiness. **b** a fault or blemish.

imperial *adjective* **1** of or characteristic of an empire or

comparable sovereign state. **2** of or characteristic of an emperor or empress. **3** (of weights and measures) used or formerly used in the UK and other Commonwealth jurisdictions: *imperial gallon*. [Say im PEERY ul]
imperial gallon *noun* = GALLON 1a.
imperialism *noun* **1** an imperial rule or system. **2** usu. *derogatory* a policy of acquiring dependent territories or extending a country's influence over less developed countries through trade, diplomacy, etc. **3** the domination or attempted domination of another country's economic, political, or cultural institutions, without actually seizing governmental control: *cultural imperialism*. **4** advocacy or support for imperial interests. [Say im PEERY a lism]
imperialist • *noun* usu. *derogatory* a person who supports or practises imperial rule or imperialism. • *adjective* of or relating to imperialism or imperialists. ▶ *adjective* [Say im PEERY a list, im peery a LISS tick]
Imperial Order Daughters of the Empire *noun* a Canadian women's organization founded in 1900, focusing on community affairs.
imperil *verb* (**imperils, imperilled, imperilling**) bring or put into danger.
imperious *adjective* overbearing, domineering, expecting obedience: *I am beginning to grow tired of his imperious demands*. ▶ **imperiously** *adverb* **imperiousness** *noun* [Say im PEERY us]
impermanence *noun* lack of permanence.
impermanent *adjective* not permanent. ▶ **impermanently** *adverb*
impermeable *adjective* **1** that cannot be penetrated: *impermeable rock*. **2** that does not permit the passage of fluids: *an impermeable membrane*. [Say im PERMY a bull]
impersonal *adjective* **1** not influenced by, showing or involving human emotions: *a vast impersonal organization*. **2** having no personal reference; objective: *an impersonal assessment*. **3** having no personality; not existing as a person: *an impersonal deity*. **4** (of a verb) used only with a formal subject (usu. *it*) and expressing an action not attributable to a definite subject (e.g. *it is snowing*). ▶ **impersonality** *noun* **impersonally** *adverb*
impersonate *verb* (**impersonates, impersonated, impersonating**) **1** pretend to be (another person) in order to deceive others: *impersonated a police officer*. **2** mimic the speech, behaviour, etc. of (another person) in order to entertain others. ▶ **impersonation** *noun* **impersonator** *noun*
impertinent *adjective* rude or insolent; lacking proper respect: *an impertinent question* ◊ *would it be impertinent to ask why you're leaving?* ▶ **impertinence** *noun* **impertinently** *adverb*
imperturbable *adjective* not excitable; calm: *you must stay calm, portray an imperturbable tranquility — no matter what*. ▶ **imperturbably** *adverb*
impervious *adjective* **1** not responsive (to an argument, outside influence, etc.): *he worked on, apparently impervious to the heat*. **2** not allowing water, gas, etc. to pass through: *an impervious layer of clay*. **3** able to withstand wear and tear; resistant. ▶ **imperviousness** *noun*
impetigo *noun* a contagious bacterial skin infection forming pustules and yellow crusty sores. [Say impa TIE go]
impetuous *adjective* acting or done rashly or with sudden energy: *an impetuous young woman* ◊ *an impetuous decision*. ▶ **impetuously** *adverb* **impetuousness** *noun* [Say im PETCH oo us]
impetus *noun* (*plural* **impetuses**) **1** a driving force or impulse: *the debate seems to have lost much of its initial*

impetus ◊ *his articles provided the main impetus for change*. **2** the force or energy with which a body moves. [Say IMPA tuss]
impiety *noun* (*plural* **impieties**) **1** a lack of piety or reverence: *he blamed the fall of the city on the impiety of the people*. **2** an act etc. showing this: *one impiety will cost me my eternity in Paradise*. [Say im PIE a tee]
impinge *verb* (**impinges, impinged, impinging**) **1** have an effect or impact, esp. a damaging or negative one: *Nora was determined the tragedy would impinge as little as possible on Constance's life*. **2** advance over an area belonging to someone or something else; encroach: *the proposed fencing would impinge upon a public beach*. **3** strike, come into forcible contact; collide: *the gases impinge on the surface of the liquid*. [Say im PINDGE]
impious *adjective* **1** not pious; lacking reverence for God or a god: *the emperor's impious attacks on the Church*. **2** wicked, profane: *this is the work of impious villains*. ▶ **impiously** *adverb* **impiousness** *noun* [Say IM pee us]
impish *adjective* mischievous. ▶ **impishness** *noun*
implacable *adjective* that cannot be appeased: *he was an implacable enemy of Ted's*. ▶ **implacably** *adverb* [Say im PLACK a bull]
implant • *verb* **1** (often foll. by *in*) instill (a principle, idea, etc.) in a person's mind. **2** *Medical* **a** insert (tissue, a substance, or an artificial object) in a living body. **b** (of a fertilized ovum) become attached to the wall of the uterus. • *noun* a thing implanted in something else, esp. a piece of tissue, a device, or another object implanted in the body: *a silicone breast implant*. ▶ **implantation** *noun*
implausibility *noun* (*plural* **implausibilities**) the quality or condition of being implausible: *this theory clearly must be scrapped on the grounds of implausibility*.
implausible *adjective* not seeming reasonable or likely to be true: *a highly implausible claim* ◊ *her explanation is not implausible*. ▶ **implausibly** *adverb*
implement • *noun* **1** a tool, instrument, or utensil. **2** a piece of farm machinery, e.g. a plow, combine, etc. • *verb* put (a decision, plan, etc.) into effect. ▶ **implementation** *noun* **implementer** *noun*
implicate *verb* (**implicates, implicated, implicating**) **1** show (a person or thing) to be concerned or involved (in a charge, crime, etc.): *she avoided saying anything that would implicate him further*. **2** be affected or involved: *several cabinet ministers have been implicated in the scandal* ◊ *a chemical implicated in ozone depletion*. [Say IMPLA kate]
implication *noun* **1** what is involved in or implied by something else. **2** the act of implicating or implying. PHRASES **by implication** by what is implied or suggested rather than by formal expression. [Say impla KAY sh'n]
implicit *adjective* **1** implied though not plainly expressed: *her comments were seen as implicit criticism of the government's policies*. **2** essentially or very closely connected with; always to be found in: *the ability to listen is implicit in the teacher's role*. **3** absolute, unquestioning: *implicit obedience* ◊ *she had the implicit trust of her parents*. ▶ **implicitly** *adverb* **implicitness** *noun* [Say im PLISS it]
implied *adjective* contained or stated by implication; involved in what is expressed; necessarily intended though not expressed: *the implied author of this work*.
implode *verb* (**implodes, imploded, imploding**) **1** burst or cause to burst inwards. **2** collapse or disintegrate internally: *factors which caused the Soviet Union to implode*.
implore *verb* (**implores, implored, imploring**) **1** entreat (a person): *I implore you to forgive me*. **2** beg

earnestly for (help, forgiveness, etc.). ▶**imploringly** *adverb*

implosion *noun* a bursting or collapsing inward.

WRITING TIP
imply, infer

imply should not be confused with **infer**. **imply** means "to suggest indirectly", as in *I didn't tell Sonja I was angry but I implied it and I think she understood*. **Infer** means "to reach an opinion based on available information or evidence", as in *From these statistics our researchers inferred a connection between smoking and heart disease* or *From your enthusiastic response, I infer that you did indeed enjoy the movie*. The use of **infer** to mean **imply**, as in *I didn't tell Sonja I was angry, but I inferred it*, is generally considered wrong.

---

imply *verb* (**implies, implied, implying**) **1** strongly suggest the truth or existence of (a thing not expressly asserted). **2** involve as a necessary consequence: *the forecasted traffic increase implied more roads and more air pollution*. **3** insinuate, hint: *what are you implying?*

impolite *adjective* rude. ▶**impolitely** *adverb* **impoliteness** *noun*

imponderable • *adjective* that cannot be estimated or assessed in any definite way: *an imponderable problem of metaphysics*. • *noun* (often in *plural*) something difficult or impossible to assess: *there are too many imponderables for an overall prediction*.

import • *verb* **1** bring in (esp. foreign goods or services) to a country. **2** bring or introduce from an external source or from one use etc. to another: *theories imported from the business world*. **3** *Computing* bring (files etc.) from one application program into another. • *noun* **1** the process of importing. **2** an imported article or service. **3** what is implied; meaning: *the import of her message is clear*. **4** importance: *pronouncements of world-shaking import*. **5** *Cdn Sport* **a** a player who is enlisted from elsewhere to play for a team representing a city, school, etc. **b** any player who is not from the area his or her team represents. **c** *Football* a professional player who learned to play football outside of Canada (usu. in the US) before the age of seventeen, or who started to learn football after the age of seventeen outside Canada. **6** esp. *Cdn* a person recently arrived in one country from another.

importance *noun* **1** the state of being important. **2** significance. **3** personal consequence; dignity: *a woman of great importance*.

WRITING TIP
more importantly

Some people consider it incorrect to use **more importantly** instead of **more important** in sentences like *Paolo brought the party hats and the balloons and, more importantly, the cake*. However, **more importantly** is overwhelmingly more common than **more important** in this kind of construction and is perfectly acceptable.

---

important *adjective* **1** of great effect or consequence; significant. **2** (of a person) having high rank or status, or great authority. **3** pretentious, pompous. **4** of great concern to; highly prized: *my family is very important to me*. **5** what is a more, or most, significant point or matter: *they are willing and, more important, able*. ▶**importantly** *adverb*

importation *noun* The action of importing or bringing in something, esp. goods from another country.

imported *adjective* (of goods etc.) that have been brought into a country: *a ban on imported sausages*.

importer *noun* a person, company, etc. that buys goods from another county to sell them in their own country: *a Toronto-based importer of British foodstuffs*.

importunate *adjective* persistent, esp. to the point of annoyance or intrusion: *importunate telemarketers asking for donations* ◊ *importunate demands*. ▶**importunately** *adverb* [Say im PORCH a nit]

importune *verb* (**importunes, importuned, importuning**) ask (a person) pressingly and persistently for or to do something; beg or demand insistently. ▶**importunity** *noun* (*plural* **importunities**) [Say im pore TOON or im pore TYOON]

impose *verb* (**imposes, imposed, imposing**) **1** (often foll. by *on, upon*) require (a tax, duty, charge, or obligation) to be paid or undertaken (by a person etc.). **2** enforce compliance with: *imposed his will*. **3** demand the attention or commitment of (a person); take advantage of: *she realized that she had imposed on his kindness* ◊ *I don't wish to impose, but may I stay at your place?*

imposing *adjective* impressive, esp. in appearance. ▶**imposingly** *adverb*

imposition *noun* **1** the action or process of imposing something or of being imposed: *the imposition of martial law*. **2** an unfair or resented demand or burden. **3** *Christianity* **a** the ritual placing of a cleric's hand on a person in blessing, ordination, etc. **b** the placing of ashes upon a person's forehead on Ash Wednesday.

impossibility *noun* (*plural* **impossibilities**) **1** the fact or condition of being impossible. **2** an impossible thing or circumstance.

impossible *adjective* **1** not possible; that cannot occur, exist, or be done: *it is impossible to alter them*. **2** (loosely) extremely difficult, inconvenient, or implausible. **3** *informal* (of a person or thing) outrageous, intolerable. ▶**impossibly** *adverb*

imposter *noun* (also **impostor**) a person who assumes a false character or pretends to be someone else.

impotence *noun* **1** lack of strength or power; helplessness: *a feeling of impotence in the face of an apparently insoluble problem*. **2** (in a male) inability, esp. for a prolonged period, to achieve an erection or orgasm. [Say IMPA tince]

impotent *adjective* **1** unable to take effective action; helpless or powerless: *she was filled with an impotent anger* ◊ *without the chairman's support, the committee is impotent*. **2** (of a male) unable, esp. for a prolonged period, to achieve an erection or orgasm. ▶**impotently** *adverb* [Say IMPA t'nt]

impound *verb* **1** confiscate; take legal possession of. **2** shut up (animals) in a pound. ▶**impoundment** *noun*

impoverish *verb* (**impoverishes, impoverished, impoverishing**) (often as **impoverished** *adjective*) **1** make poor. **2** exhaust the natural fertility of. **3** weaken or reduce the quality of; deprive of some quality; affect adversely: *this decision will degrade the environment and impoverish biodiversity*. ▶**impoverishment** *noun*

impoverished *adjective* **1** very poor; without money: *the impoverished areas of the city*. **2** poor in quality, because something is missing: *a culturally impoverished climate*.

impracticable *adjective* impossible in practice: *he was prepared to agree to anything, no matter how impracticable*. ▶**impracticably** *adverb* [Say im PRACK tick a bull]

impractical *adjective* **1** not sensible or realistic: *it was totally impractical to think that we could finish the job in two months*. **2** (of people) **a** not good at doing things that

involve using the hands or paying attention to financial matters etc. **b** not good at planning or organizing things: *he was a wonderful companion but hopelessly impractical*. **3** impossible to do. ▶ **impracticality** *noun* (*plural* **impracticalities**) **impractically** *adverb*

imprecation *noun* a spoken curse: *she hurled her imprecations at anyone who might be listening*. [Say impra KAY sh'n]

imprecise *adjective* not precise. ▶ **imprecisely** *adverb* **impreciseness** *noun* **imprecision** *noun*

impregnable[1] *adjective* **1** (of a fortress etc.) that cannot be taken by force: *the castle, with its impregnable walls, may be the best preserved in Europe*. **2** resistant to attack or criticism: *an industry that had seemed impregnable was under siege from lawyers seeking millions in damages*. **3** unable to be broken down or overcome: *impregnable shyness*. ▶ **impregnably** *adverb* [Say im PREGNA bull]

impregnable[2] *adjective* that can be impregnated. [Say im PREGNA bull]

impregnate *verb* (**impregnates**, **impregnated**, **impregnating**) **1 a** make (a female) pregnant. **b** *Biology* fertilize (a female reproductive cell or ovum). **2** fill or saturate: *steel wool pads that are impregnated with soap*. **3** fill (with feelings, moral qualities, etc.): *an atmosphere impregnated with tension*. ▶ **impregnation** *noun* [Say im PREG nate, im preg NAY sh'n]

impresario *noun* (*plural* **impresarios**) an organizer or promoter of public entertainments esp. by performing arts companies. [Say impra SAR ee oh or impra SARE ee oh]

impress ● *verb* (**impresses**, **impressed**, **impressing**) **1 a** affect or influence deeply. **b** evoke a favourable opinion or reaction from (a person): *was most impressed with your efforts*. **2** emphasize (an idea etc.): *must impress on you the need to be prompt*. **3** apply (a mark) to something with pressure: *the publisher's crest was impressed on the front cover of the volume*. ● *noun* (*plural* **impresses**) a mark made by a seal, stamp, etc.

impression *noun* **1 a** an effect produced (esp. on the mind, conscience, or feelings). **b** a striking or positive effect: *made an impression on the talent scout*. **2** a notion or belief (esp. a vague or mistaken one): *my impression is they are afraid*. **3** an imitation of a person or sound, esp. done to entertain. **4 a** the impressing of a mark. **b** a mark impressed. **5** a mould (from which a positive cast is usu. made) of the teeth or mouth made by pressing them into a soft substance.

impressionable *adjective* easily influenced; susceptible to impressions. ▶ **impressionably** *adverb*

Impressionism *noun* (also **impressionism**) **1** an artistic style or movement originating in France in the late 19th century, characterized by a concern with depicting the visual impression of the moment, esp. in terms of the shifting effect of light and colour. **2** a style of music or writing that seeks to describe a feeling or experience rather than achieve accurate depiction or systematic structure.

impressionist ● *noun* **1** an entertainer who impersonates famous people etc. **2** (**Impressionist**) a painter, writer, or composer who uses an Impressionistic style. ● *adjective* (**Impressionist**) of or relating to Impressionism or Impressionists.

impressionistic *adjective* **1** (**Impressionistic**) in the style of Impressionism: *an Impressionistic portrait*. **2** based on subjective reactions presented unsystematically: *an impressionistic view of the war*. ▶ **impressionistically** *adverb*

impressive *adjective* impressing the mind or senses, esp. so as to cause approval or admiration. ▶ **impressively** *adverb* **impressiveness** *noun*

imprimatur *noun* **1** *Catholicism* an official licence to print (an ecclesiastical book etc.). **2** official approval: *the original recording enjoyed the imprimatur of the composer*. [Say impra MAT er or impra MATE er]

imprint ● *verb* **1** (often foll. by *on*) impress or establish firmly, esp. on the mind. **2** (often foll. by *on*) make a stamp or impression of a figure etc. on a thing. **3** cause (a young animal etc.) to recognize another as a parent or object of habitual trust: *there are many species of mammals who imprint on their offspring, and fishes who imprint on the eggs*. ● *noun* **1** a mark produced by pressure on a surface; an impression or stamp. **2** a lasting impression or sign of some emotion, experience, action, etc.; an influence, an effect. **3 a** the printer's or publisher's name and other details printed in a book, usu. on the title page or at the foot of a single sheet. **b** a line of specific titles issued by a publishing company.

imprison *verb* **1** put into prison. **2** confine; shut up: *many young mothers feel imprisoned in their homes*. ▶ **imprisonment** *noun*

improbability *noun* (*plural* **improbabilities**) **1** the quality of being difficult to believe. **2** a thing or circumstance that is difficult to believe.

improbable *adjective* **1** not likely to be true or to happen. **2** difficult to believe. ▶ **improbably** *adverb*

impromptu ● *adjective* & *adverb* without preparation; on the spur of the moment. ● *noun* **1** an improvised performance or speech. **2** a short piece of usu. solo instrumental music, often song-like. [Say im PROMP too]

improper *adjective* **1 a** unseemly; indecent. **b** not in accordance with accepted rules of behaviour. **2** wrong or incorrect: *improper use of a tool*. **3** dishonest, irregular: *improper business practices*. ▶ **improperly** *adverb*

impropriety *noun* (*plural* **improprieties**) **1** lack of propriety; indecency. **2** an action or language that is improper, dishonest, or morally wrong. [Say impra PRY a tee]

improv *noun* *informal* improvisation, esp. as a theatrical technique.

improve *verb* (**improves**, **improved**, **improving**) **1 a** make or become better. **b** (foll. by *on*, *upon*) produce something better than. **2** make (land) more productive or valuable by cultivation, clearing, etc. ▶ **improved** *adjective*

improvement *noun* **1** the act or process of making something better or becoming better. **2** something that improves, esp. an addition or alteration that adds to value: *home improvements*. **3** something that has been improved.

Improvement District *noun* *Cdn* (*Alberta*, *Ont.*, & *BC*) a sparsely populated region which does not have a municipal government and is therefore administered by provincial officials. Abbreviation: **I.D.**

improver *noun* a person or thing that improves something, esp. a person who makes improvements to increase the quality or value of something.

improvident *adjective* not having or showing foresight; spendthrift or thoughtless: *an improvident drunken parent who took little account of the children's welfare*. [Say im PROV a d'nt]

improvisation *noun* something done or produced on the spur of the moment, esp. a piece of improvised music or verse. ▶ **improvisational** *adjective*

improvisatory *adjective* of, relating to, or like improvisation or an improvisation: *the infinite possibilities of improvisatory dance*. [Say im PROV a zuh tory]

improvise *verb* (**improvises**, **improvised**, **improvising**) **1 a** compose or perform (music, dialogue, etc.) on the spur of the moment, not working

from a text or score. **b** say or do (something) without preparation: *I didn't know the answer, so I had to improvise.* **2** provide or construct (a thing) from whatever is available, without preparation: *improvised a costume out of an old blue dress.* ▶ **improviser** *noun*

imprudence *noun* the quality or state of being rash or indiscreet. [Say im PRUDENCE]

imprudent *adjective* not showing care for the consequences of an action: *it would be imprudent to leave her winter coat behind.* ▶ **imprudently** *adverb* [Say im PRUDENT]

impudence *noun* the quality of not showing due respect for another person. [Say IMP yoo dince]

impudent *adjective* not showing due respect for another person: *he could have strangled this impudent upstart.* ▶ **impudently** *adverb* [Say IMP yoo d'nt]

impugn *verb* challenge or call in question (a statement, action, someone's character, etc.): *there were no real grounds for impugning the decision ◊ I'm sure he did not mean to impugn your integrity.* [Say im PYOON]

impulse *noun* **1** impetus: *gave an impulse to industrial expansion.* **2** incitement or stimulus to action arising from a state of mind or feeling: *a selfish impulse.* **3** a sudden desire or tendency to act without reflection: *did it on impulse.* **4** *Physics* **a** an indefinitely large force acting for a very short time but producing a finite change of momentum (e.g. the blow of a hammer). **b** the change of momentum produced by this or any force. **5** a stimulating force in a nerve or an electric circuit that causes a reaction.

impulsive *adjective* **1** (of a person or conduct etc.) apt to be affected or determined by sudden impulse. **2** *Physics* acting as an impulse: *impulsive low frequency signals.* ▶ **impulsively** *adverb* **impulsiveness** *noun*

impunity *noun* exemption from punishment or from the injurious consequences of an action: *the impunity enjoyed by military officers implicated in civilian killings.* PHRASES **with impunity** without having to suffer the normal injurious consequences (of an action): *protesters burned flags on the streets with impunity.* [Say im PYOON a tee]

impure *adjective* **1** mixed with foreign matter: *impure metals.* **2 a** dirty or contaminated. **b** ceremonially unclean. **3** not chaste; not morally pure: *impure thoughts.* **4** (of a colour) mixed with another colour. ▶ **impurely** *adverb*

impurity *noun* (*plural* **impurities**) **1** the quality or condition of being impure. **2 a** an impure thing or constituent. **b** *Electronics* a trace element deliberately added to a semiconductor.

imputation *noun* the action of imputing or attributing something, esp. a fault or crime, to a person: *asked for a chance to clear his name of any imputation of disloyalty that might have been attached to it.* [Say imp yoo TAY sh'n]

impute *verb* (**imputes**, **imputed**, **imputing**) (foll. by *to*) regard (esp. something undesirable) as being done or caused or possessed by: *the crimes imputed to Richard.* [Say im PYOOT]

In *symbol* indium.

in • *preposition* **1** expressing inclusion or position within limits of space, time, circumstance, etc. **2** during the time of. **3** within the time of. **4 a** with respect to. **b** as a kind of. **5** as a proportionate part of. **6** with the form or arrangement of. **7** as a member of. **8** concerned with. **9** as or regarding the content of. **10** within the ability of. **11** having the condition of; affected by. **12** having as a purpose. **13** by means of or using as material. **14 a** using as the language of expression. **b** (of music) having as its key. **15** wearing as dress. • *adverb* expressing position within limits, or

motion to such a position: **1** into a room, house, etc. **2** at home, in one's office, etc. **3** so as to be enclosed or confined. **4** in a publication. **5** in or to the inward side. **6 a** in fashion, season, or office. **b** elected. **7** exerting favourable action or influence. **8** *Sport* **a** (of a shot, serve, etc.) within the boundary of the playing area. **b** (of a player on side) having the turn to play a (of a hockey puck, soccer ball, etc.) between and behind the goalposts. **d** (of a baseball infielder or outfielder) playing closer to home plate than usual. **9** (in *combination*) *informal* denoting prolonged or concerted action, esp. by large numbers. • *adjective* **1** internal; living in; inside: *in-patient.* **2** fashionable: *the in thing to do.* **3** confined to or shared by a group of people: *in-joke.* • *noun* (foll. by *with*) *informal* an introduction to, or influence with, a person of power or authority. PHRASES **in at** present at; contributing to: *in at the kill.* **in for 1** about to undergo (esp. something unpleasant). **2** competing in or for. **3** involved in; committed to. **in on** sharing in; privy to (a secret etc.). **ins and outs** (often foll. by *of*) all the details (of a procedure etc.). **in that** because; in so far as. **in with** on good terms with.

in. *abbreviation* inch(es).

in- *prefix* **1** adjectives, meaning "not": *inedible ◊ insane.* **2** nouns, meaning "without, lacking": *inaction.*

inability *noun* (*plural* **inabilities**) the state of being unable to do something: *his inability to accept new ideas.*

in absentia *adverb* in (his, her, or their) absence: *two foreign suspects will be tried in absentia.* [Say in ab SEN shuh]

inaccessibility *noun* **1** the quality or condition of being inaccessible or unreachable. **2** the quality or condition of being unapproachable or not open to advances or influence: *her loneliness was intensified by her husband's inaccessibility.*

inaccessible *adjective* **1** not accessible; that cannot be reached: *spent the whole summer in a nearly inaccessible cottage on a northern lake.* **2** (of a person) not open to advances or influence; unapproachable: *he remained elusive and inaccessible.* **3** (of language or a work of art) difficult to understand or appreciate: *in its current form, the text is totally inaccessible.* ▶ **inaccessibly** *adverb*

inaccuracy *noun* (*plural* **inaccuracies**) **1** the quality of not being accurate: *a weapon of notorious inaccuracy.* **2** a feature or aspect of something that is not accurate: *reference works full of inaccuracies.*

inaccurate *adjective* not accurate; inexact, imprecise, incorrect. ▶ **inaccurately** *adverb*

inaction *noun* lack of action where some is expected or appropriate.

inactivate *verb* (**inactivates**, **inactivated**, **inactivating**) make inactive or inoperative. ▶ **inactivation** *noun*

inactive *adjective* **1** not active or inclined to act. **2** passive. **3** sedentary: *an inactive lifestyle.* **4** not participating fully in a club, team, etc.: *an inactive member.* ▶ **inactivity** *noun*

inadequacy *noun* (*plural* **inadequacies**) **1** the quality of not being enough or good enough: *the inadequacy of our resources.* **2** a state of not being able or confident to deal with a situation: *a feeling of inadequacy.* **3** (usu. in *plural*) a weakness; a lack of something: *gross inadequacies in the data ◊ he had to face up to his own inadequacies as a father.* [Say in ADDA kwuh see]

inadequate *adjective* **1** not enough; not good enough: *inadequate resources.* **2** (of a person) not able, or not confident enough, to deal with a situation. ▶ **inadequately** *adverb* [Say in ADDA quit]

inadmissible *adjective* that cannot be admitted or allowed: *inadmissible evidence.* [Say in ad MISSA bull]

inadvertent *adjective* not resulting from or achieved through deliberate planning; unintentional: *several*

pictures didn't turn out owing to inadvertent movement of the camera. ▶ **inadvertently** adverb [Say in ad VUR t'nt]

inadvisable adjective not advisable.

inalienable adjective that cannot be transferred to another or taken away. [Say in ALIEN a bull]

inane adjective silly, senseless: inane remarks. ▶ **inanely** adverb [Say in ANE]

inanimate adjective **1** not alive, esp. not in the manner of animals and humans: Suzie paints stones and other inanimate objects. **2** showing no sign of life, spirit, or vitality: an assembly line of inanimate workers. [Say in ANNA mitt]

inanity noun (plural **inanities**) **1** the quality of something that is silly or senseless: puzzled by the inanity of his argument. **2** something silly or senseless: the inanities of tabloid journalism. [Say in ANNA tee]

inapplicable adjective not applicable; unsuitable: these regulations are inapplicable to international students. [Say in a PLICK a bull or in APP lick a bull]

inappropriate adjective not appropriate; unsuitable. ▶ **inappropriately** adverb **inappropriateness** noun

inarticulate adjective **1** unable to speak distinctly or express oneself clearly or fluently. **2** not expressed clearly or with clear words: an inarticulate reply ◊ inarticulate cries of pain. **3** not expressed; unspoken: mention of her mother filled her with inarticulate irritation. [Say in ar TICK yoo lit]

inasmuch adverb (foll. by as) **1** seeing or considering that: Henry was a most unusual musician inasmuch as he was deaf. **2** in so far as: each group replicated the architecture of their homeland inasmuch as this was possible.

inattention noun lack of attention: they complained about his inattention to his patients ◊ the accident was the result of a moment's inattention.

inattentive adjective **1** not paying due attention; heedless. **2** neglecting to show courtesy. ▶ **inattentively** adverb **inattentiveness** noun

inaudible adjective not audible; not able to be heard. ▶ **inaudibly** adverb

inaugural • adjective marking the beginning of an institution, activity, or period of political office: the president's inaugural address ◊ women's long jump is the inaugural event of the competition. • noun an inaugural speech, esp. one made by an incoming US president. [Say in OGG yur ul or in OGG ur ul]

inaugurate verb (**inaugurates**, **inaugurated**, **inaugurating**) **1** admit (a person) formally to office. **2** open or dedicate (a building etc.) to public use by a ceremony. **3** begin, introduce, or initiate (a system, policy, or period): the moon landing inaugurated a new era in space exploration. ▶ **inauguration** noun [Say in OGG yur ate or in OGG ur ate]

inauspicious adjective showing signs that the future will not be good or successful: an inauspicious beginning. [Say in oss PISH us]

inauthentic adjective not authentic; not genuine.

in-basket noun a tray on an office desk etc. for incoming documents, letters, etc.

in-between • adjective informal intermediate. • noun informal a person or thing that fills, occupies, or takes up an intermediate space, position, or attitude.

inboard • adjective situated within or towards the centre of a boat, aircraft, vehicle, etc.; interior. • adverb within the sides of or towards the centre of a boat, aircraft, or vehicle. • noun **1** a boat equipped with a motor mounted within the hull. **2** a motor so mounted.

inborn adjective **1** (of a quality etc.) innate, existing from birth. **2** (of a disorder etc.) congenital and hereditary.

inbound • adjective coming in, headed inward, or homeward bound. • verb Basketball throw (the ball) in bounds from the sidelines.

inbounds adjective Basketball (of a pass) thrown in bounds from the sidelines.

inbred adjective **1** produced by breeding among closely related members of a group: an inbred racehorse. **2** existing in a person or animal from birth: an inbred hockey sense.

inbreed verb (**inbreeds**, **inbred**, **inbreeding**) breed from closely related people or animals, esp. over many generations.

inbreeding noun breeding between closely related animals or persons, often resulting in decreased size, vigour, and fertility, or various disabilities.

Inc. abbreviation **1** Incorporated. **2** (**inc.**) including, included.

Inca noun (plural **Inca** or **Incas**) a member of a South American Aboriginal people who established an empire in the central Andes before the Spanish conquest in the early 16th century. ▶ **Incan** adjective

incalculable adjective **1** very large or very great, esp. too great to calculate: the treasures are of incalculable value ◊ the oil spill has caused incalculable damage to the environment. **2** that cannot be measured, estimated, or calculated: the chances of such a rare event happening twice are so low that they are almost incalculable. [Say in CAL cue luh bull]

incandescence noun the emission of light by a heated object or body. [Say in can DESS ince]

incandescent adjective **1** (of an electric or other light) produced by a glowing white-hot filament. **2** glowing with heat. **3 a** brilliant, exciting: an incandescent poet. **b** extremely angry: I fought him for six weeks in incandescent fury. [Say in can DESS'nt]

incantation noun a series of words spoken or chanted as a magic spell or charm; the act of speaking these: an incantation to raise the dead. ▶ **incantatory** adjective [Say in can TAY sh'n, in CAN tuh tory]

incapable adjective **1 a** incompetent, not capable. **b** lacking the required quality or characteristic (favourable or adverse) for a specified purpose, action, etc.: incapable of hurting anyone. **2** not, esp. legally, capable of rational conduct or of managing one's own affairs. ▶ **incapably** adverb

incapacitate verb (**incapacitates**, **incapacitated**, **incapacitating**) prevent (a person) from functioning in a normal way: he was incapacitated by a stroke. ▶ **incapacitation** noun [Say inca PASSA tate]

incapacity noun (plural **incapacities**) **1** inability; lack of the necessary power or resources. **2** legal disqualification. [Say in CAPACITY]

incarcerate verb (**incarcerates**, **incarcerated**, **incarcerating**) imprison or confine. ▶ **incarceration** noun [Say in KARSA rate]

incarnate • adjective **1** (esp. of a god or spirit) embodied in flesh, esp. in human form: Damian is the devil incarnate. **2** (of a quality or trait) represented in a typical or the most extreme form: my aunt is generosity incarnate. • verb (**incarnates**, **incarnated**, **incarnating**) **1** embody or represent (a deity or spirit) in human form: the belief that God incarnates himself in man. **2** put (an idea etc.) into concrete form: she is driven to make things that will incarnate her personality. **3** (of a person etc.) be the living embodiment or type of (a quality etc.): he incarnates the kind of thinking that will destroy the environment. [Say in CAR nit for the adjective, in CAR nate for the verb]

incarnation noun **1 a** the form, appearance, or mode of presentation assumed by a person or thing at a particular time: the party's present incarnation. **b** the period of time spent in such an incarnation: he often

wrote for the popular magazine during its first incarnation as a business journal. **2 a** the embodiment of a deity etc. in esp. human flesh. **b (the Incarnation)** (in Christian theology) the embodiment of God the Son in human flesh as Jesus Christ. **3** a living embodiment (of a quality etc.): *she's the incarnation of femininity.*

incendiary • *adjective* **1** designed to cause fires: *incendiary bombs rained down night after night.* **2** tending to stir up conflict: *the final vote followed a long and incendiary debate.* **3** *informal* powerful, impressive: *an incendiary guitar solo.* • *noun* (plural **incendiaries**) an incendiary bomb or device. [Say in SENDY airy]

incense *noun* **1** a gum or spice producing a sweet smell when burned. **2** the smoke or perfume of this, used esp. in religious ceremonies. [Say IN sense]

incensed *adjective* enraged, angry: *locals are incensed by the plan to build a new four-lane road through the town* ◊ *incensed environmentalists plan to protest.* [Say in SENSED]

incentive • *noun* **1** (often foll. by *to*) a thing that motivates or encourages a person to do something: *salaried employees have less incentive to sell the company's products than those on commission.* **2** a payment or concession to stimulate greater output or investment: *the government offers tax incentives to developers willing to restore heritage properties.* • *adjective* serving to motivate: *a contract with incentive clauses.* [Say in SEN tiv]

inception *noun* the establishment or starting point of an institution or activity: *she has worked for the organization since its inception.* [Say in SEP sh'n]

incessant *adjective* unceasing, continual, repeated. ▶ **incessantly** *adverb* [Say in SESS'nt]

incest *noun* sexual intercourse between parent and child or grandchild, or siblings or half-siblings.

incestuous *adjective* **1** involving incest. **2** unwholesomely interconnected: *the incestuous literary world.* ▶ **incestuously** *adverb* **incestuousness** *noun* [Say in SESS choo us]

inch • *noun* (plural **inches**) **1** a unit of linear measure equal to one-twelfth of a foot (2.54 cm). **2** (as a unit of rainfall) a quantity that would cover a horizontal surface to a depth of 1 inch. **3** a small amount: *would not budge an inch.* • *verb* (**inches**, **inched**, **inching**) move gradually in a specified way: *inched forward.* PHRASES **by inches 1** only just: *missed me by inches.* **2** gradually: *dying by inches.* **every inch 1** (often foll. by *a, the*) entirely: *looked every inch a lady.* **2** (usu. foll. by *of*) the whole distance or area: *combed every inch of the garden.* **give a person an inch and he** (or **she**) **will take a mile** a person once conceded to will demand much. **inch by inch** gradually; bit by bit. **within an inch of** almost to the point of. **within an inch of one's life** completely, thoroughly: *cleaned the house to within an inch of its life.* **2** almost to death; severely: *beaten to within an inch of his life.*

inchoate *adjective* **1** just begun or starting to develop: *the inchoate nation is slowly maturing.* **2** not fully formed or developed; incoherent: *his thoughts on the issue are confused and inchoate.* [Say in CO it or in CO ate]

inchworm *noun* the caterpillar of the geometer moth, which moves by alternately hunching and stretching its body.

incidence *noun* **1** the occurrence, rate, or frequency of a disease, crime, or something else undesirable: *a high incidence of suicide* ◊ *osteoporosis has an unusually high incidence in the community.* **2** *Physics* the way in which esp. a ray of light strikes a surface. [Say INSA dince]

incident • *noun* **1 a** an event or occurrence. **b** a minor or detached event attracting general attention or noteworthy in some way. **2 a** a hostile clash, esp. of troops of countries at war: *a border incident.* **b** an accident, public disturbance, or other trouble: *the night*

passed without incident. **3** a distinct piece of action in a play or a poem. • *adjective* **1 a** apt or liable to happen: *changes incident to economic development.* **b** naturally connected with or forming an expected part of something: *the treasurer is authorized to pay all expenses incident to incorporation.* **2** (of light etc.) falling upon or striking against a surface: *the device measures radiant energy from the sun incident on the earth's magnetosphere.*

incidental • *adjective* **1** having a minor role in relation to a more important thing, event, etc.: *skipped over the incidental issues and addressed our main concern.* **2** happening by chance in connection with something else: *the discovery was an incidental result of their research.* **3** (of an expense or charge) incurred apart from the main sum disbursed. • *noun* (usu. in *plural*) a minor detail, expense, event, etc.

incidentally *adverb* **1** by the way; as a further thought or unconnected remark. **2** in an incidental way; as a chance occurrence: *the penalty for infringing on a copyright incidentally is fairly lenient.*

incinerate *verb* (**incinerates**, **incinerated**, **incinerating**) destroy completely by burning; reduce to ashes. ▶ **incineration** *noun* [Say in SINNA rate]

incinerator *noun* a furnace or apparatus for burning esp. waste to ashes. [Say in SINNA rate er]

incipient *adjective* at an initial stage; just beginning to happen or develop: *incipient signs of unrest.* [Say in SIPPY int]

incise *verb* (**incises**, **incised**, **incising**) **1** cut into or make a cut in: *the wound was incised and drained.* **2** engrave (letters, an inscription, etc.): *the pot is incised with a floral design.* ▶ **incised** *adjective* [Say in SIZE]

incision *noun* **1** the esp. initial cut through the surface of the body made during surgery. **2** a mark or decoration cut into a surface. [Say in SIZH un]

incisive *adjective* **1** intelligently analytical and clear-thinking: *an incisive critic.* **2** clear, accurate, and sharply focused: *an incisive interview.* **3** (of a comment etc.) cutting, penetrating: *an incisive parody.* ▶ **incisively** *adverb* **incisiveness** *noun* [Say in SIGH siv]

incisor *noun* a sharp cutting tooth, esp., in humans, any of the eight at the front of the mouth. [Say in SIZE er]

incite *verb* (**incites**, **incited**, **inciting**) urge or stir up: *they were accused of inciting the crowd to violence.* ▶ **incitement** *noun* [Say in SITE]

inclement *adjective* (of the weather or climate) severe, esp. cold, rainy, or stormy. [Say in CLEM'nt]

inclination *noun* **1** (often foll. by *to*) a disposition, tendency, or propensity. **2** (often foll. by *for*) a liking or affection. **3 a** a leaning, slope, or slant. **b** the amount of the deviation (of a surface etc.) from the normal horizontal or vertical position. **4** the act or action of bending towards something, esp. a bending of the body or head in a bow. **5** *Math* the difference of direction of two lines or planes, esp. as measured by the angle between them. **6** the dip of the needle in a magnetic compass. [Say in kluh NATION]

incline • *verb* (**inclines**, **inclined**, **inclining**) **1 a** make (a person, feelings, etc.) willing or favourably disposed: *am inclined to think so.* **b** give a specified tendency to (a thing): *the door is inclined to bang.* **2** be disposed; tend: *the government would incline towards a peaceful resolution* ◊ *some countries incline to agriculture rather than manufacturing.* **3** lean in or away from a given direction: *pennants hang from a 37-storey mast inclining over the stadium.* **4** bend (the head, body, or oneself) forward, downward, or toward a thing. • *noun* **1** a slope, esp. on a road or railway. **2** a sloping plane or surface.

inclined *adjective* **1** sloping, slanted. **2** having a natural ability in a specified subject: *musically inclined*.

include *verb* (**includes, included, including**) **1** involve, comprise, or reckon in as part of a whole. **2** treat or regard as part of the whole.

including *preposition* if one takes into account, inclusive of.

inclusion *noun* **1** the action or state of including or being included within a group or structure: *criticism of the new cabinet focused upon its inclusion of two non-elected members*. **2** a person or thing that is included within a larger group or structure.

inclusive *adjective* **1** (often foll. by *of*) including, comprising. **2** with the inclusion of the extreme limits stated: *pages 7 to 26 inclusive*. **3** including all the normal services etc.: *a hotel offering inclusive terms*. **4 a** not excluding any section of society. **b** (of language) deliberately non-sexist, esp. avoiding the use of masculine pronouns to cover men and women. ▶ **inclusively** *adverb* **inclusiveness** *noun*

incognito • *adjective & adverb* with one's name or identity kept secret: *travelling incognito*. • *noun* (*plural* **incognitos**) **1** a person who is incognito. **2** the pretended identity or anonymous character of such a person. [Say in cog NEAT oh]

incoherence *noun* **1** the quality or condition of being unable to speak intelligibly: *having lapsed into complete incoherence, he fell silent*. **2** the quality or condition of being disjointed or of lacking logic or consistency: *his essay combines irrelevant arguments with digressive anecdotes, resulting in incoherence*. [Say in co HEAR ince]

incoherent *adjective* **1** (of a person) unable to speak intelligibly: *he was drunk and incoherent*. **2** (of speech, thought, etc.) disjointed, lacking logic or consistency: *she was upset and her explanation was incoherent*. ▶ **incoherently** *adverb* [Say in co HEAR int]

income *noun* the money or other assets received, esp. periodically or in a year, from one's business, work, investments, etc.

income tax *noun* a tax levied on income.

incoming *adjective* **1 a** coming in: *incoming calls*. **b** starting, beginning: *incoming students*. **2** succeeding another person or persons: *the incoming tenant*.

incommensurable *adjective* **1** (often foll. by *with*) having no common standard of measurement; that is so different from something else that the two cannot be compared: *one can argue that the experience of women is so different from that of men that the two are incommensurable*. **2** *Math* (of numbers) that cannot be expressed as a ratio of two integers. [Say in kuh MEN shurra bull]

incommunicado *adjective & adverb* not wanting, able, or allowed to communicate with others: *is incommunicado till he gets back from China* ◊ *the prisoners were separated and detained incommunicado*. [Say in kuh myoona KODDO or in kuh myoona KADDO]

incomparable *adjective* **1** without an equal in quality or extent; matchless: *a city of incomparable beauty*. **2** (often foll. by *with, to*) unable to be compared; totally different in nature or extent: *censorship still exists, but it is now incomparable with what it was*. ▶ **incomparably** *adverb* [Say in COM purra bull]

incompatibility *noun* (*plural* **incompatibilities**) **1** the property or condition of being incompatible: *negotiators are trying to iron out the last areas of incompatibility*. **2** an incompatible thing or quality: *divorced because of their incompatibilities*.

incompatible *adjective* **1** opposed in character. **2** (often foll. by *with*) not consistent or in logical agreement. **3** (of persons) unable to live, work, etc., together in harmony. **4** (of drugs) not suitable for

taking at the same time. **5** (of equipment etc.) not capable of being used in combination with some other item.

incompetence *noun* the lack of skill or ability to do one's job or a task as it should be done: *managerial incompetence* ◊ *government incompetence*.

incompetent • *adjective* **1** not having or showing the necessary skills to do something successfully: *an incompetent builder* ◊ *an incompetent performance*. **2** *Law* not qualified to act in a particular role or capacity: *the patient is legally incompetent*. • *noun* an incompetent person. ▶ **incompetently** *adverb*

incomplete *adjective* **1** not complete, finished, or fully formed. **2** imperfect, lacking something. **3** *Football* (of a forward pass) not completed. ▶ **incompletely** *adverb* **incompleteness** *noun* **incompletion** *noun*

incomprehensible *adjective* that cannot be understood. [Say in compra HENCE a bull]

incomprehension *noun* failure to understand. [Say in compra HEN shun]

inconceivable *adjective* impossible to imagine or believe: *it is inconceivable that the officer was unaware of the problem* ◊ *they behaved with inconceivable rudeness*. ▶ **inconceivably** *adverb*

inconclusive *adjective* (of an argument, evidence, or action) not leading to a definite conclusion or result. ▶ **inconclusively** *adverb* **inconclusiveness** *noun*

incongruity *noun* (*plural* **incongruities**) **1** something incongruous: *the analysis is full of incongruities*. **2** the quality or state of being incongruous: *she was struck by the incongruity of the situation*. [Say in cun GREW it ee]

incongruous *adjective* not in harmony or in keeping with the surroundings or other aspects of something: *the track shoes looked incongruous with Rhoda's black dress and diamonds* ◊ *a plain modern building with incongruous Victorian details*.

inconnu *noun* (*plural* **inconnu**) a predatory freshwater game fish of the North American Arctic. [Say IN canoe]

inconsequential *adjective* trivial, unimportant, of no consequence: *inconsequential details* ◊ *inconsequential chatter*. [Say in consa KWEN shull]

inconsiderable *adjective* of small size, value, etc.: *we have spent a not inconsiderable amount of money already*.

inconsiderate *adjective* **1** lacking or showing a lack of consideration or regard for the feelings of others. **2** (of a person or action) thoughtless, rash. ▶ **inconsiderately** *adverb* **inconsiderateness** *noun*

inconsistency *noun* (*plural* **inconsistencies**) **1** the fact or state of being inconsistent: *inconsistency between his expressed attitudes and his actual behaviour*. **2** an inconsistent element or an instance of being inconsistent: *the single glaring inconsistency in the argument*.

inconsistent *adjective* **1** acting in a manner that is not in keeping with one's usual principles or former conduct: *parents must not become inconsistent in the way they discipline their children*. **2** (often foll. by *with*) not compatible or in keeping with: *the election results are inconsistent with predictions that were based on polls* ◊ *the witnesses' statements are inconsistent*. **3** (of a single thing) not staying the same throughout; having self-contradictory parts: *interpretation of this law has often been inconsistent* ◊ *the pace of the movie is inconsistent*. **4** erratic in behaviour or action: *the team's defence has been inconsistent this season*. ▶ **inconsistently** *adverb*

inconsolable *adjective* (of a person, grief, etc.) that cannot be consoled or comforted. ▶ **inconsolably** *adverb* [Say in cun SOLE a bull]

inconspicuous *adjective* not conspicuous; not easily noticed. ▶ **inconspicuously** *adverb* [Say in cun SPICK yoo us]

inconstant *adjective* **1** (of a person) fickle,

changeable. **2** frequently changing; variable, irregular. ▶ **inconstantly** *adverb*

incontestable *adjective* unquestionable, not open to argument. ▶ **incontestably** *adverb*

incontinence *noun* the inability to control the bladder and bowels.

incontinent *adjective* **1** unable to control movements of the bowels or bladder or both. **2** lacking self-restraint; uncontrolled: *sexually incontinent* ◊ *emotionally incontinent*.

incontrovertible *adjective* indisputable: *incontrovertible evidence*. ▶ **incontrovertibly** *adverb* [Say in contra VERTA bull]

inconvenience • *noun* **1** trouble or problems, esp. concerning what one needs or would like: *we apologize for the delay and regret any inconvenience it may have caused*. **2** a person or thing that causes problems or difficulties: *I can put up with minor inconveniences*. • *verb* (**inconveniences**, **inconvenienced**, **inconveniencing**) cause trouble or difficulty for someone: *I hope that we haven't inconvenienced you*.

inconvenient *adjective* causing trouble, difficulty, or discomfort; not convenient. ▶ **inconveniently** *adverb*

incorporate *verb* (**incorporates**, **incorporated**, **incorporating**) **1** include something so that it forms a part of something: *the new car design incorporates all the latest safety features* ◊ *we have incorporated all the latest safety features into the design*. **2** combine or form into an organization, esp. constitute as a legal corporation: *all banks have been incorporated under the federal Bank Act*. [Say in CORE pur ate]

incorporated *adjective* forming a legal corporation. [Say in CORE pur ate id]

incorporation *noun* **1** the action or process of joining or combining two or more things, or one thing with another: *the incorporation of black history as part of the school's curriculum*. **2** the process of forming into a company or community: *every year the community celebrates the anniversary of the incorporation of their town*.

incorrect *adjective* **1** not in accordance with fact. **2** not in accordance with accepted standards: *incorrect behaviour*. ▶ **incorrectly** *adverb* **incorrectness** *noun*

incorrigible • *adjective* (of a person or their behaviour) not able to be corrected, improved, or reformed: *an incorrigible flirt*. • *noun* an incorrigible person. ▶ **incorrigibly** *adverb* [Say in CORE idge a bull]

incorruptible *adjective* **1** unable to be corrupted, esp. unable to be bribed. **2** not susceptible to decay; everlasting. [Say in CORRUPT a bull]

increase • *verb* (**increases**, **increased**, **increasing**) **1** make or become greater in size, amount, etc., or more numerous. **2** advance (in quality, attainment, etc.). **3** intensify (a quality). • *noun* **1** the act or process of becoming greater or more numerous; growth, enlargement. **2** (of people, animals, or plants) growth in numbers; multiplication. **3** the amount or extent of an increase. PHRASES **on the increase** increasing, esp. in frequency. ▶ **increasingly** *adverb*

incredible *adjective* **1** that cannot be believed. **2** *informal* amazing, extraordinary: *we had an incredible time in Scotland*. ▶ **incredibly** *adverb*

incredulity *noun* the state of being unwilling or unable to believe something: *general reaction to the judge's decision ranged from incredulity to outrage*. [Say in kruh DYOOLA tee]

incredulous *adjective* **1** unwilling to believe, skeptical. **2** showing disbelief: *an incredulous look*. ▶ **incredulously** *adverb* [Say in CRED yoo luss]

increment *noun* **1 a** the action or process of increasing or becoming greater, esp. gradually. **b** an increase or addition, esp. one of a series on a fixed scale.

c the amount of this. **2** *Math* a small amount by which a variable quantity increases. ▶ **incremental** *adjective*

incrementally *adverb* [Say IN kruh m'nt, in kruh MENTAL]

incriminate *verb* (**incriminates**, **incriminated**, **incriminating**) **1** (esp. as **incriminating** *adjective*) tend to prove the guilt of: *incriminating evidence*. **2** involve in an accusation. **3** charge with a crime. ▶ **incrimination** *noun* [Say in CRIM in ate, in crim in AY sh'n]

incubate *verb* (**incubates**, **incubated**, **incubating**) **1** sit on or artificially heat (eggs) in order to bring forth young birds etc. **2** maintain (cells, micro-organisms, etc.) in a controlled environment suitable for growth and development. **3** undergo incubation. **4** develop or grow slowly: *incubate a plan*. [Say INK yoo bate]

incubation *noun* **1** the act of incubating. **2 a** (also **incubation period**) the period between exposure to an infection and the appearance of the first symptoms. **b** the processes occurring during this. [Say ink yoo BAY sh'n]

incubator *noun* **1** an apparatus used to provide a suitable temperature and environment for a premature baby or one of low birth weight. **2** an apparatus used to hatch eggs or grow micro-organisms under artificially controlled conditions. **3** a place, esp. with support staff and equipment, made available at low rent to new small businesses. [Say INK yoo bate er]

incubus *noun* (*plural* **incubi**) **1** a male demon believed to have sexual intercourse with sleeping women. **2** a person or thing that oppresses or troubles like a nightmare: *debt is an incubus of developing countries*. [Say INK yoo bus for the singular, INK yoo bye for the plural]

inculcate *verb* (**inculcates**, **inculcated**, **inculcating**) urge or impress (a fact, habit, idea, etc.) persistently: *inculcate in young people a respect for the law*. ▶ **inculcation** *noun* [Say IN cull kate, in cull KAY sh'n]

incumbency *noun* (*plural* **incumbencies**) **1** the position of an incumbent. **2** the period during which this position is held. [Say in CUM b'n see]

incumbent • *adjective* **1** currently holding office: *the incumbent prime minister*. **2** resting or falling upon a person as a duty or obligation: *it is incumbent on you to warn them*. • *noun* the holder of an office or post: *defeated the riding's Liberal incumbent*. [Say in CUM b'nt]

incur *verb* (**incurs**, **incurred**, **incurring**) suffer, experience, or become subject to (something unpleasant) as a result of one's own behaviour etc.: *incurred huge debts*. [Say in CUR]

incurable *adjective* **1** unable to be cured. **2** not likely to change: *an incurable romantic*. ▶ **incurably** *adverb*

incursion *noun* **1** an invasion or attack, esp. when sudden or brief: *officials fear that another military incursion into the region is imminent*. **2** an interruption or disturbance: *the incursion of government regulations into more and more facets of life*. [Say in CUR zh'n]

indebted *adjective* (usu. foll. by *to*) **1** owing gratitude or obligation. **2** owing money. ▶ **indebtedness** *noun* [Say in DET id]

indecency *noun* (*plural* **indecencies**) **1** behaviour that is thought to be morally or sexually offensive. **2** an indecent act, expression, etc. [Say in DEE sin see]

indecent *adjective* **1** offending against recognized standards of decency: *that skirt of Ann's is positively indecent*. **2** unbecoming; highly unsuitable: *remarried with indecent haste*. ▶ **indecently** *adverb* [Say in DEE s'nt]

indecent exposure *noun* the intentional act of publicly and indecently exposing one's body, esp. the genitals.

indecipherable *adjective* that cannot be read or understood: *his handwriting is indecipherable*. [Say in duh SIGH fur a bull]

indecision *noun* lack of decision; hesitation.

indecisive *adjective* **1** not decisive or conclusive: *an indecisive battle*. **2** unable to make decisions. ▶ **indecisively** *adverb* **indecisiveness** *noun*

indeed *adverb* **1** in truth; really: *they are, indeed, a remarkable family*. **2** expressing emphasis or intensification: *indeed it is*. **3** admittedly: *there are indeed exceptions*. **4** in point of fact: *if indeed such a thing is possible*. **5** expressing an approving or ironic echo: *who is this Mr. Smith? — who is he indeed?*

indefatigable *adjective* (of a person, quality, etc.) that cannot be tired out: *an indefatigable defender of human rights*. ▶ **indefatigably** *adverb* [Say in duh FATTA guh bull]

indefensible *adjective* that cannot be defended, justified, or maintained in argument: *their policy was morally indefensible*. [Say in duh FENCE a bull]

indefinable *adjective* that cannot be defined or exactly described: *she reminds me, in some indefinable way, of my grandmother*. [Say in duh FINE a bull]

indefinite *adjective* **1** not clearly defined or stated; vague. **2** of undetermined extent, amount, or number; unlimited. **3** *Grammar* not determining the person, thing, time, etc., referred to. [Say in DEFFA nit]

indefinite article *noun Grammar* a word (*a* or *an* in English) preceding a noun and implying lack of specificity (as in *bought me a book*; *government is an art*).

indefinitely *adverb* for an unlimited time: *was postponed indefinitely*. [Say in DEFFA nit lee]

indefinite pronoun *noun* a pronoun indicating a person, amount, etc., without being definite or particular, e.g. *any*, *some*, *anyone*.

indelible *adjective* **1** not able to be forgotten or removed: *the story made an indelible impression on me*. **2** (of ink or a pen) that makes marks that cannot be removed. ▶ **indelibly** *adverb* [Say in DELLA bull]

indelicate *adjective* **1** coarse, unrefined. **2** tactless. **3** tending to indecency. ▶ **indelicately** *adverb*

indemnify *verb* (**indemnifies**, **indemnified**, **indemnifying**) **1** protect or secure (a person) against harm, loss, etc. **2** secure (a person) against legal responsibility for actions: *the servant would be indemnified for any damage caused by his negligence*. **3** compensate (a person) for a loss, expenses, etc.: *you can be indemnified against breach of contract*. [Say in DEMNA fie]

indemnity *noun* (*plural* **indemnities**) **1 a** compensation for loss incurred. **b** a sum paid for this, esp. a sum exacted by a victor in war etc. as one condition of peace. **2** security against loss: *no indemnity will be given for loss of cash*. **3** legal exemption from penalties etc. incurred. **4** *Cdn* the salary paid to a Member of Parliament or of a Legislative Assembly. [Say in DEMNA tee]

indent • *verb* **1** start (a line of print or writing) further from the margin than other lines, e.g. to mark a new paragraph. **2** form deep recesses in (a coastline etc.): *a heavily indented coastline*. **3** make a dent in the surface of (a thing). • *noun* an indentation in printing or writing.

indentation *noun* **1** the action of indenting something or the process of being indented. **2** a cut or notch. **3** a deep recess in a coastline etc.

indenture • *noun* (usu. in *plural*) **1** a sealed agreement or contract. **2** a contract binding a person to service. • *verb* (**indentures**, **indentured**, **indenturing**) bind (a person) by indentures, esp. as an apprentice or servant. ▶ **indentured** *adjective*

indépendantiste *Cdn* • *noun* a person who supports the idea of Quebec independence; a sovereignist. • *adjective* of or relating to the sovereignist movement in Quebec. [Say an day pon don TEEST]

independence *noun* **1** the state of being independent. **2** the fact or process of becoming independent.

independent • *adjective* **1 a** (often foll. by *of*) not depending on authority or control. **b** (of a state) self-governing. **2 a** not depending on another person for one's opinion or livelihood. **b** (of income or resources) making it unnecessary to earn one's living: *a woman of independent means*. **3** unwilling to be under an obligation to others. **4** *Politics* not belonging to or supported by a party. **5** not depending on something else for its validity, efficiency, value, etc.: *independent proof*. **6** impartial; conducted or originating outside a given institution, group, etc.: *an independent inquiry*. **7** (of broadcasting, a school, etc.) not supported by public funds. **8 a** (of a film, recording, etc.) produced without the support of a major studio, record label, etc. **b** (of a store, business, businessperson, etc.) not part of a chain or larger corporate structure: *an independent bookstore ◊ an independent contractor*. **9** *Grammar* (of a clause) able to stand alone as a complete sentence. • *noun* **1** a person who or thing which is independent, esp. a retailer whose store is not part of a chain. **2** a person who is politically independent. ▶ **independently** *adverb*

independent variable *noun Math* a variable whose variation does not depend on that of another.

in-depth *adjective* thorough; done in depth.

indescribable *adjective* **1** too unusual or extreme to be described. **2** vague, indefinite. ▶ **indescribably** *adverb* [Say in DESCRIBE a bull]

indestructibility *noun* the quality or condition of being unable to be destroyed.

indestructible *adjective* that cannot be destroyed.

indeterminacy *noun* the quality of being vague, or not fixed, or not limited. [Say in DETERMINE a see]

indeterminate *adjective* **1** that cannot be identified easily or exactly: *her eyes were an indeterminate colour ◊ he was a tall man of indeterminate age*. **2** *Math* (of a quantity) not limited to a fixed value by the value of another quantity. **3** (of a judicial sentence) such that the convicted person's conduct determines the date of release. [Say in DETERMINE it]

index • *noun* (*plural* **indexes** or esp. in technical use **indices**) **1** an alphabetical list of names, subjects, etc. with page references, usu. at the end of a book. **2** a catalogue or similar collection of information in which each item is entered on a separate card and the cards are arranged in a particular order, typically alphabetical. **3** a scale relating the level of prices, wages, etc. at a particular time to those at a date taken as a base: *consumer price index*. **4** *Math* **a** the exponent of a number. **b** the power to which it is raised. **5 a** a pointer, esp. on an instrument, showing a quantity, a position on a scale, etc. **b** (usu. foll. by *of*) a sign, token, or indication of something. **6** a number expressing a physical property etc. in terms of a standard: *UV index*. • *verb* (**indexes**, **indexed**, **indexing**) **1** provide (a book etc.) with an index. **2** enter in an index. **3** relate (wages etc.) to the value of a price index: *pension benefits will be fully indexed to inflation*. [For *indices* say INDA seez]

indexation *noun* the adjustment in rates of payment etc. to reflect variations in the cost-of-living index or other economic indicators.

index card *noun* a small rectangular card made of heavy paper, used in writing or recording notes etc.

index finger *noun* the forefinger.

WRITING TIP
Indian

The use of **Indian** to refer to the indigenous people of North and South America has declined recently because it is thought to reflect Columbus's mistaken idea that he had landed in India in 1492. However, in Canada it is still common in the usage of many Aboriginal people and embedded in legislation that is still in effect. It is also the only clear way to distinguish among the three general categories of Canadian Aboriginal people (Indians, Inuit, and Metis), and is therefore acceptable.

Indian • *noun* **1 a** a native or national of India. **b** a person of Indian descent. **2 a** a member of the Aboriginal peoples of North and South America other than the Inuit and Metis, or their descendants. **b** any of the languages of the non-Inuit and non-Metis Aboriginal peoples of North and South America. **c** *Cdn* a status Indian. • *adjective* **1** of or relating to India, or to the subcontinent comprising India, Pakistan, and Bangladesh. **2** of the Aboriginal peoples of North and South America.

Indian agent *noun Cdn hist.* a person appointed by the Department of Indian Affairs to supervise government programs on a reserve or in a specific region.

Indian elephant *noun* the elephant of India, which is smaller than the African elephant.

Indian ice cream *noun Cdn (BC)* a dessert or drink made from whipped soapberries, sugar, and water.

Indian paintbrush *noun* (*plural* **Indian paintbrushes**) a chiefly North American plant with flowers hidden by brightly coloured bracts.

Indian summer *noun* **1** a period of unusually dry warm weather sometimes occurring in late autumn. **2** a late period (of life, of an epoch, etc.) characterized by comparative calm: *he would have liked to remain forever in the Indian summer of graduate school*.

Indian title *noun Cdn* the claim by Indians to rights of ownership of land by virtue of its being occupied by Indians before the arrival of Europeans.

India rubber *noun* = RUBBER 1.

Indic • *adjective* of a group of Indo-European languages comprising Sanskrit and the modern Indian languages which are its descendants. • *noun* this language group.

indicate *verb* (**indicates, indicated, indicating**) **1** point out; make known; show. **2** be a sign or symptom of; express the presence of. **3** suggest; call for; require or show to be necessary: *stronger measures are indicated*. **4** admit to or state briefly: *indicated his disapproval*. **5** (of a gauge etc.) give as a reading.

indication *noun* **1** something that suggests or indicates; a sign or symptom. **2** something indicated or suggested. **3** a reading given by a gauge or instrument.

indicative • *adjective* **1** suggestive; serving as an indication. **2** *Grammar* designating the common mood or form of a verb when it states a simple fact, as opposed to the subjunctive mood, which expresses uncertainty. • *noun Grammar* **1** the indicative mood. **2** a verb in this mood. [Say in DICKA tiv]

indicator *noun* **1** a person or thing that indicates, esp. performance, change, etc.: *economic indicators*. **2 a** a device indicating the condition of a machine etc. **b** a pointer, light, etc., which draws attention to or gives warning. **3** a recording instrument attached to an apparatus. **4** a substance which changes to a characteristic colour in the presence of a particular concentration of an ion, so indicating e.g. acidity. **5** *Biology* a species or group which acts as a sign of particular environmental conditions.

indices *plural of* INDEX. [Say INDA seez]

indict *verb* charge with a crime, esp. formally by legal process: *he was indicted on 42 drug charges*. [Say in DITE]

indictable *adjective* **1** (of an offence) rendering the person who commits it liable to be charged with a crime. **2** (of a person) so liable. [Say in DITE a bull]

indictable offence *noun Cdn & Brit.* a more serious criminal offence, such as murder, which is triable by way of indictment (*compare* SUMMARY CONVICTION OFFENCE).

indictment *noun* **1** the act of indicting or the state of being indicted. **2** a formal accusation. **3** something that serves to condemn: *the book is an indictment of the government*. [Say in DITE m'nt]

indie *informal* • *noun* **1** an independent record or film company. **2 a** a musician or band whose music is recorded by an independent company. **b** a film produced by an independent company. • *adjective* **1** (of a pop group, record label, film, etc.) independent, not belonging to one of the major record companies or film studios. **2** characteristic of the deliberately unpolished or uncommercialized style of indie bands.

indifference *noun* **1** lack of interest or attention. **2** unimportance: *a matter of indifference*.

indifferent *adjective* **1** (foll. by *to*) having no particular interest or sympathy; unconcerned: *she seemed indifferent rather than angry* ◊ *most workers were indifferent to foreign affairs*. **2** neither good nor bad; average, mediocre: *a man of indifferent abilities and limited imagination*. **3** not especially good; fairly bad: *a pair of indifferent watercolours*. **4** (often preceded by *very*) decidedly inferior. ▸ **indifferently** *adverb*

indigene *noun* a native or aboriginal inhabitant of a region etc. [Say INDA jean]

indigenization *noun* the act or process of making predominantly indigenous, esp. the increased use of indigenous people in government, employment, etc. [Say in didge a nize AY sh'n]

indigenize *verb* (**indigenizes, indigenized, indigenizing**) make indigenous; subject to native influence: *suggestions for indigenizing the criminal justice system*. [Say in DIDGE a nize]

indigenous *adjective* **1** originating or occurring naturally in a particular place; native: *the indigenous music of Siberia* ◊ *the indigenous plants of Newfoundland*. **2** (foll. by *to*) belonging naturally to a place: *coriander is indigenous to southern Europe*. **3** of or concerned with the aboriginal inhabitants of a region: *sampled some indigenous food*. ▸ **indigenously** *adverb* [Say in DIDGE a nus]

indigent • *adjective* poor: *caring for indigent families*. • *noun* an indigent person. [Say INDA j'nt]

indigestible *adjective* **1** difficult or impossible to digest. **2** too complex or awkward to read or comprehend easily. [Say inda JESTA bull]

indigestion *noun* stomach discomfort associated with difficulty in digesting food. [Say inda JES chun]

indignant *adjective* feeling or showing scornful anger. ▸ **indignantly** *adverb* [Say in DIG nint]

indignation *noun* scornful anger at supposed unjust or unfair conduct or treatment. [Say in dig NATION]

indignity *noun* (*plural* **indignities**) **1** unworthy treatment. **2** a slight or insult. **3** the humiliating quality of something: *the indignity of my position*. [Say in DIGNA tee]

indigo *noun* (*plural* **indigos**) **1** a tropical plant of the pea family, which was formerly widely cultivated as a source of dark blue dye. **2** a blue dye obtained from this plant or synthetically. **3** *noun & adjective* (also **indigo blue**) a colour between blue and violet in the spectrum. [Say INDA go]

indigo bunting *noun* a North American finch, the male of which has bright blue plumage.

indirect *adjective* **1 a** not going straight to the point: *an indirect answer*. **b** not acting or exercised with direct force; roundabout. **2** (of a route etc.) not straight; circuitous. **3** not directly sought or aimed at: *indirect result*. **4** (of lighting) from a concealed source and diffusely reflected. ▶ **indirection** *noun* **indirectly** *adverb* **indirectness** *noun*

indirect object *noun* Grammar a person or thing affected by a verbal action but not primarily acted on, e.g. *him* in *give him the book*.

indirect question *noun* Grammar a question in reported speech, e.g. *they asked who I was*.

indirect speech *noun* (also **indirect discourse**) a description of a speaker's words as opposed to a direct quotation, with the necessary changes of person, tense, etc., e.g. *she said that she would go* instead of *she said, "I will go"* (opp. DIRECT SPEECH).

indirect tax *noun* (plural **indirect taxes**) a tax that is paid to the government by the taxpayer through an intermediary rather than directly, e.g. sales tax.

indiscreet *adjective* not discreet; revealing secrets: *an indiscreet comment* ◊ *it was indiscreet of him to disclose that information*. ▶ **indiscreetly** *adverb*

indiscretion *noun* **1** lack of discretion; indiscreet conduct. **2** an indiscreet action, remark, etc.

indiscriminate *adjective* **1** (of an action etc.) done at random or without careful judgement: *terrorist gunmen engaged in indiscriminate killing*. **2** acting without careful judgment: *I love music, but I am not indiscriminate in my listening*. ▶ **indiscriminately** *adverb* [Say in dis CRIM in ut]

indispensability *noun* the quality or condition of being necessary. [Say in dis pence a BILLA tee]

indispensable *adjective* **1** essential; too important to be without: *cars have become an indispensable part of our lives* ◊ *she made herself indispensable to the department* ◊ *a good dictionary is indispensable for learning a foreign language*. **2** (of a law, duty, etc.) that is not to be set aside. [Say in dis PENCE a bull]

indisposed *adjective* **1** slightly unwell. **2** averse or unwilling.

indisputable *adjective* that cannot be disputed; unquestionable. ▶ **indisputably** *adverb*

indissoluble *adjective* **1** that cannot be dissolved or decomposed. **2** lasting, stable: *an indissoluble bond*. ▶ **indissolubly** *adverb* [Say in dis SAWL yoo bull]

indistinct *adjective* **1** not distinct. **2** confused, obscure. ▶ **indistinctly** *adverb*

indistinguishable *adjective* (often foll. by *from*) not distinguishable. [Say in dis TING wish a bull]

indium *noun* a soft silvery-white metallic element used for electroplating and in semiconductors. [Say IN dee um]

individual • *adjective* **1** single, separate. **2** particular, special; not general. **3** having a distinct character. **4** characteristic of a particular person. **5** designed for use by one person: *individual portions*. • *noun* **1** a single human being as distinct from a family or group. **2** a person: *a most unpleasant individual*. **3** a person who does not conform to the majority. **4** a single member of a class or group.

individualism *noun* **1** the habit or principle of being independent and self-reliant. **2** a social theory favouring the free action of individuals. **3** self-centred feeling or conduct; egoism. **4** = INDIVIDUALITY 1. ▶ **individualist** *noun* **individualistic** *adjective*

individuality *noun* (plural **individualities**) **1** the sum of the attributes which distinguish one person or thing from others of the same kind; strongly marked individual character. **2** the fact or condition of separate existence.

individualize *verb* (**individualizes, individualized, individualizing**) **1** give an individual character to. **2** (esp. as **individualized** *adjective*) personalize or tailor to suit the individual: *individualized training*.

individually *adverb* **1** personally; in an individual capacity. **2** in a distinctive manner. **3** one by one; not collectively.

individuate *verb* (**individuates, individuated, individuating**) distinguish from others of the same kind: *individuating details of personal history*. ▶ **individuation** *noun* [Say inda VIDGE oo ate]

indivisible *adjective* **1** not divisible. **2** not distributable among a number. [Say inda VIZZA bull]

Indo-Canadian • *noun* a Canadian born in the Indian subcontinent, esp. India, or one of Indian descent. • *adjective* of or relating to Indo-Canadians.

indoctrinate *verb* (**indoctrinates, indoctrinated, indoctrinating**) teach (a person or group) to accept a doctrine or set of beliefs, esp. when this is considered unfair or wrong: *they had been indoctrinated from an early age with their parents' beliefs*. ▶ **indoctrination** *noun* [Say in DOCTRINE ate, in doctrine AY sh'n]

Indo-European • *adjective* **1** of the family of languages spoken over the greater part of Europe and Asia as far as northern India. **2** of the hypothetical parent language of this family. • *noun* **1** the Indo-European family of languages. **2** the hypothetical parent language of all languages belonging to this family.

indolence *noun* laziness; love of ease. [Say INDA lince]

indolent *adjective* **1** lazy; wishing to avoid activity or exertion: *the bureaucrats were accused of being exceptionally indolent*. **2** Medical causing no pain: *an indolent tumour*. ▶ **indolently** *adverb* [Say INDA lint]

indomitable *adjective* impossible to subdue or defeat; unyielding, persistent: *a woman of indomitable spirit*. [Say in DOMMA tuh bull]

Indonesian • *noun* **1 a** a native or national of Indonesia in Southeast Asia. **b** a person of Indonesian descent. **2** the western branch of the Austronesian language family. • *adjective* of or relating to Indonesia or its people or language. [Say inda NEE zhun]

indoor *adjective* situated, carried on, or used within a building or under cover.

indoor-outdoor *adjective* designating a sturdy carpet that can be used both inside and outside of a house etc.

indoors *adverb* into or within a building.

indubitable *adjective* that cannot be doubted: *indubitable proof*. ▶ **indubitably** *adverb* [Say in DOO bit a bull or in DYOO bit a bull]

induce *verb* (**induces, induced, inducing**) **1** persuade: *nothing could induce Maggie to go*. **2** Medical bring on (labour) artificially, esp. by use of drugs. **3** Electricity produce (a current) by induction. **4** Physics cause (radioactivity) by bombardment. ▶ **inducer** *noun*

inducement *noun* **1** (often foll. by *to*) an attraction that leads one on. **2** something that is offered to persuade someone to do something; an incentive: *a financial inducement*.

induct *verb* **1** formally give someone a job or position of authority, esp. as part of a ceremony. **2** introduce, initiate: *inducted into a secret brotherhood*. **3** admit as a new member: *inducted him into the band*.

inductance *noun* Electricity **1** the property of an electric circuit that causes an electromotive force to be generated by a change in the current flowing. **2** INDUCTOR.

inductee *noun* a person who is being, or who has just been, introduced into a special group of people,

especially one who has just been elected to a hall of fame etc. [Say in duck TEE]

induction *noun* **1** the process of introducing someone to a new job, skill, organization, etc.; a ceremony at which this takes place: *induction into the local business community*. **2** *Medical* the process of bringing on (esp. labour) by artificial means. **3** *Logic* **a** the inference of a general law from particular instances (*compare* DEDUCTION 2). **b** *Math* a way of proving a theorem by showing that if it is true of any particular case it is true of the next case in a series, and then showing that it is indeed true in one particular case. **4** *Electricity* **a** the production of an electric or magnetic state by the proximity (without contact) of an electrified or magnetized body. **b** the production of an electric current in a conductor by a change of magnetic field. **5** the drawing of a fuel mixture into the cylinders of an internal combustion engine.

inductive *adjective* **1** (of reasoning etc.) of or based on induction. **2** of electric or magnetic induction. ▶ **inductively** *adverb*

inductor *noun* *Electricity* a component (in a circuit) which possesses inductance.

indulge *verb* (**indulges**, **indulged**, **indulging**) **1** (often foll. by *in*) allow oneself to enjoy the pleasure of something. **2** yield freely to (a desire etc.). **3** gratify the wishes of; favour: *indulged them with money*. **4 indulge oneself** give free rein to one's inclination or liking. **5** *informal* take alcoholic liquor.

indulgence *noun* **1 a** the act of indulging. **b** the state of being indulgent. **c** lenient or liberal treatment. **2** something indulged in. **3** *Catholicism* the remission of punishment in purgatory, still due for sins even after sacramental absolution. **4** a privilege granted.

indulgent *adjective* **1** ready or too ready to overlook faults etc. **2** indulging or tending to indulge. ▶ **indulgently** *adverb*

industrial • *adjective* **1** of, relating to, or employed in industry or industries: *industrial workers*. **2** designed or suitable for industrial use: *industrial alcohol*. **3** characterized by highly developed industries: *the industrial nations*. • *noun* (in *plural*) shares in industrial companies. ▶ **industrially** *adverb*

industrial arts *plural noun* woodworking, metalwork, etc., esp. as taught in schools etc.

industrial design *noun* the act or art of designing objects for manufacture. ▶ **industrial designer** *noun*

industrialism *noun* a social or economic system in which manufacturing industries are prevalent.

industrialist *noun* a person engaged in the management of an industrial enterprise.

industrialization *noun* the action or process of introducing industries to a country, region, etc., or of becoming industrialized.

industrialize *verb* (**industrializes**, **industrialized**, **industrializing**) **1** introduce industries to (a country or region etc.). **2** become industrialized.

Industrial Revolution *noun* the dramatic transformation of society resulting from the bulk of the working population turning from agriculture to industry, esp. in Britain from about 1750–1850.

industrial-strength *adjective* often *jocular* strong, powerful: *industrial-strength coffee*.

industrious *adjective* hard-working. ▶ **industriously** *adverb* **industriousness** *noun*

industry *noun* (*plural* **industries**) **1 a** a branch of trade or manufacture. **b** trade and manufacture collectively. **c** any commercial undertaking that provides services: *hospitality industry*. **2** the quality of working hard; diligence: *we were impressed by their industry*.

inebriated *adjective* drunk. [Say in EE bree ate id]

inebriation *noun* drunkenness. [Say in ee bree AY sh'n]

inedible *adjective* not edible, esp. not suitable for eating (*compare* UNEATABLE). [Say in EDDA bull]

ineffable *adjective* **1** unutterable; too great for description in words; indefinable: *the ineffable mysteries of the soul*. **2** that must not be uttered. ▶ **ineffably** *adverb* [Say in EFFA bull]

ineffective *adjective* **1** not producing any effect or the desired effect. **2** (of a person) inefficient; not achieving results. ▶ **ineffectively** *adverb* **ineffectiveness** *noun*

ineffectual *adjective* **1 a** without effect. **b** not producing the desired or expected effect. **2** (of a person) lacking the ability to achieve results: *an ineffectual leader*. ▶ **ineffectually** *adverb*

inefficiency *noun* (*plural* **inefficiencies**) **1** lack of efficiency; ineffectiveness: *is frustrated by inefficiency* ◊ *was dismissed for inefficiency*. **2** something that is not efficient: *eliminated inefficiencies*. [Say in i FISHIN see]

inefficient *adjective* **1** (of a machine, process, etc.) wasting time or resources: *an inefficient heating system*. **2** (of a person or organization) failing to make the best use of the available time and resources. ▶ **inefficiently** *adverb* [Say in i FISH int]

inelastic *adjective* **1** not elastic. **2** inflexible, unyielding, not adaptable: *their inelastic minds proved inadequate*. **3** *Economics* (of demand or supply) not responsive to, or varying less than in proportion to, changes in price.

inelegant *adjective* not attractive or graceful: *an inelegant fall* ◊ *an inelegant phrase*. ▶ **inelegantly** *adverb*

ineligibility *noun* the quality or condition of not being eligible or of not having the appropriate or necessary qualifications (for an office, position, etc.). [Say in ella juh BILLA tee]

ineligible *adjective* not eligible; not having the appropriate or necessary qualifications (for an office, position, etc.). [Say in ELLA juh bull]

ineluctable *adjective* unable to be resisted or avoided; inescapable: *ineluctable fate*. ▶ **ineluctably** *adverb* [Say inna LUCK tuh bull]

inept *adjective* unskilful, incompetent. ▶ **ineptitude** *noun* **ineptly** *adverb* **ineptness** *noun*

inequality *noun* (*plural* **inequalities**) **1 a** lack of equality between persons or things; disparity in size, number, quality, etc. **b** an example of this: *the widening inequalities in income*. **2 a** difference of rank or circumstance; social or economic disparity: *inequality between rich and poor*. **b** unfairness, inequity. **3** *Math* a formula affirming that two expressions are not equal.

inequitable *adjective* unfair, unjust: *an inequitable distribution of wealth*. ▶ **inequitably** *adverb* [Say in ECKWA tuh bull]

SPELL CHECK
inequity, iniquity

Wickedness is **iniquity**.

---

inequity *noun* (*plural* **inequities**) unfairness, bias: *inequities in school financing* ◊ *policies aimed at redressing racial inequity*. [Say in ECKWA tee]

ineradicable *adjective* unable to be eradicated or rooted out: *his experience had driven into him the ineradicable feeling that the employer was always wrong*. ▶ **ineradicably** *adverb* [Say inna RAD ick a bull]

inert *adjective* **1** without power to move or act; lacking vigour: *she lay inert with half-closed eyes* ◊ *the president has to operate within an inert political system*. **2** without active chemical or other properties.

inert gas *noun* (*plural* **inert gases**) any gaseous

element of a group that almost never combine with other elements (*also called* NOBLE GAS).

inertia *noun* **1** *Physics* a property of matter by which it continues in its existing state of rest or uniform motion in a straight line, unless that state is changed by an external force. **2 a** inertness; lack of vigour or will to move. **b** a tendency to remain unchanged. ▶**inertial** *adjective* [Say in URSH uh]

inertly *adverb* in an inert or inactive manner.

inescapability *noun* inevitability; the quality of being unavoidable.

inescapable *adjective* that cannot be escaped or avoided. ▶**inescapably** *adverb*

inessential • *adjective* not necessary; dispensable. • *noun* an inessential thing.

inestimable *adjective* too great, intense, precious, etc., to be estimated: *the information was of inestimable value*. ▶**inestimably** *adverb* [Say in ESS timma bull]

inevitability *noun* the quality or condition of being inevitable or unavoidable: *the inevitability of revolution*. [Say in evva tuh BILLA tee]

inevitable • *adjective* **1 a** unavoidable; sure to happen. **b** that is bound to occur or appear. **2** *informal* that is tiresomely familiar: *the English and their inevitable cups of tea*. • *noun* (**the inevitable**) that which is inevitable. ▶**inevitably** *adverb* [Say in EVVA tuh bull]

inexact *adjective* not exact. ▶**inexactly** *adverb*

inexactness *noun*

inexcusable *adjective* (of a person, action, etc.) that cannot be excused or justified. ▶**inexcusably** *adverb*

inexhaustible *adjective* that cannot be used up: *an inexhaustible resource*. [Say in ex OSS tuh bull]

inexorable *adjective* (of a process) that cannot be stopped or changed: *there was no inexorable march to modernism*. ▶**inexorably** *adverb* [Say in EX ur a bull]

inexpensive *adjective* not expensive, cheap. ▶**inexpensively** *adverb* **inexpensiveness** *noun*

inexperience *noun* lack of experience, or of the resulting knowledge or skill. ▶**inexperienced** *adjective*

inexpert *adjective* not skilful; lacking expertise. ▶**inexpertly** *adverb*

inexplicable *adjective* that cannot be explained or accounted for. ▶**inexplicably** *adverb* [Say in ex PLICK a bull]

inexpressible *adjective* that cannot be expressed in words. ▶**inexpressibly** *adverb*

in extremis *adjective* **1** at the point of death: *suffered from the malady in extremis yet returned to tell the tale*. **2** in great difficulties: *they suddenly found themselves in extremis 20 miles out to sea*. [Say in ex TREM iss or in ex TREEM iss]

inextricable *adjective* too closely linked to be separated: *for her, living and writing were inextricable ◊ it was here that our inextricable bond with the game was made*. ▶**inextricably** *adverb* [Say in EX trick a bull or in ex TRICK a bull]

infallibility *noun* the quality or condition of being unfailing or incapable of error. [Say in fal a BILLA tee]

infallible *adjective* **1** incapable of error: *our leaders are not infallible*. **2** (of a method, test, proof, etc.) unfailing; sure to succeed: *an infallible way to catch cheaters*. **3** *Catholicism* (of the Pope) unable to err in pronouncing dogma as doctrinally defined. ▶**infallibly** *adverb* [Say in FAL a bull]

infamous *adjective* well-known for being bad, wicked, etc.: *Hitler's infamous storm troopers*. ▶**infamously** *adverb* [Say in IN fuh muss]

infamy *noun* **1** the state of being well known for something bad or evil: *a day that will live in infamy*. **2** evil behaviour: *scenes of horror and infamy*. [Say IN fuh mee]

infancy *noun* (*plural* **infancies**) **1** early childhood; babyhood. **2** an early state in the development of an idea, undertaking, etc.: *our project is still in its infancy*. **3** *Law* the state of being a minor. [Say IN fan see]

infant *noun* **1** a child during the earliest period of its life. **2** a person or thing in an early stage of its development. **3** *Law* a minor; a person under 18.

infanticide *noun* **1** the practice of killing newborn infants: *suspected cases of infanticide*. **2** a person who kills an infant. [Say in FANTA side]

infantile *adjective* **1** like or characteristic of a child. **2** childish, immature: *infantile humour*. [Say IN f'n tile]

infant mortality *noun* death before the age of one.

infant mortality rate *noun* the ratio of the number of deaths of children under the age of one to the total number of children born.

infantry *noun* (*plural* **infantries**) foot soldiers collectively. [Say IN fun tree]

infantryman *noun* (*plural* **infantrymen**) a soldier of an infantry regiment.

infatuated *adjective* affected by an intense but usu. passing fondness or admiration. [Say in FATCH oo ate id]

infect *verb* **1** contaminate (air, water, etc.) with harmful organisms or noxious matter. **2 a** affect (a person) with disease etc; introduce a disease-causing micro-organism into. **b** affect (a computer system) with a virus.

infection *noun* **1 a** the process of infecting or state of being infected. **b** an infectious disease. **c** the presence of a virus in, or its entry into, a computer system. **2** communication of disease, esp. through the air or water etc.

infectious *adjective* **1** infecting with disease. **2** (of a disease) liable to be transmitted by air, water, etc. **3** (of emotions etc.) apt to spread; quickly affecting others. ▶**infectiously** *adverb* **infectiousness** *noun*

infective *adjective* capable of infecting with disease.

WRITING TIP
infer, imply

Infer should not be used to mean **imply**. **Infer** means "to reach an opinion based on available information or evidence", as in *From these statistics our researchers inferred a connection between smoking and heart disease* or *From your enthusiastic response, I infer that you did indeed enjoy the movie*. **Imply** means "to suggest indirectly", as in *I didn't tell Sonja I was angry but I implied it and I think she understood*. The use of **infer** to mean **imply**, as in *I didn't tell Sonja I was angry, but I inferred it*, is generally considered wrong.

---

infer *verb* (**infers**, **inferred**, **inferring**) (often foll. by *that* + clause) **1** deduce or conclude from facts and reasoning. **2** *disputed* imply, suggest.

inference *noun* **1** a conclusion reached on the basis of evidence and reasoning. **2** the process of reaching such a conclusion: *his emphasis on order and health, and by inference cleanliness*. [Say IN fur ince]

inferior • *adjective* **1** of lower rank, quality, etc. **2** poor in quality. **3** (of a planet) having an orbit within the earth's. **4** *Botany* situated below an ovary or calyx. • *noun* a person inferior to another, esp. in rank.

inferiority *noun* the state of being inferior. [Say in feary OR a tee]

inferiority complex *noun* an unrealistic feeling of general inadequacy caused by actual or supposed inferiority in one sphere, sometimes marked by aggressive behaviour in compensation.

infernal *adjective* **1 a** of hell or the underworld: *the infernal regions presided over by Pluto*. **b** hellish, fiendish.

2 *informal* detestable, tiresome: *nothing in this infernal building worked*. ▶ **infernally** *adverb* [Say in FUR null]

inferno *noun* (*plural* **infernos**) **1** a raging fire. **2** hell. [Say in FUR no]

infertile *adjective* not fertile. ▶ **infertility** *noun* [Say in FUR tile or in FURTLE, in fur TILLA tee]

infest *verb* (of harmful persons or things, esp. vermin or disease) overrun (a place) in large numbers. ▶ **infestation** *noun*

infidel • *noun* **1** usu. *derogatory* a person who does not believe in religion or in a particular religion; an unbeliever. **2** *hist.* an adherent of a religion other than one's own, esp.: **a** (from a Christian point of view) a Muslim. **b** (from a Muslim point of view) a Christian. **c** (from a Jewish point of view) a Gentile. • *adjective* that is an infidel. [Say IN fuh del]

infidelity *noun* (*plural* **infidelities**) the action or state of being unfaithful to a spouse or other sexual partner: *her infidelity continued after her marriage* ◊ *I ought not to have tolerated his infidelities*. [Say in fuh DELLA tee]

infield *noun* **1** *Baseball* **a** the area bounded by the baselines. **b** the fielders positioned along the baseline from first base to third base. **c** a team's defensive ability in the infield. **2** the area enclosed by a racetrack.

infielder *noun* *Baseball* any of the fielders, i.e. the first baseman, second baseman, third baseman, and shortstop, stationed in the infield.

infighting *noun* hidden conflict or competitiveness within an organization.

infill • *noun* (also **infilling**) **1** material used to fill a hole, gap, etc. **2** the placing of buildings to occupy the space between existing ones. **3 a** the building of a house on a lot cleared by demolishing an existing, usu. smaller house. **b** a house built where the previous one has been demolished. • *verb* fill in (a cavity etc.).

infiltrate *verb* (**infiltrates**, **infiltrated**, **infiltrating**) **1** enter a place or an organization secretly, especially in order to get information that can be used against it: *the headquarters had been infiltrated by enemy spies*. **2** (of liquids or gases) pass slowly into something: *only a small amount of the rainwater actually infiltrates into the soil*. ▶ **infiltration** *noun* **infiltrator** *noun* [Say IN fill trate, in fill TRAY sh'n]

infinite • *adjective* **1** boundless, endless. **2** very great. **3** innumerable; very many: *infinite resources*. **4** *Math* **a** greater than any assignable quantity or countable number. **b** (of a series) that may be continued indefinitely. • *noun* **1** (**the Infinite**) God. **2** (**the infinite**) infinite space. ▶ **infinitely** *adverb* [Say IN fuh nit]

infinitesimal • *adjective* infinitely or very small. • *noun* an infinitesimal amount. [Say in finna TESS'm ul]

infinitesimal calculus *noun* the differential and integral calculi regarded as one subject.

infinitesimally *adverb* in an infinitesimal or very small degree. [Say in finna TESS'm ul lee]

infinitive • *noun* a form of a verb expressing the verbal notion without reference to a particular subject, tense, etc. (e.g. *see* in *we came to see*, or *let her see*). • *adjective* having this form.

infinity *noun* (*plural* **infinities**) **1** the state of being infinite. **2** an infinite number or extent. **3** infinite distance. **4** *Math* infinite quantity. Symbol: ∞.

infirm *adjective* physically weak, esp. through age.

infirmary *noun* (*plural* **infirmaries**) **1** a place for those who are ill in a boarding school, prison, etc. **2** a hospital. [Say in FIRM a ree]

infirmity *noun* (*plural* **infirmities**) physical or mental weakness: *old age and infirmity come to men and women alike* ◊ *the infirmities of old age*. [Say in FIRM tee]

inflame *verb* (**inflames**, **inflamed**, **inflaming**) **1** provoke or become provoked to strong feeling, esp. anger: *all that kind of language does is inflame members on both sides*. **2** make a situation worse or more difficult to deal with: *the situation was further inflamed by the arrival of the security forces*. **3** *Medical* cause inflammation or fever in (a body etc.).

inflamed *adjective* (of a part of the body) red, painful, and often swollen, esp. as a reaction to injury or infection.

> **WRITING TIP**
> **inflammable, flammable**
>
> Both **inflammable** and **flammable** mean "easily set on fire". The opposite of **inflammable** and **flammable** is **non-flammable**.

inflammable • *adjective* **1** easily set on fire; flammable. **2** likely to provoke strong feelings; volatile: *the most inflammable issue in politics today*. • *noun* (usu. plural) an inflammable substance.

inflammation *noun* a localized physical condition with heat, swelling, redness, and usu. pain, esp. as a reaction to injury or infection.

inflammatory *adjective* (esp. of speeches, leaflets, etc.) tending to cause anger etc. **2** of or causing inflammation of the body.

inflammatory bowel disease *noun* either of two diseases, Crohn's disease and ulcerative colitis, which cause an inflammation of the bowel.

inflatable • *adjective* that can be inflated. • *noun* an inflatable object, esp. an inflatable boat.

inflate *verb* (**inflates**, **inflated**, **inflating**) **1** distend (a balloon etc.) with air. **2** puff up (a person's ego). **3 a** bring about inflation (of the currency). **b** raise (prices) artificially. **4** exaggerate or embellish: *I satirize their inflated claims and nationalistic rhetoric*. **5** become inflated.

inflated *adjective* **1** swollen or distended. **2** (esp. of language, sentiments, etc.) high sounding but with little meaning; bombastic. **3** (of prices, costs, etc.) unreasonably increased in amount, level, etc. **4** (of a person's ego) puffed up. **5** *Botany & Zoology* having a bulging form and hollow interior, as if filled with air.

inflation *noun* **1** *Economics* **a** a general increase in prices and fall in the purchasing value of money. **b** an increase in available currency regarded as causing this. **2** the act or condition of inflating or being inflated. ▶ **inflationary** *adjective*

inflect *verb* **1** change the pitch of (the voice, a musical note, etc.). **2** *Grammar* **a** change the form of (a word) to express tense, gender, number, mood, etc. **b** (of a word, language, etc.) undergo such change. **3** bend inwards; curve. **4** influence or modify, esp. by the addition of characteristics of another culture, musical style, etc.: *a jazz-inflected style of singing*.

inflection *noun* **1** *Grammar* **a** the process or practice of inflecting words. **b** an inflected form of a word. **c** a suffix etc. used to inflect, e.g. *-ed*. **2** a modulation of the voice. ▶ **inflectional** *adjective*

inflexibility *noun* the quality of being unable or unwilling to change or adapt or be changed or adapted: *the inflexibility of the federal government on this issue*.

inflexible *adjective* **1** that cannot be changed or adapted to particular circumstances: *an inflexible system*. **2** (of a person) unwilling to change or adapt: *inflexible in their attitudes*. ▶ **inflexibly** *adverb*

inflict *verb* (usu. foll. by *on*, *upon*) **1** cause (injury, defeat, damage, punishment etc.). **2** often *jocular* impose (something objectionable or unwelcome) on: *you're not going to inflict another family story on us, are you?*

infliction *noun* the action of inflicting something unpleasant or painful: *the repeated infliction of pain*.

inflight *adjective* occurring or provided during an aircraft flight.

inflorescence *noun* **1** *Botany* **a** the complete flower head of a plant including stems, stalks, bracts, and flowers. **b** the arrangement of this. **2** the process of flowering. [Say in flor ESSENCE]

inflow *noun* **1** a flowing in. **2** something, e.g. a liquid, money, etc., that flows in. ▶ **inflowing** *noun & adjective*

influence • *noun* **1 a** the effect a person or thing has on another: *the influence of the climate on agricultural production*. **b** the power that someone has to make someone behave in a particular way: *her parents no longer have any real influence over her*. **c** a thing or person exercising such power: *is a good influence on them*. **2** the ability to obtain favourable treatment by means of acquaintance, wealth, status, etc. **3** *Astrology* an ethereal fluid supposedly flowing from the stars and affecting character and destiny. • *verb* (**influences, influenced, influencing**) **1** exert influence on; have an effect on. **2** persuade or induce (a person) to do or think something. PHRASES **under the influence** *informal* affected by alcoholic drink.

influence peddler *noun* a person who uses his or her position or political influence in exchange for money or favours. ▶ **influence peddling** *noun*

influential *adjective* having great influence or power. ▶ **influentially** *adverb* [Say in floo EN shull]

influenza *noun* a highly contagious virus infection causing fever, severe aching, weakness, and coughing; the flu. [Say in flu ENZA]

influx *noun* (*plural* **influxes**) **1** a continual entry of people (esp. visitors or immigrants) into a place, esp. in large numbers. **2** (usu. foll. by *into*) a flowing in of a substance, esp. in large quantities. **3** the point at which a stream or river flows into another body of water.

info *noun & combining form informal* information.

info centre *noun* *Cdn* a booth or office etc. providing information to the public on a subject or region.

infomercial *noun* a television commercial made to look like a regular program, so as to disguise the fact that it is a paid advertisement. [Say INFO mur shull]

inform *verb* **1** tell: *informed them of their rights*. **2** make an accusation. **3** give or supply information or knowledge: *the book's task is to inform*. **4** have an influence on something: *religion informs every aspect of their lives* ◊ *these guidelines will inform any future decisions*.

informal *adjective* **1** without ceremony or formality: *just an informal chat*. **2** (of clothing etc.) everyday; casual. **3** (of language, writing, etc.) relaxed or conversational in style; not formal. ▶ **informality** *noun* (*plural* **informalities**) **informally** *adverb*

informant *noun* **1** a person who gives information. **2** a person who informs against another, esp. in criminal matters; an informer. **3** a person from whom a linguist, anthropologist, etc., obtains information about language, dialect, or culture.

information *noun* **1** something told; knowledge; news: *the latest information on the crisis*. **2** a booth, office, or agency providing information, esp. on a specific subject or location: *go and ask at information*. **3** *Law* (usu. foll. by *against*) a charge or complaint lodged with a court or magistrate. **4** data as processed or stored etc. by a computer system. ▶ **informational** *adjective*

information science *noun* the study of the processes for storing and retrieving information.

information superhighway *noun* (also **information highway**) a means of rapid transfer of information in different digital forms (e.g. video, sound, and graphics) via a vast electronic network.

information technology *noun* the study or use of systems (esp. computers, telecommunications, etc.) for storing, retrieving, and sending information.

informative *adjective* giving information; instructive.

informed *adjective* **1** with knowledge of the facts: *ill-informed*. **2** educated; knowledgeable: *informed readers*.

informer *noun* **1** a person who informs against another. **2** a person who informs or advises.

infotainment *noun* broadcast material intended both to entertain and to inform. [Say info TAIN m'nt]

infra- *combining form* below.

infraction *noun* esp. *Law* a violation or infringement.

infrared • *adjective* **1** having a wavelength just greater than the red end of the visible light spectrum but less than that of radio waves. **2** of or using such radiation. • *noun* the infrared part of the spectrum. [Say infra RED]

infrastructure *noun* **1 a** the basic structural foundations of a society or enterprise; a substructure or foundation. **b** roads, bridges, sewers, etc., regarded as a country's economic foundation. **2** permanent installations as a basis for military etc. operations. ▶ **infrastructural** *adjective* [Say INFRA structure]

infrequency *noun* the quality or condition of not being frequent: *the infrequency of her sons' visits*.

infrequent *adjective* not frequent. ▶ **infrequently** *adverb*

infringe *verb* (**infringes, infringed, infringing**) **1 a** act contrary to; violate (a law, an oath, etc.): *it does not infringe the freedom of religion section of the charter*. **b** act in defiance of (another's rights etc.): *the action would infringe the rights of minorities*. **2** (usu. foll. by *on*, *upon*) affect something so as to limit or restrict it; encroach on: *they are infringing on our privacy*. ▶ **infringement** *noun*

infuriate *verb* (**infuriates, infuriated, infuriating**) fill with fury; enrage. ▶ **infuriating** *adjective* **infuriatingly** *adverb* [Say in FYOORY ate]

infuse *verb* (**infuses, infused, infusing**) **1** fill; have an effect on all parts of something: *her work is infused with an anger born of pain and oppression*. **2** steep (herbs, tea, etc.) in liquid to extract the content. **3** (usu. foll. by *into*) instill (grace, spirit, life, etc.). **4** undergo infusion: *let it infuse for five minutes*. [Say in FYOOZ]

infusion *noun* **1 a** a drink, remedy, or extract prepared by soaking the leaves of a plant or herb in liquid. **b** the process of preparing such a drink, remedy, or extract. **2** the introduction of someone or something new that will have a positive influence: *an infusion of cash*. **3** *Medical* a slow injection of a substance into a vein or tissue. [Say in FEW zh'n]

ingenious *adjective* **1** clever at inventing, constructing, organizing, etc.; skilful; resourceful. **2** (of a machine, theory, etc.) cleverly contrived. ▶ **ingeniously** *adverb* [Say in GENIUS]

ingenue *noun* **1** an innocent or unsophisticated young woman. **2 a** such a part in a play. **b** the actress who plays this part. [Say on zhuh NOO]

WRITING TIP
ingenuity

Ingenuity is related to the word **ingenious**, not to **ingenuous**.

ingenuity *noun* (*plural* **ingenuities**) skill in devising or contriving. [Say in juh NOO a tee or in juh NYOO a tee]

Ingenuous should not be confused with **ingenious**. **Ingenuous** means "open, frank, innocent", as in *How was Lisa to know that her ingenuous admission to liking Edgar would result in months of teasing from her friends?* **Ingenious** means "clever, resourceful", as in *Willy devised an ingenious science experiment.*

ingenuous *adjective* **1** innocent; artless. **2** open; frank. ▶ **ingenuously** *adverb* **ingenuousness** *noun* [Say in JEN yoo us]

ingest *verb* take in (food etc.); eat. ▶ **ingestion** *noun* [Say in JEST]

inglorious *adjective* causing feelings of shame: *an inglorious chapter in our history.* ▶ **ingloriously** *adverb*

ingot *noun* a usu. oblong piece of cast metal, esp. of gold, silver, or steel. [Say IN gut]

ingrain *verb* implant (a habit, belief, or attitude) ineradicably in a person.

ingrained *adjective* **1** deeply rooted: *property rights are ingrained in our legal system.* **2** (of dirt etc.) deeply embedded.

ingrate *noun* an ungrateful person. [Say IN grate]

ingratiate *verb* (**ingratiates**, **ingratiated**, **ingratiating**) PHRASES **ingratiate oneself with** try to gain favour with someone by doing things to please them, praising them, etc.: *a social climber who had tried to ingratiate herself with the city gentry.* ▶ **ingratiating** *adjective* **ingratiatingly** *adverb* [Say in GRAY shee ate]

ingratitude *noun* a lack of due gratitude.

ingredient *noun* **1** any of the foods that are combined to make a particular dish. **2** any of the things or qualities of which something is made: *the ingredients of a good mystery story.*

in-group *noun* a small exclusive group of people with a common interest.

ingrowing *adjective* growing inwards, esp. (of a toenail) growing into the flesh.

ingrown *adjective* (of a toenail etc.) grown into the flesh.

inhabit *verb* (**inhabits**, **inhabited**, **inhabiting**) (of a person or animal) dwell in; occupy (a region, town, house, etc.). ▶ **inhabitable** *adjective* **inhabitant** *noun*

inhabited *adjective* having inhabitants; lived-in: *an inhabited planet.*

inhalant *noun* **1** a medicinal preparation for inhaling. **2** a substance inhaled by drug abusers. [Say in HAY l'nt]

inhalation *noun* the act of inhaling or breathing in: *the inhalation of airborne particles ◊ with every inhalation air passes over the vocal cords.* [Say in huh LAY sh'n]

inhale *verb* (**inhales**, **inhaled**, **inhaling**) **1** breathe in. **2** take (esp. tobacco smoke) into the lungs. **3** *informal* devour (food etc.) rapidly: *inhaled the meal.*

inhaler *noun* a portable device for administering a medicinal or anaesthetic gas or vapour, esp. to relieve nasal or bronchial congestion, e.g. in asthmatics.

inherent *adjective* existing in something, esp. as a permanent or characteristic attribute: *the inherent dangers of mountain climbing ◊ an inherent weakness in the design of the machine.* **2** (of a right) vested in a person or group: *the inherent right of self-government.* ▶ **inherently** *adverb* [Say in HAIR int]

inherit *verb* (**inherits**, **inherited**, **inheriting**) **1** receive (property, rank, title, etc.) by legal descent or succession. **2** receive or have from a predecessor or predecessors in office etc.: *inherited a lot of problems.* **3** come into possession of (clothing, etc.) from someone else: *inherits all her clothes from her sisters.*

4 derive (a characteristic, disorder, etc.) genetically from one's ancestors.

inheritance *noun* **1** something that is inherited. **2** the action of inheriting.

inheritor *noun* an heir; a person who inherits.

inhibit *verb* (**inhibits**, **inhibited**, **inhibiting**) **1** hinder, restrain, or prevent (an action or progress): *a lack of oxygen may inhibit brain development in the unborn child.* **2** prevent from acting freely: *the manager's presence inhibited them from airing their problems.*

inhibited *adjective* unable to express feelings or impulses.

inhibition *noun* **1** *Psychology* a restraint on the direct expression of an instinct. **2** a feeling of nervousness or embarrassment which prevents one from relaxing or behaving naturally: *has inhibitions about singing in public.* [Say in huh BISH'n]

inhibitor *noun* **1** a thing which inhibits someone or something. **2** a substance which slows down or prevents a particular chemical reaction or other process or reduces the activity of a particular reactant, catalyst, or enzyme. ▶ **inhibitory** *adjective*

inhospitable *adjective* **1** not hospitable. **2** (of a region, coast, etc.) not providing shelter etc. [Say in hoss PITTA bull]

in-house • *adjective* done or existing within an institution, company, etc.: *an in-house project.* • *adverb* internally, without outside assistance.

inhuman *adjective* **1** (of a person, conduct, etc.) brutal; unfeeling; barbarous. **2** not seeming to be produced by a human being and therefore frightening: *there was a strange inhuman sound.* **3** not suitable for humans: *miraculous survival in inhuman conditions.*

inhumane *adjective* not humane. ▶ **inhumanely** *adverb*

inhumanity *noun* (*plural* **inhumanities**) **1** brutality; barbarousness; callousness. **2** an inhumane act.

inhumanly *adverb* in an inhuman manner.

inimical *adjective* harmful: *these measures are inimical to society's well-being.* [Say in IMM ick ul]

inimitable *adjective* impossible to imitate. [Say in IMM it a bull]

iniquitous *adjective* very unfair or wrong; wicked: *an iniquitous system of government.* [Say in ICKWA tus]

Unfairness or inequality is **inequity**.

iniquity *noun* (*plural* **iniquities**) **1** wickedness. **2** a gross injustice. [Say in ICKWA tee]

initial • *adjective* of, existing at, or occurring at the beginning; first: *initial stage.* • *noun* **1** (usu. in *plural*) the first letters of two or more names of a person, or of words forming any name or phrase. **2** (also **initial letter**, **initial consonant**) a letter or consonant at the beginning of a word. • *verb* (**initials**, **initialled**, **initialling**) mark or sign with one's initials.

initialization *noun* *Computing* **1** the act or process of initializing an operation or program. **2** the computer operations involved in this.

initialize *verb* (**initializes**, **initialized**, **initializing**) **1** *Computing* **a** set to the value or put in the condition appropriate to the start of an operation. **b** format (a disk). **2** designate by or use an initial or initials instead of the full name.

initially *adverb* at first: *initially, he was excited.*

initiate • *verb* (**initiates**, **initiated**, **initiating**) **1** begin, introduce; set going; originate. **2 a** (usu. foll. by *into*) admit (a person) into a society, an office, a secret, etc., esp. with a ritual. **b** (usu. foll. by *in, into*) instruct (a

person) in science, art, etc. • *noun* a person who has been newly initiated; a beginner, a novice. ► **initiation** *noun* [Say i NISHY ate for the verb, i NISHY it for the noun and adjective; for *initiation* say i nishy AY sh'n]

initiative *noun* **1** the ability to initiate things: *he lacks initiative*. **2** the action of initiating something or of taking the first step or the lead. **b** a proposal made by one group, nation, etc. to another, with a view to improving relations between them: *a peace initiative*. PHRASES **on one's own initiative** without being prompted by others. **take the initiative** (usu. foll. by *in* + verbal noun) be the first to take action. [Say i NISHA tiv]

initiator *noun* a person or thing that initiates someone or something.

inject *verb* **1 a** (usu. foll. by *into*) drive or force (a fluid, medicine, etc.) under pressure into a passage, cavity, or solid material. **b** (usu. foll. by *with*) introduce by injection. **c** administer medicine etc. to (a person) by injection. **2** introduce suddenly, with force, or by way of interruption; interject: *injected a note of realism*. **3** introduce (a new quality, element, etc.): *inject some fresh ideas* ◊ *inject $200,000 of new money into the community centre*. ► **injectable** *adjective & noun*

injection *noun* **1 a** the act of injecting. **b** an instance of this. **2** a liquid or solution (to be) injected. **3** = FUEL INJECTION.

injection-moulded *adjective* made by injecting heated material into a mould.

injection moulding *noun* the shaping of rubber or plastic articles by injecting heated material into a mould.

injector *noun* **1** a person or thing that injects something. **2** (also **fuel injector**) (in an internal combustion engine) the nozzle and valve through which fuel is sprayed into the combustion chamber.

in-joke *noun* a joke which can be appreciated by only a limited group because of shared experiences etc.

injudicious *adjective* showing lack of judgment or discretion: *her feelings were hurt by the injudicious remark*. ► **injudiciously** *adverb* [Say in joo DISH us]

injunction *noun* **1** an authoritative warning or order: *specific religious injunctions about proper behaviour*. **2** *Law* an official order given by a court of law which demands that something must or must not be done.

injure *verb* (**injures**, **injured**, **injuring**) **1** do esp. physical harm or damage to; hurt. **2** harm or impair: *injured her reputation*. **3** do injustice or wrong to.

injured *adjective* **1** harmed or hurt: *the injured passengers*. **2** offended; wronged: *in an injured tone*.

injurious *adjective* **1** hurtful. **2** (of language) insulting. ► **injuriously** *adverb* [Say in JURY us]

injury *noun* (*plural* **injuries**) **1** physical harm or damage: *suffered head injuries* ◊ *escaped without serious injury*. **2** esp. *Law* wrongful action or treatment, esp. the violation of another's rights. **3** damage to one's feelings, reputation, etc.

injustice *noun* **1** a lack of fairness or justice. **2** an unjust act. PHRASES **do a person an injustice** judge a person unfairly.

ink • *noun* **1** a coloured fluid used for writing, drawing, printing, etc. **2** a black liquid ejected by a cuttlefish, octopus, etc. to confuse a predator. **3** *informal* press coverage; publicity. • *verb* **1** (usu. foll. by *in*, *over*, etc.) a mark with ink. **b** go over or trace around with ink. **2** apply ink to. **3** *informal* sign, put one's signature to (a contract etc.). PHRASES **ink out** obliterate with ink.

ink blot test *noun* a Rorschach test.

ink-jet printer *noun* a printer that creates characters and graphics by firing a stream of minute ink drops at a surface from one or more banks of tiny nozzles.

inkling *noun* (often foll. by *of*) a slight knowledge or

suspicion; a hint: *he had no inkling of what was going on* ◊ *the first inkling I had that something was wrong*.

ink pad *noun* = STAMP PAD.

inky *adjective* (**inkier**, **inkiest**) of, as black as, or stained with ink.

inlaid • *verb* past and past participle of INLAY. • *adjective* (of a piece of furniture etc.) ornamented by inlaying.

inland • *adjective* **1** pertaining to or situated in the interior of a country. **2** inhabiting the interior of a country: *inland Algonquians*. **3** esp. *Cdn & Brit.* carried on within the limits of a country; domestic: *inland trade*. • *noun* **1** the parts of a country remote from the coast or borders; the interior. **2** *Cdn hist.* (as an *adjective*) denoting persons, places, or things involved with the inland fur trade: *an inland post*. • *adverb* **1** in or towards the interior of a country. **2** conducted or occurring away from the coast or borders: *inland fishing*. ► **inlander** *noun*

inland navigation *noun* transportation by rivers and canals.

Inland Tlingit *noun* (*plural* **Inland Tlingit**) **1** a member of an Aboriginal group living in northern BC and the southern Yukon Territory. **2** the Tlingit language of this people.

in-law • *noun* (usu. in *plural*) a relative by marriage. • *combining form* denoting a relation by marriage: *father-in-law* ◊ *sister-in-law*.

in-law suite *noun* (also **in-law apartment**) an extension added or a room, suite, etc. renovated to form a small apartment within an existing house.

inlay • *verb* (**inlays**, **inlaid**, **inlaying**) **1** (usu. foll. by *in*) embed (a thing in another) so that the surfaces are even. **2** (usu. foll. by *with*) ornament (a thing) by inserting another material in its surface in a decorative design. • *noun* **1** inlaid work. **2** a piece of material inlaid or prepared for inlaying. **3** a filling shaped to fit a tooth cavity.

inlet *noun* **1** a small arm of the ocean, a lake, or a river. **2** a place or means of entry: *an air inlet*.

in-line *adjective* **1 a** having parts arranged in a line. **b** (of an internal combustion engine) having usu. vertical cylinders arranged in one or more rows. **2** involving, employing, or forming part of a continuous, usu. linear, sequence of operations or machines, as in an assembly line.

in-line skate *noun* a skate resembling an ice skate, but having a line of usu. four rubber wheels instead of a blade, for use on paved surfaces etc. ► **in-line skater** *noun* **in-line skating** *noun*

inmate *noun* a person confined in a prison, hospital, etc.

in memoriam • *preposition* in memory of (a dead person). • *noun* a written article or notice etc. in memory of a dead person. [Say in muh MORY um]

inmost *adjective* **1** most inward. **2** most intimate.

inn *noun* **1** a small hotel, esp. in the country. **2** a tavern.

innards *plural noun* *informal* **1** entrails. **2** the inner workings (of an engine etc.). [Say IN urdz]

innate *adjective* **1** inborn; natural: *an innate sense of style*. **2** originating in the mind. ► **innately** *adverb* [Say in ATE]

inner • *adjective* **1** further in; inside; interior: *the inner compartment*. **b** further inshore, nearer the land: *inner islands*. **2** (of thoughts, feelings, etc.) deeper, more secret. **3** designating the mind or soul; mental; spiritual. **4** closest to the centre of power etc.: *inner cabinet* ◊ *inner circle*. • *noun* the inner part of something.

inner child *noun* **1** a person's supposed original or authentic self, esp. regarded as damaged or concealed by negative childhood experiences. **2** that part of an

individual's personality which manifests itself in or enjoys childish activities.

inner city *noun* the central area of a city, esp. if dilapidated, overcrowded, impoverished, etc.

inner ear *noun* the semicircular canals and cochlea, which form the organs of balance and hearing and are embedded in the temporal bone.

innermost *adjective* **1** (of thoughts or feelings) most private and deeply felt: *innermost beliefs and convictions*. **2** furthest in; closest to the centre: *the innermost layer*.

inner tube *noun* an inflatable rubber tube in a tire.

inning *noun* each of the divisions of a baseball game during which both sides have a turn at bat.

innkeeper *noun* a person who manages or owns an inn.

innocence *noun* **1** the state, quality, or fact of being innocent of a crime or offence: *they must prove their innocence*. **2** lack of guile or corruption; purity: *the healthy bloom in her cheeks gave her an aura of innocence*.

innocent • *adjective* **1** free from moral wrong; sinless. **2** (usu. foll. by *of*) not guilty (of a crime etc.). **3** free from responsibility for an event yet suffering its consequences: *innocent bystanders*. **4** simple; guileless; naive. **5** not intending to hurt or offend: *an innocent question*. **6** (foll. by *of*) *informal* without, lacking: *produced a textbook innocent of analysis*. • *noun* **1** an innocent person, esp. a young child. **2** a person involved by chance in a situation, esp. a victim of crime or war. **3** (in *plural*) the young children killed by Herod after the birth of Jesus. ▶ **innocently** *adverb*

innocuous *adjective* not harmful or offensive: *it was an innocuous question*. ▶ **innocuously** *adverb* [Say i NOCK yoo us]

innovate *verb* (**innovates, innovated, innovating**) **1** bring in new methods, ideas, etc. **2** (often foll. by *in*) make changes: *the car manufacturer must innovate in design*. **3** introduce (a product) for the first time, esp. to the market: *innovating powerful antibiotics*. ▶ **innovation** *noun* **innovative** *adjective* **innovatively** *adverb* **innovativeness** *noun* **innovator** *noun*

inn-to-inn *adjective* designating a network of trails for cross-country skiing, snowmobiling, etc. on which inns are strategically located as rest stops.

Innu • *noun* (*plural* **Innu**) **1** a member of an Aboriginal people living in Labrador and northern Quebec (*see also* MONTAGNAIS, NASKAPI). **2** the Cree language of this people. • *adjective* of this people. [Say IN oo]

innuendo *noun* (*plural* **innuendoes** or **innuendos**) an indirect remark or hint, typically a suggestive or disparaging one: *she's always making sly innuendoes ◊ a constant torrent of innuendo, gossip, lies, and half-truths*. [Say in yoo END oh]

innumerable *adjective* too many to be counted. ▶ **innumerably** *adverb* [Say i NOO mur a bull or i NYOO mur a bull]

inoculate *verb* (**inoculates, inoculated, inoculating**) **1 a** treat (a person or animal) with a vaccine containing a dead or modified disease-causing agent, usu. by injection, to promote immunity against the disease. **b** introduce (an infective agent) into an organism. **c** introduce (cells or organisms) into a culture medium. **2** indoctrinate (a person) with ideas or opinions: *Americans are inoculated at birth against such values*. ▶ **inoculation** *noun* [Say i NOCK yoo late]

inoffensive *adjective* not objectionable or harmful: *a shy, inoffensive, and sensitive young girl*. ▶ **inoffensively** *adverb* **inoffensiveness** *noun*

inoperable *adjective* **1** *Surgery* that cannot be operated on successfully: *inoperable cancer*. **2** that cannot be operated; inoperative: *the airfield was bombed and made*

inoperable. **3** impractical, unworkable: *the procedures were inoperable*. [Say in OPERA bull]

inoperative *adjective* **1** not working or taking effect: *the radio was still inoperative*. **2** *Law* without practical force, invalid: *these regulations were made inoperative by the decision of the Supreme Court*. [Say in OPERA tiv]

inopportune *adjective* not appropriate, esp. as regards time; inconvenient: *the storm blew up at an inopportune moment*. ▶ **inopportunely** *adverb*

inordinate *adjective* beyond proper or normal limits; excessive: *inordinate delays*. ▶ **inordinately** *adverb* [Say in OR din it]

inorganic • *adjective* **1** not arising from natural growth: *asbestos is an inorganic fibre mined from rocks*. **2** of or denoting compounds which are not organic (broadly, compounds not containing carbon): *recent advances in inorganic chemistry*. **3** without organized physical structure. • *noun* an inorganic chemical.

in-patient *noun* a patient who stays in hospital for a period of days while receiving treatment.

input • *noun* **1 a** what is put in or taken in, or operated on by any process or system. **b** the total resources including raw materials, manpower, etc. necessary to production, which are deducted from output in calculating profits. **2** *Electronics* **a** a place where, or a device through which, energy, information, etc., enters a system. **b** energy supplied to a device or system; an electrical signal. **3** the information fed into a computer. **4** the action or process of putting in or feeding in. **5** a contribution of information etc. • *verb* (**inputs**; *past* and *past participle* **input** or **inputted**; **inputting**) (often foll. by *into*) **1** put in. **2** supply (data, programs, etc., to a computer, program, etc.).

input/output *adjective* *Computing etc.* of, relating to, or for input and output. Abbreviation: **I/O**.

inquest *noun* **1** *Law* an inquiry by a coroner's court into the cause of a sudden, unexplained, or suspicious death. **2** *informal* a discussion analyzing the outcome of a game etc.

inquire *verb* (**inquires, inquired, inquiring**) **1 a** (often foll. by *of*) seek information; ask a question (of a person). **b** ask for information as to: *inquired my name ◊ inquired whether we were coming*. **2** seek information formally; make a formal investigation. **3** (foll. by *after, for*) ask about a person, a person's health, etc. ▶ **inquirer** *noun* **inquiring** *adjective* **inquiringly** *adverb*

inquiry *noun* (*plural* **inquiries**) **1** an act or process of asking or seeking information. **2** a question, a query. **3** a formal or judicial investigation into a matter of public concern. [Say in QUIRE ee or IN kwuh ree]

inquisition *noun* **1** usu. *derogatory* **a** an intensive search or investigation. **b** a relentless, sustained, or unwelcome questioning of a person. **2** (**the Inquisition**) *Catholicism hist.* **a** an ecclesiastical court established *c.*1232 for the detection of heretics, at a time when certain heretical groups were regarded as enemies of society. **b** (also **Spanish Inquisition**) a similar but separate body, established by the Spanish crown in 1478 and directed originally against converts from Judaism and Islam. [Say in kwuh ZISH'n]

inquisitive *adjective* **1** seeking knowledge; inquiring. **2** unduly curious; prying. ▶ **inquisitively** *adverb* **inquisitiveness** *noun* [Say in KWIZZA tiv]

inquisitor *noun* **1** a person making an inquiry, esp. one seen to be excessively harsh or searching: *the professional inquisitors of the press*. **2** *hist.* an officer of the Inquisition. [Say in KWIZZA tur]

inroad *noun* (usu. in *plural*) **1** an encroachment; a using up of resources etc.: *makes inroads on my time*. **2** an advance: *making inroads into a difficult market*.

inrush *noun* (*plural* **inrushes**) a rushing in; an influx. ▶ **inrushing** *adjective & noun*

insane *adjective* **1 a** mentally deranged; not of sound mind. **b** characteristic of an insane person: *an insane laugh*. **2** (of an action) extremely foolish; irrational. ▶ **insanely** *adverb* **insanity** *noun* (*plural* **insanities**)

insatiable *adjective* unable to be satisfied: *has an insatiable appetite ◊ an insatiable desire for success*. ▶ **insatiably** *adverb* [Say in SAY shuh bull]

inscribe *verb* (**inscribes**, **inscribed**, **inscribing**) **1 a** (usu. foll. by *in*, *on*) write or carve (words etc.) on stone, metal, paper, a book, etc. **b** (usu. foll. by *with*) mark (a sheet, tablet, etc.) with characters. **2** (usu. foll. by *to*) write an informal dedication (to a person) in or on (a book etc.). **3** *Math* draw (a figure) within another so that some or all of their boundaries touch but do not intersect (*compare* CIRCUMSCRIBE).

inscription *noun* **1** words inscribed, esp. on a monument, coin, stone, or in a book etc. **2** the act or action of inscribing, esp. the informal dedication of a book etc.

inscrutable *adjective* impossible to understand or interpret: *Guy looked blankly inscrutable*. ▶ **inscrutably** *adverb* [Say in SCREW tuh bull]

inseam *noun* the inner seam on the leg of a pair of pants, extending from crotch to cuff.

insect *noun* **1** any arthropod of the class Insecta, having a head, thorax, abdomen, two antennae, three pairs of thoracic legs, and usu. one or two pairs of thoracic wings. **2** (loosely) any other small invertebrate animal esp. with several pairs of legs.

insecticidal *adjective* used for killing insects. [Say in secta SIDE ul]

insecticide *noun* a substance used for killing insects. [Say in SECTA side]

insectivore *noun* **1** any animal that feeds on insects, esp. a mammal of the order Insectivora, including shrews, hedgehogs, and moles. **2** any plant which captures and absorbs insects. ▶ **insectivorous** *adjective* [Say in SECTA vore, in sec TIVVA russ]

insecure *adjective* **1** (of a person or state of mind) uncertain; lacking confidence. **2 a** unsafe, not firm or fixed. **b** (of ice, ground, etc.) not providing good support; liable to give way. ▶ **insecurely** *adverb* **insecurity** *noun* (*plural* **insecurities**)

inseminate *verb* (**inseminates**, **inseminated**, **inseminating**) introduce semen into (a female) by natural or artificial means. ▶ **insemination** *noun* [Say in SEMMA nate, in semma NATION]

insensibility *noun* (*plural* **insensibilities**) **1** unconsciousness: *why do we continue to watch a sport where two people try to punch each other into a state of insensibility?* **2** a lack of mental feeling or emotion; hardness: *I am tired of his touchiness and insensibility*. **3** indifference: *I am tired of your insensibility to my needs*.

insensible *adjective* **1 a** without one's mental faculties; unconscious: *they knocked each other insensible with their fists ◊ was insensible with drink*. **b** (of the extremities etc.) numb; without feeling: *the insensible tip of the beak*. **2** unaware; indifferent: *insensible to her needs*. **3** without emotion; callous. ▶ **insensibly** *adverb*

insensitive *adjective* (often foll. by *to*) **1** showing or feeling no sympathetic or emotional response; indifferent, callous. **2** not sensitive to physical stimuli. **3** (of a substance, device, etc.) not susceptible or responsive to some physical influence, e.g. light etc. ▶ **insensitively** *adverb* **insensitivity** *noun*

inseparability *noun* the quality or condition of being unable to be separated. [Say in sepper a BILLA tee]

inseparable *adjective* unable or unwilling to be

separated: *inseparable friends*. ▶ **inseparably** *adverb* [Say in SEPPER a bull]

insert ● *verb* **1** place, fit, or thrust (a thing) into another: *insert the key in the lock*. **2** introduce (a letter, word, etc.) into a piece of text etc.: *inserted a new paragraph*. ● *noun* something inserted, e.g. an additional section in a magazine, a piece of cloth in a garment, a shot in a film, etc. ▶ **insertable** *adjective*

insertion *noun* **1 a** the action of inserting something: *the insertion of a line or two into the script*. **b** something that is inserted. **2** each appearance of an advertisement in a newspaper etc.

in-service ● *adjective* (of training) intended for those actively engaged in the profession or activity concerned. ● *noun* an in-service training session.

inset ● *noun* **1** something set in or inserted: *an inset photo*. **2 a** a small map, photograph, etc., inserted within the border of a larger one. **b** an extra page or pages inserted in a folded sheet or in a book; an insert. **3** a piece set into a garment as decoration etc. ● *verb* (**insets**, **inset**, **insetting**) **1** set or put in as an inset; insert. **2** decorate with an inset.

inshallah *interjection* if Allah wills it. [Say in SHALA]

inshore ● *adjective* **1** situated at sea close to the shore. **2** of or pertaining to fishing conducted from small boats in coastal waters. ● *adverb* **1** at sea but close to the shore. **2** towards the shore.

inside ● *noun* **1 a** the inner side or surface of a thing. **b** the inner part; the interior. **2 a** the side of a path or sidewalk furthest away from the road. **b** the part of a track or curving road nearest to the inner or shorter side of the curve. **3** (usu. in *plural*) *informal* **a** the stomach and bowels: *something wrong with my insides*. **b** the operative part of a machine etc. **4** *informal* a position affording information not available to outsiders: *knows someone on the inside*. ● *adjective* **1** situated on or in, or derived from, the inside. **2** (of information etc.) available only to those on the inside. **3** *Baseball* **a** (of a pitched ball) missing the plate on the batter's side. **b** (of the strike zone) nearest the batter. ● *adverb* **1 a** on, in, or to the inside. **b** indoors. **2** *slang* in prison. **3** *Cdn* (*North*) within one of the Territories. ● *preposition* **1** on the inner side of; within. **2** in less than: *inside an hour*. PHRASES **inside of** *informal* in less than (a week etc.).

inside job *noun* *informal* a crime committed by or involving the help of a person living or working on the premises burgled etc.

inside out ● *adverb* with the inner surface turned outwards. ● *adjective* (**inside-out**) in this condition. PHRASES **know a thing inside out** know a thing thoroughly. **turn inside out 1** turn the inner surface outwards. **2** *informal* cause confusion or a mess in.

insider *noun* **1** a person who is within a society, organization, etc. **2** a person privy to a secret, esp. when using it to gain advantage.

insider trading *noun* *Stock Market* the illegal use of confidential information as a basis for share trading.

inside track *noun* **1** a position of advantage. **2** the track of a racecourse etc. which is shorter, because of the curve.

insidious *adjective* proceeding or progressing inconspicuously but harmfully: *an insidious disease ◊ the insidious effects of polluted water*. ▶ **insidiously** *adverb* **insidiousness** *noun* [Say in SIDDY us]

insight *noun* **1 a** the capacity of understanding hidden truths etc., esp. of character or situations. **b** an understanding of this kind. **2** a sudden perception of the solution to a problem. ▶ **insightful** *adjective*

insignia *noun* (treated as *singular* or *plural*) a badge or distinguishing mark of military rank, office, or membership in an organization; an official emblem:

had the insignia of a captain on his hat ◊ leather jackets with biker insignia. [Say in SIG nee uh]

insignificance *noun* the quality or condition of being unimportant, undistinguished, or meaningless.

insignificant *adjective* **1** unimportant; trifling. **2** (of a person) undistinguished. **3** meaningless.

insincere *adjective* not sincere; not candid. ▶ **insincerely** *adverb* **insincerity** *noun*

insinuate *verb* (**insinuates**, **insinuated**, **insinuating**) **1** convey indirectly or obliquely; hint: *insinuated that she was lying*. **2 a** introduce (oneself, a person, etc.) into favour, office, etc., by subtle manipulation: *in the first act, the villain insinuates himself into the household of the man he intends to kill*. **b** slide (a thing, oneself, etc.) slowly and smoothly into a position: *she insinuated her right hand under his arm*. ▶ **insinuation** *noun* [Say in SIN yoo ate]

insipid *adjective* **1** lacking vigour or interest; dull, boring: *after an hour of insipid conversation, I left*. **2** lacking flavour: *a cup of insipid coffee*. [Say in SIP id]

insist *verb* maintain or demand positively and assertively: *insisted that he was innocent*. PHRASES **insist on** insistently maintain or make a persistent demand for (something): *I insist on being present*.

insistence *noun* the act of insisting on something: *Sally's insistence on doing the dishes right after the meal*.

insistent *adjective* **1** insisting; demanding positively or continually. **2** regular and repeated; demanding attention: *the insistent rattle of the window*. ▶ **insistently** *adverb*

in situ *adverb* in its original or proper place: *mosaics and frescoes have been left in situ*. [Say in SIT yoo]

insofar *adverb* to the extent that: *insofar as aboriginal people are concerned, our justice system needs to be modified*.

insole *noun* **1** a removable sole worn in a boot or shoe for comfort, warmth, etc. **2** the fixed inner sole of a boot or shoe.

insolence *noun* rudeness, disrespect. [Say in SUH lince]

insolent *adjective* rude, disrespectful; offensively contemptuous or arrogant: *nothing but insolent, brazen, American tourists ◊ her face broke into an insolent grin*. ▶ **insolently** *adverb* [Say IN suh l'nt]

insoluble *adjective* **1** (of a difficulty, problem, etc.) incapable of being solved: *the problem is not insoluble*. **2** incapable of being dissolved in a liquid: *once dry, the paint becomes insoluble in water*. [Say in SAUL yoo bull]

insolvency *noun* (*plural* **insolvencies**) the state or condition of being unable to pay one's debts. [Say in SOLVE in see]

insolvent • *adjective* unable to pay one's debts: *the $150-million debt of the insolvent department store chain*. • *noun* a debtor. [Say in SOLVE int]

insomnia *noun* habitual sleeplessness; inability to sleep. ▶ **insomniac** *noun* & *adjective* [Say in SOMNY uh, in SOMNY ack]

insouciance *noun* lack of concern: *she hid her worries behind an air of insouciance*. [Say in SOO see ince]

insouciant *adjective* carefree; unconcerned: *he remained insouciant, convinced that his scheme would work*. ▶ **insouciantly** *adverb* [Say in SOO see int]

inspect *verb* **1** look closely at or into, esp. to assess quality or check for shortcomings. **2** examine (a document etc.) officially. ▶ **inspection** *noun*

inspector *noun* **1** a person who inspects. **2** an official employed to supervise a service, system, machine, etc., and make reports: *building inspector*. **3** *Cdn* (in most police forces) a middle-ranking officer.

inspiration *noun* **1 a** a supposed force or influence on poets, artists, musicians, etc., stimulating creativity, ideas, etc. **b** a person, principle, faith, etc. as a source of esp. artistic creativity or moral fervour. **c** a similar

divine influence supposed to have led to the writing of Scripture etc. **2** a sudden brilliant, creative, or timely idea etc. **3** a drawing in of breath; inhalation. ▶ **inspirational** *adjective* **inspirationally** *adverb*

inspire *verb* (**inspires**, **inspired**, **inspiring**) **1** stimulate or arouse (a person) to esp. creative activity or moral fervour: *inspired her to write ◊ inspired by God*. **2 a** (usu. foll. by *with*) animate (a person) with a feeling. **b** (usu. foll. by *in*) create (a feeling) in a person. **3** prompt; give rise to: *the poem was inspired by the autumn*.

inspired *adjective* **1** (of a work of art etc.) as if prompted by or emanating from a supernatural source; characterized by inspiration: *an inspired speech*. **2** (of a guess) intuitive but accurate.

inspirer *noun* a person or thing that inspires someone or something: *this car is a real confidence inspirer*.

inspiring *adjective* exciting and encouraging one to do or feel something: *Laura is an inspiring teacher ◊ the book is less than inspiring*. ▶ **inspiringly** *adverb*

SPELL CHECK
in spite

Warning: the phrase **in spite** is always spelled as two words.

---

instability *noun* (*plural* **instabilities**) **1 a** a lack of stability. **b** an example of instability. **2** *Psychology* a tendency to unpredictable behaviour or erratic changes of mood. **3** a meteorological tendency towards precipitation, high winds, etc.

install *verb* (**installs**, **installed**, **installing**) **1** place (equipment, machinery, etc.) in position ready for use. **2** take (software), e.g. from a floppy disk, CD-ROM, etc., and place it in its permanent location from where it will be executed. **3** place (a person) in an office or rank with ceremony. **4** establish (a person etc.) in a place, condition, etc.: *installed herself at the head of the table*.

installation *noun* **1** the action or process of installing something or someone, or of being installed: *the installation of a central air conditioner ◊ the use of the system could be followed by installations on other vehicles*. **2** a piece of apparatus, a machine, etc. installed. **3 a** a large work of art, esp. a sculpture or mixed media piece, specially created or constructed for display in a gallery, museum, or other site. **b** an exhibition of such works. **4** a subsidiary military or industrial establishment.

installer *noun* **1** a person who installs machinery, equipment, etc.: *a qualified telephone installer*. **2** *Computing* a program which installs another program: *insert the CD-ROM and run the installer*.

instalment *noun* (also **installment**) **1** one of several usu. equal payments for something, spread over an agreed period of time. **2** any of several parts, esp. of a television or radio series or magazine story, broadcast or published in sequence at intervals.

instance • *noun* **1** an example or illustration of: *another instance of his lack of determination*. **2** a particular case: *that's not true in this instance*. **3** *Law* a legal suit. • *verb* (**instances**, **instanced**, **instancing**) cite (a fact, case, etc.) as an instance: *I refer to the situation instanced above*. PHRASES **for instance** as an example. **in the first** (or **second** etc.) **instance** in the first (or second etc.) place; at the first (or second etc.) stage of a proceeding.

instant • *adjective* **1 a** occurring immediately: *instant results*. **b** designed to produce quick or immediate results: *instant camera*. **2 a** (of food etc.) processed to allow quick preparation. **b** prepared hastily and with little effort: *I have no instant solution*. • *noun* **1** a precise moment of time, esp. the present: *come here this instant*.

2 a short space of time: *was there in an instant*. **3** an instant food or beverage, esp. instant coffee.

instantaneous *adjective* **1** occurring or done in an instant or instantly. **2** *Physics* existing at a particular instant: *measurement of the instantaneous velocity*. ▶ **instantaneously** *adverb* [Say in st'n TAY nee us]

instantly *adverb* immediately; at once.

instant replay *noun* **1** the recording and immediate rebroadcasting of part of a televised sports event, often in slow motion. **2** the part recorded and rebroadcast. **3** any immediate recollection, re-enactment, or review of an event, conversation, etc.

instead *adverb* **1** (foll. by *of*) as a substitute or alternative to; in place of: *stayed instead of going*. **2** as an alternative: *took me instead* (compare STEAD).

instep *noun* **1** the inner arch of the foot between the toes and the ankle. **2** the part of a shoe etc. fitting over or under this.

instigate *verb* (**instigates, instigated, instigating**) **1** bring about by incitement or persuasion; provoke: *accused of instigating racial violence*. **2** urge on, incite (a person etc.) to esp. a foolhardy or drastic act: *arrested on charges of instigating landless peasants to violence*. ▶ **instigation** *noun* **instigator** *noun* [Say INSTA gate]

instill *verb* (**instills, instilled, instilling**) **1** introduce (a feeling, idea, etc.) into a person's mind etc. gradually: *the Quiet Revolution instilled a sense of pride and accomplishment among Quebeckers* ◊ *instill confidence into her students*. **2** put (a liquid) into something in drops.

instinct *noun* **1 a** an innate, usu. fixed, pattern of behaviour in most animals in response to certain stimuli. **b** a similar propensity in human beings to act without conscious intention. **2** (usu. foll. by *for*) unconscious skill; intuition.

instinctive *adjective* **1** relating to or prompted by instinct. **2** apparently unconscious or automatic: *an instinctive reaction*. ▶ **instinctively** *adverb*

instinctual *adjective* *Psychology* based on natural instinct in response to a basic biological need; not learned. ▶ **instinctually** *adverb*

institute • *noun* **1 a** a society or organization for the promotion of science, education, etc. **b** a building used by an institute. **2** a unit within a university, college, etc. devoted to advanced teaching and research in a specialized field. • *verb* (**institutes, instituted, instituting**) **1** establish; found. **2 a** initiate (an inquiry etc.). **b** begin (proceedings) in a court.

institution *noun* **1** the action of instituting something: *a delay in the institution of proceedings*. **2 a** a society or organization founded esp. for charitable, religious, educational, or social purposes. **b** a business or governmental establishment providing a service to the public, e.g. a bank, prison, etc.: *financial institution*. **c** a building used by an institution. **3** a residential centre for the care of psychiatric or disabled patients etc. **4** an established law, practice, or custom: *the institution of marriage*. **5** *informal* a well-established and familiar person, custom, or object: *he soon became something of a national institution*.

institutional *adjective* **1** of or like an institution. **2** typical of institutions, esp. in being regimented or not imaginative. **3** (of religion) expressed or organized through institutions (churches etc.).

institutionalization *noun* **1** the process of establishing a practice or activity as a convention or norm in an organization or culture: *new courses focusing on women in history have led to the institutionalization of women's studies at the university level*. **2** an act of placing someone in an institution: *the government is seeking alternatives to institutionalization for mental health patients*.

institutionalize *verb* (**institutionalizes,**

institutionalized, institutionalizing) **1** place or keep (a person) in an institution. **2** convert into an institution; make institutional.

institutionalized *adjective* **1** (of a prisoner, long-term patient, etc.) made apathetic and dependent after a long period in an institution. **2** established in practice or custom: *institutionalized racism*.

institutionally *adverb* as an institution: *the Church was institutionally weak*.

in-store • *adjective* available or occurring inside a store: *an in-store promotion*. • *adverb* inside a store.

instruct *verb* **1** teach (a person) a subject etc.: *instructed her in French*. **2** command: *instructed him to fill in the hole*. **3** (of a judge) advise (a jury), prior to its deliberations, of the legal principles applicable to the case.

instruction *noun* **1** a direction; an order: *read the instructions*. **2** teaching: *individualized instruction*. **3** (in *plural*) a judge's directions to a jury, prior to its deliberations, on the legal principles applicable to the case under consideration. **4** a direction in a computer program defining and effecting an operation. ▶ **instructional** *adjective*

instructive *adjective* tending to instruct; conveying a lesson; enlightening: *found the experience instructive*.

instructor *noun* **1** a person who instructs. **2** a university teacher ranking below assistant professor.

instrument *noun* **1** a tool or implement, esp. for delicate or scientific work. **2** (also **musical instrument**) a device for producing musical sounds by vibration, wind, percussion, etc. **3** a thing used in performing an action: *drama as an instrument of learning*. **4** a measuring device, esp. in a car or aircraft, serving to gauge position, speed, etc. **5** a formal, esp. legal, document. **6** an investment option such as derivatives, stocks, bonds, etc.

instrumental • *adjective* **1** serving as a means: *was instrumental in finding the money*. **2** (of music) performed on instruments, without singing (compare VOCAL *adjective* 3). **3** of, or arising from, an instrument: *instrumental error*. • *noun* a piece of music performed by instruments. ▶ **instrumentalist** *noun*

instrumentation *noun* **1 a** the arrangement or composition of music for a particular group of musical instruments. **b** the instruments used in any one piece of music. **2 a** the design, provision, or use of instruments in industry, science, etc. **b** such instruments collectively.

insubordinate *adjective* refusing to obey instructions or show respect. ▶ **insubordination** *noun* [Say in suh BOR duh nit, in suh bor duh NAY sh'n]

insubstantial *adjective* **1** lacking solidity or substance; weak, flimsy. **2** not real; imaginary: *an insubstantial vision*. **3** not large in size or amount: *an insubstantial raise*. ▶ **insubstantiality** *noun*

insufferable *adjective* **1** intolerable. **2** unbearably arrogant or conceited etc. ▶ **insufferably** *adverb*

insufficiency *noun* (*plural* **insufficiencies**) **1** the condition of being insufficient: *insufficiency of adequate housing* ◊ *there have been demands to redress such insufficiencies*. **2** the inability of a bodily organ to perform its normal function: *renal insufficiency*.

insufficient *adjective* not sufficient; inadequate. ▶ **insufficiently** *adverb*

insular *adjective* **1** of or like an island: *the forests of insular Newfoundland*. **2** ignorant of or indifferent to cultures, peoples, etc., outside one's own experience: *a stubbornly insular farming people*. ▶ **insularity** *noun* [Say IN sue ler, in sue LERRA tee]

insulate *verb* (**insulates, insulated, insulating**) **1** prevent the passage of electricity, heat, or sound from (a wire, room, etc.) by interposing non-

conductors. **2** detach (a person or thing) from its surroundings; isolate: *we in the West are totally insulated from real life*.

insulation *noun* **1** the action of insulating or the condition of being insulated against the passage of electricity, heat, or sound. **2** materials used for this, such as foam or fibreglass.

insulator *noun* **1** a thing or substance used for insulation against electricity, heat, or sound. **2** an insulating device to support telephone wires etc. **3** a device preventing contact between electrical conductors.

Insulbrick *noun Cdn* simulated-brick asphalt siding used on houses etc. [Say IN sul brick]

insulin *noun* **1** a hormone produced in the pancreas, which controls the amount of sugar absorbed by the body. **2** a commercial preparation of this, used in the treatment of diabetes. [Say IN suh lin or IN syuh lin]

insult • *verb* **1** speak to or treat with scornful abuse or indignity. **2** offend the self-respect or modesty of. • *noun* **1** an insulting remark or action. **2** something so worthless or contemptible as to be offensive: *an insult to his intelligence*. PHRASES **add insult to injury** behave offensively as well as harmfully. ▶ **insulting** *adjective* **insultingly** *adverb*

insuperable *adjective* **1** (of a barrier) impossible to surmount. **2** (of a difficulty etc.) impossible to overcome: *the problem isn't insuperable*. [Say in SUPER uh bull]

insurable *adjective* denoting income on which employment insurance premiums are paid, or the work for which one receives such income. [Say in SURE uh bull]

insurance *noun* **1** the act or an instance of insuring property, life, etc. **2 a** a sum paid for this; a premium. **b** a sum paid out as compensation for theft, damage, loss, etc. **3** the business of providing insurance policies. **4** = INSURANCE POLICY. **5** a measure taken to provide for a possible contingency: *take an umbrella as insurance*. **6** a system of contributions from workers and employers, or one funded entirely by tax revenue, to provide government assistance in sickness, unemployment, etc.: *health insurance*.

insurance policy *noun* a contract of insurance.

insure *verb* (**insures, insured, insuring**) **1** secure the payment of a sum of money in the event of loss or damage to (property, life, a person, etc.) by regular payments or premiums: *insured the house for $250,000* ◊ *we have insured against flood damage*. **2** = ENSURE.

insured • *adjective* covered by insurance. • *noun* (usu. as **the insured**) a person etc. covered by insurance.

insurer *noun* a person or company offering insurance policies for premiums; an underwriter.

insurgency *noun* (*plural* **insurgencies**) an attempt to take control of a country by force; revolt, rebellion: *the army called for a state of emergency to fight against the Communist insurgency*. [Say in SURGE see]

insurgent • *adjective* rising in active revolt; rebellious. • *noun* a rebel; a revolutionary: *US support for anti-government insurgents in Nicaragua*. [Say in SURGE int]

insurmountable *adjective* unable to be surmounted or overcome.

insurrection *noun* a rising in open resistance to established authority; a rebellion.

intact *adjective* entire; undamaged.

intake *noun* **1** the action of taking something in. **2 a** a number (of people etc.) or the amount taken in or received: *this year's intake of students*. **b** such people etc. **3** a place where water is taken into a channel or pipe from a river, or fuel or air enters an engine etc.

intangible • *adjective* **1** that exists but that is difficult to describe, understand, or measure: *the building had an*

intangible air of sadness ◊ *the benefits are intangible*. **2** (of a business asset, e.g. a patent, trademark, or copyright) saleable, but having no value in itself. • *noun* something that cannot be precisely measured or assessed. ▶ **intangibly** *adverb* [Say in TAN juh bull]

integer *noun* a whole number. [Say INTA jur]

integral • *adjective* **1 a** of a whole or necessary to the completeness of a whole. **b** forming a whole: *integral design*. **c** having all the parts that are necessary for something to be complete: *an integral system*. **d** included as part of the whole, rather than supplied from outside: *a machine with an integral power source*. **2** *Math* **a** of or denoted by an integer. **b** involving only integers, esp. as coefficients of a function. • *noun Math* **1** a quantity of which a given function is the derivative, i.e. which yields that function when undifferentiated, and which may express the area under the curve of a graph of the function. **2** a function satisfying a given differential equation. [For the adjective say INTA grul or in TEG rul; for the noun say INTA grul]

integral calculus *noun* mathematics concerned with finding integrals, their properties and application, etc. (*compare* DIFFERENTIAL CALCULUS).

integrally *adverb* **1** in an integral way; constituting or resulting in a whole: *our well-being is integrally connected with the natural world*. **2** in a permanent manner, so that things that are joined cannot be detached or separated: *an integrally bonded adhesive inner lining*. [Say in TEGRA lee]

integrate *verb* (**integrates, integrated, integrating**) **1** combine (parts) into a whole: *efforts to integrate federal and provincial taxes*. **2** bring or come into equal participation in or membership of society, a school, etc.: *made no effort to integrate with the local community*. **3** desegregate, esp. racially (a school etc.).

integrated *adjective* **1** combined into a whole; united; undivided: *integrated policies of forestry and wildlife management*. **2** (of an institution, group, etc.) not divided by considerations of race, culture, ability, etc.; not segregated.

integrated circuit *noun* a small chip etc. of material replacing several separate components in a conventional electrical circuit.

integrated school *noun Cdn* (*Nfld*) a public school established, maintained, and operated jointly by members of the Anglican, United, and Presbyterian Churches and the Salvation Army.

integrated services digital network *noun* a telecommunications network through which sound, images, and data can be transmitted as digitized signals. Abbreviation: **ISDN**.

integration *noun* **1** the act or an instance of integrating. **2** the intermixing of persons previously segregated. **3** the combination of the diverse elements of perception etc. in a personality. **4** *Math* the process or an instance of obtaining the integral of a function.

integrative *adjective* causing or involving the combination of parts so that they become a whole: *by considering both human and physical aspects of the region, geographers have developed an integrative approach to the study of our world*. [Say INTA grate iv]

integrator *noun* a person or thing that integrates esp. computer systems. [Say INTA grate er]

integrity *noun* **1** moral uprightness; honesty: *a man of complete integrity*. **2** wholeness: *upholding territorial integrity and national sovereignty*. **3** the condition of being unified, unimpaired, or sound in construction: *the structural integrity of the novel*. [Say in TEGRA tee]

intellect *noun* **1 a** the faculty of reasoning, knowing, and thinking, as distinct from feeling. **b** the understanding or mental powers (of a particular person etc.). **2** a clever or knowledgeable person.

intellectual • *adjective* **1** of or relating to the intellect. **2 a** possessing a high level of understanding or intelligence. **b** valuing or interested in matters appealing to the intellect. **3** requiring, appealing to, or engaging the intellect. • *noun* **1** a person of superior intelligence. **2** a person who is interested in intellectual matters. **3** a person professionally engaged in intellectual activity.

intellectualism *noun* the exercise of the intellect at the expense of the emotions; an overemphasis on the intellect.

intellectualize *verb* (**intellectualizes**, **intellectualized**, **intellectualizing**) make intellectual; give an intellectual character to: *a tendency to intellectualize faith*.

intellectually *adverb* in terms of a person's mind or ability to think in a logical manner: *these students are intellectually gifted* ◊ *an intellectually stimulating book*.

intellectual property *noun* Law non-tangible property that is the result of creativity, such as patents, copyrights, etc.

intelligence *noun* **1 a** the intellect; the understanding. **b** (of a person or an animal) quickness of understanding and reasoning; wisdom. **2 a** the collection of information, esp. of military or political value: *intelligence operation*. **b** a group or agency that collects such information. **c** information so collected. **d** information in general; news.

intelligence quotient *noun* a number denoting the ratio of a person's intelligence to the statistical norm, 100 being average. Abbreviation: **IQ**.

intelligent *adjective* **1** having the faculty of understanding; possessing or showing intelligence, esp. of a high level: *intelligent life* ◊ *an intelligent remark*. **2 a** (of a device or machine) able to vary its behaviour in response to varying situations and requirements and past experience. **b** (esp. of a computer terminal) having its own data-processing capability (*opp.* DUMB *adjective* 5). **c** (of a building, office, etc.) equipped with sophisticated telecommunications and computer technology.

intelligent agent *noun* a computer program which can seek or sort information with minimal supervision by the user.

intelligently *adverb* in an intelligent manner.

intelligentsia *noun* **1** the class of intellectuals regarded as possessing culture and political initiative. **2** people doing intellectual work. [Say in tella GENT see uh]

intelligibility *noun* the ability of something to be understood: *the author's use of shorter sentences enhances the intelligibility of her work*. [Say in tella juh BILLA tee]

intelligible *adjective* (often foll. by *to*) able to be understood; comprehensible. ▶ **intelligibly** *adverb* [Say in TELLA juh bull]

Intelsat *noun* an international organization of countries operating a system of commercial communication satellites. [Say IN tell sat]

intemperance *noun* **1** a lack of moderation or self-control. **2** a tendency to overindulge, esp. in alcohol. [Say in TEMPER ince]

intemperate *adjective* **1** showing a lack of moderation or self-control: *a man given to brash, intemperate outbursts*. **2** characterized by excessive indulgence esp. in alcohol. ▶ **intemperately** *adverb* [Say in TEMPER it]

intend *verb* **1** have as one's purpose; propose: *we intend to go*. **2** design or destine (a person or a thing): *nature never intended us to fly*. **3** (often foll. by *as*) mean: *intended it as a warning*. **4 a** be meant for a person to have or use

etc.: *they are intended for the children*. **b** be designed for: *intended for a small child's hand*.

intendant *noun* (often **Intendant**) *hist.* a high-ranking administrative official in French, Portuguese, and Spanish provinces and colonies, responsible for economic development, settlement, and justice.

intended • *adjective* **1** done on purpose; intentional. **2** designed, meant: *the intended audience*. **3** future; prospective: *my intended spouse*. • *noun* *informal* one's fiancé or fiancée: *is this your intended?*

intense *adjective* **1** (of a quality, feeling, etc.) existing in a high degree; extremely strong, esp. so severe as to be difficult to withstand or endure: *intense cold*. **2 a** (of an emotion) deeply or strongly felt. **b** (of a person) extremely earnest and serious: *very intense about her music*. **c** (of an activity) characterized by emotional tension. **d** expressing strong emotion. **3** (of a colour) very strong or deep. **4** (of an action etc.) requiring a great deal of emotional, intellectual, or physical effort concentrated in a short time: *intense thought*. ▶ **intensely** *adverb*

intensification *noun* the process of becoming more intense: *Canada's participation in the Great War sparked a sudden intensification of nationalistic pride*.

intensifier *noun* **1** a word or prefix used to give force or emphasis, e.g. *really* in *my feet are really cold*. **2** a thing that intensifies.

intensify *verb* (**intensifies**, **intensified**, **intensifying**) **1 a** make (esp. something that causes stress) more intense. **b** increase the quantity or strength of (something). **2** (of any activity, esp. a conflict; also of emotions, colours, physical sensations) become much stronger, esp. rapidly.

intensity *noun* (*plural* **intensities**) **1** the quality of being intense. **2** concentration of feeling, emotional depth, earnestness, or passion. **3** esp. *Physics* the measurable amount of some quality, e.g. brightness etc.

intensive • *adjective* **1** characterized by a great deal of concentrated effort, usu. over a short period of time: *intensive study*. **2** (of agriculture) aiming to achieve the highest possible level of production within a limited area, esp. by using chemical and technological aids: *intensive farming methods*. **3** *Economics* making much use of: *labour-intensive*. **4** *Grammar* (of an adjective, adverb, etc.) expressing intensity; giving force, as *really* in *my feet are really cold*. • *noun* *Grammar* an intensifier.

intensive care *noun* **1** medical treatment with constant monitoring etc. of a dangerously ill patient. **2** a part of a hospital devoted to this.

intensively *adverb* **1** with a concentration of efforts on a single area or subject or in a short time: *we have negotiated intensively to resolve this dispute by the deadline*. **2** *Agriculture* with the goal of achieving the highest possible level of production within a limited area: *this land was once intensively farmed*.

intent • *noun* intention; a purpose. • *adjective* **1 a** resolved; bent; determined: *was intent on succeeding*. **b** attentively occupied: *intent on her books*. **2** (of a look) earnest; eager; meaningful. PHRASES **to** (or **for**) **all intents and purposes** practically; virtually.

intention *noun* **1** a thing intended; an aim or purpose: *have no intention of staying*. **2** the action or fact of intending: *done without intention*. **3** *informal* (usu. in *plural*) a person's, esp. a man's, designs in respect to marriage: *are his intentions honourable?*

intentional *adjective* done with an aim or purpose. ▶ **intentionality** *noun* **intentionally** *adverb*

intentional walk *noun* *Baseball* a tactical play in which a pitcher deliberately walks a batter.

-intentioned *combining form* motivated by the kind of

intentions described: *the efforts of our best-intentioned volunteers ◊ a well-intentioned gesture.*

intently *adverb* in an attentive, alert, or interested manner; with great concentration: *the children watched the magician intently ◊ he was typing away intently.*

inter *verb* (**inters, interred, interring**) deposit (a corpse etc.) in the earth, a tomb, etc.; bury.

inter- *combining form* **1** between, among: *intercontinental.* **2** mutually, reciprocally: *interbreed.* [Say IN tur]

Interac *noun Cdn proprietary* a system of payment by means of a debit card, in which funds are transferred electronically from the cardholder's bank account to the account of a merchant etc.

interact *verb* **1** act reciprocally; act on each other: *all transportation sectors interact.* **2** (of people) work together or communicate: *it is in the way the characters interact that the book excels.*

interaction *noun* **1** reciprocal action or influence: *the long history of interaction between the two civilizations.* **2** *Physics* the action of atomic and subatomic particles on each other.

interactive *adjective* **1** reciprocally active; acting upon or influencing each other: *fully sighted children in interactive play with others.* **2** (of a computer, television, etc.) allowing a two-way flow of information between it and a user, responding to the user's input. ▶ **interactively** *adverb* **interactivity** *noun*

inter alia *adverb* among other things: *the book covers, inter alia, such topics as architectural history and settlement patterns.* [Say inter AY lee uh or inter AL ee uh]

interbreed *verb* (**interbreeds, interbred, interbreeding**) breed or cause to breed with members of a different stock, race, or species to produce a hybrid.

intercalate *verb* (**intercalates, intercalated, intercalating**) insert (an extra day etc.) into a calendar, e.g. Feb. 29 in a leap year. ▶ **intercalation** *noun* [Say in TURCA late, in turca LAY sh'n]

intercede *verb* (**intercedes, interceded, interceding**) (usu. foll. by *with*) try to persuade someone to show pity on someone else; try to settle a dispute: *they interceded with the authorities for her release.*

intercellular *adjective* located or occurring between cells.

intercept • *verb* **1** seize, catch, or stop (a person, message, vehicle, ball, puck, etc.) going from one place to another. **2** check or stop (motion etc.). **3** overtake and destroy (an aircraft, missile, etc.). **4** *Math* mark off (a space) between two points etc. • *noun Math* the part of a line between two points of intersection with usu. the coordinate axes or other lines. ▶ **interception** *noun*

interceptor *noun* **1** an aircraft used to intercept enemy aircraft. **2** a person or thing that intercepts.

intercession *noun* **1** the act of trying to persuade someone to show pity on someone else. **2** a prayer on behalf of another. ▶ **intercessor** *noun* **intercessory** *adjective*

interchange • *verb* (**interchanges, interchanged, interchanging**) **1** (of two people) exchange (things) with each other. **2** put each of (two things) in the other's place; alternate. • *noun* **1** a reciprocal exchange between two people etc.: *a voluminous correspondence and interchange of documents.* **2** an intersection of two or more highways designed on several levels to allow vehicles to go from one road to another without crossing a flow of traffic. ▶ **interchangeability** *noun* **interchangeable** *adjective* **interchangeably** *adverb*

intercity *adjective* existing or travelling between cities.

intercollegiate *adjective* between colleges or universities.

intercolonial *adjective* existing or conducted between colonies.

intercom *noun* a system of or instrument for reciprocal communication by radio or telephone between or within offices, aircraft, etc.

interconnect *verb* connect with each other. ▶ **interconnected** *adjective* **interconnectedness** *noun* **interconnecting** *adjective* **interconnection** *noun* **interconnectivity** *noun*

intercontinental *adjective* connecting or travelling between continents.

intercontinental ballistic missile *noun* a ballistic missile able to be sent from one continent to another.

intercourse *noun* **1** = SEXUAL INTERCOURSE. **2** communication or dealings between individuals etc.: *without tact, social intercourse would break down.*

intercultural *adjective* taking place between cultures; belonging to or derived from different cultures.

intercut *verb* (**intercuts, intercut, intercutting**) *Film* **1** alternate (scenes or shots) with contrasting scenes or shots to make one composite scene. **2** switch from one shot or scene to another.

inter-denominational *adjective* concerning more than one (religious) denomination.

interdepartmental *adjective* concerning more than one department.

interdependent *adjective* dependent on each other. ▶ **interdependence** *noun*

interdict • *noun* an authoritative prohibition. • *verb* **1** prohibit (an action). **2 a** impede (an enemy force), esp. by bombing lines of communication or supply. **b** intercept (a prohibited commodity etc.); prevent (its movement): *efforts to interdict drug smugglers.* ▶ **interdiction** *noun*

interdisciplinary *adjective* of or between more than one branch of learning.

interest • *noun* **1 a** a concern; curiosity: *have no interest in fishing.* **b** a quality exciting curiosity or holding the attention: *this magazine lacks interest.* **c** the power of an issue, action, etc. to hold the attention; significance, importance: *findings of no particular interest.* **2** a subject, hobby, etc., in which one is concerned. **3** advantage or profit, esp. when financial: *it is in your interest to go.* **4 a** money paid for the use of money lent, or for not requiring the repayment of a debt. **b** = INTEREST RATE. **5** (usu. foll. by *in*) **a** a financial stake (in an undertaking etc.). **b** a legal concern, title, or right (in property). **6 a** a party or group having a common interest: *the brewing interest.* **b** a principle in which a party or group is concerned. **7** self-interest. • *verb* **1** excite the curiosity or attention of. **2** (usu. foll. by *in*) cause (a person) to take a personal interest or share: *can I interest you in a drink?* PHRASES **declare an** (or **one's**) **interest** make known one's financial etc. interests in an undertaking before it is discussed. **in the best interests of** to the greatest advantage or benefit of. **in the interest** (or **interests**) **of** as something that is advantageous to. **with interest 1** with interest charged or paid. **2** with increased force etc.: *returned the blow with interest.*

interested *adjective* **1** showing or having curiosity or concern: *I'm interested in history.* **2** having a personal interest in something because one may benefit or be affected by it; not impartial or disinterested: *he failed to recognize the efforts of the bank, among other interested parties, in working out a solution.* ▶ **interestedly** *adverb*

interest group *noun* a group of people sharing a common identifying interest, concern, or purpose.

interesting *adjective* causing curiosity; holding the attention. ▶ **interestingly** *adverb*

interest rate *noun* a charge made for borrowing a sum of money, expressed as a percentage of the total sum loaned, for a stated period of time.

inter-ethnic *adjective* occurring or existing between ethnic groups.

interface • *noun* **1** esp. *Physics* a surface forming a common boundary between two regions. **2** a point where interaction occurs between two systems, processes, subjects, etc.: *the interface between psychology and education*. **3** *Computing* **a** an apparatus for connecting two pieces of equipment or systems so that they can be operated jointly or communicate with each other. **b** the way in which a program accepts information from or presents information to the user, e.g. the layout of the screen, command structure, etc. • *verb* (**interfaces, interfaced, interfacing**) **1** connect with (another piece of equipment etc.) by an interface. **2** interact with (another person etc.).

interfacing *noun* **1** a stiffish material between two layers of fabric in collars etc. **2** *in senses of* INTERFACE *verb*.

interfaith *adjective* of, relating to, or between different religions or members of different religions.

interfere *verb* (**interferes, interfered, interfering**) **1** obstruct a process or activity: *she never allows her personal feelings to interfere with her work*. **2** take part or intervene, esp. without invitation or necessity: *the police are very unwilling to interfere in family problems*. **3** *Sport* (foll. by *with*) unlawfully obstruct an opposing player. **4** (foll. by *with*) *Cdn* & *Brit.* molest or assault sexually. **5** *Physics* (of light or other waves) combine so as to cause interference.

interference *noun* **1** the action of interfering or the process of being interfered with: *he denied that there had been any interference in the country's internal affairs* ◊ *an unwarranted interference with personal liberty*. **2 a** the fading or disturbance of received radio signals by the interference of waves from different sources, or esp. by atmospherics or unwanted signals. **b** the distorted reception caused by this. **3** *Physics* the combination of two or more wave motions to form a resultant wave in which the displacement is reinforced or cancelled. **4 a** *Football* the legal blocking of an opposing player to clear a way for the ball carrier. **b** *Sport* the illegal blocking or hindering of an opponent. PHRASES **run interference** intervene on someone's behalf, esp. to protect them from distraction, annoyance, etc.

interfering *adjective* involving oneself in an annoying way in other people's private lives.

interferon *noun* any of various proteins released by cells, usu. in response to a virus, and able to inhibit viral replication. [Say inter FEAR on]

intergalactic *adjective* of or situated between two or more galaxies. [Say inter GALACTIC]

intergenerational *adjective* **1** existing or occurring between different generations of people. **2** involving more than one generation.

interglacial *adjective* of or relating to a period of milder climate between ice ages. [Say inter GLAY shull]

intergovernmental *adjective* concerning or conducted between two or more governments.

inter-group *adjective* existing or occurring between different groups or members of different groups, esp. different social or political groups.

interim • *noun* the intervening time: *in the interim she died*. • *adjective* provisional, temporary: *an interim arrangement*. [Say INTER im]

interior • *adjective* **1** inner (opp. EXTERIOR). **2** remote from the coast or frontier; inland. **3** connected with a country's own affairs rather than those that involve other countries (opp. FOREIGN): *the interior minister*. **4** situated further in or within: *the layer of muscle lying*

interior to the epidermis. **5** existing in the mind or soul; inward. **6** drawn, photographed, etc. within a building. **7** coming from inside. • *noun* **1** the interior part; the inside. **2** the interior part of a country or region. **3 a** a country's own affairs rather than those that involve other countries. **b** a department dealing with these: *Minister of the Interior*. **4** the inside of a building, room, etc.

interior design *noun* (also **interior decoration**) the decoration or design of the interior of a building etc. ▶ **interior designer** *noun* (also **interior decorator**).

interiority *noun* **1** the quality of being interior or inward: *the plain room has no curves or niches, nothing that gives it a sense of privacy or interiority*. **2** inner character or nature; subjectivity: *the profound interiority of faith*. [Say in teery ORRA tee]

interject *verb* remark parenthetically or as an interruption: *she interjected the odd question here and there*.

interjection *noun* an exclamation, esp. as a part of speech (e.g. *hey!*, *dear me!*).

interlace *verb* (**interlaces, interlaced, interlacing**) **1** bind or cross intricately together; interweave: *interlacing branches* ◊ *her hair was interlaced with ribbons and flowers*. **2** mingle, intersperse: *discussion interlaced with esoteric mathematics*.

interleave *verb* (**interleaves, interleaved, interleaving**) **1** insert (usu. blank) leaves between the leaves of (a book etc.). **2** insert something at regular intervals between (the parts of): *pasta interleaved with strips of zucchini and carrot*.

interleukin *noun* any of several glycoproteins produced by leukocytes for regulating the reaction of the body to substances that can cause disease. Abbreviation: **IL**. [Say inter LOO kin]

interlink *verb* link or be linked together. ▶ **interlinkage** *noun* **interlinked** *adjective*

interlock • *verb* **1** engage with each other by overlapping or by the fitting together of projections and recesses. **2** be intimately connected: *interlocking responsibilities*. • *adjective* (of a fabric) knitted with closely interlocking stitches. • *noun* **1** a device for connecting or coordinating the function of different components. **2** a knitted fabric with closely interlocking stitches. **3** = INTERLOCKING BRICK.

interlocking brick *noun* (also **interlocking stone**) a paving material formed into shapes that interlock.

interlocutor *noun* a person who takes part in a dialogue or conversation. [Say inter LOCK you ter]

interloper *noun* a person who is present in a place or a situation where they do not belong: *I had the sense that we were merely interlopers at school*.

interlude *noun* **1 a** an intervening time, space, or event that contrasts with what goes before or after: *apart from a brief interlude of peace, the war lasted nine years*. **b** a temporary amusement or entertaining episode. **2** a piece of music played between other pieces or between acts of a play.

intermarriage *noun* **1** marriage between people of different races, tribes, religions, etc. **2** marriage between near relations.

intermarry *verb* (**intermarries, intermarried, intermarrying**) (foll. by *with*) (of people belonging to different races, tribes, religions, etc.) become connected by marriage.

intermediary • *noun* (plural **intermediaries**) **1** a person who acts as a link or helps to negotiate between two or more others: *intermediaries between borrowers and lenders*. **2** something acting between persons or things: *messenger RNA forms the intermediary between DNA and protein synthesis*. • *adjective* coming between two or

more people or things in time or place: *an intermediary stage*. [Say inter MEEDY airy]

intermediate • *adjective* coming between two people or things in time, place, character, etc. • *noun* an intermediate person or thing: *beginners, intermediates, and advanced skiers will all find challenging runs*.

interment *noun* burial. [Say in TUR mint]

intermezzo *noun (plural* **intermezzi** or **intermezzos**) **1** a short connecting instrumental movement in an opera or other musical work. **2** a similar piece performed independently. **3** a short piece for a solo instrument. [Say inter METSO]

interminable *adjective* **1** endless; having no prospect of an end. **2** tediously long or habitual. ▶ **interminably** *adverb* [Say in TERM in a bull]

intermingle *verb* (**intermingles, intermingled, intermingling**) (often foll. by *with*) mix together.

intermission *noun* **1** a pause or break between parts of a play, film, concert, etc. **2** a period of time during which something stops before continuing again: *the daily work goes on without intermission*.

intermittent *adjective* occurring at intervals; not continuous or steady. ▶ **intermittently** *adverb* [Say inter MIT int]

intermix *verb* (**intermixes, intermixed, intermixing**) mix together. ▶ **intermixture** *noun*

intermodal *adjective* involving two or more different modes, esp. modes of transport in conveying goods.

intern • *noun* **1** a recent medical graduate, resident and working under supervision in a hospital as part of his or her training. **2** a person in any profession gaining practical experience under supervision. • *verb* **1** serve as an intern. **2** confine; oblige (a prisoner, alien, etc.) to reside within prescribed limits. [Say IN turn for the noun, in TURN for the verb]

internal • *adjective* **1** of or situated in the inside or invisible part. **2** relating or applied to the inside of the body: *internal injuries*. **3** of or relating to political, economic, etc. activity happening entirely within a country rather than with other countries; domestic: *internal flight*. **4** used or applying within an organization. **5** experienced in one's mind; inner rather than expressed: *internal dialogue*. • *noun* (in *plural*) inner parts or features: *all the weapon's internals are well finished and highly polished*.

internal combustion engine *noun* an engine in which motive power is generated by the expansion of exhaust gases from the burning of fuel (e.g. gasoline, diesel, etc.) with air inside the engine.

internalization *noun* the act or process of making attitudes or behaviour part of one's nature by learning or unconscious assimilation.

internalize *verb* (**internalizes, internalized, internalizing**) **1** make (attitudes, behaviour, etc.) part of one's nature by learning or unconscious assimilation: *minority groups tend to internalize the values of the dominant society*. **2** *Economics* incorporate (costs) as part of the internal structure, esp. social costs resulting from the manufacture and use of a product: *several countries are trying to internalize costs of conventional agriculture*.

internally *adverb* **1** on or in the inside of something. **2** inside the body: *smugglers often carry drugs internally*. **3** within a country. **4** within a company or organization: *the job was advertised internally*.

internal medicine *noun* the branch of medicine that deals with the diagnosis and treatment, by non-surgical means, of diseases of internal organs.

international • *adjective* **1** existing, involving, or carried on between two or more nations. **2** agreed on or used by all or many nations: *international money order*.

3 of or pertaining to relations between nations: *international law*. **4** available for the use of all nations: *international waters*. • *noun* (**International**) **1** any of four associations founded (1864–1936) to promote socialist or communist action. **2** a member of any of these.

International Court of Justice *noun* an international judicial court of the UN, which meets at The Hague and adjudicates disputes between nations in accordance with international law.

International Date Line *noun* see DATELINE *noun* 1.

internationalism *noun* **1** the belief that countries should work together in a friendly way. **2** the quality or state of being international. ▶ **internationalist** *noun & adjective*

internationalization *noun* the process of making something international.

internationalize *verb* (**internationalizes, internationalized, internationalizing**) make something international.

international law *noun* a body of rules established by custom or treaty and recognized as binding by nations in their relations with one another.

internationally *adverb* **1** in, among, or throughout two or more nations: *an internationally acclaimed recording artist*. **2** outside of a particular country; abroad: *the company plans to expand internationally*.

International Monetary Fund *noun* see IMF.

international system of units *noun* a system of physical units based on the metre, kilogram, second, ampere, kelvin, candela, and mole, with prefixes to indicate multiplication or division by a power of ten.

internecine *adjective* **1** mutually destructive. **2** of or relating to conflict within a group or organization etc.: *their dispute is internecine, not a conflict between civilizations* ◊ *the Balkans' history of savage internecine warfare*. [Say inter NESS een]

internee *noun* a person who is confined as a prisoner, esp. for political or military reasons: *worked to help internees and prisoners of war*. [Say intern EE]

Internet *noun* an international computer network linking computers from educational institutions, government agencies, industry, etc.

internetwork *noun* several computer networks connected together to form a single, higher-level network. ▶ **internetworking** *noun*

internist *noun* a specialist in internal medicine.

internment *noun* confinement; the act of interning someone or state of being interned: *police ordered their arrest and internment* ◊ *internment camp*. [Say in TURN mint]

internship *noun* **1** the position of an intern. **2** the period of such a position.

interoperability *noun* the ability of different computer systems to use the same software. [Say inter opera BILLA tee]

interoperable *adjective* able to operate in conjunction: *interoperable computer systems*. [Say inter OPERA bull]

interpenetrate *verb* (**interpenetrates, interpenetrated, interpenetrating**) **1** (of two things) penetrate each other: *two interpenetrating pyrite cubes*. **2** pervade; penetrate thoroughly: *the building is interpenetrated by natural light*. ▶ **interpenetration** *noun*

interpersonal *adjective* **1** (of relations) occurring between persons, esp. reciprocally. **2** of or relating to relationships between people: *interpersonal skills*.

interplanetary *adjective* **1** between planets. **2** relating to travel between planets.

interplay *noun* the way in which two or more things

influence or affect each other: *the interplay between auctioneer and bidder*.

Interpol *noun* the International Criminal Police Organization, which coordinates investigations with an international dimension made by the police forces of member countries. [Say INTER pole]

interpolate *verb* (**interpolates**, **interpolated**, **interpolating**) **1** interject (a remark) in a conversation: *"How dreadful," interpolated the cashier*. **2** insert as something additional or different: *illustrations were interpolated in the text*. **3** estimate (values) from known ones in the same range (*compare* EXTRAPOLATE 2). **4** insert words in a book etc., esp. to give false impressions as to its date etc.: *the interpolated fragments of dialogue have been removed from the current edition*. ▶ **interpolation** *noun* [Say in TERPA late]

interpose *verb* (**interposes**, **interposed**, **interposing**) **1** (often foll. by *between*) place or insert (a thing) between others: *he interposed himself between her and the door* ◊ *a peacekeeping unit interposed between the two belligerents*. **2** say (words) as an interruption: *"What makes you so sure?" Charles interposed*. **3** exercise or advance (a veto or objection) so as to interfere: *the board interposes no objection to the recommendation*.

interpret *verb* (**interprets**, **interpreted**, **interpreting**) **1** explain the meaning of. **2** perform a piece of music, a dramatic role, etc. **3** translate orally or in sign language from one language into another. **4** explain or understand (behaviour etc.) in a specified manner. ▶ **interpretable** *adjective*

interpretation *noun* **1** the particular way in which something is understood or explained: *her evidence suggests a different interpretation of the events leading to his death* ◊ *dreams are open to interpretation*. **2** the particular way in which someone chooses to perform a piece of music, a role in a play, etc.: *a modern interpretation of "Romeo & Juliet"*. ▶ **interpretational** *adjective*

interpretative *adjective* = INTERPRETIVE.

interpreter *noun* **1** a person who translates from one language to another either orally or using sign language. **2** a person who explains the meaning of or performs (a role, music, etc.): *his reputation as an interpreter of Beethoven's piano sonatas* ◊ *the first and best interpreter of Stephen Leacock*. **3** *Computing* a program that can analyze and execute a program line by line. **4** an employee of a park, museum, etc. who gives tours, answers visitors' questions, etc.

interpretive *adjective* providing an interpretation: *interpretive dance*. ▶ **interpretively** *adverb*

interpretive centre *noun* a building or complex at a historic site, national park, etc., which contains a variety of displays and exhibits related to the site.

interprovincial *adjective* between provinces.

interracial *adjective* existing between or affecting different races. [Say inter RACIAL]

interrelate *verb* (**interrelates**, **interrelated**, **interrelating**) relate or connect to another or others: *a discussion of how the mind and body interrelate* ◊ *a number of interrelated problems*. ▶ **interrelatedness** *noun* **interrelation** *noun* **interrelationship** *noun*

interrogate *verb* (**interrogates**, **interrogated**, **interrogating**) **1** ask questions of (a person) esp. closely, thoroughly, or formally: *we interrogated the prisoner for nearly two hours*. **2** obtain data from (a computer file, database, etc.). [Say in TERRA gate]

interrogation *noun* the act or an instance of interrogating; the process of being interrogated. [Say in terra GAY sh'n]

interrogative • *adjective* **1** of or like a question; used in questions. **2** (of an adjective or pronoun) asking a question (e.g. *who?, which?*). **3** suggesting inquiry: *an interrogative gaze*. • *noun* an interrogative word (e.g. *what?, why?*). ▶ **interrogatively** *adverb* [Say inter OGGA tiv]

interrogator *noun* a person who questions someone closely, aggressively, or formally. [Say in TERRA gate er]

interrupt • *verb* **1 a** act so as to break the continuous progress of (something) temporarily. **b** stop (someone) speaking, by speaking oneself or causing some other disturbance. **2** obstruct (a person's view etc.). **3** break an even or continuous line, surface, etc. • *noun* *Computing* a signal causing an interruption of a program, e.g. to allow immediate execution of another program.

interrupter *noun* **1** a person or thing that interrupts. **2** a device for interrupting, esp. an electric circuit.

interruption *noun* **1** something that temporarily stops an activity or a situation; a time when an activity is stopped: *an interruption in blood flow to the brain* ◊ *I can't work with all these interruptions* ◊ *we played for four hours without interruption*. **2** the act of interrupting someone and of stopping them from speaking: *he continued to speak in spite of her interruptions*.

intersect *verb* **1** divide (a thing) by passing or lying across it: *the landscape is intersected by deep escarpments*. **2** (of lines, roads, etc.) cross or cut each other: *about 10 km south of where Highways 49 and 74 intersect*. **3** *Geometry* have one or more points in common.

intersection *noun* **1 a** a place where two or more roads intersect. **b** the place where two things intersect or cross. **2** a point or line common to lines or planes that intersect. **3** *Math & Logic* the set which comprises all the elements common to two or more given sets, and no others. **4** the act of intersecting.

intersession *noun Cdn* a short university term, usu. in May and June, in which the course material usually covered in thirteen weeks is condensed into five or six weeks of intensive study. [Say INTER session]

intersperse *verb* (**intersperses**, **interspersed**, **interspersing**) **1** scatter; place here and there: *practical demonstrations will be interspersed among the lectures*. **2** diversify (a thing or things with others so scattered): *open fields interspersed with pine forests*.

interstate • *adjective* existing or carried on between states, esp. of the US or Australia. • *noun US* each of a system of highways between states.

interstellar *adjective* occurring or situated between stars.

interstice *noun* **1** an intervening space: *the interstices between recollections*. **2** a chink or crevice: *the interstices between the closely spaced timbers are filled with clay*. [Say in TUR stiss]

interstitial *adjective* of, forming, or occupying small gaps: *the loon flattens its feathers to remove interstitial air*. [Say inter STISH'll]

intertextual *adjective* **1** having to do with the relationship between esp. literary texts. **2** denoting literary criticism that considers a text in light of its relation to other texts.

intertextuality *noun* the relationship between esp. literary texts; the fact of relating or alluding to other texts.

intertidal *adjective* of or relating to the area which is under water at high tide and exposed at low tide.

inter-tribal *adjective* existing or occurring between different tribes.

intertwine *verb* (**intertwines**, **intertwined**, **intertwining**) **1** (often foll. by *with*) entwine (together). **2** become entwined.

interval *noun* **1** an intervening time or space: *he knocked on the door and after a brief interval it was opened* ◊ *she's delirious, but has lucid intervals*. **2** the difference in

pitch between two sounds: *an interval of one octave.* PHRASES **at intervals** here and there; now and then.

intervale *noun* (*Maritimes, Nfld & New England*) a low, level tract of land, esp. along a river. [Say INTER vail]

interval house *noun Cdn* = WOMEN'S SHELTER.

intervene *verb* (**intervenes, intervened, intervening**) **1** occur in time between events: *in the intervening months she took a job in sales.* **2** interfere; come between so as to prevent or modify the result or course of events: *he intervened in the dispute.* **3** be situated between things: *from island to island across the intervening expanses of water.* **4** come in as an extraneous factor or thing: *they were planning to get married and then the war intervened.* **5** Law interpose in a lawsuit as a third party: *federal lawyers intervened in the case.* ▶ **intervenor** *noun* (also **intervener**)

intervention *noun* **1** the act or an instance of intervening. **2** interference, esp. by one country in another's affairs.

interventionism *noun* the principle or practice of intervention, esp. by a government in its domestic economy or by one state in the affairs of another. ▶ **interventionist** *noun & adjective*

intervertebral *adjective* between vertebrae. [Say inter VER tuh brul]

interview ● *noun* **1** a meeting at which a job applicant, student, etc. is questioned to determine their suitability. **2** a conversation between a reporter etc. and a person of public interest, used as a basis of a broadcast or publication. **3** a meeting of persons face to face, esp. for consultation. **4** a session of formal questioning by the police. ● *verb* **1** hold an interview with. **2** question to discover the opinions or experience of (a person). **3** participate in an interview; perform (well etc.) at an interview. ▶ **interviewee** *noun* **interviewer** *noun*

interwar *adjective* existing in the period between two wars, esp. the two world wars.

interweave *verb* (**interweaves**; *past* **interwove**; *past participle* **interwoven**; **interweaving**) **1** weave together: *the blue fabric was interwoven with red and gold thread.* **2** link or blend closely: *she has interwoven her political ideas with her religious beliefs.* **3** be or become interwoven: *sometimes the lives of historical figures interweave with our own.*

interwoven *adjective* **1** woven together; interlaced: *the nest is made of interwoven twigs.* **2** closely blended or linked: *interwoven narratives.*

intestate ● *adjective* not having made a will before death. ● *noun* a person who has died intestate. [Say in TEST ate]

intestine *noun* (in *singular* or *plural*) **1** the lower part of the alimentary canal from the end of the stomach to the anus. **2** Zoology (esp. in invertebrates) the whole alimentary canal. ▶ **intestinal** *adjective* [Say in TESS tine or in TESS tin, in TESS tin ul]

intifada *noun* a movement of Palestinian uprising in the Israeli-occupied West Bank, along the Jordanian border, and Gaza Strip, on the Mediterranean coast, beginning in 1987. [Say inta FODDA]

intimacy *noun* (*plural* **intimacies**) **1** close familiarity or friendship. **2** an intimate act, esp. sexual intercourse. **3** a private cozy atmosphere. **4** an intimate remark; an endearment: *his letters contain few intimacies.*

intimate¹ ● *adjective* **1** closely acquainted; familiar, close: *an intimate friend.* **2** private and personal: *intimate thoughts.* **3** (usu. foll. by *with*) having sexual relations. **4** (of knowledge) detailed, thorough. **5** (of a relationship between things) close: *the house's intimate relationship to the landscape.* **6** (of a place etc.) cozy;

suggesting intimacy: *an intimate restaurant.* ● *noun* a very close friend.

intimate² *verb* (**intimates, intimated, intimating**) state or make known, esp. in an indirect way; imply, hint: *he has already intimated that he intends to retire* ◊ *he has intimated his intention to retire.* [Say INTA mate]

intimately *adverb* **1** in a detailed and thorough way from first-hand knowledge: *she knows this neighbourhood intimately.* **2** in a very friendly or personal way: *there are few who know him intimately.* **3** very closely: *the group's religious and political concerns are intimately related.*

intimation *noun* the act of stating something or making something known, esp. in an indirect way; a hint, sign, or indication: *there was no intimation from his doctor that his condition was serious.* [Say inta MAY sh'n]

intimidate *verb* (**intimidates, intimidated, intimidating**) frighten or overawe, esp. to subdue or influence. ▶ **intimidating** *adjective* **intimidatingly** *adverb* **intimidation** *noun* **intimidator** *noun*

into *preposition* **1** expressing motion or direction to a point on or within. **2** expressing direction of attention or concern: *will look into it.* **3** expressing a change of state: *turned into a dragon* ◊ *separated into groups.* **4** *informal* interested in; knowledgeable about: *is really into ballet.* **5** after the beginning of: *five minutes into the game.* **6** Math expressing the relationship of a divisor to a dividend: *8 into 24 is 3.*

intolerable *adjective* that cannot be endured. ▶ **intolerably** *adverb*

intolerance *noun* **1** lack of tolerance for difference of opinion or practice, esp. in political or religious matters. **2** severe sensitivity or allergy to a substance, esp. a food or drug: *lactose intolerance.*

intolerant *adjective* **1** not tolerant, esp. of views, beliefs, or behaviour differing from one's own. **2** (usu. foll. by *of*) not having the capacity to tolerate or endure a specified thing: *a plant that is intolerant of shade.* ▶ **intolerantly** *adverb*

intonation *noun* **1** modulation of the voice; accent. **2** the act of intoning. **3** accuracy of pitch in playing or singing. [Say inta NAY sh'n]

intone *verb* (**intones, intoned, intoning**) **1** recite (prayers etc.) with prolonged sounds, esp. in a monotone. **2** chant (psalms etc.). **3** utter in a solemn or pompous tone.

in toto *adverb* completely: *the council must accept or reject the revisions in toto.* [Say in TOE toe]

intoxicant *noun* an intoxicating substance.

intoxicate *verb* (**intoxicates, intoxicated, intoxicating**) **1** make drunk. **2** excite or exhilarate beyond self-control: *intoxicated with power.* ▶ **intoxicating** *adjective* **intoxicatingly** *adverb* **intoxication** *noun*

intra- *prefix* forming adjectives usu. from adjectives, meaning "on the inside, within": *intramural.*

intracellular *adjective* Biology located or occurring within a cell or cells.

intractable *adjective* **1** hard to control or deal with: *intractable economic problems.* **2** (of a disease or condition) not easily treated: *intractable epilepsy.* **3** (of a person or animal) not manageable or docile; stubborn: *the union's intractable position.* [Say in TRACTA bull]

intramural ● *adjective* **1** taking place within a single (esp. educational) institution: *intramural floor hockey league.* **2** forming part of normal university or college studies. ● *noun* (in *plural*) intramural sports. [Say intra MURAL]

intranet *noun* Computing a communications network within an organization, employing the same technology as the Internet.

intransigence *noun* unwillingness to change one's

views or behaviour in a way that would be helpful to others; stubbornness: *the two sides have failed to reach a deal, each accusing the other of intransigence*. [Say in TRANSA jince]

intransigent *adjective* uncompromising, stubborn: *an intransigent attitude*. [Say in TRANSA jint]

intransitive *adjective* (of a verb or sense of a verb) that does not take or require a direct object (whether expressed or implied), e.g. *look* in *look at the sky* (*opp.* TRANSITIVE). ▶ **intransitively** *adverb*

intrauterine *adjective* within the uterus. [Say intra YOO tuh rin or intra YOO tuh rine]

intrauterine device *noun* a contraceptive device fitted inside the uterus and physically preventing the implantation of fertilized ova. Abbreviation: **IUD**.

intravenous • *adjective* in or into a vein or veins. • *noun* an intravenous injection or feeding. ▶ **intravenously** *adverb* [Say intra VENUS]

in-tray *noun* = IN-BASKET.

intrepid *adjective* fearless; very brave. ▶ **intrepidly** *adverb* [Say in TREP id]

intricacy *noun* (*plural* **intricacies**) the quality of something that is very complicated or detailed: *his jewellery designs are admired for their intricacy* ◊ *the intricacies of government policy*. [Say IN tricka see]

intricate *adjective* very complicated; perplexingly detailed. ▶ **intricately** *adverb* [Say INTRA kit]

intrigue • *verb* (**intrigues, intrigued, intriguing**) **1** provoke (a person's) interest or curiosity: *what you say intrigues me*. **2** (foll. by *with*) make and carry out secret plans, often with other people, with the aim of causing someone harm, doing something illegal, etc. • *noun* **1** the making of secret plans to cause somebody harm, do something illegal, etc.: *a novel of mystery and intrigue*. **2 a** a secret plan to cause someone harm, etc.: *political intrigues*. **b** a secret arrangement: *amorous intrigues*. ▶ **intriguer** *noun* **intriguing** *adjective* (esp. in sense 1 of *verb*). **intriguingly** *adverb* [Say in TREEG for the verb, IN treeg or in TREEG for the noun]

intrinsic *adjective* belonging to or forming part of the real nature of a person or thing: *small local stores are intrinsic to the town's character* ◊ *tedious tasks lacking any intrinsic interest*. ▶ **intrinsically** *adverb* [Say in TRIN zick]

intro *informal* • *noun* (*plural* **intros**) an introduction. • *adjective* introductory.

intro- *combining form* into: *introspection*.

introduce *verb* (**introduces, introduced, introducing**) **1** make (a person or oneself) known by name to another, esp. formally. **2** announce or present to an audience. **3** bring (a custom, idea, etc.) into use. **4** bring (a piece of legislation) before a legislative assembly. **5** (foll. by *to*) draw the attention or extend the understanding of (a person) to a subject, activity, etc. **6** insert; place in. **7** bring in; usher in; bring forward. **8** begin; occur just before the start of. **9** bring (a plant, animal, disease, etc.) to a place where it does not normally occur. ▶ **introducer** *noun*

introduction *noun* **1** the act or an instance of introducing; the process of being introduced. **2 a** formal presentation of one person to another. **3** an explanatory section at the beginning of a book etc. **4** a preliminary section in a piece of music. **5** an introductory treatise on a subject. **6** a thing introduced.

introductory *adjective* **1** written or said at the beginning of something as an introduction to what follows: *introductory paragraph* ◊ *introductory remarks*. **2** intended as an introduction to a subject or an activity: *an introductory course in Russian*. **3** intended to persuade someone to purchase something for the first time: *as an introductory offer, the first issue is free*.

introspection *noun* the examination or observation of one's own mental and emotional processes etc. ▶ **introspective** *adjective* **introspectively** *adverb*

introversion *noun* **1** a predominant concern with one's own thoughts and feelings rather than with external things. **2** the manner of someone who is shy and withdrawn.

introvert • *noun* **1** *Psychology* a person predominantly concerned with his or her own thoughts and feelings rather than with external things. **2** a shy, inwardly thoughtful person (*compare* EXTROVERT). • *adjective* (also **introverted**) typical or characteristic of an introvert. [Say INTRA vert]

intrude *verb* **1** come without being invited or wanted; force oneself abruptly on others. **2** *Geology* **a** thrust or force (esp. molten rock material) into. **b** (of rock material) be forced or thrust into as an intrusion.

intruder *noun* a person who intrudes, esp. into a building with criminal intent.

intrusion *noun* **1** the act or an instance of intruding. **2** an unwanted interruption etc. **3** *Geology* an influx of molten rock between or through strata etc. but not reaching the surface.

intrusive *adjective* **1** coming or tending to come without being invited or wanted: *an intrusive background hum*. **2** formed by or having to do with an influx of molten rock between or through strata: *intrusive rocks*. ▶ **intrusively** *adverb* **intrusiveness** *noun*

intuit *verb* understand or work out by instinct: *I intuited his real identity*. [Say in TOO it or in TYOO it]

intuition *noun* **1** the power of understanding situations or people's feelings immediately, without the need for conscious reasoning or study: *use your intuition*. **2** an idea or piece of knowledge gained by this power: *had an intuition you were here*. [Say into ISH'n]

intuitive *adjective* **1** of, characterized by, or possessing intuition. **2** perceived by intuition. **3** capable of being easily understood or grasped by intuition. ▶ **intuitively** *adverb* **intuitiveness** *noun* [Say in TOO it iv or in TYOO it iv]

in-turn *noun* *Curling* **1** an inward turn of the elbow and an outward turn of the hand made in delivering a stone, thus giving it a clockwise rotation. **2** a stone delivered with such a motion.

Inuit • *noun* (*plural* **Inuit**) **1** any of several Aboriginal peoples inhabiting the Arctic coasts of Canada and Greenland. **2** the language of the Inuit; Inuktitut. • *adjective* of the Inuit. [Say IN you it or IN oo it]

Inuk *noun* (*plural* **Inuit**) a member of any of the Inuit peoples. [Say in OOK (with OOK as in *BOOK*)]

inukshuk *noun* a figure of a human made of stones, originally used to scare caribou into an ambush, and now as a marker to guide travellers. [Say in OOK shook (with OOK as in *BOOK*)]

Inuktitut *noun* the language of the Inuit. [Say in OOK ti tut (TUT rhymes with *PUT*)]

inundate *verb* (**inundates, inundated, inundating**) **1** flood: *flood waters inundate the river plain each spring*. **2** overwhelm: *inundated with inquiries*. ▶ **inundation** *noun* [Say IN un date, in un DAY sh'n]

Inupiaq *noun* an Inuit language spoken in Canada, Alaska, and Greenland. [Say in OO pee ack]

Inupiat (*plural* **Inupiat**) • *noun* **1** a member of an Inuit people inhabiting areas of northern Alaska. **2** the Inuit language spoken by the Inupiat. • *adjective* of or relating to the Inupiat. [Say in OO pee at]

inure *verb* (**inures, inured, inuring**) accustom (a person) to something esp. unpleasant: *citizens long inured to the pain of disillusionment*. [Say in YUR]

in utero *adverb* in the womb; before birth: *others will*

spend their lives contending with the damage inflicted in utero by their mothers' drug use. [Say in YOOTER oh]

Inuvialuit • noun an Inuit people of the western Canadian Arctic, speaking Inuvialuktun. • adjective of or relating to this people. [Say in oovy AL oo it]

Inuvialuktun noun an Inuit language of the western Arctic. [Say in oovy uh LOOK toon]

invade verb (**invades, invaded, invading**) 1 enter (a country etc.) under arms, with intent to control or subdue it. 2 enter in large numbers; swarm into: every summer tourists invade the city. 3 (of a disease) attack (a body etc.). 4 encroach upon (a person's rights, esp. privacy). ▶ **invader** noun

invalid[1] noun a person weakened or disabled by illness or injury, esp. chronically or permanently. [Say INVA lid]

invalid[2] adjective 1 not officially acceptable or usable, esp. having no legal force. 2 not true or logical: an invalid argument. [Say in VALID]

invalidate verb (**invalidates, invalidated, invalidating**) 1 make (esp. an argument etc.) invalid: this new piece of evidence invalidates his version of events. 2 remove the validity or force of (a treaty, contract, etc.): an earlier decision that invalidated a statute regulating hours of work. ▶ **invalidation** noun [Say in VALID ate]

invalidity noun (plural **invalidities**) 1 lack of validity. 2 the condition of being an invalid; bodily infirmity. [Say inva LIDDA tee]

invaluable adjective extremely useful; having a value so great that it can't be expressed: an invaluable source of information. ▶ **invaluably** adverb

invariable adjective 1 unchangeable; always the same. 2 Math constant, fixed. ▶ **invariably** adverb

invasion noun 1 the act of invading or process of being invaded. 2 an entry of a hostile army into a country or territory. 3 the entry or arrival of a large number of people in a place: an invasion of tourists. 4 the spreading to new sites of pathogenic micro-organisms or malignant cells already in the body. 5 intrusion; encroachment upon a person's property, rights, privacy, etc.

invasive adjective 1 (of weeds, cancer cells, etc.) tending to spread. 2 (of medical procedures etc.) involving the introduction of instruments into the body. 3 tending to encroach on the privacy, rights, etc., of others. ▶ **invasiveness** noun

invective noun rude language and unpleasant remarks shouted in anger: the gesture infuriated him and he let out a stream of invective ◊ a speech full of invective against the government.

inveigh verb criticize strongly: inveighed against the evils of drugs and alcohol. [Say in VAY]

inveigle verb (**inveigles, inveigled, inveigling**) achieve control over someone in a clever and dishonest way, esp. so that they will do what one wants: Mary inveigled him into going with her. [Say in VAY gull]

invent verb 1 create by thought; devise; originate (a new method, an instrument, etc.). 2 concoct (a false story etc.).

invention noun 1 the process of inventing. 2 a thing invented; a contrivance, esp. one for which a patent is granted. 3 a fictitious statement or story; a fabrication. 4 creativity, inventiveness.

inventive adjective 1 (of a person) having the ability to create or design new things or to think originally: she's the most inventive painter around. 2 (of a product, process, action, etc.) showing creativity or original thought: methods of communication during the war were diverse and inventive. 3 of or pertaining to invention. ▶ **inventively** adverb **inventiveness** noun

inventor noun a person who invents things, esp. as an occupation.

inventory • noun (plural **inventories**) 1 a a complete list of goods in stock, house contents, etc. b the goods listed in this. c the action of compiling such a list. 2 any list, catalogue, or detailed account: an inventory of jobs to do. 3 the total of a firm's commercial assets. 4 a way of taking stock of the quality, characteristics, and growth of various forest areas through aerial mapping and sampling on the ground. • verb (**inventories, inventoried, inventorying**) 1 make an inventory of. 2 enter (goods) in an inventory. [Say IN v'n tory]

inverse • adjective inverted in position, order, or relation: an inverse U-shaped curve. • noun 1 (often foll. by of) a thing that is the opposite or reverse of another: a high risk company should pay higher premiums; the inverse of this is true as well: the more secure the institution, the less the premium should be. 2 Math an element which, when combined with a given element in an operation, produces the identity element for that operation. ▶ **inversely** adverb

inverse proportion noun (also **inverse ratio**) a relation between two quantities such that one increases in proportion as the other decreases.

inversion noun 1 a the act of turning upside down, inside out, or inward. b the state of being so turned. 2 the reversal of a normal order, position, sequence, or relation. 3 the reversal of the normal order of words, for rhetorical effect, e.g. sweetly blew the breeze. 4 a the reversal of the normal variation of air temperature with altitude, i.e. an increase of temperature with height instead of the normal decrease. b a layer of air having such a reversed gradient. 5 the reversal of direction of rotation of a plane of polarized light. 6 the conversion of direct current into alternating current.

invert verb 1 turn upside down, inside out, or inward. 2 reverse the position, order, sequence, or relation of.

invertebrate • adjective (of an animal) not having a backbone or spinal column. • noun an invertebrate animal. [Say in VERTA brate or in VERTA brit]

inverter noun an apparatus that converts direct electrical current into alternating current.

invert sugar noun a mixture of glucose and fructose.

invest verb 1 use or apply money with the expectation of achieving a profit or material result by putting it into shares, property, or financial schemes, or by using it to develop a commercial venture: we're investing in RRSPs ◊ the company is investing $10 million to improve its manufacturing plant in Hamilton. 2 informal buy (something useful): invested in a new car. 3 devote (time, effort etc.) to an enterprise. 4 a (foll. by with) give someone power or authority, esp. as part of a job: the new position invested her with a good deal of responsibility ◊ she was invested as the Yukon's first Poet Laureate on Canada Day 1994. b provide or endow someone or something with (a particular quality or attribute): being a model invests her with a certain glamour. ▶ **investable** adjective

investigate verb (**investigates, investigated, investigating**) find out information or facts about a person, thing, event, etc.: the RCMP has been called in to investigate ◊ this is not the first time he has been investigated by the police for fraud ◊ scientists are investigating the effects of diet on fighting cancer. ▶ **investigator** noun

investigation noun 1 the process or an instance of investigating. 2 a formal examination or study.

investigative adjective 1 (of journalism or broadcasting) investigating and seeking to expose malpractice, miscarriage of justice, etc. 2 (of a

journalist etc.) engaged in this. [Say INVEST uh gate iv or INVEST uh guh tiv]

investiture *noun* the formal investing of a person with honours or rank: *in 1918, in an investiture ceremony at Buckingham Palace, he was awarded a Military Cross for distinguished action under enemy fire.* [Say INVEST uh chur]

investment *noun* **1 a** the act or process of investing money, time, effort, etc. **b** an instance of this. **2** money etc. invested. **3** property etc. in which money is or may be invested.

investment bank *noun* a financial institution that specializes in financing commercial loans, mergers and acquisitions, foreign trade, etc. ▶ **investment banker** *noun* **investment banking** *noun*

investment company *noun* (plural **investment companies**) a company that invests the funds provided by shareholders in a variety of securities, its profits being made from the income and capital gains provided by these securities.

investment dealer *noun* *Cdn* **1** = INVESTMENT COMPANY. **2** a person who is a broker for an investment company.

investor *noun* a person who spends money for profit, esp. by purchasing property or shares in a company.

inveterate *adjective* **1** (of a person) confirmed in an esp. undesirable habit etc.: *an inveterate gambler.* **2** (of a bad feeling or habit) done or felt for a long time and unlikely to change: *inveterate hostility.* ▶ **inveterately** *adverb* [Say in VETTER it]

invidious *adjective* unpleasant and unfair; likely to offend someone or make them jealous because of real or seeming injustice: *we were in the invidious position of having to choose whether to break the law or risk lives ◊ it would be invidious to single out any one person to thank.* ▶ **invidiously** *adverb* [Say in VIDDY us]

invigorate *verb* (**invigorates**, **invigorated**, **invigorating**) give vigour or strength to. ▶ **invigorating** *adjective* **invigoratingly** *adverb* **invigoration** *noun* [Say in VIGGER ate]

SPELL CHECK	ABC
invigorate	✓

Note that **invigorate** is never spelled with a *u* after the *o* the way **vigour** is.

invincible *adjective* too powerful to be defeated or overcome: *the team seemed invincible ◊ an invincible belief in his own ability.* ▶ **invincibly** *adverb* [Say in VINSA bull]

inviolability *noun* the condition of something that must be respected and is never to be dishonoured or violated: *the inviolability of the Charter of Rights and Freedoms.*

inviolable *adjective* not to be violated, dishonoured, or profaned: *inviolable rights.* [Say in VIE uh luh bull]

inviolate *adjective* free or safe from injury or violation: *can a timeless tradition stand inviolate and unimpaired through today's demands?* [Say in VIOLET]

invisibility *noun* **1** the quality of something that cannot be seen. **2** the condition of someone or something that is not noticed or properly acknowledged or considered: *we would like to thank those who work behind the scenes in relative invisibility.*

invisible *adjective* **1 a** unable to be seen; that by its nature is not perceivable by the eye. **b** not in sight; hidden, obscured, secret. **2** too small or inconspicuous to be seen or noticed; imperceptible. **3** artfully concealed: *invisible mending.* ▶ **invisibly** *adverb*

invitation *noun* **1** the process of inviting or fact of

being invited, esp. to a social occasion. **2** the spoken or written form in which a person is invited. **3** the action or an act of enticing; attraction, allurement: *the job was an open invitation to illicit wealth.*

invitational • *adjective* (of a tournament, contest etc.) open only to those invited. • *noun* an invitational contest etc.

invite • *verb* (**invites**, **invited**, **inviting**) **1** ask (a person) courteously to come, or to do something: *invited her to lunch.* **2** make a formal courteous request for: *invited comments.* **3** tend to call forth unintentionally (something unwanted): *inviting trouble.* • *noun* informal an invitation. ▶ **invitee** *noun* **inviter** *noun*

inviting *adjective* **1** attractive. **2** enticing, tempting. ▶ **invitingly** *adverb*

in vitro *adverb* (of processes or reactions) performed, obtained, or occurring in a test tube, culture dish, or elsewhere outside a living organism. [Say in VEE troe]

in vitro fertilization *noun* a method of fertilizing an ovum in a test tube, culture dish, etc. and then implanting it in a uterus for gestation.

invocation *noun* **1** the act or an instance of invoking an authority, a precedent, etc.: *the invocation by the federal government of the War Measures Act shattered Canadians' assumptions about their civil liberties.* **2** the act or an instance of calling upon God, a deity, etc. in prayer: *hours of recitation of sutras, invocations, and prayers.* **3** an appeal or reference to a person or thing for inspiration: *fascinated by the novel's explicit invocation of General Wolfe and the Battle of the Plains of Abraham on at least three occasions.* **4** *Christianity* the words "In the name of the Father" etc. used at the beginning of a religious service, as the preface to a sermon, etc. [Say in voe KAY sh'n]

invoice • *noun* a list of goods shipped or sent, or services rendered, with prices and charges; a bill. • *verb* (**invoices**, **invoiced**, **invoicing**) **1** make an invoice of (goods and services). **2** send an invoice to (a person).

invoke *verb* (**invokes**, **invoked**, **invoking**) **1** mention or use (a law, rule, etc. as a reason for doing something: *it is unlikely that libel laws will be invoked.* **2** mention a person, a theory, an example, etc. to support one's opinions or ideas, or as a reason for something: *she invoked several eminent scholars to back up her argument.* **3** mention someone's name to make people feel a particular thing or act in a particular way: *his name was invoked as a symbol of the revolution.* **4** make someone have a particular feeling or imagine a particular scene; evoke: *the opening paragraph invokes a vision of England in the early Middle Ages.* **5** make a request (for help) to someone, especially a god. **6** *Computing* begin to run a program, etc.: *this command will invoke the HELP system.*

involuntarily *adverb* **1** against one's will; not by choice: *he submitted involuntarily to the drug test.* **2** without control from the will: *I shuddered involuntarily.*

involuntary *adjective* **1** not done willingly or by choice; unintentional. **2** (of a nerve, muscle, or movement) not under the control of the will.

involve *verb* (**involves**, **involved**, **involving**) **1** cause (a person or thing) to participate, or share the experience or effect (of a situation, activity, etc.). **2** imply, entail, make necessary. **3** implicate (a person in a charge, crime, etc.). **4** include or affect in its operations.

involved *adjective* **1 a** connected or associated with: *involved in biotechnology.* **b** implicated: *involved in drug*

dealing. **2** complicated in thought or form: *an involved process.* **3** engaged in a romantic relationship: *involved with a married man.*

involvement *noun* (often foll. by *in*, *with*) **1** the action or process of involving something or someone. **2** the fact or condition of being involved.

invulnerability *noun* the condition of a person or thing that cannot be harmed or defeated: *Gord had a false sense of invulnerability that made him fearless.* [Say in vull ner uh BILLA tee]

invulnerable *adjective* that cannot be harmed or defeated; safe: *an invulnerable position* ◊ *the sub is invulnerable to attack while at sea.* [Say in VULL ner uh bull]

-in-waiting *combining form* **1** attending another person: *lady-in-waiting.* **2** future: *leader-in-waiting.*

inward • *adjective* **1** directed toward the inside; going in. **2** situated within; that is the inner or innermost part. **3** mental, spiritual. • *adverb* (also **inwards**) **1** towards the inside. **2** in the mind or soul.

inwardly *adverb* **1** towards the inside: *the sides curved inwardly.* **2** in one's mind; secretly: *she groaned inwardly.*

in-your-face *adjective* slang aggressively blatant or provocative: *an in-your-face attitude.*

I/O *abbreviation* Computing = INPUT/OUTPUT.

IOC *abbreviation* International Olympic Committee.

IODE *abbreviation* Cdn IMPERIAL ORDER DAUGHTERS OF THE EMPIRE.

iodine *noun* **1** a non-metallic element of the halogen group, forming black crystals and a violet vapour, used in medicine and photography, and important as an essential element for living organisms. **2** a solution of this in alcohol used as an antiseptic. [Say EYE uh dine]

iodize *verb* (**iodizes**, **iodized**, **iodizing**) treat or impregnate with iodine: *iodized salt.* [Say EYE uh dize]

ion *noun* an atom, molecule, or group that has lost one or more electrons (= CATION), or gained one or more electrons (= ANION). [Say EYE on]

ion exchange *noun* the exchange of ions of the same charge between a usu. aqueous solution and a solid, used in water-softening, separation of chemical compounds, etc. ▶ **ion exchanger** *noun*

Ionic • *adjective* **1** of the order of Greek architecture characterized by a column with scroll shapes on either side of the capital. **2** of the ancient Greek dialect used in Ionia, the central part of the west coast of Asia Minor. • *noun* the Ionic dialect. [Say eye ON ick]

ionic *adjective* of or using ions. [Say eye ON ick]

ionization *noun* conversion of an atom, molecule, or substance into an ion, esp. by the removal of one or more electrons. [Say eye uh nize AY sh'n]

ionize *verb* (**ionizes**, **ionized**, **ionizing**) convert or be converted into an ion or ions. [Say EYE uh nize]

ionizer *noun* any thing which produces ionization, esp. a device used to improve air quality in a room etc. [Say EYE uh nize er]

ionizing radiation *noun* radiation consisting of particles, X-rays, or gamma rays with sufficient energy to cause ionization in the medium through which it passes. [Say EYE uh nize ing]

ionosphere *noun* an ionized region of the atmosphere above the stratosphere, extending to about 1 000 km above the earth's surface. [Say eye ONNA sphere]

iota *noun* **1** the ninth letter of the Greek alphabet (*I*, *ι*). **2** the smallest possible amount: *it doesn't make one iota of difference to me.* [Say eye OAT uh]

IOU *noun* (*plural* **IOUs**) a signed document acknowledging a debt.

ips *abbreviation* (also **i.p.s.**) inches per second.

ipso facto *adverb* **1** by that very fact or act: *as owner of*

the Toronto Maple Leafs he is ipso facto a celebrity. **2** thereby. [Say ipso FACTO]

IQ *abbreviation* (*plural* **IQs**) = INTELLIGENCE QUOTIENT.

IR *abbreviation* infrared.

Ir *symbol* iridium.

IRA *abbreviation* = IRISH REPUBLICAN ARMY.

Iranian • *adjective* **1** of or relating to Iranians or Iran, a country in the Middle East. **2** of the Indo-European group of languages including Persian, Pashto, Avestan, and Kurdish. • *noun* **1 a** a native or national of Iran. **b** a person of Iranian descent. **2** the Iranian languages. [Say i RAINY in]

Iraqi • *adjective* of or relating to Iraqis or Iraq, a country on the Persian Gulf. • *noun* (*plural* **Iraqis**) **1 a** a native or national of Iraq. **b** a person of Iraqi descent. **2** the form of Arabic spoken in Iraq. [Say i RACKY or i ROCKY]

irascible *adjective* easily provoked to anger or resentment: *his actions further irritated his irascible sister.* ▶ **irascibly** *adverb* [Say i RASSA bull]

irate *adjective* angry; characterized by, arising from, or exhibiting anger: *an irate letter* ◊ *an irate reader wrote in to complain.* [Say eye RATE]

IRC *abbreviation* Computing Internet Relay Chat.

ire *noun* anger, wrath: *by reopening the constitutional debate, we risk raising the ire of Quebec.*

iridescence *noun* the quality of something that shows luminous colours that seem to change when seen from different angles: *we admired the shimmery iridescence of the dragonfly's wings.* [Say ir uh DESS'nce]

iridescent *adjective* **1** showing rainbow-like luminous or gleaming colours. **2** changing colour with position. ▶ **iridescently** *adverb* [Say ir uh DESS'nt]

iridium *noun* a hard white metallic element, used esp. in alloys. [Say ir IDDY um]

iris *noun* (*plural* **irises**) **1** the flat circular coloured membrane behind the cornea of the eye, with a circular opening (pupil) in the centre. **2** a herbaceous plant with tuberous roots, sword-shaped leaves, and showy flowers. **3** (also **iris diaphragm**) an adjustable diaphragm of thin overlapping plates for regulating the size of a central hole esp. for the admission of light to a lens.

Irish • *adjective* of or relating to Ireland, its people, or the Celtic language of Ireland. • *noun* **1** (**the Irish**; treated as *plural*) the people of Ireland, or their immediate descendants in other countries, esp. those of Celtic origin. **2** the Celtic language of Ireland.

Irish coffee *noun* hot coffee mixed with Irish whiskey and served with whipped cream on top.

Irishman *noun* (*plural* **Irishmen**) a man who is Irish by birth or descent.

Irish moss *noun* = CARRAGEEN.

Irishness *noun* Irish qualities or character.

Irish Republican Army *noun* the military arm of Sinn Fein, the political party aiming for union between the Republic of Ireland and Northern Ireland.

Irish setter *noun* a breed of dog with a long silky dark red coat and a long feathered tail.

Irish terrier *noun* a rough-haired, light reddish-brown breed of terrier.

Irish whiskey *noun* a whisky made in Ireland from malted barley and seldom blended.

Irish wolfhound *noun* a breed of large, rough-coated hound, often grey in colour.

Irishwoman *noun* (*plural* **Irishwomen**) a woman who is Irish by birth or descent.

irk *verb* annoy: *the bylaw will irk some lakefront owners.*

irksome *adjective* annoying or irritating: *he found it irksome to have to remember his password.* ▶ **irksomeness** *noun*

iron • *noun* **1** a silver-white metallic element occurring naturally as hematite, magnetite, etc., much used for tools and implements, and an essential element in all living organisms. **2** this as a type or symbol of firmness, strength, or resistance: *will of iron*. **3** a tool or implement made of iron: *branding iron*. **4** a household appliance with a flat base which uses dry heat or steam to remove wrinkles from fabric when passed over it. **5** a golf club with an iron or steel sloping head which is angled in order to loft the ball (often with a number indicating the degree of angle: *seven-iron*). **6** a preparation of iron as a tonic or dietary supplement, used to treat anemia etc.: *iron pills.* **7** (usu. in *plural*) shackles or chains on a prisoner's feet: *clapped in irons.* • *adjective* **1 a** consisting or made of iron. **b** resembling iron, esp. in appearance or hardness. **2** firm, inflexible, stubborn, unyielding: *iron determination.* • *verb* **1 a** smooth (clothes etc.) with an iron. **b** (of a garment, material, etc.) become smooth by being pressed with an iron. **2** shackle with irons. PHRASES **in irons** handcuffed, chained, etc. **iron in the fire** an undertaking, opportunity, or commitment: *too many irons in the fire.* **iron out** remove or smooth over (difficulties etc.).

Iron Age *noun* the period following the Bronze Age when iron replaced bronze in the making of implements and weapons, lasting in Europe from about 1000 BC until the Roman period.

ironclad *adjective* strict, rigorous, hard and fast: *an ironclad guarantee.*

Iron Curtain *noun* the notional barrier to the passage of people and information which existed between the West and the countries of the former Soviet bloc until the decline of Communism.

iron fist *noun* firmness or ruthlessness: *he ruled over Haiti with an iron fist and a heart of steel.*

iron hand *noun* = IRON FIST. ▶ **ironhanded** *adjective*

> WRITING TIP
> **ironic**
>
> **Ironic** is used to describe a comment, facial expression, or gesture that is used to express the opposite of what it usually means, as in *"Ha ha, very funny," was Roger's ironic reply to Angie's joke about his new boots* or *Alicia looked at the D on her essay and gave an ironic smile.* It is also used to describe a situation or event that happens in a completely opposite way to what one would have expected, as in *It is ironic that Maeve became a teacher, since she always hated school when she was a girl.* **Ironic** should not be used to describe a state of affairs that is mildly coincidental or paradoxical. Uses such as *It's ironic that it's sunny since they said it was going to rain on the news* or *It's ironic that you should mention Carl: I was just thinking about him* are not recommended.

ironic *adjective* (also **ironical**) **1** using or displaying irony. **2** in the nature of irony. ▶ **ironically** *adverb*

ironing *noun* **1** the pressing and smoothing of clothes etc. with a heated iron. **2** clothes etc. which are to be or have just been ironed.

ironist *noun* a person who uses irony. ▶ **ironize** *verb* (**ironizes, ironized, ironizing**)

Ironman *noun* a multi-event sporting contest demanding stamina, esp. a consecutive triathlon of swimming, cycling, and running.

iron-on *adjective* able to be fixed to the surface of a fabric etc. by ironing.

iron ore *noun* any rock or mineral from which iron is or may be extracted.

ironwood *noun* any of various trees with very hard wood, esp. the hornbeam.

ironwork *noun* things made of iron. ▶ **ironworker** *noun*

ironworks *noun* (as *singular* or *plural*) a place where iron is smelted or iron goods are made.

> WRITING TIP
> **irony**
>
> **Irony** is the expression of meaning with words or gestures that usually mean the opposite, as in *"That was smart," said Lydia, with irony, to James, who had just locked his keys in the car.* It is also a situation or event that seems deliberately contrary to what one expects, as in *The irony is that although Simone has worked all her life for the Humane Society, she has never liked animals.* **Irony** should not be used for any state of affairs that is mildly odd, coincidental, or paradoxical, as in *The irony is that we've been co-workers for five years and only just realized that we live on the same street.*

irony *noun* (*plural* **ironies**) **1 a** the expression of meaning using language that normally expresses the opposite. **b** an instance of this; an ironic utterance or expression. **2** a discrepancy between the expected and actual state of affairs. **3** a literary technique in which the audience can perceive hidden meanings unknown to the characters.

Iroquoian • *noun* **1** a major Aboriginal linguistic group, including Cayuga, Mohawk, Oneida, Onondaga, Seneca, and Tuscarora. **2** a member of the Iroquois. • *adjective* of the Iroquois or the Iroquoian linguistic group or one of its members. [Say irra KWOY in]

Iroquois • *noun* (*plural* **Iroquois**) **1 a** a confederacy of Iroquoian peoples (originally including the Cayuga, Mohawk, Oneida, Onondaga, and Seneca, and later the Tuscarora) living in Ontario, Quebec, and New York. **b** a member of any of the peoples of this confederacy. **2** any of the languages of these peoples. • *adjective* of the Iroquois or their languages. [Say IRRA kwah]

irradiate *verb* (**irradiates, irradiated, irradiating**) **1** subject to any form of radiation. **2** make brighter, light up: *faces irradiated with joy.*

irradiation *noun* **1** the process or fact of irradiating or being irradiated. **2 a** the use of radiation for diagnostic or therapeutic purposes. **b** the process of exposing food to gamma rays to kill micro-organisms.

irrational *adjective* **1** illogical; unreasonable. **2** not capable of reasoning. **3** *Math* (of a root etc.) not rational; not expressible as a ratio of two integers, e.g. a non-terminating decimal. ▶ **irrationality** *noun* ▶ **irrationally** *adverb*

irreconcilable *adjective* **1** relentlessly hostile. **2** (of ideas, actions, etc.) incompatible, unable to be made consistent or brought into harmony: *irreconcilable differences.* ▶ **irreconcilably** *adverb* [Say i reck un SILE uh bull]

irrecoverable *adjective* that cannot be retrieved or remedied; lost: *irrecoverable costs* ◊ *irrecoverable loss of sight.* ▶ **irrecoverably** *adverb*

irredeemable *adjective* too bad to be corrected, improved or saved: *their irredeemable vulgarity* ◊ *the environmental situation is irredeemable.* ▶ **irredeemably** *adverb*

irreducible *adjective* that cannot be made smaller or simpler: *cut staff to an irreducible minimum* ◊ *an irreducible fact.* ▶ **irreducibly** *adverb* [Say i re DUCE uh bull]

irrefutable *adjective* that cannot be refuted or disproved: *irrefutable evidence.* ▶ **irrefutably** *adverb* [Say i re FUTE uh bull]

WRITING TIP
regardless, irrespective

Note that there is no such word as *irregardless*; appropriate alternatives include *regardless* and *irrespective*: *We'll go regardless of the weather*; *My constituents expect all their politicians, irrespective of political stripe or political agenda, to work together to improve their lives.*

irregular • *adjective* **1** not regular; not symmetrical, uneven; varying in form. **2** (of a surface) uneven. **3** contrary to a rule, moral principle, or custom. **4** uneven in duration, order, etc.; not occurring at regular intervals. **5** (of troops) not belonging to the regular or established army. **6** *Grammar* (of a verb, noun, etc.) not conjugated, pluralized, etc. according to the usual rules. **7** (of clothing, cloth, etc.) flawed or damaged, and thus often offered for sale at a reduced price. **8** (of a flower) having unequal petals etc. **9** (of a galaxy) having an irregular shape, esp. lacking any apparent axis of symmetry or central nucleus. **10** not having regular bowel movements or menstrual periods. • *noun* **1 a** (in *plural*) irregular troops. **b** a member of an irregular military force. **2** (usu. in *plural*) an imperfect piece of merchandise, esp. cloth or clothing, often sold at a reduced price. ▶ **irregularity** *noun* (*plural* **irregularities**) **irregularly** *adverb*

irrelevance *noun* lack of importance or connection with a situation: *the irrelevance of plot to a successful horror movie.*

irrelevancy *noun* **1** (*plural* **irrelevancies**) an irrelevant or unimportant detail: *you mustn't be distracted by irrelevancies.* **2** = IRRELEVANCE.

irrelevant *adjective* not relevant; not applicable (to a matter in hand): *that evidence is irrelevant to the case.* ▶ **irrelevantly** *adverb*

irreligious *adjective* **1** indifferent or hostile to religion. **2** lacking a religion. ▶ **irreligiousness** *noun*

irreparable *adjective* (of an injury, loss, etc.) that cannot be rectified or made good: *he died young, an irreparable loss to Canadian scholarship.* ▶ **irreparably** *adverb* [Say i REP ruh bull]

irreplaceable *adjective* that cannot be replaced if lost or damaged: *an irreplaceable vase.* ▶ **irreplaceably** *adverb*

irrepressible *adjective* that cannot be repressed or restrained: *full of irrepressible confidence.* ▶ **irrepressibly** *adverb*

irreproachable *adjective* faultless, blameless. ▶ **irreproachability** *noun* **irreproachably** *adverb*

irresistible *adjective* **1** too strong or convincing to be resisted. **2** delightful; alluring. ▶ **irresistibly** *adverb*

irresolute *adjective* hesitant, undecided: *she stood irresolute outside the door.* ▶ **irresolutely** *adverb* **irresolution** *noun*

irrespective *adjective* not taking into account; regardless of: *my constituents expect all their politicians, irrespective of political stripe or political agenda, to work together to improve their lives.* ▶ **irrespectively** *adverb*

irresponsibility *noun* the failure or inability to behave in a mature, reliable, trustworthy, and independent manner: *the company has been accused of fiscal irresponsibility.*

irresponsible *adjective* **1** acting or done without due sense of responsibility. **2** not responsible for one's conduct. ▶ **irresponsibly** *adverb*

irretrievable *adjective* that cannot be retrieved or restored. ▶ **irretrievably** *adverb*

irreverence *noun* a lack of respect for people or things that are generally taken seriously: *the magazine satirizes politicians with wit and irreverence.*

irreverent *adjective* lacking reverence; disrespectful. ▶ **irreverently** *adverb*

irreversibility *noun* the condition of a process, decision, medical procedure, etc. that cannot be reversed, altered, or undone.

irreversible *adjective* not reversible or alterable. ▶ **irreversibly** *adverb*

irrevocable *adjective* not able to be changed, reversed, or recovered: *an irrevocable decision.* ▶ **irrevocably** *adverb* [Say i REV uh kuh bull or i re VOKE uh bull]

irrigate *verb* (**irrigates**, **irrigated**, **irrigating**) **1** supply (land or a crop) with water, esp. by means of specially constructed channels or pipes. **2** *Medical* supply (a wound etc.) with a constant flow of liquid. ▶ **irrigation** *noun* **irrigator** *noun*

irritability *noun* a tendency to be easily annoyed or made angry.

irritable *adjective* **1** easily annoyed or angered. **2** (of an organ etc.) very sensitive to contact. **3** *Biology* responding actively to physical stimulus. ▶ **irritably** *adverb*

irritable bowel syndrome *noun* a condition involving abdominal pain and diarrhea or constipation, associated with stress, depression, etc.

irritant • *adjective* causing slight inflammation or other discomfort to the body. • *noun* **1** a substance that causes slight inflammation or other discomfort to the body: *chemical irritants.* **2** a thing that is continually annoying or distracting: *In 1966 Vietnam was becoming an irritant to the government.*

irritate *verb* (**irritates**, **irritated**, **irritating**) **1** excite to anger; annoy. **2** stimulate discomfort or pain in (a part of the body). **3** *Biology* stimulate (an organ) to action. ▶ **irritating** *adjective* **irritatingly** *adverb* **irritation** *noun*

is *3rd singular present of* BE.

ISBN *abbreviation* (*plural* **ISBNs**) international standard book number.

ISDN *abbreviation* (*plural* **ISDNs**) INTEGRATED SERVICES DIGITAL NETWORK.

-ish *suffix* forming adjectives: **1** from nouns, meaning: **a** having the qualities or characteristics of: *boyish.* **b** of the nationality of: *Danish.* **2** from adjectives, meaning "somewhat": *thickish.* **3** *informal* denoting an approximate age or time of day: *fortyish* ◊ *six-thirtyish.*

Islam *noun* **1** the religion of Muslims, a faith regarded as revealed through Muhammad as the Prophet of Allah, the one God. **2** the Muslim world. ▶ **Islamist** *noun* [Say IZ lam or IZ lom]

Islamic *adjective* having to do with Islam. [Say iz LAM ick or iz LOM ick]

island • *noun* **1** a piece of land surrounded by water. **2** anything compared to an island, esp. in being isolated or surrounded in some way. **3** a free-standing cupboard unit with a countertop, esp. in a kitchen, allowing access from all sides. **4** (in full **traffic island**) a paved or grassed area in a road to divert traffic, provide a refuge for pedestrians, etc. **5** a clump of woodland surrounded by prairie. **6 a** a detached or isolated thing. **b** *Physiology* a detached portion of tissue or group of cells (*compare* ISLET 2). • *verb* isolate: *this house where she has been islanded, thinking herself safe.*

islander *noun* **1** a native or inhabitant of an island. **2** (**Islander**) (in Canada) a native or resident of Prince Edward Island, Vancouver Island, etc.

island-hop *verb* (**island-hops**, **island-hopped**, **island-hopping**) move from one island to another, esp. as a tourist in an area of small islands. ▶ **island-hopping** *noun*

SPELL CHECK
isle, aisle

A passageway is an **aisle**.

---

isle *noun* an island, esp. a small one. [Say I'll]

islet *noun* **1** a small island. **2** *Anatomy* a portion of tissue structurally distinct from surrounding tissues. [Say EYE lit]

islets of Langerhans *plural noun* groups of cells in the pancreas secreting insulin. [Say LONG er onz]

ism *noun informal* usu. *derogatory* any distinctive but unspecified doctrine or practice of a kind with a name ending in *-ism*.

-ism *suffix* forming nouns, esp. denoting: **1** a system, principle, or ideological movement: *Conservatism* ◊ *feminism*. **2** a basis of prejudice or discrimination: *racism*. **3** a peculiarity or characteristic of a nation, individual, etc., esp. in language: *Canadianism*.

Ismaili *noun* (*plural* **Ismailis**) a member of a Shiite Muslim branch that seceded from the main group in the 8th century over the question of succession to the position of imam. [Say iz MAY lee]

isn't *contraction* is not.

ISO *abbreviation* **1** International Organization for Standardization. **2** the numerical exposure index assigned to a photographic film to indicate its sensitivity to light.

iso- *combining form* **1** equal: *isometric*. **2** *Chemistry* isomeric, esp. of a hydrocarbon with a branched chain of carbon atoms: *isobutane*. [Say ICE oh]

isobar *noun* **1** a line on a map connecting positions having the same atmospheric pressure at a given time or on average over a given period. **2** each of two or more isotopes of different elements, with the same atomic weight. [Say ICE oh bar]

isolate *verb* (**isolates**, **isolated**, **isolating**) **1 a** place apart or alone, cut off from society. **b** place (a patient thought to be contagious or infectious) in quarantine. **2 a** identify and separate for attention: *isolated the problem*. **b** *Chemistry* separate (a substance) from a mixture. **3** insulate (electrical apparatus).

isolated *adjective* **1** lonely; cut off from society or contact; remote: *feeling isolated* ◊ *an isolated farmhouse*. **2** not typical; single: *an isolated incident*.

isolation *noun* **1** the act or an instance of isolating. **2** the state of being isolated or separated. **3** designating a hospital ward etc. for patients with contagious or infectious diseases: *isolation ward*. **PHRASES** **in isolation** considered singly and not relatively.

isolationism *noun* the policy of holding aloof from the affairs of other countries or groups esp. in politics. ▶ **isolationist** *noun & adjective*

isolation pay *noun* *Cdn* a financial supplement to the salary of an employee who works in an isolated area.

isolator *noun* a thing that isolates.

isomer *noun* **1** *Chemistry* one of two or more compounds with the same molecular formula but a different arrangement of atoms and different properties. **2** *Physics* one of two or more atomic nuclei that have the same atomic number and the same mass number but different energy states. ▶ **isomeric** *adjective* [Say ICE uh mer, ice uh MAIR ick]

isometric *adjective* **1** of or having equal dimensions. **2 a** of, relating to, or denoting muscular action in which tension is developed without contraction of the muscle. **b** (of an exercise) involving contraction of a muscle group against a fixed, immovable resistance, e.g. pushing one's hands against the bottom of a desk and contracting the biceps. **3** connected with a style of drawing in three dimensions without perspective: *an isometric view of a cube*. ▶ **isometrically** *adverb* [Say ice uh METRIC]

isopropyl alcohol *noun* a colourless secondary alcohol used in antifreeze and as a solvent. [Say ice uh PRO pull]

isosceles *adjective* (of a triangle) having two sides equal. [Say eye SOSSA leez]

isotherm *noun* **1** a line on a map connecting places having the same temperature at a given time or on average over a given period. **2** a curve for changes in a physical system at a constant temperature. ▶ **isothermal** *adjective* [Say ICE uh therm]

isotonic *adjective* **1** designating or relating to a solution having the same osmotic pressure as some particular solution (esp. that in a cell, or a body fluid). **2** of or relating to a solution having the same salt concentration as blood, used esp. by athletes to restore lost salt. **3** *Physiology* (of muscle action) taking place with normal contraction. [Say ice oh TONIC]

isotope *noun* *Chemistry* each of two or more forms of the same element that contain equal numbers of protons but different numbers of neutrons in their nuclei, and hence differ in relative atomic mass but not in chemical properties; in particular, a radioactive form of an element. ▶ **isotopic** *adjective* [Say ICE uh tope, ice uh TOPIC]

Israeli • *adjective* of or relating to the modern state of Israel. • *noun* (*plural* **Israelis**) **1** a native or national of Israel. **2** a person of Israeli descent. [Say iz RAY lee]

Israelite • *noun* a member of the ancient Hebrew nation or people, esp. in the 12th to 6th centuries BC. • *adjective* of the Israelites. [Say IZ ree uh lite]

Issei *noun* (*plural* **Issei**) a member of the first generation of Japanese immigrants to North America, who immigrated in the late 19th and early 20th centuries. [Say EE say]

issue • *noun* **1 a** a giving out or circulation of shares, notes, stamps, etc. **b** a quantity of coins, supplies, copies of a newspaper or book etc., circulated or put on sale at one time. **c** an item or amount given out or distributed, esp. by a military force. **d** each of a regular series of a magazine etc.: *the May issue*. **2 a** an outgoing, an outflow. **b** a way out, an outlet, esp. the place of the emergence of a stream etc. **3** a point in question; an important subject of debate or litigation. **4** a result, outcome, or decision. **5** *Law* children: *died without issue*. • *verb* (**issues**, **issued**, **issuing**) **1** (often foll. by *out*, *forth*) *literary* go or come out. **2 a** send forth; publish; put into circulation. **b** (foll. by *to*, *with*) supply, esp. officially or authoritatively: *issued them with passports* ◊ *issued orders to the staff*. **3 a** (often foll. by *from*) be derived or result. **b** (foll. by *in*) end, result. **4** (foll. by *from*) emerge from a condition. **PHRASES** **at issue 1** under discussion; in dispute. **2** at variance. **make an issue of** make a fuss about; turn into a subject of contention. **take issue** (foll. by *with*) disagree. ▶ **issuance** *noun*
issuer *noun*

-ist *suffix* forming personal nouns (and in some senses related adjectives) denoting: **1** an adherent of a system etc. in *-ism* (see *-ISM* 1): *Marxist* ◊ *fatalist*. **2** a person who subscribes to a prejudice or practises discrimination: *racist* ◊ *sexist*.

isthmus *noun* (*plural* **isthmuses**) **1** a narrow piece of land connecting two larger bodies of land. **2** *Anatomy* a narrow part connecting two larger parts. [Say ISS muss or ISTH muss]

IT *abbreviation* information technology.

it *pronoun* **1** the thing (or occas. the animal or child) previously named or in question: *took a stone and threw it*. **2** the person in question: *Who is it? It is I ◊ is it a boy or a girl?* **3** as the subject of an impersonal verb: *it is raining ◊ it is Tuesday ◊ it is two kilometres to Whitehorse*. **4** as a substitute for a deferred subject or object: *it is silly to talk like that ◊ I take it that you agree*. **5** as a substitute for a vague object: *run for it!* **6** as the antecedent to a relative word: *it was an owl I heard*. **7** exactly what is needed: *absolutely it*. **8** the extreme limit of achievement. **9** *informal* **a** a sexual intercourse. **b** sex appeal. **10** (in children's games) a player who has to perform a required feat, esp. to catch the others. PHRASES **that's it** *informal* that is: **1** what is required. **2** the difficulty. **3** the end, enough. **this is it** *informal* **1** the expected event is at hand. **2** this is the difficulty.

ital. *abbreviation* italic (type).

Italian • *noun* **1 a** a native or national of Italy, a country in S Europe. **b** a person of Italian descent. **2** the Romance language used in Italy and parts of Switzerland. • *adjective* of or relating to Italy or its people or language.

Italianate *adjective* (esp. of architecture) of Italian style or appearance: *an Italianate villa*. [Say ITALIAN ate]

italic • *adjective* **1 a** *Typography* of the sloping kind of letters now used esp. for emphasis or distinction and in foreign words. **b** (of handwriting) compact and pointed. **2** (**Italic**) of ancient Italy. • *noun* **1** a letter in italic type. **2** this type. [Say eye TAL ick or i TAL ick]

italicize *verb* (**italicizes, italicized, italicizing**) print in italics. [Say eye TALA size or i TALA size]

Italo- *combining form* Italian; Italian and. [Say ITTA low]

itch • *noun* (*plural* **itches**) **1** an irritation in the skin. **2** an impatient desire; a hankering. **3** (**the itch**) (in general use) scabies. • *verb* (**itches, itched, itching**) **1** feel an irritation in the skin, causing a desire to scratch it. **2** (of a person) feel a desire to do something: *am itching to tell you the news*.

itchiness *noun* an itchy feeling: *one of the side effects of the medication is itchiness*.

itchy *adjective* (**itchier, itchiest**) having or causing an itch. PHRASES **have itchy feet** *informal* **1** be restless. **2** have a strong urge to travel.

it'd *contraction* **1** it had. **2** it would.

-ite *suffix* forming nouns meaning "a person or thing connected with": **1** as natives or residents of a country, city, etc.: *Israelite ◊ Vancouverite*. **2** often *derogatory* as followers of a movement etc.: *Trotskyite*.

item *noun* **1 a** any of a number of enumerated or listed things. **b** an entry in an account. **2** an article, esp. one for sale: *household items*. **3** a separate or distinct piece of news, information, etc. **4** *informal* a couple in a romantic or sexual relationship.

itemize *verb* (**itemizes, itemized, itemizing**) state or list item by item.

iteration *noun* the repetition of a process or utterance: *the fifth iteration of the Reform Party platform on the GST*. [Say itta RAY shun]

iterative *adjective* characterized by repeating or being repeated. [Say ITTER uh tive or ITTER ay tive]

itinerant • *adjective* **1** travelling from place to place: *itinerant workers*. **2** (of a judge, minister, etc.) travelling within a circuit. **3** (of a teacher) working at more than one school. • *noun* a person who travels from place to place, esp. as a minister etc. [Say eye TINNER int]

itinerary *noun* (*plural* **itineraries**) **1** a detailed route. **2 a** a record of a journey. **b** a listing of the departure and arrival times etc. of aircraft, trains, or other means of transport taken on a journey, usu. accompanying the ticket. **3** a guidebook. [Say eye TINNER airy]

-itis *suffix* forming nouns, esp.: **1** names of inflammatory diseases: *bronchitis*. **2** *informal* in extended uses with reference to conditions compared to diseases: *electionitis*. [Say ITE iss]

it'll *contraction* it will; it shall.

ITO *abbreviation* International Trade Organization.

its *possessive adjective* of it; of itself: *can see its advantages*.

it's *contraction* **1** it is. **2** it has.

itself *pronoun* emphatic and reflexive form of IT. PHRASES **by itself** apart from its surroundings, automatically. **in itself** viewed in its essential qualities: *not in itself a bad thing*.

itsy-bitsy *adjective* (also **itty-bitty**) *informal* usu. *derogatory* tiny, insubstantial, slight.

IU *abbreviation* (*plural* **IUs**) international unit, a standard quantity of a vitamin etc.

IUD *abbreviation* (*plural* **IUDs**) INTRAUTERINE DEVICE.

IV *abbreviation* (*plural* **IVs**) intravenous.

I've *contraction* I have.

IVF *abbreviation* in vitro fertilization.

ivory (*plural* **ivories**) • *noun* **1** a hard creamy-white substance composing the main part of the tusks of an elephant, hippopotamus, walrus, or narwhal. **2** the colour of this. **3** a substance resembling ivory, or made in imitation of it. **4** (usu. in *plural*) **a** an article made of ivory. **b** *slang* a piano key or a tooth. • *adjective* of the colour of ivory; creamy white. PHRASES **tickle (or tinkle) the ivories** *informal* play the piano.

ivory tower *noun* a state or place of seclusion or separation from the ordinary world and the harsh realities of life.

ivy *noun* (*plural* **ivies**) **1** a climbing evergreen plant with usu. shiny, dark green, five-pointed leaves. **2** any of various other climbing plants including poison ivy.

Ivy League • *noun* a group of universities in the eastern US, with a reputation for scholastic and social prestige. • *adjective* of or relating to the schools of the Ivy League or their students.

-ize *suffix* forming verbs, meaning: **1** make or become such: *Canadianize ◊ realize*. **2** treat in such a way: *monopolize ◊ pasteurize*. **3 a** follow a special practice: *economize*. **b** have a specified feeling: *sympathize*. **4** affect with, provide with, or subject to: *oxidize ◊ hospitalize*. ▶**-izer** *suffix*.

Jj

J¹ *noun* (also **j**) (*plural* **Js** or **J's**) **1** the tenth letter of the alphabet. **2** (as a Roman numeral) = *i* in a final position: *ij* ◊ *vj*.

J² *abbreviation* (also **J.**) **1** Judge. **2** Justice. **3** (in cards) jack.

J³ *symbol* joule(s).

jab • *verb* (**jabs, jabbed, jabbing**) **1** pierce or poke with the end or point of something. **2** punch, esp. with a short, sharp blow. **3** (foll. by *into*) thrust (a thing) hard or abruptly. **4** punch or poke with short, sharp blows: *jabbed at it with a stick*. • *noun* **1** an abrupt blow with one's fist etc. **2** *informal* a satirical or cutting remark or comment.

jabber • *verb* **1** chatter volubly and incoherently. **2** utter (words) fast and indistinctly. • *noun* meaningless jabbering; a gabble. ▶ **jabberer** *noun*

jacaranda *noun* **1** a tropical American tree with trumpet-shaped blue flowers. **2** any tropical American tree of the genus *Dalbergia*, with hard scented wood. [Say jacka RANDA]

jack • *noun* **1** a device for lifting heavy objects, esp. the axle of a vehicle off the ground while changing a wheel etc. **2** a playing card with a picture of a soldier, servant, etc. **3** a ship's flag, esp. one flown from the bow and showing nationality. **4** a female connecting device in an electrical circuit: *telephone jack*. **5** a small white ball in lawn bowling, at which the players aim. **6 a** a small starlike piece of metal or plastic used in tossing games. **b** (in *plural*) a game using jacks and a ball. **7** *informal* = LUMBERJACK. **8 a** any of various perch-like marine fish, including the amberjack. **b** a pike or pickerel. **9** a species or variety of animal smaller than other similar kinds. **10** (also **jack boat**) *Cdn* (*Nfld*) *hist.* a small fishing schooner with two masts. • *verb* **1** (usu. foll. by *up*) **a** raise (a car, etc.) with or as with a jack (in sense 1). **b** *informal* increase (prices, volume, etc.): *jacked up the rent*. **2** hunt or fish using a jacklight. PHRASES **every man jack** each and every person. **jack around** *slang* deal deceitfully or dishonestly with. **jack into** *slang* access (the Internet, a home page, etc.).

jackal *noun* a slender, long-legged, wild dog found in Africa and southern Asia, usu. hunting or scavenging for food in packs. [Say JACK'll]

Jack and Jill • *adjective* **1** open to both men and women. **2** designating a party held for a couple soon to be married, to which both men and women are invited. • *noun* (*plural* **Jack and Jills**) a Jack and Jill party.

jackass *noun* (*plural* **jackasses**) **1** a male donkey or ass. **2** a stupid person.

jackboot *noun* **1** a large boot reaching above the knee worn chiefly by soldiers, e.g. those under the Nazi regime. **2** this as a symbol of fascism or military oppression: *a country under the jackboot of a dictatorial regime*. ▶ **jackbooted** *adjective*

jacket • *noun* **1 a** a sleeved short outer garment. **b** a thing worn esp. round the torso for protection or support: *life jacket*. **2** a casing or covering, e.g. as insulation around a boiler. **3** = DUST JACKET. **4** the skin of a potato, esp. when baked whole. **5** an animal's coat. • *verb* (**jackets, jacketed, jacketing**) cover with a jacket. ▶ **jacketed** *adjective* **jacketless** *adjective*

Jack Frost *noun* frost personified.

jackhammer • *noun* a portable pneumatic hammer or drill. • *verb* drill or break up using a jackhammer.

jack-in-the-box *noun* (*plural* **jack-in-the-boxes**) a toy in the form of a box with a figure inside on a spring that jumps up when the lid is opened.

jack-in-the-pulpit *noun* any of several small North American woodland plants of the arum family.

jackknife • *noun* (*plural* **jackknives**) **1** a large pocket knife. **2** a dive in which the body is first bent at the waist and then straightened. • *verb* (**jackknifes, jackknifed, jackknifing**) **1** (of an articulated vehicle) fold against itself in an accidental skidding movement. **2** fold like a jackknife. **3** perform a jackknife dive.

jacklight • *noun* a light used illegally as a lure when hunting or fishing at night. • *verb* (**jacklights, jacklighted, jacklighting**) hunt or fish using a jacklight. ▶ **jacklighting** *noun*

jack of all trades *noun* (*plural* **jacks of all trades**) a person who can do many different kinds of work.

jack-o'-lantern *noun* a lantern made esp. from a hollowed-out pumpkin carved to resemble a face.

Jack pine *noun* a hardy pine with short needles, found in northern North America.

jackpot *noun* a large prize or amount of winnings, esp. accumulated in a game or lottery etc. PHRASES **hit the jackpot** *informal* **1** win a large prize. **2** have remarkable luck or success.

jackrabbit *noun* any of various large North American prairie hares with very long ears and hind legs.

Jacobean • *adjective* **1** of the reign of James I of England (1603–25): *Jacobean drama*. **2** (of furniture) in the style prevalent then, esp. of the colour of dark oak. • *noun* a person of the time of James I. [Say jacka BEE un]

Jacobin *noun* *hist.* a member of a democratic club established in Paris in 1789. The Jacobins were the most radical and ruthless of the political groups formed in the wake of the French Revolution, and in association with Robespierre they instituted the Terror of 1793–4 (see TERROR 4). [Say JACKA bin]

Jacobite *noun* a supporter of the deposed James II and his descendants in their claim to the British throne after the Revolution of 1688. Jacobites drew most of their support from Catholic clans of the Scottish Highlands. [Say JACKA bite]

Jacob's ladder *noun* **1** a plant with flat-topped clusters of blue or white flowers, and rows of slender pointed leaves suggesting a ladder. **2** *Nautical* a rope or chain ladder.

jacquard *noun* **1** an apparatus with perforated cards, fitted to a loom to facilitate the weaving of figured fabrics. **2** (also **jacquard loom**) a loom fitted with this. **3** a fabric or article made with this, with an intricate variegated pattern. [Say JACK ard]

Jacuzzi *noun* (*plural* **Jacuzzis**) *proprietary* **1** = WHIRLPOOL 2. **2** = HOT TUB. [Say juh COOZY]

jade • *noun* **1 a** a hard usu. green stone composed of silicates of calcium and magnesium, or of sodium and aluminum, used for ornaments etc. **b** an ornament etc. made of jade. **2** the green colour of jade. **3** an inferior or worn-out horse. **4** *derogatory* a disreputable woman. • *adjective* of the colour jade.

jaded *adjective* tired and bored, usually because you have had too much of something: *I felt terribly jaded after working all weekend* ◊ *it was a meal to tempt even the most jaded palate*. ▶ **jadedly** *adverb* **jadedness** *noun*

jade plant *noun* a succulent plant with thick shiny dark green leaves, frequently grown as a houseplant.

jaeger *noun* a seabird of the skua family, esp. one of the smaller kinds. [Say JAY ger]

jag¹ *noun* a sharp projection of rock etc.

jag² *noun informal* **1** a drinking bout. **2** a period of indulgence in an activity, emotion, etc.

jagged *adjective* **1** with an unevenly cut or torn edge. **2** deeply indented; with sharp points. **3** having a harsh or irregular quality; not smooth. ▶ **jaggedly** *adverb* **jaggedness** *noun*

jaguar *noun* a large carnivorous feline of Central and South America, mainly yellowish-brown with dark spots grouped in rosettes. [Say JAG war (WAR rhymes with FAR)]

jail • *noun* **1** a public prison for the detention of persons committed by process of law. **2** confinement in a jail. • *verb* put in jail.

jailbird *noun* a prisoner or habitual criminal.

jailbreak *noun* an escape from jail.

jailer *noun* (also **jailor**) **1** a person in charge of a jail or of the prisoners in it. **2** a person who keeps another person forcibly confined.

jailhouse *noun* a prison.

Jain • *noun* an adherent of a religion founded in India in the 6th century BC, characterized by its stress on non-violence and teaching that salvation comes by perfection through successive lives. • *adjective* of or relating to this religion. ▶ **Jainism** *noun* **Jainist** *noun* [Say JINE]

jake *adjective slang* all right; satisfactory.

jalapeno *noun* (*plural* **jalapenos**) (also **jalapeno pepper**) a very hot green chili pepper, used esp. in Mexican-style cooking. [Say hala PEE no or hala PAY nyo or hala PEE nyo]

jalopy *noun* (*plural* **jalopies**) *informal* a dilapidated old car, truck, etc. [Say juh LOPPY]

SPELL CHECK
jam, jamb   ABC ✓

Part of a door frame is a **jamb**.

---

jam • *verb* (**jams**, **jammed**, **jamming**) **1 a** squeeze or wedge into a space. **b** bruise or crush by pressure: *jammed my finger in the drawer*. **c** become wedged. **2 a** cause (machinery etc.) to become wedged or immovable so that it cannot work. **b** become jammed in this way. **3** push or cram together in a compact mass. **4** push or crowd: *they jammed on to the bus*. **5 a** block (a passage, road, etc.) by crowding or obstructing. **b** obstruct the exit of: *we were jammed in*. **c** (of ice, logs, etc.) form an obstruction in a river, stream, etc. **6** apply (brakes etc.) forcefully or abruptly. **7** make (a radio transmission) unintelligible by causing interference. **8** *informal* improvise with other musicians. • *noun* **1** a conserve of fruit and sugar boiled to a thick consistency. **2** a squeeze or crush. **3** a crowded mass: *traffic jam*. **4** *informal* an awkward situation or predicament. **5** a stoppage (of a machine etc.) due to jamming. **6** (also **jam session**) *informal* improvised playing by a group of jazz etc. musicians.

Jamaican • *adjective* of or relating to Jamaica, an island country in the Caribbean Sea, or the Jamaicans. • *noun* **1** a native or inhabitant of Jamaica. **2** the variety of English spoken in Jamaica. [Say juh MAKE in]

Jamaican patty *noun* (*plural* **Jamaican patties**) a half-moon shaped turnover of yellow pastry with a spicy filling of ground meat.

jamb *noun* a side post or surface of a doorway, window, or fireplace. [Say JAM]

jambalaya *noun* a Cajun dish of rice with shrimps, chicken, etc. [Say jam buh LIE uh]

jamboree *noun* **1** a large celebration or party, esp. a lavish and boisterous one: *the film industry's annual jamboree in Cannes*. **2** a large rally of Scouts. [Say jam buh REE]

jambuster *noun Cdn* (*Man. & NW Ont.*) a jelly-filled doughnut.

jammies *plural noun slang* = PYJAMAS 1.

jam-packed *adjective informal* full to capacity.

Jan. *abbreviation* January.

jangle • *verb* (**jangles**, **jangled**, **jangling**) **1** make, or cause (a bell etc.) to make, a harsh metallic sound. **2** irritate (the nerves etc.) by discordant sound or speech etc. • *noun* a harsh metallic sound. ▶ **jangly** *adjective*

janitor *noun* a caretaker of a school, office building, etc., responsible for its cleaning, heating, etc. ▶ **janitorial** *adjective*

janny *noun* (*plural* **jannies**) (also **janney**, *plural* **janneys**) *Cdn* (*Nfld*) a mummer. ▶ **jannying** *noun*

January *noun* (*plural* **Januaries**) the first month of the year.

japan • *noun* a hard usu. black varnish, esp. of a kind originally from Japan. • *verb* (**japans**, **japanned**, **japanning**) varnish with japan.

Japanese • *noun* (*plural* **Japanese**) **1 a** a native or national of Japan, a country in eastern Asia occupying an archipelago in the Pacific. **b** a person of Japanese descent. **2** the language of Japan. • *adjective* of or relating to Japan, its people, or its language.

jape *noun* a jest or joke: *the childish jape of filling her locker with water balloons*. ▶ **japery** *noun* (*plural* **japeries**)

japonica *noun* a flowering shrub of the rose family, with round white, green, or yellow edible fruits and bright red flowers. [Say juh PONNA cuh]

jar¹ *noun* **1 a** a container of glass, earthenware, plastic, etc., usu. cylindrical. **b** the contents of this. **2** *Brit. & Cdn informal* a glass of beer etc.

jar² • *verb* (**jars**, **jarred**, **jarring**) **1** (often foll. by *on*) (of sound, words, manner, etc.) sound discordant or grating (on the nerves etc.). **2** (foll. by *against*, *on*) strike or cause to strike with vibration or a grating sound. **3** send a shock through (a part of the body): *the fall jarred his neck*. **4** (often foll. by *with*) (of an opinion, fact, etc.) be at variance; be in conflict or in dispute. • *noun* a physical shock or jolt.

jargon *noun* **1** words or expressions used by a particular group or profession: *medical jargon*. **2** language marked by affected or convoluted syntax, vocabulary, or meaning. **3** unintelligible or meaningless talk or writing; gibberish. **4** a pidgin: *Chinook Jargon*. ▶ **jargony** *adjective*

jarring *adjective* **1** striking the body or mind with a sudden painful shock: *the boxer pounded his opponent with jarring blows* ◊ *the news of her death was jarring*. **2** (of sound) harsh and grating. **3** consisting of elements that clash or are inconsistent: *some of his outfits are absolutely jarring*. **4** marked by an abrupt and unsettling interruption to the flow or consistency of something: *a jarring shift in tone from comic to tragic*.

jasmine *noun* (also **jasmin**) an ornamental shrub or climbing plant with fragrant white or yellow flowers, which are used in perfumes and in tea. [Say JAZZ min]

jasper *noun* an opaque variety of quartz, usu. red, yellow, or brown in colour.

J

Jat *noun* a member of an Indic people widely distributed in northwestern India.

jaundice • *noun* **1** *Medical* a condition with yellowing of the skin or whites of the eyes, often caused by obstruction of the bile duct or by liver disease. **2** envy, resentment, jealousy: *if they want to maintain goodwill, they will have to be generous, or jaundice will set in*. • *verb* (**jaundices, jaundiced, jaundicing**) **1** affect with jaundice. **2** (esp. as **jaundiced** *adjective*) affect (a person) with envy, resentment, or disillusionment: *in my more jaundiced moments I have often said that Canada is a paradise for humbugs*. [Say JOHN diss]

jaunt • *noun* a short excursion for enjoyment. • *verb* take a jaunt.

jauntily *adverb* in a lively, cheerful, and self-confident manner: *he set off jauntily, whistling to himself*.

jauntiness *noun* a lively, cheerful, and self-confident manner.

jaunty *adjective* (**jauntier, jauntiest**) **1** cheerful and self-confident; carefree. **2** dashing, pert: *a jaunty hat*.

Java *noun* proprietary a programming language used esp. for creating applications for the Internet and other networks. [Say JAV uh]

java *noun* slang coffee. [Say JAV uh or JOV uh]

Javanese (also **Javan**) • *noun* (*plural* **Javanese**) **1 a** a native or inhabitant of Java, a large island in the Malay Archipelago. **b** a person of Javanese descent. **2** the Austronesian language of central Java. • *adjective* of Java, its people, or its language. [Say java NEEZ]

javelin *noun* **1** a light spear thrown in a competitive sport or as a weapon. **2** the athletic event or sport of throwing the javelin. [Say JAVA lin or JAV lin]

Javex *noun* Cdn proprietary chlorine bleach.

jaw • *noun* **1 a** each of the upper and lower bony structures in vertebrates forming the framework of the mouth and containing the teeth. **b** the parts of certain invertebrates used for the ingestion of food. **2 a** (in *plural*) the mouth with its bones and teeth. **b** the narrow mouth of a valley, channel, etc. **c** the gripping parts of a tool or machine. **d** gripping power: *jaws of death*. **3** *informal* **a** talkativeness; tedious talk: *hold your jaw*. **b** a conversation. • *verb* informal speak esp. at tedious length; gossip.

jawbone *noun* a bone of the jaw, esp. that of the lower jaw (the mandible), or either half of this.

jawbreaker *noun* informal **1** a word that is very long or hard to pronounce. **2** a large, round, hard candy.
▶ **jawbreaking** *adjective*

jawed *adjective* (usu. in *combination*) having a jaw or the kind of jaw described: *jawed fish* ◊ *slack-jawed yokels*.

jawline *noun* the outline of the jaw.

Jaws of Life *noun* a powerful hydraulic tool that can pry apart twisted metal, used esp. to rescue people trapped in wrecked vehicles.

jay *noun* any of various medium-sized birds of the crow family, with varied, often colourful, plumage, e.g. a blue jay.

Jaycee *noun* a member of a Junior Chamber of Commerce, a civic organization for young business and community leaders. [Say jay SEE]

jaywalk *verb* (of a pedestrian) cross a street at a place other than an intersection, crosswalk, etc. or against a red light, esp. with disregard for traffic. ▶ **jaywalker** *noun* **jaywalking** *noun*

jazz • *noun* **1 a** a type of music of African-American origin, characterized by improvisation, syncopated phrasing, and a regular rhythm. **b** (as an *adjective*) designating a style of music containing elements of jazz: *jazz-rock*. **2** (also **jazz ballet, jazz dance**) a style of theatrical dance performed to jazz or popular music, and incorporating elements of popular dance. **3** *slang*

energy, excitement. • *verb* (**jazzes, jazzed, jazzing**) play or dance to jazz. PHRASES **all that jazz** all that sort of thing. **jazz up** brighten or enliven. ▶ **jazzer** *noun*

jazzman *noun* (*plural* **jazzmen**) a male jazz musician.

jazzy *adjective* (**jazzier, jazziest**) **1** of or like jazz. **2** *slang* spirited, lively, exciting. **3** *slang* flashy, showy: *a jazzy car*.

Jct. *abbreviation* JUNCTION 2.

jealous *adjective* **1** (often foll. by *of*) envious or resentful (of a person or a person's advantages etc.). **2** suspicious or resentful of rivalry in love or affection. **3** fiercely protective (of rights etc.): *they are very jealous of their good reputation*. **4** (of God) intolerant of disloyalty. ▶ **jealously** *adverb*

jealousy *noun* (*plural* **jealousies**) the state or feeling of being jealous: *a sharp pang of jealousy* ◊ *resentments and jealousies festered*.

SPELL CHECK
jean, gene

Part of a chromosome is a **gene**.

---

jean *noun* **1** a heavy twilled cotton fabric, now usu. denim: *jean jacket*. **2** (usu. in *plural*) hard-wearing pants made of this fabric.

Jeep *noun* proprietary a sturdy, four-wheel drive motor vehicle, suitable for off-road travel.

jeepers *interjection* (also **jeepers creepers**) *slang* expressing surprise etc.

jeer • *verb* **1** (usu. foll. by *at*) speak or call out in derision or mockery; scoff derisively. **2** (usu. foll. by *down, from, out, etc.*) drive or force away by jeering. • *noun* a scoff or taunt. ▶ **jeeringly** *adverb*

Jeez *interjection* slang a mild expression of surprise, discovery, etc.

jeezly *adjective* Cdn slang used as an intensifier: *you're a jeezly fool!*

jehad *noun* = JIHAD. [Say juh HAD]

Jehovah *noun* a form of the Hebrew name of God used in some translations of the Bible. [Say juh HOVE uh]

Jehovah's Witness *noun* (*plural* **Jehovah's Witnesses**) a member of a fundamentalist Christian sect rejecting the supremacy of the state and religious institutions over personal conscience, faith, etc., and expecting the return of Christ to reign on earth.

Jekyll and Hyde *noun* a person alternately displaying opposing good and evil personalities. [Say JECK'll and HIDE]

SPELL CHECK ABC
jell, gel

A jellylike substance is a **gel**.

---

jell *verb* informal **1 a** set as a jelly. **b** (of ideas etc.) take a definite form. **2** (of people) readily co-operate or reach an understanding.

jellied *adjective* **1** set into a jelly: *jellied chicken stock*. **2** containing jelly as an ingredient: *jellied salad*.

Jell-O *noun* proprietary **1** a fruit-flavoured gelatin dessert. **2** the powder used to make this.

jelly • *noun* (*plural* **jellies**) **1 a** a type of jam made of fruit juice boiled with sugar and cooled to a semi-solid consistency. **b** a dessert made of juice, fruit-flavoured water, etc., sugar and gelatin, set to a soft semi-solid consistency, often in a mould. **c** a similar preparation derived from meat, bones, etc., and gelatin. **2** any substance of a similar consistency: *petroleum jelly*. • *verb* (**jellies, jellied, jellying**) **1** set or cause to set as a jelly, congeal. **2** set (food) in a jelly.

jelly bean *noun* a bean-shaped candy with a gelatinous centre and a hard sugar coating.

jelly doughnut *noun* a round jam-filled doughnut, usu. coated in icing sugar.

jellyfish *noun* (*plural* **jellyfish** or **jellyfishes**) a marine animal having an umbrella-shaped jellylike body and stinging tentacles.

jelly roll *noun* a thin, flat, rectangular sponge cake spread with jam or other filling and rolled up to form a cylindrical cake with a spiral cross-section.

je ne sais quoi *noun* an indefinable something: *she has that je ne sais quoi that distinguishes a professional from an amateur.* [Say zhuh nuh say KWAH]

jeopardize *verb* (**jeopardizes, jeopardized, jeopardizing**) endanger; put into jeopardy: *he would never do anything to jeopardize his career.* [Say JEP er dize]

jeopardy *noun* **1** danger, esp. of severe harm or loss: *the civil war has put thousands of lives in jeopardy ◊ the future of the school and 50 jobs are in jeopardy.* **2** *Law* the risk of being convicted and punished for a criminal offence. [Say JEP er dee]

jeremiad *noun* a doleful complaint or lamentation; a list of woes: *we hope that his jeremiad did not make readers too anxious about Canada's future.* [Say jerra MY ud]

jerk[1] • *noun* **1** a sharp sudden pull, twist, twitch, etc. **2** a spasmodic muscular twitch. **3** *slang* a fool; a stupid or annoying person. **4** (**the jerk**) the raising of a barbell to above the head by a rapid extension of the arms, following an initial lift to shoulder level. • *verb* **1** move with a jerk. **2** pull, thrust, twist, etc., with a jerk. **3** throw with a suddenly arrested motion. **4** (in weightlifting) raise (a weight) from shoulder level to above the head. PHRASES **jerk around** *slang* deal with unfairly; deceive or mislead.

jerk[2] • *verb* cure (meat) by cutting it in slices and drying it in the sun. • *noun* designating an originally Jamaican method of preparing meat by cutting it into strips, seasoning highly with pepper and spices, and barbecuing: *jerk chicken.*

jerkily *adverb* in a jerky manner, with spasmodic movements or abrupt starts and stops.

jerkin *noun* a sleeveless jacket.

jerkwater *adjective informal* (of a town etc.) small and remote; insignificant.

jerky[1] *adjective* (**jerkier, jerkiest**) having sudden abrupt movements; spasmodic.

jerky[2] *noun* jerked meat.

jerry-built *adjective* badly or hastily built with materials of poor quality: *did business in tents and jerry-built shacks.*

jerry can *noun* a kind of gasoline or water can.

jersey *noun* (*plural* **jerseys**) **1** a soft, fine, usu. stretchy knitted fabric. **2** a knitted usu. woollen pullover or similar garment. **3** a distinguishing sweater or shirt worn by members of a hockey, soccer, etc. team. **4** (**Jersey**) a light brown dairy cow of a breed originally from Jersey in the Channel Islands.

Jerusalem artichoke *noun* **1** a species of sunflower with edible underground tubers. **2** this tuber used as a vegetable.

jest • *noun* **1** **a** a joke. **b** fun. **2** **a** banter. **b** an object of derision: *a standing jest.* • *verb* joke; make jests. PHRASES **in jest** in fun.

jester *noun hist.* a professional joker or fool at a medieval court etc., traditionally wearing a cap and bells.

Jesuit *noun* a member of the Society of Jesus, a Catholic order of priests founded in 1534 to do missionary work. The order was zealous in opposing the Protestant Reformation and in spearheading the reforms of the Counter-Reformation, and has retained an important influence in Catholic thought and education. [Say JEZH yoo it or JEZZ oo it]

jet[1] • *noun* **1** a stream of liquid, gas, or (more rarely) solid particles shot out, esp. from a small opening. **2** a spout or nozzle for emitting water etc. in this way. **3 a** a jet engine. **b** an aircraft powered by one or more jet engines. • *verb* (**jets, jetted, jetting**) **1** spurt out or cause to spurt out in jets. **2** send or travel by jet plane.

jet[2] *noun* **1** a hard black variety of coal capable of being carved and highly polished. **2** *noun & adjective* (also **jet black**) a deep glossy black.

jet boat *noun* a small boat without a propeller, the engine of which expels a jet of water to provide thrust. ▶ **jet boater** *noun* **jet boating** *noun*

jet engine *noun* an engine (esp. of an aircraft) which for forward thrust uses the backward ejection of a high-speed jet of gas.

jet lag *noun* extreme tiredness and disrupted biological rhythms felt after a long flight in which different time zones are crossed in a relatively short time. ▶ **jet-lagged** *adjective*

jetliner *noun* a commercial airplane equipped with jet engines.

jet-propelled *adjective* propelled by a jet engine.

jetsam *noun* discarded material washed ashore, esp. that thrown overboard to lighten a ship etc. (*compare* FLOTSAM). [Say JET sum]

jet set *noun informal* wealthy people frequently travelling by air, esp. for pleasure. ▶ **jet-setter** *noun* **jet-setting** *adjective*

Jet Ski • *noun* (*plural* **Jet Skis**) *proprietary* a jet-propelled watercraft ridden like a motorbike. • *verb* (**jet ski, jet skis, jet skied, jet skiing**) ride on a jet ski. ▶ **jet skier** *noun* **jet skiing** *noun*

jet stream *noun* **1** a narrow current of very strong winds encircling the globe several miles above the earth. **2** the stream from a jet engine.

jettison • *verb* **1** throw (esp. heavy material) overboard to lighten an aircraft, ship, hot-air balloon, etc. **2** release or drop from a spacecraft in flight. **3** abandon; get rid of (something no longer wanted): *the scheme was jettisoned.* • *noun* the act of jettisoning. [Say JETTA sun]

jetty *noun* (*plural* **jetties**) **1** a landing pier. **2** a pier or breakwater constructed to protect or defend a harbour, coast, etc.

Jew *noun* a person of Hebrew descent or whose religion is Judaism.

jewel • *noun* **1 a** a precious stone; a gem. **b** this as used for its hardness as a bearing in watchmaking. **2** a personal ornament containing a jewel or jewels. **3** something of great beauty or worth. **4** (as an *adjective*) cut or shaped like a jewel: *a jewel neckline.* **5** (as an *adjective*) having the intense colour of a jewel: *jewel tones.* • *verb* (**jewels, jewelled, jewelling**) **1** (esp. as *adjective* **jewelled**) adorn or set with jewels. **2** (in watchmaking) set with jewels. PHRASES **jewel in the crown** the best in a particular class of assets.

jewel box *noun* (*plural* **jewel boxes**) **1** (also **jewellery box**) a small, usu. ornamental box for storing jewellery or other valuables. **2** (also **jewel case**) the hinged plastic case in which a compact disc is packaged.

jeweller *noun* (also esp. *US* **jeweler**) a person who makes or sells jewels or jewellery.

jewellery *noun* (also **jewelry**) ornamental objects for personal adornment, e.g. rings and necklaces, esp. made of precious metal and set with jewels. [Say JEW luh ree or JEW ul ree or JULE ree]

Jewish *adjective* **1** of or relating to Jews. **2** of Judaism. ▶ **Jewishness** *noun*

Jewry noun (plural **Jewries**) the Jewish people, nation, or community; Jews collectively.

Jew's harp noun a small lyre-shaped musical instrument held between the teeth and struck with the finger.

J.H.S. abbreviation JUNIOR HIGH SCHOOL.

jib • noun **1** a triangular sail in front of the large sail on a boat or ship. **2** the projecting arm of a crane. • verb (**jibs, jibbed, jibbing**) (of a sail etc.) pull or swing round from one side of the ship to the other; gybe.

jibe[1] • noun an instance of mocking or taunting. • verb (**jibes, jibed, jibing**) **1** (often foll. by at) jeer, mock. **2** sneer at, taunt, mock.

jibe[2] verb & noun (**jibes, jibed, jibing**) = GYBE.

jibe[3] verb (**jibes, jibed, jibing**) (usu. foll. by with) informal agree; be in accord.

jiffy noun (plural **jiffies**) (also **jiff**) informal a short time; a moment: in a jiffy.

jig • noun **1 a** a lively dance with springs and hops. **b** the music for this, usu. in triple time. **2** a device that holds a piece of work and guides the tools operating on it. **3** a device for catching fish that is jerked up and down through the water. • verb (**jigs, jigged, jigging**) **1** dance a jig. **2** move quickly and jerkily up and down. **3** work on or equip with a jig or jigs. **4** fish (for) or catch with a jig or jigger. PHRASES **in jig time** informal extremely quickly; in a short time. **the jig is up** informal the scheme is revealed or foiled.

jigger[1] • noun **1 a** a small tackle consisting of a double and single block with a rope. **b** a small sail at the stern. **c** a small fishing boat having this. **2 a** a small glass or metal cup marked for measuring liquor. **b** the quantity of liquor contained in this. **3** Cdn **a** a device upon which a gill net is hung underneath ice. **b** a piece of lead shaped like a fish, with two hooks in the mouth, fastened on the end of a heavy fishing line. **4** a person or thing that jigs. • verb (usu. in phr. **I'll be jiggered**) slang confound, damn.

jigger[2] noun = CHIGOE.

jiggle • verb (**jiggles, jiggled, jiggling**) **1** shake lightly; rock jerkily. **2** fidget. • noun a light shake. ▶**jiggly** adjective

Jiggs' dinner noun Cdn (Nfld) a boiled dinner of corned beef, potatoes, and other vegetables, esp. cabbage.

jigsaw noun **1 a** (also **jigsaw puzzle**) a puzzle consisting of a picture on board or wood etc. cut into irregular interlocking pieces to be reassembled. **b** a mental puzzle resolvable by assembling various pieces of information. **2** a machine saw with a fine blade enabling it to cut curved lines in a sheet of wood, metal, etc.

jihad noun **1** a holy war undertaken by Muslims for the propagation or defence of Islam. **2** a campaign or crusade in some cause: the long jihad against the unions needs to end. [Say juh HAD]

jillion noun informal a great many, an extremely large quantity. ▶**jillionth** adjective

jilt • verb abruptly reject or abandon (a lover etc.). • noun a person (esp. a woman) who jilts a lover.

Jim Crow noun US the practice of segregating or discriminating against blacks: Jim Crow laws. ▶**Jim Crowism** noun

jim-dandy • adjective excellent; outstanding. • noun (plural **jim-dandies**) an excellent person or thing.

jim-jams plural noun slang a fit of depression or nervousness.

jimmy • noun (plural **jimmies**) a burglar's short crowbar, usu. made in sections. • verb (**jimmies, jimmied, jimmying**) force open with a jimmy.

jingle • noun **1 a** a mixed noise as of bells or light metal objects being shaken together. **b** a thing that jingles, esp. a bell. **2 a** a repetition of the same sound in words, esp. as an aid to memory or to attract attention. **b** a short verse of this kind used in advertising etc. • verb (**jingles, jingled, jingling**) **1** make or cause to make a jingling sound. **2** proceed or move with such a sound. **3** (of writing) be full of alliterations, rhymes, etc. PHRASES **give a person a jingle** informal telephone a person. ▶**jingly** adjective (**jinglier, jingliest**)

jingo noun (plural **jingoes**) a supporter of policy favouring war; a blustering patriot. PHRASES **by jingo!** a mild oath. ▶**jingoism** noun **jingoist** noun **jingoistic** adjective

jink • verb move elusively; dodge. • noun an act of dodging or eluding.

jinni noun (also **jinnee, jinn**) (plural **jinn**) (in Muslim mythology) an intelligent being lower than the angels, able to appear in human and animal forms, and having power over people. [Say jin EE or JIN ee]

jinx informal • noun (plural **jinxes**) a person or thing that seems to cause bad luck. • verb (**jinxes, jinxed, jinxing**) (often in passive) subject (a person) to an unlucky force.

JIT abbreviation Business just-in-time.

jitter informal • noun **1** (**the jitters**) extreme nervousness. **2** Electronics **a** slight random or irregular variation, esp. in the shape or timing of a regular pulse. **b** unsteadiness of an image etc. due to this. • verb be or act nervous.

jitterbug • noun **1** hist. a fast dance popular in the 1940s, performed chiefly to swing music. **2** a person fond of dancing this. • verb (**jitterbugs, jitterbugged, jitterbugging**) dance the jitterbug.

jittery adjective **1** anxious and nervous. **2** characterized by slight irregular variation in a sound or image.

jiu-jitsu noun a Japanese system of unarmed combat using an opponent's strength and weight to his or her disadvantage, now also practised to improve physical fitness. [Say joo JIT soo]

jive • noun **1** a jerky lively style of dance esp. popular in the 1950s, performed to jazz or rock'n'roll music. **2** music for this dance. **3** a variety of American black English associated esp. with jazz musicians and enthusiasts. • verb (**jives, jived, jiving**) **1** dance the jive. **2** play jive music. **3** slang a mislead, fool: are you jiving me? **b** fool around; talk nonsense. **4** informal = JIBE[3]. ▶**jiver** noun

JK abbreviation (plural **JKs**) Cdn (Ont.) JUNIOR KINDERGARTEN.

Jnr. abbreviation Junior.

job • noun **1** a piece of work, esp. one done for hire or profit. **2** a paid position of employment. **3 a** anything one has to do. **b** responsibility: it's your job to do the dishes. **c** a specified operation or other matter, esp. an operation involving plastic surgery: nose job ◊ paint job. **4 a** informal a difficult task: had a job to find them. **b** performance: did a poor job on the exam. **5** slang an example of its type: that car's a neat little job. **6** Computing an item of work regarded separately. **7** slang a crime, esp. a robbery. **8** a transaction in which private advantage prevails over duty or public interest. **9** informal a state of affairs or set of circumstances: is a bad job. • verb (**jobs, jobbed, jobbing**) **1 a** do jobs; do piecework. **b** (usu. foll. by out) let or deal with for profit; subcontract. **2 a** deal in stocks. **b** buy and sell (stocks or goods) as a middleman. **3 a** turn a position of trust to private advantage. **b** deal corruptly with (a matter). **4** slang swindle. PHRASES **do the job** succeed in doing what is required or desired. **get on with the job** proceed with one's work; continue with one's affairs.

on the job at work; in the course of doing a piece of work. **out of a job** unemployed.

job action *noun* an organized protest by employees, such as a work slowdown.

jobber *noun* **1** a wholesaler. **2** a pieceworker. **3** a person who uses a public office or position of trust for private or party advantage.

jobbie *noun slang* = JOB *noun* 5.

jobbing *adjective* working on separate or occasional jobs.

job-hunt *verb* seek employment. ▶**job-hunter** *noun* **job-hunting** *noun*

jobless *adjective* unemployed. ▶**joblessness** *noun*

job-share • *verb* (**job-shares, job-shared, job-sharing**) (of two part-time employees) jointly do a full-time job, sharing the pay. • *noun* a job-sharing situation or arrangement. ▶**job-sharer** *noun*

job-sharing *noun* an arrangement by which a full-time job is done jointly by two or more part-time employees who share the remuneration etc.

jock *noun informal* **1** = JOCKSTRAP. **2** an esp. male athlete or sports fan, esp. one not interested in intellectual or artistic pursuits. **3** a disc jockey. **4** an enthusiast or devotee of some activity: *computer jock*. **5** a jockey.

jockey • *noun* (*plural* **jockeys**) **1** a rider in horse races, esp. a professional one. **2** *informal* (usu. in *combination*) a person having control, guidance, or direction of something: *desk jockey*. • *verb* (**jockeys, jockeyed, jockeying**) **1** (usu. foll. by *for*) try to gain an advantageous position esp. by skilful manoeuvring or unfair action: *jockey for position*. **2** ride (a horse) as a jockey.

Jockey Club *noun* (also **jockey club**) a club or association for the promotion and regulation of horse racing.

Jockey shorts *plural noun proprietary* men's or boys' close-fitting underpants with elasticized waist and leg openings and a triangular flap at the front.

jock itch *noun* a fungal infection of the groin area.

jockstrap *noun* a close-fitting undergarment providing support or protection for the male genitals.

jocular *adjective* **1** (of speech, action, etc.) of the nature of a joke; said, done, etc. jokingly: *a jocular comment*. **2** (of a person, disposition, etc.) fond of joking; speaking or acting in jest or merriment. ▶**jocularity** *noun* **jocularly** *adverb* [Say JOCK you ler, jock you LAIR uh tee]

jodhpurs *plural noun* long breeches for riding etc., wide around the hips and thighs but close-fitting from the knee to the ankle. [Say JOD purrs]

joe *noun slang* **1** a fellow or average man: *the average joe*. **2** coffee.

Joe Blow *noun informal* a hypothetical average man.

joe job *noun Cdn informal* a menial or monotonous task.

Joe Public *noun informal* (a member of) the general public.

joey *noun* (*plural* **joeys**) a young kangaroo.

jog¹ • *verb* (**jogs, jogged, jogging**) **1** run at a slow pace, esp. as exercise. **2** (of a horse) move at a slow regular pace. **3** (often foll. by *on, along*) proceed, go on one's way, get through the time, esp. at a slow and steady pace: *the industry is jogging along at a respectable growth rate*. **4** nudge (a person), esp. to arouse attention. **5** shake or bump with a push or jerk. **6** give a gentle reminder to (a person's or one's own memory). • *noun* **1 a** a slow walk or trot. **b** a gentle run taken as a form of exercise. **2** a shake, push, or nudge.

jog² • *noun* **1** a short bend, turn, or change of direction in a road etc., after which the road continues in its original direction. **2** a notch, step, or jag in an otherwise level surface or straight line. • *verb* (**jogs,**

jogged, jogging) bend, turn, or suddenly change course or direction.

jogger *noun* **1** a person who jogs, esp. regularly for exercise. **2** *Cdn & Brit.* = RUNNING SHOE.

jogging *noun* running at a gentle, regular pace as a form of exercise.

joggle • *verb* (**joggles, joggled, joggling**) shake or move by or as if by repeated jerks. • *noun* a slight shake or jerking movement.

john *noun informal* **1** a toilet. **2** a washroom. **3** a prostitute's customer.

John Doe *noun* **1 a** a person whose real name is unknown. **b** *Law* an anonymous party, usu. the plaintiff, in a legal action. **2** *informal* = JOE BLOW.

johnnycake *noun* a cornmeal bread usu. baked or fried on a griddle.

Johnny Canuck *noun Cdn informal* **1** a native, inhabitant, or citizen of Canada. **2** a Canadian soldier, esp. during the world wars. **3** Canada personified.

johnny-come-lately *noun* (*plural* **johnny-come-latelies**) *informal* a person who has recently arrived or come to prominence; an upstart.

joie de vivre *noun* a feeling of healthy and exuberant enjoyment of life. [Say zhwah duh VEEVRA]

join • *verb* **1** (often foll. by *to, together*) put together; fasten, unite. **2** connect (points) by a line etc. **3** become a member of (an association, society, organization, etc.). **4** take one's place with or in (a company, group, etc.). **5 a** come into the company of (a person). **b** (foll. by *in*) take part with (others) in an activity etc.: *join me in eating*. **c** (foll. by *for*) share the company of (a person) for a specified occasion: *may I join you for lunch?* **6** (often foll. by *with, to*) come together, be united, esp. in action or purpose. **7** (often foll. by *in*) take part with others in an activity etc. **8** be or become connected or continuous with: *the Liard joins the Mackenzie at Fort Simpson*. **9** link or unite (people etc. together) in marriage, friendship, or other alliance. • *noun* a point, line, or surface at which two or more things are joined. PHRASES **join battle** begin fighting. **join forces** combine efforts. **join hands 1 a** clasp each other's hands. **b** clasp one's hands together. **2** combine in an action or enterprise. **join up 1** enlist for military service. **2** (often foll. by *with*) unite, connect. ▶**joinable** *adjective*

joiner *noun* **1** *informal* a person who readily joins groups, associations, etc. **2** a device used for making carpentry joints.

joinery *noun* **1** the construction of wooden furniture etc. **2** carpentry joints collectively.

joint • *noun* **1 a** a place at which things or parts are joined together. **b** a point at which, or a contrivance by which, two parts of an artificial structure are joined either rigidly or so as to allow movement. **2 a** a structure in an animal body by which two bones are fitted and held together, usu. so that relative movement is possible. **b** the point of connection of two movable parts in an invertebrate, esp. an arthropod. **3 a** any of the parts into which an animal carcass is divided for food. **b** a part of a plant, animal, etc. connected by a joint to an adjacent part, esp. such a part of a digit or limb. **4** *slang* **a** often *derogatory* a place where people go for eating, drinking, entertainment, etc.: *burger joint*. **b** a residence or establishment. **c** prison. **5** *slang* a marijuana cigarette. **6** the part of a stem from which a leaf or branch grows. • *adjective* **1** (of a single thing) held or done by, or belonging to, two or more persons etc. in conjunction: *a joint venture*. **2** (of a person or persons) sharing with another in some action, state, etc.: *joint author*. **3** of, concerning, or involving both houses of a bicameral parliament. • *verb*

1 connect or fasten by joints. **2** divide (a body or member) at a joint or into joints. PHRASES **joint and several** (of a bond etc.) signed by more than one person, of whom each is liable for the whole sum. **out of joint 1** (of a bone) dislocated. **2** disordered, out of order: *feels that the times are hideously out of joint*.

Joint Chiefs of Staff *plural noun* (in the US) the chief military advisory body to the President, consisting of a chairperson, the Chiefs of Staff of the Army and Air Force, the Commandant of the Marine Corps, and the Chief of Naval Operations.

joint committee *noun* a committee composed of members nominated by two or more distinct bodies.

jointed *adjective* **1** provided with, constructed with, or having joints. **2** having joints of a specified kind. **3** *Botany* **a** having or appearing to have joints. **b** separating readily at the joints.

jointly *adverb* together, in partnership or collaboration: *the two countries are working jointly to address the issue* ◊ *we completed the project jointly with a Japanese firm* ◊ *the program, jointly financed by the province and the municipalities, will be launched in May*.

joint-stock company *noun* (*plural* **joint-stock companies**) a company, usu. unincorporated, that has its members' capital pooled in a common fund.

joint venture *noun* a commercial enterprise undertaken jointly by two or more parties otherwise retaining their separate identities.

joist *noun* each of a series of parallel supporting beams of timber, steel, etc., used in floors, ceilings, etc.

jojoba *noun* an evergreen shrub or tree of the southwestern US, which produces seeds yielding an extract used in cosmetics. [Say ho HO buh]

joke • *noun* **1 a** a thing said or done to excite laughter. **b** a witticism, jest, or short humorous anecdote. **2 a** ridiculous thing, person, or circumstance. **3 a** something trifling; a matter that is not serious, true, or worthy of concern: *that theory is a joke*. **b** *informal* something easy: *that exam was a joke*. • *verb* (**jokes, joked, joking**) **1 a** make a joke or jokes. **b** utter as a joke. **2** make the object of a joke, poke fun at; banter. • PHRASES (**all**) **joking aside** speaking seriously. **no joke** *informal* a serious matter.

joker *noun* **1** a person who jokes. **2** a person who is considered foolish or inept and so not treated seriously. **3** a playing card usu. with a figure of a jester, used in some games esp. as a wild card. **4** an unexpected factor or resource.

jokey *adjective* lighthearted and amusing: *instead of responding to the criticism with anger, he was quite jokey about it* ◊ *the teacher's jokey approach is quite popular with the students*. ▶ **jokiness** *noun*

jokingly *adverb* in a way that is intended to be amusing: *we jokingly call her "Anna Banana"*.

jollity *noun* **1** the quality or condition of being jolly, cheerful, or festive. **2** merrymaking; festiveness. [Say JOLLA tee]

jolly[1] • *adjective* (**jollier, jolliest**) **1** cheerful and good-humoured. **2** lively and very pleasant; delightful or enjoyable. • *verb* (**jollies, jollied, jollying**) **1** (usu. foll. by *up, along*) *informal* keep or make (a person) jolly or cheerful by friendly behaviour etc. **2** poke fun at, tease. • *noun* (*plural* **jollies**) *informal* (usu. in *plural*) a thrill or cause of excitement or pleasure.

jolly[2] *noun* (*plural* **jollies**) (also **jolly boat**) a small light boat carried aboard a ship.

Jolly Jumper *noun Cdn proprietary* an infant swing which suspends a baby in a harness in a standing position just above the floor, allowing the child to jump, exercise its legs, etc.

Jolly Roger *noun* a pirates' black flag, usu. with a skull and crossbones.

jolt • *verb* **1** disturb or shake from the normal position with a jerk. **2** give a mental shock to; perturb. **3** invigorate suddenly or abruptly. **4 a** move with a jolt. **b** (of a vehicle) move along with jerks, as on a rough road. • *noun* **1** an abrupt movement or jerk. **2** a surprise or mental shock. **3** a sudden invigorating sensation: *caffeine provides a jolt*.

Jordanian • *adjective* of or relating to the kingdom of Jordan in the Middle East. • *noun* a native or inhabitant of Jordan. [Say jor DAINY in]

josh *verb slang* (**joshes, joshed, joshing**) **1** tease or joke with. **2** indulge in banter. ▶ **joshing** *noun*

joss *noun* (*plural* **josses**) **1** a Chinese figure of a god. **2** (also **joss stick**) a stick of fragrant tinder mixed with clay, burned as incense.

jostle • *verb* (**jostles, jostled, jostling**) **1** push, bump, or collide, esp. in a crowd: *passengers jostle on the subway* ◊ *she jostled my elbow and I spilt my tea*. **2** (foll. by *for, with*) vie, struggle, or compete forcefully in order to gain something. • *noun* **1** the act or an instance of jostling. **2** a collision, rough push, or thrust. ▶ **jostler** *noun* [Say JOSSLE]

jot • *verb* (**jots, jotted, jotting**) (usu. foll. by *down*) write briefly or hastily. • *noun* a very small amount: *not one jot or tittle*.

jotting *noun* **1** (usu. in *plural*) a note; something jotted down. **2** the act or an instance of hastily writing something down.

joual *noun* a variety of Canadian French considered to be uneducated, characterized by non-standard grammar and syntax and, esp. in cities, numerous English borrowings. [Say zhoo ALL]

joule *noun* the SI unit of work or energy equal to the work done by a force of one newton when its point of application moves one metre in the direction of action of the force. Symbol: **J**. [Say JOOL]

jounce *verb* (**jounces, jounced, jouncing**) bump, bounce, jolt. ▶ **jouncing** *noun & adjective* [Rhymes with BOUNCE]

journal *noun* **1** a daily record of events; a diary. **2 a** a periodical, esp. an academic one dealing with a specialized subject. **b** an esp. daily newspaper. **3** a book in which business transactions are entered, with a statement of the accounts to which each is to be debited and credited. **4** (**the Journals**) a record of daily proceedings in a legislative assembly.

journalese *noun* a hackneyed style of language characteristic of some newspaper writing.

journalism *noun* **1** the work of collecting, writing, and reporting news items in the press or on television etc. **2** the news media collectively. **3** material broadcast etc. by the news media. ▶ **journalist** *noun* **journalistic** *adjective* **journalistically** *adverb*

journey • *noun* (*plural* **journeys**) **1** an act of going from one place to another, esp. at a long distance. **2** the distance travelled in a specified time: *a day's journey*. **3** the travelling of a vehicle along a route at a stated time. **4** one's passage or progress through life. • *verb* (**journeys, journeyed, journeying**) make a journey. ▶ **journeyer** *noun*

journeyman *noun* (*plural* **journeymen**) **1** a person who, having served an apprenticeship, is qualified to work in a craft or trade under the direction of a more qualified person. **2** a reliable but not outstanding worker.

joust • *noun* **1** *hist.* a combat between two knights on horseback with lances. **2** a verbal, political, etc. encounter or contest, esp. between two individuals: *the candidates squared off in a televised joust*. • *verb* engage in

a joust: *the guerrillas jousted for supremacy*. ▶ **jouster** *noun*

Jove *noun* PHRASES **by Jove!** an exclamation of surprise or approval.

jovial *adjective* cheerful and friendly: *a jovial mood*. ▶ **joviality** *noun* **jovially** *adverb* [Say JOE vee ul, joe vee ALA tee]

Jovian *adjective* of the planet Jupiter. [Say JOE vee in]

jowl *noun* **1** (often in *plural*) the cheek, esp. when this is loose and fleshy and sags below a person's jaw or chin. **2 a** *Cdn* (*Nfld*) the meat of the cheek of cod eaten as food. **b** the meat of the cheek of a pig eaten as food. **3** the dewlap of oxen, wattle of a bird, etc. **4** the jaw or jawbone. PHRASES **cheek by jowl** close together; side by side. [Rhymes with *HOWL*]

jowly *adjective* (of a person or a person's face) having cheeks that are loose and fleshy and sag below the jaw or chin.

joy *noun* **1** a vivid emotion of pleasure; extreme gladness. **2** a thing that causes joy. **3** *informal* satisfaction, success: *got no joy*. PHRASES **wish a person joy of** *ironic* be gladly rid of (what that person has to deal with).

joyful *adjective* full of, showing, or causing joy. ▶ **joyfully** *adverb* **joyfulness** *noun*

joyless *adjective* bringing no happiness; without joy: *a joyless encounter with his ex-girlfriend*. ▶ **joylessly** *adverb*

joyous *adjective* (of an occasion, circumstance, etc.) characterized by pleasure or joy; joyful. ▶ **joyously** *adverb* **joyousness** *noun*

joyride *informal* • *noun* **1** a car ride taken for fun and excitement, usu. without the owner's permission. **2** a pleasurable, often exciting, and usu. brief experience. • *verb* (only in progressive tenses) go for a joyride: *they had been joyriding in a stolen car*. ▶ **joyrider** *noun* **joyriding** *noun*

joystick *noun* **1** a lever that can be moved in several directions to control the movement of an image on a video or computer screen. **2** the control column of an aircraft.

JP *abbreviation* (*plural* **JPs**) JUSTICE OF THE PEACE.

Jr. *abbreviation* Junior.

jubilant *adjective* rejoicing, joyful. ▶ **jubilantly** *adverb* [Say JOOBA lint]

jubilation *verb* (**jubilates**, **jubilated**, **jubilating**) a feeling of great happiness and triumph. ▶ **jubilation** *noun* [Say joo buh LAY sh'n]

jubilee *noun* **1** an anniversary, esp. the 25th, 50th, or 60th. **2** a time or season of rejoicing. **3** a *Jewish Hist.* a year of emancipation and restoration, kept every 50 years. **b** a time of restitution, remission, or release. **4** *Catholicism* a period, usu. every 25 years, during which indulgences are granted under certain conditions. [Say jooba LEE or JOOBA lee]

Judaeo- *combining form* = JUDEO-.

Judaic *adjective* of or characteristic of the Jews or Judaism. [Say joo DAY ick]

Judaica *plural noun* (treated as *singular*) **1** the literature, customs, ritual objects, artifacts, etc. which are of particular relevance to Jews or Judaism. **2** such items or aspects of Jewish life individually. [Say joo DAY ick uh]

Judaism *noun* **1** the religion of the Jews, based on the law of God as revealed to Moses and recorded in the first five books of the Hebrew scriptures. **2** the cultural practices, social identity, etc. based on this religion. [Say JOO day ism]

Judas *noun* (*plural* **Judases**) a person who betrays a friend. [Say JOO dis]

judder • *verb* (esp. of a mechanism) shake or vibrate noisily or violently. • *noun* **1** an instance of juddering. **2** the condition of juddering. ▶ **juddery** *adjective*

Judeo- *combining form* **1** pertaining to the Jews, Judaism, or things Jewish. **2** Jewish and: *Judeo-Christian*. [Say joo DAY oh]

judge • *noun* **1** a public officer appointed to hear and try causes in a court of justice. **2** a person appointed to decide a competition, contest, dispute, etc. **3 a** a person who decides anything in question. **b** a person regarded in terms of capacity to decide on the merits of a thing or question: *am no judge of that*. **4** *Jewish Hist.* a leader having temporary authority in Israel in the period between Joshua and the Kings. • *verb* (**judges**, **judged**, **judging**) **1 a** try (a cause) in a court of justice. **b** pronounce sentence on (a person). **2** form an opinion about; estimate, appraise. **3** act as a judge of (a dispute or contest). **4** conclude, consider, or suppose: *I judged her to be about 50* ◊ *Mom judged that the trip would take us about 6 hours*. **5 a** form a judgment. **b** act as judge. ▶ **judgeship** *noun*

judgment *noun* (also **judgement**) **1** the critical faculty; discernment: *an error of judgment*. **2** good sense. **3** an opinion or estimate: *in my judgment*. **4 a** the sentence of a court of justice. **b** judicial decision or order in court. **5 a** a divine decree, decision, or sentence. **b** often *jocular* a misfortune viewed as a deserved recompense: *it is a judgment on you for getting up late*. **6** (**Judgment**) = LAST JUDGMENT. PHRASES **against one's better judgment** contrary to what one really feels to be advisable. **pass judgment 1** (of a judge) give a verdict. **2** criticize or condemn someone from a position of assumed moral superiority.

judgmental *adjective* (also **judgemental**) **1** of, concerning, or by way of judgment. **2** condemning, critical, esp. in moral matters. ▶ **judgmentally** *adverb*

judgment call *noun* a decision made on personal observation, by subjective determination, etc., esp. when the facts of a situation are indeterminate.

Judgment Day *noun* the day on which the Last Judgment is believed to take place; doomsday.

judicare *noun* *Cdn* a form of legal aid in which lawyers bill the province for services to poor clients rather than receiving a salary. [Say JOODA care]

judicial *adjective* **1** of, done by, or proper to a court of law. **2** invested with the authority to judge causes: *a judicial assembly*. **3** of or having to do with a judge: *judicial review*. [Say joo DISH'll]

Judicial Committee *noun* *Cdn* a committee made up of chief judges, either nationally or from a specific province or territory, which considers proposed appointments of judges to a superior court.

Judicial Committee of the Privy Council *noun* esp. *hist.* the final court for the disposal of appeals made to the King or Queen in Council from colonial countries; it was the final court of appeal for Canadians until 1949.

judicial district *noun* *Cdn* (in certain provinces) a territory, county, or district subdivided for purposes of holding district or county courts, with a judge having jurisdiction over each subdivision.

judicially *adverb* by a judge or court of law: *a judicially issued search warrant*.

judicial review *noun* *Law* a procedure by which a superior judicial body may pronounce on (in Canada) the conduct of an inferior court, committee, etc. to ensure the conduct was proper.

judiciary *noun* (*plural* **judiciaries**) the judges of a nation collectively: *independence of the judiciary is a cornerstone of our legal system*. [Say joo DISHA ree or joo DISHY airy]

judicious *adjective* having, showing, or done with good judgment or sense: *a judicious use of funds*.

J

▶**judiciously** *adverb* **judiciousness** *noun* [Say joo DISH us]

judo *noun* a refined form of jiu-jitsu using principles of movement and balance, practised as a sport or form of exercise. ▶**judoist** *noun* [Say JOO doe]

jug *noun* **1 a** a large, deep vessel, usu. of glass or earthenware, with a narrow neck and usu. a handle. a handle. **b** *Cdn & Brit.* a deep vessel for holding liquids, with a handle and often with a spout or lip shaped for pouring. **2** the contents of a jug. **3** *slang* prison. **4** (in *plural*) *slang* a woman's breasts.

jug band *noun* a folk or blues band in which jugs are played by blowing across the opening to produce bass notes, usu. accompanied by other makeshift or simple instruments.

juggernaut *noun* a large and powerful force, institution, or movement whose growth or progress cannot be controlled: *Japan's relentless industrial juggernaut.* [Say JUGGER not]

juggle • *verb* (**juggles, juggled, juggling**) **1** perform feats of dexterity, esp. by tossing objects in the air and catching them, keeping several in the air at the same time. **2** continue to deal with (several activities) at once, esp. with ingenuity. **3 a** change the arrangement of something adroitly to achieve a more viable or satisfactory result: *juggle bookings.* **b** manipulate or misrepresent (facts etc.), esp. to deceive or cheat. • *noun* an act or instance of juggling.

juggler *noun* a person who juggles.

jughead *noun* *slang* a stupid person.

jug milk *noun* (also **jug milk store, jug milk outlet,** etc.) *Cdn* (*Ont.*) a convenience store at which milk may be bought in returnable plastic jugs.

jugular • *adjective* **1 a** of the neck or throat. **b** designating or pertaining to any of several large veins of the neck. **2** (of fish) having its belly fins farther forward than the fins on its back, in the throat region. • *noun* **1** (also **jugular vein**) any of several large veins of the neck which carry blood from the face, head, brain, etc. **2** the weakest point in an opponent's argument etc., esp. when subject to fierce attack: *a go-for-the-jugular campaign.* [Say JUG yuh ler]

juice • *noun* **1** the extractable liquid part of a vegetable or fruit, commonly containing its characteristic flavour etc. **2 a** the fluid part of an animal body or substance, esp. a secretion. **b** the fluid naturally contained in or coming from anything. **3 a** (in *plural*) a person's vitality or creative, expressive, etc. faculties. **b** strength or vigour. **4** *informal* gasoline or electricity. **5** *slang* influence or money, esp. that obtained by or used in corrupt or criminal activities. **6** *slang* gossip, rumour, scandal. **7** *slang* alcoholic drink; liquor. • *verb* (**juices, juiced, juicing**) extract the juice from (a fruit etc.). ▪ PHRASES **juice up 1** increase the power, potential, or performance of. **2** heighten the enthusiasm, energy, or style of.

juice bar *noun* **1** a café-style establishment serving esp. freshly squeezed fruit juices. **2** a nightclub for teenagers, where only non-alcoholic beverages are served.

juiced *adjective* **1** *slang* intoxicated. **2** *slang* (of a baseball, card deck, etc.) being inexplicably and perhaps illicitly altered and enhanced for superior results. **3** (of fruit etc.) having had its juice extracted.

juicer *noun* **1** an appliance or device used to extract juice from fruit or vegetables. **2** an alcoholic.

juicy *adjective* (**juicier, juiciest**) **1** full of juice. **2** *informal* **a** substantial or interesting: *always gets the juicy roles.* **b** racy, scandalous: *juicy gossip.* **3** *informal* profitable.

ju-jitsu (also **ju-jutsu**) *noun* = JIU-JITSU. [Say joo JIT soo]

juju *noun* (*plural* **jujus**) **1** a magic object or charm of some West African peoples. **2** a supernatural power attributed to this. **3** *Music* a flowing, sonorous, and complex musical style of Yoruba origin, usu. combining numerous interrelating drums, guitars, and call-and-response singing. [Say JOO joo]

jujube *noun* **1 a** a shrub or tree native to the warmer regions of Eurasia, which produces edible berry-like fruits formerly taken as a cough remedy. **b** this fruit. **2** a small, flavoured, jellylike candy. [Say JOO joob]

juke • *noun* (*plural* **jukes**) *US* **1** (in full **juke joint**) a roadhouse, nightclub, etc., esp. one providing food, drinks, and music for dancing. **2** = JUKEBOX. • *verb* (**jukes, juked, juking**) **1** make a fake movement to deceive and pass an opponent: *he juked right, then ran left past the defender.* **2** dance, esp. to the music of a jukebox.

jukebox *noun* **1** a machine that automatically plays a selected musical recording when a coin is inserted. **2** a device for holding a number of CD-ROMs in such a way that any of them can be played or assessed.

Jul. *abbreviation* July.

julep *noun* = MINT JULEP. [Say JOO lip]

Julian *adjective* **1** of or associated with the Roman general and statesman Julius Caesar (100–44 BC). **2** of or pertaining to the calendar reform instituted by him in 46 BC. [Say JOO lee in]

Julian calendar *noun* a calendar introduced by Julius Caesar, in which the year consisted of 365 days, every fourth year having 366 (compare GREGORIAN CALENDAR).

julienne • *noun* **1** food, esp. vegetables, cut into short thin strips. **2** a dish of assorted vegetables cut into thin strips. • *adjective* **1** (of a vegetable etc.) cut into thin strips. **2** (of a dish or garnish) consisting of or containing such strips. • *verb* (**juliennes, julienned, julienning**) slice (esp. vegetables) into short, thin strips. ▶**julienned** *adjective* [Say joo lee EN]

July *noun* (*plural* **Julys**) the seventh month of the year.

jumble • *noun* a confused state or heap; a muddle. • *verb* (**jumbles, jumbled, jumbling**) (often foll. by *up*) **1** mix or mingle (objects etc.) in a confused and disordered way. **2** confuse or mix up (memories etc.) mentally. ▶**jumbled** *adjective*

jumbo *informal* • *noun* (*plural* **jumbos**) **1** a large animal (esp. an elephant), person, or thing. **2** (also **jumbo jet**) a large airliner with capacity for several hundred passengers. • *adjective* **1** very large of its kind. **2** extra large.

jump • *verb* **1** move off the ground or other surface by sudden muscular effort in the legs. **2** (often foll. by *up, from, in, out,* etc.) move suddenly or hastily in a specified way. **3** give a sudden bodily movement from shock or excitement etc. **4** undergo a rapid change, esp. an advance in status. **5** (often foll. by *around, about*) change or move rapidly from one idea or subject to another, omitting intermediate stages. **6 a** rise or increase suddenly: *prices jumped.* **b** cause to do this. **7 a** pass over (an obstacle, barrier, etc.) by jumping. **b** move or pass over (an intervening thing) to a point beyond. **8** skip, ignore, or pass over (a passage in a book etc.). **9** cause (a thing, or an animal, esp. a horse) to jump. **10** (foll. by *to, at*) reach a conclusion hastily, esp. without examining the premises. **11** (of a train) leave (the rails). **12 a** anticipate and respond prematurely to (permission or a signal to act). **b** ignore and pass (a red traffic light etc.). **13** get on or off (a train etc.) quickly, esp. illegally or dangerously. **14** pounce on or attack (a person) unexpectedly. **15** start (a car) using jumper cables. **16** (often foll. by *in, into*) join in eagerly and enthusiastically. **17** parachute from a flying plane. **18 a** (of a nightclub, etc.) be full of excitement, pulsate

with activity: *the joint was jumping.* **b** (of jazz or similar music) have a strong or exciting rhythm. • *noun* **1** the act or an instance of jumping. **2** *Sport* **a** an act or type of jumping, as an athletic performance. **b** a distance jumped. **c** a place to be jumped from, as in ski jumping etc. **3** an obstacle to be jumped, esp. by a horse. **4** a sudden bodily movement caused by shock or excitement. **5** an abrupt rise in amount, price, value, status, etc. **6 a** a sudden transition from one thing, idea etc. to another, omitting intermediate stages. **b** an interval or gap in argument, technological development, etc. PHRASES **get** (or **have**) **the jump on** *informal* get (or have) an advantage over (a person) by prompt action. **jump at** accept eagerly. **jump down a person's throat** *informal* berate, reprimand, or contradict a person fiercely. **jump for joy** be joyfully excited; show one's delight by excited movements. (**go**) **jump in the lake** *informal* (usu. in *imper.*) go away and stop being a nuisance. **jump on** *informal* attack or criticize severely and without warning. **jump out at 1** grab the attention; be blatantly apparent. **2** suddenly spring out and surprise (a person). **jump out of one's skin** *informal* be extremely startled. **jump the queue** take unfair precedence over others. **jump rope** skip with a skipping rope. **jump ship 1** abandon an organization, effort, etc. before one's commitment is up, an undertaking is finished, etc. **2** (of a seaman) desert. **jump to it** *informal* act promptly and energetically. **one jump ahead** one stage further on than a rival etc.

jump ball *noun* *Basketball* a ball thrown vertically between two opposing players by the referee to start or resume play.

jump-cut *Film* • *noun* **1** the excision of part of a shot in order to break its continuity of action and time. **2** the abrupt transition from one scene to another which is discontinuous in time. • *verb* (**jump-cuts, jump-cut, jump-cutting**) join (a scene) to others via a jump-cut.

jumped-up *adjective* *informal* newly or suddenly risen in status or importance, esp. when presumptuously arrogant.

jumper¹ *noun* a collarless, sleeveless dress worn over a blouse or sweater.

jumper² *noun* **1** a person or animal that jumps, esp.: **a** a horse trained for show jumping. **b** an athlete in a sport such as ski jumping, high jump, etc. **c** *informal* a person who commits suicide by leaping from a bridge, tall building, etc. **2** *Electricity* **a** a short wire used to make or break a circuit. **b** (usu. in *plural*) = JUMPER CABLE. **3** *Basketball slang* **a** = JUMPSHOT. **b** = JUMP BALL. **4** *Cdn* = JOLLY JUMPER.

jumper cable *noun* either of a pair of heavy electric cables with metal clips, used for conveying current from the battery of one motor vehicle to boost (or recharge) another.

jumpiness *noun* nervousness or uneasiness.

jumping jack *noun* **1** an exercise performed by standing with legs together and arms at one's side, jumping to a position with legs spread and arms fully extended above the head, then returning to the initial stance. **2** a toy figure with movable limbs esp. attached to strings.

jumping-off point *noun* (also **jumping-off place** etc.) **1** the place or point from where a journey, plan, campaign, etc. is begun or launched. **2** a place regarded as being the furthest limit of civilization or settlement. **3** a place from which a person moves into another, esp. remote region beyond.

jump rope *noun* **1** a skipping rope. **2** an exercise or child's game done or played with a skipping rope.

jump seat *noun* a folding extra seat in a motor vehicle, aircraft, etc.

jumpshot *noun* *Basketball* a shot at the net made at the apex of a vertical leap.

jump-start • *verb* **1** start (a motor vehicle) with jumper cables. **2** revitalize, energize, or stimulate (a team effort, etc.): *ways to jump-start the economy.* • *noun* the action of jump-starting.

jumpsuit *noun* a one-piece garment for the whole body, of a kind originally worn by paratroopers.

jumpy *adjective* (**jumpier, jumpiest**) **1** nervous; easily startled. **2** making sudden movements, esp. of nervous excitement.

Jun. *abbreviation* **1** June. **2** (also **jun.**) Junior.

junco *noun* (*plural* **juncos**) any of several small songbirds of Central and North America, with mainly grey and brown plumage. [Say JUNK oh]

junction *noun* **1** a point at which two or more things are joined. **2** a place where two or more railway lines or roads meet, unite, or cross. **3** *Electronics* a region of transition in a semiconductor between regions where conduction is mainly by electrons and regions where it is mainly by holes. ▶ **junctional** *adjective*

junction box *noun* (*plural* **junction boxes**) a rigid box or casing used to enclose and protect junctions of electrical wires, cables, etc.

juncture *noun* **1** a critical convergence of events; a critical point of time: *at this juncture.* **2** a place where things join: *the juncture of the Ottawa River and the Rideau Canal.* [Say JUNK chur]

June *noun* the sixth month of the year.

Juneberry *noun* (*plural* **Juneberries**) **1** a North American shrub of the rose family, with showy white flowers. **2** the fruit of this shrub.

June bug *noun* (also **June beetle**) any of various large beetles that appear in early summer.

Jungian • *adjective* having to do with the system of analytical psychology of Carl Jung (1875–1961), who originated the concept of introvert and extrovert personality, differentiated the four psychological functions of sensation, intuition, thinking, and feeling, and developed theories about dreams, which led to his identification of the collective unconscious. • *noun* a supporter of Jung or of his system. [Say YOONG ee in (with OO as in BOOK)]

jungle *noun* **1 a** a land overgrown with undergrowth or tangled vegetation, esp. in the tropics. **b** the luxuriant and often almost impenetrable vegetation covering such land. **2** a wild tangled mass: *a jungle of computer cord and cable.* **3 a** a scene or place of ruthless competition, struggle, or exploitation: *urban jungle.* **b** a place of bewildering complexity or confusion. **4** (also **jungle music**) a type of fast dance music with an exaggerated bass line, influenced by reggae and soul. PHRASES **law of the jungle** a state of ruthless competition.

Jungle Gym *noun* *proprietary* monkey bars for a children's playground, usu. having various bars, tubes, slides, etc.

jungly *adjective* resembling the climate or lush, tangled vegetation of a jungle: *a jungly forest.*

junior • *adjective* **1 a** (foll. by *to*) inferior in age, standing, or position. **b** of less or least standing; of the lower or lowest position: *junior partner.* **2 a** less advanced in age. **b** intended for children or young people: *junior dictionary.* **3** the younger (esp. appended to a name for distinction from an older person of the same name). **4** smaller than usual. **5** *Sport* of, or pertaining to (usu. amateur) athletes under 20 years of age. **6** esp. *US* of the year before the final year at university, high school, etc. • *noun* **1** a person who

holds a low rank in a profession, is inferior in length of service, etc. **2** a person who is a specified number of years younger than another: *10 years his junior*. **3** *Sport* **a** a junior athlete. **b** the level of competition for junior athletes: *spent three years playing junior*. **4** esp. *US* a student in the third year of a four-year program at high school, college, or university. **5** *informal* a young male child, esp. in relation to his family. **6** (in *plural*) a range of garment sizes, odd-numbered from 5 to 15, for well-proportioned, short-waisted women of slightly less than average height.

Junior A *noun Hockey* the highest level of amateur competition, for players under 20 years of age.

Junior B *noun Hockey* the second-highest level of amateur competition, for players under 20 years of age.

Junior C *noun Hockey* the third-highest level of amateur competition, for players under 20 years of age.

junior college *noun* **1** *Cdn (Que.) informal* a CEGEP. **2** *US* a college offering the first two years of a university education.

junior high school *noun* (also *informal* **junior high**) a school intermediate between elementary school and high school, usu. from Grade 7 to Grade 9.

junior kindergarten *noun Cdn (Ont.)* a class for young children, usu. ages 3 to 4, which prepares them for kindergarten through games, socialization, etc.

junior matriculation *noun* (also *informal* **junior matric**) *Cdn hist.* (in certain provinces) completion of secondary education to a level one year short of the requirements for admission to university.

junior minister *noun Cdn & Brit.* a cabinet minister with responsibility for certain matters within a larger portfolio, assisting and reporting to the minister in charge.

juniper *noun* an evergreen shrub or tree with prickly leaves and dark blue berry-like cones. [Say JOONA purr]

junk[1] • *noun* **1** anything regarded as useless or of little value. **2** old or unwanted articles that are discarded or sold cheaply. **3** *slang* a narcotic drug, esp. heroin. **4** *Baseball* a pitch effective because of unpredictable movement rather than speed, e.g. a knuckleball. **5** *Cdn* (esp. *Maritimes & Nfld*) a short log, esp. cut to fit a stove, fireplace, etc. **6** = JUNK FOOD. **7** (also **junk bond**) a high-yielding high-risk security, esp. one issued to finance a takeover. **8** a lump of fibrous tissue in the sperm whale's head, containing spermaceti. • *verb* discard as junk.

junk[2] *noun* a flat-bottomed sailing vessel with a four-sided sail, used in the China seas.

Junker *noun hist.* a member of the aristocracy in Prussia, a kingdom occupying much of modern northeastern Germany and Poland, who exercised considerable political power in the late nineteenth and early twentieth centuries. The Junkers supported the Prussian monarchy and favoured conservative policies, including protective tariffs for agriculture. [Say YOON ker (with OO as in BOOK)]

junker *noun informal* **1** an old, dilapidated automotive vehicle, boat, etc. **2** a junk dealer. [Say JUNK er]

junket • *noun* **1 a** an extensive tour taken esp. for promotional purposes, usu. with the traveller's expenses paid. **b** a pleasure outing, esp. with eating, drinking, etc. **2** a dish of sweetened and flavoured curds, often served with fruit or cream. • *verb* (**junkets, junketed, junketing**) go on a pleasure excursion. [Say JUNK it]

junketeer • *noun* a person who goes on an extravagant trip or promotional tour paid for by someone else. • *verb* go on this kind of trip or tour: *the media has been critical of government officials junketeering at public expense*. ▶ **junketeering** *noun & adjective* [Say junk it EER]

junk food *noun* food with low nutritional value.

junkie *noun informal* **1** a drug addict. **2** *informal* an aficionado of some specified activity: *a music junkie*.

junk mail *noun* unsolicited advertising material etc. sent to large numbers of people by mail.

junky • *adjective* (**junkier, junkiest**) of or like junk. • *noun* (*plural* **junkies**) = JUNKIE.

junkyard *noun* a place where junk is collected for storage or resale.

Juno *noun Cdn* (*plural* **Junos**) **1** any of several awards presented by the Canadian Academy of Recording Arts and Sciences for excellence in Canadian music recording. **2** any of the statuettes symbolizing such an award. [Say JOO no]

junta *noun* **1** a political or military clique or faction taking power after a revolution or coup. **2** a secretive group; a cabal. [Say HOONTA (with OO as in BOOK)]

Jurassic • *adjective* of or relating to the second period of the Mesozoic era, between 213 and 144 million years ago, between the Triassic and Cretaceous periods, with evidence of many large dinosaurs, the first birds, and mammals. • *noun* the Jurassic period or geological system. [Say jur ASS ick]

juridical *noun* of judicial proceedings or the law: *the two juridical systems in Canada, common law and civil law*. ▶ **juridically** *adverb* [Say jur IDDA cull]

juried *adjective* judged or selected by a jury or panel: *a juried fine arts and crafts festival*.

jurisdiction *noun* **1** the authority that an official organization has to make legal decisions about someone or something: *the Court of Appeal exercised its jurisdiction to order a review of the case ◊ these matters do not fall within our jurisdiction ◊ the Canadian court had no jurisdiction over the defendants*. **2** an area or a country in which a particular system of laws has authority: *practice varies between different provincial jurisdictions*. [Say jur iss DICTION]

jurisprudence *noun* **1** the theory or philosophy of law: *dilemmas of feminist jurisprudence*. **2** a legal system: *Aboriginal concepts of the land are in conflict with Anglo-Saxon jurisprudence*. **3** legal decisions collectively: *a principle found throughout the Criminal Code and criminal law jurisprudence that repeat offenders should be treated differently*. [Say jur iss PRUDENCE]

jurist *noun* a person who is knowledgeable in legal matters.

juror *noun* a member of a jury. [Say JUR er]

jury • *noun* (*plural* **juries**) **1** a body of usu. twelve persons sworn to render a verdict on the basis of evidence submitted to them in a court of justice. **2** a body of persons selected to award prizes in a competition. • *verb* (**juries, juried, jurying**) select or judge (entries etc.) by a jury. ▢PHRASES▢ **the jury is** (or **is still**) **out** (often foll. by *on*) a decision has not yet been reached.

jury-rig *verb* (**jury-rigs, jury-rigged, jury-rigging**) (often as **jury-rigged** *adjective*) assemble (something) hastily, using materials at hand: *jury-rig a padded canoe roof rack with rags or scrap carpeting and duct tape ◊ the man had jury-rigged sling on one shoulder*.

just • *adjective* **1** acting or done in accordance with

what is morally right or fair. **2** (of treatment etc.) deserved: *a just reward*. **3** (of feelings, opinions, etc.) well-grounded: *just resentment*. • *adverb* **1** exactly: *just what I need*. **2** exactly or nearly at this or that moment; a little time ago: *I have just seen them*. **3** *informal* simply, merely: *we were just good friends*. **4** barely; no more than: *I just managed it*. **5** *informal* positively: *it is just splendid*, **6** quite. not just yet. **7** *informal* as an intensifier: *just you wait!* **8** in questions, seeking precise information: *just how did you manage?* PHRASES **just about** almost exactly; almost completely. **just as well** convenient; fortunate: *it is just as well that I checked*. **just in case** as a precaution. **just now 1** at this moment. **2** a little time ago. **just so 1** exactly arranged: *likes everything just so*. **2** it is exactly as you say.

justice *noun* **1** just conduct; fairness. **2** the law and its administration: *the criminal justice system*. **3** judgment by legal process: *was brought to justice*. **4** a judge, esp. of a court of appeal. **b** (**Justice**) a title given to an appeal court judge: *Madam Justice Bertha Wilson of the Supreme Court* ◊ *an inquiry conducted by Mr. Justice Dubin*. PHRASES **do justice to** treat fairly or appropriately; show due appreciation of. **do oneself justice** perform in a manner worthy of one's abilities. **in justice to** out of fairness to. **with (some) justice** reasonably.

Justice of the Peace *noun* a local public official appointed to hear minor cases, take oaths, etc.

Justice of the Peace Court *noun Cdn* (in the NWT) a court presided over by a Justice of the Peace, with jurisdiction to hear all summary conviction matters, offences against municipal bylaws, etc.

justifiable *adjective* that can be justified or defended. ▶ **justifiably** *adverb*

justification *noun* a good or legitimate reason; acceptable grounds for or defence of a person's actions, conduct, or decision: *I can see no justification for further tax increases* ◊ *the exciting ending is the only justification for renting this movie* ◊ *she was angry, and not without justification — he forgot her birthday*.

justified *adjective* **1** right; having a good reason: *is a business justified in dismissing its employee without notice?* **2** declared or made free from sin in the sight of God. **3** (of text) having been adjusted so that the print fills a space evenly or forms a straight edge at the margin.

justify *verb* (**justifies, justified, justifying**) **1** show that someone or something is right or reasonable: *how*

can they justify paying such huge salaries? ◊ *her success had justified the faith her teachers had put in her*. **2** give an explanation or excuse for something or for doing something: *the Prime Minister has been asked to justify the decision to Parliament* ◊ *you don't need to justify yourself to me* ◊ *an increase in prices can't be justified*. **3** (of God) free (a person) from the consequences of sin: *some Christians believe that people are justified by faith alone*. **4** adjust (a line of type) to fill a space evenly.

just-in-time *noun* **1** a manufacturing system in which production is operated in very small batches. **2** a factory system in which materials are delivered immediately before they are required in order to minimize storage costs: *just-in-time delivery*.

justly *adverb* with good reason: *the restaurant has justly developed an excellent reputation* ◊ *parents are justly nervous about letting their young children walk home alone*.

jut *verb* (**juts, jutted, jutting**) (often foll. by *out, into*) protrude, project.

Jute *noun* a member of a Germanic tribe that settled in Britain in the 5th–6th centuries. [Say JOOT]

jute *noun* **1** a rough fibre made from the bark of a jute plant, used for making twine and rope, and woven into sacking, mats, etc. **2** an Asian plant yielding this fibre. [Say JOOT]

juvenile • *adjective* **1 a** young, youthful. **b** of or for young persons: *juvenile fiction*. **2** suited to or characteristic of youth. **3** often *derogatory* immature: *behaving in a very juvenile way*. **4** (of a sports team, league, player, etc.) involving teenagers, esp. between the ages of 15 and 19. **5** of or relating to a juvenile bird, animal, etc.: *juvenile feathers*. • *noun* **1** a young person. **2** a young bird, animal, etc., esp.: **a** a bird in its first full plumage, but not yet having adult plumage. **b** a two-year-old racehorse.

juvenile court *noun* = YOUTH COURT.

juvenile delinquency *noun* offences committed by a person or persons below the age of legal responsibility. ▶ **juvenile delinquent** *noun*

juvenile diabetes *noun* (also **juvenile-onset diabetes**) a type of diabetes mellitus in which insulin is not produced by the body in sufficient quantities and must therefore be injected.

juxtapose *verb* (**juxtaposes, juxtaposed, juxtaposing**) place or deal with close together, esp. to highlight a contrast: *in the exhibition, abstract paintings are juxtaposed with shocking photographs*. ▶ **juxtaposition** *noun* [Say JUXTA pose or juxta POSE]

J

Kk

K¹ *noun* (also **k**) (*plural* **Ks** or **K's**) the eleventh letter of the alphabet.

K² *abbreviation* (also **K.**) **1** kelvin(s). **2** King, King's. **3** Köchel, indicating a number given to each of Mozart's compositions. **4** (also **k**) (preceded by a numeral) **a** *Computing* a unit of 1,024 (i.e. 2^{10}) bytes or bits, or loosely 1,000. **b** 1,000. **5** *informal* one thousand dollars: *earns 50 K.* **6** kindergarten. **7** kilometre: *ran 30 K.* **8** (in *plural*) kilometres per hour.

K³ *symbol* **1** potassium. **2** *Baseball* strikeout.

K⁴ *noun* (*plural* **Ks**) a strikeout.

k¹ *abbreviation* knot(s).

k² *symbol* **1** kilo-. **2** *Math* a constant.

K-9 *abbreviation* designating police canine units.

Kabbalah *noun* (also **Kabbala, Cabbala**) **1** a Jewish mystical tradition. **2** any obscure doctrine or occult lore. ▶**Kabbalism** *noun* **Kabbalist** *noun* **Kabbalistic** *adjective* [Say kuh BOLLA or CABBA luh]

kabloona *noun* (*plural* **kabloona** or **kabloonas** or **kabloonat**) a person who is not Inuit, esp. a white person. [Say kuh BLUE nuh]

kabob *noun* = KEBAB. [Say ka BOB]

kaboodle *noun* = CABOODLE.

kaboom *noun* a sudden loud sound, as of an explosion.

kabuki *noun* a form of popular traditional Japanese drama with highly stylized song, acted by males only. [Say ka BOO kee]

Kaddish *noun* **1** a Jewish mourner's prayer. **2** a formula of praise used in the synagogue service. [Say CAD ish]

Kaffir *noun* **1** *hist.* a member of the Xhosa-speaking peoples of South Africa. **2** the language of these peoples. [Say CAFFER]

Kafir *noun* a native of the Hindu Kush mountains of NE Afghanistan. [Say CAFFER]

Kafkaesque *adjective* (of a situation etc.) impenetrably oppressive, nightmarish, in a manner characteristic of the fictional world of the Czech novelist Franz Kafka (1883–1924): *a Kafkaesque story about a clerk who joins a posse to hunt a murderer and finds himself pursued as a suspect.* [Say kafka ESK]

kafuffle *noun* Cdn = KERFUFFLE.

kahuna *noun* see BIG KAHUNA. [Say kuh HOONA]

Kaigani *noun* (*plural* **Kaigani** or **Kaiganis**) a member of a division of the Haida, who left the Queen Charlotte Islands in the early 18th century and settled on the southern shores of Prince of Wales Island. [Say ky GANNY]

kaiser *noun* **1** *hist.* an emperor, esp. the German Emperor, the Emperor of Austria, or the head of the Holy Roman Empire. **2** (also **kaiser roll**) a large crusty bread roll made by folding the corners of a square of bread dough into the centre, resulting in a pinwheel pattern when baked.

kalamata *noun* a medium-sized, firm, flavourful, Greek variety of purplish-black olive. [Say kala MATA]

Kalashnikov *noun* a type of rifle or submachine gun made in Russia. [Say kuh LASH ni koff]

kale *noun* a variety of cabbage which forms no compact head.

kaleidoscope *noun* **1** a tube containing mirrors and pieces of coloured glass or paper, whose reflections produce changing patterns when the tube is rotated. **2** a constantly and quickly changing pattern: *the dancers moved in a kaleidoscope of colour.* ▶**kaleidoscopic** *adjective* [Say kuh LIE duh scope]

kamik *noun* a traditional Inuit boot made from seal or caribou skin. [Say COMIC or CAMIC]

kamikaze • *noun* *hist.* (during WW II) **1** a Japanese aircraft loaded with explosives and deliberately crashed on its target. **2** the pilot of such an aircraft. • *adjective* **1** of or relating to a kamikaze. **2** reckless, dangerous, potentially self-destructive: *he made a kamikaze run across three lanes of traffic.* [Say comma COZZY]

Kamloops trout *noun* Cdn a bright silvery rainbow trout found in lakes.

Kampuchean *noun & adjective* = CAMBODIAN. [Say cam poo CHEE in]

kangaroo *noun* (*plural* **kangaroos**) **1** a plant-eating marsupial native to Australia and New Guinea, with a long tail and strongly developed hindquarters enabling it to travel by jumping. **2** Cdn designating a hooded garment, usu. of fleece material, with a front pouch: *kangaroo jacket.*

kangaroo court *noun* **1** an illegal court formed by a group of prisoners, strikers, etc. to settle disputes among themselves. **2** any trial, court, public hearing, or disciplinary proceeding operating unfairly and rendering an unjust verdict. **3** a mock trial, usu. for comic effect and often to raise funds for a charity, where participants are tried for trivial offences and given comic punishments.

kanji *noun* Japanese writing using Chinese characters. [Say CAN jee]

kaolin *noun* a fine soft white clay produced by the decomposition of other clays or feldspar, used esp. for making porcelain and in medicines. [Say KAY uh lin]

Kaposi's sarcoma *noun* a form of cancer involving multiple tumours of the lymph nodes or skin, occurring esp. in people with depressed immune systems, e.g. as a result of AIDS. Abbreviation: **KS**. [Say kuh POE sees]

kapow *noun* *informal* a sudden sharp sound, like a gunshot or explosion. [Say kuh POW]

kappa *noun* the tenth letter of the Greek alphabet (K, κ).

kaput *adjective* *slang* broken, ruined; done for. [Say kuh PUT]

karaoke *noun* a form of entertainment in which people sing popular songs as soloists against a pre-recorded backing. [Say carry OAKY]

SPELL CHECK
karat, carat

Diamonds are measured in **carats**.

---

karat *noun* a measure of purity of gold, pure gold being 24 karats. Abbreviation: **kt**. [Sounds like CARROT]

karate *noun* a Japanese system of unarmed combat using the hands and feet as weapons. [Say kuh ROTTY]

karate chop • *noun* a forceful, usu. downward motion with the side of the hand. • *verb* (**karate-chop**,

karate-chops, **karate-chopped**, **karate-chopping**) strike with a karate chop.

Karen • *noun* (*plural* **Karen** or **Karens**) **1** a member of a non-Burmese Mongoloid people, most of whom live in eastern Burma (Myanmar). **2** the language spoken by this people, which is probably of the Sino-Tibetan family. • *adjective* of or relating to the Karens. [Say kuh REN]

karma *noun* **1 a** *Buddhism* & *Hinduism* the sum of a person's actions in previous states of existence, viewed as deciding his or her fate in future existences. **b** *Jainism* subtle physical matter which binds the soul as a result of bad actions. **2** destiny. **3** the positive or negative feelings or energy felt to be produced by a person or thing. ▶ **karmic** *adjective*

karst *noun* a limestone region with underground drainage and many cavities and passages caused by the dissolution of the rock.

kart *noun* = GO-KART.

kasha *noun* a soft food made of boiled or baked grain, esp. buckwheat. [Say COSH uh]

SPELL CHECK
Kashmiri, cashmere

The spelling is **cashmere** for the soft wool.

Kashmiri • *adjective* of or relating to Kashmir, a region on the northern border between India and Pakistan, or its people or language. • *noun* **1** a native or inhabitant of Kashmir. **2** the Indic language of Kashmir. [Say cash MEERY]

Kashrut *noun* = KASHRUTH. [Say CASH root]

Kashruth *noun* *Judaism* **1** the body of religious laws relating to the suitability of food, ritual objects, etc. **2** the condition of being fit for ritual use. [Say CASH rooth]

Kaska • *noun* (*plural* **Kaska** or **Kaskas**) **1** a member of a Dene Aboriginal group living in northwestern BC. **2** the Athapaskan language of this people. • *adjective* of or relating to this people or their culture or language. [Say CASS kuh]

katydid *noun* any of various green North American grasshoppers, the male of which makes a characteristic sound that resembles its name. [Say KATY did]

kayak • *noun* **1** an Inuit one-man canoe consisting of a light wooden frame covered with sealskins. **2** a small covered canoe modelled on this, used for touring or sport. • *verb* (**kayaks**, **kayaked**, **kayaking**) **1** travel by kayak. **2** paddle a kayak on or along (a river, the ocean, etc.). ▶ **kayaker** *noun* **kayaking** *noun*

kayo *informal* • *verb* (**kayoes**, **kayoed**, **kayoing**) knock out; stun by a blow. • *noun* (*plural* **kayos**) a knockout.

Kazakh (also **Kazak**) • *noun* **1** a member of a Turkic people of central Asia, esp. of Kazakhstan. **2** the language of this people. • *adjective* of or relating to the Kazakhs or their language. [Say kuh ZOCK]

kazillion *noun* = GAZILLION.

kazoo *noun* a toy or jazz musical instrument consisting of a tube with a membrane at each end or over a hole in the side, which produces a buzzing noise when hummed into.

KB *abbreviation* **1** kilobyte(s). **2** KING'S BENCH.

Kb *abbreviation* kilobit(s).

KBps *abbreviation* kilobytes per second.

Kbps *abbreviation* kilobits per second.

kbyte *abbreviation* kilobyte(s).

KC *abbreviation* KING'S COUNSEL.

kcal *abbreviation* kilocalorie(s).

kebab *noun* a dish of pieces of marinated meat and vegetables cooked and served on a skewer. [Say kuh BOB]

keel *noun* **1** the lengthwise timber or steel structure along the base of a ship, airship, or some aircraft, on which the framework of the whole is built up. **2** a ridge along the breastbone of many birds. PHRASES **keel over 1** fall down; faint. **2** fall over sideways. **3** die. **4** capsize. **on an even keel 1** (of a ship or aircraft) not listing. **2** (of a plan or person) untroubled.

keelhaul *verb* **1** drag (a person) through the water under the keel of a ship as a punishment. **2** scold or rebuke severely.

keen¹ *adjective* **1** (of a person, desire, or interest) eager, ardent: *a keen curler*. **2** (foll. by *on*) much attracted by; fond of or enthusiastic about. **3 a** (of the senses) sharp; highly sensitive. **b** (of feelings) intense, strong, deep. **4** intellectually acute. **5 a** having a sharp edge or point. **b** (of an edge etc.) sharp. **6** (of a sound, light, etc.) penetrating, vivid, strong. **7** (of a wind, frost, etc.) piercingly cold. **8** (of a pain etc.) acute, bitter. **9** *informal* excellent.

keen² • *noun* an Irish funeral song accompanied with wailing. • *verb* **1** make a high-pitched sound like wailing. **2** utter in a wailing tone.

keener *noun* *Cdn informal* a person, esp. a student, who is extremely eager, zealous, or enthusiastic.

keenly *adverb* **1** in an intense or thorough manner: *Georgia was keenly aware of the danger* ◊ *the principal felt keenly the urgency of this financial problem*. **2** in an eager or enthusiastic manner: *a keenly awaited verdict*.

keenness *noun* **1** enthusiasm, zeal. **2** intensity, strength: *keenness of hearing*.

keep • *verb* (**keeps**, **kept**, **keeping**) **1** have continuous charge of; retain possession of. **2** (foll. by *for*) retain or reserve for a future occasion or time. **3** retain or remain in a specified condition, position, course, etc.: *keep them happy*. **4** put or store in a regular place. **5** (foll. by *from*) cause to avoid or abstain from something: *will keep you from going too fast*. **6** detain; cause to be late: *what kept you?* **7 a** observe or pay due regard to (a law, custom, etc.). **b** honour or fulfill (a commitment, undertaking, etc.): *keep one's word*. **c** respect the commitment implied by (a secret etc.). **d** act fittingly on the occasion of: *keep the Sabbath*. **8** own and look after (animals) for amusement or profit: *keeps bees*. **9 a** provide for the sustenance of (a person, family, etc.). **b** (foll. by *in*) maintain (a person) with a supply of. **10** carry on; manage (a shop, business, etc.). **11 a** maintain (accounts, a diary, etc.) by making the requisite entries. **b** maintain (a house) in proper order. **12** have (a commodity) regularly on sale: *we don't keep that book in stock*. **13** guard or protect (a person or place, a goal in hockey, etc.). **14** preserve in being; continue to have: *keep order*. **15** continue or do repeatedly or habitually: *why do you keep saying that?* **16** continue to follow (a way or course). **17 a** (esp. of perishable commodities) remain in good condition. **b** (of news or information etc.) admit of being withheld for a time. **18** remain in (one's bed, room, house, etc.). **19** retain (one's seat, ground, etc.) against opposition or difficulty. **20** maintain (a person) in return for sexual favours. • *noun* **1** food, clothes, and other things needed for living: *earn your keep*. **2** the strongest or central tower of a castle, acting as a final refuge. PHRASES **for keeps** *informal* permanently, indefinitely. **how are you keeping?** how are you? **keep at** persist or cause to persist with. **keep away** (often foll. by *from*) **1** avoid being near. **2** prevent from being near. **keep back 1** remain or keep at a distance. **2** retard the progress of. **3** conceal; decline to disclose. **4** retain, withhold: *kept back $50*. **keep one's balance** remain

K

stable; avoid falling. **keep down 1** hold in subjection.
2 keep low in amount. **3** lie low; stay hidden.
4 manage not to vomit (food eaten). **keep one's feet**
manage not to fall. **keep in 1** confine or restrain (one's
feelings etc.). **2** remain or confine indoors. **keep off**
1 stay or cause to stay away from. **2** ward off; avert.
3 abstain from. **4** avoid (a subject). **keep on**
1 continue to do something; do continually.
2 continue to use or employ. **3** (foll. by *at*) pester or
harass. **keep out 1** keep or remain outside. **2** exclude.
keep one's temper control one's anger. **keep to**
1 adhere to (a course, schedule, etc.). **2** observe (a
promise). **3** confine oneself to. **keep to oneself**
1 avoid contact with others. **2** refuse to disclose or
share. **keep together** remain or keep in harmony.
keep under hold in subjection. **keep up 1** maintain
(progress etc.). **2** prevent (prices, one's spirits, etc.) from
sinking. **3** keep in repair, in an efficient or proper state,
etc. **4** carry on (a correspondence etc.). **5** prevent (a
person) from going to bed, esp. when late. **6** (often foll.
by *with*) manage not to fall behind. **keep up with the**
Joneses strive to compete socially with one's
neighbours.

keeper *noun* **1** a person who keeps or looks after
something or someone (also in *combination*: *zookeeper*).
2 a device for keeping something in place, esp. a loop
securing the end of a buckled strap. **3** a fruit or other
product that keeps in a specified way. **4** *Football* an
offensive play in which the quarterback runs with the
ball. **5** *informal* something that one wishes to keep. **6** a
fish that is large enough that it need not be released if
caught. **7 a** a plain stud or ring worn to preserve a hole
in a pierced earlobe. **b** a ring worn to guard against the
loss of a more valuable one.

keeping *noun* the action of owning, maintaining, or
protecting something: *the keeping of dogs ◊ careful record
keeping is essential.* PHRASES **in someone's keeping**
being taken care of by someone: *her secrets were safe in his
keeping.* **in keeping (with something)** appropriate or
expected in a particular situation; in agreement with
something: *the latest results are in keeping with our earlier
findings.* **out of keeping (with something)** not
appropriate or expected in a particular situation; not
in agreement with something: *the painting is out of
keeping with the rest of the room.*

keepsake *noun* a thing kept for the sake of or in
remembrance of the giver.

keg *noun* a small barrel.

keister *noun slang* the buttocks. [Say KEE stir]

kelp *noun* **1** any of several large broad-bladed brown
seaweeds suitable for use as fertilizer. **2** the ashes of
seaweed used for the salts of sodium, potassium, and
iodine which they contain.

Kelt *noun* = CELT.

kelt *noun* a salmon or sea trout after spawning.

kelvin *noun* the SI unit of thermodynamic
temperature, equal in magnitude to the degree celsius.
Abbreviation: **K**.

Kelvin scale *noun* a scale of temperature with
absolute zero as zero.

kendo *noun* a Japanese form of fencing with two-
handed bamboo swords. [Say KEN doe]

kennel • *noun* **1** a small shelter for a dog. **2** (in *plural*) a
breeding or boarding establishment for dogs. **•** *verb*
(**kennels, kennelled, kennelling**) **1** put into or keep
in a kennel. **2** live in or go to a kennel.

keno *noun* a game of chance resembling bingo, based
on the drawing of numbers and covering of
corresponding numbers on cards. [Say KEEN oh]

Kentuckian • *noun* a native or inhabitant of the US
state of Kentucky. **•** *adjective* of or relating to Kentucky.
[Say k'n TUCKY in]

Kenyan • *adjective* of or relating to Kenya in E Africa.
• *noun* a native or inhabitant of Kenya. [Say KEN yin or
KEEN yin]

kept *past and past participle of* KEEP.

keratin *noun* a fibrous protein which occurs in hair,
feathers, hooves, claws, horns, etc. [Say KERRA tin]

kerchief *noun* a cloth used to cover the head; a head
scarf or babushka. ▶ **kerchiefed** *adjective* [Say KER chiff
or KER chief]

kerf • *noun* a slit made by cutting, esp. with a saw.
• *verb* make a kerf in (a piece of wood etc.).

kerfuffle *noun* *Cdn, Brit., & Austral. informal* a fuss or
commotion. [Say ker FUFFLE]

kermode *noun* (also **kermode bear**) a subspecies of
the black bear with either black or white fur, found in
the coastal mainland and some islands of BC. [Say
ker MOE dee]

kern *verb* *Printing* adjust the spacing between
(characters). ▶ **kerned** *adjective*

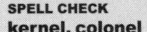

SPELL CHECK
kernel, colonel
A military officer is a **colonel**.

kernel *noun* **1** a central, softer, usu. edible part within
a hard shell of a nut, fruit stone, seed, etc. **2** the whole
seed of a cereal. **3** the nucleus or essential part of
anything: *the kernel of her argument ◊ there may be a kernel
of truth in what she said.* **4** *Computing* the lowest layer into
which a large operating system is subdivided,
responsible for allocating hardware resources to
processes etc.

kerosene *noun* a petroleum distillate widely used as a
fuel and solvent.

kestrel *noun* a small falcon that is capable of hovering
while searching for prey on the ground. [Say KESS trul]

keta *noun* = CHUM 3. [Say KEETA]

kétaine *adjective* *Cdn (Que.)* in poor taste; tacky. [Say
kay TEN]

ketamine *noun* an anaesthetic and painkilling drug,
also used (illicitly) as a hallucinogen. [Say KEETA meen]

ketch *noun* (*plural* **ketches**) a two-masted fore-and-aft-
rigged sailing boat with a mizzen-mast located forward
of the rudder and smaller than its forward mast.

ketchup *noun* a thick sauce made from tomatoes,
vinegar, sugar, etc., used as a condiment.

ketone *noun* any of a class of organic compounds in
which two hydrocarbon groups are linked by a carbonyl
group, e.g. acetone. [Say KEE tone]

kettle *noun* **1** a vessel with a spout and handle, for
boiling water in. **2** a large usu. open pot for cooking
foods, boiling liquids, etc. **3** = KETTLE HOLE. PHRASES **a**
different kettle of fish a different matter altogether.
a pretty (or **fine**) **kettle of fish** an awkward state of
affairs.

kettledrum *noun* a large drum shaped like a bowl
with a membrane adjustable for tension (and so pitch)
stretched across. ▶ **kettledrummer** *noun*

kettle hole *noun* a depression in the ground resulting
from the melting of an ice block trapped in glacial
deposits.

keV *abbreviation* kilo-electron volt.

Kevlar *noun proprietary* a synthetic fibre of high tensile
strength used esp. as a reinforcing agent in the
manufacture of rubber products, e.g. tires. [Say KEV lar]

kewpie doll *noun* (also **kewpie**) a small chubby doll
with a curl or topknot. [Say CUE pee]

K

key[1] • *noun* (*plural* **keys**) **1** an instrument, usu. of metal, for moving the bolt of a lock forwards or backwards to lock or unlock. **2** a similar implement for operating a switch in the form of a lock. **3** an instrument for grasping screws, pegs, nuts, etc., e.g. one for winding a clock etc. **4** a lever depressed by the finger in playing the organ, flute, etc. **5** (often in *plural*) each of several buttons for operating a typewriter, computer terminal, etc. **6** what gives or precludes the opportunity for or access to something. **7** a place that by its position gives control of a sea, territory, etc. **8 a** a solution or explanation. **b** a word or system for solving a cipher or code. **c** an explanatory list of symbols used in a map, table, etc. **d** a book of solutions to mathematical problems etc. **e** a literal translation of a book written in a foreign language. **9** *Music* a system of notes definitely related to each other, based on a particular note, and predominating in a piece of music: *a study in the key of C major*. **10** a tone or style of thought or expression. **11** a piece of wood or metal inserted between others to secure them. **12** the samara of a maple etc. **13** a mechanical device for making or breaking an electric circuit, e.g. in telecommunications. **14** (in basketball) the area beneath each basket, extending from the end line to a circle surrounding the free throw line. • *adjective* essential: *the key element ◊ productivity is key*. • *verb* (**keys**, **keyed**, **keying**) **1** (often foll. by *in*) enter (data) by means of a keyboard. **2** (foll. by *to*) link (one thing to another). PHRASES **key** (**in**) **on** focus on; zero in on. **key up** make (a person) nervous or tense; excite.

key[2] *noun* (*plural* **keys**) a low-lying island or reef, esp. off the coast of Florida or in the W Indies.

keyboard • *noun* **1** a set of keys on a typewriter, computer, piano, etc. **2** an electronic musical instrument with keys arranged as on a piano. • *verb* **1** enter (data) by means of a keyboard. **2** work at a keyboard. ▶**keyboarder** *noun* (in sense 1 of *noun*). **keyboardist** *noun* (in sense 2 of *noun*).

key chain *noun* a short, often decorated chain for carrying keys.

keyhole *noun* **1** a hole by which a key is put into a lock. **2** something shaped like a keyhole, with a circle above a vertical oblong, often flared at the bottom.

keyless *adjective* not having or operating by means of a key: *the car features power locks with keyless remote entry ◊ the drill has a keyless chuck that is tightened by hand*.

key lime *noun* a small yellowish tart lime.

Keynesian • *adjective* of or relating to the theories of the English economist J. M. Keynes (1883–1946), esp. regarding state control of the economy through money and taxation. • *noun* an advocate or supporter of these theories. [Say KAIN zee in]

keynote *noun* **1** a prevailing tone or idea: *choice is the keynote of the new education policy*. **2** (as an *adjective*) intended to set the prevailing tone at a meeting or conference: *keynote address ◊ keynote speaker*. **3** *Music* the note on which a key is based.

keypad *noun* a miniature keyboard or set of buttons for operating an electronic device, telephone, etc.

key ring *noun* a ring for keeping keys on.

key signature *noun* any of several combinations of sharps or flats after the clef at the beginning of each staff indicating the key of a piece of music.

keystone *noun* **1** the central principle of a policy, etc., on which all the rest depends: *changes to the welfare system are the keystone of the government's reforms*. **2** a central stone at the summit of an arch locking the whole together.

keystroke *noun* a single depression of a key on a keyboard.

keyword *noun* **1** the key to a cipher etc. **2 a** a word of great significance. **b** a significant word used in searching a computer database.

kg *abbreviation* kilogram(s).

KGB *abbreviation* the Soviet secret police (1953–91).

khaki • *adjective* dust-coloured; dull brownish yellow. • *noun* (*plural* **khakis**) **1** khaki fabric of twilled cotton or wool, used esp. in military dress. **2** the dull brownish-yellow colour of this. **3** (in *plural*) esp. military clothing made from this. [Say CACKY or COCKY or CARKY]

Khalsa *noun* the fraternity of warriors into which Sikh males are initiated at puberty. [Say COLLSA]

khan *noun* **1** a title given to rulers and officials in Central Asia etc. **2** *hist.* **a** the supreme ruler of the Turkish, Tartar, and Mongol tribes. **b** the emperor of China in the Middle Ages. [Say CON or CAN]

khat *noun* **1** the leaves of an Arabian shrub, which are chewed or drunk as an infusion as a stimulant. **2** the shrub that produces these leaves, growing esp. in mountainous regions. [Say COT]

Khmer • *noun* **1** a native of the ancient Khmer kingdom in SE Asia, or of modern Cambodia. **2** the language of this people. • *adjective* of the Khmers or their language. [Say k'MAIR]

Khoisan *noun* **1** a collective term for the Nama and the San (Bushmen) of southern Africa. **2** a southern African language family, the smallest in Africa, spoken mainly by the Nama and the San. [Say KOY sawn]

kHz *abbreviation* kilohertz.

KIA *abbreviation* killed in action.

kibble *noun* ground meal shaped into pellets esp. for pet food.

kibbutz *noun* (*plural* **kibbutzim**) a collective esp. farming settlement in Israel. [Say ki BUTS for the singular, ki buts EEM for the plural (BUTS rhymes with PUTS)]

kibitz *verb* (**kibitzes**, **kibitzed**, **kibitzing**) *informal* chat or joke lightheartedly. ▶**kibitzer** *noun* [Say KIB its]

kibosh *verb* *slang* (**kiboshes**, **kiboshed**, **kiboshing**) put an end to; dispose of. PHRASES **put the kibosh on** put an end to; finally dispose of. [Say KYE bosh]

kick • *verb* **1** strike or propel forcibly with the foot or hoof etc. **2** (usu. foll. by *at*, *against*) **a** strike out with the foot. **b** extend the leg and foot forcefully out from the body. **c** express annoyance at or dislike of (treatment, a proposal, etc.); rebel against. **3** *informal* give up (a habit). **4** (often foll. by *out* etc.) expel or dismiss forcibly. **5 kick oneself** be annoyed with oneself, esp. for missing an opportunity or doing something stupid: *I know I'll kick myself if I don't go*. **6** (in soccer, football, etc.) score (a goal or field goal) by a kick. • *noun* **1 a** a blow with the foot or hoof etc. **b** the delivery of such a blow. **c** an instance of extending the leg and foot forcefully out from the body. **2** *informal* **a** a sharp stimulant effect, esp. of alcohol: *a cocktail with a kick*. **b** (often in *plural*) a pleasurable thrill: *did it just for kicks*. **3** *informal* a specified temporary interest or enthusiasm: *on a jogging kick*. **4** the recoil of a gun when discharged. PHRASES **kick around** (or **about**) *informal* **1 a** drift idly from place to place. **b** be unused or unwanted. **2 a** treat roughly or scornfully. **b** discuss (an idea) unsystematically. **kick (some) ass** (or **butt**) *slang* act forcefully or in a domineering manner; dominate. **kick at the can** (or **cat**) *Cdn informal* an opportunity to achieve something. **kick back 1** recoil. **2** relax: *kick back in the Florida keys and enjoy more than just world-class*

K

fishing and diving. **kick the bucket** *slang* die. **kick in 1** knock down (a door etc.) by kicking. **2** *slang* contribute (esp. money); pay one's share. **3** *informal* become activated, start. **kick in the pants** *informal* **1** a reprimand or setback seen as an incentive. **2** (also **in the teeth, ass,** etc.) a humiliating punishment or setback. **kick off 1 a** (in football or soccer) begin or resume a match. **b** *informal* begin. **2** remove (shoes etc.) by kicking. **kick up** stir up; cause to move upward. **kick up a fuss** *informal* create a disturbance; object or register strong disapproval. **kick up one's heels** have a lively, enjoyable time. ▶ **kickable** *adjective*

kickback *noun informal* **1** the force of a recoil. **2** money paid illegally to someone in return for work or help; a bribe.

kick-boxer *noun* a person who takes part in the sport of kick-boxing, which combines elements of karate (e.g., kicking with bare feet) with boxing.

kick-boxing *noun* a form of martial art that combines boxing with elements of karate, esp. kicking with bare feet.

kicker *noun* **1** a person or thing that kicks, esp. a football player. **2** *informal* a surprising fact, circumstance, etc. which comes as a conclusion, often as a disappointment: *"But I thought employers are not allowed to ask such questions". Now here's the kicker. "You aren't allowed to ask," he replied, "but you're supposed to know".* **3** a small, electrically powered outboard motor.

kicking *adjective slang* lively, exciting; excellent.

kickoff *noun* **1** (in football or soccer) the start or resumption of a match. **2** the kick marking this. **3** an event marking the beginning of a campaign etc.

kickplate *noun* a protective covering for the lowest portion of a door.

kickstand *noun* a rod attached to a bicycle or motorcycle and kicked into a vertical position to support the vehicle when stationary.

kick-start ● *noun* **1** (also **kick-starter**) a device to start the engine of a motorcycle etc. by the downward thrust of a pedal. **2** an act of starting a motorcycle etc. in this way. **3** an impetus given to get a thing started or restarted: *black pepper and rosemary are powerful stimulants and tonics and help to give the metabolism a kick-start.* ● *verb* **1** start (a motorcycle etc.) in this way. **2** start or restart (a process etc.) by providing some initial impetus: *his quest to kick-start the economy and revive government revenues.*

kick the can *noun* a children's game involving chasing and capturing, in which a can must be kicked to set free those captured.

kid¹ *noun* **1** a young goat. **2** the leather made from its skin. **3** *informal* a child or young person. **4** (as a form of address) any person: *here's lookin' at you, kid!* PHRASES **kids'** (or **kid's**) **stuff** *informal* something very simple. **new kid on the block** a person, company, etc., newly arrived within a group.

kid² *verb* (**kids, kidded, kidding**) *informal* **1** (**kid oneself**) deceive, trick: *don't kid yourself.* **2** tease, joke with: *only kidding.* PHRASES **no kidding** (also **I kid you not**) *informal* that is the truth. ▶ **kidder** *noun*

kiddie *noun* (also **kiddy**) (*plural* **kiddies**) *informal* = KID¹ *noun* 3.

kiddingly *adverb* in a teasing or joking manner: *he kiddingly pretended he didn't know it was her birthday.*

kiddo *noun* (*plural* **kiddos**) *informal* (esp. as a form of address) = KID¹ *noun* 3, 4.

kid glove *noun* **1** a glove made from kid leather. **2** (as an *adjective*) delicate: *kid glove treatment.* PHRASES **handle with kid gloves** handle in a gentle or delicate manner.

kidnap (**kidnaps, kidnapped, kidnapping**) ● *verb*

carry off (a person etc.) by illegal force or deception, esp. to obtain a ransom. ● *noun* an instance of kidnapping. ▶ **kidnapper** *noun* **kidnapping** *noun*

kidney *noun* (*plural* **kidneys**) **1** either of a pair of organs in the abdominal cavity of mammals, birds, and reptiles, which remove wastes from the blood and excrete urine. **2** the kidney of a pig etc. as food.

kidney bean *noun* an edible esp. dark red kidney-shaped bean.

kidney-shaped *adjective* shaped like a kidney, with one side curving inward and the other curving outward.

kidskin *noun* = KID¹ *noun* 2.

kielbasa *noun* a type of highly seasoned sausage of Eastern European origin, usu. containing garlic. [Say keel BOSSA]

Kikuyu ● *noun* (*plural* **Kikuyu** or **Kikuyus**) **1** a member of a Bantu-speaking people constituting the largest ethnic group in Kenya. **2** the language of this people. ● *adjective* of or relating to this people. [Say kee KOO you]

kilim ● *noun* a carpet or rug woven with no pile, made in Turkey, Kurdistan, and neighbouring areas. ● *adjective* designating such a rug etc. [Say ki LEEM or KEEL im]

kill ● *verb* **1** deprive of life or vitality. **2** destroy; put an end to (feelings etc.). **3 kill oneself a** commit suicide. **b** *informal* overexert oneself. **c** *informal* laugh heartily. **4** *informal* overwhelm (a person) with amusement, disbelief, etc.: *the things he says really kill me.* **5** switch off (a spotlight, engine, etc.). **6** *Computing* **a** delete (a line, paragraph, etc.) from a computer file. **b** cause (a process) to stop running. **7** *informal* cause pain or discomfort to: *my feet are killing me.* **8** pass (time, or a specified amount of it) usu. while waiting for a specific event: *had an hour to kill before the interview.* **9** defeat (a bill in a legislative assembly). **10** *informal* consume the entire contents of (a bottle of wine etc.). **11** *Hockey* **a** (often foll. by *off*) (of a team) endure (a penalty) without being scored on. **b** (of a player) play during (a penalty) while the team is short-handed. **12 a** *Tennis etc.* hit (the ball) so skilfully that it cannot be returned. **b** stop (the ball) dead. **13** neutralize or render ineffective (taste, sound, etc.): *thick carpet killed the sound of footsteps.* **14** cancel publication or broadcast (of a news story etc.). ● *noun* **1** an act of killing (esp. an animal). **2** an animal or animals killed, esp. by a hunter. **3** *informal* the destruction or disablement of an enemy aircraft etc. PHRASES **dressed to kill** dressed showily, alluringly, or impressively. **in at the kill** present at or benefiting from the successful conclusion of an enterprise. **kill off 1** get rid of or destroy completely (esp. a number of persons or things). **2** (of an author) bring about the death of (a fictional character). **kill two birds with one stone** achieve two aims at once. **kill with kindness** spoil (a person) with overindulgence.

killdeer *noun* a large North American plover with a plaintive song.

killer *noun* **1 a** a person, animal, or thing that kills. **b** *informal* a murderer. **2** *informal* **a** an impressive, formidable, or excellent thing. **b** a decisive blow.

killer whale *noun* a predatory toothed whale with black and white markings and a high narrow dorsal fin.

killifish *noun* (**killifish** or **killifishes**) **1** a small, often brightly coloured fish found esp. in sheltered rivers and estuaries of eastern North America. **2** a brightly-coloured tropical aquarium fish.

killing ● *noun* **1** in senses of KILL *verb*. **2** a great (esp. financial) success: *make a killing.* ● *adjective* **1** that kills: *a killing frost.* **2** *informal* overwhelmingly funny. **3** *informal* exhausting; very strenuous.

killjoy *noun* a person who throws gloom over or prevents other people's enjoyment.

kiln *noun* a furnace or oven for burning, baking, or drying, esp. for firing pottery, drying lumber, etc.

kilo *noun* (*plural* **kilos**) **1** a kilogram. **2** a kilometre.

kilo- *combining form* denoting a factor of 1,000 (esp. in metric units). Abbreviation: **k**, or **K** in *Computing*.

kilobit *noun* *Computing* a unit of memory size equal to 1,024 (i.e. 2^{10}) bits.

kilobyte *noun* *Computing* 1,024 (i.e. 2^{10}) bytes as a measure of memory size. Abbreviation: **KB** or **kbyte**.

kilocalorie *noun* = CALORIE 1.

kilogram *noun* the SI unit of mass, equivalent to the international standard kept at Sèvres near Paris (approx. 2.205 lb.). Abbreviation: **kg**.

kilohertz *noun* a measure of frequency equivalent to 1,000 cycles per second. Abbreviation: **kHz**.

kilojoule *noun* 1,000 joules, esp. as a measure of the energy value of foods. Abbreviation: **kJ**.

kilolitre *noun* (also **-liter**) 1 000 litres. Abbreviation: **kl**.

kilometre *noun* (also **kilometer**) a metric unit of measurement equal to 1 000 metres. Abbreviation: **km**. [Say kuh LOMMA ter or KILLA metre, killa METRIC]

kilopascal *noun* a metric unit of pressure equal to 1,000 pascals. Abbreviation: **kPa**. [Say KILLO pask'll or killo pass KAL]

kiloton *noun* a unit of explosive power equivalent to 1,000 tons of TNT. Abbreviation: **kt**.

kilowatt *noun* 1,000 watts. Abbreviation: **kW**.

kilowatt hour *noun* a measure of electrical energy equivalent to a power consumption of 1,000 watts for one hour. Abbreviation: **kWh**.

kilt ● *noun* **1** a skirtlike garment, usu. of pleated tartan cloth and reaching to the knees, as worn by Highland men traditionally. **2** a similar garment worn by women and children. ● *verb* tuck up (skirts) around the body.

kilted *adjective* **1** provided with or wearing a kilt. **2** gathered in vertical pleats.

kilter *noun* good working order: *out of kilter* ◊ *off-kilter*.

kimberlite *noun* a rare igneous blue-tinged rock sometimes containing diamonds, found in northern Canada, South Africa, and Siberia.

kimono *noun* (*plural* **kimonos**) **1** a long loose Japanese robe worn with a sash. **2** a wraparound dressing gown. [Say ki MOE no]

kin ● *noun* **1** one's relatives or family. **2** a related or similar thing: *Brontosaurus and its close kin Diplodocus*. ● *adjective* **1** (of a person) related: *we are kin*. **2** similar; of the same sort as: *at that time I was a free spirit, kin to the bold, independent souls that the story extols*.

kinaesthesia *noun* = KINESTHESIA. [Say kin ess THEEZ ee uh or kin ess THEEZH uh]

kinase *noun* any of various enzymes that catalyze the transfer of a phosphate group from ATP to another molecule. [Say KINE ace or KIN ace]

GRAMMAR CHECK
kind ⚠

Expressions like **these kind** and **those sort** are ungrammatical. The recommended forms are **this** (or **that**) **kind**, **these** (or **those**) **kinds**. In Canadian English, when **kind** is singular, the noun following tends to be singular: *this kind of car*; *that kind of person*. When **kind** is made plural, the noun following it tends to be plural also: *these kinds of cars*; *those sorts of people*.

---

kind¹ *noun* **1 a** a race or species: *human kind*. **b** a natural group of animals, plants, etc.: *the wolf kind*. **2** type: *what kind of job are you looking for?* **3** each of the elements (bread and wine) of the Eucharist: *at the service*

we received communion in both kinds. **4** the manner natural to a person etc.: *true to its kind, the Chianti displayed a lot of dryness*. **5** character, quality: *differ in degree but not in kind*. PHRASES **all kinds of** very many, esp. of different varieties. **in kind 1** in the same form, likewise: *was insulted and replied in kind*. **2** (of payment) in goods or labour as opposed to money received than wages in kind. **kind of** *informal* to some extent. **a** (or **some**) **kind of** used to imply looseness, vagueness, exaggeration, etc., in the term used: *a kind of Jane Austen of our times* ◊ *some kind of doctor*. **nothing of the kind 1** not at all like the thing in question. **2** (expressing denial) not at all. **of a kind 1** similar in some important respect: *they're two of a kind*. **2** derogatory scarcely deserving the name: *a choir of a kind*. **something of the kind** something like the thing in question.

kind² *adjective* **1** of a friendly, generous, or gentle nature. **2** (usu. foll. by *to*) showing friendliness, affection, or consideration. **3** showing kindness: *kind words*.

kindergarten *noun* a class or school for young children, usu. five-year-olds, in preparation for grade one. Abbreviation: **K**. ► **kindergartner** *noun*

kind-hearted *adjective* of a kind disposition. ► **kind-heartedly** *adverb* **kind-heartedness** *noun*

kindle *verb* (**kindles**, **kindled**, **kindling**) **1** light or set on fire (a flame, fire, substance, etc.), esp. gradually. **2** catch fire, burst into flame. **3** arouse or inspire: *kindle enthusiasm*. **4** become animated, glow with passion etc.: *her imagination kindled*. **5** make or become bright: *kindle the embers to a glow*. ► **kindler** *noun* [Say KIN d'll]

kindling *noun* small sticks etc. for lighting fires. [Say KIND ling (KIND rhymes with PINNED)]

kindly¹ *adverb* **1** in a kind manner. **2** often *ironic* used in a polite request or demand: *kindly leave me alone*. PHRASES **look kindly upon** regard sympathetically. **take a thing kindly** like or be pleased by it. **take kindly to** be pleased or be endeared to (a person or thing). **thank kindly** thank very much.

kindly² *adjective* (**kindlier**, **kindliest**) kind, kind-hearted.

kindness *noun* (*plural* **kindnesses**) **1** the state or quality of being kind. **2** a kind act.

kindred ● *noun* **1** one's relatives, referred to collectively. **2** a relationship by blood: *ties of kindred*. ● *adjective* **1** related by blood or marriage. **2** allied or similar in character: *I was sure we were kindred souls*. [Say KIN drid]

kindred spirit *noun* a person whose character and outlook have much in common with one's own.

kinesiology *noun* the study of the mechanics of esp. human body movements. [Say kuh nee see OLLA jee or kuh nee zee OLLA jee]

kinesis *noun* **1** movement, motion. **2** *Biology* undirected movement of an organism in response to a stimulus. [Say kuh NEE sis]

kinesthesia *noun* a sense of awareness of the position and movement of the voluntary muscles of the body. ► **kinesthetic** *adjective* [Say kin ess THEEZ ee uh or kin ess THEEZH uh, kin ess THET ick]

kinetic *adjective* of, relating to, or due to motion: *she's turned a cascade of water into a kinetic sculpture*. ► **kinetically** *adverb* [Say kin ET ick]

kinetic energy *noun* energy which a body possesses by virtue of being in motion.

kinetics *plural noun* (usu. treated as *singular*) **1** = DYNAMICS 1a. **2** the branch of physical chemistry or biochemistry concerned with measuring and studying

the rates of chemical or biochemical reactions. [Say kin ET icks]

Kinette *noun Cdn* a member of a women's organization associated with the Kinsmen. [Say kin ET]

kinfolk *plural noun* people to whom one is related by blood.

king • *noun* **1** (as a title usu. **King**) a male sovereign, esp. the hereditary ruler of an independent state. **2** a person or thing pre-eminent in a specified field or class: *railway king.* **3** a large (or the largest) kind of plant, animal, etc.: *king penguin.* **4** *Chess* **a** a piece on each side which can move only one square in any direction, and which the opposing side has to checkmate to win. **b** (**king's**) designating pieces that start on the king's side of the board. **5** a piece in checkers with extra capacity of moving, made by crowning an ordinary piece that has reached the far end of the board. **6** a playing card bearing a representation of a king and usu. ranking next below an ace. **7** (**the King**) (in Canada and the UK) the anthem "God Save the King". • *adjective* denoting a king-size bed, mattress, sheets, etc. (see KING-SIZE 2).

kingbird *noun* a large North American tyrant flycatcher, esp. with a grey head and black and yellowish or white underparts.

king cobra *noun* a brownish cobra of the Indian subcontinent, which has an orange-cream throat patch and is the largest of all venomous snakes.

king crab *noun* **1** = HORSESHOE CRAB. **2** a large edible crab of the North Pacific, which resembles a spider crab.

kingdom *noun* **1** an organized community headed by a king or queen. **2** the territory subject to a king or queen. **3** *Christianity* **a** the spiritual reign attributed to God. **b** the sphere of this: *kingdom of heaven.* **4** a domain belonging to a person, animal, etc. **5** a province of nature: *the vegetable kingdom.* **6** a specified mental or emotional province: *kingdom of the heart.* **7** *Biology* the highest category in taxonomic classification.

kingdom come *noun informal* eternity; the next world: *if lightning were to strike, that thing would get blown to kingdom come.* PHRASES **till kingdom come** forever; for an indefinitely long period.

king eider *noun* an Arctic eider duck, distinguished by the orange bill and frontal shield of the male.

kingfisher *noun* a stocky bird with a crested head and a long sharp beak, which dives for fish in rivers.

King James Version *noun* (also **King James Bible**) a 1611 English translation of the Bible made under James I and still widely used. Abbreviation: **KJV**.

kingly *adjective* **1** having to do with a king; royal. **2** like or suitable for a king: *a kingly salary.*

kingmaker *noun* a person who makes kings, leaders, etc., through the exercise of political influence.

King of the Castle *noun Cdn & Brit.* a children's game consisting of trying to displace a rival from an elevated position.

kingpin *noun* **1** an essential person or thing, esp. in a complex system. **2 a** a main or large bolt in a central position. **b** a vertical bolt used as a pivot.

king salmon *noun* = CHINOOK 2.

King's Bench *noun see* QUEEN'S BENCH.

King's Counsel *noun see* QUEEN'S COUNSEL.

kingship *noun* the office of king; the fact of ruling as a king.

king-size *adjective* (also **king-sized**) **1** larger than normal. **2** designating the largest standard size of mattress, usu. 193 by 203 cm (76 by 80 in.), or the sheets etc. designed for such a mattress.

kink • *noun* **1 a** a short twist or bend in wire or tubing etc. such as may cause an obstruction. **b** a tight wave in

human or animal hair. **2** a flaw or glitch in a mechanism, plan, etc. **3** a crick or stiffness in the neck or back. **4** an esp. mental twist or quirk. • *verb* form or cause to form a kink.

kinkiness *noun informal* **1** bizarre or unusual sexual behaviour. **2** the quality of something that is sexually provocative in an unusual way.

kinky *adjective* (**kinkier, kinkiest**) **1** *informal* **a** given to or involving bizarre or unusual sexual behaviour. **b** (of clothing etc.) bizarre in a sexually provocative way. **2** strange, eccentric. **3** having kinks or twists.

kinnikinnick *noun* **1** a mixture formerly used by some Aboriginal peoples of North America as a substitute for tobacco or for mixing with it, usu. consisting of dried bearberry or sumac leaves and the inner bark of dogwood or willow. **2** any of the various plants used for this, esp. bearberry. [Say kinny kin ICK]

kinsfolk *plural noun* = KINFOLK.

kinship *noun* **1** blood relationship. **2** the sharing of characteristics or origins.

kinsman *noun* (*plural* **kinsmen**) **1** a blood relative or a relative by marriage. **2** a member of one's own tribe or people. **3** (**Kinsman**) *Cdn* a member of a fraternal organization for esp. businessmen and professionals, founded in 1920. ▶ **kinswoman** *noun* (*plural* **kinswomen**)

kiosk *noun* a light open-fronted booth or cubicle from which refreshments, newspapers, tickets, etc. are sold or information for tourists is provided. [Say KEE osk]

kipper • *noun* **1** a fish, esp. herring, that has been cured by splitting, salting, and drying in the open air or smoke. **2** a male salmon in the spawning season. • *verb* cure (a herring etc.) by splitting open, salting, and drying in the open air or smoke.

kirk *noun* **1** *esp. Scot.* a church. **2** (**the Kirk** or **the Kirk of Scotland**) the Church of Scotland (Presbyterian).

kirk session *noun* (in Presbyterian churches) = SESSION 6.

kirpan *noun* the dagger or sword worn by Sikhs as a religious symbol. [Say ker PAN or ker PON]

kirsch *noun* (*plural* **kirsches**) a colourless brandy distilled from the fermented juice of cherries. [Say KEERSH]

kismet *noun* destiny, fate. [Say KIZZ met]

kiss • *verb* (**kisses, kissed, kissing**) **1** touch with the lips, esp. as a sign of love, greeting, or reverence. **2** express (greeting or farewell) in this way. **3** (of two persons) touch each others' lips in this way. **4** touch very lightly or briefly. • *noun* (*plural* **kisses**) **1** a touch with the lips in kissing. **2** a very light or brief touch. **3** a bite-sized baked meringue or esp. chocolate candy. PHRASES **kiss and tell** recount one's romantic encounters or sexual exploits. **kiss away** remove (tears etc.) by kissing. **kiss goodbye to** *informal* accept the loss of. **kiss the ground** prostrate oneself as a token of homage. **kiss off** *slang* dismiss, get rid of, esp. roughly or abruptly. **kiss up to** *slang* act obsequiously toward in order to obtain something. ▶ **kissable** *adjective*

kiss-and-cry *noun* (*plural* **kiss-and-cries**) the area beside the ice in which figure skaters and their coaches etc. await the posting of the judges' marks at a competition: *waited in the kiss-and-cry area.*

kiss-and-tell *adjective* revealing confidential material.

kisser *noun* **1** a person who kisses. **2** *slang* the mouth; the face.

kiss of death *noun* an act or situation (often apparently friendly) which causes ruin.

kiss-off *noun slang* an abrupt or rude dismissal.

kiss of life *noun* **1** mouth-to-mouth resuscitation. **2** an act or thing which revitalizes.

kissy *adjective informal* pertaining to or given to kissing: *not the kissy type*.

kit¹ *noun* **1** a set of articles, equipment, documents, or clothing needed for a specific purpose: *first aid kit* ◊ *press kit*. **2** a container for such a set. **3** the clothing, gear, etc. needed for any activity: *battle kit*. **4** a set of all the parts needed to assemble an item, e.g. a piece of furniture, a model, etc. **5** (in full **drum kit**) a set of drums, cymbals, etc.

kit² *noun* **1** a kitten. **2** a young fox, beaver, etc.

Kitamaat *noun* a Haisla-speaking Aboriginal people of the northern coast of BC. [Say KITTA mat]

kit bag *noun* a large, often cylindrical bag or sack used for carrying the equipment of a soldier, traveller, etc.

kitchen *noun* **1 a** a room or area where food is prepared and cooked. **b** kitchen appliances, fixtures, etc., esp. as sold together. **2** the staff working in the kitchen of a restaurant etc. PHRASES **everything but the kitchen sink** everything imaginable.

kitchen cabinet *noun* a group of unofficial advisers thought to be unduly influential.

kitchenette *noun* a small kitchen or part of a room, boat, etc. fitted as a kitchen.

kitchen garden *noun* a garden where vegetables and sometimes fruit or herbs are grown for personal use.

kitchen midden *noun* a prehistoric refuse heap which marks an ancient settlement.

kitchen party *noun* (*plural* **kitchen parties**) *Cdn* (*Maritimes*) an informal entertainment held in a person's home, at which participants play music, sing, dance, etc.

kitchen racket *noun Cdn* (*Nfld & Cape Breton*) = KITCHEN PARTY.

kitchen-sink *adjective* (in art forms) depicting extreme realism, esp. drab or sordid: *kitchen-sink drama*.

kitchenware *noun* the utensils used in the kitchen.

kite • *noun* **1** a toy consisting of a light frame with thin material stretched over it, flown in the wind at the end of a long string. **2** a medium-sized bird of prey with long wings and usu. a forked tail, which often soars in flight on updrafts of air. **3** *slang* a fraudulent cheque, bill, or receipt. • *verb* (**kites, kited, kiting**) **1** soar like a kite: *kited into England on a 747 just in time for the game*. **2** originate or pass (fraudulent cheques, bills, or receipts). **3** raise (money) by dishonest means: *kite a loan*. PHRASES **go fly a kite** *informal* get lost; go away. **high as a kite** *informal* **1** intoxicated by alcohol or drugs. **2** excited; happy.

kith and kin *noun* friends and relations.

kiting *noun* **1** the hobby or activity of flying a kite. **2** the practice of writing or passing fraudulent cheques.

kitsch *noun* (often as an *adjective*) art or articles that are considered tacky, dated, or overly sentimental, but which are sometimes appreciated in an ironic or knowing way: *Donna's living room was like a shrine to 1960s kitsch, from the groovy retro lava lamp to the shag rug*. [Say KITCH]

kitschiness *noun* the quality of something considered tacky, dated, or overly sentimental, but which is sometimes appreciated in an ironic or knowing way: *he loves the early sci-fi classics, in spite of their kitschiness*. [Say KITCHY niss]

kitschy *adjective* (**kitschier, kitschiest**) tacky, garish, dated, or overly sentimental, but in a way that is sometimes appreciated in an ironic or knowing way: *a remarkable collection of kitschy commemorative plates*. [Say KITCHY]

Kitselas *noun* (*plural* **Kitselas**) **1** a member of an Aboriginal people living along the Skeena River in northwestern BC. **2** the Tsimshian language of this people. [Say KIT sul us]

kitten • *noun* **1** a young cat. **2** the young of certain other animals, as the fox, ferret, etc. • *verb* (of a cat etc.) give birth or give birth to. PHRASES **have kittens** *informal* be extremely upset, anxious, or nervous.

kittenish *adjective* **1** like a young cat; playful and lively. **2** flirtatious.

kittiwake *noun* a small gull that nests in colonies on sea cliffs. [Say KITTY wake]

kitty¹ *noun* (*plural* **kitties**) **1** a fund of money for communal use. **2** a pool of money in some card games made up of contributions from each player and used as winnings or for refreshments etc.

kitty² *noun* (*plural* **kitties**) a pet name or a child's name for a kitten or cat.

kitty-corner • *adjective* placed or situated diagonally. • *adverb* diagonally.

Kitty Litter *noun proprietary* = CAT LITTER.

Kiwanis *noun* a society of business and professional people founded in 1915 for the maintenance of commercial ethics and as a social and charitable organization. [Say ki WON iss (WON rhymes with DON)]

kiwi *noun* (*plural* **kiwis**) **1** a flightless New Zealand bird with hairlike feathers and a long bill. **2 a** a climbing plant bearing fruits with a thin hairy skin, green flesh, and black seeds. **b** (also **kiwi fruit**) this fruit. **3** (**Kiwi**) *informal* a New Zealander.

kJ *abbreviation* kilojoule(s).

KJV *abbreviation* KING JAMES VERSION.

KKK *abbreviation* KU KLUX KLAN.

kl *abbreviation* kilolitre(s).

Klan *noun* (usu. as **the Klan**) KU KLUX KLAN.

Klansman *noun* (*plural* **Klansmen**) a member of the Ku Klux Klan.

Kleenex *noun* (*plural* **Kleenex** or **Kleenexes**) *proprietary* an absorbent disposable paper tissue, used esp. as a handkerchief.

kleptomania *noun* a recurrent urge to steal, usu. without regard for need or profit. ▶ **kleptomaniac** *noun & adjective*

klezmer *noun* **1** a member of a group of musicians playing traditional eastern European Jewish music. **2** (also **klezmer music**) this type of music. [Say KLEZZ mer]

klick *noun slang* a kilometre.

Klondike *noun* a source of valuable material or wealth: *the dot-com Klondike of the Internet*.

Klondiker *noun hist.* a prospector who took part in the gold rush to the Klondike River valley, in west central Yukon Territory, in 1897–8.

klutz *noun* (*plural* **klutzes**) *informal* a clumsy, awkward person. ▶ **klutzy** *adjective* (**klutzier, klutziest**)

km *abbreviation* kilometre(s).

km/h *abbreviation* kilometres per hour.

knack *noun* **1** an acquired or intuitive faculty of doing a thing adroitly. **2** a trick or habit of action or speech etc.: *he has a knack of offending people*.

knapsack *noun* a bag of canvas, nylon, or other weatherproof material, carried strapped on the back by hikers, students, soldiers, etc.

knave *noun* **1** *archaic* a dishonest or unscrupulous man. **2** = JACK *noun* 2. ▶ **knavery** *noun* **knavish** *adjective*

knead *verb* **1 a** work (dough, clay, etc.) into a smooth mass by pressing and folding. **b** make (bread, pottery, etc.) in this way. **2** blend or weld together: *kneaded them into a unified group*. **3** massage or pummel (muscles etc.) as if kneading.

knee • *noun* **1 a** the joint between the thigh and the

K

lower leg in humans. **b** the corresponding joint in other animals. **c** the area around this. **d** the upper surface of the thigh of a sitting person; the lap: *held her on his knee.* **2** the part of a garment covering the knee. **3** anything resembling a knee in shape or position, esp. a piece of wood or iron bent at an angle, a sharp turn in a graph, etc. • *verb* (**knees, kneed, kneeing**) touch or strike with the knee: *kneed him in the groin.* PHRASES **bring to its** (or **his** or **her**) **knees** reduce (a thing or person) to a state of weakness or submission. **learn** (**something**) **at one's mother's knee** learn something at an early age. **on bended knee** (also **on one's bended knees**) kneeling, esp. in supplication, submission, or worship. **on one's knees 1** kneeling. **2** seriously weakened, just short of total collapse.

kneeboard • *noun* a short surfboard ridden in a kneeling position. • *verb* ride a kneeboard. ▶ **kneeboarder** *noun* **kneeboarding** *noun*

kneecap • *noun* the convex bone in front of the knee; the patella. • *verb* (**kneecaps, kneecapped, kneecapping**) shoot (a person) in the knee or leg as a punishment, esp. for betraying a terrorist group. ▶ **kneecapping** *noun*

knee-deep *adjective* **1** (usu. foll. by *in*) **a** immersed up to the knees. **b** deeply involved. **c** having more than one needs or wants of a specified thing. **2** (of water, snow, mud, etc.) so deep as to reach the knees.

knee-high • *adjective* **1** reaching as high as the knees. **2** (of a person) very small or very young. • *noun* (usu. in *plural*) a sock reaching just below the knee: *Carolyn was dressed in an attractive skirt and knee-highs.* PHRASES **knee-high to a grasshopper** very small or very young.

knee-jerk • *noun* a sudden involuntary kick caused by a blow on the tendon just below the knee. • *adjective* predictable, automatic, stereotyped: *a knee-jerk reaction.*

knee joint *noun* **1** = KNEE *noun* 1a, b. **2** a joint made of two pieces hinged together.

kneel *verb* (**kneels;** *past* and *past participle* **knelt** or **kneeled; kneeling**) fall or rest on the knees or a knee.

knee-length *adjective* reaching the knees.

kneeler *noun* **1** a low padded bench or cushion used for kneeling, esp. in church. **2** a person who kneels.

knee sock *noun* (usu. in *plural*) a sock covering the lower leg to just below the knee.

knell • *noun* **1** the sound of a bell, esp. when rung solemnly for a death or funeral. **2** used with reference to an announcement, event, or sound that is regarded as a solemn warning of the end of something: *the decision will probably sound the knell for the facility.* • *verb* (of a bell) ring solemnly, esp. for a death or funeral.

knelt *past* and *past participle* of KNEEL.

Knesset *noun* the parliament of modern Israel, established in 1949. [Say k'NESS it]

knew *past* of KNOW.

knickerbocker *noun* **1** (in *plural*) loose-fitting breeches gathered at the knee or calf. **2** (**Knickerbocker**) **a** a New Yorker. **b** a descendant of the original Dutch settlers in New York.

knickers *plural noun* **1** knickerbockers. **2** a boy's short trousers. PHRASES **get one's knickers** (or **shirt**) **in a knot** (or **twist**) become agitated or upset.

knick-knack *noun* a small decorative object, esp. a household ornament.

knife • *noun* (*plural* **knives**) **1 a** a metal blade used as a cutting tool with usu. one long sharp edge fixed rigidly in a handle or hinged. **b** a similar tool used as a weapon. **2** a cutting blade forming part of a machine. • *verb* (**knifes, knifed, knifing**) **1** cut or stab with or as with a knife. **2** *slang* bring about the defeat of (a person) by underhand means. **3** (usu. foll. by *through*) cut

or move through like a knife. PHRASES **go under the knife** *informal* have surgery. **like a** (**hot**) **knife through butter** easily; without meeting any resistance or difficulty. **that one could cut with a knife** *informal* (of an accent, atmosphere, etc.) very obvious, oppressive, etc.

knife-edge *noun* **1** the edge of a knife. **2** a position of extreme danger or uncertainty. **3** a sharp narrow mountain ridge formed by the meeting of adjacent glacial valleys.

knifelike *adjective* resembling a knife in shape or sharpness.

knifepoint • *noun* PHRASES **at knifepoint** under threat of being stabbed.

knifing *noun* a stabbing with a knife.

knight • *noun* **1** a man awarded a non-hereditary title (*Sir*) by a sovereign in recognition of merit or service. **2** *hist.* **a** a man, usu. noble, raised esp. by a sovereign to honourable military rank after service as a page and squire. **b** a military follower or attendant, esp. of a lady as her champion in a war or tournament. **3** *Chess* a piece usu. shaped like a horse's head. • *verb* confer a knighthood on.

knight errant *noun* (*plural* **knights errant**) *hist.* a medieval knight wandering in search of chivalrous adventures.

knighthood *noun* the title, rank, or status of a knight.

knightly *adjective* having to do with knights: *the knightly class.*

knish *noun* (*plural* **knishes**) a dumpling of flaky dough filled with cheese etc. and baked or fried. [Say k'NISH]

---

knit • *verb* (**knits;** *past* and *past participle* **knitted** or (esp. in senses 2–4) **knit; knitting**) **1 a** make (a garment, blanket, etc.) by interlocking loops of yarn with knitting needles or by machine. **b** make (a plain stitch) in knitting: *knit one, purl one.* **2 a** contract (the forehead) in vertical wrinkles. **b** (of the forehead) contract; frown. **3** (often foll. by *together*) make or become close or compact esp. by common interests etc.: *a close-knit group.* **4** (often foll. by *together*) (of parts of a broken bone) become joined; heal. • *noun* knitted material or a knitted garment: *T-shirts in cotton knit.* PHRASES **knit up 1 a** make or repair by knitting. **b** *Cdn* (*Nfld & PEI*) knot twine into meshes to make a fishnet or the heads on a lobster trap. **2** conclude, finish, or end. ▶ **knitter** *noun*

knitting *noun* **1** a garment etc. in the process of being knitted. **2** the act of knitting.

knitting needle *noun* a thin pointed rod of steel, wood, plastic, etc., used esp. in pairs for knitting.

knitwear *noun* knitted garments.

knives *plural* of KNIFE.

knob *noun* **1 a** a rounded protuberance, esp. at the end or on the surface of a thing. **b** a handle of a door, drawer, etc., shaped like a knob. **c** a knob-shaped attachment for pulling, turning, etc.: *press the knob under the desk.* **2 a** a small, usu. round, piece (of butter, coal, etc.). **b** *Cdn* (*Nfld*) a hard candy. **3** a prominent round hill. ▶ **knob-like** *adjective*

knobbed *adjective* having a knob or knobs: *his leg was knobbed and bumpy.*

knobbly *adjective* having many small knobs.

knobby *adjective* (**knobbier, knobbiest**) having, resembling, or consisting of round lumps or knobs: *knobby knees* ◊ *the knobby tires give the bike good traction.*

knock • *verb* **1 a** strike (a hard surface) with an

audible sharp blow. **b** strike, esp. a door to gain admittance: *can you hear someone knocking?* **2** make (a hole, dent, etc.) by knocking: *knock a hole in the fence.* **3** drive (a thing, a person, etc.) by striking: *knocked the ball into the hole* ◊ *knocked her hand away.* **4** *informal* criticize. **5** come into collision with something: *he knocked into the desk.* **6** cause (a person) to be in a certain state or position by striking: *knocked me senseless.* **7** (of a motor or other engine) make a thumping or rattling noise, esp. due to faulty combustion. • *noun* **1** an act of knocking. **2** a sharp rap, esp. at a door. **3** an audible sharp blow. **4** the sound of knocking in an engine, esp. in a motor engine. **5 a** a misfortune, a setback. **b** adverse criticism. PHRASES **knock around** (or **about**) **1** strike repeatedly; treat roughly: *knocked him around.* **2** lead a wandering adventurous life; wander aimlessly. **3** be present without design or volition: *there's a cup knocking about somewhere.* **4** discuss casually: *knocked a couple of ideas around.* **knock against** collide with. **knock back 1** *informal* eat or drink, esp. quickly. **2** *Brit. & Cdn informal* disconcert. **3** reverse the progress of. **knock down 1** strike (esp. a person) to the ground with a blow. **2** demolish. **3** (usu. foll. by *to*) (at an auction) dispose of (an article) to a bidder by a knock with a hammer: *knocked the Picasso down to him for a million.* **4** *informal* lower the price of (an article). **5** take (machinery etc.) apart for transportation. **knock one's head against** come into collision with (unfavourable facts or conditions). **knock into the middle of next week** *informal* send (a person) flying, esp. with a blow. **knock it off!** stop it! **knock off 1** strike (off) with a blow. **2** *informal* **a** finish work: *knocked off at 5:30.* **b** finish (work): *knocked off work early.* **3** *informal* rapidly produce (a work of art, verses, etc.). **4** (often foll. by *from*) deduct (a sum) from a price, bill, etc. **5** *slang* a steal or burglarize: *knocked off a convenience store.* **b** copy, plagiarize. **6** *slang* kill. **7** *slang* defeat: *knocked off the top team in the league.* **8** remove or reduce by: *knocked a second off the previous world record.* **knock on the head** stun or kill (a person) by a blow on the head. **knock (on) wood** knock on something wooden with the hand to avert bad luck. **knock out 1** make (a person) unconscious by a blow on the head. **2** knock down (a boxer) for a count of 10, thereby winning the contest. **3 a** defeat, esp. in a knockout competition. **b** get rid of; destroy: *a computer program to knock out viruses.* **4** *informal* astonish, esp. by unexpected excellence, generosity, etc. **5 knock oneself out** *informal* exhaust: *knocked themselves out swimming.* **6** *informal* make or write (a plan etc.) hastily. **knock over 1** cause to fall, spill, or overturn. **2** *slang* rob, burglarize. **knock one's socks off** *slang* astound, amaze. **knock together** put together or assemble hastily or roughly. **knock up** *slang* make pregnant. **take a knock** be distressed financially or emotionally.

knock-down • *adjective* **1** (of a blow, misfortune, argument, etc.) overwhelming. **2** *informal* (of a price) very low. **3** (of furniture etc.) easily dismantled and reassembled. **4** (of an insecticide) rapidly immobilizing. • *noun* an act or instance of knocking down.

knocker *noun* **1** a metal or wooden instrument hinged to a door for knocking to call attention. **2** a person or thing that knocks. **3** (in *plural*) *slang* a woman's breasts. **4** *informal* a person who continually finds fault.

knock-kneed *adjective* having legs that curve inwards at the knees.

knock knees *plural noun* an abnormal condition with the legs curved inwards at the knees.

knock-off *noun informal* a copy or imitation made esp. for commercial gain.

knockout *noun* **1** the act of making unconscious by a blow. **2** *Boxing etc.* a blow that knocks an opponent out. **3** a competition in which the loser in each round is eliminated. **4** *informal* an outstanding or irresistible person or thing.

knoll *noun* a small hill or mound. [Say NOLE]

knot • *noun* **1 a** an intertwining of a rope, string, tress of hair, etc., with another, itself, or something else to join or fasten together. **b** a set method of tying a knot: *a reef knot.* **c** a ribbon etc. tied as an ornament and worn on a dress etc. **d** a tangle in hair, knitting, etc. **2 a** a unit of a ship's or aircraft's speed equivalent to one nautical mile per hour (see NAUTICAL MILE). **b** a division marked by knots on a line or rope attached to a ship's log, used as a measure of speed. **c** *informal* a nautical mile. **3** (usu. foll. by *of*) a group or cluster. **4** something forming or maintaining a union; a bond or tie, esp. of wedlock. **5** a hard lump of tissue in an animal or human body. **6 a** a knob or protuberance in a stem, branch, or root. **b** a hard mass formed in a tree trunk at the intersection with a branch. **c** a round cross-grained piece in timber where a branch has been cut through. **d** a node on the stem of a plant. **7** a difficulty; a problem. **8** a central point in a problem or the plot of a story etc. **9** a sensation of contortion felt in the stomach or throat, caused by stress or nervousness. • *verb* (**knots**, **knotted**, **knotting**) **1 a** tie (a string etc.) in a knot. **b** secure (something) with a knot. **2 a** entangle. **b** become entangled. **3** form lumps, knobs, or knots on or in; make knotty. **4** *slang* tie (a score, game, etc.). PHRASES **tie in knots** *informal* baffle or confuse completely. **tie the knot** *informal* get married.

knothole *noun* **1** a hole in a piece of timber where a knot has fallen out. **2** a hollow formed in a tree trunk by the decay of a branch.

knotty *adjective* (**knottier**, **knottiest**) **1** full of knots. **2** hard to explain; puzzling: *a knotty problem.*

know • *verb* (**knows**; *past* **knew**; *past participle* **known**; **knowing**) **1 a** have in the mind; have learned; be able to recall: *knows a lot about cars* ◊ *knows what to do.* **b** be aware of (a fact): *she knows I am waiting.* **c** have a good command of (a subject or language): *knew German* ◊ *knows her times tables.* **2** be acquainted or friendly with (a person or thing). **3 a** recognize; identify: *I knew him at once.* **b** be aware of (a person or thing) as being or doing what is specified: *knew them to be thugs.* **c** (foll. by *from*) be able to distinguish (one from another): *did not know him from Adam.* **4** be subject to: *her joy knew no bounds.* **5** have personal experience of (fear etc.). **6** have understanding or knowledge. • *noun* (in phr. **in the know**) *informal* well informed; having special knowledge. PHRASES **before one knows it** with baffling speed. **be not to know 1** have no way of learning: *wasn't to know they'd arrive late.* **2** be not to be told: *she's not to know about the party.* **don't I know it!** *informal* an expression of rueful assent. **don't you know** *informal* or *jocular* an expression used for emphasis: *such a bore, don't you know.* **for all I know** so far as my knowledge extends: *they have been known to turn up late.* **I knew it!** I was sure that this would happen. **I know what** I have a new idea, suggestion, etc. **know about** have information about. **know best** be correct or claim to be better informed etc. than others. **know better than** be wise, well informed, or well-mannered enough to avoid (specified behaviour etc.): *she knows better than to stay out this late.* **know by name 1** have heard the name of. **2** be able to give the name of. **know by sight** recognize the appearance (only) of. **know how** know the way to do something. **know of** be aware

of; have heard of: *not that I know of*. **know one's own mind** be decisive, not vacillate. **know the ropes** (or **one's stuff**) be fully knowledgeable or experienced. **know a thing or two** be experienced or shrewd. **know what's what** have adequate knowledge of the world, life, etc. **know who's who** be aware of who or what each person is. **not know from** not know anything about. **not know that ...** *informal* be fairly sure that ... not: *I don't know that I want to go*. **not know the meaning of the word** behave as if one does not know such an idea exists. **not know what hit one** be suddenly injured, killed, disconcerted, etc. **not want to know** refuse to take any notice of. **what do you know** (or **know about that)?** *informal* an expression of surprise. **you know** *informal* **1** an expression implying something generally known or known to the hearer: *you know, the restaurant on the corner*. **2** an expression used as a gap-filler in conversation. **you know something** (or **what)?** I am going to tell you something. **you never know** nothing in the future is certain. ▶ **knowable** *adjective* **knower** *noun*

know-how *noun* **1** practical knowledge; technique, expertise. **2** natural skill or invention.

knowing • *noun* the state of being aware or informed of any thing. • *adjective* **1** usu. derogatory cunning; sly. **2** showing knowledge or awareness. PHRASES **there is no knowing** no one can tell.

knowingly *adverb* **1** consciously; intentionally: *had never knowingly injured him*. **2** in a knowing manner: *smiled knowingly*.

knowingness *noun* an implied or apparent knowledge or understanding of something that is secret or known only to a few people: *lacked the swagger and knowingness of big men on campus*.

know-it-all *noun* *informal* a person who seems or pretends to know everything.

knowledge *noun* **1 a** (usu. foll. by *of*) awareness or familiarity gained by experience (of a person, fact, or thing). **b** a person's range of information. **2 a** (usu. foll. by *of*) a theoretical or practical understanding of a subject, language, etc.: *has a good knowledge of Greek*. **b** the sum of what is known: *every branch of knowledge*. PHRASES **come to one's knowledge** become known to one. **to (the best of) my knowledge 1** so far as I know. **2** as I know for certain.

knowledgeable *adjective* well-informed; intelligent. ▶ **knowledgeably** *adverb* [Say KNOWLEDGE uh bull]

knowledge-based *adjective* **1** (of an industry etc.) producing information rather than manufactured goods, natural resources, etc. **2** (of a computer system) incorporating a set of facts, assumptions, or inference rules derived from human knowledge.

known • *verb* past participle of KNOW. • *adjective* **1** publicly acknowledged: *a known thief* ◊ *a known fact*. **2** *Math* (of a quantity etc.) having a value that can be stated.

know-nothing *noun* an ignorant person.

knuckle *noun* **1** the bone at a finger joint, esp. that adjoining the hand. **2 a** a projection of the carpal or tarsal joint of a quadruped. **b** a joint of meat consisting of this with the adjoining parts, esp. of bacon or pork. **3** something shaped, angled, or protruding like a knuckle. PHRASES **knuckle down** (often foll. by *to*) **1** apply oneself seriously (to a task etc.). **2** (also **knuckle under**) give in; submit.

knuckleball *noun* *Baseball* a slow pitch which moves erratically, made by gripping the ball with the knuckles or fingernails and throwing it with little spin. ▶ **knuckleballer** *noun*

knucklebone *noun* **1** bone forming a knuckle. **2** the

bone of a sheep or other animal corresponding to or resembling a knuckle. **3** a knuckle of meat.

knucklehead *noun* *informal* a stupid or dull-witted person. ▶ **knuckleheaded** *adjective*

knuckler *noun* *slang* a knuckleball.

knurl • *noun* a small projecting knob, ridge, etc. • *verb* make knurls on the edge of (a coin etc.). ▶ **knurled** *adjective*

KO • *noun* (plural **KOs**) a knockout in boxing etc. • *verb* (**KO's**, **KO'd KO'ing**) **1** knock out (an opponent) in boxing etc. **2** *informal* destroy, defeat. • *abbreviation* knockout.

koala *noun* (also **koala bear**) an Australian bearlike marsupial, which has grey fur and feeds on eucalyptus leaves. [Say kuh WOLLA]

Kodiak *noun* (also **Kodiak bear**) a large variety of grizzly found in Alaska. [Say KOE dee ack]

kohl *noun* a black powder, usu. antimony sulphide or lead sulphide, used as eye makeup esp. in Eastern countries. [Say KOLE]

kohlrabi *noun* (plural **kohlrabies**) a variety of cabbage with an edible turnip-like swollen stem. [Say kole RABBY or kole ROBBY]

koi *noun* (plural **koi**) (also **koi carp**, plural **koi carp**) a carp of a large ornamental variety bred in Japan.

kokanee *noun* (plural **kokanee**) a non-migratory form of sockeye salmon found in lakes in western North America. [Say CO canny or co CANNY]

kola *noun* = COLA 1.

kolbassa *noun* a type of highly seasoned sausage, usu. containing garlic. [Say co baw SAW or COO buh saw or ko BASSA]

komatik *noun* an Inuit sled consisting of two parallel wooden runners connected by wooden slats, usu. pulled by a dog team. [Say COMMA tick]

Komodo dragon *noun* (also **Komodo monitor**) a large, heavily built, East Indian monitor lizard, which captures large prey such as pigs by ambush. [Say kuh MOE doe]

kook *noun* *slang* a strange or eccentric person.

kookiness *noun* an odd or peculiar manner; eccentricity.

kooky *adjective* (**kookier**, **kookiest**) *slang* strange, eccentric.

Kool-Aid *noun* *proprietary* **1** a fruit-flavoured powder mixed with water and sugar to make a drink. **2** such a drink.

Kootenay (plural **Kootenay**) (also **Kootenai**, plural **Kootenai**) = KUTENAI. [Say COO tuh nay]

Koran *noun* the Islamic sacred book, believed to be the word of God as dictated to Muhammad and written down in Arabic. ▶ **Koranic** *adjective* [Say core ANN or kuh RAN, core ANN ick or kuh RAN ick]

Korean • *noun* **1** a native or national of North or South Korea in Southeast Asia. **2** the language of Korea. • *adjective* of or relating to Korea or its people or language. [Say kuh REE in]

kosher • *adjective* **1** (of food or premises in which food is sold, cooked, or eaten) fulfilling the requirements of Jewish law. **2** *informal* correct; genuine; legitimate. • *noun* **1** kosher food. **2** the Jewish law regarding food: *keep kosher*. [Say CO sher]

Kosovar • *noun* an esp. Albanian-speaking native or inhabitant of Kosovo, in S Yugoslavia. • *adjective* of or relating to Kosovo or its inhabitants. [Say COSSA var]

kowtow • *noun* *hist.* the Chinese custom of kneeling and touching the ground with the forehead in worship or submission. • *verb* (usu. foll. by *to*) act obsequiously. [Say COW tow (TOW rhymes with COW)]

kPa *abbreviation* kilopascal(s).

K

k.p.h. *abbreviation* kilometres per hour.

Kr *symbol* krypton.

kraft *noun* (also **kraft paper**) a kind of strong smooth brown wrapping paper.

kremlin *noun* **1** a citadel within a Russian town. **2 (the Kremlin) a** the citadel in Moscow, the capital of Russia. **b** the Russian or (formerly) USSR government housed within it.

krill *noun* **1** a small shrimp-like planktonic crustacean of the open seas, important as food for fish, and for some whales and seals. **2** these collectively.

krypton *noun* an inert gaseous element, forming a small portion of the earth's atmosphere and used in fluorescent lamps etc. [Say CRIP tonn]

KS *abbreviation* **1** Kansas (in official postal use). **2** KAPOSI'S SARCOMA.

Kt. *abbreviation* Knight.

kt. *abbreviation* **1** knot. **2** karat. **3** kiloton.

Ktunaxa Kinbasket • *noun* (*plural* **Ktunaxa Kinbasket**) **1** a member of an Aboriginal people living in southeastern BC and northeastern Washington. **2** the language of this people. • *adjective* of or relating to this people. [Say k'too NOCK aw KIN basket]

Ku *symbol* kurchatovium.

kubasa *noun* Cdn a garlic sausage of Ukrainian origin. [Say co baw SAW or COO buh saw or ko BASSA]

kudlik *noun* an Inuit soapstone seal oil lamp, providing both light and heat. [Say COOD lick]

kudos *noun* informal (often treated as *plural*) expressions of praise received for an achievement: *thanks and kudos to our volunteer instructors ◊ she has been getting kudos for the way she handled the problem.* [Say COO doze or COO dose]

kugel *noun* a baked sweet or savoury dish of potatoes or noodles mixed with eggs, cottage cheese, etc. and served as a separate course or as a side dish. [Say COO gull]

Ku Klux Klan *noun* a secret society of white people in the United States, originally formed in the southern states after the Civil War and revived in 1915 to harass and intimidate Blacks and other ethnic or religious minorities through violence, terrorism, and murder. ▶**Ku Klux Klansman** *noun* (*plural* **Ku Klux Klansmen**)

kumquat *noun* **1** an orange-like fruit with a sweet rind and acid pulp, used in preserves. **2** the East Asian shrub or tree that yields this fruit. [Say KUM kwot]

kundalini *noun* **1** (in yoga) the latent, female energy thought to lie coiled at the base of the spine. **2** (also **kundalini yoga**) a type of meditation which aims to direct and release this energy. [Say COON duh leeny]

Kung • *noun* (*plural* **Kung**) **1** a member of a San (Bushman) people of the Kalahari Desert in southern Africa, maintaining to some extent a nomadic way of life dependent on hunting and gathering. **2** the Khoisan language of the Kung. • *adjective* of or relating to the Kung or their language.

kung fu *noun* the Chinese form of unarmed combat similar to karate. [Say kung FOO]

kurchatovium *noun* = RUTHERFORDIUM. [Say kertcha TOE vee um]

Kurd *noun* a member of a mainly pastoral Muslim people living chiefly in eastern Turkey, northern Iraq, western Iran, and eastern Syria. [Rhymes with BIRD]

Kurdish • *adjective* of or relating to the Kurds or their language. • *noun* the Iranian language of the Kurds. [Say KURD ish]

Kutchin *noun* (*plural* **Kutchin**) = GWICH'IN. [Say coo CHIN]

Kutenai *noun & adjective* (*plural* **Kutenai**) = KTUNAXA KINBASKET. [Say COO tuh nay]

Kuwaiti • *noun* **1** (*plural* **Kuwaitis**) a native or inhabitant of Kuwait, a country on the northwestern coast of the Persian Gulf. **2** the dialect of Arabic spoken in Kuwait. • *adjective* of or relating to Kuwait or the Kuwaitis. [Say coo WAIT ee]

kvetch *slang* • *verb* (**kvetches**, **kvetched**, **kvetching**) complain and whine, esp. continually. • *noun* (*plural* **kvetches**) (also **kvetcher**) a person who complains a great deal. ▶**kvetching** *noun* [Say k'VETCH]

kW *abbreviation* kilowatt(s).

Kwagiulth • *noun* (*plural* **Kwagiulth**) **1** a member of an Aboriginal people living in parts of coastal BC and northern Vancouver Island. **2** the Kwa-kwa-la language of this people. • *adjective* of or relating to this people. [Say kwah GHEE oolt]

Kwakiutl *noun & adjective* (*plural* **Kwakiutl**) = KWAGIULTH. [Say kwocky OOTLE]

Kwakwaka'wakw • *noun* (*plural* **Kwakwaka'wakw**) a member of an Aboriginal people living in southwestern BC. • *adjective* of or relating to this people. [Say kwah KWOCKY wock]

Kwa-kwa-la *noun* the Wakashan language of the Kwakwaka'wakw and Kwagiulth. [Say kwah KWOLLA]

Kwanza *noun* (also **Kwanzaa**) a festival observed from 26 Dec. to 1 Jan. in celebration of black cultural heritage. [Say KWONZA]

kwashiorkor *noun* a form of malnutrition caused by a severe dietary protein deficiency, esp. in young children in the tropics. [Say kwoshy OR core]

kWh *abbreviation* kilowatt hour(s).

KWIC *noun* Computing etc. keyword in context. [Say QUICK]

KY *abbreviation* Kentucky (in official postal use).

Kyrie *noun* (also **Kyrie eleison**) **1** a short repeated invocation (in Greek or translated) beginning with the words "Lord, have mercy" used in many Christian liturgies, esp. at the beginning of the Eucharist or as a response in a litany. **2** a musical setting of the Kyrie. [Say KEERY ay (ay LAY ee sonn)]

LI

L¹ *noun* (also **l**) (*plural* **Ls** or **L's**) **1** the twelfth letter of the alphabet. **2** (as a Roman numeral) 50. **3** a thing shaped like an L, esp. a joint connecting two pipes.

L² *abbreviation* (also **L.**) **1** Lake. **2** (esp. on clothing etc.) large. **3** Liberal. **4** litre.

l *abbreviation* (also **l.**) **1** left. **2** line. **3** litre(s). **4** length. **5** (esp. *plural* **ll.**) (of poetry) line. **6** liquid.

La *symbol* lanthanum.

la *noun Music* **1** (in tonic sol-fa) the sixth note of a major scale. **2** the note A in the fixed-do system.

Lab *noun* a Labrador retriever.

Lab. *abbreviation* Labrador.

lab *noun informal* a laboratory.

lab coat *noun* a coat of a light, usu. white fabric, worn over clothing to protect it, esp. in a laboratory etc.

label • *noun* **1** a small piece of paper, fabric, etc. attached to an object and giving information about it. **2** the name or trademark of a fashion company. **3** a company that produces recorded music. **4** a classifying name applied to a person or thing. **5** *Biology & Chemistry* a radioactive isotope, fluorescent dye, or enzyme used to make something identifiable. • *verb* (**labels**, **labelled**, **labelling**) **1** attach a label to. **2** assign to a category. **3** *Biology & Chemistry* make (a substance, cell, etc.) identifiable using a label.

labial *adjective* **1 a** of the lips. **b** *Zoology* pertaining to, of the nature of, associated with, or situated on a lip or labium. **2** designating the surface of a tooth adjacent to the lips. [Say LAY bee ul]

labium *noun* (*plural* **labia**) **1** each of the two pairs of skin folds that enclose the vulva. **2** the lower lip in the mouthparts of an insect or crustacean. **3** a lip, esp. a structure resembling a lip on a plant. [Say LAY bee um]

labor etc. = LABOUR etc.

laboratory *noun* (*plural* **laboratories**) **1** a room or building fitted out for scientific experiments, research, teaching, or the manufacture of drugs and chemicals. **2** a class in which students engage in learning activities such as language drills, mapping, conducting experiments, etc. [Say LABRA tory or luh BORA tory]

laboratory animal *noun* any animal, such as a rat, monkey, mouse, etc. commonly used for experiments.

laborious *adjective* **1** needing hard work or toil: *a laborious task*. **2** (esp. of speech or writing style) showing obvious signs of effort and lacking fluency: *Americans didn't go in for long captions; they invented the one-liner while we were still being clumsy and laborious*. ▶ **laboriously** *adverb* **laboriousness** *noun* [Say luh BORY us]

labour (also **labor**) • *noun* **1 a** physical or mental work; exertion; toil. **b** such work considered as supplying the needs of a community. **2** workers, esp. manual, considered as a class or political force. **3** the process of childbirth, esp. the period from the start of uterine contractions to delivery. **4** a particular task, esp. of a difficult nature. **5** (**Labour**) = LABOUR PARTY. • *verb* **1 a** work hard or exert oneself physically or mentally. **b** do esp. manual work to earn one's living. **2** strive for a purpose: *laboured to fulfill his promise*. **3** treat or insist upon at excessive length; elaborate needlessly: *I will not labour the point*. **4** suffer under (a disadvantage or delusion): *laboured under universal disapproval*. **5** proceed with trouble or difficulty:

laboured slowly up the hill. **6** (of an engine) work noisily and with difficulty, esp. when under load. **labour in vain** make a fruitless effort. **labour of love** a task done for pleasure, not reward.

labour board *noun* (also **Labour Relations Board**) a tribunal, either provincial or federal, empowered to mediate and resolve labour disputes.

labour camp *noun* **1** a prison camp enforcing a regime of hard labour. **2** a camp providing shelter for migratory workers, esp. farm labourers.

Labour Day *noun* a holiday in celebration of working people, observed in Canada and the US on the first Monday in September and elsewhere on 1 May.

laboured *adjective* **1** not natural or spontaneous; showing signs of too much effort. **2** (esp. of breathing) slow and difficult.

labourer *noun* (also **laborer**) a person doing unskilled, usu. manual, work for wages.

labour-intensive *adjective* (of a process or industry) having labour as the largest factor or cost.

Labour Party *noun* **1** a British political party formed to represent the interests of ordinary working people. **2** any similar political party in other countries.

labour relations *plural noun* the relations between management and employees.

labour-saving *adjective* (of an appliance etc.) reducing or eliminating the work needed to do something.

labour union *noun* an organized association of workers formed to protect and further their rights and interests and bargain collectively with employers.

Labrador *noun* (also **Labrador dog**, **Labrador retriever**) a breed of retriever with a black or golden coat often used as a gun dog or guide dog.

Labradorian • *noun* a native or inhabitant of Labrador. • *adjective* of or relating to Labrador or Labradorians.

Labrador Inuit *noun* **1** the Inuit people living in N Labrador. **2** the language of this people.

labradorite *noun* a kind of feldspar often showing iridescence from internal reflective planes. [Say LABRADOR ite]

Labrador tea *noun* **1** a shrub of the heath family, with fragrant leathery evergreen leaves used to make a herbal tea. **2** a tea made from these leaves.

laburnum *noun* a small tree with racemes of golden flowers yielding poisonous seeds. [Say luh BURN um]

labyrinth *noun* **1** a complicated irregular network of passages or paths etc.; a maze. **2 a** an intricate or tangled arrangement, esp. of streets or buildings: *we lost our way in the labyrinth of streets*. **b** a complex or confusing situation: *a labyrinth of rules and regulations*. **3** *Anatomy* the complex arrangement of canals and chambers of the inner ear which constitute the organs of hearing and balance. **4** any of various devices containing or consisting of winding passages, esp. a series of chambers designed to absorb unwanted vibrations in a loudspeaker. [Say LABBER inth]

labyrinthine *adjective* **1** (of a network or layout) like a labyrinth or maze; irregular and twisting: *labyrinthine corridors*. **2** (of a system) intricate and confusing:

labyrinthine plots and counterplots ◊ *labyrinthine tax legislation*. [Say labber INTH ine]

lac *noun* a resinous substance secreted as a protective covering by an Asian insect (called the lac insect), and used to make varnish and shellac. [Say LACK]

lace • *noun* **1** a fine open fabric, esp. of cotton or silk, made by weaving thread in patterns and used esp. as a trim or to make tablecloths. **2** a cord or leather strip passed through eyelets or hooks on opposite sides of a shoe, skate, garment, etc., pulled tight and fastened. **3** braid used for trimming esp. dress uniforms. • *adjective* made of lace. • *verb* (**laces, laced, lacing**) **1** (usu. foll. by *up*) **a** fasten or tighten (a shoe, garment, etc.) with a lace or laces usu. passed alternately through two rows of eyelet holes or around two rows of hooks, studs, etc. **b** fasten (a person) into a garment etc. by means of a lace or laces. **2 a** (usu. foll. by *with*) add an ingredient to (a drink, dish, substance, etc.) to enhance or adulterate flavour, strength, effect, etc. **b** intermingle: *ribaldry laced with philosophy*. **3** (usu. foll. by *with*) with a streak (a sky etc.) with colour: *cheek laced with blood*. **b** interlace or embroider (fabric) with thread etc. **4** *informal* thrash, beat, or abuse, physically or verbally. **5** (often foll. by *through*) pass (a shoelace etc.) through. **6** pass (film, tape, etc.) between the guides and other parts of a projector, tape recorder, etc. so it runs from one spool to the other.

laced *adjective* **1 a** (of shoes etc.) made to be fastened or tightened with a lace or laces. **b** (of a shoe etc.) so fastened. **2 a** (of a drink etc.) mixed with a small measure of some other substance such as liquor etc. **b** marked with streaks of colour. **3** ornamented or trimmed with lace or laces.

lacerate *verb* (**lacerates, lacerated, lacerating**) **1** tear or cut (esp. flesh or tissue). **2** distress or cause pain to (the feelings etc.): *Mackenzie was still lacerated by his estrangement from his wife*. ▶ **lacerated** *adjective* **laceration** *noun* [Say LASSA rate]

lace-up • *noun* a shoe, boot, etc. fastened with a lace. • *adjective* (of a shoe etc.) fastened by a lace or laces.

lacewing *noun* a predatory insect with delicate lacelike wings.

lacing *noun* **1** the action of lacing something. **2** something that laces or fastens, esp. a laced fastening on a shoe etc. **3** ornamental lace trimming or braiding. **4** *informal* a beating.

lack • *noun* (usu. foll. by *of*) an absence, want, or deficiency. • *verb* be without or deficient in: *lacks courage*. [PHRASES] **for lack of** owing to the absence of: *went hungry for lack of money*. **lack for** lack: *never lacks for odd jobs*.

lackadaisical *adjective* unenthusiastic, lacking vigour. ▶ **lackadaisically** *adverb* [Say lacka DAZE ick ul]

lackey *noun* (*plural* **lackeys**) **1** *derogatory* a person who is obsequiously willing to obey or serve another person or group of people: *because she maintained this peace between her people, the Cherokee, and the British, she was seen by some as a traitor and lackey to the British*. **2** a servant, esp. a liveried footman or manservant. [Say LACKY]

lacking *adjective* **1** (of a thing) not available, missing: *money was lacking*. **2** inadequate or deficient: *is lacking in determination*.

lacklustre *adjective* (also esp. *US* **lackluster**) **1** lacking in vitality, force, or conviction. **2** (of the eye, hair, etc.) dull. [Say LACK luster]

laconic *adjective* using only a few words to say something: *his laconic reply suggested a lack of interest in the topic*. ▶ **laconically** *adverb* [Say luh CONNIC]

lacquer • *noun* **1** a sometimes coloured varnish made of shellac dissolved in alcohol, or of synthetic substances, that dries to form a hard protective coating for wood, brass, etc. **2** any of the various resinous wood varnishes capable of taking a hard polish, esp. the sap of the lacquer tree. • *verb* coat with lacquer. ▶ **lacquered** *adjective* [Say LACKER]

lacquer tree *noun* an East Asian tree with white sap that is used as a varnish for wood.

lacrosse *noun* a game in which a ball is thrown, carried and caught with a lacrosse stick. [Say luh CROSS]

lacrosse stick *noun* the stick used in lacrosse, having a curved L-shaped or triangular frame at one end with a piece of shallow netting in the angle.

lactase *noun* any of a group of enzymes which catalyze the hydrolysis of lactose. [Say LACK tace]

lactate[1] *verb* (**lactates, lactated, lactating**) (of mammals) secrete milk. [Say LACK tate]

lactate[2] *noun* any salt or ester of lactic acid. [Say LACK tate]

lactating *adjective* (of a mammal) producing and secreting milk. [Say LACK tate ing]

lactation *noun* **1** the secretion of milk by the mammary glands. **2 a** the period of milk secretion normally following childbirth. **b** the suckling of young. [Say lack TAY sh'n]

lactic *adjective* of or obtained from milk.

lactic acid *noun* a clear odourless syrupy carboxylic acid formed in sour milk, and produced in the muscle tissues during strenuous exercise.

lactobacillus *noun* (*plural* **lactobacilli**) a rod-shaped bacterium producing lactic acid from the fermentation of carbohydrates. [Say lacto buh SILL us for the singular, lacto buh SILL eye for the plural]

lactose *noun* a sugar that occurs in milk, and is less sweet than sucrose. [Say LACK tose or LACK toze]

lacuna *noun* (*plural* **lacunae**) **1** an unfilled space; a gap: *the journal has filled a lacuna in Middle Eastern studies*. **2 a** a missing portion or empty page, esp. in an ancient manuscript, book, etc. **b** something missing or left out, esp. by oversight, incompetence, etc.: *Pound's cryptic style serves to obscure the lacunae in his political and economic arguments*. **3** a space, cavity, or depression within or between the tissues of an organism, esp. in bone. [Say luh CUE nuh for the singular, luh CUE nee for the plural]

lacy *adjective* (**lacier, laciest**) of, trimmed with, or resembling lace.

lad *noun* **1 a** a boy or youth. **b** a young son. **2** (esp. in *plural*) *informal* a man; a fellow, esp. a workmate, drinking companion, etc.: *he's one of the lads*.

ladder *noun* **1 a** a fixed or portable device usu. made of wood, metal, or rope, consisting of a series of bars, rungs, or steps fixed between two supports and used as a means of climbing up or down. **b** anything resembling a ladder in appearance or function: *fish ladder*. **2** a series of stages by which one can make progress in a career or an organization: *merchants and innkeepers stood high on the social ladder* ◊ *employees on their way up the career ladder*.

ladderback *noun* an upright chair with a back formed of horizontal pieces of wood, resembling a ladder.

laddie *noun* *informal* a young boy or lad.

lade *verb* (**lades**; *past* **laded**; *past participle* **laden**; **lading**) **1 a** put cargo on board (a ship). **b** ship (goods) as cargo. **2** take on cargo.

laden *adjective* **1** (in *combination*) having a high proportion of the specified quality, substance, etc.: *debt-laden* ◊ *sugar-laden*. **2** (usu. foll. by *with*) heavily loaded, abundantly filled. **3** (of the conscience, spirit, etc.) painfully burdened with guilt etc.

la-di-da *adjective* *informal* (also **la-de-da**, **lah-di-dah**) affectedly genteel or refined.

ladies *plural* of LADY.

Ladies' Aid *noun* (also **Ladies' Aid Society**) an

organization of women who support the work of a church by fundraising, arranging social activities, etc.

ladies' room *noun* a women's washroom.

ladle • *noun* **1** a long-handled spoon with a cup-shaped bowl for serving or transferring liquids. **2** a vessel for transporting molten metal in a foundry. • *verb* (**ladles, ladled, ladling**) (often foll. by *out*) transfer (liquid) from one receptacle to another. PHRASES **ladle out** distribute, esp. lavishly. ▶**ladleful** *noun* (*plural* **ladlefuls**) [Rhymes with *CRADLE*]

lady *noun* (*plural* **ladies**) **1 a** a woman regarded as being of superior social status or as having the refined manners associated with this (*compare* GENTLEMAN). **b** (**Lady**) a title used by peeresses, female relatives of peers, the wives and widows of knights, etc. **2** any woman: *ask that lady over there.* **b** often *offensive* as a form of address: *hey, lady, move your car.* **3** *informal* **a** a wife or consort. **b** a man's girlfriend or mistress. **4** the female head of a household: *lady of the house.* **5** (in *plural* as a form of address) a female audience or the female part of an audience. **6** *hist.* a woman who is the object of chivalrous devotion, esp. one loved and courted by a knight. **7** an honorific title, used preceding the names of goddesses, allegorical figures, personifications, etc.: *Lady Luck.* PHRASES **the Ladies** (or **Ladies'**) a women's public washroom.

ladybug *noun* (also esp. *Brit.* **ladybird**) a small beetle with domed wing covers, usu. of a reddish-brown colour with black spots.

ladyfinger *noun* a finger-shaped sponge cake.

lady friend *noun* a regular female companion or lover.

lady-in-waiting *noun* (*plural* **ladies-in-waiting**) a lady attending a queen etc.

ladylike *adjective* with the modesty, comportment, etc., thought characteristic of a well-brought-up lady.

lady of the house *noun* the female head of a household.

lady of the night *noun* a prostitute.

ladyship *noun* PHRASES **her** (or **your** or **their**) **ladyship** (or **ladyships**) **1** a respectful form of reference or address to a Lady or Ladies. **2** *ironic* a form of reference or address to a woman thought to be giving herself airs.

lady's mantle *noun* a plant of the rose family with yellowish-green clustered flowers.

lady's slipper *noun* an orchid with a slipper-shaped lip on its flowers.

lag • *verb* (**lags, lagged, lagging**) (often foll. by *behind*) fall behind; not keep pace. • *noun* **1 a** = LAG TIME. **b** a delay. **2** *Physics* **a** retardation in a current or movement. **b** the amount of this.

lager *noun* (also **lager beer**) a kind of beer, light in colour and body. [Sounds like *LOGGER*]

laggard • *noun* a person, organization, etc. who makes slow progress and falls behind others: *staff were under enormous pressure and there was no time for laggards.* • *adjective* slower than desired or expected: *nor have innovations spread as rapidly in laggard regions as in areas of economic growth.* [Say LAG erd]

lagoon *noun* **1** a bay separated from the sea, a large lake, etc. by a low sandbank or similar barrier. **2** the enclosed water of an atoll or inside a barrier reef. **3** an artificial pool for the treatment of waste or to accommodate an overspill from surface drains during heavy rain.

lag time *noun* a period of time separating two events, esp. an action and its effect.

lah = LA.

laid *past and past participle of* LAY[1].

laid-back *adjective* *informal* relaxed, unconcerned, easygoing.

laid up *adjective* **1** (of a person) confined to bed or the house, esp. because of illness or injury. **2** (of a ship, vehicle, etc.) taken out of service. **3** (of goods, provisions, etc.) saved, stored up, or put away for safety.

lain *past participle of* LIE[1].

lair *noun* **1** a wild animal's den or resting place. **2** a person's hiding place, retreat, or secret base.

laissez-faire *noun* **1** the theory or practice of governmental abstention from interference in the workings of the market etc.: *laissez-faire capitalism.* **2** a policy or attitude of leaving things to take their course, without interfering: *they have a laissez-faire approach to bringing up their children.* [Say less ay FAIR]

laity *noun* (usu. as **the laity**; usu. treated as *plural*) **1** the non-ordained people in the church, as distinct from clergy: *mutual support between the clergy and the laity.* **2** ordinary people, as distinct from professionals or experts: *the soldiers knew that the laity were getting a sanitized account of the war.* [Say LAY uh tee]

lake[1] *noun* **1** a large body of water surrounded by land. **2** an expanse or surplus of liquid.

lake[2] *noun* **1** a reddish colouring. **2** an insoluble pigment made by combining a soluble organic dye and an insoluble mordant.

lake boat *noun* *Cdn* a boat or ship designed for sailing on the Great Lakes.

lake effect *noun* the influence of a lake on weather patterns, esp. increasing snowfall on its leeward side and moderating the temperature of surrounding areas: *lake effect snow.*

lakefront *noun* the shore of a lake (also as an *adjective*: *lakefront cottages*).

lakehead *noun* *Cdn* the area along a lakeshore farthest from the lake's outlet.

lakeland *noun* an area with many lakes.

laker *noun* *informal* **1** = LAKE TROUT. **2** a ship designed for sailing on lakes, esp. the Great Lakes.

lakeshore *noun* the shore of a lake.

lakeside *adjective* beside a lake.

lake trout *noun* an important sport fish of the salmon family, living in North American lakes.

lakeview *adjective* overlooking a lake: *lakeview suite.*

la-la land *noun* *informal* **1** a fanciful state or dream world. **2** (**La-La Land**) a California, esp. the world of movies and television based there. **b** *Cdn* British Columbia.

lalapalooza *noun* = LOLLAPALOOZA.

lam[1] *verb* (**lams, lammed, lamming**) *slang* hit (someone) hard.

lam[2] *noun* PHRASES **on the lam** *slang* in flight, esp. from the police.

lama *noun* (*plural* **lamas**) a Tibetan or Mongolian Buddhist monk. [Say LOMMA or LAMMA]

Lamaze *noun* designating a method of childbirth which emphasizes the use of psychological and physical preparation and breathing routines to control pain and minimize the need for drugs. [Say luh MOZZ]

lamb • *noun* **1** a young sheep. **2** the flesh of a lamb as food. **3** a mild or gentle person, esp. a young child. **4** = LAMB OF GOD 1. • *verb* **1 a** (in *passive*) (of a lamb) be born. **b** (of a ewe) give birth to lambs. **2** tend (lambing ewes). PHRASES **like a lamb** meekly, obediently.

lambada *noun* (*plural* **lambadas**) a fast erotic Brazilian dance which couples perform with their stomachs touching. [Say lum BODDA]

lambaste *verb* (**lambastes**, **lambasted**, **lambasting**) criticize severely. [Say lam BASTE]

lambda *noun* **1** the eleventh letter of the Greek alphabet (*Λ*, *λ*). **2** (as *λ*) the symbol for wavelength. [Say LAM duh]

lambent *adjective* **1** (of a flame or a light) playing on a surface with a soft radiance but without burning. **2** (of the eyes, sky, etc.) softly radiant. **3** (of wit etc.) lightly brilliant. [Say LAM bint]

Lamb of God *noun* **1** a name for Christ. **2 a** a prayer or hymn beginning with the words "Lamb of God" said or sung before or during Communion in some Christian liturgies. **b** a musical setting of this.

lambskin prepared skin from a lamb, with the wool on or as leather.

lamb's lettuce *noun* a plant native to Europe and the Mediterranean, sometimes used in salad. *Also called* MÂCHE.

lamb's quarters *noun* a European plant of the goosefoot family, naturalized in North America.

lambswool *noun* soft fine wool from a young sheep used in knitted garments etc.

lame • *adjective* **1 a** disabled, esp. in the foot or leg, so as to walk awkwardly or with difficulty. **b** limping; unable to walk normally. **2** (of an argument, story, excuse, etc.) unconvincing; unsatisfactory; weak. **3** pathetic or contemptible, esp. because unfashionable. • *verb* (**lames**, **lamed**, **laming**) make lame.

lamé • *noun* a fabric with gold or silver threads interwoven. • *adjective* (of fabric, a dress, etc.) having such threads. [Say lam AY or LAM ay]

lamebrain *noun informal* a stupid person. ▶ **lamebrained** *adjective*

lame duck *noun* **1** a disabled or powerless person or thing. **2** (in the US) the President in the final period of office, after the election of a successor. **3** any person or thing soon to be replaced.

lamely *adverb* **1** (walk, limp, etc.) in an awkward manner because of a foot or leg disability. **2** in a weak or unconvincing manner.

lameness *noun* **1** an inability to walk without difficulty as a result of an injury or disability affecting the leg or foot. **2** a weak or unconvincing quality.

lament • *noun* **1** a passionate expression of grief. **2** a song or poem of mourning or sorrow. • *verb* **1** express or feel grief (for or about). **2** regret: *lamented the lack of information*. PHRASES **lament for** (or **over**) mourn or regret.

lamentable *adjective* (of an event, fate, condition, character, etc.) deplorable; regrettable. ▶ **lamentably** *adverb* [Say luh MENTA bull]

lamentation *noun* **1** the action of lamenting. **2** a lament. [Say lam in TAY sh'n]

lamented *adjective* a conventional expression referring to a recently dead person: *your late lamented father*.

lamina *noun* (*plural* **laminae**) a thin plate or scale, e.g. of bone, stratified rock, etc. [Say LAM uh nuh for the singular, LAM uh nee for the plural]

laminate • *verb* (**laminates**, **laminated**, **laminating**) **1** beat or roll (metal) into thin plates. **2** overlay with a thin plastic layer, metal plates, etc. **3** manufacture by placing layer on layer. **4** split or be split into layers or leaves. • *noun* a laminated structure or material, esp. of layers fixed together to form rigid or flexible material. • *adjective* in the form of lamina or laminae. ▶ **lamination** *noun* [Say LAMMA nate for the verb, LAMMA nit for the noun and adjective]

lamp *noun* **1** a device for producing a steady light, esp.: **a** an electric bulb, and usu. its holder and shade or cover: *bedside lamp*. **b** an oil lamp. **c** a usu. glass holder for a candle. **2** a device producing ultraviolet, infrared,

or other radiation, for tanning skin, keeping food warm, etc.

lampblack *noun* a black pigment made from soot.

lamplight *noun* light given by a lamp or lamps. ▶ **lamplit** *adjective*

lampoon • *noun* a satirical attack. • *verb* satirize.

lamppost *noun* (also **lamp standard**) a tall post supporting a street light.

lamprey *noun* (*plural* **lampreys**) an eel-like aquatic vertebrate without scales, paired fins, or jaws, but having a sucker mouth with horny teeth and a rough tongue. [Say LAM pree]

lampshade *noun* a cover for a lamp, used to soften or direct its light.

LAN *noun Computing* local area network.

lance • *noun* **1 a** a long weapon with a wooden shaft and a pointed steel head, used by a horseman in charging. **b** a similar weapon used for spearing a fish, killing a harpooned whale, etc. **2** = LANCET. • *verb* (**lances**, **lanced**, **lancing**) **1** prick or cut open with a lancet. **2** pierce with or as with a lance: *the teenager had been lanced by a wooden splinter*. **3** (of a ray of light etc.) pierce through a narrow opening: *there were wet gleams of sunshine lancing through the woods*. PHRASES **lance the boil** relieve simmering tension or an unpleasant situation, esp. by taking drastic or painful measures.

lancer *noun hist.* a soldier of a cavalry regiment armed with lances.

lancet *noun* **1** a small broad double-edged surgical knife with a sharp point. **2** (also **lancet arch**, **lancet window**) a narrow arch or window with a pointed head. ▶ **lanceted** *adjective* [Say LANCE it]

land • *noun* **1 a** the solid part of the earth's surface, as opposed to large bodies of water or air. **b** (as an *adjective*) designating armies rather than navies or air forces: *land forces*. **2 a** an expanse of country; ground; soil. **b** such land in relation to its use, quality, etc., or (often as **the land**) as a basis for agriculture: *building land* ◊ *good land*. **3** a country, nation, or state: *our home and native land*. **4 a** landed property. **b** (in *plural*) estates. **5** a figurative domain or sphere: *TV land*. • *verb* **1** a set or go ashore. **b** (often foll. by *at*) disembark: *landed at the harbour*. **2** bring (an aircraft, its passengers, etc.) to the ground or the surface of water. **3** (of an aircraft, bird, parachutist, etc.) alight on the ground or water. **4** bring (a fish) to land, esp. with a hook or net. **5** *informal* bring to, reach, or find oneself in a certain situation, place, or state: *landed her in trouble*. **6** *informal* deal (a person etc. a blow etc.): *landed him one in the eye*. **7** set down (a person, cargo, etc.) from a vehicle, ship, etc. **8** *informal* win or obtain (a prize, job, etc.) esp. against strong competition. PHRASES **how the land lies** what the state of affairs is. **in the land of the living** *jocular* still alive. **land of Nod** sleep. **land on one's feet** emerge unharmed from a difficult situation.

land agent *noun Cdn hist.* an agent who helped settlers find homesteads, esp. on the Prairies.

landau *noun* **1** a four-wheeled horse-drawn carriage, with folding front and rear hoods enabling it to travel open, half-open, or closed. **2** a car with a folding leather hood over the rear seats. [Say LAN dow (DOW rhymes with *HOW*)]

land bank *noun* **1** a bank issuing banknotes on the securities of landed property. **2** land held in trust, esp. for future development.

land base *noun* esp. *Cdn* a territory under the control of a specified group, e.g. a logging company or Aboriginal group.

land bridge *noun* a neck of land joining two large land masses.

land claim *noun* esp. *Cdn* a legal claim by an Aboriginal group concerning the use of an area of land.

landed *adjective* **1** *Cdn* denoting official recognition of immigration to Canada: *landed immigrant* ◊ *landed status*. **2** owning land: *landed gentry*. **3** consisting of, including, or relating to land: *landed property*.

lander *noun* a spacecraft designed to land on the surface of a planet or moon.

landfall *noun* the first sight of or approach to land after a journey by sea or by air over open water.

landfast *adjective* (of ice covering a frozen body of water) firmly attached to the shore.

landfill • *noun* **1** the disposal of refuse by burying it under layers of earth. **2** refuse disposed of in this way. **3** an area filled in by this process. • *verb* **1** dispose of (refuse) in this way. **2** fill (a piece of land) with refuse in this way.

Land Forces Command *noun* *Cdn* the official name for the Canadian army.

landform *noun* a natural feature of the earth's surface.

land grant *noun* **1** the donation of land by a government to an individual, institution, etc. **2** the land so granted. **3** the agreement, treaty, etc. authorizing the grant.

landholder *noun* the owner or the tenant of land.

landholding *noun* **1** a piece of land owned or rented. **2** the owning or renting of land.

landing *noun* **1 a** the action or process of coming to land or the ground, floor, etc. **b** a place in a harbour for disembarking, loading, unloading, etc. **2** a level place between two flights of stairs, or at the top or bottom of a flight. **3** *Cdn* an area where logs are piled before transportation.

landing craft *noun* any of several types of craft esp. designed for putting troops and equipment ashore.

landing gear *noun* the undercarriage of an aircraft.

landing light *noun* **1** a light on a runway to guide an aircraft in a night landing. **2** (usu. in *plural*) a powerful light attached to an aircraft to illuminate the landing path ahead.

landing stage *noun* a platform, often floating, on which goods and passengers are disembarked.

landlady *noun* (*plural* **landladies**) **1** a woman who rents land, a building, part of a building, etc., to a tenant. **2** a woman who keeps a boarding or rooming house.

landless *adjective* not owning land.

landlocked *adjective* **1** almost or entirely enclosed by land. **2** (of fish, esp. salmon) living in fresh water cut off from the sea.

landlord *noun* **1** a person who rents land, a building, part of a building, etc., to a tenant. **2** a person who keeps a boarding or rooming house.

landlubber *noun* a person unfamiliar with the sea or sailing.

landmark *noun* **1 a** a conspicuous object in a district etc. **b** an object marking the boundary of an estate, country, etc. **c** an important building, monument, etc. **2** an event, change, etc. marking a stage or turning point in history etc.: *a landmark decision*.

land mass *noun* (*plural* **land masses**) a large area of land.

land mine *noun* an explosive mine laid in or on the ground.

land office *noun* an office recording dealings in public land. PHRASES **a land office business** very brisk business: *Katherine is doing a land office business selling jams and jellies as a fundraiser*.

landowner *noun* an owner of land. ▶ **landownership** *noun* **landowning** *adjective & noun*

land registry office *noun* *Cdn* (in the Atlantic provinces, Quebec, and parts of Ontario and Manitoba) a government office where documents concerning property are kept but where the government does not guarantee their validity (*compare* LAND TITLES OFFICE).

landscape • *noun* **1** natural or imaginary scenery, as seen in a broad view. **2** a picture representing this; the genre of landscape painting. **3** (of a page, book, etc., or the manner in which it is set or printed) having or in a rectangular shape with the width greater than the height (*compare* PORTRAIT 3). **4** the general characteristics of an activity, field, sphere, etc.: *the political landscape*. • *verb* (**landscapes**, **landscaped**, **landscaping**) alter (a piece of land) by landscape gardening. ▶ **landscaper** *noun* **landscaping** *noun*

landscape architect *noun* a person who designs outdoor environments, esp. parks or gardens together with buildings and roads.

landscape architecture *noun* the art or practice of planning and designing the outdoor environment, esp. parks or gardens together with buildings and roads.

landscape gardener *noun* a person who lays out grounds in a way that is ornamental or that imitates natural scenery.

landscape gardening *noun* the art or practice of laying out ornamental grounds or grounds imitating natural scenery.

landslide *noun* **1 a** the sliding down of a mass of land from a mountain, cliff, etc. **b** the mass of land which has so fallen. **2** an overwhelming majority for one side in an election.

land titles office *noun* *Cdn & Austral.* a government agency which keeps track of ownership of property by maintaining documents pertaining to the property once it has determined their validity (*compare* LAND REGISTRY OFFICE).

landward • *adjective* facing the land, as opposed to the sea. • *adverb* (also **landwards**) towards the land.

landwash *noun* (*plural* **landwashes**) *Cdn* (*Nfld*) the area along a shore between the high-water mark and the sea.

lane *noun* **1** a narrow road, street, or path. **2** a division of a road for a stream of traffic: *four-lane highway* ◊ *bicycle lane*. **3** a strip of track or water for a runner, rower, or swimmer, usu. marked out and separated from parallel ones by lines or ropes. **4** a path or course prescribed for or regularly followed by a ship, aircraft, etc.: *ocean lane*. **5** the long alley down which a bowling ball is thrown. **6** a gangway between crowds of people, objects, etc. **7** *Basketball* **a** = KEY[1] *noun* 14. **b** any open area on the court through which a player can move towards the hoop: *drive the lane*.

laneway *noun* **1** = LANE 1. **2** *Cdn* a narrow urban street, esp. behind houses or stores; a back alley.

language *noun* **1** the method of human communication, either spoken or written, consisting of the use of words in an agreed way. **2** the language of a particular community or country etc.: *speaks several languages*. **3** any method of expression: *body language*. **4 a** a style of expression; the use of words, etc.: *his language was poetic* ◊ *explained the process in simple, everyday language*. **b** (also **bad language**) coarse, crude, or abusive speech: *didn't like his language*. **5** a system of symbols and rules for writing computer programs or algorithms. **6** a professional or specialized vocabulary. **7** literary style. PHRASES **speak the same language** understand; have a similar outlook, manner of expression, etc.

language arts *plural noun* those subjects (as reading, writing, spelling, etc.) taught in schools to develop oral and written communication skills.

language police *noun derogatory* **1** *Cdn (Que.)* the officials of the Commission de Protection de la Langue Française responsible for ensuring that Quebec's language laws are enforced. **2** a group, often self-appointed, which criticizes what it considers to be unacceptable language.

languid *adjective* **1** (of a person, manner, or gesture) very slow and relaxed: *a languid wave of the hand*. **2** (of an occasion or period of time) pleasantly lazy and peaceful: *the terrace was perfect for languid afternoons in the sun*. **3** weak or faint from illness or fatigue: *she was pale, languid, and weak.* ▶**languidly** *adverb* [Say LANG gwid]

languish *verb* (**languishes, languished, languishing**) **1** be or grow feeble; lose or lack vitality: *plants may appear to be languishing simply because they are dormant.* **2** be forced to stay somewhere or suffer something unpleasant for a long time: *she continues to languish in a foreign prison.* **3** become weaker or fail to make progress: *share prices languished at $1.97.* [Say LANG gwish]

languor *noun* **1** the state or feeling, often pleasant, of being lazy or tired and lacking energy: *he remembered the languor and warm happiness of those golden afternoons.* **2** an oppressive stillness of the air: *the afternoon was hot, quiet, and heavy with languor.* ▶**languorous** *adjective* **languorously** *adverb* [Say LANG grr]

lank *adjective* **1** (of hair, grass, etc.) long, limp, and straight. **2** thin and tall: *he sprawled his long, lank figure over a chair.*

lanky *adjective* (**lankier, lankiest**) (of limbs, a person, etc.) ungracefully thin and long or tall.

lanolin *noun* a fat found naturally on sheep's wool and used purified for cosmetics etc. [Say LANNA lin]

lantern *noun* **1 a** a portable lamp with a transparent or translucent case, e.g. of glass or paper, protecting a flame. **b** a similar electric lamp. **c** its case. **2 a** a raised structure on a dome, room, etc., with windows to admit light. **b** a similar structure for ventilation etc. **3** the light chamber of a lighthouse.

lanthanide *noun* any element of the lanthanide series, 15 metallic elements in the periodic table having similar chemical properties. [Say LANTH uh nide]

lanthanum *noun* a silvery metallic element used in the manufacture of alloys and catalysts. [Say LANTH uh num]

Laotian • *noun* **1 a** a native or national of Laos in SE Asia. **b** a person of Laotian descent. **2** the language of Laos. • *adjective* of Laos or its people or language. [Say LOW sh'n (with LOW rhying with HOW) or luh OH sh'n]

lap¹ *noun* **1 a** the front of the body from the waist to the knees of a sitting person: *sat on her lap ◊ caught it in his lap.* **b** the clothing, esp. a skirt, covering the lap. **c** the front of a skirt held up to catch or contain something. **2** care, charge, etc.: *thrown into the laps of the teachers.* **3** a condition or region of extreme comfort, ease, etc.: *in the lap of luxury.* PHRASES **in the lap of the gods** (of an event etc.) open to chance; beyond human control.

lap² • *noun* **1 a** one circuit of a racetrack etc. **b** a swim from one end of a pool to the other and back again; two lengths. **c** a swim from one end of a pool to the other; a length. **d** a section of a journey etc.: *finally we were on the last lap.* **2 a** an amount of overlapping. **b** an overlapping or projecting part. • *verb* (**laps, lapped, lapping**) lead or overtake (a competitor in a race) by one or more laps.

lap³ • *verb* (**lapped, lapping**) **1 a** (usu. of an animal) drink (liquid) with the tongue. **b** (usu. foll. by *up, down*) consume (liquid) greedily. **c** (usu. foll. by *up*) consume (gossip, praise, etc.) greedily. **2 a** (of water) move or

beat upon (a shore) with a rippling sound as of lapping. **b** (of waves etc.) move in ripples; make a lapping sound. • *noun* the sound of wavelets on a beach.

laparoscope *noun* a fibre optic instrument inserted through the abdominal wall to give a view of the organs in the abdomen. ▶**laparoscopic** *adjective* **laparoscopy** *noun* (*plural* **laparoscopies**) [Say LAPPA ruh scope, lappa ruh SCOP ick, lappa ROSCA pee]

lapdog *noun* a small pet dog.

lapel *noun* the part of the front of a coat, jacket, etc., which is folded over towards either shoulder. [Say luh PELL]

lapidary *adjective* **1** concerned with stone or stones. **2** engraved upon stone. **3** (of writing style) dignified and concise, suitable for inscriptions: *a lapidary statement.* [Say LAPPA derry]

lapis lazuli *noun* (also **lapis**) **1 a** a blue mineral containing sodium aluminum silicate and sulphur, used as a gemstone. **2** a bright blue pigment formerly made from this. **3** its colour. [Say lappis LAZOO lee]

Lapp • *noun* **1** a member of the indigenous population of the extreme north of Scandinavia. **2** the language of this people. • *adjective* of or relating to the Lapps or their language.

lapse • *noun* **1** a slight error; a slip of memory etc. **2** a weak or careless decline into an inferior state. **3** (foll. by *of*) an interval or passage of time: *after a lapse of three years.* **4** *Law* the termination of a right or privilege through disuse or failure to follow appropriate procedures. • *verb* (**lapses, lapsed, lapsing**) **1** fail to maintain a position or standard. **2** (foll. by *into*) fall back into an inferior or previous state. **3** (of a right or privilege etc.) become invalid because it is not used or claimed or renewed.

lapsed *adjective* designating a person who has abandoned a formerly adhered-to religion, philosophy, etc.

laptop *noun* a portable microcomputer.

lapwing *noun* a plover with black and white plumage, crested head, and a shrill cry.

larceny *noun* (*plural* **larcenies**) the theft of personal property. [Say LAR suh nee]

larch *noun* (*plural* **larches**) **1** a coniferous tree with bunches of soft, bright green needles, grown for its tough timber and its resin, which yields turpentine. **2** (also **larchwood**) its wood.

lard • *noun* the internal fat of the abdomen of pigs, esp. when rendered and clarified for use in cooking. • *verb* **1** insert strips of fat or bacon in (meat etc.) before cooking. **2** (foll. by *with*) embellish or enrich (esp. talk or writing) with extraneous material, esp. to excess: *a booklet larded with advertisements.*

larder *noun* **1** a room or cupboard for storing food. **2** a store of food.

large • *adjective* (**larger, largest**) **1** of considerable or relatively great size or extent. **2** of the larger kind: *the large intestine.* **3** of wide range; comprehensive. **4** pursuing an activity on a large scale: *large manufacturer.* • *noun* **1** a garment of a size suited for people moderately larger than average. **2** a large serving of a beverage or food that is sold in more than one size. PHRASES **at large 1** at liberty; not confined. **2** as a body or whole: *popular with the people at large.* **3** (of a narration etc.) at full length and with all details. **4** without a specific target: *scatters insults at large.* **in large measure** (or **part**) to a significant extent.

large calorie *noun* see CALORIE 1.

large intestine *noun* the cecum, colon, and rectum collectively.

largely *adverb* to a great extent; principally.

largemouth *noun* (also **largemouth bass**) a North

American freshwater bass of the sunfish family, an important sport fish.

largeness *noun* the quality of being large.

large-print *adjective* designating a book etc. printed in large type.

large-scale *adjective* made or occurring on a large scale or in large amounts.

largesse *noun* (also **largess**) **1** generosity in giving money or gifts to others: *dispensing her money with such largesse*. **2** money or gifts given generously: *the distribution of largesse to the local population*. [Say lar JESS]

largetooth aspen *noun* a poplar of eastern North America, similar to the trembling aspen, with leaves with jagged edges.

largish *adjective* somewhat large. [Say LARGE ish]

largo *Music* • *adverb & adjective* in a slow tempo and dignified in style. • *noun* (*plural* **largos**) a largo passage etc. [Say LAR go]

lariat *noun* **1** a lasso. **2** a tethering rope, esp. used by cowboys. [Say LERRY it]

lark¹ *noun* **1** a small songbird with brown plumage and elongated hind claws which sings while flying, esp. the Eurasian skylark or the horned lark. **2** any of various birds resembling but not related to the true larks, e.g. the meadowlark.

lark² *informal* • *noun* a carefree frolic or spree; an amusing incident; a practical joke. • *verb* (usu. foll. by *about*) enjoy oneself by behaving in a playful and mischievous way.

larkspur *noun* **1** a plant of the buttercup family, which bears spikes of spurred flowers. **2** a delphinium.

larky *adjective* **1** lighthearted and amusing; done for fun or as a joke: *larky holiday pictures*. **2** (of a person) daring or mischievous in a harmless, playful way.

larva *noun* (*plural* **larvae**) **1** the stage of development of an insect between egg and pupa, e.g. a caterpillar. **2** an immature form of other animals that undergo some metamorphosis, e.g. a tadpole. ▶ **larval** *adjective* [Say LAR vuh for the singular, LAR vee for the plural]

laryngitis *noun* inflammation of the larynx, typically resulting in huskiness or loss of the voice, harsh breathing, and a painful cough. [Say lair in JITE us]

larynx *noun* (*plural* **larynges**) the hollow muscular organ forming an air passage to the lungs and holding the vocal cords in humans and other mammals. [Say LAIR inx for the singular, luh RIN jeez for the plural]

lasagna *noun* (also **lasagne**) **1** pasta in the form of wide ribbons. **2** a baked dish made from layers of lasagna, usu. filled with tomato sauce, cheese, and ground meat. [Say luh ZON yuh]

lascivious *adjective* lustful; feeling or showing strong sexual desire: *lascivious thoughts* ◊ *a lascivious remark*. ▶ **lasciviously** *adverb* **lasciviousness** *noun* [Say luh SIVVY us]

laser • *noun* a device that generates an intense beam of light with rays that are parallel and of the same wavelength. • *verb* **1** remove or treat (cells, tissue, etc.) with a laser. **2** inscribe or engrave (words, a design, etc.) onto a surface using a laser. **3** travel with great speed and precision: *the ball lasered toward his head*.

laser disc *noun* a disc on which signals and data are recorded digitally as a series of pits and bumps under a protective coating, and which is read optically by a laser beam reflected from the surface.

laser printer *noun* a high-speed computer printer in which a laser is used to form a pattern of dots on a photosensitive drum corresponding to the pattern of print required on the page.

lash • *verb* (**lashes**, **lashed**, **lashing**) **1** make a sudden whip-like movement: *lashed his tail*. **2** beat with a whip, rope, etc. **3** (of wind, rain, etc.) pour or rush

with great force; strike violently: *the great gale that races through the forests and lashes the cliffs* ◊ *the rain came down heavily, the water lashing against the panes*. **4** urge on as with a lash. **5** (foll. by *down, together,* etc.) fasten with a cord, rope, etc. • *noun* (*plural* **lashes**) **1 a** a sharp blow made by a whip, rope, etc. **b** (**the lash**) punishment by beating with a whip etc. **c** something that goads or hurts like a blow from a whip: *the lash of her tongue*. **d** a powerful impact: *the lash of the storm*. **2** the flexible end of a whip. **3** (usu. in *plural*) an eyelash. PHRASES **lash out** (often foll. by *at*) speak or hit out angrily.

lashing *noun* **1 a** a beating. **b** a scolding; reprimand. **2** cord used for lashing.

LASIK *noun* laser in situ keratomileusis, a form of eye surgery which uses a laser to carve the interior of the cornea (*compare* PRK). [Say LAY zick]

lass *noun* (*plural* **lasses**) *Scot. & Northern England or literary* a girl or young woman.

lassie *noun informal* = LASS.

lassitude *noun* weariness in mind or body; lack of energy. [Say LASSA tude]

lasso • *noun* (*plural* **lassos** or **lassoes**) a rope with a noose at one end, used esp. in North America for catching cattle etc. • *verb* (**lassoes**, **lassoed**, **lassoing**) catch with or as with a lasso. [Say la SOO or LASS oh]

last¹ • *adjective* **1** after all others; coming at or belonging to the end. **2 a** most recent; next before a specified time: *last Christmas* ◊ *last week*. **b** preceding; previous in a sequence: *got on at the last station*. **3** only remaining; final: *our last chance*. **4** (**the last**) least likely or suitable: *the last person I'd want*. **5** the lowest in rank: *the last place*. **6** individual, single: *I'll fail every last one of them!* • *adverb* **1** after all others: *last-mentioned*. **2** on the last occasion before the present: *when did you last see her?* **3** (esp. in enumerating) lastly. • *noun* **1** a person or thing that is last, last-mentioned, most recent, etc. **2** (**the last**) the last mention or sight etc.: *shall never hear the last of it*. **3** the last performance of certain acts: *breathed his last*. **4** (**the last**) **a** the end or last moment. **b** death. PHRASES **at last** (or **long last**) in the end; after much delay. **last but not least** last in order of mention or occurrence but not of importance. **to** (or **till**) **the last** till the end; esp. till death.

last² *verb* **1** remain unexhausted or adequate or alive for a specified or considerable time; suffice: *enough food to last us a week*. **2** continue for a specified time: *the journey lasts an hour*. PHRASES **last out** remain adequate or in existence for the whole of a period previously stated or implied.

last³ *noun* a shoemaker's model for shaping or repairing a shoe or boot.

last-ditch *adjective* (of an effort etc.) made at the last minute in an attempt to avert disaster.

last gasp • *noun* **1** the final attempt to draw breath before dying. **2** the final hours, days etc. of an event, season, etc.: *the last gasp of winter*. • *adjective* (**last-gasp**) last-minute: *last-gasp negotiations*.

last hurrah *noun* **1** any final performance, effort, or success. **2** the final act in a politician's career.

lasting *adjective* **1** continuing, permanent. **2** durable. ▶ **lastingly** *adverb* **lastingness** *noun*

Last Judgment *noun* (in some beliefs) the judgment of humankind expected to take place at the end of the world, when each person is rewarded or punished according to his or her merits.

lastly *adverb* finally; in the last place.

last minute • *noun* (also **last moment**) the time just before an important event. • *adjective* (**last-minute**) done at the last minute: *last-minute shopping*.

last name *noun* surname.

last post *noun Brit. & Cdn* **1** the last of several bugle calls giving notice of the hour of retiring at night. **2** this call blown at military funerals etc.

last rites *noun* sacred rites for a person about to die.

Last Supper *noun* the supper eaten by Christ and his disciples on the eve of the Crucifixion, as recorded in the New Testament.

last word *noun* (**the last word**) **1** a final or definitive statement: *always has the last word.* **2** (often foll. by *in*) the latest fashion.

lat *noun* (usu. in *plural*) *slang* = LATISSIMUS DORSI.

lat. *abbreviation* latitude.

latch • *noun* **1** a bar with a catch and lever used as a fastening for a gate etc. **2** a spring lock preventing a door from being opened from the outside without a key after being shut. • *verb* fasten or be fastened with a latch. PHRASES **latch on** (often foll. by *to*) *informal* **1** attach oneself (to). **2** obtain, get. **3** associate oneself strongly with. **4** become very interested in.

latchkey *noun* (*plural* **latchkeys**) a key of an outer door.

latchkey child *noun* (also **latchkey kid**) a child who is alone at home after school until a parent returns from work.

late • *adjective* (**later**, **latest**) **1** acting, arriving, or happening after the due or usual time. **2** far on in the day or night or in a specified time or period: *the late 1500s.* **3** no longer alive or having the specified status: *my late husband* ◊ *the late president.* • *adverb* (**later**, **latest**) **1** after the due or usual time. **2** far on in time: *this happened later on.* **3** at or till a late hour. **4** at a late stage of development. **5** formerly but not now: *late of Halifax.* **6** (in *comparative*) subsequently: *later in the book* ◊ *three months later.* PHRASES **at the latest** as the latest time envisaged: *will have done it by six at the latest.* **late in the day** (or **game**) *informal* at a late stage in the proceedings, esp. too late to be useful. **of late** lately, recently. **the latest** the most recent news, fashion, etc.: *have you heard the latest?*

latecomer *noun* **1** a person who arrives late. **2** a recent arrival; a newcomer.

late Loyalist *noun Cdn hist.* an American settler who came to Canada between 1790 and 1800.

lately *adverb* not long ago; recently; in recent times.

late-model *adjective* (of a car, electronic component, etc.) of a recent make.

latency *noun* (*plural* **latencies**) the condition of something that exists but is not yet active, well developed, or noticeable: *after a period of latency, the virus will begin to affect the infected person.* [Say LAY tin see]

lateness *noun* the fact or habit of being late.

latent *adjective* (of a quality or state) existing but not yet developed or manifest; hidden: *goods may have latent defects that render them more susceptible to breakage* ◊ *the request would arouse all their latent opposition to the privileged position.* ▶ **latently** *adverb* [Say LAY tint]

lateral • *adjective* **1** of, at, toward, or from the side or sides: *the lateral branches of a tree* ◊ *lateral eye movements.* **2** of or pertaining to a new job which is neither a promotion nor a demotion: *a lateral move.* • *noun* **1** a side part etc., esp. a lateral shoot or branch. **2** (also **lateral pass**) *Football* a sideways pass. • *verb* (**laterals**, **lateralled**, **lateralling**) *Football* **1** make a sideways pass. **2** throw (the ball) in a lateral pass. ▶ **laterally** *adverb* [Say LATTER ul]

lateral thinking *noun* a method of solving problems indirectly or by apparently illogical methods.

latex *noun* (*plural* **latexes**) **1** a milky fluid of mixed composition found in various plants and trees, esp. the rubber tree, and used for commercial purposes. **2** a synthetic product resembling this, used in paints etc.

3 (also **latex paint**) paint having latex as its binding medium. [Say LAY tex for the plural]

lath *noun* (*plural* **laths**) **1** a thin flat strip of wood, esp. each of a series forming a framework or support for plaster etc. **2** (esp. in phr. **lath and plaster**) laths collectively as a building material, esp. as a foundation for supporting plaster.

lathe *noun* a machine for shaping wood, metal, etc., by means of a rotating drive which turns the piece being worked on against changeable cutting tools. [Rhymes with BATHE]

lather • *noun* **1** a froth produced by agitating soap etc. and water. **2** frothy sweat, esp. of a horse. **3** a state of agitation. • *verb* **1** (of soap etc.) form a lather. **2** cover with lather. **3** (of a horse etc.) develop or become covered with lather. ▶ **lathery** *adjective*

Latin • *noun* **1** the Italic language of ancient Rome and its empire. **2** *Roman History* an inhabitant of ancient Latium in Central Italy. **3** a native or inhabitant of any of the various countries in Europe (France, Italy, Spain, etc.) and Latin America whose language is developed from Latin. • *adjective* **1** of or in Latin. **2 a** of the countries or peoples using languages developed from Latin. **b** Latin American. **3** of or relating to ancient Latium or its inhabitants. **4** of the Roman Catholic Church. **5** of or relating to the Latin alphabet.

Latina *noun* a female Latin American in North America. [Say luh TFFNA]

Latin America *noun* the parts of the Americas where Spanish or Portuguese is the main language. ▶ **Latin American** *adjective & noun*

Latino *noun* (*plural* **Latinos**) a Latin American in North America. [Say luh TEENO]

latissimus dorsi *noun* (*plural* **latissimi dorsi**) either of a pair of large, roughly triangular muscles covering the lower part of the back. [Say luh TISSA mus DORE sigh for the singular, luh TISSA my DORE sigh for the plural]

latitude *noun* **1** *Geography* **a** the angular distance on its meridian of any place on the earth's surface from the equator, expressed in degrees and minutes north or south of the equator. **b** (usu. in *plural*) regions or climes, esp. with reference to temperature: *warm latitudes.* **2** freedom to choose what one does or the way that one does it: *they allow their children far too much latitude.* ▶ **latitudinal** *adjective*

latke *noun* (in Jewish cooking) a pancake made with grated potato. [Say LAT kuh]

latrine *noun* a communal lavatory, esp. in a camp etc. [Say luh TREEN]

latte *noun* espresso coffee with hot milk. [Say LAT ay or LOT ay]

> **WRITING TIP**
> ## latter
>
> **Latter** should only be used to refer to the last-mentioned of two things, as in *I like both vanilla and chocolate, but I prefer the latter.* The use of **latter** to refer to the last of three or more things, as in *We could see a movie, go out for dinner, or catch a hockey game — I'd most enjoy the latter* is considered incorrect by some people and is not recommended. It would be better to say either — *I'm leaning towards catching a hockey game* or — *I'm leaning towards the last option.*

latter • *noun* (**the latter**) the second-mentioned or disputed last-mentioned person or thing (*opp.* FORMER *noun*). • *adjective* **1** nearer to the end: *the latter part of the year.* **2** second of two things mentioned: *the latter point is the more important.*

latter-day *adjective* modern, contemporary: *one of the Yukon's latter-day victims of gold fever.*

Latter-day Saint *noun* a member of the Mormon Church (officially called the Church of Jesus Christ of Latter-day Saints).

latterly *adverb* **1** in the latter part of life or of a period. **2** recently.

lattice *noun* **1 a** a structure of crossed laths or bars with spaces between, used as a screen, fence, etc. **b** = LATTICEWORK. **2** something with an open interlaced structure like that of a lattice. **3** a regular periodic arrangement of atoms, ions, or molecules in a crystalline solid. ▶ **latticed** *adjective* [Say LAT iss]

lattice window *noun* a window with small panes set in diagonally crossing strips of lead.

latticework *noun* laths arranged in lattice formation. [Say LAT iss work]

Latvian • *noun* **1 a** a native or inhabitant of Latvia, a country on the eastern shore of the Baltic Sea. **b** a person of Latvian descent. **2** the language of Latvia. • *adjective* of or relating to Latvia or its people.

laud *verb* praise: *though lauded by some critics, the show bombed in the ratings.* [Say LOD]

laudable *adjective* commendable, praiseworthy: *the goal is laudable but impossible to achieve.* ▶ **laudably** *adverb* [Say LOD uh bull]

laudanum *noun* a solution containing morphine, formerly used as a painkiller. [Say LOD uh num]

laudatory *adjective* expressing praise: *the overall editorial tone was laudatory, if not exultant.* [Say LOD uh tory]

laugh • *verb* **1 a** make the spontaneous sounds and movements usual in expressing lively amusement, scorn, derision, etc. **b** have the emotion expressed by laughing: *laughed inwardly at his foolishness.* **2** express by laughing. **3** (foll. by *at*) ridicule, make fun of: *laughed at us for going.* **4** (in phr. **be laughing**) *informal* be in a fortunate or successful position. • *noun* **1** the sound or act or manner of laughing. **2** *informal* a comical, entertaining or ridiculous person or thing: *the party was a laugh.* PHRASES **for laughs** for amusement or enjoyment. **have the last laugh** be the ultimate winner. **laugh all the way to the bank** be in an enviable financial position. **a laugh a minute** very funny or amusing. **laugh in a person's face** show open scorn for a person. **laugh off** get rid of (embarrassment or humiliation) by joking. **laugh out of the other side of one's face** (or **mouth**) change from enjoyment or amusement to displeasure, shame, apprehension, etc. **laugh out of court** deprive of a hearing by ridicule. **laugh over** discuss with laughter or amusement. **laugh up one's sleeve** be secretly or inwardly amused.

laughable *adjective* ludicrous; highly amusing. ▶ **laughably** *adverb*

laugher *noun* **1** a person who laughs. **2** *Sport slang* an easily won game; a walkover.

laughing • *noun* laughter. • *adjective* in senses of LAUGH *verb*. PHRASES **no laughing matter** something serious.

laughing gas *noun* nitrous oxide as an anaesthetic, formerly used without oxygen and causing an exhilarating effect when inhaled.

laughingly *adverb* **1** with amused ridicule or ludicrous inappropriateness: *we stayed in a dilapidated shack, which the brochure laughingly calls a "Victorian cottage".* **2** in an amused way; with laughter.

laughingstock *noun* a person or thing open to general ridicule.

laugh-line *noun* **1** (usu. in *plural*) a wrinkle around the eye or mouth formed over the years by smiling or laughing. **2** a line in a play, movie, etc. designed to make the audience laugh.

laughter *noun* the act or sound of laughing.

laugh track *noun* pre-recorded laughter added to a radio or television show to simulate or encourage audience response.

launch • *verb* (**launches, launched, launching**) **1 a** set (a vessel) afloat. **b** set afloat (a newly built vessel) for the first time, often with ceremonies. **c** (often foll. by *out*) (of a vessel) put out to sea etc. **2** hurl or send forth (a weapon, rocket, etc.). **3** start or set in motion (an enterprise, a person on a course of action, etc.). **4** formally introduce (a new product) with publicity etc. **5 a** (foll. by *out, into*) make a start, esp. on an ambitious enterprise. **b** (foll. by *into*) begin suddenly (a tirade, speech, song, etc.). • *noun* **1 a** the action of launching something. **b** an event at which something is launched. **2** a large motorboat, used esp. for pleasure.

launcher *noun* a structure or device to hold a rocket, missile, etc. during launching.

launching pad *noun* (also **launch pad**) **1** a platform with a supporting structure, from which rockets are launched. **2** a starting point for a career, enterprise, etc.

launder *verb* **1 a** wash and dry (clothes etc.). **b** bear laundering without damage. **2** *informal* transfer (funds) to conceal a dubious or illegal origin. **3** treat or process (something) to make it appear acceptable: *his newly-laundered image.* ▶ **launderer** *noun*

launderette *noun* (also **laundrette**) a laundromat. [Say lon DRET]

laundromat *noun* an establishment with coin-operated washers and dryers for public use.

laundry *noun* (*plural* **laundries**) **1** clothes etc. to be laundered or just laundered. **2 a** a room or building for washing clothes etc. **b** a business washing clothes etc. commercially. **3** the action of laundering.

laundry list *noun* a long list of assorted items: *a laundry list of complaints.*

laureate *noun* **1** a person who is honoured for outstanding creative or intellectual achievement: *Nobel laureate.* **2** = POET LAUREATE. [Say LORRY it]

laurel *noun* **1** = BAY² 1. **2 a** (in *singular* or *plural*) the foliage of the bay tree used as an emblem of victory or distinction in poetry, usu. formed into a wreath or crown. **b** (in *plural*) honour or distinction: *she has won laurels for this brilliantly perceptive first novel.* **3** any plant with dark green glossy leaves like a bay tree. PHRASES **rest on one's laurels** be satisfied with what one has done and not seek further success. [Say LORE ul]

Laurentian *adjective* **1** designating or pertaining to a geological region in eastern Canada of Precambrian age or the period in which it was formed, esp. designating a group of granites found northwest of the St. Lawrence River. **2** of or pertaining to the Laurentian Mountains. [Say luh REN sh'n]

lava *noun* **1** the molten matter which flows from a volcano. **2** the solid substance which it forms on cooling.

lava lamp *noun* a lamp designed as an upright tube containing coloured liquid which swirls and separates like lava when the lamp is plugged in.

lavatory *noun* (*plural* **lavatories**) **1** = TOILET 1. **2** a room or compartment containing one or more toilets. [Say LAV uh tory]

lavender • *noun* **1 a** a small evergreen shrub with narrow leaves and blue, purple, or pink aromatic flowers. **b** its flowers and stalks dried and used to scent clothes etc. **2** (also **oil of lavender** or **lavender oil**) the oil obtained by distillation of the blossoms of

L

cultivated lavender, used in medicine and perfume. **3** a pale blue colour with a trace of mauve. • *adjective* of the colour or fragrance of lavender flowers.

lavish • *adjective* **1** giving or doing something generously: *he was lavish in his praise for her paintings.* **2** great in extent, rich in quality, and usu. expensive: *a lavish new production.* • *verb* (**lavishes, lavished, lavishing**) bestow or spend (money, effort, praise, etc.) abundantly: *this woman was lavishing upon him her gratitude, respect and love* ◊ *lavished them with gifts.* ▶ **lavishly** *adverb* **lavishness** *noun*

law *noun* **1** a rule or system of rules recognized by a country or community as regulating the actions of its members and enforced by the imposition of penalties. **2** such rules as a subject of study or as the basis of the legal profession. **3** statute law and the common law. **4** a statement of fact to the effect that a particular natural or scientific phenomenon always occurs if certain conditions are present. **5** a rule defining correct procedure or behaviour in a sport. **6** something having binding force or effect: *his word was law.* **7** (**the law**) *informal* the police. PHRASES **be a law unto oneself** do what one feels is right; disregard custom. **go to law** take legal action. **in** (or **at**) **law** according to the laws. **lay down the law** be dogmatic or authoritarian. **take the law into one's own hands** redress a grievance by one's own means, esp. by force.

law-abiding *adjective* obedient to the laws.

law-breaker *noun* a person who breaks the law. ▶ **law-breaking** *noun & adjective*

law clerk *noun* **1** a judge's research assistant. **2** a law student who is articling.

law court *noun* a court of law.

lawful *adjective* conforming with, permitted by, or recognized by law; not illegal or (of a child) illegitimate. ▶ **lawfully** *adverb* **lawfulness** *noun*

lawgiver *noun* a person who lays down laws.

lawless *adjective* **1** having no laws or enforcement of them. **2** disregarding laws. ▶ **lawlessness** *noun*

lawmaker *noun* a legislator. ▶ **lawmaking** *adjective & noun*

lawman *noun* (*plural* **lawmen**) esp. *US* a law-enforcement officer, esp. a sheriff or police officer.

lawn *noun* **1** an area of grass kept mown and smooth. **2** a fine linen or cotton fabric used for clothes.

lawn bowling *noun* any of several bowling games played on grass or dirt surfaces in which players attempt to roll a ball as close as possible to a smaller ball.

lawn mower *noun* a machine for cutting the grass on a lawn.

lawn tennis *noun* the usual form of tennis, played with a soft ball on outdoor grass or a hard court.

lawrencium *noun* an artificially made radioactive metallic element. [Say luh RENCY um]

law reports *plural noun* a publication of accounts of judicial proceedings and judgments.

law school *noun* an institution of higher education, usu. part of a university, at which lawyers are trained.

Law Society *noun Cdn & Brit.* a professional body representing lawyers.

lawsuit *noun* the process of bringing a dispute, claim, etc. before a law court for settlement.

lawyer • *noun* a member of the legal profession. • *verb* (esp. as **lawyering** *noun*) follow the profession of lawyer; act as a lawyer. ▶ **lawyerly** *adjective*

lax *adjective* not strict or severe enough: *lax enforcement of environmental standards.*

laxative • *adjective* promoting bowel movements. • *noun* a laxative medicine. [Say LAXA tiv]

laxity *noun* a lack of strictness in enforcing or adhering to rules or standards of behaviour: *laxity in religious observance.*

> **WRITING TIP**
> **lay, lie**
>
> The following examples are considered incorrect: *Perhaps you should lay down for a while* (correct form is **lie**); *The dog was laying on the floor* (correct form is **lying**); *She lay the blanket over the sleeping baby* (correct form is **laid**); *She had laid on the couch for hours* (correct form is **lain**); *We have lain a clever plan* (correct form is **laid**).

lay¹ • *verb* (**lays, laid, laying**) **1** place on a surface, esp. horizontally in a position of rest: *laid the book on the table.* **2 a** put or bring into a certain or the required position or state: *lay a carpet.* **b** deposit (a corpse) in a grave; bury. **3** *disputed* lie. **4** make by laying: *lay the foundations.* **5** (of a female bird) produce (an egg). **6** a cause to subside or lie flat. **b** deal with to remove (a ghost, fear, etc.). **7** place or present for consideration (a case, proposal, etc.). **8** set down as a basis or starting point. **9** (usu. foll. by *on*) attribute or impute (blame etc.). **10** prepare or make ready (a plan or a trap). **11** prepare (a table) for a meal. **12** place or arrange the material for (a fire). **13** put down as a wager; stake. **14** *slang offensive* have sexual intercourse with. • *noun* the way, position, or direction in which something lies. PHRASES **lay aside 1** put to one side. **2** cease to practise or consider. **3** save (money etc.) for future needs. **lay back** cause to slope back from the vertical. **lay bare** expose, reveal. **lay a charge** make an accusation. **lay claim to** claim as one's own. **lay down 1** put on the ground or other surface. **2** relinquish; give up (an office). **3** formulate or insist on (a rule or principle). **4** pay or wager (money). **5** begin to construct (a ship or railway). **6** store (wine) in a cellar. **7** set down on paper. **8** sacrifice (one's life). **9** record (esp. popular music). **lay hands on 1** seize or attack. **2** place one's hands on or over, esp. in confirmation, ordination, or spiritual healing. **3** (also **lay one's hands on**) obtain, acquire, locate. **lay hold of** seize or grasp. **lay in** provide oneself with a stock of. **lay into** *informal* attack violently with words or blows. **lay it on** (**thick** or **with a shovel**) *informal* flatter or exaggerate grossly. **lay low 1** overthrow, kill, or humble. **2** incapacitate by illness. **3** *disputed* lie low. **lay off 1** discharge (workers) temporarily or permanently because of a shortage of work; make redundant. **2** *informal* (often in *imper.*) stop bothering (a person). **3** *informal* stop working: *laid off around 4:00.* **4** abstain from or stop using (something): *lay off beer.* **lay on 1** provide (a facility, amenity, etc.). **2** impose (a penalty, obligation, etc.). **3** inflict (blows, damage, etc.). **4** spread on (paint etc.). **lay open 1** break the skin of. **2** (foll. by *to*) expose (to criticism etc.). **lay out 1** spread out. **2** expose to view. **3** prepare (a corpse) for burial. **4** *informal* knock unconscious. **5** dispose (grounds etc.) according to a plan. **6** expend (money). **7** reveal or explain in detail: *she laid out the rules for us.* **lay up 1** store, save. **2** put (a ship etc.) out of service. **3** (usu. in *passive*) confine to bed through illness, injury, etc.; be taken ill: *was laid up with a cold.*

lay² *adjective* **1 a** non-clerical. **b** designating a person who has taken the vows of a religious order but is not ordained and is employed in ancillary or manual work: *lay sister.* **2 a** not professionally qualified, esp. in law or medicine. **b** of or done by such persons.

lay³ *noun* **1** a short lyric or narrative poem meant to be sung. **2** a song.

lay⁴ *past of* LIE¹.

layabout *noun* a habitual loafer or idler.

layaway *noun* a system of purchasing an article by making usu. monthly payments until the entire cost has been paid, at which point the article is released to the customer.

layer • *noun* **1** a thickness of matter, esp. one of several, laid over a surface or forming a horizontal division: *wore layers of clothing* ◊ *ozone layer*. **2** a hen that lays eggs, esp. with reference to its productivity: *a good layer*. • *verb* **1 a** arrange in layers. **b** cut (hair) in layers. **2** form layers. ▶ **layered** *adjective* **layering** *noun*

layette *noun* a set of clothing, toilet articles, and bedclothes for a newborn child. [Say lay ET]

layman *noun* (*plural* **laymen**) **1** any non-ordained member of a church. **2** a person without professional or specialized knowledge in a subject.

layoff *noun* **1** a temporary or permanent dismissal of workers. **2** a period when this is in force. **3** a rest or respite: *came back from a six-month layoff to win the race*.

layout *noun* **1** the disposing or arrangement of a site, ground, etc. **2** the way in which plans, printed matter, etc., are arranged or set out. **3** something arranged or set out in a particular way. **4** the makeup of a book, newspaper, etc.

layover *noun* a period of rest or waiting before a further stage in a journey etc.; a stopover.

layperson *noun* (*plural* **lay people** or **laypersons**) a layman or laywoman.

layup *noun* **1** *Basketball* a shot made close to the basket, in which the shooter often lays the ball against the backboard so it will rebound into the basket. **2** plies or layers assembled for the manufacture of plywood or other laminated material.

laywoman *noun* (*plural* **laywomen**) **1** any non-ordained female member of a church. **2** a woman without professional or specialized knowledge in a subject.

laze *verb* (**lazes**, **lazed**, **lazing**) **1** spend time lazily or idly. **2** (often foll. by *away*) pass (time) in this way.

lazily *adverb* **1** in an idle or inactive manner. **2** in a slow or relaxed manner: *we strolled lazily along the path*. **3** in a sloppy or careless manner.

laziness *noun* **1** an unwillingness to work or be active. **2** sloppiness or carelessness.

lazy *adjective* (**lazier**, **laziest**) **1** unwilling to work or be active; doing as little as possible. **2** not involving much energy or activity; slow and relaxed: *a lazy day on the beach*. **3** showing a lack of effort or care: *a lazy piece of work*. **4** (of a river etc.) slow-moving.

lazybones *noun* (*plural* **lazybones**) *informal* a lazy person.

lazy eye *noun* an eye with poor vision that is mainly caused by underuse, esp. the unused eye in a misaligned pair.

Lazy Susan *noun* **1** a revolving stand on a table to hold condiments etc. **2** an esp. kitchen cupboard or shelf designed to revolve in order to provide easy access to its contents.

lb. *abbreviation* a pound or pounds (weight).

LC *abbreviation* Cdn LIQUOR COMMISSION.

l.c. *abbreviation* **1** in the passage etc. cited. **2** lower case.

LCD *abbreviation* **1** LIQUID CRYSTAL DISPLAY. **2** lowest common denominator.

LCM *abbreviation* lowest (or least) common multiple.

LD *abbreviation* learning disability.

LDL *abbreviation* LOW-DENSITY LIPOPROTEIN.

lea *noun* literary a piece of meadow or arable land. [Say LEE]

leach *verb* (**leaches**, **leached**, **leaching**) **1** (of chemicals, minerals, etc.) be removed from soil etc. by the action of rainwater: *nitrates leach from the soil into rivers*. **2** (of a liquid) remove chemicals, minerals, etc. from soil: *the nutrient is quickly leached away* ◊ *a layer of iron which develops from the leaching of the upper layers of the soil*. ▶ **leachable** *adjective*

leachate *noun* a quantity of liquid that has percolated through a solid and leached out some of the constituents. [Say LEACH ate]

leaching *noun* **1** the percolation of a liquid through a solid, which results in the removal of some of the solid's constituents. **2** the movement of soluble chemicals or minerals from soil to a lower level or to a body of water, caused by the drainage of rain and groundwater and resulting in less fertile soil or contaminated lakes, streams, and reservoirs.

lead¹ • *verb* (**leads**, **led**, **leading**) **1** cause to go with one. **2 a** direct the actions or opinions of: *what led you to that conclusion?* ◊ *what led her to do that, I wonder?* **b** (of a lawyer) put a question to (a witness) in such a way as to suggest the answer desired. **3** provide access to: *this door leads into a small room* ◊ *the road leads to Moncton*. **4** pass or go through (a life etc. of a specified kind): *led a miserable existence*. **5** have the first place in: *led the parade* ◊ *leads the world in sugar production*. **6** be in charge of: *leads a team of researchers*. **7** direct by example. **8** *Cards* begin a round of card play. **9** (foll. by *to*) have as an end or outcome; result in: *what does all this lead to?* **10** (foll. by *with*) (of a newspaper, newscast, etc.) use a particular item as the main story: *led with the stock market crash*. • *noun* **1** guidance given by going in front; example: *follow her lead*. **2 a** a leading place; the leadership: *is in the lead* ◊ *take the lead*. **b** the amount by which a competitor is ahead of the others: *a lead of ten points*. **3** a clue, esp. an early indication of the resolution of a problem: *is the first real lead in the case*. **4** = LEASH *noun*. **5** a conductor (usu. a wire) conveying electric current from a source to an appliance. **6 a** the chief part in a play etc. **b** the person playing this. **c** the chief performer or instrument of a specified type: *lead guitar*. **7** (also **lead story**) the item of news given the greatest prominence in a newspaper, magazine, or newscast. **8** the member of a curling rink who delivers the first two rocks for their rink in each end. **9 a** the act or right of playing first in a game or round of cards. **b** the card led. **10 a** an artificial watercourse, esp. one leading to a mill. **b** a channel of water in an icefield. **11** Cdn (Nfld) a stretch of low, open land passing through an area covered with lakes, trees, or hills. [PHRASES] **lead by the nose** cajole (a person) into compliance. **lead off 1** begin; make a start. **2** *Baseball* be the first batter for a team in (an inning or game). **lead on 1** entice into going further than was intended. **2** mislead or deceive. [Say LEED]

lead² • *noun* **1** a heavy bluish-grey soft ductile metallic element occurring naturally in galena and other minerals. **2 a** graphite. **b** a thin length of this for use

in a pencil. **3** a lump of lead used in sounding water. **4** (in *plural*) lead frames holding the glass of a lattice or stained glass window. **5** (as an *adjective*) made of lead. **6** bullets collectively. • *verb* **1** cover, weight, or frame (a roof or windowpanes) with lead. **2** add a lead compound to (gasoline etc.). PHRASES **get the lead out** *slang* hurry up; move or work more quickly. **go over like a lead balloon** *slang* (**of** an idea etc.) fail to generate enthusiasm or interest. [Say LED]

lead crystal *noun* leaded crystal.

leaded *adjective* **1** (of gasoline) containing tetraethyl lead as an additive. **2** (of glass or crystal) containing a high proportion of lead oxide, making it more refractive. **3** (of a window) containing panes of glass set in lead strips.

leaden *adjective* **1** of or like lead. **2** heavy, slow, burdensome: *leaden limbs*. **3** dull or depressing: *leaden phrases*. **4** lead-coloured: *leaden skies*.

leader *noun* **1** a a person or thing that leads. **b** a person followed by others. **2 a** the principal player in a music group. **b** a conductor, esp. of a small musical group. **3** a short strip of non-functioning material at each end of a reel of film or recording tape for connection to the spool. **4** a shoot of a plant at the apex of a stem or of the main branch. **5** the horse or dog placed at the front of a team. **6** a length of line or wire connecting the end of a fishing line to a hook or fly.

leaderboard *noun* a scoreboard, esp. at a golf course, showing the names etc. of the leading competitors.

leaderless *adjective* without a leader.

leadership *noun* **1** the action of leading a group of people or an organization: *different styles of leadership*. **2** the state or position of being a leader: *the leadership of the party*. **3** the leaders of an organization, country, etc.: *the team's owner felt that a change of leadership was necessary*.

leadership convention *noun Cdn* a convention held by a political party to elect a new leader.

lead-footed *adjective* **1** slow or sluggish: *a lead-footed skater*. **2** tending to drive too quickly: *a lead-footed driver*.

lead-free *adjective* (of gasoline) without added tetraethyl lead.

lead head *noun* (also **lead head jig**) a simple fishing lure consisting of a single hook extending horizontally from a blob of lead. [Say LED]

lead-in *noun* **1** an introduction, opening, etc. **2** a wire leading in from outside, esp. from an antenna to a receiver or transmitter.

leading • *adjective* **1** chief; most important: *a leading cause of death*. **2** first in position: *the leading runner*. **3** bestselling; most popular: *the leading brand*. **4** most likely to succeed, win, etc.: *the leading candidate*. • *noun* guidance, leadership.

leading lady *noun* (*plural* **leading ladies**) the actress who plays the principal female part in a play or film.

leading man *noun* (*plural* **leading men**) the actor who plays the principal male part in a play or film.

leading question *noun* **1** *Law* a question that prompts the answer wanted. **2** a craftily worded question intended to lead the questioned person to say something incriminating.

leading seaman *noun* **1** (also **Leading Seaman**) a member of the Canadian Navy of the rank above able seaman and below master seaman. Abbreviation: **LS**. **2** a person of similar rank in other navies.

leadoff • *noun* an action beginning a process. • *adjective* **1** *Baseball* of or relating to the player who bats first in the batting order or an inning: *leadoff hitter*. **2** of or relating to something that serves as a beginning or introduction: *a leadoff news story*.

lead poisoning *noun* acute or chronic poisoning by absorption of lead into the body.

lead shot *noun* = SHOT[1] **6**. [Say LED]

lead time *noun* the time between the initiation and completion of a process. [Say LEED]

leaf • *noun* (*plural* **leaves**) **1 a** each of several flattened usu. green structures of a plant, usu. on the side of a stem or branch and the main organ of photosynthesis. **b** other similar plant structures, e.g. bracts, sepals, and petals. **2 a** foliage regarded collectively. **b** the state of having leaves out: *a tree in leaf*. **3** a single thickness of paper, esp. in a book with each side forming a page. **4** a very thin sheet of metal, esp. gold or silver. **5 a** the hinged part or flap of a door, shutter, table, etc. **b** an extra section inserted to extend a table. • *verb* put forth leaves. PHRASES **leaf through** turn over the pages of (a book etc.). **take a leaf out of a person's book** imitate a person. **turn over a new leaf** improve one's conduct or performance.

leafcutter *noun* **1** (also **leafcutter ant**) a tropical ant that cuts pieces from leaves for use as a culture medium for growing food fungi. **2** (also **leafcutter bee**) a solitary bee that lines its nest with leaf fragments.

-leafed *combining form* having the kind or number of leaves described: *broad-leafed weeds*.

leaf-green *noun & adjective* the colour of green leaves.

leafless *adjective* without leaves: *leafless snow-covered branches*.

leaflet • *noun* **1** a printed sheet of paper, usu. folded and free of charge, containing information. **2** a young leaf. **3** any division of a compound leaf. • *verb* (**leaflets, leafleted, leafleting**) distribute leaflets to.

leaf lettuce *noun* lettuce with loose leaves.

leaflike *adjective* resembling a leaf or leaves in shape or arrangement.

leaf mould *noun* soil consisting chiefly of decayed leaves.

leaf spring *noun* a spring consisting of a number of strips of metal curved slightly upwards and clamped together one above the other.

leaf stalk *noun* the slender stalk joining a leaf to a stem.

leafy *adjective* (**leafier, leafiest**) **1 a** having many leaves. **b** (of a place) having many trees and bushes: *leafy suburban streets*. **2** producing broad-bladed leaves, as distinct from other types of foliage: *green leafy vegetables*. **3** resembling a leaf.

league[1] • *noun* **1** a collection of people, countries, groups, etc., combining for a particular purpose, esp. mutual protection or co-operation. **2** an agreement to combine in this way. **3** a group of sports teams of a similar level organized to compete among themselves. **4** a class or category: *I'm not in your league*. • *verb* (**leagues, leagued, leaguing**) (often foll. by *together*) join in a league. PHRASES **in league** allied, conspiring.

league[2] *noun archaic* a variable measure of distance, usu. about three miles (4.8 km).

League of Nations *noun* an association of countries established in 1919 to promote international co-operation and achieve international peace and security; it was replaced after World War II by the UN.

leaguer *noun* a member of a league: *minor-leaguer*.

L

SPELL CHECK	
leak, leek	ABC ✓

The vegetable is a **leek**.

---

leak • *noun* **1 a** a hole in a pipe, container, etc. caused by wear or damage, through which matter, esp. liquid or gas, passes accidentally in or out. **b** the matter

passing in or out through this. **c** the action of leaking.
2 a a similar escape of electrical charge. **b** the charge
that escapes. **3** the intentional disclosure of secret
information. • *verb* **1 a** (of liquid, gas, etc.) pass in or
out through a leak. **b** lose or admit (liquid, gas, etc.)
through a leak. **2** intentionally disclose (secret
information). **3** (often foll. by *out*) (of a secret, secret
information) become known. PHRASES **take a leak**
slang urinate.

leakage *noun* **1** the action or result of leaking. **2** what
leaks in or out. **3** an intentional disclosure of secret
information.

leaker *noun* a person who gives secret information to
the public, esp. through the media.

leak-proof *adjective* designed so as to prevent leakage.

leaky *adjective* (**leakier, leakiest**) having a leak or
leaks.

lean¹ • *verb* (**leans**; *past* and *past participle* **leaned** or
(*esp. Brit.*) **leant; leaning**) **1** be or place in a sloping
position; incline from the perpendicular. **2** rest or
cause to rest for support against etc. **3** rely on; derive
support from: *he leans heavily on his family.* **4** be inclined
or partial to; have a tendency toward: *leaning toward
taking the train.* • *noun* a deviation from the
perpendicular; an inclination: *has a lean to the right.*
PHRASES **lean on** *informal* put pressure on (a person) to
act in a certain way.

lean² • *adjective* **1** (of a person or animal) thin; having
no superfluous fat. **2** (of meat) containing little fat.
3 meagre; of poor quality: *lean crop.* **4** (of a business,
sector of the economy, etc.) rendered more efficient or
competitive through the reduction of unnecessary
costs or expenditure. **5** (of a period of time) not
prosperous; marked by austerity and restraint. **6** (of a
vaporized fuel mixture) having a high proportion of air
(*compare* RICH 7). • *noun* the lean part of meat.

leaning *noun* a tendency or partiality.

leanness *noun* the condition of being thin or lean.

lean-to *noun* (*plural* **lean-tos**) **1** a usu. temporary
shelter consisting of an inclined roof supported at one
side by trees or posts and covered with canvas,
branches, etc. **2** a roof that has a single slope and is
supported at its upper end by a wall or building etc. **3** a
room or building with such a roof.

leap • *verb* (**leaps**; *past* and *past participle* **leaped** or
leapt; leaping) **1** jump or spring forcefully. **2** jump
across. **3** (of prices etc.) increase dramatically. **4** move
quickly or suddenly; rush: *leaped into the car.* **5** spring or
arise quickly, as if by a leap: *the idea just leapt into my
mind.* **6** (foll. by *up*) spring suddenly to one's feet; rise
with a bound from a sitting or reclining position.
7 (often foll. by *at*) accept something eagerly: *leaped at
the chance to go to Yellowknife.* • *noun* **1** a forceful jump.
2 a large, sudden increase: *a leap in prices.* **3** a sudden or
dramatic transition: *made a huge leap from TV sitcoms to
Broadway.* PHRASES **by leaps and bounds** with
startlingly rapid progress. **leap in the dark** a daring
step or enterprise whose consequences are
unpredictable. **leap to the eye** be immediately
apparent. ▶ **leaper** *noun*

leapfrog • *noun* a game in which players in turn vault
with parted legs over another who is bending down.
• *verb* (**leapfrogs, leapfrogged, leapfrogging**)
1 (foll. by *over*) perform such a vault. **2** vault over in this
way. **3** (of two or more people, vehicles, etc.) overtake
alternately. **4** (of a person, corporation, etc.) overtake or
surpass a competitor or competitors.

leap of faith *noun* (*plural* **leaps of faith**) the action or
an example of accepting or believing something that
cannot be proven.

leap year *noun* a year, occurring once in four, with

366 days (with Feb. 29 as an extra day to make the
calendar coincide with the solar year).

> **WRITING TIP**
> **learn**
>
> The use of **learn** to mean **teach** is unacceptable in
> spoken and written English except in humorous and
> very informal contexts and phrases, such as *That'll
> learn you!*

learn *verb* (**learns**; *past* and *past participle* **learned** or
learnt; learning) **1** gain knowledge of or skill in by
study, experience, or being taught. **2** acquire or
develop a particular ability: *learn to swim.* **3** commit to
memory: *will try to learn your names.* **4** become aware of
by information or from observation: *learned of the
accident* ◊ *the Sun has learned that she plans to resign.*
5 receive instruction; acquire knowledge or skill.
▶ **learnability** *noun* **learnable** *adjective*

learned *adjective* **1** (of a person) having much
knowledge acquired by study. **2** showing or requiring
learning: *a learned work.* **3** studied or pursued by
learned persons. **4** concerned with the interests of
learned persons; scholarly: *a learned journal.* **5** acquired
by learning or experience; not innate: *learned behaviour.*
6 *Cdn & Brit.* as a courteous description of a lawyer in
certain formal contexts: *my learned friend.* ▶ **learnedly**
adverb **learnedness** *noun* [Say LEARN id, except for
sense 5, which is pronounce LEARND]

learner *noun* **1** a person who is learning a subject,
language, or skill. **2** a person who is learning to drive a
motor vehicle and has not yet passed a driving test.

learning *noun* **1** knowledge acquired by study. **2** the
act or process of learning: *learning experience.*

learning curve *noun* **1** the rate of progress in
learning or gaining experience. **2** a graph of this.

learning disability *noun* (*plural* **learning
disabilities**) a difficulty in learning caused by a
physical or psychological dysfunction. ▶ **learning
disabled** *adjective*

lease • *noun* **1** an agreement by which the owner of a
building, apartment, vehicle, piece of land, etc. allows
another to use it for a specified time in return for
payment. **2** the period of time for which such an
agreement is made. • *verb* (**leases, leased, leasing**)
grant or take on lease. PHRASES **a new lease on life** a
substantially improved prospect of living, or of use
after repair.

leasehold • *noun* **1** the holding of property by lease.
2 property held by lease. • *adjective* held by lease.
▶ **leaseholder** *noun*

leash • *noun* (*plural* **leashes**) a strip of rope etc. for
leading or controlling a dog. • *verb* (**leashes,
leashed, leashing**) **1** put a leash on. **2** restrain: *the
outspoken candidate won't be leashed.* PHRASES **keep a
person on a long** (or **short**) **leash** give a person
considerable (or little) freedom of action. **straining at
the leash** eager to begin.

least • *adjective* **1** smallest, slightest, most
insignificant. **2** (**the least**; esp. with *neg.*) any at all: *it
does not make the least difference.* **3** (of a species or variety)
very small: *least bittern.* • *noun* the least amount.
• *adverb* in the least degree. PHRASES **at least 1** at all
events; anyway; even if there is doubt about a more
extended statement. **2** (also **at the least**) not less
than. **in the least** (or **the least**) (usu. with *neg.*) in the
smallest degree; at all: *not in the least offended.* **to say
the least** (or **the least of it**) used to imply the
moderation of a statement: *that is doubtful to say the least.*

least common denominator *noun* = LOWEST
COMMON DENOMINATOR.

leather • *noun* **1** material made from the skin of an animal by tanning or a similar process. **2** a thing made wholly or partly of leather. **3** dried puréed fruit cut into sheets: *fruit leather*. • *adjective* **1** made of or resembling leather. **2** of or relating to leather clothing or persons wearing such clothing. • *verb* cover with leather: *a leathered punker*.

leatherback *noun* a very large turtle that has a thick leathery shell, living esp. in tropical seas.

leather-bound *adjective* (esp. of a book) bound in leather.

leatherette *noun* imitation leather.

leathery *adjective* **1** like leather. **2** (esp. of meat etc.) tough.

leave¹ *verb* (**leaves, left, leaving**) **1** go away from. **2** cause to or let remain; depart without taking. **3** cease to reside at or attend or belong to or work for. **4** abandon, forsake, desert. **5** have remaining after one's death. **6** bequeath. **7** allow (a person or thing) to do something without interference or assistance: *leave the future to take care of itself*. **8** (foll. by *to*) commit or refer to another person: *leave that to me*. **9 a** abstain from consuming or dealing with. **b** remain over. **10** deposit something to be collected or attended to. **11** allow to remain or cause to be in a specified state or position: *left the door open ◊ the performance left them unmoved*. **12** have a particular amount remaining after subtraction: *six from seven leaves one*. **PHRASES** **be left with 1** retain (a feeling etc.). **2** be burdened with (a responsibility etc.). **have left** have remaining: *has no friends left*. **leave alone 1** refrain from disturbing, not interfere with. **2** not have dealings with. **3** = LET ALONE (see LET¹). **leave be** *informal* refrain from disturbing, not interfere with. **leave behind 1** go away without. **2** leave as a consequence or a visible sign of passage. **3** pass. **leave go** *informal* relax one's hold. **leave hold of** cease holding. **leave it at that** *informal* abstain from comment or further action. **leave much** (or **a lot** etc.) **to be desired** be highly unsatisfactory. **leave off 1** come to or make an end. **2** discontinue: *leave off work*. **3** omit from: *was left off the list*. **4** cease to wear. **leave out** omit, not include. **leave a person to himself** or **herself 1** not attempt to control a person. **2** leave a person solitary. **leave for dead** abandon as being beyond rescue.

leave² *noun* **1** permission: *gave me leave to go*. **2 a** (also **leave of absence**) permission to be absent from duty, work, etc. **b** the period for which this lasts. **PHRASES** **on leave** legitimately absent from duty, work, etc. **take one's leave** bid farewell. **take one's leave of** bid farewell to. **take leave to** venture or presume to.

leaved *adjective* **1** having leaves. **2** having a leaf or leaves of a specified kind or number: *broad-leaved*.

leaven • *noun* **1** *archaic* a substance added to dough to make it ferment and rise, esp. yeast. **2 a** a pervasive transforming influence: *the newcomers acted as a leaven, raising religious consciousness*. **b** *archaic* a small amount of a specified quality: *a leaven of malice*. • *verb* **1 a** ferment (dough) with leaven. **b** cause dough to rise with a leavening substance. **2** modify with a tempering element: *her speech was leavened with humour*. [Say LEV in]

leavening *noun* **1** a substance, e.g. yeast or baking powder, that causes dough or batter to rise. **2** the action or process of causing fermentation by using leaven. **3** a small amount of a specified quality: *the play had a good leavening of well-targeted jokes*. [Say LEV in ing]

leaves *plural of* LEAF.

leave-taking *noun* the act of taking one's leave.

leavings *plural noun* things left over, esp. as worthless.

Lebanese • *adjective* of or relating to Lebanon, a

country in the Middle East, or its inhabitants. • *noun* a native or inhabitant of Lebanon. [Say lebba NEEZ]

lech *informal* • *verb* (**leches, leched, leching**) feel lecherous; behave lustfully. • *noun* (*plural* **leches**) a lecher. [Say LETCH]

lecher *noun* a lecherous man.

lecherous *adjective* lustful; having excessive sexual desire. ▶ **lecherously** *adverb* **lecherousness** *noun*

lechery *noun* unrestrained indulgence of sexual desire.

lecithin *noun* **1** a substance widely distributed in animal tissues, egg yolk, and some plants. **2** a preparation of this used in the commercial production of food to help ingredients of different thicknesses combine to form a smooth mixture. [Say LESS i thin]

lectern *noun* **1** a stand for holding a book in a church, esp. for a Bible from which readings are made. **2** a similar stand for a lecturer etc.

lectionary *noun* (*plural* **lectionaries**) **1** a list of portions of Scripture for reading at a religious service. **2** a book containing such portions of Scripture.

lector *noun* *Catholicism* a person designated to read aloud certain readings, prayers, etc. at Mass.

lecture • *noun* **1** a speech or talk giving information about a subject to a class or other audience. **2** a long serious speech esp. as a scolding or reprimand. • *verb* (**lectures, lectured, lecturing**) **1** (often foll. by *on*) deliver a lecture or lectures. **2** talk seriously or reprovingly to (a person). **3** instruct or entertain (a class or other audience) by a lecture.

lecturer *noun* **1** a person who lectures, esp. as a teacher in post-secondary education. **2** a university professor ranking below assistant professor.

lectureship *noun* a position as a lecturer.

LED *abbreviation* light-emitting diode, a semiconductor diode which glows when a voltage is applied: *LED display*.

SPELL CHECK	
led, lead	

The metal is **lead**.

led *past and past participle of* LEAD¹.

ledge *noun* **1** a narrow horizontal surface projecting from a wall etc. **2** a shelf-like projection on the side of a rock or mountain. **3** a ridge of rocks, esp. below water. ▶ **ledged** *adjective*

ledger *noun* a book or computer document in which a business, bank, etc. records its financial accounts.

lee *noun* **1** shelter given by a neighbouring object: *camped under the lee of the forest*. **2** (also **lee side**) the side away from the wind.

SPELL CHECK	
leech, leach	

Soil that has lost its nutrients has been **leached**.

leech *noun* (*plural* **leeches**) **1** a land or freshwater worm with suckers at both ends, certain species of which are bloodsucking parasites of vertebrates, once used medically to bleed patients. **2** a person who extorts profit from or sponges on others. **PHRASES** **like a leech** constantly present and clingy.

SPELL CHECK	
leek, leak	

A hole through which something escapes is a **leak**.

leek *noun* a plant, related to the onion, with flat overlapping leaves forming an elongated cylindrical bulb, which is eaten as a vegetable.

leer • *verb* look at someone in an unpleasant way with sexual interest or evil intent: *leered at the waitress*. • *noun* a leering look.

leery *adjective* (**leerier, leeriest**) (usu. foll. by *of*) wary.

lees *plural noun* the sediment of wine etc.: *drink to the lees*. [Say LEEZ]

leeward • *adjective & adverb* on or toward the side sheltered from the wind (opp. WINDWARD). • *noun* the leeward region, side, or direction: *to leeward*. [Say LEE werd or *Nautical* LOO erd]

leeway *noun* **1 a** allowable deviation or freedom of action: *parents should give children some leeway.* **b** additional time, materials, etc.: *the government had several months' leeway to introduce reforms.* **2** the sideways drift of a ship to leeward of the desired course.

left¹ • *adjective* **1 a** on or toward the side of the human body which corresponds to the position of west if one regards oneself as facing north. **b** on or toward the part of an object which is analogous to a person's left side or (with opposite sense) which is nearer to an observer's left hand. **2** (also **Left**) *Politics* denoting or having to do with a person or group favouring radical, reforming, or socialist views. • *adverb* on or to the left side. • *noun* **1** the left side or area: *on my left.* **2 a** the road etc. on the left: *take the next left.* **b** a left turn. **3** *Boxing* **a** the left hand. **b** a blow with this. **4** (often **Left**) *Politics* a group or section favouring socialism; socialists collectively. **5** = STAGE LEFT. PHRASES **have two left feet** *informal* be clumsy. **left and right** (also **left, right, and centre**) on all sides.

left² *past and past participle of* LEAVE¹.

left brain *noun* the left cerebral hemisphere, which controls the right side of the body; in humans, it normally controls language skills and numerical calculations.

left field *noun* **1** *Baseball* **a** the part of the outfield to the left of the batter as he or she faces the pitcher. **b** the position of the fielder who covers this area: *playing left field.* **2** *informal* a position, state, experience, etc., that is removed from the mainstream or ordinary: *the proposal came from left field.* PHRASES **out in left field** *slang* completely wrong or mistaken. ▶ **left fielder** *noun*

left-hand *adjective* **1** on or toward the left side of a person or thing: *left-hand drawer.* **2** to the left: *a left-hand turn.* **3** done with the left hand: *left-hand blow.*

left-handed • *adjective* **1** using the left hand by preference as more serviceable than the right. **2** (of a tool etc.) designed for use by left-handed people. **3** (of a blow) struck with the left hand. **4 a** turning to the left; toward the left. **b** (of a screw) advanced by turning counter-clockwise. • *adverb* with the left hand or to the left side: *writes left-handed.* ▶ **left-handedly** *adverb* **left-handedness** *noun*

left-hander *noun* **1** a left-handed person. **2** a left-handed blow.

leftie = LEFTY.

leftish *adjective* tending to favour socialism and radical social change.

leftism *noun* *Politics* the principles of the political left, including the promotion of socialism and radical social change. ▶ **leftist** *noun & adjective*

left-of-centre *adjective* (of political parties, voters, etc.) having somewhat leftist views, policies, etc.

leftover • *noun* (usu. in *plural*) an item (esp. of food) remaining after the rest have been used. • *adjective* remaining over, surplus.

leftward • *adverb* (also **leftwards**) toward the left. • *adjective* going toward or facing the left.

left wing • *noun* **1** the radical or socialist section of a political party. **2** *Hockey* **a** the forward position to the left of centre (facing the opponent's goal). **b** the player

at this position. **3** the left side of an army. • *adjective* (usu. **left-wing**) socialist or radical. ▶ **left-winger** *noun*

lefty • *noun* (*plural* **lefties**) *informal* **1** a left-handed person. **2** *Politics* a left-winger. • *adjective* (of a person) **1** left-handed. **2** leftist. • *adverb* esp. *Baseball* with the left hand or to the left side: *batting lefty.*

leg *noun* **1** each of the limbs on which a person or animal walks and stands. **2 a** part of a garment covering a leg or part of a leg. **3** a support of a chair, table, bed, etc. **4** a section of a journey or relay race. **5** one branch of a forked object: *the leg of a compass.* **6** one of the sides of a triangle other than the base or hypotenuse. PHRASES **find one's legs 1** gain momentum. **2** acquire or regain mastery of a skill. **give a person a leg up** help a person to mount a horse etc. or get over an obstacle or difficulty. **have no legs** *informal* (of a golf ball etc.) have not enough momentum to reach the desired point. **leg it** *informal* walk or run hard. **not have a leg to stand on** be unable to support one's argument by facts or sound reasons. **on one's last legs** near death or the end of one's usefulness etc.

legacy *noun* (*plural* **legacies**) **1** a gift left in a will. **2** something handed down by a predecessor: *future generations will be left with a legacy of pollution.* [Say LEGGA see]

legal *adjective* **1** of or based on law; concerned with law; falling within the province of law. **2** appointed or required by law. **3** permitted by law, lawful. **4** *Sport* permitted by the rules: *a legal tackle.* **5** designating a size of paper 22 by 35.5 cm (8½ by 14 inches).

legal aid *noun* payment from public funds allowed, in cases of need, to help pay for legal advice.

legal clinic *noun* a clinic offering legal advice and assistance, paid for by legal aid.

legalese *noun* *informal* the technical language of legal documents. [Say legal EEZ]

legal holiday *noun* = STATUTORY HOLIDAY.

legalism *noun* excessive adherence to law or formula. ▶ **legalist** *noun*

legalistic *adjective* obeying the law very strictly or too strictly: *a legalistic approach to family disputes.*

legality *noun* (*plural* **legalities**) **1** lawfulness. **2** (in *plural*) obligations imposed by law. [Say li GAL a tee or lee GAL a tee]

legalization *noun* the action of making something illegal permissible by law: *the government has approved the legalization of marijuana for medicinal purposes.*

legalize *verb* (**legalizes, legalized, legalizing**) make lawful.

legally *adverb* according to the law: *they are legally entitled to compensation* ◊ *we are legally married.*

legal tender *noun* currency that cannot legally be refused in payment of a debt.

legate *noun* a member of the clergy representing the Pope. [Say LEG it]

legation *noun* **1** the position and staff of a diplomatic minister (esp. when not having ambassadorial rank). **2** the official residence of a diplomatic minister. [Say li GAY sh'n]

legato *adverb & adjective* *Music* in a smooth flowing manner, without breaks between notes. [Say luh GOT toe]

legend *noun* **1 a** a traditional story sometimes popularly regarded as historical but not proven to be true; a myth. **b** such stories collectively. **c** a popular but unfounded belief. **d** *informal* a subject of such beliefs: *became a legend in her own lifetime.* **2 a** an inscription, esp. on a coin or medal. **b** a caption. **c** a key to the symbols used on a map etc.

legendarily *adverb* according to legend, popular

belief, or reputation: *a biography of the legendarily lunatic lexicographer.*

legendary *adjective* **1** of or connected with legends. **2** described in a legend. **3** remarkable enough to be a subject of legend. **4** based on a legend.

legerdemain *noun* **1** sleight of hand; conjuring or juggling: *feats of legerdemain.* **2** trickery: *financial legerdemain.* [Say lezh er duh MAIN]

legged *adjective* having legs, esp. of a specified kind or number: *long-legged.*

legging *noun* (usu. in *plural*) **1** close-fitting stretch trousers for women or children. **2** an outer garment for keeping the legs warm.

leggy *adjective* (**leggier, leggiest**) **1 a** long-legged. **b** (of a woman) having attractively long legs. **2** long-stemmed.

leghold trap *noun* (also **leghold**) a type of trap which catches and holds an animal by one of its legs.

leghorn *noun* **1** (**Leghorn**) a chicken of a small, hardy domestic breed. **2 a** fine braided straw. **b** a hat of this.

legibility *noun* the condition of being clear enough to read.

legible *adjective* (of handwriting, print, etc.) clear enough to read; readable. ▶ **legibly** *adverb*

legion • *noun* **1** a vast host, multitude, or number. **2** (**Legion**) any of various national associations of ex-servicemen and ex-servicewomen: *Royal Canadian Legion.* **3** = LEGION HALL. **4** *Roman History* a division of 3,000–6,000 soldiers, including a complement of cavalry. **5** a large military force. • *adjective* great in number: *her good works have been legion.*

legionary • *adjective* of a legion or legions. • *noun* (*plural* **legionaries**) a soldier of a legion.

legion hall *noun* a building serving as the headquarters for a local Legion branch, usu. incorporating facilities for entertainment, e.g. an auditorium, banquet hall, bar, etc.

legionnaire *noun* **1** a member of a foreign legion. **2** a member of a Legion. [Say lee juh NAIR]

legionnaires' disease *noun* a form of bacterial pneumonia spread esp. by water droplets through air conditioning systems etc.

legislate *verb* (**legislates, legislated, legislating**) **1** make laws. **2** create or control by means of legislation: *the government is legislating pay equity.*

legislation *noun* **1** the process of making laws. **2** a law or series of laws.

legislative *adjective* of or empowered to make legislation.

legislative assembly *noun* (*plural* **legislative assemblies**) **1** the national or provincial etc. body empowered to make laws. **2** (in Canada) an elected provincial or (*hist.*) colonial legislature.

legislative building *noun* *Cdn* the building in which a provincial legislature meets.

legislative council *noun* *Cdn hist.* **1** the upper house of a provincial legislature, consisting of members appointed by the government. **2** (in colonial governments) a body of advisers appointed by the governor, serving either as a unicameral legislature or as the upper house of a bicameral legislature.

legislatively *adverb* in terms or by means of legislation: *the practice has been sanctioned legislatively.*

legislator *noun* **1** a member of a legislative body. **2** a person who makes laws.

legislature *noun* **1** the legislative body of a nation, province, etc. **2** *Cdn* = LEGISLATIVE BUILDING. [Say LEDGE iss lay chur]

legit *adjective* *informal* legitimate. [Say li JIT]

legitimacy *noun* **1** the condition of conforming to the law or to rules; legality: *reports of bribery and vote-buying have led to questions about the legitimacy of the election.* **2** the ability to be defended with logic or justification: *he questioned the legitimacy of my excuse.* **3** official status or credibility based on the sanction of a respected authority or on popular support or acceptance: *the growing number of converts to homeopathy has brought legitimacy to alternative medicine* ◊ *reports of UFO sightings over Winnipeg gained some legitimacy when the federal space agency decided to investigate.* [Say li JITTA muh see]

legitimate • *adjective* **1 a** (of a child) born of parents lawfully married to each other. **b** (of a parent, birth, descent, etc.) with, of, through, etc., a legitimate child. **2 a** sanctioned or authorized by law or principle; lawful: *the gang's legitimate and illegitimate sources of income.* **b** conforming to a recognized standard. **3** sanctioned by the laws of reasoning; logical: *a legitimate excuse for being late.* **4** (of a monarch, sovereignty, etc.) justified or validated by the strict principle of hereditary right. **5** designating or pertaining to art considered to have aesthetic merit or serious intent, esp.: **a** conventional theatre or drama as distinct from musical comedy, farce, etc. **b** classical music as distinct from jazz or other popular music. • *verb* (**legitimates, legitimated, legitimating**) make legitimate; justify or make lawful: *the new regime was not legitimated by popular support.* ▶ **legitimately** *adverb* **legitimating** *adjective* **legitimation** *noun* [Say li JITTA mit for the adjective, li JITTA mate for the verb]

legitimize *verb* (**legitimizes, legitimized, legitimizing**) **1** make something that is wrong or unfair seem acceptable: *the movie has been criticized for legitimizing violence.* **2** make something legal: *voters legitimize the government through the election of public officials.* [Say li JITTA mize]

legless *adjective* having no legs.

Lego *noun* *proprietary* a construction toy consisting of interlocking plastic building blocks.

legroom *noun* the space available for the legs of a seated person in a car, theatre, etc.

legume *noun* **1** any seed, pod, or other edible part of a leguminous plant used as food: *research has shown that legumes help to control blood sugar levels.* **2** a leguminous plant. **3** the long seed pod of a leguminous plant. [Say LEG yume]

leguminous *adjective* of or like the family Leguminosae, including peas and beans, having seeds in pods and usu. root nodules able to fix nitrogen. [Say luh GYUME in us]

legwork *noun* work which involves a lot of walking, travelling, or physical activity to collect information, deliver messages, etc.

lei *noun* (*plural* **leis**) a Polynesian garland of flowers, feathers, shells, etc. often given as a symbol of affection. [Say LAY or LAY ee]

leisure *noun* **1** free time; time at one's own disposal. **2** enjoyment of free time. PHRASES **at leisure 1** not occupied. **2** in an unhurried manner. **at one's leisure** when one has time. [Say LEEZH er or LEZH er]

leisured *adjective* **1** having ample leisure: *the leisured classes.* **2** leisurely. [Say LEEZH erd or LEZH erd]

leisurely • *adjective* **1** relaxed, having leisure, able to proceed without haste. **2** (of an action or agent) performed or operating at leisure or without haste; unhurried. • *adverb* without haste or hurry. [Say LEEZH ur lee or LEZH ur lee]

L

leitmotif *noun* (also **leitmotiv**) **1** a recurrent theme associated throughout a musical, literary, etc. composition with a particular person, idea, or situation. **2** any recurring theme, symbol, image, etc.: *there is a leitmotif of futility about the process*. [Say LITE mo teef]

Lekwiltok *noun* (*plural* **Lekwiltok**) **1** a member of a large group of the Kwakwaka'wakw living between Knight and Bute Inlets, on the west coast of BC. **2** the Kwa-kwa-la language of the Lekwiltok, of the Wakashan linguistic group. [Say LECK will tock]

lemme *informal* let me.

lemming *noun* **1** any of several short-tailed esp. Arctic rodents noted for their fluctuating populations and periodic mass migrations. The popular myth that herds of lemmings leap over cliffs to their death is not based on fact. **2** a person who unthinkingly joins a mass movement, esp. a headlong rush to destruction. ▶ **lemming-like** *adjective*

lemon • *noun* **1 a** a pale-yellow thick-skinned oval citrus fruit with acidic juice. **b** the tree that produces this fruit. **2** = LEMON YELLOW. **3** *informal* a thing which is bad, unsatisfactory, or disappointing, esp. a substandard or defective car. • *adjective* of or resembling the colour, flavour, or fragrance of a lemon.

lemonade *noun* a drink made of lemon juice and water, usu. sweetened with sugar.

lemon grass *noun* a tropical grass yielding an oil smelling of lemon, widely used in Asian cooking and in perfumes and medicine.

lemony *adjective* having the taste or aroma of lemons.

lemon yellow *noun & adjective* a pale yellow colour.

lemur *noun* a tree-dwelling primate with a pointed snout and long tail, native to Madagascar. [Say LEE mer]

lend *verb* (**lends**, **lent**, **lending**) **1** (usu. foll. by *to*) grant (to a person) the use of (a thing) on the understanding that it or its equivalent shall be returned. **2** allow the use of (money) at interest. **3** bestow or contribute (something temporary): *lend assistance* ◊ *lends a certain charm*. PHRASES **lend an ear** (or **one's ears**) listen. **lend itself to** (of a thing) allow, be suitable for. **lend oneself to** accommodate oneself to (a policy or purpose). **lend one's name to** allow one's self, name, or reputation to be associated with some cause etc. ▶ **lender** *noun* **lending** *noun & adjective*

length *noun* **1 a** the linear extent of a thing from end to end. **b** the greater of two or the greatest of three dimensions of a body or figure. **c** the quality or fact of being long. **2 a** extent from beginning to end, esp. of a period of time, etc.: *the length of a speech*. **b** a period or duration of time, esp. a long period: *a stay of some length*. **3** the distance a thing extends. **4 a** the length of a swimming pool as a measure of the distance swum. **b** the length of a horse, boat, etc., as a measure of the lead in a race. **c** the length of a car, usu. as a measure of separation from the vehicle in front. **5** a long stretch, piece, or extent of land, hair, tubing, etc. **6** a degree of thoroughness in action: *went to great lengths* ◊ *prepared to go to any length*. **7** a piece of material of a certain or distinct length: *a length of cloth*. **8** the quantity, esp. long quantity, of a vowel or syllable. **9** the extent of a garment, curtains, etc. in a vertical direction when worn or hung: *a floor-length veil*. **10** the full extent of one's body. PHRASES **at length 1** (also **at full** or **great** etc. **length**) in detail, without curtailment. **2** after a long time, at last. **length and breadth** the whole area; all places or directions.

lengthen *verb* make or become longer. ▶ **lengthener** *noun* **lengthening** *noun & adjective*

lengthwise • *adverb* in a direction parallel with a thing's length. • *adjective* lying or moving lengthwise.

lengthy *adjective* (**lengthier**, **lengthiest**) **1** (of a period of time) long, extended, of unusual length. **2** (of speech, writing, etc.) tedious, excessively detailed.

leniency *noun* mercy or tolerance, esp. in enforcing the law or punishing an offender: *he appealed to the judge for leniency*. [Say LEENY in see]

lenient *adjective* (of punishment or a person in authority) merciful: *a lenient sentence* ◊ *the judge was far too lenient with him*. ▶ **leniently** *adverb* [Say LEENY int]

Leninism *noun* Marxism as interpreted and applied by Vladimir Ilyich Lenin (1870–1924), the first premier of the Soviet Union. Leninism stresses the role of the central institutions of the Communist Party in controlling and organizing the political and economic life of a state. ▶ **Leninist** *noun & adjective*

lens • *noun* (*plural* **lenses**) **1** a piece of a transparent substance with one or usu. both sides curved for concentrating or dispersing light rays esp. in optical instruments, eyeglasses, etc. **2** (also **compound lens**) such a lens or combination of lenses used in photography. **3** = CRYSTALLINE LENS. **4** a device for focusing or otherwise modifying the direction of movement of light, sound, electrons, etc. **5** = CONTACT LENS. **6** a biconvex body of any material, as rock, ice, water, etc. **7** a viewpoint, perspective: *see life through a new lens*. • *verb* (**lenses**, **lensed**, **lensing**) **1** film (a movie etc.). **2** (of a movie etc.) be filmed.

Lent *noun* *Christianity* the period leading up to Easter, from Ash Wednesday to Holy Saturday, of which the 40 weekdays are devoted to fasting and penitence.

lent *past and past participle of* LEND.

Lenten *adjective* of, in, or appropriate to Lent.

lentil *noun* **1** a leguminous plant, native to the Mediterranean and Africa, that is grown for fodder and for its edible seeds. **2** this seed, esp. used as food with the husk removed. [Say LENT'll]

lento *Music* • *adjective* slow. • *adverb* slowly. [Say LEN toe]

leopard *noun* **1** a large African or Asian flesh-eating cat with either a black-spotted yellowish or all black coat. **2** (as an *adjective*) spotted like a leopard: *leopard moth*. [Say LEP erd]

leopard frog *noun* **1** a North American frog that is green with black pale-ringed blotches. **2** any of various similar North American frogs.

leopard skin *noun* **1** the skin of a leopard. **2** (also **leopard print**) fabric printed in imitation of a leopard skin, with tawny colours and brown blotches.

leotard *noun* **1** a close-fitting one-piece garment worn by dancers, gymnasts, etc. **2** (usu. in *plural*) heavy tights. [Say LEE uh tard]

leper *noun* **1** a person suffering from leprosy. **2** a person who is shunned, esp. on moral grounds: *smokers are the new lepers of society*. [Say LEP er]

leprechaun *noun* a small, usu. mischievous being of human form in Irish folklore. [Say LEPRA con]

leprosy *noun* a contagious bacterial disease that affects the skin, mucous membranes, and nerves, causing disfigurement. [Say LEPRA see]

lesbian • *noun* a woman who is sexually attracted to other women. • *adjective* of or pertaining to lesbians. ▶ **lesbianism** *noun*

lesion *noun* *Medical* a region in an organ or tissue which has suffered damage through injury or disease, such as a wound, ulcer, abscess, tumour, etc.: *developed hideous skin lesions on my face and a violent cough*. [Say LEE zh'n]

less • *adjective* **1** smaller in extent, degree, number, etc.: *of less importance*. **2** of smaller quantity, not so much (*opp.* MORE): *find less difficulty* ◊ *eat less meat*. **3** of lower rank, status, etc.: *no less a person than* ◊ *St. James the Less*. • *adverb* to a smaller extent, in a lower degree. • *pronoun* a smaller amount, quantity, or number: *cannot take less* ◊ *is little less than disgraceful*. • *preposition* minus: *made $1,000 less GST*. PHRASES **in less than no time** *informal* very quickly or soon. **less of** to a smaller extent. **much** (or **still**) **less** with even greater force of denial: *do not suspect him of negligence, much less of dishonesty*. **no less** (as an intensifier) what's more.

-less *suffix* forming adjectives and adverbs: **1** from nouns, meaning "not having, without, free from": *doubtless*. **2** from verbs, meaning "not affected by or doing the action of the verb": *fathomless* ◊ *tireless*.

lessee *noun* a person to whom a lease is granted or who holds a property by lease, esp. a tenant. [Say less EE]

lessen *verb* make or become less, diminish.

lesser *adjective* **1** a not so great or much as the other or the rest: *the lesser evil* ◊ *they nest mostly in Alaska and to a lesser extent in Siberia*. **b** smaller, inferior, or of lower status or worth: *Jean always looks down on us lesser mortals*. **2** designating the smaller of two similar or related plants, animals, anatomical parts, or places: *Lesser Slave Lake*.

lesser-known *adjective* known less well than others of the same kind.

-lessly *suffix* forming adverbs from nouns and verbs, meaning in a manner free from or not influenced by: *harmlessly* ◊ *carelessly* ◊ *relentlessly* ◊ *tirelessly*.

-lessness *suffix* forming nouns from nouns and verbs, meaning the state or condition of being without: *fearlessness* ◊ *homelessness*.

lesson *noun* **1** a continuous portion of teaching given to a student or class at one time. **2** an occurrence, example, rebuke, or punishment, that serves or should serve to warn or encourage: *let that be a lesson to you*. **3** a passage from the Bible read aloud during a church service. PHRASES **learn one's lesson** be wiser as a result of an unpleasant, painful, etc. experience. **teach a person a lesson** punish a person, esp. as a deterrent.

lessor *noun* a person who lets a property by lease. [Say less OR]

lest *conjunction* **1** in order that not, for fear that: *lest we forget*. **2** that: *afraid lest we should be late*.

let¹ *verb* (**lets**, **let**, **letting**) **1** allow to. **2** allow or cause (liquid or air) to escape: *let blood*. PHRASES **let alone** (also **leave alone**) **1** not to mention, far less or more: *hasn't got a television, let alone a VCR*. **2** = LET BE. **let be** not interfere with, attend to, or do. **let down 1** lower. **2** fail to support or satisfy, disappoint. **3** lengthen (a garment). **4** loosen, untie, or allow to hang freely. **let down gently** avoid disappointing or humiliating abruptly. **let fly 1** (often foll. by *at*) attack physically or verbally. **2** (often foll. by *with*) throw, hurl, or hit vigorously. **let go 1** release, set at liberty. **2 a** (often foll. by *of*) relax or relinquish one's hold. **b** lose hold of. **3 a** cease to think or talk about; dismiss from one's thoughts. **b** cease to attend to or control; take no further action concerning. **c** dismiss (an employee). **let oneself go 1** give way to enthusiasm, impulse, etc. **2** cease to take trouble, neglect one's appearance or habits. **let in 1** allow to enter: *let the dog in* ◊ *this would let in all sorts of evils*. **2** (usu. foll. by *for*) involve (a person, often oneself) in loss or difficulty. **3** (foll. by *on*) allow (a person) to share privileges, information, etc. **let oneself in** enter someone else's residence etc. by means of a key. **let it drop** (usu. in *imper.*) let the matter end there, not continue with the matter. **let know** inform (a person). **let loose 1** release or unleash. **2** loosen. **3** (also foll. by *with*) emit abruptly (a scream, tirade, etc.). **4** (often foll. by *on*) allow (a person) free access to: *once they're trained, we'll let them loose on the new computers*. **let off 1 a** fire (a gun). **b** explode (a bomb or firework). **2** allow or cause (steam, liquid, etc.) to escape. **3** allow to alight from a vehicle etc. **4 a** not punish or compel. **b** (foll. by *with*) punish lightly. **c** excuse, free: *was let off work early*. **let on** *informal* **1** reveal a secret. **2** pretend: *let on that he had succeeded*. **let out 1** allow to go out, esp. through a doorway. **2** release from restraint. **3** (often foll. by *that* + clause) reveal (a secret etc.). **4** make (a garment) looser esp. by adjustment at a seam. **5** (of a class, meeting, etc.) finish, come to an end. **let (a person) have it 1** direct a blow or shot at a person. **2** assail with blows or words. **let through** allow to pass. **let up** *informal* **1** become less intense or severe. **2** relax one's efforts. **to let** esp. *Brit.* available for rent.

let² *noun* (in tennis, squash, etc.) an obstruction of a ball or a player in certain ways, e.g. by hitting the net, requiring the ball to be served again.

letdown *noun* a disappointment, drawback, or disadvantage.

lethal *adjective* **1** causing or sufficient to cause death. **2** harmful, injurious, destructive. ▶**lethality** *noun* **lethally** *adverb* [Say LEETH'll, lee THALA tee]

lethargic *adjective* sluggish, lacking energy or enthusiasm: *I felt tired and lethargic*. ▶**lethargically** *adverb* [Say luh THAR jick]

lethargy *noun* **1** a lack of energy and enthusiasm: *only a few guest conductors have roused the orchestra out of its customary lethargy*. **2** *Medical* a pathological state of sleepiness or deep unresponsiveness and inactivity. [Say LETH er jee]

let's *contraction* let us: *let's go now*.

letter • *noun* **1 a** a character representing one or more of the simple or compound sounds used in speech; any of the alphabetic symbols. **b** (in *plural*) *informal* the initials of a degree etc. after the holder's name. **2 a** a written, typed, or printed communication, usu. sent by mail or messenger. **b** (in *plural*) an addressed legal or formal document for any of various purposes. **3** the precise terms or strict verbal interpretation of a statement or document (*opp.* SPIRIT *noun* 6): *according to the letter of the law*. **4** (in *plural*) **a** literature in general. **b** acquaintance with books, erudition: *a man of letters*. **c** authorship: *the profession of letters*. **5 a** designating a size of paper 22 by

28 cm ($8\frac{1}{2}$ by 11 inches). **b** designating office supplies, e.g. files etc., designed to hold this size of paper. • *verb* **1** write, paint, inscribe, etc. letters on. **2** write, paint, inscribe, etc. (a word or words) on. PHRASES **to the letter 1** with adherence to every detail. **2** in accordance with a strict literal interpretation.

letter bomb *noun* a terrorist explosive device disguised as a letter and sent through the mail.

letterbox • *noun* (*plural* **letterboxes**) **1** esp. *Brit.* a public mailbox into which letters are deposited for delivery by the postal service. **2** esp. *Brit.* **a** a private mailbox to which letters etc. are delivered. **b** = MAIL SLOT. **3** designating an adaptation of a motion picture for showing on television, with black borders above and below the picture so that the original theatre ratio of width to height is maintained. • *verb* (**letterboxes**, **letterboxed**, **letterboxing**) adapt a film for television broadcast in this format. ▶ **letterboxed** *adjective* **letterboxing** *noun*

letter carrier *noun* a person who delivers mail for the postal service.

lettered *adjective* **1** printed, marked, inscribed, etc. with or as with letters. **2** well-read or educated; literate, learned.

letter grade *noun* a grade given for school work expressed as a letter (A, B, C, etc.).

letterhead *noun* **1** a printed heading on stationery, containing the address etc. of an organization or individual. **2** stationery with this.

lettering *noun* **1** the process of writing, inscribing, etc. letters. **2** letters written, painted, etc. on something.

letter of intent *noun* a document containing a declaration of the intentions of the writer.

letter opener *noun* a knife with a long, narrow, blunt blade for slitting open envelopes etc.

letter-perfect *adjective* **1 a** literally correct, verbally exact. **b** flawless. **2** knowing one's part perfectly.

letters patent *plural noun* an open document issued by a sovereign or government in order to record a contract, authorize or command an action, or confer a right, privilege, title, etc.

lettuce *noun* **1** a plant with crisp edible leaves used in salads. **2** any of various plants resembling this, with edible green leaves.

let-up *noun* *informal* **1** a reduction in intensity or severity. **2** a relaxation of effort.

leukemia *noun* (also esp. *Brit.* **leukaemia**) any of a group of malignant diseases in which the bone marrow and other blood-forming organs produce increased numbers of leukocytes. [Say loo KEEMY uh]

leukocyte *noun* (also **leucocyte**) **1** a white blood cell. **2** any blood cell that contains a nucleus. [Say LOOKA site]

SPELL CHECK ABC✓
levee, levy

A collection is a **levy**.

---

levee[1] *noun* **1** *Cdn* a New Year's Day reception held by the Governor General, a Lieutenant-Governor, a mayor, etc. **2** an assembly of visitors or guests, esp. at a formal reception. [Say LEVVY]

levee[2] *noun* **1 a** an embankment against river floods. **b** any of a series of continuous embankments surrounding irrigated fields. **2** a natural embankment built up by a river. **3** a landing place, a pier, or a quay. [Say LEVVY]

level • *noun* **1** a horizontal plane or line with respect to the distance above or below a given point. **2** a height or distance from the ground or another base. **3** a position

or stage on a scale of quantity, extent, rank, or quality. **4** a floor within a multi-storey building. **5** a flat area of land. **6** an instrument giving a line parallel to the plane of the horizon for testing whether things are horizontal. • *adjective* **1** having a flat, horizontal surface. **2** at the same height as someone or something else. **3** having the same relative position; not in front or behind. **4** calm and steady. • *verb* (**levels**, **levelled**, **levelling**) **1** make or become level. **2** aim or direct a weapon, criticism, or accusation. **3** (foll. by *with*) *informal* be frank or honest with. PHRASES **do one's level best** *informal* do one's utmost; make all possible efforts. **find its level** (or **its own level**) **1** (of a liquid) reach the same height in containers etc. which communicate with each other. **2** reach a stable level, value, position, etc. with respect to something else: *the dollar found its level against the yen.* **find one's level** reach the right social, intellectual, etc. place in relation to others. **level down** bring down to a standard. **level off 1** make or become level or smooth. **2** cease or cause to cease ascending or descending, increasing or decreasing. **level out** make or become level, remove differences, irregularities, etc. from. **on the level** *informal* **1** honest(ly), truthful(ly). **2** on a given plane, horizontal, etc. **on a level with 1** equal with. **2** in the same horizontal plane as.

level crossing *noun* *Cdn & Brit.* a place at which a road and a railway cross each other at the same level.

level-headed *adjective* mentally balanced, cool, sensible. ▶ **level-headedly** *adverb* **level-headedness** *noun*

leveller *noun* **1 a** a person who advocates the abolition of social distinctions. **b** a thing which brings all people to a common level: *death the great leveller.* **2** (**Leveller**) *hist.* an extreme radical dissenter in the English Civil War (1642–9), calling for the abolition of the monarchy, social and agricultural reforms, and religious freedom. **3** a person or thing that levels.

levelly *adverb* in a calm and steady way.

level playing field *noun* a situation in which everyone has the same opportunities: *insuring everyone who works helps to ensure a level playing field in terms of premium payments and access to jobs.*

lever • *noun* **1** a projecting handle moved to operate a mechanism. **2** a bar resting on a pivot, used to help lift or dislodge a heavy or firmly fixed object. **3** *Mechanics* a mechanism consisting of a rigid bar pivoted about a fulcrum (fixed point) which can be acted upon by a force (effort) in order to move a load. **4** a means of exerting pressure on someone to act in a particular way: *rich countries should use foreign aid as a lever to promote civil rights.* • *verb* **1** use a lever. **2** (often foll. by *away*, *out*, *up*, etc.) lift, move, or act on with or as with a lever. [Say LEAVE er or LEV er]

leverage • *noun* **1** the action of a lever; a way of applying a lever. **2** the power of a lever. **3** advantage for accomplishing a purpose; increased power or influence of action: *political leverage* ◊ *retailers can exert leverage over producers by threatening to take their business elsewhere.* **4** *Business* **a** the earning potential created by the ratio of capital to shares. **b** the use of borrowed capital to enhance this. **5** *Business* **a** the ratio of a company's loan capital (debt) to the value of its common shares (equity). **b** the effect of this on share prices. • *verb* use borrowed capital for (an investment), expecting the profits made to be greater than the interest payable: *a leveraged takeover bid.* [Say LEVVER idge or LEAVER idge]

leveraged buyout *noun* the buyout of a company by its management using outside capital.

leviathan *noun* **1** an imaginary or real aquatic animal

of enormous size. **2** anything monstrously large: *the leviathan of government bureaucracy*. [Say luh VYE uh thun]

levitate *verb* (**levitates**, **levitated**, **levitating**) **1** rise and float in the air (esp. with reference to spiritualism). **2** cause to do this. **3** cause (something heavier than the surrounding medium) to rise or remain suspended without visible means, e.g. using magnetic forces. ▶ **levitation** *noun* [Say LEVVA tate]

levity *noun* the treatment of a serious matter with humour or irreverence: *with the exception of a few moments of levity, the work is dull*. [Say LEVVA tee]

levy • *verb* (**levies**, **levied**, **levying**) **1 a** raise (contributions, taxes) or impose (a rate, toll, fee, etc.) as a levy. **b** impose a tax, fee, or fine on: *there will be powers to levy property owners*. **2** *archaic* enlist or enrol (troops etc.). • *noun* (*plural* **levies**) **1 a** the collecting of a contribution, tax, etc. **b** a contribution, tax, etc., levied. **2** *archaic* **a** an act of enlisting troops. **b** (in *plural*) troops enrolled. **c** a body of troops enlisted. [Say LEVVY]

lewd *adjective* **1** lustful. **2** indecent, obscene. ▶ **lewdly** *adverb* **lewdness** *noun* [Say LUDE]

lexical *adjective* of the words of a language. ▶ **lexically** *adverb*

lexicographer *noun* a person who writes and edits dictionaries. [Say lexa COGRA fer]

lexicography *noun* the compiling, writing, or editing of dictionaries. [Say lexa COGRA fee]

lexicon *noun* **1** a dictionary, esp. of Greek, Hebrew, or Arabic. **2 a** the vocabulary of a person, language, branch of knowledge, etc. **b** a book listing this vocabulary. [Say LEXA con]

LF *abbreviation* low frequency.

Lhasa *noun* (*plural* **Lhasas**) (also **Lhasa Apso** *plural* **Lhasa Apsos**) a breed of small long-coated dog, often gold or grey and white. [Say LASSA (AP so)]

Li *symbol* lithium.

liability *noun* (*plural* **liabilities**) **1** the state of being legally responsible for something: *the company cannot accept liability for any damage caused by natural disasters*. **2** a person or thing that causes one problems or puts something at risk: *since his injury, Allan has become more of a liability than an asset to the team*. **3** what a person or company is liable for, esp. (in *plural*) debts or financial obligations: *calculating the company's liabilities and assets*. [Say lie uh BILLA tee]

liability insurance *noun* insurance that covers compensation payments and court costs for which a policyholder is legally liable because of claims for injury to other people or damage to their property resulting from the policyholder's negligence.

liable *adjective* **1** legally responsible; subject by law: *the supplier of goods can become liable for breach of contract* ◊ *non-resident trustees are liable to the basic rate of tax*. **2** (foll. by *to*) exposed or open to (something undesirable). **3** likely: *these sorts of people are liable to suffer from depression*. **4** (foll. by *for*) answerable. [Say LIE uh bull]

liaise *verb* (**liaises**, **liaised**, **liaising**) establish co-operation, act as a link: *federation members have to liaise with government departments and agencies*. [Say lee AYZ]

liaison *noun* **1 a** communication or co-operation, esp. between groups within an organization. **b** a person or association coordinating the co-operation of different groups. **2** an illicit sexual relationship. [Say lee AY zon]

liar *noun* a person who tells a lie or lies, esp. habitually.

Lib. *abbreviation* Liberal

lib *noun* *informal* **1** liberation: *women's lib*. **2** a liberal. **3** (**Lib**) a Liberal.

libation *noun* **1** a drink poured out as an offering to a god. **2** *jocular* a drink. [Say BAY sh'n]

libber *noun* *informal* an advocate of women's liberation.

libel • *noun* **1** *Law* **a** a published false statement damaging to a person's reputation (*compare* SLANDER 1). **b** the act or crime of publishing this. **2 a** a false written statement that harms someone's reputation. **b** (foll. by *on*) a thing that brings discredit by misrepresentation etc.: *the book is a libel on human nature*. • *verb* (**libels**, **libelled**, **libelling**) **1** harm someone's reputation by libellous statements. **2** accuse falsely and maliciously. **3** *Law* publish a libel against. ▶ **libeller** *noun* **libellous** *adjective* **libellously** *adverb* [Say LIE bull]

liberal • *adjective* **1** given freely or in ample or abundant quantity: *scooped out liberal portions of ice cream for us*. **2** (often foll. by *with*) giving freely, generous, not sparing. **3** open-minded, not prejudiced. **4** not strict or rigorous; (of interpretation) not literal: *they could have given the law a more liberal interpretation*. **5** for general broadening of the mind, not professional or technical: *liberal education*. **6 a** favouring a relaxing of social traditions and a significant role for the state in matters of economics and social justice. **b** favouring individual liberty and limited government involvement in economic affairs. **7** (**Liberal**) of or characteristic of Liberals or a Liberal Party. **8** *Theology* regarding many traditional beliefs as dispensable, invalidated by modern thought, or liable to change: *liberal Protestant*. • *noun* **1** a person of liberal views. **2** (**Liberal**) a supporter or member of a Liberal Party.

liberal arts *plural noun* the humanities, esp. as studied at university, leading to a broad general education.

liberalism *noun* **1** a political and social philosophy emphasizing the freedom of the individual, democratic government characterized by progress and reform, and the protection of civil liberties. **2** the quality of being open-minded. **3** (**Liberalism**) principles and practices of a Liberal party.

liberality *noun* **1** respect for political, religious or moral views, even if one does not agree with them: *treating people with justice and liberality*. **2** the quality of being generous: *immigrants attracted by the liberality of a Canadian government eager to attract new settlers*.

liberalization *noun* **1** the process of making something liberal or less strict: *the liberalization of divorce laws*. **2** the process of removing or loosening restrictions on something, esp. a political or economic system: *NAFTA promotes the liberalization of trade in North America*.

liberalize *verb* (**liberalizes**, **liberalized**, **liberalizing**) make or become more liberal or less strict. ▶ **liberalizer** *noun*

liberally *adverb* in a liberal manner; lavishly, profusely.

Liberal Party *noun* (in Canada) one of the two historically most important political parties, generally advocating a centrist position.

liberate *verb* (**liberates**, **liberated**, **liberating**) **1** (often foll. by *from*) set at liberty, set free. **2** free (a country etc.) from an oppressor or an enemy occupation. **3** (often as **liberated** *adjective*) free (a

person or group) from rigid social conventions or stigmas. **4** *slang jocular* steal. **5** *Chemistry* release (esp. a gas) from a state of combination.

liberation *noun* **1** the action of liberating: *the liberation of Normandy by Canadian troops.* **2** the freeing of a person or group from restrictive social conventions: *women's liberation.* ▶ **liberationist** *noun & adjective*

liberator *noun* a person who frees a people or a country from an oppressor or enemy occupation.

Liberian • *adjective* of or relating to Liberia, a country on the Atlantic coast of Africa, or its people. • *noun* a native or inhabitant of Liberia. [Say lie BEERY in]

libertarian • *noun* an advocate of liberty, esp. of an almost absolute freedom of expression and action. • *adjective* believing in free will. ▶ **libertarianism** *noun* [Say libber TAIRY in]

libertine • *noun* a person, esp. a man, who behaves without moral principles or a sense of responsibility, esp. in sexual matters. • *adjective* characterized by a disregard of morality, esp. in sexual matters. ▶ **libertinism** *noun* [Say LIBBER teen or LIBBER tine]

liberty *noun* (*plural* **liberties**) **1 a** freedom from captivity, imprisonment, slavery, or despotic control. **b** a personification of this. **2** the right or power to do as one pleases. **3** setting aside of rules or convention, esp. concerning intimacy: *permitted no liberties.* PHRASES **at liberty 1** free, not imprisoned: *set at liberty.* **2** entitled, permitted: *you are at liberty to leave now.* **3** available, disengaged. **take liberties 1** (often foll. by *with*) behave in an unduly familiar manner. **2** (foll. by *with*) deal freely or superficially with rules or facts. **take the liberty** presume, venture: *took the liberty of recording your poem.*

libidinal *adjective* of or pertaining to the sex drive. [Say luh BID in ul]

libidinous *adjective* lustful. [Say luh BID in us]

libido *noun* (*plural* **libidos**) the sexual drive or instinct. [Say luh BEE doe]

Libra *noun* **1** a constellation near Virgo, traditionally regarded as contained in the figure of scales. **2 a** the seventh sign of the zodiac. **b** a person born when the sun is in this sign, usu. between Sept. 23 and Oct. 22. ▶ **Libran** *noun & adjective* [Say LEE bruh]

librarian *noun* **1** a person professionally trained in the collection, organization, use, and dissemination of information resources. **2** a person in charge of, or an assistant in, a library. ▶ **librarianship** *noun*

library *noun* (*plural* **libraries**) **1 a** a collection of books, periodicals, recordings, electronic reference materials, etc. for use by the public or by members of a group. **b** a person's collection of books. **2** a room or building containing a collection of books (for reading or reference rather than for sale). **3 a** a similar collection of films, records, computer routines, etc. **b** the place where these are kept. **4** a series of books issued by a publisher in similar bindings etc., usu. as a set.

librettist *noun* a person who writes the words for an opera or a musical.

libretto *noun* (*plural* **librettos** or **libretti**) the text of an opera or other long musical vocal work. [Say lib RETTO for the singular, lib RETTOS or lib RETTY for the plural]

Libyan • *adjective* **1** of or relating to modern Libya, a country in northern Africa. **2** of ancient northern Africa west of Egypt. **3** of or relating to the Berber group of languages. • *noun* **1 a** a native or national of modern Libya. **b** a person of Libyan descent. **2** an ancient language of the Berber group. [Say LIBBY in]

lice *plural of* LOUSE 1.

licence *noun* (also esp. *US* **license**) **1** a permit from an authority to own or use something (esp. a dog, gun, or vehicle), do something (esp. construct a building, drive a motor vehicle, or marry), or carry on a trade (esp. in liquor). **2** freedom to do or say whatever one wants, often something bad or unacceptable: *lack of punishment seems to give youngsters licence to break the law.* **3** a writer's or artist's irregularity in grammar, metre, perspective, etc., or deviation from fact, esp. for effect: *poetic licence.*

licence plate *noun* a plate fixed prominently to all licensed motor vehicles, bearing a sequence of numbers and letters to identify the vehicle.

license *verb* (**licenses**, **licensed**, **licensing**) (also **licence**, **licences**, **licenced**, **licencing**) **1** grant a licence to (a person). **2** authorize the use of (premises) for a certain purpose, esp. the sale and consumption of alcoholic liquor. **3** authorize the use of a logo or proprietary name on (merchandise).

licensed *adjective* (also **licenced**) **1** having a specified or appropriate licence: *licensed mechanic.* **2** (of a restaurant etc.) having a licence to sell alcoholic drinks. **3** (of a consumer product) bearing a logo, trademark, etc. which the manufacturer was licensed to use. **4** (of a Baptist preacher) authorized by the Church to preach but not ordained.

licensed practical nurse *noun* a person who has a licence to perform basic nursing tasks under the direction of a physician or registered nurse.

licensee *noun* the holder of a licence.

licensor *noun* a person who licenses something.

licentious *adjective* sexually promiscuous or immoral: *pursued by all the vices a licentious city can bestow on the innocent.* ▶ **licentiousness** *noun* [Say lie SEN shus]

lichee *noun* = LYCHEE. [Say LEE chee]

lichen *noun* a slow-growing, greenish or yellowish plant composed of a fungus and an alga living off one another in symbiotic association, usu. forming a low crust-like, leaflike, or branching growth on rocks, walls, and trees. ▶ **lichened** *adjective* [Say LIKE in]

licit *adjective* not forbidden; lawful: *usage patterns differ between licit and illicit drugs.* [Say LISS it]

lick • *verb* **1** pass the tongue over, esp. to taste, eat, moisten, or (of animals) clean. **2** (of a flame, waves, etc.) touch or move over lightly: *flames were soon licking the curtains.* **3** *informal* a defeat. **b** surpass the comprehension of: *has got me licked.* **4** *informal* thrash. **5** *informal* solve (a problem); overcome (a difficulty). • *noun* **1** an act of licking with the tongue. **2** = SALT LICK. **3** *informal* a fast pace: *at a lick.* **4** *informal* a small amount: *doesn't make a lick of sense.* **5** *slang Music* a short ornamental solo passage. PHRASES **a lick and a promise** *informal* a hasty performance of a task, esp. of housecleaning etc. **lick a person's boots** (or **shoes**) show too much respect for someone in authority in an effort to please them. **lick one's lips** (or **chops**) **1** look forward to something eagerly. **2** show one's satisfaction. **lick one's wounds** try to recover one's strength or confidence after defeat or disappointment. ▶ **licker** *noun*

lickety-split *informal* • *adverb* at full speed; headlong. • *adjective* quick.

licking *noun informal* **1** a thrashing. **2** a defeat.

licorice *noun* **1** a plant that produces a sweet, chewy, black substance, which is extracted from the root and used in candy and medicine. **2** candy flavoured with this, usu. in long black rubbery strips. **3** a rubbery candy similar to this, in any of several flavours and colours. [Say LICKER ish]

licorice root *noun* **1** a leguminous plant, *Glycyrrhiza lepidota*, of western and central North America. **2** a leguminous plant, *Hedysarum alpinum*.

lid *noun* **1** a hinged or removable cover, esp. for the top of a container. **2** = EYELID. **3** *informal* a restraint: *keep a lid on the information.* **4** *slang* a hat or helmet. PHRASES **blow the lid off** *informal* expose (a scandal etc.). **put a lid on it** *informal* stop talking. ▶ **lidded** *adjective* (also in combination). **lidless** *adjective*

> **WRITING TIP**
> **lie, lay**
>
> The following examples are considered incorrect: *Perhaps you should lay down for a while* (correct form is **lie**); *The dog was laying on the floor* (correct form is **lying**); *She lay the blanket over the baby* (correct form is **laid**); *She had laid on the couch for hours* (correct form is **lain**); *We have lain a clever plan* (correct form is **laid**).

lie¹ • *verb* (**lies**; *past* **lay**; *past participle* **lain**; **lying**) **1** be in or assume a horizontal position or at rest on a supporting surface; be at rest on something. **2** (of a thing) rest flat on a surface: *snow lay on the ground.* **3** (of abstract things) remain undisturbed or undiscussed etc.: *let matters lie.* **4 a** be kept or remain or be in a specified, esp. concealed, state or place: *lie hidden ◊ malice lay behind those words ◊ they lay dying.* **b** (of abstract things) exist, reside; be in a certain position or relation: *my sympathies lie with the family.* **5 a** be situated or stationed: *the village lay to the east.* **b** (of a road, route, etc.) lead: *the road lies over mountains.* **c** be spread out to view: *the desert lay before us.* **6** (of the dead) be buried in a grave. **7** (foll. by *with*) *archaic* have sexual intercourse. • *noun* the way or direction or position in which a thing lies. PHRASES **as far as in me lies** to the best of my power. **let lie** not raise (a controversial matter etc.) for discussion etc. **lie ahead** be going to happen; be in store. **lie around** (or **about**) be left carelessly out of place. **lie back** recline so as to rest. **lie down** assume a lying position; have a short rest. **lie heavy** cause discomfort or anxiety. **lie in state** (of a deceased great personage) be laid in a public place of honour before burial. **lie low 1** keep quiet or unseen. **2** be discreet about one's intentions. **lie off** *Nautical* be positioned some distance from shore or from another ship. **lie with** be the responsibility of (a person): *it lies with you to answer.* **take lying down** (usu. with *neg.*) accept (defeat, rebuke, etc.) without resistance or protest etc.

lie² • *noun* **1** an intentionally false statement. **2** deception; false belief: *live a lie.* • *verb* (**lies**, **lied**, **lying**) **1** tell a lie or lies. **2** (of a thing) be deceptive: *the camera cannot lie.* PHRASES **give** (or **put**) **the lie to** serve to show the falsity of (a supposition etc.): *he continues to put the lie to the idea that the 80s were a conservative age.* **lie through one's teeth** lie brazenly.

lied *noun* (*plural* **lieder**) a type of German song, esp. of the Romantic period, usu. for solo voice with piano accompaniment. [Say LEED or LEET for the singular, LEEDER for the plural]

lie detector *noun* an instrument for determining whether a person is telling the truth by testing for

physiological changes considered to be symptomatic of lying.

liege usu. *hist.* • *adjective* entitled to receive or bound to give feudal service or allegiance. • *noun* (also **liege lord**) a feudal superior or sovereign. [Say LEEJ or LEEZH]

lien *noun* *Law* the right to keep someone's property until a debt is paid. [Say LEEN]

lieu *noun Cdn* designating time taken off work in compensation for overtime worked: *lieu time.* PHRASES **in lieu 1** instead: *we work on Saturdays and have a day off in lieu during the week.* **2** (foll. by *of*) in the place of: *they took cash in lieu of the prize they had won.* [Say LOO or LYOO]

Lieut. *abbreviation* Lieutenant.

lieutenancy *noun* (*plural* **lieutenancies**) the position, rank, office, or authority of a lieutenant. [Say lef TEN un see or loo TEN un see]

> **SAY IT RIGHT**
> **lieutenant**
>
> Many Canadians object to pronouncing **lieutenant** loo TENNANT, regarding this pronunciation as American. However, outside of the Armed Forces, it is probably somewhat more common among Canadians than lef TENNANT, except in the word *Lieutenant-Governor*, where usage is more equally divided.

lieutenant *noun* **1** a deputy or substitute acting for a superior: *the prime minister's Quebec lieutenant.* **2** (also **Lieutenant**) **a** (in the Canadian Army and Air Force and the British Army) an officer next in rank below captain. **b** (in the Canadian Navy and other navies) an officer next in rank below lieutenant commander, equivalent to a captain in the other commands. **3** (in Quebec and the US) a police officer next in rank below captain. **4** (in the Royal Newfoundland Constabulary) an officer of a rank between staff sergeant and inspector. [Say lef TENNANT or loo TENNANT]

lieutenant colonel *noun* (also **Lieutenant Colonel**) an officer ranking next below colonel and above major.

lieutenant commander *noun* (also **Lieutenant Commander**) a naval officer ranking below a commander and above a lieutenant.

lieutenant general *noun* (also **Lieutenant General**) (in the Canadian or US Army or Air Force and other armies) an officer ranking above a major general.

lieutenant-governor *noun* (*plural* **lieutenant-governors**) **1** (**Lieutenant-Governor**) *Cdn* the representative of the Crown in a province. **2** the acting or deputy governor of a state, province, etc., under a governor or Governor General.

life *noun* (*plural* **lives**) **1** the condition which distinguishes active animals and plants from inorganic matter, including the capacity for growth, functional activity, and continual change preceding death. **2 a** living things and their activity: *insect life ◊ is there life on Mars?* **b** human presence or activity: *no sign of life.* **c** the human condition; existence: *such is life.* **3 a** the period during which life lasts, or the period from birth to the present time or from the present time to death: *have done it all my life.* **b** the duration of a thing's existence or of its ability to function; validity, efficacy, etc.: *the battery has a life of two years.* **4** a person's state of existence as a living individual: *took many lives.* **5 a** an individual's occupation, actions, or fortunes; the manner of one's existence: *that would make life easy.* **b** a particular aspect of this: *how's your love life?* **c** one's romantic life: *is there someone in your life?* **6** the active part of existence; the business and pleasures of the world: *travel is the best way to see life.* **7** earthly or

supposed future existence: *this life and the next.* **8 a** energy, liveliness, animation: *put some life into it!* **b** an animating influence: *was the life of the party.* **9** the living, esp. nude, form or model: *life drawing classes.* **10** a biography. **11** *informal* a sentence of imprisonment for life: *serving life.* **12** a chance; a fresh start. PHRASES **come to life 1** emerge from unconsciousness or inactivity; begin operating. **2** (of an inanimate object) assume an imaginary animation. **for dear** (or **one's**) **life** as if or in order to escape death; as a matter of extreme urgency: *hang on for dear life* ◊ *run for your life.* **for the life of** even if (one's) life depended on it: *cannot for the life of me remember.* **get a life** *informal* begin to live a meaningful or useful life. **large as life** *informal* in person, esp. prominently: *stood there large as life.* **larger than life 1** exaggerated. **2** (of a person) having an exuberant personality. **life and limb** life and personal health and safety: *she would risk life and limb to save him.* **lose one's life** be killed. **not on your life** *informal* most certainly not. **save a person's life 1** prevent a person's death. **2** save a person from serious difficulty. **take one's life in one's hands** take a crucial personal risk. **to the life** true to the original.

life-and-death *adjective* **1** determining life or death: *a life-and-death struggle.* **2** vitally important.

life assurance *noun* esp. *Brit.* = LIFE INSURANCE.

lifebelt *noun* a belt of buoyant or inflatable material for keeping a person afloat in water.

lifeblood *noun* **1** the blood, as being necessary to life. **2** the vital factor or influence.

lifeboat *noun* a small rescue or safety boat for use during emergencies.

lifebuoy *noun* a buoyant support (usu. a ring) for keeping a person afloat in water, esp. in an emergency.

life cycle *noun* **1** the series of developmental stages through which an organism passes, from one state to the same state in the next generation. **2** the series of developmental stages of any thing, from beginning to end.

life expectancy *noun* (*plural* **life expectancies**) the average period that a person at a specified age etc. may expect to live.

life form *noun* a living thing such as a plant or animal.

life-giving *adjective* that sustains life or uplifts and revitalizes.

lifeguard *noun* an expert swimmer employed to rescue swimmers from drowning.

life history *noun* (*plural* **life histories**) the story of the development of a person or thing, from beginning to end.

life insurance *noun* insurance for a sum to be paid to named beneficiaries on the death of the insured person.

life jacket *noun* a buoyant jacket for keeping a person afloat in water, esp. in an emergency.

lifeless *adjective* **1** lacking life; no longer living; dead. **2** unconscious. **3** lacking movement or vitality. ▶ **lifelessly** *adverb* **lifelessness** *noun*

lifelike *adjective* closely resembling the person or thing represented.

lifeline *noun* **1 a** a rope etc. used for lifesaving, e.g. that attached to a lifebuoy. **b** a diver's signalling line. **2 a** a sole means of communication or transport. **b** a vital source of aid or sustenance. **3** a fold in the palm of the hand, regarded as significant in palmistry. **4** an emergency telephone counselling service.

lifelong *adjective* lasting a lifetime.

life member *noun* a person who has lifelong membership of a society etc.

life-or-death *adjective* = LIFE-AND-DEATH.

life partner *noun* a person engaged in a permanent sexual and romantic relationship with another.

life preserver *noun* a life jacket etc.

lifer *noun slang* **1** a person serving a life sentence. **2** a person seemingly destined to remain in the same job, position, etc. for life.

life raft *noun* an inflatable or timber etc. raft for use in an emergency instead of a boat.

lifesaver *noun* **1** a buoyant ring for keeping a person afloat in an emergency. **2** *informal* a thing that saves one from serious difficulty. ▶ **lifesaving** *noun & adjective*

life sciences *plural noun* biology and related subjects.

life sentence *noun* **1** a sentence of imprisonment for life. **2** (in Canada) a jail sentence of 25 years. **3** an illness or commitment etc. perceived as a continuing threat to one's freedom: *she ran away from the life sentence at the hamburger joint, tired of coming home stinking of fries.*

life-sized *adjective* (also **life-size**) of the same size as the person or thing represented.

life skills *plural noun* the basic skills needed to function normally in society.

lifespan *noun* the length of time for which a person or creature lives, or for which a thing exists or is functional.

life story *noun* (*plural* **life stories**) the story of a person's life, esp. told at tedious length.

lifestyle *noun* **1** the particular way of life of a person or group. **2** (as an *adjective*) of or relating to a particular way of living, esp. designating advertising, products, etc. designed to appeal to a consumer by association with a particular, desirable lifestyle.

life-support • *adjective* (of equipment or a system of machines) allowing vital functions, such as breathing, to continue in an adverse environment or during severe disability. • *noun* a life-support system.

life-threatening *adjective* (of an illness etc.) that endangers life.

lifetime *noun* **1** the duration of a person's life. **2** the duration of a thing or its usefulness. **3** *informal* an exceptionally long time. PHRASES **of a lifetime** such as does not occur more than once in a person's life.

lifeway *noun* esp. *Anthropology* a way of life or lifestyle, esp. of a specific group or community.

lift • *verb* **1** raise or be raised to a higher position or level. **2** pick up and move to a different position. **3** formally remove or end a legal restriction, decision, etc. **4** *informal* steal. • *noun* **1** an act or instance of lifting. **2** a free ride in another person's vehicle. **3** a device for carrying people up or down a mountain. **4** a feeling of increased cheerfulness. **5** upward force exerted by the air on an airfoil or other structure. PHRASES **lift down** pick up and bring to a lower position. **lift a finger** (or **hand** etc.) (in *neg.*) make the slightest effort: *didn't lift a finger to help.* **lift off 1** (of a spacecraft or rocket) rise from the launching pad. **2** (of an aircraft) rise from the runway during takeoff. ▶ **lifter** *noun*

liftoff *noun* **1** the vertical takeoff of a spacecraft etc. **2** an aircraft's rising from the runway during takeoff.

lift ticket *noun* a ticket or tag entitling the bearer to use a ski lift.

ligament *noun* **1** a short band of tough flexible fibrous connective tissue linking bones together. **2** any membranous fold keeping an organ in position. [Say LIGGA mint]

ligate *verb* (**ligates**, **ligated**, **ligating**) tie up (a bleeding artery etc.). ▶ **ligation** *noun* [Say li GATE, li GAY sh'n]

ligation *noun* the surgical procedure of tying a ligature tightly around a tube or duct of the body, esp. the Fallopian tubes as a sterilization procedure.

ligature • *noun* **1** a tie or bandage, esp. in surgery for a

L

bleeding artery etc. **2** *Music* a curved line joining two or more notes, indicating that they are to be played legato, sung to one syllable, or combined into one note. **3** *Printing* two or more letters joined, e.g. *æ*. • *verb* bind or connect with a ligature. [Say LIGGA chur]

light¹ • *noun* **1** the natural agent (electromagnetic radiation of wavelength between about 390 and 740 nm) that stimulates sight and makes things visible. **2** the medium or condition of the space in which this is present. **3** an appearance of brightness: *saw a distant light.* **4 a** a source of light, e.g. the sun, a lamp, fire, etc. **b** an illuminated, usu. coloured electrical device used as a signal. **5 a** a flame or spark serving to ignite: *struck a light.* **b** a device producing this: *have you got a light?* **6** the aspect in which a thing is regarded or considered: *in a new light.* **7 a** mental illumination. **b** hope, happiness; a happy outcome. **8** vivacity, enthusiasm, or inspiration visible in a person's face, esp. in the eyes. **9** an eminent person: *a leading light.* **10** a window or pane of glass. • *verb* (**lights**; *past* **lit**; *past participle* **lit** or **lighted**; **lighting**) **1** set burning or begin to burn; ignite. **2** provide with light or lighting. • *adjective* **1** well provided with light; not dark. **2** (of a colour) pale: *light blue.* • *combining form* forming compounds designating the distance travelled by light in a specified time: *light-year.* PHRASES **bring** (or **come**) **to light** reveal or be revealed. **in a good** (or **bad**) **light** giving a favourable (or unfavourable) impression. **in (the) light of** considering; in view of; drawing information from. **light at the end of the tunnel** a long-awaited sign that a period of hardship or adversity is coming to an end. **light of one's life** usu. *jocular* a much-loved person. **light up 1** *informal* begin to smoke a cigarette etc. **2** switch on lights or lighting; illuminate a scene. **3** (of a light or a panel etc. covered with lights) become illuminated. **4** (of the face or eyes) brighten with animation. **out like a light** deeply asleep or unconscious. **throw** (or **shed**) **light on** help to explain.

light² • *adjective* **1** of little weight; not heavy; easy to lift. **2 a** relatively low in weight, amount, density, intensity, etc.: *light traffic* ◊ *a light breeze.* **b** deficient in weight: *light coin.* **c** (of an isotope etc.) having not more than the usual mass. **3 a** carrying or suitable for small loads: *light aircraft.* **b** (of a ship) not laden. **c** carrying only light arms, armaments, etc.: *light infantry.* **d** (of a locomotive) with no train attached. **4 a** (of food, a meal, etc.) small in amount; easy to digest: *a light lunch.* **b** (of a foodstuff) low in fat, cholesterol, or sugar, etc. **c** (of a foodstuff) lower in calories, fat, etc. than a comparable product. **d** (of drink) not heavy on the stomach or not strongly alcoholic. **5 a** (of entertainment, music, etc.) intended for amusement, rather than edification; not profound. **b** frivolous, thoughtless, trivial: *a light remark.* **6** (of sleep or a sleeper) easily disturbed. **7** easily borne or done: *light housekeeping.* **8** nimble; quick-moving: *a light step.* **9** (of a building etc.) graceful, elegant, delicate. **10** (of type) not heavy or bold. **11 a** free from sorrow; cheerful: *a light heart.* **b** giddy: *light in the head.* **12** (of soil) not dense; porous. **13** (of a dessert) fluffy and well-aerated. • *adverb* **1** in a light manner: *sleep light.* **2** with a minimum load or minimum luggage: *travel light.* • *verb* (**lights**; *past* and *past participle* **lit** or **lighted**; **lighting**) (foll. by *on*, *upon*) come upon or find by chance. PHRASES **light into** *informal* attack. **light out** *informal* depart. **make light of** treat as unimportant. **make light work of** do a thing quickly and easily.

light box *noun* any apparatus with a translucent surface lit from behind, used to view slides, film, transparencies, etc.

light bulb *noun* a glass bulb containing an inert gas and a metal filament, providing light when an electric current is passed through.

light cream *noun* **1** *Cdn* a table cream having 7% fat. **2** esp. *US* a table cream generally with 18% fat.

light-emitting diode *noun* = LED.

lighten¹ *verb* **1** make or become lighter in weight. **2** bring relief to (the heart, mind, etc.). PHRASES **lighten up** *informal* become less earnest or intense; relax.

lighten² *verb* **1** shed light on; make less dark. **2 a** shine brightly; flash. **b** emit lightning: *it is lightening.*

lighter *noun* **1** a device for lighting cigarettes, barbecues, etc. **2** a boat, usu. flat-bottomed, for transferring goods from a ship to a wharf or another ship.

lighter-than-air *adjective* (of an aircraft) weighing less than the air it displaces, e.g. a blimp.

light-footed *adjective* nimble.

light-handed *adjective* having a light, delicate, or deft touch.

light-headed *adjective* giddy, faint. ▶ **light-headedness** *noun*

lighthearted *adjective* **1** intended to be amusing or easily enjoyable rather than too serious: *a lighthearted speech.* **2** cheerful and without problems: *he looked so happy, I could almost feel lighthearted again.* ▶ **lightheartedly** *adverb* **lightheartedness** *noun*

lighthouse *noun* a tower or other structure containing a beacon light to warn or guide ships.

light industry *noun* (*plural* **light industries**) the manufacture of small or light articles, esp. consumer goods.

lighting *noun* **1** equipment for producing light. **2** the arrangement or effect of lights.

lightkeeper *noun* a person in charge of a lighthouse.

lightless *adjective* **1** receiving no light; dark. **2** giving or producing no light.

lightly *adverb* **1** gently; with very little force or effort: *he kissed her lightly on the cheek* ◊ *she ran lightly up the stairs.* **2** to a small degree; not much: *it began to snow lightly.* **3** in a way that suggests one is not particularly worried or interested. PHRASES **get off lightly** escape with little or no punishment. **take lightly** not be serious about (a thing).

lightness¹ *noun* **1** the condition or state of being light or illuminated. **2** the quality of being light or pale in colour.

lightness² *noun* **1** the quality or fact of having little weight. **2** (of food) **a** the quality of incorporating air: *the lightness of the pastry.* **b** the quality of being easy to digest: *Vietnamese cuisine is known for its lightness and subtlety.* **3** agility, nimbleness: *Ethiopian marathoners are noted for their lightness and grace.* **4** freedom from depression or sorrow; cheerfulness. **5** absence of force or pressure in action or movement; delicacy: *lightness of touch.* **6** elegance: *the bulk and massiveness of Romanesque architecture contrasts with the lightness of Gothic.*

lightning • *noun* a flash of bright light produced by an electric discharge between clouds or between clouds and the ground. • *adjective* very quick: *lightning speed.*

lightning rod *noun* **1** a metal rod or wire fixed to an exposed part of a building or to a mast to divert lightning into the earth or sea. **2** a person or thing that attracts criticism: *if this became public, it would become a lightning rod for the opposition.*

light of day *noun* **1** daylight, sunlight. **2** general notice; public attention.

light opera *noun* = OPERETTA.

light pen *noun* **1** a pen-like photosensitive device held to the screen of a computer terminal for passing

information on to it. **2** a light-emitting device used for reading bar codes.

light pollution *noun* excessive brightening of the night sky by street lights etc., esp. as obscuring the stars etc.

lightproof *adjective* (of a container, barrier, etc.) not permitting the passage of light.

lights *plural noun* the lungs of sheep, pigs, steers, etc., used as a food esp. for pets. PHRASES **punch a person's lights out** beat a person soundly.

light show *noun* a display of changing coloured lights for entertainment.

light station *noun* = LIGHTHOUSE.

light touch *noun* delicate or tactful treatment.

lightweight • *adjective* **1** (of a person, garment, etc.) of below average weight. **2** of little importance or influence. • *noun* **1** a lightweight person, animal, or thing. **2 a** a weight in certain sports intermediate between featherweight and welterweight, in the amateur boxing scale 57–60 kg but differing for professionals and wrestlers. **b** an athlete of this weight. **3** a person of little influence or significance.

light-year *noun* **1** the distance light travels in one mean solar year, approximately 9.46×10^{12} km (5.88 × 10^{12} miles). **2** (in *plural*) a long distance or great amount.

lignin *noun* a substance produced by many plants to strengthen their tissues and make them rigid and woody. [Say LIG nin]

lignite *noun* a soft brown coal showing traces of plant structure, intermediate between bituminous coal and peat. [Say LIG nite]

likable *adjective* = LIKEABLE.

> **GRAMMAR CHECK**
> **like, as** ⚠️
>
> Although it is quite common in casual speech to use comparisons such as *He holds his guitar like Rosa does*, and *They were playing like they were professionals*, in formal contexts **like** should not be used when the comparison is being made to a statement with a verb in it (statements such as "Rosa *does*" and "they *were* professionals" in the examples above). **Like** would only be appropriate if the sentences were *He holds his guitar like Rosa*, and *They were playing like professionals*. The sentences could also be rewritten using **as** or **as if** instead of **like**: *He holds his guitar as Rosa does*; *They were playing as if they were professionals*.

---

like¹ • *adjective* (**more like, most like**) having some or all of the qualities of another or each other or an original; alike: *in like manner ◊ is very like her brother*. • *preposition* **1** resembling or characteristic of. **2** in a suitable state or mood for (doing or having something): *felt like working ◊ felt like a cup of tea*. • *adverb* *slang* so to speak: *like, I'm no Shakespeare*. • *conjunction informal disputed* **1** as: *cannot do it like you do*. **2** as if: *ate like they were starving*. • *noun* **1** a counterpart; an equal; a similar person or thing: *shall not see its like again*. **2** (**the like**) a thing or things of the same kind: *never did the like again*. PHRASES **like** (or **as like**) **as not** *informal* probably. **like so** *informal* like this; in this manner. **the likes of** *informal* a person such as. **more like it** *informal* nearer what is required. **of like** (or **of a like**) **mind** = LIKE-MINDED. **what is he** (or **she or it** etc.) **like?** what sort of characteristics does he (or she, or it, etc.) have?

like² • *verb* (**likes, liked, liking**) **1 a** find agreeable or enjoyable or satisfactory: *like reading ◊ like to dance*. **b** be fond of (a person). **2** feel about; regard: *how would you like it if it happened to you?* **3** feel inclined; choose: *we could go out if you like*. • *noun* (in *plural*) the things one

likes or prefers. PHRASES **like it or not** *informal* whether it is acceptable or not.

-like *combining form* forming adjectives from nouns, meaning "similar to, characteristic of": *doglike ◊ shell-like ◊ tortoise-like*.

likeable *adjective* pleasant; easy to like. ▶ **likeability** *noun* **likeably** *adverb*

likelihood *noun* probability; the quality or fact of being likely. PHRASES **in all likelihood** very probably.

likely • *adjective* (**likelier, likeliest**) **1** probable; such as well might happen or be true: *it is not likely that they will come ◊ the most likely place is Saskatoon*. **2** to be reasonably expected: *he is not likely to come now*. **3** promising; apparently suitable: *this is a likely spot*. • *adverb* probably: *is very likely true*. PHRASES **as likely as not** probably. **not likely** *informal* certainly not.

like-minded *adjective* having the same tastes, opinions, etc.

liken *verb* (foll. by *to*) represent as similar; point out the resemblance of (a person or thing to another).

likeness *noun* (*plural* **likenesses**) **1** (foll. by *between, to*) resemblance. **2** a semblance or guise: *in the likeness of a ghost*. **3** a portrait or representation: *a good likeness*.

likewise *adverb* **1** also, moreover, too. **2** similarly.

liking *noun* **1** what one likes; one's taste: *is it to your liking?* **2** (foll. by *for*) regard or fondness; taste or fancy.

li'l *adjective informal jocular* little.

lilac *noun* **1** a shrub or small tree with fragrant purple, mauve, pink, or white blossoms. **2** *noun & adjective* a pale pinkish-violet colour. **3** the scent of lilac. [Say LIE l'k or LIE lock or LIE lack]

Lilliputian *adjective* tiny, diminutive: *Lilliputian trees for a model railway*. [Say lilla PYOO shin]

Lillooet *noun* (*plural* **Lillooet** or **Lillooets**) **1** a member of an Aboriginal people living in southwestern BC, northeast of Vancouver. **2** the Salishan language of this people. [Say LILL oo et]

lilt • *noun* a characteristic rising and falling cadence or inflection (of a voice, accent, music, etc.). • *verb* speak or sing etc. with a lilt: *a lilting melody*.

lily *noun* (*plural* **lilies**) **1** a plant with large trumpet-shaped, often spotted, flowers on a tall, slender stem. **2** the water lily.

lily of the valley *noun* (*plural* **lilies of the valley**) a plant of the lily family, with broad oval leaves and arching stems of fragrant white bell-shaped fragrant flowers.

lily pad *noun* a floating leaf of a water lily.

lily-white *adjective* **1** as white as a lily. **2** faultless: *with so many churches it was dubbed the "lily-white town"*. **3** in favour of, committed to, or pertaining to a policy excluding non-whites: *a lily-white hiring policy*.

lima bean *noun* **1** a large edible flat whitish bean. **2** the tropical American plant that yields this bean. [Say LIE muh]

limb • *noun* **1** a projecting part of a person's or animal's body such as an arm, leg, or wing. **2** a large branch of a tree. **3** a projecting part of a thing, e.g. the branch of a cross. • *verb* remove branches from (a tree). PHRASES **out on a limb** in or into a vulnerable or risky position where one is not supported by others. **tear limb from limb** violently dismember. ▶ **limbed** *adjective* (also in *combination*).

limber • *adjective* **1** lithe, agile, nimble. **2** flexible. • *verb* (usu. foll. by *up*) **1** make (oneself or a part of the body etc.) supple. **2** warm up in preparation for athletic etc. activity. [Say LIM burr]

limbic *adjective* of a part of the brain concerned with basic emotions and instinctive actions. [Say LIM bick]

limbless *adjective* having no limbs, or fewer than the normal number of limbs.

L

limbo[1] *noun* (*plural* **limbos**) **1** (in some Christian beliefs) the supposed abode of the souls of unbaptized infants, and of the just who died before Christ. **2** an intermediate state or condition of awaiting a decision etc.: *refugees in limbo while awaiting their immigration trials*. **3** a state of neglect or oblivion: *the former star was in limbo, playing minor roles in B movies*.

limbo[2] *noun* (*plural* **limbos**) a West Indian dance in which the dancer bends backwards to pass under a horizontal bar which is progressively lowered to a position just above the ground.

Limburger *noun* a soft white cheese with a characteristic strong smell. [Say LIM burger]

lime[1] • *noun* **1** (also **quicklime**) a white caustic alkaline substance obtained by heating limestone and used for making mortar or as a fertilizer or bleach etc. **2** (also **slaked lime**) a white substance (calcium hydroxide) made by adding water to quicklime, used esp. in cement. **3** calcium or calcium salts, esp. calcium carbonate in soil etc. • *verb* (**limes, limed, liming**) treat (wood, skins, land, etc.) with lime.

lime[2] *noun* **1 a** a rounded citrus fruit resembling a lemon but greener, smaller, and more acid. **b** (also **lime tree**) the evergreen tree that bears this fruit. **2** (also **lime juice**) the juice of limes, used in drinks and cooking. **3** *noun & adjective* (also **lime green**) a bright pale green colour.

lime[3] *noun* **1** (also **lime tree**) a deciduous ornamental tree with heart-shaped leaves and fragrant yellow blossoms. **2** the wood of this.

limelight *noun* **1** an intense white light used formerly in theatres. **2** (**the limelight**) the full glare of publicity; the focus of attention: *basking in the limelight after her gold-medal victory*.

limerick *noun* a humorous or comic form of five-line poem. [Say LIMMA rick]

limestone *noun* a sedimentary rock composed mainly of calcium carbonate, used as building material and in the making of cement.

Limey *slang offensive* • *noun* (*plural* **Limeys**) a British person or ship. • *adjective* British. [Say LIME ee]

liminal *adjective* occupying a position on a boundary or threshold: *books occupying a liminal zone between science fiction and other genres*. ▶ **liminality** *noun* [Say LIMMA nul, limma NALA tee]

limit • *noun* **1** a point, line, or level beyond which something does not or may not extend or pass. **2** (often in *plural*) the boundary of an area. **3** *Cdn* an area of forested land in which an individual or company has the right to fell and remove timber. **4** the greatest or smallest amount permissible or possible: *lower limit*. • *verb* (**limits, limited, limiting**) **1** set or serve as a limit to. **2** (foll. by *to*) restrict. PHRASES **be the limit** *informal* be intolerable or extremely irritating. **go (to) the limit** behave in an extreme way. **off limits** out of bounds; forbidden. **within limits** to a moderate extent. **without limit** with no restriction. ▶ **limitable** *adjective*

limitation *noun* **1** the action of limiting something: *the limitation of their powers*. **2** (often in *plural*) a condition of limited ability: *know one's limitations*. **3** (often in *plural*) a limiting rule or circumstance: *severe limitations on water use* ◊ *this technique is good but it has its limitations*. **4** a legally specified period beyond which an action cannot be brought, or a property right is not to continue: *statute of limitations*.

limited *adjective* **1** confined within limits. **2** not great in scope or talents: *has limited experience*. **3 a** few, scanty, restricted: *a limited budget*. **b** restricted to a few examples: *limited printing*. **4** (**Limited**) *Cdn & Brit.* (after a company name) being a limited company. **5** (of a

monarchy, government, etc.) exercised under limitations of power prescribed by a constitution. **6** making few stops; express.

limited company *noun* (*plural* **limited companies**) (also **limited liability company**) *Cdn & Brit.* a company whose owners are legally responsible only to a limited amount for its debts.

limited edition *noun* an edition of a book, or reproduction of an object, limited to some specific number of copies.

limited liability *noun* *Cdn & Brit.* the status of being legally responsible only to a limited amount for debts of a trading company.

limited partner *noun* a partner in a company or venture whose liability towards its debts is legally limited to the extent of his or her investment.

limited partnership *noun* a partnership in which the liability of some partners is legally limited to the extent of their investment.

limiting *adjective* putting limits on what is possible: *lack of cash is a limiting factor*.

limitless *adjective* **1** extending or going on indefinitely: *a limitless expanse*. **2** unlimited: *limitless generosity*. ▶ **limitlessly** *adverb*

limn *verb* **1** paint or draw (a picture or portrait); portray (a subject): *a black top with a panther limned across the front*. **2** portray or represent (esp. a person) in words: *the portrait limned in the poem*. [Say LIM]

limo *noun* (*plural* **limos**) *informal* a limousine.

limousine *noun* **1** a large luxurious automobile, often with a partition behind the driver. **2** a large sedan or minibus for carrying people over a fixed route to and from an airport etc. [Say limma ZEEN or LIMMA zeen]

limp[1] • *verb* **1** walk lamely. **2** (of a damaged ship, aircraft, etc.) proceed with difficulty. **3** (of a business, an event, etc.) progress slowly or weakly: *the company limped along for years*. • *noun* a lame walk.

limp[2] *adjective* **1** not stiff or firm. **2** without energy or will: *it left my commitment quite limp*.

limpet *noun* **1** a marine mollusc with a shallow conical shell and a broad muscular foot that sticks tightly to rocks. **2** a clinging person. [Say LIM pit]

limpid *adjective* **1** (of water, eyes, etc.) clear, transparent: *the stream was a net of limpid ripples*. **2** (of writing) clear and easily comprehended: *limpid prose*. **3** calm, tranquil: *the song's limpid rhythms*. ▶ **limpidity** *noun* [Say LIM pid, lim PIDDA tee]

limply *adverb* in a limp manner; in a way that lacks strength, rigidity or conviction: *her hair hung limply* ◊ *"There's nothing to be done," he concluded limply*.

limy *adjective* (**limier, limiest**) consisting of or containing lime.

SPELL CHECK

liniment

Warning: the vowel in the second syllable of **liniment** is an *i*, not an *a*.

LINC *abbreviation* *Cdn* Language Instruction for Newcomers to Canada. [Sounds like *LINK*]

linchpin *noun* **1** a pin passed through the end of an axle to keep a wheel in position. **2** a person or thing vital to an enterprise, organization, etc.: *the linchpin of his economic strategy is living at home*. [Say LINCH pin]

lindane *noun* a toxic colourless benzene compound used as an insecticide. [Say LIN dane]

linden *noun* **1** a basswood tree. **2** an ornamental European tree with heart-shaped leaves and fragrant yellow blossoms. [Say LIN din]

lindy (also **lindy hop**) • *noun* a dance originating as a

form of the jitterbug among blacks in Harlem, New York. • *verb* dance the lindy.

line¹ • *noun* **1** a long, narrow mark or band. **2** a length of cord, wire, etc. serving a purpose. **3** a row or connected series of people or things. **4** a row of written or printed words. **5** a direction, course, or channel. **6** a telephone connection. **7** a railway track or route. **8** a notional limit or boundary. **9** a connected series of military defences facing an enemy force. **10** an arrangement of soldiers or ships in a column or line formation. **11** a wrinkle in the skin. **12** a contour or outline considered as a feature of design or composition. **13** a range of commercial goods. **14** a sphere of activity. **15** (**lines**) a way of doing something: *thinking along the same lines*. **16** (**lines**) the words of an actor's part. **17** (**lines**) a number of repetitions of a sentence written out as a school punishment. • *verb* (**lines, lined, lining**) **1** stand or be positioned at intervals along. **2** mark or cover with lines. PHRASES **all along the line** at every point. **bring into line** make conform. **come into line** conform. **end of the line** **1** the point at which further effort is unproductive or one can go no further. **2** the terminus of a rail, subway, or bus route. **get a line on** *informal* learn something about. **in line 1** arranged or standing in a line. **2** under control. **in line for** likely to receive. **in the line of** in the course of (esp. duty). **in** (or **out of**) **line with** in (or not in) accordance with. **keep in line** control: *kept me in line*. **lay** (or **put**) **it on the line** **1** speak frankly. **2** pay money. **line up** **1** arrange or be arranged in a line or lines. **2** have ready; organize: *had a job lined up*. **on the line** **1** at risk: *put my reputation on the line*. **2** speaking on the telephone. **out of line 1** not in alignment; discordant. **2** failing to conform to a rule or convention; behaving inappropriately.

line² *verb* (**lines, lined, lining**) **1** cover the inside surface of something with a layer of usu. different material. **2** cover as if with a lining: *shelves lined with books*. PHRASES **line one's pocket** make money, usu. by corrupt means.

lineage *noun* the series of families that one is descended from; ancestry: *a French nobleman of ancient lineage*. [Say LINNY idge]

lineal *adjective* **1** in the direct line of descent or ancestry: *a lineal descendant*. **2** linear; of or in lines: *the park features 3,000 lineal feet of beachfront*. [Say LINNY ul]

linear *adjective* **1 a** of or in lines; in lines rather than masses: *linear development*. **b** of length: *linear extent*. **2** long and narrow and of uniform breadth. **3** involving one dimension only. **4** progressing in a single series of steps or stages; sequential: *linear thinking*. [Say LINNY er]

Linear B *noun* a form of Bronze Age writing found in Crete and parts of Greece and recording a form of Mycenaean Greek: an earlier form (**Linear A**), not yet deciphered, also exists.

linear equation *noun* an equation between two variables that gives a straight line when plotted on a graph.

linearity *noun* **1** the quality or condition of being linear; a linear arrangement or formation. **2** the property of being representable by a line; proportionality of two related qualities (such as output and input). [Say linny AIR uh tee]

linearly *adverb* **1** in a way that involves only terms of one dimension; in a linear or proportional manner. **2** in a linear direction; by linear measurement; by means of lines. [Say LINNY er lee]

linear measure *noun* a measure of length (metres, miles, etc.).

linebacker *noun* *Football* a player or position just behind the defensive line.

line dance • *noun* a type of country-and-western dancing in which dancers line up side by side without partners and follow a choreographed pattern of steps to music. • *verb* (**line dances, line danced, line dancing**) perform this dance. ▶ **line dancer** *noun* **line dancing** *noun*

line drive *noun* *Baseball* a ball hit straight and low above the ground.

line graph *noun* a graph in which the values of the variables are represented by a continuous line.

lineman *noun* (*plural* **linemen**) **1 a** a person who repairs and maintains telephone or electrical etc. lines. **b** a person who tests the safety of railway lines. **2** *Football* a centre, guard, tackle, or end.

linemate *noun* *Hockey* a player who plays on the same line as another.

linen • *noun* **1** cloth woven from flax. **2** (*collect.*) articles made or originally made of linen, cotton, etc., as sheets, cloths, shirts, undergarments, etc. • *adjective* made of linen or flax: *linen cloth*. PHRASES **wash** (or **air**) **one's dirty linen in public** be indiscreet about one's domestic quarrels etc. [Say LIN in]

line of credit *noun* (*plural* **lines of credit**) an amount of credit extended to a borrower by a financial institution, enabling a person or company to borrow money as often as needed up to a pre-set limit without having to apply each time for a loan.

line of scrimmage *noun* *Football* the imaginary line separating two teams at the beginning of a scrimmage.

liner¹ *noun* **1** a ship or aircraft etc. carrying passengers on a regular line. **2** = EYELINER. **3** = LINE DRIVE.

liner² *noun* **1** a lining in an appliance, device, or container, esp. a removable one. **2** a lining of a garment, esp. one made of a synthetic fibre.

linesman *noun* (*plural* **linesmen**) **1** *Hockey* an on-ice official whose tasks include making offside and icing calls, breaking up fights, etc. **2** (in games played on a field or court) an umpire's or referee's assistant who decides whether a ball falls within the playing area or not. **3** *Football* an official who marks the distances won or lost on each play.

lineup *noun* **1** a line of people formed for a particular reason, e.g. to buy tickets etc. **2** the personnel or configuration of persons on a team, in a musical group, etc. **3** (in police work) a line of persons from whom a suspect is to be identified. **4** a schedule of television programs, events, etc. **5** a line of items or services offered by a company.

ling *noun* **1** any of a number of long slender predatory fishes, esp. a large East Atlantic food fish related to the cod. **2** a burbot.

ling cod *noun* a large food fish found in the North Pacific.

linger *verb* **1 a** be slow or reluctant to depart. **b** stay about. **c** (foll. by *over, on,* etc.) dally: *lingered over dinner*. **2** (foll. by *on*) (of an action or condition) be protracted; drag on: *the memory lingers on*. **3** (foll. by *on*) (of a dying person or custom) be slow in dying; drag on feebly.

lingerie *noun* women's underwear and nightclothes. [Say LAWN zhuh ray or lawn zhuh RAY]

lingering *adjective* slow to end or disappear: *a painful and lingering death* ◊ *a last lingering look* ◊ *lingering doubts* ◊ *a lingering smell of skunk*. ▶ **lingeringly** *adverb*

lingo *noun* (*plural* **lingos** or **lingoes**) *informal* **1** the vocabulary of a special subject or group of people. **2** a foreign language.

lingonberry *noun* (*plural* **lingonberries**) **1** the cowberry of northern regions, esp. of Scandinavia, where the berries are used in cooking. **2** an Arctic

variety of this occurring in Russia and North America. [Say LING gun berry]

lingua franca *noun* (*plural* **lingua francas**) **1** a common language adopted by speakers whose native languages are different. **2** a system of communication providing mutual understanding: *HTML is the lingua franca of the Internet*. [Say ling gwuh FRANKA]

lingual *adjective* of or formed by the tongue. [Say LING gwul]

linguine *plural noun* (also **linguini**) pasta in the form of narrow ribbons. [Say ling GWEENY]

linguist *noun* a person skilled in languages or linguistics. [Say LING gwist]

linguistic *adjective* of language or the study of languages. ▶ **linguistically** *adverb* [Say ling GWISS tick]

linguistics *noun* the scientific study of language and its structure. [Say ling GWIST icks]

liniment *noun* a medicated lotion, usu. made with oil, for rubbing onto the body to relieve pain. [Say LINNA mint]

lining *noun* **1** a layer of material used to line a surface etc. **2** an inside layer or surface etc.: *stomach lining*. **3** the technique of guiding or controlling a canoe or boat from the bank or shore of a stretch of inland water by means of a rope or ropes.

link • *noun* **1** one loop or ring of a chain etc. **2** a connecting part, esp. a thing or person that unites or provides continuity; one in a series. **3** a means of contact by radio, telephone, television, or computer between two points. **4** a means of travel or transport between two places: *a link to the mainland*. **5** = CUFFLINK. **6** a measure equal to one-hundredth of a surveying chain (20.12 cm or 7.92 inches). **7** (usu. in *plural*) any of the divisions of a chain of sausages. • *verb* **1** connect or join (two things or one to another). **2** connect causally, associate in speech, thought, etc.: *many diseases have been linked to smoking*. **3** clasp or intertwine (hands or arms). **4** be joined; attach oneself to (a system, company, etc.). PHRASES **link up** connect or combine.

linkage *noun* the action of linking; a link or system of links: *a complex linkage of nerves ◊ the linkage between economic development and the environment*.

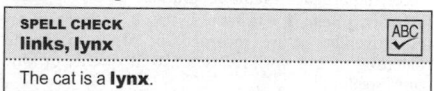

SPELL CHECK	
links, lynx	ABC ✓

The cat is a **lynx**.

links *plural noun* (treated as *singular* or *plural*) a golf course, esp. one having undulating ground, coarse grass, etc.

link-up *noun* an act or result of linking up.

linoleic acid *noun* a polyunsaturated fatty acid occurring as a glyceride in linseed and other oils and essential in the human diet. [Say linna LEE ick]

linolenic acid *noun* a polyunsaturated fatty acid (with one more double bond than linoleic acid) occurring as a glyceride in linseed and other oils and essential in the human diet. [Say linna LEN ick]

linoleum *noun* a floor covering consisting of a canvas backing thickly coated with a preparation of linseed oil and powdered cork etc. [Say lin OLE ee um]

linseed *noun* the seed of flax.

linseed oil *noun* oil extracted from linseed and used in paint and varnish.

lint *noun* **1** tiny threads or fibres of fabric; fluff. **2** a soft material used esp. for dressing wounds. **3** an accumulation of dirt, dead skin cells, etc. in the navel.

lintel *noun* a horizontal supporting piece of timber, stone, concrete, etc., across the top of a door or window.

Linux *noun* Computing a freely available Unix-like operating system. [Say LIN ux or LINE ux or LEEN ux]

lion *noun* **1** a large tawny-coloured cat that lives in prides, found in Africa and northwest India; the male has a flowing shaggy mane and takes little part in hunting, which is done co-operatively by the females. **2** a brave or celebrated person: *a literary lion*.

lioness *noun* (*plural* **lionesses**) a female lion.

lionization *noun* the act of treating as a celebrity.

lionize *verb* (**lionizes**, **lionized**, **lionizing**) treat as a celebrity: *one of the most lionized surfers in history*.

lion's share *noun* the largest or best part.

lip • *noun* **1** a either of the two fleshy parts forming the edges of the mouth. **b** a thing resembling these. **c** = LABIUM. **2** a the edge of a cup, vessel, etc., esp. the part shaped for pouring from. **b** the edge of an opening or cavity, e.g. of a canyon, the crater of a volcano, etc. **3** *informal* impudent talk: *that's enough of your lip!* • *verb* (**lips**, **lipped**, **lipping**) **1** touch with the lips; apply lips to. **2** *informal* insult, abuse; be impudent to (someone). PHRASES **bite one's lip** repress an emotion; stifle laughter, a retort, etc. **curl one's lip** express scorn. **pass a person's lips** be eaten, drunk, spoken, etc. **smack one's lips** open and close the lips noisily in relish or anticipation, esp. of food.

lipid *noun* any of a group of organic compounds that are insoluble in water but soluble in organic solvents, including fatty acids, oils, waxes, etc. [Say LIP id]

lipless *adjective* having no lips.

lipliner *noun* a cosmetic applied as a line around the lips, to accentuate them and keep lipstick from bleeding.

lipoprotein *noun* any of a group of soluble proteins that combine with and transport fat or other lipids in the blood plasma. [Say lippo PROTEIN or lie po PROTEIN]

liposome *noun* a minute artificial spherical sac usu. of a phospholipid membrane enclosing an aqueous core, esp. used to carry drugs to specific tissues. [Say LIPPA soam or LIE po soam]

liposuction *noun* a technique in cosmetic surgery for removing excess fat from under the skin by suction. [Say LIPPO suction or LIE po suction]

lipped *adjective* (also in *combination*) having the type of lips mentioned: *thin-lipped ◊ thick-lipped*.

lippy *adjective* (**lippier**, **lippiest**) *informal* **1** insolent, impertinent. **2** having large lips.

lip-read *verb* (**lip-reads**, **lip-read**, **lip-reading**) (esp. of a deaf person) understand (speech) entirely from observing a speaker's lip movements. ▶ **lip-reader** *noun* **lip-reading** *noun*

lip service *noun* an insincere expression of support etc.: *they merely pay lip service to the environmentalists*.

lip-smacking *adjective* **1** (of food etc.) delicious. **2** tantalizing; tempting: *a lip-smacking account of the latest scandal*.

lipstick *noun* a small stick of cosmetic for colouring the lips, usu. a shade of red or pink. ▶ **lipsticked** *adjective*

lip-synch (also **lip-sync**) • *noun* (in film acting etc.) the movement of a performer's lips in synchronization with a pre-recorded soundtrack. • *verb* perform (esp. a song) on film using this technique. ▶ **lip-synching** *noun* [Say LIP sink]

liquefaction *noun* the action or process of liquefying; the state of being liquefied; reduction to a liquid state. [Say lickwa FACTION]

liquefy *verb* (**liquefies**, **liquefied**, **liquefying**) make or become liquid. [Say LICKWA fie]

L

SPELL CHECK
liqueur, liquor

Liqueur refers only to sweet flavoured alcohol such as Irish cream, amaretto, etc.; the general word for distilled alcohol is **liquor**.

liqueur *noun* any of several strong sweet alcoholic spirits, variously flavoured, usu. drunk after a meal. [Say li CURE]

liquid • *adjective* **1** (of a material substance) having a consistency like that of water or oil, flowing freely but of constant volume. **2** (of light, fire, the eyes, etc.) like water in appearance; clear, bright, translucent: *a liquid lustre*. **3** (of a gas, e.g. oxygen) reduced to a liquid state by intense cold or high pressure. **4 a** (of sounds) clear and pure; harmonious, fluent. **b** (of movement) unconstrained. **5 a** (of assets) easily converted into cash. **b** having ready cash or liquid assets: *prompting investors to stay liquid*. **6** not fixed; fluid: *liquid opinions*. • *noun* **1** a liquid substance. **2** (usu. in *plural*) liquid food.

liquidate *verb* (**liquidates, liquidated, liquidating**) **1 a** wind up the affairs of (a company or firm) by ascertaining liabilities and apportioning assets. **b** (of a company) be liquidated, go into liquidation. **2** clear or pay off (a debt). **3** put an end to or get rid of (esp. by violent means); kill.

liquidation *noun* **1 a** the process of liquidating a company etc. **b** the state or condition of being wound up. **2** the action or process of abolishing or eliminating something or someone, esp. the doing away with or killing of unwanted people. PHRASES **go into liquidation** (of a company etc.) be wound up and have its assets apportioned.

liquidator *noun* **1** a person called in to wind up the affairs of a company etc. **2** a person who implements a policy of liquidation.

liquid crystal display *noun* a form of visual display in electronic devices, esp. of segmented numbers or letters, in which liquid crystals are made visible by temporarily modifying their capacity to reflect light.

liquidity *noun* (*plural* **liquidities**) **1** the state of being liquid. **2** availability of liquid assets. [Say li KWIDDA tee]

liquify *verb* = LIQUEFY.

SPELL CHECK
liquor, liqueur

A sweet flavoured liquor such as Irish cream or amaretto is a **liqueur**.

liquor • *noun* **1** an alcoholic drink, esp. produced by distillation. **2** a liquid of a particular kind used or produced in a chemical or industrial process etc. **3** other liquid, esp. that produced in cooking. • *verb* become drunk or make someone else drunk: *a sad sight of a bunch of grown men getting liquored up and putting sheets on their heads*. [Say LICKER]

liquor commission *noun* **Cdn** **1** (in the territories and certain provinces) a regulatory body controlling the sale and distribution of alcoholic beverages. **2** a liquor store operated by this body. Abbreviation: **LC**.

liquor control board *noun* (also **liquor board**) *Cdn* (in certain provinces) a regulatory body controlling the sale and distribution of alcoholic beverages.

liquorice *noun* = LICORICE. [Say LICKER ish]

LIRA *noun* (*plural* **LIRAs**) *Cdn* LOCKED-IN RETIREMENT ACCOUNT. [Say LEE ruh]

lira *noun* (*plural* **lire**) **1** the chief monetary unit of Italy, used also in San Marino and the Vatican City. **2** the chief monetary unit of Turkey. [Say LEE ruh]

LISP *abbreviation* a high-level programming language devised for list processing.

lisp • *noun* **1 a** a speech defect in which *s* is pronounced like *th* in thick and *z* is pronounced like *th* in *this*. **b** the action of lisping; a lisping pronunciation. **2** a sound resembling a lisp, e.g. the rippling of waters, rustling of leaves, etc. • *verb* speak or utter with a lisp. ▶ **lisper** *noun* **lisping** *adjective & noun*

list¹ • *noun* **1** a number of connected items, names, etc., written or printed together usu. consecutively to form a record or aid to memory: *shopping list*. **2** the books published, or to be published, by a particular publisher. **3** *Computing* a formalized representation of the concept of a list, used for the storage of data or in list processing. **4** (in *plural*) the scene of a contest. **5** LIST PRICE. • *verb* **1** make a list of. **2** enter in a list. **3** place (a property) in the hands of a real estate agent for sale or rent. **4** enter (a name and address) in a telephone directory. **5** *Computing* display or print out (a program, the contents of a file, etc.). **6** be specified in a list of prices: *the fishing reel lists at $4.95*. PHRASES **enter the lists** issue or accept a challenge: *at election time he entered the lists as a battler who genuinely enjoyed a scrap*.

list² • *verb* **1** (of a ship etc.) lean over to one side, esp. owing to a leak or shifting cargo (*compare* HEEL²). **2** (of a building etc.) lean over, tilt. • *noun* an instance of leaning over in this way: *had a distinct list to starboard*.

listed *adjective* **1** included in a list, directory, or catalogue. **2** (of securities etc.) approved for dealings on a stock exchange.

listen • *verb* **1 a** make an effort to hear something. **b** pay attention to (a person speaking or an utterance). **2** (also **listen out**) (often foll. by *for*) be eager or make a careful effort to catch the sound of. • *noun* an act of listening: *have a good listen*. PHRASES **listen in 1** listen secretly to or tap a private communication by telephone etc. **2** listen to a broadcast radio program etc. **3** listen to the conversation of others, often covertly and usu. without contributing. **listen up** *informal* pay attention.

listenable *adjective* easy or pleasant to listen to.

listener *noun* **1** a person who listens. **2** a person receiving broadcast radio programs.

listening *noun* **1** in senses of LISTEN. **2** (with qualifying adjective) broadcast, recorded, or other matter for listening to, esp. with reference to its quality or kind: *easy listening*.

listening post *noun* **1 a** a point near an enemy's lines for detecting movements by sound. **b** a station for intercepting electronic communications. **2** a place for the gathering of information from reports etc.

listeria *noun* any motile rod-like bacterium of the genus *Listeria*. [Say liss TEERY uh]

listeriosis *noun* infection with, or a disease caused by, listeria, contracted esp. by the ingestion of contaminated food or silage. [Say liss teery O sis]

listing¹ *noun* **1** a list or catalogue (see LIST¹ 1). **2 a** the drawing up of a list. **b** an entry in a catalogue, telephone directory, or other list. **3 a** the placing of a property on the list of a real estate agent. **b** a real estate agent's register of properties available for sale. **c** property so listed. **4** *Computing* a printed or displayed copy of a program or the contents of a file.

listing² *adjective* (of a ship etc.) inclining to one side.

listless *adjective* lacking energy or enthusiasm; disinclined for exertion. ▶ **listlessly** *adverb* **listlessness** *noun*

list price *noun* the price shown for an article in a printed list issued by the maker, or by the general body of makers of the particular class of goods.

list processing *noun* Computing the manipulation of data organized as lists.

listserv *noun* an e-mail system which automatically sends messages to all subscribers on specific mailing lists, in special interest groups, etc. [Say LIST serve]

lit[1] past and past participle of LIGHT[1],[2].

lit[2] *noun informal* literature.

litany *noun* (plural **litanies**) **1** a series of prayers or entreaties for use in church services or processions, usu. recited by the clergy and responded to in a recurring formula by the people. **2 a** a continuous repetition or long enumeration; a repeated formula. **b** a tedious recital: *a litany of woes.* [Say LITTA nee]

litchi *noun* = LYCHEE. [Say LEE chee]

lit crit *noun informal* literary criticism.

SPELL CHECK
lite, light

Don't use **lite** except for the senses indicated here; the standard spelling of the word is **light**.

---

lite • *adjective* **1** (also *proprietary* **Lite**) applied to low-fat or low-sugar versions of manufactured food or drink products, esp. to low-calorie beer. **2** *informal* lacking in substance; over-simplified: *the lite news on television has even less taste than tofu.* • *noun* **1** (also *proprietary* **Lite**) a light beer with relatively few calories. **2** a light, esp. a courtesy light in a motor vehicle. **3** a pane of glass, esp. in a door: *a tri-lite screen door.*

liter *noun* esp. US = LITRE.

literacy *noun* **1** the ability to read and write. **2** competence in some field of knowledge, technology, etc.: *computer literacy.*

WRITING TIP
literal, literally

In writing and formal speech, do not use *literal* and *literally* simply to add emphasis, as in *It was a literal flood of tears* and *Mamud ran like a jet, literally* — in these sentences the expressions "flood" and "like a jet" are *not* being used literally (i.e. they are not being used with their primary meanings), but *figuratively*.

---

literal *adjective* **1** taking words in their usual or primary sense without metaphor or allegory: *literal interpretation.* **2 a** (of a translation, version, transcript, etc.) following the letter, text, or exact or original words. **b** (of a representation in art or literature) exactly copied, true to life, realistic. **3** (also **literal-minded**) (of a person) apt to take what is spoken or written at face value, missing irony, humorous exaggeration, etc.; matter of fact. **4 a** without metaphor, exaggeration, or inaccuracy: *the literal truth.* **b** so called without exaggeration: *a literal extermination.* **5** *informal* disputed (as an intensifier) so called with some exaggeration or using metaphor: *a literal avalanche of mail.*

literalism *noun* **1** insistence on a literal interpretation; adherence to the letter: *insisted on the literalism of the scriptures.* **2** literal representation in art or literature: *the literalism of the battle scenes was disturbing.* ▶ **literalist** *noun* **literalistic** *adjective*

literally *adverb* **1** in a literal way; exactly: *the word planet literally means "wandering body"* ◊ *when I told you to "get lost" I didn't expect to be taken literally.* **2** used to emphasize the truth of something that may seem surprising: *there are literally hundreds of prizes to be won.* **3** *informal* used to emphasize a word or phrase that is being used in a figurative way: *I literally jumped out of my skin.*

literalness *noun* the quality or fact of being literal.

literariness *noun* the quality or fact of being literary.

literary *adjective* **1** of, constituting, or occupied with books or literature or written composition, esp. of the kind valued for quality of form. **2** well informed about literature. **3** (of a word or idiom) used chiefly in literary works or other formal writing. **4** (of painting, sculpture, etc.) depicting or representing a story.

literary critic *noun* a person who engages in literary criticism. ▶ **literary-critical** *adjective*

literary criticism *noun* the art or practice of judging and commenting on the qualities and character of literary works.

literary device *noun* any literary technique deliberately employed to achieve a specific effect, e.g. figures of speech etc.: *dramatic foreshadowing is an effective literary device.*

literate *adjective* **1** able to read and write. **2 a** well-read, cultured. **b** educated. **3** competent or well-versed in a specified area: *computer literate.* [Say LITTER it]

literati *plural noun* educated and intelligent people who produce or are well-versed in literature. [Say litter OTTY]

literature *noun* **1** written works, esp. those whose value lies in beauty of language or in emotional effect. **2** literary work or production as a whole. **3** the body of writings produced in a particular country or period. **4** printed matter, leaflets, etc. **5** the material in print on a particular subject.

lithe *adjective* **1** moving or bending easily and gracefully. **2** gracefully slim and muscled. ▶ **lithely** *adverb* [With LI as in LIE and THE as in BATHE]

lithium *noun* a soft silver-white metallic element, the lightest metal, used in alloys and in batteries. [Say LITH ee um]

litho *informal* • *noun* (plural **lithos**) **1** = LITHOGRAPHY. **2** = LITHOGRAPH. • *verb* (**lithoes**, **lithoed**, **lithoing**) produce by lithography. [Say LITH oh]

lithograph • *noun* a lithographic print. • *verb* print by lithography. [Say LITH uh graph]

lithographer *noun* a person who practises lithography. [Say lith OGGRA fur]

lithographic *adjective* of, pertaining to, or produced by lithography; engraved on stone. [Say lith uh GRAPHIC]

lithography *noun* a process of obtaining prints from a stone or metal surface so treated that what is to be printed can be inked but the remaining area rejects ink. [Say lith OGGRA fee]

lithosphere *noun* the rigid outer portion of the earth including the crust and the outermost mantle. ▶ **lithospheric** *adjective* [Say LITH us fear, lith us FEAR ick]

Lithuanian • *noun* **1 a** a native or inhabitant of Lithuania, a country on the shore of the Baltic Sea. **b** a person of Lithuanian descent. **2** the language of Lithuania. • *adjective* of or relating to Lithuania or its people or language. [Say lith oo AY nee in or lith you AY nee in]

litigant *noun* a party to a lawsuit. [Say LITTA gint (with G as in GIVE)]

litigate *verb* (**litigates**, **litigated**, **litigating**) **1** take a claim or dispute to a law court; be a party to a lawsuit: *the dilemma has focused on the kind of interest necessary for a plaintiff to be allowed to litigate.* **2** contest (a point) in a lawsuit: *the interests of the parties are always best served by settling rather than by litigating issues.* [Say LITTA gate]

litigation *noun* the action or process of carrying on a lawsuit: *the matter is in litigation.* [Say litta GAY sh'n]

litigator *noun* a person who litigates, esp. a trial lawyer. [Say LITTA gator]

litigious *adjective* too ready to take disputes to a court of law: *especially litigious members of the public may choose to litigate many matters in which they have no direct interest.*

▶**litigiously** *adverb* **litigiousness** *noun* [Say luh TIDGE us]

litmus *noun* a dye obtained from lichens that is red under acid conditions and blue under alkaline conditions. [Say LIT mus]

litmus paper *noun* a paper stained with litmus to be used as a test for acids or alkalis.

litmus test *noun* **1** *informal* a circumstance, phenomenon, question, etc., one's reaction to which serves to establish decisively the true character of an individual etc.: *they invoked a particular understanding of scripture as a litmus test for orthodoxy.* **2** a test for acids or alkalis using litmus paper.

litre *noun* a metric unit of capacity, formerly defined as the volume of one kilogram of water under standard conditions, now equal to 1 cubic decimetre (about 35 oz.).

litter • *noun* **1 a** garbage discarded in an open or public place. **b** odds and ends lying about. **2** a state of untidiness, disorderly accumulation of papers etc. **3** a group of young mammalian animals comprising all those born at one birth. **4** decomposing but still recognizable vegetable debris from plants etc. forming a distinct layer above the soil, esp. in a forest. **5** esp. *hist.* a vehicle containing a couch shut in by curtains and carried on men's shoulders or by beasts of burden. **6** a stretcher or portable bed for transporting the sick and wounded. **7 a** straw, rushes, etc., as bedding, esp. for animals. **b** straw and dung in a farmyard. **8** = CAT LITTER. • *verb* **1 a** make (a place) untidy with litter. **b** leave paper, garbage, etc. lying about, esp. in a public place. **2 a** scatter (paper etc.) untidily and leave lying about. **b** (of things) lie about untidily on: *old car parts littered the premises.* **3** (of an animal) give birth to.

litter box *noun* a tray for cat litter.

litterbug *noun* a person who carelessly leaves litter in a public place.

little • *adjective* (**littler**, **littlest**; **less** or **lesser**; **least**) **1** small in size, amount, degree, etc. **2** (preceded by *a*) a certain though small amount of: *a little cream.* **3** trivial; relatively unimportant: *exaggerates every little difficulty.* **4** (of a town, district, etc.) less large or important, later established, or suggestive of another or others of that name: *Little Italy.* **5** young or younger: *a little boy* ◊ *my little sister.* • *noun* **1** not much; only a small amount: *got very little out of it.* **2 a** a certain but no great amount: *knows a little of everything.* **b** a short time or distance: *after a little.* • *adverb* (**less**, **least**) **1 a** to a small extent only: *little-known authors* ◊ *is little more than speculation.* **b** infrequently, rarely. **2** (preceded by *a*) somewhat: *is a little deaf.* **3** not at all; hardly: *they little thought.* PHRASES **little by little** by degrees; gradually. **little or nothing** hardly anything. **no little** considerable, a good deal of: *took no little trouble over it.* **not a little 1** much; a great deal. **2** extremely: *not a little concerned.* **quite a little** a lot, much, considerably.

little-bitty *adjective informal* very small; tiny.

little black book *noun* a record or list of information, esp. of names and addresses of sexual partners.

little ice age *noun* any period of comparatively cold climate occurring outside the major ice ages, esp. (**Little Ice Age**) such a period which reached its peak in the 17th century.

Little League *noun* a baseball league for children between ages 8 and 12.

littleneck *noun* (also **littleneck clam**) a small variety of quahog.

little red schoolhouse *noun* **1** a one-room schoolhouse, esp. one of red brick, of a design that was typical throughout North America, esp. in rural areas, from the 19th to the mid-20th century. **2** (**the little red schoolhouse**) this as a symbol of old-fashioned educational practice, with all grades taught in the same room, emphasis on basics, rote learning, etc.

littoral • *adjective* of or on the shore of the sea, a lake, etc.: *the littoral sheikhdoms looked to the sea, not to the turbulent, decaying interior.* • *noun* a region lying along a shore: *the land expeditions made their way towards the Arctic littoral.* [Say LITTER ul]

liturgical *adjective* of liturgies or public religious worship. ▶**liturgically** *adverb* [Say li TUR ji cull]

liturgy *noun* (*plural* **liturgies**) **1 a** a form according to which public esp. Christian religious worship is conducted: *St James's proudly retained the Anglo-Catholic liturgy.* **b** a religious service conducted according to such a form: *his funeral was one of the first liturgies to be celebrated in the church.* **2** the Communion office of the Orthodox Church. [Say LITTER jee]

livability *noun* suitability for habitation.

livable *adjective* **1** (of a house, room, climate, etc.) fit to live in. **2** (of a life) bearable; worth living. **3** (of a person) companionable; easy to live with.

live[1] *verb* (**lives**, **lived**, **living**) **1** remain alive. **2** be alive at a specified time. **3** spend one's life in a particular way or under particular circumstances: *they are living in fear.* **4** make one's home in a particular place or with a particular person. **5** supply oneself with the means of subsistence: *they live by hunting and fishing.* **6** survive in someone's mind. **7** enjoy life intensely or to the full: *you haven't lived till you've seen Robert Tewsley dance.* PHRASES **live and breathe** be utterly absorbed or consumed by (an interest). **live and learn** expressing surprise at some new or unexpected information. **live and let live** be tolerant towards others of different opinions, lifestyles, etc. **live dangerously** take risks habitually. **live down** (usu. with *neg.*) cause (past guilt, embarrassment, etc.) to be forgotten by different conduct over a period of time: *you'll never live that down!* **live for** regard as the aim or purpose of one's life: *she lives for her work.* **live in the past** behave as though circumstances, values, etc. have not changed from what they were previously. **live it up** *informal* pursue pleasure, live extravagantly. **live off the land** subsist on the produce of the land. **live one's own life** follow one's own plans or principles; live independently. **live out 1** spend the rest of (one's life): *will I live out my days as a lexicographer?* **2** experience or execute in reality (one's fantasies, ideas, etc.). **live together** (esp. of an unmarried couple) share a home and have a sexual relationship. **live up to 1** honour or fulfill; put into practice (principles etc.). **2** reach and maintain an expected standard, either good or bad. **live with 1** share a home with. **2** share a home and have a sexual relationship with. **3** tolerate; endure. **live with oneself** retain one's self-respect. **long live…!** an exclamation of support, loyalty, or endorsement (to a person etc. specified). **where one lives** at, to, or in the right, vital, or most vulnerable spot: *hits me where I live.*

live[2] • *adjective* **1** living. **2** (of a musical performance) given in concert; not recorded. **3** (of a broadcast) transmitted at the time of occurrence; not recorded. **4** of current or continuing interest and importance. **5** (of a wire or device) connected to a source of electric current. **6** of, containing, or using undetonated explosive. **7** (of coals) burning. **8** (of a vaccine) containing living but weakened disease-causing micro-organisms. • *adverb* in order to make a live broadcast; as a live performance: *going over live now to the House of Commons.* PHRASES **go live** *Computing* (of a system) become operational.

liveable *adjective* = LIVABLE.

live action *noun Film* action involving real people or animals, as opposed to animation etc.

lived-in *adjective* **1** (of a room etc.) showing signs of habitation. **2** *informal* (of a face) marked by experience.

live-in • *adjective* **1** (of a sexual partner) cohabiting. **2** (of a servant etc.) residing on the premises of one's work. • *noun* a live-in employee, lover, etc.

livelihood *noun* a way of earning a living; an occupation. [Say LIVELY hood]

liveliness *noun* the quality of being lively; energy, excitement. [Say LIVELY ness]

livelong *adjective* in its entire length or apparently so: *the livelong day*. [Say LIVE long]

lively *adjective* (**livelier, liveliest**) **1** full of life; vigorous, energetic. **2** brisk: *a lively pace* ◊ *a lively tune*. **3** vivid, stimulating: *a lively discussion* ◊ *a lively imagination*. **4** (of a person, group, etc.) vivacious, jolly, sociable. **5** *jocular* exciting, dangerous, difficult: *the press is making things lively for them*. **6** (of a colour) bright and vivid. **7 a** (of an image, picture, etc.) lifelike, realistic, animated: *a lively description*. **b** (of feelings, impressions, memories, etc.) strong, intense, striking. **8** (of a narrative) full of action and incident. **9** (of food) tasty, esp. spicy. PHRASES **step** (or **look**) **lively** move (more) quickly or energetically.

liven *verb* (usu. foll. by *up*) *informal* **1** make or become more lively. **2** cheer; brighten. [Say LIVE in (LIVE rhymes with *DIVE*)]

liver¹ *noun* **1 a** a large, lobed, glandular organ in the abdomen of vertebrates, functioning in many metabolic processes including the regulation of toxic materials in the blood, secreting bile, etc. **b** a similar organ in other animals. **2** the flesh of an animal's liver as food. **3** a dark reddish brown.

liver² *noun* a person who lives in a specified way: *a clean liver*.

liveried *adjective* (of a servant) wearing the distinctive uniform of a household. [Say LIVER eed]

liver spots *plural noun* brown spots or patches of melanin on the skin, characteristic of any of several medical conditions. ▶ **liverspotted** *adjective*

liverwurst *noun* (also **liver sausage**) a cooked sausage having a high proportion of esp. pork liver. [Say LIVER wurst]

livery *noun* (*plural* **liveries**) **1** a distinctive uniform worn by servants in a particular household etc. **2** a distinctive marking or outward appearance: *birds in their winter livery*. **3** an emblem, design, or distinctive colour scheme on a vehicle, product, etc. indicating its owner or manufacturer. **4** a place where horses can be hired. [Say LIVER ee]

livery stable *noun* (also **livery barn**) a stable where horses are kept for their owners in return for payment, or from which horses may be rented.

lives *plural of* LIFE.

livestock *noun* (usu. treated as *plural*) animals kept esp. on a farm for use or profit, e.g. cattle etc. [With LIVE rhyming with *DIVE*]

live trap • *noun* a box-like trap for catching esp. wild animals alive and without hurting them. • *verb* (**live-trap, live-traps, live-trapped, live-trapping**) catch (an animal) in such a trap for relocation etc.

livewell *noun* a tub-like container of water in a fishing boat, often aerated and sunk flush with the deck, in which caught fish are kept alive and fresh. [With LIVE rhyming with *DIVE*]

live wire *noun* **1** an energetic and forceful person. **2** a wire conveying an electric current.

liveyer *noun Cdn (Nfld)* = LIVYER. [Say LIV yer]

livid *adjective* **1** *informal* furiously angry: *he became livid* and grabbed the wire fence and yelled at the fans to shut up. **2** of an intense reddish colour: *the livid torches illuminating their picturesque costumes*. **3** of a bluish leaden colour, like a bruise. ▶ **lividly** *adverb* [Say LIV id]

living • *noun* **1** means of keeping alive or living in a certain style: *made my living as a journalist*. **2** the action of leading one's life in a particular moral, physical, etc. manner. **3** (preceded by *the*; treated as *plural*) those who are alive. • *adjective* **1 a** that lives or has life; not dead or extinct. **b** contemporary; now existent: *the greatest living poet*. **2** (of a likeness or image of a person) exact. **3** (of a language) still in vernacular use. **4** (of water) perennially flowing. **5** (of rock etc.) still forming part of the earth's mass. **6** *informal* complete, entire: *scared the living daylights out of him*. PHRASES **within living memory** within the memory of people still living.

living colour *noun* vivid or true-to-life colour.

living museum *noun* (also **living history museum**) **1** a historic site, or a recreation of one, at which historical interpreters dress in period costume, perform period-specific tasks and trades, etc. **2** a place where plants that have been wiped out everywhere else can still be found growing naturally.

living room *noun* a room in a private home for general use during the daytime.

living standard *noun* the level of consumption in terms of food, clothing, services, etc. estimated for a person, group, or nation.

living wage *noun* the lowest wage on which a person can afford a reasonable standard of living without undue hardship.

living will *noun* a written declaration, morally though in many jurisdictions not legally binding, by a person setting out the circumstances in which artificial means of maintaining his or her life should be withdrawn.

livre *noun* an old French monetary unit, worth one pound of silver. [Say LEEV ruh]

livyer *noun Cdn (Nfld)* a resident or permanent settler in Newfoundland or Labrador. [Say LIV yer]

lizard *noun* **1** a reptile that typically has a long body and tail, four legs, movable eyelids, and a rough or scaly hide. **2** leather made from lizard skin.

ll. *abbreviation* lines (in references).

'll *verb* **1** (usu. after pronouns) shall, will: *I'll* ◊ *that'll*. **2** *informal* (usu. after verbs) till: *wait'll they see me!*

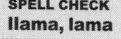
SPELL CHECK
llama, lama

A Buddhist monk is a **lama**.

llama *noun* (*plural* **llamas**) **1** a South American animal of the camel family, kept as a beast of burden and for its soft woolly fleece. **2** the wool from this animal, or cloth made from it. [Say LAMMA or LOMMA]

LL.B. *abbreviation* Bachelor of Laws.

LNG *abbreviation* liquefied natural gas.

lo¹ *interjection archaic* or *jocular* calling attention to an amazing sight. PHRASES **lo and behold** a formula introducing a surprising or unexpected fact.

lo² *adjective* low, used esp. in advertising etc.: *lo-cal*.

SPELL CHECK
load, lode

A vein of ore or a rich supply source is a **motherlode**.

load • *noun* **1** a heavy or bulky thing being or about to be carried. **2** a weight or source of pressure. **3** the total number or amount carried in a vehicle or container. **4 (a load/loads of)** *informal* a lot of. **5** the amount of work to be done by a person or machine. **6** the amount

of power supplied by a source. **7** a burden of responsibility, worry, or grief. • *verb* **1** put a load on or in. **2** place a load or large quantity on or in a vehicle, container, etc. **3** insert something into a device so that it will operate. **4** charge a firearm with ammunition. **5** bias toward a particular outcome. PHRASES **a load off one's mind** (or **back** etc.) a source of anxiety removed. **get a load of** *slang* listen attentively to; notice. **load the bases** *Baseball* place baserunners on all three bases. **take a load off (one's feet)** *informal* sit or lie down; take the body's weight off the feet. ▶ **loadable** *adjective*

loaded *adjective* **1** bearing or carrying a load. **2** *slang* **a** wealthy. **b** drunk. **c** drugged. **3** (of dice etc.) weighted or given a bias to enable cheating. **4** (of a question or statement) charged with some hidden or improper implication. **5** *informal* (of a car etc.) equipped with optional extras. PHRASES **loaded for bear** *slang* fully prepared, esp. for a fight.

loader *noun* **1 a** a machine or device for loading things. **b** = FRONT-END LOADER. **2** *Computing* a program which controls the loading of other programs. **3** a gun, machine, vessel, etc. that is loaded in a specified way. ▶ **-loading** *adjective* (in *combination*) (in sense 3).

loading *noun* **1** the application of a load to something. **2** the amount of load applied. **3** an increase in an insurance premium due to an extra factor of risk. **4** *informal* massive consumption of a particular substance etc. to enhance one's performance: *carbo-loading*.

loaf¹ *noun* (*plural* **loaves**) **1** a portion of baked bread, usu. of a standard size or shape. **2** a quantity of other food formed into a particular, usu. oblong shape: *meat loaf*. **3** (also **loaf cake**) a plain cake, usu. including fruit or nuts, baked in an oblong shape. PHRASES **half a loaf is better than none** (or **no bread**) **1** having to accept less than one expects or feels entitled to is better than having nothing at all. **2** it is better to compromise in one's demands than to risk losing all.

loaf² *verb* **1** (often foll. by *about*, *around*) spend time idly; hang about. **2** move slowly or easily: *I'm content to loaf along in a backstroke rather than churning out laps*.

loafer *noun* **1** an idle person. **2** (**Loafer**) *proprietary* a leather shoe shaped like a moccasin with a flat heel.

loam *noun* **1** a fertile soil of clay and sand containing decayed vegetable matter. **2** a paste of clay and water with sand, chopped straw, etc., used in making bricks, plastering, etc. ▶ **loamy** *adjective*

loan • *noun* **1** something lent, esp. a sum of money to be returned, normally with interest. **2** the act of lending or state of being lent. **3** a word, custom, etc., adopted by one people from another. • *verb* lend (esp. money). PHRASES **on loan** acquired or given as a loan.

loaner *noun* **1** a car, computer, etc. lent to a customer while the customer's is kept for repair or service: *loaner car*. **2** a lender.

loan shark *noun informal* a person who lends money at exorbitant rates of interest. ▶ **loansharking** *noun*

loath *adjective* disinclined, reluctant, unwilling: *was loath to admit it*. [With TH as in *BATH*]

loathe *verb* (**loathes, loathed, loathing**) regard with disgust; detest: *in high school I was subjected to dancing lessons, which I loathed*. ▶ **loather** *noun* **loathing** *noun* [With TH as in *BATHE*]

loathsome *adjective* arousing hatred or disgust; offensive, repulsive. ▶ **loathsomeness** *noun* [Say LOTHE sum (with LOTHE either like *LOATH* or like *LOATHE*)]

loaves *plural of* LOAF¹.

LOB *abbreviation Baseball* left on base.

lob • *verb* (**lobs, lobbed, lobbing**) **1** hit or throw (a ball etc.) slowly or in a high arc. **2** fire (a rocket or other missile) in a high arc. **3** send (an opponent) a lobbed ball. **4** direct (questions, insults, accusations, etc.) at a person. • *noun* **1 a** a ball struck or thrown in a high arc. **b** a stroke producing this result. **2** *Cdn* (also **lob ball**) a question that is easy to answer, esp. one that is made intentionally so in order to make the respondent look competent, articulate, etc.: *the speaker was accused of permitting too many lobs from backbenchers*.

lobby • *noun* (*plural* **lobbies**) **1** a usu. large area inside the main entrance of a building leading to other rooms, or to the auditorium in a theatre etc. **2 a** a body of persons seeking to influence legislators on behalf of a particular interest: *the anti-abortion lobby*. **b** an organized attempt by members of the public to influence legislators. **3** (also **division lobby**) each of two areas on either side of the Commons chamber in which MPs may relax or discuss party strategy and in which they assemble before a vote. • *verb* (**lobbies, lobbied, lobbying**) **1** solicit the support of (an influential person). **2 a** (of members of the public) seek to influence (the members of a legislature). **b** attempt to persuade a politician to support or oppose changes in the law: *fishermen lobbying for higher quotas*. ▶ **lobbying** *noun & adjective* **lobbyist** *noun*

lobe *noun* **1** a roundish and flattish projecting or pendulous part, often each of two or more such parts divided by a fissure: *lobes of the brain*. **2** = EARLOBE. ▶ **lobed** *adjective*

lobelia *noun* (*plural* **lobelias**) a popular low-growing garden plant with blue, scarlet, white, or purple flowers and a deeply cleft corolla. [Say lo BEELY uh]

lobotomize *verb* (**lobotomizes, lobotomized, lobotomizing**) **1** perform a lobotomy on. **2** (usu. as **lobotomized** *adjective*) make (a person) apathetic or zombie-like. [Say luh BOTTA mize]

lobotomy *noun* (*plural* **lobotomies**) a rare medical operation that cuts into the frontal lobe of the brain, formerly used to treat mental illness. [Say luh BOTTA mee]

lobster *noun* **1** any large marine crustacean with a cylindrical body, stalked eyes, and two pincer-like claws as the first of five pairs of limbs. **2** its flesh as food.

lobstering *noun* the catching of lobsters, esp. by commercial fishermen.

lobsterman *noun* (*plural* **lobstermen**) a person who traps lobster for a living.

lobster pot *noun* a device for trapping lobster, esp. one made of wooden slats.

lobster pound *noun* a place where lobsters trapped during the season are kept alive until they are sold and shipped.

lobster roll *noun* a long bread roll stuffed with a mixture of lobster meat, celery, onion, mayonnaise, etc.

lobster supper *noun Cdn* (*Maritimes*) a meal, usu. served in a community hall, featuring boiled lobster, salads, bread rolls, clam chowder, and cake or pie.

lobster thermidor *noun* a mixture of lobster meat, mushrooms, cream, egg yolks, and sherry, cooked in a lobster shell. [Say THERMA dore]

local • *adjective* **1** belonging to, existing in, or pertaining to a particular locality as opposed to the country as a whole. **2** limited, peculiar to, or only encountered in a particular place or places. **3 a** of or belonging to the neighbourhood: *the local doctor*. **b** (of a train, bus, etc.) serving a particular district or stopping at all or most stations or stops on the line or route. **4** of or affecting a part and not the whole, esp. of the body: *local pain* ◊ *a local anaesthetic*. **5** (of a telephone call) to a nearby place and not subject to long-distance charges. • *noun* **1** an inhabitant of a particular place regarded

with reference to that place. **2** a local train, bus, etc. **3** a local branch of a trade union. **4** a local anaesthetic.

local area network *noun* a computer network in which computers in close proximity are able to communicate with each other and share resources.

local bus *noun* (*plural* **local buses**) **1** a bus service operating over short distances. **2** a computer connection from a microprocessor to an adjacent peripheral device such as a video system, allowing rapid transmission of data.

local colour *noun* the typical things, customs, etc. in a place that make it interesting, and that are used in a picture, story, or film to make it seem real: *through the use of local colour and culturally identifiable still-life objects, she entered into the consciousness of the Mediterranean world.*

locale *noun* a scene or locality, esp. with reference to an event etc. taking place there: *he has acquired orchids from Hawaii and other exotic locales.* [Say lo CAL]

localism *noun* **1 a** preference for what is local or attachment to the place where one lives: *radio broadcasters are fearful that satellite broadcasting will destroy localism in favour of stations with a national reach.* **b** a limitation of ideas, sympathies, and interests resulting from such attachment. **2** a local idiom, custom, etc.: *her parents drilled the localisms out of her speech.*

locality *noun* (*plural* **localities**) **1** an area or district considered as the site occupied by certain people or things or as the scene of certain activities; a neighbourhood. **2** the site or scene of something, esp. in relation to its surroundings. **3** the situation or position of an object, esp. the geographical place or situation of a plant, mineral, etc.

localization *noun* an action or an act of localizing; the state of being localized.

localize *verb* (**localizes**, **localized**, **localizing**) **1** restrict or assign to a particular place. **2** (foll. by *in*) (of a disease or causative agent of disease) be confined to (a specified area of the body). ▶ **localized** *adjective*

locally *adverb* with regard to a particular place or part; in certain districts; in the locality specified or alluded to: *do you live locally?* ◊ *locally grown fruit.*

local time *noun* **1** the time as reckoned in a particular place. **2** time measured from the sun's transit over the meridian of a place.

locate *verb* (**locates**, **located**, **locating**) **1** discover the exact place or position of: *locate the enemy's camp.* **2** establish in a place or in its proper place. **3** state the locality of. **4** (in *passive*) be situated. **5** (often foll. by *in*) take up residence or business (in a place).

location *noun* **1** a particular place; the place or position in which a person or thing is. **2** the act of locating or process of being located. **3** an actual place or natural setting featured in a film or broadcast, as distinct from a simulation in a studio: *filmed on location.* **4** *Computing* = ADDRESS 1c, 1d. ▶ **locational** *adjective*

location ticket *noun* Cdn hist. a certificate entitling a settler to take possession of a piece of land as a homestead, but not conveying legal title.

locator *noun* a device which locates or is used for locating something, e.g. downed aircraft.

loc. cit. *abbreviation* in the passage already cited.

loch *noun* (in Scotland) **1** a lake. **2** an arm of the sea, esp. when narrow or partially landlocked. [Say LOCK]

loci[1] *plural of* LOCUS. [Say LO sigh]

loci[2] *noun* (*plural* **locis**) (also **locie**, *plural* **locies**) Cdn informal an engine used in logging or mining. [Say LO key]

lock[1] • *noun* **1** a device for fastening a door, lid, etc., which can only be opened by means of a key, combination, code, etc. **2** a confined section of a canal or river where the level can be changed for raising and lowering boats between adjacent sections by the use of gates and sluices. **3 a** the turning of the front wheels of a vehicle to change its direction of motion. **b** the maximum extent of this. **4** an interlocked or jammed state. **5** *Wrestling* a hold that keeps an opponent's limb fixed. **6** an appliance to keep a wheel from revolving or slewing. **7** a mechanism for exploding the charge of a gun. **8** = AIRLOCK 2. **9** *informal* a sure thing; a person or thing that is certain to succeed: *she is a lock to win the election.* • *verb* **1 a** fasten with a lock. **b** (of a door, window, box, etc.) have the means of being locked. **2** (foll. by *up*, *in*, *into*) enclose (a person or thing) by locking or as if by locking. **3** (often foll. by *up*, *away*) store or allocate inaccessibly: *capital locked up in land.* **4** make or become rigidly fixed or immovable. **5** become or cause to become jammed or caught. **6** (often in *passive*; foll. by *in*) entangle in an embrace or struggle. **7** interlace or intertwine: *the protesters locked arms.* PHRASES **lock down** subject (a prisoner or prisoners) to a lockdown. **have a lock on** *informal* have an unbreakable hold on or total control over: *she has a lock on her seat in the legislature.* **lock horns** come into conflict; engage in an argument. **be locked into** be irrevocably committed to: *am locked into going to this stupid party.* **lock in 1** (usu. in *passive*) convert (a mortgage) from a floating to a fixed rate of interest. **2** (of an investor) be unable to sell or convert (investments). **3** fix (a pension, investment, etc.) so that it cannot be transferred or sold. **lock on to** locate or cause to locate by radar, a heat-seeking device, etc., and then track. **lock oneself out** accidentally prevent oneself from entering a place, esp. by losing the key or locking it inside: *locked myself out of my car.* **lock out 1** keep (a person) out by locking the door. **2** (of an employer) submit (employees) to a lockout. **lock up 1** shut and secure (a building) by locking: *I'll lock up.* **2** imprison: *locked up for life.* **3** commit to a psychiatric institution. **4** (of a computer or computer screen) cease to respond to input from the keyboard or mouse. **5** (esp. of a turning object) cease to move; seize: *slammed on the brakes and her wheels locked up.* **6** store; hold in reserve: *Canada's forests lock up huge amounts of carbon.* **7** have complete control of; be assured of success in: *her party has locked up Ontario.* **under lock and key** securely locked up.

lock[2] *noun* **1** a portion of hair that coils or hangs together. **2** (in *plural*) the hair of the head. ▶ **-locked** *adjective* (in *combination*).

lockable *adjective* that can be locked.

lockdown *noun* the confining of prisoners to their cells, esp. to gain control during a riot etc.

locked-in retirement account *noun* Cdn a retirement savings account created with money transferred out of a registered pension plan and from which funds can only be transferred to a life income fund, a locked-in retirement income fund, or a life annuity. Abbreviation: **LIRA**.

locked-in retirement income fund *noun* Cdn a tax-sheltered savings plan which provides retirement income. Abbreviation: **LRIF**.

locker *noun* **1 a** small lockable cupboard or compartment, esp. one of several in a school, bus

station, locker room, etc. **2** *Nautical* a chest or compartment for clothes, stores, ammunition, etc. **3** a person or thing that locks.

locker room • *noun* a change room at a swimming pool, fitness club, etc., with lockers for storing one's clothes etc. • *adjective* (usu. **locker-room**) (of language etc.) characteristic of or suited to a men's locker room, esp. as being vulgar or containing rude or irreverent reference to sexual matters: *locker-room humour*.

locket *noun* a small ornamental case holding a portrait, lock of hair, etc., and usu. hung from the neck.

lockjaw *noun* a variety of tetanus with sustained contractions of the jaw muscles causing the mouth to remain tightly closed.

lockout *noun* the exclusion of employees by their employer from their place of work until certain terms are agreed to.

locksmith *noun* a person who makes, repairs, and replaces locks. ▶ **locksmithing** *noun*

lockstep • *noun* marching with each person as close as possible to the one in front. • *adjective* rigid; inflexible: *boring, lockstep critics*. ▰ PHRASES **in lockstep** exactly parallel; in exact synchronism: *the universities were in lockstep with fascism* ◊ *the trio marched in lockstep*.

lock, stock, and barrel • *noun* the whole of a thing. • *adverb* completely: *he sold the business lock, stock, and barrel*.

lock-up *noun* **1** *informal* = JAIL *noun* 1. **2** *Cdn* a type of press conference where members of the media are allowed to examine a government budget in a locked room before it is brought down in the legislature, but are not allowed to leave the room or file any reports until the budget is officially brought down. **3** the locking up of premises for the night.

loco¹ *noun* (*plural* **locos**) *informal* a locomotive engine.

loco² • *adjective* *slang* crazy. • *noun* (*plural* **locos**) (also **locoweed**) a poisonous plant of North America causing brain disease in cattle eating it.

locomotion *noun* motion or the power of motion from one place to another. [Say lo kuh MOTION]

locomotive • *noun* an engine, powered by diesel fuel or electricity, used for pulling trains. • *adjective* of or relating to or effecting locomotion: *locomotive power*. [Say lo kuh MOTIVE]

locus *noun* (*plural* **loci**) **1** the centre or source of something: *the locus of power has shifted*. **2** *Math* a curve etc. formed by all the points satisfying a particular equation of the relation between coordinates, or by a point, line, or surface moving according to mathematically defined conditions. **3** the position of a gene, mutation, etc. on a chromosome. **4** a position or point: *shallow inward dips toward a locus beneath the central plateau*. [Say LO cuss for the singular, LO sigh for the plural]

locust *noun* **1** a large grasshopper with great flying ability, which sometimes migrates in swarms, causing extensive damage to crops. **2** a cicada. **3** (also **locust bean**) the large edible pod of certain plants, esp. a carob bean. **4** (also **locust tree**) **a** any of a number of pod-bearing trees of the pea family, esp. the carob tree. **b** a North American tree bearing fragrant white flowers and black pods, grown as an ornamental. [Say LO kist]

locution *noun* **1** a word or phrase, esp. considered in regard to style or idiom: *attacked his adversary with several colourful locutions*. **2** style of speech: *a Dylan Thomas-like locution*. ▶ **locutionary** *adjective* [Say lo CUE sh'n]

lode *noun* **1** a vein of metal ore: *the company bought up 23 lode claims*. **2** a rich source or plentiful supply: *your book is a lode of wisdom*.

lodestone *noun* **1** a piece of magnetite or any other

naturally magnetized mineral, able to be used as a magnet. **2** a thing that attracts: *he set off to reach the goal that would be his abiding lodestone*.

lodge • *noun* **1** a hotel or inn, esp. in a resort area. **2** the main building in a resort or summer camp, usu. containing a dining area etc. **3** *Cdn* (esp. in proper names) an old people's home. **4** a house occupied in the hunting or fishing season. **5** a North American Indian's tent or wigwam. **6** a small house at the gates of a park or in the grounds of a large house, occupied by a gatekeeper, gardener, etc. **7 a** the meeting place of a branch of a society such as the Freemasons. **b** the members of such a local branch. **8** a beaver's or otter's lair. • *verb* (**lodges**, **lodged**, **lodging**) **1** deposit in court or with an official a formal statement of (complaint or information). **2** deposit (money etc.) for security. **3** bring forward (an objection etc.). **4** (foll. by *in, with*) place (power etc.) in a person or group. **5** make or become fixed or caught without further movement: *the bullet lodged in his spine* ◊ *the plans are securely lodged in her brain*. **6 a** provide with sleeping quarters. **b** receive as a guest or inhabitant. **c** establish as a resident in a house or room or rooms. **7** reside or live, esp. as a guest paying for accommodation. **8** serve as a habitation for.

lodgepole *noun* **1** a pole used to support a teepee or wigwam. **2** (also **lodgepole pine**) a pine native to mountainous regions of northwestern North America.

lodger *noun* a person receiving accommodation in another's house for payment.

lodging *noun* **1** temporary accommodation: *a lodging for the night*. **2** (in *plural*) a room or rooms rented for lodging in on a relatively long-term basis. **3** a dwelling.

lods et ventes *plural noun* *Cdn* (*Que.*) *hist.* a seigneurial right to one-twelfth of the purchase price of an estate changing hands by sale or transfer. [Say loze ay VONT]

loess *noun* a deposit of fine light-coloured wind-blown dust found esp. in the basins of large rivers and very fertile when irrigated. [Say LO ess]

loft • *noun* **1** a room or space directly under the roof of a house, used as storage or living space. **2** a space under the roof of a barn or stable etc., used esp. for storing hay and straw. **3** a gallery or upper level in a church or hall: *choir loft*. **4 a** an upper room or floor of a large building, factory, etc., sometimes converted into apartments, studios, etc. **b** an apartment built into a former warehouse or office building, esp. one having high ceilings and an open concept design. **5** the resilience of a fabric, esp. wool. **6** the thickness of insulating matter in something, e.g. a sleeping bag or down-filled coat. **7** *Golf* **a** a backward slope on the head of a club. **b** a lofting stroke. • *verb* **1 a** send (a ball etc.) high up. **b** clear (an obstacle) in this way. **2** (esp. as **lofted** *adjective*) give a loft to (a golf club).

loftily *adverb* haughtily, condescendingly: *our leader loftily informed us he had outgrown such kid stuff*.

lofty *adjective* (**loftier**, **loftiest**) **1** (of things) of imposing height, towering, soaring: *lofty heights*. **2** consciously haughty, aloof, or dignified: *lofty contempt*. **3** exalted or noble; sublime: *lofty ideals*.

log¹ • *noun* **1 a** a part of the trunk of a tree or of a large branch that has fallen or been cut down. **b** something long and cylindrical: *shape the dough into a log*. **2 a** *hist.* a float attached to a line wound on a reel for gauging the speed of a ship. **b** any other apparatus for the same purpose. **3** a record of events occurring during and affecting the voyage of a ship or aircraft. **4** = LOGBOOK. **5** any systematic record of things done, experienced, etc. • *verb* (**logs**, **logged**, **logging**) **1** clear (a region) of trees. **2** cut (a tree) into logs. **3** fell timber and cut the wood into logs. **4 a** enter (the distance made or other details) in a ship's logbook. **b** enter details about (a

person or event) in a logbook. **c** (of a ship) achieve (a certain distance). **5 a** enter (information) in a regular record. **b** attain (a cumulative total of time etc. recorded in this way): *logged 50 hours.* PHRASES **log off** (or **out**) go through the procedures to conclude use of a computer system. **log on** (or **in**) go through the procedures to begin use of a computer system.

log² *noun* a logarithm (esp. prefixed to a number or algebraic symbol whose logarithm is to be indicated).

logan *noun Cdn* (*Nfld*) a leather boot with a rubber foot, reaching to below the knee, worn in winter or when working in the bush. [Say LO gun]

loganberry *noun* (*plural* **loganberries**) **1** a hybrid between a blackberry and a raspberry, with dark red acid fruits. **2** the fruit of this plant. [Say LO gun berry]

logarithm *noun* a figure representing the power to which a fixed number or base must be raised to produce a given number: *the logarithm of 1,000 to base 10 is 3*, used to simplify calculations as the addition and subtraction of logarithms is equivalent to multiplication and division. ▶ **logarithmic** *adjective* [Say LOGGA rhythm, logga RHYTHMIC]

logbook *noun* **1** a book containing a detailed record of things done or experienced. **2** a book in which particulars of aircraft flights etc. are recorded.

log boom *noun* = BOOM² 2b.

log bronc *noun Cdn* (*BC*) a tugboat used to direct a log boom or to gather logs in the booming grounds.

log cabin *noun* **1** (also **log house**) a house or cabin with walls made of logs. **2** designating a quilt pattern in which square blocks are made up of a small square centre section surrounded by rectangular strips of increasing length.

log chute *noun Cdn* a chute constructed to allow logs being driven down a river to bypass a waterfall etc.

log drive *noun Cdn* the transporting of logs from the bush to the mills by floating them down rivers etc. ▶ **log driver** *noun*

log dump *noun* a place where logs are piled, such as on a riverbank, near a road or railway, etc., in preparation for being moved to the mill.

logged-over *adjective* (also **logged-off**, **logged-out**) (of a tract of forest) that has been logged.

logger *noun* a person who fells trees and prepares timber for milling.

loggerhead *noun* any of various large-headed animals, esp.: **1** a reddish-brown turtle found esp. in warm seas. **2** a North American shrike with mainly grey plumage and a black tail and wings. PHRASES **at loggerheads** disagreeing or disputing.

loggia *noun* (*plural* **loggias**) **1** an open-sided gallery or arcade. **2** an open-sided extension of a house. [Say LO juh or LODGE uh]

logging *noun* the work of cutting and preparing forest timber.

logging division *noun Cdn* a tract of forest being logged by loggers resident in a single logging camp.

logging road *noun* an unimproved road into a forest area, used for logging purposes.

logic *noun* **1 a** a way of thinking or explaining something: *I don't follow your logic* ◊ *your logic is flawed*. **b** sensible reasons for doing something: *there is no logic to their claims*. **2** the science of reasoning, proof, thinking, or inference. **3** the course of action or line of reasoning suggested or made necessary by something: *an economic system driven by the logic of supply and demand*. **4 a** a system or set of principles underlying the arrangements of elements in a computer or electronic device so as to perform a specified task. **b** logical operations collectively.

-logic *combining form* (also **-logical**) forming adjectives corresponding esp. to nouns in -*logy*: *geologic*.

logical *adjective* **1** based on or demonstrating the rules of logic or clear, sound reasoning: *she met his emotional appeal with logical arguments* ◊ *a logical mind*. **2** (of an action, decision, etc.) natural or sensible given the circumstances: *she was the logical choice for the position*. ▶ **logically** *adverb*

logician *noun* a person who studies or is skilled in the science of reasoning. [Say luh JISH'n]

log-in *noun Computing* **1** the action of logging in. **2** a code, password, etc. used in logging in.

-logist *combining form* forming nouns denoting a person skilled or involved in a branch of study etc. with a name in -*logy*: *archaeologist*.

logistical *adjective* (also **logistic**) related to or involving the practical organization of a plan, esp. one involving a lot of people and equipment: *provided logistical support for the expedition*. ▶ **logistically** *adverb* [Say luh JISS tickle]

logistics *plural noun* **1** the detailed coordination of a complex operation involving many people, facilities, or supplies: *was responsible for the logistics of the film shoot*. **2** the organization of moving, lodging, and supplying military troops and equipment. [Say luh JIST icks]

log-jam *noun* **1** a crowded mass of logs in a river. **2** a deadlock. **3** *Sport* a situation in which several contestants are tied at the same place in the standings.

logo *noun* (*plural* **logos**) a symbol designed for and used by a company or organization as its special sign, e.g. in advertising and packaging.

log-on *noun* = LOG-IN.

log-rolling *noun* **1** *informal* the practice of exchanging favours, esp. (in politics) of exchanging votes to mutual benefit: *have gained political leverage by combining ready money with a talent for log-rolling*. **2** the action of causing a floating log to rotate by treading, esp. as a competitive sport.

log scaler *noun Cdn* a person who measures cut logs and calculates the amount of lumber that they contain.

logy *adjective* (**logier**, **logiest**) *informal* dull and heavy in motion or thought; sluggish. [Say LO ghee]

-logy *combining form* forming nouns denoting: **1** (usu. as **-ology**) a subject of study or interest: *zoology*. **2** a characteristic of speech or language: *tautology*. **3** discourse: *trilogy*.

loin *noun* **1** (in *plural*) the part of the body on both sides of the spine between the ribs and the hip bones. **2** (in *plural*) the region of the sexual organs, esp. as the source of erotic or reproductive power: *felt a stirring in his loins*. **3** a cut of meat that includes the loin vertebrae.

loincloth *noun* a cloth worn around the loins, esp. as a sole garment.

loiter *verb* **1** hang about; linger idly. **2** linger indolently on the way when on an errand, journey, etc. ▶ **loiterer** *noun*

loll *verb* **1** (often foll. by *about*, *around*) stand, sit, or recline in a lazy attitude. **2** hang loosely: *he slumped in the seat and let his head loll back*. [Rhymes with DOLL]

lollapalooza *noun* (*plural* **lollapaloozas**) *slang* an excellent or attractive person or thing. [Say lolla puh LOOZA]

lollipop *noun* a large flat or round candy on a small stick, held in the hand and sucked.

lolly *noun Cdn* (*Nfld & Maritimes*) slush consisting of small ice crystals formed in water too turbulent to freeze over.

Lombard ● *noun* **1** a native of Lombardy in northern Italy. **2** a member of a Germanic people who conquered Italy in the 6th century. **3** the dialect of Lombardy.

• *adjective* of or relating to the Lombards or Lombardy. [Say LOM bard]

Lombardy poplar *noun* a variety of poplar with an especially tall slender form. [Say LOM bur dee]

Londoner *noun* a native or inhabitant of London, England, or London, Ontario.

lone *adjective* **1** (of a person) solitary; without a companion or supporter: *a lone figure stands on the hill.* **2** single, only: *scored the team's lone goal.* **3** (of a place) uninhabited, lonely: *the lone prairie.* **4** unmarried, single: *lone parent.*

loneliness *noun* the quality or fact of being lonely.

lonely *adjective* (**lonelier, loneliest**) **1** sad because without friends or company: *felt very lonely after her husband died.* **2** (of a place) where only a few people come or visit: *a lonely farmhouse.* **3** dreary; causing one to feel sad and alone: *lonely nights at home watching TV.*

lonely heart *noun* (usu. in *plural*) a lonely person, esp. one seeking companionship by advertising in a newspaper etc.: *a lonely hearts column.*

loner *noun* a person who prefers not to associate with others.

lonesome *adjective* **1** solitary, lonely. **2** feeling lonely or forlorn. **3** causing such a feeling. PHRASES **by** (or **on**) **one's lonesome** all alone. ▶ **lonesomeness** *noun*

long¹ • *adjective* (**longer; longest**) **1** of a great distance or duration. **2** relatively great in extent. **3** having a specified length, distance, or duration. **4** (of a ball in sport) travelling a great distance, or further than expected. **5** *Phonetics* (of a vowel) categorized as long with regard to quality and length (e.g. in *food*). **6** (of odds or a chance) reflecting or representing a low level of probability. **7** (of a drink) large and refreshing, and in which alcohol, if present, is not concentrated. **8** (**long on**) *informal* well supplied with. • *noun* a long time. • *adverb* (**longer; longest**) **1** by or for a long time. **2** throughout a specified time. **3** after an implied point of time. **4** esp. *Sport* at or to a great distance: *kick the ball long.* PHRASES **as** (or **so**) **long as 1** during the whole time that. **2** provided that; only if. **before long** fairly soon. **be long** take a long time; be slow: *was long in coming* ◊ *I won't be long.* **in the long run 1** over a long period. **2** eventually; finally. **long ago** in the distant past. **the long and the short of it 1** all that can or need be said. **2** the eventual outcome. **long in the tooth** rather old. **long time no see** *informal* (used as a greeting) it is a long time since we last met.

long² *verb* have a strong wish or desire for: *longed for a cup of tea* ◊ *I long to go to Scotland again.*

long. *abbreviation* longitude.

long- *combining form* forming adverbs meaning "for or lasting for a long time": *long-expected* ◊ *long-lasting.*

SPELL CHECK
long-ago, long ago

Note the difference in spelling between *long-ago events* and *events that happened long ago.* There is no hyphen when the latter structure is used.

long-ago *adjective* that is in the distant past.

long-awaited *adjective* that has been awaited for a long time.

longboat *noun* a sailing ship's largest boat.

longbow *noun* a bow drawn by hand and shooting a long feathered arrow.

long-chain *adjective* (of a molecule) containing a chain of many carbon atoms.

long-dead *adjective* that has been dead for a long time.

long-distance • *adjective* **1** (of a telephone call) made between places that are sufficiently far apart as to require extra payment. **2** of, relating to, or providing such service: *a long-distance company.* **3** covering relatively great distances: *long-distance race* ◊ *long-distance trucker.* • *adverb* (also **long distance**) between distant places: *phone long-distance.* • *noun* (usu. **long distance**) long-distance telephone service: *the company offers lower rates for long distance.*

long-drawn-out *adjective* (also **long-drawn**) prolonged, esp. unduly.

longer *noun* (usu. in *plural*) *Cdn* (*Nfld & Maritimes*) a long pole, esp. from the trunk of a conifer, used for building fences, fishing stages, roofs, floors, etc.

longevity *noun* **1** long life: *ways to improve health and achieve longevity.* **2** duration of life: *studying longevity.* **3** duration or length of service, employment, etc.: *his longevity as a head coach is impressive.* [Say lon JEVVA tee]

long face *noun* a dismal or disappointed expression. ▶ **long-faced** *adjective*

longhair *noun* **1** *informal* a person with long hair or characteristics associated with it, such as a hippie or an intellectual. **2** a long-haired cat.

longhand *noun* ordinary handwriting (as opposed to shorthand or typing or printing).

long haul *noun* **1** the transport of goods or passengers over a long distance: *long-haul flights* ◊ *I first noticed him on the dusty long haul by troop train across India.* **2** a prolonged effort or task: *it will be a long haul to change people's behaviour and practices.* PHRASES **over the long haul** over a long period; in the long run.

longhorn *noun* **1** a breed of cattle with long horns. **2** an elongated beetle with very long, slender, backwardly flexed antennae, and found worldwide esp. in woodland.

longhouse *noun* a dwelling shared by several nuclear families, esp. among the Iroquois and the Aboriginal peoples of the northwest coast of North America.

longing • *noun* a feeling of intense desire. • *adjective* having or showing this feeling. ▶ **longingly** *adverb*

longish *adjective* somewhat long.

longitude *noun* **1** *Geography* the angular distance east or west from a standard meridian such as Greenwich to the meridian of any place. Symbol: λ. **2** *Astronomy* the angular distance of a celestial body north or south of the ecliptic measured along a great circle through the body and the poles of the ecliptic. [Say LON ji tude or LONGGA tude]

longitudinal *adjective* **1** of or in length: *measures 48 inches in longitudinal circumference.* **2** running lengthwise: *longitudinal stripes.* **3** of longitude; measured east to west: *longitudinal positions.* **4** (of research, a study, etc.) involving information about an individual or group at different times throughout a long period: *longitudinal data.* ▶ **longitudinally** *adverb* [Say lon ji TUDE in ul or longga TUDE in ul]

long john *noun* **1** (in *plural*) *informal* close-fitting cotton or wool knit underpants with full-length legs. **2** a long, cream-filled doughnut, usu. iced.

long jump *noun* an athletic contest of jumping as far as possible along the ground in one leap. ▶ **long-jumper** *noun*

long-lasting *adjective* that lasts, or has lasted, for a long time.

long-legged *adjective* having long legs.

long-life *adjective* **1** (of perishable foods etc.) treated to preserve freshness. **2** (esp. of batteries etc.) manufactured in such a way as to last for a long time.

longline *noun* a deep-sea fishing line with a large number of baited hooks.

L

longliner *noun* a fishing boat using longlines.

longlining *noun* fishing using longlines.

long-lived *adjective* having a long life; durable.

long-lost *adjective* that has been lost or not seen for a long time.

long lot *noun* Cdn hist. a long narrow farm lot extending back from a river, esp. one along the St. Lawrence River or in the Red River Settlement.

long-playing *adjective* (of a record) designed to be played at 33¹/₃ revolutions per minute.

long-range *adjective* **1** (of a missile, aircraft, etc.) having a long range. **2** of or relating to a period of time far into the future.

long-run *adjective* occurring or running over a long period of time: *long-run costs*.

long-running *adjective* continuing for a long time.

longshore *adjective* **1** existing on or frequenting the shore. **2** directed along the shore.

longshoreman *noun* (*plural* **longshoremen**) a person employed to load and unload ships.

long shot *noun* **1** a competitor or team etc. that is unlikely to succeed. **2** an undertaking or venture that has great potential but little chance of success. **3** a wild guess. **4** a bet at long odds. **5** *Film* a shot including objects at a distance. **PHRASES** **by a long shot** by any means: *it isn't over by a long shot*.

long-sleeved *adjective* with sleeves reaching to the wrist.

longspur *noun* a North American songbird related to the buntings, with brownish plumage and a boldly marked head in the male.

long-standing *adjective* that has long existed; not recent: *a long-standing agreement*.

long-suffering *adjective* bearing provocation patiently.

SPELL CHECK
long-term, long term ✅ABC

Note the difference in spelling between *long-term plans* and *plans for the long term*. There is no hyphen when the latter kind of structure is used.

---

long-term *adjective* **1** of or for a long period of time: *long-term plans*. **2** (of an investment, loan, etc.) maturing or coming due after a long period of time.

long-time *adjective* that has been such for a long time.

long ton *noun* a unit of weight equal to 2,240 lb. avoirdupois (1016 kg).

long view *noun* a broad and forward-looking assessment of circumstances etc.: *in his long view, it is perseverance that will eventually bring about integration*. **PHRASES** **take the long view** consider what is likely to happen, be relevant, etc. over the long term.

long wave *noun* a radio wave of frequency less than 300 kHz.

longways *adverb* (also **longwise**) = LENGTHWISE.

long weekend *noun* a three-day weekend consisting of Saturday, Sunday, and a statutory holiday on the Friday or Monday.

long-winded *adjective* **1** (of speech or writing) tediously lengthy. **2** (of a person) verbose; given to long discourses. ▶**long-windedly** *adverb* **long-windedness** *noun*

loo *noun* (*plural* **loos**) esp. Brit. informal a toilet or washroom.

loofah *noun* **1** a climbing gourd-like plant, native to Asia, producing edible squash-like fruits. **2** the dried fibrous interior of this fruit used as a sponge. [Say LOOFA]

look • *verb* **1** direct one's gaze in a specified direction. **2** have an outlook in a specified direction. **3** have the appearance or give the impression of being. • *noun* **1** an act of looking. **2** an expression of a feeling or thought by looking at someone. **3** the appearance of someone or something. **4** (**looks**) a person's facial appearance considered aesthetically. **5** a style or fashion. • *interjection* (also **look here!**) calling attention, expressing a protest, etc. **PHRASES** **look after 1** take care of. **2** follow with the eye. **look alive** (or **lively**) informal be brisk and alert. **look around 1** look in every or another direction. **2** examine the objects of interest in a place. **3** examine the possibilities etc. with a view to deciding on a course of action. **look back 1** (foll. by *on, upon, to*) turn one's thoughts to (something past). **2** cease to progress: *since then we have never looked back*. **look before you leap** avoid precipitate action. **look down on** (or **upon** or **look down one's nose at**) regard with contempt or a feeling of superiority. **look forward to** await (an expected event) eagerly or with specified feelings. **look in** make a short visit or call. **look a person in the eye** (or **eyes** or **face**) look directly and unashamedly at him or her. **look like 1** have the appearance of. **2** indicate the presence of: *it looks like mice*. **3** threaten or promise: *it looks like rain*. **look on 1** regard: *looks on you as a friend*. **2** be a spectator; avoid participation. **look oneself** appear in good health (esp. after illness etc.). **look out 1** direct one's sight or put one's head out of a window etc. **2** (often foll. by *for*) be vigilant or prepared. **3** (foll. by *on, over*, etc.) have or afford a specified outlook. **4** search for and produce: *shall look one out for you*. **look over 1** inspect or survey: *looked over the house*. **2** examine (a document etc.) esp. cursorily. **look sharp** act promptly; make haste. **look through 1** examine the contents of, esp. cursorily. **2** ignore by pretending not to see: *I waved, but you just looked through me*. **look up 1** search for (esp. information in a book). **2** informal go to visit (a person): *had intended to look them up*. **3** raise one's eyes: *Mary Jane looked up when I went in*. **4** improve, esp. in price, prosperity, or well-being: *things are looking up all over*. **look a person up and down** scrutinize a person keenly or contemptuously. **look up to** respect or venerate. **not like the look of** find alarming or suspicious.

look-alike • *noun* a person or thing closely resembling another: *an Elvis look-alike*. • *adjective* closely similar, esp. in appearance; identical.

looker *noun* **1** a person having a specified appearance: *a good-looker*. **2** informal an attractive person, esp. a woman. **3** a person who looks.

look-in *noun* informal an informal call or visit.

-looking *adjective* (in *combination*) having a specified appearance: *good-looking* ◊ *silly-looking*.

looking glass *noun* (*plural* **looking glasses**) archaic a mirror.

lookit *interjection* informal **1** demanding attention or protesting. **2** look at (someone or something).

lookout *noun* **1** a watch or looking out: *on the lookout for bargains*. **2 a** a post of observation. **b** a person or party or boat stationed to keep watch. **3** a view over a landscape. **4** a prospect of luck: *it's a bad lookout for them*. **5** informal a person's own concern.

look-see *noun* informal a survey or inspection.

looky *verb* informal (in *imper.*; usu. as *looky here*) demanding attention.

loom¹ *noun* an apparatus in which yarn or thread is woven into fabric by the crossing of vertical and horizontal threads.

loom² *verb* (often foll. by *up*) **1** come into sight dimly, esp. as a vague and often magnified or threatening shape. **2** (of an event or prospect) be ominously close: *there is a crisis looming in the school system*. **3** (often foll. by *over*) be ominously above: *the castle loomed over us*. PHRASES **loom large** figure significantly.

loon *noun* **1** an aquatic diving bird with a long slender body and a sharp bill, esp. the common loon, with a haunting yodel-like call, red eyes, bands of alternating black and white on the collar, and a checkered black and white back. **2** *informal* a crazy person. **3** *Cdn* = LOONIE.

loonie *noun* (*plural* **loonies**) *Cdn* **1** the Canadian one-dollar coin. **2** *informal* the Canadian dollar: *the loonie rose a tenth of a cent today against the American dollar*.

looniness *noun* craziness, silliness.

loony *slang* • *noun* (*plural* **loonies**) a mad or silly person; a lunatic. • *adjective* (**loonier, looniest**) crazy, silly.

loony bin *noun slang* a mental home or hospital.

loony-tune *informal* • *adjective* (also **loony-tunes**) crazy, silly; bizarre. • *noun* a crazy or silly person.

loop • *noun* **1** a shape produced by a curve that bends round and crosses itself. **2** (also **loop-the-loop**) a manoeuvre in which an aircraft describes a vertical circle in the air. **3** *Figure Skating* a jump from the back outside edge of one foot, landing on the back outside edge of the same foot, with rotation in the air. **4** *Electricity* a complete circuit for a current. **5** an endless strip of tape or film allowing continuous repetition. **6** *Computing* a programmed sequence of instructions that is repeated until or while a particular condition is satisfied. **7** the circle of influential people or those keeping up to date: *has been out of the loop for a while now*. • *verb* **1** form (thread etc.) into a loop or loops. **2** enclose with or as with a loop. **3** (often foll. by *up, back, together*) fasten or join with a loop or loops. **4 a** form a loop. **b** move in loop-like patterns. PHRASES **loop the loop** perform the feat of circling an aircraft in a vertical loop. **throw** (or **knock**) **one for a loop** surprise, astonish; catch off guard.

looped *adjective* **1** coiled or wreathed in loops. **2** consisting of a loop: *looped hiking trails*. **3** *slang* drunk.

looper *noun* an inchworm.

loophole *noun* **1** a means of evading a rule etc. without infringing the letter of it. **2** a narrow vertical slit in a wall for shooting or looking through or to admit light or air.

loop-the-loop *noun* the feat of circling in an aircraft in a vertical loop.

loopy *adjective* (**loopier, loopiest**) **1** *slang* crazy. **2** having many loops: *large, loopy handwriting*.

SPELL CHECK
loose, lose

You can **lose** money, weight, a game, a glove, your job, your temper, or your balance.

loose • *adjective* (**looser, loosest**) **1 a** not or no longer held by bonds or restraint. **b** (of an animal) not confined or tethered etc. **2** detached or detachable from its place: *has come loose*. **3** not held together or contained or fixed: *loose papers ◊ had her hair loose ◊ a loose end*. **4** slack, relaxed; not tense or tight. **5** (of a person's joints) easily moved. **6** not compact or dense: *loose soil*. **7** (of language, concepts, etc.) inexact; conveying only the general sense. **8** morally lax; dissolute: *loose living*. **9 a** (of talk) indiscreet. **b** (of the tongue) likely to speak indiscreetly. **10** (of the bowels) afflicted with diarrhea. **11** *Sport* **a** (of a ball, puck, etc.) in play but not in any player's possession. **b** (of play etc.) with the players not close together. **12** (of a partnership, coalition, etc.) allowing for substantial

independence among its members. • *adverb* (**looser, loosest**) **1** (in *combination*) loosely: *loose-fitting*. **2** without constraint: *the dog runs loose*. **3** without attachment: *pried her fingers loose*. • *verb* (**looses, loosed, loosing**) **1** release; set free; free from constraint: *his speech loosed a tide of nationalist sentiment*. **2** untie or undo (something that constrains): *he loosed the straps that bound her arms*. **3** detach from moorings. **4** relax: *loosed my hold on it*. **5** discharge (a gun or arrow etc.). PHRASES **on the loose 1** escaped from captivity. **2** having a free enjoyable time. **stay loose** remain relaxed.

loose cannon *noun* a reckless person or thing causing unintentional or misdirected damage.

loose end *noun* an unfinished detail. PHRASES **at loose ends** (of a person) with nothing to do; unsettled, without a place or purpose.

looseleaf • *adjective* **1** (of a notebook, manual, etc.) with each leaf separate and removable. **2** pertaining to or for use with a looseleaf binder etc.: *looseleaf paper*. • *noun* looseleaf paper.

loosely *adverb* **1** not firmly or tightly: *she fastened the belt loosely around her waist*. **2** in a way that is not exact: *use a term loosely ◊ the play is loosely based on his childhood*.

loosen *verb* **1** make or become less tight or compact or firm. **2** release (the bowels) from constipation. PHRASES **loosen a person's tongue** make a person talk freely. **loosen up 1** warm up in preparation for an activity: *arrive early to loosen up and hit some practice balls*. **2** make or become relaxed: *they taught me to have fun at work and loosen up*.

looseness *noun* the quality of being loose: *jazz has a looseness that is not found in classical music*.

loosestrife *noun* any of a number of tall plants that bear upright spikes of flowers and grow by water and in wet ground. [Say LOOSE strife]

loosey-goosey *adjective* *informal* laid back; very relaxed.

SPELL CHECK
loot, lute

The musical instrument is a **lute**.

loot • *noun* **1** goods taken from an enemy. **2** stolen property or valuables: *two men wearing masks, each carrying a bag of loot*. **3** *slang* money: *twenty thousand dollars is a lot of loot*. **4** *informal* a collection or mass of recently-obtained goodies: *Halloween loot*. • *verb* **1** rob (premises) or steal (goods) left unprotected, esp. after riots or other violent events. **2** plunder (a city, building, etc.).

loot bag *noun* a bag containing candy, trinkets, etc., given to each child at a birthday party etc.

looter *noun* a person who steals things left unprotected after a riot, fire, or other violent event.

looting *noun* the act of stealing things left unprotected after a riot, fire, or other violent event.

lop¹ *verb* (**lops, lopped, lopping**) **1** (often foll. by *off, away*) cut or remove (a part or parts) from a whole, esp. branches from a tree. **2** (often foll. by *off, away*) remove (something regarded as unnecessary or burdensome: *this route lops an hour off the journey*. **3** (foll. by *at*) make lopping strokes on (a tree etc.).

lop² *noun* **1** a state of the sea in which the waves are short and choppy. **2** the sea or its surface when in this condition. ▶ **loppy** *adjective* (**loppier, loppiest**)

lope • *verb* (**lopes, loped, loping**) **1** run with a long bounding stride. **2** move with long, easy strides. • *noun* a long bounding stride.

loppet *noun* a long-distance cross-country ski race in which all competitors start together. [Say LOPPIT]

lopsided *adjective* **1** with one side lower or smaller than the other; unevenly balanced. **2** *Sport* (of a score, victory, etc.) with one side greatly outscoring the other. ▸ **lopsidedly** *adverb* **lopsidedness** *noun*

loquacious *adjective* talkative: *she was loquacious and eager to share her past filled with horrid stories.* ▸ **loquacity** *noun* [Say lo KWAY shus, lo KWASSA tee]

lord • *noun* **1 a** a master or ruler. **b** a powerful person in a specified field or group: *drug lord*. **2** *hist.* a feudal superior, esp. of a manor. **3** (**Lord**) (often as **the lord**) **a** a name for God. **b** a name for Christ. **4** (in the UK) a peer of the realm or a person entitled to the title *Lord*, esp. a marquess, earl, viscount, or baron. **5** (**Lord**) (in the UK) **a** a prefixed as the designation of a marquess, earl, viscount, or baron. **b** prefixed to the first name of the younger son of a duke or marquess. **c** (**the Lords**) = HOUSE OF LORDS. • *interjection* (**Lord**) expressing surprise, dismay, etc. PHRASES **lord it over 1** domineer. **2** adopt an attitude of superiority over. **lord over** (usu. in *passive*) rule over.

lord and lady *noun* (*plural* **lords and ladies**) esp. *Cdn* (usu. in *plural*) the harlequin duck.

lordly *adjective* (**lordlier, lordliest**) of, characteristic of, or suitable for a lord: *lordly titles ◊ they were putting on lordly airs.*

Lord's Day *noun* Sunday.

lordship *noun* supreme power or rule: *his lordship over the other gods.* PHRASES **his** (or **your**) **Lordship** (or **lordship**) (*plural* **their** (or **your**) **Lordships** or **lordships**) **1** *Brit.* a respectful form of reference or address to a Lord or a bishop. **2** *Cdn & Brit.* a respectful form of reference or address to a judge. **3** *ironic* a form of reference or address to a man thought to give himself airs.

Lord's Prayer *noun* the prayer taught by Christ to his disciples, beginning with the words "Our Father".

Lord's Supper *noun* Christianity the sacrament commemorating the Last Supper, in which bread and wine are consecrated and consumed.

Lordy *interjection* expressing surprise, dismay, etc.

lore *noun* a body of traditions and knowledge on a subject or held by a particular group: *herbal lore*.

lorikeet *noun* any of various small brightly coloured parrots. [Say LORA keet]

> **SPELL CHECK**
> **lose, loose**
>
> The opposite of *tight* is **loose**. If you release something you **loose** it: *loosed the dogs on them.*

lose *verb* (**loses**, *past* and *past participle* **lost; losing**) **1** be deprived of or cease to have, esp. by negligence or misadventure. **2 a** be deprived of (a person, esp. a close relative or patient) by death. **b** suffer the death of (a baby) in childbirth or through miscarriage. **3** become unable to find; fail to keep in sight or follow or mentally grasp: *lose one's way*. **4** let or have pass from one's control or reach: *lose one's chance ◊ lose one's bearings*. **5** be defeated in (a game, race, lawsuit, battle, etc.). **6** evade; get rid of: *lost our pursuers*. **7** fail to apprehend by sight or hearing; not catch (words etc.). **8** forfeit (a stake, deposit, right to a thing, etc.). **9** spend (time, efforts, etc.) to no purpose: *lost no time in raising the alarm*. **10 a** suffer loss or detriment; incur a disadvantage. **b** be worse off, esp. financially. **c** experience a deficit of expenditure over income: *lost

money on her house*. **11** cause (a person) the loss of: *will lose you your job*. **12** (of a timepiece) **a** become slow. **b** become slow by (a specified amount of time). **13** (in *passive*) disappear, perish; be dead: *was lost in the war ◊ is a lost art*. **14** *informal* get rid of; discard. **15** undergo a reduction of; shed (weight). **16** vomit: *lost my lunch*. PHRASES **lose one's balance** fail to remain stable; fall. **lose one's cool** *informal* lose one's composure. **lose face** be humiliated; lose one's credibility. **lose heart** be discouraged. **lose it 1** lose one's composure suddenly and completely. **2** lose one's mind, sense of reality, sanity, etc. **3** cease to excel or be proficient in a specified field. **lose one's nerve** become timid or irresolute. **lose out** *informal* **1** (often foll. by *on*) be unsuccessful; not get a fair chance or advantage (in). **2** (foll. by *to*) be beaten in competition or replaced by. **lose one's temper** become angry. **lose time** allow time to pass with something unachieved etc. **lose the** (or **one's**) **way** become lost.

lose-lose *adjective* *informal* designating a condition, settlement, etc. which is damaging or disadvantageous to everyone involved: *a lose-lose situation*.

loser *noun* **1** a person or thing that loses or has lost (esp. a contest or game): *is a poor loser ◊ the loser pays*. **2** *informal* **a** a person who regularly fails: *a born loser*. **b** a socially awkward person; a misfit: *rejects and losers*. **3** a person or thing that is put at a disadvantage by a particular situation or course of action: *children are the losers when politicians keep fiddling around with education*.

losing • *noun* the action of LOSE: *hates losing*. • *adjective* that loses or results in loss: *a losing proposition ◊ a losing team ◊ a money-losing company*.

losing battle *noun* a contest or effort in which failure seems inevitable.

loss *noun* (*plural* **losses**) **1 a** the fact or process of no longer having something or as much of something: *weight loss ◊ funding cuts will lead to job losses ◊ loss of sleep*. **b** the fact of feeling grief when deprived of a person by death, estrangement, etc.: *when she died I felt a terrible sense of loss*. **2** a person, thing, or amount lost: *he will be a great loss to many people*. **3** the death of a person: *his wife's death was a great loss to him ◊ troops suffered heavy losses ◊ the epidemic has caused widespread loss of life*. **4** the disadvantage caused when someone leaves or when a useful or valuable object is taken away: *that is no great loss ◊ if he doesn't want to go out with you, that's his loss ◊ her departure is a big loss to the school*. PHRASES **at a loss 1** puzzled or uncertain what to think, do, or say: *she became popular, and was at a loss to know why ◊ Clarke was at a loss for words*. **2** making less money than is spent buying, operating, or producing something: *the airline has been running at a loss*.

loss leader *noun* an item sold at a loss to attract customers.

lost • *verb* *past* and *past participle* of LOSE. • *adjective* **1** unable to find one's way; not knowing where one is. **2** confused or in difficulties. **3** that cannot be found or recovered. **4** suffering damnation: *lost souls*. PHRASES **be lost for words** be so surprised, confused, etc. that one cannot think what to say. **be lost in** be engrossed in. **be lost on** be wasted on, or not noticed or appreciated by. **be lost to** be no longer affected by or accessible to: *is lost to the world*. **be lost without** have great difficulty if deprived of: *am lost without my address book*. **get lost** (usu. in *imper.*) *slang* go away.

lost and found *noun* (*plural* **lost and founds**) a place where misplaced items are collected for retrieval by their owners.

lost cause *noun* **1** an enterprise etc. with no chance of success. **2** a person one can no longer hope to influence.

lost generation *noun* the generation reaching maturity c.1915–25, a high proportion of whose men were killed in the First World War, characterized by disillusionment.

lot • *noun* **1** *informal* **a** a large number or amount: *a lot of people* ◊ *lots of chocolate*. **b** *informal* much: *a lot warmer* ◊ *is lots better*. **2 a** each of a set of objects used in making a chance selection. **b** this method of deciding: *chosen by lot*. **3** a share, or the responsibility resulting from it. **4** a person's destiny, fortune, or condition. **5 a** a portion of land assigned to a particular owner; each of the portions into which a tract of land is divided when offered for sale. **b** land near a film studio where outside filming may be done. **c** a plot of land used for parking vehicles. **d** the area at a car dealership where cars for sale are kept. **6** an article or set of articles for sale at an auction etc. **7** a number or quantity of associated persons or things. • *verb* (**lots, lotted, lotting**) divide into lots. PHRASES **cast** (or **draw**) **lots** decide by means of lots. **throw in one's lot with** decide to share the fortunes of. **the** (or **the whole**) **lot** the whole number or quantity. **a whole lot** *informal* very much: *is a whole lot better*.

Lothario *noun* (*plural* **Lotharios**) a man known for many sexual conquests. [Say luh THAIR ee oh or luh THAR ee oh (with TH as in *THIN*)]

lotion *noun* a medicinal or cosmetic liquid preparation applied externally.

lottery *noun* (*plural* **lotteries**) **1 a** a means of raising money, usu. on a large scale and government-operated, by selling numbered tickets and giving prizes to the holders of numbers drawn at random. **b** any game of chance involving the sale of tickets. **c** a process of selection relying on random drawing: *visas are awarded through a lottery*. **2** an enterprise, process, etc., whose outcome is governed by chance: *life is a lottery*.

lotto *noun* (*plural* **lottos**) **1** (also esp. *Que.* **loto**, *plural* **lotos**) a lottery. **2** a game of chance like bingo, but with numbers drawn by the players instead of being called.

lotus *noun* (*plural* **lotuses**) **1** (in Greek mythology) a legendary plant whose fruit induces a dreamy forgetfulness and an unwillingness to depart. **2** either of two large water lilies, an Indian lily with large pink flowers, which is used symbolically in Hinduism and Buddhism, or a white-flowered lily regarded as sacred in ancient Egypt. **3** any plant of the genus *Lotus*. [Say LO tis]

lotus land *noun* **1** a place of lazy relaxation and enjoyment: *a lotus land of ever-bigger cars, expensive apartments, and more exotic vacations*. **2** (**Lotus Land**) *Cdn jocular* southern British Columbia.

lotus position *noun* a cross-legged position of meditation with both feet resting on the thighs.

loud • *adjective* **1 a** strongly audible, esp. noisily or oppressively so. **b** able or liable to produce loud sounds: *a loud engine*. **c** clamorous, insistent: *loud complaints*. **2** (of colours, design, etc.) gaudy, obtrusive. **3** (of behaviour) aggressive and noisy. • *adverb* in a loud manner. PHRASES **loud and clear 1** loudly and clearly: *speak loud and clear*. **2** without misunderstanding: *got the hint loud and clear*. **out loud 1** aloud. **2** loudly: *laughed out loud*.

loud hailer *noun* a megaphone.

loudly *adverb* in a way that causes a great deal of noise.

loudmouth *noun* *informal* a noisily self-assertive or vociferous person. ▶ **loudmouthed** *adjective*

loudness *noun* **1** the quality or condition of being loud: *the loudness of the music drove her to distraction*. **2** the (great or small) extent to which a thing is heard: *varied in loudness and pitch*.

loudspeaker *noun* an apparatus that converts electrical impulses into sound, esp. music and voice.

Lou Gehrig's disease *noun* = AMYOTROPHIC LATERAL SCLEROSIS. [Say loo GAIR ig]

lounge • *verb* (**lounges, lounged, lounging**) **1** recline comfortably and casually; loll. **2** (often foll. by *around, about*) stand or move about idly. • *noun* **1** a place where people may sit and relax, esp.: **a** a public room or bar, e.g. in a hotel. **b** a place in an airport etc. with seats for waiting passengers. **c** a room where staff, students, etc. may congregate informally. **2** designating live, easy-listening musical entertainment characteristic of lounges: *lounge singer*.

lounge chair *noun* a chair for lounging or reclining in.

lounge lizard *noun* *informal* **1** an idle person who frequents lounges. **2** a singer or other performer of esp. pop songs in lounges.

lounger *noun* **1** a person who lounges. **2** a piece of furniture for relaxing on. **3** a casual garment for wearing when relaxing.

lour *verb* = LOWER³. [Rhymes with *HOUR*]

louse • *noun* (*plural* **lice**) **a** a parasitic insect that infests the human hair and skin and transmits various diseases. **b** any similar insect that is a parasite of mammals, birds, fish, or plants. **2** (*plural* **louses**) *slang* a contemptible or unpleasant person. • *verb* (**louses, loused, lousing**) remove lice from. PHRASES **louse up** *slang* mess up.

lousy *adjective* (**lousier, lousiest**) **1** infested with lice. **2** *informal* very bad; disgusting (also as a term of general disparagement). **3** *informal* (often foll. by *with*) well supplied, teeming.

lout *noun* a rough, crude, or ill-mannered person (usu. a man). ▶ **loutish** *adjective* **loutishness** *noun*

louvre *noun* (also **louver**) **1** each of a set of overlapping slats, esp. in a door, designed to admit air and some light. **2** a domed structure on a roof with side openings for ventilation etc. ▶ **louvred** *adjective* [Say LOOVER]

lovable *adjective* inspiring or deserving love or affection.

lovage *noun* a Mediterranean herb of the parsley family, used esp. for flavouring liqueurs. [Say LUV idge]

love • *noun* **1** an intense feeling of deep affection or

fondness for a person or thing; great liking. **2** sexual passion. **3** sexual relations. **4** a beloved one; a sweetheart (often as a form of address). **5** *informal* a person of whom one is fond. **6** affectionate greetings: *give him my love*. **7** (in some sports) no score; nil. **8** a formula for ending an affectionate letter etc. • *verb* (**loves, loved, loving**) **1** feel love or deep fondness (for). **2** delight in; admire; greatly cherish. **3** like very much; love's books **4** be inclined, esp. as a habit; greatly enjoy; find pleasure in: *loves to find fault*. PHRASES **fall in love** (often foll. by *with*) develop a great (esp. sexual) love (for). **for love** for pleasure not profit. **for the love of** for the sake of. **in love** (often foll. by *with*) deeply enamoured (of). **make love 1** (often foll. by *to, with*) have sexual intercourse (with). **2** (often foll. by *to*) *archaic* pay amorous attention (to). **no love lost between** mutual dislike between (two people etc.). **not for love or money** *informal* not in any circumstances.

loveable *adjective* = LOVABLE.

love affair *noun* **1** an esp. extramarital romantic or sexual relationship between two people in love. **2** an intense enthusiasm or liking for something.

lovebird *noun* **1** a very small African parrot with mainly green plumage and usu. a red or black face, noted for the affectionate behaviour of mated birds. **2** (in *plural*) *informal* lovers.

love handles *plural noun slang* excess fat at the waist.

love-hate relationship *noun* **1** an intensely emotional relationship in which one or each party has ambivalent feelings of love and hate for the other. **2** a situation in which feelings of liking and disliking are combined: *our love-hate relationship with raccoons*.

love-in *noun* (*plural* **love-ins**) *informal* **1** a gathering (esp. of hippies) expressing or advocating love and peace. **2** *jocular* a gathering of like-minded people: *the so-called "debate" was really a love-in*.

love interest *noun* a person or character in a film etc. in whom another has a romantic or sexual interest.

loveless *adjective* without love; unloving or unloved or both. ▶ **lovelessness** *noun*

love letter *noun* a letter expressing feelings of sexual love.

love life *noun* (*plural* **love lives**) a person's life with regard to relationships with lovers.

loveliness *noun* the quality of being very attractive.

lovelorn *adjective* (of a person) unhappy because the person they love does not love them: *a lonely, lovelorn man, sitting at home by himself*.

lovely • *adjective* (**lovelier, loveliest**) **1** exquisitely beautiful. **2** pleasing, delightful. • *noun* (*plural* **lovelies**) *informal* a pretty woman.

lovemaking *noun* amorous sexual activity, esp. sexual intercourse.

lover *noun* **1** a person in love with another. **2** a person with whom another is having sexual relations. **3** (in *plural*) a couple in love or having sexual relations. **4** a person who likes or enjoys something specified: *a music lover* ◊ *a lover of words*.

loveseat *noun* a small sofa for two.

lovesick *adjective* languishing with romantic love.

lovestruck *adjective* completely smitten by love.

love triangle *noun* a situation in which one person is romantically involved with two others.

lovey *informal adjective* (also **lovey-dovey**) fondly affectionate, esp. unduly sentimental.

loving • *adjective* feeling or showing love. • *noun* affection; active love.

loving-kindness *noun* tenderness and consideration.

lovingly *adverb* in a loving manner: *he gazed lovingly at his children* ◊ *the house has been lovingly restored*.

low¹ • *adjective* **1** of less than average height. **2** situated not far above the ground, horizon, etc. **3** below average in amount, extent, or intensity. • *noun* **1** a low point, level, or figure. **2** an area of low barometric pressure. • *adverb* **1** in or into a low position or state. **2** quietly or at low pitch. **3** at or to a moral position considered contemptible: *how low can you stoop?*

low² • *noun* a sound made by cattle; a moo. • *verb* utter (with) this sound.

Low Arctic *noun* the part of the Canadian Arctic south of the Arctic Circle.

lowball *informal* • *adjective* **1** designating a deceptively or unrealistically low price or estimate. **2** inexpensive. • *verb* deceptively offer someone an unrealistically low price or estimate: *that's lowballing the increase in fan interest since his last performance here*.

low beam *noun* (usu. in *plural*) a headlight beam used for short-range illumination.

low blow *noun* **1** a cruel or unfair criticism or attack. **2** a punch below the belt in boxing.

low-born *adjective* born to a family that has a low social status.

lowboy *noun* a low chest or table with drawers and short legs.

lowbrow • *adjective* not highly intellectual or cultured. • *noun* a lowbrow person. [With LOW rhyming with *SHOW* and BROW rhyming with *COW*]

low-budget *adjective* produced or operated with a limited amount of money: *a low-budget film*.

low-cal *adjective* (also **low-calorie**) (of food, a diet, etc.) low in calories.

Low Church *noun* a tradition within Anglicanism stressing the authority of the Bible and the importance of personal conversion and giving relatively little emphasis to ritual, priestly authority, and the sacraments.

low-cut *adjective* **1** (of a dress etc.) having a low neckline. **2** (of a running shoe etc.) not covering the ankle.

low-density lipoprotein *noun* the form of lipoprotein in which cholesterol is transported in the blood. Abbreviation: **LDL**.

lowdown • *noun* *informal* (usu. foll. by *on*) the relevant information (about). • *adjective* *informal* dishonourable, contemptible.

low-E *adjective* (also **low-emissivity**) designating a window which has been coated to prevent the escape or entry of heat, yet which permits the passage of light.

low-end *adjective* designating or pertaining to relatively cheap models of consumer products, services, etc.: *bought low-end equipment*.

lower¹ • *adjective* (*comparative* of LOW¹) **1** less high in position or status. **2** situated below another part: *lower lip* ◊ *lower atmosphere*. **3 a** situated on less high land: *the lower town*. **b** situated to the south: *Lower California*. **c** situated along or pertaining to the downstream part of a river, esp. the part closest to the mouth: *the Lower St. Lawrence*. **4** (of an animal or plant) showing relatively primitive characteristics, e.g. a platypus or a fungus. **5** denoting the early part or division of a period, system, formation, etc.: *during the lower Paleozoic era*. • *adverb* in or to a lower position, status, etc.

lower² *verb* **1** let or haul down. **2** make or become lower. **3** reduce the height or pitch or elevation of: *lower your voice*. **4** degrade. **5** diminish. PHRASES **lower the boom on** *slang* **1** inflict a physical defeat on (a person). **2** treat (a person) severely. **3** put a stop to (an activity).

lower³ *verb* **1** frown; look sullen. **2** (of the sky etc.) look dark and threatening: *huge clouds lowered over the lake*. [Rhymes either with *FLOWER* or with *BLOWER*]

Lower Canadian *Cdn hist.* • *noun* a native or inhabitant of the former British colony of Lower Canada (1791–1841), now Labrador and southern Quebec. • *adjective* of or relating to the colony of Lower Canada.

lower case • *adjective* designating letters that are not capitals. • *noun* lower case letters.

lower class • *noun* the poor or underprivileged class of society. • *adjective* (**lower-class**) of this class.

lower house *noun* the usu. larger and more representative body of a bicameral legislature, esp. (in Canada) the House of Commons.

lower middle class • *noun* the class of society between the lower and middle classes. • *adjective* (**lower-middle-class**) of the lower middle class.

lowest common denominator *noun* 1 the lowest common multiple of the denominators of several fractions. 2 the least desirable common feature of members of a group: *the school curriculum seems aimed at the lowest common denominator*.

lowest common multiple *noun* the lowest quantity that is a multiple of two or more given quantities.

low frequency *noun* (in radio) 30–300 kilohertz.

low gear *noun* a gear such that the driven end of a transmission revolves slower than the driving end.

Low German *noun* the group of dialects of Germany spoken in the lowland areas of the north, most closely related to Dutch and Frisian.

low-grade *adjective* of low quality or strength.

low-impact *adjective* 1 designating esp. aerobic exercises designed to put little or no potentially harmful stress on the body. 2 (of camping etc.) affecting or altering the natural environment as little as possible.

low-income *adjective* of or relating to the income group comprising those earning relatively low wages.

low-intensity *adjective* (of warfare, conflicts, etc.) relatively restrained, localized, or small-scale.

low-key *adjective* (also **low-keyed**) lacking intensity or prominence; restrained.

lowland • *noun* 1 (usu. in *plural*) low-lying country. 2 (**Lowland**) (usu. in *plural*) the region of Scotland lying south and east of the Highlands. • *adjective* of or in lowland or the Scottish Lowlands. ▶ **lowlander** *noun* (also **Lowlander**)

low latitudes *plural noun* regions near the equator.

low-level *adjective* 1 designating an activity conducted on or at a low level: *low-level negotiations* ◊ *low-level flight*. 2 *Computing* (of a programming language) close in form to machine language.

low-life *noun* (*plural* **low-lifes**) (also **low-lifer**) 1 a degenerate person or a member of the underworld. 2 such people collectively.

lowlight *noun* 1 a monotonous or dull period; a feature of little prominence: *the lowlights of the evening*. 2 (usu. in *plural*) a dark tint in the hair produced by dyeing.

lowly *adjective* (**lowlier**, **lowliest**) humble in feeling, behaviour, or status: *he was just a lowly office worker*.

low-lying *adjective* (of land) at low altitude (above sea level etc.).

low maintenance *adjective* requiring little or infrequent maintenance, attention, etc.: *a low maintenance machine*.

lowness *noun* the quality or condition of being low.

low-pitched *adjective* 1 (of a sound) low. 2 (of a roof) having only a slight slope.

low post *noun* *Basketball* the area below the opponent's basket.

low-pressure • *adjective* 1 characterized by or exerting below-average pressure. 2 (of a job, situation, etc.) not demanding or stressful. • *noun* (**low pressure**) an atmospheric condition with pressure below 101.3 kilopascals.

low profile *noun* an attitude or manner characterized by the avoidance of attention or publicity.

low relief *noun* see RELIEF 7.

low-rent *adjective* 1 (also **low-rental**) designating housing or a neighbourhood for tenants with relatively low incomes. 2 *informal* inferior; second-rate; cheap: *she was earning her living in low-rent films like The Stud*.

low-rise • *adjective* (of a building) having few storeys. • *noun* a low-rise building.

low-risk *adjective* that does not constitute a troubling risk.

low season *noun* the period during which the fewest people travel, book accommodation, etc.

low-slung *adjective* 1 suspended; sagging: *the dress had a low-slung sash on which hung a cluster of silk rosebuds*. 2 a with a low and wide profile: *low-slung houses*. b close to the ground: *low-slung furniture*.

low spirits *plural noun* dejection, depression.

low-tech *noun* (also **low-technology**) relatively unsophisticated tools, machines, procedures, etc.: *a low-tech kitchen*.

low tide *noun* (also **low water**) the time or level of the tide at its ebb.

low-water mark *noun* 1 the level reached at low water. 2 a minimum recorded level or value etc.: *the stock market was approaching its low-water mark*.

lox¹ *noun* liquid oxygen.

lox² *noun* smoked salmon.

loyal *adjective* 1 true or faithful (to duty, a friend, cause, etc.). 2 steadfast in allegiance; devoted to the sovereign or government of one's country.

loyalism *noun* the principles, practices, or actions of a loyalist or Loyalists.

loyalist *noun* 1 a person who remains loyal to the existing sovereign, government, etc., esp. in the face of rebellion or usurpation. 2 (**Loyalist**) a any of the colonists of the American revolutionary period who supported the British cause, many of whom afterwards migrated to Canada. b *Cdn* a descendant of such a person. 3 a person loyal to a specific person, cause, etc.

loyally *adverb* in a loyal and faithful manner.

loyal Opposition *noun* = OFFICIAL OPPOSITION.

loyalty *noun* (*plural* **loyalties**) 1 the state of being loyal. 2 (often in *plural*) a feeling of loyalty: *arguments with in-laws are distressing because they cause divided loyalties*.

lozenge *noun* 1 a rhombus or diamond figure. 2 a small candy or medicinal tablet for dissolving in the mouth, esp for soothing sore throats or relieving coughs. 3 a diamond-shaped pane in a window. 4 the diamond-shaped facet of a cut gem. [Say LOZ inj]

LP *noun* a long-playing record.

LPG *abbreviation* liquefied petroleum gas.

LPN *noun* (*plural* **LPNs**) LICENSED PRACTICAL NURSE.

Lr *symbol* lawrencium.

LRB *abbreviation* Labour Relations Board.

LRC *abbreviation* (of trains) light, rapid, comfortable.

LRIF *noun* (*plural* **LRIFs**) *Cdn* LOCKED-IN RETIREMENT INCOME FUND. [Say ELL riff]

LRT *abbreviation* light rail (or rapid) transit.

LS *abbreviation* *Cdn* LEADING SEAMAN.

LSAT *abbreviation* Law School Admission Test. [Say ELL sat]

LSD *noun* lysergic acid diethylamide, a powerful hallucinogenic drug.

LSI *abbreviation* *Computing* large-scale integration; the

technology integrating several thousand circuits on one chip.

Lt *abbreviation* **1** (also **Lt.**) LIEUTENANT. **2** (**Lt.**) light.

Ltd. *abbreviation* Limited.

Lt.-Gov. *abbreviation* Lieutenant-Governor.

Lu *symbol* lutetium.

luau *noun* (*plural* **luaus**) a Hawaiian party or feast usu. accompanied by some form of entertainment. [Jay LOO uw (OW rhymes with *HOW*)]

Lubavitcher • *noun* a member of a group of Hasidic Jews founded in the 18th century, stressing increased religious observance and missionary work. • *adjective* (also **Lubavitch**) of or pertaining to Lubavitchers. [Say LOOBA vitcher or loo BAW vuh chur]

lubber *noun* **1** a big clumsy fellow; a lout. **2** = LANDLUBBER. ▶ **lubberly** *adjective & adverb*

lube *informal* • *noun* **1** = LUBRICANT. **2** an application of lubricant (esp. to a motor vehicle). • *verb* (**lubes**, **lubed**, **lubing**) = LUBRICATE.

Lubicon *noun* (*plural* **Lubicon** or **Lubicons**) **1** an Aboriginal group living near Peace River, Alberta. **2** the Algonquian language of the Lubicon. [Say LOOBA con]

lubricant • *noun* a substance used to reduce friction. • *adjective* lubricating.

lubricate *verb* (**lubricates**, **lubricated**, **lubricating**) **1** reduce friction in (machinery etc.) by applying oil or grease etc. **2** make slippery or smooth by applying an oily substance. **3** (usu. as **lubricated** *adjective*) *informal* drunk. ▶ **lubrication** *noun* **lubricator** *noun*

lubricious *adjective* **1** showing a great interest in sex in a way that is considered unpleasant or unacceptable. **2** slippery, smooth, oily. ▶ **lubricity** *noun* [Say loo BRISH us, loo BRISSA tee]

lucid *adjective* **1 a** expressing or expressed clearly; easy to understand: *a lucid account* ◊ *write in a clear and lucid style*. **b** (of a dream) vivid; clear. **2** able to think clearly, esp. during or after a period of illness, confusion, or insanity: *he has a few lucid moments every now and then*. ▶ **lucidity** *noun* **lucidly** *adverb* [Say LOO sid, loo SIDDA tee]

Lucifer *noun* Satan. [Say LOOSSA fur]

Lucite *noun* *proprietary* a solid transparent plastic. [Say LOO site]

luck • *noun* **1** chance regarded as the bringer of good or bad fortune. **2** circumstances of life (beneficial or not) brought by this. **3** good fortune; success due to chance: *in luck* ◊ *out of luck*. • *verb* *informal* **1** (foll. by *into*) acquire by good fortune. **2** (foll. by *out, in*) achieve success or advantage by good luck. **3** (foll. by *out*) fail or be disadvantaged by bad luck. PHRASES **as luck would have it** by chance; because of luck. **for luck** to bring good fortune. **no such luck** *informal* unfortunately not. **try one's luck** make a venture. **with luck** if all goes well. **worse luck** *informal* unfortunately.

luckily *adverb* (qualifying a whole sentence or clause) fortunately: *luckily there was enough food*.

luckiness *noun* the quality of being lucky.

luckless *adjective* having no luck; unfortunate.

lucky *adjective* (**luckier**, **luckiest**) **1** having or resulting from good luck, esp. as distinct from skill or design or merit. **2** bringing good luck: *a lucky charm*. **3** fortunate, appropriate: *a lucky guess*. PHRASES **get lucky** *informal* have sex, esp. with a date. **thank one's lucky stars** be extremely grateful to fate.

lucrative *adjective* profitable, yielding financial gain: *a lucrative career as a stand-up comedian*. [Say LOO cruh tiv]

lucre *noun* *derogatory* financial profit or gain: *people would risk their lives far more readily for their closely held beliefs than for filthy lucre*. [Say LOO cur]

Luddism *noun* opposition to increased industrialization or new technology. [Say LUD ism]

Luddite • *noun* **1** *hist.* a member of any of the bands of English artisans who rioted against mechanization and destroyed machinery (1811–16). **2** a person opposed to increased industrialization or new technology: *a man with marked Luddite tendency, Billy Roh gets twitchy around certain everyday conveniences.* • *adjective* of the Luddites or their beliefs. [Say LUD ite]

'lude *noun* (also **lude**) *slang* a Quaalude.

ludicrous *adjective* absurd or ridiculous; laughable: *Bill wears a red plaid jacket and a ludicrous straw hat.* ▶ **ludicrously** *adverb* [Say LOODA cruss]

luff • *noun* the edge of a fore-and-aft sail next to the mast or stay. • *verb* **1** steer (a ship) nearer the wind. **2** turn (the helm) so as to achieve this. **3** raise or lower (the jib of a crane or derrick). **4** (of a sail) flap from being set too close to the wind.

Luftwaffe *noun* *hist.* the German air force up to the end of World War II. [Say LOOFT voffa]

lug • *verb* (**lugs**, **lugged**, **lugging**) **1** drag or tug (a heavy object) with effort or violence. **2** (usu. foll. by *around, about*) carry (something heavy) around with one. • *noun* **1** a projection on an object by which it may be carried, fixed in place, etc. **2** a ridge on the sole of a shoe or boot, or on a tire, designed to provide traction. **3** *slang* an awkward or stupid person, esp. a man. **4** either of two flaps of a hat, for covering the ears.

luge • *noun* **1** a light sled with runners for one or two people, ridden in a sitting position or a lying position with face upwards. **2** the sport in which these are raced. • *verb* (**luges**, **luged**, **luging**) ride on a luge. ▶ **luger** *noun* [Say LOOZH]

Luger *noun* *proprietary* a type of German automatic pistol. [Say LOOG er]

luggage *noun* suitcases, bags, etc. to hold a traveller's belongings.

lugubrious *adjective* mournful, dismal: *lugubrious rock bands who spawned a fashion trend for basic black clothing and a general gloominess of demeanour*. ▶ **lugubriously** *adverb* **lugubriousness** *noun* [Say loo GOO bree us]

lukewarm *adjective* **1** moderately warm; tepid. **2** unenthusiastic, indifferent. ▶ **lukewarmly** *adverb* **lukewarmness** *noun*

lull • *verb* **1** soothe or send to sleep gently. **2** (usu. foll. by *into*) deceive (a person) into confidence: *lulled into a false sense of security*. **3** allay (suspicions etc.) usu. by deception. **4** (of noise, a storm, etc.) abate or fall quiet. • *noun* a temporary quiet period in a storm or in any activity.

lullaby • *noun* (*plural* **lullabies**) **1** a soothing song to send a child to sleep. **2** the music for this. • *verb* (**lullabies**, **lullabied**, **lullabying**) sing to sleep.

lulling *adjective* calming, soothing, esp. in a manner that makes one sleepy: *the lulling rhythm of the train*.

lulu *noun* (*plural* **lulus**) *slang* a remarkable, incredible, or memorable person or thing, esp. for its unpleasantness: *a lulu of a nightmare*.

lumbar *adjective* Anatomy relating to the lower back area. [Say LUMBER or LUM bar]

lumber • *noun* **1** partly or fully prepared timber. **2** *slang* a hockey stick. • *verb* **1 a** perform the labour or carry on the business of cutting and preparing timber. **b** (often foll. by *over*) go over (ground) cutting down timber. **2** burden or leave (a person etc.) with something unwanted or unpleasant: *I always get lumbered with the chores*. **3** move in a slow clumsy noisy way. PHRASES **lay on the lumber** *slang* check heavily with a hockey stick.

lumber camp *noun* a camp in which loggers live.

lumbering • *noun* **1** the lumber or timber trade. **2** the

work of cutting and preparing forest timber. • *adjective* slow and clumsy or awkward: *opponents fear the big, lumbering defenceman from Cut Knife, Saskatchewan*.

lumberjack *noun* esp. *hist.* = LOGGER.

lumberjack jacket *noun* (also **lumberjacket**) a jacket, usu. of warm, red and black checked material, originally worn by loggers.

lumberjack shirt *noun* a long-sleeved shirt of brushed cotton or flannel, usu. in red and black check.

lumberman *noun* (plural **lumbermen**) **1** a lumber company owner or manager. **2** = LOGGER.

lumber mill *noun* a factory where logs and lumber are processed.

lumber road *noun* = LOGGING ROAD.

lumberyard *noun* **1** a place where lumber is stored and sold. **2** a business operating such a place.

luminance *noun* Physics **1** the state or quality of reflecting light. **2** the intensity of light emitted from a surface per unit area in a given direction. [Say LOO min ince]

luminary *noun* (plural **luminaries**) **1** a prominent or influential member of a group or gathering: *business luminaries*. **2** a lamp or artificial light. [Say LOOMA nerry]

luminescence *noun* **1** the emission of light by a substance that has not been heated, e.g. by a firefly. **2** the light emitted by a luminescent object or surface. ▶ **luminescent** *adjective* [Say looma NESS ince]

luminosity *noun* (plural **luminosities**) **1** the quality of being luminous; brightness, radiance: *Halley's Comet was an impressive sight rivalling the brightest stars in overall luminosity*. **2** Physics the rate of emission of radiation. [Say looma NOSSA tee]

luminous *adjective* **1** full of or shedding light; radiant, bright, shining: *the luminous dial on his watch*. **2** (of a colour) very bright: *luminous paint ◊ he wore luminous green socks*. **3** (of a person's complexion or eyes) glowing with health, vigour, or a particular emotion: *her eyes were luminous with joy*. **4** of visible radiation: *luminous intensity*. ▶ **luminously** *adverb* [Say LOOM in us]

lummox *noun* (plural **lummoxes**) *informal* a clumsy or stupid person. [Say LUM ucks]

lump[1] • *noun* **1 a** a compact shapeless or unshapely mass: *a lump of dirt*. **b** a cube of sugar for putting in tea or coffee. **2** *slang* a quantity or heap. **3** a tumour, swelling, or bruise. **4** a heavy, dull, or ungainly person. **5** (in *plural*) *slang* hard knocks, attacks, defeats: *take one's lumps*. • *verb* (usu. foll. by *together, with, in with, under*, etc.) mass together or group indiscriminately. PHRASES **lump in the throat** a feeling of pressure in the throat, caused by emotion.

lump[2] *verb* *informal* endure or suffer (a situation); tolerate reluctantly. PHRASES **like it or lump it** put up with something whether one likes it or not.

lumpectomy *noun* (plural **lumpectomies**) the surgical removal of a usu. cancerous lump from the breast. [Say lump ECTA mee]

lumpen *adjective* *derogatory* ignorantly contented, boorish, stupid; uninterested in revolutionary advancement: *there will always be some lumpen layabouts who will rip off the system*. [Say LUMP in]

lumpiness *noun* the condition of something that is full of or covered with lumps.

lumpish *adjective* **1** heavy and clumsy. **2** stupid, lethargic. **3** shaped like a lump; lumpy.

lump sum *noun* **1** a sum covering a number of items. **2** money paid down at once (*opp.* INSTALMENT 1).

lumpy *adjective* (**lumpier, lumpiest**) **1** full of or covered with lumps. **2** (of water) cut up by the wind into small waves.

lun *noun* Cdn (*Nfld*) a lee; a sheltered spot.

lunacy *noun* (plural **lunacies**) **1** insanity (originally of the intermittent kind attributed to changes of the moon); the state of being a lunatic. **2** great folly or eccentricity; a foolish act. [Say LOONA see]

lunar *adjective* **1** of, relating to, resembling, or determined by the moon. **2** concerned with travel to the moon and related research.

lunar eclipse *noun* an eclipse of the moon.

lunar month *noun* the period of the moon's revolution, esp. the interval between new moons of about 29$\frac{1}{2}$ days.

lunar orbit *noun* **1** the orbit of the moon around the earth. **2** an orbit around the moon.

lunar year *noun* a period of 12 lunar months.

lunatic • *noun* **1** an insane person. **2** someone foolish or eccentric. • *adjective* mad, foolish.

lunch • *noun* (plural **lunches**) **1** the meal eaten in the middle of the day. **2** a light meal eaten at any time. • *verb* (**lunches, lunched, lunching**) eat one's lunch. PHRASES **do lunch** *informal* have lunch with a person, esp. a business associate. **out to lunch** *slang* out of touch with reality; unaware; crazy.

lunch box *noun* (plural **lunch boxes**) a plastic or metal container with a handle, for carrying a packed meal to school or work.

lunch bucket • *noun* = LUNCH BOX. • *adjective* (**lunch-bucket**) = LUNCH-PAIL *adjective*

lunch counter *noun* **1** a counter in a department store etc., where light lunches and snacks are served. **2** = LUNCHEONETTE.

luncheon *noun* a lunch, esp. a formal one. [Say LUNCH in]

luncheonette *noun* a small restaurant or snack bar serving light lunches. [Say lunch in ET]

luncheon meat *noun* a usu. tinned block of ground meat, usu. sliced and eaten cold in sandwiches etc.

luncher *noun* a person who eats or is eating lunch: *a light luncher may prefer one of our salads*.

lunch hour *noun* a break from work, usu. around the middle of the day, when lunch is eaten.

lunch pail • *noun* = LUNCH BOX. • *adjective* (**lunch-pail**) working-class; blue-collar: *lunch-pail town*.

lunchroom *noun* **1** a room in a school, office, etc. where lunch is served or where people may eat lunches brought from home. **2** = LUNCHEONETTE.

lunchtime *noun* the time around the middle of the day when lunch is usually eaten.

lung *noun* either of the pair of respiratory organs which bring air into contact with the blood in humans and many other vertebrates.

lunge[1] • *noun* **1** a sudden movement forward. **2** a thrust with a sword etc., esp. the basic attacking move in fencing. **3** a movement forward by bending the front leg at the knee while keeping the back leg straight. • *verb* (**lunges, lunged, lunging**) **1** make a lunge. **2** Fencing make a thrust with a foil or rapier.

lunge[2] *noun* = MUSKELLUNGE.

lungfish *noun* (plural **lungfish** or **lungfishes**) a freshwater fish with gills and a modified swim bladder used as lungs.

lungful *noun* (plural **lungfuls**) the amount of something, esp. air, needed to fill the lungs.

lunker *noun* *slang* an animal, esp. a fish, which is an exceptionally large example of its species; a whopper.

lunkhead *noun* (also **lunk**) *slang* a slow-witted, unintelligent person. ▶ **lunkheaded** *adjective*

lupine[1] *noun* (also **lupin**) a plant with long tapering spikes of blue, purple, pink, white, or yellow flowers. [Say LOO pin]

lupine[2] *adjective* of or like a wolf or wolves. [Say LOO pine]

L

lupus *noun* any of various diseases producing skin ulcers, esp. lupus erythematosus. [Say LOO pus]

lupus erythematosus *noun* an inflammatory disease of the skin giving rise to scaly red patches, esp. on the face, and sometimes also involving internal organs. [Say loo pus air uh theema TOE sis]

lurch • *noun* (*plural* **lurches**) a sudden unsteady movement or leaning; a stagger • *verb* (**lurches, lurched, lurching**) 1 (of a person etc.) stagger, move unsteadily. 2 (of a ship etc.) move suddenly to one side. PHRASES **leave in the lurch** desert (a friend etc.) in difficulties.

lure • *verb* (**lures, lured, luring**) 1 (usu. foll. by *away, into*) entice (a person, an animal, etc.) usu. with some form of bait. 2 attract back again or recall (a person, animal, etc.) with the promise of a reward. • *noun* 1 a thing used to entice. 2 (usu. foll. by *of*) the attractive or compelling qualities (of a pursuit etc.). 3 live or esp. artificial bait used to entice fish or animals; a decoy.

lurid *adjective* 1 sensational, horrifying, or terrible: *lurid details*. 2 showy, gaudy: *paperbacks with lurid covers*. 3 vivid or glowing in colour: *lurid orange*. 4 of an unnatural glare: *lurid nocturnal brilliance*. 5 ghastly, wan: *lurid complexion*. ▶ **luridly** *adverb* [Say LOOR id]

lurk *verb* 1 linger furtively or unobtrusively. 2 a lie in ambush. b (usu. foll. by *in, under, about,* etc.) hide, esp. for sinister purposes. 3 exist latently or semi-consciously: *a lurking suspicion*. 4 *Computing* read messages on an on-line bulletin board without contributing messages oneself. ▶ **lurker** *noun*

luscious *adjective* 1 delicious; having a rich, sweet taste: *luscious pepper squash soup*. 2 (of fabric, colours or music) soft and deep or heavy in a way that is pleasing to feel, look at or hear: *luscious silks and velvets ◊ luscious harmonies*. 3 voluptuously attractive. ▶ **lusciously** *adverb* **lusciousness** *noun*

lush[1] *slang noun* (*plural* **lushes**) an alcoholic, a drunkard.

lush[2] *adjective* 1 (of plants, gardens, etc.) growing thickly and strongly in a way that is attractive; covered in healthy grass and plants: *lush vegetation ◊ the lush, green countryside*. 2 luxurious, opulent: *a lush apartment*. 3 (of colour, sound, etc.) very rich and providing great pleasure to the senses: *lush orchestrations*. ▶ **lushly** *adverb* **lushness** *noun*

lust • *noun* 1 strong sexual desire. 2 a passionate desire for: *a lust for power*. 3 (usu. in *plural*) a sensuous appetite regarded as sinful: *the lusts of the flesh*. • *verb* (usu. foll. by *after, for*) have a strong or excessive (esp. sexual) desire. ▶ **lustful** *adjective* **lustfully** *adverb*

lustily *adverb* in a healthy, strong, and vigorous manner: *three sailors singing lustily ◊ the fans booed lustily*.

lustre (esp. *US* **luster**) • *noun* 1 the shining quality of a surface: *her hair had lost its lustre ◊ the shell had a beautiful pearly lustre*. 2 a shiny or reflective surface. 3 a thin metallic coating giving an iridescent glaze to ceramics. 4 the quality of being special in a way that is exciting; splendour, distinction: *the presence of the prince added lustre to the occasion*. • *verb* (**lustres, lustred, lustring**) put lustre on (pottery, a cloth, etc.). ▶ **lustreless** *adjective* **lustrous** *adjective* [Say LUSTER]

lusty *adjective* (**lustier, lustiest**) 1 healthy and strong. 2 vigorous or lively. 3 lustful; full of sexual desire. 4 (of a meal etc.) hearty, abundant.

lute *noun* a guitar-like instrument with a long neck and a pear-shaped body, much used in the 14th–17th centuries.

lutetium *noun* a silvery metallic element. [Say loo TEECY um]

Lutheran • *noun* a member of the Church which accepts the Augsburg Confession of 1530, whose theology (esp. the doctrine that people are justified by their faith in God rather than by the good works they may do) was inspired by the German religious reformer Martin Luther (1483–1546). • *adjective* 1 of or relating to Lutherans or the Lutheran church. 2 of or characterized by the theology of Luther. ▶ **Lutheranism** *noun* [Say LOOTH er in]

Lutz *noun* (*plural* **Lutzes**) *Figure Skating* a jump in which the skater takes off from the back outside edge of one skate, using the toe of the free foot to assist the takeoff, and lands, after at least one complete rotation in the air, on the back outside edge of the other skate.

lux *noun* (*plural* **lux**) *Physics* the SI unit of illumination. Abbreviation: **lx**. [Say LUCKS]

luxe • *noun* luxury: *gold paint adds instant luxe*. • *adjective* deluxe, sumptuous: *the excitement of luxe fabrics*. [Sounds like LUCKS]

luxuriance *noun* the condition of vegetation or hair that is rich and profuse in growth: *the luxuriance of the rainforest*. [Say lug ZHURRY ince or luck SHURRY ince]

> **WRITING TIP**
> **luxuriant, luxurious**
>
> **Luxuriant** is *not* another word for **luxurious**. It refers to lush growth of plants or hair, not to luxury.

luxuriant *adjective* (of vegetation, hair, etc.) lush, profuse in growth: *the most luxuriant coniferous forest in Canada*. [Say lug ZHURRY int or luck SHURRY int]

luxuriantly *adverb* 1 abundantly; in a lush or profuse manner: *wildflowers grow luxuriantly in the garden*, 2 in a self indulgently pleasurable or comfortable manner: *she bathed luxuriantly in the warm pool*. [Say lug ZHURRY int lee or luck SHURRY int lee]

luxuriate *verb* (**luxuriates, luxuriated, luxuriating**) enjoy (something) as a luxury; take self-indulgent delight in: *she was luxuriating in a long bath*. [Say lug ZHURRY ate or luck SHURRY ate]

luxurious *adjective* 1 characterized by luxury; sumptuous, rich: *a luxurious estate*. 2 extremely comfortable; self-indulgent: *a luxurious bath*. ▶ **luxuriously** *adverb* **luxuriousness** *noun* [Say lug ZHURRY us or luck SHURRY us]

luxury *noun* (*plural* **luxuries**) 1 choice or costly surroundings, possessions, food, etc.; luxuriousness: *a life of luxury*. 2 (often in *plural*) something desirable for comfort or enjoyment, but not indispensable. 3 a means of indulging one's tastes and desires: *the luxury of only having to work when one wants to*. 4 (as an *adjective*) providing great comfort, expensive: *luxury holiday*. [Say LUCK shur ee or LUG zhur ee]

Lw *symbol* lawrencium.

lx *abbreviation* lux.

-ly[1] *suffix* forming adjectives esp. from nouns, meaning: 1 having the qualities of: *princely*. 2 recurring at intervals of: *daily ◊ hourly*.

-ly[2] *suffix* forming adverbs from adjectives, denoting esp. manner or degree: *boldly ◊ happily ◊ deservedly*.

lychee *noun* 1 a sweet fleshy fruit with a thin spiny skin. 2 the tree, originally from China, bearing this fruit. [Say LEE chee]

Lycra *noun proprietary* an elastic polyurethane fibre or fabric used esp. for close-fitting sports clothing and foundation garments; spandex. [Say LIKE ruh]

lye *noun* 1 any strong alkaline solution, esp. of potassium hydroxide used for washing or cleansing. 2 water that has been made alkaline by percolation through vegetable ashes. [Say LIE]

lying[1] *pres. part. of* LIE[1].

lying[2] • *verb pres. part. of* LIE[2]. • *adjective* deceitful, false.

Lyme disease *noun* a form of arthritis which mainly

L

affects the large joints and is caused by spirochete bacteria transmitted by ticks. [Say LIME]

lymph *noun* a colourless liquid containing white blood cells that cleans the tissues of the body and helps to prevent infections from spreading. [Say LIMF]

lymphatic • *adjective* of or secreting or conveying lymph. • *noun* a vein-like vessel conveying lymph. [Say lim FAT ick]

lymphatic system *noun* a network of vessels conveying lymph.

lymph node *noun* (also **lymph gland**) a small mass of tissue in the lymphatic system where lymph is purified and lymphocytes are formed.

lymphocyte *noun* a form of leukocyte (white blood cell) with a single round nucleus, occurring esp. in the lymphatic system. [Say LIMF uh site]

lymphoid *adjective* denoting or having to do with the tissue responsible for producing lymphocytes and antibodies. [Say LIMF oid]

lymphoma *noun* (plural **lymphomas**) any malignant tumour of the lymph nodes, excluding leukemia. [Say lim FOME uh]

lynch *verb* (**lynches, lynched, lynching**) (of a body of people) put (a person) to death, esp. by hanging, for an alleged offence without a legal trial. ▶ **lyncher** *noun* **lynching** *noun* [Say LINCH]

lynch mob *noun* **1** a mob intent on lynching someone. **2** any unruly, angry crowd of people.

lynchpin *noun* = LINCHPIN. [Say LINCH pin]

lynx *noun* (plural **lynxes** or **lynx**) **1** any of various small to medium-sized members of the cat family typically having a short tail, tufted ears, and mottled or spotted fur, found esp. in the northern latitudes of North America and Eurasia. **2** its fur. [Say LINKS]

lyre *noun* an ancient stringed instrument like a small U-shaped harp, played usu. with a plectrum and accompanying the voice. [Sounds like *LIAR*]

lyric • *adjective* **1** (of poetry) expressing the writer's emotions, usu. briefly and in stanzas or recognized forms. **2** (of a poet) writing in this manner. **3** meant to be sung, fit to be expressed in song, song-like: *lyric opera*. **4** (of a singing voice) using a light register: *a lyric soprano*. • *noun* **1** a lyric poem or verse. **2** (in *plural*) lyric verses. **3** (usu. in *plural*) the words of a song. [Say LEAR ick]

lyrical *adjective* **1** = LYRIC 1, 2, 4. **2** resembling, couched in, or using language appropriate to, lyric poetry. **3** *informal* highly enthusiastic: *Debbie began to wax lyrical about the food, telling me how wonderful it was going to be*. ▶ **lyrically** *adverb* [Say LEAR ick ul]

lyricism *noun* the character or quality of being lyric or lyrical: *towards the end of the novel, lyricism inundates the prose*. [Say LEAR uh sism]

lyricist *noun* a person who writes the words to a song. [Say LEAR uh sist]

-lysis *combining form* forming nouns denoting disintegration or decomposition: *electrolysis*. [Say luh sis]

Lysol *noun* proprietary a disinfectant. [Say LICE oll]

L

Mm

M¹ *noun* (also **m**) (*plural* **Ms** or **M's**) **1** the thirteenth letter of the alphabet. **2** (as a Roman numeral) 1,000.

M² *abbreviation* (also **M.**) **1** Monsieur. **2** (in sizes) medium. **3** *Chemistry* molar. **4** Middle. **5** Monday.

M³ *symbol* mega-.

m¹ *abbreviation* (also **m.**) **1 a** masculine. **b** male. **2** married. **3** mile(s). **4** million(s). **5** minute(s). **6** month.

m² *symbol* **1** metre(s). **2** milli-. **3** *Physics* mass.

'm *abbreviation informal* am: *I'm sorry*.

M-16 *noun* (*plural* **M-16s**) a lightweight, automatic or semi-automatic magazine-fed rifle.

M.A. *noun* (*plural* **M.A.'s**) Master of Arts.

ma *noun* (*plural* **mas**) *informal* mother.

ma'am *noun* madam. [Say MAM]

ma-and-pa *adjective* = MOM-AND-POP.

Mac *noun informal* **1** a form of address to a male stranger. **2** a McIntosh apple.

macabre *adjective* grim, gruesome, esp. in having to do with death: *a macabre tale of cannibalism*. [Say muh COBBRA or muh COB or muh CABBRA]

macadam *noun* **1** material for road building with successive layers of compacted broken stone. **2** a material of stone or slag bound with tar, used in paving. [Say muh CAD um]

macadamia *noun* an evergreen tree with slender, glossy leaves and globular edible nut-like seeds. [Say macka DAY mee uh]

macaque *noun* a medium-sized, forest-dwelling monkey, which has a long tail and prominent cheek pouches for holding food. [Say muh CACK]

macaroni *noun* a tubular variety of pasta, usu. cut into short pieces.

macaroon *noun* a small light cookie made with egg whites, sugar, and ground almonds or coconut. [Say macka ROON]

macaw *noun* a long-tailed brightly coloured parrot native to South and Central America. [Say muh KAW]

Mace • *noun proprietary* an irritant chemical preparation used in aerosol form as a disabling weapon. • *verb* (**Maces, Maced, Macing**) (also **mace, maces, maced, macing**) spray (a person) with Mace.

mace¹ *noun* **1** a staff of office, esp. the symbol of the Speaker's authority in the House of Commons. **2** *hist.* a heavy club usu. having a metal head and spikes. **3** (also **mace-bearer**) an official who carries a mace on ceremonial occasions.

mace² *noun* the dried outer covering of the nutmeg, used as a spice.

macerate *verb* (**macerates, macerated, macerating**) make or become soft by soaking: *let the currants macerate in port for 12 hours*. ▶**maceration** *noun* [Say MASSA rate, massa RAY sh'n]

Mach *noun* (also **Mach number**) the ratio of the speed of a body to the speed of sound in the surrounding medium; it is often used with a numeral (e.g., *Mach 1*, *Mach 2*, etc.) to indicate the speed of sound, twice the speed of sound, etc. [Sounds like MOCK or MACK]

mâche *noun* = LAMB'S LETTUCE. [Say MOSH]

machete *noun* a broad heavy knife, originally used in Central America and the West Indies as an implement and weapon. [Say muh SHETTY]

Machiavellian • *adjective* **1** elaborately cunning; scheming, unscrupulous: *an account of the benefits to be derived from Machiavellian manipulation*. **2** of or characteristic of the Italian statesman and political philosopher Niccolò di Bernardo dei Machiavelli (1469–1527) or his principles, esp. that the acquisition and effective use of power may necessitate unethical methods that are not in themselves desirable. • *noun* a person who is scheming and unscrupulous, esp. in politics or advancing their career. ▶**machiavellianism** *noun* [Say macky a VELLY in]

machination *noun* (usu. in *plural*) a cunning plot or scheme: *political machinations*. [Say masha NATION or macka NATION]

machine • *noun* **1** an apparatus using or applying mechanical power, having several parts, each with a definite function which together perform certain kinds of work. **2** a particular kind of machine, e.g. a vehicle, piece of electrical or electronic apparatus, etc. **3** an instrument that transmits a force or directs its application. **4 a** the controlling system of a political party, a similar organization, etc.: *Ontario continued in the grip of the "Big Blue Machine" that controlled the province throughout the post-war period*. **b** a well-organized group acting with often ruthless efficiency: *Cincinnati's Big Red Machine won four World Series between 1970 and 1976*. **5** a person who acts mechanically and with apparent lack of emotion. **6** a coin-operated dispenser: *pop machine*. • *verb* (**machines, machined, machining**) **1** cut, make, form, or operate on by means of a machine. **2** engrave, shape, print, or sew (a thing) by means of a machine.

machine code *noun* (also **machine language**) a language that a particular computer can handle or act on directly, without further translation (*compare* SOURCE CODE).

machine gun • *noun* **1** a mounted or portable gun which is mechanically loaded and fired, giving continuous fire while the trigger is pressed. **2** (**machine-gun**) (as an *adjective*) like a machine gun, esp. in rapidly and usu. noisily repeated action: *machine-gun coughing fits*. • *verb* (**machine-gun, machine-guns, machine-gunned, machine-gunning**) shoot at with a machine gun. ▶**machine-gunner** *noun*

machine-readable *adjective* (of data) in a form that a computer can process.

machinery *noun* (*plural* **machineries**) **1** machines collectively or in general. **2** the moving parts or mechanism of a machine. **3** (foll. by *of*) an organized system: *the machinery of government*. **4** (foll. by *for*) the means or procedures devised or available: *the machinery for decision-making*.

machine shed *noun* *Cdn* (*West*) a small, auxiliary structure or outbuilding in which machines, equipment, implements, etc. are kept.

machine shop *noun* a workshop for making or repairing machines or parts of machines.

machine tool *noun* a mechanically operated tool for working on metal, wood, or plastics.

machining *noun* the working of material such as cloth or metal using a machine.

machinist *noun* **1** a person who operates machinery or a machine, esp. a machine tool. **2** a person who makes or invents machines or machinery.

machismo *noun* **1** exaggerated or aggressive pride in being male. **2** a show of such assertive manliness or masculinity. [Say muh CHIZ mo or muh KIZ mo]

Mach number *noun see* MACH.

macho • *adjective* showing aggressive pride in one's masculinity. • *noun* = MACHISMO. [Say MOTCH oh or MATCH oh]

mackerel *noun* (*plural* **mackerel** or **mackerels**) a swift-swimming predatory fish esp. of the North Atlantic and Mediterranean, which approaches the shore in summer for spawning and is commercially important as a food fish. [Say MACK rull]

mackinaw *noun* **1 a** a heavy, napped and felted woollen cloth, now usu. with a plaid design. **b** (also **mackinaw coat** or **mackinaw jacket**) a thick, double-breasted jacket, usu. short and often belted, made of this cloth. **2** (**Mackinaw**; in full **Mackinaw trout**) = LAKE TROUT. [Say MACK in awe]

> **SPELL CHECK**
> **mackintosh, McIntosh**
>
> The apple is a **McIntosh**.

mackintosh *noun* (*plural* **mackintoshes**) esp. *Brit.* a raincoat.

macramé *noun* **1** the art of knotting cord or string in patterns to make decorative articles. **2** articles made in this way. [Say MACRA may]

macro • *noun* (*plural* **macros**) *Computing* a series of abbreviated instructions expanded automatically when required. • *adjective* **1** large-scale: *a macro virus* ◊ *take extreme close-ups with a macro lens*. **2** overall, comprehensive: *the analysis of events at the macro level*.

macro- *combining form* **1** long, large: *macromolecule*. **2** large-scale, comprehensive: *macroeconomics*.

macrobiotic • *adjective* relating to or following a dietary system intended to prolong life, usu. comprised of pure vegetable foods, brown rice, etc. • *noun* (**macrobiotics**; treated as *singular*) the use or theory of such a dietary system. [Say macro bye OTT ick]

macrocosm *noun* **1** the universe; the whole of all nature: *the law of the macrocosm*. **2** a complex structure or whole, esp. one considered to be epitomized by some constituent portion or microcosm: *the family is a microcosmic unit of the macrocosm of the state*. ▶**macrocosmic** *adjective* [Say MACRO kozzum, macro COSMIC]

macroeconomic *adjective* having to do with large-scale or general economics. [Say macro ECONOMIC]

macroeconomics *noun* the study of large-scale or general economic factors, e.g. national productivity. [Say macro ECONOMICS, macro ECONOMIST]

macromolecule *noun* a molecule containing a very large number of atoms and having a very high molecular weight. [Say macro MOLECULE]

macronutrient *noun* a chemical required in relatively large amounts for the growth and development of living organisms. [Say macro NUTRIENT]

macrophage *noun* a large white blood cell responsible for engulfing and digesting bacteria and cell debris at points of infection or injury, esp. in the spleen, lymph nodes, liver, and lungs. [Say MACRO fage (FAGE rhymes with *CAGE*)]

> **WRITING TIP**
> **mad, very mad**
>
> Instead of saying that someone is **mad** or **very mad**, try to use more precise and interesting adjectives:
>
> *Angry demonstrators protested outside the building.*
> I was **annoyed** at her for hanging up on me.
> He became **enraged** when the other children teased him.
> After an hour of trying to assemble the barbecue, I became **exasperated** and gave up.
> Passengers grew **frustrated** as the delay continued.
> The more they argued, the more **furious** they became.
> Workers were **incensed** by the arbitrator's decision.
> She's still **indignant** about not being invited.
> The politician was **infuriated** by the verbal attack.
> **Irate** callers jammed the phone lines to complain.
> I get **irritated** when he starts to whine.
> He forgot her birthday again and she's **livid.**
> The public was **outraged** when he was let out on parole.

mad *adjective* (**madder, maddest**) **1** insane; having a disordered mind. **2** (of a person, conduct, or an idea) wildly foolish. **3** carried away by enthusiasm or desire: *mad about hockey* ◊ *is power-mad*. **4** *informal* a beside oneself with anger; furious. **b** annoyed, exasperated. **5** (of an animal) **a** suffering from rabies. **b** abnormally furious. **6 a** frantic, wild, desperate: *a mad dash*. **b** wildly lighthearted. **7** (of a storm, wind, etc.) wild, violent. PHRASES **like mad** *informal* with great energy, intensity, or enthusiasm.

madam *noun* **1** a polite or respectful form of address or mode of reference to a woman. **2** a woman who keeps a brothel. [Say MAD um]

Madame *noun* (*plural* **Mesdames**) a title or form of address used of or to a French-speaking woman, corresponding to Mrs. or madam. **2** (**madame**) = MADAM 1. [Say muh DAM or MAD um for the singular, may DAM for the plural]

madcap *adjective* **1** (of a person) reckless, wildly impulsive. **2** (of an endeavour etc.) undertaken without forethought.

mad cow disease *noun informal* bovine spongiform encephalopathy, a usu. fatal virus disease of cattle involving the central nervous system.

> **SPELL CHECK**
> **maddening, madding**
>
> A secluded place is sometimes described as *far from the madding crowd*. This is also the title of a novel by Thomas Hardy. It is wrong to say "far from the maddening crowd"

madden *verb* **1** make or become mad. **2** irritate intensely. ▶**maddening** *adjective* **maddeningly** *adverb*

madder *noun* **1** a plant with yellowish flowers. **2** a reddish-purple dye obtained from the root of the madder, or its synthetic substitute.

madding *adjective* PHRASES **far from the madding crowd** (of a place) secluded, removed from public notice.

> **SPELL CHECK**
> **made, maid**
>
> A female servant or young woman is a **maid**.

made • *verb* past and past participle of MAKE. • *adjective*

(usu. in *combination*) **1** (of a person or thing) built or formed artificially or in a specified manner: *well-made*. **2** successful: *a self-made man*. PHRASES **be made for** be ideally suited to. **be made of** consist of. **have it made** *informal* be sure of success.

made beaver *noun* *Cdn hist.* (*plural* **made beaver** or **made beavers**) **1** a unit of exchange formerly used among fur traders, equivalent to the value of the prepared skin of one adult beaver in prime condition. **2** a coin or token equivalent to this.

made-for-TV *adjective* (also **made-for-television**) **1** (of a film etc.) specially made for first showing on television, not in theatres. **2** (of a set, event, sound bite, etc.) ideally suited to television.

Madelinot *noun* *Cdn* a resident or native of the Magdalen Islands. [Say madda leen OH]

made man *noun* (*plural* **made men**) a man who has attained success or whose success in life is assured.

made-to-measure *adjective* **1** (of clothing, draperies, etc.) made to a specific customer's measurements, specifications, etc. **2** conceived, designed, or particularly suited for a specific situation etc.: *a made-to-measure solution*.

made up *adjective* **1** invented, not true. **2** (of a person) wearing makeup. **3** (of a meal etc.) already prepared.

madhouse *noun* **1** esp. *hist.* a home or hospital for the mentally ill. **2** *informal* a scene of extreme confusion or uproar.

Madison Avenue *noun* **1** a street in New York where many American advertising agencies have their offices. **2** the American advertising industry: *consumers are easily swayed by the Madison Avenue approach that promotes perception rather than reality.*

madly *adverb* **1** in a mad, insane, or foolish manner. **2** a passionately, fervently. **b** extremely, very.

madman *noun* (*plural* **madmen**) an insane, wildly foolish, or furious man.

madness *noun* the quality or state of being mad.

Madonna *noun* *Christianity* **1** (**the Madonna**) a name for the Virgin Mary. **2** (usu. **madonna**) a picture or statue of the Madonna.

madras *noun* **1** a strong cotton fabric with brightly coloured or white stripes, checks, etc. **2** (**Madras**; in full **Madras curry**) a hot spiced curry dish usu. made with chicken or beef. [Say muh DRASS]

madrigal *noun* a song for several singers usu. without instrumental accompaniment, having a secular rather than a religious theme and featuring interwoven melodies and the use of many nonsense syllables like *fah-lah-lah*. [Say MADRA gull]

madroño *noun* (*plural* **madroños**) (also **madroña**, *plural* **madroñas**) an evergreen tree of western North America, with peeling red bark, white flowers, red berries, and glossy leaves; an arbutus. [Say muh DRO nyo, muh DRO nya]

mad scientist *noun* a wildly eccentric or dangerously insane scientist, esp. as a stock figure in melodramatic horror stories.

madwoman *noun* (*plural* **madwomen**) an insane, wildly foolish, or furious woman.

maelstrom *noun* **1** a great whirlpool. **2** a state of turbulence or confusion: *she is at the centre of an academic maelstrom*. [Say MAIL strum]

maestoso *adjective & adverb* *Music* to be performed majestically. [Say my STO zo]

maestro *noun* (*plural* **maestros**) (often as a form of address) **1** a distinguished musician, esp. a conductor or performer. **2** a great performer in any sphere, esp. artistic: *a movie maestro*. [Say MY stro]

Mafia *noun* **1** an organized secret society of criminals, originating in Sicily but now operating internationally,

esp. in the US. **2** (**mafia**) **a** a similar criminal organization based in another country and sometimes operating internationally: *Russian mafia*. **b** any closely united group regarded as exerting a secret and often sinister influence: *the prison mafia*. [Say MOFFY uh or MAFFY uh]

Mafioso *noun* (*plural* **Mafiosi**) a member of the Mafia. [Say moffy OH so or maffy OH so for the singular, moffy OH see or maffy OH see for the plural]

mag *noun* **1 a** *informal* a magazine (periodical). **b** *informal* a magazine (in a rifle etc.). **2** *informal* **a** magnesium. **b** magnetic. **3** magnitude.

magazine *noun* **1** a periodical publication containing articles, stories, etc. by various writers, usu. with photographs, illustrations, etc. **2** a chamber for holding a supply of cartridges to be fed automatically to the breech of a repeating rifle, machine gun, etc. **3** a similar device feeding a camera, slide projector, etc. **4 a** a building for the storage of arms, ammunition, and provisions for use in war. **b** a store for large quantities of explosives. **5** a regular television or radio broadcast format comprising a variety of entertainment or news items.

Magen David *noun* = STAR OF DAVID. [Say maw GIN daw VID (with G as in *GONE*)]

magenta *noun & adjective* brilliant mauvish-crimson. [Say muh JENTA]

maggot *noun* any soft-bodied limbless larva, esp. of a fly, typically found in decaying organic matter. ▶ **maggoty** *adjective*

magi *plural of* MAGUS. [Say MAY jie]

magic • *noun* **1 a** the supposed art of influencing events by the occult control of nature or spirits. **b** witchcraft. **2** the art of producing by sleight of hand, optical illusion, etc. apparently inexplicable phenomena. **3** an inexplicable or remarkable influence producing surprising results. **4** an enchanting quality or phenomenon. **5** *informal* exceptional skill or talent. • *adjective* **1 a** of, pertaining to, working, or produced by magic. **b** (of a material object) used or usable in magic rites; having supernatural powers: *magic wand*. **2** producing surprising results, like those attributed to magic. **3** *informal* wonderful, exciting, fantastic. • *verb* (**magics**, **magicked**, **magicking**) change or create by magic, or apparently so: *the TV genius who magicked up three hit shows*. PHRASES **like magic 1** very rapidly. **2** without any apparent explanation.

magical *adjective* **1** of or relating to magic. **2 a** resembling magic in action or effect. **b** produced as if by magic. **3** wonderful, enchanting. ▶ **magically** *adverb*

magic bullet *noun* *informal* a cure-all or universal remedy, esp. any usu. undiscovered highly specific and highly successful drug.

magic carpet *noun* a mythical carpet able to transport a person on it to any desired place.

magician *noun* **1** a person skilled in or practising magic or sorcery. **2** a conjuror. **3** a person with exceptional skill: *is a magician with the puck*.

Magic Marker *noun* *proprietary* a felt-tipped indelible marker pen.

magic mushroom *noun* a mushroom that causes hallucinations when ingested.

magic realism *noun* (also **magical realism**) a literary or artistic genre in which realism and narrative are combined with surreal, fantastic, dreamlike, or mythological elements. ▶ **magical realist** *noun & adjective*

magic word *noun* a word or phrase the utterance of which effects magic or creates a desired effect.

M

magisterial *adjective* **1** having or showing power or authority: *magisterial advice* ◊ *a magisterial authority figure*. **2** showing great knowledge, understanding, or skill: *a magisterial text* ◊ *performs with magisterial focus and seriousness*. **3** having to do with a magistrate: *magisterial office*. ▶ **magisterially** *adverb* [Say madge iss TEERY ul]

magistrate *noun* **1** an official conducting a court for minor cases and preliminary hearings. **2** a civil officer administering the law. [Say MADGE iss trate]

Magistrate's Court *noun Cdn* = PROVINCIAL COURT.

maglev *noun* magnetic levitation, a system in which magnetic repulsion supports a train above the rail or rails on which it runs, allowing it to glide along in a magnetic field: *maglev trains*. [Say MAG lev]

magma *noun* **1** a hot fluid or semi-liquid material beneath the crust of the earth or other planet, which erupts as lava and from which igneous rock is formed by cooling. **2** a crude pasty mixture of mineral or organic matter. ▶ **magmatic** *adjective* [Say MAG muh, mag MAT ick]

Magna Carta *noun* (also **Magna Charta**) **1** a charter of political rights that King John of England was forced to sign by his rebellious barons in 1215, effectively redefining the limits of royal power; over time, the rights granted to nobles were extended to all citizens, making it an important and influential document in later English constitutional practice. **2** any similar document: *the Quebec Act of 1774 is sometimes described as the Magna Carta for French Canada*.

magna cum laude *adverb & adjective* (of a degree, diploma, etc.) with or of great distinction; of a higher standard than average, though not the highest (compare SUMMA CUM LAUDE). [Say magna koom LOUD ay]

magnanimity *noun* noble generosity, esp. towards a rival or enemy: *her magnanimity in sharing insights is a model for all scholars*. [Say magna NIM it ee]

magnanimous *adjective* nobly generous; not petty in feelings or conduct: *the company reaped magnanimous praise from tough critics*. ▶ **magnanimously** *adverb* [Say mag NANA muss]

magnate *noun* a wealthy and influential person, esp. in business: *shipping magnate*. [Say MAG nate or MAG nit]

magnesia *noun* **1** magnesium oxide, a white solid compound with a high melting point, used to line furnaces and fireplaces. **2** (in general use) hydrated magnesium carbonate, a white powder used as an antacid and laxative. [Say mag NEEZHA]

magnesium *noun* a naturally occurring silvery metallic element, used for making light alloys and an essential element in living organisms. [Say mag NEEZY um]

 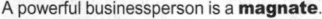
magnet *noun* **1** a piece of iron, steel, alloy, ore, etc., usu. in the form of a bar or horseshoe, having properties of attracting or repelling iron. **2** a person or thing that attracts.

magnetic *adjective* **1** having the properties of a magnet or pertaining to a magnet or magnetism. **2** capable of being attracted by or acquiring the properties of a magnet. **3** very attractive or alluring: *a magnetic personality*. **4** (of a bearing, direction, etc.) measured relative to magnetic north. ▶ **magnetically** *adverb*

magnetic disk *noun* see DISK 1a.

magnetic field *noun* a region of variable force around magnets or current-carrying conductors.

magnetic flux *noun* a measure of the quantity of magnetism, taking account of the strength and extent of a magnetic field.

magnetic north *noun* the north magnetic pole, usu. the point indicated by a compass needle.

magnetic pole *noun* **1** each of the points of the earth's surface, near to but not corresponding to the geographical poles, where the lines of force of the earth's magnetic fields are vertical. **2** a point at which magnetic force is concentrated, esp. either of two such opposite points or regions of a magnet.

magnetic resonance imaging *noun* a form of medical imaging using the nuclear magnetic resonance of protons in the body. Abbreviation: **MRI**.

magnetic stripe *noun* (also **magnetic strip**) a strip of magnetized material on the back of a credit card etc. containing electronically coded information.

magnetic tape *noun* a tape coated with magnetic material for recording sound or pictures or for the storage of information.

magnetism *noun* **1 a** the characteristic properties of magnetic phenomena, esp. attraction. **b** the property of matter producing these phenomena. **2** an attractive power or influence, esp. personal charm: *his personal magnetism attracted students from all over Europe*.

magnetite *noun* magnetic iron oxide, an important ore of iron.

magnetization *noun* the act of making something into a magnet or of becoming a magnet.

magnetize *verb* (**magnetizes**, **magnetized**, **magnetizing**) **1** give magnetic properties to; make into a magnet. **2** attract as if by a magnet: *they are magnetized into the whirling climax of the dance*.

magnetometer *noun* an instrument measuring magnetic forces, esp. the earth's magnetism. [Say magna TOM it er]

magnetosphere *noun* the not necessarily spherical region surrounding a planet, star, etc. in which its magnetic field is effective and prevails over other magnetic fields. ▶ **magnetospheric** *adjective* [Say mag NEETA sphere, mag neeta SPHERE ick]

magnification *noun* **1 a** the action or process of magnifying by or as by a lens. **b** the process of being so magnified. **2** the amount or degree of magnification. **3** a magnified reproduction.

magnificence *noun* splendidness, grandeur, nobility, impressiveness: *at the top of our climb we sat and enjoyed the magnificence of the view*. [Say mag NIFFA since]

magnificent *adjective* splendid; impressive. ▶ **magnificently** *adverb* [Say mag NIFFA s'nt]

magnifier *noun* a piece of equipment used to make things look larger.

magnify *verb* (**magnifies**, **magnified**, **magnifying**) **1** make (a thing) appear larger than it is, as with a lens. **2** exaggerate: *she tends to magnify the imperfections of those she doesn't like*. **3** intensify: *the sound was magnified by the low roof*. **4** *archaic* glorify, esp. render honour to (God): *my soul doth magnify the Lord*.

magnifying glass *noun* a convex lens used to increase the apparent size of an object viewed through it.

magnitude *noun* **1** great size or extent: *the magnitude of their task*. **2** importance: *discoveries of great magnitude*. **3 a** each of a set of classes into which stars are arranged according to their brilliance, stars of the first magnitude being the most brilliant, those of the sixth barely visible to the naked eye. **b** the relative brightness of a star according to this scale. **4** the intrinsic size of an earthquake or underground explosion, as distinct from local intensity. PHRASES **of the first magnitude** very important.

magnolia *noun* **1** a tree or shrub with dark green foliage and large, creamy-pink, wax-like flowers in spring. **2** a pale, creamy pink colour. [Say mag NO lee uh]

magnum *noun* (*plural* **magnums**) **1 a** a wine bottle of about twice the standard size. **b** the quantity of liquor held by such a bottle. **2** (**Magnum**) *proprietary* **a** a gun cartridge or shell that is especially powerful or large. **b** a cartridge or gun adapted so as to be more powerful than its calibre suggests.

magnum opus *noun* **1** a great and usu. large work of art, literature, etc. **2** the most important work of an artist, writer, etc. [Say magnum OPE us]

magpie *noun* **1** a European and North American bird of the crow family, with a long pointed tail, black and white plumage, and a noisy chattering call, proverbial for its habit of taking and hoarding bright objects. **2** a person who collects things indiscriminately.

magus *noun* (*plural* **magi**) **1** a member of a priestly caste of ancient Persia. **2** a sorcerer. **3** *Christianity* (**the** (**three**) **Magi**) the "wise men" from the East who brought gifts to the infant Christ. [Say MAY gus for the singular, MAY jie for the plural]

mag wheel *noun* a lightweight, steel wheel for a motor vehicle, often with an intricate pattern of holes and spokes.

Magyar • *noun* **1** a member of the predominant cultural group in Hungary, who migrated from Russia in the 9th century. **2** the language of this people; Hungarian. • *adjective* of or relating to this people or language. [Say MAG yar]

maharaja *noun* (also **maharajah**) *hist.* a title of some Indian princes of high rank. [Say maw huh RAW juh]

maharishi *noun* **1** a great Hindu sage or spiritual leader. **2** a popular leader of spiritual thought. [Say maw huh REESHY]

mahatma *noun* **1** (in India etc.) a person regarded with reverence, love, and respect. **2 a** each of a class of persons in India and Tibet supposed by some to have supernatural powers. **b** a wise or holy person. [Say muh HATMA or muh HOTMA]

Mahayana *noun* one of the two major traditions of Buddhism, now practised in a variety forms in esp. China, Japan, Tibet, and Korea. [Say maw huh YAWN uh]

Mahdi *noun* (*plural* **Mahdis**) **1** a spiritual and temporal messiah expected by Muslims. **2** a leader claiming to be this Messiah. ▶ **Mahdist** *noun* [Say MODDY, MOD ist]

mahi mahi *noun* the common dolphin, eaten as food. [Say MAW hee maw hee]

mah-jong *noun* (also **mah-jongg**) a Chinese game for four, resembling rummy and played with 136 or 144 pieces called tiles. [Say maw JONG]

mahogany • *noun* (*plural* **mahoganies**) **1** a rich, reddish-brown wood used for furniture. **2** a tropical tree yielding this wood. **3** a deep rich reddish-brown. • *adjective* of a rich reddish-brown colour. [Say muh HOGGA nee]

maid *noun* **1** a female domestic servant. **2** *literary* a girl or young woman.

maiden • *noun* *literary* a girl; a young unmarried woman. • *adjective* **1** unmarried: *maiden aunt*. **2** being or involving the first attempt or occurrence: *maiden voyage*. **3 a** (of soil etc.) that has never been disturbed; unworked. **b** (of a plant or tree) grown from seed as opposed to a stock; not pruned or transplanted.

maidenhair *noun* (also **maidenhair fern**) a tropical fern that has fine hairlike stalks and delicate fronds.

maidenhead *noun* **1** virginity. **2** the hymen.

maidenly *adjective* of or suggesting a girl or young unmarried woman: *charmed by her maidenly beauty*.

maiden name *noun* a wife's surname before marriage.

maid of honour *noun* **1** an unmarried woman who acts as a bride's principal bridesmaid (*compare* MATRON OF HONOUR). **2** an unmarried lady attending a queen or princess.

> **SPELL CHECK**
> **mail, male**
>
> The opposite of female is **male**.

mail¹ • *noun* **1 a** letters, parcels, etc. conveyed by the postal system. **b** the postal system. **c** one complete delivery or collection of mail. **d** one delivery of letters to one place, esp. to a business on one occasion. **2 a** = E-MAIL. **b** = VOICE MAIL. **3** a vehicle carrying mail. **4** (**the mails**) the postal service, esp. serving remote areas as the North etc. • *verb* send (a letter etc.) through the postal service.

mail² • *noun* **1** armour made of interlaced rings or chains, or overlapping plates, joined together flexibly. **2** the protective shell, scales, etc., of an animal. • *verb* clothe with or as if with mail.

mailbag *noun* **1** a large sack or bag for carrying mail. **2** the correspondence, comments, etc. received by a radio station, television program, etc.

mail bomb • *noun* **1** an explosive device disguised as a letter or package and sent through the mail. **2** a huge, useless file sent by e-mail to take up a large amount of the recipient computer's memory, disk space, etc. • *verb* send a mail bomb.

mailbox *noun* **1 a** a public receptacle into which letters are dropped for delivery by the postal service. **b** a private receptacle to which letters are delivered. **2** the file etc. in which electronic or voice mail is received and stored.

mailed *adjective* wearing or protected by armour of interlaced chains or flexibly joined metal plates.

mailer *noun* **1** an advertising pamphlet, brochure, or catalogue sent out in the mail. **2** a container such as a cardboard tube etc. for the conveyance of items, esp. papers, by mail. **3** a person or thing which dispatches messages etc. by mail, electronic mail, etc.

mailing *noun* **1 a** the action or process of sending something by mail. **b** a letter or parcel sent by mail. **2** a batch of mail or a number of items mailed at one time, esp. as part of a publicity campaign, survey, etc.

mailing address *noun* the address to which one has one's mail sent, esp. if different from that of one's office, home, etc.

mailing list *noun* a list of people to whom advertising matter, information, etc. is to be mailed regularly.

mailman *noun* (*plural* **mailmen**) a postman.

mail merge *noun* *Computing* **1** a program that draws on a file of names and addresses and a text file to produce multiple copies of a letter, each addressed to a different recipient. **2** the facility for doing this.

mail order • *noun* **1** an order for goods sent by mail. **2** a system of buying and selling goods by mail. • *verb* (**mail-order**) buy through mail-order catalogues etc.

mailroom *noun* a room in a company etc. where mail is collected, sorted, or otherwise dealt with.

mail slot *noun* a slit in the door of a house, apartment, etc. through which letters are delivered.

maim *verb* **1** cripple, disable, mutilate. **2** harm, impair, render powerless or essentially incomplete: *emotionally maimed by neglect*.

M

---

main • *adjective* **1** chief in size, importance, extent, etc.; principal: *the main part* ◊ *the main point*. **2** (of strength etc.) exerted to the full; sheer: *by main force*. • *noun* **1** a principal channel, duct, etc., for water, sewage, etc.: *water main*. **2** esp. *Brit*. (**the mains**) **a** the central distribution network for electricity, gas, water, etc. **b** a domestic electricity supply as distinct from batteries. **3** *literary* **a** the ocean or oceans: *the Spanish Main*. **b** the mainland. ⬛PHRASES⬛ **in the main** for the most part. **with might and main** with all one's strength.

main chance *noun* ⬛PHRASES⬛ **an eye for** (or **to**) **the main chance** consideration for one's own interests.

main clause *noun* *Grammar* a clause that alone forms a complete sentence (*compare* SUBORDINATE CLAUSE).

main course *noun* (also **main dish**) **1** the chief course of a meal. **2** any of a number of substantial dishes in a large menu.

main drag *noun* *informal* = MAIN STREET.

mainframe *noun* **1** a large or general-purpose computer, esp. one supporting numerous peripherals etc. **2** the central processing unit and primary memory of a computer.

mainland *noun* **1** a large continuous extent of land, including the greater part of a country or territory and excluding neighbouring islands, peninsulas, etc. **2** (**Mainland**) *Cdn* (*Nfld*) **a** the provinces of Canada other than Newfoundland. **b** (to those on the coastal islands) the coast of Labrador. **3** (**Mainland**) *Cdn* (*BC*) (usu. as **the Mainland**) the heavily populated lowland region of southwestern BC, around the city of Vancouver. ▶ **mainlander** *noun*

mainline • *adjective* (of an institution etc.) well established and adhering to norms of conduct or belief; moderate in opinions, attitudes, etc.: *mainline churches*. • *noun* **1** (usu. **main line**) a principal railway line. **2** *Forestry* the primary, heavy cable used to haul logs from the forest to the landing. **3** *slang* a principal vein, esp. as a site for a drug injection. • *verb* *slang* take drugs intravenously.

mainly *adverb* for the most part; chiefly.

main man *noun* (*plural* **main men**) **1** a principal figure on a team, in a political campaign, etc. **2** the principal performer in a band. **3** *slang* a close and usu. trusted friend or companion.

mainmast *noun* the principal mast of a ship.

main memory *noun* *Computing* random access memory.

mainsail *noun* **1** (in a square-rigged vessel) the lowest sail on the mainmast. **2** (in a fore-and-aft-rigged vessel) a sail set on the after part of the mainmast. [Say MAIN sail or MAIN sull]

mainsheet *noun* *Nautical* the rope which controls the boom of the mainsail when set.

mainspring *noun* **1** a chief motive, reason, or incentive: *the mainspring of the plot of the play is incest*. **2** the principal spring of a mechanical clock etc.

main squeeze *noun* *slang* a lover.

mainstage *noun* the stage of the principal theatre operated by a theatrical company, usu. the one on which major works are performed.

mainstay *noun* a chief support or principal element: *Swan Lake is a mainstay of the repertoire*.

mainstream • *adjective* **1** belonging to or characteristic of an established field of activity. **2** of or pertaining to the mainstream. • *noun* **1** the prevailing trend in opinion, fashion, etc. **2** the stream of education or a class at school etc. for students without special needs. **3** a type of jazz based on the swing style of the 1930s and consisting esp. of solo improvisation on chord sequences. **4** the principal current of a river. • *verb* **1 a** place (a child with a disability) in a school or class for those without special needs for all or part of the school day. **b** educate in such an integrated environment. **2** incorporate into the mainstream. ▶ **mainstreamer** *noun* **mainstreaming** *noun*

main street *noun* the principal street of a town or city.

mainstreet *verb* *Cdn* campaign in main streets to win political support: *all day long he mainstreeted in downtown Kelowna*.

mainstreeting *noun* *Cdn* political campaigning in main streets to win support.

maintain *verb* **1** cause to continue; keep up, preserve (a state of affairs, an activity, etc.): *maintained friendly relations*. **2** support (life, a condition, etc.) by work, nourishment, expenditure, etc.: *maintained him in comfort*. **3** support or uphold, esp. in speech or argument: *maintained that she was the best*. **4** preserve or provide for the preservation of (a building, machine, road, etc.) in good repair. **5** give aid to (a cause, party, etc.). **6** pay for the upkeep, repair, or equipping of (a garrison etc.).

maintenance *noun* **1 a** the action or process of maintaining or being maintained. **b** the state or fact of being maintained. **2 a** the provision of the means to support life, esp. by work etc. **b** a husband's or wife's provision for a spouse after separation or divorce. **3** (as an *adjective*) (of a drug, dosage, treatment, etc.) sufficient to sustain an esp. beneficial effect on the body.

maintenance man *noun* a man employed for caretaking and janitorial duties.

maison de la culture *noun* (*plural* **maisons de la culture**) *Cdn* (*Que*.) a cultural centre, usu. containing a library, theatre, and exhibition space for visual arts. [Say ZON duh la kool toor (with ON as in French and with OO as in *WOOL* and *POOR*)]

maître d' *noun* (*plural* **maître d's**) = MAÎTRE D'HOTEL. [Say may truh DEE or may tur DEE]

maître d'hotel *noun* (*plural* **maîtres d'hotel**) **1** the manager etc. of a hotel. **2** a head waiter. [Say may truh doe TELL or mettra doe TELL]

maize *noun* esp. *Brit*. = CORN[1] 1.

Maj *abbreviation* (also **Maj.**) MAJOR *noun* 1.

majestic *adjective* showing majesty; stately and dignified; grand, imposing. ▶ **majestically** *adverb*

majesty *noun* (*plural* **majesties**) **1** impressive dignity or beauty. **2 a** royal power. **b** (**Majesty**) (preceded by *your*, *her*, *his*, *their*, etc.) a title used to refer to or address a sovereign or a sovereign's wife or widow.

majolica *noun* earthenware with coloured decoration on a white glaze. [Say muh JAW lick uh or muh YAW lick uh]

major • *adjective* **1** important, large, serious, significant: *a major road* ◊ *the major consideration must be their health*. **2** *Music* **a** (of a scale) having intervals of a semitone between the third and fourth, and seventh and eighth degrees. **b** (of an interval) greater by a semitone than a minor interval: *major third*. **c** (of a key) based on a major scale, tending to produce a bright or joyful effect: *D major*. **3** legally adult. • *noun* **1** *Military* **a** (in the Canadian or US Army and Air Force and other armies) an officer of a rank next below lieutenant colonel and above captain. Abbreviation: **Maj** *Cdn* or **Maj. b** an officer in charge of a section of band instruments. **2** a person considered legally an adult. **3** *Music* a major key etc. **4 a** the principal subject or course of a student at university or college. **b** a student specializing in a specified subject: *a philosophy major*. **5** (in *plural*) the major leagues. **6** *Hockey* = MAJOR PENALTY.

7 designating levels of amateur hockey for competitors between the ages of 18 and 21, or for younger players if their skills are adequate to compete with older players. • *verb* (foll. by *in*) study or qualify in a subject: *majored in history*.

majorette *noun* = DRUM MAJORETTE.

major general *noun* (in the Canadian or US Army and Air Force and other armies) an officer of a rank next below a lieutenant general and above brigadier general or brigadier.

majoritarian • *adjective* **1** governed by or believing in majority rule: *prevents true majoritarian politics from operating in America*. **2** of, relating to, or constituting a majority: *the majoritarian will as expressed by the state*. • *noun* a person who supports majority rule. ▶ **majoritarianism** *noun* [Say muh jorra TERRY in]

majority *noun* (*plural* **majorities**) **1** (usu. foll. by *of*) the greater number or part. **2** *Politics* **a** the number by which the votes cast for one party, candidate, etc. exceed those of the next in rank: *won by a majority of 151* (compare PLURALITY 3). **b** a party etc. receiving the greater number of votes. **3** full legal age: *attained her majority*. PHRASES **in the majority** belonging to or constituting a majority party etc.

majority government *noun* *Cdn, Brit., Austral., & NZ* a government that has more than half of the total number of parliamentary seats.

majority leader *noun* (in the US) the floor leader of the party having the majority in a legislature.

majority rule *noun* the principle that the greater number should exercise greater power.

major junior *noun* *Cdn* the highest level of amateur hockey competition.

major league • *noun* **1** either of the two principal professional baseball leagues in North America, the American League and the National League. **2** a similar league in other sports. **3** a category in any field considered to be the most demanding, most professional, or of the highest calibre. • *adjective* (usu. **major-league**) **1** of or relating to a major league: *set a major-league record*. **2** of the highest order. ▶ **major-leaguer** *noun*

majorly *adverb* *slang* to a great extent.

major penalty *noun* (*plural* **major penalties**) *Hockey* a five-minute penalty, given esp. for fighting.

major planet *noun* see PLANET 1.

major prophet *noun* each of the prophets (Isaiah, Jeremiah, and Ezekiel) for whom the longer prophetic books of the Bible are named and whose prophecies they record.

make • *verb* (**makes**, **made**, **making**) **1** form by putting parts together or combining substances. **2** cause to be or come about. **3** force to do something. **4** alter (something) so that it forms (something else). **5** constitute, amount to, or serve as. **6** estimate as or decide on. **7** gain or earn (money or profit). **8** arrive at or achieve. **9** prepare to go in a particular direction or do a particular thing: *he made toward the car*. **10** arrange bedclothes tidily on (a bed) ready for use. • *noun* **1** (esp. of a product) a type, origin, brand, etc. of manufacture. **2** a kind of mental, moral, or physical structure or composition. PHRASES **make as if** (or **though**) act as if the specified circumstances applied: *made as if she had not noticed*. **make away** (or **off**) depart hastily. **make away with 1** get rid of; kill. **2** squander. **make a day** (or **night** etc.) **of it** devote a whole day (or night etc.) to an activity. **make do 1** manage with the limited or inadequate means available. **2** (foll. by *with*) manage with (something) as an inferior substitute. **make for 1** tend to result in (happiness etc.). **2** proceed towards (a place). **make it** *informal* **1** succeed in reaching, esp. in

time. **2** be successful. **3** (usu. foll. by *with*) *slang* have sexual intercourse (with). **make it up 1** be reconciled, esp. after a quarrel. **2** fill in a deficit. **make it up to** remedy negligence, an injury, etc. to (a person). **make like** *informal* pretend to be; imitate. **make much** (or **little**) **of 1** derive much (or little) advantage from. **2** give much (or little) attention, importance, etc., to. **make of 1** construct from. **2** conclude to be the meaning or character of: *can you make anything of it?* **make off** = MAKE AWAY. **make off with** carry away; steal. **make or break** cause the success or ruin of. **make out 1 a** distinguish by sight or hearing. **b** decipher (handwriting etc.). **2** understand: *can't make him out*. **3** assert; pretend: *made out she liked it*. **4** *informal* make progress; fare: *how did you make out?* **5** (usu. foll. by *to*) draw up; write out: *made out a cheque to her*. **6** *informal* indulge in sexual activity usu. stopping short of intercourse. **7** prove or try to prove: *how do you make that out?* **make over 1** transfer the possession of (a thing) to a person. **2** refashion (a garment etc.). **3** change (a person, institution, etc.) to fit a new image. **make up 1** serve or act to overcome (a deficiency). **2** complete (an amount, a party, etc.). **3** compensate. **4** be reconciled. **5** put together; compound; prepare. **6** sew (parts of a garment etc.) together. **7** get (a sum of money, a company, etc.) together. **8** concoct (a story). **9** (of parts) compose (a whole). **10 a** apply cosmetics. **b** apply cosmetics to. **11** settle (a dispute). **12** prepare (a bed) for use with fresh sheets etc. **13** compile (a list, an account, a document, etc.). **make up to** curry favour with; court. **on the make** *informal* **1** intent on gain. **2** looking for sexual partners.

make-believe • *noun* pretense. • *adjective* pretended.

make-do *adjective* makeshift.

make-over *noun* a complete transformation or remodelling.

maker *noun* **1** (often in *combination*) a person or thing that makes. **2** a manufacturer. **3** (**our**, **the**, etc. **Maker**) God. PHRASES **meet one's maker** *informal* die.

makeshift *adjective* temporary: *a makeshift arrangement*.

makeup *noun* **1** cosmetics for the face etc., either generally or to create a performer's appearance or disguise. **2** the appearance of the face etc. when cosmetics have been applied: *his makeup was not convincing*. **3** a person's character, temperament, etc. **4** the composition or constitution (of a thing). **5** a supplementary test or assignment given to a student who missed or failed the original one: *makeup exam*.

make-work *noun* **1** work or activity of little or no value, devised mainly to keep someone busy: *a make-work project*. **2** *Cdn* designating an esp. government-sponsored project, program, grant, etc. intended to create jobs: *make-work programs*.

making *noun* **1** in senses of MAKE *verb*. **2** (in *plural*) **a** earnings; profit. **b** (usu. foll. by *of*) essential qualities or ingredients: *has the makings of a general* ◊ *we have the makings of a meal*. **c** *informal* paper and tobacco for rolling a cigarette. PHRASES **be the making of** ensure the success or favourable development of. **in the making** in the course of being made or formed.

mako *noun* (*plural* **makos**) a large blue shark of tropical and temperate oceans worldwide. [Say MACK oh]

malachite *noun* a bright green mineral of hydrous copper carbonate, taking a high polish and used ornamentally. [Say MALA kite]

maladaptive *adjective* (of an individual, species, etc.) failing to adjust adequately to the environment, and undergoing emotional, behavioural, physical, or mental repercussions: *his resistance to entering therapy*

M

was part of the same maladaptive pattern that maintained the family's problems in the first place.

maladjusted *adjective* **1** not correctly adjusted. **2** (of a person) unable to adapt to or cope with the demands of a social environment. ▶ **maladjustment** *noun*

maladroit *adjective* clumsy; bungling: *both parties are unhappy about the maladroit handling of the whole affair.* ▶ **maladroitly** *adverb* [Say MALA droit]

malady *noun* (*plural* **maladies**) **1** a disease or ailment: *an incurable malady.* **2** something that is wrong or is a cause for complaint: *the nation's maladies.* [Say MALA dee]

Malagasy • *adjective* of or relating to Madagascar, an island country off the eastern coast of Africa. • *noun* (*plural* **Malagasies**) **1** the language of Madagascar. **2** a native or inhabitant of Madagascar. [Say mala GASSY]

malaise *noun* **1** he problems affecting a particular situation or group of people that are difficult to explain or identify: *economic malaise ◊ the latest crime figures are merely symptomatic of a wider malaise in society.* **2** a general feeling of being ill, unhappy, or not satisfied, without signs of any particular problem: *a serious malaise among the staff.* [Say mu LAZE]

malamute *noun* a dog of a breed developed in Alaska, with a thick grey or black and white coat, pointed ears, and a plumed tail curling over the back. [Say MALA mute]

malapropism *noun* (also **malaprop**) the use of a word in mistake for one sounding similar, to comic effect, e.g. *consummated* for *consommé.* [Say MALA prop ism]

malaria *noun* an intermittent and remittent fever caused by a protozoan parasite of the genus *Plasmodium*, introduced by the bite of a mosquito. ▶ **malarial** *adjective* [Say muh LAIRY uh]

malarkey *noun* *informal* humbug; nonsense. [Say muh LARKY]

malathion *noun* an insecticide containing phosphorus, with low toxicity to other animals. [Say mala THIGH un]

Malay • *noun* **1 a** a member of a people inhabiting Malaysia and Indonesia in Southeast Asia. **b** a person of Malay descent. **2** the language of this people, the official language of Malaysia. • *adjective* of or relating to this people or language. [Say muh LAY]

Malayan • *noun* = MALAY *noun* 1. • *adjective* of or relating to Malays or Malaya (now part of Malaysia). [Say muh LAY un]

Malayo-Polynesian • *adjective* of or relating to the Malays and the Polynesians, or to Malayo-Polynesian. • *noun* a family of languages (also called **Austronesian**) extending from Madagascar in the west to the Pacific islands in the east, including Indonesian, Tagalog, Malagasy, Micronesian, Melanesian, and Polynesian. [Say muh LAY yo polla NEE zhun]

Malaysian • *noun* a native or inhabitant of Malaysia in Southeast Asia. • *adjective* of or relating to Malaysia or its people. [Say muh LAY zhun]

malcontent • *noun* a discontented person; a rebel: *the strike was engineered by a handful of malcontents.* • *adjective* discontented or rebellious: *a malcontent hanger-on at Kate's café.* [Say MAL kun tent]

> **SPELL CHECK** **male, mail** ABC ✓
>
> The spelling is **mail** for the sending of letters or messages and for a type of armour.

male • *adjective* **1** of the sex that can beget offspring by fertilization or insemination. **2** of men or male animals, plants, etc.; masculine: *playing a male role ◊ male choir.* **3** (of plants or their parts) containing only fertilizing organs. **4** (of parts of machinery etc.)

designed to enter or fill the corresponding female part: *a male plug.* • *noun* a male person, animal, or plant.

male bonding *noun* the formation of friendship and loyalty between males, esp. between a particular pair of male associates.

male chauvinism *noun* the attitude of some men that regards women as inferior.

male chauvinist *noun* (also **male chauvinist pig**) *derogatory* a man who is prejudiced against women or regards women as inferior.

Malecite *noun & adjective* = MALISEET. [Say MALA site]

malefactor *noun* a criminal; an evildoer: *some malefactors have escaped without being punished.* [Say MALA factor]

malemute *noun* = MALAMUTE. [Say MALA mute]

maleness *noun* the essence or quality of being male; masculinity.

malevolence *noun* the desiring of evil for someone else; hostility, ill will: *breaking their windows was an act of pure malevolence.* [Say muh LEVVA lince]

malevolent *adjective* wishing evil to others: *the glint of dark, malevolent eyes ◊ some malevolent force of nature.* ▶ **malevolently** *adverb* [Say muh LEVVA l'nt]

malfeasance *noun* *Law* evildoing; illegal action: *the auditor cited numerous instances of bad spending, if not outright malfeasance.* [Say mal FEEZ ince]

malformation *noun* faulty formation. ▶ **malformed** *adjective*

malfunction • *noun* a failure to function in a normal or satisfactory manner. • *verb* fail to function normally or satisfactorily.

malice *noun* the intention to do evil or to injure another person. [Say MAL iss]

malice aforethought *noun* *Law* the intention to commit a crime, esp. murder.

malicious *adjective* characterized by malice; intending or intended to do harm. ▶ **maliciously** *adverb* **maliciousness** *noun* [Say mu LISH us]

malign • *adjective* evil in nature or effect; malevolent: *she had a strong and malign influence over him.* • *verb* speak ill of; slander: *don't you dare malign her in my presence.* [Say muh LINE]

malignancy *noun* (*plural* **malignancies**) **1** a tumour; a malignant mass of tissue in the body. **2** the state of being malevolent: *her eyes sparkled with renewed malignancy.* [Say muh LIG nun see]

malignant *adjective* **1 a** (of a disease) very virulent or infectious: *malignant cholera.* **b** (of a tumour) tending to invade normal tissue and recur after removal; cancerous. **2** harmful; feeling or showing intense ill will: *his future was left in the hands of malignant fate.* ▶ **malignantly** *adverb* [Say muh LIG nint]

malinger *verb* exaggerate or feign illness in order to escape duty, work, etc. ▶ **malingerer** *noun* [Say muh LINGER]

Maliseet (*plural* **Maliseet**) • *noun* **1** a member of an Aboriginal people now occupying northwestern New Brunswick and eastern Quebec. **2** the Algonquian language of this people. • *adjective* of or relating to this people or their language or culture. [Say MALA seet]

> **SPELL CHECK** **mall, maul** ABC ✓
>
> An animal which attacks someone **mauls** them.

mall *noun* **1** a retail complex containing several stores, restaurants, etc., in a single building or adjacent buildings. **2** a sheltered walk or promenade.

mallard *noun* (*plural* **mallards**) a common wild duck or drake of the northern hemisphere, the male of which

has a green head, narrow white collar, chestnut breast, and a blue patch on the wings. [Say MAL urd or MAL ard]

malleable *adjective* **1** (of metal etc.) able to be hammered or pressed permanently out of shape without breaking or cracking. **2** (of a person) adaptable: *younger actresses with more malleable identities.* [Say MAL I Y uh bull]

mallet *noun* **1** a type of hammer, usu. made of wood and having a relatively large head, used for driving chisels, beating metal, etc. **2** a light hammer used for playing the vibraphone etc. **3** a long-handled wooden hammer for striking a croquet or polo ball.

mallow *noun* **1** a plant with hairy stems, pink or purple flowers, and disc-shaped fruit, naturalized in North America and often grown as an ornamental. **2** any of several plants resembling or related to this.

mall rat *noun informal* a person, esp. a teenager, who frequents malls to socialize etc.

malnourished *adjective* suffering from malnutrition.

malnutrition *noun* (also **malnourishment**) a dietary condition resulting from the absence of some foods or essential elements necessary for health.

malodorous *adjective* foul smelling. [Say mal ODOROUS]

Malpeque oyster *noun Cdn* a large edible oyster raised in Malpeque Bay in PEI. [Say MAUL peck]

malpractice *noun* careless, wrong, or illegal behaviour while in a professional job: *medical malpractice ◊ a malpractice suit ◊ he is currently standing trial for alleged malpractices.*

malt • *noun* **1** barley or other grain that is steeped, germinated, and dried, esp. for brewing or distilling and vinegar making. **2 a** = MALT WHISKY. **b** = MALT LIQUOR. **3** = MALTED MILK. • *verb* **1** convert (grain) into malt. **2** (of seeds) become malt when germination is checked by drought.

malted • *adjective* **1** converted into malt. **2** mixed with malt or a malt extract. • *noun* = MALTED MILK.

malted milk *noun* **1** a powder made from dried milk and malted cereals. **2** a drink made of this and milk, usu. with ice cream and flavouring.

Maltese • *noun* **1** (*plural* **Maltese**) **a** a native or national of Malta, an island country in the central Mediterranean. **b** a person of Maltese descent. **2** the Semitic language of Malta, heavily influenced by Italian. • *adjective* of Malta or its people. [Say maul TEASE]

Maltese cross *noun* a cross with arms of equal length broadening from the centre, often indented at the ends.

Malthusian • *adjective* of or relating to T. R. Malthus, English clergyman and economist (1766–1834) or his theories, esp. that without the practice of "moral restraint" the population tends to increase at a greater rate than its ability to feed itself, resulting in the population checks of war, famine, and epidemic. • *noun* a follower of Malthus. ▶ **Malthusianism** *noun* [Say mal THOOZEY un]

malt liquor *noun* alcoholic liquor made from malt by fermentation as opposed to distillation, e.g. beer etc.

maltreat *verb* ill-treat. ▶ **maltreatment** *noun*

malt whisky *noun* (*plural* **malt whiskies**) whisky made from malted barley.

malty *adjective* (**maltier, maltiest**) of, containing, or resembling malt.

mama *noun informal* (esp. as a child's term) mother.

mama's boy *noun informal* a boy or man who is excessively influenced by or devoted to his mother.

mambo • *noun* (*plural* **mambos**) **1** a Latin American dance like the rumba. **2** the music for this. • *verb*

(**mamboes, mamboed, mamboing**) perform the mambo.

mamma¹ *noun informal* = MAMA.

mamma² *noun* (*plural* **mammae**) **1** a milk-secreting organ of female mammals, e.g. the breast in human females. **2** a corresponding structure in male mammals, which does not secrete milk. [Say MAM uh for the singular, MAM ee for the plural]

mammal *noun* any warm-blooded animal of the vertebrate class Mammalia, members of which are characterized by the possession of mammary glands in the female and a four-chambered heart. ▶ **mammalian** *adjective & noun* [For *mammalian* say muh MAIL yun]

mammary *adjective* of the human female breasts or milk-secreting organs of other mammals. [Say MAM ur ee]

mammogram *noun* an image obtained by mammography. [Say MAM a gram]

mammography *noun* an X-ray technique of diagnosing and locating abnormalities (esp. tumours) of the breasts. [Say muh MOGRA fee]

Mammon *noun* wealth regarded as an idol or as an evil influence: *gamblers worshipping at the temple of Mammon.* ▶ **Mammonism** *noun* [Say MAM un]

mammoth • *noun* a large extinct elephant with a hairy coat and curved tusks. • *adjective* huge.

mammy *noun* (*plural* **mammies**) dated a child's word for mother.

Man. *abbreviation* Manitoba.

WRITING TIP
man

Because the most common meaning of **man** is "a male human being", the use of the word to mean "any person" or "the human race", as in *All men are created equal* or *man's astounding technical achievements*, is often perceived as excluding women. To avoid accusations of sexism, it may be safest to use alternative constructions, e.g. *All people are created equal*, or *humankind's astounding technical achievements*.

---

man • *noun* (*plural* **men**) **1** an adult human male. **2** a male member of a workforce, team, etc. **3** a husband or lover. **4** a person. **5** human beings in general. **6** a figure or token used in a board game. • *verb* (**mans, manned, manning**) provide (a place or machine) with the personnel to run, operate, or defend it. • *interjection informal* expressing surprise, admiration, etc. PHRASES **as one man** in unison; in agreement. **be a man** be courageous; not show fear. **be one's own man** be free to act; be independent. **man to man** with candour; honestly. **separate** (or **sort out**) **the men from the boys** *informal* find those who are truly virile, competent, etc. **to a man** all without exception.

man about town *noun* (*plural* **men about town**) a sophisticated man who frequently goes to fashionable clubs, parties, theatres, etc.

manacle • *noun* (usu. in *plural*) a fetter or shackle for the hand; a handcuff. • *verb* (**manacles, manacled, manacling**) fetter with manacles. [Say MAN a cull]

manage *verb* (**manages, managed, managing**) **1** be in charge of (a business, household, team, a person's career, etc.). **2** succeed in achieving; contrive: *managed a smile ◊ managed to ruin the day.* **3 a** (often foll. by *with*) succeed in one's aim, esp. against heavy odds: *managed with one assistant.* **b** meet one's needs with limited resources etc.: *just about manages on her pension.* **4** gain influence with or maintain control over (a person etc.): *cannot manage their teenage son.* **5 a** cope

with; make use of: *couldn't manage another bite* ◊ *can you manage by yourself?* **b** be free to attend on (a certain day) or at (a certain time): *can you manage Thursday?* **6** handle or wield (a tool, weapon, etc.).

manageability *noun* the quality of being manageable.

manageable *adjective* able to be easily managed, controlled, or accomplished etc. ▶ **manageably** *adverb*

management *noun* **1** the action or process of managing or being managed. **2 a** the professional administration of business concerns, public undertakings, etc. **b** the people engaged in this. **c** (**the management**) a governing body; a board of directors or the people in charge of running a business, regarded collectively. **3** the technique of treating a disease etc.

manager *noun* **1** a person controlling or administering a business or part of one. **2** a person controlling the affairs, training, etc. of a person or team in sports, entertainment, etc. **3** a person regarded in terms of skill in household or financial or other management: *a good manager*. ▶ **managerial** *adjective* [For *managerial* say manna JEERY ul]

managing *adjective* (in *combination*) having executive control or authority: *managing director*.

mañana • *adverb* in the indefinite future (esp. to indicate procrastination). • *noun* an indefinite future time. [Say mun YONNA]

manatee *noun* any large aquatic plant-eating mammal, with paddle-like forelimbs, no hind limbs, and a powerful tail. [Say manna TEE]

Manchu • *noun* (*plural* **Manchus**) **1** a member of a people in China, descended from a Tartar people, who formed the last imperial dynasty (1644-1912). **2** the language of the Manchus, now spoken in parts of northeast China. • *adjective* of or relating to the Manchu people or their language. [Say man CHOO]

mandala *noun* **1** a symbolic circular figure representing the universe in Hinduism and Buddhism. **2** *Psychology* such a symbol in a dream, held to represent the dreamer's search for completeness and self-unity. [Say MANDA luh]

mandarin *noun* **1** (**Mandarin**) the most widely spoken form of Chinese and the official language of China. **2** *hist.* a Chinese official in any of nine grades of the pre-Communist civil service. **3 a** a bureaucrat: *the memoirs of various diplomats, politicians, and mandarins*. **b** a powerful member of the establishment: *the changes in ice dancing were inserted into the books by the mandarins of the sport*. **4** (also **mandarin orange**) **a** a small flattish deep-coloured orange with a loose skin. **b** the tree yielding this. [Say MANDA rin]

mandate • *noun* **1** an order given to a person, organization, etc. to carry out a certain task: *the committee's mandate is to report on all options*. **2 a** a support for a policy or course of action, regarded by a victorious party, candidate, etc., as derived from the wishes of the people in an election: *a referendum or election seeking a mandate to negotiate a deal with Quebec*. **b** *Cdn* the period during which a government is in power: *halfway through its mandate, the government wanted to give the impression that it had new projects*. **3** a commission to act for another. • *verb* (**mandates, mandated, mandating**) **1** require, esp. by law; make mandatory. **2** instruct (a delegate) to act or vote in a certain way.

mandatory *adjective* compulsory; required by law or regulation: *it is mandatory for blood banks to test all donated blood for the virus*. [Say MANDA tory]

mandatory supervision *noun Cdn Law* supervision by a parole officer of a convict serving the last part of a sentence in the community after being released from prison, usu. because of good behaviour in the first two-thirds of the sentence.

man-day *noun* a day of work etc. by one person, as a unit of measure.

mandible *noun* **1** the jaw, esp. the lower jaw in mammals and fishes. **2** the upper or lower part of a bird's beak. **3** either of the two parts that are at the front and on either side of an insect's mouth, used especially for biting and crushing food. ▶ **mandibular** *adjective* [Say MANDA bull, man DIB yoo lur]

mandolin *noun* **1** a musical instrument resembling a lute, having paired metal strings plucked with a pick. **2** (also **mandoline**) a kitchen utensil fitted with cutting blades and used for slicing vegetables. ▶ **mandolinist** *noun* (in sense 1). [Say manda LIN]

mandrake *noun* a poisonous plant with white or purple flowers and large yellow fruit, causing vomiting and sleepiness and possessing a root once thought to resemble the human form and to shriek when plucked.

mandrel *noun* **1** a shaft inserted into a workpiece to secure it to a lathe (*compare* CHUCK *noun* 2). **2** a cylindrical rod round which metal or other material is forged or shaped. [Say MAN drull]

mandrill *noun* a large West African baboon, the adult of which has a bright red and blue face and blue buttocks. [Say MAN drill]

SPELL CHECK
mane, main

The spelling is **main** in "the main reason" and "water main".

---

mane *noun* **1** long hair growing in a line on the neck of a horse, lion, etc. **2** a person's long, thick hair.

man-eater *noun* **1** an animal, esp. a shark or tiger, that eats human flesh. **2** *informal* a woman who has many men as lovers and is perceived as using them for her own advantage.

maned *adjective* having a mane or long thick hair, esp. of a specified kind: *his silver-maned, handsome face*.

maneuver *noun* = MANOEUVRE.

man Friday *noun* a male helper or follower; a right-hand man.

manful *adjective* brave; resolute. ▶ **manfully** *adverb*

manganese *noun* **1** a grey brittle metallic element used with steel to make alloys. **2** (also **manganese oxide**) the black mineral oxide of this used in the manufacture of glass. [Say MANGA neez]

mange *noun* a skin disease in hairy and woolly animals, caused by a parasite and occasionally communicated to humans. [Rhymes with *RANGE*]

manger *noun* a long open box or trough in a barn etc. for livestock to eat from.

manger scene *noun* = NATIVITY SCENE.

mangia-cake *noun Cdn derogatory* or *jocular* (among Italian-Canadians) a non-Italian white person, esp. of British stock, with characteristically North American traits or customs. [Say MUNJA cake]

mangle[1] *noun* esp. *Brit. hist.* a machine having two or more cylinders usu. turned by a handle, between which wet clothes etc. are squeezed and pressed; a wringer.

mangle[2] *verb* (**mangles, mangled, mangling**) **1** crush, bend, break, or mutilate (something), esp. so that it is difficult to ascertain its original form. **2** spoil (a quotation, text, etc.) by misquoting, mispronouncing, etc. ▶ **mangler** *noun*

mango *noun* (*plural* **mangoes** or **mangos**) **1** a fleshy yellowish-red fruit, eaten ripe or used green for pickles etc. **2** the Indian evergreen tree bearing this fruit.

mangrove *noun* **1** a tropical tree or shrub that grows in shore mud with many tangled roots above ground.

2 any of various other trees or shrubs resembling this. [Say MANG grove]

mangy *adjective* (**mangier, mangiest**) **1** (esp. of a domestic animal) having mange. **2** in poor condition; shabby: *mangy, withered vegetables*. [Say MAIN jee]

manhandle *verb* (**manhandles, manhandled, manhandling**) **1** move (heavy objects) by human effort. **2** *informal* handle (a person) roughly.

manhattan *noun* a cocktail made of vermouth, whisky, etc.

Manhattanite *noun* a native or inhabitant of Manhattan, a borough of New York City occupying an island at the mouth of the Hudson River.

manhole *noun* a covered opening allowing access to a sewer, tunnel, boiler, etc.

manhood *noun* **1** the state of being a man rather than a child or woman. **2 a** manliness; courage. **b** a man's sexual potency. **c** *informal euphemism* the penis. **3** men collectively. **4** the state of being human.

man-hour *noun* an hour regarded in terms of the amount of work that could be done by one person within this period.

manhunt *noun* an organized search for a person, esp. a criminal.

mania *noun* **1** *Psychology* mental illness marked by periods of great excitement and violence. **2** (often foll. by *for*) an extreme or abnormal desire or enthusiasm: *has a mania for jogging*.

-mania *combining form* **1** *Psychology* denoting a special type of mental abnormality or obsession: *megalomania* ◊ *nymphomania*. **2** denoting extreme enthusiasm or admiration: *Trudeaumania*.

maniac • *noun* **1** a person exhibiting extreme symptoms of wild behaviour etc.; an insane person. **2** an obsessive enthusiast. • *adjective* of or behaving like a maniac. ▶ **-maniac** *combining form*

maniacal *adjective* wild or violent, esp. suggesting insanity: *a maniacal laugh*. ▶ **maniacally** *adverb* [Say muh NYE a cull]

manic *adjective* **1** of or affected by mania. **2** frenzied, elated, or abnormally energetic as if affected by a manic disorder. ▶ **manically** *adverb* [Say MAN ick]

manic depression *noun* a mental disorder characterized by alternating periods of great happiness and depression.

manic-depressive • *adjective* affected by or relating to a mental disorder with alternating periods of great happiness and depression. • *noun* a person having such a disorder.

Manichean • *noun* an adherent of a religious system of the 3rd–5th centuries, representing Satan, evil, or darkness in a state of everlasting conflict with God, goodness, or light. • *adjective* **1** of or relating to Manicheans. **2** of or characterized by contrast or conflict between opposites: *a very Manichean view, where you have the artists on one side, who are very pure, and on the other side you have the world, which is Satanic*. ▶ **Manicheism** *noun* [Say manna KEY un, manna KEY ism]

manicotti *noun* large tubular pasta, usu. served stuffed with ricotta cheese and covered with tomato sauce. [Say manna COTTY]

manicure • *noun* a usu. professional cosmetic treatment of the hands and fingernails. • *verb* (**manicures, manicured, manicuring**) **1** apply a manicure to (the hands or a person). **2** trim or cut neatly: *manicured the lawn*. ▶ **manicured** *adjective*

manicurist *noun* a person who manicures hands and fingernails professionally.

manifest • *adjective* clear or obvious to the eye or mind: *her distress was manifest*. • *noun* a list of the cargo or passengers carried by a ship, truck, aircraft, etc. • *verb* **1** display or show (a quality, feeling, etc.) by one's acts etc.: *this confidence is manifested in a willingness to revive cultural traditions*. **2** show plainly to the eye or mind. **3** (of a thing) reveal itself: *the symptoms of the disease manifested themselves ten days later*. **4** (of a ghost) appear. ▶ **manifestation** *noun*

manifest destiny *noun* the esp. 19th-century belief that the US was intended by God to expand to the Pacific coast, and eventually to cover all of North America.

manifestly *adverb* clearly, obviously, evidently: *I thought the show was great, but he was manifestly bored*.

manifesto *noun* (*plural* **manifestos** or **manifestoes**) a public declaration of principles, intentions, purposes, etc.: *his party's manifesto proposes that Quebec become sovereign before entering into a new relationship with the rest of Canada*. [Say manna FESS toe]

manifold • *adjective* *literary* **1** many and various: *the possibilities were manifold*. **2** having various forms, parts, applications, etc.: *the appeal of the crusade was manifold*. • *noun* a pipe or chamber branching into several openings: *the exhaust manifold*. [Say MANNA fold]

SPELL CHECK
manikin, mannequin

A model for displaying clothing is a **mannequin**.

---

manikin *noun* **1** a little person; a dwarf. **2** a dummy or jointed figure of a human body used by artists for arranging drapery on etc. **3** an anatomical model of the body. [Say MANNA kin]

manila *noun* **1** (also **manila hemp**) the strong fibre of a Philippine tree, used for rope etc. **2** a strong brown paper made from manila hemp or other material and used for wrapping paper, envelopes, etc. [Say muh NILLA]

man in the street *noun* an ordinary average person, as distinct from an expert.

manioc *noun* a plant with starchy tuberous roots from which tapioca is obtained. *Also called* CASSAVA. [Say MANNY ock]

manipulable *adjective* that may be manipulated. [Say muh NIP yoo luh bull]

manipulate *verb* (**manipulates, manipulated, manipulating**) **1** handle, treat, or use, esp. skilfully (a tool, question, material, etc.). **2** manage (a person, situation, etc.) to one's own advantage, esp. unfairly or unscrupulously. **3** manually examine and treat (a part of the body). **4** *Computing* alter, edit, or move (text, data, etc.). ▶ **manipulation** *noun* [Say muh NIP yoo late]

manipulative *adjective* **1** characterized by unscrupulous exploitation of a situation, person, etc. for one's own ends. **2** of, concerning, or causing manipulation. [Say muh NIP yoo luh tiv]

manipulator *noun* a person who manipulates, esp. one who is skilful at influencing people or situations in order to get what he or she wants.

Manitoba maple *noun* a fast-growing North American maple with leaflets arranged in pairs on either side of the stem, found east of the Rockies.

Manitoban • *adjective* of or relating to Manitoba. • *noun* a resident or native of Manitoba.

manitou *noun* (esp. among the Cree and Ojibwa) **1** a good or evil spirit as an object of reverence. **2** something regarded as having supernatural power. [Say MANNA too]

M

mankind *noun* **1** the human species. **2** male people, as distinct from female.

manlike *adjective* **1** having the qualities of a man. **2** (of an animal, shape, etc.) resembling a human being.

manliness *noun* the quality of being manly or of having qualities regarded as admirable in a man.

manly *adjective* (**manlier, manliest**) **1** having qualities regarded as admirable in a man, such as courage, frankness, strength, etc. **2** (of things, qualities, etc.) befitting a man.

man-made *adjective* made by humans; synthetic.

manna *noun* **1** *Bible* the substance miraculously supplied as food to the Israelites in the wilderness. **2** (also **manna from heaven**) an unexpected benefit: *the abundant federal manna that blanketed the provinces on the eve of the election*.

manned *adjective* (of an aircraft, spacecraft, etc.) having a human crew.

mannequin *noun* **1** a three-dimensional model of a human body, used when making clothes or esp. for displaying them in stores. **2** a model employed by a couturier etc. to show clothes to customers. [Say MANNA kin]

manner *noun* **1** a way a thing is done or happens: *always dresses in that manner*. **2** (in *plural*) **a** the social habits and customs, esp. of a particular group: *18th-century aristocratic manners*. **b** polite or well-bred behaviour: *has no manners*. **3** a person's outward bearing, way of speaking, etc.: *has an imperious manner*. **4** a style in literature, art, etc.: *in the manner of Leacock*. **5** a kind or sort: *what manner of man is he?* PHRASES **all manner of** many different kinds of. **in a manner of speaking** in some sense; to some extent; so to speak. **to the manner born 1** *informal* naturally at ease in a specified job, situation, etc. **2** destined by birth to follow a custom or way of life.

mannered *adjective* **1** behaving in a specified way: *ill-mannered*. **2** (of behaviour, art, writing, etc.) trying to impress people by being formal and not natural: *his prose style is far too mannered and self-conscious*.

mannerism *noun* **1** a particular habit or way of speaking or behaving that someone has but is not aware of: *toying with a strand of hair is a mannerism that men studiously avoid*. **2** too much use of a particular style in painting or writing: *he indulges in the annoying mannerism of overloading his text with exclamation marks*. **3** (usu. **Mannerism**) a style of 16th-century Italian art preceding the Baroque, characterized by unusual and often bizarre effects of scale, lighting, and perspective, and the use of bright colours, e.g. the works of Bronzino and Caravaggio. ► **mannerist** *noun*

mannerly *adjective* well-mannered; polite.

mannikin *noun* = MANIKIN. [Say MANNA kin]

manning depot *noun* *Cdn hist.* (during World War II) a training depot for recruits to the Royal Canadian Air Force.

mannish *adjective* **1** usu. *derogatory* (of a woman) masculine in appearance or manner. **2** characteristic of a man. ► **mannishness** *noun*

manoeuvrability *noun* the quality of being manoeuvrable: *I like the manoeuvrability of smaller cars*.

manoeuvrable *adjective* able to be manoeuvred easily.

manoeuvre (also **maneuver**) • *noun* **1** a planned and controlled movement or series of moves: *you will be asked to perform some standard manoeuvres during your driving test*. **2** (in *plural*) a large-scale exercise of troops, warships, etc.: *the army is on manoeuvres in the Arctic*. **3** an often deceptive planned or controlled action designed to gain an objective: *diplomatic manoeuvres*. • *verb* (**manoeuvres, manoeuvred, manoeuvring**) **1** perform or cause to perform a manoeuvre: *manoeuvred the car into the space*. **2** perform or cause (troops etc.) to perform military manoeuvres. **3** (usu. foll. by *into, out, away*) force, drive, or manipulate (a person, thing, etc.) by scheming or skill: *she manoeuvred her way to the top of the company*. ► **manoeuvrer** *noun*

man of the cloth *noun* a clergyman.

man-of-war *noun* *hist.* an armed sailing ship.

man on the street *noun* = MAN IN THE STREET.

manor *noun* **1** (also **manor house**) a large house with lands. **2** *Brit.* **a** a unit of land consisting of a lord's estate and lands rented to tenants etc. **b** *hist.* a feudal lordship over lands. ► **manorial** *adjective* [For *manorial* say muh NORRY ul]

manpower *noun* **1** the power generated by a person working, as opposed to by a machine etc. **2** people available for work, service, etc. **3** *Cdn hist.* (often **Manpower**) a government department offering job referral services for the unemployed: *manpower centre*.

manqué *adjective* (placed after noun) that might have been but is not: *a comic actor manqué*. [Say mong KAY]

mansard *noun* a roof which has four sloping sides, each of which becomes steeper halfway down. [Say MAN sard]

manse *noun* the house, owned by a congregation, of an esp. Presbyterian or United Church minister. PHRASES **son** (or **daughter**) **of the manse** a child of an esp. Presbyterian minister.

manservant *noun* (*plural* **menservants**) a male servant.

mansion *noun* a large house.

man-sized *adjective* (also **man-size**) **1** of the size of a man. **2** big enough for a man: *a man-sized sandwich*. **3** *informal* very large: *a man-sized project*.

manslaughter *noun* **1** the killing of a human being. **2** *Law* the unlawful killing of a human being without the intention to do so.

manta *noun* a large ray living in all tropical seas, with wing-like pectoral fins and a whip-like tail.

mantel *noun* (also **mantelpiece**) **1** a structure of wood, marble, etc. above and around a fireplace. **2** (also **mantelshelf**) a shelf above a fireplace.

M

mantis *noun* (*plural* **mantis** or **mantises**) a slender insect related to the cockroach, which feeds on other insects.

> **SPELL CHECK**
> **mantle, mantel**
>
> The shelf over a fireplace is a **mantel**.

mantle • *noun* **1** a loose sleeveless cloak. **2** a covering: *a mantle of snow*. **3** a fragile lacelike tube fixed around a jet of burning gas to give an incandescent light. **4** the plumage of the back and folded wings of a bird, esp. if distinct in colour. **5** the region between the crust and the core of the earth. • *verb* (**mantles, mantled, mantling**) clothe in or as if in a mantle; cover, conceal: *heavy mists mantled the forested slopes behind the village*.

mantra *noun* **1** a word or sound repeated to aid concentration in meditation. **2** a hymn or text from the Vedas, the most ancient Hindu scriptures. **3** a frequently repeated word, phrase, etc; a slogan: *"axe the tax" was the Liberals' mantra before they were elected*.

manual • *adjective* **1** of or relating to the hand or hands. **2** done or performed with the hands. **3** involving physical rather than mental effort: *manual labour*. **4** worked by hand, not by automatic equipment or with electronic assistance etc.: *manual transmission*. **5** not involving computers or electronic transmission of data etc. • *noun* **1 a** a book of instructions, esp. for operating a machine or learning a subject; a handbook: *a computer manual*. **b** any small book. **2** an organ keyboard played with the hands not the feet. ▶ **manually** *adverb*

manufacture • *noun* **1 a** the making of articles esp. in a factory etc. **b** a branch of an industry: *woollen manufacture*. **2** a manufactured item or product: *a major importer of cotton manufactures*. • *verb* (**manufactures, manufactured, manufacturing**) **1** make (articles), esp. on an industrial scale. **2** invent or fabricate (evidence, a story, etc.): *a news story manufactured by an unscrupulous journalist*. ▶ **manufacturer** *noun*

manure • *noun* **1** animal dung used for fertilizing land. **2** any compost or artificial fertilizer. *See also* GREEN MANURE. • *verb* apply manure to (land etc.).

manuscript • *noun* **1** a book, document, etc. written by hand. **2** an author's text submitted for publication. **3** handwritten form: *produced in manuscript*. • *adjective* written by hand.

Manx • *adjective* **1** of or relating to the Isle of Man, a British Crown possession in the Irish Sea. **2** designating a tailless cat. • *noun* **1** the now extinct Celtic language formerly spoken in the Isle of Man. **2** (**the Manx**; treated as *plural*) the Manx people.

many • *adjective* great in number; numerous. • *noun* (as *plural*) a large number: *many like skiing*. PHRASES **have one too many** become drunk. **as many** the same number of: *six mistakes in as many lines*. **as many again** the same number additionally: *sixty here and as many again there*. **be too** (or **one too**) **many for** outwit, baffle. **a good** (or **great**) **many** a large number. **many's the time** often: *many's the time we saw it*. **many a time** many times.

many-sided *adjective* having many sides, aspects, interests, capabilities, etc. ▶ **many-sidedness** *noun*

Maoism *noun* the Communist doctrines of the Chinese statesman Mao Zedong (1893–1976) as formerly practised in China, having as a central idea permanent revolution and stressing the importance of the peasantry, of small-scale industry, and of agricultural collectivization. ▶ **Maoist** *noun* & *adjective* [Say MOW ism (MOW rhymes with COW)]

Maori • *noun* (*plural* **Maori** or **Maoris**) **1** a member of the Polynesian aboriginal people of New Zealand. **2** the language of the Maori. • *adjective* of or concerning the Maori or their language. [Rhymes with *FLOWERY*]

map • *noun* **1 a** a usu. flat representation of the earth's surface, or part of it, showing physical features, cities, etc. (*compare* GLOBE 2). **b** a diagrammatic representation of a route etc.: *drew a map of the journey*. **2** a two-dimensional representation of the stars, the heavens, etc., or of the surface of a planet, the moon, etc. **3** a diagram showing the arrangement or components of a thing, esp. of the sequence of genes on a chromosome or of bases in a DNA or RNA molecule. **4** *Math* a correspondence by which each element of a given set has associated with it one or more elements of a second set. • *verb* (**maps, mapped, mapping**) **1** represent (a country etc.) on a map. **2** *Math* associate each element of (a set) with one element of another set. **3** record in detail the spatial distribution of something: *the project to map the human genome*. PHRASES **all over the map** disorganized; lacking a central focus: *the presentation was all over the map*. **map out** arrange in detail; plan (a course of conduct etc.). **put on the map** *informal* establish as prominent or important. **wipe off the map** *informal* obliterate.

maple *noun* **1** a tree or shrub with usu. lobed leaves and colourful fall foliage, frequently grown for shade, ornament, wood, or its sugar. **2** the wood of the maple. **3** the flavour of maple syrup or maple sugar.

maple bush *noun Cdn* = SUGAR BUSH.

maple butter *noun Cdn* **1** a spread made by heating maple syrup, then rapidly cooling it while stirring until it has a creamy consistency. **2** butter blended with maple syrup or maple sugar.

maple leaf *noun* **1** (*plural* **maple leaves**) the leaf of the maple, used as an emblem of Canada. **2** (**Maple Leaf**) the Canadian flag. **3** (**Maple Leaf**; *plural* **Maple Leafs**) a one-ounce gold coin, bearing the image of a maple leaf, produced by the Royal Canadian Mint.

maple sugar *noun* a sugar produced by evaporating the sap of the sugar maple etc.

maple syrup *noun* a syrup produced from the sap of the sugar maple etc.

map-maker *noun* a person who makes maps; a cartographer. ▶ **map-making** *noun*

map-reading *noun* the inspection and interpretation of a map.

map reference *noun* a set of numbers and letters specifying a location as represented on a map.

maquiladora *noun* a Mexican factory taking advantage of cheap labour, run by a foreign company and exporting its products to the country of that company. [Say macky la DORE uh]

Mar. *abbreviation* March.

mar *verb* (**mars, marred, marring**) ruin; spoil: *the game was marred by the behaviour of drunken fans*.

maraca *noun* (*plural* **maracas**) a hollow gourd or gourd-shaped container filled with beans, pebbles, etc. and usu. shaken in pairs as a percussion instrument. [Say muh ROCKA or muh RACKA]

maraschino *noun* (*plural* **maraschinos**) a strong sweet liqueur made from a small black cherry. [Say mare a SHEE no or mare a SKEE no]

maraschino cherry *noun* a cherry preserved in maraschino or maraschino-flavoured syrup.

marasmus *noun* severe loss of weight in a person, esp. an undernourished child. [Say muh RAZ muss]

marathon *noun* **1** a long-distance running race, usu. of 26 miles 385 yards (42.195 km). **2** a long-lasting or difficult task, operation, etc.: *a marathon shopping expedition*. ▶ **marathoner** *noun*

maraud *verb* go about in search of things to steal or

M

people to attack: *marauding gangs of looters*.
▶ **marauder** *noun* [Say muh ROD]

marble • *noun* **1** limestone in a metamorphic crystalline (or granular) state, capable of taking a polish, used in sculpture and architecture. **2** anything resembling marble in hardness, coldness, durability, etc.: *her features were marble*. **3 a** a small ball of marble, glass, clay, etc., used as a toy. **b** (in *plural*; treated as *singular*) a game using these. **4** (in *plural*) *slang* one's mental faculties: *he's lost his marbles*. **5** (as an *adjective*) (esp. of a food) made with two or more colours swirled together: *marble cheese*. **6** a marble sculpture. • *verb* (**marbles, marbled, marbling**) stain or colour (paper, the edges of a book, soap, etc.) to look like marble.

marbled *adjective* **1** (of meat) streaked with alternating layers of lean and fat. **2** stained or coloured to look like variegated marble.

marbling *noun* **1** colouring or markings like marble. **2** streaks of fat in lean meat.

marc *noun* **1** the residue of pressed grapes etc. **2** a brandy made from this.

March *noun* the third month of the year.

march[1] • *verb* (**marches, marched, marching**) **1** walk in a military manner with a regular measured tread. **2** cause to march or walk: *marched the cadets back to camp* ◊ *marched him out of the room*. **3 a** walk somewhere quickly in a determined way: *she marched over to me and demanded an apology*. **b** (of events etc.) continue unrelentingly: *time marches on*. **4** take part in a protest march. • *noun* (*plural* **marches**) **1 a** an act of marching; a journey made by marching: *the army began the long march to the coast*. **b** the uniform step of troops etc.: *a slow march*. **2** a long difficult walk. **3** a procession as a protest or demonstration. **4** (usu. foll. by *of*) progress or continuity: *the march of events*. **5 a** a piece of music composed to accompany a march. **b** a composition of similar character and form. PHRASES **march on 1** advance towards (a military objective). **2** proceed. **on the march 1** marching. **2** in steady progress.

march[2] *noun* hist. **1** (usu. in *plural*) a boundary, a frontier (esp. between England and Scotland or Wales). **2** a tract of often disputed land between two countries.

March break *noun* Cdn a school holiday, usu. about a week long, in March.

marcher *noun* a person who marches or takes part in a march.

March hare *noun* a hare in the breeding season, characterized by excessive leaping, strange behaviour, etc.: *mad as a March hare*.

marching orders *plural noun* **1** a dismissal: *gave him his marching orders*. **2** instructions or directions given authoritatively: *he announces the musical marching orders for the next fortnight*. **3** Military the direction for troops to depart for war etc.

marchioness *noun* (*plural* **marchionesses**) **1** the wife or widow of a marquess. **2** a woman holding the rank of marquess in her own right (*compare* MARQUISE 1). [Say marsha NESS]

march past *noun* (*plural* **march pasts**) the marching of troops past a saluting point at a review.

Mardi Gras *noun* **1** the last Tuesday before Lent, celebrated in some areas (esp. New Orleans) as a day of great revelry. **2** the period of festivities culminating in this. [Say MARDY graw]

mare[1] *noun* a female horse.

mare[2] *noun* (*plural* **maria** or **mares**) any of a number of large dark flat areas on the surface of the moon or Mars, once thought to be seas. [Say MAR ay or MAR ee for the singular, MAR ee uh for the plural]

margarine *noun* a butter substitute made from vegetable oils or animal fats with milk etc.

margarita *noun* a cocktail made with tequila, lime juice, and orange liqueur, typically served in a glass with a salt-coated rim. [Say marga REETA]

margin *noun* **1 a** the edge or border of a surface. **b** (in *plural*) the ignored or unimportant sections of a group etc.: *people living on the margins of society*. **2 a** the blank border on each side of the print on a page etc. **b** a line ruled esp. on exercise paper, marking off a margin. **3** an amount (of time, money, etc.) by which a thing exceeds, falls short, etc.: *won by a narrow margin* ◊ *a margin of profit*. **4** a sum deposited with a stockbroker to cover the risk of loss on a transaction on account.

marginal *adjective* **1 a** of or written in a margin. **b** having marginal notes. **2 a** of or at the edge; not central. **b** not significant or decisive: *the work is of merely marginal interest*. **3** Cdn, Brit., Austral., & NZ (of a parliamentary seat or constituency) having a small majority at risk in an election. **4** close to the limit, esp. of profitability. **5** (of the sea) adjacent to the shore of a country. **6** (of land) that cannot produce enough to be profitable except when prices of farm products are high. **7** barely adequate; not provided for: *living a marginal existence*. **8** (of a person) not fitting into the mainstream. **9** (of a rate of taxation) imposed on the portion of income exceeding the limit of a tax bracket, rather than on the total income.

marginalia *plural noun* marginal notes. [Say margin AILY uh]

marginality *adjective* the quality or state of being marginal, esp. of not being considered significant or of not fitting into the mainstream.

marginalization *noun* the act of treating someone or a group as insignificant: *the marginalization of the elderly*.

marginalize *verb* (**marginalizes, marginalized, marginalizing**) make or treat as insignificant: *many institutions continue to marginalize and exclude female students* ◊ *members of marginalized ethnic groups*.

marginally *adverb* very slightly; not very much: *the latest results are only marginally better*.

margin of error *noun* a usu. small difference allowed for miscalculation, change of circumstances, etc.

maria *plural of* MARE[2]. [Say MAR ee uh]

mariachi *noun* **1** an itinerant Mexican folk band. **2** a member of such a band. [Say merry ATCH ee or merry OTCH ee]

Marian *adjective* of or relating to the Virgin Mary: *Marian devotion*. [Say MERRY un]

marigold *noun* a plant of the daisy family, with golden or bright yellow flowers.

marijuana *noun* **1** the dried leaves, flowering tops, and stems of hemp, used as an intoxicating drug usu. smoked in cigarettes; cannabis. **2** the plant yielding these.

marimba *noun* (*plural* **marimbas**) a kind of deep-toned xylophone, originating in Africa and consisting of wooden keys on a frame with a tuned resonator beneath each key. [Say muh RIMBA]

marina *noun* (*plural* **marinas**) a specially designed harbour with moorings for pleasure boats etc. [Say muh REENA]

marinade • *noun* **1** a mixture of wine, vinegar, oil, spices, etc., in which meat, fish, etc., is soaked before cooking, esp. to tenderize or add flavour. **2** meat, fish, etc., soaked in such a mixture. • *verb* (**marinades, marinaded, marinading**) = MARINATE. [Say MARE a nade]

marinara *adjective* designating a sauce made from tomatoes, onions, herbs, etc., usu. served with pasta. [Say mare a NAIR uh or mar a NAR uh]

M

marinate *verb* (**marinates, marinated, marinating**) soak (meat, fish, etc.) in a marinade. ▶ **marination** *noun* [Say MARE a nate, mare a NATION]

marine • *adjective* **1 a** of, found in, or produced by the sea. **b** of, found in, or produced by any esp. large body of water. **2 a** of or relating to shipping or naval matters: *marine insurance.* **b** for use at sea. • *noun* **I a** country's shipping, fleet, or navy: *mercantile marine* ◊ *merchant marine.* **2 a** a member of a body of troops trained to serve on land or sea. **b** (**Marine**) (in the US) a member of the Marine Corps, a branch of the armed forces trained to attack land targets from the sea.

marine park *noun* **1** an area of an ocean or other body of water set aside as an ecological preserve. **2** a theme park featuring marine wildlife.

mariner *noun* a sailor. [Say MARE in ur]

marionette *noun* a puppet worked from above by strings. [Say marry ANNETTE]

mariposa lily *noun* any of various lilies of western North America with showy flowers of three petals. [Say mare a POZE uh]

marital *adjective* of marriage or the relations between husband and wife. ▶ **maritally** *adverb*

marital status *noun* a person's situation as regards being single, married, divorced, separated, or in a common-law relationship.

maritime *adjective* **1** connected with the sea or seafaring: *maritime insurance.* **2** living or found near the sea. **3** (**Maritime**) *Cdn* of or relating to the Maritime provinces.

maritime climate *noun* a climate of coastal regions, having mild, wet weather with little variation in seasonal temperatures, owing to the influence of the sea.

Maritime Command *noun Cdn* the official name for the Canadian navy.

Maritimer *noun Cdn* a native or resident of the Maritime provinces.

Maritimes *plural noun* (also **Maritime provinces**) New Brunswick, Nova Scotia, and Prince Edward Island.

marjoram *noun* **1** either of two aromatic plants of the mint family, wild marjoram or sweet marjoram. **2** the fresh or dried leaves of sweet marjoram used as a flavouring in cooking. [Say MAR juh rum]

mark¹ • *noun* **1** a small area on a surface having a different colour from its surroundings. **2** something that indicates position or acts as a pointer. **3** a line, figure, or symbol made to identify or record something. **4** a sign or indication of a quality or feeling. **5** a characteristic feature or property of something. **6** a level or stage. **7** a point awarded for a correct answer or for proficiency in an examination. **8** a particular model or type of a vehicle or machine. • *verb* **1** make a mark on. **2** write a word or symbol on (an object) in order to identify it. **3** indicate the position of. **4** indicate or acknowledge (a significant event). **5** assess and give a mark to (written work). **6** notice or pay careful attention to. PHRASES **hit** (or **miss**) **the mark** succeed (or fail) in an attempt to do something. **leave** (or **make**) **one's mark on** have a long-lasting (often harmful) effect on. **make one's mark** attain distinction. **mark down 1** mark (goods etc.) at a lower price. **2** make a written note of. **3** choose (a person) as one's victim. **4** reduce the examination marks of. **mark off** (often foll. by *from*) separate (one thing from another) by a boundary etc.: *marked off the subjects for discussion.* **mark out 1** plan (a course of action etc.). **2** appoint: *marked out for success.* **3** trace out boundaries, a course, etc. **mark time** *Military* march on the spot, without moving forward. **2** act routinely; go through the motions. **3** await an opportunity to advance. **mark up 1** mark (goods etc.) at a higher price.

2 mark or correct (text etc.) for typesetting or alteration. **off the mark 1** having made a start. **2** (also **wide of the mark**) not accurate. **quick** (or **slow**) **off the mark** fast (or slow) in responding to a situation or understanding something. **on the mark 1** accurate. **2** ready to start. **on your mark** (or **marks**) (as an instruction) get ready to start (esp. a race). **up to the mark** reaching the usual or normal standard, esp. of health.

mark² *noun* = DEUTSCHMARK.

markdown *noun* a reduction in price.

marked *adjective* **1** having a visible mark. **2** clearly noticeable; evident: *a marked difference.* **3** (of playing cards) having distinctive marks on their backs to assist cheating. **4** designating a person whose conduct is watched with suspicion or hostility: *marked man.* ▶ **markedly** *adverb* noticeably. [Say MARK id lee]

marker *noun* **1** a stone, post, etc., used to mark a position etc. **2** a person or thing that marks. **3** a felt-tipped pen with a broad tip. **4** a person who records a score, esp. in billiards. **5** a flare etc. used to direct a pilot to a target. **6** a bookmark. **7** any distinguishing characteristic or mark. **8** a person who marks school assignments or examination papers. **9** *slang* a promissory note.

market • *noun* **1** the gathering of people for the purchase and sale of provisions, livestock, etc., esp. with a number of different vendors. **2** an open space or covered building used for this. **3 a** (often foll. by *for*) a demand for a commodity or service: *a ready market.* **b** a place or group providing such a demand: *Canada is a small market.* **4** conditions as regards, or opportunity for, buying or selling. **5** the rate of purchase and sale, market value: *the market fell.* **6** (**the market**) the trade in a specified commodity: *the market in soft drinks.* **7** = STOCK MARKET. • *verb* (**markets, marketed, marketing**) **1** sell. **2 a** offer for sale. **b** promote an item for sale. **3** buy or sell goods in a market. PHRASES **be in the market for** wish to buy. **be on** (or **come into**) **the market** be offered for sale. **put on the market** offer for sale.

marketability *noun* the quality of being marketable.

marketable *adjective* **1** able or fit to be sold. **2** (of an attribute, skill, etc.) in demand.

market-driven *adjective* determined solely by consumer demand: *a market-driven program.*

market economy *noun* an economy subject to and determined by free competition.

marketeer *noun* **1** a person involved in or promoting a usu. specified market: *black marketeer.* **2** = MARKETER. ▶ **marketeering** *noun*

marketer *noun* a person trained in the marketing of products etc.

market garden *noun* a small farm growing fruit, vegetables, flowers, and other high-value crops destined for sale at nearby urban centres. ▶ **market gardener** *noun* **market gardening** *noun*

marketing *noun* **1** the action or business of promoting and selling products, including market research and advertising. **2** in senses of MARKET *verb*.

marketing board *noun Cdn & Brit.* an association of agricultural producers controlling the marketing of a specific commodity, often setting prices and imposing production quotas.

marketplace *noun* **1** an open space where a market is held in a town. **2** the world of commerce or trade. **3** any place or environment where ideas etc. are exchanged or evaluated: *allowing great choice in the education marketplace.*

market price *noun* the current price which a commodity or service fetches in the market.

M

market research *noun* the study of consumers' needs and preferences. ▶ **market researcher** *noun*

market share *noun* a single company's or product's proportion of the total sales of a commodity or service.

market value *noun* the value of a product or service as determined by consumer demand (*opp.* BOOK VALUE).

marking *noun* (usu. in *plural*) **1** an identification mark, esp. a symbol on an aircraft. **2** the colouring of an animal's fur, feathers, etc. **3** the action of MARK¹ *verb*.

marksman *noun* (*plural* **marksmen**) a person skilled in shooting, esp. with a pistol or rifle. ▶ **marksmanship** *noun*

markup *noun* **1** the amount added to the cost price of goods to cover overhead charges, profit, etc. **2** the action or process of increasing the price of goods. **3** the corrections made in marking up text. **4** a system of tagging used to identify the structure of a text held electronically.

marl • *noun* soil consisting of clay and lime, with fertilizing properties. • *verb* apply marl to (the ground).

marlin *noun* any of several large marine game fishes and food fishes of the swordfish family, with the upper jaw elongated to form a pointed snout.

marmalade • *noun* **1** a citrus fruit jam, usu. made with oranges. **2** a preserve made of other fruits or vegetables, esp. ginger, or onions stewed with sugar and vinegar. • *adjective* (esp. of a cat) orange tabby.

marmoset *noun* a small tropical American monkey with a silky coat and a long bushy tail. [Say MARMA zet]

marmot *noun* a burrowing rodent with a heavy-set body and short bushy tail. [Say MAR mutt]

maroon¹ *adjective & noun* brownish crimson.

maroon² *verb* leave (someone) trapped and isolated in an inaccessible place, especially an island: *a novel about schoolboys marooned on a desert island* ◊ *we were marooned by the blizzard*.

marque *noun* a make or brand, esp. of motor vehicle. [Sounds like MARK]

marquee *noun* **1** a canopy over the entrance to a large building. **2 a** a usu. brightly lit sign over the entrance to a theatre etc., listing the names of featured performers. **b** (as an *adjective*) popular enough to be listed on a marquee; famous: *a marquee player* ◊ *marquee status*. **3** a large tent used for social or commercial functions. [Say mar KEY]

marquess *noun* a British nobleman ranking between a duke and an earl (*compare* MARQUIS). [Say MAR kwiss]

marquetry *noun* inlaid work in wood, ivory, etc., esp. as used for the decoration of furniture. [Say MARKA tree]

marquis *noun* (*plural* **marquises**) a European nobleman ranking between a duke and a count (*compare* MARQUESS). [Say mar KEY]

marquise *noun* **1 a** the wife or widow of a marquis. **b** a woman holding the rank of marquis in her own right (*compare* MARCHIONESS). **2** a pointed oval-shaped cut of diamond, usu. with 58 facets. [Say mar KEEZ]

Marquis wheat *noun* a variety of wheat which ripens in a relatively short growing season, allowing wheat to be grown further north in Canada. [Say MAR kwiss]

marram *noun* a coarse shore grass that binds sand with its tough rhizomes. [Say MARE um]

marriage *noun* **1** the legal or religious union of a man and a woman in order to live together and often to have children. **2** an act or ceremony establishing this union. **3** one particular union of this kind: *by a previous marriage*. **4** a legal union between two people of the same sex: *gay marriages are a hot button topic everywhere these days*. **5** a close association or intimate union: *the marriage of true minds*. **6** a combination of different elements.

marriageable *adjective* **1** (of a person) fit for marriage, esp. of an appropriate age. **2** (of age) fit for marriage.

marriage commissioner *noun* Cdn (in some provinces) an official who conducts civil marriages.

marriage of convenience *noun* (*plural* **marriages of convenience**) a marriage concluded to achieve some practical purpose, esp. financial or political.

married • *adjective* **1** united in marriage. **2** of or relating to marriage: *married name* ◊ *married life*. **3** bound by strong, almost irrevocable ties: *married to her job*. • *noun* a married person: *young marrieds*.

married quarters *plural noun* housing provided to married personnel and their families by the armed forces, usu. for a low rent.

marrow *noun* **1** = BONE MARROW. **2** (also **vegetable marrow**) **a** a large usu. white-fleshed gourd used as food. **b** the plant that yields this gourd.

marrow bone *noun* a bone containing edible marrow.

marry *verb* (**marries, married, marrying**) **1 a** take as one's wife or husband in marriage. **b** (of a person authorized to perform marriages) join (persons) in marriage. **c** (of a parent or guardian) give (a son, daughter, etc.) in marriage. **2 a** enter into marriage. **b** (foll. by *into*) become a member of (a family, a social group) by marriage. **3** combine or be combined successfully with something else: *the show marries poetry with art*. █PHRASES█ **marry money** marry a rich person. **marry off** find a wife or husband for.

Marsala *noun* a dark sweet fortified dessert wine. [Say mar SALA or mar SOLLA]

marsh *noun* (*plural* **marshes**) low land flooded in wet weather and usu. watery at all times.

> **SPELL CHECK**
> **marshal, martial**
>
> The word pertaining to fighting is **martial**: *martial arts*. **Marshal** is spelled with only one *l*, except in the forms *marshalled* and *marshalling*.

---

marshal • *noun* **1 a** (in titles of ranks) a high-ranking officer in the armed forces of some countries. **b** an officer of the highest rank in the armies of some countries. **c** a high-ranking officer of state. **2** a person arranging ceremonies or controlling procedure at parades, races, etc. **3** US **a** a federal or municipal law officer. **b** the head of a fire department. • *verb* (**marshals, marshalled, marshalling**) **1** arrange or draw up (armed forces) in order for fighting, exercise, or review. **2** arrange (people) in a body or procession or for a race etc. **3** dispose, arrange, or set (things, material or immaterial) in methodical order, esp. in preparation for something: *marshalling my thoughts*.

marshland *noun* land consisting of marshes.

marshmallow *noun* **1** a very soft, fluffy, usu. white candy made of sugar, egg white, gelatin, etc. **2** an excessively tender-hearted or unassertive person.

marsh marigold *noun* a golden-flowered plant of the buttercup family, which grows esp. in moist meadows.

marshy *adjective* (**marshier, marshiest**) (of ground) like a marsh.

marsupial *noun* any mammal of an order whose members are born incompletely developed and are usu. carried and suckled in a pouch on the mother's belly. [Say mar SOUPY ul]

mart *noun* (usu. in proper names) a store: *Drug Mart*.

> **SPELL CHECK**
> **marten, martin**
>
> The bird is a **martin**.

---

marten *noun* **1** any of various weasel-like carnivores

found in forests of Eurasia and North America, esp. the pine marten. **2** the pelt or fur of the marten.

martial *adjective* **1** of or appropriate to warfare or the military. **2** brave; fond of fighting. [Say MAR shull]

martial art *noun* any of various fighting techniques or sports including judo and karate.

martial law *noun* military government, involving the suspension of ordinary law.

Martian • *adjective* of the planet Mars. • *noun* a hypothetical inhabitant of Mars. [Say MAR sh'n]

> **SPELL CHECK**
> **martin, marten**
>
> The weasel-like mammal is a **marten**.

---

martin *noun* any of several birds belonging to the swallow family, e.g. the purple martin, a voracious eater of insects.

martini *noun* a cocktail made of dry vermouth and usu. gin. [Say mar TEENY]

Martin Luther King Day *noun* (in some US states) a holiday on the third Monday in January, commemorating the civil rights activist Martin Luther King (1929–68).

martyr • *noun* **1 a** a person who is put to death for refusing to renounce a faith or belief. **b** a person who suffers for adhering to a principle, cause, etc. **c** a person who suffers or pretends to suffer in order to obtain sympathy or pity. **2** (foll. by *to*) a constant sufferer from (an ailment etc.). • *verb* put to death as a martyr. [Say MAR tur]

martyrdom *noun* the sufferings or death of a martyr. [Say MAR tur dum]

martyred *adjective* **1** (of a person) having been martyred: *a martyred saint.* **2** (of an attitude or manner) showing feigned or exaggerated suffering to obtain sympathy or admiration: *he gave her a martyred look and walked away.* [Say MAR tur dum]

marvel • *noun* a wonderful or astonishing person or thing: *the marvels of modern technology* ◊ *you're a marvel!* • *verb* (**marvels, marvelled, marvelling**) feel or express surprise or wonder.

marvellous *adjective* (also esp. *US* **marvelous**) **1** astonishing. **2** excellent. ▶ **marvellously** *adverb* **marvellousness** *noun*

Marxism *noun* the political and economic theories based on the writings of Karl Marx (1818–83), predicting the overthrow of capitalism, the taking over of the means of production by the proletariat or wage earners, and the eventual attainment of a classless society, in accordance with scientific laws determined by dialectical materialism (a theory that political and historical events result from a conflict of social forces). ▶ **Marxist** *noun & adjective*

Marxist-Leninist • *noun* an advocate of Marxism as developed by Lenin and as implemented in the Soviet Union and subsequently in China. • *adjective* of or relating to this form of Marxism.

Mary Jane *noun* **1** a flat, low-cut shoe for girls, with a single strap across the top. **2** *slang* marijuana.

marzipan *noun* a paste of ground almonds, sugar, etc., moulded into decorative shapes or used to coat large cakes. [Say MARZA pan]

mas *noun* (originally in Trinidad) a masquerade, esp. one held as part of an annual carnival parade.

Masai • *noun* (*plural* **Masai** or **Masais**) **1 a** a people living in Kenya and Tanzania, traditionally subsisting by herding cattle. **b** a member of this people. **2** the language of the Masai. • *adjective* of or relating to the Masai. [Say MASS eye]

masala *noun* **1** any of various spice mixtures ground into a paste or powder for use in Indian cooking. **2** a dish flavoured with this. [Say muh SALA]

mascara *noun* (*plural* **mascaras**) a cosmetic applied to the eyelashes to make them look darker and thicker. ▶ **mascaraed** *adjective*

mascarpone *noun* a soft mild Italian cream cheese. [Say mass car PONY]

mascot *noun* **1** a person, animal, or thing that is supposed to bring good luck to or represent a team, school, etc. **2** a costumed figure representing a sports team, usu. leading cheers among the spectators watching games.

masculine • *adjective* **1** of or characteristic of men. **2** manly, vigorous. **3** (of a woman) having qualities considered appropriate to a man. **4** *Grammar* of or denoting the gender proper to certain words or grammatical forms, including those referring to males. • *noun* *Grammar* the masculine gender; a masculine word. ▶ **masculinity** *noun*

masculinize *verb* (**masculinizes, masculinized, masculinizing**) **1** induce male physiological characteristics in. **2** cause to appear or seem masculine: *a slightly masculinized swagger.* [Say MASCULINE ize]

maser *noun* a device using the stimulated emission of radiation by atoms in a state of high energy to amplify or generate coherent monochromatic electromagnetic radiation in the microwave range (*compare* LASER). [Say MAY zur]

mash • *noun* **1** a soft mixture. **2** a mixture of boiled grain, bran, etc., given warm to horses etc. **3** a mixture of malt grains and hot water which is then fermented for brewing beer. **4** a soft pulp made by crushing, mixing with water, etc. • *verb* (**mashes, mashed, mashing**) **1** reduce (potatoes etc.) to a uniform mass by crushing. **2** crush or pound to a pulp. ▶ **masher** *noun*

> **SPELL CHECK**
> **mask, masque**
>
> A dramatic entertainment popular in Shakespeare's time was a **masque**.

---

mask • *noun* **1** a covering for all or part of the face: **a** worn as a disguise, as part of a costume, or to amuse or terrify. **b** made of wire, gauze, paper, etc., and worn for protection, e.g. by an athlete, or by a medical practitioner to prevent infection of a patient. **c** worn to conceal the face at balls etc. and usu. made of velvet or silk. **2** a respirator used to filter inhaled air or to supply gas for inhalation. **3** a likeness of a person's face, esp. one made by taking a mould from the face: *death mask.* **4** a disguise or pretense: *hid his shady business dealings behind a mask of respectability.* **5** a hollow model of a human head worn by ancient Greek and Roman actors. **6** the face or head of an animal, esp. a fox. **7** = FACE MASK **2**. • *verb* **1** cover (the face etc.) with a mask. **2** disguise or conceal (a taste, one's feelings, etc.). **3** cover (an object or surface) so as to protect it from a process, esp. painting: *mask off doors and cupboard with sheets of plastic.*

masked *adjective* **1** wearing a mask; disguised or hidden by or as by a mask. **2** (of an animal etc.) having facial markings or features suggesting a mask.

masked ball *noun* a ball at which masks are worn.

masking tape *noun* usu. cream coloured adhesive tape used in painting to cover areas on which paint is not wanted, and in various household tasks.

masochism *noun* **1** the condition or state of deriving (esp. sexual) gratification from one's own pain or humiliation. **2** the enjoyment of what appears to be painful or tiresome. ▶ **masochist** *noun* **masochistic**

adjective **masochistically** *adverb* [Say MASSA kism, MASSA kist, massa KISS tick]

mason *noun* **1** a person who builds with stone or brick. **2** (**Mason**) a Freemason.

Masonic *adjective* of or relating to Freemasons. [Say muh SONIC]

Masonite *noun* *proprietary* fibreboard made from wood fibre pulped under steam at high pressure.

masonry *noun* **1 a** the work of a mason. **b** stonework or brickwork. **2** (**Masonry**) Freemasonry.

masque *noun* a dramatic and musical entertainment esp. of the 16th and 17th centuries, originally of pantomime, later with dialogue in poetic verse. [Sounds like MASK]

masquerade • *noun* **1** a false show or pretense. **2** a masked ball. • *verb* (**masquerades, masqueraded, masquerading**) (often foll. by *as*) have or assume a false appearance. ▶**masquerader** *noun* [Say maska RAID]

Mass. *abbreviation* Massachusetts.

Mass *noun* (*plural* **Masses**) (also **mass**) **1** the sacrament commemorating the Last Supper, in which bread and wine are consecrated and consumed, esp. in the Catholic Church. **2** a celebration of this. **3** the words or form of service used in the Mass. **4** a musical setting of parts of this.

mass • *noun* (*plural* **masses**) **1** a coherent body of matter of indefinite shape. **2** a dense aggregation of objects: *a mass of fibres*. **3** a large number or amount. **4** an unbroken expanse (of colour etc.). **5** covered or abounding in: *was a mass of cuts and bruises*. **6** a main portion (of a painting etc.) as perceived by the eye. **7** (**the mass**) **a** the majority. **b** (in *plural*) the ordinary people. **8** *Physics* the quantity of matter a body contains. **9** (as an *adjective*) relating to, done by, or affecting large numbers of people or things; largescale: *mass murder*. • *verb* (**masses, massed, massing**) (usu. as **massed** *adjective*) **1** assemble into a mass or as one body: *massed bands*. **2** *Military* (with reference to troops) concentrate or be concentrated. PHRASES **in the mass** collectively: *I hear very nice voices, untrained but, in the mass, having a nice effect.*

massacre • *noun* **1** a general slaughter (of persons, occasionally of animals). **2** *informal* an utter defeat or destruction. • *verb* (**massacres, massacred, massacring**) **1** murder (esp. a large number of people) cruelly or violently. **2** *informal* defeat heavily; destroy. **3** *informal* perform (a piece of music, a play, etc.) very ineptly: *the choir was massacring "In the Bleak Midwinter".* [Say MASSA cur]

Massacre of the Innocents *noun* the killing of all male infants in Bethlehem on Herod's orders, in an unsuccessful attempt to kill the infant Jesus.

massage • *noun* the action of rubbing and pressing a person's body with the hands to reduce pain in the muscles and joints: *massage will help the pain ◊ a back massage ◊ gave her a massage*. • *verb* (**massages, massaged, massaging**) **1** apply massage to. **2** (usu. foll. by *into, onto*) apply (a lotion etc.) by rubbing. **3** manipulate (statistics etc.) to give an acceptable result. **4** flatter (a person's ego etc.). ▶**massager** *noun* [Say muh SOZH]

massasauga *noun* (*plural* **massasaugas**) (also **massasauga rattlesnake**) a small spotted venomous North American rattlesnake. [Say massa SOGGA]

mass communication *noun* the communication of information to a large audience, esp. by means of newspapers and broadcasting.

masseur *noun* a person who provides massage professionally. [Say ma SUR]

masseuse *noun* a woman who provides massage professionally. [Say ma SOOSE or ma SUHZ]

massif *noun* a large mountain mass; a compact group of mountain heights. [Say ma SEEF or MASS if]

massive *adjective* **1** large and heavy or solid. **2** (of the features, head, etc.) relatively large in scale; of solid build. **3** exceptionally large, substantial, or far-reaching. **4** (of a mineral) not visibly crystalline. **5** (of architectural or artistic style) presenting great, solid masses. ▶**massively** *adverb* **massiveness** *noun*

massless *adjective* (of a subatomic particle) having no mass.

mass market • *noun* the market for mass-produced goods. • *adjective* (**mass-market**) designed for or appealing to a large segment of the population. • *verb* (**mass-market, mass-markets, mass-marketed, mass-marketing**) market (a product) on a mass scale. ▶**mass-marketed** *adjective* **mass-marketing** *noun*

mass media *noun* = MEDIA 2.

mass murder *noun* the killing of several people, esp. at once by one person. ▶**mass murderer** *noun*

mass noun *noun* a noun that is not countable and cannot be used with the indefinite article ("a") or in the plural, e.g. *luggage, china, happiness*.

mass number *noun* the total number of protons and neutrons in an atomic nucleus.

mass-produce *verb* (**mass-produces, mass-produced, mass-producing**) manufacture by mass production. ▶**mass-produced** *adjective*

mass production *noun* the production of large quantities of a standardized article, esp. by a standardized mechanical process.

mass transit *noun* public transportation, esp. in urban areas.

mast[1] *noun* **1** a long upright post of timber, iron, etc., set up on a ship's keel, esp. to support sails. **2** a post or latticework upright for supporting a radio or television antenna. **3** a flagpole: *half-mast*. PHRASES **before the mast** *hist.* serving as an ordinary seaman in a sailing ship.

mast[2] *noun* the fruit of the beech, oak, chestnut, and other forest trees, esp. as food for pigs.

mastectomy *noun* (*plural* **mastectomies**) the surgical removal of all or part of a breast. [Say mass TECKTA me]

-masted *combining form* (of a ship) having a specified number of masts: *a two-masted schooner*.

master • *noun* **1** a person having control of persons or things, e.g. a household, merchant ship, college, school, pet, etc. **2** a person who has or gets the upper hand: *we shall see which of us is master*. **3 a** a person skilled in a particular trade and able to teach others: *master carpenter*. **b** a person highly accomplished in a particular skill, activity, etc.: *a master of manipulation*. **4** (also **master's degree**) a graduate degree, usu. awarded after at least one full year of study beyond the undergraduate level. **5** a revered teacher in philosophy etc. **6 a** an artist of great skill, esp. one regarded as a model of excellence. **b** a work of painting or sculpture by such an artist. **7 a** *Chess etc.* a player of proven ability at the international level. **b** *Sport* (in *plural*) a class for competitors over the usual age for the highest level of competition: *Masters tournament*. **8** the original copy of a sound recording, film, data file, etc. from which a series of copies can be made. **9** (**Master**) a title prefixed to the name of a boy not old enough to be called Mr. **10** (in Ontario) a judicial officer with jurisdiction over decrees given provisionally in legal actions. **11** *Mechanics* a machine, device, or component directly controlling another (*compare* SLAVE 5). • *adjective* **1** main, principal: *master bedroom*. **2 a** (of a material or

immaterial thing) controlling, supreme: *master plan*. **b** designating a device or component which directly controls the action of others: *master switch*. **3** designating the copy of a tape, disc, file, etc. which is the authoritative source for copies. **4** commanding, superior, great, leading: *a master spirit*. • *verb* **1** overcome, defeat, get the better of in a contest or struggle. **2** break, tame, reduce to subjection, or compel to obey. **3** acquire complete knowledge of (a subject), facility in using (an instrument etc.), or skill at (performing a task). **4** rule as a master. PHRASES **be master of 1** know how to control. **2** have at one's disposal. **be one's own master** be independent or free to do as one wishes.

master bedroom *noun* the largest bedroom in a dwelling, usu., in a family dwelling, the one intended for the parents.

master corporal *noun* (also **Master Corporal**) *Cdn* (in the Canadian Army and Air Force) a non-commissioned officer of a rank above corporal and below sergeant.

masterful *adjective* **1** powerful and able to control others: *he looked masculine and masterful*. **2** highly skilled: *a masterful assessment of the difficulties*. ► **masterfully** *adverb* **masterfulness** *noun*

master key *noun* a key that opens several locks, each of which also has its own key that will not open any of the rest.

masterly *adjective* worthy of a master; very skilful: *a masterly piece of work*.

mastermind • *noun* **1** the person directing an intricate operation. **2** a person with an outstanding intellect. • *verb* plan and direct (a scheme or enterprise).

master of ceremonies *noun* **1** a person introducing speakers at a banquet, entertainers in a variety show, etc. **2** a person in charge of ceremonies at a state or public occasion. Abbreviation: **MC**.

masterpiece *noun* **1** an outstanding piece of artistry or workmanship. **2** a person's best work.

master seaman *noun* (also **Master Seaman**) *Cdn* (in the Canadian Navy) a non-commissioned officer of a rank above leading seaman and equivalent to a master corporal in other commands.

master stroke *noun* an outstandingly skilful act of policy etc.

master switch *noun* a switch controlling the supply of electricity etc. to an entire system.

masterwork *noun* = MASTERPIECE.

mastery *noun* **1** (often foll. by *of*) comprehensive knowledge or use of a subject or instrument. **2** masterly skill. **3** control or power: *human mastery of the natural world* ◊ *he struggled for mastery over his emotions*.

masthead *noun* **1 a** the title of a newspaper etc. at the head of the front or editorial page. **b** a box in a newspaper or magazine listing the names of owners and staff etc. **2** the highest part of a ship's mast, esp. that of a lower mast as a place of observation or punishment.

mastic *noun* **1** a gum or resin exuded from the bark of the mastic tree, used in making varnish. **2** (also **mastic tree**) the evergreen tree yielding this gum or resin. **3** a waterproof, putty-like filler and sealant used in building. [Say MASS tick]

masticate *verb* (**masticates**, **masticated**, **masticating**) grind or chew (food) with one's teeth. ► **mastication** *noun* [Say MASTA kate, masta KAY sh'n]

mastiff *noun* a large strong dog with drooping ears, often used as a guard dog. [Say MASS tiff]

mastitis *noun* an inflammation of the mammary gland (the breast or udder). [Say mas TITE iss]

mastodon *noun* a large extinct mammal resembling the elephant but having teeth of a relatively primitive form and number. [Say MASTA don]

mastoid • *adjective* of or pertaining to the mastoid process or bone. • *noun* (also **mastoid process**) a conical prominence on the temporal bone behind the ear, to which muscles are attached.

masturbate *verb* (**masturbates**, **masturbated**, **masturbating**) arouse oneself sexually or cause (another person) to be aroused by manual stimulation of the genitals. ► **masturbation** *noun* **masturbatory** *adjective* [Say MASTER buh tory]

mat¹ • *noun* **1** a small piece of carpeting or other heavy material, used as a covering on a floor. **2** a usu. thin piece of cork, rubber, plastic, etc., to protect a surface from the heat or moisture of an object placed on it. **3** a piece of padded, resilient material for landing on in gymnastics, wrestling, etc. **4** a thick tangled mass of hair, vegetation, etc., esp. forming a layer. • *verb* (**mats**, **matted**, **matting**) **1** become matted. **2** cover or furnish with mats. PHRASES **go to the mat** vigorously engage in an argument or contention, esp. on behalf of a particular person or cause.

mat² • *noun* **1** a sheet of cardboard forming a margin around a picture inside a frame. **2** a sheet of cardboard on which a picture etc. is mounted. • *verb* (**mats**, **matted**, **matting**) **1** mount (a print etc.) on a cardboard backing. **2** provide (a print etc.) with a border.

mat³ *noun* = MATRIX 2.

matador *noun* a bullfighter whose task is to kill the bull. [Say MATTA door]

match¹ • *noun* (*plural* **matches**) **1** a person, thing, action, etc. equal to another in some quality: *this river is a match for the most skilled anglers*. **2** a person or thing exactly like or corresponding to another: *this vase is an exact match for the one that was broken*. **3** a person or thing that associates or combines well with another: *ginger and peaches are a wonderful match*. **4** a contest or game of skill etc. in which persons or teams compete against each other. **5 a** a marriage. **b** a close association of two people: *as partners they are a perfect match*. **6** a person viewed in regard to his or her eligibility for marriage, esp. as to rank or fortune: *an excellent match*. **7** *Computing* a record, string, etc. that matches the requirements of a search or is identical with a given record etc. **8** an incident in which the participants vie to outdo each other: *slanging match*. • *verb* (**matches**, **matched**, **matching**) **1 a** combine well with, esp. in colour: *the curtains match the wallpaper*. **b** (often foll. by *with*) correspond; harmonize: *his socks do not match*. **2** (foll. by *against*, *with*) place (a person, aptitudes etc.) in competition with (another): *match your skill against the experts*. **3** find material etc. that matches (another): *can you match this paint?* **4** find a person or thing suitable for another: *matching unemployed workers with vacant positions*. **5** be equal to: *the players are well matched*. **6** find or provide something equal to: *can you match that story?* **7** (of a donor, government, etc.) provide funds to equal donations provided by others: *Walter Carsen generously matched all new donations to the ballet*. PHRASES **match up** (often foll. by *with*) pair up; fit to form a coherent whole or relation. **match up to** be as good as or equal to. **meet one's match** meet someone who has as much skill, determination, etc. as oneself, and perhaps more. **to match** corresponding in some essential respect with what has been mentioned: *yellow dress with gloves to match*.

M

match² *noun* **1** a short thin piece of wood, paper, etc., tipped with a composition that can be ignited by friction. **2** a piece of wick, cord, etc., designed to burn at a uniform rate, for firing a cannon, igniting a trail of gunpowder, etc. PHRASES **put a match to** set fire to.

matchbook *noun* a small folder, usu. with a striking surface on the back, containing paper matches.

matchbox *noun* (*plural* **matchboxes**) **1** a small box for holding matches. **2** something very small, esp. a very small house or apartment.

matching *adjective* **1** that matches: *shoes and matching gloves*. **2** (of financial grants) of an amount based on the amount raised from other sources: *matching grant*.

matchless *adjective* without an equal; incomparable. ▶ **matchlessly** *adverb*

matchmaker *noun* **1 a** a person who schemes to bring couples together. **b** a person who arranges marriages. **2** a person who arranges matches between employers and prospective employees, corporate deal makers, etc. ▶ **matchmaking** *noun & adjective*

match penalty *noun* (*plural* **match penalties**) *Hockey* = GAME MISCONDUCT.

match point *noun* *Tennis etc.* **1** the state of a game when one side needs only one more point to win the match. **2** this point.

matchstick • *noun* the stem of a match. • *adjective* **1** very thin, skeletal. **2** made of or as though of matchsticks.

matchup *noun* **1** the action of pairing or setting in opposition. **2** (esp. in sports or politics) **a** two suited or equal persons, teams, or things. **b** a pair so matched. **c** a contest between such a pair.

mate¹ • *noun* **1** (in *combination*) a fellow member or joint occupant of: *roommate*. **2** a partner in marriage or a lover. **3** either of a pair of mated animals. **4** either of a pair of things: *I have the left shoe, but I can't find its mate*. **5 a** an officer on a merchant ship subordinate to the master. **b** an assistant to an officer on board ship: *boatswain's mate*. **6** an assistant to a skilled worker: *plumber's mate*. • *verb* (**mates, mated, mating**) (often foll. by *with*) **1 a** bring (animals or birds) together for breeding. **b** (of animals or birds) come together for breeding. **2 a** join (persons) in marriage. **b** (of persons) be joined in marriage. **c** copulate.

mate² *noun & verb* (**mates, mated, mating**) *Chess* = CHECKMATE.

material • *noun* **1** the matter from which a thing is made. **2** cloth, fabric. **3** (in *plural*) things needed for an activity: *building materials* ◊ *writing materials*. **4** a person or thing suitable for a specific role or purpose: *officer material*. **5** (in *singular* or *plural*) information, ideas, evidence, etc. to be used in creating an artistic or literary work, drawing a conclusion, etc.: *materials for a biography*. **6** (in *singular* or *plural*, often foll. by *of*) the elements or constituent parts of a substance. • *adjective* **1** formed or consisting of matter: *the material world*. **2 a** concerned with bodily comfort etc.: *material well-being*. **b** relating to the physical, not intellectual or spiritual, aspect of things. **3 a** (often foll. by *to*) pertinent, essential, relevant: *at the material time*. **b** serious, important, of consequence: *the insects did not do any material damage to the crop*. **4** *Law* (of evidence, a fact, etc.) significant, influential, esp. to the extent of determining a cause, affecting a judgment, etc.: *a material witness*.

material culture *noun* the physical objects (tools, articles of domestic and religious use, dwelling places, etc.) which give evidence of the type of culture developed by a social group.

materialism *noun* **1 a** a tendency to prefer material possessions and physical comfort to spiritual values.

b a way of life based on material interests. **2** *Philosophy* the doctrine that nothing exists but matter and its movements and modifications. **3** *Art* a tendency to lay stress on the material aspect of objects represented. ▶ **materialist** *noun & adjective* **materialistic** *adjective* **materialistically** *adverb*

materiality *noun* the quality of being material or physical. [Say muh teery ALA tee]

materialization *noun* an act of materializing.

materialize *verb* (**materializes, materialized, materializing**) **1** take place or start to exist as expected or planned: *the predicted increase did not materialize*. **2** appear, arrive, or be present when expected: *the train failed to materialize*.

materially *adverb* **1** substantially, considerably: *Whitehorse is not materially colder than Prince Albert or even Winnipeg*. **2** in terms of wealth or material possessions: *a materially and culturally rich area*.

matériel *noun* available means or resources, esp. materials and equipment used in warfare (opp. PERSONNEL 1): *the costs in men and matériel paled beside the political costs of the misadventure*. [Say muh teery EL]

maternal *adjective* **1** of or like a mother. **2** motherly, having the instincts of motherhood. **3 a** related through the mother: *maternal uncle*. **b** inherited from the mother: *maternal chromosome*. **4** of or pertaining to the mother in pregnancy and childbirth. ▶ **maternalistic** *adjective* **maternally** *adverb*

maternity *noun* **1** (as an *adjective*) **a** for women during and just after childbirth: *maternity ward* ◊ *maternity leave*. **b** designed for a pregnant woman: *maternity dress*. **2** a maternity ward or hospital. **3** motherhood.

matey *adjective* (**matier, matiest**) *informal* (often foll. by *with*) sociable; familiar and friendly.

math *noun* *informal* mathematics.

mathematical *adjective* **1** of or relating to mathematics. **2 a** (of a concept, object, etc.) as understood or defined in mathematics. **b** (of a proof etc.) rigorously precise. ▶ **mathematically** *adverb*

mathematician *noun* an expert in or student of mathematics. [Say math emma TISH in]

mathematics *noun* **1** the abstract, deductive science of number, quantity, space, and arrangement studied in its own right (**pure mathematics**), or as applied to other disciplines such as physics, engineering, etc. (**applied mathematics**). **2** (as *plural*) the use of mathematics in calculation etc.

matinee *noun* an afternoon performance at a theatre, concert hall, etc. [Say mat in AY]

mating • *noun* the action or process of matching, marrying, or pairing (animals etc.) for breeding purposes. • *adjective* of or pertaining to the act of mating: *mating season*.

matriarch *noun* **1 a** a woman who is the head of a family or tribe. **b** a woman who dominates an organization: *they hooked me up with Alexandra Spaulding, the matriarch of the show for twenty-two years*. **2** an elderly woman who is highly respected. ▶ **matriarchal** *adjective* [Say MAY tree ark, may tree ARK'll]

matriarchy *noun* (*plural* **matriarchies**) **1** a form of social organization in which the mother is the head of the family and descent is reckoned through the female line. **2 a** a society etc. governed by a woman or women. **b** government by a woman or women. [Say MAY tree arky]

matriculate *verb* (**matriculates, matriculated, matriculating**) **1** be enrolled at a college or university. **2** admit (a student) to membership of a college or university. [Say muh TRICK yoo late]

matriculation *noun* **1** the action or process of matriculating, esp. formal admission into a university,

M

college, etc. **2** *Cdn see* JUNIOR MATRICULATION, SENIOR MATRICULATION. [Say muh trick you LAY sh'n]

matrilineal *adjective* of or based on kinship with the mother or the female line: *the Minangs have a matrilineal social system; family names and property are passed along through the female line from generation to generation ◊ each pod of whales is an extended family comprised of matrilineal groups*. ▶ **matrilineally** *adverb* [Say matra LINNY ul]

matrimonial *adjective* of or relating to marriage or married people. [Say matra MOANY ul]

matrimonial cake *noun Cdn* (*Prairies*) = DATE SQUARE.

matrimony *noun* marriage: *joined in holy matrimony*. [Say MATRA moany]

matrix *noun* (*plural* **matrices** or **matrixes**) **1** an environment or substance in which a thing is developed: *the European cultural matrix*. **2 a** a mould in which a thing is cast or shaped, such as printing type, an engraved die to strike coins, etc. **b** a positive or negative copy of an original disc recording used in making other copies. **3 a** the rock material in which a gem, fossil, etc. is embedded. **b** any relatively fine or homogeneous substance in which coarser or larger particles are embedded. **4** *Math* a rectangular array of symbols, elements, etc. in rows and columns that is treated as a single element. **5** *Computing* a grid-like array of interconnected circuit elements. [Say MAY trix for the singular, MAY truh seez or MAY trixes for the plural]

matron *noun* **1** a middle-aged or elderly married woman, esp. a dignified, staid, or portly one of high social standing. **2** a female prison officer. [Say MAY trun]

matronly *adjective* like or characteristic of a matron, esp. as regards stuffiness or portliness. [Say MAY trun lee]

matron of honour *noun* a married woman attending the bride at a wedding.

Matsqui *noun* (*plural* **Matsqui**) a member of a Salishan Aboriginal people, a subdivision of the Halkomelem, living in the Lower Fraser valley of BC. [Say MAT skwee]

matte (also *esp. Brit.* **matt**) • *adjective* **1** (of a colour, surface, etc.) dull, without lustre. **2** (of lipstick, face powder, paint, etc.) having a flat, not shiny or glossy, finish. • *noun* paint formulated to give a dull flat finish (*compare* GLOSS[1] 3, SEMIGLOSS). [Say MAT]

matted *adjective* **1** (esp. of plants, hair, etc.) tangled and interlaced. **2** covered with a dense growth. **3** (of a picture) provided with a mat.

matter • *noun* **1 a** physical substance in general, as distinct from mind and spirit. **b** that which has mass and occupies space. **2** an affair or situation under consideration; a topic. **3** (**the matter**) the reason for a problem. **4** written or printed material. **5** *Law* something to be tried or proved in court; a case. • *verb* be important or significant. PHRASES **as a matter of course** as a regular habit or usual procedure. **be another** (or **a different**) **matter** be completely different. **for that matter 1** as far as that is concerned. **2** and indeed also. **in the matter of** as regards. **make matters worse** make an already difficult situation more difficult. **a matter of 1** approximately: *a matter of hours*. **2 a** thing that relates to, depends on, or is determined by: *it's simply a matter of experience*. **a matter of life and death** a matter of vital importance. **it's all** (or **only**) **a matter of time** (**before...**) this consequence is inevitable though it may not happen immediately. **no matter 1** (foll. by *when*, *how*, etc.) regardless of: *will do it no matter what the consequences*. **2** it is of no importance. **take matters into one's own hands** act decisively and independently. **what is the matter with** surely there is no objection to. **what matter?** that need not worry us.

matter of fact • *noun* (*plural* **matters of fact**) **1** what

belongs to the sphere of fact as distinct from opinion etc. **2** *Law* the part of a judicial inquiry concerned with the truth of alleged facts. • *adjective* (**matter-of-fact**) **1** unimaginative. **2** unemotional. **3** pertaining to, having regard to, or depending on actual fact as distinct from what is speculative or fanciful. PHRASES **as a matter of fact** actually, in reality (esp. to correct a falsehood or misunderstanding). ▶ **matter-of-factly** *adverb* **matter-of-factness** *noun*

matting *noun* **1** fabric of hemp, grass, etc., for mats: *coconut matting*. **2** *in senses of* MAT[1],[2] *verb*.

mattock *noun* an agricultural tool shaped like a pickaxe, with an adze and a chisel edge as the ends of the head. [Say MAT uck]

mattress *noun* (*plural* **mattresses**) a large fabric case stuffed with soft, firm, or springy material, or a similar case filled with air or water, used on or as a bed.

maturation *noun* **1** the action or process of maturing. **2** the state of being matured. [Say match oo RAY sh'n]

mature • *adjective* (**maturer**, **maturest**) **1 a** with fully developed powers of body and mind; adult. **b** sensible, wise. **c** middle-aged or elderly. **2 a** complete in natural development or growth. **b** (of wine, cheese, etc.) ready for consumption. **c** (of fruit) ripe. **3** (of thought, intentions, etc.) careful and thorough: *on mature reflection, he decided they should not go*. **4** fully developed or established; at a point after which further development, expansion, or improvement is unlikely or impossible: *mature technology*. **5** (of a bond etc.) due for payment. **6 a** (in Alberta) a film classification which requires that viewers under 14 years of age be accompanied by an adult. **b** (in BC) a film classification which advises of content which may be inappropriate for young viewers, without indicating an age restriction. • *verb* (**matures**, **matured**, **maturing**) **1 a** bring to or reach a mature state; develop fully. **b** ripen. **c** come to maturity. **2** perfect (a plan etc.). **3** (of a bond etc.) become due for payment. ▶ **maturely** *adverb* **maturity** *noun*

matzo *noun* (also **matzoh**, **matzah**) (*plural* **matzos**, **matzohs**, **matzahs** or **matzoth**) **1** a flat, crisp, unleavened bread for the Passover. **2** a slab of this. [Say MOTT so or MOTT suh for the singular, MOTT soze or MOTT sawth for the plural]

matzo ball *noun* a small dumpling made of seasoned matzo meal bound together with egg and chicken fat, typically served in chicken soup.

maudlin *adjective* **1** (of a book, movie, or song) expressing or causing exaggerated emotions, especially in a way that is not sincere: *a maudlin ballad*. **2** talking in a silly, emotional way, often full of self-pity, especially when drunk: *he gets very maudlin after a few drinks*. [Say MOD lin]

maul *verb* **1** (of an animal) tear and mutilate (a person, prey, etc.). **2 a** beat and bruise (a person). **b** handle roughly or carelessly; damage by rough handling. **3** subject to damaging criticism; injure by criticizing. ▶ **mauling** *noun* [Sounds like MALL]

maunder *verb* talk in a rambling manner: *the idea that art may give access to the spiritual realm is not necessarily to be dismissed as New Age maundering*. [Say MAWN dur]

Maundy Thursday *noun* the Thursday before Easter, observed in the Christian Church as a commemoration of the Last Supper. [Say MAWN dee]

mausoleum *noun* **1** a large and grand tomb. **2** a very large and sombre building. [Say mozza LEE um]

mauve pale purple. ▶ **mauvish** *adjective* [Rhymes with COVE]

mauzy *adjective* (**mauzier**, **mauziest**) (also **mausy**, **mausier**, **mausiest**) *Cdn* (*Nfld*) (of weather) foggy,

M

damp, or misty, esp. producing condensation on objects. [Say MOZZY]

maven *noun informal* an expert or connoisseur. [Say MAY v'n]

maverick *noun* **1** an independent-minded or unorthodox person: *maverick politicians*. **2** a calf or yearling not branded with its owner's mark. [Say MAV rick]

maw *noun* **1** the jaws or throat of a greedy or ravenous animal or person: *a gigantic wolfhound with a fearful, gaping maw ◊ I was cramming large pieces of toast down my maw*. **2** a thing perceived as a consuming mouth or entrance: *the voracious maw of the publicity machine*.

mawkish *adjective* expressing or sharing emotion in a way that is exaggerated or embarrassing: *a mawkish poem*. ▶ **mawkishly** *adverb* **mawkishness** *noun*

max *slang* • *noun* (a) maximum. • *adjective* maximal. • *adverb* maximally; at most. • *verb* (**maxes, maxed, maxing**) (foll. by *out*) **1** achieve or attain a maximum in something: *prices max out at fifty thousand*. **2** spend to the limit of (a credit card). PHRASES **to the max 1** completely. **2** to the furthest possible extreme.

max. *abbreviation* maximum.

maxi *noun* (*plural* **maxis**) *informal* **1** a maxi-coat, -skirt, etc. **2** = MAXI-PAD.

maxi- *combining form* very large or long: *maxi-coat*.

maxilla *noun* (*plural* **maxillae**) **1** the jaw or jawbone, esp. the upper jaw in most vertebrates. **2** the mouthpart of many arthropods used in chewing. ▶ **maxillary** *adjective* [Say mac SILLA for the singular, mac SILLY for the plural; mac SILLA ree]

maxim *noun* a general truth or rule of conduct expressed in a sentence: *the maxim that actions speak louder than words*.

maximal *adjective* **1** being or relating to a maximum. **2** the greatest possible in size, duration, etc.

maximally *adverb* to the maximum extent; very: *a maximally clear audio system*.

maximization *noun* an act of maximizing.

maximize *verb* (**maximizes, maximized, maximizing**) increase or enhance to the utmost. ▶ **maximizer** *noun*

maximum • *noun* (*plural* **maximums** or **maxima**) the highest possible or attainable amount or magnitude. • *adjective* of or pertaining to a maximum; that is a maximum.

maximum-security *adjective* (of a correctional institution) intended for offenders who require the greatest degree of physical security and so usu. having not only bars on the windows, but high walls, double fences, security posts with armed guards, electronic monitoring systems, etc.

maxi-pad *noun* a sanitary pad designed to absorb heavy menstrual flow.

maxwell *noun* a unit of magnetic flux, equal to that induced through one square centimetre by a perpendicular magnetic field of one gauss.

May *noun* **1** the fifth month of the year. **2** (**may**) the hawthorn or its blossom.

> **WRITING TIP**
> **may, can**
>
> Both **can** and **may** are used to express permission: *Can I go now? May I go now?* But because **can** is also used to indicate capability (*Can I sing? = Am I able to sing?*), in formal contexts **may** tends to be used to express permission (*May I sing? = Am I allowed to sing?*).

may *auxiliary verb* (*3rd singular present* **may**; *past* **might**) **1** (often foll. by *well* for emphasis) expressing

possibility: *it may be true ◊ you may well lose your way*. **2** expressing permission: *may I come in?* **3** expressing a wish: *may he live to regret it*. **4** expressing uncertainty or irony in questions: *who may you be? ◊ who are you, may I ask?* **5** in purpose clauses and after *wish*, *fear*, etc.: *take such measures as may avert disaster ◊ hope she may succeed*. PHRASES **be that as it may** (or **that is as may be**) despite the fact that it may be so: *be that as it may, I still want to go*. **may as well** = MIGHT AS WELL (see MIGHT[1]).

Maya • *noun* **1** (*plural* **Maya** or **Mayas**) a member of an Indian people of Central America. The Maya civilization developed over an extensive area of southern Mexico, Guatemala, and Belize from the 2nd millennium BC, reaching its peak *c.*300–*c.*900 AD. The Mayas had a cumbersome system of pictorial writing and an extremely accurate calendar system. **2** the language of this people. • *adjective* of or relating to this people or language. [Say MY uh]

maya *noun* **1** *Hindu Philosophy* illusion, magic, the supernatural power wielded by gods and demons. **2** *Hinduism & Buddhism* the power by which the universe becomes manifest; the illusion or appearance of the phenomenal world. [Say MY uh]

Mayan • *adjective* of or relating to the Mayas. • *noun* a Maya. [Say MY un]

maybe • *adverb* perhaps, possibly. • *noun* (*plural* **maybes**) an uncertain response, a possibility.

May Day *noun* **1** May esp. as a festival with dancing, or as an international holiday in honour of workers.

mayday *noun* an international radio distress signal used esp. by ships and aircraft.

mayflower *noun* any of various flowers that bloom in May.

mayfly *noun* (*plural* **mayflies**) **1** a slender aquatic insect with delicate transparent wings and two or three long filaments on the tail, which lives briefly in spring in the adult stage. **2** an imitation mayfly used by anglers.

mayhem *noun* violent or damaging action.

mayn't *contraction* may not.

mayo *noun informal* mayonnaise.

mayonnaise *noun* a thick creamy dressing made of egg yolks, oil, vinegar, etc.

mayor *noun* the head of a municipal corporation, esp. of a city or town. ▶ **mayoral** *adjective*

mayoralty *noun* (*plural* **mayoralties**) **1** the office of mayor. **2** a mayor's period of office. [Say MAY ur ul tee]

maypole *noun* a tall pole painted and decked with flowers and ribbons, for dancing around on May Day.

maze *noun* **1 a** a network of paths and passages arranged in bewildering complexity, usu. with a correct path concealed by blind alleys etc. **b** such a pattern, represented on paper by a pattern of lines, designed as a puzzle. **2** any complex system, arrangement, etc. that bewilders, confuses, or perplexes.

mazel tov *interjection* good luck, congratulations. [Say MOZZLE tov or MOZZLE toff or MOZZLE tove]

mazurka *noun* **1** a usu. lively Polish dance in triple time, usu. with a slide and hop. **2** a piece of music for this dance or composed in its rhythm, usu. with accentuation of the second or third beat. [Say muh ZURKA]

MB *abbreviation* **1** (also **Mb**) *Computing* megabyte. **2** Manitoba (in official postal use). **3** *Cdn* MEDAL OF BRAVERY. **4** Mennonite Brethren.

M.B.A. • *abbreviation* Master of Business Administration. • *noun* (*plural* **M.B.A.'s**) a person who holds this degree.

Mbps *abbreviation* megabytes per second.

Mbyte *abbreviation* megabyte.

MC • *noun* (*plural* **MC's**) a master of ceremonies. • *verb* (**MC's, MC'd, MC'ing**) act as master of ceremonies for.

Mc *abbreviation* megacycle(s).

McCarthyism *noun* **1** *hist.* (esp. in the US) the policy of hunting out suspected Communists and removing them from government departments or other positions, esp. as pursued by the Republican politician Joseph McCarthy in the period 1950–4. Many of the accused were blacklisted or lost their jobs, though most did not in fact belong to the Communist Party. **2** any use of unfair or unsubstantiated accusations to hound, harass, or investigate: *ever more dangerous signs of McCarthyism on the part of the Israeli ruling establishment*.
▶ **McCarthyite** *adjective & noun*

McCoy *noun informal* PHRASES **the real McCoy** the real thing.

mCi *abbreviation* millicurie(s).

McIntosh *noun* (*plural* **McIntoshes**) a medium-sized, deep red apple with green blotches.

Mc/s *abbreviation* megacycles per second.

MD *abbreviation* **1** (*plural* **MDs**) Doctor of Medicine. **2** *Cdn* (*Prairies & North*) MUNICIPAL DISTRICT. **3** Mini Disc.

Md *symbol* mendelevium.

Md. *abbreviation* Maryland.

MDA *abbreviation* methylenedioxyamphetamine, a synthetic hallucinogenic drug.

MDMA *abbreviation* methylenedioxymeth-amphetamine, an amphetamine-based drug that causes euphoria and hallucinations; ecstasy.

MDT *abbreviation* Mountain Daylight Time.

GRAMMAR CHECK
me, I

The use of **me** instead of **I** after the verb "to be", as in *It's me again*, is now considered acceptable in writing as well as speech. In sentences like *It is I who knows you best*, however, **I** must be used instead of **me**. To avoid sounding excessively formal, such a sentence could be reworded *I'm the one who knows you best*, which is much more natural. *See also usage note at* THAN.

---

me¹ • *pronoun* **1** *objective case of* I²: *he saw me*. **2** *informal* myself, to or for myself: *I got me a gun*. **3** *informal* used in exclamations: *dear me!* • *adjective* of or displaying an excessive preoccupation with personal fulfillment and gratification: *the me generation*. • *noun* one's personality, the ego: *the real me*.

GRAMMAR CHECK
me, I

Never use **I** in sentences like *The teacher spoke to my father and I*; *The bus picked up my sister and I*; or *just between you and I*. In all these cases **I** should be replaced by **me**: *The teacher spoke to my father and me*; *The bus picked up my sister and me*; *just between you and me*. To know whether to use **I** or **me**, try saying the sentence as though it referred only to you, and then just add *my father and..* or *my sister and..* etc.

---

me² *noun* = MI.

mea culpa • *noun* (*plural* **mea culpas**) an acknowledgement of fault or error: *the minister's mea culpa, his admission that the government was not fulfilling its promise, was inadequate*. • *interjection* expressing such an acknowledgement. [Say may a KOOL puh or may a CULL puh (KOOL rhymes with WOOL)]

mead *noun* an alcoholic drink of fermented honey and water.

meadow *noun* **1** a piece of grassland, esp. one used for

hay or for grazing animals. **2** a piece of low well-watered ground, esp. near a river.

meadowland *noun* land used for the cultivation of grass, esp. for hay.

meadowlark *noun* any of several North American songbirds related to the blackbirds but speckled brown with yellow underparts, esp. the eastern meadowlark or the western meadowlark, which has a characteristic bubbling song.

meagre *adjective* (also **meager**) small in quantity and poor in quality: *a meagre diet of bread* ◊ *a meagre salary*.
▶ **meagrely** *adverb* **meagreness** *noun* [Say MEE gur]

meal¹ *noun* **1** an occasion when food is eaten. **2** the food eaten on one occasion. PHRASES **make a meal of** consume as a meal.

meal² *noun* **1** the edible part of any grain or pulse (usu. other than wheat) ground to powder. **2** any powdery substance made by grinding.

Meals on Wheels *plural noun* (usu. treated as *singular*) a service by which meals are delivered to old people, invalids, etc.

meal ticket *noun* **1** a ticket entitling one to a meal, esp. at a specified place with reduced cost. **2** *informal* a person or thing that is a source of food or income: *he was booking blues artists, giving them a meal ticket and a guitar*.

mealtime *noun* any of the usual times of eating.

mealy *adjective* (**mealier, mealiest**) **1** of or like meal; soft and powdery. **2** containing meal. **3** covered with or as with meal, flour, or any fine dust or powder.

mealy bug *noun* a small insect whose body is covered with white powder, and which infests vines and is a pest of citrus trees and greenhouses.

mealy-mouthed *adjective* not willing to speak directly.

mean¹ *verb* (**means, meant, meaning**) **1** intend to express or refer to. **2** (of a word) have as its explanation in the same language or its equivalent in another language. **3** intend to occur or be the case. **4** have as a consequence. **5** intend or design for a particular purpose. **6** be of specified importance. PHRASES **mean it** not be joking or exaggerating. **mean to say** really admit: *do you mean to say you have lost it?* **mean well** (often foll. by *by*) have good intentions.

mean² *adjective* **1** uncooperative, unkind, or unfair. **2** stingy; not generous. **3 a** malicious, ill-tempered. **b** vicious or aggressive in behaviour. **4 a** low in the social hierarchy; humble: *mean origins*. **b** (of housing etc.) shabby; characterized by poverty: *her home was mean and small*. **5** (of a person's capacity, understanding, etc.) inferior, poor: *this should be clear even to the meanest intelligence*. **6** *informal* **a** (of a person) skilful, formidable: *is a mean fighter*. **b** (of a thing) excellent, impressive: *a mean batch of chili*. PHRASES **no mean** a very good: *that is no mean achievement*.

mean³ • *noun* **1** a quality, condition, or way of doing something that is in the middle of two extremes and better than either of them: *he needed to find a mean between frankness and rudeness*. **2** *Math* **a** the term or one of the terms midway between the first and last terms of an arithmetical or geometrical etc. progression. **b** the quotient of the sum of several quantities and their number; the average. • *adjective* **1** (of a quantity) equally far from two extremes: *hope is the mean virtue between despair and presumption*. **2** calculated as a mean.

meander • *verb* **1** wander at random: *aimlessly meandering now, checking out the record stores, watching the passing tourists*. **2** (of a stream or road) wind about: *Highway 13 meanders east through the undulating, mid-Alberta prairie*. • *noun* (often in *plural*) a curve in a

winding river. ▶**meandering** *adjective & noun* [Say mee ANDER]

meanie *noun informal* a mean, stingy, or ill-tempered person.

meaning • *noun* **1** what is meant by a word, action, idea, etc. **2** significance: *he gave me a look full of meaning*. **3** the quality or sense of purpose that makes one feel that one's life is valuable: *her life seemed to have lost all meaning* ◊ *having a child gave new meaning to their lives.* • *adjective* expressive, significant: *a meaning glance*. ▶**meaningly** *adverb*

meaningful *adjective* **1** full of meaning; significant. **2** able to be interpreted. **3** intended to communicate something not directly expressed: *a meaningful look*. ▶**meaningfully** *adverb*

meaningless *adjective* having no meaning or significance. ▶**meaninglessly** *adverb* **meaninglessness** *noun*

meanly *adverb* unkindly, unfairly.

meanness *noun* nastiness; the quality of being mean.

means *plural noun* **1** (often treated as *singular*) an action, object, system, etc. by which a result is brought about; a method or methods: *an effective means of communication*. **2 a** money resources: *live beyond one's means*. **b** wealth: *a man of means*. PHRASES **by all means** certainly. **by any means** in any way: *not by any means rich*. **by means of** by the agency or instrumentality of (a thing or action). **by no means** (or **not by any manner of means**) not at all; certainly not.

means of production *plural noun* (in Marxist doctrine) the raw materials and means of labour (machines, implements, etc.) used in the production process.

mean-spirited *adjective* petty; spiteful; selfish. ▶**mean-spiritedness** *noun*

means test • *noun* an official inquiry to establish need before financial assistance from public funds is given. • *verb* (**means-test**) **1** assess (a grant etc.) by a means test: *means-tested programs for seniors*. **2** subject (a person) to a means test.

mean streets *plural noun* **1** streets where the poor or socially deprived live or work. **2** streets noted for violence and crime.

meant *past and past participle of* MEAN[1].

meantime • *noun* the intervening period: *in the meantime*. • *adverb =* MEANWHILE.

meanwhile • *adverb* **1** in the intervening period of time. **2** at the same time. • *noun* the intervening period: *in the meanwhile*.

measles *plural noun* (also treated as *singular*) **1** an acute infectious viral disease marked by red spots on the skin. **2** the spots of measles.

measly *adjective* (**measlier, measliest**) **1** *informal* ridiculously small in size, amount, or value. **2** *informal* inferior, contemptible, worthless. **3** of or affected with measles.

measurable *adjective* **1** that can be measured. **2** noticeable; definite: *a measurable improvement*. ▶**measurably** *adverb*

measure • *noun* **1** a size or quantity found by measuring. **2** a system of measuring: *linear measure*. **3** a rod or tape etc. for measuring. **4** a vessel of standard capacity for transferring or determining fixed quantities of liquids etc.: *a pint measure*. **5 a** the degree, extent, or amount of a thing. **b** (foll. by *of*) some degree of: *gained a measure of acceptance*. **6** a unit of capacity, e.g. a bushel: *20 measures of wheat*. **7** a factor by which a person or thing is reckoned or evaluated: *their success is a measure of their determination*. **8** suitable action to achieve some end: *a stop-gap measure* ◊ *drastic measures*. **9** a legislative enactment. **10** a quantity contained in

another an exact number of times. **11** a prescribed extent or quantity. **12** a bar of music. • *verb* (**measures, measured, measuring**) **1 a** ascertain the extent or quantity of (a thing) by comparison with a fixed unit or with an object of known size. **b** take measurements; use a measuring instrument. **2** be of a specified size: *it measures six centimetres*. **3** ascertain the size and proportion of (a person) for clothes. **4** estimate (a quality, person's character, etc.) by some standard or rule. **5** (often foll. by *off*) mark (a line etc. of a given length). **6** (foll. by *out*) deal or distribute (a thing) in measured quantities. **7** (foll. by *with, against*) bring (oneself or one's strength etc.) into competition with. PHRASES **beyond measure** very greatly. **for good measure** as something beyond the minimum; as a finishing touch. **have** (or **get**) **the measure of** have an accurate opinion of the abilities or character of. **in a** (or **some**) **measure** partly. **measure up 1 a** determine the size etc. of by measurement. **b** take comprehensive measurements. **2** (often foll. by *to*) have the necessary qualifications (for).

measured *adjective* **1** ascertained by measurement. **2** rhythmical; regular in movement: *a measured pace*. **3** (of language) carefully considered; restrained.

measureless *adjective* not measurable; infinite.

measurement *noun* **1** the action or process of measuring something: *accurate measurement is essential* ◊ *a telescope with which precise measurements can be made*. **2** a size, quantity, or extent determined by measuring. **3** (in *plural*) **a** detailed dimensions. **b** the measured circumference or length of the parts of a person's body used in fitting clothes, esp. the chest, waist, and hips. **4** a system of measuring or of measures: *metric measurement*.

SPELL CHECK
meat, meet, mete

To come together with is to **meet**. The spelling is also **meet** in "meet the recommendations". The spelling is **mete** in "mete out punishment".

meat *noun* **1** the flesh of animals (esp. mammals) as food. **2 a** the essence or chief part of: *the answers to these questions provide the meat of the book*. **b** significant content; substance: *he had some strong meat in his programs, including the Boston premiere of Poulenc's Gloria*. **3** the edible part of fruits, nuts, eggs, shellfish, etc. **4** *informal* human flesh.

meat and potatoes • *noun* basics; ordinary but fundamental things. • *adjective* (**meat-and-potatoes**) basic, fundamental, down-to-earth.

meatball *noun* **1** minced meat compressed into a small round ball. **2** a stupid, clumsy, or ineffectual person.

meathead *noun* a stupid person.

meathook *noun* **1** a hook on which to hang meat carcasses etc. **2** *slang* an arm or hand.

meatiness *noun* the quality of being full of meat or like meat: *we savoured the meatiness of the mushrooms*.

meatless *adjective* (of a meal) without meat.

meat loaf *noun* a dish of ground meat mixed with onion, bread crumbs, etc., baked in a loaf pan.

meat market *noun* **1** a butcher's shop. **2** *slang* a place, esp. a bar, club, etc., where people seek to meet others for sexual encounters.

meat packer *noun* a person or business engaged in meat packing.

meat packing *noun* the business of processing and packing meat and distributing it to retailers.

meaty *adjective* (**meatier, meatiest**) **1** full of meat; fleshy. **2** of or like meat. **3** full of substance.

M

mecca *noun* (*plural* **meccas**) (also **Mecca**) a place which attracts people of a particular group: *tourist mecca*.

mechanic *noun* a skilled worker who makes or uses or repairs machinery, esp. engines.

mechanical • *adjective* **1** of or relating to machines or mechanisms. **2** working or produced by machinery. **3** (of a person or action) like a machine; automatic; lacking originality. **4 a** (of an agency, principle, etc.) belonging to mechanics. **b** (of a theory etc.) explaining phenomena by the assumption of mechanical action. **5** of or relating to mechanics as a science. • *noun* (in *plural*) the working parts of a machine, esp. of an automobile.

mechanical engineering *noun* the branch of engineering that deals with the design, construction, and maintenance of machines. ▶ **mechanical engineer** *noun*

mechanically *adverb* **1** by mechanical means: *a mechanically powered vehicle.* **2** in a machine-like manner: *she spoke mechanically, as if thinking of something else.* **3** of or pertaining to machines or mechanisms: *they've always been mechanically-minded* ◊ *the car was found to be mechanically sound.*

mechanics *plural noun* **1** (treated as *singular*) the branch of applied mathematics dealing with motion and tendencies to motion. **2** (treated as *singular*) the science of machinery. **3** (usu. treated as *plural*) **a** the construction, workings, or routine operation of a thing: *mechanics of a lawn mower.* **b** the practicalities or details of a thing: *mechanics of laundering money.*

mechanism *noun* **1** the structure or adaptation of parts of a machine. **2** a system of mutually adapted parts working together in or as in a machine. **3** the mode of operation of a process. **4** a means: *no mechanism for complaints.* **5** Philosophy the doctrine that all natural phenomena, including life, allow mechanical explanation by physics and chemistry. **6** an unconscious, structured set of mental processes underlying a person's behaviour or responses: *defence mechanism.*

mechanistic *adjective* designating theories or views which consider phenomena as physical processes: *a mechanistic view of the brain.* ▶ **mechanistically** *adverb* [Say mecka NISS tick]

mechanization *noun* an act of mechanizing.

mechanize *verb* (**mechanizes**, **mechanized**, **mechanizing**) **1** make mechanical; give a mechanical character to. **2** introduce machines or machinery in or into (a factory, process, etc.). **3** *Military* equip with tanks, armoured cars, etc.

mechoui *noun* (*plural* **mechouis**) *Cdn* (*Que.*) **1** a meal of meat, esp. lamb or mutton, roasted on a spit over a fire. **2** a party, usu. outdoors and for large numbers of people, at which meat, usu. a whole animal, is cooked in this way and served. [Say MAY shwee]

M.Ed. *abbreviation* Master of Education.

med *informal* • *adjective* medical: *med school.* • *noun* (usu. in *plural*) medication: *take your meds!*

med. *abbreviation* medium.

medal • *noun* **1** a piece of metal, usu. in the form of a disc, struck or cast with an inscription or device to commemorate an event etc., or awarded as a distinction to a soldier, scholar, athlete, etc., for services rendered, for proficiency, etc. **2** a similar object marked with a religious image, inscription, etc. **3** (as an *adjective*) designating the part of a competition that will determine the medal winners or a sport eligible for medals: *curling is now a medal sport.* • *verb* (**medals**, **medalled**, **medalling**) **1** (usu. in *passive*)

decorate or honour with a medal. **2** (esp. of an athlete) receive a medal. ▶ **medalled** *adjective*

medallion *noun* **1** a large medal. **2** a thing shaped like this, e.g. a decorative panel or tablet, portrait, etc. **3** a small, flat, round or oval cut of meat or fish. [Say muh DAL yun]

medallist *noun* (also esp. *US* **medalist**) **1** a recipient of a (specified) medal: *gold medallist.* **2** an engraver or designer of medals.

Medal of Bravery *noun* Canada's third highest decoration for bravery. Abbreviation: **MB**.

meddle *verb* (**meddles**, **meddled**, **meddling**) (often foll. by *with*, *in*) interfere in or busy oneself unduly with others' concerns. ▶ **meddler** *noun*

meddlesome *adjective* fond of meddling; interfering.

Mede *noun* hist. a member of an Indo-European people which established an empire in Media in Persia (modern Iran) in the 7th century BC.

medevac • *noun* the transportation of sick or wounded patients by air to hospital, esp. from a remote location, a battlefield, etc. • *verb* (**medevacs**, **medevacked**, **medevacking**) transport by medevac. [Say MEDDA vac]

media *plural noun* **1** plural of MEDIUM. **2** (usu. preceded by *the*; treated as *plural* or *singular*) the main means of mass communication (esp. newspapers and broadcasting) regarded collectively: *media coverage.*

mediaeval esp. *Brit.* = MEDIEVAL. [Say med EVIL or meddy EVIL]

Median *adjective* of or relating to the Medes, an Indo-European people who established an empire in Persia in the 7th century BC. [Say MEEDY un]

median • *adjective* **1** situated in the middle: *the surface is predominantly undulating in the median area, and rolling to steep around the periphery.* **2** *Statistics* referring to the middle term of a series of values: *the median duration of this treatment was four months.* **3** *Anatomy, Botany, & Zoology* of, pertaining to, or designating the plane which divides a body, organ, or limb into roughly symmetrical halves. • *noun* **1** *Math* the middle value of a series of values arranged in order of size. **2** (also **median strip**) a paved or landscaped strip of ground, or a physical barrier such as a raised curb, dividing a street or highway. **3** *Math* a straight line drawn from any vertex of a triangle to the middle of the opposite side. [Say MEEDY un]

mediate *verb* (**mediates**, **mediated**, **mediating**)

1 intervene (between parties in a dispute) to produce agreement or reconciliation: *an independent body was brought in to mediate between staff and management.* **2** find a solution to a disagreement between people or groups: *they help the parties identify the issues and work toward mediating a settlement.* [Say MEEDY ate]

mediation *noun* Law the process or action of mediating between parties in a dispute to produce agreement or reconciliation. [Say meedy AY sh'n]

mediator *noun* a person or an organization that tries to bring about agreement between people or groups who disagree with each other. [Say MEEDY ate ur]

medic *noun* informal a doctor or medical student.

Medicaid *noun* US a federal and state system of health insurance for those requiring financial assistance. [Say MEDDA kade]

medical • *adjective* **1** of or relating to the science or practice of medicine in general. **2** of or relating to conditions requiring medical and not surgical treatment: *medical ward.* **3** of or relating to the condition of one's health: *medical leave.* • *noun* informal a medical examination.

medical doctor *noun* a physician.

medical examiner *noun* **1** a medically qualified public officer who investigates unusual or suspicious deaths, performs post-mortems, and initiates inquests. **2** a doctor who performs medical examinations.

medicalization *noun* an act of medicalizing.

medicalize *verb* (**medicalizes, medicalized, medicalizing**) involve medicine in; view in medical terms, esp. unwarrantedly: *medicalize menopause.*

medically *adverb* from a medical viewpoint; in a medical sense: *he was found to be medically unfit for the job.*

medical officer *noun* a doctor appointed by a company or public authority to attend to matters relating to health.

medical officer of health *noun* (*plural* **medical officers of health**) Cdn & Brit. a person in charge of a public health department, responsible for enforcing public health regulations. Abbreviation: **MOH.**

medical practitioner *noun* a physician or surgeon.

medicare *noun* **1** (in Canada) a national health care program financed by taxation and administered by the provinces and territories. **2** (**Medicare**) (in the US) a federal system of health insurance for persons over 65 years of age.

medicate *verb* (**medicates, medicated, medicating**) **1** treat medically; administer medication to. **2** add a medicinal substance to: *medicated shampoo.*

medication *noun* **1** a substance used for medical treatment. **2** treatment using drugs.

medicinal • *adjective* **1** (of a substance) having healing properties. **2** (of a taste, smell, etc.) resembling that of medicine. • *noun* a medicinal substance. ▶ **medicinally** *adverb* [Say muh DISSA null]

medicine *noun* **1** the science or practice of the diagnosis, treatment, and prevention of disease, esp. as distinct from surgical methods. **2** any drug or preparation used for the treatment or prevention of disease, esp. one taken by mouth. **3** a spell, charm, or fetish which is thought to cure afflictions. **4** (as an *adjective*) (in Aboriginal societies) used to designate the healing power that may reside in physical objects or in the knowledge and techniques of healing rites. PHRASES **a taste** (or **dose**) **of one's own medicine** treatment such as one is accustomed to giving others. **take one's medicine** submit to something disagreeable.

medicine ball *noun* a large heavy stuffed usu. leather ball thrown and caught for exercise.

medicine bundle *noun* a collection of objects, often wrapped in hide, which have sacred and personal power for the owner, used by Plains Aboriginal peoples as a religious object.

medicine cabinet *noun* (also **medicine chest**) a small cupboard containing medicines, items for first aid, etc.

Medicine Line *noun* Cdn (West) esp. hist. the Canada-US border, esp. from Ontario westward.

medicine man *noun* a person believed to have magical powers of healing, esp. among some North American Aboriginal peoples.

medicine wheel *noun* a wheel-shaped arrangement of stones at which acts of ritual and meditation were or are performed by certain Aboriginal peoples, located at various places throughout North America.

medieval *adjective* **1** of, or in the style of, the Middle Ages. **2** informal old-fashioned, archaic: *medieval attitudes about class structure.* [Say med EVIL or meddy EVIL]

medievalist *noun* a student of or expert in the Middle Ages. [Say med EVIL ist or meddy EVIL ist]

medina *noun* (*plural* **medinas**) the old Arab or non-European quarter of a northern African town. [Say muh DEENA]

mediocre *adjective* **1** of middling quality, neither good nor bad. **2** second-rate. [Say meedy OAKER]

mediocrity *noun* (*plural* **mediocrities**) **1** the state of being mediocre. **2** a mediocre person or thing. [Say meedy OCKRA tee]

meditate *verb* (**meditates, meditated, meditating**) **1 a** exercise the mind in (esp. religious) contemplation. **b** (usu. foll. by *on, upon*) focus on a subject in this manner. **2** plan mentally; design. ▶ **meditation** *noun* **meditator** *noun*

meditative *adjective* **1** inclined to meditate. **2** indicative of meditation. ▶ **meditatively** *adverb* [Say MEDDA tay tiv]

Mediterranean • *noun* **1** (**the Mediterranean**) **a** the Mediterranean Sea. **b** the countries bordering on the Mediterranean Sea. **2** a native of a country bordering on the Mediterranean. • *adjective* **1** of or characteristic of the Mediterranean, countries bordering it, or their inhabitants: *Mediterranean cooking.* **2** (of climate) characterized by hot dry summers and warm wet winters. **3** designating scrubby, dense, drought-resistant vegetation that is adapted to this climate, including broad-leaved evergreen shrubs and small thorn trees. [Say medda tuh RAINY un]

medium • *noun* (*plural* **media** or **mediums**) **1** the middle quality, degree, etc. between extremes: *find a happy medium.* **2** the means by which something is communicated: *the medium of television.* **3** the intervening substance through which impressions are conveyed to the senses etc.: *light passing from one medium into another.* **4** the physical environment or conditions of growth, storage, or transport of a living organism. **5** an agency or means of doing something: *the medium through which money is raised.* **6** the material or form used by an artist, composer, etc. **7** the liquid, e.g. oil or gel, with which pigments are mixed for use in painting. **8** (*plural* **mediums**) a person claiming to be in contact with the spirits of the dead and to communicate between the dead and the living. **9 a** a garment size designed to fit the average figure. **b** an article of clothing in this size. • *adjective* **1** between two qualities, degrees, etc. **2** average; moderate: *of medium height.*

medium of exchange *noun* (*plural* **mediums of exchange**) a standard item exchanged in commercial transactions, e.g. money.

medium-range *adjective* (of an aircraft, missile, etc.) able to travel a medium distance.

medium-security *adjective* (of a correctional institution) having perimeter security, ranging from fences to armed posts.

mediumship *noun* the practice of being a spiritual medium: *mediumship and telepathic powers*.

medium-sized *adjective* of average size.

medivac *noun & verb* = MEDEVAC. [Say MEDDA vac]

medley *noun* (*plural* **medleys**) **1** a varied mixture: *a sanctuary for a medley of wildlife and plant species*. **2** a collection of musical items from one work or various sources arranged as a continuous whole. **3** a dish of assorted vegetables. **4** (also **medley relay**) a relay race between teams in which each team member runs a different distance, swims a different stroke, etc.

medulla *noun* **1** the inner region of certain organs or tissues usu. when it is distinguishable from the outer region or cortex, as in hair or a kidney. **2** (also **medulla oblongata**) the continuation of the spinal cord within the skull, forming the lowest part of the brain stem. **3** the soft internal tissue of plants. [Say muh DULLA (oblong GATTA)]

medusa *noun* (*plural* **medusae**) a free-swimming form of a cup-shaped aquatic invertebrate, having stinging tentacles around the edge of a jellylike body, e.g. a jellyfish. [Say muh DOO suh or muh DYOO suh for the singular, muh DOO see or muh DYOO see for the plural]

meek *adjective* **1** humble and submissive; suffering injury etc. tamely. **2** piously gentle in nature. ▶ **meekly** *adverb* **meekness** *noun*

SPELL CHECK
meet, meat, mete   ABC✓

The food is spelled **meat**. The spelling is **mete** in "mete out punishment".
---

meet¹ • *verb* (**meets, met, meeting**) **1** come together with at the same place and time. **2** see or be introduced to for the first time. **3** come into contact with; touch or join. **4** encounter (a situation). **5** fulfill or satisfy (a requirement). • *noun* the assembly of competitors for various sporting activities: *track meet*. PHRASES **meet the eye** (or **the ear**) be visible (or audible). **meet a person's eye** check if another person is watching and look into his or her eyes in return. **meet a person halfway** make a compromise; respond in a friendly way to the advances of another person. **meet up** (often foll. by *with*) informal meet or make contact, esp. by chance. **meet with 1** see sense 8 of *v*. **2** receive (a reaction): *met with the committee's approval*. **3** = sense 1a of *v*. **more (to it) than meets the eye** hidden qualities or complications.

meet² *adjective* archaic suitable, fit, proper.

meeting *noun* **1** in senses of MEET¹. **2** an assembly of people, esp. the members of a society, committee, etc., for discussion or entertainment. **3** an assembly (esp. of Quakers) for worship. **4** the persons assembled: *address the meeting*.

meeting house *noun* **1** a place of worship for Quakers. **2** hist. a Protestant place of worship.

meeting place *noun* a place where people often meet.

meg *noun* slang megabyte(s).

mega slang • *adjective* of enormous size, importance, etc. • *adverb* extremely: *mega famous*.

mega- *combining form* **1** large. **2** denoting a factor of one million (10^6) in the metric system of measurement. **3** to a great degree, extent, etc.

megabit *noun* 1,048,576 (i.e. 2^{20}) bits as a measure of data capacity, or loosely 1,000,000 bits.

megabuck *noun* informal **1** a million dollars: *megabuck salary*. **2** (in plural) a huge sum of money.

megabyte *noun* 1,048,576 (i.e. 2^{20}) bytes as a measure of data capacity, or loosely 1,000,000 bytes.

megacity *noun* (*plural* **megacities**) **1** a very large city, esp. one with a population of over 10 million. **2** a large city formed by combining separate cities in a metropolitan area into one corporate entity.

megadeal *noun* a business transaction involving large amounts of money, property, etc. [Say MEGA deal]

megadose *noun* a very large dose, esp. of a vitamin etc. [Say MEGA dose]

megafauna *noun* the large animals, esp. the large vertebrates, of a given area, habitat, or epoch.

megaflop *noun* **1** a unit of computing speed equal to one million floating-point operations per second. **2** slang a complete failure.

megahertz *noun* (*plural* **megahertz**) one million hertz, esp. as a measure of frequency of radio transmissions.

megahit *noun* a highly successful enterprise, product, etc. [Say MEGA hit]

megalithic *adjective* Archaeology made of or marked by the use of large stones: *famous for its huge megalithic tombs*. [Say mega LITH ick]

megalomania *noun* **1** lust for power: *the Tories reveal their megalomania, insecurity, and arrogant intolerance for dissent*. **2** a mental disorder producing an exaggerated belief in one's own importance or power. ▶ **megalomaniac** *adjective* & *noun* **megalomaniacal** *adjective* [Say mega loh MANIA, mega loh MANIAC, mega loh muh NYE A cull]

megalopolis *noun* (*plural* **megalopolises**) **1** a very large city. **2** an urban region consisting of a city and its environs. [Say mega LOPPA liss]

mega-mall *noun* an extremely large shopping mall, usu. including elaborate entertainment facilities.

megaphone *noun* a large funnel-shaped device for amplifying the sound of the voice.

megaproject *noun* a very large-scale, costly construction or engineering project, e.g. the building of a dam, the development of a transportation infrastructure, etc.

megastar *noun* a very famous person, esp. in the world of entertainment. ▶ **megastardom** *noun* [Say MEGA star]

megastore *noun* a large store, selling many different types of goods, usu. situated on the outskirts of a town or city.

megaton *noun* **1** a unit of explosive power equal to one million tons of TNT. **2** informal a very large or heavy amount: *sold megatons of albums*. ▶ **megatonnage** *noun* [Say MEGA tun]

megavolt *noun* one million volts, esp. as a unit of electromotive force.

megawatt *noun* one million watts, esp. as a measure of electrical power as generated by power stations.

Meiji • *noun* the period of the rule of the Japanese emperor Meiji Tenno (1852–1912, emperor 1867–1912), which saw the country's emergence as a major world power. • *adjective* pertaining to or characteristic of this period. [Say MAY jee]

meiosis *noun* (*plural* **meioses**) a type of cell division that results in daughter cells with half the chromosome number of the parent cell (compare MITOSIS). ▶ **meiotic** *adjective* [Say my OH sis for the singular, my OH seez for the plural; for *meiotic* say my OTT ick]

-meister *combining form* often jocular a person skilled in or famous for something specified by the initial element: *schlockmeister*.

M

melamine *noun* a hard plastic material, used especially for covering other materials. [Say MELLA mean]

melancholia *noun* **1** a mental illness marked by depression and ill-founded fears. **2** = MELANCHOLY *noun* 1. ▶ **melancholic** *adjective* & *noun* **melancholically** *adverb* [Say melon COALY uh, melon CAWL ick]

melancholy • *noun* (*plural* **melancholies**) **1 a** a pensive sadness. **b** a tendency to this. **2** *hist.* black bile, one of the four humours which were once thought to determine a person's physical and mental qualities; a dominance of melancholy made a person sad (*see* HUMOUR *noun* 5). • *adjective* **1** (of a person) sad, gloomy. **2** (of a thing) saddening, depressing. **3** (of words, a tune, etc.) expressing sadness. [Say MELON cawly]

Melanesian • *noun* **1** a member of the dominant Negroid people of Melanesia, a region of the western Pacific, south of Micronesia and west of Polynesia. **2** any of the Malayo-Polynesian languages of this people. • *adjective* of or relating to this people or their language. [Say mella NEE zhun]

mélange *noun* a mixture, a medley: *a mélange of meat, vegetables, and rice.* [Say may LAWNZH]

melanin *noun* a dark brown to black pigment occurring in the hair, skin, and iris of the eye, that is responsible for tanning of the skin when exposed to sunlight. [Say MELLA nin]

melanoma *noun* (*plural* **melanomas**) a usu. malignant tumour of melanin-forming cells, usu. in the skin. [Say mella NOMA]

melatonin *noun* a substance formed in the pineal gland of various mammals, which inhibits melanin formation and is thought to be concerned with regulating the reproductive cycle. [Say mella TOE nin]

Melba toast *noun* very thin crisp toast.

meld • *verb* merge, blend, combine: *the influences melded into a single, unified and unique conception.* • *noun* a thing formed by merging or blending: *an electrifying meld of olive oil, tomatoes, black olives, garlic, capers, and chilies.*

melee *noun* **1** a confused fight, skirmish, or scuffle: *he was suspended for his part in a melee near the Toronto bench.* **2** a confused mass of people: *the melee of people that were always thronging the streets.* [Say MAY lay or MEL ay or mel AY]

mellifluent *adjective* = MELLIFLUOUS. [Say muh LIFF loo int]

mellifluous *adjective* (of a voice, words, etc.) pleasing, musical, flowing. [Say muh LIFF loo us]

mellow • *adjective* **1** (of sound, colour, light) soft and rich, free from harshness. **2** (of character) softened or matured by age or experience. **3** good-humoured, relaxed, genial. **4** *informal* partly intoxicated, esp. pleasantly. **5** (of fruit) soft, sweet, and juicy with ripeness. **6** (of wine, cheese, etc.) well-matured, smooth. **7** (of earth) rich, loamy. • *verb* **1** make or become mellow. **2** *informal* (often foll. by *out*) relax, become less intense. ▶ **mellowness** *noun*

melodic *adjective* relating to melody: *melodic inventiveness* ◊ *the melodic line.* ▶ **melodically** *adverb* [Say muh LOD ick]

melodious *adjective* **1** of, producing, or having melody: *a melodious contralto voice.* **2** sweet-sounding: *a melodious Southern drawl.* ▶ **melodiously** *adverb* **melodiousness** *noun* [Say muh LODEY us]

melodrama *noun* (*plural* **melodramas**) **1** a sensational dramatic piece with crude appeals to the emotions and usu. a happy ending. **2** the genre of drama of this type. **3** language, behaviour, or an occurrence suggestive of this. ▶ **melodramatic** *adjective* [Say MELLOW drama, mellow DRAMATIC]

melodramatics *plural noun* melodramatic behaviour, action, or writing. [Say mellow DRAMATICS]

melody *noun* (*plural* **melodies**) **1** an arrangement of single notes in a musically expressive succession. **2** the principal part in harmonized music. **3** a musical arrangement of words; a song. **4** sweet music, either vocal or instrumental: *the haunting melody of the meadowlark.*

melon *noun* **1** the sweet fruit of various gourds. **2** the gourd producing this. **3 a** a mass of waxy material in the head of some toothed whales, thought to focus acoustic signals. **b** the dome this forms on the forehead. **4** a yellowish pink colour.

melt • *verb* **1** make or become liquid by heat. **2** soften or liquefy, esp. by the action of moisture; dissolve. **3 a** (of a person, feelings, the heart, etc.) be softened as a result of pity, love, etc. **b** dissolve into tears. **4** soften (a person, feelings, the heart, etc.): *a look to melt a heart of stone.* **5** (usu. foll. by *into*) change or merge imperceptibly into another form or state: *night melted into dawn.* **6** (often foll. by *away*) (of a person) leave or disappear unobtrusively: *melted into the background.* **7** *informal* (of a person) perspire excessively, suffer extreme heat. • *noun* **1** an act of melting. **2 a** a period of melting. **b** the snow in spring: *the precipitation falls as snow and is released during the spring melt.* **b** = MELTWATER. **3** a sandwich, hamburger, or other dish having melted cheese on top: *tuna melt.* **4** metal etc. in a melted condition. PHRASES **melt away** disappear or make disappear by or as if by liquefaction. **melt down 1** melt (esp. metal articles) in order to reuse the raw material. **2** become liquid and lose structure. **3** (of a part of a nuclear reactor) lose structural integrity, creating a potential for the catastrophic release of radiation (*compare* MELTDOWN 1). **melt in the mouth** (of food) be delicious and esp. very light.

meltdown *noun* **1** the melting of (and consequent damage to) a structure, esp. the overheated core of a nuclear reactor. **2 a** any uncontrolled and usu. disastrous transformation with far-reaching repercussions. **b** a collapse or reversal of fortune, esp. a sudden rapid drop in the value of assets, shares, etc.

melter *noun* a machine that melts something: *snow melter.*

melting *adjective* **1** that melts or is in the process of melting. **2** yielding to emotion, esp. feeling or showing pity, love, etc. **3** (of sound) soft and liquid: *melting chords.* ▶ **meltingly** *adverb*

melting point *noun* the temperature at which any given solid will melt.

melting pot *noun* **1** a place or situation where people from different ethnic or cultural backgrounds are integrated and mixed together, often resulting in conformity and a loss of individuality: *a Franco-American who lost his French tongue in the American melting pot.* **2** a place where theories, ideas, etc. are mixed together: *my closet is a melting pot of fashion.* **3** a pot in which metals etc. are melted and mixed.

melt-in-the-mouth *adjective* (also **melt-in-your-mouth**) (of food) delicious and of a very fine texture.

meltwater *noun* water formed by the melting of snow and ice, esp. from a glacier.

member *noun* **1** a person or organization belonging to a group or society. **2** a part of a complex structure. **3 a** any part or organ of the body, esp. a limb. **b** the penis.

membership *noun* **1** the state or condition of being a member. **2** the number of members in a particular body. **3** the body of members collectively.

membrane *noun* **1** any pliable sheet-like structure acting as a boundary, lining, or partition in an organism. **2** a thin pliable sheet or skin of various

M

kinds. ▶**membranous** *adjective* [Say MEM brain, MEM brun us]

meme *noun Biology* an element of a culture or system of behaviour that is passed from one individual to another by non-genetic means, esp. imitation.

memento *noun (plural* **mementoes** or **mementos)** an object kept as a reminder or souvenir of a person or event. [Say muh MENTOE]

memo *noun (plural* **memos)** a memorandum.

memoir *noun* **1** (in *plural*) an autobiography or a written account of one's memory of certain events or people. **2** a historical account or biography written from personal knowledge or special sources. ▶**memoirist** *noun* [Say MEM warr, MEM warr ist (WARR rhymes with *FAR*)]

memorabilia *plural noun* souvenirs of memorable events, people, periods, etc. [Say memmer a BEEL yuh]

memorable *adjective* **1** worth remembering, not to be forgotten. **2** easily remembered. ▶**memorably** *adverb* [Say MEMMER a bull]

memorandum *noun (plural* **memoranda) 1 a** a written note or communication esp. in business between people working for the same organization. **b** an informal diplomatic message, esp. summarizing the state of a question etc. **2** a note or record made for future use. **3** *Law* a document summarizing or embodying the terms of a contract or other legal details: *memorandum of agreement.* [Say memma RANDOM for the singular, memma RANDA for the plural]

memorial • *noun* an object, institution, or custom established in memory of a person or event: *the Terry Fox Memorial.* • *adjective* intending to commemorate a person or thing: *memorial service.*

Memorial Cup *noun* a trophy awarded annually to the Canadian major junior amateur hockey champions.

Memorial Day *noun* **1** *Cdn (Nfld)* a statutory holiday, 1 July, commemorating losses to the Newfoundland Regiment at the battle of the Somme. **2** *US* a day on which those who died on active service are remembered, usu. the last Monday in May.

memorialize *verb* (**memorializes, memorialized, memorializing**) produce something that will preserve the memory of a person or thing: *a poem memorializing a dead cat ◊ the town is about to memorialize him with a statue.*

memorial service *noun* a service of commemoration of the dead, usu. without the body or bodies being present.

memorization *noun* an act of memorizing.

memorize *verb* (**memorizes, memorized, memorizing**) commit to memory, learn by heart. ▶**memorizing** *noun*

memory *noun (plural* **memories) 1 a** the faculty by which things are recalled to or kept in the mind. **b** an individual's capacity to remember things: *my memory is poor.* **2** one's store of things remembered: *buried deep in my memory.* **3** a recollection or remembrance: *the memory of better times.* **4 a** the capacity of a computer or other electronic machinery to store data or program instructions in such a way that they may be retrieved when required. **b** a device in which data or program instructions may be stored and from which they may be retrieved when required. **c** = MEMORY BOARD. **5** the remembrance of a person or thing: *his mother's memory haunted him.* **6 a** the reputation of a dead person: *Dad's memory lives on.* **b** in formulaic phrases used of a dead sovereign etc.: *of blessed memory.* **7** the length of time over which the memory or memories of any given person or group extends. **8 a** the capacity of a substance etc. for manifesting effects of its previous state, behaviour, or treatment. **b** the capacity of a substance etc. for returning to a previous state when the cause of the transition from that state is removed.

c such effects or such a state. PHRASES **commit to memory** learn (a thing) so as to be able to recall it at will. **down memory lane** through a succession of sentimental memories deliberately pursued. **from memory** without reading from or referring to books etc. **in memory of** to keep alive the remembrance of.

memory bank *noun* **1** the memory device of a computer etc. **2** *informal* the store of memories of an individual or group.

memory board *noun* a detachable storage device, containing additional memory capacity, which can be installed in a computer.

memory card *noun* a memory chip housed in a rectangular plastic case which plugs into a computer enabling data storage and retrieval.

memory chip *noun Computing* a semiconductor chip made as a memory, e.g. a ROM or a RAM, containing many separately addressable locations.

men *plural of* MAN.

menace • *noun* **1** a dangerous thing or person. **2** *jocular* a pest, a nuisance. **3** a threat. • *verb* threaten, esp. in a malignant or hostile manner. ▶**menacing** *adjective* **menacingly** *adverb* [Say MEN iss]

ménage *noun* a family or group living together as a household: *the Winshaw ménage.* [Say may NAZH]

ménage à trois *noun (plural* **ménages à trois)** a sexual relationship involving three people, esp. in one household. [Say may nazh a TRWAH]

menagerie *noun* **1** a collection of wild animals in captivity for exhibition etc. **2** a collection of different animals: *shares her apartment with a menagerie of pets.* **3** a collection of strange or outlandish people etc.: *some other specimens in the television menagerie.* [Say muh NAZH a ree]

mend • *verb* **1** restore to a sound condition; repair (a broken article, a damaged road, torn clothes, etc.). **2** regain health; heal. **3** improve or put right (a fault, something wrong, etc.): *mend matters.* • *noun* a darn or repair in material etc.: *a mend in my shirt.* PHRASES **mend (one's) fences** make peace with a person; reconcile differences. **mend one's manners** improve one's behaviour. **mend one's ways** reform, improve one's habits. **on the mend** improving in health or condition.

mendacious *adjective* untruthful; false: *a mendacious account of the incident.* ▶**mendaciously** *adverb* **mendacity** *noun* [Say men DAY shuss, men DASSA tee]

mendelevium *noun* an artificially made radioactive metallic element. [Say menda LEEVY um]

mender *noun* a person who mends things.

mendicant • *adjective* **1** begging: *fed french fries to the mendicant gulls.* **2** designating or belonging to any of the religious orders, e.g. the Franciscans, Dominicans, etc., whose members support themselves by work and charitable contributions. • *noun* **1** a beggar. **2** a mendicant friar. [Say MENDA k'nt]

mending *noun* **1** the action of a person who mends. **2** things, esp. clothes, to be mended.

menfolk *plural noun informal* **1** men in general. **2** the men of one's family.

menial • *adjective* (of work) not requiring much skill and usu. low-paying with little prestige: *menial factory jobs.* • *noun* a domestic servant. [Say MEENY ul]

meninges *plural noun* the three membranes that line the skull and vertebral canal and enclose the brain and spinal cord. [Say men IN jeez]

meningitis *noun* an inflammation of the meninges of the brain or spinal cord due to infection by viruses or bacteria. [Say men in JITE us]

meningococcus *noun* a bacterium involved in some forms of meningitis and cerebrospinal infection.

M

▶ **meningococcal** adjective [Say men inga COCKUS, men inga COCKLE]

meniscus noun (plural **menisci**) **1** the curved upper surface of a liquid in a tube etc., caused by surface tension etc. **2** a lens that is convex on one side and concave on the other, esp. one thickest in the middle, with a crescent-shaped section. **3** a thin fibrous cartilage between the surfaces of some joints, e.g. the knee. [Say muh NISK us for the singular, muh NISK eye for the plural]

Mennonite • noun a member of a Protestant denomination originating in Friesland in the 16th century, emphasizing adult baptism and rejecting military service and the holding of public office. • adjective of or pertaining to Mennonites. ▶ **Mennonitism** noun [Say MENNA nite]

menopausal adjective **1** (of a woman) undergoing menopause. **2** characteristic of menopause: menopausal symptoms. [Say menna PAUSE ul]

menopause noun **1** the final cessation of menstruation. **2** the period in a woman's life, usu. between 45 and 50, when this occurs. [Say MENNA pause]

menorah noun Judaism **1** a candelabrum with usu. seven branches, used at home and in the synagogue on Sabbaths and holidays. **2** a candelabrum used during Hanukkah, having eight branches and a holder for the candle used to light the others. **3** a representation of either as a symbol of Judaism. [Say men ORE uh]

mensch noun informal an admirable or honourable person.

menservants plural of MANSERVANT.

menses plural noun **1** blood and mucosal tissue etc. discharged from the uterus at menstruation. **2** the time of menstruation. [Say MEN seez]

Menshevik noun a member of a minority faction of the Russian Socialist Party; they were defeated by the Bolsheviks in the power struggle following the overthrow of the czar in 1917. [Say MEN shuh vick]

men's room noun (also **men's**) a public washroom for men.

menstrual adjective of or relating to the menses or menstruation. [Say MEN strull or MEN stroo ul]

menstrual cycle noun the process of ovulation and menstruation in sexually mature women and female primates.

menstruate verb (**menstruates**, **menstruated**, **menstruating**) (of a woman) discharge blood and mucus from the uterus through the vagina; undergo menstruation. [Say MEN strait]

menstruation noun the process of discharging blood and mucosal tissue etc. from the uterus through the vagina that occurs in sexually mature, non-pregnant women, normally at intervals of about one lunar month, until menopause. [Say men STRAY sh'n]

menswear noun clothes for men.

-ment suffix **1** forming nouns expressing the means, product, or result of the action of a verb: abridgement. **2** forming nouns from adjectives: merriment.

mental adjective **1** of or pertaining to the mind. **2** carried on or performed by, or taking place in, the mind. **3** informal crazy: this is driving me mental. **4** designating a medical establishment for the care and treatment of the mentally ill: mental institution.

mental block noun a sudden and temporary inability to continue a thought process or mental link, esp. due to subconscious emotional factors.

mental case noun informal derogatory a person suffering from some kind of mental impairment, esp. one under or requiring medical care for mental illness.

mental handicap noun the condition or fact of being of such low intelligence, or having the intellectual capacities so underdeveloped, esp. through illness or injury, as to inhibit normal social functioning.

mentality noun (plural **mentalities**) **1** mental character or disposition. **2** outlook; what is in or of the mind. **3** kind or degree of intelligence. [Say men TALA tee]

mentally adverb **1** relating to a person's mental state: he's mentally unwell. **2** in one's head or mind; using one's mind: I added it up mentally.

mentally handicapped adjective (of a person) having such a learning disability as to inhibit normal social functioning.

mentally ill adjective (of a person) having a mental illness.

mentally incompetent adjective (of a person) mentally ill or mentally handicapped to an extent that care, supervision, and control are required.

mentally retarded adjective (of a person) suffering from mental retardation.

mental note noun a fixing of something in one's mind, to be remembered subsequently.

mental retardation noun a developmental disorder in which a person has impaired learning ability and a lower than normal IQ.

menthol noun a mint-tasting organic alcohol found in oil of peppermint etc., used as a flavouring and to relieve local pain. [Say MENTH awl]

mentholated adjective treated with or containing menthol. [Say MENTHA late id]

mention • verb **1** refer to or remark on incidentally. **2** specify by name or otherwise. **3** reveal or disclose: do not mention this to anyone. **4** (in dispatches) award (a person) a minor honour for meritorious, usu. gallant, military service. • noun **1** an incidental reference, esp. by name, to a person or thing. **2** (in dispatches) a military honour awarded for outstanding conduct. PHRASES **don't mention it** said in polite dismissal of an apology or thanks. **make mention** (or **no mention**) **of** refer (or not refer) to. **not to mention** introducing a fact or thing of secondary or (as a rhetorical device) of primary importance. ▶ **mentionable** adjective & noun

mentor • noun an experienced and trusted adviser or guide: he was a mentor to many young lawyers. • verb act as a mentor to (a person): she has mentored several graduate students. ▶ **mentoring** noun & adjective **mentorship** noun [Say MEN tore]

menu noun **1 a** a list of dishes to be served at a meal, available in a restaurant, etc. **b** a card, folder, etc. on which such a list is written or printed. **c** the food served or available. **2** a list of available commands, options, etc., displayed on a television or computer screen, for selection by the operator.

menu bar noun a graphically represented bar in which the primary menus and menu options for a software program are displayed and from which these can be accessed.

menu-driven adjective (of a program or computer) used by making selections from menus.

meow • noun one of the characteristic sounds made by a domestic cat. • verb make this sound.

Mephistophelian adjective devilish, fiendish. [Say muh fista FEELY un]

mercantile adjective **1** having to do with the exchange of goods or merchandise; commercial: a mercantile society ◊ mercantile buildings. **2** hist. having to do with mercantilism: in the 1840s, Britain abandoned the mercantile system of preferential trade with colonies in favour of free trade. [Say MURK'n tile]

mercantilism noun hist. the economic theory that trade generates wealth and is stimulated by the

accumulation of precious metals, which a government should encourage by promoting exports and restricting imports. ▶ **mercantilist** *noun* [Say mur CANTA lism]

Mercator projection *noun* (also **Mercator's projection**) a cylindrical map projection in which all parallels of latitude have the same length and meridians are represented by equidistant straight lines at right angles to the equator and any course that follows a constant compass bearing is represented by a straight line. [Say mur CATER]

mercenary • *adjective* primarily concerned with money or other material reward: *mercenary motives*. • *noun* (*plural* **mercenaries**) **1** a professional soldier serving a foreign power for money. **2** a person whose services are available for money: *intellectual mercenaries with knowledge for sale*. [Say MURSE a nerry]

merchandise • *noun* goods to be bought and sold. • *verb* (**merchandises**, **merchandised**, **merchandising**) **1** put on the market, promote the sale of (goods etc.). **2** advertise, publicize (an idea or person). ▶ **merchandiser** *noun* **merchandising** *noun & adjective* [Say MURCH'n dice or MURCH'n dize for the noun, MURCH'n dize for the verb]

merchant • *noun* **1** a person whose occupation is the purchase and sale of goods for profit. **2** a wholesale trader, esp. with foreign countries. **3** a retail trader, a store keeper. **4** *informal* usu. *derogatory* a person showing a partiality for a specified activity or practice: *speed merchant*. • *adjective* **1** connected with or relating to trade or commerce: *the merchant class*. **2** (of a ship, fleet, etc.) serving for or involved in the transport of merchandise.

merchant bank *noun* esp. *Brit.* a bank dealing primarily in long-term commercial loans and financing; an investment bank. ▶ **merchant banker** *noun* **merchant banking** *noun*

merchant marine *noun* a fleet or number of ships used in trade and not for purposes of war; a nation's commercial shipping. ▶ **merchant mariner** *noun*

merchant navy *noun* = MERCHANT MARINE.

merchant ship *noun* a ship conveying merchandise.

merciful *adjective* having, showing, or feeling mercy.

mercifully *adverb* **1** in a merciful manner. **2** (qualifying a whole sentence) fortunately.

merciless *adjective* **1** unrelenting. **2** showing no mercy. ▶ **mercilessly** *adverb* **mercilessness** *noun*

mercurial *adjective* **1** lively, quick to react and often changing: *the moody and mercurial musician* ◊ *mercurial stock prices*. **2** of or containing mercury: *mercurial particles*. ▶ **mercurially** *adverb* [Say mur CURE ee ul]

mercuric *adjective* of or containing mercury in the divalent state. [Say mur CURE ick]

mercury *noun* **1** a toxic silvery-white heavy liquid metallic element used in barometers, thermometers, and amalgams. **2 a** the column of mercury in a thermometer or barometer. **b** the temperature or barometric pressure indicated by this, esp. as rising or falling. **3** any of various weedy plants of the spurge family, naturalized in North America.

mercury vapour *noun* a vapour of mercury atoms or ions above liquid mercury or at low pressure.

mercury vapour lamp *noun* (also **mercury vapour light**) a lamp in which bluish light is produced by an electric discharge through mercury vapour.

mercy • *noun* (*plural* **mercies**) **1** compassion or forbearance shown to a powerless person, esp. an offender or one with no claim to kindness. **2** the disposition to forgive or show compassion. **3** an act of mercy. **4** (as an *adjective*) administered or performed out of mercy or pity for a suffering person: *mercy killing*.

5 something to be thankful for: *small mercies*. • *interjection* expressing surprise or fear. **PHRASES** **at the mercy of 1** wholly in the power of. **2** liable to danger or harm from.

mere *adjective* **1** that is nothing more than what is specified. **2** (**the merest**) the smallest or slightest. ▶ **merely** *adverb*

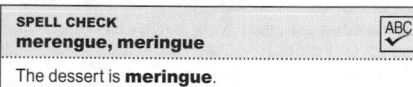
merengue *noun* **1** a dance of Dominican and Haitian origin, with alternating long and stiff-legged steps. **2** a piece of music for this dance, usu. with two and three beats to the bar. [Say muh RENG gay]

meretricious *adjective* (of decorations, literary style, etc.) showily attractive but valueless: *meretricious souvenirs* ◊ *meretricious promises*. ▶ **meretriciously** *adverb* **meretriciousness** *noun* [Say mare a TRISH us]

merganser *noun* a diving fish-eating duck with a long narrow serrated hooked bill. [Say mur GANSE ur]

merge • *verb* (**merges**, **merged**, **merging**) **1** (often foll. by *with*) **a** combine or be combined. **b** join or blend gradually. **2** (foll. by *in*) lose or cause to lose character and identity by absorption in (something else). **3** combine (multiple files, sets of data, etc.) to produce only one file, set, etc., usu. in an ordered sequence. **4 a** (of lanes of traffic etc.) be gradually integrated into fewer lanes. **b** (of a vehicle) join a lane of traffic. **5** (of two or more companies) combine to form a single commercial organization in order to increase efficiency and reduce competition. • *noun* **1** a merger. **2 a** *Computing* a function that enables file or data merging: *merge facility*. **b** = MAIL MERGE. **3** an instance or the site of merging traffic. ▶ **merged** *adjective*

merger *noun* the combining of two commercial companies etc. into one.

meridian *noun* **1 a** a great circle passing through the celestial poles and zenith of a given place on the earth's surface. **b** the circle of the earth which lies on the same plane. **2 a** half the circle of the earth which extends from pole to pole through a place, corresponding to a line of longitude. **b** a line on a map, globe, etc. representing one of these. **3** any of the pathways in the body along which energy is said to flow, esp. each of twelve associated with specific organs for acupuncture etc. **4 a** any great circle of a sphere that passes through the poles. **b** any line on a surface of revolution that is in a plane with its axis. [Say mur IDDY un]

meringue *noun* **1** a mixture of stiffly beaten egg white and sugar. **2** this used as a topping for pies or cakes, browned on top but still soft inside. **3** a round of this mixture, baked until crisp, usu. decorated or filled with whipped cream etc. [Say muh RANG]

merino *noun* (*plural* **merinos**) **1** (also **merino sheep**) a variety of sheep with long fine wool. **2** a soft woollen or wool-and-cotton material like cashmere, originally of merino wool. **3** a fine woollen yarn. [Say muh REENO]

merit • *noun* **1** the quality of being entitled to reward or gratitude. **2** excellence, worth. **3** (usu. in *plural*) **a** a thing that entitles one to reward or gratitude. **b** claim or title to commendation or esteem. **4** esp. *Law* intrinsic rights and wrongs or excellences and defects: *the merits of a case*. • *verb* (**merits**, **merited**, **meriting**) deserve or be worthy of (reward, punishment, consideration, etc.).

M

PHRASES **on its merits** with regard only to its intrinsic worth.

meritocracy *noun* (*plural* **meritocracies**) **1** government or the holding of power by persons selected competitively according to merit. **2** a group of persons selected in this way. **3** a society governed by meritocracy. ▶ **meritocratic** *adjective* [Say merit OCK ruh see, merit a CRAT ick]

meritorious *adjective* having merit; deserving reward, praise, or gratitude: *meritorious public service*. [Say mare a TORY us]

merlin *noun* a small European or North American falcon that hunts small birds.

Merlot *noun* **1** a variety of black grape used in winemaking. **2** a red wine made from Merlot grapes. [Say mur LO or mare LO]

mermaid *noun* an imaginary half-human sea creature, with the head and trunk of a woman and tail of a fish.

merman *noun* (*plural* **mermen**) an imaginary half-human sea creature, with the head and trunk of a man and the tail of a fish.

merrily *adverb* joyously, happily.

merriment *noun* **1** exuberant enjoyment; being merry. **2** mirth, fun.

merriness *noun* happiness, gaiety, mirth, joy.

merry *adjective* (**merrier, merriest**) **1** joyous. **2** full of laughter or gaiety. **PHRASES** **make merry** be festive; enjoy oneself.

merry-go-round *noun* **1** a revolving platform with wooden horses, cars, etc. for people to ride on at a fair etc.; a carousel. **2** a cycle of bustling activities.

merrymaker *noun* a person who participates in festivities; a reveller.

merrymaking *noun* festivity, fun.

mesa *noun* an isolated flat-topped hill with steep sides, found in arid and semi-arid regions esp. of Mexico and the southwestern US. [Say MAY suh]

mescal *noun* **1 a** any of various succulent plants of Mexico and the southwestern US, used as sources of fermented liquor, food, or fibre. **b** a strong liquor distilled from the sap of this (*compare* TEQUILA). **2 a** a peyote cactus. **b** a preparation of this used as a hallucinogenic drug (*compare* MESCALINE, PEYOTE). [Say MESS cal]

mescaline *noun* (also **mescalin**) a hallucinogenic alkaloid present in the peyote cactus. [Say MESKA leen or MESKA lin]

mesclun *noun* a kind of green salad made from a selection of lettuces, typically with other edible leaves and flowers. [Say MESK lun]

mesh • *noun* (*plural* **meshes**) **1** material made of a network of wire or thread. **2** the spacing of the strands of a net. **3** a complex or constricting situation. • *verb* (**meshes, meshed, meshing**) **1 a** (often foll. by *with*, *together*) fit in, be harmonious, combine. **b** bring together, harmonize, reconcile. **2** (often foll. by *with*) (of the teeth of a wheel) be engaged (with another piece of machinery). **3** entangle, catch in or as in a net. ▶ **meshed** *adjective* **meshing** *noun* & *adjective*

mesmeric *adjective* hypnotic; having such a strong effect on people that they cannot give their attention to anything else: *a mesmeric performance*. [Say mez MARE ick]

mesmerism *noun* **1** the process or practice of inducing a hypnotic state by the influence of an operator over the will and nervous system of the patient. **2** the state so induced. ▶ **mesmerist** *noun* [Say MEZMER ism]

mesmerize *verb* (**mesmerizes, mesmerized, mesmerizing**) **1** fascinate, hold spellbound. **2** hypnotize. [Say MEZMER ize]

meso- *combining form* middle, intermediate. [Say MESSO or MEZO]

Meso-American • *adjective* of or relating to Meso-America, the central region of America from central Mexico to Nicaragua, esp. as a region of ancient civilizations and Aboriginal cultures. • *noun* a member of a Meso-American people. [Say mezo AMERICAN]

mesolithic (also **Mesolithic**) • *adjective* of or concerning the part of the Stone Age between the paleolithic and neolithic periods, from about 8500 to 2700 BC, when people lived by hunting, gathering, and fishing. • *noun* the mesolithic period. [Say mezo LITH ick]

meson *noun* any of a class of elementary particles believed to participate in the forces that hold nucleons together in the atomic nucleus. [Say MEZ on or MEEZ on]

Mesopotamian • *adjective* of or relating to Mesopotamia, an ancient region of southwest Asia in present-day Iraq, between the Tigris and Euphrates rivers, where the civilizations of Akkad, Sumer, Babylonia, and Assyria were situated. • *noun* a native or inhabitant of Mesopotamia. [Say messa puh TAMEY un]

mesosphere *noun* the region of the atmosphere extending from the top of the stratosphere to an altitude of about 50 miles. ▶ **mesospheric** *adjective* [Say MEZO sphere, mezo SFEER ick]

Mesozoic • *adjective* of or relating to the geological era between the Paleozoic and Cenozoic, comprising the Triassic, Jurassic, and Cretaceous periods and lasting from about 248 to 65 million years BP, when reptiles were dominant on land and sea, vegetation had become abundant, and the first mammals, birds, and flowering plants appeared. • *noun* this geological era. [Say mezo ZO ick]

mesquite *noun* **1** a spiny leguminous tree of the southwestern US and Mexico. **2** the wood of this used for grilling food. [Say mes KEET]

mess • *noun* (*plural* **messes**) **1 a** a dirty, untidy state of affairs: *the room is a mess ◊ made such a mess*. **b** a bungled state of affairs. **2** a state of confusion, embarrassment, or trouble: *my life's a mess*. **3** something causing a mess, e.g. spilled liquid etc. **4 a** a person whose life or affairs are confused. **b** a dirty or unkempt person. **5** excrement, esp. of a domestic animal or child. **6** a place providing meals and recreational facilities for members of the armed forces. **7** *informal* a large quantity of something: *a whole mess of preconceptions*. • *verb* (**messes, messed, messing**) **1** *informal* (foll. by *with*) interfere or get involved with. **2** take one's meals, esp. as the member of a mess. **3** *informal* (esp. of an animal or infant) defecate or soil by defecating. **PHRASES** **make a mess of** bungle (an undertaking). **mess around** (or **about**) **1** act desultorily; putter. **2** *informal* make things awkward for; cause arbitrary inconvenience to (a person). **3** *informal* **a** engage in sexual activity. **b** engage in adulterous sexual activity. **mess up 1** make a mess of; dirty. **2** make a mess of a situation. **3** make unhappy, confused, or dysfunctional: *messed-up kids*. **4** ruin or damage.

message *noun* **1** a usu. brief oral or written communication. **2** an inspired or significant communication from a prophet, writer, or preacher. **3** the central import of something; an implicit esp. polemical meaning in an artistic work etc. **PHRASES** **get the message** *informal* understand what is meant. **send a message** make a significant statement, esp. implicitly or by one's actions.

message board *noun* **1** = BULLETIN BOARD 1. **2** a computerized bulletin board on the Internet for the posting of electronic messages. **3** an electronic board in an arena, train station, etc., which displays instructions to fans, information to travellers, etc.

M

messaging *noun* the sending and processing of electronic mail by computer.

messenger *noun* **1** a person who carries a message. **2** a person employed to carry messages. **3** *Biology* a molecule or substance that carries (esp. genetic) information.

mess hall *noun* a military dining area.

Messiah *noun* **1 a** the promised deliverer of the Jews, as prophesied in the Hebrew Bible. **b** (usu. as **the Messiah**) (in Christian theology) Jesus Christ regarded as fulfilling this prophecy, and as saviour of humankind. **2** (usu. **messiah**) a liberator or would-be liberator of an oppressed people, country, etc.: *in 1971 when Albertans dumped Social Credit for the messiah of economic and cultural modernization.* [Say muh SIGH uh]

messianic *adjective* (also **Messianic**) **1** of, pertaining to, or characteristic of the Messiah or a messiah: *a messianic prophecy.* **2** inspired by hope or belief in the Messiah or a messiah: *her zeal at promoting dance is just short of messianic: "I believe the arts are essential and can save the world," she says.* ▶ **messianism** *noun* [Say messy ANNICK, muh SIGH a nism]

Messieurs *plural of* MONSIEUR. [Say mess SYUH]

messily *adverb* in a messy way.

messiness *noun* the state of being messy.

Messrs. *plural of* MR. [Say MESSERS]

mess-up *noun* a mess, a muddle; a confused situation.

messy *adjective* (**messier, messiest**) **1** untidy or dirty. **2** causing or accompanied by a mess. **3** difficult to deal with; full of awkward complications. *a messy divorce.*

mestiza *noun* (*plural* **mestizas**) a woman who is a mestizo. [Say mess TEEZA]

mestizo *noun* (*plural* **mestizos**) (in Latin and South America) the offspring of a European and an American Indian. [Say mess TEEZO]

met *past and past participle of* MEET[1].

metabolic *adjective* pertaining to, involving, or characterized by metabolism. ▶ **metabolically** *adverb* [Say meta BAWL ick]

metabolism *noun* all the chemical processes that occur within a living organism, resulting in energy production (**destructive metabolism**) and growth (**constructive metabolism**). [Say muh TABBA lism]

metabolite *noun* a substance formed in or necessary for metabolism. [Say muh TABBA lite]

metabolize *verb* (**metabolizes, metabolized, metabolizing**) process or be processed by metabolism. [Say muh TABBA lize]

metacarpal *noun* any of the five bones of the hand, between the wrist and the fingers. [Say meta CAR pull]

metafiction *noun* a work of fiction in which the author self-consciously alludes to the artificiality or literariness of a work by parodying or departing from novelistic conventions and traditional narrative techniques. ▶ **metafictional** *adjective* [Say META fiction]

metal • *noun* **1 a** any of a class of substances (including many chemical elements) which are in general lustrous, malleable, fusible, ductile solids and good conductors of heat and electricity, e.g. gold, iron, brass, steel. **b** a material of this kind. **2** material used for making glass, in a molten state. **3** = HEAVY METAL 1. • *adjective* made of metal. • *verb* (**metals, metalled, metalling**) provide or fit with metal.

metalanguage *noun* a language used for the description or analysis of another language. [Say META language]

metalhead *noun* *slang* a fan of heavy metal music.

metallic • *adjective* **1** of, consisting of, or characteristic of metal or metals. **2** sounding sharp and ringing, like struck metal. **3** having the sheen or lustre of metals. • *noun* (usu. in *plural*) **1** an article or substance made of or containing metal, esp. a fabric. **2** a paint or colour having the sheen or lustre of metal.

metallurgical *adjective* of or concerning the production, purification, and properties of metals and their application. [Say meta LURGE ick'll]

metallurgist *noun* a person who studies or is an expert in metallurgy. [Say META lurge ist]

metallurgy *noun* the science concerned with the production, purification, and properties of metals and their application. [Say META lurge ee]

metalwork *noun* **1** the art of working in metal. **2** metal objects collectively. ▶ **metalworker** *noun* **metalworking** *noun & adjective*

metamorphic *adjective* (of rock) that has undergone transformation by natural agencies such as heat and pressure. ▶ **metamorphism** *noun* [Say meta MORF ick, meta MORF ism]

metamorphose *verb* (**metamorphoses, metamorphosed, metamorphosing**) **1** change completely in form or nature: *a father seeing his daughter metamorphosing from girl into woman.* **2** (of an insect or amphibian) undergo metamorphosis, esp. transform from an immature to an adult form: *feed the larvae to your fish before they metamorphose into adults.* [Say meta MORF oze]

metamorphosis *noun* (*plural* **metamorphoses**) **1** a process in which someone or something changes completely into something different: *she had undergone an amazing metamorphosis from awkward schoolgirl to beautiful woman.* **2** the transformation between an immature form and an adult form, e.g. from a pupa to an insect. [Say meta MORFA sis or meta more FOE sis for the singular, meta MORFA seez or meta more FOE seez for the plural]

WRITING TIP
metaphor, simile

Metaphor is the imaginative use of a word or phrase to describe something else, to show that the two have the same qualities: *All the world's a stage/ And all the men and women merely players.* In **simile** the comparison between the two things is made explicit by the use of the words "as" or "like": *I wandered lonely as a cloud; Like as the waves make towards the pebbled shore,/ So do our minutes hasten to their end.*

---

metaphor *noun* **1 a** a figure of speech in which a word or phrase is applied to an object or action to which it is not literally applicable: *"I had fallen through a trap door of depression," said Mark, who was fond of theatrical metaphors.* **b** the use of such words and phrases: *her poetry depends on suggestion and metaphor.* **2** a thing regarded as representative or symbolic of something else, esp. something abstract: *the company was a metaphor for an industry in danger of collapse.* ▶ **metaphoric** *adjective* **metaphorical** *adjective* **metaphorically** *adverb* [Say META fore, meta FORE ick]

metaphysical • *adjective* **1** of or relating to metaphysics: *the essentially metaphysical question of the nature of mind.* **2** based on abstract general reasoning; theoretical: *a metaphysical view of law.* **3** transcending physical matter or the laws of nature; supernatural: *Good and Evil linked in a metaphysical battle across time and*

M

space. **4** of or relating to a group of 17th-century poets whose work is characterized by complex and elaborate imagery and subtlety of thought, including John Donne, George Herbert, and Andrew Marvell. • *noun* (**the Metaphysicals**) the metaphysical poets. ▶ **metaphysically** *adverb* [Say meta PHYSICAL]

metaphysics *plural noun* (usu. treated as *singular*) **1** the branch of philosophy that deals with the first principles of things, including such concepts as being, knowing, substance, essence, cause, identity, time, and space. **2** *informal* abstract or subtle talk with no basis in reality; mere theory: *Roz finds Charis an endearing nincompoop and mostly dismisses her gauzy metaphysics*. [Say meta PHYSICS]

metastasis *noun* **1** the transfer of a disease, etc. from one part of the body to another; esp. the development of secondary tumours at a distance from a primary site of cancer. **2** a secondary tumour. ▶ **metastasize** *verb* (**metastasizes**, **metastasized**, **metastasizing**) **metastatic** *adjective* [Say muh TASTA sis for the singular, muh TASTA size, meta STATIC]

metatarsal *noun* any of the five bones of the foot, between the ankle and the toes. [Say meta TAR sull]

mete *verb* (**metes**, **meted**, **meting**) (usu. foll. by *out*) apportion or allot (a punishment or reward): *justice must be meted out in accordance with the crime*.

meteor *noun* a small body of matter from outer space that becomes incandescent as a result of friction with the earth's atmosphere and is visible as a streak of light.

meteoric *adjective* **1** of meteors or meteorites. **2** rapid like a meteor; dazzling, transient: *meteoric rise to fame*.

meteorite *noun* a rock or metal fragment formed from a meteor of sufficient size to reach the earth's surface without burning up completely in the atmosphere.

meteoroid *noun* any small body moving in the solar system that becomes visible as it passes through the earth's atmosphere as a meteor.

meteorological *adjective* of or relating to the weather or atmospheric conditions. [Say meteor a LOGICAL]

meteorologist *noun* a person who studies the earth's atmosphere and its changes, esp. to forecast the weather. [Say meteor OLLA jist]

meteorology *noun* the study of the processes and phenomena of the atmosphere, esp. as a means of forecasting the weather. [Say meteor OLLA jee]

meteor shower *noun* a group of meteors appearing to come from one point in the sky, esp. around a particular date each year.

meter¹ • *noun* **1** a thing that measures, esp. an instrument for recording a quantity of gas, electricity, etc. supplied, present, or needed, or a device in a taxi measuring the time and distance travelled and the fare payable. **2** = PARKING METER. • *verb* **1** measure by means of a meter. **2** deliver in measured amounts: *metered doses of medication*. **3** provide with a meter or meters.

meter² = METRE¹, METRE².

meth *noun slang* methamphetamine.

methadone *noun* a potent drug used to relieve severe pain, and as a substitute for morphine or heroin.

methamphetamine *noun* an amphetamine derivative with quicker and longer action, used as a stimulant. [Say meth am FETTA mean]

methane *noun* a colourless odourless inflammable gaseous hydrocarbon, the main constituent of natural gas. [Say METH ane]

methanol *noun* a colourless volatile inflammable liquid, used as a solvent. [Say METH a nawl]

methinks *verb* (*past* **methought**) *archaic* or *jocular* it seems to me.

methionine *noun* an amino acid which is an important constituent of proteins. [Say meth EYE uh nine]

method *noun* **1** a mode of procedure; a defined or systematic way of doing a thing. **2** orderliness of thought or behaviour: *was criticized for his lack of method*. **PHRASES** **method in one's madness** sense in what appears to be foolish or strange behaviour.

methodical *adjective* characterized by method or order. ▶ **methodically** *adverb* [Say muh THODDICK'll]

Methodism *noun* any of various branches of a Protestant denomination originating in the 18th-century evangelistic movement of Charles and John Wesley and George Whitefield. Methodism has a strong tradition of missionary work and concern for social welfare, and emphasizes the believer's personal relationship with God. In Canada, the Methodist Church merged with part of the Presbyterian Church to form the United Church of Canada. ▶ **Methodist** *noun* & *adjective* [Say METHA dism, METHA dist]

methodological *adjective* pertaining to the application of a specific method to a particular field. [Say method a LOGICAL]

methodology *noun* (*plural* **methodologies**) **1** a body of methods used in a particular branch of activity. **2** the branch of knowledge that deals with method and its application in a particular field. [Say method OLLA jee]

methought *past* of METHINKS.

methyl *noun* the monovalent hydrocarbon radical — CH_3, present in many organic compounds. [Say METH'll]

methyl alcohol *noun* = METHANOL.

methylate *verb* (**methylates**, **methylated**, **methylating**) **1** mix or impregnate with methanol. **2** introduce a methyl group into (a molecule or compound). [Say METH'll ate]

methylated spirits *noun* (also **methylated spirit**) alcohol to which about 10 percent methanol has been added to make it unfit for drinking.

methylene *noun* the highly reactive divalent group of atoms CH_2. [Say METH'll een]

meticulous *adjective* giving great attention to details; very careful and precise: *meticulous planning* ◊ *my father was meticulous about his appearance*. ▶ **meticulously** *adverb* **meticulousness** *noun* [Say muh TICK yoo luss]

métier *noun* a person's work, especially when they have a natural skill or ability for it: *he followed many unsuccessful paths before finding his true métier*. [Say mate YAY]

Metis *noun* (*plural* **Metis**) (esp. in Canada) a person of mixed Aboriginal and European descent. [Say may TEE]

metonym *noun* a word used in metonymy. ▶ **metonymic** *adjective* [Say META nim, meta NIM ick]

metonymy *noun* the substitution of the name of an attribute or adjunct for that of the thing meant, e.g. *Crown* for *monarch*. [Say muh TAWNA mee]

metre¹ *noun* (also **meter**) a metric unit and the base SI unit of linear measure, equal to about 39.4 inches.

metre² *noun* (also **meter**) **1 a** any form of poetic

M

rhythm, determined by the number and length of feet in a line. **b** a metrical group or measure. **2** the basic pulse and rhythm of a piece of music.

metre-kilogram-second *adjective* denoting a system of measure using the metre, kilogram, and second as the basic units of length, mass, and time. Abbreviation: **mks**.

metric • *adjective* **1** of or pertaining to the metre or metric system. **2** of or relating to measurement; metrical. • *noun* = METRIC SYSTEM.

metrical *adjective* **1** of, relating to, or composed in metre: *metrical psalms*. **2** of or involving measurement: *metrical geometry.* ▶ **metrically** *adverb*

metric system *noun* the decimal measuring system with the metre, litre, and gram (or kilogram) as units of length, volume, and mass.

metric ton *noun* (also **metric tonne**) 1,000 kilograms (2205 lb.).

Metro *noun* **1** an informal name for (Metropolitan) Toronto. **2** an informal name for the urban area of Halifax-Dartmouth.

metro¹ *noun* (*plural* **metros**) a subway system in some cities, e.g. Montreal and Paris.

metro² *adjective* metropolitan: *metro council*.

metronome *noun* Music an instrument marking time at a selected rate by giving a regular tick. [Say METRA nome]

metropolis *noun* **1** a large, busy city, esp. the main city of a country or region. **2** a city or town which is a local centre of activity. [Say muh TROPPA liss]

metropolitan • *adjective* **1** of or relating to a metropolis. **2** encompassing a city and its suburbs: *metropolitan Toronto*. **3** belonging to, forming, or forming part of, a mother country as distinct from its colonies etc.: *metropolitan France*. **4** of an ecclesiastical metropolis. • *noun* **1** (also **metropolitan bishop**) a bishop having authority over the bishops of a province, in the Western Church equivalent to archbishop, in the Orthodox Church ranking above archbishop and below patriarch. **2** an inhabitant of a metropolis. ▶ **metropolitanism** *noun* [Say metra POLLA tun]

SPELL CHECK
mettle, metal, meddle

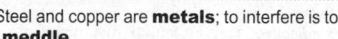

Steel and copper are **metals**; to interfere is to **meddle**.

---

mettle *noun* a person's ability to cope well with difficulties or to face a demanding situation in a spirited and resilient way: *she really showed her mettle under pressure ◊ disasters often test the mettle of a community*.

MeV *abbreviation* mega-electron volt(s).

mew • *verb* (of a cat, gull, etc.) utter its characteristic cry. • *noun* this sound, esp. of a cat.

mewl *verb* cry feebly; whimper.

Mexican • *noun* **1** a native or national of Mexico. **b** a person of Mexican descent. **2** an indigenous language of Mexico, esp. Nahuatl. • *adjective* **1** of or relating to Mexico or its people or indigenous languages. **2** of Mexican descent.

mezuzah *noun* (*plural* **mezuzahs**) a parchment inscribed with religious texts and attached in a case to the doorpost of a Jewish house as a sign of faith. [Say muh ZOO zuh]

mezzanine *noun* **1** a low storey between two others (usu. between the ground floor and the second floor). **2** the lowest balcony or foremost part of a single balcony in a theatre. [Say MEZZA neen]

mezzo *noun* (*plural* **mezzos**) (also **mezzo-soprano**, *plural* **mezzo-sopranos**) **1 a** a female voice between soprano and contralto. **b** a singer with this voice. **2** a part written for mezzo-soprano. [Say METSO]

mezzo-forte *adjective* & *adverb* fairly loud. Abbreviation: **mf**. [Say metso FOR tay]

mezzo-piano *adjective* & *adverb* fairly soft. Abbreviation: **mp**. [Say metso PIANO]

MF *abbreviation* milk fat.

mf *abbreviation* mezzo-forte.

mfg. *abbreviation* manufacturing.

MFN *abbreviation* (*plural* **MFNs**) MOST FAVOURED NATION.

mfr. *abbreviation* manufacturer's.

Mg *symbol* magnesium.

mg *abbreviation* milligram(s).

Mgr. *abbreviation* **1** Manager. **2** Monsignor.

MHA *noun* (*plural* **MHAs**) (in Newfoundland and Australia) Member of the House of Assembly.

MHz *abbreviation* megahertz.

mi *noun* (also **me**) Music **1** (in tonic sol-fa) the third note of a major scale. **2** the note E in the fixed-do system.

mi. *abbreviation* mile(s).

MIA *abbreviation* missing in action.

miasma *noun* (*plural* **miasmas**) **1** a highly unpleasant or unhealthy smell: *a miasma of stale alcohol and cigarette smoke hung around him*. **2** an oppressive or unpleasant atmosphere which surrounds or comes from something: *a miasma of despair rose from the workshops*. [Say mee AZMA or my AZMA]

mic *noun* microphone. [Say MIKE]

mica *noun* (*plural* **micas**) any of a group of silicate minerals with a layered structure, esp. muscovite. [Say MIKE uh]

mice *plural of* MOUSE.

Mich. *abbreviation* Michigan.

mickey *noun* (*plural* **mickeys**) *Cdn* a half bottle of liquor, usu. 375 ml.

Mickey Mouse *adjective informal* **1** of inferior quality. **2** ridiculous, trivial. **3** (of a university course etc.) requiring little work or intellectual ability.

Micmac *noun* & *adjective* = MI'KMAQ.

micro *informal* • *noun* (*plural* **micros**) **1** = MICROCOMPUTER. **2** = MICROPROCESSOR. **3** = MICROWAVE. • *adjective* **1** microscopic; very small. **2** small-scale: *carbon emissions cannot be dealt with at the micro level*.

micro- *combining form* **1** small: *microchip*. **2** denoting a factor of one millionth (10^{-6}): *microgram*. Symbol: μ. **3** (in names of instruments, techniques, and disciplines) dealing with small effects or small quantities. **4** involving the use of a microscope. **5** pertaining to or obtained by micrography: *microtext*.

microbe *noun* a minute living being; a micro-organism (esp. a bacterium causing disease or fermentation). ▶ **microbial** *adjective* [Say MIKE robe, my CROW bee ul]

microbiological *adjective* of or pertaining to micro-organisms such as bacteria and viruses.

microbiologist *noun* a person who studies or is an expert in micro-organisms such as bacteria and viruses.

microbiology *noun* the scientific study of micro-organisms, e.g. bacteria, viruses, and fungi.

microbrew *noun* a beer produced on a small scale by a relatively small brewer. ▶ **microbrewer** *noun*

microbrewery *noun* (*plural* **microbreweries**) a brewery which produces beer on a small scale, usu. specializing in high-quality brands made without chemical preservatives. ▶ **microbrewing** *noun*

microcassette *noun* a small audio cassette for use in a tape recorder, answering machine, etc.

microchip • *noun* a tiny wafer of semiconducting material used to make an integrated circuit. • *verb*

M

implant a microchip under the skin of (a pet) for identification purposes.

microcircuit *noun* a minute electric circuit, esp. an integrated circuit. ▶ **microcircuitry** *noun*

microclimate *noun* the climate of a small local area or enclosed space, esp. as differing from the surroundings.

microcomputer *noun* a small computer that contains a microprocessor as its central processing unit.

microcosm *noun* a community, place, or situation regarded as embodying in miniature the characteristic qualities or features of something much larger: *the longhouse was a microcosm of Iroquoian society* ◊ *the island at the centre of the story is obviously, in microcosm, Quebec in the middle of the North American sea*. ▶ **microcosmic** *adjective* [Say MICRO kozzum, micro COSMIC]

microdot *noun* **1** a tiny photograph of a document etc., about the size of a dot. **2** a tiny capsule or tablet of LSD. [Say MICRO dot]

microeconomic *adjective* having to do with the branch of economics that deals with small-scale economic factors.

microeconomics *noun* the branch of economics that deals with small-scale economic factors such as individual commodities, producers, consumers, etc. (*compare* MACROECONOMICS).

microelectronic *adjective* having to do with microchips and microcircuits.

microelectronics *noun* the design, manufacture, and use of microchips and microcircuits.

microenvironment *noun* *Biology & Botany* the immediate small-scale environment of a thing, esp. as a distinct part of a larger environment.

microfibre *noun* a lightweight, water-resistant polyester used esp. for outerwear, swimsuits, etc.

microfiche *noun* (*plural* **microfiche** or **microfiches**) a flat rectangular piece of film bearing very small photographs of the pages of a printed text or document. [Say MICRO feesh]

microfilm • *noun* a length of film bearing very small photographs of documents etc. • *verb* photograph (a document etc.) on microfilm.

microform *noun* very small photographic reproduction on film or paper of a manuscript etc.

microgram *noun* one-millionth of a gram.

micrograph *noun* a photograph taken by means of a microscope.

microgravity *noun* very weak gravity, as in an orbiting spacecraft.

micromanage *verb* (**micromanages**, **micromanaged**, **micromanaging**) supervise or control with excessive attention to small details. ▶ **micromanagement** *noun* **micromanager** *noun*

micrometer *noun* a gauge for accurately measuring small distances, thicknesses, etc. [Say my KROM it ur]

micrometre *noun* one-millionth of a metre. [Say MICRO meet ur]

micron *noun* one-millionth of a metre. Symbol: μ. [Say MY kron]

Micronesian • *adjective* of or relating to Micronesia, a region of the west Pacific to the north of Melanesia, or its people or their languages. • *noun* **1** a native of Micronesia. **2** the group of Austronesian languages spoken in Micronesia. [Say micro NEE zhun]

micronutrient *noun* a chemical element or substance required in trace amounts for the growth and development of living organisms.

micro-organism *noun* any of various microscopic organisms, esp. a bacterium or virus.

microphone *noun* an instrument for converting sound waves into electrical energy variations which may be reconverted into sound after transmission by wire or radio or after recording.

microprocessor *noun* an integrated circuit that contains all the functions of a central processing unit of a computer.

microscope *noun* an instrument magnifying small objects by means of a lens or lenses so as to reveal details invisible to the naked eye. ▤ PHRASES **under the microscope** examined in great detail.

microscopic *adjective* **1** so small as to be visible only with a microscope. **2** extremely small. **3** of the microscope. ▶ **microscopically** *adverb*

microscopy *noun* the use of the microscope. ▶ **microscopist** *noun* [Say my CROSS kuh pee]

microsecond *noun* one-millionth of a second.

microstructural *adjective* having to do with the structure on a microscopic scale. [Say micro STRUCTURAL]

microstructure *noun* (in a metal or other material) the arrangement of crystals etc. which can be made visible and examined with a microscope. [Say MICRO structure]

microsurgery *noun* intricate surgery performed using microscopes, enabling the tissue to be operated on with miniaturized precision instruments. [Say MICRO surgery]

microswitch *noun* (*plural* **microswitches**) a switch that can be operated rapidly by a small movement. [Say MICRO switch]

microwave • *noun* **1** an electromagnetic wave with a wavelength in the range 0.001–0.3m. **2** (also **microwave oven**) an oven that uses microwaves to cook or heat food. • *verb* (**microwaves**, **microwaved**, **microwaving**) cook in a microwave oven. ▶ **microwaveable** *adjective*

mid[1] *adjective* **1** (usu. in *combination*) that is the middle of: *mid-air*. **2** that is in the middle; medium, half.

mid[2] *preposition* *literary* = AMID.

mid-air *noun* some part or section of the air above ground level or above another surface: *suspended in mid-air* ◊ *mid-air collision*.

midday *noun* the middle of the day; noon.

midden *noun* **1** a refuse heap near a dwelling. **2** = KITCHEN MIDDEN.

middle • *adjective* **1** at an equal distance from the extremities of a thing. **2** (of a member of a group) so placed as to have the same number of members on each side. **3** intermediate in rank, quality, order, etc. **4** average: *of middle height*. **5** (of a language) of the period between the old and modern forms. • *noun* **1** (often foll. by *of*) the middle point or position or part. **2** a person's waist. **3** a position between two rivals, subject to attack from both: *caught in the middle*. ▤ PHRASES **in the middle of** (often foll. by *verbal noun*) in the process of; during.

middle age *noun* the period between youth and old age, about 40 to 60. ▶ **middle-aged** *adjective*

Middle Ages *plural noun* the period of European history generally considered as beginning either with the fall of the Roman Empire in the West (5th century) or with the end of the Dark Ages (*c.* 1000), and ending either with the start of the Renaissance in Italy (14th century) or with the fall of Constantinople (1453).

Middle America *noun* **1** the middle class in the US, esp. seen as having conventional attitudes, tastes, etc. **2** Mexico and Central America.

middlebrow *informal* • *adjective* claiming to be or regarded as only moderately intellectual. • *noun* a middlebrow person.

middle C *noun* the C near the middle of the piano

M

keyboard, the note between the treble and bass staffs, at about 260 Hz.

middle class • *noun* the class of society between the upper and the lower, including professional and business workers and their families. • *adjective* (**middle-class**) of the middle class.

middle distance *noun* **1** (in a painted or actual landscape) the part between the foreground and the background. **2** *Athletics* a race distance of esp. 400, 800, or 1500 metres: *middle-distance runner*.

middle ear *noun* the cavity of the central part of the ear behind the drum.

Middle East *noun* a term applied to an extensive area of southwestern Asia and northern Africa, stretching from the Mediterranean to Pakistan, including the Arabian peninsula, and having a predominantly Muslim population. ▶ **Middle Eastern** *adjective*

Middle English *noun* the English language *c.*1150–1500, during which many French words entered English as a result of the Norman Invasion and subsequent French rule.

middle-income *adjective* of or relating to the group of people earning average salaries.

middleman *noun* (*plural* **middlemen**) **1** any of the traders who handle a commodity between its producer and the retailer or consumer. **2** a person who helps to arrange things between people who do not want to talk directly to each other: *he acted as a middleman in discussions between the two companies*. **3** *Cdn hist.* any of several canoemen positioned in the middle of a canoe, between the bowman and the steersman.

middle name *noun* **1** a person's name placed after the first name and before the surname. **2** a characteristic quality of a person etc.: *punctuality is my middle name*.

middle-of-the-road *adjective* **1** (of a person etc.) moderate; avoiding extremes. **2** (of music) intended to appeal to a wide audience.

middle school *noun* = JUNIOR HIGH SCHOOL.

middle-sized *adjective* of medium size.

middleweight *noun* **1** a weight in certain sports above welterweight, in the amateur boxing scale 71-5 kg but differing for professionals and wrestlers. **2** an athlete of this weight.

middling *adjective* **1** moderate or average in size, amount or rank: *the economies of these two middling British Columbia centres, Kamloops and Nanaimo, were dissimilar*. **2** *informal* (of a person's health) fairly good. [Say MID ling]

Mideast *noun* = MIDDLE EAST.

midfield *noun* **1** (in football, soccer, etc.) the central part of the playing field, away from the goals or end zones. **2** (in soccer) the players positioned in the midfield. ▶ **midfielder** *noun*

midge *noun* **1** any gnat-like insect. **2 a** a tiny, two-winged, non-biting insect that is often seen in swarms near water or marshy areas where it breeds. **b** a similar insect with piercing mouthparts for sucking blood or eating smaller insects.

midget *noun* **1** an extremely small person or thing. **2** (as an *adjective*) very small. **3** *Cdn* **a** a level of amateur sport, usu. involving players aged 16 to 17. **b** a player in this age group.

MIDI *noun* a standard system for transferring data between electronic musical instruments, synthesizers, computers, etc., allowing them to be used simultaneously. [Say MIDDY]

midi *noun* (*plural* **midis**) a garment of medium length, usu. reaching to mid-calf. [Say MIDDY]

midland • *noun* **1** (**the Midlands**) the inland counties of central England. **2** the middle part of a country. • *adjective* of or in the midland or Midlands.

mid-life *noun* middle age: *mid-life planning*.

mid-life crisis *noun* (*plural* **mid-life crises**) an emotional crisis of self-confidence that can occur in early middle age.

midline • *noun* a line down the middle of something, dividing it into halves that are mirror images: *the abdomen was opened by midline incision*. • *adjective* (**midline**) designating or pertaining to consumer products or services that are of a general quality, neither expensive nor cheap; mid-range.

midnight *noun* **1** 12 o'clock at night. **2** the middle of the night.

midnight blue *noun* & *adjective* very dark blue.

midnight Mass *noun* esp. *Catholicism* a Mass beginning at midnight on Christmas Eve.

midpoint *noun* the middle point.

mid-range • *adjective* (esp. of a consumer product etc.) mid-priced; of average cost, capability, etc. • *noun* the middle part of the range of audible frequencies: *mid-range speakers*.

Midrash *noun* (*plural* **Midrashim**) an ancient commentary on part of the Hebrew scriptures. [Say MID rash for the singular, mid rash EEM for the plural]

midriff *noun* the region of the front of the body between the chest and the waist. [Say MID riff]

midsection *noun* **1** the middle part of something. **2** the middle part of the human torso; midriff.

midship *noun* the middle part of a ship or boat.

midshipman *noun* (*plural* **midshipmen**) (in the Royal Navy) and *hist.* in the Royal Canadian Navy) a naval officer ranking below sub-lieutenant.

midships *adverb* = AMIDSHIPS.

midshore *adjective* *Cdn* designating the fishery an intermediate distance from shore, between the inshore and the offshore fisheries.

mid-size • *adjective* (also **mid-sized**) **1** (of a car) of a size between compact and full-size, usu. having a wheelbase of 100 to 105 inches and a four- or six-cylinder engine from 2 to 3.5 litres in size. **2** of intermediate size. • *noun* a mid-size car.

midsole *noun* a shock-absorbing layer in the sole of a running shoe etc.

midst PHRASES **in the midst of** among; in the middle of. **in our** (or **your** or **their**) **midst** among us (or you or them).

midstream • *noun* the middle of a stream, river, etc. • *adverb* (also **in midstream**) in the middle of an action etc.: *abandoned the project midstream*.

midsummer *noun* the period of or near the summer solstice, about June 21.

mid-term • *adjective* occurring in the middle of a term. • *noun* a mid-term exam.

midtown *noun* an area of a city at a moderate distance from the downtown area.

midway • *adverb* in or toward the middle of the distance or interval between two points. • *noun* a fair or an area with amusements, sideshows, rides, etc.

mid-week • *noun* the middle of the week. • *adjective* occurring at mid-week. • *adverb* at mid-week.

Midwest *noun* a region of the northern US west of the Great Lakes comprising the states of Illinois, Iowa, Indiana, Kansas, Michigan, Minnesota, Missouri, Nebraska, North Dakota, Ohio, South Dakota, and Wisconsin. ▶ **Midwestern** *adjective* **Midwesterner** *noun*

midwife *noun* (*plural* **midwives**) **1** a person (usu. a woman) trained to assist women in childbirth. **2** a person or thing that brings about change: *cults may serve as midwives for new sensibilities*. ▶ **midwifery** *noun* [Say MID wife, mid WIF ur ee]

mid-winter *noun* **1** the middle of the winter: *mid-*

M

winter blues. **2** the period of or near the winter solstice, about Dec. 22.

mien *noun* a person's look or bearing, as showing character or mood: *his cold eyes and forbidding mien reminded me of every teacher who had ever stared at me for doing something wrong*. [Sounds like MEAN]

miffed *adjective informal* put out of humour; offended.

might¹ *auxiliary verb* (*3rd. singular* **might**) *past of* MAY, used esp.: **1** in reported speech, expressing possibility: *said he might come* or permission: *asked if I might leave* (*compare* MAY 1, 2). **2** expressing a possibility based on a condition not fulfilled: *if you'd looked you might have found it*. **3** expressing complaint that an obligation or expectation is not or has not been fulfilled: *they might have asked*. **4** expressing a request: *you might give them a call*. **5** *informal* **a** = MAY 1: *it might be true*. **b** (in tentative questions) = MAY 2: *might I have the pleasure of this dance?* **c** = MAY 4: *who might you be?* PHRASES **might as well** expressing that it is probably at least as desirable to do a thing as not to do it: *might as well go to lunch ◊ won't win but might as well try*.

might² *noun* great and impressive power or strength, esp. on account of size: *a convincing display of military might*. PHRASES **might is right** those who are powerful can do what they wish unchallenged, even if their action is in fact unjustified. **with all one's might** to the utmost of one's power.

might-have-been *noun informal* **1** a past possibility that no longer applies. **2** a person or thing that could have been more eminent.

mightily *adverb* **1** very; very much: *we're mightily impressed*. **2** with great strength or effort: *we have struggled mightily to win back lost trade*.

mightiness *noun* the state or condition of being mighty; great strength or power.

mightn't *contraction* might not.

mighty • *adjective* (**mightier, mightiest**) **1** powerful or strong, in body, mind, or influence. **2** massive, bulky. **3** *informal* great, considerable. • *adverb informal* very: *a mighty difficult task*.

migraine *noun* a recurrent throbbing headache that usually affects one side of the head, often accompanied by nausea and disturbance of vision. [Say MY grain]

migrant • *adjective* that migrates. • *noun* a migrant person or animal, esp. a bird. [Say MY grunt]

migrate *verb* (**migrates, migrated, migrating**) **1** (of people) move from one place of residence to another, esp. in a different country. **2** (of an animal, esp. a bird or fish) change its area of habitation with the seasons. **3** (of a cell, atom, molecule, etc.) move in a non-random manner from one position or region to another or in a particular direction. ▶ **migration** *noun* **migratory** *adjective* [Say MY grate, my GRAY sh'n, MY gruh tory]

mike *informal* • *noun* **1** a microphone. **2** a microwave oven. • *verb* (**mikes, miked, miking**) put a microphone near, in, or on (a person, place, etc.) in order to transmit, amplify, or record sounds.

Mi'kmaq • *noun* (*plural* **Mi'kmaq** or **Mi'kmaqs**) **1** a member of an Aboriginal people living in Nova Scotia, New Brunswick, PEI, and the Gaspé Peninsula. **2** the Algonquian language of this people. • *adjective* of or relating to this people or their culture or language. [Say MICK mack or MIG maw or MEE maw]

mikveh *noun* (*also* **mikvah, mikva**) a bath in which certain Jewish ritual purifications are performed. [Say MIK vuh]

mil¹ *noun* one thousandth of an inch (0.0254 mm), as a unit of measure for the diameter of wire, thickness of a film, etc.

mil² *noun* (*plural* **mil**) (usu. in *plural* *informal* a million dollars (or pounds).

Milanese • *adjective* of or relating to Milan in northwestern Italy. • *noun* (*plural* **Milanese**) a native or inhabitant of Milan. [Say milla NEEZ]

mild *adjective* **1** (esp. of a person) gentle and not easily provoked. **2** moderate; not severe or harsh. **3** (of the weather, esp. in winter) moderately warm. **4** (of food, tobacco, etc.) not sharp or strong in taste etc. **5** (of medicine, soap, etc.) operating gently; not harsh. **6** not keenly felt or seriously intended: *mild surprise*.

mildew • *noun* **1** a destructive growth of minute fungi on plants. **2** a similar growth on paper, leather, etc. exposed to damp. • *verb* taint or be tainted with mildew. ▶ **mildewed** *adjective* [Say MIL doo or MIL dyoo]

mildly *adverb* in a mild fashion; to a limited extent. PHRASES **to put it mildly** as an understatement (implying the reality is more extreme).

mild-mannered *adjective* = MILD *adjective* 1.

mildness *noun* gentleness; the quality of being mild: *the mildness of a spring day ◊ her mildness of manner*.

mile *noun* **1** (*also* **statute mile**) a unit of linear measure equal to 1,760 yards (approx. 1.609 kilometres). **2** (in *plural*) *informal* a great distance or amount: *miles better*. **3** a race extending over a mile. PHRASES **miles away** *informal* lost in thought; preoccupied. (**talk** etc.) **a mile a minute** (talk etc.) very quickly. **go the extra mile** extend or exert oneself for another's benefit, esp. beyond what is strictly necessary.

mileage *noun* **1 a** the distance travelled. **b** the distance a vehicle is capable of travelling per unit of fuel. **2** expenses per distance travelled. **3** *informal* use, benefit, advantage: *got good mileage out of that story*.

miler *noun informal* a person or horse qualified or trained specially to run a mile.

milestone *noun* (*also* **milepost**) **1** a stone (or post) set up beside a road to mark a distance in miles. **2** a significant event or stage in a life, history, project, etc.

milieu *noun* (*plural* **milieux** or **milieus**) one's environment or social surroundings: *many novels upheld the rural milieu as the cradle of French-Canadian spiritual values*. [Say mil YOO for the singular, mil YOOS for the plural (with OO as in HOOD)]

militancy *noun* the condition of being aggressively active esp. in support of a cause: *their quiet protests have given way to dangerous militancy*. [Say MILLA t'n see]

militant • *adjective* aggressively active esp. in support of a (usu. political) cause, typically favouring extreme, violent, or confrontational methods: *militant environmentalists*. • *noun* a militant person, esp. a political activist. ▶ **militantly** *adverb* [Say MILLA t'nt]

militarism *noun* the belief or desire of a people or government that a country should maintain a strong military capability and be prepared to use it aggressively to defend or promote national interests. ▶ **militarist** *noun & adjective* **militaristic** *adjective* [Say MILLA tuh rism]

militarization *noun* an act of militarizing. [Say milla tuh rize AY sh'n]

militarily *adverb* **1** in a military or warlike manner: *we*

may have to intervene militarily. **2** from a military point of view: *a militarily superior country.* [Say milla TARE a lee]

militarize *verb* (**militarizes, militarized, militarizing**) **1** equip or supply with soldiers and other military resources: *a militarized security zone.* **2** make similar to an army: give a military character to: *a militarized police force.* [Say MILLA tuh rize]

military • *adjective* of, relating to, or characteristic of soldiers or armed forces. • *noun* (as *singular* or *plural*; **the military**) members of the armed forces, as distinct from civilians and the police.

military-industrial complex *noun* a nation's military and the industries supplying it, esp. as a single powerful influence on public policy.

militate *verb* (usu. foll. by *against*) (of a fact or circumstance) be a powerful or conclusive factor in preventing: *drug use, alcoholism and crime militate against stable life in a nuclear family.* [Say MILLA tate]

militia *noun* (*plural* **militias**) **1** a military force raised from the civilian population and supplementing a regular army in an emergency. **2** any usu. small military force not sanctioned by a nation or government. [Say muh LISHA]

militiaman *noun* (*plural* **militiamen**) a member of a militia. [Say muh LISHA m'n]

milk • *noun* **1** an opaque white fluid secreted by female mammals for the nourishment of their young. **2** the milk of cows, goats, or sheep as food. **3** the milk-like juice of plants, e.g. in the coconut. **4** a milk-like preparation of herbs, drugs, etc. • *verb* **1** draw milk from (a cow, ewe, goat, etc.). **2 a** exploit (a person or thing) esp. financially. **b** get all possible advantage from (a situation or thing). **3** extract sap, venom, etc. from. **4** (of a cow etc.) yield milk. PHRASES **cry over spilt milk** waste time worrying about something that has happened that cannot be remedied. **land of** (or **flowing with**) **milk and honey** a place where prosperity and abundance are easily available: *while Canada is not the land of milk and honey, it offers immigrants more worldly wealth and freedom than China ever could.*

milker *noun* **1** an animal, esp. a cow, yielding milk or kept for milking. **2** a person who, or a machine which, milks.

milk fat *noun* = BUTTERFAT. Abbreviation: **MF**.

milkiness *noun* a milky quality.

milkmaid *noun* a girl or woman who milks cows or works in a dairy.

milkman *noun* (*plural* **milkmen**) a person who sells or delivers milk.

milk of magnesia *noun* a white suspension of magnesium hydroxide usu. in water as an antacid or laxative.

milk powder *noun* milk dehydrated by evaporation.

milk run *noun* **1** the regular route followed by a person delivering milk. **2** a routine trip or train route with many regular stops.

milkshake *noun* a frothy drink, usu. cold, of milk, flavouring, and usu. ice cream, mixed in a blender.

milk snake *noun* a harmless, usu. brightly coloured North American snake.

milk store *noun Cdn* = CONVENIENCE STORE.

milk tooth *noun* a temporary tooth in young mammals; a baby tooth.

milkweed *noun* **1** a North American plant with milky juice and seeds plumed with long silky hairs. **2** any of various other plants with milky juice.

milk-white *adjective* white like milk.

milky *adjective* (**milkier, milkiest**) **1** of, like, or mixed with milk. **2** (of a gem, liquid, etc.) cloudy; not clear.

Milky Way *noun* **1** (also **Milky Way Galaxy**) the galaxy of which the solar system is part. **2** this viewed

as a faintly luminous band of light encircling the heavens, formed of countless indistinguishable stars.

mill¹ • *noun* **1 a** a building fitted with a mechanical apparatus for grinding grain. **b** such an apparatus. **2** an apparatus for grinding any solid substance to powder or pulp: *pepper mill.* **3 a** a building fitted with machinery for manufacturing processes etc.: *paper mill.* **b** such machinery. **4 a** any group etc. generating something specified: *rumour mill.* **b** any institution etc. operating impersonally or inhumanely and concerned solely with output: *puppy mill.* • *verb* **1 a** grind (grain), produce (flour), or hull (seeds) in a mill. **b** extract (a mineral) from rock by crushing the rock in a mill. **2** produce regular ribbed markings on the edge of (a coin). **3** cut or shape (metal) with a rotating tool. **4** (often foll. by *about, around*) (of people or animals) move in an aimless manner, esp. in a confused mass. PHRASES **go** (or **put** or **run**) **through the mill** undergo (or cause to undergo) intensive work or a difficult ordeal.

mill² *noun* one thousandth of a dollar, esp. in calculating tax rates.

millenarian • *adjective* **1** relating to or believing in a future (and typically imminent) thousand-year age of blessedness, beginning with or culminating in the Second Coming of Christ. **2** believing in the imminence or inevitability of a golden age of peace, justice, and prosperity: *millenarian Marxists.* • *noun* a person with millenarian views. ▶ **millenarianism** *noun* [Say milla NAIRY un]

millennial *adjective* having to do with a millennium. [Say mil ENNY ul]

millennium *noun* (*plural* **millennia** or **millenniums**) **1 a** a period of 1,000 years. **b** any millennium reckoned from the supposed date of the birth of Christ: *the third millennium.* **2** the period of 1,000 years during which (according to one interpretation of Revelation 20:1–5) Christ will reign in person on earth. **3** a period of good government, great happiness, and prosperity. [Say mil ENNY um]

miller *noun* **1** the proprietor or tenant of a grain mill. **2** a person who works or owns a mill.

millet *noun* a fast-growing cereal plant widely grown in warm countries for its large crop of small nutritious seeds, which can be used to make flour or alcohol.

milli- *combining form* a thousand, esp. denoting a factor of one thousandth. Abbreviation: **m**.

milligram *noun* one thousandth of a gram.

millilitre *noun* one thousandth of a litre.

millimetre *noun* one thousandth of a metre (0.039 in.).

milliner *noun* a person who makes or sells women's hats. ▶ **millinery** *noun* [Say MILLA nur, MILLA nur ee]

milling frolic *noun Cdn (NS)* **1** *hist.* a gathering at which participants pound new wool to raise the nap, usu. with singing etc. **2** a cultural event at which songs traditionally sung at these are performed.

million *cardinal number* **1** a thousand thousand. **2** (often in *plural*) *informal* a very large number: *millions of years* ◊ *thanks a million.* **3** (**the millions**) the bulk of the population. PHRASES **look** (or **feel** etc.) (**like**) **a million bucks** (or **dollars** etc.) *informal* look (or feel) extremely good.

millionaire *noun* **1** a person whose assets are worth at least one million dollars, pounds, etc. **2** a person of great wealth.

millionth *adjective, noun & adverb* the ordinal number corresponding to one million.

millipede *noun* an arthropod with a long segmented body having two pairs of legs on each segment.

millisecond *noun* one thousandth of a second.

millpond *noun* a pool of water retained by a dam for

M

the operation of a mill. PHRASES **like a millpond** (of a stretch of water) very calm.

millstone *noun* **1** each of two circular stones used for grinding grain. **2** a heavy burden or responsibility: *unemployment was an economic millstone around the country's neck*.

mill wheel *noun* a wheel used to drive a mill, e.g. a water wheel.

millwork *noun* **1** work done in a mill. **2** wood products manufactured in a mill, e.g. trim.

millwright *noun* **1** a person who maintains or repairs mill machinery. **2** a person who designs or builds mills.

milo *noun* a drought-resistant variety of sorghum grown esp. in the central US. [Say MY lo]

milquetoast *noun* a timid person. [Say MILK toast]

milt *noun* **1 a** a sperm-filled reproductive gland of a male fish. **b** the semen of a male fish. **2** the spleen in mammals. **3** an analogous organ in other vertebrates.

mime • *noun* **1** the theatrical technique of suggesting action, character, etc. by gesture and expression without using words. **2** a theatrical performance using this technique. **3** (also **mime artist**) a practitioner of mime. • *verb* (**mimes**, **mimed**, **miming**) **1** convey (an idea or emotion) by gesture without words. **2** (often foll. by *to*) (of singers etc.) mouth (the words of a song etc.) along with a soundtrack.

mimesis *noun* **1** *Biology* = MIMICRY 3. **2** the representation of the real world in art, poetry, etc. [Say muh MEE sis or my MEE sis]

mimetic *adjective* of, relating to, constituting, or habitually practising imitation: *mimetic patterns in butterflies ◊ the mimetic connection between art and life*. [Say mim ETT ick]

mimic • *verb* (**mimics**, **mimicked**, **mimicking**) **1** imitate (a person, gesture, etc.) esp. to entertain or ridicule. **2** (of a thing) resemble closely: *the robot was programmed to mimic a series of human movements ◊ the creation of a vaccine that mimics the virus*. • *noun* a person skilled in imitation. ▶ **mimicker** *noun*

mimicry *noun* (*plural* **mimicries**) **1** the act or art of mimicking. **2** a thing that mimics another. **3** *Biology* a close external resemblance of an animal (or part of one) to another animal or to a plant or inanimate object; a similar resemblance in a plant. [Say MIMIC ree]

mimosa *noun* (*plural* **mimosas**) **1** a shrub with globular flowers and leaves that droop when touched. **2** any of various acacia plants with showy yellow flowers. **3** a drink of champagne and orange juice. [Say mim OH zuh or mim OH suh]

Min *noun* any of the Chinese languages or dialects spoken in the Fukien province in southeastern China and parts of Taiwan.

Min. *abbreviation* **1** Minister. **2** Ministry.

min *abbreviation* **1** minute(s). **2** (**min.**) minimum.

minaret *noun* a slender turret connected with a mosque and having a balcony from which the muezzin calls at hours of prayer. [Say minna RET]

mince *verb* (**minces**, **minced**, **mincing**) **1 a** cut up into very small pieces. **b** grind (meat). **2** walk with an affected delicacy, typically with quick short steps. PHRASES **not mince words** speak candidly and directly, esp. when criticizing someone or something.

mincemeat *noun* a mixture of currants, raisins, sugar, apples, candied peel, spices, and often suet, used as a pie filling. PHRASES **make mincemeat of** utterly defeat (a person, argument, etc.).

mince pie *noun* a pie containing mincemeat.

mincing *adjective* (of a way of walking or speaking) very delicate, and not natural: *short mincing steps*.

mind • *noun* **1** the faculty of consciousness and thought. **2** a person's intellect or memory. **3** a person

identified with their intellectual faculties. **4** a person's attention or will. • *verb* **1** be distressed or annoyed by; object to. **2** remember or take care to do. **3** give attention to; watch out for. **4** take care of temporarily. **5** (in *passive*) be inclined to do. **6** (also **mind you**) introducing a qualification to a previous statement. PHRASES **be in** (or **of**) **two minds** be unable to decide between alternatives. **be of one mind** share the same opinion. **give someone a piece of one's mind** rebuke someone. **have** (**half**) **a mind to** be inclined to. **have in mind 1** be thinking of. **2** intend to do. **in one's mind's eye** in one's imagination. **mind one's Ps & Qs** be careful to be polite and avoid giving offence. **never mind 1** do not be concerned or distressed. **2** let alone. **out of one's mind** having lost control of one's mental faculties. **put one in mind of** remind one of. **to my mind** in my opinion.

mind-altering *adjective* (of a drug) hallucinogenic.

mind-bending *adjective informal* (esp. of a psychedelic drug) influencing or altering one's state of mind.

mind-blowing *adjective slang* **1** overwhelming, bewildering. **2** (esp. of drugs etc.) inducing hallucinations. ▶ **mind-blowingly** *adverb*

mind-boggling *adjective informal* overwhelming, startling. ▶ **mind-bogglingly** *adverb*

minded *adjective* **1** (in *combination*) **a** inclined to think in some specified way: *mathematically minded ◊ fair-minded*. **b** having a specified kind of mind: *high-minded*. **c** interested in or enthusiastic about a specified thing: *car-minded*. **2** disposed or inclined (to an action). ▶ **mindedly** *adverb* **mindedness** *noun*

minder *noun* a person whose job it is to attend to a person or thing (often in *combination*: *netminder*).

mindful *adjective* (often foll. by *of*) taking heed or care. ▶ **mindfully** *adverb* **mindfulness** *noun*

mind game *noun* **1** (usu. in *plural*) *informal* a series of deliberate actions or responses planned for psychological effect on another, typically for amusement or competitive advantage. **2** a game designed to test or exercise the intellect.

mindless *adjective* **1** lacking intelligence; stupid. **2** not requiring thought or skill: *totally mindless work*. **3** (of an action, condition, thing, etc.) characterized by a lack of thought. **4** (usu. foll. by *of*) heedless of (advice etc.). ▶ **mindlessly** *adverb* **mindlessness** *noun*

mind-numbing *adjective* (esp. of tedium) that numbs the mind. ▶ **mind-numbingly** *adverb*

mind reader *noun* a person capable of discerning the thoughts of another. ▶ **mind reading** *noun*

mindscape *noun* reality as imagined in one's mind, and often as portrayed in art.

mindset *noun* a frame of mind, a mental attitude.

mind's eye *noun informal* the mind as viewer of memories or things imagined. PHRASES **in one's mind's eye** in one's imagination or mental view.

mine¹ *possessive pronoun* **1** the one or ones belonging to or associated with me: *it is mine ◊ mine are over there*. **2** *archaic* = MY: *mine eyes have seen*. PHRASES **of mine** of or belonging to me: *a friend of mine*.

mine² • *noun* **1** an excavation in the earth for extracting metal, coal, salt, etc. **2** an abundant source (of information etc.). **3** a receptacle filled with explosive and placed in the ground or in the water for destroying enemy personnel, ships, etc. **4** a subterranean gallery in which explosive is placed to blow up fortifications. • *verb* (**mines**, **mined**, **mining**) **1** obtain (metal, coal, etc.) from a mine. **2** (often foll. by *for*) dig in (the earth etc.) for ore etc. **3 a** dig or burrow in (usu. the earth). **b** make (a hole, passage, etc.) underground. **4** lay explosive mines under or in. **5** = UNDERMINE.

minefield *noun* **1** an area planted with explosive mines. **2** a subject or situation presenting unseen hazards.

miner *noun* **1** a person who works in a mine. **2** any burrowing insect or grub.

mineral • *noun* **1** a substance that occurs naturally in the earth and is not formed from animal or vegetable matter. **2** a substance obtained by mining. **3** any of the elements, e.g. calcium, iron, etc., that are essential for good nutrition. • *adjective* **1** of or containing a mineral or minerals. **2** obtained by mining.

mineralization *noun* an act of mineralizing.

mineralize *verb* (**mineralizes**, **mineralized**, **mineralizing**) **1** change wholly or partly into a mineral. **2** introduce a mineral substance into (water etc.). **3** change (a metal) into an ore.

mineralogical *adjective* having to do with the minerals: *a mineralogical study of the lava*. [Say minner a LOGICAL]

mineralogist *noun* a person who studies or is an expert in mineralogy. [Say minner OLLA jist]

mineralogy *noun* the scientific study of minerals. [Say minner OLLA jee]

mineral oil *noun* a colourless odourless oily liquid obtained from petroleum and used as a lubricant, laxative, etc.

mineral rights *plural noun* ownership rights to the minerals located on or below a property.

mineral water *noun* water found in nature with some dissolved salts present.

mine shaft *noun* a shaft giving access to a mine.

minestrone *noun* a soup containing vegetables and pasta, beans, or rice. [Say minna STRONE ee]

minesweeper *noun* a ship for clearing away floating and submerged mines.

mineworker *noun* = MINER 1.

Ming *noun* **1** the Chinese dynasty founded in 1368 after the collapse of Mongol authority in China, and ruling until succeeded by the Manchus in 1644. **2** Chinese porcelain made during this dynasty.

mingle *verb* (**mingles**, **mingled**, **mingling**) (often foll. by *with*) **1** mix, blend. **2** socialize, esp. at a party etc.

mingy *adjective* (**mingier**, **mingiest**) *informal* **1** mean, stingy. **2** small. [Say MIN jee]

mini *noun* (*plural* **minis**) **1** *informal* a miniskirt. **2** a garment, e.g. a dress, with a miniskirt.

mini- *combining form* miniature; very small or minor of its kind: *minibus* ◊ *mini-budget*.

miniature • *adjective* **1** much smaller than normal. **2** represented on a small scale. • *noun* **1** any object reduced in size. **2** a small-scale minutely finished portrait. PHRASES **in miniature** on a small scale. [Say MINNA chur or MINNY a chur]

miniature golf *noun* a game patterned on golf, but played on a small obstacle course.

miniaturist *noun* a person who produces or is interested in miniature paintings, objects, etc. [Say MINNA chur ist or MINNY a chur ist]

miniaturization *noun* an act of making something smaller. [Say minna chur ize AY sh'n or minny a chur ize AY sh'n]

miniaturize *verb* (**miniaturizes**, **miniaturized**, **miniaturizing**) produce in a smaller version; make small. [Say MINNA chur ize or MINNY a chur ize]

mini-bar *noun* a small fridge containing drinks and snacks placed in a hotel room for the use of guests, the contents being charged to the bill if used.

mini-blind *noun* a type of narrow-slatted venetian blind.

mini-budget *noun* an interim budget, usu. limited in scope, brought down by a government.

minibus *noun* (*plural* **minibuses**) a small bus for about twelve passengers.

mini-cam *noun* a hand-held video camera.

Mini Disc *noun* *proprietary* a small recordable version of a compact disc.

minigolf *noun* = MINIATURE GOLF.

minim *noun* *Music* = HALF NOTE.

minima *plural of* MINIMUM.

minimal *adjective* **1** as small as possible; minimum. **2 a** *Art etc.* characterized by the use of simple or primary forms or structures etc., often geometric or massive: *huge minimal forms in a few colours*. **b** *Music* characterized by the repetition of short phrases which change very gradually as the music proceeds.

minimalism *noun* a minimalist attitude or style.

minimalist • *adjective* **1** (esp. of an aesthetic style) constituting or characterized by the minimum required; not elaborate. **2** of or relating to minimal art or music. • *noun* **1** a person advocating minor or moderate reform in politics. **2** a person who advocates or practises minimal art or music. ▶ **minimalistic** *adjective*

mini-mall *noun* a mall containing a relatively small number of stores etc. and with access to each store from the outdoors rather than from an interior hallway.

minimally *adverb* to a small or the smallest extent: *minimally invasive surgery* ◊ *the decision affects us minimally*.

mini-mart *noun* = CONVENIENCE STORE.

mini-mill *noun* a small steel plant, esp. one that produces steel by melting down scrap.

minimization *noun* an act of minimizing.

minimize *verb* (**minimizes**, **minimized**, **minimizing**) **1** reduce (something, esp. something unwanted or unpleasant) to the smallest possible amount or degree: *the aim is to minimize costs*. **2** estimate or represent at less than the true value or importance: *he always tried to minimize his own faults, while exaggerating those of others*. ▶ **minimizer** *noun*

minimum (*plural* **minimums** or **minima**) • *noun* **1** the least possible or attainable amount: *reduced to a minimum*. **2** the lowest amount of a varying quality, e.g. temperature, pressure, etc., attained or recorded within a particular period. • *adjective* that is a minimum.

minimum-security *adjective* (of a correctional institution) having no extraordinary security measures such as perimeter fences, barred windows, etc.

minimum wage *noun* the lowest wage permitted by law or special agreement.

mining *noun* the process or industry of removing metals, coal, etc. from a mine.

minion *noun* *derogatory* an unimportant person in an organization who has to obey orders; a servant: *while I was waiting to see him, a minion brought me some tea* ◊ *whenever the director needed more information, his minions were sent scurrying in all directions to obtain it*. [Say MIN yun]

mini-putt *noun* *Cdn* = MINIATURE GOLF.

miniseries *noun* a film shown on television in several segments broadcast within a few days of each other.

M

miniskirt *noun* a very short skirt.

minister • *noun* **1** (in Canada, the UK, and other Commonwealth countries) a head of a government department. **2** (also **minister of religion**) a member of the clergy, esp. in some Protestant denominations. **3** a diplomatic agent, usu. ranking below an ambassador. • *verb* **1** render aid or service (to a person, cause, etc.). **2** serve as or perform the functions of a minister of religion: *ministered there for 17 years*.

ministerial *adjective* **1** of a government minister. **2** of a minister of religion or a minister's office. [Say min iss TEERY ul]

Minister of the Crown *noun* (*plural* **Ministers of the Crown**) (in Canada, the UK, and other Commonwealth countries) a member of the Cabinet.

minister without portfolio *noun* (*plural* **ministers without portfolio**) a government minister who has Cabinet status, but is not in charge of a specific department or ministry.

ministration *noun* (usu. in *plural*) aid or service: *the kind ministrations of her neighbours*. [Say min iss TRAY sh'n]

ministry *noun* (*plural* **ministries**) **1** a government department headed by a minister. **2 a** (**the ministry**) the vocation or profession of a religious minister: *called to the ministry*. **b** a form of Christian service effected by a layperson: *an organist and choirmaster in charge of the parish's music ministry*. **3** (**the ministry**) the body of ministers of a government or of a religion. **4** a period of government under one prime minister. **5** the act of ministering to someone: *the soldiers were no less in need of his ministry*. [Say MIN iss tree]

minivan *noun* a small passenger van, usu. having side windows and removable rear seats.

mink *noun* **1** either of two small semiaquatic ermine-like animals of North America and Europe. **2** the thick brown fur of these. **3** a coat made of this.

minke *noun* a small baleen whale with a pointed snout. [Say MIN kuh]

Minn. *abbreviation* Minnesota.

Minnesotan • *noun* a native or inhabitant of the US state of Minnesota. • *adjective* of or relating to Minnesota.

minnow *noun* any of various small freshwater fish, esp. of the carp family.

Minoan • *adjective* of or relating to the Bronze Age civilization centred on Crete (*c.*3000–1100 BC), whose remains include large urban centres dominated by palaces. • *noun* **1** an inhabitant of Minoan Crete or the Minoan world. **2** the language or scripts associated with the Minoans. [Say min OWEN]

minor • *adjective* **1** lesser or comparatively small in size or importance: *minor poet ◊ minor operation*. **2** *Music* **a** (of a scale) having intervals of a semitone between the second and third, fifth and sixth, and seventh and eighth degrees. **b** (of an interval) less by a semitone than a major interval. **c** (of a key) based on a minor scale, tending to produce a melancholy effect. **3** *Cdn* designating organized amateur team sport for children: *minor hockey*. • *noun* **1** a person under the legal age limit or majority: *no unaccompanied minors*. **2** *Music* a minor key etc. **3** a student's subsidiary subject or course (*compare* MAJOR 1). **4** *Hockey* = MINOR PENALTY. **5** (in *plural*) the minor leagues. • *verb* (foll. by *in*) (of a student) undertake study in (a subject) as a subsidiary to a main subject. PHRASES **in a minor key** (of novels, events, people's lives, etc.) understated, subdued, often with a melancholy tinge.

minority *noun* (*plural* **minorities**) **1** a smaller number or part, esp. within a political party or structure. **2** the state of having less than half the votes or of being supported by less than half of the body of opinion: *in the*

minority. **3 a** (also **minority group**) a relatively small group of people differing from others in the society of which they are a part in race, religion, language, political persuasion, etc. **b** a member of such a group. **4** (as an *adjective*) relating to or done by the minority: *minority interests*. **5 a** the state of being under full legal age. **b** the period of this. [Say my NORRA tee or min ORRA tee]

minority government *noun* *Cdn*, *Brit.*, *Austral.*, & *NZ* a government that has fewer seats in parliament than the total number held by all other parties.

minority leader *noun* (in the US) the floor leader of the party having a minority in a legislature.

minor league • *noun* **1** (esp. in hockey and baseball) a league of professional clubs other than the major leagues. **2** *Cdn* an amateur league for children and youth, esp. in hockey, football, etc. • *adjective* (usu. **minor-league**) **1** of a minor league: *set a minor-league record*. **2** of inferior quality; small-time: *a career of minor-league, dead-end jobs*. ► **minor-leaguer** *noun*

minor penalty *noun* (*plural* **minor penalties**) *Hockey* a two minute penalty given for lesser infractions.

minor planet *noun* see PLANET 2.

minor prophet *noun* any of the Hebrew prophets after whom the shorter prophetic books of the Bible are named: Hosea, Joel, Amos, Obadiah, Jonah, Micah, Nahum, Habakkuk, Zephaniah, Haggai, Zechariah, and Malachi.

Minotaur *noun* (in Greek mythology) a man with a bull's head, kept in a Cretan labyrinth and fed with human flesh. [Say MIN a tore or MINE a tore]

minoxidil *noun* a drug used to treat high blood pressure which can also promote hair growth when applied on the skin. [Say min OXA dill]

minstrel *noun* **1** a medieval singer or musician, esp. singing or reciting poetry. **2** *hist.* a person who entertained patrons with singing, buffoonery, etc.

mint¹ • *noun* **1** an aromatic plant growing in temperate regions, often used as a herb in cooking. **2** a mint-flavoured candy. **3** the flavour or scent of mint. • *adjective* having the flavour of mint: *mint icing*.

mint² • *noun* **1** a place where money is coined under governmental control. **2** a vast sum of money: *making a mint*. • *adjective* in perfect condition; as new: *the bike was in mint condition*. • *verb* **1** make (coin) by stamping metal. **2** invent, coin (a word, phrase, etc.).

minted¹ *adjective* flavoured with mint.

minted² *adjective* recently created: *newly minted MBAs*.

mint green *noun* & *adjective* a pale pastel green.

mint julep *noun* a sweet iced alcoholic drink of bourbon flavoured with mint.

minty *adjective* (**mintier**, **mintiest**) having a taste or aroma suggesting mint.

minuet *noun* **1** a slow stately dance for two in triple time, popular esp. in the 17th and 18th centuries. **2** the music for this, or music in the same rhythm and style, often as a movement in a suite, sonata, or symphony. [Say min yoo ETT]

minus • *preposition* **1** with the subtraction of: *7 minus 4 equals 3*. Symbol: –. **2** (of temperature) below zero: *minus 2°*. **3** lacking; deprived of: *Stephen returned minus the dog*. • *adjective* **1** *Math* negative. **2** *Electronics* having a negative charge. **3** (after a grade etc.) of a standard slightly lower than the one stated: *got a B minus*. • *noun* (*plural* **minuses**) **1** = MINUS SIGN. **2** *Math* a negative quantity. **3** a disadvantage.

minuscule • *adjective* **1** extremely small or unimportant. **2** (of a letter) lower case. • *noun* a lower case letter. [Say MINNA skyool]

minus sign *noun* the symbol –, indicating subtraction or a negative value.

M

minute[1] • *noun* **1** the sixtieth part of an hour. **2 a** a short time. **b** as soon as: *call me the minute you get back.* **3** the sixtieth part of an angular degree. **4** (in *plural*) a brief summary of the proceedings at a meeting. • *verb* (**minutes, minuted, minuting**) record (proceedings) in the minutes. PHRASES **in a minute 1** very soon. **2** very readily: *she'd marry him in a minute.* **just (or wait) a minute 1** a request to wait for a short time. **2** as a prelude to a query or objection. **not for a minute** not at all: *I never thought for a minute that you would refuse.*

minute[2] *adjective* (**minutest**) **1** very small. **2** very detailed, careful and thorough: *a minute examination.* [Say my NYOOT or my NOOT]

minutely *adverb* to smallest detail: *the agreement has been examined minutely.* [Say my NYOOT lee or my NOOT lee]

Minuteman *noun* (*plural* **Minutemen**) *US* **1** a type of three-stage intercontinental ballistic missile. **2** *hist.* an American militiaman of the revolutionary period. [Say MINNIT man]

minuteness *noun* the quality of being very small or detailed; small size.

minutiae *plural noun* precise, trivial, or minor details: *studied the minutiae of the contract.* [Say min OOSH uh or min OOSHY uh]

minx *noun* (*plural* **minxes**) a mischievous or pert girl.

minyan *noun* the quorum of ten males over thirteen years of age required for traditional Jewish public worship. [Say MIN yun or min YAWN]

Miocene • *adjective* of or relating to the fourth epoch of the Tertiary period, between the Oligocene and the Pliocene, lasting from about 24.6 to 5.1 million years ago; during this time the Alps and Himalayas were being formed and apes underwent great development. • *noun* this geological epoch. [Say MY a seen]

MIPS *noun* a unit of computing speed equivalent to a million instructions per second. [Say MIPS]

miracle *noun* **1** an act or event that does not follow the laws of nature and is believed to be caused by God. **2 a** any remarkable occurrence. **b** a remarkable development in some specified area: *an economic miracle.* **3** (usu. foll. by *of*) a remarkable or outstanding specimen: *the plan was a miracle of ingenuity.*

miraculous *adjective* **1** of the nature of a miracle; supernatural. **2** remarkable, surprising. **3** having the power to work miracles. ▶**miraculously** *adverb* **miraculousness** *noun*

mirage *noun* **1** an optical illusion caused by atmospheric conditions, esp. the appearance of a sheet of water in a desert or on a hot road from the reflection of light. **2** an illusory thing: *network news constructs a mirage of objectivity.* [Say mur AWZH]

mire • *noun* **1** a stretch of swampy or boggy ground. **2** wet or soft mud; muck. **3** a difficult situation from which it is difficult to extricate oneself: *he has been left to squirm in a mire of new allegations.* • *verb* (**mires, mired, miring**) (esp. as **mired**) **1** plunge or sink in a mire: *struggling to free a cart mired down in the muddy street.* **2** involve in difficulties: *the economy is mired in the longest recession in decades.*

mirror • *noun* **1** a polished surface, usu. of amalgam-coated glass or metal, which reflects an image. **2** anything regarded as giving an accurate reflection or description of something else. • *verb* reflect as in a mirror.

mirrored *adjective* **1** fitted with a mirror or mirrors: *a mirrored wall.* **2** having a reflective surface: *mirrored sunglasses.*

mirror image *noun* **1** an identical image, but with the structure reversed, as in a mirror. **2** a phenomenon or occurrence which is identical to another.

mirth *noun* merriment, laughter. ▶**mirthful** *adjective* **mirthless** *adjective* **mirthlessly** *adverb*

MIS *abbreviation* *Computing* management information systems.

mis- *prefix* added to verbs and verbal derivatives: meaning "amiss", "badly", "wrongly", unfavourably : *mislead* ∪ *misshapen.*

misadventure *noun* **1** bad luck or a small accident: *the repetition of previous political misadventures.* **2** *Law* an accident without concomitant crime or negligence: *death by misadventure.*

misalign *verb* give the wrong alignment to. ▶**misaligned** *adjective* **misalignment** *noun* [Say miss a LINE]

misanthrope *noun* (also **misanthropist**) **1** a person who hates humans. **2** a person who avoids human society. [Say MISS un thrope, miss ANTHRA pist]

misanthropic *adjective* hating and avoiding other people. [Say miss un THROP ick]

misanthropy *noun* a dislike of other people. [Say miss ANTHRA pee]

misapplication *noun* the use of something for the wrong purpose or in the wrong way.

misapply *verb* (**misapplies, misapplied, misapplying**) apply (a theory, a term, funds, etc.) wrongly.

misapprehend *verb* misunderstand.

misapprehension *noun* a mistaken belief about or interpretation of something: *I was under the misapprehension that the course was for complete beginners.*

misappropriate *verb* (**misappropriates, misappropriated, misappropriating**) apply (usu. another's money) to one's own use or to a wrong use: *he is accused of misappropriating money from the company's pension fund.* ▶**misappropriation** *noun* [Say missa PRO pree ate, missa pro pree AY sh'n]

misbegotten *adjective* **1** contemptible: *get back here, you misbegotten swine!* **2** badly designed or planned: *someone's misbegotten idea of a country house.* **3** (of a child) illegitimate.

misbehave *verb* (**misbehaves, misbehaved, misbehaving**) (of a person, machine, etc.) behave badly. ▶**misbehaviour** *noun*

misc. *abbreviation* miscellaneous.

miscalculate *verb* (**miscalculates, miscalculated, miscalculating**) calculate wrongly. ▶**miscalculation** *noun*

miscarriage *noun* the expulsion of a fetus from the womb before it can survive independently, esp. before the 28th week of pregnancy.

miscarriage of justice *noun* (*plural* **miscarriages of justice**) any failure of the judicial system to attain the ends of justice: *documented cases of miscarriage of justice where innocent people have been executed.*

miscarry *verb* (**miscarries, miscarried, miscarrying**) **1** (of a woman or female animal) have a miscarriage. **2** (of a business, plan, etc.) fail, be unsuccessful: *carefully laid plans will miscarry because the unexpected will happen.*

miscast *verb* (**miscasts, miscast, miscasting**) assign an unsuitable role to (a performer).

miscegenation *noun* **1** the interbreeding of races, esp. of whites and non-whites. **2** marriage between people of different races. [Say miss EDGE in ay sh'n]

miscellaneous *adjective* **1** composed of elements of different kinds: *a miscellaneous assortment of tools too numerous to mention.* **2** of various kinds: *the director, maybe five producers, the casting director, and miscellaneous assistants.* [Say missa LAY nee us]

miscellany *noun* (*plural* **miscellanies**) a group or collection of different kinds of things: *a bewildering*

M

miscellany of agencies, boards, and committees. [Say MISSA lay nee]

mischief *noun* **1** conduct which is troublesome, but not malicious, esp. in children: *keep out of mischief.* **2** playfulness that is intended to tease, mock, or create trouble: *her eyes were full of mischief.* **3** harm or injury caused by a person or thing. **4** a person or thing responsible for harm or annoyance: *that loose connection is the mischief.* PHRASES **do a person a mischief** wound or kill a person. **get up to** (or **make**) **mischief** cause trouble. [Say MISS chiff]

SAY IT RIGHT
mischievous

Although the pronunciation miss CHEE vee us is very common, it is not considered standard by many people.

---

mischievous *adjective* **1** (of a person) disposed to mischief. **2** (of conduct etc.) teasing; playfully malicious. [Say MISS chiv us or miss CHEE vee us]

misconceived *adjective* badly planned, organized, etc.: *a misconceived education policy.*

misconception *noun* a misunderstanding; a wrong idea: *traditional misconceptions and prejudices.*

misconduct *noun* **1** improper or unprofessional behaviour: *alleged police misconduct.* **2** bad management: *shareholders claiming misconduct or ineffectiveness on the part of the directors.* **3** *Hockey* a penalty, usu. lasting for five minutes or more, called against a player for fighting or arguing with the referee etc.

misconstrue *verb* (**misconstrues, misconstrued, misconstruing**) interpret (a word, action, etc.) wrongly: *I sincerely hope my letter was not misconstrued.*

miscount • *verb* count wrongly. • *noun* a wrong count.

miscreant *noun* an immoral or criminal person: *they expelled 30 miscreants and chained the school doors to keep out the dope pushers and other undesirables.* [Say MISS kree int]

miscue • *noun* **1** an error or blunder. **2** (in pool etc.) the failure to strike the ball properly with the cue. • *verb* (**miscues, miscued, miscueing** or **miscuing**) make a miscue.

misdeal • *verb* (**misdeals, misdealt, misdealing**) make a mistake in dealing (cards). • *noun* **1** a mistake in dealing cards. **2** a misdealt hand.

misdeed *noun* an evil deed, a wrongdoing; a crime.

WRITING TIP
misdemeanour

Misdemeanour is not used officially in Canadian law, where the term **summary conviction offence** is used instead.

---

misdemeanour *noun* (also **misdemeanor**) **1** a minor wrongdoing: *misdemeanours or small deceits might merit a cuff round the ears or an angry scolding.* **2** *Law* a minor criminal offence, esp. (in the US) one less serious than a felony. [Say miss duh MEAN er]

misdiagnose *verb* (**misdiagnoses, misdiagnosed, misdiagnosing**) diagnose incorrectly. ▸ **misdiagnosis** *noun* (*plural* **misdiagnoses**) [Say miss die ug NOCE]

misdirect *verb* **1** direct (a person, letter, blow, etc.) wrongly. **2** (of a judge) instruct (the jury) wrongly.

misdirected *adjective* **1** sent in the wrong direction: *a misdirected pass.* **2** used or applied wrongly or inappropriately: *misdirected energies.* **3** undeserved by its target or victim: *misdirected anger.*

misdirection *noun* wrong direction or guidance.

miser *noun* a person who hoards wealth and lives miserably.

miserable *adjective* **1** wretchedly unhappy or uncomfortable: *felt miserable.* **2** contemptible. **3** causing wretchedness or discomfort: *miserable weather.* **4** *informal* (of a person) gloomy, morose. ▸ **miserableness** *noun* **miserably** *adverb*

miserly *adjective* like a miser, stingy.

misery *noun* (*plural* **miseries**) **1** great discomfort of mind or body. **2** a thing causing this. PHRASES **put out of its** etc. **misery 1** release (a person, animal, etc.) from suffering or suspense. **2** kill (an animal in pain).

misfire • *verb* (**misfires, misfired, misfiring**) **1** (of a gun, motor engine, etc.) fail to go off or start or function regularly. **2** (of an action etc.) fail to have the intended effect. • *noun* a failure of function or intention.

misfit *noun* **1** a person unsuited to a particular kind of environment, occupation, etc. **2** something that does not fit or suit well.

misfortune *noun* **1** bad luck: *the project was dogged by misfortune.* **2** an unfortunate condition or event: *never laugh at other people's misfortunes.*

misgivings *plural noun* mistrust or apprehension.

misguided *adjective* mistaken in thought or action: *a misguided attempt to rescue the hostages.* ▸ **misguidedly** *adverb* **misguidedness** *noun*

mishandle *verb* (**mishandles, mishandled, mishandling**) **1** deal with incorrectly or ineffectively: *the officer had mishandled the situation.* **2** handle (a person or thing) roughly or carelessly: *the equipment could be dangerous if mishandled.*

mishap *noun* an unlucky accident.

mishear *verb* (**mishears, misheard, mishearing**) hear incorrectly or imperfectly.

mis-hit • *verb* (**mis-hits, mis-hit, mis-hitting**) hit (a ball etc.) faultily. • *noun* a faulty or bad hit.

mishmash *noun* a confused mixture.

Mishnah *noun* an authoritative collection of Jewish oral law, forming the first part of the Talmud. [Say MISH nuh]

misidentification *noun* the wrong identification of somebody or something.

misidentify *verb* (**misidentifies, misidentified, misidentifying**) identify wrongly.

misinform *verb* give wrong information to, mislead. ▸ **misinformation** *noun*

misinformed *adjective* **1** (of a person) incorrectly informed; having an incorrect or imperfect knowledge of or acquaintance with the facts. **2** (of an argument etc.) based on incorrect information.

misinterpret *verb* (**misinterprets, misinterpreted, misinterpreting**) interpret wrongly; draw a wrong inference from. ▸ **misinterpretation** *noun*

misjudge *verb* (**misjudges, misjudged, misjudging**) **1** judge wrongly. **2** have a wrong opinion of. ▸ **misjudgment** *noun* (also **misjudgement**)

mislabel *verb* (**mislabels, mislabelled, mislabelling**) **1** attach an incorrect label to. **2** describe or designate wrongly.

mislay *verb* (**mislays, mislaid, mislaying**) **1** unintentionally put (a thing) where it cannot readily be found. **2** lose.

mislead *verb* (**misleads, misled, misleading**) cause to have a wrong idea or impression about something.

misleading *adjective* giving the wrong idea or impression. ▸ **misleadingly** *adverb*

mismanage *verb* (**mismanages, mismanaged,**

mismanaging) manage badly or dishonestly. ▶**mismanagement** *noun*
mismatch • *verb* (**mismatches**, **mismatched**, **mismatching**) match unsuitably or incorrectly. • *noun* (*plural* **mismatches**) a bad match.
misname *verb* (**misnames**, **misnamed**, **misnaming**) call by a wrong or inappropriate name.
misnomer *noun* a name or term used wrongly: *"great hall" was a misnomer — it may have been large, but it was by no means great.* [Say miss NOME er]
miso *noun* (in Japanese cooking) a paste made from fermented soybeans and barley or rice malt. [Say MEE so]
misogyny *noun* disdain or contempt for women: *the omnipresent misogyny of the locker room.* ▶**misogynist** *noun* **misogynistic** *adjective* [Say miss AWE juh nee, miss AWE juh nist, miss awe juh NISS tick]

SPELL CHECK
misspell

Warning: **misspell** is spelled with two *s*'s.

---

misperception *noun* a wrong or incorrect perception.
misplace *verb* (**misplaces**, **misplaced**, **misplacing**) (usu. as **misplaced** *adjective*) **1** put in the wrong place. **2** bestow (affections, confidence, etc.) on an inappropriate object.

GRAMMAR CHECK
misplaced modifiers

In the sentence *as a single woman, he found her very interesting*, the phrase *as a single woman* should be modifying *her*, but its position in the sentence makes it sound like it is modifying *he*, which is silly. To guard against misplacing modifiers, try to keep them as close as possible to the person or thing they are modifying: *He found her, as a single woman, interesting*.

---

misplaced modifier *noun* a word, phrase, or clause which sounds like it refers to a person or thing other than the one intended.
misplay • *verb* play (a ball, card, etc.) in a wrong or ineffective manner. • *noun* an instance of playing the ball or a card in such a way.
misprint • *noun* a mistake in printing. • *verb* print wrongly.
mispronounce *verb* (**mispronounces**, **mispronounced**, **mispronouncing**) pronounce (a word etc.) wrongly. ▶**mispronunciation** *noun*
misquote *verb* (**misquotes**, **misquoted**, **misquoting**) quote wrongly.
misread *verb* (**misreads**, **misread**, **misreading**) read or interpret (text, a situation, etc.) wrongly. ▶**misreading** *noun*
misrepresent *verb* represent wrongly; give a false or misleading account of. ▶**misrepresentation** *noun*
misrule *noun* **1** bad government. **2** disorder: *it was a feast of misrule, with pranks like the tipping of privies.*
miss¹ • *verb* (**misses**, **missed**, **missing**) **1** fail to hit, reach, or come into contact with. **2** be too late for. **3** fail to notice, hear, or understand. **4** fail to be present. **5** avoid. **6** (often foll. by *out*) omit. **7** notice or feel the loss or absence of. • *noun* (*plural* **misses**) a failure to hit, reach, attain, connect, etc. PHRASES **be missing** not have (*see also* MISSING *adjective*). **give** (a **thing**) **a miss** avoid, leave alone: *gave the party a miss.* **miss a beat** (usu. with *neg.*) hesitate in making a transition from one activity to another or in conversation: *she carried on without missing a beat.* **miss**

the boat 1 lose an opportunity. **2** fail to understand the point. **a miss is as good as a mile** the fact of failure, escape, or success is not affected by the narrowness of the margin. **not miss much** be alert. **not miss a trick** never fail to seize an opportunity, advantage, etc.
miss² *noun* (*plural* **misses**) **1** (**Miss**) a title for an unmarried woman or girl. **2 a** the title of a young woman representing a country, group, etc., esp. in a beauty contest: *Miss Canada*. **b** *ironic* or *jocular* a mock title of a young woman supposedly personifying a particular state, condition, etc.: *little Miss Innocent*. **3 a** a girl or unmarried woman. **b** usu. *derogatory* or *jocular* a girl, esp. a schoolgirl, with implications of silliness etc. **4** used as a term of address to a waitress, female schoolteacher, sales clerk, etc. **5** (in *plural*) = MISSY 1.
missable *adjective* that can be passed over or skipped, esp. because it is not worth seeing etc.

SPELL CHECK
missal, missile

A type of weapon is a **missile**.

---

missal *noun* Catholicism a book containing the texts used in the Mass throughout the year. [Say MISS'll]
misshape *verb* (**misshapes**, **misshaped**, **misshaping**) give a bad, ugly, or wrong shape or form to; distort. [Say mis SHAPE]
misshapen *adjective* ill-shaped, deformed, distorted.

SPELL CHECK
missile, missal

A book used by Catholics at Mass is a **missal**.

---

missile *noun* **1** a destructive, self-propelling projectile, esp. a nuclear weapon, that is directed automatically or by remote control. **2** an object or weapon suitable for throwing at a target or discharging from a machine: *police used shields as protection against missiles thrown by pickets.* [Say MISS'll or MISS ile]
missing *adjective* **1** not in its place; lost. **2** not present, absent. **3** (of a person) not yet traced or confirmed as alive but not known to be dead. PHRASES **go missing** become lost, esp. under unusual or suspicious circumstances: *$20 has gone missing from my wallet.*
missing link *noun* **1** a thing lacking to complete a series. **2** a hypothetical intermediate animal assumed to be an evolutionary link between humans and apes.
mission *noun* **1 a** a particular task or goal assigned to a person or group. **b** a journey with a purpose. **c** a person's duty, vocation, or work, esp. that enthusiastically accepted or assumed: *mission in life*. **2** a military or scientific operation or expedition for a particular purpose. **3** a body of persons sent, esp. to a foreign country, to conduct negotiations, establish political or commercial relations, etc. **4 a** members of a religious organization sent to spread their faith abroad. **b** a missionary post or organization. **c** a body of people established to do missionary, evangelical, or humanitarian work in their own country, esp. among the poor or disadvantaged. **5** a particular, usu. intensive, course or period of preaching, services, etc., undertaken to stimulate interest in the work of a parish, a community, the faith, etc.
missionary • *adjective* **1** of, concerned with, or characteristic of, religious missions. **2** characteristic of a person engaged in a religious mission: *missionary zeal*. • *noun* (*plural* **missionaries**) a person doing missionary work.
mission statement *noun* a declaration made by a company etc. of its general principles of operation.

M

missis *noun* (*plural* **missises**) = MISSUS.

Mississauga *noun* (*plural* **Mississauga** or **Mississaugas**) **1** a member of an Ojibwa Aboriginal people living in southern Ontario. **2** the Algonquian language of this people. [Say missa SOGGA]

Mississippian • *noun* **1** a native or resident of the US state of Mississippi. **2** *Geology* **a** the Mississippian period. **b** the system of rocks dating from this time. **•** *adjective* **1** of or pertaining to the state of Mississippi or its inhabitants. **2** designating or pertaining to the period of the Paleozoic era in North America following the Devonian and preceding the Pennsylvanian, from about 360 to 320 million years BP, characterized as a time of near tropical conditions, when amphibians and insects, including grasshoppers, cockroaches, silverfish, termites, beetles, and giant dragonflies, were abundant. **3** designating a culture which flourished in the Mississippi basin from about AD 800 until the arrival of the Europeans, based on intensive agriculture, esp. of corn, and characterized by large towns in river valleys. [Say miss i SIPPY in]

missive *noun* **1** an esp. official letter. **2** *jocular* a letter, esp. a long and serious one.

misspell *verb* (**misspells**; *past* and *past participle* **misspelled** or **misspelt**; **misspelling**) spell wrongly. ▶ **misspelled** *adjective* **misspelling** *noun*

misspend *verb* (**misspends**, **misspent**, **misspending**) spend amiss or wastefully.

misspent *adjective* wastefully or irresponsibly spent, passed, etc.: *misspent money* ◊ *misspent youth*.

misstate *verb* (**misstates**, **misstated**, **misstating**) state wrongly or inaccurately. ▶ **misstatement** *noun*

misstep *noun* an inappropriate or clumsy action.

missus *noun* (*plural* **misstuses**) **1** a form of address to a woman. **2** *slang* or *jocular* a wife.

missy *noun* (*plural* **missies**) **1** (also **misses'**) a standard size of clothing designed for well-proportioned and well-developed women, usu. around 5 feet 6 inches. **2** an affectionate or derogatory form of address to a young girl.

mist • *noun* **1 a** a diffuse cloud of water droplets on or near the ground that limits visibility, but to a lesser degree than fog. **b** any condensed vapour settling in fine droplets on a surface and obscuring glass etc. **2** dimness or blurring of the sight caused by tears etc. **3 a** a diffuse cloud of small particles resembling mist. **b** a haze or haziness produced by distance, time, etc.: *lost in the mists of time.* **•** *verb* **1** (usu. foll. by *up, over*) cover or become covered with mist or as with mist. **2** spray (a plant, one's hair, etc.) with vaporized moisture.

mistake • *noun* **1 a** a misconception about the meaning of something; an incorrect idea or opinion. **b** a thing incorrectly done or thought. **2** an error of judgment. **•** *verb* (**mistakes**; *past* **mistook**; *past participle* **mistaken**; **mistaking**) **1** misunderstand the meaning or intention of (a person, a statement, etc.). **2** (foll. by *for*) wrongly take or identify: *mistook me for you.* **3** choose wrongly: *mistake one's vocation.* PHRASES **and** (or **make**) **no mistake** *informal* undoubtedly; have no doubt about. **by mistake** accidentally; in error. **there is no mistaking** one is sure to recognize (a person or thing).

mistaken *adjective* **1** wrong in opinion or judgment. **2** based on or resulting from an error, misapprehension, etc.: *mistaken identity.* ▶ **mistakenly** *adverb*

Mistassini Cree *noun* (*plural* **Mistassini Cree** or **Mistassini Crees**) a member of a Cree people living on the shores of Lac Mistassini in north central Quebec. [Say mista SEENY]

mister¹ *noun* **1** = MR. **2** *slang* or *jocular* a form of address to an adult male stranger.

mister² *noun* device for producing or dispensing mist, esp. for misting plants, hair, etc.

mistily *adverb* **1** in or as through a mist: *a ship glimpsed mistily in the distance.* **2** sentimentally: *they sat mistily recalling the early days.*

mistime *verb* (**mistimes**, **mistimed**, **mistiming**) say or do at the wrong time.

mistiness *noun* a misty condition; haze, vapour, mist.

mistletoe *noun* **1 a** a parasitic plant growing on apple and other trees and bearing white glutinous berries in winter. **b** a sprig of this hung as a Christmas decoration, under which people are supposed to kiss. **2** a parasitic plant resembling this, native to North America. [Say MISS'll toe]

mistranslate *verb* (**mistranslates**, **mistranslated**, **mistranslating**) translate incorrectly. ▶ **mistranslation** *noun*

mistreat *verb* treat wrongly, badly, or abusively. ▶ **mistreatment** *noun*

mistress *noun* (*plural* **mistresses**) **1** a woman (other than his wife) with whom a married man has a (usu. prolonged) sexual relationship. **2** (often foll. by *of*) a woman with power to control, use, or dispose of something at will: *mistress of the situation.* **3** a female head of a household. **4 a** a woman in authority over others. **b** the female owner of a pet. **5** *literary* a woman loved and courted by a man.

mistrial *noun* **1** a trial rendered invalid through some error in the proceedings. **2** *US* a trial in which the jury cannot agree on a verdict.

mistrust • *verb* **1** be suspicious of; doubt the truth, validity, or genuineness of. **2** feel no confidence in (a person, oneself, one's powers, etc.). **•** *noun* **1** suspicion. **2** lack of confidence.

mistrustful *adjective* **1** (foll. by *of*) distrustful, suspicious. **2** lacking confidence or trust.

misty *adjective* (**mistier**, **mistiest**) **1 a** clouded, obscured, or accompanied by mist. **b** consisting of or covered with mist or fine particles resembling mist. **2** not clear; vague, obscure, or indistinct: *four misty figures silhouetted by the fire* ◊ *they talked of marriage in a misty abstract way.*

misty-eyed *adjective* **1** emotional: *misty-eyed memories.* **2** having eyes blurred by tears.

mistype *verb* (**mistypes**, **mistyped**, **mistyping**) type wrongly.

misunderstand *verb* (**misunderstands**, **misunderstood**, **misunderstanding**) fail to understand correctly.

misunderstanding *noun* **1** a failure to understand correctly. **2** a slight disagreement or quarrel.

misunderstood *adjective* **1** (of word, actions, etc.) misinterpreted. **2** (of a person) not appreciated, not valued sympathetically.

misuse • *verb* (**misuses**, **misused**, **misusing**) **1** use wrongly or improperly; apply to the wrong purpose. **2** subject to ill-treatment; maltreat. **•** *noun* **1 a** wrong or improper use or application of power, a word, etc. **b** the non-therapeutic use of a drug. **2** the wrong or improper use of something.

SPELL CHECK
mite, might

The word for strength is **might**. **Might** is also the spelling in "They said they might be late".

---

mite • *adverb* (usu. preceded by *a*) *informal* somewhat: *is a mite shy.* **•** *noun* **1** a small object or person, esp. a child. **2 a** an initiation level of sports competition for young children, usu. between the ages of 5 and 8. **b** a player at this level. **3** any of various small arachnids having four

pairs of legs when adult, many of which live in the soil or are parasitic on plants or animals. **4** a modest contribution; the best one can do: *offered my mite of comfort.* **5** any small monetary unit.

miter *esp. US* = MITRE.

mitigate *verb* (**mitigates**, **mitigated**, **mitigating**) make milder or less intense or severe; moderate or give relief from: *how can we mitigate the suffering?* ◊ *environmental effects are mitigated by modifying the design of the project.* [Say MITTA gate]

mitigating circumstances *noun Law* extenuating circumstances which, while not excusing a crime etc., permit greater leniency in sentencing or imposing penalties.

mitigation *noun* the action of reducing the severity, seriousness, or painfulness of something: *a meeting to discuss noise mitigation measures.* [Say mitta GAY sh'n]

mitochondrial *adjective* having to do with a mitochondrion or mitochondria. [Say mite uh CON dree ul]

mitochondrion *noun* (*plural* **mitochondria**) *Biology* an organelle found in large numbers in the cytoplasm of most cells, containing enzymes that are responsible for energy production during respiration. [Say mite uh CON dree un for the singular, mite uh CON dree uh for the plural]

mitosis *noun* a type of cell division that results in two daughter cells each having the same number and kind of chromosomes as the parent nucleus (*compare* MEIOSIS). [Say my TOE sis]

mitre (*also esp. US* **miter**) • *noun* **1** a tall, deeply-cleft headdress worn by bishops and abbots, forming in outline the shape of a pointed arch. **2** (*also* **mitre joint**) a place where the edges of two pieces of wood or metal etc., each cut at a 45° angle, are joined to make a 90° angle. **3** a diagonal seam of two pieces of fabric that meet at a corner, made by folding. • *verb* (**mitres**, **mitred**, **mitring**) join by means of a mitre. ▶ **mitred** *adjective* [Say MITE er]

mitt *noun* **1** a covering for the hand with two sections, one for the thumb and the other for all four fingers. **2** *Baseball* a protective glove worn by the catcher or first baseman for catching the ball. **3** a padded cloth mitten worn as protection from heat etc.: *oven mitt.* **4** *slang* a hand or fist. **5** *slang* (*in plural*) boxing gloves.

mitten *noun* **1** = MITT 1. **2** a glove leaving the tips of the fingers and thumb exposed. ▶ **mittened** *adjective*

mitzvah *noun* (*plural* **mitzvoth**) *Judaism* **1** a a precept or commandment. **b** a religious obligation. **2** a good deed or considerate act. [Say MITS vuh for the singular, MITS vot for the plural]

-miut *suffix* meaning "the people of" designating subgroups of the Inuit: *Sadlermiut.* [Say mee oot]

mix • *verb* (**mixes**, **mixed**, **mixing**) **1** combine or put together. **2** be sociable, esp. at a party. **3** *Film* **a** blend (two pictures or sounds) temporarily by fading one out as the other is faded in. **b** combine (two or more sound signals) into one, with or without modulation, in a mixer. **4** produce (a recording) by combining a number of separate recordings or soundtracks. • *noun* (*plural* **mixes**) **1** the result of mixing or combining. **2** a a number of ingredients mixed together: *trail mix.* **b** the proportion or combination of different components that make up a product, plan, policy, or other integrated whole. **3** a commercially prepared mixture of ingredients for making a cake etc., or for a process such as making concrete. **4** a the action or process of combining or merging film pictures or soundtracks. **b** a transition between two pictures or sounds in which one fades out as the other fades in; a dissolve. **5** *Music* **a** a version of a recording in which the component tracks are mixed in a different way. **b** a recording made

by mixing other recordings. **6** the soft drink, fruit juice, etc. with which an alcoholic drink is diluted. **7** a crossbred animal: *a Labrador-collie mix.* PHRASES **be** (or **get**) **mixed up in** be or become involved in (esp. something undesirable). **be** (or **get**) **mixed up with** be or become associated with (esp. someone dishonest). **mix in 1** combine, blend. **2** (of a person) blend sociably or harmoniously with a group. **mix and match** select from a range of alternative combinations. **mix it up** *informal* **1** fight, argue; cause trouble. **2** interact vigorously, boisterously, or roughly. **mix up 1** mix thoroughly. **2** confuse; mistake the identity of. ▶ **mixable** *adjective*

mix-and-match • *adjective* **1** suitable for or selected by mixing and matching. **2** coordinating. • *noun* (*plural* **mix-and-matches**) a combination of coordinating items.

mixed *adjective* **1** a consisting of diverse qualities or elements. **b** formed by mingling, blending, or combining different substances, individuals, etc. **2** containing persons from various backgrounds etc. **3** for or involving persons of both sexes: *mixed curling.* **4** (of wooded land) consisting of several species of trees. **5** a (of reactions, reviews, results, etc.) having both negative and positive aspects. **b** (of a message, a signal, etc.) ambiguous, unclear.

mixed-blood • *adjective* (of a person) having parents or ancestors from two or more races. • *noun* (**mixed blood**) a person having parents or ancestors from two or more races.

mixed breed *noun* a crossbreed.

mixed doubles *plural noun Tennis* a doubles game with a man and a woman as partners on each side.

mixed drink *noun* an alcoholic beverage consisting liquor with fruit juice or a soft drink etc.

mixed farm *noun* a farm with both crops and livestock.

mixed farming *noun* farming of both crops and livestock.

mixed feelings *plural noun* (also **mixed emotions**) a mixture of pleasure and dismay about something.

mixed grass *noun* (*plural* **mixed grasses**) grass combining a variety of species, esp. blue grama and wheat grass: *mixed-grass prairie.*

mixed marriage *noun* a marriage between persons of different races or religions.

mixed media • *noun* the use of a variety of mediums in a work of art, public performance, show, etc. • *adjective* (also **mixed-media**) = MULTIMEDIA *adjective*.

mixed metaphor *noun* a combination of inconsistent metaphors, e.g. *this tower of strength will forge ahead.*

mixed race *adjective* = MIXED-BLOOD *adjective*.

mixed-up *adjective informal* **1** mentally or emotionally confused. **2** socially ill-adjusted.

mixed-use *adjective* (of a building etc.) designed to accommodate diverse functions, usu. including residential units, work places, public areas, etc.

M

mixer *noun* **1 a** a kitchen appliance for mixing or beating foods, usu. one with two rotating beaters. **b** a machine or device for mixing or processing other materials. **2 a** a person who manages socially in a specified way: *a good mixer*. **b** a social gathering to enable people to get to know one another. **3** = MIX *noun* 6. **4 a** a device for merging input signals to produce a combined output in the form of sound or pictures. **b** a person who operates this.

Mixmaster *noun* **1** *proprietary* a type of electric food mixer. **2** a sound-recording engineer or disc jockey who mixes music for recording, raves, etc.

mixture *noun* **1** the result of mixing; something mixed; a combination. **2** *Chemistry* the product of the mechanical mixing of substances without chemical change, as opposed to a chemical compound. **3** a medicinal or other preparation consisting of two or more ingredients mixed together, esp. a liquid medicine as opposed to pills, powders, etc.: *cough mixture*. **4 a** a gas, vaporized gasoline, or oil mixed with air, forming an explosive charge in an internal combustion engine. **b** a combination of gasoline with a small proportion of oil, used as a combined fuel and lubricant in some two-stroke engines. **5** the process of mixing or being mixed.

mix-up *noun* a confusion, misunderstanding, or mistake.

mizzen *noun* (also **mizzen-sail**) the lowest fore-and-aft sail of a fully rigged ship's mizzen-mast. [Say MIZZ in]

mizzen-mast *noun* the mast next aft of the mainmast on a sailing ship.

Mk. *abbreviation* **1** the German mark. **2** (also **Mk**) mark: *the Mk III version*.

mks *abbreviation* metre-kilogram-second.

ml *abbreviation* **1** (also **mL**) millilitre(s). **2** mile(s).

MLA *abbreviation* (*plural* **MLAs**) Member of the Legislative Assembly.

mm *abbreviation* millimetre(s).

Mme *abbreviation* (*plural* **Mmes**) Madame.

MMM *abbreviation* *Cdn* Member of the Order of Military Merit.

mmm *interjection* expressing hesitation or inarticulate interrogation, assent, reflection, or satisfaction.

MMR *abbreviation* measles, mumps, and rubella (vaccine).

MMT *abbreviation* methylcyclopentadienyl manganese tricarbonyl, an octane-boosting gasoline additive.

Mn *symbol* the element manganese.

MNA *abbreviation* (*plural* **MNAs**) *Cdn* (in Quebec) Member of the National Assembly.

mnemonic • *noun* a device, such as a pattern of letters, ideas, or associations, which assists in remembering something, e.g., the phrase *Every Good Boy Deserves Fudge* to remember the order of notes on the lines in the staff of a treble clef. • *adjective* of or designed to aid the memory. [Say nuh MONN ick]

MO *abbreviation* (*plural* **MOs**) **1** Missouri (in official postal use). **2** = MODUS OPERANDI. **3** Medical Officer.

Mo *symbol* molybdenum.

mo. *abbreviation* month.

moa *noun* (*plural* **moas**) an extinct flightless New Zealand bird that resembles the ostrich. [Say MOE uh]

moan • *noun* **1** a long, low mournful sound expressing physical or mental suffering etc. **2** a low plaintive sound made by wind etc. **3** a complaint or grievance. • *verb* **1** make a moan. **2** *informal* complain or grumble. **3** utter with moans. ▶ **moaner** *noun*

moat • *noun* a deep defensive ditch around a castle, town, etc., usu. filled with water. • *verb* surround with or as with a moat.

mob • *noun* **1 a** a disorderly crowd; a rabble. **b** an assembly of people; a crowd or group. **2** (**the mob**) usu. derogatory the ordinary people. **3** (**the Mob**) *informal* the Mafia or a similar criminal organization. • *verb* (**mobs**, **mobbed**, **mobbing**) **1 a** crowd round in order to attack or mob. **b** (of a mob) attack. **c** crowd into (a building). **2** assemble in a mob.

mobile • *adjective* **1 a** movable; not fixed; free or able to move or flow easily. **b** (of troops, police patrols, etc.) that may be easily and rapidly moved from place to place. **2 a** (of a person) able to move into different social levels or change environments, fields of employment, etc. **b** (of a society) not rigidly stratified, able to accommodate social or professional movement. **3** (of the face etc.) readily changing its expression. **4** (of a service, library, etc.) accommodated in a vehicle so as to serve various places. • *noun* a decorative structure, usu. consisting of pieces of metal, plastic, etc., hung so as to turn freely. [Say MOE bile; for the adjective you can also say MOE bull]

mobile home *noun* a large, transportable structure equipped with living accommodations, permanently parked, and used as a residence.

mobile phone *noun* (also **mobile telephone**) = CELLULAR PHONE.

mobility *noun* **1** the ability to move easily from one place, social class, or job to another: *career mobility*. **2** the ability to move or travel around easily: *an electric wheelchair has given her greater mobility*. [Say mo BILLA tee]

mobilization *noun* the act of organizing people, troops, etc., for action.

mobilize *verb* (**mobilizes**, **mobilized**, **mobilizing**) **1 a** organize or make ready for service or action (originally troops in time of war). **b** be organized or made ready for action. **2** render movable or capable of movement; bring into circulation. ▶ **mobilizer** *noun*

Möbius strip *noun* (also **Möbius loop**) **1** *Math* a surface with only one side and one edge, formed by twisting a long, narrow, rectangular strip through 180° and joining the ends. **2** a stylized version of this used as a symbol for recycling etc. [Say MOE bee us]

mob rule *noun* rule imposed and enforced by a mob.

mobster *noun* *slang* a gangster.

moccasin *noun* **1** a type of soft leather slipper or shoe with combined sole and heel, as originally worn by some North American Aboriginal peoples. **2** a hard-soled shoe with a low heel resembling this. **3** a kind of venomous North American snake, including the semiaquatic water moccasin of the southern US. ▶ **moccasined** *adjective*

moccasin telegraph *noun* esp. *Cdn* (esp. *North*) *informal* **1** a means of transmitting rumours or unofficial information by word of mouth; the grapevine. **2** information so relayed.

mocha *noun* **1** a coffee of fine quality. **2** a flavouring made from this, often with chocolate added, used in cakes etc. [Say MOE kuh]

mock • *verb* **1 a** ridicule; scoff at. **b** (foll. by *at*) act or speak with scorn or contempt for; use ridicule. **2** mimic contemptuously. **3** jeer or defy contemptuously. • *adjective* **1** sham, imitation (esp. without intention to deceive). **2** pretended, fake: *a mock battle* ◊ *mock chicken*. ▶ **mocker** *noun*

mockery *noun* (*plural* **mockeries**) **1** derision, ridicule: *the government has left itself open to mockery and ridicule* ◊ *there was mockery in her voice*. **2** (often foll. by *of*) something that makes a person or thing seem foolish, absurd, or worthless: *the trial was decried as a mockery of justice*. PHRASES **make a mockery of something** make something appear foolish, absurd, or worthless: *his infidelity makes a mockery of marriage*.

M

mock-heroic • *adjective* (of a literary work or style) imitating the style of heroic literature in a humorous way in order to parody it. • *noun* such a style.

mocking *adjective* (of behaviour, and expression, etc.) showing that one thinks somebody or something is ridiculous: *a mocking smile*.

mockingbird *noun* a long-tailed songbird with greyish plumage, which mimics the calls of other birds.

mockingly *adverb* in a mocking manner.

mock orange *noun* a bushy shrub that is cultivated for its strongly scented white flowers.

mocktail *noun* a drink consisting of the same mixes etc. as the various cocktail recipes and usu. served in the same glasses, but without the alcohol.

mock-up *noun* an experimental model or replica of a proposed structure, page layout, etc.

mod[1] *adjective* modern, esp. in style of dress.

mod[2] *noun* (in Scotland, Cape Breton, etc.) an event at which Gaelic music, poetry, and dancing are performed, often with a competitive element.

modal *adjective* **1** of or relating to mode or form as opposed to substance. **2** *Grammar* **a** of or denoting the mood of a verb. **b** (of an auxiliary verb, e.g. *would*) used to express the mood of another verb. **3** *Statistics* **a** of, pertaining to, or of the nature of a mode. **b** (of a value etc.) occurring most frequently in a sample or population. **4** *Music* denoting a style of music using a particular mode. [Say MOE dull]

modality *noun* (*plural* **modalities**) **1** a particular mode in which something exists or is experienced or expressed: *modalities of literary expression*. **2** a prescribed method or technique of procedure, treatment, behaviour, etc.: *massage is an important modality in helping to manage pain*. [Say muh DALA tee]

mode *noun* **1** a way or manner in which a thing is done; a method of procedure. **2** a prevailing fashion, custom, or style, esp. of a particular place or period. **3 a** any of a number of distinct ways in which a machine, computer system, etc. operates: *print mode*. **b** *informal* or *jocular* a specified way in which a person functions, behaves, etc., esp. by conscious choice: *as soon as this is over I'm switching into holiday mode*. **4** *Statistics* the value or range of values that occurs most frequently in a given set of data etc. **5** *Music* **a** each of the scale systems that result when the white notes of the piano are played consecutively over an octave. **b** each of the two main modern scale systems, the major and minor: *minor mode*. **6** *Physics* any of the distinct kinds or patterns of vibration that an oscillating system can sustain. **7** *Grammar* = MOOD[2] 1.

model • *noun* **1** a representation in three dimensions of an existing person or thing or of a proposed structure, esp. in smaller scale: *model airplane* ◊ *architect's model*. **2** a simplified description of a system, process, etc. put forward as a basis for theoretical or empirical understanding; a conceptual or mental representation of a thing. **3** a figure in clay, wax, etc. to be reproduced in another, usu. more durable material. **4 a** a car etc. of a particular design or produced in a specified year. **b** each of a series of varying designs of the same type of structure, commodity, or object. **5** an exemplary person or thing: *a model of self-discipline*. **6** (often foll. by *for*) a person or thing used, or for use, as an example to copy or imitate: *the Canadian model of federalism*. **7 a** a person employed to pose for an artist, photographer, etc. **b** a person employed to display clothes etc. by wearing them. **8** an actual person, place, etc. on which a fictional character, location, etc. is based. • *adjective* **1** serving as an example; exemplary, ideally perfect. **2** designating a small-scale model of the object or kind of object specified. • *verb* (**models,**

modelled, modelling) **1 a** act or pose as an esp. fashion or photographic model. **b** (of a person acting as a model) display (a garment). **2 a** shape (a figure) in clay, wax, etc. **b** (foll. by *after*, *on*, etc.) give shape to (a document, argument, other immaterial object, etc.), esp. in imitation of another. **3** devise a (usu. mathematical) model or simplified description of (a phenomenon, system, etc.). **4** *Art* (in drawing, painting, etc.) form with or assume the appearance of natural relief; cause to appear three-dimensional.

model home *noun* a finished house, sometimes furnished and decorated, used to give potential buyers an idea of what other houses of its type would look like when finished.

modeller *noun* a person who makes models of objects.

modelling *noun* **1** the work of a fashion model: *a career in modelling*. **2** the activity of making models of objects: *clay modelling*.

modem *noun* a device that connects one computer system to another using a telephone line so that data can be sent.

moderate • *adjective* **1** avoiding extremes in conduct, opinions, or expression. **2** of medium quantity, quality, size, or extent. **3** (of prices, charges, etc.) reasonable, fairly low. • *noun* a person who holds moderate views, esp. in politics, religion, etc. • *verb* (**moderates, moderated, moderating**) **1** make or become less violent, intense, rigorous, etc. **2** preside over (a deliberative body) or at (a debate etc.). **3** *Physics* retard (neutrons), esp. with a moderator. ▶**moderately** *adverb* [Say MODDER it for the adjective and noun, MODDER ate for the verb]

moderation *noun* **1** the action of making something less extreme, intense, or violent: *the union's approach was based on increased dialogue and the moderation of demands*. **2** the quality of being moderate, esp. in conduct, opinion, etc.: *she urged the police to show moderation*. **3** *Physics* the action or process of slowing down neutrons by the use of a moderator. PHRASES **in moderation** in a moderate manner or degree.

moderato *Music* • *adjective & adverb* performed at a moderate pace. • *noun* (*plural* **moderatos**) a piece of music to be performed in this way. [Say modder OTTO]

moderator *noun* **1** a chairperson of a discussion on television or radio. **2** a person chosen to preside over a meeting or assembly and conduct its business. **3** (in the United Church) a person elected to serve as the head of the church. **4** (in the Presbyterian Church) **a** a person elected by the General Assembly to moderate the Assembly. **b** a person appointed or elected by a synod or presbytery to preside over meetings, officiate at services, etc. **5** *Physics* a substance used in a nuclear reactor to retard neutrons and control the rate of fission. **6** an arbitrator or mediator.

modern • *adjective* **1** of the present and recent times. **2** (of a person) up-to-date in lifestyle, outlook, opinions, etc. **3** designating or pertaining to art, architecture, etc. marked by a departure from traditional styles and values. **4** belonging to a comparatively recent period in the history of the earth. • *noun* **1** (usu. in *plural*) a person living in or belonging to modern times. **2** a person with modern tastes or opinions. **3** = MODERN DANCE.

modern dance *noun* a style of theatrical dance developed in the 20th century, not constrained by the rules and techniques of classical ballet.

modern-day *adjective* of the present; contemporary.

modern English *noun* English from about 1500 onward, with the period from 1500–1750 known as **early modern English**.

modernism *noun* **1** (**Modernism**) the methods, style, or attitudes of modern artists, writers, architects,

M

composers, etc., esp. a style of art etc. rejecting classical and traditional methods of expression. **2** a movement towards modifying traditional religious beliefs and doctrines in accordance with modern ideas. **3 a** modern character or quality of thought, expression, etc. **b** a modern term or expression. ▶ **modernist** noun **modernistic** adjective

modernity noun the quality or condition of being modern: *suburban sprawl and other signs of modernity*. [Say muh DUR nuh tee or muh DAIR nuh tee]

modernization noun an act of modernizing.

modernize verb (**modernizes**, **modernized**, **modernizing**) **1** make modern; adapt to modern needs, habits, standards, or styles. **2** adopt modern ways, views, styles, etc. ▶ **modernizer** noun

modern Latin noun Latin since 1500, used esp. in scientific classification.

modernness noun the quality of being modern.

modest adjective **1 a** having or expressing a humble or moderate estimate of one's own merits or achievements. **b** (of an action, attribute, etc.) proceeding from or indicating such a quality. **2** diffident, bashful, not bold or forward. **3 a** decorous in manner and conduct, avoiding impropriety or indecency. **b** reserved in sexual matters. **4** moderate or restrained in amount, extent, severity, etc.; not excessive or exaggerated: *a modest sum*. **5** (of a thing) unpretentious in appearance etc.; not showy or ostentatious. ▶ **modestly** adverb

modesty noun the quality of being modest.

modicum noun (foll. by *of*) a small quantity: *plenty of ambition, but just a modicum of talent*. [Say MOD i kum]

modifiable adjective able to be modified.

modification noun **1** the action of modifying something. **2** a change made.

modifier noun **1** a person or thing that modifies or alters something. **2** a word, esp. an adjective or noun, that qualifies the sense of another word, e.g. *good* and *family* in *a good family house*.

modify verb (**modifies**, **modified**, **modifying**) **1** make partial or minor changes in. **2** make less severe or extreme; tone down: *modify one's demands*. **3** Grammar (esp. of an adjective or adverb) restrict or add to the meaning of another word or phrase: in *"the playful kitten"*, *"playful"* modifies *"kitten"*. **4** Chemistry change or replace all the substituent radicals of a polymer, thereby changing its physical properties such as solubility etc.: *modified starch*.

modish adjective fashionable. ▶ **modishly** adverb **modishness** noun [Say MODE ish]

modular adjective **1** of or pertaining to modules. **2 a** employing or involving a module or modules as the basis of design, measurement, or construction. **b** part of a system so designed or constructed. **3 a** (of an educational course) designed as a series of units or separate sections. **b** (of a facility, service, etc.) provided in a number of separate stages. ▶ **modularity** noun **modularization** noun [Say MOD you ler or MODGE oo ler, mod you LERRA tee or modge oo LERRA tee]

modulate verb (**modulates**, **modulated**, **modulating**) **1 a** regulate or adjust: *the device automatically modulates airflow*. **b** moderate: *modulate pain with heat or ice*. **2** adjust or vary the tone or pitch of (the speaking voice etc.). **3** alter the amplitude or frequency of (a wave) by a wave of a lower frequency to convey a signal. **4** Music (often foll. by *from*, *to*) change or cause to change from one key to another. ▶ **modulation** noun **modulator** noun [Say MOD you late or MODGE oo late]

module noun **1** a standardized part or independent unit used in construction or assembly, esp. of furniture, a building, or an electronic system. **2** an independent self-contained unit of a spacecraft: *lunar module*. **3** a distinct unit or period of training or education which can be combined with others to make up a course. **4** Computing any of a number of distinct but interrelated units from which a program may be built up or into which a complex activity may be analyzed. **5 a** a standard or unit of measurement. **b** a length chosen as a basis for the dimension of parts of a building, items of furniture, etc. so that all lengths are integral multiples of it. [Say MOD yool or MODGE ool]

modus operandi noun the particular way in which a person or thing performs a task or action: *burglary was not part of the killer's modus operandi*. [Say moe dus oppa RANDY]

modus vivendi noun **1** an arrangement or agreement allowing conflicting parties to coexist peacefully, either indefinitely or until a settlement is reached: *English Canada sought a modus vivendi with Quebec*. **2** a way of living or coping: *literature is more than a modus vivendi*. [Say moe dus viv ENDY for the singular, moe dee viv ENDY for the plural]

mogul¹ noun **1** informal an important or influential person: *media mogul*. **2** (**Mogul**) hist. **a** = MUGHAL. **b** (often **the Great Mogul**) any of the emperors of Delhi in the 16th–19th centuries. [Say MOE gull]

mogul² noun **1** a mound of hard snow on a ski slope. **2** (in plural) a freestyle skiing event in which skiers negotiate the moguls on a run with as much speed and élan as possible. [Say MOE gull]

MOH abbreviation MEDICAL OFFICER OF HEALTH.

mohair • noun **1** the hair of the angora goat. **2** a yarn or fabric from this, either pure or mixed with wool or cotton. • adjective made or consisting of mohair.

Mohawk noun **1 a** (plural **Mohawk** or **Mohawks**) a member of an Iroquois people, one of the five of the original Iroquois federation, now inhabiting parts of southern Ontario and northern New York. **b** the Iroquoian language of this people. **2** (**mohawk**) a haircut, supposedly resembling that worn by the Mohawk, in which the head is shaved except for a brushlike strip of hair over the top of the head to the back of the neck.

Mohegan • noun (plural **Mohegan** or **Mohegans**) **1** a member of an Algonquian people formerly inhabiting part of Connecticut. **2** the language of this people. • adjective designating or pertaining to this people or their language. [Say moe HEEG in]

mohel noun Judaism a person trained to perform ritual circumcisions. [Say maw HELL or MOE hell]

moi interjection jocular as a tongue-in-cheek rejoinder to being accused of something of which one knows one is guilty; what, me?: *pretentious? moi?* [Say MWAH]

moil • verb **1** toil, work hard, drudge: *toil and moil*. **2** swirl, mill about; move around in agitation or confusion. • noun turmoil, confusion, trouble: *the moil of his intimate thoughts*.

moiré • noun **1** a fabric, often silk, having a pattern of glossy wavy bars. **2** a variegated or clouded appearance like that of this fabric. • adjective having a moiré pattern. [Say more AY]

moist adjective **1** slightly wet. **2 a** (of the season, climate, etc.) having some or considerable rainfall. **b** (of the eyes) wet with tears, ready to shed tears.

moisten verb wet superficially or moderately.

moistly adverb in a moist manner.

moistness noun the quality of being moist.

moisture noun water or other liquid diffused in a small quantity as vapour, or within a solid, or condensed on a surface.

moisturize verb (**moisturizes**, **moisturized**,

moisturizing) make less dry (esp. the skin by use of a cosmetic). ▶**moisturizer** *noun* **moisturizing** *adjective*

mojo *noun* (*plural* **mojos**) esp. *US* **1** magic, voodoo. **2** a charm or amulet.

mol *abbreviation* = MOLE⁴.

mol. *abbreviation* **1** molecular. **2** molecule.

molar¹ • *adjective* **1** (of a tooth) serving to grind, esp. designating any of the back teeth of mammals. **2** of or pertaining to a molar tooth. • *noun* a molar tooth.

molar² *adjective* **1** of or relating to mass. **2** acting on or by means of large masses or units.

molar³ *adjective* *Chemistry* **1** of a mass of substance usu. per mole: *molar latent heat*. **2** (of a solution) containing one mole, or a specified number of moles, of solute per litre of solvent. ▶**molarity** *noun* [Say muh LERRA tee]

molasses *noun* **1** a thick, dark, uncrystallized syrup drained from raw sugar during refining. **2** a lighter, sweeter version of this substance combined with invert sugar and corn syrup for use as a table syrup, in baking, etc. [Say muh LASS iss or muh LASS izz]

mold etc. = MOULD etc.

mole¹ *noun* **1** any small burrowing insect-eating mammal with dark velvety fur and very small eyes. **2** *informal* **a** a spy who achieves over a long period an important position within the security defences of a country. **b** someone within an organization who anonymously betrays confidential information: *there seems to be a mole in the Prime Minister's Office*. **3** a remotely operated or automatic machine capable of tunnelling through rock.

mole² *noun* a small often slightly raised dark blemish on the skin caused by a high concentration of melanin.

mole³ *noun* **1** a massive structure serving as a pier, breakwater, or causeway. **2** an artificial harbour.

mole⁴ *noun* *Chemistry* the SI unit of amount of substance equal to the quantity containing as many elementary units as there are atoms in 0.012 kg of carbon-12.

mole⁵ *noun* a highly spiced Mexican sauce made chiefly from chili peppers and chocolate, served with meat. [Say MOE lay]

molecular *adjective* of, relating to, or consisting of molecules. ▶**molecularly** *adverb* [Say muh LECK yuh ler]

molecular weight *noun* the ratio of the average mass of one molecule of an element or compound to one twelfth of the mass of an atom of carbon-12.

molecule *noun* the smallest fundamental unit (usu. a group of atoms) of a chemical compound that can take part in a chemical reaction. [Say MOLLA cule]

molehill *noun* a small mound thrown up by a mole in burrowing. PHRASES **make a mountain out of a molehill** exaggerate a minor difficulty.

moleskin *noun* **1 a** a kind of twilled cotton cloth with its surface shaved before dyeing. **b** (in *plural*) clothes, esp. trousers, made of this. **2** an adhesive-backed felt put on parts of the feet to reduce abrasion from shoes.

molest *verb* **1** attack or interfere with (a person), esp. sexually. **2** annoy or pester (a person) in a hostile or injurious way. ▶**molestation** *noun* **molester** *noun* [Say muh LEST, maul ess TAY sh'n]

moll *noun* *slang* a gangster's female companion.

mollify *verb* (**mollifies, mollified, mollifying**) appease, pacify: *his explanation failed to mollify her*. [Say MOLLA fie]

mollusc *noun* (also esp. *US* **mollusk**) any of various animals living in aquatic or damp habitats and having soft, unsegmented bodies and usu. hard shells, including snails, slugs, mussels, and octopuses.

molly *noun* (also **mollie**) a small American freshwater fish bearing live young, bred in many colours for aquariums.

Molotov cocktail *noun* a simple homemade bomb, usu. consisting of a bottle filled with gasoline with a rag stuffed in the neck that is ignited just before throwing. [Say MOLLA toff]

Molson muscle *noun* *Cdn slang* a beer belly.

molt *verb & noun* esp. *US* = MOULT.

molten *adjective* melted, esp. made liquid by heat. [Say MOLE tin]

molto *adverb* *Music* very: *allegro molto*.

molybdenum *noun* a silver-white brittle metallic element occurring naturally and used in steel to give strength and resistance to corrosion. [Say muh LIBDA num]

mom *noun* *informal* mother. [Say MUM or MOM]

mom-and-pop *adjective* designating a store, restaurant, etc. run by a married couple or other members of a family.

moment *noun* **1** a very brief portion of time; an instant. **2** a short period of time: *wait a moment*. **3 a** an exact or particular point of time: *I came the moment you called*. **b** a brief period of time marked by a particular quality or experience: *a revolutionary moment*. **4** importance: *of no great moment*. **5** *Physics & Mechanics* etc. **a** the turning effect produced by a force acting at a distance on an object. **b** this effect expressed as the product of the force and the distance from its line of action to a point. PHRASES **at the moment** at this time; now. **have one's moments** be impressive, happy, etc., on occasions. **in a moment 1** very soon. **2** instantly. **man** (or **woman** etc.) **of the moment** the one of importance at the time in question.

momentarily *adverb* **1** for a moment; fleetingly. **2 a** at any moment; very soon. **b** instantly.

momentary *adjective* **1** lasting only a moment. **2** short-lived; transitory.

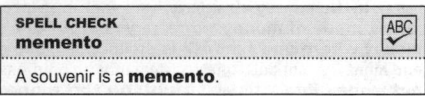

SPELL CHECK
memento

A souvenir is a **memento**.

momentous *adjective* having great importance. ▶**momentously** *adverb* **momentousness** *noun*

momentum *noun* **1** *Physics* the quantity of motion of a moving body, measured as a product of its mass and velocity. **2** the impetus gained by movement. **3** the impetus and driving force gained by the development of a process or course of events: *the investigation gathered momentum in the spring*. [Say moe MEN tum]

momma *noun* = MAMA¹.

mommy *noun* (*plural* **mommies**) *informal* mother.

mommy track *noun* *informal* a career path for women who sacrifice some promotions and pay raises in order to devote more time to raising their children. ▶**mommy tracker** *noun* **mommy tracking** *noun*

Mon. *abbreviation* Monday.

monarch *noun* **1** a sovereign with the title of king, queen, emperor, empress, or the equivalent. **2** (also **monarch butterfly**, *plural* **monarch butterflies**) a large migrating orange and black butterfly found mainly in North America. **3** (also **monarch flycatcher**) a flycatcher found in Africa, Asia, and Australasia, typically having boldly marked or colourful plumage.

monarchical *adjective* having to do with or involving a monarchy: *monarchical government*. [Say muh NAR kick'll]

monarchism *noun* the advocacy of or the principles of monarchy. ▶**monarchist** *noun & adjective*

monarchy *noun* (*plural* **monarchies**) **1** a form of government with a monarch at the head. **2** a state with this.

monastery *noun* (*plural* **monasteries**) the residence

of a religious community, esp. of monks living in seclusion. [Say MONNA sterry]

monastic • *adjective* **1** of or relating to monasteries or the religious communities living in them. **2** resembling these or their way of life; austere, solitary or celibate: *she set her things around the monastic student dorm room.* • *noun* a monk or other follower of a monastic rule. ▶ **monastically** *adverb* **monasticism** *noun* [Say muh NASS tick, muh NASSTA sism]

Monday • *noun* the second day of the week, following Sunday. • *adverb* **1** on Monday. **2** (**Mondays**) on Mondays; each Monday.

mondo *slang* • *adjective* big, large, considerable: *mondo waves.* • *adverb* very, extremely: *mondo cool.*

monetarily *adverb* in a monetary sense. [Say monna TERRA lee]

monetarism *noun* the policy of controlling the amount of money available in a country as a way of keeping the economy strong. ▶ **monetarist** *noun & adjective* [Say MONNA tuh rism]

monetary *adjective* **1** of or pertaining to coinage or currency. **2** of or pertaining to money. [Say MONNA terry]

monetary policy *noun* the means by which a government tries to affect macroeconomic conditions by increasing or decreasing the supply of money.

monetary unit *noun* a standard unit of currency in a country, related to monetary units of other countries by a foreign exchange rate.

money *noun* **1** a current medium of exchange in the form of coins and banknotes. **2** (*plural* **monies** or **moneys**) (in *plural*) sums of money. **3** wealth. **4 a** money as a resource: *time is money.* **b** profit, remuneration: *in it for the money.* **c** a salary, wage: *makes good money.* PHRASES **for my money** in my opinion or judgment; for my preference: *is too aggressive for my money.* **in the money** *informal* having or winning a lot of money. **made of money** *informal* very rich. **put one's money where one's mouth is** produce, bet, or pay out money to support one's statements or opinions. **put money into** invest in. (**right**) **on the money 1** on target; carried out with skill and precision. **2** correct in a prediction, observation, etc.

moneybags *plural noun* (treated as *singular*) usu. *derogatory* a wealthy person.

moneybelt *noun* a belt with a compartment for carrying money, passports, etc., worn underneath clothing esp. by tourists.

money bill *noun* a government bill to impose, change, or regulate taxation, to supply government monetary requirements, etc.

money-changer *noun* a person whose business it is to change money, esp. at an official rate. ▶ **money-changing** *noun & adjective*

moneyed *adjective* **1** having much money; wealthy. **2** consisting of money: *moneyed assistance.*

money-grubber *noun informal* a person greedily intent on amassing money. ▶ **money-grubbing** *adjective & noun*

money launderer *noun* a person who transfers funds to conceal their dubious or illegal origin.

money laundering *noun* the practice or system of transferring funds to conceal their dubious or illegal origin.

moneylender *noun* a person who lends money, esp. as a business, at interest. ▶ **moneylending** *noun & adjective*

money-loser *noun* an unprofitable business venture etc. ▶ **money-losing** *adjective*

money-maker *noun* **1** a person who earns much money. **2** a thing, idea, etc. that produces much money. ▶ **money-making** *noun & adjective*

money market *noun* the trade in short-term loans between banks and other financial institutions.

money order *noun* an order for payment of a specified sum, issued by a bank or post office.

money pit *noun informal* **1** a project, program, etc. that eats up large amounts of money and is often perceived as wasteful and unnecessary. **2** = PIT[1] *noun* 7.

money supply *noun* the total amount of money in circulation or in being in a country.

money's worth *noun* (preceded by *your*, *my*, *one's*) good value for one's money.

monger *noun* (usu. in *combination*) **1** a dealer or trader: *fishmonger.* **2** usu. *derogatory* a person who promotes or deals in something specified: *warmonger.* ▶ **-mongering** *combining form.* [Say MONG grr or MUNG grr]

Mongol • *adjective* **1** of or relating to the Asian people now inhabiting Mongolia or their language. **2** resembling this people, esp. in appearance. • *noun* **1** a Mongolian. **2** the Mongolian language. [Say MONG gull]

Mongolian • *noun* **1** a native or inhabitant of Mongolia, a country in eastern Asia bordered by Russia and China. **2** the language of Mongolia. • *adjective* of or relating to Mongolia or its people or language. [Say mong GOALIE in]

Mongoloid • *adjective* of or relating to the division of humankind including the indigenous peoples of eastern Asia, southeastern Asia, and the Arctic region of North America, characteristically having dark eyes, straight hair, pale ivory to dark skin, and little facial or body hair. • *noun* a person of Mongoloid physical type. [Say MONG guh loyd]

mongoose *noun* (*plural* **mongooses**) a short-legged carnivorous mammal, native to southern Asia and Africa, and noted for the ability to kill venomous snakes. [Say MONG goose]

mongrel • *noun* **1** a dog of no definable type or breed. **2** any other animal or plant resulting from the crossing of different breeds or types. **3** *offensive* a person of mixed race. • *adjective* of mixed origin, nature, or character: *Scotland is a mongrel nation, a collection of different peoples bound together by common geography.* ▶ **mongrelize** *verb* **mongrelization** *noun* [Say MONG grul]

monied *adjective* = MONEYED. [Say MUN eed]

monies see MONEY 2. [Say MUN ees]

moniker *noun* (also **monicker**) *slang* a name. [Say MONNA curr]

monitor • *noun* **1** any of various persons or devices for checking or warning about a situation, operation, etc.: *fetal monitor.* **2** a school pupil with disciplinary or other special duties. **3 a** a television receiver used in a studio to select or verify the picture being broadcast. **b** a loudspeaker used in a studio for listening to what is being recorded. **c** any large or powerful speaker, esp. one used on stage by a band. **4** *Computing* a component displaying data as characters on a screen. **5** a detector of radioactive contamination. **6** (also **monitor lizard**) a large tropical lizard formerly believed to give warning of the approach of crocodiles. • *verb* **1** watch and check something over a period of time. **2** maintain regular surveillance over. **3** regulate the strength of (a recorded or transmitted signal). ▶ **monitoring** *noun & adjective*

monk *noun* a member of a religious community of men living under certain vows esp. of poverty and chastity.

monkey • *noun* (*plural* **monkeys**) **1** any of various mainly long-tailed, agile primates that live in trees in tropical countries. **2** a mischievous person, esp. a child: *young monkey.* • *verb* (**monkeys**, **monkeyed**,

monkeying) **1** (often foll. by *with*) tamper or play mischievous tricks. **2** (foll. by *around*, *about*) fool around. PHRASES **have a monkey on one's back** *slang* **1** be a drug addict. **2** have a burdensome problem.

monkey bars *plural noun* a playground structure of joined bars for children to climb on.

monkey business *noun* *informal* **1** mischief. **2** suspicious or dishonest activities or behaviour.

monkey suit *noun* *informal* **1** a tuxedo. **2** any uniform.

monkey wrench *noun* (*plural* **monkey wrenches**) a wrench with an adjustable jaw. PHRASES **throw a monkey wrench into** (**the works etc.**) cause confusion or disruption.

monkfish *noun* (*plural* **monkfish**) **1** a variety of anglerfish. **2** a large bottom-dwelling shark with a flattened body and large pectoral fins.

monkish *adjective* suggestive of a monk or the monastic life, as in austerity or isolation.

monkshood *noun* a cultivated aconite with hood-shaped blue or purple flowers. [Say MONK's hood]

mono *informal* • *adjective* monophonic. • *noun* **1** (*plural* **monos**) a monophonic record, reproduction, etc. **2** = MONONUCLEOSIS. **3** = MONOFILAMENT 2.

mono- *combining form* (usu. **mon-** before a vowel) **1** one, alone, single. **2** *Chemistry* (forming names of compounds) containing one atom or group of a specified kind.

monobloc *adjective* made as, contained in, or involving a single casting: *a monobloc chair*.

monochromatic *adjective* **1** (of light or other radiation) of a single wavelength or frequency. **2** containing only one colour. **3** (of a musical performance etc.) lacking any distinguishing or inspiring characteristics. ▶ **monochromatically** *adverb*

monochrome • *noun* **1** a photograph or picture done in one colour or different tones of this, or in black and white only. **2** *Photography etc.* black and white. • *adjective* having or using only one colour or in black and white only.

monocle *noun* a single eyeglass, kept in position by the muscles around the eye. ▶ **monocled** *adjective* [Say MONNA cull]

monoclonal *adjective* forming a single clone; derived from a single individual or cell.

monocoque *noun* an aircraft or vehicle structure in which the chassis is integral with the body. [Say MONNA cock]

monocultural *adjective* designating the agricultural practice of cultivating a single crop to the exclusion of others.

monoculture *noun* **1 a** the cultivation of a single crop to the exclusion of others. **b** an area in which such a practice prevails. **2** a society which is ethnically or culturally homogeneous: *progress reduces the cultures of the Third World to a single monoculture*.

monofilament *noun* **1** a single strand of synthetic fibre. **2** a type of fishing line using this.

monogamous *adjective* characterized by monogamy. [Say muh NOGGA muss]

monogamy *noun* **1 a** the practice or state of being married to one person at a time. **b** the practice or state of having a sexual relationship with only one partner. **2** *Zoology* the habit of having only one mate at a time. [Say muh NOGGA mee]

monogram *noun* two or more letters, esp. a person's initials, combined in one design and marked on items of clothing etc. ▶ **monogrammed** *adjective*

monograph *noun* a detailed written study of a single specialized subject or an aspect of it.

monolingual • *adjective* **1** knowing or using only one language. **2** written in a single language. • *noun* a person who knows only one language. [Say mono LING gwul or mono LING gyoo ul]

monolith *noun* **1** a single block of stone, esp. shaped into a pillar or monument. **2** a large, impersonal political, corporate, or social structure regarded as uniform and immovable: *small states struggling to break away from the communist monolith*. **3** a large block of concrete, brickwork, etc., sunk in water, e.g. in the building of a dock. ▶ **monolithic** *adjective*

monolithically *adverb* [Say MONNA lith]

monologist *noun* a person who delivers a monologue, e.g. the host of a talk show. [Say MONNA log ist]

monologue *noun* **1 a** a long speech in a play, film, etc. spoken by one actor, esp. when alone. **b** a dramatic composition, esp. in verse, told or performed by one person. **2** a long speech by one person in a conversation etc. **3** a stand-up comedy routine, esp. one performed at the beginning of a talk show by the host. [Say MONNA log]

monologuist *noun* = MONOLOGIST. [Say MONNA log ist or mu NOLLA gist]

monomania *noun* exaggerated or obsessive enthusiasm for or preoccupation with one thing: *at an early age Katherine developed a monomania about ballet*. ▶ **monomaniac** *noun* **monomaniacal** *adjective* [Say monna MAY nee uh, monna muh NIE uh cull]

monomer *noun* **1** a unit in a dimer, polymer, etc. **2** a molecule or compound that can be polymerized (compare DIMER). [Say MONNA mer]

monomial *Math* • *adjective* (of an algebraic expression) consisting of one term. • *noun* a monomial expression. [Say muh NOME ee ul]

mononucleosis *noun* an abnormally high proportion of white blood cells with a simple nucleus, esp. glandular fever, an infectious viral disease characterized by swelling of the lymph glands and prolonged weariness. [Say monno nuke lee OH sis]

monophonic *adjective* **1** (of sound reproduction) using only one channel of transmission (compare STEREOPHONIC). **2** *Music* having a simple melodic line predominating over other parts.

monopolist *noun* a person who has or advocates a monopoly. ▶ **monopolistic** *adjective* [Say muh NOPPA list]

monopolize *verb* (**monopolizes**, **monopolized**, **monopolizing**) **1** obtain exclusive possession or control of (a trade or commodity etc.). **2** dominate or prevent others from sharing in (a conversation, person's attention, etc.). ▶ **monopolization** *noun* **monopolizer** *noun* [Say muh NOPPA lize]

monopoly *noun* (*plural* **monopolies**) **1 a** the exclusive possession or control of the trade in a commodity or service. **b** this conferred as a privilege by the state. **2 a** a commodity or service that is subject to a monopoly. **b** a company etc. that possesses a monopoly. **3** (foll. by *of*, *on*) exclusive possession, control, or exercise.

monorail *noun* a railway in which the track consists of a single rail, usu. elevated with the train units suspended from it.

monosaccharide *noun* a sugar that cannot be hydrolyzed to give a simpler sugar, e.g. glucose. [Say monna SACKA ride]

monosodium glutamate *noun* a chemical compound used in foods as a flavour enhancer. [Say monna sodium GLOOTA mate]

monosyllabic *adjective* **1** having only one syllable: *a monosyllabic word*. **2** (of a person) using brief words to signify reluctance to engage in conversation: *Ralph grew increasingly monosyllabic as the evening progressed*. [Say monna sil AB ick]

M

monosyllable *noun* a word of one syllable. PHRASES **in monosyllables** in simple direct words. [Say monna SYLLABLE]

monotheism *noun* the doctrine or belief that there is only one God. ▶**monotheist** *noun* **monotheistic** *adjective* [Say monna THEE ism, monna thee ISS tick (with TH as in THICK)]

monotone • *noun* **1** a sound or utterance continuing or repeated on one note without change of pitch. **2** sameness of style in writing, expression, etc. • *adjective* **1** without change of pitch or tone. **2** containing only one tone of one colour.

monotonous *adjective* **1** lacking in variety; tedious through sameness. **2** (of a sound or utterance) without variation in tone or pitch. ▶**monotonously** *adverb* [Say muh NOTTA niss]

monotony *noun* **1** lack of interesting variety; dull or tedious routine. **2** sameness of tone or pitch; lack of variety in cadence or inflection. [Say muh NOTTA nee]

monounsaturated *adjective* (of a compound, esp. a fat or oil molecule) containing one double bond.

monovalent *adjective* *Chemistry* having a valence of one. [Say monna VAY lint]

monoxide *noun* *Chemistry* an oxide containing one oxygen atom.

Monseigneur *noun* a title given to an eminent French person, esp. a prince, cardinal, archbishop, or bishop. [Say moe sen YUR]

Monsieur *noun* (*plural* **Messieurs**) the title or form of address used of or to a French-speaking man, corresponding to Mr. or sir. [Say muh SYUH for the singular, may SYUH for the plural]

Monsignor *noun* **1** a title in the Roman Catholic Church bestowed by the Pope on priests, either in conjunction with an office or as an honorary title for distinguished service. **2** a person holding this title. [Say mun SEEN yur]

monsoon *noun* **1** a wind in south Asia, esp. in the Indian Ocean, blowing from the southwest in summer (**wet monsoon**) and the northeast in winter (**dry monsoon**). **2** a rainy season accompanying a wet monsoon. **3** any other wind with periodic alternations. ▶**monsoonal** *adjective* [Say mon SOON]

monster *noun* **1** an imaginary creature, usu. large and frightening. **2** an inhumanly cruel or wicked person. **3** a misshapen or ugly person, animal, or plant. **4** a large animal or thing. **5** (as an *adjective*) **a** huge; extremely large of its kind: *monster home*. **b** very successful: *had a monster season*.

monstrance *noun* *Catholicism* a receptacle, usu. of gold or silver, with an open or transparent compartment in which the consecrated Host is exposed for veneration. [Say MON strince]

monstrosity *noun* (*plural* **monstrosities**) **1** a huge, hideous, or outrageous thing, esp. an unsightly building. **2** the condition or fact of being monstrous. **3** = MONSTER 3. [Say mon STROSSA tee]

monstrous *adjective* **1** of or like a monster in appearance, fearsomeness, etc. **2** huge. **3 a** outrageously wrong or absurd. **b** atrocious; horrible: *a monstrous crime*. ▶**monstrously** *adverb* **monstrousness** *noun*

Mont. *abbreviation* Montana.

montage • *noun* **1** *Film* combination of images in quick succession to compress background information or provide atmosphere. **2 a** the technique of producing a new composite whole from fragments of pictures, words, music, etc. **b** a composition produced in this way. • *verb* (**montages**, **montaged**, **montaging**) make or integrate into a montage: *montaging bits and pieces of different songs to create an entirely new sound*. [Say mon TOZH]

Montagnais • *noun* (*plural* **Montagnais**) **1** a member of an Innu people living in the barrens between Hudson Bay and the Labrador coast. **2** the Cree language of this people. • *adjective* of or relating to this people or their culture or language. [Say MON tun yay]

Montagnais-Naskapi *noun* (*plural* **Montagnais-Naskapi**) = INNU *noun*.

montane *adjective* **1** of or inhabiting mountainous country: *the rolling hills and montane villages*. **2** designating or pertaining to the belt of upland vegetation below the timberline: *montane meadows*.

Monterey Jack *noun* a mild white cheddar cheese. [Say monta RAY]

Montessori *noun* the system of education (esp. of young children) propounded by the Italian physician and educator Maria Montessori (1870–1952) that seeks to develop natural interests and activities rather than use formal teaching methods. [Say monta SORRY]

Montezuma's revenge *noun* diarrhea suffered by travellers, esp. visitors to Mexico. [Say monta ZOOMA's]

month *noun* **1 a** (also **calendar month**) each of usu. twelve periods into which a year is divided. **b** a period of time between the same dates in successive calendar months. **2** a period of 30 days or of four weeks. **3** = LUNAR MONTH. **4** the period of a woman's menstrual cycle. PHRASES **month of Sundays** a very long period.

monthly • *adjective* done, produced, or occurring once a month. • *adverb* once a month; from month to month. • *noun* (*plural* **monthlies**) **1** a monthly periodical. **2** (in *plural*) *informal* a menstrual period.

Montreal bagel *noun* *Cdn* a type of bagel, originally made in Montreal, which is lighter, thinner, and sweeter than other kinds of bagel.

Montreal canoe *noun* *Cdn* = CANOT DU MAÎTRE.

Montrealer *noun* a native or inhabitant of Montreal.

Montreal smoked meat *noun* *Cdn* = SMOKED MEAT 2.

monument *noun* **1** anything enduring that serves to commemorate or make celebrated, esp. a structure or building. **2** a stone or other structure placed over a grave or in a church etc. in memory of the dead. **3** an ancient building or site etc. that has survived or been preserved. **4** an outstanding, enduring, and memorable example of something: *recordings that are a monument to the art of playing the piano*.

monumental *adjective* **1 a** extremely great; stupendous: *a monumental achievement*. **b** (of a literary work etc.) impressive and of lasting importance. **2** of or serving as a monument. **3** *informal* calamitous: *a monumental blunder*. ▶**monumentality** *noun* **monumentally** *adverb*

moo • *verb* (**moos**, **mooed**, **mooing**) make the characteristic vocal sound of cattle. • *noun* (*plural* **moos**) this sound.

mooch *informal* • *verb* (**mooches**, **mooched**, **mooching**) **1 a** (often foll. by *off*) beg, scrounge. **b** steal. **2** loiter or saunter desultorily. **3** fish with light tackle allowed to drift. • *noun* (*plural* **mooches**) a person who mooches. ▶**moocher** *noun*

mood[1] *noun* **1** a state of mind or feeling. **2** a fit of melancholy or bad temper. **3** (as an *adjective*) inducing a particular mood: *mood music*. **4** the atmosphere or pervading tone of a place, event, composition, etc. PHRASES **in the** (or **no**) **mood** inclined (or disinclined).

mood[2] *noun* *Grammar* **1** a form or set of forms of a verb serving to indicate whether it is to express a fact, command, wish, etc.: *subjunctive mood*. **2** the distinction of meaning expressed by different moods.

moodily *adverb* in a gloomy or sullen way.

M

moodiness *noun* a moody character or quality.

moody *adjective* (**moodier, moodiest**) given to changes of mood; gloomy, sullen.

moolah *noun* (also **moola**) *slang* money.

moon • *noun* **1 a** the natural satellite of the earth, orbiting it monthly, illuminated by the sun and reflecting some light to the earth. **b** this regarded in terms of its waxing and waning in a particular month: *new moon*. **c** moonlight: *there is no moon tonight*. **2** a satellite of any planet. **3** (**the moon**) something desirable but unattainable: *promised them the moon*. **4** a month. • *verb* **1** (often foll. by *about, around,* etc.) move or look listlessly. **2** (foll. by *over*) act aimlessly or inattentively from infatuation for (a person). **3** *slang* expose one's buttocks to (another person): *mooned the crowd*. PHRASES **many moons ago** a long time ago. **over the moon** extremely happy or delighted.

moonbeam *noun* a ray of moonlight.

moon face *noun* a round face.

moon-faced *adjective* having a round face.

Moonie *noun* *slang* a member of the Unification Church, a religious organization founded in Korea in 1954.

moonless *adjective* without the moon; not lit by the moon: *a moonless night*.

moonlight • *noun* **1** the light of the moon. **2** (as an *adjective*) lighted by the moon: *a moonlight stroll*. • *verb* (**moonlights, moonlighted, moonlighting**) *informal* have a second job, esp. at night, in addition to one's regular day job. ▶ **moonlighter** *noun*

moonlit *adjective* lighted by the moon.

moonscape *noun* **1** the surface or landscape of the moon. **2** an area resembling this; a wasteland.

moonshine *noun* **1** *slang* illicitly distilled alcoholic liquor. **2** foolish or unrealistic talk or ideas.

moonshiner *noun* *slang* an illicit distiller of alcoholic liquor.

moonstone *noun* any of various milky stones, esp. feldspar, which seem to change colour depending on the viewer's position, used in jewellery.

moonstruck *adjective* **1** romantically captivated. **2** mentally deranged.

moonwalk *noun* **1** a walk by an astronaut on the surface of the moon. **2** a dance step in which a person moves backwards while making the motions of walking forwards. ▶ **moonwalk** *verb*

moony *adjective* (**moonier, mooniest**) listless; stupidly dreamy.

Moor *noun* a member of a Muslim people of mixed Berber and Arab descent inhabiting northwest Africa, who conquered the Iberian peninsula in the 8th century and retained control of portions of Spain until the 15th century. [Say MOOR or MORE]

moor[1] *noun* a tract of open, uncultivated, usu. poorly drained upland. [Say MOOR or MORE]

moor[2] *verb* make fast (a boat, buoy, etc.) by attaching a cable etc. to a fixed object. ▶ **moorage** *noun*

mooring *noun* **1 a** a fixed object to which a boat, buoy, etc., is moored. **b** (often in *plural*) a place where a boat etc. is moored. **2** (in *plural*) a set of permanent anchors and chains laid down for ships to be moored to. **3** (in *plural*) a source of stability or security: *spiritual moorings*.

Moorish *adjective* having to do with the Moors, a Muslim people of northwestern Africa who conquered Spain and Portugal several centuries ago. [Say MOOR ish or MORE ish]

moorland *noun* esp. *Brit.* an extensive area of moor.

moose *noun* (*plural* **moose**) **1** the largest living deer, found in northern parts of North America, Europe, and Asia, and having a growth of skin hanging from the neck and (in males) very large antlers. **2** (also **moose meat**) the flesh of the moose as food.

moosehair *noun* stiff, pale hair from the shoulders, back, rump, and chest of a moose, dyed and used by some Aboriginal peoples to form decorative patterns on garments.

moosehide *noun* the skin of a moose, esp. when tanned: *moosehide leggings*.

moose milk *noun* *Cdn* **1** a drink including alcoholic liquor (usu. rum), milk, and often eggs etc. **2** *informal* home-distilled liquor. **3** *informal* any alcoholic drink.

moot • *adjective* **1** debatable, undecided: *whether this should be enforced by law or not is a moot point*. **2** unlikely to happen and therefore not worth considering: *he argued that the issue had become moot since the board had changed its policy*. **3** *Law* designating a discussion of a hypothetical case as an academic exercise: *moot court*. • *verb* raise (a question) for discussion: *the idea of applying for recognition as a historic site was mooted*.

moot point *noun* **1** a statement or question that is not or is no longer of any practical purpose. **2** a statement or question that is undecided or debatable.

mop • *noun* **1** a tool for cleaning floors etc., consisting of a bunch of thick strings or soft material fastened to a long handle. **2 a** a similarly-shaped large or small implement for various purposes. **3** anything resembling a mop, esp. a thick mass of hair. **4** an act of mopping or being mopped: *gave it a mop*. • *verb* (**mops, mopped, mopping**) **1** wipe or clean with or as with a mop. **2 a** wipe tears or sweat etc. from (one's face or brow etc.). **b** wipe away (tears etc.). PHRASES **mop up 1** wipe up with or as with a mop. **2** *informal* absorb (profits etc.). **3** dispatch; make an end of.

mope • *verb* (**mopes, moped, moping**) **1** be gloomily depressed or listless; behave sulkily. **2** wander about listlessly. • *noun* **1** a person who mopes. **2** (**the mopes**) low spirits.

moped *noun* a small motorcycle equipped with both a low-powered engine and pedals. [Say MOE ped]

moper *noun* a person who is gloomily depressed or sulky, or who is wandering around listlessly.

mopey *adjective* (also **mopy**) (**mopier, mopiest**) characterized by moping.

moppet *noun* *informal* (esp. as a term of endearment) a baby or small child.

MOR *abbreviation* MIDDLE-OF-THE-ROAD.

moraine *noun* a ridge or mound of rock debris etc. carried and deposited by a glacier. ▶ **morainic** *adjective* [Say muh RAIN]

moral • *adjective* **1 a** concerned with goodness or badness of human character or behaviour, or with the distinction between right and wrong. **b** concerned with accepted rules and standards of human behaviour. **2 a** conforming to accepted standards of general conduct. **b** capable of moral action: *humans are moral creatures*. **3** concerned with morals or ethics: *moral philosophy*. **4** concerned with or leading to a psychological effect associated with confidence in a right action: *moral support* ◊ *moral victory*. • *noun* **1 a** a moral lesson (esp. at the end) of a fable, story, event, etc. **b** a moral maxim or principle. **2** (in *plural*) moral behaviour, e.g. in sexual conduct.

morale *noun* the amount of confidence, enthusiasm,

M

etc. that a person or group has at a particular time: *the first signs of spring help boost our morale*. [Say more AL]

moralism *noun* the practice of moralizing, esp. showing a tendency to make judgments about others' morality: *the patriotic moralism of many political leaders*.

moralist *noun* **1** a person who has strong ideas about moral principles, especially one who tries to tell other people how they should behave. **2** a person who teaches or writes about moral principles.

moralistic *adjective* having or showing very fixed ideas about what is right and wrong, esp. when this causes one to judge other people's behaviour. ▶ **moralistically** *adverb*

morality *noun* (*plural* **moralities**) **1** the degree of conformity of an idea, practice, etc., to moral principles: *debating the morality of possession of nuclear weapons*. **2** right moral conduct: *these past few years have seen a sharp decline in morality*. **3** a particular system of morals: *commercial morality*.

morality squad *noun Cdn* a police unit dealing with infractions of legislation concerning prostitution, pornography, drugs, gambling, etc.

moralize *verb* (**moralizes**, **moralized**, **moralizing**) tell other people what is right and wrong, especially in order to emphasize that one's own opinions are correct: *he's always moralizing about "young people today"*. ▶ **moralizer** *noun*

morally *adverb* according to principles of good behaviour and what is considered to be right or wrong: *to act morally* ◊ *morally wrong* ◊ *felt morally responsible*.

moral pressure *noun* persuasion by appealing to a person's moral sense.

moral sense *noun* the ability to distinguish right and wrong.

morass *noun* (*plural* **morasses**) **1** a disordered situation, esp. one impeding progress: *a legal morass that hinders justice*. **2** a bog or marsh. [Say muh RASS]

moratorium *noun* (*plural* **moratoriums** or **moratoria**) **1** (often foll. by *on*) a temporary prohibition or suspension (of an activity). **2 a** a legal authorization to debtors to postpone payment. **b** the period of this postponement. [Say mora TORY um]

Moravian • *noun* **1** a native of Moravia, a region of the Czech Republic. **2** a member of a Protestant denomination founded in northern Germany by emigrants from Moravia, accepting the Bible as the only source of faith. • *adjective* **1** of, relating to, or characteristic of Moravia or its people. **2** of or relating to the Moravian Church. [Say muh RAVE ee in]

moray *noun* a tropical predatory eel-like fish of warm seas, which typically hides in crevices with just the head protruding. [Say MORE ay]

morbid *adjective* **1** (of the mind, ideas, etc.) having or showing an unusual interest in sad or unpleasant things, esp. death. **2** gruesome, grisly. **3** *Medical* of the nature of or indicative of disease. ▶ **morbidity** *noun* **morbidly** *adverb*

mordant • *adjective* **1** (of sarcasm etc.) critical and unkind, but funny: *his mordant wit appealed to students*. **2** (of a substance) serving to fix colouring matter or gold leaf on another substance. • *noun* a mordant substance. ▶ **mordantly** *adverb*

more • *adjective* existing in a greater or additional quantity, amount, or degree. • *noun* a greater quantity, number, or amount. • *adverb* **1** in a greater degree. **2** forming the comparative of adjectives and adverbs, esp. those of more than one syllable: *more absurd* ◊ *more easily*. **3** again: *once more*. PHRASES **more and more** in an increasing degree. **more of** to a greater extent: *more of a poet than a musician*. **more or less 1** in a greater or

less degree. **2** approximately; an estimate. **more so** of the same kind to a greater degree.

morel *noun* an edible fungus with a honeycombed cap. [Say muh RELL]

moreover *adverb* what's more.

mores *plural noun* the customs and behaviour that are considered typical of a particular social group or community: *this is a dramatic change to our country's social mores and should be considered very carefully*. [Say MORE aze]

morgue *noun* **1** a room or building in which dead bodies may be kept until burial or cremation; a mortuary. **2** (esp. in a newspaper office or television studio) a room or file of miscellaneous cuttings, photographs, videotape, etc. for future use. [Say MORG]

moribund *adjective* **1** at the point of death: *a project to restore and save a moribund trout river*. **2** lacking vitality: *the provincial party had long been moribund*. [Say MORE i bund]

Mormon • *noun* a member of the Church of Jesus Christ of Latter-day Saints, a religion founded in the US in 1830 by Joseph Smith (1805–44), who claimed to have found and translated the Book of Mormon, which is taken as scriptural alongside the Bible. • *adjective* of or relating to the Mormons or their beliefs. ▶ **Mormonism** *noun* [Say MORE m'n]

SPELL CHECK ABC ✓
morn, mourn

To show sorrow is to **mourn**.

---

morn *noun literary* morning.

morning *noun* **1** the early part of the day, esp. from sunrise to noon. **2** a time compared with the morning, esp. the early part of one's life etc.

morning coat *noun* a coat with tails, and with the front cut away below the waist.

morning glory *noun* (*plural* **morning glories**) any of various climbing and twining plants with trumpet-shaped flowers that fade in the afternoon.

morning sickness *noun* nausea experienced during early pregnancy, often in the morning.

morning star *noun* a planet, usu. Venus, seen in the east before sunrise.

Moroccan • *noun* **1** a native or national of Morocco in N Africa. **2** a person of Moroccan descent. • *adjective* of or relating to Morocco. [Say muh ROCKIN]

morocco *noun* (*plural* **moroccos**) **1** a fine flexible leather made (originally in Morocco) from goatskins tanned with sumac, used esp. in bookbinding and shoemaking. **2** an imitation of this in grained calf etc. [Say muh ROCKO]

moron *noun informal* a very stupid or foolish person. ▶ **moronic** *adjective* [Say MORE on, muh RON ick]

morose *adjective* sullen and ill-tempered: *it lifted morale around the normally morose headquarters of the NFB*. ▶ **morosely** *adverb* **moroseness** *noun* [Say muh ROACE]

morph[1] *noun* a variant form of an animal or plant.

morph[2] *verb* **1** alter or transform (an image) by computer. **2** *slang* be transformed.

morpheme *noun Linguistics* the smallest unit of meaning that a word can be divided into (e.g. *table* includes just one morpheme, but *unlikable* contains three: *un-*, *like*, and *-able*). [Say MORE feem]

morphine *noun* a drug obtained from opium and used medicinally to relieve pain. [Say MORE feen]

morphing *noun* a technique that changes a film image into a numerical code, enabling it to be manipulated by a computer so that the effect can be created of transforming an image smoothly into another.

M

morphological *adjective* relating to morphology. ▶**morphologically** *adverb* [Say morfa LOGICAL]

morphology *noun* (*plural* **morphologies**) **1** *Biology* the study of the forms of organisms. **2** *Linguistics* **a** the study of the forms of words. **b** the system of forms in a language. **3** the shape, form, or external arrangement of something, esp. as an object of study. [Say mor FOLLA jee]

morrow *noun* (usu. as **the morrow**) *literary* the following day.

Morse *noun* (also **Morse code**) an alphabet or code in which letters are represented by combinations of long and short light or sound signals.

morsel *noun* a small amount or piece of something, esp. food.

mortadella *noun* a large spiced sausage usu. made of pork and pork fat and eaten cold. [Say morta DELLA]

mortal • *adjective* **1** subject to death. **2** causing death; fatal. **3** (of a battle) fought to the death. **4** associated with death: *mortal agony*. **5** (of an enemy) not reconcilable until death. **6** (of pain, fear, an affront, etc.) intense, very serious. **7** *informal* **a** very great: *in a mortal hurry*. **b** long and tedious: *for two mortal hours*. **8** *informal* conceivable, imaginable: *of no mortal use*. • *noun* **1** a mortal being, esp. a human. **2** *jocular* a person described in some specified way: *a thirsty mortal*. ▶**mortally** *adverb*

mortality *noun* (*plural* **mortalities**) **1** the state of being subject to death. **2** loss of life on a large scale. **3 a** the number of deaths in a given period etc. **b** (also **mortality rate**) = DEATH RATE.

mortal sin *noun* a grave sin involving a deliberate turning away from God in a serious matter, regarded as depriving the soul of God's grace and incurring damnation unless repented of.

mortar • *noun* **1** a mixture of lime with cement, sand, and water, used in building to bond bricks or stones. **2** a short large-bore cannon for firing shells at high angles: *mortar fire*. **3** a device for firing a lifeline or firework. **4** a rounded bowl made of hard material, in which ingredients are pounded with a pestle. • *verb* **1** plaster or join with mortar. **2** attack or bombard with mortar shells. [Say MORTER]

mortarboard *noun* **1** an academic cap with a stiff flat square top. **2** a flat board with a handle on the undersurface, for holding mortar in bricklaying etc. [Say MORTER board]

mortgage • *noun* an agreement by which money is lent by a bank, trust company, etc. for buying a house or other property, the property itself being the security. • *verb* (**mortgages**, **mortgaged**, **mortgaging**) **1** give a bank, trust company, etc. the legal right to take possession of (a house or some other property) as a security for money lent. **2** expose to future risk for the sake of immediate advantage: *have mortgaged our future to foreign investment*. ▶**mortgageable** *adjective* [Say MORE gidge]

mortgagee *noun* the creditor in a mortgage, e.g. a bank, trust company, etc. [Say more gidge EE]

mortgagor *noun* (also **mortgager**) the debtor in a mortgage. [Say MORE gidge or]

mortician *noun* an undertaker. [Say more TISH'n]

mortification *noun* **1** the controlling of the passions by self-denial or discipline. **2** a humiliation; something that causes shame or humiliation. [Say morta fuh CAY sh'n]

mortify *verb* (**mortifies**, **mortified**, **mortifying**) **1** cause (a person) to feel shamed or humiliated: *she was mortified to realize he had heard every word she said*. **2** bring (the body, the flesh, the passions, etc.) into subjection by self-denial or discipline: *she mortifies her palate, taking less than she would like*. ▶**mortifying** *adjective*

mortifyingly *adverb*

mortise (also **mortice**) • *noun* a hole in a piece of wood etc. designed to receive the end of another part, esp. a tenon. • *verb* (**mortises**, **mortised**, **mortising**) **1** join securely, esp. by mortise and tenon. **2** cut a mortise in. [Say MORE tiss]

mortuary • *noun* (*plural* **mortuaries**) a room or building in which dead bodies may be kept until burial or cremation. • *adjective* of death or burial.

Mosaic *adjective* of or associated with Moses. [Say moe ZAY ick]

mosaic *noun* **1 a** a picture or pattern produced by an arrangement of small variously coloured pieces of glass or stone etc. **b** the process of producing such a work. **2** something that resembles a mosaic, esp. in its diversity of composition: *the Canadian cultural mosaic*. **3** (also **mosaic disease**) a virus disease causing mottled leaves in plants, esp. tobacco, corn, and sugar cane. [Say moe ZAY ick]

Mosaic Law *noun* the laws attributed to Moses and listed in the Pentateuch (the first five books of the Bible).

mosasaur *noun* (also **mosasaurus**, *plural* **mosasauruses**) any large extinct marine reptile with a long slender body and flipper-like limbs. [Say MOE suh sore, moe suh SORE us]

mosey *verb* (**moseys**, **moseyed**, **moseying**) *informal* walk in a leisurely or aimless manner. [Say MOZE ee]

mosh *verb* (**moshes**, **moshed**, **moshing**) *slang* dance in a violent manner, involving jumping up and down and deliberately hitting other dancers, esp. at a rock concert. ▶**mosher** *noun* **moshing** *noun*

mosh pit *noun* *slang* the area in front of the stage at a rock concert, where moshing usually takes place.

Moslem *noun & adjective* = MUSLIM. [Say MOZZ lum]

mosque *noun* a Muslim place of worship. [Say MOSK]

mosquito *noun* (*plural* **mosquitoes** or **mosquitos**) **1** any of various slender biting insects, the female of which punctures the skin of humans and other animals with a long proboscis to suck their blood and transmits diseases such as malaria and encephalitis. **2** *Cdn* **a** an initiation level of sports competition for young children. **b** a player at this level.

mosquito net *noun* (also **mosquito netting**) a net to keep off mosquitoes.

moss *noun* (*plural* **mosses**) **1** a small, flowerless, green plant, growing in low carpets or rounded cushions in damp habitats, covering the surface of tree trunks, stones, etc. **2** (in full **Irish moss**) = CARRAGEEN.

mossy *adjective* like or covered in moss.

most • *adjective* **1** existing in the greatest quantity or degree: *the most noise*. **2** the majority of; nearly all of: *most people*. • *noun* **1** the greatest quantity or number: *the most I can do*. **2** (**the most**) *slang* the best of all. **3** the majority: *most of them*. • *adverb* **1** in the highest degree: *this is most interesting*. **2** forming the superlative of adjectives and adverbs, esp. those of more than one syllable: *most certain* ◊ *most easily*. **3** *informal* almost. PHRASES **at most** no more or better than. **at the most 1** as the greatest amount. **2** not more than. **for the most part 1** as regards the greater part. **2** usually. **make the most of 1** employ to the best advantage. **2** represent at its best or worst.

Most Favoured Nation *noun* a country which is afforded beneficial trade terms with another, e.g. lower import tariffs than others.

mostly *adverb* **1** as regards the greater part. **2** usually.

Most Reverend *noun* the official title of certain high-ranking clergy, e.g. archbishops and bishops.

mote *noun* a speck of dust.

M

motel *noun* a hotel designed for motorists, usu. having direct access from each room to the parking lot.

motet *noun* a short sacred choral composition. [Say moe TET]

moth *noun* **1** an insect with two pairs of broad wings covered in microscopic scales, distinguished from a butterfly (in most instances) by its nocturnal activity, its thick body and hairlike antennae, and the folded position of its drably coloured wings when at rest. **2** a small insect that breeds in clothing and other domestic textiles, on which its larva feeds.

mothball • *noun* a ball of naphthalene etc. placed in stored clothes to keep away moths. • *verb* **1** place in mothballs. **2 a** take out of use or active service. **b** put in storage for an indefinite time. PHRASES **in mothballs** stored unused for a considerable time.

moth-eaten *adjective* **1** damaged or destroyed by moths. **2** antiquated, time-worn.

mother • *noun* **1 a** a woman in relation to a child or children to whom she has given birth. **b** a woman who serves as a mother, e.g. a stepmother, adoptive mother, or foster mother. **2** any female animal in relation to its offspring. **3** a quality or condition etc. that gives rise to another: *necessity is the mother of invention*. **4** (also **Mother Superior**) the head of a female religious community. **5** (as an *adjective*) **a** designating an institution etc. regarded as having maternal authority: *Mother Church ◊ mother earth*. **b** designating the main ship, spacecraft, etc., in a convoy or mission: *the mother craft*. **6** *slang* a person or thing that is very large, powerful, etc. • *adjective* **1** that is a mother: *a mother bird*. **2** characteristic of a mother: *mother love*. **3** inherited or learned from, or as if from, one's mother; native: *mother tongue*. • *verb* **1** give birth to; be the mother of. **2** protect as a mother. PHRASES **every mother's son** *informal* every man; everyone. **the mother of all …** the largest … of all.

motherboard *noun* a printed circuit board containing the principal components of a microcomputer etc.

Mother Carey's chicken *noun* = STORM PETREL.

mother country *noun* (*plural* **mother countries**) **1** the country which colonized or settled a particular place. **2** one's native country.

mother figure *noun* an older woman who is regarded as a source of nurture, support, etc.

Mother Goose *noun* the fictitious author of a collection of nursery rhymes first published in England in the late 18th century.

motherhood *noun* **1** the state or condition of being a mother. **2** the qualities or attributes characteristic of a mother. **3** (as an *adjective*) having an inherent goodness or fairness that is obvious or cannot be disputed: *cleaning up the park was a motherhood issue*.

mother-in-law *noun* (*plural* **mothers-in-law**) the mother of one's husband or wife.

mother-in-law suite *noun* = IN-LAW SUITE.

motherland *noun* **1** one's native country. **2** the land in which one's ancestors lived.

motherless *adjective* without a mother.

motherlike *adjective & adverb* (in a manner) suggestive or characteristic of a mother, as in affection, care, etc.

motheriness *noun* the quality of being motherly.

motherlode *noun* **1** *Mining* the main vein of a system. **2** a rich or important source of something: *the spectacular motherlode of grayling that Chris discovered*.

motherly *adjective* **1** like or characteristic of a mother in affection, care, etc. **2** of or relating to a mother.

mother-of-pearl *noun* a smooth iridescent substance forming the inner layer of the shell of some molluscs.

mother's allowance *noun* *Cdn hist.* = FAMILY ALLOWANCE 1.

Mother's Day *noun* the second Sunday in May as a day to honour mothers.

mother ship *noun* **1** a ship escorting or having charge of a number of other, smaller vessels. **2** an aircraft or spacecraft from which another aircraft or spacecraft is launched or controlled.

Mother Superior *noun* the head of a female religious community.

mother-to-be *noun* (*plural* **mothers-to-be**) a woman who is expecting a baby.

mother tongue *noun* one's native language.

mothproof • *adjective* (of clothes) treated so as to repel moths. • *verb* treat (clothes) in this way.

motif *noun* (*plural* **motifs**) **1** a distinctive feature or dominant idea in artistic or literary composition: *the literary motif of sibling rivalry*. **2** *Music* a short succession of notes producing a single impression; a brief melodic or rhythmic formula out of which longer passages are developed. **3** a decorative design or pattern: *the colourful hand-painted motifs which adorn the boats*. [Say moe TEEF]

motile *adjective* *Zoology & Botany* capable of motion. ▶ **motility** *noun* [Say MOE tile, moe TILLA tee]

motion • *noun* **1** the act or process of moving or of changing position. **2** a particular manner of moving the body in walking etc. **3** a change of posture. **4** a gesture. **5** a formal proposal put to a committee, legislature, etc. **6** *Law* an application for a rule or order of court. • *verb* **1** direct (a person) by a sign or gesture. **2** (often foll. by *to* a person) make a gesture directing: *motioned to me to leave*. PHRASES **go through the motions** make a pretense; do something perfunctorily or superficially. **in motion** moving; not at rest. **put** (or **set**) **in motion** set going or working. ▶ **motionless** *adjective* **motionlessly** *adverb*

motion picture *noun* a continuous picture of events obtained by projecting a sequence of photographs taken at very short intervals.

motion sickness *noun* nausea induced by motion, esp. by travelling in a vehicle.

motivate *verb* (**motivates, motivated, motivating**) **1** supply a motive to; be the motive of. **2** cause (a person) to act in a particular way. **3** stimulate the interest of (a person in an activity). ▶ **motivation** *noun* **motivational** *adjective* **motivator** *noun*

motive • *noun* **1** a factor or circumstance that induces a person to act in a particular way. **2** a distinctive feature or dominant idea in artistic, musical, or literary composition; a motif. • *adjective* **1** producing motion: *the charge of gas is the motive force for every piston stroke*. **2** motivating, causing: *the motive principle of a writer's work*. ▶ **motiveless** *adjective*

motive power *noun* a moving or impelling power, esp. a source of energy used to drive machinery.

mot juste *noun* (*plural* **mots justes**) the most appropriate expression: *the writer in need of the mot juste may find a thesaurus useful*. [Say moe ZHOOST]

motley *adjective* (**motlier, motliest**) of varied character: *a motley crew*.

motocross *noun* cross-country racing on motorcycles. ▶ **motocrosser** *noun*

M

motor • *noun* **1** a thing that imparts motion. **2** a machine (esp. one using electricity or internal combustion) supplying motive power for a vehicle etc. or for some other device with moving parts. • *adjective* **1** driven by a motor. **2** of or for motor vehicles. **3** of or for motorists: *a federation of motor clubs*. **4** relating to muscular movement or the nerves activating it: *motor skills*. • *verb* **1** travel by or in a motor vehicle. **2** move under motor power in a boat.

motorbike noun informal **1** = MOTORCYCLE. **2** = DIRT BIKE.

motorboat • noun a motor-driven boat. • verb travel in or by motorboat.

motorcade noun a procession of motor vehicles.

motorcoach noun (plural **motorcoaches**) a bus that is comfortably equipped for long journeys.

motorcycle noun a two-wheeled motor-driven road vehicle without pedal propulsion. ▶ **motorcycling** noun **motorcyclist** noun

motorhome noun a large motor vehicle equipped as a self-contained home for camping or long trips.

motorist noun the driver of a car.

motorization noun the introduction or use of motor vehicles.

motorize verb (**motorizes, motorized, motorizing**) **1** provide with a motor. **2** equip (troops etc.) with motor transport.

motormouth noun slang a person who talks incessantly and trivially.

motor nerve noun a nerve carrying impulses from the brain or spinal cord to a muscle.

motor scooter noun see SCOOTER.

motorsport noun (also **motor racing**) the racing of motorized vehicles, esp. cars, as a sport.

motor vehicle noun a road vehicle powered by an internal combustion engine.

Motown noun music with rhythm and blues and soul elements, associated with Detroit. [Say MOE town]

mottled adjective marked with spots or patches of colour: mottled brown plumage. ▶ **mottling** noun

motto noun (plural **mottoes**) a short sentence or phrase chosen and used as a guide or rule of behaviour or as an expression of the aims or ideals of a family, a country, an institution, etc.

mould¹ • noun **1** a hollow container into which molten metal etc. is poured or soft or liquid material is pressed or poured to harden into a required shape. **2** something formed in a mould. **3** a usual or expected type of something: Martha doesn't fit into the traditional mould of an academic. • verb **1** make (an object) in a required shape or from certain ingredients: was moulded out of clay. **2** give a shape to. **3** influence the formation or development of: consultation helps to mould policies. **4** (esp. of clothing) fit closely to: the gloves moulded his hands. **5** (foll. by to) conform to the shape of: the shoe moulds to my foot. PHRASES **break the mould 1** (also **break out of the mould**) change people's expectations of something, esp. in a dramatic or challenging way. **2** make impossible the repetition of a certain type of creation: they broke the mould when Alex was born.

mould² noun a woolly, furry, or staining growth of minute fungi, as that which forms on food, textiles, etc., esp. in moist conditions.

mould³ noun **1** loose earth. **2** the upper soil of cultivated land, esp. when rich in organic matter.

mouldable adjective capable of being moulded.

mouldboard noun the curved board or blade in a plow that turns over the furrow.

moulded adjective **1** formed, shaped. **2** made from a mould.

moulder¹ verb slowly decay or deteriorate, esp. from neglect: old cookies mouldering in the cupboard ◊ boxes of books left to moulder away in a warehouse.

moulder² noun a person who moulds something; a machine for moulding things.

mouldiness noun the quality of being mouldy.

moulding noun a strip of wood, metal, etc. used as an ornamental or structural architectural feature around

doors and windows etc. or for other esp. decorative purposes, e.g., to frame pictures.

mouldy adjective (**mouldier, mouldiest**) **1** covered with mould; smelling of mould. **2** old and decaying. **3** old-fashioned.

moult • verb shed feathers, hair, a shell, etc., in the process of renewing plumage, a coat, etc. • noun a loss of plumage, skin, or hair, esp. as a regular feature of an animal's life cycle: is in moult once a year. [Say MOLT]

mound • noun **1** a raised mass of earth, stones, or other compacted material. **2** a heap or pile. **3** a hillock. **4** Baseball a slight elevation on which the pitcher stands. • verb **1** heap up in a mound or mounds. **2** cover with a pile or mound of something: the desk was mounded with papers. PHRASES **take the mound** Baseball (of a pitcher) start or enter a game.

mount¹ • verb **1** climb up or on to. **2** get up on (an animal or bicycle) to ride it. **3** (in passive) be on horseback; be provided with a horse. **4** increase in size, number, or intensity. **5** organize and initiate. **6** put or fix in place or on a support. **7** set in or attach (a picture) to a backing. • noun **1** something on which an object is mounted for support or display. **2** a horse used for riding. PHRASES **mount guard** (often foll. by over) perform the duty of guarding; take up sentry duty.

mount² noun mountain, hill: Mount Everest.

mountable adjective that may be mounted on a specified surface: a wall-mountable unit.

mountain noun **1** a large natural elevation of the earth's surface rising abruptly from the surrounding level; a large or high and steep hill. **2** a large heap or pile; a huge quantity: a mountain of work. PHRASES **move mountains 1** achieve spectacular results. **2** make every possible effort.

mountain ash noun (plural **mountain ash** or **mountain ashes**) a small deciduous tree of the rose family, with compound leaves, white flowers, and scarlet berries.

mountain avens noun (plural **mountain avens**) a creeping alpine plant with white or yellow flowers, a species of which is the floral emblem of the Northwest Territories.

mountain bike noun a bicycle with a light sturdy frame, broad deep-treaded tires, and multiple gears, originally designed for riding on mountainous terrain. ▶ **mountain biker** noun **mountain biking** noun

mountaineer • noun a mountain climber. • verb climb mountains as a sport. ▶ **mountaineering** noun

mountain goat noun **1** (also **Rocky Mountain goat**) a North American goat-antelope with shaggy white hair and backward curving horns, living in the Rocky Mountains. **2** any goat that lives on mountains, proverbial for agility.

mountain lion noun a cougar.

mountainous adjective **1** (of a region) having many mountains. **2** huge.

mountain range noun a line of mountains connected by high ground.

mountain sheep noun (plural **mountain sheep**) a sheep native to mountain regions, esp. a bighorn sheep or a Dall sheep.

mountainside noun the side of a mountain; slope.

Mountain Time noun the time in a zone including Alberta, the US states in or near the Rocky Mountains, and Mexico. **Mountain Standard Time** is seven hours behind GMT; **Mountain Daylight Time** is six hours behind GMT.

mountaintop noun the top of a mountain.

mounted • adjective **1** in senses of MOUNT¹ verb. **2** serving on horseback: mounted police. • noun Cdn a mounted police force: officers of the mounted.

M

Mountie *noun informal* a member of the RCMP.

Mountie hat *noun Cdn* the characteristic tan hat of the RCMP, with a broad flat encircling brim.

mounting *noun* **1** = MOUNT¹ *noun* 1. **2** *in senses of* MOUNT¹ *verb*.

mourn *verb* **1** feel or show deep sorrow or regret for (a dead person, a lost thing, a past event, etc.). **2** show conventional signs of grief after a person's death.

mourner *noun* a person who mourns, esp. at a funeral.

mournful *adjective* **1** sad, sorrowing. **2** expressing or suggestive of mourning. ▶ **mournfully** *adverb*

mourning *noun* **1** the expression of deep sorrow, esp. for a loss, death, etc. **2** the wearing of solemn clothing as a convention to indicate sorrow after a death. **3** the clothes worn in mourning. PHRASES **in mourning** assuming the signs of mourning, esp. in dress.

mourning dove *noun* a small slender North American dove with a long pointed tail and a plaintive call.

mouse • *noun* (*plural* **mice**) **1 a** a small rodent with a pointed snout, a long tail, and relatively large ears and eyes. **b** any of several similar rodents, such as a small shrew or vole. **2** a timid or feeble person. **3** a small hand-held device moved over a flat surface to produce a corresponding movement of a cursor or arrow on a computer screen, usu. having fingertip controls for selecting a function or entering a command. • *verb* (**mouses, moused, mousing**) **1** (esp. of a cat, owl, etc.) hunt for or catch mice. **2** use a mouse to move a cursor on a computer screen: *moused over to the window and clicked on it.* ▶ **mouselike** *adjective & adverb* **mouser** *noun*

mouse pad *noun* a flat pad across which a computer mouse is moved.

mousetrap *noun* **1** a trap with bait for catching and usu. killing mice. **2** cheese of poor quality: *mousetrap cheddar*.

mousey (**mousier, mousiest**) = MOUSY. [Say MOUSE ee]

moussaka *noun* a Greek and eastern Mediterranean baked dish of ground meat, eggplant, etc. with white sauce. [Say muh SOCK uh]

mousse • *noun* **1 a** a dessert of whipped cream, eggs, etc., usu. flavoured with fruit or chocolate. **b** a meat or fish purée made with whipped cream etc. **2** a foamy preparation applied to the hair enabling it to be styled more easily. • *verb* (**mousses, moussed, moussing**) apply mousse to (hair). [Say MOOSE]

moustache *noun* **1** the hair on the upper lip, esp. as left to grow by men. **2** a similar growth around the mouth of some animals. ▶ **moustached** *adjective*

moustachio *noun* = MUSTACHIO. [Say muh STASHY oh]

mousy *adjective* (**mousier, mousiest**) **1** of or like a mouse. **2** (of a person) shy or timid; ineffectual. **3** (esp. of hair) nondescript light brown. **4** dark grey with a yellow tinge.

mouth • *noun* (*plural* **mouths**) **1** an external opening in the head, through which most animals admit food and emit communicative sounds. **2 a** the opening of a bag, sack, cave, volcano, etc. **b** the muzzle of a gun. **3 a** the place where a river enters a sea or lake. **b** the expanse of water connecting a bay or harbour with a lake or the sea. **4** *informal* **a** talkativeness. **b** impudent talk; cheek. **c** boastful talk. **5** an individual regarded as needing sustenance: *an extra mouth to feed.* • *verb* **1** utter or speak solemnly or with affectations: *mouthing platitudes.* **2** say (words) with movement of the mouth but no sound. **3** utter very distinctly. **4** move the lips silently. **5** take (food) in the mouth. **6** touch with the mouth. PHRASES **have a big mouth** talk indiscreetly. **keep one's mouth shut** *informal* refrain from saying something inappropriate. **mouth off 1** (often foll. by *at*) talk insolently or disrespectfully. **2** talk loudly; express one's opinions forcefully. **put words into a person's mouth** inaccurately represent a person as having said something. **take the words out of a person's mouth** say what another was about to say. **watch one's mouth** be careful not to say something offensive. ▶ **mouthed** *adjective* (also in *combination*)

mouthful *noun* (*plural* **mouthfuls**) **1** a quantity, esp. of food, that fills or is in the mouth. **2** a small quantity. **3** a long or complicated word or phrase. PHRASES **say a mouthful** say something important.

mouthguard *noun* a piece of esp. sports equipment protecting the mouth, teeth, etc.

mouth organ *noun* (also **mouth harp**) = HARMONICA.

mouthpart *noun* any of the (usu. paired) organs surrounding the mouth of an insect or other arthropod and adapted for feeding.

mouthpiece *noun* **1** the part of a musical instrument, a telephone, a tobacco pipe, etc. placed in or near the mouth. **2** any apparatus or part of one that fits into the mouth, e.g. of scuba equipment, a bridle, etc. **3** a person, organization, etc. that speaks for another or others.

mouth-to-mouth *noun* a method of resuscitation in which a person breathes into a subject's lungs through the mouth.

mouthwash *noun* (*plural* **mouthwashes**) a liquid antiseptic etc. for rinsing the mouth or gargling.

mouth-watering *adjective* **1** (of food etc.) having a delicious smell or appearance; appetizing. **2** tempting, alluring: *mouth-watering deals*.

mouthy *adjective* (**mouthier, mouthiest**) *informal* impudent, cheeky.

movable (also **moveable**) • *adjective* **1** that can be moved. **2** *Law* (of property) able to be taken from one house etc. to another, e.g., furniture, as distinct from land or buildings. **3** (of a religious feast or festival) variable in date from year to year. • *noun* **1** an article of furniture that may be removed from a house, as distinct from a fixture. **2** (in *plural*) personal property.

movable type *noun hist.* individually cast pieces of metal, each with a raised letter, which could be arranged for use in a printing press.

SPELL CHECK **mauve**	ABC ✓

The pale purple colour is **mauve**.

move • *verb* (**moves, moved, moving**) **1** go or cause to go in a specified direction or manner. **2** change or cause to change position. **3** change one's place of residence. **4** change from one state, sphere, or activity to another. **5** take or cause to take action. **6** make progress. **7** provoke compassion, affection, or other feelings in. **8** propose for discussion and resolution at a meeting or legislative assembly. **9** empty (the bowels). • *noun* **1** an instance of moving. **2** an action taken towards achieving a purpose. **3** a manoeuvre in a sport or game. **4** a player's turn during a board game. PHRASES **get a move on** *informal* **1** hurry up. **2** make a start. **get moving** *informal* begin, leave, etc. quickly: *it's late — we'd better get moving.* **get something moving** *informal* cause something to make vigorous progress. **move along** (or **on**) change to a new position, esp. to avoid crowding, getting in the way, etc. **move house** esp. *Cdn & Brit.* transfer one's furniture, goods, etc. from one residence to another. **move in 1** take possession of a new house etc. **2** get into a position of influence, interference, etc. **3** (often foll. by *on*) get into a position of readiness or proximity (for an offensive action etc.). **move in with** start to share accommodation with (an

M

existing resident). **move on** move to another place, topic, job, etc. **move out 1** leave one's home; change one's place of residence. **2** leave a position, job, etc. **move over** adjust one's position to make room for another. **move up 1** improve one's position or condition, esp. in a career. **2** *Baseball* (of a baserunner) move to the next base. **on the move 1** progressing. **2** moving around. **put the move** (or **moves**) **on** make sexual advances towards.

movement *noun* **1 a** an act of changing physical location or position or of having this changed. **b** a planned and controlled move by armed forces. **2** (usu. in *plural*) a person's activities and whereabouts, esp. at a particular time. **3** a body of persons with a common object: *the peace movement*. **4** a direction of thought or opinion; a social trend. **5** a change in amount. **6 a** the moving parts of a mechanism (esp. a clock or watch). **b** a particular group of these. **7** *Music* **a** a principal division of a longer musical work, self-sufficient in terms of key, tempo, structure, etc. **b** rhythmical character in music; tempo. **8** the progressive development of a poem, story, etc. **9** (of the bowels) the action of discharging feces. **10 a** an activity in a market for some commodity. **b** a rise or fall in price.

mover *noun* **1** a person or thing that moves. **2** a person or company that transports furniture etc. for clients changing residence or business location. **3** a person who makes a motion in a formal meeting etc. **4** (esp. in **movers and shakers**) a person who incites or instigates to action; an enterprising person.

movie *noun informal* a motion-picture film.

moviegoer *noun* a person who attends movies. ▶**moviegoing** *noun*

movieland *noun informal* the motion-picture industry.

moviemaker *noun* a filmmaker. ▶**moviemaking** *noun*

moving *adjective* **1** that moves or causes to move. **2** affecting with emotion. ▶**movingly** *adverb* (in sense 2)

moving picture *noun* = MOTION PICTURE.

moving sidewalk *noun* a structure like a conveyor belt for pedestrians.

moving target *noun* **1** a target that is in motion when aimed at. **2** a person, thing, or phenomenon that changes character so frequently as to be difficult to assess, deal with, etc.

mow[1] *verb* (**mows**; *past* **mowed**; *past participle* **mowed** or **mown**; **mowing**) cut down grass, hay, etc. with a machine or scythe. PHRASES **mow down** kill or destroy randomly or in great numbers. [Rhymes with SHOW]

mow[2] *noun* **1** a pile or heap of hay, grain, etc. **2** a place in a barn where hay or straw is stored. [Rhymes with COW]

mower *noun* **1** = LAWN MOWER. **2** a person who mows lawns.

moxie *noun slang* force of character, energy, ingenuity.

Mozambican • *noun* a native or inhabitant of Mozambique, a country on the east coast of southern Africa. • *adjective* of or relating to Mozambique. [Say moe zam BEAK in]

mozzarella *noun* a very mild white Italian cheese originally made of buffalo milk. [Say motsa RELLA]

MP *abbreviation* (*plural* **MPs**) **1** Member of Parliament. **2 a** military police. **b** military policeman.

mp *abbreviation* mezzo-piano.

m.p. *abbreviation* melting point.

mph *abbreviation* miles per hour.

MPP *abbreviation* (*plural* **MPPs**) *Cdn* (*Ont.*) Member of Provincial Parliament.

MPV *abbreviation* (*plural* **MPVs**) multi-purpose vehicle, a minivan.

Mr. *noun* (*plural* **Messrs.**) **1** a title prefixed to the name of a man not having a higher, honorific, or professional title. **2** a title prefixed to a designation of office etc.: *Mr. Speaker*. **3** a title prefixed to a characteristic of a certain man: *Mr. Nice Guy*.

MRI *abbreviation* MAGNETIC RESONANCE IMAGING.

Mr. Right *noun jocular* the man who would make the ideal husband for a particular woman.

Mrs. *noun* (*plural* **Mrs.** or **Mesdames**) a title prefixed to the name of a married woman not having a higher, honorific, or professional title.

MS *abbreviation* (*plural* **MSS**) manuscript. **2** MULTIPLE SCLEROSIS. **3** *Cdn* MASTER SEAMAN.

Ms. *noun* a title prefixed to the name of a woman regardless of her marital status.

ms *abbreviation* millisecond(s).

M.Sc. *abbreviation* (*plural* **M.Sc.'s**) Master of Science.

MSG *abbreviation* MONOSODIUM GLUTAMATE.

Msgr. *abbreviation* **1** Monseigneur. **2** Monsignor.

MSRP *abbreviation* manufacturer's suggested retail price.

MSS *abbreviation* manuscripts.

MST *abbreviation* Mountain Standard Time.

M.S.W. *abbreviation* (*plural* **M.S.W.'s**) Master of Social Work.

MT *abbreviation* MOUNTAIN TIME.

Mt. *abbreviation* **1** Mount: *Mt. Logan*. **2** Mountain.

MTB *abbreviation* (*plural* **MTBs**) **1** motor torpedo boat. **2** mountain bike.

Mtl. *abbreviation* Montreal.

mu *noun* **1** the twelfth Greek letter (M, μ). **2** (μ, as a symbol) = MICRO- 2. [Say MYOO]

much • *adjective* **1** existing or occurring in a great quantity. **2** (preceded by *as*, *how*, *that*, etc.) with relative rather than distinctive sense: *I don't know how much money you want*. • *noun* **1** a great quantity. **2** (preceded by *as*, *how*, *that*, etc.) with relative rather than distinctive sense: *we do not need that much*. **3** (usu. in *neg.*) a noteworthy or outstanding example: *not much of a party*. • *adverb* **1 a** in a great degree: *much to my surprise ◊ is much the same*. **b** (qualifying a verb or past participle) greatly: *they much regret the mistake ◊ much annoyed*. **c** qualifying a comparative or superlative adjective: *much better*. **2** for a large part of one's time: *is much away from home*. • *interjection informal* expressing strong disagreement. PHRASES **as much** the extent or quantity just specified; the idea just mentioned: *I thought as much ◊ as much as that?* **a bit much** *informal* somewhat excessive or immoderate. **much as** even though: *cannot come, much as I would like to*. **too much** *informal* an intolerable situation etc.: *that really is too much*. **too much for 1** more than a match for. **2** beyond what is endurable by. ▶**muchly** *adverb jocular*

mucho *adjective & adverb jocular* much. [Say MOOCH oh]

muck • *noun* **1** mud. **2** very dark and highly organic soil. **3** *informal* dirt or filth; anything disgusting. **4** farmyard manure. **5** *informal* an untidy state; a mess. **6** waste material removed during mining or civil engineering operations. • *verb* **1** (usu. foll. by *up*) *informal* ruin, spoil, mess up. **2** make dirty. **3** manure with muck. **4** (in hockey) play tenaciously and physically, esp. along the boards in an attempt to gain control of the puck. PHRASES **muck about** (or **around**) *informal* **1** putter or fool about. **2** (foll. by *with*) fool or interfere with. **muck out** clean (a barn etc.) of manure.

mucker *noun slang* **1** a person or machine that removes mining waste. **2** a person, esp. a hockey player, known more for tenacity and hard work than for talent.

M

muckrake *verb* (**muckrakes**, **muckraked**, **muckraking**) search out and reveal scandal, esp. among famous people. ▶**muckraker** *noun* **muckraking** *noun*

mucky *adjective* (**muckier**, **muckiest**) **1** covered with muck. **2** dirty.

mucky-muck *noun* (also **muckamuck**, **muckety-muck**) *slang* a person of great self-importance.

mucosa *noun* (*plural* **mucosae**) a mucous membrane. ▶**mucosal** *adjective* [Say myoo CO suh for the singular, myoo CO see for the plural]

mucous *adjective* of, resembling, secreting, or covered with mucus. [Say MYOO cuss]

mucous membrane *noun* a mucus-secreting tissue lining many body cavities and tubular organs.

mucus *noun* **1** a slimy substance, usu. not mixable with water, secreted by a mucous membrane or gland. **2** a gummy substance found in plants. [Say MYOO cuss]

mud *noun* **1** wet soft earthy matter. **2** hard ground from the drying of an area of this. PHRASES **as clear as mud** *informal* not at all clear. **drag through the mud** denigrate publicly. **fling** (or **sling** or **throw**) **mud** speak disparagingly or slanderously. **here's mud in your eye!** *informal* a toast made when drinking. **one's name is mud** one is unpopular or in disgrace.

mudbank *noun* a bank of mud, esp. on the bed of a river or the bottom of the sea.

mud bath *noun* **1** a bath in the mud of mineral springs, esp. to relieve rheumatism etc. **2** a muddy scene or occasion.

mudcat *noun* **1** Cdn = BULLHEAD 1. **2** a large North American catfish with a long slender body and a flat head.

muddiness *noun* the quality of being muddy.

muddle • *verb* (**muddles**, **muddled**, **muddling**) **1** (often foll. by *up*) bring into disorder. **2** bewilder, confuse. **3** mismanage (an affair). **4** (often foll. by *with*) busy oneself in a confused and ineffective way. • *noun* **1** a state of disorder. **2** mental confusion. PHRASES **make a muddle of 1** bring into disorder. **2** bungle. **muddle along** (or **on**) progress in a haphazard way. **muddle through** succeed by perseverance rather than skill or efficiency.

muddle-headed *adjective* stupid, confused.

muddler *noun* a type of fly used in trout fishing.

muddy • *adjective* (**muddier**, **muddiest**) **1** like mud. **2** covered in or full of mud. **3** (of liquid) turbid. **4** mentally confused. **5** obscure. **6** (of light) dull. **7** (of colour) impure. • *verb* (**muddies**, **muddied**, **muddying**) make muddy. PHRASES **muddy the waters** confuse matters.

mud flat *noun* a stretch of muddy land left uncovered at low tide.

mudguard *noun* a curved strip or cover over a wheel of a bicycle, motorcycle, etc. to reduce the amount of mud etc. thrown up from the road.

mudhole *noun* **1** a water hole dried so as to become mud. **2** a muddy hole in a road.

mud pie *noun* **1** mud made into a pie shape by a child. **2** a rich chocolate ice cream pie.

mud room *noun* a small room, often a vestibule, in a house, in which wet or muddy footwear and outer clothes are removed.

mudslide *noun* an avalanche of mud etc.

mudslinger *noun* a person who criticizes others to ruin their reputation; a slanderer.

mudslinging *noun informal* abuse, slander, or malevolent criticism.

mud-wrestle *verb* (**mud-wrestles**, **mud-wrestled**,

mud-wrestling) engage in mud wrestling. ▶**mud wrestler** *noun*

mud wrestling *noun* an activity in which usu. female contestants wrestle in a mud-filled ring.

muesli *noun* a breakfast food of crushed cereals (usu. oats), dried fruits, nuts, etc., eaten with milk. [Say MYOOZ lee]

muezzin *noun* a Muslim crier who proclaims the hours of prayer usu. from a minaret. [Say moo EZZ in]

muff[1] *noun* **1** a fur or other covering, usu. in the form of a tube with an opening at each end for the hands to be inserted for warmth. **2** = EARMUFF.

muff[2] • *verb* **1** bungle; deal clumsily with. **2** fail to catch or receive (a ball etc.). **3** blunder in (a theatrical part etc.). • *noun* a failure, esp. to catch a ball.

muffin *noun* a cupcake-like sweet bread.

muffle *verb* (**muffles**, **muffled**, **muffling**) **1** (often foll. by *up*) wrap or cover for warmth. **2** cover or wrap up (a source of sound) to reduce its loudness. **3** (usu. as **muffled** *adjective*) stifle (an utterance, e.g. a curse). **4** prevent from speaking.

muffler *noun* **1** a device attached to a motor vehicle's exhaust system to reduce noise. **2** a scarf worn for warmth. **3** any of various devices used to deaden sound in musical instruments.

mufti[1] *noun* a Muslim legal expert empowered to give rulings on religious matters. [Say MUFF tee]

mufti[2] *noun* plain clothes worn by a person who also wears (esp. military) uniform: *in mufti*. [Say MUFF tee]

mug • *noun* **1 a** a drinking vessel, usu. cylindrical and with a handle and used without a saucer. **b** its contents. **2** *slang* the face or mouth of a person. • *verb* (**mugs**, **mugged**, **mugging**) **1** rob (a person) with violence esp. in a public place. **2** *slang* make faces, esp. before an audience, camera, etc. PHRASES **a mug's game** *informal* a foolish or unprofitable activity. ▶**mugful** *noun* (*plural* **mugfuls**) **mugger** *noun* (in sense 1 of *v.*).

mugginess *noun* oppressive humidity.

mugging *noun* a violent robbery of a person in a public place.

muggy *adjective* (**muggier**, **muggiest**) (of the weather etc.) oppressively damp and warm; humid.

Mughal • *noun* a member of the Muslim dynasty of Mongol origin that ruled much of India from the 16th to the 19th century (*compare* MOGUL[1] 2b). • *adjective* of or having to do with this dynasty. [Say MOOG'll]

mug shot *noun slang* a photograph of a face, esp. for official purposes.

mug-up *noun* Cdn (esp. Nfld) a break for a hot drink (esp. tea) and snacks, esp. while on a hike, journey, etc.

mujahedeen *plural noun* (also **mujahideen**) guerrilla fighters in Islamic countries, esp. supporting Muslim fundamentalism. [Say mooja huh DEEN]

mukluk *noun* **1** a winter boot with a heavy rubber sole and a high fabric upper, usu. with laces. **2** a traditional Inuit boot, usu. made from seal or caribou skin. [Say MUCK luck]

mulatto *noun* (*plural* **mulattoes**) *dated* a person of mixed white and black parentage. [Say muh LATTO]

mulberry *noun* (*plural* **mulberries**) **1** (also **mulberry tree** or **mulberry bush**) a kind of small deciduous tree with broad leaves, esp. the white mulberry, grown originally for feeding silkworms, and the red mulberry of eastern North America, which bears juicy edible fruit. **2** the dark red or white berry of such a tree. **3** *noun & adjective* a dark red or purple colour.

mulch • *noun* a mixture usu. of vegetable matter spread around or over a plant to enrich or insulate the soil or suppress weeds. • *verb* (**mulches**, **mulched**, **mulching**) treat with mulch.

M

mule[1] *noun* **1** the offspring (usu. sterile) of a donkey and a horse, used as a beast of burden. **2** a stupid or obstinate person. **3** a hybrid and usu. sterile plant or animal: *mule canary*. **4** *slang* a person acting as a courier for illicit drugs. **5** (also **spinning mule**) a kind of spinning machine producing yarn on spindles.

mule[2] *noun* a light shoe or slipper without a back.

mule deer *noun* (*plural* **mule deer**) a long-eared black-tailed deer of prairies and mountains of western North America.

muley *noun* (*plural* **muleys**) (also **mulie**, *plural* **mulies**) *informal* = MULE DEER.

mulish *adjective* **1** like a mule. **2** stubborn. ▶ **mulishly** *adverb* **mulishness** *noun*

mull[1] *verb* (often foll. by *over*) ponder or consider.

mull[2] *verb* (esp. as **mulled** *adjective*) warm (wine or beer) with added sugar, spices, etc.

mullah *noun* a Muslim learned in Islamic theology and sacred law. [Say MULLA or MOOLA (with OOL as in *WOOL*)]

mullein *noun* a plant with woolly leaves and tall spikes of yellow flowers. [Say MULL'n]

mullet *noun* a fish with a thick body and a large blunt-nosed head, commonly used as food. [Say MULL it]

mulligan *noun* (also **mulligan stew**) a stew made from odds and ends of food. [Say MULLA g'n]

mulligatawny *noun* a highly seasoned soup originally from India. [Say mulla guh TONNY]

mullion *noun* a vertical bar dividing the lights in a window. ▶ **mullioned** *adjective* [Say MULL yin]

multi- *combining form* many; more than one.

multicellular *adjective* *Biology* having or involving many cells.

multicoloured *adjective* (also **multicolour**) of many colours.

multiculti *adjective* (also *Cdn* **multicult**) *informal* = MULTICULTURAL.

multicultural *adjective* **1** designating or pertaining to a society consisting of many culturally distinct groups. **2 a** (of a person etc.) advocating or receptive to the establishment of a multicultural society. **b** (of a group etc.) consisting of individuals from various, culturally distinct groups. ▶ **multiculturalism** *noun* **multiculturalist** *noun & adjective* **multiculturally** *adverb*

multi-dimensional *adjective* of or involving more than three dimensions.

multidisciplinary *adjective* combining or involving many separate disciplines or fields of endeavour.

multi-ethnic *adjective* composed of or involving several ethnic groups.

multi-faceted *adjective* having several facets, aspects, etc.

multifarious *adjective* **1** many and various: *multifarious activities*. **2** having great variety or diversity: *a vast, multifarious organization*. ▶ **multifariously** *adverb* **multifariousness** *noun* [Say multi FERRY us]

multi-function *adjective* (also **multi-functional**) having or fulfilling several functions.

multi-grain *adjective* (of baked goods, cereals, etc.) incorporating many grains.

multilateral *adjective* **1** (of an agreement, treaty, conference, etc.) in which three or more parties participate. **2** performed by more than one party: *multilateral disarmament*. ▶ **multilateralism** *noun* **multilaterally** *adverb*

multi-layered *adjective* (also **multi-layer**) composed of, occurring in, or having many layers.

multi-level *adjective* **1** having, involving, or operating on many levels. **2** designating a method of direct selling in which buyers at each level of a hierarchy

secure the participation of further buyers at a level below them. ▶ **multi-levelled** *adjective*

multilingual *adjective* **1** in or using several languages. **2** (of a person) speaking several languages fluently. ▶ **multilingualism** *noun*

multimedia • *adjective* (of art, education, etc.) using more than one medium of expression, communication, etc. • *noun* an extension of hypertext allowing the provision of audio and video material cross-referenced to a computer text: *multimedia applications*.

multi-millionaire *noun* a person with a fortune of several million dollars, pounds, etc.

multinational • *adjective* **1** (of a business organization) operating in several countries. **2** relating to or including several nationalities or ethnic groups. • *noun* a multinational company.

multi-party *adjective* **1 a** comprising members of several esp. political parties: *multi-party talks*. **b** sponsored by or involving more than one person, interest group, etc.: *multi-party lawsuit*. **2** designating or pertaining to an electoral system in which the interests of the electorate are represented by three or more political parties. ▶ **multi-partyism** *noun*

multiple • *adjective* **1** having many parts, elements, or individual components. **2** (foll. by *plural noun*) many and various. **3** *Medical* (of a disease or symptom) affecting several parts, organs, etc. • *noun* a number that may be divided by another a certain number of times without a remainder: *56 is a multiple of 7*.

multiple-choice *adjective* **1** (of a question) accompanied by several possible answers from which the correct one is to be chosen. **2** (of a test, questionnaire, etc.) consisting of multiple-choice questions.

multiple personality *noun* (*plural* **multiple personalities**) (also **multiple personality disorder**) a condition in which an individual's personality is apparently split into two or more distinct sub-personalities, each of which may become dominant at different times.

multiple sclerosis *noun* a chronic, progressive disease of the nervous system, in which sclerosis occurs in patches in the brain and spinal cord, resulting in tremor, paralysis, speech and sight defects, etc.

multiplex • *adjective* **1** manifold; of many elements; having many related features: *multiplex ties of work and friendship*. **2** involving simultaneous transmission of several messages along a single channel of communication. **3** of or relating to a single-site complex of two or more cinemas. • *noun* (*plural* **multiplexes**) **1** a multiplex cinema. **2** a multiplex system or signal. • *verb* (**multiplexes**, **multiplexed**, **multiplexing**) incorporate into a multiplex signal or system. ▶ **multiplexing** *noun & adjective*

multiplication *noun* **1** the arithmetical process of multiplying. **2** the act or process of multiplying. **3** the reproduction of people or animals, or the propagation of plants.

multiplication sign *noun* the sign ($\times$) to indicate that one quantity is to be multiplied by another, as in 2×3.

multiplication table *noun* a list of multiples of a particular number, usu. from 1 to 12.

multiplicity *noun* (*plural* **multiplicities**) a great number and variety of something: *this situation can be influenced by a multiplicity of different factors.* [Say multi PLISSA tee]

multiplier *noun* **1 a** a thing which or person who multiplies or causes something to increase. **b** a quantity by which a given number is multiplied. **2** *Economics* the factor by which an increase in income, employment, etc., is a multiple of the change in

M

investment or (esp. government) spending producing it: *this graph shows the tourism income multiplier for selected countries*. **3** *Electricity* an instrument for increasing by repetition the intensity of a current, force, etc.

multiplier effect *noun* the total impact on the economy that results when money spent or invested in one area is used, in turn, to buy or invest in something else, and so on.

multiply[1] *verb* (**multiplies, multiplied, multiplying**) **1** obtain from (a number) another that is a specified number of times its value: *multiply 6 by 4 and you get 24*. **2 a** increase in number by accumulation or repetition. **b** increase in number by reproduction or procreation. **3** produce a large number of (instances etc.). **4 a** breed (animals). **b** propagate (plants). [Say MULTA ply]

multiply[2] *adverb* in several different ways or respects: *multiply injured patients*. [Say MULL tip lee]

multipolar *adjective* consisting of or divided into more than two esp. political alliances, parties, etc.: *what we have now is a multipolar world with tremendous uncertainties*. ▶**multipolarity** *noun*

multiprocessing *noun* *Computing* processing by a number of processors sharing a common memory and common peripherals.

multiprocessor *noun* a computer capable of performing multiprocessing.

multiprogramming *noun* *Computing* the execution of two or more independent programs concurrently.

multi-purpose *adjective* having many purposes.

multiracial *adjective* relating to or made up of many human races.

multi-sensory *adjective* pertaining to or affecting more than one of the five senses.

multi-stage *adjective* consisting of, occurring in, or involving many stages.

multi-task *verb* do several different things at once.

multi-tasking • *noun* the execution of a number of tasks at once. • *adjective* capable of multi-tasking.

multi-track • *adjective* **1** relating to or made by the mixing of separately recorded soundtracks. **2** (of a school) having students divided into several groups on overlapping schedules esp. to ease overcrowding. • *noun* a multi-track recording. • *verb* **1** record using multi-track recording. **2** divide a student body into several groups on overlapping schedules to ease overcrowding etc. ▶**multi-tracked** *adjective* **multi-tracking** *noun*

multitude *noun* **1** (often foll. by *of*) a great number: *a multitude of medical conditions are due to being overweight*. **2** a large gathering of people; a crowd: *the prime minister addressed the multitude*. **3** (**the multitude**) the common people: *placing political power in the hands of the multitude*.

multitudinous *adjective* **1** very numerous: *multitudinous blankets kept us warm*. **2** consisting of many individuals or elements: *the multitudinous array of chemical substances that exist in the natural world*. [Say multi TUDE in us]

multi-use *adjective* serving many uses.

multi-user *adjective* **1** having many users. **2** (of a computer system) able to be used by more than one person and accessed from more than one terminal concurrently.

multivalence *noun* the condition of being multivalent. [Say multi VAY lince]

multivalent *adjective* **1** having or able to have many applications, interpretations, meanings, or values: *a complex, multivalent fiction* ◊ *a multivalent vaccine*. **2** *Chemistry* **a** having a valence of more than two. **b** having a variable valence. [Say multi VAY lint]

multivariate *adjective* *Statistics* involving or having two or more variable quantities. [Say multi VERY it]

multivitamin • *noun* a nutritional supplement, esp. a pill, incorporating several vitamins. • *adjective* designating a nutritional supplement of this sort.

multi-year *adjective* lasting or covering many years.

mum[1] *noun* *Cdn & Brit. informal* mother.

mum[2] *adjective* *informal* silent: *keep mum*. PHRASES **mum's the word** say nothing.

mum[3] *verb* (**mums, mummed, mumming**) play as a mummer.

mum[4] *noun* *informal* = CHRYSANTHEMUM.

mumble • *verb* (**mumbles, mumbled, mumbling**) speak or utter indistinctly. • *noun* an indistinct utterance. ▶**mumbler** *noun* **mumbling** *noun & adjective* **mumblingly** *adverb*

mumbo-jumbo *noun* (*plural* **mumbo-jumbos**) **1** meaningless or ignorant ritual. **2** obscure language or action intended to mystify or confuse.

mummer • *noun* **1** an actor in a traditional masked mime. **2** (in Newfoundland) a person participating in Christmas mumming. • *verb* (in Newfoundland) participate in mumming activities.

mummification *noun* an act of mummifying.

mummified *adjective* embalmed and preserved as or like a mummy.

mummify *verb* (**mummifies, mummified, mummifying**) **1** embalm and preserve (a body) in the form of a mummy (see MUMMY[2]). **2** shrivel or dry up (tissues etc.).

mumming *noun* (also **mummering**) **1** a performance, esp. of a folk play, by disguised actors, often accompanied by an outdoor procession or visits to private houses. **2** (in Newfoundland) the visiting of private houses by disguised merrymakers during the twelve days of Christmas.

mummy[1] *noun* (*plural* **mummies**) *Cdn & Brit. informal* mother.

mummy[2] *noun* (*plural* **mummies**) **1** (esp. in ancient Egypt) a body of a human being or animal that has been ceremonially preserved by removal of the internal organs, treatment with resin, and wrapping in bandages. In Egypt the preservation of the body was regarded as important for the afterlife. **2** a dried-up body.

mumps *plural noun* (treated as *singular*) an acute contagious and infectious viral disease, esp. of children, characterized by fever and swelling of the parotid glands.

munch *verb* (**munches, munched, munching**) eat steadily and usu. audibly with a marked action of the jaws, esp. with great enjoyment.

muncher *noun* a person who munches.

munchies *plural noun* *informal* **1** snacks; food suitable for snacks. **2** (**the munchies**) hunger, esp. desire for snack food.

munchkin *noun* *informal* **1** a small or dwarf-like person, animal, etc. **2** a child.

mundane *adjective* **1** dull, routine; of or pertaining to everyday life: *seeking a way out of his mundane, humdrum existence*. **2** of this earthly world rather than a heavenly or spiritual one: *encompasses the secular with the spiritual, and the mundane with the celestial*. ▶**mundanely** *adverb* **mundanity** *noun* (*plural* **mundanities**) [Say mun DANE or MUN dane, mun DANNA tee]

mung *noun* (also **mung bean**) the small round green bean of a widely cultivated leguminous plant, commonly grown as a source of bean sprouts.

municipal *adjective* of, concerning, or operated by a municipality. [Say myoo NISSA pull]

M

municipal court *noun* a lower court with limited jurisdiction, usu. extending to bylaw infractions, certain civil matters, etc.

municipal district *noun Cdn (Prairies & North)* a large, lightly populated rural area administered by a regional municipal government. Abbreviation: **MD**.

municipality *noun* (*plural* **municipalities**) **1** a city, town, or district having local government. **2** the governing body of this area.

municipally *adverb* with regard to a municipality: *a municipally owned park*. [Say myoo NISSA plee]

munificence *noun* great generosity: *the university asked for $1,000,000, which was an amount exceeding even Douglas's munificence*. [Say myoo NIFFA since]

munificent *adjective* (of a giver or a gift) splendidly generous: *a munificent gesture ◊ he enjoys being munificent on a princely scale*. ▶ **munificently** *adverb* [Say myoo NIFFA sint]

munition *noun* (usu. in *plural*) military weapons, ammunition, equipment, and stores. [Say myoo NISH'n]

muon *noun Physics* an unstable elementary particle like an electron, but with a much greater mass. [Say MYOO on]

mural • *noun* a painting executed directly on a wall. • *adjective* placed or painted on a wall. ▶ **muralist** *noun*

murder • *noun* **1** the unlawful premeditated killing of a human being by another (*compare* MANSLAUGHTER). **2** *informal* an unpleasant, troublesome, or dangerous state of affairs: *it was murder here*. **3** *informal* something very damaging: *chlorine is murder on hair*. • *verb* **1** kill (a human being) unlawfully, esp. wickedly or inhumanly. **2** *Law* kill (a human being) with malice and a premeditated motive. **3** *informal* **a** put an end to or destroy. **b** spoil by bad execution, performance, mispronunciation, etc.: *murdered the soliloquy*. **4** *slang* conclusively defeat (an opponent etc.), esp. at a game or sport. PHRASES **scream** (or **shout, yell,** etc.) **bloody** (or **blue**) **murder** *slang* shout loudly. **get away with murder** *informal* do whatever one wishes and escape punishment. **murder will out** murder cannot remain undetected.

murderball *noun Cdn* a game in which players in opposing teams attempt to hit their opponents with a large, inflated ball.

murderer *noun* a person who has murdered someone.

murderess *noun* (*plural* **murderesses**) a woman who has murdered someone.

murder mystery *noun* (*plural* **murder mysteries**) a novel, play, etc. about a murder in which the murderer's identity is concealed until the denouement.

murderous *adjective* **1** (of a person, weapon, action, etc.) capable of, intending, or involving murder or great harm. **2** *informal* extremely arduous or unpleasant. ▶ **murderously** *adverb* **murderousness** *noun*

murk *noun* **1** darkness, gloom; poor visibility. **2 a** air obscured by fog, dense vapour, etc. **b** confusion, obscurity, vagueness, or incomprehensibility.

murkiness *noun* the quality of being murky.

murky *adjective* (**murkier, murkiest**) **1** dark, gloomy. **2** (of darkness) thick, dense. **3** suspiciously obscure: *a murky past*. **4** indistinct, confused, not easily understood.

murmur • *noun* **1** a softly spoken or nearly inarticulate utterance. **2** the quiet or subdued expression of a particular feeling by a group of people: *there was a murmur of approval from the crowd*. **3** a recurring sound heard in the heart and usu. indicating abnormality. **4** a subdued continuous sound, as made by waves, a brook, etc. • *verb* **1** utter (words) in a low voice. **2** make a subdued continuous sound. **3** (usu. foll. by *at, against*)

complain in low tones, grumble. ▶ **murmurer** *noun* **murmuring** *adjective & noun* **murmurous** *adjective*

Murphy's Law *noun jocular* any of various maxims about the apparent perversity of things, esp. the principle that if anything can go wrong, it will.

murre *noun* an auk or guillemot. [Rhymes with *HER*]

murrelet *noun* any of several small auks of the north Pacific. [Say MUR lit]

muscat *noun* **1** a sweet fortified white wine made from musk-flavoured grapes. **2** such a grape. [Say MUSS cat]

muscle • *noun* **1** a fibrous tissue with the ability to contract, producing movement in or maintaining the position of an animal body. **2** the part of an animal body that is composed of muscles. **3 a** physical power or strength. **b** force, influence: *more marketing muscle*. **4** *slang* a person employed to threaten or use violence. • *verb* (**muscles, muscled, muscling**) **1** *informal* **a** move by the exercise of physical power. **b** make one's way by the exercise of physical power: *muscled through the crowds*. **c** *Baseball* (of a batter) propel (the ball) forcefully with the part of the bat nearest the hands, relying more on muscle strength than on swing momentum. **2** *slang* coerce by violence, intimidation, etc., esp. by economic or political pressure: *he was eventually muscled out of his market*. PHRASES **not move a muscle** be completely motionless. **muscle in** (**on**) *informal* involve oneself in something when one has no right to do so, for one's own advantage.

muscle-bound *adjective* **1** with muscles stiff and inelastic through excessive exercise or training. **2** *informal* usu. *derogatory* (of a person) very, esp. excessively muscular.

muscle car *noun informal* a powerful car, esp. a hot rod.

muscled *adjective* having well-developed muscles or the kind of muscles described.

muscle fibre *noun* each of the elongated cells of which muscular tissue is composed, which have the ability to contract.

muscleman *noun* (*plural* **musclemen**) **1** a man with highly developed muscles. **2** a person who employs or threatens violence on behalf of another, esp. a professional criminal.

muscly *adjective* with well-developed muscles; strong.

Muscovite • *noun* a native or citizen of Moscow. • *adjective* of or relating to Moscow, the capital of Russia. [Say MUSKA vite]

muscovite *noun* a silver-grey form of mica with a sheetlike crystalline structure that is used in the manufacture of electrical equipment etc. [Say MUSKA vite]

muscular *adjective* **1** having well-developed muscles. **2** of or affecting the muscles. **3** robust, vigorous.

muscular dystrophy *noun* a hereditary progressive weakening and wasting of the muscles.

muscularity *noun* **1** the fact of having well-developed muscles. **2** strength or vigour: *the remedy for such widespread discrimination must match the problem in both scope and muscularity*. [Say muss cue LERRA tee]

musculature *noun* **1** the muscular system of a body or organ. **2** a person's or animal's muscles collectively, esp. if well-developed. [Say MUSS cue luh chur]

musculoskeletal *adjective* of or relating to the musculature and skeleton together. [Say muss cue lo SKELETAL]

muse[1] *noun* **1** (**Muse**) *Greek & Roman Myth* any of the nine

goddesses who encourage such artistic and scientific pursuits as poetry, history, dancing, song, tragedy, comedy, hymns, and astronomy. **2** a person or spirit that gives a writer, painter, musician, etc. ideas and the desire to create: *he felt that his muse had deserted him*.

muse[2] *verb* (**muses**, **mused**, **musing**) **1 a** ponder, reflect: *he was musing on the problems he faced*. **b** gaze meditatively (on a scene etc.): *sat musing on her hands*. **2** say or murmur meditatively.

museologist *noun* a person who organizes and manages a museum. [Say muse ee OLLA jist]

museology *noun* the science or practice of organizing and managing museums. [Say muse ee OLLA jee]

museum *noun* a building used for storing, preserving, and exhibiting objects considered to be of lasting historical, scientific, or cultural interest.

museum piece *noun* **1** a specimen of art etc. fit for a museum. **2** *derogatory* an old-fashioned or quaint person or object: *his car is practically a museum piece*.

mush[1] • *noun* (*plural* **mushes**) **1** a soft pulpy or formless mass. **2** feeble sentimentality. **3** *US* cornmeal boiled in water until it thickens. • *verb* (**mushes**, **mushed**, **mushing**) reduce to mush; mash.

mush[2] • *verb* (**mushes**, **mushed**, **mushing**) **1 a** travel through snow with a dogsled. **b** (of dogs) pull a sled. **2** used as a command to dogs pulling a sled to urge them forward. • *noun* (*plural* **mushes**) a journey across snow with a dogsled. ▶ **musher** *noun*

mushiness *noun* **1** the quality of being soft and pulpy like mush. **2** feeble sentimentality.

mushing *noun* the activity or sport of travelling through snow with a dogsled.

mushroom • *noun* **1** the usu. edible spore-producing body of various fungi, typically with a stalk and domed cap, proverbial for its rapid growth. **2** the pinkish-brown colour of this. **3** any item resembling a mushroom in shape. • *verb* **1** appear or develop rapidly. **2** expand and flatten like a mushroom cap. **3** gather mushrooms. ▶ **mushrooming** *adjective & noun*

mushroom cloud *noun* a cloud of smoke, vapour, etc. suggesting the shape of a mushroom, esp. from a nuclear explosion.

mushy *adjective* (**mushier**, **mushiest**) **1** like mush, soft and pulpy. **2** feebly sentimental.

music *noun* **1** the art of combining vocal or instrumental sounds (or both) to produce beauty of form, harmony, and expression of emotion. **2** the sounds so produced. **3** musical compositions collectively. **4** the written or printed score of a musical composition. **5** certain pleasant sounds, e.g. birdsong, the sound of a stream, etc. PHRASES **face the music** *informal* put up with or stand up to unpleasant consequences, esp. criticism. **music to one's ears** something very pleasant to hear.

musical • *adjective* **1** of or relating to music. **2** (of sounds, a voice, etc.) melodious, harmonious. **3** fond of or skilled in music: *the musical one of the family*. **4** set to or accompanied by music. **5** (of a dancer, choreographer, etc.) able to suit or fit dance steps to music particularly pleasingly. • *noun* a musical comedy or music theatre.

musical chairs *plural noun* **1** a party game in which the players compete in successive rounds for a decreasing number of chairs, sitting down on a chair whenever the music stops. **2** a series of esp. minor changes, manoeuvres, etc. after the manner of the game.

musical comedy *noun* (*plural* **musical comedies**) a light drama on stage or film, consisting of dialogue, songs, and dancing.

musicality *noun* **1** the quality or character of being

musical. **2** (of a dancer, choreographer, etc.) the ability to suit or fit dance steps to music particularly pleasingly. [Say music ALLA tee]

musically *adverb* **1** in a way that is connected with music: *musically gifted*. **2** with musical skill: *he plays very musically*. **3** in a way that is pleasing to listen to: *speaks musically*.

musical ride *noun* *Cdn* an exhibition in which riders on horseback (usu. members of a mounted police force) perform choreographed manoeuvres to music.

music box *noun* (*plural* **music boxes**) **1** a mechanical instrument playing a tune by causing a toothed cylinder to strike a comblike metal plate within a box. **2** a figurine, toy, or other decorative item incorporating a music box.

music hall *noun* **1** a public hall or theatre used for musical performances. **2** variety entertainment, popular *c.*1850–1914, consisting of singing, dancing, and novelty acts; vaudeville.

musician *noun* a person who performs esp. instrumental music, esp. professionally. ▶ **musicianship** *noun*

musicological *adjective* having to do with musicology. [Say music uh LOGICAL]

musicologist *noun* an academic who specializes in the study of music. [Say music OLLA jist]

musicology *noun* the branch of knowledge that deals with music as a subject of study rather than as a skill or performing art, esp. academic research in music. [Say music OLLA jee]

music stand *noun* a rest or frame on which sheet music or a score is supported.

music theatre *noun* in late 20th-century music, the combination of elements from music and drama in new forms distinct from traditional opera, esp. as designed for small groups of performers.

music video *noun* a dramatization of a song or piece of music on videotape, esp. for broadcast on television.

musing *noun* **1** an act or instance of being absorbed in thought: *fell into a state between musing and dozing*. **2** (often in *plural*) an expression of one's thoughts or opinions: *his melancholy musings on life and loss*. ▶ **musingly** *adverb*

musk *noun* **1 a** a strong-smelling reddish-brown substance produced by a gland in the male musk deer and used as an ingredient in perfumes. **b** any of various similar substances secreted by other animals, esp. for scent marking. **2 a** a substance designed to imitate musk, esp. for use in perfumes. **b** an aromatic odour resembling that of musk, esp. worn as a fragrance. **3** a plant with pale-green oval leaves and yellow flowers, formerly grown for its musky perfume.

musk deer *noun* (*plural* **musk deer**) a small deer-like East Asian mammal without antlers, the male having long protruding canine teeth.

muskeg *noun* **1** a swamp or bog in northern North America, consisting of a mixture of water and partly dead vegetation, often covered by a layer of sphagnum or other mosses. **2** terrain characterized by such swamps.

muskellunge *noun* (*plural* **muskellunge**) a large North American pike that occurs only in the Great Lakes region. [Say MUSKA lunge]

musket *noun* *hist.* an infantryman's usu. smoothbore light gun, fired from shoulder level.

musketeer *noun* *hist.* **1** a soldier armed with a musket. **2** a member of either of two bodies forming part of the household troops of the French king in the 17th and 18th centuries.

muskie *noun* (*plural* **muskie** or **muskies**) = MUSKELLUNGE.

M

muskmelon *noun* a yellow or green melon, having a raised network of markings on the skin.

Muskogean • *noun* a language family of southeastern North America, including Creek, Seminole, and Choctaw. • *adjective* of or pertaining to this language family. [Say muska JEE in or muh SKO jee in]

Muskogee • *noun* (*plural* **Muskogee** or **Muskogees**) **1** a member of a North American Aboriginal people forming part of the Creek Confederacy, now living esp. in Oklahoma. **2** the Muskogean language of this people. • *adjective* of or relating to this people. [Say muh SKO jee]

Muskoka chair *noun* Cdn a slatted wooden lawn chair with a fan-shaped back and broad arms. [Say muh SKO kuh]

muskox *noun* (*plural* **muskox** or **muskoxen**) a large goat-antelope of the tundra, esp. in Canada and Greenland, with a thick shaggy coat and small curved horns.

muskrat *noun* **1** a large semiaquatic North American rodent with a musky smell, valued for its fur. **2** the fur of this.

musky *adjective* (**muskier**, **muskiest**) smelling of or like musk: *a musky perfume*.

Muslim • *noun* a follower of the Islamic religion. • *adjective* of or relating to Muslims or their religion. [Say MUZZ lim]

muslin *noun* a fine cotton fabric that is almost transparent, used, especially in the past, for making clothes and curtains. [Say MUZZ lin]

muss *informal* • *verb* (**musses**, **mussed**, **mussing**) (often foll. by *up*) mess, make untidy: *don't muss my hair*. • *noun* (*plural* **musses**) a mess; a state of confusion or untidiness.

SPELL CHECK
mussel, muscle

Body tissue is **muscle**.

---

mussel *noun* **1** a bivalve mollusc with a brown or purplish-black shell, living in sea water and often used for food. **2** a similar freshwater mollusc, which forms small pearls.

must[1] • *auxiliary verb* (*3rd singular present* **must**; *past* **had to** or in indirect speech **must**) **1** be obliged to; should. **2** expressing insistence. **3** expressing an opinion about something that is very likely. • *noun informal* a thing that should not be overlooked or missed: *if you go to Halifax the Citadel is a must*. PHRASES **I must say** often *ironic* I cannot refrain from saying: *a fine way to behave, I must say*.

must[2] *noun* grape juice before or during fermentation.

must[3] *noun* mustiness, mould.

must[4] • *adjective* (of a male elephant or camel) in a state of dangerous frenzy, associated with the rutting season. • *noun* this state.

mustache *noun* = MOUSTACHE.

mustachio *noun* (*plural* **mustachios**) (often in *plural*) a moustache, esp. a large one. ▶ **mustachioed** *adjective* [Say muh STASHY oh]

mustang *noun* a small wild horse of the American plains.

mustard • *noun* **1** a spicy yellow or brown paste made from the crushed seeds of certain plants and used as a condiment. **2 a** the yellow-flowered plant of the cabbage family whose seeds are used to make this paste. **b** any of various other plants resembling this plant in appearance or taste. **3** (also **mustard yellow**) the brownish-yellow colour of the condiment mustard. • *adjective* of a brownish-yellow colour.

mustard gas *noun* a colourless oily liquid, whose vapour is a powerful irritant, used in chemical warfare.

mustardy *adjective* made with mustard or reminiscent of the taste, smell, or colour of mustard.

muster • *verb* **1** collect, gather together. **2** collect or assemble (originally soldiers) for inspection, to check numbers, etc. **3** (often foll. by *up*) summon up (courage, strength, etc.). • *noun* a group of people, especially soldiers, that have been brought together, e.g. for inspection: *ready for muster at 6:00 a.m.* PHRASES **pass muster** come up to the required standard.

must-have • *noun* an item regarded as indispensable. • *adjective* indispensable.

mustiness *noun* the quality of being musty or fusty.

mustn't *contraction* must not.

must-see • *noun* a site, event, film, etc. that must be seen. • *adjective* that must be seen.

musty *adjective* (**mustier**, **mustiest**) **1** mouldy; having a smell or taste indicative or suggestive of mouldiness or decay. **2** stale-smelling or fusty. **3** having lost newness, interest, or liveliness.

mutability *noun* the quality of being mutable; the ability to change or be changed: *the mutability of life in the Arctic zone is a major theme.* [Say mute uh BILLA tee]

mutable *adjective* literary **1** liable or subject to change or alteration: *the mutable nature of fashion.* **2** fickle: *mutable nature of modern youth.* [Say MUTE uh bull]

mutagen *noun* an agent causing or promoting mutation, e.g. radiation. ▶ **mutagenesis** *noun* **mutagenic** *adjective* [Say MUTE uh jin, mute uh GENESIS, mute uh JEN ick]

mutant • *adjective* **1** resulting from mutation. **2** having the characteristics or attributes of a mutant. • *noun* **1** an individual, gene, etc. which has arisen by or undergone mutation. **2** (esp. in science fiction) an individual with freak or grossly abnormal anatomy, abilities, etc.

mutate *verb* (**mutates**, **mutated**, **mutating**) **1** change or cause to change in form or nature: *technology continues to mutate at an alarming rate* ◊ *each side is mutating their image of the opposing culture into something evil and sinister.* **2** Biology (with reference to a cell, DNA molecule, etc.) undergo or cause to undergo change in a gene or genes: *the virus is able to mutate into new forms that are immune to the vaccine* ◊ *certain nucleotides were mutated.* ▶ **mutated** *adjective*

mutation *noun* **1** the action or process of mutating: *the mutation of ethnic politics into nationalist politics* ◊ *her novel went through several mutations.* **2 a** a genetic change which, when transmitted to offspring, gives rise to heritable variations: *a link between the mutation and the disease.* **b** the process by which such changes arise: *cells affected by mutation.* **3** a distinct form produced by genetic change; a mutant. ▶ **mutational** *adjective*

WRITING TIP
mute, moot

An issue that is undecided or debatable or that is no longer of practical importance or relevance is **moot**: *The question of whether or not stores should be allowed to sell toy guns remains a moot point*; *The final score was 6-0, so whether or not the first goal should have counted is moot.*

---

mute • *adjective* **1** silent, refraining from, or temporarily incapable of speech. **2** (of a person) lacking the faculty of speech. **3** (of an animal) naturally lacking the power of articulate speech. **4 a** not expressed in speech: *mute protest.* **b** characterized by an absence of sound: *the mute forest.* **5** (of a letter) not pronounced. • *noun* **1** a person who cannot or will not speak: *a deaf*

M

mute. **2 a** a clip placed over the bridge of a violin etc. to dampen the resonance without affecting the vibration of the strings. **b** a pad or cone inserted into the bell of a wind instrument to soften the sound. **3** = MUTE BUTTON 2. • *verb* (**mutes, muted, muting**) **1 a** deaden, muffle, or soften the sound of (a thing, esp. a musical instrument). **b** suppress the volume of (a loudspeaker) or the output of (an amplifier or other circuit component). **2** tone down, make less intense.

mute button *noun* **1** a device on a telephone etc. to temporarily prevent the caller from hearing what is being said at the receiver's end. **2** a device on a television etc. that temporarily suppresses all sound.

muted *adjective* **1** (of colours etc.) subdued: *a muted green*. **2** (of a musical instrument) having a muffled tone or employing a mute. **3 a** silent, quiet, muffled: *they discussed the accident in muted voices*. **b** understated: *muted anger*.

mutely *adverb* without speaking; silently.

muteness *noun* inability or refusal to speak; silence.

mutilate *verb* (**mutilates, mutilated, mutilating**) **1** injure or damage (a person or animal or a part of the body) very severely, e.g. by removal of a limb or organ. **2** inflict serious damage on: *intruders slashed and mutilated several paintings*. ▶**mutilation** *noun* **mutilator** *noun* [Say MUTE uh late]

mutinous *adjective* rebellious, tending to mutiny: *mutinous soldiers* ◊ *a mutinous two-year-old*. ▶**mutinously** *adverb* [Say MUTE in us]

mutiny • *noun* (*plural* **mutinies**) an open revolt against authority, esp. by soldiers or sailors against their officers. • *verb* (**mutinies, mutinied, mutinying**) revolt; engage in mutiny: *the government finally toppled when soldiers deserted and sailors mutinied*. [Say MUTE in ee]

mutt *noun* **1** *derogatory* or *jocular* a dog, esp. a mongrel. **2** *slang* an ignorant, stupid, or blundering person.

mutter • *verb* **1** speak in a barely audible manner. **2** murmur or grumble about. **3** say or express (complaints etc.), esp. in secret. **4** make a low rumbling sound. • *noun* **1** low, indistinct muttered words or sounds. **2** an act of muttering. ▶**mutterer** *noun* **muttering** *noun & adjective* **mutteringly** *adverb*

mutton *noun* the flesh of sheep used for food. PHRASES **mutton dressed as lamb** *informal* a usu. middle-aged or elderly woman dressed or made up to appear younger. [Say MUTT in]

mutton chop *noun* **1** (usu. in *plural*) (also **mutton chop whiskers**) the whiskers on a man's cheek when shaped like a meat chop, narrow at the top and broad and rounded at the bottom. **2** a piece of mutton, usu. the rib and half vertebra to which it is attached.

mutual *adjective* **1** (of feelings, actions, etc.) experienced or done by each of two or more parties with reference to the other or others; reciprocal: *mutual affection*. **2** held in common or shared between two or more persons: *mutual friend* ◊ *a mutual interest*. **3** (of people) having the same specified relationship to each other: *mutual well-wishers*.

mutual fund *noun* a fund in which contributions from many persons combined are invested in various securities and in which dividends are paid in proportion to the contributors' holdings.

mutuality *noun* the quality of being mutual or reciprocal: *a mutuality of respect between them*. [Say myoo choo ALA tee]

mutually *adverb* **1** with mutual action or feeling; reciprocally: *a mutually beneficial solution* ◊ *athletics and good study habits are not mutually exclusive*. **2** in co-operation; by mutual agreement; jointly: *it was mutually agreed that we all would go*.

mutuel *noun* = PARIMUTUEL. [Sounds like MUTUAL]

muzak *noun* **1** recorded light background music. **2** bland, undemanding music. [Say MYOO zack]

muzzle • *noun* **1** the projecting part of an animal's face, including the nose and mouth. **2** a guard, usu. made of straps or wire, fitted over an animal's nose and mouth to stop it biting or feeding. **3** the open end of a firearm. • *verb* (**muzzles, muzzled, muzzling**) **1** put a muzzle on (an animal etc.). **2** impose silence upon.

muzzleloader *noun* a gun that is loaded through the muzzle. ▶**muzzle-loading** *adjective & noun*

muzzy *adjective* (**muzzier, muzziest**) **1 a** mentally hazy; dull. **b** dazed or fuddled from drinking alcohol. **2** blurred, indistinct.

MV *abbreviation* **1** motor vessel. **2** megavolt(s).

MVA *abbreviation Cdn* market value assessment (of property values for tax purposes).

MVP *abbreviation* (*plural* **MVPs**) *Sport* most valuable player.

MW *abbreviation* megawatt(s).

Mx. *abbreviation* maxwell(s).

my • *possessive adjective* **1** of or belonging to me or myself. **2** as a form of address in affectionate, sympathetic, respectful, jocular, or patronizing contexts. • *interjection* expressing surprise, admiration, etc.: *my, she's beautiful!*

myalgia *noun* a pain in a muscle or group of muscles. ▶**myalgic** *adjective* [Say my AL juh or my AL jee uh]

mycelium *noun* (*plural* **mycelia**) the vegetative part of a fungus, consisting of a network of fine white filaments. [Say my SEELY um]

Mycenaean • *noun* an inhabitant of the ancient Greek city of Mycenae or of the late Bronze Age civilization represented by finds at Mycenae and depicted in the poetry of Homer; the Mycenaeans controlled the Aegean from about 1400 to 1100 BC and built fortified citadels and impressive palaces. • *adjective* of or relating to Mycenae or the civilization of which it was the centre. [Say my suh NEE in]

mycologist *noun* a person who studies fungi. [Say my COLLA jist]

mycology *noun* **1** the study of fungi. **2** the fungi of a particular region. [Say my COLLA jee]

myelin *noun* a white substance which forms a sheath around certain nerve fibres. ▶**myelinated** *adjective* **myelination** *noun* [Say MY uh lin]

myeloma *noun* (*plural* **myelomas**) a malignant tumour of the bone marrow. [Say my uh LO muh]

Mylar *noun proprietary* a polyester film used to make audio tapes, insulation, etc. [Say MY lar]

myna *noun* (also **mynah**) a Southeast Asian starling that is able to mimic the human voice. [Say MY nuh]

myocardial *adjective* having to do with the myocardium. [Say my oh CARDY ul]

myocardium *noun* (*plural* **myocardia**) the muscular tissue of the heart. [Say my oh CARDY um for the singular, my oh CARDY um for the plural]

myopia *noun* **1** short-sightedness. **2** lack of imagination or intellectual insight: *most people are guilty of ethnocentric myopia*. ▶**myopic** *adjective* **myopically** *adverb* [Say my OPE ee uh, my OP ick]

myriad • *noun* an indefinitely great number: *myriads of Arctic spring flowers*. • *adjective* **1** of an indefinitely great number: *the myriad lights of the city*. **2** having countless phases or aspects: *myriad diversity*. [Say MEARY add]

myrrh *noun* **1** a sticky substance with a sweet smell that comes from several trees of the genus *Commiphora*, used in perfume, medicine, incense, etc. **2** *Cdn* (*Nfld*) fir or spruce resin, often used as a component of home remedies. [Rhymes with HER]

myrtle *noun* **1** an evergreen shrub with glossy

aromatic foliage, white flowers, and purple-black oval berries. **2** the lesser periwinkle, a trailing evergreen plant with lilac-blue flowers. [Rhymes with *TURTLE*]

GRAMMAR CHECK
myself

Do not misuse **myself**. Sentences like *Ivan, Marty, and myself went out to a movie* and *They were very kind to my wife and myself* are not recommended. It is better to say *Ivan, Marty, and I went out for dinner* and *They were very kind to my wife and me*. Reserve **myself** for reflexive uses like *I'll just help myself to a drink* or emphatic ones like *I myself was not offended, but they were*.

---

myself *pronoun* **1** *emphatic form of* I[2] *or* ME[1]: *I saw it myself* ◊ *I like to do it myself*. **2** *reflexive form of* ME[1]: *able to dress myself*. **3** *in my normal state of body and mind*: *I'm not myself today*. **PHRASES I myself** I for my part: *I myself am doubtful*.

mysterious *adjective* **1** full of or wrapped in mystery. **2** puzzling; enigmatic. ► **mysteriously** *adverb* **mysteriousness** *noun*

mystery *noun* (*plural* **mysteries**) **1** a secret, hidden, or inexplicable matter: *the reason remains a mystery*. **2** secrecy or obscurity: *wrapped in mystery*. **3** (as an *adjective*) secret, undisclosed: *mystery guest*. **4** the practice of making a secret of (esp. unimportant) things: *engaged in mystery and intrigue*. **5** a fictional work dealing with a puzzling event, esp. a crime: *a well known mystery writer*. **6 a** a religious truth divinely revealed, esp. one beyond human reason. **b** *Catholicism* a decade of the rosary. **PHRASES make a mystery of** treat as an impressive secret.

mystic • *noun* a person who tries to become united with God through prayer and meditation and so understand important things that are beyond normal human understanding. • *adjective* = MYSTICAL. [Say MISS tick]

mystical *adjective* **1** having to do with mystics or mysticism: *mystical contemplation* ◊ *mystical doctrine*. **2** having to do with ancient religious mysteries or other occult or esoteric rites: *the Chinese mystical art of feng shui* ◊ *mystical powers*. **3** of hidden meaning: *a mystical inscription*. **4** spiritually allegorical or symbolic:

the mystical body of Christ. **5** inspiring a sense of spiritual mystery, awe, and fascination: *the mystical forces of nature*. ► **mystically** *adverb* [Say MISS tick ul]

mysticism *noun* the belief that knowledge of God and of real truth can be found through prayer and meditation. [Say MIST i sism]

mystification *noun* an act of mystifying. [Say miss tiffa KAY sh'n]

mystify *verb* (**mystifies**, **mystified**, **mystifying**) bewilder, confuse: *scientists are mystified by the phenomenon*. ► **mystifying** *adjective* **mystifyingly** *adverb* [Say MISSTA fye]

mystique *noun* an atmosphere of mystery and importance evoking admiration, surrounding some activity or person; charisma. [Say miss TEEK]

myth *noun* **1** a traditional narrative usu. involving supernatural or imaginary persons and embodying popular ideas on natural or social phenomena etc. **2** such narratives collectively. **3** a widely held but false notion. **4** a fictitious person, thing, or idea. **5** an idealized version of the past, esp. as embodying significant cultural realities: *during the early 1870s the Canadian prairie came as close as it ever did to the myth of the "Wild West"*. ► **mythic** *adjective* **mythical** *adjective* **mythically** *adverb*

mythmaker *noun* a creator of myths or folklore. ► **mythmaking** *noun*

mythological *adjective* **1** having to do with ancient myths or mythology: *Zeus and other mythological beings*. **2** fictitious or idealized: *some mythological notion of our past*. ► **mythologically** *adverb*

mythologize *verb* (**mythologizes**, **mythologized**, **mythologizing**) convert into myth; make mythical: *the 1950s TV sitcom mythologized the nuclear family*. ► **mythologizer** *noun*

mythology *noun* (*plural* **mythologies**) **1** a body of myths: *Greek mythology*. **2** the study of myths. **3** a body of traditions or stories, usu. somewhat idealized, concerning a particular person, institution, event, etc.: *cowboy mythology*.

mythopoeic *adjective* having to do with the making of myths: *the mythopoeic aspect of literature*. [Say myth oh PEE ick]

mythos *noun* **1** *literary* a myth; a body of myths: *the Arthurian mythos*. **2** a narrative theme or pattern: *the novel is related to the mythos visible in the plots and situations of the poems*. [Say MITH oss or MY thoss]

Nn

N¹ *noun* (also **n**) (*plural* **Ns** or **N's**) the fourteenth letter of the alphabet.

N² *abbreviation* (also **n**) **1 a** North. **b** Northern. **2** New. **3** nuclear.

N³ *symbol Chemistry* **1** nitrogen. **2** newton(s).

n¹ *abbreviation* (also **n.**) **1** name. **2** neuter. **3** noon. **4** note. **5** noun.

n² *symbol* **1** *Math* an indefinite number. **2** nano-. **PHRASES** **to the nth** (or **nth degree**) **1** *Math* to any required power. **2** to any extent; to the utmost: *lawyers who go to the nth degree to make the law more lenient*.

'n *conjunction* (also **'n'**) *informal* and.

NA *abbreviation* **1** North America. **2** North American.

Na *symbol* sodium.

n/a *abbreviation* **1** not applicable. **2** not available.

naan *noun* = NAN².

nab *verb* (**nabs**, **nabbed**, **nabbing**) *informal* **1** arrest; catch in wrongdoing. **2** capture, catch.

nabob *noun informal* a very rich or influential person: *the article takes a dim view of Hollywood nabobs*. [Say NAY bob]

nacho *noun* (*plural* **nachos**)) a tortilla chip topped with cheese, salsa, etc. and broiled. [Say NOTCH oh]

nada *noun informal* nothing: *has said nada*. [Say NODDA]

nadir *noun* **1** the part of the celestial sphere directly below an observer (*opp.* ZENITH). **2** the lowest point in the fortunes of a person or thing: *the period 1920–60 constituted a nadir for flamenco, with declining public interest* ◊ *a nadir in US–Soviet relations*. [Say NAY deer]

NAFTA *abbreviation* North American Free Trade Agreement.

nag¹ • *verb* (**nags**, **nagged**, **nagging**) **1** annoy or irritate (a person) with persistent fault-finding or continuous urging. **2** (of a pain) ache dully but persistently. **3 a** worry or preoccupy (a person, the mind, etc.): *his mistake nagged him*. **b** (often foll. by *at*) worry. • *noun* a persistently nagging person.

nag² *noun* **1** an old or broken-down horse. **2** *informal* a horse, esp. a racehorse. **3** a small riding horse or pony.

nagging • *noun* the action of persistent fault-finding or urging. • *adjective* **1** worrying or preoccupying: *a nagging feeling*. **2** aching dully and persistently: *a nagging headache*. ▶ **naggingly** *adverb*

Nahuatl • *noun* **1** a member of a group of Aboriginal peoples of southern Mexico and Central America, including the Aztecs. **2** the language of these people. • *adjective* of the Nahuatl peoples or language. [Say nuh WOTTLE]

naïf • *adjective* = NAIVE. • *noun* a naive person. [Say naw EEF]

nail • *noun* **1** a small usu. sharpened metal spike with a broadened flat head, driven in esp. with a hammer to join things together. **2 a** a horny covering on the upper surface of the tip of the human finger or toe. **b** a claw or talon. • *verb* **1** fasten with a nail or nails. **2** fix or hold (one's eyes, attention, etc.) on something. **3** hit, strike, or punch (a person, ball, etc.). **4 a** secure, catch, or get hold of (a person or thing). **b** arrest (a person). **5** *Baseball* put (a runner) out: *nailed him at first*. **6** complete or perform (something) well or perfectly: *nailed a triple somersault*. **PHRASES** **hard as nails** **1** callous; unfeeling. **2** in good physical condition. **nail**

one's colours to the mast persist; refuse to give in. **nail down 1** bind (a person) to a promise etc. **2** define precisely. **3** fasten (a thing) with nails. **nail in the coffin** something to make imminent a person's death or the end or failure of something.

nail-biter *noun* **1** something that causes anxiety or tension: *the game was a real nail-biter*. **2** a person who habitually bites his or her fingernails.

nail-biting • *adjective* causing severe anxiety or tension. • *noun* the habit of biting one's fingernails.

nailed *adjective* having nails or the kind of fingernails described.

nail file *noun* a roughened metal or emery strip used for smoothing the nails.

nailhead *noun* the flat head of a nail.

nail set *noun* a tool for sinking a nailhead below a surface.

naive *adjective* **1** showing a lack of experience, wisdom, or judgment: *it's naive of you to think that such things only happen in other countries* ◊ *a naive and impractical suggestion*. **2** (of a person) natural and unaffected; innocent: *had a sweet, naive look when he smiled*. **3** (of art etc.) produced in a sophisticated society but deliberately rejecting conventional expertise. ▶ **naively** *adverb* **naiveness** *noun* [Say nigh EEV]

naïveté *noun* **1** lack of experience, wisdom, or judgment. **2** innocence and lack of affectation. [Say nigh ee vuh TAY or nigh EEVA tee]

naivety *noun* = NAÏVETÉ. [Say nigh EEVA tee]

naked *adjective* **1** unclothed. **2** plain; undisguised: *the naked truth*. **3 a** (of a flame etc.) unprotected from the wind etc. **b** (of a light bulb) unshaded. **4** defenceless. **5 a** (of landscape) barren; treeless. **b** (of rock) exposed; without soil etc. **6** (of a sword etc.) unsheathed. **7** without leaves, hairs, scales, a shell, etc. **8** (of a room, wall, etc.) without decoration, furnishings, etc.; empty, plain. **PHRASES** **the naked eye** unassisted vision, e.g. without a telescope, microscope, etc. ▶ **nakedly** *adverb* **nakedness** *noun*

Nama • *noun* (*plural* **Nama** or **Namas**) **1** a member of a people of South Africa and Namibia. **2** the language of this people. • *adjective* of or relating to this people or their language. [Say NOMMA]

namby-pamby • *adjective* **1** lacking vigour or drive; weak. **2** insipidly pretty or sentimental. • *noun* (*plural* **namby-pambies**) a namby-pamby person.

name • *noun* **1** the word by which an individual person, family, animal, place, or thing is known, spoken of, etc. **2 a** a usu. abusive term used of a person etc.: *called me names*. **b** a word denoting an object or esp. a class of objects, ideas, etc. **3** a famous person. **4** a reputation, esp. a good one. **5** something existing only nominally (*opp.* FACT, REALITY). • *verb* (**names, named, naming**) **1** give a usu. specified name to. **2** call (a person or thing) by the right name. **3** mention: *named a time*. **4** nominate, appoint, etc. **5** *Cdn & Brit.* Parliament (of the Speaker) mention (a member of a legislative assembly) as disobedient to the chair, thus banning her or him from the House. • *adjective* **1** famous; widely-known: *a name band*. **2** designating the person that gives his or her name to a firm, theatrical production, etc.: *one of the name partners*. **PHRASES** **by name**

1 called: *Erin by name.* **2** using the name or names of someone: *knows all her students by name.* **give a bad name** cause disrepute to: *this kind of behaviour gives students a bad name.* **have one's name on a thing** be destined or particularly suited to receive that thing: *a bullet out there with my name on it.* **(have) to one's name** (possess) as one's own. **in all but name** virtually. **in name** (or **in name only**) as a mere formality; hardly at all: *was the manager in name only.* **in the name of 1** calling to witness; invoking: *in God's name, what are you doing?* **2** by the authority of: *stop in the name of the law.* **3** for the sake of: *they did it all in the name of friendship.* **in one's own name** independently; without authority. **make a name for oneself** (also **make one's name**) become famous. **name after** (also **name for**) call (a person) by the name of (a specified person): *named him after his grandfather.* **name the day** arrange a date for one's wedding. **name names** mention specific names, esp. in accusation. **name of the game** *informal* the purpose or essence of an action etc. **what's in a name?** names are arbitrary labels. **you name it** *informal* no matter what; whatever you like. ▶ **nameable** *adjective*

name brand *noun* = BRAND NAME.

name-calling *noun* abusive language.

name-dropping *noun* the practice of casually mentioning the names of famous people one knows or pretends to know in order to impress others. ▶ **name-drop** *verb* (**name-drops, name-dropped, name-dropping**) **name-dropper** *noun*

nameless *adjective* **1** having no name or inscription. **2** inexpressible; indefinable: *a nameless sensation.* **3** anonymous, esp. deliberately: *our informant, who shall be nameless.* **4** individually indistinguishable: *a series of nameless nightclubbing bimbos.* **5** too loathsome or horrific to be named: *nameless vices.* ▶ **namelessly** *adverb* **namelessness** *noun*

namely *adverb* that is to say; in other words.

nameplate *noun* **1** a plate or panel bearing the name of an occupant of a room etc. **2 a** a plate attached to a car, computer, etc. bearing the name of the manufacturer or model. **b** a line of products produced under a single name.

namer *noun* a person who gives a name to something.

namesake *noun* a person or thing having the same name as another: *was her aunt's namesake.*

Namibian • *noun* a native or inhabitant of Namibia, a country in southern Africa. • *adjective* of or relating to Namibia or the Namibians. [Say nuh MIBBY in]

nam pla *noun* a pungent, salty fish sauce used in Thai cooking. [Say NAM pla]

nan[1] *noun* *Brit. & Cdn informal* grandmother.

nan[2] *noun* (in Indian cooking) a type of flat, oval, leavened bread cooked esp. in a clay oven.

nana *noun* *informal* grandmother.

Nanaimo bar *noun* *Cdn* a dessert consisting of a crust of chocolate and cookie crumbs, usu. also including coconut and nuts, covered with a usu. vanilla buttercream filling and a chocolate glaze, served cut into squares. [Say nuh NIME oh]

nanny • *noun* (*plural* **nannies**) **1 a** a person employed, esp. on a full-time basis, to care for a child, usu. in the child's home. **b** an unduly protective person, institution, etc. **2** = NAN[1]. **3** (also **nanny goat**) a female goat. • *verb* (**nannies, nannied, nannying**) be unduly protective towards.

nano- *combining form* **1** denoting a factor of 10^{-9}: *nanosecond.* **2** very small; minute.

nanometre *noun* (also **nanometer**) one billionth of a metre. Abbreviation: **nm**.

nanosecond *noun* **1** one billionth of a second. **2** an extremely short interval.

nanotechnology *noun* the branch of technology that deals with dimensions and tolerances of less than 100 nanometres, esp. the manipulation of individual atoms and molecules.

nap[1] • *verb* (**naps, napped, napping**) sleep lightly or briefly. • *noun* a short sleep or doze, esp. by day. **PHRASES catch a person napping 1** find a person asleep or off guard. **2** detect in negligence or error.

nap[2] • *noun* **1** the raised pile on textiles, esp. velvet. **2** a soft downy surface. • *verb* (**naps, napped, napping**) raise a nap on (cloth).

nap[3] (**naps, napped, napping**) (usu. in *passive*) cover (food) with a sauce: *clams napped with a white sauce.*

napa[1] *noun* a soft leather made by a special process from the skin of sheep or goats. [Say NAPPA]

napa[2] *noun* a plant with a long, dense head of whitish, broad leaves used in salads and Oriental cooking. [Say NAPPA]

napalm • *noun* a jellied gasoline used in incendiary bombs. • *verb* attack with napalm bombs. [Say NAY palm]

nape *noun* the back of the neck.

naphtha *noun* a colourless, flammable petroleum distillate used as a fuel and solvent. [Say NAP thuh or NAF thuh]

naphthalene *noun* a white crystalline aromatic substance produced by the distillation of coal tar and used in mothballs and the manufacture of dyes etc. [Say NAF thuh leen or NAP thuh leen]

napkin *noun* (also **table napkin**) a square piece of linen, paper, etc. used for wiping the lips, fingers, etc. at meals; a serviette.

napoleon *noun* *hist.* a gold twenty-franc piece minted in the reign of Napoleon I (1769–1821), emperor of France.

Napoleonic *adjective* of, relating to, or characteristic of Napoleon I (1769–1821), emperor of France, or his time. [Say nuh poley ON ick]

nappa *noun* = NAPA[1].

napped *adjective* (of a textile) having a nap or pile of a specified kind.

nappy *noun* (*plural* **nappies**) a small, shallow, glass or ceramic bowl for serving fruit, ice cream, etc.

narc *noun* *slang* a police narcotics officer.

narcissism *noun* excessive or erotic interest in oneself, one's physical features, etc.: *exhibitionists indulging in rampant narcissism.* ▶ **narcissist** *noun* **narcissistic** *adjective* [Say NARSA sism]

narcissus *noun* (*plural* **narcissi**) any bulbous plant of a genus that includes the daffodil, esp. one with flowers that have white or pale outer petals and a shallow orange or yellow cup in the centre. [Say nar SISS us for the singular, nar SISS eye for the plural]

narcolepsy *noun* a disease with fits of sleepiness and drowsiness. ▶ **narcoleptic** *adjective & noun* [Say NARKA lepsy]

narcosis *noun* (*plural* **narcoses**) a state of drowsiness or unconsciousness induced by a narcotic drug. [Say nar CO sis]

narcotic • *noun* **1** a drug or other substance affecting mood or behaviour and sold for non-medicinal purposes, esp. an illegal one. **2** a drug that induces drowsiness, stupor, or unconsciousness, and relieves pain. • *adjective* denoting or having to do with narcotics or their effects or use: *a narcotic effect.*

nark *noun* = NARC.

narrate *verb* (**narrates, narrated, narrating**) **1** give a continuous story or account of. **2** provide a spoken commentary or accompaniment for (a film etc.).

N

3 recount or relate a story, events, experiences, etc. ▶ **narration** *noun* [Say NAIR ate or nuh RATE]
narrative • *noun* **1** a spoken or written account of connected events in order of happening. **2** the practice or art of narration. • *adjective* in the form of, or concerned with, narration: *narrative verse.* ▶ **narratively** *adverb* [Say NERRA tiv]
narratological *adjective* having to do with narratology. [Say nerra tuh LOGICAL]
narratology *noun* the study of the structure and function of narrative. [Say nerra TOLLA jee]
narrator *noun* **1** a character in a play, film, etc., who relates part of the plot to the audience. **2** a person who speaks a commentary in a film, broadcast, etc. **3** a character who recounts the events in a plot, esp. that of a novel or narrative poem. **4** the imagined voice recounting a story in a novel etc., as distinct from the author: *the omniscient narrator.* [Say NAIR ate er or nuh RATE er]
narrow • *adjective* (**narrower**, **narrowest**) **1 a** of small width in proportion to length. **b** confined or confining: *within narrow bounds.* **2** of limited scope: *in the narrowest sense.* **3** with little margin: *a narrow escape.* **4** searching: *a narrow examination.* **5** = NARROW-MINDED. • *noun* **1** (usu. in *plural*) the narrow part of a strait, river, sound, etc. **2** a narrow pass or street. • *verb* **1** become narrow; diminish; contract; lessen. **2** make narrow; constrict; restrict. PHRASES **narrow down** reduce the number of possibilities or choices, esp. by eliminating those that are less appropriate or desirable.
narrowcast • *verb* (**narrowcasts**; *past* and *past participle* **narrowcast** or **narrowcasted**; **narrowcasting**) transmit (a television program etc.), esp. by cable, to an audience targeted by interests or location. • *noun* **1** transmitting in this way. **2** a transmission or program of this kind. ▶ **narrowcaster** *noun* **narrowcasting** *noun*
narrowly *adverb* **1** only by a small amount: *the car narrowly missed a cyclist.* **2** in a way that is limited: *a narrowly defined task.* **3** closely; carefully: *she looked at him narrowly.*
narrow-minded *adjective* rigid or restricted in one's views; intolerant, prejudiced. ▶ **narrow-mindedly** *adverb* **narrow-mindedness** *noun*
narrowness *noun* the quality of being narrow: *a narrowness of mind.*
narthex *noun* (*plural* **narthexes**) a lobby inside the main entrance to a church building. [Say NARTH ex]
narwhal *noun* a white Arctic whale, the male of which has a long straight spirally fluted tusk developed from one of its teeth. [Say NAR wull]
nary *adjective* *informal* or *jocular* not a; no: *nary a one.* [Rhymes with *HAIRY*]
NASA *abbreviation* (in the US) National Aeronautics and Space Administration. [Say NASS uh]
nasal • *adjective* **1** of, for, or relating to the nose. **2** (of a letter or a sound) pronounced with the breath passing through the nose, e.g. *m*, *n*, *ng*, or French *en*, *un*, etc. **3** (of the voice or speech) having an intonation caused by breathing through the nose. • *noun* a nasal letter or sound. ▶ **nasally** *adverb*
nascent *adjective* **1** just beginning to be; not yet mature: *nascent talents.* **2** *Chemistry* just being formed and therefore unusually reactive: *nascent hydrogen.* [Say NAY sint or NASS int]
NASDAQ *noun* (in the US) National Association of Securities Dealers Automated Quotations, a system for quoting prices on over-the-counter securities. [Say NASS dack or NAZZ dack]
Naskapi • *noun* (*plural* **Naskapi** or **Naskapis**) **1** a member of an Innu people living along the north shores of the Gulf of St. Lawrence and the St. Lawrence River. **2** the Cree language of this people. • *adjective* of or relating to this people. [Say nuh SKAPPY]
Nass-Gitksan *noun* an Aboriginal language spoken by the Nisga'a and Gitksan. [Say nass git k'SAN]
nastily *adverb* in a nasty manner; in a mean way, spitefully.
nastiness *noun* **1** the quality of being nasty. **2** nasty behaviour.
nasturtium *noun* a trailing plant with rounded edible leaves and bright orange, yellow, or red flowers. [Say nuh STIR shum]
nasty • *adjective* (**nastier**, **nastiest**) **1 a** highly unpleasant: *a nasty experience.* **b** annoying; objectionable: *has a nasty habit of breaking.* **2** difficult to negotiate; dangerous, serious: *a nasty question* ◊ *a nasty illness.* **3** (of a person or animal) ill-natured, ill-tempered: *nasty to her mother.* **4** (of the weather) unpleasant because of cold, wind, precipitation, etc. **5 a** disgustingly dirty, filthy. **b** unpalatable; disagreeable: *nasty smell.* **6** obscene. • *noun* (*plural* **nasties**) *informal* a nasty person, animal, thing, etc. PHRASES **a nasty bit** (or **piece**) **of work** *informal* an unpleasant or contemptible person.
Nat. *abbreviation* **1** National. **2** Natural.
natal *adjective* of or pertaining to the place or time of one's birth: *no one knows whether young adult loons return to their natal areas.* [Say NATE ul]
natch *adverb* *informal* = NATURALLY.
nation *noun* **1 a** a community of people forming a state or inhabiting a territory. **b** the state or territory itself. **2** a group of Aboriginal people with common ancestry who are socially, culturally, and linguistically united.
national • *adjective* **1** of or pertaining to a nation or the nation, esp. as a whole. **2** peculiar to or characteristic of a particular nation. **3** owned, controlled, or financially supported by the nation: *a national library.* • *noun* **1** a citizen of a specified country, usu. entitled to hold that country's passport: *French nationals.* **2** (in *plural*) a national tournament or competition.
national anthem *noun* a song adopted by a nation, expressive of its identity etc. and intended to inspire patriotism.
National Assembly *noun* **1** *Cdn* the provincial legislature of Quebec. **2** an elected house of legislature in various countries.
National Guard *noun* (in the US) a militia recruited on a state-by-state basis but serving as the primary reserve force of the US army, and available for federal use in emergencies.
National Historic Site *noun* (in Canada) a place designated by the federal government as historically significant, identified by an associated building, archaeological remains, or commemorative statue, cairn, or plaque.
national income *noun* the total annual money value of the goods and services produced by a country.
nationalism *noun* **1 a** patriotic feeling, principles, etc. **b** an extreme form of this. **2** a policy of national independence. ▶ **nationalist** *noun* & *adjective* **nationalistic** *adjective* **nationalistically** *adverb*
nationality *noun* (*plural* **nationalities**) **1 a** the status of belonging to a particular nation: *what is your nationality?* **b** a nation: *the architects represented three different nationalities—the US, Canada, and Britain.* **2** an ethnic group forming a part of one or more political nations. **3** existence as a nation; nationhood.
nationalization *noun* the act of nationalizing an industry etc.

nationalize *verb* (**nationalizes, nationalized, nationalizing**) **1** take over (an industry, transportation service, land, etc.) from private ownership on behalf of the state. **2** make national.

nationally *adverb* referring to a country as a whole: *crime figures are down nationally* ◊ *a nationally run health system*.

national park *noun* an area of natural beauty or ecological or historical significance, protected by the nation for the use of the general public.

National Policy *noun* *Cdn hist.* a policy of tariff protection for Canadian manufacturers brought into effect in 1879 by Sir John A. Macdonald and espoused by subsequent Conservative prime ministers.

national service *noun* service in the armed forces under conscription for a specified period.

National Socialism *noun* *hist.* the doctrines of nationalism, racial purity, etc., adopted by the Nazis. ▶ **National Socialist** *noun & adjective*

nationhood *noun* the state or fact of being a nation: *a parade to celebrate their nationhood*.

Nation of Islam *noun* a black Islamic organization founded *c.* 1930 in Detroit.

nation-state *noun* a sovereign state of which most of the citizens or subjects are united also by factors such as language, common descent, etc., which define a nation.

nationwide *adjective & adverb* extending over the whole nation.

native • *noun* **1 a** a person born in a specified place: *a native of Kamloops*. **b** a local inhabitant. **2** a member of an indigenous people of a country, region, etc., as distinguished from settlers, immigrants, etc. or their descendants. **3** (usu. foll. by *of*) an indigenous animal or plant. • *adjective* **1** (usu. foll. by *to*) belonging to a person or thing by nature; inherent; innate: *native intelligence*. **2** of one's birth or birthplace: *our home and native land*. **3** belonging to one by right of birth: *native language*. **4** (usu. foll. by *to*) belonging to a specified place: *the anteater is native to South America*. **5** (also **Native**) **a** (of a person) indigenous; descended from the original inhabitants of a region or country. **b** of, pertaining to, or characteristic of the indigenous people of a place: *native customs*. **6** *Computing* designed for or built into a given system. **PHRASES go native** (of a settler, traveller, etc.) adopt the way of life of the indigenous inhabitants of a place.

Native American *noun* an American Indian, esp. of the US.

native-born *adjective* belonging to a particular place or country by birth.

Native Canadian *noun* an Aboriginal Canadian; a Canadian Indian, Inuit, or Metis.

native friendship centre *noun* *Cdn* = FRIENDSHIP CENTRE.

native son *noun* a male native of a particular city, province or state, etc.: *when the former leader died in his sleep, Newfoundland lost a renowned native son*.

native speaker *noun* a person who has spoken a specified language from early childhood.

nativism *noun* **1** the attitude, practice, or policy of protecting the interests of native-born or existing inhabitants against those of immigrants. **2** *Anthropology* a return to or emphasis on a way of life or customs under threat from outside influences. ▶ **nativist** *adjective & noun*

nativity *noun* (*plural* **nativities**) **1** (esp. **the Nativity**) **a** the birth of Christ. **b** the festival of Christ's birth; Christmas. **2** a picture of the Nativity. **3** birth. **4** the birth of the Virgin Mary or St. John the Baptist. [Say nuh TIVVA tee]

nativity scene *noun* a usu. three-dimensional depiction of Christ's birth in a stable, with Mary and Joseph, farm animals, visiting shepherds, etc.

NATO *abbreviation* North Atlantic Treaty Organization. [Say NAY toe]

natter *informal* • *verb* **1** chatter idly. **2** grumble; talk frothily. • *noun* **1** aimless chatter. **2** grumbling talk.

nattily *adverb* in a natty or smart manner: *nattily dressed youths*.

nattiness *noun* the quality of being neatly dressed or dapper.

natty *adjective* (**nattier, nattiest**) *informal* **1** smartly or neatly dressed; dapper. **2** neat and fashionable: *a natty suit*.

natural • *adjective* **1** existing in or derived from nature; not made, caused, or processed by humankind. **2** in accordance with nature; normal or to be expected: *a natural death*. **3** born with a particular skill or quality: *a natural leader*. **4** relaxed and unaffected. **5** (of a parent or child) related by blood. **6** *archaic* illegitimate. **7** *Music* (of a note) not sharpened or flattened. • *noun* **1** a person with an innate gift or talent. **2** an off-white colour. **3** *Music* a natural note or a sign (♮) denoting one. **4** a pale fawn colour.

natural-born *adjective* having a character or position by birth: *a natural-born entertainer*.

natural childbirth *noun* childbirth with minimal medical or technological intervention.

natural death *noun* death by age or disease, not by accident, violence, etc.

natural gas *noun* an inflammable, mainly methane gas found in the earth's crust, not manufactured.

natural historian *noun* a person who compiles a natural history.

natural history *noun* (*plural* **natural histories**) **1** the study of animals or plants, esp. as set forth for popular use. **2** an aggregate of the facts concerning the flora and fauna etc. of a particular place or class: *a natural history of Vancouver Island*.

naturalism *noun* **1** the theory or practice in art and literature of representing nature, character, etc. realistically and in great detail. **2** action based on natural instincts.

naturalist • *noun* **1** an expert or student of natural history. **2** a person who believes in or practises naturalism. • *adjective* = NATURALISTIC.

naturalistic *adjective* **1** imitating nature closely; lifelike. **2** of or according to naturalism.

naturalization *noun* an act of naturalizing something.

naturalize *verb* (**naturalizes, naturalized, naturalizing**) **1** admit (a person of foreign birth) to the citizenship of a country. **2** introduce (an animal, plant, etc.) into another region so that it flourishes in the wild. **3** adopt (a foreign word, custom, etc.). **4** become naturalized.

natural law *noun* **1** unchanging moral principles common to all people by virtue of their nature as human beings. **2 a** an observable law relating to natural phenomena. **b** these collectively: *where they saw chance, we see natural law*.

natural life *noun* (*plural* **natural lives**) the duration of one's life on earth.

natural logarithm *noun* a logarithm to the base e (2.71828.....). Abbreviation: $\log_e$.

naturally *adverb* **1** in a natural manner: *spoke very naturally*. **2** as a natural result. **3** (qualifying a whole sentence) as might be expected; of course. **4** by nature; instinctively: *a naturally talented actor*. **5** without artificial help, special treatment, etc.: *her hair curls naturally*.

N

naturalness *noun* **1** the quality of being like real life: *the naturalness of the dialogue made the book so true to life.* **2** the quality of behaving in a normal, relaxed, or innocent way: *teenagers lose their childhood simplicity and naturalness.* **3** the quality of happening in a normal, expected way: *the naturalness of her reaction.*

natural numbers *noun* the integers 1, 2, 3, etc., sometimes with the addition of 0.

natural philosophy *noun hist.* natural science, esp. physical science.

natural resources *noun* materials or conditions occurring in nature and capable of economic exploitation.

natural science *noun* **1** the sciences used in the study of the physical world, e.g. physics, chemistry, geology, biology, botany. **2** any one of these sciences.

natural selection *noun* the Darwinian theory of the survival and propagation of organisms best adapted to their environment.

nature *noun* **1** a thing's or person's innate or essential qualities or character: *not in their nature to be cruel ◊ is the nature of iron to rust.* **2** (often **Nature**) **a** the physical power causing all the phenomena of the material world: *Nature is the best physician.* **b** these phenomena, including plants, animals, landscape, etc. **3** a kind, sort, or class: *things of this nature.* **4** = HUMAN NATURE. **5** a specified element of human character: *our animal nature.* **6** an uncultivated or wild area, condition, community, etc. PHRASES **against nature** unnatural; immoral. **back to nature** returning to a pre-industrial or natural state. **by nature** innately. **from nature** *Art* using natural objects as models. **in nature 1** actually existing. **2** anywhere; at all. **3** in the natural world. **in (or of) the nature of** characteristically resembling or belonging to the class of: *the answer was in the nature of an excuse.* **in the nature of things** inevitably. **in a state of nature** in an uncivilized or uncultivated state. **one's better nature** the good side of one's character; one's capacity for tolerance, generosity, etc.

natured *adjective* (in *combination*) having a specified disposition: *good-natured.*

nature reserve *noun* a tract of land managed so as to preserve its flora, fauna, physical features, etc.

naturism *noun* the practice of not wearing any clothes because of a belief that this is more natural and healthy. ▶ **naturist** *noun & adjective*

naturopath *noun* a person who uses or promotes naturopathy. ▶ **naturopathic** *adjective* [Say NATCH er uh path or NAY chur uh path]

naturopathy *noun* the treatment or prevention of disease etc. without drugs, usu. involving diet, exercise, massage, etc. [Say natch er OP uth ee or nay chur OP uth ee]

Naugahyde *noun proprietary* a material used in upholstery, consisting of a fabric base coated with a layer of rubber or vinyl resin and finished with a leather-like grain. [Say NOGGA hide]

naught *noun archaic* or *literary* nothing, nought. PHRASES **come to naught** be ruined or unsuccessful: *French attempts to trade with the Iroquois came to naught, and Champlain moved to strengthen the colony's defences.*

naughtily *adverb* in a naughty manner.

naughtiness *noun* **1** the quality or state of being naughty. **2** naughty activity.

naughty *adjective* (**naughtier**, **naughtiest**) **1** (esp. of children) disobedient; badly behaved. **2** *informal* jocular connected with sex in a rude or funny way: *a naughty postcard.*

nausea *noun* a feeling of sickness with an inclination to vomit. [Say NOZZY uh or NOZH uh]

nauseate *verb* (**nauseates**, **nauseated**, **nauseating**) **1** affect with nausea; cause to feel sick: *was nauseated by the smell.* **2** disgust; appall: *I was nauseated by the violence in the movie.* ▶ **nauseated** *adjective* **nauseating** *adjective* **nauseatingly** *adverb* [Say NOZZY ate]

> **WRITING TIP**
> **nauseous**
>
> It is perfectly fine to use **nauseous** to mean "queasy", as in *The smell made me nauseous.* Some people argue that it can only mean "causing nausea", as in *The nauseous smell made me queasy,* but the first sense is by far the most common, even in edited writing.

nauseous *adjective* **1** affected with nausea, sick: *felt nauseous all day.* **2** causing nausea, offensive to the taste or smell: *the nauseous scent of the leaves when crushed.* [Say NOSH us]

nautical *adjective* of or concerning sailors or ships; naval; maritime. ▶ **nautically** *adverb* [Say NOT ick ul]

nautical mile *noun* a unit of approx. 1 852 metres (2,025 yards).

nautilus *noun* (*plural* **nautiluses** or **nautili**) a mollusc with a light brittle spiral shell and numerous short tentacles around the mouth. [Say NOT ill us for the singular, NOT ill eye for the plural]

nav. *abbreviation* **1** navigation. **2** naval.

nav *noun informal* **1** navigation: *nav lights.* **2** navigator.

Navajo (also **Navaho**) • *noun* (*plural* **Navajo** or **Navajos**, **Navaho** or **Navahos**) **1** a member of an Athapaskan people of Arizona, Utah, and New Mexico. **2** the Athapaskan language of this people. • *adjective* of this people. [Say NAVVA hoe]

> **SPELL CHECK**
> **naval, navel**
>
> The belly button is the **navel**.

naval *adjective* **1** of, in, for, etc. the navy or a navy. **2** of or concerning ships or boats: *a naval battle.*

> **SPELL CHECK**
> **nave, knave**
>
> A scoundrel is a **knave**.

nave *noun* the central longitudinal part of a church, usu. from the main entrance to the chancel and excluding the side aisles.

> **SPELL CHECK**
> **navel, naval**
>
> The word pertaining to fighting ships is **naval**.

navel *noun* **1** a rounded depression in the centre of the belly caused by the detachment of the umbilical cord. **2** a central point.

navel-gazing *noun* usu. profitless meditation; self-absorption: *the classic directive to "write about what you know" is to blame for a lot of navel-gazing.*

navel orange *noun* a large seedless orange with a navel-like formation at the top.

navigable *adjective* (of a river, the sea, etc.) that ships can sail on. [Say NAVVA guh bull]

navigate *verb* (**navigates**, **navigated**, **navigating**) **1 a** manage or direct the course of (a ship, aircraft, etc.). **b** find one's way; steer the correct course. **2 a** sail on or across (a sea, river, etc.). **b** travel or fly through (the air). **3** (of a passenger in a vehicle) assist the driver by map-reading etc. **4** *informal* steer (oneself, a course, etc.) through a crowd etc.

navigation *noun* **1** the act or process of navigating.

2 any of several methods of determining or planning a ship's or aircraft's position and course by geometry, astronomy, radio signals, etc. ▶ **navigational** *adjective*

navigator *noun* **1** a person skilled or engaged in navigation. **2** an explorer by sea: *Prince Henry the Navigator*.

navvy *noun* (*plural* **navvies**) *Brit. & Cdn informal* a labourer excavating or constructing roads, canals, railways, etc.

navy • *noun* (*plural* **navies**) **1 a** the whole body of a nation's ships of war, including crews, maintenance systems, and related material such as aircraft etc. **b** the officers and other ranks of a navy. **2** (also **navy blue**) a dark blue colour as used in naval uniform. • *adjective* (also **navy blue**) dark blue.

navy bean *noun* **1** a variety of French bean with small white seeds. **2** the dried seed of this used as a vegetable.

nay • *adverb* or rather; and even; and more than that: *impressive, nay, magnificent*. • *interjection Parliament* or *archaic* = NO *interjection*. • *noun* **1** the word "nay". **2** a negative vote.

naysayer *noun* a person who expresses negative, cynical, or gloomy views: *he desperately tried to keep the naysayers from crushing his vision before he began*. ▶ **naysaying** *noun*

Nazarene • *noun* **1** (**the Nazarene**) Christ. **2** a native or inhabitant of Nazareth, a town in the northern part of the modern state of Israel. **3 a** a member of an early Jewish-Christian sect living in Syria. **b** a member of a Protestant denomination called the Church of the Nazarene. • *adjective* of or concerning Nazareth, the Nazarenes, etc. [Say NAZZA reen]

Nazi • *noun* (*plural* **Nazis**) **1** *hist.* a member of the authoritarian and racist German National Socialist party, which ruled Germany from 1933–45 under the dictatorial leadership of Adolf Hitler and whose militaristic foreign policies resulted in the Second World War. **2** *derogatory* a person holding extreme racist or authoritarian views or behaving brutally. **3** a person belonging to any organization similar to the Nazis. • *adjective* of or concerning the Nazis, Nazism, etc. ▶ **Nazism** [Say NOTSY or NATSY, NOTSY ism or NATSY ism]

NB *abbreviation* **1** New Brunswick. **2** *nota bene*.

Nb *symbol* niobium.

NBA *abbreviation* National Basketball Association.

NBC *abbreviation* (of armaments or warfare) nuclear, biological, and chemical.

NCM *abbreviation* (*plural* **NCMs**) *Cdn* non-commissioned member.

NCO *abbreviation* (*plural* **NCOs**) non-commissioned officer.

Nd *symbol* neodymium.

n.d. *abbreviation* no date.

NDP *abbreviation* *Cdn* NEW DEMOCRATIC PARTY. ▶ **NDPer** *noun* (*plural* **NDPers**)

NDT *abbreviation* Newfoundland Daylight Time.

NE *abbreviation* **1** northeast. **2** northeastern.

Ne *symbol* the element neon.

né *adjective* born (indicating a man's previous name): *Lord Beaconsfield, né Benjamin Disraeli*. [Say NAY]

Neanderthal • *adjective* **1** of or belonging to the type of human widely distributed in paleolithic Europe, with a retreating forehead and massive brow ridges. **2** (also **neanderthal**) *jocular* or *derogatory* **a** primitive, uncivilized, uncouth: *from a hick mining town, she recalls dating neanderthal boys beneath the glow of molten slag heaps*. **b** reactionary; extremely conservative. • *noun* **1** a Neanderthal hominid. **2** (also **neanderthal**) *jocular* or *derogatory* **a** a primitive, uncivilized, or uncouth person: *no self-respecting girl would be caught dead tearing around the countryside with such neanderthals*. **b** a reactionary or extremely conservative person: *cultural neanderthals in Congress*. [Say nee ANDER tholl]

neap *noun* (also **neap tide**) a tide just after the first and third quarters of the moon when there is least difference between high and low water.

Neapolitan • *noun* a native or citizen of Naples, Italy. • *adjective* of or relating to Naples. [Say nee uh POLLA tin]

Neapolitan ice cream *noun* ice cream made in layers of chocolate, vanilla, and strawberry.

near • *adverb* **1** (often foll. by *to*) to or at a short distance in space or time; close by: *the time drew near* ◊ *dropped near to them*. **2** closely: *as near as one can guess*. **3** *informal* almost, nearly: *damn near died*. • *preposition* **1** to or at a short distance (in space, time, condition, or resemblance) from: *stood near the back* ◊ *occurs nearer the end*. **2** (in *combination*) **a** that is almost: *near-hysterical*. **b** intended as a substitute for; resembling: *near-beer*. • *adjective* **1** close at hand; close to, in place or time: *the end is near* ◊ *in the near future*. **2 a** closely related: *a near relation*. **b** intimate: *a near friend*. **3** close; narrow: *a near escape* ◊ *a near guess*. **4** similar (to): *is nearer the original*. **5** stingy. • *verb* approach; draw near to: *neared the harbour*. PHRASES **come near** be on the point of, almost succeed in: *came near to falling*. **near at hand 1** within easy reach. **2** in the immediate future. **nearest and dearest** one's closest friends and relatives collectively.

nearby • *adjective* situated in a near position: *a nearby hotel*. • *adverb* (also **near by**) close; not far away.

Nearctic • *adjective* of or relating to the Arctic and the temperate parts of North America as a wildlife region. • *noun* the Nearctic region. [Say nee ARCTIC]

near-death experience *noun* an out-of-body experience taking place on the brink of death, recounted by a person on recovery.

Near East *noun* (**the Near East**) **1** = MIDDLE EAST. **2** *hist.* the Balkans. ▶ **Near Eastern** *adjective*

nearly *adverb* **1** almost: *nearly there*. **2** closely: *nearly related*. **3** with a close degree of approximation. PHRASES **not nearly** far from: *not nearly enough*.

near miss *noun* (*plural* **near misses**) **1** a bomb etc. falling close to the target. **2** a narrowly avoided collision. **3** an attempt that is almost but not quite successful.

nearness *noun* closeness, proximity.

Near North *noun* *Cdn* the southern edge of the Subarctic, extending across Canada in a band just north of the heavily settled areas of the Fraser Valley, the Prairies, southern Ontario, and the St. Lawrence Valley.

nearsighted *adjective* **1** unable to distinguish objects clearly at a distance; myopic. **2** lacking imagination, foresight, or proper consideration. ▶ **nearsightedly** *adverb* **nearsightedness** *noun*

near-term *adjective* occurring in or pertaining to the near future.

neat *adjective* **1 a** (of a room etc.) tidy; clean; in an orderly condition. **b** (of a person) liking to keep things in order; fastidious: *a neat worker*. **2** elegantly simple in form etc.; well-proportioned. **3** (of language, style, etc.) brief, clear, and pointed. **4 a** cleverly executed: *a neat piece of work*. **b** deft; dexterous. **5** (of esp. alcoholic liquor) undiluted. **6** *slang* (as a general term of approval) good, pleasing, excellent.

neaten *verb* make neat.

'neath *preposition* (also **neath**) *archaic* beneath.

neatly *adverb* in a neat way: *neatly folded clothes* ◊ *the box fitted neatly inside* ◊ *she summarized the plan very neatly*.

neatness *noun* the quality of being neat.

neat-o *adjective* *slang* = NEAT[1] *adjective* 6.

nebbish *informal* • *noun* an ineffectual or timid person. • *adjective* ineffectual; timid. ▶ **nebbishy** *adjective*

nebula *noun* (*plural* **nebulae** or **nebulas**) **1** a cloud of

N

gas and dust in space, sometimes glowing and sometimes appearing as a dark silhouette against other glowing matter. **2** a clouded spot on the cornea causing defective vision. ▶ **nebular** *adjective* [Say NEB you luh for the singular; for *NEBULAE* say NEB you lee]

nebulous *adjective* **1** hazy, indistinct, vague: *nebulous ideas*. **2** *Astronomy* of or like a nebula or nebulae. ▶ **nebulously** *adverb* [Say NEB you lus]

necessarily *adverb* **1** as a necessary result; inevitably. **2** by force of necessity: *we don't necessarily have to leave*.

necessary • *adjective* **1** requiring to be done, achieved, etc.; requisite, essential: *it is necessary to work* ◊ *lacks the necessary documents*. **2** determined, existing, or happening by natural laws, predestination, etc., not by free will; inevitable: *a necessary evil*. • *noun* (*plural* **necessaries**) (usu. in *plural*) any of the basic requirements of life, such as food, warmth, etc. PHRASES **the necessary** an action, item, etc., needed for a purpose: *they will do the necessary*.

necessitate *verb* (**necessitates**, **necessitated**, **necessitating**) make necessary (esp. as a result): *will necessitate some sacrifice*. [Say nuh SESSA tate]

necessity *noun* (*plural* **necessities**) **1 a** (often in *plural*) an indispensable thing: *central heating is a necessity* ◊ *the necessities of life*. **b** (usu. foll. by *of*) indispensability: *the necessity of a warm overcoat*. **2** a state of affairs or circumstances enforcing a certain course: *there was a necessity to hurry*. **3** imperative need: *necessity is the mother of invention*. **4** want; poverty; hardship: *stole because of necessity*. PHRASES **of necessity** unavoidably.

neck • *noun* **1 a** the part of the body connecting the head to the shoulders. **b** the part of a shirt, dress, etc. around or close to the neck. **c** = NECKLINE. **2 a** something resembling a neck, such as the narrow part of a cavity or vessel, a passage, channel, pass, isthmus, etc. **b** the narrow part of a bottle, vase, etc. near the mouth. **3** the part of a violin, guitar, etc. bearing the fingerboard. **4** the length of a horse's head and neck as a measure of its lead in a race. • *verb informal* kiss and caress amorously. PHRASES **get it in the neck** *informal* **1** receive a severe reprimand or punishment. **2** suffer a fatal or severe blow. **neck and neck** very close in a race, competition, etc. **up to one's neck** (often foll. by *in*) *informal* very deeply involved; very busy.

neckband *noun* a strip of material around the neck of a garment.

-necked *combining form* having a neck of the kind described: *ring-necked pheasant*.

neckerchief *noun* a square of cloth worn around the neck. [Say NECKER chiff or NECKER cheef]

necklace *noun* a chain or string of beads, precious stones, etc., worn as an ornament around the neck.

neckless *adjective* without a neck.

neckline *noun* the edge or shape of the opening of a garment at the neck: *a square neckline*.

neck of the woods *noun informal* a community or locality.

necktie *noun* = TIE *noun* 2.

necromancer *noun* a person who predicts the future by supposedly communicating with the dead. [Say NECK ruh mance er]

necromancy *noun* **1** the prediction of the future by the supposed communication with the dead. **2** witchcraft. ▶ **necromantic** *adjective* [Say NECK ruh mancy]

necrophilia *noun* a morbid and esp. erotic attraction to corpses. ▶ **necrophiliac** *noun* **necrophilic** *adjective* [Say neck ruh FILLY uh]

necropolis *noun* (*plural* **necropolises**) **1** an ancient

cemetery or burial place. **2** a cemetery, esp. a large one in or near a city. [Say nuh CROPPA liss]

necrosis *noun* the death or decay of part or all of an organ or tissue due to disease, injury, or deficiency of nutrients, esp. as one of the symptoms of gangrene or pulmonary tuberculosis. [Say nuh CROW sis]

nectar *noun* **1** a sugary substance produced by plants to attract pollinating insects and made into honey by bees. **2 a** (in Greek and Roman mythology) the drink of the gods. **b** a drink compared to this. **3** a drink of usu. undiluted fruit juice or a blend of fruit juices.

nectarine *noun* **1** a variety of peach with a thin smooth skin and firm flesh. **2** the tree bearing this.

née *adjective* (also **nee**) (used in adding a married woman's maiden name after her surname) born: *Mrs. Patricia Barber, née Clarke*. [Say NAY]

SPELL CHECK
need, knead ✓ABC

To work dough or clay is to **knead** it.

---

need • *verb* **1** stand in want of; require: *needs a new coat* ◊ *this needs revising*. **2 a** be under a necessity or obligation: *it needs to be done carefully*. **b** (3rd singular present **need**) (without *to*) be under the necessity or obligation: *he need not come*. • *noun* **1 a** a want or requirement: *my needs are few*. **b** a thing wanted: *my greatest need is a car*. **2** circumstances requiring some course of action; necessity: *there is no need to worry*. **3 a** a condition of lacking or requiring some necessary thing, either physically or psychologically. **b** destitution; poverty. **4** a crisis, time of difficulty, distress, or trouble; an emergency: *failed them in their need*. PHRASES **have need of** require; want. **have no need to** not be obliged to: *I have no need to prove my manhood*. **if need be** if necessary. **in need** requiring help. **in need of** requiring. **need not have** did not need to (but did).

needful • *adjective* **1** necessary; indispensable. **2** having a need or needs. • *noun* **1** (**the needful**) what is necessary. **2** *informal* money or action needed for a purpose.

neediness *noun* the quality of being needy.

needle • *noun* **1 a** a very thin small piece of smooth steel etc. pointed at one end and with a slit (eye) for thread, used in sewing. **b** a larger plastic, wooden, etc. slender stick without an eye, used in knitting. **2** a slender, usu. pointed, indicator on a dial or other measuring instrument. **3** any of several small thin pointed instruments, esp.: **a** a surgical instrument for stitching. **b** the end of a hypodermic syringe. **c** a thin metal rod used in acupuncture. **d** = STYLUS 3. **e** an etching tool. **4 a** a hypodermic syringe. **b** an injection of a drug, vaccine, etc. through the needle of such a syringe. **5** a pointed peak or mass of rock. **6** any of the sharp, stiff, slender leaves on a conifer. • *verb* (**needles**, **needled**, **needling**) *informal* **1** incite or irritate; provoke. **2** tease, harass. PHRASES **needle in a haystack** something almost impossible to find because it is concealed by so many other things etc. ▶ **needled** *adjective* (also in *combination*)

needle-nose *adjective* (of pliers) having long, thin, pincers suitable for gripping in very narrow spaces.

needlepoint • *noun* embroidery worked over canvas etc., esp. using small stitches. • *verb* work or create through needlepoint.

needless *adjective* unnecessary, uncalled for, not needed or wanted. PHRASES **needless to say** of course; it goes without saying. ▶ **needlessly** *adverb*

needlework *noun* **1** the action of producing

something with a needle, esp. by embroidery, tapestry, etc. **2** a piece of work so produced: *needlework cushion*.
needling *noun* an act of irritating or provoking an opponent etc.
needn't *contraction* need not.
needs *adverb* of necessity: *must needs decide*.
need-to-know *adjective* designating the principle or practice of telling people only what is necessary for them to carry out a task effectively.
needy *adjective* (**needier**, **neediest**) **1** (of a person) **a** poor; destitute. **b** lacking some essential emotional or psychological quality, experience, etc. **2** (of circumstances) characterized by poverty or need.
neem *noun* a tree of the mahogany family, whose leaves and bark are used medicinally in the Indian subcontinent.
ne'er *adverb literary* = NEVER. [Say NAIR]
ne'er-do-well • *noun* a good-for-nothing person. **• *adjective*** good-for-nothing.
nefarious *adjective* wicked; immoral: *a nefarious, cigar-smoking lobbyist who bribes public officials*. ▶ **nefariousness** *noun* [Say nuh FERRY us]
neg *noun informal* a photographic negative.
neg. *abbreviation* negative.
negate *verb* (**negates, negated, negating**) **1** make ineffective, invalidate: *alcohol negates the effects of the medicine*. **2** imply, involve, or assert the non-existence of; deny: *another example of the government's efforts to negate the state of Quebec*. **3** *Grammar* make (a clause, sentence, etc.) negative in meaning. [Say nuh GATE]
negation *noun* **1** a contradiction, denial, or refusal: *the Loyalists' negation of the American Revolution*. **2** the absence or opposite of something actual or positive: *death is the negation of life*. **3** *Grammar* denial of the truth of a clause or sentence, typically involving the use of a negative word (e.g. *not, no, never*), or a word or affix with negative force (e.g. *nothing, non-*).
negative • *adjective* **1** expressing or implying denial, prohibition, or refusal: *a negative vote ◊ a negative answer*. **2 a** (of a person, attitude, etc.) unhelpful, critical, or destructive; pessimistic, defeatist. **b** not having or showing an interested attitude, aiming to improve something, etc.; uncooperative. **3** (of an effect) harmful: *eliminate the negative side effects of the drug*. **4 a** (of the results of a test or an experiment) indicating that a substance or condition is not present: *the biopsy was negative*. **b** (in *combination*) (of a person, blood, etc.) not having a specified condition, substance, etc.: *HIV-negative*. **5** marked by the absence rather than the presence of qualities. **6** of the opposite nature to a thing regarded as positive: *debt is negative capital*. **7** *Grammar* (of a word, clause, etc.) expressing negation. **8** *Algebra* (of a quantity) less than zero, to be subtracted from others or from zero (*opp.* POSITIVE). **9** *Electricity* **a** of the kind of charge carried by electrons (*opp.* POSITIVE). **b** containing or producing such a charge. **10** (of a visual image, esp. a photograph) showing the lights, shades, and colour values reversed from those of the original. **• *noun*** **1** a negative statement or reply. **2** an image with black and white reversed or colours replaced by complementary ones, from which positive pictures are obtained. **3** *Grammar* a word or particle expressing negation, e.g. *not, don't*. **4** (**the negative**) the side or aspect of a question which is opposed to the affirmative or positive. **5 a** a negative quality or characteristic. **b** an absence of something. **6** a negative result on a medical test, experiment, etc. **• *interjection*** no. ◼ PHRASES **in the negative** in rejection of a proposal or suggestion, with negative effect; no: *the answer was in the negative*. ▶ **negatively** *adverb*
negativism *noun* **1** the tendency to be negative in

attitude, action, or position. **2** extreme skepticism, criticism, etc. ▶ **negativist** *noun*
negativity *noun* a negative attitude towards a situation or person. [Say negga TIVVA tee]
neglect • *verb* **1** fail to care for or to do; be remiss about: *neglected their duty ◊ neglected his children*. **2** fail; overlook or forget the need to: *neglected to inform them*. **3** not pay due attention to; disregard: *this area of research has been largely neglected*. **• *noun*** **1** lack of caring; negligence: *the house suffered from neglect*. **2 a** the act or fact of neglecting. **b** the state or condition of being neglected: *the house fell into neglect*. **3** (usu. foll. by *of*) disregard. ▶ **neglected** *adjective* **neglectful** *adjective*
negligee *noun* a woman's light dressing gown, usu. made of delicate, semi-transparent fabric and trimmed with lace etc. [Say NEG li zhay]
negligence *noun* **1** a lack of reasonable or proper care and attention; carelessness. **2** *Law* **a** (in full **contributory negligence**) failure on the part of an injured party to take adequate precautions to prevent accident or injury. **b** (in full **criminal negligence**) an offence involving a wanton or reckless disregard for the lives or safety of others. ▶ **negligent** *adjective* **negligently** *adverb* [Say NEG luh jince]
negligible *adjective* not worth considering or noticing; insignificant: *the cost was negligible ◊ a negligible amount*. [Say NEG lidge uh bull]
negotiability *noun* the quality of being negotiable. [Say nuh go shuh BILLA tee]
negotiable *adjective* **1** open to discussion or modification: *the price is negotiable*. **2** (of a bill, draft, cheque, etc.) that can be exchanged for money. **3** (of an obstacle) that may be crossed or got over, around, or through. [Say nuh GO shuh bull]
negotiate *verb* (**negotiates, negotiated, negotiating**) **1** (usu. foll. by *with*) confer with others in order to reach a compromise or agreement. **2** arrange or settle (a matter) or bring about (a result) by negotiating: *negotiated a settlement ◊ negotiate a loan*. **3** find a way over, through, etc. (an obstacle, difficulty, etc.). ▶ **negotiated** *adjective* **negotiating** *noun* [Say nuh GO she ate]
negotiating table *noun* a place or meeting etc. at which disputes, esp. labour disputes, armed conflicts, constitutional matters, etc., are negotiated.
negotiation *noun* formal discussion between people who are trying to reach an agreement: *peace negotiations ◊ the details are still under negotiation ◊ the price is open to negotiation*. [Say nuh go she AY sh'n]
negotiator *noun* a person who negotiates esp. on behalf of an institution etc. [Say nuh GO she ate er]

WRITING TIP
Negro
Avoid using **Negro**; use **black** instead.

Negro • *noun* (*plural* **Negroes**) a member of the black or dark-skinned group of human populations that exist or originated in Africa south of the Sahara, now distributed around the world. **• *adjective*** of or concerning this people.
Negroid • *adjective* **1** denoting, concerning, or belonging to one of the group of human populations having dark skin, tightly curled hair, and a broad flattish nose, indigenous to sub-Saharan Africa and parts of Melanesia. **2** (of features etc.) characteristic of these peoples. **• *noun*** a member of one of these peoples. [Say NEE groid]
Negro spiritual *noun* = SPIRITUAL *noun*.
neigh • *noun* **1** the high whinnying sound of a horse.

2 any similar sound, e.g. a laugh. • *verb* **1** make such a sound. **2** utter with such a sound. [Say NAY]

neighbour *noun* (also **neighbor**) **1** a person, institution, etc., resident or established next door to or near or nearest another. **2 a** a person or thing near or next to another: *my neighbour at dinner*. **b** a country etc. adjacent to or near another: *Canada and the US are neighbours*. **c** (in *plural*) a resident of such a country etc.: *our neighbours to the South*. **3** a person regarded as a fellow human being, esp. as entitled to kindness, compassion, consideration, etc. **4** (as an *adjective*) **a** neighbouring: *a neighbour nation*. **b** living in the vicinity or next door: *neighbour kids*.

neighbourhood *noun* (also **neighborhood**) **1 a** a district, esp. considered in reference to the character or circumstances of its inhabitants. **b** a small but relatively self-contained section of a larger urban area. **2** the people of a district; one's neighbours. **3** (often foll. by *of*) the nearby or surrounding area, the vicinity. ▓PHRASES▓ **in the neighbourhood of** roughly; about: *paid in the neighbourhood of $100*.

neighbourhood watch *noun* systematic local vigilance by householders to discourage crime.

neighbouring *adjective* situated next or near to a place or person: *neighbouring buildings*.

neighbourliness *noun* the quality of being a good neighbour: *a sense of community and neighbourliness*.

neighbourly *adjective* (also **neighborly**) characteristic of a good neighbour.

> **GRAMMAR CHECK** ⚠️
> **neither**
>
> Although **neither** is often treated as a plural in informal spoken English, as in *Neither of them are very good*, in careful writing it is better to use singular verbs in such cases: *Neither of them is very good*. When using the construction, **neither... nor...**, the verb can be either singular or plural, though if either subject is plural the verb tends to be plural: *Neither he nor she has been there*; *Neither he nor his sisters have been there*.

---

neither • *adjective & pronoun* not the one nor the other (of two things); not either. • *adverb* **1** (foll. by *nor*) not either; not on the one hand: *would neither come in nor go out*. **2** not either; also not: *if you do not, neither shall I*. • *conjunction* nor yet; nor: *I do not know, neither can I guess*. [Say NYE ther or NEE ther]

nelson *noun* a wrestling hold in which one arm is passed under the opponent's arm from behind and the hand is applied to the neck (**half nelson**), or both arms and hands are applied (**full nelson**).

nematode *noun* any of various often parasitic worms which have slender, unsegmented, cylindrical bodies and are found abundantly in soil and water. [Say NEMMA tode]

nemesis *noun* (*plural* **nemeses**) **1** a long-standing or persistent rival, enemy, or tormentor: *Kirk hoped to catch his nemesis off guard*. **2 a** punishment or defeat that is deserved and cannot be avoided: *knowledge that I was heading towards my nemesis*. **b** divine punishment for a mortal's wrongdoing or excessive pride, esp. in Greek drama. [Say NEMMA sis for the singular, NEMMA seez]

neo- *combining form* **1** new, modern. **2** a new or revived form of. [Say NEE oh]

neoclassical *adjective* (also **neoclassic**) **1** of or relating to a revival or development of a classical style or treatment in art, literature, music, etc. **2** *Economics* of, pertaining to, or characteristic of a body of theory primarily concerned with supply and demand rather than with the source and distribution of wealth. ▶ **neoclassicism** *noun* **neoclassicist** *noun*

neo-colonialism *noun* the use of economic, political, or other pressures to control or influence other countries, esp. former dependencies. ▶ **neo-colonialist** *noun & adjective*

neo-con *adjective & noun* = NEO-CONSERVATIVE.

neo-conservatism *noun* an approach to politics, economics, etc. which represents a return to a modified form of a conservative viewpoint, in contrast to more radical or liberal schools of thought.

neo-conservative • *adjective* of or pertaining to an approach to politics, economics, etc. which represents a return to a modified form of a conservative viewpoint, in contrast to more radical or liberal schools of thought. • *noun* an advocate or supporter of neo-conservative principles or beliefs.

neocortex *noun* (*plural* **neocortices**) the most recently evolved part of the cerebral cortex, involved in sight and hearing in advanced reptiles and in mammals. [Say neo CORTEX]

neodymium *noun* a silver-grey naturally-occurring metallic element used in colouring glass etc. [Say neo DIMMY um]

neo-Gothic *adjective* of or relating to a revival of the medieval Gothic style in art or architecture.

neo-liberal • *adjective* relating to or denoting a modified form of liberalism tending to favour free-market capitalism. • *noun* an adherent or advocate of such a belief or movement. ▶ **neo-liberalism** *noun*

neolithic (also **Neolithic**) • *adjective* of or relating to the later Stone Age, when ground or polished stone weapons and implements prevailed. • *noun* the neolithic period. [Say neo LITH ick]

neologism *noun* **1** a new word or expression. **2** the coining or use of new words. [Say nee OLLA jism]

neon • *noun* **1** an inert gaseous element occurring in traces in the atmosphere and giving an orange glow when electricity is passed through it in a sealed low-pressure tube, used in lights and illuminated advertisements: *neon sign*. **2** a neon lamp or tube; neon lighting. • *adjective* **1** of, pertaining to, or involving neon. **2 a** resembling a neon light in colour or brilliance. **b** harshly bright, gaudy, or glowing.

neonatal *adjective* having to do with children immediately after birth: *a hospital's neonatal unit* ◊ *neonatal care*. [Say neo NATE ul]

neo-Nazi • *noun* (*plural* **neo-Nazis**) a person holding extreme racist views or belonging to an organization modelled on Nazism. • *adjective* of or relating to neo-Nazis or neo-Nazism. ▶ **neo-Nazism** *noun*

neophyte *noun* **1** a beginner; a novice: *neophyte sailor*. **2** a new convert, esp. to a religious faith. **3** *Catholicism* **a** a novice of a religious order. **b** a newly ordained priest. [Say neo FITE]

Neoplatonic *adjective* having to do with Neoplatonism. [Say neo pluh TONIC]

Neoplatonism *noun* a philosophical and religious system based on Platonic ideas, which emphasizes the distinction between a supposed eternal world and the changing physical world, and combines this with a mystic possibility of union with the supreme being from which all reality is supposed to derive. ▶ **Neoplatonist** *noun* [Say neo PLAY t'n ism]

neoprene *noun* any of various strong synthetic rubbers which are resistant to oil, heat, and weathering. [Say NEO preen]

neotropical *adjective* of or relating to tropical and South America as a biogeographical region.

Nepalese *adjective & noun* (*plural* **Nepalese**) = NEPALI. [Say neppa LEEZ]

Nepali • *noun* (*plural* **Nepali** or **Nepalis**) **1 a** a native or national of Nepal, a country in southern Asia, in the Himalayas. **b** a person of Nepali descent. **2** the language of Nepal. • *adjective* of Nepal or its language or people. [Say nuh POLLY]

nephew *noun* a son of one's brother or sister, or of one's brother-in-law or sister-in-law.

nepotism *noun* favouritism shown to relatives in bestowing employment or conferring privileges. ▶ **nepotistic** *adjective* [Say NEPPA tism]

neptunium *noun* a radioactive metallic element produced from uranium. [Say nep TUNE ee um]

nerd *noun slang* a foolish, feeble, or uninteresting person, esp. one ridiculed as studious, puny, or not fashionable. ▶ **nerdiness** *noun* **nerdish** *adjective* **nerdy** *adjective* (**nerdier, nerdiest**)

nerve • *noun* **1 a** a fibre or bundle of fibres that transmits impulses of sensation or motion between the brain or spinal cord and other parts of the body. **b** the material constituting these. **2 a** coolness in danger; bravery; assurance. **b** *informal* impudence, audacity: *they've got nerve.* **3** (in *plural*) **a** the bodily state in regard to physical sensitiveness and the interaction between the brain and other parts. **b** a state of heightened nervousness or sensitivity; a condition of mental or physical stress: *need to calm my nerves.* **4** a rib of a leaf. • *verb* (**nerves, nerved, nerving**) brace (oneself) to face danger, suffering, etc.: *she nerved herself to enter the room.* PHRASES **get on a person's nerves** irritate or annoy a person. **have nerves of steel** (of a person etc.) be not easily upset or frightened. **hit** (or **touch**) **a nerve** remark on or draw attention to a sensitive subject or point.

nerve cell *noun* an elongated branched cell transmitting impulses in nerve tissue.

nerve centre *noun* **1** a group of closely connected nerve cells associated in performing some function. **2** the centre of control of an organization etc.

nerved *adjective* having nerves esp. of the kind indicated: *she was steely-nerved.*

nerve ending *noun* the branched or specialized end of a nerve fibre.

nerve gas *noun* a poisonous gas or vapour that disrupts the functioning of the nervous system, esp. for use in warfare.

nerve impulse *noun* a signal transmitted along a nerve fibre.

nerveless *adjective* **1** inert, lacking vigour or spirit: *their playing was correct but nerveless.* **2** *Anatomy & Zoology* without nerves.

nerve-racking *adjective* (also **nerve-wracking**) stressful, frightening; straining the nerves.

nervily *adverb* in an impudent or audacious manner; cheekily.

nervous *adjective* **1 a** worried, anxious. **b** timid, reluctant, afraid. **c** resulting from or reflecting these feelings: *nervous smile.* **2 a** excitable; high-strung. **b** resulting from this temperament, from a disorder of the nervous system, etc.: *a nervous headache.* **3** pertaining to or affecting the nerves: *a nervous disorder.*

nervous breakdown *noun* a period of incapacitating mental and emotional disturbance, severe depression, etc.

nervously *adverb* in a nervous manner.

nervousness *noun* the state of being nervous: *he tried to hide his nervousness.*

nervous system *noun* the body's network of specialized cells which transmit nerve impulses between parts of the body.

nervous wreck *noun informal* a person suffering from mental stress, emotional exhaustion, etc.

nervy *adjective* (**nervier, nerviest**) impudent, audacious.

-ness *suffix* forming nouns from adjectives, and occasionally other words, expressing: **1** state or condition, or an instance of this: *happiness ◊ a kindness.* **2** something in a certain state: *wilderness.*

nest • *noun* **1** a structure or place where a bird lays eggs and shelters its young. **2** an animal's or insect's breeding ground or lair. **3** a snug or secluded retreat, shelter, home, etc. **4** (often foll. by *of*) a place fostering something undesirable: *a nest of vice.* **5** a group or set of similar objects, often of different sizes and fitting together for storage: *a nest of tables.* **6** a group of machine guns, snipers, etc. • *verb* **1** use or build a nest. **2** take or collect wild birds' nests or eggs. **3 a** (of objects) fit together or one inside another. **b** place or fit (a thing) inside another, similar one, esp. in a hierarchical arrangement. ▶ **nested** *adjective*

nest egg *noun* a sum of money saved for the future.

nester *noun* a bird that builds a nest in the place or way indicated: *a tree nester.*

nestle *verb* (**nestles, nestled, nestling**) **1** place or lie in a partly hidden, snug, or sheltered position. **2** settle down in a snug or comfortable manner. **3** rest or settle (a head, shoulder, etc.) in a snug or affectionate manner. **4** draw or press close to a person or thing, esp. in an affectionate manner.

nestling *noun* a bird that is too young to leave its nest. [Say NEST ling]

Net *noun informal* (also **net**) (usu. **the Net**) the Internet.

net¹ • *noun* **1** an open-meshed material of twine or cord. **2** a piece or structure of net for catching fish or insects. **3** a fine fabric with a very open weave. **4** *Sport* a goal. **5** a trap. **6** a system for selecting or recruiting someone. **7** a communications or computer network. • *verb* (**nets, netted, netting**) **1** catch or obtain with or as if with a net. **2** (in sport) score (a goal). **3** cover with a net.

net² • *adjective* **1** (esp. of money) remaining after all necessary deductions, or free from deductions: *net income.* **2** (of a price) to be paid in full; not reducible. **3** (of a weight) excluding that of the packaging or container etc. **4** (of an effect, result, etc.) ultimate. **5** after all factors have been calculated: *a net importer of oil.* • *noun* a net sum, income, result, etc. • *verb* (**nets, netted, netting**) gain or yield (a sum) as net profit.

nether *adjective* esp. *literary* or *jocular* = LOWER¹ *adjective* 1, 2.

Netherlander *noun* a native or national of the Netherlands. ▶ **Netherlandish** *adjective*

nethermost *adjective* lowest; farthest down.

nether regions *plural noun* **1** *jocular* the parts of the human body below the waist, esp. the buttocks and genitals. **2** the deepest or farthest parts of a place, esp. referring to hell or the underworld.

netherworld *noun* **1** the infernal regions; hell. **2** the world of the criminal underground. **3** a state of neglect or oblivion: *the arcane netherworld of Canada's constitutional history.*

netiquette *noun informal* the informal code of conduct governing effective and polite use of the Internet. [Say NET i kit]

net-like *adjective* resembling a net or mesh.

netminder *noun* a goaltender. ▶ **netminding** *noun*

net profit *noun* the effective profit; the actual gain after working expenses have been paid.

Net surf *verb* browse through the Internet.

Net surfer *noun* (also **net surfer**) a person who uses

N

the Internet, esp. habitually. ▶ **Net surfing** *noun & adjective*

netter *noun* a person or boat that fishes using a net esp. of a specified kind.

netting *noun* **1** netted fabric. **2** a piece of this. **3** the action of fishing with a net or nets. **4** the action or process of making a net, nets, or a network.

nettle • *noun* **1** a plant with jagged leaves covered with stinging hairs. **2** any of various plants resembling this. • *verb* (**nettles, nettled, nettling**) irritate, provoke, annoy.

net ton *noun see* TON *noun* 5b.

network • *noun* **1** an arrangement of intersecting horizontal and vertical lines. **2** a complex system of railways, roads, etc. **3** a group of broadcasting stations that connect to broadcast a program simultaneously. **4** a number of interconnected computers, operations, etc. **5** a group of people who interact together. • *verb* **1** connect as or operate with a network **2** interact with others to exchange information and develop contacts.

network computer *noun* a low-cost personal computer without local disk storage, designed to be connected to the Internet, a local area network, etc., from which it would access applications and data.

networked *adjective* (of a computer etc.) joined to others as part of an interconnected group.

networker *noun* **1** *Computing* a member of an organization or computer network who operates from home or from an external office. **2** a member of a professional or social network.

networking *noun* **1** a system of trying to meet and talk to other people who may be useful in one's work. **2** the linking of computers to share data and improve the efficient use of resources.

net worth *noun* the monetary value of something when debts etc. have been deducted from the value of assets.

neural *adjective* of or relating to a nerve or the central nervous system. [Say NYUR ul or NUR ul]

neuralgia *noun* an intense intermittent pain along the course of a nerve, esp. in the head or face. ▶ **neuralgic** *adjective* [Say nyur AL juh or nur AL juh]

neural network *noun* (also **neural net**) **1** a system of interconnections which resembles or is based on the arrangement of neurons in the brain and nervous system. **2** a configuration of computers designed to simulate this.

neural tube *noun* a hollow structure from which the brain and spinal cord develop.

neural tube defect *noun* any of a range of congenital abnormalities, including spina bifida, resulting from incomplete fusion of the neural tube.

neuro- *combining form* a nerve or nerves. [Say NYURO, NURO]

neurobiology *noun* the biology of the nervous system.

neurochemical • *adjective* of or pertaining to the chemistry of the nervous system. • *noun* a drug or other substance that acts on the nervous system. ▶ **neurochemist** *noun* **neurochemistry** *noun*

neurological *adjective* having to do with the anatomy, functions, and organic disorders of nerves and the nervous system. ▶ **neurologically** *adverb*

neurologist *noun* a specialist in the anatomy, functions, and organic disorders of nerves and the nervous system. [Say nyur OLLA jist or nur OLLA jist]

neurology *noun* the branch of biology or esp. medicine that deals with the anatomy, functions, and organic disorders of nerves and the nervous system. [Say nyur OLLA jee or nur OLLA jee]

neuromuscular *adjective* pertaining to, consisting of, or resembling both nerves and muscle tissue.

neuron *noun* a specialized cell transmitting nerve impulses; a nerve cell. [Say NUR on or NYUR on]

neuropsychology *noun* the study of the relationship between the nervous system (esp. the brain) and behaviour.

neuroscience *noun* any or all of the sciences dealing with the structure and function of the nervous system and brain. ▶ **neuroscientist** *noun*

neurosis *noun* (*plural* **neuroses**) **1** a mild mental illness characterized by symptoms of stress such as anxiety, hypochondria, depression, obsessive behaviour, etc., without loss of contact with reality. **2** any more or less specific anxiety or malaise experienced by an individual, group, nation, etc.: *the feeling that Canada has left undone what it ought to have done amounts to a national neurosis.* [Say nyur OWE sis or nur OWE sis for the singular, nyur OWE sees or nur OWE sees for the plural]

neurosurgeon *noun* a surgeon who operates on the nervous system, esp. the brain and spinal cord.

neurosurgery *noun* surgery performed on the nervous system, esp. the brain and spinal cord.

neurotic • *adjective* **1** caused by or suffering from neurosis: *neurotic fears.* **2** *informal* abnormally sensitive or obsessive: *she became neurotic about keeping the house clean.* • *noun* a neurotic person. ▶ **neurotically** *adverb* [Say nur OT ick or nyur OT ick]

neurotoxic *adjective* poisonous to the nervous system. ▶ **neurotoxicity** *noun*

neurotransmission *noun* the transfer of an impulse from one nerve to another.

neurotransmitter *noun* a chemical substance released from a nerve fibre that effects the transfer of an impulse to another nerve or muscle.

neuter • *adjective* **1** *Grammar* (of a noun etc.) neither masculine nor feminine. **2** (of a plant) having neither pistils nor stamen. **3** (of an insect) having no functional sexual organs, sterile. **4** having no sexual characteristics, being neither male or female. • *noun* **1** *Grammar* the neuter gender. **2 a** a non-fertile insect, esp. a worker bee or ant. **b** a castrated animal. • *verb* **1** castrate or spay (an animal). **2** deprive of potency, vigour, or force: *fixing the exchange rate effectively neuters the Bank of Canada.* ▶ **neutered** *adjective* **neutering** *noun* [Say NOOTER or NYOOTER]

Neutral *noun* a member of an Iroquoian people formerly living on the shores of Lake Erie.

neutral • *adjective* **1** not helping or supporting either of two opposing sides, esp. countries at war or in dispute; impartial. **2** belonging to a neutral party, nation, etc.: *neutral ships.* **3** indistinct, vague, indeterminate: *the tone was neutral, devoid of sentiment.* **4** occupying a middle position with regard to two extremes. **5** (of colours, esp. white, beige, or grey) not strong or intense; harmonizing well with most other colours. **6** *Chemistry* neither acid nor alkaline. **7** having neither a positive nor a negative electrical charge. **8** *Physics* designating or situated at a point, on a line or plane, etc. where opposing forces are in equilibrium. **9** (in *combination*) having neither a positive nor a negative effect: *revenue-neutral.* **10** (in *combination*) specifying neither male nor female characteristics: *gender-neutral.* • *noun* **1 a** a neutral country or person. **b** a citizen of a neutral country. **2** a position of the driving and driven parts in a gear mechanism in which no power is transmitted. **3** a state in which no progress is made: *this government seems to be stuck in neutral on this issue.* **4** a neutral colour. ▶ **neutrality** *noun*

neutralize *verb* (**neutralizes, neutralized, neutralizing**) **1** counterbalance; render ineffective by an opposite force or effect. **2 a** make (an acidic or

alkaline solution etc.) chemically neutral. **b** eliminate a charge difference in; make electrically neutral. **3** *euphemism* kill or make (a person) harmless or ineffective. ▶ **neutralization** *noun* **neutralizer** *noun*

neutrally *adverb* in a neutral manner, esp. so as not to support one side or the other in a dispute.

neutral zone *noun* **1** *Hockey* the central area of a rink, extending from blue line to blue line. **2** an esp. demilitarized area acting as a buffer between two belligerents.

neutrino *noun* (*plural* **neutrinos**) any of a group of stable elementary particles with zero electric charge and probably zero mass, which travel at the speed of light. [Say noo TREE no or nyoo TREE no]

neutron *noun* an elementary particle of about the same mass as a proton but without an electric charge, present in all atomic nuclei except those of ordinary hydrogen. [Say NOO tron or NYOO tron]

neutron bomb *noun* a kind of atomic bomb producing large numbers of neutrons but little blast, so causing great damage to life but little property damage.

neutron star *noun* a very small, dense star composed mainly of closely packed neutrons.

never *adverb* **1** at no time. **2** not at all: *never fear*. **3** *informal* (expressing surprise or incredulity) surely not: *you never left the key in the lock!* PHRASES **well I never!** expressing great surprise.

never-ending *adjective* never coming to an end, endless.

nevermore *adverb* at no future time; never again.

never-never land *noun* an imaginary, utopian or illusory place.

nevertheless *adverb* in spite of that; all the same.

new *adjective* **1** not existing before; made, introduced, or discovered recently or now for the first time. **2** not previously used or owned. **3** seen, experienced, or acquired recently or now for the first time. **4** inexperienced at or unaccustomed to. **5** reinvigorated, restored, or reformed. **6** (in place names) discovered or founded later than and named after.

New Age *noun* a broad movement characterized by alternative approaches to traditional Western culture, with interest in spiritual matters, mysticism, holistic ideas, environmentalism, etc. ▶ **New Ager** *noun*

newbie *noun* *slang* a novice on the Internet. [Say NEW bee]

newborn ● *adjective* **1** (of a child etc.) recently born. **2** newly created or formed: *the newborn lobby group*. ● *noun* a newborn child.

New Brunswicker *noun* a native or inhabitant of New Brunswick.

newcomer *noun* **1** a person who has recently arrived. **2** a beginner in some activity.

New Criticism *noun* an approach to the analysis of literary texts which concentrates on the organization of the text itself, with particular emphasis on irony, ambiguity, etc., rather than on its historical or biographical context.

new deal *noun* **1** new arrangements or conditions, esp. when better than the earlier ones. **2** (**New Deal**) the economic measures introduced by US President Franklin D. Roosevelt in 1933 to counteract the effects of the Great Depression; it involved a massive public works program, complemented by the large-scale granting of loans, and succeeded in reducing unemployment by between 7 and 10 million. ▶ **New Dealer** *noun*

New Democrat *noun* *Cdn* a member or supporter of the New Democratic Party.

New Democratic *adjective* *Cdn* of, belonging to or constituted by the New Democratic Party.

New Democratic Party *noun* (in Canada) a left-of-centre political party, more successful provincially than federally, formed from the Co-operative Commonwealth Federation in 1961. Abbreviation: **NDP.**

newel *noun* **1** the supporting central post of winding stairs. **2** (also **newel post**) a post at the head or foot of a staircase supporting a handrail. [Say NEW ul]

newfangled *adjective* *derogatory* different from what one is used to; objectionably new.

Newfie (also **Newf**) *informal* ● *noun* **1** a Newfoundlander. **2** Newfoundland. **3** a Newfoundland dog. ● *adjective* of or relating to Newfoundland or Newfoundlanders.

new-found *adjective* newly discovered.

Newfoundland *noun* (also **Newfoundland dog**) a very large breed of dog with a thick coarse coat and webbed feet, noted for its intelligence, strength, and swimming ability. [Say new f'n LAND or NEW f'nd l'nd or NEW f'nd land or new FOUND l'nd]

Newfoundlander *noun* a native or inhabitant of Newfoundland.

Newfoundland Time *noun* the time in a zone including the island of Newfoundland. **Newfoundland Standard Time** is three and a half hours behind GMT; **Newfoundland Daylight Time** is two and a half hours behind GMT.

newish *adjective* somewhat new.

New Jerusalem *noun* **1** *Christianity* the abode of the saints in heaven. **2** *informal* an ideal place or situation: *democratic capitalism has not built a New Jerusalem*.

New Left *noun* an international political movement initiated in the 1960s by young left-wing radicals opposed to the philosophy of the old liberal society; beginning mainly as an anti-capitalist and anti-war movement, the New Left grew with its opposition to US involvement in the Vietnam War and expanded to promote such causes as women's liberation, education, and environmentalism. ▶ **New Leftist** *noun*

new look ● *noun* **1** a new or revised appearance or presentation, esp. of something familiar. **2** (often **New Look**) a style of women's clothing introduced after World War II, featuring long full skirts and a generous use of material. ● *adjective* (**new-look**) having a new image; restyled.

newly *adverb* **1** recently. **2** afresh, anew: *newly painted*. **3** in a new or different manner: *newly arranged*.

newlywed *noun* a recently married person.

new money *noun* *informal* **1** recently acquired money or wealth. **2** the recently wealthy: *old money lives here alongside the mansions of uppity new money*.

new moon *noun* **1 a** the moon when first seen as a crescent after conjunction with the sun. **b** the time of its appearance. **2** *Astronomy* the time at which the moon is in conjunction with the sun.

newness *noun* the quality of being new.

New Right *noun* a political movement characterized by rejection of all forms of socialism and an emphasis on traditional conservative values.

news *noun* **1** information about important or interesting recent events, esp. when published or broadcast. **2** (**the news**) a broadcast report of news. **3** newly received or noteworthy information. **4** (foll. by *to*) *informal* information not previously known (to a person): *that's news to me*.

news agency *noun* (*plural* **news agencies**) an organization that collects and distributes news items.

newsboy *noun* esp. *hist.* a boy who sells or delivers newspapers.

news bulletin *noun* a short broadcast or published news item or collection of news items.

newscast *noun* a radio or television broadcast of news reports.

newscaster *noun* a person who reads news broadcasts.

news conference *noun* a press conference.

news flash *noun* (*plural* **news flashes**) a single item of important news broadcast separately and often interrupting other programs.

newsgroup *noun* *Computing* (on the Internet or other network) a forum for the discussion of, and exchange of information about, a particular subject.

newshound *noun* *informal* a newspaper reporter, esp. an aggressive one.

newsletter *noun* a usu. informal printed report issued periodically by a society, business, organization, etc.

newsmagazine *noun* **1** a publication reporting and commenting on current events, usu. issued weekly on glossy paper, typically with many photographs. **2** a television news program consisting of in-depth reports on selected current events.

newsmaker *noun* a person or thing at the centre of newsworthy events. ▶ **newsmaking** *noun*

newsman *noun* (*plural* **newsmen**) a reporter, newscaster, or journalist.

newspaper *noun* a printed publication (usu. daily or weekly) containing news, advertisements, correspondence, etc.

newspapering *noun* the business etc. of producing newspapers.

newspaperman *noun* (*plural* **newspapermen**) a journalist.

newspaperwoman (*plural* **newspaperwomen**) *noun* a female journalist.

Newspeak *noun* ambiguous euphemistic language used esp. in political propaganda.

newsprint *noun* a type of low-quality paper on which newspapers are printed.

news reader *noun* = NEWSCASTER.

newsreel *noun* *hist.* a short motion picture of recent events.

news release *noun* = PRESS RELEASE.

newsroom *noun* a room in a newspaper or broadcasting office where news is processed.

news service *noun* = NEWS AGENCY.

newsstand *noun* a stall for the sale of newspapers.

New Style *noun* dating reckoned by the Gregorian Calendar (*compare* OLD STYLE).

newsweekly *noun* (*plural* **newsweeklies**) a weekly newspaper or newsmagazine.

news wire *noun* a service transmitting the latest news stories, e.g. via teleprinter, satellite, or the Internet.

newswoman *noun* (*plural* **newswomen**) a female reporter, newscaster, or journalist.

newsworthiness *noun* the quality of being newsworthy: *newsworthiness never justifies violating someone's privacy*.

newsworthy *adjective* of sufficient interest to the public to warrant mention in the news; topical.

newsy *adjective* (**newsier**, **newsiest**) **1** (of a newspaper etc.) full of esp. gossipy news. **2** (of a news item) light, gossipy.

newt *noun* a small, rough-skinned amphibian with a well-developed tail, usu. spending its adult life on land and returning to water to breed.

New Testament *noun* the second part of the Christian Bible concerned with the life and teachings of Christ and his earliest followers.

newton *noun* *Physics* the SI unit of force that, acting on a mass of one kilogram, increases its velocity by one metre per second every second along the direction that it acts. Abbreviation: **N**.

new wave *noun* **1** a recent trend in a given field: *the new wave in fitness ◊ a new wave diet*. **2** (often as **the new wave**) a movement in French cinema of the late 1950s and early 1960s, characterized by frequent use of jump-cuts, on-location shooting, hand-held cameras, etc. **3** a style of pop music of the late 1970s and early 1980s, influenced by punk but characterized by a greater use of synthesizers and a more mainstream sound.

New World *noun* North and South America regarded collectively in relation to Europe.

new world order *noun* often *ironic* a state of co-operation, peace, and justice among all nations.

new year *noun* the calendar year just begun or about to begin.

New Year's *noun* **1** (also **New Year's Eve**) the evening of Dec. 31. **2** (also **New Year's Day**) the first day of the year, Jan. 1.

New Yorker *noun* a native or inhabitant of New York State or New York City. • *adjective* of or relating to New York State or New York City.

New York steak *noun* (also **New York strip**) a steak cut from the outer side of a T-bone.

New Zealander *noun* a native or inhabitant of New Zealand, an island country in the South Pacific.

next • *adjective* **1** coming immediately after the present one in time, space, or order. **2** (of a day of the week) nearest (or the nearest but one) after the present. **3** beside. • *adverb* **1** immediately afterwards. **2** following in the specified order: *the next oldest*. • *noun* the next person or thing. PHRASES **as good** (or **well** or **much** etc.) **as the next person** as good, well, etc. as the average person: *I can take a joke as well as the next guy*. **next to 1** adjacent to. **2** almost: *next to nothing left*. **3** following in order after: *next to skiing her favourite sport was skating*.

SPELL CHECK	
next door, next-door	

Note the difference in spelling between *the boy next door* and *the next-door neighbour*. There is a hyphen when the latter kind of structure is used.

next door *adverb & adjective* in or to the next house, room, etc. PHRASES **next door to 1** in the next house etc. to. **2** nearly, almost, near to.

next-generation *adjective* designating an imminent technology, style, model, etc.

next of kin *noun* the closest living relative or relatives.

next-to-last *adjective* penultimate.

next world *noun* a supposed life after death.

nexus *noun* (*plural* **nexuses**) **1** a connected group, series, or network: *a nexus of ideas*. **2** a connection: *the nexus between industry and political power*. [Say NEX us]

NF *abbreviation* Newfoundland (in official postal use).

NFB *abbreviation* National Film Board of Canada.

NFL *abbreviation* (in the US) National Football League.

Nfld. *abbreviation* Newfoundland.

NGO *abbreviation* (*plural* **NGOs**) non-governmental organization.

Nguni • *noun* **1** (*plural* **Nguni**) a member of a group of Bantu-speaking peoples living mainly in southern Africa. **2** the group of closely related Bantu languages spoken by these peoples. • *adjective* of or relating to these peoples or this group of languages. [Say 'n GOONY]

NGV *abbreviation* (*plural* **NGVs**) natural gas vehicle.

NHL *abbreviation* National Hockey League. ▶**NHLer** *noun* (*plural* **NHLers**)

Ni *symbol* the element nickel.

niacin *noun* a vitamin of the vitamin B complex, found in milk, liver, and yeast. [Say NIGH uh sin]

Niagara *noun* (also **niagara**; usu. foll. by *of*) an outpouring, a deluge: *a Niagara of fan mail*.

nib • *noun* **1** the point of a pen, which touches the writing surface. **2** (in *plural*) shelled and crushed coffee or cocoa beans. **3** the point of a tool etc. • *verb* (**nibs, nibbed, nibbing**) provide with a nib.

nibble • *verb* (**nibbles, nibbled, nibbling**) **1 a** take small bites at. **b** eat in small amounts. **c** bite at gently or cautiously or playfully. **2** (often foll. by *at*) show cautious interest in. • *noun* **1** an instance of nibbling something. **2 a** a very small amount of food. **b** (also **nibbly**, *plural* **nibblies**) (usu. in *plural*) a small food item. **3** a tentative display of interest. PHRASES **nibble away** (**at**) consume or wear away slowly or gradually. ▶**nibbler** *noun*

niblet *noun* a small piece of food, e.g. a kernel of corn.

NIC *abbreviation* (*plural* **NICs**) newly industrialized (or industrializing) country.

nicad *noun* a battery, often rechargeable, with a nickel anode and a cadmium cathode. [Say NYE cad]

Nicaraguan • *adjective* of or relating to Nicaragua, the largest country in Central America. • *noun* a native or inhabitant of Nicaragua. [Say nicka ROG win]

WRITING TIP
nice, very nice

Instead of saying that something is **nice** or **very nice**, try to use more precise and interesting adjectives to describe things:

we had a **delightful/splendid/enjoyable** time
a **satisfying/delicious/exquisite** meal
a **fashionable/stylish/elegant/chic** outfit
this is a **cozy/comfortable/attractive** room
she is **kind/friendly/likeable/amiable**
our adviser is **compassionate/understanding/sympathetic**
a **thoughtful/considerate/caring** gesture
When describing the weather, you can use words like **pleasant**, **fair**, **mild**, and **fine** instead of **nice**.

---

nice *adjective* (**nicer, nicest**) **1** pleasant, agreeable, satisfactory. **2** (of a person) kind, good-natured. **3** *ironic* bad or awkward: *a nice mess*. **4 a** fine or subtle: *a nice distinction*. **b** requiring careful thought or attention: *a nice problem*. **5** scrupulous: *were not too nice about their methods*. **6** satisfactory or adequate in terms of the quality described: *nice and warm*.

nice-guy *adjective* characteristic of a nice, agreeable person: *a nice-guy image*.

nicely *adverb* **1** in an attractive or satisfactory way; well: *the room was nicely furnished*. **2** in a kind, friendly, or polite way: *if you ask her nicely she might say yes*. **3** carefully; exactly: *his novels nicely describe life in Canada between the wars*. PHRASES **do nicely** be appreciated or welcome: *some ice cream right now would do nicely*.

Nicene Creed *noun* a formal statement of Christian belief that is very widely used in Christian liturgies. It is based on the creed adopted at the first Council of Nicaea (in modern Turkey) in 325, and asserts a belief in Christ's dual nature as at once human and divine and equal with God. [Say NICE een or nice EEN]

niceness *noun* pleasantness, politeness; the quality of being nice.

nicety *noun* (*plural* **niceties**) **1** a subtle distinction or detail: *legal niceties* ◊ *the car lacks such niceties as air bags*. **2** a minor aspect of polite social behaviour; a detail of

etiquette: *social niceties*. **3** precision, accuracy: *regulated with exact nicety*. [Say NICE uh tee]

niche *noun* **1** a shallow recess, esp. in a wall to contain a statue etc. **2** a comfortable or suitable position in life or employment: *Japanese immigrants found their niche in farming*. **3** (a relatively small consumer group sharing a common profession or interest, targeted by a company or advertiser as a viable market for a specialized product or line of products: *niche marketing* ◊ *the magazine is aimed at a profitable new niche for advertisers in print media — Chinese-Canadian readers*. **4** *Ecology* a position or role taken by a kind of organism within its community. [Say NEESH or NITCH]

nick • *noun* **1** a small cut or notch. **2** a scratch or light wound. • *verb* make a nick or nicks in. PHRASES **in the nick of time** only just in time; just at the right moment. **nick** (**someone**) **for** *informal* defraud someone of (a sum): *insurance companies will be nicked for an extra $40 million*.

nickel • *noun* **1** a silvery-white metallic element, occurring naturally in various minerals and chiefly used in alloys, esp. with iron, to which it imparts strength and resistance to corrosion, and with copper for coinage. **2 a** a five-cent coin. **b** five cents. • *verb* (**nickels, nickelled, nickelling**) coat with nickel.

nickel and dime • *verb* (**nickels and dimes, nickelled and dimed, nickelling and diming**) put a financial strain on (someone) by charging small amounts for many minor services etc.: *a bad contractor may nickel and dime you with extra charges*. • *adjective* (**nickel-and-dime**) petty, insignificant: *had been arrested for various nickel-and-dime offences*.

nicker *verb* neigh.

nickname • *noun* a familiar, shortened, or humorous name given to a person or thing instead of or as well as the real name. • *verb* (**nicknames, nicknamed, nicknaming**) give a nickname to.

niçoise *adjective* designating food (esp. a salad) garnished with tomatoes, capers, anchovies, etc. [Say nee SWOZZ]

nicotiana *noun* = TOBACCO 2. [Say nick oh tee ANNA or nick oh shee ANNA]

nicotine *noun* a poisonous alkaloid present in tobacco. [Say NICKA teen or nicka TEEN]

niece *noun* a daughter of one's brother or sister, or of one's brother-in-law or sister-in-law.

niftily *adverb* cleverly, skilfully: *a niftily executed deke*.

nifty *adjective* (**niftier, niftiest**) *informal* **1** cleverly designed, executed, etc. **2** clever. **3** stylish.

Nigerian • *noun* a native or inhabitant of Nigeria, a country on the southern coast of West Africa. • *adjective* of or relating to Nigeria or the Nigerians. [Say nigh JEERY in]

niggardliness *noun* stinginess, cheapness. [Say NIG erd lee niss]

WRITING TIP
niggardly

Niggardly has absolutely no racial connotations and is a perfectly acceptable word.

---

niggardly *adjective* **1** stingy: *a niggardly attitude*. **2** meagre, scanty: *a niggardly 1.4 percent pay increase*. [Say NIG erd lee]

niggle • *verb* (**niggles, niggled, niggling**) **1** find fault in a petty way. **2** *informal* irritate. • *noun* a trifling complaint or criticism; a worry or annoyance.

niggling *adjective* **1** troublesome or irritating in a petty way. **2** trifling or petty.

nigh often *jocular* • *adjective* (esp. of a momentous event) near; approaching: *the end of the world is nigh*. • *adverb*

almost: *nigh impossible*. PHRASES **nigh on** almost: *but that was nigh on three days ago*.

night *noun* **1** the period of darkness between one day and the next; the time from sunset to sunrise. **2** a night or evening appointed for some activity, or spent or regarded in a certain way: *parent-teacher night ◊ a great night out.* PHRASES **night and day** all the time; unceasingly.

nightcap *noun* **1** *hist.* a cap worn in bed. **2** a hot or alcoholic drink taken at bedtime. **3** *Baseball* the second game of a doubleheader when played in the evening.

nightclothes *noun* clothes for wearing in bed.

nightclub *noun* a club that is open at night for drinking, eating, dancing, entertainment, etc. ▶**nightclubber** *noun* **nightclubbing** *noun*

night crawler *noun* an earthworm.

nightfall *noun* the onset of night; the end of daylight.

nightgown *noun* (also **nightdress**, *plural* **nightdresses**) a woman's or girl's loose garment worn in bed.

nighthawk *noun* **1** a nocturnal insect-eating North American bird. **2** a person who is active at night.

nightie *noun informal* a nightgown.

nightingale *noun* a small reddish-brown Old World bird noted for the melodious song of the male, often heard at night.

nightlife *noun* activity or entertainment occurring at night in a city, as in nightclubs etc.

night light *noun* **1** a dim light kept on in a room or hallway at night. **2** any light at night, e.g. a street light.

nightly • *adjective* **1** happening, done, or existing in the night. **2** recurring every night. • *adverb* every night.

nightmare *noun* **1** a frightening or unpleasant dream. **2** a terrifying or very unpleasant experience or situation. **3** a haunting or obsessive fear. ▶**nightmarish** *adjective* **nightmarishly** *adverb*

night owl *noun* a person active at night.

nightshade *noun* **1** a plant with red or black usu. poisonous berries, some varieties of which are also used in herbal medicines. **2** (also **deadly nightshade**) = BELLADONNA.

night shift *noun* a shift of workers employed during the night.

nightshirt *noun* a long shirt worn in bed.

nightspot *noun* a nightclub.

nightstick *noun* a police officer's truncheon.

night table *noun* (also **nightstand**) a small low bedside table, often with drawers.

nighttime *noun* the time between evening and morning; the time of night or darkness.

night vision *noun* **1** the faculty of seeing during the night or in the dark. **2** (**night-vision**) (as an *adjective*) designating equipment enabling one to see in the dark: *night-vision goggles.*

night watchman *noun* (*plural* **night watchmen**) a person whose job is to keep watch by night.

nightwear *noun* clothing suitable for wearing in bed.

nihilism *noun* **1** the rejection of all moral and religious principles, often in the belief that life is meaningless: *lawlessness and moral nihilism.* **2** an extreme form of skepticism maintaining that nothing has a real existence: *the nihilism of a disillusioned revolutionary.* ▶**nihilist** *noun* **nihilistic** *adjective* [Say NIGH ill ism]

-nik *suffix* forming nouns denoting a person associated with a specified thing or quality: *beatnik.*

Nikkei *noun* (also **Nikkei index**, **Nikkei average**) a figure indicating the relative price of representative shares on the Tokyo Stock Exchange. [Say NEE kay]

nil *noun* nothing; no number or amount (often as a score in games).

Nilotic *adjective* **1** of or relating to the Nile or the Nile region of Africa. **2** of or relating to a group of East African Negroid peoples, or the languages spoken by them. [Say nye LOT ick]

nimble *adjective* (**nimbler**, **nimblest**) **1** quick and light in movement or action; agile. **2** (of the mind) quick to comprehend; clever, versatile. ▶**nimbleness** *noun* **nimbly** *adverb*

nimbostratus *noun* cloud forming a low diffuse dark grey layer, often with falling rain or snow. [Say nimbo STRAT us]

nimbus *noun* (*plural* **nimbuses** or **nimbi**) **1 a** a bright cloud or halo surrounding a supernatural being or saint. **b** the halo of a saint etc. **2** a rain cloud. [Say NIM bus for the singular, NIM bye for the plural]

NIMBY *noun* (*plural* **NIMBYs**) a person who objects to unwanted groups or developments appearing in his or her neighbourhood.

nimrod *noun* **1** *slang* an inept person. **2** often *humorous* or *ironic* a skilled hunter: *December brings visions of trophy whitetail to a million Pennsylvania nimrods.*

nincompoop *noun* an idiot.

nine *cardinal number* one more than eight. PHRASES **dressed to the nines** dressed very elaborately or elegantly. **have nine lives** appear to recover repeatedly from disastrous circumstances. **nine-tenths** nearly all: *possession is nine-tenths of the law.* **nine times out of ten** nearly always.

ninefold *adjective & adverb* **1** nine times as much or as many. **2** consisting of nine parts.

900 number *noun* a telephone number, with the digits "900" in place of an area code, used to access information or entertainment provided for a fee charged by the minute.

ninepin *noun* **1** (in *plural*; usu. treated as *singular*) a game in which nine pins are set up at the end of an alley and bowled at in an attempt to knock them down. **2** a pin used in this game. PHRASES **go down** (or **drop** or **fall**) **like ninepins** topple or succumb in large numbers.

niner *noun Cdn* (esp. *Ont.*) *slang* a student in grade nine, the first year of high school.

nineteen *cardinal number* one more than eighteen. ▶**nineteenth** *ordinal number*

ninetieth *ordinal number* constituting number ninety in a series.

nine-to-five *adjective* of or involving standard office hours (typically 9 a.m. to 5 p.m.). ▶**nine-to-fiver** *noun*

ninety *cardinal number* (*plural* **nineties**) ten more than eighty. PHRASES **ninety-first, -second**, etc. the ordinal numbers between ninetieth and a hundredth. **ninety-one, -two**, etc. the cardinal numbers between ninety and a hundred.

ninja *noun* **1** a person skilled in an originally Japanese martial art characterized by stealthy movement and camouflage. **2** *informal* any fanciful warrior using acrobatics and various bladed weapons.

ninny *noun* (*plural* **ninnies**) a foolish or stupid person.

ninth *ordinal number* constituting the number nine in a series. ▶**ninthly** *adverb*

niobium *noun* a rare grey-blue metallic element used in alloys for superconductors. [Say nigh OH bee um]

nip • *verb* (**nips**, **nipped**, **nipping**) **1** pinch, squeeze, or bite sharply. **2** (of the cold, frost, etc.) cause pain or harm to. **3** (foll. by *in*, *out*, etc.) *informal* go quickly.

4 *informal* (of an athlete, team, etc.) overtake or defeat (an opponent) by a narrow margin. **5** make (the waist of a garment) very narrow in comparison to the shoulders, bust, and hips. • *noun* **1 a** a pinch, a sharp squeeze. **b** a bite. **2** biting cold. **3** *Cdn* (*Man. & NW Ont.*) a hamburger. **4** *informal* a small drink of alcohol. PHRASES **nip at someone's heel** (or **heels**) pursue someone very closely. **nip in the bud** suppress or destroy (esp. an idea) at an early stage.

nip and tuck • *noun* (*plural* **nips and tucks**) *informal* **1** a cosmetic surgical operation. **2** a minor renovation or improvement. • *adjective* (of a competition) not decided until the last possible moment.

nipper *noun* **1** a person or thing that nips. **2** *Cdn* (*Maritimes & Nfld*) a glove worn while handling lines to protect the hands from friction. **3** *Cdn* (*Nfld*) a large mosquito. **4** the claw of a crab, lobster, etc. **5** (in *plural*) any tool for gripping or cutting, e.g. forceps or pincers.

nipping *adjective* causing sharp pain; stinging.

nipple *noun* **1 a** a small projection in which the mammary ducts of female mammals terminate and from which milk is secreted for the young. **b** an analogous structure in the male. **2** a rubber device shaped like this on a baby's or animal's feeding bottle. **3** a small projection on a device or machine, esp. one from which oil, grease, or other fluid is dispensed in small amounts. **4** a nipple-like protuberance.

nippy *adjective* (**nippier**, **nippiest**) *informal* **1** chilly, cold. **2** (of food, esp. cheese) piquant, sharp.

nirvana *noun* **1** an enlightened state of freedom from worldly attachments and desires and release from the continuous cycle of suffering and rebirth, attained by the extinction of individuality; it represents the final goal of Buddhism. **2** *informal* a state of perfection: *Australia is diving and snorkelling nirvana.* [Say nur VONNA]

Nisei • *noun* (*plural* **Nisei**) a Canadian or American whose parents were immigrants from Japan. • *adjective* of or relating to the Nisei. [Say nee SAY]

Nisga'a (also **Nishga**) • *noun* (*plural* **Nisga'a** or **Nisga'as**, or **Nishga** or **Nishgas**) **1** a member of a Tsimshian Aboriginal people living in the Skeena River valley in northwestern BC. **2** the language of this people, a dialect of Nass-Gitksan. • *adjective* of or relating to this people or their language. [Say NISS guh; for *Nishga* say NISH guh]

nit *noun* the egg or young form of a louse or other parasitic insect, esp. of human head lice or body lice. PHRASES **pick nits** search for and criticize small, esp. insignificant faults or errors; nitpick.

Nitinat • *noun* (*plural* **Nitinat** or **Nitinats**) **1** a member of an Aboriginal people, part of the Nuu-chah-nulth, living on southern Vancouver Island. **2** the Wakashan language of this people. • *adjective* of or relating to this people. [Say NITTA nat]

nitpick *verb* search for and criticize small, esp. insignificant faults or errors. ▶ **nitpicker** *noun*

nitpicking *noun & adjective* *informal* searching for and criticizing small, esp. insignificant faults or errors. ▶ **nitpicky** *adjective*

nitrate *noun* **1** any salt or ester of nitric acid. **2** potassium or sodium nitrate when used as a fertilizer. ▶ **nitration** *noun* [Say ny TRATE, ny TRAY sh'n]

nitre *noun* saltpetre, potassium nitrate. [Say NITE er]

nitric *adjective* of or containing nitrogen. [Say NY trick]

nitric acid *noun* a colourless corrosive poisonous liquid.

nitric oxide *noun* a colourless toxic gas, involved in physiological processes in minute quantities, and forming nitrogen dioxide in air.

nitrite *noun* any salt or ester of nitrous acid. [Say NY trite]

nitro *noun* *informal* nitroglycerine. [Say NY tro]

nitro- *combining form* **1** of or containing nitric acid, nitre, or nitrogen. **2** made with or by use of any of these. **3** of or containing the monovalent $-NO_2$ group.

nitrogen *noun* a colourless odourless unreactive gaseous element that forms four-fifths of the earth's atmosphere and is an essential constituent of proteins, nucleic acids, and other biological molecules.

nitrogen dioxide *noun* a reddish brown poisonous gas.

nitrogenous *adjective* containing nitrogen. [Say ny TRODGE in us]

nitroglycerine *noun* (also **nitroglycerin**) an explosive yellow liquid made by reacting glycerol with a mixture of concentrated sulphuric and nitric acids, used as an explosive and medically to dilate blood vessels. [Say ny tro GLISSA rin]

nitrous *adjective* of, like, or impregnated with nitrogen, esp. in the trivalent state. [Say NY truss]

nitrous acid *noun* a weak acid existing only in solution and in the gas phase.

nitrous oxide *noun* a colourless gas used as an anaesthetic and as an aerosol propellant.

nitty-gritty *noun* *slang* the realities or practical details of a matter.

nitwit *noun* *informal* a stupid person.

nix • *verb* (**nixes**, **nixed**, **nixing**) *slang* **1** cancel. **2** reject. • *adverb* no.

Nlaka'pamux • *noun* (*plural* **Nlaka'pamux**) **1** a member of an Aboriginal people living near the Thompson River in the Fraser River Valley of BC. **2** their Salishan language. • *adjective* of this people or their culture or language. [Say 'n thlaw COP'm]

nm *abbreviation* **1** nanometre. **2** nautical mile.

NMR *abbreviation* nuclear magnetic resonance.

NNE *abbreviation* north-northeast.

NNW *abbreviation* north-northwest.

No^1 *symbol* nobelium.

No^2 *noun* traditional Japanese drama with dance and song, evolved from Shinto rites.

No. *abbreviation* number.

no • *adjective* **1** not any. **2** quite the opposite of. **3** hardly any. • *interjection* used to give a negative response. • *adverb* not at all. • *noun* (*plural* **noes**) **1** an utterance of the word *no*. **2** a denial or refusal. **3** a negative vote. PHRASES **no two ways about it** (or **that**) *informal* there is no question; undoubtedly. **no way** *informal* **1** it is impossible. **2** I will not agree etc. **3** you're kidding. **... or no ...** regardless of the ...: *rain or no rain, I shall go out.* **there is no ...ing** it is impossible to ...: *there was no mistaking what they meant.*

no-account *adjective* unimportant, worthless.

Noah's ark *noun* **1** the ship in which Noah, his family, and the animals were saved from a Flood that destroyed the rest of the world, according to the biblical account in the Old Testament book of Genesis. **2** an imitation of this as a child's toy.

nob *noun* *slang* the head.

Nobelist *noun* a winner of a Nobel Prize. [Say no BELL ist]

nobelium *noun* an artificially produced radioactive metallic element. [Say no BEELY um]

Nobel Prize *noun* (also **Nobel**) any of six international

prizes awarded annually for physics, chemistry, physiology or medicine, literature, economics, and the promotion of peace.

nobility *noun* **1** nobleness of character, mind, birth, or rank. **2** an aristocracy.

noble • *adjective* (**nobler, noblest**) **1** belonging by rank, title, or birth to the aristocracy. **2** of excellent character; having lofty ideals; free from pettiness and meanness. **3** of imposing appearance. **4** (of a metal or element) unreactive; inert. **5** excellent, admirable. • *noun* a nobleman or noblewoman.

noble gas *noun* (*plural* **noble gases**) any gaseous element of a group that almost never combine with other elements.

nobleman *noun* (*plural* **noblemen**) a man of noble rank or birth.

nobleness *noun* the quality of being noble.

noble savage *noun* an idealized concept, prevalent esp. in European Romantic literature of the late 18th and early 19th centuries, of the native peoples outside Europe as innately good and uncorrupted by exposure to civilization.

noblesse oblige *noun* the moral obligation incumbent upon rich or noble people to act generously and honourably. [Say no bless oh BLEEZH]

noblewoman *noun* (*plural* **noblewomen**) a woman of noble rank or birth.

nobly *adverb* in a noble or admirable manner: *they struggled nobly to hold on to what they had.* [Say NO blee]

nobody • *pronoun* no person. • *noun* (*plural* **nobodies**) a person of no importance, authority, or position.

no-brainer *noun* *informal* something that requires a minimum of thought or mental effort.

nock • *noun* **1** *Archery* a notch at either end of a bow for holding the string. **2 a** a notch at the butt-end of an arrow for receiving the bowstring. **b** a notched piece of metal or plastic etc. serving this purpose. • *verb* set (an arrow) on the string.

no-confidence motion *noun* a non-confidence motion.

nocturnal *adjective* **1** of or relating to the night. **2** done at night. **3** active at night. ▶**nocturnally** *adverb* [Say nock TURN ul]

nocturne *noun* *Music* a short composition of a romantic nature, usu. for piano. [Say NOCK turn]

nod • *verb* (**nods, nodded, nodding**) **1** incline one's head slightly and briefly in greeting, assent, or command. **2** let one's head fall forward in drowsiness. **3** (of flowers, plumes, etc.) bend downwards and sway, or move up and down. **4** make a mistake due to a momentary lack of alertness or attention. • *noun* **1** a nodding of the head. **2** an indication of approval, acceptance, or merit. **3** a passing or superficial reference, allusion, or acknowledgement: *a nod to the 1960s.* PHRASES **get the nod** be chosen or approved. **nod off** *informal* fall asleep.

nodal *adjective* of or pertaining to a node or nodes. [Say NO dull]

noddy *noun* (*plural* **noddies**) **1** a simpleton. **2** a tropical seabird with mostly dark plumage, resembling a tern. **3** *Cdn* (*Nfld*) the Atlantic fulmar. **4** *Cdn* (*Nfld*) *derogatory* = BAYMAN 1b.

node *noun* **1 a** the part of a plant stem from which one or more leaves emerge. **b** a knob on a root or branch. **2** a natural swelling or bulge in a bodily organ. **3** either of two points at which a planet's orbit intersects the plane of the ecliptic or the celestial equator. **4** *Math* **a** a point at which a curve intersects itself. **b** a vertex in a graph. **5** a point in a computer network where information is received and distributed among various communication lines.

nodule *noun* **1** a small rounded lump of anything. **2** a small swelling or aggregation of cells, e.g. a small tumour, node, or ganglion, or a swelling on a root of a legume containing bacteria. [Say NOD yul or NODGE ul]

Noel *noun* (also **Noël**) Christmas. [Say no ELL]

noes *plural* of NO *noun*.

no-fault *adjective* **1** (of automobile insurance) valid regardless of the allocation of blame for an accident etc. **2** not assigning responsibility to either party: *a no-fault divorce.*

no-fly zone *noun* an area where esp. military aircraft are forbidden to fly.

no-frills *adjective* **1** providing only the strict minimum necessary: *no-frills flights.* **2** lacking ornament or embellishment.

noggin *noun* **1** *informal* the head. **2** a small mug.

no go • *noun* (*plural* **no goes**) **1** a project, proposal, etc. that cannot proceed. **2** an athlete who cannot play, esp. because of injury. • *interjection* indicating impossibility or that something is not advisable.

no-go area *noun* (also **no-go zone**) an area forbidden to unauthorized people.

no-good *informal* • *adjective* useless. • *noun* a useless person or thing.

Noh *noun* = No².

no-hitter *noun* *Baseball* a game in which a team's pitchers yield no hits.

no-hoper *noun* *slang* a useless person; a person who has no chance of succeeding.

nohow *adverb* in no way; by no means.

noise *noun* **1** a sound, esp. a loud or unpleasant or undesired one. **2** a series of loud sounds, esp. shouts; a confused sound of voices and movements. **3 a** irregular fluctuations accompanying a transmitted signal but not relevant to it. **b** *Computing* a signal that interrupts a program, usu. causing an error. **4** (in *plural*) remarks expressing a specified feeling, which may or may not be genuine: *made sympathetic noises.* PHRASES **make noises** (usu. foll. by *about*) speak indirectly about one's attitude or intentions: *management is making noises about layoffs.* **noises off** sounds made off stage to be heard by the audience.

noiseless *adjective* **1** silent. **2** making no avoidable noise. ▶**noiselessly** *adverb* **noiselessness** *noun*

noisemaker *noun* a device for making a loud noise at a party, celebration, etc.

noisily *adverb* in a noisy way.

noisiness *noun* the quality of being noisy.

noisy *adjective* (**noisier, noisiest**) **1** full of or attended with noise. **2** making or given to making much noise.

no-load *adjective* (of a mutual fund share) sold without a commission being charged to the buyer.

nomad • *noun* **1** a member of a people roaming from place to place for food or fresh pasture: *the land claimed by the agrarians was the same land traversed by the nomads in their quest for food.* **2** a wanderer: *Edward was a nomad, flitting from sparsely furnished rooms in Mexico to houses in Hollywood and hotel rooms worldwide.* • *adjective* **1** living as a nomad: *encounters of nomad peoples with settled ones.* **2** wandering. ▶**nomadic** *adjective* **nomadically** *adverb* **nomadism** *noun* [Say NO mad, no MAD ick]

no man's land *noun* **1** *Military* the space between two opposing armies. **2** an area not assigned to any owner. **3** an area not clearly belonging to any one subject etc.

nom de guerre *noun* (*plural* **noms de guerre** *pronunc.* same) an assumed name under which a person fights, plays, writes, etc. [Say nom duh GAIR]

nom de plume *noun* (*plural* **noms de plume** *pronunc.*

same) an assumed name under which a person writes. [Say nom duh PLOOM]

nomenclature *noun* a set or system of names, esp. as used in a particular science etc.: *the nomenclature of botany*. [Say NO m'n clay chur or NOM'n clay chur]

nomenklatura *noun* (in the former Soviet Union) a select list or group of people from whom upper-level government positions were filled. [Say no m'n kluh TOOR uh]

nominal *adjective* **1** existing in name only; not real or actual: *Thailand retained nominal independence under Japanese military occupation*. **2** (of a sum of money, rent, etc.) virtually nothing; much below the actual value of a thing: *the legislation provided for land to be given to new homesteaders in return for a nominal fee*. **3** of or as or like a noun. ▶ **nominally** *adverb*

nominal value *noun* the face value (of a coin, shares, etc.).

nominate *verb* (**nominates**, **nominated**, **nominating**) **1 a** propose (a candidate) for election. **b** propose (a person or thing) formally for an honour, office, or task: *was nominated for six Genies*. **2** appoint to an office: *a board of six nominated and six elected members*. **3** name or appoint (a date or place).

nomination *noun* **1** the action of nominating or state of being nominated: *women's groups opposed the nomination of the judge* ◊ *the film received five nominations*. **2** a person or thing nominated: *send your nominations in by November 30*.

nominative • *noun* Grammar the case of nouns, pronouns, and adjectives, expressing the subject of a verb. • *adjective* **1** Grammar of or in this case. **2** of, or appointed by, nomination (as distinct from election). [Say NOM in a tiv for the grammar sense, NOM in ay tiv for the nomination sense]

nominator *noun* a person who proposes another for an honour, office, etc.

nominee *noun* **1 a** a person who is nominated for an office. **b** a person, creative work, etc. nominated for an award. **2** Commerce a person (not necessarily the owner) in whose name a stock etc. is registered. [Say nomma NEE]

no more • *noun* nothing further: *have no more to say*. • *adjective* not any more: *no more wine?* • *adverb* **1** no longer. **2** never again. **3** to no greater extent: *could no more do it than fly in the air*. **4** just as little, neither: *you did not come, and no more did she*.

non- *prefix* giving the negative sense of words with which it is combined, esp.: **1** not doing or having or involved with: *non-productive* ◊ *nonpayment*. **2 a** not of the kind or class described: *non-member*. **b** forming terms used adjectivally: *non-union*. **3** a lack of. **4** (with adverbs) not in the way described: *non-verbally*. **5** forming adjectives from verbs, meaning "that does not" or "that is not meant to (or to be)": *non-skid*. **6** used to form a neutral negative sense when a form in *in-* or *un-* has a special sense or (usu. unfavourable) connotation: *non-controversial* ◊ *non-effective*.

non-aggression *noun* a lack of or restraint from aggression or military conflict: *non-aggression pact*. ▶ **non-aggressive** *adjective*

nonagon *noun* a plane figure with nine sides and angles. [Say NONNA gon]

non-aligned *adjective* (of a country etc.) not providing support for or receiving support from any of the powerful countries in the world: *the non-aligned countries*. ▶ **non-alignment** *noun*

non-allergenic *adjective* not causing allergy or an allergic reaction.

no-name • *adjective* **1** designating a person or thing that is not well known or famous: *a movie starring no-name actors*. **2** designating an item not bearing a well-known brand name, usu. costing less than better-known brands: *no-name computers*. • *noun* a no-name person or thing: *a team of no-names*.

non-believer *noun* a person who does not believe or has no (esp. religious) faith.

non-binding *adjective* (of arbitration, a vote, an agreement, etc.) not legally binding on any of the parties involved.

non-biodegradable *adjective* not able to be decomposed by bacteria or other living organisms.

nonce *noun* designating a word or phrase etc. coined for one specific occasion: *nonce formation*. �**PHRASES** **for the nonce** for the time being; for the present occasion. [Rhymes with *RESPONSE*]

nonchalance *noun* a calm and casual, unexcited or indifferent attitude: *he heard the news with a casual nonchalance*. [Say non shuh LONCE]

nonchalant *adjective* calm and casual, unmoved, unexcited, indifferent. ▶ **nonchalantly** *adverb* [Say non shuh LONT]

non-com *noun* informal a non-commissioned officer.

non-combatant *noun* **1** a member of a military force who is not engaged in combat, e.g. a doctor, chaplain, etc. **2** a person not fighting in a war, esp. a civilian.

non-commercial *adjective* not commercial: *approved for non-commercial use*.

non-commissioned officer *noun* Military a corporal or sergeant.

noncommittal *adjective* avoiding commitment to a definite opinion or course of action: *his attitude is not, on the whole, hostile: it is better described as noncommittal*. ▶ **noncommittally** *adverb* [Say non kuh MIT'll]

non-competitive *adjective* not competitive.

non-compliance *noun* failure to comply; a lack of compliance. ▶ **non-compliant** *adjective*

non-conductor *noun* a substance that does not conduct heat or electricity.

non-confidence *noun* Cdn a lack of majority support for a government, policy, etc. expressed by a legislature: *a non-confidence motion*.

nonconformist • *noun* **1** a person who does not conform to a prevailing principle: *Montreal is a mecca for artists and nonconformists who gather here to slip the stifling bonds of provincialism*. **2** (usu. **Nonconformist**) (in the UK) a Protestant belonging to a denomination other than the Church of England (Anglican) or the Church of Scotland (Presbyterian). • *adjective* of or relating to a nonconformist.

nonconformity *noun* **1** the fact of not following normal ways of thinking and behaving: *their films champion nonconformity and question authority*. **2** the beliefs and practices of Nonconformist Churches.

non-custodial *adjective* **1** (of a parent) not having custody of a child or children, e.g. after a divorce. **2** (of a criminal sentence) served outside of a traditional correctional institution.

non-dairy *adjective* containing no milk products: *a non-dairy creamer*.

non-denominational *adjective* not restricted as regards religious denomination.

nondescript *adjective* lacking distinctive characteristics; dull: *a four-room apartment in a nondescript Toronto suburb*. [Say non duh SCRIPT]

non-destructive *adjective* that does not involve destruction or damage.

> **GRAMMAR CHECK**
> **none** ⚠
>
> Despite claims that **none** must always be followed by a singular verb, the verb may in fact be either singular or plural: *None of my friends* **was** *more upset than Isabel; I looked for my friends, but none of them* **were** *at the party.*

none • *pronoun* **1** not any of. **2** no person: *none but fools have ever believed it.* • *adjective* not any. • *adverb* by no amount; not at all: *none the wiser* ◊ *none too fond of it.* PHRASES **none other** (usu. foll. by *than*) no other person.

nonentity *noun* (*plural* **nonentities**) a person or thing of no importance: *the college transformed him from a feeble, obscure nonentity into a highly envied officer.* [Say non ENTITY]

nones *plural noun* in the ancient Roman calendar, the ninth day before the ides by inclusive reckoning, i.e. the 7th day of March, May, July, October, the 5th of other months. [Rhymes with *BONES*]

nonetheless *adverb* nevertheless.

non-event *noun* an unimportant or anticlimactic occurrence.

non-existence *noun* the condition of not existing: *complained about the non-existence of adequate care.*

non-existent *adjective* not existing.

non-ferrous *adjective* (of a metal) other than iron or steel.

non-fiction *noun* literary work other than fiction, including biography and reference books. ▶ **non-fictional** *adjective*

non-flammable *adjective* not flammable.

non-functional *adjective* **1** not having a function. **2** not functioning; out of order.

non-governmental *adjective* not belonging to or associated with a government.

non-import *noun* Cdn Football a player who is a Canadian or who has played with a Canadian team for five years or more.

non-infectious *adjective* (of a disease) not infectious.

non-interference *noun* a lack of interference.

non-intervention *noun* the principle or practice of not becoming involved in others' affairs, esp. by one country in regard to another. ▶ **non-interventionist** *adjective & noun*

non-invasive *adjective* **1** (of a medical procedure) not requiring incision into the body or the removal of tissue. **2** (of an infection etc.) not tending to spread.

non-issue *noun* something that is of little or no importance: *the debate was a non-issue.*

non-judgmental *adjective* not judgmental; avoiding moral judgments.

non-linear *adjective* not linear; not pertaining to, involving, or arranged in a straight line: *Joyce's stream-of-consciousness, non-linear narrative.*

non-member *noun* a person who is not a member (of a particular association, club, etc.).

non-military *adjective* not military; not involving armed forces; civilian.

non-negotiable *adjective* that cannot be negotiated.

non-nuclear *adjective* **1** not involving nuclei or nuclear energy. **2** not having nuclear weapons.

no-no *noun* (*plural* **no-nos**) informal something that is not possible or acceptable.

no-nonsense *adjective* serious, sensible; without flippancy.

non-operational *adjective* **1** that does not operate. **2** out of order.

nonpareil • *adjective* unrivalled or unique: *the kitchen,* that universal, nonpareil source of food. • *noun* such a person or thing: *as a body puncher he is the nonpareil, a relentless, two-fisted aggressor.* [Say non pur AY]

non-partisan *adjective* not partisan.

nonpayment *noun* failure to pay; a lack of payment.

non-performing *adjective* (of an investment, loan, etc.) producing no income.

non-person *noun* a person regarded as non-existent or insignificant.

nonplussed *adjective* **1** perplexed. **2** unfazed. [Say non PLUSST]

non-political *adjective* not political; not involved in politics.

non-prescription *adjective* (of medication) available without a prescription.

non-productive *adjective* not productive. ▶ **non-productively** *adverb*

non-professional • *adjective* not professional (esp. in status). • *noun* a non-professional person.

non-profit *adjective* (of an organization, institution, event, etc.) not involving or making a profit.

non-proliferation *noun* the prevention of an increase in something, esp. possession of nuclear weapons: *nuclear non-proliferation treaty.*

non-reactive *adjective* (of a substance, container, etc.) that does not react or cause a reaction.

non-refundable *adjective* that cannot be refunded.

non-renewable *adjective* (esp. of a resource) not renewable.

non-resident • *adjective* (of a person) not residing in a particular place. • *noun* a non-resident person.

nonresistance *noun* failure to resist; a lack of resistance. ▶ **nonresistant** *adjective*

non-returnable *adjective* that may or need or will not be returned.

non-scientific *adjective* not involving science or scientific methods. ▶ **non-scientist** *noun*

non-sectarian *adjective* not sectarian; non-denominational.

nonsense *noun* **1** spoken or written words that have no meaning, or make no sense. **2** foolish talk, ideas, etc. **3** unacceptable behaviour: *she tolerates a lot of nonsense from her staff.* **4** a form of literature meant to amuse by absurdity: *nonsense verse.* ▶ **nonsensical** *adjective* **nonsensically** *adverb*

non sequitur *noun* a conclusion, remark, response, etc. not logically following from what has gone before. [Say non SECKWA tur]

non-sexist *adjective* (of language, an attitude, etc.) not sexist.

non-sexual *adjective* not based on or involving sex.

non-slip *adjective* **1** that does not slip. **2** that inhibits slipping.

non-smoker *noun* a person who does not smoke. ▶ **non-smoking** *adjective & noun*

non-specialist *noun* a person who is not a specialist (in a particular subject).

non-specific *adjective* that cannot be specified.

non-standard *adjective* **1** not standard. **2** (of language) containing features which are widely used but generally considered incorrect.

non-starter *noun* **1** a person or animal that does not start in a race. **2** informal a person or thing that is unlikely to succeed or be effective.

non-status *adjective* (in Canada) designating a person of Indian ancestry who is not registered as an Indian under the Indian Act.

non-steroidal *adjective* of or relating to a drug etc. that is not a steroid but which has similar effects.

non-stick *adjective* **1** that does not stick. **2** that does not allow things to stick to it.

non-stop • *adjective* **1** (of a train, flight, journey, etc.) without any stops: *a non-stop flight to Victoria*. **2** without any breaks or pauses: *a non-stop meeting*. • *adverb* without stopping or pausing: *cried non-stop for three hours*. • *noun a non-stop train, flight, etc.*

nonsuch *noun* a person or thing that is unrivalled (used esp. in the names of things): *a replica of the Nonsuch, the ketch that Groseilliers sailed into Hudson Bay*.

non-surgical *adjective* (of a medical procedure) performed without surgery: *a non-surgical treatment*.

non-tariff barrier *noun* something, such as a system of grants to domestic manufacturers, that has the effect of limiting imports without the use of tariffs.

non-technical *adjective* **1** not technical. **2** without technical knowledge.

non-toxic *adjective* not toxic.

non-traditional *adjective* not traditional.

non-transferable *adjective* that may not be transferred.

non-treaty *adjective* designating status or non-status Indian people who have not signed a treaty with the Canadian government.

non-uniform *adjective* not uniform.

non-union *adjective* **1** not belonging to a trade union. **2** not done or produced by members of a trade union. ▶ **non-unionized** *adjective*

non-use *noun* failure to use.

non-verbal *adjective* not involving words or speech. ▶ **non-verbally** *adverb*

non-violence *noun* the avoidance of violence, esp. as a principle. ▶ **non-violent** *adjective*

non-volatile *adjective* (esp. of a substance) not volatile.

non-voter *noun* a person who does not vote or is not entitled to vote.

non-voting *adjective* not having or using a vote.

non-white • *adjective* **1** (of a person) not white. **2** of or relating to non-white people. • *noun* a non-white person.

noodle • *noun* **1** a long, thin strip of pasta, usu. eaten with a sauce or in a soup. **2** *informal* a foolish person. **3** *informal* the head: *use your noodle!* • *verb* (**noodles, noodled, noodling**) *informal* **1** improvise or play esp. jazz music in a casual or desultory manner. **2** do or say something in an unproductive or undirected way: *I wish he'd stop noodling around*.

nook *noun* **1** a corner or recess; a secluded place. **2** a small or inaccessible place: *every nook and cranny*. [Rhymes with *LOOK*]

nookie *noun* (also **nooky**) *slang* sexual activity. [Rhymes with *COOKIE*]

noon *noun* twelve o'clock in the day, midday.

noonday *noun* midday: *noonday meal*.

no one *noun* (also **no-one**) no person; nobody.

noontime *noun* midday: *noontime concert*.

noose *noun* a loop with a knot that tightens as the rope or wire is pulled, esp. in a snare, lasso, or hangman's halter. PHRASES **put one's head in a noose** bring about one's own downfall.

Nootka *noun & adjective* (*plural* **Nootka**) = NUU-CHAH-NULTH. ▶ **Nootkan** *adjective* [Say NOOT kuh]

nope *interjection informal* = NO *interjection*.

no place *adverb* nowhere.

nor *conjunction* **1** and not; and not either: *I said I had not seen it, nor had I* ◊ *can neither read nor write*. **2** and no more; neither: *"I cannot go" – "Nor can I"*.

nor' (esp. in compounds) = NORTH: *nor'wester*.

NORAD *abbreviation* North American Aerospace Defence Command, an alliance of US and Canadian air defence forces under joint command in Colorado Springs, Colorado. [Say NOR add]

Nor-Am *adjective* esp. *Skiing* North American.

Nordic • *adjective* **1** of or relating to a physical type of northern Germanic peoples characterized by tall stature and fair colouring. **2** of or relating to Scandinavia or Finland. **3** of or relating to cross-country skiing or ski jumping (compare ALPINE *adjective* 3). • *noun* a Nordic person, esp. a native of Scandinavia or Finland.

nordicity *noun* *Cdn* a measure of the degree of northernness of a high-latitude place, calculated by assigning values to ten criteria, including latitude, summer heat, and annual cold. [Say nor DISSA tee]

nor'easter *noun* = NORTHEASTER.

norepinephrine *noun* a hormone released by the adrenal medulla and by sympathetic nerve endings as a neurotransmitter, used as a drug to raise blood pressure. [Say nor eppa NEFF rin]

norm *noun* **1** something that is usual, typical, or standard: *child labour is the norm in some countries* ◊ *the village is the norm against which the neighbouring town is measured*. **2** customary behaviour, appearance, etc.: *social norms*. **3** the average or general level: *temperature well below the seasonal norm*.

normal • *adjective* **1** constituting or conforming to a standard; regular, usual, typical. **2 a** physically or mentally sound; healthy. **b** about average in intelligence, emotional development, ability, etc. • *noun* **1 a** the normal value of a temperature etc. **b** the usual state, level, etc.: *things have returned to normal*. **2** a person or thing that is normal.

normalcy *noun* = NORMALITY.

normality *noun* a situation or condition where everything is normal or as one would expect it to be.

normalization *noun* the process of making something fit a normal pattern or condition.

normalize *verb* (**normalizes, normalized, normalizing**) bring or return to a normal or standard condition or state: *Vietnam and China agreed to normalize diplomatic relations* ◊ *the editor has normalized archaic spellings*.

normally *adverb* **1** in a normal manner. **2** usually.

normal school *noun* *hist.* a school or college for training teachers.

Norman • *noun* **1** a native or inhabitant of Normandy. **2** a descendant of the people of mixed Scandinavian and Frankish origin established there in the 10th century, who conquered England in 1066. **3** Norman French. **4** the style of Romanesque architecture found in Britain under the Normans. **5** any of the English kings from William I (*c.*1027–87) to Stephen (*c.*1097–1154). • *adjective* **1** of or relating to the Normans or Normandy. **2** of or relating to the Norman style of architecture.

Norman French *noun* French as spoken by the Normans or (after 1066) in English law courts.

normative *adjective* establishing, relating to, or deriving from a standard or norm, esp. of behaviour: *a normative approach* ◊ *the normative force of the Canadian Bill of Rights*. [Say NORMA tiv]

Norse • *noun* **1 a** the Norwegian language. **b** the Scandinavian language group. **2** (**the Norse**; treated as *plural*) **a** the Norwegians. **b** the Vikings. • *adjective* **1** of or relating to Norway or the Norse language. **2** of or relating to ancient Scandinavia or its inhabitants. ▶ **Norseman** *noun* (*plural* **Norsemen**)

north • *noun* **1** the point of the horizon 90° counter-clockwise from east. **2** (usu. **the North**) **a** the Arctic. **b** (in Canada) (from Labrador to the west) the northern part of a province. **c** the part of the world or a country

N

or a town lying to the north. **d** the industrialized nations. • *adjective* **1** towards, at, near, or facing north. **2** coming from the north: *north wind*. • *adverb* **1** towards, at, or near the north. **2** (foll. by *of*) further north than. **3** *informal* (foll. by *of*) more than: *paid him north of $40,000*. [PHRASES] **north by east** (or **west**) between north and north-northeast (or north-northwest). **up north** to or in the north.

North American • *adjective* of or relating to North America. • *noun* a native or inhabitant of North America, esp. a citizen of the US or Canada.

North American Free Trade Agreement *noun* an agreement which came into effect in January 1994 between Canada, the US, and Mexico to remove barriers to trade between the three countries over a ten-year period. Abbreviation: **NAFTA**.

North Americanism *noun* **1** a word or expression originating in Canada and the US. **2** a word or expression used only in Canada and the US.

North Atlantic Treaty Organization *noun* an association of European and North American nations, formed in 1949 for the defence of Europe and the North Atlantic against the perceived threat of Soviet aggression.

northbound *adjective* travelling or leading northwards.

north canoe *noun Cdn hist.* a birchbark canoe of the fur trade, about 9 m (30 ft.) long, used on the rivers and lakes northwest of Lake Superior.

northeast • *noun* **1** the point of the horizon midway between north and east. **2** (**Northeast**) the part of a country, city, etc. lying to the northeast. • *adjective* of, towards, or coming from the northeast. • *adverb* towards, at, or near the northeast.

northeaster *noun* a northeast wind.

northeasterly • *adjective & adverb* = NORTHEAST. • *noun* (*plural* **northeasterlies**) a northeast wind.

northeastern *adjective* located or existing in the northeast of a geographical region: *Robert's family comes from northeastern Italy*.

northeastward *adjective & adverb* (also **northeastwards**) towards the northeast.

northerly • *adjective & adverb* **1** in a northern position or direction. **2** (of wind) blowing from the north. • *noun* (*plural* **northerlies**) (usu. in *plural*) a wind blowing from the north.

northern • *adjective* **1** of or in the north; inhabiting the north. **2** lying or directed towards the north. **3** (of a wind) blowing from the north. • *noun* = NORTHERN PIKE.

northerner *noun* a native or inhabitant of the north.

Northern Games *noun Cdn* a festival of arts and crafts, dancing, and games held in a different Arctic community every year.

northern hemisphere the half of the earth north of the equator.

northern lights *plural noun* a natural luminous phenomenon of shimmering streamers of greenish or reddish light in the sky, esp. near the northern magnetic pole, caused by the interaction of charged solar particles with atmospheric gases, under the influence of the earth's magnetic field.

northernmost *adjective* furthest to the north.

northernness *noun* the condition of being from or situated in the north of a geographical region.

northern pike *noun* (*plural* **northern pike**) a large species of pike found in northern waters and valued as a game fish.

Northern States *plural noun* the states in the north of the US, esp. those lying roughly north of the southern boundary of Pennsylvania and the Ohio river forming the Union side in the Civil War.

North Korean • *adjective* of or relating to North Korea, a country in the Far East, occupying the northern part of the peninsula of Korea. • *noun* a native or inhabitant of North Korea.

northland *noun* (also **northlands**) the northern lands; the northern part of a country.

Northman *noun* (*plural* **Northmen**) **1** a Viking. **2** *Cdn hist.* a voyageur who spent winters in the interior.

north-northeast • *noun* the point or direction midway between north and northeast. • *adjective & adverb* in, from, or towards this direction.

north-northwest • *noun* the point or direction midway between north and northwest. • *adjective & adverb* in, from, or towards this direction.

north of 60 *noun Cdn informal* the areas of Canada north of 60 degrees latitude.

North Pole *noun* see POLE^2 1.

north-south *adjective* of or relating to countries of the north and south: *north-south divide*.

North Star *noun* Polaris.

northward • *adverb* (also **northwards**) towards the north. • *adjective* **1** situated or directed towards the north. **2** moving or facing towards the north. • *noun* a northward direction or region.

northwest • *noun* **1** the point of the horizon midway between north and west. **2** (**Northwest**) the part of a country, city, etc. lying to the northwest. • *adjective* of, towards, or coming from the northwest. • *adverb* towards, at, or near the northwest.

northwester *noun* **1** a northwest wind. **2** (**Northwester**) *Cdn hist.* = NOR'WESTER 3.

northwesterly • *adjective & adverb* = NORTHWEST. • *noun* (*plural* **northwesterlies**) a northwest wind.

northwestern *adjective* located or existing in the northwest of a geographical region.

North West Mounted Police *noun Cdn hist.* a federal police force established in 1873, renamed the Royal North West Mounted Police in 1904 and the Royal Canadian Mounted Police in 1920. Abbreviation: **NWMP**.

Northwest Rebellion *noun Cdn* an armed uprising of Metis, Indians, and white settlers in Saskatchewan in 1885, led by Louis Riel (1844–85), who proclaimed a provisional government for Western Canada with the capital at Batoche.

northwestward *adjective & adverb* (also **northwestwards**) towards the northwest.

Norway maple *noun* a European maple tree with leaves similar to the sugar maple, which is frequently planted in eastern North America.

Norway spruce *noun* a large Eurasian spruce, with many cultivated varieties planted both as a forest tree and as an ornamental.

Norwegian • *noun* **1 a** a native or national of Norway. **b** a person of Norwegian descent. **2** the language of Norway. • *adjective* of or relating to Norway or its people or language. [Say nor WEEGE un]

nor'wester *noun* **1** a northwest wind. **2** an oilskin hat. **3** (**Nor'Wester**) *Cdn hist.* an employee of the North West Company, esp. a stockholding member stationed year-round at a trading post in the northern interior to negotiate the acquisition of furs. The North West Company engaged in the fur trade in the late eighteenth and early nineteenth centuries before it was absorbed by the Hudson's Bay Company in 1821.

Nos. *abbreviation* (also **nos.**) numbers.

nose • *noun* **1** an organ above the mouth on the face or head of a human or animal, containing nostrils and used for smelling and breathing. **2 a** the sense of smell: *dogs have a good nose*. **b** the ability to detect a particular thing: *a nose for scandal*. **3** the odour or

perfume of wine, tea, tobacco, hay, etc. **4** the open end or nozzle of a tube, pipe, etc. **5** the front end or projecting part of a thing, e.g. of a car or aircraft. **6** *Cdn* the northeast portion of the Grand Banks of Newfoundland, lying outside Canada's 320-km (200-mile) fishing zone. • *verb* (**noses, nosed, nosing**) **1 a** perceive the smell of, discover by smell. **b** detect. **2 a** thrust or rub one's nose against or into, esp. in order to smell. **b** smell or sniff (wine etc.). **3** pry or search. **4** move forward slowly and cautiously. PHRASES **as plain as the nose on your face** easily seen. **by a nose** by a very narrow margin: *won the race by a nose.* **count noses** count those present, one's supporters, etc.; decide a question by mere numbers. **cut off one's nose to spite one's face** disadvantage oneself in the course of trying to disadvantage another. **have one's nose in (a book** etc.) *informal* read intently. **keep one's nose clean** *slang* stay out of trouble, behave properly. **nose out** defeat by a narrow margin. **on the nose** *slang* precisely. **poke** (or **stick**) **one's nose into** *informal* pry or intrude into (esp. a person's affairs). **put a person's nose out of joint** *informal* upset or annoy a person. **see no further than one's nose** be short-sighted, esp. in foreseeing the consequences of one's actions etc. **turn up one's nose** (usu. foll. by *at*) *informal* show disdain. **under a person's nose** *informal* right before a person (esp. of defiant or unnoticed actions). **with one's nose in the air** haughtily.

nosebleed • *noun* an instance of bleeding from the nose. • *adjective informal* **1** (of seats in an arena, theatre, etc.) situated in a high level. **2** (of a price etc.) very high.

nose cone *noun* the cone-shaped nose of a rocket etc.

-nosed *combining form* having the kind of nose described: *a broken-nosed bully.*

nose-dive • *noun* **1** a steep downward plunge by an aircraft. **2** a sudden plunge, drop, or decline: *his career took a nose-dive.* • *verb* (**nose-dives, nose-dived, nose-diving**) make a nose-dive.

no-see-um *noun* a small bloodsucking insect, esp. a midge.

nosegay *noun* a small bunch of flowers; a posy.

nose ring *noun* a ring fixed in the nose of an animal (esp. a bull) for leading it, or of a person for ornament.

nose tackle *noun* Football **1** the defensive player who lines up in the centre of the linemen in formation. **2** this field position.

nosh *slang* • *verb* (**noshes, noshed, noshing**) **1** eat or drink. **2** eat between meals; snack. • *noun* (*plural* **noshes**) **1** food or drink. **2** a snack. ▶ **nosher** *noun*

no-show *noun* a person who is expected at an event, has a ticket reserved for a trip, etc. but does not appear for it.

nosily *adverb* in a way that shows too much curiosity in other people's affairs.

nosiness *noun* an excessive and unwelcome curiosity in other people's affairs.

nostalgia *noun* **1** (often foll. by *for*) sentimental yearning for a period of the past; regretful or wistful memory of an earlier time. **2** something that evokes these feelings: *the house my father built is full of nostalgia and recollections.* ▶ **nostalgic** *adjective* **nostalgically** *adverb* **nostalgist** *noun* [Say nuh STAL juh]

nostril *noun* either of two external openings of the nose.

nostrum *noun* **1** a quack remedy, esp. one prepared by the person recommending it: *herbal nostrums.* **2** a pet scheme, esp. for political or social reform: *they have become prey to a far right whose economic nostrums run to demonizing taxes.* [Say NOSS trum]

nosy *adjective* (also **nosey**) (**nosier, nosiest**) *informal* inquisitive, prying.

Nosy Parker *noun informal* a nosy person.

not *adverb* expressing negation. PHRASES **not at all** (in polite reply to thanks) there is no need for thanks. **not least** with considerable importance, notably. **not quite 1** almost: *am not quite there.* **2** noticeably not: *not quite proper.* **not in the slightest** not at all.

nota bene *verb* (as *imperative*) observe what follows, take notice. [Say note a BEN ay]

notable • *adjective* worthy of note; striking, remarkable, eminent. • *noun* a famous or important person or thing: *literary notables.* ▶ **notably** *adverb*

notarize *verb* (**notarizes, notarized, notarizing**) certify (a document) as a notary. [Say NOTE a rize]

notary *noun* (*plural* **notaries**) **1** (also **notary public,** *plural* **notaries public**) a person authorized to perform certain legal formalities, esp. to draw up or certify contracts, deeds, etc. **2** *Cdn* (*Que.*) a member of the legal profession not authorized to plead in court but qualified to draft deeds, contracts, and other legal documents, e.g. wills, real estate transactions, etc. [Say NOTE a ree]

notate *verb* (**notates, notated, notating**) write in notation. ▶ **notated** *adjective*

notation *noun* **1 a** the representation of numbers, quantities, pitch and duration etc. of musical notes, dance movements, chess moves, etc. by symbols. **b** any set of such symbols. **2** a note or annotation.

notch • *noun* (*plural* **notches**) **1** a V-shaped indentation on an edge or surface. **2** one of a series of holes for the tongue of a buckle on a belt, shoe, etc. **3** each of a series of indentations marking graduated points on a regulating dial etc. **4** a nick made on a stick etc. in order to keep count. **5** *informal* a step or degree: *move up a notch.* **6** a deep gorge. • *verb* (**notches, notched, notching**) **1** make notches in. **2** (often foll. by *up*) record or score with or as with notches. **3** secure or insert by notches: *the notched corners of the log house.* ▶ **notched** *adjective*

note • *noun* **1** a brief record of facts, topics, thoughts, etc., as an aid to memory, for use in writing, public speaking, etc. (often in *plural*: *spoke without notes*). **2** an observation, usu. unwritten, of experiences etc.: *compare notes.* **3** a short or informal letter. **4** a formal diplomatic or parliamentary communication. **5** a short annotation or additional explanation in a book etc.; a footnote. **6 a** = BANKNOTE: *a five-pound note.* **b** a written promise or notice of payment of various kinds. **7 a** notice, attention: *worthy of note.* **b** distinction, eminence: *a person of note.* **8 a** a written sign representing the pitch and duration of a musical sound. **b** a single tone of definite pitch made by a musical instrument, the human voice, etc. **c** a key of a piano etc. **9 a** a bird's song or call. **b** a single tone in this. **10** a quality or tone of speaking, expressing mood or attitude etc.; a hint or suggestion: *ended on a note of optimism.* **11** a characteristic; a distinguishing feature. • *verb* (**notes, noted, noting**) **1** observe, notice; give or draw attention to. **2** (often foll. by *down*) record as a thing to be remembered or observed. **3** (in *passive*; often foll. by *for*) be famous or well known (for a quality, activity, etc.). PHRASES **hit** (or **strike**) **the right** (or **a false**) **note** speak or act in an appropriate (or

N

inappropriate) manner. **take note** (often foll. by *of*) observe; pay attention (to).

notebook *noun* **1** a small book for making or taking notes. **2** (also **notebook computer**) a portable computer smaller than a laptop.

noted *adjective* well known; famous: *the restaurant is noted for its desserts* ◊ *a noted author*.

notepad *noun* **1** a pad of paper for writing notes on. **2** a small hand-held computer taking input from an electronic stylus rather than a keyboard.

notepaper *noun* paper for writing letters.

noteworthy *adjective* worthy of attention; remarkable.

not-for-profit *adjective* = NON-PROFIT.

nothing • *noun* **1** not anything. **2** an unimportant person or thing. • *adverb* **1** not at all, in no way: *is nothing like enough*. **2** *informal* not at all: *Is he ill?—Ill nothing, he's dead*. PHRASES **be nothing to 1** not concern. **2** not compare with. **3** have no claim on a person's affections. **be** (or **have**) **nothing to do with 1** have no connection with. **2** not be involved or associated with. **for nothing 1** at no cost; without payment. **2** with no reward or result; to no purpose: *did all that work for nothing*. **have nothing on 1** be naked. **2** have no engagements. **have nothing on a person 1** have much less of a certain quality or ability than something else: *his previous movies have nothing on his new one*. **2** (of the police etc.) have no information that could show a person to be guilty of something. **make nothing of 1** do without hesitation. **2** treat as a trifle. **3** be unable to understand, use, or deal with. **no nothing** *informal* (concluding a list of negatives) nothing at all. **nothing doing** *informal* **1 a** there is no prospect of success or agreement. **b** I refuse. **2** nothing is happening. **nothing** (or **nothing else**) **for it** no alternative: *nothing for it but to pay up*. **nothing less than** at least: *nothing less than a disaster*. **nothing** (or **not much**) **to it 1** untrue or unimportant. **2** simple to do. **think nothing of it** do not apologize or feel bound to show gratitude.

nothingness *noun* **1** non-existence; the non-existent. **2** worthlessness, triviality, insignificance.

notice • *noun* **1** attention, observation: *it escaped my notice*. **2** a displayed sheet etc. bearing an announcement or other information. **3 a** an intimation or warning, esp. a formal one to allow preparations to be made: *give notice* ◊ *at a moment's notice*. **b** a formal announcement or declaration of intention to end an agreement or leave employment at a specified time: *hand in one's notice*. **4 a** a short published review or comment about a new play, book, etc. **b** a small advertisement or announcement in a newspaper or magazine: *death notices*. • *verb* (**notices**, **noticed**, **noticing**) **1** perceive, observe; take notice of. **2** remark upon; speak of. **3** treat (a person) with some degree of attention, favour, or politeness; recognize or acknowledge (a person). PHRASES **at short** (or **a moment's**) **notice** with little warning. **put on notice** alert or warn (a person). **take notice** (or **no notice**) show signs (or no signs) of interest. **take notice of 1** observe; pay attention to. **2** act upon.

noticeable *adjective* **1** easily seen or noticed; perceptible. **2** worthy or deserving notice. ▶ **noticeably** *adverb*

notice board *noun* a board for displaying notices.

notification *noun* the act of giving or receiving information about something, esp. in a formal or official manner.

notify *verb* (**notifies**, **notified**, **notifying**) inform or give notice to (a person): *must notify your doctor of any change in your condition*.

notion *noun* **1** an idea, a belief or an understanding of something: *rejected the notion that greed is a necessary evil* ◊ *has the notion that people are honest* ◊ *you have no notion of the trouble you've caused*. **2** an impulse or desire, esp. one of a whimsical kind: *had a notion to visit her in Moose Jaw*. **3** (in *plural*) small articles related to sewing, such as thread, ribbons, buttons, etc.

notional *adjective* **1** existing only in the imagination. **2** existing only in theory or as a suggestion or idea. ▶ **notionally** *adverb*

notoriety *noun* fame for an unpleasant quality or deed: *he gained notoriety for his involvement in the death of Stella Duane* ◊ *the town achieved notoriety as the site of a railway crash*. [Say no tuh RYE a tee]

notorious *adjective* well known, esp. unfavourably: *a notorious criminal* ◊ *notorious for its climate*. ▶ **notoriously** *adverb* [Say no TORY us]

notwithstanding • *preposition* in spite of; without prevention by: *notwithstanding your objections*. • *adverb* nevertheless; all the same. • *conjunction* (usu. foll. by *that* + clause) although. [Say not with STANDING]

notwithstanding clause *noun Cdn* Section 33 of the Canadian Charter of Rights and Freedoms, which allows Parliament and the provincial legislatures to override Charter clauses covering fundamental freedoms and legal and equality rights.

nougat *noun* a candy made from sugar or honey, nuts, and egg white. [Say NOO g't]

SPELL CHECK
nought, naught

The spelling is **naught** in "all for naught" and "come to naught".

---

nought *noun literary* or *archaic* nothing.

noun *noun Grammar* a word (other than a pronoun) or group of words used to name or identify any of a class of persons, places, or things (**common noun**), or a particular one of these (**proper noun**).

nourish *verb* (**nourishes**, **nourished**, **nourishing**) **1 a** sustain with food. **b** enrich; promote the development of (the soil etc.). **c** provide with intellectual or emotional sustenance or enrichment. **2** foster or cherish (a feeling etc.): *had nourished the lifelong hope of finding a theory*.

nourishing *adjective* (esp. of food) containing much nourishment; sustaining.

nourishment *noun* **1** substances necessary for growth, health, and good condition, esp. food. **2** something of intellectual or emotional benefit: *intellectual nourishment*.

nouveau *adjective* **1** *derogatory* or *jocular* (of a person) having recently become the thing specified: *nouveau gentry*. **2** modern; up-to-date: *nouveau chic*. [Say NOO voe]

nouveau riche • *noun* (also **nouveaux riches**) people who have recently acquired wealth, esp. those perceived as ostentatious or lacking in good taste. • *adjective* having to do with such people. [Say noo voe REESH]

nouvelle *adjective* of, pertaining to, or characteristic of nouvelle cuisine. [Say noo VELL]

nouvelle cuisine *noun* a modern style of (esp. French) cooking that avoids traditional rich sauces and emphasizes the freshness of the ingredients and attractive presentation. [Say noo VELL quiz EEN]

Nov. *abbreviation* November.

nova *noun* (*plural* **novae** or **novas**) a star showing a sudden increase of brightness and then subsiding. [Say NO vee or NO vuz for the plural]

Nova Scotian • *noun* a native or inhabitant of Nova Scotia. • *adjective* of or relating to Nova Scotia.

novel¹ *noun* **1** a fictitious prose story of considerable length and complexity, esp. one representing character and action with some degree of realism. **2** (**the novel**) this type of literature.

novel² *adjective* of a new kind or nature; strange; previously unknown: *a novel approach to doing research*.

novelette *noun* a short novel.

novelist *noun* a writer of novels. ▶**novelistic** *adjective*

novelization *noun* a movie that has been made into a novel.

novelize *verb* (**novelizes, novelized, novelizing**) make into a novel.

novella *noun* (*plural* **novellas**) a short novel or narrative story. [Say nuh VELLA]

novelty • *noun* (*plural* **novelties**) **1** newness, originality: *waitressing was fun at first, but the novelty soon wore off*. **2** a new or unusual thing or occurrence: *in 1914 air travel was still a novelty*. **3** a small toy or decoration etc. of novel design. **4** (as an *adjective*) having novelty; appealing through newness; faddish: *novelty song*.

November *noun* the eleventh month of the year.

novena *noun* *Catholicism* a devotion consisting of special prayers or services on nine successive days. [Say no VEENA]

novice *noun* **1** a beginner; an inexperienced person: *novice programmer*. **2** a person who has entered a religious order and is under probation, before taking vows. **3** a horse, dog, etc. that has not won a major prize in a competition. **4** *Cdn* **a** a level of children's sports, usu. involving children aged 8 to 9. **b** a player in this age group.

novitiate *noun* **1** the period of being a novice: *has not advanced beyond his novitiate in philosophy*. **2** a religious novice: *a monk praying with two novitiates*. [Say no VISHY it or no VISHY ate]

Novocaine *noun* *proprietary* a local anaesthetic derived from benzoic acid. [Say NOVA cane]

now • *adverb* **1** at the present time. **2** at or from this precise moment. **3** under the present circumstances. • *conjunction* as a consequence of the fact. **PHRASES** **now and again** (or **then**) from time to time; intermittently. **now now** used to reprimand or pacify a person.

nowadays *adverb* at the present time or age; in these times.

nowhere • *adverb* in, at, or to no place; not anywhere. • *noun* **1** no place. **2** a remote, dull, or nondescript place. • *adjective* *slang* **1** remote, insignificant. **2** unsatisfactory, dull: *a nowhere job*. **PHRASES** **come out of** (or **from**) **nowhere** be suddenly evident or successful. **get nowhere** make or cause to make no progress. **in the middle of nowhere** *informal* remote from urban life. **nowhere near** not nearly.

no win *adjective* of or designating a situation in which success is impossible.

noxious *adjective* **1** harmful, injurious: *noxious fumes*. **2** unpleasant, repugnant: *a kernel of noxious idealism*. [Say NOCK shuss]

noxious weed *noun* a plant considered harmful to animals or the environment.

nozzle *noun* **1** a spout on a hose etc. through which a stream of air or liquid issues. **2** a duct in a jet or rocket engine in which the speed of the ejected fuel is increased.

NP *abbreviation* **1** Notary Public. **2** NURSE PRACTITIONER.

Np *symbol* neptunium.

NPT *abbreviation* Non-Proliferation Treaty.

NS *abbreviation* Nova Scotia.

ns *abbreviation* nanosecond.

NSAID *abbreviation* non-steroidal anti-inflammatory drug. [Say EN sed]

NSF *abbreviation* not sufficient funds, used to denote a cheque written for an amount that exceeds the total funds of a person's bank account, which is therefore not honoured by the bank.

NST *abbreviation* Newfoundland Standard Time.

NSW *abbreviation* New South Wales.

NT *abbreviation* **1** New Testament. **2** NEWFOUNDLAND TIME. **3** Northwest Territories (in official postal use).

nth *see* N². [Say ENTH]

nuance • *noun* a subtle difference in or shade of meaning, feeling, colour, etc.: *the various nuances expressed by a single word*. • *verb* (**nuances, nuanced, nuancing**) give a nuance or nuances to: *most of their language was nuanced through their body language*. ▶**nuanced** *adjective* [Say NOO awnce or NYOO awnce]

nub *noun* **1** the point or gist (of a matter or story): *the nub of the argument*. **2** a small lump or stub: *the candle burned to a nub*.

nubbin *noun* a small lump or stub.

nubby *adjective* (**nubbier, nubbiest**) **1** (of fabric) coarse or knobbly in texture: *a warm, nubby blanket*. **2** covered with tiny knobs or lumps.

nubile *adjective* (of a girl or young woman) sexually attractive. [Say NOO bile or NYOO bile]

nuclear *adjective* **1** of, relating to, or constituting a nucleus. **2** using, producing, or resulting from nuclear energy: *nuclear reactor*. **3** of, involving, or possessing nuclear weapons. [Say NOO klee er or NYOO kloo or]

nuclear bomb *noun* a bomb using the release of energy by nuclear fission or fusion or both.

nuclear energy *noun* = ATOMIC ENERGY.

nuclear family *noun* a couple and their children, regarded as a basic social unit.

nuclear fission *noun* a nuclear reaction in which a heavy nucleus splits spontaneously or on impact with another particle, with the release of energy.

nuclear force *noun* a strong attractive force between nucleons in the atomic nucleus that holds the nucleus together.

nuclear fuel *noun* a substance that will sustain a fission chain reaction so that it can be used as a source of nuclear energy.

nuclear fusion *noun* a nuclear reaction in which atomic nuclei of low atomic number fuse to form a heavier nucleus with the release of energy.

nuclear magnetic resonance *noun* the absorption of electromagnetic radiation by a nucleus in an external magnetic field, which is used to provide information about and create images of solids and liquids exposed to this radiation in a diagnostic medical procedure called magnetic resonance imaging. Abbreviation: **NMR**.

nuclear physicist *noun* a person who studies nuclear physics.

nuclear physics *noun* the physics of atomic nuclei and their interactions, esp. in the generation of nuclear energy.

nuclear power *noun* **1** electric or motive power generated by a nuclear reactor. **2** a country that has nuclear weapons. ▶**nuclear-powered** *adjective*

nuclear reactor *noun* see REACTOR 2.

nuclear war *noun* a war in which nuclear weapons are used.

nuclear waste *noun* radioactive waste material e.g. from the use or reprocessing of nuclear fuel.

nuclear weapon *noun* a missile, bomb, etc., using the release of energy by nuclear fission or fusion or both.

N

nuclear winter *noun* a period of abnormal cold and darkness predicted to follow a nuclear war.

nucleate *verb* (**nucleates, nucleated, nucleating**) **1** form a nucleus. **2** form around a central area: *a nucleated village*. [Say NOO klee ate or NYOO klee ate]

nucleic acid *noun* either of two complex organic substances (DNA and RNA), whose molecules consists of many nucleotides linked in a long chain, and present in all living cells. [Say noo CLAY ick or nyoo CLAY ick]

nucleon *noun* a proton or neutron. [Say NOO klee on or NYOO klee on]

nucleoside *noun* an organic compound consisting of a purine or pyrimidine base linked to a sugar, e.g. adenosine. [Say NOO klee aside or NYOO klee aside]

nucleotide *noun* an organic compound consisting of a nucleoside linked to a phosphate group. [Say NOO klee a tide or NYOO klee a tide]

nucleus *noun* (*plural* **nuclei**) **1** the central and most important part of an object, movement, or group, forming the basis for its activity and growth: *the students became the nucleus of a national militia*. **2** the solid part of a comet's head. **3** the positively charged central core of an atom that contains most of its mass. **4** a large dense organelle of eukaryotic cells, containing the genetic material. **5** a discrete mass of grey matter in the central nervous system. **6** *Chemistry* a ring structure or other arrangement of atoms which is characteristic of a group of compounds. [Say NOO klee us or NYOO klee us for the singular, NOO klee eye or NYOO klee eye for the plural]

nude • *adjective* **1 a** (of a person, body part, etc.) naked, unclothed, bare. **b** (of performance etc.) involving a naked or scantily clad person or persons. **c** (of a thing) lacking natural coverage, foliage, etc. **2** (of hosiery etc.) flesh-coloured and very sheer. **3** (of beaches etc.) used by nudists. • *noun* **1** a painting, sculpture, etc. of a nude human figure. **2** a nude person. **3** (**the nude**) an unclothed state: *sleeps in the nude*.

nudge • *verb* (**nudges, nudged, nudging**) **1** prod gently esp. with the elbow to attract attention. **2** push gently or gradually. **3** coax or give a gentle reminder or encouragement to (a person). **4** move slightly or slowly, esp. by gradual pushing: *we nudged through the bushes*. • *noun* **1** a light touch or push. **2** a gentle reminder. PHRASES **nudge, nudge, wink, wink** used to imply a sexual innuendo in the preceding phrase or clause.

nudie *noun* *informal* a film, photograph, etc. featuring nudity: *nudie magazine*.

nudist *noun* a person who advocates or practises going unclothed.

nudity *noun* nakedness.

nuff *noun* *slang* enough: *nuff said*.

nugget *noun* **1 a** a lump of gold, platinum, etc., as found in the earth. **b** a lump of anything compared to this. **2** a small, valuable, and esp. abstract thing concealed in a larger mass: *a nugget of information*. **3** a small piece of chicken etc. covered with batter and deep-fried.

nuisance *noun* **1** a person, thing, or circumstance causing trouble, annoyance, or inconvenience. **2** anything harmful or offensive to the community or a member of it and for which a legal remedy exists: *a barking dog that bothers the neighbours would be considered a public nuisance and you could be fined for disturbing the peace*. [Say NOOSE ince or NYOOSE ince]

nuisance grounds *plural noun* *Cdn* (*West*) *informal* a garbage dump.

nuke *informal* • *noun* **1** a nuclear weapon. **2** a nuclear power station. • *verb* (**nukes, nuked, nuking**) **1** bomb or destroy with nuclear weapons. **2** *informal* cook (food) in a microwave. **3** *slang* destroy.

null • *adjective* **1** (esp. **null and void**) invalid; having no legal or binding force: *if bribery was proved — and it often was — the election was declared null and void*. **2** associated with, producing, or having the value zero: *a null result*. **3** (of a class or set) **a** empty; having no elements: *null list*. **b** all the elements of which are zeros: *null matrix*. • *noun* *Computing* (also **null character**) a character denoting nothing, usu. represented by a zero.

nullification *noun* an act of making something legally null and void; invalidation.

nullify *verb* (**nullifies, nullified, nullifying**) **1** make legally null and void; invalidate: *in one 1984 ruling, the Canadian courts nullified these reforms*. **2** make of no value or use; cancel out, neutralize: *periodic epidemics nullified any natural population growth*. [Say NULL if eye]

nullity *noun* (*plural* **nullities**) **1** *Law* the fact of being null and void; invalidity, esp. of marriage. **2 a** nothingness: *that nullity of demeanour which we so pathetically accept as a substitute for true dignity*. **b** a mere nothing; a nonentity: *he had the intimate conviction that he was a nullity*. [Say NULL it ee]

numb • *adjective* **1** deprived of feeling or the power of motion: *numb with cold*. **2** unable to experience emotion: *I felt numb after his death*. • *verb* **1** make numb. **2** stupefy, paralyze: *we sat there in silence, numbed by the shock of her death*.

> **GRAMMAR CHECK**
> **a number of**
>
> Use a plural verb after **a number of**, e.g. *A number of people were seen* (not *was seen*).

number • *noun* **1** a quantity or value expressed by a word, symbol, or figure. **2** a quantity or amount of something countable. **3** (**a number of**) several. **4** a single issue of a magazine. **5** a song, dance, or other musical item. **6** *informal* an item of clothing of a particular type, regarded with approval: *a little black number*. **7** a grammatical classification of words that consists typically of singular and plural. • *verb* **1** amount to. **2** mark with a number or give a number to. **3** count or estimate. **4** include as a member of a group. PHRASES **any number of 1** *informal* a large unspecified number of. **2** any particular whole quantity of. **by (the) numbers** following simple instructions (as if) identified by numbers. **one's days are numbered** one does not have long to live, prosper, etc. **do a number on** (**a person**) *slang* **1** disparage, speak, or write of with contempt. **2** deceive. **have a person's number** *informal* understand a person's real motives, character, etc. **have a person's number on it** (of a bomb, bullet, etc.) be destined to hit a specified person. **one's number is up** *informal* one is finished or doomed to die. **without number** innumerable.

number cruncher *noun* *slang* **1** *Computing* & *Math* a machine capable of complex calculations etc. **2** a person, esp. an accountant or statistician, whose primary concern is with numbers, statistics, etc. ▶ **number crunching** *noun*

numbered *adjective* having been assigned or marked with a number, esp. to indicate position in a series: *the limited-edition print is for sale, signed and numbered*.

numbered company *noun* *Cdn* a corporation the name of which is simply its registration number followed by the province in which it is registered.

numbered treaty *noun* any of a number of land cession treaties signed from 1871 to 1921 between the Canadian government and Aboriginal nations throughout the north and west of Canada.

numbering *noun* the process or method of assigning

numbers to a series of things: *some word processors feature automatic numbering for pages*.

numberless *adjective* **1** innumerable, countless. **2** without a number or numbers.

number one *informal* • *noun* **1** oneself, one's own person and interests: *always takes care of number one*. **2** the best; the finest quality: *we're number one!* **3** *euphemism* an act of urination. • *adjective* **1** leading; most important: *number one priority*. **2** finest quality.

numbers game *noun* **1** (also **numbers**, **numbers racket**) a lottery based on the occurrence of unpredictable numbers in the results of races etc. **2** a comparison, contest, etc. regarded merely in terms of numerical statistics: *the numbers game that is played to show how well a language is doing often makes no distinction between the number of people who can speak the language and the number who actually do*.

number theory *noun* the branch of mathematics that deals with the properties and relationships of numbers, esp. the positive integers.

number two *noun* **1** (often as an *adjective*) something second-rate. **2** a second-in-command. **3** *euphemism* an act of defecation.

numbing *adjective* (of an experience or a situation) so intense that one's senses become less responsive: *the numbing cold* ◊ *a numbing variety of choices*. ▶ **numbingly** *adverb*

numbness *noun* a numb feeling.

numbskull *noun* a stupid or foolish person.

numeracy *noun* a good basic knowledge of math; the ability to understand and work with numbers. [Say NOOMER a see or NYOOMER a see]

numeral • *noun* a word, figure, or group of figures denoting a number. • *adjective* expressing or denoting a number or numbers.

numerate *adjective* acquainted with the basic principles of mathematics, esp. arithmetic. [Say NOOMER it or NYOOMER it]

numerator *noun* the number above the line in a fraction showing how many of the parts indicated by the denominator are taken (e.g. 2 in $^2/_3$). [Say NOOMER ate er or NYOOMER ate er]

numerical *adjective* (also **numeric**) **1** of, pertaining to, or characteristic of a number or numbers: *numerical superiority*. **2** (of a figure, symbol, etc.) expressing a number. ▶ **numerically** *adverb* [Say noo MARE ick ul or nyoo MARE ick ul]

numerology *noun* the study of the supposed occult or esoteric significance of numbers. [Say noomer OLLA jee or nyoomer OLLA jee]

numero uno *noun informal* **1** oneself, one's own person and interests: *always takes care of numero uno*. **2** the best; the finest quality: *all it will take is a .500 season, and they're back to numero uno in this town*. [Say noomer oh OON oh]

numerous *adjective* **1** (with *plural*) great in number. **2** consisting of many: *a numerous family*.

numinous *adjective* having a strong spiritual quality; indicating or suggesting the presence of a divinity; awe-inspiring: *the world was alive with numinous rocks, springs, and peaks*. [Say NOO min us or NYOO min us]

numismatic *adjective* of or relating to coins or medals. [Say noo miz MAT ick or nyoo miz MAT ick]

numismatics *plural noun* (usu. treated as *singular*) the study of coins or medals, esp. from an archaeological or historic standpoint. ▶ **numismatist** *noun* [Say noo miz MAT icks or nyoo miz MAT iks, noo MIZ muh tist or nyoo MIZ muh tist]

nummy *adjective* (**nummier**, **nummiest**) *informal* delicious.

numskull *noun* = NUMBSKULL.

nun *noun* a member of a Christian community of women living under vows of poverty, chastity, and obedience, according to the rule of a particular order.

nunatak *noun* an isolated peak of rock projecting above a surface of inland ice or snow. [Say NUN attack]

Nunavummiut *plural noun* the people inhabiting the territory of Nunavut. [Say noona VOOMY it]

nunnery *noun* (*plural* **nunneries**) *hist.* a convent.

nuptial • *adjective* **1** of or relating to marriage or weddings. **2** *Zoology* of or pertaining to mating or the breeding season, esp. designating characteristic breeding coloration or behaviour. • *noun* (usu. in *plural*) a wedding: *celebrated our nuptials*. [Say NUP shull]

nurse • *noun* **1** a person professionally trained to care for the sick or infirm, assist in surgery, treat minor medical problems, and give medical advice. **2** (formerly) a person employed or trained to take charge of young children. **3** *archaic* = WET NURSE. • *verb* (**nurses**, **nursed**, **nursing**) **1 a** work as a nurse. **b** care for (a person) during sickness or infirmity. **c** give medical attention to (an illness or injury). **2 a** (of a woman) breast-feed (a baby). **b** feed or be fed at the breast or teat; suckle. **3** harbour or nurture (a grievance, hatred, etc.). **4 a** foster; promote the development of. **b** tend or cultivate (a plant) carefully. **5** consume (a drink) slowly. **6** hold or treat carefully or caressingly: *stood nursing the teapot*.

nurse practitioner *noun* a specially trained registered nurse who is qualified to diagnose and treat common diseases, minor injuries, etc.

nursery *noun* (*plural* **nurseries**) **1 a** a room or place equipped for young children. **b** = DAYCARE **3**. **2 a** a place where plants, trees, etc., are reared for sale or transplantation. **b** a place which breeds or supports animals, esp. a pond etc. where young fry are reared. **3** an environment in which certain types of people or qualities are fostered or bred: *Toronto's Horseshoe Tavern, the nursery of many country performers*.

nursery rhyme *noun* a simple traditional song or story in rhyme for children.

nursery school *noun* a school for children below the age for compulsory education, usu. between the ages of three and five.

nurse's aide *noun* a person who assists registered nurses in hospital or home care by performing basic tasks such as making beds, serving meals, etc.

nursing *noun* **1 a** the practice or profession of providing health care as a nurse. **b** the duties of a nurse. **2** (as an *adjective*) concerned with or suitable for nursing the sick or infirm etc.: *nursing care*. **3** the action of breast-feeding.

nursing assistant *noun* a person who is trained to provide nursing care for patients who are not acutely ill, and to assist nurses in the care of the acutely ill.

nursing home *noun* an institution providing long-term health care, esp. for the elderly.

nursing mother *noun* a mother who is breast-feeding her baby.

nursing station *noun* **1** *Cdn* a clinic or small hospital in a remote community, staffed by nurses and visited regularly by a doctor. **2** the central desk on a hospital floor or ward where nurses complete paperwork, store medications, etc.

nurture • *noun* **1** the process of bringing up or training (esp. children): *Roger's birth and nurture preoccupied both of them for the next couple of months*. **2** the social environment as an influence on or determinant of personality: *crime is usually the product of bad nurture, not a bad nature, he says*. • *verb* (**nurtures**, **nurtured**, **nurturing**) **1** foster the development of; encourage: *my father nurtured my love of art*. **2** bring up to maturity: *my*

N

wife and I work very hard to create a family home in which to nurture our children. ▶ **nurturer** *noun*

nut *noun* **1 a** a fruit consisting of a hard or tough shell around an edible kernel. **b** this kernel. **2** a small usu. square or hexagonal flat piece of metal or other material with a threaded hole through it for screwing on the end of a bolt to secure it. **3** *slang* **a** an obsessive enthusiast or devotee: *a health-food nut.* **b** a crazy or eccentric person. **4** (in *plural*) *coarse slang* the testicles. **5** *slang* a person's head. PHRASES **off one's nut** *slang* crazy. **a tough** (or **hard**) **nut to crack** a problem resisting easy solution.

nutbar *noun* **1** *informal* an eccentric or crazy person. **2** (also **nut bar**) a bar made from chopped nuts and other vegetarian ingredients.

nut brown *noun & adjective* a dark brown colour.

nutcase *noun* *slang* a crazy, eccentric, or foolish person.

nutcracker *noun* a device for cracking the shell of a nut to reach the edible kernel.

nuthatch *noun* (*plural* **nuthatches**) a small bird that climbs up and down tree trunks to feed on nuts, insects, etc. [Say NUT hatch]

nuthouse *noun* *slang* a mental home or hospital.

nutmeg *noun* **1** an evergreen East Indian tree yielding a hard aromatic seed. **2** the seed of this grated or ground and used as a spice.

nutrient *noun* any substance that provides essential nourishment for the maintenance of life.

nutrient cycle *noun* the transfer of elements essential for the nutrition of living organisms, from the organisms to their physical surroundings and back again, in a continuous cycle.

nutrition *noun* **1** the process by which humans or animals utilize food for the proper functioning of the organism. **2** the scientific study of this and of dietary requirements. ▶ **nutritional** *adjective* **nutritionally** *adverb*

nutritionist *noun* a person who studies or is an expert on the processes of esp. human nourishment.

nutritious *adjective* rich in nutrients.

nutritive *adjective* **1** of or pertaining to nutrition. **2** serving as nutritious food. [Say NOOTRA tiv or NYOOTRA tiv]

nuts *informal* • *adjective* crazy, mad, eccentric. • *interjection* an expression of contempt or derision: *nuts to you.* PHRASES **be nuts about** be enthusiastic about or very fond of.

nuts and bolts • *plural noun* the practical details. • *adjective* (usu. **nuts-and-bolts**) pertaining to the practical details.

nutshell *noun* the hard exterior covering of a nut. PHRASES **in a nutshell** in a few words; concisely stated.

nutso *informal* • *noun* (*plural* **nutsos**) a crazy or eccentric person. • *adjective* crazy, eccentric.

nutsy *adjective* (**nutsier, nutsiest**) *informal* = NUTSO *adjective*.

nuttiness *noun* **1** a crazy or eccentric manner. **2** a rich, mellow flavour resembling the taste of nuts.

nut tree *noun* any tree bearing nuts, esp. a hazel.

nutty *adjective* (**nuttier, nuttiest**) **1 a** tasting like nuts. **b** having a rich mellow flavour. **2** *informal* crazy, eccentric. **3** enthusiastic: *nutty about boats.* **4** full of or having many nuts. PHRASES **nutty as a fruitcake** *informal* crazy, extremely eccentric.

Nuu-chah-nulth • *noun* (*plural* **Nuu-chah-nulth**) **1** a member of a major linguistic group of the Wakashan living on the west coast of Vancouver Island. **2** the Wakashan language of this people. • *adjective* of this people or their culture or language. [Say noo CHAW nool]

Nuxalk • *noun* (*plural* **Nuxalk**) **1** a member of a Salishan Aboriginal people of the central BC coast. **2** the Salishan language of this people. • *adjective* of or relating to this people or their culture or language. [Say noo HAWLK]

nuzzle *verb* (**nuzzles, nuzzled, nuzzling**) **1** touch or rub gently with the nose. **2** press the nose or mouth gently. **3** move so as to touch; snuggle.

NW *abbreviation* **1** northwest. **2** northwestern.

NWC *abbreviation* Cdn hist. North West Company.

NWMP *abbreviation* Cdn hist. = NORTH WEST MOUNTED POLICE.

NWO *abbreviation* Northwestern Ontario.

NWT *abbreviation* (also **N.W.T.**) Northwest Territories.

nylon *noun* **1** any of various synthetic polyamide fibres with tough, lightweight, elastic properties, used for textiles, cord, etc. **2** a nylon fabric. **3** (in *plural*) pantyhose or stockings made of nylon.

nymph *noun* **1** any of various mythological semi-divine spirits regarded as maidens and associated with aspects of nature, esp. rivers and woods. **2** esp. *literary* a beautiful young woman. **3 a** an immature form of some insects. **b** a young dragonfly or damselfly. **4** a fishing fly made to resemble the aquatic larva of a mayfly.

nymphet *noun* *informal* a sexually attractive girl or young woman. [Say nim FETT or NIMF it]

nympho *noun* (*plural* **nymphos**) *informal* a nymphomaniac.

nymphomania *noun* excessive or uncontrollable sexual desire in women. ▶ **nymphomaniac** *noun & adjective* [Say nimfa MANIA]

NYSE *abbreviation* New York Stock Exchange.

Oo

O¹ *noun* (also **o**) (*plural* **Os** or **O's**) **1** the fifteenth letter of the alphabet. **2** (**0**) = OH². **3** a human blood type of the ABO system. **4** a round thing, as a circle, spot, etc.

O² *symbol* the element oxygen.

O³ *interjection* **1** = OH¹. **2** prefixed to a name in the vocative: *O Canada*.

o' *preposition* of, on: *o'clock ◊ will-o'-the-wisp*.

OAC *abbreviation* **1** (also **o.a.c.**) on approved credit. **2** *Cdn* (*Ont.*) Ontario Academic Credit, a senior level high school course, undertaken after Grade 12, usu. as preparation for university.

oaf *noun* (*plural* **oafs**) an awkward or stupid lout. ▶ **oafish** *adjective* **oafishness** *noun*

oak *noun* **1** a large tree or shrub that bears acorns and usu. has lobed deciduous leaves. **2** the hard, durable wood of this tree, used esp. for furniture and in building.

oak apple *noun* (also **oak gall**) a spherical growth or gall that forms on oak trees in response to the developing larvae of certain wasps.

oaken *adjective* made of oak: *oaken church pews*.

oaky *adjective* (**oakier, oakiest**) (of wine etc.) having the coconut-like aroma or flavour of oak, acquired from the wood of the barrel in which it is aged.

OAP *abbreviation Cdn* Old Age Pension.

SPELL CHECK [ABC✓]
oar, ore

Rocks from which minerals are extracted are **ore**.

---

oar *noun* **1** a pole with a wide, flat blade at one end used for rowing or steering a boat by leverage against the water. **2** a rower. PHRASES **put one's oar in** interfere, meddle. **rest on one's oars** relax one's efforts. ▶ **oared** *adjective* (also in *combination*)

oarlock *noun* a device on a boat's gunwale serving as a fulcrum for an oar and keeping it in place.

oarsman *noun* (*plural* **oarsmen**) a rower.

oarswoman *noun* (*plural* **oarswomen**) a female rower.

OAS *abbreviation* **1** *Cdn* OLD AGE SECURITY. **2** Organization of American States.

oasis *noun* (*plural* **oases**) **1** a fertile spot in a desert, where water is found. **2** an area or period of calm in the midst of turbulence. [Say oh ACE iss for the singular, oh ACE eez for the plural]

oat *noun* **1 a** a cereal plant cultivated in cool climates. **b** (in *plural*) the grain yielded by this, used as food. **2** any other cereal of the genus *Avena*, esp. the wild oat, *A. fatua*. PHRASES **feel one's oats** *informal* **1** be lively or frisky. **2** revel in one's own power. **sow one's oats** (or **wild oats**) indulge in youthful excess or promiscuity.

oatcake *noun* a thin, unleavened, biscuit made of oatmeal, common in Scotland and northern England.

oat grass *noun* any of various grasses resembling the oat plant.

oath *noun* (*plural* **oaths**) **1** a solemn declaration or undertaking (often naming God) as to the truth of something or as a commitment to future action. **2** a statement or promise contained in an oath: *oath of allegiance*. **3** a swear word. PHRASES **under** (or **on**) **oath** having sworn a solemn oath. **take** (or **swear**) **an oath** make such a declaration or undertaking.

oatmeal *noun* **1 a** rolled oats: *oatmeal cookies*. **b** meal made from ground oats. **2** porridge made from oats. **3** *noun & adjective* a greyish-fawn colour flecked with brown.

OB *abbreviation* **1** obstetric. **2** obstetrics. **3** obstetrician.

O/B *abbreviation* (also **o/b**) outboard.

obdurate *adjective* stubborn, unyielding: *they were obdurate in their opposition to the policy*. ▶ **obdurately** *adverb* [Say OB dyoor it or OB door it]

obeah *noun* a kind of sorcery or witchcraft practised esp. in the West Indies. [Say OH be uh]

obedience *noun* **1** the act or practice of obeying. **2** submission to another's rule or authority. **3** compliance with a law or command. **4** designating courses, trials, etc. pertaining to the training of dogs to obey orders: *sent Sleuth to obedience school*. PHRASES **in obedience to** prompted by or in accordance with.

obedient *adjective* obeying or ready to obey. ▶ **obediently** *adverb*

obeisance *noun* **1** deferential respect: *they paid obeisance to the prince*. **2** a bow, curtsy, or other respectful or submissive gesture. [Say oh BAY since]

obelisk *noun* **1** a tapering usu. four-sided stone pillar set up as a monument or landmark etc. **2** a symbol (†) used as a reference mark in printed matter or to indicate that a person is deceased. [say OBBA lisk]

obese *adjective* very fat; corpulent. ▶ **obesity** *noun* [say oh BEESE, oh BEESE it ee]

obey *verb* **1 a** carry out the command of: *you will obey me*. **b** carry out (a command): *obey orders*. **2** do what one is told to do. **3** be prompted by, respond to (a force or impulse).

obfuscate *verb* (**obfuscates, obfuscated, obfuscating**) make something less clear and more difficult to understand, usu. deliberately: *he was suspicious of the lingo of psychologists, which he thought was designed to obfuscate and not to explain*. ▶ **obfuscation** *noun* [Say OB fuss kate, ob fuss KAY sh'n]

OB/GYN *abbreviation* (also **ob-gyn**) **1** obstetrics and gynecology. **2** obstetrician-gynecologist.

obi *noun* (*plural* **obis**) a sash worn with a Japanese kimono. [Say OH be]

obit *noun informal* an obituary. [Say OH bit]

obiter dictum *noun* (*plural* **obiter dicta**) **1** a judge's expression of opinion uttered in court or giving judgment, but not essential to the decision and therefore without binding authority. **2** an incidental remark. [Say ob it ur DICK tum]

obituary *noun* (*plural* **obituaries**) a notice of a death, esp. in a newspaper, usu. comprising a brief biographical sketch of the deceased. [Say oh BIT chew airy]

object • *noun* **1** a material thing that can be seen or touched. **2** (foll. by *of*) a person or thing to which action or feeling is directed: *the object of attention*. **3** a thing sought or aimed at; a purpose. **4** *Grammar* a noun or its equivalent governed by an active transitive verb or by a preposition, e.g. *us* in *she likes us* and *he's with us*. **5** *derogatory* a person or thing of esp. a pathetic or ridiculous appearance. • *verb* **1** express or feel opposition, disapproval, or reluctance; protest: *I object to being treated like this*. **2** have an objection: *I object!*

PHRASES **no object** not forming an important or restricting factor: *money is no object*. **object of the exercise** the main point of an activity.

objectification *noun* the act of treating people as if they are objects, without rights or feelings.

objectify *verb* (**objectifies**, **objectified**, **objectifying**) **1** express (something abstract) in a concrete form: *good poetry objectifies feeling*. **2** treat or regard a person as an object, as if they have no rights or feelings: *a sexist attitude that objectifies women*.

objection *noun* **1** an expression or feeling of opposition or disapproval; a reason for disagreeing. **2** the act of objecting.

objectionable *adjective* unpleasant, offensive, undesirable, disapproved of: *I myself didn't find her behaviour objectionable*. ▶ **objectionably** *adverb*

objective • *adjective* **1** (of a person, an opinion, etc.) not influenced by feelings or personal bias (*compare* SUBJECTIVE 1). **2 a** (of writing, art, etc.) concerned with outward things or events; dealing with or laying stress on what is external to the mind. **b** external to or independent of the mind: *objective reality*. **3** (of symptoms) observed by another and not only felt by the patient. • *noun* something sought or aimed at; a target, goal, or aim. ▶ **objectively** *adverb*

objectivity *noun* an approach to considering, judging, or presenting facts that is not influenced by personal feelings, opinions, or bias; impartiality: *some readers felt that the article lacked objectivity ◊ even though her son was one of the candidates, she was able to judge the competition with objectivity*. [Say ob jeck TIVVA tee]

object lesson *noun* a practical example or illustration of some principle.

objector *noun* a person who objects to something.

objet *noun* an object displayed as an ornament. [Say ob ZHAY]

objet d'art *noun* (*plural* **objets d'art**) a small decorative or artistic object. [Say ob zhay DAR]

Oblate • *noun* a member of the Oblates of Mary Immaculate, a Roman Catholic missionary order of priests and brothers founded in France in 1816. • *adjective* of or pertaining to the Oblates of Mary Immaculate. [Say OB late or OBE late]

oblation *noun* **1** a thing offered to a divine being. **2** *Christianity* the presentation of bread and wine to God in the Eucharist. [Say oh BLAY sh'n]

obligate *verb* (**obligates**, **obligated**, **obligating**) bind (a person) legally or morally: *I am obligated to help*.

obligation *noun* **1** a duty; what one is morally or legally required to do. **2** the constraining power of a law, precept, duty, contract, etc. **3** a binding agreement, esp. one enforceable under legal penalty. **4 a** a service, benefit, or kindness done or received: *repay an obligation*. **b** indebtedness for this: *be under an obligation*. **PHRASES** **day of obligation** *Catholicism* a day on which all are required to attend Mass.

obligatory *adjective* **1** required by rule, law, or custom. **2** legally or morally binding. [Say uh BLIGGA tory]

oblige *verb* (**obliges**, **obliged**, **obliging**) **1** constrain, compel: *they obliged her to go with them*. **2** be binding on. **3 a** make indebted by conferring a favour: *I'm obliged to you for your help ◊ I don't want you to feel obliged*. **b** gratify: *oblige me by leaving*. **c** perform a service for: *will you oblige?* **4** *informal* (foll. by *with*) make a contribution of a specified kind: *Beth obliged with a song*. **PHRASES** **much obliged** an expression of thanks.

obliging *adjective* courteous, accommodating. ▶ **obligingly** *adverb*

oblique • *adjective* **1 a** slanting; declining from the vertical or horizontal. **b** diverging from a straight line or course. **2** not going straight to the point; roundabout, indirect: *he issued an oblique attack on the prime minister*. **3** *Math* **a** (of a line, plane figure, or surface) inclined at other than a right angle. **b** (of an angle) acute or obtuse. **c** (of a cone, cylinder, etc.) an axis not perpendicular to the plane of its base. • *noun* an oblique stroke (/). ▶ **obliquely** *adverb* **obliqueness** *noun* [Say oh BLEAK]

obliterate *verb* (**obliterates**, **obliterated**, **obliterating**) **1** destroy utterly; wipe out: *the memory was so painful that he obliterated it from his mind ◊ radiation therapy is administered in an attempt to obliterate the malignant cells*. **2** cause to become invisible or indistinct; blot out: *clouds were darkening, obliterating the sun*. ▶ **obliteration** *noun* [Say oh BLITTER ate]

oblivion *noun* **1** a state in which one is no longer aware or conscious of what is happening: *drink oneself into oblivion*. **2** the state of being forgotten or disregarded: *rescued from oblivion*. [Say oh BLIVVY un]

oblivious *adjective* unaware or unconscious of: *she became totally absorbed, oblivious to the passage of time*. ▶ **obliviously** *adverb* **obliviousness** *noun* [Say oh BLIVVY us]

oblong • *adjective* **1** deviating from a square form by having one long axis, esp. rectangular with adjacent sides unequal. **2** greater in breadth than in height. • *noun* an oblong figure or object.

obnoxious *adjective* annoying, irritating. ▶ **obnoxiously** *adverb* [Say ob NOCK shuss]

OBO *abbreviation* or best offer.

oboe *noun* **1** a woodwind double-reed treble instrument with a plaintive tone. **2** its player. ▶ **oboist** *noun*

obscene *adjective* **1** offensively or repulsively indecent, esp. by offending accepted sexual morality. **2** *informal* highly offensive or repugnant: *an obscene accumulation of wealth*. ▶ **obscenely** *adverb*

obscenity *noun* (*plural* **obscenities**) **1** an obscene word, action, etc. **2** the state or quality of being obscene. [Say ub SENNA tee]

obscurantism *noun* the practice of deliberately making something difficult to understand: *literary criticism and the social sciences are often guilty of obscurantism*. ▶ **obscurantist** *noun & adjective* [Say OBSCURE int ism]

obscure • *adjective* **1** not clearly expressed or easily understood. **2** unexplained, doubtful. **3** dark, dim. **4** indistinct; not clear. **5** hidden; remote from observation. **6 a** unnoticed. **b** undistinguished, hardly known. **7** (of a colour) dingy, dull, indefinite. • *verb* (**obscures**, **obscured**, **obscuring**) **1** prevent from being seen, heard, detected, understood, etc. **2** dim the glory of; outshine. **3** conceal from sight. ▶ **obscurely** *adverb*

obscurity *noun* (*plural* **obscurities**) **1** the state of not being well-known. **2** an obscure thing, esp. one that is difficult to understand. **3** darkness; poor light.

obsequious *adjective* trying too hard to please someone, especially someone who is important: *an obsequious manner*. ▶ **obsequiously** *adverb* **obsequiousness** *noun* [Say ub SEE kwee us]

observable *adjective* that can be seen or noticed: *Saturn's rings are observable in a telescope*.

observance *noun* **1** the act or process of keeping or performing a law, duty, custom, ritual, etc.: *strict observance of the rules ◊ the decline in religious observance*. **2** an act of a religious or ceremonial character; a customary rite: *official anniversary observances*. **3** the rule of a religious order: *monastic observances*.

observant *adjective* **1** quick to notice things: *her observant eye took in every detail ◊ a very observant child*.

2 adhering strictly to the rules of a particular religion, esp. Judaism: *many families in this community are no longer observant*. ▶ **observantly** *adverb*

observation *noun* **1 a** the action or process of observing something or someone carefully or in order to gain information: *she was brought into hospital for observation ◊ detailed observations were carried out on the students' behaviour*. **b** an observed truth or fact; a thing learned by observing. **2** perception; the faculty of taking notice. **3** a remark or statement, esp. one that is of the nature of a comment. **4 a** the accurate watching and noting of a phenomenon etc. for the purpose of scientific investigation. **b** a measurement or other result so obtained. **c** the noting of the symptoms of a patient, the behaviour of a suspect, etc. **5** the taking of the sun's or another celestial body's altitude to find a latitude or longitude. **6** *Military* the watching of an enemy's position or movements: *an observation post*. PHRASES **under observation** being watched or monitored. ▶ **observational** *adjective*

observation deck *noun* a platform or area designed for viewing e.g. animals at a wildlife sanctuary etc.

observatory *noun* (*plural* **observatories**) a room or building equipped for the observation of natural, esp. astronomical or meteorological, phenomena.

observe *verb* (**observes**, **observed**, **observing**) **1** perceive, note; take notice of; become conscious of. **2** watch carefully. **3 a** follow or adhere to (a law, command, method, principle, etc.). **b** keep or adhere to (an appointed time). **c** maintain (silence). **d** duly perform (a rite). **e** celebrate (an anniversary). **4** examine and note (phenomena) without the aid of experiment. **5** say, observe. by way of comment.

observer *noun* **1** a person who observes. **2** a person who attends a conference etc. to note the proceedings but does not participate.

obsess *verb* (**obsesses**, **obsessed**, **obsessing**) **1** preoccupy, haunt; fill the mind of (a person) continually: *he was obsessed with thoughts of death*. **2** be continually preoccupied with: *her husband, who is obsessing about the wrongs that have been done to him*. ▶ **obsessed** *adjective* (also in *combination*)

obsession *noun* **1** a state of being obsessed with someone or something: *she cared for him with a devotion bordering on obsession*. **2** an idea or thought that continually preoccupies or intrudes on a person's mind: *he was in the grip of an obsession he was powerless to resist*. ▶ **obsessional** *adjective*

obsessive • *adjective* **1** demonstrating a troubling and intrusive preoccupation with one particular person or thing: *the popular TV star was stalked by an obsessive fan ◊ lately, his interest in fireworks has become obsessive*. **2** extremely dedicated, thorough, or careful: *she approaches her work with an obsessive attention to detail ◊ parents with an obsessive concern about their children's education*. • *noun* a person who demonstrates an unhealthy or intrusive preoccupation with a person or activity: *some gamblers and other obsessives are advised by their doctors to exercise ◊ hip-hop obsessives*.

obsessive-compulsive *adjective* designating or pertaining to a disorder in which a person has an obsessive compulsion to perform meaningless acts, e.g. handwashing, repeatedly.

obsessively *adverb* **1** in a manner that demonstrates a troubling and intrusive preoccupation with one particular person or thing: *she is obsessively jealous*. **2** in a dedicated, thorough, or extremely careful way: *her handwriting is obsessively neat*.

obsidian *noun* a dark glassy volcanic rock formed from hardened lava. [Say ub SIDDY un]

obsolescence *noun* the state of becoming old-fashioned, out of date, or no longer used: *tape recorders are on their way to obsolescence*. [Say obsa LESS ince]

obsolescent *adjective* becoming obsolete; going out of use or date: *was forced to work with obsolescent equipment ◊ obsolescent slang*. [Say obsa LESS'nt]

obsolete *adjective* disused, out of date. [Say obsa LEET]

obstacle *noun* a person or thing that obstructs progress.

obstacle course *noun* (also **obstacle race**) **1** a course or race in which various obstacles have to be negotiated. **2** an endeavour in which there are many problems to overcome.

obstetric *adjective* (also **obstetrical**) of or relating to pregnancy and childbirth. ▶ **obstetrically** *adverb* [Say ub STET rick]

obstetrician *noun* a physician specializing in obstetrics. [Say obsta TRISH un]

obstetrics *noun* the branch of medicine concerned with pregnancy and childbirth. [Say ub STET ricks]

obstinacy *noun* a stubborn unwillingness to change one's opinion or chosen course of action, despite the advice of others to do so. [Say OB stinna see]

obstinate *adjective* **1** stubbornly refusing to change one's opinion or chosen course of action, despite attempts to persuade one to do so. **2** (of an unwelcome phenomenon or situation) very difficult to change or overcome: *the obstinate problem of unemployment*. ▶ **obstinately** *adverb* [Say OB stin it]

obstreperous *adjective* noisy and difficult to control: *the boy is unruly and obstreperous*. ▶ **obstreperously** *adverb* **obstreperousness** *noun* [Say ub STREPPER us]

obstruct *verb* **1** block up; make hard or impossible to pass along or through: *you can't park here, you're obstructing my driveway ◊ first check that the accident victim doesn't have an obstructed airway*. **2** prevent the progress of; impede: *they were charged with obstructing the police ◊ terrorists attempting to obstruct the peace process*. **3** block (a view): *the pillar obstructed our view of the stage*.

obstruction *noun* **1** the fact of trying to prevent something or someone from making progress: *the obstruction of justice ◊ he was arrested for obstruction of a police officer*. **2** the fact of blocking a road, an entrance, a passage, etc.: *obstruction of the factory gates ◊ the abandoned car was causing an obstruction*. **3** something that blocks a road, an entrance, etc.: *it is my job to make sure that all pathways are clear of obstructions*. **4** something that blocks a passage or tube in the body; a medical condition resulting from this: *he had an operation to remove an obstruction in his throat ◊ a bowel obstruction*. **5** *Sport* the act of unlawfully obstructing another player.

obstructive *adjective* causing or intended to cause an obstruction: *of course she can do it — she's just being deliberately obstructive ◊ obstructive lung disease*.

obtain *verb* **1** acquire, secure; have granted to one. **2** be prevalent, customary, or established: *the price of silver fell to that obtaining elsewhere in the world*. ▶ **obtainable** *adjective*

obtrusive *adjective* unpleasantly or unduly noticeable: *the set designs in this production are obtrusive*. ▶ **obtrusively** *adverb* **obtrusiveness** *noun* [Say ub TRUCE iv]

obtuse *adjective* **1 a** dull-witted; slow to understand. **b** difficult to understand; obscure. **2** of blunt form; not sharp-pointed or sharp-edged. **3** (of an angle) more than 90° and less than 180°. ▶ **obtusely** *adverb* **obtuseness** *noun* [Say ub TOOSE or ub TYOOSE]

obverse • *noun* **1 a** the side of a coin or medal etc. bearing the head or principal design. **b** this design (*compare* REVERSE 7). **2** the counterpart of a fact or truth

etc.: *true solitude is the obverse of true society.* • *adjective* that is an obverse.

obviate *verb* (**obviates, obviated, obviating**) get around or do away with (a need, inconvenience, etc.): *farming methods that are designed to strengthen the plant and obviate the need for pesticides.* [Say OB vee ate]

obvious *adjective* **1** easily seen or recognized or understood. **2** not subtle; revealing sentiments, intentions, etc. clearly. ▶ **obviously** *adverb* **obviousness** *noun*

OC *abbreviation* Officer of the Order of Canada.

occasion • *noun* **1 a** a special or noteworthy event or happening. **b** the time or occurrence of this: *on the occasion of their marriage.* **2** a reason or justification: *there is no occasion to be angry.* **3** a juncture suitable for doing something; an opportunity. **4** an immediate but subordinate or incidental cause: *the assassination was the occasion of the war.* • *verb* be the occasion or cause of; bring about esp. incidentally. PHRASES **on occasion** now and then; when the need arises. **rise to the occasion** produce the necessary will, energy, ability, etc., in unusually demanding circumstances. **take the** (or **this** etc.) **occasion** make use of the opportunity: *I'd like to take this occasion to thank you all.*

occasional *adjective* **1** happening, done, consumed, etc. infrequently. **2** made or meant for, or associated with, a special occasion: *an occasional poem.* **3** (of furniture etc.) used from time to time and for various purposes: *an occasional table.* ▶ **occasionally** *adverb*

Occident *noun literary* **1** (**the Occident**) the West. **2** western Europe. **3** Europe, the Americas, or both, as distinct from the Orient. **4** European in contrast to Oriental civilization. [Say OCK suh d'nt]

occidental • *adjective* **1** of the Occident, as distinct from oriental. **2** western. **3** of western Europe. **4** relating to European or Western (in contrast to oriental) civilization. • *noun* (**Occidental**) a native or inhabitant of the Occident. [Say ock suh DENTAL]

occipital *adjective* situated at the back of the head. [Say ock SIPPA tull]

occiput *noun* the back of the head. [Say OXA put]

occlude *verb* (**occludes, occluded, occluding**) **1** stop up or close (pores, an orifice, a passage, etc.): *thick makeup can occlude the pores.* **2** *Chemistry* absorb and retain (gases or impurities). [Say uh KLUDE]

occluded front *noun Meteorology* a front that results when the cold front of a rotating low-pressure system overtakes the leading warm front, causing upward displacement of warm air between them.

occlusion *noun* **1** *Meteorology* a phenomenon in which the cold front of a depression overtakes the warm front, causing upward displacement of warm air between them. **2** *Dentistry* the position of the teeth when the jaws are closed. **3** the blockage or closing of a hollow organ etc.: *coronary occlusion.* ▶ **occlusive** *adjective* [Say uh CLUE zh'n, uh CLUE siv]

occult • *adjective* **1** involving the supernatural; mystical, magical. **2** communicated only to the initiated: *the typically occult language of the time.* **3** mysterious; beyond the range of ordinary knowledge: *a weird occult sensation of having experienced the situation before.* • *noun* (**the occult**) supernatural, mystical, or magical beliefs, practices, or phenomena. • *verb* (of a celestial body) conceal (an apparently smaller body) from view by passing or being in front of it.

occultation *noun Astronomy* the concealment of one celestial body by another passing between it and the observer, as when a star or planet is concealed by the moon. [Say ock'll TAY sh'n]

occultism *noun* belief or involvement in supernatural, mystical, or magical practices or phenomena. ▶ **occultist** *noun*

occupancy *noun* (*plural* **occupancies**) **1** the act, condition, or fact of occupying something or of being occupied. **2** the number of people occupying or meant to occupy a room, vehicle, etc.: *high-occupancy vehicle.*

occupant *noun* **1** a person who lives or works in a particular house, room, building, etc. **2** a person who is in a vehicle, seat, etc. at a particular time.

occupation *noun* **1** what occupies one; a means of passing one's time. **2** a person's temporary or regular employment; a business, calling, or pursuit. **3** the act of occupying or state of being occupied. **4 a** the act of taking or holding possession of (a country, district, etc.) by military force. **b** the state or time of this.

occupational *adjective* **1** of or in the nature of an occupation or occupations. **2** (of a disease, etc.) rendered more likely by one's occupation.

occupational hazard *noun* **1** a risk or danger connected with a particular job. **2** an unpleasant but not necessarily dangerous consequence of one's job, hobby, etc.: *the low pay is an occupational hazard of a career in city politics.*

occupational therapist *noun* a person whose job is to help people maximize their capabilities, independence, or recuperation from physical or mental illness.

occupational therapy *noun* mental or physical activity designed to help people maximize their capabilities, independence, or recuperation from physical or mental illness.

occupier *noun* **1** a member of a group that takes possession of a country by force. **2** a person or company residing in or using a property as its owner or tenant.

occupy *verb* (**occupies, occupied, occupying**) **1** reside in; be the tenant of. **2** take up or fill (space or time or a place). **3** hold (a position or office). **4** take military possession of (a country, region, town, strategic position). **5** place oneself in (a building etc.) forcibly or without authority. **6** (usu. in *passive*; often foll. by *in, with*) keep busy or engaged.

occur *verb* (**occurs, occurred, occurring**) **1** come into being as an event or process at or during some time; happen. **2** exist or be encountered in some place or conditions: *fossils occur throughout this area.* **3** come into the mind of, esp. as an unexpected or casual thought: *suddenly it occurred to me that I had forgotten to pay the hydro bill.*

occurrence *noun* **1** an incident or event: *vandalism used to be a rare occurrence.* **2** the fact or frequency of something happening: *the occurrence of cancer increases with age.* **3** the fact of something existing or being found in a place or under a particular set of conditions: *the occurrence of natural gas fields.*

ocean *noun* **1 a** a large expanse of sea, esp. each of the main areas called the Atlantic, Pacific, Indian, Arctic, and Antarctic Oceans. **b** these regarded cumulatively as the body of water surrounding the land of the globe. **2** (usu. as **the ocean**) the sea. **3** (often in *plural*) a very large expanse or quantity of anything: *oceans of time.*

oceanfront • *adjective* on the shore of an ocean. • *noun* a property or land on the shore of an ocean.

ocean-going *adjective* (of a ship) able to cross oceans.

oceanic *adjective* **1** of, like, or near the ocean. **2** (of a climate) affected by the closeness of the ocean. **3** *Biology & Geology* of the part of the ocean beyond the edge of the continental shelf. **4** *informal* of enormous size or extent; huge, vast: *grew up among oceanic fields of wheat.* [Say oh shee ANNICK or oh see ANNICK]

oceanographer *noun* a person who studies the physical and biological properties and phenomena of oceans. [Say ocean OGRA fur]

oceanographic *adjective* having to do with the study

of the physical and biological properties and phenomena of oceans. [Say ocean a GRAPHIC]

oceanography *noun* the study of the physical and biological properties and phenomena of oceans. [Say ocean OGRA fee]

ocean perch *noun* (*plural* **ocean perch** or **ocean perches**) 1 the flesh of various species of redfish marketed as food. 2 any of various fish of the scorpion fish family.

oceanside *adjective* near, by, on or along the shore of an ocean: *oceanside resort*.

ocelot *noun* 1 a medium-sized cat native to South and Central America, with a deep yellow or orange coat and black stripes and spots. 2 its fur. [Say AW suh lot]

ochre • *noun* 1 a mineral of clay and ferric oxide, used as a pigment varying from light yellow to brown or red. 2 a pale brownish yellow. • *adjective* pale brownish yellow. [Say OH cur]

o'clock *adverb* 1 of the clock (used to specify the hour): *6 o'clock*. 2 used after a numeral to indicate direction or bearing with reference to an imaginary clock face, twelve o'clock being directly above or in front of the observer or at the top of a circular target etc.

OCR *abbreviation* optical character recognition.

Oct. *abbreviation* October.

octa- *combining form* (also **oct-** before a vowel) eight.

octagon *noun* 1 a plane figure with eight sides and angles. 2 an object or building with this cross-section. ▶ **octagonal** *adjective* [Say OCTA gon, ock TAGGA null]

octahedron *noun* (*plural* **octahedrons** or **octahedra**) 1 a solid figure contained by eight (esp. triangular) plane faces. 2 a body, esp. a crystal, in the form of a regular octahedron. ▶ **octahedral** *adjective* [Say octa HEED run for the singular, octa HEED runs or octa HEED ruh for the plural]

octane *noun* a colourless inflammable hydrocarbon of the alkane series.

octave *noun* 1 *Music* a a series of eight notes occupying the interval between (and including) two notes, one having twice or half the frequency of vibration of the other. b this interval. c each of the two notes at the extremes of this interval. 2 a group or stanza of eight lines. 3 a the seventh day after a church festival. b a period of eight days including a festival and its octave. [Say OCK tiv]

octavo *noun* (*plural* **octavos**) 1 a size of book or page given by folding a standard sheet three times to form a quire of eight leaves. 2 a book or sheet of this size. Abbreviation: **8vo**. [Say ock TOV oh]

octet *noun* 1 *Music* a a composition for eight voices etc. b the performers of such a piece. 2 a group of eight. 3 the first eight lines of a sonnet. [Say OCK tet]

octo- *combining form* (also **oct-** before a vowel) eight.

October *noun* the tenth month of the year.

October Crisis *noun* *Cdn* the kidnapping of the British diplomat James Cross and the Quebec labour and immigration minister Pierre Laporte by cells of the Front de Libération du Québec in October of 1970, resulting in the federal government's invoking of the War Measures Act to allow for the detention of some 450 suspected FLQ members.

octogenarian • *noun* a person from 80 to 89 years old. • *adjective* 1 of this age. 2 of octogenarians. [Say octa juh NAIRY un]

octopus *noun* (*plural* **octopuses** or **octopi**) a mollusc with eight suckered arms, a soft saclike body, and

strong beak-like jaws. [Say OCTA pusses or OCTA pie for the plural]

ocular • *adjective* of or connected with the eyes or sight; visual. • *noun* the eyepiece of an optical instrument. ▶ **ocularly** *adverb* [Say OCK yoo lur]

OD *slang* • *noun* (*plural* **ODs**) an overdose, esp. of a narcotic drug. • *verb* (**OD's**, **OD'd**, **OD'ing**) take an overdose.

O.D. *abbreviation* Doctor of Optometry.

Odawa (*plural* **Odawa** or **Odawas**) • *noun* 1 a member of an Aboriginal people formerly living along the Ottawa River, and now living esp. on Manitoulin Island. 2 the Ojibwa dialect of this people. • *adjective* of this people or their language. [Say oh DAH wah]

odd *adjective* 1 strange. 2 additional; beside the reckoning: *earned the odd dollar*. 3 a (of numbers such as 3 and 5) not integrally divisible by two. b (of things or persons numbered consecutively) bearing such a number: *no parking on odd dates*. 4 left over when the rest have been distributed or divided into pairs: *odd socks*. 5 detached from a set or series: *a few odd volumes*. 6 (appended to a number, sum, etc.) somewhat more than: *forty odd* ◊ *forty-odd people*. 7 by which a round number, given sum, etc., is exceeded: *we have 102 — what'll we do with the odd 2?*

oddball *informal* • *noun* an odd or eccentric person. • *adjective* strange, bizarre.

oddity *noun* (*plural* **oddities**) 1 a strange person, thing, or occurrence. 2 a peculiar trait. 3 the state of being odd.

odd jobs *plural noun* small, esp. domestic, jobs of various types, usu. done for others.

oddly *adverb* 1 in a strange or unusual way: *she's behaving very oddly lately*. 2 used to show that something is surprising: *Mr. Lewis was oddly cheerful after the accident* ◊ *oddly enough, the most expensive tickets sold fastest*.

odd man out *noun* (also **odd one out**) 1 a person or thing differing from all the others in a group in some respect. 2 a method of selecting one of three or more persons e.g. by tossing a coin.

odd-man rush *noun* (*plural* **odd-man rushes**) *Hockey* a situation in which the players leading an offensive rush outnumber the skaters defending against it.

oddment *noun* 1 an odd article; something left over. 2 (in *plural*) miscellaneous articles.

oddness *noun* strange or unusual qualities or behaviour.

odds *plural noun* 1 the ratio between the amounts staked by the parties to a bet, based on the expected probability either way. 2 a the chances or balance of probability in favour of or against some result: *the odds are against it* ◊ *the odds are that it will rain*. b this probability expressed as a ratio: *the odds against winning are 50 to 1*. 3 the balance of advantage: *the odds are in your favour* ◊ *against all odds*. 4 an equalizing allowance to a weaker competitor; a handicap. 5 a difference giving an advantage: *it makes no odds*. PHRASES **at odds** (often foll. by *with*) in conflict or at variance. **by all odds** certainly. **take odds** accept a bet.

odds and ends *plural noun* miscellaneous articles or remnants.

odds-on *adjective* designating the outcome or chance most favoured by the odds: *odds-on favourite*.

ode *noun* 1 a lyric poem, usu. rhymed and in the form of an address, in varied or irregular metre. 2 *hist.* a

poem meant to be sung. **3** an artistic or literary creation praising or exalting something: *this film is an ode to fly fishing*.

odious *adjective* extremely unpleasant: *what an odious man!* ▶ **odiously** *adverb* [Say OH dee us]

odometer *noun* an instrument for measuring the distance travelled by a vehicle. [Say oh DOMMA tur]

odorous *adjective* having a scent or odour.

odour *noun* (also **odor**) **1** a distinctive, usu. unpleasant smell. **2** a lasting esp. unpleasant quality or trace attaching to something: *an odour of intolerance*. **3** the state of being held in a specified regard: *a decade of bad odour between Britain and the European Community*. ▶ **odourless** *adjective* (in sense 1).

odyssey *noun* (*plural* **odysseys**) a series of wanderings; a long adventurous journey: *his odyssey from soldier to politician*.

OECD *abbreviation* Organization for Economic Co-operation and Development.

Oedipal *adjective* having to do with an Oedipus complex. [Say EEDA pull]

Oedipus complex *noun* *Psychology* (according to Freud etc.) the complex of emotions aroused in a young (esp. male) child by a subconscious sexual desire for the parent of the opposite sex and wish to exclude the parent of the same sex. [Say EEDA puss]

o'er *adverb & preposition* *literary* = OVER.

oesophagus (*plural* **oesophagi** or **oesophaguses**) esp. *Brit.* = ESOPHAGUS. [Say i SOFFA gus]

oestrogen *Brit.* = ESTROGEN. [Say ESTRA jen]

oeuvre *noun* (*plural* **oeuvres**) **1** the works of an author, painter, composer, etc., esp. regarded collectively: *the complete oeuvre of Mozart*. **2** a work of art, music, etc. [Say OOV ruh (with OO as in HOOD)]

GRAMMAR CHECK
might have

Use **have**, not **of**, in expressions like **might have**, **could have**, **would have**, and **should have**: *I should have been more careful* (not *I should of been more careful*).

---

of *preposition* **1** expressing the relationship between a part and a whole. **2** belonging to; coming from. **3** expressing the relationship between a scale or measure and a value. **4** made from. **5** expressing the relationship between a direction and a point of reference. **6** expressing the relationship between a general category and something which belongs to such a category. **7** expressing time in relation to the following hour: *a quarter of three*.

WRITING TIP
off, off of

In careful writing avoid using **off of** when **off** by itself would do, as in *The plate fell off of the table*, which would be better written as *The plate fell off the table*.

---

off • *adverb* **1** away from the place in question. **2** so as to be removed or separated. **3** starting a journey or race. **4** so as to bring to an end or be discontinued. **5** (of an electrical appliance or power supply) not functioning or so as to cease to function. **6** having specified material goods or wealth: *badly off*. • *preposition* **1** moving away and often down from. **2** situated or leading in a direction away from. **3** so as to be removed, separated, or absent from. • *adjective* **1 a** *Brit. & Cdn* unwell: *am feeling a bit off*. **b** (of food etc.) unfit for consumption; no longer fresh. **2** not up to par; disappointing, weak: *his game was off*. **3** decreased in

price, quantity etc.: *tourism is off this summer*. • *verb* *slang* kill, murder. • *noun* (in *combination*) a competition: *cook-off*. PHRASES **off and on** intermittently; now and then. **off of** *slang disputed* = OFF *preposition* 1a: *picked it up off of the floor*.

WRITING TIP
off

Although sentences like *I bought the guitar off my neighbour* are common, this construction is best avoided in formal writing and speech. It is better to say *I bought the guitar from my neighbour*.

---

off-air *adjective & adverb* **1** involving or by the transmission of programs by broadcasting. **2** associated with a radio or television program but not broadcast: *off-air comments*.

offal *noun* **1** the less valuable edible parts of a carcass, esp. the entrails and internal organs. **2** refuse or waste: *plastic bags, old shoes, all the indestructible offal of industrial society*. [Sounds like AWFUL]

offbeat • *adjective* **1** eccentric, unconventional. **2** *Music* not coinciding with the beat. • *noun* *Music* any of the normally unaccented beats in a bar.

off-Broadway • *noun* New York City theatres, theatrical productions, or theatre life outside the area of Broadway, characteristically being more experimental and less commercial. • *adverb* occurring outside New York City's main theatre district.

off-camera *adjective & adverb* out of the range of a film or television camera.

off-campus *adjective & adverb* away from a university or college campus.

off-centre • *adjective* **1** slightly away from the centre; not quite coinciding with a central position. **2** unconventional, eccentric: *off-centre ideas*. • *adverb* positioned away from the centre.

off chance *noun* (**the off chance**) the slight possibility.

off-colour *adjective* slightly indecent or obscene: *an off-colour joke*.

offcut *noun* a remnant of wood, paper, etc., after cutting.

off-day *noun* **1** a day when one is not at one's best. **2** a day off from work, sports training, etc.

off-duty *adjective* **1** not engaged in one's regular work: *an off-duty police officer*. **2** pertaining to or during the time when one is not at work: *off-duty activities*.

offence *noun* (also **offense**) **1** an illegal act. **2** a wounding of the feelings: *no offence was meant and no offence was taken*. **3** the act of attacking or taking the offensive. **4** a thing that constitutes a violation of what is judged to be right or natural: *an offence to morality*. **5** *Sport* **a** the role of scoring points, goals, etc. for one's team: *he plays offence*. **b** the plays, moves, or tactics for achieving this. **c** the players on a team who perform this role.

offend *verb* **1** cause offence to or resentment in; wound the feelings of. **2** displease or anger. **3** commit an illegal act. **4** (often foll. by *against*) do wrong; transgress. ▶ **offender** *noun* **offending** *adjective*

offensive • *adjective* **1** giving or meant or likely to give offence; insulting: *offensive language*. **2** disgusting, foul-smelling, repulsive. **3 a** aggressive, attacking. **b** (of a weapon) meant for use in attack. **4** *Sport* of or relating to a team in possession of the ball, puck, etc.: *offensive line*. • *noun* **1** (usu. as **the offensive**) an aggressive action or attitude: *take the offensive*. **2** an attack, an offensive campaign or stroke. **3** aggressive or forceful action in pursuit of a cause: *a peace offensive*. ▶ **offensively** *adverb* **offensiveness** *noun*

offer • *verb* **1** present for acceptance, refusal, or consideration. **2** express willingness to do something for someone. **3** provide (access or opportunity). **4** present (a prayer or sacrifice) to a deity. **5** (foll. by *up*) place in the desired position for fixing. • *noun* **1** an expression of readiness to do or give something. **2** an amount of money that someone is willing to pay for something. **3** a specially reduced price. **4** a proposal of marriage.

offering *noun* **1** a contribution, esp. of money, to a church. **2** a thing offered as a religious sacrifice or token of devotion. **3** anything contributed or offered.

offertory *noun* (plural **offertories**) **1** *Christianity* **a** the offering of the bread and wine at the Eucharist. **b** a hymn accompanying this. **2 a** the collection of money at a religious service. **b** music played or sung while this is collected. **c** the money collected. [Say OFFER tory]

off-gas • *noun* (plural **off-gases**) a gas which is given off, esp. one emitted as the by-product of a chemical process. • *verb* (**off-gas**, **off-gassed**, **off-gassing**) emit a chemical, esp. a harmful one, in the form of a gas. ▶ **off-gassing** *noun*

offhand • *adjective* curt or casual in manner. • *adverb* **1** in an offhand manner. **2** without preparation or premeditation. ▶ **offhanded** *adjective* **offhandedly** *adverb* **offhandedness** *noun*

off-hour *noun* an hour when one is not working.

off-ice *adjective & adverb* *Hockey etc.* not occurring or positioned on the ice: *off-ice training* ◊ *off-ice official*.

office *noun* **1** a room, set of rooms, or building used as a place for non-manual work. **2** a position of authority or service. **3** tenure of an official position. **4** (in *plural*) service done for others: *the good offices of the rector*. **5** (also **divine office**) *Christianity* the prayers and psalms said daily by Catholic priests or other clergy.

office block *noun* a large building designed to contain business offices.

office-holder *noun* an esp. elected official.

office hours *noun* the hours during which business is normally conducted.

officer *noun* **1** a person holding a position of authority or trust, esp. one with a commission in the armed services, in the mercantile marine, or on a passenger ship. **2** a policeman or policewoman. **3** a holder of a post in a society or organization, e.g. the president or secretary. **4** a holder of a public, civil, or ecclesiastical office; an appointed or elected functionary (usu. with a qualifying word: *probation officer* ◊ *returning officer*). **5** a person who acts in an official capacity in a company. **6** a bailiff: *the sheriff's officer*. **7** (**Officer**) a member of the grade below Companion in the Order of Canada.

official • *adjective* **1 a** having to do with an authority or public body and its tenure, duties, actions, and responsibilities: *the prime minister's official engagements*. **b** having the approval or authorization of such a body or authority: *the official cause of death* ◊ *the government has not made it official, but it looks like minimum wage is going up*. **2** (often *derogatory*) characteristic of officials and bureaucracy: *what a lot of red tape and questions and official guffaw*. **3** holding office; employed in a public capacity. **4** formal; ceremonial: *an official reception* ◊ *the queen's official birthday*. • *noun* a person holding office or engaged in official duties.

officialdom *noun* people who are in positions of authority in large organizations, when they seem to be more interested in following rules than in being helpful or efficient: *the report is critical of attempts by officialdom to deal with the problem of homelessness*.

official language *noun* the language or languages under which government services etc. must be provided to citizens upon their request.

officially *adverb* **1** in a formal and public way: *the library will be opened officially by the mayor*. **2** with the authority of the government or some other organization: *the event is officially sponsored by the province*. **3** according to information that has been given to the public but that may not be true: *there is speculation he was murdered, although officially he died in a car crash*.

official opposition *noun* *Cdn & Brit.* (in a legislature) the opposition party which has the most seats and is thereby granted certain parliamentary privileges.

official secrets *plural noun* *Cdn & Brit.* confidential information involving national security.

officiate *verb* (**officiates**, **officiated**, **officiating**) **1** act in an official capacity, esp. on a particular occasion. **2** perform a religious service or ceremony. **3** act as a referee, umpire, etc. at a competition or game. ▶ **officiator** *noun* [Say oh FISHY ate]

officious *adjective* asserting authority aggressively, esp. with regard to petty or trivial matters; domineering: *the team leader issues orders in an officious manner*. ▶ **officiously** *adverb* **officiousness** *noun* [Say oh FISH us]

offing *noun* the more distant part of the sea in view. **PHRASES** **in the offing** not far away; likely to appear or happen soon.

off-island • *adjective* situated or occurring away from an island, esp. (in Canada) PEI. • *adverb* away from an island, esp. (in Canada) PEI: *travelled off-island*.

off-key *adjective* out of tune.

off-line • *adjective* **1** *Computing* (of a computer terminal or process) not directly controlled by or connected to a central processing unit. **2** designating or relating to the initial stage of video editing, in which the material is viewed and the desired selections are made. • *adverb* with a delay between the production of data and its processing; while not directly controlled by or connected to a central processing unit.

off-load *verb* **1** get rid of (esp. something unpleasant) by giving it to someone else. **2** unload (cargo etc.).

off-peak • *adjective* used or for use at times other than those of greatest demand. • *adverb* at times other than those of greatest demand.

off-piste *adjective & adverb* *Skiing* away from prepared ski runs. [Say off PEEST]

off-putting *adjective* **1** disconcerting; disturbing. **2** repellent; unpleasant. ▶ **off-puttingly** *adverb*

off-ramp *noun* a sloping one-way road leading off a highway.

off-reserve *Cdn* • *adjective* located on or inhabiting land which is not part of a designated reserve for Aboriginal people: *off-reserve housing*. • *adverb* not on a reserve: *lives off-reserve*.

off-road • *adjective* (of a vehicle etc.) designed for rough terrain or for cross-country driving. • *adverb* away from the road, on rough terrain.

off-roader *noun* a vehicle or bicycle designed for use over rough terrain.

off-roading *noun* the activity of driving over rough terrain, esp. as a sport.

off-sale *Cdn* (*BC, Alberta, & North*) • *noun* **1** the sale of liquor for consumption elsewhere than at the place of sale. **2** (usu. in *plural*) an alcoholic drink sold for consumption elsewhere. • *adjective* designating a place where liquor is sold in this manner: *an off-sale outlet*.

off-screen *adjective & adverb* **1** not appearing on a movie, television, or computer screen. **2** in private life or in real life as opposed to a film or television role.

off-season *noun* **1** *Sport* the period following the conclusion of the regular season and playoffs, during

which no competition takes place. **2** a time when business etc. is slack: *off-season prices*.

offset • *noun* **1** a side shoot from a plant serving for propagation. **2** a method of printing in which ink is transferred from a plate or stone to a uniform rubber surface and from there to paper etc.: *offset litho*. • *verb* (**offsets, offset, offsetting**) **1** counterbalance, compensate. **2** place out of line. **3** print by the offset process.

offshoot *noun* **1** a side shoot or branch. **2** a thing which originated as a branch of something else; a derivative.

offshore • *adjective* **1 a** situated at sea some distance from the shore. **b** of or pertaining to fishing conducted from large vessels on the grounds and banks at some distance from the shore. **2** (of the wind) blowing seawards. **3 a** (of goods, funds, etc.) made or registered abroad. **b** (of a person) living abroad: *offshore investors*. • *adverb* **1** at some distance from the shore. **2** in a direction away from the shore. **3** abroad.

offside • *adjective* Hockey, Soccer, etc. **1** (of a player) in a position, usu. ahead of the ball or puck, that is not allowed if it affects play. **2** of or relating to such a position: *offside pass*. • *adverb* in an offside position: *caught offside*. • *noun* the infraction of being offside.

off-site *adjective & adverb* away from a site; removed from the premises: *off-site storage*.

off-speed *adjective* Baseball (of a pitch or ball) delivered at less than full speed.

offspring *noun* (*plural* **offspring**) **1** a person's child or children or descendant(s). **2** an animal's young or descendant(s). **3** something derived or descended from another: *ringette is an offspring of hockey*.

offstage *adjective & adverb* **1** not on the stage and so not visible or audible to the audience. **2** in private or real life as opposed to a theatre etc. role.

off-the-rack *adjective* (esp. of clothes) ready-made.

off-the-shelf • *adjective* (of goods) supplied ready-made; available from existing stock: *the store sells off-the-shelf and custom-made equipment*. • *adverb* (**off the shelf**) that can be obtained easily from existing stock: *firearms are available off the shelf*.

off-the-wall *adjective* slang crazy, absurd, outlandish.

off-track *adjective* **1** situated or taking place away from a racetrack: *off-track betting*. **2** (of skiing, hiking, etc.) not performed on a groomed trail. **3** situated or taking place away from a railway track. **4** (**off track**) away from the subject, goal, etc.: *the economy is seriously off track*.

off-white *noun & adjective* a white colour with a grey or yellowish tinge.

oft *adverb* often: *oft-recurring ◊ oft-quoted*.

often *adverb* (**oftener, oftenest**) **1 a** frequently; many times. **b** at short intervals. **2** in many instances: *vocabulary often reflects social standing*. PHRASES **as often as not** in roughly half the instances: *I had two homes, really, because as often as not I was at her place*. **more often than not** in more than (roughly) half the instances: *food is scarce and more often than not they go hungry*. [Say OFF'n or OFT'n]

oftentimes *adverb* often. [Say OFF'n times or OFT'n times]

ogle • *verb* (**ogles, ogled, ogling**) **1** stare at someone in an offensive way, esp. with sexual interest: *they came to ogle the sunbathers*. **2** watch, stare at; keep an eye on: *ogling the local geological wonders*. • *noun* an amorous or lecherous look. ▶ **ogler** *noun* [Say OH gull]

ogre *noun* **1** a man-eating giant in folklore etc. **2** a cruel, irascible, or ugly person. ▶ **ogreish** *adjective* [Say OH gur]

oh¹ *interjection* (also **O**) expressing surprise, pain, entreaty, etc.: *oh, what a mess ◊ oh for a holiday*. PHRASES

oh boy expressing surprise, excitement, etc. **oh well** expressing resignation.

oh² *noun* zero: *the big four oh ◊ the Jays are five and oh*.

OHIP *abbreviation* Cdn Ontario Health Insurance Plan. [Say OH hip]

ohm *noun* Electricity the SI unit of resistance, transmitting a current of one ampere when subjected to a potential difference of one volt. Symbol: Ω. ▶ **ohmic** *adjective* [Say OME]

-oholic *combining form* -AHOLIC.

-oid *suffix* forming adjectives and nouns, denoting form or resemblance: *asteroid ◊ rhomboid ◊ thyroid*. ▶ **-oidal** *suffix* **-oidally** *suffix*

oil • *noun* **1** any of various thick, viscous, usu. inflammable liquids insoluble in water but soluble in organic solvents, obtained from animal, plant, or mineral sources. **2** petroleum. **3** vegetable oil used in cooking. **4 a** (usu. in *plural*) = OIL PAINT. **b** a picture painted in oil paints. **5** any of various thick liquids used on the hair, skin, etc.: *suntan oil*. • *verb* **1** apply oil to. **2** impregnate or treat with oil: *oiled silk*. PHRASES **oil the wheels** help make things go smoothly.

oil and water *noun* two elements or factors which do not agree or blend together.

oil can *noun* a can containing oil, esp. one with a long nozzle for oiling machinery.

oilcloth *noun* **1** a fabric waterproofed with oil. **2** a canvas coated with linseed or other oil and used to cover a table or floor.

oiler *noun* **1** an oil can for oiling machinery. **2** an oil tanker. **3** a person who oils machinery. **4 a** an oil well. **b** (in *plural*) oilskins.

oil field *noun* an area of land or seabed underlain by strata which contain oil, usu. in amounts that justify commercial exploitation.

oiliness *noun* the condition of containing or being covered with oil: *my skin is prone to oiliness*.

oil lamp *noun* a lamp using oil as fuel.

oilman *noun* (*plural* **oilmen**) an owner or employee of an oil company.

oil paint *noun* a mix of ground colour pigment and oil.

oil painting *noun* **1** the art of painting in oils. **2** a picture painted in oils.

oil pan *noun* (in an internal combustion engine) the bottom part of the crankcase, in which the oil used to lubricate the engine collects.

oil patch *noun* (*plural* **oil patches**) slang **1** a petroleum-rich region in a country etc. **2** the petroleum industry.

oil rig *noun* a structure with equipment for drilling an oil well. ▶ **oil rigger** *noun*

oil sand *noun* (usu. in *plural*) a deposit of loose sand or partially consolidated sandstone containing bitumen.

oilseed *noun* any of various seeds from cultivated crops yielding oil, e.g. rape, peanut, or cotton.

oilskin *noun* **1** cloth waterproofed with oil. **2** (often in *plural*) a garment made of this.

oil slick *noun* a smooth patch of floating oil, esp. one on the sea.

oil tanker *noun* a ship designed to carry oil in bulk.

oil well *noun* a well from which petroleum is drawn.

oily *adjective* (**oilier, oiliest**) **1** of, like, or containing much oil. **2** covered or soaked with oil. **3** trying to be too polite or flattering, in a way that is annoying and not genuine; smarmy: *she is oily and too quick to please*.

oink • *verb* **1** (of a pig) make its characteristic grunt. **2** (of a person) grunt like a pig. • *noun* the grunt of a pig or a sound resembling this.

ointment *noun* a smooth greasy healing or cosmetic preparation for the skin.

OJ *noun* informal orange juice.

Ojibwa (also **Ojibway**, **Ojibwe**) • *noun* (*plural* **Ojibwa** or **Ojibwas**) **1** a member of an Algonquian people living esp. around Lake Superior and certain adjacent areas. **2** the Algonquian language of this people. • *adjective* of or relating to the Ojibwa. [Say oh JIB way]

Oji-Cree *noun* a mixture of the Cree and Ojibwa languages spoken in northwestern Ontario and Manitoba. [Say AW gee cree]

OK (also **okay**) *informal* • *adjective* all right; satisfactory. • *adverb* well, satisfactorily: *that worked out OK.* • *noun* (*plural* **OKs** or **okays**) approval, sanction. • *interjection* all right, yes. • *verb* (**OK's** or **okays**, **OK'd** or **okayed**, **OK'ing** or **okaying**) give an OK to; approve, sanction. **Oka** *noun Cdn* a variety of semi-soft cured cheese originally made by Trappist monks. [Say OH kuh]

Okanagan *noun* (*plural* **Okanagan**) **1** a member of an Aboriginal people living in southern BC. **2** the Salishan language of this people. [Say oh kuh NOGGIN]

okey-doke *adjective, interjection, & adverb* (also **okey-dokey**) *slang* = OK[1].

Okie *noun informal* **1** a native or inhabitant of the US state of Oklahoma. **2** a migrant agricultural worker, esp. one from Oklahoma who was forced to leave a farm during the Great Depression. [Sounds like *OAKY*]

Oklahoman • *noun* a native or inhabitant of Oklahoma. • *adjective* of Oklahoma. [Say oak luh HOME un]

okra *noun* (*plural* **okras**) **1** an African plant yielding long ridged seed pods. **2** the seed pods eaten as a vegetable and used to thicken soups and stews. [Say OAK ruh]

Oktoberfest *noun* **1** an annual beer festival celebrated in Munich, Germany in late September and early October. **2** a similar autumn festival held elsewhere.

old *adjective* (**older**, **oldest**) **1** having lived for a long time; no longer young. **2** made or built long ago. **3** possessed or used for a long time. **4** dating from far back; long-established. **5** former; previous. **6** of a specified age. **7** *informal* expressing affection, familiarity, or contempt: *good old Mum.* **8** *Cdn* (of cheddar) aged 10-24 months. **PHRASES of old** formerly; long ago.

old age *noun* the later part of normal life.

old-age home *noun* = OLD PEOPLE'S HOME.

old-age pension *noun* a pension paid by the state to citizens above a certain age. ▶ **old-age pensioner** *noun*

old age security *noun Cdn* a system of government-funded pensions for those over 65. Abbreviation: **OAS**.

old bat *noun derogatory* an older woman, esp. one regarded as unattractive or unpleasant.

old boys' network *noun informal* (also **old boy network**) an informal network through which men from the same social background, profession, school, etc. help each other in business, politics, etc.

old country *noun* (**the old country**) the native country of an immigrant, settler, etc.

old dear *noun informal* an elderly woman.

olden *adjective archaic* or *literary* of old; of a former age: *in the olden days.*

Old English *noun* the language spoken in England by the Anglo-Saxons up to about 1150, an ancestor of, but very different from, modern English.

old-fashioned • *adjective* **1** in or according to the style, fashion, or tastes of an earlier period; antiquated. **2** believing in old ways, customs, etc.; conservative. • *noun* a cocktail consisting chiefly of whisky, bitters, water, and sugar.

old folks' home *noun informal* = OLD PEOPLE'S HOME.

Old French *noun* the French language up to *c.*1400.

old girl *noun* **1** esp. *Brit.* a former female pupil of a school. **2** *informal* **a** an elderly woman. **b** an affectionate term of address to a girl or woman.

old-growth *adjective* (of a tree etc.) mature, never felled.

old guard *noun* the original or past or conservative members of a group.

old hand *noun* a person with much experience.

old hat *adjective informal* tediously familiar or out of date.

old home week *noun informal* **1** a festival during which former residents of a town return home for the festivities. **2** any event attended by people who have not seen each other for a long time.

oldie *noun informal* **1** a thing that is old or familiar, esp. an old song or film. **2** an elderly person.

old lady *noun informal* or *offensive* one's mother, wife, or girlfriend.

old-line *adjective* **1** conservative: *old-line companies.* **2** well established: *old-line New England families.*

old man *informal* **1** one's father, husband, or boyfriend. **2** an affectionate form of address to a boy or man.

old man's beard *noun* any of various plants with plumed seeds, including some species of clematis.

Old Master *noun* **1** a great artist of former times, esp. of the 13th–17th centuries in Europe. **2** a painting by such a painter.

old money *noun* **1** wealth accumulated in a family over several generations. **2** people endowed with this.

Old Order *adjective* of or relating to various sects of the Mennonite church in North America, which strictly observe the oldest forms of worship and preserve the most conservative codes of behaviour, dress, etc.

old people's home *noun* an institution providing accommodation and nursing care for the elderly, esp. for those too infirm to live alone.

old school *noun* **1** traditional attitudes. **2** people having such attitudes.

oldsquaw *noun* a duck that breeds in Arctic regions of North America and Eurasia, the male of which has very long tail feathers and mainly white plumage in winter.

oldster *noun* an old person.

Old Style • *noun* dating reckoned by the Julian calendar (*compare* NEW STYLE). • *adjective* (**old-style**) of an old style, outmoded: *old-style communists.*

Old Testament *noun* the first part of the Christian Bible containing the scriptures of the Hebrews.

old-time *adjective* belonging to or typical of former times: *old-time rock'n'roll.* ▶ **old-timey** *adjective*

old-timer *noun* **1** a person who has lived in a place or been associated with an organization, job, etc. for a long time. **2** an elderly person. **3** *Sport* **a** a retired professional player, esp. one who participates in sports charity events: *NHL old-timers.* **b** a member of a team of middle-aged or elderly amateur players.

Old West *noun* the western US and Canada before the influx of settlers and establishment of government.

old wives' tale *noun* a foolish or unscientific tradition or belief.

old woman *noun informal* or *offensive* **1** one's wife, mother, or girlfriend. **2** a fussy or timid man.

Old World *noun* Europe, Asia, and Africa, regarded collectively as the part of the world known before the European discovery of the Americas.

old-world *adjective* belonging to or associated with old times: *a restaurant with old-world charm.*

old year *noun* the year just ended or about to end.

oleander *noun* an evergreen poisonous shrub native to the Mediterranean and bearing clusters of white, pink, or red flowers. [Say oh lee ANDER]

olfactory *adjective* of or relating to the sense of smell: *olfactory nerves*. [Say OLLA gark] [Say ole FACTORY or awl FACTORY]

oligarch *noun* (*plural* **oligarchs**) a member of an oligarchy. [Say OLLA gark]

oligarchic *adjective* based on or having to do with the political control of a country, organization, or institution by a small group of people: *an oligarchic regime.* ▶ **oligarchical** *adjective* [Say olla GARK ick]

oligarchy *noun* (*plural* **oligarchies**) **1** a small group of people having control of a country, organization, or institution: *both cities were once ruled by an oligarchy.* **2** a state governed in this way: *he believed that Britain was an oligarchy.* [Say OLLA garky]

Oligocene • *adjective* of or relating to the third epoch of the Tertiary period, between the Eocene and the Miocene, lasting from about 38 to 24.6 million years ago; it was a time of falling temperatures, with evidence of the first primates. • *noun* this geological epoch. [Say AWL ig a seen]

oligopolistic *adjective* based on, involved in, or having to do with a state of limited competition, in which a market is shared by a small number of producers or sellers. [Say olla goppa LISS tick]

oligopoly *noun* (*plural* **oligopolies**) a state of limited competition between a small number of producers or sellers. [Say olla GOPPA lee]

olive • *noun* **1** a small oval fruit with a hard stone and bitter flesh, green when unripe and bluish black when ripe, eaten or used as a source of oil used in cooking. **2** (also **olive green**) the greyish-green colour of an unripe olive. **3** (also **olive tree**) the evergreen tree that produces this fruit, which has dark green lance-shaped leathery leaves with silvery undersides. **4** the wood of the olive tree. • *adjective* **1** (also **olive green**) coloured like an unripe olive. **2** (of the complexion) yellowish brown, sallow.

olive branch *noun* **1** the branch of an olive tree as a symbol of peace. **2** a gesture of reconciliation or friendship: *following the election, the triumphant candidate extended an olive branch to her opponent.*

olive drab *noun & adjective* the dull olive green colour used in certain army uniforms.

olive oil *noun* an oil extracted from olives, used esp. in cooking.

-ology *combining form* see -LOGY.

Olympiad *noun* **1 a** a period of four years between Olympic Games, used by the ancient Greeks in dating events. **b** a four-yearly celebration of the ancient Olympic Games. **2** a celebration of the modern Olympic Games. **3** a regular international contest in chess, bridge, etc. [Say a LIMPY ad]

Olympian • *adjective* **1** of or associated with Mount Olympus in Greece, traditionally the home of the Greek gods. **2** resembling or appropriate to a god, esp. in superiority and aloofness: *the opinions of the Department of Justice are usually invested with an Olympian authority.* **3** of great size: *confidence reached Olympian proportions.* • *noun* **1** *Greek & Roman Myth* any of the twelve gods regarded as living on Olympus, usu. including Zeus (Jupiter), Aphrodite (Venus), Apollo, Ares (Mars), Artemis (Diana), Athena (Minerva), Demeter (Ceres), Dionysus (Bacchus), Hephaestus (Vulcan), Hera (Juno), Hermes (Mercury), and Poseidon (Neptune). **2** a competitor in the Olympic Games. [Say a LIMPY un]

Olympic • *adjective* **1** of or pertaining to the modern Olympic Games. **2** of ancient Olympia or the ancient Olympic Games. • *noun* (**the Olympics**) the Olympic Games.

Olympic Games *noun* **1** a modern international sports competition, traditionally held every four years since 1896 in different venues. Since 1992, the Summer and Winter Games have alternated every second year. **2** *hist.* an ancient Greek festival held at Olympia every four years, with athletic, literary, and musical competitions.

Olympic-sized *adjective* (also **Olympic-size**) of the dimensions prescribed for modern Olympic competitions: *an Olympic-sized pool*.

om *noun* *Hinduism & Buddhism* a mystic syllable used as a mantra and at the beginning and end of prayers. [Say OME]

oma *noun* (*plural* **omas**) (among people of German descent) grandmother. [Say OH muh]

Omaha • *noun* (*plural* **Omaha** or **Omahas**) **1** a member of an Aboriginal people of northeastern Nebraska. **2** the Siouan language of this people. • *adjective* of or pertaining to the Omaha or their language. [Say OH muh haw]

ombudsman *noun* (*plural* **ombudsmen**) (also **ombudsperson**) **1** an official appointed by a government to investigate individuals' complaints against public authorities etc. **2** an official within an institution who investigates complaints from employees, students, etc. [Say OMM budz mun]

omega *noun* (*plural* **omegas**) **1** the last (24th) letter of the Greek alphabet (Ω, ω). **2** the last of a series. [Say oh MAY guh]

omega-3 fatty acid *noun* a long-chain polyunsaturated fatty acid found esp. in fish oil, believed to help reduce blood cholesterol levels.

omelette *noun* a dish of beaten eggs cooked in a frying pan and served plain or with a filling.

omen *noun* **1** an occurrence or object regarded as portending good or evil. **2** indication of good or evil to come: *ravens are traditionally stigmatized as bearers of ill omen.*

omicron *noun* the fifteenth letter of the Greek alphabet (O, o). [Say OMM uh kron or OME uh kron]

ominous *adjective* giving the worrying impression that something bad or unpleasant is going to happen; threatening: *dark, ominous clouds* ◊ *an ominous ticking sound.* ▶ **ominously** *adverb* **ominousness** *noun*

omission *noun* **1** someone or something that has been left out or excluded: *there are glaring omissions in the report.* **2** the action of excluding or leaving out someone or something: *the omission of recent publications from her bibliography.* **3** a failure to do something, esp. something that one has a moral or legal obligation to do: *pay compensation for a wrongful act or omission.*

omit *verb* (**omits**, **omitted**, **omitting**) **1** leave out; not insert or include. **2** fail or neglect: *omitted to say.*

omni- *combining form* **1** all; of all things. **2** in all ways or places.

omnibus • *noun* (*plural* **omnibuses**) **1** *hist.* = BUS *noun* 1. **2** a volume containing several novels etc. previously published separately. • *adjective* serving several purposes at once or comprising several items: *this omnibus bill deals with various tax acts.*

omnidirectional *adjective* of equal sensitivity or power in all (esp. horizontal) directions: *omnidirectional microphone.*

OMNIMAX *noun* *proprietary* a technique of wide-screen cinematography in which 70mm film is projected through a fish-eye lens onto a hemispherical screen.

omnipotence *noun* great or absolute power or influence: *the omnipotence of God.* [Say omm NIPPA tince]

omnipotent *adjective* having great or absolute power or influence: *more than ten splinter groups have emerged from the wreckage of the once-omnipotent Communist Party.* ▶ **omnipotently** *adverb* [Say omm NIPPA t'nt]

omnipresent *adjective* **1** present everywhere at the same time: *an omnipresent danger.* **2** widely or

constantly encountered: *the omnipresent voice of his brother-in-law*. [Say OMNI present]

omniscience *noun* infinite or extensive knowledge: *his mere appointment to the board does not infuse him with some godlike omniscience*. [Say omm NISHY ince]

omniscient *adjective* having infinite or very extensive knowledge. [Say omm NISHY unt]

omniscient narrator *noun* a narrator of a story who seems to know all that is happening, including the thoughts of all the characters, as opposed to a narrator who tells the story only from the point of view of one character.

omnivore *noun* an animal or a person that eats all types of food, esp. both plants and meat. [Say OMNI vore]

omnivorous *adjective* **1** feeding on many kinds of food, esp. on both plants and meat. **2** taking in or using just about anything available: *an omnivorous reader*. [Say omm NIVVER us]

ON *abbreviation* Ontario (in official postal use).

on • *preposition* **1** in contact with and supported by (a surface). **2** on to. **3** in the possession of. **4** forming a distinctive part of the surface of. **5** about; concerning. **6** as a member of (a committee, jury, etc.). **7** having (the thing mentioned) as a target, aim, or focus. **8** stored in or broadcast by. **9** in the course of or while travelling in. **10** indicating the day or time when something takes place. **11** engaged in. **12** regularly taking (a drug or medicine). **13** paid for by. • *adverb* **1** in contact with and supported by a surface. **2** (of clothing) being worn. **3** further forward; with continued movement or action. **4** taking place or being presented. **5** (of an electrical appliance or power supply) functioning. **6** on duty or on stage. PHRASES **be on about** refer to or discuss esp. tediously or persistently: *what are they on about?* **be on at** *informal* nag or grumble at. **be on to 1** realize the significance or intentions of. **2** get in touch with (esp. by telephone). **on and off** intermittently; now and then. **on and on** continually; at tedious length. **on side** *see* ONSIDE. **on time** punctual, punctually. **on to** to a position or state on or in contact with.

on-again, off-again *adjective* operating or occurring at irregular and often unpredictable intervals.

on-air *adjective* on the air; broadcasting.

on-base percentage *noun* Baseball a statistic indicating the number of times a player reaches base in relation to his or her at-bats.

on-board *adjective* provided or situated on board a vehicle, ship, etc.: *on-board computer* (compare ON BOARD (see BOARD)).

on-camera *adjective & adverb* within the range of a film or television camera: *an on-camera interview*.

once • *adverb* **1** on one occasion or for one time only: *did not once say please ◊ have read it once*. **2** at some point or period in the past: *could once play chess*. **3** ever or at all: *if you once forget it*. **4** by one degree: *a cousin once removed*. • *conjunction* as soon as: *once they have gone we can relax*. • *noun* one time or occasion: *just the once*. PHRASES **all at once 1** without warning; suddenly. **2** all together. **at once 1** immediately. **2** simultaneously. **for once** on this (or that) occasion, even if at no other. **once again** (or **more**) another time. **once and for all** (or **once for all**) (done) in a final or conclusive manner, esp. so as to end hesitation

or uncertainty. **once and future** that has been in the past and will be again. **once** (or **every once**) **in a while** from time to time; occasionally. **once or twice** a few times. **once upon a time 1** at some vague time in the past. **2** formerly.

once-in-a-lifetime *adjective* (of an experience, opportunity, etc.) so extraordinary that it is not likely to be repeated in one's lifetime.

once-over *noun* informal a rapid preliminary inspection or piece of work.

oncologist *noun* a doctor who diagnoses and treats cancerous tumours. [Say on COLLA jist]

oncology *noun* the branch of medicine dealing with the diagnosis and treatment of cancerous tumours. [Say on COLLA jee]

oncoming *adjective* approaching from the front.

on-deck circle *noun* Baseball a circular area outside the team's dugout where the next batter warms up etc.

one • *cardinal number* **1** the lowest cardinal number; 1. **2** single, or a single person or thing. **3** (before a person's name) a certain. **4** a noteworthy example of. **5** identical; the same. • *pronoun* **1** used to refer to a person or thing previously mentioned or easily identified. **2** a person of a specified kind. **3** used to refer to the speaker, or any person, as representing people in general. PHRASES **at one** in agreement. **for one** being one, even if the only one: *I for one do not believe it*. **for one thing** as a single consideration, ignoring others. **one and all** everyone. **one and only 1** unique. **2** superb, unequalled. **one by one** singly, successively. **one day 1** on an unspecified day. **2** at some unspecified future date. **one thing and another** informal various events, items, matters, tasks, etc.

one-and-a-half *noun* (plural **one-and-a-halfs**) Cdn (Que.) an apartment having one room plus a bathroom.

one another *pronoun* each the other or others (esp. as a formula of reciprocity): *love one another*.

one-armed bandit *noun* informal a slot machine worked by a long handle at the side.

one-dimensional *adjective* **1** having or pertaining to a single dimension. **2** lacking depth or scope; superficial: *the story was one-dimensional*.

one-handed • *adjective* **1** having only one hand, or only one hand capable of use. **2** used, worked, or performed with one hand. • *adverb* using only one hand: *he pulled himself one-handed to the deck*.

one-horse *adjective* **1** using a single horse. **2** informal small, unimportant; obscure: *a one-horse town*.

Oneida (plural **Oneida** or **Oneidas**) • *noun* **1** a member of an Iroquois people formerly living in New York State, and now living near London, Ont. **2** the Iroquoian language of this people. • *adjective* of or relating to this people. [Say oh NIDE uh]

one-liner *noun* informal a short witty remark; a joke consisting of only one sentence.

one-man *adjective* **1** involving, done, or operated by

only one man. **2** committed or attached to one man only: *Katherine is a one-man woman.*

one-man band *noun* **1** an entertainer who plays a number of musical instruments at the same time. **2** a person who does everything personally or operates without assistance.

oneness *noun* **1** the fact or state of being one: *efforts to promote the racial unity and the oneness of mankind.* **2** identity or harmony with someone or something: *a strong sense of oneness with all things.*

one-night stand *noun* **1** *informal* a sexual relationship lasting only one night. **2** a single performance of a play etc. in a place.

one-off *informal* • *adjective* made or happening only once; not repeated. • *noun* a thing that is made or happens only once.

one-on-one • *adjective* involving direct communication, competition, confrontation, etc. between two people. • *adverb* in direct communication, confrontation, etc.: *spoke one-on-one.* • *noun* a one-on-one meeting, encounter, confrontation, etc.

one percent *noun* (also **1 percent**, **1%**) partly skimmed milk containing one percent milk fat.

one-piece • *noun* **1** (of a bathing suit, snowsuit, etc.) made as a single garment. **2** made or consisting of a single piece. • *noun* a thing that is made or consists of one piece.

one-room schoolhouse *noun* (also **one-room school**) *esp. hist.* a school in which all grades are taught by one teacher in a single classroom.

onerous *adjective* burdensome; causing or requiring trouble: *an onerous responsibility.* [Say OWN er us or ON er us]

oneself *pronoun* the reflexive and emphatic form of *one*: *hurt oneself* ◊ *one has to do it oneself.*

one-shot *adjective* **1** achieved or done with a single attempt, stroke, etc. **2** occurring, produced, used, etc. only once: *a one-shot deal.*

one-sided *adjective* **1** favouring one side in a dispute; unfair, partial. **2** having or occurring on one side only. **3** larger or more developed on one side. ▶ **one-sidedness** *noun*

one-size-fits-all *adjective* **1** (of clothing) available in one size only. **2** *informal* suitable for or used in all circumstances: *a one-size-fits-all solution.*

one-step *adjective* done or made etc. in a single step: *one-step installation process.*

one-stop *adjective* (of a store etc.) capable of supplying all a customer's needs within a particular range of goods or services: *a one-stop building supply centre.*

one-time • *adjective* **1** former: *the one-time champion.* **2** done or occurring etc. only once: *a one-time payment.* • *verb* (**one-times**, **one-timed**, **one-timing**) *Hockey* shoot (a moving puck) without stopping it first.

one-timer *noun* *Hockey* a shot that has been one-timed.

one-to-one *adjective* **1** with each member of a group corresponding to a member of another group. **2** = ONE-ON-ONE *adjective*.

one-track mind *noun* a mind preoccupied with one subject.

one-two *informal* • *noun* (plural **one-twos**) *Boxing* the delivery of two punches in quick succession. • *adjective* (of two teams, competitors, etc.) holding first and second place.

one-up *informal* • *adjective* having a particular advantage. • *verb* (**one-ups**, **one-upped**, **one-upping**) do better than (someone): *always trying to one-up me.*

one-upmanship *noun* *informal* the art or practice of maintaining an advantage in a competitive relationship.

one-way *adjective* **1** allowing movement or travel in one direction only. **2** characterized by or entailing no reciprocal feeling, communication, responsibility, etc.: *a one-way relationship.* **3** (of a window, etc.) permitting vision from one side only.

one-way street *noun* **1** a street on which vehicular travel is allowed in only one direction. **2** a situation, relationship, etc., in which there is no reciprocity or possibility of returning to a previous state.

one-woman *adjective* **1** involving, done, or operated by only one woman: *a one-woman show.* **2** committed or attached to one woman only.

ongoing *adjective* **1** continuing to exist or be operative etc. **2** that is or are in progress: *ongoing discussions.*

on-ice *adjective* & *adverb* *Hockey* & *Curling* occurring or positioned on the ice: *on-ice violence.*

onion *noun* **1** a swollen edible bulb with a pungent taste and smell, used as a vegetable. **2** the plant that produces this bulb, with long rolled or strap-like leaves and spherical heads of greenish-white flowers.

onion dome *noun* a bulbous dome, esp. on an Eastern Orthodox church etc. ▶ **onion-domed** *adjective*

onion ring *noun* a ring of onion coated in batter and deep-fried.

onion skin *noun* **1** the brown outermost skin or any outer skin of an onion. **2** thin smooth translucent paper.

on-line • *adjective* (of equipment or a process) directly controlled by or connected to a central processing unit. • *adverb* while thus controlled or connected.

onlooker *noun* a non-participating observer; a spectator. ▶ **onlooking** *adjective*

WRITING TIP
only

In normal speech it is standard to place **only** just before the verb, as in *I only wanted to talk to you.* In careful writing, however, you should consider placing **only** where it is least ambiguous. Consider the possible meanings of *The loon can only be heard in the morning mist.* It can mean that *the morning mist* is the only place the loon can be heard, or that the loon can be *heard* there but not seen; if the first sense was intended, the sentence could have been written less ambiguously as *Only in the morning mist can the loon be heard.*

---

only • *adverb* **1** and no one or nothing more besides. **2** no longer ago than. **3** not until. **4** with the negative or unfortunate result that. • *adjective* **1** alone of its or their kind; single or solitary. **2** alone deserving consideration. • *conjunction* *informal* except that. **PHRASES** **only too** extremely: *only too willing.*

on-off *adjective* (of a switch) having two positions, "on" and "off".

onomatopoeia *noun* **1** the formation of a word from a sound associated with what is named (e.g. *sizzle*). **2** the use of such words. ▶ **onomatopoeic** *adjective* [Say onna matta PEE uh]

Onondaga (plural **Onondaga** or **Onondagas**) • *noun* **1** a member of an Iroquois people now living esp. on the Six Nations reserve near Brantford, Ont. **2** the Iroquoian language of this people. • *adjective* of or relating to this people. [Say on on DOGGA]

on-ramp *noun* a sloping one-way road leading onto a highway.

on-reserve *Cdn* • *adjective* located on or inhabiting land which is part of a designated reserve for Aboriginal people. • *adverb* on a reserve: *works on-reserve.*

onrush *noun* (*plural* **onrushes**) an onward rush.
▶ **onrushing** *adjective*

onscreen • *adjective* appearing on a movie, television, or computer screen. • *adverb* **1** on or by means of a screen. **2** within the view presented by a motion picture scene.

onset *noun* the beginning of some esp. unpleasant operation, situation, condition, etc.

on-set *adjective* taking place or occurring on the set of a play or film.

onshore • *adjective* **1** on the shore. **2** (of the wind) blowing from the sea towards the land. • *adverb* on or towards the land.

onside *adjective & adverb* **1** *Sport* (of a player) in a legal position; not offside. **2** (also **on side**) in or into a position of agreement with (another person or thing): *it would be helpful to have the minister onside*.

on-site *adjective* taking place or available on a site or premises.

onslaught *noun* a fierce attack. [Say ON slot]

onstage *adjective & adverb* on the stage; visible to the audience.

Ont. *abbreviation* Ontario.

Ontarian • *noun* a native or inhabitant of Ontario. • *adjective* of or relating to Ontario. [Say on TERRY un]

on-the-job *adjective* done or occurring while a person is at work.

onto *preposition* to a position or state on or in contact with.

ontological *adjective* based on or having to do with the branch of metaphysics dealing with the nature of being. ▶ **ontologically** *adverb* [Say onta LOGICAL]

ontology *noun* the branch of metaphysics dealing with the nature of being. [Say on TOLLA jee]

onus *noun* a burden, duty, or responsibility: *the onus is on employers to follow health and safety laws*. [Say OH nus]

onward • *adverb* (also **onwards**) **1** further on. **2** towards the front. **3** with advancing motion. **4** into the future: *from 1998 onward*. • *adjective* directed onward.

onyx *noun* (*plural* **onyxes**) a semi-precious variety of agate with different colours in layers. [Say ON ix]

oodles *plural noun* *informal* a very great amount.

ooh • *interjection* expressing surprise, delight, pain, etc. • *noun* an exclamation of "ooh". • *verb* (**oohs, oohed, oohing**) (in phr. **ooh and aah**) express delight, a favourable reaction, etc.

Ookpik *noun* *Cdn proprietary* a doll resembling an owl, originally handcrafted of sealskin by Inuit artisans, now mass-produced and sold as a souvenir.

oolichan *noun* (**oolichan** or **oolichans**) = EULACHON. [Say OOLA con]

oomiak *noun* (*plural* **oomiaks**) = UMIAK. [Say OOMY ack]

oompah *noun* (also **oompahpah**) a representation of the repetitive rhythmical playing of lower brass instruments, esp. in German and eastern European dance music.

oomph *noun* *slang* **1** energy, liveliness. **2** attractiveness, esp. sexual appeal.

oops *interjection* *informal* expressing surprise or apology, esp. on making an obvious mistake.

oopsy daisy *interjection* = UPSY-DAISY.

ooze • *verb* (**oozes, oozed, oozing**) **1** (of fluid) pass slowly through the pores of something; trickle or leak slowly out. **2** (of a substance) exude moisture. **3** give a powerful impression of (a quality): *she walked into the party oozing confidence*. • *noun* **1** a sluggish flow of liquid. **2** a deposit of wet mud or slime, esp. at the bottom of a river, lake, or estuary. ▶ **oozy** *adjective*

OP *abbreviation* **1** *Catholicism* Order of Preachers (used

after the name of a member of the Dominican order). **2** *Military* observation post. **3** out of print.

Op. *abbreviation* *Music* opus.

op *noun* *informal* operation (in surgical and military senses).

opa *noun* (*plural* **opas**) (among people of German descent) grandfather; grandpa. [Say OH puh]

opacity *noun* (*plural* **opacities**) **1** the state of being difficult to see through: *sheets of frosted glass with varying degrees of opacity*. **2** the state of being difficult to understand: *the opacity of the poet's language*. [Say oh PASSA tee]

opal *noun* a quartz-like form of hydrated silica, usu. white or colourless and sometimes showing changing colours, often used as a gemstone. [Say OH pull]

opalescent *adjective* showing changing colours like an opal. [Say oh puh LESS'nt]

opaque *adjective* **1** (of glass, liquid, etc.) not clear enough to see through or allow light through: *opaque glass*. **2** obscure; not easy to understand: *this is a very complicated book, too often maddeningly opaque*. ▶ **opaqueness** *noun* [Say oh PAKE]

op. cit. *abbreviation* in the work already quoted. [Say OPP sit]

OPEC *abbreviation* Organization of Petroleum Exporting Countries. [Say OH peck]

op-ed *noun* a newspaper page usu. located opposite the editorial page and containing signed opinion pieces, letters to the editor, etc.: *op-ed article*.

open • *adjective* **1** allowing access, passage, or view; not closed, fastened, or restricted. **2** exposed to view or attack; not covered or protected. **3** (foll. by *to*) vulnerable or subject to. **4** spread out, expanded, or unfolded. **5** officially admitting customers or visitors; available for business. **6** (of an offer or opportunity) still available. **7** frank and communicative. **8** not finally settled; still admitting of debate. **9** (often foll. by *to*) accessible, receptive, or available. **10** (foll. by *to*) admitting of; making possible. **11** *Music* (of a string) allowed to vibrate along its whole length. **12** *Phonetics* (of a vowel) produced with a relatively wide opening of the mouth and the tongue kept low. **13** (of an electric circuit) having a break in the conducting path. **14** *Cdn* (of a mortgage etc.) that may be paid off in full. • *verb* **1** make or become open **2** spread out; unfold or be unfolded. **3** formally begin or establish. **4** make available or more widely known. **5** break the conducting path of (an electric current). • *noun* **1** (**the open**) fresh air or open countryside. **2 Open** a championship or competition with no restrictions on who may compete. PHRASES **be open with** speak frankly to. **open fire** start shooting. **open on to** give access to. **open out 1** unfold; spread out. **2** develop, expand. **3** accelerate. **open up 1** unlock (premises). **2** make accessible. **3** reveal; bring to notice. **4** accelerate esp. a motor vehicle. **5** begin shooting or sounding. **6** talk or speak openly. ▶ **openable** *adjective*

open air • *noun* (**the open air**) a free or unenclosed space outdoors. • *adjective* (**open-air**) **1** out of doors. **2** open to the air; having no covering: *an open-air vehicle*.

open-and-shut *adjective* (of an argument, case, etc.) straightforward and conclusive.

open bar *noun* a bar, e.g. at a reception etc., where the drinks are paid for by the host or through an admission fee rather than purchased directly by the guests.

open book • *noun* a person or thing that is easily understood. • *adjective* (usu. **open-book**) (of an examination etc.) written with the use of a textbook, one's notes, etc.: *an open-book exam*.

open concept *adjective Cdn* (of a house, office, etc.) having few or no internal walls or partitions.

open custody *noun Cdn* custody in a correctional facility that has relatively little supervision or security, e.g. a group home.

open door *noun* **1** a policy or practice of allowing trade with all nations on an equal basis. **2** free or unrestricted admittance, esp. for immigration etc.: *open door policies*.

open-ended *adjective* **1** having no predetermined limit or boundary. **2** (of a question etc.) not limiting the respondent in the range of his or her answer. ▶ **open-endedness** *noun*

opener *noun* **1** a person or thing that opens (something). **2** a device for opening cans, bottles, etc. **3** the first item in a program, series, season, etc. PHRASES **for openers** *informal* to start with.

open-faced *adjective* (also **open-face**) (of a sandwich etc.) without an upper layer of bread etc.

open-heart *adjective* of or relating to surgery in which the heart has been temporarily bypassed and opened.

open house *noun* **1** a reception or party during which guests are invited to drop in to a person's home. **2** a time during which an institution, such as a school, is open to visitors. **3** a time during which a house etc. that is for sale may be viewed by prospective buyers without an appointment.

opening • *noun* **1** an aperture or gap, esp. one allowing access. **2** a favourable situation or opportunity. **3** an available position or opportunity in a business or company etc. **4** a beginning; an initial part. **5** the process of becoming open or making something open: *the long-awaited opening of a new library*. **6** a ceremony to celebrate a new building, facility, etc. being ready for use. **7** the first performance of a theatrical production etc. **8** a tract of land that is thinly wooded in comparison to the surrounding forest. **9** *Cdn* a period of fixed length determined by the government during which herring fishing may be undertaken. **10** a counsel's preliminary statement of a case in a law court. • *adjective* initial, first.

opening line *noun* **1** the first line of a book, movie, etc. **2** a phrase or sentence initiating a conversation, esp. with someone to whom one is sexually attracted.

open letter *noun* a letter, esp. of protest, addressed to an individual and published in a newspaper etc.

open-line *adjective* designating a radio or television program in which the public can participate by phone.

openly *adverb* **1** frankly, honestly. **2** publicly; without concealment.

open market *noun* an unrestricted market with free competition of buyers and sellers.

open-minded *adjective* accessible to new ideas; unprejudiced. ▶ **open-mindedly** *adverb* **open-mindedness** *noun*

open-mouthed *adjective* with the mouth open, esp. in surprise.

open-necked *adjective* (of a shirt) worn with the top button unfastened.

openness *noun* **1** the quality of being honest and not hiding information or feelings. **2** the quality of being receptive to different ideas or people. **3** the quality of not being enclosed or covered.

open-pit mine *noun* a large pit excavated in the ground from which minerals are mined.

open-pit mining *noun* the process of extracting minerals situated just below the earth's surface from a large pit excavated in the ground.

open-plan *adjective* = OPEN CONCEPT.

open question *noun* a matter not yet decided: *whether Americans will find her to their liking is an open question*.

open season *noun* **1** the season when restrictions on the killing of game etc. are lifted. **2** a time when there appear to be no restrictions on criticizing particular groups of people or treating them unfairly: *appears to be open season on unions*.

open shop *noun* **1** a business etc. where employees do not have to be members of a labour union (*opp.* CLOSED SHOP). **2** this system.

open skies *noun* a system allowing unrestricted access to the airspace over a country: *open skies agreement*.

open society *noun* a society with wide availability of information and freedom of belief.

open stock *noun* merchandise, e.g. dishes, which may be purchased as individual pieces rather than as a set.

open system *noun* (often in *plural*) a computer system in which the components conform to non-proprietary standards rather than to the standards of a specific supplier of hardware or software, thus allowing greater compatibility.

open university *noun* (often **Open University**) a university that teaches mainly by broadcasting and correspondence, and is open to those without formal academic qualifications.

openwork *noun* a pattern with intervening spaces in metal, leather, lace, etc.

opera[1] *noun* (*plural* **operas**) **1 a** a dramatic work in one or more acts, set to music for singers (usu. in costume) and instrumentalists. **b** this as a genre. **c** the score for an opera. **d** a performance of an opera. **2** a building for the performance of opera. **3** a company performing opera.

opera[2] *plural of* OPUS.

operable *adjective* **1** that can be operated. **2** suitable for treatment by surgical operation. [Say OPERA bull]

opera glasses *plural noun* small binoculars for use in a theatre.

opera house *noun* **1** a theatre for the performance of opera, also often used for ballet performances. **2** a theatre, esp. in a small town.

operate *verb* (**operates**, **operated**, **operating**) **1** manage, work, control; put or keep in a functional state. **2** be in action; function. **3** produce an effect; exercise influence: *the tax operates to our disadvantage*. **4 a** perform a surgical operation. **b** conduct a military or naval action. **c** be active in business etc., esp. dealing in stocks and shares. **5** (foll. by *on*) influence or affect (feelings etc.). **6** bring about; accomplish.

operatic *adjective* **1** of or relating to opera. **2** resembling or characteristic of opera. [Say opper ATTIC]

operating profit *noun* gross profit before deduction of expenses.

operating room *noun* (also **operating theatre**) a room for surgical operations.

operating system *noun* the basic software that enables the running of a computer program.

operating table *noun* a table on which surgical operations are performed.

operation *noun* **1 a** the action or process or method of working or operating. **b** the state of being active or functioning: *not yet in operation*. **c** the scope or range of effectiveness of a thing's activity. **2** an active process; a discharge of a function: *the operation of breathing*. **3** a piece of work, esp. one in a series (often in *plural*: *begin operations*). **4** an act of surgery performed on a patient. **5** a strategic movement of troops, ships, etc. for military action: *Operation Overlord*. **6** a financial transaction. **7** a business or enterprise: *owned a dairy operation near Goderich*. **8** *Math* the subjection of a

number or quantity or function to a process affecting its value or form, e.g. multiplication, differentiation.
operational *adjective* **1 a** of or used for operations. **b** engaged or involved in operations. **2** able or ready to function. ▶ **operationally** *adverb*

operations room *noun* a room etc. from which military or police operations are directed.

operative • *adjective* **1** in operation; having effect: *the station will be fully operative again in January* ◊ *the law becomes operative immediately*. **2** most relevant: *I was in love with her — "was" being the operative word*. **3** of or by surgery. • *noun* **1** a worker, esp. a skilled one. **2** a secret service agent; a spy. [Say OPPER a tiv]

operator *noun* **1** a person operating a machine etc., esp. one who operates a telephone switchboard. **2** a person operating or engaging in business: *tour operators in Vancouver offer trips to the Gulf Islands*. **3** *informal* a person acting in a specified way: *a smooth operator*. **4** *Math* a symbol or function denoting an operation (e.g. ×, +).

operetta *noun* a theatrical production, usu. of a comic nature, combining songs with spoken dialogue. [Say opper ETTA]

ophthalmia *noun* an inflammation of the eye, esp. conjunctivitis. [Say off THALMY uh or opp THALMY uh]

ophthalmic *adjective* of or relating to the eye and its diseases. [Say off THAL mick or opp THAL mick]

ophthalmological *adjective* having to do with medical treatment of the eye. [Say off thuh muh LOGICAL or opp thuh muh LOGICAL]

ophthalmologist *noun* a doctor who studies and treats diseases of the eye. [Say off thuh MOLLA jist or opp thuh MOLLA jist]

ophthalmology *noun* the branch of medicine concerned with the study and treatment of disorders and diseases of the eye. [Say off thuh MOLLA jee or opp thuh MOLLA jee]

opiate • *noun* **1** a drug containing or derived from opium, usu. to ease pain or induce sleep. **2** a thing which soothes or stupefies. • *adjective* containing opium. [Say OH pee it]

opine *verb* (**opines, opined, opining**) hold or express as an opinion: *she opined that the commission had no mandate to look at the alleged cover-up*. [Say oh PINE]

opinion *noun* **1** a belief or assessment based on grounds short of proof. **2** a view held as probable. **3** (often foll. by *on*) what one thinks about a particular topic or question: *my opinion on capital punishment*. **4 a** a formal statement of professional advice: *get a second opinion*. **b** *Law* a formal statement of reasons for a judgment given. **5** an estimation: *had a low opinion of it*. PHRASES **be of the opinion that** believe or maintain that. **in one's opinion** according to one's view or belief. **a matter of opinion** a disputable point.

opinionated *adjective* conceitedly assertive or dogmatic in one's opinions.

opinion poll *noun* = GALLUP POLL.

opium *noun* **1** a heavy-scented addictive drug prepared from the juice of the opium poppy, used in medicine as an analgesic and narcotic; it is the source of both morphine and heroin. **2** anything regarded as soothing or stupefying. [Say OH pee um]

opium den *noun* a place where opium may be purchased and used.

opium poppy *noun* a poppy native to Europe and East Asia, with white, red, pink, or purple flowers.

opossum *noun* **1** a North American mainly tree-living marsupial that can grasp things with its tail and has hind feet with opposable thumbs. **2** a similar animal, suited to an aquatic habitat and having webbed hind feet. [Say a POSSUM]

OPP *abbreviation* (in Canada) Ontario Provincial Police.

opp. *abbreviation* opposite.

opponent *noun* a person who opposes or belongs to an opposing side.

opportune *adjective* **1** (of a time) well-chosen or especially favourable or appropriate. **2** (of an action or event) done or occurring at a favourable or useful time. ▶ **opportunely** *adverb* **opportuneness** *noun*

opportunism *noun* **1** the adaptation of policy or judgment to circumstances or opportunity, esp. regardless of principle. **2** the seizing of opportunities when they occur. ▶ **opportunist** *noun* [Say opper TUNE ism]

opportunistic *adjective* **1** of or relating to opportunism. **2** *Ecology* (of a species) able to spread quickly in a previously unoccupied habitat. **3** *Medical* **a** (of a micro-organism) rarely causing disease except in unusual circumstances, e.g. in patients with depressed immune systems. **b** (of an infection) caused by such a micro-organism. ▶ **opportunistically** *adverb* [Say opper too NISS tick or opper tyoo NISS tick]

opportunity *noun* (*plural* **opportunities**) **1** a good chance; a favourable occasion. **2** a chance or opening offered by circumstances. PHRASES **opportunity knocks** an opportunity occurs.

opposable *adjective* **1** able to be opposed. **2** (of the thumb in primates) capable of facing and touching the other digits on the same hand.

oppose *verb* (**opposes, opposed, opposing**) **1** resist; set oneself against; argue against. **2** be hostile (to). **3** take part in a game, sport, etc., against (another competitor or team). **4** (foll. by *to*) place in opposition or contrast: *the dispute that opposed Spain to Canada* ◊ *the film unremittingly opposes Miami Beach to New York City*.

opposed *adjective* **1** anxious to prevent or put an end to; disapproving of or disagreeing with: *was opposed to discrimination*. **2** in conflict or disagreement with: *parties opposed to the government*. **3** (of two or more things) contrasting or conflicting: *diametrically opposed political views*. PHRASES **as opposed to** in contrast with.

opposing *adjective* **1** in conflict or competition with a specified or implied subject: *the opposing team*. **2** (of two or more subjects) differing from or in conflict with each other: *the brothers fought on opposing sides in the war*. **3** facing; opposite: *on the opposing page*.

opposite • *adjective* **1** (often foll. by *to*) having a position on the other or further side, facing or back to back. **2** (often foll. by *to, from*) **a** of a contrary kind; diametrically different. **b** being the other of a contrasted pair. **3** (of angles) between opposite sides of the intersection of two lines. **4** (of leaves etc.) placed at the same height on the opposite sides of the stem, or placed straight in front of another organ. • *noun* an opposite thing or person or term. • *adverb* **1** in an opposite position: *the tree stands opposite*. **2** (of a leading theatrical etc. part) in a complementary role to (another performer). • *preposition* in a position opposite to.

opposite field *noun* *Baseball* the part of the diamond on the opposite side of the plate from the batter, e.g. right field for right-handed hitters.

oppositely *adverb* in an opposite way: *oppositely charged particles*.

opposite number *noun* a person holding an equivalent position in another group or organization.

opposition *noun* **1** resistance, antagonism. **2** the state of being hostile or in conflict or disagreement. **3** contrast. **4** a group or party of opponents or competitors. **5** *Cdn, Brit., Austral. & NZ* **a** (**the Opposition**) the principal parliamentary party

opposed to that in office (*see also* OFFICIAL OPPOSITION). **b** (often **Opposition**) all the members of a parliament who are not of the governing party. **6** the act of opposing or placing opposite. **7 a** diametrically opposite position. **b** *Astrology & Astronomy* the position of two heavenly bodies when their longitude differs by 180°, as seen from the earth. ▶ **oppositional** *adjective*

oppress *verb* (**oppresses**, **oppressed**, **oppressing**) **1** treat someone in a cruel and unfair way, esp. by not giving them the same freedom, rights, etc. as others: *the state functioned to oppress women*. **2** cause someone to feel distressed, anxious, or uncomfortable: *oppressed by worry* ◊ *oppressed by the heat*. ▶ **oppressed** *adjective*

oppression *noun* **1** prolonged cruel or unjust treatment or exercise of control or authority: *a region shattered by oppression and killing*. **2** the state of being subject to such treatment or exercise of authority: *a response to poverty and oppression*. **3** mental pressure or distress: *Beatrice's mood had initially been alarm and a sense of oppression*.

oppressive *adjective* **1** oppressing; harsh or cruel. **2** difficult to endure. **3** (of weather) hot and humid. ▶ **oppressively** *adverb* **oppressiveness** *noun*

oppressor *noun* a person or group of people that treats someone in a cruel and unfair way, esp. by not giving them the same freedom, rights, etc. as other people.

opprobrium *noun* **1** harsh criticism or censure: *wondered why the public feels such opprobrium for the legal profession*. **2** public disgrace arising from some act or conduct: *my views are not sufficient justification for continuing to bring opprobrium upon my colleagues*. [Say a PRO bree um]

opt *verb* exercise an option; make a choice: *opted for the red one* ◊ *opted to go to Bermuda instead*. PHRASES **opt out** (often foll. by *of*) **1** choose not to participate. **2** (in Canada) (of a doctor, health clinic, etc.) operate with private rather than government funding. **opt in** choose to participate.

opted-out *adjective* designating a person or thing that has opted out: *an opted-out clinic*.

optic • *adjective* of or relating to the eye, vision, or light: *optic nerve*. • *noun* a lens etc. in an optical instrument.

optical *adjective* **1** of sight; visual. **2 a** of or concerning sight or light in relation to each other. **b** belonging to optics. **3** (esp. of a lens) constructed to assist sight or on the principles of optics.

optical character recognition *noun* the identification of printed characters using photoelectric devices and computer software.

optical disk *noun see* DISK *noun* 1b.

optical fibre *noun* thin glass fibre through which signals can be transmitted as modulated light.

optical illusion *noun* **1** an experience of seeming to see something which does not exist or is other than it appears to one. **2** something that deceives one's eyes and causes such an experience.

optically *adverb* in terms or by means of optics, light, or eyesight.

optical microscope *noun* a microscope using the direct perception of light (*compare* ELECTRON MICROSCOPE).

optical scanner *noun* a device that performs optical character recognition and produces coded signals corresponding to the characters identified. ▶ **optical scanning** *noun*

optician *noun* a person qualified to make and supply glasses and contact lenses. [Say opp TISH'n]

optic nerve *noun* each of the second pair of cranial nerves, transmitting impulses to the brain from the retina at the back of the eye.

optics *plural noun* **1** (treated as *singular*) the scientific study of sight and the behaviour of light, or of other radiation or particles: *electron optics*. **2** the optical components of an instrument or apparatus.

optimal *adjective* best or most favourable, esp. under a particular set of circumstances: *optimal growing conditions for this kind of plant*. ▶ **optimally** *adverb* [Say OPP tim'll]

optimism *noun* **1** an inclination to hopefulness and confidence; a tendency to take a favourable view of circumstances or prospects. **2** *Philosophy* **a** the doctrine that this world is the best of all possible worlds. **b** the theory that good must ultimately prevail over evil in the universe (*opp.* PESSIMISM 2).

optimist *noun* **1** a person inclined to or professing optimism. **2** (**Optimist**) a member of an international social and charitable association founded in 1911, dedicated esp. to helping children and youth, e.g. by sponsoring sports clubs etc. ▶ **optimistic** *adjective* **optimistically** *adverb*

optimization *noun* **1** the process of making the best or most effective use of a situation, opportunity, or resource. **2** the process of improving something to the utmost.

optimize *verb* (**optimizes**, **optimized**, **optimizing**) **1 a** make the best or most effective use of (a situation, an opportunity, etc.): *an approach that optimizes recycling opportunities*. **b** make optimal; improve to the utmost: *optimize a patient's chance for survival*. **2** make (a computer program) as efficient as possible. ▶ **optimizer** *noun*

optimum • *noun* (*plural* **optima** or **optimums**) the most favourable conditions for growth, reproduction, or success: *27°C is the optimum for banana growing*. • *adjective* = OPTIMAL.

option • *noun* **1** a thing that is or may be chosen. **2** the liberty of choosing; freedom of choice. **3 a** the right, obtained by payment, to buy, sell, etc. specified stocks etc. at a specified price within a set time. **b** the provision in a contract allowing one to extend the terms of the contract for a specified time: *option year*. **4** (also **option play**) *Football* a play in which a player, esp. the quarterback, has the option of throwing the ball or running with it. • *verb* buy or sell under option; have an option on. PHRASES **have no option but to** must. **keep** (or **leave**) **one's options open** not commit oneself. ▶ **optional** *adjective* **optionally** *adverb*

optometrist *noun* a person qualified to prescribe and dispense eyeglasses and contact lenses, and to detect eye diseases. [Say opp TOMMA trist]

optometry *noun* the science or profession of measuring eyesight, detecting eye disease, and prescribing corrective lenses (but not drugs or medicines). [Say opp TOMMA tree]

opt-out *adjective* designating a provision in a contract etc. allowing one to opt out: *opt-out clause*.

opulence *noun* extravagance, wealth, or luxury. [Say OPP yoo lince]

opulent *adjective* **1** made or decorated with expensive materials: *the opulent hotel lobby*. **2** abundant: *opulent dogwoods flourish in the slope by the house* ◊ *an opulent array of fresh fish*. ▶ **opulently** *adverb* [Say OPP yoo l'nt]

opus *noun* (*plural* **opuses** or **opera**) **1** *Music* **a** a separate composition or set of compositions: *notes for an unfinished opus*. **b** used before a number given to a composer's work, usu. indicating the order of publication. Abbreviation: **Op.**: *the Brahms Piano Quintet, opus 34*. **2** any artistic or creative work (*compare* MAGNUM OPUS): *her three-volume, 1,800-page opus is a defence of this*

theory. [Say OH pus for the singular, OH pus is or OPPER uh for the plural]
OR *abbreviation* **1** (**O.R.**) operating room. **2** other ranks.
or *conjunction* **1** used to link alternatives. **2** introducing a synonym or explanation of a preceding word or phrase. **3** otherwise. PHRASES **not A or B** not A, and also not B. **one or two** (or **two or three** etc.) *informal* a few. **or else 1** otherwise: *do it now, or else you will have to do it tomorrow*. **2** *informal* expressing a warning or threat: *hand over the money or else*. **or so** (after a quantity or a number) or thereabouts: *send ten or so*.
-or *suffix* forming nouns denoting a person or thing performing the action of a verb: *actor*.
oracle *noun* **1 a** a place where advice or prophecy was sought from the gods in classical antiquity: *the site of the famous oracle*. **b** the usu. ambiguous or obscure response given at an oracle: *"the human head once struck off does not regrow like the rose" was the oracle he received*. **c** a prophet or prophetess at an oracle: *consulted the oracle of Apollo at Delphi*. **2** a person or thing regarded as an infallible authority on a subject or guide to future action: *casting the Attorney General as the oracle for the public interest is impossible* ◊ *musings of an investment oracle*. [Say ORE a cull]
oracular *adjective* **1** of or concerning an oracle or oracles: *an oracular priestess*. **2** (esp. of advice etc.) mysterious or ambiguous: *she was given to oracular utterances*. **3** prophetic: *"We believe our competitive position will continue to improve," said an oracular CEO*. [Say ore ACK yu lur]

> **SPELL CHECK**
> **oral, aural**
>
> The word pertaining to hearing or the ear is **aural**.

oral • *adjective* **1 a** by word of mouth; spoken; not written: *the oral tradition*. **b** designating a society or culture which has not reached the stage of literacy. **2** done or taken by the mouth: *oral contraceptive*. **3** of the mouth. **4** *Psychology* of or concerning a supposed stage of infant emotional and sexual development, in which the mouth is of central interest. • *noun* (usu. in plural) *informal* a spoken examination, test, etc. ▶ **orally** *adverb*
-orama *combining form* = -RAMA.
orang *noun* = ORANGUTAN. [Say a RANG]
Orange *adjective* **1** of or relating to Orangemen. **2** of or relating to the House of Orange, the Dutch royal house, which was originally a princely dynasty of the principality centred on the town of Orange in the 16th century. In 1689, William of Orange, a Protestant, became King William III of Great Britain and Ireland.
orange • *noun* **1 a** a large round juicy citrus fruit with a bright reddish-yellow tough rind. **b** any of the esp. white-flowered trees or shrubs that bear this fruit. **2 a** fruit or plant resembling this. **3 a** the reddish yellow colour of an orange. **b** orange pigment. • *adjective* **1** orange coloured; reddish yellow. **2** tasting like an orange; orange flavoured.
Orangeman *noun* (plural **Orangemen**) a member of the Orange Order.
Orange Order *noun* (also **Orange Lodge**) a society formed in 1795 to support Protestantism in Ireland, established in Canada in the 19th century, where its anti-Catholic and conservative attitudes had a considerable political and social influence.
orange pekoe *noun* a black tea made from very small leaves.
orange roughy *noun* (plural **orange roughies**) an orange-coloured fish much prized for food.
orangewood *noun* the wood of the orange tree.

orangey *adjective* **1** somewhat orange in colour. **2** having the taste or smell of oranges.
orangutan *noun* a large red long-haired tree-living ape, native to Borneo and Sumatra, with long arms and hooked hands and feet. [Say a RANG oo tan]
oration *noun* **1** a formal speech, discourse, etc., esp. when ceremonial: *florid funeral orations*. **2** a way of speaking; language: *there is nothing like his style of messianic oration*. [Say ore AY sh'n]
orator *noun* **1** a person making a speech. **2** an eloquent public speaker. [Say ORE a tur]
oratorical *adjective* involving the use of exaggerated, eloquent, or highly coloured language: *he spoke with oratorical passion*. [Say ore a TORE a cull]
oratorio *noun* (plural **oratorios**) a semi-dramatic work for orchestra and voices esp. on a sacred theme, performed without costume, scenery, or action, e.g. Handel's *Messiah*. [Say ore a TORY oh]
oratory *noun* (plural **oratories**) **1** the art or practice of formal speaking, esp. in public: *skilled in traditional oratory*. **2** exaggerated, eloquent, or highly coloured language: *earnest citizens under the spell of his patriotic oratory*. **3** a small chapel, esp. for private worship. **4** (**Oratory**) *Catholicism* **a** (also **Institute of the Oratory of St. Philip Neri**) a religious society of priests living in community without vows. **b** a church, branch, or house of this society. [Say ORE a tory]
orb *noun* **1** a globe surmounted by a cross esp. carried by a sovereign at a coronation. **2** a sphere; a globe: *the tomato plants died before ripening one red orb*. **3** *literary* a heavenly body, esp. the sun or moon.
orbit • *noun* **1 a** the regularly repeated elliptical course of a celestial object, spacecraft, etc. about a star or a planet. **b** (preceded by *in*, *into*, *out of*, etc.) the state of motion in an orbit. **c** one complete passage around an orbited body. **2** the path of an electron around an atomic nucleus. **3** a range or sphere of action or influence: *audiences drawn from outside the Party orbit*. **4 a** the eye socket. **b** the area around the eye of a bird or insect. • *verb* (**orbits**, **orbited**, **orbiting**) **1 a** (of a satellite etc.) go around in orbit. **b** fly in a circle. **2** move in orbit around. **3** put into orbit. PHRASES **into orbit** into a state of heightened performance, frenzy, etc.: *sales went into orbit*. ▶ **orbital** *adjective*
orbital sander *noun* a sander having a circular motion.
orbiter *noun* a spacecraft designed to remain in orbit without landing.
orca *noun* (plural **orcas**) the killer whale.
orchard *noun* a piece of enclosed land with fruit trees. ▶ **orchardist** *noun*
orchestra *noun* **1 a** usu. large group of instrumentalists, esp. combining strings, woodwinds, brass, and percussion: *symphony orchestra*. **2 a** (also **orchestra pit**) the part of a theatre, opera house, etc., where the orchestra plays, usu. in front of the stage and on a lower level. **b** the seats on the ground floor in a theatre: *bought a ticket in the front orchestra*. ▶ **orchestral** *adjective* [Say ORE kiss truh, ore KESS trull]
orchestrate *verb* (**orchestrates**, **orchestrated**, **orchestrating**) **1** arrange, score, or compose (music) for orchestral performance. **2** combine, arrange, or build up (elements of a situation etc.) for maximum effect. ▶ **orchestration** *noun* **orchestrator** *noun* [Say ORE kess trate]
orchid *noun* **1** a plant that bears flowers in fantastic shapes and brilliant colours, usu. having one petal larger than the others. **2** a flower of this plant. [Say ORE kid]
ordain *verb* **1** bestow the office of minister, priest, or deacon on (a person). **2** (in the Presbyterian church)

bestow the office of elder on (a person). **3 a** order or decree something officially: *custom ordained that the empress should be brought in first*. **b** (of God, fate, etc.) prescribe, determine: *could not change what nature had ordained*.

ordeal *noun* a painful or trying experience.

order • *noun* **1** the arrangement of people or things according to a particular sequence or method. **2** a state in which everything is in its correct place. **3** a state in which the laws and rules regulating public behaviour are observed. **4** an authoritative command or direction. **5** a request for something to be made, supplied, or served. **6** the prescribed procedure followed in a meeting, law court, or religious service. **7** quality or nature: *poetry of the highest order*. **8** a social class or system. **9** a rank in the Christian ministry. **10** (**orders** or **holy orders**) the rank of an ordained minister of the Christian Church. **11** a society of monks, nuns, or friars living under the same rule. **12** (esp. **Order**) a company of distinguished people to which appointments are made as an honour or reward: *Order of Canada*. **13** *Biology* a principal taxonomic category that ranks below class and above family. **14** any of the five classical styles of architecture (Doric, Ionic, Corinthian, Tuscan, and Composite). • *verb* **1** give an order. **2** request that (something) be made, supplied, or served. **3** arrange methodically. PHRASES **by order** according to the proper authority. **in bad** (or **good** etc.) **order** not working (or working properly etc.). **in order 1** one after another according to some principle. **2** ready or fit for use. **3** according to the rules (of procedure at a meeting etc.). **in order that** with the intention; so that. **in order to** with the purpose of doing; with a view to. **keep order** enforce orderly behaviour. **made to order 1** made according to individual requirements, measurements, etc. (opp. READY-MADE 1). **2** exactly what is wanted. **of** (or **in** or **on**) **the order of 1** approximately. **2** having the order of magnitude specified by: *of the order of one in a million*. **on order** (of goods etc.) ordered but not yet received. **order about 1** dominate; command officiously. **2** send hither and thither. **Order! Order!** a call for silence or calm, esp. by the Speaker of a legislative assembly. **order out** (or **in**) order food to be delivered to one's home etc. **out of order 1** not working properly. **2** not in the correct sequence. **3** not according to the rules (of a meeting, organization, etc.). **4** *informal* **a** not behaving in an acceptable fashion. **b** (of behaviour) not acceptable. **take orders 1** accept commissions. **2** accept and carry out commands. **3** (also **take holy orders**) be ordained.

order book *noun* **1** a listing or record of orders for a product etc. **2** the level of incoming orders: *a total order book of about 500 planes*.

order form *noun* a printed form on which customers enter details concerning their orders.

Order-in-Council *noun* (*plural* **Orders-in-Council**) *Cdn & Brit.* an administrative order determined by the cabinet and formally issued by the sovereign or the sovereign's representative, usu. to deal with routine matters or to establish detailed regulations concerning acts passed by Parliament.

orderliness *noun* a neat appearance or methodical arrangement.

orderly • *adjective* **1** methodically arranged; regular. **2** obedient to discipline; well-behaved; not unruly. • *noun* (*plural* **orderlies**) **1** an attendant in a hospital responsible for the non-medical care of patients and the maintenance of order and cleanliness. **2** a soldier who carries orders for an officer etc.

order of business *noun* a subject or task requiring attention, esp. in a series: *the first order of business when we arrived at the studio was to talk to the cast*.

Order of Canada *noun* an order of merit established in 1967 to honour Canadians for exemplary achievement, awarded in three ranks.

order of magnitude *noun* a class in a system of classification determined by size, usu. by powers of 10.

Order of Military Merit *noun* an order of merit established in 1972 to honour members of the Canadian Forces in recognition of special achievement, awarded in three grades.

order of the day *noun* **1** the prevailing state of affairs: *confusion would seem to be the order of the day*. **2** a program, agenda, or procedure: *before working out, warm-ups should be the order of the day*. **3** what is called for by necessity, fashion, etc.: *on Sundays, a black suit was the order of the day*.

Order Paper *noun* esp. *Parliament* an agenda, esp. a daily list of topics etc. to be discussed or voted on in a legislature. PHRASES **die on the Order Paper** *Cdn* (of a bill) fail to be voted on before the end of a legislative session.

ordinal • *noun* (also **ordinal number**) a number defining a thing's position in a series, e.g. "first", "second", "third", etc. (*compare* CARDINAL NUMBER). • *adjective* **1 a** of or relating to an ordinal number. **b** defining a thing's position in a series etc. **2** *Biology* of or concerning an order.

ordinance *noun* **1** an authoritative order; a decree. **2** an enactment by a local authority. [Say ORE din ince]

ordinarily *adverb* used to say what normally happens in a particular situation, esp. because something different is happening this time: *ordinarily I don't pay by cheque* ◊ *we're ordinarily quite busy*.

ordinariness *noun* the quality of something that is normal, with no special or distinctive features.

ordinary *adjective* **1** regular, normal, customary, usual: *in the ordinary course of events*. **2** boring; commonplace: *an ordinary little man*. PHRASES **out of the ordinary** unusual.

ordinary seaman *noun* a sailor of the lowest rank, that below able seaman. Abbreviation: **OS**.

ordinate *noun* *Math* **1** a straight line from any point drawn parallel to one coordinate axis and meeting the other, usually a coordinate measured parallel to the vertical. **2** the distance of a point from the horizontal axis measured parallel to the vertical axis.

ordination *noun* the act of ordaining or conferring holy orders on a priest, minister, etc.

ordnance *noun* **1** mounted guns; cannon. **2** a branch of government service or the military dealing esp. with military stores and materials. [Say ORD nince]

Ordovician *Geology* • *adjective* of or relating to the second period of the Paleozoic era, lasting from about 505 to 438 million years ago, between the Cambrian and Silurian periods, marked by the diversification of many groups of invertebrates and the appearance of the first vertebrates (jawless fish). • *noun* this geological period or system. [Say orda VISH'n]

ordure *noun* excrement; dung. [Say ORE dyoor]

Ore. *abbreviation* Oregon.

SPELL CHECK
ore, oar

A boat is propelled with **oars**.

---

ore *noun* a naturally occurring solid material from which metal or other valuable minerals may be extracted.

ore body *noun* a large mass of mineral-bearing rock etc.

oregano *noun* **1** the dried leaves of wild marjoram used as a herb in cooking (*compare* MARJORAM). **2** the aromatic, purple-flowered plant producing these leaves. [Say a REGGA no]

org *noun* organization.

organ *noun* **1 a** a usu. large musical instrument having pipes supplied with air from bellows, sounded by keys, and distributed into sets or stops which form partial organs, each with a separate keyboard. **b** a smaller instrument without pipes, producing similar sounds electronically. **c** a smaller keyboard wind instrument with metal reeds; a harmonium. **d** = BARREL ORGAN. **2 a** a usu. self-contained part of an organism having a special vital function: *digestive organs*. **b** esp. *jocular* the penis. **3** a medium of communication, esp. a newspaper or periodical that represents the views of a political party or movement. **4** a department or organization that performs a specified function: *actions may be brought only by an organ of government on behalf of the public*.

organdy *noun* (*plural* **organdies**) a fine translucent cotton muslin, usu. stiffened. [Say ORGAN dee]

organelle *noun* any of various organized or specialized structures which form part of a cell. [Say orga NELL]

organ grinder *noun* the player of a barrel organ.

organic • *adjective* **1** of or relating to plants or animals. **2** a *Physiology* of or relating to a bodily organ or organs. **b** *Medical* (of a disease) affecting the structure of an organ. **3** (of a plant or animal) having organs or an organized physical structure. **4** produced or involving production without the use of chemical fertilizers, pesticides, etc.: *organic farming*. **5** (of a compound etc.) containing carbon (*opp.* INORGANIC). **6** denoting a relation between elements of something such that they fit together harmoniously as necessary parts of a whole: *theory and practice in organic unity* ◊ insists that the independent republics constitute an organic whole. **7** characterized by or designating continuous or natural development: *the company expanded through organic growth rather than acquisitions*. • *noun* (esp. in plural) an organic substance, esp. a fertilizer, pesticide, etc. ▶ **organically** *adverb*

organism *noun* **1** a living individual consisting of a single cell or of a group of interdependent parts sharing the life processes; an individual plant or animal. **2** a whole with interdependent parts compared to a living being.

organist *noun* the player of an organ.

organization *noun* **1** the action of organizing something: *the organization of conferences and seminars*. **2** the structure or arrangement of related or connected items: *the spatial organization of the cells*. **3** an efficient and orderly approach to tasks: *his lack of organization*. **4** an organized body, esp. a business, government department, charity, etc.: *a research organization*. ▶ **organizational** *adjective* **organizationally** *adverb*

organize *verb* (**organizes, organized, organizing**) **1 a** give an orderly structure to, systematize. **b** bring the affairs of (another person or oneself) into order; make arrangements for (a person). **2 a** arrange for or initiate (a scheme etc.). **b** provide; take responsibility for: *organized some sandwiches*. **3** enrol new members in a trade union, political party, etc. **4** form different elements into an organic whole.

organized crime *noun* widespread criminal activity organized under powerful leadership.

organizer *noun* **1** a person who organizes an event, the creation of a trade union, a political party, etc. **2** a thing used for organizing objects, such as a handbag or

folder with many compartments. **3** a hand-held electronic device serving as a diary, address book, etc.

organ loft *noun* a gallery in a church etc. for an organ.

organ stop *noun* **1** a set of pipes of a similar tone in an organ. **2** the handle of the mechanism that brings it into action.

organza *noun* (*plural* **organzas**) a thin stiff transparent silk or synthetic dress fabric. [Say ore GAN zuh]

orgasm *noun* a sexual climax characterized by feelings of pleasure centred in the genitals and (in men) experienced as an accompaniment to ejaculation. ▶ **orgasmic** *adjective*

orgy *noun* (*plural* **orgies**) **1** a wild party, esp. one with excessive drinking and sex. **2** excessive indulgence in an activity: *a brief orgy of spending*. [Say ORE jee]

orient • *noun* (**the Orient**) **1** the Far East. **2** (formerly) the Middle East. • *verb* **1 a** establish one's position in relation to one's surroundings, the points of the compass, etc.: *tried to orient themselves by the stars*. **b** bring (oneself, different elements, etc.) into a clearly understood position or relationship, esp. to known facts or principles: *it took him some time to orient himself in his new school*. **c** place, align, or determine exactly the position of (a structure etc.), esp. with the aid of a compass; find the bearings of. **2** direct (a person) toward a particular interest, action, career, etc. **3** direct or aim (something) at: *programs oriented toward the immigrant community*.

oriental • *adjective* **1** (often **Oriental**) of, relating to, or characteristic of East Asia, or Asiatic countries generally. **2** (often **Oriental**) of or characteristic of Eastern civilizations etc. generally. **3** (often **Oriental**) designating a person of East Asian origin. • *noun* (esp. **Oriental**) *offensive* a person of East Asian origin.

orientalism *noun* **1** (often **Orientalism**) **a** the representation or concept of the Orient, esp. the Middle East, in Western academic writing, art, or literature. **b** this representation perceived as romanticized, idealized, or stereotyped, esp. as embodying a colonial attitude. **2** the study or knowledge of Oriental languages, literatures, etc. ▶ **orientalist** *noun*

oriental rug *noun* (also **oriental carpet**) a rug or carpet hand-knotted in or as in the Orient.

orientate *verb* (**orientates, orientated, orientating**) = ORIENT *verb*.

orientation *noun* **1 a** a person's esp. political or psychological attitude or adjustment in relation to circumstances, ideas, etc. **b** = SEXUAL ORIENTATION. **2** an introduction to a subject or situation; a briefing. **3** the position of a building, object, etc. relative to specific defined data, the points of the compass, etc. **4** the faculty by which birds etc. find their way home from a distance.

oriented *adjective* **1** (with preceding noun or adverb) having a specified emphasis, bias, or interest: *job-oriented*. **2** having a particular orientation.

orienteer • *noun* a competitor in the sport of orienteering. • *verb* participate in the sport of orienteering.

orienteering *noun* a competitive sport in which participants have to find their way on foot, skis, etc. across rough country with the aid of map and compass.

orifice *noun* a usu. small opening, esp. the mouth of a bodily organ or other cavity, e.g. a nostril. [Say ORE a fiss]

origami *noun* the Japanese art of folding paper into decorative shapes and figures. [Say ore a GAMMY]

origin *noun* **1 a** a beginning, cause, or ultimate source of something. **b** that from which a thing is derived; a source or starting point: *a word of Latin origin*. **2** (often

in *plural*) a person's social background, family, etc.: *middle-class origins*.

original • *adjective* **1** existing from the beginning or earliest stages. **2** inventive: *has an original mind*. **3 a** that is the origin or source of something. **b** (of a picture, text, etc.) from which another is copied, translated, etc.: *in the original Greek* ◊ *an original Rembrandt*. **c** not derivative or imitative, esp. made, composed, etc. by a person himself or herself: *an original poem*. • *noun* **1 a** an original model, pattern, picture, etc. from which another is copied or translated. **b** a person represented in a picture or upon whom a literary character is based. **2** an unusual or eccentric person. **3 a** a garment specially designed for a fashion collection. **b** a copy of such a garment made to order.

originality *noun* **1** the quality or fact of being original, esp. the power of creating or thinking creatively. **2** newness or freshness, esp. of literary or artistic style.

originally *adverb* in or from the beginning; at first: *the house was originally blue*.

original sin *noun* *Christianity* the innate tendency to evil of all humans, traditionally held to be inherited from generation to generation since Adam and Eve's first sin in the Garden of Eden.

originate *verb* (**originates**, **originated**, **originating**) **1** (usu. foll. by *from, in, with*) begin, arise, be derived, take its origin. **2** cause to begin; initiate. **3** (of an aircraft, bus, etc.) begin a scheduled trip at a particular place. ▶ **origination** *noun* **originator** *noun*

oriole *noun* **1** a bird of the American blackbird family, with black and orange or yellowish-orange feathers. **2** an Old World bird related to the starling, often having brightly coloured plumage. [Say ORE ee ul or ORE ee ole]

ormolu *noun* gilded bronze; a gold-coloured alloy of copper, zinc, and tin used to decorate furniture, make ornaments, etc. [Say ORMA loo]

ornament • *noun* **1 a** a thing used or serving to adorn, esp. a small trinket, vase, figure, etc.: *a mantelpiece crowded with ornaments* ◊ *her only ornament was a brooch*. **b** a person who adds honour or distinction to his or her sphere, time, etc.: *an ornament to her profession*. **2** decoration added to embellish esp. a building. • *verb* adorn, beautify, provide with ornaments.

ornamental • *adjective* serving as an ornament; decorative. • *noun* a thing considered to be ornamental rather than essential, esp. a cultivated plant.

ornamentation *noun* things added to something to provide decoration: *a plain brick house without ornamentation* ◊ *instrumental ornamentation*.

ornate *adjective* highly decorated: *Victorian buildings clustered around an ornate church*. ▶ **ornately** *adverb* **ornateness** *noun* [Say ore NATE]

ornery *adjective* *informal* **1** grumpily stubborn. **2** crotchety, cantankerous. [Say ORNER ee]

ornithological *adjective* having to do with the scientific study of birds. [Say ore nitha LOGICAL]

ornithologist *noun* a person who studies birds. [Say ore nith OLLA jist]

ornithology *noun* the study of birds. [Say ore nith OLLA jee]

orographic *adjective* **1** having to do with mountains, esp. with regards to their features and formation. **2** (of clouds or rainfall) resulting from moist air being forced upwards by mountains. [Say or a GRAPHIC]

orphan • *noun* **1 a** a child or young animal deprived by death of one or usu. both parents. **b** a child bereft of parental care, esp. through abandonment or neglect. **2** the first line of a paragraph at the foot of a page or

column (*compare* WIDOW *noun* 3). • *verb* bereave (a child etc.) of its parents or a parent.

orphanage *noun* a usu. residential institution for the care and education of orphans.

orphaned *adjective* (of a child) deprived by death of one or usu. both parents.

ortho- *combining form* **1** straight, rectangular, upright. **2** normal, proper, correct.

orthodontic *adjective* having to do with the treatment of crooked alignment of the teeth and jaws. [Say ortha DON tick]

orthodontics *noun* the branch of dentistry that deals with treatment of crooked teeth and misaligned jaws. ▶ **orthodontist** *noun* [Say ortha DON ticks, ortha DON tist]

orthodox *adjective* **1** (of people, views, beliefs, or practices) conforming to what is generally or traditionally accepted as right or true: *orthodox economics* ◊ *orthodox medical treatment* ◊ *orthodox Marxism*. **2** (of a person) conventional, not independent-minded: *a relatively orthodox artist*. **3** (usu. **Orthodox**) (of Judaism or Jews) adhering strictly to the rabbinical interpretation of Jewish law and its traditional observances. **4** (**Orthodox**) of or relating to the Orthodox Church. [Say ORTHA docks]

Orthodox Church *noun* the family of Eastern Churches, having the Patriarch of Constantinople as its head, and including the national Churches of Russia, Romania, Greece, etc.

orthodoxy *noun* (*plural* **orthodoxies**) **1 a** the quality or character of being orthodox. **b** belief in or agreement with what is, or is currently held to be, right, esp. in religious matters. **c** the body of orthodox doctrine. **2** an authorized or generally accepted theory, doctrine, etc.: *the uninitiated who do not live up to prevailing political orthodoxies*. **3** (also **Orthodoxy**) **a** the Orthodox practice of Judaism. **b** the body of Orthodox Jews. **4 a** the Orthodox Church or Churches. **b** the body of Orthodox Christians. [Say ORTHA docksy]

orthogonal *adjective* of, involving, or at right angles; rectangular. [Say orth OGGA n'l]

orthographic *adjective* having to do with spelling. ▶ **orthographical** *adjective* [Say ortha GRAPHIC]

orthography *noun* (*plural* **orthographies**) **1** correct or conventional spelling. **2** spelling with reference to its correctness: *dreadful orthography*. [Say orth OGGRA fee]

orthopaedic *adjective* (also **orthopedic**) **1** pertaining to or concerned with orthopaedics. **2 a** (of a bed etc.) designed to relieve back problems, usu. having a very firm mattress or board. **b** (of footwear etc.) designed to ease or correct deformities of the feet. [Say ortha PEED ick]

orthopaedics *noun* (also **orthopedics**) the branch of medicine dealing with the correction of deformities of bones or muscles or the treatment of impairments of the skeletal system. ▶ **orthopaedist** (also **orthopedist**) *noun* [Say ortha PEED icks, ortha PEED ist]

orthotic *noun* (usu. in *plural*) **1** a moulded insert for a shoe etc. designed to improve posture and gait. **2** an artificial external device, as a brace or splint, serving to prevent or assist relative movement of the limbs. [Say orth OTT ick]

Orwellian *adjective* of or characteristic of the writings of George Orwell (1903–50), esp. with reference to the totalitarian development of the state as depicted in *Nineteen Eighty-four* and *Animal Farm*: *in true Orwellian tradition, because the four-storey complex of cells and torture chambers had no name, it did not exist*. [Say ore WELLY un]

oryx *noun* (*plural* **oryx** or **oryxes**) a large straight-horned antelope native to Africa and Arabia. [Say ORE icks]

orzo *noun* a variety of pasta shaped like grains of rice or barley.

OS *abbreviation* **1** *Computing* operating system. **2** old style. **3** ORDINARY SEAMAN. **4** outsize. **5** out of stock.

Os *symbol* osmium.

Oscar *noun* any of the statuettes awarded annually by the US Academy of Motion Picture Arts and Sciences for excellence in film acting, directing, etc.

oscillate *verb* (**oscillates, oscillated, oscillating**) **1** move to and fro between points: *in the stifling heat each periodic sweep of the oscillating fan was a cool caress.* **2** vacillate; vary between extremes of opinion, action, etc.: *the populace oscillated between security and reassurance on the one hand, and threat and menace on the other.* **3** *Physics* move with periodic regularity. **4** *Electricity* (of a current) undergo high-frequency alternations. ▶ **oscillating** *adjective* **oscillation** *noun* **oscillator** *noun* [Say OSSA late]

oscilloscope *noun* a device for viewing oscillations by a display on the screen of a cathode ray tube. [Say aw SILLA scope]

osier *noun* any of various willows with long flexible shoots used in basketwork. [Say OZE ee er]

osmium *noun* a hard bluish-white element, the heaviest known metal, occurring naturally in association with platinum and used in certain alloys. [Say OZ mee um]

osmosis *noun* **1** the passage of a solvent through a semi-permeable partition into a more concentrated solution, so as to make the concentration on the two sides more nearly equal. **2** gradual, usu. unconscious assimilation or absorption of ideas, knowledge, etc.: *she learned Dutch through osmosis while living in Holland.* ▶ **osmotic** *adjective* [Say oz MOE sis, oz MOT ick]

osprey *noun* (*plural* **ospreys**) a large bird of prey with a brown back and white markings, feeding on fish, which it catches in its claws after making a spectacular dive from the air. [Say OSS pray or OSS pree]

Ossie *noun* & *adjective* = AUSSIE.

ossification *noun* the process of turning into bone or bony tissue. [Say ossa fuh KAY sh'n]

ossify *verb* (**ossifies, ossified, ossifying**) **1** turn into bone or bony tissue; harden. **2** make or become rigid, fixed, or unprogressive in attitude: *an ossified, bureaucratized system.* [Say OSSA fie]

osso bucco *noun* (also **osso buco**) an Italian dish of veal shanks containing marrow bone stewed in wine with vegetables. [Say oh so BOOK oh]

ostensible *adjective* stated or appearing to be true, but not necessarily so: *the real dispute which lay behind the ostensible complaint.* ▶ **ostensibly** *adverb* [Say oss TEN sib ul]

ostentation *noun* an exaggerated display of wealth, knowledge or skill that is made in order to impress people: *the house was spacious but without any trace of ostentation.* [Say oss ten TAY sh'n]

ostentatious *adjective* characterized by a vulgar or pretentious display, esp. of wealth, designed to impress people and attract notice: *ostentatious gold jewellery* ◊ *we watched them make a noisy and ostentatious entrance.* ▶ **ostentatiously** *adverb* [Say oss ten TAY shuss]

osteo- *combining form* bone.

osteoarthritis *noun* a degenerative disease of joint cartilage causing pain and stiffness esp. in those middle-aged and older. [Say OSS tee oh ARTHRITIS]

osteology *noun* the study of the structure and function of the skeleton. [Say oss tee OLLA jee]

osteopath *noun* a person who treats medical disorders through the manipulation and massage of the skeleton and musculature. ▶ **osteopathic** *adjective* [Say OSS tee a path, oss tee a PATH ick]

osteopathy *noun* a system of complementary medicine involving the treatment of medical disorders through the manipulation and massage of the skeleton and musculature. [Say oss tee OPPA thee]

osteoporosis *noun* a condition of fragile, porous bones caused by loss of the protein and mineral content of bone tissue, esp. as a result of hormonal changes, or deficiency of calcium or vitamin D. [Say OSS tee oh puh ROE sis]

ostracism *noun* the action of deliberately excluding someone from a society or group; the state of not being included: *the consequences of revealing his co-workers' corruption were harassment and ostracism.* [Say OSTRA sism]

ostracize *verb* (**ostracizes, ostracized, ostracizing**) exclude (a person) from a society, favour, privileges, etc. by common consent; refuse to associate with: *in those days, even in the universities, socialists were often ostracized.* [Say OSTRA size]

ostrich *noun* (*plural* **ostriches**) a large African swift-running flightless bird, with two toes on each foot and long legs.

OT *abbreviation* **1 a** overtime. **b** *Football* offensive tackle. **2 a** occupational therapy. **b** occupational therapist. **3** Old Testament.

OTC *abbreviation* = OVER-THE-COUNTER.

other *adjective* & *pronoun* **1** used to refer to a person or thing that is different from one already mentioned or known. **2** additional. **3** alternative of two. **4** those not already mentioned. **5** (usu. **the Other**) *Philosophy* & *Sociology* that which is distinct from, different from, or opposite to something or oneself. **PHRASES** **the other day** (or **night** or **week** etc.) a few days etc. ago: *heard from him the other day.* **other things being equal** if conditions are or were alike in all but the point in question. **someone** (or **something** or **somehow** etc.) **or other** some unspecified person, thing, manner, etc.

other half *noun* **1** *jocular* one's wife or husband. **2** *informal* (**the other half**) a group of people having different, esp. markedly superior or inferior, social, cultural, or economic standing: *how the other half lives.* **3** the rest, the remainder, or esp. the second of two equal parts.

otherness *noun* **1** the state or fact of being other or different. **2** a thing or existence separate from or other than the thing mentioned and the thinking subject.

other ranks *plural noun* *Cdn, Brit., Austral., & NZ* non-commissioned officers and ordinary soldiers, sailors, etc.

otherwise *adverb* **1** or else. **2** in other respects. **3** in another way, differently. **4** as an alternative: *otherwise known as Josh.* **PHRASES** **and** (or **or**) **otherwise** the negation or opposite (of a specified thing): *experiences pleasant and otherwise.*

other world *noun* **1** a supposed life after death: *the god who escorts the dead to the other world.* **2** (also **otherworld**) **a** an alternate reality or state of consciousness: *the plant was frequently consumed by shamans to journey to the other world.* **b** (esp. in science fiction etc.) a world or culture in fantasy or outer space: *the temple was invisible to the men, lying in some strange otherworld.*

otherworldliness *noun* a concern with spiritual thoughts and ideas rather than with ordinary life.

otherworldly *adjective* **1** concerned with spiritual matters, life after death, etc. **2** of or pertaining to an

imaginary, ideal, or fantastic world. **3** unworldly; impractical.

Ottawa *noun & adjective* (plural **Ottawa** or **Ottawas**) = ODAWA.

Ottawan • *noun* a native or inhabitant of Ottawa. • *adjective* of or relating to the city of Ottawa.

otter *noun* **1 a** a semiaquatic fish-eating mammal with strong claws and webbed feet, noted for its agile swimming. **b** its fur or pelt. **2** = SEA OTTER.

Ottoman • *adjective* hist. **1** of or concerning the dynasty of Osman or Othman I (late 13th century), the branch of the Turks to which he belonged, or the empire ruled by his descendants. **2** Turkish. • *noun* an Ottoman person; a Turk. [Say OTTA m'n]

ottoman *noun* **1** an upholstered seat, usu. square and without a back or arms, sometimes a box with a padded top. **2** a footstool of similar design. [Say OTTA m'n]

ouananiche *noun* (plural **ouananiche**) *Cdn* a landlocked lake variety of Atlantic salmon, found in Newfoundland and Labrador, Quebec, and Ontario. [Say WANNA nish]

ouch *interjection* expressing pain or annoyance.

ought *auxiliary verb* **1** expressing duty or rightness. **2** expressing shortcoming. **3** expressing advisability or prudence. **4** expressing esp. strong probability

oughtn't *contraction* ought not.

Ouija *noun* (also **Ouija board**) *proprietary* a board having letters or signs at its rim to which a pointer under supposedly spiritualistic influence points in answer to questions from attenders at a seance etc. [Say WEE jee or WEE juh]

ounce¹ *noun* **1 a** a unit of weight of one-sixteenth of a pound avoirdupois (approx. 28 grams). Abbreviation: **oz. b** a unit of one-twelfth of a pound troy or apothecaries' measure, equal to 480 grains (approx. 31 grams). **2** = FLUID OUNCE. **3** a small quantity.

ounce² *noun* = SNOW LEOPARD.

ouncer *noun* (in combination) a thing that weighs or consists of a specified number of ounces: a forty-ouncer of rye.

our *possessive adjective* **1** of or belonging to us or ourselves. **2** (esp. as **Our**) of Us the king or queen, emperor or empress, etc.: given under Our seal. **3** of us, the editorial staff of a newspaper etc.: a foolish adventure in our view.

Our Father *noun* Christianity **1** the prayer taught by Christ to his disciples, beginning with the words "Our Father". **2** God.

Our Lady *noun* Christianity **1** the Virgin Mary. **2** an image or representation of the Virgin Mary.

Our Lord *noun* **1** Christianity Jesus Christ. **2** God.

ours *possessive pronoun* the one or ones belonging to or associated with us: it is ours ◊ ours are over there. PHRASES **of ours** of or belonging to us: a friend of ours.

ourself *pronoun* **1** archaic a word formerly used instead of myself by a sovereign, newspaper editorial staff, etc. (compare OUR 2, 3). **2** disputed= OURSELVES.

ourselves *pronoun* **1 a** emphatic form of WE or US: we ourselves did it ◊ made it ourselves. **b** reflexive form of US: are pleased with ourselves. **2** in our normal state of body or mind: not quite ourselves today. PHRASES **be ourselves** act in our normal unconstrained manner.

oust *verb* remove (a person) from a job or position of power, esp. by forcing oneself in: the reformists were ousted from power. ▶ **ousted** *adjective*

ouster *noun* a removal (of a person), esp. from a position of power, as a result of political manoeuvring or upheaval: a showdown which led to his ouster as the head of the film festival ◊ blamed his ouster from the board of directors on a former vice-president's resentment.

out • *adverb* **1 a** a moving away from a place, esp. from one that is open. **b** Cdn (North) in or to the more southern or heavily populated part of the country. **2** away from one's usual base or residence. **3** outdoors. **4** so as to be revealed, heard, or known. **5** at or to an end: the romance fizzled out. **6** at a specified distance from the target. **7** to sea, away from the land. **8** (of the tide) falling or at its lowest level. **9** no longer in prison. • *preposition* out of. • *noun* **1** informal a way of escape; an excuse. **2** Baseball the action or an act of putting a player out. • *adjective* **1** not at home or one's place of work. **2** in existence, use, or the public domain. **3** open about one's homosexuality. **4** not possible or worth considering. **5** no longer existing, current, or prevalent. **6** unconscious. **7** mistaken. **8** (of the ball in tennis, squash, etc.) outside the playing area. **9** Baseball no longer batting or on base. • *interjection* a peremptory dismissal, reproach, etc. • *verb* informal reveal the homosexuality of. PHRASES **on the outs** at variance or enmity. **out and about** (of a person, esp. after an illness) engaging in normal activity. **out for** having one's interest or effort directed to; intent on. **out of 1** from within. **2** not within. **3** from among. **4** beyond the range of. **5** without or so as to be without. **6** from. **7** owing to; because of. **8** by the use of (material). **9** at a specified distance from (a town, port, etc.). **10** beyond. **11** as depicted in (a fictional work). **out of it** informal **1** dazed, dopey. **2** out of touch; not up to date. **out to** keenly striving to do. **out with** an exhortation to expel or dismiss (an unwanted person). **out with it** say what you are thinking.

out- *prefix* added to verbs and nouns, meaning: **1** so as to surpass or exceed: outnumber. **2** external, separate: outline. **3** out of; away from; outward: outgrowth.

outage *noun* an interruption in supply, esp. of electricity.

out-and-out • *adjective* in every respect; complete: an out-and-out crook. • *adverb* completely; totally.

outback *noun* esp. Austral. the remote and usu. uninhabited inland districts. ▶ **outbacker** *noun*

out basket *noun* a tray or basket, esp. on a person's desk, for outgoing documents etc.

outbid *verb* (**outbids, outbid, outbidding**) bid higher than (another person) at an auction etc.

outboard • *adjective* **1** (of a motor) portable and attachable to the outside of the stern of a boat. **2** (of a boat) having an outboard motor. **3** located on, near, or towards the outside of an aircraft, ship, etc. • *adverb* on, towards, or near the outside of a ship, aircraft, etc.

• *noun* **1** an outboard engine. **2** a boat with an outboard engine.

outbound *adjective* outward bound.

outbreak *noun* a usu. sudden eruption of emotion, war, disease, rebellion, etc.

outbuilding *noun* a detached building, e.g. a shed, barn, garage, etc., that is separate from but within the grounds of a main building.

outburst *noun* **1** an explosion of anger etc., expressed in words. **2** a sudden burst of activity etc.

outcast • *noun* **1** a person cast out from or rejected by his or her home, country, society, etc. **2** a tramp or vagabond. • *adjective* rejected; homeless; friendless.

outclass *verb* (**outclasses**, **outclassed**, **outclassing**) **1** belong to a higher class than. **2** defeat easily. **3** be superior to.

outcome *noun* a result; a visible effect.

outcrop • *noun* (also **outcropping**) **1** the emergence of a stratum, vein, or rock, at the surface. **2** a stratum etc. emerging. • *verb* (**outcrops**, **outcropped**, **outcropping**) appear as an outcrop; crop out.

outcry *noun* (*plural* **outcries**) a strong expression of public disapproval or anger: *the public outcry over the bombing*.

outdated *adjective* out of date; obsolete.

outdistance *verb* (**outdistances**, **outdistanced**, **outdistancing**) **1** leave (a competitor) behind completely. **2** be vastly superior to.

outdo *verb* (**outdoes**; *past* **outdid**; *past participle* **outdone**; **outdoing**) exceed or surpass in doing or performance.

outdoor *adjective* **1** done, existing, or used out of doors. **2** fond of the open air: *an outdoor type*.

outdoors • *adverb* in or into the open air; out of doors. • *adjective* = OUTDOOR adjective 2. • *noun* the world outside buildings; the open air.

outdoorsman *noun* (*plural* **outdoorsmen**) a person who enjoys or frequently participates in outdoor activities, esp. in the wilderness.

outdoorswoman *noun* (*plural* **outdoorswomen**) a woman who enjoys or frequently participates in outdoor activities, esp. in the wilderness.

outdoorsy *adjective* **1** associated with or characteristic of the outdoors. **2** (of a person) fond of an outdoor life or outdoor activities, esp. in the wilderness.

outer *adjective* **1** external: *pierced the outer layer*. **2** farther from the centre or inside; relatively far out.

outermost *adjective* furthest from the inside; the most far out.

outer space *noun* the universe beyond the earth's atmosphere.

outerwear *noun* clothing, such as a coat, that is worn over other clothing to provide warmth or protection while outdoors.

outfall *noun* the outlet of a river, drain, sewer, etc.

outfield *noun* **1** the part of a baseball field that lies outside of the baseline. **2** the positions in this space, i.e. right, left, and centre field. **3** the players who occupy these positions. ▶ **outfielder** *noun*

outfit • *noun* **1** a set of clothes worn or esp. designed to be worn together. **2** a complete set of equipment etc. for a specific purpose. **3** a business or company engaged in a particular type of work: *a construction outfit*. **4** a military unit. **5** a group of musicians: *a jazz outfit*. • *verb* (**outfits**, **outfitted**, **outfitting**) provide with an outfit, e.g. of clothes or equipment.

outfitter *noun* **1** a supplier of equipment for outdoor activities such as hiking trips etc. **2** a person who acts as guide on wilderness trips etc.

outflank *verb* **1 a** extend one's flank beyond that of (an enemy). **b** outmanoeuvre (an enemy) in this way. **2** get the better of (an opponent).

outflow *noun* **1** an outward flow. **2** the amount that flows out.

outfox *verb* (**outfoxes**, **outfoxed**, **outfoxing**) *informal* outwit.

outgas *verb* (**outgases**, **outgassed**, **outgassing**) **1** release or give off a gas or vapour. **2 a** release or give off (a substance) as a gas or vapour. **b** drive off a gas or vapour from.

outgoing • *adjective* **1** friendly; sociable; extrovert. **2** retiring from office. **3** going out or away. • *noun* **1** (in *plural*) expenditure. **2** an instance of going out: *the deliveries and outgoings of raw materials*.

outgroup *noun* a group perceived as outsiders by members of an in-group.

outgrow *verb* (**outgrows**; *past* **outgrew**; *past participle* **outgrown**; **outgrowing**) **1** grow too big for (one's clothes). **2** leave behind (a childish habit, taste, ailment, etc.) as one matures. **3** grow faster or taller than (a person, plant, etc.).

outgrowth *noun* **1** something that grows out. **2** an offshoot; a natural product. **3** the process of growing out.

outgun *verb* (**outguns**, **outgunned**, **outgunning**) **1** surpass in military or other power or strength. **2** shoot better than.

outharbour *noun* Cdn (Nfld) = OUTPORT 1.

outhouse *noun* **1** an outdoor toilet that is enclosed but separate from the main building. **2** an outbuilding.

outing *noun* **1** a short holiday away from home, esp. of one day or part of a day; a pleasure trip, an excursion. **2** any brief journey from home. **3** a public appearance in a game, race, etc. **4** *informal* the practice or policy of revealing the homosexuality of a prominent person.

outlander *noun* a foreigner, alien, or stranger.

outlandish *adjective* bizarre, strange, unfamiliar.

outlast *verb* last longer than or beyond; survive: *outlasted its usefulness*.

outlaw • *noun* **1** a fugitive from the law. **2** a person who does not conform to traditional or established practices: *arrests on drug-related charges have underlined their status as outlaws of popular culture*. • *verb* **1** make illegal; prohibit. **2** declare (a person) an outlaw.

outlay *noun* **1** an amount of money spent; an expenditure. **2** an act or instance of spending money.

outlet *noun* **1** a means of exit or escape. **2** a socket in a wall etc. for connecting an electrical appliance to a wiring system. **3** a means of expression (of a talent, emotion, etc.): *an outlet for tension*. **4 a** a place that sells merchandise made by a particular company or of a particular type. **b** = FACTORY OUTLET. **5 a** a stream, river, or channel flowing out of and draining a larger body of water, e.g. a lake. **b** the mouth of a river.

outline • *noun* **1** a rough statement of the main facts or points to be presented in a piece of writing, etc. **2** a sketch containing only contour lines. **3** (in *singular* or *plural*) **a** lines enclosing or indicating an object: *the outline of a shape under the blankets*. **b** a contour. **c** an external boundary. **4** (in *plural*) the main features or general principles: *the outlines of a plan*. • *verb* (**outlines**, **outlined**, **outlining**) **1** describe the main features of; summarize. **2** draw in outline. **3** draw a line around: *outlined in red*. ▮PHRASES▮ **in outline** sketched or represented as an outline.

outlive *verb* (**outlives**, **outlived**, **outliving**) **1** live longer than (another person). **2** live beyond (a specified date or time). **3** live through (an experience).

outlook *noun* **1** the prospect for the future: *the outlook is bleak*. **2** one's mental attitude or point of view: *narrow in their outlook*. **3** a view on which one looks out: *a pleasant outlook over the valley*.

outlying *adjective* situated far from a centre; remote.

outmanoeuvre *verb* (**outmanoeuvres**, **outmanoeuvred**, **outmanoeuvring**) **1** use skill and cunning to secure an advantage over (a person). **2** outdo in manoeuvring.

out-migration *noun* the action of migrating from one place to another, esp. in the same country.

outmoded *adjective* **1** no longer in fashion. **2** obsolete.

outnumber *verb* exceed in number.

out-of-body experience *noun* a sensation of being outside one's body, esp. of floating and being able to observe oneself from a distance.

out-of-court *adjective* (esp. of a settlement) made or done outside or without the intervention of a court.

out of date *adjective* old-fashioned, obsolete.

out-of-pocket *adjective* (of costs etc.) paid out in cash.

out of print *adjective* (of a book) no longer available from the publisher.

out-of-province *adjective Cdn* in, from, or pertaining to another province: *out-of-province health insurance*.

out-of-sight *adjective* **1** not visible. **2** *informal* excellent.

out-of-the-way *adjective* **1** remote; far from a main road or centre of population. **2** unusual; extraordinary.

out-of-town *adjective* **1** originating from outside of a particular place: *out-of-town visitors*. **2** occurring in another place: *an out-of-town hockey tournament*. ▶ **out-of-towner** *noun*

> **SPELL CHECK**
> **out-of-work, out of work**
>
> Note the difference in spelling between *out-of-work actors* and *thousands of people were out of work*. There is no hyphen when the latter kind of structure is used.

out-of-work *adjective* unemployed.

outpace *verb* (**outpaces**, **outpaced**, **outpacing**) **1** go faster than. **2** outdo in a contest.

outpatient *noun* a person receiving treatment at a hospital without being hospitalized.

outperform *verb* **1** perform better than. **2** surpass in a specified field or activity. ▶ **outperformance** *noun*

outplacement *noun* the act or process of finding new employment for esp. executive workers who have been dismissed or made redundant.

outplay *verb* surpass in playing; play better than.

outpoll *verb* receive more votes than (an opponent) in an election, opinion poll, etc.: *outpolled her closest competitor three to one*.

outport *noun* **1** *Cdn* **a** (in Newfoundland) any port other than St. John's, esp. an isolated fishing village. **b** (*Maritimes*) a coastal fishing village. **2** a subsidiary port.

outporter *noun Cdn* an inhabitant or native of an outport.

outpost *noun* **1** a detachment set at a distance from the main body of an army, esp. to prevent surprise. **2** a distant branch or settlement.

outpost camp *noun Cdn* a remote hunting or fishing camp.

outpouring *noun* **1** a large amount of something produced in a short time: *a remarkable outpouring of new ideas*. **2** (usu. in *plural*) an expression of very strong feelings: *outpourings of public grief*. **3** something that pours out: *an outpouring of water from the lake*.

output • *noun* **1** the product of a process, esp. of manufacture, or of mental or artistic work. **2** the quantity or amount of this. **3** the printout, results, etc. supplied by a computer. **4** the power etc. delivered by an apparatus. **5** *Electronics* a place where energy, information, etc. leaves a system. • *verb* (**outputs**; *past* and *past participle* **output** or **outputted**; **outputting**) **1** put or send out. **2** (of a computer) supply (results etc.).

outrage • *noun* **1** an extreme or shocking violation of others' rights, sentiments, etc. **2** a gross offence or indignity. **3** fierce anger or resentment: *a feeling of outrage*. • *verb* (**outrages**, **outraged**, **outraging**) **1** subject to outrage. **2** injure, insult, etc. flagrantly. **3** shock and anger. ▶ **outraged** *adjective*

outrageous *adjective* **1** deeply shocking and unacceptable. **2** grossly cruel. **3** immoral, offensive. **4** highly unusual or unconventional. ▶ **outrageously** *adverb* [Say out RAGE us]

outran *past of* OUTRUN.

outrank *verb* **1** be superior in rank to. **2** take priority over.

outré *adjective* outside the bounds of what is usual or proper: *the image of rock stars in the public's mind is, of course, the young and exhibitionistic, the outré and the promiscuous, visible and shocking*. [Say oo TRAY]

outreach • *verb* (**outreaches**, **outreached**, **outreaching**) **1** reach further than. **2** surpass. • *noun* **1** the activity of an organization in contacting, educating, and providing services, advice, etc. to people in the community, esp. outside its usual centres. **2** the extent or length of reaching out.

outrider *noun* **1** a mounted attendant riding ahead of, or with, a carriage etc. **2** a motorcyclist acting as a guard in a similar manner. ▶ **outriding** *noun*

outrigger *noun* **1** a beam, spar, or framework, rigged out and projecting from or over a ship's side for various purposes. **2** a similar projecting beam etc. in a building. **3** a log etc. fixed parallel to a canoe to stabilize it. **4** a chassis extension supporting the body of a motor vehicle.

outright • *adverb* **1** altogether, entirely: *proved outright*. **2** not gradually, nor by degrees, nor by instalments: *bought it outright*. **3** without reservation, openly: *denied the charge outright*. • *adjective* **1** downright, direct, complete: *outright anger*. **2** undisputed, clear: *the outright winner*.

outrun *verb* (**outruns**; *past* **outran**; *past participle* **outrun**; **outrunning**) **1 a** run faster or farther than. **b** escape from: *it's harder than anyone imagines to outrun destiny*. **2** go beyond (a specified point or limit): *spiralling costs outran initial estimates*.

outscore *verb* (**outscores**, **outscored**, **outscoring**) score more than (an opponent) in a game etc.

outsell *verb* (**outsells**; *past* and *past participle* **outsold**; **outselling**) **1** sell more than. **2** be sold in greater quantities than.

outset *noun* the start, beginning. PHRASES **at** (or **from**) **the outset** from the beginning.

outshine *verb* (**outshines**; *past* and *past participle* **outshone**; **outshining**) **1** shine brighter than. **2** surpass in ability, excellence, etc.

outshoot *verb* (**outshoots**, **outshot**, **outshooting**) **1** shoot better or further than (another person). **2** *Hockey* record more shots on goal than the opposing team: *the Senators outshot the Sabres 18-6 in the first period*.

outside • *noun* **1** the external side or surface of something. **2** the external appearance of someone or something. **3** the part of a path nearer to a road. **4** the side of a curve where the edge is longer. **5** *Cdn (North)* the rest of the world, esp. a more heavily populated or urban area. • *adjective* **1** situated on or near the outside. **2** not of or belonging to a particular group. **3** *Cdn (North)* of or relating to the rest of the world, esp. to a more heavily populated or urban area. • *preposition & adverb* **1** situated or moving beyond the boundaries of. **2** beyond the limits or scope of. **3** not being a member of. **4** *Cdn (North)* in or to the rest of the world, esp. a more heavily populated or urban area. [PHRASES] **at the outside** (of an estimate etc.) at the most. **get outside of** *slang* eat or drink. **outside and in** outside and inside. **outside in** = INSIDE OUT. **outside of** *informal* apart from.

outsider *noun* **1 a** a non-member of some circle, party, profession, etc. **b** an uninitiated person, a layman. **2** a competitor, applicant, etc. thought to have little chance of success.

outsize • *adjective* **1** unusually large. **2** (of garments etc.) of an exceptionally large size. • *noun* an exceptionally large person or thing, esp. a garment. ▶ **outsized** *adjective*

outskirts *plural noun* the outer border or fringe of a town, district, subject, etc.

outsmart *verb* outwit, be cleverer than.

outsold *past and past participle of* OUTSELL.

outsole *noun* the outer sole of a boot or shoe, esp. a sports shoe.

outsource *verb* (**outsources**, **outsourced**, **outsourcing**) **1** obtain (goods etc.) by contract from an outside source. **2** contract (work) out. ▶ **outsourcing** *noun*

outspend *verb* (**outspends**, **outspent**, **outspending**) spend more than (one's resources or another person).

outspoken *adjective* given to or involving plain speaking; frank in stating one's opinions. ▶ **outspokenness** *noun*

outspread • *adjective* spread out; fully extended or expanded. • *verb* (**outspreads**, **outspread**, **outspreading**) spread out; expand.

outstanding *adjective* **1 a** conspicuous, eminent, esp. because of excellence. **b** (usu. foll. by *at*, *in*) remarkable in (a specified field). **2** (esp. of a debt) not yet settled. ▶ **outstandingly** *adverb*

outstay *verb* **1** stay beyond the limit of (one's welcome, invitation, etc.). **2** stay or endure longer than (another person etc.).

outstep *verb* (**outsteps**, **outstepped**, **outstepping**) step outside or beyond.

outstretch *verb* (**outstretches**, **outstretched**, **outstretching**) **1** (usu. as **outstretched** *adjective*) reach out or stretch out (esp. one's hands or arms). **2** go beyond the limit of: *their good intentions far outstretched their capacity to offer help*.

outstrip *verb* (**outstrips**, **outstripped**, **outstripping**) **1** pass in running etc. **2** surpass in competition or relative progress or ability. **3** be or become faster than: *demand is outstripping supply*.

outta *preposition informal* out of.

outtake *noun* a length of film etc. rejected in editing.

out-think *verb* (**out-thinks**, **out-thought**, **out-thinking**) outwit; outdo in thinking.

out-thrust • *adjective* extended; projected: *ran forward with out-thrust arms*. • *verb* (**out-thrusts**, **out-thrust**, **out-thrusting**) thrust out. • *noun* a thing which projects or is extended outward: *root hairs are out-thrusts from the root surface*.

out to lunch *adjective informal* out of touch with reality; unaware; crazy.

out tray *noun* = OUT BASKET.

out-turn *noun Curling* **1** an inward turn of the elbow and an outward turn of the hand made in delivering a stone, giving it a clockwise rotation. **2** a stone delivered with such a motion.

outvote *verb* (**outvotes**, **outvoted**, **outvoting**) defeat by a majority of votes.

outward • *adjective* **1** situated on or directed towards the outside. **2** going out: *on the outward voyage*. **3** bodily, external, apparent, superficial: *in all outward respects*. • *adverb* (also **outwards**) in an outward direction; towards the outside. • *noun* the outward appearance of something; the exterior. ▶ **outwardly** *adverb*

outward bound *adjective* **1** (of a ship, passenger, etc.) going away from home. **2** (**Outward Bound**) a movement to provide adventure training, naval training, and other outdoor activities for young people.

outwash *noun* (*plural* **outwashes**) the material carried from a glacier by meltwater and deposited beyond the moraine.

outweigh *verb* exceed in weight, value, importance, etc.

outwit *verb* (**outwits**, **outwitted**, **outwitting**) be too clever or crafty for; deceive by greater ingenuity.

outwork • *verb* work harder or faster than. • *noun* an advanced or detached part of a fortification.

outworn *adjective* obsolete; out-of-date: *outworn sexual clichés*.

ouzo *noun* (*plural* **ouzos**) a Greek aniseed-flavoured spirit. [Say OOZE oh]

ova *plural of* OVUM. [Say OVE uh]

oval • *adjective* having a rounded and slightly elongated outline or shape like that of an egg. • *noun* **1** a body, object, or design with such a shape or outline. **2** an oval speed skating rink, racetrack, etc.

Oval Office *noun* the office of the US President in the White House.

ovarian *adjective* affecting or having to do with the ovaries: *ovarian cyst*. [Say oh VERY un]

ovary *noun* (*plural* **ovaries**) **1** each of the female reproductive organs in which ova are produced. **2** the hollow base of the carpel of a flower, containing one or more ovules. [Say OVE a ree]

ovation *noun* an enthusiastic reception, esp. spontaneous and sustained applause. [Say oh VAY sh'n]

oven *noun* **1** an enclosed compartment, e.g. as part of a stove, used for baking, roasting, heating, etc. **2** a small furnace or kiln used in chemistry etc.

ovenproof *adjective* suitable for use in an oven.

oven-ready *adjective* (of food) prepared before sale so as to be ready for immediate cooking in the oven.

ovenware *noun* dishes that can be used for cooking food in the oven.

over • *preposition* **1** extending upwards from or above. **2** above so as to cover or protect. **3** expressing movement or a route across. **4** beyond and falling or hanging from. **5** expressing duration. **6** at a higher level, layer, or intensity than. **7** higher or more than. **8** expressing authority or control. **9** on the subject of.

0

• *adverb* **1** expressing movement or a route across an area. **2** beyond and falling or hanging from a point. **3** in or to the place indicated. **4** expressing action and result. **5** finished. **6** expressing repetition of a process. PHRASES **not over** not very; not at all: *not over friendly*. **over again** once again. **over against** in an opposite situation to; adjacent to, in contrast with. **over all** taken as a whole. **over and above** in addition to; not to mention: *$100 over and above the asking price*. **over and over** so that the same thing or the same point comes up again and again: *said it over and over*. **over with** (also **over and done with**) (esp. of an unpleasant or disagreeable task, experience, etc.) finished, completed: *let's get it over with*. **start** (or **begin** etc.) **over** begin again.

over- *prefix* added to verbs, nouns, adjectives, and adverbs, meaning: **1** excessively; to an unwanted degree: *overheat*. **2** upper, outer, extra: *overcoat* ◊ *overtime*. **3** "over" in various senses: *overhang* ◊ *overshadow*. **4** completely, utterly: *overjoyed*.

overabundance *noun* an excessive quantity of something.

overabundant *adjective* in excessive quantity. ▶ **overabundantly** *adverb*

overachieve *verb* (**overachieves, overachieved, overachieving**) **1** do more than might be expected (esp. scholastically). **2** achieve more than (an expected goal or objective etc.). ▶ **overachievement** *noun* **overachiever** *noun*

overact *verb* act in an exaggerated manner.

overactive *adjective* excessively active. ▶ **overactivity** *noun*

over-age *adjective* over a certain age limit; too old.

overall • *adjective* **1** total, inclusive of all: *overall cost*. **2** taking everything into account, general: *overall improvement*. **3** from end to end: *overall length*. • *adverb* **1** taken as a whole: *overall, the performance was excellent*. **2** when everything is included: *finished second in their division and eighth overall*. • *noun* (in *plural*) loose-fitting pants with fabric extending up to cover the front torso, fastened around the neck or over the shoulders. ▶ **overalled** *adjective*

overarching *adjective* **1** all-embracing; comprehensive: *the diversity of Canadians' backgrounds has made it difficult for an overarching national political culture to emerge*. **2** forming an arch over: *North Vancouver is annexed to Vancouver by the overarching Lions Gate Bridge*.

overarm *adjective & adverb* **1** = OVERHAND 1. **2** *Swimming* with one or both arms lifted out of the water during a stroke.

overate *past of* OVEREAT.

overawe *verb* (**overawes, overawed, overawing**) cause (a person) to feel a great deal of fear, respect, etc.

overbalance *verb* (**overbalances, overbalanced, overbalancing**) **1** cause (a person or thing) to lose its balance and fall. **2** fall over, capsize. **3** outweigh.

overbearing *adjective* unpleasantly overpowering: *an overbearing, ill-tempered brute*.

overbite *noun* the overlapping of the lower teeth by the upper.

overblown *adjective* **1** excessively inflated or pretentious: *a world of overblown egos*. **2** (of a flower etc.) past its prime.

overboard *adverb* from on a ship into the water: *fall overboard*. PHRASES **go overboard 1** be highly enthusiastic. **2** behave immoderately; go too far. **throw overboard** abandon, discard.

overbook *verb* accept too many bookings or reservations for (an aircraft, hotel, etc.).

overburden • *verb* burden (a person, thing, etc.) to excess. • *noun* **1** rock etc. that must be removed prior to

mining the mineral deposit beneath it. **2** an excessive burden.

overcapacity *noun* the resources to produce more goods, handle more business, etc. than is needed at a particular time.

overcast • *adjective* **1** (of the sky, weather, etc.) covered with cloud; dull and gloomy. **2** (in sewing) edged with stitching to prevent fraying. • *noun* a covering, esp. of clouds.

overcautious *adjective* excessively cautious. ▶ **overcautiously** *adverb* **overcautiousness** *noun*

overcharge • *verb* (**overcharges, overcharged, overcharging**) **1** charge too high a price to (a person) or for (a thing). **2** put too much charge into (a battery, gun, etc.). **3** put exaggerated or excessive detail into (a description, picture, etc.). • *noun* an excessive charge (of explosive, money, etc.).

overcoat *noun* **1** a heavy coat, esp. one worn over indoor clothes for warmth outdoors in cold weather. **2** a protective coat of paint etc.

overcome • *verb* (**overcomes**; *past* **overcame**; *past participle* **overcome**; **overcoming**) **1** prevail over. **2** be victorious. • *adjective* (usu. foll. by *with, by*) **1** exhausted, made helpless. **2** affected by (emotion etc.).

overcompensate *verb* (**overcompensates, overcompensated, overcompensating**) **1** (usu. foll. by *for*) compensate excessively for (something). **2** strive for power etc. in an exaggerated way, esp. to make allowance or amends for a real or fancied grievance, defect, handicap, etc. ▶ **overcompensation** *noun*

overconfidence *noun* excessive confidence.

overconfident *adjective* excessively confident. ▶ **overconfidently** *adverb*

overcook *verb* cook too much or for too long. ▶ **overcooked** *adjective*

overcrowd *verb* fill (a space, object, etc.) beyond what is usual or comfortable. ▶ **overcrowded** *adjective* **overcrowding** *noun*

overcut *verb* (**overcuts, overcut, overcutting**) cut too many trees in an area of forest at one time.

overcutting *noun* the act or an instance of cutting too many trees in an area of forest at one time.

overdevelop *verb* (**overdevelops, overdeveloped, overdeveloping**) **1** develop too much. **2** *Photography* treat with developer for too long. ▶ **overdevelopment** *noun*

overdo *verb* (**overdoes**; *past* **overdid**; *past participle* **overdone**; **overdoing**) carry to excess, go too far, exaggerate: *overdid the sarcasm*. PHRASES **overdo it** (or **things**) exhaust oneself.

overdone *adjective* **1** overcooked. **2** excessive, exaggerated.

overdose • *noun* an excessive dose (of a drug, sensation, etc.). • *verb* (**overdoses, overdosed, overdosing**) **1** (often foll. by *on*) take an overdose of a drug. **2** give an excessive dose of (a drug etc.) or to (a person).

overdraft *noun* **1** a deficit in a bank account caused by drawing more money than is credited to it. **2** the amount of this.

overdramatize *verb* (**overdramatizes, overdramatized, overdramatizing**) express or react to in an excessively dramatic way.

overdrawn *adjective* **1** (of a bank account) having an overdraft. **2** (of a person) having overdrawn one's bank account.

overdress • *verb* (**overdresses, overdressed, overdressing**) **1** dress (a person, esp. a child) too warmly. **2** dress with too much display or formality. **3** overdress oneself. • *noun* (*plural* **overdresses**) a dress

worn over another dress or a blouse etc. ▶ **overdressed** *adjective*

overdrive *noun* **1** an extra high gear in a vehicle, used when driving at high speeds. **2** (usu. preceded by *in*, *into*) a state of high or excessive activity.

overdub • *verb* (**overdubs**, **overdubbed**, **overdubbing**) impose (additional sounds) on an existing recording. • *noun* an instance of overdubbing: *a guitar overdub*.

overdue *adjective* **1** past the time when due or ready. **2** not yet paid, arrived, etc., though after the expected time. **3** (of a library book etc.) retained longer than the period allowed. **4 a** (of a baby) not yet born, though past the due date. **b** (of a pregnant woman) having passed her due date without having given birth.

overeager *adjective* excessively eager.

over easy *adjective* (of a fried egg) flipped when almost cooked and fried lightly on the other side, so that the yolk remains slightly liquid.

overeat *verb* (**overeats**; *past* **overate**; *past participle* **overeaten**; **overeating**) eat too much. ▶ **overeater** *noun* **overeating** *noun*

overemphasis *noun* excessive emphasis. ▶ **overemphasize** *verb* (**overemphasizes**, **overemphasized**, **overemphasizing**)

overenthusiasm *noun* excessive enthusiasm. ▶ **overenthusiastic** *adjective*

overestimate • *verb* (**overestimates**, **overestimated**, **overestimating**) form too high an estimate of (a person, ability, cost, etc.). • *noun* too high an estimate. ▶ **overestimation** *noun*

overexcite *verb* (**overexcites**, **overexcited**, **overexciting**) excite excessively. ▶ **overexcited** *adjective*

overexert *verb* exert too much. ▶ **overexertion** *noun*

overexpose *verb* (**overexposes**, **overexposed**, **overexposing**) **1** expose too much, esp. to the public eye. **2** *Photography* expose (film) for too long a time. ▶ **overexposure** *noun*

overextend *verb* **1** extend (a thing) too far. **2** **overextend oneself** take on oneself an excessive burden of work etc. ▶ **overextended** *adjective*

overfeed *verb* (**overfeeds**, **overfed**, **overfeeding**) feed excessively.

overfill *verb* fill to excess or to overflowing.

overfish *verb* (**overfishes**, **overfished**, **overfishing**) deplete (a body of water) by too much fishing. ▶ **overfishing** *noun*

overflight *noun* an instance of overflying.

overflow • *verb* **1 a** flow over the brim or limits of. **b** fill (a container) so full that the contents spill out. **2 a** (of a receptacle etc.) be so full that the contents overflow it. **b** (of contents) overflow a container. **3** (of a crowd etc.) extend beyond the limits of (a room etc.). **4** flood (a surface or area). **5** (foll. by *with*) be full of. **6** (of kindness, a harvest, etc.) be very abundant. • *noun* **1** what overflows or is superfluous: *an overflow crowd*. **2** the flowing over of a liquid: *there was some overflow after a heavy rainfall* ◊ *an overflow of sewage*. **3** (esp. in a bathtub or sink) an outlet for excess water etc. **4** an excess: *an overflow of ideas*. PHRASES **to overflowing** so as to be more than full; so as to overflow.

overfly *verb* (**overflies**; *past* **overflew**; *past participle* **overflown**; **overflying**) fly over or beyond (a place or territory).

overfull *adjective* filled excessively or to overflowing.

overgraze *verb* (**overgrazes**, **overgrazed**, **overgrazing**) allow (grassland) to be so heavily grazed, or (of livestock) feed on (grassland) so heavily, that the vegetation is damaged and ground becomes liable to erosion. ▶ **overgrazed** *adjective* **overgrazing** *noun*

overgrown *adjective* **1** abnormally large: *he's like an overgrown child*. **2** wild; grown over with vegetation.

overgrowth *noun* **1** growth that is excessive or too rapid. **2** a growth over or on something.

overhand *adjective & adverb* **1** (in tennis, baseball, etc.) thrown or played with the hand above the shoulder. **2** *Swimming* = OVERARM **2**. **3 a** with the palm of the hand downward or inward. **b** with the hand above the object held.

overhang • *verb* (**overhangs**, **overhung**, **overhanging**) project or hang over. • *noun* **1** the overhanging part of a structure etc. **2** the amount by which this projects. **3** an excess or buildup of any factor in an economy or market which has, or is likely to have, an undesirable effect upon it. ▶ **overhanging** *adjective*

overharvest *verb* kill too many trees, animals, fish, etc., by logging, hunting, fishing, etc. ▶ **overharvesting** *noun*

overhaul • *verb* **1** take to pieces in order to examine. **2** examine the condition of (and improve or repair as necessary). • *noun* a thorough examination, with adjustments or repairs as necessary.

overhead • *adverb* above one's head. • *adjective* **1** placed overhead. **2** (of a driving mechanism etc.) above the object driven. **3** (of expenses) arising from general running costs, as distinct from particular business transactions. • *noun* **1** (also in *plural*) overhead expenses. **2** (also **overhead projector**) a device that projects an enlarged image of a transparency onto a screen or wall. **3** a transparency for use on an overhead projector.

overhear *verb* (**overhears**, **overheard**, **overhearing**) hear as an eavesdropper or as an unobserved or unintentional listener.

overheat *verb* **1** make or become too hot; heat to excess. **2** *Economics* suffer, or cause to suffer, from marked inflation as a result of placing excessive pressure on resources at a time of expanding demand. ▶ **overheating** *noun*

overheated *adjective* **1** excessively hot. **2** excessively passionate about a matter: *an overheated editorial*. **3** (of an economy etc.) suffering from marked inflation.

overhype *verb* (**overhypes**, **overhyped**, **overhyping**) promote with excessive hype. ▶ **overhyped** *adjective*

overindulge *verb* (**overindulges**, **overindulged**, **overindulging**) indulge to excess. ▶ **overindulgence** *noun* **overindulgent** *adjective*

overjoyed *adjective* filled with great joy.

overkill *noun* **1** an excess of what is necessary or appropriate. **2** the amount by which destruction or the capacity for destruction exceeds what is necessary for victory or annihilation.

overland *adjective & adverb* by land.

Overlander *noun* *Cdn hist.* one of a group of people who journeyed overland from Ontario to the Cariboo goldfields in BC in 1862.

overlap • *verb* (**overlaps**, **overlapped**, **overlapping**) **1** (of part of an object) partly cover (another object). **2** cover and extend beyond. **3** (of two things) partly coincide; not be completely separate: *where psychology and philosophy overlap*. • *noun* **1** a part or amount which overlaps: *an overlap of about two centimetres*. **2** a common area of interest, responsibility, etc.: *there are many overlaps between the approaches* ◊ *there is some overlap in requirements*. **3** a period of time in which two events or activities happen together. ▶ **overlapping** *noun & adjective*

overlay • *verb* (**overlays**, **overlaid**, **overlaying**) **1** lay over. **2** cover the surface of (a thing) with (a

coating etc.): *their fingernails had been overlaid with silver or gold.* **3** overlie: *a third screen will overlay the others.* • *noun* **1** a thing laid over another. **2** (in printing etc.) a transparent sheet to be superimposed on another sheet.

overlie *verb* (**overlies**; *past* **overlay**; *past participle* **overlain**; **overlying**) lie on top of: *soft clays overlie the basalt rock* ◊ *the national situation was overlain by sharp regional differences.*

overload • *verb* (esp. in *passive*) **1** put too great a load on or into something. **2** (often foll. by *with*) give (a person or thing) too much of something. **3** put too great a demand on a computer, electrical system, etc., causing it to fail. • *noun* an excessive quantity; a demand etc. which surpasses capability or capacity.

overlong *adjective & adverb* too or excessively long.

overlook • *verb* **1 a** miss or fail to see or notice (a thing). **b** see (a mistake, wrongdoing, etc.) but decide officially to ignore it: *we have overlooked your persistent lateness.* **c** consider (a person or thing) not good or important enough and so ignore them or it: *was repeatedly overlooked for promotion.* **2** have a view from above, be higher than. • *noun* a place giving a view of the scene below.

overlord *noun* **1** a lord superior to other lords or rulers. **2** a person in a position of superiority or supreme power.

overly *adverb* excessively; too.

overmatch *verb* (**overmatches, overmatched, overmatching**) be more than a match for; defeat by superior strength etc.

overmuch *adverb* to too great an extent; excessively.

overnight • *adverb* **1** for the duration of a night: *stay overnight.* **2** during the course of a night. **3** suddenly, immediately: *the situation changed overnight.* • *adjective* **1** done, happening, operating, etc. overnight: *an overnight stop.* **2** staying for one night: *an overnight guest.* **3** for use overnight: *an overnight bag.* **4** lasting or valid for one night. **5** (of a delivery etc.) occurring before opening time the next business day. **6** sudden, instant: *an overnight success.* • *verb* **1** send (a package etc.) by overnight delivery. **2** stay for the night at or in: *overnighted at Kingston.*

over-optimism *noun* excessive or unjustifiabe optimism.

over-optimistic *adjective* excessively or unjustifiably optimistic.

overpackaged *adjective* (of a product) wrapped in excessive packaging.

overpackaging *noun* excessive packaging of a product, e.g. consisting of several layers of wrapping.

overpass *noun* (*plural* **overpasses**) a road or railway line that passes over another by means of a bridge.

overpay *verb* (**overpays, overpaid, overpaying**) **1** recompense (a person etc.) too highly. **2** pay more than (an amount owing). ▶ **overpayment** *noun*

overplay *verb* **1** play (a part) to excess. **2** give undue importance to. ▮PHRASES▮ **overplay one's hand 1** be unduly optimistic about one's capabilities. **2** spoil a good case by exaggerating its value.

overpopulated *adjective* having too large a population. ▶ **overpopulation** *noun*

overpower *verb* **1** reduce to submission, subdue: *he overpowered his unarmed guard.* **2** make (a thing) ineffective or imperceptible by greater intensity. **3** (of heat, emotion, etc.) be too intense for, overwhelm.

▶ **overpowering** *adjective* **overpoweringly** *adverb*

over-prescribe *verb* (**over-prescribes, over-prescribed, over-prescribing**) prescribe an excessive amount of (a drug) or too many (drugs). ▶ **over-prescription** *noun*

overpriced *adjective* **1** (of a product) too expensive; costing more than it is worth. **2** (of a store etc.) selling merchandise that is too expensive.

overprint • *verb* print further matter on a surface already printed, esp. a postage stamp. • *noun* **1** the words etc. overprinted. **2** an overprinted postage stamp.

overproduce *verb* (**overproduces, overproduced, overproducing**) **1** produce more of (a commodity) than is wanted. **2** produce to an excessive degree. ▶ **overproduction** *noun*

overprotective *adjective* excessively protective, esp. of a person in one's charge.

overqualified *adjective* too highly qualified (esp. for a particular job etc.).

overran *past of* OVERRUN.

overrate *verb* (**overrates, overrated, overrating**) rate or esteem too highly. ▶ **overrated** *adjective*

overreach *verb* (**overreaches, overreached, overreaching**) **1** exceed (the limits of a person's authority etc.). **2 a** strain oneself by reaching too far: *never lean sideways from a ladder or overreach.* **b** defeat one's object by attempting what is beyond one's abilities: *a stock market trader who tried to go too far, and overreached himself.* ▶ **overreacher** *noun* **overreaching** *noun & adjective*

overreact *verb* respond more forcibly etc. than is justified. ▶ **overreaction** *noun*

overreliance *noun* excessive reliance.

overrepresent *verb* cause to be present in numbers higher than would be expected statistically.

override • *verb* (**overrides**; *past* **overrode**; *past participle* **overridden**; **overriding**) **1** use one's authority to reject someone's decision, order, etc.; overrule: *the chairman overrode the committee's objections and signed the agreement.* **2** be more important than something: *considerations of safety override all other concerns.* **3** interrupt the action of (an automatic device) esp. to take manual control: *a special code is needed to override the time lock.* • *noun* **1** the action or process of suspending an automatic function. **2** a device for this.

overriding *adjective* foremost; taking precedence: *accuracy is our overriding concern.*

overripe *adjective* (esp. of fruit etc.) past its best; excessively ripe. ▶ **overripeness** *noun*

overrule *verb* (**overrules, overruled, overruling**) **1** set aside (a decision, argument, proposal, etc.) by exercising a superior authority. **2** annul a decision by or reject a proposal of (a person) in this way.

overrun • *verb* (**overruns**; *past* **overran**; *past participle* **overrun**; **overrunning**) **1** (esp. of something undesirable) swarm or spread over. **2** conquer or ravage (territory) by force. **3** (of time, expenditure, production, etc.) exceed (a fixed limit). **4** *Printing* carry over (a word etc.) to the next line or page. **5** *Mechanics* rotate faster than. • *noun* **1** an instance of something exceeding an expected or allowed time or cost: *the cost overrun caused the company's share price to fall* ◊ *an increase in the budgeted fee due to overrun of the project.* **2** the amount of this. **3** the movement of a vehicle at a speed greater than is imparted by the engine.

oversampling *noun* a process used in CD players by which each component of the signal is repeated electronically so as to increase the apparent sampling frequency, making it easier to remove spurious signals introduced by the original sampling process.

overseas • *adverb* abroad: *was sent overseas.* • *adjective* (also **oversea**) **1** foreign; across or beyond the sea. **2** of or connected with movement or transport over the sea: *overseas postage rates.*

oversee *verb* (**oversees**; *past* **oversaw**; *past participle* **overseen**; **overseeing**) officially supervise (workers, work, etc.).

overseer *noun* a person who supervises others, esp. workers.

oversell *verb* (**oversells**, **oversold**, **overselling**) **1** sell more of (a commodity etc.) than one can deliver. **2** exaggerate the merits of.

oversexed *adjective* having unusually strong sexual desires.

overshadow *verb* **1** appear much more prominent or important than. **2** cast into the shade; shelter from the sun. **3** make an occasion less happy than it should be: *victory was overshadowed by the terrible loss of life*.

overshoe *noun* a shoe worn over another as protection from wet, cold, etc.

overshoot • *verb* (**overshoots**, **overshot** **overshooting**) **1** pass or send beyond (a target or limit). **2** (of an aircraft) fly beyond or taxi too far along (the runway) when landing or taking off. • *noun* **1** the act of overshooting. **2** the amount of this. PHRASES **overshoot the mark** go beyond what is intended or proper.

oversight *noun* **1** a failure to notice something. **2** an inadvertent mistake. **3** the action of overseeing something: *effective oversight of the financial reporting process*.

oversimplification *noun* an explanation of a situation, problem, etc. that is too simple and ignores some of the facts.

oversimplified *adjective* (of a problem or situation etc.) explained in such a simple way that some facts are ignored and a distorted impression is given.

oversimplify *verb* (**oversimplifies**, **oversimplified**, **oversimplifying**) distort (a problem etc.) by stating it in too simple terms.

oversized *adjective* (also **oversize**) of more than the usual size.

overskate *verb* (**overskates**, **overskated**, **overskating**) (of a hockey player) skate faster than or past the puck.

oversleep *verb* (**oversleeps**, **overslept**, **oversleeping**) sleep too long.

oversold *past and past participle of* OVERSELL.

overspend *verb* (**overspends**, **overspent**, **overspending**) **1** spend too much. **2** spend more than (a specified amount). ▶ **overspending** *noun*

overspill *noun* **1** what is spilled over or overflows. **2** the surplus population leaving a country or city to live elsewhere.

overstate *verb* (**overstates**, **overstated**, **overstating**) **1** state (esp. a case or argument) too strongly. **2** exaggerate. ▶ **overstatement** *noun*

overstay *verb* stay longer than (one's welcome, a time limit, etc.).

overstep *verb* (**oversteps**, **overstepped**, **overstepping**) **1** pass beyond (a boundary or mark). **2** violate (certain standards of behaviour etc.). PHRASES **overstep the mark** (or **bounds**) violate conventions of behaviour.

overstimulate *verb* (**overstimulates**, **overstimulated**, **overstimulating**) stimulate or excite excessively. ▶ **overstimulation** *noun*

overstock • *verb* stock excessively. • *noun* a supply in excess of demand or requirement.

overstorey *noun* (*plural* **overstoreys**) (also **overstory** *plural* **overstories**) the uppermost canopy level of a forest ecosystem, formed by the taller trees.

overstress • *verb* (**overstresses**, **overstressed**, **overstressing**) stress too much. • *noun* an excessive degree of stress.

overstretch • *verb* (**overstretches**, **overstretched**, **overstretching**) **1** stretch too much. **2** (esp. as **overstretched** *adjective*) make excessive demands on (resources, a person, etc.). • *noun* the fact or an instance of overstretching.

overstuffed *adjective* (of furniture) made soft and comfortable by thick upholstery.

oversubscribed *adjective* subscribed for more than the amount available of (a commodity offered for sale etc.): *the offer was oversubscribed*.

oversupply • *verb* (**oversupplies**, **oversupplied**, **oversupplying**) supply with too much. • *noun* an excessive supply.

overt *adjective* unconcealed; done openly: *an overt act of aggression*. ▶ **overtly** *adverb* **overtness** *noun* [Say oh VURT or OH vurt]

overtake *verb* (**overtakes**; *past* **overtook**; *past participle* **overtaken**; **overtaking**) **1** catch up with and pass in the same direction. **2** (of a storm, misfortune, etc.) come suddenly or unexpectedly upon. **3** become level with and exceed (a compared value etc.).

overtax *verb* (**overtaxes**, **overtaxed**, **overtaxing**) **1** make excessive demands on (a person's strength etc.). **2** tax too heavily.

> **SPELL CHECK**
> **over-the-counter, over the counter**
>
> Note the difference in spelling between *an over-the-counter drug* and *this medication is available over the counter*. There is no hyphen when the latter kind of structure is used.

over-the-counter *adjective* obtainable from a store, esp. (of drugs) without a prescription.

over-the-top *adjective informal* (esp. of behaviour, dress, etc.) outrageous, excessive.

overthrow • *verb* (**overthrows**; *past* **overthrew**; *past participle* **overthrown**; **overthrowing**) **1** remove forcibly from power. **2** put an end to (an institution etc.). **3** conquer, overcome. **4** knock down, upset. **5 a** throw (a ball) too far. **b** throw a ball past or over (a person, base, spot, etc.). • *noun* **1** a defeat or downfall. **2** the act or an instance of overthrowing.

overtime • *noun* **1** the time during which a person works at a job in addition to the regular hours. **2** payment for this. **3** a further period of play at the end of a game when the score is tied. • *adjective* **1** pertaining to overtime: *overtime pay*. **2** happening in overtime: *an overtime goal*. • *adverb* in addition to regular hours.

overtired *adjective* excessively tired.

overtone *noun* **1** a subtle or elusive quality or implication: *sinister overtones*. **2** *Music* any of the tones above the lowest in a harmonic series.

overtook *past of* OVERTAKE.

overtop • *verb* (**overtops**, **overtopped**, **overtopping**) **1** be or become higher than. **2** surpass. • *preposition* above. • *adverb* over the top of.

overture *noun* **1** an orchestral piece opening an opera, ballet, etc. **2** a one-movement composition in this style. **3** (usu. in *plural*) an approach or proposal made to a person with the aim of starting a discussion, establishing a relationship, etc. **4** something that serves as an introduction. [Say OVER chur]

overturn *verb* **1** cause to fall down or over; upset. **2** overthrow; destroy. **3** reverse; invalidate: *overturned the verdict*. **4** turn over; capsize.

overuse • *verb* (**overuses**, **overused**, **overusing**) use too much or too frequently. • *noun* excessive use.

overvalue *verb* (**overvalues**, **overvalued**,

overvaluing) value too highly; have too high an opinion of.

overview *noun* a general survey.

overwater • *verb* water (a plant etc.) too much. • *adjective* situated above the water.

overweening *adjective* arrogant, presumptuous, conceited: *had an overweening ambition to rule the world*.

overweight • *adjective* **1** in excess of a weight considered normal or desirable. **2** beyond an allowed or suitable weight. • *noun* excessive or extra weight.

overwhelm *verb* **1** overpower with emotion. **2** (usu. foll. by *with*) overpower with an excess of work, responsibility, etc. **3** bring to sudden ruin or destruction; crush. **4** bury or drown beneath a huge mass; submerge utterly.

overwhelming *adjective* **1** very great or very strong; overpowering: *your affection is overwhelming*. **2** complete; total, or nearly so: *an overwhelming success* ◊ *the overwhelming majority*. ▶ **overwhelmingly** *adverb*

overwind *verb* (**overwinds**, **overwound**, **overwinding**) wind (a mechanism, esp. a watch) beyond the proper stopping point.

overwinter *verb* **1** spend the winter. **2** (of insects, fungi, etc.) live through the winter. **3** keep (animals, plants, etc.) alive through the winter.

overwork • *verb* **1** work too hard. **2** cause (another person) to work too hard. **3** weary or exhaust with too much work. **4** make excessive use of. • *noun* excessive work. ▶ **overworked** *adjective*

overwrite *verb* (**overwrites**; *past* **overwrote**; *past participle* **overwritten**; **overwriting**) **1** write on top of (other writing). **2** *Computing* destroy (data) in (a file etc.) by entering new data. **3** (esp. as **overwritten** *adjective*) write too elaborately or too ornately.

overwrought *adjective* **1** overexcited, nervous, distraught. **2** overdone; too elaborate. [Say over ROT]

overzealous *adjective* too zealous in one's attitude, behaviour, etc.; too enthusiastic. [Say over ZELL us]

ovoid • *adjective* **1** (of a solid or of a surface) egg-shaped. **2** oval, with one end more pointed than the other. • *noun* an ovoid body or surface. [Say OVE oid]

ovulate *verb* (**ovulates**, **ovulated**, **ovulating**) produce ova or ovules, or discharge them from the ovary. ▶ **ovulation** *noun* [Say OV yoo late, ov yoo LAY sh'n]

ovule *noun* the part of the ovary of seed plants that contains the germ cell; an unfertilized seed. [Say OVE yool]

ovum *noun* (*plural* **ova**) **1** a mature reproductive cell of female animals, produced by the ovary. **2** the egg cell of plants. [Say OVE um for the singular, OVE uh for the plural]

ow *interjection* expressing sudden pain.

owe *verb* (**owes**, **owed**, **owing**) **1** be under obligation (to a person etc.) to pay or repay (money etc.). **2** render (honour, gratitude, etc.) to a person: *owe grateful thanks to my father*. **3** be indebted to a person or thing for: *we owe the discovery of insulin to Banting and Best*. PHRASES **owe it to oneself** need (to do) something in order to avoid unfairness to oneself: *I owe it to myself to go*.

owing *adjective* **1** owed; yet to be paid: *the balance owing*. **2** (foll. by *to*) **a** caused by; attributable to: *the cancellation was owing to lack of public interest*. **b** (foll. by *to*) because of: *delayed owing to bad weather*.

owl *noun* **1** a nocturnal bird of prey with large eyes and a hooked beak, and usu. a loud hooting call. **2** informal a person compared to an owl, esp. in looking solemn or wise. ▶ **owlish** *adjective*

own • *adjective* **1** belonging to oneself or itself. **2** used to emphasize identity rather than possession: *cooks his own meals*. • *pronoun* **1** private property: *is it your own?* **2** kindred: *among my own*. • *verb* **1** have as property;

possess. **2 a** confess; admit as valid, true, etc.: *owns he did not know*. **b** (foll. by *to*) confess to: *owned to a prejudice*. **3** acknowledge paternity, authorship, or possession of. PHRASES **come into one's own 1** receive one's due. **2** achieve recognition. **get one's own back** (often foll. by *on*) *informal* get revenge. **hold one's own** maintain one's position; not be defeated or lose strength. **on one's own 1** alone. **2** independently, without help. **own up** (often foll. by *to*) confess frankly. ▶ **-owned** *adjective* (in *combination*)

owner *noun* a person who owns something. ▶ **ownerless** *adjective* **ownership** *noun*

ox *noun* (*plural* **oxen**) **1** a large usu. horned domesticated bovine animal kept for milk or meat; a cow or bull. **2** a castrated male of this, typically used as a draft animal. **3** a foolish, clumsy person.

oxbow *noun* **1** a U-shaped collar of an ox yoke. **2 a** a loop formed by a horseshoe bend in a river. **b** (also **oxbow lake**) a lake formed when the river cuts across the narrow end of the loop.

Oxbridge *noun* **1** Oxford and Cambridge universities regarded together, esp. in contrast to newer institutions. **2** the characteristics of these universities or of their students, often stereotyped as being of the British upper classes and having had a private school education: *an Oxbridge accent*.

oxen *plural* of ox.

ox-eye daisy *noun* (*plural* **ox-eye daisies**) a daisy that has flowers with white petals and a yellow centre.

oxford *noun* (also **oxford shoe**) a low, sturdy shoe laced over the instep.

oxidant *noun* a substance that brings about oxidization by being reduced and gaining electrons. [Say OX id unt]

oxidase *noun* any of a class of enzymes that react with molecular oxygen to form water or hydrogen peroxide. [Say OX id ace or OX id aze]

oxide *noun* a binary compound of oxygen.

oxidize *verb* (**oxidizes**, **oxidized**, **oxidizing**) **1** combine or cause to combine with oxygen. **2** cover (metal) or (of metal) become covered with a coating of oxide etc.; make or become rusty or tarnished. **3** *Chemistry* undergo or cause to undergo a loss of electrons. ▶ **oxidized** *adjective* **oxidizer** *noun* [Say OX id ize]

oxtail *noun* the tail of an ox, esp. as an ingredient in soup.

oxygen *noun* a colourless tasteless odourless gaseous element, occurring naturally in air, water, and most minerals and organic substances, and essential to plant and animal life.

oxygenate *verb* (**oxygenates**, **oxygenated**, **oxygenating**) **1** supply, treat, or mix with oxygen; oxidize. **2** charge (blood) with oxygen by respiration. ▶ **oxygenation** *noun* [Say OXYGEN ate, oxygen AY sh'n]

oxygen mask *noun* a mask placed over the nose and mouth through which oxygen or oxygen-enriched air is supplied to relieve breathing difficulties.

oxygen tent *noun* a tent-like enclosure containing oxygen-enriched air, placed over a patient to aid breathing.

oxymoron *noun* a figure of speech in which apparently contradictory terms appear in conjunction, e.g. *bittersweet* or *living death* or *a deafening silence*. ▶ **oxymoronic** *adjective* [Say oxy MORE on, oxy muh RON ick]

oxytocin *noun* **1** a hormone released by the pituitary gland that causes increased contraction of the uterus during labour and stimulates the ejection of milk into the ducts of the breasts. **2** a synthetic form of this used to induce labour etc. [Say oxy TOE sin]

oy *interjection* calling attention or expressing alarm, dismay, exasperation, etc.

oyster *noun* **1** any of various bivalve molluscs with rough irregular shells, several kinds of which are eaten (esp. raw) as a delicacy and may be farmed for food or pearls. **2** something regarded as containing all that one desires: *the world is my oyster*.

oyster bed *noun* a part of the sea floor where oysters breed or are bred.

oystercatcher *noun* a usu. coastal wading bird with a strong orange-coloured bill, which feeds on shellfish.

oystering *noun* the activity of fishing for or gathering oysters.

oyster mushroom *noun* an edible fungus with an oyster-shaped cap, which grows on trees.

oyster sauce *noun* a dark brown sauce made from soy sauce and oyster extract, used in Asian cooking.

oy vey *interjection* an exclamation of dismay etc. [Say OI vay]

Oz *slang* • *noun* **1** Australia. **2** an Australian. • *adjective* Australian.

oz. *abbreviation* ounce(s).

ozone *noun* **1** a colourless unstable toxic gas with a pungent odour and powerful oxidizing properties, formed from normal oxygen by electrical discharges or ultraviolet light. **2** = OZONE LAYER. [Say OH zone]

ozone-friendly *adjective* (of manufactured articles) containing chemicals that are not destructive to the ozone layer.

ozone hole *noun* a region of marked thinning of the ozone layer, esp. above each pole.

ozone layer *noun* a layer of ozone in the stratosphere that absorbs most of the sun's ultraviolet radiation.

Ozzie *noun & adjective* = AUSSIE.

O

Pp

P¹ *noun* (also **p**) (*plural* **Ps** or **P's**) the sixteenth letter of the alphabet.

P² *abbreviation* (also **P.**) **1 a** (on road signs) parking. **b** (on an automatic transmission display) park. **2** (of a grade) pass. **3** *Baseball* pitcher. **4** president.

P³ *symbol* **1** phosphorus. **2** *Physics* **a** poise (unit). **b** proton.

p *abbreviation* (also **p.**) **1** (*plural* **pp**) page. **2** pico-. **3** piano (softly).

PA¹ *abbreviation* *Cdn* (*Sask.* & *Man.*) PARENTAL ACCOMPANIMENT.

PA² *noun* (*plural* **PAs**) a public address system.

Pa *symbol* protactinium.

pa *noun informal* father.

p.a. *abbreviation* per annum.

paan *noun* the leaf of the betel palm wrapped around a preparation of betel nuts and lime and chewed. [Sounds like *PAN*]

Pablum *noun* **1** *proprietary* a soft cereal for infants. **2** (**pablum**) bland or insipid intellectual fare, entertainment, etc.

pace • *noun* **1 a** a single step in walking or running. **b** the distance covered in this. **c** the distance between two successive stationary positions of the same foot in walking. **2** speed in walking or running. **3** speed or tempo in theatrical or musical performance. **4 a** the rate at which something progresses: *learn at your own pace.* **b** the speed at which life is led: *the pace of city life.* **5 a** a manner of walking or running. **b** any of various gaits, esp. of a trained horse etc. • *verb* (**paces, paced, pacing**) **1 a** walk (esp. repeatedly or methodically) with a slow or regular pace: *pacing up and down.* **b** (of a horse) = AMBLE *verb* 2. **2** traverse by pacing. **3** set the pace for (a rider, runner, etc.). **4** (often foll. by *off*) measure (a distance) by pacing. **5 pace oneself** distribute one's energy, efforts, etc. equally over the time allotted for a task, so as not to exhaust oneself too soon. PHRASES **change of pace** a change from what one is used to. **keep pace** (often foll. by *with*) advance at an equal rate (as). **off the pace 1** slower than the leading horse in a race. **2** behind the leader in any race or contest. **put a person through his** (or **her**) **paces** test a person's qualities in action etc. **set the pace** determine the speed, esp. by leading.

-paced *combining form* happening or changing at the speed or pace described: *a fast-paced action movie* ◊ *a relaxed, slow-paced lifestyle.*

pacemaker *noun* **1** a device which supplies electrical signals to the heart, stimulating it to beat at an appropriate rate. **2** the part of the heart which determines the rate at which it contracts and where the contractions begin. **3** a competitor who sets the pace for another in racing etc. **4** = PACESETTER 1.

pacer *noun* **1** a horse bred to take part in harness racing. **2** a person who paces or sets the pace.

pacesetter *noun* **1** a person etc. serving as a model for others. **2** = PACEMAKER 3. ▶ **pace-setting** *adjective* & *noun*

pachyderm *noun* any thick-skinned mammal, esp. an elephant or rhinoceros. [Say PACKY durm]

pacific *adjective* **1** characterized by or tending to peace: *NATO, it is felt, should embrace both the Germanys, even before its character has altered into something more pacific and reflective of European unity.* **2** (**Pacific**) of or adjoining the Pacific Ocean.

pacification *noun* the act of pacifying or the process of being pacified. [Say passa fuh KAY sh'n]

Pacific dogwood *noun* an ornamental dogwood tree of the west coast of North America, with white floral bracts and red fruits; it is the floral emblem of BC.

Pacific Rim *noun* (usu. as **the Pacific Rim**) the countries and regions bordering the Pacific Ocean, esp. regarded collectively as a group with shared political, economic, and environmental interests.

Pacific salmon *noun* any of the five species constituting the genus *Oncorhynchus*, of the North Pacific: the pink salmon, chum salmon, coho salmon, sockeye salmon, and chinook salmon.

Pacific Scandal *noun Cdn hist.* a scandal surrounding financial contributions to Sir John A. Macdonald's 1872 election campaign by businessmen who were subsequently granted the charter to build the Canadian Pacific Railway.

Pacific Time *noun* the time in a zone including BC and the Pacific states of the US. **Pacific Standard Time** is eight hours behind GMT; **Pacific Daylight Time** is seven hours behind GMT.

Pacific yew *noun* a small yew tree of the west coast of North America.

pacifier *noun* **1** a person or thing that pacifies. **2** a baby's soother. [Say PASSA fie er]

pacifism *noun* the belief that all disputes should be settled by peaceful means rather than war. ▶ **pacifist** *noun* & *adjective* **pacifistic** *adjective* [Say PASSA fism, PASSA fist, pass FISS tick]

pacify *verb* (**pacifies, pacified, pacifying**) **1** appease (a person, anger, etc.). **2** bring (a country etc.) to a state of peace. [Say PASSA fie]

pacing *noun* **1** in senses of PACE *verb*. **2** = PACE *noun* 3. **3** the tempos and overall rhythm, taken as a whole, selected by a conductor for a performance of a work.

pack¹ • *noun* **1** a cardboard or paper container and the items inside it. **2** a set of playing cards. **3** a collection of related documents. **4** a group of animals that live and hunt together. **5** usu. *derogatory* a group or set of similar things or people. **6** the main body of competitors following the leader in a race or competition. **7** *Cdn* & *Brit.* an organized group of Cubs, Brownies, etc. **8** a backpack. **9** pack ice. **10** a hot or cold pad of absorbent material, used for treating an injury. • *verb* **1** fill (a suitcase or bag) with clothes and other items needed for travel. **2** place in a container for transport or storage. **3** be capable of being folded up for transport or storage. **4** cram a large number of things into. **5** crowd or fill with people. **6** cover, surround, or fill. **7** *informal* carry (a gun). **8** form a hard thick mass: *the wind had packed the snow against the door.* • *adjective* (of an animal) used for carrying a load: *pack dog.* PHRASES **pack in** *informal* stop, give up: *packed in his job.* **pack it in** (or **up**) *informal* end or stop it. **pack off** *informal* send (a person) away, esp. abruptly or promptly. **pack one's bags** prepare to leave. **send packing** *informal* dismiss (a person) summarily.

pack² *verb* select (a jury etc.) or fill (a meeting) so as to secure a decision in one's favour.

package • *noun* **1 a** an object or objects wrapped in paper or packed in a box; a parcel. **b** a box etc. in which things are packed. **2** (also **package deal**) a set of things offered or agreed to as a whole. **3** a portfolio, folder, etc., containing publicity materials: *information package*. **4** a group of related objects viewed or organized as a unit. **5** *Computing* a piece of software suitable for various applications rather than one which is custom-built. **6** (also **package tour**, **package holiday**) a tour, vacation, etc. with all arrangements made at an inclusive price. • *verb* (**packages**, **packaged**, **packaging**) **1** put together in a package. **2** present (a product, person, or message) to appeal to the public. ▸ **packager** *noun*

packaging *noun* **1** a wrapping or container for goods. **2** the action or process of packing goods. **3** the creation of an image for promotional purposes; the style and context in which a particular product, person, or idea is marketed.

pack animal *noun* an animal for carrying packs.

packed *adjective* **1** full to capacity: *a packed auditorium*. **2** filled with something packed in. **3 a** (of a person) having finished packing for a trip: *are you all packed?* **b** (of a suitcase etc.) that has been packed. **4** having a specified quality in abundance: *an action-packed movie*. **5** compressed into a hardened mass: *packed snow*. **6** (of a food) packed in a specified substance for preservation: *oil-packed tuna*.

packer *noun* **1** a person or thing that packs, esp. a dealer who prepares and packs food for transportation and sale. **2 a** a pack animal. **b** a person who transports goods by means of pack animals. **c** a person who carries goods on his or her back.

packet • *noun* **1** a small package. **2** *Computing* a unit of data transmitted over a network. **3** = PACKAGE *noun* 3. • *verb* make up into or wrap up in a packet.

packet switching *noun* *Computing* a method of data transmission in which a message is broken down into a number of parts that are sent independently, over whatever route is optimum for each packet, and reassembled at the destination.

pack horse *noun* a horse for carrying loads.

pack ice *noun* an area of large crowded pieces of floating ice in the sea.

packing *noun* **1** the process of packing. **2** material used to fill up space around or in something, esp. to protect a fragile article in transit. **3** material used to seal a joint or lubricate an axle.

packing plant *noun* a factory where meat or fish is processed and packaged for shipping and sale.

packing snow *noun* wet snow that holds together when compressed, good for making snowballs, snowmen, etc.

pack rat *noun* **1** a North American rat that accumulates hoards of litter in its den. **2** a person who hoards things.

packsack *noun* a knapsack.

packsaddle *noun* a saddle adapted for supporting packs.

pack train *noun* a train of pack animals with their loads.

pact *noun* an agreement or treaty between two or more people, groups, or countries.

pad¹ • *noun* **1 a** a piece of material used to reduce friction or jarring, fill out hollows, hold or absorb liquid, etc. **b** = SANITARY PAD. **2** a number of sheets of paper fastened together at one edge. **3** = STAMP PAD. **4** the fleshy underpart of an animal's foot or of a human finger. **5** a guard for the leg, elbow, etc. in

sports. **6 a** a flat surface for helicopter takeoff or rocket-launching. **b** a broad, flat expanse of concrete etc. used as a floor or foundation. **7** *informal* an apartment. **8** the floating leaf of a water lily. **9** = CUSHION *noun* 3. **10** = TOUCHPAD. • *verb* (**pads**, **padded**, **padding**) **1** provide with a pad or padding; stuff. **2** lengthen or fill out (a book etc.) with unnecessary material. **3** inflate or falsify figures in an expense account, budget, etc.

pad² • *verb* (**pads**, **padded**, **padding**) **1** (often foll. by *around*, *over*, etc.) walk with a soft dull steady step. **2** travel on foot. • *noun* the sound of soft steady steps.

PA day *abbreviation* *Cdn* = PROFESSIONAL DEVELOPMENT DAY.

padding *noun* **1** soft material used to pad or stuff with. **2** superfluous matter added to lengthen a book, essay, etc. **3** inflated or fraudulent entries in a budget etc.

paddle • *noun* **1** a short broad-bladed oar used without a rowlock. **2** a paddle-shaped instrument or part of a machine, esp. one used for beating or mixing food. **3 a** *Sport* a short-handled bat used esp. in table tennis. **b** a numbered bat shaped like this, used to signal bids in an auction. **4** *Zoology* a fin or flipper. **5** each of the boards fitted around the circumference of a paddlewheel or mill wheel. **6** the action of paddling; a period spent paddling. **7** a plastic-covered electrode used in cardiac stimulation. • *verb* (**paddles**, **paddled**, **paddling**) **1** move or propel over water by means of paddles. **2** row gently. **3** transport (a person) by paddling: *we paddled her to the island*. **4** *informal* spank. **5** stir or mix with or as with a paddle. **6** dog-paddle. **7** *Brit.* & *Cdn* walk, esp. barefoot, in shallow water. **8** dabble the feet or hands in shallow water. PHRASES **paddle one's own canoe** manage one's own affairs.

paddleboat *noun* **1** a boat propelled by a paddlewheel. **2** = PEDAL BOAT. ▸ **paddleboating** *noun*

paddler *noun* a person who paddles a canoe or kayak etc.

paddlewheel *noun* a wheel with blades fitted around its circumference, which propels a boat when revolved by pushing backwards against the water.

paddlewheeler *noun* a steamer propelled by paddlewheels.

paddling *noun* the sport or activity of moving over water by means of paddles in a canoe, kayak, raft, etc.

paddock • *noun* **1** a small field, esp. for keeping horses in. **2** an enclosure adjoining a racetrack where horses or cars are gathered before a race. • *verb* keep or enclose in a paddock. [Say PAD ick]

paddy *noun* (*plural* **paddies**) **1** (also **paddy field**) a field where rice is grown. **2** rice before threshing or in the husk.

paddy wagon *noun* *slang* a police van for transporting prisoners or people who have been arrested.

padlock • *noun* a detachable lock hanging by a pivoted hook on the object fastened. • *verb* secure with a padlock.

Padlock Law *noun* *Cdn hist.* a 1937 Quebec statute allowing the Attorney General to close any premises suspected of being used to propagate communism.

padre *noun* **1** a Christian clergyman, esp. a Roman Catholic priest. **2** a chaplain in any of the armed services. [Say POD ray or PAD ray]

pad Thai *noun* a spicy Thai dish of rice noodles and shrimp, chicken, vegetables, etc. [Say pad TIE]

paean *noun* **1** a song of praise or triumph. **2** a thing that expresses enthusiastic praise: *there is little of the sappily sentimental in these paeans to her family*. [Say PEE un]

paediatrics *esp. Brit.* = PEDIATRICS. [Say peedy AT ricks]

paedophile *esp. Brit.* = PEDOPHILE. ▸ **paedophilia** [Say PEDDA file or PEEDA file, pedda FILLY uh or peeda FILLY uh]

P

paella *noun* (*plural* **paellas**) a Spanish dish of rice, saffron, chicken, seafood, etc. [Say pie AY uh or pie ELLA]

pagan • *noun* **1** usu. *derogatory* a person holding religious beliefs other than those of any of the main religions of the world. **2** a person considered to be irreligious. • *adjective* **1** of or associated with pagans: *a pagan god*. **2** irreligious. ▶ **paganism** *noun* [Say PAY g'n]

page[1] • *noun* **1 a** a leaf of a book etc. **b** each side of this. **c** what is written or printed on this. **2** *Computing* **a** a section of stored data, esp. that can be displayed on a screen at one time. **b** a hypertext document containing text and/or images which can be accessed by users of a network, esp. the Internet. **3 a** an episode that might fill a page in written history etc. **b** a memorable event. • *verb* (**pages, paged, paging**) **1** (foll. by *through*) leaf through (a book etc.). **2** (foll. by *through, up, down*) *Computing* display (text etc.) one page at a time.

page[2] • *noun* **1 a** an attendant of a person of rank, a bride, etc., esp. a boy. **b** a person employed in a legislative assembly to deliver members' messages. **2** a boy or man, usu. in livery, employed to run errands, attend to a door, etc. **3** *hist.* a boy in training for knighthood and attached to a knight's service. • *verb* (**pages, paged, paging**) **1** summon by making an announcement or by sending a messenger. **2** summon by means of a pager.

pageant *noun* **1 a** a brilliant spectacle or parade. **b** a procession or play depicting historical events: *Christmas pageant*. **c** a contest or show: *beauty pageant*. **2** a tableau etc. on a fixed stage or moving vehicle. **3** something resembling a pageant in its grandeur, sweep, etc.: *the pageant of history*. [Say PADGE int]

pageantry *noun* elaborate display or ceremony. [Say PADGE in tree]

pageboy *noun* **1** a woman's hairstyle with the hair reaching to the shoulder and rolled under at the ends. **2** a youth employed as a page.

page break *noun* **1** the point in a piece of continuous text where a page ends and its successor begins. **2** *Computing* a special character which, inserted into a text, causes a computer to display or print a new page.

pager *noun* a radio device with a beeper, activated from a central point to alert the person wearing it.

page-turner *noun* **1** a book so exciting or engrossing that one is compelled to read it quickly. **2** a person who turns the pages of a musical score for a pianist etc. ▶ **page-turning** *adjective*

paginate *verb* (**paginates, paginated, paginating**) assign numbers to the pages of a book etc. ▶ **pagination** *noun* [Say PADGE in ate, padge in AY sh'n]

paging *noun* the action of contacting or summoning someone by means of a pager, esp. as a feature of an electronic device or as a service offered by a telecommunications company.

pagoda *noun* (*plural* **pagodas**) **1** a Hindu or Buddhist temple or sacred building, esp. a many-tiered tower, in India and the Far East. **2** an ornamental imitation of this. [Say puh GO duh]

pah *interjection* expressing disgust or contempt.

paid • *verb* past and past participle of PAY. • *adjective* recompensed or reimbursed: *paid vacation*.

SPELL CHECK
pail, pale

The spelling is **pale** for something lacking colour or weak, and in "beyond the pale".

pail *noun* **1** a bucket. **2** an amount contained in this.

SPELL CHECK
pain, pane

A sheet of glass is a **pane**.

pain • *noun* **1 a** physical suffering or discomfort caused by illness or injury: *she's in great pain*. **b** a feeling of marked discomfort in a particular part of the body: *he had a severe pain in his stomach* ◊ *stomach pains* ◊ *labour pains*. **2** mental suffering or distress. **3** (in *plural*) careful effort; trouble taken: *take pains*. **4** (also **pain in the neck** etc.) *informal* a nuisance. • *verb* cause pain to. **PHRASES** **be at** (or **take**) **pains** take great care in doing something: *took great pains not to wake her*. **no pain, no gain** one cannot make progress (esp. in physical activity) without experiencing some pain. **on** (or **under**) **pain of** with (death etc.) as the penalty.

pained *adjective* expressing pain: *a pained expression*.

painful *adjective* **1** causing bodily or mental pain or distress. **2** (esp. of part of the body) suffering pain. **3** causing trouble or difficulty; laborious: *a painful climb*. **4** very bad: *painful jokes*. ▶ **painfully** *adverb*

painkiller *noun* a medicine or drug for alleviating pain. ▶ **painkilling** *adjective*

painless *adjective* **1** not causing or suffering pain. **2** effortless; easy. ▶ **painlessly** *adverb*

painstaking *adjective* careful, industrious, thorough. ▶ **painstakingly** *adverb*

paint • *noun* **1 a** a colouring matter, esp. in liquid form, for imparting colour to a surface. **b** this as a dried film or coating: *the paint peeled off*. **2** *jocular* or *archaic* makeup, esp. rouge or nail polish. **3** *Basketball* = KEY[1] 14. • *verb* **1** cover the surface of (a wall, object, etc.) with paint esp. of a specified colour: *paint the door green*. **2** depict (an object, scene, etc.) with paint; produce (a picture) by painting. **3** describe vividly as if by painting. **4 a** apply makeup to (the face, skin, etc.). **b** apply nail polish to (fingernails or toenails). **5** apply (a liquid) to a surface with a brush etc. **6** practise the art of painting. **7** cause (text, images, etc.) to be displayed or represented on a computer screen. **PHRASES** **paint a picture** describe in vivid detail. **paint into a corner** force (a person, oneself) into a situation from which it is not easy to escape. **paint over** (or **out**) efface with paint. **paint the town red** *informal* enjoy oneself flamboyantly.

paintball *noun* a game in which participants simulate military combat using air guns to shoot capsules of paint at each other. ▶ **paintballer** *noun*

paintbox *noun* (*plural* **paintboxes**) a box holding dry paints for painting pictures.

paintbrush *noun* (*plural* **paintbrushes**) **1** a brush for applying paint. **2** a plant of western North America that bears brightly coloured flowering spikes with a brush-like appearance. **3** = HAWKWEED.

paint-by-number *adjective* **1** denoting a painting set or book in which the pictures are divided into sections with numbers indicating the colour to be used. **2** unoriginal; lacking individuality.

paint chip *noun* **1** a card showing a colour or a range of related colours available in a type of paint. **2** a small area on a painted surface where the paint has been chipped away.

painted *adjective* **1** that has been painted. **2** (of a plant or animal) brightly coloured; variegated.

painted lady *noun* a migratory butterfly with mostly orange-red wings and black or white markings.

painted turtle *noun* a small North American freshwater turtle that is black or olive with red and yellow markings on the head and shell.

painter[1] *noun* **1** a person who paints pictures. **2** a

person who applies paint for decoration and protection to walls, doors, etc.

painter² *noun* a rope attached to the bow of a boat for tying it to a quay etc.

painterly *adjective* **1** like, characteristic of, or pertaining to a painter or paintings; artistic. **2** (of a painting or style of painting) characterized by qualities of colour, stroke, and texture rather than of contour or line.

painting *noun* **1** the process or art of using paint. **2** a painted picture.

paint stripper *noun* a heating device or a solvent for removing paint.

paint thinner *noun* a volatile liquid, e.g. turpentine, Varsol, etc., used to dilute paint, clean paintbrushes, etc.

paintwork *noun* **1** a painted surface or area in a building, on a car, etc. **2** the work of painting.

> **SPELL CHECK**
> **pair, pear, pare**
>
> The fruit is a **pear**. To trim is to **pare**.

pair • ** *noun* **1 a set of two persons or things used together or regarded as a unit: *a pair of gloves*. **2** an article, e.g. scissors, pants, etc., consisting of two joined or corresponding parts not used separately. **3 a** a dating or married couple. **b** a mated couple of animals. **4** two horses harnessed side by side. **5** the second member of a pair in relation to the first: *cannot find its pair*. **6** two playing cards of the same denomination. **7** (in *plural*) **a** = PAIRS SKATING. **b** a sporting event, e.g. synchronized swimming or rowing, performed by teams of two. **•** *verb* **1** (often foll. by *off*) arrange or be arranged in couples. **2** match or be matched together: *pair a wool vest with a silk shirt*. **3 a** join or be joined in marriage, close friendship, etc. **b** (of animals) mate. **PHRASES in pairs** in twos.

paired *adjective* occurring in pairs or as a pair.

pairing *noun* an arrangement or match resulting from organizing or forming into pairs.

pairs skater *noun* a figure skater who performs with a partner a choreographed routine of jumps, lifts, throws, etc. to music.

pairs skating *noun* a type of figure skating in which a couple perform together a choreographed routine of jumps, lifts, throws, etc. to music.

paisley *noun* **1** a distinctive detailed pattern of curved feather-shaped figures. **2** a soft woollen fabric having this pattern. [Say PAZE lee]

pajamas *plural noun* = PYJAMAS.

pak *noun* (esp. in *combination*) = PACK¹ *noun*: *econo-pak*.

Pakistani • ** *adjective* of or relating to Pakistan. **• *noun* (*plural* **Pakistanis**) a person of Pakistani nationality or descent. [Say packa STANNY]

pakora *noun* a piece of cauliflower, carrot, etc. in seasoned batter and deep-fried. [Say puh CORE uh]

pal • ** *noun informal* **1 a friend. **2** a form of address to an esp. male stranger. **•** *verb* (**pals, palled, palling**) (usu. foll. by *around*) associate; form a friendship.

palace *noun* **1** the official residence of a sovereign, president, archbishop, or bishop. **2** a splendid mansion. **3** a spacious building used for exhibitions, concerts, etc.: *cow palace*. **4** an establishment noted for the provision of a specified thing: *movie palace*.

palace coup *noun* (also **palace revolution**) the (usu. non-violent) overthrow of a sovereign, government, etc. by senior officials.

paladin *noun* **1** *hist.* a knight renowned for heroism and chivalry. **2** a dedicated advocate or supporter of a

cause: *the foremost paladin of states' rights and a bitter foe of federal supremacy*. [Say PAL a din]

Palaearctic *esp. Brit.* = PALEARCTIC. [Say paily ARC tick or pally ARC tick]

palaeo- *esp. Brit.* = PALEO-. [Say PAILY oh or PALLY oh]

Palaeocene *esp. Brit.* = PALEOCENE. [Say PAILY oh seen or PAILY oh noon]

Palaeozoic *esp. Brit.* = PALEOZOIC. [Say paily a ZO ick or pally a ZO ick]

palatability *noun* the degree to which something is pleasant to taste: *food that is high in palatability*. [Say pala tuh BILLA tee]

palatable *adjective* **1** pleasant to taste. **2** (of an idea, suggestion, etc.) acceptable, satisfactory: *some of the dialogue has been changed to make it more palatable to an American audience*. [Say PALA tuh bull]

palatal • ** *adjective* **1 of the palate. **2** (of a sound) made by placing the surface of the tongue against the hard palate, e.g. *y* in *yes*. **•** *noun* a palatal sound. [Say PALA tull]

> **SPELL CHECK**
> **palate, palette, pallet**
>
> A board for mixing paint is a **palette**. The spelling is **pallet** for a bed and for a shipping skid.

palate *noun* **1** a structure closing the upper part of the mouth cavity in vertebrates. **2** a person's sense of appreciation of taste and flavour, esp. when sophisticated and discriminating: *a menu to tempt even the most jaded palate*. **3** flavour, taste, esp. of wine or beer. **4** a mental taste or inclination; liking: *the suggestions may not suit everyone's palate*. [Say PAL it]

palatial *adjective* (of a building) like a palace, esp. spacious and splendid. [Say puh LAY shull]

palaver • ** *noun* prolonged and tedious fuss or discussion: *the newspaper has pronounced the palaver over prayer in the schools over, but the battle rages on*. **• *verb* **1** talk unnecessarily at length. **2** confer. [Say puh LAV er]

palazzo • ** *noun* (*plural* **palazzos) **1** a large palatial building or mansion. **2** loose, wide-legged pants worn by women. **•** *adjective* denoting a loose, wide-legged garment. [Say puh LAT so or puh LOT so]

> **SPELL CHECK**
> **pale, pail**
>
> A bucket is a **pail**.

pale¹ • ** *adjective* **1 (of a person or complexion) of a whitish or ashen appearance. **2 a** (of a colour) not dark or deep. **b** faintly coloured. **3** of faint lustre; dim. **4** feeble; weak: *a pale imitation*. **•** *verb* (**pales, paled, paling**) **1** grow or make pale. **2** (often foll. by *before*, *beside*) be feeble in comparison (with).

pale² ** *noun* **1 a pointed piece of wood for fencing etc.; a stake. **2** an enclosed or delimited area, e.g. the areas of Russia to which Jewish residence was historically restricted: *the vast majority of Jews who emigrated to Canada between 1881 and 1921 had come from a part of the Russian Empire known as the Pale of Settlement ◊ for the Romans, the Celts were outside the pale of civilization*. **PHRASES beyond the pale** outside the bounds of acceptable behaviour. ▶ **paling** *noun*

Palearctic *adjective* Zoology of the Arctic and temperate parts of the Old World. [Say pailey ARCTIC]

paleface *noun* a name supposedly used by the North American Indians for the white man.

palely *adverb* in a dim, whitish, or faintly coloured way.

paleness *noun* a dim, faint, or whitish quality.

paleo- *combining form* of ancient (esp. prehistoric) times. [Say PAILY oh or PALLY oh]

Paleocene *Geology* • *adjective* of or relating to the earliest epoch of the Tertiary period, between the Cretaceous period and the Eocene epoch, lasting from about 65 to 55 million years BP, characterized by a sudden diversification of mammals. • *noun* this geological epoch or system. [Say PAILEY oh seen]

paleolithic • *adjective* of or relating to the early phase of the Stone Age, when primitive stone implements were used, lasting for about 2.5 million years until the end of the last ice age. • *noun* the paleolithic period. [Say pailey oh LITH ick]

paleontological *adjective* having to do with the scientific study of extinct and fossil animals and plants. [Say pailey onta LOGICAL]

paleontologist *noun* a scientist who studies extinct and fossil animals and plants. [Say pailey un TOLLA jist]

paleontology *noun* the branch of science that deals with extinct and fossil animals and plants. [Say pailey un TOLLA jee]

Paleozoic *Geology* • *adjective* of or relating to the geological era between the Precambrian and the Mesozoic, lasting from about 590 to 248 million years ago. The era began with the first invertebrates with hard external skeletons, notably trilobites, and ended with mass extinctions and the rise to dominance of the reptiles. • *noun* this geological era. [Say pailey a ZO ick]

Palestinian • *adjective* of or relating to Palestine, an area in the Middle East on the eastern coast of the Mediterranean Sea. • *noun* 1 a native of Palestine in ancient or modern times. 2 an Arab, or a descendant of one, born or living in the area formerly called Palestine, the land west of the Jordan in which the state of Israel was established in 1948. [Say pala STINNY un]

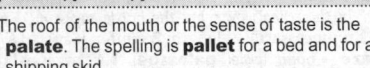

SPELL CHECK
palette, palate, pallet

The roof of the mouth or the sense of taste is the **palate**. The spelling is **pallet** for a bed and for a shipping skid.

palette *noun* 1 a thin board or slab or other surface, usu. with a hole for the thumb, on which an artist lays and mixes colours. 2 the range of colours used by an artist. 3 the range or variety of tonal or instrumental colour in a musical piece, composer's work, etc.: *he commands the sort of tonal palette that this music needs.* 4 *Computing* the range of colours or shapes available to a user of a computer graphics card. [Say PAL it]

Pali • *noun* an Indic language used in the canonical books of Buddhists. • *adjective* of this language. [Say PALLY]

palimony *noun* *informal* an allowance made by one member of an unmarried couple to the other after separation. [Say PALA moe nee]

palindrome *noun* a word or phrase that reads the same backwards as forwards, e.g. *rotator*, or *nurses run*.
▶ **palindromic** *adjective* [Say PAL in drome, pal in DROM ick]

palisade • *noun* 1 a fence of pales or iron railings. 2 a strong pointed stake used in a close row for defence. • *verb* (**palisades**, **palisaded**, **palisading**) enclose or provide with a palisade. [Say pala SAYD]

pall • *noun* 1 a cloth spread over a coffin, hearse, or tomb. 2 a dark or gloomy covering: *a pall of black smoke hung over the quarry.* 3 something regarded as enveloping a situation with an air of gloom, heaviness, or fear: *torture and murder have cast a pall of fear over the villages.* • *verb* become uninteresting or less appealing through familiarity: *the novelty of the quiet life palled after a while.* [Rhymes with WALL]

Palladian *adjective* in the neo-classical style of the Italian architect Andrea Palladio (1508–80), favouring clarity, order, and symmetry, and the use of classical motifs such as pillared porticoes with pediments.
▶ **Palladianism** *noun* [Say puh LADY in]

palladium *noun* a white metallic element occurring naturally and used in chemistry as a catalyst and for making jewellery. [Say puh LADY um]

pallbearer *noun* a person helping to carry or officially escorting a coffin at a funeral.

SPELL CHECK
pallet, palate, palette

The roof of the mouth or the sense of taste is the **palate**. The board for mixing paint is a **palette**.

pallet *noun* 1 a a straw mattress. b a makeshift or small, uncomfortable bed. 2 a portable platform for transporting and storing loads. [Say PAL it]

palliative • *noun* 1 anything used to alleviate pain without eliminating its source: *aromatherapy can be used as a palliative.* 2 an action, a decision, etc. that is designed to make a difficult situation seem better without actually solving the cause of the problems: *grants by themselves provide little more than a temporary palliative to ailing industries.* • *adjective* serving to alleviate pain, anxiety, etc., esp. without eliminating its source: *short-term, palliative measures had been taken.* [Say PAL ee uh tiv]

palliative care *noun* medical care provided for the terminally ill, aimed at relieving symptoms.

pallid *adjective* 1 pale: *her face pallid from illness* ◊ *a pallid ray of winter sun.* 2 feeble, lacking in vitality: *her part of the book, her Scandinavian-Canadian angst, seems pallid and banal.* [Say PAL id]

pallor *noun* paleness. [Say PAL er]

pally *adjective* (**pallier**, **palliest**) *informal* friendly. [Say PAL ee]

palm[1] *noun* 1 a tropical unbranched evergreen tree with a crown of very long feathered or fan-shaped leaves, usu. having old leaf scars forming a regular pattern on the trunk. 2 a the leaf of this tree as a symbol of victory or excellence. b a prize for this.

palm[2] • *noun* 1 the inner surface of the hand between the wrist and fingers. 2 the part of a glove that covers this. • *verb* 1 conceal in the hand. 2 take or pass on stealthily. 3 touch, move, etc. with the palm. PHRASES **in the palm of one's hand** under one's control or influence. **palm off 1** (often foll. by *on*) a impose or thrust fraudulently (on a person). b cause a person to accept unwillingly or unknowingly: *palmed my old computer off on him.* 2 (often foll. by *with*) cause (a person) to accept unwillingly or unknowingly: *palmed him off with my old computer.*

palmate *adjective* (also **palmated**) 1 shaped like an open hand. 2 having lobes etc. like spread fingers. [Say PAL mate]

palmcorder *noun* a small, hand-held camcorder.

palmed *adjective* having or using the kind of palm or palms described: *leather-palmed gloves* ◊ *an open-palmed slap in the face.*

palmetto *noun* (*plural* **palmettos**) a kind of small palm tree. [Say pal METTO or pol METTO]

palmist *noun* a person who claims to be able to interpret a person's character and predict their future by examining the lines and other features of the hand, esp. the palm and fingers.

palmistry *noun* the art or practice of interpreting a person's character or predicting their future by examining the lines and other features of the hand, esp. the palm and fingers. [Say PALM iss tree]

palm reader *noun* a person who practises palmistry.

P

Palm Sunday *noun* Christianity the Sunday before Easter, celebrating Christ's entry into Jerusalem.

palmtop *noun* a computer small and light enough to be held in one hand.

palmy *adjective* (**palmier**, **palmiest**) **1** of or like or abounding in palms. **2** prosperous: *palmy days*.

palomino *noun* (*plural* **palominos**) a golden or tan-coloured horse with a light-coloured mane and tail, originally bred in the southwestern US. [Say pala MEE no]

palooka *noun* (*plural* **palookas**) *slang* an oaf or lout. [Say puh LOO kuh]

palpable *adjective* **1** that can be touched or felt: *the palpable bump at the bridge of the nose*. **2** clear to the mind or plain to see; obvious: *to speak of dawn raids in the circumstances is palpable nonsense*. **3** (of a feeling or atmosphere) so intense as to be almost touched or physically felt: *a palpable sense of loss*. ▶ **palpably** *adverb* [Say PAL puh bull]

palpate *verb* (**palpates**, **palpated**, **palpating**) examine (esp. medically) by touch. ▶ **palpation** *noun* [Say PAL pate]

palpitate *verb* (**palpitates**, **palpitated**, **palpitating**) **1** (of the heart) beat rapidly, strongly or irregularly. **2** tremble, quiver: *she was palpitating with terror*. [Say PAL puh tate]

palpitation *noun* (often in *plural*) increased beating or fluttering of the heart due to exertion, excitement, or disease. [Say pal puh TAY sh'n]

palsied *adjective* affected with palsy. [Say POL zeed]

palsy *noun* (*plural* **palsies**) *dated* paralysis, esp. with involuntary tremors. [Say POL zee]

paltry *adjective* (**paltrier**, **paltriest**) **1** (of an amount) very small or meagre: *funding of the arts is paltry*. **2** having no value or useful qualities: *a paltry excuse*. [Say POL tree]

pampas *plural noun* (*singular* **pampa**) large treeless plains in South America. [Say PAM pus]

pamper *verb* treat (a person or animal) with abundant or excessive kindness or comfort. ▶ **pampered** *adjective* **pampering** *noun*

pamphlet *noun* **1** a small booklet or leaflet containing information. **2** a short treatise on a controversial, esp. political subject.

pamphleteer • *noun* a writer or issuer of (esp. political) pamphlets. • *verb* write or issue pamphlets. ▶ **pamphleteering** *noun*

pan[1] • *noun* **1 a** a cooking vessel of metal, earthenware, heat-resistant glass, etc. **b** the contents of this. **2** a panlike vessel in which substances are heated etc. **3** any similar shallow container such as the bowl of a pair of scales. **4** = ICE PAN. **5** a hollow in the ground. **6** a hard substratum of soil. **7 a** a metal drum in a steel band. **b** steel-band music and the associated culture. • *verb* (**pans**, **panned**, **panning**) **1** *informal* criticize severely. **2 a** (often foll. by *off*, *out*) wash (gold-bearing gravel) in a shallow pan. **b** search for gold by panning gravel. **c** (foll. by *out*) (of gravel) yield gold. PHRASES **pan out** (of an action etc.) turn out well or in a specified way.

pan[2] • *verb* (**pans**, **panned**, **panning**) **1** swing (a movie camera) horizontally to give a panoramic effect or to follow a moving object. **2** (of a movie camera) be moved thus. • *noun* a panning movement.

pan- *combining form* **1** all; the whole of. **2** relating to the whole or all the parts or members of: *pan-American*.

panacea *noun* (*plural* **panaceas**) a cure for all ills: *that time-honoured panacea, cod liver oil* ◊ *tree planting to combat desertification is far from being a panacea but it is a positive development*. [Say panna SEE uh]

panache *noun* flamboyant confidence of style or manner: *not everyone can do the amazing jumps that these dancers executed with panache*. [Say puh NASH]

Panamanian • *adjective* of or relating to the Republic of Panama, in Central America. • *noun* a person of Panamanian nationality or descent. [Say panna MAY nee in]

pancake • *noun* **1** any of various thin, flat, usu. round cakes of batter, grated potatoes, etc., fried on both sides, esp. one made of flour, milk, eggs, and leavening, served with butter and maple syrup. **2** (also **pancake makeup**) a thick layer of makeup, esp. foundation. **3** (also **pancake landing**) an emergency landing in which an aircraft levels out close to the ground and drops vertically with its undercarriage retracted. • *verb* (**pancakes**, **pancaked**, **pancaking**) **1 a** make a pancake landing. **b** cause (an aircraft) to pancake. **2** *informal* flatten. PHRASES **flat as a pancake** completely flat.

Pancake Day *noun* Shrove Tuesday, the day before Ash Wednesday, when pancakes are traditionally eaten, originally to consume any remaining eggs before the fast of Lent began.

pancetta *noun* cured belly of pork, usu. in a long casing. [Say pan CHETTA]

pancreas *noun* (*plural* **pancreases**) a gland near the stomach supplying the duodenum with digestive fluid and secreting insulin into the blood. ▶ **pancreatic** *adjective* [Say PAN cree us, pan cree ATTIC]

pancreatitis *noun* inflammation of the pancreas. [Say pan cree uh TITE iss]

panda *noun* (*plural* **pandas**) **1** (also **giant panda**) a bearlike mammal with black and white markings, native to China and Tibet. **2** (also **red panda**) a reddish-brown Himalayan raccoon-like mammal with a long bushy tail.

pandemic • *adjective* (of a disease or something seen as one) prevalent over a whole country or the world: *the fascination with the rich and powerful was pandemic*. • *noun* a pandemic disease: *North America experienced three principal cholera pandemics in 1832, 1848, and 1866*. [Say pan DEM ick]

pandemonium *noun* wild and noisy disorder or confusion. [Say panda MOE nee um]

pander *verb* (foll. by *to*) gratify or indulge a person, a desire or weakness, etc., esp. when these are not considered acceptable: *the media are pandering to people's baser instincts*. ▶ **panderer** *noun* **pandering** *noun*

P & H *abbreviation* postage and handling.

pandit *noun* = PUNDIT 1.

P & L *abbreviation* profit and loss.

Pandora's box *noun* (*plural* **Pandora's boxes**) a process that generates many difficult problems as the result of unwise interference in something: *a Pandora's box of political and judicial horrors*. [Say pan DORE uh's]

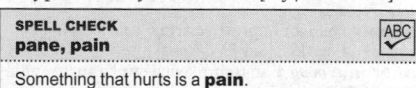

> **SPELL CHECK**
> **pane, pain**
>
> Something that hurts is a **pain**.

pane *noun* a single sheet of glass in a window or door. ▶ **paned** *adjective*

panegyric *noun* a speech or piece of writing etc. expressing high praise: *an editorial panegyric to the efficiency of the local police* ◊ *a panegyric on friendship*. [Say panna JYE rick]

panel • *noun* **1 a** a distinct, usu. rectangular, section of a surface, e.g. of a wall, door, or vehicle. **b** a board on which a number of electrical switches, controls or dials are fixed. **2** a strip of material as part of a garment. **3** a group of people invited to decide on or discuss a matter. **4** a list of available jurors. • *verb* (**panels**, **panelled**,

P

panelling) **1** fit or provide with panels. **2** cover or decorate with panels.

panelling *noun* (also esp. *US* **paneling**) panels collectively, esp. wooden panels used for a decorative wall covering.

panellist *noun* (also esp. *US* **panelist**) a member of a panel (esp. in broadcasting).

panel truck *noun* a robust small truck capable of carrying heavy loads, with an enclosed compartment behind the driver's cab.

panfish *noun* (*plural* **panfish**) any small freshwater fish suitable for frying whole in a pan, esp. one caught by an angler rather than bought. ▶ **panfishing** *noun*

pan-fried *adjective* fried or sautéed in a shallow pan with little fat or oil. ▶ **pan-fry** *verb* (**pan-fries**, **pan-fried**, **pan-frying**)

pang *noun* a sudden sharp pain or painful emotion.

Pangaea *noun* a single vast continent comprising all of the earth's land masses, which is believed to have existed in late Paleozoic and Mesozoic times (about 250 million years ago) before breaking up to eventually become the modern continents and islands of the earth. [Say pan JEE uh]

Pangnirtung hat *noun* *Cdn* (*North*) a knitted wool hat in bright colours, with a tassel at the crown and earflaps, traditional in the eastern Arctic. [Say PANG nur tung]

panhandle • *noun* a narrow strip of territory surrounded on three sides by the territory of another country or state. • *verb* (**panhandles**, **panhandled**, **panhandling**) *informal* beg for money in the street. ▶ **panhandler** *noun*

panic • *noun* **1** sudden uncontrollable fear or alarm leading to unthinking behaviour, esp. that which may suddenly spread through a crowd. **2** widespread apprehension in relation to financial and commercial matters leading to hasty measures to guard against loss: *panic selling*. **3** an agitated busyness as when making hurried preparations for something. • *verb* (**panics**, **panicked**, **panicking**) affect or be affected with panic.

panic button *noun* a button for summoning help in an emergency. PHRASES **push** (or **press**) **the panic button** react in an unduly alarmed manner.

panicky *adjective* anxious or worried; affected by or showing panic: *a panicky voice*.

panic-stricken *adjective* affected with panic.

panjandrum *noun* a person claiming to have great importance or authority: *our great panjandrum, the Assistant Deputy Minister for Parks Canada*. [Say pan JAN drum]

pannier *noun* **1** a basket, esp. one of a pair carried by a beast of burden. **2** each of a pair of bags or boxes on either side of the rear wheel of a bicycle or motorcycle. [Say PAN yer]

panoply *noun* an impressive array: *a panoply of positive feminist role models*. [Say PANNA plee]

panorama *noun* **1** an unbroken view of a surrounding region. **2** a complete survey or presentation of a subject, sequence of events, etc. **3** a picture or photograph containing a wide view. **4** a continuous passing scene. ▶ **panoramic** *adjective*

pan pipe *noun* (in *singular* or *plural*) a musical instrument made of a series of short pipes graduated in length and fixed together with the mouthpieces in line.

pansy *noun* (*plural* **pansies**) a garden plant with richly coloured flowers, related to the violet. [Say PAN zee]

pant¹ • *verb* **1** breathe with short quick breaths, as from exertion or excitement. **2** utter breathlessly. **3** (often foll. by *for*) yearn or crave: *producers are panting for material to fill their programs*. • *noun* a panting breath.

pant² *noun* = PANTS (often used before another noun: *pant leg*).

pantaloon *noun* **1** (in *plural*) *hist.* men's close-fitting breeches fastened below the calf or at the foot. **2** *informal* pants. **3** baggy pants (esp. for women) gathered at the ankles. [Say panta LOON]

pantheism *noun* **1** the belief or philosophical theory that God and the universe are identical (implying that God does not exist apart from and in a superior relation to the universe); the identification of God with the forces of nature and with natural substances. **2** worship that admits or tolerates all gods. ▶ **pantheist** *noun* **pantheistic** *adjective* [Say PANTH ee ism]

pantheon *noun* **1** a building in which famous dead people are buried or have memorials. **2** the deities of a people collectively: *the gods of the Hindu and Shinto pantheons*. **3** a temple dedicated to the gods, esp. (**the Pantheon**) the circular one in Rome. **4** a group of famous or respected people: *she has won her place in the pantheon of popular culture*. [Say PANTH ee on]

panther *noun* **1** a cougar. **2** a leopard, esp. with black fur.

panties *plural noun* legless underwear for women and girls.

pantingly *adverb* **1** while panting. **2** in an enthusiastic manner: *the media will now pantingly pursue all the rumours about his predilections*.

pantomime • *noun* **1 a** the use of gestures and facial expression to convey meaning, esp. in drama and dance. **b** a performance of this. **2** an esp. British theatrical entertainment based on a fairy tale, with music, jokes, etc., usu. produced around Christmas. **3** *informal* an absurd or exaggerated piece of behaviour: *the authorities went through a pantomime of execution and read the reprieve at the last moment*. • *verb* (**pantomimes**, **pantomimed**, **pantomiming**) represent by pantomime: *Jeff assumes the dialect of the stereotypical Hollywood showbiz shyster, even pantomiming a cigar for extra theatrics*. [Say PANTA mime]

pantry *noun* (*plural* **pantries**) a small room or cupboard in which food, dishes, cutlery, table linen, etc., are kept.

pants *plural noun* any of various garments reaching from the waist at least as far as the thighs, but usu. to the ankles, divided into two parts to cover each leg separately. PHRASES **scare** (or **beat** etc.) **the pants off** *informal* scare, beat, etc., thoroughly. **with one's pants down** *informal* in an embarrassingly unprepared state.

pantsuit *noun* a women's suit of pants and a matching jacket.

panty *noun* = PANTIES.

pantyhose *plural noun* very thin or sheer nylon tights for women.

panzer *noun* a German armoured unit or tank: *panzer division*.

panzerotto *noun* (*plural* **panzerotti**) *Cdn* a baked pizza-like turnover, consisting of dough folded into a sealed pocket, filled with tomato sauce, cheese, etc. [Say panza ROTTO]

pap *noun* **1 a** soft or semi-liquid food for infants or invalids. **b** a mash or pulp. **2** unchallenging or trivial reading matter, ideas, entertainment, etc.; nonsense.

papa *noun* (*plural* **papas**) *archaic* father (esp. as a child's word).

papacy *noun* **1** the office or authority of the Pope: *nuns taught their charges the importance of prayer and promoted loyalty to the papacy*. **2** the time during which a Pope is in office: *during the papacy of John XXIII*. [Say PAPE uh see]

papal *adjective* of a pope or the papacy. [Say PAPE ul]

paparazzo *noun* (*plural* **paparazzi**) (usu. in *plural*) a

freelance photographer who pursues celebrities to get photographs of them. [Say pappa RAT so for the singular, pappa RAT see for the plural]

papaw noun = PAWPAW. [Say puh PAW]

papaya noun (plural **papayas**) **1** an elongated melon-shaped fruit with edible orange flesh and small black seeds. **2** the tropical tree that produces this fruit. [Say puh PIE uh]

paper • noun **1 a** a material manufactured in thin sheets from the pulp of wood or other fibrous substances, used for writing or drawing or printing on, or as wrapping material etc. **b** a piece of this. **2** = NEWSPAPER. **3 a** a document printed on paper. **b** (in plural) personal documents, esp. verifying identity or credentials. **4** Commerce **a** negotiable documents, e.g. bills of exchange. **b** (as an adjective) recorded on paper though not existing: paper profits. **5** = WALLPAPER 1. **6 a** a scholarly essay or dissertation. **7** Theatre slang free tickets or the people admitted by them: the house is full of paper. **8 a** a set of questions in an exam. **b** the written answers to these. • verb **1** apply paper to, esp. decorate (a wall etc.) with wallpaper. **2** (foll. by over) **a** cover (a hole or blemish) with paper. **b** disguise or try to hide (a fault etc.). **3** Theatre fill (a theatre) by giving free tickets. PHRASES **on paper 1** in writing. **2** in theory; to judge from written or printed evidence. **push paper** engage in office work.

paperback • adjective (of a book) bound in stiff paper, not boards. • noun a paperback book.

paperbark noun any of various trees with peeling papery bark, esp. the paperbark maple.

paperboard noun a sheet of stiff material made by pasting and pressing together sheets of paper.

paper boy noun (also **paper girl**) a boy or girl who delivers or sells newspapers.

paper chase noun **1** informal any process involving much paperwork. **2** a cross-country run in which runners follow a trail marked by torn-up paper.

paper clip • noun a clip of bent wire or of plastic for holding several sheets of paper together. • verb (**paper-clip**) (**paper-clips, paper-clipped, paper-clipping**) attach with a paper clip.

paperless adjective using computers rather than paper to record or exchange information: a paperless office.

papermaker noun a person who makes paper for a living. ▶ **papermaking** noun & adjective

paper-pusher noun informal a menial clerical or office worker. ▶ **paper-pushing** noun

paper route noun **1** a job of regularly delivering newspapers. **2** a route taken doing this.

paper-thin adjective & adverb very thin.

paper tiger noun an apparently threatening but ineffectual person or thing: history suggests that Russian-equipped foreign forces are paper tigers formidable in numbers but ineffective.

paper trail noun documentation linking a person or group to an esp. incriminating event or series of events.

paperweight noun a small heavy object for keeping loose papers in place.

paperwork noun **1** routine clerical or administrative work. **2** paper documents collectively.

paperworker noun a person employed in the pulp and paper industry.

papery adjective resembling paper in texture or thinness: papery petals.

papier mâché noun paper pulp or strips of paper mixed with glue, used for making moulded figures etc. [Say paper ma SHAY or pap yay ma SHAY]

papilla noun (plural **papillae**) **1** a small nipple-like protuberance in a part or organ of the body. **2** Botany a

small fleshy projection on a plant. [Say puh PILLA for the singular, puh PILLY for the plural]

papilloma noun (plural **papillomas**) a wart-like usu. benign tumour. [Say pap uh LOW muh]

papoose noun a North American Indian child. [Say puh POOSE]

pappardelle plural noun pasta in the form of broad flat ribbons, usu. served with a meat sauce. [Say pap ar DEL ay]

pappy noun (plural **pappies**) esp. US father.

paprika noun a spice made from dried ground red sweet peppers. [Say PAP rick uh or puh PREE kuh]

Pap smear noun (also **Pap test**) a procedure for detecting cervical cancer involving the scraping and microscopic examination of cells from the cervix.

Papuan • noun **1** a native or inhabitant of Papua, the southeastern part of the island of New Guinea in the W Pacific. **2** a group of around 750 languages spoken in New Guinea and neighbouring islands. • adjective of or relating to Papua or its people or to Papuan. [Say PAP oo in or POP oo in]

papyrus noun (plural **papyri**) **1** a grasslike aquatic plant with tall, dark green stems. **2 a** a material prepared in ancient Egypt from the pithy stem of this plant, used in sheets throughout the ancient Mediterranean world for writing or painting on and also for making articles such as rope, sandals, and boats. **b** a document written on this material. [Say puh PIE rus for the singular, puh PIE rye for the plural]

par • noun **1** the average or normal amount, degree, condition, etc.: feel below par. **2** an equal standing: this home cooking is on a par with the best in the world. **3** Golf the number of strokes a first-class player should normally require for a hole or course. **4** the face value of a stock or bond. **5** the recognized value of one country's currency in terms of another's: the Australian dollar was almost at par with the Canadian dollar. • verb (**pars, parred, parring**) Golf complete (a hole or course) with a score equal to par. PHRASES **par for the course** informal what is normal or expected in any given circumstances.

par. abbreviation (also **para.**) paragraph.

para- combining form of or using parachutes: parasailing.

parable noun **1** a simple story used to illustrate a moral or spiritual lessons: the parable of the Prodigal Son. **2** an allegory: the latter poem takes the form of an ironic parable about art and reality. [Say PERRA bull]

parabola noun (plural **parabolas**) a symmetrical curve like the path of a projectile under the influence of gravity. [Say puh RABBA luh]

parabolic adjective of or like a parabola: a row of parabolic arches of red brick. [Say perra BOLL ick]

parachute • noun a cloth canopy that fills with air and allows a person etc. attached to it to fall from an airplane at a safe rate, or which is released from the rear of a landing aircraft as a brake. • verb (**parachutes, parachuted, parachuting**) **1** drop or land by parachute. **2** appoint or be appointed as an outsider to a position, candidacy, etc.: Elaine had leapfrogged over most of her co-workers and parachuted into a senior position in a new agency. ▶ **parachutist** noun

parade • noun **1 a** a public procession, usu. celebrating a special day. **b** a series of people or things in succession: a parade of players to the penalty box. **2 a** a formal or ceremonial march or assembling of troops for inspection or display. **b** = PARADE GROUND. • verb (**parades, paraded, parading**) **1** march in or assemble for a parade. **2** display (something) publicly in order to impress or attract attention: she paraded her knowledge. **3** pass by or cause to pass by in procession.

P

PHRASES **on parade 1** on display. **2** taking part in a parade.

parade ground *noun* (also *Cdn* **parade square**) an outdoor area where soldiers etc. gather for inspection, roll call, etc.

paradichlorobenzene *noun* a crystalline compound used in mothballs. [Say pair a die klor oh BEN zeen]

paradigm *noun* **1** a typical example or pattern; a model: *there is a new paradigm for public art in this country.* **2** a mode of viewing the world which underlies the theories and methodology of science etc. in a particular period of history: *the publication of his book provided a new paradigm for the study of literature.* **3** a list serving as an example or pattern of the inflections of a noun, verb, etc. ▶ **paradigmatic** *adjective* [Say PERRA dime, perra dig MAT ick]

paradigm shift *noun* a fundamental change (in approach, philosophy, etc.): *a paradigm shift away from large families toward smaller ones.*

paradisal *adjective* ideal, wonderful, heavenly: *a paradisal garden of beautiful flowers.* [Say PERRA dice ul]

paradise *noun* **1** (in some religions) heaven as the final resting place of those who have lived a morally good life. **2 a** an idyllic place or state. **b** an ideal or perfect place: *a walker's paradise.* **3** the abode of Adam and Eve in the Biblical account of Creation; the garden of Eden.

paradox *noun* (*plural* **paradoxes**) **1 a** a seemingly absurd or self-contradictory statement which, when investigated or explained, may prove to be well-founded or true: *"more haste, less speed" is a well-known paradox* ◊ *it's a work full of paradox and ambiguity.* **b** a statement that is actually self-contradictory, absurd, or false. **2** a situation, person, or thing that combines contradictory qualities or features: *he was a paradox — a loner who loved to chat to strangers* ◊ *it is a curious paradox that professional comedians often have unhappy personal lives.*

paradoxical *adjective* **1** of or involving paradox, esp. apparently inconsistent with itself or with reason, though in fact true: *it is paradoxical that some of the poorest people live in some of the richest areas of the country.* **2** (of a person etc.) characterized by paradox. ▶ **paradoxically** *adverb*

paraffin *noun* **1** a translucent, inflammable, waxy or oily substance distilled from petroleum and shale and used esp. in candles, cosmetics, and polishes, and for coating and sealing. **2** *Chemistry* = ALKANE. [Say PERRA fin]

paraffin wax *noun* paraffin in its solid form.

paraglider *noun* a participant in the sport of paragliding.

paragliding *noun* a sport resembling hang-gliding, using a wide, parachute-like canopy attached to the body by a harness, allowing a person to glide after jumping from or being hauled to a height.

paragon *noun* **1** a person or thing seen as a model of excellence: *the cook in this restaurant is a paragon.* **2** a model (of virtue etc.): *it would have taken a paragon of virtue not to feel viciously jealous.* [Say PERRA gon]

paragraph • *noun* **1 a** a distinct passage of a text, dealing with one particular point of the subject, the words of one speaker, etc., and beginning on a new, usu. indented line. **b** a distinct, usu. numbered, article or section of a legal document. **2** a symbol (usu. ¶) used to mark a new paragraph or section of a text, introduce an editorial comment, or as a reference mark. • *verb* arrange (text) in paragraphs.

Paraguayan • *adjective* of or relating to Paraguay, a country in northern South America. • *noun* a native or inhabitant of Paraguay. [Say pa ra GWAY in]

parakeet *noun* a small usu. long-tailed parrot.

paralegal • *noun* a person trained in subsidiary legal matters, but not fully qualified as a lawyer; a legal aide. • *adjective* of or relating to auxiliary aspects of the law. [Say perra LEGAL]

parallax *noun* (*plural* **parallaxes**) **1 a** the apparent difference in the position or direction of an object caused when the observer's position is changed. **b** such a difference or change in the position of a celestial object as seen from different points on the earth's surface or opposite points in its orbit. **2** the angular amount of such a difference or change. [Say PERRA lax]

parallel • *adjective* **1 a** (of lines or planes) side by side with the same distance continuously between them. **b** (foll. by *to, with*) (of a line or plane) having this relation (to another). **2** (of circumstances etc.) precisely similar, analogous, or corresponding. **3** running through the same period of time, contemporary in duration: *parallel universe.* **4** *Computing* **a** involving the concurrent performance of multiple operations: *parallel processing.* **b** of or involving the simultaneous transmission of data over separate wires: *parallel port.* **5** (of a text etc.) having two or more translations etc. printed in a format which allows direct comparison, usu. on facing or consecutive pages: *a parallel Bible.* • *noun* **1 a** comparison. **2** a person or thing precisely analogous or equal to another in essential particulars. **3** (also **parallel of latitude**) **a** each of the imaginary parallel circles of constant latitude on the earth's surface. **b** a corresponding line on a map. • *verb* (**parallels, paralleled, paralleling**) **1** be parallel to; correspond to. **2** run parallel with, alongside of, or in the same general direction as. • *adverb* in a parallel direction or manner: *main streets ran parallel to the shoreline.* PHRASES **in parallel 1** (of electric circuits) arranged so as to join at common points at each end. **2** concurrently, simultaneously, contemporaneously.

parallel bars *plural noun* **1** a gymnastics event in which participants perform feats on a pair of parallel rails on posts. **2** these rails.

parallelism *noun* **1 a** the state, position or character of being parallel. **b** an example of this. **c** a parallel case, passage, etc. **2** correspondence, in sense or esp. construction, of successive clauses or passages in writing. **3** *Computing* **a** the execution of operations concurrently by separate parts of a computer, esp. separate microprocessors. **b** the capability of a computer to operate in this way.

parallelogram *noun* a plane figure having four straight sides with opposite sides parallel. [Say perra LELLA gram]

parallel park *verb* park a vehicle parallel to the sidewalk or roadside.

parallel parking *noun* the parking of a vehicle parallel to the sidewalk or roadside.

> **GRAMMAR CHECK**
> **parallel structure**
>
> The failure to use parallel structure makes writing awkward and potentially unclear. For example, the sentence *As a result of abuse, children may become withdrawn, too eager to please, aggressive, demanding, or have suicidal tendencies* is much less awkward if it is rewritten as *As a result of abuse, children may become withdrawn, fawning, aggressive, demanding, or suicidal.*

parallel structure *noun* sentence structure in which related parts of a sentence have the same grammatical function (e.g. all nouns, all adjectives, etc.).

Paralympian *noun* a disabled athlete who participates in the Paralympics. [Say perra LIM pee in]

Paralympic *adjective* having to do with the Paralympics. [Say perra LIM pick]

Paralympics *plural noun* (also **Paralympic Games**) an international athletic competition for disabled athletes. [Say perra LIM picks]

paralysis *noun* (*plural* **paralyses**) **1** loss of the ability to move a part of the body, usu. as a result of disease or injury to the nervous system. **2** a state of utter powerlessness; inability to act or function: *the paralysis gripping the country*. [Say puh RALLA sis]

paralytic *adjective* of, causing, or suffering from paralysis. [Say perra LIT ick]

paralyze *verb* (**paralyzes, paralyzed, paralyzing**) (also **paralyse, paralyses, paralysed, paralysing**) **1** affect with paralysis. **2** render incapable of action. **3** bring to a standstill.

paramecium *noun* any freshwater protozoan of the genus *Paramecium*, of a characteristic slipper-like shape covered with cilia. [Say perra MEE see um]

paramedic *noun* a paramedical worker, trained in first aid, esp. one who works in ambulances.

paramedical *adjective* (of services etc.) supplementing and supporting medical work.

parameter *noun* **1** a limit or boundary which defines the scope of a particular process or activity: *the parameters within which the media works*. **2** *Math* a quantity constant in the case considered but varying in different cases. [Say puh RAMMA ter]

paramilitary • *adjective* (of forces etc.) organized similarly to military forces. • *noun* (*plural* **paramilitaries**) **1** a paramilitary force or organization. **2** a member of such a force or organization.

paramount *adjective* **1** superior to others in importance, influence, etc.: *this matter is of paramount importance ◊ safety is paramount ◊ the welfare of the child must always be the court's paramount consideration*. **2** (of a person, nation, etc.) above others in rank or order; highest in power or jurisdiction: *China's paramount leader*.

paramour *noun* **1** an illicit lover of a married person. **2** any lover; a sweetheart. [Say PERRA moor]

paranoia *noun* (*plural* **paranoias**) **1** a mental illness characterized by delusions of persecution, unwarranted jealousy, or exaggerated self-importance. **2** unjustified suspicion and mistrust of others. ▶ **paranoiac** *adjective & noun* [Say perra NOYA]

paranoid • *adjective* **1** resulting or suffering from a mental illness characterized by delusions of persecution, unwarranted jealousy, or exaggerated self-importance: *paranoid delusions ◊ paranoid schizophrenic*. **2** unreasonably or obsessively anxious, suspicious, or mistrustful: *the threat of corporate downsizing has made a lot of employees paranoid ◊ she's paranoid about getting wrinkles*. • *noun* a person who is paranoid. [Say PERRA noyd]

paranormal *adjective* of phenomena or powers whose operation is outside the scope of known laws of nature or normal objective investigation. [Say perra NORMAL]

parapet *noun* **1** a low wall at the edge of a roof, balcony, etc., or along the sides of a bridge etc. **2** a bank of earth or stone erected to provide protection from observation and attack, esp. one on top of a wall or rampart, or in front of a trench. [Say PERRA pet]

paraphernalia *plural noun* (also treated as *singular*) miscellaneous belongings, items of equipment, accessories, etc.: *skiing paraphernalia ◊ an electric kettle and all the paraphernalia for making tea and coffee ◊ the legal paraphernalia of court hearings and appeals*. [Say perra fuh NAILY uh]

paraphrase • *noun* rewording. • *verb* (**paraphrases,**

paraphrased, paraphrasing) express the meaning of in other words.

paraplegia *noun* paralysis of the legs and part or all of the torso. ▶ **paraplegic** *adjective & noun* [Say perra PLEE juh, perra PLEE jick]

paraprofessional • *noun* a person without professional training to whom a particular aspect of a professional task is assigned. • *adjective* of or designating such a person.

parapsychologist *noun* a person who studies mental phenomena outside the sphere of orthodox scientific psychology, e.g. hypnosis, telepathy, etc.

parapsychology *noun* the study of mental phenomena outside the sphere of the orthodox scientific psychology, e.g. hypnosis, telepathy, etc.

parasail • *verb* participate in the sport of parasailing. • *noun* an open parachute used in parasailing.

parasailing *noun* a sport in which participants wearing open parachutes glide through the air while being towed by a speedboat.

parasite *noun* **1** an organism living in or on another and benefiting at the expense of the other. **2** a person who lives off others. ▶ **parasitic** *adjective* **parasitically** *adverb* **parasitism** *noun* [Say PERRA site, perra SIT ick, PERRA site ism]

parasitize *verb* (**parasitizes, parasitized, parasitizing**) infest or exploit (an organism or part) as a parasite: *Canada has six different types of ticks that parasitize people*. [Say PERRA suh tize]

parasitologist *noun* a person who studies parasitic organisms. [Say perra sit OLLA jist]

parasitology *noun* the branch of biology or medicine concerned with the study of parasitic organisms. [Say perra sit OLLA jee]

parasol *noun* a light umbrella used to give shade from the sun. [Say PERRA sol]

parasympathetic *adjective* relating to one of the major divisions of the autonomic nervous system, whose nerves leave the spinal cord in the cranial or sacral region, and which is associated more with calmness and rest than with alertness (compare SYMPATHETIC 8).

parathyroid • *noun* a gland next to the thyroid, secreting a hormone that regulates calcium and phosphate levels in the body. • *adjective* of this gland.

paratrooper *noun* a soldier who has been trained to be dropped by parachute from an aircraft.

paratroops *plural noun* troops equipped to be dropped by parachute from aircraft.

parboil *verb* partly cook by boiling.

parcel • *noun* **1** an item or quantity of goods etc. wrapped up in a single package. **2** a piece of land. **3** (esp. in **part and parcel**) an integral part. • *verb* (**parcels, parcelled, parcelling**) **1** (foll. by *up*) wrap as a parcel. **2** (foll. by *out*) divide into portions.

parch *verb* (**parches, parched, parching**) **1** make or become hot and dry with heat. **2** roast (peas, grain, etc.) lightly.

parched *adjective* **1** dried out, esp. by heat. **2** thirsty.

parchment *noun* **1 a** an animal skin, esp. that of a sheep or goat, prepared as a writing or painting surface. **b** a manuscript written on this. **2** (also **parchment paper**) high-grade translucent paper made to resemble parchment, used for lampshades, as a writing surface, and in baking. **3** a diploma.

pardner *noun* *jocular* a partner or comrade.

pardon • *noun* **1** the action of forgiving or being forgiven for an error or offence: *she obtained pardon for her actions*. **2 a** a remission or cancellation of the legal consequences of a crime or conviction: *offered a full pardon to the five convicted men*. **b** a document conveying

a legal pardon. **3** *Catholicism hist.* the remission of punishment in purgatory, still due for sins even after sacramental absolution. • *verb* **1** release from the consequences of a legal offence or sin. **2** forgive or excuse (a person, error, or offence). **3** make esp. courteous allowances for, excuse (a person, fact, or action). • *interjection* (also **pardon me** or **I beg your pardon**) **1** a formula of apology or disagreement. **2** a request to repeat something said. ▶ **pardonable** *adjective* **pardonably** *adverb*

SPELL CHECK
pare, pair, pear

The spelling is **pair** for a set of two and in "au pair".
The fruit is a **pear**.

---

pare *verb* (**pares, pared, paring**) **1 a** cut away the skin or outer covering of (esp. fruit or vegetables). **b** trim by cutting away the surface or edge: *pared his nails.* **c** (often foll. by *off, away*) cut off (the surface or edge). **2** (usu. foll. by *down*) gradually reduce in size, extent, or number, esp. so as to arrive at the essentials.

pared-down *adjective* simplified, reduced esp. to a minimum: *pared-down companies.*

parent • *noun* **1** a biological father or mother. **2** a person who holds the position or exercises the function of such a parent, e.g. by adopting a child. **3** an animal or plant considered in relation to its offspring. **4** a thing from which another is derived or has its existence: *Quebec was founded by immigrants who came here in the 17th and 18th centuries from a parent culture that was largely feudal.* **5 a** an initiating organization or enterprise. **b** = PARENT COMPANY. • *verb* **1** be or act as a parent to (a child). **b** beget, produce. **2** be a parent; take care of one's children.

parentage *noun* descent from or through parents: *their parentage is unknown.*

parental *adjective* having to do with a parent: *parental authority* ◊ *parental consent* ◊ *parental involvement.*

Parental Accompaniment *noun* **1** (in Manitoba) a film classification which recommends that viewers under 15 years of age be accompanied by a parent or guardian. **2** (in Saskatchewan) a film classification which requires that viewers under 14 years of age be accompanied by a parent or guardian. Abbreviation: **PA**.

Parental Guidance *noun* **1** (in Alberta, Saskatchewan, and Ontario) a film classification which advises of content that should be subject to parental discretion, without specifying an age restriction. **2** (in Manitoba and the Maritimes) a film classification which advises of content most suitable for mature viewers over 12 years of age. Abbreviation: **PG**.

parent company *noun* a company of which other companies are subsidiaries.

parenthesis *noun* (*plural* **parentheses**) **1** a word, clause, or sentence inserted as an explanation or afterthought into a passage, usu. set off in text by brackets, dashes, or commas. **2** (usu. in *plural*) either of a pair of round brackets ( ) used for this.

parenthetical *adjective* of or by way of a parenthesis: *ignore the parenthetical references to the author's childhood.* ▶ **parenthetically** *adverb* [Say pair in THETTA cull]

parenthood *noun* the state of being a parent: *the joys of parenthood.*

parenting *noun* the occupation or concerns of parents, esp. taking care of one's children.

parent-teacher association *noun* a local organization of parents and teachers for promoting closer relations and improving educational facilities at a school. Abbreviation: **PTA**.

parer *noun* a paring knife.

pareve *adjective Judaism* (of food) being or containing neither meat nor dairy and so kosher for use with either, according to the dietary laws (includes fruit, vegetables, fish, etc.). [Say PAR uh vuh or PAR vuh]

par excellence *adjective* being the supreme example of its kind: *the short story par excellence.* [Say par eck sel LONCE]

parfait *noun* **1** ice cream, sauces, crushed fruit, etc. layered in a tall glass. **2** a frozen dessert made with egg whites, sugar, whipped cream, and flavouring. [Say par FAY]

parfleche *noun* a hide, esp. of buffalo, from which the hair has been removed and which has been dried on a frame: *parfleche bag.* [Say PAR flesh]

parge *verb* (also **parget**) (**parges, parged, parging** or **pargets, pargeted, pargeting**) **1** apply parging to (a wall, brickwork, etc.). **2** plaster (a wall etc.) esp. with an ornamental pattern.

parging *noun* **1** a thin layer of mortar, plaster, etc. covering a wall for protection or to create a smooth surface. **2** the mortar used for parging. [Say PAR jing]

pariah *noun* **1** a social outcast: *they were treated as social pariahs.* **2** a despised person: *made myself into a pariah by sitting down at a table for six.* **3** (also **pariah state**) a country against which political or diplomatic sanctions are in force: *the Foreign Minister said Serbia would be made a pariah by the world until policies of ethnic cleansing were stopped.* [Say puh RYE uh]

parietal *adjective* **1** *Anatomy* **a** of the wall of the body or the lining of any of its cavities. **b** of or near the **parietal bones**, the pair of bones forming the central part of the sides and top of the skull. **2** *Botany* of the wall of a hollow structure, esp. an ovary. [Say puh RYE it ul]

parimutuel *noun* **1** a form of betting in which those backing the first three places divide the losers' stakes (less the operator's commission). **2** a booth etc. for placing bets under this system. [Say perry MYOO choo el]

paring *noun* **1** (often in *plural*) a thin portion cut or peeled from a surface; a shaving. **2** an act of cutting, shaving, or peeling such a strip. [Say PAIR ing]

paring knife *noun* a kitchen knife with a short, firm, pointed blade used for paring fruit, vegetables, etc.

parish *noun* (*plural* **parishes**) **1 a** an area of ecclesiastical jurisdiction having a church and clergy. **b** the people who are members of a parish. **2** *Cdn* **a** (*Que.*) a county subdivision functioning as both a political and an ecclesiastical unit. **b** (*NB*) a county subdivision, the unit of representation at county councils.

parish hall *noun* **1** a large meeting room, usu. part of or connected to a parish church, in which social events, meetings, etc. are held. **2** the building in which this is housed, if separate from the church.

parishioner *noun* **1** a member or attendee of a particular church. **2** an inhabitant of a parish. [Say puh RISHA ner]

Parisian • *adjective* of or typical of the people or city of Paris, France. • *noun* **1** a native or inhabitant of Paris. **2** the kind of French spoken in Paris. [Say puh REE zhin]

parity *noun* (*plural* **parities**) **1** equality or equal status. **2 a** equivalence of pay for jobs or categories of work perceived as being comparable or analogous: *striking factory workers are seeking parity with their colleagues in sales and marketing.* **b** the practice or system of setting pay levels according to such perceived comparability. **3** *Math & Computing* **a** the property of an integer by virtue of which it is odd or even numbers. **b** the property of employing odd or even numbers. **4** *Computing* a function whose being odd or even provides a check on a set of binary values. **5** *Physics* (of a quantity) the fact of changing its

sign or remaining unaltered under a given transformation of coordinates etc. **6** equivalence of one currency with another. [Say PERRA tee]

park • *noun* **1** a piece of land with lawns, gardens, etc. in a town or city, maintained at public expense for recreational use. **2** a large area of government land kept in its natural state for recreational use, wildlife conservation, etc. **3** a large enclosed area of land, either public or private, used to accommodate wild animals in captivity: *wildlife park*. **4** an area developed for a specified purpose or form of recreation: *industrial park* ◊ *water park* ◊ *theme park*. **5** a stadium etc. for sports events: *ballpark*. **6** an area for motor vehicles etc. to be left in: *trailer park*. **7** the gear position or function in automatic transmission in which the gears are locked, preventing the vehicle's movement. **8** a large enclosed piece of ground, usu. with woodland and pasture, attached to a stately home etc. • *verb* **1** leave (a vehicle) temporarily, in a parking lot, by the side of the road, etc. **2** *informal* leave, deposit, or settle (a person or thing) in a convenient place, usu. temporarily. **PHRASES park oneself** *informal* sit down.

parka *noun* (*plural* **parkas**) a warm, hooded coat extending to the thighs or calves.

parkade *noun Cdn* a parking garage.

park-and-ride *noun* a system whereby commuters, shoppers, etc. travel by car to parking lots on the outskirts of a city and continue into the city by public transportation.

park belt *noun Cdn* (*West*) the lightly wooded grasslands between the open prairie and the northern forests in Manitoba, Saskatchewan, and Alberta.

parkette *noun Cdn* (*S Ont.*) a small park in a city.

parking *noun* **1** the act of stopping a vehicle at a place and leaving it for a time: *parking attendant*. **2** an area for leaving vehicles: *underground parking*. **3** *slang* the act of indulging in sexual activity, usu. stopping short of intercourse, while in a parked car.

parking brake *noun* = EMERGENCY BRAKE.

parking garage *noun* a structure with space for parking vehicles.

parking light *noun* a small light on either side of the front and rear of a vehicle.

parking lot *noun* a usu. outdoor area for parking vehicles.

parking meter *noun* a coin-operated meter which receives fees for vehicles parked in the street and indicates the time available.

parking stall *noun Cdn* (*West*) & *US* a parking space in a parking garage or parking lot.

parking ticket *noun* a notice of a fine etc. imposed for parking illegally.

Parkinson's disease *noun* (also **Parkinsonism**) a progressive disease of the nervous system which produces tremor, muscular rigidity, as well as slowness and imprecision of movements.

parkland *noun* **1 a** open grassland scattered with clumps of trees etc. **b** *Cdn* the lightly wooded grasslands between the open prairie and the northern forests in Manitoba, Saskatchewan, and Alberta. **c** *Cdn* the grassy region between the Prairies and the foothills of the Rockies. **2** a piece of land set aside by the government for public recreation, wildlife conservation, etc.

parks officer *noun Cdn* = PARK WARDEN.

park warden *noun* (also **park ranger**) an official responsible for patrolling and maintaining a national, provincial, etc. park, having the powers of a peace officer in matters of park regulations.

parkway *noun* a highway or main road with trees, grass, etc. planted alongside.

parlance *noun* a particular way of speaking, esp. as regards choice of words, idiom, etc.: *dated terms that were once in common parlance* ◊ *medical parlance*. [Say PAR lince]

parlay • *verb* **1** transform (an advantage etc.) into something greater: *she hopes to parlay her success as a model into an acting career*. **2** use (money won on a bet) as a further stake. **3** turn an initial stake or winnings from a previous bet into (a larger amount) by gambling: *it involved parlaying a small bankroll into big winnings*. • *noun* a bet made by parlaying. [Say par LAY or PAR lay]

parley • *noun* (*plural* **parleys**) an informal conference, under truce, with an enemy, for discussing the mutual arrangement of matters such as terms for armistice, exchange of prisoners, etc. • *verb* (**parleys, parleyed, parleying**) (often foll. by *with*) hold a parley. [Say PARLY]

parliament *noun* **1** (usu. **Parliament**) the highest legislative body in certain countries, including Canada. **2** a legislative body of a province, state, etc.: *provincial parliament*. **3** the members of a parliament. **4** a period during which the members of a parliament are assembled, following a general election and until dissolution. **5** a place where parliament meets. **6** the House of Commons.

parliamentarian *noun* **1** a member of a parliament, esp. one well-versed in its procedures. **2** *hist.* (**Parliamentarian**) a member or supporter of the party opposing Charles I in the English Civil War (1642–9).

parliamentary *adjective* **1** of or relating to a parliament. **2** enacted or established by a parliament. **3** according to the constitution of a parliament: *parliamentary democracy*. **4** (of language) admissible in a parliament; polite.

parliamentary committee *noun* a group of people drawn from the upper or lower houses of a legislature, appointed to consider the details of a proposed bill after its second reading.

parliamentary government *noun* a government in which a prime minister (or premier) chooses MPs, usu. from his or her own party, to be Ministers of the Crown who will form the Cabinet and be responsible to Parliament for the conduct of the government.

parliamentary secretary *noun* (*plural* **parliamentary secretaries**) an MP belonging to the party in government, appointed by the prime minister to assist a senior cabinet minister.

parliament building *noun* **1** a building in which a parliament meets. **2** a complex of buildings housing the parliament and offices of its members and staff, esp. (**Parliament Buildings**) (in Canada) those in Ottawa.

Parliament Hill *noun Cdn* the hill in Ottawa on which the Parliament Buildings stand.

parlour *noun* (also **parlor**) **1** a sitting room in a house. **2 a** a business providing specified goods or services: *beauty parlour*. **b** *Cdn* = BEER PARLOUR. **3** (also **milking parlour**) a room or building equipped for milking cows. **4** a room in a hotel, club, etc. for the private use of guests. **5** a room in a convent or monastery set aside for conversation.

Parmesan *noun* hard dry cheese used esp. in grated form. [Say PARMA zon or PARMA zan]

parmigiana *adjective* made or served with Parmesan cheese. [Say parma JONNA]

parmigiano *noun* Parmesan cheese, esp. grated. [Say parma JONNO]

parochial *adjective* **1** of a parish: *the parochial church council*. **2** (of views etc.) merely local, narrow or restricted in scope: *parochial attitudes* ◊ *their interests are too parochial*. ▶ **parochialism** *noun* [Say puh ROKEY ul]

P

parochial school *noun* a primary or secondary school established and run by a religious body.

parodic *adjective* imitating something or someone in a deliberately exaggerated and often humorous manner, usu. in order to ridicule the subject: *the actor's parodic portrayal of an aging rock star.* ▶ **parodically** *adverb* [Say puh ROD ick]

parodist *noun* a person who writes parodies. [Say PERRA dist]

parody • *noun* (*plural* **parodies**) **1** an imitation of the style of a particular writer, artist, genre, or person with deliberate exaggeration for comic effect: *this film is a parody of the horror genre* ◊ *her provocative use of parody.* **2** a thing done so badly that it seems to be an intentional mockery of what it should be: *the trial was a parody of justice.* • *verb* (**parodies**, **parodied**, **parodying**) **1** produce a humorously exaggerated imitation of (a person, writer, artist, or genre): *she led a rally in songs parodying government attitudes toward the poor.* **2** mimic humorously: *he parodied his friend's voice.* [Say PERRA dee]

parole • *noun* **1** the release of a prisoner, temporarily for a special purpose or completely, before the expiry of a sentence, on the promise of good behaviour. **2** the system or practice of granting or accepting such a conditional release. • *verb* (**paroles**, **paroled**, **paroling**) put (a prisoner) on parole. PHRASES **on parole** released esp. from a custodial sentence on the terms of parole. ▶ **parolee** *noun* [Say puh ROLE]

parotid • *adjective* of or situated near the parotid glands. • *noun* (also **parotid gland**) a salivary gland in front of the ear. [Say puh ROT id]

paroxysm *noun* **1** (often foll. by *of*) a sudden attack or outburst (of rage, laughter, etc.): *a paroxysm of laughter* ◊ *this could drive people to paroxysms of frustration.* **2** a sudden attack, recurrence, or worsening of disease etc.: *its paroxysms occur, like the paroxysms of many diseases, at certain periods.* [Say PAIR uck sism]

parquet *noun* a flooring of short strips or blocks of wood arranged in a pattern, usu. sold in square, interlocking tiles. [Say par KAY or PAR kay]

parr *noun* a young salmon between the stages of fry and smolt, distinguished by dark rounded patches evenly spaced along its sides.

parrot • *noun* a vividly coloured esp. tropical bird with a short down-curved bill, grasping feet, and a raucous voice, some varieties of which can mimic the human voice. • *verb* (**parrots**, **parroted**, **parroting**) repeat the words or actions of another mindlessly or mechanically: *encouraging students to parrot back information.*

parrotfish *noun* (*plural* **parrotfish** or **parrotfishes**) a brightly coloured fish with a mouth like a parrot's hooked bill, which is used to scrape food from coral and other hard surfaces.

parry • *verb* (**parries**, **parried**, **parrying**) **1** ward off (a weapon or attack), esp. with a countermove: *he parried the blow by holding his sword vertically.* **2** deal skilfully with (an awkward question etc.): *she parried questions from reporters outside the building.* • *noun* (*plural* **parries**) an act of parrying: *her question was met with a polite parry.*

parse *verb* (**parses**, **parsed**, **parsing**) **1** analyze (a word) grammatically, stating its inflection, relation to the sentence, etc. **2** resolve (a sentence) into its component parts and describe them grammatically. **3** *Computing* analyze (a string) into syntactic components. ▶ **parser** *noun* [Say PARCE]

Parsi *noun* (*plural* **Parsis**) (also **Parsee**, *plural* **Parsees**) an adherent of Zoroastrianism, esp. a descendant of the

Zoroastrian Persians who fled to India in the 7th–8th centuries to escape Muslim persecution. [Say par SEE]

parsimonious *adjective* very unwilling to spend money or use resources: *even the parsimonious Chester paid for a round of drinks.* ▶ **parsimoniously** *adverb* [Say parsa MOE nee us]

parsimony *noun* extreme unwillingness to use money or other resources: *a great tradition of public art has been shattered by government parsimony.* [Say PARSA moe nee]

parsley *noun* a biennial herb with white flowers and flavourful leaves, used for seasoning and garnishing food.

parsnip *noun* **1** a biennial plant of the parsley family with a large, tapering, pale-yellow root. **2** this root eaten as a vegetable.

parson *noun* **1** any (esp. Protestant) member of the clergy. **2** an Anglican parish priest.

parsonage *noun* a church house provided for a minister. [Say PAR s'n idge]

part • *noun* **1** a piece or segment which is combined with others to make up a whole. **2** some but not all of something. **3** a specified fraction of a whole. **4** a measure allowing comparison between the amounts of different ingredients used in a mixture. **5** a role played by an actor or actress. **6** a person's contribution to an action or situation. **7** (in *plural*) *informal* a region. **8** *Music* melody or other constituent of harmony assigned to a particular voice or instrument. **9** (in *plural*) abilities: *a man of many parts.* • *verb* **1** move apart or divide to leave a central space. **2** leave or cause to leave someone's company. **3** (foll. by *with*) give up possession of; hand over. • *adverb* partly: *part jazz, part blues.* PHRASES **for one's part** as far as one is concerned. **in part** (or **parts**) to some extent; partly. **look the part** have an appearance suitable for a role, job, or position. **on the part of** proceeding from: *an error on my part.* **part and parcel** (usu. foll. by *of*) an essential part. **play a part** **1** be significant or contributory. **2** perform a dramatic role. **take part** (often foll. by *in*) participate (in). **take the part of** support; back up.

partake *verb* (**partakes**; *past* **partook**; *past participle* **partaken**; **partaking**) **1** (foll. by *in*, *of*) participate in: *partook in the festivities.* **2** (foll. by *of*) eat or drink a part or amount (of a thing). **3** (foll. by *of*) have some (of a quality etc.): *the book is neither historical nor purely literary, yet partakes of both.* ▶ **partaker** *noun*

parter *combining form* something having a specified number of parts, esp. a radio or television production in a specified number of episodes: *three-parter.*

parterre *noun* **1** a level space in a garden occupied by flower beds arranged formally. **2** the ground floor of a theatre auditorium, esp. the section overhung by balconies. [Say par TAIR]

parthenogenesis *noun* *Biology* reproduction from an ovum without fertilization, esp. as a normal process in invertebrates and lower plants. [Say parth uh no GENESIS]

partial • *adjective* **1** forming only part: *a partial success.* **2** biased, unfair: *the judge may be clearly partial to one side or the other in the lawsuit.* **3** having a liking for: *loved carrot cake and was partial to peanut butter pie.* • *noun* a denture replacing some but not all of the teeth.

partiality *noun* bias, favouritism: *declared her partiality to Tolstoy.* [Say parshy ALA tee]

partially *adverb* in part; to some degree; not fully: *fatigue partially accounts for his poor performance* ◊ *the building was partially destroyed by fire.*

participant *noun* a person who participates in something.

participate *verb* (**participates**, **participated**, **participating**) (usu. foll. by *in*) share or take part. ▶ **participation** *noun*

participatory *adjective* **1** characterized by participation, esp. in decision-making in an organization, community, or society: *participatory democracy*. **2** (esp. of forms of entertainment or art) allowing members of the general public to take part. **3** that participates, esp. in a role that is usu. one of observation only: *a participatory audience*.

participial *adjective* involving a participle; for example, the word *cutting* in *a cutting remark* is a **participial adjective**, because *cutting* is the present participle of the verb *to cut*. [Say parta SIPPY ul]

participle *noun* Grammar a word formed from a verb, e.g. *going*, *gone*, *being*, *been*, and used in compound verb forms, e.g. *is going*, *has been*, or as an adjective, e.g. *working woman*, *burnt toast*. [Say PARTA sipple]

particle *noun* **1** a very small bit or piece of something: *dirt particles*. **2** Physics any of numerous subatomic constituents of the physical world that interact with each other, including electrons, neutrinos, and photons. **3** the least possible amount: *pure sand without a particle of dirt in it*. **4** Grammar **a** a minor part of speech, esp. a short word that does not change its form. **b** a common prefix or suffix such as *in-*, *-ness*.

particle accelerator *noun* an apparatus for accelerating subatomic particles to high velocities by means of electric or electromagnetic fields.

particle beam *noun* a stream of subatomic particles produced by a particle accelerator, used for studying nuclear structure etc., or as a military weapon.

particleboard *noun* a rigid sheet made from compressed wood chips, splinters, sawdust, and resin.

particle physics *noun* the branch of physics concerned with the properties and interactions of subatomic particles.

parti-coloured *adjective* of several colours.

particular • *adjective* **1** relating to or considered as one thing or person as distinct from others; individual: *in this particular case*. **2** more than is usual; exceptional: *took particular trouble*. **3** paying close attention to detail; fastidious. • *noun* **1** a detail; an item: *all documents must conform in every particular to the requirements*. **2** (in *plural*) points of information; a detailed account: *the particulars of the plan*. PHRASES **in particular** especially, specifically.

particularism *noun* **1** exclusive devotion to one party, sect, etc. **2** the principle of leaving political independence to each state in an empire or federation. **3** the theological doctrine that some but not all people are redeemed. ▶ **particularist** *noun & adjective* **particularistic** *adjective*

particularity *noun* (*plural* **particularities**) **1** the quality of being individual or particular: *objects lost their particularity to become part of the overall design*. **2** fullness or minuteness of detail in a description: *present their argument with accuracy and particularity*. **3** (usu. in *plural*) **a** a small detail: *the tedious particularities of daily life*. **b** a distinctive feature: *regional particularities*.

particularize *verb* (**particularizes**, **particularized**, **particularizing**) mention or describe particularly; treat individually or in detail: *particularized answers to special concerns*.

particularly *adverb* **1** especially, very. **2** specifically.

particulate • *adjective* in the form of separate particles. • *noun* matter in this form. [Say par TICK you lit or par TICK you late]

partier *noun* **1** a person who parties. **2** slang a person who drinks or uses drugs recreationally.

parting • *noun* **1** a leave-taking or departure: *they exchanged a few words on parting* ◊ *broken promises and unkind partings*. **2** a division; an act of separating: *parting of the Red Sea*. **3** a point at which things part or

are parted. • *adjective* done or said etc. as one is leaving: *parting words* ◊ *a parting glance*.

parting shot *noun* a remark or glance etc. reserved for the moment of departure.

Parti Québécois *noun* Cdn a political party in Quebec, founded in 1968 and dedicated to achieving Quebec sovereignty. Abbreviation: **PQ**.

Parti Rouge *noun* Cdn hist. a radical French-Canadian political party founded about 1848 and first led by Louis-Joseph Papineau.

partisan • *noun* **1** an esp. zealous supporter of a party, person, or cause. **2** a guerrilla. • *adjective* **1** of partisans. **2** biased towards a particular cause. ▶ **partisanship** *noun* [Say PAR ti zan or PAR ti zun]

partition • *noun* **1** division into parts, esp. of a country with separate areas of government. **2** a structure dividing a space into two parts, esp. a light interior wall. **3** Computing **a** a self-contained part of a program, or a group of programs within a program library. **b** each of a number of blocks into which some operating systems divide memory in order to facilitate storage and retrieval of information. • *verb* **1** divide into parts. **2** (foll. by *off*) separate (part of a room etc.) with a partition. **3** Computing divide (memory) into partitions. ▶ **partitioned** *adjective*

partly *adverb* to some extent; not completely.

partner • *noun* **1 a** a person, organization, country, etc. who shares or takes part with another or others in some activity: *Canada's trading partners*. **b** a person who is associated with another or others in the carrying on of a business with shared risks and profits. **2** a colleague or associate. **3** a dancer, figure skater, tennis player, etc. paired with another. **4 a** either member of a married couple or an established unmarried couple. **b** a person with whom one has sexual relations. • *verb* **1** be or act as the partner of. **2** (foll. by *with*) associate as partners. ▶ **partnering** *noun* **partnerless** *adjective*

partnership *noun* **1** the state of being a partner or partners. **2** a joint business. **3** a pair or group of partners.

part of speech *noun* (*plural* **parts of speech**) each of the categories to which words are assigned according to their grammatical and semantic functions (e.g. noun, verb).

partook *past of* PARTAKE.

partridge *noun* (*plural* **partridge** or **partridges**) **1** a short-tailed game bird with mainly brown plumage, native to Europe and Asia and introduced in North America. **2** any of various related birds, esp. the ruffed grouse or the ptarmigan.

partridgeberry *noun* (*plural* **partridgeberries**) **1** either of two North American plants with edible red berries. **2** the fruit of these plants.

part-time • *adjective* employed, occurring, or lasting less than full-time: *part-time student*. • *adverb* on a part-time basis: *Daniel works part-time at the IGA*. ▶ **part-timer** *noun*

partway *adverb* **1** part of the way. **2** partly: *stood with her robe partway open*.

party • *noun* (*plural* **parties**) **1** a social gathering, usu. of invited guests. **2** a group of people engaged in an activity or travelling together: *search party*. **3** a political group organized to campaign for election. **4** a person or people forming one side in an agreement or dispute. **5** (foll. by *to*) Law an accessory (to an action). **6** informal a person. • *verb* (**parties**, **partied**, **partying**) **1** go to parties frequently. **2** revel, carouse: *partied all night*.

party animal *noun* informal a person who parties.

partyer *noun* = PARTIER.

party-goer *noun* a person who attends a party or parties.

partying *noun* the activity of going to parties or revelling.

party line *noun* **1** the official policies adopted by a political party. **2** an official position or interpretation of events etc. put forth publicly by members of an organization, institution, etc. **3** a telephone line shared by two or more subscribers.

party politics *plural noun* political activity carried out through, by, or for political parties.

party-pooper *noun* (also **party-poop**) *slang* a person whose manner or behaviour inhibits other people's enjoyment; a killjoy.

parvenu • *noun* (*plural* **parvenus**) **1** a person of obscure origin who has gained wealth or position: *he knows who has wealth and how much and he can advise the parvenu how to get on in society.* **2** an upstart: *a student who takes up philosophy becomes vain and aggressive, with all the reactions of a parvenu.* • *adjective* **1** associated with or characteristic of such a person. **2** upstart. [Say PARVA noo]

parvovirus *noun* (*plural* **parvoviruses**) any of a class of small viruses affecting vertebrate animals, esp. one which causes contagious disease in dogs. [Say PARVO virus]

pascal *noun* **1** the SI unit of pressure, equal to one newton per square metre. **2** (**Pascal**) a programming language esp. used in education. [Say PASS cull for sense 1, pass CAL for sense 2]

paschal *adjective* **1** of or relating to Easter. **2** of or relating to Passover. [Say PASS cull]

pas de deux *noun* (*plural* **pas de deux**) **1** a theatrical dance for two persons, esp. a man and a woman. **2** an encounter or interaction between two people or things: *a grim pas de deux of escalating nastiness between the two characters.* [Say paw duh DUH for the singular, paw duh DUH or paw duh DUHS for the plural]

pasha *noun* (*plural* **pashas**) **1** *hist.* the title (placed after the name) of a Turkish officer of high rank, e.g. a military commander, the governor of a province, etc. **2** *informal* a powerful or wealthy person: *the last of the great Hollywood pashas.* [Say PASH uh]

Pashto • *noun* the language of the Pathans, the official language of Afghanistan, also spoken in northwestern Pakistan. • *adjective* of this language. [Say PASH toe]

paska *noun* (*plural* **paskas**) *Cdn* a rich, usu. decorated, egg bread, often containing dried fruits, traditional at Easter among people of Ukrainian origin. [Say PASS kuh]

pasque flower *noun* either of two spring-flowering anemones with purple flowers, esp. the prairie crocus of North America. [Say PASK]

pass¹ • *verb* (**passes**, **passed**, **passing**) **1** move or go onward, past, through, or across. **2** change from one state or condition to another. **3** transfer (something) to someone. **4** propel, kick, hit, or throw (the puck or ball) to a teammate. **5** (of time) go by. **6** occupy or spend (time). **7** be done or said: *not another word passed between them.* **8** come to an end. **9** be successful in (an examination, test, or course). **10** declare to be satisfactory. **11** approve or put into effect (a proposal or law) by voting. **12** utter (remarks) or pronounce (a judgment or sentence). **13** forgo one's turn or an opportunity to do or have something. **14** discharge (urine or feces) from the body. • *noun* (*plural* **passes**) **1** an act of passing. **2** a success in an examination. **3** an official document authorizing the holder to have access to, use, or do something. **4** *informal* an amorous or sexual advance. **5** a particular state of affairs. **6** *Computing* a single scan through a set of data or a program. PHRASES **in passing 1** by the way. **2** in the course of speech, conversation, etc. **make a pass at** *informal* make amorous or sexual advances to. **pass**

around 1 distribute. **2** send or give to each of a number in turn. **pass away** *euphemism* die. **pass by 1** go past. **2** disregard, omit. **pass one's eye over** read (a document etc.) cursorily. **pass off** (foll. by *as*) misrepresent (a person or thing) as something else. **pass on 1** transmit to the next person in a series. **2** *euphemism* die. **3** proceed on one's way. **pass out 1** become unconscious. **2** distribute. **pass over 1** omit, ignore, or disregard. **2** ignore the claims of (a person) to promotion or advancement. **pass through 1** experience. **2** be in a place temporarily while on the way to somewhere else. **pass up** *informal* refuse or neglect (an opportunity etc.).

pass² *noun* (*plural* **passes**) **1** a narrow passage through mountains. **2** a navigable channel, esp. at the mouth of a river. **3** a way by which to pass or get through; a road or route. **4** *Cdn* a migration route followed by animals: *deer pass.* PHRASES **head** (or **cut**) **off at the pass** deter (a person) or prevent (a problem) early on.

passable *adjective* **1** barely satisfactory; just adequate. **2** (of a road etc.) that can be passed. ▶ **passably** *adverb*

passage *noun* **1** the process, action, or means of passing: *the passage of time* ◊ *a passage through the crowd.* **2 a** a sea route around a large land mass, usu. between two oceans: *Northwest Passage.* **b** a narrow strait between islands etc. **3** the liberty or right to pass through. **4 a** the right of conveyance as a passenger, esp. by sea. **b** a journey, esp. by sea. **5 a** a short extract from a book etc. **b** a section of a piece of music. **6** = PASSAGEWAY. **7** a transition from one state to another. **8** the passing of a bill etc. into law. **9** *Anatomy* a duct etc. in the body: *nasal passages.*

passageway *noun* a narrow way for passing along, esp. with walls on either side; a corridor.

Passamaquoddy • *noun* (*plural* **Passamaquoddy**) **1** a member of a North American Aboriginal people inhabiting parts of southeastern Maine and (formerly) southwestern New Brunswick. **2** the Algonquian language of this people. • *adjective* of this people or their language. [Say passa muh QUODDY]

passbook *noun* a small book issued by a financial institution to an account holder recording sums deposited and withdrawn.

pass card *noun* a plastic card with an encoded magnetic strip, which, when passed through a scanner, acts as a key to open a locked door etc.

passé *adjective* **1** no longer fashionable or topical; out of date. **2** past one's prime. [Say pass AY]

passed ball *noun Baseball* a pitch dropped by the catcher, allowing a runner to advance one or more bases.

passenger *noun* a traveller in or on a public or private conveyance (other than the driver, pilot, crew, etc.).

passenger pigeon *noun* a wild pigeon of North America, noted for migrating in huge flocks and hunted to extinction by 1914.

passer *noun* a person who passes something, esp. the puck or ball.

passerby *noun* (*plural* **passersby**) a person who goes past, esp. by chance.

passerine • *noun* any one of a large order of birds that have feet adapted for perching, including sparrows and most land birds. • *adjective* of or relating to this order. [Say PASSA reen]

passim *adverb* (of allusions or references in a published work) to be found at various places throughout the text. [Say PASS im]

passing • *adjective* **1** transient, fleeting: *a passing glance.* **2** incidental: *a passing reference.* • *noun* the death of a person.

passing lane *noun* a traffic lane in which drivers may pass other vehicles.

passion *noun* **1** strong barely controllable emotion. **2** intense sexual love or desire. **3** strong enthusiasm: *a passion for football*. **4** a person or thing arousing passion. **5** an outburst of anger: *flew into a passion*. **6** (**the Passion**) **a** *Christianity* the suffering of Christ during his last days. **b** a narrative of this from the Gospels.

passionate *adjective* **1** dominated by or easily moved to strong feeling, esp. love or anger. **2** showing or caused by passion. ▶ **passionately** *adverb*

passion flower *noun* a climbing plant of warm regions, which bears distinctive flowers with parts that supposedly resemble the instruments of the Crucifixion.

passion fruit *noun* the edible purple fruit of some species of passion flower.

passionless *adjective* without emotion or enthusiasm: *he spoke in a passionless voice*.

Passion play *noun* (also **passion play**) a play depicting the events of Christ's Passion, usu. performed during Lent.

Passion Sunday *noun* the fifth Sunday in Lent.

passive • *adjective* **1** suffering action; acted upon. **2** offering no opposition; submissive. **3** **a** not active; inert. **b** (of a metal) abnormally unreactive owing to a surface coating of oxide. **4** *Grammar* designating the voice in which the subject undergoes the action of the verb, e.g. in *they were killed*. **5** of or designating a system in which energy for heating etc. is obtained by the absorption of existing radiant energy, usu. sunlight. **6** (of radar, a satellite, etc.) not generating its own signal; receiving or reflecting radiation from a transmitter etc. • *noun* the passive voice or form of a verb. ▶ **passively** *adverb*

passive smoke *noun* = SECOND-HAND SMOKE.

passive smoking *noun* the involuntary inhaling, esp. by a non-smoker, of smoke from others' cigarettes etc.

passivity *noun* the state of accepting what happens without reacting to it or trying to fight against it. [Say pass IVVA tee]

Passover *noun* the Jewish spring festival commemorating the liberation of the Israelites from slavery in Egypt, held from the 15th to the 22nd day of the seventh month of the Jewish year. The festival (also called Pesach) commences with a ceremonial dinner (the Seder) and involves the observance of strict dietary laws, e.g., requiring that matzo be eaten instead of bread and prohibiting the consumption of any leaven.

passport *noun* **1** a document issued by a government certifying the holder's identity and citizenship, and entitling the holder to travel abroad under its protection. **2** (foll. by *to*) a thing that ensures admission or attainment: *a passport to success*.

pass rush *noun* *Football* the elements of a team's defensive play aimed at thwarting the quarterback's pass attempts. ▶ **pass rusher** *noun* **pass-rushing** *adjective*

pass-through • *noun* an opening in a wall between two rooms, esp. a kitchen and a dining area, through which dishes etc. are passed. • *adjective* (of costs) chargeable to the customer.

---

password *noun* **1** a selected word or phrase securing recognition, admission, etc., when used by those to whom it is disclosed. **2** a confidential sequence of characters that has to be typed in order to gain access to a particular computer, network, etc.

---

past • *adjective* **1** gone by in time and no longer existing: *in past years* ◊ *the time is past*. **2** recently completed or gone by: *the past month*. **3** relating to a former time: *past president*. **4** *Grammar* expressing a past action or state. • *noun* **1** (**the past**) **a** a past time. **b** what has happened in past time: *cannot undo the past*. **2** a person's past life or career, esp. if discreditable: *a man with a past*. **3** a past tense or form. • *preposition* **1** beyond in time or place: *is past two o'clock* ◊ *ran past the house*. **2** beyond the range, duration, or compass of: *past belief*. • *adverb* so as to pass by: *hurried past*. PHRASES **not put it past a person** believe it possible of a person. **past it** *informal* old and useless.

pasta *noun* (*plural* **pastas**) **1** a type of dough extruded or stamped into various shapes for cooking, e.g. lasagna or spaghetti. **2** a dish made from this.

paste • *noun* **1** a moist thick mixture, esp. of powder and liquid. **2** an adhesive, esp. for sticking paper and other light materials. **3** a puréed preparation of ground meat, fish, vegetable, etc.: *tomato paste*. **4 a** a hard glasslike composition used in making imitation gems. **b** imitation jewellery made of this. **5** a mixture of clay, water, etc., used in making ceramics. • *verb* (**pastes**, **pasted**, **pasting**) **1** fasten or coat with paste. **2** *Computing* insert or reproduce (already existing text) at a new location in a document, file, etc. **3** *slang* **a** beat or thrash. **b** bomb or bombard heavily.

pasteboard *noun* a sheet of stiff material made by pasting together sheets of paper.

pastel • *noun* **1** a crayon consisting of powdered pigments bound with a gum solution. **2 a** the art or technique of drawing with pastels. **b** a work of art in pastel. **3 a** light and subdued shade of a colour. • *adjective* of a light and subdued shade or colour.

pastern *noun* **1** the part of a horse's foot between the fetlock and the hoof. **2** a similar part in other animals. [Say PASS turn]

pasteurization *noun* the process of partially sterilizing milk or wine etc. by heating or irradiation in order to make it safe for consumption. [Say pass chur ize AY sh'n]

pasteurize *verb* (**pasteurizes**, **pasteurized**, **pasteurizing**) subject (milk, wine, etc.) to the process of partial sterilization by heating or irradiation in order to make it safe for consumption. [Say PASS chur ize]

pastiche • *noun* **1** a medley, esp. a picture or a musical composition, made up from or imitating various sources: *often opts for pastiche, a string of melodies culminating in conventional sax solos*. **2** a literary or other work of art composed in the style of a well-known writer, artist, etc.: *opening like a high-budget slasher flick, it drifts into Hitchcock pastiche*. • *verb* (**pastiches**, **pastiched**, **pastiching**) copy or imitate the style of (an artist, author, time period, etc.): *the poems seem not to parody but to pastiche the flamenco world*. [Say pass TEESH]

pastille *noun* a small candy, lozenge, or chocolate. [Say pass TEAL]

pastime *noun* a recreational activity or hobby.

pastiness *noun* an unhealthy pale colour, esp. of a person's face or complexion.

pasting *noun* *informal* a severe beating or defeat.

pastor • *noun* (also **Pastor**) (often as a title or form of address) a minister or priest in charge of a church or a congregation. • *verb* be pastor of (a church).

pastoral • *adjective* **1** having to do with the keeping or grazing of sheep or cattle: *pastoral lands* ◊ *pastoral activities can lead to major environmental problems*. **2** of or associated with country life; rural: *a pastoral scene*. **3** (of art) portraying country life, usu. in a romantic or idealized form: *the pastoral drama is an authentic look at the Sioux nation in the 1860s*. **4** of or pertaining to a pastor or the spiritual care of a congregation. • *noun* **1** a pastoral poem, play, etc. **2** (also **pastoral letter**) a letter from a pastor (esp. a bishop) to the clergy or people. ▶ **pastoralism** *noun* [Say PASS tur ul]

pastoralist • *noun* a farmer of sheep or cattle. • *adjective* involved in the keeping and grazing of sheep or cattle. [Say PASS tur ul ist]

past perfect *noun* = PLUPERFECT.

pastrami *noun* seasoned smoked beef brisket, usu. cut in thin slices for sandwiches. [Say pus TROMMY]

pastry *noun* (*plural* **pastries**) **1** a dough of flour, fat, and water baked and used as a base and covering for pies etc. **2 a** food made wholly or partly of this. **b** a piece or item of this food. **3** a sweet bread or cake.

pasture • *noun* **1** (also **pasture land**) an area of land covered with grass etc. suitable for grazing animals, esp. cattle or sheep. **2** grass and other growing plants for animals. **3** the circumstances of a person's life, work, etc.: *find greener pastures*. • *verb* (**pastures, pastured, pasturing**) graze in a pasture. ▌PHRASES▐ **out to pasture 1** out to graze. **2** *informal* **a** (of a person) in retirement. **b** (of a thing) out of service.

pasty[1] *noun* (*plural* **pasties**) esp. *Brit.* a savoury turnover. [Say PAST ee]

pasty[2] *adjective* (**pastier, pastiest**) **1** unhealthily pale. **2** like paste. [Say PASTE ee]

PA system *noun* = PUBLIC ADDRESS SYSTEM.

pat[1] • *verb* (**pats, patted, patting**) **1 a** tap gently with the hand or a flat surface. **b** tap (a person) gently, esp. as a sign of affection, sympathy, or congratulation. **2** flatten or mould by patting. **3** (foll. by *on, upon*) tap or beat lightly on (a surface), esp. making a gentle sound. • *noun* **1** a light tap, esp. with the hand. **2** the sound made by this, or by light footsteps. **3** a small mass (esp. of butter) formed by patting.

pat[2] *adjective* too quick, easy, or simple; not seeming natural or realistic: *a pat answer* ◊ *the pat jokes of a TV sitcom*. ▌PHRASES▐ **have down pat** know or have memorized perfectly. **stand pat** stick stubbornly to one's opinion or decision.

pat. *abbreviation* patent.

patch • *noun* (*plural* **patches**) **1** a piece of material used to mend or reinforce clothing etc. **2** a pad or shield worn over an eye or eye socket. **3** a dressing etc. put over a wound. **4** a small area or piece of ground, esp. one that contrasts with a surrounding area: *a patch of ice* ◊ *a vegetable patch*. **5** a small scrap, piece, or remnant: *fog patches*. **6** an adhesive patch worn on the skin, which releases measured amounts of a drug into the bloodstream. **7** *Cdn* (*Nfld*) a herd of seals. **8** *informal* a period of time: *went through a bad patch*. **9 a** a temporary electrical connection. **b** *Computing* a small piece of code inserted to correct or enhance a program. • *verb* (**patches, patched, patching**) **1 a** (often foll. by *up*) mend with a patch or patches. **b** repair the damage to: *patch a pothole*. **2** (often foll. by *together*) construct hastily or in a makeshift way. **3** (foll. by *up*) settle (differences etc.) after a quarrel or dispute. **4** (often foll. by *through, into*) connect or be connected by a temporary electrical, radio, etc. connection.

5 *Computing* correct or enhance (a routine, program, etc.) by inserting a patch. ▶ **patcher** *noun*

patchily *adverb* in an incomplete or uneven manner: *the fish are patchily distributed in the lake*.

patchiness *noun* an uneven or incomplete quality: *there is a patchiness in the writing style that makes the novel difficult to follow*.

patchouli *noun* **1** a strongly scented East Indian plant of the mint family. **2** an aromatic oil obtained from this, used esp. in perfume. [Say puh CHOOLY]

patchwork • *noun* **1** needlework in which small pieces of cloth in different designs are sewn together to form a quilt etc. **2** a thing composed of different pieces or elements. • *adjective* **1** composed of patchwork pieces. **2 a** resembling patchwork: *patchwork fields*. **b** pieced together with lack of uniformity: *patchwork political philosophy*.

patchy *adjective* (**patchier, patchiest**) **1** uneven in quality. **2** having or existing in patches.

pate *noun* *jocular* the head, esp. if bald.

pâté *noun* a rich paste of finely ground or puréed and seasoned meat or fish etc., served as an appetizer. [Say pat AY or PAT ay]

pâté de foie gras *noun* see FOIE GRAS.

patella *noun* (*plural* **patellas** or **patellae**) the kneecap. ▶ **patellar** *adjective* [Say puh TELLA for the singular, puh TELLAS or puh TELLY for the plural]

patent • *noun* **1** a government licence conferring a right or title, esp. the sole right to make, use, or sell some invention. **2** an invention or process protected by this. **3** the right or title to an area of public land granted to an individual by the government. • *adjective* **1** obvious, plain: *the patent absurdity of the charges*. **2** made and marketed under a patent; proprietary. **3** concerning patents: *patent law*. **4** made of patent leather. • *verb* **1** obtain a patent for (an invention). **2** grant (an area of public land) by a patent. ▶ **patentable** *adjective* [Say PAT int or PATE int]

patent leather *noun* leather with a glossy varnished surface, used for shoes and accessories.

patently *adverb* clearly, plainly, without a doubt: *it was patently obvious that Ted was lying* ◊ *her apology was patently insincere*. [Say PATE int lee or PAT int lee]

paternal *adjective* **1** fatherly. **2** related through the father: *paternal grandmother*. **3** inherited from the male parent: *paternal chromosome*. **4** (of an organization, government etc.) limiting freedom and responsibility by well-meant regulations.

paternalism *noun* the system in which a government or an employer protects the people who are governed or employed by providing them with what they need without giving them the freedom or responsibility of deciding themselves, in their supposed interest. ▶ **paternalist** *adjective & noun* **paternalistic** *adjective* **paternalistically** *adverb*

paternity *noun* **1** fatherhood. **2** one's paternal origin: *the government went to great lengths to determine the paternity of each child*.

paternity leave *noun* a leave of absence taken by a father to care for a new baby.

paternity suit *noun* a lawsuit held to determine whether a certain man is the father of a certain child.

path *noun* (*plural* **paths**) **1 a** a track laid down for walking or made by continual treading. **b** a track laid for a special purpose: *bike path*. **2** the line along which a person or thing moves: *flight path*. **3** a course of action or conduct: *career path*. **4** *Computing* a sequence of movements or operations taken by a system.

Pathan *noun* a member of a Pashto-speaking people inhabiting northwestern Pakistan and southeastern Afghanistan. [Say puh TAN]

path-breaking *adjective* = GROUNDBREAKING *adjective* 1.

pathetic *adjective* **1** arousing pity or sadness or contempt. **2** *informal* miserably inadequate: *a pathetic performance*. ▶ **pathetically** *adverb*

pathetic fallacy *noun* a literary device involving metaphor, in which natural phenomena that cannot feel as humans do are described as if they could, in sympathy with the mood of the narrator or speaker, e.g. *the clouds wept as the coffin was brought to the church*.

pathfinder *noun* **1** a person who explores new territory, investigates a new subject, etc. **2** an aircraft or its pilot sent ahead to locate and mark the target area for bombing. **3** (**Pathfinder**) *Cdn* a member of the branch of the Girl Guides for 12- to 15-year-olds.

pathogen *noun* a bacterium, virus, or other micro-organism that can cause disease. ▶ **pathogenic** *adjective* [Say PATH uh jin, path uh JEN ick]

pathogenesis *noun* the manner of development of a disease. [Say path uh GENESIS]

pathological *adjective* (also **pathologic**) **1** of pathology. **2** of or caused by a physical or mental disorder: *pathological depression*. **3** *informal* **a** extreme and unreasonable: *pathological fear of spiders*. **b** compulsive: *pathological liar*. ▶ **pathologically** *adverb* [Say path uh LOGICAL]

pathologist *noun* a doctor who studies the causes and effects of bodily disease, esp. one who examines dead bodies to find out the cause of death. *See also* SPEECH-LANGUAGE PATHOLOGIST. [Say puh THOLLA jist]

pathology *noun* (*plural* **pathologies**) **1** the science of the causes and effects of bodily diseases, esp. the branch of medicine that deals with the laboratory examination of samples of body tissue for diagnostic or forensic purposes. **2** the symptoms or typical behaviour of a disease. **3** any abnormal or unhealthy condition. *See also* SPEECH-LANGUAGE PATHOLOGY. [Say puh THOLLA jee]

pathos *noun* a quality in speech, writing, events, etc. that excites pity or sadness. [Say PAY thoss]

pathway *noun* **1** a path or course. **2** *Biochemistry* a sequence of reactions undergone in a living organism.

patience *noun* the capacity to accept or endure delay, provocation, or hardship calmly without anger. PHRASES **have no patience with** (or **for**) be unable to tolerate; be irritated by.

patient • *adjective* having or showing patience. • *noun* a person receiving medical treatment. ▶ **patiently** *adverb*

patina *noun* (*plural* **patinas**) **1** a film, usu. green, formed on the surface of old bronze. **2** a similar film on other surfaces. **3** a gloss produced by age on woodwork etc. **4** a superficial appearance: *the film festival retains a patina of respectability*. [Say puh TEENA or PAT uh nuh]

patio *noun* (*plural* **patios**) a paved usu. roofless area adjoining a house, used for outdoor recreation.

patisserie *noun* **1** a bakeshop where fancy, esp. French, pastries are made, sold, and usu. served. **2** esp. French pastries collectively. [Say puh TEECE uh ree]

patly *adverb* in a simple and somewhat unnatural or unconvincing manner: *a patly symbolic gesture*.

patois *noun* (*plural* **patois**) a non-standard local dialect. [Say pat WAH for the singular, pat WAHS for the plural]

patriarch *noun* **1** the male head of a family or tribe. **2** (often in *plural*) *Bible* **a** each of the twelve sons of Jacob, from whom the tribes of Israel were descended. **b** Abraham, Isaac, and Jacob, and their forefathers. **3 a** the title of a chief bishop, esp. those presiding over the Churches of Antioch, Alexandria, Constantinople, Jerusalem, and Rome; now also the title of the heads of certain Orthodox Churches. **b** *Catholicism* a bishop ranking next above primates and metropolitans, and

immediately below the pope. **4 a** a venerable old man. **b** the oldest member of a group: *at seventy-seven, he's Hollywood's reigning patriarch*. [Say PAY tree ark]

patriarchal *adjective* of a patriarch or patriarchy. [Say pay tree ARK ul]

patriarchy *noun* (*plural* **patriarchies**) **1** a system of society, government, etc., ruled by a man and with descent through the male line. **2** the attitudes, structures, etc. of a society seen as ensuring male dominance. [Say PAY tree arky]

patriate *verb* (**patriates, patriated, patriating**) *Cdn* bring (legislation, esp. a constitution) under the authority of the autonomous country to which it applies, used with reference to laws passed on behalf of that country by its former mother country. ▶ **patriation** *noun* [Say PAY tree ate]

patrician • *noun* **1** *hist.* a member of the ancient Roman nobility (*compare* PLEBEIAN *noun* 1). **2** an aristocrat. **3** a refined or well-bred person. • *adjective* **1** noble, aristocratic. **2** *hist.* of the ancient Roman nobility. **3** refined, well-bred. [Say puh TRISH'n]

patrilineal *adjective* of or based on kinship with the father or descent through the male line. [Say patra LINNY ul]

patrimony *noun* (*plural* **patrimonies**) **1** a heritage: *the Nazca lines were declared part of the patrimony of humanity by Unesco*. **2** property inherited from one's father or ancestor: *owners refuse to part with their patrimony in the interests of agricultural development*. [Say PATRA moe nee]

patriot *noun* a person who is ardently devoted to the well-being or interests of his or her country. [Say PAY tree it]

Patriote *noun* *Cdn hist.* a supporter of Louis-Joseph Papineau (1786–1871) in the Rebellion of Lower Canada in 1837. [Say pat ree OT]

patriotic *adjective* having or expressing devotion to and vigorous support for one's country. ▶ **patriotically** *adverb* [Say pay tree OT ick]

patriotism *noun* ardent devotion to the well-being and interests of one's country. [Say PAY tree uh tism]

patristic *adjective* of the early Christian theologians or their writings. [Say puh TRISS tick]

patrol • *noun* **1** the act of going around an area, esp. at regular intervals, in order to protect or supervise it. **2** one or more persons or vehicles sent out on patrol. **3 a** a detachment of troops sent out to reconnoitre. **b** such reconnaissance. **4** a routine operational voyage of a ship or aircraft. **5** a unit of six to eight Scouts or Guides. • *verb* (**patrols, patrolled, patrolling**) **1** carry out a patrol of. **2** act as a patrol.

patrol car *noun* a police car used in patrolling roads and streets.

patroller *noun* a member of a patrol: *volunteer park patrollers*.

patrolman *noun* (*plural* **patrolmen**) a police officer on a patrol.

patron *noun* **1** a person who gives financial or other support to a person, cause, arts organization, work of art, etc. **2** a usu. regular customer of a store etc. **3** = PATRON SAINT. [Say PAY trin]

patronage *noun* **1** the support, promotion, or encouragement given by a patron. **2 a** the control of appointments to office, privileges, etc., esp. in public service. **b** the appointing of friends, supporters, etc. to office etc. **3** a customer's support for a store etc. [Say PAY truh nidge or PATTRA nidge]

patroness *noun* a woman who gives financial or other support to a person, cause, arts organization, work of art, etc. [Say PAY truh niss]

patronize *verb* (**patronizes, patronized, patronizing**) **1** treat a person with apparent kindness

that betrays a feeling of superiority. **2** act as a patron towards (a person, cause, artist, etc.); support; encourage. **3** frequent (a store etc.) as a customer. ▶ **patronizing** *adjective* **patronizingly** *adverb* [Say PAY truh nize or PATTRA nize]

patron saint *noun* a saint who has been chosen as the special protector of a particular place, occupation, or person (who may be named after this saint): *St. Joseph, Canada's patron saint ◊ St. Vincent's parish celebrated the feast of its patron saint last week*.

patronymic • *noun* a name derived from the name of a father or ancestor, e.g. *Johnson, O'Brien, Ivanovich*. • *adjective* **1** (of a name) so derived. **2** (of an affix) indicating such a derivation. [Say pattra NIM ick]

patsy *noun* (*plural* **patsies**) *slang* a person who is deceived, ridiculed, tricked, etc.

patter • *verb* **1** make a rapid succession of taps, as of rain on a window. **2** run with quick short steps. • *noun* **1** a rapid succession of taps, light steps, etc. **2** rapid speech used by a comedian, a comic singer, or a salesman.

pattern • *noun* **1** a repeated decorative design on fabric, paper, etc. **2** an esp. regular or logical form, order, or arrangement. **3** a model or design from which copies, garments, etc. can be made. **4** an example of excellence: *a pattern of elegance*. **5** a wooden or metal figure from which a mould is made for a casting. **6** a sample (of cloth, wallpaper, etc.). **7** a random combination of shapes or colours. • *verb* **1** (usu. foll. by *after, on*) model (a thing) on a design etc. **2** decorate with a pattern. ▶ **patterning** *noun* **patternless** *adjective*

patty *noun* (also **pattie**) (*plural* **patties**) **1** a quantity of any substance formed into a disc-like shape, esp. ground meat etc. **2 a** a little pie or pastry. **b** = JAMAICAN PATTY.

patty cake *noun* a child's game in which partners clap their own and each other's hands to the rhythm of a recited rhyme or song.

paucity *noun* smallness of number or quantity: *she was complaining about the paucity of parts for older actors*. [Say POSSA tee]

paunch *noun* (*plural* **paunches**) the belly or stomach, esp. when protruding. ▶ **paunchy** *adjective*

pauper *noun* a very poor person. ▶ **pauperization** *noun* **pauperize** *verb* (**pauperizes**, **pauperized**, **pauperizing**)

pause • *noun* **1** a temporary stop or break. **2** (also **pause button**) a control allowing the interruption of the operation of a VCR, CD player, etc. • *verb* (**pauses, paused, pausing**) **1** make a pause; wait. **2** (usu. foll. by *upon*) linger over (a word etc.). PHRASES **give pause to** cause (a person) to hesitate.

pave *verb* (**paves, paved, paving**) **1** cover (a street etc.) with asphalt, concrete, stone, etc. **2** cover or strew (a floor etc.) with anything: *paved with flowers*. PHRASES **pave the way for** prepare a situation conducive to: *legislation paving the way for economic growth*.

pavement *noun* **1** a paved area or surface, as a roadway, playground, etc. **2** the asphalt, concrete, or densely packed stones etc. used to pave a surface.

paver *noun* **1** a person or machine that paves roads etc. **2** a stone, brick, etc. used in paving a surface.

pavilion *noun* **1** a summer house or other decorative building in a garden. **2** a usu. large tent at a show, fair, etc. **3** a building at a fair or exhibition housing displays or exhibits esp. on a common theme. [Say puh VILL yin]

paving *noun* the material used to pave a surface: *paving stones*.

Pavlovian *adjective* **1** of or relating to the Russian physiologist I. P. Pavlov (1849–1936) or his work, esp. on conditioned reflexes. **2** of the nature of a reaction or

response made unthinkingly or under the influence of others. [Say pav LOE vee in]

paw • *noun* **1** a foot of an animal having claws or nails. **2** *informal* a person's hand. • *verb* **1** strike or scrape (the ground) with a paw, hoof, or foot. **2** *informal* fondle awkwardly or indecently.

pawn[1] *noun* **1** *Chess* a piece of the lowest value. **2** a person used by others for their own purposes.

pawn[2] • *verb* deposit an object, esp. with a pawnbroker, as security for money lent. • *noun* an object left as security for money etc. lent. PHRASES **in pawn** (of an object etc.) held as security. **pawn off** pass off (a responsibility, something unwanted).

pawnbroker *noun* a person who lends money at interest on the security of personal property pawned. ▶ **pawnbroking** *noun*

pawnshop *noun* a shop where pawnbroking is conducted and often where property collected from defaulted loans is sold.

pawpaw *noun* **1** a North American tree with purple flowers and edible fruit. **2** = PAPAYA.

pax *noun* (often **Pax**; usu. foll. by Latin or Modern Latin adjective) the peace or political stability due to the dominance of one state or power: *Pax Romana ◊ Pax Americana*.

pay • *verb* (**pays, paid, paying**) **1** give (someone) money due for work, goods, or an outstanding debt. **2** give (money) thus owed. **3** be profitable or advantageous: *crime doesn't pay*. **4** suffer or account for a fault etc.: *you'll pay! ◊ paid the penalty*. **5 a** give (attention, respect, a compliment, etc.) to. **b** make (a visit, call, etc.). • *noun* wages; payment. • *adjective* designating a service or object the use of which requires payment: *pay phone*. PHRASES **pay back 1** return (money). **2** take revenge on (a person). **3** recompense. **pay dearly 1** obtain at a high cost, great effort, etc. **2** suffer for a wrongdoing etc. **pay down** reduce (debt etc.) by repayment. **pay one's dues 1** fulfill one's obligations. **2** undergo hardship to succeed or gain experience. **pay for 1** hand over the price of. **2** bear the cost of. **3** suffer or be punished for (a fault etc.). **pay into** pay (money) into a bank account, savings plan, etc. **pay one's (own) way** cover costs; not be indebted. **pay one's last respects** show respect towards a dead person by attending the funeral home or funeral. **pay off 1** *informal* yield good results; succeed. **2** pay (a debt) in full. **3** dismiss (workers) with a final payment. **pay out** pay (money) from funds under one's control; spend. **pay the piper (and call the tune)** pay the cost of (and so have the right to control) an activity or undertaking. **pay a** (or **the**) **price** suffer a disadvantage or loss in return for a gain. **pay one's respects** make a polite visit. **pay through the nose** *informal* pay much more than a fair price. **pay up** pay the full amount. **put paid to** *informal* **1** eliminate. **2** terminate; negate. **3** deal effectively with (a person).

payable • *adjective* **1** that must be paid; due: *payable in April*. **2** that may be paid. • *noun* (in *plural*) debts owed by a business; liabilities.

pay-as-you-go *noun* a system or the practice of paying debts and meeting costs as they arise.

payback *noun* **1** a financial return; a reward. **2** the profit from an investment etc., esp. one equal to the initial outlay. **3** (also **payback period**) the length of time required for an investment to pay for itself in terms of profits or savings. **4** an act of revenge or retaliation.

paycheque *noun* **1** an esp. regular payment given to an employee. **2** a cheque for this.

payday *noun* **1** a day on which payment, esp. of wages,

is collected or expected to be collected. **2** *informal* the winning or gaining of a large sum, as from gambling, a contest, etc.

pay dirt *noun Mining* ground worth working for ore. **PHRASES** **hit** (or **strike**) **pay dirt** find or reach a source of profit or reward.

payee *noun* a person who is paid, esp. one to whom a cheque is made payable. [Say pay EE]

pay equity *noun* the practice of ensuring that men and women in occupations of equal or comparable value receive equal pay.

payer *noun* a person who pays or who has to pay for something.

payload *noun* **1 a** the part of a transport vehicle's load from which revenue is derived. **b** goods transported. **2 a** the explosive warhead carried by an aircraft or rocket. **b** the instruments etc. carried by a spaceship.

paymaster *noun* an official who pays troops, workers, etc.

payment *noun* **1** the action or process of paying someone or something or of being paid. **2** an amount paid. **3** reward, recompense.

payoff *noun informal* **1** an act of payment. **2** a deserved benefit, reward, or punishment. **3** a bribe.

payola *noun* (*plural* **payolas**) bribery or a bribe offered for unofficial promotion of a product etc. in the media, esp. paid to radio disc jockeys for the playing of specific recordings. [Say pay OH luh]

payout *noun* a large payment of money, esp. as compensation or a dividend: *an insurance payout*.

pay-per-view *noun* a television service requiring viewers to pay a fee in order to watch a specific broadcast: *a pay-per-view movie*.

pay phone *noun* a telephone operated by the insertion of coins, a credit card, a phone card, etc.

payroll *noun* **1** a list of employees receiving regular pay. **2** the personnel costs of a company etc.

payroll tax *noun* (*plural* **payroll taxes**) a tax paid by an employer calculated as a percentage of employees' salaries, the percentage being determined by the size of the payroll.

pay stub *noun* (also **pay slip**, **pay statement**) a note given to an employee when paid detailing the amount of pay and deductions for tax etc.

pay-TV *noun* (also **pay television**) any television service requiring payment from viewers, esp. one in which viewers subscribe to a specific channel.

PB *noun informal* peanut butter.

Pb *symbol* the element lead.

PC *abbreviation* **1** (*plural* **PCs**) PERSONAL COMPUTER. **2** *Cdn* Progressive Conservative. **3** politically correct; political correctness. **4** *Cdn* postal code. **5** *Cdn & Brit.* privy councillor. **6** police constable. **7** protective custody.

pc. *abbreviation* (also **pce.**) piece: *3 pc. bath*.

PCB *noun* (*plural* **PCBs**) polychlorinated biphenyl, any of several toxic aromatic compounds containing two benzene molecules in which hydrogens have been replaced by chlorine atoms, formed as industrial waste.

PCMCIA *abbreviation* Personal Computer Memory Card International Association, denoting a standard specification for memory cards and interfaces in small computers.

PCO *abbreviation Cdn* PRIVY COUNCIL OFFICE.

PCP *abbreviation* **1** = PHENCYCLIDINE. **2** *Medical* pneumocystis carinii pneumonia, a fatal lung infection esp. of immunodeficient patients.

PCR *abbreviation* polymerase chain reaction, a means of detecting and reproducing nucleic acid.

Pd *symbol* palladium.

pd. *abbreviation* paid.

PD day *noun Cdn* PROFESSIONAL DEVELOPMENT DAY.

PDQ *abbreviation informal* pretty damn quick.

PDT *abbreviation* Pacific Daylight Time.

PE *abbreviation* **1** physical education. **2** (in official postal use) Prince Edward Island.

pea *noun* **1** a round green seed that is widely eaten as a vegetable. **2** a hardy climbing plant, which produces pods containing these. **3** any of several similar leguminous plants or seeds: *sweet pea* ◊ *chickpea*.

pea brain *noun informal* a stupid or dim-witted person. ▶ **pea-brained** *adjective*

peace *noun* **1 a** quiet: *needs peace to work well.* **b** mental calm: *peace of mind.* **2 a** freedom from or the cessation of war: *peace talks.* **b** (esp. **Peace**) a peace treaty between countries at war: *the Peace of Paris.* **3 a** freedom from civil disorder: *peace, order, and good government.* **b** freedom from quarrels or dissension between individuals. **4** *Christianity* a ritual liturgical greeting. **PHRASES** **at peace 1** in a state of friendliness. **2** serene. **3** *euphemism* dead. **hold one's peace** keep silence. **keep the peace** prevent, or refrain from, strife. **make one's peace** (often foll. by *with*) re-establish friendly relations. **make peace** bring about peace; reconcile.

peaceable *adjective* **1** not warlike. **2** free from disturbance; peaceful. ▶ **peaceably** *adverb*

peace bond *noun* a written undertaking to a court of law to keep the peace, esp. to refrain from damaging property or inflicting personal injury.

peace dividend *noun* public money which becomes available when spending on defence is reduced.

peaceful *adjective* **1** characterized by peace; tranquil. **2** not violating or infringing peace: *peaceful coexistence.* **3** pertaining to a state of peace. ▶ **peacefully** *adverb* **peacefulness** *noun*

peacekeeper *noun* a person, esp. a member of an international military force, involved in the active maintenance of a truce between nations or communities.

peacekeeping *noun* the active maintenance of a truce between nations or communities, esp. by international military forces: *peacekeeping mission*.

peacemaker *noun* a person, group, or nation who brings about peace. ▶ **peacemaking** *noun & adjective*

peace officer *noun* a civil officer, e.g. a police officer, appointed to preserve the public peace.

peace pipe *noun* = CALUMET.

peace process *noun* (*plural* **peace processes**) a process of negotiation toward a peace treaty.

peace sign *noun* **1** a sign of peace made by holding up the hand with the palm outwards and the first two fingers forming a V. **2** a symbol consisting of a circle divided into thirds by lines, with the central line extended to cover the whole diameter of the circle.

peacetime *noun* a period without war.

peach[1] • *noun* (*plural* **peaches**) **1 a** a round juicy fruit with downy cream or yellow skin flushed with red. **b** (also **peach tree**) the tree that bears this fruit. **2** the orange-pink colour of a peach. **3** *informal* an impressive or attractive person or thing. • *adjective* of an orange-pink colour.

peach[2] *verb* (**peaches**, **peached**, **peaching**) (usu. foll. by *against*, *on*) *informal* turn informer; inform.

peaches and cream *noun* **1** (usu. with *neg.*) an excellent or desirable situation: *it wasn't all peaches and cream.* **2** a fair complexion characterized by creamy skin and pink cheeks. **3** a variety of corn with alternating white and yellow kernels.

peach fuzz *noun informal* the down on the chin of an adolescent boy whose beard has not yet developed.

peachy *adjective* (**peachier**, **peachiest**) **1** like a

peach in colour or flavour. **2** (also **peachy-keen**) *informal* attractive, outstanding.

peacock *noun* a male peafowl, having brilliant plumage and a tail (with eyelike markings) that can be expanded erect in display like a fan.

peafowl *noun* (*plural* **peafowl**) a large crested pheasant.

pea green *noun & adjective* a bright green colour.

peahen *noun* a female peafowl.

SPELL CHECK

peak, peek, pique

A peep or quick look is a **peek**. The spelling is **pique** in "it piqued my interest".

---

peak • *noun* **1** a projecting usu. pointed part. **2 a** the highest point in a curve: *on the peak of the wave*. **b** the time of greatest success (in a career etc.). **c** the highest point on a graph etc. • *verb* reach the highest value, quality, etc. • *adjective* of or at the highest value, quality, frequency, rate, level, etc.: *peak shopping times*.

peaked[1] *adjective* having a peak. [Say PEEKT]

peaked[2] *adjective* = PEAKY. [Say PEAK id]

peaky *adjective* (**peakier, peakiest**) **1** sickly. **2** white-faced.

SPELL CHECK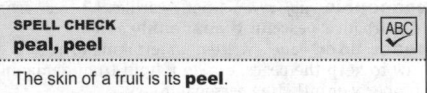

peal, peel

The skin of a fruit is its **peel**.

---

peal • *noun* **1 a** the loud ringing of a bell or bells. **b** a set of bells. **2** a loud repeated sound, esp. of thunder, laughter, etc. • *verb* **1** sound forth in a peal. **2** ring (bells) in peals.

peameal bacon *noun Cdn* back bacon rolled in a coating of fine cornmeal.

peanut *noun* **1** the oval seed of a plant native to South America, which yields an oil used in cooking and which is often roasted and eaten as a snack. **2** the plant of the pea family that bears these seeds, which develop in pods that ripen underground. **3** (in *plural*) *informal* a paltry or trivial thing or amount, esp. of money.

peanut butter *noun* a paste of ground roasted peanuts.

peanut gallery *noun slang* **1** the uppermost balcony in a theatre, where the cheapest seats are. **2** a group of hecklers or rowdy spectators.

peanutty *adjective* having the taste of peanuts.

SPELL CHECK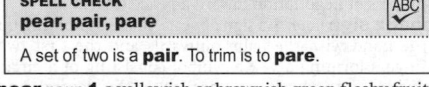

pear, pair, pare

A set of two is a **pair**. To trim is to **pare**.

---

pear *noun* **1** a yellowish or brownish-green fleshy fruit, tapering towards the stalk. **2** any of various trees bearing this fruit.

SPELL CHECK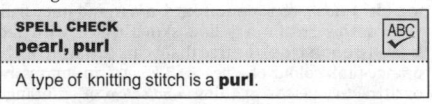

pearl, purl

A type of knitting stitch is a **purl**.

---

pearl • *noun* **1** a usu. white or bluish-grey hard mass formed within the shell of a pearl oyster or other bivalve mollusc, highly prized as a gem for its lustre. **2** a precious thing; the finest example: *Odessa is known as the pearl of the Black Sea*. **3** anything resembling a pearl. **4** an iridescent off-white colour. • *adjective* of the colour of pearl. • *verb* form pearl-like drops. **PHRASES** **pearls before swine** something valuable offered to a person unable to appreciate it.

pearl onion *noun* a very small onion, usu. pickled.

pearl oyster *noun* any of various tropical marine bivalve molluscs that are important commercial sources of pearls.

pearly *adjective* (**pearlier, pearliest**) **1** resembling a pearl; lustrous. **2** containing pearls or mother-of-pearl. **3** adorned with pearls.

Pearly Gates *plural noun informal* the gates of Heaven.

pearly whites *plural noun informal* the teeth.

Peary caribou *noun* a small caribou of the Arctic islands of Canada. [Say PEERY]

peasant • *noun* **1** (esp. formerly or in poorer countries) a member of a class of farm labourers or small farmers dependent on subsistence farming. **2** *derogatory* an ignorant, stupid, or unsophisticated person. • *adjective* **1** of or characteristic of peasants. **2** (of a style of dress, art, etc.) inspired by Western folk traditions. ▶ **peasanty** *adjective*

peasantry *noun* peasants collectively. [Say PEZZ'n tree]

peashooter *noun* a toy weapon consisting of a small tube through which peas, rolled paper, or other pellets are propelled by blowing.

pea soup *noun* **1** a thick soup, usu. dull yellow or green, made from dried split peas. **2** (also **pea-souper**) *informal* a thick yellowish fog.

peat *noun* vegetable matter partly decomposed in wet acid conditions to form a brown deposit like soil, used for fuel, in gardening, etc.

peat moss *noun* **1** any of various absorbent mosses that grow in dense masses on boggy ground and form peat as they decay. **2** such moss when dried, used esp. in gardening for packing plants and for compost.

peaty *adjective* composed of or covered in peat: *peaty bogs* ◊ *wet, peaty ground*.

peavey *noun* (also **peavy**) (*plural* **peaveys, peavies**) a logging implement consisting of a long pole ending in a metal spike and hinged hook. [Say PEE vee]

pebble • *noun* **1** a small smooth stone worn by the action of water. **2** a dimpled texture, as of leather, the ice surface in curling, etc. **3** an agate or other gem, esp. when found as a pebble in a stream etc. • *verb* (**pebbles, pebbled, pebbling**) give a dimpled texture to (leather, the ice surface in curling, etc.). ▶ **pebbled** *adjective* **pebbly** *adjective*

pec *noun* (usu. in *plural*) *informal* a pectoral muscle.

pecan *noun* **1** a pinkish-brown smooth nut with an edible kernel. **2** a hickory of the southern US that produces this. [Say PEE can or pee CAN]

peccadillo *noun* (*plural* **peccadilloes** or **peccadillos**) a trifling offence; a minor sin: *living a fishbowl existence, with all your domestic peccadilloes on display*. [Say pecka DILLO]

peccary *noun* (*plural* **peccaries**) any of several dark-furred pig-like mammals inhabiting forest and forest scrub in Central and South America. [Say PECKA ree]

peck[1] • *verb* **1** strike or bite (something) with a beak or pointed instrument. **2** kiss (esp. a person's cheek) hastily or perfunctorily. **3 a** make (a hole) by pecking. **b** (foll. by *out, off*) remove or pluck out by pecking. **4** (also foll. by *away, out*) type at a typewriter etc. • *noun* **1** a stroke or bite with a beak or pointed instrument. **2** a hasty or perfunctory kiss. **PHRASES** **peck at 1** eat (food) listlessly; nibble. **2** strike (a thing) repeatedly with a beak.

peck[2] *noun* **1 a** (in Britain and other Commonwealth countries) a measure of capacity for dry goods, equal to 2 imperial gallons (9.09 litres). **b** (in the US) a measure of capacity for dry goods, equal to 8 US quarts (8.81 litres). **2** a vessel used to contain this amount. **PHRASES** **a peck of** a large number or amount of (troubles, dirt, etc.).

pecking order *noun* **1** a hierarchy based on rank or status: *teachers were so low in the social and economic*

pecking *order that their voices were rarely heeded*. **2** a pattern of behaviour observed among social animals in which those of high rank attack those of lower rank without provoking an attack in return.

peckish *adjective informal* moderately hungry.

pecorino *noun* (*plural* **pecorinos**) an Italian cheese made from ewes' milk. [Say pecka REENO]

pectin *noun* a substance similar to sugar that forms in ripe fruit and causes jam or jelly to become firm as it is cooked.

pectoral • *adjective* of, relating to, or worn on the chest: *pectoral muscle* ◊ *pectoral cross*. • *noun* **1** (esp. in *plural*) a pectoral muscle. **2** a pectoral fin. [Say PECK tuh rul]

peculiar *adjective* **1** strange: *a peculiar flavour*. **2 a** (usu. foll. by *to*) belonging exclusively: *a particular type of mace considered to be peculiar to Japan has surfaced in Ecuador*. **b** belonging to the individual: *their own peculiar brand of art*. **3** particular: *a point of peculiar interest*.

peculiarity *noun* (*plural* **peculiarities**) **1** an odd or unusual feature or habit: *for all his peculiarities, she finds his personality quite endearing*. **2** a distinguishing characteristic or habit: *it is a peculiarity of North America today that culture is absorbed into society mainly through the university classroom*. **3** the state of being peculiar: *the peculiarity of their upbringing*. [Say puh cue lee ERRA tee]

peculiarly *adverb* **1** in a way that relates to or is especially typical of one particular person, thing, place, etc.: *Canadians are wrong to see this as a peculiarly American problem*. **2** more than usually; especially: *some patients were peculiarly difficult to cure*. **3** in an odd or unusual manner: *most were peculiarly dressed in great big hats and great big boots and all of them shouting*.

pecuniary *adjective* **1** of, concerning, or consisting of, money: *pecuniary aid*. **2** (of an offence) entailing a money penalty or fine. [Say puh CUE nee airy]

pedagogic *adjective* having to do with teaching or teaching methods. ▶ **pedagogical** *adjective* **pedagogically** *adverb* [Say pedda GODGE ick]

pedagogue *noun* a teacher. [Say PEDDA gog]

pedagogy *noun* (*plural* **pedagogies**) the science of teaching. [Say PEDDA godge ee]

pedal • *noun* any of several types of foot-operated levers or controls for mechanisms, esp.: **1** either of a pair of levers for transmitting power to a bicycle or tricycle wheel etc. **2** any of the foot-operated controls in a motor vehicle. **3** a bar on a musical instrument, e.g. a piano, organ, or harp, that is operated by the foot in order to produce or affect sound. • *verb* (**pedals, pedalled, pedalling**) **1** operate a bicycle, organ, etc. by using the pedals. **2** work (a bicycle etc.) with the pedals. PHRASES **pedal to the metal** *informal* **1** full speed, full out. **2** with the gas pedal of a vehicle pressed completely to the floor.

pedal boat *noun* a small recreational pontoon boat usu. with pedal-operated paddlewheels.

pedant *noun* a person who is excessively concerned with minor details and rules or with displaying academic learning: *pedants who observed that the 21st century did not begin until January 1st 2001*. ▶ **pedantic** *adjective* **pedantically** *adverb* **pedantry** *noun* (*plural* **pedantries**) [Say PED'nt, puh DAN tick, PED'n tree]

peddle *verb* (**peddles, peddled, peddling**) **1** sell (goods); sell goods as a peddler, i.e. in small quantities and from place to place: *a new consumer publication chiefly peddling clothing and cosmetics*. **2** advocate or promote (ideas, a way of life, etc.): *the party's members peddle dubious ideas that start people worrying*. **3** sell (drugs) illegally.

peddler *noun* **1** a travelling seller of small items esp. carried in a pack etc. **2** a person who sells drugs illegally.

pedestal *noun* **1** a base supporting a column, statue, etc. **2** either of the two supports at either end of the writing surface of a desk, usu. containing drawers. **3** an upright, column-like support for a seat, machine, etc.: *pedestal sink*. PHRASES **put** (or **set**) **on a pedestal** admire disproportionately, idolize.

pedestrian • *noun* a person on foot rather than in a vehicle. • *adjective* **1** (esp. of writing) dull: *her latest play is more pedestrian and less ambitious than her earlier work*. **2** of, relating to, or for walkers or walking: *pedestrian mall* ◊ *pedestrian crossing*.

pediatric *adjective* involved in or having to do with the treatment of children's illnesses and disease: *pediatric care unit* ◊ *pediatric dentist*. [Say peedy AI rick]

pediatrician *noun* a doctor who studies and treats children's illnesses and diseases. [Say peedy uh TRISH'n]

pediatrics *plural noun* (treated as *singular*) the branch of medicine dealing with children and their diseases. [Say peedy AT ricks]

pedicure • *noun* **1** remedial or cosmetic treatment of the feet. **2** a session of such treatment. ▶ **pedicured** *adjective* [Say PED i cure]

pedigree *noun* **1** a recorded line of descent of a person or esp. a purebred animal. **2** the history of a person, thing, idea, etc., esp. a list of achievements: *the verandah, which already had a long pedigree in Canadian architecture, was a feature characteristic of Queen Anne Revival houses*. **3** a genealogical table. ▶ **pedigreed** *adjective*

pediment *noun* **1** the triangular part crowning the front of a building in the classical style. **2** a similar part of a building in other styles, irrespective of shape. **3** a similar feature surmounting a door etc. [Say PED i mint]

pedlar *noun* = PEDDLER. [Say PED ler]

pedophile *noun* a person who desires children sexually. ▶ **pedophilia** *noun* [Say PEDDA file or PEEDA file, pedda FILLY uh or peeda FILLY uh]

pee *informal* • *verb* (**pees, peed, peeing**) **1** urinate. **2 pee oneself** urinate into one's clothes. **3** wet (esp. bedclothes, one's clothing) by urinating. • *noun* **1** an act of urination. **2** urine. PHRASES **peed off** annoyed.

peek • *verb* (usu. foll. by *in, out, at*) look quickly or furtively. • *noun* a quick or furtive look.

peekaboo • *noun* the game of hiding one's face and suddenly revealing it, as played with a young child. • *interjection* the utterance made when doing this. • *adjective* (of a garment etc.) transparent or having a pattern of small holes so as to reveal the body.

P

P

peel • *verb* **1 a** strip the skin etc. from. **b** strip (skin, peel, wrapping, etc.) from a fruit etc. **2 a** (of a tree, an animal's or person's body, a painted surface, etc.) have the outer layer of bark, skin, paint, etc. flake off. **b** (often foll. by *off*) (of bark, a person's skin, paint, etc.) flake off. **3 a** remove or separate (a label, a banknote, etc.) from the outside or top of something. **b** turn back so as to expose something underneath. **4** separate from a body of people, vehicles, etc.: *peeled away from the line of cars.* **5 a** (often foll. by *off*) *informal* (of a person) take off (a garment). **b** (foll. by *down*) undress. **6** (of a vehicle etc.) move quickly, leave a place, etc. suddenly: *peeled out of her driveway.* **7** *Curling* remove (a rock) from play with a rock that itself also goes out of play. • *noun* **1** the outer covering of a fruit, vegetable, shrimp, etc. **2** the chemical removal of superficial layers of skin on the face, usu. to remove scars etc.

peeler *noun* **1 a** a utensil for peeling fruit etc. **b** a person who or thing which peels trees etc. **2** (also **peeler crab**) a crab when it casts its shell.

peeling *noun* a strip of the outer skin of a vegetable, fruit, etc.: *potato peelings.*

peen *noun* the wedge-shaped or thin or curved end of a hammerhead (*opp.* FACE *noun* 5a).

peep¹ • *verb* **1** (usu. foll. by *at, in, out, into*) look quickly and secretly, esp. through a small opening. **2** (usu. foll. by *out*) come slowly into view; emerge. • *noun* a furtive or peering glance.

peep² • *verb* make a shrill feeble sound as of young birds, mice, etc. • *noun* **1** such a sound. **2** a slight sound, utterance, or complaint: *not a peep out of them.* **3** any of several sandpipers.

pee-pee *noun informal* **1** urine. **2** the penis.

peeper¹ *noun* **1** a person who peeps. **2** *informal* (usu. in *plural*) an eye. **3** *slang* a private investigator.

peeper² *noun* = SPRING PEEPER.

peephole *noun* a small hole to be looked through.

peeping Tom *noun* a person who secretly observes others, esp. women undressing.

peep show *noun* **1** a show of live nudes or an erotic film viewed from a coin-operated booth. **2** a series of small pictures viewed through a magnifying lens placed in a small opening of a box etc.

peer¹ *verb* look keenly or with difficulty: *peered into the fog.*

peer² *noun* **1** a person who is equal in ability, standing, rank, or value: *children are worried about failing in front of their peers.* **2** a noble or person of high rank: *dukes and earls are hereditary peers.* PHRASES **without peer** unequalled, unrivalled.

peerage *noun* **1** the nobility: *increasingly, the amateur politicians who make up the hereditary peerage are coming to represent the common man.* **2** the rank of peer or peeress: *a life peerage.* **3** a book containing a list of peers with their genealogy etc. [Say PEER idge]

peeress *noun* (*plural* **peeresses**) **1** the wife or widow of a noble. **2** a woman having the rank of a noble by creation or descent.

peer group *noun* a group of people of the same age, status, interests, etc.

peerless *adjective* superior to all others of its kind; unequalled, unrivalled: *many of the photos were contributed by peerless nature photographer Teresa Torres.*

peer pressure *noun* influence from members of one's peer group.

peeve *informal* • *noun* a cause of annoyance. • *verb* (**peeves**, **peeved**, **peeving**) (usu. in *passive*) annoy.

peevish *adjective* **1** easily annoyed, esp. by unimportant things. **2** (of a quality, action, etc.) characterized by or exhibiting petty vexation or spite. ▶ **peevishly** *adverb* **peevishness** *noun*

peewee • *noun* **1** *Cdn* **a** a level of amateur sport, usu. involving children aged 12–13: *peewee hockey.* **b** a player in this age group. **2** a very small or young person or thing. • *adjective* very small.

peg • *noun* **1 a** a usu. cylindrical pin or bolt of wood, metal, etc., often tapered at one end, and used for: **a** holding esp. two things together. **b** hanging garments etc. on. **c** fastening a rope for holding up a tent etc. **d** tightening or loosening the strings of a violin etc. **e** inserting into a cribbage board to keep score. **2** *Baseball informal* a strong, long, low throw, esp. at a base. **3** an occasion, pretext, excuse, theme, etc.: *used the incident as a peg for the article.* **4** a short blunt structure or outgrowth in a plant, animal, etc. • *verb* (**pegs**, **pegged**, **pegging**) **1 a** (usu. foll. by *down, in, out,* etc.) fix (a thing) with a peg. **b** drive or insert a peg or pegs into. **2** *informal* identify, categorize, form an opinion of (a person etc.). **3** *informal* **a** throw (a ball) hard and low. **b** *Baseball* stop or put out (a runner) with such a throw. **4** *informal* measure, mark, set: *the cost was pegged at $5.5 million.* **5 a** fix (prices, wages, exchange rates, etc.) at a certain level or in line with a certain standard. **b** prevent the price of (stock etc.) from falling or rising by freely buying or selling at a given price. PHRASES **peg out 1** *slang* die. **2** measure, extend, or mark the boundaries of (land etc.). **3** score the winning point in cribbage. **a round** (or **square**) **peg in a square** (or **round**) **hole** a person in a situation unsuited to his or her capacities, disposition, etc.; a misfit. **take a person down a peg or two** humble a person.

Pegboard *noun* *proprietary* a type of perforated board having a regular pattern of small holes for pegs.

pegged *adjective* **1** in senses of PEG *verb.* **2** (of a garment) wide at the top and narrow at the bottom.

peg leg *informal* • *noun* **1** an artificial leg, esp. a wooden leg. **2** *offensive* a person with an artificial leg. • *adjective* **1** (also **peg-legged**) *informal* having a peg leg. **2** = PEGGED 2.

Peguis *noun* (*plural* **Peguis**) a member of a Cree- and Ojibwa-speaking Aboriginal group living about 200 km north of Winnipeg. [Say PEG wis]

PEI *abbreviation* Prince Edward Island.

Peigan • *noun* (*plural* **Peigan** or **Peigans**) **1** a member of an Aboriginal people, a part of the Blackfoot Confederacy, living in southern Alberta and northwestern Montana. **2** the Algonquian language of this people. • *adjective* of or relating to this people or their culture or language. [Say pee GAN]

pejorative • *adjective* (of a word, an expression, etc.) expressing contempt and criticism or disapproval: *their reasons were political, in the pejorative sense of the word.* • *noun* a derogatory word or form: *disgusted by their continual use of pejoratives.* ▶ **pejoratively** *adverb* [Say puh JORRA tiv]

Peking duck *noun* a Chinese dish consisting of duck hung to dry, coated with honey so that it turns a deep-reddish brown, dried again, and then roasted, and served in shreds with vegetables, sauce, and small pancakes.

Pekingese (also **Pekinese**) • *noun* (*plural* **Pekingese**) **1** a lapdog of a short-legged breed with long hair and a snub nose. **2** a citizen of Peking (Beijing). **3** the form of the Chinese language used in Beijing. • *adjective* of or concerning Beijing or its language or citizens. [Say pee king EEZ or pee kin EES]

Peking man *noun* the fossilized remains of an extinct human species of the middle Pleistocene period, found in 1926 in China and now usu. classified as a late form of *Homo erectus*.

pekoe *noun* a high-quality black tea. [Say PEE co]

pelagic *adjective* of, performed on, or inhabiting the open sea: *pelagic snails*. [Say puh LADGE ick]

pelargonium *noun* a tender shrubby plant that is widely cultivated for its red, pink, or white flowers and fragrant leaves, commonly called a geranium. [Say peller GO nee um]

pelican *noun* any large water bird with a large bill and a pouch in the throat for storing fish.

pellet *noun* **1** a small, hard, compressed mass of something. **2 a** a bullet or piece of small shot. **b** an imitation bullet for a toy gun: *pellet gun*. **3 a** a small mass of bones, feathers, etc. regurgitated by a bird of prey. **b** a small hard piece of animal feces.

pell-mell • *adverb* **1** headlong, recklessly. **2** in disorder or confusion. • *adjective* confused, tumultuous: *in the pell-mell rush to get the bill through, people on both sides feel somewhat trampled*.

pellucid *adjective* very clear: *high up in a blue sky pellucid as crystal*. [Say puh LUCID]

pelt[1] *verb* **1** (usu. foll. by *with*) **a** hurl many small objects at. **b** strike repeatedly with esp. many small things. **c** assail (a person etc.) with insults, abuse, etc. **2** (usu. foll. by *down*) (of rain etc.) fall quickly and torrentially. **3** move or run fast or vigorously. PHRASES **(at) full pelt** as fast as possible.

pelt[2] *noun* the dressed or undressed skin of a fur-bearing mammal with hair, wool, etc. still on.

pelvic *adjective* involving, situated in, or having to do with the pelvis: *pelvic bones*.

pelvic inflammatory disease *noun* an inflammation of the female reproductive organs, caused by bacterial infection. Abbreviation: **PID**.

pelvis *noun* (*plural* **pelvises** or **pelves**) **1 a** the wide curved set of bones at the bottom of the torso that the legs and spine are connected to. **b** the part of the abdomen containing the pelvis. **2** the basin-like cavity of the kidney.

pemmican *noun* pounded, dried meat (usu. buffalo) mixed to a paste with melted fat, berries, etc. originally made by North American Indians and adapted by fur traders etc. [Say PEM ick in]

Pen. *abbreviation* Peninsula.

pen[1] • *noun* **1** an instrument for writing or drawing with ink. **2** (usu. as **the pen**) the occupation or practice of writing. **3** an instrument resembling a pen in form or function. **4** an electronic pen-like device used with a writing surface to enter commands or data into a computer. • *verb* (**pens, penned, penning**) **1** write. **2** compose and write. PHRASES **the pen is mightier than the sword** persuasion, legislation, and education can achieve more than the use of armed force. **put pen to paper** begin writing.

pen[2] • *noun* **1 a** a small enclosure for cows, sheep, poultry, etc. **b** a number of animals in a pen or sufficient to fill a pen. **2** a place of confinement. **3** an enclosure for sheltering submarines. • *verb* (**pens, penned, penning**) enclose or shut in a pen.

pen[3] *noun* a female swan.

pen[4] *noun slang* = PENITENTIARY.

penal *adjective* of or concerning legal punishment or its infliction: *Australia was a penal colony*. [Say PEEN'll]

penal code *noun* a system of laws relating to crime and its punishment.

penalize *verb* (**penalizes, penalized, penalizing**) **1** subject to a penalty for breaking a rule etc. **2** put at a comparative disadvantage; handicap unfairly. [Say PEEN'll ize or PEN'll ize]

penalty *noun* (*plural* **penalties**) **1** a punishment, esp. a fine, for a breach of law, contract, etc. **2** a disadvantage, loss, etc., esp. as a result of one's own actions: *paid the penalty for forgetting*. **3 a** a disadvantage imposed on a competitor for a breach of the rules etc. **b** (as an *adjective*) awarded against a side incurring a penalty: *penalty kick*. PHRASES **under** (or **on**) **penalty of** under the threat of (dismissal etc.).

penalty area *noun Soccer* the ground in front of the goal in which a foul by defenders involves the award of a penalty kick.

penalty box *noun* (*plural* **penalty boxes**) *Hockey & Lacrosse* an area of seating reserved for players temporarily withdrawn from play as a penalty.

penalty kick *noun Soccer* a free kick at the goal, given after a foul in the penalty area.

penalty killer *noun Hockey* a player who plays while the team's strength is reduced by a penalty, esp. one skilled at stopping the other team from scoring. ▶ **penalty killing** *noun*

penalty shootout *noun* = SHOOTOUT 2.

penalty shot *noun Hockey* **1** a shot by an offensive player on a goal defended only by the goaltender, allowed as a penalty for certain infractions. **2** such a shot used esp. to decide the outcome of a tied game.

penance *noun* **1** an act of self-punishment as reparation for guilt. **2 a** (in the Catholic and Orthodox Churches) a sacrament including confession of one's sins, feeling sorry for having committed them, and forgiveness. **b** a punishment or discipline imposed esp. by a priest, or undertaken voluntarily, to make up for a sin. **3** an unpleasant task or situation, esp. one regarded as a punishment for something: *she regards living in New York as a penance; she hates big cities*. [Say PEN ince]

pen and ink • *noun* **1** the instruments of writing or drawing. **2** writing. **3** a drawing made using pen and ink. • *adjective* (**pen-and-ink**) (esp. of a drawing) done in ink.

pen-based *adjective* (of a computer etc.) taking input from an electronic pen rather than a keyboard.

pence *noun Brit.* **1** *plural of* PENNY. **2** *informal* a penny, esp. in British decimal currency.

penchant *noun* an inclination; a strong or habitual liking: *this author has a penchant for cute phrases*. [Say PEN ch'nt]

pencil • *noun* **1 a** an instrument for writing or drawing, usu. consisting of a thin rod of graphite etc. enclosed in a cylinder. **b** a cosmetic or medication in pencil form: *eyebrow pencil*. **2** (as an *adjective*) **a** resembling a pencil in shape: *pencil bomb*. **b** for, with, or of a pencil: *pencil sketch ◊ pencil stub*. • *verb* (**pencils, pencilled, pencilling**) **1** write, sketch, etc. with or as if with a pencil. **2** (usu. foll. by *in*) **a** note down or arrange tentatively or provisionally: *have pencilled in the wedding*. **b** fill (an area) with thin or delicate pencil strokes: *pencilled in her eyebrows*.

pencil crayon *noun Cdn* a pencil with a coloured core used for art, colouring, etc.

pencilled *adjective* **1** written in pencil: *she read the pencilled queries and suggestions*. **2** (of an area) filled in with pencil strokes: *she had pencilled eyebrows*.

pencil-pusher *noun informal derogatory* a person, esp. a clerk, whose job involves a lot of boring paperwork. ▶ **pencil-pushing** *noun & adjective*

pencil-thin *adjective* very thin or narrow.

pendant *noun* **1 a** a hanging jewel etc., esp. one attached to a necklace, bracelet, etc. **2** a light fixture, ornament, etc., hanging from a ceiling. [Say PEN dint]

pending • *adjective* **1** awaiting decision or settlement, undecided: *a settlement was pending.* **2** about to come into existence: *patent pending.* • *preposition* **1** until: *pending his return.* **2** during: *pending these negotiations.*

pendulous *adjective* **1** (of a part of the body) tending to droop heavily. **2** (of flowers, bird's nests, etc.) hanging down and esp. swinging. [Say PEND you luss]

pendulum *noun* **1** a weight suspended so as to swing freely, esp. a rod with a weighted end regulating the movement of a clock's works. **2** popular opinion etc. characterized by oscillation or regular movement from one extreme to another. [Say PEND you lum]

penetrable *adjective* **1** able to be penetrated or entered; accessible: *a savage land of rocks and forests only penetrable by the patient explorer.* **2** able to be understood: *the scriptural passage is not readily penetrable.* [Say PENNA truh bull]

penetrate *verb* (**penetrates, penetrated, penetrating**) **1** find access into or through, esp. forcibly. **2** see into, find out, or discern (a person's mind, the truth, etc.). **3** see through (darkness, fog, etc.). **4** be understood, fully realized, or absorbed by the mind. **5** breach or get through (an opponent's defence). **6** enter (a market) to establish a new brand, product, etc. **7** (usu. foll. by *into, through, to*) make a way. **8** (of a male) put the penis into the vagina or anus of (a sexual partner).

penetrating *adjective* **1** that permeates, gets or forces a way into or through something. **2** having or suggesting sensitivity or insight: *a penetrating remark.* **3 a** (of a voice etc.) easily heard through or above other sounds. **b** (of a smell) sharp, pungent. **4** capable of penetrating an opponent's defence.

penetration *noun* **1** the action or process of making a way through or into something: *the drywall has been damaged from moisture penetration* ◊ *the rugged and forbidding landscape made penetration and colonization of northern regions difficult.* **2** the selling or buying of a brand or type of product in a particular market or area: *the penetration of UNIX systems into the PC market.* **3** the insertion by a man of his penis into the vagina or anus of a sexual partner. **4** the perceptive understanding of complex matters: *the survey shows subtlety and penetration.*

penetrative *adjective* **1** (of sexual activity) involving the insertion of a man's penis into the anus or vagina of a sexual partner. **2** able to make a way into or through something: *penetrative weapons.* **3** having or showing deep understanding and insight: *a thorough and penetrative survey of the organization's work.*

penetrator *noun* a person or thing that penetrates something.

penguin *noun* any black-and-white flightless seabird of the southern hemisphere, with wings developed into scaly flippers for swimming underwater.

penicillin *noun* any of various antibiotics produced naturally by moulds of the genus *Penicillium*, or synthetically, and able to prevent the growth of certain disease-causing bacteria. [Say penna SILL in]

penile *adjective* of or concerning the penis. [Say PEE nile]

peninsula *noun* (*plural* **peninsulas**) a piece of land almost surrounded by water or projecting far into a sea or lake etc. ▶ **peninsular** *adjective* [Say puh NIN sul uh or puh NIN sul uh]

penis *noun* (*plural* **penises** or **penes**) the male genital organ which carries the duct for the emission of sperm, in mammals consisting largely of erectile tissue and serving also for the elimination of urine.

penitence *noun* a feeling of regret and a wish to atone for a wrongdoing or sin; repentance. [Say PEN it ince]

penitent • *adjective* regretting and wishing to atone for sins etc. • *noun* **1** a person who repents, a repentant sinner. **2** a person doing penance under the direction of a confessor. ▶ **penitential** *adjective* **penitentially** *adverb* [Say PEN it int, penna TEN shul]

penitentiary *noun* (*plural* **penitentiaries**) **1** *Cdn* a federal corrections institution for convicted offenders serving a sentence of two years or more. **2** *US* a state or federal prison, esp. for serious offenders. [Say penna TEN shuh ree]

penknife *noun* (*plural* **penknives**) a small folding knife, esp. for carrying in a pocket.

penlight *noun* a small, pen-shaped flashlight.

penmanship *noun* **1** handwriting. **2** the skill or art of handwriting.

Penn. *abbreviation* (also **Penna.**) Pennsylvania.

pen name *noun* a literary pseudonym.

pennant *noun* **1 a** a tapering flag, esp. that flown at the masthead of a vessel in commission. **b** such a flag identifying a team, club, cause, etc. **2** *Sport* **a** a flag symbolizing a league championship, esp. in professional baseball. **b** such a championship.

pennant race *noun* *Baseball* an esp. close competition among professional teams for the league pennant.

penne *noun* pasta in the form of short tubes with the ends cut diagonally. [Say PEN ay]

penniless *adjective* having no money. ▶ **pennilessness** *noun*

Pennsylvania Dutch (also **Pennsylvania German**) • *noun* **1** a dialect of High German spoken by German and Swiss immigrants to Pennsylvania in the 17th and 18th centuries, still spoken by some of their descendants in Pennsylvania and nearby areas and southern Ontario, esp. the Amish. **2** (as *plural*) these settlers or their descendants. • *adjective* of, pertaining to, or designating these people or their dialect.

Pennsylvanian • *noun* **1** a native or inhabitant of the US state of Pennsylvania. **2** (**the Pennsylvanian**) the upper Carboniferous period (320–286 million years ago) or system; this period was characterized by swamp forests and the formation of much of the world's coal, as well as by the appearance of reptiles. • *adjective* **1** of or relating to Pennsylvania. **2** of or relating to the upper Carboniferous period or system.

penny *noun* (*plural* for separate coins **pennies**, *Brit.* for a sum of money **pence**) **1** a one-cent coin. **2** *Brit.* a coin and monetary unit equal to one-hundredth of a pound. **3** *Brit. hist.* a former coin and monetary unit equal to one-two-hundred-and-fortieth of a pound. **4** a usu. small sum of money; a very little or the least amount of wealth, money, etc.: *worth every penny.* PHRASES **in for a penny, in for a pound** an exhortation to total commitment to an undertaking. **like a bad penny** continually returning when unwanted. **pennies from heaven** unexpected esp. financial benefits. **a penny for your thoughts** a request to a person to confide in the speaker. **a pretty penny** a considerable sum of money.

penny auction *noun* **1** a fundraising auction where items are sold for very small sums. **2** an auction of goods repossessed or seized as collateral, in which the bidders collude to pay absurdly low prices so that the repossessor sees no financial gain from the sale and the owner can regain the property at little or no cost.

penny-pincher *noun* a person who is extremely or excessively careful with money: *penny-pinchers will appreciate this store's low prices* ◊ *she didn't want to work for penny-pinchers who pay their employees poorly.*

penny-pinching • *adjective* extremely or excessively careful with money; thrifty or cheap. • *noun* extreme or excessive care with money; thrift, stinginess.

pennyroyal *noun* either of two small-leaved plants of the mint family, cultivated for use in herbal medicine.

penny stock *noun* common stock valued at less than a dollar a share, and therefore highly speculative.

pennywhistle *noun* a tin pipe with six holes, which may be variously covered to give different notes.

penny-wise *adjective* careful, esp. overly careful, in saving small amounts or in small expenditures. PHRASES **penny-wise and pound foolish** thrifty in small expenditures but careless or wasteful in large ones.

pen pal *noun* a person with whom one builds a friendship by exchanging letters, esp. someone in a foreign country whom one has never met.

pen-pusher *noun informal derogatory* = PENCIL-PUSHER ▶ **pen-pushing** *noun*

pension • *noun* **1** a regular payment made by a government to people above a specified age, to the disabled, or to such a person's surviving dependants. **2** a similar payment made by an employer etc. to a retired employee. **3** a regular payment from a fund etc. to which the recipient has contributed (usu. with an employer) as an investment during his or her working life in order to realize a return upon retirement: *pension plan*. • *verb* grant a pension to. PHRASES **pension off 1** dismiss with a pension. **2** cease to employ or use.

pensionable *adjective* **1** entitled to a pension. **2** (of a service, job, etc.) entitling an employee to a pension. **3** of, pertaining to, or affecting a person's pension: *pensionable earnings*.

pensioner *noun* a recipient of (esp. an old-age) pension.

pensive *adjective* engaged in, involving, or reflecting deep or serious thought: *a pensive mood ◊ she is quiet and pensive*. ▶ **pensively** *adverb*

penstemon *noun* a North American plant with stems of showy flowers like snapdragons. [Say pen STEE min or PENSTA min]

pent *adjective* (usu. foll. by *up*) closely confined; shut in.

penta- *combining form* five.

pentagon *noun* **1** a plane figure with five sides and angles. **2** (**the Pentagon**) **a** a pentagonal building in Arlington, Virginia, containing the headquarters of the US armed forces. **b** the leaders of the US armed forces. ▶ **pentagonal** *adjective* [Say PENTA gon, pen TAGGA nul]

pentahedron *noun* (*plural* **pentahedrons** or **pentahedra**) a solid figure with five faces. [Say penta HEE drun for the singular, penta HEE druns or penta HEE druh for the plural]

pentameter *noun* a verse of five metrical feet, e.g. English iambic verse of ten syllables. [Say pen TAMMA ter]

pentamidine *noun* a drug used to treat protozoal infections, esp. in AIDS patients. [Say pen TAMMA deen]

Pentateuch *noun* the first five books of the Bible (Genesis, Exodus, Leviticus, Numbers, and Deuteronomy), called the Torah by Jews, and traditionally ascribed to Moses. ▶ **Pentateuchal** *adjective* [Say PENTA tuke]

pentathlete *noun* an athlete who participates in a pentathlon. [Say pen TATH leet]

pentathlon *noun* **1** (in full **modern pentathlon**) an athletic competition in which participants engage in five different events, including fencing, shooting, swimming, riding, and cross-country running. **2** any athletic event comprising five different events. [Say pen TATH lon]

Pentecost *noun* **1** a Christian festival observed on the seventh Sunday after Easter, commemorating the descent of the Holy Spirit on the disciples. **2 a** the Jewish harvest festival, on the fiftieth day after the second day of Passover. **b** a synagogue ceremony on the anniversary of the giving of the Law on Mount Sinai. **3** (in some Christian denominations) the liturgical season extending from Pentecost to the beginning of Advent. [Say PENTA cost]

Pentecostal • *adjective* (also **pentecostal**) **1** of or relating to Pentecost. **2** of or designating Christian denominations and individuals who emphasize charismatic forms of worship, e.g. speaking in tongues, healing, etc., and are often fundamentalist in outlook. • *noun* a member of a Pentecostal denomination. ▶ **Pentecostalism** *noun* [Say penta COST ul]

penthouse *noun* **1** an apartment or suite on the top floor of a tall building. **2** a structure on the roof of a building to house elevator machinery etc.

pentobarbital *noun* a barbiturate formerly used to relieve insomnia. [Say penta BARBA tawl]

WRITING TIP
penultimate

Penultimate does *not* mean "absolutely ultimate" or "not surpassable". It means "second-last".

---

penultimate *adjective* last but one; second-last. [Say pen ULTIMATE]

penumbra *noun* (*plural* **penumbrae** or **penumbras**) **1** the partly shaded region around the shadow of an opaque body, esp. that around the total shadow of the moon or earth in an eclipse. **2** a partial shadow. ▶ **penumbral** *adjective* [Say pen UMM bruh for the singular, pen UMM bree or pen UMM bruhs for the plural]

penury *noun* (*plural* **penuries**) extreme poverty: *wild spending followed by extreme penury*. [Say PEN yur ee]

peon *noun* **1** a menial or drudge: *I was a peon in the department*. **2 a** a Spanish American farm worker. **b** a poor or destitute South American. [Say PEE on]

peony *noun* (*plural* **peonies**) a perennial plant with large showy red, pink, or white flowers. [Say PEE uh nee]

people • *noun* **1** (treated as *plural*) a human beings, esp. as opposed to animals etc. **b** persons in general: *people do not like rudeness*. **2** (usu. as *plural*) persons composing a community, race, nation, etc. **3** (**the people**) treated as *plural*) **a** the mass of people in a country etc. not having special rank or position. **b** these considered as an electorate. **4** (treated as *plural*) family: *my people came from Scotland*. • *verb* (**peoples, peopled, peopling**) **1** fill with people; populate. **2** (esp. as **peopled** *adjective*) inhabit; occupy as inhabitants, fictional characters etc.: *a novel peopled with unlovable characters*.

peoplehood *noun* the condition, state, or awareness of being a people.

people person *noun* a person who enjoys or is particularly good at interacting with other people.

people power *noun* **1** political or other pressure applied by the people, esp. through the public demonstration of popular opinion. **2** physical power exerted by people as opposed to machines etc.

people skills *plural noun* character traits that allow one to deal effectively with other people.

pep *informal* • *noun* liveliness; energy and enthusiasm. • *verb* (**peps, pepped, pepping**) (usu. foll. by *up*) fill with energy or liveliness.

pepper • *noun* **1 a** the hot-tasting aromatic berries of certain plants, dried and then ground or used whole as a spice or condiment to flavour food. **b** the climbing vine that yields these berries. **2 a** the bell-shaped, smooth-skinned, mildly pungent fruit of a tropical American plant of the nightshade family. **b** the plant bearing this fruit. **3** = CAYENNE. • *verb* **1** sprinkle or treat with or as if with pepper. **2** sprinkle liberally: *peppered with quotations from Shakespeare*. **3** pelt with missiles.

peppercorn *noun* the dried pepper berry as a condiment.

pepper mill *noun* (also **pepper grinder**) a device for grinding pepper by hand.

peppermint *noun* **1 a** a mint plant grown for the strong-flavoured oil obtained from its leaves. **b** the oil from this. **2** a candy flavoured with peppermint.

pepperoni *noun* a hard, highly-seasoned sausage made with beef and pork.

pepper spray *noun* an aerosol spray of oils derived from cayenne pepper, used to overcome an assailant.

pepper squash *noun* (*plural* **pepper squash** or **pepper squashes**) *Cdn* a variety of winter squash with dark green to orange skin and yellow flesh.

pepper steak *noun* **1** a dish of beef steak coated in coarsely crushed peppercorns before cooking. **2** steak coated with peppercorns as a basis for this dish. **3** a stew-like dish of steak with bell peppers.

peppery *adjective* **1** of, like, or containing much pepper. **2** hot-tempered. **3** pungent.

peppy *adjective* (**peppier, peppiest**) *informal* vigorous, energetic.

pep rally *noun* (*plural* **pep rallies**) a meeting or gathering to inspire enthusiasm, esp. before a sports event.

pep talk *noun* a usu. short talk intended to enthuse, encourage, etc.

peptic ulcer *noun* an ulcer in the stomach or duodenum.

peptide *noun* any of a group of organic compounds consisting of two or more amino acids bonded in sequence.

Péquiste *noun Cdn* a supporter or member of the Parti Québécois. [Say pay KEEST]

per *preposition* **1** for each. **2** by means of. **3** (also **per**) in accordance with: *as per instructions*. PHRASES **as per usual** *informal* as usual.

perambulate *verb* (**perambulates, perambulated, perambulating**) walk through, over, or around a place, esp. for pleasure and in a leisurely way: *I perambulate the summer streets*. ▶ **perambulation** *noun* [Say purr AM byoo late]

per annum *adverb* for each year: *a growth rate of 2.7% per annum*.

per capita *adverb & adjective* per person: *the province with more cars on the road per capita* ◊ *per capita income*.

perceivable *adjective* that can be noticed, observed, or understood.

perceive *verb* (**perceives, perceived, perceiving**) **1** notice or become aware of something, esp. through the sight; observe: *I began to perceive a change in Mila's attitude*. **2** come to realize or understand. **3** interpret or look on (someone or something) in a particular way; regard as: *she did not perceive herself as disabled* ◊ *it's generally perceived to be one of the best mystery novels ever written*. ▶ **perceiver** *noun*

percent • *adverb* in every hundred. • *noun* **1** percentage: *service revenues have increased as a percent of total revenues*. **2** one part in every hundred: *half a percent*.

percentage *noun* **1** a rate or proportion percent. **2** a proportion. **3** *informal* personal benefit or advantage: *explain to me the percentage in looking like a hoodlum*.

percentile *noun Statistics* one of the 100 equal groups that a larger group of people can be divided into, according to their place on a scale measuring a particular value: *overall these students rank in the 21st percentile on the tests — that is, they did worse than 79 percent of all children taking the test*. [Say purr SEN tile]

perceptible *adjective* capable of being perceived by the senses or mind. ▶ **perceptibly** *adverb*

perception *noun* **1** the ability to see, hear, or become aware of something through the senses: *the normal limits to human perception*. **2** the state of being or process of becoming aware of something in such a way: *the perception of pain*. **3** a way of regarding, understanding, or interpreting something; a mental impression: *Hollywood's perception of the tastes of the American public* ◊ *we need to challenge many popular perceptions of old age*. **4** intuitive understanding and insight: *"He wouldn't have accepted," said my mother, with unusual perception*.

perceptive *adjective* **1** capable of perceiving. **2** sensitive; discerning; observant: *a perceptive remark*. ▶ **perceptively** *adverb* **perceptiveness** *noun*

perceptual *adjective* having to do with the ability to interpret or become aware of something through the senses: *a patient with perceptual problems who cannot judge distances*. ▶ **perceptually** *adverb*

perch[1] • *noun* (*plural* **perches**) **1** a usu. horizontal bar, branch, etc. used by a bird to rest on. **2** a usu. high or precarious place for a person or thing to rest on. • *verb* (**perches, perched, perching**) (usu. foll. by *on*) settle or rest, or cause to settle or rest on or as if on a perch etc.: *the bird perched on a branch* ◊ *a town perched on a hill*. PHRASES **knock something off its perch** cause someone to lose a position of superiority or security: *the disaster could be enough to knock the country off its seemingly unshakable economic perch*.

perch[2] *noun* (*plural* **perch** or **perches**) **1** a spiny-finned edible freshwater fish of North America. **2** = OCEAN PERCH.

percolate *verb* (**percolates, percolated, percolating**) **1** (often foll. by *through*) **a** (of liquid etc.) filter or ooze gradually (esp. through a porous surface). **b** (of an idea etc.) spread gradually through an area or a group of people: *such worry can percolate down to children*. **2 a** prepare (coffee) by repeatedly passing boiling water through ground beans. **b** (of coffee) be or become made by percolating. ▶ **percolation** *noun* [Say PERK uh late]

percolator *noun* a machine for making coffee by circulating boiling water through ground beans. [Say PERK uh later]

percussion *noun* **1 a** the playing of music by striking instruments with sticks etc. **b** the section of such instruments in an orchestra. **2** the forcible striking of one esp. solid body against another: *make sure the drill has a percussion or hammer action*. ▶ **percussionist** *noun* **percussive** *adjective* **percussively** *adverb*

per diem • *adverb & adjective* for each day. • *noun* (*plural* **per diems**) an allowance or payment for each day. [Say purr DEE em]

peregrine *noun* (also **peregrine falcon**) a powerful falcon much prized for hawking on account of its fast and accurate flight. [Say PERRA grin]

peremptorily *adverb* in a sudden or abrupt manner that allows no opportunity for discussion or refusal: *Mandy peremptorily rejected the request* ◊ *Wiggins and Singh were peremptorily fired on Tuesday*. [Say purr emp TORA lee]

peremptory *adjective* (of a person or their manner or actions) expecting to be obeyed immediately and without question or refusal: *a peremptory command* ◊ *the letter was peremptory in tone*. [Say purr EMP ter ee]

perennial • *adjective* **1** denoting a plant that usu. lives for more than two seasons and, after an initial period, produces flowers annually. **2** constantly occurring; recurring: *a perennial problem*. **3** lasting for a long time: *a perennial source of hope*. **4** (of a stream) flowing through all seasons of the year. • *noun* a perennial plant. ▶ **perennially** *adverb* [Say puh RENNY ul]

perestroika *noun* (in the former Soviet Union) the policy or practice of restructuring or reforming the

economic and political system, esp. under Mikhail Gorbachev 1985–91. [Say perra STROY kuh]

perfect • *adjective* **1** complete. **2** flawless. **3** very satisfactory: *a perfect evening*. **4** exact; precise: *a perfect circle*. **5** entire; unqualified: *a perfect stranger*. **6** *Grammar* (of a tense) denoting a completed action or event in the past, formed in English with *have* or *has* and the past participle, as in *they have eaten*. **7** *Baseball* **a** designating a game or inning in which no member of the opposing team has reached first base safely. **b** designating a pitcher who has not allowed an opposing batter to reach first base safely: *has been perfect over four innings*. **8** eminently suitable: *sausage is perfect in this dish*. • *verb* **1** make perfect; improve. **2** carry through; complete. • *noun Grammar* the perfect tense. ▶ **perfectibility** *noun* **perfectible** *adjective*

perfection *noun* **1** the act or process of making perfect. **2** the state of being perfect; faultlessness. **3** a perfect person, thing, or example. **4** full development; completion.

perfectionism *noun* the uncompromising pursuit of perfection. ▶ **perfectionist** *noun & adjective* **perfectionistic** *adjective*

perfectly *adverb* **1** completely; absolutely: *I understand you perfectly*. **2** quite, completely: *is perfectly capable of doing it*. **3** in a perfect way.

perfect pitch *noun* = ABSOLUTE PITCH.

perfidious *adjective* deceitful and untrustworthy; treacherous: *he is less transparent and more perfidious than she thought*. [Say purr FIDDY us]

perfidy *noun* actions that betray someone; deceitfulness, untrustworthiness: *in Act II he learns of Giovanni's perfidy and swears revenge*. [Say PURR fi dee]

perforate *verb* (**perforates**, **perforated**, **perforating**) **1** make a hole or holes through; pierce. **2** make a row of small holes in (paper etc.) so that a part may be torn off easily. ▶ **perforated** *adjective* **perforation** *noun* [Say PURR fur ate]

perforce *adverb* unavoidably; necessarily: *each flat had a sink and running water in its tiny kitchen, which was perforce also the bathroom*. [Say purr FORCE]

perform *verb* **1 a** carry out, execute, or do. **b** carry out or do something. **2** fulfill or carry into effect (a promise etc.). **3** act in an official way; conduct (a ceremony etc.): *performed the marriage*. **4 a** act, dance, or stage (a role, ballet, play, etc.). **b** play or sing (a piece of music etc.) for an audience. **c** accomplish (a feat, act of skill, etc.), esp. for an audience. **5** give a performance to entertain an audience: *is performing in Saint John*. **6** function, esp. in a specified way: *the car performs well*. **7** (of an investment) yield a return; be profitable. **8** *slang* have sexual intercourse (esp. satisfactorily).

performance *noun* **1 a** the act or process of performing or carrying out. **b** the execution or fulfillment (of a duty etc.). **2 a** a staging or production (of a drama, piece of music, etc.). **b** the action of performing a part, a piece of music, etc. **3** a person's achievement: *put up a good performance*. **4** *informal* a fuss; a scene; a public exhibition: *made such a performance about leaving*. **5 a** the capabilities of a machine, esp. a car or aircraft. **b** (as an *adjective*) of high capability: *a performance car*. **6** the return on an investment, esp. in stocks and shares etc.

performance art *noun* a kind of visual art in which the activity of the artist forms a central feature. ▶ **performance artist** *noun*

performer *noun* **1** a person who performs for an audience in a show, concert, etc. **2** a person or thing that functions, operates, or behaves in the manner described: *this epoxy was the best performer of all the glues we tested* ◊ *this model is our best seller and top performer*.

performing arts *plural noun* the arts, e.g. drama, music, and dance, that require performance for their realization.

perfume • *noun* **1** a sweet smell. **2** a scented liquid. • *verb* (**perfumes**, **perfumed**, **perfuming**) (usu. as **perfumed** *adjective*) impart a sweet scent to.

perfumer *noun* a maker or seller of perfumes. ▶ **perfumery** *noun* (*plural* **perfumeries**)

perfumy *adjective* having a sweet, pleasant scent like that of perfume: *a perfumy fragrance*.

perfunctorily *adverb* without interest, enthusiasm, or sincerity, and often out of habit or as part of a routine: *he kissed her perfunctorily before leaving for work*. [Say pur FUNK tora lee]

perfunctory *adjective* done as a matter of duty or habit, without real interest, attention, or feeling: *after a perfunctory bag check the guard waved us through*. [Say purr FUNK tuh ree]

pergola *noun* (*plural* **pergolas**) an arbour or covered walk, formed of growing plants trained over trellises. [Say PURR guh luh]

perhaps *adverb* **1** possibly: *perhaps it is lost*. **2** introducing a polite request: *perhaps you would open the window?*

pericardial *adjective* having to do with the membrane enclosing the heart. [Say perra CARDY ul]

pericardium *noun* (*plural* **pericardia**) the membrane enclosing the heart, consisting of an outer fibrous layer and an inner double layer. [Say perra CARDY um]

pericarp *noun* the part of a fruit formed from the wall of the ripened ovary.

perigee *noun* the point in the orbit of a celestial body or satellite where it is nearest the earth (*opp.* APOGEE 1). [Say PERRA jee]

peril *noun* **1** serious and immediate danger. **2** a thing that causes or may cause damage or loss, esp. as covered by an insurance policy. ▐PHRASES▌ **at one's peril** at one's own risk.

perilous *adjective* dangerous. ▶ **perilously** *adverb* **perilousness** *noun*

perimeter *noun* **1 a** the circumference or outline of a closed figure. **b** the length of this. **2** the outer edges of an area, away from the centre of activity, population, interest, etc. **3 a** the outer boundary of an enclosed area. **b** a defended boundary. [Say puh RIMMA ter]

perinatal *adjective* of or relating to the time immediately before and after birth. [Say perra NATE ul]

perineal *adjective* having to do with the area of the body between the anus and the scrotum or vulva. [Say perra NEE ul]

perineum *noun* the region of the body between the anus and the scrotum or vulva. [Say perra NEE ul]

period • *noun* **1** a length or portion of time: *sunny with cloudy periods*. **2** a distinct portion of history, a person's life, etc.: *the pre-Confederation period*. **3** a time forming part of a geological era: *the Quaternary period*. **4 a** an interval between recurrences of an astronomical or other phenomenon. **b** the time taken by a planet to rotate about its axis. **5** a division of an academic day allotted to a particular subject, course, etc. **6** each of the intervals into which the playing time of a sporting event, etc. is divided. **7** an occurrence of menstruation. **8 a** a punctuation mark (.) used at the end of a sentence or an abbreviation. **b** used at the end of a sentence etc. to indicate finality, absoluteness, etc.: *we want the best, period*. • *adjective* belonging to or characteristic of some past period: *period furniture*.

periodic *adjective* **1** appearing or occurring at regular intervals. **2** intermittent; appearing or occurring at irregular intervals: *periodic outbreaks of meningitis*. **3** of

P

or concerning the period of a celestial body: *periodic motion*.

periodical • *noun* a magazine etc. that is published at regular intervals, e.g. monthly or weekly. • *adjective* **1** published at regular intervals. **2** of or relating to periodicals: *a periodical article*. ▶ **periodically** *adverb*

periodic function *noun* *Math* a function returning to the same value at regular intervals.

periodicity *noun* the condition of being periodic; the tendency to recur at intervals: *the discovery of the comet's periodicity by Halley*. [Say period ISSA tee]

periodic table *noun* an arrangement of chemical elements in order of increasing atomic number and in which elements of similar chemical properties appear at regular intervals.

periodization *noun* the division of history into periods: *the periodization of nineteenth-century British culture*. [Say period ize AY sh'n]

periodontal *adjective* affecting or having to do with the gums and other structures surrounding and supporting teeth: *periodontal disease*. [Say perry uh DON tul]

periodontics *noun* the branch of dentistry concerned with the gums and other structures surrounding and supporting the teeth. [Say perry uh DON ticks]

period piece *noun* a work of art, furniture, literature, etc., considered in relation to its associations with or evocativeness of a past period.

peripatetic • *adjective* **1** (of a teacher) working in more than one school or college etc. **2** going from place to place: *a peripatetic huckster of curios*. • *noun* a peripatetic person, esp. a teacher. [Say perra puh TET ick]

peripheral • *adjective* **1** of minor importance: *the central focus of this bill has been distorted by peripheral issues*. **2** of the periphery: *Confederation favoured Central Canada, making it dominant and the peripheral areas dependent*. **3** near the surface of the body, with special reference to the circulation and nervous system: *a peripheral vein*. **4** (of equipment) used with a computer etc. but not an integral part of it: *all computers need programs to control the various peripheral devices, such as printers*. • *noun* a peripheral device or piece of equipment, e.g. a keyboard, printer, disk or tape drive, etc. ▶ **peripherally** *adverb* [Say puh RIFFA rul]

peripheral vision *noun* that which is visible to the eye from the main area of focus.

periphery *noun* (*plural* **peripheries**) **1** the boundary of an area or surface: *stores of the mall were accessed not from an internal courtyard but from the parking lot on the periphery*. **2** an outer or surrounding region: *around Ottawa, in its periphery, are a number of smaller centres*. **3** a marginal or secondary position in, or part or aspect of, a group, subject, or sphere of activity: *the key factor is transferring power from Ottawa — the political power core — to the politically weak periphery*. [Say puh RIFFA ree]

periscope *noun* an apparatus with mirrors or prisms in a tube so that the user can view the area above, e.g. the surface of the sea from a submerged submarine.

perish *verb* (**perishes**, **perished**, **perishing**) **1** be destroyed; suffer death or ruin. **2** fade away; disappear. **PHRASES** **perish the thought** an exclamation of horror against an unwelcome idea.

perishable • *adjective* liable to perish; subject to decay. • *noun* (in *plural*) a thing, esp. a foodstuff, subject to speedy decay. ▶ **perishability** *noun*

peritoneum *noun* (*plural* **peritoneums** or **peritonea**) the membrane lining the cavity of the abdomen. [Say perra tuh NEE um, perra tuh NEE uh]

peritonitis *noun* an inflammatory disease of the peritoneum (the membrane lining the cavity of the abdomen). [Say perra tuh NITE iss]

periwinkle¹ • *noun* **1** an evergreen trailing plant with blue or white flowers and glossy leaves. **2** a tropical shrub native to Madagascar. **3** a purple-blue colour like that of the periwinkle flower. • *adjective* of the colour of a periwinkle. [Say PAIR i winkle]

periwinkle² *noun* = WINKLE *noun*. [Say PAIR i winkle]

> **SPELL CHECK**
> **pejorative**
>
> Note that there is no r before the j in *pejorative*, a word used as a put-down.

perjure *reflexive verb* (**perjures**, **perjured**, **perjuring**) *Law* **perjure oneself** wilfully tell a lie when under oath. ▶ **perjurer** *noun* **perjury** *noun* [Say PURR jurr]

perk¹ *verb* (often foll. by *up*) raise (esp. one's ears) briskly. **PHRASES** **perk up 1** recover confidence, liveliness, etc. **2** restore confidence or courage or liveliness in (esp. another person). **3** smarten up: *perk up an outfit with a scarf*.

perk² *noun* *informal* a perquisite; a benefit, or privilege, e.g. the use of a company car.

perk³ *informal* • *verb* **1** (of coffee) percolate. **2** percolate (coffee). • *noun* *Cdn* a coffee percolator.

perkily *adverb* **1** in a cheerful and energetic manner. **2** in a self-assertive manner.

perkiness *noun* **1** a cheerful and energetic manner. **2** a self-assertive manner.

perky *adjective* (**perkier**, **perkiest**) **1** lively; cheerful. **2** bright, attractive. **3** self-assertive.

perlite *noun* a glassy type of vermiculite, expandable to a solid form by heating, used for insulation, as a plant growth medium, etc. [Say PURR lite]

perm • *noun* a way of changing a hairstyle by using chemicals to create curls that last for several months. • *verb* treat (a person's hair) in such a way.

permaculture *noun* the development of agricultural ecosystems meant to be self-sustaining and complete.

permafrost *noun* subsoil which remains below freezing point all year, as in polar regions.

permanence *noun* the state of lasting or remaining unchanged indefinitely: *we used colourfast dyes for permanence* ◊ *we no longer talk about the permanence of marriage*.

permanency *noun* = PERMANENCE.

permanent • *adjective* **1** lasting, or intended to last or function, indefinitely without change: *his permanent address*. **2** persistent, enduring: *a permanent stoop*. **3 a** (of hair dye) producing colour that lasts until the hair grows out. **b** (of ink etc.) indelible. **4** (of an employee or position) not having a specified date of termination; not contractual. • *noun* a perm. ▶ **permanently** *adverb*

permanent magnet *noun* a magnet retaining its magnetic properties in the absence of an inducing field or current.

permanent press *noun* **1** a process for producing fabrics which retain their crease, press, shape, etc. **2** a fabric treated by this process.

permanent resident *noun* an immigrant deemed to have settled in a country permanently and entitled to all privileges of citizenship except voting rights; a landed immigrant.

permeability *noun* the ability of a membrane or other material to allow liquids or gases to pass through it. [Say purr me uh BILLA tee]

permeable *adjective* capable of being permeated. [Say PURR me uh bull]

permeate *verb* (**permeates**, **permeated**, **permeating**) penetrate throughout; pervade; saturate: *living next door to 250 million Americans whose*

linguistic and cultural influences permeate our society. ▶ **permeation** *noun* [Say PURR me ate]

permethrin *noun* a synthetic compound used as an insecticide, esp. against disease-carrying insects. [Say purr MEETH rin]

Permian • *adjective* of or relating to the final period of the Paleozoic era, lasting from about 286–248 million years ago, between the Carboniferous and Triassic periods, characterized by the development of reptiles, including the appearance of warm-blooded, mammal-like reptiles. • *noun* this geological period or system. [Say PURMY in]

permissibility *noun* the condition of being allowed or permitted.

permissible *adjective* acceptable according to the law or a particular set of rules; permitted, allowed. ▶ **permissibly** *adverb*

permission *noun* consent; authorization.

permissive *adjective* tolerant; liberal, esp. in sexual matters: *the permissive society.* ▶ **permissively** *adverb* **permissiveness** *noun*

permit • *verb* (**permits, permitted, permitting**) **1** give permission or consent to: *permit me to say.* **2 a** allow; give an opportunity to: *the new design permits easier storage.* **b** give an opportunity: *circumstances permitting.* **3** (foll. by *of*) admit; allow for: *the camp permits of no really successful defence.* • *noun* **1** a document granting legal permission: *liquor permit.* **2** a document etc. which allows entry into a specified zone.

permutate *verb* (**permutates, permutated, permutating**) change the order or arrangement of. [Say PURR myoo tate]

permutation *noun* **1 a** an ordered arrangement or grouping of a set of numbers, items, etc. **b** any one of the range of possible groupings: *the permutations of x, y, and z are xyz, xzy, yxz, yzx, zxy, and zyx.* **2** any combination or selection of a specified number of things from a larger group. ▶ **permutational** *adjective* [Say purr myoo TAY sh'n]

pernicious *adjective* having a very harmful effect, especially in a way that is gradual and not easily noticed: *the pernicious influence of TV violence on children.* ▶ **perniciously** *adverb* [Say purr NISH us]

pernickety *adjective informal* = PERSNICKETY. [Say purr NICKA tee]

SPELL CHECK
prerogative ✓ABC

Note that there are two r's in *prerogative*.

---

perogy *noun* (*plural* **perogies**) (also **perogie, perogi**) a dough dumpling stuffed with potato, cheese, etc., boiled and then optionally fried, and usu. served with onions, sour cream, etc. [Say purr OH ghee]

peroxide • *noun* **1 a** = HYDROGEN PEROXIDE. **b** a solution of hydrogen peroxide used to bleach the hair or as an antiseptic. **2** a compound of oxygen with another element containing the greatest possible proportion of oxygen. **3** any salt or ester of hydrogen peroxide. • *verb* (**peroxides, peroxided, peroxiding**) bleach (the hair) with peroxide. [Say purr OXIDE]

perp *noun slang* the perpetrator of a crime.

perpendicular • *adjective* **1 a** at right angles to the plane of the horizon. **b** (usu. foll. by *to*) *Geometry* at right angles (to a given line, plane, or surface). **2** upright, vertical. **3** (of a slope etc.) very steep. **4** *jocular* in a standing position. • *noun* **1** a perpendicular line. **2 a** perpendicular line or direction: *is out of the perpendicular.* ▶ **perpendicularly** *adverb*

perpetrate *verb* (**perpetrates, perpetrated,**

perpetrating) commit or perform (a crime, blunder, etc.). ▶ **perpetration** *noun* **perpetrator** *noun*

perpetual *adjective* **1** eternal; lasting indefinitely. **2** uninterrupted; continuous: *the perpetual noise of traffic.* **3** frequent, much repeated: *perpetual interruptions.* **4** permanent during life: *he was elected perpetual president.* ▶ **perpetually** *adverb*

perpetuate *verb* (**perpetuates, perpetuated, perpetuating**) make perpetual; make continue indefinitely: *the system perpetuated itself for several centuries.* ▶ **perpetuation** *noun*

perpetuity *noun* the state or quality of being perpetual. PHRASES **in perpetuity** forever. [Say purr puh CHOO uh tee]

perplex *verb* (**perplexes, perplexed, perplexing**) puzzle, disconcert. ▶ **perplexed** *adjective* **perplexing** *adjective* **perplexingly** *adverb*

perplexity *noun* (*plural* **perplexities**) **1** the state of being perplexed: *this question caused more perplexity than any other.* **2** a thing which perplexes: *a multitude of minor problems and perplexities within the college.* [Say purr PLEXA tee]

perquisite *noun* **1** a benefit received in addition to one's salary for taking a job, e.g. the use of a company car. **2** something to which someone has a special right because of their social position: *politics used to be the perquisite of the property-owning classes.* [Say PURR kwuh zit]

per se *adverb* by or in itself: *distance per se is not always a good indicator of an island's isolation.* [Say purr SAY]

persecute *verb* (**persecutes, persecuted, persecuting**) **1** subject (a person etc.) to hostility or ill-treatment, esp. because of their race or their political or religious views. **2** harass; annoy persistently: *a three-year-old who ran up and down the hallways persecuting his grandmother's lodgers.*

persecution *noun* hostility or ill-treatment of a person, esp. because of their race or their political or religious views: *refugees fleeing religious persecution in their homeland.*

persecutor *noun* a person who persecutes another.

perseverance *noun* determination in doing something despite difficulty or delay in achieving success: *he's shown remarkable perseverance in coming back from a career-threatening injury.* [Say pursa VEER ince]

persevere *verb* (**perseveres, persevered, persevering**) continue steadfastly or determinedly; persist. [Say pursa VEER]

Persian • *noun* **1 a** a native or inhabitant of ancient or modern Persia (now Iran). **b** a person of Persian descent. **2** the language of ancient Persia (Iranian) or modern Iran (Farsi). **3** (also **Persian cat**) a cat of a breed with a broad round head, long silky hair and a thick tail. **4** *Cdn* (*NW Ont.*) an oblong doughnut covered with pink or white icing. • *adjective* of or relating to Persia or its people or language.

Persian carpet *noun* (also **Persian rug**) a carpet or rug of a traditional pattern, made by hand in the Near East from silk or wool.

persimmon *noun* **1** a pulpy edible fruit that resembles a large tomato and has very sweet flesh. **2** the evergreen tree bearing this fruit. [Say purr SIMMIN]

persist *verb* **1** (often foll. by *in*) continue firmly or obstinately (in an opinion or a course of action) esp. despite obstacles, objections, etc. **2** (of a custom, institution, phenomenon, etc.) survive. **3** be insistent with a statement or question.

persistence *noun* **1** firm or stubborn continuance in a course of action in spite of difficulty or opposition: *her persistence was finally rewarded when the insurance company agreed to pay for the damage.* **2** the continued or prolonged existence of something: *governments*

addressed the persistence of unemployment with new job-creation programs.

persistent *adjective* **1** continuing in spite of obstacles, attempts at control, etc. **2** enduring. **3** constantly repeated: *persistent nagging.* **4** (of horns, leaves, etc.) remaining instead of falling off in the normal manner. **5** (of a chemical) remaining within the environment for a long time after its introduction. ▶ **persistently** *adverb*

persnickety *adjective informal* fussy; fastidious: *you had to do it accurately and concisely because my father was extremely persnickety about that.* [Say purr SNICKA tee]

person *noun* **1** an individual human being. **2** the living body of a human being: *hidden about your person.* **3** *Grammar* a category used in the classification of pronouns, verb forms, etc., according to whether they indicate the speaker (**first person**), the addressee (**second person**), or a third party (**third person**). **4** (in *combination*) used to replace -*man* in offices open to either sex: *salesperson.* **5** an individual as distinguished from a thing, a type, or an animal, esp. an individual regarded as having human dignity, personality, or responsibility. PHRASES **in one's own person** oneself; as oneself. **in person** physically present.

persona *noun* (*plural* **personas** or **personae**) **1** the aspects of a person's character that are presented to other people, esp. when the real character is different: *his public persona is quite different from the private man we know.* **2** a character assumed by an author, performer, etc. in his or her writing, work, etc.: *Gibson loses the Aussie accent and slides seamlessly into the persona of Bret Maverick.* **3** a character in a fictional work. [Say purr SO nuh for the singular; for *personae* say purr SO nigh or purr SO nee]

personable *adjective* (of a person) pleasant, likeable, agreeable: *a personable young man who gave us a most attractive presentation.* ▶ **personably** *adverb*

personage *noun* **1** a person, esp. of rank or importance. **2** a character in a play etc.

personal • *adjective* **1** one's own; individual; private. **2** done or made in person. **3** directed to or concerning an individual. **4 a** referring (esp. in a hostile way) to an individual's private life or concerns. **b** close, intimate. **5** of the body and clothing. **6** existing as a person, not as an abstraction or thing. **7** *Grammar* of or denoting one of the three persons: *personal pronoun.* **8** intended for a particular person rather than a group. • *noun* (also **personal ad**) an advertisement or notice regarding companionship etc., esp. in a newspaper or on a computer bulletin board.

personal computer *noun* a general-purpose microcomputer designed for use by one person at a time, esp. in the home or office. Abbreviation: **PC**. ▶ **personal computing** *noun*

personal digital assistant *noun* a small hand-held computer, often pen-based, containing information such as addresses and appointments.

personal flotation device *noun* a life jacket or other buoyant or inflatable device for keeping a person afloat in water, esp. in an emergency.

personal identification number *noun* a number serving as a password esp. for a bank machine, automatic debit terminal, etc. Abbreviation: **PIN**.

personality *noun* (*plural* **personalities**) **1 a** all the qualities or characteristics which make a person a distinctive individual: *an attractive personality.* **b** socially attractive qualities: *has no personality.* **c** the unique characteristics of a place, situation, or thing. **2** a famous person: *a TV personality.* **3** a person who stands out from others by virtue of his or her character: *is a real personality.* **4** the condition of being a person.

personality cult *noun* the extreme public admiration of or devotion to a famous person, esp. a politician.

personality disorder *noun* any of several psychiatric disorders characterized by a tendency to behave in certain abnormal ways that cause harm to oneself or others.

personalization *noun* **1** the process of designing something to meet a person's individual needs: *personalization is a key selling feature of many software packages.* **2** the process of marking something with a person's name or initials etc. so that it can be identified more easily: *the Centre promotes the personalization of firearms to make identification of lost or stolen handguns easier.* **3** the process of causing something to become concerned with personal matters or feelings rather than with general issues: *the personalization of politics.*

personalize *verb* (**personalizes**, **personalized**, **personalizing**) **1** make personal; adapt to individual persons' needs etc. **2** mark or inscribe with a particular person's name, initials, etc. **3** cause (a discussion etc.) to become concerned with personal matters or feelings rather than with general issues.

personally *adverb* **1** in person: *see to it personally.* **2** for one's own part: *speaking personally.* **3** as a person: *I don't know him personally, but I've read his books.* PHRASES **take personally** be offended by.

personal organizer *noun* **1** a looseleaf notebook with sections for various kinds of information, such as appointments, addresses, etc. **2** a hand-held microcomputer serving the same purpose.

personal pronoun *noun* each of the pronouns *I, you, he, she, it, we, they, me, him, her, us, them.*

personal property *noun Law* all one's property except land and those interests in land that pass to one's heirs (compare REAL *adjective* 5).

personal space *noun* **1** the immediate area around a person where encroachment is considered threatening or uncomfortable. **2** space for an individual's use.

personal stereo *noun* a small portable audio cassette player, often with radio, or compact disc player, used with lightweight headphones.

personal touch *noun* (*plural* **personal touches**) **1** a characteristic or individual approach to a situation. **2** a personal element added to something otherwise impersonal.

personal trainer *noun* a fitness expert hired to come to a person's home etc. to plan and supervise workouts.

personal watercraft *noun* (*plural* **personal watercraft**) a jet-propelled recreational boat for one or two persons, ridden like a motorcycle.

persona non grata *noun* (*plural* **personae non gratae**) an unacceptable or unwelcome person: *on his return he found that he was persona non grata with the government.* [Say non GRATTA for the singular, non GRAT eye or non GRATTY for the plural]

personhood *noun* the quality or condition of being an individual person.

personification *noun* **1** the practice of representing objects, qualities, etc. as human beings, in art and literature; an object, quality, etc. that is represented in this way: *the personification of autumn in Keats's poem.* **2** (foll. by *of*) a person or thing viewed as a striking example of (a quality etc.): *the personification of ugliness.* [Say purr sonna fuh CAY sh'n]

personify *verb* (**personifies**, **personified**, **personifying**) **1** attribute a human nature or characteristics to (an abstraction or thing): *the river was personified as a goddess.* **2** symbolize (a quality etc.) by a figure in human form: *a drama in which the virtues and vices were personified.* **3** (usu. as **personified** *adjective*)

P

embody (a quality) in one's own person: *is love personified*. [Say purr SONNA fye]

personnel *noun* **1** a body of employees, persons involved in a public undertaking, armed forces, etc. **2** (also **personnel department**) the part of an organization concerned with the hiring, training, and welfare of employees. [Say person ELL]

personnel carrier *noun* an armoured vehicle for transporting troops etc.

perspective • *noun* **1 a** the art of drawing solid objects on a two-dimensional surface so as to give the right impression of relative positions, size, etc. **b** a picture drawn in this way. **2** the apparent relation between visible objects as to position, distance, etc. **3 a** a point of view: *a Marxist perspective*. **b** a mental view of the relative importance of things: *keep the right perspective*. • *adjective* of or in perspective. PHRASES **in** (or **out of**) **perspective 1** drawn or viewed according (or not according) to the rules of perspective. **2** correctly (or incorrectly) regarded in terms of relative importance.

perspiration *noun* **1** = SWEAT *noun* 1. **2** sweating.

perspire *verb* (**perspires, perspired, perspiring**) sweat.

persuadable *adjective* able to be persuaded.

persuade *verb* (**persuades, persuaded, persuading**) **1** cause (another person or oneself) to believe; convince: *persuaded them that it would be helpful* ◊ *tried to persuade me of its value*. **2** induce (another person or oneself): *persuaded us to join them*. ▶ **persuader** *noun*

persuasion *noun* **1** persuading: *yielded to persuasion*. **2** persuasiveness: *use all your persuasion*. **3** a belief or conviction: *my private persuasion*. **4** a religious or political belief, or the group holding it: *of a different persuasion*. **5** *informal* or *jocular* **a** any group or party: *the male persuasion*. **b** kind or type.

persuasive *adjective* able to persuade; convincing. ▶ **persuasively** *adverb* **persuasiveness** *noun* [Say purr SWAY siv]

SPELL CHECK
pursue

Warning: **pursue** is spelled with two *u*'s.

---

pert *adjective* **1** (of a girl or young woman) lively or cheeky in a way that is attractive. **2 a** (of clothes) neat and suggesting jauntiness. **b** (of a bodily feature) shapely and attractive. **3** (of a person or their speech or behaviour) disrespectful, rude.

pertain *verb* (foll. by *to*) relate or have reference to: *evidence pertaining to the case*.

pertinence *noun* relevance or applicability to a particular matter: *I'm not convinced of the pertinence of the issue*.

pertinent *adjective* relevant to the matter in hand: *please keep your comments pertinent to the topic under discussion*. ▶ **pertinently** *adverb*

perturb *verb* (usu. in *passive*) make worried or anxious: *her sudden appearance did not seem to perturb him in the least* ◊ *I was perturbed by his lack of interest*.

perturbation *noun* **1** anxiety; mental uneasiness: *she sensed her friend's perturbation*. **2** a slight alteration of a physical system, e.g. of the electrons in an atom, caused by a secondary influence. **3** a minor deviation in the course of a celestial body, caused by the attraction of a neighbouring body. [Say purr turb AY sh'n]

pertussis *noun* whooping cough. [Say purr TUSS iss]

perusal *noun* the action of reading or examining something: *the agreement was signed after careful perusal*. [Say purr OOZE ul]

WRITING TIP
peruse

Peruse has two nearly opposite meanings. Its traditional sense is "to examine thoroughly or in detail", as in *The editor perused the article to find every mistake*. The more recent sense is "to skim quickly", as in *I only had time to peruse the newspaper before leaving for work*. Readers should be aware that **peruse** may be used in either of these senses, and it is best avoided in writing because of its possible ambiguity.

---

peruse *verb* (**peruses, perused, perusing**) **1** read or study thoroughly or carefully. **2** read in a casual manner. **3** examine (a person's face etc.) carefully. [Say purr OOZE]

Peruvian • *noun* **1** a native or national of Peru in South America. **2** a person of Peruvian descent. • *adjective* of or relating to Peru. [Say purr OOVY in]

perv *noun slang* a sexual pervert.

pervade *verb* (**pervades, pervaded, pervading**) **1** spread throughout: *the smell of stale cabbage pervaded the air*. **2** (of influences etc.) become widespread among, in, or through: *the sense of crisis which pervaded Europe in the 1930s*. ▶ **pervasion** *noun*

pervasive *adjective* existing in all parts of a place or thing; spreading gradually to affect all parts of a place or thing: *a pervasive musty smell* ◊ *the pervasive influence of US pop*. ▶ **pervasively** *adverb* **pervasiveness** *noun*

SPELL CHECK
proverbial

Warning: the first three letters of **proverbial**, as in *the proverbial cloud with a silver lining*, are *pro*, not *per*; **proverbial** is derived from the word **proverb**.

---

perverse *adjective* **1** (of a person or action) showing deliberate determination to behave in a way that most people find unacceptable, wrong, or unreasonable: *he finds a perverse pleasure in upsetting his parents*. **2** persistent in error. ▶ **perversely** *adverb*

perversion *noun* **1** the alteration of something from its original course, meaning, or state to a distortion or corruption of what was first intended: *some people argue that the use of slang in English is a perversion of the language*. **2** sexual behaviour or desire that is considered abnormal or unacceptable.

perversity *noun* (*plural* **perversities**) **1** activity or behaviour that seems to be deliberately opposed to what most people find proper, acceptable, or reasonable: *in her teenage years, Gloria went through a period of rebelliousness and perversity*. **2** a perverse action, element, or quality: *the dorm is no longer host to the Friday-night perversities that made it infamous*.

pervert • *verb* **1** alter (something) from its original course, meaning, or state to a distortion or corruption of what was first intended: *pervert the course of justice* ◊ *clichés and jargon which pervert meaning*. **2** corrupt: *some people believe that television can pervert the minds of children*. • *noun* a person showing sexual perversion. ▶ **perverted** *adjective*

Pesach *noun Judaism* Passover. [Say PAY sack]

peskily *adverb* in an annoying or irritating way.

peskiness *noun* annoying or irritating behaviour.

pesky *adjective* (**peskier, peskiest**) *informal* annoying.

peso *noun* (*plural* **pesos**) the basic monetary unit of several Latin American countries and the Philippines. [Say PAY so]

pessimism *noun* **1** a tendency to take a gloomy view of circumstances or expect the worst outcome.

P

2 *Philosophy* a belief that this world is as bad as it could be or that all things tend to evil (*opp.* OPTIMISM 2). ▶ **pessimist** *noun* **pessimistic** *adjective* **pessimistically** *adverb*

pest *noun* **1** a troublesome or annoying person or thing; a nuisance. **2** a destructive animal, esp. an insect which attacks crops, livestock, etc.

pester *verb* trouble or annoy, esp. with frequent or persistent requests.

pesticide *noun* a chemical preparation for destroying insects or other organisms harmful to cultivated plants or to animals.

pestilence *noun* a fatal epidemic disease, esp. bubonic plague: *high death rates due to famine, pestilence, and war.* [Say PESTA lince]

pestilential *adjective* **1** of or relating to pestilence: *pestilential diseases.* **2** annoying or troublesome: *a pestilential nuisance.*

pestle *noun* a club-shaped instrument for pounding substances in a mortar. [Say PESSLE]

pesto *noun* (*plural* **pestos**) a sauce of crushed basil leaves, pine nuts, garlic, Parmesan cheese, and olive oil, usu. served with pasta.

PET *abbreviation* **1** POSITRON EMISSION TOMOGRAPHY. **2** polyethylene terephthalate, a plastic used in recyclable packaging.

pet • *noun* **1** a domestic or tamed animal kept for pleasure or companionship. **2** a darling, a favourite (often as a term of endearment). • *adjective* **1** kept as a pet: *pet lamb.* **2** of or for pets: *pet food.* **3** often *jocular* favourite or particular: *pet peeve.* **4** expressing fondness or familiarity: *pet name.* • *verb* (**pets**, **petted**, **petting**) **1** treat as a pet. **2** stroke (an animal). **3** engage in erotic caressing.

SPELL CHECK
petal, pedal

A foot-operated lever is a **pedal**.

---

petal *noun* each of the parts of the corolla of a flower. ▶ **petalled** *adjective* (also in *combination*)

petard *noun* PHRASES **hoist with one's own petard** adversely affect oneself by schemes against others. [Say puh TARD]

peter *verb* (foll. by *out*) decrease, diminish, or fade gradually towards to an end.

Peterborough canoe *noun* *Cdn* a type of all-wood canoe originally built at Peterborough, Ontario. [Say PETER burro]

Peterhead *noun* *Cdn* a decked launch or large whaleboat with a sail and a small motor, used in the eastern Arctic.

Peter Pan *noun* a person who retains youthful features, or who is immature.

Peter Principle *noun* *jocular* the principle that members of a hierarchy are promoted until they reach a level at which they are no longer competent.

petiole *noun* **1** *Botany* the slender stalk joining a leaf to a stem. **2** *Zoology* a slender stalk between two structures, as that connecting the abdomen and thorax in wasps, ants, and other insects. [Say PETTY ole]

petit bourgeois • *noun* (*plural* **petits bourgeois**) a member of the lower middle class. • *adjective* pertaining to or characteristic of the lower middle class. [Say petty BOOR zhwah]

petite • *adjective* **1** (of a woman) of small and dainty build. **2** (of a thing) small in size. **3** designating a size in women's clothing for shorter women. • *noun* a petite size in women's clothing. [Say puh TEET]

petite bourgeoisie *noun* the lower middle class. [Say petty boor zhwah ZEE]

petition • *noun* **1** a formal written request, esp. one signed by many people, appealing to authority in some cause. **2** an application to a court for a writ etc. **3** a formal prayer to God or request to someone in authority: *down-to-earth prayers contrast with aching thoughts for times of bereavement and other petitions.* • *verb* **1** make or address a petition to: *petition your MP.* **2** make a solemn or humble appeal to (a figure of authority): *although repeatedly petitioned by Johnson, he remained unconvinced.* ▶ **petitioner** *noun*

pet name *noun* an affectionate nickname.

petrel *noun* any of various seabirds with mainly black (or brown) and white plumage and a hooked bill, usu. flying far from land. [Say PET rul]

Petri dish *noun* (*plural* **Petri dishes**) a shallow covered dish used for the culture of bacteria etc. [Say PEE tree]

petrify *verb* (**petrifies**, **petrified**, **petrifying**) (usu. as **petrified** *adjective*) **1** paralyze with fear, astonishment, etc. **2** change (organic matter) into a stony substance. **3** deprive or become deprived of vitality or the capacity for change: *the inner life of the communist parties petrified.*

petrochemical • *noun* a substance industrially obtained from petroleum or natural gas. • *adjective* of or relating to petrochemistry or petrochemicals.

petrochemistry *noun* **1** the branch of chemistry dealing with petroleum and natural gas. **2** the branch of chemistry dealing with rocks.

petrodollar *noun* a unit of currency earned by a country etc. from petroleum exports.

petroglyph *noun* a rock carving, esp. a prehistoric one. [Say PETRO gliff]

petroleum *noun* a dark viscous hydrocarbon oil found in the upper strata of the earth, refined for use as a fuel for heating and in internal combustion engines, for lighting, as a solvent, etc. [Say puh TROLL ee um]

petroleum jelly *noun* a soft, greasy, translucent semi-solid mixture of hydrocarbons used as a lubricant, ointment, etc.

petticoat *noun* an undergarment in the form of a skirt or a skirt and bodice. [Say PETTY coat]

pettily *adverb* in a way that shows an unreasonable or spiteful concern with trivial or unimportant matters: *they argued pettily about whose turn it was to wash the dishes.*

pettiness *noun* an unreasonable concern with trivial or unimportant matters, esp. one that is motivated by spite.

petting zoo *noun* (also **petting farm**) a collection of wild or farm animals displayed so that visitors, esp. children, may walk among the animals to pet or feed them etc.

petty *adjective* (**pettier**, **pettiest**) **1** unimportant. **2** small-minded. **3** on a small scale: *petty princes.* **4** (of a crime) of lesser importance (*compare* GRAND 9).

petty bourgeois *noun* (*plural* **petty bourgeois**) = PETIT BOURGEOIS.

petty bourgeoisie *noun* = PETITE BOURGEOISIE.

petty cash *noun* a small amount of money kept from or for small payments.

petty officer *noun* (also **Petty Officer**) **1** *Cdn* (in the Canadian navy) an officer of either of two ranks: petty officer first class, ranking below chief petty officer second class, equivalent to warrant officer in the other commands; or petty officer second class, ranking next below it, equivalent to sergeant in the other commands. **2** a non-commissioned officer in other navies.

petulance *noun* childishly sulky, bad-tempered, or unreasonable behaviour: *he threw the plate to the floor in a fit of petulance.* [Say PET you lince or PETCH oo lince]

petulant *adjective* (of a person or their manner)

childishly sulky, bad-tempered, or unreasonable, esp. because one cannot have or do what one wants: *he behaved like a petulant child and refused to co-operate ◊ her tone of voice became abrupt and petulant.* ▶ **petulantly** *adverb* [Say PET you lint or PETCH oo lint]

Petun • *noun* **1** a member of an Aboriginal people formerly living in southwestern Ontario; defeated by the Iroquois in the mid 17th century, they were absorbed into neighbouring Aboriginal groups. **2** the Iroquoian language of this people. • *adjective* of or relating to this people or their culture or language. [Say puh TOON]

petunia *noun* (*plural* **petunias**) a plant that has esp. white, purple, or red funnel-shaped flowers, with many ornamental varieties.

pew *noun* **1** (in a church) a long bench with a back. **2** an enclosed compartment or section in a church, for a family or other group. PHRASES **take a pew** have a seat. [Say PYOO]

pewter • *noun* **1** a grey alloy of tin, antimony and copper (formerly, tin and lead). **2** utensils made of this. **3** a bluish or silvery grey. • *adjective* of a bluish or silvery grey colour. [Say PYOO ter]

peyote *noun* **1** a small blue-green Mexican cactus with no spines. **2** a hallucinogenic drug containing mescaline prepared from this cactus, taken sacramentally by some American Indians. [Say pay OH tee]

PFD *noun* (*plural* **PFDs**) PERSONAL FLOTATION DEVICE.

PG *abbreviation* (of films) classified as suitable for children subject to parental guidance.

PGA *abbreviation* Professional Golfers' Association.

PGP *abbreviation* "Pretty Good Privacy", a computer program which encrypts and decrypts messages for secure transmission over digital circuits.

pH *noun* a measure of acidity or alkalinity; a pH of 7 corresponds to a neutral solution, one less than 7 to an acidic solution, and one greater than 7 to an alkaline solution.

phagocyte *noun* a type of cell capable of engulfing and absorbing foreign matter, esp. a leukocyte ingesting bacteria in the body. ▶ **phagocytic** *adjective* [Say FAGGA site, fagga SIT ick]

phalanx *noun* (*plural* **phalanxes** or **phalanges**) **1** a set of people etc. forming a compact mass, or banded for a common purpose: *a phalanx of elegant apartment buildings.* **2** a bone of the finger or toe. **3** a bundle of stamens united by filaments. [Say FAL anx or FAIL anx for the singular, fuh LAN jeez for the plural]

phalarope *noun* any small wading or swimming bird with a straight bill and lobed feet. [Say FALA rope]

phallic *adjective* **1** of or resembling a phallus. **2** *Psychology* denoting the stage of male sexual development characterized by preoccupation with the genitals. [Say FAL ick]

phallocentric *adjective* **1** centred on a belief in male superiority. **2** centred on the phallus. ▶ **phallocentrism** *noun* [Say fal oh SEN trick]

phallus *noun* (*plural* **phalluses** or **phalli**) **1** the (esp. erect) penis. **2** an image of this as a symbol of generative power in nature. [Say FAL us for the singular, FAL us iz or FAL eye for the plurals]

phantasm *noun* a figment of the imagination; an illusion or apparition: *the cart seemed to glide like a terrible phantasm.* [Say FAN tasm]

phantasmagoria *noun* a shifting series of real or imaginary figures as seen in a dream or as created as an effect in a film etc.: *what happened next was a phantasmagoria of horror and mystery.* ▶ **phantasmagoric** *adjective* **phantasmagorical** *adjective* [Say fan tazzma GORY uh]

phantom • *noun* **1** a ghost; an apparition. **2** a form

without substance or reality; a mental illusion. • *adjective* merely apparent; illusory.

Pharaoh *noun* **1** a ruler in ancient Egypt. **2** the title of this ruler. ▶ **Pharaonic** *adjective* [Say FAIR oh, fair ay ON ick]

Pharisee *noun* **1** a member of an ancient Jewish sect, distinguished by strict observance of the traditional and written law, and commonly held to have pretensions to superior sanctity. **2** a self-righteous person; a hypocrite: *what she calls heroes, I remember as a crowd of self-important Pharisees.* [Say FAIR uh see]

pharmacare *noun* *Cdn* (in some provinces) a system of subsidization of drug costs, esp. by the government.

pharmaceutical • *adjective* **1** of or engaged in pharmacy. **2** pertaining to the preparation, use, or sale of medicinal drugs. • *noun* a medicinal drug. ▶ **pharmaceutically** *adverb* [Say farma SUIT uh cull]

pharmacist *noun* a person qualified to prepare and dispense drugs and to give expert advice on their use and effects.

pharmacological *adjective* based on, having to do with, or involved in the study of drugs and their use in medicine. ▶ **pharmacologically** *adverb* [Say farma cuh LOGICAL]

pharmacologist *noun* a person who studies drugs and their use in medicine. [Say farma COLLA jist]

pharmacology *noun* the scientific study of drugs and their use in medicine. [Say farma COLLA jee]

pharmacy *noun* (*plural* **pharmacies**) **1** the preparation and the dispensing of (medicinal) drugs. **2** a pharmacist's store or dispensary.

pharynx *noun* (*plural* **pharynges**) a cavity, with enclosing muscles and mucous membrane, behind the nose and mouth, and connecting them to the esophagus. [Say FAIR inx for the singular, fuh RIN jeez for the plural]

SPELL CHECK
phase, faze

If something doesn't bother you, it doesn't **faze** you.

---

phase • *noun* **1** a distinct period or stage in a process of change or development. **2** each of the aspects of the moon or a planet, according to the amount of its illumination. **3** *Physics* a particular stage or point in the cycle of a periodic phenomenon, esp. an alternating current or a light wave. **4** a difficult or unhappy period, esp. in adolescence. **5** a genetic or seasonal variety of an animal's coloration etc. • *verb* (**phases**, **phased**, **phasing**) **1** carry out (a program etc.) in phases or stages. **2** adjust the phase of; bring into phase, synchronize. PHRASES **in phase** having the same phase at the same time. **out of phase** not in phase. **phase in** (or **out**) bring gradually into (or out of) use.

phase-in *noun* the process of bringing something into use or availability gradually: *phase-in period.*

phase-out *noun* the gradual removal of something from use or availability.

phaser *noun* (esp. in science fiction) a usu. hand-held weapon incorporating a laser beam whose "phase" can supposedly be altered to create different effects (such as stunning, annihilation, etc.) on the target.

phat *adjective* (**phatter**, **phattest**) *slang* excellent.

Ph.D. *abbreviation* Doctor of Philosophy.

pheasant *noun* a large, long-tailed game bird originally from Asia, the male of which typically has very showy plumage.

phencyclidine *noun* a veterinary anaesthetic and a hallucinogenic drug. Abbreviation: **PCP**. [Say fen SIKE luh deen]

phenobarbital *noun* a narcotic and sedative

barbiturate drug used esp. to treat epilepsy. [Say feeno BARBA tawl]

phenol *noun* **1** a white moisture-absorbing mildly acidic crystalline solid, used diluted as an antiseptic and disinfectant. **2** any hydroxyl derivative of an aromatic hydrocarbon. [Say FEE nawl]

phenolic • *adjective* **1** of the nature of, derived from, or containing a phenol, esp containing or designating a hydroxyl group bonded directly to a benzene ring. **2 a** designating a large class of polymeric materials that have wide industrial applications as plastics or resins and are prepared from phenols by condensation with aldehydes. **b** made of such a material. • *noun* **1** a phenolic plastic or resin. **2** any compound containing a hydroxyl group bonded directly to a benzene ring, esp. in plants. [Say fuh NAWL ick]

phenom *noun informal* an unusually gifted person, a prodigy. [Say FEE nom]

phenomenal *adjective* **1** extraordinary: *the company has experienced phenomenal growth in sales.* **2** perceptible by, or perceptible only to, the senses: *the phenomenal world.* ▶ **phenomenally** *adverb* [Say fuh NOMMA nul]

phenomenological *adjective* based on a philosophical approach that concentrates on the study of what is seen, heard, felt, etc. in contrast to what may actually be real or true about the world. [Say fuh nomma nuh LOGICAL]

phenomenology *noun* Philosophy **1** the science of the objects of a person's perception as distinct from that of being (ontology). **2** a philosophical approach that concentrates on the study of what is seen, heard, felt, etc. in contrast to what may actually be real or true about the world. [Say fuh nomma NOLLA jee]

> **WRITING TIP**
> **phenomenon, phenomena**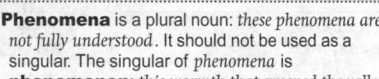
>
> **Phenomena** is a plural noun: *these phenomena are not fully understood*. It should not be used as a singular. The singular of *phenomena* is **phenomenon**: *this warmth that greened the valley was not so much a season as a brief phenomenon*.

phenomenon *noun* (*plural* **phenomena**) **1** a fact, circumstance, or occurrence that appears or is perceived: *glaciers are natural phenomena.* **2** a renowned, remarkable person or thing. [Say fuh NOMMA non or fuh NOMMA nun for the singular, fuh NOMMA nuh for the plural]

phenotype *noun* Biology a set of observable characteristics of an individual or group as determined by its genotype and environment. ▶ **phenotypic** *adjective* [Say FEENO type, feeno TIP ick]

phenylalanine *noun* Biochemistry an amino acid widely distributed in plant proteins and essential in the human diet. [Say fennel ALA neen or fee nul ALA neen]

phenylketonuria *noun* an inherited inability to metabolize phenylalanine, ultimately leading to mental deficiency if untreated. Abbreviation: **PKU**. [Say fennel keeta NURY uh or fee nul keeta NURY uh]

pheromonal *adjective* having to do with pheromones. [Say ferra MONE ul]

pheromone *noun* a chemical substance produced and released into the environment by an animal, esp. a mammal or an insect, for detection and response by another usu. of the same species. [Say FERRA mone]

phew *interjection* an expression of relief, discomfort, astonishment, or disgust.

phial *noun* a small glass bottle, esp. for liquid medicine. [Sounds like FILE]

phil- *combining form* = PHILO-.

-phil *combining form* = -PHILE.

philander *verb* have casual affairs with many women. ▶ **philanderer** *noun* **philandering** *adjective* [Say fill ANDER, fil ANDER er]

philanthropic *adjective* (of a person or organization) seeking to promote the welfare of others; generous and charitable: *they receive financial support from philanthropic bodies.* ▶ **philanthropically** *adverb* [Say fill un THROP ick]

philanthropist *noun* a person who seeks to promote the welfare of others, esp. by the generous donation of money to good causes. [Say fill ANTHRA pist]

philanthropy *noun* **1** a love of humankind. **2** the disposition or effort to promote the happiness and well-being of one's fellow people, esp. by gifts of money, work, etc. [Say fill ANTHRA pee]

philatelic *adjective* having to do with the collection and study of postage stamps. [Say filla TELL ick]

philatelist *noun* a person who collects and studies postage stamps. [Say fill ATTA list]

philately *noun* the collection and study of postage stamps. [Say fill ATTA lee]

-phile *combining form* forming nouns and adjectives with the sense "lover of, that loves" something specified, designating either a fondness or affection, e.g. *bibliophile*, or an esp. sexual obsession, e.g. *pedophile*. [Say FILE]

philharmonic *adjective* devoted to music (chiefly used in the names of orchestras, choirs, etc.). [Say fill har MON ick or filler MON ick]

> **SPELL CHECK**
> **Philippine, Filipina/Filipino, Pilipino**
>
> A person from the Philippines is a **Filipina** or a **Filipino**; the language of the Philippines is **Pilipino**.

Philippine *adjective* of or relating to the Philippines, an archipelago and nation in the South China Sea, or their people. [Say FILLA peen]

Philistine • *noun* **1** a member of a people opposing the Israelites in ancient Palestine. **2** (usu. **philistine**) a person who is hostile or indifferent to culture, the arts, etc., or one whose interests or tastes are commonplace or material: *some philistine acquired a "priceless" painting he will use as collateral in his next leveraged buyout.* • *adjective* hostile or indifferent to culture; commonplace, prosaic: *his party's platform appeals to philistine middle-class suburbanites.* ▶ **philistinism** *noun* [Say FILLA steen or FILLA stine, FILLA stin ism]

Phillips *noun* proprietary denoting a screw with a cross-shaped slot for turning, or a corresponding screwdriver.

philo- *combining form* denoting a liking for what is specified. [Say FYE loe]

philodendron *noun* (*plural* **philodendrons**) a tropical American climbing plant with bright foliage, often grown as a houseplant. [Say filla DEN drun]

philological *adjective* **1** having to do with the study of the structure, historical development, and relationships of a language or languages. **2** having to do with the linguistic, historical, interpretative, and critical aspects of literature. [Say filla LOGICAL]

philologist *noun* **1** a person who studies the structure, historical development, and relationships of a language or languages. **2** a person who studies the linguistic, historical, interpretative, and critical aspects of literature. [Say fill OLLA jist]

philology *noun* **1** the branch of knowledge that deals with the structure, historical development, and relationships of a language or languages. **2** the branch of knowledge that deals with the linguistic, historical,

interpretative, and critical aspects of literature. [Say fill OLLA jee]

philosopher *noun* a person engaged or learned in philosophy or a branch of it, esp. as an academic discipline.

philosophical *adjective* (also **philosophic**) **1** of or according to philosophy: *philosophical discussions about free will.* **2** skilled in or devoted to philosophy: *was a member of the university Philosophical Society.* **3** having or showing a calm attitude toward disappointments or difficulties: *she was philosophical about losing the contract.* ► **philosophically** *adverb*

philosophize *verb* (**philosophizes, philosophized, philosophizing**) **1** reason like a philosopher. **2** speculate; theorize: *she paused for a while to philosophize on racial equality.* ► **philosophizer** *noun*

philosophy *noun* (*plural* **philosophies**) **1** the use of reason and argument in seeking truth and knowledge of reality, esp. of the causes and nature of things and of the principles governing existence, the material universe, perception of physical phenomena, and human behaviour. **2 a** a particular system or set of beliefs reached by this. **b** a personal rule of life. **3** serenity; calmness. **4** the branch of knowledge that deals with the principles of a particular field or subject: *philosophy of science.*

phlegm *noun* **1** the thick sticky substance secreted by the mucous membranes of the respiratory passages, discharged by coughing. **2** coolness and calmness of disposition: *phlegm and determination carried them through many difficult situations.* [Say FLEM]

phlegmatic *adjective* (of a person) having an unemotional and calm disposition. [Say fleg MAT ick]

phlegmy *adjective* (of a cough, laughter, etc.) having a sound affected by the presence of phlegm in the respiratory passages. [Say FLEMMY]

phloem *noun* the tissue conducting food material in plants (*compare* XYLEM). [Say FLOE em]

phlox *noun* (*plural* **phlox** or **phloxes**) a North American plant with dense clusters of esp. white, blue, or red scented flowers, popular as a garden plant. [Say FLOX]

-phobe *combining form* forming nouns and adjectives denoting a person having a fear or dislike of what is specified: *xenophobe.*

phobia *noun* (*plural* **phobias**) an abnormal fear or hatred.

-phobia *combining form* forming abstract nouns denoting a fear of or aversion to what is specified: *agoraphobia.*

phobic • *adjective* characterized by a strong or unreasonable fear or hatred of something: *a phobic state* ◊ *Wendy is phobic about germs.* • *noun* a person with a strong and unreasonable fear of something: *cat phobics.*

-phobic *combining form* having a strong or unreasonable fear or hatred of the thing described: *claustrophobic* ◊ *technophobic* ◊ *camera-phobic.*

phoebe *noun* a small North American tyrant flycatcher with mainly grey-brown or blackish plumage. [Say FEEBY]

Phoenician • *noun* **1** a member of a people of ancient Phoenicia in southern Syria or of its colonies, esp. Carthage in northern Africa. **2** the Semitic language of the Phoenicians. • *adjective* of or relating to Phoenicia, its colonies, its people, or their language. [Say fuh NEESH in]

phoenix *noun* (*plural* **phoenixes**) a mythical bird that, after living for centuries in the Arabian desert, burned itself on a funeral pyre and rose from the ashes with renewed youth to live through another cycle. [Say FEE nix]

phone • *noun* a telephone. • *verb* (**phones, phoned,**

phoning) **1** speak to (a person) by telephone. **2** send (a message) by telephone. **3** make a telephone call. **4** dial (a telephone number). **5** make a telephone call to (a place). PHRASES **phone in** call a radio show etc. on the telephone to participate in a broadcast discussion. **phone up** call (somebody) on the telephone.

phone book *noun* a book listing telephone subscribers in a particular area, their telephone numbers, and usu. their addresses.

phone booth *noun* = TELEPHONE BOOTH.

phone card *noun* a prepaid card for use with a public telephone.

phone-in *noun* a broadcast program during which the listeners or viewers phone the studio etc. and participate: *phone-in show.*

phoneme *noun* any of the units of sound in a specified language that distinguish one word from another, e.g. *p, b, d, t* as in pad, pat, bad, bat, in English. ► **phonemic** *adjective* [Say FOE neem, fuh NEEM ick]

phone phreak *noun see* PHREAK.

phonetic *adjective* **1** representing vocal sounds. **2 a** designating the difference between any two sounds; e.g. in English the *b* of *bin*, the *p* of *pin*, and the *p* of *spin* are phonetically different. **b** (of a system of spelling etc.) reflecting phonetic differences; having a direct correspondence between symbols and sounds. **3** of or relating to phonetics. ► **phonetically** *adverb* [Say fuh NET ick]

phonetics *plural noun* (usu. treated as *singular*) **1** vocal sounds and their classification. **2** the study of these. [Say fuh NET icks]

phoney *adjective & noun* = PHONY.

phonic *adjective* of, designating, or pertaining to phonics. [Say FON ick]

phonics *plural noun* (treated as *singular*) a method of teaching reading by associating letters or groups of letters with particular sounds. [Say FON icks]

phoniness *noun* **1** the quality of something that is not real or genuine and is intended to deceive others. **2** the manner of a person who behaves in an artificial or insincere way in order to deceive others.

phono • *noun* = PHONOGRAPH (esp. on a button or as a setting on a stereo system). • *adjective* designating a type of plug (and the corresponding socket) used with audio and video equipment, in which one conductor is cylindrical and the other is a central part that extends beyond it. [Say FOE no]

phonograph *noun* a record player. [Say FONE uh graph]

phonological *adjective* based on or having to do with the study of speech sounds in a language. ► **phonologically** *adverb* [Say fone uh LOGICAL]

phonology *noun* **1** the study of speech sounds in a language. **2** the system of speech sounds in a specific language. [Say fuh NOLLA jee]

phony *informal* • *adjective* (**phonier, phoniest**) **1** sham; counterfeit; fake. **2** insincere. • *noun* (*plural* **phonies**) a phony person or thing.

phony-baloney *adjective & noun slang* = PHONY.

phooey *interjection* an expression of disgust or contempt. [Say FOO ee]

phosphate *noun* any salt or ester of phosphoric acid. [Say FOSS fate]

phospholipid *noun* any lipid consisting of a phosphate group and one or more fatty acids, including those forming cell membranes. [Say foss fuh LIPID]

phosphor *noun* **1** a synthetic fluorescent or phosphorescent substance esp. used in cathode ray tubes. **2** (in *combination*) = PHOSPHORUS. [Say FOSS fur]

phosphorescence *noun* **1** radiation similar to fluorescence but detectable after excitation ceases.

2 the emission of light without combustion or perceptible heat. ▶ **phosphorescent** *adjective* [Say foss fuh RESS ince]

phosphoric acid *noun* a crystalline solid which has many commercial uses, e.g. in fertilizer and soap manufacture and food processing. [Say foss FOR ick]

phosphorous *adjective Chemistry* containing phosphorus, esp. in its lower valence of three: *phosphorous acid*. [Say FOSS fur us]

phosphorus *noun* a chemical element found in several different forms, including as a poisonous, pale yellow substance that shines in the dark and starts to burn as soon as it is placed in air. [Say FOSS fur us]

photo *noun* (plural **photos**) = PHOTOGRAPH *noun*.

photo- *combining form* denoting: **1** light: *photosensitive*. **2** photography.

photo-aging *noun* skin damage such as wrinkles, brown spots, changes in texture, etc. caused by the sun's ultraviolet light.

Photo CD *noun* (plural **Photo CDs**) *proprietary* **1** a compact disc from which still photographs can be displayed on a television screen. **2** the technology for storing and reproducing photographs in this way.

photochemical *adjective* of or relating to the chemical action of light. ▶ **photochemically** *adverb*

photochemical smog *noun* a condition caused by the action of sunlight on pollutants in the air, resulting in haze and high levels of ozone and nitrogen oxide.

photocopied *adjective* (of printed or written pages, documents, etc.) reproduced by photocopier.

photocopier *noun* an electrical machine for producing immediate photographic copies of text or graphic matter by a process usu. involving the electrical or chemical action of light.

photocopy • *noun* (plural **photocopies**) a photographic copy of printed or written material produced by a process involving the action of light on a specially prepared surface. • *verb* (**photocopies**, **photocopied**, **photocopying**) make copies of printed or written material using this process.

photoelectric *adjective* marked by or using emissions of electrons from substances exposed to light.

photoelectric cell *noun* a device which generates an electric current or voltage dependent on the degree of illumination.

photo essay *noun* an essay consisting of text matter and numerous photographs.

photo finish *noun* (plural **photo finishes**) a close finish of a race or contest, esp. one where the winner is distinguishable only on a photograph.

photofinisher *noun* a person or store involved in the commercial development and printing of films.

photofinishing *noun* the commercial development and printing of films.

photogenic *adjective* **1** (esp. of a person) having an appearance that looks pleasing in photographs. **2** producing or emitting light. [Say photo JEN ick]

photogrammetric *adjective* based on or having to do with the use of photography for surveying and mapping. [Say photo gruh METRIC]

photogrammetry *noun* the use of photography for surveying and mapping. [Say photo GRAMMA tree]

photograph • *noun* a picture formed by means of the chemical action of light or other radiation on sensitive film. • *verb* **1** take a photograph of (a person etc.). **2** appear (in a particular way) when in a photograph.

photographer *noun* a person who takes pictures.

photographic *adjective* involving or having to do with photography or pictures: *photographic equipment*. ▶ **photographically** *adverb*

photographic memory *noun* a memory allowing the precise recall of images with the accuracy of a photograph.

photography *noun* **1** the process or art of taking photographs. **2** the business of producing and printing photographs.

photo ID *noun* identification containing a photograph of the bearer.

photojournalism *noun* the art or practice of relating news through the use of photographs, with or without an accompanying text, esp. in magazines etc. ▶ **photojournalist** *noun*

photometer *noun* an instrument for measuring light or for comparing the intensities of light from different sources. ▶ **photometric** *adjective* **photometry** *noun* [Say foe TOMMA ter, photo METRIC, foe TOMMA tree]

photon *noun* an elementary particle with energy and momentum but no charge or mass, consisting of a quantum of electromagnetic radiation, such as light; the energy of a photon is proportional to the frequency of radiation. ▶ **photonic** *adjective* [Say FOE tawn, foe TONNIC]

photo opportunity *noun* (plural **photo opportunities**) (also *informal* **photo op**, plural **photo ops**) an opportunity for media photographers to take pictures of a politician, celebrity, etc.

photoperiod *noun* the period of daily illumination which an organism receives.

photo radar *noun* a computer-operated radar system which takes a photograph of the licence plate of a speeding car, the picture and a ticket being subsequently delivered in the mail to the car's owner.

photo-realism *noun* detailed and not idealized representation in art, esp. of mundane or sordid aspects of life. ▶ **photo-realist** *noun* **photo-realistic** *adjective*

photoreceptor *noun* a structure in a living organism, esp. a sensory cell or sense organ, that reacts to the presence of light, usu. containing a pigment that undergoes a chemical change when light is absorbed, thus stimulating a nerve.

photosensitive *adjective* reacting chemically, electrically, etc., to light. ▶ **photosensitivity** *noun*

photosynthesis *noun* the process in which the energy of sunlight is used by organisms, esp. green plants, to synthesize carbohydrates from carbon dioxide and water. ▶ **photosynthesize** *verb* (**photosynthesizes**, **photosynthesized**, **photosynthesizing**) **photosynthetic** *adjective*

photovoltaic *adjective* relating to the production of electric current at the junction of two substances exposed to light. Abbreviation: **PV**. [Say photo vol TAY ick]

photovoltaics *noun* the branch of science and technology dealing with photovoltaic effects and devices. [Say photo vol TAY icks]

phr. *abbreviation* phrase.

phrasal *adjective Grammar* of the nature of or consisting of a phrase. [Say FRASE ul]

phrasal verb *noun* an idiomatic phrase consisting of a verb and an adverb, e.g. *break down*, or a verb and a preposition, e.g. *see to*.

phrase • *noun* **1** a small group of words forming a conceptual unit, but not a sentence, esp. such a group without a predicate or finite verb, e.g., "the green car" and "on Friday morning". **2** an idiomatic or short pithy expression. **3** a manner or mode of expression: *a nice turn of phrase*. **4** *Music* a group of notes forming a more or less distinct unit within a larger passage or piece. • *verb* (**phrases**, **phrased**, **phrasing**) **1** express in words: *phrased the reply badly*. **2** divide (music) into

phrases etc. in performance; play so as to give due expression to phrasing.

phrase book *noun* a book for tourists etc. listing useful expressions translated into another language.

phraseology *noun* a particular mode of expression, esp. one characteristic of a particular speaker or writer. *Mrs Roper's inelegant phraseology* ◊ *legal phraseology*. [Say fray zee OLLA jee]

phrasing *noun* **1** the words used to express something. **2** *Music* the way in which a musician or singer divides a piece of music into phrases by pausing in suitable places.

phreak • *noun* (also **phone freak**) a person who makes fraudulent use of a telephone system by electronic means, esp. for computer hacking etc. • *verb* use an electronic device to obtain (a telephone call) without payment. ▶ **phreaking** *noun* [Say FREAK]

phrenological *adjective* based on or having to do with the study of the shape and size of the skull as a supposed indication of character and mental faculties. [Say frenna LOGICAL]

phrenologist *noun* a person who studies the shape and size of a person's skull as a supposed indication of character and mental faculties. [Say fruh NOLLA jist]

phrenology *noun* the study of the shape and size of the skull as a supposed indication of character and mental faculties. [Say fruh NOLLA jee]

phyla *plural* of PHYLUM. [Say FYE luh]

phylactery *noun* (*plural* **phylacteries**) either of two small leather boxes containing Biblical texts in Hebrew, worn by Jewish men during morning prayer on all days except the Sabbath as a reminder to keep the law. [Say fill ACTER ee]

phyllo *noun* **1** a kind of dough capable of being stretched into very thin leaves which may then be layered to make pastries, e.g. baklava. **2** pastry made this way. [Say FEE loe]

phylum *noun* (*plural* **phyla**) **1** a taxonomic rank below kingdom comprising a class or classes and subordinate taxa. **2** a group of languages related to each other less closely than those of a family. [Say FYE lum for the singular, FYE luh for the plural]

phys. ed. *noun* = PHYSICAL EDUCATION.

physical • *adjective* **1 a** of or concerning the body: *physical exercise* ◊ *physical abuse*. **b** of or concerning observable aspects or features of the environment. **2** of or pertaining to matter, the world of the senses, or things material as opposed to things mental or spiritual. **3 a** of or in accordance with the laws of nature: *a physical impossibility*. **b** of or pertaining to physics. **4 a** (of a person or action) inclined to be aggressive or violent, making frequent use of bodily contact, etc. **b** (of an attribute etc.) involving the body rather than the mind: *physical charms*. • *noun* (also **physical examination**) a medical examination to determine health or physical fitness. PHRASES **get physical 1** become violent or physically aggressive. **2** become sexually involved. **3** exercise, become physically fit or toned.

physical change *noun* **1** a change that affects the body or structure of a person or thing. **2** *Chemistry* a usu. reversible change in which the chemical composition of the starting material is not altered and no new chemical substance is formed; water turning into ice during freezing is a physical change (*compare* CHEMICAL CHANGE).

physical chemistry *noun* the application of the techniques and theories of physics to the study of chemical systems, behaviour, etc.

physical education *noun* instruction in physical exercise and sports, esp. in schools.

physical force *noun* **1** material or corporal rather than moral means of persuasion etc. **2** the use of armed power to effect or repress political changes.

physical geography *noun* the branch of geography dealing with natural features and forces of the earth's surface, such as landforms and climate.

physicality *noun* the quality of being physical esp. rather than emotional or spiritual: *he ascribed his dislocated shoulder to the ballet's brutal physicality*.

physically *adverb* **1** in a way that is concerned with a person's body rather than their mind: *physically and emotionally exhausted* ◊ *exercise keeps me physically fit* ◊ *I don't find him physically attractive*. **2** according to the laws of nature or what is probable: *it is physically impossible to finish by the end of the week*.

physically challenged *adjective* *euphemism* (of a person) having a physical disability.

physical science *noun* any branch of the sciences that deals with inanimate matter and energy, e.g. physics, chemistry, geology, astronomy, etc.

physical therapist *noun* esp. *US* = PHYSIOTHERAPIST.

physical therapy *noun* esp. *US* = PHYSIOTHERAPY.

physician *noun* a person legally qualified to practise medicine, esp. a specialist in non-surgical medical diagnosis and treatment.

physicist *noun* an expert in or student of physics.

physics *noun* the science dealing with the properties and interactions of matter and energy.

physio *noun* *Cdn & Brit. informal* **1** (*plural* **physios**) a physiotherapist. **2** physiotherapy.

physiognomy *noun* (*plural* **physiognomies**) **1** a person's face or expression, esp. viewed as indicative of character or ethnic background: *he studied their physiognomies and body language*. **2** the external features of a landscape, plant community, etc.: *the town's pre-war physiognomy*. [Say fizzy ONNA me]

physiographic region *noun* a region that is defined by its natural geographical features, such as mountains, lakes, vegetation, etc. [Say fizzy uh GRAPHIC]

physiologic *adjective* = PHYSIOLOGICAL.

physiological *adjective* having to do with the normal functions and parts of living organisms: *physiological differences between adults and children*. ▶ **physiologically** *adverb* [Say fizzy uh LOGICAL]

physiologist *noun* a person who studies the normal function of living organisms and their parts. [Say fizzy OLLA jist]

physiology *noun* **1** the branch of biology that deals with the normal functions of living organisms and their parts. **2** the way in which a living organism or bodily part functions: *the physiology of the brain*. [Say fizzy OLLA jee]

physiotherapist *noun* a person who treats diseases by physiotherapy.

physiotherapy *noun* esp. *Cdn & Brit.* the treatment of disease, injury, or weakness in the joints or muscles by physical methods that include manipulation, massage, infrared heat treatment, and exercise, instead of by drugs or surgery.

physique *noun* the form, size, and development of a person's body. [Say fizz EEK]

phytoplankton *noun* plankton consisting of microscopic plants. [Say fight oh PLANK tun]

PI *abbreviation* private investigator.

pi *noun* **1** the sixteenth letter of the Greek alphabet (Π, π). **2** (as π) the symbol of the ratio of the circumference of a circle to its diameter (approx. 3.14159). [Say PIE]

pianissimo *Music* • *adjective* performed very softly. • *adverb* very softly. [Say pee uh NISS i moe]

P

pianist *noun* a person who plays the piano, esp. professionally. [Say PEE uh nist or pee ANN ist]

pianistic *adjective* having to do with the art, skill, or technique of playing the piano. ▸ **pianistically** *adverb* [Say pee uh NISS tick]

piano[1] *noun* (*plural* **pianos**) **1** a large musical instrument played by pressing down keys on a keyboard and causing hammers to strike metal strings, the vibration from which is stopped by dampers when the keys are released. **2** an instrument operated in the same way and producing the same tone electronically.

piano[2] *adjective* Music performed softly. • *adverb* softly.

piano bar *noun* a cocktail lounge having a piano and featuring live entertainment.

pianoforte *noun* formal a piano. [Say piano FOR tay]

piano wire *noun* a special kind of strong steel wire used for the strings of pianos.

piazza *noun* (*plural* **piazzas**) a public square or marketplace esp. in an Italian town. [Say pee AT suh]

pic *noun* (*plural* **pix** or **pics**) *informal* **1** a motion picture. **2** a picture, painting, or photograph.

pica *noun* (*plural* **picas**) **1** a unit of type size equal to 12 points (approximately $^1/_6$ inch). **2** a size of letters in typewriting (10 per inch). [Say PIKE uh]

picaresque *adjective* having to do with a style of fiction that is structured as a series of episodes involving a central figure, esp. a rough or dishonest hero involved in a series of adventures, e.g. Byron's *Don Juan*. [Say picka RESK]

picayune *adjective* petty, insignificant: *picayune criticisms* ◊ *disagreement over picayune points*. [Say picka YUNE]

piccolo *noun* (*plural* **piccolos**) **1** a small flute sounding an octave higher than the ordinary flute. **2** its player. [Say PICKA loe]

pick[1] • *verb* **1** (often foll. by *up*) take hold of and move. **2** remove (a flower or fruit) from where it is growing. **3** choose from a number of alternatives. **4** remove unwanted matter from (one's nose or teeth) with a finger or a pointed instrument. • *noun* **1** an act of selecting something. **2** (usu. foll. by *of*) *informal* the best person or thing in a particular group. PHRASES **pick and choose** select carefully or fastidiously. **pick apart 1** find fault, criticize harshly. **2** break up or dismantle. **pick at 1** eat (food) without interest; nibble. **2** = PICK ON 1 (see below). **pick a person's brains** extract ideas, information, etc., from a person for one's own use. **pick a fight** (or **quarrel**) start an argument or a fight deliberately. **pick holes in 1** find fault with (an idea etc.). **2** make holes in (material etc.) by plucking, poking, etc. **pick a lock** open a lock with an instrument other than the proper key, esp. with intent to steal. **pick off 1** pluck (leaves etc.) off. **2** shoot (people etc.) one by one without haste. **3** eliminate (opposition etc.) singly. **4** Baseball put out (a runner) by throwing the ball to a base. **pick on 1** find fault with; nag at. **2** single out (a person) for criticism, victimization, etc. **pick out 1** take from a larger number, esp. with care and deliberation: *picked him out from the others*. **2** distinguish from surrounding objects or at a distance. **3** play (a tune) by ear on the piano etc. **4** accentuate (decoration etc.) with a contrasting colour: *trim picked out in diamonds*. **pick over** select the best from. **pick a person's pockets** steal the contents of a person's pockets. **pick to pieces** = PICK APART. **pick up 1** grasp and raise (from the ground etc.). **2 a** learn or acquire with little effort. **b** catch (an illness). **c** buy (a thing) cheaply or luckily. **d** hear or learn (news etc.). **3 a** fetch (a person, animal, or thing) left in another's charge. **b** stop for and take along with one, esp. in a vehicle. **4** make the

acquaintance of (a person) casually, esp. as a sexual overture. **5** (of one's health, the weather, share prices, etc.) recover, prosper, improve. **6 a** gather (speed); accelerate (a pace). **b** (of the wind) become stronger. **7** (of the police etc.) take into charge; arrest. **8** detect by scrutiny or with a telescope, searchlight, radio, etc. **9 a** (often foll. by *with*) form or renew a friendship. **b** resume, take up anew: *pick up where we left off*. **10** (esp. in phr. **pick up the tab**) accept the responsibility of paying (a bill etc.). **11 pick oneself up** raise or recover oneself after a fall, setback, etc. **12** (esp. in phrase **pick up your feet**) raise (the feet) clear of the ground so as to walk without stumbling. **13** *informal* tidy or clean up (a room etc.). **pick up on** become aware of. **pick up the gauntlet** = TAKE UP THE GAUNTLET (see TAKE). **pick up the pieces** restore to normality or make better (a situation, one's life, etc.), esp. after a setback. **take one's pick** make a choice.

pick[2] *noun* **1** a long-handled tool having a usu. curved iron bar pointed at one or both ends, used for breaking up hard ground, masonry, etc. **2** a plectrum. **3** (usu. in *combination*) an instrument with a sharp point, used for a specified purpose: *toothpick* ◊ *ice pick*. **4** a comb with long, widely spaced teeth used esp. for curly hair. **5** Figure Skating = TOE PICK.

pickaxe • *noun* = PICK[2] noun 1. • *verb* (**pickaxes, pickaxed, pickaxing**) strike or break with a pick.

picker *noun* a person or machine that picks, gathers, or collects something.

pickerel *noun* (*plural* **pickerel** or **pickerels**) **1** a walleye. **2 a** a northern pike. **b** any of various other smaller North American pikes. **3** a sauger. [Say PICKER ul]

picket • *noun* **1 a** a person or group of people outside a place as a protest or to persuade esp. workers not to enter during a strike etc. **b** an occasion on which people act as pickets: *a mass picket of the embassy*. **2 a** pointed stake or peg driven into the ground to form a fence etc. **3** Military a small body of troops sent out to watch for the enemy. • *verb* (**pickets, picketed, picketing**) **1 a** form a picket outside (a place of work etc.). **b** demonstrate as a picket. **2** post or station (soldiers) as a picket. ▸ **picketer** *noun*

picket fence *noun* **1** a fence consisting of vertical pickets nailed to horizontal rails between fence posts. **2** (also **white picket fence**) this as a symbol of conventional middle-class esp. suburban domesticity and contentment.

picket line *noun* a boundary established by workers on strike, esp. at the entrance to the place of work, which others are asked not to cross.

pickings *plural noun* **1** profits or gains that are easily or dishonestly obtained. **2** remaining scraps.

pickle • *noun* **1 a** a vegetable, esp. a small cucumber, preserved in brine, vinegar, etc. **b** a condiment of chopped vegetables preserved in brine, vinegar, mustard, etc. **c** the brine, vinegar, etc. in which food is preserved. **2** *informal* a difficult or unpleasant predicament: *in a pickle*. • *verb* (**pickles, pickled, pickling**) **1** preserve (food) in brine, vinegar, etc. **2** treat (metal, wood, etc.) with an acid or other chemical for cleaning, bleaching, etc.

pickled *adjective* **1** (of food) preserved in brine or vinegar. **2** *slang* drunk. **3** (of wooden furniture etc.) artificially aged with acid or other chemicals.

pick-me-up *noun* **1** an esp. alcoholic drink taken as a tonic or restorative when feeling weak, tired, ill, etc. **2** a good experience, good news, etc. that cheers.

pickoff *noun* Baseball a play in which a runner is caught off base and tagged out.

pickpocket • *noun* a person who steals from the

pockets of others. • *verb* steal from the pockets of (a person). ▶ **pickpocketing** *noun*

pickup *noun* **1** (also **pickup truck**) a light truck having a usu. open bed with low sides. **2** a device that produces an electrical signal in response to some other kind of signal or change, esp.: **a** a device on a musical instrument which converts sound vibrations into electrical signals for amplification. **b** the part of a record player carrying the stylus. **c** an analogous part of a compact disc player. **3** *slang* a person met casually, esp. for sexual purposes. **4 a** the act or action of picking up: *free pickup and delivery*. **b** something picked up. **5 a** the capacity for increasing speed; acceleration. **b** an increase in or recovery of health, prosperity, etc. **6** (as an *adjective*) **a** impromptu, done on the spur of the moment or with whatever components, people, etc. are at hand: *pickup hockey*. **b** (of a performing group, esp. musicians or dancers) assembled for a particular performance, tour, etc. rather than as a permanent ensemble. **7** the tendency to pick up or absorb a substance: *prevents dirt pickup*. **8** *Music* a note or series of notes before a bar line, esp. as the beginning of a phrase. **9** *Fishing* a semicircular loop of metal for guiding the line back on to the spool as it is reeled in.

pick-up sticks *noun* a game in which players use two small thin sticks to try to remove other sticks from a jumbled pile without disturbing it.

picky *adjective* (**pickier, pickiest**) *informal* excessively choosy.

picnic • *noun* **1** an outing including a packed meal eaten outdoors: *picnic basket*. **2** any meal eaten outdoors or without tables, chairs, etc. **3** *informal* something agreeable or easily accomplished.: *work was no picnic*. • *verb* (**picnics, picnicked, picnicking**) take part in a picnic. ▶ **picnicker** *noun*

picnic table *noun* a rectangular table with benches attached along each long side.

pico- *combining form* denoting a factor of 10^{-12}. [Say PEEKO]

Pict *noun* a member of an ancient people of northern Britain who resisted the Roman invaders and eventually amalgamated with the Scots. ▶ **Pictish** *adjective*

pictograph *noun* (also **pictogram**) **1 a** a pictorial symbol or sign. **b** an ancient record consisting of pictorial symbols, as in cave paintings etc. **2** a pictorial representation of statistics etc. on a chart, graph, etc. ▶ **pictographic** *adjective* [Say PICTA graph]

pictorial *adjective* **1** of or expressed in a picture or pictures. **2** containing or illustrated by a picture or pictures. ▶ **pictorially** *adverb* [Say pick TORY ul]

picture • *noun* **1** a painting, drawing, or photograph. **2** an image on a television screen. **3** a film. **4** an impression formed from an account or description. • *verb* (**pictures, pictured, picturing**) **1** represent in a picture. **2** form a mental image of. PHRASES **get the picture** *informal* grasp or become aware of a particular situation, set of circumstances, etc. **in the picture 1** actively involved. **2** fully informed or noticed. **out of the picture** no longer involved; inactive; irrelevant.

picture-perfect *adjective* **1** ideal, perfectly ordered in every detail. **2** precisely accurate.

picture postcard • *noun* a postcard with a picture or view on one side. • *adjective* (**picture-postcard**) (of a view etc.) conventionally attractive.

picturesque *adjective* **1 a** (of landscape, buildings, etc.) beautiful or striking, esp. in a quaint way. **b** (of a route etc.) affording views of this kind. **2** (of language etc.) vivid. **3** *informal* (of a person, appearance, manner, etc.) unique, strange, or unusual; eccentric.

▶ **picturesquely** *adverb* **picturesqueness** *noun* [Say picture ESK]

picture tube *noun* the cathode ray tube of a TV set.

picture window *noun* a large window, esp. one consisting of one pane of glass without mullions.

PID *abbreviation* = PELVIC INFLAMMATORY DISEASE.

piddle • *verb* (**piddles, piddled, piddling**) **1** *informal* urinate. **2 a** work or act in a petty or trifling way. **b** while or fritter away time etc. • *noun* *informal* **1** urination. **2** urine.

piddling *adjective* (also **piddly**) *informal* trivial; trifling.

SPELL CHECK
pidgin, pigeon

A small city bird is a **pigeon**.

---

pidgin *noun* a form of a language altered by non-native speakers, with vocabulary from two or more languages, used for communication between people not having a common language. [Say PIDGE in]

pie *noun* **1** any of various dishes with a pastry crust or topping or both, with a filling of fruit, meat, etc. **2** anything resembling a pie in form: *a mud pie*. **3** *informal* wealth, market share, etc. considered as something to be shared out: *they each claimed a piece of the pie*. PHRASES **easy as pie** *informal* very easy. **pie in the sky** *informal* **1** an extravagant promise unlikely to be fulfilled. **2** an unrealistic prospect of future happiness, esp. after present suffering.

piebald • *adjective* having irregular patches of two colours, esp. black and white. • *noun* a piebald animal, esp. a horse. [Say PIE bald]

piece • *noun* **1** a portion separated from or regarded distinctly from the whole. **2** an item used in constructing something or forming part of a set. **3** a musical or written work. **4** a figure or token used to make moves in a board game. **5** a coin of specified value. **6** *informal* a firearm. • *verb* (**pieces, pieced, piecing**) (usu. foll. by *together*) assemble from individual parts. PHRASES **break to pieces** break into fragments. **by the piece** (paid) according to the quantity of work done. **go to pieces 1** break up, lose cohesion. **2** collapse emotionally or mentally; suffer a breakdown. **in one piece 1** (of a thing) unbroken; consisting of a single piece or mass. **2** (of a person etc.) whole, unharmed, without injury or loss. **in pieces** broken, in fragments. (**all**) **of a piece** (often foll. by *with*) uniform, consistent, in keeping. **piece by piece** with one piece or part after another in succession; gradually. **a piece of the action** *slang* **1** a share in the profits accruing from something. **2** a share in the excitement. **a piece of one's mind** a sharp rebuke or lecture. **a piece of the puzzle** an item of information that helps to understand a larger problem. **say one's piece** give one's opinion or make a statement. **take to pieces** = PICK APART (see PICK[1]).

pièce de résistance *noun* (*plural* **pièces de résistance**) the most important or remarkable item: *the pièce de résistance of the auction is an eighteenth-century grandfather clock*. [Say pyess duh ray zis TONCE]

piecemeal • *adverb* piece by piece; gradually; separately: *the agreement was written piecemeal*. • *adjective* consisting of pieces; done bit by bit; gradual; unsystematic: *a piecemeal approach to solving the unemployment issue*.

piece of work *noun* (*plural* **pieces of work**) **1** a thing made by working. **2** a task, a difficult thing. **3** a person of a specified and usu. unpleasant kind: *he's a nasty piece of work*.

piecework *noun* work paid for by the amount produced. ▶ **pieceworker** *noun*

pie chart *noun* a circle divided into sectors to represent relative quantities.

pied *adjective* having several colours: *the pied flycatcher.* [Rhymes with *RIDE*]

piedmont *noun* a gentle slope leading from the foot of mountains to a region of flat land: *the town's setting, where tidewater meets the piedmont.* [Say PEED mont]

Pied Piper *noun* **1** (in German legend) a piper who rid the town of Hamelin (Hameln) of rats by enticing them away with his music. **2** a person enticing followers esp. to their doom.

pie-eyed *adjective slang* drunk.

Piegan *noun & adjective* = PEIGAN. [Say pee GAN]

pie plate *noun* (also **pie pan**) a shallow usu. round dish with sloping sides, in which pies are baked.

pier *noun* **1** a structure raised on piles and leading out into the sea, a lake, etc., used as a landing stage and promenade. **2** a support of an arch or of the span of a bridge.

pierce *verb* (**pierces**, **pierced**, **piercing**) **1 a** (of a sharp instrument etc.) penetrate the surface of. **b** (often foll. by *with*) prick with a sharp instrument, esp. to make a hole in. **c** make a hole, opening, or tunnel into or through (something); bore through: *pierced a hole in the belt.* **d** (of cold, grief, etc.) affect keenly or sharply. **e** (of a light, glance, sound, etc.) penetrate keenly or sharply. **2** force (a way etc.) through or into (something): *pierced their way through the undergrowth.*

pierced *adjective* **1** having a hole or holes. **2** (of a part of the body) having a hole in which a ring etc. is worn: *pierced ears.* **3** (of an earring) designed to be worn in a pierced ear.

piercer *noun* **1** a sharp device used to pierce holes in something. **2** a person whose job is to pierce holes for rings and other jewellery in another person's body; a body piercer.

piercing *adjective* **1** (of voices, sounds, etc.) very high and loud; shrill. **2 a** (of eyes) very bright and seeming to see through the person they are looking at. **b** (of a look) very direct; searching. **3** (of a feeling, comment, etc.) very perceptive. **4** (of wind, cold, etc.) bitter; penetrating. ▶ **piercingly** *adverb*

pierogi *noun* = PEROGY. [Say puh ROE ghee]

pie-shaped *adjective* shaped like a triangular piece cut out of a round pie, having one curved side.

piety *noun* (*plural* **pieties**) **1** the quality of being religious or reverent: *her saintly deference and humble piety.* **2** a belief or point of view which is accepted with unthinking conventional reverence: *the accepted pieties of our time.* [Say PIE uh tee]

piezoelectric *adjective* having to do with a **piezoelectric effect**, in which mechanical pressure is applied to certain crystals, e.g. quartz, to produce a positive charge on one crystal face and a negative charge on the opposite crystal face, resulting in an electric field between the two faces. Piezoelectric substances are used widely in microphones, earphones, and cigarette lighters. [Say pie eezo ELECTRIC]

piffle *informal* • *noun* nonsense; empty speech. • *verb* (**piffles**, **piffled**, **piffling**) talk or act feebly; trifle.

piffling *adjective* trivial, unimportant.

pig *noun* **1** a domesticated hoofed mammal with a large head, a broad flat snout, and a stout often almost hairless body, raised as a source of meat. **2** *informal* **a** a selfish and greedy person. **b** an ill-mannered, insensitive, or vulgar person. **c** a fat person. **3** an oblong mass of metal (esp. iron or lead) from a smelting furnace. **4** *slang derogatory* a police officer. **PHRASES buy a pig in a poke** buy, accept, etc. something without knowing its value or esp. seeing it. **make a pig of**

oneself overeat. **pig out** (**pigs**, **pigged**, **pigging**) *informal* eat gluttonously: *pigging out on cookies.*

SPELL CHECK
pigeon, pidgin ☑ ABC

A type of language is a **pidgin**.

---

pigeon *noun* a stout, usu. grey and white bird with a small head, short legs, and a cooing voice, commonly found nesting in buildings in cities and towns.

pigeonhole • *noun* **1** each of a set of compartments in a cabinet or on a wall for papers, letters, etc. **2** a small recess for a pigeon to nest in. • *verb* (**pigeonholes**, **pigeonholed**, **pigeonholing**) **1** deposit (a document) in a pigeonhole. **2** put (a matter) aside for future consideration or to forget it. **3** assign (a person or thing) to a preconceived category.

piggish *adjective* **1** of or relating to pigs. **2** having a quality associated with pigs, esp. greed, dirtiness, or stubbornness. ▶ **piggishness** *noun*

piggy • *noun* (also **piggie**) (*plural* **piggies**) *informal* **1** a little pig. **2** a child's word for a pig. • *adjective* (**piggier**, **piggiest**) **1** like a pig; piggish. **2** (of features etc.) like those of a pig: *little piggy eyes.*

piggyback • *noun* (also **piggyback ride**) a ride on the back and shoulders of another person. • *verb* **1** ride on a person's back and shoulders. **2 a** give a piggyback ride to. **b** carry or mount on top of another thing: *they've piggybacked their own networks on to the system.* **3** (usu. foll. by *on*) use an already established situation as a basis so as to gain an advantage: *we were piggybacking on their training program.* • *adverb* **1** on the back and shoulders of another person. **2** on top of a larger object.

piggy bank *noun* a container, esp. in the shape of a pig with a slot in the top, used for saving coins in.

pigheaded *adjective* obstinate.

pig iron *noun* crude iron from a smelting furnace.

pig Latin *noun* a jocular or secret language formed from English by transferring the initial consonant or consonant cluster of each word to the end of the word and adding usu. AY, e.g. *ixnay* from *nix*.

piglet *noun* a young pig.

pigment • *noun* **1** colouring matter used as paint or dye. **2** the natural colouring matter of animal or plant tissue, e.g. chlorophyll, hemoglobin. • *verb* colour with or as if with pigment.

pigmentation *noun* **1** the natural colouring of plants, animals, etc. **2** the colouring of tissue by the deposition of pigment.

pigmy *noun* (*plural* **pigmies**) = PYGMY.

pig-out *noun slang* an instance of eating a large amount of food.

pigskin *noun* **1** the hide of a pig. **2** leather made from this. **3** a football.

pigsty *noun* (*plural* **pigsties**) **1** (also **pigpen**) a pen or enclosure for a pig or pigs. **2** a filthy room etc. [Say PIG stye]

pigtail *noun* **1** the tail of a pig. **2** a braid of hair hanging from the back of the head, or either of a pair at the sides. ▶ **pigtailed** *adjective* (in sense 2)

pigweed *noun* **1** a herbaceous plant that grows as a weed or is grown for grain or fodder. **2** = GOOSEFOOT.

pika *noun* (*plural* **pikas**) a small rabbit-like mammal with small ears and no tail, found in the mountains and deserts of western North America. [Say PIKE uh]

pike *noun* (*plural* **pike**) **1 a** a large voracious freshwater fish with a long narrow snout and sharp teeth. **b** any of various similar predatory fishes with large teeth. **2** *hist.* an infantry weapon with a pointed steel or iron head on a long wooden shaft. **3** a jackknife position in

diving or gymnastics. PHRASES **come down the pike** appear on the scene: *together they can veto any constitutional proposal that comes down the pike*.

pike-perch *noun* (*plural* **pike-perch** or **pike-perches**) a predatory pike-like freshwater fish of the perch family, e.g. the walleye.

pike pole *noun* Cdn a long pole with a sharp point and hook, used for moving floating logs.

piker *noun informal* **1** a cheap or stingy person. **2** a cautious or timid person.

pilaf *noun* a Middle Eastern or Indian dish of spiced rice or wheat with meat, fish, vegetables, etc. [Say PEE laff]

pilaster *noun* a rectangular column, esp. projecting from a wall. [Say pill ASTER]

Pilates *noun* a system of exercises, sometimes using specialized apparatus, designed to improve strength, flexibility, and posture, and enhance mental awareness and control of body movement. [Say puh LOT eez]

pilau *noun* = PILAF. [Say pi LAU (LAU rhymes with HOW)]

pilchard *noun* **1** a small European marine fish of the herring family, the young of which are often marketed as sardines. **2** a sardine of the Pacific coast of North America, esp. as tinned and sold as food. [Say PILL churd]

pile¹ • *noun* **1** a heap of things laid or gathered upon one another. **2 a** a large imposing building: *a Victorian Gothic pile*. **b** a large group of tall buildings. **3** *informal* **a** a large quantity. **b** a large amount of money; a fortune. **4 a** a series of plates of dissimilar metals laid one on another alternately to produce an electric current. **b** (in full **atomic pile**) a nuclear reactor. • *verb* (**piles, piled, piling**) **1 a** (often foll. by *up, on*) heap up. **b** (foll. by *with*) load: *piled the bed with coats*. **2** crowd hurriedly or tightly: *piled into the car*. PHRASES **pile it on** *informal* exaggerate. **pile up 1** accumulate; heap up. **2** *informal* cause (a vehicle etc.) to crash.

pile² *noun* a heavy beam driven vertically into the bed of a river, soft ground, etc., to support the foundations of a superstructure.

pile³ *noun* **1** the soft projecting surface on velvet, plush, etc., or esp. on a carpet; nap. **2** soft hair or down, or the wool of a sheep.

pileated *noun* (of a bird) having a conspicuous cap or crest. [Say PILLY ate ed]

pileated woodpecker *noun* a North American woodpecker with a red-topped head.

piledriver *noun* a machine for driving piles into the ground.

piles *plural noun* hemorrhoids.

pileup *noun informal* **1** a multiple crash of road vehicles. **2** an accumulation (of things, tasks, etc.). **3** a confused mass of people fallen on top of one another.

pilfer *verb* steal (objects of little value) esp. in small quantities. ▶ **pilferage** *noun* **pilferer** *noun*

pilgrim *noun* **1** a person who journeys to a sacred place for religious reasons. **2** (usu. **Pilgrim**) one of a group of 102 people who pioneered British colonization of North America, sailing in the *Mayflower* and founding a settlement at Plymouth, Massachusetts, in 1620.

pilgrimage *noun* **1** a journey to a holy place for religious reasons: *go on a pilgrimage*. **2** life viewed as a journey. **3** any journey taken for nostalgic or sentimental reasons: *a pilgrimage to his native village in Quebec and to the tombs of his ancestors*. [Say PILGRIM idge]

piling *noun* **1** a group or mass of heavy beams piled into the ground. **2** a structure made of heavy beams driven into the ground.

Pilipino *noun* the national language of the Philippines. [Say pilla PEE no]

pill¹ *noun* **1 a** a solid medicine formed into a ball or a flat disc for swallowing whole. **b** (usu. as **the pill**) a

contraceptive pill. **2** an unpleasant or painful necessity: *to make this bitter pill easier to swallow in Quebec, the federal government is announcing a one-year delay*. **3** *informal* an objectionable annoying person. PHRASES **sugar** (or **sweeten**) **the pill** make an unpleasant necessity acceptable.

pill² *verb* (of esp. knitted fabric) form balls of fluff on the surface: *this sweater is pilling*.

pillage • *verb* (**pillages, pillaged, pillaging**) steal or rob with violence, esp. during war; plunder. • *noun* the action of pillaging a place or property, esp. in wartime. ▶ **pillager** *noun* [Say PILL idge]

pillar *noun* **1** a tall upright column used as a support for a building or as an ornament or monument etc. **2 a** a strong supporter or important member of something: *a pillar of society*. **b** a fundamental part or feature of a system, organization, etc.: *dismantled the pillars of the welfare state*. **3** an upright mass of air, water, rock, etc.: *pillar of salt*. PHRASES **pillar of strength** a person regarded as showing or giving great moral support, fortitude, etc. ▶ **pillared** *adjective*

pillbox *noun* (*plural* **pillboxes**) **1** a small shallow cylindrical box for pills. **2** a hat of a similar shape. **3** a small partly underground enclosed concrete fort.

pillion *noun* seating for a passenger behind a motorcyclist. PHRASES **ride pillion** travel seated behind a motorcyclist etc.

pillory • *noun* (*plural* **pillories**) *hist.* a wooden framework with holes for the head and hands, enabling the public to assault or ridicule a person so imprisoned. • *verb* (**pillories, pilloried, pillorying**) **1** expose (a person) to ridicule or public contempt: *I went from being pilloried to having people be nice to me*. **2** *hist.* put in the pillory. [Say PILLER ee]

pillow • *noun* **1** a usu. oblong support for the head, esp. in bed, with a cloth cover stuffed with feathers, flock, foam rubber, etc. **2** any pillow-shaped block or support. • *verb* **1** rest (the head etc.) on or as if on a pillow: *pillowed his head on his arms*. **2** serve as a pillow for: *moss pillowed her head*.

pillowcase *noun* (also **pillow slip**) a washable fabric cover for a pillow.

pillow talk *noun* intimate conversation in bed.

pillowy *adjective* resembling a pillow in softness, shape, or fluffiness.

pill-popper *noun* **1** a person who takes pills in abundance. **2** a drug addict. ▶ **pill-popping** *noun* & *adjective*

pilot • *noun* **1** a person who operates the flying controls of an aircraft. **2** a person qualified to take charge of a ship entering or leaving harbour, moving through dangerous waters, etc. **3 a** an experimental undertaking or test, esp. in advance of a larger one: *a pilot project*. **b** a test episode of a television series used to assess audience reaction etc. **4** = PILOT LIGHT 1. • *verb* (**pilots, piloted, piloting**) **1** act as a pilot on (a ship) or of (an aircraft). **2** conduct or lead; guide: *piloted the new bill through the Commons*. **3** produce a pilot or test for (an idea, scheme, etc.); try out.

pilot hole *noun* a small hole drilled into something to receive a nail or screw, or to guide a larger drill bit.

pilothouse *noun* = WHEELHOUSE 1.

pilotless *adjective* (esp. of an aircraft) operated without a pilot.

pilot light *noun* **1** a small flame that burns continuously, e.g. on a gas stove or oil furnace, and lights a larger flame when the valve controlling the fuel opens. **2** an electric indicator light or control light.

pilot whale *noun* a small black whale with a low dorsal fin and a square bulbous head, found in temperate or subtropical waters.

Pilsner *noun* (also **Pilsener**) a pale lager beer with a strong flavour of hops. [Say PILLS ner or PILCE ner]

pimento *noun* (*plural* **pimentos**) **1** = SWEET PEPPER. **2** a small tropical tree, native to Jamaica. **3** the dried unripe berries of this, usu. crushed for use in cooking. *Also called* ALLSPICE. [Say pi MENTO]

pimiento *noun* = PIMENTO. [Say pimmy ENTO or pim YENTO]

pimp • *noun* a man who lives off the earnings of a prostitute or a brothel. • *verb* **1** act as a pimp. **2** cause to act as a prostitute. ▶ **pimping** *noun*

pimple *noun* a small, hard, inflamed, usu. raised spot on the skin. ▶ **pimpled** *adjective* **pimply** *adjective*

PIN *noun* a confidential identification number issued by a bank etc. to validate electronic transactions.

pin • *noun* **1** a thin piece of metal with a sharp point at one end and a round head at the other, used for fastening pieces of cloth, paper, etc. **2** a metal projection from a plug or an integrated circuit. **3** a small brooch or badge. **4** *Medicine* a steel rod used to join the ends of fractured bones while they heal. **5** a club-shaped usu. wooden peg used as a target in bowling. **6** *Wrestling* a throw which keeps one's opponent on the mat for a specified period of time. **7** *Golf* a stick with a flag placed in a hole to mark its position. **8** a metal peg in a hand grenade that prevents it from exploding. • *verb* (**pins, pinned, pinning**) **1** attach or fasten with a pin or pins. **2** hold someone firmly so they are unable to move. **3** *Wrestling* capture (one's opponent) in a pin. **4** (foll. by *on*) fix (blame or responsibility) on. PHRASES **neat as a pin** very tidy. **pin down 1** (often foll. by *to*) bind (a person etc.) to a promise, arrangement, etc. **2** force (a person) to declare his or her intentions. **3** restrict the actions or movement of (an enemy etc.). **4** specify (a thing) precisely: *could not pin down my unease to a particular cause*. **5** hold (a person etc.) down by force. **pin one's hopes** (or **faith** etc.) **on** rely implicitly or completely on.

pina colada *noun* (*plural* **pina coladas**) a drink made from pineapple juice, rum, and coconut. [Say peena kuh LODDA or peenya kuh LODDA]

pinafore *noun* an apron-like garment, usu. fastened at the back, worn over a dress, esp. by small girls.

pinata *noun* (*plural* **pinatas**) a brightly decorated papier mâché figure filled with small treats and suspended overhead to be broken by a blindfolded person waving a stick. [Say pin YOTTA or peen YOTTA]

pinball *noun* a game in which small metal balls are shot across a board and score points by striking pins with lights etc.: *pinball machine*.

pince-nez *noun* (*plural* **pince-nez**) a pair of eyeglasses held in place only by a clip on the nose. [Say PANCE nay]

pincers *plural noun* **1** (also **pair of pincers**) a gripping tool resembling scissors but with blunt usu. concave jaws to hold a nail etc. for extraction. **2** the front claws of lobsters and some other crustaceans.

pinch • *verb* (**pinches, pinched, pinching**) **1 a** grip (esp. skin or flesh) tightly, e.g. between finger and thumb, two hard surfaces, etc. **b** (of a shoe, garment, etc.) constrict (the flesh) painfully. **2** *slang* **a** steal; take without permission. **b** arrest (a person). **3** remove (leaves, buds, etc.) to encourage bushy growth. • *noun* (*plural* **pinches**) **1** an act of gripping the skin of someone's body between the finger and the thumb. **2** an amount that can be taken up with fingers and thumb: *a pinch of salt*. **3** the stress or pain caused by poverty, cold, hunger, etc. **4** *Baseball* (as an *adjective*) (of a hit, run, etc.) made by a pinch hitter: *pinch homer*. **5** *slang* **a** an arrest. **b** a theft. PHRASES **feel the pinch** experience the effects of poverty. **in a pinch** in an emergency; if necessary. **pinch oneself** check to make

sure that one is awake and not dreaming. **pinch pennies** live frugally.

pinched *adjective* (of the features) drawn, as with cold, hunger, worry, etc.

pin cherry *noun* (*plural* **pin cherries**) a wild North American cherry tree bearing very small fruit.

pinch-hit • *verb* (**pinch-hits, pinch-hit, pinch-hitting**) **1** *Baseball* substitute for another hitter, esp. at a critical point in the game: *I was sent in to pinch-hit for Manny*. **2** act as a substitute for another person in an emergency: *I was sent to the Calgary office to pinch-hit for George while he was recovering from hip surgery*. • *noun* (usu. **pinch hit**) *Baseball* a single, double, etc. hit while pinch-hitting: *Brad leads the team in pinch hits*.

pinch-hitter *noun* **1** a baseball player who bats instead of another. **2** a person acting as a substitute for another, esp. in an emergency.

pinch-run *verb* *Baseball* (**pinch-runs, pinch-ran, pinch-run, pinch-running**) substitute for another runner, esp. at a critical point in the game. ▶ **pinch-runner** *noun*

pincushion *noun* a small cushion for holding pins.

pine[1] *noun* **1** an evergreen tree native to northern temperate regions, with needle-shaped leaves that grow in clusters, often grown for its soft timber or for tar and turpentine. **2** the soft timber of this tree, often used to make furniture. **3** *Sport informal* the bench: *warming the pine*.

pine[2] *verb* (**pines, pined, pining**) **1** (often foll. by *away*) decline or waste away, esp. from grief, disease, etc. **2** long eagerly; yearn: *pining to go home* ◊ *pined for him*.

pineal gland *noun* a pea-sized conical mass of tissue in the brain, secreting a hormone-like substance in some mammals. [Say PINNY ul or PINE ee ul]

pineapple *noun* **1** a large juicy tropical fruit consisting of aromatic yellow flesh surrounded by a tough segmented skin and topped with a tuft of stiff leaves. **2** the widely cultivated tropical plant that bears this fruit, which is low-growing, with a spiral of sword-shaped leaves and a thick stem.

pine cone *noun* the cone-shaped fruit of the pine tree.

pine marten *noun* **1** a weasel-like mammal with predominantly dark brown fur with a splash of orange on the chest, the most common marten of North America. **2** the European marten, which has a dark brown coat and white throat and stomach.

pine nut *noun* the edible seed of various pine trees.

pine tar *noun* a sticky, dark liquid obtained by distilling pinewood, used in making paints, roofing, etc.

pinewood *noun* **1** the timber of the pine. **2** a forest of pines.

piney *adjective* of, like, or full of pines.

ping • *noun* **1** a single short high ring. **2** the sound of an engine thumping or rattling esp. due to faulty combustion. • *verb* **1** make a ping. **2** (of a motor or other engine) make a thumping or rattling noise, esp. due to faulty combustion.

pingo *noun* (*plural* **pingos**) a dome-shaped mound found in permafrost areas, consisting of a layer of soil over a large core of ice.

ping-pong *noun* *proprietary* = TABLE TENNIS.

pinhead *noun* **1** the head of a pin. **2** a very small thing. **3** *informal* a stupid or foolish person.

pinhole *noun* a hole made by a pin.

pinion • *noun* **1** the outer part of a bird's wing, usu. including the feathers that support it in flight. **2 a** small cogwheel engaging with a larger one. **b** a cogged spindle engaging with a wheel. • *verb* **1** cut off the pinion of (a wing or bird) to prevent flight. **2** bind the

arms of a person: *they were pinioned against the wall*. [Say PIN yin]

pink[1] • *noun* **1** a pale red colour. **2** a type of small carnation with sweet-smelling white, pink, or crimson flowers and slender, usu. grey-green leaves. **3** *informal* often *derogatory* a person with socialist tendencies. **4** = PINK SALMON. **5** (**the pink**) the most perfect condition etc.: *the pink of elegance*. • *adjective* **1** (often in *combination*) of a pale red colour of any of various shades: *salmon-pink*. **2** esp. *derogatory* tending to socialism. **3** (of wine) rosé. PHRASES **in the pink** *informal* in very good health.

pink[2] *verb* cut a scalloped or zigzag edge on (esp. fabric).

pink-collar *adjective* (of a profession etc.) traditionally associated with women.

pink eye *noun* **1** contagious ophthalmia in humans and some livestock. **2** a contagious fever in horses.

pinking shears *plural noun* a dressmaker's serrated shears for cutting a zigzag edge.

pinkish *adjective* somewhat pink.

pinkly *adverb* with a pink colour.

pinko *noun* (*plural* **pinkos**) *derogatory* a socialist.

pink salmon *noun* a medium-sized pink-fleshed migratory salmon of the Pacific and, more recently, Atlantic Oceans, the male of which has a humped back at spawning time.

pink slip • *noun* a notice of dismissal from employment. • *verb* (**pink-slip, pink-slips, pink-slipped, pink-slipping**) dismiss (a person) from employment: *was pink-slipped last week*.

pinky • *noun* (also **pinkie**) (*plural* **pinkies**) the little finger. • *adjective* somewhat pink; pinkish.

pin money *noun* a very small sum of money, esp. for spending on inessentials.

pinnacle *noun* **1** the culmination or climax (e.g. of success). **2** a natural peak, e.g. of rock etc. **3** a small ornamental turret usu. ending in a pyramid or cone, crowning a buttress, roof, etc. [Say PINNA cull]

pinnate *adjective* **1** (of a compound leaf) having leaflets arranged on either side of the stem, usu. in pairs opposite each other. **2** having branches, tentacles, etc., on each side of an axis. [Say PIN ate]

PIN number *noun* = PIN.

pinochle *noun* **1** a card game with a double pack of 48 cards (nine to ace only). **2** the combination of queen of spades and jack of diamonds in this game. [Say PEE nuckle]

Pinot *noun* **1** any of several varieties of black or white grape used in winemaking. **2** a red or white wine made from these grapes. [Say pee NO]

pinpoint • *noun* **1** the point of a pin. **2** something very small or sharp. • *adjective* **1** very small. **2** precise, accurate. • *verb* locate or determine with precision or accuracy: *pinpointed the problem*.

pinprick *noun* **1** a prick caused by a pin. **2** a trifling irritation.

pins and needles *plural noun* a tingling sensation in a limb recovering from numbness. PHRASES **on pins and needles** in an agitated state of suspense.

pinstripe *noun* **1** a very narrow white stripe in the design of cloth: *pinstripe suit*. **2** a pinstripe suit: *came wearing pinstripes*. ▶ **pinstriped** *adjective*

pint *noun* **1** a measure of capacity for liquids etc., equal to one-eighth of a gallon (0.568 litre in Imperial measure, or 0.473 litre in US measure). **2** a dry measure, equal to a half quart or (in the US) one sixty-fourth of a bushel (0.5506 litre). **3** *Cdn* (*Maritimes*) a mickey of liquor. **4** esp. *Brit. informal* a pint of beer. [Say PINT with the *I* as in *PIKE*]

pintail *noun* a duck with a pointed tail.

pinto • *adjective* having irregular patches of two colours. • *noun* (*plural* **pintos**) **1** a horse with irregular patches of two colours. **2** (also **pinto bean**) a variety of kidney bean with mottled seeds.

pint-sized *adjective* (also **pint-size**) *informal* very small.

pin-up *noun* **1** a photograph of a popular or sexually attractive person, affixed to a wall. **2** a person shown in such a photograph.

pinwheel • *noun* **1** a hand-held toy consisting of a stick with a small vaned wheel which rotates. **2** a firework which can be fixed at the centre and which rotates rapidly when lit. **3** something shaped like a pinwheel: *pastry pinwheels*. • *verb* rotate or cause to rotate like a pinwheel.

pinworm *noun* a small parasitic nematode worm.

piny *adjective* = PINEY. [Say PINE ee]

pion *noun* *Physics* a meson having a mass approximately 270 times that of an electron. [Say PIE on]

pioneer • *noun* **1** an initiator of a new enterprise; an inventor etc. **2** a settler in a previously unsettled land. • *verb* **1** initiate or originate (an enterprise etc.). **2** act or prepare the way as a pioneer. ▶ **pioneering** *adjective*

pious *adjective* **1** devout; religious. **2** hypocritically virtuous; sanctimonious: *very little of the party's actions supports its pious promises*. ▶ **piously** *adverb* [Say PIE us]

pip[1] *noun* the seed of an apple, orange, grape, etc.

pip[2] *noun* **1** any of the spots on a playing card, dice, or domino. **2** a diamond-shaped segment of the surface of a pineapple.

pipe • *noun* **1** a tube of metal, plastic, wood, etc. used to convey water, gas, exhaust, etc. **2 a** a narrow wooden or clay etc. tube with a bowl at one end containing burning tobacco, opium, etc., the smoke from which is drawn into the mouth. **b** the quantity of tobacco etc. held by this: *smoked a pipe*. **3** *Music* **a** a wind instrument consisting of a single tube. **b** any of the tubes by which sound is produced in an organ. **c** (in *plural*) bagpipes. **4** a tubal organ, vessel, etc. in an animal's body. **5** (in *plural*) *informal* or *jocular* the voice or vocal cords, esp. in reference to singing. **6** a high note or song, esp. of a bird. **7** a cylindrical vein of ore. **8 a** a boatswain's whistle. **b** the sounding of this. • *verb* (**pipes, piped, piping**) **1** play (a tune etc.) on a pipe or pipes. **2 a** convey (oil, water, gas, etc.) by pipes. **b** provide with pipes. **3** (often foll. by *in*) transmit (music, a radio program, etc.) by wire or cable. **4** (usu. foll. by *up, on, to*, etc.) signal the arrival of (an officer etc.) on board a ship. **5** utter in a shrill voice; whistle. **6** arrange (icing, cream, etc.) in decorative lines or twists on a cake etc. **7** lead or bring (a person etc.) by the sound of a pipe. PHRASES **pipe down** *informal* be quiet or less insistent. **pipe up** begin to play, sing, speak, etc. **put that in your pipe and smoke it** *informal* a challenge to another to accept something frank or unwelcome.

pipe band *noun* a band consisting of bagpipers and drummers.

pipe bomb *noun* a homemade bomb contained in a metal tube.

pipe cleaner *noun* a piece of flexible covered wire, used for cleaning a tobacco pipe and for crafts.

pipe dream *noun* an unattainable or fanciful hope.

pipeful *noun* (*plural* **pipefuls**) the amount of tobacco that can be held by a pipe.

pipeline • *noun* **1** a long, usu. underground, pipe for conveying oil, gas, etc. **2** a channel supplying goods, information, etc.: *the plan includes $100 million to pay for a food and medical pipeline to fight Somalia's famine*. • *verb* (**pipelines, pipelined, pipelining**) convey by a pipeline. PHRASES **in the pipeline** being planned, worked on, or produced.

P

pipe organ *noun Music* an organ using pipes instead of or as well as reeds.

piper *noun* **1** a bagpiper. **2** a person who plays a pipe, esp. an itinerant musician.

pipe-stone *noun* a hard red clay of the central US, used by Aboriginal peoples to make tobacco pipes.

pipette *noun* a slender tube for transferring or measuring small quantities of liquids esp. in chemistry. [Say pipe ET or pip ET]

pipe wrench *noun* (*plural* **pipe wrenches**) a wrench with one fixed and one movable jaw, designed so as to grip a pipe etc. when turned in one direction only.

piping • *noun* **1** the sound of a pipe or pipes being played. **2** lengths of pipe, or a system of pipes, esp. in domestic use. **3** a thin pipe-like fold used as trim or edging on fabric. **4** ornamental lines of icing, cream, mashed potato, etc. on a cake or other dish. • *adjective* (of a noise) high; whistling.

piping hot *adjective & adverb* very or suitably hot (esp. as required of food, water, etc.).

piping plover *noun* a small buff-coloured North American bird with a whistling call.

pipit *noun* a mainly ground-dwelling songbird, which is found worldwide and has brown streaky plumage.

pippin *noun* **1** an apple grown from seed. **2** a red and yellow dessert apple.

pipsqueak *noun informal* a contemptibly small, weak, or insignificant person or thing.

piquancy *noun* the quality of being agreeably sharp or stimulating: *the tart cranberries add piquancy ◊ the secret adds piquancy to the tale.* [Say PEEK'n see]

piquant *adjective* **1** having a pleasant sharp taste or appetizing flavour: *a piquant blend of tamarind, chilies, garlic, and coconut.* **2** pleasantly exciting and stimulating to the mind: *a piquant bit of gossip.* [Say pee CONT or pee CANT or PEE cant]

pique • *verb* (**piques, piqued, piquing**) **1** wound the pride of, irritate: *he was piqued by the accusation.* **2** arouse (curiosity, interest, etc.): *our taste buds were piqued by the '88 Chardonnay.* • *noun* enmity; resentment: *huffed off in a fit of pique.* [Say PEEK]

piracy *noun* (*plural* **piracies**) **1** the practice or an act of robbery of ships at sea. **2** a similar practice or act in other forms, esp. hijacking. **3** the infringement of copyright by unauthorized reproduction or use of a book, recording, computer program, etc.

piranha *noun* (*plural* **piranhas**) a predatory South American freshwater fish, which has very sharp teeth that are used to tear flesh from prey. [Say puh RONNA or puh RANNA]

pirate • *noun* **1** a person who commits piracy. **2** a person who infringes another's copyright or other business rights. **3** a person, organization, etc., that broadcasts without official authorization: *pirate radio station.* • *verb* (**pirates, pirated, pirating**) use or reproduce another's work or ideas without permission for one's own benefit, usu. in contravention of patent or copyright. ▶ **pirated** *adjective*

piratical *adjective* of or characteristic of a pirate: *a black piratical fisherman's hat.* [Say pie RAT uh cull]

pirogi *noun* = PEROGY. [Say puh ROE ghee]

pirogue *noun* a long narrow canoe made from a single tree trunk. [Say pi ROAG]

pirouette • *noun* a rapid turn or spin on the point of the toe or the ball of the foot, made esp. by a dancer. • *verb* (**pirouettes, pirouetted, pirouetting**) perform a pirouette. [Say pir oo ET]

piscatorial *adjective* of or concerning fish, fishermen, or fishing: *the fishing resort is billed as a "piscatorial treasure trove".* [Say piska TORY ul]

Piscean *noun* a person born under the astrological

sign of Pisces, usu. between Feb. 19 and Mar. 20. [Say PICE ee in]

Pisces *noun* (*plural* **Pisces**) **1** a large constellation between Aries and Aquarius, traditionally regarded as contained in the figure of a pair of fish. **2 a** the twelfth sign of the zodiac. **b** a person born when the sun is in this sign, usu. between Feb. 19 and Mar. 20. [Say PICE eez]

piss *coarse slang* • *verb* (**pisses, pissed, pissing**) **1** urinate. **2 a** discharge (blood etc.) when urinating. **b** wet with urine. **3 piss oneself** a wet one's clothing with urine. **b** be very frightened, amused, or excited. • *noun* **1** urine. **2** an act of urinating. **3** an unpalatable drink. [PHRASES] **piss around** fool or mess around. **piss away** squander; waste: *pissed away his money.* **piss down** rain heavily. **piss in** (or **into** or **against**) **the wind** do something to no effect or against one's own interests. **piss off 1** go away. **2** (often as **pissed off** *adjective*) annoy; anger. **piss on** show utter contempt for, esp. by humiliating; defeat heavily.

piss and vinegar *noun coarse slang* energy; aggression.

pissed *adjective slang* **1** drunk. **2** annoyed; angry.

pissy *adjective* (**pissier, pissiest**) *coarse slang* **1** disagreeable; foul: *a pissy mood.* **2** second-rate.

pistachio • *noun* (*plural* **pistachios**) **1** an evergreen tree with small brownish-green flowers, which bears an oval reddish fruit. **2** (also **pistachio nut**) the edible pale green seed of this tree. **3** (also **pistachio green**) a pale green colour. • *adjective* (also **pistachio green**) pale green. [Say piss TASHY oh]

piste *noun* a ski run of compacted snow. [Say PEEST]

pistil *noun* the female organs of a flower, comprising the stigma, style, and ovary. [Say PISS tul]

pistol *noun* a small hand-held firearm. [Say PISS tul]

pistol-grip *noun* a handle shaped like the butt of a pistol.

pistol-whip *verb* (**pistol-whips, pistol-whipped, pistol-whipping**) beat with a pistol.

piston *noun* **1** a disc or short cylinder fitting closely within a tube in which it moves up and down against a liquid or gas, used in an internal combustion engine to impart motion, or in a pump to receive motion. **2** a sliding valve in a trumpet etc.

pit • *noun* **1 a** a usu. large deep hole in the ground. **b** a hole made in digging for industrial purposes: *gravel pit.* **c** a mine, esp. a coal mine. **d** a covered hole as a trap for esp. wild animals. **2 a** an indentation left after smallpox, acne, etc. **b** a hollow in a plant or animal body or on any surface. **3** the stone of a fruit. **4** (in full **orchestra pit**) the part of a theatre, opera house, etc. where the orchestra plays, usu. in front of the stage and on a lower level. **5 a** (**the pit** or **bottomless pit**) hell. **b** (**the pits**) *slang* a wretched or the worst imaginable place, situation, person, etc. **6 a** an area at the side of a track where race cars are serviced and refuelled. **b** a sunken area in a garage floor for access to a car's underside. **7** the area of a stock market or commodity exchange in which a particular stock or commodity is traded, esp. one in which dealers shout their bids and contracts on certain commodities aloud: *wheat pit.* **8** = MOSH PIT. • *verb* (**pits, pitted, pitting**) **1** (usu. foll. by *against*) **a** set (people or things) in opposition or rivalry. **b** match (one's wits, strengths, etc.) against an opponent. **2** make or develop pits, scars, or indentations: *rain pitted the bare earth ◊ the cooktop will pit if sugar is spilled on it.* **3** remove pits from (fruit).

pita *noun* (*plural* **pitas**) a flat round hollow unleavened bread which can be split and filled. [Say PEETA]

pit bull *noun* **1** (also **pit bull terrier**) an American variety of bull terrier, noted for its ferocity. **2 a** a tenacious or aggressive person: *a political pit bull.* **b** (as

an *adjective*) aggressive; fierce: *had a reputation as a pit bull prosecutor*.

pitch¹ • *verb* (**pitches, pitched, pitching**) **1** erect and fix (a tent, camp, etc.). **2** throw; fling. **3** *Baseball* throw (the ball) to the batter. **4** fix or plant (a thing) in a definite position. **5 a** express in a particular style or at a particular level: *pitched his argument at the most basic level*. **b** *informal* promote (a product, idea, etc.); attempt to win sales or approval for: *pitched his outline to the editor*. **c** make a bid or offer for business. **6** (often foll. by *against, into*, etc.) fall heavily, esp. headlong. **7** (of a ship etc.) plunge in a longitudinal direction. **8** *Music* set at a particular pitch. **9** move with a vigorous jogging motion, as in a train, carriage, etc.; lurch. • *noun* (*plural* **pitches**) **1** height, degree, intensity, etc.: *builds to a pitch of excitement* ◊ *keep our enthusiasm at a fever pitch*. **2** the steepness of a slope, esp. of a roof, stratum, etc. **3** *Baseball* the act or manner of pitching the ball to a batter. **4** *Music* **a** the degree of highness or lowness of a tone. **b** a standard scale of this used in performance etc. **5** the pitching motion of a ship etc. **6** *informal* behaviour or speech intended to influence or persuade, esp. for the purpose of sales or advertising. **7** (also **pitch shot**) *Golf* a high approach shot with a short run. **8** *Mechanics* the distance between successive corresponding points or lines, e.g. between the teeth of a cogwheel etc. **9** the density of characters on a line, usu. per inch. **PHRASES pitch in** *informal* **1** assist, co-operate. **2** set to work vigorously. **pitch into** *informal* attack forcibly with blows, words, etc.

pitch² • *noun* (*plural* **pitches**) **1** a sticky resinous black or dark brown substance obtained by distilling tar or turpentine, semi-liquid when hot, hard when cold, used for waterproofing. **2** any of various similar substances, such as asphalt or bitumen. **3** the resin or crude turpentine which exudes from pine and fir trees. • *verb* (**pitches, pitched, pitching**) cover, coat, or smear with pitch.

pitch-black *adjective* (also **pitch-dark**) very or completely dark.

pitchblende *noun* a mineral form of uranium oxide occurring in pitch-like masses and yielding radium. [Say PITCH blend]

pitched battle *noun* **1** a vigorous fight, argument etc. **2** *Military* a battle planned beforehand and fought on chosen ground.

pitched roof *noun* a sloping roof.

SPELL CHECK
pitcher, picture

A painting or photograph is a **picture**.

pitcher¹ *noun* **1** *Baseball* the player who throws the ball to the batter. **2** a person or thing that pitches.

pitcher² *noun* **1** a vessel with a lip and a handle, for holding and pouring liquids. **2** the amount of liquid contained in this: *a pitcher of lemonade*. ▸ **pitcherful** *noun* (*plural* **pitcherfuls**)

pitcher plant *noun* a red-flowered plant of eastern North America, which has pitcher-shaped leaves that can hold liquids to trap and drown insects, so that nutrients can be absorbed from the insects' bodies by the plant.

pitchfork • *noun* a long-handled fork for pitching hay etc. • *verb* **1** throw or lift with a pitchfork. **2** thrust (a person etc.) forcibly into a position, office, etc.: *the $1.2 billion construction program will pitchfork this slummy city into the present*.

pitchman *noun* (*plural* **pitchmen**) a person delivering a sales pitch, esp. in a radio or television commercial.

pitchout *noun* **1** *Baseball* a pitch purposely thrown

wide of the plate, to make it easier for the catcher to throw out a baserunner who is attempting to steal. **2** *Football* a short lateral pass thrown behind the line of scrimmage.

pitch pine *noun* any of various pine trees with hard, heavy timber that yields much resin.

pitch pipe *noun* a small pipe blown to set the pitch for singing or tuning.

piteous *adjective* deserving or causing pity; wretched: *piteous cries* ◊ *a piteous sight*. ▸ **piteously** *adverb* [Say PITY us]

pitfall *noun* **1** a danger or difficulty, esp. one that is hidden or not obvious at first. **2** a covered pit for trapping animals etc.

pith *noun* **1** spongy white tissue lining the rind of an orange, lemon, etc. **2** the essential part: *the pith and substance of the bill*. **3** *Botany* the spongy cellular tissue in the stems and branches of dicotyledonous plants. **4** force; energy, esp. of words or speech: *writes with a combination of pith, élan, and exactitude*.

pithead *noun* **1** the top of a mine shaft. **2** the area surrounding this. [Say PIT head]

pith helmet *noun* a light helmet made from the dried pith of certain swamp plants, worn by explorers etc. in the tropics for protection from the sun.

pithily *adverb* in a short but well-expressed way: *the excitement surrounding the prime minister was pithily expressed by the term "Trudeaumania"*. [Say PITH uh lee]

pithiness *noun* the quality of an expression or remark that is short but is expressed well and is full of meaning. [Say PITH ee niss]

pithy *adjective* (**pithier, pithiest**) **1** (of an expression, remark, etc.) short but expressed well and full of meaning: *a collection of famous quotations and pithy sayings*. **2** of, like, or containing much pith. [Say PITH ee]

pitiable *adjective* **1** deserving or arousing pity: *wanted the actor to make his character as pitiable as possible*. **2** contemptible: *a pitiable lack of talent*. [Say PITY a bull]

pitiful *adjective* **1** deserving of or arousing pity: *a pitiful call for help*. **2** contemptible: *a pitiful excuse for a man*. ▸ **pitifully** *adverb* [Say PITTA full]

pitiless *adjective* **1** showing no pity; cruel: *a pitiless tyrant*. **2** very harsh or severe; unrelenting: *the pitiless heat of the desert*. ▸ **pitilessly** *adverb* [Say PITY less]

pit-lamping *noun* *Cdn* (*BC*) the hunting practice of using strong portable lights to blind an animal temporarily so that it freezes in its tracks, thus allowing the hunter an easy shot.

piton *noun* a peg or spike driven into a rock or crack to support a climber or a rope. [Say PEE tawn]

pit socks *plural noun* *Cdn* (*Cape Breton*) standard grey work socks, esp. worn by miners.

pit stop *noun* **1** *Motor Racing* a stop at a pit for servicing and refuelling. **2 a** a brief stop during a trip for a snack, rest, etc. **b** a place where one makes such a stop.

pittance *noun* a very small or inadequate amount of money paid to someone as an allowance, wage, etc.: *paid him a mere pittance*.

pitted *adjective* **1** having pits or indentations in the surface of: *his pitted face*. **2** (of a fruit) having the pit or stone removed: *pitted olives*.

pitter-patter • *adverb* **1** with a sound like quick light steps. **2** with a rapid beat: *her heart went pitter-patter*. • *noun* such a sound.

pituitary • *noun* (*plural* **pituitaries**) a small ductless gland at the base of the brain secreting various hormones essential for growth and other bodily functions. • *adjective* of or relating to this gland. [Say pi TOO a terry or pi TYOO a terry]

pit viper *noun* any of various American and Asian

venomous snakes that have sensory pits on the head to detect the heat of prey.

pity • *noun* **1** sorrow and compassion aroused by another's condition. **2** something to be regretted; grounds for regret or mild annoyance: *what a pity!* • *verb* (**pities, pitied, pitying**) feel (often contemptuous) pity for: *I pity you if you think that.* PHRASES **for pity's sake** an exclamation of urgent supplication, anger, etc. **take** (or **have**) **pity on** feel or act compassionately towards. ▶ **pitying** *adjective* **pityingly** *adverb*

pivot • *noun* **1** a short shaft or pin on which something turns or swings. **2** a crucial or essential person, point, etc., in a scheme or enterprise: *the men at the pivot of the revolution.* **3** a pivoting movement. **4** *Basketball* **a** a movement in which the ball carrier may take one or more paces in any direction with one foot, while keeping the other foot in place. **b** an offensive position in the frontcourt, usu. played by the centre, in which the player stands facing away from the basket. **c** the player who plays in the pivot position. **5** *Hockey* a centre. • *verb* (**pivots, pivoted, pivoting**) **1** turn on or as if on a pivot. **2** (foll. by *on, upon*) depend on: *the film's success pivots on the smooth execution of the climactic scene.* **3** provide with or attach by a pivot: *the dampers are pivoted on wires instead of hinges.* [Say PIV it]

pivotal *adjective* of crucial importance in relation to the development or success of something else: *played a pivotal role in helping the two sides reach an agreement.*

pix *plural noun informal* **1** pictures, esp. photographs. **2** movies.

pixel *noun Electronics* any of the minute areas of uniform illumination of which an image on a television or computer screen is composed. [Say PIX ul]

pixie *noun* (also **pixy**) (*plural* **pixies**) **1** a small fairy, often portrayed with pointed ears and a pointed hat. **2** a small, mischievous person. ▶ **pixieish** *adjective* [Say PIXY, PIXY ish]

pizza *noun* a food consisting of a flat round base of dough baked with a topping of tomato sauce and cheese and other garnishes, e.g. meat, vegetables, etc.

pizzazz *noun* (also **pizazz**) *informal* an attractive combination of liveliness and style or glamour: *add pizzazz to the outfit with a matching belt.* [Say puh ZAZZ]

pizzeria *noun* a place where pizzas are made or sold.

pizzicato *Music* • *adverb* plucking the strings of a violin etc. with the finger. • *adjective* (of a note, passage, etc.) performed pizzicato. [Say pits i CATTO or pits i COTTO]

PJs *plural noun informal* = PYJAMAS 1.

pkg. *abbreviation* package.

PKU *abbreviation* PHENYLKETONURIA.

pl. *abbreviation* plural.

placard *noun* a printed or handwritten poster used esp. as an advertisement, in protest demonstrations, picket lines, etc. [Say PLACK ard or PLACK erd]

placate *verb* (**placates, placated, placating**) make less angry; calm: *the landlord is trying to placate tenants.* ▶ **placatingly** *adverb* [Say pluh KATE or PLACK ate or PLAY kate]

place • *noun* **1** a particular position or location. **2** a portion of space occupied by or set aside for someone or something. **3** a vacancy or available position. **4** a position in a sequence or hierarchy. **5** the position of a figure in a series indicated in decimal notation. **6** (in place names) a square or short street. **7** *informal* a person's home. **8 a** any of the first three or sometimes four positions in a race. **b** the second position, esp. in a horse race. • *verb* (**places, placed, placing**) **1** put in a particular position or situation. **2** find an appropriate place or role for. **3** allocate or award a specified position in a sequence or hierarchy.

4 remember the relevant background or circumstances of. **5** arrange for the implementation of (an order, bet, etc.). **6 a** finish second in a horse race. **b** finish among the first three or sometimes four in a race. PHRASES **all over the place** *informal* **1** everywhere: *companies are going bankrupt all over the place.* **2** in disorder; chaotic. **give place to 1** make room for. **2** yield precedence to. **3** be succeeded by. **go places** *informal* be successful. **in place 1** in the right position; suitable. **2** not moving; on the spot: *running in place.* **in place of** in exchange for; instead of. **in places** at some places or in some parts, but not others. **keep a person in his** or **her place** suppress a person's aspirations or pretensions. **out of place 1** in the wrong position. **2** unsuitable. **put oneself in another's place** imagine oneself in another's position. **put a person in his** (or **her**) **place** deflate or humiliate a person. **take place** occur. **take one's place** go to one's correct position, be seated, etc. **take the place of** be substituted for; replace.

placebo *noun* (*plural* **placebos**) a pill, medicine, etc. with no active ingredient, prescribed to bring about improvement in the psychological condition of patients who do not need medicine but think that they do; placebos are also used in drug studies in which their effects are compared with the effects of an experimental drug. [Say pluh SEE bo]

place kick *noun Football* a kick in which the ball is placed on the ground and held upright. ▶ **place-kick** *verb* **place-kicker** *noun*

placeless *adjective* not confined to a place; not having a specific location: *a placeless plot.*

placemat *noun* a small mat used to protect and keep clean a table on which dishes and eating utensils are set.

placement *noun* **1** the act of finding somebody a suitable job or place to live: *a job placement service.* **2** a job, often as part of a course of study or for gaining experience: *has a placement with a communications company in Waterloo.* **3** the act of placing something somewhere.

place name *noun* the name of a city, hill, lake, etc.

placenta *noun* (*plural* **placentas**) **1** a flattened circular organ in the uterus of some pregnant mammals, nourishing and maintaining the fetus through the umbilical cord and expelled after birth. **2** (in flowers) part of the ovary wall carrying the ovules. ▶ **placental** *adjective* [Say pluh SENTA]

placer *noun* a deposit of sand, gravel, etc., in the bed of a stream etc., containing minerals, e.g. gold, in particles. [Say PLASS er]

placer mining *noun* a type of mining in which particles of gold and other minerals are recovered from deposits of gravel and sand etc. found in riverbeds and stream beds. [Say PLASSER mining]

place setting *noun* a set of plates, cutlery, etc. for one person at a meal.

placid *adjective* **1** (of a person) not easily aroused or disturbed; peaceful. **2** calm; serene. ▶ **placidly** *adverb* [Say PLASS id]

placing *noun* **1** the fact or condition of being placed, esp. of being ranked in a race or of being found in a situation. **2** an instance of being placed.

placket *noun* **1** an opening or slit in a garment, for fastenings or access to a pocket. **2** the flap of fabric under this.

plagiarism *noun* the practice of taking someone else's work or ideas and passing them off as one's own. [Say PLAY juh rism]

plagiarist *noun* a person who plagiarizes. [Say PLAY juh rist]

plagiarize *verb* (**plagiarizes**, **plagiarized**, **plagiarizing**) **1** take and use (the thoughts, writings, inventions, etc. of another person) as one's own. **2** pass off the thoughts etc. of (another person) as one's own. ▶ **plagiarizer** *noun* [Say PLAY juh rize]

plague • *noun* **1 a** (**the plague**) a contagious bacterial disease characterized by fever and delirium, with the formation of buboes (**bubonic plague**) and sometimes infection of the lungs (**pneumonic plague**). **b** any severe or fatal contagious disease spreading rapidly over a wide area. **2** (foll. by *of*) an unusual infestation of a pest etc.: *a plague of frogs.* **3 a** great trouble. **b** an affliction, esp. as regarded as divine punishment. **4** *informal* a nuisance. • *verb* (**plagues**, **plagued**, **plaguing**) **1** afflict, torment: *plagued by war.* **2** *informal* pester or harass continually. [Say PLAIG]

plaice *noun* (*plural* **plaice**) a North Atlantic flatfish with a brown back and a white underside, which is a commercially important food fish. [Sounds like *PLACE*]

plaid *noun* **1 a** checkered or tartan, esp. woollen, twilled cloth. **b** a checkered or tartan pattern. **2** a long piece of plaid worn over the shoulder as part of Highland Scottish costume. [Say PLAD]

SPELL CHECK
plain, plane

The spelling is **plane** for an airplane and a flat surface.

---

plain • *adjective* **1** not decorated or elaborate; simple or ordinary. **2** without a pattern; in only one colour. **3** unmarked; without identification. **4** easy to perceive or understand; clear. **5** (of language) clearly expressed; direct. **6** (of a woman or girl) not beautiful or attractive. **7** sheer; simple: *plain stupidity.* • *adverb* simply: *plain stupid.* • *noun* **1** a level tract of esp. treeless and flat grassland; prairie. **2** (**the Plains**) the region of western North America originally characterized by such grassland. PHRASES **be plain with** speak bluntly to.

plainchant *noun* = PLAINSONG.

plain clothes • *plural noun* ordinary clothes worn esp. as a disguise by police officers etc. • *adjective* (**plainclothes**) not wearing a uniform: *a plainclothes officer.*

plain-Jane • *adjective* ordinary, simple, not remarkable: *a plain-Jane dress.* • *noun* (**plain Jane**) a plain or unattractive girl or woman.

plainly *adverb* **1** in a way that is easy to see, hear, understand or believe; clearly: *the sea was plainly visible in the distance* ◊ *something was plainly wrong.* **2** using simple words to say something in a direct and honest way: *to put it plainly, he's a crook.* **3** in a simple way, without decoration: *she was plainly dressed.*

plainness *noun* **1** the quality of being simple, unembellished, or unadorned. **2** the quality of not being beautiful, or of being drab or ordinary.

plains bison *noun* (*plural* **plains bison**) (also **plains buffalo** *plural* **plains buffalo** or **plains buffaloes**) a subspecies of the North American bison, distinguished by a yellow-ochre cape of hair over the shoulders.

Plains Cree *noun* (*plural* **Plains Cree**) **1** a member of a Cree people who moved west to the Plains in the 18th century and now live in Manitoba, southern Saskatchewan, and central Alberta. **2** the dialect of Cree spoken by this people.

Plains Indian *noun* (*plural* **Plains Indians**) a member of any of a number of Aboriginal peoples inhabiting the Plains of western North America, including the Assiniboine, Blackfoot, Gros Ventres, Peigan, Blood, and Sarcee.

plainsong *noun* church music, usu. unaccompanied, sung in unison in medieval modes and in free rhythm corresponding to the accentuation of the words (*also called* GREGORIAN CHANT).

plain-spoken *adjective* outspoken; blunt.

plaintiff *noun* Law a person who brings a case against another into court (*opp.* DEFENDANT).

plaintive *adjective* expressing sorrow; mournful, sad: *a plaintive melody.* ▶ **plaintively** *adverb*

plain-vanilla *adjective* **1** ordinary, plain, unexciting. **2** (esp. of a computer, program, or other product) having no interesting or unusual feature.

plait • *noun* a length of hair, straw, etc., in three or more interlaced strands; a braid. • *verb* **1** form (hair etc.) into a plait. **2** make something by weaving strands of straw, rope, etc. into a plait or plaits: *plaited baskets and rugs.* [Sounds like *PLATE*]

plan • *noun* **1** a detailed proposal for doing or achieving something. **2** an intention or decision about what one is going to do. **3** a scheme for the regular payment of contributions towards a pension, insurance policy, etc. **4** a map or diagram. **5** a scale drawing of a horizontal section of a building. • *verb* (**plans**, **planned**, **planning**) **1** decide on and arrange in advance. **2** (foll. by *for*) make preparations for. **3** make a plan of (something to be made or built). PHRASES **go according to plan** proceed as expected or planned. **plan on** *informal* **1** aim at doing; intend. **2** (also **plan for**) anticipate, expect; work under a specified assumption.

planar *adjective* Math of, relating to, or in the form of a plane. [Say PLANE er]

SPELL CHECK
plane, plain

The spelling is **plain** for something simple or ordinary and for a prairie.

---

plane[1] • *noun* **1 a** a flat surface on which a straight line joining any two points on it would wholly lie. **b** imaginary flat surface through or joining etc. material objects. **2** a level surface. **3** = AIRPLANE. **4** a flat surface producing lift by the action of air or water over and under it (usu. in *combination: hydroplane*). **5** (often foll. by *of*) a level of attainment, knowledge, etc.: *it lifted Queen's to the plane of a first-class teaching institution.* **6** a flat thin object such as a tabletop. • *adjective* **1** (of a surface etc.) perfectly level. **2** (of an angle, figure, etc.) lying in a plane. • *verb* (**planes**, **planed**, **planing**) (of a speedboat etc.) skim over water: *the boat's efficient foil shape gives very good balance when planing.*

plane[2] • *noun* **1** a tool consisting of a wooden or metal block with a projecting steel blade, used to smooth a wooden surface by paring shavings from it. **2** a similar tool for smoothing metal. • *verb* (**planes**, **planed**, **planing**) **1** smooth (wood, metal, etc.) with a plane. **2** pare (irregularities) with a plane.

plane[3] *noun* a tall tree with maple-like leaves and bark that peels in uneven patches.

planeload *noun* as much as can be carried in an airplane.

planer *noun* = PLANE[2] *noun* 1.

planet *noun* **1** a celestial body moving in an elliptical orbit around a star, esp. (also **major planet**) any of the nine large rocky or gaseous bodies orbiting the sun. **2** (also **minor planet**) an asteroid. **3** (**the planet**) the earth.

planetarium *noun* (*plural* **planetariums** or **planetaria**) **1** a domed building in which images of stars, planets, constellations, etc. are projected for

public entertainment or education. **2** the device used for such projection.

planetary *adjective* **1** of or like planets: *planetary influence*. **2** global, worldwide: *the greatest planetary catastrophe known to have occurred*. **3** of or involving a gear in which one wheel travels around the outside or the inside of another wheel with which it meshes.

planetwide *adjective* taking place all over the world; involving the whole planet; worldwide.

plangent *adjective* (of a sound) plaintive; sad: *the plangent melancholy of late romanticism.* ▶ **plangently** *adverb* [Say PLAN jint]

plank • *noun* **1** a long flat piece of timber used esp. in building etc. **2** a single item of a political or other program (*compare* PLATFORM 4). • *verb* **1** provide, cover, or floor with planks. **2** (usu. foll. by *down*) *informal* put (a thing etc.) down roughly or violently: *we ran and planked ourselves down on the riverbank just in time.* PHRASES **walk the plank** *hist.* (of a pirate's captive etc.) be made to walk along a plank over the side of a ship to one's death in the sea. ▶ **planked** *adjective*

plank house *noun* a large rectangular dwelling framed with timbers and covered with planks, used esp. by the Aboriginal peoples of the Pacific coast of North America.

planking *noun* planks as flooring etc.

plank road *noun Cdn* a road of planks laid across logs running end to end over rough ground.

plankton *noun* the chiefly microscopic organisms drifting or floating in the sea or fresh water. ▶ **planktonic** *adjective* [Say PLANK tun, plank TONIC]

planned *adjective* in accordance with a plan: *his planned arrival* ◊ *planned parenthood*.

planned economy *noun* (*plural* **planned economies**) an economy in which production, prices, incomes, etc. are determined centrally by government.

planner *noun* **1** = URBAN PLANNER. **2** a person who makes plans. **3** a list, table, organizer, etc., with information helpful in planning.

planning *noun* **1** in senses of PLAN *verb*. **2** the coordinating of land use and development.

plant • *noun* **1 a** any living organism of the kingdom Plantae, usu. containing chlorophyll enabling it to live wholly on inorganic substances and lacking specialized sense organs and the power of voluntary movement. **b** a small organism of this kind, as distinguished from a shrub or tree. **2 a** machinery, fixtures, etc., used in industrial processes. **b** a factory. **c** (also **physical plant**) the premises, fittings, and equipment of a business or institution. **3** *informal* **a** something, esp. incriminating or compromising, positioned or concealed so as to be discovered later. **b** a person stationed as a spy or source of information. • *verb* **1** place (a seed, bulb, or growing thing) in the ground so that it may take root and flourish. **2** (often foll. by *in, on,* etc.) **a** put or fix in position. **b plant oneself** take up a position: *planted myself by the door.* **3** deposit (young fish, spawn, oysters, etc.) in a river or lake. **4** station (a person etc.), esp. as a spy or source of information. **5** cause (an idea etc.) to be established, esp. in another person's mind. **6** deliver (a blow, kiss, etc.) with a deliberate aim. **7** *informal* position or conceal (something incriminating or compromising) for later discovery. **8** settle or establish (a colony, city, etc.).

Plantagenet *hist.* • *adjective* belonging to or having to do with the English royal dynasty that held the throne from the accession of Henry II in 1154 until the death of Richard III in 1485. • *noun* a member of this dynasty. [Say plan TADGE a nit]

plantain *noun* **1** a low-growing plant with a rosette of leaves and seeds used as food for birds, occurring widely as a lawn weed. **2 a** a kind of banana that contains high levels of starch and little sugar, used esp. in cooking. **b** the plant that bears this fruit. [Say plan TANE or PLAN tane]

plantar *adjective* relating to the sole of the foot: *plantar warts*. [Sounds like *PLANTER*]

plantation *noun* **1** a large farm, esp. in tropical or subtropical areas, on which cotton, tobacco, sugar, etc. is cultivated, usu. by resident farm workers. **2** an area planted with trees etc., esp. as part of a reforestation program.

planter *noun* **1** a large container for growing plants, usu. outdoors. **2** the owner or manager of a coffee, cotton, tobacco, etc. plantation. **3** a person employed to plant seedlings in reforestation programs. **4** a machine for planting seeds etc.

planting *noun* **1** in senses of PLANT *verb*. **2** an arrangement of plants in a garden or other setting.

plantlet *noun* an undeveloped or small plant.

plantlike *adjective* resembling or similar to a plant.

plaque *noun* **1** an ornamental usu. metal tablet, esp. affixed to a building in commemoration. **2** a sticky deposit on teeth where bacteria proliferate. [Say PLACK]

plasma *noun* **1 a** the colourless fluid in blood, lymph, or milk, in which corpuscles or fat globules are suspended. **b** this taken from donated blood for use in transfusions. **2** = PROTOPLASM. **3** a gas of positive ions and free electrons with an approximately equal positive and negative charge. [Say PLAZMA]

plasma membrane *noun* a membrane in a cell which regulates the passage of molecules in and out of the cytoplasm.

plaster • *noun* **1** a soft pliable mixture esp. of lime or gypsum with sand and water for spreading on walls, ceilings, etc., to form a smooth hard surface when dried. **2** = PLASTER OF PARIS. **3** a protective substance spread on a bandage etc. • *verb* **1** cover (a wall etc.) with plaster or a similar substance. **2** (often foll. by *with*) cover (a surface, etc.) with a lot of something: *pictures plastered all over her office*. **3** stick or apply (a thing) thickly like plaster: *plastered glue all over it*. **4** (often foll. by *down*) make (esp. hair) smooth with water, cream, etc.; fix flat. **5** apply a medical plaster or plaster cast to. **6** *slang* bomb or shell heavily.

plasterboard *noun* two boards with a filling of plaster used to form or line the inner walls of houses etc.

plastered *adjective slang* drunk.

plasterer *noun* a person who plasters walls, ceilings, etc. for a living.

plaster of Paris *noun* fine white plaster made of gypsum and used for making plaster casts etc.

plasterwork *noun* work done in plaster, esp. the plaster-covered surface of a wall.

plastic • *noun* **1** any of a number of light strong materials that are produced by chemical processes and can be moulded when heated. **2** *informal* (also **plastic money**) credit cards or other types of plastic card that can be used instead of money. **3** = PLASTIC WRAP. • *adjective* **1 a** made of plastic. **b** artificial, insincere: *a plastic smile*. **2** capable of being moulded; supple: *clay is a plastic substance*. ▶ **plastically** *adverb*

plastic explosive *noun* a putty-like explosive capable of being moulded by hand.

SPELL CHECK ABC✓
Plasticine, Pleistocene

The first epoch of the Quaternary period is the **Pleistocene** epoch.

Plasticine *noun proprietary* a soft plastic material used,

esp. by children, for modelling. [Say plasta SEEN or PLASTA seen]

plasticity *noun* the ability to be moulded or to undergo a permanent change: *one cannot expect imaginativeness of plasticity from a bureaucracy.* [Say plass TISSA tee]

plasticize *verb* (**plasticizes**, **plasticized**, **plasticizing**) (often as **plasticized** *adjective*) coat with plastic. ▶ **plasticizer** *noun* [Say PLASTA size]

plasticky *adjective informal* suggestive of or resembling plastic. [Say PLASTIC ee]

plastic surgeon *noun* a surgeon who reconstructs parts of the body by the transfer of tissue.

plastic surgery *noun* the process of reconstructing or repairing parts of the body by the transfer of tissue, either to treat injury or for cosmetic reasons.

plastic wrap *noun* a very thin clinging transparent plastic film, used esp. to cover food.

> SPELL CHECK
> **plate, plait** ✓ABC
>
> Something braided or woven is a **plait**.

plate • *noun* **1** a flat dish from which food is eaten or served. **2** bowls, cups, and other utensils made of gold or silver. **3** a thin, flat piece of metal used to join or strengthen or forming part of a machine. **4** a small, flat piece of metal bearing a name or inscription and fixed to a wall or door. **5** a sheet of metal or other material bearing an image of type or illustrations, from which multiple copies are printed. **6** a printed photograph or illustration in a book. **7** *Botany & Zoology* a thin, flat organic structure or formation. **8** *Geology* each of the several rigid pieces of the earth's lithosphere which together make up the earth's surface. **9** a horizontal timber laid along the top of a wall to support the ends of joists or rafters. • *verb* (**plates**, **plated**, **plating**) cover (a metal object) with a thin coating of a different metal. PHRASES **on a plate** *informal* (of receiving something) with little or no effort. **on one's plate** for one to deal with or consider.

plate armour *noun* armour of metal plates.

plateau • *noun* (*plural* **plateaus** or **plateaux**) **1** an area of fairly level high ground. **2** a state of little variation after an increase: *microwave sales have reached a plateau and will stay at about one million a year.* • *verb* (**plateaus**, **plateaued**, **plateauing**) (often foll. by *out*) reach a level or stable state after an increase: *my career plateaued once I hit my thirties.* [Say pla TOE for the singular, pla TOES for either plural]

plateful *noun* (*plural* **platefuls**) the amount of food etc. that is placed on a plate.

plate glass *noun* fine-quality glass for windows etc.

platelet *noun* a small colourless disc-shaped cell fragment without a nucleus, found in large numbers in blood and involved in clotting. [Say PLATE lit]

plate tectonics *noun* the slow movement of rigid plates on the underlying mantle of the earth's surface (*see also* TECTONIC PLATE).

platform *noun* **1** a raised level surface on which people or things can stand. **2** a raised structure along the side of a railway track where passengers get on and off trains. **3** a raised structure standing in the sea from which oil or gas wells can be drilled. **4** the declared policy of a political party or group. **5** an opportunity for the expression or exchange of views. **6** a very thick sole on a shoe. **7** *Computing* a standard for the hardware of a computer system, which determines the kinds of software it can run.

plating *noun* **1** a coating of gold, silver, etc. **2** armour consisting of metal plates.

platinum • *noun* **1** a precious silvery-white metallic element occurring naturally in nickel and copper ores, unaffected by simple acids and fusible only at a very high temperature, used in making jewellery and laboratory apparatus. **2** a greyish-white or silvery colour like that of platinum. • *adjective* **1** (of an album or other recording) having attained the highest recognition for sales exceeding a specified high figure. **2** platinum-coloured. **3** designating a group of similar metallic elements often associated in ores, comprising platinum, iridium, palladium, osmium, rhodium, and ruthenium.

platinum blond • *adjective* silvery-blond. • *noun* a person with silvery-blond hair.

platitude *noun* a trite or commonplace remark, esp. one solemnly delivered: *it is a platitude of sports that a great player makes everyone around him better.* [Say PLATTA tude]

Platonic *adjective* **1** of or associated with the Greek philosopher Plato (*c.*429–*c.*347 BC) or his philosophy (*see* PLATONISM). **2** (**platonic**) (of love or friendship) not involving sex. **3** pertaining to the perfect or ideal form of something: *excessively admiring the British constitution as the Platonic ideal of government.* [Say pluh TONIC]

Platonism *noun* the philosophy of the Greek philosopher Plato (*c.*429–*c.*347 BC) or his followers, esp. his theory of the real existence of "ideas" or "forms", which he contrasts with particular things in the material world which can only approximate them. ▶ **Platonist** *noun* [Say PLAY tin ism]

platoon • *noun* **1** *Military* a tactical unit usu. divided into three sections of ten to twelve soldiers. **2** a group of persons acting together. **3** a pair or group of players on a team who alternate at the same position. **4** *Football* a group of offensive or defensive players sent on or off the field as a unit. • *verb* *Sport* alternate (a player) with or (of a player) interchange with another player at the same position on a team.

platter *noun* **1** a large usu. oval dish or plate for presenting or serving food. **2** a serving of food on such a plate, usu. consisting of several different items: *cheese platter.* PHRASES **on a platter** *informal* available with little trouble to the recipient.

platypus *noun* (*plural* **platypuses**) an Australian egg-laying aquatic mammal, with a duck-like bill, webbed feet, and grey fur. [Say PLATTA puss]

plaudit *noun* (usu. in *plural*) an emphatic expression of approval: *the restaurant has won plaudits for its natural foods and hearty fish chowder.* [Say PLOD it]

plausibility *noun* the believability or reasonableness of an argument, statement, etc. [Say plozza BILLA tee]

plausible *adjective* (of an argument, statement, etc.) seeming reasonable, believable, or probable: *it wasn't a very plausible explanation.* ▶ **plausibly** *adverb* [Say PLOZZA bull]

play • *verb* **1** engage in games or other activities for enjoyment rather than for a serious or practical purpose. **2** take part in (a sport or contest). **3** compete against. **4** take a specified position in a sports team. **5** represent (a character) in a play or film. **6** perform on or have the skill to perform on (a musical instrument). **7** produce (notes) from a musical instrument; perform (a piece of music). **8** move (a piece) or display (a playing card) in one's turn in a game. **9** make (a record player, radio, etc.) produce sounds. **10** be co-operative: *he needs financial backing, but the banks won't play.* **11** move lightly and quickly; flicker. • *noun* **1** games and other activities engaged in for enjoyment. **2** the progress of a sporting match. **3** a move or manoeuvre in a sport or game. **4** the state of being active, operative, or effective: *luck came into play.* **5** a dramatic work for the stage or to

be broadcast. **6** the ability or freedom of movement in a mechanism. **7** light and constantly changing movement. **8** the button on a VCR, compact disc player, etc., which causes it to play when pushed. PHRASES **at play** engaged in recreation. **in play** for amusement; not seriously. **make a play for** *informal* make a conspicuous attempt to acquire. **make play with** use ostentatiously. **play along 1** co-operate, comply. **2** pretend to agree or co-operate. **play around 1** behave playfully or irresponsibly. **2** (often foll. by *with*) have casual or extramarital sexual relations. **play back** play (sounds or video images recently recorded), esp. to monitor recording quality etc. **play both ends against the middle** keep one's options open by trying to keep favour with opposing sides. **play by ear 1** perform (music) without having seen a score of it. **2** (also **play it by ear**) proceed instinctively or step by step according to results and circumstances. **play one's cards right** (or **well**) make good use of opportunities; act shrewdly. **play down** minimize the importance of. **play fast and loose** act unreliably; ignore one's obligations. **play favourites** show favouritism. **play for time** seek to gain time by delaying. **play host to** act as host to. **play a** (or **one's**) **hunch** make an instinctive choice. **play into a person's hands** act so as unwittingly to give a person an advantage. **play it cool** *informal* **1** affect indifference. **2** be relaxed or unemotional. **play the man** *Sport* focus one's attention on the opposing player, not the puck, stick, ball, etc. **play the market** speculate in stocks etc. **play off** (usu. foll. by *against*) **1** oppose (one person against another), esp. for one's own advantage. **2** play an extra match to decide a draw or tie. **play on 1** continue to play. **2** take advantage of (a person's feelings etc.). **play out 1 a** use up. **b** tire. **2** finish, bring or come to an end or resolution. **3** perform to the end. **play it safe** avoid risks. **play to the gallery** *see* GALLERY. **play up** emphasize, make the most of. **play up to 1** flatter, esp. to win favour. **2** perform as expected considering (one's capability, reputation, etc.). **play with 1** consider (an idea etc.), but not seriously. **2** touch or fondle idly: *played with her scarf.* **play with fire** take foolish risks. **play with oneself** masturbate.

playa *noun* (*plural* **playas**) a flat area of silt or sand at the bottom of a desert basin, dry except after rain. [Say PLY uh]

playability *noun* the quality of a game, musical instrument, piece of music, etc. that makes it easy to be played.

playable *adjective* (of a game, musical instrument, piece of music, etc.) easily played.

play-act *verb* behave affectedly or insincerely. ▶ **play-acting** *noun* **play-actor** *noun*

playback *noun* a playing back of a recording.

playbook *noun* **1** *Sport* (esp. *Football*) a book containing descriptions of a team's strategies and plays. **2** a set of strategies employed by a company, political party, etc.

playboy *noun* **1** a sexually promiscuous man. **2** an irresponsible, pleasure-seeking, esp. wealthy man.

play-by-play *noun* the verbal description of a sports match etc. as it unfolds, esp. as part of a broadcast: *play-by-play announcer*.

playdough *noun* a soft, malleable, coloured dough-like substance used esp. by children for modelling.

playdown *noun* (usu. in *plural*) esp. *Cdn & Scot. Sport* a playoff match in a tournament etc.

player *noun* **1** a person taking part in a sport or game. **2** a person playing a musical instrument. **3** a person who plays a part on the stage; an actor. **4** a machine that plays audio or video recordings. **5** a person or company important in an industry, activity, etc.

player piano *noun* a piano fitted with an apparatus enabling it to play automatically.

playful *adjective* **1** fond of or inclined to play. **2** done in fun; humorous. ▶ **playfully** *adverb* **playfulness** *noun*

playground *noun* **1** an outdoor area for children to play on. **2** any place of recreation, e.g. a resort: *Nova Scotia, Canada's ocean playground*.

playgroup *noun* a group of esp. preschool children who play regularly together under supervision.

playhouse *noun* **1** a theatre. **2** a toy house for children to play in.

playing card *noun* each of a set of usu. 52 cards with an identical pattern on one side and different values represented by numbers and symbols on the other, used to play various games.

playing field *noun* a field used for outdoor team games.

playlet *noun* a short play or dramatic piece.

playlist *noun* a list of pieces to be played, esp. on a radio show.

playmaker *noun* a player in a team game who leads attacks or brings other players on the same side into a position to score. ▶ **playmaking** *noun & adjective*

playmate *noun* **1** a child's companion in play. **2** a lover.

playoff *noun* *Sport* **1** (often in *plural*) a tournament played to determine a champion among competitors having advanced from preliminary competition. **2** a game or match in such a tournament. **3** a match played to decide a draw or tie.

play on words *noun* a pun.

playpen *noun* a portable enclosure for young children to play in.

playroom *noun* a room set aside for playing in.

playschool *noun* a nursery school.

plaything *noun* **1** a toy or other thing to play with. **2** a person or thing treated as a toy.

playtime *noun* time for play or recreation.

playwright *noun* a person who writes plays.

playwriting *noun* the activity of writing plays.

plaza *noun* **1** a shopping centre, mall. **2** an open square in an urban area.

plea *noun* **1** an earnest appeal or entreaty. **2** *Law* a formal statement by or on behalf of a defendant., esp. in response to a charge. **3** an argument or excuse.

plea bargain *Law* • *noun* an arrangement between a prosecutor and a defendant in which the defendant pleads guilty to a lesser charge in the expectation of a lesser sentence: *they were hoping for a first-degree murder conviction, but the charge was downgraded to manslaughter through a plea bargain*. • *verb* (of a defendant) plead guilty to a lesser charge in the expectation of a lesser sentence.

plea bargaining *noun Law* the practice of making an arrangement with a defendant in which the defendant pleads guilty to a lesser charge in the expectation of a lighter sentence: *they will not challenge any procedures related to the legal process, such as bail or plea bargaining*.

plead *verb* (**pleads**; **pleaded** or esp. *US* **pled**; **pleading**) **1 a** make an earnest appeal. **b** say pleadingly. **2** *Law* address a law court as an advocate on behalf of a party. **3** maintain (a cause) esp. in a law court. **4** *Law* declare to be one's state as regards guilt in or responsibility for a crime: *plead guilty*. **5** offer as an excuse: *pleaded forgetfulness*. ▶ **pleader** *noun*

pleading • *noun* (usu. in *plural*) a formal statement of the cause of an action or defence. • *adjective* expressing an earnest entreaty. ▶ **pleadingly** *adverb*

pleasant *adjective* **1** pleasing to the mind, feelings, or senses. **2** polite and friendly. ▶**pleasantly** *adverb* **pleasantness** *noun*

pleasantry *noun* (*plural* **pleasantries**) a pleasant or amusing remark, esp. made in casual conversation.

please • *verb* (**pleases, pleased, pleasing**) **1** be agreeable (to); make (a person) glad; give pleasure (to). **2 a** be glad or willing to: *am pleased to help*. **b** (often foll. by *about, at, with*) derive pleasure or satisfaction (from). **3** be the wish of: *it did not please them to attend*. **4** think fit; have the will or desire: *take as many as you please*. • *interjection* **1** used as a polite way of making a request or giving an order: *please come in*. **2** *informal* used to express scorn: *"He said he was too busy to help." "Oh please!"* PHRASES **if you please 1** used in making a polite request: *come this way, if you please*. **2** used to express annoyance when reporting something, esp. something unexpected. **please God** may God let it happen; if it is pleasing to God: *please God, things will improve*. **please oneself** do as one likes. ▶**pleased** *adjective* **pleasing** *adjective* **pleasingly** *adverb*

pleasurable *adjective* causing pleasure; agreeable. ▶**pleasurably** *adverb*

pleasure • *noun* **1** a feeling of satisfaction or joy. **2** enjoyment. **3** a source of pleasure or gratification. **4** *formal* the will or desire. **5** sensual gratification or enjoyment: *a life of pleasure*. **6** (as an *adjective*) done or used for pleasure: *pleasure boat*. • *verb* (**pleasures, pleasured, pleasuring**) give (esp. sexual) pleasure to.

pleat • *noun* a fold or crease, esp. a flattened fold in cloth doubled upon itself. • *verb* (usu. as **pleated** *adjective*) make a pleat or pleats in. ▶**pleating** *noun*

plebeian • *noun* **1** a commoner, esp. in ancient Rome. **2** *derogatory* a member of the lower classes, esp. an uncultured one. • *adjective* **1** of the common people: *tried to hide her plebeian origins*. **2** uncultured; unrefined: *rude, plebeian tastes*. [Say pluh BEE in]

plebiscite *noun* **1** the direct vote of all electors on an important public question, e.g. a change in the constitution. **2** the public expression of a community's opinion, with or without binding force. [Say PLEBBA site]

plectrum *noun* (*plural* **plectrums** or **plectra**) a guitar pick. [Say PLECK trum]

pled esp. *US past of* PLEAD.

pledge • *noun* **1** a solemn promise or undertaking. **2** a thing given as security for the fulfillment of a contract, the payment of a debt, etc., and liable to forfeiture in the event of failure. **3** a thing put in pawn. **4 a** the promise of a donation to charity, a fundraising campaign, etc. **b** such a donation. **5** a thing given as a token of love, favour, or something to come. **6** a toast. **7** a solemn undertaking to abstain from alcohol: *sign the pledge*. **8** the state of being pledged: *goods lying in pledge*. • *verb* (**pledges, pledged, pledging**) **1 a** deposit as security. **b** pawn. **2** promise solemnly by the pledge of (one's honour, word, etc.). **3** bind by a solemn promise. **4** promise solemnly: *we pledged our support*. **5** commit oneself to donate (a sum).

Pleistocene *Geology* • *adjective* of or relating to the first epoch of the Quaternary period, lasting from about 2,000,000 to 10,000 years ago, marked by a succession of glacial and interglacial periods and the appearance of cattle, horses, and the woolly mammoth. The epoch also saw the appearance of *Homo erectus* and, by the end of the epoch, *Homo sapiens*. • *noun* this geological epoch or system. [Say PLICE tuh seen]

plenary • *adjective* **1** entire, unqualified: *the council has plenary powers to administer the agreement*. **2** (of an assembly, presentation, etc.) to be attended by all

members or participants. • *noun* (*plural* **plenaries**) a plenary session etc. [Say PLENNA ree]

plenitude *noun* *literary* **1** abundance: *the farm boasts a plenitude of animals and birds*. **2** fullness, completeness: *he beamed with the kind of inner plenitude most people get when they talk about their successful children*. [Say PLENNA tude]

plenteous *adjective* *literary* plentiful. ▶**plenteously** *adverb* **plenteousness** *noun* [Say PLENTY us]

plentiful *adjective* abundant. ▶**plentifully** *adverb*

plenty • *noun* a situation in which there is an ample supply of food, money, etc. • *pronoun* (often foll. by *of*) a great or sufficient quantity or number. • *adjective* *informal* existing in an ample quantity. • *adverb* **1** *informal* fully, entirely: *is plenty large enough*. **2** a lot: *plenty more*.

plethora *noun* (*plural* **plethoras**) an abundance: *a plethora of useful examples* ◊ *the neighbourhood is marred by a plethora of seedy bars and nightclubs*. [Say PLETH er uh]

pleurisy *noun* inflammation of the membranes lining the thorax and enveloping the lungs, marked by pain in the chest or side, fever, etc. [Say PLURA see]

Plexiglas *noun* *proprietary* a tough light transparent acrylic thermoplastic used instead of glass.

plexus *noun* (*plural* **plexus** or **plexuses**) **1** a network of nerves or blood vessels in an animal body: *solar plexus*. **2** a structure consisting of a bundle of minute closely interwoven and interconnected fibres or tubes.

pliability *noun* the quality of bending easily: *leather is treated until it attains the desired pliability*. [Say ply a BILLA tee]

pliable *adjective* **1** bending easily; supple: *pliable plastic tubing*. **2** flexible in disposition or character; compliant: *many companies won't negotiate rates, but some are pliable*. [Say PLY a bull]

pliant *adjective* **1** flexible; able to be bent or folded: *pliant canvas*. **2** (of a person etc.) readily influenced: *the pliant media*. [Say PLY int]

pliers *plural noun* pincers with gripping jaws usu. having parallel serrated surfaces, used for holding small objects, bending wire, etc.

plight *noun* a condition, state, or predicament, esp. an unfortunate one.

plink • *verb* **1** emit a short, sharp, metallic or ringing sound. **2** play a musical instrument in this manner. • *noun* the sound or action of plinking.

plinth *noun* **1** the lower square slab at the base of a column or pedestal. **2** a base supporting a vase or statue etc. **3** *Architecture* the projecting part of a wall immediately above the ground.

Pliocene *Geology* • *adjective* of or relating to the last epoch of the Tertiary period, lasting from about 5.1 to 2 million years ago, marked by falling temperatures, the extinction of many mammals, and the appearance of the first hominids, the ancestors of humans. • *noun* this geological epoch or system. [Say PLY uh seen]

PLO *abbreviation* Palestine Liberation Organization.

plod • *verb* (**plods, plodded, plodding**) **1** (often foll. by *along, on,* etc.) walk doggedly or laboriously; trudge. **2** work slowly and steadily, esp. without inspiration or creativity. • *noun* a slow heavy walk or pace: *they slow to a plod*. ▶**plodder** *noun* **plodding** *adjective* **ploddingly** *adverb*

plonk *informal* • *verb* set down hurriedly, clumsily, or firmly. • *noun* **1** a heavy thud, as of one hard object hitting another. **2** cheap or inferior wine.

plop • *noun* an abrupt, hollow sound as of a smooth object dropping into water without a splash. • *verb* (**plops, plopped, plopping**) **1** make a plop. **2** fall or drop with a plop. PHRASES **plop down** (also **plop oneself down**) sit down abruptly.

plot • *noun* **1 a** a defined and usu. small piece of

P

ground, esp. one used for a special purpose. **b** a grave or area of graves, esp. as belonging to a particular family. **2** a plan or an outline of the main events in a novel, film, etc. **3** a conspiracy or secret plan, esp. for unlawful purposes. • *verb* (**plots, plotted, plotting**) **1** plan or contrive secretly (a crime, conspiracy, etc.). **2** make a ground plan, map, or diagram of (an existing object or a place or thing to be laid out, constructed, etc.); draw to scale. **3** mark (a point or course etc.) on a chart or diagram. **4** devise the plot of (a novel, film, etc.). ▶ **plotless** *adjective*

plot line *noun* the main features of the plot of a play, novel, film, etc.

plotter *noun* **1** a person who plots something esp. unlawful. **2** an instrument for automatically plotting a graph etc. **3** a device capable of drawing with a pen under the control of a computer.

plough *noun & verb* = PLOW. [Say PLOW]

ploughman *noun* (*plural* **ploughmen**) (also **plowman**) a person who uses a plough. [Say PLOWMAN]

ploughshare *noun* (also **plowshare**) the large cutting blade of a plough. [Say PLOW share]

plover *noun* a plump-breasted shorebird with a pigeon-like bill. [Rhymes with *LOVER*]

plow • *noun* **1** (often **plough**) a farm implement with a cutting blade for cutting furrows in the soil and turning it up. **2** an implement resembling this and having a comparable function, esp. for deflecting material against which it moves: *snowplow.* • *verb* **1** (often **plough**) make furrows in and turn up (the earth) with a plow, esp. before sowing. **2** (often **plough**) **a** (foll. by *out, up, down,* etc.) turn or extract (roots, weeds, etc.) with a plow. **b** (foll. by *under*) bury in the soil by plowing. **3 a** remove (snow) from a surface with a plow. **b** clear (a surface) of snow with a plow. **4** furrow or scratch (a surface) with or as if with a plow. **5** produce (a furrow or line) in this way. **6** (foll. by *through*) advance laboriously, esp. through work, a book, etc. **7** (of a ship etc.) **a** (often foll. by *through*) cleave the surface of the water. **b** cleave (the surface of the water); cut (a course) through the water. **8** (foll. by *through, into*) (esp. of a car etc.) travel or be propelled clumsily or violently into or through (an obstacle). **9** (foll. by *into*) invest (money, usu. a large amount) in (a project etc.). PHRASES **plow back** reinvest (profits) in the business producing them. ▶ **plowed** *adjective*

plowing match *noun* a rural fair featuring plowing competitions, farm machinery demonstrations, new product displays, and entertainment.

ploy *noun informal* a stratagem; a cunning manoeuvre to gain an advantage.

pluck • *verb* **1** (often foll. by *out, off,* etc.) remove by picking or pulling out or away. **2 a** pull off (the feathers, hair, fur, etc.) from. **b** shape or thin (the eyebrows) by removing hairs. **3** pull at, esp. abruptly or with a jerk. **4** (foll. by *at*) tug or snatch at. **5** sound (the string of a musical instrument) by doing this with the finger or pick. **6** rescue (a person) from a difficult or unpleasant situation. **7** remove (a person) from obscurity. • *noun* **1** courage, spirit, boldness. **2** an act of plucking; a twitch. PHRASES **pluck up** summon up (one's courage, spirits, etc.). ▶ **plucker** *noun*

pluckily *adverb* in a spirited manner; bravely.

plucky *adjective* (**pluckier, pluckiest**) brave, spirited.

plug • *noun* **1** a piece of solid material fitting tightly into a hole, used to fill a gap or cavity, act as a wedge, stop a sink, etc. **2 a** a device of metal pins in an insulated casing fitting into holes in a socket for making an electrical connection. **b** *informal* an electric socket. **3** = SPARK PLUG 1. **4** *informal* a piece of (often free) publicity for an idea, product, etc. **5** a mass of

solidified lava filling the neck of a volcano. **6** a stick of tobacco, esp. for chewing. **7** *Fishing* a lure with one or more hooks attached. **8** a small area of scalp with strong hair growth grafted on to a balding area. **9** *informal* a baby's pacifier. • *verb* (**plugs, plugged, plugging**) **1** (often foll. by *up*) stop, fill, or obstruct (a hole etc.) with or as if with a plug etc. **2** *informal* seek to popularize (an idea, product, etc.) by repeated recommendation; give free publicity to. **3** *slang* shoot or hit (a person etc.). PHRASES **plug away** *informal* (often foll. by *at*) work steadily away (at); persevere doggedly. **plug a gap** remedy a deficiency. **plug in 1 a** connect electrically by inserting a plug in a socket. **b** be able to be connected by a plug. **2** *informal* incorporate, account for: *must plug in the new data.* **plug into** become connected with (a source of information, a trend, etc.).

plug and play *noun* a standard of compatibility for peripherals, software, etc. that makes installation simpler by allowing automatic configuration of the system.

plugged *adjective* **1** stopped up, closed, or filled with a plug. **2** (of a coin) having a portion removed and the space filled with base material.

plugged-in *adjective* **1** connected by means of a plug. **2** *informal* aware of what is happening, in fashion, etc.

plugger *noun* **1** a person who or thing which plugs something. **2** *informal* a person who works diligently, esp. a hockey player.

plug-in • *adjective* able to be connected by means of a plug. • *noun* **1** a plug-in device or unit. **2** *Cdn* an electrical outlet in a garage, near a parking space, etc. for plugging in the block heater of a car etc.

SPELL CHECK
plum, plumb

The spelling is **plumb** in "plumb line", "plumb the depths of", and "plumb crazy".

---

plum • *noun* **1 a** an oval fleshy fruit, usu. purple, reddish, or yellow when ripe, with sweet pulp and a flattish pointed stone. **b** (also **plum tree**) the deciduous tree of the rose family that bears this fruit. **2** a deep reddish-purple colour. **3** a highly desirable thing; the pick of a collection, esp. a choice appointment etc. • *adjective* **1** (also **plum-coloured**) of a reddish-purple colour. **2** valuable, coveted.

plumage *noun* a bird's feathers. [Say PLOO midge]

plumb[1] • *noun* a ball of lead or other heavy material, esp. one attached to the end of a line for finding the depth of water or determining the vertical. • *adverb* **1** exactly: *plumb in the centre.* **2** vertically, straight down. **3** *slang* completely: *plumb crazy.* • *adjective* **1** vertical, perpendicular. **2** downright, sheer: *plumb nonsense.* • *verb* **1 a** measure the depth of (water) with a plumb. **b** determine (a depth). **2 a** test (an upright surface) to determine the vertical. **b** make vertical. **3** explore or experience fully or in detail: *plumb the depths of fear* ◊ *plumbed the files for evidence.* PHRASES **out of** (or **off**) **plumb** not vertical. [Say PLUM]

plumb[2] *verb* **1** provide (a building or room etc.) with plumbing. **2** (often foll. by *in*) fit as part of a plumbing system. **3** work as a plumber. [Say PLUM]

plumb bob *noun* = PLUMB[1] 1.

plumber *noun* a person who fits and repairs the water pipes, water tanks, etc. in a building. [Say PLUMMER]

plumbing *noun* **1** the system of water pipes etc. in a building. **2** *jocular* **a** the excretory system. **b** the reproductive system. **3** the work of a plumber. [Say PLUMMING]

plumb line *noun* a line with a plumb attached.

plume • *noun* **1** a feather, esp. a large one used for

ornament. **2** a trail of vapour etc. issuing from a localized source and spreading out as the trail travels: *a plume of smoke*. **3** an ornament of feathers etc. attached to a headdress etc., usu. symbolizing dignity or rank. **4** a feather-like part or formation. • *verb* (**plumes, plumed, pluming**) **1** decorate or provide with a plume or plumes. **2** (of a trail of smoke, vapour, etc.) form a plume. **3** (of a bird) preen (itself or its feathers). ▶ **plumed** *adjective*

plummet • *verb* (**plummets, plummeted, plummeting**) drop, fall, or plunge rapidly. • *noun* a plumb or plumb line. [Say PLUM it]

plummy *adjective* (**plummier, plummiest**) **1 a** resembling a plum or plums, esp. in taste or colour. **b** consisting of or rich in plums. **2** *informal* (of a voice) deep, thick-sounding, esp. as supposedly characteristic of the British upper classes. **3** *informal* good, desirable.

plump¹ • *adjective* having a full rounded shape; filled out. • *verb* (often foll. by *up, out*) make or become plump.

plump² *verb* **1** drop, fall, or set down abruptly, esp. heavily or with a dull thud: *plumped down on the chair*. **2** decide in favour of (one of two or more possibilities): *offered a choice of drinks, he plumped for brandy*.

plumpish *adjective* somewhat plump.

plumpness *noun* the quality of being plump.

plum pudding *noun* a rich boiled or steamed suet pudding with raisins, currants, spices, etc., traditionally served at Christmas.

plum tomato *noun* a plum-shaped tomato, usu. used in cooking rather than eaten raw.

plunder • *verb* **1** rob (a place or person), esp. systematically or as in war. **2** steal or embezzle (goods). **3** steal from (another's writings etc.). • *noun* **1** the violent or dishonest acquisition of property. **2** property acquired by plundering. ▶ **plunderer** *noun*

plunge • *verb* (**plunges, plunged, plunging**) **1** (usu. foll. by *in, into*) **a** thrust forcefully or abruptly. **b** dive; propel oneself forcibly. **c** enter or cause to enter a certain condition or embark on a certain course abruptly or impetuously: *plunged into a lively discussion* ◊ *the room was plunged into darkness*. **2** immerse completely. **3 a** move suddenly and dramatically downward. **b** (foll. by *down, into*, etc.) move with a rush: *plunged down the stairs*. **c** diminish rapidly. **4** (of currency, prices, etc.) drop sharply in value or amount. **5** (of a horse) start violently forward. **6** (of a ship) pitch. • *noun* **1** a sudden violent movement or fall. **2** an act of jumping or diving. PHRASES **take the plunge** *informal* **1** take a decisive first step; commit oneself irrevocably to a course of action. **2** get married.

plunge pool *noun* **1** a deep basin excavated at the foot of a waterfall by the falling water. **2** a cold water pool, esp. forming part of the equipment of a sauna.

plunger *noun* **1** a part of a mechanism that works with a plunging or thrusting movement. **2** a rubber cup on a handle for clearing blocked pipes by a plunging and sucking action. [Say PLUN jer]

plunk • *noun* **1** the sound made by the sharply plucked string of a stringed instrument. **2** the sound of something dropping, esp. heavily. • *verb* **1** (often foll. by *down*) drop down heavily or abruptly. **2 a** cause (a string) to sound with a plunk; play (a note) with a plunk. **b** sound with a plunk. PHRASES **plunk down** spend (money).

pluperfect • *adjective* Grammar **1** (of a tense) denoting an action completed prior to some past point of time specified or implied, formed in English by *had* and the past participle, as: *he had gone by then*. **2** *informal* more than perfect; complete, thorough: *a state of pluperfect sobriety*. • *noun* the pluperfect tense. [Say ploo PERFECT]

plural • *adjective* **1 a** more than one in number. **b** (of a

society etc.) composed of or reflecting different ethnic groups or cultural traditions. **2** *Grammar* (of a word or form) denoting more than one, or (in languages with dual number) more than two. • *noun* Grammar **1** a plural word or form. **2** the plural number.

pluralism *noun* **1 a** a form of society in which the minorities maintain their independent cultural traditions. **b** the toleration or acceptance of a diversity of opinions, values, theories, etc. **2** a political system in which power is shared among a number of political parties. ▶ **pluralist** *noun* **pluralistic** *adjective*

plurality *noun* (*plural* **pluralities**) **1** the state or fact of being plural. **2 a** a large number or quantity: *a plurality of interests*. **b** the greater number or part; more than half of the whole. **3 a** the number of votes cast for a candidate who receives more than any other but does not receive an absolute majority. **b** the number by which this exceeds the number of votes cast for the candidate placing second. [Say plur ALA tee]

pluralize *verb* (**pluralizes, pluralized, pluralizing**) **1** make or become plural. **2** express in or form the plural. [Say PLURAL ize]

WRITING TIP
plus

Do not use **plus** as a conjunction, as in sentences like *We saw clowns, plus there were lions and elephants*. Such usage is not standard. An acceptable alternative might be *We saw clowns, and there were lions and elephants too*.

---

plus • *preposition* **1 a** *Math* made more by, increased by: *3 plus 4 equals 7*. Symbol: +. **b** with the addition of, inclusive of: *five plus me*. **2** (of temperature) above zero: *plus 2°C*. **3** *informal* with; having gained; newly possessing: *returned plus a new car*. • *adjective* **1** (after a number) at least; more than indicated: *fifteen plus*. **2 a** (after a grade etc.) rather better than: *B plus*. **b** *informal* of superior quality, excellent in its kind. **3** *Math* positive. **4** having a positive electrical charge. **5** (of a women's clothing size) designed for people larger and usu. heavier than most. • *noun* (*plural* **pluses**) **1** = PLUS SIGN. **2** *Math* an additional or positive quantity. **3** an advantage; a positive quality: *experience is a plus*. • *conjunction* *informal* disputed and furthermore: *they arrived late, plus they were hungry*. PHRASES **on the plus side** as an advantage. **plus or minus 1** give or take, add or subtract. **2** more or less, roughly.

Plus-15 *noun* (*plural* **Plus-15s**) *Cdn* (in Calgary) an enclosed overhead walkway between buildings.

plus ça change *interjection* used to express resigned acknowledgement of the fact that human nature and institutions remain fundamentally unchanged in spite of superficial alterations over time; the more things change, the more they stay the same: *this is why successful revolutions go on to produce regimes as authoritarian as the ones the revolutionaries rebelled against. Plus ça change ....* [Say ploo suh SHONZH]

plush • *noun* a type of cloth with a cut pile surface like, but longer and smoother than, velvet. • *adjective* **1** made of or resembling plush. **2** stylish, luxurious. ▶ **plushness** *noun* **plushy** *adjective* (**plushier, plushiest**)

plus-minus *noun* Hockey (also **plus/minus**) a statistic indicating a player's effectiveness on offence and defence, adjusted every time an even-strength goal is scored while the player is on the ice, with 1 added to the cumulative total if the player's team scores and 1 subtracted if the opponents score.

plus sign *noun* the symbol +, indicating addition or a positive value.

P

plutocracy *noun* (*plural* **plutocracies**)
1 a government by the wealthy: *the Patriotes demanded an end to the plutocracy that governed both Upper and Lower Canada at the time.* **b** a nation governed in this way: *America was a mongrel plutocracy of little account.* **2** a wealthy elite or ruling class: *the Yankees outbid the Braves and the Red Sox — all members of the baseball plutocracy — to get the talented pitcher.* [Say ploo TOCKRA see]

plutocrat *noun* often *derogatory* a wealthy and influential person: *a bloated Wall Street plutocrat.*
▶ **plutocratic** *adjective* [Say PLUTO crat]

plutonium *noun* a dense silvery radioactive metallic element used in some nuclear reactors and weapons. [Say ploo TONY um]

ply¹ *noun* (*plural* **plies**) **1** a thickness or layer of certain materials, esp. wood, cloth, or tissue paper: *three-ply.* **2** = PLYWOOD. **3** a strand or twist of rope, yarn, or thread. **4** a reinforcing layer of fabric in a tire.

ply² *verb* (**plies**, **plied**, **plying**) **1** work steadily at (one's business or trade). **2** (of a vehicle, esp. a ship) travel regularly (to and fro between two points). **3** (foll. by *with*) **a** supply (a person) continuously (with food, drink, etc.). **b** approach repeatedly (with questions, demands, etc.). **4** use or wield vigorously (a tool, weapon, etc.). **5** (of a taxi driver etc.) attend regularly for custom: *ply for trade.*

plywood *noun* a strong warp-resistant board consisting of two or more layers of wood glued and pressed together with the directions of the grains alternating.

PM *abbreviation* (*plural* **PMs**) **1** Prime Minister. **2** postmortem.

Pm *symbol* promethium.

p.m. *abbreviation* (also **P.M.**) after noon.

PMO *abbreviation* Cdn PRIME MINISTER'S OFFICE.

PMS *abbreviation* premenstrual syndrome.

PNE *abbreviation* Cdn Pacific National Exhibition.

pneumatic *adjective* **1** of or relating to air, wind, or gases. **2** containing or operated by compressed air.
▶ **pneumatically** *adverb* [Say new MAT ick]

pneumonia *noun* a bacterial or other infection causing inflammation of the lungs causing the air sacs to fill with pus and become solid. [Say new MOANY uh]

pneumonic plague *noun* a contagious bacterial disease characterized by fever and delirium and associated with infection of the lungs. [Say new MON ick]

PO *abbreviation* **1** Post Office. **2** postal order. **3** purchase order. **4** PETTY OFFICER.

Po *symbol* polonium.

poach *verb* (**poaches**, **poached**, **poaching**) **1** cook (a shelled egg, fish, etc.) in simmering water. **2 a** catch (game or fish) illegally. **b** (often foll. by *on*) trespass or encroach (on another's property, ideas, etc.). **c** take illicitly or unfairly (a person, thing, idea, etc.).

poacher *noun* **1** a person who illegally hunts or fishes on somebody else's property. **2** a special pan for poaching eggs.

pock • *noun* **1** a small pus-filled spot on the skin, esp. caused by chicken pox etc. **2 a** a scar or pit left by a pustule, pimple, etc. **b** any small disfiguring mark, hole, or pit. • *verb* mark with pocks or disfiguring spots: *rain pocks the surface of the water* ◊ *the buildings have been pocked by gunfire.* ▶ **pocked** *adjective*

pocket • *noun* **1** a small bag sewn into or on clothing, for carrying small articles. **2 a** a pouch-like compartment in a suitcase, car door, etc. **b** any small bag-like pouch, esp. made of pastry etc. **3** one's financial resources. **4 a** an isolated group or area contrasted with or differing from its surroundings: *a few pockets of resistance.* **b** a wide or deep hollow among hills or mountains; a distinct area of depth within a pond or lake etc. **5** a cavity in a rock or stratum. **6** a

pouch at the corner or on the side of a pool table into which balls are driven. **7 a** = AIR POCKET. **b** a local atmospheric condition. **8** (as an *adjective*) **a** of a suitable size and shape for carrying in a pocket. **b** smaller than the usual size. • *verb* (**pockets**, **pocketed**, **pocketing**) **1** put into one's pocket. **2** take possession of, esp. dishonestly. **3** *Billiards etc.* drive (a ball) into a pocket. PHRASES **dig into one's pockets** spend or provide money. **in pocket 1** having gained in a transaction. **2** (of money) available. **in a person's pocket 1** under a person's control. **2** close to or intimate with a person. **out of pocket** having lost in a transaction.

pocketbook *noun* **1** one's stock of cash or financial resources. **2** (**pocket book**) a small book.

pocketful *noun* (*plural* **pocketfuls**) an amount held in a pocket.

pocket knife *noun* (*plural* **pocket knives**) a knife with a folding blade.

pocket money *noun* **1** money for minor expenses. **2** esp. *Brit.* an allowance of money made to a child.

pocket protector *noun* **1** a plastic insert for a shirt pocket, designed to protect the garment from rips and ink stains caused by pens. **2** this viewed as typical of the attire of a computer nerd.

pocket-sized *adjective* (also **pocket-size**) **1** small enough to be carried in a pocket. **2** small-scale: *a pocket-sized revolution.*

pocket watch *noun* (*plural* **pocket watches**) a watch intended to be carried in the pocket of a waistcoat, jacket, etc.

pockmark *noun* = POCK *noun* 2. ▶ **pockmarked** *adjective*

PO'd *adjective* slang annoyed.

pod • *noun* **1** a long seed vessel esp. of a leguminous plant, e.g. a pea. **2 a** a streamlined compartment suspended under an aircraft for an engine, fuel tanks, equipment, etc. **b** a detachable compartment in a spacecraft. **3** any protruding, detachable, or more or less enclosed part of a tool, craft, vehicle, etc. **4** the cocoon of a silkworm. **5** a small group of marine animals, esp. whales. • *verb* (**pods**, **podded**, **podding**) **1** bear, form, or have a pod or pods. **2** remove (peas etc.) from pods.

podded *adjective* (of a plant) having pods or the kind of pods described: *flat-podded peas.*

podiatrist *noun* a doctor who treats foot disorders. [Say puh DIE a trist]

podiatry *noun* a medical specialty involving the care of the feet and treatment of foot disorders. [Say puh DIE a tree]

podium *noun* (*plural* **podiums** or **podia**) **1** a raised platform at the front of a hall or stage. **2** a platform from which a conductor conducts an orchestra etc. **3** a lectern. **4** a desk at an airport departure gate.

poem *noun* **1** a metrical composition of words expressing facts, thoughts, feelings, or imaginative description. **2** an esp. non-metrical composition of words having some esp. aesthetic quality or qualities in common with poetry. **3** something, other than a composition of words, with poetic qualities.

poesy *noun* archaic poetry. [Say POE uh zee]

poet *noun* **1** a writer of poems. **2** a person possessing high powers of imagination or expression etc.: *he is infinitely more than a teller of sentimental tales; he is a poet.*

poetess *noun* (*plural* **poetesses**) often *offensive* a female poet.

poetic *adjective* (also **poetical**) **1 a** of, like, or pertaining to poetry or poets. **b** written in verse. **2** elevated or sublime in expression. ▶ **poetically** *adverb*

poetic justice *noun* well-deserved unforeseen retribution or reward.

poetic licence *noun* a writer's or artist's transgression of established rules of language for effect.

poetics *noun* **1** the art of writing poetry. **2** the study of poetry and its techniques.

Poet Laureate *noun* a person honoured by a state as its pre-eminent or most representative poet.

poetry *noun* **1 a** the expression or embodiment of beautiful or elevated thought, imagination, or feeling, in language and a form adapted to stir the imagination and the emotions. **b** composition in verse, metrical language, or some equivalent patterned arrangement of language. **2** poems collectively. **3** a poetic or tenderly pleasing quality. **4** anything compared to poetry.

pogey *noun* (also **pogy**) *Cdn informal* **1** unemployment insurance benefits. **2** welfare benefits. [Say POE ghee]

pogo • *noun* (*plural* **pogos**) **1** (also **pogo stick**) a toy consisting of a spring-loaded stick with rests for the feet, for jumping about on. **2** (**Pogo**) *Cdn proprietary* (also **Pogo stick**) a hot dog covered in cornmeal batter, deep-fried or baked, and served on a stick. **3** a dance with movements suggestive of jumping on a toy pogo stick. • *verb* (**pogoes, pogoed, pogoing**) move or jump up and down as if on a toy pogo stick, esp as a form of dancing to certain types of rock music, esp. punk.

pogrom *noun* **1** an organized massacre of a particular ethnic group, esp. that of Jews in Russia or eastern Europe: *beginning in 1881, pogroms and anti Jewish laws in Russia left 100,000 Jews homeless.* **2** an organized, officially tolerated attack on any community or group: *concern that the massive screening will lead to pogroms of gays in the military.* [Say poe GROM]

poignancy *noun* evocative sadness; the quality of being moving: *the poignancy of parting and separation.* [Say POIN yin see]

poignant *adjective* deeply moving, esp. in a way that arouses sadness or regret: *the final scene is especially poignant.* ▶ **poignantly** *adverb* [Say POIN yint]

poinsettia *noun* a small shrub native to Mexico, with large esp. scarlet bracts surrounding small yellow flowers, popular as a houseplant at Christmas. [Say poin SETTA or poin SETTY uh]

SPELL CHECK
point, pointe

Ballerinas dance *on pointe* in *pointe shoes*.

---

point • *noun* **1** the tapered, sharp end of a tool, weapon, or other object. **2** a particular spot, place, or moment. **3** an item, detail, or idea in a discussion, text, etc. **4** (**the point**) the most significant or relevant factor or element. **5** advantage or purpose: *what's the point of it all?* **6** a positive feature or characteristic. **7** a unit of scoring or of measuring value, achievement, or extent. **8** a period or decimal point. **9** a very small dot or mark on a surface. **10** (in geometry) something having position but not spatial extent, magnitude, dimension, or direction. **11** each of thirty-two directions marked at equal distances around a compass. **12** a narrow piece of land jutting out into the sea, a lake, etc. **13** *Printing* a unit of measurement for type sizes and spacing. **14** each of a set of electrical contacts in the distributor of a motor vehicle. **15** a marking woven into a Hudson's Bay blanket to indicate weight. **16 a** *Hockey* either of two areas to the left and right of the net, just inside the blue line where it meets the boards: *a shot from the point.* **b** *Basketball* a frontcourt position, usu. manned by the guard who sets up the

team's defence. **17** *Lacrosse* **a** a player stationed a short distance in front of the goalkeeper and behind the cover-point. **b** this position. • *verb* **1** direct someone's attention in a particular direction by extending one's finger. **2** direct or aim (something). **3** face in or indicate a particular direction. **4** (often foll. by *to*) cite or function as evidence. **5** give a sharp, tapered point to. **6** fill in or repair the joints of (brickwork) with smoothly finished mortar or cement. PHRASES **at** (or **in**) **all points** in every part or respect. **at the point of** on the verge of; about to do (the action specified). **beside the point** irrelevant or irrelevantly. **case in point** an instance that is relevant or under consideration. **have a point** be correct or effective in one's contention. **make** (or **prove**) **a** (or **one's**) **point** establish a proposition; prove one's contention. **make a point of** (often foll. by verbal noun) **1** insist on; treat or regard as essential. **2** make a special project of (doing). **on** (or **upon**) **the point of** (foll. by verbal noun) about to do (the action specified). **point out** (often foll. by *that* + clause) indicate, show; draw attention to. **point up** emphasize; show as important. **score points off** get the better of in an argument etc. **take a person's point 1** concede that a person has made a valid contention. **2** understand the import or significance of what a person is saying. **to the point** relevant or relevantly. **to the point of** to the stage of; to such a degree as to justify. **up to a** (**certain**) **point** to some extent, but by no means completely.

point-and-click *noun* designating computer interfaces where the user selects an action by pointing the cursor to an icon on the screen and clicks with a mouse to initiate the action.

point-and-shoot • *adjective* designating a camera which does not require any manual adjustments to advance the film or take properly exposed and focused photographs. • *noun* a point-and-shoot camera.

point-blank • *adjective* **1** (of a shooting distance or shot) very close to the target. **2** (of a remark, question, etc.) straightforward, blunt, direct. • *adverb* **1** at very close range. **2** directly, bluntly, straightforwardly.

point blanket *noun* a type of Hudson's Bay blanket with distinctive markings or points, usu. in the form of short black lines, woven in to indicate weight.

point-counterpoint *noun* a situation in which opposing views etc. are heard in alternation: *journalism has become dominated by point-counterpoint, which allows just two points of view for every issue.*

pointe *noun* *Ballet* **1** the tip of the toe or toes, or the toe of a pointe shoe. **2** (also **pointe work**) dance performed on the tips of the toes. [Say POINT]

pointed *adjective* **1** sharpened or tapering to a point. **2** (of a remark etc.) **a** having particular force. **b** precisely aimed, exactly directed. **3** emphasized; made evident: *pointed ideas on education.* **4** having a point of a specified kind. ▶ **pointedly** *adverb*

pointer *noun* **1** a thing that points, e.g. the index hand of a gauge etc. **2** a rod for pointing to features on a map, chart, etc. **3** *informal* a hint, clue, or indication; a suggestion. **4** a dog of a breed that on scenting game stands rigid looking toward it. **5** *Cdn* a flat-bottomed rowboat, pointed at both ends and having a shallow draft, used by loggers. **6** a movable image on a computer screen, often in the shape of an arrow, used to activate a window, point to an icon, etc. **7** a thing having or earning so many points: *a three-pointer*.

pointe shoe *noun* a soft heelless shoe worn by female ballet dancers, with a stiffened toe allowing the dancer to dance on the tip of the toes.

point form *noun* an abbreviated form of writing, not using full sentences or developed paragraphs.

point guard *noun Basketball* a small fast guard with good ball-handling skills who directs the team's offence.

pointillism *noun* a neo-Impressionist painting technique using tiny dots of various pure colours, which become blended in the viewer's eye; it was developed by the French artist Georges Seurat (1859–91) with the aim of producing a greater degree of luminosity and brilliance of colour. ▶ **pointillist** *noun & adjective* [Say PWANT ill ism]

pointing *noun* **1** in senses of POINT verb. **2 a** cement or mortar filling the joints of brickwork. **b** facing produced by this. **c** the process of producing this.

pointless *adjective* **1** lacking force, purpose, or meaning. **2** without a sharp or tapering point; having a rounded or blunt end. **3** (in games) without a point scored. ▶ **pointlessly** *adverb* **pointlessness** *noun*

point man *noun* (*plural* **point men**) **1** the soldier at the head of a patrol. **2** a person who leads a new endeavour etc. **3** *Hockey* the player taking a position at the point during a power play.

point of departure *noun* **1** an initial assumption or the starting point of a thought, action, etc. **2** a time or place at which a journey begins.

point of no return *noun* a point in a journey or enterprise at which it becomes essential or more practical to continue to the end.

point of order *noun* a query in a debate etc. as to whether correct procedure is being followed.

point of reference *noun* a basis or standard for evaluation, assessment, or comparison.

point-of-sale *noun* (also **point-of-purchase**) designating, pertaining to, for use at, or associated with the place at which goods are retailed.

point of view *noun* **1** a position from which a thing is viewed. **2** a particular way of considering a matter. **3** (in fiction etc.) the narrator's position relative to the story being told: *first-person point of view*.

point source *noun* a source of light or pollution etc. of negligible dimensions: *this wasn't a point source: it was spread out over a huge area* ◊ *point source pollution*.

point spread *noun* the number of points constituting the margin by which a stronger team is expected to defeat a weaker one, for betting purposes.

point-to-point *adjective* (of a dedicated communication link etc.) joining only two nodes in a network.

pointy *adjective* having a noticeably sharp end.

poise • *noun* **1** a calm and confident manner with control of one's feelings or behaviour: *his performance was full of maturity and poise* ◊ *she seemed embarrassed for a moment but quickly recovered her poise*. **2** the ability to move or stand in a graceful way with good control of one's body: *poise and good deportment can be cultivated*. • *verb* (**poises**, **poised**, **poising**) (usu. in *passive*) **1** balance; hold suspended or supported. **2** carry (one's head etc.) in a specified way. **3** hover in the air etc.

poised *adjective* **1** composed, self-assured. **2** ready for action: *the economy is poised for a recovery* ◊ *the Leafs are poised to win the Stanley Cup*.

poison • *noun* **1** a substance that when absorbed by a living organism causes death or injury, esp. quickly. **2** a harmful influence or principle etc. • *verb* **1** administer poison to. **2** kill or injure or infect (a person or animal) with poison. **3** infect (air, water, etc.) with poison. **4** (esp. as **poisoned** *adjective*) treat (a weapon) with poison. **5** corrupt or pervert (a person or mind). **6** spoil or destroy (a person's pleasure etc.). **7** render (land etc.) unusable, e.g. by the accumulation of chemicals or toxins etc. **PHRASES** **what's your poison?** *informal* what can I get you to drink? ▶ **poisoner** *noun* **poisoning** *noun*

poison ivy *noun* a North American climbing plant that secretes an irritant oil from its leaves.

poison oak *noun* either of two North American shrubs related to poison ivy and having similar properties.

poisonous *adjective* **1** causing death or illness if swallowed or absorbed into the body; toxic: *poisonous chemicals*. **2** (of animals) producing a poison that can cause death or illness if the animal bites; venomous. **3** extremely unpleasant or unfriendly: *a poisonous atmosphere in the staff room*. ▶ **poisonously** *adverb*

poison pill *noun* **1** a pill containing esp. fast-acting poison. **2** any of various ploys used by a company threatened with an unwelcome takeover bid to make itself unattractive to the bidder.

> **SPELL CHECK**
> **polka, polka dot**
>
> Warning: both the dance called the **polka** and **polka dots** are spelled with an *l*.

poke • *verb* (**pokes**, **poked**, **poking**) **1** (foll. by *in*, *up*, *down*, etc.) **a** a thrust or push with the hand, point of a stick, etc. **b** be thrust forward. **2** (foll. by *at* etc.) make thrusts with a stick etc. **3 a** thrust the end of a finger etc. against. **b** *informal* punch, hit. **4** (foll. by *in*) produce (a hole etc. in a thing) by poking. **5** thrust forward, esp. obtrusively: *poked her head out of the window*. **6** (often foll. by *along*) move or go slowly or in an aimless manner. **7** (foll. by *around*, *about*) pry; search casually. • *noun* **1 a** an act of poking someone or something. **b** a thrust or nudge. **2** *hist.* a small miners' bag for nuggets etc. **3** = POKEWEED. **PHRASES** **poke fun at** ridicule, tease.

poke check *noun Hockey* a defensive play in which a player holds his or her stick low along the ice and pokes the puck out of the puck carrier's control. ▶ **poke-check** *verb* **poke-checking** *noun*

poker[1] *noun* a stiff metal rod for stirring an open fire.

poker[2] *noun* a card game in which bluff is used as players bet on the value of their hands.

poker face *noun* a facial expression that hides one's true feelings. ▶ **poker-faced** *adjective*

poker run *noun* (also **poker derby** *plural* **poker derbies**) *Cdn* a contest in which participants race to a series of points (usu. over a large area) collecting one playing card at each, the winner being determined by a combination of time taken and the poker hand collected.

pokeweed *noun* a North American plant with red stems, spikes of cream flowers, and purple berries.

pokey *noun* (*plural* **pokeys**) *slang* prison.

poky *adjective* (**pokier**, **pokiest**) **1** (of a room etc.) small and cramped. **2** annoyingly slow.

pol *noun informal* a politician.

polar *adjective* **1 a** of or near a pole of the earth or a celestial body, or of the celestial sphere. **b** (of a species or variety) living in the north polar region. **2** having magnetic polarity. **3 a** (of a molecule) having a positive charge at one end and a negative charge at the other. **b** (of a compound) having electric charges. **4** *Math* of or relating to a pole. **5** directly opposite in character.

polar bear *noun* a very large white Arctic bear, which lives mainly on pack ice.

polar bear swim *noun* (also **polar bear dip**) an organized swim in cold or partially ice-covered water, esp. on a holiday such as New Year's Day.

polar cap *noun* a region of ice or other frozen matter surrounding a pole of a planet.

polar climate *noun* the prevailing weather conditions of the Arctic and Antarctic regions, characterized by low levels of precipitation, average monthly

temperatures not exceeding 10°C, and very little sunlight in winter.

Polar Fleece *noun* *proprietary* a thick fleece fabric.

polar ice cap *noun* = POLAR CAP.

Polaris *noun* a type of submarine-launched ballistic missile. [Say po LAIR iss]

polarity *noun* (*plural* **polarities**) **1** the tendency of a magnet to point with its extremities to the magnetic poles of the earth. **2** the condition of having two poles with contrary qualities. **3** the state of having two opposite tendencies, opinions, etc.: *the polarity between male and female* ◊ *the cold war's neat polarities could not be carried on*. **4** the electrical condition of a body (positive or negative). [Say puh LAIR uh tee]

polarization *noun* **1** an act of restricting the vibrations of light to one direction. **2** the state of division into two groups representing extremes of opinion, wealth, etc.: *the polarization of society into rich and poor*. [Say poe luh rise AY sh'n]

polarize *verb* (**polarizes**, **polarized**, **polarizing**) **1** restrict the vibrations of (a wave of light) to one direction. **2** give magnetic or electric polarity to (a substance or body). **3** divide into two groups of opposing opinion etc.: *the cultural sphere has polarized into two competing ideological positions* ◊ *the war in Vietnam polarized political opinion*. ▶ **polarizer** *noun*

Polaroid *noun* *proprietary* **1** a type of camera with internal processing that produces a finished print rapidly after each exposure. **2** a photograph taken with such a camera.

polder *noun* a piece of low-lying land reclaimed from the sea or a river and protected by dikes, esp. in the Netherlands. [Say POLE dur]

Pole *noun* **1** a native or national of Poland. **2** a person of Polish descent.

SPELL CHECK
pole, poll ABC☑

A vote or survey is a **poll**. A tax on every adult is a **poll tax**.

---

pole[1] • *noun* **1** a long slender rounded piece of wood, metal, etc., esp. with the end placed in the ground as a support etc. **2** a long slender flexible rod used by a competitor in pole vaulting. **3** = FISHING ROD. • *verb* (**poles**, **poled**, **poling**) use poles, esp. to propel a boat or oneself on skis.

pole[2] *noun* **1 a** (also **north pole, south pole**) each of the two points in the celestial sphere about which the stars appear to revolve. **b** (also **North Pole, South Pole**) each of the extremities of the axis of rotation of the earth or another body. **c** *see* MAGNETIC POLE. **2** each of the two opposite points on the surface of a magnet at which magnetic forces are strongest. **3** each of two terminals (positive and negative) of an electric cell or battery etc. **4** each of two opposed principles or ideas: *Miriam and Rebecca represent two poles in the argument*. **5** *Math* each of two points in which the axis of a circle cuts the surface of a sphere. PHRASES **be poles apart** differ greatly, esp. in nature or opinion.

poleaxe • *noun* a battle-axe. • *verb* (**poleaxes**, **poleaxed**, **poleaxing**) **1** hit or kill with or as if with a poleaxe. **2** *informal* affect (a person) very greatly with surprise, distress, etc.: *I was poleaxed by the news that she had cheated on the exams*.

polecat *noun* a skunk. [Say POLE cat]

polemic • *noun* **1** a controversial discussion. **2** a verbal or written attack, esp. on a political opponent. **3** (in *plural*; also treated as *singular*) the art of controversial discussion, esp. in theology. • *adjective* (also **polemical**) of, relating to, or involving strongly

critical or controversial writing or speech: *a polemic essay*. ▶ **polemicist** *noun* [Say puh LEMMICK, puh LEMMA sist]

polenta *noun* cornmeal boiled in water and often baked or fried. [Say puh LENTA]

pole position *noun* the most favourable position at the start of a motor race.

pole vault *noun* the sport of vaulting over a high bar with the aid of a long flexible pole. ▶ **pole-vault** *verb*
pole vaulter *noun*

police • *noun* (treated as *plural*) **1** (usu. as **the police**) a force responsible for enforcing the law, maintaining public order, etc. **2** a group, often self-appointed, which criticizes or attempts to stop practices that it considers unacceptable: *fashion police*. • *verb* (**polices**, **policed**, **policing**) **1** control (a country or area) by means of police. **2** provide with police. **3** keep order in; control.

police constable *noun* = CONSTABLE 1.

police force *noun* the body of police of a city etc.

policeman *noun* (*plural* **policemen**) a member of a police force.

police officer *noun* a policeman or policewoman.

police state *noun* a totalitarian state or country controlled by political police supervising the citizens' activities.

police station *noun* the office of the police in a certain district or community.

policewoman *noun* (*plural* **policewomen**) a female member of a police force.

policy *noun* (*plural* **policies**) **1** a course or principle of action adopted or proposed by a government, party, individual, etc. **2** a contract of insurance.

policyholder *noun* a person or body holding an insurance policy.

policy wonk *noun* = WONK 2.

polio *noun* = POLIOMYELITIS. [Say POE lee oh]

poliomyelitis *noun* an infectious viral disease that affects the central nervous system and which can cause permanent paralysis. [Say poe lee oh my uh LITE iss]

polis *noun* (*plural* **poleis**) a city state in ancient Greece. [Say POE liss for the singular, POE leece for the plural]

poli-sci *noun* *informal* political science: *poli-sci class*. [Say polly SIGH]

Polish • *adjective* **1** of or relating to Poland. **2** of the Poles or their Slavic language. • *noun* this language.

polish • *verb* (**polishes**, **polished**, **polishing**) **1** make or become smooth or glossy by rubbing. **2** (esp. as **polished** *adjective*) refine or improve; add finishing touches to. • *noun* (*plural* **polishes**) **1** a substance used for polishing. **2** smoothness or glossiness produced by friction. **3** an act of rubbing something to give it a shiny surface: *I could give the silver a polish*. **4** refinement or elegance of manner, conduct, etc. PHRASES **polish off 1** finish (esp. food) quickly. **2** get rid of (an enemy, etc.). **polish up** revise or improve (a skill etc.). ▶ **polisher** *noun*

Polish sausage *noun* = KIELBASA.

politburo *noun* (*plural* **politburos**) the principal policy-making committee of a Communist party. [Say PAUL it byoor oh]

polite *adjective* (**politer**, **politest**) **1** having good manners; courteous. **2** of or relating to people who regard themselves as more cultured and refined than others: *not used in polite society*. ▶ **politely** *adverb*
politeness *noun*

politic • *adjective* **1** seeming sensible in the circumstances: *I did not think it politic to express my reservations*. **2** political: *body politic*. • *verb* (**politics,**

P

politicked, politicking) engage in politics. [Say PAUL uh tick]

political *adjective* **1 a** of or concerning the state or its government, or public affairs generally. **b** of, relating to, or engaged in politics. **c** belonging to or forming part of a civil administration. **2** having an organized form of society or government. **3** taking or belonging to a side in politics. **4** relating to or affecting interests of status or authority rather than matters of principle.

political asylum *noun* protection given by a country to a political refugee from another country.

political correctness *noun* the avoidance of forms of expression or action that exclude, marginalize, or insult certain racial or cultural groups.

politically *adverb* in a way related to politics: *a politically sensitive issue* ◊ *politically motivated crimes* ◊ *it makes sense politically as well as economically*.

politically correct *adjective* exhibiting political correctness.

politically incorrect *adjective* failing to exhibit political correctness.

political science *noun* the study of the state and systems of government. ▶ **political scientist** *noun*

political will *noun* support by the public for policies.

politician *noun* **1** a person engaged in or concerned with politics. **2** a person skilled in politics.

politicization *noun* the act or an instance of giving a political character to: *the politicization of education*. [Say puh litta size AY sh'n]

politicize *verb* (**politicizes, politicized, politicizing**) **1** cause to become political in character: *wage bargaining in the public sector became more politicized*. **2** make politically aware: *we successfully politicized an entire generation of women*. [Say puh LITTA size]

politicking *noun* political activity, especially to win support. [Say PAULA ticking]

politico *noun* (*plural* **politicos**) *informal* a politician or political enthusiast. [Say puh LITTA co]

politics *plural noun* **1** (treated as *singular* or *plural*) **a** the art and science of government. **b** public life and affairs as involving authority and government. **2** (usu. treated as *plural*) **a** a particular set of ideas, principles, or commitments in politics: *what are their politics?* **b** activities concerned with the acquisition or exercise of authority or power: *office politics*. **c** an organizational process or principle affecting authority, status, etc.: *the politics of the decision*.

polity *noun* (*plural* **polities**) **1** a form or process of civil government or constitution. **2** an organized society; a state as a political entity: *this legislation serves not only the needs of the polity but also the needs of the individual*. [Say PAULA tee]

polka • *noun* **1** a lively dance for couples, performed to music with two beats to the bar. **2** the music for this. • *verb* dance the polka. [Say POLE kuh or POE kuh]

polka dot *noun* a round dot as one of many forming a regular pattern on fabric etc. ▶ **polka-dot** *adjective* **polka-dotted** *adjective* [Say POKE a dot]

SPELL CHECK
poll, pole
[ABC ✔]

The spelling is **pole** for a post and in "North Pole" and "pole position". A person from Poland is a **Pole**.

---

poll • *noun* **1** an assessment of public opinion by questioning a representative sample. **2 a** the process of voting at an election. **b** (usu. in *plural*) a place where votes are cast. **3 a** a human head. **b** the part of this on which hair grows. **4** a hornless animal, esp. one of a breed of hornless cattle. **5** the part of an animal's (esp. a horse's) head between the ears. • *verb* **1** take the vote or votes of. **2** record the opinion of (a person or group) in an opinion poll. **3** give one's vote. **4** cut off the top of (a tree or plant), esp. make a pollard of. **5** (esp. as **polled** *adjective*) cut the horns off (cattle). **6** *Computing* check the status of (a computer system) at intervals. [PHRASES] **go to the polls** have an election: *the province goes to the polls next week*.

pollack *noun* (*plural* **pollack**) = POLLOCK. [Say PAUL uck]

pollard • *noun* **1** an animal that has lost its horns; an ox, sheep, or goat of a hornless breed. **2** a tree with branches cut off to encourage the growth of new young branches. • *verb* make (a tree) a pollard. [Say PAUL erd]

poll captain *noun* *Cdn* a person who directs an election campaign for a candidate in a given area.

pollen *noun* the fine dust-like grains discharged from the male part of a flower containing the gamete that fertilizes the female ovule.

pollinate *verb* (**pollinates, pollinated, pollinating**) fertilize (a plant) with pollen. ▶ **pollinator** *noun*

pollination *noun* the act or an instance of fertilizing a plant with pollen.

polling *noun* the registering or casting of votes.

polling station *noun* (also **polling place**) a building where voting takes place during an election.

polliwog *noun* = POLLYWOG. [Say POLLY wog]

pollock *noun* (*plural* **pollock**) an important North Atlantic food fish of the cod family. [Say PAUL uck]

pollster *noun* a person who conducts opinion polls. [Say POLE stir]

poll tax *noun* a tax levied on every adult.

pollutant *noun* a substance that pollutes air, water, etc.: *testing for pollutants in the lake water*. [Say POLLUTE int]

pollute *verb* (**pollutes, polluted, polluting**) **1** contaminate (water, air, a place, etc.) with poisonous or harmful substances: *the explosion polluted the town with dioxin*. **2** corrupt: *a society polluted by racism*.

polluted *adjective* **1** made unclean; contaminated. **2** *slang* drunk.

polluter *noun* a person, country, company, etc. that pollutes.

pollution *noun* the presence in the environment, or the introduction into it, of substances, features, etc. that have harmful or unpleasant effects.

Pollyanna *noun* (*plural* **Pollyannas**) a cheerful optimist; an excessively cheerful person. ▶ **Pollyannaish** *adjective* [Say polly ANNA]

pollywog *noun* a tadpole.

polo *noun* **1** a game in which players riding on horses try to hit a ball into a goal using long wooden mallets. **2** (also **polo shirt**) a short-sleeved casual shirt with a collar and a short buttoned placket at the neckline.

polonium *noun* a rare radioactive metallic element, occurring naturally in uranium ores. [Say puh LOANY um]

poltergeist *noun* a noisy mischievous ghost, esp. one manifesting itself by physical damage. [Say POLE tur geist (GEIST rhymes with *PRICED*)]

poly *noun* (*plural* **polys**) **1** polyester. **2** polyethylene. [Say POLLY]

polyamide *noun* any of a class of polymers produced from the interaction of an amino group of one molecule and a carboxylic acid group of another, and which includes many synthetic fibres such as nylon. [Say polly AM ide]

polybag • *noun* a bag made of polyethylene, used esp. for packaging etc. • *verb* (**polybags, polybagged, polybagging**) place or package (something) in a polybag. [Say POLLY bag]

polycarbonate *noun* any of a class of polymers in

which the units are linked through a carbonate group, mainly used in moulding. [Say polly CARBONATE]

polychlorinated biphenyl *noun see* PCB. [Say polly CHLORINATED]

polychrome • *adjective* painted or decorated in many colours. • *noun* **1** a work of art in several colours, esp. a statue. **2** varied colouring: *this carving has traces of polychrome and some undecipherable writing on it.* ▶ **polychromed** *adjective* [Say POLLY chrome]

polycotton *noun* fabric made from a mixture of cotton and polyester fibre. [Say POLLY cotton]

polycyclic *adjective* Chemistry having more than one ring of atoms in the molecule. [Say polly SIKE lick]

polyester *noun* **1** any of a group of condensation polymers used to form synthetic fibres or to make resins. **2** a fabric made from such a polymer.

polyethylene *noun* a tough light thermoplastic polymer of ethylene, used for packaging and insulating. [Say polly ETH a leen]

polygamous *adjective* **1** having more than one spouse at the same time. **2** having more than one mate. **3** bearing some flowers with stamens only, some with pistils only, some with both, on the same or different plants. ▶ **polygamy** *noun* [Say puh LIGGA muss, puh LIGGA me]

polyglot • *adjective* **1** of many languages. **2** (of a person) speaking or writing several languages. **3** (of a book, esp. the Bible) with the text translated into several languages. • *noun* **1** a polyglot person. **2** a polyglot book, esp. a Bible. [Say POLLY glot]

polygon *noun* a plane figure with usu. four or more sides and angles. ▶ **polygonal** *adjective* [Say POLLY gon, puh LIGGA nul]

polygraph *noun* **1** a machine designed to detect and record changes in physiological characteristics (e.g. rates of pulse and breathing), used esp. as a lie detector. **2** a test using a polygraph. [Say POLLY graph]

polyhedral *adjective* (of a solid figure) having many (usu. more than six) faces. [Say polly HEED rul]

polyhedron *noun* (plural **polyhedrons** or **polyhedra**) a solid figure with many (usu. more than six) faces. [Say polly HEE drun]

polymath *noun* a person of much or varied learning; a great scholar. ▶ **polymathic** *adjective* [Say POLLY math]

polymer *noun* a compound composed of one or more large molecules formed from repeated units of smaller molecules. [Say PAULA mer]

polymerase *noun* any enzyme which catalyzes the formation of a polymer, esp. of DNA or RNA. [Say PAULA mer aze]

polymerase chain reaction *noun see* PCR.

polymeric *adjective* having to do with or consisting of a polymer or polymers. [Say paula MAIR ick]

polymerization *noun* an act of polymerizing. [Say paula mer ize AY sh'n]

polymerize *verb* (**polymerizes**, **polymerized**, **polymerizing**) cause molecules to combine to form a polymer. [Say PAULA mer ize]

polymorphic *adjective* having or passing through many stages of development. [Say polly MORF ick]

polymorphism *noun* Biology the existence of various different forms in the successive stages of the development of an organism. ▶ **polymorphous** *adjective* [Say polly MORF ism]

Polynesian • *adjective* of or relating to Polynesia, a region of the central Pacific, containing the easternmost of the three great groups of Pacific Islands, including Hawaii, Samoa, and French Polynesia. • *noun* **1 a** a native of Polynesia. **b** a person of Polynesian descent. **2** the Polynesian languages as a group,

including Maori, Hawaiian, and Samoan. [Say paula NEE zh'n]

polynomial Math • *noun* an expression of more than two algebraic terms, esp. the sum of several terms that contain different powers of the same variable(s). • *adjective* of or being a polynomial. [Say polly NO me ul]

polynya *noun* (plural **polynyas**) a stretch of open water surrounded by ice, esp. in the Arctic seas. [Say puh LEEN yuh]

polyp *noun* **1** Zoology a small and very simple sea creature with a body shaped like a tube. **2** Medical a small usu. benign growth protruding from a mucous membrane. [Say PAUL ip]

polypeptide *noun* a peptide formed by the combination of about ten or more amino acids. [Say polly PEP tide]

polyphonic *adjective* (of vocal music etc.) in two or more relatively independent parts. [Say polly FON ick]

polyphony *noun* the simultaneous combination of a number of musical parts, each forming an individual melody and harmonizing with the others. [Say puh LIFFA nee]

polypropylene *noun* any of various propylene polymers including thermoplastic materials used for films, fibres, or moulding materials. [Say polly PRO puh leen]

polyrhythm *noun* Music the use of two or more different rhythms simultaneously. ▶ **polyrhythmic** *adjective* [Say POLLY rhythm]

polysaccharide *noun* any of a group of carbohydrates, including starch, cellulose, and glycogen, whose molecules consist of long chains of monosaccharides. [Say polly SACKA ride]

polystyrene *noun* a thermoplastic polymer of styrene, usu. hard or expanded with a gas to produce a lightweight rigid substance, used for insulation and in packaging. [Say polly STYE reen]

polytechnic *noun* an institution of higher education offering courses in many (esp. vocational) subjects at degree level or below. [Say polly TECK nick]

polytheism *noun* the belief in or worship of more than one god. ▶ **polytheist** *noun* **polytheistic** *adjective* [Say polly THEE ism, polly thee ISS tick (with TH as in THICK)]

polyunsaturated *adjective* (of a compound, esp. a fat or oil molecule) containing several double or triple bonds and thus not encouraging the formation of cholesterol in the blood. [Say polly un SATURATED]

polyurethane *noun* any polymer containing the urethane group, used in adhesives, paints, plastics, rubbers, foams, etc. [Say polly YURRA thane]

polyvinyl chloride *noun* a tough transparent solid polymer of vinyl chloride, easily coloured and used for a wide variety of products including pipes, flooring, etc. Abbreviation: **PVC**. [Say polly VINYL]

pomegranate *noun* **1** an orange-sized fruit with a tough golden-orange outer skin containing many seeds in a red pulp. **2** the tree bearing this fruit, native to North Africa and western Asia. [Say POMMA gran it]

pommel *noun* **1** a knob, esp. at the end of a sword hilt. **2** the upward projecting front part of a saddle. [Say PUM'll]

pomp *noun* a splendid display; splendour.

pompadour *noun* **1** a woman's hairstyle with the hair in a high turned-back roll around the face. **2** a man's hairstyle with the hair combed high off the forehead. [Say POMPA door]

pompano *noun* (plural **pompanos**) **1** a tropical food and game fish that has a flat narrow body with a row of large spiky scales along each side. **2** any of various similar fishes, e.g. the Pacific pompano, which lives along the west coast of North America. [Say POMPA no]

P

pompom *noun* (also **pompon**) **1 a** a ball or bobble made of tufts of yarn etc. used for decoration. **b** a bundle of strips of fabric, paper, etc. waved or shaken by cheerleaders or spectators at a sporting event. **2** the round tuft on a soldier's cap etc. **3** a dahlia or chrysanthemum with small tightly-clustered petals.

pomposity *noun* pretentiousness; the quality of being exaggeratedly self-important: *the prince's manner was informal, without a trace of pomposity.* [Say pom POSSA tee]

pompous *adjective* **1** self-important, affectedly grand or solemn. **2** (of language) pretentious; unduly grand in style. ▶ **pompously** *adverb* [Say POM pus]

poncho *noun* (*plural* **ponchos**) **1** a South American cloak made of a blanket-like piece of cloth with a slit in the middle for the head. **2** a garment in this style, esp. a raincoat.

pond • *noun* **1** a fairly small body of still water formed naturally or by hollowing etc. **2** (**the pond**) *jocular* the Atlantic Ocean. • *verb* (of water) form a pond.

ponder *verb* **1** weigh mentally; think over; consider. **2** (usu. foll. by *over*) think; muse.

ponderosa *noun* (*plural* **ponderosas**) a tall, slender pine tree of western North America. [Say ponder OH suh]

ponderous *adjective* **1** heavy; unwieldy: *he lifted and carried the ponderous stones as if they were so many bales of hay.* **2** laborious: *she watched the cow's ponderous progress.* **3** (of style etc.) dull; tedious: *it's a ponderous, dull film.* ▶ **ponderously** *adverb*

pond scum *noun* **1** a mass of scummy freshwater algae floating in stagnant water. **2** *slang derogatory* a worthless or contemptible person or thing.

pondweed *noun* an aquatic plant that grows in still or running water and sometimes has floating leaves.

pontiff *noun* the Pope. ▶ **pontifical** *adjective* [Say PON tiff, pon TIFFA cull]

pontificate • *verb* (**pontificates**, **pontificated**, **pontificating**) tell people what's right in a way that is pompous and arrogant: *economists who pontificate on human behaviour.* • *noun* **1** the office of bishop or pope. **2** the period of this. [Say pon TIFFA kate for the verb, pon TIFFA kit for the noun]

pontoon *noun* **1** a flat-bottomed boat. **2 a** each of several boats, hollow metal cylinders, etc., used to support a temporary bridge. **b** a hollow tube or other float for keeping a boat, float plane, etc., buoyant. [Say pon TOON]

pony *noun* (*plural* **ponies**) **1** a horse of any small breed. **2** a small drinking glass. **3** (in *plural*) *slang* a racehorses. **b** (**the ponies**) horse racing. PHRASES **pony up** *informal* hand over (money etc.) esp. in settlement of an account.

ponytail *noun* a person's hair drawn back, tied, and hanging down like a pony's tail. ▶ **ponytailed** *adjective*

Ponzi *adjective* designating a form of fraud in which belief in the success of a non-existent enterprise is fostered by payment of quick returns to the first investors from money invested by others. [Say PONZY]

poo esp. *Cdn & Brit. informal* • *noun* excrement. • *verb* (**poos**, **pooed**, **pooing**) **1** defecate. **2** defecate in (one's pants etc.). • *interjection* var of POOH.

poobah *noun* = POOH-BAH.

pooch *noun* (*plural* **pooches**) *informal* a dog.

poodle *noun* a breed of dog with a coat of usu. clipped tight curls.

poof *interjection* announcing something sudden, esp. a disappearance or appearance.

pooh • *interjection* expressing impatience or contempt. • *noun* = POO.

pooh-bah *noun* a person with much influence, esp. one seen as pompous and self-important: *the pooh-bahs of the international wine industry.*

pooh-pooh *verb* (**pooh-poohs**, **pooh-poohed**, **pooh-poohing**) express contempt for; ridicule; dismiss (an idea etc.) scornfully.

pooja *noun* (*plural* **poojas**) = PUJA. [Say POO juh]

pool • *noun* **1 a** a small body of still water or other liquid. **b** a receptacle or hole filled with water for swimming, wading, etc. **c** a deep place in a river. **2** any of various games of billiards, esp. eight ball. **3 a** a common supply of persons, commodities, resources, etc.: *gene pool.* **b** esp. *Cdn* a grain farmers' co-operative for marketing etc. **c** a group of persons sharing duties, resources, etc.: *car pool.* **4 a** the collective amount of players' stakes in gambling etc. **b** a bet in which players contribute to a pool, all of which is taken by one winner or divided among a few. **5** a group of contestants who compete against each other in a tournament for the right to advance to the next round. • *verb* **1** form into a pool. **2** (of blood) become static. **3** put (resources etc.) into a common fund. **4** share (things) in common.

pool hall *noun* a place for playing billiards.

poolroom *noun* a place for playing billiards.

poolside • *noun* the area adjoining a swimming pool: *poolside bar.* • *adverb* to, toward, or beside a swimming pool: *sat poolside.*

poop • *noun* **1** the stern of a ship; the deck that is highest and furthest aft. **2** (also **poo-poo**) = POO. **3** *slang* the latest information; news: *what's the poop?* **4** *informal* a stupid or ineffectual person. • *verb* **1** (esp. as **pooped** *adjective* or foll. by *out*) *informal* exhaust; tire out. **2** (also **poo-poo**) = POO.

pooper scooper *noun* an implement for clearing up (esp. dog) excrement.

poopy *adjective informal* soiled with or suggestive of excrement.

poor *adjective* **1** lacking adequate money. **2** deficient in (a possession or quality): *oxygen-poor.* **3 a** inadequate, unsatisfactory: *a poor crop.* **b** not good or skilled at: *a poor judge of character ◊ a poor loser.* **4** deserving pity or sympathy; unfortunate: *you poor thing.* PHRASES **poor man's** an inferior or cheaper substitute for.

poorhouse *noun hist.* an institution where poor people used to have to live if they couldn't afford living anywhere else, often with the requirement that they perform tedious manual labour in return.

poorly • *adverb* **1** scantily; defectively. **2** with no great success. • *adjective* unwell.

poor relation *noun* something that is not treated with as much respect as other similar things because it is not thought to be as good, important or successful: *many downhillers think of cross-country skiing as a poor relation — fit only for wimps who can't take speed.*

POP *abbreviation* probability of precipitation.

pop¹ • *noun* **1** a sudden sharp explosive sound as of a cork when drawn, or of a bursting toy balloon. **2** any carbonated, sweetened, non-alcoholic drink, e.g. cola. **3** a single item or instance of service for which a price is set; a person paying for such an item or service: *charged us $75 a pop.* • *verb* (**pops**, **popped**, **popping**) **1** make or cause to make a sudden short explosive sound. **2** go or come quickly or unexpectedly. **3** put or place quickly. **4** (of a person's eyes) open wide and appear to bulge. **5** *informal* take or inject (a drug). • *adjective* sudden, unexpected: *pop quiz.* PHRASES **pop off** *informal* **1** die. **2** quietly slip away (*compare* sense 2 of *verb*). **pop out** *Baseball* be put out by having one's pop-up caught. **pop the question** *informal* propose marriage. **pop up** appear, esp. unexpectedly.

pop² *informal* • *adjective* **1** in or relating to a popular or modern style. **2** performing or relating to pop music: *pop star.* • *noun* **1** (also **pop music**) commercial

popular music, esp. that since the 1950s. **2** pop art. **3** (in *plural*) pieces of light classical music, show tunes, etc.: *a pops concert*.

pop[3] *noun* esp. *US informal* father.

pop[4] *noun* a snack of flavoured frozen water, yogourt, etc. with a stick embedded in it for holding.

pop. *abbreviation* population.

pop art *noun* art based on modern popular culture and the mass media, esp. as a critical comment on traditional fine art values, e.g. the works of Andy Warhol, which often simply depict consumer products.

popcorn *noun* **1** corn which bursts open when heated. **2** these kernels when popped. **3** (as an *adjective*) resembling popcorn in appearance: *popcorn shrimp*.

pop culture *noun* commercial culture based on popular taste.

pope *noun* **1** (as a title usu. **Pope**) the Bishop of Rome as head of the Roman Catholic Church. **2** the head of the Coptic Church, the patriarch of Alexandria.

pop-eyed *adjective informal* **1** having bulging eyes. **2** wide-eyed (with surprise etc.).

pop fly *noun* = FLY BALL.

popgun *noun* a child's toy gun which shoots a pellet, cork, etc. by the compression of air with a piston.

poplar *noun* a tall, fast-growing tree with leaves that seem to tremble in the breeze, grown esp. for timber and pulp.

popout • *noun Baseball* an act of being put out on a short fly ball. • *adjective* (**pop-out**) designating a part of a machine etc. that is easily removable: *pop-out panel*.

popover *noun* **1** a food made from a thin batter of milk, eggs, and flour, which rises to form a hollow shell when baked. **2** a loose casual garment put on by slipping it over the head.

poppa *noun informal* (esp. as a child's word) **1** father. **2** grandfather.

popper *noun* **1** a person or thing that pops. **2** a pan or electric appliance for popping popcorn. **3** *informal* any of a number of inhaled muscle relaxants and blood vessel dilators used as a stimulant. **4** *Angling* a plug that makes a popping sound at the surface of the water as it moves.

pop-psych *adjective* (also **pop-psychology**) characterized by or relating to usu. superficial psychological concepts as popularly understood.

poppy[1] *noun* (*plural* **poppies**) **1** a plant with showy usu. red flowers, many varieties of which are a source of drugs such as heroin, morphine and codeine. **2** a red plastic representation of this flower worn in the period leading up to Remembrance Day.

poppy[2] *adjective* (of music, a group, etc.) having a sound characteristic of pop music.

poppycock *noun slang* nonsense.

Poppy Day *noun Brit. & Cdn* = REMEMBRANCE DAY.

poppy seed *noun* the small black seed of the poppy, used in fillings and toppings for bread, cakes, etc.

Popsicle *noun proprietary* a piece of frozen flavoured and coloured sweetened water, juice, etc. on a stick.

Popsicle stick *noun* a thin, flat stick with rounded ends on which a Popsicle is frozen, often used in arts and crafts.

popster *noun informal* a pop musician.

populace *noun* all the ordinary people of a particular country or area: *he had the support of large sections of the local populace*. [Say POP you liss]

popular *adjective* **1** liked or admired by many people or by a specified group. **2 a** of or carried on by the general public: *popular meetings*. **b** existing widely among the general public: *popular discontent*. **3** adapted to the understanding or taste of the people: *popular science*.

popular culture *noun* = POP CULTURE.

popular front *noun* a party etc. representing the populace against an esp. totalitarian government.

popularity *noun* the state of being liked, enjoyed or supported by a large number of people.

popularization *noun* an act of popularizing something.

popularize *verb* (**popularizes**, **popularized**, **popularizing**) **1** make popular. **2** cause (a person, principle, etc.) to be generally known or liked. **3** present (a technical subject etc.) in a readily understandable form. ▶ **popularizer** *noun*

popularly *adverb* **1** by a large number of people: *a popularly held belief*. **2** by the ordinary people of a country: *a popularly elected government*.

popular music *noun* **1** songs, folk tunes, etc., appealing to the tastes of a large number of people. **2** pop music.

popular vote *noun* the total number of votes cast by voters in an election: *the party failed to win a majority of the popular vote*.

populate *verb* (**populates**, **populated**, **populating**) **1** inhabit; form the population of (a town, country, etc.). **2** supply with inhabitants; people: *a densely populated district*.

population *noun* **1 a** the inhabitants of a place, country, etc. referred to collectively. **b** any specified group within this: *the Italian population of Toronto*. **2** the total number of any of these: *a population of eight million* ◊ *the seal population*. **3** the act or process of supplying with inhabitants.

population density *noun* the number of inhabitants per square kilometre of a region.

population pyramid *noun* a type of bar graph depicting the percentage of the total population falling within specified age groups, with bars stacked so that the bottom bar represents the youngest group and the top the oldest; in developing countries a greater proportion of the population tends to be younger so the lowest bars are longest, resulting in a pyramid shape for the graph, while in developed countries the birth rate is lower and the bulk of the population tends to be of working age, resulting in a barrel-shaped graph with a narrower top and bottom and fatter middle.

populism *noun* a type of politics that claims to represent the opinions and wishes of ordinary people.

populist • *noun* **1** a member or adherent of a political party seeking support mainly from the ordinary people. **2** a person who holds, or who is concerned with, the views of the populace. • *adjective* of or relating to a populist or populists.

SPELL CHECK	
populous, populace	

The people living in an area are the *populace*.

populous *adjective* having many inhabitants. [Say POP you lus]

pop-up • *adjective* **1** *Computing* (of a menu etc.) able to be superimposed on the screen and suppressed rapidly. **2** (of a toaster etc.) operating so as to move the object (toast when ready etc.) quickly upwards. **3** (of a book etc.) containing three-dimensional figures etc. that rise up when the page is turned. • *noun* **1** *Baseball* the act of hitting the ball high in the air, usu. in or just beyond the infield. **2** *Computing* a pop-up menu etc.

porcelain *noun* **1** a hard white shiny substance made by baking clay and used for making delicate chinaware. **2** objects made of this. [Say PORSA lin]

porch *noun* (*plural* **porches**) **1** a covered shelter for the entrance of a building. **2** a veranda.

P

porcine *adjective* of or like pigs. [Say POR sine]

porcini *noun* (*plural* **porcini**) a mushroom with a glossy brown cap and a fat stem. [Say por CHEENY]

porcupine *noun* **1** a large rodent with defensive spines or quills. **2** (as an *adjective*) denoting any of various animals or other organisms with spines: *porcupine fish*.

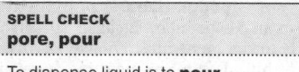

SPELL CHECK
pore, pour

To dispense liquid is to **pour**.

pore[1] *noun* a minute opening in a surface, e.g. the skin, through which gases or fluids may pass.

pore[2] *verb* (**pores, pored, poring**) (foll. by *over*) be absorbed in studying (a book etc.): *he consulted the treaty and pored over his law books*.

porgy *noun* (*plural* **porgies**) any of numerous fishes found esp. in North American Atlantic coastal waters, some of which are important food fishes. [Say PORG ee]

pork *noun* **1** the flesh of a pig, used as food. **2** esp. *US slang* an example of pork barrel politics.

pork barrel *noun informal* a source of government funds for projects designed to win votes (often as an *adjective*: *pork barrel politics*). ▶ **pork-barrelling** *noun*

pork belly *noun* (*plural* **pork bellies**) a side of pork, esp. as a commodity.

porker *noun* **1** a pig raised for food. **2** a young fattened pig.

pork pie *noun* a pie of ground pork etc. eaten cold.

porky *adjective* (**porkier, porkiest**) **1** *informal* fleshy, fat. **2** of or like pork.

porn (also **porno**) *informal* • *noun* pornography. • *adjective* pornographic.

pornographer *noun* a person who produces or sells pornography.

pornographic *adjective* showing or describing explicit sexual activity to stimulate erotic rather than aesthetic or emotional feelings: *pornographic movies*.

pornography *noun* the explicit description or exhibition of sexual activity in literature, films, etc., intended to stimulate erotic rather than aesthetic or emotional feelings.

porosity *noun* the quality or state of being porous: *the soil's porosity is so reduced that water cannot penetrate*. [Say por OSSA tee]

porous *adjective* **1** having many small holes that allow water or air to pass through slowly. **2** easy to pass through or infiltrate: *the goalie received no help from the team's porous defence*. [Say POR us]

porphyry *noun* (*plural* **porphyries**) **1** a hard rock quarried in ancient Egypt, composed of crystals of white or red feldspar in a red matrix. **2** an igneous rock with large crystals scattered in a matrix of much smaller crystals. [Say PORFA ree]

porpoise *noun* a small toothed whale with a low triangular dorsal fin and a blunt rounded snout. [Say POR pus]

porridge *noun* a dish consisting of a cereal, esp. oats, boiled in water or milk. ▶ **porridgy** *adjective*

port[1] *noun* **1** a harbour. **2** a town or place possessing a harbour where ships load or unload. PHRASES **any port in a storm** any refuge in difficult or troubled circumstances.

port[2] *noun* (also **port wine**) a strong, sweet, usu. dark red fortified wine of Portugal.

port[3] • *noun* the left-hand side (looking forward) of a ship, boat, or aircraft. • *verb* turn (the helm) to port. • *adjective* situated on or turned toward the left-hand side (looking forward) of a ship or aircraft.

port[4] • *noun* **1 a** an opening in the side of a ship for entrance etc. **b** a porthole. **2** an aperture for the passage of steam, water, etc. **3** a socket or aperture in an electronic circuit, esp. in a computer network, where connections can be made with peripheral equipment. • *verb* *Computing* transfer (software) from one operating system etc. to another.

portability *noun* the state of being portable: *the new model's biggest selling feature is its portability*.

portable • *adjective* **1 a** easily movable or transportable, convenient for carrying: *portable TV*. **b** not fixed; movable: *portable classroom*. **2** (of a right, privilege, etc.) capable of being transferred or adapted in altered circumstances: *portable pension*. **3** (of software etc.) not restricted to one machine or computer system; able to be transferred from one machine or system to another. • *noun* **1** a portable object, e.g. a radio etc. **2** a small transportable building used as a classroom.

portage • *noun* **1** the carrying of boats or goods between two navigable waters or around an impassable section of a river etc. **2 a** a place at which this is necessary. **b** the route taken during a portage. • *verb* (**portages, portaged, portaging**) **1** convey (a boat or goods) between navigable waters. **2** carry a boat or goods at (a portage). **3** circumvent (a stretch of impassable waters) by means of a portage. [Say por TOZH]

portage trail *noun* *Cdn* a trail created by people performing a portage.

portal *noun* a doorway or gate etc., esp. a large and elaborate one.

porta-potty *noun* (*plural* **porta-potties**) a portable toilet.

portend *verb* foreshadow as an omen; give warning of: *the debate portends an unwelcome future*. [Say por TEND]

portent *noun* an omen, a sign of something to come: *gloomy portents of global destruction*. [Say POR tent]

portentous *adjective* **1** like or serving as a portent: *this portentous year in Canadian history*. **2** pompously solemn: *portentous music*. ▶ **portentously** *adverb* [Say por TEN tus]

porter *noun* **1 a** a person employed to carry luggage etc., esp. a railway, airport, or hotel employee. **b** a hospital employee who moves patients, equipment, trolleys, etc. **2** a dark brown bitter beer brewed from charred or browned malt. **3** a sleeping car attendant. **4** a gatekeeper or doorman.

portfolio *noun* (*plural* **portfolios**) **1** a case for keeping loose sheets of paper, drawings, etc. **2** a range of investments held by a person, company, etc. **3** the office or responsibility of a government minister. **4** samples of an artist's or photographer's work.

porthole *noun* a usu. round window in the side of a ship or an aircraft. [Say PORT hole]

portico *noun* (*plural* **porticoes**) a roof supported by columns at regular intervals usu. attached as a porch to a building. [Say PORTA co]

portion • *noun* **1** a part or share. **2** the amount of food allotted to one person; a helping. **3** a specified or limited quantity. • *verb* **1** divide (a thing) into portions. **2** (foll. by *out*) distribute.

Portland cement *noun* a cement manufactured from chalk and clay.

portly *adjective* (**portlier, portliest**) rather fat.

portmanteau *noun* (*plural* **portmanteaus**) a travelling bag for clothes etc., esp. of leather and opening into two equal parts. [Say port man TOE]

portobello *noun* (*plural* **portobellos**) a large edible variety of the common mushroom. [Say porto BELLO]

port of call *noun* a place where a ship or a person stops on a journey.

portrait *noun* **1** a representation of a person or animal, esp. of the face, made by drawing, painting,

photography, etc. **2** a description in words of a person. **3** a person etc. resembling or typifying another: *is the portrait of his father.* **4** (in graphic design etc.) a format in which the height of an illustration etc. is greater than the width (*compare* LANDSCAPE 3).

portraitist *noun* a person who takes or paints portraits.

portraiture *noun* the art of painting or taking portraits. [Say PORTRA chur]

portray *verb* **1** make a likeness of. **2** represent, esp. dramatically: *immigrants as portrayed in the media.* ▶ **portrayal** *noun*

Portuguese • *noun* (*plural* **Portuguese**) **1 a** a native or national of Portugal. **b** a person of Portuguese descent. **2** the Romance language of Portugal, also used in Brazil etc. • *adjective* of or relating to Portugal.

Portuguese man-of-war *noun* (*plural* **Portuguese men-of-war**) a dangerous tropical or subtropical marine creature with a floating bladder-like body and very long stinging tentacles.

pose • *verb* (**poses, posed, posing**) **1** assume a certain attitude of body, esp. when being photographed or being painted for a portrait. **2** (full. by *as*) set oneself up as or pretend to be (another person etc.): *posing as a celebrity.* **3** behave affectedly in order to impress others. **4** put forward or present (a question, threat, etc.). **5** place (an artist's model etc.) in a certain attitude of position. • *noun* **1** an attitude of body, esp. assumed when being photographed etc. **2** an attitude or pretense, esp. one assumed for effect: *his generosity is a mere pose.*

poser *noun* **1** a person who behaves affectedly in order to impress others. **2** a puzzling question or problem.

SPELL CHECK   ABC ✔
possess

Note that there are two double-s's in *possess*.

---

poseur *noun* a person who poses for effect or behaves affectedly: *no longer singing himself, he calls new punk bands poseurs.* [Say poe ZER]

posh *adjective informal* luxurious. ▶ **poshness** *noun*

posit *verb* (**posits, posited, positing**) state or assume as a fact: *Darwin's theory posited immense stretches of evolutionary time.* [Say POZZ it]

position • *noun* **1** a place where someone or something is located or has been put. **2** the correct place. **3** a way in which someone or something is placed or arranged. **4** a situation or set of circumstances. **5** high rank or social standing. **6** a job. **7** a point of view or attitude. **8** a place where part of a military force is posted. • *verb* put or arrange in a particular position. PHRASES **in a position to** enabled by circumstances, resources, information, etc. to (do, state, etc.). ▶ **positional** *adjective*

position paper *noun* a written report of policy on a particular issue, prepared by a business etc.

positive • *adjective* **1** characterized by the presence rather than the absence of distinguishing features. **2** expressing or implying affirmation, agreement, or permission. **3** constructive, optimistic, or confident. **4** with no possibility of doubt; certain. **5** (of a quantity) greater than zero. **6** of, containing, or producing the kind of electric charge opposite to that carried by electrons. **7** (of a photographic image) showing light and shade or colours true to the original. **8** *Grammar* (of an adjective or adverb) expressing a quality in its basic, primary degree. **9** (of a person, blood, etc.) having a specified condition, substance, etc.: *HIV-positive.* • *noun* a positive quality, attribute, image, etc. ▶ **positively** *adverb* **positiveness** *noun*

positivism *noun* **1 a** the philosophical system of the French philosopher Auguste Comte (1798–1857), which holds that every rationally justifiable assertion can be scientifically verified or is capable of logical or mathematical proof, and which therefore rejects metaphysics and theism. **b** a humanistic religious system founded on this. **2** (in full **logical positivism**) a philosophical system that considers that the only meaningful philosophical problems are those that can be solved by logical analysis. ▶ **positivist** *noun & adjective* **positivistic** *adjective* [Say POSITIVE ism]

positivity *noun* the quality of being positive. [Say pozza TIVVA tee]

positron *noun* a subatomic particle with a positive charge equal to the negative charge of an electron. [Say POZZA tron]

positron emission tomography *noun* a form of tomography used esp. for brain scans which employs positron-emitting isotopes introduced into the body as a source of radiation.

posse *noun* **1** a body of men summoned by a sheriff etc. to find a criminal, maintain order, etc. **2** *slang* an esp. criminal gang. **3** *informal* usu. *derogatory* a band of persons acting or going about together. [Say POSSY]

possess *verb* (**possesses, possessed, possessing**) **1** hold as property; own. **2** have an ability, quality, or characteristic: *they possess a special value for us.* **3 a** (of a demon etc.) occupy; have power over (a person etc.): *possessed by the devil.* **b** (of an emotion, infatuation, etc.) dominate, be an obsession of: *possessed by fear.* **4** have sexual intercourse with (esp. a woman). PHRASES **be possessed of** own, have. **what possessed you?** an expression of incredulity.

possession *noun* **1** the act or state of possessing or being possessed. **2** the thing possessed. **3** the act or state of actual holding or occupancy. **4** *Law* **a** power or control over a thing, esp. land, which is similar to lawful ownership but which may exist separately from it. **b** *informal* the state of possessing an illegal drug or drugs: *charged with possession.* **5** (in *plural*) property, wealth, subject territory, etc. **6** *Football, Hockey, etc.* **a** temporary control of the ball or puck by a particular player or team. **b** a period of such control. PHRASES **in possession 1** (of a person) possessing. **2** (of a thing) possessed. **in possession of 1** having in one's possession. **2** maintaining control over: *in possession of one's wits.* **in the possession of** held or owned by. **take possession** (often foll. by *of*) become the owner or possessor (of a thing).

possessive • *adjective* **1** showing a desire to possess or retain what one already owns. **2** showing jealous and domineering tendencies toward another person. **3** *Grammar* indicating possession. • *noun* (also **possessive case**) the case of nouns and pronouns expressing possession. ▶ **possessiveness** *noun*

possessive adjective *noun* each of the adjectives indicating possession: *my, your, her, his, its, our, their.*

possessive pronoun *noun* each of the pronouns indicating possession: *mine, yours, hers, his, its, ours, theirs.*

possessor *noun* a person who owns or has something; an owner.

possibility *noun* (*plural* **possibilities**) **1** the state or fact of being possible, or an occurrence of this: *outside the range of possibility* ◊ *saw no possibility of going.* **2 a** a thing that may exist or happen: *there are three possibilities.* **b** a possible candidate, member of a team, etc. **3** (usu. in *plural*) the capability of being used, improved, etc.: *it has possibilities.*

possible • *adjective* **1** capable of existing or

happening; that may be managed, achieved, etc.: *came as early as possible*. **2** that is likely to happen etc.: *few thought their victory possible*. **3** that is perhaps true or a fact: *it's possible that he has left*. **4** that is or perhaps will be (what is denoted by the noun): *looking for a possible serial killer*. • *noun* **1** a possible candidate, member of a team, etc. **2 (the possible)** whatever is likely, manageable, etc.

possibly *adverb* **1** perhaps. **2** in accordance with possibility: *cannot possibly refuse*.

possum *noun* **1** *informal* = OPOSSUM 1. **2** a tree-dwelling Australian marsupial with a long tail capable of grasping. PHRASES **play possum** *informal* pretend to be asleep or unaware.

post¹ • *noun* **1** a long piece of wood or metal set upright in the ground etc. **2 a** a pole etc. marking the start or finish of a race. **b** = GOALPOST. • *verb* **1 a** attach (a paper etc.) in a prominent place; stick up. **b** announce or advertise by placard, in a published text, on a computer bulletin board, etc. **2** achieve (a score in a game, etc.).

post² • *noun* **1** esp. *Brit.* the official conveyance of parcels, letters, etc.: *send it by post*. **2** esp. *Brit.* a single collection, dispatch, or delivery of these; the letters etc. dispatched. • *verb* **1** esp. *Brit.* put (a letter etc.) in the mail. **2** (esp. as **posted** *adjective*) supply a person with information: *keep me posted*. **3** enter an item in a ledger or spreadsheet. **4** (of a rider) rise and fall in the saddle in rhythm with the horse at a trot.

post³ • *noun* **1** a job. **2** a place where a soldier is stationed or which he or she patrols. **3** a place where an official is on duty: *customs post*. **4 a** a position taken up by a body of soldiers. **b** a force occupying this. **c** a fort. **5** = TRADING POST. **6** *Basketball* the area in the vicinity of the opponent's basket. • *verb* **1** place or station (soldiers, an employee, etc.). **2** appoint to a post or command.

post⁴ *verb* put up, provide (esp. bail money).

post⁵ *noun informal* POST-PRODUCTION.

post- *prefix* after in time or order.

postage *noun* the amount charged for sending a letter etc. by post, usu. prepaid in the form of a stamp.

postage and handling *noun* a price charged for the mailing, packing, and delivery of a package etc.

postage stamp *noun* **1** an official stamp affixed to or imprinted on a letter etc. indicating the amount of postage paid. **2** (as an *adjective*) very small: *a postage-stamp lawn*.

postal *adjective* of or relating to the post office or mail delivery.

postal code *noun Cdn* a series of six alternating letters and numerals used as part of a postal address to expedite the processing of machine-sorted mail.

postal station *noun Cdn* one of a number of branch post offices in a community too large to be serviced by a single post office.

postcard *noun* **1** a card with a photograph or picture on one side, for sending a short message by mail without an envelope. **2** (as an *adjective*) picturesque: *a postcard view of the blue-green lake*.

post-coital *adjective* occurring or existing after sexual intercourse.

post-colonial *adjective* occurring or existing after the end of colonial rule. ▶ **post-colonialism** *noun*

post-Confederation *adjective Cdn* **1** of or pertaining to the period after 1867 in Canada. **2** relating to or characteristic of the period after a province or territory entered Confederation.

post-consumer *adjective* designating waste thrown away by consumers and used in recycled products.

postdate *verb* (**postdates, postdated, postdating**)

1 affix or assign a date later than the actual one to (a document, cheque, event, etc.). **2** follow in time; belong to a later date.

post-doctoral *adjective* of or relating to research undertaken after the completion of doctoral research.

poster • *noun* **1** a printed or written notice posted or displayed in a public place as an announcement or advertisement. **2** a large printed picture suitable for decorative display on a wall. **3** *Computing* a person who posts a message on a bulletin-board service. • *verb* **1** affix posters on (a wall, building, etc.). **2** place posters throughout a neighbourhood etc.

poster boy *noun* **1** a male poster child. **2** a male model who appears in a print advertisement.

poster child *noun* (*plural* **poster children**) **1** a child who appears on a poster or in an advertisement for a charitable organization. **2** a person or thing that epitomizes or represents a quality, cause, etc.: *the city is a poster child for bad government*.

poster girl *noun* **1** a female poster child. **2** a female model who appears in a print advertisement.

posterior • *adjective* situated behind or at the back. • *noun* the buttocks. [Say poss TEERY er]

posterity *noun* all succeeding generations: *is leaving her art collection for posterity*. [Say poss TERRA tee]

post-feminism *noun* post-feminist ideas, views, and attitudes.

post-feminist • *adjective* relating to or occurring in the period after the feminist movement of the 1970s or to the ideas, views, and attitudes of this period, often characterized as less rigid and dogmatic than those of traditional feminism and focused more on enjoying the privileges won by the feminist movement of the 1970s, e.g. social equality, economic independence, and sexual freedom, than on advancing traditional feminist causes. • *noun* a person who holds post-feminist ideas and attitudes.

postglacial *adjective* formed or occurring after a glacial period or ice age, esp. with reference to the period since the last glaciation, which began with a sudden rise in temperature about 10,000 years ago.

post-grad *informal* = POST-GRADUATE.

post-graduate • *adjective* **1** (of a course of study) carried on after completing a bachelor's degree. **2** of or relating to students following this course of study. • *noun* a post-graduate student.

posthole *noun* a hole for the insertion of a fence post.

posthumous *adjective* **1** occurring after death. **2** (of a book etc.) published after the author's death. **3** (of a child) born after the death of its father. ▶ **posthumously** *adverb* [Say POSS tyuh muss]

postie *noun Cdn & Brit. informal* a postal worker, esp. a letter carrier.

Post-Impressionism *noun* the work or style of a varied group of late 19th-century and early 20th-century artists including Vincent Van Gogh (1853–90), Paul Gauguin (1848–1903), and Paul Cézanne (1839–1906). They reacted against the naturalism of the Impressionists to explore colour, line, and form, intending to express the artist's emotional response to the objects represented rather than the general observer's view. ▶ **Post-Impressionist** *noun & adjective*

post-industrial *adjective* relating to or characteristic of a society or economy which no longer relies on heavy industry. ▶ **post-industrialism** *noun*

posting *noun* **1** an appointment to a position. **2** a message posted to a discussion group etc. on the Internet.

Post-it *noun* (also **Post-it Note**) *proprietary* a small sheet of paper with an adhesive strip on the bottom,

designed for easy positioning on and removal from smooth surfaces.

postman *noun* (*plural* **postmen**) a person who is employed to deliver letters etc.

postmark • *noun* an official mark stamped on a letter, esp. one giving the place, date, etc. of dispatch or arrival, and serving to cancel the stamp. • *verb* mark (an envelope etc.) with this.

postmaster *noun* a person in charge of a post office.

post-menopausal *adjective* of or occurring after menopause.

postmodern *adjective* connected with or influenced by postmodernism: *postmodern architecture*.

postmodernism *noun* a late 20th-century movement in the arts, architecture, and criticism, which represents a departure from or a rejection of modernism and the modernist emphasis on purity of technique and form. Typical features include a deliberate mixing of varied or disconnected images and artistic styles, esp. in television and advertising, the self-conscious use of earlier styles and conventions, and the frequent incorporation of images relating to the consumerism and mass communication of late 20th-century post-industrial society. ▶ **postmodernist** *adjective & noun* **postmodernity** *noun*

post-mortem • *noun* **1** an examination made after death, esp. to determine its cause. **2** *informal* a discussion analyzing the course and result of a game, election, etc. • *adverb & adjective* after death.

postnatal *adjective* characteristic of or relating to the period after childbirth. [Say post NATE ul]

post office *noun* **1** the public department or corporation responsible for postal services and (in some countries) telecommunication. **2** a building, counter in a drugstore, etc., where stamps can be bought, letters can be mailed, etc. **3** a children's game in which imaginary letters are delivered in exchange for kisses.

post office box *noun* (*plural* **post office boxes**) a numbered locked box at a post office, in which mail for an individual or company is kept until called for.

post-op *informal* • *adjective* post-operative. • *adverb* post-operatively.

post-operative *adjective* of the period following a surgical operation. ▶ **post-operatively** *adverb*

postpartum *adjective* following childbirth. [Say post PART um]

postpartum depression *noun* depression suffered by a mother following childbirth.

postpone *verb* (**postpones**, **postponed**, **postponing**) put off to a future time; arrange (an event etc.) to take place at a later time; defer. ▶ **postponement** *noun*

post-production *noun* work done on a film, broadcast, etc. after filming or recording has taken place, e.g. editing, synchronizing the soundtrack, adding digital effects, etc.

postscript *noun* **1** an additional paragraph or remark, usu. at the end of a letter after the signature and introduced by "PS". **2** any additional information, action, etc.

post-season *Sport* • *adjective* of or occurring after the conclusion of the regular season: *post-season play*. • *noun* the playoffs.

post-secondary *adjective* of or relating to education occurring after completion of high school.

post-structural *adjective* connected with or influenced by post-structuralism.

post-structuralism *noun* a movement in philosophy and literary criticism that emerged in the late 1970s, challenging the theoretical assumptions of structural-ism; it departed from the structuralist claims to scientific objectivity and comprehensiveness and emphasized instead plurality and instability of meaning, rejecting any theoretical system that claimed to have universal validity. Significant post-structuralists are the critics Jacques Derrida (b.1930) and Roland Barthes (1915–80), the psychoanalyst Jacques Lacan (1901–81), and the historian Michel Foucault (1926–84). ▶ **post-structuralist** *noun & adjective*

post-traumatic stress disorder *noun* (also **post-traumatic stress syndrome**) a condition of mental and emotional stress that sometimes follows injury or severe psychological shock, characterized by withdrawal and anxiety, and a tendency to physical illness.

postulate • *verb* (**postulates**, **postulated**, **postulating**) suggest or assume the existence, fact, or truth of something as a basis for reasoning, discussion, or belief: *the finding led scientists to postulate the existence of a sixth moon* ◊ *in an aside, we postulate that the character on stage is speaking directly to us*. • *noun* **1** a thing suggested or assumed as true as the basis for reasoning, discussion, or belief: *the postulate of Babylonian influence on Greek astronomy*. **2** *Math* an assumption used as a basis for mathematical reasoning: *Euclid's fifth postulate*. [Say POSS tyoo late for the verb, POSS tyoo lit for the noun]

postural *adjective* connected with the way the body is held when sitting or standing: *bad postural habits*. [Say POSS tyur ul or POSS chur ul]

posture • *noun* **1** the relative position of parts, esp. of the body: *in a reclining posture*. **2** the way one holds one's body: *good posture and balance*. **3** an attitude or approach: *an aggressive posture*. • *verb* (**postures**, **postured**, **posturing**) behave in a way that is intended to impress or mislead others: *his views on the environment are not sincere, he's just posturing*. ▶ **posturing** *noun*

post-war *adjective* occurring or existing after a war (esp. the most recent major war).

posy *noun* (*plural* **posies**) a small bunch of flowers. [Say POE zee]

pot • *noun* **1** a vessel, usu. rounded, for holding liquids or solids or for cooking in. **2** the contents of a pot. **3** the total amount of the bet in a game etc. **4** *informal* a fund established by a group of people for a common purpose, esp. for buying food and drinks. **5** *informal* a large sum: *pots of money*. **6** = POT-BELLY. **7** *slang* marijuana. • *verb* (**pots**, **potted**, **potting**) **1** place (a plant) in a flowerpot. **2** (usu. as **potted** *adjective*) preserve in a sealed pot: *potted shrimps*. **3** *Hockey* score (a goal). **4** shoot at, hit, or kill (an animal) with a potshot. **5** seize or secure. **6** make pottery. PHRASES **go to pot** *informal* deteriorate; be ruined. **the pot calling the kettle black** a case of accusing someone of something of which one is oneself guilty. **pot of gold** an imaginary reward; an ideal; a jackpot.

potability *noun* (esp. of water) the state of being drinkable. [Say poe tuh BILLA tee]

potable • *adjective* drinkable. • *noun* (usu. in *plural*) a drinkable substance. [Say POE tuh bull]

potash *noun* an alkaline potassium compound, usu. potassium carbonate or hydroxide, used esp. in the manufacture of fertilizer and soap. [Say POT ash]

potassium *noun* a soft silver-white metallic element occurring naturally in sea water and various minerals, an essential element for living organisms, and forming many useful compounds. [Say puh TASSY um]

potato *noun* (*plural* **potatoes**) **1** a starchy edible plant tuber that is one of the most important food crops, cooked and eaten as a vegetable. **2** the plant of the

nightshade family that produces these tubers on underground runners.

potato pancake *noun* a pancake made with grated potato.

pot-bellied *adjective* having a pot-belly.

pot-bellied stove *noun* (also **pot-belly stove**) a small stove with a rounded body, used for burning esp. wood.

pot-belly *noun* (*plural* **pot-bellies**) a protruding stomach.

potboiler *noun* a mediocre work of literature or art done merely to make the writer or artist money.

potency *noun* (*plural* **potencies**) **1 a** the powerful effect, odour, or flavour of a substance: *the unexpected potency of the fruit punch* ◊ *a garlic-like potency*. **b** the power or influence of a person or thing: *the movie's potency*. **2** a male's ability to achieve an erection. [Say POE n see]

potent *adjective* **1** powerful; strong: *the team's potent offensive attack*. **2** (of a drug, alcoholic drink, poison, etc.) having strong physical or chemical properties. **3** (of a male) capable of sexual erection or orgasm. ▶ **potently** *adverb* [Say POE tint]

potentate *noun* a person who possesses great power, esp. a monarch or ruler. [Say POE t'n tate]

potential ● *adjective* capable of coming into being or action. ● *noun* **1** the possibility of something developing or happening: *potential for error*. **2** qualities that exist and can be developed: *she has artistic potential*. **3** usable resources. **4** the quantity determining the energy of mass in a gravitational field or of charge in an electric field.

potential difference *noun* the difference of electric potential between two points.

potential energy *noun* the energy possessed by a body by virtue of its position relative to others, stresses within itself, electric charge, and other factors (*compare* KINETIC ENERGY).

potentiality *noun* (*plural* **potentialities**) the state or quality of possessing latent power capable of coming into being; potential: *ideas existing in potentiality rather than actuality*. [Say puh tenshy ALA tee]

potentially *adverb* possibly; with the indicated result possible: *it would be a potentially fatal mistake*.

potentilla *noun* a plant of a genus that includes the cinquefoils, esp. (in gardening) a small shrub with yellow or red flowers. [Say poe tun TILLA]

potful *noun* (*plural* **potfuls**) an amount that can be or is contained in a pot.

pothead *noun* *slang* a habitual user of marijuana.

pothole *noun* **1** a hole in a road surface caused by wear or extremes of weather. **2** (also **pothole lake**) a shallow pond or lake formed by a natural hollow in the ground in which water has collected. **3** a deep hole in the ground or a riverbed. **4** a deep hole or system of caves and underground riverbeds formed by the erosion of rock esp. by water. ▶ **potholed** *adjective*

potion *noun* a liquid medicine, poison, magic charm, etc.: *love potion*.

potlatch *noun* (*plural* **potlatches**) (among some Aboriginal peoples of the Pacific coast of North America) a ceremonial feast at which possessions are given away or destroyed to display wealth or enhance prestige. ▶ **potlatching** *noun*

pot light *noun* *Cdn* a light encased in a cylindrical shell, recessed into a ceiling. ▶ **pot lighting** *noun*

potluck *noun* **1** (also **potluck supper**, **potluck dinner**, etc.) a party to which each guest brings a dish to be shared. **2** whatever is available.

pot pie *noun* a pie of beef, chicken, etc. with vegetables, baked and topped with a crust.

potpourri *noun* (*plural* **potpourris**) **1** a mixture of dried petals and spices used to perfume a room etc. **2** a mixture of things, esp. a musical or literary medley: *a fast-paced potpourri of sight gags and one-liners*. [Say poe puh REE]

pot roast ● *noun* a piece of meat, esp. beef, cooked slowly in a covered dish with a small amount of liquid. ● *verb* cook (a piece of meat) in this way.

potshot *noun* **1** a random shot at a person or animal. **2** a shot aimed at an animal etc. within easy reach. **3** a piece of esp. random or opportunistic criticism.

potted *adjective* **1** (of a plant) planted or grown in a flowerpot, esp. indoors. **2** *slang* intoxicated by alcohol or drugs. **3** abridged; summarized: *a potted history*.

potter[1] *verb* esp. *Brit.* = PUTTER[3].

potter[2] *noun* a maker of ceramic vessels.

potter's wheel *noun* a flat revolving disc on which wet clay is shaped by a potter.

pottery *noun* (*plural* **potteries**) **1** vessels etc. made of fired clay. **2** a potter's work. **3** a potter's workshop.

potty[1] *adjective* (**pottier**, **pottiest**) *slang* esp. *Brit.* foolish or crazy.

potty[2] *noun* (*plural* **potties**) *informal* **1** a small seat fitting over a toilet seat, used by a young child during toilet training. **2** a child's commode.

pouch ● *noun* (*plural* **pouches**) **1** a small bag. **2 a** a pocket-like receptacle in the abdomen of female marsupials, in which the newly born young, in an immature state, are carried while they complete their development, obtaining nourishment from the mother's mammary teats. **b** any of several pocket-like structures in various other animals, e.g. in the cheeks of rodents. **3** a baggy area of skin underneath the eyes etc. **4** a soldier's leather ammunition bag. **5** a lockable bag for mail or dispatches. **6** *Botany* a bag-like cavity, esp. the seed vessel, in a plant. ● *verb* (**pouches, pouched, pouching**) put or make into a pouch.

pouf *noun* a soft projecting mass of material on a dress, headdress, etc. ▶ **poufy** *adjective* [Say POOF]

poultice ● *noun* a soft medicated and usu. heated mass applied to the body and kept in place with muslin etc., for relieving soreness and inflammation. ● *verb* (**poultices, poulticed, poulticing**) apply a poultice to. [Say POLE tiss]

poultry *noun* domestic fowls (chickens, turkeys, ducks, geese, etc.), esp. as a source of food.

pounce ● *verb* (**pounces, pounced, pouncing**) **1** spring or swoop, esp. as in capturing prey. **2** (often foll. by *on*, *upon*) **a** make a sudden attack. **b** seize eagerly upon an object, remark, etc.: *pounced on what we said*. ● *noun* a sudden swoop or spring.

pound[1] *noun* **1** a unit of weight equal to 16 oz. avoirdupois (453.6 g), or 12 oz. troy (373.2 g). **2** (also **pound sterling**) the chief monetary unit of the UK and several other countries. **3** = POUND SIGN 2.

pound[2] *verb* **1 a** crush or beat with repeated heavy blows. **b** thump or pummel, esp. with the fists. **c** grind to a powder or pulp. **2** deliver heavy blows or gunfire. **3 a** (foll. by *along*, *down*, etc.) make one's way heavily or clumsily. **b** *informal* walk (the streets etc.); cover on foot, esp. in search of work, business, etc.: *pounded the pavement*. **4 a** (of the heart) beat heavily. **b** (of the head) throb painfully. ▋PHRASES▐ **pound into** instill (an attitude, behaviour, etc.) forcefully. **pound out** produce with or as if with heavy blows: *pound out a tune*.

pound[3] *noun* **1** an enclosure, esp. one maintained by public authorities, where stray or homeless animals are kept. **2** a place where impounded vehicles are kept until redeemed. **3** *Cdn hist.* = BUFFALO POUND. **4** *hist.* = BUFFALO JUMP. **5** (also **pound net**) an enclosure of nets in the water near the shore, consisting of a long straight

wall of net leading the fish into a first enclosure, and a second enclosure from which they cannot escape.

poundage *noun* **1** a weight stated in pounds. **2** a person's weight, esp. that which is regarded as excess.

pound cake *noun* a cake made with equal weights of butter, sugar, flour, and eggs.

pounder *noun* **1** (usu. in *combination*) **a** a thing or person weighing a specified number of pounds: *a five-pounder*. **b** a gun carrying a shell of a specified number of pounds. **2** a person or thing that pounds something.

pounding *noun* a resounding defeat; an onslaught resulting in heavy losses: *our team took a pounding*.

pound sign *noun* **1** the sign #, esp. on a telephone keypad or computer keyboard. **2** the sign £, representing a pound sterling.

SPELL CHECK
pour, pore

A tiny opening in the skin is a **pore**; if you read something intently, you **pore** over it.

---

pour *verb* **1** flow or cause to flow esp. downwards in a stream or shower. **2** dispense (a drink, e.g. tea) by pouring. **3** (of rain, or with *it* as subject) fall heavily. **4** come or go in profusion or rapid succession: *the crowd poured out ◊ letters poured in*. **5** bestow or spend (money) lavishly or freely. **6** discharge or send freely. **7** (often foll. by *out*) utter at length or in a rush: *poured out their story*. **8** *informal* put or fit a person into a tight-fitting garment, esp. in such a way that every part of it is "filled out" by the wearer. ■ PHRASES **it never rains but it pours** misfortunes rarely come singly. **pour it on** proceed, work, etc. very quickly, with all one's energy. **pour oil on the waters** (or **on troubled waters**) calm a disagreement or disturbance, esp. with conciliatory words. ▶ **pourable** *adjective* **pourer** *noun*

pout ■ *verb* **1** push the lips forward as an expression of displeasure or sulking. **2** (of the lips) be pushed forward. ■ *noun* **1** such an action or expression. **2** a fit of sulking: *in a pout*.

poutine *noun* Cdn **1** a dish of french fries topped with cheese curds and a sauce, usu. gravy. **2** NB **a** a potato dumpling. **b** a pudding or pie. [Say poo TEEN]

pouty *adjective* (**poutier, poutiest**) **1** (of a person's mouth or expression) having the lips or the bottom lip pushed forward as a sign of childish annoyance or sexual allure. **2** (of a person) having such a mouth or expression: *pouty fashion models*.

poverty *noun* **1** the state of being poor. **2** the state of being inferior in quality or insufficient in amount: *the poverty of her dress ◊ a poverty of intellect*. **3** renunciation of the right to individual ownership of property, as a vow taken by members of a religious order.

poverty line *noun* an income level chosen to distinguish those who are living in poverty from those who are not, representing either a level of income deemed small in comparison to those of others in the same population or a level of income that is insufficient to purchase a specified selection of goods and services deemed essential.

poverty-stricken *adjective* extremely poor.

POW *abbreviation* (*plural* **POWs**) prisoner of war.

pow *interjection* expressing the sound of a blow or explosion.

powder ■ *noun* **1** a substance in the form of fine dry particles. **2** a medicine or cosmetic in this form. **3** = GUNPOWDER. **4** loose, usu. freshly-fallen snow, esp. when considered as a type of terrain for skiing. ■ *verb* **1 a** apply powder to. **b** sprinkle or decorate with or as with powder. **2** (esp. as **powdered** *adjective*) reduce to

a fine powder. ■ PHRASES **powder one's nose 1** apply powder to one's nose. **2** *euphemism* go to a washroom.

powder blue *noun & adjective* pale blue.

powder keg *noun* **1** a barrel of gunpowder. **2** a dangerous or volatile situation: *today the whole region is a powder keg that could explode*.

powderman *noun* (*plural* **powdermen**) (also **powder monkey**) the member of a logging crew responsible for the use of explosives.

powder-puff *noun* **1** a soft pad for applying powder to the skin, esp. the face. **2** a soft or weak person (also as an *adjective*: *a powder-puff performance*).

powder room *noun* **1** a small room containing a toilet and sink, located off a bedroom, hallway, etc. **2** *euphemism* a women's washroom, esp. in a public building.

powdery *adjective* of a powder-like consistency or composition, with fine dry particles.

powdery mildew *noun* **1** a plant disease caused by a parasitic fungus characterized by a white floury covering of spores. **2** the fungus itself.

power ■ *noun* **1** the ability to do something or act in a particular way. **2** the capacity to influence other people or the course of events. **3** a right or authority given or delegated to a person or body. **4** political authority or control. **5** physical strength or force. **6** a country viewed in terms of its international influence and military strength. **7** capacity or performance of an engine or other device. **8** energy that is produced by mechanical, electrical, or other means. **9** *Physics* the rate of doing work, measured in watts or horsepower. **10** *Math* the product obtained when a number is multiplied by itself a certain number of times. ■ *verb* **1** supply with power. **2** (foll. by *up/down*) switch (a device) on or off. **3** move or cause to move with speed or force. ■ *adjective* **1** of or relating to the generation or distribution of electricity: *power plant*. **2** driven by mechanical or electrical energy: *power steering*. **3** *informal* expressing esp. corporate power; characteristic of or involving authority or influence: *wore a power suit*. **4** *Baseball* of or relating to a player who displays power rather than finesse: *power hitter ◊ power pitcher*. **5** designating an activity engaged in with maximum intensity: *a power nap*. ■ PHRASES **in the power of** under the control of. **power behind the throne** a person who asserts authority or influence without having formal status. **the powers that be** those in authority.

power-assisted *adjective* (esp. of steering and brakes in a motor vehicle) employing a source of power to assist manual operation.

power bar *noun* an electrical cord containing a number of outlets, an on-off switch, and often a surge suppressor, used esp. for computer equipment.

power base *noun* a source of authority or support.

powerboat *noun* a powerful motorboat.

power-broker *noun* a person who exerts influence or affects the equilibrium of political power by intrigue. ▶ **power-broking** *noun & adjective*

powered *adjective* operated by or moving under mechanical or other stated power: *powered flight ◊ a water-powered sawmill*.

power forward *noun* **1** *Basketball* **a** a large forward who plays in the low post and usu. has good shot-blocking and rebounding skills. **b** this position. **2** *Hockey* an effective forward known as much for strength and toughness as for skill and scoring ability.

powerful *adjective* **1** having much power or strength. **2** politically or socially influential. **3** having a strong emotional effect: *powerful drama*. ▶ **powerfully** *adverb*

power grid *noun* a system of electricity distribution

P

over a wide area, consisting of a network of high-voltage power lines between major power stations.

powerhouse *noun* **1** = POWER STATION. **2** a very strong, energetic, or successful person, organization, or thing (also as an *adjective*: *a powerhouse performance*).

powerless *adjective* **1** without power or strength. **2** wholly unable: *powerless to help*. ▶**powerlessly** *adverb* **powerlessness** *noun*

powerlifter *noun* an athlete who does powerlifting.

powerlifting *noun* a form of competitive weightlifting emphasizing sheer strength, consisting of three types of lift: the bench press, the squat, and the two-handed dead lift.

power line *noun* a conductor supplying electrical power, esp. one supported by poles etc.

power of attorney *noun* the authority to act for another person in legal or financial matters.

power of sale *noun* the authority by which a bank, trust company, etc., may seize and sell a mortgaged property on which the mortgage is in default.

power pack *noun* **1** a unit for supplying power. **2** the equipment for converting an alternating current to a direct current at a different (usu. lower) voltage.

power plant *noun* **1** an apparatus or installation which provides power for an industry, machine, etc. **2** = POWER STATION.

power play *noun* **1** *Hockey* **a** a temporary situation in which a team has a numerical advantage over the opposing team because one or more of the opposing players are serving a penalty. **b** an offensive strategy adopted by a team having such an advantage. **2** *Football* a running play in which a number of offensive players clear a path for the ball carrier. **3** an (often underhanded) attempt to gain or maintain power in personal relationships, politics, etc.

power skating *noun Cdn* a skating technique aiming to increase a skater's power, speed, and agility by the most efficient use of the skate blades and of the muscles and alignment of the body.

power station *noun* a facility where electricity is generated for distribution.

power supply *noun* a device that provides electrical power, esp. independently of the main electrical system or at a different voltage.

power surge *noun* a sudden marked increase in voltage of an electric current.

power takeoff *noun* a device for the transmission of mechanical power from an engine, esp. that of a tractor etc.

power tool *noun* an electrically powered tool.

powertrain *noun* **1** the mechanism that transmits the drive from the engine of a vehicle to its axle. **2** this together with the engine and axle.

power trip *noun slang* something done primarily for the enjoyment of exercising power over other people: *the director is on a real power trip*.

power walker *noun* a person who takes brisk walks for exercise, esp. with vigorous arm swinging.

power walking *noun* brisk walking for exercise, often accompanied by vigorous swinging of the arms to increase the aerobic demand.

powwow • *noun* **1** a cultural gathering among some North American Aboriginal peoples, with dancing, music, eating, etc. **2** a conference or meeting for discussion. • *verb* hold a powwow. [Say POW wow]

pox *noun* **1** any virus disease producing a rash of pimples that become pus-filled and leave pockmarks on healing. **2** *informal hist.* = SYPHILIS.

pp *abbreviation* **1** pianissimo. **2** pages.

ppb *abbreviation* parts per billion.

ppm *abbreviation* parts per million.

PPS *abbreviation* additional postscript.

PPV *abbreviation* pay-per-view.

PQ *abbreviation* **1** Parti Québécois. **2** Province of Quebec.

PR *abbreviation* **1** public relations. **2** proportional representation. **3** Puerto Rico. **4** (**pr.**) pair.

Pr *symbol* praseodymium.

practicability *noun* feasibility; the quality of being workable or doable: *we were doubtful about the practicability of the plan*. [Say prack ticka BILLA tee]

practicable *adjective* **1** that can be done or used. **2** possible in practice. ▶**practicably** *adverb* [Say PRACK ticka bull]

practical *adjective* **1** of or concerned with practice or use rather than theory. **2** suited to use or action; designed mainly to fulfill a function: *practical shoes*. **3 a** (of a person) inclined to action rather than speculation. **b** sensible as regards the conduct of everyday affairs, financial matters, etc. **4 a** that is such in effect though not nominally: *for all practical purposes*. **b** virtual: *in practical control*. **5** feasible; concerned with what is actually possible: *practical politics*. ▶**practicality** *noun* (*plural* **practicalities**) [Say PRACK tick ul, prack tick ALA tee]

practical joke *noun* a trick played on a person which makes them look foolish and is intended to amuse others. ▶**practical joker** *noun*

practically *adverb* **1** virtually, almost: *practically nothing*. **2** in a practical way.

practical nurse *noun see* LICENSED PRACTICAL NURSE, REGISTERED PRACTICAL NURSE.

SPELL CHECK
practice, practise

In Canada the noun is always spelled with a *c* (*practice*) and the verb usually with an *s* (*practise*): *I'm late for soccer **practice**; I have to **practise** some more on the piano*.

---

practice • *noun* (also **practise**) **1** the actual doing of something; action as contrasted with ideas: *put a plan into practice*. **2** a way of doing something that is common, habitual, or expected: *standard practice*. **3** a habit or custom. **4** repeated exercise in an activity requiring the development of skill: *practice session*. **5** action or execution as opposed to theory. **6** the professional work or business of a doctor, lawyer, etc.: *has a practice in town*. **7** procedure generally, esp. of a specified kind: *bad practice*. • *verb* (**practices, practiced, practicing**) = PRACTISE. [PHRASES] **in practice** when actually applied; in reality. **out of practice** lacking a former skill from lack of recent practice. **put into practice** actually apply (an idea, method, etc.).

practicum *noun* a course of practical training through experience working in a particular field. [Say PRACK tick um]

practise *verb* (**practises, practised, practising**) **1** perform habitually; carry out in action: *practise the same method*. **2** do repeatedly as an exercise to improve a skill; exercise oneself in or on (an activity requiring skill). **3** pursue or be engaged in (a profession, religion, etc.). [PHRASES] **practise what one preaches** do more or less habitually what one tells others to do.

practised *adjective* **1** experienced, expert: *with a practised hand*. **2** gained or perfected through practice: *a practised accent*.

practising *adjective* currently active or engaged in (a profession or activity): *a practising Christian*.

practitioner *noun* **1** a person practising a profession,

esp. medicine. **2** a person who regularly does a particular activity, esp. one requiring skill: *an outstanding practitioner of the art of lexicography*. [Say prack TISHA ner]
pragmatic *adjective* solving problems in a practical and sensible way rather than by having fixed ideas or theories; realistic: *a pragmatic approach to management problems*. ▶ **pragmatically** *adverb* [Say prag MAT ick]
pragmatism *noun* the tendency to solve problems in a practical and sensible way rather than by having fixed ideas or theories: *the claims were based on reason, pragmatism and common sense*. ▶ **pragmatist** *noun* [Say PRAGMA tism]
prairie *noun* **1** a large area of usu. treeless and flat grassland, esp. in western Canada. **2** (also **the prairies**) the region of western North America originally characterized by such grassland. **3** (**the Prairies**) = PRAIRIE PROVINCES.
prairie chicken *noun* **1** a medium-sized grouse of the North American prairies. **2** = SHARP-TAILED GROUSE.
prairie crocus *noun* (*plural* **prairie crocuses**) *Cdn* a spring-flowering plant of the buttercup family, found from BC to Manitoba and in the US, which has leaves covered with silky hairs, purple or white crocus-like flowers, and long plumed seeds; it is the floral emblem of Manitoba.
prairie dog *noun* a North American rodent that lives in burrows and makes a barking sound.
prairie fire *noun* an uncontrolled fire that burns off the grasses etc. of the prairie.
prairie lily *noun* (*plural* **prairie lilies**) a North American lily bearing upright reddish-orange flowers with spotted petals; it is the floral emblem of Saskatchewan.
prairie oyster *noun* **1** a seasoned raw egg, swallowed without breaking the yolk. **2** the testicle of a calf eaten as a delicacy.
Prairie provinces *plural noun* Alberta, Saskatchewan, and Manitoba.
prairie schooner *noun* a covered wagon used by the 19th-century pioneers in crossing the prairies.
prairie smoke *noun* *Cdn* either of two plants with long-plumed seeds, the three-flowered avens or the prairie crocus.
prairie wool *noun* *Cdn* the natural grassy plant cover of prairie land.
praise • *verb* (**praises, praised, praising**) **1** express warm approval or admiration of. **2** glorify (God or a deity) in words. • *noun* the expression of approval or admiration for someone or something: *the audience was full of praise for the whole production*. PHRASES **praise be!** an exclamation of pious gratitude. **sing the praises of** commend (a person) highly.
praiseworthy *adjective* worthy of praise.
praline *noun* **1** a confection made by browning nuts in boiling sugar, often crushed and used as a topping or in ice cream etc. **2** a fudge-like, cookie-shaped candy. [Say PRAY leen or PRAW leen]
prance • *verb* (**prances, pranced, prancing**) **1** (of a horse) raise the forelegs and spring from the hind legs. **2** (often foll. by *about*) walk or behave in an elated or arrogant manner. • *noun* an act or instance of prancing.
prank *noun* a practical joke; a piece of mischief. ▶ **prankish** *adjective* **prankster** *noun*
praseodymium *noun* a soft silvery metallic element of the lanthanide series, occurring naturally in various minerals and used in catalyst mixtures. [Say praisy uh DIMMY um]
prate *verb* (**prates, prated, prating**) talk foolishly or at tedious length about something: *prating on and on about secret trips to France with mysterious women*.

pratfall *noun* *informal* **1** a fall on the buttocks. **2** a humiliating failure or blunder.
prattle • *verb* (**prattles, prattled, prattling**) chatter or say in a childish way. • *noun* **1** childish chatter. **2** inconsequential talk. ▶ **prattling** *adjective*
prawn • *noun* **1** any of various marine crustaceans, resembling a shrimp but usu. larger. **2** esp. *Brit.* a large shrimp. • *verb* fish for prawns.
praxis *noun* accepted practice or custom: *church doctrine, long divorced from praxis*. [Say PRAX iss]

SPELL CHECK
pray, prey

A hunter's victim is its **prey**.

pray *verb* **1** say prayers (to God etc.). **2 a** entreat, beseech. **b** ask earnestly: *prayed to be released*. PHRASES **pray tell** (used when adding emphasis to question or request, sometimes ironically) please say: *and what, pray tell, would be the point?*
prayer[1] *noun* **1 a** a solemn request or thanksgiving to God or an object of worship: *say a prayer*. **b** the act of praying: *be at prayer*. **c** a religious service consisting largely of prayers: *evening prayer*. **2 a** an entreaty to a person. **b** a thing entreated or prayed for: *my prayer is that all of us realize how important it is to appreciate every day we have*. PHRASES **not have a prayer** *informal* have no chance (of success etc.).
prayer[2] *noun* a person who prays.
prayer book *noun* a book containing prayers for use in religious services or private devotions.
prayerful *adjective* **1** (of a person) given to praying. **2** (of speech, actions, etc.) characterized by or expressive of prayer. ▶ **prayerfully** *adverb*
prayer meeting *noun* a gathering of esp. evangelical Christians to offer prayers.
prayer rug *noun* (also **prayer mat**) a small carpet used by Muslims when praying.
prayer shawl *noun* a shawl worn by Jewish men, esp. at prayer (*also called* TALLIS).
praying mantis *noun* (*plural* **praying mantis** or **praying mantises**) a mantis that holds its forelegs in a position suggestive of hands folded in prayer, while waiting to pounce on its prey.
pre- *prefix* before (in time, place, order, degree, etc.).
preach *verb* (**preaches, preached, preaching**) **1 a** deliver a sermon or religious address. **b** proclaim or expound (the Gospel etc.). **2** give moral advice in an annoying or pompously self-righteous way: *viewers want to be entertained, not preached at*. **3** advocate or try to convince people of the value of something: *I used to preach energy efficiency*. PHRASES **preach to the converted** commend an opinion to a person or persons already in agreement.
preacher *noun* a person who preaches, esp. a minister of religion. ▶ **preacherly** *adjective*
preachiness *noun* the tendency to give moral advice in an obtrusive way: *annoyed by their preachiness*.
preachy *adjective* (**preachier, preachiest**) *informal* inclined to preach or moralize.
preamble *noun* **1** a preliminary statement or introduction: *she would come down and without preamble read him an extract from one of her essays*. **2** the introductory part of a statute or deed etc. [Say PREE amble]
preamplifier *noun* (also **preamp**) an electronic device that amplifies a very weak signal (e.g. from a microphone or pickup) and transmits it to a main amplifier.
pre-arrange *verb* (**pre-arranges, pre-arranged,**

pre-arranging) arrange beforehand. ▶**pre-arranged** adjective **pre-arrangement** noun

Precambrian • adjective of the earliest geological time including the whole of the earth's history from its origin about 4,600 million years ago to the beginning of the Cambrian period about 570 million years ago. The period was characterized by the formation of the earth's crust and atmosphere, the appearance of the first single-celled organisms, and the development of the first flatworms and jellyfish. • noun this geological period. [Say pree CAME bree un or pree CAM bree un]

precarious adjective **1** (of a situation) not safe or certain; dangerous: he earned a precarious living as an artist ◊ the museum is in a financially precarious position ◊ the world is a precarious and unstable place. **2** not securely held or in position: a precarious ladder. ▶**precariously** adverb **precariousness** noun [Say pruh KERRY us]

precast adjective (of concrete) cast in its final shape before positioning.

precaution noun an action taken in advance to avoid danger, prevent problems, etc. ▶**precautionary** adjective

---

SPELL CHECK	ABC ✓
precede, proceed	

To move forwards or to continue is to **proceed**: Please proceed to the next level.

---

precede verb (**precedes, preceded, preceding**) **1** come or go before in time, order, importance, etc.: the preceding paragraph. **2** walk etc. in front of: preceded by our guide. [Say pree SEED]

precedence noun **1** priority in time, order, or importance, etc. **2** the right of preceding others on formal occasions. PHRASES **take precedence** (often foll. by over, of) have priority (over). [Say PRESSA dince]

precedent noun **1** a previous case or legal decision etc. taken as a guide for subsequent cases or as a justification: they fear the precedent could trigger similar measures elsewhere. **2** a similar event or action that occurred earlier: there is no precedent for such a study. [Say PRESSA dint]

precept noun a general rule intended to regulate behaviour or thought; a principle: the legal precept of being innocent until proven guilty. [Say PREE sept]

pre-Christian adjective before Christ or Christianity.

precinct noun **1** an enclosed or clearly defined area, e.g. around a cathedral, college, etc. **2** a specially designated area in a town, esp. with the exclusion of traffic: shopping precinct. **3 a** a subdivision of a county, city, etc., for police or electoral purposes. **b** informal the police station of such a subdivision. **c** (in plural) a neighbourhood: affluent precincts of Los Angeles. [Say PREE sinct]

precious • adjective **1** of great value or worth. **2** beloved; much prized: precious memories. **3** affectedly refined, esp. in language or manner: at the same time there was a jazz salon — too precious a word for it. **4** informal expressing contempt or disdain: you can keep your precious flowers. • adverb informal extremely, very: had precious little left. ▶**preciousness** noun

precipice noun **1** a vertical or steep face of a rock, cliff, mountain, etc.: hunters would stampede buffalo herds over the precipice. **2** a dangerous situation: it threatens global destruction by propelling mankind toward the nuclear precipice. [Say PRESSA piss]

precipitate • verb (**precipitates, precipitated, precipitating**) **1** hasten the occurrence of; cause to occur prematurely: the war was to precipitate immense changes in the life of the nation. **2** send rapidly into a certain state or condition: were precipitated into war.

3 deposit or be deposited in solid form from a solution or from suspension in a gas. • adjective **1** occurring suddenly or abruptly: the precipitate resignation of the director. **2** hasty, thoughtless: I must apologize for my staff — their actions were precipitate. • noun **1** Chemistry a substance precipitated from a solution. **2** Physics moisture condensed from vapour by cooling and depositing, e.g. rain or dew. ▶**precipitately** adverb [Say pree SIPPA tate for the verb, pree SIPPA tit for the adjective and noun]

precipitation noun **1 a** rain or snow etc. falling to the ground. **b** a quantity of this. **2** the act of precipitating or the process of being precipitated.

precipitous adjective **1 a** of or like a precipice. **b** dangerously steep. **2 a** sudden and great: a precipitous decline in exports. **b** done very quickly, without enough thought or care: a precipitous action. ▶**precipitously** adverb **precipitousness** noun [Say pruh SIPPA tus]

précis • noun (plural **précis**) a summary or abstract, esp. of a text or speech. • verb (**précises, précised, précising**) make a précis of. [Say PRAY see]

precise adjective **1 a** accurately expressed. **b** definite, exact. **2** scrupulous in being exact, observing rules, etc.: the director was precise with his camera positions. **3** identical, exact: at that precise moment. **4** (of an instrument) accurate; exact.

precisely adverb **1** in a precise manner; exactly. **2** (as a reply) quite so; as you say.

precision noun **1** the condition of being precise; accuracy. **2** the degree of refinement in measurement etc. **3** (as an adjective) marked by or adapted for precision: precision instruments.

precision skater noun a member of a team of 12 to 32 figure skaters who perform in unison.

precision skating noun Cdn figure skating performed in unison by a team of 12 to 32 skaters.

preclude verb (**precludes, precluded, precluding**) **1** (often foll. by from) prevent, exclude: the bill has been drafted in such a way as to preclude it from affecting any First Nations. **2** make impossible; remove: growing up in Canada precluded any real understanding of what it meant to face being drafted. [Say pree CLUDE]

precocious adjective **1** often derogatory (of a person, esp. a child) prematurely developed in some faculty or characteristic: she's a precocious child, but we are not made to feel that she is an adult in child's clothing. **2** (of an action etc.) indicating such development: his precocious career was helped, no doubt, by the fact that many older musicians were leaving town. **3** (of a plant) flowering or fruiting early: precocious daffodils. ▶**precociously** adverb **precocity** noun [Say pruh CO shus, pruh COSSA tee]

pre-colonial adjective of or relating to the period before a region or territory became a colony.

pre-Columbian adjective of or pertaining to the period of history in the Americas before the arrival of Columbus in 1492.

preconceived adjective (of an idea or opinion) formed before having the evidence for its truth or usefulness: the same set of facts can be tailored to fit a preconceived belief.

preconception noun **1** a preconceived idea. **2** a prejudice.

precondition noun a prior condition, that must be fulfilled before other things can be done.

pre-Confederation adjective Cdn **1** of or pertaining to the period before 1867 in Canada. **2** relating to or characteristic of the period before a province or territory entered Confederation.

pre-contact adjective of or relating to an Aboriginal society before contact with Europeans.

precook *verb* cook in advance.

precursor *noun* **1** a person or thing that comes before another of the same kind; a forerunner: *a three-stringed precursor of the violin*. **2** a substance from which another is formed by decay or chemical reaction etc. [Say pree CURSOR]

predate *verb* (**predates, predated, predating**) exist or occur at a date earlier than.

predation *noun* Zoology the natural preying of one animal on others. [Say pruh DAY sh'n]

predator *noun* **1** an animal naturally preying on others: *it survives by outrunning predators*. **2** a predatory corporation, country, individual, etc.: *protecting domestic industry from foreign predators*. [Say PREDDA ter]

predatory *adjective* **1** (of an animal) preying naturally upon others: *the predatory leopard seal is armed with powerful jaws*. **2** (of a corporation, country, individual, etc.) plundering or exploiting others: *predatory laissez-faire capitalism*. [Say PREDDA tory]

pre-dawn • *noun* the period of time just before dawn. • *adjective* relating to or occurring during this time.

predecease *verb* (**predeceases, predeceased, predeceasing**) die earlier than (another person). [Say pree duh CEASE]

predecessor *noun* **1** a former holder of an office or position with respect to a later holder: *my immediate predecessor*. **2** a thing to which another has succeeded: *the new plan resembles its predecessor*. [Say PREEDA sesser]

predestination *noun* Theology the belief that everything that happens has been decided or planned in advance by God or by fate, esp. with regard to the salvation of some and not others.

predestine *verb* (**predestines, predestined, predestining**) (often as predestined *adjective*) **1** determine beforehand: *that title predestined the book for publishing's boneyard*. **2** ordain in advance by divine will or fate: *argued that God has predestined some for heaven and others for hell*. [Say pree DES tin]

predetermination *noun* an act of predetermining.

predetermine *verb* (**predetermines, predetermined, predetermining**) **1** determine or decree beforehand. **2** predestine.

predicament *noun* a difficult, unpleasant, or embarrassing situation. [Say pree DICKA mint]

predicate • *verb* (**predicates, predicated, predicating**) (foll. by *on*) found or base (a statement etc.) on: *democracy is predicated on the assumption that the governors are not substantially different from the governed*. • *noun* Grammar what is said about the subject of a sentence etc. (e.g. *went home* in *Earl went home*). [Say PREDDA kate for the verb, PREDDA kit for the noun]

predicative *adjective* (of an adjective or noun) forming or contained in the predicate, as *old* in *the dog is old* and *house* in *there is a large house* (opp. ATTRIBUTIVE). ▶ **predicatively** *adverb* [Say pruh DICKA tiv]

predict *verb* (often foll. by *that* + clause) make a statement about the future; foretell, prophesy.

predictability *noun* the quality of being predictable: *the bland but comforting predictability of brand-name hotels*.

predictable *adjective* **1** that can be predicted or is to be expected. **2** likely to behave in a way that is easy to predict. ▶ **predictably** *adverb*

prediction *noun* **1** the art of predicting or the process of being predicted. **2** a thing predicted; a forecast.

predictive *adjective* relating to or having the effect of predicting an event or result: *predictive accuracy* ◊ *the rules are not predictive of behaviour*.

predictor *noun* something that can show what will happen in the future: *cholesterol level is not a strong predictor of heart disease in women*.

predigest *verb* **1** render (food) easily digestible before

being eaten. **2** make (reading matter, etc.) easier to read, understand, appreciate, etc.

predilection *noun* a preference or special liking: *less impressive was the director's predilection for utterly irrelevant statistics*. [Say predda LECTION]

predispose *verb* (**predisposes, predisposed, predisposing**) make someone liable or inclined to a specified attitude, action, or condition: *stress can predispose people to heart attacks* ◊ *religious societies were predisposed to interpret inexplicable happenings as portents*. ▶ **predisposition** *noun* [Say pree DISPOSE, pree dis POSITION]

SPELL CHECK
prejudice

Note that there is no *d* before the *j* in *prejudice*.

---

prednisone *noun* a synthetic drug similar to cortisone, used to relieve rheumatic and allergic conditions and to treat leukemia. [Say PREDNA zone]

predominance *noun* **1** the situation of being greater in number or amount than other things or people; preponderance: *the predominance of female teachers in elementary schools*. **2** the state of having more power or influence than others; dominance: *the ongoing struggle for global predominance*.

predominant *adjective* **1** being the main or most numerous or widespread element: *its predominant colour was white*. **2** prevailing, exerting control: *the predominant political forces*.

predominantly *adverb* mainly; for the most part.

predominate *verb* (**predominates, predominated, predominating**) **1** have or exert control: *private interest was not allowed to predominate over the public good*. **2** be the strongest, main, or most numerous or widespread element: *a garden in which dahlias predominate*.

pre-eclampsia *noun* a condition of pregnancy characterized by high blood pressure and other symptoms associated with eclampsia. [Say pree i CLAMPSY uh]

preemie *noun* informal a baby born prematurely.

pre-eminence *noun* outstanding excellence; the most eminent position: *the pre-eminence of Venetian glass-makers in the fifteenth century*.

pre-eminent *adjective* surpassing all others; very distinguished in some way: *the world's pre-eminent expert on asbestos*. ▶ **pre-eminently** *adverb*

pre-empt *verb* **1** take action in order to prevent (an anticipated event) happening: *the government pre-empted a coup attempt*. **2** act in advance of (someone) in order to prevent them doing something: *it looked as if she'd ask him for more, but he pre-empted her*. **3** (of a broadcast) interrupt or replace (a scheduled program): *the violence pre-empted regular programming*. **4** take for oneself (esp. public land) so as to have the right of pre-emption.

pre-emption *noun* **1 a** the purchase of goods or shares by one person or party before the opportunity is offered to others: *the commission had the right of pre-emption*. **b** the right to purchase (esp. public land) in this way: *Natives who had signed treaty were forbidden from acquiring lands by homestead or pre-emption*. **2** the action of pre-empting or forestalling, esp. of making a pre-emptive attack: *the US vowed damaging retaliation for any attempt at pre-emption*.

pre-emptive *adjective* **1** serving to pre-empt or forestall something, esp. to prevent attack by disabling the enemy: *pre-emptive action* ◊ *a pre-emptive strike*. **2** relating to the purchase of goods or shares by one person or party before the opportunity is offered to others: *pre-emptive rights*. ▶ **pre-emptively** *adverb*

preen *verb* **1** (of a bird) tidy (the feathers or itself) with

its beak. **2** (of a person) smarten or admire (oneself, one's hair, clothes, etc.).

pre-existing *adjective* (also **pre-existent**) existing at an earlier time or already.

prefab *informal* • *adjective* prefabricated. • *noun* a prefabricated building etc.

prefabricate *verb* (**prefabricates, prefabricated, prefabricating**) **1** manufacture sections of (a building or piece of furniture etc.) to enable quick and easy assembly on site: *prefabricated homes ◊ there are many kinds of oil rigs, but all are prefabricated inshore.* **2** produce in an artificially standardized way: *is always spouting prefabricated answers to the difficult questions of life.* [Say pree FABRICATE]

prefabrication *noun* the assembling of a building etc. from components made beforehand. [Say pree FABRICATION]

preface • *noun* **1** an introduction to a book stating its subject, scope, etc. **2** the preliminary part of a speech. • *verb* (**prefaces, prefaced, prefacing**) **1** introduce or begin (a speech or event): *prefaced my remarks with a warning.* **2** provide (a book etc.) with a preface: *the book is prefaced by a quotation from Leacock.* ▶ **prefatory** *adjective* [Say PREFF iss, PREFFA tory]

prefect *noun* **1** a chief officer, magistrate, governor, etc. **2** the chief administrative officer of certain departments in France. **3** a senior pupil in a school etc. authorized to enforce discipline. **4** *Catholicism* a cardinal presiding over a congregation of the Curia. [Say PREE fect]

prefecture *noun* **1 a** a district under the government of a prefect. **b** an administrative division of a Japanese or Chinese province. **2 a** a prefect's office or tenure. **b** the official residence of a prefect. [Say PREE feck chur]

prefer *verb* (**prefers, preferred, preferring**) **1** choose instead; like better: *would prefer to stay ◊ prefers coffee to tea.* **2** submit (information, an accusation, etc.) for consideration: *the police will prefer charges.* **3** give preference to as a creditor. [Say pruh FUR]

preferability *noun* the state of being more desirable than something else. [Say preff er a BILLA tee]

preferable *adjective* **1** to be preferred. **2** more desirable. ▶ **preferably** *adverb* [Say PREFF er a bull or pruh FURRA bull]

preference *noun* **1** a greater liking for one alternative over another or others: *a preference for long walks and tennis over jogging ◊ he chose a clock in preference to a watch.* **2** a thing preferred. **3 a** the favouring of one person etc. before others. **b** the favouring of one country by admitting its products at a lower import duty. **4** *Law* a prior right, esp. to the payment of debts.

preferential *adjective* **1** of or involving preference: *preferential treatment.* **2** (of a tariff etc.) favouring particular countries. **3** (of voting) in which the voter puts candidates in order of preference. ▶ **preferentially** *adverb* [Say preffer EN shul]

preferment *noun* promotion or appointment to a position or office: *most of her ministers owed their first preferment to her.* [Say pruh FUR mint]

preferred share *noun* (also **preferred stock**) a share in a company which yields a fixed rate of interest and takes preference over common stock in entitlement to dividends.

prefigure *verb* (**prefigures, prefigured, prefiguring**) be an early indication or version of (something): *this movement prefigured the Protestant Reformation.*

prefix • *noun* (*plural* **prefixes**) **1** a verbal element placed at the beginning of a word to adjust or qualify its meaning, e.g. *ex-, non-, re-.* **2** a title placed before a name, e.g. *Mr.* • *verb* (**prefixes, prefixed, prefixing**)

(often foll. by *to*) **1** add (something) at the beginning as a prefix or introduction: *the book is prefixed with a preface.* **2** join (a word or element) as a prefix.

preform *verb* form or shape beforehand.

preggers *adjective* *informal* = PREGNANT 1.

pregnancy *noun* (*plural* **pregnancies**) **1** the condition or period of being pregnant: *the first weeks of pregnancy.* **2** a case or situation of being pregnant: *a straightforward pregnancy.*

pregnant *adjective* **1** (of a woman or female animal) having a child or young developing in the uterus. **2** full of meaning; significant or suggestive: *a pregnant pause.* **3** (esp. of a person's mind) imaginative, inventive. **4** (foll. by *with*) plentifully provided: *a word that is pregnant with meaning.*

preheat *verb* heat beforehand.

prehensile *adjective* (of a tail or limb) capable of grasping. [Say pree HEN sile]

prehistoric *adjective* **1** of or relating to the period before written records. **2** *informal* utterly out of date. ▶ **prehistorically** *adverb* **prehistory** *noun*

pre-industrial *adjective* of or relating to the time before industrialization.

prejudge *verb* (**prejudges, prejudged, prejudging**) **1** form a premature judgment on (a person, issue, etc.). **2** pass judgment on (a person) before a trial or proper inquiry. ▶ **prejudgment** *noun*

SPELL CHECK
prejudice, prejudiced

Note that the adjective is **prejudiced**.

---

prejudice • *noun* **1 a** a preconceived opinion. **b** (foll. by *against, in favour of*) bias or partiality. **c** dislike or distrust of a person, group, etc. **2** harm or injury that results or may result from some action or judgment: *prejudice resulting from delay in the institution of the proceedings.* • *verb* (**prejudices, prejudiced, prejudicing**) **1** cause (a person) to have a prejudice. **2** have a harmful effect on something: *any delay will prejudice the child's welfare.* ▐PHRASES▌ **without prejudice** (often foll. by *to*) without detriment (to any existing right or claim). [Say PREDGE uh diss]

prejudiced *adjective* **1** not impartial: *the prejudiced referee.* **2** bigoted: *people are prejudiced against us ◊ prejudiced views.* [Say PREDGE uh dist]

prejudicial *adjective* **1** causing or characterized by prejudice: *use the words that the people themselves prefer, and avoid prejudicial, discriminatory terms.* **2** harmful to someone or something: *the proposals were considered prejudicial to the city centre.* ▶ **prejudicially** *adverb* [Say predge uh DISH'll]

prelate *noun* a high ecclesiastical dignitary, e.g. a cardinal, archbishop, etc. [Say PRELLIT]

prelim *noun* *informal* **1** (often in *plural*) a preliminary game, contest, round, etc. **2 a** a preliminary examination, hearing, or trial. [Say PREE lim or pri LIM]

preliminary • *adjective* introductory, preparatory. • *noun* (*plural* **preliminaries**) (usu. in *plural*) **1** a preliminary action or arrangement: *dispense with the preliminaries.* **2** a preliminary trial or contest. • *adverb* (foll. by *to*) preparatory to; in advance. [Say pruh LIMMA nerry]

preliterate *adjective* of or relating to a society or culture that has not developed the use of writing. [Say pre LITERATE]

preload *verb* (esp. as **preloaded** *adjective*) load (esp. software) beforehand.

prelude • *noun* **1** an action, event, or situation serving as an introduction: *education cannot simply be a prelude to a career.* **2 a** an introductory piece of music, often

preceding a fugue or forming the first piece of a suite or beginning an act of an opera. **b** a short piece of music of a similar type, esp. for the piano. **3** the introductory part of a poem etc. • *verb* (**preludes, preluded, preluding**) serve as a prelude or introduction to: *the bombardment preluded an all-out final attack*. [Say PRAY lood or PRELL yood]

premarital *adjective* existing or (esp. of sexual relations) occurring before marriage. [Say pree MERRA tul]

premature *adjective* **1 a** occurring or done before the usual or proper time; too early: *a premature decision*. **b** too hasty: *it would be premature to do so at this stage*. **2** (of a baby) born (esp. three or more weeks) before the end of the full term of gestation. ▶ **prematurely** *adverb*

pre-med *noun* **1** a program of studies taken in preparation for medical school. **2** a pre-med student.

premeditated *adjective* (of an action) thought out or planned beforehand: *premeditated murder*. ▶ **premeditation** *noun* [Say pre MEDITATE]

premenopausal *adjective* preceding menopause. [Say pre MENOPAUSAL]

premenstrual *adjective* occurring before a menstrual period: *premenstrual tension*. [Say pre MENSTRUAL]

premenstrual syndrome *noun* any of a complex of symptoms (including tension, fluid retention, etc.) experienced by some women in the days immediately before menstruation. Abbreviation: **PMS**.

SPELL CHECK
premier, premiere

The head of a province is a **premier**; the first showing of a movie is a **premiere**.

---

premier • *noun* **1** *Cdn* the first minister of a province or territory. **2** a prime minister or head of government in any of several other countries. • *adjective* first in importance, order, or time: *has a reputation as Canada's premier actor*.

premiere • *noun* the first performance or showing of a play, film, etc. • *verb* (**premieres, premiered, premiering**) **1** give a premiere of. **2** (of a play, film, etc.) be presented for the first time.

premiership *noun* the period or position of being a premier: *resigned in the second year of his premiership*.

premise • *noun* **1** (also **premiss**, *plural* **premisses**) *Logic* a previous statement or proposition from which another is inferred or follows as a conclusion. **2** the basic plot or circumstances on which a play, film, etc., is based: *the script needs rewriting but its potential is real and its premise is not so futuristic*. **3** (in *plural*) a house, building, etc., with any buildings or property near it belonging to it: *was escorted from the premises*. • *verb* (**premises, premised, premising**) (foll. by *on*) base on: *the reforms were premised on our findings*. PHRASES **on the premises** in the building etc. concerned. [Say PREM iss]

premium • *noun* **1** an amount to be paid for a contract of insurance. **2 a** a sum added to interest, wages, etc.; a bonus. **b** a sum added to ordinary charges. **3** a reward or prize. • *adjective* (of a commodity) of best quality and therefore more expensive. PHRASES **at a premium 1** highly valued; above the usual or nominal price. **2** scarce and in demand. **put a premium on 1** provide or act as an incentive to. **2** attach special value to.

premix • *verb* (**premixes, premixed, premixing**) (esp. as **premixed** *adjective*) mix beforehand. • *noun* (*plural* **premixes**) a mixture prepared beforehand of various materials, e.g. animal feed. [Say pree MIX]

premolar • *adjective* in front of a molar tooth. • *noun*

(in an adult human) each of eight teeth situated in pairs between each of the four canine teeth and each first molar.

premonition *noun* a forewarning; a vague expectation or foreboding (esp. of misfortune): *she had a premonition of imminent disaster*. ▶ **premonitory** *adjective* [Say premma NISH'n, pree MONNA tory]

prenatal *adjective* of or concerning the period before childbirth. [Say pree NATE ul]

prenup *noun* *informal* a prenuptial agreement. [Say pree NUP]

prenuptial *adjective* **1** existing or occurring before marriage. **2** (of an agreement, contract, etc.) entered into by a couple before marriage, specifying how their assets are to be split in the event of divorce. [Say pree NUP choo ul or pree NUP shoo ul or pree NUP shul]

preoccupation *noun* **1** the state of being preoccupied. **2** a thing that engrosses the mind. [Say pre OCCUPATION]

preoccupied *adjective* otherwise engrossed; mentally distracted. [Say pre OCCUPIED]

preoccupy *verb* (**preoccupies, preoccupied, preoccupying**) (of a thought etc.) dominate or engross the mind of (a person) to the exclusion of other thoughts. [Say pre OCCUPY]

pre-op *adjective* = PREOPERATIVE.

preoperative *adjective* of or related to the period or a condition before an operation. [Say pre OPERATIVE]

preordained *adjective* ordained or determined beforehand: *he believes in a divinely preordained plan of creation*. [Say pre ORDAIN]

pre-owned *adjective* second-hand, used.

prep *informal* • *noun* **1** = PREPARATION. **2** = PREPPY. • *adjective* **1** = PREPARATORY: *prep time*. **2** relating to a preparatory school: *prep athlete*. • *verb* (**preps, prepped, prepping**) *informal* **1** prepare, make ready or suitable. **2** prepare oneself for an event.

prepackaged *adjective* (of goods) packaged on the site of production or before retail.

preparation *noun* **1** the action or process of making ready or being made ready for use or consideration: *the preparation of a draft contract* ◊ *the project is in preparation*. **2** (often in *plural*) something done to make ready. **3** a specially prepared substance, esp. a food or medicine.

preparative *adjective* preparatory. [Say pruh PERRA tiv]

preparatory • *adjective* done in order to prepare for something: *preparatory meetings* ◊ *after a few preparatory drawings, she completed the portrait in one session*. • *adverb* (often foll. by *to*) in a preparatory manner: *preparatory to departure*. [Say PREP er a tory or pruh PERRA tory]

preparatory school *noun* a usu. private school preparing pupils for college or university.

prepare *verb* (**prepares, prepared, preparing**) make or get ready. PHRASES **be prepared 1** (usu. foll. by *for*) be ready or disposed: *was prepared for a legal battle*. **2** (foll. by *to*) be willing to.

preparedness *noun* a state of readiness.

preparer *noun* a person who prepares something.

prepay *verb* (**prepays, prepaid, prepaying**) **1** pay (a charge) in advance. **2** pay for (goods or a service) in advance. ▶ **prepayable** *adjective* **prepayment** *noun*

preponderance *noun* superiority in number or amount: *the restaurant now attracts a preponderance of families with children*. [Say pruh PONDER ince]

preponderant *adjective* surpassing in influence, power, number, or importance; predominant: *in most Canadian ridings, no one industry is preponderant*. ▶ **preponderantly** *adverb* [Say pruh PONDER int]

P

preposition *noun* Grammar a word governing (and usu. preceding) a noun or pronoun and expressing a relation to another word or element, as in: "the man *on* the platform", "came *after* dinner", "what did you do it *for?*". ▶ **prepositional** *adjective* [Say preppa ZISH'n]

prepositional phrase *noun* a phrase formed with a preposition, e.g. *on the hill*.

prepossessing *adjective* attractive, appealing: *he wasn't exactly handsome or even prepossessing*.

preposterous *adjective* utterly absurd; outrageous: *I find the whole idea of this book preposterous*. ▶ **preposterously** *adverb* **preposterousness** *noun* [Say pruh POSS ter us]

preppy (also **preppie**) *informal* • *noun* (*plural* **preppies**) a person attending an expensive private school or who looks like such a person (with neat and stylish hair, clothing, etc.). • *adjective* (**preppier, preppiest**) **1** of, like, or pertaining to a preppy or preppies. **2** neat and fashionable.

preprocessor *noun* a computer program that modifies data to conform with the input requirements of another program. [Say pre PROCESSOR]

pre-production *noun* work done on a film, broadcast, etc. before production begins: *pre-production discussions*.

pre-program *verb* (**pre-programs, pre-programmed, pre-programming**) program (a computer etc.) beforehand.

prep school *noun* = PREPARATORY SCHOOL.

prepubescent • *adjective* (also **prepubertal**) **1** occurring prior to puberty. **2** that has not yet reached puberty. • *noun* a prepubescent boy or girl. [Say pre pyoo BESS int]

pre-qualify *verb* (**pre-qualifies, pre-qualified, pre-qualifying**) qualify in advance, as for a mortgage, sporting event, etc.

prequel *noun* a story, film, etc., whose events or concerns precede those of an existing work. [Say PREE quil]

Pre-Raphaelite • *noun* a member of a group of English 19th-century artists whose early work was marked by bright colours, strong boundary lines, and meticulous detail; later works typically depict scenes from classical mythology or medieval romance in a dreamy style. • *adjective* **1** of or relating to the Pre-Raphaelites. **2** (**pre-Raphaelite**) (esp. of a woman) like a type painted by a Pre-Raphaelite, e.g. with long thick curly auburn hair. [Say pre RAFFY uh lite]

pre-recorded *adjective* (of a message, material for broadcasting, etc.) recorded in advance.

pre-release • *adjective* of or pertaining to the period before the release of a prisoner, consumer product, etc. • *noun* a film, record, software, etc., given restricted availability before being generally released.

prerequisite • *adjective* required as a precondition: *the student must have the prerequisite skills*. • *noun* a prerequisite thing: *absolute trust and openness is a basic prerequisite for a solid, worthwhile relationship*. [Say pre RECKWA zit]

prerogative *noun* **1** a right or privilege exclusive to an individual or class: *owning a car was once the prerogative of the very rich*. **2** the right or privilege exercised by a monarch or head of state over all other people, which overrides the law and is in theory subject to no restriction. [Say pruh ROGGA tiv]

Pres. *abbreviation* President.

presage • *noun* a sign or warning that something, esp. something bad, will happen. • *verb* (**presages, presaged, presaging**) be a warning or sign that something will happen, usually something unpleasant: *nothing had presaged the dreadful fate about to befall him* ◊ *heavy clouds were forming, presaging rain*. [Say PRESS idge for the noun, pree SAGE for the verb]

presbyter *noun* (in the Presbyterian Church) an elder. [Say PRESS buh ter]

Presbyterian • *noun* a member of a Protestant denomination in which the Church is administered locally by the minister with a group of elected elders of equal rank, and regionally and nationally by representative courts of ministers and elders. • *adjective* of Presbyterians. ▶ **Presbyterianism** *noun* [Say press buh TEERY in]

presbytery *noun* (*plural* **presbyteries**) **1 a** (in the Presbyterian and United Churches) an ecclesiastical body made up of all of the ministers from a district together with an equal number of elders, ranking next above a Session. **b** a district represented by this. **2** the house of a Catholic priest. [Say PRESS buh tree]

preschool • *adjective* of or relating to the time before a child is old enough to go to school. • *noun* = NURSERY SCHOOL. ▶ **preschooler** *noun*

prescience *noun* the ability to foresee what will happen in the future. [Say PRESSY ince]

prescient *adjective* having foreknowledge or foresight: *those prescient people who publish investment newsletters*. ▶ **presciently** *adverb* [Say PRESSY int]

pre-screen *verb* screen beforehand; make a preliminary selection among (candidates etc.).

prescribe *verb* (**prescribes, prescribed, prescribing**) **1 a** advise the use of (a medicine etc.), esp. by an authorized prescription. **b** recommend, esp. as a benefit: *prescribed a change of scenery*. **2** (used about a person or an organization with authority) to say what should be done or how something should be done: *the prescribed form must be completed and returned to this office* ◊ *the syllabus prescribes which books should be studied*.

prescription *noun* **1 a** a doctor's (usu. written) instruction for the composition and use of a medicine. **b** a medicine prescribed. **2 a** the act or an instance of prescribing. **b** a thing considered as bringing about a specified condition: *a prescription for anarchy*.

prescriptive *adjective* **1** prescribing. **2** Linguistics attempting to impose rules of correct usage, often at variance with actual usage, on the users of a language: *a prescriptive grammar book* ◊ *a good dictionary should be descriptive rather than prescriptive*. ▶ **prescriptivism** *noun* **prescriptivist** *noun & adjective*

pre-season *noun* the period before a season (esp. a sports season) begins: *pre-season game*.

presence *noun* **1** the state or condition of being

present. **2** a place where a person is: *was admitted to their presence*. **3** a person's appearance, bearing, or force of personality, esp. when imposing: *stage presence*. **4** a person, spirit, etc., that is present: *there was a presence in the room*. **5** the maintenance by a nation of political interests and influence in another country or region: *maintained a presence*. PHRASES **in the presence of** in front of; observed by.

presence of mind *noun* calmness and self-control in sudden difficulty etc.

present[1] • *adjective* **1** being or occurring in a particular place. **2** existing or occurring now. **3** *Grammar* (of a tense or participle) expressing an action now going on or habitually performed, or a condition now existing. • *noun* **1** (**the present**) the period of time now occurring. **2** *Grammar* a present tense or form of a verb. PHRASES **at present** now. **for the present 1** just now. **2** as far as the present is concerned.

present[2] *verb* **1** give formally or ceremonially. **2** offer for acceptance or consideration. **3** formally introduce (someone) to someone else. **4** put (a show or exhibition) before the public. **5** introduce and appear in (a television or radio show). **6** be the cause of (a problem). **7** exhibit (a particular appearance) to others. **8** (foll. by *with*) *Medicine* (of a patient) come forward for medical examination for (a particular condition or symptom). PHRASES **present arms** hold a rifle etc. vertically in front of the body as a salute. **present oneself 1** appear. **2** come forward for examination etc.

present[3] *noun* a gift; a thing given or presented. PHRASES **make a present of** give as a gift.

presentable *adjective* **1** of good appearance; fit to be presented to other people. **2** fit for presentation. ▶ **presentably** *adverb*

presentation *noun* **1 a** the act of showing something or of giving something to someone. **b** a thing presented. **2** the manner or quality of presenting. **3** a demonstration or display of materials, information, etc.; a lecture. **4** an exhibition or theatrical performance. **5** a formal introduction. **6** the position of the fetus in relation to the cervix at the time of delivery. **7** *Cdn* (*Prairies*) **a** a wedding at which the bride and groom receive gifts of money rather than things. **b** a gift of money at such a wedding. ▶ **presentational** *adjective*

present-day *adjective* of this time; modern.

presenter *noun* a person who presents something, e.g. an award, or gives a presentation.

presentiment *noun* a vague expectation; a foreboding (esp. of misfortune): *a presentiment of disaster*. [Say pre ZENTA mint or pre SENTA mint]

presently *adverb* **1** at the present time; now. **2** soon; after a short time.

preservation *noun* **1** the act of preserving or process of being preserved. **2** a state of being well or badly preserved: *in an excellent state of preservation*.

preservationist *noun* a supporter or advocate of preservation, esp. of historic sites, natural areas, etc.

preservative • *noun* a substance for preserving perishable foodstuffs, wood, etc. • *adjective* tending to preserve. [Say pre ZERVA tiv]

preserve • *verb* (**preserves**, **preserved**, **preserving**) **1 a** keep safe or free from harm, decay, etc. **b** keep alive (a name, memory, etc.). **2** maintain (a thing) in its existing state. **3** retain (a quality or condition). **4 a** treat or refrigerate (food) to prevent decomposition or fermentation. **b** prepare (fruit) by boiling it with sugar, for long-term storage. **5** keep (a natural area, wildlife, etc.) undisturbed for protection or private use. • *noun* (in *singular* or *plural*) **1** preserved fruit or vegetables etc.; jam, pickles, etc. **2** a place

where game or fish etc. is preserved. **3** a sphere or area of activity regarded as a person's own: *the civil service became the preserve of the educated middle class*. ▶ **preserver** *noun*

pre-set • *verb* (**pre-sets**, **pre-set**, **pre-setting**) set or fix in advance of operation or use. • *noun* (**preset**) a setting or control, esp. on an electronic instrument, configured or adjusted beforehand to facilitate use.

pre-settlement *adjective* designating the time in North America before the arrival of European settlers.

pre-shrunk *adjective* (of a fabric or garment) caused to shrink during manufacture so that it does not shrink in use.

preside *verb* (**presides**, **presided**, **presiding**) (often foll. by *at*, *over*) be in a position of authority, esp. as the chairperson or president of a meeting.

presidency *noun* (*plural* **presidencies**) **1** the office of president. **2** the period of this.

president *noun* **1** the elected head of a republican state. **2** the head of an association, union, council, etc. **3** the head of a company etc. **4** the head of a college or university. **5** a person in charge of a meeting, assembly, etc. ▶ **presidential** *adjective*

president-elect *noun* (*plural* **presidents-elect**) a president who has been elected but has not yet taken office.

press[1] • *verb* (**presses**, **pressed**, **pressing**) **1** move into a position of contact with something by exerting continuous physical force. **2** exert continuous physical force on (something), esp. to operate a device. **3** apply pressure to (something) to flatten or shape it. **4** move in a specified direction by pushing. **5** (often foll. by *on*, *ahead*) continue in one's action. **6** forcefully put forward (an opinion or claim). **7** make strong efforts to persuade or force to do something. **8** extract (juice or oil) by crushing or squeezing fruit, vegetables, etc. **9** (of time) be short. **10** (**be pressed to do**) have difficulty doing. **11** *Weightlifting* raise (a weight) by gradually pushing it upwards from the shoulders. • *noun* (*plural* **presses**) **1** a device for applying pressure in order to flatten or shape something or to extract juice or oil. **2** a printing press. **3** (**the press**) newspapers or journalists collectively. **4** coverage in newspapers and magazines. **5** a printing or publishing business. **6** a closely packed mass of people or things. **7** *Weightlifting* a raising of a weight up to shoulder height followed by its gradual extension above the head. **8** *Basketball* any of various forms of close guarding by the defending team. PHRASES **at** (or **in**) **press** (or **the press**) being printed. **be pressed for** have barely enough (time etc.). **go** (or **send**) **to press** go or send to be printed. **press the button 1** set machinery in motion. **2** *informal* initiate an action or train of events, esp. nuclear war. **press** (**the**) **flesh** shake hands.

press[2] *verb* (**presses**, **pressed**, **pressing**) **1** *hist.* force to serve in the army etc. **2** bring into use as a makeshift: *was pressed into service*.

press agent *noun* a person employed by an organization to deal with press publicity.

pressboard *noun* a material made of compressed paper laminations, used as a separator or insulator in electrical equipment.

press box *noun* (*plural* **press boxes**) a reporters' enclosure esp. at a sports event.

press conference *noun* a session to which journalists are invited to hear an announcement, ask questions, etc.

press corps *noun* a group of reporters from various publications, networks, etc. who regularly cover the same beat.

presser *noun* a person or thing that presses or operates a press.

press gallery *noun* a gallery for reporters, esp. in a legislative assembly.

press gang • *noun hist.* a group of men employed to force or coerce men to enlist in the army or navy. • *verb* (**press-gang**) force or coerce someone to perform a task or job: *she press-ganged reluctant family members to help plan the event.*

pressing • *adjective* calling for immediate attention; urgent: *pressing business.* • *noun* **1** a thing made by pressing, esp. a phonograph record. **2** a series of these made at one time. **3** the act or an instance of applying force or weight to something. ▶ **pressingly** *adverb*

press kit *noun* a portfolio, folder, etc. containing printed matter or other multimedia materials relating to a certain issue, product, etc., prepared by an organization for distribution to the media.

press office *noun* a department, e.g. of a business firm or political party, responsible for dealings with the press. ▶ **press officer** *noun*

press release *noun* an official statement issued to the media by a government department, business, etc., for information and possible publication.

press secretary *noun* (*plural* **press secretaries**) a person who deals with publicity and public relations for an individual or organization.

press time *noun* the time at which a print run of a newspaper, magazine, etc. begins.

pressure • *noun* **1 a** the exertion of continuous force on or against a body by another in contact with it. **b** the force exerted. **c** the amount of this (expressed by the force on a unit area): *atmospheric pressure.* **d** = BLOOD PRESSURE. **2** urgency; the need to meet a deadline etc.: *work under pressure.* **3** affliction or difficulty: *under financial pressure.* **4** constraining influence: *if pressure is brought to bear.* • *verb* (**pressures, pressured, pressuring**) **1** apply (esp. psychological or moral) pressure to. **2** (often foll. by *into*) persuade; coerce: *was pressured into attending.*

pressure cooker *noun* **1** an airtight pot in which food can be cooked quickly under steam pressure. **2** an environment or situation of great pressure or stress.

pressure group *noun* a group that promotes a particular interest or cause by influencing public policy.

pressure point *noun* **1** a small area on the skin especially sensitive to pressure. **2** a point where an artery can be pressed against a bone to inhibit bleeding. **3** a target for political pressure or influence.

pressure ridge *noun* a ridge caused by pressure, esp. a ridge of ice in the polar sea forced up by lateral pressure.

pressure-treated *adjective* (of wood) treated with chemical preservatives applied under high pressure to reduce rotting and insect infestation.

pressurization *noun* an act of pressurizing.

pressurize *verb* (**pressurizes, pressurized, pressurizing**) **1** (esp. as **pressurized** *adjective*) maintain normal atmospheric pressure in (an aircraft cabin etc.) at a high altitude. **2** raise to a high pressure.

prestige *noun* **1** respect, reputation, or influence derived from achievements, power, wealth, etc. **2** (as an *adjective*) having or conferring prestige. ▶ **prestigious** *adjective* [Say press TEEZH or press TEEJ, press TEE jiss or press TIDGE iss]

presto • *adverb Music* in quick tempo. • *noun* (*plural* **prestos**) *Music* a movement to be played in a quick tempo. • *interjection* (also **presto chango**) used to announce the successful completion of a magical trick or other surprising, esp. rapid, achievement. [Say PRESS toe (change oh)]

presumably *adverb* as may reasonably be presumed.

presume *verb* (**presumes, presumed, presuming**) **1 a** suppose to be true; take for granted. **b** assume (a person) to be: *presumed dead.* **2 a** take the liberty; be impudent enough: *presumed to question their authority.* **b** dare: *may I presume to ask?* **3** make unjustified demands; take liberties: *forgive me if I have presumed.* **4** take advantage of or make unscrupulous use of (a person's good nature etc.): *I felt it would be presuming on our friendship to keep asking her for help.*

presumption *noun* **1** arrogance; presumptuous behaviour. **2 a** the act of presuming a thing to be true. **b** a thing that is or may be presumed to be true. **3** a ground for presuming: *a strong presumption against their being guilty.* **4** *Law* an inference from known facts.

presumption of innocence *noun* the legal presumption that every person charged with a criminal offence is innocent until proven guilty.

presumptive *adjective* giving grounds for presumption: *presumptive evidence.*

presumptuous *adjective* unduly or overbearingly confident: *it is presumptuous of me to ask.* ▶ **presumptuously** *adverb* **presumptuousness** *noun* [Say pre ZUMP choo us]

presuppose *verb* (**presupposes, presupposed, presupposing**) **1** require as a precondition; imply: *for Aristotle, social order presupposed a measure of equality.* **2** assume beforehand: *your argument presupposes that currencies are controllable.* [Say pre SUPPOSE]

presupposition *noun* **1** the action or state of presupposing or being presupposed. **2** a thing assumed beforehand as the basis of argument etc. [Say pre SUPPOSITION]

prêt-à-porter • *adjective* (of clothes) sold ready-to-wear. • *noun* ready-to-wear clothes. [Say pret uh por TAY]

pre-tax *adjective* (of income or profits) before the deduction of taxes.

preteen • *adjective* of or relating to a child just under the age of thirteen. • *noun* a preteen child.

pretend • *verb* **1** claim or assert falsely so as to deceive. **2** imagine to oneself in play. **3** profess, esp. falsely or extravagantly: *does not pretend to be a scholar.* **4** lay claim to (a quality or title): *he cannot pretend to theological sophistication.* • *adjective informal* pretended; in pretense: *pretend money.*

pretended *adjective* false; not real or genuine: *a pretended friend* ◊ *her pretended indifference.*

pretender *noun* **1** a person who claims or aspires to a title or position: *a pretender to the English throne* ◊ *a heavyweight bout between the reigning champ and the young pretender.* **2** a person who pretends.

pretense *noun* (also **pretence**) **1 a** a pretext or excuse: *on the slightest pretense.* **b** a false show of intentions or motives: *the pretense of friendship* ◊ *false pretenses.* **2** a claim, esp. a false or ambitious one: *has no pretense to any great talent.* **3** make-believe. **4** affectation: *stripped of pretense.* [Say PREE tense or pre TENSE]

pretension *noun* **1** (usu. in *plural*) an aspiration or claim to a greater status or position or to a certain quality: *pretensions of uniqueness* ◊ *literary pretensions.* **2** the behaviour or a behavioural trait of a person who tries to impress others by affecting greater importance, talent, culture, etc. than they actually possess; pretentiousness: *she attacked the pretension of artists* ◊ *social pretensions.* **3** a claim to a title or position: *pretensions to the throne.* [Say pre TENSION]

pretentious *adjective* attempting to impress others by making something or oneself appear more important,

wealthy, talented, etc. than it or one really is: *it is pretentious of him to casually drop names of famous politicians into conversation as if he really knows them* ◊ *a pretentious poet of little talent*. ▶ **pretentiously** *adverb* **pretentiousness** *noun* [Say pre TEN shus]

preterm *adjective* born or occurring prematurely.

preternatural *adjective* beyond what is normal or natural: *preternatural shrewdness* ◊ *a preternatural shade of red*. ▶ **preternaturally** *adverb* [Say pree tur NATURAL]

pretext *noun* **1** an ostensible or alleged reason or intention. **2** an excuse offered. PHRASES **on** (or **under**) **the pretext** (foll. by *of*, or *that* + clause) professing as one's object or intention.

pretrial • *adjective* **1** of or pertaining to the period before a trial: *pretrial publicity*. **2** of or pertaining to a preliminary hearing before a trial: *pretrial testimony*. • *noun* a preliminary hearing before a trial.

prettification *noun* an act of making a thing or person pretty, esp. in an affected or superficial way. [Say pritta fuh CAY sh'n]

prettify *verb* (**prettifies, prettified, prettifying**) make (a thing or person) pretty esp. in an affected or superficial way. [Say PRITTA fye]

prettily *adverb* in a way that is pleasing to the eye, ear, etc.; attractively, charmingly.

prettiness *noun* **1** the quality of being pretty; delicate beauty. **2** affected or trivial beauty in art.

pretty • *adjective* (**prettier, prettiest**) **1** (of a person, esp. a woman or girl) attractive in a delicate, dainty, or graceful way without stateliness. **2** (of a thing) pleasing to the eye, the ear, or the aesthetic sense: *a pretty dress*. **3** *ironic* considerable, fine: *a pretty penny*. • *adverb informal* **1** fairly, moderately: *found it pretty difficult*. **2** very, considerably: *you're pretty strong!* • *noun* (*plural* **pretties**) a pretty person (esp. as a form of address to a child). • *verb* (**pretties, prettied, prettying**) (often foll. by *up*) make pretty or attractive. PHRASES **pretty much** (or **nearly** or **well**) *informal* almost; very nearly. **pretty please** an emphatic form of request. **sitting pretty** *informal* in a favourable or advantageous position.

pretzel • *noun* a crisp salted biscuit made in the shape of a knot or a stick. • *verb* (**pretzels, pretzelled, pretzelling**) twist, bend, or contort (an object, a part of the body, etc.).

prevail *verb* **1** prove more powerful than opposing forces; be victorious: *it's hard for logic to prevail over emotion*. **2** be the more usual or predominant: *the climate is dry in summer and sunny skies generally prevail*. **3** exist or occur in general use or experience; be current: *British imperial values were to prevail for more than a century*. **4** (foll. by *on, upon*) persuade: *had to prevail upon friends to lend him the money*.

prevailing *adjective* **1** most usual or widespread: *prevailing opinion*. **2** (of a wind) that blows in an area most frequently.

prevalence *noun* general or widespread occurrence or existence: *the declining prevalence of smoking*. [Say PREVVA lince]

prevalent *adjective* generally existing or occurring: *the attitude is prevalent among students* ◊ *the most prevalent disease*. ▶ **prevalently** *adverb* [Say PREVVA lint]

prevaricate *verb* (**prevaricates, prevaricated, prevaricating**) speak or act in an evasive or misleading way: *she seemed to prevaricate when questioned by the media*. ▶ **prevarication** *noun* [Say pre VERRA kate]

prevent *verb* stop from happening or doing something: *the weather prevented me from going*. ▶ **preventability** *noun* **preventable** *adjective* **preventer** *noun* **prevention** *noun*

preventive (also **preventative**) • *adjective* serving to prevent, esp. preventing disease, breakdown, etc.:

preventive maintenance. • *noun* a preventive agent, measure, drug, etc. ▶ **preventively** *adverb*

preview • *noun* **1** the act of seeing in advance. **2 a** the showing of a film, exhibition, etc., before the official opening. **b** a film trailer. **3** a foretaste, a preliminary glimpse. • *verb* see or show in advance.

previous *adjective* coming before in time or order: *previous attempts*. • *adverb* (foll. by *to*) before: *previous to writing*. ▶ **previously** *adverb*

pre-war *adjective* existing or occurring before a war (esp. the most recent major war).

prewash • *noun* (*plural* **prewashes**) a preliminary wash. • *verb* (**prewashes, prewashed, prewashing**) give a preliminary wash to, esp. before selling.

pre-wire *verb* (**pre-wires, pre-wired, pre-wiring**) wire beforehand, esp. put in during construction wiring for services such as alarms or communications that are normally installed afterwards.

> **SPELL CHECK**
> **prey, pray**
>
> To say prayers is to **pray**. The insect is a **praying mantis**.

prey • *noun* **1** an animal that is hunted or killed by another for food. **2** (often foll. by *to*) a person or thing that is influenced by or vulnerable to (something undesirable): *fell prey to morbid fears*. • *verb* (foll. by *on, upon*) **1** hunt and kill for food. **2** attack or take advantage of: *scam artists preying on elderly homeowners* ◊ *pickpockets preying on tourists*. **3** cause trouble or distress to a person: *fear preyed on his mind*.

prez *noun* (*plural* **prezzes**) *US slang* a president.

price • *noun* **1 a** the amount of money or goods for which a thing is bought or sold. **b** value or worth: *beyond price*. **2** what is or must be given, done, sacrificed, etc., to obtain or achieve something. **3** the amount of money etc. needed to bribe a person: *everyone has a price*. **4** a sum of money offered or given as a reward, esp. for the capture or killing of a person. • *verb* (**prices, priced, pricing**) **1** fix or find the price of (a thing for sale). **2** estimate the value of. PHRASES **price on a person's head** a reward for a person's capture or death. **price oneself out of the market** lose to one's competitors by charging more than customers are willing to pay. **what price ...?** (often foll. by verbal noun) *informal* **1** what is the chance of ...?: *what price your finishing the course?* **2** what is the value or use of ...?: *what price success?* ▶ **priced** *adjective*

price-fixing *noun* the maintaining of prices at a certain level by agreement between competing sellers.

price gouging *noun* the practice of charging unjustly high prices for items, services, etc.

price index *noun* (*plural* **price indexes** or **price indices**) an index showing the variation in the prices of a set of goods etc. since a chosen base period.

priceless *adjective* **1** beyond price. **2** *informal* very amusing or absurd.

price support *noun* government policy of providing support for certain basic, usu. agricultural, products to stop the price falling below an agreed level.

price tag *noun* **1** the label on an item showing its price. **2** the cost of an enterprise or undertaking.

price war *noun* a period of fierce competition between two or more firms in the same industry that are seeking to increase their shares of the market by cutting the prices of their products.

pricey *adjective* (**pricier, priciest**) *informal* expensive. ▶ **priciness** *noun* [Say PRICE ee, PRICE ee niss]

prick • *verb* **1** pierce slightly; make a small hole in.

2 trouble mentally: *my conscience is pricking me*. **3** feel a pricking sensation. • *noun* **1** an act of piercing something with a fine, sharp point: *the pin prick had produced a drop of blood*. **2** a small hole or mark made by pricking. **3** a pain caused as by pricking. **4** a mental pain: *the pricks of conscience*. PHRASES **kick against the pricks** persist in futile resistance. **prick (up) one's ears 1** (of a dog etc.) make the ears erect when on the alert. **2** (of a person) become suddenly attentive.

prickle • *noun* **1** a short spine or pointed outgrowth on a plant or animal. **2** a prickling sensation. • *verb* (**prickles, prickled, prickling**) affect or be affected with a sensation as of pricking.

prickliness *noun* the quality of being touchy or overly sensitive: *part of the problem was his prickliness over the question of his authority*.

prickly *adjective* (**pricklier, prickliest**) **1** (esp. in the names of plants and animals) having prickles. **2 a** (of a person) ready to take offence; touchy. **b** (of a topic, argument, etc.) full of contentious or complicated points; thorny. **3** tingling.

prickly pear *noun* **1** a cactus native to arid regions of North and South America, bearing barbed bristles and large pear-shaped prickly fruits. **2** the edible orange or red fruit of this plant.

pricy *adjective* (**pricier, priciest**) = PRICEY.

pride • *noun* **1 a** a feeling of elation or satisfaction at achievements or qualities or possessions etc. that do one credit. **b** (**the pride**; foll. by *of*) an object of this feeling: *the pride of the museum's collection*. **c** the foremost or best of a group. **2** a high or overbearing opinion of one's worth or importance. **3** knowledge of one's own worth or character; a sense of dignity and respect for oneself. **4** a group or company (of animals, esp. lions). • *verb* (**prides, prided, priding**) **pride oneself on** be proud of. PHRASES **one's pride and joy** a thing of which one is very proud. **take pride** (or **a pride**) **in 1** be proud of. **2** maintain in good condition or appearance. ▶ **prideful** *adjective* **pridefully** *adverb*

pride of place *noun* the most important or prominent position.

priest *noun* **1** an ordained minister of the Catholic or Orthodox Church, or of the Anglican Church (above a deacon and below a bishop), authorized to perform certain rites and administer certain sacraments. **2** an official minister of a non-Christian religion.

priestess *noun* (*plural* **priestesses**) a female priest of a non-Christian religion.

priesthood *noun* **1** the office or position of a priest: *wanted to enter the priesthood*. **2** priests collectively.

priestlike *adjective* like or suggestive of a priest.

priestly *adjective* of or associated with priests: *priestly duties*.

prig *noun* a self-righteously correct or moralistic person. ▶ **priggish** *adjective* **priggishness** *noun*

prim *adjective* (**primmer, primmest**) **1 a** (of a person or manner) stiffly formal and precise. **b** (of a thing) ordered, regular, formal: *a prim garden*. **2** (of a woman or girl) demure. **3** prudish; prissy.

prima ballerina *noun* (*plural* **prima ballerinas**) the chief female dancer in a ballet or ballet company. [Say preema balla REENA]

primacy *noun* **1** the state or position of being first in order, importance, or authority; pre-eminence: *the primacy of collective rights over individual rights* ◊ *the Constitution has primacy over all other laws*. **2** the office of a primate. [Say PRIME uh see]

prima donna *noun* (*plural* **prima donnas**) **1** the chief female singer in an opera or opera company. **2** a

temperamentally self-important person. ▶ **prima donna-ish** *adjective* [Say preema DONNA]

primaeval *adjective* = PRIMEVAL. [Say pry MEE vul]

prima facie • *adverb* at first sight; from a first impression: *chimpanzee behaviour includes many tricks that appear prima facie to be products of creative intellect*. • *adjective* (of evidence) based on the first impression: *can see a prima facie reason for it*. [Say prime uh FAY she]

primal *adjective* **1** relating to an early stage of evolutionary development and usu. basic or primitive: *primal human needs* ◊ *a primal stage*. **2** fundamental, essential: *the primal reason*. [Say PRY mul]

primal scream *noun* a scream releasing emotion.

primarily *adverb* mainly: *a course designed primarily for specialists* ◊ *the problem is not primarily a financial one*. [Say pry MERRA lee]

primary • *adjective* **1 a** of the first importance; chief: *our primary concern*. **b** fundamental, basic. **2** earliest, original; first in a series. **3** of the first rank in a series; not derived: *the primary meaning of a word*. **4** (of education) for young children, esp. below the age of 12. **5** (of a battery or cell) generating electricity by irreversible chemical reaction. **6** *Biology* belonging to the first stage of development. **7** (of an industry or type of economic activity) concerned with obtaining natural raw materials for conversion into commodities and products for the consumer: *mining, agriculture, and forestry are primary industries*. • *noun* (*plural* **primaries**) **1** a thing that is primary. **2** (also **primary election**) (in the US) a preliminary election to appoint delegates to a party conference or to select the candidates for a principal (esp. presidential) election.

primary colour *noun* any of the colours red, green, and blue, or (for pigments) red, blue and yellow, from which all other colours can be obtained by mixing.

primary school *noun* a school for young children, esp. one covering the first three or four grades and sometimes kindergarten.

primary sexual characteristics *plural noun* the physical characteristics distinctive to each sex that are essential to reproduction, including the testis in males and the ovary in females (*compare* SECONDARY SEXUAL CHARACTERISTICS).

primary source *noun* first-hand historical evidence or an original account of an event, esp. used as research material (*compare* SECONDARY SOURCE).

primate *noun* **1** any animal of the order Primates, the highest order of mammals, including lemurs, apes, monkeys, and humans. **2** an archbishop or bishop ranked first among all the bishops of a country, region, etc. [Say PRY mate; for sense 2 you can also say PRY mit]

primavera *adjective* designating a pasta dish made with lightly sautéed spring vegetables. [Say preema VERRA]

prime¹ • *adjective* **1** chief, most important: *the prime motive*. **2** of the best or highest quality or value; first-rate, excellent: *prime real estate*. **3** primary, fundamental. **4** *Math* **a** (of a number) divisible only by itself and unity, e.g. 2, 3, 11. **b** (of numbers) having no common factor but unity. • *noun* **1** the state of the highest perfection of something: *in the prime of life*. **2** (**the prime**; foll. by *of*) the best part. **3** a prime number. **4** = PRIME RATE.

prime² *verb* (**primes, primed, priming**) **1** prepare (a thing) for use or action. **2** prepare (a gun) for firing or (an explosive) for detonation. **3 a** pour (a liquid) into a pump to prepare it for working. **b** inject gasoline into (the cylinder or carburetor of an internal combustion engine). **4** prepare (wood etc.) for painting by applying a substance that prevents paint from being absorbed. **5** equip (a person) with information etc. **6** ply (a

person) with food or drink in preparation for something. **PHRASES** **prime the pump** (esp. of a government) encourage the growth of a new or weak business or industry by investing money in it.

prime meridian *noun* **1** the meridian from which longitude is reckoned, esp. that passing through Greenwich. **2** the corresponding line on a map.

prime minister *noun* the head of the executive branch of government in most countries with a parliamentary system. ▶ **prime ministerial** *adjective* **prime ministership** *noun*

Prime Minister's Office *noun Cdn* the political staff of the prime minister, responsible for scheduling engagements, overseeing press and public relations, etc.

prime mover *noun* **1** a person who originates or promotes an action, event, etc.; an initiator. **2** an initial natural or mechanical source of motive power.

primer[1] *noun* **1** a substance used to prime wood etc. **2** a cap, cylinder, etc., used to ignite the powder of a cartridge etc. **3** a molecule that serves as a starting material for a polymerization. **4** a person who primes something.

primer[2] *noun* **1** a textbook for teaching children to read. **2** an introductory book. [Say PRIME er or PRIMMER]

prime rate *noun* the lowest rate of interest at which money can be borrowed commercially, offered by banks to customers with a good history of repaying loans.

prime rib *noun* a roast or steak cut from the seven ribs immediately before the loin.

prime time *noun* the time at which a radio or television audience is expected to be at its highest, usu. between 7 and 11 p.m.

primeval *adjective* **1** of or relating to the first age of the world: *a lush primeval forest.* **2** (of feelings or actions) based on primitive instinct; raw and elementary: *primeval fear.* [Say pry MEE vul]

priming *noun* **1** a mixture used by painters for a preparatory coat. **2 a** gunpowder placed in the pan of a firearm. **b** a train of powder connecting the fuse with the charge in blasting etc.

primitive • *adjective* **1** relating to the earliest times in history or stages in development. **2** denoting a preliterate, non-industrial society of simple organization. **3** offering an extremely basic level of comfort or convenience. **4** (of behaviour or emotion) instinctive and unreasoning. • *noun* **1** a person belonging to a primitive society. **2** a painter using a simple, naive style that deliberately rejects subtlety or conventional techniques. ▶ **primitively** *adverb* **primitiveness** *noun*

primitivism *noun* **1** an unsophisticated quality or behaviour. **2** a belief in the value of what is simple and unsophisticated, expressed as a philosophy of life or through art or literature. ▶ **primitivist** *noun & adjective*

primly *adverb* **1** in a precise or stiffly formal manner. **2** in a prudish or prissy manner.

primness *noun* the quality of being precise, stiffly formal, or prudish.

primo *adjective slang* first-class; first-rate. [Say PREEMO]

primogeniture *noun* (in full **right of primogeniture**) the right of the first-born child, esp. the eldest son, to inherit the estate of his or her parents. [Say prime oh JENNA chur or preemo JENNA chur]

primordial *adjective* **1** existing at or from the beginning: *the earth's primordial atmosphere.* **2** basic and fundamental: *a primordial fear.* [Say pry MORDY ul]

primordial soup *noun* a solution rich in organic compounds in the primitive oceans of the earth, from which life is thought to have originated.

primp *verb* **1** make oneself well-groomed, esp. in a fussy or affected manner. **2** make (the hair, one's clothes, etc.) tidy.

primrose *noun* **1** any one of a large group of plants that bear flowers in a wide variety of colours during the spring. **2** a European plant of this group that produces solitary pale yellow flowers in early spring. **3** *noun & adjective* (also **primrose yellow**) pale yellow.

primula *noun* (*plural* **primulas**) = PRIMROSE 1. [Say PRIM you luh]

prince *noun* (as a title usu. **Prince**) **1** a male member of a royal family other than a reigning king. **2** a son or grandson of a British monarch. **3** a ruler of a small state, actually or nominally subject to a king or emperor. **4** (as an English rendering of foreign titles) a noble usu. ranking next below a duke. **5** *Catholicism* a title applied to a Cardinal: *Prince of the Church.* **6** (often foll. by *of*) the chief or greatest: *the prince of novelists.* **7** a powerful or influential man, esp. a magnate in a specified industry etc.: *merchant prince.* **8** *informal* an admirable or generous man. ▶ **princelike** *adjective*

princeling *noun* **1** a young prince. **2** the ruler of a small principality or domain. [Say PRINCE ling]

princely *adjective* (**princelier**, **princeliest**) **1 a** of or worthy of a prince. **b** held by a prince: *princely state.* **2** sumptuous, generous, splendid.

princess • *noun* (*plural* **princesses**) (as a title usu. **Princess**) **1** the wife of a prince. **2** a female member of a royal family other than a reigning queen. **3** a daughter or granddaughter of a British monarch. **4** a pre-eminent woman or thing personified as a woman: *the luxury cruise ship was called the Pacific Princess.* **5** *informal* a girl or woman regarded or treated as a princess, esp. one who is pampered, egocentric, demanding, etc. • *adjective* designating a style of dress, coat, etc. with a close fitted bodice and a flared skirt with a seamless waist.

SPELL CHECK
principal, principle

A fundamental truth or law is a **principle**: *Distracting your opponent is against the principles of fair play.* **Principle** is also the spelling in "I support the idea in principle" and in "they refused on principle".

---

principal • *adjective* **1** first in rank or importance; chief. **2** main, leading: *a principal cause of my success.* **3** (of money) constituting the original sum invested or lent. • *noun* **1** a head, ruler, or superior. **2** the head of some schools, colleges, and universities. **3** the leading performer in a concert, play, etc. **4** a sum of money lent or invested, on which interest is paid: *the debtor paid the full principal by instalments, but the creditor sued for the interest.* **5** a person for whom another acts as agent etc. **6** *Cdn* a lawyer who supervises an articling student. **7** the person actually responsible for a crime. **8** *Music* the leading player in each section of an orchestra: *principal horn.* **9** (also **principal dancer**) a dancer who is of the highest rank in a ballet company.

principal clause *noun Grammar* = MAIN CLAUSE.

principality *noun* (*plural* **principalities**) **1** a state ruled by a prince. **2** the government of a prince. [Say prince i PALA tee]

principally *adverb* mainly: *the book is aimed principally at beginners.*

principal meridian *noun Cdn* **1** a geographical meridian established by an authority as a meridian of reference for land surveying purposes. **2** (**Principal Meridian**) = FIRST MERIDIAN.

principalship *noun* the function or office of a school principal: *efforts to fill the vacant principalship.*

principle noun **1** a fundamental truth or law as the basis of reasoning or action: *arguing from first principles* ◊ *moral principles*. **2 a** a personal code of conduct: *a person of high principle*. **b** (in *plural*) such rules of conduct: *has no principles*. **3** a general law in physics etc. **4** a law of nature forming the basis for the construction or working of a machine etc. **5** a fundamental source; a primary element: *held water to be the first principle of all things*. PHRASES **in principle** as regards fundamentals but not necessarily in detail. **on principle** on the basis of a natural attitude: *I refuse on principle*.

principled *adjective* based on or having (esp. praiseworthy) principles of behaviour.

print • noun **1** the text appearing in a book, newspaper, etc. **2** an indentation or mark left on a surface by pressure. **3** a printed picture or design. **4** a photograph printed on paper from a negative or transparency. **5** a copy of a motion picture on film. **6** a piece of fabric or clothing with a coloured pattern or design. • *verb* **1** produce (books, newspapers, etc.) by a process involving the transfer or text or designs to paper. **2** produce (text or a picture) in such a way. **3** produce a paper copy of (information stored on a computer). **4** produce (a photographic print) from a negative. **5** write clearly without joining the letters. **6** mark with a coloured design. • *adjective* **1** (of an article of clothing) made of a printed fabric: *a print dress*. **2** of or relating to newspapers or magazines: *the print media*. PHRASES **appear in print** have one's work published. **in print 1** (of a book etc.) available from the publisher. **2** in printed form. **out of print** no longer available from the publisher. ▶ **printable** *adjective*

printed circuit *noun* an electric circuit with thin strips of conductor on a flat insulating sheet.

printer *noun* **1** a person or company that prints books, magazines, etc. **2** the owner of a printing business. **3** a device that prints, esp. as part of a computer system.

printhead *noun* the component in a printer that assembles and prints the characters on the paper.

printing *noun* **1** the production of printed books etc. **2** a single impression of a book. **3** printed letters or writing imitating them.

printing press *noun* (*plural* **printing presses**) a machine for printing from types or plates etc.

printmaker *noun* **1** a person, esp. a graphic artist, who makes prints: *a noted Inuit printmaker*. **2** a person who makes print. ▶ **printmaking** *noun*

printout *noun* computer output in printed form.

print run *noun* the number of copies of a book etc. printed at one time.

prior • *adjective* **1** earlier. **2** (often foll. by *to*) coming before in time, order, or importance. • *adverb* (foll. by *to*) before: *decided prior to their arrival*. • *noun* **1** the superior officer in a religious order. **2** *slang* a prior criminal conviction: *has three priors*.

prioress *noun* (*plural* **prioresses**) a female superior of a house of any of various orders of nuns. [Say PRIOR ess]

prioritize *verb* (**prioritizes**, **prioritized**, **prioritizing**) **1** put tasks, problems, etc. in order of importance, so that the most important can be dealt with first: *before we start, let's prioritize our goals*. **2** treat something as being more important than other things: *the need to prioritize famine relief*. [Say pry ORA tize]

priority *noun* (*plural* **priorities**) **1** something that is

given prior or special attention or considered more important. **2** precedence in rank etc.

priory *noun* (*plural* **priories**) a monastery governed by a prior or a convent governed by a prioress. [Say PRIOR ee]

prise *verb* esp. *Brit.* (**prises**, **prised**, **prising**) = PRY 1.

prism *noun* **1** a solid geometric figure whose two ends are similar, equal, and parallel rectilinear figures, whose sides are parallelograms. **2** a transparent body in this form, usu. triangular with refracting surfaces at an acute angle with each other, which separates white light into a spectrum of colours. **3** *Crystallography* a form having three or more faces that meet in edges parallel to the vertical axis.

prismatic *adjective* **1** of, like, or using a prism. **2 a** (of colours) distributed by or as if by a transparent prism. **b** (of light) displayed in the form of a spectrum. ▶ **prismatically** *adverb* [Say prizz MAT ick]

prison *noun* **1** a place in which a person is kept in captivity, esp. a building to which persons are legally committed while awaiting trial or for punishment; a jail. **2** any place of real or perceived confinement.

prison camp *noun* a camp for prisoners of war or those imprisoned for their political beliefs.

prisoner *noun* **1** a person kept in prison. **2** (also **prisoner at the bar**) a person in custody on a criminal charge and on trial. **3** a person or thing confined by illness, another's grasp, etc. **4** (also **prisoner of war**) a person who has been captured in war. PHRASES **take no prisoners** deal very aggressively with a person or thing. **take prisoner** seize and hold as a prisoner.

prissily *adverb* in a prim or prudish manner.

prissiness *noun* the quality of being prim or prudish.

prissy *adjective* (**prissier**, **prissiest**) prim, prudish.

pristine *adjective* **1** in its original condition: *a pristine copy of the book*. **2** fresh and clean, as if new: *a pristine bedroom*. **3** unspoiled: *pristine wilderness*. [Say priss TEEN]

privacy *noun* **1 a** the state of being private and undisturbed. **b** a person's right to this. **2** freedom from intrusion or public attention. **3** avoidance of publicity. [Say PRY vuh see or PRIVVA see]

Privacy Commissioner *noun* *Cdn* the official responsible for investigating the collection and storage of personal information on private citizens by federal government departments.

private • *adjective* **1** for or belonging to one particular person or group only. **2** (of a service or industry) provided by an individual or commercial company rather than the state. **3** (of thoughts, feelings, etc.) not to be shared or revealed. **4** (of a person) not choosing to share their thoughts and feelings. **5** (of a person) having no official or public position. **6** not connected with one's work or official position: *the president visited the country in a private capacity*. **7** (of a place) secluded. • *noun* **1** (also **Private**) (in the Canadian Army and Air Force and other armies) a person holding the lowest rank. **2** (in *plural*) *informal* the genitals. PHRASES **in private** privately; in private company or life.

private company *noun* (*plural* **private companies**) *Cdn, Brit., Austral.,* & *NZ* a company with restricted membership and no issue of shares.

private detective *noun* = PRIVATE INVESTIGATOR.

private enterprise *noun* **1** a business or businesses not under government control. **2** = FREE ENTERPRISE.

privateer *noun* **1** an armed vessel owned and officered by private individuals and authorized for war service. **2 a** a commander of such a vessel. **b** a crew member of such a vessel. [Say pry vuh TEER]

private eye *noun informal* a private investigator.

private investigator *noun* a usu. freelance detective carrying out investigations for a private employer.

private label *noun* a make of goods manufactured specially for a retailer and bearing the retailer's name.

privately *adverb* in a private manner: *I insist that we speak privately* ◊ *a privately run school*.

private member *noun* a member of a legislative body not holding a government office.

private member's bill *noun* a bill introduced by a private member, not part of government legislation.

private parts *plural noun* the genitals.

private school *noun* a school established and supported by a private group rather than through taxes etc.

private sector *noun* the part of the economy that is free of direct governmental control.

privation *noun* lack of the comforts or necessities of life: *suffered many privations*. [Say pry VAY sh'n]

privatization *noun* an act of privatizing a business, industry, etc. [Say pry vuh tize AY sh'n]

privatize *verb* (**privatizes, privatized, privatizing**) make private, esp. assign (a business etc.) to private as distinct from governmental control or ownership. [Say pry vuh TIZE]

privet *noun* any evergreen shrub of the olive family, bearing small white flowers and black berries, often used for hedges. [Say PRIV it]

SPELL CHECK | ABC ✓
privilege

Warning: there is no *d* before the *g* in **privilege**; do not forget the *i* before the *l*.

---

privilege • *noun* **1** a special right or advantage available only to a particular person or a group of people. **2** the rights and advantages possessed by the rich and powerful: *had led a life of luxury and privilege*. **3** (also **parliamentary privilege**) the freedom of members of a legislative assembly to speak at its meetings without risking legal action. **4** a special benefit or honour, esp. one restricted to a small group: *it is a privilege to meet you*. **5** a monopoly or patent granted to an individual, corporation, etc. • *verb* (**privileges, privileged, privileging**) **1** invest with a privilege. **2** consider or treat as more important; favour.

privileged *adjective* **1** having special rights or advantages that most people do not have: *she comes from a privileged background* ◊ *in those days, only a privileged few had the vote*. **2** honoured: *I was privileged to receive an invitation*. **3 a** legally protected from being made public: *privileged communication*. **b** (of an exchange of information) made between such people and in such circumstances that it is not actionable. **4** (of information) kept within a select group and not divulged to others.

privy • *adjective* sharing in the secret of (a person's plans etc.): *the tight-knit circle privy to departmental secrets*. • *noun* (*plural* **privies**) an outhouse. [Say PRIVVY]

Privy Council *noun* (in Canada) a (now chiefly honorary) body of advisers appointed by the Governor General, made up of current and former Cabinet ministers, provincial premiers, etc.

privy councillor *noun* (also **privy counsellor**) a member of a Privy Council.

Privy Council Office *noun* (in Canada) an administrative body which coordinates the activities of the federal Cabinet, provides advice to the prime minister, and implements government objectives.

prix fixe *noun* **1** a fixed price for a restaurant meal chosen from a usu. limited menu. **2** a meal that is served for such a price (compare À LA CARTE). [Say pree FIX]

prize¹ • *noun* **1** something that can be won in a competition or lottery etc. **2** a reward given as a symbol of victory or superiority. **3** something striven for or worth striving for: *missed all the great prizes of life*. **4** a person considered highly: *he's no prize*. **5** (as an *adjective*) **a** to which a prize is awarded: *a prize bull*. **b** supremely excellent or outstanding of its kind. **6** a ship or property captured in naval warfare. **7** a find or windfall. • *verb* (**prizes, prized, prizing**) value highly: *a prized possession*. PHRASES **keep one's eyes on the prize** remain focused on the ultimate goal. **no prizes for guessing** it is obvious.

prize² *verb* (**prizes, prized, prizing**) *US* = PRISE.

prizefight *noun* a boxing match fought for money.
▶ **prizefighter** *noun* **prizefighting** *noun*

prizewinner *noun* a winner of a prize.
▶ **prizewinning** *adjective*

PRK *abbreviation* photorefractive keratectomy, a form of eye surgery which uses a laser to carve away part of the outer surface of the cornea (compare LASIK).

pro¹ • *noun* (*plural* **pros**) a professional. • *adjective* professional.

pro² • *adjective* (of an argument or reason) for; in favour. • *noun* (*plural* **pros**) a reason or argument for or in favour. • *preposition & adverb* in favour of. PHRASES **pros and cons** reasons or considerations for and against a proposition etc.

pro-¹ *prefix* favouring or supporting: *pro-government*.

pro-² *prefix* before in time, place, order, etc.

proactive *adjective* (of a person, policy, etc.) creating or controlling a situation by taking the initiative.
▶ **proactively** *adverb*

pro-am • *adjective* (of a sports event etc.) involving professionals and amateurs. • *noun* a pro-am event.

prob *noun informal* a problem.

probability *noun* (*plural* **probabilities**) **1** the state or condition of being probable. **2** the likelihood of something happening. **3** a probable or most probable event: *the probability is that they will come*. **4** *Math* the extent to which an event is likely to occur, measured by the ratio of the favourable cases to the whole number of cases possible. PHRASES **in all probability** most probably.

probable • *adjective* that may be expected to happen or prove true; likely: *the probable explanation*. • *noun* a probable candidate, member of a team, etc.
▶ **probably** *adverb*

probate • *noun* **1** the official process of proving that a will is valid. **2** a verified copy of a will with a certificate as handed to the executors. • *verb* (**probates, probated, probating**) establish the validity of (a will).

probation *noun* **1** *Law* a system of suspending the sentence on an offender subject to a period of good behaviour under supervision. **2** a process or period of testing the character or abilities of a person in a certain role, esp. of a new employee. PHRASES **on probation** undergoing probation, esp. legal supervision.
▶ **probationary** *adjective*

probation officer *noun* an official supervising offenders on probation.

probe • *noun* **1** a penetrating investigation. **2** any small device, esp. an electrode, for measuring, testing,

etc. **3** a blunt-ended surgical instrument usu. of metal for exploring a wound etc. **4** an unmanned exploratory spacecraft transmitting information about its environment. • *verb* (**probes, probed, probing**) **1** examine or inquire into closely. **2** explore (a wound or part of the body) with a probe. **3** penetrate with a sharp instrument. **4** pierce or explore with or as with a probe. ▶ **prober** *noun* **probingly** *adverb*

probity *noun* uprightness, honesty: *a woman of probity.* [Say PRO bit ee or PROB it ee]

problem *noun* **1** a doubtful or difficult matter requiring a solution. **2** something hard to understand or accomplish or deal with. **3** (as an *adjective*) **a** causing problems; difficult to deal with: *problem child.* **b** (of a play, novel, etc.) in which a social or other problem is treated. **4** a *Physics & Math* an inquiry starting from given conditions to investigate or demonstrate a fact, result, or law. **b** *Math* a proposition in which something has to be constructed (*compare* THEOREM 1). **5** a puzzle or question for solution. PHRASES **no problem** *informal* that is simple or easy. **that's your** (or **his, her,** etc.) **problem** said to disclaim responsibility or involvement.

problematic *adjective* (also **problematical**) **1** attended by difficulty: *it has become more problematic to shoot and process black-and-white film.* **2** doubtful or questionable: *the thesis is problematic for another reason.* ▶ **problematically** *adverb* [Say prob luh MAT ick]

pro bono *adjective* **1** (of legal work) done without charge. **2** (of a lawyer) doing such work. [Say pro BONE oh]

proboscis *noun* (*plural* **proboscises** or **probosces**) **1** the long flexible trunk or snout of some mammals, e.g. an elephant or tapir. **2** the elongated mouthparts of some insects. **3** the sucking organ in some worms. **4** *jocular* the human nose. [Say pro BOSS kiss]

procedural *adjective* having to do with a procedure: *procedural rules.* ▶ **procedurally** *adverb* [Say pro SEE jer ul]

procedure *noun* **1** a way of doing something, esp. the usual or correct way: *emergency procedures* ◊ *the procedure for logging on to the network usually involves a password.* **2** the official or formal order or way of doing something, esp. in business, law or politics: *parliamentary procedure.* **3** a medical operation: *a routine surgical procedure.* **4** *Computing* = SUBROUTINE. [Say pro SEE jur]

SPELL CHECK
proceed, precede ABC ✓

To come or go before is to **precede**: *April precedes May.*

---

proceed *verb* **1** (often foll. by *to*) go forward or on further; make one's way. **2** continue; go on with an activity: *proceeded to finish the painting* ◊ *proceeded with marking the exams.* **3** (of an action) be carried on or continued: *the case will now proceed.* **4** adopt a course of action: *how shall we proceed?* **5** go on to say. **6** (foll. by *against*) start a lawsuit (against a person). **7** (often foll. by *from*) come forth or originate.

proceeding *noun* **1** an action or piece of conduct: *a high-handed proceeding.* **2** (in *plural*) (also **legal proceedings**) an action at law; a lawsuit. **3** (in *plural*) a published report of discussions or a conference.

proceeds *plural noun* money produced by a transaction or other undertaking.

process[1] • *noun* (*plural* **processes**) **1** a course of action or proceeding, esp. a series of stages in manufacture or some other operation. **2 a** the progress or course of something: *in process of construction.* **b** the course of becoming, happening, etc.:

regeneration is in process. **3** a natural or involuntary operation or series of changes: *the process of growing old.* **4** a summons or writ. **5** (as an *adjective*) (of food etc.) that has been processed: *process cheese.* **6** a natural appendage or outgrowth on an organism. • *verb* (**processes, processed, processing**) **1** put (a raw material, a food, etc.) through an industrial or manufacturing process in order to change or preserve it etc. **2** deal with (a document, request, etc.) officially. **3** operate on (data) by means of a program. **4** mix, chop, etc. (food) using a food processor. **5** = DEVELOP *verb* 7.

process[2] *verb* (**processes, processed, processing**) walk in procession. [Say pro SESS]

procession *noun* **1** a number of people or vehicles etc. moving forward in orderly succession, esp. at a ceremony, demonstration, or festivity. **2** the movement of such a group: *go in procession.*

processional • *adjective* **1** of processions. **2** used, carried, or sung in processions. • *noun* *Christianity* a hymn etc. sung during a procession.

processor *noun* **1** a person or company etc. that processes something, esp. food. **2** a machine that processes things. **3** = CENTRAL PROCESSING UNIT. **4** a piece of software that performs operations on data: *word processor.* **5** = FOOD PROCESSOR.

pro-choice *adjective* favouring the right of a woman to choose to have an abortion.

proclaim *verb* **1** announce or declare publicly or officially. **2** declare (a person) to be (a king, traitor, etc.). **3** reveal as being: *an accent that proclaims you a Scot.* ▶ **proclaimer** *noun*

proclamation *noun* **1** an official statement about something important that is made to the public. **2** an act or instance of proclaiming. [Say prock luh MAY sh'n]

proclivity *noun* (*plural* **proclivities**) a tendency or inclination: *an unfortunate proclivity for indiscretion.* [Say pro CLIVVA tee]

procrastinate *verb* (**procrastinates, procrastinated, procrastinating**) delay or postpone action. ▶ **procrastination** *noun* **procrastinator** *noun* [Say pro CRASS tuh nate]

procreate *verb* (**procreates, procreated, procreating**) bring (offspring) into existence by the natural process of reproduction. ▶ **procreation** *noun* **procreative** *adjective* [Say PRO create]

proctologist *noun* a doctor specializing in treating diseases of the anus and rectum. [Say prock TOLLA jist]

proctology *noun* the branch of medicine concerned with the anus and rectum. [Say prock TOLLA jee]

proctor • *noun* a person who supervises students in an examination etc. • *verb* supervise an examination etc.

procurable *adjective* obtainable. [Say pro CURABLE]

procure *verb* (**procures, procured, procuring**) **1** obtain, esp. by care or effort; acquire: *managed to procure a copy.* **2** bring about: *procured their dismissal.* **3** obtain (a prostitute) for another person.

procurement *noun* **1** the action of obtaining or procuring something: *financial assistance for the procurement of legal advice* ◊ *the company's procurements from foreign firms.* **2** the act of buying or purchasing, esp. by a government. [Say pro CURE mint]

prod • *verb* (**prods, prodded, prodding**) **1** poke with the finger or a pointed object. **2** stimulate to action. • *noun* **1** a poke or thrust. **2** a stimulus to action. **3** an implement, such as a pointed or electrified rod, used for herding cattle etc. ▶ **prodder** *noun*

prodigal • *adjective* **1** recklessly wasteful: *credit was granted with almost prodigal generosity.* **2** having returned after an absence: *they were welcomed back like prodigal children returning to the fold.* • *noun* **1** a prodigal

person. **2** a wasteful person who repents. **3** a person who returns back to a place, family, etc., after an absence. ▶**prodigality** *noun* [Say PRODDA gull, prodda GALA tee]

prodigious *adjective* **1** remarkably or impressively great in extent, size, or degree: *he can perform prodigious feats of memory* ◊ *a prodigious capacity for work*. **2** abnormal: *something rare and strange, possibly prodigious and terrible, was going to happen*. ▶**prodigiously** *adverb* [Say pruh DIDGE us]

prodigy *noun* (*plural* **prodigies**) **1** a person endowed with exceptional qualities or abilities, esp. a precocious child: *parent-driven tennis prodigies*. **2** (foll. by *of*) a wonderful example (of a quality): *his book is certainly a prodigy of information gathering*. [Say PRODDA jee]

produce • *verb* (**produces, produced, producing**) **1** bring (something) into existence: *produced dinner* ◊ *produced a masterpiece*. **2** manufacture (goods) from raw materials etc. **3** yield (fruit, a harvest, etc.): *grain produced in the West*. **4** give birth to (a child). **5** cause or bring about (a reaction, sensation, etc.). **6** bring forward for consideration, inspection, or use: *produced the tickets*. **7 a** bring (a play, performer, book, etc.) before the public. **b** supervise the making of (a film, broadcast, etc.). • *noun* **1** something that has been produced. **2** agricultural and natural products collectively: *the produce of Canada's oceans*. **3** fruits and vegetables.

producer *noun* **1** a person, company, country, etc. that produces goods or materials: *milk producers*. **2 a** a person in charge of a film, play, etc., who obtains the money to pay for it and arranges rehearsals, filming, publicity, etc. **b** the director of a theatrical event or broadcast program. **3** *Ecology* an organism that is able to manufacture food from simple organic compounds such as water, carbon dioxide, or nitrogen, e.g., through photosynthesis.

product *noun* **1** a thing that is grown or produced, usu. for sale. **2** a thing or substance produced during a natural, chemical, or manufacturing process: *the products of combustion*. **3** a thing or state that is the result of something: *the product of their labours*. **4** a person who has been greatly influenced by something: *a product of her times*. **5** *Math* a quantity obtained by multiplying quantities together.

production *noun* **1** the action of making or manufacturing from components or raw materials: *banning the production of chemical weapons*. **2** the process of being manufactured, esp. in large quantities: *go into production*. **3 a** a total yield. **b** the rate at which something is produced. **4 a** the process or administrative management of making a film, play, record, etc. **b** a film, play, record, etc., produced. **5** the sets, costumes, props, lighting, etc. and other physical aspects of a theatrical entertainment. **6** *informal* an exaggeratedly or needlessly complicated situation or event: *always makes such a production out of doing the housework*. **7** (as an *adjective*) (of a car etc.) mass-produced; not custom-made: *a production model*.

production line *noun* = ASSEMBLY LINE.

production values *plural noun* the quality of a film, television, or theatrical production as regards the sets, costumes, props, authenticity of period detail, music, etc. as distinct from the acting, direction, etc.

productive *adjective* **1** of or engaged in the production of goods. **2** producing much. **3** *Economics* producing commodities of exchangeable value: *productive labour*. **4** (foll. by *of*) producing or giving rise to: *their love is complex and productive of pain and disillusionment*. ▶**productively** *adverb*

productivity *noun* (*plural* **productivities**) **1** the

capacity to produce. **2** the quality or state of being productive. **3** the effectiveness of productive effort, esp. in industry. **4** production per unit of effort.

Prof. *abbreviation* Professor.

prof *noun* a professor.

pro-family *adjective* promoting or supporting traditional family life.

profane • *adjective* **1** secular; not sacred: *strong views on the need to separate the sacred from the profane*. **2 a** having or showing a lack of respect for God or holy things; irreverent: *a profane person might be tempted to violate the tomb*. **b** (of language) obscene: *movies filled with profane language*. **3** not initiated into religious rites or any esoteric knowledge. • *verb* (**profanes, profaned, profaning**) **1** treat (a sacred thing) with irreverence or disregard. **2** violate (what is entitled to respect). ▶**profanely** *adverb* **profaner** *noun* [Say pro FANE]

profanity *noun* (*plural* **profanities**) **1** profane language; blasphemy. **2** a swear word. [Say pro FANNA tee]

profess *verb* (**professes, professed, professing**) **1** claim openly to have (a quality or feeling). **2** pretend: *professed to be interested in what I was saying*. **3** declare: *profess ignorance*. **4** affirm one's faith in or allegiance to. **5** receive into a religious order under vows.

professed *adjective* **1** self-acknowledged: *a professed Christian*. **2** claimed or asserted openly but often falsely: *for all her professed populism, she was seen as remote from ordinary people*. **3** (of a monk or nun) having taken the vows of an order. ▶**professedly** *adverb* (in senses 1, 2) [Say pruh FEST, pruh FESSID lee]

profession *noun* **1** a vocation or calling, esp. one that involves some branch of advanced learning or science: *the medical profession*. **2** a body of people engaged in a profession. **3** a declaration or avowal. **4** a declaration of belief in a religion. **5 a** the declaration or vows made on entering a religious order. **b** the ceremony or fact of being professed in a religious order.

professional • *adjective* **1** of or belonging to or connected with a profession. **2 a** having or showing the skill of a professional, competent. **b** worthy of a professional: *professional conduct*. **3** engaged in a specified activity as one's main paid occupation (compare AMATEUR): *a professional lexicographer*. **4** *derogatory* engaged in a specified activity regarded with disfavour: *a professional agitator*. • *noun* **1** a person qualified or employed in one of the professions: *health professionals*. **2** a professional player or performer. **3** a highly skilled and experienced person: *Mary Jane is a real professional on stage*. **4** an expert player of a game, esp. golf or tennis, who provides instruction to members of a club etc.

professional development day *noun* esp. *Cdn* a day on which classes are cancelled so that teachers may attend seminars etc. to develop their teaching skills.

professionalism *noun* **1** the skill or qualities required or expected of members of a profession. **2** great skill and ability.

professionalization *noun* an act of professionalizing an occupation, activity, etc.

professionalize *verb* (**professionalizes, professionalized, professionalizing**) **1** make (an occupation, activity, etc.) professional, esp. by requiring certification etc. **2** become professional.

professionally *adverb* **1** in a way that is connected with a person's job or training: *you need a complete change, both personally and professionally*. **2** in a way that shows skill and experience: *the product has been marketed very professionally*. **3** as a paid job, not as a hobby: *after the injury, he never played professionally again*.

professor *noun* **1** a university teacher. **2** (often as a title) a university teacher of the highest rank.

professorial *adjective* having to do with a professor; like a professor in manner or dress: *professorial duties* ◊ *exuding an air of bearded professorial authority.* [Say proffa SORRY ul]

professorship *noun* the position of a professor or the period during which this is held.

proffer *verb* offer (a gift, services, a hand, etc.).

proficiency *noun* the quality of being proficient or skilled; expertness: *he learned the syllabic script, which he used with great proficiency.* [Say pruh FISH'n see]

proficient *adjective* (often foll. by *in*, *at*) adept, expert. ▶ **proficiently** *adverb* [Say pruh FISH'nt]

profile • *noun* 1 an outline (esp. of a human face) as seen from one side. 2 a short biographical or character sketch. 3 a representation by a graph or chart of information (esp. on certain characteristics) recorded in a quantified form. 4 the extent to which a person, company, organization, etc., attracts public notice or comment: *try to raise our profile.* 5 a vertical cross-section of a structure etc. • *verb* (**profiles**, **profiled**, **profiling**) 1 represent in profile. 2 give a profile to. **PHRASES** **in profile** as seen from one side. **keep a low profile** remain inconspicuous. ▶ **profiler** *noun*

SPELL CHECK
profit, prophet

A person who foretells is a **prophet**.

profit • *noun* 1 financial gain; excess of returns over outlay. 2 an advantage or benefit. • *verb* (**profits**, **profited**, **profiting**) 1 be beneficial to. 2 obtain an advantage or benefit: *profited by the experience.* 3 make or earn a profit. **PHRASES** **at a profit** with financial gain.

profitability *noun* the quality of being profitable; capacity to make a profit: *we need to increase profitability.*

profitable *adjective* 1 yielding profit: *a highly profitable business.* 2 beneficial; useful: *she spent a profitable afternoon in the library.* ▶ **profitably** *adverb*

profit and loss *noun* the gain and loss made in a commercial transaction or series of transactions, esp. as shown on a balance sheet: *profit and loss account.*

profit centre *noun* 1 a part of a business organization with its own profits and costs and hence ascertainable profitability. 2 a profitable part of an organization.

profiteer • *verb* make or seek to make excessive profits, esp. illegally or in black market conditions. • *noun* a person who profiteers.

profitless *adjective* producing no useful result or profit: *further argument was profitless.*

profit margin *noun* the difference between the cost of buying or producing something and the price for which it is sold: *increase the profit margin to 20 percent.*

profit-sharing *noun* the sharing of profits esp. between employer and employees: *profit-sharing plan.*

profit-taking *noun* the sale of shares etc. at a time when profit will accrue.

profligacy *noun* the state of being shamelessly immoral or recklessly extravagant and wasteful: *after his conversion from a life of profligacy, Jones preached to fellow soldiers and civilians.* [Say PROFF lig a see]

profligate *adjective* 1 shamelessly immoral: *he succumbed to drink and a profligate lifestyle.* 2 recklessly extravagant and wasteful: *profligate spending.* ▶ **profligately** *adverb* [Say PROFF lig it]

pro forma • *adjective* 1 done or produced as a matter of form: *in these ridings the elections are pro forma, and the only question is the size of the majority to support re-election.* 2 (of an invoice etc.) sent in advance of goods supplied. • *adverb* as a matter of form: *I was pro forma the runner-*

up, *but John was so far in front that second place didn't count.* [Say pro FORMA]

profound *adjective* (**profounder**, **profoundest**) 1 a having or showing great knowledge or insight: *a profound treatise.* b demanding deep study or thought: *profound doctrines.* 2 (of a state or quality) deep, intense, unqualified: *profound indifference.* 3 at or extending to a great depth: *profound crevasses.* 4 (of a sigh) deep-drawn. ▶ **profoundly** *adverb*

profundity *noun* (*plural* **profundities**) 1 the quality of understanding or dealing with a subject at a very serious level: *he lacked profundity and analytical precision.* 2 the quality of being very great, serious, or powerful: *the profundity of her misery.* 3 something said which shows great understanding: *his profundities were lost on the young audience.* [Say pruh FUNDA tee]

profuse *adjective* 1 (often foll. by *in*, *of*) lavish; extravagant: *was profuse in her praise.* 2 (esp. of something given or offered) exuberantly plentiful; abundant: *I offered my profuse apologies.* ▶ **profusely** *adverb* **profusion** *noun* [Say pro FYOOSS, pro FUSION]

prog *noun* *Cdn* (*Nfld*) food, e.g. for a meal, the winter, etc.: *prog bag.*

progenitor *noun* 1 the ancestor of a person, animal, or plant: *the plant has the resistance to heat and insects of its Indian progenitor.* 2 a person who originates an artistic, political, or intellectual movement: *the progenitors of abstract painting.* 3 something that serves as a model: *a progenitor of the building is the nearby Stanley Court Apartments.* [Say pro JENNA tur]

progeny *noun* the offspring of a person, animal, or plant: *mules are the progeny of a horse bred with a donkey.* [Say PRODGE a nee]

progesterone *noun* a steroid hormone released by the corpus luteum which stimulates the preparation of the uterus for pregnancy. [Say pro JESTER own]

progestin *noun* (also **progestogen**) 1 any of a group of steroid hormones (including progesterone) that maintain pregnancy and prevent further ovulation during it. 2 a similar hormone produced synthetically. [Say pro JESS tin, pro JESTA jin]

prognosis *noun* (*plural* **prognoses**) 1 a forecast of the likely outcome of a situation: *the prognosis for Bill C-43 appeared bleak.* 2 a forecast of the course of a disease or other medical condition: *the GP has better points of reference as regards prognosis of particular disorders.* [Say prog NO sis for the singular, prog NO seez for the plural]

prognostic *adjective* serving as an advance indication of the likely outcome of a disease, ailment, or other situation: *patients are grouped according to prognostic factors* ◊ *early delinquency is strongly prognostic of future crime.* [Say prog NOSS tick]

prognostication *noun* 1 the action of predicting future events: *given the pitfalls of prognostication, why would the magazine dedicate an issue to key technologies of the 21st century?* 2 a prediction: *economic prognostications.*

prognosticator *noun* a person who predicts future events: *our football prognosticators offer their picks for this week's games.*

program (also **programme**) • *noun* 1 a a usu. printed list of a series of events, pieces of music, performers, etc. at a public function, performance etc. b the performance itself: *a program of pieces for violin.* 2 a radio or television broadcast. 3 a a course of activities or actions undertaken to achieve a certain result: *fitness program.* b a plan of future events: *the program is dinner and a movie.* 4 a a course of study; curriculum: *a graduate of Carleton's journalism program.* b a system of extracurricular, usu. athletic activities: *football program.* 5 a plan offering subscribers certain benefits: *frequent flyer program.* 6 a series of coded instructions to

control the operation of a computer or other machine.
• verb (**programs** or **programmes**, **programmed**,
programming) **1** make a program or definite plan of.
2 provide (a computer etc.) with coded instructions for
the automatic performance of a particular task. **3** train
to behave in a predetermined way. **4** choose or
schedule (films, plays, pieces of music, etc.) for
performance. PHRASES **get with the program** *slang*
become aware of and attuned to the realities of a
situation. ▶ **programmability** *noun* **programmable**
adjective

programmatic *adjective* **1** of the nature of or
according to a program, schedule, or method;
systematic: *feminist issues were easily grafted onto the
programmatic agenda of the political left*. **2** having to do
with music that is intended to evoke images or convey a
story: *the piece includes programmatic sections and
imaginative evocations of mood*. ▶ **programmatically**
adverb

programmer *noun* **1** a person who writes computer
programs. **2** a person responsible for the programming
of broadcast programs, films, etc.

programming *noun* **1** the writing of computer
programs. **2** the choice, arrangement, or broadcasting
of radio or television programs, films, etc. **3** the action
of programming; planning for management or
administrative purposes.

progress • *noun* (*plural* **progresses**) **1** forward or
onward movement towards a destination. **2** advance or
development towards completion, betterment, etc.;
improvement: *has made little progress this term*. • *verb*
(**progresses**, **progressed**, **progressing**) **1** move or
be moved forward or onward; continue: *the argument is
progressing*. **2** advance or develop towards completion,
improvement, etc.: *science progresses*. **3** cause (a
situation, condition, person etc.) to advance or
improve. PHRASES **in progress** in the course of
developing; going on. [Say PRAW gress or PRO gress for
the noun, pruh GRESS for the verb]

progression *noun* **1** the process of developing
gradually from one stage or state to another:
opportunities for career progression ◊ *the rapid progression of
the disease* ◊ *a natural progression from childhood to
adolescence*. **2** a number of things that come in a series:
a long progression of sunny days. **3 a** = ARITHMETIC
PROGRESSION. **b** = GEOMETRIC PROGRESSION. [Say
pruh GRESH'n]

progressive • *adjective* **1** moving forward: *progressive
motion*. **2** proceeding step by step; cumulative:
progressive drug use. **3 a** (of a political party,
government, etc.) favouring or implementing rapid
progress or social reform. **b** holding liberal views;
modern: *this is a progressive company*. **c** (of music)
modern, experimental, avant-garde: *progressive jazz*.
4 (of disease, violence, etc.) increasing in severity or
extent. **5** (of taxation) at rates increasing with the sum
taxed. **6** *Grammar* (of an aspect) expressing an action in
progress, e.g. present progressive (*am writing*), past
progressive (*was writing*). **7** (of education) informal and
without strict discipline, stressing individual needs.
• *noun* an advocate of progressive political policies or
social reform. [Say pruh GRESS iv]

Progressive Conservative • *noun* a member or
supporter of the Progressive Conservative Party.
• *adjective* of or relating to the Progressive Conservative
Party or its policies.

Progressive Conservative Party *noun* (in
Canada) one of the two historically most important
political parties, advocating right-of-centre policies.

progressively *adverb* steadily and continuously: *the

situation was becoming progressively more difficult ◊ *the pain
got progressively worse*. [Say pruh GRESS iv lee]

progressivism *noun* the beliefs or principles of a
political party, government, etc. that favours or
implements rapid progress or social reform.
▶ **progressivist** *noun & adjective* [Say pruh GRESS iv ism]

prohibit *verb* (**prohibits**, **prohibited**,
prohibiting) (often foll. by *from* + verbal noun)
1 formally forbid, esp. by authority. **2** prevent; make
impossible: *his accident prohibits him from playing football*.

prohibition *noun* **1** the act of forbidding: *the
prohibition of smoking in public areas*. **2** *Law* a law or rule
that stops something being done or used: *a prohibition
against selling alcohol to people under the age of 18*. **3** (usu.
Prohibition) **a** the prevention by law of the
manufacture and sale of alcoholic drink, esp. as in the
US 1920–33. **b** the period during which such a
prohibition is in effect. ▶ **prohibitionism** *noun*
prohibitionist *noun* [Say pro hib ISH'n]

prohibitive *adjective* **1** (of prices, taxes, etc.) greater
than one is able to pay: *the cost of the books is prohibitive*.
2 intended to prevent or prohibit something:
prohibitive legislation. ▶ **prohibitively** *adverb* [Say
pro HIBBA tiv]

project • *noun* **1** a plan; a scheme. **2 a** an undertaking
that is carefully planned and designed to achieve a
particular aim. **b** any planned activity: *a do-it-yourself
project*. **3** a usu. long-term exercise or study of a set
topic undertaken by a student or group of students to
be submitted for assessment. **4** an individual or
collaborative enterprise undertaken usu. for industrial
or scientific research, or having a social purpose. **5** =
HOUSING PROJECT. • *verb* **1** plan or contrive (a course of
action, scheme, etc.). **2** protrude; jut out. **3** throw; cast;
impel: *projected the stone into the water*. **4** extrapolate
(results etc.) to a future time; forecast: *the unemployment
rate is projected to fall*. **5** cause (light, shadow, images,
etc.) to fall on a surface, screen, etc. **6 a** cause (a sound,
esp. the voice) to be heard at a distance. **b** use the voice
loudly enough to be heard in a large room etc.
7 express or convey (feelings, a particular image, etc.)
forcefully or effectively, e.g. to an audience. **8** *Geometry*
draw straight lines from a centre or parallel lines
through every point of a given figure to produce a
corresponding figure on a surface or a line by
intersecting it. **9** *Psychology* **a** attribute (an emotion
etc.) to an external object or person, esp. unconsciously.
b project oneself imagine oneself as being in
another person's place, the future, etc. [Say PRAW ject or
PRO ject for the noun, pruh JECT for the verb]

projectile • *noun* **1** a missile, esp. fired by a rocket. **2** a
bullet, shell, etc. fired from a gun. **3** any object thrown
as a weapon. • *adjective* projected with great force:
projectile vomiting. [Say pruh JECK tile]

projection *noun* **1 a** a forecast or estimate based on
present trends: *sales have exceeded our projections*. **b** this
process: *population projection is essential for planning*. **2** a
thing that projects or sticks out from a surface. **3 a** the
presentation of an image etc. on a surface or screen.
b the image etc. presented. **4** the act of making a voice
or sound audible at a distance: *actors and singers have to
have good projection*. **5 a** a mental image or
preoccupation viewed as an objective reality: *monsters
can be understood as mental projections of mankind's fears*.
b the unconscious transfer of one's own impressions or
feelings to external objects or persons. **6** *Math* the
action of projecting a figure. **7** the representation on a
flat surface of any part of the surface of the earth or a
celestial sphere: *Mercator projection*.

projectionist *noun* a person whose job is to show
films by operating a projector.

projector *noun* **1 a** an apparatus containing a source of light and a system of lenses for projecting slides or film onto a screen. **b** an apparatus for projecting rays of light. **2** a person who forms or promotes a project.

prolapse • *noun* **1** the forward or downward displacement of a part or organ. **2** the prolapsed part or organ, esp. the uterus or rectum. • *verb* (**prolapses, prolapsed, prolapsing**) undergo prolapse. [Say PRO laps]

prole *derogatory informal* • *adjective* proletarian. • *noun* a proletarian.

proletarian • *adjective* **1** belonging to or having to do with the class of wage earners, esp. (in Marxist theory) labourers engaged in industrial production, whose only asset is the labour they can sell to an employer: *the proletarian revolution*. **2** often *derogatory* belonging to or characteristic of the lowest class of citizens in a community: *cluttered back gardens of the proletarian inner city*. • *noun* a member of the proletariat: *a downtrodden proletarian struggling for equality*. [Say prole a TERRY un]

proletariat *noun* **1** the class of wage earners, esp. (in Marxist theory) labourers engaged in industrial production, whose only asset is the labour they can sell to an employer. **2** poor landless freemen constituting the lowest class of citizens in ancient Rome. [Say prole a TERRY it]

pro-life *adjective* in favour of preserving life, esp. in opposing abortion. ▶ **pro-lifer** *noun*

proliferate *verb* (**proliferates, proliferated, proliferating**) **1** increase rapidly in numbers: *large movie theatres are proliferating*. **2** produce or reproduce rapidly: *proliferating muscle cells in the artery*. ▶ **proliferation** *noun* [Say pruh LIFFER ate, pruh liffer AY sh'n]

prolific *adjective* **1** extremely productive: *a prolific writer ◊ a prolific goal scorer*. **2** (of a plant, animal, or person) producing much fruit or foliage or many offspring: *the beaver is not a remarkably prolific animal*. **3** present in large numbers; plentiful: *marine life is prolific, with large shoals of pollock*. **4** (of an area or a season) characterized by plentiful wildlife or produce: *one of the most prolific areas for birds*. ▶ **prolifically** *adverb* [Say pruh LIF ick]

prolix *adjective* (of speech or writing) using or containing too many words; lengthy and tedious: *his prose is prolix and awkward*. ▶ **prolixity** *noun* [Say PRO licks, pro LICKS a tee]

prologue *noun* **1 a** a preface or introduction to a literary or musical work, esp. an introductory speech or short poem addressed to the audience by one of the actors in a play (*compare* EPILOGUE 2). **b** the actor speaking the prologue. **2** a short preliminary time trial held before a cycling race to obtain a leader. **3** (usu. foll. by *to*) any act or event serving as an introduction.

prolong *verb* extend (an action, condition, etc.) in time or space.

prom *noun* *informal* a semi-formal or formal dance for high school or university students.

promenade • *noun* **1** a walk, or sometimes a ride or drive, taken esp. for display, leisure, etc. **2 a** esp. *Brit.* a paved public walk along the seafront at a resort. **b** any paved public walk. **3** = PROM. **4** (in square dancing) a movement resembling a march made by couples in formation. • *verb* (**promenades, promenaded, promenading**) **1** make a promenade. **2** lead (a person etc.) about a place esp. for display. **3** make a promenade through (a place). ▶ **promenader** *noun* [Say promma NAD or promma NOD]

promethium *noun* a radioactive metallic element occurring in nuclear waste material. [Say pro MEETHY um]

prominence *noun* **1** the state of being important or famous: *the band rose to prominence after the release of their second album*. **2** a thing that projects from something, esp. a projecting feature of the landscape or a protruding part of the body: *a steep, rocky prominence ◊ bony prominences*. [Say PROMMA nince]

prominent • *adjective* **1** distinguished; important: *a prominent member of city council*. **2** conspicuous: *a prominent billboard*. **3** jutting out; projecting: *her cheekbones were wide apart and prominent*. • *noun* (also **prominent moth**) a stout moth with tufts on the forewings, the caterpillars of which have fleshy growths on the back. ▶ **prominently** *adverb* [Say PROMMA n'nt]

promiscuity *noun* **1** the behaviour of a person who engages in frequent short sexual relationships with different partners: *she believes that promiscuity reduces the value of sexual relationships*. **2** an unselective, indiscriminate, or casual approach or behaviour: *attacked the opposition's supposed fiscal promiscuity*. [Say promise CUE a tee]

promiscuous *adjective* **1** having or involving frequent short sexual relationships with different partners: *not all singles are as promiscuous as he is*. **2** demonstrating or implying an unselective approach: *a shamelessly promiscuous tourist, who travelled the country stopping at random ◊ promiscuous pill-popping*. ▶ **promiscuously** *adverb* [Say pruh MISS cue us]

promise • *noun* **1** an assurance that one will or will not undertake a certain action, behaviour, etc. **2** a sign or signs of future achievements, good results, etc.: *shows great promise*. • *verb* (**promises, promised, promising**) **1** make (a person) a promise, esp. to do, give, or procure (a thing). **2** afford expectations of: *promises to be a good evening*. **3** *informal* assure, confirm: *I promise you, it won't be easy*.

promised land *noun* (**the promised land**) **1** (**Promised Land**) *Bible* Canaan, the land promised by God to Abraham and his descendants (Gen. 12:7). **2 a** any place where happiness is expected, esp. heaven. **b** any coveted situation: *a promised land of economic freedom*.

promising *adjective* likely to turn out well; hopeful; full of promise: *a promising start*. ▶ **promisingly** *adverb*

promissory note *noun* a signed document containing a written promise to pay a stated sum to a specified person or the bearer at a specified date or on demand. [Say PROMISE or ee]

promo *informal* • *noun* (*plural* **promos**) **1** an advertising or publicity campaign for a particular product. **2** a trailer for a television program, theatrical production, etc. • *adjective* of or relating to publicity for a performer, commercial product, etc.; promotional: *a promo video*.

promontory *noun* (*plural* **promontories**) a point of high land jutting out into the sea etc.; a headland. [Say PROM'n tory]

promote *verb* (**promotes, promoted, promoting**) **1** (often foll. by *to*) advance or raise (a person) to a higher office, rank, etc.: *was promoted to captain*. **2** help forward; encourage; support actively (a cause, process, desired result, etc.): *promoted women's rights ◊ rest promotes recovery*. **3** publicize and sell (a product). **4** advance (a student) to the next grade.

promoter *noun* **1** a person who promotes. **2** a person who finances, organizes, etc. a sporting event, theatrical production, etc. **3** a person involved in setting up and funding a new company.

promotion *noun* **1** activity that supports or provides active encouragement for the furtherance of a cause,

venture, or aim: *a society for the promotion of religious tolerance.* **2** the publicizing of a product, organization, or venture so as to increase sales or public awareness. **3** a publicity campaign for a particular product, organization, or venture: *the paper is reaping the rewards of a series of promotions.* **4** (usu. **promotions**) the activity or business of organizing such publicity or campaigns: *she's the promotions manager for a major record company.* **5** the action of raising someone to a higher position or rank or the fact of being so raised: *has been designated for promotion to colonel ◊ a promotion to sales manager.* ▶ **promotional** *adjective*

prompt • *adjective* **1** (of a person) acting without delay: *prompt in paying our bills.* **2** made, done, etc. readily or at once: *a prompt reply.* • *verb* **1** incite; urge: *prompted them to action.* **2 a** supply a forgotten word, sentence, etc., to (an actor etc.). **b** assist (a hesitating speaker) with a suggestion. **3** give rise to; inspire (a feeling, action, etc.). • *noun* **1 a** an act of prompting. **b** a thing said to help the memory of an actor etc. **2** an indication or sign on a computer screen to show that the system is waiting for input.

prompter *noun* **1** a person seated out of sight of the audience who prompts actors. **2** a person or thing that prompts.

prompting *noun* the action of saying something to persuade, encourage, or remind someone to do or say something: *he didn't need any prompting.*

promptly *adverb* **1** without delay: *Katherine deals with all the correspondence promptly.* **2** exactly at the correct time or at the time mentioned; punctually: *they arrived promptly at two o'clock.* **3** (before a verb) immediately: *she read the letter and promptly burst into tears.*

promptness *noun* the quality of being prompt or quick in action, performance, arrival, etc.

promulgate *verb* (**promulgates**, **promulgated**, **promulgating**) **1** make known to the public; spread, promote: *the stereotype that was promulgated in the 1940s ◊ most of the bands promulgating this philosophy broke up years ago.* **2** proclaim (a decree, news, etc.): *Muhammad promulgated a charter.* ▶ **promulgation** *noun* [Say PROM'll gate, prom'll GAY sh'n]

prone *adjective* **1 a** lying face downwards (*compare* SUPINE *adjective* 1). **b** lying flat; prostrate. **c** having the front part downwards, esp. the palm of the hand. **2** disposed or liable, esp. to a bad action, condition, etc.: *is prone to depression.* **3** more than usually likely to suffer: *accident-prone.* ▶ **proneness** *noun*

prong *noun* each of two or more projecting pointed parts at the end of a fork etc.

pronged *adjective* **1** having a prong or prongs. **2** (in *combination*) having a specified number of points of attack, perspectives, etc.: *a three-pronged theory.*

pronghorn *noun* (also **pronghorn antelope**) a small, very swift deer-like mammal with black horns that are shed and regrown annually, inhabiting the plains of Western Canada and the northwestern US.

pronoun *noun* a word used instead of and to indicate a noun already mentioned or known, esp. to avoid repetition, e.g. *we, theirs, this, ourselves.*

pronounce *verb* (**pronounces**, **pronounced**, **pronouncing**) **1** utter or speak (words, sounds, etc.), esp. in a certain way. **2 a** utter or deliver (a judgment, sentence, curse, etc.) formally or solemnly. **b** proclaim or announce officially: *I pronounce you man and wife.* **3** state or declare, as being one's opinion: *pronounced dessert excellent.* **4** pass judgment; give one's opinion: *pronounced for the defendant.*

pronounced *adjective* **1** very noticeable; marked: *a pronounced limp.* **2** (of opinions etc.) strongly felt; definite: *has very pronounced views.* **3** (of a word, sound, etc.) uttered. ▶ **pronouncedly** *adverb* [Say pruh NOUNST, pruh NOUN sid lee]

pronouncement *noun* **1** an authoritative declaration of opinion or judgment, esp. one that is regarded as self-important or condescending: *the pronouncements on drinking and sexual mores made by those in our society who are most spectacularly not with it.* **2** a formal or official statement: *an official pronouncement on changes in government policy.*

pronto *adverb informal* promptly, quickly.

pronunciation *noun* **1** the way in which a word, language, etc. is pronounced, esp. with reference to a standard. **2** a person's way of pronouncing words etc. [Say pruh nunsy AY sh'n]

proof • *noun* **1** facts, evidence, argument, etc. establishing or helping to establish a fact: *proof of their honesty ◊ no proof that he was there.* **2** *Law* the spoken or written evidence in a trial. **3** a demonstration or act of proving. **4** a test or trial: *put them to the proof.* **5** the standard of strength of distilled alcoholic liquors, in which the strongest measure is 100%. **6** a printout used for making corrections before final printing. **7** the stages in the resolution of a mathematical or philosophical problem. **8** a photographic print made for selection etc. • *adjective* **1** able or intended to withstand the damaging effects of something or a person's tampering: *the helmet is proof against concussions ◊ a childproof bottle.* **2** (of a distilled alcoholic liquor) of standard strength. • *verb* **1** make (something) proof, esp. make (fabric) waterproof. **2** proofread (printer's proofs, copy, etc.). ▶ PHRASES **the proof of the pudding is in the eating** (also **the proof is in the pudding**) the true value of something can be judged only from practical experience.

proof line *noun Cdn* (*Ont.*) = BASELINE 5.

proof positive *noun* absolutely certain proof.

proofread *verb* (**proofreads**, **proofread**, **proofreading**) read (printer's proofs, copy, etc.) and mark any errors. ▶ **proofreader** *noun* **proofreading** *noun*

prop. *abbreviation* **1** proprietor. **2** proposition.

prop • *noun* **1** a rigid support, esp. one not an integral part of the thing supported. **2** a person who supplies support, assistance, comfort, etc. **3** *Rugby* a forward at either end of the front row of a scrum. **4** a movable object used on a theatre stage etc. **5** *informal* a propeller. • *verb* (**props**, **propped**, **propping**) **1** (often foll. by *up*) support with or as if with a prop. **2** (often foll. by *against*, etc.) lean (something) against a support.

propaganda *noun* **1** usu. *derogatory* information, esp. of a biased or misleading nature, used to promote or

P

publicize a particular political cause or point of view: *the pamphlet was an obvious piece of Nazi propaganda*. **2** the action of spreading such information as a political strategy: *were accused of engaging in systematic hate propaganda*. [Say proppa GANDA]

propagandist • *noun* a person who spreads propaganda. • *adjective* consisting of or spreading propaganda: *propagandist slogans* ◊ *the journal was no propagandist organ of a political movement*. ▶**propagandistic** *adjective* [Say proppa GAN dist, proppa gan DISS tick]

propagandize *verb* (**propagandizes, propagandized, propagandizing**) **1** promote or publicize a particular cause, organization, or view, esp. in a biased or misleading way: *the photographs did not propagandize the country's poverty*. **2** attempt to influence (someone) in such a way: *he was propagandized into a set of beliefs and values he was not informed enough to understand*. [Say proppa GAN dize]

propagate *verb* (**propagates, propagated, propagating**) **1** breed by natural processes from the parent stock: *use root cuttings to propagate this variety of poppy* ◊ *certain trees need fire to propagate*. **2** spread: *movies that propagate imperialistic and racist themes* ◊ *urban legends propagate over the Net*. **3** transmit or be transmitted in a particular direction or through a medium: *visible light is electromagnetic energy propagated as radiant wave motion* ◊ *sound waves propagate through water even better than through air*. ▶**propagation** *noun* **propagator** *noun* [Say PROPPA gate, proppa GAY sh'n]

propane *noun* a gaseous hydrocarbon of the alkane series used as bottled fuel.

propel *verb* (**propels, propelled, propelling**) **1** drive or push forward. **2** urge on; encourage.

propellant • *noun* **1** a thing that propels. **2** an inert compressed fluid in which the active contents of an aerosol are dispersed. **3** an explosive that fires bullets etc. from a firearm. **4** a substance used as a reagent in a rocket engine etc. to provide thrust. • *adjective* propelling; capable of driving or pushing forward.

propeller *noun* a revolving shaft with blades, esp. for propelling a ship or aircraft.

propensity *noun* (*plural* **propensities**) an inclination or tendency: *has a propensity for wandering*. [Say pruh PENSA tee]

proper • *adjective* **1** right: *the proper amount* ◊ *at the proper time*. **2** decent; respectable, esp. excessively so: *not quite proper*. **3** belonging or relating exclusively or distinctively: *with the respect proper to them*. **4** (usu. placed after noun) strictly so called; real: *this is the crypt, not the cathedral proper*. **5** *Christianity* (of a psalm, lesson, etc.) appointed for a particular day, occasion, or season. • *noun Christianity* the part of a service that varies with the season or feast.

properly *adverb* **1** fittingly; suitably: *do it properly*. **2** accurately; correctly: *properly speaking*. **3** rightly: *he very properly refused*. **4** respectably: *behave properly*.

proper name *noun* (also **proper noun**) a name used for an individual person, place, animal, country, title, etc., and spelled with a capital letter, e.g. Jane, Whitehorse, Everest.

property *noun* (*plural* **properties**) **1 a** something owned; a possession, either tangible, e.g. a house, land, etc., or intangible, e.g. patents, copyrights, etc.: *intellectual property*. **b** possessions collectively, esp. real estate: *has money in property*. **2** an attribute, quality, or characteristic: *medicinal properties*. **3** a movable object used on a theatre stage etc. **4** an artist, performer, athlete, or work regarded as a commercial asset, success, or sensation: *Stella Duane has become a hot property since her book hit the bestseller list*.

property tax *noun* (*plural* **property taxes**) a tax based on the value of property.

prophecy *noun* (*plural* **prophecies**) **1 a** a divinely inspired utterance. **b** a prediction of future events: *a prophecy of massive inflation*. **2** the faculty, function, or practice of prophesying: *the gift of prophecy*. [Say PROFFA see]

prophesy *verb* (**prophesies, prophesied, prophesying**) foretell future events: *Jacques was prophesying a bumper harvest* ◊ *the papers prophesied that she would resign following an election defeat*. [Say PROFFA sigh]

SPELL CHECK
prophet, profit ✓ABC

The money made by a company is a **profit**.

---

prophet *noun* **1 a** a teacher or interpreter of the supposed will of God. **b** (in the Christian, Jewish and Muslim religions) a person sent by God to teach the people and give them messages from God: *an Old Testament prophet* ◊ *Hebrew prophets*. **2 a** a person who foretells events. **b** a person who advocates and speaks innovatively for a cause: *a prophet of the new order*. **3** (**the Prophet**) **a** Muhammad. **b** Joseph Smith (1805–44), founder of the Mormons, or one of his successors. ▶**prophetess** *noun* (*plural* **prophetesses**) [Sounds like PROFIT]

prophetic *adjective* **1** accurately describing or predicting what will happen in the future: *his warnings proved prophetic*. **2** of or concerning a prophet: *the prophetic books of the Old Testament*. ▶**prophetically** *adverb* [Say pruh FET ick]

prophylactic • *adjective* **1** tending to prevent disease: *prophylactic antibiotics*. **2** protective; precautionary: *interrogation law places an emphasis on prophylactic standards against unfair self-incrimination*. • *noun* **1** a preventive medicine or course of action: *malaria prophylactics*. **2** a condom. [Say proffa LACK tick]

propitious *adjective* giving or indicating a good chance for success; favourable: *a propitious moment for attack* ◊ *we hoped for propitious weather*. [Say pruh PISH us]

proponent *noun* a person advocating a motion, theory, or proposal; an advocate: *a prominent proponent of free trade*. [Say pruh PONE int]

proportion • *noun* **1 a** a comparative part or share: *a large proportion of the profits*. **b** a comparative ratio: *the proportion of births to deaths*. **2** (usu. in *plural*) a correct or ideal relationship in size, degree, etc. between one thing and another, or between the parts of a whole. **3** (in *plural*) dimensions; size: *large proportions*. **4** *Math* **a** an equality of ratios between two pairs of quantities, e.g. 3:5 and 9:15. **b** a set of such quantities. • *verb* adjust or regulate in proportion to something; make (a thing) proportional. **PHRASES in proportion 1** by the same factor. **2** without exaggerating (importance etc.): *must get the facts in proportion*. **out of (all) proportion 1** badly proportioned. **2** exaggerated, overemphasized. **3** (often foll. by *to, with*) disproportionate.

proportional *adjective* in due proportion; comparable: *a proportional increase* ◊ *resentment proportional to his injuries*. ▶**proportionally** *adverb*

proportional representation *noun* an electoral system in which all parties gain seats in proportion to the number of votes cast for them. Abbreviation: **PR**.

proportionate *adjective* = PROPORTIONAL. ▶**proportionately** *adverb* [Say PROPORTION it]

proportioned *adjective* having dimensions or a comparative relationship of parts of a specified type: *she was tall and perfectly proportioned* ◊ *gracefully proportioned structures with fine internal rhythms*.

proposal *noun* **1** a plan or suggestion, esp. a formal or written one, put forward for consideration or discussion by others: *a proposal to build an opera house* ◊ *his proposal that the system should be changed was rejected*. **2** an offer of marriage.

propose *verb* (**proposes, proposed, proposing**) **1** put forward for consideration or as a plan. **2** intend: *propose to open a restaurant*. **3** make an offer of marriage. **4** nominate (a person) as a member of a society, for an office, etc. **5** offer (a person's health, a person, etc.) as a subject for a toast.

proposed *adjective* suggested: *the proposed site*.

proposer *noun* a person who formally suggests something at a meeting etc.: *the proposer and seconder of the motion*.

proposition • *noun* **1** a plan proposed; a proposal. **2 a** an offer of terms for a business transaction. **b** an enterprise or undertaking esp. with regards to its financial success: *the company is a profitable proposition*. **3** a statement or assertion. **4** *Logic* a statement consisting of subject and predicate that is subject to proof. **5** a problem, opponent, prospect, etc. that is to be dealt with: *a difficult proposition*. **6** *Math* a formal statement of a theorem or problem, often including the demonstration. **7** *informal* a proposal to have sexual relations, esp. one made bluntly or offensively. • *verb informal* make a proposal (esp. of sexual relations) to.

propound *verb* **1** offer for consideration; propose: *some, like John Locke, propounded fundamental principles based on natural law*. **2** *Cdn & Brit. Law* produce (a will etc.) before the proper authority so as to establish its legality. ▶ **propounder** *noun*

proprietary *adjective* **1 a** (of a name) owned and used for a particular product only by a particular company. **b** (of goods) manufactured and sold by a particular firm: *proprietary medicines*. **2** of or relating to an owner or ownership: *proprietary rights*. **3** of, holding, or concerning property. [Say pruh PRY a terry]

proprietor *noun* **1** the owner of a business. **2** a holder of property. ▶ **proprietorial** *adjective* **proprietorship** *noun* [Say pruh PRY a tur, pruh pry a TORY ul]

propriety *noun* (*plural* **proprieties**) **1** moral and social behaviour that is considered to be correct and acceptable: *nobody questioned the propriety of her being there alone*. **2** (in *plural*) the details or rules of correct conduct: *they were careful to observe the proprieties*. [Say pruh PRY a tee]

propulsion *noun* **1** the action of driving or pushing forward: *they dive and use their wings for propulsion under water*. **2** the force that drives something forward: *steam propulsion*. ▶ **propulsive** *adjective*

propylene *noun* a gaseous hydrocarbon used in the manufacture of chemicals. [Say PRO puh leen]

propylene glycol *noun* either of two isomeric liquid alcohols, esp. one which is used as a solvent, in antifreeze, and in the food and plastics industries.

pro-rate *verb* (**pro-rates, pro-rated, pro-rating**) calculate or distribute proportionally: *pension pro-rated to years of service*. ▶ **pro-rated** *adjective*

prorogue *verb* (**prorogues, prorogued, proroguing**) **1** discontinue the meetings of (a parliament etc.) without dissolving it. **2** (of a parliament etc.) be prorogued. ▶ **prorogation** *noun* [Say pro ROAG, pro ruh GAY sh'n]

prosaic *adjective* **1** like prose, lacking poetic beauty. **2** dull; commonplace: *took a prosaic view of life*. ▶ **prosaically** *adverb* [Say pruh ZAY ick]

proscenium *noun* **1** (also **proscenium arch**) an arch that forms a frame at the front of a stage. **2** the part of the stage in front of the drop or curtain, usu. with the enclosing arch. [Say pro SEENY um]

prosciutto *noun* Italian cured ham, usu. served raw and thinly sliced as an hors d'oeuvre. [Say pruh SHOO toe]

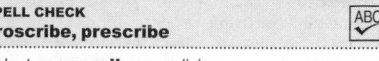
SPELL CHECK **proscribe, prescribe**
A doctor **prescribes** medicine

proscribe *verb* (**proscribes, proscribed, proscribing**) **1** reject or denounce (a practice etc.) as dangerous etc.; forbid, esp. by law.: *in the west, French was proscribed as a language of instruction*. **2** banish, exile: *proscribed from the club*. [Say pro SCRIBE]

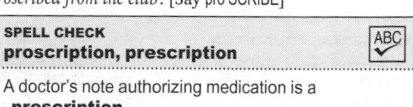
SPELL CHECK **proscription, prescription**
A doctor's note authorizing medication is a **prescription**.

proscription *noun* the action of forbidding, esp. by law. [Say pro SCRIP sh'n]

prose *noun* **1** the ordinary form of the written or spoken language; writing that is not poetry: *Milton's prose works*. **2** dull or commonplace speech, writing, etc.: *closely typed in best office prose*.

prosecute *verb* (**prosecutes, prosecuted, prosecuting**) **1 a** institute legal proceedings against (a person). **b** institute a prosecution with reference to (a claim, crime, etc.). **2** (of a lawyer) represent a person or an organization that prosecutes. **3** carry on (a war, pursuit, etc.).

prosecution *noun* **1 a** the institution and carrying on of a criminal charge in a court. **b** the carrying on of legal proceedings against a person. **c** the prosecuting party in a court case. **2** the action of carrying out or the process of being occupied with something: *the prosecution of war*.

prosecutor *noun* a person who prosecutes, esp. in a criminal court. ▶ **prosecutorial** *adjective* [Say PROSSA cute er, prossa cue TORY ul]

proselytize *verb* (**proselytizes, proselytized, proselytizing**) **1** attempt to persuade others to adopt one's own belief, esp. in religion: *proselytizing Buddhist monks strove to insert themselves into Himalayan folk belief*. **2** champion or promote a cause or opinion: *the company has been eagerly proselytizing the wonders of the plan*. ▶ **proselytizer** *noun* [Say PROSSA luh tize]

prose poem *noun* a piece of imaginative poetic writing in prose.

prosody *noun* **1** the systematic study of verses, covering the principles of metre, rhythm, rhyme, and stanza forms. **2** patterns of stress and intonation in ordinary speech. [Say PROZZA dee or PROSSA dee]

prospect • *noun* **1 a** the chance or hope that something will happen: *there's little prospect of a settlement*. **b** (often in *plural*) the chances of being successful: *her prospects for a new job were good*. **c** a vision or idea of the future: *she dreaded the prospect of the visit*. **2 a** something viewed in terms of its profitability: *a good prospect for investment*. **b** a candidate or competitor who is likely to be successful. **3** a possible or probable customer, subscriber, etc. **4** an extensive view of landscape. • *verb* **1** explore a region for minerals: *the company is also prospecting for gold*. **2** (often foll. by *for*) search around, look out for something: *prospecting for customers*. ▶ **prospecting** *noun*

prospective *adjective* **1** expected; potential: *prospective buyer*. **2** concerned with or applying to the future: *prospective analysis*. ▶ **prospectively** *adverb*

prospector *noun* a person who searches an area for gold, minerals, etc.

prospectus *noun* (*plural* **prospectuses**) **1** a document advertising or describing a commercial enterprise etc., esp. to attract investors. **2** a listing of the courses etc. of an educational institution.

prosper *verb* **1** succeed; thrive. **2** make successful: *Heaven prosper him*.

prosperity *noun* the state of being prosperous. [Say pruh SPARE a tee]

prosperous *adjective* **1** successful; rich: *a prosperous entrepreneur*. **2** thriving: *a prosperous enterprise*.

prostaglandin *noun* any of a group of hormone-like substances that cause muscle contraction and which may be used to induce labour. [Say prossta GLAND in]

prostate *noun* a gland surrounding the neck of the bladder in male mammals and releasing a fluid forming part of the semen. [Say PROSS tate]

prosthesis *noun* (*plural* **prostheses**) an artificial part supplied to remedy a deficiency, e.g. a false breast, leg, tooth, etc. ▶ **prosthetic** *adjective* [Say pross THEESIS for the singular, pross THEESEEZ for the plural, pross THETTICK]

prosthetics *plural noun* **1** (usu. treated as *singular*) the branch of surgery that deals with the replacement of defective or missing parts of the body by artificial substitutes. **2** artificial body parts. [Say pross THETTICKS]

prostitute • *noun* **1** a person who engages in sexual activity for payment. **2** a person who misuses his or her talents or skills esp. for money. • *verb* (**prostitutes, prostituted, prostituting**) **1** put oneself or one's talents to an unworthy or corrupt use for the sake of personal gain: *his willingness to prostitute himself to the worst instincts of the electorate*. **2** make a prostitute of (esp. oneself). ▶ **prostitution** *noun*

> **SPELL CHECK**
> **prostrate, prostate**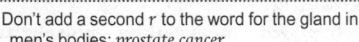
>
> Don't add a second r to the word for the gland in men's bodies: *prostate cancer*.

prostrate • *adjective* **1 a** lying face downwards. **b** lying horizontally. **2** overcome, esp. by grief, exhaustion, etc.: *prostrate with self-pity*. **3** *Botany* growing along the ground. • *verb* (**prostrates, prostrated, prostrating**) **1 prostrate oneself** throw (oneself) down in submission etc.: *she prostrated herself on the bare floor of the church*. **2** (of fatigue, illness, etc.) overcome; reduce to extreme physical weakness: *totally prostrated by pneumonia*. ▶ **prostration** *noun* [Say PROSS trate for the adjective, praw STRATE for the verb, pross TRAY sh'n]

prosy *adjective* (**prosier, prosiest**) **1** resembling or characteristic of prose. **2** tedious; commonplace: *a prosy lecture*. [Say PROSE ee]

protactinium *noun* a radioactive metallic element whose chief isotope yields actinium by decay. [Say pro tack TINNY um]

protagonist *noun* **1** the principal character in a work of fiction, film, drama, etc.: *there are at least two Canadian novels in which the protagonist is a semi-human being*. **2** (often in *plural*) the most prominent or most important individual in a situation or course of events: *in this colonial struggle the main protagonists were Great Britain and France*. **3** a leading or respected supporter of a cause, movement, etc.: *a leading protagonist of the conservation movement*. [Say pro TAGGA nist]

protease *noun* any enzyme able to hydrolyze proteins and peptides by splitting them. [Say PRO tee ace]

protect *verb* **1** keep (a person or thing) safe from harm, injury, etc. **2 a** attempt to preserve (a threatened plant or animal species) by legislating against hunting, collecting, etc. **b** restrict by law access to or development of (land) in order to preserve its wildlife or its undisturbed state. **3** *Computing* restrict access (to a file, disk, etc.) to a specified user or users. **4** shield (domestic industry) from competition by imposing import duties on foreign goods. **5** keep a person, thing, etc. safe from something: *this vaccine protects against several diseases*. ▶ **protected** *adjective*

protection *noun* **1 a** the act of protecting, or the state of being protected: *bring clothes that provide adequate protection against wind and rain* ◊ *he asked to be put under police protection*. **b** a thing that prevents someone or something suffering harm or injury: *they wore the charm as a protection against evil spirits*. **2 a** the practice of paying money to criminals so that they will not attack a business, property, or person: *ran a protection racket*. **b** (also **protection money**) the money paid for this, esp. on a regular basis. **3** insurance coverage: *health protection* ◊ *our policy provides complete protection against fire and theft*. **4** a legal or other formal measure intended to preserve civil liberties and rights: *the constitutional protections afforded under the Charter*.

protectionism *noun* the principle or practice of protecting a country's own industry by taxing foreign goods. ▶ **protectionist** *noun & adjective*

protective *adjective* **1** protecting; intended to protect: *protective equipment*. **2** having or showing the tendency to protect a person or thing: *a protective mother*.

protective custody *noun* the detention of a person for his or her own protection.

protectively *adverb* in a way that protects or is intended to protect.

protectiveness *noun* the quality or state of being protective.

protector *noun* **1** a person who protects. **2** (often in *combination*) a thing or device that protects: *surge protector*. **3** (**Protector**) (also **Lord Protector of the Commonwealth**) *Brit. hist.* the title of Oliver Cromwell 1653–58 and his son Richard 1658–59.

protectorate *noun* **1 a** a territory that is controlled and protected by a larger state. **b** such a relation of one state to another. **2** *hist.* **a** the office of the protector of a kingdom or country. **b** the period of this, esp. (**Protectorate**) in England 1653–59. [Say PROTECTOR it]

protege *noun* a person whose welfare and career are looked after by an influential person, esp. over a long period: *a protege of the great violinist Yehudi Menuhin*. [Say PRO tuh zhay or PRAW tuh zhay]

protein *noun* **1** any of a group of organic compounds composed of one or more chains of amino acids and forming an essential part of all living organisms. **2** such substances collectively, esp. as a dietary component. [Say PRO teen]

pro tem *adjective & adverb* for the time being; temporarily: *a printer which Marisa could use pro tem* ◊ *a pro tem committee*.

proteolysis *noun* the splitting of proteins or peptides by enzymes, esp. during the process of digestion. ▶ **proteolytic** *adjective* [Say pro tee AWL iss iss, pro tee a LIT ick]

Proterozoic • *adjective* of or relating to the eon constituting the later part of Precambrian time, from about 2.5 billion to 550 million years ago, when life consisted of bacteria and algae. • *noun* this time. [Say pro tur oh ZO ick]

protest • *noun* **1** a statement of dissent, disapproval, or complaint; a remonstrance: *she signed the protest condemning the sale of toy guns.* **2** a usu. public demonstration of objection to government etc. policy: *protest demonstration.* • *verb* **1 a** (usu. foll. by *against, at, about,* etc.) make a protest against an action, proposal, etc. **b** object to: *he protested their decision.* **c** maintain a difference of opinion, stubbornly disagree: *"I am not too tired," she protested.* **2** affirm (one's innocence etc.) solemnly, esp. in reply to an accusation etc. **3** *Law* write or obtain a protest in regard to (a bill). PHRASES **under protest** unwillingly.

Protestant (also **protestant**) • *noun* a member or follower of any of the western Christian Churches that are separate from the Catholic Church in accordance with the principles of the Reformation. • *adjective* of or relating to any of the Protestant Churches or their members etc. ▶ **Protestantism** *noun* [Say PROTTA st'nt]
Protestant Reformation *noun* = REFORMATION 2.

protestation *noun* **1** an emphatic declaration that something is or is not the case: *her protestations of innocence were in vain.* **2** an objection or protest: *despite the protestations from those most loyal to him, Broadbent chose to depart.* [Say protta STAY sh'n or pro tess TAY sh'n]

protester *noun* (also **protestor**) a person who participates in a protest.

protest vote *noun* a vote for a party or candidate representing a protest against the actions or policies of another party or candidate.

protist *noun* any of a group of mostly single-celled organisms, including protozoa, simple algae and fungi, and slime moulds, that have both plant and animal characteristics. [Say PRO tist]

proto- *combining form* **1** first. **2** designating the earliest attested or hypothetically-reconstructed form of a language: *Proto-Algonquian.*

protocol *noun* **1 a** official, esp. diplomatic, formality and etiquette observed on state occasions etc.: *protocol forbids the prince from making any public statement in his defence.* **b** the rules, formalities, etc. of any procedure, group, etc.. **2** the original draft of a diplomatic document, esp. of the terms of a treaty agreed to in conference and signed by the parties: *it is set out in a legally binding protocol which forms part of the treaty.* **3** *Computing* a set of rules governing the exchange and transmission of data electronically between devices.

proton *noun* *Physics* a stable elementary particle with a positive electric charge, equal in magnitude to that of an electron, and occurring in all atomic nuclei. [Say PRO tawn]

protoplasm *noun* the material comprising the living part of a cell, consisting of a nucleus embedded in membrane-enclosed cytoplasm. ▶ **protoplasmic** *adjective* [Say PRO tuh plasm, pro tuh PLASMIC]

prototype • *noun* **1** an original thing or person of which or whom copies, imitations, improved forms, representations, etc. are made. **2** a trial model or preliminary version of a vehicle, machine, etc. • *verb* (**prototypes, prototyped, prototyping**) make a prototype of (a product). [Say PRO tuh type]

prototypical *adjective* constituting the essential type of; ideal: *a prototypical folkie: bearded, amiable, peace-*

loving, full of his songs. ▶ **prototypically** *adverb* [Say pro tuh TYPICAL]

protozoan • *noun* (*plural* **protozoa** or **protozoans**) (also **protozoon**, *plural* **protozoa**) any usu. single-celled and microscopic organism of the subkingdom Protozoa, including amoebae and ciliates. • *adjective* of or relating to this phylum. [Say pro tuh ZO un]

protract *verb* prolong or lengthen esp. in time or in space: *the majority saw little point in protracting ethnic and religious hostilities.*

protracted *adjective* of excessive length or duration: *a protracted debate.*

protractor *noun* an instrument for measuring angles, usu. in the form of a semicircle graduated by degrees. [Say pruh TRACTOR or PRO tractor]

protrude *verb* (**protrudes, protruded, protruding**) extend beyond or above a surface; project: *a fin protruded from the water.* ▶ **protrusion** *noun*

protuberance *noun* **1** a thing that protrudes from something else: *some dinosaurs had protuberances on top of their heads.* **2** the fact or state of protruding: *the large size and protuberance of the incisors.* [Say pruh TOOBER ince or pruh TYOOBER ince]

protuberant *adjective* bulging out; prominent: *protuberant eyes.* [Say pruh TOOBER int or pruh TYOOBER int]

proud *adjective* **1** feeling greatly honoured or pleased. **2 a** valuing oneself, one's possessions, etc. highly, or esp. too highly: *she wasn't too proud to take the money.* **b** suitably satisfied with one's achievements: *proud of a job well done.* **3 a** (of an occasion etc.) justly arousing pride: *a proud day for us.* **b** (of an action etc.) showing pride: *a proud wave of the hand.* **4** (of a thing) imposing; distinguished: *the statue stands tall and proud.* PHRASES **do proud** *informal* **1** be a source of pride to (someone): *her achievements did her family proud.* **2** treat (a person) with lavish generosity or honour: *they did us proud on our anniversary.* ▶ **proudly** *adverb*

Prov. *abbreviation* **1** (also **prov.**) Provincial, provincial. **2** (also **prov.**) Province, province.

provable *adjective* that can be shown to be true.

prove *verb* (**proves**; *past* **proved**; *past participle* **proven** or **proved**; *proving*) **1 a** demonstrate the truth of by evidence or argument. **b** assert or reveal (something). **c** show (a thing or person) to be (right, wrong, etc.): *the facts will prove me right.* **2 a** be found: *the tool proved useless for the job.* **b** turn out to be, emerge as, become: *jealousy will prove his downfall.* **3** test the accuracy of (esp. a calculation); subject to a testing process. **4** establish the genuineness and validity of (a will). PHRASES **prove oneself** show one's abilities, courage, etc.

proven *adjective* **1** shown to be such through trial and experience: *a proven performer.* **2** (also in *combination*) demonstrated to be effective: *a time-proven technique.*

provenance *noun* **1** the place of origin or history, esp. of a work of art etc. **2** origin. [Say PROVVA nince]

Provençal • *adjective* **1** of or concerning the language, inhabitants, landscape, etc. of Provence in southeast France. **2** (also **provençale**) containing olive oil, garlic, and often tomato, and normally flavoured with mixed Provençal herbs such as tarragon, rosemary, etc. • *noun* **1** a native of Provence. **2** the Romance language of Provence, closely related to French, Italian, and Catalan. [Say praw von SAL]

proverb *noun* a short pithy saying in general use, held to embody a general truth.

proverbial *adjective* **1** (esp. of a specific characteristic etc.) as well-known as a proverb; notorious: *his proverbial honesty.* **2** of or referred to in a proverb: *the proverbial ill wind.* ▶ **proverbially** *adverb*

provide *verb* (**provides, provided, providing**) **1 a** supply, furnish. **b** offer or present (an answer,

example, opportunity, etc.): *darkness provided a chance for escape*. **2** (foll. by *that*) ensure or specify: *this agreement provides that profits will be divided equally.* PHRASES **provide for 1** supply money and other necessities, e.g. food, for: *she provides for her family.* **2** make the necessary plans to deal with something that may happen: *had not provided for rain.* **3** (of a law, etc.) make it possible for something to be done later: *freedom of speech is provided for in the constitution.*

provided *conjunction* (also **providing**) (often foll. by *that*) on the condition or understanding (that).

providence *noun* esp. *Christianity* (also **Providence**) God, or a force that some people believe controls human lives, usu. in a protective way: *trust in divine providence.* [Say PROVVA dince]

providential *adjective* **1** of or by divine intervention; caused by Providence: *believed in the providential ordering of history.* **2** occurring at a favourable time; opportune, lucky: *it's risky to depend solely on providential rainfall to water the area.* ▶**providentially** *adverb* [Say provva DEN shull]

provider *noun* **1** a person or thing that provides. **2** the breadwinner of a family etc.

province *noun* **1** a principal administrative division of a country etc., esp. (in Canada) one of the ten principal political units which, along with the Territories, constitute Canada. **2** (in *plural*) the whole of esp. a European country outside the capital city, often regarded as uncultured, unsophisticated, etc.: *they talked of French customs and habits, of Paris and the provinces.* **3** a person's particular area of knowledge, interest or responsibility: *such decisions are normally the province of higher management* ◊ *I'm afraid the matter is outside my province.* **4** an area containing a distinct group of animal or plant communities or with a distinct geology or topography. **5** (in Catholic and Anglican churches) a district under an archbishop or a metropolitan, usu. consisting of adjacent dioceses. **6** a territorial division of a religious order. **7** *Roman History* a territory outside Italy under a Roman governor.

provincehood *noun* Cdn the quality or status of being a province.

Province House *noun* the name of the legislative building in Nova Scotia and PEI.

province-wide *adjective* esp. *Cdn* extending throughout or pertaining to a whole province.

provincial • *adjective* **1** of, pertaining to, or under the jurisdiction of a province or provinces. **2** of or concerning the whole of esp. a European country outside the capital city: *French provincial furniture.* **3** *derogatory* having or showing a narrow or limited view of life and current affairs and a lack of sophistication: *a rough, provincial people were the citizens of Haworth — hostile to strangers and taciturn to a fault.* • *noun* **1** Cdn (in *plural*) a provincial tournament or championship. **2** an inhabitant of esp. a European region outside the capital city. **3** an unsophisticated or uncultured person. **4** *Christianity* the head or chief of a province or of a religious order in a province. ▶**provincially** *adverb*

provincial building *noun* Cdn a building housing provincial government offices.

provincial court *noun* Cdn a court established by provincial legislation, usu. having both criminal and civil divisions, which conducts hearings by judge alone on offences of a relatively minor nature.

provincialism *noun* **1 a** an attitude or manners reflecting a limited or restricted view of life and current events; narrow-mindedness: *he wanted to escape from the narrow-minded provincialism of the small town where he had been brought up.* **b** an unsophisticated outlook. **2** allegiance to or concern for one's province

rather than one's country: *provincialism became the dominant force to the detriment of nationalism.* ▶**provincialist** *noun & adjective*

provincialization *noun* Cdn the transfer (of responsibilities, etc.) to the provincial level: *the provincialization of labour market training seriously damages any chance for a national industrial strategy.* ▶**provincialize** *verb* (**provincializes, provincialized, provincializing**)

provincial park *noun* Cdn an area of land owned and preserved by a provincial government for public benefit and enjoyment and conservation of wildlife.

provincial parliament *noun* Cdn a provincial legislative assembly.

provincial police *noun* Cdn (esp. *Ont. & Que.*) a police force under provincial authority responsible for jurisdictions without municipal police protection.

provincial right *noun* Cdn (usu. in *plural*) the right of a province or provinces to maintain and exercise authority over specified areas under provincial jurisdiction.

proving ground *noun* any area or situation in which a person or thing is tested or proven.

provision • *noun* **1 a** the action of providing or supplying something for use: *the provision of services.* **b** something provided. **c** preparation that is made for the future: *make provision for one's old age* ◊ *no provision for a deadlock-breaking mechanism.* **2** (in *plural*) food, drink, etc., esp. for a long journey. **3** a condition or requirement in a legal document: *under the provisions of the lease, the tenant is responsible for repairs.* • *verb* supply (an expedition etc.) with provisions.

provisional • *adjective* **1** providing for immediate needs only; temporary: *he was admitted to hospital with a provisional diagnosis of intestinal obstruction.* **2** (**Provisional**) designating the unofficial wing of the IRA established in 1970, advocating terrorism. • *noun* (**Provisional**) a member of the Provisional wing of the IRA. ▶**provisionally** *adverb*

proviso *noun* (*plural* **provisos**) a condition that must be accepted before an agreement can be made: *their participation is subject to a number of important provisos* ◊ *he agreed to their visit with the proviso that they should stay no longer than one week.* [Say pruh VIZE oh]

provocateur *noun* a person who provokes a disturbance or controversy; an agitator: *Rush Limbaugh, radio's right-wing provocateur.* [Say pruh VOKKA tur]

provocation *noun* **1** action or speech that makes someone annoyed or angry, esp. deliberately: *did it under severe provocation* ◊ *bursts into tears at the slightest provocation* ◊ *attacked without provocation.* **2** Cdn & Brit. Law an action, insult, etc. deemed likely to provoke physical retaliation or an irrational response. [Say provva KAY sh'n]

provocative *adjective* **1** intentionally causing anger, annoyance, controversy, etc.: *a provocative editorial.* **2** tending to arouse sexual desire. **3** intellectually stimulating: *a provocative book.* ▶**provocatively** *adverb* **provocativeness** *noun* [Say pruh VOKKA tiv]

provoke *verb* (**provokes, provoked, provoking**) **1** annoy, disturb, or harass: *don't provoke the dog.* **2** cause a person to do something by behaving in a certain esp. annoying way: *provoked her into leaving him.* **3** cause a particular reaction in a person etc.: *provoked an angry response.* **4** give rise to: *will provoke fermentation.*

provoking *adjective* **1** exasperating, irritating, annoying. **2** prompting (thought, anxiety, laughter, etc.): *thought-provoking.* ▶**provokingly** *adverb*

provolone *noun* a type of mellow cow's-milk cheese originally made in southern Italy, often smoked after

drying and moulded into the shape of a pear. [Say pro vo LO nay, prov uh LO nee]

provost *noun* a high administrative officer in a university. [Say PROV ust]

prow *noun* the forepart or bow of a ship. ▶ **prowed** *combining form* [Rhymes with HOW]

prowess *noun* great skill; exerting prowess. [Say prow ESS or PROW iss (PROW rhymes with HOW)]

prowl • *verb* **1 a** move quietly and carefully, esp. when looking or hunting for something or with the intent to commit a crime. **b** move through or in a place in this way: *prowling the streets*. **2** walk or wander, e.g. because one is anxious or unable to relax: *prowling about the house*. • *noun* an act of prowling: *an apparently aimless prowl through downtown*. PHRASES **on the prowl** moving about secretively: *an intruder on the prowl*. ▶ **prowler** *noun*

proximate *adjective* nearest or next before or after (in place, order, time, causation, thought process, etc.): *the proximate cause of the carnage* ◊ *the failure of the proximate military power to lend assistance*. [Say PROCK sim it]

proximity *noun* nearness in space, time, etc.: *do not operate microphones in close proximity to television sets*. [Say prock SIMMA tee]

proxy *noun* (*plural* **proxies**) **1** the authority that one gives to someone to do something for one, when one cannot do it oneself: *you can vote either in person or by proxy* ◊ *a proxy vote*. **2** a person who has been given the authority to represent someone else: *your proxy will need to sign the form on your behalf* ◊ *she is acting as proxy for her husband*. **3** a document giving the power to act as a proxy, esp. in voting: *please send in your proxies for the Annual General Meeting by September 11*.

Prozac *noun* *proprietary* the antidepressant drug fluoxetine hydrochloride. [Say PRO zack]

prude *noun* a person who is or claims to be easily shocked by matters relating to sex or nudity.

prudence *noun* the quality or state of being careful or cautious, or of having good judgment.

prudent *adjective* **1** careful to provide for the future. **2** discreet or cautious. **3** having or exercising good judgment.

prudential *adjective* involving or showing care or forethought, esp. in business: *what does a prudential, realistic policy look like?* [Say proo DEN shull]

prudently *adverb* in a careful or cautious manner.

prudery *noun* the attitude or behaviour of people who seem very easily shocked by things connected with sex.

prudish *adjective* very easily shocked by things connected with sex. ▶ **prudishness** *noun*

prune¹ *noun* **1** a dried plum. **2** (also **prune plum**) a variety of plum suitable for drying.

prune² *verb* (**prunes, pruned, pruning**) **1** trim a tree etc. by cutting away dead or overgrown branches etc. **2** reduce (costs etc.): *try to prune expenses*. **3** reduce the extent of (something) by cutting or removing unnecessary parts etc.: *must prune the list*. ▶ **pruner** *noun*

prurience *noun* a tendency towards an unhealthy or excessive interest in sexual matters. [Say PROOR ee ince]

prurient *adjective* **1** having or showing an excessive interest in sexual matters. **2** encouraging such an excessive interest. [Say PROOR ee int]

Prussian • *adjective* of or relating to Prussia, a former German state, originally a small country on the southeast shores of the Baltic Sea. • *noun* a native of Prussia. [Say PRUSH'n]

pry *verb* (**pries, pried, prying**) **1** (often foll. by *open, up*, etc.) move, open, raise, etc., by leverage: *pry up the lid* ◊ *pried the box open*. **2** remove, obtain, or separate with

difficulty: *could not pry the secret out of Joelene*. **3** inquire impertinently (into a person's private affairs etc.).

pry bar *noun* a metal bar used for prying up nailed boards etc.

prying *adjective* unduly inquisitive or curious, esp. about secret, private, or personal matters.

PS *abbreviation* **1** (also **ps**) postscript. **2** Public School. **3** power steering.

PSAC *abbreviation* Public Service Alliance of Canada.

psalm *noun* **1** (also **Psalm**) any of the sacred songs contained in the Biblical Book of Psalms. **2** a musical setting for a Psalm. [Say SOM]

pseudo • *adjective* sham: *we are talking about real journalists, not the pseudo kind*. • *noun* (*plural* **pseudos**) a pretentious or insincere person. [Say SOO doe]

pseudo- *combining form* (also **pseud-** before a vowel) **1** supposed or purporting to be but not really so; not genuine: *pseudo-intellectual*. **2** resembling or imitating (often in technical applications): *pseudo-language*. [Say SOO doe]

pseudoephedrine *noun* a compound commonly used as a nasal decongestant. [Say soo doe a FED rin]

pseudonym *noun* a fictitious name, esp. one assumed by an author. [Say SOO duh nim]

pseudo-science *noun* a collection of beliefs or practices mistakenly regarded as being based on scientific method. ▶ **pseudo-scientific** *adjective* [Say SOO doe science, soo doe SCIENTIFIC]

pshaw *interjection* an expression of contempt or impatience.

psi¹ *noun* **1** the twenty-third letter of the Greek alphabet (Ψ, ψ). **2** supposed parapsychological faculties, phenomena, etc. regarded collectively. [Say SIGH or puh SIGH]

psi² *abbreviation* pounds per square inch.

psoriasis *noun* a skin disease marked by red scaly patches. ▶ **psoriatic** *adjective* [Say suh RYE a sis, sorry ATTIC]

PST *abbreviation* **1** *Cdn* provincial sales tax. **2** Pacific Standard Time.

psych *informal* • *verb* (**psychs, psyched, psyching**) **1** (usu. foll. by *up*) prepare (oneself or another person) mentally for an ordeal etc. **2** (usu. foll. by *out*) analyze (a person's motivation etc.) for one's own advantage: *trying to psych Ian out*. **3** (often foll. by *out*) influence a person psychologically, esp. negatively; intimidate, frighten. • *noun* psychology: *psych textbook*. • *adjective* psychiatric: *psych ward*. [Say SIKE]

psyche *noun* **1** the soul; the spirit. **2** the mind. [Say SIKE ee]

psychedelia *plural noun* psychedelic articles, esp. posters, paintings, music, etc. [Say sike a DELLY uh]

psychedelic • *adjective* **1 a** expanding the mind's awareness etc., esp. through the use of hallucinogenic drugs. **b** (of an experience) hallucinatory; bizarre. **c** (of a drug) producing hallucinations. **2** *informal* **a** producing an effect resembling that of a psychedelic drug; having vivid colours or designs etc. **b** (of colours, patterns, etc.) bright, bold and often abstract. • *noun* a hallucinogenic drug. ▶ **psychedelically** *adverb* [Say sike a DEL ick]

psychiatric *adjective* of or relating to mental illness or its treatment: *a psychiatric disorder*. [Say sike ee AT rick]

psychiatrist *noun* a medical doctor specializing in the diagnosis and treatment of mental illness. [Say sigh KIE a trist]

psychiatry *noun* the study and treatment of mental disease. [Say sigh KIE a tree]

psychic • *adjective* **1 a** (of a person) considered to have occult powers, such as telepathy, clairvoyance, etc. **b** (of a faculty, phenomenon, etc.) inexplicable by natural

laws. **2** of or relating to the soul or mind. • *noun* a person considered to have psychic powers; a medium. ▶ **psychical** *adjective* **psychically** *adverb* [Say SIKE ick]

psycho *informal* • *noun* (*plural* **psychos**) a psychopath. • *adjective* psychopathic. [Say SIKE oh]

psycho- *combining form* relating to the mind or psychology. [Say SIKE oh]

psychoactive *adjective* (of a drug) affecting the mind. [Say sike oh ACTIVE]

psychoanalysis *noun* a therapeutic method of treating mental disorders by investigating the interaction of conscious and unconscious elements in the mind and bringing repressed fears and conflicts into the conscious mind. [Say sike oh ANALYSIS]

psychoanalyst *noun* a person who treats patients using psychoanalysis. [Say sike oh ANALYST]

psychoanalytic *adjective* having to do with psychoanalysis. ▶ **psychoanalytical** *adjective* **psychoanalytically** *adverb* [Say sike oh ANALYTIC]

psychoanalyze *verb* (**psychoanalyzes**, **psychoanalyzed**, **psychoanalyzing**) treat (a patient) using psychoanalysis. [Say sike oh ANALYZE]

psychobabble *noun informal derogatory* writing or talk filled with psychiatric jargon, esp. concerning personality and relationships, esp. when used by lay people with little regard for accuracy. [Say SIKE oh babble]

psychodrama *noun* **1** a form of psychotherapy in which patients act out events from their past. **2** a play or film etc. in which psychological elements are the main interest. [Say SIKE oh drama]

psychodynamics *plural noun* (treated as *singular*) the study of the activity of and the interrelation between the various parts of an individual's personality or psyche. [Say sike oh DYNAMICS]

psychological *adjective* **1** of, relating to, affecting, or arising in the mind. **2** of or relating to psychology. **3** *informal* (of an ailment etc.) having a basis in the mind; imaginary. ▶ **psychologically** *adverb* [Say sike uh LOGICAL]

psychologist *noun* an expert or specialist in psychology. [Say sigh COLLA jist]

psychology *noun* (*plural* **psychologies**) **1** the scientific study of the human mind and its functions, esp. those affecting behaviour in a given context. **2 a** the mental characteristics or attitude of a person or group. **b** the mental factors governing a situation or activity: *the psychology of crime.* [Say sigh COLLA jee]

psychometric *adjective* of, relating to, or deriving from psychometry. [Say sike oh METRIC]

psychometry *noun* the measurement of mental abilities. [Say sigh COMMA tree]

psychopath *noun* **1** a person suffering from chronic mental disorder esp. with abnormal or violent social behaviour. **2** a mentally or emotionally unstable person. ▶ **psychopathic** *adjective* [Say SIKE oh path, sike oh PATH ick]

psychopathology *noun* (*plural* **psychopathologies**) **1** the scientific study of mental disorders. **2** features of people's mental health considered collectively: *ageism, family discord, and psychopathology all play their part in abuse.* **3** mental or behavioural disorder: *she showed evidence of genuine psychopathology.* [Say sike oh puh THOLLA jee]

psychopathy *noun* psychopathic or psychologically abnormal behaviour. [Say sigh COP uth ee]

psychosexual *adjective* of or involving the psychological aspects of the sexual impulse. [Say sike oh SEXUAL]

psychosis *noun* (*plural* **psychoses**) a severe mental derangement, esp. when resulting in delusions and loss of contact with external reality. [Say sigh CO sis for the singular, sigh CO seez for the plural]

psychosocial *adjective* of or involving the influence of social factors or human interactive behaviour. [Say sike oh SOCIAL]

psychosomatic *adjective* (of an illness etc.) caused or aggravated by mental conflict, stress, etc. [Say sike oh suh MAT ick]

psychotherapeutic *adjective* having to do with the treatment of mental disorders by psychological means. [Say sike oh therra PYOOT ick]

psychotherapist *noun* a medical practitioner who treats mental disorders by psychological means. [Say sike oh THERAPIST]

psychotherapy *noun* (*plural* **psychotherapies**) the treatment of mental disorder by psychological means. [Say sike oh THERAPY]

psychotic • *adjective* of, denoting, or suffering from a severe mental derangement, esp. when resulting in delusions and loss of contact with external reality: *a psychotic disorder ◊ a psychotic individual.* • *noun* a person suffering from such a mental derangement: *won an award for his role as a drunken psychotic in the off-Broadway play.* ▶ **psychotically** *adverb* [Say sigh COT ick]

psychotropic *noun* (of a drug) acting on the mind. [Say sike oh TROP ick]

Pt *symbol* the element platinum.

pt. *abbreviation* **1** part. **2** pint. **3** point. **4** port.

PTA *abbreviation* PARENT-TEACHER ASSOCIATION.

ptarmigan *noun* (*plural* **ptarmigan** or **ptarmigans**) a game bird of Arctic regions resembling a grouse but with feathered toes and predominantly white plumage in winter. [Say TAR mig un]

pterodactyl *noun* a large extinct flying bird-like reptile with a long slender head and neck. [Say tare a DACK til]

PTH *abbreviation* parathyroid hormone (*see* PARATHYROID).

PTO *abbreviation* **1** POWER TAKEOFF. **2** please turn over.

Ptolemaic *adjective* **1** of or relating to the Greek astronomer Ptolemy (2nd century) or his theories, esp. the theory that the earth is the stationary centre of the universe. **2** of or relating to the Ptolemies, Macedonian rulers of Egypt 323–30 BC. [Say tolla MAY ick]

ptooey *interjection* representing the noise of spitting, esp. in contempt, disgust, etc.

Pu *symbol* plutonium.

pub *noun* an establishment that is licensed to sell alcoholic drinks and usu. also serves light meals etc.

pubbing *noun* the action of going drinking in pubs.

pub-crawl • *noun* a drinking tour of several pubs or bars. • *verb* make such a tour.

puberty *noun* the period during which adolescents reach sexual maturity and become capable of reproduction. [Say PYOO bur tee]

pubes *noun* (*plural* **pubes**) **1** the lower part of the abdomen at the front of the pelvis, covered with hair from puberty. **2** *informal* the pubic hair. [Say PYOO beez]

pubescence *noun* the time when puberty begins. ▶ **pubescent** *adjective* [Say pyoo BESS ince, pyoo BESS'nt]

pubic *adjective* of or relating to the pubes or pubis: *pubic hair.* [Say PYOO bick]

pubis *noun* (*plural* **pubes**) either of a pair of bones forming the two sides of the pelvis. [Say PYOO biss for the singular, PYOO beez for the plural]

public • *adjective* **1** of or concerning the people as a whole: *in the public interest.* **2** open to or shared by all the people: *public meeting.* **3** done or existing openly: *made her views public.* **4 a** (of a service, funds, etc.)

provided or heavily subsidized by, or concerning a government: *public money* ◊ *public housing*. **b** (of a person) in government: *had a distinguished public career*. **5** devoted or directed to the promotion of the general welfare; patriotic: *public spirit*. **6** well-known; famous: *a public figure*. **7** *Cdn* of or relating to a public school or the public school system. • *noun* **1** the community in general, or members of the community: *the public is being denied the right to certain types of information*. **2** a section of the community having a particular interest or in some special connection: *the reading public*. PHRASES **go public 1** become a public company. **2** reveal previously unknown information etc. **in public** openly, publicly. **in the public eye** at the centre of public attention; famous or notorious.

public access *noun* (usu. as an *adjective*) designating a type of television programming that is made available to community groups or members of the public.

public accounts committee *noun Cdn & Brit.* a standing committee of a legislature, responsible for reviewing government expenditure, primarily by examining the Auditor General's report.

public address system *noun* an electronic system used to amplify sound, used at public meetings etc.

public assistance *noun* = SOCIAL ASSISTANCE.

publication *noun* **1 a** the preparation and issuing of a book, newspaper, engraving, music, etc. to the public. **b** a book etc. so issued. **2** the action of making something generally known: *a delay in the publication of exam results*.

public company *noun* (*plural* **public companies**) a company whose shares are traded freely on a stock exchange.

public corporation *noun* **1** a corporation that is owned and operated by a government to serve the public. **2** = PUBLIC COMPANY.

Public Curator *noun Cdn* (*Que.*) a provincial government official responsible for the affairs of persons legally unfit to conduct them themselves.

public debt *noun* debt incurred by a government.

public domain *noun* the legal status of a work on which copyright has expired, or which has never been copyrighted.

public enemy *noun* (*plural* **public enemies**) a notorious wanted criminal.

public health *noun* services, such as immunization, preventive medicine, etc., that are provided by a government and intended to improve the general health of citizens: *public health nurse*.

public housing *noun* housing provided for low-income families and subsidized by public funds.

publicist *noun* a person who promotes something, esp. a person employed by a company or individual to obtain publicity for products, services, etc.

publicity *noun* **1** the action or fact of publicizing someone or something or of being publicized. **2 a** the technique or the process of promoting or advertising a product, person, company, etc. **b** material or information used for this. **3** public exposure; fame or notoriety.

publicize *verb* (**publicizes**, **publicized**, **publicizing**) make publicly known; advertise.

public law *noun* the law of relations between individuals and the state.

publicly *adverb* **1** so as to be seen by other people; in public: *some weep publicly*. **2** used in reference to views expressed to others and not necessarily genuinely felt: *publicly, officials criticized the resolution, but privately they thought it tolerable*. **3** by the state rather than a privately-owned company: *a publicly owned company*.

public mischief *noun Cdn* the criminal offence of making a false accusation, reporting an offence that did not occur, etc.

public ownership *noun* ownership by the state.

public purse *noun informal* the national treasury.

public relations *plural noun* **1** the work of presenting a good image of an organization, person, etc., to the public, esp. by providing information: *she works in public relations*. **2** the state of the relationship between an organization and the public: *the company sponsors literacy groups, which is good for public relations*.

public school *noun* **1** a primary or secondary school that is supported by public funds. **2** *Cdn* (*Ont.*) **a** a school that is part of the public school system (*compare* SEPARATE SCHOOL 1). **b** an elementary school that is part of the public school system. **c** elementary schooling in the public school system.

public school board *noun Cdn* **1** an elected board of trustees responsible for the public schools of a particular area. **2** the administrative unit responsible for the public schools in a given area. **3** the area within which such a board has jurisdiction.

public school system *noun Cdn* a system of publicly-funded non-denominational schools.

public sector *noun* that part of the economy that is under direct control by the state.

public servant *noun* a government employee, esp. of a federal government.

public service *noun* **1** public servants collectively. **2** a service provided to the public without charge by a corporation etc.

public service announcement *noun* **1** free air time donated by a radio or television station to a non-profit organization. **2** a message aired by a radio or television station as a service to the public.

public speaking *noun* an act or the skill of addressing an audience effectively.

public transit *noun* (also **public transportation**, **public transport**) a system of buses, trains, etc., running on fixed routes, esp. when owned by a government agency.

Public Trustee *noun Cdn* a provincial government official who administers the estates of people who die without a will, missing persons, etc.

public utility *noun* (*plural* **public utilities**) an organization or corporation supplying water, electricity, etc. to the public.

public works *noun* building work, e.g. of roads, hospitals, etc., which is paid for by the government.

publish *verb* (**publishes**, **published**, **publishing**) **1** (of an author, publisher, etc.) prepare and issue (a book, a newspaper, computer software, etc.) for public sale. **2** (esp. as **published** *adjective*) publish the works of (a particular writer or composer): *a published poet*. **3** make generally known. **4** announce (an edict etc.) formally; read (marriage banns). **5** *Law* communicate (a libel etc.) to a third party. ▶ **publishable** *adjective*

publisher *noun* **1** a person or esp. a company that produces and distributes copies of a book, newspaper, etc. for sale. **2** a newspaper proprietor.

publishing *noun* the occupation or activity of preparing and issuing books, journals, and other material for sale.

PUC *abbreviation* public utilities commission, a government regulatory body for public utilities.

puce *noun & adjective* a dark reddish purple. [Say PYOOS]

puck *noun* **1** a hard rubber disc used in hockey. **2** *Cdn* something shaped like a hockey puck, esp. a disc of chlorine used in swimming pool systems.

puck carrier *noun Hockey* the player in possession of the puck.

pucker • *verb* (often foll. by *up*) **1** gather or cause to gather into wrinkles, folds, or bulges: *puckered her eyebrows*. **2** contract (the lips) as when preparing to kiss. • *noun* such a wrinkle, bulge, fold, etc.

puck-handler *noun* a hockey player with a usu. specified ability to control the puck while deking, stickhandling, receiving passes, etc.: *a brilliant skater and puck-handler*.

puck-handling *noun* Hockey the ability to control the puck while deking, stickhandling, receiving passes, etc.

puck hog *noun* informal a hockey player who selfishly refuses to pass the puck to his or her teammates.

puckster *noun* Cdn slang a hockey player.

pudding *noun* **1** any of various cooked desserts that are heavier and more moist than cake, esp.: **a** a steamed dessert made of flour, suet, fruit, etc.: *Christmas pudding*. **b** a cake-like dessert with a sauce on the bottom. **c** a dessert incorporating bread, rice, tapioca, etc. in a sauce made of milk, eggs, etc.: *rice pudding*. **2** (in full **milk pudding**) a dessert made of flavoured milk thickened with cornstarch.

puddle • *noun* a small pool, esp. of rainwater or melted snow on a road etc. • *verb* (**puddles, puddled, puddling**) (of liquid) form a small pool: *water ran down the wall, puddling on the floor*. ▶ **puddly** *adjective*

pudendum *noun* (*plural* **pudenda**) (usu. in *plural*) the genitals, esp. of a woman. [Say pyoo DEN dum]

pudgy *adjective* (**pudgier, pudgiest**) *informal* plump.

pueblo • *noun* (*plural* **pueblos**) **1** a town or village in Latin America, esp. an Indian settlement. **2** (**Pueblo**) a member of a North American Indian people living esp. in New Mexico and Arizona. **3** a communal dwelling consisting of a number of multi-storey adobe or stone houses joined together, used by certain Indian peoples of the southwestern US. • *adjective* (**Pueblo**) of or relating to the Pueblos or their culture. [Say PWEB lo]

puerile *adjective* trivial, childish, immature: *you're making puerile excuses*. ▶ **puerility** *noun* [Say PURE ile, pure ILLA tee]

Puerto Rican • *noun* **1** a native of Puerto Rico, an island of the Greater Antilles. **2** a person of Puerto Rican descent. • *adjective* of or relating to Puerto Rico or its inhabitants. [Say porto REEK'n or pware toe REEK'n]

puff • *noun* **1 a** a short quick blast of breath, wind, smoke, etc. **b** an inhalation or exhalation from a cigarette etc. **2** a food that is light or fluffy: *cream puff*. **3** a gathered mass of material in a dress etc. **4** a roll of hair that is cylindrical in shape. **5** (also **puff piece**) an extravagantly, esp. uncritically enthusiastic or favourable review, article, etc., esp. in a newspaper. • *verb* **1** emit a puff of air or breath; blow with short blasts. **2** (often foll. by *out, away*, etc.) send out or move with puffs of vapour, smoke, etc.: *a train puffed out of the station*. **3** make or be out of breath: *arrived somewhat puffed*. **4** (usu. foll. by *up, out*) become or cause to become inflated; swell. **5** (usu. foll. by *out, up, away*) blow or emit (dust, smoke, a light object, etc.) with a puff. **6 a** smoke (a pipe etc.) in puffs. **b** (usu. foll. by *away* etc.) take puffs at a cigarette etc. **7** advertise or promote (goods, a book, etc.) with exaggerated or false praise. PHRASES **puffed up** proud or boastful.

puffball *noun* a ball-shaped fungus that ruptures and releases a cloud of spores when ripe, some varieties of which are edible when young.

puffer *noun* **1** a person or thing that puffs. **2** = PUFFERFISH.

pufferfish *noun* (*plural* **pufferfish** or **pufferfishes**) a spiny tropical fish that is able to inflate itself like a balloon when threatened.

puffery *noun* exaggerated praise or commendation.

puffin *noun* a seabird with a large head, a brightly coloured triangular bill, and black and white plumage, native to the North Atlantic and North Pacific.

puffiness *noun* a puffed up or swollen condition.

puffy *adjective* (**puffier, puffiest**) **1** swollen. **2** soft, rounded, and light: *small puffy clouds*.

pug *noun* (also **pug dog**) a small dog with a broad flat nose and deeply wrinkled face.

pugilist *noun* a boxer, esp. a professional. ▶ **pugilistic** *adjective* [Say PYOO jil ist, pyoo jil ISS tick]

pugnacious *adjective* quarrelsome; disposed to fight. ▶ **pugnaciously** *adverb* **pugnacity** *noun* [Say pug NAY shuss, pug NASSA tee]

puh-leeze *interjection* (also **puh-lease**) please (indicating scorn or contempt at implied gullibility).

puja *noun* a Hindu rite of worship. [Say POO juh]

puke *slang* • *verb* (**pukes, puked, puking**) vomit. • *noun* vomit. ▶ **pukey** *adjective*

Pulitzer Prize *noun* each of 13 annual awards for achievements in American journalism, literature, and music. [Say PULL itz er or PYOO litz er]

pull • *verb* **1** exert force on (something) so as to move it toward oneself or the origin of the force. **2** remove by pulling. **3** *informal* bring out (a weapon) for use. **4** move steadily: *the bus pulled away*. **5** move oneself steadily with effort or against resistance: *she pulled away from him*. **6** attract as a customer. **7** strain (a muscle, ligament, etc.). **8** (often foll. by *at, on*) inhale deeply while drawing on (a cigarette). **9** *informal* cancel or withdraw (an entertainment or advertisement). **10** check the speed of (a horse) to make it lose a race. • *noun* **1** an act of pulling. **2** a deep draft of a drink or an inhalation on a cigarette, pipe, etc. **3** a force, influence, or compulsion. PHRASES **pull apart** (or **to pieces**) = PICK APART (see PICK[1]). **pull away 1** remove by pulling. **2** move away. **3** (of a competitor) increase one's lead over others. **pull back** retreat or cause to retreat. **pull down 1** demolish (esp. a building). **2** *informal* earn (a sum of money) as wages etc. **pull even** (often foll. by *with*) reach the same level as (a leading competitor); catch up. **pull a face** assume a distinctive or specified expression: *pulled a glum face*. **pull for** support; desire success for. **pull in 1** (of a bus, train, etc.) arrive to take passengers. **2** (of a vehicle) arrive at a place for stopping, refuelling, etc. **3** earn or acquire. **4** *informal* arrest. **5** rein in, hold in, check. **pull one's hair out** be anxious, exasperated, frustrated, etc. **pull a person's leg** deceive a person playfully. **pull off 1** remove by pulling. **2** succeed in achieving or accomplishing. **3** remove from participation in: *we're going to pull you off the job*. **pull oneself together** recover control of oneself. **pull out 1** take out by pulling. **2** depart. **3** withdraw from an undertaking. **4** (of a bus, train, etc.) leave with its passengers. **5** (of a vehicle) move out from the side of the road, or from its normal position to overtake. **pull out all the stops** exert extreme effort. **pull over 1** move (a vehicle) to the side of or off the road. **2** (of the police etc.) stop (a vehicle) for a traffic violation etc. **pull the plug** (often foll. by *on*) *informal* put an end to an enterprise etc.; destroy; cut off (supplies etc.). **pull punches** (usu. in *neg.*) **1** avoid using one's full force. **2** criticize less strongly than one might. **pull rank** take unfair advantage of one's seniority. **pull strings** exert (esp. clandestine) influence. **pull the strings** be the real instigator of what another does. **pull through 1** get through an illness, a dangerous situation, or a difficult undertaking. **2** enable (a person) to do this. **pull together** work in harmony. **pull up 1** stop or cause to stop moving. **2** pull out of the ground. **3** come or bring closer. **4** cause (a file etc.) to appear on a computer

screen. **pull one's (own) weight** do one's fair share of work. ▶ **puller** noun

pull-down adjective **1** that may be, or is designed to be, pulled down. **2** Computing designating a menu that need only be displayed onscreen when required.

pulley noun (plural **pulleys**) **1** a grooved wheel or set of wheels for a cord etc. to pass over, set in a block and used for changing the direction of a force. **2** a wheel or drum fixed on a shaft and turned by a belt, used esp. to increase speed or power.

pull factor noun a political, social, or economic consideration that influences an immigrant's decision to settle in a particular place (compare PUSH FACTOR).

Pullman noun **1** a railway car affording special comfort. **2** a sleeping car. **3** a large suitcase. [Say PULL m'n]

pull-off • adjective that may be, or is designed to be, pulled off. • noun **1** an act of pulling something off. **2** an area by the side of a road where vehicles may stop.

pull-on • adjective designating a garment without fasteners that is pulled on. • noun such a garment.

pullout • adjective that may be, or is designed to be, pulled out: *pullout couch*. • noun **1** something that can be pulled out, esp. a section of a magazine. **2** the act of pulling out; a withdrawal, esp. from military involvement. **3** = PULL-OFF 2.

pullover noun a knitted garment put on over the head and covering the top half of the body.

pull-up noun **1** an exercise involving raising oneself with one's arms by pulling up against a horizontal bar etc. fixed above one's head. **2** the act of pulling up; a sudden stop.

pulmonary adjective of or relating to the lungs. [Say PUL mun airy (PUL rhymes with HULL)]

pulmonary artery noun (plural **pulmonary arteries**) the artery conveying blood from the heart to the lungs.

pulmonary vein noun the vein carrying oxygenated blood from the lungs to the heart.

pulp • noun **1** the soft fleshy part of fruit etc. **2** any soft thick wet mass. **3** a soft shapeless mass made of ground wood or other vegetable fibres, etc., used in papermaking. **4** popular or sensational writing often regarded as of poor quality: *pulp fiction*. **5** vascular tissue filling the interior cavity and root canals of a tooth. **6** = PULPWOOD. • verb **1** reduce to pulp. **2** withdraw (a publication) from the market, usu. recycling the paper. **3** remove pulp from. PHRASES **beat a person to a pulp** beat a person severely.

pulp cutter noun a logger who cuts wood into short lengths for the pulping process.

pulpit noun **1** a lectern or raised usu. enclosed platform in a church etc. from which the preacher delivers a sermon. **2 (the pulpit)** preachers or preaching collectively. [Say PUL pit (PUL rhymes with HULL or FULL)]

pulpwood noun timber suitable for making pulp.

pulpy adjective (**pulpier**, **pulpiest**) **1** consisting of or resembling pulp. **2** relating to or characteristic of pulp fiction or pulp writing; sensational.

pulsar noun Astronomy a celestial object, thought to be a rapidly rotating neutron star, emitting regular pulses of radio waves etc. [Say PULSE arr]

pulsate verb (**pulsates**, **pulsated**, **pulsating**) **1** expand and contract rhythmically; throb. **2** vibrate, quiver, thrill. **3** vary in magnitude, intensity, brightness, etc. ▶ **pulsation** noun

pulse¹ • noun **1 a** a rhythmical throbbing of the arteries as blood is propelled through them, esp. as felt in the wrists, temples, etc. **b** each successive beat of the arteries or heart. **2** a throb or thrill of life or emotion. **3** a general feeling or opinion: *the pulse of the nation*.

4 a a single vibration of sound, electric current, light, etc., esp. as a signal. **b** designating a telephone system in which the number composed on a rotary dial or buttons is translated into electronic pulses corresponding in number to the digit dialled. **5** a musical beat. **6** any regular or recurrent rhythm, e.g. of the stroke of oars. **7 a** a feature or button on a blender etc. allowing the operator to pulse. **b** the action of pulsing food in a blender etc. • verb (**pulses, pulsed, pulsing**) **1** pulsate. **2** transmit etc. by rhythmical beats. **3 a** operate (a food processor, blender, etc.) in short bursts using a button that engages the mechanism only as long as the operator keeps it depressed. **b** process (food) in a blender etc. in this way.

pulse² noun **1** the edible seeds of various leguminous plants, e.g. chickpeas, lentils, beans, etc. **2** the plant or plants producing this.

pulverize verb (**pulverizes**, **pulverized**, **pulverizing**) **1** reduce to fine particles. **2** crumble to dust. **3** informal **a** demolish. **b** defeat utterly.

puma noun a cougar. [Say PYOO muh]

pumice noun (also **pumice stone**) **1** a light porous volcanic rock often used as an abrasive in cleaning or polishing substances. **2** a piece of this used for removing hard skin etc. [Say PUM iss]

pummel verb (**pummels, pummelled, pummelling**) **1** pound or thump repeatedly. **2** beat with the fists. **3** defeat thoroughly. **4** criticize harshly.

pump¹ • noun a device, usu. with rotary action or the reciprocal action of a piston or plunger, or functioning by suction, for raising or moving liquids or gases, inflating tires, etc. • verb **1** raise or remove (liquid, gas, etc.) with a pump. **2 a** (usu. foll. by *up*) fill (a tire etc.) with air. **b** increase the volume, loudness, strength, etc. of. **3** (often foll. by *out*) cause to move, pour forth, etc., in great quantities. **4** elicit information from (a person) by persistent questioning. **5 a** move vigorously up and down. **b** shake (a person's hand) effusively. **6** apply and release (brakes) quickly several times in succession, esp. to prevent skidding. **7** (foll. by *into*) cause a major input of (money, effort, etc.). PHRASES **pump iron** informal engage in bodybuilding with weights.

pump² noun a lightweight, low-cut women's shoe, with no laces or straps.

pumped adjective (also **pumped up**) **1** in senses of PUMP¹ verb. **2** informal eager, excited, or emotionally prepared for an undertaking, event, etc.

pumper noun **1** in senses of PUMP¹ verb. **2** a fire truck used to pump water or chemicals to douse a fire.

pumpernickel noun a dense, dark, sour rye bread.

pumpkin noun **1** a large rounded orange fruit with a thick rind and edible flesh. **2** the plant of the gourd family that produces this fruit. **3** a term of endearment, esp. to a child, pet, etc.

pumpkinseed noun a colourful North American sunfish with an orange belly.

pump-priming noun **1** the introduction of fluid etc. into a pump to prepare it for working. **2** esp. US the stimulation of commerce etc. by investment.

pun • noun the humorous use of a word to suggest different meanings, or of words of the same sound and different meanings. • verb (**puns, punned, punning**) (foll. by *on*) make a pun or puns with (words).

punch¹ • verb (**punches, punched, punching**) **1** strike bluntly, esp. with a closed fist. **2** prod or poke with a blunt object. **3** pierce a hole in metal, paper, a ticket, etc. **4** strike (a button on a keypad) with the fingertip. • noun (plural **punches**) **1** a blow with a fist. **2** the ability to deliver this. **3** informal vigour; effective force. **4** any of various devices or machines for punching holes in materials, e.g. paper, leather, metal,

P

P

plaster. **5** a tool or machine for impressing a design or stamping a die on a material. PHRASES **beat someone to the punch** do something before someone else is able to; anticipate or forestall the actions of another. **punch the (time) clock 1** record the time of one's arrival at or departure from work by inserting a card into a timed puncher. **2** be employed in a conventional, esp. nine-to-five job. **punch in 1** punch the clock to record the time of one's arrival at work. **2** enter (data) into a computer, calculator, etc. using a keyboard or keypad. **3** dial (a number on a telephone) by hitting the keypads with the fingertip. **punch out 1** remove or detach by punching. **2** punch the clock to record the time of one's departure from work. **3** *informal* assault with punches; beat up. **punch up 1** enter or access (data) into or from a computer, cash register, etc. using a keyboard or keypad. **2** *informal* make more punchy, vigorous, effective; enliven. **3** *informal* beat up.

punch[2] *noun* (*plural* **punches**) a drink of mixed beverages, e.g. fruit juices, carbonated drinks, etc., often including alcohol.

punch[3] *noun* PHRASES **as pleased** (or **proud**) **as punch** showing great pleasure (or pride).

punch-drunk *adjective* stupefied from or as though from a series of heavy blows to the head.

punchline *noun* the climactic final phrase of a joke etc.

punch-up *noun informal* (also **punchout**) a fist fight.

punchy *adjective* (**punchier, punchiest**) **1** having punch or vigour; forceful. **2** PUNCH-DRUNK. **3** in a state of nervous tension or extreme fatigue. **4 a** (of a sentence etc.) terse, short. **b** composed of punchy segments: *a punchy news program*.

punctilious *adjective* **1** showing great attention to detail or correct behaviour: *a punctilious draftsman* ◊ *she averted her eyes out of punctilious courtesy*. **2** precise in behaviour. ▶ **punctiliously** *adverb* [Say punk TILLY us]

punctual *adjective* **1** precisely on time. **2** habitually occurring or arriving at the appointed time. ▶ **punctuality** *noun* **punctually** *adverb*

punctuate *verb* (**punctuates, punctuated, punctuating**) **1** insert punctuation marks in. **2** interrupt at intervals: *punctuated his tale with heavy sighs*. **3** emphasize, accentuate; give force to: *his answer is definitive, punctuated by a violent shake of the head*.

punctuation *noun* the system or arrangement of marks used in writing to separate sentences and phrases etc. and to clarify meaning.

punctuation mark *noun* any of the marks, e.g. period and comma, used in writing to separate sentences and phrases etc. and to clarify meaning.

puncture • *noun* **1** a small hole in a tire resulting in an escape of air. **2** a hole in something such as the skin, caused by a sharp object: *puncture wound* ◊ *in a lumbar puncture, a needle is inserted in the lower back to extract fluid for diagnosis*. • *verb* (**punctures, punctured, puncturing**) **1** make a small hole in: *punctured the balloon* ◊ *suffered a punctured lung*. **2** suddenly make someone feel less confident, proud, etc.: *punctured his illusions*. **3** penetrate: *a volley of shots punctured the silence* ◊ *punctured the other team's defence*.

pundit *noun* **1** a Hindu learned in Sanskrit and in the philosophy, religion, and laws of India. **2** often *ironic* a learned expert or teacher, esp. one who makes authoritative pronouncements on current affairs. ▶ **punditry** *noun*

pungency *noun* **1** the quality of having a sharp or strong taste or smell. **2** the quality of writing or speech that contains harsh criticism of a person or thing: *the play is so long that it dispels any political pungency it might have*. [Say PUN jin see]

pungent *adjective* **1** having a sharp or strong taste or smell. **2** involving harsh criticism; strongly critical: *has many pungent opinions* ◊ *pungent wit*. ▶ **pungently** *adverb* [Say PUN jint]

punish *verb* (**punishes, punished, punishing**) **1** cause (an offender) to suffer for an offence: *punished for his crime*. **2** inflict a penalty for (an offence): *in those days murder was punished with the death penalty*. **3** *informal* inflict severe blows on (an opponent). **4** subject (someone) to severe, usu. exhausting, treatment: *authors on book tours have punishing schedules*. ▶ **punishable** *adjective* **punisher** *noun* **punishing** *adjective* **punishingly** *adverb*

punishment *noun* **1** the action of punishing; the condition of being punished: *the punishment for murder*. **2** *informal* severe treatment or suffering: *the carpet by the door takes the most punishment*.

punitive *adjective* inflicting or intended to inflict punishment: *punitive action will be taken*. [Say PYOON it iv]

punitive damages *plural noun Law* damages exceeding simple compensation, awarded to punish the defendant.

Punjabi • *noun* (*plural* **Punjabis**) **1 a** *hist.* a native of the Punjab in India, now divided between India and Pakistan. **b** a native of the state of Punjab in India or the province of Punjab in Pakistan. **2** the language spoken in these areas. • *adjective* of or relating to these areas, their inhabitants, or their language. [Say poon JABBY or pun JABBY]

punk • *noun* **1** a young man or boy regarded as contemptible or insignificant, esp. because of rude or violent behaviour (often as a general term of abuse). **2** a young hoodlum or ruffian. **3 a** (also **punk rock**) a loud fast-moving form of angry and aggressive rock music. **b** the subculture or style associated with this, esp. that characterized by coloured spiked hair and leather clothing decorated with safety pins etc. **c** = PUNKER. **4** an inexperienced person; a novice. **5** soft crumbly wood that has been attacked by fungus, used as tinder. • *adjective* **1** worthless, rotten. **2** denoting punk rock and its associated subculture: *punk hair*.

punker *noun* (also **punk rocker**) a person who enjoys or plays punk music; a member of the punk subculture.

punkish *adjective* characteristic of or resembling a punker.

punky *adjective* **1** containing or like soft crumbly wood that has been attacked by fungus: *a punky log*. **2** characteristic of or resembling a punker.

punt[1] • *noun* a long narrow flat-bottomed boat, square at both ends, used mainly for pleasure on rivers and propelled by a long pole. • *verb* **1** propel (a punt) with a pole. **2** travel or convey in a punt.

punt[2] • *verb* kick (a ball, esp. in football or rugby) after it has dropped from the hands and before it reaches the ground. • *noun* such a kick.

puny *adjective* (**punier, puniest**) **1** undersized. **2** weak, feeble. [Say PYOO nee]

pup • *noun* **1** a young dog. **2** a young wolf, rat, seal, etc. • *verb* (**pups, pupped, pupping**) (of a female dog etc.) bring forth (young).

pupa *noun* (*plural* **pupae**) an inactive immature form of an insect, being the resting stage between larva and adult, e.g. a chrysalis. ▶ **pupal** *adjective* [Say PYOO puh for the singular, PYOO pee for the plural]

pupil[1] *noun* a person who is taught by another, esp. a schoolchild or student in relation to a teacher.

pupil[2] *noun* the dark circular opening in the centre of the iris of the eye, varying in size to regulate the passage of light to the retina.

puppet *noun* **1** a small figure representing a human being or animal and moved by various means as entertainment, e.g. by pulling strings attached to its limbs or by putting one's hand inside it. **2** a person, state, etc. whose actions are controlled by another: *puppet government*.

puppeteer *noun* **1** (also **puppet master**) a person who works puppets. **2** a person who manipulates others: *by giving regular advice to patients, she would become more puppeteer than therapist.* ▶ **puppeteering** *noun*

puppetry *noun* the art and skill of making and using puppets.

puppy *noun* (*plural* **puppies**) **1** a young, esp. immature dog. **2** a conceited or arrogant young man. **3** *slang* a person having a specified character: *he's one sick puppy*. ▶ **puppyish** *adjective*

pup tent *noun* a small triangular tent, esp. for two people, usu. without side walls or a window.

purchase • *verb* (**purchases**, **purchased**, **purchasing**) **1** buy. **2** obtain or achieve at some cost. • *noun* **1** the action of buying: *make a purchase*. **2** something bought: *return your purchases for a refund*. **3** a firm hold on a thing to move it or to prevent it from slipping: *my feet could gain no purchase on the slippery floor* ◊ *a goalie will rough up the ice so that he can get a decent purchase with his skate blades*. ▶ **purchaser** *noun*

purchasing power *noun* **1** a person's financial ability to make purchases. **2** the amount that a sum of money etc. can purchase.

purdah *noun* a system in certain Muslim and Hindu societies of screening women from strangers by means of a veil or curtain. PHRASES **in purdah** (of a woman) screened from contact with strangers. [Say PUR duh]

pure *adjective* (**purer**, **purest**) **1** unmixed: *a pure white sheet* ◊ *pure alcohol* ◊ *the air is pure* ◊ *pure-blooded*. **2** chaste. **3** morally or sexually undefiled; not corrupt. **4** guiltless. **5** sincere. **6** mere, simple, nothing but, sheer, true: *it was pure malice*. **7** (of a sound) not discordant, perfectly in tune. **8** (of a subject of study) dealing with abstract concepts and not practical application. **9** having no complicated or unnecessary elements. PHRASES **pure and simple** plainly, indisputably, certainly; and nothing else: *they were stolen, pure and simple*.

purebred • *adjective* (of an animal) bred from parents of the same breed or variety. • *noun* such an animal.

purée • *noun* a pulp of vegetables or fruit etc. reduced to a smooth thick liquid. • *verb* (**purées**, **puréed**, **puréeing**) make a purée of. [Say pure AY or PURE ay]

pure laine *Cdn* • *adjective* **1** designating a francophone Quebecer descended from the French settlers in New France and having exclusively French ancestry. **2** of or consisting of pure laine Quebecers: *pure laine nationalism*. • *noun* such a person. [Say pure LEN]

purely *adverb* **1** in a pure manner. **2** merely, solely, exclusively. **3** entirely, completely.

pure science *noun* a science depending on deductions from demonstrated truths, e.g. math or logic, or one studied without practical applications.

purgation *noun* **1** the action of purifying or cleansing a person or thing, esp. (in Catholic doctrine) the spiritual cleansing of a soul in purgatory: *souls in a state of grace but suffering from the residual effects of sin must enter a period of purgation*. **2** purging of the bowels. [Say pur GAY sh'n]

purgative • *noun* **1** a laxative. **2** a thing that rids a person of unwanted feelings or memories: *confrontation would be a purgative*. • *adjective* strongly laxative. [Say PURGA tiv]

purgatorial *adjective* **1** having the effect of cleansing or purifying: *through purgatorial punishment the soul is rendered fit for Heaven*. **2** involving or representing a necessary period of something unpleasant leading to a happier state: *arrived downtown after a purgatorial drive through miles of urban sprawl*.

purgatory *noun* **1** the condition or supposed place of spiritual cleansing, esp. (*Catholicism*) of those dying in the grace of God but having to atone for venial sins etc. **2** a place or situation of suffering or neglect in which a person remains temporarily before moving into a more favourable place or situation: *they salvaged from the archival purgatory of film history a small trove of neglected masterpieces and made them more accessible to the public* ◊ *the coffee table is our home's purgatory, the halfway point for everything eaten, worn, or broken*. [Say PURGA tory]

purge • *verb* (**purges**, **purged**, **purging**) **1** rid someone of an unwanted feeling, memory, or condition: *she felt purged of her guilt*. **2** remove by a cleansing process: *the dam releases water to purge heavy reservoir inflows*. **3** remove unwanted people from an organization, typically in an abrupt or violent manner: *purged all but 26 of the central committee members* ◊ *purged the party of extremists*. **4** empty the stomach or bowels by vomiting or taking a laxative: *bingeing and purging is a serious eating disorder*. • *noun* an abrupt or violent removal of a group of people from an organization or place: *millions of people were executed or sent to labour camps in Stalin's purges* ◊ *a wholesale purge of reformists*. ▶ **purger** *noun*

purification *noun* **1** the action or process of making physically pure or clean. **2** the action or process of making ceremonially or ritually clean.

purifier *noun* a thing or person that purifies or refines: *installed a home water purifier*.

purify *verb* (**purifies**, **purified**, **purifying**) **1** cleanse or make pure. **2** make ceremonially clean. **3** rid something of an unwanted element: *attempts to purify the language by removing foreign influences*.

Purim *noun* a Jewish spring festival commemorating the defeat of a plot to massacre the Jews in Persia in the 5th century BC. [Say POOR im]

purine *noun* an organic nitrogenous base forming uric acid on oxidation. **2** any of a group of compounds with a similar structure, including adenine. [Say POOR een]

purism *noun* scrupulous or exaggerated observance of or insistence on traditional rules or structures, esp. in language or art.

purist *noun* a stickler for or advocate of scrupulous correctness or authenticity, e.g. in language or art.

puritan • *noun* **1** (**Puritan**) *hist.* a member of a group of English Protestants who regarded the Reformation of the Church under Elizabeth I as incomplete and sought to simplify and regulate forms of worship. **2** a person practising, affecting, or advocating extreme strictness, esp. in religion or morality: *today's puritans impede frank talk about race, class, and sexuality* ◊ *gardening puritans*. • *adjective* **1** (**Puritan**) *hist.* of or relating to the Puritans. **2** scrupulous and austere in religion or morals. ▶ **puritanism** *noun* [Say PURE a tin]

puritanical *adjective* often *derogatory* practising, affecting, or advocating strict religious or moral behaviour, esp. opposed to pleasure. ▶ **puritanically** *adverb* [Say pure a TAN ick ul]

purity *noun* (*plural* **purities**) **1** a clean and pure state; freedom from contamination: *wants to preserve the purity of our drinking water*. **2** freedom from external influences: *the history of jazz is that of creative purity gradually corrupted by success*. **3** freedom from immorality, esp. of a sexual nature: *white often represents purity and innocence*. [Say PURE it ee]

P

purl • *noun* **1** a knitting stitch made by putting the needle through the front of the previous stitch and passing the yarn around the back of the needle. **2** a babbling motion or sound. • *verb* **1** knit with a purl stitch. **2** (of a brook etc.) flow with a swirling motion and babbling sound. **3** make a babbling sound.

purlieu *noun* (*plural* **purlieus**) **1** (in *plural*) the area near or surrounding a place: *middle-class purlieus of the Bronx*. **2** a place frequented by a person: *she met her aunt in the lobby, that lofty purlieu*. [Say PURL yoo]

purloin *verb formal or jocular* steal, pilfer. [Say pur LOIN]

purple • *noun* **1** a colour intermediate between red and blue. **2** a purple robe, esp. as the dress of royalty. **3** (**the purple**) a position of rank, authority, or privilege. **4 a** the scarlet official dress of a cardinal. **b** the position or office of a cardinal. • *adjective* **1** of a purple colour. **2** (of writing, speech, etc.) excessively elaborate or ornate. • *verb* (**purples, purpled, purpling**) make or become purple.

purple gas *noun Cdn* (*Prairies*) gasoline sold with reduced taxes to farmers for farm machinery and vehicles, dyed purple for identification.

purple loosestrife *noun* a wetland plant with a long spike of purple flowers.

purplish *adjective* fairly purple in colour: *purplish lips*.

purport *verb* **1** claim or appear to be or do something, esp. falsely: *the theory does not purport to explain reality* ◊ *the purported inventor of the new technique*. **2** (of a document, speech, etc.) have as its meaning; state.

purportedly *adverb* according to what is claimed to have happened or be true, esp. when this may not be so: *the newspaper ran a picture purportedly showing the underage teen celeb downing a cold one*.

purpose • *noun* **1 a** something to be attained; a thing intended: *our purpose was to delay*. **b** the reason for which something is done or made, or for which it exists: *for tax purposes*. **2** resolution, determination. • *verb* (**purposes, purposed, purposing**) have as one's purpose; intend. PHRASES **on purpose** intentionally. **to no purpose** with no result or effect. **to the purpose 1** relevant. **2** useful.

purpose-built *adjective* (also **purpose-made, purpose-designed**, etc.) built or made for a specific purpose: *purpose-built art gallery*.

purposeful *adjective* **1** having or indicating purpose. **2** intentional. **3** resolute. ▶ **purposefully** *adverb*

purposeless *adjective* having no aim or plan. ▶ **purposelessness** *noun*

purposely *adverb* on purpose; intentionally.

purr • *verb* **1** (of a cat) make a low vibratory sound usu. expressing contentment. **2** (of a person, machinery, etc.) make a similar sound. **3** (of a person) express pleasure. **4** utter or express (words or contentment) in this way. • *noun* a purring sound.

purse • *noun* **1** a small woman's bag for holding small personal articles, e.g. wallet, keys, makeup, etc. **2** *hist.* a small pouch of leather etc. for carrying money, esp. coins. **3** a receptacle resembling a purse in form or purpose. **4** money, funds. **5** a sum collected as a present or given as a prize in a contest. • *verb* (**purses, pursed, pursing**) **1** pucker or contract (the lips). **2** become contracted and wrinkled.

purser *noun* **1** an officer on a ship who keeps the accounts. **2** the head steward in a ship or airplane.

purse seine *noun* a fishing net or seine which may be drawn into the shape of a sack, used for catching shoal fish. ▶ **purse seiner** *noun* **purse seining** *noun*

purse strings *plural noun* control of or access to funds: *tighten the purse strings*.

purslane *noun* a small, fleshy-leaved plant, used as a herb and salad vegetable. [Say PURSE lane]

pursuant *adverb* (foll. by *to*) conforming to or in accordance with: *the director has initiated an inquiry, pursuant to article 19 of the agreement*. [Say PURSUE int]

pursue *verb* (**pursues, pursued, pursuing**) **1** follow with intent to overtake or capture or do harm to. **2** continue or proceed along (a route or course of action). **3** follow or engage in (study or other activity). **4** proceed in compliance with (a plan etc.). **5** seek after, aim at. **6** continue to investigate or discuss (a topic). **7** seek the attention or acquaintance of (a person) persistently. **8** (of misfortune etc.) persistently assail. **9** persistently attend, stick to. **10 a** go in pursuit. **b** continue. ▶ **pursuer** *noun*

pursuit *noun* **1** the act of looking for or trying to find something: *the pursuit of happiness* ◊ *she travelled the world in pursuit of her dreams*. **2** an occupation or activity: *intellectual pursuits*. **3** the act of following or chasing someone: *we drove away with two police cars in pursuit*.

purvey *verb* provide or supply (food, provisions, or esp. shady or dishonest information, services, etc.) esp. as one's business. ▶ **purveyor** *noun* [Say pur VAY]

purview *noun* the range of influence, responsibilities, or concerns of a person or thing: *the senate has used its powers to influence decisions not formally within its purview* ◊ *a magazine with a global purview*. [Say PUR view]

pus *noun* a thick yellowish or greenish liquid produced from infected tissue, consisting of dead bacteria and white blood cells with tissue debris and serum.

push • *verb* (**pushes, pushed, pushing**) **1** exert force on (someone or something) so as to move them away from oneself or from the source of the force. **2** move (one's body or a part of it) forcefully into a specified position. **3** move forward by using force. **4** drive oneself or urge (someone) to greater effort. **5** (often foll. by *on*) demand persistently. **6** *informal* promote the use, sale, or acceptance of. **7** *informal* sell (a narcotic drug) illegally. **8** (**be pushing**) *informal* be nearly (a particular age). • *noun* (*plural* **pushes**) **1** an act of pushing. **2** a vigorous effort. **3** forcefulness and enterprise. PHRASES **be pushed for** *informal* have very little of (esp. time). **push around** *informal* bully. **push one's luck 1** take undue risks. **2** act presumptuously. **push off 1** push with an oar etc. to get a boat out into a river etc. **2** *informal* go away. **push through** get (a scheme, proposal, etc.) completed or accepted quickly. **when push comes to shove** when action must be taken; when a decision, commitment, etc. must be made.

push button • *noun* a button to be pushed esp. to operate an electrical device. • *adjective* (**push-button**) **1** operated by pressing a push button. **2** easily obtainable, as at the push of a button; instant.

pushcart *noun* a small handcart, esp. one used by a street vendor.

pusher *noun* **1** *informal* a person who sells (esp. prohibited) drugs illegally. **2** a person or thing that pushes.

push factor *noun* a political, social, or economic consideration that influences a person's decision to emigrate from a particular place.

pushiness *noun* the quality of being excessively or unpleasantly forward or self-assertive.

pushover *noun* *informal* **1** something easily done or won; an easy task or victory. **2** a person who can easily be overcome, persuaded, etc.

push-pin *noun* a tack with a spool-shaped, usu. plastic head, used on bulletin boards etc.

push-pull *adjective* **1** *Electronics* consisting of two valves etc. operated alternately. **2** operated by pushing and pulling.

push-start • *noun* the starting of a motor vehicle by pushing it to turn the engine. • *verb* start (a vehicle) in this way.

Pushtu *noun & adjective* = Pashto. [Say PUSH too (PUSH rhymes with *HUSH*)]

push-up • *noun* **1** an exercise in which a person lies facing the floor and, keeping the back straight, raises the upper part of the body by pressing down on the hands to straighten the arms. **2** a muskrat's resting place, formed by pushing up vegetation through a hole in the ice. • *adjective* designating a brassiere or similar garment which is underwired or padded to provide uplift for the breasts.

pushy *adjective* (**pushier**, **pushiest**) *informal* excessively or unpleasantly forward or self-assertive.

SPELL CHECK
puss, pus

Liquid matter from bodily infections is **pus**.
---

puss *noun* (*plural* **pusses**) *informal* **1** a cat (esp. as a form of address). **2** a playful or coquettish girl. **3** *slang* the face or mouth.

pussy *noun* (*plural* **pussies**) *informal* a cat.

pussycat *noun* *informal* **1** a cat. **2** a meek, mild-tempered, or amiable person.

pussyfoot *verb* (**pussyfoots**, **pussyfooted**, **pussyfooting**) **1** act cautiously or noncommittally: *as we stand here and pussyfoot around the issue, every single day more youth are taking up smoking.* **2** move stealthily or warily: *he pussyfooted close enough to a bull elk to take him with a bow.*

pussy willow *noun* a willow with soft, furry, white or yellow catkins.

pustule *noun* a pimple containing pus. [Say PUS chool or PUST yool]

SPELL CHECK   ABC
put, putt

The golf stroke is a **putt**.
---

put • *verb* (**puts**, **put**, **putting**) **1** move to or place in a particular position. **2** bring into a particular state or condition. **3** assign a value, figure, or limit to. **4** express in a particular way. **5** (of a ship) proceed in a particular direction: *the boat put out to sea.* **6** throw (a shot or weight) in an athletic competition. • *noun* a throw of the shot or weight. PHRASES **put about 1** spread (information, rumour, etc.). **2** *Nautical* turn around; put (a ship) on the opposite tack. **put across 1** make acceptable or effective. **2** express in an understandable way. **put aside 1** save (esp. a sum of money) for later use. **2** reserve an item for a customer to collect later. **3** disregard; ignore or forget: *put aside our differences.* **put away 1** put (a thing) back in the place where it is normally kept. **2** lay (money etc.) aside for future use. **3 a** confine or imprison. **b** commit to a home or mental institution. **4** *informal* consume (food and drink), esp. in large quantities. **5** = PUT DOWN 7. **put back 1** restore to its proper or former place. **2** change (a planned event) to a later date or time. **3** move back the hands of (a clock or watch). **4** check the advance of. **put down 1** suppress by force or authority. **2** *informal* snub or humiliate. **3** record or enter in writing. **4** enter the name of (a person) on a list, esp. as a member or subscriber. **5** (foll. by *as, for*) account or reckon. **6** (foll. by *to*) attribute: *put it down to bad planning.* **7** put (an old or sick animal) to death. **8** preserve or store (fruit, wine, etc.) for future use. **9** pay (a specified sum) as a deposit. **10** put (a baby) to bed. **11** land (an aircraft). **put forth 1** (of a plant) send out (buds or leaves). **2** *formal* submit or put into circulation. **put forward 1** suggest, propose, or nominate. **2 a** advance the hands of (a clock or watch). **b** move (an event etc.) to an

earlier time or date: *put forward the date of our wedding.* **3** put into a prominent position; draw attention to oneself etc. **put one's hands on** (*see* LAY¹). **put in 1 a** enter or submit (a claim etc.). **b** (foll. by *for*) submit a claim for (a specified thing). **2** (foll. by *for*) be a candidate for (an appointment, election, etc.). **3** spend (time): *put in five hours of overtime.* **4** interpose (a remark, blow, etc.). **5** (of a ship) enter or call at a port, harbour, etc. **6** plant (a crop etc.). **put it to a person** (often foll. by *that* + clause) present or submit a question, statement, etc. to (a person) for consideration or by way of appeal. **put one's mind to** devote all one's attention and energy to achieving something. **put off 1 a** postpone. **b** postpone engagement with (a person). **2** (often foll. by *with*) evade (a person) with an excuse etc. **3** hinder or distract: *the sudden noise put her off her game.* **4** offend, disconcert; cause (a person) to lose interest in something. **5** (of a vehicle or its driver) stop to let a passenger get off. **put on 1** clothe oneself with. **2** apply (makeup, lotion, etc.) to the skin. **3** cause (an electrical device, light, etc.) to function. **4** stage (a play, show, etc.). **5 a** pretend to be affected by (an emotion). **b** assume, take on (a character or appearance). **c** (**put it on**) exaggerate one's feelings etc. **6** increase one's weight by (a specified amount). **7** (foll. by *to*) make aware of or put in touch with: *put us on to her.* **8** *informal* tease, play a trick on: *are you putting me on?* **9** place (a tax etc.) on something: *put a duty on wine.* **10** bet (money) on something: *put $100 on the white horse.* **put out 1 a** (often as **put out** *adjective*) disconcert or annoy. **b** inconvenience: *don't put yourself out.* **2** extinguish (a fire or light). **3** *Baseball* cause (a player) to be out. **4** dislocate (a joint etc.): *put my back out.* **5** exert (strength etc.). **6** issue, publish, or broadcast (something). **7** blind (a person's eyes). **put one over** (foll. by *on*) *informal* get the better of; trick. **put over 1** make acceptable or effective. **2** express in an understandable way. **3** postpone. **put through 1** carry out or complete (a task or transaction). **2** (often foll. by *to*) connect (a person) by telephone to another user. **3** subject to an ordeal or trying experience: *put her parents through hell.* **4** arrange or pay for (someone) to attend university etc.: *put all his kids through college.* **put together 1** assemble (a whole) from parts. **2** combine (parts) to form a whole. **put under** render unconscious by anaesthetic etc. **put up 1** build or erect. **2 a** raise (a hand) to answer or ask a question. **b** raise (one's hands) to indicate surrender. **3** raise (a price etc.). **4** take or provide accommodation: *friends put me up for the night.* **5** engage in (a fight, struggle, etc.) as a form of resistance. **6** present (a proposal etc.). **7 a** present oneself for election. **b** propose for election. **8** provide (money) as a backer in an enterprise. **9** display (a notice). **10** preserve or can (fruit etc.). **11** offer for sale or competition. **12** arrange (long hair) in a bun or upswept hairstyle. **put upon** (usu. in *passive*) *informal* make unfair or excessive demands on; take advantage of (a person). **put up or shut up** *informal* defend or justify oneself or remain silent. **put a person up to** (usu. foll. by verbal noun) instigate a person in: *put them up to stealing the money.* **put up with** endure, tolerate; submit to.

putative *adjective* generally considered or reputed to be; supposed: *the putative Canadian ability to compromise.*
▶ **putatively** *adverb* [Say PYOOT a tiv]

put-down *noun* *informal* a snub or humiliating remark or criticism.

put-in *noun* a place on the banks of a river etc. from which to launch a canoe or other small craft.

put-on *noun* *informal* a deception or hoax.

putrefaction *noun* the process of decay or rotting in a body or other organic matter. [Say pyoo truh FACTION]

putrefy *verb* (**putrefies, putrefied, putrefying**) decay and smell very bad: *nearly choked on the stench of putrefying carcasses.* [Say PYOO truh fie]

putrid *adjective* **1** decomposed, rotten. **2** foul, noxious. **3** morally corrupt. **4** *slang* of poor quality; contemptible; very unpleasant. [Say PYOO trid]

putsch *noun* (*plural* **putsches**) an attempt at political revolution; a violent uprising: *the KGB was becoming more and more pathetic in the 1980s, as its futile putsch against Yeltsin and Gorbachev proved.* ▶**putschist** *noun* & *adjective* [Rhymes with BUTCH]

putt • *verb* (**putts, putted, putting**) strike (a golf ball) gently to get it into or nearer to a hole. • *noun* a putting stroke.

putter[1] *noun* **1** a golf club used in putting. **2** a golfer who putts.

putter[2] *noun & verb* = PUTT-PUTT.

putter[3] *verb* **1** (often foll. by *around, about*) work or occupy oneself in a desultory but pleasant manner: *puttering in the garden.* **2** go slowly, dawdle.

putt-putt • *noun* **1** the rapid intermittent sound of a small gasoline engine. **2** a small boat, car, etc. fitted with such an engine. • *verb* (**putt-putts, putt-putted, putt-putting**) make this sound.

putty • *noun* (*plural* **putties**) **1** a soft sticky substance that hardens when dry, used for fixing glass into window frames, filling holes in woodwork, etc. **2** a fine white mortar of lime and water, used in pointing brickwork etc. **3** a light shade of yellowish grey. • *verb* (**putties, puttied, puttying**) cover, fix, join, or fill up with putty. PHRASES **putty in a person's hands** someone who is too compliant, or easily influenced.

putty knife *noun* (*plural* **putty knives**) a knife with a broad blunt flexible blade for spreading putty.

put-up *adjective* fraudulently presented or devised: *a put-up job.*

putz • *noun* (*plural* **putzes**) *slang* a fool; a stupid person. • *verb* (**putzes, putzed, putzing**) (usu. foll. by *around*) waste time; fool around. [Rhymes with NUTS]

puzzle • *noun* **1** a difficult or confusing problem. **2** a problem or toy designed to test knowledge or ingenuity: *jigsaw puzzle.* • *verb* (**puzzles, puzzled, puzzling**) **1** confound or disconcert mentally. **2** (usu. foll. by *over* etc.) be perplexed (about). **3** (usu. as **puzzling** *adjective*) require much thought to comprehend: *a puzzling situation.* **4** (foll. by *out*) solve or understand by hard thought. ▶**puzzled** *adjective*
puzzlement *noun*

puzzler *noun* **1** a difficult question or problem. **2** a person who is fond of solving puzzles.

PV *abbreviation* PHOTOVOLTAIC.

PVA *abbreviation* polyvinyl acetate, a soft plastic polymer used in paints and adhesives.

PVC *abbreviation* POLYVINYL CHLORIDE.

PWC *abbreviation* (*plural* **PWCs**) PERSONAL WATERCRAFT.

pygmy *noun* (*plural* **pygmies**) **1** a member of any of several small-statured peoples of equatorial Africa and parts of Southeast Asia. **2** a very small person, animal, or thing. **3** (as an *adjective*) **a** of or relating to pygmies. **b** (of a person, animal, etc.) dwarf. [Say PIG mee]

pyjamas *plural noun* **1** a suit of loose trousers, shorts, or underpants and a top for sleeping in. **2** loose trousers tied around the waist, originally worn in some Asian countries. **3** (**pyjama**) designating parts of a suit of pyjamas: *pyjama jacket* ◊ *pyjama pants.*

pylon *noun* **1** a plastic cone used to mark areas of roads etc. **2** esp. *Brit.* a tall structure erected as a support (esp. for electric power cables). **3** a structure on the wing of an aircraft supporting an engine or weapon.

pyramid *noun* **1** a monumental structure, usu. of stone, with a square base and sloping sides meeting centrally at an apex, esp. an ancient Egyptian royal tomb. **2** a polyhedron or solid figure of this type with a base of three or more sides. **3** a pyramid-shaped thing or pile of things. **4** an organization or a system seen as a structure in which the higher the level, the fewer people or things that occupy that level. ▶**pyramidal** *adjective*

pyramid selling *noun* (also **pyramid scheme**) a system of selling goods in which the right to sell the goods is sold to an increasing number of distributors at successively lower levels, each of whom is recompensed for recruiting other distributors to the scheme.

pyre *noun* a heap of combustible material esp. on which a corpse is burned. [Rhymes with FIRE]

pyrethrum *noun* **1** an aromatic plant of the daisy family, usu. having feathery foliage and brightly coloured flowers. **2** an insecticide made from the dried flowers of this plant. [Say pie WREATH rum]

Pyrex *noun* *proprietary* a hard heat-resistant type of glass, often used for ovenware. [Say PIE rex]

pyrimidine *noun* **1** *Chemistry* a cyclic organic nitrogenous base. **2** any of a group of compounds with a similar structure. [Say pir IMMA deen]

pyrite *noun* (also **pyrites, iron pyrites**) a yellow lustrous form of iron disulphide. [Say PIE rite]

pyrogy *noun* (also **pyrohy**) = PEROGY. [Say purr OH ghee]

pyromania *noun* an obsessive desire to set things on fire. ▶**pyromaniac** *noun* [Say pie roe MAY nee uh]

pyrotechnic *adjective* of or relating to fireworks. ▶**pyrotechnical** *adjective* [Say pie roe TECK nick]

pyrotechnics *plural noun* **1** (treated as *singular*) the art of making fireworks. **2** a display of fireworks. **3** any brilliant display: *dazzled the crowd with his guitar pyrotechnics.* [Say pie roe TECK nicks]

pyrrhic *adjective* (of a victory) won at too great a cost to be of use to the victor: *they see it as a pyrrhic victory in that, while recognizing special rights for the Indians, the court implicitly acknowledged the Crown's ultimate jurisdiction.* [Say PIR ick]

pysanka *noun* (*plural* **pysanky**) *Cdn* a hand-painted Ukrainian Easter egg, usu. having elaborate and intricate designs. [Say PIS un kuh for the singular, PIS un key for the plural]

Pythagorean • *adjective* of or relating to the Greek philosopher Pythagoras (*c.*560–480 BC) or his philosophy, esp. regarding the repeated incarnation of souls, with punishments and rewards for behaviour in previous lives. • *noun* a follower of Pythagoras. [Say pie thagga REE un]

Pythagorean theorem *noun* the theorem attributed to Pythagoras that the square on the hypotenuse of a right-angled triangle is equal to the sum of the squares on the other two sides.

python *noun* a large, heavy-bodied, non-venomous snake found throughout the tropics in the Old World, killing prey by constriction and asphyxiation.

Qq

Q¹ *noun* (also **q**) (*plural* **Qs** or **Q's**) the seventeenth letter of the alphabet.

Q² *abbreviation* (also **Q.**) **1** Queen, Queen's. **2** question.

Qallunaaq *noun* (*plural* **Qallunaat**) *Cdn* (*North*) a person who is not Inuit, esp. a white person. [Say ka LOO nack for the singular, ka LOO nat for the plural]

Q & A (also **Q and A**) • *abbreviation* question and answer. • *noun* (*plural* **Q & As**) a question-and-answer session, column, etc.

QB *abbreviation* (*plural* **QBs**) **1** quarterback. **2** Queen's Bench.

QC *abbreviation* (also **Qc**) Quebec.

QC *abbreviation* **1** (also **Q.C.**) Queen's Counsel. **2** quality control.

qi *noun* the physical life force thought by some Chinese philosophers to flow through the body. [Say CHEE]

qigong *noun* a system of techniques to focus and strengthen qi, including breathing exercises, meditation, and hand and arm movements, used in alternative medicine and as a basis for training in martial arts. [Say chee GOONG]

qiviut *noun Cdn* (*North*) & *Alaska* fine, soft wool from a muskox. [Say KIVVY oot]

QPF *abbreviation Cdn* Quebec Police Force; the Sûreté du Québec.

QST *noun Cdn* Quebec Sales Tax.

qt. *abbreviation* quart(s).

q.t. *noun informal* quiet: *on the q.t.*

Quaalude *noun proprietary* **1** the tranquilizer methaqualone. **2** a tablet of this. [Say KWAY lude]

quack¹ • *noun* the harsh sound made by ducks. • *verb* **1** utter this sound. **2** *informal* talk loudly and foolishly.

quack² *noun* **1** an unqualified practitioner of medicine. **2** (as an *adjective*) of or characteristic of unskilled medical practice: *quack cure.* ▶ **quackery** *noun*

quack grass *noun* (*plural* **quack grasses**) a coarse grass with long creeping roots, commonly growing as a weed in lawns; couch grass.

quad • *noun* **1** *informal* a quadrangle. **2** *informal* = QUADRUPLET 1. **3** *informal* a quadriplegic. **4** quadraphonic. **5** (usu. in *plural*) *slang* = QUADRICEPS. **6** *Figure Skating* a quadruple jump, in which a skater completes four rotations in the air. • *adjective* quadraphonic.

quad chair *noun* (also **quad chairlift**) a chairlift with chairs that seat four people.

quadrangle *noun* **1** a four-sided plane figure, esp. a square or rectangle. **2** a four-sided court, esp. enclosed by buildings, as in some colleges, schools, etc. ▶ **quadrangular** *adjective*

quadrant *noun* **1** a quarter of a circle's circumference. **2** a plane figure enclosed by two radii of a circle at right angles and the arc cut off by them. **3** a quarter of a sphere or spherical body. **4** any of four parts of a plane divided by two lines at right angles. **5 a** a thing, esp. a graduated strip of metal, shaped like a quarter-circle. **b** an instrument graduated for taking angular measurements.

quadraphonic *adjective* (of sound reproduction) using four transmission channels. [Say kwodra FON ick]

quadrat *noun Ecology* a small area marked out for study. [Say KWOD rit]

quadratic *Math* • *adjective* involving the second and no higher power of an unknown quantity or variable: *quadratic equation.* • *noun* **1** a quadratic equation. **2** (in *plural*) the branch of algebra dealing with these. [Say kwod RAT ick]

quadriceps *noun* (*plural* **quadriceps**) a large four-headed muscle at the front of the thigh, the chief extensor of the knee. [Say KWODRA seps]

quadrilateral • *adjective* having four sides. • *noun* a four-sided figure. [Say kwodra LATERAL]

quadrille *noun* **1** a square dance usu. performed by four couples and containing five figures, each of which is a complete dance in itself. **2** the music for this. [Say kwod RILL]

quadrillion • *noun* (*plural* **quadrillion** or **quadrillions**) **1** a thousand raised to the fifth power (10^{15} and 10^{24} respectively). **2** *informal* a very large amount. • *adjective* amounting to one quadrillion in number. [Say kwod RILL yun]

quadriplegia *noun* paralysis of all four limbs. ▶ **quadriplegic** *adjective & noun* [Say kwodra PLEE juh]

quadrophonic *adjective* = QUADRAPHONIC. [Say kwodra FON ick]

quadruped • *noun* a four-footed mammal. • *adjective* four-footed. [Say KWOD ruh ped]

quadruple • *adjective* **1** fourfold. **2 a** having four parts. **b** involving four participants: *quadruple alliance.* **3** being four times as many or as much. **4** (of time in music) having four beats in a bar. • *noun* a fourfold number or amount. • *verb* (**quadruples, quadrupled, quadrupling**) multiply by four; increase fourfold. [Say kwod RUPE ul]

quadruplet *noun* **1** each of four children born at one birth. **2** a set of four things working together. [Say kwod RUPE lit]

quadruplex *noun* (*plural* **quadruplexes**) *Cdn* a building divided into four self-contained residences. [Say KWODRA plex]

quaff *verb* drink deeply or in long drafts. ▶ **quaffable** *adjective* **quaffer** *noun* [Say KWOFF]

quagmire *noun* **1** a soft boggy or marshy area that gives way underfoot. **2** a hazardous or awkward situation: *who has drawn us into this constant constitutional quagmire?* [Say KWAG mire or KWOG mire]

quahog *noun* (also **quahaug**) an edible round clam of the Atlantic coast of North America. [Say KWAH hog (with KWAH as in *SQUASH* or *QUACK*)]

quail¹ *noun* (*plural* **quail** or **quails**) **1** a small, short-tailed New World game bird resembling a partridge, e.g. the bobwhite. **2** any of a number of similar but slightly smaller Old World birds.

quail² *verb* be apprehensive with fear: *the crackdown on all political opposition was so severe that hundreds quailed and fled.*

quaint *adjective* attractively unusual or unfamiliar in character or appearance, esp. in an old-fashioned way. ▶ **quaintly** *adverb* **quaintness** *noun*

quake • *verb* (**quakes, quaked, quaking**) **1** (of the earth) shake, tremble. **2** (of a person) shake or shudder: *was quaking with fear.* • *noun* an earthquake.

Quaker • *noun* a member of the Society of Friends, a

Christian movement devoted to peaceful principles and rejecting formal doctrine, sacraments, and ordained ministers. • *adjective* of or relating to Quakers. ▶ **Quakerism** *noun*

qualification *noun* **1** the action or fact of qualifying or being eligible for something: *curling long sought qualification as an Olympic sport.* **2** a quality or accomplishment that makes someone suitable for a particular job or activity. **3** a statement or assertion that makes another less absolute: *I accept his theories, but not without certain qualifications ◊ I can say without qualification that it is the best thing they have ever done.* **4** a condition that must be fulfilled before a right can be acquired etc.: *a five-year residency qualification for presidential candidates.*

qualifier *noun* **1** a person or team that has defeated others in order to enter a particular competition. **2** a game or match that a person or team has to win in order to enter a particular competition: *a World Cup qualifier.* **3** *Grammar* a word, esp. an adjective or adverb, that describes another word in a particular way: *In "the open door," "open" is a qualifier, describing the door.*

qualify *verb* (**qualifies**, **qualified**, **qualifying**) **1** make competent or fit for a position or purpose. **2** make legally entitled. **3** (foll. by *for*) (of a person) satisfy the conditions or requirements (for a position, award, competition, etc.). **4** modify or make less absolute (a statement or assertion): *I want to qualify what I said earlier — I didn't mean he couldn't do the job, only that he would need supervision.* **5** (of a word, esp. an adjective) attribute a quality to (another word, esp. a noun). **6** (foll. by *as*) attribute a specified quality to, describe as: *the idea was qualified as absurd.*

qualifying *adjective* serving to determine those that qualify: *qualifying examination.*

qualitative *adjective* concerned with or depending on quality or qualities: *a qualitative difference.* ▶ **qualitatively** *adverb*

quality *noun* (*plural* **qualities**) **1** the standard of something when compared to other things like it: *quality of life ◊ wine of exceptional quality.* **2 a** general excellence: *we provide quality at reasonable prices.* **b** (as an *adjective*) of high quality: *a quality product.* **3** a distinctive, usu. good, attribute or characteristic. **4** the distinctive timbre of a voice or sound.

quality control *noun* a system of maintaining standards in manufactured products by testing and inspection.

quality time *noun* time spent devoting one's undivided attention to a favourite activity, such as a hobby, or to a person, esp. a child, perceived as compensating in quality for what it lacks in duration or frequency.

qualm *noun* **1** a misgiving; an uneasy doubt. **2** a scruple of conscience; a pang of doubt about one's own conduct. [Say KWOM]

quandary *noun* (*plural* **quandaries**) **1** a perplexing situation or problem that requires a solution: *is caught in a quandary over whether to start his own business or remain in his current secure position with the firm.* **2** a difficult situation; a practical dilemma. [Say KWON dree]

quantifiable *adjective* able to be expressed or measured as a quantity: *lacking any other quantifiable information, crucial decisions are often made solely on price.*

quantification *noun* the action or process of expressing or measuring as a quantity: *neighbourhood unit planning has given rise to a methodology of quantification, where population densities are exactly calculated.*

quantify *verb* (**quantifies**, **quantified**, **quantifying**) express or measure the quantity of: *the study did not try*

to quantify how frequently viruses are spread by people sharing software ◊ the price of freedom is hard to quantify.

quantitative *adjective* **1** concerned with quantity. **2** measured or measurable by quantity. ▶ **quantitatively** *adverb*

quantity *noun* (*plural* **quantities**) **1** an indefinite number or amount. **2** a specified or definite number or amount that can be measured or counted: *add the correct quantity of cream.* **3** a large amount or number; an abundance: *buys in quantity.* **4** the property of things that is measurable: *quantity is easy to measure, whereas quality is not.* **5** a person or thing viewed as having a specified value: *an unknown quantity.* **6** the length or shortness of vowel sounds or syllables. **7** *Math* a value, component, etc. that may be expressed in numbers.

quantum (*plural* **quanta**) • *noun* **1** *Physics* **a** the smallest possible quantity of radiant energy, which is proportional in magnitude to the frequency of radiation it represents; light, for example, which appears as a continuous electromagnetic wave, is actually emitted in discrete amounts or quanta (known as photons). **b** a small and distinct amount of another physical property, such as angular momentum or charge. **2** a portion or amount: *an average quantum of common sense.* • *adjective* dramatic or significant: *a quantum advance.* [Say KWON tum]

quantum leap *noun* (also **quantum jump**) **1** a sudden large increase, change, or advance: *a quantum leap in automobile design.* **2** an abrupt transition in an atom or molecule from one quantum state to another.

quantum-mechanical *adjective* of or relating to quantum mechanics.

quantum mechanics *plural noun* the branch of mechanics that deals with the mathematical description of the motion and interaction of subatomic particles, incorporating the concept that these particles can also be regarded as waves.

quantum theory *noun* (*plural* **quantum theories**) *Physics* a theory of matter and energy based on the concept of quanta.

quarantine • *noun* **1** isolation imposed on persons or animals that have arrived from elsewhere or been exposed to, and might spread, infectious or contagious disease. **2** the period of this isolation. • *verb* (**quarantines**, **quarantined**, **quarantining**) impose such isolation on; put in quarantine. [Say KWORE in teen]

quark *noun* *Physics* any of a class of subatomic particles with a fractional electric charge, of which protons, neutrons, etc. are thought to be composed. [Rhymes with *PORK* or *PARK*]

quarrel • *noun* **1** an angry argument or disagreement between individuals or with others. **2** an occasion of complaint against a person or thing: *I have no quarrel with his decision.* • *verb* (**quarrels**, **quarrelled**, **quarrelling**) **1** have a dispute. **2** (often foll. by *with*) take exception; find fault. ▶ **quarreller** *noun*

quarrelsome *adjective* given to or characterized by quarrelling.

quarry[1] • *noun* (*plural* **quarries**) **1** an open-air excavation from which stone for building etc. is or has been obtained by cutting, blasting, etc. **2** any place from which stone etc. may be extracted. **3** a supply or source of something: *a quarry of information.* • *verb* (**quarries**, **quarried**, **quarrying**) extract (stone) from a quarry.

quarry[2] *noun* (*plural* **quarries**) **1** the object of pursuit by hounds, hunters, etc.: *the party intends to ban hunting live quarry with hounds.* **2** any object of chase, aim, or attack: *the quarry of this storm hunt was a violent tornado.*

quarry tile *noun* an unglazed floor tile.

quart *noun* **1 a** a measure of capacity for liquids etc.,

equal to a quarter of an Imperial gallon (1.135 litres or 40 fl. oz.). **b** a measure of capacity for liquids etc., equal to a quarter of a US gallon (0.946 litres or 32 fl. oz.). **2** a unit of dry measure, equal to one-thirty-second of a bushel (1.1 litres). **3** a container holding a quart.

quarter • *noun* **1** each of four equal or corresponding parts into which something is or can be divided. **2** a period of three months, used esp. in reference to financial transactions. **3** a quarter-hour. **4** a Canadian or US coin worth 25 cents. **5** one fourth of a pound weight (avoirdupois, equal to 4 ounces). **6** each of four equal periods into which a game is divided in football, basketball, etc. **7** a part of a town or city with a specified character or use: *the business quarter*. **8** (in *plural*) rooms or lodgings. **9** a person, area, etc. regarded as the source of something: *help from an unexpected quarter*. **10** pity or mercy shown to an opponent: *they gave the enemy no quarter*. **11** (in *plural*) the haunches or hindquarters of a horse. **12** the direction of one of the points of the compass. **13** = QUARTER SECTION. • *verb* **1** divide into quarters. **2** *hist.* cut the body of (an executed person) into four parts. **3** (in *passive*) be stationed or lodged. **4** range over (an area) in all directions. • *adjective* forming an amount equal to or roughly equal to a quarter.

quarterback • *noun* **1** the player who directs the offence of a football team. Abbreviation: **QB**. **2** this position on a football team. • *verb* **1** play a game as a quarterback. **2** lead (a team) in the role of quarterback. **3** lead, oversee: *she was quarterbacking the development of their digital video transmission system*.

quarterdeck *noun* part of a ship's upper deck near the stern, historically reserved for officers of the ship.

quarter horse *noun* a small stocky breed of horse noted for agility and speed over short distances, often used to herd livestock.

quarterly • *adjective* produced or occurring once every quarter of a year: *a quarterly report*. • *adverb* once every quarter of a year: *dividends are calculated quarterly*. • *noun* (*plural* **quarterlies**) a quarterly review or magazine.

quartermaster *noun* **1** a regimental officer in charge of lodging, rations, etc. **2** a naval petty officer in charge of steering, signals, etc.

quarter note *noun* *Music* a note having the time value of a quarter of a whole note, drawn as a large dot with a stem.

quarter section *noun* a quarter of a square mile of esp. agricultural land, 160 acres.

quartet *noun* **1 a** a composition for four voices etc. **b** the performers of such a piece. **2** any group of four.

quarto *noun* (*plural* **quartos**) *Printing* **1** the size given by folding a (usu. specified) sheet of paper twice, yielding 4 leaves or 8 pages. **2** a book consisting of sheets folded in this way. Abbreviation: **4to**.

quartz *noun* (*plural* **quartzes**) a mineral consisting of silica, crystallizing in colourless or white hexagonal prisms, often coloured by impurities (as amethyst etc.), and found widely in igneous and metamorphic rocks.

quartzite *noun* a hard, metamorphic rock consisting mainly of granular quartz.

quasar *noun* any of a class of starlike celestial objects, apparently of great size and remoteness, often associated with a spectrum with a large red shift and intense radio emission. [Say KWAY zar]

quash *verb* (**quashes**, **quashed**, **quashing**) **1** suppress; crush (speculation, a plan, an uprising etc.): *quashed the rebellion*. **2** reject something and declare it no longer valid, esp. by a legal procedure: *the judge granted a motion to quash the charges*. [Say KWOSH]

quasi *adjective* **1** resembling: *a quasi marriage*. **2** being nearly or in part: *a quasi democracy*. [Say KWOZZY]

quasi- *combining form* **1** seemingly; apparently but not really: *quasi-scientific*. **2** being partly or almost: *quasi-independent*.

quaternary • *adjective* **1 a** having four parts. **b** fourth in a series. **2** (**Quaternary**) *Geology* of or relating to the most current period in the Cenozoic era, comprising the Pleistocene and Holocene epochs and beginning about 2 million years ago, in which humans and other mammals evolved into their present forms and were strongly affected by the ice ages of the Pleistocene. **3** (of an ammonium compound) containing a nitrogen atom bonded to four organic groups or atoms. • *noun* (*plural* **quaternaries**) **1** a set of four things. **2** (**Quaternary**) *Geology* the Quaternary period. **3** (of an industry or type of economic activity) concerned with gathering, processing, and disseminating information. [Say KWOTTER nairy or kwuh TURNER ee]

quatrain *noun* a stanza of four lines, usu. with alternate rhymes. [Say KWOT rain]

quaver • *verb* **1** (esp. of a voice or sound) vibrate, shake, tremble. **2** say or sing with a shaky or trembling voice. • *noun* a tremble in speech. [Say KWAY vur]

quavery *adjective* (of a voice etc.) tremulous. [Say KWAY vur ee]

quay *noun* a solid stationary artificial landing place lying alongside or projecting into water for loading and unloading boats, ships, etc. [Sounds like *KEY*]

quayside • *noun* the land forming or near a quay. • *adjective* at or by a quay. [Say KEY side]

Que. *abbreviation* Quebec.

queasily *adverb* in a queasy, nauseous, or uneasy manner.

queasiness *noun* the quality or condition of feeling queasy.

queasy *adjective* (**queasier**, **queasiest**) **1** feeling or tending to feel sick or nauseous. **2** slightly nervous or worried about something; uneasy. **3** feeling disgust or revulsion: *his pretentiousness made me queasy*. **4** causing nausea, anxiety, or disgust: *a queasy excursion to town for a drink*.

Quebecer (also **Quebecker**) a native or inhabitant of Quebec. [Say kwuh BECKER or kuh BECKER or kay BECKER]

Quebec heater *noun* *Cdn* a tall, cylindrical stove using coal or wood for fuel, used esp. for heating or cooking. [Say kwuh BECK or kuh BECK or kay BECK]

Québécois *Cdn* • *noun* (*plural* **Québécois**) a francophone native or inhabitant of Quebec. • *adjective* of or relating to Quebec or the Québécois. [Say kay beck WAH]

Québécoise *Cdn* • *noun* (*plural* **Québécoises**) a francophone woman who is a native or inhabitant of Quebec. • *adjective* being a Québécoise. [Say kay beck WAHZ]

Quechua • *noun* (*plural* **Quechua** or **Quechuas**) **1** a member of a South American Indian people of Peru and neighbouring countries. **2** the language of this people. • *adjective* of or relating to this people or their language. [Say KETCH wuh]

queen • *noun* **1** (as a title usu. **Queen**) a female sovereign etc., esp. the hereditary ruler of an independent nation. **2** (also **queen consort**) a king's wife. **3 a** a woman or thing pre-eminent or supreme in a specified area or of its kind: *tennis queen*. **b** a belle or mock sovereign on some occasion: *queen of the fair*. **4** the fertile female among ants, bees, etc. **5 a** the most powerful piece in chess. **b** (**queen's**) designating a chess piece or pieces starting on the queen's side of the board: *queen's knight*. **6** in a deck of playing cards, any of

Q

the four cards bearing a picture of a queen. **7 (the Queen)** (in Canada and the UK) the anthem "God Save the Queen". • *verb* make (a woman) queen. • *adjective* denoting a queen-size bed, mattress, sheets, etc. PHRASES **queen it** behave in an unpleasant and superior way towards other people.

Queen Anne *adjective* **1** (of furniture) typical of the early 18th century, esp. characterized by the use of walnut, curving lines, and upholstery. **2** (of architecture) typical of English architecture of the early 18th century, esp. characterized by quaintness and an old-fashioned quality achieved by blending diverse elements of earlier periods.

Queen Anne's lace *noun* a plant of the parsley family, with fern-like leaves and lacy clusters of small white flowers.

queen bee *noun* **1** (of bees) the fertile female in a hive. **2 a** a woman who holds a superior position in an organization etc. **b** a woman who behaves in a superior or controlling manner.

queenly *adjective* (**queenlier, queenliest**) **1** fit for or appropriate to a queen. **2** majestic.

Queen's Bench *noun* (also **Court of Queen's Bench**) (in Alberta, Saskatchewan, Manitoba, and New Brunswick) the superior-court trial division, which has the jurisdiction to hear the most serious indictable offences and civil cases.

Queen's Birthday *noun* *Cdn* (in BC and Newfoundland and Labrador) a holiday falling on the Monday immediately preceding 25 May; Victoria Day.

Queen's Counsel *noun* *Cdn*, *Brit.*, *Austral.*, & *NZ* an appointment bestowed on a barrister by the Attorney General in recognition of excellence as an advocate and following advice from the barrister's peers.

Queen's English *noun* the English language as correctly written or spoken in Britain.

queen-size *adjective* (also **queen-sized**) **1** designating the second-largest standard size of mattress, usu. 153 by 208 cm (60 by 80 in.), or the bed frame, sheets, etc. designed for such a mattress. **2** of an extra-large size, esp. designating women's hosiery for heavier than average legs.

Queen's Park *noun* **1** the grounds and building in Toronto where the Ontario legislature is situated. **2** the government of Ontario.

Queen's Printer *noun* *Cdn* an official printer of bills and reports, office stationery, bulletins, etc. for the federal or provincial governments.

WRITING TIP
queer

Although in recent years some homosexuals have been using the word *queer* to refer to themselves, its use by others is still often offensive.

---

queer • *adjective* **1** unnatural; odd; eccentric. **2** *slang* **a** (esp. of a man) homosexual. **b** of or pertaining to a homosexual or homosexuals. **3** shady; suspect; of questionable character. **4** slightly ill; giddy; faint. • *noun* *slang* a homosexual. • *verb* *slang* spoil; put out of order. ▶ **queerly** *adverb* **queerness** *noun*

quell *verb* **1 a** put an end to (something), esp. by force; suppress: *quell an uprising*. **b** cause to submit; suppress: *quell the protesters*. **2** allay or suppress (feelings, fear, anger, etc.): *quelled the doubts of supporters*.

quench *verb* (**quenches, quenched, quenching**) **1** satisfy (thirst) by drinking. **2** extinguish (a fire or light etc.). **3** esp. *Metallurgy* cool (a hot substance) in cold water, air, oil, etc. **4** stifle or suppress (desire etc.). ▶ **quencher** *noun*

querulous *adjective* of a whining, complaining, or

peevish nature or disposition: *a querulous fear rose in his voice*. ▶ **querulously** *adverb* **querulousness** *noun* [Say KWARE uh lus]

query • *noun* (*plural* **queries**) **1** a question or inquiry. **2** a question that expresses doubt or reservation: *queries about the feasibility of the project*. **3** *Computing* **a** the action of searching a string of characters in a computer database. **b** a string or set of characters searched. • *verb* (**queries, queried, querying**) **1** express in the form of a question. **2** express doubt about something: *queried the coach's abilities*. **3** ask a question of: *queried him about his preference*. [Say KWEER ee]

quesadilla *noun* a dish of vegetables and grated cheese etc., stuffed between two tortillas, usu. baked or fried and served with salsa, sour cream, etc. [Say case a DEE yuh]

quest • *noun* **1** a search or the act of seeking; an expedition. **2** the thing sought. **3** a goal sought; an attempt or endeavour: *his quest to win twenty games*. • *verb* (often foll. by *for*) go about in search of something; go on a quest. PHRASES **in quest of** seeking. ▶ **quester** *noun*

question • *noun* **1** a sentence worded or expressed so as to seek information. **2 a** doubt or uncertainty about something. **b** the raising of such doubt etc.: *his suitability is open to question*. **3** a matter or issue that needs to be settled: *the question is how should I invest the money*. **4** (foll. by *of*) a matter or concern depending on conditions: *a question of whether I can afford it*. **5** a matter to be discussed or decided or voted on: *the airport question*. • *verb* **1** ask questions of; interrogate. **2** express or feel doubt about something: *her honesty has never been questioned*. **3** challenge; argue against: *questioned the judge's ruling*. PHRASES **be a question of time** be certain to happen sooner or later. **beyond all question** undoubtedly. **come into question** be discussed; become of practical importance. **in question** that is being discussed or referred to: *the person in question*. **call into question** cast doubt on, dispute. **no question of** no possibility of: *there's no question of my giving in*. **no question that** no doubt that. **out of the question** too impracticable etc. to be worth discussing; impossible. **put the question** require supporters and opponents of a proposal to record their votes. **without question 1** undoubtedly. **2** without hesitation.

questionable *adjective* **1** doubtful as regards truth or quality: *questionable measurements*. **2** not clearly in accordance with honesty, honour, wisdom, etc.: *questionable business practices*. **3** of dubious value. ▶ **questionably** *adverb*

questioner *noun* a person who asks questions, esp. in a broadcast program or public debate.

questioning • *noun* **1** interrogation, esp. of a suspect by police officers. **2** the action of posing a question or calling into question. • *adjective* expressing or suggesting a question or doubt: *a questioning look*. ▶ **questioningly** *adverb*

question mark *noun* **1** a punctuation mark (?) indicating a question. **2** a cause for uncertainty: *public support remains a question mark*. **3** doubt or uncertainty: *a question mark looms over my plans*.

questionnaire *noun* a formulated series of questions, esp. for statistical study or market research.

question period *noun* *Cdn* a period of time set aside each day during parliamentary proceedings in which members may question government ministers.

queue • *noun* **1** a line or sequence of persons, vehicles, etc., awaiting their turn to be attended to or to proceed. **2** *Computing* a list of data items, commands, etc., stored so as to be retrievable in a definite order, usu. the order

of insertion. • *verb* (**queues, queued, queuing** or **queueing**) **1** (often foll. by *up*) (of persons etc.) form a queue; take one's place in a queue. **2** esp. *Computing* arrange in a queue. [Sounds like *CUE*]

quibble • *noun* a trivial or unimportant point of criticism, sometimes used to avoid a more important issue. • *verb* (**quibbles, quibbled, quibbling**) argue about small differences or disagreements. ▸ **quibbler** *noun* **quibbling** *adjective*

quiche *noun* a pastry shell containing eggs, milk, cream, cheese, etc., with vegetables, meat, fish, etc. [Say KEESH]

quiche lorraine *noun* a quiche with bacon in the filling. [Say keesh luh RAIN]

Quichua *noun* (*plural* **Quichua** or **Quichuas**) = QUECHUA. [Say KITCH wuh]

> **WRITING TIP**
> **quick, quickly**
>
> The use of **quick** as an adverb is usually restricted to set phrases, such as *Come quick*, *Quick — do something!*, and *Get rich quick*. Outside of such expressions, the adverb **quickly** is more standard: *We ran* **quickly**, not *We ran* **quick**.

quick • *adjective* **1** moving fast. **2** lasting or taking a short time: *a quick worker*. **3** with little or no delay; prompt. **4** intelligent. **5** (of a person's eye or ear) keenly perceptive. **6** (of temper) easily roused. • *adverb* **1** at a rapid rate; quickly: *he'll do the work as quick as he can*. **2** (as *interjection*) come, go, etc., quickly: *Quick! Get your shoes and let's go!* • *noun* **1** the tender flesh below the growing part of a fingernail or toenail. **2** the central or most sensitive part: *his laughter cut us to the quick*. **PHRASES** **be quick** act quickly. **cut to the quick** deeply offend or upset someone, hurt a person's feelings.

quick and dirty *adjective* done hastily; makeshift.

quick bread *noun* a baked good, usu. less sweet and rich than a cake or cookie, leavened with baking powder or baking soda, e.g. a muffin, scone, etc.

quicken *verb* **1** make or become quicker; accelerate. **2** enliven, animate, rouse, or become lively, animated, or roused: *his memory quickened when he saw her*. **3** (of a fetus) begin to show signs of life.

quick-fire *adjective* = RAPID-FIRE.

quickie *informal* • *noun* **1** a thing done or made quickly or hastily. **2** a brief act of sexual intercourse. **3** an alcoholic drink taken quickly. • *adjective* made or executed quickly: *quickie divorce*.

quicklime *noun* = LIME¹ *noun* 1.

quickly *adverb* **1** fast. **2** soon; after a short time.

quickness *noun* the quality of being fast, esp. at thinking etc.: *the quickness of her wit*.

quicksand *noun* **1 a** loose wet sand, easily yielding to pressure, that sucks in anything placed or falling in it. **b** a bed of this. **2** a treacherous thing or situation.

quicksilver • *noun* mercury. • *adjective* in constant flux; changeable, unpredictable: *a quicksilver temper*.

quickstep • *noun* a fast foxtrot. • *verb* (**quicksteps, quickstepped, quickstepping**) dance the quickstep.

quick study *noun* (*plural* **quick studies**) a person who adapts easily to new surroundings, a new job, etc.; a fast learner.

quick-witted *adjective* able to think quickly and issue an immediate usu. clever reply; intelligent. ▸ **quick-wittedness** *noun*

quid *noun* (*plural* **quid**) *Brit. slang* one pound sterling.

quid pro quo *noun* **1** a thing given as compensation. **2** return made (for a gift, favour, etc.).

quiescence *noun* a state or period of inactivity or dormancy: *the environment surrounding Internet stocks has entered a state of relative quiescence*. [Say kwee ESSENCE]

quiescent *adjective* in a state or period of inactivity or dormancy: *the counterculture produced a profound change in the formerly quiescent middle class*. [Say kwee ESS int]

quiet • *adjective* (**quieter, quietest**) **1** making little or no noise. **2** free from activity, disturbance, or excitement. **3** without being disturbed or interrupted: *a quiet drink*. **4** discreet, moderate, or restrained. **5** (of a person) tranquil and reserved. • *noun* an absence of noise or disturbance. • *verb* make or become quiet. **PHRASES** **be quiet** cease talking etc. **keep quiet 1** refrain from making a noise. **2** (often foll. by *about*) suppress or refrain from disclosing information etc. **on the quiet** unobtrusively; secretly.

quieten *verb* esp. *Brit.* (often foll. by *down*) = QUIET *verb*.

quietism *noun* **1** religious mysticism based on the rejection of outward forms of devotion in favour of passive contemplation and extinction of the will. **2** any philosophy emphasizing human passivity and the principle of nonresistance. ▸ **quietist** *noun & adjective*

quietly *adverb* in a quiet manner: *Marcia walked quietly across the room* ◊ *do it quietly*.

quietness *noun* the condition of being quiet or peaceful.

Quiet Revolution *noun* *Cdn* in Quebec, the period 1960–66, characterized by province-wide social, economic, and educational reforms, as well as mounting separatist sentiment and the issue of a special status for Quebec within Confederation.

quietude *noun* a state of quiet.

quill • *noun* **1** (usu. in *plural*) the spines of a porcupine. **2** (also **quill feather**) a large feather in a wing or tail. **3** the hollow stem of this. **4** (also **quill pen**) a pen made of a quill. **5** a hollow rotating sleeve of metal etc. • *verb* form into cylindrical quill-like folds.

quillwork *noun* art using porcupine quills to decorate clothing, teepees, and utilitarian items, done by a number of Aboriginal groups, esp. the Mi'kmaq.

quilt • *noun* **1** a bed cover made of padding enclosed between layers of cloth etc. and kept in place by lines of stitching. **2** a collection of diverse elements that together constitute a whole, resembling a patchwork quilt: *a ragged quilt of crossword puzzles, and horoscopes, and chess columns*. • *verb* make a quilt.

quilted *adjective* **1** covered or lined with padded material held together with lines of stitching: *quilted diapers*. **2** (of padding and cloth) stitched or sewn together in the manner of a quilt.

quilter *noun* a person who makes quilts.

quilting *noun* **1** the practice of making quilts. **2 a** the materials, such as cloth, padding, etc., used in making of quilts. **b** these materials having been quilted.

quince *noun* **1** a hard acid pear-shaped fruit used in jams and jellies. **2** the shrub or small tree bearing this fruit.

quinine *noun* **1** an alkaloid found esp. in the bark of the cinchona, an evergreen native to South America. **2** a bitter drug containing this, used as a specific remedy for malaria and as an additive to tonic water. [Say KWIN ine or KWINE ine or KWIN een]

quinoa *noun* **1** any of several annual goosefoots grown by the Indians of the Andes for their edible starchy seeds. **2** these seeds used as food. [Say KEEN wuh]

quinsy *noun* an inflammation of the throat, esp. an abscess in the region around the tonsils. [Say KWIN zee]

quint *noun informal* a quintuplet.

quintal *noun* **1** a hundredweight (112 lb.), used e.g. as a measure for dried salt cod. **2** a weight of about 100 lb. **3** a weight of 100 kg. [Say KWIN tull]

Q

quintessence *noun* **1** the purest and most perfect, or most typical, form, manifestation, or embodiment of some quality or class: *she was the quintessence of political professionalism.* **2** the most essential part of any substance: *advertising is the quintessence of marketing.* ▶ **quintessential** *adjective* **quintessentially** *adverb* [Say kwint ESSENCE, kwint ESSENTIAL]

quintet *noun* **1 a** a composition for five voices etc. **b** a group of five musicians. **2** any group of five.

quintuple • *adjective* **1** consisting of five parts. **2** involving five parties. • *noun* a fivefold number or amount. • *verb* (**quintuples,** **quintupled,** **quintupling**) multiply by five.

quintuplet *noun* each of five children born at one birth.

quinzhee *noun* (*plural* **quinzhees**) a shelter created by piling up snow, letting it settle, and then hollowing out the interior. [Say KWINZY]

quip • *noun* a clever saying; an epigram; a sarcastic remark etc. • *verb* (**quips, quipped, quipping**) **1** make quips. **2** say (something) as a quip.

quire *noun* **1** four sheets of paper etc. folded to form eight leaves, as often in medieval manuscripts. **2** any collection of leaves one within another in a manuscript or book. **3** 25 (also 24) sheets of paper.

quirk *noun* **1** a peculiarity of behaviour or character; an eccentricity. **2** a trick of fate. ▶ **quirkily** *adverb* **quirkiness** *noun* **quirky** *adjective* (**quirkier, quirkiest**)

quisling *noun* **1** a person co-operating with an occupying enemy. **2** a traitor. [Say QUIZ ling]

quit • *verb* (**quits, quit, quitting**) **1** give up; abandon (a task etc.). **2** cease; stop: *quit grumbling ◊ trying to quit smoking.* **3** give up (one's employment); resign. **4** leave or depart from (a place etc.): *she quit New York with the vow that she would never return.* • *adjective* (foll. by *of*) rid: *glad to be quit of her.*

quite *adverb* **1** completely; entirely; wholly; to the utmost extent; in the fullest sense. **2** somewhat; rather; to some extent. **3** (often foll. by *so*) said to indicate agreement. PHRASES **quite a** a remarkable or outstanding (person or thing): *it was quite an event.* **quite another** (or **other**) very different: *that's quite another matter.* **quite a few** *informal* a fairly large number of. **quite some 1** a large amount of: *quite some time ago.* **2** *informal* = QUITE A: *that was quite some movie.* **quite something** a remarkable thing.

quits *adjective* on even terms by retaliation or repayment: *then we'll be quits.* PHRASES **call it quits 1** acknowledge that things are now even; agree not to proceed further in a quarrel etc. **2** cease an activity; stop working etc.

quitter *noun* a person who gives up easily.

quiver • *verb* tremble or vibrate slightly. • *noun* **1** a quivering motion or sound. **2** a case for holding arrows.

quixotic *adjective* exceedingly idealistic or romantic; unrealistic and impractical: *some quixotic dream of establishing a traditional aboriginal homeland.* ▶ **quixotically** *adverb* [Say quick SOT ick]

quiz • *noun* (*plural* **quizzes**) **1** a short test or examination. **2** a test of knowledge, esp. between individuals or teams as a form of entertainment. • *verb* (**quizzes, quizzed, quizzing**) **1** test or examine (students). **2** examine by questioning.

quizzical *adjective* (of a person's expression or behaviour) indicating mild or amused puzzlement: *she gave me a quizzical look.* ▶ **quizzically** *adverb*

qulliq *noun* (*plural* **qulliqs**) *Cdn* (*North*) = KUDLIK. [Say CULL ick]

SPELL CHECK
quandary

Warning: **quandary** is spelled with an *a*, not an *o*.

Quonset *noun* *proprietary* (also **Quonset hut**) a prefabricated metal building with a semi-cylindrical corrugated roof. [Say KWON set]

quorum *noun* the fixed minimum number of members that must be present to make the proceedings of an assembly, society, or meeting valid. [Say KWORE um]

quota *noun* **1** the share that an individual person or company is obliged to contribute to or entitled to take from a total. **2 a** a quantity of goods etc. which a producer is obliged or entitled to produce, export, import, etc. under official controls. **b** *Cdn* authorization to produce a specified quantity of an agricultural product granted by a marketing board to a farmer. **3** the number of immigrants allowed to enter a country, students allowed to enrol for a course, etc. **4** a share or portion of something that one can normally expect to receive or give: *got my quota of sleep.*

quotable *adjective* worth, or suitable for, quoting.

quotation *noun* **1** a group of words taken from a text or speech and repeated by someone other than the original author or speaker: *a quotation from Leacock.* **2** the action of quoting from a text, speech, piece of music, or work of art: *a great argument with much quotation of Darwin.* **3** a short passage or tune taken from one piece of music to another. **4** *Stock Market* an amount stated as the current price of stocks or commodities. **5** an estimate of the cost of something.

quotation mark *noun* each of a set of punctuation marks, single (' ') or double (" "), used to mark the beginning and end of a quoted passage, a title, etc., or words regarded as slang, jargon, or unfamiliar.

quote • *verb* (**quotes, quoted, quoting**) **1** repeat or copy out (a passage or remark by another). **2** repeat a passage or remark from. **3** put forward or describe as being. **4** give someone (an estimated price). **5** name (someone or something) at (specified odds). **6** give (a company) a listing on a stock exchange. • *noun* *informal* **1** a quotation. **2** (usu. in *plural*) quotation marks. • *adverb* (in speech, reading aloud, etc.) indicating the presence of opening quotation marks: *he said, quote, "We shall never surrender".*

quotidian *adjective* commonplace, ordinary, everyday: *I acquired plates, cups, cutlery, towels and bedsheets, all the quotidian provisions that I had always taken for granted.* [Say quo TIDDY un]

quotient *noun* **1** a result obtained by dividing one quantity by another. **2** the degree or presence of a usu. specified characteristic in a thing or person. [Say QUO sh'nt]

Quran *noun* (also **Qur'an**) = KORAN. [Say kuh RAN]

q.v. *abbreviation* *quod vide*, "which see" (in cross-references).

QWERTY *adjective* (also **qwerty**) denoting the standard keyboard on English-language typewriters, word processors, etc. [Say KWUR tee]

Rr

R¹ *noun* (also **r**) (*plural* **Rs** or **R's**) the eighteenth letter of the alphabet. PHRASES **the three Rs** reading, writing, and arithmetic, as the fundamentals of learning.

R² *abbreviation* (also **R.**) **1** (of films) restricted. **2** *Regina*: *Elizabeth R.* **3** *Rex*. **4** River. **5** (also ®) registered as a trademark. **6** R-value: *R2000*. **7** radius. **8** (in a liturgy) response.

R³ *symbol* **1** roentgen. **2** electrical resistance. **3** (in chemical formulas) an organic radical or group.

r. *abbreviation* (also **r**) **1** right. **2** run(s). **3** radius.

Ra *symbol* radium.

rabbet • *noun* a step-shaped channel etc. cut along the edge or face or projecting angle of a length of wood etc., usu. to receive the edge or tongue of another piece. • *verb* (**rabbets, rabbeted, rabbeting**) **1** join or fix with a rabbet. **2** make a rabbet in.

rabbi *noun* (*plural* **rabbis**) **1** a Jewish scholar or teacher, esp. of the law. **2** a person appointed as a Jewish religious leader.

rabbinate *noun* **1** the position or office of a rabbi. **2** rabbis collectively. [Say RAB in it]

rabbinical *adjective* (also **rabbinic**) of or relating to rabbis, or to Jewish law or teaching. [Say ruh BIN ick ul]

rabbit • *noun* **1** a burrowing gregarious plant-eating mammal of the hare family, with long ears and a short tail. **2** a hare. **3** the fur of the rabbit. • *verb* (**rabbits, rabbited, rabbiting**) hunt rabbits. ▶ **rabbity** *adjective*

rabble *noun* **1** a large disorderly group of people; a mob. **2** (**the rabble**) the lower classes.

rabble-rouser *noun* a person who stirs up a crowd of people, esp. in agitation for social or political change. ▶ **rabble-rousing** *adjective & noun*

rabid *adjective* **1** (of a person, feelings, etc.) unreasonably or extremely fanatical: *a rabid anarchist*. **2** of, relating to, or affected with rabies. ▶ **rabidly** *adverb*

rabies *noun* a contagious and fatal viral disease of animals, transmissible through saliva to humans and causing madness and convulsions.

raccoon *noun* **1** a greyish-brown furry nocturnal flesh-eating mammal of North America, with a ringed bushy tail, sharp snout, and black mask-like markings across the eyes. **2** the fur of the raccoon.

race¹ • *noun* **1** a contest of speed between athletes, horses, vehicles, etc. **2** (in *plural*) a series of these for horses, dogs, etc. at a fixed time on a regular course. **3** any contest or competition: *leadership race* ◊ *arms race*. **4** a determined or urgent effort, esp. one involving a number of people etc.: *the race to find a cure*. **5 a** a strong or rapid current flowing through a narrow channel in the sea or a river: *a tide race*. **b** the channel of a stream etc., esp. one built to lead water to or from a mill, mine, etc. **6** each of two grooved rings in a ball bearing. • *verb* (**races, raced, racing**) **1** take part in a race. **2** have a race with. **3** try to surpass in speed. **4** (foll. by *with*) compete in speed with. **5** cause (a horse, car, etc.) to race. **6** go at full speed: *raced down the highway*. **7** (esp. of the heart) beat very quickly. **8 a** (of an engine, wheel, etc.) run or revolve very swiftly, without resistance, or out of control. **b** cause (an engine, wheel, etc.) to do

this. **9** move (a person or thing) very quickly: *the victim was raced to hospital*.

race² *noun* **1** each of the major divisions of humankind, having distinct physical characteristics. **2** a tribe, nation, etc., regarded as of a distinct ethnic stock. **3** the fact or concept of division into races: *discrimination based on race*. **4** a genus, species, breed, or variety of animals, plants, or micro-organisms. **5** a group of persons, animals, or plants connected by common descent. **6** descent; kindred: *of noble race*. **7** a group of persons etc. with some common feature: *the race of poets*.

race car *noun* a car built for racing on a prepared track.

racecourse *noun* = RACETRACK.

racehorse *noun* a horse bred or kept for racing.

raceme *noun* a flower cluster with the separate flowers attached by short equal stalks at equal distances along a central stem, e.g. lily of the valley. [Say ray SEEM]

racer *noun* **1** a person or thing that races. **2** a horse, yacht, bicycle, etc., of a kind used for racing.

racetrack *noun* **1** a ground or track for horse racing. **2** a track or course used for any race.

raceway *noun* **1** a racetrack, esp. one used for harness racing. **2** a track or channel along which something runs.

racial *adjective* **1** of or concerning race: *racial diversity*. **2** on the grounds of or connected with difference in race: *racial discrimination*. **3** of or relating to racism; racist: *a racial incident*. ▶ **racially** *adverb*

racialism *noun* = RACISM. ▶ **racialist** *noun & adjective*

racily *adverb* in a racy manner or style.

raciness *noun* the fact or condition of being racy.

racing car *noun* = RACE CAR.

racing stripe *noun* a thin horizontal stripe of paint along the body of a car.

racism *noun* **1** a belief in the superiority of a particular race. **2** prejudice or antagonism towards other races based on this. ▶ **racist** *noun & adjective*

rack • *noun* **1** a framework usu. with rails, bars, hooks, etc., for holding or storing things: *roof rack* ◊ *coat rack*. **2** a cogged or toothed bar or rail engaging with a wheel or pinion etc., or using pegs to adjust the position of something. **3** *hist.* an instrument of torture stretching the victim's joints by the turning of rollers to which the wrists and ankles were tied. **4 a** a triangular frame in which the balls are arranged before the opening shot of a game of pool etc. **b** the balls positioned in this way. **5** a set of antlers. **6** a frame for holding animal fodder. **7** destruction: *rack and ruin*. **8** a roast of lamb cut from the loin. • *verb* **1** (of disease or pain) inflict suffering on. **2** *hist.* torture (a person) on the rack. **3** = RACK UP 1. **4** place in or on a rack. **5** shake violently. **6** injure by straining. **7** oppress (tenants) by exacting excessive rent. PHRASES **off the rack** (of an article of clothing) available for immediate purchase; ready-made: *buys all his suits off the rack*. **on the rack** in distress or under strain. **rack one's brains** make a great mental effort. **rack up 1** place (the balls for a game of pool etc.) in the rack. **2** accumulate (points etc.): *racked up 50 goals last season*. **3** run up (a bill, debt, etc.).

rack-and-pinion *adjective* (esp. of a steering system) using a rack and pinion (*see* RACK *noun* 2, PINION *noun*2).

SPELL CHECK
racket, racquet

Racquet is the usual Canadian spelling in "tennis racquet".

racket • *noun* **1** a loud unpleasant noise. **2** *informal* a scheme for obtaining money or attaining other ends by fraudulent and often violent means. **3** a form of organized crime. **4** *informal* an occupation or line of business: *starting up a new racket*. **5** = RACQUET. • *verb* (**rackets**, **racketed**, **racketing**) (often foll. by *along*, *around*) make a racket, esp. by moving noisily.

racketball *noun* = RACQUETBALL.

racketeer *noun* a person who makes money through dishonest or illegal activities. ▶ **racketeering** *noun*

rackety *adjective* characterized by noise, excitement, etc.: *the rackety clamour of the engines*.

raconteur *noun* a teller of anecdotes. [Say rack on TUR]

racoon *noun* = RACCOON.

SPELL CHECK
racquet, racket

The spelling is **racket** in "stop making such a racket" and "a criminal racket".

racquet *noun* **1** a bat with a round or oval frame strung with catgut, nylon, etc., used in tennis, squash, etc. **2** (in *plural*) a ball game for two or four persons played with racquets in a plain four-walled court. **3** a snowshoe resembling a racquet.

racquetball *noun* a game played with a small hard ball and a short-handled racquet in a four-walled handball court.

racy *adjective* (**racier**, **raciest**) **1** lively, entertaining, and usu. mildly sexually titillating: *the wit, racy energy, and swing of the music*. **2** having characteristic qualities in a high degree: *a racy flavour*.

rad • *noun* **1** *slang* a political radical. **2** (*plural* **rad**) radian. **3** a unit of absorbed dose of ionizing radiation, corresponding to the absorption of 0.01 joule per kilogram of absorbing material. **4** *informal* radiator. • *adjective* (**radder**, **raddest**) *slang* excellent.

radar *noun* **1** a method for detecting the position and speed of aircraft, ships, or other objects, by sending out pulses of high-frequency electromagnetic waves. **2** the apparatus used for this.

radar trap *noun* = SPEED TRAP.

raddled *adjective* untidy, unkempt.

radial • *adjective* **1** of, concerning, or in rays. **2 a** arranged like rays or radii; having the position or direction of a radius. **b** having spokes or radiating lines. **c** acting or moving along lines diverging from a centre. **3** relating to the radius, the thicker and shorter of the two bones in the human forearm: *radial artery*. **4** (of a vehicle tire) having the core fabric layers arranged radially at right angles to the circumference and the tread strengthened. • *noun* **1** a radial tire. **2** the radial nerve or artery. [Say RAY dee ul]

radial arm saw *noun* (also **radial saw**) a type of circular saw mounted on an arm that can be adjusted to various angles.

radially *adverb* in a radial manner; in the form of radii or rays. [Say RAY dee a lee]

radian *noun* *Math* a unit of angle, equal to an angle at the centre of a circle the arc of which is equal in length to the radius; 1 radian is the same as 57.296°. [Say RAY dee un]

radiance *noun* **1** light or heat as emitted or reflected by something: *the sun's radiance*. **2** great joy or love, apparent in someone's expression or bearing: *the radiance of her acting*. **3** a glowing quality of the skin, esp. as indicative of good health or youth. [Say RAY dee ince]

radiant *adjective* **1** emitting rays of light. **2** (of a person, a look, etc.) beaming with joy or hope or love. **3** (of beauty) splendid or dazzling. **4** (of light) issuing in rays. **5** operating radially. **6** extending radially; radiating. [Say RAY dee unt]

radiant energy *noun* energy in the form of radiation: *the earth emits radiant energy known as thermal radiation*.

radiantly *adverb* **1** in a bright or shining manner. **2** in a way that shows great happiness, love, or health: *she smiles radiantly*.

radiate • *verb* (**radiates**, **radiated**, **radiating**) **1 a** emit rays of light, heat, or other electromagnetic waves. **b** (of light or heat) be emitted in rays. **2** emit (light, heat, or sound) from a centre. **3** transmit or demonstrate (an emotion, feeling, etc.): *radiates happiness*. **4** diverge or cause to diverge or spread from a centre. • *adjective* having divergent rays or parts radially arranged. [Say RAY dee ate]

radiation *noun* **1** the emission of energy as electromagnetic waves or as moving subatomic particles, esp. high-energy particles which cause ionization: *the link between exposure to radiation and cancer*. **2** the energy transmitted in this way, esp. invisibly: *ultraviolet radiation*.

radiation sickness *noun* illness caused by exposure of the body to ionizing radiation, accompanied by nausea, hair loss, diarrhea, bleeding, and damage to the bone marrow and central nervous system.

radiation therapy *noun* = RADIOTHERAPY.

radiator *noun* **1** a person or thing that radiates. **2 a** a device for heating a room etc., consisting of a metal case through which hot water or steam circulates. **b** a usu. portable, esp. electric heater resembling this. **3** a device in a motor vehicle or aircraft with a large surface for cooling circulating water from the engine. [Say RAIDY ate er or RADDY ate er]

radical • *adjective* **1** of the root or roots; fundamental: *a radical error*. **2** far-reaching; thorough: *a radical change in policy*. **3 a** advocating thorough reform; holding extreme political views; revolutionary. **b** (of a measure etc.) advanced by or according to principles of this kind. **4** *Math* of the root of a number or quantity. **5** *slang* excellent, outstanding. **6** (of surgery etc.) seeking to ensure the removal of all diseased tissue. **7** *Botany* of, or springing direct from, the root. • *noun* **1** a person holding radical views or belonging to a radical party. **2** *Chemistry* **a** (in full **free radical**) an uncharged atom or group of atoms with one or more unpaired electrons. **b** an element or atom or a group of these normally forming part of a compound and remaining unaltered during the compound's ordinary chemical changes. **3** the root of a word. **4** *Math* a quantity forming or expressed as the root of another. **b** a radical sign. ▶ **radicalism** *noun* **radicalization** *noun* **radicalize** *verb* (**radicalizes**, **radicalized**, **radicalizing**) **radically** *adverb*

radical sign *noun* a symbol, $\sqrt{\ }$, $\sqrt[3]{\ }$, etc., indicating the square, cube, etc., root of the number following.

radicchio *noun* (*plural* **radicchios**) a variety of chicory with dark red leaves, used esp. in salads. [Say ruh DEEKY oh]

radii *plural of* RADIUS. [Say RAY dee eye]

radio • *noun* (*plural* **radios**) **1 a** the transmission and reception of sound messages etc. by electromagnetic waves of radio frequency. **b** an apparatus for receiving, broadcasting, or transmitting radio signals. **c** a

message sent or received by radio. **2** sound broadcasting in general: *prefers radio to television*. **3** a broadcasting station or network: *CBC Radio*. • *verb* (**radioes, radioed, radioing**) **1** send (a message) by radio. **2** send a message to (a person) by radio. • *adjective* **1** of, relating to, or transmitting radio signals: *a radio station*. **2** of or using radio frequencies. **3** (of a vehicle) equipped with a two-way radio for use in communication: *radio car*.

radio- *combining form* **1** denoting radio or broadcasting. **2 a** connected with radioactivity. **b** denoting artificially prepared radioisotopes of elements: *radio-cesium*. **3** connected with rays or radiation.

radioactive *adjective* of or exhibiting radioactivity. ▸ **radioactively** *adverb*

radioactivity *noun* **1** the spontaneous disintegration of atomic nuclei, with the emission of usu. penetrating radiation or particles. **2** radioactive substances, or the radiation they emit.

radio astronomy *noun* the branch of astronomy which uses radio frequencies rather than visible light to study the universe.

radiocarbon *noun* a radioactive isotope of carbon.

radiocarbon dating *noun* a method of estimating the age of organic archaeological specimens by determining the ratio of carbon-14 (which decays at a known rate) to another isotope which remains constant.

radio collar *noun* a collar equipped with a small radio transmitter, used e.g. for tracking an animal's movement in the wild. ▸ **radio-collar** *verb*

radio-controlled *adjective* (of a model aircraft etc.) controlled from a distance by radio.

radio frequency *noun* (*plural* **radio frequencies**) the frequency band of telecommunication, ranging from 10^4–10^{11} or 10^{12} Hz.

radiograph • *noun* a picture obtained by X-rays, gamma rays, etc. • *verb* obtain a picture of by X-rays, gamma ray, etc. ▸ **radiographer** *noun* **radiographic** *adjective* **radiography** *noun* [Say RADIO graph, raidy OGRA fur, radio GRAPHIC, raidy OGRA fee]

radioisotope *noun* a radioactive isotope. [Say radio ICE uh tope]

radiological *adjective* having to do with the scientific study of X-rays and other high-energy radiation, esp. as used in medicine. [Say raidy a LOGICAL]

radiologist *noun* a medical practitioner who specializes in the scientific study of X-rays and other high-energy radiation. [Say raidy OLLA jist]

radiology *noun* the scientific study of X-rays and other high-energy radiation, esp. as used in medicine. [Say raidy OLLA jee]

radiometer *noun* an instrument for measuring the intensity or force of radioactivity. ▸ **radiometric** *adjective* [Say raidy OMMA tur, radio METRIC]

radiometric dating *noun* a method of dating geological specimens by determining the relative proportions of the isotopes of a radioactive element present in a sample.

radio telescope *noun* a directional aerial system for collecting and analyzing radiation in the radio frequency range from stars etc.

radiotherapist *noun* a doctor who treats cancer and other diseases by X-rays or other forms of radiation.

radiotherapy *noun* the treatment of cancer and other diseases by X-rays or other forms of radiation.

radish *noun* (*plural* **radishes**) a small, round, red, fleshy root with a pungent taste, eaten esp. raw in salads.

radium *noun* a radioactive metallic element originally obtained from pitchblende etc., used esp. in luminous materials and in radiotherapy. [Say RAY dee um]

radius *noun* (*plural* **radii** or **radiuses**) **1** *Math* **a** a straight line from the centre to the circumference of a circle or sphere. **b** a radial line from the focus to any point of a curve. **c** the length of the radius of a circle etc. **2** a usu. specified distance from a centre in all directions: *within a radius of 20 miles*. **3 a** the thicker and shorter of the two bones in the human forearm (*compare* ULNA). **b** the corresponding bone in a vertebrate's foreleg or a bird's wing. **4** any of the five arm-like structures of a starfish. **5 a** any of a set of lines diverging from a point like the radii of a circle. **b** an object of this kind, e.g. a spoke. **6 a** the outer rim of a composite flower head, e.g. a daisy. **b** a radiating branch of an umbel. [Say RAY dee us; for *radii* say RAY dee eye]

radon *noun* a naturally occurring gaseous radioactive inert element arising from the disintegration of radium, and used in radiotherapy. [Say RAY don]

RAF *abbreviation* (in the UK) Royal Air Force.

raffia *noun* **1** a palm tree, native to tropical Africa and Madagascar, with a short trunk and very long leaves. **2** the fibre from these leaves, used for making hats, baskets, and mats. [Say RAFFY uh]

raffish *adjective* disreputable, esp. in an attractive manner: *he had a cosmopolitan, slightly raffish air*. ▸ **raffishness** *noun*

raffle • *noun* a fundraising lottery with goods as prizes. • *verb* (**raffles, raffled, raffling**) (often foll. by *off*) dispose of by means of a raffle.

raft[1] • *noun* **1** a flat floating structure of logs, barrels, etc. tied together and used as a boat or a floating platform. **2** a lifeboat or small (often inflatable) boat, esp. for use in emergencies. **3** *Forestry* a mass of squared timber or logs fastened together for transportation on water. **4** a large floating accumulation of fallen trees, ice, etc. • *verb* **1** transport as or on a raft. **2** *Forestry* move (logs) by means of a raft. **3** cross (water) on a raft. **4** form into a raft. **5** use a raft; travel by raft. **6** engage in the sport of whitewater rafting. **7** (of an ice floe) be driven on top of or underneath another floe.

raft[2] *noun* (foll. by *of*) *informal* a large number or amount.

rafter[1] *noun* each of the usu. sloping beams forming the framework of a roof.

rafter[2] *noun* **1** a person who travels by raft, esp. to flee a country. **2** a person who engages in whitewater rafting. **3** *Forestry* a person who rafts timber.

raftered *adjective* **1** (of a room or ceiling) having exposed rafters. **2** (of ice) forced into overlapping layers.

rafting *noun* the sport or pastime of travelling down a river on a raft.

rag[1] *noun* **1** a torn, frayed, or worn piece of cloth. **2 a** (in *plural*) old or worn clothes. **b** *informal* a garment of any kind. **3** *derogatory* a newspaper or magazine, esp. one regarded as inferior or worthless. **4** an odd scrap; an irregular piece. **5** a jagged projection, esp. on metal.

rag[2] *verb* (**rags, ragged, ragging**) *slang* scold; reprove severely; criticize. ▸ PHRASES **rag on** *slang* nag, bother, scold. **rag the puck 1** *Hockey* keep possession of the puck by skilful stickhandling so as to waste time. **2** *Cdn slang* waste time intentionally.

rag[3] *noun* a ragtime composition or tune.

ragamuffin *noun* **1** a person in ragged dirty clothes, esp. a child. **2** = RAGGAMUFFIN.

rage • *noun* **1** fierce or violent anger. **2** a fit of this. **3** the violent action of a natural force: *the rage of the storm*. **4** (foll. by *for*) **a** a vehement desire or passion. **b** a widespread temporary enthusiasm or fashion. • *verb* (**rages, raged, raging**) **1** be full of anger. **2** (often foll.

by *at, against*) speak furiously or madly; rave. **3** (of wind, battle, debate, fever, etc.) be violent; be at its height; continue unchecked. PHRASES **all the rage** very popular, fashionable.

ragga *noun* a style of popular music combining elements of reggae and hip hop.

raggamuffin *noun* **1** an exponent or follower of ragga, typically dressing in ragged clothes. **2** = RAGGA.

ragged *adjective* **1** (of clothes etc.) torn; frayed. **2** rough; shaggy; hanging in tufts. **3** (of a person) in ragged clothes. **4** with a broken or jagged outline or surface. **5** *Printing* (esp. of a right margin) not justified and so uneven. **6** faulty; imperfect. **7** (of a sound) rough and uneven: *ragged breathing*. **8** exhausted: *I've been run ragged*. ▶ **raggedly** *adverb* **raggedness** *noun* **raggedy** *adjective* [Say RAG id]

ragging *noun* **1** the process or technique of decorating a wall etc. by applying or smudging paint with a rag or piece of material. **2** the effect or finish so produced.

raggle-taggle *adjective* constituted of an assortment of (often disreputable) people; ragtag.

raging *adjective* extreme, very painful: *a raging headache*.

raglan *adjective* having or denoting sleeves attached to a garment by a diagonal seam running from the neck to the underarm.

ragout *noun* a stew. [Say rag OO]

rag rug *noun* a small rug made from strips of rags woven together.

rags-to-riches *adjective* denoting a person who starts out poor and ends up rich, or a story describing such a development.

ragtag • *adjective* (also **ragtail**) **1** disorganized, not well matched, scraggly. **2** ragged or shabby; unkempt. • *noun derogatory* the rabble or riff-raff.

ragtime • *noun* a style of popular music characterized by a syncopated melodic line and regularly accented accompaniment, evolved by American black musicians in the 1890s and played esp. on the piano. • *adjective* of or resembling ragtime.

ragtop *noun* **1** a convertible car with a top made of cloth. **2** the top of such a car.

ragweed *noun* a North American plant of the daisy family, whose tiny green flowers produce much pollen, making it a major cause of hayfever in some areas.

rah *interjection informal* an expression of encouragement, approval, etc.

raid • *noun* **1** a rapid surprise attack, esp.: **a** by troops, aircraft, etc. in warfare. **b** to commit a crime or do harm. **c** *informal* as a prank or to gain food, drink, etc.: *a raid on the kitchen*. **2** a surprise attack by police etc. to arrest suspected persons or seize illicit goods. **3** *Stock Market* an attempt to lower prices by the concerted selling of shares. **4** the luring away of a competitor's workers, members, etc. • *verb* make a raid on (a person, place, or thing). ▶ **raider** *noun*

rail • *noun* **1** a level or sloping bar or series of bars in a fence, attached to a wall, etc. **2** a steel bar or continuous line of bars laid on the ground, usu. as one of a pair forming a railway track. **3** a railway: *send it by rail ◊ rail fares*. **4** (in *plural*) the inside boundary fence of a racetrack. **5** a bird with drab grey and brown plumage and a long bill, often found in marshes. • *verb* **1** furnish with a rail or rails. **2** (usu. foll. by *in, off*) enclose with rails: *a small space was railed off*. **3** (often foll. by *at, against*) complain vehemently; rant. PHRASES **off the rails** deranged.

rail fence *noun* a fence made of wooden posts and rails.

railhead *noun* **1** the furthest point reached by a

railway. **2** the point on a railway at which road transport of goods begins.

railing *noun* **1** a handrail. **2 a** (often in *plural*) a fence or barrier made of rails. **b** the material for these.

railroad • *noun* = RAILWAY. • *verb* **1** (often foll. by *to, into, through*, etc.) rush or coerce (a person or thing): *railroaded me into going ◊ railroaded it through the legislature*. **2** send (a person) to prison by means of false evidence. ▶ **railroader** *noun*

railway *noun esp. Cdn & Brit.* **1** a track or set of tracks made of steel rails upon which trains run. **2** such a system operated by a single company. **3** the organization and personnel required for its working. **4** a similar set of tracks for other vehicles etc.

railwayman *noun* (*plural* **railwaymen**) *esp. Brit. & Cdn* a railway employee.

railway yard *noun* (also **rail yard**) the area where rolling stock is kept and made up into trains.

raiment *noun literary & archaic* clothing. [Say RAY m'nt]

SPELL CHECK ABC✓
rain, rein, reign

The horse strap is a **rein**, which is also the spelling used in "rein something in". A Queen who is ruling is **reigning**. Canadian Confederation happened during the **reign** of Queen Victoria.

---

rain • *noun* **1** the condensed moisture of the atmosphere falling visibly in separate drops. **2** (in *plural*) **a** (**the rains**) the rainy season in tropical countries. **b** rainfalls. **3 a** falling liquid or solid particles or objects. **b** a large or overwhelming quantity: *a rain of congratulations*. • *verb* **1** (of rain) fall. **2 a** fall like rain: *tears rained down their cheeks*. **b** (preceded by *it* as subject) send in large quantities: *it is raining invitations*. **3** send down like rain; lavishly bestow: *rained blows upon him*. **4** (of the sky, clouds, etc.) send down rain. PHRASES **rain on someone's parade** *informal* spoil a person's good time. **rain out** (esp. in *passive*) cause (an event etc.) to be terminated or cancelled because of rain. **rain or shine** whether it rains or not.

rainbow • *noun* **1** an arch of colours (conventionally red, orange, yellow, green, blue, indigo, violet) formed in the sky (or across a waterfall etc.) opposite the sun by reflection, twofold refraction, and dispersion of the sun's rays in falling rain or in spray or mist. **2** a similar effect formed by the moon's rays. **3** a wide variety of related things: *a rainbow of colours*. **4** = RAINBOW TROUT. • *adjective* many-coloured. PHRASES **chase a rainbow** pursue an illusory goal.

rainbow coalition *noun* a loose coalition or alliance of several different left-of-centre political groups, representing social, ethnic, and other minorities.

rainbow trout *noun* (*plural* **rainbow trout**) a large trout originally of the Pacific coast of North America, but now widespread throughout the continent.

rain check *noun* **1** a ticket given for later use when a sports or other outdoor event is interrupted or postponed by rain. **2** a promise that an offer will be maintained though deferred. **3** a voucher given to a customer when a sale item sells out, entitling the customer to purchase the item at the sale price when more stock arrives. PHRASES **take a rain check on** reserve the right to take up (an offer) at a later date.

raincoat *noun* a waterproof or water-resistant coat.

raindrop *noun* a single drop of rain.

rainfall *noun* **1** a fall of rain. **2** the quantity of rain falling within a given area in a given time.

rainforest *noun* a luxuriant forest in an area of heavy rainfall with little seasonal variation.

rainmaker *noun* **1** a person who seeks to cause rain to

fall, either by magic or by a technique such as seeding. **2** *slang* a person who is highly successful esp. in business. ▶ **rainmaking** *noun*

rainout *noun* **1** the cancellation or premature ending of an event because of rain. **2** radioactive debris or other atmospheric pollution carried to the earth's surface by precipitation.

rainproof *adjective* (esp. of a building, garment, etc.) resistant to rainwater.

rainstorm *noun* a storm with heavy rain.

rainwater *noun* water obtained from collected rain, as distinct from a well etc.

rainwear *noun* clothes for wearing in the rain.

rainy *adjective* (**rainier, rainiest**) **1** (of weather, a climate, day, region, etc.) in or on which rain is falling or much rain usually falls. **2** (of cloud, wind, etc.) laden with or bringing rain.

SPELL CHECK
raise, raze

To destroy something completely or tear something down is to **raze** it.

---

raise • *verb* (**raises, raised, raising**) **1** lift or move to a higher position or level. **2** set upright. **3** increase the amount, level, or strength of. **4** promote to a higher rank. **5** cause to be heard, felt, or considered: *doubts have been raised*. **6** build (a structure). **7** collect or levy (money or resources). **8** bring up (a child). **9** breed or grow (animals or plants). **10** wake from sleep or bring back from death. **11** abandon or force to abandon (a blockade, embargo, etc.). **12** drive (an animal) from its lair. **13** (foll. by *to*) *Mathematics* multiply (a quantity) to a specified power. **14** *Curling* strike (a rock) with another rock to move it deeper on the sheet. • *noun* **1** an increase in salary. **2** *Curling* the act or an instance of striking a rock with another rock to move it deeper on the sheet. PHRASES **raise from the dead** restore to life. **raise one's glass to** drink the health of. **raise one's hand to** make as if to strike (a person). **raise one's hat** (often foll. by *to*) remove it momentarily as a gesture of courtesy or respect. **raise hell** (or **the devil**) *informal* make a disturbance. **raise a laugh** cause others to laugh. **raise a person's spirits** give him or her new courage or cheerfulness. **raise a stink** create a fuss or disturbance. **raise one's voice** speak, esp. louder. ▶ **raiser** *noun* (also in *combination*)

raisin *noun* **1** a partially dried grape. **2** the dark purplish-brown colour of raisins. ▶ **raisiny** *adjective*

raison d'être *noun* (*plural* **raisons d'être**) a purpose or reason that accounts for or justifies or originally caused a thing's existence: *NATO seemed to lose its raison d'être with the end of the Cold War*. [Say raise on DETRA (with ON as in French)]

raita *noun* an Indian side dish of chopped cucumber (or other vegetables) and spices in yogourt. [Say ruh EET uh]

Raj *noun* (**the Raj**) *hist.* the period of British rule in the Indian subcontinent before 1947. [Say RAWZH]

raja *noun* (also **rajah**) *hist.* **1** an Indian king or prince. **2** a minor official or noble in India. **3** a Malay or Javanese chief. [Say RAWZH uh]

rake¹ • *noun* **1** an implement consisting of a pole with a hooked crossbar or fine tines at the end, for drawing together fallen leaves etc. or smoothing loose soil or gravel. **2** a similar implement used for other purposes, e.g. by a croupier drawing in money at a gaming table. • *verb* (**rakes, raked, raking**) **1** collect or gather or remove with or as with a rake. **2** make tidy or smooth with a rake: *raked it level*. **3** use a rake. **4** search a place for something: *I raked through a clutter of drawers*. **5 a** direct gunfire along (a line) from end to end.

b sweep with the eyes. **6** scratch or scrape esp. in fingernails: *the cat raked his face with its claws*. PHRASES **rake in** *informal* amass (profits etc.). **rake up** (or **over**) revive the memory of (past quarrels, grievances, etc.).

rake² *noun* a man who is fashionable or stylish but immoral or promiscuous.

rake³ • *verb* (**rakes, raked, raking**) set or be set at a sloping angle. • *noun* **1** a raking position or build. **2** the amount by which a thing rakes. **3** the slope of the stage or the auditorium in a theatre.

raked *adjective* placed on a slope: *raked seating*.

raker *noun* a person or thing that rakes something.

rakish¹ *adjective* (of a man) fashionable or stylish but immoral or promiscuous. ▶ **rakishly** *adverb*

rakish² *adjective* dashing; jaunty: *a hat at a rakish angle*.

raku *noun* a kind of Japanese lead-glazed earthenware, primarily for use in the tea ceremony. [Say RACK oo]

rallentando *adverb* & *adjective* with a gradual decrease of speed. [Say ral in TAN doe]

rally¹ • *verb* (**rallies, rallied, rallying**) **1** (with reference to troops) bring or come together again so as to continue fighting. **2** bring or come together as support or for united action: *his family rallied round*. **3** recover or cause to recover in health. **4** (of share, currency, or commodity prices) increase after a fall. • *noun* (*plural* **rallies**) **1** a mass meeting held as a protest or in support of a cause. **2** a quick or marked recovery. **3** *Baseball* the scoring of two or more runs in one inning. **4** *Tennis etc.* an extended exchange of strokes between players. **5** a competition for motor vehicles, usu. over public roads or rough terrain.

rally² *verb* (**rallies, rallied, rallying**) subject to good-humoured ridicule.

rallying cry *noun* a slogan.

RAM *abbreviation* *Computing* random access memory.

ram • *noun* **1** an uncastrated male sheep. **2** *hist.* = BATTERING RAM. • *verb* (**rams, rammed, ramming**) **1** force or squeeze into place by pressure. **2** (usu. foll. by *down, in, into*) beat down or drive in by heavy blows. **3** (of a ship, vehicle, etc.) strike violently, crash against. **4** (foll. by *against, at, on, into*) dash or violently impel. **5** (foll. by *through*) push (a bill etc.) through a legislature. PHRASES **ram home** stress forcefully (an argument, lesson, etc.).

-rama *combining form* *informal* or *jocular* forming nouns denoting abundance, a spectacle, extravaganza, etc., or the place containing it: *nostalgia-rama*.

Ramadan *noun* the ninth month of the Muslim year, during which strict fasting is observed from sunrise to sunset. [Say RAMMA dan]

ramble • *verb* (**rambles, rambled, rambling**) **1** walk for pleasure, with or without a definite route. **2** (often foll. by *on*) talk or write disconnectedly and usu. at length. **3** (esp. of buildings, paths, etc.) spread in various directions with no regular pattern. • *noun* a walk taken for pleasure. ▶ **rambler** *noun*

rambling *adjective* **1** wandering. **2** disconnected, incoherent. **3** (of a house, street, etc.) irregularly arranged. **4** (of a plant) straggling, climbing.

rambunctious *adjective* *informal* **1** active; full of energy: *Maeve and Kate were too rambunctious to play in the house*. **2** boisterous; unruly; difficult to control. ▶ **rambunctiously** *adverb* **rambunctiousness** *noun*

ramen *plural noun* quick-cooking noodles, usu. served in a broth with meat and vegetables. [Say ROM in]

ramification *noun* **1** a consequence of an action or event, esp. when complex or unwelcome: *any change is bound to have legal ramifications*. **2** a subdivision of a complex structure or process perceived as comparable to a tree's branches: *an extended family with its*

ramifications of neighbouring in-laws. [Say ramma fuh KAY sh'n]

ramify *verb* (**ramifies, ramified, ramifying**) form branches or subdivisions or offshoots; branch out: *a solution that causes a ramifying series of new problems.* [Say RAMMA fie]

ramp • *noun* **1** a slope for joining two levels of ground, floor, etc.: *wheelchair ramp.* **2** a short sloping road leading on or off a highway. **3** movable stairs for entering or leaving an aircraft. **4** the apron of an airfield. **5** an access point to the Internet. • *verb* **1** (usu. as **ramped** *adjective*) furnish or build with a ramp. **2** (often foll. by *up*) increase; gradually build: *use of the term "information highway" has ramped up from zero to several hundred a month.*

rampage • *verb* (**rampages, rampaged, rampaging**) rush wildly or violently about: *a herd of rampaging elephants ◊ rioters rampaged through the city.* • *noun* a period of uncontrolled, often prolonged, unruly or violent behaviour, typically involving many people: *thugs went on the rampage and wrecked a classroom.*

rampant *adjective* **1** (of something bad) existing or spreading everywhere uncontrollably: *rampant corruption ◊ unemployment is now rampant in most of Europe.* **2** rank, luxuriant: *rich soil soon becomes home to rampant weeds.* ▶ **rampantly** *adverb* [Say RAMP int]

rampart *noun* **1 a** a defensive wall with a broad top and usu. a stone parapet, built around a castle, fort, etc. **b** a walkway on top of such a wall. **2** a defence or protection: *from now on religion would be a rallying point and a rampart against the absolutism of the occupying power.* **3** (in *plural*) *Cdn* (*BC, Alberta,* & *North*) steep rock walls, as found on either side of a river gorge.

ramrod • *noun* a rod for ramming down the charge of a muzzle-loading firearm. • *adjective* very straight: *ramrod posture.* • *adverb* like a ramrod: *ramrod straight.* • *verb* (**ramrods, ramrodded, ramrodding**) force or drive as with a ramrod: *ramrodded the bill through the legislature.*

ramshackle *adjective* **1** (of a house etc.) tumbledown, rickety. **2** (of an organization or system) poorly designed or organized.

ran *past of* RUN.

ranch • *noun* (*plural* **ranches**) **1 a** a cattle-breeding farm esp. in the western US and Canada. **b** a farm where other animals are bred: *mink ranch.* **2** (also **ranch house, ranch home,** or **ranch bungalow**) **a** a house on a cattle ranch, usu. of one storey and with a long, low design. **b** a similar type of house, usu. found in the suburbs. **3** a type of thick, white salad dressing made with sour cream. • *verb* (**ranches, ranched, ranching**) **1** work on or run a ranch. **2** breed or rear (animals) on or as on a ranch. **3** use (land) as a ranch.

rancher *noun* **1** a person who owns or works on a ranch. **2** a ranch-style house.

ranching *noun* the activity of running a ranch: *cattle ranching.*

ranchland *noun* land used for or suitable for ranching.

rancid *adjective* (of fats, oils, or fatty meats such as bacon) smelling or tasting rank and stale as a result of oxidation. [Say RAN sid]

rancorous *adjective* bitter, resentful, full of spite. ▶ **rancorously** *adverb*

SPELL CHECK
rancour, rancorous

Note that Canadians normally put a *u* in *rancour*, but always remove that *u* from *rancorous.*

rancour *noun* (also esp. *US* **rancor**) bitterness,

resentfulness, spitefulness: *she learned to accept criticism without rancour.* [Sounds like RANKER]

R & B *abbreviation* (also **r & b**) rhythm and blues.

R & D *abbreviation* (also **R and D**) research and development.

random *adjective* **1** made, done, etc., without method or conscious choice: *random selection.* **2** *Statistics* **a** with equal chances for each item. **b** given by a random process: *random sample.* PHRASES **at random** without aim or purpose or principle. ▶ **randomly** *adverb* **randomness** *noun*

random access *noun* a process that allows information in a computer to be stored or recovered quickly without reading through items stored previously.

randomize *verb* (**randomizes, randomized, randomizing**) use a method in an experiment, a piece of research, etc. that gives every item an equal chance of being considered; put things in random order.

R and R *abbreviation* (also **R & R**) **1** rest and recreation. **2** rest and relaxation. **3** rest and recuperation. **4** rescue and resuscitation.

randy *adjective* (**randier, randiest**) *informal* **1** lustful; eager for sexual gratification. **2** bawdy, risqué.

rang[1] *past of* RING[2].

rang[2] *noun* *Cdn* (*Que.*) *hist.* Surveying a row of long lots, usu. along a road. [Sounds like WRONG]

range • *noun* **1** the area of variation between limits on a particular scale: *that car's outside my price range.* **2** a set of different things of the same general type. **3** the scope or extent of a person's or thing's abilities or capacity. **4** the distance within which something is able to operate or be effective. **5 a** a row, series, line, or tier, esp. of mountains or buildings. **b** *Cdn* a row of prison cells. **6** a large area of open land for grazing or hunting. **7** an area used as a testing ground for military equipment. **8** an area with targets for shooting practice. **9** the area over which a plant or animal is distributed. **10** an electric or gas stove. **11** *Cdn* (*Que.* & *Ont.*) a row of lots forming a concession. **12** *N Amer.* (*West*) a series of townships extending north and south parallel to the principal meridian of a survey. • *verb* (**ranges, ranged, ranging**) **1 a** vary or extend between limits: *prices range between $7 and $10.* **b** run in a line: *ranges north and south.* **2 a** place or arrange in a row or ranks or in a specified order: *flowerpots ranged in rows.* **b** place or align (oneself) with a certain group, cause, etc.: *has ranged herself with the Opposition.* **3** rove, wander: *ranged through the woods.* **4** traverse in all directions: *ranging the woods.* **5** *Printing* **a** make (type) lie flush at the ends of successive lines. **b** (of type) lie flush. **6 a** (of a gun) send a projectile over a specified distance: *ranges over a mile.* **b** (of a projectile) cover a specified distance. **c** obtain the range of a target by adjustment after firing past it or short of it.

rangefinder *noun* an instrument for estimating the distance of an object, esp. one to be shot at or photographed.

rangeland *noun* an extensive area of open country used for grazing or hunting animals.

ranger *noun* **1 a** = FOREST RANGER. **b** (also **park ranger**) = PARK WARDEN. **2** a member of a body of armed men, esp. a mounted soldier. **3** (**Ranger**) *Cdn hist.* a member of the Newfoundland Rangers (1935-49), a police force which served those parts of Newfoundland and Labrador outside the jurisdiction of the St. John's police force. **4** *Cdn* (*North*) an Indian or Inuit who serves as a military scout or observer on a voluntary basis. **5** (**Ranger**) *Cdn & Brit.* a member of the senior branch of the Girl Guides, aged 15 or older.

rangy[1] *adjective* (**rangier, rangiest**) **1** (of a person) tall and slim. **2** (of an animal) having a long, slender

form. **3** having a tendency or ability to range or wander about. [Say RANGE ee]

rangy² *adjective* (**rangier, rangiest**) (of a person, esp. a child) wild; uncontrollable. [Say RANG ee]

rank¹ • *noun* **1 a** a position in a hierarchy, a grade of advancement. **b** a distinct social class: *people of all ranks*. ● a grade of dignity or achievement in the top rank of performers. **d** high social position: *persons of rank*. **e** a place in a scale. **2** a row or line. **3** a single line of soldiers drawn up abreast. **4** order, array. • *verb* **1** have rank or place: *ranks next to the king*. **2** classify, give a certain grade to. **3** arrange (esp. soldiers) in a rank or ranks. **PHRASES** **break rank** (or **ranks**) **1** fail to remain in line. **2** fail to maintain solidarity. **close ranks** maintain solidarity. **the ranks 1** the common soldiers, i.e. privates and corporals. **2** a group of people of a specified type: *joined the ranks of the unemployed*. **rise from the ranks 1** (of a private or a non-commissioned officer) receive a commission. **2** (of a self-made man or woman) advance by one's own efforts.

rank² *adjective* **1** (of vegetation) growing too thickly and coarsely: : *an area overgrown with rank grass and nettles*. **2** foul-smelling, offensive: *the bay is deceptively shallow and has a rank smell at low tide*. **3** complete, unmistakable: *rank amateur*.

rank and file *noun* (usu. treated as *plural*) **1** the ordinary soldiers who are not officers. **2** the ordinary members of any group or society as opposed to the leaders.

ranking • *noun* ordering by rank; classification. • *adjective* having a high rank or position.

rankle *verb* (**rankles, rankled, rankling**) **1** (of envy, disappointment, etc., or their cause) cause persistent annoyance or resentment. **2** (of an experience, event, etc.) cause, or continue to cause, bad, esp. bitter feelings in (a person).

ransack *verb* **1** pillage or plunder (a house, country, etc.). **2** thoroughly search (a place, a receptacle, a person's pockets, one's conscience, etc.).

ransom • *noun* a sum of money or other payment demanded or paid for the release of a prisoner or hostage. • *verb* buy the freedom or restoration of.

rant • *verb* (often foll. by *about, on*) speak vehemently or wildly, esp. at length. • *noun* a piece of ranting, a tirade. **PHRASES** **rant and rave** express anger noisily and forcefully. ▶ **ranter** *noun*

rap • *noun* **1** a quick sharp blow or knock. **2** *slang* **a** criticism, punishment. **b** a charge, accusation, or reputed fault: *a drunk driving rap ◊ pinned the rap on us*. **3** *slang* a conversation: *rap session*. **4 a** (also **rap music**) a style of popular music characterized by the rhythmic and usu. rapid reciting of rhyming lyrics against an often sampled background with a pronounced beat. **b** the reciting of lyrics in rap music. **c** a rap song. • *verb* (**raps, rapped, rapping**) **1** strike briskly. **2** knock; make a sharp tapping sound: *rapped on the table*. **3** *informal* **a** criticize adversely. **b** accuse, charge. **4** *slang* talk. **5 a** perform rap music, talk in the style of rap. **b** utter in this style. **PHRASES** **beat the rap** escape punishment. **rap a person's knuckles** (also **rap a person on the knuckles**) **1** strike a person's knuckles sharply. **2** criticize or reprimand a person. **rap on the knuckles** a reprimand or reproof. **rap out 1** utter (an oath, order, etc.) abruptly or on the spur of the moment. **2** express or reproduce (a rhythm, signal, etc.) by raps. **take the rap** suffer the consequences.

rapacious *adjective* greedy, grasping, extortionate: *a rapacious businessman*. ▶ **rapacity** *noun* [Say ruh PAY shuss, ruh PASS it ee]

rape¹ • *noun* **1** the action or an act of forcing a person, esp. a woman or girl, to have sexual intercourse unwillingly. **2** (often foll. by *of*) plunder, abuse, or violation: *the rape of our natural resources*. • *verb* (**rapes, raped, raping**) **1** commit rape on (a person, usu. a woman). **2** spoil or destroy: *polluters are raping the land*.

rape² *noun* a plant of the cabbage family, the seeds of which yield oil used in cooking etc. *See also* CANOLA. **rapeseed** *noun* **1** the seed of the rape plant. **2** the rape plant.

rapeseed oil *noun* (also **rape oil**) an oil made from rapeseed and used as a lubricant and in foodstuffs.

rape-shield *noun* (used as an *adjective*) designating legislation limiting the allowable questioning of the victim of an alleged sexual assault on matters of personal esp. sexual history.

rapid • *adjective* **1** quick, swift. **2** acting or completed in a short time. **3** (of a slope) descending steeply. **4** *Photography* fast. • *noun* (usu. in *plural*) a section of a river with a swift turbulent current.

rapid eye movement *noun* a type of jerky movement of the eyes during periods of dreaming. Abbreviation: **REM**.

rapid-fire *adjective* fired, uttered, etc., in quick succession: *a rapid-fire exchange*.

rapidity *noun* the quality of being rapid; swiftness of motion or action. [Say ruh PIDDA tee]

rapidly *adverb* quickly: *the disease spread rapidly*.

rapid transit *noun* high-speed urban transportation of passengers, usu. by rail.

rapier • *noun* a light slender sword used for thrusting. • *adjective* very quick and intelligent: *rapier wit*. [Say RAY pee er]

rapini *plural noun* the edible leaves of an immature white turnip. [Say ruh PEENY]

rapist *noun* a person who commits rape.

rappel • *verb* (**rappels, rappelled, rappelling**) descend a steep rock face by using a doubled rope coiled round the body and fixed at a higher point. • *noun* a descent made by rappelling. [Say ruh PEL]

rapper *noun* **1** a performer of rap music. **2** a person or thing that raps.

rapport *noun* a relationship or communication, esp. when useful and harmonious: *establish a rapport*. [Say ruh PORE]

rapprochement *noun* the establishment or resumption of harmonious relations, esp. between nations: *the visit may imperil the current atmosphere of rapprochement between the two superpowers*. [Say ra prosh MON (with ON as in French)]

rap sheet *noun* *slang* an official record of one's criminal activities.

rapt *adjective* fully absorbed or intent, enraptured: *listen with rapt attention*.

raptor *noun* **1** any bird of prey, e.g. an eagle, owl, falcon, or hawk. **2** *informal* = VELOCIRAPTOR.

rapture *noun* **1 a** ecstatic delight, mental transport. **b** (in *plural*) great pleasure or enthusiasm or the expression of it. **2** (**Rapture**) (in some Christian beliefs) the transporting of believers to heaven at the Second Coming of Christ. ▶ **rapturous** *adjective* **rapturously** *adverb*

rare¹ *adjective* (**rarer, rarest**) **1** seldom done or found or occurring, uncommon. **2** of less than the usual density: *the rare atmosphere of the mountaintops*.

rare² *adjective* (**rarer, rarest**) (of meat) slightly cooked.

rare earth *noun* **1** a lanthanide element. **2** an oxide of such an element.

rarefied *adjective* (also **rarified**) **1** (of air, a gas, etc.) thinner or less dense than usual: *to cope with the rarefied atmosphere at higher altitudes, the body produces more red blood cells*. **2** often *ironic* distant from the lives and

R

concerns of ordinary people: *politicians sitting in the rarefied atmosphere of Ottawa may be out of touch with economic reality ◊ was able to explain the most rarefied scientific problems with clarity*. [Say RARE a fide]

rarely *adverb* **1** seldom; not often. **2** in an unusual degree; exceptionally.

raring *adjective informal* enthusiastic, eager: *raring to go*.

rarity *noun* (*plural* **rarities**) **1** the state or quality of being rare. **2** an uncommon thing, esp. one valued for being rare.

rascal *noun often jocular* a dishonest or mischievous person, esp. a child. ▶ **rascally** *adjective*

rash¹ *adjective* reckless, hasty; acting or done without due consideration.

rash² *noun* (*plural* **rashes**) **1** an eruption of the skin in spots or patches. **2** (usu. foll. by *of*) a sudden widespread phenomenon, esp. of something unwelcome: *a rash of robberies*.

rashly *adverb* in a rash, reckless, or hasty manner.

rashness *noun* the quality of being rash; undue haste or boldness.

rasp • *noun* **1** a harsh, grating noise: *a cracking falsetto voice which veers between a squeak and a rasp*. **2** a coarse file for scraping, filing, or rubbing down objects of wood or metal etc. • *verb* **1 a** scrape something with a rasp in order to make it smoother: *we had the dog's teeth rasped*. **b** scrape or rub something in a painful or unpleasant way: *the coarse grass rasped my feet*. **2** make a harsh grating sound: *could hear a saxophone rasping in the distance*.

raspberry • *noun* (*plural* **raspberries**) **1 a** a soft edible berry consisting of a cluster of red drupelets. **b** the bramble that bears this fruit. **2** the deep red colour of a raspberry. **3** *informal* a sputtering sound made with the lips and tongue expressing dislike, derision, or disapproval. • *adjective* like a raspberry; deep red.

raspy *adjective* (**raspier**, **raspiest**) (of someone's voice) having a rough sound, as if the person has a sore throat.

Rastafarian (also **Rasta**) • *noun* a member of a sect of Jamaican origin regarding blacks as a chosen people and the former Emperor Haile Selassie of Ethiopia (d. 1975, entitled *Ras Tafari*) as God. • *adjective* of this sect. ▶ **Rastafarianism** *noun* [Say rasta FAIRY un]

raster *noun* a pattern of horizontal lines of pixels composing an image on a cathode ray tube display or for printing etc.: *raster graphics*.

rat • *noun* **1 a** a rodent resembling a large mouse, with a pointed snout and a long sparsely haired tail. **b** a muskrat or similar rodent. **2** a deserter from a party, cause, difficult situation, etc.; a turncoat or informant. **3** *informal* an unpleasant person. **4** a worker who refuses to join a strike. **5** *informal* a person frequently found in a specified place: *rink rat*. • *verb* (**rats**, **ratted**, **ratting**) *informal* **1** (usu. foll. by *on*, *out*) **a** inform on; be an informant against. **b** betray; let down. **2** (of a person, dog, etc.) hunt or kill rats. **3** *informal* desert a cause, party, etc.

ratable *adjective* = RATEABLE.

ratatouille *noun* a dish of stewed onions, zucchini, tomatoes, eggplant, and peppers. [Say ratta TOO ee]

ratchet • *noun* **1** a device or tool consisting of a bar or wheel with a set of angled teeth in which a cog or tooth engages, allowing movement in one direction only, e.g. a kind of wrench. **2** a wheel with a rim so toothed. • *verb* (**ratchets**, **ratcheted**, **ratcheting**) **1** cause something to rise or fall as a step in what is perceived to be a steady and irreversible process: *interest rates were ratcheted up another notch*. **2** operate by means of a

ratchet: *a ratcheting screwdriver*. **3** make a sound like a ratchet: *a train ratcheted by*.

rate • *noun* **1** a stated numerical proportion between two sets of things (the second usu. expressed as unity), esp.: **a** as a measure of amount or degree: *a rate of 50 miles per hour*. **b** as the basis of calculating an amount or value: *rate of taxation*. **2** a fixed or appropriate charge or cost or value; a measure of this: *postal rates*. **3** rapidity of movement or change: *prices increasing at a dreadful rate*. **4** class or rank: *first-rate*. • *verb* (**rates**, **rated**, **rating**) **1** estimate the worth or value of: *how do you rate your chances of winning?* **2** consider; regard as: *I rate them among my benefactors*. **3 a** (often foll. by as) rank or be rated. **b** rank highly; be of importance or esteemed: *I guess I don't rate*. **4** be worthy of, deserve. **5** place (a film etc.) in a category relative to its suitability for viewing. **PHRASES at any rate** in any case, whatever happens. **at this** (or **that**) **rate** if this example is typical or this assumption is true.

rateable *adjective* able to be rated or estimated.

rate of return *noun* (*plural* **rates of return**) the annual amount of income from an investment, expressed as a percentage of the original investment.

ratepayer *noun* *Cdn & Brit.* a person paying local property taxes.

rater *noun* **1** a person or thing that rates: *bond rater*. **2** a person or thing rated: *second-rater*.

rather *adverb* **1** by preference. **2** as a more likely alternative: *is stupid rather than honest*. **3 a** more precisely: *a book, or rather, a pamphlet*. **b** (often foll. by *than*) on the contrary, instead (of): *rescheduled for Friday rather than today*. **4** slightly; to some extent; somewhat: *rather drunk*. **PHRASES had rather** would rather.

rathole *noun* **1** a cramped or squalid building etc. **2** a seemingly bottomless hole, esp. one down which expenditures disappear.

ratification *noun* the action or an act or ratifying something; formal sanction or confirmation: *the agreement needed the ratification of every province*. [Say ratta fuh KAY sh'n]

ratify *verb* (**ratifies**, **ratified**, **ratifying**) confirm or accept (an agreement made in one's name) by formal consent, signature, etc.: *the province says it will refuse to ratify any constitutional amendment*. [Say RATTA fie]

rating *noun* **1** a classification or ranking of someone or something based on a comparative assessment of their quality, standard, or performance: *the hotel regained its five-star rating*. **2** the estimated standing of a person, organization, etc. as regards credit etc. **3** the relative popularity of a broadcast program as determined by the estimated size of the audience. **4 a** *Cdn & Brit.* a non-commissioned sailor. **b** a person's position or class on a ship's books.

ratio *noun* (*plural* **ratios**) **1** the quantitative relation between two similar magnitudes determined by the number of times one contains the other integrally or fractionally: *in the ratio of three to two ◊ the ratio 1:5*. **2** a proportional relationship between things not precisely measurable. [Say RAY shee oh]

ration • *noun* **1** a fixed official allowance of food, clothing, etc., in a time of shortage. **2** (foll. by *of*) a single portion of provisions, fuel, clothing, etc. **3** (usu. in *plural*) a fixed daily allowance of food, esp. in the armed forces. **4** (in *plural*) provisions. • *verb* **1** limit (persons or provisions) to a fixed ration. **2** (usu. foll. by *out*) share out (food etc.) in fixed quantities. [Say RASH'n]

rational *adjective* **1** of or based on reasoning or reason. **2** not foolish or absurd or extreme. **3** endowed with reason, reasoning. **4** rejecting what is unreasonable or cannot be tested by reason in religion or custom. **5** *Math*

(of a quantity or ratio) expressible as a ratio of whole numbers. [Say RASH'n ul]

rationale *noun* a set of reasons or a logical basis for a course of action or a particular belief: *the rationale behind the agreement* ◊ *the rationale for her decision* ◊ *I don't see the rationale of the party's policy.* [Say rasha NAL]

rationalism *noun* **1** *Philosophy* the theory that reason is the foundation of certainty in knowledge (*compare* EMPIRICISM). **2** *Theology* the practice of treating reason as the ultimate authority in religion. **3** a belief in reason rather than religion as a guiding principle in life. **4** the principle or practice of using reasoning and calculation as a basis for analysis, a course of action, etc. ▶ **rationalist** *noun* [Say RASH'n ul ism]

rationality *noun* **1** the ability to think clearly, sensibly, and logically. **2** the quality of something that is rational or based on logic or reason; a rational order, design, view, etc.: *was scrutinized for comprehensiveness, rationality, and clarity* ◊ *scientific rationality.* [Say rash'n ALA tee]

rationalization *noun* the action or an act of rationalizing: *a need for rationalization of the publishing industry* ◊ *no amount of rationalization could justify his actions.* [Say rash'n ul ize AY sh'n]

rationalize *verb* (**rationalizes**, **rationalized**, **rationalizing**) **1 a** offer or subconsciously adopt a rational but specious explanation of (one's behaviour or attitude). **b** explain one's behaviour or attitude in this way. **2** make logical and consistent. **3** make (a business etc.) more efficient by reorganizing it to reduce or eliminate waste of labour, time, or materials; downsize. **4** (often foll. by *away*) explain or explain away rationally. **5** *Math* clear of irrational numbers. **6** be or act as a rationalist. [Say RASH'n ul ize]

rationally *adverb* **1** in a rational manner; reasonably: *spoke calmly and rationally.* **2** in respect of or by means of reason: *I was scared to go, even though I was convinced rationally that there was no reason to be.* [Say RASH'n a lee]

rat pack *noun* a group of associates, friends, etc.

rat race *noun* a fiercely competitive struggle for position, power, etc.

rats *interjection* expressing annoyance, frustration, disappointment, etc.

rat-tail *noun* (also **rat's tail**) a thing shaped like the tail of a rat, i.e. long, slender, and tapering: *rat-tail haircut.* ▶ **rat-tailed** *adjective*

rattan *noun* any East Indian climbing palm with long thin jointed pliable stems used for wicker furniture etc. [Say ruh TAN]

rat-tat-tat *noun* a knocking or rapping staccato sound: *rat-tat-tat dialogue.*

rattle • *verb* (**rattles**, **rattled**, **rattling**) **1** make or cause to make a rapid succession of short sharp hard sounds, usu. through being shaken or vibrating against something. **2** move with a rattling noise. **3 a** (usu. foll. by *off*) say or recite rapidly. **b** (usu. foll. by *on*) talk in a lively thoughtless way. **4** *informal* alarm, fluster. • *noun* **1** a rattling sound. **2** an instrument or toy made to rattle esp. in order to amuse babies or to give an alarm. **3** the set of rings in a rattlesnake's tail. **4** a plant with seeds that rattle in their cases when ripe: *red rattle.* **5** *Cdn* (*Nfld & NS*) rapids or fast-flowing water.

rattlesnake *noun* (also *informal* **rattler**) a poisonous North American snake with a rattling structure of rings in its tail.

rattletrap *informal* • *noun* a rickety old vehicle etc. • *adjective* rickety.

rattling • *adjective* **1** that rattles. **2** brisk, vigorous: *a rattling pace.* • *adverb* remarkably: *a rattling good story.*

rattly *adjective* rattling; tending to rattle: *Dad drove a rattly old car for years.*

ratty *adjective* (**rattier**, **rattiest**) **1** relating to or infested with rats. **2** *informal* shabby, tattered, wretched.

raucous *adjective* harsh-sounding, loud and hoarse. ▶ **raucously** *adverb* **raucousness** *noun* [Say ROCK us]

raunch *noun* *slang* **1** earthiness, bawdiness, provocative sexuality. **2** the sound of a distorted electric guitar.

raunchy *adjective* (**raunchier**, **raunchiest**) *informal* **1** coarse, earthy; sexually provocative. **2 a** (of the sound of an electric guitar) distorted. **b** (of music) featuring raunchy guitars.

ravage • *verb* (**ravages**, **ravaged**, **ravaging**) cause severe and extensive damage to: *a country ravaged by civil war* ◊ *the recession has ravaged the textile industry* ◊ *drought-ravaged farms.* • *noun* (usu. in *plural*) destructive effect: *survived the ravages of winter.*

rave • *verb* (**raves**, **raved**, **raving**) **1** talk wildly or furiously in or as in delirium. **2** (usu. foll. by *about, over*) speak with rapturous admiration; go into raptures. **3** (of the sea, wind, etc.) howl, roar. **4** *slang* attend a rave. • *noun* **1 a** *informal* a highly enthusiastic review of a film, play, etc.: *a rave review.* **b** an enthusiastic reaction: *has won raves for her jams.* **2** a large often illegal all-night party or event, often held in a warehouse or open field, with dancing to loud fast electronic music.

raven • *noun* a large glossy blue-black crow that feeds chiefly on carrion etc., having a hoarse cry, and noted for its craftiness. • *adjective* glossy black: *raven tresses.* [Say RAVE un]

ravening *verb* (esp. of a wild animal) extremely hungry and hunting for prey. [Say RAV un ing]

ravenous *adjective* **1** very hungry, famished. **2** (of hunger, eagerness, etc., or of an animal) voracious. ▶ **ravenously** *adverb* [Say RAV un us]

raver *noun* *slang* a person who attends raves.

ravine *noun* a narrow, steep-sided valley, esp. one formed by erosion by running water.

raving • *noun* (usu. in *plural*) wild or delirious talk. • *adjective* delirious, frenzied. • *adverb* *informal* as an intensifier: *raving mad.* ▶ **ravingly** *adverb*

ravioli *noun* small squares of pasta stuffed with minced meat, cheese, spinach, etc. [Say ravvy OH lee]

ravish *verb* (**ravishes**, **ravished**, **ravishing**) **1** force a woman to have sex. **2** fill with delight: *continues to ravish us with our old favourites.* ▶ **ravisher** *noun*

ravishing *adjective* **1** entrancing, delightful. **2** (of a person) extraordinarily beautiful. ▶ **ravishingly** *adverb*

raw *adjective* **1** (of food) uncooked. **2** in the natural state; not processed: *raw sewage.* **3** (of statistics, data, etc.) not analyzed or processed. **4** (of a person) inexperienced: *raw recruits.* **5 a** stripped of skin; having the flesh exposed. **b** sensitive to the touch from having the flesh exposed. **c** abnormally sensitive: *touched a raw nerve.* **6** (of the weather) chilly and damp. **7 a** crude in artistic quality; lacking finish. **b** not controlled or refined: *raw emotion.* **8** (of the edge of cloth) without hem or selvage. **9** (of liquor) undiluted. **10** (of silk) as reeled from cocoons. **11** (of milk) not pasteurized. **12** (of leather) untanned. **13** (of film or video footage etc.) unedited. PHRASES **in the raw 1** in its natural state without mitigation: *life in the raw.* **2** naked.

raw-boned *adjective* gaunt and bony.

raw deal *noun* harsh or unfair treatment.

rawhide *noun* **1** hide that has not been tanned. **2** a rope or whip of this.

raw material *noun* material from which products are manufactured.

rawness *noun* the state or quality of being raw.

ray[1] • *noun* **1** a single line or narrow beam of light from a small or distant source. **2** a straight line in which radiation travels to a given point. **3** (in *plural*) radiation

of a specified type: *X-rays*. **4** a trace or beginning of an enlightening or cheering influence: *a ray of hope*. **5 a** any of a set of radiating lines or parts of things. **b** the part of a straight line extending from a point indefinitely in one direction. **6** the marginal portion of a composite flower, e.g. a daisy. **7 a** a radial division of a starfish. **b** each of a set of bones etc. supporting a fish's fin. • *verb* (**rays, rayed, raying**) **1** (foll. by *out, forth*) (of light, thought etc.) issue in or as if in rays. **2** radiate. PHRASES **catch** (or **get, bag,** etc.) **some rays** *informal* sunbathe.

ray² *noun* a large marine or freshwater fish with a broad flat body, wing-like pectoral fins, and a long slender tail.

ray³ *noun* = RE².

rayed *adjective* esp. *Biology* having rays of a specified number or kind: *white-rayed daisies*.

rayon *noun* any of various textile fibres or fabrics made from viscose.

raze *verb* (**razes, razed, razing**) completely destroy; tear down: *the temple was razed to the ground by the Roman emperor Titus* ◊ *the fire razed several stores*.

razor • *noun* an instrument with a sharp blade or blades used in cutting hair or bristles esp. from the skin. • *verb* **1** cut or shave with a razor. **2** cut or slice: *a closely razored lawn*.

razorback *noun* an animal with a sharp ridged back, esp. a semi-wild hog of the southern US.

razorbill *noun* (also **razor-billed auk**) an auk with a sharp-edged bill, breeding along the coasts of the North Atlantic.

razor-edged *adjective* having a sharp edge: *was fenced with razor-edged wire*.

razor's edge *noun* (also **razor edge**) **1** a sharp edge. **2** a critical situation: *had no idea of the economic razor's edge on which most African societies lived* ◊ *the razor's edge of violence*. **3** the most advanced stage of something: *in 1960, jet planes were at the razor's edge of chic*.

razor wire *noun* a type of coiled wire with extremely sharp edges or points, used as a barrier or run along the top of walls etc.

razz *slang* • *noun* (*plural* **razzes**) = RASPBERRY 3. • *verb* (**razzes, razzed, razzing**) tease, ridicule.

razzle-dazzle *noun* (also **razzle**) *informal* **1** a flamboyant often insincere display, as of publicity (often as an *adjective*: *razzle-dazzle costumes*). **2** glamorous excitement; bustle.

razzmatazz *noun informal* = RAZZLE-DAZZLE.

Rb *symbol* rubidium.

RBI *noun* (*plural* **RBIs** or **RBI**) *Baseball* **1** run batted in (*plural* **runs batted in**), a run scored because of a batter's hit, sacrifice fly, walk, etc., and counted among the batter's statistics: *leads the team with 57 RBIs*. **2** (as an *adjective*) designating a hit etc. which drives a runner home to score a run: *RBI double*. [Say arr bee EYE or RIBBY]

RC *abbreviation* **1** Roman Catholic. **2** Red Cross.

RCAF *abbreviation hist.* Royal Canadian Air Force.

RCMP • *abbreviation* Royal Canadian Mounted Police. • *noun* (*plural* **RCMPs**) *Cdn informal* an RCMP officer.

RCN *abbreviation hist.* Royal Canadian Navy.

RCNVR *abbreviation hist.* Royal Canadian Naval Volunteer Reserve.

Rd. *abbreviation* Road.

RDA *abbreviation* (*plural* **RDAs**) recommended daily allowance (for a vitamin etc.).

RDI *abbreviation* (*plural* **RDIs**) recommended daily intake (for a vitamin, mineral, etc.).

rDNA *abbreviation* RECOMBINANT DNA.

Re *symbol* rhenium.

re¹ *preposition* **1** in the matter of (as the first word in a heading). **2** *informal* about, concerning. [Say REE]

re² *noun* Music **1** (in tonic sol-fa) the second note of a major scale. **2** the note D in the fixed-do system. [Say RAY]

re- *prefix* attachable to almost any verb or its derivative, meaning: **1** once more; afresh, anew: *renumber*. **2** back; with return to a previous state: *reassemble*.

reabsorb *verb* absorb again.

reach • *verb* (**reaches, reached, reaching**) **1** stretch out an arm in order to touch or grasp something. **2** be able to touch (something) with an outstretched arm or leg. **3** arrive at or attain; extend to. **4** make contact with. **5** succeed in influencing or having an effect on. • *noun* (*plural* **reaches**) **1** an act of reaching. **2** the distance to which someone can stretch out their arm. **3** the extent or range of something's application, effect, or influence. **4** (also **reaches**) a continuous extent of land or water, esp. a stretch of river between two bends. PHRASES **out of reach** not able to be reached or attained. ▶ **reachable** *adjective* **reacher** *noun*

reacquaint *verb* (usu. foll. by *with*) make (a person or oneself) acquainted again.

react *verb* **1** act or behave in a particular way in response to something: *how did they react to the news?* **2** respond with hostility, opposition, or a contrary course of action to: *artists reacting against the conservative principles of their predecessors*. **3** (of a person) suffer from adverse physical effects after ingesting, breathing, or touching a substance: *many babies also react to soy-based formulas*. **4** interact and undergo a chemical or physical change or cause to do this: *nitrous oxide reacts with the metal*.

reactance *noun* a property of an alternating current circuit containing inductance or capacitance that together with any resistance makes up its impedance, i.e. the total opposition of the circuit to the passage of current.

reaction *noun* **1** an action performed or a feeling experienced in response to a situation or event: *Val's immediate reaction was one of relief* ◊ *a spokesman said the changes were not in reaction to the company's recent losses* ◊ *a mixed reaction to her appointment as director*. **2** a mode of thinking or behaving that is deliberately different from previous methods of thought and behaviour: *the return to traditional family values is a reaction against the permissiveness of the last decades*. **3** a response by the body, usu. a bad one, to a drug, chemical substance, etc.: *an allergic reaction*. **4** a tendency to oppose change or to advocate return to a former system, esp. in politics. **5** a chemical process in which two or more substances act mutually on each other and are changed into different substances, or one substance changes into two or more other substances. **6** *Physics* a force that is equal in magnitude but opposite in direction to some other force. **7** the ability to move quickly in response to something, esp. danger: *a driver with quick reactions*.

reactionary usu. *derogatory* • *adjective* tending to oppose (esp. political) change and advocate return to a former system. • *noun* (*plural* **reactionaries**) a reactionary person.

reactivate *verb* (**reactivates, reactivated, reactivating**) restore to a state of activity; bring into action again. ▶ **reactivation** *noun*

reactive *adjective* **1** showing reaction. **2** reacting rather than taking the initiative. **3** having a tendency to react chemically. **4** of or relating to reactance. ▶ **reactivity** *noun*

reactor *noun* **1** a person or thing that reacts. **2** (also **nuclear reactor**) an apparatus or structure in which

a controlled nuclear chain reaction releases energy. **3** *Electricity* a component used to provide reactance, esp. an inductor. **4** an apparatus for the chemical reaction of substances.

read¹ • *verb* (**reads, read, reading**) **1** look at and understand the meaning of (written or printed matter) by interpreting its characters or symbols. **2** speak (written or printed words) aloud. **3** (of a passage, text, or sign) contain or consist of specified words. **4** habitually read (a particular newspaper or magazine). **5** discover (information) by reading. **6** understand or interpret the nature or significance of: *her exclusion can be read as a backhanded compliment*. **7** inspect and record the figure indicated on (a measuring instrument). **8** hear and understand the words of (someone speaking on a radio transmitter). **9** (of a computer) copy or transfer (data). • *noun* **1** a period or act of reading. **2** a book etc. as regards its readability: *is a really good read*. PHRASES **read between the lines** look for or find hidden meaning (in a document etc.). **read a person like a book** understand a person's motives etc. **read into** find or assume meanings in the words of a speaker or writer which are not intended: *you're reading too much into her comment*. **read my lips** *informal* listen carefully: *read my lips: I'm going home!* **read back** read aloud (a message just received) so that the sender can check its accuracy. **read up on** make a special study of (a subject).

read² *adjective* (often in *combination*) educated or versed in a subject (esp. literature) by reading: *well-read*. PHRASES **take as read** accept without reading or discussing.

readability *noun* **1** legibility: *criticized the readability of his handwriting*. **2** the quality of being interesting or pleasant to read.

readable *adjective* **1** able to be read; legible. **2** interesting or pleasant to read. **3** (of data) able to be processed (by a computer, human, etc.).

reader *noun* **1** a person who reads or is reading. **2** a device that interprets data encoded on CD-ROMs, magnetic strips, bar codes, etc., usu. in order to display it in readable form on a monitor. **3 a** a book of written passages, exercises, etc. used in learning to read. **b** a collection of writings on a subject, used esp. as a supplement to a textbook. **4** a publisher's employee who reports on submitted manuscripts. **5** a person employed by a printer to correct proofs. **6** a person appointed to read aloud, esp. parts of a service in a church. **7** a device for producing an image that can be read from microfilm etc.

reader-friendly *adjective* **1** designating written material using a format and level of language that is manageable for the reader; pleasant to read. **2** (of a setting, library, etc.) conducive to reading.

readership *noun* **1** the readers of a newspaper etc. **2** the number or extent of these.

readily *adverb* **1** without showing reluctance. **2** easily, promptly; without difficulty. [Say RED a lee]

readiness *noun* **1** willingness to do something: *Spain had indicated a readiness to accept his terms*. **2** the state of being fully prepared for something: *your muscles tense in readiness for action*. [Say READY ness]

reading *noun* **1** the action or skill of reading. **2** an instance of something being read to an audience. **3** an interpretation of a text. **4** a figure recorded on a

measuring instrument. **5** a stage of debate in parliament through which a bill must pass before it can become law.

reading week *noun Cdn* a week usu. halfway through a university term during which there are no classes, intended for students to concentrate on their reading, research, etc.

readjust *verb* **1** adjust again. **2** adapt to a new or former situation or surroundings. ▶ **readjustment** *noun* [Say re ADJUST]

readmission *noun* the act or process of admitting again. [Say re ADMISSION]

readmit *verb* (**readmits, readmitted, readmitting**) admit again. [Say re ADMIT]

read-only memory *noun* (*plural* **read-only memories**) *Computing* a memory read at high speed but not capable of being changed by program instructions. Abbreviation: **ROM**.

readout *noun* **1** the display of data by an automatic device in an understandable form. **2** a record of output produced by a computer or scientific instrument.

read/write *adjective Computing* capable of reading existing data and accepting alterations or further input.

ready • *adjective* (**readier, readiest**) **1** prepared for an activity or situation. **2** made suitable and available for immediate use. **3** easily available or obtained; within reach. **4** (foll. by *to*, *for*) willing to do or having a desire for. **5** immediate, quick, or prompt. • *adverb* (done, prepared, etc.) beforehand: *ready assembled furniture*. • *verb* (**readies, readied, readying**) make ready; prepare. PHRASES **at the ready** ready for action. **get** (or **make**) **ready** prepare: *get ready for bed*.

ready-made • *adjective* **1** (esp. of clothes) made in a standard size, not to the measurements of a particular customer. **2** (esp. of food) prepared in advance. **3** ideal or very appropriate and already available: *a ready-made solution*. • *noun* something that is ready-made.

ready-mix • *adjective* (also **ready-mixed**) having some or all of the constituents already mixed together: *ready-mix cookie dough*. • *noun* concrete with some or all of the constituents mixed together.

ready-to-wear • *noun* clothing or an article of clothing that is made in standard sizes, not tailored to a particular customer. • *adjective* pertaining to this style of clothing; ready-made.

reaffirm *verb* affirm again. ▶ **reaffirmation** *noun*

reagent *noun Chemistry* **1** a substance used to test for the presence of another substance by means of the reaction which it produces. **2** any substance used in chemical reactions. [Say re AGENT]

real • *adjective* **1** actually existing. **2** genuine, sincere; not feigned: *cried real tears*. **3** not artificial: *real cream*. **4** complete, utter, serious: *that's a real shame*. **5** *Law* consisting of or relating to immovable property such as land or houses: *real estate* (compare PERSONAL PROPERTY). **6** appraised by purchasing power; adjusted for changes

in the wages of money: *real value* ◊ *income in real terms*. • *adverb informal* really, very. PHRASES **for real** *informal* **1** in earnest: *playing for real*. **2** genuine: *that's just acting, it's not for real*. **get real** *slang* get serious. **the real thing** (of an object or emotion) genuine, not illusory or inferior: *this isn't just a crush, this is the real thing*.

real estate *noun* **1** immovable property, such as land or houses, and the proprietary rights over these. **2** the business of buying and selling land, buildings, houses, etc.: *she's in real estate*. **3** Computing (esp. of memory, a disk, a screen, etc.) available space.

real estate agency *noun* (*plural* **real estate agencies**) a business that represents clients in the purchase, sale, or rental of houses etc.

real estate agent *noun* a person whose business is to represent clients in the purchase, sale, or rental of houses etc.

realign *verb* **1** adjust or alter the direction of. **2** restructure or regroup (political parties, divisions in sports, etc.). ▶ **realignment** *noun* [Say re a LINE]

realism *noun* **1** an interest in regarding things in their true nature and dealing with them as they are. **2** fidelity to nature in representation; the showing of life etc. as it is in fact, esp. in literature, theatre, or the visual arts. **3** (also **Realism**) a movement in esp. French art of the 19th century marked by a rebellion against the traditional historical, mythological, and religious subjects in favour of non-idealized scenes of modern life. ▶ **realist** *noun & adjective*

realistic *adjective* **1** having or showing a sensible and practical idea of what can be done, achieved, etc.: *a realistic solution*. **2** true to real life; resembling the original: *a realistic rubber snake*. **3** (of art) depicting things in their true nature, free from enhancement or idealization. ▶ **realistically** *adverb*

reality *noun* (*plural* **realities**) **1** what exists or is real; that which underlies appearances. **2** (foll. by *of*) the real nature or truth of (a thing): *the reality of the situation*. **3** one's true personal situation and the problems that exist in one's life: *she's lost touch with reality*. **4** a real aspect or condition of something, esp. one that cannot be avoided: *snow is one of the realities of Canadian winter*. **5** resemblance to an original: *the model was impressive in its reality*. PHRASES **in reality** in fact.

reality check *noun* an occasion on which one consciously confronts reality, esp. in contrast with one's desires, expectations, beliefs, habits, etc.

realizable *adjective* **1** able to be achieved or made to happen: *such a dream, if it is realizable at all, is one for the distant future*. **2** in or able to be converted into cash: *10 percent of realizable assets*.

realization *noun* **1** an act of becoming fully aware of something as a fact: *there was a growing realization of the need to create common economic structures* ◊ *realization dawned suddenly*. **2** the fulfillment or achievement of something desired or anticipated: *he did not live to see the realization of his dream*. **3** an actual, complete, or dramatic form given to a concept or work: *a perfect realization of the concerto on compact disc*. **4** the action of converting an asset into cash.

realize *verb* (**realizes**, **realized**, **realizing**) **1** become fully aware of; accept something as fact. **2** understand clearly. **3** make (plans, dreams, ideas) happen in reality: *she never realized her ambition of becoming a professional singer*. **4 a** convert into money: *he realized all the assets in her trust fund*. **b** acquire (profit): *she realized a profit of $100 000*. **c** be sold for (a specified price): *the paintings realized $2 million at auction*. **5** present as real; make realistic; give apparent reality to: *the story was powerfully realized on stage*.

real life • *noun* life lived by actual people as

distinguished from the world of fiction, television, theatre, etc. • *adjective* (usu. **real-life**) actually having occurred; not fictional: *based on real-life experiences*.

real live *adjective* often *jocular* actual; not pretended or simulated: *a real live burglar*.

reallocate *verb* (**reallocates**, **reallocated**, **reallocating**) allocate again or differently. ▶ **reallocation** *noun* [Say re ALOE kate, re aloe KAY sh'n]

really *adverb* **1** in actual fact; truly. **2** very: *really useful*. **3** (as a strong affirmative) seriously, I assure you. **4** an expression of disbelief, mild protest, or surprise.

realm *noun* **1** *formal* a kingdom. **2** a field of activity, or interest, or of some abstract conception: *the realm of public health* ◊ *the realm of possibility*. [Say RELM]

realness *noun* the fact or quality of being real; reality, truth.

realpolitik *noun* politics based on realities and material needs, rather than on morals or ideals: *René Lévesque came face-to-face with the bruised egos and sweaty opportunism of Canadian realpolitik*. [Say ray al paula TEEK]

real time • *noun* the actual time during which a process or event occurs. • *adjective* (usu. **real-time**) Computing **1** (of a system) in which input data is processed within milliseconds so that it is available virtually immediately as feedback to the process from which it is coming, e.g. in an airline booking system. **2** (of information, an image, etc.) responding virtually immediately to changes in the state of affairs it reflects: *real-time weather forecasting*.

Realtor *noun* **1** *proprietary* (in Canada) a member firm of the Canadian Real Estate Association. **2** (**realtor**) a real estate agent.

realty *noun* real estate.

real world • *noun* (usu. as **the real world**) **1** the world as it really exists as distinguished from any model of existence considered to be ideal, hypothetical, or fictitious. **2** real life as distinguished from any lifestyle considered to be sheltered or privileged. • *adjective* (**real-world**) **1** of or pertaining to the real world, esp. consisting of harsh realities. **2** practical: *real-world knowledge*.

ream • *noun* **1** twenty quires or 500 (formerly 480) sheets of paper. **2** (in *plural*) a large quantity of paper, writing, or printed matter: *wrote reams about it*. • *verb* **1** widen (a hole in metal etc.) with a borer. **2** extract the juice from (fruit) with a reamer. PHRASES **ream a person out** *informal* reprimand a person harshly.

reamer *noun* **1** a tool for enlarging or finishing drilled holes. **2** a kitchen implement with a central ridged dome on which a half fruit can be pressed down and turned to extract its juice.

reanalysis *noun* a second or further analysis.

reanalyze *verb* (**reanalyzes**, **reanalyzed**, **reanalyzing**) analyze again; subject to further analysis.

reanimate *verb* (**reanimates**, **reanimated**, **reanimating**) **1** resuscitate; restore to life: *cryonic suspension, in which a person is frozen after death in hopes of being reanimated in the future*. **2** restore to activity, liveliness or use; revive: *the positive poll results reanimated their campaign*. ▶ **reanimation** *noun*

reap *verb* **1** cut (a crop, esp. grain) as a harvest. **2** gather or harvest the crop of (a field etc.). **3** receive as the consequence of one's own or others' actions: *they are now reaping the rewards of all their hard work*.

reaper *noun* **1** a person who reaps. **2** esp. *hist.* a machine for reaping. **3** (**the Reaper**) = GRIM REAPER.

reappear *verb* appear again or as previously. ▶ **reappearance** *noun*

reapply *verb* (**reapplies**, **reapplied**, **reapplying**)

apply again, esp. submit a further application (for a position etc.).

reappoint *verb* appoint again to a position previously held. ▶ **reappointment** *noun*

reapportion *verb* apportion again or differently. ▶ **reapportionment** *noun*

reappraisal *noun* a reassessment of something, esp. in the light of new facts.

reappraise *verb* (**reappraises**, **reappraised**, **reappraising**) appraise or assess again.

rear¹ • *noun* 1 the back part of anything. 2 the space behind, or position at the back of, anything. 3 (also **rear end**) *informal* the buttocks. 4 the hindmost part of an army or fleet. • *adjective* at the back. PHRASES **bring up the rear** come last. **in the rear** behind; at the back.

rear² *verb* 1 a bring up and educate (children). b breed and care for (animals). 2 (usu. foll. by *up*) a (of a horse etc.) raise itself on its hind legs. b get up, rise: *she reared up from the bench*. 3 a set upright. b build. c hold up. 4 extend to a great height. PHRASES **rear back** *Baseball* (of a pitcher) lean back on one leg before lurching forward to throw a pitch. **rear** (or **raise**) **its** (**ugly**) **head** (of a situation, problem, etc.) make an (unwelcome) appearance.

rear admiral *noun* (also **Rear Admiral**) a naval officer ranking below a vice admiral.

rear-end *verb* (of a car, truck, etc., or its driver) crash into the back of (another vehicle).

rear-ender *noun* *informal* a collision in which one vehicle rear-ends another.

rearguard *noun* 1 a body of troops detached to protect the rear, esp. in retreats. 2 a defensive or conservative element in an organization etc.: *bitter battles between the left and right wings, between the vanguard and the rearguard*. 3 *Hockey slang* a defenceman.

rearing *noun* 1 the process of caring for children as they grow up, teaching them how to behave as members of society. 2 the process of breeding animals and caring for them as they grow: *livestock rearing*.

rearm *verb* arm or become armed again, esp. with improved weapons. ▶ **rearmament** *noun*

rearmost *adjective* furthest back; last.

rearrange *verb* (**rearranges**, **rearranged**, **rearranging**) arrange again in a different way. ▶ **rearrangement** *noun* **rearranging** *noun*

rear-view mirror *noun* (also **rear-view**) a mirror fixed inside the windshield of a car, truck, etc. enabling the driver to see traffic etc. behind.

rearward • *adverb* towards the rear. • *adjective* located at or towards the rear.

rear-wheel drive *noun* a drive system in a car etc. in which engine power operates through the rear wheels alone.

WRITING TIP
reason

The well-established idioms in *the reason why* I was late and *the reason is because* my car broke down continue to be strongly criticized as redundant by many teachers of composition. To avoid such criticism, you should use constructions like *the reason I* was late and *the reason is that* my car broke down.

---

reason • *noun* 1 a motive, cause, or justification. 2 a fact adduced or serving as this: *give me one good reason why I should let you*. 3 the intellectual faculty by which conclusions are drawn from premises. 4 sanity: *has lost his reason*. 5 sensible conduct. • *verb* 1 form or try to reach conclusions by connected thought. 2 (foll. by *with*) use an argument (with a person) by way of persuasion.

PHRASES **by reason of** owing to. **in** (or **within**) **reason** within the bounds of sense or moderation. **it stands to reason** (often foll. by *that* + clause) it is evident or logical. **listen to reason** be persuaded to act sensibly. **see reason** acknowledge the force of an argument. **with reason** justifiably.

reasonable *adjective* 1 having sound judgment; moderate; ready to listen to reason. 2 in accordance with reason; not absurd. 3 a inexpensive. b fairly good. ▶ **reasonableness** *noun* **reasonably** *adverb*

reasoned *adjective* (of an argument, opinion, etc.) presented in a logical way that shows careful thought.

reasoning *noun* the process of thinking about things in a logical way; opinions and ideas that are based on logical thinking: *what is the reasoning behind this decision?* ◊ *this line of reasoning is faulty*.

reassemble *verb* (**reassembles**, **reassembled**, **reassembling**) assemble again or into a former state. ▶ **reassembly** *noun*

reassert *verb* assert again. ▶ **reassertion** *noun*

reassess *verb* (**reassesses**, **reassessed**, **reassessing**) assess again, esp. differently. ▶ **reassessment** *noun* [Say re ASSESS]

reassign *verb* assign again or differently. ▶ **reassignment** *noun*

reassurance *noun* 1 the action of removing someone's doubts or fears: *children need reassurance and praise*. 2 a statement or comment that removes someone's doubts or fears: *we have been given reassurances that the water is safe to drink*.

reassure *verb* (**reassures**, **reassured**, **reassuring**) restore confidence to; dispel the apprehensions of. ▶ **reassuring** *adjective* **reassuringly** *adverb*

reattach *verb* (**reattaches**, **reattached**, **reattaching**) attach again or in a former position.

reawaken *verb* awaken again. ▶ **reawakening** *noun*

Reb *noun* a traditional Jewish courtesy title used preceding a man's first name or surname.

rebar *noun* a steel reinforcing rod in concrete. [Say REE bar]

rebate • *noun* 1 a partial refund of money paid. 2 a deduction from a sum to be paid; a discount. • *verb* (**rebates**, **rebated**, **rebating**) pay back as a rebate.

rebbe *noun* 1 a Jewish religious leader or rabbi. 2 (**Rebbe**) a title of respect used for a Hasidic religious leader. [Say REBBA]

rebel • *noun* 1 a person who fights against, resists, or refuses allegiance to, the established government. 2 a person who resists authority, control, or convention. • *adjective* 1 rebellious. 2 of or concerning rebels. 3 in rebellion. • *verb* (**rebels**, **rebelled**, **rebelling**) (often foll. by *against*) act as a rebel; revolt.

rebellion *noun* 1 an act of violent or open resistance to an established government or authority: *the north of the country rose in rebellion against the government* ◊ *the army put down the rebellion*. 2 the action or process of resisting authority, control, or convention: *an act of teenage rebellion* ◊ *the prime minister's actions provoked a backbench rebellion*.

rebellious *adjective* 1 engaged in an organized revolt against the government: *rebellious colonists*. 2 unwilling to obey rules or accept normal standards of behaviour etc.: *rebellious teens* ◊ *he has always had a rebellious streak*. 3 not easily handled or kept in place: *a rebellious lock of hair*. ▶ **rebelliously** *adverb* **rebelliousness** *noun*

rebirth *noun* 1 the process of being reincarnated or born again: *the endless cycle of birth, death, and rebirth*. 2 a revival: *the rebirth of learning*.

reboot *Computing* • *verb* boot up (a system) again. • *noun* an act of rebooting.

reborn *adjective* 1 having experienced a complete

spiritual change; born-again. **2** existing or active again; brought back to life. **3** having experienced a profound transformation.
rebound • *verb* **1** spring back after action or impact. **2** make a recovery: *gold prices are beginning to rebound.* **3** *Basketball* recover (a ball) that has bounced off the backboard or rim of the basket. **4** (foll. by *upon*) (of an action) have an adverse effect upon (the doer). • *noun* **1** a positive reaction that happens after something negative: *a big rebound in profits for last year.* **2** *Sport* a puck, ball, etc. which has bounced back from the goal, basket, etc. or been let loose by the goaltender: *blasted the rebound back into the net.* • *adjective* (of a medical condition, illness, etc.) occurring again: *a rebound earache.* PHRASES **on the rebound 1** while still recovering from an emotional shock, esp. rejection by a lover: *I was on the rebound when I met Donna.* **2** while bouncing again: *scored on the rebound.* ►**rebounder** *noun* **rebounding** *noun*

rebroadcast • *verb* (**rebroadcasts;** *past* **rebroadcast** or **rebroadcasted;** *past participle* **rebroadcast;** **rebroadcasting**) **1** broadcast (a program received from another station). **2** broadcast again. • *noun* **1** the action or act of rebroadcasting a program. **2** a repeat broadcast.

rebuff • *noun* a rejection of one who makes advances, offers help or sympathy, shows interest or curiosity, makes a request, etc.: *her offer of help was met with a sharp rebuff.* • *verb* reject, disregard, esp. in an abrupt or ungracious manner: *the federal party is considering legal action after an informal request was rebuffed last year.*

rebuild • *verb* (**rebuilds, rebuilt, rebuilding**) **1** build (a car, house, etc.) again from new or previously used parts and materials. **2** make or become successful, functional, etc. again. **3** re-establish or revive (confidence, a country's economy, etc.). • *noun* (esp. of a car or car part, such as an engine) something that has been or needs to be rebuilt.

rebuke • *verb* (**rebukes, rebuked, rebuking**) scold or reprimand harshly. • *noun* a stern reprimand.

rebus *noun* (*plural* **rebuses**) a type of puzzle or visual pun in which a word is represented by pictures etc. suggesting its parts. [Say REE bus]

rebut *verb* (**rebuts, rebutted, rebutting**) refute or disprove (evidence or a charge): *he made no attempt to rebut the treasurers's claims.* ►**rebuttal** *noun* [Say re BUT, re BUT ul]

rec *adjective* **1** recreation: *rec centre.* **2** recreational: *rec league.*

recalcitrant • *adjective* **1** resisting discipline or authority; obstinately disobedient: *a recalcitrant child.* **2** difficult to manage or operate: *a recalcitrant lock.* • *noun* a recalcitrant person. [Say re KALSA trint]

recalculate *verb* (**recalculates, recalculated, recalculating**) calculate again. ►**recalculation** *noun*

recall • *verb* **1** recollect, remember. **2 a** summon a person to return: *a player recalled from the minors.* **b** request the return of something, esp. a manufactured product with a defect. **3** bring back to memory; serve as a reminder of: *that picture recalls a funny story I once heard.* **4** revoke or annul (an action or decision). • *noun* **1** the action of recalling, esp. a summons to come back: *the recall of Parliament.* **2** a request for the return of a faulty product. **3** the ability to remember: *doesn't need notes because she has total recall.* **4** removal of an elected official from office. PHRASES **beyond recall** that cannot be brought back to the original state or cancelled: *damaged beyond recall.*

recant *verb* say publicly that one no longer holds an opinion or belief considered wrong: *when Franco*

prevailed in the Spanish Civil War, Dali publicly recanted his former contempt for family values and the church. ►**recantation** *noun* **recanter** *noun*

recap *informal* • *verb* (**recaps, recapped, recapping**) recapitulate; give a summary. • *noun* a recapitulation; a summary or review.

recapitulate *verb* (**recapitulates, recapitulated, recapitulating**) go briefly through (the main points of a speech, argument, etc.) again; summarize. [Say re kuh PITCHA late]

recapitulation *noun* **1** the act or an instance of summarizing and restating the main points of something. **2** *Music* part of a movement, esp. in a sonata, in which themes from the exposition are restated. [Say re kuh pitcha LAY sh'n]

recapture *verb* (**recaptures, recaptured, recapturing**) **1** capture again; recover or regain. **2** experience (a past emotion etc.) again.

recast *verb* (**recasts, recast, recasting**) **1** put into a new form. **2** change the cast of (a play etc.).

SPELL CHECK
recommend

Warning: **recommend** is spelled with only one *c* and two *m*'s.

recede *verb* (**recedes, receded, receding**) **1** withdraw or move backwards from a previous position or away from an observer, or appear to do so. **2** fade, become remote: *hopes of a settlement are receding.* **3** slope backwards: *a receding chin.* **4** decline in force, value, or significance. **5** (foll. by *from*) withdraw or retreat from (an engagement, promise, etc.). **6** (of a person's hair) cease to grow at the front, sides, etc.: *receding hairline.* [Sounds like *RESEED*]

receipt *noun* **1** the action of receiving something or the fact of its being received: *will pay on receipt of the goods ◊ please acknowledge receipt of this letter.* **2** a printed or written acknowledgement of the acceptance of goods or payment of money. **3** (usu. in *plural*) an amount of money etc. received: *box office receipts.* PHRASES **in receipt of** having received: *claimants in receipt of the family benefit.* [Say re SEAT]

receivable • *adjective* **1** capable of being received. **2** (of bills, accounts, etc.) for which money has not yet been received. • *noun* (in *plural*) debts owed to a business, esp. regarded as assets.

receive *verb* (**receives, received, receiving**) **1** be given, or presented with, or paid. **2** accept or take delivery of. **3** buy or accept (goods known to be stolen). **4** form (an idea or impression) from an experience. **5** detect and pick up (broadcast signals). **6** *Tennis* be the player to whom the server serves the ball. **7** serve as a receptacle for. **8** suffer, experience, or be subject to: *the event received wide media coverage.* **9** meet with (a specified reaction). **10** entertain as a guest. **11** admit as a member. **12** *Football* be the player or team to whom the offensive team kicks the ball. PHRASES **be at** (or **on**) **the receiving end** *informal* bear the brunt of something unpleasant.

received *adjective* generally accepted as authoritative or true: *much of this book attempts to counter received opinion or the party line.*

receiver *noun* **1** a person or thing that receives. **2 a** the part of a machine or instrument that receives sound, signals, etc. **b** the apparatus contained within the earpiece of a telephone. **c** the handset of a telephone. **3** (also **official receiver**) a person appointed by a court to manage the property of a bankrupt or insane person, or property under litigation. **4** an apparatus, such as a radio etc., that

receives signals transmitted as electromagnetic waves. **5** *Football* (also **wide receiver**) a player on the offensive team who is eligible to catch passes from the quarterback. **6** a person who receives stolen goods.

receiver general *noun* (*plural* **receivers general**) the official to whom all money owed to the government is sent.

receivership *noun* the state of a business having its property controlled by someone appointed by the government because it has gone bankrupt: *five hundred jobs were lost when the company went into receivership*.

recent • *adjective* **1** not long past. **2** not long established; lately begun; modern. **3** (**Recent**) *Geology* = HOLOCENE. • *noun* *Geology* = HOLOCENE. ▶ **recently** *adverb*

receptacle *noun* **1** a container in which something is stored or deposited. **2** an electrical outlet. **3** *Botany* **a** the common base of floral organs. **b** a structure supporting the reproductive organs in some algae and mosses. **4** *Zoology* an organ or structure which receives a secretion, eggs, sperm, etc. [Say re SEPTA cull]

reception *noun* **1** the action or process of receiving or being received: *transmission and reception of data* ◊ *reception of the sacraments*. **2** the manner in which a person or thing is received or welcomed: *her latest album has met with a mixed reception* ◊ *the returning champion was given a warm reception*. **3** a formal social event to which guests are invited to mark some occasion, e.g. a wedding. **4** a place where guests or clients etc. report on arrival at a hotel, office, etc. **5 a** the receiving of broadcast signals: *the v-chip allows parents to block reception of certain TV programs*. **b** the quality of this: *the reception is very good*. **6** *Football* a catch of a ball thrown by the quarterback.

receptionist *noun* a person employed in an organization to welcome and direct visitors, answer the telephone, etc.

receptive *adjective* **1** quick or able to receive impressions or ideas. **2** willing or anxious to hear, acknowledge, or accept; open: *was receptive to suggestions* ◊ *a receptive audience*. **3** concerned with receiving stimuli etc. ▶ **receptivity** *noun* [Say re SEP tiv, re sep TIVVA tee]

receptor *noun* *Biology* **1** a cell or group of cells, found in the eyes, ears, nose, etc., specialized to detect a particular stimulus, such as light, heat, or a drug, and to initiate the transmission of impulses via the sensory nerves. **2** a region in a tissue or molecule in a cell (esp. in a membrane) which specifically recognizes and responds to a complimentary molecule, such as a hormone, or other substance.

recess • *noun* (*plural* **recesses**) **1** a short break between classes, esp. in elementary school. **2** a temporary cessation from work, esp. of Parliament or a court. **3** a space set back in a wall; a niche. **4** (often in *plural*) a hidden, isolated, or secret place: *cold, dry air from the surface has already forced some animals further into the grotto's recesses*. **5** *Anatomy* a fold or indentation in an organ. • *verb* (**recesses**, **recessed**, **recessing**) **1** make a recess in. **2** place in a recess; set back. **3** take a recess; adjourn. [Say RE sess]

recessed *adjective* placed in such a way as to be flush or set back from the surface in which it is set. [Say RE sest]

recession *noun* **1** a temporary decline in economic activity or prosperity associated with lower levels of production and employment. **2** a receding or withdrawal from a place or point. **3** a receding part of an object; a recess. [Say re SESH'n]

recessional • *adjective* **1** of or pertaining to a recession or recessions. **2** (of a hymn or other piece of

music) sung or played while the clergy etc. withdraw after a service. • *noun* a recessional hymn. [Say re SESH'n ul]

recessionary *adjective* connected with a recession or likely to cause one: *recessionary conditions*. [Say re SESH'n airy]

recession-proof *adjective* (of a business, market, city, etc.) unaffected by economic recession.

recessive *adjective* **1** *Genetics* (of an inherited characteristic) appearing in offspring only when not masked by a dominant characteristic inherited from one parent. **2** tending to recede. **3** of or relating to an economic recession. [Say re SESS iv]

recharge • *verb* (**recharges**, **recharged**, **recharging**) **1** put a fresh charge in; refill. **2** restore an electric charge to (a battery or piece of equipment powered by batteries). **3** (of a battery etc.) be recharged. **4** (of a person) recover energy by resting or relaxing for a short time. • *noun* a renewed charge. ▶ **rechargeable** *adjective & noun*

recharger *noun* a device for recharging batteries or equipment powered by batteries.

recheck • *verb* check again. • *noun* a second or further check or inspection.

rechristen *verb* give a new name to: *after the US purchased Alaska from Russia in 1867, they rechristened New Archangel as Sitka*. [Say re CHRIS in]

recidivism *noun* a tendency to relapse habitually into crime: *the best way to reduce recidivism rates is by classifying offenders with a high risk of reoffending as dangerous*. [Say re SID iv ism]

recidivist *noun* a person who relapses into crime: *a recidivist who always committed the same crime: burglary without violence*. [Say re SID iv ist]

SPELL CHECK
receive
When you accept something you **receive** it.

recipe *noun* **1** a statement of the ingredients and procedure required for preparing a dish. **2** a means of achieving something: *a recipe for success*. [Say RESSA pee]

recipient • *noun* a person who receives something. • *adjective* receiving or capable of receiving something: *Canada continues to link economic aid to the recipient country's record on human rights*. [Say re SIPPY unt]

reciprocal • *adjective* **1** in return: *a reciprocal greeting*. **2** mutual: *their feelings are reciprocal*. **3** *Grammar* (of a pronoun) expressing mutual action or relation (as in *each other*). • *noun* *Math* an expression or function so related to another that their product is one: *½ is the reciprocal of 2*. ▶ **reciprocally** *adverb* [Say re SIPRA cull]

reciprocate *verb* (**reciprocates**, **reciprocated**, **reciprocating**) **1** return (affection etc.): *Broadbent's disdain for Canadian socialist intellectuals is in large degree reciprocated by the academic left*. **2** (foll. by *with*) offer or give something in return: *Claude reciprocated with observations in his own field of expertise*. **3 a** (of a part of a machine) move backwards and forwards: *a reciprocating saw*. **b** cause to do this. [Say re SIPRA kate]

reciprocity *noun* (*plural* **reciprocities**) the practice of exchanging things with others for mutual benefit, esp. privileges granted by one country or organization to another: *the permit entitles the holder to snowmobile on all official trail systems in Ontario as well as in states where trail permit reciprocity is in effect*. [Say ressa PROSSA tee]

recirculate *verb* (**recirculates**, **recirculated**, **recirculating**) circulate again, esp. make available for reuse. ▶ **recirculation** *noun*

recital *noun* **1** the performance of a program of instrumental music, song, or dance, by a soloist or

small group; *piano recital* ◊ *the ballet school's end-of-year recital*. **2** a spoken description of a series of events etc. that is often long and boring: *an interminable recital of her woes*. [Say re SITE ul]

recitation *noun* **1** the act of repeating a text from memory or of reading a text aloud before an audience. **2** an act of talking or writing about a series of things: *Leia continued her recitation of the week's events*. [Say ressa TAY sh'n]

recitative *noun* **1** declamatory speech-like singing used esp. in opera or oratorio for advancing the plot (*compare* ARIA). **2** a passage or part of a musical score given in this form. [Say ressa tuh TEEV]

recite *verb* (**recites**, **recited**, **reciting**) **1** repeat aloud or declaim (a poem or passage) from memory, esp. before an audience. **2** give a recitation. **3** mention in order; enumerate: *she recited her accomplishments*. **4** give a detailed description or account of.

reckless *adjective* disregarding the consequences or danger etc. ▶ **recklessly** *adverb* **recklessness** *noun*

reckon *verb* **1** count or compute by calculation. **2 a** conclude after calculation. **b** *informal* expect: *reckons to finish by Friday*. **c** *informal* think, suppose: *reckon it'll rain today?* **3** (foll. by *on*) rely on, count on, or base plans on: *didn't reckon on it being so hard*. **4** consider or regard: *she is reckoned an authority on the subject*. **5** (foll. by *in*) count in or include in computation. **6** make calculations; add up an account or sum. PHRASES **to be reckoned with** (or **to reckon with**) of considerable importance; not to be ignored or taken lightly: *they are a force to be reckoned with*.

reckoning *noun* **1** the action or process of calculating or estimating something: *by my reckoning, you still owe me $5* ◊ *the system of time reckoning in Babylon*. **2** an opinion or judgment: *this did not constitute a cult, by the reckoning of most scholars*. **3** the avenging or punishing of past mistakes or misdeeds: *in the final reckoning truth is rewarded* ◊ *if we continue to abuse the environment, a day of reckoning will certainly come*.

reclaim *verb* **1** seek the return of (one's property, etc.). **2** make wasteland fit for cultivating, esp. by draining it. **3** recover raw material from waste products so that it can be used again. ▶ **reclaimed** *adjective*

reclamation *noun* the action or process of reclaiming or recovering something: *a land reclamation project*. [Say reckla MAY sh'n]

reclassification *noun* the action or process of classifying something again or differently.

reclassify *verb* (**reclassifies**, **reclassified**, **reclassifying**) classify again or differently.

recline *verb* (**reclines**, **reclined**, **reclining**) lie or cause to lie backwards in a horizontal or leaning position, esp. in resting: *reclined in the chair* ◊ *reclined the seat back*. ▶ **reclining** *adjective*

recliner *noun* a comfortable chair for reclining in, usu. with adjustable back and footrest.

recluse *noun* a person preferring or living in seclusion or isolation. ▶ **reclusive** *adjective* [Say RECK loose or ruh KLOOSE, ruh KLOO siv]

recognition *noun* **1** the action or an act of recognizing a person or thing; the fact of being recognized: *changed beyond recognition*. **2** the acknowledgement or admission of a service, achievement, ability, etc.; appreciation. **3** formal approval. **4** the mental process whereby things are identified as having been previously apprehended or as belonging to a known category. **5** (also **diplomatic recognition**) the process by which a country declares that another political entity fulfills the conditions of statehood and acknowledges its willingness to deal with it as a member of the international community.

6 the identification of printed characters using photoelectric devices (*see* OPTICAL CHARACTER RECOGNITION). [Say reck ug NISH'n]

recognizable *adjective* able to be recognized from previous encounters or knowledge. ▶ **recognizably** *adverb*

recognizance *noun* **1** a commitment by which a person undertakes before a court or magistrate to observe some condition, e.g. to appear when summoned: *a police officer can release an accused on recognizance*. **2** a sum pledged as surety for this. [Say ruh COG niz ince]

recognize *verb* (**recognizes**, **recognized**, **recognizing**) **1** identify (a person or thing) as already known; know again. **2** discover the nature of, esp. by some distinctive feature: *I can always recognize a phony*. **3** realize or admit. **4** acknowledge the existence, validity, character, or claims of. **5** show appreciation of; reward. **6** (foll. by *as, for*) treat or acknowledge. **7** (of a chairperson etc.) allow (a person) to speak in a debate etc. **8** grant diplomatic recognition to (a country).

recoil • *verb* **1** suddenly move or spring back in fear, horror, or disgust: *she recoiled from his touch* ◊ *he recoiled in horror at the sight of the corpse*. **2** react to an idea or situation with strong dislike or fear: *recoiled at the very thought of betraying him* ◊ *recoils from the idea of eating meat*. **3** rebound after an impact, esp. (of a gun) move suddenly backwards when it is fired. • *noun* a sudden movement backwards, esp. of a gun when it is fired.

recollect *verb* succeed in remembering; call to mind. [Say recka LECT]

recollection *noun* **1** the ability to remember something; the act of remembering something: *I have no recollection of meeting her before* ◊ *to the best of my recollection, we said we would go on a trip this summer*. **2** a thing recollected: *her recollections of the Dirty Thirties*.

Récollet *noun* a member of the reformed branch of the Franciscan Observants, founded in France in the late 16th century, and active in New France. [Say RECKA lay]

recolonize *verb* (**recolonizes**, **recolonized**, **recolonizing**) colonize again.

recombinant *adjective* (of a gene etc.) formed by recombination. [Say re COMBA nint]

recombination *noun* the rearrangement, esp. by crossing over in chromosomes, of genes to form a combination different from that of its parents. [Say re COMBINATION]

recombine *verb* (**recombines**, **recombined**, **recombining**) combine again or differently. [Say re kum BINE]

recommence *verb* (**recommences**, **recommenced**, **recommencing**) begin again. [Say re COMMENCE]

recommend *verb* **1 a** suggest as fit for some purpose or use. **b** suggest (a person) as suitable for a particular position. **2** advise as a course of action etc.: *I recommend that you stay where you are*. **3** (of qualities, conduct, etc.) make acceptable or desirable: *a plan with little to recommend it*. ▶ **recommendable** *adjective* **recommendation** *noun*

recommit *verb* (**recommits**, **recommitted**, **recommitting**) commit again. ▶ **recommitment** *noun* [Say re COMMIT]

recompense • *verb* (**recompenses**, **recompensed**, **recompensing**) compensate a person for a loss, an expense, or for work completed: *no attempt was ever made to recompense Logan for the loss of his family* ◊ *we will recompense you for gas and incidentals*. • *noun* compensation or reward given for loss or harm suffered or for effort made: *a generous salary plus free*

board and lodging were adequate recompense for her editorial expertise. [Say reck um PENCE]

recon *noun* esp. *US slang* military reconnaissance. [Say re CON]

reconcile *verb* (**reconciles**, **reconciled**, **reconciling**) **1** restore friendly relations after an argument or estrangement: *she wanted to be reconciled with her father*. **2** make someone or oneself accept an unpleasant situation because it is impossible to change it: *I was reconciled to leaving ◊ she could not reconcile herself to the thought of leaving him*. **3** cause to coexist in harmony; show the compatibility of: *cannot reconcile your views with the facts*. **4** settle (a quarrel etc.). [Say RECK'n sile]

reconciliation *noun* **1** an end to a disagreement and the start of a good relationship again: *their change of policy brought about a reconciliation ◊ they really both long for a reconciliation*. **2** the process of making it possible for two different ideas, facts, etc. to coexist without being opposed to each other: *the reconciliation of science and religion*. **3** = PENANCE 2a. **4** the action or practice of making one account consistent with another, esp. by allowing for transactions begun but not yet completed. [Say reck'n silly AY sh'n]

recondition *verb* **1** overhaul, refit, renovate. **2** make usable again.

reconfiguration *noun* a new or modified arrangement of the parts or elements of something. [Say re configure AY sh'n]

reconfigure *verb* (**reconfigures**, **reconfigured**, **reconfiguring**) configure again or differently, esp. adapt (a computer system) to a new task by altering its configuration. [Say re CONFIGURE]

reconnaissance *noun* **1** a survey of a region, esp. a military examination to locate an enemy or ascertain strategic features. **2** a preliminary survey or inspection: *lawyers responsible for client reconnaissance*. [Say re CONNA since]

reconnect *verb* connect again. ▶**reconnection** *noun*

reconnoitre • *verb* (**reconnoitres**, **reconnoitred**, **reconnoitring**) make an observation of an area, esp. for military purposes: *they flew helicopter patrols into the region to reconnoitre landing zones for the assault ◊ Hilda left to reconnoitre a powder room*. • *noun* an observation of an area, esp. for military purposes: *a nocturnal reconnoitre of the camp*. [Say recka NOY ter]

reconsider *verb* consider again, esp. for a possible change of decision. ▶**reconsideration** *noun*

reconstitute *verb* (**reconstitutes**, **reconstituted**, **reconstituting**) **1** build up again from parts; reconstruct. **2** restore the previous constitution of (dried food etc.) by adding water. ▶**reconstitution** *noun* [Say re CONSTITUTE]

reconstruct *verb* **1** build or form again. **2 a** form a mental or visual impression of (past events) by assembling the evidence for them. **b** re-enact (a crime). **3** reorganize. ▶**reconstructive** *adjective* [Say re CONSTRUCT]

reconstruction *noun* **1** the act or a mode of reconstructing. **2** a thing reconstructed. **3** (**Reconstruction**) *US hist.* the period (1865-77) following the Civil War. **4** the rebuilding of, and restoration of economic stability to, an area devastated by war. [Say re CONSTRUCTION]

recontextualize *verb* (**recontextualizes**, **recontextualized**, **recontextualizing**) place or study something in a new or different context. [Say re kun TEXTUAL ize]

reconvene *verb* (**reconvenes**, **reconvened**,

reconvening) convene again, esp. (of a meeting etc.) after a pause in proceedings. [Say re kun VEEN]

record • *noun* **1** a piece of evidence or information constituting an account of something that has occurred, been said, etc. **2** the previous conduct or performance of a person or thing. **3** (also **criminal record**) a list of a person's previous criminal convictions. **4** the best performance or most remarkable event of its kind officially recognized. **5** a thin plastic disk carrying recorded sound in grooves on each surface, for reproduction by a record player. **6** *Computing* a number of related items of information which are handled as a unit. • *verb* **1** make a record of. **2** convert (sound, a broadcast, etc.) into permanent form for later reproduction. PHRASES **break** (or **beat**) **the record** outdo all previous performances etc. **for the record** as an official statement etc. **go on record** state one's opinion or judgment openly or officially, so that it is recorded. **a matter of record** a thing established as a fact by being recorded. **off the record** as an unofficial or confidential statement etc. **on record** officially recorded; publicly known. **set** (or **put** or **get**) **the record straight** correct a misapprehension. ▶**recordability** *noun* **recordable** *adjective*

record-breaking *adjective* that breaks a record (*see* RECORD *noun* 5).

recorder *noun* **1** an apparatus for recording, esp. a tape recorder. **2 a** a keeper of records. **b** a person who makes an official record. **3** *Music* a reedless cylindrical wind instrument, played by blowing directly into one end while covering differing combinations of holes along the cylinder.

recording *noun* **1** the process by which audio or video signals are recorded for later reproduction. **2** material or a program recorded. **3** the compact disc, record, or tape so produced.

recount¹ *verb* give an account of an event or experience: *I will recount a few of the stories ◊ recounted a dream she had*. [Say re COUNT]

recount² • *verb* count again. • *noun* a recounting, esp. of votes. [Say REE count]

recoup *verb* recover or regain something lost or spent: *hoping to recoup past losses through future profits ◊ she rested to recoup her energy*. [Say COOP]

recourse *noun* **1** the action or an act of turning to a possible source of help, advice, protection, etc. **2** a person or thing turned to. PHRASES **have recourse to** turn to (a person or thing) for help. [Say RE course]

re-cover *verb* **1** cover again. **2** provide (a chair etc.) with a new cover.

recover *verb* **1** regain possession or use or control of; reclaim. **2** return to health or consciousness or to a normal state or position: *the country never recovered from the war*. **3** obtain or secure (compensation etc.) by legal process. **4** retrieve or make up for (a loss, setback, etc.). **5 recover oneself** regain composure or consciousness or control of one's limbs. **6** retrieve (reusable substances) from industrial waste. ▶**recoverable** *adjective* **recovering** *adjective*

recovery *noun* (*plural* **recoveries**) **1** a return to a normal state of health, mind, or strength: *Robert has made a full recovery from his injury ◊ she is on the road to recovery ◊ signs of recovery in the housing market*. **2** the action or process of regaining possession or control of something stolen or lost: *a reward for information leading to recovery of the stolen goods ◊ recovery of his sight*. **3** the process of overcoming an addiction to drugs etc. or recovering from mental illness. **4** the room in a hospital where patients are kept immediately after an operation: *your mother is now in recovery*.

recreate *verb* (**recreates, recreated, recreating**) create over again. [Say re CREATE]

recreation[1] *noun* something created again; a reproduction or re-enactment: *a recreation of the historic event* ◊ *a recreation of a pioneer town*. [Say re CREATION]

recreation[2] *noun* **1** the process or means of entertaining oneself. **2** an activity or pastime pursued, esp. habitually, for the pleasure or interest it gives: *recreation centre*. [Say reck ree AY sh'n]

recreational *adjective* **1** of or pertaining to recreation. **2** used for recreation: *recreational facilities*. **3** designating or relating to the taking of a drug on an occasional basis for pleasure, esp. when socializing. ▶ **recreationally** *adverb* [Say reck ree AY sh'n ul]

recreational vehicle *noun* a van or camper used for recreational purposes, such as touring and camping, esp. a large motorhome. Abbreviation: **RV**.

recrimination *noun* an accusation in response to one from someone else: *the good relations slowly gave way to recrimination and bitterness* ◊ *peace negotiations have broken down in recriminations and acrimony*. [Say re crimmin AY sh'n]

rec room *noun* a room in a house, usu. in the basement, used for relaxation and entertainment.

recross *verb* (**recrosses, recrossed, recrossing**) cross or pass over again.

recruit • *noun* **1** a serviceman or servicewoman newly enlisted and not yet fully trained. **2** a new employee or member of a society or organization. • *verb* **1 a** enlist (a person) as a recruit. **b** attempt to hire or enrol (a person). **2** form (an army etc.) by enlisting recruits. **3** get or seek recruits. **4** (attempt to) induce (an athlete) to sign on as a student at a college or university. ▶ **recruiter** *noun* **recruitment** *noun* [Say re CROOT]

recrystallize *verb* (**recrystallizes, recrystallized, recrystallizing**) crystallize again.

recta *plural of* RECTUM.

rectal *adjective* of or relating to the rectum.

rectangle *noun* a plane figure with four straight sides and four right angles, esp. one with the adjacent sides unequal.

rectangular *adjective* **1 a** shaped like a rectangle. **b** having the base or sides or section shaped like a rectangle. **2 a** placed at right angles. **b** having parts or lines placed at right angles.

rectifiable *adjective* that can be corrected or made right: *rectifiable problems*. [Say reck ti FIE a bull]

rectification *noun* the process of adjusting something or making something right; correction. [Say reck ti fi KAY sh'n]

rectify *verb* (**rectifies, rectified, rectifying**) **1** adjust or make right; correct, amend. **2** find a straight line equal in length to (a curve). **3** convert (alternating current) to direct current. [Say RECK ti fie]

rectilinear *adjective* (also **rectilineal**) bounded, moving in, or characterized by straight lines: *fields of onions stretched out in large rectilinear blocks*. [Say reck tuh LINNY er, reck tuh LINNY ul]

rectitude *noun* morally correct behaviour or thinking: *his intelligence and rectitude keep the audience rooting for the hero*. [Say RECK ti tood or RECK ti tyood]

recto *noun* (*plural* **rectos**) **1** the right-hand page of an open book. **2** the front of a printed leaf of paper or manuscript (*opp.* VERSO 1b).

rector *noun* **1 a** (in the Church of England) a clergyman in charge of a parish who, formerly, would have been entitled to the whole of the tithes of the parish (*compare* VICAR 1a). **b** (in other Anglican churches) a member of the clergy who has charge of a parish. **2** *Catholicism* a priest in charge of a church or religious institution. **3** the head of some schools, universities, and colleges. [Say RECKTER]

rectory *noun* (*plural* **rectories**) a rector's house. [Say RECKTER ee]

rectum *noun* (*plural* **rectums** or **recta**) the final section of the large intestine, terminating at the anus. [Say RECKTER]

recumbent *adjective* lying down: *near the church door lie recumbent marble figures*. [Say re CUM bint]

recuperate *verb* (**recuperates, recuperated, recuperating**) recover from illness, exhaustion, financial loss, etc. ▶ **recuperation** *noun* **recuperative** *adjective* [Say re COOPER ate]

recur *verb* (**recurs, recurred, recurring**) **1** occur again; be repeated. **2** (of a thought, idea, etc.) come back to one's mind. [Say re CURR]

recurrence *noun* the repeated occurrence of something: *attempts to prevent the recurrence of the disease*. [Say re CURR ince]

recurrent *adjective* **1** recurring; happening repeatedly: *recurrent nightmares*. **2** (of a nerve, vein, branch, etc.) turning back so as to reverse direction. ▶ **recurrently** *adverb* [Say re CURRENT]

recut *verb* (**recuts, recut, recutting**) cut again.

recyclable • *adjective* that can be used again or converted to reusable material: *recyclable bottles*. • *noun* (usu. in *plural*) materials that can be used again or converted to reusable material.

recycle *verb* (**recycles, recycled, recycling**) **1** return material to a previous stage of a cyclic process, esp. convert waste to reusable material. **2** use again with little or no alteration: *recycle a speech*. **3** convert (an object) into something new: *recycle a wine bottle into a vase*. ▶ **recycler** *noun* **recycling** *noun*

red • *adjective* **1** of a colour at the end of the spectrum next to orange and opposite violet, as of blood, fire, or rubies. **2** (of a person's face) red due to embarrassment, anger, or heat. **3** (of hair or fur) of a reddish-brown colour. **4** (of wine) made from dark grapes and coloured by their skins. **5** *informal derogatory* communist or socialist. **6** *Cdn* of or relating to the Liberal Party. • *noun* **1** a red colour, pigment, or material. **2** *informal derogatory* communist or socialist. **3** *informal* a sockeye salmon. ▮PHRASES▮ **in the red** in debt, esp. to a bank: *the company is $5 million in the red*.

red alert *noun* **1** an urgent warning of imminent danger. **2** an instruction to prepare for an emergency. **3** a state of readiness for an emergency.

red alga *noun* (*plural* **red algae**) a seaweed with red pigment found esp. in deep water of tropical seas.

Red Army *noun* **1** *hist.* the army of the Soviet Union, created by the Communist government after the Bolshevik Revolution of 1917; the name was officially dropped in 1946. **2** the army of China or some other (esp. Communist) countries. **3** a left-wing extremist terrorist organization in Japan.

red-bait *verb* harass and persecute (a person) on account of known or suspected Communist sympathies. ▶ **red-baiter** *noun* **red-baiting** *noun*

red-berry *noun Cdn* (esp. *Nfld*) (*plural* **red-berries**) **1** any of various plants bearing red berries, e.g. partridge-berry, cranberry. **2** the fruit of any of these plants.

red blood cell *noun* (also **red cell**) = ERYTHROCYTE.

red-blooded *adjective* full of life, spirited.

red-breasted *adjective* (of a bird) having a red breast: *red-breasted merganser*.

redbud *noun* an early-flowering North American tree of the pea family, with pink flowers that grow from the trunk, branches, and twigs.

redcap *noun* a railway porter.

red carpet *noun* **1** a strip of red carpet traditionally laid down on formal occasions to greet important visitors. **2** a ceremonial welcome; a lavish reception: *rolled out the red carpet*.

red cedar *noun* **1** a North American coniferous tree with reddish-brown bark and reddish wood. **2** the wood of a red cedar.

red cent *noun* **1** the (originally copper) coin of the lowest value. **2** a trivial sum: *not one red cent of taxpayers' money*.

Red Chamber *noun* *Cdn* **1** the Senate chamber of the Parliament Buildings in Ottawa. **2** the Senate itself.

redcoat *noun* *hist.* **1** *Cdn* a member of the North West Mounted Police. **2** a British soldier.

redcurrant *noun* **1** a widely cultivated shrub bearing small, sweet, red berries. **2** this berry.

redd *noun* a hollow in a riverbed made by a trout or salmon to spawn in.

red deer *noun* (*plural* **red deer**) a large deer with a reddish-brown coat; a wapiti.

Red Delicious *noun see* DELICIOUS *noun*.

redden *verb* **1** make or become red. **2** blush.

reddish *adjective* somewhat red.

redecorate *verb* (**redecorates**, **redecorated**, **redecorating**) decorate again or differently. ▶ **redecoration** *noun* [Say re DECORATE]

rededicate *verb* (**rededicates**, **rededicated**, **rededicating**) dedicate anew. ▶ **rededication** *noun* [Say re DEDICATE]

redeem *verb* **1 a** compensate for the faults or bad aspects of: *the station's weather forecaster has professional shortcomings that no computer graphics can redeem ◊ an excellent dessert menu is the restaurant's only redeeming feature*. **b redeem oneself** compensate for past failings, esp. so as to regain favour. **2 a** save or deliver a person from sin, error, or evil: *a sinner redeemed by the grace of God*. **b** help a person recover from a life of suffering or evil: *a traumatized young man redeemed by the love of a pure young woman*. **3** exchange a coupon or gift certificate for merchandise, a discount, or money: *the vouchers can be redeemed for anything but cigarettes and alcohol*. **4** gain or regain possession of something in exchange for payment: *a mortgagor has the right to redeem the land by paying off the entire debt*. **5** pay the money required to clear a debt: *were unable to redeem their mortgage*. **6** repurchase or exchange a bond or share for money: *many of the municipal bonds will be redeemed before maturity*. ▶ **redeemable** *adjective*

redeemer *noun* **1** a person who redeems. **2** (**Redeemer**) Jesus Christ.

redefine *verb* (**redefines**, **redefined**, **redefining**) define again or differently. ▶ **redefinition** *noun*

redemption *noun* **1** the action of saving or being saved from sin, error, or evil: *God's plans for the redemption of the world from sin ◊ an act of redemption for betraying his ideals years earlier*. **2** an act or the process of erasing or compensating for the flaws of a person, a thing, or oneself: *it was a night of redemption for the goalie, who had looked awful in the team's previous game ◊ the possibility of romantic redemption*. **3** a thing that saves someone from error or evil: *his marginalization from the Hollywood jungle proved to be his redemption*. **4** the action or regaining or gaining possession of something in exchange for payment, or clearing a debt: *redemption of shares did not render the company insolvent*. PHRASES **beyond/past redemption** (of a person or thing) too bad to be saved or improved.

redemption centre *noun* *Cdn* (*Maritimes & Nfld*) a place where consumers return beer bottles, pop cans, etc. and receive back their deposit.

redemptive *adjective* **1** *Theology* acting to save or deliver a person from sin or evil: *the redemptive work of Christ*. **2** acting to erase or compensate for a person's faults or suffering: *the exceptional sufferings of Russia under the heel of Marxism may have a redemptive effect*.

Red Ensign *noun* any of several predominantly red flags having the Union Jack in the upper corner along the hoist, esp.: **1** *Cdn hist.* one used as Canada's national flag until 1965, with the Canadian coat of arms in the fly. **2** *Cdn* one used as the provincial flag of Ontario or Manitoba, with the provincial coat of arms in the fly. **3** *Cdn hist.* one used as the flag of the Hudson's Bay Company, having the initials HBC in the fly. **4** the ensign of the British merchant navy.

redeploy *verb* move (troops, workers, materials, etc.) from one area of activity to another: *intelligence agencies are fighting for bigger budgets as they redeploy forces and shift priorities*. ▶ **redeployment** *noun* [Say re duh PLOY]

redesign ● *verb* design again or differently. ● *noun* **1** the action of redesigning something. **2** a new design.

redevelop *verb* (**redevelops**, **redeveloped**, **redeveloping**) develop anew (esp. an urban area, with new buildings). ▶ **redeveloper** *noun*

redevelopment *noun*

red-eye *noun* **1** a red reflection from the blood vessels of a person's retina, seen on a colour photograph taken with a flash. **2** (also **red-eye flight**) *informal* an overnight airline flight. **3** *Cdn* a drink made with tomato juice and beer. **4** any of various fish with red eyes, e.g. the rock bass or smallmouth bass.

red-eyed *adjective* **1** having red eyes from crying etc. **2** (of a bird) having eyes surrounded by a red ring.

red-faced *adjective* embarrassed, ashamed.

Red Fife *noun* *Cdn* a high-yielding variety of wheat, with superior milling and baking qualities, developed in the 1840s near Peterborough, Ont.

redfish *noun* (*plural* **redfish** or **redfishes**) any of various reddish fishes.

red flag *noun* **1** a warning of danger. **2** (in auto racing etc.) a red flag waved as a signal to stop. **3** a symbol of revolution, socialism, or Communism.

red fox *noun* (*plural* **red foxes**) the common fox of Eurasia and North America, having a characteristic red or fawn coat.

red giant *noun* a very large star of high luminosity and low surface temperature.

Red Guard *noun* any of various radical or socialist groups, in particular a militant youth movement in China (1966–76), who carried out vicious attacks on intellectuals and other disfavoured groups as part of Mao's Cultural Revolution.

red-handed *adjective* in or just after the act of committing a crime, doing wrong, etc.: *caught red-handed*.

redhead *noun* **1** a person with red hair. **2** a North American duck with a reddish-chestnut head and grey and black body.

red-headed *adjective* **1** (of a person) having red hair. **2** (of birds etc.) having a red head: *red-headed woodpecker*.

red herring *noun* **1** dried smoked herring. **2** a misleading clue or distraction.

red-hot ● *adjective* **1 a** sufficiently hot to glow red. **b** very hot: *the stove is red-hot*. **2 a** highly exciting: *a red-hot date*. **b** sexy: *the red-hot sex revue, I Love You Baby Blue*. **3** intensely excited. **4** (of news) sensational; completely new. **5** (of a sports team, player, etc.) on a winning streak; performing exceptionally. ● *noun* (**red hot**) a hot dog.

redial ● *verb* (**redials**, **redialed** or **redialled**, **redialing** or **redialling**) dial again. ● *noun* the facility on a telephone by which (in the event of a number being busy, etc.) the number just dialed may be automatically redialed by pressing a single button.

redid *past of* REDO. [Say re DID]

red ink *noun* financial deficit or debt: *drowning in red ink*.

R

redirect *verb* **1** use (resources etc.) in a different, more desirable way: *redirect funds*. **2** send (an object, person, etc.) in a different direction: *redirect the ball*. **3** change the address of (a letter). ▶ **redirection** *noun*

rediscover *verb* discover again. ▶ **rediscovery** *noun* (*plural* **rediscoveries**)

redistribute *verb* (**redistributes, redistributed, redistributing**) distribute again or differently. ▶ **redistributive** *adjective*

redistribution *noun* **1** the action or process of redistributing something, esp. of wealth by means of taxation. **2** *Cdn* the reapportioning, made every ten years, of the number of seats in the House of Commons to reflect changes in the size of the population. ▶ **redistributionist** *noun & adjective*

red-letter day *noun* a day that is pleasantly noteworthy or memorable.

red-light district *noun* a district containing many brothels, strip clubs, etc.

red line • *noun* **1** *Hockey* the centre line on the ice surface, midway between the two blue lines. **2** a red mark on a gauge, dial, etc., indicating the maximum safe value of speed, rate of working, or other quantity. • *verb* (**redline**) (**redlines, redlined, redlining**) refuse credit, loans, or other esp. financial services to businesses or residents of a neighbourhood considered high-risk or less lucrative: *presumably the company will lay its fibre optic cable in the wealthiest communities first, redlining the city's poorer neighbourhoods*.

red maple *noun* a maple of eastern North America, with red twigs, buds, and flowers.

red mullet *noun* a red or reddish-brown marine food fish of the Mediterranean and northeastern Atlantic.

redneck *derogatory* • *noun* a person holding reactionary political views. • *adjective* reactionary; conservative.

redness *noun* the condition of being red: *he uses a mild cream to reduce skin redness and irritation*.

redo *verb* (**redoes**; *past* **redid**; *past participle* **redone**; **redoing**) **1** do again or differently. **2** redecorate or renovate.

redolence *noun* **1** the quality of something that is strongly reminiscent or suggestive of something else: *the redolence of moral blackmail that adheres to certain charitable appeals*. **2** the strong smell of something: *a distinct hemp-like redolence*. [Say REDDA lince]

redolent *adjective* **1** strongly reminiscent or suggestive or mentally associated: *traditional roller skating is redolent of unfashionable 1950s roller rinks where teenagers did their dating*. **2** having a strong fragrance or odour: *the cantor's balmy breath, redolent of mouthwash and borscht*. [Say REDDA lint]

redouble *verb* (**redoubles, redoubled, redoubling**) make or grow greater or more intense or numerous; intensify: *redoubled their efforts*.

redoubt *noun* **1** *Military* an outwork or fieldwork usu. square or polygonal and without flanking defences. **2** something serving as a refuge: *the photo department went from being a white male redoubt to one of the best integrated divisions of the organization*. [Say DOUT]

redoubtable *adjective* **1** formidable, esp. as an opponent. **2** (of a person) commanding respect. [Say re DOUT a bull]

red pepper *noun* the ripe fruit of the sweet pepper, used as a vegetable.

redpoll *noun* any of various finches with red crests.

redraw *verb* (**redraws**; *past* **redrew**; *past participle* **redrawn; redrawing**) draw again or differently.

redress • *verb* (**redresses, redressed, redressing**) remedy or rectify (a wrong or grievance etc.): *they are concerned with redressing women's unequal pay in the workforce*. • *noun* remedy or compensation for a wrong or grievance: *a crime in which the victim has no legal redress*. PHRASES **redress the balance** restore equality. [Say re DRESS or REE dress]

red ribbon *noun* **1 a** (in Canada) an award given for coming first in a contest. **b** (in the US) an award given for coming second in a contest. **2** a small loop of red ribbon worn as a symbol of AIDS awareness.

Red River cart *noun* *Cdn hist.* a sturdy two-wheeled wooden cart pulled by oxen or horses, used for transportation on the Prairies.

Red River jig *noun* *Cdn* **1** a Metis step dance originating in the Red River valley of Manitoba, combining French-Canadian dance rhythms and Aboriginal powwow steps, including an element of improvisation by dancers who compete for originality and precise footwork. **2** the music for this.

Red River Rebellion *noun* *Cdn hist.* an uprising in 1869–70 by the Metis in the Red River valley in Manitoba under Louis Riel, in response to the takeover of their territory by the government of Canada.

red shift *noun* the shift of spectral lines toward longer wavelengths, arising when a galaxy or celestial body and its observer are moving apart. ▶ **red-shifted** *adjective*

red snapper *noun* an edible marine fish of the West Atlantic.

red squirrel *noun* a small North American squirrel with reddish fur.

Red Star *noun* esp. *hist.* the emblem of some Communist countries.

redstart *noun* **1** any of various North and South American warblers with red markings. **2** a red-tailed European songbird.

red-tailed hawk *noun* a common North and Central American hawk with a russet-coloured tail.

red tape *noun* excessive bureaucracy or adherence to formalities esp. in public business.

red-throated loon *noun* a small loon of Nearctic and Palearctic regions, with a grey head, red throat patch, and plain, uncheckered back.

red tide *noun* a discoloration of marine waters caused by an outbreak of toxic red organisms called dinoflagellates.

Red Tory *noun* (*plural* **Red Tories**) *Cdn* a Progressive Conservative who holds more liberal views on certain esp. social issues than his or her fellow party members. ▶ **Red Toryism** *noun*

reduce *verb* (**reduces, reduced, reducing**) **1** make or become smaller or less in amount, degree, or size. **2** (foll. by *to*) change (something) to (a simpler or more basic form). **3** (foll. by *to*) bring to (an undesirable state or action). **4** boil (a sauce or other liquid) so that it becomes thicker and more concentrated. **5** *Chemistry* cause to combine chemically with hydrogen. **6** *Chemistry* cause to undergo a reaction in which electrons are gained from another substance or molecule. **7** restore (a dislocated body part) to its proper position. PHRASES **reduce to the ranks** demote a non-commissioned officer to the rank of private. ▶ **reducer** *noun* **reducible** *adjective*

reduced circumstances *plural noun* a poorer financial condition or situation; a state of poverty: *she is still an eye-catching dresser despite her reduced circumstances*.

reduction *noun* **1** the action or fact of making a specified thing smaller or less in amount, degree, or size: *arms reduction* ◊ *a reduction in the number of casualties*. **2** an amount by which prices etc. are reduced. **3** a copy of a picture etc. made on a smaller scale than the original. **4** an arrangement of an orchestral score for piano etc.

reductionism *noun* often *derogatory* the practice of

analyzing and describing a complex phenomenon, esp. a mental, social, or biological phenomenon, in terms of phenomena which are held to represent a simpler or more fundamental level, esp. when this is said to provide a sufficient explanation. ▶ **reductionist** *noun* **reductionistic** *adjective*

reductive *adjective* often *derogatory* that tries to explain something complicated by considering it as a combination of simple parts.

redundancy *noun* (*plural* **redundancies**) **1** the state of being no longer needed or useful. **2** (in writing etc.) the use of words or ideas that are repeated elsewhere and which can therefore be omitted without any loss of significance. **3** the condition of having one function or responsibility performed by more than one person or part: *redundancy in our parliamentary system*. **4** the inclusion, in machinery or computer equipment, of extra components that are not strictly necessary to functioning, in case of failure in other components. **5** the state of being no longer employed because there is no more work available: *the plant's 800 workers face redundancy*. [Say re DUN din see]

redundant *adjective* **1** no longer needed or useful; superfluous. **2** (of words) that can be omitted without any loss of significance. **3** (of a person) no longer needed at work and therefore unemployed. **4** *Engineering & Computing* (of a component) not needed but included in case of failure in another component. ▶ **redundantly** *adverb* [Say re DUN dint]

reduplicate *verb* (**reduplicates**, **reduplicated**, **reduplicating**) repeat (a letter or syllable or word) exactly or with a slight change, e.g. hurly-burly, see-saw. ▶ **reduplication** *noun* [Say re DUPLICATE]

redwing *noun* any of several red-winged birds, esp. the red-winged blackbird.

red-winged blackbird *noun* a very common North and Central American blackbird, the male of which has a conspicuous red patch on the wings.

redwood *noun* **1** an exceptionally large conifer of California and Oregon, yielding red wood. **2** any tree yielding red wood.

reed *noun* **1** any of various water or marsh plants of the grass family, with tall firm stems. **2** reeds growing in a mass or used as material esp. for thatching. **3** a pipe of reed or straw. **4 a** the vibrating part of the mouthpiece of some wind instruments, e.g. the oboe and clarinet, made of reed or other material and producing the sound. **b** (esp. in *plural*) a reed instrument.

re-edit *verb* (**re-edits**, **re-edited**, **re-editing**) edit again or differently.

re-educate *verb* (**re-educates**, **re-educated**, **re-educating**) educate again, esp. to change a person's views or beliefs. ▶ **re-education** *noun*

reedy *adjective* (**reedier**, **reediest**) **1** full of reeds. **2** like a reed, esp. in weakness or slenderness. **3** (of a voice) high, thin, and harsh; not resonant.

reef • *noun* (*plural* **reefs**) **1** a ridge of jagged rock, coral, or sand just above or below the surface of the sea. **2** a vein of ore, esp. one containing gold: *gold locked in underground reefs*. **3** each of several strips across a sail, for taking it in or rolling it up to reduce the surface area in a high wind. • *verb* take in a reef or reefs of (a sail).

reefer *noun* **1** *slang* a marijuana cigarette. **2** a thick close-fitting double-breasted jacket.

reef knot *noun* a double knot made symmetrically to hold securely and cast off easily.

reek • *verb* (often foll. by *of*) **1** smell strongly and unpleasantly. **2** have unpleasant or suspicious associations: *this reeks of corruption*. **3** give off smoke or fumes. • *noun* a foul or stale smell. ▶ **reeky** *adjective*

reel • *noun* **1** a cylindrical device on which film, tape, etc., is wound. **2** a device for winding and unwinding a line as required, esp. in fishing. **3** a revolving part in various machines. **4** a lively folk or Scottish dance with two or more couples facing each other. • *verb* **1** wind (thread, a fishing line, etc.) on a reel. **2** (foll. by *in*, *up*) draw (fish etc.) in or up by the use of a reel. **3** stand or walk or run unsteadily. **4** be shaken mentally or physically. **5** rock from side to side, or swing violently. **6** dance a reel. PHRASES **reel off** say or recite very rapidly and without apparent effort.

re-elect *verb* elect again, esp. to a further term of office. ▶ **re-election** *noun*

reel-to-reel *adjective* designating a tape recorder in which the tape passes between two reels mounted separately, rather than within a cassette.

re-emerge *verb* (**re-emerges**, **re-emerged**, **re-emerging**) emerge again; come back out.

re-emergence *noun* an act of emerging again; a return to view or prominence: *the re-emergence of fashion trends from the 1960s* ◊ *we awaited the re-emergence of the whale from the water*.

re-emphasize *verb* (**re-emphasizes**, **re-emphasized**, **re-emphasizing**) place renewed emphasis on.

re-enact *verb* act out (a past event). ▶ **re-enactment** *noun*

re-engineer *verb* **1** design and construct again: *a re-engineered automobile*. **2** change the structure of a business or other organization, usu. by introducing improved technology and reducing staff, to improve efficiency. ▶ **re-engineering** *noun*

re-enter *verb* **1** enter (a building etc.) again; go back in. **2** participate in (a race, politics, a contest, etc.) again. ▶ **re-entrance** *noun*

re-entrant • *adjective* **1** (of an angle) pointing inwards (*opp.* SALIENT *adjective* 2). **2** *Math* (of an interior angle in a polygon) greater than 180°. • *noun* **1** a re-entrant angle. **2** a person who re-enters (esp. the workforce).

re-entry *noun* (*plural* **re-entries**) the act of entering again, esp. (of a spacecraft, missile, etc.) re-entering the earth's atmosphere.

re-equip *verb* (**re-equips**, **re-equipped**, **re-equipping**) provide or be provided with new equipment. ▶ **re-equipment** *noun*

re-establish *verb* (**re-establishes**, **re-established**, **re-establishing**) establish again or anew. ▶ **re-establishment** *noun*

re-evaluate *verb* (**re-evaluates**, **re-evaluated**, **re-evaluating**) evaluate again or differently. ▶ **re-evaluation** *noun*

reeve *noun* *Cdn* (in Ontario and the Western provinces) the elected leader of the council of a town or other rural municipality. ▶ **reeveship** *noun*

re-examination *noun* a second or further examination, esp. of a witness after cross-examination.

re-examine *verb* (**re-examines**, **re-examined**, **re-examining**) examine again or further (esp. a witness after cross-examination).

ref *Sport informal* • *noun* a referee. • *verb* (**refs**, **reffed**, **reffing**) supervise (a game or match) as a referee.

refashion *verb* change the composition or appearance of (something); fashion again or differently.

refer *verb* (**refers**, **referred**, **referring**) (usu. foll. to) **1** allude (to) or describe: *I wasn't referring to you*. **2** represent; pertain (to): *the word "doe" can be used to refer to a female rabbit*. **3** send or direct (someone) to a person or thing for help, information, advice, etc.: *referred me to a psychiatrist*. **4** direct (questions to be answered, matters to be dealt with, issues to be resolved, etc.) to someone: *refer all questions to me*. **5** consult (notes, instructions, etc.) for information or advice. **6** trace or attribute something to a person or thing as a cause or source.

referee • *noun* **1** an official who supervises a hockey, basketball, etc. game or boxing match to ensure that the competitors obey the rules. **2** a person whose opinion or judgment is sought, esp. by mutual consent of two parties in a legal dispute. **3** a person appointed to examine and assess an academic work being considered for publication. • *verb* (**referees**, **refereed**, **refereeing**) **1** act as referee. **2** supervise (a game, match, etc.) as a referee. **3** review (an academic publication) as a referee. ▶ **refereed** *adjective* **refereeing** *noun*

reference • *noun* **1** (foll. by *to*) **a** an allusion: *made no reference to our problems*. **b** a relation or correspondence. **2 a** a direction of attention to a book or passage of a book, esp. one used as a source of information for a research paper, article, etc. **b** a useful source of information, such as a book, article, etc. **c** such sources of information considered collectively. **d** the act of looking up a passage etc. or looking in a book for information. **3 a** a testimonial supporting an applicant for employment etc. **b** a person giving this. • *verb* (**references**, **referenced**, **referencing**) **1** cite; make mention of or a reference to. **2** provide (a book etc.) with references to authorities. PHRASES **with** (or **in**) **reference to** regarding; as regards. **without reference to** not taking account of.

reference book *noun* a book meant to be consulted for information on individual matters rather than read continuously, e.g. a dictionary, atlas, etc.

reference library *noun* (*plural* **reference libraries**) a library in which the books are for consultation, not loan.

reference point *noun* a basis or standard for evaluation, assessment, or comparison.

referendum *noun* (*plural* **referendums** or **referenda**) **1** the process of referring a political question to the electorate for a direct decision by general vote. **2** a vote taken by referendum.

referent *noun* the thing in the world that a word or phrase denotes or stands for: *"the Morning Star" and "the Evening Star" have the same referent (the planet Venus)*. [Say REFFER int]

referential *adjective* **1** containing references or allusions. **2** (of art) imitating the style of or containing references to other artistic works and thus lacking originality. [Say reffer EN shul]

referral *noun* the referring of an individual to an expert or specialist for advice, esp. the directing of a patient by a general practitioner to a medical specialist. [Say re FUR ul]

refill • *verb* fill or become filled again. • *noun* **1** a replacement for something that has been used up, esp. fitting in the same container or device as the original: *lead refills for a pencil*. **2** a second serving, esp. of a beverage etc., replacing one consumed, usu. served in the same cup. ▶ **refillable** *adjective*

refinance *verb* (**refinances**, **refinanced**, **refinancing**) **1** finance again; arrange a new financial agreement or loan for: *refinance a house*. **2** repay some or all of (a loan) by obtaining fresh loans, usu. at a lower rate of interest. ▶ **refinancing** *noun* [Say re FINANCE]

refine *verb* (**refines**, **refined**, **refining**) **1** free from impurities or defects; purify, clarify. **2** make or become more polished, elegant, or cultured. **3** make or become more subtle or delicate in thought, feelings, etc. **4** fine-tune, improve or perfect: *refine the mechanism*.

refined *adjective* **1** characterized by polish, elegance, or subtlety. **2** (esp. of sugar, oil, etc.) purified, freed from impurities or extraneous matter. **3** fine-tuned, perfected: *a refined process*.

refinement *noun* **1** the process of improving something by making small changes. **2** an added development or improvement. **3** polish or elegance in behaviour, manners, or taste. **4** a fine distinction.

refiner *noun* a person or company whose business is to refine crude oil, sugar, etc.

refinery *noun* (*plural* **refineries**) a place where oil etc. is refined.

refining *noun* **1** the process of removing impurities or unwanted elements from a substance, esp. as part of an industrial process: *the petroleum refining industry*. **2** the process of improving something by making small changes.

refinish *verb* (**refinishes**, **refinished**, **refinishing**) **1** apply a new finish to (a surface). **2** remove old layers of paint or varnish from (wood, furniture, etc.) and apply new stain, varnish, etc. to.

refit • *verb* (**refits**, **refitted**, **refitting**) restore or be restored to a serviceable condition by renewals and repairs. • *noun* a restoration or repair of machinery, equipment, fittings, etc. ▶ **refitting** *noun*

reflect *verb* **1** (of an esp. smooth or polished surface) throw back or cause to rebound (heat, light, sound, etc.). **2** (esp. of a mirror, water, glass, etc.) reproduce or show an image of. **3** result from; suggest or point to something as a cause or source: *his aggressive behaviour reflects a will to win*. **4** bring credit or discredit to: *this loss reflects badly on the coaching*. **5 a** meditate on; think about. **b** consider; remind oneself. **6** (of light, heat, an image, etc.) be cast back; bounce back or off: *moonlight reflected off the water*. **7** (of an action, result, etc.) show or bring (credit, discredit, etc.).

reflection *noun* **1** the throwing back by a body or surface of light, heat, or sound without absorbing it: *the reflection of light*. **2 a** reflected light, heat, or colour: *the reflections from the street lamps gave them just enough light*. **b** a reflected image: *gazed at her reflection in the mirror*. **3** deep and careful consideration: *a week off would give him time for reflection* ◊ *on reflection, she decided to accept the offer after all*. **4** an indication of something: *your clothes are a reflection of your personality* ◊ *the increase in homelessness is a sad reflection on our society*. **5** an account or representation of something: *the article is an accurate reflection of events that day*. **6** an idea about a particular subject, esp. one that is written down or expressed: *reflections on human destiny and art*.

reflective *adjective* **1** (of a surface etc.) reflecting light, images, etc. **2** (of a person or mood etc.) given to meditation. **3** (of an account) characterized by deep thought or reflection. **4** (foll. by *of*) indicative; symptomatic. ▶ **reflectively** *adverb*

reflector *noun* **1** a piece of glass or metal etc. for reflecting light in a required direction, e.g. a red one on the back of a bicycle. **2 a** a telescope etc. using a mirror to produce images. **b** the mirror itself. **3** any surface which reflects light, heat, etc., or something considered in terms of its reflective properties.

R

reflex • *noun* (*plural* **reflexes**) **1** an involuntary or automatic response of any organ or body part to a stimulus. **2** an immediate or automatic reaction to something, esp. a habitual response: *hitting the snooze button is a reflex*. **3** (in *plural*) the ability, usu. physical, to react quickly, esp. dexterously or with coordination: *Eric has excellent reflexes*. • *adjective* **1** (of an action) independent of the will, as an automatic response to the stimulation of a nerve (e.g. a sneeze). **2** (of a response or reaction) immediate, unthinking.

reflexive *adjective* **1** triggered by, or as if by, reflex. **2** *Grammar* (of a word or form) referring back to the subject of a sentence (esp. of a pronoun, e.g. *myself*). **3** *Grammar* (of a verb) having a reflexive pronoun as its object (as in *to wash oneself*). ▶ **reflexively** *adverb* **reflexivity** *noun* [Say reflex IVVA tee]

reflexologist *noun* a person who studies reflexology. [Say reflex OLLA jist]

reflexology *noun* a system of massage used to relieve tension and treat illness, based on the theory that there are reflex points on the feet, hands, and head linked to every part of the body. [Say reflex OLLA jee]

refocus *verb* (**refocuses**, **refocused**, **refocusing**) **1** (of a camera lens) adjust the focus of. **2** change the scope or object of (attention, a study, goals, etc.).

reforest *verb* replant (former forest land) with trees. ▶ **reforestation** *noun*

reform • *verb* **1** make or become better by the removal of faults and errors; improve. **2** abolish or cure (an abuse or vice). • *noun* **1** significant changes suggested or made to something; an overhaul: *Senate reform.* **2** the removal of faults or abuses, esp. of a moral or political or social kind: *committed to reform.* **3** (**Reform**) *Cdn* = REFORM PARTY 1. **4** (**Reform**) *Cdn hist.* designating those who opposed the Family Compact in Upper Canada or the Château Clique in Lower Canada in the movement for responsible government in the 19th century. **5** (usu. **Reform**) = REFORM JUDAISM.

re-form *verb* form again.

reformat *verb* (**reformats**, **reformatted**, **reformatting**) **1** revise or represent in another format. **2** *Computing* make adjustments to (a storage medium) to enable it to receive data.

reformation *noun* **1** the act of reforming or process of being reformed, esp. a radical change for the better in political or religious or social affairs. **2** (**the Reformation**) *hist.* the 16th-century movement to reform the doctrine and practices of the Catholic Church, which resulted in the establishment of the Protestant Churches. [Say reffer MAY sh'n]

reformatory • *noun* (*plural* **reformatories**) an institution to which young offenders are sent to be reformed. • *adjective* tending or designed to reform. [Say re FORMA tory]

reformed *adjective* **1** (of a person) no longer behaving in an immoral, criminal, or self-destructive manner: *a reformed ex-con ◊ a reformed computer hacker*. **2** that has been improved through various changes: *a reformed senate*. **3** (**Reformed**) **a** designating a Church that has accepted the principles of the Reformation, esp. a Calvinist Church. **b** belonging to or falling under the influence of a Reformed Church.

reformer *noun* **1** a person who advocates or brings about (esp. political or social) reform. **2** (**Reformer**) *Cdn* a supporter or member of the Reform Party. **3** (**Reformer**) *Cdn hist.* a person who participated in the movement for responsible government in Upper and Lower Canada in the 19th century.

reformism *noun* the promotion of social, political, or religious reform.

reformist • *noun* an advocate or supporter of social,

political, or religious reform. • *adjective* of or pertaining to reformists or their policies.

Reform Judaism *noun* a branch of Judaism which has reformed or abandoned aspects of Orthodox Jewish worship and ritual in an attempt to adapt to modern social, political, and cultural changes.

Reform Party *noun* *Cdn* **1** an esp. Western Canadian right-wing political party favouring greater power for the provinces, deficit reduction, reduced power for government, and conservative social values. Founded in 1987, the party merged with some members of the Progressive Conservative Party in 2000 to form the Canadian Alliance. **2** *hist.* the party of Reformers that opposed the Tories in Upper Canada in the 1800s.

reform school *noun* = REFORMATORY.

reformulate *verb* (**reformulates**, **reformulated**, **reformulating**) formulate again or differently. ▶ **reformulation** *noun*

refract *verb* **1** (of water, air, glass, etc.) deflect (a ray of light, sound, etc.) at a certain angle when it enters obliquely from another medium. **2** change, distort, or influence (an idea, emotion, etc.) as it is passed through an intermediary: *the group refracts an entire musical spectrum into vivid new colours*. ▶ **refracted** *adjective*

refraction *noun* the process by which, or the extent to which, light, sound, etc., is refracted when passing obliquely through the interface between one medium and another or through a medium of varying density.

refractive *adjective* involving or capable of causing refraction.

refractor *noun* **1** a refracting medium or lens. **2** a telescope using a lens to produce an image. [Say re FRACTOR]

refractory *adjective* **1** stubborn, unmanageable, rebellious: *like a teacher trying to get her refractory pupils to pull themselves together*. **2** (of a wound, disease, etc.) not yielding to treatment. **3** (of a substance) hard to fuse or work. **4** temporarily unresponsive to nervous or sexual stimuli: *refractory period*. [Say re FRACTOR ee]

refrain[1] *verb* (usu. foll. by *from*) avoid doing (an action); abstain: *refrain from smoking*.

refrain[2] *noun* **1** a recurring phrase or number of lines, esp. at the ends of stanzas. **2** the music accompanying this. **3** an often repeated idea or expression.

refreeze *verb* (**refreezes**; *past* **refroze**; *past participle* **refrozen**; **refreezing**) freeze again.

refresh • *verb* (**refreshes**, **refreshed**, **refreshing**) **1 a** impart strength or energy to (a person etc.); invigorate: *the nap refreshed her*. **b** revive with food, rest, etc.: *refreshed myself with a drink*. **2** revive or stimulate (the memory), esp. by consulting the source of one's information. **3** replenish. **4** replenish or recharge the data stored in a memory device. **5** (of a monitor or screen) repeat the display of digital information on a screen or cathode ray tube at rapid intervals in order to make an image appear continuous. • *noun* the process of renewing the data stored in a memory device. ▶ **refreshed** *adjective*

refresher *noun* **1** something that refreshes, esp. a drink. **2** an update or review of previous education: *refresher course*.

refreshing *adjective* **1** serving to refresh. **2** pleasantly new or different. **3** (of food or drink) cooling or thirst-quenching. ▶ **refreshingly** *adverb*

refreshment *noun* **1** the act of refreshing or the process of being refreshed in mind or body. **2** (usu. in *plural*) food or drink, esp. provided for or sold to people in a public place or at a public event. **3** something that refreshes or stimulates the mind.

refried beans *plural noun* a Mexican dish of cooked beans which have been left to cool, then fried.

refrigerant *noun* a substance used for refrigeration.

refrigerate *verb* (**refrigerates, refrigerated, refrigerating**) **1** make or become cool or cold. **2** subject (food etc.) to cold in order to freeze or preserve it. ▶ **refrigerated** *adjective* **refrigeration** *noun*

refrigerator *noun* **1** a cabinet or room in which food etc. is kept cold. **2** (as an *adjective*) designating a truck, railway car, etc. equipped with a refrigerator.

refuel *verb* (**refuels, refuelled, refuelling**) **1** replenish a fuel supply. **2** supply with more fuel.

refuge *noun* **1** a shelter from pursuit, danger, or trouble. **2** a person or place etc. offering this. **3** a thing or course used as a means of escape from difficulties, problems, etc.: *alcohol is his refuge.* **4** a park or sanctuary in which esp. endangered animals are protected. PHRASES **take refuge in** resort to as a means of escape or shelter. [Say REF yoodge]

refugee *noun* (*plural* **refugees**) a person taking refuge, esp. in a foreign country, from war, persecution, or natural disaster: *refugee status.*

refugee determination *noun* (also **refugee determination process**) *Cdn* the process by which the validity of a claim of refugee status is assessed.

refund • *verb* **1** pay back (money or expenses). **2** reimburse (a person). • *noun* **1** an act of refunding. **2** a sum refunded. ▶ **refundable** *adjective*

refurbish *verb* (**refurbishes, refurbished, refurbishing**) **1** brighten up, redecorate. **2** restore, repair. ▶ **refurbished** *adjective* **refurbishment** *noun* [Say re FUR bish]

refusal *noun* **1** an act of indicating or showing that one is not willing to do, accept, or grant something: *their refusal to accept change.* **2** (also **first refusal**) the right or privilege of deciding to take or leave a thing before it is offered to others: *should tenants have the right of first refusal if the landlord decides to sell a property?*

refuse[1] *verb* (**refuses, refused, refusing**) **1** decline to take or accept (something offered or presented). **2** adamantly decline; be stubbornly unwilling: *the car refuses to start ◊ I refuse!* **3** withhold permission or consent: *I refuse to let you stay up past your bedtime.* **4** decline to give (to a person something requested); deny: *refused me a day off.* **5** decline to admit (a person) to a particular position or place.

refuse[2] *noun* *formal* items rejected as worthless; garbage. [Say REF yooss]

refusenik *noun* **1** *hist.* a Jew in the former Soviet Union who was refused permission to emigrate to Israel. **2** a person who refuses to comply with rules or regulations imposed by an establishment, esp. due to moral beliefs. [Say re FUZE nick]

refutation *noun* **1** the act of proving by argument that a statement or theory or the person proposing it is wrong: *this book is a definitive refutation of her thesis.* **2** the act of denying or contradicting a statement or accusation without argument or proof: *despite the prime minister's refutations of any cover-up, many Canadians believe that they are not being told the whole story.* [Say ref you TAY sh'n]

refute *verb* (**refutes, refuted, refuting**) **1** prove by argument that a statement or theory or the person proposing it is wrong; disprove, rebut: *these claims have not been convincingly refuted.* **2** deny or contradict a statement or accusation without argument or proof: *a spokesperson refuted the allegations of bias.* [Say re FYOOT]

reg *noun* *informal* (usu. in *plural*) regulation.

Reg. *abbreviation* Regina (queen).

reg. *abbreviation* **1** registered. **2** regular price.

regain *verb* **1** obtain possession or use of after loss. **2** get back to, reach (a place, position) again.

regal *adjective* of, like, or fit for a monarch: *regal splendour ◊ a regal gesture.* [Say REE gull]

regale *verb* (**regales, regaled, regaling**) **1** entertain or divert with (talk etc.): *he regaled her with a colourful account of the meeting.* **2** entertain lavishly with feasting: *I was regaled with excellent home cooking.* [Say re GAIL]

regalia *plural noun* **1** any distinctive or elaborate clothes or accoutrements. **2** the decorations or insignia of royalty used esp. at coronations. **3** the decorations or insignia of any order. [Say re GAIL yuh]

regally *adverb* **1** in the dignified manner of a king or queen: *she strolled regally along the red carpet.* **2** in a magnificent or impressive manner: *the castle stood regally upon the hill.* [Say REE guh lee]

regard • *verb* **1** look upon or view; consider: *is regarded as our best swimmer.* **2** esteem, value: *we regard your work highly.* **3** (of a thing) relate to; have some connection with: *this note is regarding our conversation of last night.* **4** gaze on steadily (usu. in a specified way): *she regarded them with apprehension.* • *noun* **1** (foll. by *for, to*) concern (for); proper consideration or appreciation (of): *lived with no regard for anyone but herself.* **2** (often foll. by *for*) esteem; opinion: *she held his work in high regard.* **3** a respect: *in this regard.* **4** (in *plural*) an expression of friendliness in a letter etc.; compliments: *give him my regards.* **5** a gaze; a steady or significant look. PHRASES **as regards** about, concerning. **with** (or **in**) **regard to** as concerns; with respect to.

regarding *preposition* about, concerning.

regardless • *adjective* (usu. foll. by *of*) without regard or consideration for: *regardless of the expense.* • *adverb* despite what might happen; anyway, nevertheless: *we must carry on regardless.*

regatta *noun* (*plural* **regattas**) a series of races of boats, yachts, etc. [Say re GATTA]

Regatta Day *noun* *Cdn* (*Nfld*) **1** a marine event held annually on usu. the first Wednesday in August on Quidi Vidi Lake in St. John's, Newfoundland, associated with a carnival. **2** (in Newfoundland) a provincial statutory holiday held on this day.

regency *noun* (*plural* **regencies**) **1 a** the office or jurisdiction of regent. **b** a commission acting as regent. **c** the period of office of a regent or regency commission. **2** (**Regency**) **a** the period (1811–20) during the reign of George III in Britain when George, Prince of Wales, was regent. **b** (as an *adjective*) designating clothing, architecture, furniture, and other decorative arts of this period, inspired by Greco-Roman models and characterized esp. by purity and simplicity of line and detail. **3** (**Regency**) **a** (in France) the period from 1715 to 1723 during the reign of Louis XV when Philip, Duke of Orleans, was regent. **b** (as an *adjective*) designating architecture and furniture typical of this period, characterized esp. by delicate finishes and curved lines. [Say REE jin see]

regenerate • *verb* (**regenerates, regenerated, regenerating**) **1** reconstitute in a new and improved form; revive: *regenerate the neighbourhood.* **2** bring or come into renewed existence, esp. of a greater spiritual or moral nature. **3** regrow or cause (new plant or animal tissue) to regrow to replace lost or damaged tissue. **4** *Chemistry* restore or be restored to an initial state of reaction or process. • *adjective* **1** spiritually born again. **2** reformed. [Say re JENNER ate for the verb, re JENNER it for the adjective]

regeneration *noun* **1** a revival; reconstitution in an improved form. **2 a** the formation of new animal tissue. **b** the natural replacement of lost parts or organs. **3** the fact or process of being reborn, esp. spiritually. **4** the natural regrowth of a forest which has been felled or thinned.

regenerative *adjective* involving regeneration, esp. capable of developing new plant or animal tissue: *the skin's regenerative properties*. [Say re JENNER uh tiv]

regent • *noun* **1** a person appointed to administer a country or state because the monarch is a minor, absent, or incapacitated. **2** a member of the governing body of a university or other academic institution. • *adjective* (placed after noun) acting as regent: *Prince Regent*. [Say REE jint]

reggae *noun* a West Indian style of popular music indigenous to the black culture of Jamaica, developed from an eclectic mix of African religious music, Christian black revival songs, New Orleans rhythm and blues, and Rastafarian liturgical music. [Say REG ay]

regie *noun Cdn* (*Que.*) (also **Régie**) (usu. as **the regie**) any of several Quebec government bodies regulating insurance, housing, language, etc. [Say ray ZHEE]

regime *noun* **1 a** a method of government or dominance of a country or state, esp. one that is or is considered to be oppressive: *a military regime*. **b** a period in which such a government is in power: *during the Nazi regime*. **2** a system of managing or organizing something: *a tax regime*. **3** a (medical) regimen. [Say ray ZHEEM]

regimen *noun* **1** *Medical* a prescribed course of exercise, way of life, or diet. **2** a strict routine or schedule, usu. imposed or suggested. [Say REDGE a men]

regiment *noun* **1** a permanent unit of an army usu. commanded by a colonel and divided into several companies, troops, or batteries and often into two battalions. **2** (usu. foll. by *of*) a large array or number. ▶ **regimental** *adjective* [Say REDGE a mint]

regimentation *noun* **1** the action of imposing order; the process by which (people etc.) are integrated in a system, institution, etc. **2** strict organization, order. [Say redge uh men TAY sh'n]

regimented *adjective* **1** characterized by strict discipline or order. **2** organized, usu. strictly or oppressively, in definite groups or according to an order or system. [Say REDGE uh ment ed]

Regina *noun* the reigning queen (following a name or in the titles of lawsuits). [Say re JYE nuh or re JEE nuh]

Regina Manifesto *noun Cdn hist.* the declaration of principles and objectives, including the goal of establishing a welfare state, adopted by the Co-operative Commonwealth Federation in 1933. [Say re JYE nuh]

Reginan • *noun* a native or inhabitant of Regina, Saskatchewan. • *adjective* of or relating to Regina. [Say re JYE nun]

region *noun* **1** a (usu. specified) area of land or division of the earth's surface without fixed limits but having definable features such as climate, fauna, flora, etc.: *wine-growing region*. **2** an area of land or division of the earth's surface marked by certain boundaries: *the region between the Ottawa and St. Lawrence rivers*. **3 a** the area of land outside a principal city: *Edmonton and surrounding regions*. **b** the area of land surrounding and including a (usu. specified) place: *the Great Lakes region*. **c** (in *plural*) esp. *Cdn* the areas of a country, province, etc. away from the political centre. **4** a part of the body near or including a (usu. specified) organ etc.: *the lower back region*. **5** a relatively large administrative division of a country or province, esp. one uniting several large municipalities. **6** an area of the world made up of neighbouring countries which are considered socially, economically, or politically interdependent: *the Baltic region*. PHRASES **in the region of** approximately.

regional • *adjective* of, pertaining to, or characteristic of a region. • *noun* **1** a thing, such as a stamp, newspaper, etc., produced or used in a particular region. **2** (in *plural*) a tournament or championship involving teams, athletes, etc. from a particular region.

regional district *noun Cdn* (*BC*) an administrative unit that coordinates the services of municipalities and rural areas within its boundaries, similar to a regional municipality.

regionalism *noun* **1** the theory or practice of regional rather than central systems of administration of economic, cultural, or political affiliation. **2** allegiance to or concern for one's region rather than one's country. **3** a linguistic feature, custom, etc. peculiar to a particular region and not found or heard elsewhere in a country. ▶ **regionalist** *noun & adjective*

regionalization *noun* **1** the process of dividing a territory, enterprise, or organization into or according to geographical regions for administrative purposes: *the regionalization of Europe*. **2** the process of bringing something under the control of a regional authority for administrative purposes: *the plan for regionalization of police services would mean that existing municipal police forces will merge to form larger, regional forces*.

regionalize *verb* (**regionalizes**, **regionalized**, **regionalizing**) **1** bring under the control of a region for administrative purposes. **2** divide into regions. [Say REGIONAL ize]

regionally *adverb* **1** on a regional basis; from region to region: *regionally diverse*. **2** in or throughout a region: *the store is regionally renowned*.

regional municipality *noun* (*plural* **regional municipalities**) *Cdn* (*Ont. & Que.*) a large municipality representing a federation of all the area municipalities within its borders. Abbreviation: **RM**.

register • *noun* **1** an official list or record of births, deaths, marriages, guests, students in attendance at school, etc. **2** a device that records information automatically, esp. a cash register. **3** a device used to store information within a computer system for high-speed access. **4** an adjustable plate for widening or narrowing an opening and regulating the passage of air, heat, smoke, etc.: *floor register*. **5 a** the range of tones of a voice or instrument. **b** a part of this range: *lower register*. **6** *Linguistics* each of several forms of a language (colloquial, formal, literary, etc.) usually used in particular circumstances. • *verb* **1** set down or record a name, an event, a sale, etc. in a list or register for official purposes. **2** a check into a hotel. **b** (foll. by *for*) enrol in a course etc. **3 a** (of a couple to be married etc.) have a list of gifts compiled and kept at a store for consultation by gift buyers. **b** (usu. in *passive*) (of a gift store) compile and maintain a list of gifts for (a couple to be married etc.): *where are you registered?* **4 a** (of an instrument) record automatically; indicate. **b** (of temperature, winds, an earthquake, etc.) be or reach a certain figure when measured. **5 a** express (an emotion) facially or by gesture: *registered surprise*. **b** (of an emotion) show in a person's face or gestures. **6** make an impression; be recognized or noted mentally: *did not register at all*. **7** entrust (a letter etc.) to a post office for transmission by registered mail.

registered *adjective* **1** recorded; officially set down, esp. in a register. **2** officially licensed; certified: *registered nurse* ◊ *registered firearm*. **3** signed up; enrolled. **4** (of dogs etc.) registered as a purebred by an authorized breeder.

Registered Education Savings Plan *noun Cdn* = RESP.

Registered Home Ownership Savings Plan *noun Cdn* = RHOSP.

registered mail *noun* **1** a postal procedure with special precautions for safety and for compensation in case of loss. **2** letters or mail sent this way.

registered nurse *noun* a nurse who is licensed to practise and is a registered member of a nurses' association.

registered nursing assistant *noun* a nursing assistant who holds a certificate issued by a professional body of nurses.

registered practical nurse *noun* a person who is registered by a professional association of nurses as being trained to perform basic nursing tasks under the direction of a physician or registered nurse.

Registered Retirement Income Fund *noun* *Cdn* = RRIF.

Registered Retirement Savings Plan *noun* *Cdn* = RRSP.

registrant *noun* a person who registers or has registered for something. [Say REDGE iss trint]

registrar *noun* **1** an official responsible for keeping a register or official records. **2** an official at an educational institution responsible for maintaining records of students' enrolment, marks, etc. **3** *Cdn & Brit. Law* a judicial and administrative officer responsible for issuing and filing court documents. [Say REDGE iss trar]

registration *noun* **1** the action of making an official record of something: *university registration starts in August* ◊ *registration fees*. **2** the form or certificate that verifies that something or someone has been registered: *asked to see my car registration*.

registry *noun* (*plural* **registries**) **1** a place or office where registers or records are kept. **2** registration. **3** a list of gifts requested e.g. by a couple to be married, and of those already purchased, kept at a store for consultation by gift buyers: *bridal registry*. **4** a ship's country of origin as indicated on its registration.

registry office *noun* *Cdn* **1** a government office where private property, such as vehicles, real estate, etc., may be registered and where records of ownership are kept. **2** a government office where records of births, deaths, and marriages are kept.

regrade *verb* (**regrades**, **regraded**, **regrading**) grade again or differently.

regress *verb* (**regresses**, **regressed**, **regressing**) **1** (esp. in abstract senses) return to a previous or less advanced state: *they would not regress to pre-technological tribalism*. **2** *Psychology* return or cause to return mentally to a former stage of life, esp. through hypnosis or mental illness. [Say re GRESS]

regression *noun* **1** a return to a former or less developed state: *regression to an underdeveloped state*. **2** *Psychology* a return to an earlier stage of development, esp. through hypnosis or mental illness. [Say re GRESH'n]

regressive *adjective* **1** becoming or making less advanced; returning to a former or less developed state: *the policy has been condemned as a regressive step* ◊ *the regressive, infantile wish for the perfect parent of early childhood*. **2** (of a tax) taking a proportionally greater amount from those on lower incomes; having less effect on the rich than on the poor. [Say re GRESS iv]

regret • *verb* (**regrets**, **regretted**, **regretting**) **1** feel or express sorrow or distress over (an action or loss etc.): *we regretted your absence*. **2** express polite apologies for (an error, an inconvenience, an inability, etc.). **3 a** acknowledge with sorrow or remorse: *I regret that I cannot attend* ◊ *regret to inform you that my father has died*. **b** be reluctant (to say something etc.) for fear of causing offence or disappointment. • *noun* **1** a feeling of sorrow, repentance, disappointment, etc., over an action or loss etc. **2** (often in *plural*) an (esp. polite or formal) expression of disappointment or sorrow at an occurrence, inability to comply, etc.: *refused with many regrets*. PHRASES **live to regret** (of an action)

eventually feel the consequences of. **give** (or **send**) **one's regrets** formally decline an invitation.

regretful *adjective* feeling or showing regret. ▶ **regretfully** *adverb* **regretfulness** *noun*

regrettable *adjective* (of events or conduct) unfortunate, unwelcome; deserving condemnation. ▶ **regrettably** *adverb*

regroup *verb* **1** group or arrange again or differently. **2** become organized before attempting something again.

regrow *verb* (**regrows**; *past* **regrew**; *past participle* **regrown**; **regrowing**) grow again, esp. after an interval. ▶ **regrowth** *noun*

regular • *adjective* **1** arranged or recurring in a constant or definite pattern, esp. with the same space between individual instances. **2** doing the same thing often or at uniform intervals: *regular worshippers*. **3** done or happening frequently. **4** conforming to or governed by an accepted standard of procedure or convention. **5** usual or customary. **6** *Grammar* (of a word) following the normal pattern of inflection. **7** (of merchandise) of average size. **8** of or belonging to the permanent professional armed forces of a country. **9** of an ordinary kind. **10** (of coffee) containing an average amount of cream and sugar. **11** *Geometry* (of a figure) having all sides and all angles equal. **12** *Christianity* subject to or bound by religious rule. **13** *informal* absolute; genuine: *a regular hero*. • *noun* **1** *informal* a regular customer, visitor, participant, member of a team, etc. **2 a** a coffee containing an average amount of cream and sugar. **b** a serving of a beverage etc. of a size between a small and a large. **3** a regular soldier. PHRASES **keep regular hours** do the same thing, esp. going to bed and getting up, at the same time each day. ▶ **regularity** *noun* **regularization** *noun* **regularize** *verb* (**regularizes**, **regularized**, **regularizing**)

regularly *adverb* **1** at regular intervals or times. **2** in a balanced or regular manner.

regular season *noun* *Sport* the schedule of games that follows the exhibition season and leads up to the playoffs.

regulate *verb* (**regulates**, **regulated**, **regulating**) **1** govern or control by law; subject to esp. legal restrictions. **2** keep (a biological function etc.) regular; maintain the health of: *drugs that regulate the immune system*. **3** adapt to requirements. **4** alter the speed of (a machine or clock) so that it may work accurately.

regulation *noun* **1** the action or process of regulating or being regulated: *the regulation of financial markets*. **2** a rule or directive made and maintained by an authority, esp. a subordinate form of legislation that may be established without the necessity of enacting a new statute: *safety regulations* ◊ *comply with the regulations* ◊ *under the new regulations they will be required to have fire alarms*. **3** (as an *adjective*) in accordance with regulations; of the correct type etc.: *a regulation tie*.

regulation time *noun* *Sport* the time normally allotted for the completion of a game which does not result in a tie (*compare* OVERTIME *noun* 3).

regulator *noun* **1** a person or thing that regulates something. **2** a person or body that supervises a particular industry or business activity. **3** a device that automatically controls speed, temperature, or pressure of machinery.

regulatory *adjective* **1** having to do with a regulation or regulations: *regulatory agency*. **2** in violation of a regulation: *a regulatory offence*. [Say REGG you luh tory]

regurgitate *verb* (**regurgitates**, **regurgitated**, **regurgitating**) **1** bring (swallowed food) up again to the mouth. **2** repeat information without analyzing or

comprehending it: *just regurgitating the facts*.
▶ **regurgitation** noun [Say re GURGE uh tate]
rehab informal • noun rehabilitation. • verb (**rehabs**,
rehabbed, **rehabbing**) rehabilitate; undergo
rehabilitation. [Say REE hab]
rehabilitate verb (**rehabilitates**, **rehabilitated**,
rehabilitating) **1 a** restore (a person) to effectiveness
or normal life by training etc., esp. after imprisonment,
injury, or illness. **b** heal (an injury etc.). **2** recondition,
overhaul. **3** restore the reputation or standing of: *the
author wishes to rehabilitate Snow's stature by demonstrating
his significance in the struggle for modernity*.
▶ **rehabilitative** adjective [Say re huh BILLA tate,
re huh BILLA tay tiv]
rehabilitation noun **1** the process of returning to
health by training and therapy after an illness, injury,
or addiction. **2** the process of preparing a criminal to
return to normal life after imprisonment. **3** an
overhaul, renovation, or refurbishment. **4** the process
of returning something, esp. an environmental
feature, to its former condition: *wildlife rehabilitation*.
5 the process of returning to former standing or
reputation after a period of critical or official
disfavour. [Say re huh billa TAY sh'n]
rehash • verb (**rehashes**, **rehashed**, **rehashing**)
put (old material) into a new form without significant
change or improvement: *rehashing the old theories*.
• noun (plural **rehashes**) the reuse of old ideas or
material without significant change or improvement:
*unless a comedian is a good writer, any book produced will be
just a limp rehash of stand-up material*.
rehearsal noun a trial performance or practice of a
play, ceremony, etc.: *rehearsals for Swan Lake ◊ wedding
rehearsal ◊ only had six days of rehearsal ◊ spent weeks in
rehearsal ◊ rehearsal studio*.
rehearse verb (**rehearses**, **rehearsed**,
rehearsing) **1** practise (a play, recital, ceremony, etc.)
for later public performance: *they are rehearsing Hamlet*.
2 hold a rehearsal: *the dancers are rehearsing till 6 p.m*.
3 train (a person) by rehearsal: *rehearsed her in the role of
Ophelia*. **4** recite or say over, esp. in preparation for
some subsequent event: *rehearsed his excuses for being
late*. **5** state a list of points, esp. those that have been
made many times before: *criticisms of the pulp and paper
industry have been rehearsed many times before*.
reheat verb heat again.
rehouse verb (**rehouses**, **rehoused**, **rehousing**)
provide with new housing.
rehydrate verb (**rehydrates**, **rehydrated**,
rehydrating) **1** absorb water again after dehydration.
2 cause (a person or thing) to absorb moisture or fluid.
▶ **rehydration** noun
Reich noun the former German nation or
Commonwealth, esp. the Third Reich. [Say RIKE]

> **SPELL CHECK**
> **reign, rein**
>
> The horse strap is a **rein**; this is also the spelling in
> "rein something in" and "give a free rein to".

reign • verb **1** hold royal office; be king or queen.
2 (often in phr. **reign supreme**) prevail; hold sway:
confusion reigns. **3** (of a winner, champion, etc.) be
currently holding the title etc. • noun **1** sovereignty,
rule: *under his reign we saw the completion of the
Shakespearian plays*. **2** the period during which a
sovereign rules. **3** a period during which a specified
person, quality, etc. holds sway: *the reign of love and
peace*. ▶ **reigning** adjective [Sounds like RAIN]
reign of terror noun (plural **reigns of terror**) **1** a
period of remorseless repression or bloodshed, during

which the general population lives in constant fear of
death or violence. **2** (**Reign of Terror**; also **the
Terror**) the period of the French Revolution between
mid 1793 and July 1794 when the ruling Jacobin faction
ruthlessly executed anyone considered a threat to their
regime; 40,000 people were guillotined.
reiki noun a supposed healing technique in which a
therapist channels energy into a patient by means of
touch, to activate the natural healing processes of the
patient's body and restore physical and emotional well-
being. [Say RAY key]
reimburse verb (**reimburses**, **reimbursed**,
reimbursing) **1** repay (a person who has expended
money). **2** repay (a person's expenses).
▶ **reimbursement** noun [Say re im BURSE]

> **SPELL CHECK**
> **rein, reign**
>
> A Queen who is ruling is **reigning**. Canadian
> Confederation happened during the **reign** of
> Queen Victoria.

rein • noun (in singular or plural) **1** a long narrow strap
with each end attached to the bit, used to guide or
check a horse etc. in riding or driving. **2** a means of
control: *took over the reins of government*. • verb **1** check
or manage with reins. **2** (foll. by *up, back*) pull up or back
with reins. **3** (foll. by *in*) hold in as with reins; restrain.
4 govern, restrain, control. **PHRASES** **free** (or **full**)
rein complete freedom of action. **keep a tight rein
on** allow little freedom to. [Sounds like RAIN]
reincarnate verb (**reincarnates**, **reincarnated**,
reincarnating) (often as **be reincarnated**) **1** cause
someone to undergo rebirth in another body: *Sebastian
thinks he will be reincarnated as a gecko*. **2** cause a person
or thing to undergo a transformation or change: *the
backyard was reincarnated as a wedding chapel for the
outdoor ceremony*. [Say re in CAR nate or re in car NATE]
reincarnation noun **1** the rebirth of a soul in a new
body. **2** a new embodiment or occurrence of a person,
idea, etc.: *the doomsayers see Vladimir Zhironovsky as the
reincarnation of Russian expansion*. [Say re in car NAY sh'n]
reindeer noun (plural **reindeer**) a subarctic deer, of
which both sexes have large antlers, domesticated in
northern Eurasia; reindeer are the same species as
caribou.
reinforce verb (**reinforces**, **reinforced**,
reinforcing) strengthen or support, esp. with
additional personnel or material or by an increase of
numbers or quantity or size etc.
reinforcement noun **1** the act of making something
stronger, esp. a feeling or an idea: *the reinforcement of
existing prejudices by the media*. **2** a thing that reinforces:
*paper reinforcements help stop the holes in looseleaf from
tearing*. **3** (in plural) extra personnel or equipment etc.
sent to increase the strength of an army or similar
force. **4** the strengthening or establishing of a response
through the repetition of a stimulus or the satisfaction
of a need: *positive reinforcement*.
reinjure verb (**reinjures**, **reinjured**, **reinjuring**)
injure again.
reinsert verb insert again. ▶ **reinsertion** noun
reinstall verb install again.
reinstate verb (**reinstates**, **reinstated**,
reinstating) **1** replace in a former position. **2** restore
to a former condition or status. ▶ **reinstatement**
noun [Say re in STATE]
reintegrate verb (**reintegrates**, **reintegrated**,
reintegrating) **1** restore wholeness or unity to.
2 integrate or be reintegrated back into society.
▶ **reintegration** noun [Say re INTA grate]

R

reinterpret *verb* (**reinterprets**, **reinterpreted**, **reinterpreting**) interpret again or differently. ▶ **reinterpretation** *noun*

reintroduce *verb* (**reintroduces**, **reintroduced**, **reintroducing**) **1** introduce again. **2** introduce (a species) to a place it formerly inhabited. ▶ **reintroduction** *noun*

reinvent *verb* **1** invent again. **2** change something so much that it appears to be something completely new. PHRASES **reinvent the wheel** waste effort by doing something that has already been done and does not need redoing. ▶ **reinvention** *noun*

reinvest *verb* invest again (esp. money made from one investment in other investments etc.). ▶ **reinvestment** *noun*

reinvigorate *verb* (**reinvigorates**, **reinvigorated**, **reinvigorating**) impart fresh vigour to.

reissue • *verb* (**reissues**, **reissued**, **reissuing**) issue again or in a different form. • *noun* a new issue, esp. of a previously published book etc.

reiterate *verb* (**reiterates**, **reiterated**, **reiterating**) say or do again or repeatedly: *let me reiterate that we are fully committed to this policy.* ▶ **reiteration** *noun* [Say re ITTER ate]

reject • *verb* **1** put aside or send back as not to be used or done or complied with etc. **2** refuse to accept or believe in (an idea). **3 a** fail to give (a person or an animal) due attention, care, or affection. **b** fail to accept (a person) into a group. **4** (of the body) not accept (a new organ) after a transplant operation. • *noun* a thing or person rejected as unfit or below standard. ▶ **rejection** *noun*

rejig *verb* (**rejigs**, **rejigged**, **rejigging**) *Cdn & Brit.* reconfigure, rearrange; reorganize.

rejoice *verb* (**rejoices**, **rejoiced**, **rejoicing**) **1** feel great joy. **2** be glad: *rejoiced to be home again ◊ I rejoice that I am able to be here this morning.* **3** (foll. by *in*, *at*) take delight. **4** celebrate some event. ▶ **rejoicing** *noun*

rejoin[1] *verb* **1** join together again; reunite. **2** join (a companion etc.) again.

rejoin[2] *verb* say in answer: *"We'll need gravel," Sam said. "Closest place is the trees," Sigfus rejoined.*

rejoinder *noun* a reply, esp. a sharp or witty one: *she would have made some cutting rejoinder but none came to mind.*

rejuvenate *verb* (**rejuvenates**, **rejuvenated**, **rejuvenating**) **1** make young or as if young again. **2** inject new vigour, liveliness, efficiency, etc. into: *rejuvenate the political process.* **3** make new or as if new again: *rejuvenated the old building.* ▶ **rejuvenation** *noun*

rekey *verb* re-enter (text or other data) using a keyboard. [Say re KEY]

rekindle *verb* (**rekindles**, **rekindled**, **rekindling**) kindle again.

┌─────────────────────────────────────┐
│ **SPELL CHECK**   ABC │
│ **renown, renowned**   ✓ │
├─────────────────────────────────────┤
│ Note that there is no *k* in **renown** or **renowned** (meaning "fame" and "famous", respectively). │
└─────────────────────────────────────┘

relabel *verb* (**relabels**, **relabelled**, **relabelling**) label again or differently.

relapse • *verb* (**relapses**, **relapsed**, **relapsing**) **1** experience a return of an illness after partial or apparently complete recovery. **2** fall back or sink again into any state, practice, etc. • *noun* **1** a deterioration in someone's physical or mental health after a temporary improvement: *suffered a relapse of tuberculosis.* **2** a lapse back into a previous less desirable state: *a relapse into old-style protectionism.* [Say REE laps]

relate *verb* (**relates**, **related**, **relating**) **1** narrate or recount (incidents, a story, etc.). **2** connect by blood or marriage. **3** (usu. foll. by *to*, *with*) bring into relation (with one another); establish a connection between: *cannot relate your opinion to my own experience.* **4** (foll. by *to*) have reference to; concern: *see only what relates to himself.* **5 a** (foll. by *to*) understand or have empathy for: *I can relate to that.* **b** understand, be connected to, or have empathy for a person etc.: *we just don't relate.*

related *adjective* **1** connected by blood or marriage. **2** associated or connected: *work-related stress.* **3** of the same type; in the same group, category, etc.: *related industries.* ▶ **relatedness** *noun*

relation *noun* **1 a** the way in which one person or thing is related to another. **b** the existence or effect of a connection, correspondence, contrast, or feeling prevailing between persons or things, esp. when qualified in some way: *bears no relation to the facts ◊ enjoyed good relations for many years.* **2** a person connected by blood or marriage; a relative. **3** (in *plural*) **a** (usu. foll. by *with*) dealings, rapport, interaction (with others). **b** sexual intercourse. **4** = RELATIONSHIP. **5 a** narration: *his relation of the events.* **b** a narrative. PHRASES **in relation to** as regards.

relational *adjective* concerning the way in which two or more people or things are connected: *a chapter dealing with the relational issues within these groups.*

relational database *noun* a database structured to recognize the relation of stored items of information.

relationship *noun* **1** the fact or state of being related. **2 a** a connection or association: *a good working relationship.* **b** an emotional (esp. sexual) association between two people. **3** kinship.

relative • *adjective* **1** considered or having significance in relation to something else; not absolute: *they live in relative comfort.* **2** (foll. by *to*) proportionate to (something else); in proportion to: *growth is relative to input.* **3 a** comparative; compared one with another: *their relative advantages.* **b** (foll. by *to*) in relation to: *move slowly relative to each other.* **4** having mutual relations; related to each other. **5** (usu. foll. by *to*) having reference; relating; relevant: *the facts relative to the issue.* • *noun* **1** a person connected by blood or marriage. **2** a species related to another by common origin: *the apes, humans' closest relatives.*

relative clause *noun* a clause attached to an antecedent by a relative pronoun, e.g. *who screamed* in *the man who screamed.*

relative humidity *noun* humidity expressed as the ratio of the mass of water vapour in a volume of air to the value for saturated air at the same temperature.

relatively *adverb* in relation or comparison to something else; fairly, quite when compared to others: *considering the price of most new cars, this one is relatively cheap ◊* . PHRASES **relatively speaking** used to compare something with all similar things: *relatively speaking, a mosquito bite is painless.*

relative pronoun *noun* a pronoun referring to an expressed or implied antecedent and attaching a subordinate clause to it, e.g. *who* in *the man who screamed;* other relative pronouns include *who, whom, which,* and *that.*

relativism *noun* the doctrine or belief that truth, knowledge, morality, etc., are relative and not absolute, i.e. that something held to be untrue or immoral by certain societies or at certain times could be true or moral in other circumstances. ▶ **relativist** *noun*

relativistic *adjective* **1** of, pertaining to, or characterized by relativism. **2** *Physics* (of phenomena etc.) accurately described only by the theory of relativity.

relativity *noun* **1** the fact or state of being relative.

2 *Physics* **a** (also **special theory of relativity**) a theory based on the principle that all motion is relative and that light has constant velocity, regarding space-time as a four-dimensional continuum, and modifying previous conceptions of geometry. **b** (also **general theory of relativity**) a theory extending this to gravitation and accelerated motion.

relaunch • *verb* (**relaunches, relaunched, relaunching**) start or present something again in a new or different way, esp. a product for sale: *relaunched the newspaper as a tabloid.* • *noun* a relaunching of something, esp. a business or product.

relax *verb* (**relaxes, relaxed, relaxing**) **1 a** make or become less stiff or rigid or tense. **b** become at ease, unperturbed, etc. **2** make or become less formal or strict: *rules were relaxed.* **3** reduce or abate (one's attention, efforts, etc.). **4** cease work or effort.

relaxant *noun* a drug etc. that reduces tension and produces relaxation, esp. of muscles.

relaxation *noun* **1** the act of relaxing or state of being relaxed. **2** recreation or rest, esp. after a period of work. **3** a partial remission or relaxing of a penalty, duty, etc. **4** a lessening of severity, precision, etc.

relaxed *adjective* free from tension and anxiety; at ease: *I felt quite relaxed during the test* ◊ *the restaurant has a comfortable and relaxed atmosphere.*

relaxer *noun* **1** something used to help a person relax. **2** a chemical product designed to straighten hair.

relaxing *adjective* conducive to relaxation: *a relaxing atmosphere* ◊ *a relaxing holiday.*

relay • *noun* **1** a set of people etc. appointed to relieve others or to operate in shifts: *operated in relays.* **2** = RELAY RACE. **3** a device activating changes in an electric circuit etc. in response to other changes affecting itself. **4 a** a device, installation, satellite, etc. which receives, amplifies, and retransmits a transmission, broadcast, etc. **b** a relayed message or transmission. **5** a fresh set of people or horses substituted for tired ones. • *verb* **1** receive (a message, broadcast, etc.) and transmit it to others. **2 a** arrange in relays. **b** provide with or replace by relays.

re-lay *verb* (**re-lays, re-laid, re-laying**) lay again or differently.

relay race *noun* a race between teams of which each member in turn covers part of the distance.

release • *verb* (**releases, released, releasing**) **1** set free from confinement. **2** free from an obligation or duty. **3** allow to move or flow freely. **4** allow (information) to be generally available. **5** make (a film or recording) available to the public. **6** make over (property, money, or a right) to another. • *noun* **1** the action or process of releasing or being released. **2** a film or other product released to the public. **3** a handle or catch that releases part of a mechanism. **4** a document making over property, money, or a right to another. **5** a document freeing a person from legal responsibility or obligation.

relegate *verb* (**relegates, relegated, relegating**) consign or dismiss to an inferior or less important position, category, etc.: *this attitude relegated philosophy to a position subordinate to science.* ▸ **relegation** *noun* [Say RELLA gate]

relent *verb* **1** finally agree to something after refusing: *finally the government relented and agreed to our request.* **2** relax one's severity; become less stern: *by evening the rain relented.* [Say re LENT]

relentless *adjective* **1** unrelenting; insistent. **2** continuous; oppressively constant: *the pressure was relentless.* ▸ **relentlessly** *adverb* **relentlessness** *noun* [Say re LENT liss]

relevance *noun* **1** connection or appropriateness to the subject or situation at hand: *what is the relevance of your comment to this debate?* **2** applicability or significance to people in their lives and the world: *the movie still has relevance in today's world.* [Say RELLA vince]

relevant *adjective* (often foll. by *to*) **1** closely connected or appropriate to the matter at hand. **2** having ideas that are valuable and useful to people in their lives and work: *the message of that speech remains relevant today.* ▸ **relevantly** *adverb* [Say RELLA vint]

reliable *adjective* **1** that may be relied on. **2** of sound and consistent character or quality. ▸ **reliability** *noun* **reliably** *adverb*

reliance *noun* (foll. by *on*) dependence; the act or state of relying on something. ▸ **reliant** *adjective*

relic *noun* **1** an object interesting because of its age or association with the past. **2** a part of a deceased holy person's body or belongings etc. kept as an object of reverence. **3 a** a surviving custom, belief, thing, etc. from a past age. **b** an old person, esp. one embodying old practices, customs, etc. **4** a memento or souvenir. **5** (in *plural*) what has survived destruction or wasting or use. [Say RELLICK]

relict *noun* a species, structure, etc., surviving from a previous age or in changed circumstances after the disappearance of related species, structures, etc. [Say RELL ict]

relief *noun* **1** a feeling of reassurance and relaxation following release from anxiety or distress. **2** a cause of relief. **3** a temporary break in a generally tense or boring situation. **4** financial or practical assistance given to those in special need or difficulty. **5** a person or group of people replacing others who have been on duty. **6** distinct appearance due to being accentuated in some way: *the sun threw the peaks into relief.* **7** a method of moulding, carving, or stamping in which the design stands out from the surface, to a greater (**high relief**) or lesser (**low relief**) extent. **8** alleviation of some burden, esp. taxation.

relief camp *noun* *Cdn hist.* one of a number of camps set up across Canada at the height of the Depression (1932–36) in which single, unemployed, homeless men were provided with lodging, food, medical care, work clothes, and minimal pay for work.

relief pitcher *noun* *Baseball* a pitcher who replaces another in mid-game.

relieve *verb* (**relieves, relieved, relieving**) **1** bring or provide aid or assistance to. **2** alleviate or reduce (pain, suffering, pressure, etc.). **3** mitigate the tedium or monotony of. **4** bring military support for (a besieged place). **5** release (a person) from a duty by acting as or providing a substitute. **6** (foll. by *of*) take (a burden or responsibility) away from (a person). **7** bring into relief; cause to appear solid or detached. ▸ PHRASES **relieve oneself** urinate or defecate.

relieved *adjective* freed from anxiety or distress: *am very relieved to hear it.*

reliever *noun* **1** in senses of RELIEVE. **2** = RELIEF PITCHER.

relight *verb* (**relights, relit, relighting**) light (a fire etc.) again.

religion *noun* **1** the belief in a superhuman controlling power, esp. in a personal God or gods entitled to obedience and worship. **2** the expression of this in worship. **3** a particular system of faith and worship. **4** a thing that one is strongly devoted to: *football is their religion.*

religiosity *noun* the condition of being esp. excessively religious: *as a whole the poem is a distinctive meditation, with only one or two lapses into religiosity.* [Say re lidge ee OSSA tee]

religious • *adjective* **1** devoted to religion; devout. **2** of or concerned with religion. **3** of or belonging to a

religious order, e.g. of monks. **4** scrupulous, conscientious: *a religious attention to detail*. • *noun* (*plural* **religious**) a person bound by religious vows, e.g. a monk, nun, etc. ▶ **religiously** *adverb*

reline *verb* (**relines, relined, relining**) line again.

relinquish *verb* (**relinquishes, relinquished, relinquishing**) voluntarily cease to keep or claim; give up, let go of: *she relinquished her position as head of the department to become their scientific adviser.* ▶ **relinquishment** *noun* [Say re LINK wish]

relish • *noun* (*plural* **relishes**) **1** great liking, enjoyment, or satisfaction: *told the story with great relish.* **2 a** an appetizing flavour. **b** an attractive quality: *fishing loses its relish in winter.* **3** a condiment eaten with plainer food to add flavour, esp. a sauce made of pickled chopped vegetables. • *verb* (**relishes, relished, relishing**) **1** get pleasure out of; enjoy greatly. **2** look forward to, anticipate with pleasure: *did not relish what lay before her.* [Say RELL ish]

relive *verb* (**relives, relived, reliving**) live (an experience etc.) over again, esp. in the imagination.

reload *verb* **1** load (a gun, camera, etc.) again. **2** load (ammunition, film, etc.) into a gun, camera, etc.

relocate *verb* (**relocates, relocated, relocating**) **1** locate in a new place. **2** move to a new place (esp. to live or work). ▶ **relocation** *noun*

reluctance *noun* **1** unwillingness or disinclination to do something: *his reluctance to wear a bike helmet nearly cost him his life.* **2** hesitancy or lack of enthusiasm in doing something: *with some reluctance he agreed to clean up the garage.*

reluctant *adjective* **1** unwilling or disinclined: *reluctant to leave.* **2** done or produced with unwillingness or disinclination: *reluctant hospitality.* ▶ **reluctantly** *adverb*

rely *verb* (**relies, relied, relying**) (foll. by *on, upon*) **1** depend on with confidence or assurance: *am relying on your judgment.* **2** be dependent on: *relies on her for everything.*

REM *abbreviation* RAPID EYE MOVEMENT.

remain *verb* **1** be left over after others or other parts have been removed or used or dealt with. **2** continue to exist or stay; be left behind: *remained at home.* **3** continue to be: *remained calm* ◊ *remained friends.* PHRASES **remain to be seen** be not yet known or certain.

remainder • *noun* **1** a part remaining or left over. **2** remaining persons or things. **3** a number left after division or subtraction. **4** a copy of a book left unsold when it is no longer in great demand, often disposed of at a reduced price. • *verb* (esp. as **remaindered** *adjective*) dispose of (books) at a reduced price.

remaining *adjective* left over after others or other parts have been completed, used, or dealt with.

remains *plural noun* **1** what remains after other parts have been removed or used etc. **2** relics of antiquity, esp. of buildings: *Roman remains.* **3** a person's body after death.

remake • *verb* (**remakes, remade, remaking**) make again or differently. • *noun* a thing that has been remade, esp. a film or recording.

remand • *verb* return (a prisoner) to custody, esp. to allow further inquiries to be made or while awaiting trial. • *noun* **1** a re-committal to custody. **2** the state of having been remanded (also as an *adjective*: *remand centre*). [Say MAND]

remark • *verb* **1** (often foll. by *that* + clause) **a** say by way of comment. **b** take notice of; regard with attention. **2** (usu. foll. by *on, upon*) make a comment. • *noun* **1** a written or spoken comment; anything said.

2 a the act of noticing or observing: *worthy of remark.* **b** the act of commenting: *let it pass without remark.*

remarkable *adjective* **1** worth notice; exceptional. **2** striking, conspicuous. ▶ **remarkably** *adverb*

remarriage *noun* the marriage of a person who has been married previously and divorced.

remarry *verb* (**remarries, remarried, remarrying**) marry again.

remaster *verb* (often as **remastered** *adjective*) rework or adjust the master of (a recording), esp. to improve the sound quality. ▶ **remastering** *noun*

rematch *noun* (*plural* **rematches**) a second match or game between the same opponents.

remedial *adjective* **1** serving or meant as a remedy: *took remedial action.* **2** (of teaching etc.) for learners requiring special attention or aid. [Say re MEEDY ul]

remedy • *noun* (*plural* **remedies**) (often foll. by *for, against*) **1** a medicine or treatment (for a disease etc.). **2** a means of counteracting or removing anything undesirable: *shopping became a remedy for personal problems.* **3** a way of dealing with a problem using the processes of the law: *holding copyright provides the only legal remedy against unauthorized copying.* • *verb* (**remedies, remedied, remedying**) rectify; make good. [Say REMMA dee]

remember *verb* **1** keep in the memory; not forget. **2 a** bring back into one's thoughts, call to mind (knowledge or experience etc.). **b** have in mind (a duty, commitment, etc.): *will you remember to lock up?* ◊ *remembered that I was to meet her at 9.* **3** think of or acknowledge (a person) in some connection, as in commemoration or in making a gift etc. **4** (foll. by *to*) convey greetings from (one person) to (another): *remember me to your mother.* **5** mention (in prayer).

remembrance *noun* **1** the act of remembering or process of being remembered. **2** a memory or recollection. **3** a thing serving to remind one of another; a keepsake or souvenir. **4** a gift made in remembrance of another.

Remembrance Day *noun* (in Canada) 11 Nov., the anniversary of the armistice at the end of World War I, on which those killed in war are commemorated.

remind *verb* **1** (foll. by *of*) cause (a person) to remember or think of. **2** cause (a person) to remember (a commitment etc.): *remind them to pay their subscriptions.*

reminder *noun* **1** a thing that reminds, esp. a letter or bill. **2** (often foll. by *of*) a memento or souvenir.

reminisce *verb* (**reminisces, reminisced, reminiscing**) (often foll. by *about*) indulge in remembering events from one's past. [Say remma NISS]

reminiscence *noun* **1** the recalling of one's past experiences or events, esp. with enjoyment. **2 a** a past fact or experience that is remembered. **b** the process of narrating this. **3** (in *plural*) a collection in literary form of incidents and experiences that a person remembers. **4** a characteristic of one thing reminding or suggestive of another. [Say remma NISS ince]

reminiscent *adjective* (foll. by *of*) tending to remind one of or suggest: *the architecture is reminiscent of a bygone era.* ▶ **reminiscently** *adverb* [Say remma NISS'nt]

remiss *adjective* careless of duty; negligent: *I would be remiss if I did not mention my parents.* [Say re MISS]

remission *noun* **1** a period during which a serious illness improves for a time and the patient seems to get better: *the patient has been in remission for the past six months* ◊ *the symptoms reappeared after only a short remission.* **2** *Cdn & Brit.* the reduction of a prison sentence on account of good behaviour etc.: *with remission for good behaviour, he could be out by the end of the year.* **3** the remitting of a debt or penalty etc.: *new*

businesses may qualify for tax remission. **4** (often foll. by *of*) forgiveness (of sins etc.). [Say re MISSION]

remit *verb* (**remits, remitted, remitting**) **1** cancel or refrain from exacting or inflicting (a debt or punishment etc.). **2** send (money etc.) in payment. **3** (foll. by *to*) refer (a matter for decision etc.) to some authority: *the request for an investigation was remitted to a special committee.* **4** *Theology* (usu. of God) pardon (sins etc.). [Say re MITT]

remittance *noun* **1** money sent, esp. by mail, for goods etc. or as an allowance. **2** the act of sending money. [Say re MITT ince]

remittent *adjective* that abates at intervals: *remittent fever.* [Say re MITT'nt]

remix • *verb* (**remixes, remixed, remixing**) mix (esp. a recording) again. • *noun* (*plural* **remixes**) a sound recording that has been remixed to produce a new version (see MIX *verb* 4). ▶ **remixer** *noun*

remnant • *noun* **1** a small remaining quantity. **2** a piece of cloth etc. left when the greater part has been used or sold. **3** (foll. by *of*) a surviving trace: *a remnant of empire.* • *adjective* remaining; leftover: *you've got remnant old growth, cutthroat trout and big fir trees.*

remodel *verb* (**remodels, remodelled, remodelling**) **1** model again or differently. **2** change the structure or shape of (esp. a room or building); reconstruct. ▶ **remodelling** *noun*

remonstrance *noun* a forcefully reproachful protest: *angry remonstrances in the House of Commons ◊ shut his ears to any remonstrance.* [Say re MON strince]

remonstrate *verb* (**remonstrates, remonstrated, remonstrating**) make a protest; argue forcibly: *remonstrated with them for being too mealy-mouthed ◊ "I'm not stupid," he remonstrated ◊ remonstrated that he was sincere.* ▶ **remonstration** *noun* [Say REM in strate]

remorse *noun* deep regret for a wrong committed. ▶ **remorseful** *adjective* **remorsefully** *adverb* [Say re MORSE]

remorseless *adjective* **1** cruel without regret or feelings of guilt: *the remorseless cruelty of their wit.* **2** (of something unpleasant) never ending or improving; relentless: *the remorseless rush of time.* ▶ **remorselessly** *adverb*

remote (**remoter, remotest**) • *adjective* **1** far away in place or time. **2** out of the way; situated away from the main centres of population, society, etc. **3** distantly related: *a remote ancestor.* **4** slight, faint: *not the remotest chance.* **5** (of a person) aloof; not friendly. **6** (foll. by *from*) widely different; separate by nature: *ideas remote from the subject.* **7** situated, occurring, operating, or performed at or from a (not necessarily great) distance: *remote camera.* • *noun*= REMOTE CONTROL 2.

remote control *noun* **1** control of a machine or apparatus from a distance by means of signals transmitted from a radio or electronic device. **2** such a device, esp. a hand-held one controlling a television etc. ▶ **remote-controlled** *adjective*

remotely *adverb* **1** in the slightest degree: *I'm not even remotely interested ◊ police wanted to speak to anyone even remotely connected with the incident.* **2** from a distance: *the device lets you turn on the car's ignition remotely.* **3** far away or apart: *remotely located users can communicate by e-mail.*

remoteness *noun* the condition of being situated far away or far from others.

remote sensing *noun* the scanning of the earth by satellite or high-flying aircraft in order to obtain information about it.

removable *adjective* that can be taken off or out of something: *a removable filter.*

removal *noun* **1** the taking away of something unwanted: *the removal of a brain tumour.* **2** dismissal, e.g.

from a job: *the removal of the President from office.* **3** the abolition of something: *removal of trade barriers.*

remove • *verb* (**removes, removed, removing**) **1** take off or away from the place or position occupied. **2 a** move or take to another place; change the situation of. **b** get rid of; eliminate: *will remove all doubts.* **3** cause to be no longer present or available: *take away: all privileges were removed.* **4** (often foll. by *from*) dismiss (a person) from office. **5** *informal* kill, assassinate. • *noun* **1** a degree of remoteness; a distance. **2** a stage in a gradation; a degree: *is several removes from what I expected.*

removed *adjective* **1** (esp. of cousins) separated by a specified number of steps of descent: *a first cousin twice removed.* **2** distant, remote, separated: *not far removed from anarchy.*

remover *noun* a substance used for getting rid of something unwanted: *hair remover ◊ paint remover.*

remunerate *verb* (**remunerates, remunerated, remunerating**) pay for services rendered: *under the new proposal, senators would be remunerated for the days on which they actually attend Parliament.* ▶ **remuneration** *noun* **remunerative** *adjective* [Say re MYOONA rate, re MYOONA ruh tiv]

Renaissance *noun* **1** the period in Western European history in the 14th–16th centuries of intensified classical scholarship and a turning away from the medieval educational tradition, marked by advances in art and literature under the influence of classical models. **2** the culture and style of art, architecture, etc. developed during this era. **3** (**renaissance**) a revival, esp. of culture. [Say RENNA sonce or re NAY sonce]

Renaissance man *noun* a person with many talents or pursuits, esp. in the humanities.

renal *adjective* of or concerning the kidneys. [Say REE null]

rename *verb* (**renames, renamed, renaming**) name again; give a new name to.

rend *verb* (**rends, rent, rending**) **1** split or divide in pieces or into factions: *a country rent by civil war.* **2** cause emotional pain to (the heart etc.). PHRASES **rend the air** sound piercingly.

render *verb* **1** cause to be or become; make: *rendered us helpless.* **2** give or pay (money, service, etc.), esp. in return or as a thing due: *render thanks.* **3** (often foll. by *to*) **a** give (assistance): *rendered aid.* **b** show (obedience) etc. **c** do (a service etc.). **4 a** submit; send in; present (an account, reason, etc.). **b** hand down (a verdict). **5 a** represent or portray artistically, musically, etc. **b** perform (a role); represent (a character, idea, etc.): *the dramatist's conception was well rendered.* **c** *Music* perform; execute. **6** translate: *rendered the poem into French.* **7** (often foll. by *down*) melt down (fat etc.) esp. to clarify; extract by melting.

rendering *noun* **1** a performance of a piece of music, drama, etc.; an interpretation: *an excellent rendering of the part.* **2** a translation: *a faithful rendering of the text.* **3** a depiction: *a proper rendering of their history ◊ an artist's rendering of the scene.*

rendezvous • *noun* (*plural* **rendezvous**) **1** an agreed or regular meeting place. **2** a meeting by arrangement. **3** a place appointed for assembling troops etc. **4** a pre-arranged meeting between spacecraft in space. • *verb* (**rendezvouses, rendezvoused, rendezvousing**) meet at a rendezvous. [Say RON day voo for the singular, RON day vooz for the plural]

rendition *noun* (often foll. by *of*) **1** an interpretation or performance of a dramatic role, piece of music, etc. **2** a translation. **3** a visual representation.

renegade • *noun* **1** a person who leaves one political, religious, etc. group to join another that has very

R

different views: *our Liberal candidate in this election is a renegade from the Conservatives*. **2** a person who opposes and lives outside a group or society that they used to belong to: *teenage renegades*. • *adjective* **1** traitorous, rebellious. **2** of changed allegiance. [Say RENNA gade]

renege *verb* (**reneges, reneged, reneging**) **1** go back on one's word; change one's mind. **2** (foll. by *on*) go back on (a promise or undertaking). [Say re NEG or re NAIG]

renegotiate *verb* (**renegotiates, renegotiated, renegotiating**) negotiate again or on different terms. ▶ **renegotiation** *noun* [Say re nuh GO she ate]

renew *verb* **1** revive; regenerate; make new again; restore to the original state. **2** reinforce; resupply; replace. **3** repeat or re-establish; resume after an interruption: *a renewed attack*. **4** get, begin, make, say, give, etc. anew. **5 a** grant or be granted a continuation of or continued validity of (a licence, subscription, lease, etc.). **b** extend the period of loan of (a library book). **6** recover (one's youth, strength, etc.).

renewable • *adjective* **1** able to be renewed. **2** (of a source of material or energy) not depleted by utilization. • *noun* a renewable source of material or energy.

renewable resource *noun* a resource, such as air, water, forests, or fish, that can be used and, if properly managed, will be replaced by natural processes at approximately the same rate and thus not run out.

renewal *noun* **1** the action of extending the period of validity of a licence, subscription, or contract: *the lease is up for renewal at the end of the month*. **2** the resumption of an activity or state after an interruption: *a renewal of hostilities*. **3** a situation in which something is replaced, improved, or made more successful: *economic renewal ◊ urban renewal*.

rennet *noun* **1** curdled milk found in the stomach of a calf, used in curdling milk for cheese, junket, etc. **2** a preparation made from the stomach membrane of a calf or from certain fungi, used for the same purpose. [Say REN it]

reno *noun* (*plural* **renos**) *Cdn informal* **1** a renovated house. **2** renovation: *reno project*. [Say RENNO]

renounce *verb* (**renounces, renounced, renouncing**) **1** consent formally to abandon; surrender; give up (a claim, right, possession, etc.). **2** refuse to recognize any longer. **3 a** decline further association or disclaim relationship with: *renounced my former friends*. **b** withdraw from; discontinue; forsake. PHRASES **renounce the world** abandon society or material affairs.

renovate *verb* (**renovates, renovated, renovating**) **1** remodel or install new fixtures etc. in (a building or part of it). **2** restore to good condition; repair. ▶ **renovation** *noun* **renovator** *noun*

renown *noun* fame; high distinction. [Say re NOWN (NOWN rhymes with *CROWN*)]

GRAMMAR CHECK
renown, renowned ⚠️

It is important not to confuse the noun **renown** and the adjective **renowned**. Note the difference between *She is a writer of great renown* and *She is a renowned writer*.

---

renowned *adjective* famous; celebrated. [Say re NOW'nd]

rent¹ • *noun* **1** a regular payment made by a tenant to an owner or landlord for the use of land or premises. **2** payment for the use of a service, equipment, etc. • *verb* **1** occupy or use (property, equipment, etc.) for a fixed, usu. temporary period, in return for payment.

2 (often foll. by *out*) allow a person to use (something) in return for rent. **3** occupy and use property in return for paying rent: *fed up with renting*. **4** be leased or hired out at a specified rate: *the apartment rents for $850 a month*. PHRASES **for rent** available to be rented.

rent² *noun* a large tear, an opening.

rent³ *past and past participle of* REND.

rent-a- *combining form* often *jocular* denoting availability for hire: *rent-a-van ◊ the CBC's usual rent-a-pundit*.

rentable *adjective* **1** available or suitable for renting. **2** giving an adequate ratio of profit to capital.

rental • *noun* **1** the amount paid or received as rent. **2** the act of renting. **3** a rented house, car, etc. • *adjective* **1** of or relating to rent. **2** available for rent; rented: *a rental car*.

rente *noun* *Cdn hist.* an annual payment made (in cash or produce) by a tenant to a landowner under the seigneurial system (*compare* CENS). [Say RONT]

renter *noun* a person who rents an apartment, a car, etc.

rent-free *adjective & adverb* with exemption from rent.

renumber *verb* change the number or numbers given or allocated to.

renunciation *noun* **1** the formal rejection of something, typically a belief, claim, or course of action: *a renunciation of violence*. **2** the act of rejecting physical pleasures, esp. for religious reasons: *days of prayer, meditation, and renunciation*. [Say re nun see AY sh'n]

reoccupy *verb* (**reoccupies, reoccupied, reoccupying**) occupy again.

reoccur *verb* (**reoccurs, reoccurred, reoccurring**) occur again or habitually. ▶ **reoccurrence** *noun*

reoffend *verb* offend again; commit a further (esp. criminal) offence.

re-offer *verb* *Cdn* (*Maritimes*) stand as a candidate for re-election: *the Halifax MP has decided not to re-offer*.

reopen *verb* open again. ▶ **reopening** *noun*

reorder • *verb* **1** put in order again; rearrange. **2** repeat an order for (a product). • *noun* a renewed or repeated order for a product etc.

reorganization *noun* **1** the action of organizing something again or differently. **2** the process of changing the structure of the management of a corporation.

reorganize *verb* (**reorganizes, reorganized, reorganizing**) **1** organize differently. **2** restructure the management of (a corporation), esp. to solve financial difficulties. ▶ **reorganizer** *noun*

reorient *verb* **1** give a new direction to (ideas etc.); redirect (a thing). **2** help (a person) find his or her bearings again. **3** change the outlook of (a person). **4 reorient oneself** adjust oneself to or come to terms with something.

reorientate *verb* (**reorientates, reorientated, reorientating**) = REORIENT. ▶ **reorientation** *noun*

Rep. *abbreviation* **1** *US* Representative. **2** *US* Republican. **3** Republic.

rep *noun informal* **1** a representative, esp. a sales representative. **2 a** repertory. **b** a repertory theatre or company. **3** reputation. **4** (usu. in *plural*) a repetition of a fitness exercise.

repack *verb* pack again.

repackage *verb* (**repackages, repackaged, repackaging**) **1** package again or differently. **2** present in a new form. ▶ **repackaging** *noun*

repaid *past and past participle of* REPAY.

repaint *verb* **1** paint again or differently. **2** restore the paint or colouring of.

repair • *verb* **1 a** restore to good condition after damage or wear. **b** renovate or mend by replacing or

fixing parts or by compensating for loss or exhaustion. **c** set right or make amends for (loss, wrong, error, etc.). **2** (foll. by *to*) go, make one's way: *repaired to the living room*. • *noun* **1** the action of fixing or mending something: *took my bike in for repairs ◊ my car is beyond repair ◊ the building is in need of repair.* **2** the result of this: *the repair is hardly visible.* **3** good or relative condition for working or using: *in good repair.* ▶ **repairable** *adjective* **repairer** *noun*
repairman *noun* (*plural* **repairmen**) a person who repairs vehicles, machinery, appliances, etc.
reparation *noun* **1** the making of amends for a wrong one has done, by paying money to or otherwise helping those who have been wronged: *the courts required a convicted offender to make financial reparation to his victim.* **2** compensation for war damage paid by the defeated country: *the country was almost crippled by the reparations payments it had to make after the war.* [Say reppa RAY sh'n]
repartee *noun* conversation or speech characterized by quick, witty comments or replies: *she engaged him in witty repartee.* [Say rep ar TAY or rep ar TEE]
repast *noun* *formal* a meal, esp. of a specified kind: *a light repast.* [Say re PAST]
repatriate • *verb* (**repatriates**, **repatriated**, **repatriating**) **1 a** restore (a person) to his or her native land. **b** return to one's own native land. **2** bring (legislation, esp. a constitution) under the authority of the autonomous country to which it applies, used with reference to laws passed on behalf of that country by its former mother country. **3** return (capital) from a foreign investment to investment in the country from which it originally came. • *noun* a person who has been repatriated. ▶ **repatriation** *noun* [Say re PAY tree ate]
repave *verb* (**repaves**, **repaved**, **repaving**) pave (a road, driveway, etc.) again.
repay *verb* (**repays**, **repaid**, **repaying**) **1** pay back (money). **2** return (a visit etc.). **3** make repayment to (a person). **4** make return for (a service, action, etc.): *the book repays close study.* **5** (often foll. by *for*) give in recompense. **6** make repayment. ▶ **repayable** *adjective* **repayment** *noun*
Rep by Pop *noun* *Cdn hist.* = REPRESENTATION BY POPULATION.
repeal • *verb* revoke or annul (a law etc.): *this bill repeals section 745 of the Criminal Code ◊ prohibition was repealed after a few years.* • *noun* the action of revoking or annulling a law or act of parliament: *a repeal of the four-cents-a-litre federal excise tax on fuel.*
repeat • *verb* **1** say or do again. **2 repeat oneself** say the same thing again. **3 repeat itself** occur again in the same way or form. **4** (of food) be tasted again after being swallowed, as a result of indigestion. **5** repeat a particular success, achievement, etc., esp. win a particular championship etc. again, esp. for the second consecutive time. • *noun* **1** an instance of repeating or being repeated. **2** a repeated broadcast. **3** (as an *adjective*) occurring, done, or used more than once: *a repeat performance.* **4** *Music* a passage intended to be repeated. • *adverb* indicating emphasis: *will not, repeat not, allow this to happen.* ▶ **repeatability** *noun* **repeatable** *adjective*
repeated *adjective* frequent; done or said again and again: *repeated attempts.* ▶ **repeatedly** *adverb*
repeater *noun* **1** a person or thing that repeats. **2** a firearm which fires several shots without reloading. **3** a device for the automatic retransmission or amplification of an electrically transmitted message.
repel *verb* (**repels**, **repelled**, **repelling**) **1** drive back; ward off; repulse. **2** refuse admission or approach or acceptance to: *repel an assailant.* **3** be repulsive or distasteful to. **4** resist mixing with or admitting: *repels moisture.* **5** (of a magnetic pole) push away from itself: *like poles repel.* [Say re PELL]
repellency *noun* the quality of being able to repel a particular thing: *water repellency.* [Say re PELL'n see]
repellent • *adjective* **1** able to repel a particular thing; impervious to a particular substance: *water-repellent nylon.* **2** disgusting, repulsive: *the idea was slightly repellent to her.* • *noun* (also **repellant**) **1** a substance that repels, esp. a chemical that repels insects. **2** a substance used to waterproof fabric etc.
repeller *noun* a device used to repel something.
repent *verb* **1** wish one had not done, regret (one's wrongdoing, omission, etc.); resolve not to continue (a wrongdoing etc.). **2** (often foll. by *of*) feel deep sorrow about one's actions etc. ▶ **repentance** *noun* **repentant** *adjective*
repercussion *noun* **1** (usu. in *plural*; often foll. by *of*) an indirect effect or reaction following an event or action: *consider the repercussions of moving.* **2** the recoil after impact. **3** an echo or reverberation. [Say ree pur KUSH'n or rep ur KUSH'n (KUSH rhymes with *MUSH*)]
repertoire *noun* **1** a stock of pieces etc. that a company or a performer knows or is prepared to perform. **2** all of the works existing in a particular artistic genre. **3** a stock of regularly performed pieces, regularly used techniques, etc.: *went through her repertoire of excuses.* [Say REPPER twar or REPPA twar (TWAR rhymes with *FAR*)]
repertory *noun* (*plural* **repertories**) **1** = REPERTOIRE. **2** the performance of various theatrical productions for short periods in rotation by one company: *will direct performances of Hamlet and Macbeth in repertory at the Elgin Theatre June 6–18.* **3 a** a company performing repertory. **b** repertory theatres regarded collectively. **4** a store or collection, esp. of information, instances, etc.: *animals possess a small repertory of sounds and gestures by which they communicate.* [Say REPPER tory or REPPA tory]
repertory theatre *noun* **1 a** a theatre at which plays are performed for short runs in sequence by the same company. **b** such theatres collectively. **2** a movie theatre at which esp. second-run films are shown for short runs, often for one showing only.
repetition *noun* **1 a** the fact of repeating something that has already been said or written: *her comments are worthy of repetition ◊ a repetition of his reply to the delegates.* **b** the recurrence of an action or event: *we want no repetition of last year's tragic events.* **2** a thing repeated: *the geometric repetitions of Islamic art.* **3** a training exercise which is repeated, e.g. a series of repeated raisings and lowerings of a weight or a series of aerobic exercises or stretches. [Say reppa TISH'n]
repetitious *adjective* (esp. of speech or writing) having much repetition, esp. when unnecessary or tiresome. ▶ **repetitiously** *adverb* [Say reppa TISH us]
repetitive *adjective* **1** saying or doing the same thing many times, so that it becomes boring: *a repetitive task.* **2** repeated many times: *repetitive patterns of behaviour.* ▶ **repetitively** *adverb* **repetitiveness** *noun* [Say re PETTA tive]
repetitive strain injury *noun* (*plural* **repetitive strain injuries**) injury arising from the prolonged use of particular muscles, esp. during keyboarding.
rephrase *verb* (**rephrases**, **rephrased**, **rephrasing**) express in an alternative way. [Say re PHRASE]
replace *verb* (**replaces**, **replaced**, **replacing**) **1** put back in place. **2** take the place of; succeed; be substituted for. **3** find or provide a substitute for. **4** (often foll. by *with*, *by*) fill up the place of. **5** (in *passive*, often foll. by *by*) be succeeded or have one's place filled by another; be superseded. ▶ **replaceable** *adjective*

replacement *noun* **1** the act of replacing one thing with another, esp. something that is better or newer: *the replacement of film with videotape ◊ the replacement of smaller family farms by larger, intensive operations.* **2** a person who replaces another in an organization: *can we ever find a replacement for Al?* **3** a thing that replaces something, esp. if old or worn-out, etc.: *a hip replacement ◊ vitamin pills are no replacement for a healthy diet.*

replant *verb* **1** transfer (a plant etc.) to a larger pot, a new site, etc. **2** plant (ground) again.

replay • *verb* **1** play back (a piece of film, sound recording, etc.). **2** play (a game etc.) again. **3** go over in one's mind, esp. an event or sequence of events: *she replayed in her mind every detail of the night before.* • *noun* **1** the playing again of a section of a recording, esp. so as to be able to watch an incident or hear a passage more closely: *watched a replay of the disputed goal.* **2** an occurrence which closely follows the pattern of a previous event: *hoped to avoid a replay of the fiasco that almost destroyed the place.*

replenish *verb* (**replenishes**, **replenished**, **replenishing**) **1** fill up again. **2** renew (a supply etc.). ▶ **replenishment** *noun* [Say re PLEN ish]

replete *adjective* **1** filled or well-supplied with: *this language is replete with acronyms.* **2** very full of or sated by food: *I went out into the sunny street again, replete and relaxed.* **3** equipped with: *a word processor replete with pull-down menus and dialogue boxes.* [Say re PLEET]

replica *noun* (*plural* **replicas**) **1** a facsimile, an exact copy. **2** a copy or model, esp. on a smaller scale. **3** a duplicate of a work made by the original artist. [Say REP li kuh]

replicate *verb* (**replicates**, **replicated**, **replicating**) **1** repeat (an experiment etc.): *these findings have been replicated by a later study.* **2** make a replica of: *it might be impractical to replicate eastern culture in the west.* **3** (of genetic material or a living organism) reproduce or give rise to a copy of (itself): *this drug prevents the virus from replicating itself ◊ an enzyme which HIV needs in order to replicate.* ▶ **replication** *noun*

replicator *noun* [Say REP lick ate]

reply • *verb* (**replies**, **replied**, **replying**) **1** (often foll. by *to*) make an answer, respond in word or action. **2** say in answer. • *noun* (*plural* **replies**) **1** the act of replying: *what did they say in reply?* **2** what is replied; a response. **3** *Law* the plaintiff's response to the defendant's plea.

repo *noun* (*plural* **repos**) *informal* the action of repossessing, e.g. of a car etc. (also as an *adjective*: *repo man*). [Say REE po]

report • *verb* **1** give a spoken or written account of something. **2** convey information about an event or situation. **3** make a formal complaint about. **4** present oneself as having arrived somewhere or as ready to do something. **5** (foll. by *to*) be responsible to (a supervisor or manager). **6** *Parliament* (of a committee chairman) announce that the committee has dealt with (a bill). • *noun* **1** an account given of a matter after investigation or consideration. **2** a piece of information about an event or situation. **3** = REPORT CARD 1. **4** the sound of an explosion or gunfire. PHRASES **report back** deliver a report to the person, organization, etc. for whom one acts etc. ▶ **reportable** *adjective*

reportage *noun* **1** the describing of events, esp. the reporting of news etc. for the press and for broadcasting. **2** the typical style of this. **3** reported news collectively: *reportage on prison life.* [Say rep or TAWZH]

report card *noun* **1** a written statement of a student's marks and behaviour at school, sent home to the parent or guardian. **2** an evaluation of performance: *a report card on health care.*

reportedly *adverb* according to what some people say: *the singer has reportedly left the band.*

reported speech *noun* the speaker's words with the changes of person, tense, etc. usual in reports, e.g. *she said that she would go* (opp. DIRECT SPEECH).

reporter *noun* **1** a person employed to report news etc. for newspapers or broadcasts. **2** a person who reports. **3** = COURT REPORTER 1.

repose • *noun* **1** the cessation of activity or excitement or toil. **2** sleep. **3** a peaceful state; stillness. • *verb* (**reposes**, **reposed**, **reposing**) **1** lie down in rest: *reposed on a sofa.* **2** (often foll. by *on*) lay (one's head etc.) to rest (on a pillow etc.). **3** (often foll. by *in*, *on*) lie; be lying or laid. **4** (foll. by *on*, *upon*) be supported or based on. **5** (foll. by *in*) place (trust etc.) in. **6** be kept in a place: *the manuscript reposes in the library.* [Say re POZE]

reposition *verb* **1** move or place in a different position. **2** adjust or alter one's position. **3** change the image of (a company, product, etc.) to target a new or wider market.

repository *noun* (*plural* **repositories**) **1** a place where things are stored or may be found, esp. a warehouse or museum. **2** a receptacle. **3** a book, person, etc. regarded as a store of information etc.: *a repository of information about language all across the country.* [Say re POZZA tory or re POZZA tree]

repossess *verb* (**repossesses**, **repossessed**, **repossessing**) regain possession of (esp. property or goods on which repayment of a debt is in arrears). ▶ **repossession** *noun* **repossessor** *noun*

repot *verb* (**repots**, **repotted**, **repotting**) put (a plant) in another, esp. larger, pot.

reprehensible *adjective* deserving condemnation or rebuke: *I believe very strongly that all acts of murder are reprehensible in the eyes of Canadians.* ▶ **reprehensibly** *adverb* [Say rep re HENSA bull]

represent *verb* **1** be entitled or appointed to act and speak for. **2** be an elected member of a legislature for. **3** constitute; amount to. **4** be a specimen or example of; typify. **5** (in *passive*) be present to a particular degree. **6** portray in a particular way. **7** depict in a work of art. **8** signify, symbolize, or embody.

representation *noun* **1** the action of speaking or acting on behalf of someone or the state of being so represented: *asylum-seekers should be guaranteed good legal advice and representation ◊ no taxation without representation.* **2** the description or portrayal of someone or something in a particular way or as being of a certain nature: *the representation of women in the media.* **3** a thing (esp. a painting etc.) that represents another: *a striking representation of a vase of flowers.* **4** (esp. in *plural*) formal statements made to a higher authority, esp. so as to communicate an opinion or register a protest: *is the Minister ready to listen to representations and make changes to the gun law?*

representational *adjective* **1** (of a painting etc.) depicting an object as it actually appears to the eye: *representational art.* **2** of or relating to representation.

Representation by Population *noun Cdn hist.* the concept, esp. in the Province of Canada after 1851, that legislative representation should be based proportionally on population, rather than divided equally between Canada East and Canada West.

representative • *adjective* **1** typical of a class or category. **2** containing typical specimens of all or many classes: *a representative sample.* **3 a** consisting of elected deputies etc. **b** based on the representation of a nation etc. by such deputies: *representative government.* **4** (foll. by *of*) serving as a portrayal or symbol of: *representative of their attitude to work.* **5** (of art) representational. • *noun* **1** (foll. by *of*) a sample, specimen, or typical

embodiment or analogue of. **2 a** the agent of a person or society. **b** a salesperson, esp. a travelling salesperson. **3** a delegate; a substitute. **4 a** a deputy in a representative assembly. **b (Representative)** (in the US) a member of the House of Representatives. ▶ **representativeness** noun

repress verb (**represses, repressed, repressing**) **1 a** subdue (someone or something) by force: *the uprisings were repressed*. **b** restrain or prevent (the expression of a feeling): *Charlotte couldn't repress a sharp cry of fear*. **2** Psychology **a** suppress or control (thoughts, desires, etc.) in oneself or another. **b** actively exclude (an unwelcome thought) from conscious awareness. ▶ **repression** noun **repressive** adjective **repressiveness** noun

repressed adjective **1** (of a person) having emotions or desires that are not allowed to be expressed: *a very repressed family*. **2** (of emotions) not expressed openly: *he suffers because of his own repressed anger*.

reprieve • verb (**reprieves, reprieved, reprieving**) **1** cancel or postpone the punishment of someone, esp. someone condemned to death: *under the new regime, prisoners under sentence of death were reprieved*. **2** abandon or postpone plans to close or put an end to. • noun **1 a** a cancellation or postponement of a punishment: *the condemned man was granted a last-minute reprieve*. **b** a warrant for this: *went through a pantomime of execution and read the reprieve at the last moment*. **2** a temporary escape from an undesirable fate or unpleasant situation: *a reprieve from all Dora's harsh words ◊ we've been given a three-month reprieve before we have to start paying the new rates*. [Say re PREEV]

reprimand • noun (often foll. by for) an official or sharp rebuke (for a fault etc.). • verb express severe disapproval of (a person or their actions), esp. officially. [Say REP ruh mand]

reprint • verb print again. • noun **1** the act of printing more copies of a work. **2** a book etc. reprinted. **3** the quantity reprinted.

reprisal noun an act of retaliation: *they did not want to give evidence for fear of reprisals ◊ they shot ten hostages in reprisal for the assassination of their leader*. [Say re PRIZE ul]

reprise • noun **1** a repeated passage in music. **2** a repeated item in a musical program. • verb (**reprises, reprised, reprising**) repeat (a performance, song, etc.): *the opera will be reprised in Toronto this fall*. [Say re PRIZE or re PREEZ]

reproach • verb (**reproaches, reproached, reproaching**) **1** express disapproval to (a person) for a fault etc. **2** scold; rebuke. • noun **1** a rebuke. **2** blame, criticism: *her behaviour was above reproach*. **3** a thing that brings disgrace or discredit: *she is a reproach to her family*. PHRASES **above** (or **beyond**) **reproach** perfect. ▶ **reproachful** adjective **reproachfully** adverb

reprobate • noun an unprincipled person; a person of highly immoral character. • adjective immoral. [Say REP ruh bate]

reprocess verb (**reprocesses, reprocessed, reprocessing**) process again or differently. ▶ **reprocessing** noun

reproduce verb (**reproduces, reproduced, reproducing**) **1** produce a copy or representation of. **2** cause to be seen or heard etc. again: *tried to reproduce the sound exactly*. **3** produce further members of the same species by natural means. **4 reproduce oneself** produce offspring: *corn cannot reproduce itself*. **5** give a specified quality or result when copied: *reproduces badly*. **6** Biology form afresh (a lost part etc. of the body). ▶ **reproducible** adjective

reproduction noun **1** the action or process of making a copy of something: *colour reproduction is very expensive*.

2 a copy of a work of art, esp. a print or photograph of a painting. **3** (as an adjective) (of furniture etc.) made in imitation of a certain style or of an earlier period. **4** the quality of reproduced sound: *digital recording gives excellent sound reproduction*. **5** the process by which a new organism is produced by or from an existing organism or organisms of the same species. *sexual reproduction*.

reproductive adjective **1** of, pertaining to, or effecting reproduction of an organism, esp. human reproduction: *reproductive technology*. **2** serving to reproduce. ▶ **reproductively** adverb

reprogram verb (**reprograms, reprogrammed, reprogramming** or **reprograms, reprogramed, reprograming**) program (esp. a computer) again or differently. ▶ **reprogrammable** adjective (also **reprogramable**)

reproof noun (plural **reproofs**) an expression of blame or disapproval: *a glance of reproof ◊ it wasn't a harsh criticism, just a mild reproof*. [Say re PROOF]

reprove verb (**reproves, reproved, reproving**) express disapproval of (a person, a person's conduct, etc.); reprimand: *he ceaselessly reproved her for her bad spelling*. ▶ **reproving** adjective **reprovingly** adverb [Say re PROOVE]

reptile noun any cold-blooded animal of a class that includes snakes, lizards, crocodiles, turtles, tortoises, and other animals distinguished by having a dry scaly skin and by laying soft-shelled eggs on land. ▶ **reptilian** adjcotivo & noun [For *reptilian* say rep TILLY in]

republic noun **1 a** a state in which supreme power is held by the people or their elected representatives or by an elected or nominated president, not by a monarch etc. **b** the system of government of such a state. **c** a period during which a state has such a government: *paper money was adopted in the closing months of the First Republic*. **2** a society with equality between its members: *the literary republic*.

republican • adjective **1** of or constituted as a republic. **2** characteristic of a republic. **3** advocating or supporting republican government. • noun **1** a person advocating or supporting republican government. **2 (Republican)** (in the US) a member or supporter of the Republican Party. **3** (also **Republican**) an advocate of a united Ireland. ▶ **republicanism** noun

Republican Party noun one of the two main US political parties, favouring only a moderate degree of central power.

republication noun the publication of a text that has been published previously, esp. in a new edition.

republish verb (**republishes, republished, republishing**) publish again or in a new edition etc.

repudiate verb (**repudiates, repudiated, repudiating**) **1** deny the truth or validity of: *they have repudiated the charges*. **2** refuse to accept or be associated with: *did not repudiate evangelical traditions ◊ rightists also repudiate the moderate camp*. **3** refuse to fulfill or honour an obligation, debt, or agreement: *attempts to repudiate the contract*. ▶ **repudiation** noun [Say re PYOODY ate]

repugnance noun intense disgust or aversion: *a repugnance to organized social life*. [Say re PUG nunce]

repugnant adjective **1** extremely distasteful; unacceptable: *overturn provincial laws deemed repugnant by the federal government*. **2** incompatible or in conflict with: *the notion of standards is repugnant to our national character*. [Say re PUG nunt]

repulse verb (**repulses, repulsed, repulsing**) **1** drive back (an attack or attacking enemy) by force of arms: *the American attempt to annex Canada during the*

R

War of 1812 was repulsed. **2 a** rebuff (friendly advances or their maker): *she repulsed his advances.* **b** refuse (a request or offer or its maker). **3** be repulsive to, repel, disgust: *audiences were repulsed by the film's brutality.*

repulsion *noun* **1** aversion; disgust: *his voice makes me shiver with repulsion.* **2** esp. *Physics* the force by which bodies tend to repel each other or increase their mutual distance (*opp.* ATTRACTION): *the electric repulsion between two positively charged protons.* ▶**repulsive** *adjective* **repulsively** *adverb* **repulsiveness** *noun*

reputable *adjective* having a good reputation; respectable. ▶**reputably** *adverb* [Say REP you tuh bull]

reputation *noun* **1** what is generally said or believed about a person's or thing's character or standing: *has a reputation for honesty.* **2** the state of being well thought of. **3** fame, credit, or notoriety for doing something. **4** a reputation for promiscuity, drunkenness, etc.

repute *noun* reputation: *an unexpected success of international repute* ◊ *houses of ill repute.* [Say re PYOOT]

reputed *adjective* **1** generally considered or reckoned: *is reputed to be the best.* **2** passing as being, but probably not being: *his reputed father.* ▶**reputedly** *adverb* [Say re PYOOT id]

request • *noun* **1** an act of asking politely or formally for something: *came at his request* ◊ *a request for information* ◊ *catalogues are available on request.* **2** a thing asked for: *my request was granted.* **3 a** a letter, phone call, etc. asking for a particular recording etc. to be played on a radio program, often with a personal message. **b** the recording etc. played in response to such a letter etc. • *verb* **1** ask to be given or allowed or favoured with: *requests your presence.* **2** ask a person to do something: *farmers are requested to sign a waiver.* **3** ask: *requested that she remain there.*

requiem *noun* **1** (**Requiem**) esp. *Catholicism* a Mass for the repose of the souls of the dead. **2** a musical setting for this. **3** (often foll. by *for*) a memorial: *his book was a fitting requiem.* [Say RECK we em]

require *verb* (**requires, required, requiring**) **1** need; depend on for success or fulfillment: *the work requires patience.* **2** lay down as an imperative: *did all that was required by law.* **3** command; instruct (a person etc.). **4** order; insist on (an action or measure). **5** (often foll. by *of, from,* or *that* + clause) demand (of or from a person) as a right. **6** wish to have: *is there anything you require?* ▶**requirement** *noun*

requisite • *adjective* required by circumstances or regulations: *failed to get the requisite number of signatures for a referendum.* • *noun* a thing needed (for some purpose): *a week when political tact was a requisite for curling* ◊ *the requisites of his appointment.* [Say RECK wuh zit]

requisition • *noun* **1** an official order for the use of property or materials, esp. by an army during a war. **2 a** a formal written demand that a duty etc. should be performed. **b** the form on which such a request is written: *filled out a requisition.* • *verb* demand the use or supply of, esp. by requisition order. [Say reck wuh ZISH'n]

reread *verb* (**rereads, reread, rereading**) read again. ▶**rereading** *noun*

re-record *verb* record again. ▶**re-recording** *noun*

re-release • *verb* (**re-releases, re-released, re-releasing**) release (a record, film, etc.) again. • *noun* a re-released record, film, etc.

reroute *verb* (**reroutes, rerouted, rerouting**) send or carry by a different route. [Say re ROOT or re ROUT]

rerun • *verb* (**reruns;** *past* **reran;** *past participle* **rerun; rerunning**) **1** show a television program, film, etc. again. **2** run (a race, computer program, etc.) again. • *noun* **1** something that is done in the same way as something in the past: *the campaign was largely a rerun of 1979.* **2** a television program etc. shown again.

res *noun* (*plural* **reses**) *informal* **1** *Cdn* a university or college residence. **2** resolution (of a computer screen etc.). **3** = REZ. [Say REZ]

resale *noun* the sale of a thing previously bought. ▶**resaleable** *adjective* (also **resalable**)

reschedule *verb* (**reschedules, rescheduled, rescheduling**) alter the schedule of; replan.

rescind *verb* revoke, cancel: *the club has rescinded its offer.* ▶**rescission** *noun* [Say re SIND, re SIZH'n]

rescue • *verb* (**rescues, rescued, rescuing**) **1** save or set free or bring away from attack, custody, danger, harm, or an unpleasant situation. **2** *informal* keep from being lost or abandoned; retrieve: *he got out of his chair to rescue his cup of coffee.* • *noun* an act of saving or being saved from danger or distress: *a wealthy benefactor came to the ballet's rescue with a million dollars* ◊ *a search and rescue team* ◊ *a daring sea rescue.* ▶**rescuer** *noun*

reseal *verb* seal again. ▶**resealable** *adjective*

research • *noun* **1** the systematic investigation into and study of materials, sources, etc., in order to establish facts and reach new conclusions. **2** (as an adjective) engaged in or intended for research: *research assistant.* • *verb* (**researches, researched, researching**) do research. ▶**researcher** *noun*

SPELL CHECK
reseed, recede

To move back gradually from a previous position is to **recede**: *The flood waters have begun to recede; a receding hairline.*

---

reseed *verb* sow (land) with seed again, esp. grass seed.

resell *verb* (**resells, resold, reselling**) sell (an object etc.) after buying it. ▶**reseller** *noun*

resemblance *noun* a likeness or similarity.

resemble *verb* (**resembles, resembled, resembling**) be like; have a similarity to, or features in common with, or the same appearance as.

resent *verb* show or feel indignation at; be aggrieved by (a circumstance, action, or person). ▶**resentful** *adjective* **resentfully** *adverb* **resentment** *noun*

reservation *noun* **1** the act of booking (a room, seat, etc.) for a particular person: *I'll call the restaurant and make a reservation.* **2** (often in *plural*) an express or tacit limitation, qualification, or exception to an agreement etc.: *had reservations about the plan.* **3** an area of land reserved for occupation by American Indians in the US, Australian Aboriginals, etc. (*compare* RESERVE *noun* 5). **4** *Cdn* a constitutional power residing with the Governor General or the Lieutenant-Governor of a province to withhold royal assent from a bill until it has been re-examined.

reserve • *verb* (**reserves, reserved, reserving**) **1** postpone, put aside, or keep back for a later occasion or special use. **2** order to be specially retained or allocated for a particular person or at a particular time. **3** retain or secure, esp. by formal or legal stipulation: *reserve the right to.* **4** postpone delivery of (judgment etc.): *reserved my comments.* **5** *Cdn* (of the Governor General or a Lieutenant-Governor) withhold royal assent from (a bill). • *noun* **1** a thing reserved for future use; an extra stock or amount: *a great reserve of strength* ◊ *energy reserves.* **2** a limitation, qualification, or exception attached to something: *accept your offer without reserve.* **3** coolness or distance of manner. **4** a place reserved for special use, esp. as a habitat for wildlife: *nature reserve.* **5** (in Canada) an area of land set aside for the use of a specific group of Aboriginal people. **6** (in *singular* or *plural*) assets kept readily available as cash or at a central bank, or as gold or foreign exchange: *reserve currency.* **7** (in *singular* or *plural*)

a troops withheld from action to reinforce or protect others. **b** forces in addition to the regular army, navy, air force, etc., but available in an emergency. **8 a** member of the military reserve. **9** an extra player chosen to be a possible substitute in a team. **10** the intentional suppression of the truth: *exercised a certain amount of reserve*. • *adjective* **1** of or pertaining to a reserve or reserves: *reserve land*. **2** kept in reserve; constituting a reserve: *reserve Chardonnay* ◊ *reserve fund*. PHRASES **in reserve** unused and available if required.

reserved *adjective* **1** reticent; slow to reveal emotion or opinions; uncommunicative. **2 a** set apart, destined for some use or fate. **b** booked in advance. **c** (often foll. by *for, to*) left by fate for; falling first or only to.

reservist *noun* a member of a country's reserve forces.

reservoir *noun* **1** a large natural or artificial lake or pool used for collecting and storing water for public and industrial use, irrigation, etc. **2 a** any natural or artificial receptacle esp. for or of fluid. **b** a place where fluid etc. collects. **3** a part of a machine etc. holding fluid. **4** a body of porous rock holding a large quantity of oil or natural gas. **5** a reserve or supply: *a reservoir of information*. [Say REZZER vwar (VWAR rhymes with FAR)]

reset • *verb* (**resets, reset, resetting**) **1** set (a broken bone, gems, a measuring gauge, etc.) again or differently. **2** cause (a device or appliance) to return to a former state, esp. to a condition of readiness. • *noun* **1** the action or an act of resetting something. **2** a device for resetting an instrument etc.

resettle *verb* (**resettles, resettled, resettling**) settle again. ► **resettlement** *noun*

reshape *verb* (**reshapes, reshaped, reshaping**) shape or form again or differently.

reshoot • *verb* (**reshoots, reshot, reshooting**) shoot (a scene in a film etc.) again. • *noun* a scene in a film etc. shot again.

reshuffle • *verb* (**reshuffles, reshuffled, reshuffling**) **1** shuffle (cards) again. **2** interchange the posts of (government ministers, employees, etc.). **3** change the position or order of; interchange. • *noun* an act of reorganizing or rearranging something: *he was brought into the government in the last cabinet reshuffle*.

reside *verb* (**resides, resided, residing**) **1** (of a person) have one's home, dwell permanently. **2** be present or situated in: *lakes that reside in areas where much of the rock is granite* ◊ *the power and magic that reside in language*. **3** (of power, a right, etc.) belong by right to a person or group: *the issue is handled by the offices of deputy ministers, where the true power resides*.

residence *noun* **1** the fact of living in a particular place: *Rome was his main place of residence* ◊ *will take up residence this fall*. **2 a** the place where a person resides; an abode. **b** a house, esp. an impressive one. **3 a** building providing accommodation for students at a university or college: *lived in residence for a year* ◊ *the university is building a new residence*. PHRASES **in residence** dwelling at a specified place. **-in-residence** (in *combination*) designating a practitioner of one of the arts, working in or associated with a university, organization, etc., in order to share professional knowledge: *artist-in-residence*.

residency *noun* (*plural* **residencies**) **1** = RESIDENCE 1. **2** a period of specialized medical training; the position of a resident. **3 a** *Brit.* & *Cdn* a regular engagement at a club, theatre, etc. for a musician, dance company, etc. **b** the position of an artist-in-residence.

resident • *noun* **1** (often foll. by *of*) **a** a permanent inhabitant (of a city, neighbourhood, building, etc.). **b** a bird belonging to a species that does not migrate. **2** a medical graduate engaged in specialized practice under supervision in a hospital. • *adjective* **1** residing;

in residence. **2 a** having quarters on the premises of one's work etc.: *resident housekeeper*. **b** working regularly in a particular place. **c** frequenting a particular place: *the resident intellectual at our table*. **3** located; inherent: *powers of feeling are resident in the nerves*. **4** (of birds etc.) non-migratory. **5** *Computing* (of a program etc.) occupying a permanent place in memory, esp. in main memory or the memory built into a particular device, and hence rapidly accessible during processing.

residential *adjective* **1** suitable for or occupied by dwellings: *residential area*. **2** used as a residence: *residential complex*. **3** based on or connected with residence: *a residential course of study*.

residential school *noun* esp. *Cdn hist.* a boarding school operated or subsidized by religious orders or the federal government to accommodate Aboriginal and Inuit students.

residual • *adjective* **1** remaining; still left: *crops are left to grow on residual moisture for three or four months after the rainy season*. **2** esp. *Chemistry* left as a residue, esp. at the end of some process. **3** *Math* resulting from subtraction. **4** (in calculation) still unaccounted for or not eliminated. • *noun* **1** a quantity left over or (*Math*) resulting from subtraction. **2** an error in calculation not accounted for or eliminated. **3** (in *plural*) a royalty paid to an actor, musician, etc., for a repeat of a television commercial, song, etc. ► **residually** *adverb* [Say re ZIDGE oo ul]

residual power *noun* a power remaining with one political group after other powers have been allocated to another group, as between a federal government and a province.

residue *noun* **1** what is left over or remains: *though thousands of the weapons are being retired, their residue — plutonium — threatens to plague society for centuries*. **2** esp. *Chemistry* a substance left after combustion, evaporation, etc.; a deposit, a sediment: *our water leaves a white, chalky residue in the kettle*. [Say REZZA due]

resign *verb* **1** voluntarily leave a job or position: *was forced to resign after the scandal* ◊ *resigned from the military* ◊ *resigned as chief executive* ◊ *will resign her Senate seat in May*. **2 resign oneself** accept and be ready to endure something as inevitable: *have resigned myself to the idea*.

re-sign *verb* **1** sign (a document etc.) again. **2** (of a sports player etc.) sign a contract for a further period.

resignation *noun* **1** an act of giving up a job or position: *calls for the minister's resignation*. **2** the document etc. conveying this intention: *handed in her resignation*. **3** the uncomplaining endurance of a sorrow or difficulty: *a shrug of resignation*.

resigned *adjective* prepared to accept something undesirable but unavoidable: *am resigned to being single* ◊ *am resigned to the fact that she won't be coming* ◊ *resigned to his fate*. ► **resignedly** *adverb* [For *resignedly* say re ZINE id lee]

resilience *noun* **1** the ability of a person or thing to withstand or recover quickly from something unpleasant, such as shock, injury, etc.: *praised the refugees for their resilience and determination* ◊ *the resilience of the German economy*. **2** the ability of a substance to return to its original shape after it has been bent, stretched, or pressed. [Say re ZILL yince]

resilient *adjective* **1** (of a substance etc.) resuming its original shape after bending, stretching, etc. **2** (of a person) readily recovering from shock, depression, etc.: *a tough and resilient enemy*. [Say re ZILL yint]

resin • *noun* **1** a sticky flammable organic substance that cannot be dissolved in water, secreted by some trees (esp. fir and pine) and other plants (compare GUM[1] *noun* 1a). **2** (also **synthetic resin**) a solid or liquid

organic compound made by polymerization etc. and used in adhesives, plastics, and varnishes. • **verb (resins, resined, resining)** rub or treat with resin. ▶ **resinous** adjective [Say REZZIN]

resist verb **1** withstand the action or effect of; repel. **2** stop the course or progress of; prevent from reaching, penetrating, etc. **3** abstain from (pleasure, temptation, etc.). **4** strive against; try to impede; refuse to comply with: *resist arrest*. **5** offer opposition; refuse to comply. PHRASES **cannot** (or **could not** etc.) **resist 1** feel obliged or strongly inclined to: *cannot resist teasing me*. **2** be certain to be amused, attracted, etc., by: *can't resist children's clothes*.

resistance noun **1** the refusal to accept or comply with something; the attempt to prevent something by action or argument: *she put up no resistance to being led away ◊ their plan met with resistance ◊ resistance to change may be our undoing*. **2** the power of resisting: *showed resistance to wear and tear*. **3 a** the ability to withstand adverse conditions, esp. a person's capacity for withstanding common infections or a plant's capacity to withstand common diseases: *resistance to cold*. **b** lack of sensitivity to a drug, insecticide, etc., esp. owing to continued exposure or genetic change: *resistance to antibiotics is a growing problem*. **4** the impeding, slowing, or stopping effect exerted by one material thing on another: *the aerodynamic design reduces wind resistance*. **5** Physics **a** the property of hindering the conduction of electricity, heat, etc. **b** the measure of this in a body. Symbol: **R**. **6 a** (also **resistance movement**) a secret organization resisting authority, esp. in an occupied country. **b** (**the Resistance**) the underground movement formed in France during World War II to fight the German occupying forces and the Vichy government. **7** armed or violent opposition: *government forces were unable to crush guerrilla-like resistance*. PHRASES **the path of least resistance** an option avoiding difficulty or unpleasantness; the easiest course of action. ▶ **resistant** adjective

resister noun a person or thing that resists something.

resistivity noun a measure of the resisting power of a specified material to the flow of an electric current. [Say re ziss TIVVA tee]

resistor noun a device having resistance to the passage of an electrical current.

resize verb (**resizes, resized, resizing**) alter the size of; make larger or smaller.

resold past and past participle of RESELL.

resolute adjective (of a person or a person's mind or action) determined; decided; not vacillating. ▶ **resolutely** adverb **resoluteness** noun [Say REZZA loot]

resolution noun **1** a formal expression of opinion or intention by a legislative body or meeting: *passed a resolution*. **2** a firm decision to do or not do something: *New Year's resolutions*. **3** the quality of being determined or resolute: *the reforms owe a lot to the resolution of one woman*. **4** the action of solving a problem, dispute, or contentious matter: *conflict resolution ◊ the government hopes for an early resolution of the hostage crisis*. **5 a** esp. Chemistry the process of reducing or separating something into constituent parts or components. **b** the replacing of a single force etc. by two or more jointly equivalent to it. **6** Physics etc. the smallest interval measurable by a scientific (esp. optical) instrument. **7 a** the degree of detail visible in a photographic or television image. **b** the amount of graphical information that can be shown on a computer screen, usu. denoted by the number of lines that can be distinguished visibly, or by the number of pixels that

can be displayed in the horizontal and vertical directions of a graphics screen.

resolvable adjective able to be solved or settled: *resolvable issues*.

resolve • verb (**resolves, resolved, resolving**) **1** settle or find a solution to a problem, dispute, doubt, etc.: *trying to resolve our differences*. **2 a** decide firmly on a course of action: *resolve to put a stop to terrorism*. **b** (of an assembly or meeting) pass a resolution by vote: *be it resolved that the federal government amend human rights legislation*. **3** separate or reduce into constituent parts or a more basic form: *growth may be resolved into radial, anterior, lateral, and vertical components*. **4** (of optical or photographic equipment) separate or distinguish between closely adjacent objects: *Hubble was able to resolve six variable stars in M31*. **5** (of something seen at a distance) turn into a different form when seen more clearly: *the streaking shapes resolved into long, thin-bodied hounds*. • noun **1** a firm mental decision or intention; a resolution. **2** resoluteness; steadfastness.

resolved adjective resolute, determined.

resonance noun **1 a** the quality of sound that is deep, full, and reverberating. **b** Physics the reinforcement or prolongation of sound by reflection from a surface or by vibrations of a similar frequency from another object. **2** Mechanics a condition in which an object or system is subjected to an oscillating force having a frequency close to its own natural frequency. **3** the ability to evoke or suggest images, memories, and emotions: *the terminology of modern marketing has a distinctly military resonance*. **4** a short-lived subatomic particle that is an excited state of a more stable particle. [Say REZZA nince]

resonant adjective **1** (of sound) deep, clear, and continuing to sound or ring; echoing. **2** (of a body, room, etc.) tending to reinforce or prolong sounds, esp. by vibrations of a similar frequency. **3** having the power to bring images, feelings, memories, etc. to mind: *a resonant poem*. **4** (often foll. by with) (of a place) resounding: *resonant with the sound of bees*. [Say REZZA nint]

resonate verb (**resonates, resonated, resonating**) **1** produce or be filled with a deep, full, reverberating sound. **2** evoke or suggest images, memories, and emotions: *words that resonate with humour and hope*. **3** make an impression on or have special significance for someone: *the statement still resonates with women ◊ an issue that resonates in western Canada*. [Say REZZA nate]

resonator noun **1** a device responding to a specific vibration frequency, and used for detecting it when it occurs in combination with other sounds. **2 a** structure or device which reinforces or amplifies sound by resonance, esp. an acoustical chamber of a musical instrument, such as the hollow body of a stringed instrument. **3** a device which displays electrical resonance, esp. one used for the detection of radio waves. [Say REZZA nate er]

resort • noun **1** a place frequented esp. for holidays or for a specified purpose or quality: *ski resort*. **2 a** a person or thing to which one has recourse; an expedient or measure: *a taxi was our best resort*. **b** recourse to; use of: *without resort to violence*. • verb turn to as an expedient: *resorted to threats*. PHRASES **in the** (or **as a**) **last resort** when all else has failed.

resound verb **1** (of a place) ring or echo: *the hall resounded with laughter*. **2** (of a voice, instrument, sound, etc.) produce echoes; go on sounding. **3 a** (of fame, a reputation, etc.) be much talked of: *her public demeanour grew to infamous proportions and resounded to such acclaim that she was the most vaunted guest*. **b** (foll. by

R

through) produce a sensation: *the scandal resounded through Europe*. [Say re ZOUND]

resounding *adjective* **1** (of a sound) loud and echoing or reverberating: *the door shut with a resounding bang*. **2** unmistakable; emphatic: *a resounding success* ◊ *won with an resounding 60% of the vote*. ▶**resoundingly** *adverb* [Say re ZOUND ing]

resource • *noun* **1** (usu. in *plural*) **a** a stock or supply of money, materials, staff, and other assets that can be drawn on by a person or organization in order to function effectively. **b** available assets. **2** (often in *plural*) a material or condition occurring in nature and capable of economic exploitation. **3** (in *plural*) a country's collective means of supporting itself or becoming wealthier, as represented by its reserves of minerals, land, and other assets. **4** (often in *plural*) a book, videotape, or other material which supplies information on a particular topic: *educational resources*. **5** (in *plural*) one's personal attributes and capabilities regarded as able to help or sustain one in adverse circumstances: *mental recreation is necessary if a person is to develop his or her inner resources* ◊ *a society increasingly content to leave many children and their parents thrown back on their own resources*. • *verb* (**resources, resourced, resourcing**) (usu. in *passive*) provide (a person or organization) with materials, money, staff, and other assets needed for effective operation: *the school is very well resourced*.

resourceful *adjective* good at finding ways of doing things and solving problems. ▶**resourcefully** *adverb* **resourcefulness** *noun*

resource teacher *noun Cdn* **1** a teacher who provides educational resources, curriculum advice, and teaching ideas to other teachers. **2** a teacher who works with special-needs or gifted children.

resourcing *noun* the action of providing a person or organization with the materials, money, staff, and other assets necessary to operate effectively: *the level of resourcing required by pupils of different ages*.

RESP *abbreviation Cdn* Registered Educational Savings Plan, a tax-sheltered plan for saving money for a child's post-secondary education.

respect • *noun* **1** a feeling of admiration for someone because of their qualities or achievements. **2** due regard for the feelings or rights of others. **3** (in *plural*) polite greetings. **4** a particular aspect, point, or detail. • *verb* **1** feel or have respect for. **2** avoid harming or interfering with. **3** agree to recognize and abide by. **PHRASES** **with** (or **with all due**) **respect** a mollifying formula preceding an expression of disagreement with another's views. **with respect to** (or **in respect of**) as concerns; with reference to.

respectability *noun* **1** the state or quality of being proper, correct, and socially acceptable. **2** the state or quality of being accepted as valid or important within a particular field: *academic respectability*.

respectable *adjective* **1** regarded by society as being proper, correct, and good. **2** of some merit or importance. **3** adequate or acceptable in number, size, or amount. ▶**respectably** *adverb*

respecter *noun* **PHRASES** **be no respecter of** a person or thing that disregards social status, legal restraints, etc.: *this disease can strike anyone and is no respecter of class or race*.

respectful *adjective* feeling or showing respect, deferential: *stood at a respectful distance*. ▶**respectfully** *adverb* **respectfulness** *noun*

respecting *preposition* with reference or regard to.

respective *adjective* concerning or appropriate to each of several individually: *go to your respective places*.

respectively *adverb* each individually or in turn, and in the order mentioned: *she and I gave $10 and $5 respectively*.

respell *verb* (**respells**; *past* and *past participle* **respelled** or **respelt**; **respelling**) spell again or differently, esp. phonetically.

respiration *noun* **1** the action of breathing. **2** *Biology* the metabolic process in animals and plants in which organic substances are broken down into simpler products and energy is produced. In animals this process requires oxygen and creates carbon dioxide; in plants the process is reversed.

respirator *noun* **1** *Medical* an apparatus for maintaining artificial breathing. **2** an apparatus worn over the face to prevent gas, air, dust particles, etc., from being inhaled. [Say RESPER ate er]

respiratory *adjective* pertaining to, affecting, or serving for breathing. [Say RESPER a tory]

respire *verb* (**respires, respired, respiring**) **1** inhale and exhale air; breathe. **2** (of living organisms) carry out respiration.

respite *noun* **1** a short period of rest or relief from something difficult or unpleasant: *the busy academic schedule offers her little respite* ◊ *a respite from their studies*. **2** a short delay permitted before an unpleasant obligation is met or a punishment is carried out: *the residents won a brief respite from eviction*. [Say RESS pite or RESS pit]

respite care *noun* temporary institutional care of a dependent elderly, ill, or handicapped person, granting a respite to the usual caregiver.

resplendent *adjective* making an attractive or impressive display, esp. by being brilliant or brightly coloured: *Murray was there, resplendent in a multi-hued sports shirt* ◊ *a white hat resplendent with red velvet flowers*. ▶**resplendently** *adverb* [Say re SPLEN dint]

respond *verb* **1** answer, give a reply. **2** act or behave in an answering or corresponding manner. **3** (usu. foll. by *to*) **a** react favourably: *animals respond to kindness*. **b** exhibit a response; react: *cells respond to stimuli*.

respondent *noun* **1** a person who answers questions, esp. for a survey or questionnaire. **2** a defendant in a lawsuit, esp. one in an appeal or divorce case.

responder *noun* a person or thing that responds.

response *noun* **1** an answer given in word or act. **2** a feeling, movement, change, etc., caused by a stimulus or influence.

response time *noun* **1** *Computing* the elapsed time between the issuing of a command by a user and the receipt of some form of response or feedback from the computer. **2** the elapsed time between the receipt of an emergency call and the arrival of police, paramedics, etc. at the scene of the emergency.

responsibility *noun* (*plural* **responsibilities**) **1 a** the state or fact of being responsible: *the church had taken responsibility for helping the sick and the homeless* ◊ *no one has yet claimed responsibility for the bombing*. **b** the ability to act independently and make decisions: *a job with more responsibility*. **2** a person, duty, or thing for which one is responsible: *the food is my responsibility*.

responsible *adjective* **1** (often foll. by *to, for*) liable to be called to account (to a person or for a thing). **2** morally accountable for one's actions; capable of rational conduct. **3** respectable; evidently trustworthy. **4** (often foll. by *for*) being the primary cause. **5** involving responsibility: *a responsible job*. ▶**responsibly** *adverb*

responsible government *noun Cdn* a form of government in which the cabinet or executive branch is held collectively responsible and accountable to an elected legislature, and may remain in power only so long as it has the support of the legislature.

R

responsive *adjective* **1** responding readily (to some influence): *is always very responsive to my needs.* **2** responding with interest or enthusiasm: *a responsive class.* ▶ **responsively** *adverb* **responsiveness** *noun*

SPELL CHECK
rest, wrest

If you take something forcibly from someone's possession, you **wrest** it from them.

---

rest¹ • *verb* **1** cease work or movement in order to relax or recover strength. **2** allow to be inactive in order to regain or save strength or energy. **3** place or be placed so as to stay in a specified position: *his feet rested on the table.* **4** (foll. by *on*) depend or be based on. **5** (foll by *in, on*) place (trust, hope, or confidence) in or on. **6** (foll. by *with*) (of power, responsibility, etc.) belong to. **7** (of a problem or subject) be left without further investigation or discussion. **8** conclude the case for the prosecution or defence in a court of law. • *noun* **1** the action or a period of resting. **2** a motionless state. **3** *Music* an interval of silence of a specified duration. **4** an object that is used to hold or support something. PHRASES **at rest 1** not moving. **2** lying dead. **3** not agitated or troubled. **give it a rest** *informal* leave (a usu. contentious or perplexing issue) for the moment. **put** (or **lay**) **to rest 1** put a decisive end to (a rumour, notion, myth, etc.). **2** bury in a grave. **rest** (or **God rest**) **his** (or **her**) **soul** may God grant his (or her) soul repose. **rest one's case** conclude one's argument etc. **rest up** rest oneself thoroughly. **set at rest** settle or relieve (a question, a person's mind, etc.).

rest² • *noun* (**the rest**) the remaining part or parts; the others; the remainder of some quantity or number: *leave the rest.* • *verb* remain in a specified state: *you can rest assured that I'll get it done.* PHRASES **rest easy** remain or become calm, relaxed.

restart • *verb* begin again. • *noun* a new beginning.

restate *verb* (**restates**, **restated**, **restating**) express again or differently, esp. more clearly or convincingly. ▶ **restatement** *noun*

restaurant *noun* a commercial establishment where meals are prepared, served, and eaten.

WRITING TIP
restaurateur, restauranteur

It is becoming increasingly common to use the form **restauranteur**, but there are still many people who consider only **restaurateur** correct.

---

restaurateur *noun* (also **restauranteur**) a person who owns or manages a restaurant. [Say ress ter a TUR, ress ter on TUR]

rested *adjective* refreshed or reinvigorated by resting.

restful *adjective* **1** favourable to quiet or repose; soothing. **2** free from disturbing influences. **3** relaxed or refreshed by rest.

rest home *noun* a home for old or infirm people that is run privately and offers special care for its residents.

Restigouche salmon *noun* (*plural* **Restigouche salmon** or **Restigouche salmons**) a variety of Atlantic salmon associated with the Restigouche River in northern New Brunswick. [Say RESTA goosh]

restitution *noun* **1** (often foll. by *of*) the restoration of something lost or stolen to its proper owner: *the restitution of property taken from aboriginal peoples.* **2** payment made for an injury or loss: *ordered to pay $5,000 in restitution* ◊ *restitution to the victims of crime.* [Say resta TOO sh'n or resta TYOO sh'n]

restive *adjective* **1** restless, impatient, uneasy, nervous: *Roman emperors kept the restive mob supplied with*

bread and circuses ◊ *the Prime Minister managed to keep his small-c conservatives loyal, if restive.* **2** (of a horse) refusing to advance, stubbornly standing still or moving backwards or sideways. **3** (of a person) unmanageable; rejecting control. ▶ **restiveness** *noun*

restless *adjective* **1** uneasy, agitated; affording no rest: *a restless night.* **2 a** (of a person) fidgeting; unable to be still. **b** (of a thing) constantly moving: *a restless camera.* ▶ **restlessly** *adverb* **restlessness** *noun*

restock *verb* stock or supply again. [Say re STOCK]

restoration *noun* **1** the return of something to a former or original state: *building restoration.* **2** the act of returning something to a former owner, place, or condition. **3** a model or drawing representing the supposed original form of a ruined building etc. **4** (**the Restoration**) *hist.* **a** the re-establishment of Charles II as king of England in 1660 after Oliver Cromwell's son, Richard, had proved incapable of maintaining the Protectorate. **b** the period marked by this event. **c** (often as an *adjective*) the literary period following this: *Restoration comedy.* [Say ress ter AY sh'n]

restorative • *adjective* **1** tending or able to restore health or strength: *I have always found beach walks restorative.* **2** *Dentistry* pertaining to the use of structures provided to replace or repair dental tissue so as to restore its form and function. • *noun* a restorative medicine, food, etc. [Say re STORA tive]

restore *verb* (**restores**, **restored**, **restoring**) **1** bring back to the original or former state by rebuilding, repairing, repainting, etc. **2** bring back to good health etc.; cure. **3** give back to the original or former owner. **4** bring back to dignity or right; reinstate. **5** put back; replace. **6** make a representation of the supposed original state of (a ruin, extinct animal, etc.). ▶ **restored** *adjective* **restorer** *noun*

restrain *verb* **1 a** prevent (someone or oneself) from doing something: *I couldn't restrain her from asking.* **b** keep (someone or oneself) under control: *tried to restrain myself.* **2** impose a limit upon: *high prices restrain sales.* **3** forcibly control or confine: *restrained her dog.*

restrained *adjective* **1** kept under control or within bounds. **2** not excessive or extravagant; characterized by restraint or reserve.

restraining order *noun* a temporary court order issued to prevent an individual from committing a particular action, such as seeing or talking with a person.

restraint *noun* **1** self-control; avoidance of excess or exaggeration. **2** reserve of manner. **3** a device that restrains, such as a harness, seat belt, etc. **4** restriction of liberty or freedom of action; confinement. **5** a controlling agency or influence. [Say re STRAINT]

restrict *verb* **1 a** limit to a specific person or group of people: *parking is restricted to customers and employees.* **b** limit (a person or thing) according to specific guidelines: *restrict your speech to the key points.* **2** control, curtail, or reduce: *restrict the use of chemical weapons.* **3** (usu. foll. by *from*) discourage, prevent: *factors restricting men from becoming nurses.*

restricted • *adjective* **1** confined, controlled, or limited in some way. **2** (of land, access, information, etc.) available or accessible only to certain authorized individuals or to a certain group. **3** of or pertaining to a movie with the classification "Restricted". • *noun* (**Restricted**) **1** *Cdn* a film classification designating movies that may contain scenes of graphic violence, sex, coarse language, etc. and which have been deemed unsuitable for people under the age of 18. **2** *US* a film classification designating movies that cannot be viewed by people under the age of 18 unless accompanied by an adult.

restricted weapon *noun Cdn* a firearm, esp. a handgun, of a category that may be used only by licensed operators under specific conditions.

restriction *noun* **1** the limitation or control of something or someone, or the state of being limited or restricted. *the restriction of government power* ◊ *laws other that prevent any restriction of movement* ◊ *restrictions on freedom of speech.* **2** a limiting condition or regulation: *planning restrictions on commercial development* ◊ *travel restrictions have been lifted.*

restrictive *adjective* **1** tending to limit, prevent, or restrict; imposing restrictions. **2** *Grammar* (of a clause or phrase) specifying which particular thing or things are being discussed, as opposed to merely describing them; in *the books which are on the table used to belong to Anna*, the clause *which are on the table* is restrictive because it tells us *which* books used to belong to Anna, but if we insert commas around the clause, *the books, which are on the table, used to belong to Anna*, it merely tells us where the books are and is therefore not restrictive. ▶ **restrictively** *adverb* **restrictiveness** *noun*

restring *verb* (**restrings, restrung, restringing**) **1** fit (a musical instrument) with new strings. **2** thread (beads etc.) on a new string.

restroom *noun* esp. *US* a public washroom in a restaurant, bar, store, etc.

restructure *verb* (**restructures, restructured, restructuring**) **1** give a new structure to; rebuild. **2** fundamentally reorganize (a business, corporation, etc.). ▶ **restructuring** *noun*

restyle *verb* (**restyles, restyled, restyling**) reshape; remake in a new style.

result • *noun* **1** a consequence or outcome of something. **2** (often in *plural*) a satisfactory outcome; a favourable result: *she doesn't just work hard, she gets results.* **3** a quantity, formula, etc., obtained by calculation. **4** (in *plural*) **a** a list of scores or winners etc. in an exam or sporting event. **b** the findings of a research study, survey, etc. • *verb* **1** (often foll. by *from*) arise as the actual consequence or follow as a logical consequence (from conditions, causes, etc.). **2** (often foll. by *in*) have a specified end or outcome: *resulted in a large profit.* PHRASES **as a result** consequently, therefore. **as a result of** because of; due (to). **without result** in vain; fruitless.

resultant *adjective* occurring as a result; consequent: *resultant unemployment.*

resume *verb* (**resumes, resumed, resuming**) **1** begin again or continue after an interruption. **2** occupy again: *the judge resumed her seat.*

resumé *noun* **1** a brief account of one's education, experience, previous employment, and interests, usu. submitted with a job application. **2** a summary. [Say REZZA may or REZZ you may]

resumption *noun* the act of beginning something again after it has stopped: *the resumption of peace talks.*

resupply • *verb* (**resupplies, resupplied, resupplying**) **1** supply again; provide with a fresh supply. **2** take on or acquire a fresh supply. • *noun* the act or resupplying something or being resupplied.

resurface *verb* (**resurfaces, resurfaced, resurfacing**) **1** rise again; turn up or appear again. **2** lay a new surface on (a road, ice rink, etc.).

resurgence *noun* **1** a renewed prominence or popularity: *the resurgence of disco.* **2** a recovery; an increase after decline: *resurgence of the economy.* ▶ **resurgent** *adjective* [Say re SURGE ince]

resurrect *verb* **1** bring back from obscurity or disrepair; revive: *efforts to resurrect rail travel in Canada.* **2** raise from the dead. [Say rezza RECT]

resurrection *noun* **1** the action or fact of rising from

the dead. **2** (usu. **Resurrection**) (in Christian belief) **a** Christ's rising from the dead. **b** the rising of the dead at the Last Judgment. **3** a revival or revitalization of something: *the resurrection of the moribund textile industry* ◊ *the resurrection of 70s fashions.* [Say rezza REC sh'n]

resuscitate *verb* (**resuscitates, resuscitated, resuscitating**) **1** revive from unconsciousness or apparent death. **2** revive or restore: *resuscitate the ailing economy.* ▶ **resuscitation** *noun* **resuscitator** *noun* [Say re SUSSA tate]

retail • *noun* the sale of goods in relatively small quantities to the public, and usu. not for resale. • *adjective* **1** of or pertaining to the retailing of goods: *retail industry.* **2** sold by retail: *retail price.* • *adverb* by retail; at a retail price: *do you buy wholesale or retail?* • *verb* **1** sell (goods) in retail trade. **2** (often foll. by *at, of*) (of goods) be sold in this way (esp. for a specified price): *retails at $4.95.* ▶ **retailer** *noun* **retailing** *noun*

retain *verb* **1** maintain possession of; keep. **2** allow to remain or prevail; preserve: *retains its shape.* **3** (often as **retaining** *adjective*) keep in place; hold fixed: *retaining wall.* **4** secure (a hotel room etc.), or professional services, esp. of a lawyer) with a preliminary payment. **5** keep in one's memory.

retainer *noun* **1** *Law* a fee for retaining a lawyer etc. **2** *a hist.* a dependant or follower of a person of rank. **b** a long-standing family friend or servant. **3** a thing that holds something in place or retains. **4** *Dentistry* **a** a device consisting of wires cemented to the teeth or a moulded plastic plate fitting over the teeth to keep teeth aligned once they have been straightened. **b** a structure cemented to a tooth to keep a bridge in place. PHRASES **on (a) retainer** with services secured by a preliminary payment: *she was available on retainer.*

retake *verb* (**retakes; past retook; past participle retaken; retaking**) **1** take again: *I had to retake my driving test.* **2** recapture; regain possession of something once lost: *in 799 the Moors retook Barcelona* ◊ *retook the lead late in the race.* **3** film (a scene) or make (a recording) again.

retaliate *verb* (**retaliates, retaliated, retaliating**) respond to an injury, insult, assault, etc. in a similar manner; attack in return. ▶ **retaliation** *noun* **retaliatory** *adjective* [Say re TALLY ate, re TALLY a tory]

retard • *verb* delay the progress, development, arrival, or accomplishment of: *the lack of a rail link retarded the town's development.* • *noun slang offensive* **1** a mentally retarded person. **2** a stupid or foolish person.

retardant • *adjective* tending to slow or resist; capable of remaining unaffected by: *fire-retardant paint.* • *noun* **1** something that slows a process: *corrosion retardant.* **2** something that remains unaffected by or resistant to something else: *flame-retardant.*

retardation *noun* a delay, esp. in mental, physical, or social development.

retarded *adjective* less developed, esp. mentally, than is normal for one's age.

SPELL CHECK	
retch, wretch	ABC ✓
An unfortunate or wicked person is a **wretch**.	

retch • *verb* make an attempt to vomit, esp. involuntarily and without effect. • *noun* such a motion or the sound of it. ▶ **retching** *noun*

retell *verb* (**retells, retold, retelling**) tell again or in a different version. ▶ **retelling** *noun*

retention *noun* **1** the continued possession, use, or control of something: *the retention of direct control by the federal government.* **2** the action of absorbing and continuing to hold a substance: *mulching improves the*

R

soil's moisture retention. **3** the ability to keep things experienced or learned in one's memory. **4** *Medical* the failure to eliminate a substance from the body: *eating too much salt can lead to fluid retention.*

retentive *adjective* **1** tending to retain (moisture etc.). **2** not forgetful: *gifted with long retentive memories.* ▶ **retentiveness** *noun*

rethink • *verb* (**rethinks, rethought, rethinking**) think about (something) again, esp. with a view to making changes. • *noun* a reassessment.

reticence *noun* the avoidance of saying all one knows or feels, or of saying more than is necessary; reserve or restraint in speech etc.: *although Reibling is a man with a message, he finds it difficult to overcome his natural reticence.* ▶ **reticent** *adjective* [Say RETTA since]

reticulum *noun* (*plural* **reticula**) **1 a** a fine network of membranes etc. in living organisms. **b** a fine network within the cytoplasm of a cell. **2** a ruminant's second stomach. [Say re TICK you lum for the singular, re TICK you luh in plural]

retina *noun* (*plural* **retinas**) a light-sensitive layer at the back of the eyeball that triggers nerve impulses through the optic nerve to the brain where the visual image is formed. ▶ **retinal** *adjective* [Say RET in uh]

retinol *noun* a vitamin found in green and yellow vegetables, egg yolk, and fish-liver oil, essential for growth and vision in dim light. [Say RETTA nawl]

retinue *noun* a group of attendants accompanying an important person. [Say RETTA new]

retire *verb* (**retires, retired, retiring**) **1 a** leave office or employment, esp. because of age. **b** cause (a person) to retire from work. **c** cease to employ or use (something), or remove it from service. **2** withdraw or retreat, esp. to another room or location. **3** go to bed. **4** *Baseball* put out (a batter); cause (a side) to end a turn at bat. **5** withdraw (a bill or note) from circulation or currency. **6** retreat; withdraw (troops).

retired *adjective* **1** having retired from employment. **2** withdrawn from society or public life; secluded.

retiree *noun* a person who has retired from work. [Say re tire EE]

retirement *noun* **1** the act or fact of leaving one's job and ceasing to work: *took early retirement* ◊ *retirement age.* **2** the act of stopping a particular type of work, esp. in sports, the arts, politics, etc.: *she came out of retirement to win a gold medal* ◊ *dancers have to prepare for an early retirement.* **3** the condition of having retired, esp. from office or employment: *how will you spend your retirement?*

retiring *adjective* shy; fond of being on one's own: *a quiet, retiring man.*

retitle *verb* (**retitles, retitled, retitling**) give a different title to.

retold *past and past participle of* RETELL.

retook *past of* RETAKE.

retool *verb* **1** equip (a factory etc.) with new tools. **2** equip or prepare oneself again or for a new challenge or task: *if they just retool their inner selves, they can find romantic love.* **3** adapt or alter something to make it more useful or suitable: *he likes to retool the old stories and make them relevant for today's kids.*

retort • *noun* a sharp, witty, or angry reply. • *verb* reply angrily or wittily. [Say re TORT]

retouch *verb* (**retouches, retouched, retouching**) **1** improve or repair (a painting, makeup, etc.) by fresh touches or alterations; touch up. **2** alter or restore a photograph, print, negative, etc. by making minor changes after development. ▶ **retouching** *noun*

retrace *verb* (**retraces, retraced, retracing**) **1** go back over (one's steps etc.). **2** go back over (the course of an event etc.) in one's memory. **3** trace back to a source or beginning.

retract *verb* **1** withdraw or revoke (a statement, accusation, proposal, etc.). **2** (of a part of the body) draw or be drawn back or in. **3 a** (of a part of a device or mechanism) draw or be drawn back. **b** draw (an undercarriage etc.) into the body of an aircraft. ▶ **retractable** *adjective* **retraction** *noun*

retractor *noun* **1** a muscle used for retracting. **2** a device for retracting. **3** *Medical* an instrument or appliance used in surgical operations to hold back skin, tissues, etc. from the area of the operation.

retrain *verb* train again or further, esp. for new work. ▶ **retraining** *noun*

retransmission *noun* the transmission of data, radio signals, or broadcast programs that have been previously transmitted.

retransmit *verb* (**retransmits, retransmitted, retransmitting**) transmit (esp. radio signals or broadcast programs) back again or to a further distance.

retread • *verb* (**retreads, retreaded, retreading**) **1** put a fresh tread on (a tire). **2** alter (a person or thing) so that it is superficially different but essentially the same as its predecessor: *secular humanists who appear to be retreading universal religion in New Age format.* • *noun* **1** a retreaded tire. **2** a superficial reworking or revival of a well-known song, story, idea, etc.: *a lacklustre retread of their debut album.* [Say re TRED]

retreat • *verb* **1** (esp. of military forces) retire or draw back from a superior force during or following defeat, turn away from difficulty or opposition. **2** relinquish or abandon a position, stance, or view; back down. **3** become smaller in size or extent; decline, recede. **4** withdraw into privacy or security, one's own thoughts, etc.; take refuge. **5** move backwards. • *noun* **1 a** the act of moving back or withdrawing: *the army was in retreat* ◊ *beat a speedy retreat.* **b** *Military* a signal for this: *sound the retreat.* **2** an act of changing one's decisions, plans, or attitude, esp. as a result of criticism from others: *the union made a retreat from its earlier position.* **3** a quiet or secluded place in which one can rest and relax: *their country retreat in the Laurentians.* **4 a** a period of seclusion for prayer and religious meditation: *went on retreat.* **b** a period during which co-workers or people sharing a common interest meet away from their home or workplace to exchange ideas.

retrench *verb* (**retrenches, retrenched, retrenching**) reduce or eliminate (costs, employees, etc.); cut down expenses: *when they see their equity plunge, they tend to retrench, spend less and pay down their other debts.* ▶ **retrenchment** *noun*

retrial *noun* a second or further (judicial) trial.

retribution *noun* **1** punishment that is considered to be morally right and fully deserved: *a life sentence is not about rehabilitation—it is about punishment and retribution.* **2** retaliation: *many CBC staffers, fearing retribution in the face of deep budget cuts, declined to speak to reporters.* ▶ **retributive** *adjective* [Say ret ri BYOO sh'n, re TRIB you tiv]

retrievable *adjective* able to be retrieved: *retrievable data.*

retrieval *noun* **1** the process of getting something back from somewhere: *the investigation was completed after the retrieval of the plane wreckage.* **2** the obtaining or consulting of material stored in a computer system, in books, on tape, etc.: *retrieval systems* ◊ *methods of information retrieval.*

retrieve *verb* (**retrieves, retrieved, retrieving**) **1** regain possession of; recover and bring back. **2** (of a dog) find and bring back (game, a ball, a stick, etc.); fetch. **3** *Computing* find or extract (information stored in

a computer). **4** reel in (a fishing line). **5** repair or set right (a loss or error etc.): *retrieved the situation*.
retriever *noun* **1** a breed of dog used for retrieving game. **2** a person or thing that retrieves something.
retro • *noun* (*plural* **retros**) style or fashion imitating the past, esp. in dress, music, etc. • *adjective* **1** imitative of a style or fashion from the past (also in *combination*: *retro-chic*). **2** nostalgic for a previous time: *a retro mood*.
retro- *combining form* **1** denoting action back, backwards, or in return: *retroactive*. **2** *Anatomy & Medical* denoting location behind.
retroactive *adjective* (of legislation etc.) applying to the past as well as to the present or future; taking effect from a past date: *the salary increases are to be made retroactive to 1992.* ▶ **retroactively** *adverb*
retrofit • *verb* (**retrofits, retrofitted, retrofitting**) **1** modify (machinery etc.) to incorporate changes and developments introduced after manufacture. **2** provide (an older building etc.) with new fixtures, equipment, etc. that did not exist at the time of construction. • *noun* **1** a modification made to a product to incorporate changes made in later products of the same type or model. **2** a retrofitted product.
retrograde • *adjective* **1** directed backwards: *a retrograde flow*. **2** reverting to a less developed or inferior state; reactionary: *the government, dominated by the old Communist-trained leadership, is capable of taking further retrograde steps to protect its position.* **3** *Astronomy* in retrograde or showing retrograde. • *noun* *Astronomy* **1** the apparent backward motion of a planet in the zodiac. **2** the apparent motion of a celestial body from east to west.
retrospect *noun* a survey of past time or events. PHRASES **in retrospect** when looked back on; with hindsight: *in retrospect, I think I was a spoiled child*.
retrospective • *adjective* (of a film series, exhibition, recital, etc.) showing an artist's development over his or her lifetime. • *noun* a retrospective film series, concert, exhibition, etc. ▶ **retrospectively** *adverb*
retroviral *adjective* having to do with a retrovirus: *retroviral infection*.
retrovirus *noun* (*plural* **retroviruses**) any of a group of RNA viruses which insert a DNA copy of their genome into the host cell in order to replicate, e.g. HIV.
retry *verb* (**retries, retried, retrying**) **1** *Law* try (a defendant or lawsuit) a second or further time. **2** *Computing* endeavour to complete (a function) or run (a program) after a failed attempt.
retune *verb* (**retunes, retuned, retuning**) **1** tune (a musical instrument) again or differently. **2** tune (a radio etc.) to a different frequency. **3** alter the tuning of (an engine etc.) to improve smoothness and efficiency.
return • *verb* **1** come or go back to a place. **2** (foll. by *to*) go back to (a particular state or activity). **3** give or send back or put back in place. **4** feel, say, or do (the same feeling, action, etc.) in response. **5** (in tennis) hit or send the (the ball) back to an opponent. **6** (of a judge or jury) state or present (a verdict). **7** yield or make (a profit). **8** (of an electorate) elect to office. **9** *Football* catch a ball that has been kicked by the opposing team and carry it back downfield. • *noun* **1** an act or the action of returning. **2** a thing returned. **3** a formal report or statement compiled or submitted by order: *an income tax return*. **4** a profit from an investment. **5** (in *plural*) decision; results: *election returns*. **6** *Computing* = ENTER *noun*. **7** (in tennis etc.) the act of hitting a ball back in the direction of the server. **8** *Football* the act of receiving a kicked ball and bringing it back downfield. • *adjective* characterized by return or returning: *return fire* ◊ *return airfare* ◊ *the return leg of our trip* ◊ *a return engagement* ◊ *return address*. • *adverb* *Cdn & Brit.* (of travel)

to a particular destination and back: *flying return to Edmonton*. PHRASES **by return** (**mail**) by the next available mail delivery in the return direction. **in return** as an exchange or reciprocal action. **many happy returns** a greeting on a birthday.
returnable • *adjective* **1** able or intended to be returned. **2** (esp. of bottles etc.) that may be returned for money, esp. a deposit paid at the time of purchase. • *noun* a bottle, can, etc. that may be returned, esp. for money.
returned *adjective* **1** that has come or been brought back. **2** *Cdn, Austral.,* & *NZ* (of a member of the armed forces) discharged after active service, esp. abroad.
returnee *noun* **1** a person who returns to or from a place or position. **2** a person who has returned home after war or service abroad. [Say return EE]
returner *noun* *Football* a player who returns punts and kickoffs.
returning office *noun* *Cdn* an office where the returning officer and other administrative staff for an election etc. work.
returning officer *noun* *Cdn, Brit., Austral.,* & *NZ* an official organizing and overseeing the conduct of an election, referendum, etc. in a constituency.
retype *verb* (**retypes, retyped, retyping**) type again, esp. to correct errors.
Reuben *noun* (also **Reuben sandwich**) a hot sandwich on rye bread, containing corned beef, sauerkraut, and usu. Swiss cheese. [Say ROO bin]
reunification *noun* the restoration of political unity to a divided territory: *the reunification of Germany*.
reunify *verb* (**reunifies, reunified, reunifying**) restore (esp. separated territories) to a political unity.
reunion *noun* **1** the act of two or more people coming together again after a period of separation: *she had a tearful reunion with her parents*. **2** a social gathering esp. of relatives, friends, or former classmates after a long separation: *a family reunion* ◊ *their high school reunion*.
reunite *verb* (**reunites, reunited, reuniting**) bring or come back together.
reupholster *verb* repair or replace the stuffing, springs, covering, etc. of (a piece of furniture). ▶ **reupholstery** *noun* [Say re up HOLSTER]
reuse • *verb* (**reuses, reused, reusing**) use again or more than once. • *noun* a second or further use. ▶ **reused** *adjective*
Rev. *abbreviation* **1** Reverend. **2** Review.
rev *informal* • *noun* (in *plural*) the number of revolutions of an engine per minute: *running at 3,000 revs*. • *verb* (**revs, revved, revving**) (often foll. by *up*) **1 a** (of an internal combustion engine) revolve with increasing speed. **b** (of a vehicle) operate with increasing revolution of the engine, esp. with the clutch disengaged. **2** increase the speed of revolution of an internal combustion engine. **3** stimulate, activate, or accelerate: *rev up your love life*. **4 a** (of a person) become enthusiastic or excited: *revving up for the game*. **b** (of a thing) increase in activity or pace: *the industry is revving up for spring*.
revaluation *noun* an assessment of the value of something whose value has been assessed previously.
revalue *verb* (**revalues, revalued, revaluing**) *Economics* **1** assess the value of something again. **2** give a different or esp. higher value to (a currency) in relation to other currencies or gold (*opp.* DEVALUE 2).
revamp • *verb* **1** repair, restore: *revamp a damaged reputation*. **2** renovate, overhaul: *completely revamp the education system*. • *noun* **1** a revamped version; an overhaul or revision. **2** an act of revamping something.
RevCan *noun* *Cdn slang* Revenue Canada.
reveal *verb* **1** display, show, or expose; allow to appear. **2** disclose, divulge, betray: *revealed her plans*. **3** (esp. of

God) make known by inspiration or supernatural means. **4** appear or become apparent; come into view: *after several listens each record reveals itself as a self-contained masterpiece.* ▶ **revealer** *noun*

revealing *adjective* **1** providing insight esp. into something obscure or private: *her autobiography is quite revealing.* **2** (of an article of dress etc.) allowing more of the body to be seen than is usual or conventional: *a revealing blouse.* ▶ **revealingly** *adverb*

reveille *noun* a signal given in the morning, usu. on a drum or bugle, to waken soldiers and indicate that it is time to rise. [Say REVVA lee]

réveillon *noun* (among francophones) a festive meal on Christmas morning after midnight Mass or on New Year's Eve. [Say REV ay on (with on as in French)]

revel • *verb* (**revels, revelled, revelling**) take great delight in: *revelled in her new-found freedom.* • *noun* (usu. in *plural*) a lively and noisy festivity, esp. one involving drinking and dancing: *needed a day to recuperate from their revels.* [Say REV'll]

revelation *noun* **1** the making known of something that was previously secret or unknown: *the revelation of an alleged plot to assassinate the queen.* **2** a surprising and previously unknown fact, esp. one that is made known in a dramatic way: *revelations about her life.* **3** the divine or supernatural disclosure to humans of something relating to human existence or the world: *an attempt to reconcile Darwinian theories with biblical revelation* ◊ *a divine revelation.* **4** a completely new or surprising experience: *my trip to the Yukon was a revelation to me* ◊ *the idea came as a revelation.* [Say revva LAY sh'n]

revelatory *adjective* serving to reveal, esp. something significant: *scenes which should be terrifying, tragic, or revelatory feel poetic and contrived.* [Say REVVA luh tory]

reveller *noun* a person who engages in lively and noisy festivities, esp. involving drinking and dancing: *after the bars close in Ottawa, late-night revellers move across to Hull.*

revelling *noun* the action of enjoying oneself in a noisy, enthusiastic way: *a night of drunken revelling.*

revelry *noun* (*plural* **revelries**) the action of revelling or merrymaking; boisterous gaiety or mirth: *after all the revelry, the feast ended with men asleep on their chairs, children sprawled on the floor, and bottles everywhere.*

revenge • *noun* **1** retaliation for an offence or injury. **2 a** an act of retaliation. **b** the opportunity to retaliate or avenge a loss etc. **3** the desire for this; a vindictive feeling. • *verb* (**revenges, revenged, revenging**) **1** take revenge for (an offence). **2** retaliate on behalf of (a person).

revenge of the cradle *noun* Cdn (**the revenge of the cradle**) the extremely high birth rate of French Canadians from the 19th to the mid-20th centuries, perceived as a means of retaliation against the English.

revenue *noun* **1 a** income, esp. of a large amount, from any source. **b** (in *plural*) items constituting this. **2** a government's annual income from which public expenses are met. **3** the department of the civil service collecting this.

reverb *noun* Music informal **1** reverberation. **2** a device to produce this. [Say re VERB or REE verb]

reverberant *adjective* **1** (of sound) vibrating or repeating several times, creating an echo or tremolo: *the song ends with a reverberant fade-out.* **2** (of a place) allowing sound to echo or reverberate; having poor acoustics: *the band played a sold-out show in the tiny, reverberant arena.* [Say re VERB a rint]

reverberate *verb* (**reverberates, reverberated, reverberating**) **1 a** (of sound, light, or heat) be returned or echoed or reflected repeatedly. **b** return (a sound etc.) in this way. **2 a** (of a story, rumour, etc.) be heard much or repeatedly. **b** (of an event) have

continuing effects. ▶ **reverberation** *noun* [Say re VERB a rate]

revere *verb* (**reveres, revered, revering**) hold in deep and usu. affectionate or religious respect: *a trumpeter revered by fellow musicians* ◊ *she is now revered as a national hero.* [Say re VEER]

reverence • *noun* **1** a feeling of great respect or admiration for a person or thing: *the poem conveys his deep reverence for nature* ◊ *the crowd knelt in reverence and worship.* **2** (**Reverence**) a title used of or to some members of the clergy. • *verb* (**reverences, reverenced, reverencing**) regard or treat with reverence: *the many divine beings reverenced by Hindu tradition.* [Say REVVER ince]

Reverend • *adjective* (as the title of a member of the clergy): *the Reverend Robert M. Bisset.* Abbreviation: **Rev.** • *noun* informal (also **reverend**) a clergyman. [Say REVVER und]

reverent *adjective* feeling or showing great respect or admiration: *a reverent silence.* [Say REVVER unt]

reverential *adjective* full of respect or admiration: *his name was always mentioned in almost reverential tones.* ▶ **reverentially** *adverb* [Say revver EN shull]

reverently *adverb* in a reverent or respectful manner. [Say REVVER unt lee]

reverie *noun* a state of absent-minded meditation or musing; a daydream: *was lost in a reverie.* [Say REVVER ee]

reversal *noun* **1** a change to an opposite direction, position, situation, or course of action: *a dramatic reversal in population decline* ◊ *government policy reversal.* **2** a situation in which two or more people exchange positions or functions: *in a peculiar role reversal, the cats were chasing the dog around the house.* **3** a change from success or fortunate circumstances to failure or misfortune: *a reversal of fortune.*

reverse • *verb* (**reverses, reversed, reversing**) **1** turn the other way around or up or inside out. **2** change to the opposite character or effect: *reversed the decision.* **3** move backwards or in the opposite direction. **4** make (an engine etc.) work in a contrary direction. **5** revoke or annul (a verdict, decree, act, etc.). • *adjective* **1** placed or turned in an opposite direction or position. **2** opposite or contrary in character or order; inverted. • *noun* **1** the opposite or contrary: *is the reverse of the truth.* **2** the contrary of the usual manner. **3** an occurrence of misfortune; a disaster, esp. a defeat in battle: *suffered a reverse.* **4** reverse gear or motion. **5** the reverse side of something. **6** Football a play in which one offensive player hands the ball off to a player running in the opposite direction. **7 a** the side of a coin or medal etc. bearing the secondary design. **b** this design (compare OBVERSE 1). **8** the verso of a leaf. **9** a device, as on a tape player, that turns something over or backwards. ▶ PHRASES **reverse the charges** make the recipient of a telephone call responsible for payment.

reverse discrimination *noun* discrimination against men or white people that results from policies intended to end discrimination against women or racial minorities.

reverse psychology *noun* the principle or practice of suggesting to a person that he or she do the opposite of what one really wants him or her to do.

reverser *noun* a person or thing that reverses something, esp. a device for reversing the flow of gas from a jet engine to produce a retarding backward force: *thrust reverser.*

reverse video *noun* a mode on a computer monitor in which the colours normally used for the background and characters are reversed.

reversible *adjective* **1** (of clothes or fabrics) that can be turned inside out and worn or that can be used with

either side showing: *Janet wears a reversible vest, with stripes on one side and a leopard print on the other*. **2** (of a process, action, or disease) that can be changed so that it returns to its original situation or condition: *fortunately, Rafael's condition is reversible*. **3** (of an electric motor, fan, drill, etc.) that can operate in either direction.

reversing falls *noun* *Cdn* a set of rapids on a tidal river, the flow of which reverses regularly due to the pressure of the incoming tide.

reversion *noun* **1** a return to a previous state, habit, etc.: *called for a reversion to the two-party system*. **2** *Biology* the action of returning to a former or ancestral type. **3** the legal right (esp. of the original owner, or his or her heirs) to possess or succeed to property on the death of the present possessor. **4** a sum payable on a person's death, esp. by way of life insurance. [Say re VERSION]

revert *verb* **1** (foll. by *to*) **a** return to a former state or condition. **b** return to a former practice or habit. **c** return to an earlier topic of conversation or thought. **2** (of property, an office, etc.) return by reversion. **3** fall back into a wild state.

SPELL CHECK
review, revue   ABC ✓

A theatrical entertainment is a **revue**.
---

review • *noun* **1** a general survey or assessment of a subject or thing: *a review of recent developments in education*. **2** a retrospective survey or report on past events: *our end-of-year review*. **3** a reconsideration or examination, with the possibility or intention of change if desirable or necessary: *our defence policy is under review ◊ rent review ◊ his parole application is up for review*. **4** an action of reviewing a subject or material already learned: *we need a review of irregular verbs*. **5** *Law* consideration of a judgment, sentence, etc., by some higher court or authority. **6** a display and formal inspection of troops etc. **7** an account or criticism of a book, performance, restaurant, etc., esp. when published or broadcast. **8** a periodical publication with critical articles on current events, the arts, etc. • *verb* **1** survey or look back on. **2** reconsider or revise. **3 a** go over (a lesson, or series of lessons) to reinforce a subject already learned. **b** present or study material again, e.g. to prepare for a test. **4** hold a review of (troops etc.). **5 a** publish or broadcast a review of (a book, performance, etc.). **b** write a review of (a scholarly article) to assess its suitability for publication. **6** *Law* submit (a sentence, decision, etc.) to review. **7** view again. ▶ **reviewable** *adjective*

reviewer *noun* a person who writes or broadcasts reviews of books, performances, etc.; a critic.

revile *verb* (**reviles, reviled, reviling**) criticize abusively: *she was now reviled by the party she had once led*.

revise *verb* (**revises, revised, revising**) **1** examine or re-examine and improve or amend (esp. written or printed matter). **2** consider and alter (an opinion etc.). ▶ **reviser** *noun*

revision *noun* **1** the action of changing something, or examining it with the intention of changing it: *the plan needs drastic revision*. **2** a change or set of changes made to something: *the second print run includes revisions*.

revisionism *noun* often *derogatory* **1** a reinterpretation of classical Marxist theory. **2** the theory or practice of revising one's attitude to or description of a previously accepted situation or point of view: *they feel the need for some discreet but deliberate revisionism of their pasts*. ▶ **revisionist** *noun & adjective*

revisit *verb* (**revisits, revisited, revisiting**) **1** visit again. **2** take up (a subject etc.) again; reconsider.

revitalization *noun* the action of making something stronger, healthier, or more active: *revitalization of the BC salmon industry*.

revitalize *verb* (**revitalizes, revitalized, revitalizing**) make something stronger, healthier, or more active: *a plan to revitalize the city's harbourfront*.

revival *noun* **1** an improvement in the condition or strength of something; a recovery. **2** the process of bringing something back into existence, use, fashion, etc. **3 a** a reawakening of religious fervour. **b** a series of evangelistic meetings to promote this. **4** a new production of an old play etc. **5** restoration to bodily or mental vigour or to life or consciousness.

revivalism *noun* **1** belief in or the promotion of a revival, esp. of religious fervour. **2** a tendency or desire to revive a former custom or practice: *Seventies revivalism*. ▶ **revivalist** *noun & adjective*

revive *verb* (**revives, revived, reviving**) **1** come or bring back to consciousness or life or strength. **2** come or bring back to existence, use, notice, etc. **3** produce (a play etc.) that has not been performed for some time.

revivification *noun* the process of giving new life or vigour to something: *ever since the branch plant closed down, this manufacturing town has been in desperate need of revivification*. [Say re vivva fuh KAY sh'n]

revivify *verb* (**revivifies, revivified, revivifying**) restore to activity, vigour, or life: *they revivified a wine industry that had all but vanished*. [Say re VIVVA fie]

revocable *adjective* (of a promise, agreement, etc.) that can be cancelled or revoked: *a proxy will not be valid at the expiration of 11 months, and will be revocable*. [Say re VOKE a bull or REV ick a bull]

revocation *noun* the action of cancelling or revoking an agreement, privilege, etc.: *the court upheld the revocation of the doctor's licence*. [Say revva KAY sh'n]

revoke *verb* (**revokes, revoked, revoking**) withdraw or cancel (a licence, decision, promise, etc.): *the Board of Governors voted to revoke the contract*.

revolt • *verb* **1** rise in rebellion against authority. **2** (often in *passive*) affect with strong disgust; nauseate: *was revolted by the thought of it*. • *noun* **1** an act of rebelling. **2** a state of insurrection: *in revolt*. **3** a sense of loathing. **4** a mood of protest or defiance.

revolting *adjective* disgusting, horrible. ▶ **revoltingly** *adverb*

revolution *noun* **1 a** the forcible overthrow of a government or social order, in favour of a new system: *the French Revolution ◊ a country on the brink of revolution*. **b** (in Marxism) the replacement of one ruling class by another; the class struggle which is expected to lead to political change and the triumph of communism. **2** any fundamental change or reversal of conditions: *the Industrial Revolution ◊ a revolution in the way people thought*. **3** a circular movement made by something fixed to a central point: *one revolution per second*. **4 a** motion in orbit or a circular course or around an axis or centre; rotation. **b** the single completion of an orbit or rotation. **c** the time taken for this.

revolutionary • *adjective* **1** involving a complete or dramatic change. **2** of or causing political revolution. **3** (**Revolutionary**) of or relating to a particular revolution, esp. the American Revolution. • *noun* (*plural* **revolutionaries**) an instigator or supporter of esp. political revolution.

revolutionize *verb* (**revolutionizes, revolutionized, revolutionizing**) introduce fundamental change to.

Révolution tranquille *noun* *Cdn* = QUIET REVOLUTION. [Say ray voll oo SYON tron KEEL (with SYON as in French)]

revolve *verb* (**revolves, revolved, revolving**) **1** turn or cause to turn around, esp. on an axis; rotate. **2** move in a circular orbit. **3** (foll. by *around*) have as its chief concern; be centred upon: *my life revolves around my job.*

revolver *noun* a pistol with revolving chambers enabling several shots to be fired without reloading.

revolving door *noun* **1** a door with usu. four partitions turning around a central axis. **2 a** a situation, organization, etc. in which new arrivals depart again almost immediately, usu. without due care or attention given them, and often return again very soon: *the revolving door of psychiatric care.* **b** (as an *adjective*) (usu. **revolving-door**) designating or describing an institution etc. where people are processed quickly or through which people pass constantly: *a revolving-door workplace.*

revue *noun* a theatrical entertainment of a series of short usu. satirical sketches and songs. [Say re VIEW]

revulsion *noun* a sense of loathing: *news of the attack will be met with sorrow and revulsion.* [Say re VULL sh'n]

reward • *noun* **1 a** a thing given in recognition of service, effort, or achievement: *the holiday was a reward for 40 years' service with the company* ◊ *the emotional rewards of being a parent.* **b** a fair return for good or bad behaviour: *a slap on the face was his reward for his impudence.* **2 a** sum offered for the detection of a criminal, the restoration of lost property, etc. **3 a** benefit provided in return for frequent use of a commercial service, as in a frequent flyer program. • *verb* **1** give a reward to (a person) or for (a service etc.). **2** make return for (an action): *the book rewards a close reading.* PHRASES **go to one's reward** die.

rewarding *adjective* (of an activity etc.) well worth doing; providing satisfaction. ▶ **rewardingly** *adverb*

rewind • *verb* (**rewinds, rewound, rewinding**) wind (a film or tape etc.) back to the beginning. • *noun* **1** a mechanism for doing this. **2** the action or process of doing this. ▶ **rewinder** *noun*

rewire *verb* (**rewires, rewired, rewiring**) provide (a building etc.) with new wiring.

reword *verb* change the wording of.

rework *verb* revise; refashion. ▶ **reworking** *noun*

rewrite • *verb* (**rewrites**; *past* **rewrote**; *past participle* **rewritten; rewriting**) **1** write again or differently. **2** present or depict (history or a historical event) in a new or different light, esp. to further one's own interests: *it is wrong to try to rewrite history and claim that this was a government policy.* • *noun* the action of rewriting something so as to improve it: *the script went through several rewrites.*

Rex *noun* the reigning king (following a name or in the titles of lawsuits).

rez *noun* (*plural* **rezzes**) *informal* an Indian reserve or reservation.

rezone *verb* (**rezones, rezoned, rezoning**) classify (a property, area, etc.) as belonging to a different zone or subject to a different set of zoning regulations.

Rf *symbol* rutherfordium.

Rh[1] *symbol* rhodium.

Rh[2] *abbreviation* rhesus factor.

rhapsodic *adjective* enthusiastic or ecstatic in language or manner: *you have no doubt heard rhapsodic stories of miracle cures for baldness.* [Say RAP sod ick]

rhapsodize *verb* (**rhapsodizes, rhapsodized, rhapsodizing**) talk or write about a person or thing with great enthusiasm: *when he first viewed Victoria, he rhapsodized about the site.* [Say RAPSA dize]

rhapsody *noun* (*plural* **rhapsodies**) **1** a highly enthusiastic or ecstatic expression of feeling: *rhapsodies of praise.* **2** a piece of music in one extended movement, usu. emotional in character. [Say RAPSA dee]

rhea *noun* (*plural* **rheas**) a South American flightless bird, similar to but smaller than an ostrich. [Say REE uh]

Rhenish • *adjective* of the Rhine River in western Europe, and the regions adjoining it. • *noun* wine from this area. [Say REE nish or REN ish]

rhenium *noun* a rare metallic element, occurring naturally in molybdenum ores and used in the manufacture of superconducting alloys. [Say REENY um]

rheostat *noun* *Electricity* an instrument used to control a current by varying the resistance. ▶ **rheostatic** *adjective* [Say REE uh stat, ree uh STATIC]

rhesus factor *noun* = RH FACTOR.

rhesus monkey *noun* (*plural* **rhesus monkeys**) a small monkey common in northern India, often kept in captivity and widely used in medical research. [Say REE sus]

rhetoric *noun* **1** the art of effective or persuasive speaking or writing: *rhetoric embraces the rules of good writing and speaking but goes beyond mere correctness.* **2** language designed to persuade or impress (often with an implication of insincerity or exaggeration etc.): *all we have from the Opposition is empty rhetoric.* [Say RETTER ick]

rhetorical *adjective* **1** expressed with a view to persuasive or impressive effect; artificial or extravagant in language: *the rhetorical commitment of the government to give priority to primary education.* **2** of the nature of rhetoric. **3** of or relating to the art of rhetoric: *repetition is a common rhetorical device.* ▶ **rhetorically** *adverb* [Say ruh TORA cull]

rhetorical question *noun* a question asked not for information but to produce an effect, e.g. *who cares?*

rheumatic • *adjective* **1** of, relating to, or suffering from rheumatism. **2** producing or produced by rheumatism: *rheumatic fever.* • *noun* a person suffering from rheumatism. ▶ **rheumatically** *adverb* [Say roo MAT ick]

rheumatism *noun* any disease marked by inflammation and pain in the joints, muscles, or fibrous tissue, esp. rheumatoid arthritis. [Say ROOMA tism]

rheumatoid arthritis *noun* a chronic progressive disease causing inflammation and stiffening of the joints. [Say ROOMA toid]

Rh factor *noun* (also **rhesus factor**) an antigen occurring on the red blood cells of most humans and some other primates. Red blood cells that have this antigen are called **Rh-positive**; those that do not have it are called **Rh-negative**.

rhinestone *noun* an imitation diamond. [Say RINE stone]

rhino *noun* (*plural* **rhino** or **rhinos**) **1** *informal* a rhinoceros. **2** (**Rhino**) *Cdn slang* a member of the Rhinoceros Party.

rhinoceros *noun* (*plural* **rhinoceros** or **rhinoceroses**) **1** a large thick-skinned plant-eating mammal of Africa and South Asia, with one or two horns on the nose and plated or folded skin. **2** (**Rhinoceros**) *Cdn* a member of the Rhinoceros Party.

Rhinoceros Party *noun* *Cdn* a spoof political party which first ran candidates in the 1960s; the party's goal is to demonstrate the supposed shortcomings of the traditional Canadian political parties.

rhinoplasty *noun* (*plural* **rhinoplasties**) plastic surgery of the nose. [Say RYE no plasty]

rhizomatous *adjective* bearing or consisting of an underground rootlike stem with both roots and shoots. [Say rye ZOE muh tus]

rhizome *noun* an underground rootlike stem bearing both roots and shoots, e.g. in irises. [Say RYE zome]

Rh-negative *adjective* see RH FACTOR.

Rhodes Scholar *noun* a student attending Oxford

University on any of several scholarships awarded annually on the basis of merit to students from certain Commonwealth countries, the US, and Germany. ▶ **Rhodes Scholarship** noun [Sounds like ROADS]

rhodium noun a hard white metallic element, occurring naturally in platinum ores and used in making alloys and plating jewellery. [Say ROADY um]

rhododendron noun an evergreen shrub or small tree of the heather family, with usu. large clusters of trumpet-shaped flowers, widely grown as an ornamental. [Say ROAD uh DEN drun]

rhombic adjective having the shape of a rhombus. [Say ROM bick]

rhomboid • adjective having or nearly having the shape of a rhombus. • noun a quadrilateral of which only the opposite sides and angles are equal. [Say ROM boyd]

rhombus noun (plural **rhombuses** or **rhombi**) Math a parallelogram with oblique angles and equal sides. [Say ROM bus for the singular; for RHOMBI say ROM bye]

RHOSP abbreviation Cdn Registered Home Ownership Savings Plan, a tax-sheltered account in which a first-time homebuyer may save money for a down payment. [Say AR hosp]

Rh-positive adjective see RH FACTOR.

rhubarb noun 1 a a large-leaved plant producing long fleshy dark red stalks that can be cooked and eaten. b these leaf stalks. 2 slang a heated dispute. [Say ROO barb]

rhumba noun & verb = RUMBA. [Say RUMBA]

rhyme • noun 1 the quality shared by words or syllables that have or end with the same sound as each other, esp. when such words etc. are used at the ends of lines of poetry. 2 (in singular or plural) verse having rhymes. 3 a poem having rhymes. 4 a word that has the same sound as another. • verb (**rhymes**, **rhymed**, **rhyming**) 1 a (of words or lines) produce a rhyme. b (foll. by with) act as a rhyme (with another). 2 make or write rhymes. 3 (foll. by with) treat (a word) as rhyming with another. PHRASES **rhyme or reason** (usu. in negative expressions) sense or logic: there's no rhyme or reason to it. ▶ **rhymer** noun

rhyme scheme noun the ordered pattern of rhymes at the ends of the lines of a poem or verse.

rhythm noun 1 a measured flow of words and phrases in verse or prose determined by various relations of long and short or accented and unaccented syllables. 2 the aspect of musical composition concerned with periodical accent and the duration of notes. 3 movement with a regular succession of strong and weak elements. 4 a regularly recurring sequence of events. 5 a sense of rhythm. 6 Art a harmonious correlation of parts.

rhythm and blues noun popular music with a blues theme and strong rhythm.

rhythmic adjective (also **rhythmical**) relating to or characterized by rhythm. ▶ **rhythmically** adverb

rhythm method noun birth control by avoiding sexual intercourse when ovulation is likely to occur.

rhythm section noun the part of a band etc. mainly supplying rhythm, usu. consisting of drums, bass, etc.

rib • noun 1 each of the curved bones articulated in pairs to the spine and protecting the thoracic cavity and its organs. 2 a a roast of meat from this part of an animal. b (usu. in plural) = SPARERIBS. 3 a ridge or long raised piece often of stronger or thicker material across a surface or through a structure serving to support or strengthen it. 4 any of a ship's transverse curved timbers forming the framework of the hull. 5 Knitting a combination of plain and purl stitches producing a ribbed, somewhat elastic fabric. 6 a vein of a leaf or an

insect's wing. 7 a structural member in an airfoil. • verb (**ribs**, **ribbed**, **ribbing**) 1 provide with ribs; act as the ribs of. 2 informal tease. 3 mark with ridges.

ribald adjective (of language or its user) referring to sexual matters in a rude but humorous way. [Say RYE b'ld or RIBBLED]

ribaldry noun ribald talk or behaviour. [Say RYE b'll dree or RIBBLE dree]

ribbed adjective 1 having ribs or riblike markings. 2 Knitting having ribbing.

ribbing noun 1 ribs or a riblike structure. 2 a pattern in knitting of alternate ridges and depressions. 3 informal good-natured teasing.

ribbit noun the sound made by a frog.

ribbon noun 1 a a narrow strip or band of fabric, used esp. for trimming or decoration. b material in this form. 2 a ribbon of a special colour etc. worn to indicate some honour, allegiance, or membership of a sports team etc. 3 a long narrow strip of anything, e.g. impregnated material forming the inking agent in a typewriter or printer. 4 (in plural) ragged strips: torn to ribbons. ▶ **ribboned** adjective

rib cage noun the wall of bones formed by the ribs around the chest.

rib-eye noun (also **rib-eye steak**) a roundish steak cut from the rib.

riboflavin noun a vitamin of the vitamin B complex, found in liver, milk, and eggs, essential for energy production. [Say rye bo FLAY vin]

ribonucleic acid noun a nucleic acid present in living cells, esp. in ribosomes where it is involved in protein synthesis. Abbreviation: **RNA**. [Say rye bo new CLAY ick]

ribosomal adjective found in or having to do with a ribosome or ribosomes: ribosomal RNA. [Say rye buh SOAM ull]

ribosome noun each of the minute particles consisting of RNA and associated proteins found in the cytoplasm of living cells, concerned with the synthesis of proteins. [Say RYE buh soam]

rice • noun 1 the grain of a widely cultivated swamp grass, a major world cereal. 2 the plant producing this grain, grown in warmer parts of the world, usu. in standing water. • verb pass (cooked potatoes etc.) through a coarse sieve to produce long strands.

rice cake noun a round, crisp biscuit made of puffed rice.

rice paper noun 1 edible paper made from the pith of an oriental tree and used for painting and in cookery. 2 paper made wholly or partly from the straw of rice.

ricer noun a utensil with small holes through which boiled potatoes or other soft food can be pushed to form particles of a similar size to grains of rice.

rich adjective 1 having much wealth. 2 splendid, costly, elaborate: rich tapestries ◊ rich with lace. 3 valuable: rich offerings. 4 ample: a rich harvest. 5 abundantly supplied with: rich with wildlife. 6 (of food or diet) containing a large amount of fat, butter, eggs, sugar, etc. 7 (of the mixture in an internal combustion engine) containing a high proportion of fuel (compare LEAN² 6). 8 (of colour or sound or smell) mellow and deep, strong and full. 9 (of an incident or assertion etc.) highly ludicrous. 10 (of soil) very fertile; abounding in nutrients. 11 (of a country, region, etc.) abounding in natural resources or means of production.

-rich combining form having or containing much; abundant in: oil-rich ◊ vitamin-rich.

Richardson's ground squirrel noun a ground squirrel of western North America, commonly called a gopher.

riches *plural noun* wealth; money and valuable possessions.

richly *adverb* **1** in a rich way. **2** fully, thoroughly.

Richter scale *noun* a scale for representing the strength of an earthquake, beginning at near 0 for the smallest. The more destructive earthquakes typically have magnitudes between about 5.5 and 8.9; it is a logarithmic scale and a difference of one represents an approximate thirtyfold difference in magnitude. [Say RICK ter]

rick • *noun* a stack of hay, straw, etc., built into a regular shape and usu. covered or thatched. • *verb* form into a rick or ricks.

rickets *noun* a disease of children characterized by softening of the bones (esp. the spine) and bow legs, caused by vitamin D deficiency.

rickettsia *noun* (*plural* **rickettsiae** or **rickettsias**) a parasitic micro-organism causing typhus and other diseases. ▶ **rickettsial** *adjective* [Say ri KETSY uh]

rickety *adjective* insecure or shaky in construction; likely to collapse.

rickey *noun* (*plural* **rickeys**) a drink of lime juice, soda water, and usu. gin.

rickrack *noun* (also **ricrac**) a zigzag braided trimming for garments.

rickshaw *noun* a light, two-wheeled, usu. hooded vehicle drawn by one or more persons.

ricochet • *noun* the action of a projectile, esp. a shell or bullet, in rebounding off a surface. • *verb* (**ricochets, ricocheted, ricocheting**) rebound one or more times from a surface. [Say RICK a shay]

ricotta *noun* a soft Italian cheese with a texture resembling that of fine cottage cheese, used esp. in pasta dishes and desserts. [Say ri COTTA]

rid *verb* (**rids, rid, ridding**) (foll. by *of*) make (a person or place) free of something unwanted. PHRASES **be** (or **get**) **rid of** be freed or relieved of (something unwanted); dispose of.

riddance *noun* PHRASES **good riddance** expressing welcome relief from an unwanted person or thing.

ridden • *verb* past participle of RIDE. • *adjective* (in combination) infested or afflicted: *a rat-ridden cellar*.

riddle¹ • *noun* **1** a question or statement testing ingenuity in divining its answer or meaning. **2** a puzzling fact, thing, or person. • *verb* (**riddles, riddled, riddling**) speak in or propound riddles.

riddle² *verb* (**riddles, riddled, riddling**) (usu. foll. by *with*) **1** make many holes in, esp. with gunshot. **2** fill; spread through: *was riddled with errors*.

RIDE *noun* Cdn (Ont.) a program to reduce impaired driving, in which police stop vehicles randomly and check drivers for signs of intoxication, esp. during the holiday season: *a RIDE checkpoint*.

ride • *verb* (**rides**; *past* **rode**; *past participle* **ridden**; **riding**) **1** sit on and control the movement of (a horse, bicycle, or motorcycle). **2** travel in or on a vehicle or horse. **3** travel over on horseback or on a bicycle or motorcycle: *ride the scenic trail*. **4 a** be carried or supported by: *surfers rode the waves*. **b** be animated, stimulated, or spurred on by circumstances etc.: *riding a wave of popularity*. **5** sail or float: *a ship rode at anchor in the dock*. **6** yield to (a blow) so as to reduce its impact. **10** (in *passive*) be full of or dominated by: *ridden by guilt*. • *noun* **1** an act of riding. **2** a roller coaster, merry-go-round, etc. ridden at a fair. **3** a demonstration of (esp. horse) riding as entertainment: *musical ride*. **4** a person giving a lift in a vehicle. PHRASES **come** (or **go** etc.) **along for the ride** participate disinterestedly or just for fun. **let a thing ride** leave it alone; let it take its natural course. **ride again** reappear, esp. unexpectedly and reinvigorated. **ride down** overtake or trample on

horseback. **ride high** be elated or successful. **ride on** be dependent on or conditioned by: *so much is riding on the outcome*. **ride out** come safely through; endure, bear (a storm etc. or a danger or difficulty). **ride shotgun 1** travel as a guard in the seat next to the driver of a vehicle. **2** ride in the passenger seat of a vehicle. **3** act as a protector. **ride the pine** (or **bench**) Sport (of an athlete) not participate, esp. because of poor performance; be benched. **ride up** (of a garment) work or move upwards out of its proper position: *these pants ride up at the back*. **take for a ride** informal hoax or deceive.

rider *noun* **1** a person who rides (a horse, bus, bicycle, etc.). **2 a** an additional clause amending or supplementing a document. **b** a condition, proviso, qualification, etc. ▶ **riderless** *adjective*

ridership *noun* the number of passengers using a particular form of mass transportation.

ridge *noun* **1** the line of the junction of two surfaces sloping upwards towards each other: *the ridge of a roof*. **2** a long narrow hilltop, mountain range, or watershed. **3** any narrow elevation across a surface. **4** Meteorology an elongated region of high barometric pressure. **5** Agriculture a raised strip of arable land, usu. one of a set separated by furrows.

ridged *adjective* with a surface marked by ridges.

ridgepole *noun* **1** the horizontal pole of a long tent. **2** a beam along the ridge of a roof.

ridicule • *noun* derision or mockery. • *verb* (**ridicules, ridiculed, ridiculing**) make fun of; subject to ridicule.

ridiculous *adjective* **1** unreasonable, absurd. **2** deserving or inviting ridicule. **3** outrageous. ▶ **ridiculously** *adverb* **ridiculousness** *noun*

riding¹ *noun* **1** in senses of RIDE verb. **2** the practice or skill of riders of horses.

riding² *noun* (in Canada) a district whose voters elect a representative member to a legislative body; a constituency or electoral district.

riding association *noun* Cdn a unit of organization of a political party at the level of the riding, responsible for nominating a candidate for election and conducting the election campaign in the riding.

Riel Rebellion *noun* Cdn **1** = RED RIVER REBELLION. **2** = NORTHWEST REBELLION. **3** these collectively. [Say ree ELL]

Riesling *noun* **1** a kind of dry white wine produced in Germany, Austria, and elsewhere. **2** the variety of grape from which this is produced. [Say REEZ ling]

rife *adjective* **1** (esp. of something undesirable) widespread: *corruption is rife in the organization*. **2** full of (esp. something undesirable): *the organization is rife with corruption*.

riff • *noun* **1** a short repeated phrase in rock, jazz, etc., often played over changing chords or harmonies or used as a background to a solo: *a guitar riff*. **2** informal any commentary, improvisation, etc. on a theme: *launched into a riff on old movies*. • *verb* **1** play riffs. **2** informal (foll. by on) comment or expound: *no meeting is complete without him riffing on topics ranging from euthanasia to Elmer Fudd*.

riffle • *verb* (**riffles, riffled, riffling**) **1 a** turn (pages) in quick succession. **b** shuffle (playing cards) esp. by flicking up and releasing the corners or sides of two piles of cards so that they intermingle and may be slid together to form a single pile. **2** (often foll. by through) leaf quickly (through pages etc.). **3** (esp. of wind) disturb the smoothness of or cause ripples in or on; ruffle: *wind-riffled hair*. • *noun* **1** a quick or casual leaf or search through something. **2 a** a shallow part of a stream where the water flows brokenly. **b** a patch of waves or ripples on water.

riff-raff *noun* (often as **the riff-raff**) the rabble.

rifle • *noun* **1** a gun with a long rifled barrel, esp. one fired from shoulder level. **2** (in *plural*) infantry armed with rifles: *the Royal Winnipeg Rifles*. • *verb* (**rifles, rifled, rifling**) **1** (esp. as **rifled** *adjective*) make spiral grooves in (a gun or its barrel or bore) to make a bullet spin. **2** shoot, throw, launch, etc. forcefully in a straight line. **3** (foll. by *through*) search through something in a hurried way in order to steal or find something.

rifling *noun* the arrangement of grooves on the inside of a gun's barrel.

rift • *noun* **1 a** a crack or split in an object. **b** an opening in a cloud etc. **2** a cleft or fissure in earth or rock. **3 a** a large fault bounding a rift valley. **b** = RIFT VALLEY. **4** a disagreement; a breach in friendly relations. • *verb* split or move apart: *rifting opened the basin that is Lake Tanganyika*.

rift valley *noun* (*plural* **rift valleys**) a steep-sided valley formed by the downward displacement of a long block of the earth's crust between two nearly parallel faults.

rig • *verb* (**rigs, rigged, rigging**) **1 a** provide (a ship) with sails, rigging, etc. **b** prepare (a sailing ship) for sailing. **2** (often foll. by *out, up*) fit with clothes or other equipment. **3** (foll. by *up*) set up hastily, esp. by making do with what is available. **4** (often foll. by *to*) connect with ropes, wires, etc. **5** assemble and adjust the parts of (an aircraft etc.). **6** *Forestry* prepare (a spar tree) by attaching guy lines, skylines, and the mainline. **7** manage or conduct fraudulently; fix: *they rigged the election*. • *noun* **1** the arrangement of masts, sails, rigging, etc. of a sailing ship. **2** equipment for a special purpose, e.g. a radio transmitter or fishing tackle; gear. **3** = OIL RIG, DRILLING RIG. **4** a large vehicle, esp. a transport truck or tractor-trailer. **5** an outfit, uniform, or style of dress.

rigamarole *noun* = RIGMAROLE. [Say RIGGA muh role]

rigatoni *noun* pasta in the form of short broad hollow fluted tubes. [Say rigga TONY]

rigged *adjective* **1** (often in *combination*) having sails or rigging, esp. of the kind described: *a square-rigged sailing ship*. **2** arranged or influenced in a dishonest way in order to achieve a particular result: *rigged elections* ◊ *a rigged poker game*.

rigger *noun* **1** a person who rigs or who arranges rigging. **2** *Forestry* = HIGH RIGGER. **3** a ship rigged in a specified way. **4** a worker on an oil rig. **5** a person who manages an election etc. fraudulently.

rigging *noun* **1** a ship's spars, ropes, etc., supporting and controlling the sails. **2** an arrangement of ropes, wires, etc. in any structure or system, e.g. on an airship. **3** the lines, blocks, hooks, and other equipment used in yarding logs by means of cables.

rigging crew *noun* the work crew in charge of rigging trees.

SPELL CHECK
right, rite, write, wright

A religious observance is a **rite**. To put words on paper is to **write**. The maker of something is a **wright**.

---

right • *adjective* **1** on, towards, or relating to the side of a human body or of a thing which is to the east when the person or thing is facing north. **2** morally good, justified, or acceptable. **3** factually correct. **4** most appropriate: *the right person for the job*. **5** in a satisfactory, sound, or normal condition. **6** relating to a right-wing person or group. • *noun* **1** that which is morally right. **2** (in *plural*) the authority to perform, publish, or film a particular work or event. **3** the right-hand part, side, or direction. **4** a right turn. **5** a person's right fist, or a blow given with it. **6** (often

Right) a group or political party favouring conservative views. • *verb* **1** restore to a normal or upright position. **2** restore to a normal or correct condition. **3** make amends for (a wrong). • *adverb* **1** on or to the right side. **2** to the furthest or most complete extent or degree. **3** exactly; directly. **4** correctly or satisfactorily. **5** immediately. • *interjection informal* **1** expressing agreement or assent. **2** *ironic* expressing scorn. PHRASES **as right as rain** perfectly sound and healthy. **by right** (or **rights**) justly, in fairness, properly. **do right by** act dutifully towards (a person). **in one's own right** on account of one's own status, effort, etc.; independently of one's relationship with others. **in the right** having justice or truth on one's side. **in one's right mind** sane; competent to think and act. **on the right side of 1** not violating (a law etc.). **2** in the favour of (a person etc.). **put** (or **set**) **right 1** restore to order, health, etc. **2** correct the mistaken impression etc. of (a person or thing). **put** (or **set**) **to rights** make correct or well ordered. **right and left** (or **right, left, and centre**) on all sides. **right away** (also **right off**) immediately. **right enough** *Cdn & Brit. informal* certainly, indeed, undeniably, sure enough. **right on** *informal* **1** an expression of strong approval or encouragement. **2** absolutely to the point: *the speech was right on*. **right you are!** *informal* an exclamation of assent. **too right** *informal* an expression of agreement. **within one's rights** not exceeding one's authority or entitlement.

right angle *noun* a 90° angle. PHRASES **at right angles** (**to**) placed to form a right angle (with). ▶ **right-angled** *adjective*

right brain *noun* the right half of the cerebrum, controlling the left side of the body, in humans often associated with spatial perception and intuition.

righteous *adjective* **1** (of a person or conduct) morally right; virtuous: *the film is Spielberg's memorial homage to a righteous gentile*. **2** = SELF-RIGHTEOUS: *I don't know how the government members can sit here with such righteous indignation at our request that they simply live up to the promises they made*. ▶ **righteously** *adverb* **righteousness** *noun* [Say RYE chuss]

right fielder *noun* the fielder who plays in the part of the outfield to the right of the batter as he or she faces the pitcher.

rightful *adjective* **1 a** (of a person) having status etc. legitimately or justly: *the rightful owner*. **b** (of status, position, property, etc.) that one is entitled to: *has assumed its rightful place*. **2** (of an action etc.) equitable, fair. ▶ **rightfully** *adverb* **rightfulness** *noun*

right-hand *adjective* **1** on or towards the right side of a person or thing: *right-hand corner*. **2** done with the right hand: *right-hand blow*. **3** (of a screw) = RIGHT-HANDED 4b.

right-handed • *adjective* **1 a** using the right hand by preference as more serviceable than the left. **b** using a tool etc. by preference on one's right side: *right-handed batter*. **2** (of a tool, instrument, etc.) made to be used by right-handed people: *right-handed guitar*. **3** (of a blow) struck with the right hand. **4 a** turning to the right; towards the right. **b** (of a screw) advanced by turning to the right (clockwise). • *adverb* with the right hand or to the right side: *plays right-handed*. ▶ **right-handedly** *adverb* **right-handedness** *noun*

right-hander *noun* **1** a right-handed person. **2** a right-handed blow etc.

right-hand man *noun* an indispensable or chief assistant.

Right Honourable *adjective* (in Canada) a title given for life to the Governor General, the prime minister, and the chief justice. Abbreviation: **Rt. Hon.**

rightist • *adjective* professing or supporting the

principles or policies of the right. • *noun* a person or thing supporting or professing such principles or policies.

rightly *adverb* justly, properly, correctly, justifiably.

rightness *noun* the condition of being proper, acceptable, or correct.

right-of-centre *adjective* (of political parties, voters, etc.) having somewhat conservative views, policies, etc.

right-of-way *noun* (*plural* **rights-of-way**) **1** a right established by usage to pass over another's ground. **2** a path subject to such a right. **3** the right of one vehicle to proceed before another. **4** a strip of land reserved for a road, railway, hydro lines, etc.

rightsize *verb* (**rightsizes, rightsized, rightsizing**) = DOWNSIZE.

rightsizing *noun* **1** the reducing of something in size or scope, esp. of a company (by firing workers, eliminating positions, etc.); downsizing. **2** the replacing of a larger computer with a smaller one or a network of smaller ones.

right-thinking *adjective* **1** having sound views and principles. **2** having views in accord with what might be expected.

right-to-life *adjective* = PRO-LIFE. ▶ **right-to-lifer** *noun*

rightward • *adverb* (also **rightwards**) towards the right. • *adjective* going towards or facing the right.

right whale *noun* a baleen whale with a large head and a deeply curved jaw, of Arctic and temperate waters.

right wing • *noun* **1** the conservative or reactionary section of a political party or system. **2** *Hockey* **a** the forward position to the right of centre. **b** the player at this position. **3** the right side of an army. • *adjective* (usu. **right-wing**) conservative or reactionary. ▶ **right winger** *noun*

righty *informal* • *noun* (*plural* **righties**) **1** a right-handed person. **2** *Politics* a right winger. • *adverb* esp. *Baseball* with the right hand or to the right side: *bats righty*.

rigid *adjective* **1** that cannot be bent: *a rigid frame*. **2** (of a person, conduct, etc.) inflexible, strict: *a rigid disciplinarian*. ▶ **rigidity** *noun* **rigidly** *adverb*

rigmarole *noun* **1** a lengthy and complicated procedure. **2** a long and complicated story or talk: *all she could do was listen to his rigmaroles*. [Say RIG muh role]

rigor mortis *noun* stiffening of the body after death. [Say rigger MORE tiss]

rigorous *adjective* **1** characterized by or showing rigour; strict. **2** strictly exact or accurate. **3** (of the weather) cold, severe. ▶ **rigorously** *adverb* **rigorousness** *noun* [Say RIGGER us]

rigour *noun* (also **rigor**) **1 a** severity, strictness, harshness. **b** (in *plural*) harsh measures or conditions. **c** (often in *plural*) severity of weather or climate; extremity of cold. **2** logical exactitude. **3** strict enforcement of rules etc.: *the utmost rigour of the law*. **4** austerity of life; puritanical discipline. [Say RIGGER]

Rig-Veda *noun* the oldest and principal of the Hindu Vedas (see VEDA). [Say rig VAY duh or rig VEE duh]

rile *verb* (**riles, riled, riling**) **1** *informal* (often foll. by *up*) anger, irritate. **2** make (water) turbulent or muddy.

rill *noun* **1** a small stream. **2** a shallow channel cut in the surface of soil or rocks by running water.

rim • *noun* **1 a** a raised edge or border. **b** a margin or verge, esp. of something circular. **2** the part of a pair of eyeglasses surrounding the lenses. **3** the outer edge of a wheel, on which the tire is fitted. **4** a boundary line: *the rim of the horizon*. • *verb* (**rims, rimmed, rimming**) form an edge around something; border: *mountains that rim the city*.

rime *noun* **1** frost, esp. formed from cloud or fog. **2** *literary* hoarfrost.

rimless *adjective* not having a border or rim: *rimless glasses*.

rimmed *adjective* (often in *combination*) having a rim or the kind of rim described: *steel-rimmed glasses*.

rimrock *noun* an outcrop of resistant rock, esp. one forming a cliff at the edge of a plateau.

rind • *noun* **1** the tough outer layer or covering of fruit and vegetables, cheese, bacon, etc. **2** the bark of a tree or plant. • *verb* strip the bark from. [Rhymes with FIND]

SPELL CHECK
ring, wring

If you extract something by pressure, you **wring** it; you can **wring** clothes, someone's hand, or a chicken's neck; you can also **wring** someone's heart or concessions from someone.

---

ring[1] • *noun* **1** a small circular band, typically of precious metal, worn on a finger. **2** a circular band, object, or mark. **3** an enclosed space in which a sport, performance, or show takes place. **4** a group of people or things arranged in a circle. **5** a group of people with a shared interest or goal, esp. one involving illegal activity: *a drug ring*. **6** *Chemistry* a number of atoms bonded together to form a closed loop in a molecule. **7** (in *plural*) a gymnastics event in which the gymnast holds on to two suspended rings. • *verb* **1** surround. **2** draw a circle around. **PHRASES** **run** (or **make**) **rings around** *informal* outclass or outwit (another person).

ring[2] • *verb* (**rings**; *past* **rang**; *past participle* **rung**; **ringing**) **1** make or cause to make a clear resonant or vibrating sound. **2** (foll. by *with*) reverberate with (a sound). **3 a** (of a telephone) emit a ring, buzz, beep, or other sound indicating an incoming call. **b** esp. *Brit.* call by telephone. **4** call for attention by sounding a bell. **5** sound (the hour, a peal, etc.) on a bell or bells. **6** (foll. by *in* or *out*) usher (someone or something) in (or out) by or as if by ringing a bell. **7** (of the ears) be filled with a buzzing or humming sound due to a blow or loud noise. **8** convey a specified impression or quality: *her honesty rings true*. • *noun* **1** an act or instance of ringing. **2** a loud clear sound or tone. **3** *informal* a telephone call: *give me a ring*. **4** a quality conveyed by something heard: *the tale had a ring of truth*. **PHRASES** **ring down** (or **up**) **the curtain 1** cause the curtain to be lowered (or raised). **2** (foll. by *on*) mark the end (or the beginning) of (an enterprise etc.). **ring in one's ears** (or **heart** etc.). linger in the memory. **ring off** end a telephone call by replacing the receiver; hang up. **ring off the hook** (of a telephone) ring incessantly. **ring true** (or **false**) convey an impression of truth (or falsehood). **ring up 1** record (an amount spent or earned) on or as on a cash register. **2** accomplish; record (a victory etc.).

ring-billed gull *noun* a small grey North American gull with black wing tips and a black band across a yellow bill.

ringed *adjective* (often in *combination*) having or marked with a ring or rings, esp. of the kind described.

ringed seal *noun* an Arctic seal with irregular ring-shaped markings.

SPELL CHECK
ringer, wringer

The spelling is **wringer** in "put through the wringer".

---

ringer *noun* *slang* **1 a** a fraudulent substitute, esp. in sports. **b** a person resembling another, esp. an imposter. **2** a person who rings a bell; a bell-ringer. **3** a device for ringing a bell, esp. on a telephone. **PHRASES** **be a ringer** (or **dead ringer**) **for** resemble (a person) exactly.

ringette *noun* *Cdn* a game resembling hockey, played (esp. by women and girls) with a straight stick and a rubber ring.

ring finger *noun* the finger next to the little finger, esp. of the left hand, on which the wedding ring is usu. worn.

ringing • *adjective* **1** having or emitting a clear resonant sound: *a ringing voice*. **2** (of a statement) clear, forceful, and emphatic: *a ringing endorsement*. • *noun* a clear resonant sound, esp. one that affects the ears and makes it difficult to hear other things.

ringleader *noun* a leading instigator in an esp. illicit or illegal activity.

ringlet *noun* a curly lock of hair, esp. a long one. ▶ **ringleted** *adjective*

ringmaster *noun* **1** the person directing a circus performance. **2** *informal* a leader or director.

ringneck *noun* any of various ring-necked birds, esp. the ring-necked pheasant, which has a white ring around the neck.

ring-necked *adjective* (of an animal, bird, etc.) having a band or bands of colour around the neck.

ringside *noun* the area immediately beside a boxing ring, circus ring, or other centre of attention.

ring-tailed *adjective* **1** (of monkeys, lemurs, raccoons, etc.) having a tail ringed in alternate colours. **2** with the tail curled at the end.

ringworm *noun* any of various fungous infections of the skin causing circular inflamed patches.

rink *noun* **1** an area of natural or artificial ice for skating, playing hockey, curling, etc. **2** an area for roller skating. **3** a building containing either of these. **4** a team in curling.

rink rat *noun see* RAT *noun* 5.

rinkside • *noun* the area adjacent to the ice at a rink: *rinkside seats*. • *adverb* along the edge of the ice at a rink: *sat rinkside*.

rinky-dink *adjective* *informal* second-rate, small-time, inferior, amateurish: *a rinky-dink production*.

rinse • *verb* (**rinses, rinsed, rinsing**) (often foll. by *out*) wash with clean water, esp. to remove soap or detergent. • *noun* **1** an act of rinsing something: *give it a rinse*. **2** a dye for the temporary tinting of hair: *a blue rinse*. **3** a solution for cleansing the mouth.

riot • *noun* **1** an esp. violent disturbance of the peace by a crowd; an occurrence of serious public disorder. **2** a lavish display: *a riot of colour*. **3** *informal* a very amusing thing or person. • *verb* (**riots, rioted, rioting**) make or engage in a riot. PHRASES **run riot 1** throw off all restraint. **2** (of plants) grow or spread uncontrolled.

Riot Act *noun* a proclamation in the Criminal Code of Canada which is read to order rioters to disperse. PHRASES **read the riot act** give someone a severe warning that they must improve their behaviour.

rioter *noun* a person who takes part in a riot.

riotous *adjective* **1** marked by or involving rioting. **2** uproarious, characterized by boisterous revelry: *a riotous party*. ▶ **riotously** *adverb* **riotousness** *noun* [Say RYE uh tus]

RIP *abbreviation* may he or she or they rest in peace.

rip¹ • *verb* (**rips, ripped, ripping**) **1** tear (a thing) quickly or forcibly away or apart: *ripped the book up*. **2 a** make (a hole etc.) by ripping. **b** make a long tear or cut in. **c** cut (wood) along the grain. **3** come violently apart; split. **4** rush along. **5** *informal* criticize. • *noun* **1** a long tear or cut. **2** an act of ripping. **3** the sound of something being ripped. **4** *informal* a fraud or swindle: *what a rip!* PHRASES **let rip** *informal* **1** act or proceed without restraint. **2** speak violently. **3** not check the speed of or interfere with (a person or thing). **rip into**

attack verbally. **rip off** *informal* **1 a** defraud (a person etc.). **b** steal (a thing). **2** rob (a store).

rip² *noun* a stretch of rough water in the sea or in a river, caused by the meeting of currents.

riparian *adjective* of or on a riverbank: *the riparian forest along the Tat's banks teemed with birds*. [Say ri PERRY in]

rip cord *noun* a cord for releasing a parachute from its pack.

ripe *adjective* **1** (of grain, fruit, cheese, etc.) ready to be reaped or picked or eaten. **2** mature; fully developed: *a ripe beauty*. **3** (of a person's age) advanced. **4** (often foll. by *for*) fit or ready: *land ripe for development*. **5** (of the complexion etc.) red and full like ripe fruit. ▶ **ripely** *adverb*

ripen *verb* make or become ripe.

ripeness *noun* the quality of fruit, vegetables, cheese, wine, etc. that is fully developed or matured and is ready to be consumed.

rip-off *noun* *informal* **1** a fraud or swindle, esp. something that is grossly overpriced: *designer label clothes are just expensive rip-offs*. **2** an inferior imitation of something: *the episode was a rip-off of a famous movie*.

riposte • *noun* a quick sharp reply or retort: *the witty riposte brought down the house*. • *verb* (**ripostes, riposted, riposting**) deliver a riposte. [Say ri POST (POST rhymes with *LOST*)]

ripped *adjective* **1** in senses of RIP¹. **2** *informal* drunk, intoxicated; high.

ripper *noun* **1** a person or thing that rips. **2** a murderer who rips the victims' bodies.

ripple • *noun* **1** a ruffling of the water's surface; a small wave or series of waves. **2** a gentle lively sound that rises and falls, e.g. of laughter or applause. **3** a wavy appearance in hair, material, etc. **4** ice cream with added syrup giving a coloured ripple effect: *raspberry ripple*. **5** a riffle in a stream. **6** (usu. as an *adjective*) designating potato chips having a corrugated appearance. • *verb* (**ripples, rippled, rippling**) **1 a** form ripples; flow in ripples. **b** cause to do this. **2** show or sound like ripples.

ripple effect *noun* the continuous and spreading results or consequences of an event or action.

ripply *adjective* having or causing small waves or ripples.

rip-rap *noun* a collection of loose stone as a foundation for a breakwater, embankment, etc.

rip-roaring *adjective* **1** wildly noisy or boisterous. **2** excellent, first-rate. ▶ **rip-roaringly** *adverb*

ripstop • *adjective* (of fabric, clothing, etc.) woven so that a tear will not spread. • *noun* ripstop fabric.

riptide *noun* **1** a strong surface current from the shore. **2** a stretch of rough water in the sea or in a river, caused by the meeting of currents.

RISC *noun* **1** a computer designed to perform a limited set of operations at high speed. **2** computing using this kind of computer. [Say RISK]

rise • *verb* (**rises**; *past* **rose**; *past participle* **risen; rising**) **1** come or go up. **2** get up from lying, sitting, or kneeling. **3** increase in number, size, intensity, or quality. **4** (of land) slope upwards. **5** (of the sun, moon, or stars) appear above the horizon. **6** reach a higher social or professional position. **7** (foll. by *to*) respond adequately to (a challenge). **8** (foll. by *up*) rebel. **9** (of a river) have its source. **10** be restored to life. • *noun* **1** an act or instance of rising. **2** an upward slope or hill. **3** the vertical height of a step, arch, or incline. PHRASES **get a rise out of** *informal* provoke an emotional reaction from (a person), esp. by teasing. **on the rise** on the increase. **rise above 1** be superior to (petty feelings etc.). **2** show dignity or strength in the

face of (difficulty, poor conditions, etc.). **rise and shine** (usu. as *imper.*) *informal* get out of bed; wake up.

riser *noun* **1** a person who rises, esp. from bed: *an early riser*. **2** a vertical section between the treads of a staircase. **3** a vertical pipe for the flow of liquid or gas. **4 a** a low platform on a stage etc. **b** one of a series of these arranged in step-like fashion, usu. for seating.

risible *adjective* deserving to be laughed at rather than taken seriously: *Eastwood's outdated tough-guy act seems risible, even pathetic.* [Say RIZZA bull]

rising • *adjective* **1** going up; getting higher. **2** increasing: *rising costs.* **3** advancing to maturity or high standing: *a rising young lawyer.* **4** (of ground) sloping upwards. • *noun* a revolt or insurrection.

risk • *noun* **1** a chance or possibility of danger, loss, injury, or other adverse consequences: *a health risk.* **2** a person or thing causing a risk or regarded in relation to risk: *is a poor risk.* • *verb* **1** expose to risk. **2** accept the chance of: *could not risk getting wet.* **3** venture on. PHRASES **at risk** exposed to danger. **at one's (own) risk** accepting responsibility, agreeing to make no claims. **at the risk of** with the possibility of (an adverse consequence). **put at risk** expose to danger. **risk one's neck** put one's own life in danger. **run a (or the) risk** (often foll. by *of*) expose oneself to danger or loss etc. **take (or run) a risk** chance the possibility of danger etc.

riskiness *noun* the possibility of danger, failure, or loss involved in an undertaking.

risky *adjective* (**riskier, riskiest**) **1** involving risk. **2** = RISQUÉ.

risotto *noun* (*plural* **risottos**) an Italian dish of esp. arborio rice cooked in broth with various other ingredients, as meat, onions, etc. [Say ri ZOTTO]

risqué *adjective* slightly indecent: *he doesn't see a contradiction between his faith and his risqué humour.* [Say riss KAY]

Ritalin *noun* *proprietary* a drug which stimulates the central nervous system, used esp. to treat attention deficit disorder. [Say RITTA lin]

SPELL CHECK
rite, right, write, wright

The opposite of *left* is **right**; something just or correct is **right**; **right** is also the spelling in "right away" and "right angle". To put words on paper is to **write**. The maker of something is a **wright**.

---

rite *noun* **1** a religious or solemn observance or act: *burial rites.* **2** an action or procedure required or usual in this. **3** a body of customary observances characteristic of a Church or a part of it: *Eastern rite.*

rite of passage *noun* (often in *plural*) a ritual or event marking a stage of a person's advance through life, e.g. marriage.

ritual • *noun* **1** a prescribed order of performing rites. **2** a procedure regularly followed. • *adjective* of or done as a ritual or rites: *ritual dance.*

ritualism *noun* the regular or excessive practice of ritual. ▶ **ritualistic** *adjective* **ritualistically** *adverb*

ritualize *verb* (**ritualizes, ritualized, ritualizing**) make something into a ritual by following a pattern of action or behaviour.

ritually *adverb* **1** as part of a religious or formal ceremony: *prior to certain religious festivals males ritually wash their bodies.* **2** in or as part of a regularly followed procedure or pattern of behaviour: *she works out ritually in the morning before going to work.*

ritz *noun* esp. showy or gaudy luxury: *in southwest Palm Beach, he's removed from all the ritz and glitz.* PHRASES **put**

on the ritz make a show of luxury or extravagance: *why should we have to put on the ritz for the Frasers?*

ritzy *adjective* (**ritzier, ritziest**) *informal* **1** high-class, luxurious. **2** fashionable in a showy or gaudy way.

rival • *noun* **1** a person, team, organization, etc. competing with another for the same objective. **2** a person or thing that equals another in quality etc. **3** (as an *adjective*) being a rival or rivals: *a rival firm.* • *verb* (**rivals, rivalled, rivalling**) **1** be the rival of or comparable to. **2** seem or claim to be as good as.

rivalrous *adjective* prone to or subject to rivalry; competitive: *rivalrous siblings.* [Say RIVAL russ]

rivalry *noun* (*plural* **rivalries**) competition for the same objective or for superiority in the same field: *commercial rivalry ◊ a friendly rivalry between the two teams.*

river *noun* **1** a natural stream of water flowing in a channel to the ocean or a lake etc. **2** a copious flow: *rivers of blood.* **3** (as an *adjective*) (in the names of animals, plants, etc.) living in or associated with the river. PHRASES **sell down the river** *informal* betray or let down. **up the river** *informal* to or in prison: *the cop confronts a man he sent up the river.*

riverbank *noun* the raised or sloping edge of a river.

riverbed *noun* the bed or channel in which a river flows.

riverboat *noun* a boat designed for use on rivers.

river drive *noun* *Cdn* a log drive down a river. ▶ **river driver** *noun*

riverfront • *noun* land adjacent to a river. • *adjective* situated or occurring beside a river.

riverine *adjective* of or on a river or riverbank: *fish collected from small riverine populations.* [Say RIVER ine]

river lot *noun* *Cdn hist.* a long narrow farm lot extending back from a river, esp. one along the St. Lawrence River or in the Red River Settlement.

river otter *noun* a North American otter noted for its agile swimming and playful behaviour.

riverside *noun* the ground along a riverbank: *riverside path.*

rivet • *noun* a nail or bolt for holding together metal plates etc., its headless end being beaten out or pressed down when in place. • *verb* (**rivets, riveted, riveting**) **1 a** join or fasten with rivets. **b** beat out or press down the end of (a nail or bolt). **c** fix; make immovable. **2 a** (foll. by *on, upon*) direct intently (one's eyes or attention etc.). **b** (esp. as **riveting** *adjective*) engross (a person or the attention). ▶ **riveter** *noun*

rivulet *noun* **1** a small stream or brook. **2** a thin stream of liquid: *rivulets of sweat.* [Say RIV yuh lit]

RM *abbreviation* *Cdn* **1** RURAL MUNICIPALITY. **2** REGIONAL MUNICIPALITY.

rm. *abbreviation* room.

RN *abbreviation* **1** Registered Nurse. **2** (in the UK) Royal Navy.

Rn *symbol* radon.

RNA *abbreviation* **1** ribonucleic acid. **2** = REGISTERED NURSING ASSISTANT.

roach[1] *noun* (*plural* **roach** or **roaches**) **1** a small edible European freshwater fish of the carp family. **2** any of various freshwater fishes of North America.

roach[2] *noun* (*plural* **roaches**) **1** *informal* a cockroach. **2** *slang* the butt of a marijuana cigarette.

road • *noun* **1** a path or way with a specially prepared surface, used by motor vehicles, cyclists, etc.; a street. **2 a** one's way or route: *our road took us through unexplored territory.* **b** a method or means of accomplishing something. **3** (usu. in *plural*) a partly sheltered piece of water near the shore in which ships can ride at anchor. • *adjective* *Sport* of or relating to a game or games played at an opponent's venue: *a poor*

road record. PHRASES **get out of the** (or **my** etc.) **road** *informal* cease to obstruct a person. **go down the road** *Cdn* leave one's hometown in search of employment, adventure, etc., esp. leave the Maritimes for central or western Canada. **in the** (or **my** etc.) **road** *informal* obstructing a person or thing. **one for the road** *informal* a final (esp. alcoholic) drink before departure. **on the road 1** travelling, esp. as a sales representative or a performer. **2** (of a car etc.) in working condition; able to be driven. **the road to** the way of getting to or achieving: *the road to Owen Sound ◊ the road to ruin*. **take to the road** set out.

road allowance *noun Cdn* **1** a strip of land retained by government authorities for the construction of a road. **2** an area at either side of a road which remains a public right-of-way.

road apple *noun slang* (usu. in *plural*) **1** a piece of horse manure. **2** *Cdn hist.* a frozen piece of horse manure used as a hockey puck, esp. on the Prairies.

roadblock *noun* **1** a barrier or barricade on a road, esp. one set up by police or military personnel to stop and check vehicles. **2** any obstruction: *roadblocks to peace*. **3** the action of blocking a road as a protest.

road hockey *noun Cdn* (esp. S Ont.) = STREET HOCKEY.

roadholding *noun* the capacity of a moving vehicle to remain stable when cornering at high speeds etc.

roadhouse *noun* **1** a restaurant or bar located on a major road usu. on the outskirts of a town or city. **2** a theatre designed for touring companies.

roadie *noun informal* a person employed by a touring pop group etc. to set up and maintain equipment. [Say ROAD ee]

roadkill *noun* **1** the killing of an animal by a vehicle on a road. **2** an animal killed in this way.

roadless *adjective* not having roads: *a roadless wilderness*.

road rage *noun* violent anger caused by the stress and frustration of driving.

roadrunner *noun* a bird of Mexican and US deserts, related to the cuckoo, which flies poorly but runs fast.

road salt *noun* coarse salt used to melt ice on roads etc.

road show *noun* **1 a** a performance given by a group of touring entertainers, esp. a theatre company. **b** a company giving such performances. **2** a radio or television program done on location, usu. a series of programs each from a different venue. **3** a touring political or advertising campaign.

roadside *noun* the strip of land beside a road: *a roadside stand*.

roadster *noun* **1** an open two-seater car. **2** a motorcycle for use on roads.

road test ● *noun* **1** a test of the performance of a vehicle on the road. **2** a test of any new product. ● *verb* (**road-test**) **1** test (a vehicle) on the road. **2** test (any new product). **3** perform a preliminary version of (a new song, play, etc.) before an audience to gauge reaction to it.

road trip *noun* **1** a series of games played away from home. **2** any journey made by car, bicycle, bus, etc.

roadway *noun* **1** a road. **2** the main or central portion of a road, esp. that part used by vehicles. **3** the part of a bridge or railway used for traffic.

roadwork *noun* **1** the construction or repair of roads, or other work involving digging up a road. **2** athletic exercise or training involving running on roads.

roadworthiness *noun* the condition of a vehicle that is fit to be used on the road.

roadworthy *adjective* fit to be used on the road.

roam ● *verb* ramble; wander over, through, or about. ● *noun* an act of roaming; a ramble.

roan ● *adjective* (of an animal, esp. a horse) having a coat of which the prevailing colour is interspersed with hairs of another colour, esp. bay or sorrel or chestnut mixed with white or grey. ● *noun* a roan animal.

roar ● *noun* **1** a loud deep hoarse sound, as made by a lion, a loud engine, thunder, a person in pain or rage or excitement, etc. **2** a loud laugh. ● *verb* **1 a** utter or make a roar. **b** utter loud laughter. **2** travel in a vehicle at high speed, esp. with the engine roaring. **3** (often foll. by *out*) say, sing, or utter (words, an oath, etc.) in a loud tone.

roaring *adjective* in senses of ROAR *verb*. PHRASES **roaring drunk** *informal* very drunk and noisy. **roaring success** *informal* a great success. **roaring trade** (or **business**) *informal* very brisk trade or business.

Roaring Twenties *plural noun informal* the decade of the 1920s.

roast ● *verb* **1 a** cook (food, esp. meat) in an oven or by exposure to open heat. **b** heat (coffee beans) before grinding. **2** criticize severely, denounce. **3** honour (a person) with a roast. **4** undergo roasting. ● *adjective* (of meat or a potato, chestnut, etc.) roasted. ● *noun* **1 a** roast meat. **b** a dish of this. **c** a piece of meat for roasting. **2** the process of roasting. **3** a party where roasted food is eaten: *pig roast*. **4** a mock-serious ceremonial tribute at which friends of the guest of honour offer short speeches of praise and good-natured insult. PHRASES **roast alive** subject to intense heat. **roast in hell** suffer damnation.

roaster *noun* **1** a person or thing that roasts. **2 a** an oven or dish for roasting food in. **b** a coffee-roasting apparatus. **3** something fit for roasting, e.g. a fowl etc.

roasting ● *adjective* **1** very hot. **2** used for or fit for roasting: *roasting pan ◊ roasting chicken*. ● *noun* **1** in senses of ROAST *verb*. **2** a severe criticism or denunciation.

rob *verb* (**robs, robbed, robbing**) (often foll. by *of*) **1** take unlawfully from, esp. by force or threat of force: *robbed the safe ◊ robbed her of her jewels*. **2** deprive of what is due or normal: *was robbed of my sleep*. **3** commit robbery. **4** *informal* overcharge (a customer). PHRASES **rob Peter to pay Paul** take away from one to give to another, discharge one debt by incurring another: *the minister's plan to pay down the deficit by $5 million at the expense of the unemployed is essentially a case of robbing Peter to pay Paul*.

robber *noun* a person who commits robbery.

robbery *noun* (*plural* **robberies**) **1** the action or process of robbing, esp. with force or threat of force: *armed robbery*. **2** unashamed swindling or overcharging: *set us back $50 — it was sheer robbery*.

robe ● *noun* **1** a long loose outer garment. **2** a dressing gown or bathrobe. **3** (often in *plural*) a long outer garment worn as an indication of the wearer's rank, office, profession, etc. **4** a blanket or wrap of fur. ● *verb* (**robes, robed, robing**) **1** clothe (a person) in a robe; dress. **2** put on one's robes or vestments.

Robertson *noun proprietary* **1** a type of screw with a square notch on the head. **2** a type of screwdriver with a square tip designed to fit into this.

robin *noun* **1** a red-breasted thrush. **2** (also **robin redbreast**) a small brown European bird, the adult of which has a red throat and breast. **3** a bird similar in appearance etc. to either of these.

Robin Hood *noun* a person who acts illegally or unfavourably toward the rich for the benefit of the poor.

robin's egg blue *noun & adjective* a pale greenish-blue colour.

robot *noun* **1** a machine with a human appearance or functioning like a human. **2** a machine capable of carrying out a complex series of actions automatically. **3** a person who works mechanically and efficiently but

R

insensitively. ▶**robotic** *adjective* **robotically** *adverb* [Say ROE bot, roe BOT ick]

roboticist *noun* an expert in designing and operating robots. [Say roe BOTTA sist]

robotics *plural noun* (usu. treated as *singular*) the study of robots; the art or science of their design and operation. [Say roe BOT icks]

robotize *verb* (**robotizes, robotized, robotizing**) convert (a production system, factory, etc.) to operation by robots. [Say ROE bot ize]

robust *adjective* (**robuster, robustest**) **1 a** strong and sturdy, esp. in physique or construction. **b** healthy, vigorous; not readily damaged or weakened: *a robust industry*. **2** (of exercise, discipline, etc.) vigorous, requiring strength. **3** (of intellect or mental attitude) straightforward, not given to nor confused by subtleties. **4** (of a statement, reply, etc.) bold, firm, unyielding. **5** (of wine etc.) rich and full-bodied.

robusta *noun* **1** coffee or coffee beans from a widely grown African species of coffee plant. **2** the West African bush that produces these beans.

robustly *adverb* **1** in a strong and sturdy manner: *the house is robustly constructed*. **2** in a healthy, vigorous, or energetic manner: *we sang robustly*. **3** in a bold and straightforward manner: *she robustly rebutted her colleague's argument*. **4** in a rich and full-bodied way: *a robustly flavourful dish*.

robustness *noun* **1** strength, health, and vigour. **2** sturdiness of construction. **3** a bold and straightforward manner or approach. **4** a strong and rich flavour or smell.

ROC *abbreviation Cdn* the "rest of Canada"; the parts of Canada outside the province of Quebec. [Say ROCK]

rock[1] *noun* **1** the hard mineral material of the earth's crust, exposed on the surface or underlying soil. **2** a mass of rock projecting out of the ground or water. **3** a boulder. **4** (**the Rock**) **a** *Cdn* the island of Newfoundland. **b** Gibraltar. **5** a large polished circular stone with a handle on top, used in the game of curling. **6** *Geology* any natural material with a distinctive composition of minerals. **7** *informal* a diamond or other precious stone. PHRASES **between a rock and a hard place** in a dilemma. **on the rocks** *informal* **1** (esp. of a marriage) in danger of breaking up. **2** (of a drink) served undiluted with ice cubes.

rock[2] *verb* **1** move to and fro: *rocked by the waves* ◊ *an earthquake rocked the house*. **2** distress, perturb. **3** dance to or play rock music. **4** (of popular music) possess a strong beat, esp. in 2/4 or 4/4 time; exhibit the characteristics of rock music. **5** *slang* be cool or impressive: *the latest version really rocks*. • *noun* **1** a rocking movement: *gave the chair a rock*. **2** a period of rocking: *had a rock in his chair*. **3** (often as an *adjective*) **a** = ROCK 'N' ROLL. **b** a form of popular music which evolved from rock 'n' roll and pop music, usu. characterized by a harsher sound. PHRASES **rock the boat** *informal* disturb the equilibrium of a situation.

rockabilly *noun* a type of popular music combining elements of rock 'n' roll and hillbilly music. [Say ROCKA billy]

rock and roll *noun & verb* = ROCK 'N' ROLL.

rock bass *noun* a North American freshwater fish frequenting rocky shallows in weedy lakes and streams.

rock-bottom • *adjective* the very lowest: *rock-bottom prices*. • *noun* (**rock bottom**) the very lowest level.

rocker *noun* **1** a person or thing that rocks. **2** a curved bar or similar support, on which something can rock. **3** a rocking chair. **4 a** a person who performs, dances to, or enjoys rock music. **b** a popular song that rocks; a rock song. **5** a skate with a highly curved blade. **6** any

rocking device forming part of a mechanism. PHRASES **off one's rocker** *slang* crazy.

rockery *noun* (*plural* **rockeries**) = ROCK GARDEN.

rocket • *noun* **1** a cylindrical projectile that can be propelled to a great height or distance by combustion of its contents, used esp. as a firework or signal. **2** (also **rocket engine** or **rocket motor**) an engine using a similar principle but not dependent on air intake for its operation. **3** a rocket-propelled missile, spacecraft, etc. **4** anything that moves very quickly, e.g. a train, ball, etc.: *hit a rocket to left field*. **5** any of various fast-growing plants of the mustard family. **6** = ARUGULA. • *verb* (**rockets, rocketed, rocketing**) **1** bombard with rockets. **2 a** move quickly: *a young boy rocketed past her on Rollerblades*. **b** increase rapidly: *stock prices rocketed in May*. **3** propel (someone or something) with great speed: *rocketed a shot off the post*.

rocket science *noun* a difficult or complicated matter: *fixing a leaky faucet isn't exactly rocket science*.

rocket scientist *noun* *jocular* a person who is highly intelligent, esp. in scientific and mathematical matters: *you don't have to be a rocket scientist to know that smoking isn't good for you*.

rocket ship *noun* a spaceship powered by rockets.

rock face *noun* a vertical surface of natural rock.

rockfall *noun* **1** a descent of loose rocks. **2** a mass of fallen rock.

rockfish *noun* any of various fishes frequenting rocks or rocky bottoms, e.g. the striped bass.

rock garden *noun* a garden composed of large stones with plants growing between them.

rockhound *noun* *informal* **1** a geologist. **2** an amateur collector or student of rocks and minerals. ▶**rockhounding** *noun*

rockiness *noun* **1** the condition of something that is formed of rocks or has many rocks. **2** the condition of something that is unsteady or full of problems.

rocking chair *noun* a chair mounted on rockers or springs for gently rocking in.

rocking horse *noun* a wooden or plastic horse mounted on rockers or springs for a child to rock on.

rocklike *adjective* resembling a rock in appearance or hardness.

rock 'n' roll • *noun* a type of popular music originating in the 1950s, characterized by a heavy beat and simple melodies. • *verb* *informal* get down to business; make progress. ▶**rock 'n' roller** *noun*

rock ptarmigan *noun* a ptarmigan found in extreme northern regions, distinguished by its black tail feathers in winter.

rock salt *noun* common salt as a solid mineral.

rock slide *noun* **1** the sliding down of a mass of rock from a mountain, cliff, etc. **2** the mass of rock fragments which has so fallen.

rock-solid *adjective* very solid or firm.

rock-steady • *adjective* unlikely to collapse, be changed, etc.; rock-solid. • *noun* (**rocksteady**) a style of popular music originating in Jamaica, characterized by a slow tempo and accentuated offbeat.

rockumentary *noun* (*plural* **rockumentaries**) a documentary about rock music and musicians. [Say rock you MENTA ree]

rocky[1] *adjective* (**rockier, rockiest**) **1** of or like rock. **2** full of or abounding in rock or rocks.

rocky[2] *adjective* (**rockier, rockiest**) *informal* **1** fraught with difficulties, disagreements, etc.: *the marriage got off to a rocky start*. **2** unsteady, tottering.

rocky road *noun* **1** (as an *adjective*) designating a mixture of chocolate chips, marshmallow, and nuts used in ice cream or as a topping for brownies etc. **2** a

course of action fraught with difficulties, obstacles, etc.

rococo • *noun* a baroque style of art, architecture, and interior design prevalent in 18th-century Continental Europe. The style began in Paris as a reaction against heavy and grandiose baroque ornamentation and is characterized esp. by lightness, daintiness, and elegance. • *adjective* **1** (of furniture or architecture) elaborately ornate and characterized by light pastel and gold colours, asymmetrical patterns, curving and interlacing forms and scrollwork, and shell motifs and other natural shapes. **2** (of art) light, delicate, and highly ornamented, and (esp. in painting) tending to feature common rather than significant subjects, typified esp. by the painting of Antoine Watteau (1684–1721) and the early music of Joseph Haydn (1732–1809) and Wolfgang Amadeus Mozart (1756–91). [Say ruh CO co]

rod *noun* **1** a slender straight bar esp. of wood or metal. **2** this as a symbol of office. **3 a** a stick or bundle of twigs used in caning or flogging. **b (the rod)** the use of this. **4 a** = FISHING ROD. **b** an angler using a rod. **5 a** a slender straight round stick growing as a shoot on a tree. **b** this when cut. **6** *slang* = HOT ROD *noun*. **7** any of numerous rod-shaped structures in the eye, detecting dim light. **8** a metal shaft in an internal combustion engine etc.: *piston rod*. **9** a long slender piece of fuel for a nuclear reactor. PHRASES **ride the rods** *hist. informal* ride surreptitiously and without paying on a freight train.

rode *past of* RIDE.

rodent • *noun* a gnawing animal of an order that includes rats, mice, squirrels, beavers, porcupines, and other mammals with strong incisors and no canine teeth. • *adjective* of this order. ▶ **rodent-like** *adjective*

rodeo • *noun* (*plural* **rodeos**) **1** a display or competition exhibiting the skills of riding broncos, roping cattle, wrestling steers, etc. **2** a similar (usu. competitive) exhibition of other skills, e.g. motorcycle riding, cycling, etc. **3** a roundup of cattle on a ranch for branding etc. • *verb* (**rodeos, rodeoed, rodeoing**) compete in a rodeo. [Say ROADY oh]

rod-like *adjective* having the thin, straight shape of a rod.

roe *noun* **1** (also **hard roe**) the mass of eggs in a female fish's ovary, esp. when ripe and used as food. **2** (also **soft roe**) the ripe testes of a male fish, esp. when used as food.

roentgen *noun* a unit of ionizing radiation, the amount producing one electrostatic unit of positive or negative ionic charge in one cubic centimetre of air under standard conditions. [Say RONT gun or RUNT gun]

roger *interjection* **1** your message has been received and understood (used in radio communication etc.). **2** *slang* all right; OK.

rogue *noun* **1** a dishonest or unprincipled person. **2** *jocular* a mischievous person, esp. a child. **3** (usu. as an *adjective*) **a** a wild animal driven away or living apart from the herd and of fierce temper: *rogue elephant*. **b** a stray, irresponsible, or undisciplined person or thing: *intercontinental ballistic missiles in the hands of rogue nations could threaten the US within 20 years*. [Say ROAG]

rogues' gallery *noun* **1** a collection of photographs of known criminals etc., used for identification of suspects. **2** any collection of people notable for a certain shared quality or characteristic, esp. a disreputable one.

roguish *adjective* **1** playfully mischievous: *a roguish smile*. **2** characteristic of a dishonest or unprincipled person: *a roguish lifestyle*. ▶ **roguishly** *adverb* **roguishness** *noun* [Say ROE gish]

'roid *noun* *slang* an anabolic steroid, when taken for its muscle-building properties by an athlete.

roil *verb* **1** make (a liquid) muddy by agitating it and disturbing the sediment: *winds roil these waters*. **2** (esp. of liquid) move in a turbulent, swirling manner: *queasiness roiled in my belly*. [Sounds like ROYAL]

roistering • *adjective* enjoying oneself or celebrating in a noisy or boisterous way: *the roistering lumberjack of snowy northern woods was one of Hollywood's favourite characters in movies with a Canadian setting*. • *noun* noisy or boisterous celebration or revelling.

role *noun* **1** a performer's part in a play, film, etc. **2** a person's or thing's characteristic or expected function. **3** the part played or assumed by a person in society, life, etc., influenced by his or her conception of what is appropriate.

role model *noun* a person looked to by others as an example in a particular role or situation.

role-play • *verb* act as one would expect another person to behave in a particular situation, esp. as part of a learning activity or training exercise. • *noun* (usu. **role play**) = ROLE-PLAYING.

role player *noun* a player whose playing time with a team is limited to certain specific situations, esp. as a substitute.

role-playing *noun* a learning activity or training exercise in which a person acts as they would expect another person to behave in a particular situation.

role-playing game *noun* a game in which players take on the roles of imaginary characters who engage in adventures, usu. in a fantasy setting created by a referee.

roll • *verb* **1** move by turning over and over on an axis. **2** move forward on wheels or with a smooth, undulating motion. **3** (of a moving ship, aircraft, or vehicle) sway on an axis parallel to the direction of motion. **4** (of a machine or device) begin operating. **5** (often foll. by *up*) turn (something flexible) over and over on itself to form a cylindrical or spherical shape. **6** flatten (something) by passing a roller over it or by passing it between rollers. **7** (of a loud, deep sound such as that of thunder) reverberate. **8** pronounce (a consonant, typically an *r*) with a trill. **9** (as **rolling** *adjective*) steady and continuous. **10** throw (dice). **11** set out; start moving, working, etc.: *let's roll*. • *noun* **1** a cylinder formed by rolling flexible material. **2** a rolling movement. **3** a gymnastic exercise in which the body is rolled into a tucked position and turned in a forward or backward circle. **4** a prolonged, deep, reverberating sound. **5** (in drumming) a sustained, rapid alternation of single or double strokes of each stick. **6** a very small loaf of bread. **7** an official list or register of names. **8** a document in scroll form. **9** a quantity of banknotes rolled together. **10** a bout of success or progress. PHRASES **be rolling** *informal* be very rich. **be rolling in** *informal* have plenty of (esp. money). **on a roll** *slang* experiencing a bout of success or progress; engaged in a period of intense activity. **roll back 1** cause (esp. prices or wages) to decrease; reduce. **2** turn or force back or further away: *roll back Communism*. **3** cancel; annul: *roll back a decision*. **rolled into one** combined in one person or thing. **roll in** arrive in great numbers or quantity. **roll in the aisles** *informal* laugh uproariously. **roll on** put on or apply by rolling. **roll out 1 a** unveil (a new aircraft or spacecraft). **b** launch (a new product, campaign, etc.). **2** *slang* get out of bed. **roll over 1** send (a person) sprawling or rolling. **2** *Economics* reinvest (stocks, bonds, mutual funds, etc.). **roll up 1** *informal* arrive in a vehicle; appear on the scene. **2** make into or form a roll. **roll**

R

with the punches *informal* adapt oneself to difficult circumstances.

rollaway • *adjective* (of a bed etc.) that can be removed on wheels or casters. • *noun* a rollaway bed etc.

rollback *noun* **1** a reduction or decrease in prices, wages, etc. **2** the action or an act of rolling backwards.

roll bar *noun* an overhead metal bar strengthening the frame of a vehicle (esp. in racing) and protecting the occupants if the vehicle overturns.

roll call *noun* **1** a process of calling out a list of names to establish who is present. **2** a distinguished list of persons, things, etc.: *a roll call of former champions*.

rolled oats *plural noun* oats that have been husked and crushed.

roller *noun* **1 a** a hard revolving cylinder for smoothing the ground, spreading ink or paint, crushing or stamping, rolling up cloth on, etc., used alone or as a rotating part of a machine. **b** a cylinder for diminishing friction when moving a heavy object. **2** a small cylinder on which hair is rolled for setting. **3** a long swelling wave.

Rollerblade • *noun proprietary* an in-line skate. • *verb* (**rollerblade, rollerblades, rollerbladed, rollerblading**) skate using in-line skates. ▶**rollerblader** *noun*

roller coaster • *noun* **1** a ride at an amusement park etc., having small open railway cars which travel in a linked line on an elevated, winding track up and down steep hills and around sharp corners. **2** any experience, time, etc. marked by sudden ups and downs or changes: *an emotional roller coaster*. • *adjective* (**roller-coaster**) that goes up and down, or changes, suddenly and repeatedly: *a roller-coaster economy*. • *verb* (**roller-coaster**) (also **rollercoast**) go up and down or change in this way.

roller hockey *noun* hockey played on in-line skates.

roller rink *noun* **1** a rink used for roller skating. **2** a building containing such a rink.

roller skate • *noun* each of a pair of boots with wheels attached (or metal or plastic frames with small wheels, fitted to shoes) for riding on paved surfaces etc. • *verb* (**roller skates, roller skated, roller skating**) move on roller skates. ▶**roller skater** *noun*

rollicking *adjective* lively, fast-paced, and amusing: *a rollicking musical free-for-all*.

rolling pin *noun* a cylinder made of wood or plastic for rolling out pastry, dough, etc.

rolling stock *noun* the locomotives, cars, or other vehicles used on a railway.

rolling stone *noun* a person who is unwilling to settle for long in one place.

rollout *noun* **1 a** the official wheeling out of a new aircraft or spacecraft. **b** the official launch of a new product. **2** the part of a landing during which an aircraft travels along the runway losing speed.

rollover *noun* **1** *Economics* the extension or transfer of a debt or other financial relationship, esp. the reinvestment of stocks, bonds, mutual funds, etc. **2** *informal* the overturning of a vehicle etc.

Rolodex *noun* (*plural* **Rolodexes**) *proprietary* a desktop card index mounted on a rotating axis, used for storing addresses and telephone numbers. [Say ROLA dex]

roly-poly *adjective* pudgy, plump.

ROM *noun Computing* read-only memory. [Say ROM]

romaine *noun* a variety of lettuce with crisp narrow leaves forming a long upright head. [Say roe MAIN]

Roman • *adjective* **1** of ancient Rome or its territory or people. **2** of medieval or modern Rome. **3** of papal Rome, esp. = ROMAN CATHOLIC *adjective*. **4** surviving from a period of Roman rule: *Roman road*. **5** (**roman**) (of type) of a plain upright kind used in ordinary print. **6** (of the

alphabet etc.) based on the ancient Roman system with letters A–Z. • *noun* **1 a** a citizen of the ancient Roman Republic or Empire. **b** a soldier of the Roman Empire. **2** a citizen of modern Rome. **3** = ROMAN CATHOLIC *noun*. **4** (**roman**) roman type.

Roman Catholic • *adjective* of or relating to the part of the Christian Church acknowledging the Pope as its head. • *noun* a member of this Church. ▶**Roman Catholicism** *noun*

romance • *noun* **1 a** a love affair. **b** sentimental or idealized love: *Don asked Carolyn for a date and romance blossomed*. **c** a prevailing sense of wonder or mystery surrounding the mutual attraction in a love affair: *has the romance gone out of your marriage?* **2** a feeling of excitement and adventure: *the romance of travel*. **3 a** a literary genre with romantic love or highly imaginative unrealistic episodes forming the central theme: *a master of romance fiction*. **b** a work of this genre: *likes to read historical romances*. **4** a medieval tale, usu. in verse, of some hero of chivalry, of the kind common in the Romance languages: *the courtly romances about King Arthur and his knights*. • *adjective* (**Romance**) of any of the languages descended from Latin (e.g. French, Italian, Spanish, Portuguese, Catalan, Romansh, Romanian, Friulian). • *verb* (**romances, romanced, romancing**) **1** attempt to win the attention or affection of someone: *women say they want to be romanced*. **2** describe or imagine something in an idealized or unrealistic way; romanticize: *romancing the past*.

Romanesque • *noun* a style of architecture prevalent in Europe *c.* 900–1200, with massive vaulting and round arches (compare NORMAN *adjective* 4). • *adjective* of the Romanesque style of architecture. [Say roman ESK]

Romanian • *noun* **1 a** a native or national of Romania in eastern Europe. **b** a person of Romanian descent. **2** the Romance language of Romania. • *adjective* of Romania or its people or language. [Say roe MAINY in]

romanization *noun* **1** the process of bringing a region or a people under Roman influence. **2** the representation or reproduction of text in the Roman alphabet or in roman type.

romanize *verb* (**romanizes, romanized, romanizing**) **1** bring something (esp. a region or people) under Roman influence or authority. **2** put (text) into the Roman alphabet or into roman type.

Roman numeral *noun* any of the Roman letters representing numbers: I = 1, V = 5, X = 10, L = 50, C = 100, D = 500, M = 1000.

Romano *noun* a strong-tasting hard cheese, originally made in Italy. [Say roe MAN oh]

Romansh • *noun* a Romance language spoken in the Swiss canton of Grisons. It has several dialects and is an official language of Switzerland. • *adjective* having to do with this language. [Say roe MANSH]

romantic • *adjective* **1** inclined towards or suggestive of romance in love: *a romantic woman ◊ romantic words*. **2** of, characterized by, or suggestive of an idealized, sentimental, or fantastic view of reality: *a romantic picture*. **3** (of a person) imaginative, visionary, idealistic. **4 a** (of style in art, music, etc.) concerned more with feeling and emotion than with form and aesthetic qualities; preferring grandeur or picturesqueness to finish and proportion. **b** (also **Romantic**) of or relating to the Romanticism of the 18th and 19th centuries. **5** (of a project etc.) not practical, fantastic. • *noun* **1** a romantic person. **2** a writer or artist of the Romantic school. ▶**romantically** *adverb*

romanticism *noun* **1** (also **Romanticism**) adherence to a romantic style in art, music, etc. **2** a tendency towards romance or romantic views.

3 (Romanticism) a movement in the arts and literature, originating in the late 18th century, characterized by a rejection of rationalism and the order and restraint of classicism and neoclassicism, favouring instead inspiration, irrationality, subjectivity, and the primacy of the individual.

romanticization *noun* the process of dealing with or describing something in an idealized or unrealistic fashion, making it seem better or more appealing than it really is: *the romanticization of the past*.

romanticize *verb* (**romanticizes, romanticized, romanticizing**) deal with or describe something in an idealized or unrealistic fashion; make something seem better or more appealing or interesting than it really is: *a romanticized account of war*.

Romany • *noun* (*plural* **Romanies**) **1** a gypsy. **2** the Indo-European language of the gypsies. • *adjective* of or relating to gypsies or their language. [Say ROMMA nee]

Romeo *noun* (*plural* **Romeos**) a passionate male lover or seducer.

romp • *verb* **1** play about roughly and energetically. **2** *informal* proceed easily or rapidly. **3** win a race, contest, etc. with ease. • *noun* **1** a period of romping or boisterous play. **2** a song, play, etc. that is lively, energetic, and lighthearted. **3** a playful and lighthearted journey or excursion. **4** *Sport* an easy victory. **5** a sexual encounter that is usu. spontaneous, playful, lighthearted, and carefree.

romper *noun* **1** (also **romper suit**, **rompers** *plural noun*) a young child's one-piece garment covering the legs and trunk. **2 a** a loose-fitting woman's garment combining esp. a short-sleeved or sleeveless top and wide-legged shorts. **b** a similar garment worn in bed.

rondo *noun* (*plural* **rondos**) *Music* a form of composition with a recurring theme, often found in the final movement of a sonata or concerto etc. [Say RON doe]

roof • *noun* (*plural* **roofs**) **1 a** the upper outside covering of a building, esp. a house, usu. supported by its walls. **b** any external covering forming a shelter or top: *the roof of the car*. **2 a** the overhead inner surface of a room, cavity, etc.: *the roof of a cave*. **b** the top inner surface of a compartment or opening: *the roof of the mouth*. • *verb* **1** (often foll. by *over*) cover with or as with a roof. **2** put (something) on top of a roof, accidentally or intentionally: *roofed a tennis ball*. PHRASES **go through the roof** *informal* (of prices etc.) reach extreme or unexpected heights. **hit** (or **go through**) **the roof** *informal* become very angry. **raise the roof** make a lot of noise inside a building, esp. by cheering or shouting. **a roof over one's head** somewhere to live. **under one roof** in the same building. **under a person's roof** in a person's home. ▶ **roofed** *adjective* (also in *combination*).

roofer *noun* a person who constructs or repairs roofs.

roofing *noun* **1** the material for making or covering roofs: *roofing shingles*. **2** the process of building roofs.

roofless *adjective* without a roof: *the roofless ruins of a medieval church*.

roofline *noun* the outline or silhouette of a roof or roofs.

roof rack *noun* a frame that can be mounted on the roof of a car, truck, etc. for carrying luggage, skis, etc.

rooftop *noun* the outer surface of a roof, esp. the roof of a house.

rook • *noun* **1** in chess, each of the four pieces set in the corner squares at the beginning of a game, moving in a straight line forwards, backwards, or sideways over any number of unoccupied squares. Also called CASTLE. **2** a black Eurasian bird of the crow family, nesting in colonies in treetops. **3** *informal* = ROOKIE. • *verb* **1** charge (a customer) extortionately. **2** *informal* win money from (a person) at cards etc. esp. by swindling.

rookery *noun* (*plural* **rookeries**) **1 a** a colony of seabirds (esp. penguins) or seals. **b** a place where seabirds, sea lions, seals, etc. breed. **2 a** a colony of rooks. **b** a clump of trees having rooks' nests.

rookie *noun* *informal* **1** an athlete who is playing his or her first full season in a particular league (also as an *adjective*: *rookie season*). **2** a new recruit, esp. in an army or police force. **3** (usu. as an *adjective*) a novice: *a rookie politician*.

room • *noun* **1** space viewed in terms of its capacity to accommodate contents or allow action: *there was no room to move*. **2** opportunity or scope: *room for improvement*. **3 a** a part of a building enclosed by walls, floor, and ceiling. **b** a bedroom. **4** (in *plural*) a set of rooms rented out to lodgers. • *verb* rent a room or rooms; lodge, board. PHRASES **make room** (often foll. by *for*) clear a space (for a person or thing) by removal of others. **not enough** (or **no**) **room to swing a cat** not enough space to live or work in.

room and board *noun* **1** accommodation and meals. **2** the cost of this.

-roomed *combining form* (of a building) having the number of rooms described: *a one-roomed shack*.

roomer *noun* **1** a lodger occupying a room or rooms without meals. **2** a house or apartment having a specified number of rooms: *a one-roomer*.

roomette *noun* a private single compartment in the sleeping car of a train. [Say room ETT]

roomful *noun* (*plural* **roomfuls**) the number of people filling a room.

roomie *noun* *informal* a roommate.

roominess *noun* the quality of being spacious or having ample space for people or things.

rooming house *noun* a house or building divided into furnished rooms or apartments for rent.

roommate *noun* a person who lives in the same apartment, room, etc. as another.

room service *noun* **1** (in a hotel etc.) drinks or a meal served in a guest's room. **2** the department that provides this service.

room temperature *noun* a temperature that would be considered comfortable for a normal room in a house, usu. approx. 20° C or 68° F.

roomy *adjective* (**roomier, roomiest**) having plenty of room to contain people or things; spacious.

roost • *noun* **1** a branch, perch, etc. where birds or bats regularly settle, esp. to sleep. **2** a place where domestic fowl perch at night, esp. in a henhouse. • *verb* (of a bird) settle for rest or sleep. PHRASES **come home to roost** (of a scheme etc.) have negative or unfavourable consequences for the person who originated it.

rooster *noun* a male chicken.

rooster tail *noun* the spray of water, dust, or snow thrown up behind a moving vehicle etc.

SPELL CHECK
root, route

The path you follow to reach a destination is a **route**, which is also the spelling in "paper route".

---

root • *noun* **1** a part of a plant normally below ground, which acts as a support and collects water and nourishment. **2** the embedded part of a bodily organ or structure such as a hair. **3** a turnip, carrot, or other vegetable which grows as the root of a plant. **4** the basic cause, source, or origin: *money is the root of all evil*. **5** (in *plural*) family, ethnic, or cultural origins. **6** *Linguistics* the part of a word that has the main meaning, on which its other forms are based: *"Talk" is the root of "talks", "talked" and "talking".* **7** *Music* the lowest note of a chord in its original (uninverted) form.

R

8 *Math* a number or quantity that when multiplied by itself one or more times gives a specified number or quantity. • *verb* **1** develop roots and become firmly established. **2 a** fix firmly with roots or as if with roots: *fear rooted him to the spot*. **b** be based in: *fear is rooted in ignorance*. **3** (usu. foll. by *out*, *up*) dig up by the roots. **4** (of an animal, esp. a pig) turn up (the ground) with the snout, beak, etc., in search of food. **5 a** (foll. by *around*, *in*, etc.) rummage around or look for something. **b** (foll. by *out* or *up*) find or extract by rummaging. **6** (foll. by *for*) *informal* **a** *Sport* encourage with cheering, applause, etc. **b** offer support to. PHRASES **put down roots 1** begin to draw nourishment from the soil. **2** become settled or established. **strike at the root** (or **roots**) **of** set about destroying. **take root 1** begin to grow and draw nourishment from the soil. **2** become fixed or established. **root out** find and get rid of.

root beer *noun* a carbonated drink made from an extract of roots.

root canal *noun* **1** the pulp-filled cavity in the root of a tooth. **2** a procedure to replace the infected pulp of a tooth with an inert material.

root cellar *noun* an underground room in a house for storing esp. vegetables and fruit.

rooted *adjective* **1** firmly established: *her affection was deeply rooted*. **2 a** having a root or roots. **b** (in *combination*) having roots of a specified type, number, or quality. ▶ **rootedness** *noun*

rooter *noun* a fan or supporter: *the play brought the crowd of Ticat rooters to their feet*.

rootin' tootin' *adjective informal* **1** resembling or characteristic of the Wild West or an inhabitant of the Wild West. **2** boisterous, noisy, rip-roaring: *a rootin' tootin' good time*.

rootless *adjective* **1** having no settled home or family ties: *a rootless, free-spirited musician*. **2** (of a plant) not having roots. ▶ **rootlessness** *noun*

rootlet *noun* a slender root or division of a root.

rootlike *adjective* resembling a root in appearance or function.

rootstock *noun* **1** a stock onto which another variety has been grafted or budded. **2** a rhizome, esp. one from which new leaves and shoots grow annually. **3** a primary form from which offshoots have arisen.

rootsy *adjective* (**rootsier**, **rootsiest**) *informal* (esp. of music) uncommercialized, full-blooded, esp. showing traditional origins.

rope • *noun* **1 a** a strong thick cord made by twisting together strands of hemp, cotton, nylon, wire, or similar material. **b** a piece of this. **2** (foll. by *of*) **a** a quantity of similar things held together by or as if by a string passed through the middle of each: *a rope of pearls*. **b** a strand of a semi-liquid substance: *a rope of saliva*. **3** (**the ropes**) **a** the rules and procedures of a business, operation, etc.: *learning the ropes*. **b** the ropes enclosing a boxing or wrestling ring etc. **4** (**the rope**) **a** a halter for hanging a person. **b** execution by hanging. **5** a lasso. • *verb* (**ropes**, **roped**, **roping**) **1** fasten, secure, or catch with rope. **2** (usu. foll. by *off*) enclose (a space) with rope. **3** (usu. foll. by *in*, *into*) persuade or entice someone to join or participate in an activity: *I got roped into doing the dishes*. PHRASES **give a person plenty of rope** (or **enough rope to hang himself**) give a person enough freedom of action to bring about his or her own downfall. **on the ropes 1** *Boxing* forced against the ropes by the opponent's attack. **2** near defeat. ▶ **ropelike** *adjective*

roper *noun* a person who uses a lasso to catch and secure cattle etc.

rope tow *noun* a type of ski lift consisting of an endless moving rope driven by a motor.

roping *noun* the sport or activity of using a lasso to catch and secure cattle etc.

ropy *adjective* having the strong, thin, flexible nature or appearance of rope: *ropy muscles*.

Roquefort *noun proprietary* **1** a soft blue cheese made from ewes' milk. **2** a salad dressing made of this. [Say ROKE furt]

rorqual *noun* any of various baleen whales characterized by a pleated throat and small dorsal fin, esp. the finback or the minke whale. [Say ROAR kwull]

Rorschach *adjective* designating or pertaining to a type of personality test in which a standard set of ink blots is presented one by one to the subject, who is asked to describe what they suggest or resemble. [Say ROAR shack or ROAR shock]

rosary *noun* (*plural* **rosaries**) **1** *Catholicism* **a** a form of devotion accompanying the contemplation of fifteen events in the life of Christ and the Virgin Mary (now usu. in groups of five) in which fifteen decades of Hail Marys are repeated, each decade preceded by an Our Father. **b** a string of beads divided into sets used for keeping count in the recital of this. **2** a similar string of beads or knotted cord used for counting prayers in other religions. [Say ROZA ree]

rose[1] • *noun* **1** a prickly bush or shrub that bears red, pink, yellow, or white fragrant flowers, and is widely grown as an ornamental. **2** the flower of this bush or shrub. **3** any flowering plant resembling this. **4 a** a light crimson colour; pink. **b** (usu. in *plural*) a rosy complexion: *roses in her cheeks*. **5 a** (as an *adjective*) representing or designating something resembling a rose: *rose diamond*. **b** a rose-shaped design, e.g. on a compass. • *adjective* pink or pale red. PHRASES **come up roses** develop in a very favourable way. **come up smelling of roses** emerge in a very favourable light, esp. from a difficult situation.

rose[2] *past of* RISE.

rosé *noun* any pale red or pink wine, coloured by only brief contact with the skins of red grapes. [Say roe ZAY]

roseate *adjective* **1** having a partly pink plumage: *roseate tern*. **2** rose-coloured: *he jabbed a stiff forefinger at the large roseate scar high on his right breast*. [Say ROZY it]

rose-breasted grosbeak *noun* a grosbeak that breeds across most of North America east of the Rockies, the male of which is black and white with a red patch on its breast.

rosebud *noun* **1** a bud of a rose. **2** (often as an *adjective*) representing or designating something resembling a rosebud in nature or appearance: *rosebud mouth*.

rose-coloured *adjective* **1** of the colour of a pale red rose; rose-pink. **2** optimistic, sanguine, cheerful: *a rose-coloured view of things*. PHRASES **see through rose-coloured glasses** regard (circumstances etc.) with unfounded optimism or naïveté.

rosehip *noun* = HIP[2].

rosemary *noun* **1** a fragrant shrub of the mint family, native to southern Europe. **2** the leaves of this plant used as a flavouring.

rose pink *noun & adjective* the colour of a pale red rose, warm pink.

rose red *noun & adjective* the colour of a red rose; dark red, crimson.

rosette *noun* **1** an ornament or other object carved, moulded, shaped, or arranged to resemble or represent a rose: *a rosette of butter*. **2 a** a naturally occurring circular arrangement of horizontally spreading leaves, esp. about the base of a stem. **b** a similar but abnormal cluster of leaves on the stem, a symptom of disease. **3** a rose-shaped arrangement of ribbon worn esp. as a badge of membership or support, or as a symbol of a

prize won in a competition. **4** markings resembling a rose, esp. on the skin of a leopard. [Say rose ETT]

rosewater *noun* water distilled from roses, or scented with the essence of roses, used as a perfume and as a flavouring in cooking.

rosewood *noun* any of several fragrant woods derived esp. from tropical leguminous trees of the genus *Dalbergia* used in making furniture.

Rosh Hashanah *noun* the festival celebrating the Jewish New Year marked by penitence, self-reflection, and an examination of one's relationship with and responsibilities to God. [Say rosh huh SHONNA]

rosin • *noun* the solid amber residue obtained after the distillation of crude turpentine, or of naphtha extract from pine stumps, used in adhesives, varnishes, inks, etc. or used, esp. powdered, to prevent slipping when applied to the bows of stringed instruments, the hands of baseball players, dancers' shoes, etc. • *verb* (**rosins, rosined, rosining**) treat with rosin. [Say ROZZIN]

roster • *noun* **1** *Sport* a list of players belonging or available to a team. **2** (often foll. by *of*) **a** any list of people or things belonging to a specified group: *a roster of experts.* **b** a group of people or things considered as being on a roster: *the whole roster will be performing.* **3** a list or plan showing turns of duty or leave for individuals or groups in any organization, originally a military force. • *verb* place on a roster.

rostrum *noun* (*plural* **rostra** or **rostrums**) a platform or pulpit for public speaking. [Say ROSS trum]

rosy *adjective* (**rosier, rosiest**) **1** a coloured like a pink or red rose. **b** pink as an indication of health or youth: *rosy cheeks.* **2 a** promising: *a rosy future.* **b** optimistic, esp. unjustifiably so: *painted a rosy picture of the situation.*

> **SPELL CHECK**
> **rot, wrought**
>
> Black iron used to make decorative fences and gates is **wrought** iron.

---

rot • *verb* (**rots, rotted, rotting**) **1 a** (of animal or vegetable matter) lose its original form by the chemical action of bacteria, fungi, etc.; decay. **b** (foll. by *away*) decay to the point of falling apart: *the old barn was rotting away.* **c** (foll. by *off*) separate from the main body because of decay: *dead branches rotted off.* **d** (of ice on lakes etc.) disintegrate into a honeycombed structure due to thawing. **2** (of society, institutions, etc.) deteriorate; become corrupt or degenerate due to neglect or abuse. **3** (of a person) languish, waste away: *he was left to rot in prison.* **4** cause to rot, make rotten: *too much candy will rot your teeth.* • *noun* **1 a** the process or state of rotting. **b** rotten or decayed matter. **2** *Botany* any of various diseases in plants characterized by the weakening or decay of tissue. **3** a decline or breakdown in standards or behaviour: *the rot has set in.* **4** *slang* nonsense: *her ideas were nothing but rot.*

rotary • *adjective* **1** acting by rotation: *a rotary blade.* **2** operating through the rotation of some part: *a rotary mower.* • *noun* (*plural* **rotaries**) *US & Cdn* (*NS, Nfld, & BC*) a traffic circle or roundabout. [Say ROE tuh ree]

rotatable *adjective* capable of being rotated. [Say ROTATE a bull]

rotate *verb* (**rotates, rotated, rotating**) **1** move around an axis or centre; spin, revolve. **2 a** change the position, responsibility, etc. of a person or thing in a regularly recurring order: *rotate the tires.* **b** act or occur in turns or in a particular order: *you wash, I'll dry, and tomorrow we'll rotate.*

rotation *noun* **1** the action of rotating about an axis or centre: *the moon moves in the same direction as the earth's*

rotation ◊ *performed three rotations.* **2** a regular organized sequence of things or events. **3 a** a regular succession of members of a group through positions or duties etc.: *the teachers acted as department head in rotation.* **b** (also **starting rotation**) *Baseball* the group of usu. four or five pitchers on a team that start games in succession. **4** a system of growing different crops in regular order to avoid exhausting the soil. ▶ **rotational** *adjective*

rotator *noun* **1** a muscle that rotates a limb etc. **2** a machine or device for causing something to rotate. **3** a revolving apparatus or part.

rotator cuff *noun* the muscles associated with a capsule with fused tendons that supports the arm at the shoulder joint.

rote *adjective* by routine or mechanical repetition etc.: *rote learning.* **PHRASES** **by rote 1** in a mechanical or repetitious manner. **2** acquired through memorization without proper understanding or reflection.

rotgut *noun* *slang* cheap usu. inferior alcoholic liquor, often with other ingredients mixed in.

roti *noun* (*plural* **rotis**) a dish of Indian origin, common in the Caribbean, consisting of a flat pancake or unleavened bread folded over usu. a spicy meat filling with chickpeas. [Say ROE tee]

rotini *noun* a variety of pasta in small spirals. [Say roe TEENY]

rotisserie • *noun* **1** a usu. motor-driven rotating spit for roasting meat esp. over a barbecue or in an oven. **2** (also **rotisserie league baseball**) a game in which fans draft imaginary baseball teams of usu. 23 players by bidding on actual players with a set amount of money, and collect points for each home run, RBI, stolen base, etc. their players compile. **3** (as an *adjective*) designating things pertaining to rotisserie or to any similar esp. baseball fantasy league: *rotisserie player.* • *verb* cook meat with a rotisserie. [Say roe TISSER ee]

rotor *noun* **1** a rotary part of a machine, esp. in the distributor of an internal combustion engine. **2** a hub with a set of radiating airfoils on a helicopter etc. that provides lift when rotated in an approximately horizontal plane.

rototill *verb* till or break up soil using a Rototiller. [Say ROE toe till]

Rototiller *noun* a machine with rotating blades and prongs used for breaking up or tilling the soil. [Say ROE toe tiller]

rotten *adjective* (**rottener, rottenest**) **1 a** in a state of decomposition or decay. **b** falling to pieces or liable to break from age or use. **2** miserable, wretched, unfortunate: *I feel rotten today.* **3** despicable, vile, loathsome: *rotten scoundrel* ◊ *what a rotten thing to do!* **4** (also **rotting**) *Cdn* designating ice or snow which, in the course of melting, has become granular and weak; disintegrating. **5** morally, socially, or politically corrupt. **PHRASES** **spoil someone rotten** spoil or indulge a person excessively. ▶ **rottenness** *noun*

Rottweiler *noun* **1** a large, stocky, powerful dog having short coarse hair with black and tan markings, a broad head with drooping ears, and usu. a docked tail. **2** a very tenacious person. [Say ROT wile er]

rotund *adjective* (of a person) fat. [Say roe TUND]

rotunda *noun* **1 a** a circular hall or room. **b** the main hall of a public building. **2** a building with a circular ground plan, esp. one with a dome. [Say roe TUNDA]

rouge • *noun* **1** a red powder or cream used for colouring the cheeks. **2** (*rouge*) *Cdn* esp. *hist.* a Quebec supporter of a Liberal party. **3** *Cdn Football* a single point scored when the receiving team fails to run a kick out of the end zone, such as on a punt, kickoff, or missed field goal. • *verb* (**rouges, rouged, rouging**) colour with rouge. [Say ROOZH]

rough • *adjective* **1** having an uneven or irregular surface, not smooth or level or polished. **2** not gentle; violent or boisterous: *rough treatment*. **3 a** (of the sea, weather, etc.) violent, stormy, turbulent. **b** (of a flight, landing, trip, etc.) turbulent, bumpy. **4** lacking sophistication or refinement. **5** not finished tidily; plain and basic. **6** harsh in sound or taste. **7** not worked out or correct in every detail; approximate: *a rough guess*. **8** *informal* difficult and unpleasant. • *adverb* **1** in a rough manner: *he likes to play rough*. **2** (live or sleep etc.) outdoors, without a proper bed or accommodation; on the street. • *noun* **1** a rough, preliminary state: *jot things down in rough first*. **2** *Golf* the area of longer grass around the fairway and the green. • *verb* (foll. by *out*) shape or plan roughly. PHRASES **rough and ready** simple or crude but effective; not elaborate but adequate. **rough around the edges 1** (of a person) irritable. **2** (of a thing) having a few imperfections, unpolished. **rough in 1** install (wiring, plumbing, ductwork, etc.) for a room that is planned but is not yet built. **2** lay the groundwork or make preliminary arrangements for (a room): *rough in a bedroom*. **rough it** live in rough accommodation without basic comforts or conveniences. **rough up** *slang* treat (a person) with violence or abuse.

roughage *noun* **1** = DIETARY FIBRE. **2** coarse fodder. [Say RUFF idge]

rough-and-tumble • *adjective* disregarding rules or convention. • *noun* a situation without rules or organization; a free-for-all: *needed a break from the rough-and-tumble of political life*.

roughcast *noun* plaster of lime and gravel, used on outside walls.

rough cut • *noun* the first version of a film after preliminary editing. • *adjective* (usu. **rough-cut**) (of a log etc.) having been cut with a coarse blade to an approximate size before a more precise, finished cut is made.

roughen *verb* make or become rough.

rough-hew *verb* (**rough-hews**; *past* **rough-hewed**; *past participle* **rough-hewed** or **rough-hewn**; **rough-hewing**) shape out roughly; give crude form to.

rough-hewn *adjective* **1** uncouth, unrefined: *a large rough-hewn sailor approaches*. **2** (of timber, stone, etc.) cut or shaped out roughly.

roughhouse • *noun* boisterous or rambunctious play or wrestling, esp. indoors. • *verb* (**roughhouses**, **roughhoused**, **roughhousing**) engage in rambunctious behaviour or roughhouse. ▶ **roughhousing** *noun* [Say RUFF house]

rough ice *noun* *Cdn* a large bank of ice that has accumulated on the shore of a river from the freezing of successive tides.

roughing *noun* *Hockey* an unnecessary or excessive use of force for which a player is given a penalty.

rough-legged hawk *noun* a hawk of boreal regions. having legs covered with feathers to the base of the toes.

roughly *adverb* **1** approximately: *roughly 20*. **2** in a coarse or uneven manner: *roughly cut timbers*. **3** in a harsh manner: *she spoke roughly*. PHRASES **roughly speaking** in an approximate sense.

roughneck *informal* • *noun* **1** a rough or rowdy person. **2** a worker on an oil rig. • *verb* work as a roughneck on an oil-drilling operation.

roughness *noun* **1** the quality of something that has a coarse, uneven, or irregular surface: *the handle has a slight roughness that enables you to hold onto it without losing your grip*. **2** a rugged, aggressive, or violent manner or quality: *there's too much roughness in the sport* ◊ *he seems to have lost some of his roughness over the years*.

roughrider *noun* a person who breaks in or can ride unbroken horses.

roughshod *adjective* (of a horse) having shoes with nailheads projecting to prevent slipping. PHRASES **ride roughshod over** domineer over; treat with disrespect or disregard. [Say RUFF shod]

roughy *noun* (*plural* **roughies**) a kind of rough-skinned marine fish, esp. the orange roughy. [Say RUFFY]

roulette *noun* a gambling game in which a ball is dropped onto a revolving wheel with numbered compartments, players betting on the number at which the ball will come to rest. [Say roo LET]

round • *adjective* **1** shaped like a circle or cylinder. **2** shaped like a sphere. **3** having a curved surface with no sharp projections. **4** (of a person's shoulders) bent forward. **5** (of a voice or musical tone) rich and mellow. **6** (of a number) expressed in convenient units rather than exactly, e.g. to the nearest whole number. • *noun* **1** a circular piece or section. **2** a route or sequence by which a number of people or places are visited or inspected in turn: *a doctor's rounds*. **3** a regularly recurring sequence of activities: *the daily round*. **4** each of a sequence of sessions in a process, esp. in a sports contest. **5** a single division of a boxing or wrestling match. **6** a song for three or more unaccompanied voices or parts, each singing the same theme but starting one after another. **7** the amount of ammunition needed to fire one shot. **8** a set of drinks bought for all the members of a group. **9** a single distinct outburst of applause. • *adverb & preposition* esp. *Brit.* = AROUND. • *verb* **1** make or become round. **2** pass around (a corner, cape, etc.). **3** (usu. foll. by *off*) express (a number) in a less exact but more convenient form (also foll. by *down* when the number is decreased and *up* when it is increased). PHRASES **go the rounds** (of news etc.) be passed on from person to person. **in the round 1** with all features shown; all things considered. **2** *Theatre* with the audience around at least three sides of the stage. **3** (of sculpture) with all sides shown; not in relief. **4** (of undressed timber or logs) trimmed on only two sides. **5** (of a fish) not gutted; whole. **make** (or **do**) **the rounds of** go around from place to place. **make one's rounds** take a customary route for inspection etc. **round about 1** in a ring (about); all round; on all sides (of). **2** with a change to an opposite position. **3** approximately: *cost round about $50*. **round and round** several times round. **round off 1** bring to a complete or symmetrical or well-ordered state. **2** smooth out; blunt the corners or angles of. **3** = ROUND *verb* 3. **round on a person** make a sudden verbal attack on or unexpected retort to a person. **round out 1** = ROUND OFF 1. **2** provide more detail about. **round peg in a square hole** *see* PEG. **round up 1** collect or bring together (members of a group, suspects, cattle, etc.). **2** express a number in a less exact but more convenient form by increasing it.

roundabout *adjective* indirect.

rounded *adjective* **1** that has been rounded. **2** having a circular, spherical, or curving shape. **3** possessing a pleasing depth or wide range of characteristics etc.: *a rounded flavour*.

roundel *noun* **1** a small circular object, esp. a decorative medallion. **2** a circular identifying mark, usu. incorporating the colours of the national flag, painted on military aircraft. **3** a poem of eleven lines in three stanzas. [Say ROUND ul]

rounder *noun* **1** *slang* a person who makes the rounds of prisons or bars; a habitual criminal or drunkard. **2** (in *combination*) a boxing match of a specified number of rounds.

Roundhead *noun* a member or supporter of the party opposing Charles I in the English Civil War (1642–9).

roundhouse *noun* **1** a circular repair shed for railway locomotives, built around a turntable. **2** *slang* a punch given with a wide sweep of the arm.

roundish *adjective* somewhat round; roughly having the shape of a circle: *the tree has large, roundish leaves.*

roundly *adverb* **1** bluntly, in plain language, severely: *was roundly criticized.* **2** vigorously; energetically: *was roundly applauded.* **3** in a circular way.

roundness *noun* **1** the quality being circular or spherical. **2** the quality of a person's body or part of the body that is round or plump: *his face has a cheerful roundness.* **3** the quality of being complete or fully developed.

round robin *noun* a tournament in which each competitor plays in turn against every other.

round-shouldered *adjective* with shoulders bent forward so that the back is rounded.

round table *noun* an assembly for discussion, esp. at a conference.

round-the-clock *adjective* lasting or covering all day and usu. all night: *round-the-clock care.*

round trip *noun* a trip to a place and back to the point of origin.

roundup *noun* **1** a systematic rounding up of people or things, esp.: **a** the arrest of people suspected of a particular crime or crimes. **b** the rounding up of cattle etc. usu. for the purpose of registering ownership, counting, etc. **2** the people and horses engaged in the rounding up of cattle etc. **3** a summary.

roundwood *noun* timber used in the round without being squared by sawing or hewing, such as logs, posts, and pilings.

roundworm *noun* a nematode worm, esp. a parasitic one infesting the gut of a mammal or bird.

rouse *verb* (**rouses**, **roused**, **rousing**) **1** (often foll. by *from*, *out of*) bring out of sleep; wake. **2** (often foll. by *up*) stir up, make active or excited, startle out of inactivity or confidence or carelessness: *was roused to protest.* **3** provoke to anger: *is terrible when roused.* **4** evoke (feelings). PHRASES **rouse oneself** overcome one's laziness or inaction; become active.

rousing *adjective* exciting, stirring. ▶ **rousingly** *adverb*

roust *verb* rouse, stir up: *Dad would roust me out of bed at 5:20 to bring in the cows for milking.*

rout[1] • *noun* **1** a disorderly retreat of defeated troops. **2** a decisive defeat. • *verb* **1** cause to retreat in disorder: *in a matter of minutes the attackers were routed.* **2** defeat decisively: *the Leafs routed the Habs 6–1.* PHRASES **put to rout** put to flight, defeat utterly.

rout[2] *verb* **1** = ROOT *verb* 4, 5. **2** cut a groove, or any pattern not extending to the edges, in (a wooden or metal surface). PHRASES **rout out** force or fetch out of bed or from a house or hiding place.

route • *noun* **1 a** a way or course taken (esp. regularly) in getting from a starting point to a destination: *drove home by the quickest route.* **b** a series of steps taken to achieve something: *the route to success.* **c** (esp. in the US) (with following numeral) a specific highway: *Route 66.* **2** a round of stops regularly travelled in delivering, selling, or collecting goods: *paper route.* • *verb* (**routes**,

routed, **routing**) send or forward or direct to be sent by a particular route. [Rhymes with *SHOOT* or *SHOUT*]

router *noun* a tool for cutting grooves etc. [Rhymes with *SHOUTER*]

routine • *noun* **1** a regular course or procedure, an unvarying performance of certain acts. **2** a set sequence in a performance, esp. a dance, comedy act, etc. **3** *informal* a hackneyed, predictable response or formula of speech: *went into her overprotective mother routine.* **4** *Computing* a sequence of instructions for performing a task. • *adjective* **1** performed as part of a routine: *routine duties.* **2** of a customary or standard kind: *routine surgery.* ▶ **routinely** *adverb*

rove *verb* (**roves**, **roved**, **roving**) **1** wander without a settled destination, roam, ramble. **2** (of eyes) look in changing directions. **3** wander over or through.

rover *noun* **1** a roving person; a wanderer. **2** *Football* a defensive linebacker assigned to move around in anticipation of opponents' play. **3** a remote-controlled surface vehicle for extraterrestrial exploration. **4** (**Rover**) *Cdn* a member of the senior level (ages 18-26) in Scouting.

roving *adjective* **1** wandering, roaming. **2** (of a journalist etc.) required to travel to locations to deal with events as they occur. **3** characterized by roving; inclined to wander: *a roving life.*

roving eye *noun* (esp. in a man) a tendency to flirt or to be constantly looking to start a new sexual relationship: *if his wife wasn't around, he had a roving eye.*

R

row[1] *noun* **1** a number of persons or things in a more or less straight line. **2** a line of seats across a theatre etc.: *in the front row.* **3** a street with a continuous line of houses along one or each side. **4** a line of plants in a field or garden. **5** a horizontal line of entries in a table etc. **6** a complete line of stitches in knitting or crochet. PHRASES **a hard** (or **long etc.**) **row to hoe** a difficult task. **in a row 1** forming a row. **2** in succession: *two Sundays in a row.*

row[2] • *verb* **1** propel a boat with oars. **2** convey (a passenger) in a boat in this way. • *noun* a period of rowing.

row[3] *informal* • *noun* **1** a fierce quarrel or dispute. **2** esp. *Brit.* a loud noise or commotion. • *verb* make or engage in a row. PHRASES **make** (or **kick up**) **a row** make a vigorous protest. [Rhymes with *NOW*]

rowan *noun* **1** (also **rowan tree**) = MOUNTAIN ASH. **2** (also **rowanberry** *plural* **rowanberries**) the scarlet berry of this tree. [Say ROW un (ROW rhymes with *CROW* or *COW*)]

rowboat *noun* a small boat propelled by oars.

rowdily *adverb* in a noisy and disorderly manner.

rowdiness *noun* a noisy and disorderly manner or behaviour.

rowdy • *adjective* (**rowdier**, **rowdiest**) noisy and disorderly. • *noun* (*plural* **rowdies**) a rowdy person. ▶ **rowdyism** *noun*

rower *noun* **1** a person who takes part in the sport or activity of propelling a boat by oars. **2** a rowing machine.

row house *noun* any of a number of usu. similar houses joined in a row.

rowing machine *noun* an exercise machine for simulating the action of rowing.

royal • *adjective* **1** of or suited to or worthy of a king or queen. **2** in the service or under the patronage of a king or queen: *Royal Winnipeg Ballet.* **3** of the family of a king

or queen. **4** kingly, majestic, stately, splendid. **5** on a great scale, of exceptional size or quality, first-rate: *gave us a royal send-off*. **6** *informal* extreme; of the highest degree: *a royal pain*. • *noun informal* a member of the royal family. PHRASES **royal road to** a way of attaining without trouble: *by itself, observation offers no royal road to success in studies of social learning*.

Royal Air Force *noun* the British air force.

royal assent *noun* (in Canada, the UK, and other Commonwealth countries) the formal consent of the sovereign or his or her representative to a bill passed by Parliament, which thus becomes law.

royal blue *noun & adjective* a deep vivid blue.

Royal Canadian Air Force *noun hist.* Canada's permanent air force between 1924 and unification of the armed forces in 1968.

Royal Canadian Legion *noun see* LEGION 2.

Royal Canadian Mounted Police *noun* Canada's national police force, which enforces federal statutes and provides policing for jurisdictions without municipal police protection in all provinces and territories except Ontario and Quebec.

Royal Canadian Navy *noun hist.* Canada's permanent naval force between 1910 and unification of the Armed Forces in 1968.

Royal Commission *noun* (in Canada, the UK, and other Commonwealth countries) a commission of inquiry appointed by the Crown at the request of the government to investigate and report on a particular matter.

royal flush *noun (plural **royal flushes**)* a poker hand consisting of the five highest cards in one suit.

royalist • *noun* **1** a supporter of monarchy. **2** *hist.* a supporter of the King against Parliament in the English Civil War (1642–9). • *adjective* of or pertaining to royalists.

royal jelly *noun (plural **royal jellies**)* a substance secreted by honeybee workers and fed by them to future queen bees.

royally *adverb* **1** in the manner of or fit for a king or queen. **2** *slang* to a considerable degree; extremely.

Royal Marine *noun* a British marine (*see* MARINE *noun* 2a).

Royal Navy *noun* the British navy.

royalty *noun (plural **royalties**)* **1** the office or dignity or power of a king or queen. **2 a** royal persons. **b** a member of a royal family. **3** a sum paid to a patent-holder for the use of a patent or to an author etc. for each copy of a book etc. sold or for each public performance of a work. **4 a** a royal right (now esp. over minerals) granted by the sovereign to an individual or corporation. **b** a payment made by a producer of minerals, oil, or natural gas to the owner of the site or of the mineral rights over it.

royal "we" *noun* the use of "we" instead of "I" by a single person (as traditionally by a sovereign).

rpm *abbreviation* revolutions per minute.

RPN *abbreviation (plural **RPNs**)* **1** REGISTERED PRACTICAL NURSE. **2** Registered Psychiatric Nurse.

RR *abbreviation* **1** railroad. **2** RURAL ROUTE.

RRIF *abbreviation (plural **RRIFs**)* Cdn Registered Retirement Income Fund, a tax-sheltered savings plan which provides retirement income. [Say RIFF]

RRSP *abbreviation (plural **RRSPs**)* Cdn Registered Retirement Savings Plan, a tax-sheltered plan for saving for retirement.

R.S.C. *abbreviation Cdn* Revised Statutes of Canada.

RSI *abbreviation (plural **RSIs**)* REPETITIVE STRAIN INJURY.

RSP *abbreviation (plural **RSPs**)* Cdn Retirement Savings Plan.

RSVP • *noun (plural **RSVPs**)* a reply to an invitation. • *verb* (**RSVP's**, **RSVP'd**; **RSVP'ing**) reply to an invitation.

rt. *abbreviation* right.

Rte. *abbreviation* route.

Rt. Hon. *abbreviation* Right Honourable.

Rt. Rev. *abbreviation* Right Reverend.

RU-486 *noun* a name for the drug mifepristone, which is used to induce abortion in early pregnancy.

Ru *symbol* ruthenium.

rub • *verb* (**rubs**, **rubbed**, **rubbing**) **1** apply firm pressure to (a surface) with a repeated back and forth motion. **2** move to and fro against a surface while pressing or grinding against it. **3** apply with a rubbing action. **4** (foll. by *in*, *into*, *through*) use rubbing to make (a substance) go into or through something. **5** reproduce the design of (a carving on a grave marker) by rubbing paper laid on it with coloured chalk etc. • *noun* **1** an act of rubbing. **2** an impediment or difficulty: *there's the rub*. **3** a substance applied by rubbing. **4** a massage. PHRASES **not have two coins to rub together** have no money. **rub down 1** dry or smooth or clean by rubbing. **2** massage. **rub elbows** (or **shoulders**) **with** associate or come into contact with (another person or thing). **rub one's hands** rub one's hands together usu. in sign of keen satisfaction, or for warmth. **rub it in** (or **rub a person's nose in it**) emphasize or repeat an embarrassing fact etc. **rub noses** (of two people) touch noses in greeting, as a sign of friendship in some societies. **rub off 1** (usu. foll. by *on*) be transferred by contact: *some of his attitudes have rubbed off on me*. **2** remove by rubbing. **rub out 1** erase. **2** *slang* kill, eliminate. **rub salt into** (or **in**) **the wound** (or **wounds**) behave or speak so as to aggravate a hurt already inflicted. **rub the wrong way** irritate or repel as by stroking a cat against the lie of its fur.

rubber *noun* **1** a tough elastic polymeric substance made from the latex of plants or synthetically. **2** a piece of this or another substance for erasing pencil or ink marks. **3** *informal* a condom. **4** (in *plural*) **a** galoshes. **b** Cdn (Nfld) long, waterproof boots worn esp. by fishermen and sealers. **5** a person who rubs; a masseur or masseuse. **6** an implement used for rubbing. **7** (**the rubber**) Hockey slang the puck. **8** Baseball an oblong piece of rubber embedded in the pitcher's mound on which the pitcher stands to deliver the ball. **9 a** a match of three or five successive games between the same sides or persons at bridge, lawn tennis, etc. **b** a deciding game when scores are even. PHRASES **burn** (or **lay**) **rubber 1** travel very quickly in a car; speed. **2** leave tire tracks on a surface, usu. by accelerating or braking rapidly.

rubber band *noun* a loop of rubber for holding papers etc. together.

rubber cement *noun* an adhesive containing rubber in a solvent.

rubberize *verb* (**rubberizes**, **rubberized**, **rubberizing**) treat or coat with rubber.

rubberneck *informal* • *noun* a person who stares inquisitively or stupidly. • *verb* act in this way. ▶ **rubbernecker** *noun*

rubber plant *noun* **1** an evergreen plant with dark green shiny leaves, often cultivated as a houseplant. **2** (also **rubber tree**) any of various tropical trees yielding latex used to make rubber.

rubber stamp • *noun* **1** a device for inking and imprinting on a surface. **2 a** a person who mechanically copies or agrees to others' actions: *this House is merely acting as a rubber stamp regarding the request of the Government of Newfoundland*. **b** an

indication of such agreement: *the Constituent Congress has provided the necessary rubber stamp for a coup against the elected government*. • *verb* (**rubber-stamp**) approve automatically without proper consideration: *the parliament merely rubber-stamped the decisions of the party*.

rubbery *adjective* **1** resembling rubber in appearance, texture, or feel. **2** feeling weak and unable to support one's own weight: *I got up on rubbery legs*.

rubbing *noun* **1** in senses of RUB *verb*. **2** an impression or copy made by rubbing (see RUB *verb* 5).

rubbing alcohol *noun* alcohol made unfit for drinking and used in massaging, as an antiseptic, etc.

rubbish *noun* **1** esp. *Brit.* waste material; refuse. **2** worthless material or articles. **3** absurd ideas or suggestions; nonsense. ▶ **rubbishy** *adjective*

rubble *noun* rough fragments of stone or brick etc., esp. from demolished or decaying buildings.

rubby *noun* (*plural* **rubbies**) *Cdn slang* a person who drinks rubbing alcohol, aftershave, etc. mixed with cheap wine etc.; a derelict alcoholic.

rub-down *noun* a massage.

rube *noun* *informal* a country bumpkin.

rubella *noun* German measles. [Say roo BELLA]

rubidium *noun* a soft silvery element occurring naturally in various minerals and as the radioactive isotope rubidium-87. [Say roo BIDDY um]

ruble *noun* the chief monetary unit of Russia and some other former republics of the USSR. [Say ROO bull]

rubric *noun* a category or designation: *the buildings have demonstrable links with the revival of Greek and Roman architecture, and therefore fit easily under the rubric of Neoclassicism*. [Say ROO brick]

ruby *noun* (*plural* **rubies**) **1** a rare precious stone consisting of corundum with a colour varying from deep crimson or purple to pale rose. **2** *noun & adjective* a glowing purplish-red colour.

ruche *noun* a frill or gathering of lace etc. as a trimming. ▶ **ruched** *adjective* **ruching** *noun* [Say ROOSH]

ruck *noun* (**the ruck**) **1** an undistinguished crowd of persons or things: *what differentiates it from the ruck of contemporary fiction is that its narrative unfolds in reverse*. **2** (in racing) the main body of competitors not likely to overtake the leaders.

rucked up *adjective* creased or folded; wrinkled.

rucksack *noun* a backpack.

ruckus *noun* (*plural* **ruckuses**) *informal* a noisy disturbance; an uproar.

rudbeckia *noun* (*plural* **rudbeckias**) a North American plant of the daisy family, bearing yellow or orange flowers with a dark conelike centre, e.g. the black-eyed Susan. [Say rud BECKY uh]

rudder *noun* **1 a** a flat piece hinged vertically to the stern of a vessel for steering. **b** a vertical airfoil pivoted from the tailplane of an aircraft, for controlling its horizontal movement. **2** a guiding principle etc. ▶ **rudderless** *adjective*

ruddiness *noun* redness, esp. of a person's complexion.

ruddy *adjective* (**ruddier, ruddiest**) **1** (of a person or complexion) freshly or healthily red. **2** reddish.

rude *adjective* (**ruder, rudest**) **1** (of a person, remark, etc.) impolite or offensive. **2** roughly made or done; lacking subtlety or accuracy: *a rude plow*. **3** primitive or unsophisticated: *exchanged their rude shanty for a real frame house*. **4** abrupt, sudden, startling, violent: *a rude awakening*. **5** *informal* indecent, lewd: *a rude joke*. ▶ **rudely** *adverb* **rudeness** *noun*

rudiment *noun* **1** (in *plural*) the elements or first principles of a subject. **2** (in *plural*) an imperfect

beginning of something undeveloped or yet to develop. **3** *Biology* an undeveloped or immature part or organ, esp. a structure in an embryo or larva which will develop into a limb etc. [Say ROODA m'nt]

rudimentary *adjective* **1** involving basic principles; fundamental: *urban reformers wanted a rudimentary welfare state with better public health protection*. **2** incompletely developed: *health care in the village is still quite rudimentary*. [Say rooda MENTA ree]

rue[1] *verb* (**rues, rued, rueing** or **ruing**) repent of; bitterly feel the consequences of; wish to be undone or non-existent: *I rue the day I took this job*.

rue[2] *noun* a perennial evergreen shrub with bitter leaves formerly used in medicine.

rueful *adjective* expressing sorrow or regret in a genuine or humorous way. ▶ **ruefully** *adverb*

ruff *noun* **1** a projecting starched frill worn around the neck esp. in the 16th century. **2** a projecting or conspicuously coloured ring of feathers or hair around a bird's or animal's neck. **3** a fringe of fur around the hood or along the edges of a jacket.

ruffed grouse *noun* (*plural* **ruffed grouse**) a North American woodland grouse, which has a black or reddish ruff on the sides of the neck and is much prized as a game bird.

ruffian *noun* a violent lawless person.

ruffle • *verb* (**ruffles, ruffled, ruffling**) **1** disturb the smoothness or tranquility of. **2** upset the calmness of (a person). **3** gather (fabric) into a ruffle. **4 a** (of a bird) erect (its feathers) in anger, display, etc. **b** disorder or disarrange (hair). **5** undergo ruffling. • *noun* an ornamental frill of fabric, lace, etc. used to decorate the edge of a garment, pillowcase, etc. PHRASES **ruffle feathers** (or **a person's feathers**) *informal* upset or annoy (a person).

rufous *adjective* (esp. of animals) reddish brown. [Say ROO fuss]

rug *noun* **1** a piece of thick material, usu. with a deep or shaggy pile or woven in a pattern of colours, or a piece of dressed animal skin, placed as a covering or decoration on part of a floor. **2** *slang* a toupée, a wig. PHRASES **pull the rug (out) from under** deprive of support; weaken, unsettle.

rugby *noun* (also **rugby football**) a team game played with an oval ball that may be kicked, carried, and passed from hand to hand.

rugby shirt *noun* a men's usu. cotton casual shirt with a collar and a few buttons at the neck.

rugged *adjective* **1** (of ground or terrain) having a rough uneven surface. **2** (of features) strongly marked; irregular in outline. **3 a** unpolished; lacking gentleness or refinement: *rugged grandeur*. **b** austere, unbending: *rugged honesty*. **c** involving hardship: *a rugged life*. **4** (esp. of a machine) robust, sturdy. ▶ **ruggedly** *adverb* **ruggedness** *noun*

rug rat *noun* *slang* a small child.

ruin • *noun* **1** a destroyed or wrecked state: *the palace fell to ruin*. **2** a person's or thing's downfall or elimination: *the ruin of my hopes*. **3** the complete loss of one's property or position: *bring to ruin*. **4** (in *singular* or *plural*) the remains of a building etc. that has suffered ruin: *ancient ruins*. **5** a cause of ruin; a destructive thing or influence: *will be the ruin of us*. • *verb* **1 a** bring to ruin: *your extravagance has ruined me*. **b** utterly impair or wreck: *the rain ruined my hat*. **2** (esp. as **ruined** *adjective*) reduce to ruins. PHRASES **in ruins 1** in a state of ruin. **2** completely wrecked: *their hopes were in ruins*.

ruination *noun* **1** the act of bringing to ruin. **2** the act of ruining or the state of being ruined.

ruinous *adjective* **1** bringing ruin: *at ruinous expense*. **2** in ruins; dilapidated. ▶ **ruinously** *adverb*

rule • noun 1 a principle to which an action, procedure, etc. conforms or is required to conform. 2 a prevailing custom or standard; the normal state of affairs. 3 government or dominion: *under British rule.* 4 the period of time during which a government or monarch holds power. 5 = RULER 2. 6 a code of discipline of a religious order. • verb (**rules, ruled, ruling**) 1 exercise decisive influence over; keep under control. 2 have sovereign control of: *rules over a vast kingdom.* 3 pronounce authoritatively: *was ruled out of order.* 4 a make parallel lines across (paper). b make (a straight line) with a ruler etc. 5 be customary or prevalent: *apathy rules in this organization.* 6 slang be superior or pre-eminent: *hockey rules!* 7 (of a court etc.) make a formal decision or ruling: *waiting for the Supreme Court to rule.* PHRASES **as a rule** usually; more often than not. **by rule** in a regulation manner; mechanically. **rule out** 1 exclude; pronounce irrelevant or ineligible. 2 prevent; make impossible. **rule the roost** be in control.

rule of thumb noun a rule for general guidance, based on experience or practice rather than theory.

ruler noun 1 a person exercising government or dominion. 2 a straight-edged strip of rigid material marked at regular intervals, used to draw lines or measure distance.

ruling • noun an authoritative decision or announcement. • adjective prevailing; currently in force.

rum noun a liquor distilled from sugar cane residues or molasses.

rumba • noun 1 an Afro-Cuban dance. 2 a a ballroom dance imitative of this, danced on the spot with a pronounced movement of the hips. b the music for it. • verb (**rumbas, rumbaed** or **rumba'd, rumbaing**) dance the rumba.

rumble • verb (**rumbles, rumbled, rumbling**) 1 make a continuous deep resonant sound as of distant thunder. 2 (of a person or vehicle) move with a rumbling noise. 3 utter or say with a rumbling sound. 4 slang engage in a street fight. • noun 1 a rumbling sound. 2 slang a street fight between gangs.

rumblings plural noun early indications of some state of affairs or the initial stages of change: *rumblings of discontent.*

rumen noun the first stomach of a ruminant, in which food, esp. cellulose, is partly digested by bacteria. [Say ROO mun]

ruminant • noun an animal that chews the cud regurgitated from its rumen, e.g. a cow. • adjective of or belonging to ruminants. [Say ROOMA n'nt]

ruminate verb (**ruminates, ruminated, ruminating**) 1 meditate, ponder. 2 (of ruminants) chew the cud. ▶**rumination** noun **ruminative** adjective [Say ROO min ate, roo min AY sh'n, ROO min a tiv]

rummage • verb (**rummages, rummaged, rummaging**) search, esp. untidily and unsystematically: *rummaged through the drawers ◊ was rummaging around in her bag looking for keys.* • noun an unsystematic and untidy search: *found it after a rummage through my purse.*

rummage sale noun a sale of miscellaneous usu. second-hand articles, esp. for charity.

rummy noun a card game in which the players try to form sets and sequences of cards.

rumour (also **rumor**) • noun 1 general talk or hearsay of doubtful accuracy. 2 a current but unverified statement or assertion: *heard a rumour that you are leaving.* • verb report by way of rumour: *it is rumoured that he is leaving ◊ you are rumoured to be sick.* PHRASES **rumour has it** it is rumoured: *rumour has it that she is resigning.*

rump noun 1 the hind part of a mammal, esp. the buttocks. 2 a small remnant of a parliament or similar body: *he leaves behind the rump of an administration that saw more than 200 appointees forced from office.*

rumple verb (**rumples, rumpled, rumpling**) make or become creased. ▶**rumpled** adjective

rumpus noun (plural **rumpuses**) informal a disturbance, brawl, row, or uproar.

rumpus room noun a room, usu. in the basement of a house, for games and play.

rum-runner noun a person or ship engaged in smuggling alcohol, esp. during Prohibition. ▶**rum-running** noun

run • verb (**runs**; past **ran**; past participle **run**; **running**) 1 move at a speed faster than a walk, never having both or all feet on the ground at the same time. 2 move about in a hurried and hectic way. 3 pass or cause to pass: *she ran her fingers through her hair.* 4 move forcefully: *the tanker ran aground.* 5 (of a bus, train, etc.) make a regular journey on a particular route. 6 be in charge of; manage or organize. 7 continue, operate, or proceed. 8 function or cause to function. 9 pass into or reach a specified state or level: *inflation is running at 11 percent.* 10 (of a liquid) flow. 11 emit or exude a liquid. 12 (of dye or colour) dissolve and spread when wet. 13 stand as a candidate; enter or be entered as a competitor. 14 publish or be published in a newspaper or magazine. 15 be suffering from (a fever). 16 (esp. of the eyes or nose) exude liquid matter. 17 Computing a (of a computer or computer user) execute (a program or series of commands). b (often foll. by *under*) (of a computer program or system) operate within a specified environment. 18 navigate (rapids, a waterfall, etc.) in a boat. 19 transport in a car. 20 smuggle (goods). 21 (of stockings) develop a run. • noun 1 an act or instance of running. 2 a running pace. 3 a journey or route. 4 a short excursion in a car. 5 a course or track made or regularly used: *a ski run.* 6 a length, spell, or stretch of something: *a run of bad luck.* 7 an enclosed area in which animals may run freely in the open. 8 a rapid series of musical notes. 9 a sequence of cards of the same suit. 10 (**the run of**) free and unrestricted use of or access to. 11 Baseball a point scored by the batter returning to home plate after touching the bases. 12 a vertical strip of unravelled fabric in hosiery. 13 (**the runs**) informal diarrhea. 14 Cdn (Nfld & Maritimes) a narrow passage of water. 15 = BUFFALO RUN. PHRASES **at a run** running. **on the run** 1 escaping, running away. 2 hurrying about from place to place. **run across** 1 happen to meet. 2 (foll. by *to*) make a brief journey or a flying visit (to a place). **run after** 1 pursue with attentions; seek the society of. 2 give much time to (a pursuit etc.). 3 pursue at a run. **run along** informal depart. **run around** 1 bustle; hurry from one place to another. 2 deceive or evade repeatedly. 3 (often foll. by *with*) informal engage in sexual relations (esp. casually or illicitly). **run at** attack by charging or rushing. **run away** 1 get away by running; flee, abscond. 2 elope. 3 (of a child) leave the parental home. **run away with** 1 carry off (a person, stolen property, etc.). 2 win (a prize) easily. 3 leave home to have a relationship with. 4 deprive of self-control or common sense: *lets her ideas run away with her.* **run down** 1 knock down or collide with. 2 reduce the strength or numbers of (resources). 3 (of an unwound clock etc.) stop. 4 (of a person or a person's health) become feeble from overwork or undernourishment. 5 discover after a search. 6 disparage. **run dry** cease to flow, be exhausted. **run for it** seek safety by fleeing. **a run** (or **a good run**) **for one's money** 1 vigorous competition. 2 pleasure derived from an activity.

3 return for outlay or effort. **run afoul** (or **foul**) **of** act contrary to; go against. **run high 1** (of feelings) be strong. **2** (of the sea) have a strong current with a high tide. **run in 1** *informal* arrest. **2** incur (a debt). **run in the family** (of a trait) be common in the members of a family. **run into 1** collide with. **2** encounter. **3** reach as many as (a specified figure). **4** be continuous or coalesce with. **run into the ground** *informal* bring (a person) to exhaustion etc. **run its course** follow its natural progress; be left to itself. **run low** (or **short**) become depleted, have too little: *supplies ran low ◊ ran short of sugar*. **run off 1** flee. **2** produce (copies etc.) on a machine. **3** decide (a race or other contest) after a series of heats or in the event of a tie. **4** flow or cause to flow away. **5** write or recite fluently. **6** digress suddenly. **run off at the mouth** *informal* talk indiscreetly or incessantly. **run off one's feet** very busy. **run on 1** (of written characters) be joined together. **2** continue in operation. **3** elapse. **4** speak volubly. **5** talk incessantly. **run out 1** come to an end; become used up. **2** (foll. by *of*) exhaust one's stock of. **3** escape from a container. **4** (of rope) pass out; be paid out. **run out on** *informal* desert (a person). **run over 1** overflow. **2** study or repeat quickly. **3** (of a vehicle or its driver) pass over; knock down or crush. **4** touch (the keys of a piano etc.) in quick succession. **5** (often foll. by *to*) go quickly by a brief journey or for a flying visit. **run ragged** exhaust (a person). **run the show** *informal* dominate in an undertaking etc. **run through 1** examine or rehearse briefly. **2** peruse. **3** deal successively with. **4** consume (an estate etc.) by reckless or quick spending. **5** pass through by running. **6** pervade. **7** pierce with a sword etc. **run to 1** have the money or ability for. **2** reach (an amount or number). **3** (of a person) show a tendency to: *runs to fat*. **4 a** be enough for (some expense or undertaking). **b** have the resources or capacity for. **5** fall into (ruin). **run to earth** (or **to ground**) **1** *Hunting* chase to its lair. **2** discover after a long search. **run up 1** accumulate (a debt etc.) quickly. **2** build or make hurriedly. **3** raise (a flag). **4** grow quickly. **run up against** meet with (a difficulty or difficulties). **run wild 1** grow unchecked or untrained. **2** act or behave without any control or restraint. **run with 1** proceed with: *if she agrees to the idea we'll run with it*. **2** associate with: *runs with a rough crowd*.

runabout *noun* **1** a light car. **2** a small pleasure boat.

runaround *noun* deceit or evasion: *gave me the runaround*.

runaway • *adjective* **1** (of a person) having run away: *runaway children*. **2** (of an animal or vehicle) no longer under the control of its rider or owner: *a runaway freight train*. **3** happening very rapidly; out of control: *runaway inflation*. **4** happening very easily: *a runaway victory*. • *noun* **1** a person who has run away: *teenage runaways*. **2** an animal or vehicle that is running out of control. **3** an easy victory. **4** a fugitive.

rundown • *noun* **1** a reduction in numbers. **2** a detailed analysis. **3** *Baseball* a play in which usu. two fielders try to tag out a runner caught between bases. • *adjective* **1** decayed after prosperity. **2** enfeebled through overwork etc. **3** dilapidated.

rune *noun* any of the letters of the earliest Germanic alphabet used by Scandinavians and Anglo-Saxons from about the 3rd century and formed by modifying Roman or Greek characters to suit carving.

rung[1] *noun* **1** each of the horizontal supports of a ladder. **2** a strengthening crosspiece in the structure of a chair etc. **3** a level or rank in society, an organization, one's career, etc.

rung[2] *past participle of* RING[2].

runic *adjective* (of writing) using the letters of the earliest Germanic alphabet, used by Scandinavians and Anglo-Saxons from about the 3rd century: *runic inscriptions*. [Say RUNE ick]

run-in *noun* (*plural* **run-ins**) a quarrel.

runner *noun* **1** a person, horse, etc., that runs, esp. in a race or for fitness. **2 a** *Baseball* = BASERUNNER. **b** *Football* the ball carrier. **3** *Cdn & Irish* = RUNNING SHOE. **4 a** a creeping plant stem that can take root. **b** a twining plant. **5** each of the long pieces on the underside of a sleigh etc. that forms the contact in sliding. **6** a rod or groove or blade on which a thing slides. **7** a long narrow ornamental cloth or rug. **8 a** a messenger, collector, or agent for a bank, stockbroker, etc. **b** a messenger or agent for a bookmaker, drug dealer, etc. **9** (also **runner bean**) any of several cultivated climbing varieties of bean or their edible pods, esp. the scarlet runner bean, which has red flowers and long green pods. **10** a roller for moving a heavy article.

runner-up *noun* (*plural* **runners-up**) **1** the competitor or team taking second place. **2** a competitor or team that comes close to winning.

running • *noun* **1** the action of runners in a race etc. **2** management or operation: *the day-to-day running of the office ◊ the running costs for the car*. **3** an act or an instance of racing. • *adjective* **1** continuing on an essentially continuous basis though changing in detail: *a running joke ◊ have had a running battle with the neighbours about the fence*. **2** consecutive; one after another: *three days running*. **3** done with a run: *a running jump*. **4** (of water) flowing naturally or supplied to a building through pipes and taps. **5** (of a sore or part of the body) exuding liquid or pus. **PHRASES in** (or **out of**) **the running** (of a competitor) with a good (or poor) chance of winning. **make** (or **take up**) **the running** take the lead; set the pace. **take a running jump** *slang* used when angrily rejecting or disagreeing with someone: *not a good idea to tell your teacher to take a running jump*. **up and running** in operation.

running back *noun* *Football* a back whose main task is to run carrying the ball.

running dog *noun* a person who follows a political system unthinkingly: *refused to let the team play against any teams which he considered running dogs of capitalism*.

running mate *noun* **1** *US* a candidate for a supporting position in an election, esp. for the vice presidency. **2** a horse entered in a race in order to set the pace for another horse from the same stable.

running shoe *noun* any of various shoes having an upper made of cloth and a rubber or synthetic sole.

runny *adjective* (**runnier**, **runniest**) **1** tending to run or flow. **2** excessively fluid.

runoff *noun* **1** an amount of rainfall or melted snow that is carried off an area by streams and rivers. **2** the spring thaw. **3** an amount of water coming off a roof etc. **4** an additional competition, election, race, etc., after a tie.

run-of-the-mill *adjective* ordinary, undistinguished.

runt *noun* **1** a small pig, esp. the smallest in a litter. **2** a weakling; an undersized person.

run-through *noun* (*plural* **run-throughs**) **1** a rehearsal, usu. of a whole production, complete act, etc., with as few stops as possible. **2** a brief survey.

runty *adjective* small and weak.

run-up *noun* (*plural* **run-ups**) **1** (often foll. by *to*) the period preceding an important event. **2** *Golf* a low approach shot.

runway *noun* **1** a specially prepared surface along which aircraft take off and land. **2** a trail to an animals' watering hole. **3** an incline down which logs are slid. **4** a long raised platform in a theatre etc.

rupee *noun* the basic monetary unit of India, Pakistan, Sri Lanka, and several other countries. [Say roo PEE]

rupture • *noun* **1** a sudden and complete breaking or bursting: *the patient died after the rupture of an aneurysm.* **2** an ending of agreement or good relations between people: *the rupture with his father would never be healed.* **3** an abdominal hernia: *almost gave myself a rupture lifting it.* • *verb* (**ruptures, ruptured, rupturing**) **1** cause to break or burst suddenly: *a ruptured appendix* ◊ *the impact ruptured both fuel tanks.* **2** suffer the bursting of a bodily part. **3** undergo a rupture: *if the main artery ruptures, he could die.*

rural *adjective* **1** of, relating to, living in, or suggesting the country (*opp.* URBAN). **2** of or concerning agriculture. ▶ **rurally** *adverb*

rural municipality *noun* (*plural* **rural municipalities**) *Cdn* **1** *Prairies & Que.* a usu. sparsely populated municipality outside of urban municipalities that is administered by an elected council or the provincial government. Abbreviation: **RM.** **2** *NS* one of the 24 districts that contain incorporated cities and towns.

rural route *noun* a mail delivery route in an area outside of a town or city. Abbreviation: **RR.**

ruse *noun* a stratagem or trick. [Say ROOZ]

rush¹ • *verb* (**rushes, rushed, rushing**) **1** move or act with urgent haste. **2** transport or produce with urgent haste. **3** deal with hurriedly. **4** (of air or a liquid) flow strongly. **5** dash towards in an attempt to attack or capture. **6** *Hockey* bring the puck up the ice, esp. into the opposing team's zone. **7** *Football* move the ball forward by carrying it rather than by passing etc. **8** flow, fall, spread, or roll impetuously or fast: *the blood rushed to my face.* • *noun* (*plural* **rushes**) **1** an act or instance of rushing. **2 a** a period of great activity. **b** = RUSH HOUR. **3** (as an *adjective*) done with great haste or speed: *a rush job.* **4** *informal* a thrill or feeling of excitement. **5** (foll. by *on, for*) a sudden strong demand for a commodity. **6** (as an *adjective*) designating a seat at a performance purchased at a reduced price on the day of the performance, or a ticket purchased for such a seat: *a rush ticket.* **7** *Hockey* the action of bringing the puck up the ice. **8** *Football* the action of rushing the football. **9** a sudden migration of large numbers: *gold rush.*

rush² *noun* (*plural* **rushes**) **1** a marsh or waterside plant with inconspicuous greenish or brownish flowers and slender stem-like pith-filled leaves, used for making chair seats and baskets etc. **2** a stem of this plant. **3** rushes as a material.

rusher *noun* *Football* **1** an offensive player, usu. a running back or quarterback, who advances the ball by carrying it rather than by passing or receiving it: *the team's quarterback is their leading rusher.* **2** a defensive player whose role is to charge the quarterback and prevent him or her from throwing the football.

rush hour *noun* a time of day when traffic is at its heaviest.

russet • *adjective* reddish brown. • *noun* **1** a reddish-brown colour. **2** a kind of rough-skinned russet-coloured apple. **3** a variety of potato with a reddish skin.

Russian • *noun* **1 a** a native or national of Russia or the Russian Federation. **b** a person of Russian descent. **2** *hist.* a native or national of the former Soviet Union. **3** the official language of Russia and the former Soviet Union. • *adjective* **1** of Russia. **2** of or in Russian.

Russian doll *noun* a set of hollow and usu. decorated wooden doll figures of differing sizes, each one made so as to nest inside the next largest.

Russian Orthodox *adjective* having to do with the national Church of Russia (see ORTHODOX CHURCH).

Russian roulette *noun* **1** an act of daring in which one (usu. with others in turn) squeezes the trigger of a revolver held to one's head with one chamber loaded, having first spun the chamber. **2** a potentially dangerous enterprise: *unless you want to play Russian roulette, find an effective method of contraception.*

Russian thistle *noun* a prickly tumbleweed, native to Eurasia and accidentally introduced into North America, where it has become a pest.

Russo- *combining form* Russian; Russian and. [Say RUSS oh]

rust • *noun* **1** a reddish-brown or yellowish-brown coating formed on iron or steel by oxidation, esp. as a result of moisture. **2 a** any of various plant diseases with rust-coloured spots caused by fungi. **b** the fungus causing this. **3** an impaired state due to disuse or inactivity: *vowed to scrape the rust off the machinery of government.* **4** a reddish-brown or brownish-red colour. • *adjective* of a reddish-brown or brownish-red colour. • *verb* **1** affect or be affected with rust; undergo oxidation. **2** lose quality or efficiency by disuse or inactivity: *I've been sitting in this office rusting for years now.*

rust belt *noun* *informal* an area of once profitable heavy industry, esp. (**Rust Belt**) in the US Midwest and northeastern states.

rustbucket *noun* *informal* an old and rusty car, ship, etc.

rustic • *adjective* **1** having the characteristics of or associations with the country or country life. **2** unsophisticated, simple, unrefined. **3** constructed or made in a plain or simple fashion: *a rustic oak bench.* • *noun* a person from or living in the country, esp. a simple unsophisticated one.

rusticate *verb* (**rusticates, rusticated, rusticating**) go to, live in, or spend time in the country: *a place to rusticate while other people worked.*

rustle • *verb* (**rustles, rustled, rustling**) **1** make or cause to make a gentle sound as of dry leaves blown in a breeze. **2** (often foll. by *along* etc.) move with a rustling sound. **3** steal (cattle or horses). • *noun* a rustling sound or movement. PHRASES **rustle up** *informal* produce quickly when needed.

rustler *noun* a person who steals cattle or horses etc.

rustproof • *adjective* (of a metal) not susceptible to corrosion by rust. • *verb* make rustproof.

rusty *adjective* (**rustier, rustiest**) **1** rusted or affected by rust. **2** stiff with age or disuse. **3** (of knowledge etc.) faded or impaired by neglect: *my French is a bit rusty.* **4** rust-coloured. **5** looking or being antiquated. **6** (of a voice) croaking or creaking.

rut¹ • *noun* **1** a deep track made by the passage of wheels. **2** any groove, furrow, etc. **3** an established (esp. tedious) mode of practice or procedure. • *verb* (**ruts, rutted, rutting**) mark with ruts. PHRASES **in a rut** following a fixed (esp. tedious or dreary) pattern of behaviour that is difficult to change.

rut² • *noun* **1** the periodic sexual excitement or activity of a male deer, goat, ram, etc. **2** the period during which this happens. • *verb* (**ruts, rutted, rutting**) be affected with rut.

rutabaga *noun* (*plural* **rutabagas**) **1** a large, round, yellow-fleshed root that is eaten as a vegetable. **2** the plant of the cabbage family that produces this root. [Say ROOTA bay guh or ROOTA bag uh]

ruthenium *noun* a rare hard white metallic element, occurring in platinum ores, used as a chemical catalyst and in some alloys. [Say roo THEENY um]

rutherfordium *noun* a name variously proposed for the artificial radioactive elements of atomic number

104 and 106. [Say ruther FORDY um (RUTHER rhymes with *MOTHER*)]

ruthless *adjective* having no pity or compassion.
▶ **ruthlessly** *adverb* **ruthlessness** *noun*

RV *abbreviation* (*plural* **RVs**) RECREATIONAL VEHICLE.

R-value *noun* a measure of the insulating capability of a wall, building material, etc., with greater numbers indicating greater resistance to heat loss.

Rwandan • *adjective* a native or inhabitant of Rwanda, a country in central Africa. • *adjective* of or relating to Rwanda or its people. [Say roo ON dun]

Rx *abbreviation* **1** prescription. **2** (in prescriptions) take.

rye *noun* **1 a** a cereal plant with spikes bearing wheat-like grains. **b** the grain of this used for bread and fodder. **2** (also **rye whisky**) **a** a whisky blended from rye and other grains. **b** whisky distilled from fermented rye. **3** rye bread.

ryegrass *noun* (*plural* **ryegrasses**) a kind of grass that is a valuable fodder and lawn grass.

SPELL CHECK
rhyme, rhythm

Warning: **rhyme** and **rhythm** are spelled with an *h*.

R

Ss

S¹ *noun* (also **s**) (*plural* **Ss** or **S's**) **1** the nineteenth letter of the alphabet. **2** an S-shaped object or curve.

S² *abbreviation* (also **S.**) **1** small. **2 a** Saturday. **b** Sunday. **3** soprano. **4** South, Southern. **5** *Cdn* Senate. **6** Saint. **7** Society.

S³ *symbol Chemistry* **1** the element sulphur. **2** siemens.

s *abbreviation* (also **s.**) **1** second(s). **2** shilling(s). **3** singular. **4** son. **5** section.

Saanich *noun* (*plural* **Saanich**) **1** a member of a division of Straits people living on the Saanich Peninsula of Vancouver Island. **2** the dialect spoken by the Saanich. [Say SAN itch]

sabayon *noun* = ZABAGLIONE. [Say SAB eye yon]

Sabbath *noun* **1** a day of rest and worship kept by Jews and some Christians on Saturday. **2** a day of worship celebrated by most Christians on Sunday, in commemoration of Christ's resurrection.

sabbatical • *adjective* (of leave) granted at intervals to a professor or teacher for study or travel, originally every seventh year. • *noun* a period of sabbatical leave. [Say suh BAT ick ul]

saber *noun* esp. *US* = SABRE.

Sabine's gull *noun* an Arctic gull with a forked tail, dark grey head, and black and yellow bill. [Say SAB ine]

Sabin vaccine *noun* an oral vaccine giving immunity against polio. [Say SAY bin]

sable¹ *noun* **1** a small brown-furred flesh-eating mammal of northern Europe and parts of northern Asia, related to the marten. **2** its skin or fur.

sable² • *noun* **1** esp. *literary* black. **2** (also **sable antelope**) a large African antelope with long curved horns, the males of which are mostly black in old age. • *adjective* black: *a tall woman with long sable hair*.

sabotage • *noun* deliberate damage to or destruction of property, esp. in order to disrupt the production of goods or as a political or military act. • *verb* (**sabotages, sabotaged, sabotaging**) **1** commit sabotage on. **2** make useless: *sabotaged my plans*. [Say SABBA tawzh]

saboteur *noun* a person who sabotages. [Say sabba TUR]

sabre *noun* (also esp. *US* **saber**) **1** a cavalry sword with a curved blade. **2** a light fencing sword with a tapering blade.

sabre-rattling *noun* a display or threat of force.

sabre-toothed *adjective* designating any of various extinct mammals with long sabre-shaped upper canines.

sac *noun* **1** a bag-like cavity, enclosed by a membrane, in an animal or plant. **2** the distended membrane surrounding a hernia, cyst, tumour, etc.

saccharide *noun Chemistry* = SUGAR 2. [Say SACK a ride]

saccharin *noun* a very sweet substance, used as a substitute for sugar. [Say SACK a rin]

saccharine • *adjective* **1** sweet; sugary. **2** unpleasantly over-polite, sentimental, etc.: *horribly saccharine American sitcoms*. • *noun* something that is excessively sweet, sentimental, etc.: *contemporary commercial art styles ranging from heavy metal to birthday card saccharine*. [Say SACK a rin]

sachem *noun* the supreme chief of some North American Aboriginal peoples. [Say SAY chum]

sachet *noun* **1** a small perfumed bag or packet of potpourri used to scent clothes. **2** a small sealed bag or packet: *a sachet of sugar*. [Say sash AY]

sack¹ • *noun* **1 a** a large strong bag, esp. one made of heavy fabric, for storing or conveying goods. **b** this with its contents: *a sack of potatoes*. **2** (**the sack**) *informal* dismissal, esp. from employment. **3** (**the sack**) *slang* bed. **4** *Baseball* a base. **5** *Football* a tackle of a quarterback behind the line of scrimmage. **6** a woman's short loose dress with a sack-like appearance. **7** a man's or woman's loose-hanging coat not shaped to the back. • *verb* **1** *informal* dismiss esp. from employment. **2** *Football* tackle (the quarterback) behind the line of scrimmage before he is able to throw the ball. PHRASES **hit the sack** *informal* go to bed. **sack out** *informal* go to bed; go to sleep.

sack² • *verb* plunder and destroy (a captured town etc.): *the city was sacked and burned in 390 BC*. • *noun* the sacking of a captured place: *the sack of Rome*.

sackcloth *noun* **1** a coarse fabric, as of flax or hemp. **2** clothes of this, formerly worn as a penance or in mourning.

sacking *noun* material for making sacks; sackcloth.

sacral *adjective* **1** of or relating to the **sacrum**, a triangular bone situated between the two hip bones. **2** *Anthropology* of or for sacred rites. [Say SAKE rul]

sacrament *noun* **1** a religious ceremony or act of the Christian Churches regarded as an outward and visible sign of inward and spiritual grace, e.g. baptism, confirmation, or the Eucharist. **2** (also **the Blessed Sacrament**) the consecrated elements of the Eucharist, esp. the bread or Host. **3** a thing of mysterious and sacred significance: *there is evidence of the ritual consumption of peyote as a sacrament by some native North Americans*. [Say SACKRA m'nt]

sacramental • *adjective* constituting or having to do with a sacrament. • *noun* an observance that has a significance similar to that of the sacraments but which is not counted among the sacraments, e.g. the use of holy water or the sign of the cross. ▶ **sacramentally** *adverb* [Say sackra MENTAL]

sacred *adjective* **1 a** connected with a god or dedicated to a religious purpose and so made holy by association. **b** religious rather than secular: *sacred music*. **2** regarded with great respect or reverence by a particular religion, group, or individual: *the eagle is a very sacred bird*. **3** (of writings etc.) embodying the laws or doctrines of a religion. **4** regarded as too important or valuable to be interfered with; sacrosanct: *waterfront access is sacred in Vancouver: nobody violates it* ◊ *for many journalists, nothing is sacred*.

sacred cow *noun informal* an idea or institution unreasonably held to be above criticism: *even health care — one of this country's sacred cows — has been subjected to cutbacks*.

sacredness *noun* **1** the condition of being connected with a god or dedicated to a religious purpose; holiness. **2** the state of being regarded with great respect or reverence.

sacrifice • *noun* **1 a** the act of giving up something valued for the sake of something else more important or worthy. **b** a thing given up in this way. **c** the loss entailed in this. **2 a** the slaughter of an animal or person or the surrender of a possession as an offering to a deity. **b** an animal, person, or thing offered in this way. **3** an act of prayer, thanksgiving, or penitence performed to honour or appease a god. **4** *Christianity* **a** Christ's offering of himself in the Crucifixion. **b** the Eucharist regarded either as a symbolic offering of the body and blood of Christ or as an act of thanksgiving. **5** *Baseball* a play in which a batter deliberately hits the ball solely to advance a baserunner and is himself put out (usu. as an *adjective*: *sacrifice fly*). **6** (in games) a loss incurred deliberately to avoid a greater loss or to obtain a compensating advantage. • *verb* (**sacrifices**, **sacrificed**, **sacrificing**) **1** give up or offer as a sacrifice. **2** devote or give over to. **3** *Baseball* advance (a baserunner) by hitting a sacrifice fly, bunt, etc. ▶ **sacrificial** *adjective* [Say SACKRA fice, sackra FISH ul]

sacrificial lamb *noun* **1** a lamb offered as a religious sacrifice. **2** a person, principle, etc. sacrificed to achieve an end: *everyone seemed to know there was going to be a big war and that I was going to be the sacrificial lamb.*

sacrilege *noun* a violation or misuse of what is regarded as sacred or deserving great respect: *putting church vestments to secular use was considered sacrilege ◊ using anything but olive oil would be a sacrilege.* ▶ **sacrilegious** *adjective* **sacrilegiously** *adverb* [Say SACKRA lidge, sackra LIDGE us]

sacristy *noun* (*plural* **sacristies**) a room in a church where the vestments, sacred vessels, etc., are kept. [Say SACK riss tee]

sacrosanct *adjective* (of a person, place, law, etc.) most sacred; exempt from criticism etc.: *in the fashion world, major designers are a sacrosanct group.* [Say SACK roe sankt]

SAD *abbreviation* SEASONAL AFFECTIVE DISORDER.

sad *adjective* (**sadder**, **saddest**) **1** unhappy. **2** causing or suggesting sorrow: *a sad story.* **3** regrettable. **4** shameful, deplorable: *is in a sad state.* **5** *slang* contemptible, pathetic, unfashionable.

sadden *verb* make or become sad.

saddle • *noun* **1** a seat of leather etc., usu. raised at front and rear, fastened on a horse etc. for riding. **2** a seat for the rider of a bicycle etc. **3** a cut of meat consisting of the two loins. **4** a ridge rising to a summit

at each end. **5** a part of an animal's back resembling a saddle in shape or marking. • *verb* (**saddles**, **saddled**, **saddling**) **1** put a saddle on (a horse etc.). **2** burden (a person) with a task, responsibility, debt, etc. **3** (of a trainer) enter (a horse) for a race. PHRASES **in the saddle 1** mounted. **2** in office or control. **saddle up** put a saddle on (a horse) in preparation for riding.

saddleback *noun* **1** a thing, esp. a hill or ridge, with a concave upper outline. **2** any of various animals or birds with saddle-like markings on the back.

saddlebag *noun* **1** each of a pair of bags laid across a horse etc. behind the saddle. **2** a bag attached behind the saddle of a bicycle, motorcycle, snowmobile, etc. **3** (as an *adjective*) *Cdn hist.* designating a preacher, doctor, etc., who travelled from place to place to work.

saddle horn *noun* a pommel on a saddle.

saddle horse *noun* a horse for riding.

saddler *noun* a maker of or dealer in saddles and other equipment for horses.

saddlery *noun* (*plural* **saddleries**) the saddles, other equipment, or business premises of a saddler.

saddle shoe *noun* a two-tone oxford shoe with a band of leather in the second colour across the instep, originally popular in the 1950s.

saddle stitch • *noun* (*plural* **saddle stitches**) a stitch of thread or a wire staple passed through the centre of a magazine or booklet. • *verb* (**saddle-stitch**, **saddle-stitches**, **saddle-stitched**, **saddle-stitching**) bind (a booklet etc.) with saddle stitches. ▶ **saddle-stitched** *adjective* **saddle-stitching** *noun*

Sadducee *noun* a member of a Jewish sect or party of the time of Christ that denied the resurrection of the dead, the existence of spirits, and the obligation of the traditional oral law. [Say SAD yoo see]

sadhu *noun* (*plural* **sadhus**) (in India) a wise and holy man, esp. one who lives apart from people and society. [Say SAW doo]

sadism *noun* **1** a form of sexual perversion characterized by the enjoyment of inflicting pain or suffering on others. **2** *informal* the enjoyment of cruelty to others. ▶ **sadist** *noun* **sadistic** *adjective* **sadistically** *adverb* [Say SAY dism, SAY dist, suh DIS tick]

sadly *adverb* **1** showing or feeling sadness: *he smiled sadly as the store closed its doors for the last time.* **2** unfortunately: *sadly, I had to miss the party because I was sick.* **3** greatly, to a regrettable extent: *she will be sadly missed ◊ if you think I'm falling for that one, you're sadly mistaken.*

sadness *noun* a sad feeling or quality.

sado-masochism *noun* sexual gratification achieved through inflicting and receiving pain. ▶ **sado-masochist** *noun* **sado-masochistic** *adjective* [Say say doe MASSA kism, say doe massa KISS tick]

sad sack *noun* *informal* a very inept person.

safari *noun* (*plural* **safaris**) **1** a hunting or scientific expedition, esp. in East Africa: *go on safari.* **2** a sightseeing trip esp. to see African animals in their natural habitat.

safe • *adjective* (**safer**, **safest**) **1 a** free of danger or injury. **b** out of or not exposed to danger: *safe from their enemies.* **2** affording security or not involving danger or risk: *put it in a safe place.* **3 a** reliable, certain: *a safe investment ◊ a safe method.* **b** *Cdn & Brit.* (of a riding, seat in Parliament, etc.) usually won easily by a particular party. **4** prevented from escaping or doing harm: *safe behind bars.* **5** (also **safe and sound**) uninjured; with no harm done. **6 a** cautious and unenterprising; consistently moderate. **b** (of an action etc.) moderate, cautious, conservative: *a safe estimate.* **7** *Baseball* having reached a base without being put out: *safe at second.* **8 a** resistant to damage etc. by the specified object or

S

condition: *microwave-safe*. **b** not harmful to something specified: *child-safe*. • *noun* **1** a strong lockable cabinet etc. for valuables. **2** a cupboard etc. for storing food: *pie safe*. **3** (esp. *Cdn*) *slang* a condom. • *adverb informal* in a safe manner: *play safe*. PHRASES **on the safe side** with a margin of security against risks.

safe deposit *noun* = SAFETY DEPOSIT.

safeguard • *noun* a proviso etc. that tends to prevent something undesirable. • *verb* guard or protect (rights etc.) by a precaution or stipulation.

safe harbour *noun* **1** a harbour offering protection to ships. **2** any place or circumstance offering protection: *the law also provides a safe harbour that allows companies to make predictions about their business without being legally liable if those predictions don't come true*.

safe house *noun* a place of refuge or rendezvous for spies, criminals, police informants, etc.

safekeeping *noun* preservation in a safe place.

safely *adverb* **1** without being harmed, damaged, or susceptible to loss. **2** without much possibility of being wrong: *we can safely assume it won't rain today*. **3** without any possibility of the situation changing: *once she was safely in power, she was free to break her election promises*. **4** without any problems being caused; with no risk: *the recommendations can be safely ignored*.

safe sex *noun* (also **safer sex**) sexual activity in which precautions are taken to reduce the risk of spreading sexually transmitted diseases, esp. AIDS.

safety *noun* (*plural* **safeties**) **1** the condition of being safe; freedom from danger or risks. **2 a** any of various devices for preventing injury from machinery (also as an *adjective*: *safety feature*). **b** (as an *adjective*) designating items of protective clothing: *safety helmet*. **3** *Football* **a** a defensive back who plays in a deep position. **b** a play in which the offensive team moves the ball into its own end zone and either downs the ball or is tackled there or moves it out of bounds, resulting in two points being awarded to the defensive team. **c** the two points so awarded. **4** *Baseball* = BASE HIT. PHRASES **safety first** a motto advising caution.

safety belt *noun* **1** = SEAT BELT. **2** a belt or strap securing a person to prevent injury.

safety deposit *noun* (also **safe deposit**) a place in which valuables are stored: *safety deposit box*.

safety glass *noun* glass that will not splinter when broken.

safety glasses *plural noun* eyeglasses with reinforced lenses to protect the eyes.

safety net *noun* **1** a net placed to catch an acrobat etc. in case of a fall. **2** any means of protection against difficulty or loss: *the social safety net*.

safety pin • *noun* a pin with a point that is bent back to the head and is held in a guard when closed. • *verb* (**safety-pin, safety-pins, safety-pinned, safety-pinning**) fasten with a safety pin.

safety touch *noun* (*plural* **safety touches**) *Cdn Football* = SAFETY 3b.

safety valve *noun* **1** a valve opening automatically to relieve excessive pressure. **2** a means of giving harmless vent to excitement, energy, etc.

safflower *noun* an orange-flowered thistle-like plant, whose seeds yield an edible oil.

saffron • *noun* **1** an orange-yellow flavouring and food colouring made from the dried stigmas of the crocus. **2** the orange-yellow colour of this. • *adjective* of an orange-yellow colour.

sag • *verb* (**sags, sagged, sagging**) **1 a** sink or subside under weight or pressure, esp. unevenly. **b** droop, hang down loosely. **2** have a downward bulge or curve in the middle. **3** decline, weaken, diminish. **4** fall in price. • *noun* **1 a** the amount that a rope etc.

sags. **b** the distance from the middle of its curve to a straight line between its supports. **2** a sinking condition. **3** a fall in price.

saga *noun* **1** a long story of heroic achievement, esp. a medieval Icelandic or Norwegian prose narrative. **2** a series of connected books giving the history of a family etc. **3** a long involved story. [Say SAG uh or SAW guh]

sagacious *adjective* wise, esp. on practicalities: *a sagacious political aide*. ▶ **sagaciously** *adverb*

sagacity *noun* [Say suh GAY shuss, suh GASSA tee]

sagamore *noun* = SACHEM. [Say SAG a more]

sage[1] *noun* **1** an aromatic plant with dull greyish-green leaves that are used as a herb in cooking, e.g. in poultry stuffing. **2** *noun & adjective* (also **sage green**) the dull greyish-green colour of sage leaves.

sage[2] • *noun* a profoundly wise person: *the sages of Alexandria* ◊ *the network sages are considering cancelling the show*. • *adjective* (**sager, sagest**) having, showing, or indicating profound wisdom: *sage remarks* ◊ *sage advice*.

sagebrush *noun* **1** a shrubby aromatic plant of North America. **2** scrub that is dominated by such shrubs, occurring esp. in semi-arid regions of western North America.

sagely *adverb* in a way that shows great wisdom.

saggy *adjective* tending to sag.

Sagittarian *noun* a person born under the astrological sign of Sagittarius, between 22 Nov. and 21 Dec. [Say sadge a TERRY un]

Sagittarius *noun* **1** a large constellation, said to represent a centaur carrying a bow and arrow. **2 a** the ninth sign of the zodiac. **b** a person born when the sun is in this sign, usu. between Nov. 22 and Dec. 21. [Say sadge a TERRY us]

sago *noun* (*plural* **sagos**) **1** a kind of starch, made from the powdered pith of the sago palm and used in puddings etc. **2** (also **sago palm**) any of several palms and cycads from which sago is made, growing in freshwater swamps of Southeast Asia. [Say SAY go]

Saharan *adjective* of or relating to the Sahara Desert in North Africa. [Say suh HAIR un or suh HAR un]

sahib *noun* (*plural* **sahibs**) **1** (in India) a polite form of address, often placed after a person's name or title. **2** a gentleman: *they wore red saris when attending on the sahibs*. [Say SAW hib]

Sahtu Dene • *noun* (*plural* **Sahtu Dene**) **1** a member of a Dene people living near Great Bear Lake, NWT. **2** the Athapaskan language of this people. • *adjective* of or relating to this people or their culture or language. [Say saw too DEN ay]

said • *verb* past and past participle of SAY. • *adjective* (**the said**) the previously mentioned: *the said witness*.

SPELL CHECK   ABC✓
sail, sale

Something being sold is for **sale**.

---

sail • *noun* **1** a piece of material extended on rigging to catch the wind and propel a boat or ship. **2** a ship's sails collectively. **3** a voyage or excursion in a sailing ship. **4** a ship, esp. as discerned from its sails. **5** a wind-catching apparatus, usu. a set of boards, attached to the arm of a windmill. • *verb* **1** travel on water by the use of sails or engine power. **2 a** navigate (a ship etc.). **b** travel on (a sea). **3** glide or move smoothly or in a stately manner. **4** (often foll. by *through*) *informal* move or succeed easily: *sailed through the exams*. PHRASES **make sail** *Nautical* **1** spread a sail or sails. **2** start a voyage. **sail close to the wind 1** sail as nearly against the wind as possible. **2** come close to indecency or dishonesty; risk overstepping the mark: *as an author I've had a reputation*

for sailing close to the wind, but I don't think this new book is really offensive. **under sail** with sails set; sailing.

sailboard *noun* a board with a mast and sail, used in windsurfing. ▶ **sailboarder** *noun* **sailboarding** *noun*

sailboat *noun* a boat driven by sails.

sailcloth *noun* **1** canvas for sails. **2** a dress material like canvas.

sailer *noun* a sailing vessel, esp. one that sails in a specified way.

sailfish *noun* (*plural* **sailfish** or **sailfishes**) a kind of fish with a large dorsal fin that resembles a sail.

sailing ship *noun* (also **sailing craft**, **sailing vessel**, etc.) a vessel driven by sails.

sailor *noun* **1** a member of a ship's crew, esp. one below the rank of officer. **2** a person who sails for recreation. **3** a person considered as liable or not to be seasick: *a good sailor*.

sailplane *noun* a glider designed for sustained flight.

saint *noun* **1** a holy or (in some Churches) a canonized person regarded as having a place in heaven. **2** (**Saint** or **St.**) the title of a saint or archangel. **3** a very virtuous person; a person of great real or affected holiness. **4** a soul in heaven: *with all the angels and saints.* **5** (*Bible, archaic,* and used by Puritans, Mormons, etc.) one of God's chosen people; a member of the Christian Church or one's own branch of it.

St. Bernard *noun* a breed of very large dog originally kept to rescue travellers by the monks of the Hospice on the Great St. Bernard Pass in the Alps.

sainted *adjective* sacred; of a saintly life; worthy to be regarded as a saint: *the story of his sainted sister, Emily.*

sainthood *noun* the state of being a saint.

St. James Street *noun* *Cdn* **1** a street in Montreal where the offices of many financial institutions are located. **2** the moneyed interests of Montreal, esp. as opposed to other regions of Canada.

Saint-Jean-Baptiste Day *noun* *Cdn* (in Quebec) the former official name (still commonly in use) for the Fête nationale, June 24. [Say san zhon ba TEEST]

saintliness *noun* a very holy or virtuous manner or behaviour.

saintly *adjective* (**saintlier**, **saintliest**) very holy or virtuous; befitting a saint.

St. Patrick's Day *noun* March 17, the feast day of St. Patrick, on which Irish heritage is celebrated.

saint's day *noun* (*plural* **saints' days**) a Church festival in memory of a saint.

sake[1] *noun* (esp. **for the sake of** or **for one's sake**) **1** out of consideration for; in the interest of; because of; owing to: *for my own sake as well as yours.* **2** in order to please, honour, get, or keep: *for the sake of uniformity.* ▪ PHRASES **for Christ's** (or **God's** or **goodness'** or **Heaven's** or **Pete's** etc.) **sake** an expression of urgency, impatience, supplication, anger, etc. **for old times' sake** in memory of former times.

sake[2] *noun* a Japanese alcoholic drink made from fermented rice. [Say SACKY or SOCKY]

salaam • *noun* **1** (in Muslim countries and India) the greeting "Peace". **2** a low bow of the head and body with the right palm on the forehead used with or without this greeting. • *verb* make a salaam. [Say suh LOM]

salable esp. *US* = SALEABLE.

salacious *adjective* **1** lustful; lecherous: *the magazine caters to millions of salacious male readers.* **2** (of writings, pictures, talk, etc.) tending to cause sexual desire: *an exchange of salacious e-mails.* ▶ **salaciously** *adverb* **salaciousness** *noun* [Say suh LAY shuss]

salad *noun* **1** a cold dish of various mixtures of raw or cooked vegetables, esp. lettuce, tomatoes, etc., or pasta,

sometimes combined with meat or cheese, and usu. seasoned with oil and vinegar or other dressing. **2** a mixture of fish, meat, etc. with mayonnaise and other seasonings, often as a sandwich filling: *egg salad.* **3** a vegetable or herb suitable for eating raw, e.g. lettuce.

salad days *plural noun* a period of youthful inexperience: *judging by their growing list of impressive clients, the company's salad days may be over.*

salal *noun* a shrub of western North America, with pink or white flowers and edible purple-black berries. [Say suh LAL]

salamander *noun* **1** a tailed scaleless newt-like amphibian, usu. with bright markings. **2** a mythical lizard-like creature thought able to endure fire. **3** an elemental spirit living in fire. [Say SAL a mander]

salami *noun* (*plural* **salamis**) a highly seasoned dried sausage often flavoured with garlic.

salaried *adjective* receiving a salary instead of a wage: *white-collar salaried employees* ◊ *salaried positions.*

salary *noun* (*plural* **salaries**) a fixed regular payment made by an employer to an employee, esp. payment made for professional or non-manual work, usu. expressed as an annual sum: *a $35,000 salary.*

salbutamol *noun* a drug used to widen the bronchi in the treatment of asthma. [Say sal BYOOT a maul]

Salchow *noun* *Figure Skating* a jump from the backward inside edge of one skate to the backward outside edge of the other, with a full turn in the air. [Say SOW cow (SOW rhymes with COW)]

> **SPELL CHECK** [ABC✓]
> **sale, sail**
>
> The wind-catching sheet on a boat is a **sail**.

sale *noun* **1** the exchange of a commodity for money etc.; the action of selling: *the sale of the house.* **2** the amount sold: *the sales were enormous.* **3** (in *plural*) the branch of a company etc. concerned with the selling of goods: *sales staff* ◊ *director of sales.* **4** an offering of goods or services at reduced prices for a period, e.g. at the end of a season etc. **5 a** an event at which goods are sold. **b** a public auction. ▪ PHRASES **for sale** offered for purchase. **on sale** for sale, esp. at a reduced price.

saleable *adjective* fit to be sold.

salesman *noun* (*plural* **salesmen**) a man employed to sell goods or services in a store etc. or as an agent between the producer and retailer; a sales representative.

salesmanship *noun* **1** skill in selling. **2** selling techniques.

salesperson *noun* (*plural* **salespeople** or **salespersons**) a salesman or saleswoman.

sales pitch *noun* (*plural* **sales pitches**) an argument used to persuade someone, esp. to buy something.

sales representative *noun* (also *informal* **sales rep**) a person who represents a business to prospective customers and solicits orders.

sales talk *noun* persuasive talk to promote the sale of goods or the acceptance of an idea etc.

sales tax *noun* a tax on sales or on the receipts from sales, added to the cost of a purchase.

saleswoman *noun* (*plural* **saleswomen**) a woman employed to sell goods or services in a store etc. or as an agent between the producer and retailer.

salicylate *noun* a salt or ester of salicylic acid. [Say suh LISSA late]

salicylic acid *noun* a bitter chemical used as a fungicide and in the production of acetylsalicylic acid and dyes. [Say sal a SILL ick]

salience *noun* great importance or prominence: *with*

S

the onset of puberty, the father archetype begins to lose its salience. [Say SAY lee ince]

salient • adjective **1** most important or notable: the salient features. **2** (of an angle etc.) pointing outwards (opp. RE-ENTRANT adjective 1). • noun **1** a salient angle or part of a work in fortification. **2** an outward bulge in a line of military attack or defence. [Say SAY leent]

saline • adjective containing salt or salts. • noun (also **saline solution**) a solution of salt in water. ▶ **salinity** noun [Say SAY leen, suh LINNA tee]

Salisbury steak noun a patty of minced beef mixed with milk, bread crumbs, and seasoning, and cooked. [Say SAWLZ bur ee]

Salish noun (plural **Salish**) = SNE NAY MUXW. [Say SAL ish]

Salishan • noun an Aboriginal language group of the west coast of North America, including Comox, Halkomelem, Lillooet, Nuxalk, Okanagan, Sechelt, Shuswap, Squamish, Straits, and Nlaka'pamux. • adjective of or relating to this language group. [Say SAL ish un]

saliva noun liquid secreted into the mouth by glands to provide moisture and facilitate chewing and swallowing; spittle. ▶ **salivary** adjective [For salivary say SAL iv airy]

salivate verb (**salivates**, **salivated**, **salivating**) secrete or discharge saliva esp. in excess or in anticipation. [Say SAL iv ate]

sallow adjective (**sallower**, **sallowest**) (of the skin) of a sickly yellow or pale brown. ▶ **sallowness** noun

Sally noun informal (usu. as **the Sally**) the Salvation Army.

sally • noun (plural **sallies**) **1 a** a lively remark esp. by way of attack upon a person or thing or of a diversion in argument: responds to the egg-tossing with a verbal sally. **b** a sudden charge from a fortification upon its besiegers: the forces in the cluster of fortresses were depleted by the desperate sallies from the gate. **2** an excursion: her energetic sallies into the fields during harvesting. • verb (**sallies**, **sallied**, **sallying**) **1** go for a walk, set out on a journey, etc.: the men sally out on stage as girls. **2** (usu. foll. by out) make a military sally: a base from which to sally out to observe or clobber foe.

Sally Ann noun Cdn & Brit. informal (usu. as **the Sally Ann**) the Salvation Army.

salmon • noun (plural **salmon** or (esp. of types) **salmons**) **1** a large, edible food and sport fish that is much prized for its pink flesh. **2** any of various similar but unrelated fishes. **3** (also **salmon pink**) the colour of salmon flesh, usu. pink with a tinge of orange. • adjective (also **salmon pink**) of the colour of salmon.

salmonberry noun (plural **salmonberries**) **1** any of several pink- or orange-fruited North American brambles, esp. the pink-flowered variety found on the west coast. **2** the fruit of such a shrub.

salmonella noun (plural **salmonellae** or **salmonellas**) **1** a bacterium comprising rod-shaped forms, some of which cause food poisoning and typhoid in people and various diseases in animals. **2** food poisoning caused by this. [Say salma NELLA for the singular, salma NELLY or salma NELLAS for the plural]

salmonid • adjective of or relating to the family that includes salmon and trout. • noun a fish of this family. [Say SALMA nid]

salmon trout noun a lake trout or Dolly Varden trout.

salon noun **1** a boutique or parlour specializing in fashionable products such as clothes, or services such as hairdressing. **2** the reception room of a mansion or large house. **3 a** an exhibition of painting, sculpture, books, etc. **b** (**Salon**) an annual exhibition in Paris of the work of living artists. **4** a gathering of intellectuals etc. hosted by a celebrity or socialite.

saloon noun **1** hist. a bar found esp. in mining, logging, and ranching communities of the Old West, often associated with heavy drinking, gambling, prostitution, and fighting. **2** a bar or tavern, esp. one modelled after a saloon of the Old West.

salsa noun (plural **salsas**) **1** a Latin American spicy sauce made with tomatoes and chilies etc. and used usu. as a dip or garnish. **2 a** a kind of dance music of Latin American origin, incorporating jazz and rock elements. **b** a dance performed to this. [Say SAWL suh]

salsa verde noun **1** an Italian sauce made with olive oil, garlic, capers, anchovies, vinegar or lemon juice, and a large quantity of chopped parsley, usu. served with fish. **2** a Mexican sauce of finely chopped onion, garlic, coriander, parsley, and hot peppers. [Say sal suh VAIR day]

SALT abbreviation Strategic Arms Limitation Talks (or Treaty).

salt • noun **1 a** a substance, sodium chloride, found esp. in water or as a reddish brown mineral. **b** this substance, esp. in a white, granular form, used esp. for seasoning and preserving food. **c** = ROAD SALT. **2** a chemical compound formed from the reaction of an acid with a base, with all or part of the hydrogen of the acid replaced by a metal or metal-like radical. **3** (often in plural) a substance resembling common salt, used esp. as a medicine or cosmetic: bath salts. **4** an experienced sailor. • adjective **1** containing or tasting of salt: salt air. **2** (of beef, fish, etc.) treated, cured, or preserved with salt: salt cod. **3** (of a plant) growing in the sea or in salt marshes. • verb **1** cure or preserve (meat or fish etc.) with salt or brine. **2** season with salt. **3** sprinkle with salt, esp. in order to melt snow or ice. **4 a** make (a geological sample etc.) appear to be more valuable a source than it is by depositing extraneous ore etc. in it. **b** fraudulently increase the figures represented in (the books, accounts, etc.). PHRASES **salt away** informal save or stash (money, information, etc.) for the future. **the salt of the earth 1** a person or people of great worthiness, reliability, honesty, etc. **2** those people whose qualities are a model for the rest. **take with a grain** (or **pinch**) **of salt** be justifiably skeptical of; believe only in part. **worth one's salt** deserving what one earns; capable.

salt and pepper adjective having dark and light (esp. grey) colours interspersed.

saltbox • adjective designating a house etc. with two storeys at the front and one at the back, having a steep pitched roof sloping towards the back. • noun (plural **saltboxes**) a saltbox house.

saltcellar noun a small container for holding salt.

saltchuck noun (BC, Alaska, & US Northwest) informal the ocean, or an inlet, canal, or bay, etc. of salt water.

Salteaux (plural **Salteaux**) = SAULTEAUX. [Say SO toe]

salted adjective seasoned, treated, or preserved with salt.

salter noun esp. Cdn a truck which dispenses salt on roads to melt snow and ice.

salt fish noun preserved cod that has been split, salted, and dried.

saltie noun Cdn informal an ocean-going ship.

saltine noun a salted cracker. [Say sawl TEEN]

saltiness noun **1** the quality of something that has the flavour or smell of salt. **2** the quality of language or humour that is coarse or rude.

salting noun **1 a** the action of applying salt as a seasoning. **b** the process of covering meat, fish, etc. in salt or soaking it in brine in order to preserve it. **2** (esp. in plural) a salt marsh.

salt lick noun **1** a place where animals go to lick naturally occurring salt from the ground. **2** a block of

salt or a preparation of salt given to domestic horses and cattle etc. to lick.

salt marsh *noun* (also **saltwater marsh**) a marsh that has been flooded by the tide, sometimes used as a pasture or for collecting water for making salt.

saltpetre *noun* potassium nitrate, a white crystalline salty substance used esp. in manufacturing gunpowder and wrongly believed to curb sexual desire. [Say salt PETER]

salt pork *noun* cured pork fat, highly salted.

salt water • *noun* **1** water with a high concentration of salt, esp. sea water. **2** the ocean, sea, etc. • *adjective* (usu. **saltwater**) **1** of, pertaining to, or consisting of salt water. **2** living in or by a body of salt water.

saltwater taffy *noun* a candy made by boiling sugar or molasses and butter in sea water or salted fresh water.

salty *adjective* (**saltier**, **saltiest**) **1** tasting of, containing, or preserved with salt. **2 a** (of humour etc.) racy, risqué. **b** (of language) coarse, vulgar.

salubrious *adjective* **1** favourable to good health: *the regular entertainment had a salubrious effect on the troops* ◊ *she enjoyed the clean air and salubrious mineral springs*. **2** pleasant; agreeable: *many of what are now gentrified and salubrious areas were overcrowded, dank dark slums only 50 years ago*. [Say suh LOOB ree us]

salutary *adjective* producing good effects: *a review process open to the public and the press would be salutary because it would generate crucial information to help root out environmental boondoggles*. [Say SAL yoo terry]

salutation *noun* **1** a sign or expression of greeting or recognition of another's arrival or departure: *no one returned our salutations*. **2** the initial words of a letter used to address the person being written to, e.g. "Dear Sir". **3** a gesture of respect: *he raised his glass in salutation*. [Say sal yoo TAY sh'n]

salute • *noun* **1** a gesture of respect, courteous recognition, or solidarity, esp. when arriving or departing. **2** *Military & Nautical* a prescribed or specified movement of the hand, weapons, or flags as a sign of respect or recognition. **3** the discharge of a gun or guns as a formal or ceremonial sign of respect or celebration. **4** a tribute or testimonial (to). • *verb* (**salutes**, **saluted**, **saluting**) **1 a** make a salute to. **b** (often foll. by *to*) perform a salute. **2** (foll. by *with*) receive or greet with (a smile, handshake, etc.). PHRASES **in salute** as a form of salute: *we raised our glass in salute*.

Salvadoran (also **Salvadorean**) • *adjective* of or relating to El Salvador, a republic in Central America. • *noun* a native or national of El Salvador. [Say salva DOOR un, salva DOOR ee un]

salvage • *verb* (**salvages**, **salvaged**, **salvaging**) **1** save or recover (materials) from a shipwreck, fire, etc. **2** recover, save, or preserve (something) from the brink of loss or ruin: *tried to salvage their marriage*. • *noun* **1** the rescue of a ship, its cargo, or other property from loss at sea, destruction by fire, etc. **2** the retrieval or saving of waste materials for recycling. **3** property or materials that have been salvaged. ▶ **salvageable** *adjective* **salvager** *noun*

salvation *noun* **1** the act of saving or being saved. **2** preservation from destruction, harm, etc. **3** the saving of the soul through deliverance from sin and its consequences. **4** a person or thing that saves: *her policies were the salvation of the country's economy*.

Salvation Army *noun* an international evangelical organization with a military structure, which assists the poor and homeless.

salvationism *noun* **1** (**Salvationism**) the principles or methods of the Salvation Army. **2** a religious teaching laying particular stress on individual

salvation. ▶ **salvationist** *noun & adjective* (also **Salvationist**)

salve • *noun* **1** a healing ointment. **2** a thing that soothes (hurt feelings, an uneasy conscience, etc.): *an hour in the department store was the perfect salve for my wounded ego*. • *verb* (**salves**, **salved**, **salving**) soothe or calm (pride, conscience, etc.): *some even salve their conscience about the hungry and hopeless by saying they contribute by buying charity sweepstakes tickets*. [Say SALV]

salver *noun* a tray usu. of silver or other metal, on which drinks, letters, etc. are presented. [Say SAL vur]

salvia *noun* (*plural* **salvias**) a plant of the mint family with red or blue flowers. [Say SAL vee uh]

salvo *noun* (*plural* **salvoes** or **salvos**) **1** the simultaneous or concentrated discharge of artillery or other weapons in battle or as a salute. **2** a sudden vigorous or aggressive act or series of acts: *it was the latest salvo in a bitter political battle that could influence US justice for years to come*. [Say SAL vo]

SAM *abbreviation* (*plural* **SAMs**) surface-to-air missile.

samara *noun* (*plural* **samaras**) the wing-like structure containing the seeds of a maple tree etc. [Say SAMMER uh]

Samaritan • *noun* **1** (also **good Samaritan**) a charitable or helpful person. **2** a native of Samaria in western Jordan. • *adjective* of Samaria or the Samaritans. [Say suh MARE a tun]

samarium *noun* a soft silvery metallic element, used in making alloys. [Say suh MERRY um]

Sama-Veda *noun* an ancient collection of sacred Hindu hymns and incantations, traditionally called the third Veda but originating outside Vedic society. [Say samma VAY duh]

samba • *noun* (*plural* **sambas**) **1** a rhythmically complex Brazilian dance of African folk origin. **2** a related ballroom dance of moderate tempo. **3** the music for this. • *verb* (**sambas**, **sambaed** or **samba'd**, **sambaing**) dance the samba. [Say SAM buh]

sambuca *noun* (*plural* **sambucas**) an Italian aniseed-flavoured liqueur traditionally served aflame with a coffee bean floating on them. [Say sam BOOK uh]

same • *adjective* **1** (often as **the same**) not different. **2** unvarying: *always serves the same dish*. **3** (of a person or thing) previously alluded to: *this same medical student went on to become a doctor*. • *pronoun* (**the same**) the same person or thing. • *adverb* (usu. as **the same**) similarly; in the same way: *I hope you feel the same*. PHRASES **all** (or **just**) **the same** nevertheless; anyway. **at the same time 1** simultaneously. **2** notwithstanding. **be all** (or **just**) **the same to** be a matter of indifference, or of little importance or interest: *if it's all the same to you, I'd rather go out*. **same difference** *informal* no difference, the same thing. **same here** *informal* the same applies to me. **the same to you!** may you do, have, find, etc., the same thing; likewise. **the very same** emphatically the same.

same-day *adjective* **1** designating a service provided on the day of purchase etc. **2** occurring on the same day as another related event: *a same-day news conference*.

sameness *noun* the quality of being the same; a lack of variety.

same-sex *adjective* designating or pertaining to a sexual relationship in which both partners are of the same sex: *same-sex couple*.

Sami • *noun* the Lapps collectively. • *adjective* of or relating to the Lapps. [Say SOMMY]

Samoan • *adjective* of or relating to Samoa, a group of islands in Polynesia. • *noun* a native or inhabitant of Samoa. [Say suh MOE un]

samosa *noun* (*plural* **samosas**) an Indian snack consisting of a triangular pastry stuffed with a spicy

mixture of diced vegetables or meat, fried in ghee or oil. [Say suh MOE suh]

samovar noun a metal, usu. ornate, Russian urn for making tea, with an internal heating tube to keep water at boiling point. [Say SAMMA varr]

Samoyed noun a breed of white dog, once used for working in the Arctic, having a thick shaggy coat, stocky build, pricked ears, and a tail curling over the back. [Say SAMMA yed]

sampan noun a small boat or skiff with a flat bottom usu. propelled by a scull or oars set in the stern, used along the coasts and rivers of the Far East. [Say SAM pan]

sample • noun **1** a small part or quantity intended to show what the whole is like. **2** a small amount of a product given usu. free of charge to prospective customers. **3** a specimen, esp. one taken for scientific testing or analysis: a blood sample. **4** Statistics a portion selected from a population, the study of which is intended to provide statistical estimates relating to the whole. **5** a unit of sound or piece of music that has been digitalized. **6** an illustrative or typical example: provide a writing sample. • verb (**samples, sampled, sampling**) **1** try or examine (something) by experiencing it or taking a sample: sample our down-home cooking. **2 a** ascertain the momentary value of (an analog signal) many times a second so that these values may be represented digitally; convert (an analog signal) to a digital one. **b** record (sound) digitally for subsequent electronic processing.

sampler noun **1** a piece of embroidery sewn in various stitches as a demonstration of skill, usu. containing the alphabet or mottos and often displayed on a wall. **2** an electronic device used to digitalize analog sound or music. **3** a collection of representative items etc. **4** a device for obtaining samples for scientific study.

sampling noun **1** the action or process of testing the quality of something from a sample or samples. **2** a representative selection of items: a sampling of Italian dishes. **3** the technique or process of digitally encoding analog sound and reusing it as part of a composition or recording.

samurai noun (plural **samurai**) **1** (in feudal Japan) a member of a military caste. **2** a Japanese army officer. [Say SAM uh rye]

San • noun (plural **San**) **1** a member of the aboriginal Bushmen of southern Africa. **2 a** the group of Khoisan languages spoken by the San. **b** any of these languages. • adjective of the San or their languages. [Sounds like SAWN]

sanatorium noun (plural **sanatoriums** or **sanatoria**) an establishment for the treatment of convalescents and those suffering chronic mental or physical disorders, tuberculosis, etc. [Say sanna TORY um]

sanctification noun **1** the process of making or becoming holy or free from sin. **2** the process of making something seem right, good, or legitimate: the sanctification of the market principle. [Say sank tiffa KAY sh'n]

sanctify verb (**sanctifies, sanctified, sanctifying**) **1** consecrate; make holy. **2** purify or free from sin. **3** give a person or thing the appearance of being right or good; legitimize: I don't know why we have this need in our culture to sanctify the role of the writer. [Say SANK tif eye]

sanctimonious adjective pretending piety, sanctity, or holiness; hypocrisy: sanctimonious corporate jargon about "our employees being our most valuable resource". ▶ **sanctimoniously** adverb **sanctimoniousness** noun **sanctimony** noun [Say sankta MOANY us, SANKTA moany]

sanction • noun **1** approval or encouragement granted for a particular action. **2** the action of making something legally binding; official ratification. **3** (esp. in plural) military or esp. economic action by a country to coerce another to conform to an international agreement or norms of conduct. **4** a penalty or reward enacted to enforce obedience to a law or rule. • verb authorize, ratify, or agree to (an action etc.).

sanctity noun **1** the state or quality of being holy, sacred, or saintly: a life of sanctity, like that of St Francis. **2** the quality of something considered too important to subject to dishonour or to violate: an intrusion into the sanctity of our homes. [Say SANKTA tee]

sanctuary noun (plural **sanctuaries**) **1** a holy place such as a church or temple etc. **2 a** esp. Jewish Hist. the inmost recess or holiest part of a temple etc.; the holy of holies. **b** the part of a church containing the altar. **3** a place where birds, wild animals, etc., are bred and protected. **4** a place of refuge, esp. a church or sacred building. **5** immunity from arrest. PHRASES **take sanctuary** resort to a place of refuge.

sanctum noun (plural **sanctums, sancta**) **1** a holy place: from the vessel of ashes placed in the sanctum's doorway, he smeared a pinch onto his forehead. **2** informal a person's private room, or den: Sheppard worked out of a sanctum behind a large outer room.

Sanctus noun (plural **Sanctuses**) **1** a prayer praising the glory and power of God, beginning "Holy, holy, holy", said or sung during some Christian liturgies. **2** a musical setting of this.

sand • noun **1** a loose granular substance resulting from the weathering of rocks, found on beaches, deserts, etc. **2** (in plural) an area predominantly of sand. **3** a light yellow-brown colour like that of sand. • verb **1** smooth or grind by rubbing with sandpaper. **2** sprinkle or cover with, or bury under, sand. PHRASES **sand down** sand (a usu. painted surface) down to the bare wood etc. **sands of time** the moments or passage of time. **the sands are running out** the allotted time is nearly at an end.

sandal noun a light open shoe consisting of a sole with light straps, worn esp. in warm weather.

sandalwood noun the scented wood of a widely cultivated Indian tree that yields fragrant oil and timber used esp. in carving and incense.

sandbag • noun a bag filled with sand, esp.: **1** stacked with others to make temporary fortifications for the defence of a military camp against enemy fire. **2** used to protect buildings etc. against flood waters, heavy winds, etc. **3** used as a weapon to inflict a heavy blow without leaving a mark. **4** used as ballast esp. for a boat or balloon. • verb (**sandbags, sandbagged, sandbagging**) **1 a** place sandbags around or against (a building, river, etc.) in order to fortify it. **b** build protective dikes with sandbags. **2** knock down with a blow from a sandbag. **3** informal coerce by harsh means; bully: each will try to sandbag the Liberals into adopting its policies. **4** informal lull (an opponent) into overconfidence by downplaying one's chances or abilities. ▶ **sandbagger** noun

sandbank noun a deposit of sand formed in shallow water by the action of tides and currents.

sandbar noun a large bank of sand forming in a river or sea, often exposed at low tide.

sandblast verb roughen, treat, or clean with a jet of sand driven by compressed air or steam.

sandbox noun (plural **sandboxes**) **1** a shallow pile of sand enclosed on four sides for children to play in. **2** (as an adjective) jocular designating juvenile behaviour or an attitude characteristic of a child at play: sandbox diplomacy.

sandcastle noun a shape like a castle made in sand, usu. by a child on a beach.

sandcherry noun (plural **sandcherries**) any of several

shrubby wild cherries of North America, purple-leaved varieties of which are often cultivated in gardens.

sand dollar *noun* a flattened sea urchin that lives partly buried in sand.

sand dune *noun* a shifting mound or ridge of sand formed by the wind.

sand eel *noun* = SAND LANCE.

sander *noun* **1** a power tool using sandpaper to smooth surfaces, remove layers of paint, etc. **2** a vehicle that sprinkles sand on icy streets and highways.

sanderling *noun* a small wading bird of the sandpiper family.

sandfly *noun* (*plural* **sandflies**) **1** a blackfly. **2** a small hairy biting fly that transmits a number of diseases.

S&H *abbreviation* shipping and handling.

sandhill *noun* a hill of sand, esp. a dune on a shore.

sandhill crane *noun* a grey North American crane with a bare reddish patch on the forehead.

sand lance *noun* (also **sand launce**) a small elongated eel-like fish that lives in shallow waters of the northern hemisphere and is often found burrowing in the sand.

sandlot *noun* a small plot of unoccupied land used by children for games and sports.

S&M *abbreviation* sexual gratification achieved through inflicting and receiving pain; sadism and masochism or sado-masochism.

sandman *noun* a make-believe figure that is supposed to make children sleep by sprinkling sand or sleep in their eyes; a personification of tiredness.

sandpaper • *noun* strong paper coated with sand or another abrasive, used for smoothing or roughening up a surface. • *verb* smooth or grind by rubbing with sandpaper. ▶ **sandpapery** *adjective*

sandpiper *noun* a wading bird with a long bill and long legs.

sandpit *noun* a pit from which sand is or has been excavated.

sandstone *noun* **1** any of various sedimentary rocks of consolidated grains of sand, esp. of quartz, red, yellow, brown, grey, or white in colour. **2** any rock composed of clearly visible broken pieces of older rocks.

sandstorm *noun* a storm, esp. in a desert, of wind with clouds of sand.

sand trap *noun* a shallow pit of fine sand serving as an obstacle or hazard on a golf course.

sandwich • *noun* (*plural* **sandwiches**) **1** two or more slices of usu. buttered bread with a filling. **2** anything resembling a sandwich in composition or appearance: *an ice cream sandwich.* • *verb* (**sandwiches**, **sandwiched**, **sandwiching**) **1** place or insert (a thing) between two dissimilar ones. **2** squeeze in between others. **3** trap or crush (an opposing player) between oneself and a teammate, the boards, etc. [Say SAND witch or SAN witch or SAM witch]

sandwich board *noun* **1** a pair of signs, usu. bearing advertisements, joined at the top by straps and suspended from the shoulders so that one sign is displayed over the front of the wearer, the other over the back. **2** a similar pair of signs joined at the top and forming a tent so that they may be free-standing.

sandwich generation *noun* the generation of adults in their late 20s or early 30s trying to raise children while also having to care for aged parents.

sandy *adjective* (**sandier**, **sandiest**) **1** composed of or containing a large proportion of sand. **2** having the texture of sand. **3 a** (of hair) light reddish-blond. **b** (of a person) having sandy hair.

sane *adjective* (**saner**, **sanest**) **1** of sound mind; not

mad. **2** (of views etc.) sensible, reasonable; moderate. ▶ **sanely** *adverb*

sang *past of* SING.

sang-froid *noun* coolness of mind or action, esp. in the face of danger or adversity: *with complete sang-froid she ignored the snake and walked right by.* [Say sang FRWAH]

sangria *noun* a drink of esp. red wine with sugar, fruit juice, sliced citrus fruit, and usu. soda. [Say san GREE uh]

sanguine *adjective* **1** optimistic; confident: *Evelyn's counsel was not as sanguine as his client during the hours in court.* **2** (in medieval science and medicine) of or having the constitution associated with the predominance of blood among the bodily humours, supposedly marked by a ruddy complexion and a courageous, amorous disposition. [Say SANG gwin]

sanitarium *noun* = SANATORIUM. [Say sanna TERRY um]

sanitary *adjective* **1** of or pertaining to the conditions affecting health, the promotion of good health, or protection against infection. **2** hygienic; free from or designed to kill or prevent germs, infection, etc.

sanitary pad *noun* (also **sanitary napkin**) an absorbent pad worn during menstruation.

sanitation *noun* **1** systems designed to protect or promote health. **2** the maintenance or improving of these. **3** the disposal of sewage and garbage.

sanitize *verb* (**sanitizes**, **sanitized**, **sanitizing**) **1** make (something) hygienic or thoroughly free from germs. **2** make (information etc.) more acceptable by removing indecent or disturbing material: *Lowry is presenting a carefully edited and sanitized version of these details.* ▶ **sanitizer** *noun*

sanity *noun* **1 a** the state of being sane. **b** mental health. **2** reasonableness, moderation.

sank *past of* SINK.

sans *preposition* *jocular* without a: *I tried to start the car, which had sat outside sans block heater.* [Say SONZ]

sans-culotte *noun* *hist.* a lower-class Parisian republican in the French Revolution. [Say sawn cue LOT]

Sansei *noun* (*plural* **Sansei**) a North American whose grandparents were immigrants from Japan. [Say SAN say]

Sanskrit • *noun* the ancient language of the Indian subcontinent, the principal language of religious writings and scholarship, the source of some of the modern languages of the area, and one of the languages recognized for official use in India. • *adjective* of or in this language. ▶ **Sanskritic** *adjective* [Say SAN scrit, san SCRIT ick]

sans serif • *noun* a form of type without serifs. • *adjective* without serifs. [Say san SAIR if]

Santa Claus (*plural* **Santa Clauses**) (also **Santa**, *plural* **Santas**) a folk figure, usu. represented as a fat, white-bearded old man in a red suit, said to bring presents on Christmas Eve.

Santee *noun* (*plural* **Santee** or **Santees**) **1** a member of a Dakota group originally inhabiting Minnesota, now also living in Manitoba and Saskatchewan. **2** the Siouan language of this people. [Say san TEE]

sap • *noun* **1** the fluid, chiefly water with dissolved sugars and mineral salts, that circulates in a plant and is essential to its growth. **2** the sap of the sugar maple, used for making maple syrup etc. **3** a tunnel or trench to conceal assailants' approach to a fortified place. **4** *slang* a foolish person. • *verb* (**saps**, **sapped**, **sapping**) gradually weaken or destroy a person's strength, power, confidence, etc.: *my energy had been sapped.*

sapient *adjective* *literary* wise, intelligent: *Spock was unable to determine whether any sapient life forms existed on the planet.* [Say SAY pee int]

sapling *noun* a young tree.

sapper *noun* **1** a person who digs tunnels and trenches. **2** a military engineer who lays or detects and disarms mines. **3** (also **Sapper**) *Cdn & Brit.* a soldier having the rank of private in regiments of engineers.

sapphire • *noun* **1** a transparent blue precious stone consisting of corundum. **2** precious transparent corundum of any colour. **3** (also **sapphire blue**) an intense blue colour. • *adjective* **1** (also **sapphire-blue**) of sapphire blue. **2** set with a sapphire or sapphires. [Say SAFF ire]

sappy *adjective* (**sappier, sappiest**) **1** *informal* too sentimental. **2** full of sap.

sapsucker *noun* a small woodpecker that pecks holes in trees and visits them for sap and insects.

sapwood *noun* the soft outer layers of recently formed wood between the heartwood and the bark.

SAR *abbreviation* SEARCH AND RESCUE.

Saracen *hist.* • *noun* **1** an Arab or Muslim at the time of the Crusades. **2** a nomad of the Syrian and Arabian desert. • *adjective* of the Saracens. [Say SARAH sun]

Saran *noun* (also **Saran Wrap**) *proprietary* clear thin plastic film, used to wrap foods. [Say suh RAN]

sarcasm *noun* **1** the use of bitter or wounding, esp. ironic, remarks; language consisting of such remarks. **2** such a remark: *his speeches were always laced with jokes and wry sarcasms*. ▸ **sarcastic** *adjective* **sarcastically** *adverb* [Say SAR kaz um, sar KASS tick]

Sarcee (*plural* **Sarcee** or **Sarcees**) • *noun* **1** a member of a small Athapaskan group living on the Bow River near Calgary. **2** the language of this people. • *adjective* of or relating to this people or their culture or language. [Say SAR see]

sarcoma *noun* a malignant tumour of connective or other non-epithelial tissue. [Say sar CO muh]

sarcophagus *noun* (*plural* **sarcophagi**) a stone coffin, esp. one adorned with a sculpture or inscription. [Say sar COFFA gus for the singular, sar COFFA guy for the plural]

sardine *noun* **1** any of various fish of the herring family. **2** a young Atlantic or Pacific herring preserved in oil or brine and canned. **3** a young European pilchard likewise preserved. PHRASES **like sardines** crowded close together (as sardines are in cans).

Sardinian • *noun* **1** a native or inhabitant of Sardinia, a large island in the Mediterranean Sea. **2** the Romance language of Sardinia. • *adjective* of or relating to Sardinia or its people or language. [Say sar DINNY un]

sardonic *adjective* mocking or sarcastic, esp. in a disdainful or superior way: *she is sardonic in her attitude towards "the little woman"* ◊ *sardonic humour*. ▸ **sardonically** *adverb* [Say sar DON ick]

sarge *noun* *slang* sergeant.

SPELL CHECK
sergeant
An officer in the military or in certain police forces is a **sergeant**.

sari *noun* (*plural* **saris**) (also **saree** *plural* **sarees**) a length of cotton or silk draped around the body, traditionally worn as a main garment by Indian women. [Say SAR ee]

sarong *noun* **1** a Malay and Javanese garment, worn by both sexes, consisting of a long strip of (often striped) cloth worn tucked around the waist or under the armpits. **2** a woman's garment resembling this. [Say suh RONG]

sarsaparilla *noun* (*plural* **sarsaparillas**) **1** a preparation of the dried roots of various tropical American shrubs, used to flavour some drinks and medicines and formerly used as a tonic. **2** any of the

plants used to make this preparation. **3** a soft drink flavoured with sarsaparilla. [Say saspa RILLA]

SAR Tech *noun* (*plural* **SAR Techs**) *Cdn* a search and rescue technician, a non-commissioned member of the Canadian Forces specialized in performing rescue operations and highly trained in such related skills as parachuting, mountain climbing, first aid, etc.

sartorial *adjective* having to do with clothes or clothing: *sartorial elegance* ◊ *their new uniforms made them the sartorial talk of the league*. ▸ **sartorially** *adverb* [Say sar TORY ul]

sash *noun* (*plural* **sashes**) **1** a long strip of cloth worn tied around the waist or over one shoulder. **2** a frame holding the glass in a sash window, esp. one that slides up and down in the grooves of a window aperture.

SPELL CHECK
sashay, sachet
A small packet of perfume or seasonings is a **sachet**.

sashay *verb* *informal* **1** walk or move casually or nonchalantly; saunter. **2** walk or move so as to attract attention. [Say sash AY]

sashimi *noun* a Japanese dish of garnished raw fish in thin slices. [Say sa SHEE mee]

sash window *noun* a window consisting of two frames of glass, one or both of which can slide up and down to create or close an opening.

Sask. *abbreviation* Saskatchewan.

Saskatchewan Day *noun* *Cdn* (*Sask.*) a statutory holiday occurring on the first Monday in August.

Saskatchewanian • *adjective* of or relating to Saskatchewan. • *noun* a native or inhabitant of Saskatchewan. [Say suh scatch a WONNY un]

Saskatchewan Party *noun* a political party of Saskatchewan formed in 1997 by the Conservatives and some Liberals.

saskatoon *noun* *Cdn* (*Prairies*) **1** a shrub of western North America, which produces sweet purple edible berries. **2** (also **saskatoon berry**) this berry.

sasquatch *noun* (*plural* **sasquatch** or **sasquatches**) a mythical large, hairy, ape-like creature said to live in northwestern North America. [Say SASK watch]

sass *informal* • *noun* impudence, cheek. • *verb* (**sasses, sassed, sassing**) be impudent to.

sassafras *noun* (*plural* **sassafrases**) **1** a small North American tree, with aromatic leaves and bark. **2** a preparation of oil extracted from the leaves or bark of this tree, used in medicines and perfumes. [Say SASSA frass]

sassiness *noun* *informal* **1** cheekiness. **2** liveliness and confidence. **3** stylishness.

sassy *adjective* (**sassier, sassiest**) *informal* **1** showing a lack of respect; cheeky. **2** lively, bold, and confident. **3** stylish, fashionable.

SAT *abbreviation* *proprietary* SCHOLASTIC APTITUDE TEST.

Sat. *abbreviation* Saturday.

sat past and past participle of SIT.

Satan the Devil; Lucifer. [Say SAY tun]

satanic *adjective* **1** having to do with Satan or Satanism. **2** extremely evil or wicked: *satanic madness*. [Say suh TAN ick]

Satanism *noun* the worship of Satan, typically involving a distortion of Christian practices and symbols, such as placing a cross upside down. ▸ **Satanist** *noun* [Say SAY tun ism]

satay *noun* (also **saté**) an Indonesian and Malaysian dish of small pieces of meat grilled on a skewer and usu. served with spicy peanut sauce. [Say sa TAY or SAT ay]

SATB *abbreviation Music* soprano, alto, tenor, and bass.

satchel *noun* a small bag usu. of leather and hung from the shoulder with a strap, for carrying books etc. esp. to and from school.

sate *verb* (**sates, sated, sating**) satisfy a person or their desire or appetite etc. fully: *stocked to sate your cravings at any time of the day or night* ◊ *they sated themselves with music as if it were a kind of drug.*

satellite • *noun* **1** a celestial body orbiting the earth or another planet, e.g. the moon. **2** an artificial body placed in orbit around the earth or another planet, esp. for observation or remote sensing of the earth's surface, for astronomical observation, or as a relay for telecommunication. **3** something that is subordinate to or reliant on another place or thing: *lives in a satellite of Toronto.* • *adjective* **1** transmitted by satellite: *satellite television.* **2** (of a region etc.) subordinate to another body etc.

satellite dish *noun* (*plural* **satellite dishes**) a saucer-shaped aerial for receiving broadcasting signals transmitted by satellite.

sati *noun* (*plural* **satis**) = SUTTEE. [Say suh TEE or SUT ee]

satiate *verb* (**satiates, satiated, satiating**) satisfy a person or their desire or appetite etc. fully: *had nothing better to do than satiate his vanity by lying under a sun lamp.* ▶ **satiation** *noun* [Say SAY shee ate, say shee AY sh'n]

satin • *noun* **1** a smooth, glossy fabric. **2** a paint with a low lustre. • *adjective* **1** smooth as satin. **2** made of satin.

satinwood *noun* **1** a glossy yellow timber, valued for use in cabinetmaking. **2** either of two hardwood trees producing this timber, native either to India and Ceylon or to the Caribbean and Florida.

satiny *adjective* resembling the smooth, glossy look or feel of satin.

satire *noun* **1** the use of humour, irony, exaggeration, or ridicule to expose and criticize people's vices or foolishness, esp. in the context of contemporary politics or other topical issues. **2** a work or composition using satire. **3** this genre of literature. ▶ **satiric** *adjective* (also **satirical**) **satirically** *adverb* **satirist** *noun* **satirize** *verb* (**satirizes, satirized, satirizing**) [Say SAT ire, suh TEER ick, SAT er ist, SAT er ize]

satisfaction *noun* **1** fulfillment of one's wishes, expectations, or needs, or the pleasure derived from this: *job satisfaction* ◊ *didn't want to give them the satisfaction of knowing they had hurt her.* **2** a thing that settles an obligation or pays a debt: *in full and final satisfaction of the claim.* **3** what is felt to be owed or due to one, esp. in reparation of an injustice or wrong: *I complained to the manager but I didn't get any satisfaction.* PHRASES **to one's satisfaction** so that one is content, pleased, or convinced: *the affair was settled to the client's complete satisfaction* ◊ *can you prove it to our satisfaction?*

satisfactorily *adverb* in an acceptable manner: *our questions have been answered satisfactorily.* [Say satis FACTOR a lee]

satisfactory *adjective* satisfying expectations or needs; leaving no room for complaint.

satisfied *adjective* content or pleased: *satisfied customers* ◊ *was satisfied with the results.*

satisfy *verb* (**satisfies, satisfied, satisfying**) **1** meet the expectations, needs, or desires of. **2** fulfill (a desire or need). **3** provide with adequate information about or proof of something. **4** comply with (a condition, obligation, or demand). PHRASES **satisfy oneself** be certain in one's own mind. ▶ **satisfying** *adjective* **satisfyingly** *adverb*

satrap *noun* **1** a provincial governor in the ancient Persian Empire. **2** a minor or subordinate ruler: *in* attendance were the prime minister and a rich broth of cabinet ministers and provincial satraps. [Say SAT rap]

saturate *verb* (**saturates, saturated, saturating**) **1** soak something thoroughly with liquid so that no more can be absorbed: *constant rain saturated the soil.* **2** fill a person or thing with something until no more can be held or absorbed: *the electronic media have saturated the airwaves with sensational stories about violent crimes.* **3** cause a substance to absorb, hold, or combine with the greatest possible amount of another substance: *the groundwater is saturated with calcium hydroxide.* **4** supply (a market) beyond the point at which the demand for a product is satisfied **5** permeate, inspire, or imbue something with a particular influence, quality, etc.: *his postmodern approach is saturated with art references.*

saturated *adjective* **1** completely wet. **2** filled with the greatest possible amount of something: *auto-saturated countries* ◊ *media-saturated culture.* **3 a** (of an organic molecule) containing the greatest number of hydrogen atoms. **b** (of fat) containing a high proportion of fatty acid molecules, considered less healthy in the diet than unsaturated fats. **4** (of a solution) containing the greatest amount of a dissolved substance that it can hold for the temperature it is at: *a saturated solution of sodium chloride.* **5** (of colour) very strong or bright: *the filter gave the sky a saturated blue colour.* [Say SATCH a rate id]

saturation point *noun* the stage beyond which no more can be absorbed or accepted.

Saturday • *noun* the day of the week following Friday. • *adverb* **1** on Saturday. **2** (**Saturdays**) on Saturdays; each Saturday.

satyr *noun* **1** one of a class of Greek woodland gods with a horse's ears and tail, or (in Roman representations) with a goat's ears, tail, legs, and budding horns. **2** a man with strong sexual desires. [Say SAT er or SATE er]

sauce • *noun* **1** any of various liquid or semi-liquid preparations eaten with food. **2** stewed fruit, e.g. apples, eaten as dessert or used as a garnish. **3** *informal* impudence, impertinence. **4** *informal* alcohol. • *verb* (**sauces, sauced, saucing**) *informal* be impudent to.

sauced *adjective* **1** served with a sauce. **2** *slang* drunk.

saucepan *noun* a usu. round metal pot, often with a lid and long handle, used for cooking over heat.

saucer *noun* **1** a shallow circular dish, esp. for standing a teacup on. **2** something saucer-shaped: *flying saucer.*

saucily *adverb* **1** in a cheeky sexually suggestive manner. **2** in a bold and lively manner.

saucy *adjective* (**saucier, sauciest**) **1 a** sexually suggestive, esp. in a way intended to be lighthearted and humorous: *saucy stories.* **b** cheeky, rude. **2** (of a person) bold, lively, and full of spirit. **3** covered with sauce: *saucy barbecued ribs.*

Saudi (also **Saudi Arabian**) • *adjective* of Saudi Arabia, a country in southwestern Asia occupying most of the Arabian peninsula, or its ruling dynasty. • *noun* (*plural* **Saudis**) **1** a person of Saudi nationality or descent. **2** a member of the ruling dynasty of Saudi Arabia. [Say SOWDY or SODDY (SOWDY rhymes with HOWDY)]

sauerkraut *noun* pickled cabbage. [Say SOUR krout]

sauger *noun* a large-mouthed North American fish of the perch family. [Say SOGGER]

Saulteaux (*plural* **Saulteaux**) • *noun* **1** a member of an Aboriginal people formerly living on the shore of Lake Superior north of Sault Ste. Marie, now esp. in Manitoba. **2** the Ojibwa dialect of this people. • *adjective* of or relating to this people or their language. [Say SO toe]

S

sauna *noun* **1** a special room filled with steam to clean and refresh the body. **2** a period spent in a sauna.

saunter • *verb* walk or go slowly; amble, stroll. • *noun* a leisurely ramble.

sauropod *noun* any of a group of plant-eating dinosaurs with a long neck and tail, and four thick limbs. [Say SORE oh pod]

sausage *noun* **1 a** ground meat seasoned and often mixed with other ingredients, usu. encased in cylindrical form in a skin. **b** a length of this. **2** a sausage-shaped object.

sausage roll *noun* minced pork enclosed in pastry and baked.

sauté • *verb* (**sautés**, **sautéed**, **sautéing**) fry (food) quickly in a little hot fat. • *noun* food cooked in this way. [Say SAW tay or saw TAY or so TAY]

Sauvignon *noun* (also **Sauvignon Blanc**) **1** a variety of white grape used in winemaking. **2** a dry white wine made from these grapes. [Say SO veen yon, so veen yon BLONK (with ON as in French)]

savage • *adjective* **1** fierce; cruel. **2** wild: *a savage animal.* **3** *archaic offensive* uncivilized; primitive. **4** *informal* angry; bad-tempered: *in a savage mood.* • *noun* **1** *archaic offensive* a member of a primitive tribe. **2** a cruel or barbarous person. • *verb* (**savages**, **savaged**, **savaging**) **1** attack and bite or maul etc. **2** criticize fiercely. ▶ **savagely** *adverb* **savagery** *noun*

savannah *noun* (also **savanna**) a grassy plain in the tropics and subtropics with few or no trees.

savant *noun* a learned person or expert in some field, esp. a distinguished scientist etc.: *writers and painters and savants of other kinds.* [Say sa VONT]

save[1] • *verb* (**saves**, **saved**, **saving**) **1** rescue, protect, etc. from danger, discredit, etc. **2** keep for future use; refrain from spending or using. **3 a** relieve from spending (money, time, trouble, etc.); prevent exposure to (annoyance etc.): *saved myself $50* ◊ *a word processor saves time.* **b** obviate the need or likelihood of: *soaking saves scrubbing.* **4** preserve from damnation; convert: *saved her soul.* **5** preserve (one's strength etc.): *save your energy.* **6** *Computing* store (data) on a hard drive etc. **7 a** avoid losing (a game, match, etc.). **b** prevent an opponent from scoring (a goal etc.). **c** stop (a ball etc.) from entering the goal. • *noun* **1** *Hockey etc.* an act of preventing an opponent from scoring. **2** *Baseball* **a** a statistical credit given to a relief pitcher for maintaining a team's winning lead. **b** the action of maintaining such a lead. PHRASES **save one's breath** not waste time speaking to no effect. **save the day** (or **situation**) find or provide a solution to difficulty or disaster. **save face** preserve esteem; avoid humiliation. **save it** *slang* shut up. **save one's neck** (or **skin** or **ass** or **bacon**) avoid loss, injury, or death; escape from danger. **save the trouble** avoid useless or pointless effort.

save[2] *preposition* & *conjunction archaic* or *literary* except: *the cats are all gone save one.*

saver *noun* a person or thing that saves esp. something described: *energy-saver* ◊ *money-saver.*

saving • *adjective* making economical use of: *labour-saving.* • *noun* **1** anything that is saved. **2** an economy. **3** (usu. in *plural*) money saved. • *preposition* **1** except: *all saving that one.* **2** without offence to: *saving your presence.*

saving grace *noun* a redeeming quality: *even the corniest westerns usually had one saving grace: the scenery.*

savings account *noun* an interest-paying bank account on which cheques may not usually be drawn.

savings and loan *noun* (in the US) a co-operative association which accepts savings at interest and lends money to savers for houses or other purchases.

savings bond *noun* a certificate issued by a government or a public company promising to repay borrowed money at a fixed rate of interest at a specified time.

saviour *noun* (also **savior**) **1** a person who saves or delivers from danger, destruction, etc.: *the country's saviour.* **2** (**Saviour**) *Christianity* Christ.

savoir faire *noun* the ability to act suitably in any situation: *if only I had Norman's poise, savoir faire, and sophistication.* [Say sav warr FAIR (WARR rhymes with CAR)]

savory *noun* (*plural* **savories**) either of two aromatic plants of the mint family, summer savory and winter savory, used as a herb in cooking.

savour (also **savor**) • *verb* **1** appreciate and enjoy the taste of (food): *we savoured the feast.* **2** enjoy or appreciate (an experience etc.): *savour every moment of the victory.* • *noun* **1** a characteristic taste, flavour, etc.: *her cooking unites the savour and freshness of the South with a northern sophistication.* **2** a quality suggestive of or containing a small amount of another: *bring a savour of drama into our daily lives.*

savoury (also **savory**) • *adjective* **1** having an appetizing taste or smell. **2** (of food) salty or piquant, not sweet: *a savoury omelette.* **3** pleasant; acceptable: *didn't possess the most savoury of reputations.* • *noun* (*plural* **savouries**) a savoury dish served as an appetizer or at the end of dinner.

savvy *slang* • *noun* shrewdness and practical knowledge, esp. in politics or business: *behind the success of the fund is a balance of trading savvy and economic foresight.* • *adjective* (**savvier**, **savviest**) having or showing shrewdness and practical knowledge, esp. in politics or business: *the savvy angler also stays in constant motion* ◊ *a media-savvy financial wizard.*

saw[1] • *noun* a tool for cutting with a toothed blade. • *verb* (**saws**; *past* **sawed**; *past participle* **sawn** or **sawed**; *saving*) **1** cut with a saw. **2** move to and fro with a motion as of a saw or person sawing: *sawing away on his violin.* PHRASES **saw logs** *slang* snore. **saw off** *Cdn* compromise by trading concessions: *they sawed off over wages and job security.* **saw up** saw into pieces.

saw[2] *past of* SEE[1].

saw[3] *noun* a short phrase or sentence that states a general truth about life or gives advice: *the old saw about doing unto others as you would have them do to you.*

sawdust *noun* powdery wood particles produced in sawing.

sawed-off *adjective* **1** (of a gun) having part of the barrel sawn off to make it easier to handle and give a wider field of fire. **2** *informal* (of a person) short.

sawhorse *noun* a rack supporting wood for sawing.

sawlog *noun* a felled tree suitable for cutting into timber.

sawmill *noun* a factory in which wood is sawn mechanically into planks, boards, etc. ▶ **sawmilling** *adjective*

sawn *past participle of* SAW[1].

saw-off *noun* *Cdn* **1** an arrangement between political rivals in which each agrees not to contest a seat etc. held by the other: *these saw-offs are a fascinating element in Canadian democracy.* **2** any compromise involving mutual concessions: *management and the union agreed to a saw-off.* **3** a tie, deadlock, stalemate, etc.: *the talks ended in a saw-off.*

sawtooth *adjective* (also **sawtoothed**) (esp. of a roof, wave, etc.) shaped like the teeth of a saw, esp. with one steep and one slanting side.

saw-whet owl *noun* a small brown North American owl of coniferous and deciduous woods.

sawyer *noun* **1** a person who saws timber. **2** a large

longhorn beetle whose larvae bore tunnels in the wood of injured or recently felled trees. [Say SOY er or SAW yur]

sax *noun* (*plural* **saxes**) *informal* **1** a saxophone. **2** a saxophone player.

saxifrage *noun* a plant that grows on rocky or stony ground and bears small white, yellow, or red flowers. [Say SAXA frayge or SAXA fradge]

Saxon • *noun* **1** *hist.* **a** a member of a Germanic people originally of northern Germany, of which a portion conquered and occupied parts of England in the 5th–6th centuries. **b** the language of the Saxons. **2** = ANGLO-SAXON *noun*. **3** a native of modern Saxony in northern Germany. • *adjective* **1** *hist.* of the Saxons. **2** of modern Saxony or Saxons.

saxophone *noun* **1** a metal woodwind reed instrument in several sizes and registers, the most recognizable form of which has an upturned bell, used esp. in jazz and popular music. **2** its player. ▶ **saxophonist** *noun*

say • *verb* (**says**, **said**, **saying**) **1** utter words so as to convey information, an opinion, an instruction, etc. **2** (of a text or symbol) convey information or instructions. **3** (of a clock or watch) indicate (a time). **4** (in *passive*) be asserted or reported. **5** (foll. by *for*) present (a consideration) in favour of or excusing: *he had nothing to say for himself*. **6** assume as a hypothesis. • *interjection* esp. *US* an exclamation of surprise, to attract attention, etc. • *noun* **1** an opportunity to state one's opinion or feelings. **2** an opportunity to influence events. • *adverb* selecting, assuming, or taking as an example or (a specified number etc.) as near enough: *paid, say, $20*. PHRASES **not to say** and indeed; or possibly even: *his language was near not to say offensive*. **say much** (or **something**) **for** indicate the high quality of. **says you!** *informal* I disagree. **say what?** *slang* an expression of astonishment. **say when** *informal* indicate when enough drink or food has been given. **say the word 1** indicate that you agree or give permission. **2** give the order etc. **that is to say 1** in other words, more explicitly. **2** or at least. **they say** it is rumoured. **to say nothing of** = NOT TO MENTION (see MENTION). **what do** (or **would**) **you say to?** would you like? **when all is said and done** after all, in the long run. **you can say that again!** (or **you said it!**) *informal* I agree emphatically. **you don't say** *informal* an expression of amazement or disbelief.

saying *noun* a short, pithy, commonly known expression which generally offers advice or wisdom. PHRASES **go without saying** be too well known or obvious to need mention. **there is no saying** it is impossible to know.

sayonara *interjection* goodbye. [Say sigh a NARR uh]

say-so *noun* **1** the power or act of deciding or allowing something: *no new employees come into the organization without his say-so*. **2** a person's arbitrary or unauthorized assertion or instruction: *I don't stop on the say-so of anybody's assistant*.

Sb *symbol* antimony.

Sc *symbol* scandium.

Sc. *abbreviation* science.

scab • *noun* **1** a dry rough crust formed over a cut, sore, etc. in healing. **2** *informal derogatory* a person who refuses to strike or join a trade union, or who tries to break a strike by working. • *verb* (**scabs**, **scabbed**, **scabbing**) **1** act as a scab. **2** (of a wound etc.) form a scab; heal over.

scabbard *noun* *hist.* a sheath for a sword, bayonet, etc. [Say SCAB urd]

scabby *adjective* covered in scabs.

scabies *noun* a contagious skin disease causing severe itching. [Say SKAY beez]

scabrous *adjective* **1** having a rough surface; bearing short stiff hairs, scales, etc. **2** unpleasant; unattractive: *lived in a scabrous hovel*. **3** indecent; scandalous: *scabrous details included being regularly being seen with a mistress*. [Say SKAB russ]

scad *noun* a fish with an elongated body and very large spiky scales.

scads *plural noun* *informal* large quantities.

scaffold *noun* **1** = SCAFFOLDING 1. **2 a** *hist.* a raised wooden platform used for the execution of criminals. **b** any similar raised platform. **3** (**the scaffold**) death by execution. [Say SKAFF old]

scaffolding *noun* **1** a temporary structure formed of poles, planks, etc., used by workers while building or repairing a house etc. **2** materials used for this. **3** any supporting framework. [Say SKAFF old ing]

scag *noun* = SKAG.

scalable *adjective* **1** capable of being scaled or climbed. **2** *Computing* able to be used or produced at different ranges of size, capability, etc.

scalar *Math & Physics* • *adjective* (of a quantity) having only magnitude, not direction. • *noun* a scalar quantity (*compare* VECTOR 1). [Say SKAY lur]

scalawag *noun* a scamp; a rascal. [Say SKAL a wag]

scald • *verb* **1** burn (the skin etc.) with hot liquid or steam. **2** heat (esp. milk) to near boiling point. **3** clean (a pan etc.) by rinsing with boiling water. **4** treat (food, poultry, etc.) with boiling water in preparation for cooking etc. • *noun* a burn etc. caused by scalding. [Rhymes with *BALD*]

scalding *adjective* **1** extremely hot. **2** producing an effect like that of scalding: *scalding truths*. [Rhymes with *BALDING*]

scale[1] • *noun* **1** each of the small thin bony or horny overlapping plates protecting the skin of fish and reptiles. **2** a thick white deposit formed in a kettle, boiler, etc. by the action of heat on water. **3** plaque formed on teeth. **4 a** (in full **scale insect**) any of various insects which cling to plants and secrete a shieldlike scale as covering. **b** the diseased condition of plants infested with these insects. • *verb* (**scales**, **scaled**, **scaling**) **1** remove scale or scales from. **2** remove plaque from (teeth) by scraping. PHRASES **scales fall from a person's eyes** a person is no longer deceived.

scale[2] *noun* **1** (also in *plural*) a weighing machine or device: *bathroom scale*. **2** (**the Scales**) the zodiacal sign or constellation Libra. PHRASES **tip the scales 1** weigh. **2** affect the result of something in one way rather than another: *cost and convenience tip the scales in favour of emergency aerosol can tire sealers*.

scale[3] • *noun* **1** a series of degrees; a graded classification system: *pay fees according to a prescribed scale* ◊ *seven points on the Richter scale*. **2 a** (often as an *adjective*) a relation between the actual size of something and a map, diagram, etc. which represents it: *on a scale of one centimetre to the kilometre* ◊ *a scale model*. **b** relative dimensions or degree: *generosity on a grand scale*. **3** a set of marks on a line used in measuring, reducing, enlarging, etc. **4** an arrangement of all the notes in any system of music in ascending or descending order. **5** *Math* the ratio between units in a numerical system. **6** the minimum pay rate for a particular job, as determined by a union contract. • *verb* (**scales**, **scaled**, **scaling**) **1 a** climb (a wall, height, etc.). **b** climb (the social scale, heights of ambition, etc.). **2** represent in proportional dimensions; reduce to a common scale. **3** *Forestry* **a** estimate the amount of (standing timber). **b** measure (a log) to estimate how much cut timber it will yield. PHRASES **in scale** (of

drawing etc.) in proportion to the surroundings etc. **scale back** reduce the scale, scope, or size of. **scale down** make smaller in proportion; reduce in size. **scale up** make larger in proportion; increase in size. **to scale** with a uniform reduction or enlargement.

scaled-down *adjective* reduced in size, number, or extent: *a scaled-down version of our original plan*.

scaleless *adjective* not having scales: *a scaleless reptile*.

scalene • *adjective* **1** (of a triangle) having three unequal sides. **2** (of a cone or cylinder) with the axis not perpendicular to the base. • *noun* a scalene triangle. [Say SKAY leen or skay LEEN]

scaler *noun* a person who scales timber or logs.

scallion *noun* a shallot or green onion; any long-necked onion with a small bulb. [Say SKAL yun]

scallop • *noun* **1** an edible bivalve mollusc with a ribbed fan-shaped shell. **2** (also **scallop shell**) a single valve from the fan-shaped shell of a scallop, which is edged with small rounded lobes. **3** (in *plural*) an ornamental edging cut in material in imitation of the edge of a scallop shell. • *verb* (**scallops, scalloped, scalloping**) **1 a** ornament (an edge or material) with scallops or scalloping. **b** cut or shape in the form of a scallop. **2** (esp. as **scalloped** *adjective*) bake (food, esp. potatoes) in a cream sauce. [Say SKAL up or SKAWL up]

scalloper *noun* (also **scallop dragger**) a boat for fishing for scallops. [Say SKAL up er or SKAWL up er]

scallywag *noun* = SCALAWAG.

scaloppine *noun* (also **scallopini**) thin, boneless slices of meat, esp. veal, sautéed or fried. [Say skal a PEENY]

scalp • *noun* **1** the skin covering the top of the head, with the hair etc. attached. **2 a** *hist.* the scalp of an enemy cut or torn away as a trophy. **b** a trophy or symbol of conquest. • *verb* **1** *hist.* take the scalp of (an enemy). **2** *informal* resell (esp. tickets) at inflated prices.

scalpel *noun* a surgeon's small sharp knife shaped for holding like a pen.

scalper *noun* a person who buys tickets for concerts, sporting events, etc. and resells them at inflated prices.

scaly *adjective* **1** covered in or having many scales or flakes. **2** of or like a deposit of scale.

scam *slang* • *noun* a trick or swindle. • *verb* (**scams, scammed, scamming**) **1** swindle. **2** obtain in a manner not considered ethical or proper: *scammed four tickets to the game*. ▶ **scammer** *noun*

scamp *noun informal* a rascal; a rogue.

scamper *verb* **1** run and skip impulsively or playfully. **2** move quickly, go hastily.

scampi *plural noun* **1** large prawns. **2** (often treated as *singular*) a dish of these, usu. fried.

scan • *verb* (**scans, scanned, scanning**) **1** look at intently or quickly: *scanned the text for errors*. **2 a** scan (a particular region) to be traversed or swept by a radar etc. beam. **b** examine all parts of (a surface etc.) to detect radioactivity etc. **3 a** resolve (a picture) into its elements of light and shade in a pre-arranged pattern esp. for the purposes of television transmission. **b** use a beam or detector to convert (an image, text, etc.) into a sequence of signals for processing, transmission, etc. **4 a** make a scan of (the body or part of it). **b** examine (a patient etc.) with a scanner. **5** test the metre of (a line of verse etc.) by reading with the emphasis on its rhythm. **6** (of a verse etc.) have a regular rhythm according to fixed rules: *this line doesn't scan*. • *noun* **1** the act of looking quickly through something written or printed: *a quick scan of the sports pages*. **2** an image obtained by scanning or with a scanner.

scandal *noun* **1** a person or circumstance etc. causing general public outrage or indignation. **2** the outrage etc. so caused, esp. as a subject of common talk.

scandalize *verb* (**scandalizes, scandalized, scandalizing**) offend the moral feelings, sensibilities, etc. of; shock.

scandalous *adjective* **1** causing general public outrage by a perceived offence against morality or law: *the couple's scandalous behaviour at the wedding*. **2** (of a state of affairs) disgracefully bad, esp. as a result of someone's negligence or mismanagement: *a scandalous waste of taxpayers' money*. ▶ **scandalously** *adverb*

Scandinavian • *noun* **1 a** a native or inhabitant of Scandinavia. **b** a person of Scandinavian descent. **2** the family of languages of Scandinavia. • *adjective* of or relating to Scandinavia or its people or languages. [Say skanda NAVY un]

scandium *noun* a rare soft silver-white metallic element. [Say SKANDY um]

scanner *noun* **1** a device for scanning, systematically examining, reading, or monitoring something. **2** a device for converting text, an image, etc. into a sequence of signals for processing, transmission, etc. **3** a machine for measuring the intensity of radiation, ultrasound reflections, etc., from the body as a diagnostic aid. **4** a person who scans or examines critically.

scant *adjective* **1** barely sufficient; deficient: *with scant regard for the truth* ◊ *scant of breath*. **2** barely amounting to, hardly reaching (a specified quantity): *a scant 150 kilograms* ◊ *a scant cup of flour*.

scantily *adverb* **1** in a barely sufficient or adequate manner: *the program is scantily funded*. **2** (dressed etc.) in a very revealing manner: *the sunbathers were scantily clad in skimpy bikinis*.

scanty *adjective* (**scantier, scantiest**) **1** of small extent or amount. **2** barely sufficient.

-scape *combining form* forming nouns denoting a view or a representation of a view: *seascape*.

scapegoat • *noun* **1** a person who is blamed for the wrongdoings, mistakes, or faults of others: *she felt she had been made a scapegoat for her boss's incompetence*. **2** *Bible* a goat sent into the wilderness after the Jewish chief priest had symbolically laid the sins of the people upon it. • *verb* make a scapegoat of: *prostitutes are being scapegoated by the AIDS scare*. ▶ **scapegoating** *noun*

scapula *noun* (*plural* **scapulae** or **scapulas**) the shoulder blade. [Say SKAP yoo luh for the singular, SKAP yoo lee for the plural]

scapular • *adjective* of or relating to the shoulder or shoulder blade. • *noun* **1 a** a monastic cloak consisting of a piece of cloth covering the shoulders and extending in front and behind almost to the feet. **b** two small rectangles of woollen cloth joined by tapes or strings passing over the shoulders, worn under one's clothing as a symbol of affiliation to a religious order or as a form of devotion. **2** a feather growing near the insertion of a bird's wing. [Say SKAP yoo lur]

scar • *noun* **1** a usu. permanent mark on the skin left after the healing of a wound etc. **2** the lasting effect of grief etc. on a person's character. **3** a mark left by damage etc.: *the table bore many scars*. **4** a mark left on the stem etc. of a plant by the fall of a leaf etc. **5** a steep craggy outcrop of a mountain or cliff. • *verb* (**scars, scarred, scarring**) **1** (esp. as **scarred** *adjective*) mark with a scar or scars: *was scarred for life*. **2** heal over; form a scar. **3** form a scar on.

scarab *noun* **1** the sacred dung beetle of ancient Egypt. **2** any beetle of the family that includes the dung beetle. **3** a gem or other ornament made to resemble this beetle. [Say SCARE ub]

scarce • *adjective* (**scarcer, scarcest**) **1** (esp. of food, money, etc.) insufficient for the demand; scanty: *we abandoned the plan because money was scarce*. **2** hard to find; rare. • *adverb* *archaic* or *literary* scarcely: *scarce able to*

see through the mist of tears. PHRASES **make oneself scarce** *informal* keep out of the way.

scarcely *adverb* **1** hardly; barely; only just: *I scarcely know him*. **2** surely not: *he can scarcely have said so*.

scarcity *noun* (*plural* **scarcities**) (often foll. by *of*) a lack or inadequacy. [Say SCARCE a tee]

scare • *verb* (**scares**, **scared**, **scaring**) **1** frighten, esp. suddenly. **2** drive away by frightening. **3** become scared. • *noun* **1** a sudden attack of fright or worry. **2** a general, esp. baseless, fear of war, invasion, epidemic, etc. **3** (as an *adjective*) denoting an effort to influence others by highlighting or exaggerating a perceived threat: *scare tactics*. **4** a financial panic causing share selling etc. PHRASES **scare up** (or **out**) **1** frighten (game etc.) out of cover. **2** *informal* manage to find: *see if we can scare up a meal*.

scarecrow *noun* **1** an object, esp. a human figure dressed in old clothes, set up in a field to scare birds away. **2** *informal* a badly dressed, grotesque-looking, or very thin person.

scared *adjective* frightened; terrified.

scaremonger *noun* a person who spreads frightening reports or rumours: *government officials blasted scaremongers for overhyping the Y2K problem*. ▶ **scaremongering** *noun* [Say SCARE mong gur or SCARE mung gur]

scarf¹ *noun* (*plural* **scarves** or **scarfs**) **1** a square, triangular, or esp. oblong strip of material worn around the neck, over the shoulders, or tied around the head, for warmth or ornament. **2** a cloth or other covering for a table, dresser, etc.

scarf² *verb* *informal* eat or drink greedily.

scarification *noun* **1** a shallow incision or series of these made in the skin, esp. as part of a medical procedure or for decoration. **2** the process of loosening or breaking up soil with a scarifier. [Say scare a fuh KAY sh'n]

scarifier *noun* **1** a machine with spikes or prongs used for loosening soil, esp. in reforestation. **2 a** a spiked machine for breaking up the surface of a paved road. **b** a machine or implement for roughening up the iced surface of a road. **3** a tool for cutting and removing debris from a lawn.

scarify¹ *verb* (**scarifies**, **scarified**, **scarifying**) **1** make cuts in the surface of: *she scarified the snakebite with a paring knife*. **2** loosen (esp. soil) with a scarifier. **3** nick or make an incision in (a hard seed) to facilitate its germination. [Say SCARE a fie]

scarify² *verb* (**scarifies**, **scarified**, **scarifying**) *informal* scare; terrify. [Say SCARE a fie]

scarily *adverb* **1** in a frightening way: *the toboggan hill is scarily steep*. **2** in a striking, surprising, or alarming way: *Gilda's predictions have been scarily accurate*.

scarlet • *noun* **1** a brilliant red tinged with orange. **2** clothes or material of this colour. • *adjective* **1** of a scarlet colour. **2** immoral; promiscuous: *a scarlet woman*.

scarlet fever *noun* an infectious bacterial fever, affecting esp. children, with a scarlet rash.

scarlet runner *noun* a cultivated climbing variety of bean which has red flowers and long green edible pods.

scarves *plural* of SCARF¹.

scary *adjective* (**scarier**, **scariest**) **1** scaring, frightening. **2** striking, surprising, or alarming: *she is so much like her mother that it's scary*.

scat • *noun* **1** the droppings of an animal, esp. a carnivore. **2** improvised jazz singing using sounds imitating instruments, instead of words. • *verb* (**scats**, **scatted**, **scatting**) **1** sing scat. **2** depart quickly. • *interjection* go!

scathing *adjective* witheringly scornful; severe:

scathing sarcasm. ▶ **scathingly** *adverb* [Rhymes with SUNBATHING]

scatological *adjective* marked by a preoccupation with or reference to excretion and human waste: *toilet jokes and other scatological humour*. [Say scatta LOGICAL]

scatter • *verb* **1 a** throw here and there. **b** cover by scattering. **2** disperse or cause (objects, hopes, clouds, etc.) to disperse. **3** *Physics* deflect or diffuse (light, particles, etc.). **4** (of esp. a shotgun) fire a charge of shot diffusely. • *noun* an esp. small amount scattered: *a scatter of catalogues on the living room floor*.

scatterbrain *noun* a person given to silly or disorganized thought with lack of concentration. ▶ **scatterbrained** *adjective*

scattered *adjective* **1** not clustered together; wide apart: *scattered villages*. **2** scatterbrained.

scatter graph *n. Statistics* (also called **scatter plot**) a kind of graph that is used to determine if there is a correlation between two variables, e.g. a person's age and their shoe size; if the values of the two variables form a pattern like a line when they are plotted on the graph, then a correlation between the two variables has been established.

scattergun • *noun* a shotgun. • *adjective* (also **scattershot**) random, haphazard: *takes a scattergun approach when it comes to making travel plans*.

scattering *noun* **1** a quantity or amount scattered. **2** a small number or amount.

scatty *adjective* (**scattier**, **scattiest**) *informal* scatterbrained; disorganized.

scaup *noun* a kind of duck, the male of which has a dark head and breast and a white-sided body. [Say SCOP]

scavenge • *verb* (**scavenges**, **scavenged**, **scavenging**) **1** search for and collect (useful items) from among usu. discarded material. **2** (of an animal or bird) feed on (carrion) or search for food in (garbage etc.): *scavenging back road dumps*. • *noun* the action or process of scavenging. ▶ **scavenger** *noun*

scavenger hunt *noun* a game in which people try to collect certain miscellaneous objects, usu. outdoors over a wide area.

scenario *noun* (*plural* **scenarios**) **1** an outline of the plot of a play etc., with details of the scenes, situations, etc. **2** a postulated sequence of future events. **3** *informal* a situation or scene. [Say sen AIRY oh or sen ARR ee oh]

scene *noun* **1** a place in which events in real life, drama, or fiction occur; the locality of an event etc.: *the scene of the disaster*. **2** an incident in real life, fiction, etc.: *distressing scenes occurred*. **3** a public incident displaying emotion, temper, etc., esp. when embarrassing to others: *made a scene in the restaurant*. **4** a continuous portion of a theatrical production in a fixed setting and usu. without a change of performers; a subdivision of an act. **b** a similar section of a film, book, etc. **5** a landscape or a view: *a desolate scene*. **6** *informal* **a** an area of action or interest: *not my scene*. **b** a way of life; a milieu: *the jazz scene*. PHRASES **behind the scenes 1** among the performers, scenery, etc. offstage. **2** not known to the public; secret. **behind-the-scenes** secret, using secret information: *a behind-the-scenes investigation*. **change of scene** (or **scenery**) a move to different surroundings esp. through travel. **come on the scene** arrive. **quit the scene** depart. **set the scene 1** describe the location of events. **2** give preliminary information.

scenery *noun* **1** the general appearance of the natural features of a landscape, esp. when picturesque. **2** the painted representations of landscape, rooms, etc., used as the background in a play etc.

scenic *adjective* **1 a** (esp. of natural scenery)

picturesque; impressive or beautiful. **b** of or concerning natural scenery. **2** *Theatre* of or on the stage: *the scenic art*.

scent • *noun* **1** a distinctive, esp. pleasant, smell. **2 a** a scent trail left by an animal perceptible to hounds etc. **b** clues etc. that can be followed like a scent trail: *once their interest is aroused they follow the scent with sleuth-like persistence*. **c** a feeling of the presence of something: *a scent of danger*. **3** esp. *Brit.* = PERFUME 2. • *verb* **1 a** discern by scent: *the dog scented game*. **b** sense the presence of; detect: *scent victory*. **2** make fragrant. **3** apply the sense of smell to: *scented the air*. PHRASES **on the scent** in possession of a useful clue in an investigation. **put** (or **throw**) **off the scent** deceive by false clues etc.

scented *adjective* having esp. a pleasant smell.

scentless *adjective* having no odour or scent: *scentless flowers*.

scent marking *noun* the depositing by a mammal of a chemical substance that can be detected by others, either to attract them or to repel them.

sceptic etc. = SKEPTIC.

sceptre *noun* (*US* **scepter**) a staff borne esp. at a coronation as a symbol of sovereignty. ▶**sceptred** *adjective* [Say SEP tur]

schedule • *noun* **1** a list or plan of intended events, times, etc.; a timetable. **2** any list, form, or tabular statement. **3** any of a number of forms attached to a tax return, which are completed if necessary to provide details of information summarized on the return. • *verb* (**schedules**, **scheduled**, **scheduling**) **1** include in a schedule; arrange (an event etc.) for a certain time. **2** make a schedule of. PHRASES **according to** (or **on**) **schedule** as planned; on time. **behind schedule** behind time. ▶**scheduler** *noun* **scheduling** *noun* [Say SKED zhoo ul or SHED zhool or SHED jool]

schema *noun* (*plural* **schemata** or **schemas**) a representation of a plan or theory in the form of an outline or model: *his international schema in which Canada stood prominently amongst those at the centre of the world political economy*. [Say SKEEM uh for the singular, SKEEM a tuh or SKEEM uhs for the plural]

schematic • *adjective* **1** of or concerning a scheme or schema. **2** representing objects by symbols etc. • *noun* a schematic diagram, esp. of an electronic circuit. ▶**schematically** *adverb* [Say skeem AT ick or skim AT ick]

scheme • *noun* **1 a** a systematic plan or arrangement for work, action, etc. **b** a proposed or operational systematic arrangement: *a colour scheme*. **2** an artful or deceitful plot. **3** a timetable, outline, syllabus, etc. • *verb* (**schemes**, **schemed**, **scheming**) make plans, esp. in a devious way or with intent to do something illegal or wrong: *his colleagues, meanwhile, were busily scheming to get rid of him* ◊ *schemed their downfall*. PHRASES **scheme of things** the way things are or are planned: *has little influence in the overall scheme of things*. ▶**schemer** *noun*

scheming • *adjective* cunning or deceitful. • *noun* plots; intrigues. ▶**schemingly** *adverb*

schemozzle *noun* = SHEMOZZLE. [Say shuh MOZZLE]

scherzo *noun* (*plural* **scherzos**) a vigorous, light, or playful composition, usu. as a movement in a symphony, sonata, etc. [Say SKAIRT so]

schism *noun* **1** the division of a group into opposing sections or parties: *a social rift, an irreparable and continuing schism between cultures and peoples in Canada's north*. **2** the separation of a Church into two Churches or the secession of a group owing to doctrinal, disciplinary, etc., differences: *they had fallen into schism and separated themselves from the church*. [Say SKIZ um]

schist *noun* a metamorphic rock composed of layers of different minerals and splitting into thin irregular plates. [Say SHIST]

schizo *informal offensive* • *adjective* schizophrenic. • *noun* (*plural* **schizos**) a schizophrenic. [Say SKITS oh]

schizoid • *adjective* **1** (of a person or personality etc.) tending to or resembling schizophrenia or a schizophrenic, but usu. without delusions. **2** having inconsistent or contradictory elements: *what are the reasons for this schizoid relationship we have with science?* • *noun* a schizoid person. [Say SKITS oid]

schizophrenia *noun* **1** a mental disease marked by a breakdown in the relation between thoughts, feelings, and actions, frequently accompanied by delusions and retreat from social life. **2** *informal* a mentality or approach characterized by inconsistent or contradictory elements: *the political schizophrenia that has Americans preferring a Republican President and a Democrat Congress*. ▶**schizophrenic** *adjective & noun* [Say skitsa FREENY uh, skitsa FREN ick]

schlemiel *noun informal* an awkward or unlucky person: *he dressed so sloppily, looked so ugly, sounded like such a poor schlemiel, it seemed impossible that a woman would fall for him*. [Say shluh MEAL]

schlep *informal* • *verb* (**schleps**, **schlepped**, **schlepping**) **1** carry (esp. something burdensome). **2** go or work tediously or effortfully. • *noun* **1** a tedious journey; a trek. **2** an inept or stupid person. ▶**schlepper** *noun* [Say SHLEP]

schlock *noun informal* **1** cheap, shoddy or defective goods. **2** junk (esp. applied to inferior art or entertainment). ▶**schlocky** *adjective* (**schlockier**, **schlockiest**) [Say SHLOCK]

schlockey *noun Cdn* a children's game played on a four-foot by eight-foot framed plywood sheet stationed between two players, in which each player, using a cut-off hockey stick, attempts to score by shooting a puck past a centre barrier and through a hole in the framing board at the opposing end. [Say SHLOCK ee]

schlub *noun slang* a clumsy, stupid, or untidy person. ▶**schlubby** *adjective* [Say SHLUB]

schlump *noun slang* a slow or slovenly person; a slob, a fool. [Say SHLUMP]

schm- *prefix* (also **shm-**) *slang* used in the second element of a reduplication to express contemptuous dismissal: *fancy-schmancy* ◊ *Harvard Schmarvard*.

schmaltz *noun informal* sentimentality, esp. in music, drama, etc. ▶**schmaltzy** *adjective* (**schmaltzier**, **schmaltziest**) [Rhymes with *WALTZ*]

schmo *noun slang* (*plural* **schmoes**) an ordinary, unremarkable person. [Say SHMO]

schmooze *informal* • *verb* (**schmoozes**, **schmoozed**, **schmoozing**) **1** talk, chat, esp. at a social function. **2** talk to (a person, esp. an important or influential one). • *noun* conversation, esp. at a social function. ▶**schmoozer** *noun* [Say SHMOOZ]

schmuck *slang* • *noun* an objectionable or contemptible person. • *verb Cdn* hit, flatten.

schmucky *adjective* (**schmuckier**, **schmuckiest**) unpleasant, objectionable.

schnapps *noun* any of various strong usu. colourless spirits made from grain, with added flavourings such as peppermint, peach, etc. [Say SHNAPS or SHNOPPS]

schnauzer *noun* a German breed of dog with a close wiry coat and heavy whiskers round the muzzle. [Say SHNOW zur or SHNOUT zur (SHNOW rhymes with *NOW*)]

schnitzel *noun* a thin cutlet, esp. of veal or pork, breaded and fried. [Say SHNIT zul]

schnozz *noun* (*plural* **schnozzes**) (also **schnozzle**, **schnozzola**) *slang* the nose.

scholar *noun* **1** a learned person, esp. in language, literature, etc.; an academic. **2** the holder of a

scholarship: *Rhodes scholar.* **3 a** a person with specified academic ability. **b** a person who learns: *am a scholar of life.* ▶ **scholarly** *adjective*

scholarship *noun* **1 a** academic achievement; learning of a high level. **b** the methods and standards characteristic of a good scholar: *shows great scholarship.* **2** a payment to maintain a student in full-time education, awarded on the basis of scholarly achievement.

scholastic *adjective* of or concerning universities, schools, education, teachers, etc. [Say skuh LASS tick]

scholastically *adverb* with regard to schools or education: *she has always excelled scholastically.*

Scholastic Aptitude Test *noun* *proprietary* a standardized test of a student's verbal and mathematical skills, used for admission to American colleges. Abbreviation: **SAT**.

school¹ • *noun* **1** an institution for educating children. **2** a day's work at school; lessons. **3** any institution at which instruction is given in a particular discipline. **4** a department or faculty of a university. **5** a college or university. **6** a group of artists, philosophers, etc. sharing similar ideas, methods, or style. • *verb* send to school; provide for the education of. **PHRASES** **of the old school** according to former and esp. better tradition: *a gentleman of the old school.* **school of hard knocks** experience gained from adversity.

school² • *noun* a large number of fish, whales, etc. swimming together. • *verb* form schools.

school age *noun* the age range in which children normally attend school. ▶ **school-aged** *adjective*

school board *noun* **1** an elected board responsible for decisions and policy concerning the schools in a given area. **2** the administrative unit responsible for the schools in a given area. **3** the area under the jurisdiction of a school board.

schoolboy *noun* a boy attending school.

schoolchild *noun* (*plural* **schoolchildren**) a child attending school.

school commission *noun* *Cdn* (*Que.*) = SCHOOL BOARD 1.

school district *noun* **1** an administrative unit responsible for the schools in a given area. **2** the area under the jurisdiction of a school district.

school division *noun* *Cdn* (*Man.*) = SCHOOL DISTRICT.

schooler *noun* (usu. in *combination*) a person attending a school: *high-schooler.*

schoolgirl *noun* a girl attending school.

schoolhouse *noun* a building used as a school, esp. a small one in a village or rural area.

schooling *noun* **1** education, esp. at school. **2** training or discipline, esp. of an animal.

school inspector *noun* (in the UK and Canada) an official appointed to inspect and report on the efficiency, teaching standards, etc. of schools.

schoolmarm *noun* **1** a prim and fussy female schoolteacher. **2** *slang* a tree which has forked to form two trunks. ▶ **schoolmarmish** *adjective* (in sense 1).

schoolmaster *noun* a male teacher in an esp. private school. ▶ **schoolmasterly** *adjective*

schoolmate *noun* a companion at school.

schoolroom *noun* a room where students are taught; a classroom.

school section *noun* *Cdn* (*Ont.*) esp. *hist.* a subdivision of a school district.

schoolteacher *noun* a person who teaches in a school.

school unit *noun* *Cdn* (*PEI*) = SCHOOL DISTRICT.

schoolyard *noun* a playing area beside a school.

school year *noun* = ACADEMIC YEAR.

schooner *noun* **1** a fore-and-aft-rigged ship with two or more masts, the forward mast being smaller than the other masts. **2** a tall beer glass. **3** *hist.* = PRAIRIE SCHOONER. [Say SKOONER]

schtick *noun* = SHTICK.

schuss • *noun* (*plural* **schusses**) a straight downhill run on skis. • *verb* (**schusses**, **schussed**, **schussing**) **1** make a schuss. **2** move rapidly downwards: *his mother's Oldsmobile schussed down Jill's driveway.* [Rhymes with PUSS]

schwa *noun* **1** the indistinct unstressed vowel sound as in *a moment ago.* **2** the symbol [@] representing this in the International Phonetic Alphabet. [Say SHWAH]

sciatica *noun* neuralgia of the hip and thigh; a pain in the sciatic nerve. [Say sigh ATTIC uh]

sciatic nerve *noun* the largest nerve in the human body, running from the pelvis to the thigh. [Say sigh ATTIC]

science *noun* **1** a branch of knowledge conducted on objective principles involving the systematized observation of and experiments with phenomena, esp. concerned with the material and functions of the physical universe. **2** systematic and formulated knowledge, esp. of a specified type or on a specified subject: *political science.* **3** skilful technique: *has house cleaning down to a science.*

science fair *noun* an esp. competitive fair in which elementary school or high school students design and exhibit science projects.

science fiction *noun* fiction based on imagined future scientific or technological advances, major social or environmental changes, etc., frequently portraying space or time travel, life on other planets, etc.

scientific *adjective* **1 a** (of an investigation etc.) according to rules laid down in science for performing observations and testing the soundness of conclusions. **b** systematic, accurate. **2** used in, engaged in, or relating to (esp. natural) science. **3** constituted of scientists. ▶ **scientifically** *adverb*

scientific method *noun* a method of procedure consisting of systematic observation, measurement, and experiment, and the formulation, testing, and modification of hypotheses.

scientist *noun* **1** a person with expert knowledge of a (usu. physical or natural) science. **2** a person using scientific methods.

Scientologist *noun* an adherent of Scientology. [Say sigh un TOLLA jist]

Scientology *noun* *proprietary* a religious system whose adherents seek self-knowledge and spiritual fulfillment through graded courses of study and training. [Say sigh un TOLLA jee]

sci-fi *noun* *informal* science fiction.

scimitar *noun* an oriental curved sword usu. broadening towards the point. [Say SIM it er]

scintillate *verb* (**scintillates**, **scintillated**, **scintillating**) **1** talk cleverly or wittily; be brilliant. **2** sparkle; twinkle; emit sparks. [Say SINT a late]

scintillating *adjective* **1** sparkling or shining brightly: *the reflection from the scintillating snow hurt her eyes.* **2** brilliantly and excitingly clever or skilful: *a scintillating conversation ◊ the team produced a scintillating second-half performance.* ▶ **scintillatingly** *adverb*

scintillation *noun* **1** the process or state of scintillating. **2** the twinkling of a star. [Say sinta LAY sh'n]

scion *noun* **1** a shoot of a plant etc., esp. one cut for grafting or planting. **2** a descendant; a younger member of a (esp. distinguished) family: *the idealistic scion of a noble family.* [Say SIGH un]

S

scissor *verb* **1** cut with or as with scissors. **2** move or cause to move like scissors.

scissor kick *noun Swimming* a movement, esp. in the side stroke, in which the legs are parted slowly and brought together forcefully.

scissors *plural noun* **1** (also **pair of scissors** *singular*) an instrument for cutting, having two pivoted blades with finger and thumb holes in the handles. **2** (treated as *singular*) **a** a method of high jump with a forward and backward movement of the legs. **b** a hold in wrestling in which the opponent's body or esp. head is gripped between the legs.

sclerosis *noun* (*plural* **scleroses**) **1** an abnormal hardening of body tissue. **2** rigidity; excessive resistance to change: *there are few signs of long-term economic sclerosis.* [Say skluh ROE sis]

sclerotic *adjective* **1** of or having sclerosis. **2** of or relating to the white of the eye. **3** rigid; unchanging in views or opinions. [Say skluh ROT ick]

scoff *informal* • *verb* **1** speak derisively, esp. of serious subjects; mock; be scornful. **2** eat greedily. • *noun* **1** food; a meal. **2** *Cdn* (*Maritimes & Nfld*) a big meal, esp. of seafood, served in conjunction with a party.

scoffer *noun* a person who talks about something in a scornfully derisive or mocking way.

scofflaw *noun informal* a person who flouts the law, esp. a person not complying with various laws which are difficult to enforce effectively.

scold • *verb* rebuke or reprimand (esp. a child): *I was forever being scolded for eating with my hands.* • *noun* a nagging or grumbling person, esp. a woman. ▶ **scolder** *noun* **scolding** *noun* **scoldingly** *adverb*

sconce *noun* **1** a semicircular or triangular lighting fixture attached to a wall. **2** a bracket to support a candle, attached to a wall. [Rhymes with *FONTS*]

scone *noun* a tea biscuit often containing raisins or currants, usu. served with butter and jam. [Rhymes with *CON* or *CONE*]

scoop • *noun* **1** any of various objects resembling a spoon, for transferring substances. **2** a quantity taken up by a scoop. **3** a movement of or resembling scooping. **4 a** a piece of news published by a newspaper etc. in advance of its rivals. **b** *informal* the latest information; news: *what's the scoop on why she quit?* • *verb* **1** hollow out with or as if with a scoop. **2 a** lift with a scoop. **b** pick up rapidly in the hands or arms. **3** forestall (a rival newspaper, reporter, etc.) with a scoop. **4** (usu. foll. by *up*) secure (something of monetary value) esp. suddenly. ▶ **scooper** *noun*

scoop neck *noun* a rounded low-cut neckline on a garment. ▶ **scoop-necked** *adjective*

scoot *verb informal* move quickly.

scooter *noun* **1** (also **motor scooter**) a light motorcycle with a low seat and a curved metal shield protecting the driver's legs. **2** a motorized cart used by a disabled or elderly person. **3** a means of transport consisting of a footboard mounted on two wheels and a steering column with handles, propelled by resting one foot on the footboard and pushing the other against the ground. **4** *Cdn* a snowmobile.

scope • *noun* **1** the extent to which it is possible to range: *this is beyond the scope of our research.* **2** the sweep or reach of mental activity, observation, or outlook: *an intellect limited in its scope.* **3** space or freedom to act: *doesn't leave us much scope.* **4** *informal* a telescope, microscope, or other device designated by a word ending in *-scope.* • *verb* (often foll. by *out*) *slang* investigate or assess (a person, situation, etc.); check out, examine.

scorch • *verb* (**scorches**, **scorched**, **scorching**) **1 a** burn the surface of with flame or heat so as to

discolour, parch, injure, or hurt. **b** affect with the sensation of burning. **2** become discoloured etc. with heat. **3** *informal* (of a motorist etc.) go at excessive speed. • *noun* (*plural* **scorches**) **1** a mark made by scorching. **2** a scorching effect.

scorched earth policy *noun* a military strategy of burning or destroying an area's crops and other resources that would otherwise sustain the enemy.

scorcher *noun informal* **1** a very hot day. **2** *Sport* an extremely fast shot or hit. **3** a scathing or harsh rebuke, attack, etc. **4** a book or play that is risqué or erotic.

scorching *adjective* **1** *informal* very hot. **2** (of criticism etc.) stringent; harsh. ▶ **scorchingly** *adverb*

score • *noun* **1** the number of points, goals, runs, etc. achieved by an individual or side in a game. **2** (*plural* **score**) a group or set of twenty. **3** (**scores of**) a large amount or number of. **4** a written representation of a musical composition showing all the vocal or instrumental parts. **5** a notch or line cut or scratched into a surface. **6** (**the score**) *informal* the state of affairs; the real facts. • *verb* (**scores**, **scored**, **scoring**) **1** gain (a point, goal, run, etc.) in a competitive game. **2** be worth (a number of points). **3** record the score during a game. **4** cut or scratch a mark on (a surface). **5** (foll. by *out, through*) delete (text) by drawing a line through it. **6** orchestrate or arrange (a piece of music). **7** *informal* succeed in obtaining (illegal drugs). **8** *informal* succeed in attracting a sexual partner. PHRASES **keep score** register the score as it is made. **know the score** *informal* be aware of the essential facts. **on that score** so far as that is concerned. **settle a score** avenge an injury. **score off** (or **score points off**) *Brit. & Cdn informal* humiliate, esp. verbally in repartee etc. **score points** outdo another person; make a more favourable impression.

scoreboard *noun* a large board in an arena etc., for publicly displaying the score in a game etc.

scorecard *noun* (also **scoresheet**) a printed card on which esp. sports scores are recorded.

scorekeeper *noun* an official who records the score at a game, contest, etc. ▶ **scorekeeping** *noun*

scoreless *adjective Sport* without a goal, run, or point scored: *the game ended in a scoreless tie.*

scorer *noun Sport* **1** a player who scores goals or points: *the sophomore power forward is the team's leading scorer.* **2** an official responsible for keeping score.

scoring *noun* the action of scoring goals or points: *some fans complain that there isn't enough scoring in soccer.*

scorn • *noun* disdain, contempt. • *verb* **1** hold in contempt or disdain. **2** abstain from or refuse to do as unworthy: *scorns lying* ◊ *scorns to lie.* PHRASES **pour scorn on** express contempt or disdain for.

scornful *adjective* full of scorn; contemptuous. ▶ **scornfully** *adverb*

Scorpio *noun* (*plural* **Scorpios**) **1** (usu. **Scorpius**) a large constellation between Sagittarius and Libra, traditionally regarded as contained in the figure of a scorpion. **2 a** the eighth sign of the zodiac. **b** a person born when the sun is in this sign, usu. between Oct. 23 and Nov. 21. [Say SCORE pee oh]

scorpion *noun* **1** an arachnid with lobster-like pincers and a jointed tail that is capable of inflicting a poisonous sting on prey. **2** (also **false scorpion**) a similar, smaller arachnid with pincers but no tail. **3** (**the Scorpion**) the zodiacal sign or constellation Scorpio. [Say SCORE pee un]

Scot *noun* **1** a native of Scotland or person of Scottish descent. **2** *hist.* a member of a Gaelic people that migrated from Ireland to Scotland around the 6th century.

Scotch • *adjective* = SCOTTISH or SCOTS. • *noun* **1** = SCOTTISH or SCOTS **2**. **2** Scotch whisky.

scotch *verb* (**scotches, scotched, scotching**) put an end to: *injury scotched his attempt.*

Scotch pine *noun* a pine tree, native to Eurasia, that is extensively planted for its timber and other products.

Scotch Tape • *noun* proprietary transparent adhesive tape. • *verb* (**Scotch-tape, Scotch-tapes, Scotch-taped, Scotch-taping**) fasten with Scotch Tape.

Scotch whisky *noun* (*plural* **Scotch whiskies**) whisky distilled in Scotland, esp. from malted barley.

scoter *noun* (*plural* **scoter** or **scoters**) a northern duck that breeds in the Arctic and Subarctic and overwinters off coasts further south. [Say SCOTE er]

scot-free *adverb* without being punished or harmed.

Scotland Yard *noun* (in the UK) **1** the headquarters of the London Metropolitan Police. **2** its Criminal Investigation Department.

Scots • *adjective* **1** = SCOTTISH. **2** in the dialect, accent, etc., of (esp. Lowlands) Scotland. • *noun* the form of English spoken in (esp. Lowlands) Scotland.

Scotsman *noun* (*plural* **Scotsmen**) **1** a native of Scotland. **2** a person of Scottish descent.

Scotswoman *noun* (*plural* **Scotswomen**) **1** a Scottish woman. **2** a woman of Scottish descent.

Scottish • *adjective* of Scotland or its inhabitants or their descendants. • *noun* (**the Scottish**; treated as *plural*) the people of Scotland or their descendants. ▶ **Scottishness** *noun*

Scottish terrier *noun* (also informal **Scottie, Scottie dog**) a breed of small terrier with a rough coat and short legs.

scoundrel *noun* a person who shows no moral principles or conscience.

scour • *verb* **1** cleanse or brighten esp. metal by rubbing, esp. with soap, chemicals, or an abrasive substance. **2** (of water, or a person with water) clear out (a pipe, channel, etc.) by flushing through. **3** wear away, erode: *as the ice sheet moved over the Canadian Shield, the ice scoured its massive rock surface.* **4** hasten over (an area etc.) searching thoroughly: *scoured the pages of the newspaper.* • *noun* (also in *plural*, treated as *singular*) diarrhea in livestock.

scourge • *noun* **1** a whip used for punishment, esp. of people. **2** a person or thing that causes trouble or suffering: *the scourge of graffiti has become widespread in the city.* • *verb* (**scourges, scourged, scourging**) **1** whip. **2** punish; afflict. [Say SKURGE]

scout • *noun* **1** a person, esp. a soldier, sent out to get information about the enemy's position, strength, etc. **2 a** = TALENT SCOUT. **b** *Sport* a person who travels ahead of the team in order to gain information about future opponents. **c** a person employed by a mining company to find new mining opportunities or report on the activities of competitors. **3** a car, ship, aircraft, etc. designed or sent out for reconnoitring. **4** (**Scout**) a boy (usu. aged 11-14) who is a member of a Scouting organization. • *verb* **1** act as a scout. **2** make a search. **3** *informal* explore to get information about (territory, an organization, etc.). **4 a** look for (new talent etc.). **b** discover or examine (a prospective recruit). ▶ **scouter** *noun* **scouting** *noun*

Scouting *noun* an international movement, founded in England in 1908 by Robert Baden-Powell, aiming to develop character and promote responsible behaviour in young people, usu. through outdoor activities.

scoutmaster *noun* a person in charge of a group of Scouts.

scout's honour *interjection* professing honesty or genuineness.

scow *noun* a flat-bottomed boat used as a barge etc. [Rhymes with COW]

scowl • *noun* a severe frown producing a sullen, bad-tempered, or threatening look on a person's face. • *verb* make a scowl.

scrabble • *verb* (**scrabbles, scrabbled, scrabbling**) **1** scratch or grope to find or collect or hold on to something. **2** scramble on hands and feet. • *noun* **1** an act of scrabbling. **2** (**Scrabble**) proprietary a game in which players use lettered tiles to form words on a special board.

scraggly *adjective* sparse and irregular; ragged.

scraggy *adjective* (**scraggier, scraggiest**) **1** thin and bony. **2** = SCRAGGLY.

scram *verb* (**scrams, scrammed, scramming**) (esp. in *imperative*) *informal* go away.

scramble • *verb* (**scrambles, scrambled, scrambling**) **1** move or make one's way quickly and awkwardly, typically by using one's hands as well as one's feet. **2** make or become jumbled or muddled. **3** make (a broadcast transmission or telephone conversation) unintelligible unless received by an appropriate decoding device. **4** cook (beaten eggs with a little liquid) in a pan. **5** (with reference to a fighter aircraft) take off or cause to take off immediately in an emergency or for action. **6** (informal) act in a hurried, disorderly, or undignified manner: *firms scrambled to win contracts.* **7** (of a quarterback) move quickly to dodge or evade tacklers while waiting for an opportunity to throw the ball. **8** distribute by scattering randomly to a crowd. • *noun* **1** an act of scrambling. **2** a difficult climb or walk. **3** (foll. by *for*) an eager or disorganized struggle or competition. **4** an emergency takeoff by fighter aircraft.

scrambler *noun* **1** a person or thing that scrambles. **2** a device used to scramble television signals, telephone conversations, etc.

scrap • *noun* **1** a fragment or remnant; a small detached piece. **2** rubbish or waste, usu. of some value for the material it contains. **3** an extract or cutting from something written or printed. **4** discarded metal or paper for reuse. **5** the smallest piece or amount: *not a scrap of food left.* **6** (in *plural*) **a** odds and ends. **b** bits of uneaten food. **7** *informal* a fight or rough quarrel, esp. a spontaneous one. • *verb* (**scraps, scrapped, scrapping**) **1** discard, esp. as useless. **2** get rid of; cancel. **3** make scrap of. **4** engage in a fight or quarrel.

scrapbook *noun* a book of blank pages for sticking clippings, drawings, photographs, etc. in.

scrape • *verb* (**scrapes, scraped, scraping**) **1** move a hard or sharp edge across (a surface), as to make something smooth or clean. **2** rub (a surface) harshly against or with another. **3** make (a hollow) by scraping. **4 a** draw or move with a sound of, or resembling, scraping. **b** emit or produce such a sound. **5** move or pass along almost touching close or surrounding features, obstacles, etc. **6** just manage to achieve (a living etc.). **7** (often foll. by *by, through*) **a** barely manage. **b** pass (an examination etc.) with difficulty. **8** (foll. by *together, up*) contrive to bring or provide; amass with difficulty. • *noun* **1** the act or sound of scraping. **2** a scraped place (on the skin etc.). **3** a scrap; a fight or quarrel. **4** *informal* an awkward predicament, esp. resulting from an escapade. ▮PHRASES▮ **scrape (the bottom of) the barrel** *informal* be obliged to use one's last resources.

scraper *noun* a tool etc. used for scraping, esp. for removing ice, paint, etc. from a surface.

scrap heap *noun* a collection of discarded or cancelled things.

scrapie *noun* a disease of sheep involving the central

nervous system and characterized by lack of coordination, thought to be caused by a virus-like agent. [Say SCRAPE ee]

scraping *noun* **1** in senses of SCRAPE *verb & noun.* **2** (esp. in plural) a fragment produced by this.

scrapper *noun* *informal* **1** a person who fights. **2** a competitive or tenacious person.

scrappiness *noun* **1** a feisty, pugnacious, or determined manner or behaviour: *the low-scoring forward is valued for his scrappiness.* **2** the quality of something that is carelessly arranged or incomplete.

scrappy *adjective* (**scrappier**, **scrappiest**) **1** pugnacious or tenacious. **2** consisting of scraps. **3** incomplete; carelessly arranged or put together.

scratch • *verb* (**scratches**, **scratched**, **scratching**) **1** score or mark the surface of with a sharp or pointed object. **2** make a long narrow superficial wound in (the skin). **3** scrape (something) without marking, esp. with the hand to relieve itching: *stood there scratching.* **4** make or form by scratching. **5** write hurriedly or awkwardly: *scratched a quick reply.* **6** (often foll. by *together, up,* etc.) obtain or achieve (a thing, a living, etc.) by scratching or with difficulty. **7** cancel or strike (out) with or as with a pencil etc. **8 a** withdraw (a competitor, candidate, etc.). **b** (of a competitor) withdraw from a race. **9 a** scratch the ground etc. in search. **b** look around haphazardly: *they were scratching around for evidence.* • *noun* **1** a mark or wound made by scratching. **2** a sound of scratching. **3** an act of scratching oneself. **4** *informal* a superficial wound. **5** a line from which competitors in a race (esp. those not receiving a handicap) start. **6** *slang* money. **7** an athlete or competitor withdrawn from a competition etc. • *adjective* **1** collected by chance. **2 a** collected or made from whatever is available: *a scratch crew.* **b** made from basic or rudimentary ingredients, not from prefabricated components: *scratch cake.* **3** with no handicap given: *a scratch race.* PHRASES **from scratch 1** from the beginning. **2** (of food) prepared from the basic ingredients, without the use of prepared mixes etc. **3** without help or advantage. **scratch along** make a living etc. with difficulty. **scratch one's head** be perplexed. **scratch my back and I will scratch yours 1** do me a favour and I will return it. **2** used in reference to mutual aid or flattery. **scratch the surface 1** understand or deal with a matter only superficially. **2** investigate further. **up to scratch** up to the required standard.

scratch-and-sniff *adjective* designating a perfumed card etc. whose perfume is released when the card is scratched.

scratch-and-win *noun* a lottery ticket coated with an opaque substance which is scratched away to reveal whether the ticket holder wins a prize.

scratcher *noun* a person or thing that scratches.

scratch pad *noun* **1** a pad of paper for scribbling. **2** *Computing* a small fast memory for the temporary storage of data.

scratchproof *adjective* that cannot be marred with scratches.

scratchy *adjective* (**scratchier**, **scratchiest**) **1** tending to make scratches or a scratching noise. **2** (esp. of a garment) tending to itch: *a scratchy sweater.* **3** demanding relief by or as if by scratching: *a scratchy throat.* **4** (of a drawing etc.) done in scratches.

scrawl • *verb* write in a hurried untidy way. • *noun* **1** a piece of hurried writing. **2** a scrawled note. **3** a careless, illegible style of handwriting.

scrawniness *noun* unattractive skinniness.

scrawny *adjective* (**scrawnier**, **scrawniest**) unattractively skinny.

scream • *noun* **1** a loud high-pitched piercing cry expressing fear, pain, etc. **2** a similar sound, e.g. of sirens. **3** *informal* an irresistibly funny thing, person, etc. • *verb* **1** emit a scream. **2** speak or sing (words etc.) in a screaming tone. **3** make or move with a shrill sound like a scream. **4** laugh uncontrollably. **5** *informal* move very quickly. **6** be blatantly obvious or conspicuous.

screamer *noun* **1** a person or thing that screams. **2** *informal* a person or thing that raises screams of laughter, excitement, fear, etc. **3** *Sport* something moving very fast, esp. a powerful base hit, slapshot, etc.

screamingly *adverb* **1** extremely: *screamingly funny.* **2** blatantly: *screamingly obvious.*

scree *noun* (in *singular* or *plural*) **1** small loose stones. **2** a mountain slope covered with these.

screech • *noun* (*plural* **screeches**) **1** a harsh high-pitched scream etc. **2** (in Canada) a potent dark rum of Newfoundland. • *verb* (**screeches**, **screeched**, **screeching**) utter with or make a screech. PHRASES **screech in** *Cdn* (*Nfld*) initiate (a visitor) by means of a screech-in: *tourists were screeched in at a seaside ceremony.* ▶ **screecher** *noun*

screech-in *noun* *Cdn* (*Nfld*) a jocular ritual by which visitors to Newfoundland are "initiated", involving the drinking of screech and performing acts such as dipping a foot in the ocean, kissing a cod, etc.

screech owl *noun* **1** any of various small North American eared owls. **2** any owl that screeches instead of hooting, esp. a barn owl.

screechy *adjective* (**screechier**, **screechiest**) (of a sound) harsh and piercing: *screechy guitars.*

screed *noun* a long usu. tiresome piece of writing or speech: *the screed against gamblers and drinkers was typical of his gospel compositions.*

screen • *noun* **1** a fixed or movable upright partition for separating, concealing, or sheltering. **2** a thing used as a shelter, esp. from observation. **3 a** a measure adopted for concealment. **b** the protection afforded by this: *under the screen of night.* **4 a** a blank usu. white or silver surface on which a photographic image is projected. **b** (**the screen**) the film industry. **5 a** the surface of a cathode ray tube or similar electronic device, esp. of a television, computer, etc., on which images appear. **b** the collection of images etc. displayed on a computer screen at one time: *move to the next screen.* **6** a frame with fine wire netting to keep out flies, mosquitoes, etc. **7** a system of checking for the presence or absence of a disease, ability, attribute, etc. • *verb* **1 a** afford shelter to; hide partly or completely. **b** protect from detection, censure, etc. **2** shut off or hide behind a screen. **3** *Hockey* obstruct the view of (a goalie) by being positioned in front of him or her. **4 a** show (a film etc.) on a screen. **b** broadcast (a television program). **5** prevent from causing, or protect from, electrical interference. **6 a** test (a person or group) for the presence or absence of a disease. **b** check on (a person) for the presence or absence of a quality, esp. reliability, suitability, etc. **c** find out details about (an incoming telephone call) to determine whether it should be answered.

screen door *noun* a light outer door of a house, with a screen for keeping out insects while letting in air.

screener *noun* a person or thing that screens something, esp. a person who gets information about people to determine if they are suitable for or can be trusted in a particular situation or job: *works as a call screener for a phone-in show.*

screening *noun* **1** the showing of a film. **2** the testing of a group of people for a disease etc.

screenplay *noun* the script of a film, with acting instructions, scene directions, etc.

screen-print • *verb* (usu. as **screen-printed** *adjective*) force ink onto a surface through a prepared screen of fine material in order to create a picture or pattern. • *noun* (**screen print**) a design or picture created by screen-printing.

screen-printing *noun* a process like stencilling with ink forced through a prepared sheet of fine material.

screen saver *noun Computing* a program which, after a set time, replaces an unchanging screen display with a moving image to prevent damage to the phosphor.

screen test *noun* a filmed audition of a prospective film or television actor.

screenwriter *noun* a person who writes a screenplay.
▶ **screenwriting** *noun*

screw • *noun* **1** a thin cylinder or cone with a spiral ridge or thread running around the outside, used esp. for fastening. **2** (also **screw propeller**) a form of propeller with twisted blades acting like a screw on the water or air. **3** *slang* a prison guard. • *verb* **1** fasten or tighten with a screw or screws. **2** *slang* (often in *passive*) cheat or take advantage of; treat unfairly. **3** (foll. by *out of*) *slang* extort (consent, money, etc.) from (a person). **4** *coarse slang* (as an exclamation) used to express frustration, anger, dismissive contempt, etc. PHRASES **have one's head screwed on (straight)** *informal* have common sense. **have a screw loose** *informal* be slightly crazy. **put the screws on** *informal* exert pressure, esp. to extort or intimidate. **screw around** *slang* **1** be promiscuous. **2** fool around; waste time. **3** (foll. by *with*) toy with someone psychologically. **screw up 1** *slang* **a** bungle or mismanage; handle something badly; make a mistake. **b** spoil or ruin (an event, opportunity, etc.). **2** *slang* (usu. as **screwed-up** *adjective*) disturb mentally. **3** summon up (one's courage etc.). **4** contract or contort (one's face etc.). **5** contract and crush into a tight mass (a piece of paper etc.).

screwball • *noun* **1** *Baseball* a ball pitched so that it curves towards the side from which it was thrown. **2** *slang* a crazy or eccentric person. • *adjective* **1** *slang* crazy, eccentric. **2** designating a style of zany fast-moving comedy film with eccentric characters or ridiculous situations.

screw cap *noun* = SCREW-TOP.

screwdriver *noun* **1** a tool with a shaped tip to fit into the head of a screw to turn it. **2** a cocktail of vodka and orange juice.

screwed *adjective* **1** *slang* ruined; rendered ineffective; in a hopeless state: *now we're screwed!* **2** twisted.

screw eye *noun* a screw with a loop for passing cord etc. through instead of a slotted head.

screw-top *noun* (also as an *adjective*) a cap or lid that can be screwed on to a bottle, jar, etc.: *screw-top jar.*

screw-up *noun slang* a bungle, muddle, mess.

screwy *adjective* (**screwier, screwiest**) *slang* **1** crazy or eccentric. **2** absurd. **3** messed up, confused.

scribal *adjective* having to do with a scribe or the work of a scribe: *scribal errors.*

scribble • *verb* (**scribbles, scribbled, scribbling**) **1** write carelessly or hurriedly. **2** often *derogatory* be an author or writer. **3** draw carelessly or meaninglessly. • *noun* **1** a scrawl. **2** a hasty note etc. **3** careless handwriting.

scribbler *noun* **1** *informal* a person or thing that scribbles, esp. a professional writer. **2** *Cdn* a small, soft-covered booklet for writing in; a student's notebook.

scribblings *plural noun* scribbled writing.

scribe *noun* **1** a person who writes out documents, esp. an ancient or medieval copyist of manuscripts. **2** *Jewish Hist.* an ancient Jewish record-keeper or, later, professional theologian and jurist. **3** (also **scriber**) a

pointed instrument for making marks on wood, bricks, etc., to guide a saw, or in sign writing. **4** *informal* a writer, esp. a journalist.

scrim *noun* **1** a theatrical drop made of an open-weave fabric that looks opaque when lit from in front but becomes transparent when lit from behind. **2** the fabric of which such drops are made.

scrimmage • *noun* **1** a rough or confused struggle: *an open scrimmage for power and authority and prestige.* **2** *Football* **a** a sequence of play beginning with a backward pass from the centre to put the ball in play and continuing until the ball is declared dead. **b** (also **scrimmage line**) = LINE OF SCRIMMAGE. **3** *Sport* a session or informal game in which a team's various squads practise plays against each other. • *verb* (**scrimmages, scrimmaged, scrimmaging**) engage in a scrimmage.

scrimp *verb* **1** spend money carefully in order to save: *workers who had scrimped to achieve lower-middle-class status.* **2** spend too little money on something: *tenants claim the landlord scrimped on repairs to the building.* PHRASES **scrimp and save** practise thrift to save money or in order to pay for something else.

scrimshaw • *verb* adorn (whalebone, ivory, shells, etc.) with carved or coloured designs. • *noun* work or a piece of work of this kind.

scrip¹ *noun* **1** a provisional certificate of money subscribed to a bank or company etc. entitling the holder to a formal certificate and dividends. **2** such certificates collectively. **3** temporary paper currency.

scrip² *noun* (also **land scrip**) **1** a certificate entitling the holder to acquire possession of certain portions of public land. **2** *Cdn hist.* a certificate issued to Metis entitling the bearer to 240 acres or money for the purchase of land, issued in compensation for lands lost by the Metis after the Northwest Rebellion.

script • *noun* **1** handwriting as distinct from print; written characters. **2** type imitating handwriting. **3** an alphabet or system of writing: *the Russian script.* **4 a** the text of a play, film, or broadcast. **b** a predictable or planned series of statements, actions, etc.: *the solicitor general followed the script to the letter, as it had been set out in a cabinet minute, and accepted the amendment on property rights ◊ ordered every member of his team to stick to the script when discussing policy matters.* **5** *Computing* a file containing commands or other actions that could have been entered from the keyboard, used to replay often-used sequences of actions. • *verb* write a script for a film, show, event, etc.: *the 1990 version was scripted by Desmond Donaldson ◊ tightly scripted photo opportunities.*

scriptural *adjective* **1** of or relating to a scripture, esp. the Bible. **2** having the authority of a scripture.

scripture *noun* writings sacred to a religion or group, esp. (as **Scripture** or **the Scriptures**) the Bible.

scriptwriter *noun* a person who writes a script for a film, broadcast, etc. ▶ **scriptwriting** *noun*

scritch *noun* a quiet scraping or scratching sound.
▶ **scritching** *noun & adjective*

scroll • *noun* **1** a roll of parchment or paper esp. with writing on it. **2** a book in the ancient roll form. **3** an ornamental design or carving imitating a roll of parchment. • *verb* **1** (often foll. by *down, up,* etc.) *Computing* move (displayed text etc.) up, down, or across on a screen or in a window in order to display different parts of it. **2** curl up like paper.

scroll bar *noun* a long thin section at the edge of a computer display by which material can be scrolled using a mouse.

scroll saw *noun* a narrow-bladed saw for cutting along curved lines in ornamental work.

S

scrollwork *noun* decoration of spiral lines, esp. as cut by a scroll saw.

Scrooge *noun* a mean or miserly person.

scrotum *noun* a pouch of skin containing the testicles. [Say SKROTE um]

scrounge *informal* • *verb* (**scrounges**, **scrounged**, **scrounging**) **1** (often foll. by *up*) search or forage for; obtain by or as by foraging. **2** search about to find something at no cost. **3** obtain (things) illicitly or by cadging. • *noun* an act of scrounging. ▶**scrounger** *noun*

scrub¹ • *verb* (**scrubs**, **scrubbed**, **scrubbing**) **1** rub a surface hard so as to clean, esp. with a hard brush. **2** (often foll. by *up*) (of a surgeon etc.) thoroughly clean the hands and arms by scrubbing, before operating. **3** *informal* scrap or cancel. **4** use water to remove impurities from (gas etc.). • *noun* **1** an act of scrubbing: *give the floor a good scrub*. **2** a substance, implement, etc., used in scrubbing: *facial scrub*.

scrub² *noun* **1 a** vegetation consisting mainly of brush or stunted forest growth. **b** an area of land covered with this. **2** an animal of inferior breed or physique (often as an *adjective*: *scrub horse*). **3** a small or dwarf variety (often as an *adjective*: *scrub pine*). **4** *Sport* **a** *informal* a team or player not of the first class. **b** *Cdn* (as an *adjective*) designating an informal match played by children, amateurs, etc; a pickup game: *scrub baseball*.

scrubbable *adjective* (of a surface or finish) that is easily cleaned and is not likely to be damaged by scrubbing or washing.

scrubber *noun* a person or thing that scrubs, esp. apparatus for purifying gases, removing excess pollutants from exhaust, etc.

scrubby *adjective* (**scrubbier**, **scrubbiest**) **1** covered with small bushes and trees: *a scrubby hillside*. **2** (of plants) small and not fully developed: *scrubby vegetation*.

scrubland *noun* land consisting of scrub vegetation.

scruff *noun* the back of the neck as used to grasp and lift or drag an animal or person by (esp. *scruff of the neck*).

scruffiness *noun* a messy or untidy appearance.

scruffy *adjective* (**scruffier**, **scruffiest**) *informal* shabby, slovenly, untidy; ragged.

scrum • *noun* **1** *Rugby* an arrangement of the forwards of each team in opposing groups, each with arms interlocked and heads down, with the ball thrown in between them to restart play. **2** *Brit. & Cdn informal* a disorderly crowd. **3** *Cdn* **a** a situation where a crowd of reporters surround and interrogate a politician in an impromptu, informal, or disorderly manner. **b** the crowd of reporters in such a situation. • *verb* (**scrums**, **scrummed**, **scrumming**) **1** (often foll. by *down*) *Rugby* form a scrum. **2** *Cdn* **a** (of a politician or reporter) engage in a scrum. **b** (of reporters) surround and interrogate (a politician) in a scrum.

scrumptious *adjective informal* **1** delicious. **2** pleasing. ▶**scrumptiously** *adverb* **scrumptiousness** *noun*

scrunch *verb* (**scrunches**, **scrunched**, **scrunching**) **1 a** make or become crushed or crumpled. **b** squeeze oneself into a compact shape; crouch. **2** make or cause to make a crunching sound. **3** style (hair) by squeezing or crushing in the hands to give a tousled look.

scruncheon *noun Cdn* (*Nfld*) (in *plural*) small pieces of pork fat fried crisp and usu. eaten with fish and brewis. [Say SKRUN sh'n]

scrunchy *noun* (also **scrunchie**) (*plural* **scrunchies**) an elastic band covered in loose fabric, used to fasten the hair in a ponytail etc.

scruple • *noun* (in *singular* or *plural*) **1** regard to the morality or propriety of an action: *there would be no limit to what he could do with the money provided he had no* scruples. **2** a feeling of doubt or hesitation caused by this: *he hadn't the slightest scruple in using terror*. • *verb* (**scruples**, **scrupled**, **scrupling**) be reluctant because of scruples: *a man who would not scruple to murder children*. [Say SCREW pull]

scrupulosity *noun* **1** extreme care and attention to details: *I appreciate scrupulosity in money matters*. **2** great care in the avoidance of doing wrong: *she scorns scrupulosity as a wasted effort since everything is inherently corrupt*. [Say screw pyoo LOSSA tee]

scrupulous *adjective* **1** conscientious or thorough even in small matters. **2** careful to avoid doing wrong. **3** over-attentive to details. ▶**scrupulously** *adverb* **scrupulousness** *noun* [Say SCREW pyoo lus]

scrutineer *noun* esp. *Cdn & Brit.* a person who scrutinizes or examines something, esp. the conduct and result of a ballot. [Say screw tin EAR]

scrutinize *verb* (**scrutinizes**, **scrutinized**, **scrutinizing**) look closely at; examine with close scrutiny. [Say SCREW tin ize]

scrutiny *noun* (*plural* **scrutinies**) **1** a critical investigation or examination: *his actions have come under scrutiny* ◊ *the incident became the focus of intense media scrutiny*. **2** an official examination of ballot papers to check their validity or accuracy of counting. [Say SCREW tuh nee]

SCSI *noun* (*plural* **SCSIs**) a standard interface connecting peripheral devices, such as disk storage units, to small and medium-sized computers. [Sounds like SCUZZY]

scuba *noun* (*plural* **scubas**) a portable breathing apparatus for divers, consisting of cylinders of compressed air strapped on the back, feeding air automatically through a mask or mouthpiece: *scuba diving* ◊ *scuba diver* ◊ *learn to scuba dive*.

scud • *verb* (**scuds**, **scudded**, **scudding**) **1** be driven swiftly in a straight course by the wind: *tattered clouds scudded across the sky*. **2** fly or run straight, fast, and lightly; skim along: *a rock scudded past his ear*. • *noun* (usu. **Scud**) a type of long-range surface-to-surface missile originally developed in the former USSR.

scuff • *verb* **1** graze or brush against. **2** mark or wear the surface off (leather, esp. of shoe uppers, a floor, etc.) by scratching or grazing with or against something. **3** *Baseball* scratch or roughen up the surface of (the ball) illicitly to increase its movement when pitched. **4 a** walk with dragging feet. **b** drag (one's feet) across a surface. • *noun* a mark of scuffing. ▶**scuffed** *adjective*

scuffle • *noun* **1** a confused struggle or disorderly fight at close quarters; a tussle. **2** the shuffling of feet. • *verb* (**scuffles**, **scuffled**, **scuffling**) **1** engage in a scuffle. **2** move with a shuffling gait. **3** scarify or stir the surface of the ground, esp. between rows of crops. ▶**scuffler** *noun*

SPELL CHECK
scull, skull

The head of a skeleton is the **skull**.

---

scull¹ • *noun* **1** either of a pair of small oars used by a single rower. **2** an oar placed over the stern of a boat to propel it, usu. by a twisting motion. **3** a small boat propelled with a scull or sculls. **4** (in *plural*) a race between boats with two oars per rower. • *verb* propel (a boat) with sculls. ▶**sculler** *noun*

scull² *noun Cdn* (*Nfld*) the seasonal migration of caplin from the sea to inshore waters to spawn.

scullery *noun* (*plural* **sculleries**) a small kitchen or room at the back of a house for washing dishes etc.

sculpin *noun* any of numerous fish native to non-tropical regions, having large spiny heads.

S

sculpt *verb* **1** create or represent something by carving, casting, or other shaping techniques. **2** provide something with a particular shape: *a carefully sculpted beard ◊ a valley sculpted by glaciers*. ▶ **sculpting** *noun*

sculptor *noun* an artist who makes sculpture.

sculptress *noun* a female artist who makes sculptures.

sculptural *adjective* having to do with sculpture. ▶ **sculpturally** *adverb*

sculpture • *noun* **1** the art of making forms, often representational, in stone, wood, clay, metal, etc. **2** a work or works of sculpture. • *verb* (**sculptures**, **sculptured**, **sculpturing**) **1** represent in or adorn with sculpture. **2** (esp. as **sculptured** *adjective*) give a markedly contoured form to: *rocks sculptured by the waves ◊ the dancers' sculptured bodies*.

scum • *noun* **1** a layer of dirt, froth, etc. forming at the top of liquid, esp. in boiling or fermentation or on stagnant water. **2** the most worthless part of something. **3** *informal* a worthless, despicable person or group. • *verb* (**scums**, **scummed**, **scumming**) **1** remove scum from. **2** be or form a scum on. **3** (of a liquid) develop scum.

scumbag *noun* (also **scumball**, **scum-bucket**) *slang* a contemptible, despicable, or disgusting person.

scummy *adjective* (**scummier**, **scummiest**) **1** despicable, worthless. **2** disgusting. **3** having a floating layer of dirt or froth: *a scummy fish pond*.

scupper • *noun* (often in *plural*) a hole in a ship's side to carry off water from the deck. • *verb slang* **1** sink (a ship or its crew). **2** defeat or ruin (a plan etc.): *her testimony scuppered his chance for early parole*.

scurf *noun* **1** flakes on the skin's surface, cast off as fresh skin develops below, esp. those of the head. **2** any scaly matter on a surface. ▶ **scurfy** *adjective*

scurrility *noun* an excessive interest in scandal and desire to damage reputations: *the scurrility of professional journalism*. [Say skur ILLA tee]

scurrilous *adjective* **1** making or spreading scandalous claims about someone with the intention of damaging their reputation: *scurrilous attacks on his integrity*. **2** given to or expressed with rude and insulting humour: *a collection of bawdy and scurrilous writings*. ▶ **scurrilously** *adverb* [Say SKUR a lus]

scurry • *verb* (**scurries**, **scurried**, **scurrying**) run or move hurriedly, esp. with short quick steps. • *noun* (*plural* **scurries**) a scurrying movement.

S-curve *noun* two curves in a road etc., one following the other in the opposite direction.

scurvy *noun* a disease caused by lack of vitamin C, with swollen, bleeding gums and the opening of previously healed wounds.

scuttle • *verb* (**scuttles**, **scuttled**, **scuttling**) **1** abandon, thwart, or dismiss (a plan, rumour, etc.). **2** let water into (a ship) to sink it. **3** run or move hurriedly with short quick steps, esp. furtively or busily. • *noun* **1** a hole with a lid in a ship's deck or side. **2** an opening in the ceiling, floor, or wall of a building; a trap door. **3** a small bucket, usu. with a sloping lip, for pouring, carrying, and holding coal. **4** a hurried pace.

scuttlebutt *noun* **1** *informal* rumour, gossip. **2** a barrel of drinking water kept on the deck of a ship.

scuzz *noun* *slang* something sleazy, disgusting, or despicable.

scuzzball *noun* (also **scuzzbag**) *slang* a filthy, sleazy, or shady person.

scuzziness *noun* *slang* a sleazy, disgusting, or despicable manner or behaviour.

scuzzy *adjective* (**scuzzier**, **scuzziest**) *slang* squalid, sleazy, abhorrent, or disgusting.

scythe • *noun* an agricultural tool consisting of a pole with two short handles projecting from it and a long thin curving blade at the bottom, which is swung over the ground to cut grass, grain, etc. • *verb* (**scythes**, **scythed**, **scything**) cut with, or as if with, a scythe. [Say SYTHE (with TH as in *SOOTHE*)]

SDI *abbreviation* Strategic Defence Initiative, a projected US satellite system designed to defend against nuclear weapons.

SE *abbreviation* **1** southeast. **2** southeastern.

Se *symbol* selenium.

sea *noun* **1** the expanse of salt water that covers most of the earth's surface and surrounds its land masses. **2** a particular (usu. named) tract of salt water partly or wholly enclosed by land. **3** a vast expanse or quantity: *a sea of faces*. ▨PHRASES▧ **at sea 1** in a ship on the sea. **2** (also **all at sea**) perplexed, confused. **by sea** in a ship or ships. **go to sea** become a sailor. **on the sea 1** in a ship at sea. **2** situated on the coast. **put** (or **put out**) **to sea** leave land or port.

sea bass *noun* (*plural* **sea bass** or **sea basses**) any of various marine fishes resembling or related to the bass.

seabed *noun* = SEA FLOOR.

seabird *noun* any bird that lives on or near the sea.

seaboard *noun* the coastal region or land along the sea.

sea change *noun* a notable or unexpected transformation; a radical change: *there is a real sea change occurring in the world economic system*.

seacoast *noun* the border of land near the sea.

sea cucumber *noun* any of several hundred species of wormlike marine invertebrate.

sea dog *noun* **1** an old or experienced sailor. **2** *informal* a harbour seal.

Sea-Doo *noun* (*plural* **Sea-Doos**) *proprietary* = PERSONAL WATERCRAFT.

seafarer *noun* **1** a sailor. **2** a traveller by sea.

seafaring • *adjective* **1** travelling by sea. **2** related to or involved in the occupation or business of a sailor. • *noun* **1** travel by sea. **2** the business or occupation of a sailor. [Say SEA fare ing]

sea floor *noun* the bottom of the sea.

seafoam • *noun* **1** foam formed on the sea. **2** (also **seafoam green**) a pastel bluish-green. • *adjective* of the colour of seafoam green.

seafood *noun* any edible animal obtained from the sea, including fish, crustaceans, and molluscs.

seafront *noun* an area or esp. the part of a coastal town directly facing the sea.

sea-going *adjective* **1** fit for crossing the sea. **2 a** travelling by sea. **b** involved in the occupation of a sailor. **3** of or related to the occupation or lifestyle of a sailor.

seagrass *noun* (*plural* **seagrasses**) any of various grasslike plants growing in or by the sea, esp. eelgrass.

sea green *noun* & *adjective* the colour of the sea, a pale bluish green.

seagull *noun* a gull, esp. a herring gull.

sea horse *noun* any of various small upright marine fishes that have a body suggestive of the head and neck of a horse.

sea ice *noun* a large expanse of ice formed from frozen salt water, esp. occurring in the sea.

sea kayak • *noun* a usu. fibreglass kayak with a rudder. • *verb* travel by sea kayak, esp. for recreation. ▶ **sea kayaker** *noun* **sea kayaking** *noun*

seal[1] • *noun* **1** a device or substance used to join two things together or make something impervious. **2** a piece of wax or lead with an individual design stamped into it, attached to a document as a guarantee of

authenticity. **3** a confirmation or guarantee: *a seal of approval.* **4** an engraved device used for stamping a seal. • **verb 1** fasten or close securely. **2** (foll. by *off*) isolate (an area) by preventing entrance to and exit from it. **3** apply a non-porous coating to (a surface) to make it impervious. **4** conclude, establish, or secure definitively. **5** authenticate (a document) with a seal. **PHRASES** **one's lips are sealed** one promises to keep a secret. **set one's seal to** (or **on**) authorize, endorse, or confirm.

seal² • **noun 1** a fish-eating amphibious sea mammal with a streamlined body and limbs developed as flippers. **2** sealskin. • **verb** hunt for seals.

sealant **noun 1** a material or substance used to fill a gap or crack so that air, liquid, etc. cannot enter or escape. **2** a substance applied to a surface to make it impervious or resistant to water, dirt, stains, etc.

sea legs **noun** the ability to keep one's balance and avoid becoming sick while at sea.

sealer¹ **noun 1** (also **sealer jar**) *Cdn* (esp. *Prairies* & *BC*) **a** a preserving jar with a glass or metal lid secured by a metal band screwed onto the mouth of the jar. **b** the contents of a sealer. **2** an undercoat of paint etc. used to give porous building materials a surface more receptive to finishing coats. **3** a device or substance used to make something airtight or impervious to water, oil, etc.

sealer² **noun 1** a person who hunts seals. **2** a ship used for hunting seals.

sea level **noun** the average level of the sea's surface, used as an international standard in calculating altitude and as a barometric standard.

sealift **noun** a large-scale transportation of supplies, troops, etc. by sea.

sealing **noun** the hunting of seals.

sealing wax **noun** a mixture of shellac, rosin, turpentine, and pigment, softened by heating and used to make seals.

sea lion **noun** any of several large-eared seals having broader muzzles and sparser fur than the fur seals.

seal of approval **noun 1** a seal or stamp on a product etc. indicating that it has been approved by an authority. **2** an expression of endorsement etc.

seal oil **noun** oil obtained from the fat of seals.

seal-oil lamp **noun** = KUDLIK.

sealskin **noun 1** the skin or prepared fur of a seal. **2** (often as an *adjective*) a garment made from this.

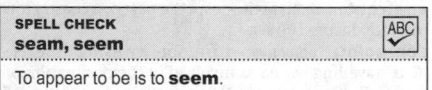

SPELL CHECK	ABC ✓
seam, seem	
To appear to be is to **seem**.	

seam • **noun 1** a line along which two pieces of cloth etc. are stitched together. **2** a line or ridge where two parallel edges meet, e.g. of floorboards fitted edge to edge. **3** a stratum of coal etc. **4** a wrinkle or scar. • **verb 1** join with a seam. **2** (esp. as **seamed** *adjective*) mark or score (a surface) with lines or indentations. **PHRASES** **come apart at the seams** collapse emotionally.

seaman **noun** (*plural* **seamen**) **1** a person whose occupation is on the sea; a sailor. **2** an enlisted member of the navy below the rank of petty officer.

seamanship **noun** the art and skill of managing, handling, and maintaining a ship or boat.

seamless **adjective 1** without a seam. **2** uninterrupted, smooth. ▶ **seamlessly** *adverb* **seamlessness** *noun*

seamstress **noun** (*plural* **seamstresses**) a woman who makes and mends clothing, esp. professionally. [Say SEAM struss or SEM struss]

seamy *adjective* (**seamier**, **seamiest**) **1** marked with or showing seams. **2** disreputable: *a seamy sex scandal.*

seance **noun** a meeting at which spiritualists attempt to make contact with the dead. [Say SAY awnce]

sea otter **noun** a Pacific otter with thick dark fur.

seaplane **noun** an aircraft designed to take off from and land and float on water.

seaport **noun 1** a harbour or port for sea-going ships. **2** a town or city having such a harbour or port.

sear • **verb 1** burn or scorch the surface of. **2** cause great pain or anguish (to). **3** brown (meat) quickly at a high temperature so that it will retain its juices in cooking. **4** leave an esp. disturbing impression etc. on or in: *verbal abuse can sear into a child's self-worth, leaving deep psychological scars.* • **adjective** = SERE¹. [Rhymes with HEAR]

search • **verb** (**searches**, **searched**, **searching**) **1** look through, examine, or go over thoroughly to find something. **2** *Computing* locate a specified piece of information or text in a table, file, document, etc. **3** examine or question (one's mind, conscience, etc.) thoroughly: *search your heart.* **4** (foll. by *out*) look probingly for. • **noun** (*plural* **searches**) **1** an act of searching; an investigation. **2** *Computing* the locating of a specified piece of information or text. **PHRASES** **in search of** trying to find. **search me!** *informal* I don't know. ▶ **searchable** *adjective*

search and replace **noun** a computer function which allows a user to find a string of characters in a text and replace it automatically or interactively with another string.

search and rescue **noun** an operation designed to find the survivors of a disaster, people who are lost or in danger, etc. and bring them to safety.

search engine **noun** a program for the retrieval of data, files, etc. from a database or network.

searcher **noun** a person who searches for something.

searching *adjective* (of an examination etc.) thorough, penetrating. ▶ **searchingly** *adverb*

searchlight **noun 1** a powerful outdoor electric light with a concentrated beam that can be turned in any direction. **2** the light or beam from this.

searchmaster **noun** *Cdn* an air force officer in charge of coordinating a search and rescue operation, usu. from the airfield nearest the missing person etc.

search party **noun** (*plural* **search parties**) a group of people organized to look for a lost person or thing.

search warrant **noun** a judge's order authorizing a person to enter and search a building and to seize evidence.

searing *adjective* **1** very hot; scorching. **2** very painful; agonizing: *felt this searing pain in my shoulder.* **3** (of words or speech) powerful and critical: *the article was a searing attack on the government.* ▶ **searingly** *adverb* [Rhymes with HEARING]

sea salt **noun** salt produced by evaporating sea water.

seascape **noun 1** a picturesque view or prospect of the sea. **2** a representation of such a view, esp. a painting.

seashell **noun** the shell of a marine mollusc.

seashore **noun** land close to or bordering on the sea.

seasick *adjective* suffering from dizziness or nausea from the motion of a ship at sea. ▶ **seasickness** *noun*

seaside **noun** the seacoast, esp. when visited for a holiday or pleasure.

season • **noun 1** each of the four periods (spring, summer, fall, and winter) into which the year is divided, associated with a type of weather and a stage of vegetation. **2** a time of year characterized by climatic features: *the dry season.* **3** a time when something is plentiful, in vogue, or regularly indulged in: *tourist*

season. **4** a schedule of shows, sporting events, or performances. **5** (also **Season**) the time of year surrounding a particular holiday: *Season's greetings*. **6** the time of year when a usu. specified animal breeds or is hunted or fished: *salmon season*. **7** a period of indefinite or varying length: *the season of her youth*. • *verb* **1** flavour (food) with salt, herbs, etc. **2 a** make or become suitable or conditioned, esp. by exposure to the air or weather: *seasoned hardwood*. **b** make or become mature or experienced: *a seasoned pro*. **3** enhance with wit, excitement, etc.: *her conversation is seasoned liberally with exclamation points and punch lines*. PHRASES **for all seasons 1** ready for any situation or emergency. **2** welcome or appropriate at any time under any conditions: *shoes for all seasons*. **in season 1** (of food) available in quantity and in good condition. **2** (of an animal) in heat.

seasonable *adjective* usual for or appropriate to a particular season of the year: *seasonable temperatures ◊ serenaded the guests with seasonable tunes*.

seasonal *adjective* **1** of, depending on, or characteristic of the seasons of the year or a particular season: *a selection of seasonal fresh fruit*. **2** varying with the season: *there are companies whose markets are seasonal ◊ seasonal rainfall*. **3** (of a person) employed only during a particular season.

seasonal affective disorder *noun* a depressive state associated with late fall and winter and thought to be caused by a lack of light. Abbreviation: **SAD**.

seasonality *noun* the fact of varying with the seasons: *monsoon areas are characterized by marked seasonality*.

seasonally *adverb* **1** at a certain time of year; during some seasons: *local strawberries are available seasonally*. **2** according to the season or seasons: *temperatures in the region vary seasonally*.

seasoning *noun* **1** an ingredient added to food to enhance its flavour. **2** the flavouring of a dish achieved by adding such ingredients.

season ticket *noun* (usu. in *plural*) (also esp. *Cdn* **season's ticket**) tickets or a pass for esp. a schedule of sporting or cultural events during a specified period, usu. bought at a reduced rate.

sea star *noun* = STARFISH.

seat • *noun* **1 a** a thing made or used for sitting on. **b** the part of a chair etc. on which one actually sits. **2** a place for one person to sit in a theatre, vehicle, etc. **3 a** the right to sit as a member of a deliberative or administrative body. **b** *Cdn & Brit.* a Member of Parliament's constituency. **c** = COUNTY SEAT. **4** the buttocks. **5** the part of the pants etc. covering the buttocks. **6** the part of a thing on which it rests or appears to rest; the base. **7** the manner of sitting on a horse etc. **8** a site or location of something specified: *a seat of learning*. • *verb* **1** find, and guide a person or oneself to, an available seat. **2** provide sitting accommodation for. **3** place or fit in position. PHRASES **be seated** sit down. **by the seat of one's pants** *informal* by instinct rather than logic or knowledge. **take a** (or **one's**) **seat** sit down.

seat belt *noun* a strap or set of straps designed to secure a person in a seat of a vehicle, aircraft, etc.

seated *adjective* **1** sitting. **2** positioned.

-seater *noun* (in *combination*) a car, aircraft, piece of furniture, auditorium, etc. having a specified seating capacity.

seating *noun* **1** seats collectively: *seating area*. **2** sitting accommodation: *seating capacity*.

seatmate *noun* a person sitting in a nearby seat.

seat-of-the-pants *adjective* based on instinct or intuition rather than logic or knowledge: *had nothing but success with his seat-of-the-pants style of managing*.

sea trout *noun* (plural **sea trout** or **sea trouts**) **1** any of various migratory trout, esp. a large silvery race of the trout *Salmo trutta*. **2** any of various marine fishes that resemble trout.

seat sale *noun* *Cdn & Brit.* a sale of esp. airline tickets at a reduced price.

sea urchin *noun* a small marine creature with a spherical or flattened spiny shell.

seawall *noun* a wall or embankment erected as a breakwater to prevent encroachment by the sea.

seaward • *adverb* (also **seawards**) towards the sea. • *adjective* **1** going out to sea. **2** directed or facing towards the sea; situated on the side nearest the sea. • *noun* the direction or position in which the sea lies.

seaway *noun* an inland waterway for sea-going ships.

seaweed *noun* any of various algae growing in the sea or on the rocks on a shore. ▶ **seaweedy** *adjective*

seaworthiness *noun* the condition of a ship that is in a suitable condition to undergo a sea voyage.

seaworthy *adjective* (esp. of a ship) in a suitable condition to undergo a sea voyage.

sec *noun* *informal* an instant or moment; a second: *wait just a sec*.

sec. *abbreviation* second(s).

secateurs *plural noun* *Cdn & Brit.* a pair of pruning shears that can be used with one hand to clip usu. thin branches and flowers etc. [Say sekka TURZ]

WRITING TIP
secede, succeed
When somebody becomes the rightful holder of a title or position, they **succeed** the person who formerly held the title or they **succeed to** the position itself: *Jamal succeeded Tracey as budget chief; Elizabeth succeeded to the throne in 1558*.

secede *verb* (**secedes**, **seceded**, **seceding**) withdraw formally from an alliance, an association, a federal union, or a political or religious organization: *Belgium seceded from the Netherlands in 1830*. ▶ **seceder** *noun* [Say suh SEED]

WRITING TIP
secession, succession
The process in which a person takes over an official position or title is **succession**: *She's third in order of succession to the throne*.

secession *noun* **1** the action of withdrawing formally from membership of a federation or organization, esp. a political state: *in the event of Quebec's secession*. **2** (**Secession**) *hist.* the withdrawal of eleven southern States from the US Union in 1860, leading to the Civil War. [Say suh SESSION]

secessionism *noun* the principles of those in favour of secession. ▶ **secessionist** *noun & adjective* [Say suh SESSION ism]

Sechelt • *noun* (plural **Sechelt**) **1** a member of an Aboriginal people living on the coast of BC, north of Vancouver. **2** their Sne Nay Muxw language. • *adjective* of or relating to this people or their language. [Say SEE shash]

seclude *verb* (**secludes**, **secluded**, **secluding**) keep (a person) sequestered or shut up in order to prevent access or influence from outside.

secluded *adjective* **1** remote; hidden from view. **2** isolated or withdrawn from human contact.

seclusion *noun* a secluded state; confinement, isolation, privacy.

second[1] • *ordinal number* **1** coming next after the first. **2** coming next in rank, quality, or importance to a

person or thing regarded as first. **3** (in *plural*) *informal* a second helping of food at a meal. **4** a slightly flawed or inferior-quality item. **5** an assistant or attendant, esp. in a boxing match or duel. **6** *Curling* the second player on a curling rink. **7** *Cdn & Brit.* (in Scouts, Girl Guides, etc.) a boy or girl chosen by their pack to assist the Sixer and replace him or her if absent. **8** an interval or chord spanning two consecutive notes in the diatonic scale e.g. C to D. • *verb* **1** support, assist; offer backing to. **2** formally support or endorse (a nomination, resolution, motion, etc., or its proposer). PHRASES **in the second place** as a second consideration etc. **second to none** superior; better than the rest.

second² *noun* **1** a sixtieth part of a minute of time or angular measurement. **2** *informal* a brief moment or instant: *I'll be there in a second.*

second³ *verb* transfer a military officer or other official or worker temporarily to other employment or another position: *he was seconded from his job with the city of Toronto to a two-year assignment with the feds.* [Say suh KOND]

secondarily *adverb* second in order of importance; in the second place: *she was a poet first and secondarily a dramatist ◊ we're primarily concerned with solving the problems and only secondarily concerned with the cost.*

secondary • *adjective* **1** second in rank, sequence, importance, etc. to what is primary. **2** derived from, based on, or supplementing something else that is primary; not original. **3** designating, relating to, or involved in education above primary or elementary education, below college or university, usu. for students in their mid to late teens. **4** arising after or in consequence of an earlier symptom, infection, etc. **5** (of a cell or battery) generating electricity by a reversible chemical reaction and therefore able to store applied energy. **6** (of a current) induced, not supplied directly from a source; of, pertaining to, or carrying the output of electrical power in a transformer etc. **7** (of an industry or type of economic activity) concerned with the conversion of the raw materials provided by primary industry into the commodities and products for the consumer; of the manufacturing industry. • *noun* (*plural* **secondaries**) **1** a secondary person or thing. **2** = SECONDARY SCHOOL. **3** *Football* **a** the defensive backs collectively. **b** the area of the field they cover; the defensive backfield. **4** a secondary coil, current, etc.

secondary colour *noun* a colour derived from the mixing of two primary colours.

secondary school *noun* a school offering secondary education.

secondary sexual characteristics *plural noun* the physical characteristics distinctive to each sex but not essential to reproduction, which typically develop, in humans, during puberty, e.g. facial hair in human males (compare PRIMARY SEXUAL CHARACTERISTICS).

secondary source *noun* an account of events based on someone else's evidence or original report (compare PRIMARY SOURCE): *based essentially on secondary sources, the book makes no claim to originality.*

second ballot *noun* a deciding ballot taken between a candidate who has won a previous ballot without securing an absolute majority and the candidate with the next highest number of votes.

second banana *noun* *informal* **1** a supporting comedian in a show or vaudeville skit etc. **2** a person who plays a subordinate or secondary role.

second base *noun* *Baseball* **1** the second of the three bases, located directly beyond the pitcher's mound from home plate. **2** the position of the player covering this base and the area of the infield between it and first

base. ▶ **second baseman** *noun* (*plural* **second basemen**)

second-best • *adjective* next in quality to the best or first. • *noun* **1** a second-best person or thing. **2** a less adequate or desirable alternative.

second chamber *noun* the upper house of a bicameral legislature, usu. having the function of revising measures prepared and passed by the lower, e.g. the Senate of the Canadian Parliament.

second class • *noun* **1** a set of persons or things grouped together as second-best. **2** the second-best accommodation in a train, ship, etc., usu. available at a lower rate. • *adjective* (usu. **second-class**) **1** belonging to or travelling by the second class. **2** inferior in quality, standard, status, etc. • *adverb* (usu. **second-class**) by second class.

second-class citizen *noun* **1** a person deprived of normal civic and legal rights. **2** a person treated as socially inferior.

second coming *noun* **1** (usu. **Second Coming**) the prophesied return of Christ to earth. **2** the return of a person or thing, esp. in a new incarnation.

second cousin *noun* a child of one's parent's first cousin.

second-degree *adjective* **1 a** designating the second-most serious category of crime. **b** (of murder) next in seriousness to first-degree murder, committed with intent but without premeditation and with certain mitigating circumstances. **2** denoting burns severe enough to cause blistering but not permanent scarring.

Second Empire • *noun* *hist.* **1** the French imperial government of Napoleon III, 1852–70. **2** this period in France. • *adjective* designating a style of architecture prominent during this time, influenced by French Renaissance architecture and characterized esp. by use of the mansard roof.

second fiddle *noun* see FIDDLE.

second gear *noun* the second (and next to lowest) in a sequence of gears of a car, bicycle, etc.

second generation • *noun* **1** the grandchildren of immigrants who have settled in a country; the offspring of the first generation born in a country. **2** (of technology) an advanced or refined stage of development. • *adjective* (usu. **second-generation**) **1** designating the offspring of a first generation. **2** designating something in an improved stage of development.

second-growth • *noun* a growth of trees etc. replacing one that has been destroyed by fire, removed by logging, etc. • *adjective* **1** designating a forest, trees, etc. replacing vegetation that has been destroyed. **2** designating timber etc. that has been removed from a second-growth.

second-guess *verb* (**second-guesses, second-guessed, second-guessing**) **1** anticipate or predict by guesswork. **2** question or judge with hindsight.

second hand *noun* the hand on an analog clock or watch that indicates the passing of seconds.

second-hand • *adjective* **1 a** previously owned or used; not new. **b** selling goods that have been previously owned or used. **2 a** not heard or obtained directly from the original source, but accepted on another's authority. **b** not undergone or felt personally, but vicariously through another. • *adverb* **1** through an intermediary; not from the original source. **2** after being previously owned or used; not new: *she buys second-hand.*

second-hand smoke *noun* the smoke from a smoker's cigarette etc. inhaled unwillingly by others.

second-in-command *noun* **1** the officer next in

rank to the commanding or chief officer. **2** a person next in authority to the person in charge.

second language *noun* a language spoken or used in addition to one's native language.

second-last • *adjective* immediately preceding the final or most recent. • *adverb* occurring or finishing immediately before the person or thing that is last or most recent. • *noun* the penultimate person or thing.

secondly *adverb* **1** furthermore; in the second place. **2** as a second item.

secondment *noun* the temporary transfer of an official or worker to another department or position of employment: *the banker spent two years on secondment to the Department of Industry*. [Say suh KOND m'nt]

second nature *noun* an acquired ability or habit etc. that has become instinctive.

second-rate *adjective* of mediocre quality; inferior. ▶ **second rater** *noun*

second reading *noun* the second of three successive occasions on which a bill must be presented to a legislature before it becomes law.

second-run *noun* (as an *adjective*) designating a movie theatre showing films after their first release.

second sight *noun* the ability to perceive future or distant events; clairvoyance.

second string • *noun* *Sport* **1** a roster of backup players available to replace players from the starting lineup if they become unable to play, esp. due to injury. **2** a backup player or substitute on this roster. • *adjective* (**second-string**) **1** designating a player etc. who is a backup or substitute: *second-string defenceman*. **2** designating a person or thing not of the first class or rank: *a second-string composer*. ▶ **second stringer** *noun*

second thoughts *plural noun* **1** a new opinion or resolution reached after further consideration. **2** apprehension or doubt about a decision, action, etc. that has already been made.

Second Vatican Council = VATICAN II (*see* VATICAN COUNCIL).

second wind *noun* **1** recovery of the power of normal breathing during exercise after initial breathlessness. **2** a renewed energy or vigour needed to continue an effort.

secrecy *noun* **1** the ability or tendency to withhold information or keep things secret. **2** a state or condition in which disclosure of facts and events is strictly limited. PHRASES **sworn to secrecy** having been made to promise to keep a secret. [Say SEE kruh see]

secret • *adjective* **1** kept or meant to be kept private, unknown, or hidden from others: *no one knew about her secret life*. **2** (of a person) **a** having a role unknown to others: *secret agent*. **b** able to preserve secrecy. • *noun* **1** a fact, matter, or action kept private or shared only with those concerned. **2** a thing known only to a few, though not intentionally concealed: *this cozy restaurant is one of the city's best kept secrets*. **3** a mystery: *the secrets of the universe*. **4** the best or only way to achieve something; the way a particular person achieves something: *careful planning is the secret of success* ◊ *She still looks so young. What's her secret?* PHRASES **in secret** without others knowing. **in on the secret** among the number of those who know it.

secret agent *noun* a person operating covertly or engaged on secret service; a spy.

secretarial *adjective* involving or having to do with the work of a secretary: *secretarial college* ◊ *secretarial work*. [Say sekra TERRY ul]

secretariat *noun* a permanent administrative and executive department of a government or similar organization. [Say sekra TERRY it]

secretary *noun* (*plural* **secretaries**) **1** a person employed to manage or assist with files and correspondence, make appointments, etc. **2** an official appointed by an organization to conduct its correspondence, keep its records, etc. **3** *Cdn* & *Brit.* = PARLIAMENTARY SECRETARY. **4** a civil servant employed as the chief assistant to an ambassador.

Secretary-General *noun* (*plural* **Secretaries-General**) the principal administrator of an organization, such as the UN.

Secretary of State *noun* (*plural* **Secretaries of State**) **1** *Cdn* **a** *hist.* (until 1993) a department responsible for a variety of matters, esp. those falling outside of existing jurisdictions but not considered important enough for the creation of a new department, e.g. citizenship, bilingualism. **b** (usu. *secretary of state* when not used as a title) a government minister responsible for a specific area within a department, such as scientific research, the status of women, etc. **2** *US* the chief government official responsible for foreign affairs.

secrete *verb* (**secretes**, **secreted**, **secreting**) **1** (of a cell, organ, etc.) produce and discharge (a substance): *insulin is secreted in response to rising levels of glucose in the blood*. **2** conceal; put into hiding: *the assets had been secreted in Swiss bank accounts*. [Say suh KREET]

secretion *noun* **1** the process by which substances are produced and discharged from a cell, gland, or organ for a particular function in the organism or for excretion: *the secretion of bile by the liver*. **2** the secreted substance: *bodily secretions*. [Say suh KREE shun]

secretive *adjective* inclined to make or keep secrets. ▶ **secretively** *adverb* **secretiveness** *noun* [Say SEE kruh tiv]

secretly *adverb* in a way that is known about by only one person or a few people but is hidden to others.

secretory *adjective* involving or having to do with the process by which substances are produced and discharged from a cell, gland, or organ. [Say suh KREET a ree]

secret police *noun* a police force operating in secret for political purposes.

secret service *noun* **1** a government department concerned with espionage and national security. **2** (**Secret Service**) (in the US) a branch of the Treasury Department dealing with counterfeiting and providing protection for the President etc.

secret society *noun* (*plural* **secret societies**) an organization formed to promote a cause covertly and whose members are sworn to secrecy about its existence and proceedings.

SecState *noun* *Cdn slang* = SECRETARY OF STATE.

sect *noun* **1** a body of people holding religious doctrines usu. different from those of a larger group from which they have separated. **2** usu. *derogatory* a religious faction or group regarded as heretical or as deviating from orthodox tradition. **3** the system or body of adherents of a particular philosopher or philosophy, or school of thought in politics etc.

sectarian *adjective* **1** of or concerning a sect. **2** pertaining to or created by differences of religion or denomination: *sectarian violence in Ireland*. **3** bigoted or narrow-minded esp. in following the doctrines of one's sect. ▶ **sectarianism** *noun* [Say sec TERRY un]

section • *noun* **1** a part cut off or separated from something. **2** a group of musicians playing similar instruments forming part of a band or orchestra. **3** a subdivision of a newspaper, book, document, statute, etc. **4** a (*West*) one square mile of esp. agricultural land, 640 acres (approx. 260 hectares). **b** a particular district or community of a town: *residential section*. **5** a department of a store, library, etc. in which similar

S

items may be found together: *produce section*. **6** one of the naturally divided segments of a citrus fruit, such as an orange. **7** *Cdn* = SCHOOL SECTION. **8** a subdivision of an army platoon. **9 a** the cutting of a solid along a plane. **b** the resulting figure or the area of this. **10 a** a representation of the internal structure of something as it would appear if cut across a vertical or horizontal plane. • *verb* arrange in or divide into sections.

sectional • *adjective* **1** of or relating to a section. **2 a** relating to a section or sections of a country, society, community, etc. **b** concerned with local or regional matters as opposed to general ones. **3** assembled or made from several sections: *sectional table*. • *noun* a piece of furniture, such as a couch, composed of sections which can be used separately.

section road *noun* (*West*) a road bordering a section of land.

sector *noun* **1** a distinct part or branch of an economy: *the tourism sector*. **2** the plane figure enclosed by two radii of a circle, ellipse, etc., and the arc between them. **3** a subdivision of an area for military operations, controlled by one commander or headquarters. ▶ **sectoral** *adjective*

secular *adjective* **1** concerned with or belonging to the material world and the affairs of this world as opposed to the eternal or spiritual world. **2** (of literature, music, an artist, etc.) not concerned with or promoting religious belief. **3** (of clergy) not bound by a religious or monastic rule.

secular humanism *noun* a political and social philosophy emphasizing the freedom of the individual, esp. with regard to the belief that religion should not be taught or practised within a publicly funded education system. ▶ **secular humanist** *noun & adjective*

secularism *noun* the belief that religion should not be involved in the organization of society, education, etc. ▶ **secularist** *noun*

secularization *noun* the act or process of removing the influence or power that religion has over something: *the secularization of education*.

secularize *verb* remove something from the control or influence of religion.

secure • *adjective* **1** assured, confident. **2** reliable, certain not to fail. **3** fixed or fastened so as not to give way or yield under strain: *made the door secure*. **4** not likely to be lost or stolen etc. **5** (of a place) **a** affording protection or safety. **b** difficult to escape from. • *verb* (**secures, secured, securing**) **1** make secure or safe; fortify. **2** fasten or close securely. **3** obtain or achieve. **4** ensure (a situation, outcome, result, etc.): *the final goal secured the victory*. **5** guarantee against loss: *a loan secured by property*. **6** seize and hold (a person) in custody.

secure custody *noun* *Cdn* custody in a correctional facility designed and designated for the detention of young offenders.

securely *adverb* **1** so as not to give way, become loose, escape, or be lost: *he locked the door securely behind him* ◊ *the ropes are securely fastened*. **2** in such a way that one is free from or protected against danger or risk: *the software allows users to send data securely over the Internet*. **3** in a way that is unlikely to be changed or altered: *the bill has become securely established*. **4** in a way that is comfortable, stable, and free from fear or anxiety.

securities commission *noun* an agency established to supervise and regulate the selling and trading of securities.

security *noun* (*plural* **securities**) **1 a** the condition of being protected from or not exposed to danger; safety. **b** freedom from care etc. **2** something that provides protection or safety. **3 a** measures taken to ensure safety and prevent crime or other danger in a building, office, country, etc. **b** the department or members responsible for ensuring safety. **4** measures taken to ensure confinement of a prisoner etc.: *maximum-security prison*. **5** the guarantee or assurance of something: *job security*. **6** (often in *plural*) **a** a certificate attesting the ownership of, or interest in, the capital, assets, property, profits, earnings, or royalties of any person or company. **b** a document, such as a bond, debenture, or note, acknowledging a debt. **7** something valuable (e.g. a home etc.) given or promised as a guarantee of the fulfillment of an obligation, such as an appearance in court or the payment of a debt, and given up in the event of a default: *his home and business are being held as security for the loan*.

security blanket *noun* **1** a familiar blanket or other object given to or esp. clung to by a child for comfort or reassurance. **2** *informal* something comforting or reassuring: *my jeans are a security blanket — I feel less anxious when I have them on*.

Security Council *noun* a permanent body of the UN seeking to maintain peace and security.

security guard *noun* a person employed to ensure the security of a person, building, vehicles, etc.

Secwepemc *noun & adjective* (*plural* **Secwepemc**) = SHUSWAP. [Say SHWEP muh]

sedan *noun* **1** a car for four or more people. **2** (also **sedan chair**) *hist.* an enclosed chair for conveying one person, carried on poles by two porters.

sedate • *adjective* calm, dignified, and unhurried: *his rowdy friends turned the sedate, champagne-sipping gathering into a foot-stomping celebration of rock 'n' roll*. • *verb* (**sedates, sedated, sedate**) make sleepy or quiet by means of drugs; administer a sedative to. ▶ **sedately** *adverb* **sedation** *noun* [Say suh DATE, suh DAY sh'n]

sedative • *noun* a drug, influence, etc., that tends to calm or soothe. • *adjective* calming, soothing. [Say SEDDA tiv]

sedentary *adjective* **1** (of work etc.) characterized by much sitting and little physical exercise. **2** (of a person) spending much time seated. [Say SED'n terry]

Seder *noun* a Jewish ritual service and ceremonial dinner for the first night or first two nights of the Passover. [Say SAY dur]

sedge *noun* **1** any of various grasslike plants growing esp. in wet areas. **2** an expanse of this plant.

sediment *noun* **1** matter that settles to the bottom of a liquid; dregs. **2** matter that is carried by water or wind and deposited on the surface of the land.

sedimentary *adjective* **1** of or like sediment. **2** (esp. of rocks) formed from sediment, usu. laid down in strata which are initially horizontal or nearly so. [Say sedda MENTA ree]

sedimentation *noun* the process of depositing sediment. [Say sedda mun TAY sh'n]

sedition *noun* conduct or speech inciting people to rebel against the authority of a government or monarch: *the rebellion revealed that the local gentry, far from upholding law and order, might lead the forces of sedition and separatism*. ▶ **seditious** *adjective* [Say suh DISH'n, suh DISH us]

seduce *verb* (**seduces, seduced, seducing**) **1** tempt or entice a person into sexual activity. **2 a** attract someone to a belief or into a course of action that is inadvisable or foolhardy; lead astray: *seduced into a life of crime*. **b** deceive: *the unwary might find themselves seduced by the intriguing title*. **3** attract powerfully: *the California trio have seduced grunge fans*.

seducer *noun* a person, esp. a man, who sexually seduces, esp. habitually.

seduction *noun* **1** the action of seducing someone: *she was a timid woman, with little experience in seduction*. **2** a tempting or attractive thing: *the seductions of life in the big city*. ▶ **seductive** *adjective* **seductively** *adverb* **seductiveness** *noun*

seductress *noun* (*plural* **seductresses**) a female seducer.

sedulous *adjective* showing dedication and diligence: *watched him with the most sedulous care*. ▶ **sedulously** *adverb* [Say SED yoo lus]

sedum *noun* a widely distributed plant with fleshy leaves and star-shaped yellow, pink, or white flowers, popular as a garden plant. [Say SEED um]

see¹ • *verb* (**sees**; *past* **saw**; *past participle* **seen**; **seeing**) **1** perceive with the eyes. **2** experience or witness. **3** deduce after reflection or from information. **4** regard in a specified way. **5** regard as a possibility; envisage. **6** meet (someone one knows) socially or by chance. **7** meet regularly as a boyfriend or girlfriend. **8** consult (a specialist or professional). **9** give an interview or consultation to. **10** escort to a specified place. **11** (foll. by *to*) attend to. **12** (foll. by *that*) ensure that. PHRASES **as far as I can see** to the best of my understanding or belief. **as I see it** in my opinion. **has seen better days** has declined from former prosperity, good condition, etc. **let me see** an appeal for time to think before speaking etc. **see about** attend to. **see after 1** take care of. **2** = SEE ABOUT. **see here!** = LOOK HERE! (*see* LOOK *interjection*). **see into** investigate. **see life** gain experience of the world, often by enjoying oneself. **see the light 1** realize one's mistakes etc. **2** suddenly see the way to proceed. **3** undergo religious conversion. **see the light of day** (usu. with *neg.*) come into existence. **see off** be present at the departure of (a person). **see out 1** accompany out of a building etc. **2** finish (a project etc.) completely. **3** remain awake, alive, etc., until the end of (a period). **4** last longer than; outlive. **see red** become suddenly enraged. **see a person right** make sure that a person is rewarded, safe, etc. **see stars** *informal* see lights before one's eyes as a result of a blow to the head, dizziness, etc. **see things** have hallucinations or false imaginings. **see through 1** not be deceived by; detect the true nature of. **2** penetrate visually. **see a person through** support a person during a difficult time. **see a thing through** persist with it until it is completed. **see to it** ensure: *see to it that I am not disturbed*. **see one's way clear to** feel able or entitled to. **see you** (or **see you later**) *informal* an expression on parting. **we shall see 1** let us await the outcome. **2** a formula for declining to act at once. **will see about it** a formula for declining to act at once. **you see 1** you understand. **2** you will understand when I explain.

see² *noun* **1** the area under the authority of a bishop or archbishop; a diocese. **2** the office or jurisdiction of a bishop or archbishop.

seed • *noun* **1** a flowering plant's unit of reproduction. **2** a prime cause or beginning: *seeds of doubt*. **3** *archaic* semen or sperm. **4** *archaic* offspring, progeny, descendants: *the seed of Abraham*. **5** *Sport* a seeded player. • *verb* **1** sow seeds. **2** produce or drop seed. **3** remove seeds from (fruit etc.). **4** place a crystal or crystalline substance in (a solution etc.) to cause crystallization or condensation (esp. in a cloud to produce rain). **5** *Sport* **a** assign to (a strong competitor in a competition) a position in an ordered list so that strong competitors do not meet each other in early rounds: *is seeded seventh*. **b** arrange (the order of play) in this way. **6** go to seed. • *adjective* (of funding etc.) intended to initiate a

project etc.; *seed capital*. PHRASES **go** (or **run**) **to seed 1** cease flowering as seed develops. **2** become degenerate, unkempt, ineffective, etc.

seedbed *noun* **1** a bed of fine soil in which to sow seeds. **2** a place of development.

seeder *noun* **1** a person or thing that seeds. **2** a machine for sowing seed, esp. a drill.

seed head *noun* a flower head in seed.

seediness *noun* **1** a filthy, shabby, sleazy, or disreputable appearance or manner. **2** the condition of a place that is dilapidated, shabby, or rundown and possibly associated with immoral or illegal activities.

seedless *adjective* (of fruit) having no seeds: *seedless grapes*.

seedling *noun* a young plant, esp. one raised from seed and not from a cutting etc.

seed money *noun* money allocated to initiate a project.

seed pod *noun* a long seed vessel that splits when ripe.

seedy *adjective* (**seedier**, **seediest**) **1** having a filthy, shabby, sleazy, or disreputable manner or appearance. **2** (of a place) shabby, rundown and possibly associated with immoral or illegal activities: *a seedy hotel*.

seeing • *conjunction* considering that, because. • *noun* the sense or faculty of sight.

Seeing Eye dog *noun proprietary* a dog that is specially trained to guide a blind person.

seek *verb* (**seeks**, **sought**, **seeking**) **1** make a search or inquiry (for). **2** a try or want to find or get. **b** ask for; request: *sought help from him*. **3** endeavour or try: *sought to convince her not to go*. **4** make for or resort to (a place or person, for advice, health, etc.): *sought her bed*. PHRASES **seek out 1** search for and find. **2** single out for companionship etc. **far to seek** difficult to find: *the reason is not far to seek*. ▶ **seeker** *noun*

SPELL CHECK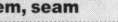
seem, seam

Two pieces of cloth are joined at a **seam**.

---

seem *verb* **1** give the impression or sensation of being: *seems ridiculous*. **2** appear or be perceived or ascertained: *they seem to have left*. PHRASES **can't seem to** *informal* seem unable to. **it seems** (or **would seem**) it appears to be true or the fact (in a hesitant, guarded, or ironical statement).

seeming *adjective* **1** apparent but not genuine: *the medical examiner has turned a seeming suicide into murder* ◊ *her seeming indifference*. **2** giving the impression of having the quality specified: *familiar-seeming lyrics*. ▶ **seemingly** *adverb*

seemliness *noun* the quality of being proper or suitable in a particular social situation: *constraints of propriety and seemliness limit the topics a judge may address*.

seemly *adjective* (**seemlier**, **seemliest**) conforming to propriety or good taste; suitable: *I felt it was not seemly to watch too closely*.

seen *past participle of* SEE¹.

seep • *verb* **1** ooze, filter, or percolate slowly. **2** permeate. **3** pass gradually: *her anger seeped away*. • *noun* a place where water, petroleum, etc. oozes out of the ground.

seepage *noun* **1** the act of seeping. **2** the quantity that seeps out.

seer *noun* **1** a person who sees. **2** a person of supposed supernatural insight esp. as regards the future.

seersucker *noun* material of linen, cotton, etc., with a puckered surface.

see-saw • *noun* **1** a long plank balanced on a central support for children to sit on at each end and move up and down by pushing the ground with their feet. **2** an

S

up-and-down or to-and-fro motion. **3** a contest or situation with each of the opposing forces repeatedly gaining the advantage. • *verb* **1** play on a see-saw. **2** move up and down as on a see-saw. **3** vacillate in policy, emotion, etc. • *adjective* **1** with up-and-down or backward-and-forward motion. **2** characterized by vacillation or progress alternating in two opposite directions.

seethe *verb* (**seethes, seethed, seething**) **1** boil, bubble over. **2** be very agitated, esp. with anger.

see-through *adjective* (esp. of clothing) translucent.

segment • *noun* **1** each of several parts into which a thing is or can be divided or marked off. **2** *Math* a part of a figure cut off by a line or plane intersecting it, esp.: **a** the part of a circle enclosed between an arc and a chord. **b** the part of a line included between two points. **c** the part of a sphere cut off by any plane not passing through the centre. **3** an item within a broadcast program. **4** each of the longitudinal sections of the body of certain animals (e.g. worms). • *verb* **1** divide into segments. **2** (of a cell) undergo cleavage or divide into many cells. ▶ **segmental** *adjective* **segmentation** *noun* [Say SEG m'nt, seg MENTAL, seg men TAY sh'n]

S **segregate** *verb* (**segregates, segregated, segregating**) **1** set apart from the rest or from each other; separate or divide: *the journal added a fiction section, at first segregated on newsprint from the rest of the magazine* ◊ *baseball slowly segregated towns into divisions of equal strength and commercial ability*. **2** separate or divide people, activities, or institutions along racial, sexual, or religious lines: *the public school system attempted to segregate the Chinese from other students* ◊ *was among the first musicians to refuse to play before segregated audiences*. [Say SEGRA gate]

segregation *noun* **1** enforced separation of racial groups in a community etc. **2** the act of separating people or things from a larger group: *the segregation of smokers and non-smokers in restaurants*. ▶ **segregationist** *noun & adjective* [Say segra GAY sh'n]

segue • *verb* (**segues, segued, segueing** or **seguing**) **1** *Music* (usu. foll. by *into*) go on without a pause into the next section. **2** move smoothly from one thing or topic to another: *night segued into morning*. • *noun* an uninterrupted transition from one musical section or melody to another. [Say SEG way]

sei *noun* a small whale with dark skin and white grooves on the belly. [Say SAY]

seigneur *noun* **1** *Cdn hist.* a holder of land under the seigneurial system. **2** a feudal lord; the lord of a manor. ▶ **seigneurial** *adjective* [Say seen YUR, seen YURI ul]

seigneurial system *noun* *Cdn hist.* a system of land tenure established in New France, based on the feudal system, under which land was owned by seigneurs who rented it to tenant farmers and provided mills, a court system, and other services.

seigneury *noun* (*plural* **seigneuries**) **1** *Cdn hist.* **a** a tract of land held by a seigneur under the seigneurial system. **b** a grant of land in the interior, esp. for the harvesting of furs, fish, etc. **2** a seigneur's domain. [Say SENIOR ee]

seine • *noun* (also **seine net**) a net for encircling fish, with floats at the top and weights at the bottom edge, and usu. hauled ashore (also as an *adjective*: *seine boat*). • *verb* (**seines, seined, seining**) fish or catch with a seine. ▶ **seiner** *noun* **seining** *noun* [Sounds like *SANE*]

seismic *adjective* **1** of or relating to an earthquake or earthquakes or other vibrations of the earth and its crust, produced either naturally or artificially by explosions. **2** of enormous proportions or effect: *seismic*

shifts in the global economy. ▶ **seismically** *adverb* [Say SIZE mick]

seismograph *noun* an instrument that records the force, direction, etc. of earthquakes. [Say SIZE muh graph]

seismological *adjective* having to do with the scientific study and recording of earthquakes and related phenomena. [Say size muh LOGICAL]

seismologist *noun* a scientist who studies earthquakes and related phenomena. [Say size MOLLA jist]

seismology *noun* the scientific study and recording of earthquakes and related phenomena. [Say size MOLLA jee]

seismometer *noun* = SEISMOGRAPH. [Say size MOMMA tur]

seize *verb* (**seizes, seized, seizing**) **1** take hold of forcibly or suddenly. **2** take possession of forcibly: *seized power*. **3** take possession of (contraband goods, documents, etc.) by warrant or legal right; confiscate. **4** affect suddenly: *panic seized us* ◊ *was seized with remorse*. **5** take advantage of (an opportunity). **6** comprehend quickly or clearly. **7** (usu. foll. by *on, upon*) **a** take hold forcibly or suddenly. **b** take advantage eagerly: *seized on a pretext*. **8** (usu. foll. by *up*) **a** (of a moving part in a machine) become stuck or jammed from undue heat, friction, etc. **b** (of part of the body etc.) become stiff.

seizure *noun* **1** the action of capturing someone or something using force: *the army's seizure of power*. **2** the use of legal authority to take something from someone: *the largest ever seizure of cocaine by the RCMP* ◊ *the court ordered the seizure of his assets*. **3** a sudden attack of epilepsy etc.

Sekani • *noun* (*plural* **Sekani** or **Sekanis**) **1** a member of an Aboriginal group living on the western slope of the Rocky Mountains in north central BC. **2** the Athapaskan language of this people. • *adjective* of or relating to this people or their language. [Say suh CANNY]

seldom *adverb* rarely, not often.

select • *verb* **1** choose, esp. as the best or most suitable. **2** choose or pick out something from a number. • *adjective* **1** chosen for excellence or suitability. **2** (of a society etc.) exclusive, cautious in admitting members. ▶ **selectable** *adjective*

select committee *noun* a small parliamentary committee appointed for a special purpose.

selection *noun* **1** the action or fact of carefully choosing someone or something as being the best or most suitable: *the selection of candidates* ◊ *selection criteria*. **2** a number of people or things that have been chosen from a larger group: *a selection of his poems was published last year* ◊ *the choir will sing selections from its repertoire*. **3** a range of things from which a choice may be made: *we offer a wide selection of desserts*. **4** *Biology* the process in which environmental and genetic influences determine which types of organism thrive better than others, regarded as a factor in evolution.

selection committee *noun* a committee that chooses a person or thing, esp. a person for a job.

selective *adjective* **1** using or characterized by selection. **2** able to select, esp. (of a radio receiver) able to respond to a chosen frequency without interference from others. **3** (of one's memory, hearing, etc.) selecting what is convenient. **4** (of a herbicide etc.) affecting only a particular species.

selective cutting *noun* (also **selective logging**) *Forestry* a method of removing trees from a forest in which only selected trees are harvested, usu. mature trees of a certain species.

selectively *adverb* in a way that affects or involves only those people or things chosen as being most

suitable, relevant, important, etc.: *Hamish selectively sent applications to universities across the country*.

selectivity *noun* **1** the quality of carefully choosing someone or something as the best or most suitable: *schools are tending towards greater selectivity*. **2** the property of affecting some things and not others.

selector *noun* a person or thing that selects something, esp. a device for selecting a particular setting on a machine.

selenium *noun* a non-metallic element characterized by the variation of its electrical resistivity with intensity of illumination. [Say suh LEENY um]

self • *noun* (*plural* **selves**) **1** a person's or thing's own individuality or essence: *showed his true self*. **2** one's own interests or pleasure: *cares for nothing but self*. **3** used in phrases equivalent to *myself*, *yourself*, *himself*, etc.: *his very self*. • *pronoun informal* myself, yourself, himself, herself, etc.: *ticket admitting self and guest*. PHRASES **one's better self** one's nobler impulses. **one's former** (or **old**) **self** oneself as one formerly was.

self- *combining form* expressing reflexive action: **1** of or directed towards oneself or itself: *self-respect ◊ self-cleaning*. **2** by oneself or itself, esp. without external agency: *self-evident*. **3** on, in, for, or relating to oneself or itself: *self-absorbed*.

self-absorbed *adjective* preoccupied with one's own emotions, interests, or situation.

self-absorption *noun* **1** preoccupation with one's own emotions, interests, or situation. **2** the absorption, by a body, of radiation emitted within it.

self-actualization *noun* the realization of one's talents and potentialities, esp. considered as a drive or need present in everyone. ▶ **self-actualize** *verb* (**self-actualizes**, **self-actualized**, **self-actualizing**)

self-addressed *adjective* (of an envelope etc.) having one's own address on for return communication.

self-aggrandizement *noun* the act or process of making oneself more important in appearance or reality. ▶ **self-aggrandizing** *adjective*

self-appointed *adjective* designated so by oneself, not authorized by another: *a self-appointed expert*.

self-assertion *noun* the aggressive promotion of oneself, one's views, etc. ▶ **self-assertive** *adjective* **self-assertiveness** *noun*

self-assessment *noun* assessment or evaluation of oneself, or one's actions, attitudes, or performance.

self-assurance *noun* confidence in one's own abilities etc. ▶ **self-assured** *adjective*

self-aware *adjective* conscious of one's character, feelings, motives, etc. ▶ **self-awareness** *noun*

self-censorship *noun* the censoring of oneself.

self-centred *adjective* preoccupied with one's own personality or affairs. ▶ **self-centredness** *noun*

self-cleaning *adjective* (of an oven) equipped with a mechanism that allows heating to sufficiently high temperatures to burn off grease, dirt, etc.

self-confessed *adjective* openly admitting oneself to be: *a self-confessed thief*.

self-confidence *noun* = SELF-ASSURANCE. ▶ **self-confident** *adjective* **self-confidently** *adverb*

self-congratulation *noun* = SELF-SATISFACTION. ▶ **self-congratulatory** *adjective*

self-conscious *adjective* **1** nervous or awkward because one is shy or worried about what others think. **2** strongly aware of who one is or what one is doing. ▶ **self-consciously** *adverb* **self-consciousness** *noun*

self-contained *adjective* **1** independent. **2** (esp. of living accommodation) complete in itself. **3** (of a person) uncommunicative.

self-contradictory *adjective* containing two ideas or statements that cannot both be true: *your argument is self-contradictory*.

self-control *noun* the power of controlling one's external reactions, emotions, etc. ▶ **self-controlled** *adjective*

self-correcting *adjective* correcting itself without external help.

self-created *adjective* created by oneself or itself.

self-critical *adjective* critical of oneself, one's abilities, etc. ▶ **self-criticism** *noun*

self-deception *noun* deceiving oneself esp. concerning one's true feelings etc.

self-defeating *adjective* (of an attempt etc.) doomed to failure because of internal inconsistencies etc.

self-defence *noun* **1** a defence of oneself, one's rights or position, esp. through the use of physical force: *acted in self-defence*. **2** the skill of being able to protect oneself from physical attack without using weapons: *took self-defence classes*.

self-delusion *noun* the action of deluding oneself; failure to recognize reality: *he retreats into a world of fantasy and self-delusion*.

self-denial *noun* the denial of one's own interests or needs, often for moral or religious reasons. ▶ **self-denying** *adjective*

self-deprecating *noun* modest about or critical of oneself, esp. humorously so: *self-deprecating jokes*. ▶ **self-deprecatingly** *adverb* **self-deprecation** *noun* **self-deprecatory** *adjective*

self-destruct • *verb* **1** (of a spacecraft, bomb, etc.) explode or disintegrate automatically, esp. when pre-set to do so. **2** destroy oneself. • *adjective* enabling a thing to self-destruct: *hit the self-destruct button*.

self-destruction *noun* **1** the process or an act of destroying oneself or itself. **2** the process or an act of self-destructing. **3** *informal* suicide. ▶ **self-destructive** *adjective* **self-destructively** *adverb*

self-determination *noun* **1** the freedom of a people to decide their own allegiance or form of government. **2** the freedom to live or act as one chooses, without needing to consult others. ▶ **self-determining** *adjective*

self-directed *adjective* **1** designating an investment trust, such as an RSP, in which the investment instruments are selected by the trust holder. **2** exercising personal control over one's own life, career, etc. **3** (of criticism, a joke, etc.) directed towards oneself.

self-discipline *noun* the act of or ability to apply oneself, control one's feelings, etc.; self-control. ▶ **self-disciplined** *adjective*

self-discovery *noun* (*plural* **self-discoveries**) the process of acquiring insight into oneself, one's character, desires, etc.

self-doubt *noun* lack of confidence in oneself, one's abilities, etc. ▶ **self-doubting** *adjective*

self-educated *adjective* taught by oneself by reading etc., without formal instruction.

self-effacing *adjective* retiring; modest; timid. ▶ **self-effacingly** *adverb*

self-employed *adjective* working for oneself, as a freelancer or owner of a business etc.; not employed by an employer. ▶ **self-employment** *noun*

self-esteem *noun* a good opinion of one's own character and abilities.

self-evident *adjective* obvious; without the need of evidence or explanation. ▶ **self-evidently** *adverb*

self-examination *noun* **1** the study of one's own conduct, reasons, etc. **2** the examining of one's body or a part of one's body for signs of illness etc.

self-explanatory *adjective* easily understood; not needing explanation.

self-expression *noun* the expression of one's feelings, thoughts, etc., esp. in writing, painting, music, etc.

self-financing *adjective* that finances itself, esp. (of a project or undertaking) that pays for its own implementation or continuation.

self-flagellation *noun* **1** the flogging of oneself, esp. as a form of religious discipline. **2** excessive self-criticism.

self-fulfilling *adjective* **1** (of a prophecy, forecast, etc.) bound to come true as a result of actions brought about by its being made. **2** causing or bringing about self-fulfillment.

self-fulfillment *noun* the fulfillment of one's own hopes and ambitions.

self-governing *adjective* exercising control over its or one's own affairs; independent: *a self-governing republic located within Russia*.

self-government *noun* government of a country or region by its own people.

self-guided *adjective* **1** (of a hike, visit to a tourist attraction, etc.) performed without the supervision of a tour guide. **2** (of a hiking trail, scenic route, etc.) equipped with informative signs, plaques, etc., so as to be suitable for a self-guided tour.

self-hatred *noun* (also **self-hate**) intense dislike of oneself.

self-help *noun* **1** the theory that individuals should provide for their own support and improvement in society. **2** the act or faculty of providing for or improving oneself (also as an *adjective*: *self-help book*).

selfhood *noun* separate and conscious existence.

self-image *noun* one's own idea or picture of oneself, esp. in relation to others.

self-immolation *noun* **1** the offering of oneself as a sacrifice. **2** an act of suicide by setting oneself on fire, as a protest.

self-importance *noun* a high opinion of oneself. ▶ **self-important** *adjective* **self-importantly** *adverb*

self-imposed *adjective* (of a task or condition etc.) imposed on and by oneself, not externally.

self-improvement *noun* the improvement of one's own position or disposition by one's own efforts.

self-induced *adjective* induced by oneself or itself.

self-indulgence *noun* **1** the quality of being self-indulgent. **2** a self-indulgent act: *Saturday's simple minded pleasures and self-indulgences*.

self-indulgent *adjective* indulging or tending to indulge in pleasure, idleness, etc. ▶ **self-indulgently** *adverb*

self-inflicted *adjective* (of a wound, damage, etc.) inflicted on oneself, esp. deliberately.

self-interest *noun* **1** one's personal interest or advantage. **2** concern for one's own interest or advantage. ▶ **self-interested** *adjective*

selfish *adjective* **1** deficient in consideration for others; concerned chiefly with one's own personal profit or pleasure. **2** (of a motive etc.) appealing to self-interest. ▶ **selfishly** *adverb* **selfishness** *noun*

self-justification *noun* the justification or excusing of oneself, one's actions, etc. ▶ **self-justifying** *adjective*

self-knowledge *noun* the understanding of oneself, one's motives, etc.

selfless *adjective* disregarding oneself or one's own interests. ▶ **selflessly** *adverb* **selflessness** *noun*

self-loathing *noun* = SELF-HATRED.

self-love *noun* **1** selfishness; self-indulgence. **2** regard for one's own well-being and happiness.

self-made *adjective* **1** successful or rich by one's own effort. **2** made by oneself.

self-medicate *verb* (**self-medicates**, **self-medicated**, **self-medicating**) medicate oneself without seeking any medical supervision.

self-medication *noun* the use of medication to treat oneself without seeking any medical supervision.

self-mockery *noun* the action or process of mocking oneself or itself.

self-mocking *adjective* mocking oneself or itself.

self-motivated *adjective* acting on one's own initiative without external pressure. ▶ **self-motivation** *noun*

self-parody *noun* (*plural* **self-parodies**) the intentional or inadvertent parodying or exaggeration of one's usual behaviour or speech. ▶ **self-parodying** *adjective*

self-perpetuating *adjective* perpetuating itself or oneself without external intervention: *the self-perpetuating power of the bureaucracy*. ▶ **self-perpetuation** *noun*

self-pity *noun* extreme sorrow for one's own troubles etc. ▶ **self-pitying** *adjective* **self-pityingly** *adverb*

self-portrait *noun* a portrait or description of an artist, writer, etc., by himself or herself.

self-possessed *adjective* calm and confident, esp. at times of stress or difficulty. ▶ **self-possession** *noun*

self-preservation *noun* the preservation of one's own life, safety, best interests, etc., esp. as a basic instinct.

self-proclaimed *adjective* proclaimed by oneself or itself to be such.

self-propelled *adjective* moving or able to move without external propulsion.

self-protection *noun* the act of protecting oneself or itself. ▶ **self-protective** *adjective*

self-realization *noun* **1** the development of one's faculties, abilities, etc. **2** this as an ethical principle.

self-referential *adjective* (esp. of a literary or other creative work) making reference to itself, its author or creator, or to other works of the author or creator: *self-referential elements in Donne's poems*.

self-regard *noun* **1** a proper regard for oneself; self-respect. **2** vanity, conceit. ▶ **self-regarding** *adjective*

self-regulating *adjective* regulating oneself or itself without intervention. ▶ **self-regulation** *noun* **self-regulatory** *adjective*

self-reliance *noun* reliance on one's own resources etc.; independence. ▶ **self-reliant** *adjective*

self-respect *noun* respect for oneself; a feeling that one is behaving with honour, dignity, etc. ▶ **self-respecting** *adjective*

self-restraint *noun* = SELF-CONTROL.

self-righteous *adjective* excessively confident of one's own righteousness or virtue, esp. in comparison to others. ▶ **self-righteously** *adverb* **self-righteousness** *noun*

self-rule *noun* = SELF-GOVERNMENT.

self-sacrifice *noun* the negation of one's own interests, wishes, etc., in favour of those of others. ▶ **self-sacrificing** *adjective*

selfsame *adjective* the very same: *the selfsame thing*.

self-satisfaction *noun* excessive and unwarranted satisfaction with oneself, one's achievements, etc. ▶ **self-satisfied** *adjective*

self-seeking *adjective* seeking one's own welfare before that of others.

self-serve (also **self-service**) • *adjective* **1** (esp. of a

gas station) where customers serve themselves and pay at a checkout counter etc. **2** (of a machine) serving goods after the insertion of coins. • *noun informal* a self-serve gas station etc.

self-serving *adjective* = SELF-SEEKING.

self-starter *noun* **1** an ambitious person who needs no external motivation. **2** = STARTER 2.

self-styled *adjective* called so by oneself: *a self-styled artist*.

self-sufficiency *noun* the quality or condition of being independent or able to supply one's needs for a commodity, esp. food, from one's own resources.

self-sufficient *adjective* **1** needing nothing; independent. **2** (of a person, nation, etc.) able to supply one's needs for a commodity, esp. food, from one's own resources. ▶ **self-sufficiently** *adverb*

self-supporting *adjective* **1** capable of maintaining oneself or itself financially. **2** staying up or standing without external aid.

self-sustaining *adjective* sustaining oneself or itself.

self-taught *adjective* educated or trained by oneself.

self-will *noun* one's own will or desire.

self-willed *adjective* obstinately pursuing one's own wishes.

self-worth *noun* = SELF-ESTEEM.

Selkirk settler *noun Cdn hist.* an early esp. Scottish settler at the Red River Settlement in what is now Manitoba, founded by the Earl of Selkirk (1771–1820).

sell • *verb* (**sells**, **sold**, **selling**) **1** exchange (goods, services, etc.) for money. **2** keep a stock of for sale or be a dealer in. **3 a** (of goods) be purchased. **b** (of a publication or recording) attain sales of (a specified number of copies). **4** (foll. by *for*) have a specified price. **5** betray for money or other reward. **6 a** advertise or publish the merits of. **b** give (a person) information on the value of something, inspire with a desire to buy or acquire or agree to something. **7** cause to be sold. • *noun* **1** a manner of selling. **2** *informal* a deception or disappointment. PHRASES **sell off** sell the remainder of (goods) at reduced prices. **sell one's body** work as a prostitute. **sell oneself 1** promote one's own abilities. **2 a** offer one's services dishonourably for money or other reward. **b** be a prostitute. **sell out 1 a** sell all one's stock of a commodity. **b** (of a commodity) be completely or all sold. **c** (of a performance etc.) sell all its tickets. **d** dispose of the whole of (one's property, shares, etc.) by sale. **2 a** (often foll. by *to*) abandon one's principles, honourable aims, etc. for personal gain. **b** betray (a person etc.). **sell short** disparage, underestimate. ▶ **sellable** *adjective*

SPELL CHECK
seller, cellar

A basement is a **cellar**. A container for holding salt is a **saltcellar**.

---

seller *noun* **1** a person who sells. **2** a commodity that sells well or badly.

seller's market *noun* an economic position in which goods are scarce and expensive and sellers have the advantage over buyers.

selling point *noun* a feature of something that makes it attractive, esp. to buyers or customers.

sell-off *noun* **1** the privatization of a state company by a sale of shares. **2** a sale or disposal of bonds, shares, etc., usu. causing a fall in price. **3** a sale, esp. to dispose of property.

sellout *noun* **1** a commercial success, esp. the selling of all tickets for a show. **2** a betrayal.

seltzer *noun* (also **seltzer water**) **1** natural

effervescent mineral water. **2** an artificial substitute for this; soda water. [Say SELT sir]

selvage *noun* (also **selvedge**) an edging that prevents cloth from unravelling (either an edge along the warp or a specially woven edging). [Say SELL vidge]

selves *plural of* SELF.

semantic *adjective* **1** relating to meaning in language; relating to the denotations and connotations of words: *"brain-dead" – the proper medical term – has undergone a semantic shift and is now used informally to mean "stupid".* **2** of or relating to semantics: *a semantic theorist.* ▶ **semantically** *adverb* [Say suh MAN tick]

semantics *plural noun* (usu. treated as *singular*) **1** the branch of linguistics concerned with meaning. **2** the interpretation or meaning of a sentence, word, etc.: *what teachers call fidgeting, scientists know as "micro-movements," and semantics aside, such motion appears to be a healthy thing.* [Say suh MAN ticks]

semaphore • *noun* **1** a system of sending messages by holding the arms or two flags in certain positions according to an alphabetic code. **2** a signalling apparatus consisting of a post with a movable arm or arms esp. for use on railways. • *verb* (**semaphores**, **semaphored**, **semaphoring**) signal or send by semaphore. [Say SEMMA for]

semblance *noun* the outward or superficial appearance of something: *Effie's struggle to maintain a semblance of calm only increased John's hostility.* [Say SEM blince]

semen *noun* the reproductive fluid of male animals, containing spermatozoa in suspension.

semester *noun* an academic session occupying half of the academic year, lasting usu. for 15 to 18 weeks.

semestered *adjective Cdn* (of a school) operating under a system in which the school year is divided into two terms having school days with a reduced number of longer periods, with the whole year's course material in any given subject concentrated into one or the other term. ▶ **semestering** *noun*

semi *noun* (*plural* **semis**) *informal* **1** *Cdn & Brit.* a semi-detached house. **2** a semifinal. **3** a semi-trailer.

semi- *prefix* **1** half: *semicircle*. **2** partly; in some degree or particular: *semi-detached*. **3** almost. **4** occurring or appearing twice in a specified period: *semi-annual*. [Say SEMMY]

semi-annual *adjective* occurring, published, etc., twice a year. ▶ **semi-annually** *adverb*

semiaquatic *adjective* **1** (of an animal) living partly on land and partly in water. **2** (of a plant) growing in very wet ground.

semi-arid *adjective* having slightly more precipitation than an arid climate, and characterized by coarse grasses and scrub.

semi-automatic • *adjective* **1** partially automatic. **2** (of a firearm) having a mechanism for continuous loading but not for continuous firing. • *noun* a semi-automatic firearm.

semi-autonomous *adjective* **1** partly self-governing. **2** acting to some degree independently or having the partial freedom to do so.

semicircle *noun* **1** half of a circle or of its circumference. **2** a set of objects ranged in, or an object forming, a semicircle. ▶ **semicircular** *adjective*

semicircular canal *noun* one of three fluid-filled channels in the ear giving information to the brain to help maintain balance.

semicolon *noun* a punctuation mark (;) of intermediate value between a comma and a period. [Say SEMI co lin]

semiconductor *noun* a solid substance that is a non-conductor when pure or at a low temperature but has a

S

conductivity between that of insulators and that of most metals when containing a suitable impurity or at a higher temperature and is used in integrated circuits, transistors, diodes, etc.

semi-conscious *adjective* partly conscious. ▶ **semi-consciousness** *noun*

semi-desert *noun* a semi-arid area intermediate between grassland and desert.

semi-detached • *adjective* (of a house) joined to another by a shared wall on one side only. • *noun* a semi-detached house.

semifinal *noun* a match or round immediately preceding the final. ▶ **semifinalist** *noun*

semi-formal • *adjective* (esp. of clothing) having some formal elements. • *noun* a dance or other social occasion to which semi-formal dress is worn.

semigloss • *adjective* (of a paint or painted surface) having or producing such a finish. • *noun* a paint that has or produces a moderately satiny finish.

semi-independent *adjective* **1 a** partially independent of control or authority. **b** partially self-governing. **2** partially independent of financial support from public funds.

semi-liquid • *adjective* of a consistency between solid and liquid. • *noun* a semi-liquid substance.

semi-monthly • *adjective* occurring, published, etc., twice a month. • *adverb* twice a month.

seminal *adjective* **1** (of a work, event, moment, or figure) strongly influencing later research or developments: *a seminal work in the history of women's poetry* ◊ *Jeremy Brett plays the seminal detective, Sherlock Holmes.* **2** of or relating to semen: *seminal fluid.* [Say SEMMA nul]

seminar *noun* a small group, esp. at a university, meeting to discuss or study a particular topic.

seminarian *noun* a student in a seminary. [Say semma NERRY in]

seminary *noun* (*plural* **seminaries**) **1** a training college for priests, rabbis, etc. **2** a place of education or development. [Say SEMMA nerry]

Seminole • *noun* (*plural* **Seminoles**) **1** a member of any of several groupings of North American Aboriginal peoples comprising Creek Confederacy emigrants to Florida or their descendants in Florida and Oklahoma. **2** the Muskogean language of the Seminoles. • *adjective* of this people or their language. [Say SEM in ole]

semi-opaque *adjective* partially transparent.

semiotic *adjective* of semiotics. [Say semmy OTT ick]

semiotics *noun* the study of signs and symbols in various fields, esp. language. [Say semmy OTT icks]

semi-permanent *adjective* rather less than permanent. ▶ **semi-permanently** *adverb*

semi-permeable *adjective* (of a membrane etc.) allowing small molecules, but not large ones, to pass through.

semi-precious *adjective* (of a gem) less valuable than a precious stone.

semi-private *adjective* **1** partially or somewhat private. **2** (of a hospital room) shared by two patients.

semi-professional • *adjective* **1** receiving payment for an activity but not relying on it for a living. **2** involving semi-professionals. • *noun* a semi-professional musician, sportsman, etc. ▶ **semi-professionally** *adverb*

semi-retired *adjective* (of a person) partially but not completely retired. ▶ **semi-retirement** *noun*

semi-skilled *adjective* (of work or a worker) having or needing some training but less than for a skilled worker.

semi-soft *adjective* (of cheese) having a consistency between firm and soft.

semi-solid *adjective* & *noun* = SEMI-LIQUID.

semi-sweet *adjective* (esp. of chocolate) slightly sweetened.

semi-synthetic *adjective* Chemistry (of a substance) that is prepared synthetically but derives from a naturally occurring material.

Scmite *noun* a member of any of the peoples supposed to be descended from Shem, son of Noah, including esp. the Jews, Arabs, Assyrians, and Phoenicians. [Say SEM ite or SEEM ite]

Semitic • *adjective* **1** of or relating to the Semites, esp. the Jews. **2** of or relating to the languages of the family including Hebrew and Arabic. • *noun* the Semitic language family. [Say suh MIT ick]

semitone *noun* the smallest interval used in classical European music; half a tone. [Say SEMMY tone]

semi-trailer *noun* a trailer having wheels at the back but supported at the front by a towing vehicle.

semi-transparent *adjective* partly transparent.

semi-vowel *noun* **1** a sound intermediate between a vowel and a consonant (e.g. *w*, *y*). **2** a letter representing this.

semi-weekly • *adjective* occurring, published, etc., twice a week. • *adverb* twice a week.

semolina *noun* the hard grains left after the milling of flour, used esp. in making pasta. [Say semma LEENA]

senate *noun* **1** (**Senate**) **a** (in Canada) the upper chamber of Parliament, consisting of senators appointed to represent the regions of Canada. **b** (in the US) the upper, elected, house of Congress or of a state legislature. **c** a similar legislative body in other countries, e.g. France. **2** the governing body of a university or college.

senator *noun* a member of a senate. ▶ **senatorial** *adjective* **senatorship** *noun*

send *verb* (**sends**, **sent**, **sending**) **1 a** order or cause to go or be conveyed: *sent me a book.* **b** propel; cause to move: *sent him flying.* **c** cause to go or become: *his dancing sends her into raptures.* **d** dismiss with or without force. **2** (of God, providence, etc.) grant or bestow or inflict. **3** *slang* affect emotionally, put into ecstasy. PHRASES **send away for** send an order to a dealer for (goods). **send for 1** summon. **2** order by mail. **send in 1** cause to go in. **2** submit (an entry etc.) for a competition etc. **send off 1** get (a letter, parcel, etc.) dispatched. **2** attend the departure of (a person) as a sign of respect etc. **3** *Sport* (of a referee) order (a player) to leave the field and take no further part in the game. **send off for** = SEND AWAY FOR. **send on** transmit to a further destination or in advance of one's own arrival. **send out for** order delivery of (food). **send up 1** cause to go up. **2** transmit to a higher authority. **3** *informal* satirize or ridicule, esp. by mimicking. **send word** send a message. ▶ **sender** *noun*

send-off *noun* a demonstration of goodwill etc. at a person's departure, the start of a project, etc.

send-up *noun* *informal* a satire or parody.

Seneca • *noun* (*plural* **Seneca** or **Senecas**) **1 a** member of one of the founding peoples of the Iroquois Five Nations confederacy, now living in Ontario and New York. **2** the Iroquoian language of this people. • *adjective* of or relating to this people or their culture or language. [Say SENNA kuh]

Senegalese • *adjective* of or relating to Senegal, a country on the coast of West Africa. • *noun* (*plural* **Senegalese**) a native or inhabitant of Senegal. [Say senna guh LEEZ]

senile *adjective* **1** of or characteristic of old age.

2 having the weaknesses or diseases of old age. [Say SEE nile]

senile dementia *noun* a severe form of mental deterioration in old age, characterized by loss of memory and control of bodily functions.

senility *noun* mental or physical infirmity due to old age; the condition of being senile. [Say suh NILLA too]

senior • *adjective* **1** more or most advanced in age, standing, rank, etc. **2** of high or highest position: *senior management*. **3** (placed after a person's name) senior to another of the same name. **4** (of a school) having students in an older age range (esp. over 11). **5** esp. *US* of the final year at a university, high school, etc. • *noun* **1 a** = SENIOR CITIZEN. **b** a person of comparatively long service etc. **2** one's elder, or one's superior in length of service, membership, etc. **3** esp. *US* a student in the final year at a university, high school, etc.

senior citizen *noun* an elderly person, esp. a person over 65.

senior government *noun Cdn* the federal or a provincial government, or both, as opposed to a municipal government.

senior high school *noun* a secondary school comprising usu. the three highest grades.

seniority *noun* **1** the fact of being older or of a higher rank than others: *a position of seniority*. **2** the rank that one has in a company because of the length of time one has worked there: *an assistant with five years' seniority* ◊ *should promotion be based on merit or seniority?*

senior matriculation *noun* (also *informal* **senior matric**) *Cdn hist.* (in certain provinces) completion of secondary education to a level required for admission to university.

senna *noun* **1** a cassia tree. **2** a laxative prepared from the dried pods of this.

señor *noun* (*plural* **señores**) a title used of or to a Spanish-speaking man. [Say sen YOUR for the singular, sen YOUR ez for the plural]

señora *noun* a title used of or to a Spanish-speaking married woman. [Say sen YOUR uh]

señorita *noun* (*plural* **señoritas**) a title used of or to a Spanish-speaking unmarried woman. [Say sen yuh REETA]

sensation *noun* **1** the consciousness of perceiving or seeming to perceive some state or condition of one's body or its parts or of the senses: *lost all sensation in my arm* ◊ *the sensation of falling*. **2** an awareness or impression: *a sensation of being watched*. **3 a** a stirring of emotions or intense interest, esp. among a large group of people: *his arrest caused a sensation*. **b** a person, event, etc., causing such interest: *she was a sensation, the talk of the evening*.

sensational *adjective* **1 a** causing a sensation: *a sensational crime*. **b** deliberately trying to provoke interest by including material that is exciting, shocking, salacious, etc.: *sensational journalism*. **2** very good: *a sensational singer*. **3** of or causing sensation.

sensationalism *noun* the use of or interest in sensational material in journalism, political agitation, etc. ▶ **sensationalist** *noun* **&** *adjective* **sensationalistic** *adjective*

sensationalize *verb* (**sensationalizes, sensationalized, sensationalizing**) (esp. of a newspaper) present information about (something) in a way that provokes public interest and excitement, at the expense of accuracy: *the papers want to sensationalize the tragedy that her family has suffered*.

sensationally *adverb* **1** in a very good way or to a high degree: *she's sensationally good looking*. **2** in a sensational way: *the incident was reported sensationally in the media*.

sense • *noun* **1** any of the special bodily faculties by which sensation is roused: *has keen senses* ◊ *the sense of smell*. **2** the ability to perceive or feel or to be conscious of the presence or properties of things. **3** consciousness: *sense of one's own importance*. **4** an appreciation, understanding, or instinct regarding a specified matter: *the moral sense* ◊ *my sense is that they won't come*. **5** the instinctive or acquired capacity to comprehend or appreciate a specified quality, subject, etc.: *has no fashion sense*. **6** practical wisdom or judgment, common sense. **7** a meaning; the way in which a word etc. is to be understood: *the sense of the word is clear*. **8** the prevailing opinion among a number of people. • *verb* (**senses, sensed, sensing**) **1** perceive by a sense or senses. **2** be vaguely aware of. **3** realize. **4** (of a machine etc.) detect. **PHRASES** **bring a person to his** or **her senses 1** cure a person of folly. **2** restore a person to consciousness. **come to one's senses 1** regain consciousness. **2** become sensible after acting foolishly. **in a** (or **one**) **sense** if the statement is understood in a particular way: *is true in a sense*. **make sense** be intelligible, reasonable, or practicable. **make sense of** show or find the meaning of. **out of one's senses** in or into a state of madness: *frightened him out of his senses*. **take leave of one's senses** go mad.

senseless *adjective* **1** unconscious. **2** wildly foolish. **3** without meaning or purpose. **4** incapable of sensation. ▶ **senselessly** *adverb* **senselessness** *noun*

sense organ *noun* a bodily organ conveying external stimuli to the sensory system.

sensibility *noun* (*plural* **sensibilities**) **1** openness to emotional impressions: *sensibility to kindness*. **2 a** (in *plural*) emotional capacities or feelings: *was limited in his sensibilities*. **b** a person's moral, emotional, or aesthetic ideas or standards: *offended the sensibilities of believers*.

sensible *adjective* **1** having or showing wisdom or common sense: *a sensible person* ◊ *a sensible compromise*. **2 a** perceptible by the senses: *sensible phenomena*. **b** great enough to be perceived; appreciable: *a sensible difference*. **3** (of clothing etc.) practical and functional. ▶ **sensibleness** *noun* **sensibly** *adverb*

sensitive *adjective* **1** (often foll. by *to*) very open to or acutely affected by external stimuli or mental impressions. **2** (of a person) **a** easily offended or emotionally hurt. **b** attuned to others' emotions. **c** deeply and easily affected by emotion, beauty, etc. **3** (often foll. by *to*) (of an instrument etc.) responsive to or recording slight changes. **4** (often foll. by *to*) **a** (of photographic materials) prepared so as to respond (esp. rapidly) to the action of light. **b** readily affected by or responsive to external influences: *an environmentally sensitive area*. **5 a** (of a topic etc.) needing careful handling to avoid causing offence, embarrassment, etc. **b** involved with or likely to affect (esp. national) security. **6** (of a market) liable to quick changes of price. ▶ **sensitively** *adverb* **sensitivity** *noun* (*plural* **sensitivities**)

sensitize *verb* (**sensitizes, sensitized, sensitizing**) **1** make sensitive. **2** *Photography* make sensitive to light. **3** make (an organism etc.) abnormally sensitive to a foreign substance.

SPELL CHECK	
sensor, censor	

To remove something objectionable from a book or movie is to **censor** it.

sensor *noun* a device giving a signal for the detection or measurement of a physical property to which it responds.

sensory *adjective* of sensation or the senses. [Say SENSA ree]

sensual *adjective* **1 a** of or depending on the senses only and not on the intellect or spirit: *sensual pleasures*. **b** given to the pursuit of sensual pleasures or the gratification of the appetites; self-indulgent sexually or in regard to food and drink. **c** suggesting an interest in physical esp. sexual pleasure: *he was darkly sensual and mysterious*. **2** of sense or sensation, sensory. ▶ **sensualism** *noun* **sensualist** *noun* [Say SEN shoo ul]

sensuality *noun* **1** the state or quality of being pleasing to the senses: *life can dazzle with its sensuality, its colour*. **2** the enjoyment, expression, or pursuit of physical, esp. sexual, pleasure: *he ate the grapes with surprising sensuality*. [Say sen shoo ALA tee]

sensually *adverb* **1** with regard to or suggestive of physical pleasure or gratification of the senses: *their arrangements are faintly jazzy and sensually funky*. **2** in a way that can be perceived by the senses. [Say SEN shoo ul ee]

> **SPELL CHECK**
> **sensual, sensuous**
>
> Both *sensual* and *sensuous* are normally used to refer to pleasures of the senses, and nowadays both usually suggest sexuality. Traditionally *sensuous* has been the more neutral term, used to describe the pleasures that music and other arts give to the senses, but today there seems to be little distinction made between the words.

sensuous *adjective* **1** of or derived from or affecting the senses, esp. aesthetically rather than sensually. **2** attractive or gratifying physically, esp. sexually: *her voice was rather deep but very sensuous*. ▶ **sensuously** *adverb* **sensuousness** *noun* [Say SEN shoo us]

> **SPELL CHECK**
> **sent, cent, scent**
>
> A penny is a **cent**; a smell is a **scent**.

sent *past and past participle of* SEND.

sentence • *noun* **1** a set of words complete in itself as the expression of a thought. **2** a decision of a law court, esp. the punishment allotted to a person convicted in a criminal trial. • *verb* (**sentences**, **sentenced**, **sentencing**) **1** declare the sentence of (a convicted criminal etc.). **2** (foll. by *to*) declare (such a person) to be condemned to a specified punishment. PHRASES **under sentence of** having been condemned to. ▶ **sentencing** *noun*

sentience *noun* the condition or quality of having the power of perception by the senses: *artificial intelligences reaching for true sentience*. [Say SEN shince]

sentient *adjective* having the power of perception by the senses: *you always have the feeling that the land is somehow sentient, watching you*. [Say SEN shint]

sentiment *noun* **1** an opinion or point of view: *I agree with your sentiment regarding the project*. **2** an opinion or feeling as distinguished from the words meant to convey it; an emotional feeling conveyed in literature, art, etc. **3 a** emotional or tender feelings collectively, esp. when considered excessive or inappropriate: *there is no room for sentiment in business*. **b** the display of this. **4** a mental feeling: *the sentiment of pity*.

sentimental *adjective* **1** of or characterized by sentiment. **2** showing or affected by emotion rather than reason. **3** appealing to esp. excessive sentiment. ▶ **sentimentalism** *noun* **sentimentalist** *noun* **sentimentality** *noun* **sentimentalize** *verb*

(**sentimentalizes**, **sentimentalized**, **sentimentalizing**) **sentimentally** *adverb*

sentimental value *noun* the value of a thing to a particular person because of its associations.

sentinel *noun* a sentry or lookout; a guard. [Say SEN tin ul]

sentry *noun* (*plural* **sentries**) a soldier etc. stationed to keep guard.

sepal *noun* Botany each of the divisions or leaves of the calyx. [Say SEEPLE or SEPPLE]

separability *noun* the condition or quality of being able to be separated.

separable *adjective* able to be separated. ▶ **separably** *adverb*

separate • *adjective* **1** (often foll. by *from*) forming a unit that is or may be regarded as apart or by itself. **2** *Cdn* of or relating to a separate school or the separate school system. • *noun* (in *plural*) separate articles of clothing suitable for wearing together in various combinations. • *verb* (**separates**, **separated**, **separating**) **1** make separate. **2 a** prevent union or contact of. **b** part by occupying an intervening space: *a river separates the two counties*. **3** go different ways, disperse. **4** cease to live together as a married couple. **5** (often foll. by *from*) secede. **6 a** divide or sort (milk, ore, fruit, light, etc.) into constituent parts or sizes. **b** (often foll. by *out*) extract or remove (an ingredient, waste product, etc.) by such a process for use or rejection. **7** (of a substance) stop being combined; divide into constituent parts. ▶ **separately** *adverb* **separateness** *noun*

separate school *noun* Cdn **1** (in Ontario) a publicly funded school for Catholic students (*compare* PUBLIC SCHOOL 2a). **2** (in Alberta and Saskatchewan) a publicly funded school for children belonging to the religious minority (usu. Catholics) in a given district.

separate school board *noun* Cdn **1** a board of trustees responsible for the separate schools of a particular area. **2** the administrative unit responsible for the separate schools in a given area. **3** the area within which a separate school board has jurisdiction.

separate school district *noun* Cdn (in Alberta and Saskatchewan) the area within which a separate school board has jurisdiction.

separate school system *noun* Cdn a system of publicly funded denominational (usu. Catholic) schools operated alongside a public school system.

separation *noun* **1** the action or state of moving or being moved apart: *the damage that may arise from the separation of parents and children ◊ reunited after a separation of 20 years*. **2** an arrangement by which a husband and wife remain married but live apart: *agreed to a trial separation*. **3** any of three or more one-colour reproductions of a coloured picture which can combine to reproduce the full colour of the original. **4** the process of dividing something into constituent or distinct elements: *the separation of church and state*. **5** the process by which one part of a country breaks away from the country and establishes itself as independent: *Quebec separation*.

separation anxiety *noun* anxiety provoked in a child by the threat of separation from its parents etc.

separatism *noun* the advocacy or practice of separation of a certain group of people from a larger body, esp. for political or ecclesiastical independence; (in Canada) the advocacy of the secession of Quebec or the Western provinces from Canada. [Say SEPRA tism]

separatist • *noun* a person who favours separation, esp. for political or ecclesiastical independence; (in Canada) a person who favours the secession of Quebec or the Western provinces from Canada. • *adjective* of,

pertaining to, or characteristic of separatists or their views. [Say SEPRA tist]

separator *noun* a machine or device for separating, e.g. cream from milk or egg yolk from egg white.

SPELL CHECK
separate   ABC✓

Warning: **separate**, with a following the p, is the only correct spelling for the adjective and the verb.

Sephardi *noun* (*plural* **Sephardim**) a Jew of Spanish or Portuguese descent. ▶ **Sephardic** *adjective* [Say suh FARDY for the singular, suh FAR dim for the plural]

sepia • *noun* (*plural* **sepias**) **1** a dark reddish-brown colour. **2 a** a brown pigment prepared from a black fluid secreted by cuttlefish, used in monochrome drawing and in watercolours. **b** a brown tint used in photography. **3** a drawing done in sepia. • *adjective* of a dark reddish-brown colour. [Say SEEPY uh]

Sept. *abbreviation* September.

septa *plural of* SEPTUM.

September *noun* the ninth month of the year.

septet *noun* **1** *Music* **a** a composition for seven performers. **b** the performers of such a composition. **2** any group of seven. [Say sep TET]

septic • *adjective* **1** contaminated with bacteria from a festering wound etc. **2** of or relating to a septic system. • *noun* = SEPTIC SYSTEM.

septic field *noun* (also **septic bed**) a bed of gravel and tile laid underneath the ground to serve as a drainage area for the effluent from a septic tank.

septic system *noun* an underground sewage disposal system consisting of a septic tank and septic field.

septic tank *noun* a tank in which the organic matter in sewage is decomposed through bacterial activity.

septuagenarian • *noun* a person from 70 to 79 years old. • *adjective* of this age. [Say sept wuh juh NERRY in]

Septuagint *noun* a Greek version of the Hebrew Scriptures including the Apocrypha, said to have been made about 270 BC. [Say SEPT wuh jint]

septum *noun* (*plural* **septa**) *Anatomy, Botany, & Zoology* a partition, such as that between the nostrils.

sepulchral *adjective* **1** of a tomb or interment. **2** funereal, gloomy, dismal: *sepulchral look.* [Say se PUL krul (PUL rhymes with *HULL*)]

sepulchre *noun* a tomb esp. cut in rock or built of stone or brick, a burial vault or cave. [Say SEPPLE cur]

sequel *noun* **1** what follows after or as a result of an earlier event: *famine is the sequel to war.* **2** a novel, film, etc., that continues the story of an earlier one.

sequence • *noun* **1** succession, coming after or next. **2** order of succession: *shall follow the sequence of events* ◊ *historical sequence.* **3** a set of things belonging next to one another on some principle of order; a series without gaps. **4** a part of a film dealing with one scene or topic. **5** a set of poems on one theme: *sonnet sequence.* **6** a set of three or more playing cards next to one another in value. **7** *Music* repetition of a phrase or melody at a higher or lower pitch. • *verb* (**sequences**, **sequenced**, **sequencing**) arrange in a definite order.

sequencer *noun* **1** a programmable electronic device for storing sequences of musical notes, chords, rhythms, etc. and transmitting them when required to an electronic musical instrument. **2** an apparatus for performing or initiating operations in the correct sequence, esp. one forming part of the control system of a computer.

sequential *adjective* **1** following in a sequence or as a logical conclusion: *using sequential aerial photography, he*

noted that logs identified on 1944 photos showed little evidence of movement in 1952 photos but had significantly changed in distribution prior to 1970. **2** esp. *Computing* occurring or performed in a particular order. ▶ **sequentially** *adverb* [Say si KWEN shul]

sequester *verb* seclude, isolate, set apart: *the jury, which was sequestered overnight, returned to court once during its deliberations.* [Say si KWESS ter]

sequin *noun* a circular spangle attached to clothing as an ornament. ▶ **sequined** *adjective* [Say SEEK win]

sequoia *noun* (*plural* **sequoias**) a Californian redwood tree of very great height and breadth. [Say suh KWOY uh]

sera *plural of* SERUM. [Say SEE ruh]

seraph *noun* (*plural* **seraphim** or **seraphs**) *Bible* a supernatural being with three pairs of wings. **2** *Christianity* a member of the highest order of the nine ranks of heavenly beings, gifted esp. with love and associated with light, ardour, and purity. [Say SAIR uff for the singular, SERRA fim for the plural]

Serb • *noun* **1** a native of Serbia, a country in the Balkans. **2** a person of Serbian descent. • *adjective* of or relating to the Serbs or their dialect.

Serbian • *noun* **1** the dialect of the Serbs. **2** = SERB. • *adjective* of or relating to the Serbs or their dialect.

Serbo-Croat (also **Serbo-Croatian**) • *noun* the Slavic language of the Serbs and Croats, written in the Cyrillic alphabet by Serbs and the Roman alphabet by Croats. • *adjective* of or relating to this language. [Say sir bo CROW at, sir bo crow AY sh'n]

sere[1] *adjective* *literary* (esp. of a plant etc.) withered: *spring will arrive and turn this sere landscape into an oasis of green.* [Say SEER]

sere[2] *noun* *Ecology* a natural succession of plant (or animal) communities, esp. a full series from uncolonized habitat to the appropriate climax vegetation. [Say SEER]

serenade • *noun* **1** a piece of music sung or played in the open air, esp. by a lover at night under the window of his beloved. **2** a suite of diverse pieces for an instrumental ensemble, esp. a string orchestra or wind ensemble. • *verb* (**serenades**, **serenaded**, **serenading**) sing or play a serenade to. [Say serra NADE]

serendipitous *adjective* (of an event, discovery, meeting, etc.) occurring by (esp. fortunate) chance: *the body remained undisturbed for centuries because of a serendipitous series of climatic occurrences.* ▶ **serendipitously** *adverb* [Say sair un DIPPA tus]

serendipity *noun* (*plural* **serendipities**) the fact of something interesting or pleasant happening by chance; good fortune: *her rise might look like serendipity, but she actually left very little to chance.* [Say sair un DIPPA tee]

serene *adjective* (**serener**, **serenest**) **1** placid, tranquil. **2 a** (of the sky etc.) clear and calm. **b** (of the sea etc.) unruffled. ▶ **serenely** *adverb* **serenity** *noun* [Say suh REEN, suh RENNA tee]

serf *noun* (*plural* **serfs**) **1** *hist.* (under the feudal system) a labourer who was not free to move from the land on which he worked. **2** an oppressed person, a drudge. ▶ **serfdom** *noun*

serge *noun* a durable twilled woollen or worsted fabric used mainly for clothing. [Say SURGE]

sergeant *noun* **1** (in the Canadian Army and Air Force and other armies) a non-commissioned officer ranking above corporal. **2** (in some Canadian police forces) = STAFF SERGEANT. **3** (in some Canadian police forces) an officer ranking above the lowest ranks. [Say SAR jint]

sergeant-at-arms *noun* (*plural* **sergeants-at-arms**) an official of a court or city or parliament, with ceremonial duties.

sergeant major *noun* **1** (in the RCMP) an officer

S

ranking above staff sergeant major. **2** (in the OPP) an officer ranking below inspector.

serial • *noun* **1** a story, play, or film which is published, broadcast, or shown in regular instalments. **2** a periodical. • *adjective* **1** of or in or forming a series. **2** (of a story etc.) in the form of a serial. **3** (of a publication) appearing in successive parts published usu. at regular intervals, periodical. **4** *Computing* **a** performed or used in sequence, sequential. **b** (of a device) involving the transfer of data as a single sequence of bits: *serial port*. **5** (of a person, action, etc.) habitual, given to or characterized by the repetition of certain behaviour in a sequential pattern: *serial rapist*.

serialization *noun* **1** the act or process of serializing something. **2** a serial version of a story etc.: *a 50-part animated serialization of Anne of Green Gables*.

serialize *verb* (**serializes, serialized, serializing**) publish or produce in instalments.

serial killer *noun* a person who murders repeatedly, often with no apparent motive and usually following a characteristic, predictable pattern of behaviour. ▶ **serial killing** *noun*

serially *adverb* in a series; in serial form or arrangement: *the novel was first issued serially*.

serial number *noun* a number showing position in a series, esp. one printed on a banknote or manufactured article by which it can be individually identified.

series *noun* (*plural* **series**) **1** a number of similar or related things coming one after another. **2 a** a set of programs with the same actors etc. or on related subjects but each complete in itself. **b** a set of performances offered for purchase by subscription. **3** *Geology* a range of strata corresponding to an epoch in time. **4** *Math* a set of quantities constituting a progression or having values determined by a common relation. PHRASES **in series 1** in ordered succession. **2** *Electricity* (of a set of circuits or components) arranged so that the current passes through each successively.

serif *noun* **1** a slight projection finishing off a stroke of a letter, as in T contrasted with T (*compare* SANS SERIF). **2** a form of type with serifs. [Say SAIR if]

serious *adjective* **1** thoughtful, earnest, responsible, not reckless or given to trifling. **2** important, demanding consideration: *this is a serious matter*. **3** not slight or negligible: *a serious injury*. **4** sincere, in earnest: *are you serious?* **5** (of music and literature) not merely for amusement (*opp.* LIGHT^2 5a). **6** not perfunctory: *serious thought*. **7** not to be trifled with: *a serious opponent*. **8** (of a relationship or the people involved in it) involving profound love, the intention to marry, etc. **9** *informal* large in size or amount: *serious money*. **10** *informal* remarkable; impressive.

seriously *adverb* **1** in a serious manner (esp. introducing a sentence, implying that irony etc. is now to cease). **2** to a serious extent. **3** *informal* very, really: *seriously rich*.

seriousness *noun* the state of being serious: *he spoke with a seriousness that was unusual in him*.

sermon *noun* **1** a spoken or written discourse on a religious or moral subject, esp. a discourse based on a text or passage of Scripture and delivered in a service by way of religious instruction or exhortation. **2** an esp. long talk that tries to present moral advice: *we had to listen to a long sermon on the evils of wasting time*.

seronegative *adjective* giving a negative result in a

test of blood serum, e.g. for presence of a virus. ▶ **seronegativity** *noun* [Say seero NEGATIVE]

seropositive *adjective* giving a positive result in a test of blood serum, e.g. for presence of a virus. ▶ **seropositivity** *noun* [Say seero POSITIVE]

serotonin *noun* a compound present in blood platelets and serum, which constricts the blood vessels and acts as a neurotransmitter. [Say serra TOE nin]

serpent *noun* **1** usu. *literary* a snake, esp. of a large kind. **2** a sly or treacherous person, esp. one who exploits a position of trust. **3** (**the Serpent**) *Bible* Satan.

serpentine *adjective* **1** of or like a serpent. **2** coiling, meandering, writhing: *on the rough, serpentine roads Michael drove impatiently*. **3** cunning: *the conspiracy gets ever more serpentine*. [Say SIRP'n tine or SIRP'n teen]

serrated *adjective* with a saw-like edge: *a serrated knife*. ▶ **serration** *noun* [Say suh RATE id]

serum *noun* (*plural* **sera** or **serums**) **1** the amber-coloured protein-rich liquid in which blood cells are suspended and which separates out when blood coagulates. **2** the blood serum of an animal used esp. to provide immunity to a pathogen or toxin by inoculation or as a diagnostic agent. **3** a watery fluid in animal bodies. [Say SEER um for the plural, SEER uh for the plural]

servant *noun* **1** a person hired to carry out the orders of an individual or corporate employer, esp. a person employed in a house on domestic duties or as a personal attendant. **2** a devoted follower, a person willing to serve another: *a servant of Jesus*. **3** a person employed by a government: *civil servant*.

serve • *verb* (**serves, served, serving**) **1** perform duties or services for. **2** be employed as a member of the armed forces. **3** spend (a period) in office, in an apprenticeship, or in prison. **4** present food or drink to. **5** attend to (a customer in a shop). **6** be of use in fulfilling (a purpose). **7** treat in a specified way. **8** (of food or drink) be enough for. **9** *Law* formally deliver (a summons or writ). **10** (in tennis etc.) hit the ball etc. to begin or resume play. **11** (of a male breeding animal) copulate with (a female). • *noun* (in tennis, volleyball, etc.) an act of hitting the ball or shuttlecock to start play. PHRASES **serve one's needs** be adequate. **serve the purpose of** take the place of, be used as. **serve a person right** be a person's deserved punishment or misfortune. **serve** (or esp. **serve out**) **one's time 1** hold office for the normal period. **2** (also **serve time**) undergo imprisonment, apprenticeship, etc. **serve up** offer for acceptance.

server *noun* **1** a person who serves or attends to the requirements of another, esp. a waiter. **2** (in tennis etc.) the player who serves the ball. **3** *Christianity* a person assisting the celebrant at a service, esp. the Eucharist. **4** *Computing* **a** a program which manages shared access to a centralized resource or service in a network. **b** a device on which such a program is run. **5** a utensil for serving food: *salad servers*.

service • *noun* (often as an *adjective*) **1** the action or process of serving. **2** a period of employment with an organization. **3** an act of assistance. **4** a ceremony of religious worship according to a prescribed form. **5** a system supplying a public need such as transport, or utilities such as water. **6** (in *plural*) the armed forces. **7** a set of matching crockery used for serving a particular meal. **8** (in tennis etc.) a serve. **9** a periodic routine inspection and maintenance of a vehicle or other machine. **10** the sector of the economy that supplies the needs of the consumer but produces no tangible goods, as banking or tourism. **11 a** the act or process of serving customers in a store. **b** assistance or advice given to customers after the sale of goods. • *verb*

S

(**services**, **serviced**, **servicing**) **1** provide service or services for, esp. maintain. **2** maintain or repair (a car etc.). **3** pay interest on (a debt). **4** supply with a service. **5** (of a male animal) copulate with (a female animal). PHRASES **at a person's service** ready to serve or assist a person. **be of service** be available to assist. **in service 1** employed as a servant. **2** available for use. **on active service** serving in the armed forces in wartime. **out of service** not available for use. **see service 1** have experience of service, esp. in the armed forces. **2** (of a thing) be much used.

serviceability *noun* usefulness; readiness for use. [Say service a BILLA tee]

serviceable *adjective* **1** useful or usable. **2** able to render service. **3** durable; capable of withstanding difficult conditions. **4** suited for ordinary use rather than ornament. [Say SERVICE a bull]

service area *noun* **1** the area served by a broadcasting station, public utility, etc. **2** the area in a store, garage, etc. set aside for the maintenance and repair of machines, cars, etc.

service bay *noun* a space in an auto repair shop designed to accommodate one car at a time.

serviceberry *noun* (*plural* **serviceberries**) **1** a North American shrub of the rose family, with showy white flowers. **2** the edible fruit of this.

service centre *noun* **1** a registered commercial operation where cars, appliances, etc. can be taken for maintenance and repair. **2** *Cdn* a town or city which serves as a shopping and distribution centre for a surrounding sparsely populated area.

service club *noun* an association of business or professional people having the aims of promoting community welfare and goodwill.

serviced *adjective Cdn & Brit.* hooked up to utilities such as gas, water, and hydro: *a serviced campsite*.

service industry *noun* (*plural* **service industries**) an industry engaged in providing services rather than the manufacture of goods.

service line *noun* (in tennis etc.) a line marking the limit of the area into which the ball must be served.

serviceman *noun* (*plural* **servicemen**) **1** a man serving in the armed forces. **2** a man providing service etc.

service provider *noun* a company, organization, etc. which provides a service to customers, esp. one which provides access to the Internet.

service road *noun* a road parallel to a main road, giving access to houses, stores, etc.

service station *noun* a gas station.

servicewoman *noun* (*plural* **servicewomen**) a woman serving in the armed forces.

serviette *noun Cdn & Brit.* a napkin for use at table, esp. a paper one. [Say servy ET]

servile *adjective* **1** having or showing an excessive willingness to serve or please others: *some historians have accused Bishop Briand of servile compliance with the English*. **2** of or being or like a slave or slaves: *a servile task*. ▶ **servilely** *adverb* **servility** *noun* [Say SIR vile, sir VILLA tee]

serving *noun* **1** the action of SERVE *verb*. **2** a quantity of food served to one person. **3** (as an *adjective*) used for serving food: *serving spoons*.

servitude *noun* **1** slavery. **2** the state of being subject to someone more powerful: *lifetimes of sweat and servitude*.

servo *noun* (*plural* **servos**) **1** (also **servo-mechanism**) a powered mechanism producing motion or forces at a higher level of energy than the input level, e.g. in the brakes and steering of large motor vehicles, esp. where feedback is employed to make the control automatic.

2 (also **servo-motor**) the motive element in a servo-mechanism. **3** (in *combination*) of or involving a servo-mechanism: *servo-assisted*. [Say SIR vo]

sesame *noun* **1** an East Indian plant that produces seeds used as food and yielding an edible oil. **2** its seeds. [Say SESSA me]

sesquicentennial • *noun* a one-hundred-and-fiftieth anniversary. • *adjective* of or relating to a sesquicentennial. [Say sess kwi sen TENNY ul]

sessile *adjective* **1** *Botany & Zoology* (of a flower, leaf, eye, etc.) attached directly by its base without a stalk. **2** (of an organism, e.g. a barnacle) fixed in one place; immobile. [Say SESS ile]

session *noun* **1** the process of assembly of a deliberative or judicial body to conduct its business. **2** a single meeting for this purpose. **3** a period during which such meetings are regularly held. **4 a** an academic year or term. **b** the period during which a school etc. has classes. **5** a period devoted to an activity. **6** the governing body of a Presbyterian or United Church congregation, composed of the minister and the elders. PHRASES **in session** assembled for business; not on vacation. ▶ **sessional** *adjective*

set[1] *verb* (**sets**, **set**, **setting**) **1** put, lay, or stand (a thing) in a certain position or location. **2** put, bring, or place into a specified state. **3** cause or instruct (someone) to do something. **4** give someone (a task). **5** decide on or fix (a time, value, price, etc.). **6** establish as (an example or record). **7** adjust (a device) as required. **8** prepare (a table) for a meal by placing cutlery, crockery, etc., on it. **9** harden into a solid, semi-solid, or fixed state. **10** arrange (damp hair) into the required style. **11** put (a broken or dislocated bone or limb) into the correct position for healing. **12** (of the sun, moon, etc.) appear to move towards and below the earth's horizon as the earth rotates. **13** *Printing* arrange (type or text) as required. **14** provide (words) with music for singing. **15** (of a tide or current) take or have a specified direction or course. **16** (of blossoms or a tree)form into or produce (fruit). PHRASES **set about 1** begin or take steps towards. **2** *informal* attack. **set back 1** place further back in place or time. **2** impede or reverse the progress of. **3** *informal* cost (a person) a specified amount. **set down 1** record in writing. **2** allow to alight from a vehicle. **3** (foll. by *to*) attribute to. **4** (foll. by *as*) explain or describe to oneself as. **set forth 1** begin a journey. **2** make known; expound. **set forward** begin to advance. **set free** release. **set one's heart** (or **hopes**) **on** want or hope for eagerly. **set in** (of weather, a condition, etc.) begin (and seem likely to continue), become established. **set little by** consider to be of little value. **set much by** consider to be of much value. **set off 1** begin a journey. **2** detonate (a bomb etc.). **3** initiate, stimulate. **4** cause (a person) to start laughing, talking, etc. **5** serve as an adornment or foil to; enhance. **6** (foll. by *against*) use as a compensating item. **set on** (or **upon**) **1** attack violently. **2** cause or urge to attack. **set out 1** begin a journey. **2** aim or intend: *set out to hurt her*. **3** demonstrate, arrange, or exhibit. **4** mark out. **5** declare. **set sail 1** hoist the sails. **2** begin a sea voyage. **set one's teeth 1** clench them. **2** summon one's resolve. **set to** begin doing something vigorously, esp. fighting, arguing, or eating. **set up 1** place in position or view. **2** organize or start (a business etc.). **3** establish in some capacity. **4** supply the needs of. **5** cause or make arrangements for (a condition or situation). **6** prepare (a task etc.) for another. **7** *informal* put (a person) in a dangerous or vulnerable position. **set oneself up as** make pretensions to being.

S

set² *noun* **1** a number of things or people grouped together as similar or forming a unit. **2** a group of people with common interests or occupations: *the literary set*. **3** the way in which something is set, disposed, or positioned: *that cold set of his jaw*. **4** a radio or television receiver. **5** (in tennis, darts, and other games) a group of games counting as a unit towards a match. **6** a collection of scenery, stage furniture, etc., used for a scene in a play or film. **7** *Math* a collection of distinct entities satisfying specified conditions and regarded as a unit. **8 a** a sequence of songs or pieces performed by a musical ensemble before or after an intermission. **b** the period during which such a sequence is played.

set³ *adjective* **1** *in* senses of SET¹. **2** prescribed or determined in advance. **3** fixed, unchanging, unmoving. **4** (of a phrase or speech etc.) having invariable or predetermined wording; not extempore. **5** prepared for action. **6** (foll. by *on*, *upon*) determined to acquire or achieve etc. **7** (of a book etc.) specified for reading in preparation for an examination.

set-aside *noun* **1** the action of setting something aside for a special purpose. **2** the policy of taking land out of production to reduce crop surpluses (often as an *adjective*: *set-aside land*).

setback *noun* **1** a reversal or arrest of progress. **2** a relapse. **3** the distance by which a building or a part of a building is set back from the property line.

set-off *noun* **1** a thing set off against another. **2** a thing of which the amount or effect may be deducted from that of another or opposite tendency.

set piece *noun* **1** a formal or elaborate arrangement, esp. in art or literature. **2** a sequence of rehearsed movements etc., as in sports or military operations.

settee *noun* a seat (usu. upholstered), with a back and usu. arms, for more than one person. [Say set EE]

setter *noun* **1** a large, long-haired dog trained to stand rigid when scenting game. **2** a person or thing that sets.

setting *noun* **1** the position or manner in which a thing is set. **2** the immediate surroundings (of a house etc.). **3** the surroundings of any object regarded as its framework; the environment of a thing. **4 a** the place and time in which a story, drama, etc. is set. **b** the scenery and stage properties etc. used in a play, film, etc. **5** a frame in which a jewel is set. **6** the music to which words of a poem, song, etc., are set. **7** a set of cutlery, dishes, etc. for one person. **8** the way in which or level at which a machine is set to operate.

settle¹ *verb* (**settles**, **settled**, **settling**) **1** reach an agreement or decision about (an argument or problem). **2** (often foll. by *down*) adopt a more steady or secure life, esp. through establishing a permanent home. **3** sit, come to rest, or arrange comfortably or securely. **4** become or make calmer or quieter. **5** (foll. by *down to*) apply oneself to. **6** pay (a debt or account). **7** (foll. by *for*) accept or agree to (something less than satisfactory). **8** (of suspended particles) sink slowly in a liquid to form sediment. **9 a** people (a place) with inhabitants. **b** take up residence in a new place: *our family settled here in 1834.* **10** sink down gradually, as by its own weight: *the foundations are settling.* **11** (of the ground etc.) become firm or compact. **12** dispose of or arrange for the disposal of (an estate, etc.). PHRASES **settle in 1** become established in a new home etc. **2** become accustomed to a new home, new surroundings, etc. **3** dispose oneself comfortably for remaining indoors. **settle up 1** pay (an account, debt, etc.). **2** finally arrange (a matter). **settle with 1** pay all or part of an amount due to (a creditor). **2** get revenge on.

settle² *noun* a bench with a high back and arms and often with a box fitted below the seat.

settled *adjective* **1** that has settled or been settled; fixed, unchanging, established. **2** (of a person's expression or bearing) indicating a settled mind, character, or disposition. **3** (of weather) calm and fair.

settlement *noun* **1** an official agreement intended to resolve a dispute or conflict: *the union succeeded in reaching a wage settlement* ◊ *negotiated a peace settlement* ◊ *the terms of the divorce settlement.* **2 a** the process of establishing a community of fixed homes in a place: *the settlement of the West.* **b** a place or area established in this way: *the Red River Settlement.* **c** a small village. **3** the process of paying money owed: *the settlement of the debt.*

settler *noun* a person who goes to settle in a new country or place.

set-to *noun* (*plural* **set-tos**) *informal* a fight or argument.

set-up *noun* **1** an arrangement or organization: *would you be comfortable with a team-teaching set-up?* **2** an act of setting up. **3** *informal* a conspiracy or trick whereby a person is caused to incriminate himself or herself or to look foolish, or a criminal is caught red-handed. **4** *Sport* a pass or play intended to provide an opportunity for another player to score. **5** a plan or course of action. **6** a set or collection of the equipment etc. needed for a particular activity or purpose. **7** *informal* an event or activity with a pre-arranged conclusion.

seven *cardinal number* one more than six, or three less than ten.

seven deadly sins *plural noun* (in Christian tradition) pride, covetousness (greed for material things), lust, envy, gluttony (overindulgence in food), anger, and sloth (laziness), regarded as the basic human vices.

sevenfold *adjective & adverb* **1** seven times as much or as many. **2** consisting of seven parts.

seventeen *cardinal number* one more than sixteen. ▶ **seventeenth** *ordinal number*

seventh *ordinal number* **1** constituting number seven in a sequence. **2** one of seven equal parts of a thing. **3** *Music* an interval or chord spanning seven consecutive notes in the diatonic scale (e.g. C to B).

Seventh-day Adventist • *noun* a member of a branch of the Adventists with beliefs based rigidly on faith and the Scriptures and the imminent return of Christ to earth, and observing the Sabbath on Saturday. • *adjective* of or relating to the Seventh-day Adventists.

seventieth *ordinal number* corresponding to seventy.

seventy *cardinal number* ten less than eighty. PHRASES **seventy-first, -second**, etc. the ordinal numbers between seventieth and eightieth. **seventy-one, -two**, etc. the cardinal numbers between seventy and eighty.

seventy-eight *noun* *hist.* a gramophone record played at 78 rpm.

sever *verb* **1** (often foll. by *from*) divide, break, or make separate, esp. by cutting. **2** end (a relationship or connection); break off something: *sever ties.* **3** separate (a piece of land) from a larger lot. **4** end the employment contract of (a person). [Say SEV er]

several *adjective* **1** more than two but not many. **2** separate or respective; distinct: *all went their several ways.* ▶ **severally** *adverb*

severance *noun* **1** the action of ending a connection or relation: *a complete severance of all links with them.* **2** (also **severance pay**) an amount paid to an employee who is dismissed (also as an *adjective*: *severance package*). **3** the act or an instance of severing a piece of land from a larger lot. [Say SEV er ince]

severe *adjective* **1** rigorous, strict, and harsh in attitude or treatment: *severe discipline.* **2** serious, critical: *a severe shortage.* **3** forceful: *a severe storm.*

4 extreme (in an unpleasant quality): *a severe winter*. **5** making great demands on energy, skill, etc.: *severe competition*. **6** unadorned; plain: *severe dress*. ▶**severely** *adverb* **severity** *noun* [Say suh VEER, suh VERRA tee]

SPELL CHECK
sew, sow   ABC✓

To plant seeds in a field is to **sow**.

---

sew *verb* (**sews**; *past* **sewed**; *past participle* **sewn** or **sewed**; **sewing**) **1** fasten, join, attach, etc., by making stitches with a needle and thread or a sewing machine. **2** make (a garment etc.) by sewing. PHRASES **sew up 1** join or enclose by sewing. **2** *informal* (esp. in *passive*) bring to a desired conclusion or condition. **3** gain complete control of: *we've sewn up the market*.
sewage *noun* waste matter, esp. excrement, conveyed in sewers.
sewer[1] *noun* a conduit, usu. underground, for carrying off drainage water and sewage. ▶**sewerage** *noun*
sewer[2] *noun* a person that sews.
sewing *noun* **1** a piece of material or work to be sewn: *put down her sewing*. **2** the action of sewing.
sewing machine *noun* a machine for sewing or stitching.
sex • *noun* (*plural* **sexes**) **1** either of the main divisions (male and female) into which living things are placed on the basis of their reproductive functions. **2** the fact of belonging to one of these. **3** males or females collectively. **4** sexual intercourse. **5** sexual instincts, desires, etc., or their manifestation: *all you ever think about is sex!* • *adjective* **1** of or relating to sex: *sex education*. **2** arising from a difference or consciousness of sex: *sex discrimination*. • *verb* (**sexes**, **sexed**, **sexing**) determine the sex of.
sex act *noun* the (or an) act of sexual intercourse.
sexagenarian • *noun* a person from 60 to 69 years old. • *adjective* of this age. [say sexa juh nerry in]
sex appeal *noun* sexual attractiveness.
sex change *noun* an apparent change of sex by surgical means and hormone treatment.
sex chromosome *noun* a chromosome concerned in determining the sex of an organism, which in most animals are of two kinds, the x chromosome and the y chromosome.
sexed *adjective* **1** having a sexual appetite: *highly sexed*. **2** having sexual characteristics.
sex hormone *noun* a hormone affecting sexual development or behaviour.
sexily *adverb* **1** in a sexually attractive or stimulating way: *walked sexily across the floor*. **2** excitingly; trendily.
sexiness *noun* **1** the quality or condition of being sexually attractive or stimulating. **2** trendiness.
sexism *noun* **1** prejudice or discrimination, esp. against women, on the grounds of sex. **2** behaviour or attitudes derived from a traditional stereotype of sexual roles. ▶**sexist** *adjective & noun*
sexless *adjective* **1** *biology* neither male nor female. **2** lacking in sexual desire or attractiveness.
sex life *noun* a person's sexual activities viewed collectively: *has an active sex life*.
sex object *noun* a person regarded mainly in terms of sexual attractiveness.
sex offender *noun* a person who commits a sexual crime.
sexology *noun* the study of sexual life or relationships. ▶**sexologist** *noun*
sexpot *noun informal* a sexy person (esp. a woman).
sex symbol *noun* a person widely noted for sex appeal.

sextant *noun* an instrument with a graduated arc of 60° used in navigation and surveying for measuring the angular distance of objects by means of mirrors.
sextet *noun* **1** a musical composition for six voices etc. **2** the performers of such a piece. **3** any group of six.
sexton *noun* a person who looks after a church and churchyard, often acting as bell-ringer etc.
sex trade *noun* = SEX WORK.
sextuple • *adjective* **1** sixfold. **2** having six parts. **3** being six times as many or much. • *noun* a sixfold number or amount. • *verb* multiply by six. [Say sex TUPPLE]
sextuplet *noun* each of six children born at one birth. [Say sex TUP lit]
sexual *adjective* **1** of or relating to sex or the desire for sex: *sexual fantasies*. **2** of or relating to the sexes or the relations between them: *sexual discrimination*. **3** *Botany* (of classification) based on the distinction of sexes in plants. **4** *Biology* having a sex.
sexual abuse *noun* the forcing of a person, esp. a child, to engage in sexual activity or relations; the making of unwanted sexual advances etc.
sexual assault *noun* threatened or actual sexual contact with another person without consent.
sexual harassment *noun* harassment (esp. of a woman) in a workplace etc. involving the making of unwanted sexual advances, obscene remarks, demands for sexual favours etc.
sexual intercourse *noun* genital contact between individuals, esp. involving the insertion of a man's penis into a woman's vagina.
sexual interference *noun Law* the act or an instance of touching directly or indirectly any part of the body of a person under 14 years of age for sexual purposes.
sexuality *noun* **1** possession of sexual powers; capacity for sexual feelings. **2** sexual feelings, desires, etc. collectively. **3** = SEXUAL ORIENTATION.
sexualize *verb* (**sexualizes**, **sexualized**, **sexualizing**) **1** make sexual. **2** attribute sex or a sexual role to.
sexually *adverb* **1** by sexual activity: *sexually transmitted disease*. **2** in a sexual capacity: *sexually attractive* ◊ *sexually active*.
sexually transmitted disease *noun* a disease transmitted by sexual contact, e.g. AIDS, gonorrhea.
sexual orientation *noun* (also **sexual preference**) the fact of being attracted to people of the opposite sex, of one's own sex, or both sexes.
sex work *noun* prostitution. ▶**sex worker** *noun*
sexy *adjective* (**sexier**, **sexiest**) **1** sexually attractive or stimulating. **2** sexually aroused. **3** concerned with or engrossed in sex. **4** *informal* (of a project etc.) exciting, appealing, trendy.
SF *abbreviation* science fiction.
SG *abbreviation* **1** Solicitor General. **2** specific gravity.
SGML *abbreviation Computing* Standard Generalized Mark-up Language, a form of generic coding used for producing printed material in electronic form.
Shabbat *noun* (also **Shabbos**, **Shabbes**) the Jewish Sabbath. [Say shaw BOT]
shabbily *adverb* in a shabby manner or fashion: *shabbily dressed* ◊ *had been treated shabbily*.
shabbiness *noun* the quality or condition of being shabby: *lived in a state of perpetual shabbiness*.
shabby *adjective* (**shabbier**, **shabbiest**) **1** in bad repair or condition; faded and worn. **2** dressed in old or worn clothes. **3** of poor quality. **4** contemptible, dishonourable: *a shabby trick*.
shack *noun* a roughly built hut or cabin. PHRASES

S

shack up *slang* live together in a sexual relationship without being married.

shackle • *noun* **1** a fetter enclosing the ankle or wrist. **2** (usu. in *plural*) a restraint or impediment: *society is going to throw off the shackles of racism and colonialism*. **3** a metal loop or link, closed by a bolt, to connect chains etc. **4** the U-shaped part of a padlock. • *verb* (**shackles**, **shackled**, **shackling**) **1** impede, restrain: *they seek to shackle the oil and gas companies by imposing new controls*. **2** (often foll. by *to*) fasten with a shackle.

shacktown *noun Cdn* a community or section of one composed of shacks or other temporary housing.

shacky *adjective* resembling a shack; dilapidated, ramshackle.

shad *noun* (*plural* **shad** or **shads**) a deep-bodied edible fish of the herring family, usu. living or breeding in fresh water.

shade • *noun* **1** comparative darkness (and usu. coolness) caused by shelter from direct light and heat. **2** a place or area sheltered from the sun. **3** a darker part of a picture etc. **4** a colour, esp. with regard to its depth or as distinguished from one nearly like it. **5** a slight amount: *a shade better*. **6 a** = LAMPSHADE. **b** (also **window shade**) a blind. **7** something that excludes or moderates light. **8** (in *plural*) *informal* sunglasses. **9** a slightly differing variety: *many shades of opinion*. **10** *literary* **a** a ghost. **b** (in *plural*) the underworld. • *verb* (**shades**, **shaded**, **shading**) **1** screen from light. **2** cover, moderate, or exclude the light of. **3** darken, esp. with parallel pencil lines to represent shadow etc. **4** (often foll. by *away*, *off*, *into*) pass or change by degrees. PHRASES **put in the shade** appear or be very superior to (a person or thing). **shades of** suggesting reminiscence or unfavourable comparison: *shades of fascism*.

shading *noun* **1** the representation of light and shade, e.g. by pencilled lines, on a map or drawing. **2** the graduation of tones from light to dark to create a sense of depth.

shadow • *noun* **1** shade or a patch of shade. **2** a dark figure projected by a body intercepting rays of light. **3** an inseparable attendant or companion. **4** a person secretly following another. **5** the slightest trace: *a shadow of a doubt*. **6** a weak or insubstantial remnant or thing: *a shadow of my former self*. **7** (as an *adjective*) *Cdn & Brit.* denoting members of a political party in opposition holding responsibilities parallel to those of the government: *shadow cabinet*. **8** the shaded part of a picture. **9** = EYESHADOW. **10** gloom or sadness. • *verb* **1** cast a shadow over. **2** secretly follow and watch the movements of. **3** accompany (a person) at work either as training or to obtain insight into a profession. PHRASES **in the shadow of 1** close to; very near. **2** under the influence or power of. **3** dominated or eclipsed by the personality of.

shadowbox *verb* (**shadowboxes**, **shadowboxed**, **shadowboxing**) box against an imaginary opponent as a form of training. ▶ **shadowboxing** *noun*

shadowless *adjective* **1** (of a lamp etc.) constructed in such a way as to cast no shadow. **2** having no shadows: *the shadowless surface of the road*.

shadowy *adjective* **1** like or having a shadow. **2** full of shadows. **3** vague, indistinct.

shady *adjective* (**shadier**, **shadiest**) **1** giving shade. **2** situated in shade. **3** (of a person or behaviour) disreputable; of doubtful honesty.

shaft • *noun* **1** the stem or handle of a tool, implement, etc. **2** a column, esp. between the base and capital. **3** a long narrow space, usu. vertical, for access to a mine, an elevator in a building, for ventilation, etc. **4** a long and narrow part supporting or connecting or driving a part or parts of greater thickness etc. **5** each of the pair of poles between which an animal is harnessed to a vehicle. **6 a** an arrow or spear. **b** the long slender stem of these. **7** a remark intended to hurt or provoke. **8** (foll. by *of*) **a** a ray (of light). **b** a bolt (of lightning). **9** the central stem of a feather. **10** *Mechanics* a large axle or revolving bar transferring force by belts or cogs. **11** *informal* (**the shaft**) harsh or unfair treatment. • *verb informal* treat unfairly.

shag¹ *noun* **1** a rough growth or mass of hair etc. **2** a hairstyle in which the hair is cut in layers from the top. **3** a carpet with a long rough pile (also as an *adjective*: *shag carpet*). **4** a cormorant, esp. the crested cormorant.

shag² *verb* (**shags**, **shagged**, **shagging**) *Baseball informal* retrieve and throw back (fly balls), esp. in batting practice.

shaganappi *esp. Cdn (West)* • *noun* (*plural* **shaganappis**) **1** thread, cord, or thong made of rawhide. **2** a rough pony. • *adjective informal* of inferior quality. [Say shagga NAPPY]

shaggy *adjective* (**shaggier**, **shaggiest**) **1** hairy, rough-haired. **2** unkempt. **3** (of the hair) coarse and abundant. **4** (of cloth) having a long and coarse nap. **5** *Biology* having a hairlike covering.

shaggy-dog story *noun* a long rambling story, more amusing to the teller than the audience or amusing only by its pointlessness.

shah *noun* a title of the former monarch of Iran.

shake • *verb* (**shakes**; *past* **shook**; *past participle* **shaken**; **shaking**) **1** move forcefully or quickly up and down or to and fro. **2 a** tremble or vibrate markedly. **b** cause to do this. **3 a** agitate or shock. **b** upset the composure of. **4** weaken or impair; make less convincing or firm or courageous: *shook their confidence*. **5** (of a voice, note, etc.) make tremulous or rapidly alternating sounds: *his voice shook with emotion*. **6** brandish; make a threatening gesture with (one's fist, a stick, etc.). **7** shake hands. **8** *informal* = SHAKE OFF. • *noun* **1** an act of shaking: *give it a shake* ◊ *a shake of the head*. **2** (in *plural*; **the shakes**) a fit of or tendency to trembling or shivering, esp. caused by fear or withdrawal from drugs or alcohol. **3** = MILKSHAKE. **4** = CEDAR SHAKE. PHRASES **in two shakes (of a lamb's tail)** very quickly. **more than you can shake a stick at** more than one can count, a considerable amount or number. **no great shakes** *informal* not very good or significant. **shake a person by the hand** = SHAKE HANDS. **shake down 1** settle or cause to fall by shaking. **2** settle down. **3** become established; get into harmony with circumstances, surroundings, etc. **4** *slang* extort money from. **shake hands** (often foll. by *with*) clasp right hands at meeting or parting, in reconciliation or congratulation, or over a concluded bargain. **shake one's head** move one's head from side to side in refusal, denial, disapproval, incredulity, or concern. **shake in one's shoes** tremble with apprehension. **shake a leg 1** hurry. **2** begin dancing. **shake off 1** get rid of (something unwanted). **2** manage to evade (a person who is following or pestering one). **shake out 1** empty by shaking. **2** spread or open (a sail, flag, etc.) by shaking. **shake up 1** mix (ingredients) by shaking. **2** restore to shape by shaking. **3** disturb or make uncomfortable. **4** rouse from lethargy, apathy, conventionality, etc.

shakedown *noun* **1** a period or process of adjustment or change. **2** *slang* a swindle; a piece of extortion. **3** a search. **4** (as an *adjective*) denoting a voyage, flight, etc., to test a new ship or aircraft and its crew.

shaker *noun* **1** a person or thing that shakes. **2** a container, usu. with a perforated top, from which something is shaken: *pepper shaker*. **3** a container for shaking together the ingredients of cocktails etc.

4 (Shaker) a a member of an American religious sect living simply, in celibate mixed communities. **b** (as an *adjective*) (of furniture etc.) produced by or of a type produced by Shakers, characterized by simplicity and lack of ornamentation. **5** (as an *adjective*) (also **shaker knit**) designating a style of knitting, used esp. in sweaters, having parallel rows of ribbing. ▶ **Shakerism** *noun* (in sense 4)

Shakespearean (also **Shakespearian**) • *adjective* **1** of or relating to the English poet and dramatist William Shakespeare (1564–1616). **2** in the style of Shakespeare. • *noun* a student of Shakespeare's works etc.

shakeup *noun* an upheaval or drastic reorganization.

shakily *adverb* in a shaky manner; unsteadily: *got shakily to his feet.*

shakiness *noun* the condition of being shaky; unsteadiness: *the shakiness of the ladder made him nervous.*

shaking tent *noun* (among some Algonquian peoples) a tent or lodge in which a shaman consulted the spirits for advice or assistance.

shaky *adjective* (**shakier, shakiest**) **1** unsteady; apt to shake; trembling. **2** unsound, infirm. **3** unreliable, wavering: *got off to a shaky start.*

shale *noun* soft finely layered rock that splits easily, consisting of consolidated mud or clay. ▶ **shaley** *adjective* (also **shaly**)

shall *auxiliary verb* **1** indicating future predictions. **2** indicating will or determination. **3** indicating or offering suggestions. **4** indicating orders or instructions.

shallot *noun* **1** a variety of onion that forms clumps of small bulbs. **2** the bulb of this, esp. as used in cooking. [Say shuh LOT or SHALL it]

shallow • *adjective* **1** of little depth. **2** superficial, trivial: *a shallow mind.* • *noun* (often in *plural*) shallow waters. ▶ **shallowly** *adverb* **shallowness** *noun*

shalom *noun* & *interjection* a Jewish salutation at meeting or parting. [Say shuh LOM]

sham • *noun* **1 a** a person or thing pretending or pretended to be what he or she or it is not. **b** fraudulent deception; pretense. **2** a decorative cover for a bed pillow when not in use. • *adjective* pretended, counterfeit. • *verb* (**shams, shammed, shamming**) **1** feign, pretend. **2 a** pretend to be. **b** simulate: *is shamming sleep.*

shaman *noun* a person regarded as having access to the world of good and evil spirits, esp. among some peoples of northern Asia and North America. ▶ **shamanic** *adjective* **shamanism** *noun* **shamanistic** *adjective* [Say SHAY min, shuh MAN ick]

shamble • *verb* (**shambles, shambled, shambling**) walk or run with a shuffling or awkward gait. • *noun* a shambling gait.

shambles *noun* a scene or situation of complete disorder; a mess: *the economy was a shambles.*

shame • *noun* **1** a feeling of distress or humiliation caused by consciousness of the guilt or foolishness of oneself or an associate. **2** a capacity for experiencing this feeling: *has no sense of shame.* **3** a state of disgrace, discredit, or intense regret. **4 a** a person or thing that brings disgrace etc. **b** a thing or action that is wrong or regrettable. • *verb* (**shames, shamed, shaming**) **1** bring shame on. **2** (foll. by *into, out of*) force by shame: *was shamed into confessing.* PHRASES **put to shame** disgrace or humiliate by revealing superior qualities etc. **shame on you!** you should be ashamed.

shamefaced *adjective* feeling or showing shame or embarrassment: *James came home, shamefaced at his lack of success.* ▶ **shamefacedly** *adverb* [Say SHAME faced, shame FACE id lee]

shameful *adjective* worthy of or causing shame or disgrace: *a shameful accusation.* ▶ **shamefully** *adverb*

shameless *adjective* **1** having or showing no sense of shame. **2** impudent, brazen. ▶ **shamelessly** *adverb* **shamelessness** *noun*

shampoo • *noun* (*plural* **shampoos**) **1** liquid or cream used to lather and wash the hair. **2** a similar substance for washing a car or carpet etc. **3** an act of cleaning something, esp. the hair, with shampoo: *a shampoo and set.* • *verb* (**shampoos, shampooed, shampooing**) wash with shampoo. ▶ **shampooer** *noun*

shamrock *noun* a low-growing clover-like plant with a three-lobed leaf on each stem, used as the national emblem of Ireland or the Irish.

shanghai *verb* (**shanghais, shanghaied, shanghaiing**) trick or force (a person) into doing something or going somewhere.

Shangri-La *noun* (*plural* **Shangri-Las**) an imaginary paradise on earth.

shank • *noun* **1 a** the leg. **b** the lower part of the leg; the leg from knee to ankle. **c** the shin bone. **2 a** the lower part of an animal's foreleg, esp. that of a horse. **b** the upper part of the foreleg or hind leg of an animal as a cut of meat. **3** a shaft or stem. **4 a** the long narrow part of a tool etc. joining the handle to the working end. **b** the stem of a key, spoon, anchor, etc. **c** the straight part of a nail or fish hook. **5** the narrow middle of the sole of a shoe. **6** *slang* an improvised knife, esp. as made by a prison inmate. • *verb* **1** *Golf* mis-hit (the ball) with the heel of the club. **2** *slang* slash with a knife. ▶ **shanked** *adjective*

shan't *contraction* shall not.

shanty[1] *noun* (*plural* **shanties**) **1** a crudely built shack or cabin. **2** a hut or cabin. **3** esp. *Cdn hist.* a lumberjack's log cabin or shack. **4** esp. *Cdn hist.* a logging camp.

shanty[2] *noun* (*plural* **shanties**) (also **sea shanty**) a song with alternating solo and chorus, of a kind originally sung by sailors while hauling ropes etc.

shantyman *noun* (*plural* **shantymen**) *Cdn hist.* a lumberjack; a worker at a lumber camp.

shantytown *noun* a poor or depressed area of a city or town, consisting of shanties.

shape • *noun* **1** the external form or appearance of a person or thing. **2** a description or sort or way: *not tolerated in any way, shape, or form.* **3** a definite or proper arrangement: *must get our ideas into shape.* **4 a** condition, as qualified in some way: *in good shape.* **b** (when unqualified) good condition: *back in shape.* **c** the nature, qualities, or characteristics of something: *the shape of things to come.* **5** a person or thing as seen, esp. indistinctly or in the imagination. **6** a mould or pattern. **7** a piece of material, paper, etc., made or cut in a particular form. • *verb* (**shapes, shaped, shaping**) **1** give a certain shape or form to. **2** give signs of a future shape or development. **3** imagine. **4** assume or develop into a shape. **5** direct (one's life, course, etc.). PHRASES **lick into shape** make presentable or efficient. **shape up 1** take a (specified) form or suggest that such a form will be taken: *shaping up to be a cold winter.* **2** show promise; make good progress; improve: *were told to shape up.* **shape up or ship out** achieve a satisfactory performance or be dismissed. **take shape** assume a distinct form; develop into something definite. **whip into shape** make presentable or efficient, esp. severely.

shaped *adjective* having the type of shape mentioned: *an L-shaped room.*

shapeless *adjective* lacking definite or attractive shape. ▶ **shapelessness** *noun*

shapely *adjective* (**shapelier, shapeliest**) **1** well

formed or proportioned. **2** of elegant or pleasing shape or appearance.

shaper *noun* a person or thing that makes something to a required shape or form.

shape-shifter *noun* (in folklore, science fiction, etc.) any creature capable of changing its form, e.g. a werewolf. ▶ **shape-shifting** *noun*

shard *noun* **1** a broken piece of pottery or glass etc. **2** a fragment of something shattered, broken, etc.

share[1] • *noun* **1** a portion that a person receives from or gives to a common amount. **2 a** a part that is or ought to be contributed by an individual to an enterprise or commitment. **b** a part that is or ought to be received by an individual from this: *a share of the credit*. **3** part-proprietorship of property held by joint owners, esp. any of the equal parts into which a company's capital is divided entitling its owner to a proportion of the profits. • *verb* (**shares**, **shared**, **sharing**) **1** get or have or give a share of. **2** use or benefit from jointly with others. **3** have in common: *I share your opinion*. **4** have a share; be a sharer: *must learn to share*. **5** (foll. by *in*) participate. **6** (often foll. by *out*) **a** divide and distribute. **b** give away part of. **7 a** tell, recount (a story, joke, one's feelings, etc.). **b** tell others an esp. personal story, one's feelings, etc. PHRASES **share and share alike** make an equal division.

share[2] *noun* = PLOUGHSHARE.

shareable *adjective* able to be shared: *shareable courseware*.

sharecropper *noun* a tenant farmer who gives a part of each crop as rent. ▶ **sharecropping** *noun*

shareholder *noun* an owner of shares in a company. ▶ **shareholding** *noun*

sharer *noun* a person who shares (in) something.

shareware *noun* software that is available free of charge and often distributed informally for evaluation, after which a fee is requested for continued use.

shark *noun* **1** any of various large usu. voracious marine fish with a long body and prominent dorsal fin. **2** *informal* a person who unscrupulously exploits or swindles others: *loan shark*.

sharkskin *noun* **1** the rough scaly skin of a shark. **2** a smooth slightly lustrous fabric.

sharp • *adjective* **1** having an edge or point able to cut or pierce. **2** tapering to a point or edge. **3** abrupt, steep, angular: *a sharp turn*. **4** well defined, clean-cut: *in sharp contrast*. **5 a** severe or intense: *a sharp pain*. **b** (of food or its flavour) pungent, acid. **c** keen: *has a sharp ear*. **d** (of a frost) severe, hard. **6** (of a voice or sound) shrill and piercing. **7** (of words, temper, a person, etc.) harsh: *had a sharp tongue*. **8** (of a person) quick to perceive or comprehend. **9** *derogatory* quick to take advantage. **10** vigorous or brisk. **11** *Music* **a** above the desired or true pitch. **b** (of a key) having a sharp or sharps in the signature. **c** (as **C sharp** etc.) a semitone higher than C etc. **12** *informal* stylish or flashy with regard to dress. • *noun* **1** *Music* **a** a note raised a semitone above natural pitch. **b** the sign (♯) indicating this. **2** *informal* a swindler or cheat. **3** a fine sewing needle. • *adverb* **1** punctually: *at nine o'clock sharp*. **2** suddenly, abruptly, promptly: *pulled up sharp*. **3** at a sharp angle. **4** *Music* above the true pitch: *sings sharp*. PHRASES **keep a sharp eye on** (or **out for**) watch carefully (for). **sharp as a tack** extremely quick, clever, astute, alert, etc.

sharp-edged *adjective* **1** having a sharp edge. **2** biting, caustic; harsh or cutting in speech.

Shar-Pei *noun* (*plural* **Shar-Peis**) a compact squarely built dog of Chinese origin, with a characteristic

wrinkly skin and short bristly coat of a fawn, cream, black, or red colour. [Say shar PAY]

sharpen *verb* make or become sharp. ▶ **sharpener** *noun*

sharp-featured *adjective* (of a person) having well-defined facial features.

sharpie *noun* a swindler.

sharply *adverb* **1** in a critical, harsh, or severe way: *the report was sharply critical of the police* ◊ *"is there a problem?" he asked sharply*. **2** suddenly and by a large amount; dramatically: *profits fell sharply following the takeover* ◊ *the road fell sharply to the sea*. **3** in a way that clearly shows the differences between two things: *their experiences contrast sharply with those of the other children*. **4** quickly and suddenly or loudly: *she moved sharply across the room to block his exit* ◊ *rapped sharply on the table*. **5** used to emphasize that something has a sharp point or edge: *sharply pointed*. ▶ **sharpness** *noun*

sharp-shinned hawk *noun* (also **sharp-shin**) a small North American hawk.

sharpshooter *noun* a skilled shooter or marksman. ▶ **sharpshooting** *noun & adjective*

sharp-tailed grouse *noun* a medium-sized grouse of grasslands in western North America, with a short pointed tail.

shasta *noun* (*plural* **shastas**) (also **shasta daisy**, *plural* **shasta daisies**) a tall European plant that bears a single daisy-like flower.

shatter *verb* **1** break suddenly in pieces. **2** severely damage or utterly destroy: *shattered hopes* ◊ *shattered the myth*. **3** greatly upset or discompose. ▶ **shattering** *adjective* **shatteringly** *adverb*

shatterproof *adjective* (of glass etc.) designed to resist shattering.

shave • *verb* (**shaves**; *past* **shaved**; *past participle* **shaved** or (as *adjective*) **shaven**; **shaving**) **1** remove bristles or hair with a razor. **2** reduce by a small amount. **3** cut thin slices from the surface of (wood etc.). **4** pass close to without touching; miss narrowly. **5** cut (hair, grass, etc.) very short. • *noun* **1** an act of shaving or the process of being shaved. **2** a close approach without contact.

shaver *noun* **1** a person or thing that shaves. **2** an electric razor. **3** *informal* a young boy.

shaving *noun* **1** a thin, curled strip cut off the surface of wood, chocolate, etc. **2** (as an *adjective*) used in shaving: *shaving cream*.

Shavuot *noun* = PENTECOST 2. [Say shuh VOO us or shaw voo OTT]

shawl *noun* a piece of fabric, usu. rectangular and often folded into a triangle, worn over the shoulders or head or wrapped around a baby. ▶ **shawled** *adjective*

Shawnee • *noun* (*plural* **Shawnee** or **Shawnees**) **1** a member of an Algonquian people formerly resident in the eastern US and now chiefly in Oklahoma. **2** the language of this people. • *adjective* of or pertaining to the Shawnee. [Say shaw NEE]

she • *pronoun* **1** the woman or girl or female animal previously named or in question. **2** a thing regarded as female, e.g. a vehicle or ship. **3** a person etc. of unspecified sex, esp. referring to one already named or identified: *ask any doctor and she will tell you*. • *noun* **1** a female; a woman. **2** (in *combination*) female: *she-goat*.

s/he *pronoun* a written representation of "he or she" used to indicate both sexes.

sheaf • *noun* (*plural* **sheaves**) **1** a pile or bundle of things, esp. paper. **2** a bundle of stalks and ears of grain tied after reaping. • *verb* make into sheaves.

shear • *verb* (**shears**; *past* **sheared**; *past participle* **shorn** or **sheared**; **shearing**) **1** clip the wool off (a sheep etc.). **2** remove or take off by cutting. **3** cut with scissors or shears etc. **4** (foll. by *of*) **a** strip bare. **b** deprive. **5** (often foll. by *off*) distort or be distorted, or break, from a structural strain. • *noun* **1** a strain produced by pressure in the structure of a substance, when its layers are shifted sideways in relation to each other. **2** (in *plural*) large scissors for use in gardens etc. **3** a hydraulically powered cutter used in logging to fell trees. **4** = WIND SHEAR. ▶ **shearer** *noun*

shearling *noun* **1** a sheep that has been shorn once. **2** a fleece or wool from a shearling, esp. the tanned fleece used to make garments, with the wool to the inside. [Say SHEER ling]

shearwater *noun* **1** any of a number of seabirds related to petrels, which habitually skim low over the open sea with wings outstretched. **2** = SKIMMER 3.

sheath *noun* **1** a close-fitting cover, esp. for the blade of a knife or sword. **2** a condom. **3** *Botany*, *Anatomy*, & *Zoology* an enclosing case or tissue. **4** the protective covering round an electric cable. **5** a woman's close-fitting dress.

sheathe *verb* (**sheathes**, **sheathed**, **sheathing**) **1** put into a sheath. **2** encase; protect with a sheath or sheathing.

sheathing *noun* **1** a protective casing or covering. **2** a layer of plywood etc. covering the frame.

shebang *noun slang* PHRASES **the whole shebang** the whole situation, thing, etc. [Say shuh BANG]

shed[1] *noun* **1** a one-storeyed structure usu. of simple construction used for storage, as shelter for animals, or as a workshop etc. **2** a large roofed structure often with one side or more sides open, for storing or maintaining machinery, vehicles, etc.: *drive shed*.

shed[2] *verb* (**sheds**, **shed**, **shedding**) **1 a** let or cause to fall off: *trees shed their leaves*. **b** (of an animal) lose hair, feathers, etc. **2** take off (clothes). **3** reduce (an electrical power load) by disconnection etc. **4** cause to fall or flow: *shed tears*. **5** disperse, diffuse, radiate: *shed light*. **6** remove or get rid of: *has shed 25 pounds*.

she'd *contraction* **1** she had. **2** she would.

sheen *noun* **1** a gloss or lustre on a surface. **2** radiance, brightness.

sheep *noun* (*plural* **sheep**) **1** a ruminant mammal with a thick woolly coat and (esp. in the male) curving horns, of which domesticated varieties are kept in flocks for wool or meat. **2** a bashful, defenceless, or esp. easily led person. PHRASES **might as well be hanged for a sheep as a lamb** might as well attempt the bolder of two strategies if the consequences of failure are the same. **separate the sheep from the goats** divide into desirable and undesirable groups.

sheepdog *noun* **1** a dog trained to guard and herd sheep. **2** a dog of various breeds suitable for this.

sheepish *adjective* **1** embarrassed through shame or foolishness. **2** bashful, shy, reticent. ▶ **sheepishly** *adverb* **sheepishness** *noun*

sheeplike *adjective* resembling a sheep, esp. in being bashful, defenceless, or esp. easily led.

sheepskin *noun* **1** a garment or rug of sheep's skin

with the wool on. **2** leather from a sheep's skin used in bookbinding.

sheer • *adjective* **1** complete; nothing more than: *sheer luck*. **2** (of a cliff or ascent etc.) perpendicular; very steep. **3** (of a textile) very thin. • *noun* **1 a** a sheer fabric. **b** (in *plural*) curtains made of sheer fabric. **c** (in *plural*) sheer nylon hosiery. **2** a deviation from a course. • *verb* **1** esp. *Nautical* swerve or change course. **2** (foll. by *away*, *off*) go away, esp. from a person or topic one dislikes or fears.

sheerly *adverb* **1** directly, outright. **2** perpendicularly.

sheesh *interjection* expressing mild frustration, exasperation, surprise, embarrassment, etc.

sheet[1] • *noun* **1** a large rectangular piece of fabric used esp. in pairs as inner bedclothes. **2 a** a broad usu. thin flat piece of material, e.g. paper or metal. **b** (as an *adjective*) made in sheets: *sheet metal*. **3** the long rectangular ice surface on which curling is played. **4** a wide continuous surface or expanse of water, ice, flame, falling rain, etc. **5** a set of unseparated postage stamps. **6** *derogatory* a newspaper, esp. a disreputable one. **7** a large shallow pan, used for baking: *cookie sheet*. • *verb* **1** provide or cover with sheets. **2** form into sheets. **3** (of rain etc.) fall in sheets. PHRASES **between the sheets** in bed, esp. engaged in sexual activity.

sheet[2] *noun* a rope or chain attached to the lower corner of a sail for securing or controlling it. PHRASES **three sheets to the wind** *slang* drunk.

sheeting *noun* **1** material for making bed linen. **2** material covering another in sheets: *covered with plastic sheeting*.

sheet lightning *noun* a lightning flash whose bolt is unseen, observed as a sudden flash of brightness illuminating a wide area.

sheet music *noun* **1** printed musical scores. **2** music published in single or interleaved sheets, not bound.

she/he *pronoun* a written representation of "he or she" used to indicate both sexes.

sheik *noun* (also **sheikh**) **1** a chief or head of an Arab tribe, family, or village. **2** a Muslim leader. ▶ **sheikdom** *noun* [Say SHEEK or SHAKE]

shekel *noun* **1** the chief monetary unit of modern Israel. **2** (of a cliff or ascent etc.) a silver coin and unit of weight used in ancient Israel etc. **3** (in *plural*) *informal* money; riches. [Say SHECK'll]

shelf *noun* (*plural* **shelves**) **1** a thin flat piece of wood or metal etc. projecting from a wall, or as part of a unit, used to support books etc. **2 a** a projecting horizontal ledge in a cliff face etc. **b** a reef or sandbank under water. **c** = CONTINENTAL SHELF. PHRASES **off the shelf** (of goods) available immediately from a retailer's stock, as opposed to custom-made. **on the shelf 1** put away indefinitely; set aside. **2** no longer active or of use. **3** *informal derogatory* (of a woman) past the age when she might expect to be married.

shelf ice *noun* floating ice permanently attached to a land mass.

shelf life *noun* **1** the amount of time for which a stored item of food etc. remains usable. **2** the length of time during which an idea, practice, etc. is fashionable or practicable.

shell • *noun* **1** the hard outer covering of molluscs,

eggs, nuts, turtles, etc. **2 a** an explosive projectile or bomb for use in a big gun or mortar. **b** a hollow metal or paper case used as a container for fireworks, explosives, cartridges, etc. **c** a cartridge. **3** a mere semblance or outer form without substance. **4** any of several things resembling a shell in being an outer case, esp.: **a** a light racing boat. **b** a hollow pastry case. **c** the metal framework of a vehicle body etc. **d** the walls of an unfinished or gutted building, ship, etc. **5** a very light all-weather jacket, often with a removable lining. **6** (also **shell program**) a program which provides an interface between the user and the operating system. **7** something resembling a seashell: *pasta shells*. • *verb* **1** remove the shell or pod from. **2** bombard (a town, troops, etc.) with shells. PHRASES **come out of one's shell** cease to be shy; become communicative. **shell out** *informal* **1** pay (money). **2** hand over (a required sum etc.).

she'll *contraction* she will; she shall.

shellac • *noun* **1** lac resin melted into thin flakes and used for making varnish. **2** varnish made from this. • *verb* (**shellacs**, **shellacked**, **shellacking**) **1** varnish with shellac. **2** *slang* defeat or thrash soundly. [Say shuh LACK]

shellacking *noun slang* a severe defeat or beating. [Say shuh LACKING]

shelled *adjective* **1** (of an animal, nut, etc.) having a shell or shells, esp. of a specific kind: *hard-shelled nuts*. **2** (of an edible animal, nut, etc.) that has had its shell removed: *shelled shrimp*.

shellfish *noun* (*plural* **shellfish** or **shellfishes**) **1** an aquatic shelled mollusc, e.g. an oyster, scallop, etc. **2** a crustacean, e.g. a crab etc.

shell game *noun* **1** a sleight-of-hand game or trick in which a small object is concealed under a walnut shell etc., with bystanders encouraged to place bets or to guess as to which shell the object is under. **2** *informal* a confidence trick; a deception.

shell-like *adjective* resembling a shell in shape or appearance.

shell shock *noun* a nervous breakdown or other psychological disturbance resulting from exposure to battle.

shell-shocked *adjective* **1** suffering from shell shock. **2** *informal* having received stunning news etc., or having been overwhelmingly defeated.

shelter • *noun* **1** a structure built to give protection, esp. from the weather or from attack: *bus shelter* ◊ *bomb shelter*. **2 a** a place of refuge provided for the homeless, abused women, etc. **b** an animal sanctuary. **3** a shielded condition; protection: *took shelter under a tree*. **4** (also **tax shelter**) a financial arrangement, such as an investment, intended to avoid or minimize taxes. • *verb* **1 a** provide (a person or thing) with protection from the weather, danger, etc.: *sheltered them from the storm*. **b** protect (a person or thing) from unpleasantness or difficulty. **2** find refuge; take cover: *sheltered under a tree*. **3** protect (invested income) from taxation; invest (money) with this purpose.

shelter belt *noun* a line of trees etc. serving to break the force of the wind.

sheltered *adjective* **1** (of a place) not greatly exposed to bad weather, sun, etc. **2** kept away from or not exposed to unpleasant circumstances, harmful influences, or the normal difficulties of life: *a sheltered upbringing*. **3** (of a course of study, activity, etc.) provided for people with some sort of disability.

shelve *verb* (**shelves**, **shelved**, **shelving**) **1** put (books etc.) on a shelf. **2 a** abandon or defer (a plan etc.). **b** remove (a person) from active work etc. **3** (of

ground etc.) slope in a specified direction: *land shelved away to the horizon*.

shelves *plural of* SHELF.

shelving *noun* **1** *in senses of* SHELVE. **2** a set of shelves; shelves collectively.

shemozzle *noun slang* **1** a brawl or commotion. **2** a muddle. [Say shuh MOZZLE]

shenanigans *plural noun informal* **1** high-spirited behaviour; mischief: *he watched the other students in their horseplay and shenanigans*. **2** secret or dishonest activity or manoeuvres: *the company's chairman stood accused of financial shenanigans* ◊ *political shenanigans*. [Say shuh NANNA gun]

shepherd • *noun* **1** a person employed to tend sheep, esp. at pasture. **2** a person, esp. a member of the clergy etc., who guides, cares for, or watches over a group of people. **3** = GERMAN SHEPHERD. • *verb* **1 a** tend (sheep etc.) as a shepherd. **b** guide (followers etc.). **2** marshal, drive, or direct the movement of. [Say SHEP erd]

shepherdess *noun* a woman employed to tend sheep, esp. at pasture. [Say SHEP erd ess]

shepherd's pie *noun* a dish of ground meat under a layer of mashed potato.

sherbet *noun* **1** a frozen dessert, similar to ice cream, made from water, milk, and sugar, usu. fruit-flavoured. **2** a flavoured sweet powder eaten as a candy or used to make an effervescing drink. [Say SHUR bit or SHUR bert]

sheriff *noun* **1** *Cdn* an appointed official responsible for court administration and trial preparation, the selection of jury panels, the serving of legal documents, and the seizure and sale of property to settle damage claims. **2** *US* an officer in a county, usu. elected, responsible for keeping the peace, administering justice, etc.

Sherpa *noun* (*plural* **Sherpa** or **Sherpas**) a member of a Himalayan people living on the border of Nepal and Tibet renowned for their skill in mountaineering. [Say SHUR puh]

sherry *noun* (*plural* **sherries**) a fortified wine originally from southern Spain.

she's *contraction* **1** she is. **2** she has.

Shetland • *adjective* of or pertaining to the Shetland Islands off the northern coast of Scotland. • *noun* (also **Shetland wool**) a fine loosely twisted wool from Shetland sheep. [Say SHET lind]

Shetland sheepdog *noun* a small collie-like breed of dog.

Shia (also **Shiah**, **Shi'a**) • *noun* (*plural* **Shia** or **Shias**) **1** one of the two main branches of Islam, esp. in Iran, that rejects the first three Sunni caliphs and regards Ali, the fourth caliph, as Muhammad's first successor. **2** an adherent of the Shia branch of Islam. • *adjective* of or relating to Shia. [Say SHEE uh]

shiatsu *noun* a kind of therapy of Japanese origin, in which pressure is applied with the fingers or palms to certain points of the body. [Say she AT soo]

shibboleth *noun* **1** an old or old-fashioned idea, principle, or phrase that is considered outdated or no longer important: *certain rules of grammar are helpful and should be preserved, but beware of the shibboleth masquerading as a rule*. **2** a custom, word, phrase, pronunciation, etc. that distinguishes a particular class or group of people: *the usual Canadian pronunciation of "out and about" is considered a shibboleth that distinguishes a Canadian speaker from an American*. [Say SHIBBA leth]

shied *past and past participle of* SHY.

shield • *noun* **1 a** a piece of metal, wooden, acrylic, etc. armour, carried on the arm or in the hand to deflect blows from the head or body. **b** a thing serving to protect: *insurance is a shield against disaster*. **2** a thing resembling a shield, esp.: **a** a trophy in the form of a

shield. **b** a protective plate or screen in machinery etc. **c** a shield-like part of an animal, esp. a shell. **d** a similar part of a plant. **3** a piece of fabric etc. worn as a liner to protect part of a garment from staining: *dress shield*. **4** Geology **a** a large rigid area of the earth's crust, usu. of Precambrian rock, which has been unaffected by later geological episodes. **b** (**the Shield**) (in Canada) the Canadian Shield. **5** a stylized representation of a shield, characteristically of a flat-topped heart shape, used for displaying a coat of arms etc. ● *verb* protect, shelter, or screen with or as with a shield from attack, danger, exposure, etc., or from blame or lawful punishment; cover or hide with a shield.

Shield country *noun* Cdn the area covered by the Canadian Shield, characterized by thin soil, rock outcrops, countless lakes and rivers, and, in the southern areas, vast coniferous forests.

shift ● *verb* **1** change or move or cause to change or move from one position or state to another. **2** change gear in a vehicle. **3** contrive or manage as best one can. ● *noun* **1 a** a slight change in position, direction, or tendency: *a shift of wind took us by surprise* ◊ *a shift in public opinion*. **b** the substitution of one thing for another; a rotation. **2 a** one of two or more recurring periods in which different groups of workers, players on a hockey team, etc. do the same jobs in relay: *works the night shift* ◊ *scored on his last shift*. **b** a group of workers, players, etc. who work in this way: *the day shift was just leaving*. **3 a** a woman's straight unwaisted dress. **b** a woman's loose-fitting undergarment; a slip. **4** a displacement of spectral lines (see also RED SHIFT). **5** a key on a keyboard used to switch between lower and upper case, conduct special operations, etc. **6** a gear lever or gear-changing mechanism in a motor vehicle. PHRASES **make shift** manage or contrive; get along somehow: *made shift without it*. **shift for oneself** rely on one's own efforts. **shift gears** change one's course of action, strategy, intensity, etc. **shift (one's) ground** take up a new position in an argument etc.

shifter *noun* **1** a person or thing that shifts. **2** = GEARSHIFT.

shiftily *adverb* in an evasive or deceitful way: *glanced shiftily from side to side*.

shiftiness *noun* the character or quality of being evasive or deceitful.

shifting agriculture *noun* = SHIFTING CULTIVATION.

shifting cultivation *noun* a form of agriculture, used esp. in tropical Africa, in which an area of land is cleared of vegetation and cultivated for a few years and then abandoned for a new area until its fertility has been naturally restored.

shifting sand *noun* (also **shifting sands** *plural noun* or **shifting ground**) a changing or unstable state of affairs: *the shifting sand of fashion trends*.

shiftless *adjective* lacking resourcefulness; lazy; inefficient: *her vocation is to blithely harbour a host of shiftless, worthless, temporary lovers*. ▶ **shiftlessly** *adverb* **shiftlessness** *noun*

shift work *noun* work conducted in often variable periods independent of a standard workday, usu. at night. ▶ **shift worker** *noun*

shifty *adjective* (**shiftier, shiftiest**) *informal* not straightforward; evasive; deceitful.

Shiism *noun* (also **Shi'ism**) the doctrines or principles of the Shia branch of Islam. [Say SHEE ism]

shiitake *noun* an edible mushroom that grows on fallen timber, cultivated in Japan and China. [Say shi TOCKY or shi TACKY]

Shiite (also **Shi'ite**) ● *noun* an adherent of the Shia branch of Islam. ● *adjective* of or relating to Shia. [Say SHEE ite]

shiksa often *offensive* ● *noun* **1** a Gentile girl or woman. **2** a Jewish girl or woman not observing traditional Jewish behaviour. ● *adjective* (of a girl or woman) Gentile. [Say SHICK suh]

shill ● *noun* **1** an accomplice, esp. one posing as an enthusiastic or successful customer to encourage or entice potential buyers, gamblers, etc. **2** an adherent of a party or point of view etc. posing as a disinterested advocate. ● *verb* **1** (often foll. by *for*) promote a cause, esp. with pretended objectivity: *even The New Republic, which from the beginning shilled shamelessly for Clinton's candidacy, is becoming disillusioned*. **2** act as an accomplice or shill in a scam.

shillelagh *noun* a thick stick or club of blackthorn or oak used in Ireland esp. as a weapon. [Say shi LAY lee or shi LAY luh]

shilling *noun* hist. a former British coin and monetary unit equal to one-twentieth of a pound or twelve pence.

shilly-shally *verb* (**shilly-shallies, shilly-shallied, shilly-shallying**) act with indecision or hesitation. ▶ **shilly-shallying** *noun*

shim ● *noun* a thin strip, wedge, or washer of metal, wood, rubber, etc. inserted in a space in machinery etc. to make parts fit or align. ● *verb* (**shims, shimmed, shimming**) wedge, raise, or fill up with a shim.

shimmer ● *verb* **1** shine with a tremulous or faint diffused light. **2** quiver or tremble, or appear to do so, esp. when distorted by heat waves: *the asphalt shimmered*. ● *noun* a faint tremulous light or image. ▶ **shimmering** *adjective* **shimmery** *adjective*

shimmy ● *noun* (*plural* **shimmies**) an abnormal vibration of esp. the front wheels of a car or truck etc. ● *verb* (**shimmies, shimmied, shimmying**) **1** shake or sway the body, esp. with a rolling of the hips and shaking of the shoulders and breasts. **2** (esp. of a car etc.) shake or vibrate abnormally.

shin *noun* **1** the front of the leg below the knee. **2** the front or sharp edge of the tibia. **3** a cut of beef from the lower part of an animal's foreleg.

shin bone *noun* = TIBIA 1.

shindig *noun* (also **shindy** *plural* **shindies**) *informal* **1** a lively or festive gathering; a party. **2** a brawl, commotion, or noisy disturbance.

shine ● *verb* (**shines, shone, shining**) **1 a** emit, give off, or reflect light. **b** (of the sun, a star, etc.) not be obscured by clouds etc.; be visible: *the sun is shining today*. **2** (of a person's eyes or face) be unusually bright, vibrant, or animated, esp. with excitement, joy, etc. **3** direct (light or a source of light) in a particular direction: *shone the flashlight in my eyes*. **4** (*past* and *past participle* **shined**) make bright; polish. **5** be brilliant in some respect; excel. ● *noun* **1** brightness or radiance emanating from a light or source of light. **2** a lustre or glow of light reflecting off a surface, esp. the result of cleaning or polishing: *the shine of chrome*. **3** an act of rubbing something to give it a shiny surface: *my shoes need a shine*. **4** *slang* = MOONSHINE 1. PHRASES **shine through** be clearly evident. **take the shine off** spoil the brilliance or newness of. **take a shine to** *informal* take a fancy to; like.

shiner *noun* **1** *informal* a black eye. **2** any of various silvery fishes, esp. a North American minnow.

shingle ● *noun* **1** a thin rectangular tile, usu. made of asphalt or wood, used to cover esp. walls or roofs. **2** a small sign or nameplate hanging outside a store or esp. the office of a doctor or lawyer etc. **3** small rounded pebbles, esp. on a seashore. ● *verb* (**shingles, shingled, shingling**) install shingles on (a roof or wall etc.). PHRASES **hang out one's shingle** set up a practice or profession. ▶ **shingled** *adjective*

shingles *plural noun* (usu. treated as *singular*) a disease

caused by a herpesvirus and characterized by a rash of minute blisters on the skin, often in a band across the body, and accompanied by localized pain.

shininess *noun* glossiness; smoothness.

shining *adjective* **1** having a shine; gleaming, radiant. **2** conspicuously excellent; distinguished, brilliant: *a shining example of co-operation*.

shinny • *verb* (**shinnies, shinnied, shinnying**) (usu. foll. by *up* or *down*) *informal* climb up or down a tree etc. by clasping it with the arms and legs and hauling oneself up. • *noun* Cdn **1** (also **shinny hockey**) informal pickup hockey played usu. without nets, referees, or equipment except for skates, sticks, and a ball or puck etc. **2** = STREET HOCKEY. **3** *informal* hockey.

shin splints *plural noun* (usu. treated as *singular*) acute pain in the shin and lower leg caused esp. by prolonged running on hard surfaces.

Shinto *noun* a religious system incorporating the worship of ancestors, nature spirits and other divinities, and prior to 1945 the state religion of Japan, founded on a belief in the divinity of the Japanese emperor. ▶ **Shintoism** *noun* **Shintoist** *noun*

shiny *adjective* (**shinier, shiniest**) **1** full of brightness; having a polished or gleaming surface. **2** noticeably or apparently new.

ship • *noun* **1** a large sea-going vessel propelled by engine or sail. **2** an aircraft. **3** a spacecraft. • *verb* (**ships, shipped, shipping**) **1** transport, deliver, or convey (goods, passengers, sailors, etc.) by or on a ship. **2 a** transport (goods) by truck, rail, or other means. **b** *informal* send (a person) away; dispatch: *shipped the kids off to school*. **3** (often foll. by *out*) **a** (of a sailor) become employed on a ship. **b** (of a ship or passenger etc.) set out on a journey, esp. by sea. **4 a** take in (water or waves) over the side of a ship. **b** take or draw (an anchor, oars, etc.) into the ship or boat to which it belongs. **c** put (an oar etc.) in its correct position in readiness to function. PHRASES **run a tight ship** manage a company or organization etc. with strict authority. **when a person's ship comes in** (or **home**) when a person's fortune is made.

-ship *suffix* forming nouns denoting: **1** a quality or condition: *friendship*. **2** status, title, or office: *authorship*. **3** a skill in a certain capacity: *workmanship*. **4** the collective individuals of a group: *membership*.

shipboard *adjective* occurring or used on board a ship: *a shipboard romance*. PHRASES **on shipboard** on board ship.

shipbuilder *noun* a person or company whose occupation or business is the design and construction of ships. ▶ **shipbuilding** *noun*

shiplap *noun* a type of wooden siding consisting of horizontal boards with overlapping L-shaped notches along their edges to allow for flush placement against the wall.

shipmate *noun* a fellow member of a ship's crew.

shipment *noun* **1** an amount of goods transported, delivered, or received: *haven't received the latest shipment*. **2** the action of shipping goods: *logs waiting for shipment*.

shipowner *noun* a person owning a ship or ships.

shipper *noun* a person or company that transports or receives goods by land, sea, or air.

shipping *noun* **1** the transport of goods by sea, land, or air: *high shipping costs*. **2** ships collectively, esp. the ships of a country, frequenting a particular port, or used for a particular purpose.

ship's biscuit *noun* hist. a hard coarse kind of cracker kept and eaten on board ship.

shipshape *adjective* in good order; tidy and neat.

ship-to-shore • *adjective* **1** from a ship to land. **2** (of radio telephones etc.) capable of transmitting communication from a point at sea to a point on land. • *noun* a ship-to-shore radio telephone.

shipwreck • *noun* **1 a** the destruction of a ship by a storm, sinking, etc. **b** the remains of a ship so destroyed. **2** (often foll. by *of*) the destruction of hopes, dreams, etc.; total loss or ruin. • *verb* **1** cause (a person or ship etc.) to suffer shipwreck. **2** destroy or cause the loss of (a person's hopes, dreams, fortunes, etc.).

shipyard *noun* a large enclosed area adjoining the sea or a major river in which ships are built or repaired.

shiraz *noun* (*plural* **shirazes**) a variety of red wine produced in Australia and South Africa. [Say shuh RAZZ]

shire *noun* Brit. a county.

shirk *verb* **1** avoid, evade, or attempt to get out of (duty, work, responsibility, fighting, etc.). **2** make a habit or practice of avoiding work or responsibility etc. ▶ **shirker** *noun*

shirt *noun* **1** a garment for the upper body with sleeves, a collar, and buttons down the front. **2** any of a number of articles of clothing designed to cover the upper body, having short or long sleeves, and which may or may not have buttons or a collar. PHRASES **get one's shirt in a knot** become agitated or upset. **keep one's shirt on** *informal* refrain from becoming excited, anxious, or impatient. **lose one's shirt** *informal* lose all one's money, esp. in a bet, investment, etc. **the shirt off one's back** *informal* one's last remaining possessions.

shirted *adjective* wearing a shirt.

shirtless *adjective* not wearing a shirt.

shirt sleeve *noun* (usu. in *plural*) **1** the sleeve of a shirt. **2** (as an *adjective*; usu. **shirt-sleeve**) **a** designating weather that is warm enough that a jacket is not required: *shirt-sleeve days*. **b** designating an environment etc. that is casual, informal, or relaxed. **c** designating a person etc. that is hard-working or working-class: *a shirt-sleeve crowd*. PHRASES **in shirt sleeves** wearing a shirt with no jacket etc. over it.

shirt-tail • *noun* (also in *plural*) the lower curved part of a shirt below the waist. • *adjective* designating someone of remote relationship: *shirt-tail cousin*.

shish kebab *noun* pieces of marinated meat and vegetables cooked and served on a skewer. [Say SHISH kuh bob]

shiv *noun* slang a knife, switchblade, or razor.

shiva *noun* (*plural* **shivas**) (also **shivah**, *plural* **shivahs**) *Judaism* a period of seven days' mourning for the dead beginning immediately after the funeral. PHRASES **sit shiva** mourn. [Say SHIVVA]

shiver • *verb* **1** tremble with cold, fear, etc. **2** suffer a quick trembling movement of the body; shudder. **3** break into splinters. • *noun* **1** a momentary quivering or trembling of the body. **2** (in *plural*) **a** an attack of shivering, esp. from fear or awe. **b** excitement, fear, or disquiet: *his appearance sent shivers through the room*. **3** (esp. in *plural*) each of the small pieces into which esp. glass is shattered when broken; a splinter.

shivery *adjective* shivering with cold, fear, illness, etc.

shlemiel *noun* = SCHLEMIEL. [Say shluh MEAL]

shlep *verb & noun* = SCHLEP.

shlock *noun* = SCHLOCK.

shlub *noun* = SCHLUB.

shlump *noun* = SCHLUMP.

shm- *prefix* = SCHM-.

shmaltz *noun* = SCHMALTZ.

shmooze *verb & noun* = SCHMOOZE.

shmuck *noun* = SCHMUCK *noun*.

shoal[1] • *noun* **1** a school of fish, porpoises, etc. **2** a large number. • *verb* (of fish) gather in schools.

shoal[2] • *noun* **1** an area of shallow water. **2** a submerged sandbank visible at low tide. **3** (esp. in *plural*)

hidden danger or difficulty: *the shoals of constitutional reform.* • *verb* **1** (of water) become increasingly shallow. **2** (of a ship etc.) move into shallower waters. • *adjective* (of water) shallow. [Rhymes with *GOAL*]

shock[1] • *noun* **1** a sudden and usu. disturbing effect on the mind, feelings, or emotions, resulting in surprise, distress, depression, etc. **2** the condition associated with circulatory failure and a sudden drop in blood pressure, characterized esp. by pallor, sweating, a fast but weak pulse, and occasionally fainting, usu. caused by pain, fright, disease, or an injury resulting in severe blood loss. **3** a sudden and violent collision, impact, tremor, etc. **4** = ELECTRIC SHOCK 1. **5** = SHOCK ABSORBER. • *verb* **1 a** arouse surprise or bewilderment etc. (in a person). **b** arouse outrage, disgust, anger, etc. (in a person): *I'm shocked to hear you say it.* **2** experience shock: *I don't shock easily.* **3** affect with an electric or physical shock.

shock[2] *noun* **1** a small stack of bales of hay or straw, or sheaves of grain, collected in a field, esp. to hasten drying. **2** an unkempt or shaggy mass of hair.

shock absorber *noun* **1** a device used on a car etc. to compensate for the roughness of a road by absorbing mechanical shock and vibrations. **2** anything that absorbs shocks. ▶ **shock-absorbing** *adjective*

shocked *adjective* scandalized, horrified, disgusted.

shocker *noun informal* a revelation, rumour, news item, result, etc. that causes surprise or outrage etc.

shocking *adjective* causing indignation, scandal, or disgust. ▶ **shockingly** *adverb*

shock jock *noun slang* a radio personality that expresses outrageous or controversial views.

shock resistant *adjective* able to withstand light abuse without breaking etc.

shock treatment *noun* (also **shock therapy**) **1** a method of treating depressive patients by artificially inducing convulsions using anaphylactic or electric shock or by drugs. **2** sudden and harsh or drastic measures taken to improve a situation: *shock treatment economics.*

shock troops *plural noun* troops trained for assault.

shock wave *noun* **1** a sharp change of pressure in a narrow region travelling through air etc. caused by explosion or by a body moving faster than sound. **2** a series of reactions to or repercussions of an event.

shod • *verb past and past participle of* SHOE. • *adjective* having or wearing shoes or other footwear.

shoddily *adverb* in an inferior manner; poorly: *the house was shoddily constructed.*

shoddiness *noun* the state or condition of being of poor or inferior quality.

shoddy *adjective* (**shoddier**, **shoddiest**) of poor or inferior quality.

shoe • *noun* **1** one of a matching pair of protective coverings for the foot having a sturdy sole and made esp. of leather ending below, at, or just above the ankle. **2** a band of iron shaped to the hard part of the hoof of an animal, esp. a horse, and secured by nails to the underside to prevent wear or injury. **3** anything resembling a shoe in shape or use. **4** = BRAKE SHOE. • *verb* (**shoes**; *past and past participle* **shod** or **shoed**; **shoeing**) **1** fit (esp. a horse etc.) with a shoe or shoes. **2** cover or protect with a shoe or shoes. PHRASES **be in a person's shoes** be in his or her situation, predicament, etc. **fill** (or **step into**) **a person's shoes** adequately fill a person's position or role. **if the shoe fits** if a criticism or description seems applicable, one should be guided by it. **the shoe is on the other foot** the situation is reversed.

shoebox *noun* (*plural* **shoeboxes**) **1** the oblong box in

which a new pair of shoes is packaged. **2** a small or cramped room, apartment, etc.

-shoed *combining form.* wearing shoes of a specified kind or colour: *white-shoed ◊ pointy-shoed.*

shoehorn • *noun* a curved piece of metal, plastic, etc., used to ease the heel into a shoe. • *verb* force into a tight, inadequate, or unsuitable space or position: *a hundred people would have to be shoehorned into the hall.*

shoelace *noun* a short length of string used for tying shoes and boots etc.

shoeless *adjective* not having or wearing shoes.

shoemaker *noun* a person who makes and repairs shoes and boots. ▶ **shoemaking** *noun*

shoepack *noun* (also **shoepac**) **1** a moccasin with an extra sole. **2** a commercially manufactured oiled leather boot, esp. with a rubber sole.

shoeshine *noun* an act of cleaning and polishing shoes.

shoestring *noun* **1** a shoelace. **2** *informal* a small esp. inadequate amount of money: *living on a shoestring.* **3** (as an *adjective*) designating a business, project, plan, etc. based on or conducted with a limited amount of money: *a shoestring budget.*

shofar *noun* (*plural* **shofars** or **shofroth**) a trumpet made of a ram's horn used by Jews in religious ceremonies and, in Biblical times, as a war trumpet. [Say SHOW fur for the singular, SHOW frot for the plural]

shogun *noun* any of a succession of hereditary commanders-in-chief in feudal Japan who were generally the real rulers of the country until 1867. [Say SHOW gun]

shone *past and past participle of* SHINE. [Say SHON]

shoo • *interjection* an exclamation used to frighten or drive away. • *verb* (**shoos**, **shooed**, **shooing**) drive or urge (a person, animal, etc.) in a desired direction.

shoo-in *noun informal* something sure to succeed or win; a certainty.

GRAMMAR CHECK
shook, shaken

Note that while it's common to hear *they were shook up after the accident*, the standard past participle of *shake* is **shaken**: *the accident left them shaken.*

---

shook • *verb past of* SHAKE. • *adjective informal* (foll. by *up*) emotionally or physically disturbed; upset.

SPELL CHECK
shoot, chute

A channel, rapid, or parachute is a **chute**; garbage is sent down a **chute**.

---

shoot • *verb* (**shoots**, **shot**, **shooting**) **1** kill or wound (a person or animal) with a bullet or arrow. **2** cause (a gun) to fire. **3** move suddenly and rapidly. **4** direct (a glance, question, or remark) at someone. **5** film or photograph (a scene, film, etc.). **6** (of a boat) sweep swiftly down or under (rapids, a waterfall, or a bridge). **7 a** (in hockey, basketball, etc.) direct (a puck or ball) toward the net, basket, etc. **b** *Basketball* successfully make or score (a basket, three-pointer, etc.). **c** *Basketball* practise taking shots at (a basket). **8** send out buds or shoots; germinate. **9** *informal* make (a specified score) in a round of golf. • *noun* **1** a competition in shooting. **2** a film or photography session. **3** a young branch or new growth of a plant. • *interjection informal* **1** an invitation for a comment, question, etc. **2** an exclamation of disappointment, anger, frustration, etc. PHRASES **shoot down 1** kill (a person) by shooting. **2** cause (an aircraft, its pilot, etc.) to crash by shooting. **3** reject (a person, argument,

proposal, etc.). **shoot from the hip** *informal* speak or act spontaneously or hastily, usu. without proper consideration. **shoot it out** *slang* engage in a decisive confrontation. **shoot a line** *slang* speak misleadingly. **shoot oneself in the foot** *informal* inadvertently make a situation worse, esp. while trying to make it better. **shoot one's mouth off** *slang* talk too much or indiscreetly. **shoot the breeze** (or **bull**) *slang* chat idly. **shoot up 1** grow rapidly, esp. (of a person) grow taller. **2** rise suddenly. **3** terrorize (a district) by indiscriminate shooting.

shoot-'em-up *noun slang* **1** a fast-moving movie which features extensive shooting and gunplay. **2** (as an *adjective*) designating movies, games, etc. based on or featuring abundant use of weapons etc.

shooter *noun* **1** a person who discharges a firearm. **2** a (*in combination*) a gun or other device for shooting: *peashooter*. **b** *slang* a firearm. **3** a player who takes a shot or is in position to take a shot in hockey, basketball, etc. **4** a small drink of alcohol, esp. liquor. **5** *slang* a person who takes drugs intravenously.

shooting • *noun* **1** a the wounding or killing of esp. a person by gunfire. **b** the discharge of a firearm: *heard shooting*. **2** a the hobby or sport of hunting game. **b** the hobby or sport of firing at targets: *skeet shooting*. **3** (in hockey and basketball etc.) the ability to shoot accurately. • *adjective* (of a pain etc.) sharp and spreading quickly. PHRASES **the whole shooting match** *informal* everything.

shooting gallery *noun* (*plural* **shooting galleries**) **1** a long room or fairground booth used for recreational shooting at usu. moving targets with real or simulated guns. **2** *slang* a place where addictive drugs may be illicitly obtained and injected.

shooting guard *noun Basketball* **1** the second guard on a team, usu. having strong ball-handling skills and good three-point shooting. **2** the position played by this guard (*compare* POINT GUARD).

shooting star *noun* **1** a small meteor burning up upon entering the earth's atmosphere. **2** a plant of the primrose family, with pink, swept-back petals.

shootout *noun* **1** a decisive gunfight. **2** (also **penalty shootout**) (in soccer, hockey, etc.) a method of deciding games ending in a tie in which each team takes a specified number of penalty shots, the team scoring the most being declared the winner. **3** esp. *Hockey* a close high-scoring game.

shop • *noun* **1** a place where goods are sold. **2** a place where repairs or manufacturing takes place. **3** a a room in a school equipped for teaching woodworking or mechanical skills etc. for use in a workshop. **b** (also **shop class**) the study of these skills as a course. **4** one's trade, profession, or business, esp. as a subject of conversation: *talk shop*. • *verb* (**shops, shopped, shopping**) **1** a go to one or several stores or shops to buy goods. **b** visit shops to look at merchandise without the express intention of making a purchase. **2** order and buy merchandise by mail, by phone, on-line, etc. **3** shop at (a particular store), esp. regularly. **4** sell or propose (an idea, information, etc.) to several prospective buyers: *she shopped her script around to potential producers*. PHRASES **set up shop** establish oneself in business etc. **shop around** visit several stores, service providers, etc. in search of the best price or service. **shop till one drops** *informal* shop excessively, esp. to the point of exhaustion.

shopaholic *noun jocular* an avid or compulsive shopper. [Say a HOL ick]

shop floor *noun Cdn & Brit.* **1** the working environment in a factory, esp. as distinct from a management environment. **2** the workers in a factory etc. **3** (as an

adjective) (usu. **shop-floor**) working or occurring in or pertaining to a factory etc.: *shop-floor productivity*.

shopkeeper *noun* a person who owns or manages a shop or store. ▶ **shopkeeping** *noun*

shoplift *verb* steal (merchandise) from a store by posing as a customer. ▶ **shoplifter** *noun* **shoplifting** *noun*

shopper *noun* **1** a person who makes purchases in a shop. **2** an advertising supplement; a flyer.

shopping *noun* **1** the purchase of merchandise etc. **2** goods purchased.

shopping centre *noun* a shopping mall (*see* MALL 1).

shopping channel *noun* a television station whose programming features items for sale that may be ordered by telephone.

shopping mall *noun* = MALL 1.

shopping plaza *noun* = PLAZA 1.

shop steward *noun* a person elected by workers in a factory etc. to represent them in dealings with management.

shop talk *noun* conversation about one's job etc.

shop window *noun* a large window in a storefront; the place behind this, in which items are displayed.

shopworn *adjective* **1** (of an item for sale) faded or dirty from being on display in a store. **2** (of a person, idea, etc.) no longer fresh or new; hackneyed or stale: *he wastes little time on shopworn notions that the Cold War was triggered by President Truman's atomic diplomacy*.

shore[1] *noun* **1** the land at the edge of the sea or a large body of water; a coast. **2** land, as opposed to sea: *ship-to-shore*. **3** (usu. in *plural*) a country, esp. one bounded by a coast: *travelled to foreign shores*.

shore[2] • *verb* (**shores, shored, shoring**) (often foll. by *up*) **1** reinforce; strengthen or fortify: *a plan to shore up the economy*. **2** support a wall etc. with a beam or beams set at an angle. • *noun* a beam of timber, steel, etc. set obliquely against an unsafe wall, tree, ship, etc., as a support.

shorebird *noun* a bird which frequents the shore, e.g. a plover or a sandpiper.

shore dinner *noun* **1** a dinner served by a restaurant, community group, etc., including usu. abundant quantities of shellfish. **2** = SHORE LUNCH.

shoreline *noun* the line along which a stretch of water, esp. a sea or lake, meets the shore.

shore lunch *noun* (*plural* **shore lunches**) *Cdn* a meal cooked on a lakeshore or riverbank etc. as part of a fishing or other boating excursion, featuring freshly caught fish, pan-fried.

shoring *noun* props used to support or hold up something weak or unstable.

shorn • *verb* past participle of SHEAR. • *adjective* **1** (of a person or animal) having had all or most of the hair of the head, wool, etc. removed. **2** (usu. foll. by *of*) deprived: *a terrace of row houses, shorn of their gables and gingerbread, facades covered with dark, imitation brick*.

short • *adjective* **1** of a small length or duration. **2** relatively small in extent. **3** (of a person) small in height. **4** (usu. foll. by *of, on*) not having enough of. **5** in insufficient supply. **6** (of a person) terse; uncivil. **7** (of a ball in sport) travelling only a small distance, or not far enough. **8** *Baseball* (of a position in the field) near, close; shallow: *short centre field*. **9** (of odds or a chance) reflecting or representing a high level of probability. **10** (of a vowel) characterized as short with regard to quality and length. **11** (of pastry) containing a high proportion of fat to flour and therefore crumbly. • *adverb* (in sport) at, to, or over a short distance, or not as far as the point aimed at. • *noun* **1** a short-circuit. **2** a short film. **3** *Baseball* **a** = SHORTSTOP 2. **b** the area of the field covered by the shortstop. • *verb* **1** short-circuit.

2 *informal* cheat (a person) out of something; shortchange. PHRASES **be caught** (or **taken**) **short 1** be put at a disadvantage, esp. by being without something one badly needs. **2** *informal* urgently need to urinate or defecate. **fall** (or **come**) **short of** fail to reach or amount to. **for short** as an abbreviation: *I'm Richard, but you can call me Rick for short*. **go short** (often foll. by *of*) not have enough. **in short** to use few words; briefly. **in short supply** scarce. **in the short term** (or **run**) over a short period of time. **make short work of** accomplish, dispose of, consume, etc. quickly. **pull up** (or **bring up**) **short** stop or pause abruptly or before the expected destination. **short and sweet** esp. *ironic* brief and enjoyable. **short end of the stick** the less favourable part of a deal. **short for** an abbreviation for: *"Bob" is short for "Robert"*. **short of 1** having a partial or total lack; deficient: *short of spoons*. **2** without going so far as; except: *did everything short of destroying it*. **3** distant from: *two miles short of home*. **short of breath** panting, out of breath.

shortage *noun* (often foll. by *of*) a deficiency or lack of something needed: *a shortage of funds ◊ oil shortage*.

shortbread *noun* a crisp rich crumbly type of cookie made with butter, flour, and sugar.

shortcake *noun* a cake with a filling of fruit and whipped cream: *strawberry shortcake*.

shortchange *verb* (**shortchanges, shortchanged, shortchanging**) **1** cheat (a customer), accidentally or intentionally, by giving insufficient change. **2** cheat or treat unfairly.

short-circuit • *noun* a faulty electrical connection resulting in a condition of low resistance between two points in a circuit, often causing a flow of excess current which could damage an appliance or cause a fuse to blow. • *verb* **1** (of an electrical appliance or apparatus) fail or cease working as a result of a short-circuit. **2** collapse or self-destruct. **3** bypass or avoid (a task etc.) by taking a more direct route or course of action: *others said the motion was an attempt to short-circuit debate on the controversial issue*.

shortcoming *noun* a fault, e.g. in a person's character, a plan, or system.

shortcut *noun* **1** a route that shortens the distance travelled or the time required to make a journey. **2** a quick or easy way of accomplishing something.

short-eared owl *noun* a medium-sized whitish owl with brown streaks, which has very short ear tufts and which is found esp. in open country.

shorten *verb* **1** become or make shorter or short; curtail. **2** *Nautical* reduce the amount of (sail spread).

shortening *noun* **1** a soft fat that produces a crisp flaky effect in baked products, such as pastry, esp. a solid white fat made from hydrogenated vegetable oils, sometimes combined with lard. **2** an act of making something short or shorter.

shortfall *noun* **1** a failure to reach esp. a financial goal or expectations; a failure to meet budget. **2** an esp. financial loss or deficit below what was expected.

short fuse *noun informal* a quick temper.

shortgrass *noun* (*plural* **shortgrasses**) any of a number of short grasses especially resistant to drought.

shorthair *noun* a short-haired domestic cat or dog.

short-haired *adjective* (of a dog or cat) having short hair.

shorthand *noun* **1** a method of writing or typing in abbreviations and symbols esp. for taking dictation quickly. **2** (often foll. by *for*) any abbreviated or symbolic mode of expression.

short-handed • *adjective* **1** not having the usual number of workers etc; understaffed. **2** *Hockey* playing or occurring with fewer than six players on the ice, esp.

because one or more players is serving a penalty. • *adverb* with fewer players, workers, etc. than usual: *playing short-handed*.

short haul *noun* the transport of goods or passengers over a short distance.

Shorthorn *noun* a breed of cattle with short horns.

shortish *adjective* somewhat short.

short list • *noun* a list of selected candidates for a position from which a final choice is made. • *verb* (usu. **shortlist**) add (a person) to a list of candidates for a position.

short-lived *adjective* lasting only for a short time; ephemeral.

shortly *adverb* **1** in a short time; before long; soon: *we will be arriving shortly*. **2** (foll. by *before* or *after*) a short time (before or after); not long: *they arrived shortly before noon*. **3** in a few words; briefly or curtly.

shortness *noun* the quality or fact of being short in duration, extent, etc.

short notice *noun* an announcement or warning of an event etc. made only briefly before its occurrence: *she gave him such short notice before leaving*. PHRASES **on** (or **at**) **short notice** with little advance warning.

short-order *adjective* of or designating restaurant food that can be prepared and served quickly: *a short-order cook*. PHRASES **in short order** immediately.

short-range *adjective* **1** operating or capable of operating within a small or limited area: *short-range missile*. **2** relating to a fairly immediate future time: *short-range forecast*.

short rib *noun* **1** any of the lower ribs which are not attached to the breastbone. **2** a piece of meat containing one or more of these ribs.

shorts *plural noun* **1** a pair of pants extending only as far as the knees or higher. **2** men's underpants.

short shrift *noun* brusque or dismissive treatment: *the latter are given red-carpet presidential welcomes, while the former are unceremoniously given short shrift ◊ the newspapers give science woefully short shrift*.

short-sighted *adjective* **1** unable to focus except on comparatively near objects. **2** lacking imagination, foresight, or proper consideration: *a short-sighted plan*. ▶ **short-sightedly** *adverb* **short-sightedness** *noun*

short-sleeved *adjective* (of a shirt etc.) with sleeves not reaching below the elbow.

short-staffed *adjective* having insufficient staff.

shortstop *noun* *Baseball* **1** the player that covers the part of the infield between second and third. **2** this position.

short story *noun* (*plural* **short stories**) a prose narrative shorter than a novel usu. involving only a few characters and concentrating on a single event or theme.

short temper *noun* a tendency to lose one's temper quickly or easily.

short-tempered *adjective* quick to lose one's temper; easily irritable; irascible.

short-term *adjective* **1** lasting for, occurring in, or pertaining to a relatively short period of time: *short-term solution*. **2** maturing or becoming effective after a short period: *short-term deposit*. PHRASES **in the short term** for the near or immediate future.

short ton *noun* a unit of weight equal to 2,000 lb. avoirdupois (907.19 kg).

short-track speed skating *noun* a form of speed skating competition performed on a standard-size hockey rink rather than on a speed skating oval.

short-wave *noun* a radio wave with a wavelength of less than about 100 metres, a frequency of three to 30 MHz.

S

shorty *noun* (*plural* **shorties**) *informal* or *derogatory* a person shorter than average.

shot[1] *noun* **1** the firing of a gun or cannon. **2** a person with a specified level of ability in shooting: *he was an excellent shot.* **3** a hit, stroke, or kick of the ball in sports, esp. an attempt to score. **4** *informal* an attempt to do something. **5** (*plural* **shot**) a ball of metal or stone fired from a large gun or cannon. **6** (also **lead shot**) tiny lead pellets used in a single charge or cartridge in a shotgun. **7** a heavy ball thrown by a shot putter. **8** a photograph. **9** a film sequence photographed continuously. **10** the launch of a rocket: *a moon shot.* **11** *informal* a small drink of alcohol. **12** *informal* an injection of a drug or vaccine. PHRASES **have** (or **take**) **a shot at** *informal* make an attempt at; try. **give something a shot** try something. **like a shot** *informal* without hesitation; willingly. **shot in the arm** *informal* stimulus or encouragement. **shot in the dark** a mere guess.

shot[2] • *verb* past and past participle of SHOOT. • *adjective* **1** (of coloured material) woven so as to show different colours at different angles: *shot silk.* **2** *informal* **a** ruined; worn out: *the transmission's shot.* **b** exhausted. PHRASES **shot through** permeated or suffused.

shot[3] *noun* *informal* a sum of money owed or due; a bill.

shot glass *noun* a small, often graduated, typically 2-oz. glass for measuring liquor.

shotgun • *noun* a smoothbore gun for firing small shot at short range, used esp. for hunting. • *adjective* **1** of, pertaining to, or resembling a shotgun. **2** wide-ranging, but random: *our family used a shotgun approach, spraying our after-tax charitable dollars towards every charity that asked.* • *verb* (**shotguns**, **shotgunned**, **shotgunning**) shoot with a shotgun.

shotgun marriage *noun* (also **shotgun wedding**) *informal* **1** an enforced or hurried wedding, esp. because of the bride's pregnancy. **2** any enforced alliance, partnership, etc.: *the shotgun marriages of America's largest companies spurred growth through the 1980s.*

shot put *noun* an athletic contest in which a very heavy ball is thrown as far as possible. ▶ **shot putter** *noun*

shot rock *noun* Curling the rock lying nearest to the centre of the rings.

should *auxiliary verb* past of SHALL, used esp.: **1 a** to express a duty, obligation, or likelihood. **b** (in the 1st person) to express a tentative suggestion. **2** forming a conditional or indefinite clause: *if you should see him.* **3** expressing purpose = MAY, MIGHT[1]: *in order that we should not worry.*

shoulder • *noun* **1** the joint where a person's arm or an animal's wing or foreleg is attached to the body. **2** the upper foreleg and shoulder blade of a pig, lamb, etc. when butchered. **3** (often in *plural*) **a** the upper part of the back and arms. **b** this part of the body regarded as capable of bearing a burden or blame, providing comfort, etc.: *a shoulder to cry on.* **4** a strip of ground bordering a road, where vehicles may stop in an emergency. **5** a part of a garment covering the shoulder. **6** a part of anything resembling a shoulder in form or function, as in a bottle, mountain, tool, etc. • *verb* **1 a** push with the shoulder; jostle. **b** make one's way by jostling: *shouldered through the crowd.* **2** take (a burden etc.) on one's shoulders: *shouldered the family's problems.* PHRASES **put one's shoulder to the wheel** make an effort. **shoulder to shoulder 1** side by side. **2** with closed ranks or united effort.

shoulder blade *noun* either of the large flat bones of the upper back; the scapula.

shouldered *adjective* having shoulders of a specified type: *broad-shouldered.*

shoulder-length *adjective* (of hair) reaching to the shoulders.

shouldn't *contraction* should not.

shout • *verb* **1** make a loud cry or vocal sound; speak loudly. **2** say or express loudly; call out. • *noun* a loud cry expressing joy etc. or calling attention. **shout at** speak loudly to etc. **shout down** reduce to silence by shouting. **shout for** call for by shouting. ▶ **shouter** *noun*

shove • *verb* (**shoves**, **shoved**, **shoving**) **1** push vigorously. **2** *informal* put somewhere: *shoved it in the drawer.* • *noun* an act of shoving or of prompting a person into action. PHRASES **shove it** *slang* used for expressing contemptuous rejection or dismissal. **shove off 1** start from the shore in a boat. **2** *slang* depart; go away: *told him to shove off.* **shove over** *informal* move over.

shovel • *noun* **1** a spade-like tool for shifting quantities of snow, earth, etc., esp. having the sides curved upwards. **2** a machine or part of a machine having a similar form or function. **3** Cdn the wide flat part of a moose's antler. • *verb* (**shovels**, **shovelled**, **shovelling**) **1** shift or clear (snow etc.) with or as if with a shovel. **2** clear (an area) of snow etc. using a shovel: *shovelled the driveway.* **3** use a shovel. **4** *informal* move (esp. food) in large quantities or roughly: *shovelled peas into his mouth.* ▶ **shovelful** *noun* (*plural* **shovelfuls**)

shoveller *noun*

show • *verb* (**shows**; *past* **showed**; *past participle* **shown**; *showing*) **1** be, allow, or make visible. **2** exhibit or produce for inspection or viewing. **3** represent or depict in art. **4** display or allow to be perceived (a quality, emotion, or characteristic). **5** demonstrate or prove. **6** treat (someone) with a specified quality. **7** explain or demonstrate something to. **8** conduct or lead: *show them in, please.* **9** finish third or in the first three in a race. • *noun* **1** a spectacle or display. **2** a play or other stage performance, esp. a musical. **3** a radio or television program . **4** an event or competition involving the public display of animals, plants, or products. **5** *informal* an undertaking, project, or organization: *I run the show.* **6** an outward appearance or display of a quality or feeling. **7** the third position, esp. in a horse race. **8** Cdn a logging operation. PHRASES **get this show on the road** *informal* get moving; make a start. **show around** take (a person) to places of interest; act as guide for (a person) in a building etc. **show cause** Law allege with justification. **show one's colours** make one's opinion clear. **show a person the door** dismiss or eject a person. **show one's face** make an appearance; let oneself be seen. **show one's hand** (or **cards**) **1** disclose one's plans. **2** reveal one's cards. **show off 1** display to advantage. **2** act pretentiously; ostentatiously display one's knowledge, talent, etc. **show oneself** be seen in public. **show through 1** be visible through a covering. **2** (of real feelings etc.) be revealed inadvertently. **show up 1** make or be conspicuous or clearly visible. **2** expose (a fraud, impostor, inferiority, etc.). **3** *informal* appear; be present; arrive. **4** *informal* embarrass or humiliate. **show the way 1** indicate what has to be done etc. by attempting it first. **2** show others which way to go etc.

show and tell *noun* **1** an elementary school activity in which each student brings an object from home and describes it to his or her classmates. **2** any informative display and discussion of assembled objects.

showbiz *noun* *informal* = SHOW BUSINESS.

showboat • *noun* **1** a river steamer on which theatrical performances are given. **2** *informal* a show-off: *a charming showboat and crowd-pleaser.* • *verb* act

pretentiously; show off: *instead of just scoring and vanishing he had to stick around and showboat.*

show business *noun informal* the entertainment industry, esp. theatre, movies, and television.

showcase • *noun* **1** a glass case used for exhibiting goods etc. **2** a place or medium for presenting (esp. attractively) to general attention. • *verb* (**showcases, showcased, showcasing**) exhibit or display.

show-cause hearing *noun* a judicial hearing where a party involved in litigation must show cause why something must or must not be done, esp. a hearing at which the prosecution shows cause why an accused should be kept in custody rather than granted bail.

showdown *noun* a final test or confrontation; a decisive situation.

shower • *noun* **1** a brief fall of esp. rain, snow, hail, etc. **2 a** a cubicle, bath, etc. in which one stands under a spray of water. **b** the apparatus etc. used for this. **c** the act of washing oneself in a shower. **3 a** a brisk flurry of bullets, stones, sparks, etc. **b** a similar flurry of gifts, letters, praise, etc. **4** a party for giving presents to a prospective bride, pregnant woman, etc. • *verb* **1** discharge (water, missiles, etc.) in a shower. **2** use a shower. **3** lavishly bestow (gifts, praise, etc.). **4** descend or come in a shower: *it showered on and off all day.*

showery *adjective* (of weather or a period of time) characterized by frequent showers of rain.

showgirl *noun* an actress who sings and dances in musicals, variety shows, etc.

show home *noun* (also **show house**) = MODEL HOME.

showily *adverb* in a gaudy or ostentatious way.

showiness *noun* the quality or condition of being gaudy or ostentatious, esp. excessively so.

showing *noun* **1** the action of showing something. **2** a usu. specified quality of performance: *made a poor showing.*

show jumper *noun* a horse or rider competing in show jumping.

show jumping *noun* the sport of riding horses over a course of fences and other obstacles, with penalty points for errors.

showman *noun* (*plural* **showmen**) **1** a person who presents or produces an esp. theatrical show. **2** an entertainer who performs with panache and style. **3** a person skilled in self-promotion or publicity. ▶ **showmanship** *noun*

shown *past participle of* SHOW.

show-off *informal* • *noun* a person who shows off. • *adjective* ostentatious, showy. ▶ **show-offy** *adjective*

show of hands *noun* (*plural* **shows of hands**) raised hands as a means of voting, showing interest, etc.

showpiece *noun* **1** an item of work presented for exhibition or display. **2** an outstanding example or specimen.

showplace *noun* a place serving to display something to its best advantage.

showroom *noun* a room in a factory, office building, etc. used to display goods for sale.

showstopper *noun informal* **1** a performance receiving prolonged applause. **2** anything which draws great attention and admiration. ▶ **show-stopping** *adjective*

showtime *noun* the time at which a movie, concert, etc. is scheduled to begin.

show tune *noun* a popular tune from a musical.

showy *adjective* (**showier, showiest**) having a striking appearance or style, esp. by being extremely or excessively bright, colourful, large, etc.

shrank *past of* SHRINK.

shrapnel *noun* **1** fragments of a bomb etc. thrown out by an explosion. **2** a shell containing bullets or pieces of metal timed to burst short of impact. [Say SHRAP nul]

shred • *noun* **1** a scrap, fragment, or strip of esp. cloth, paper, etc. **2** the least amount, remnant: *not a shred of evidence.* • *verb* (**shreds, shredded, shredding**) tear or cut into shreds. PHRASES **tear to shreds** completely refute (an argument etc.).

shredder *noun* **1** a machine used to reduce documents to shreds. **2** any device used for shredding. **3** *slang* a snowboarder.

shrew *noun* **1** a small usu. insect-eating mouselike mammal with a long pointed snout and tiny eyes. **2** a bad-tempered or scolding woman.

shrewd *adjective* **1** having good judgment; astute: *a shrewd businesswoman.* **2** (of a face etc.) shrewd-looking. ▶ **shrewdly** *adverb* **shrewdness** *noun*

shriek • *verb* **1** utter a shrill screeching sound or words esp. in pain or terror. **2** indicate clearly or blatantly. • *noun* a high-pitched piercing cry or sound; a scream. PHRASES **shriek with laughter** laugh uncontrollably. [Say SHREEK]

shrike *noun* a bird with a strong hooked and toothed bill, which impales small birds and insects on thorns.

shrill • *adjective* **1** piercing and high-pitched in sound. **2** (of a person, argument, etc.) sharp, unrestrained, not reasoning. • *verb* **1** (of a cry etc.) sound shrilly. **2** (of a person etc.) utter or send out (a song, complaint, etc.) shrilly. ▶ **shrillness** *noun* **shrilly** *adverb*

shrimp • *noun* **1** (*plural* **shrimp** or **shrimps**) any of various small (esp. marine) edible crustaceans, with ten legs, grey-green when alive and pink when cooked. **2** *informal* a very small slight person. • *verb* go catching shrimps. ▶ **shrimper** *noun*

shrine *noun* **1 a** a chapel, church, altar, etc., sacred to a saint, holy person, relic, etc. **b** the tomb of a saint etc. **c** a niche containing a holy statue etc. **2** a place associated with or containing memorabilia of a particular person, event, etc. **3** a Shinto place of worship.

Shriner *noun* a member of the Order of Nobles of the Mystic Shrine, a charitable society founded in the US in 1872. [Say SHRINE er]

shrink • *verb* (**shrinks**; *past* **shrank** or **shrunk**; *past participle* **shrunk**; **shrinking**) **1 a** make or become smaller, esp. by the action of moisture, heat, or cold. **b** make or become reduced in size or number: *the workforce has shrunk considerably.* **2** (usu. foll. by *from, back*) recoil: *shrank from her touch.* **3** be averse from doing: *shrinks from meeting them.* • *noun informal* a psychiatrist. ▶ **shrinkable** *adjective* **shrinkage** *noun*

shrinking violet *noun informal* a very shy person.

shrink wrap • *noun* thin transparent plastic film wrapped around and then shrunk tightly on to an article as packaging, protection, etc. • *verb* (**shrink-wrap, shrink-wraps, shrink-wrapped, shrink-wrapping**) enclose (an article) in shrink wrap.

shrink-wrapped *adjective* **1** packaged in shrink wrap. **2** (of software) readily available commercially, and usu. standardized for a mass market.

shrivel *verb* (**shrivels, shrivelled, shrivelling**) contract or wither into a wrinkled, folded, rolled-up, contorted, or dried-up state.

shroom *noun slang* = MAGIC MUSHROOM.

shroud • *noun* **1** a sheet-like garment for wrapping a corpse for burial. **2** anything that conceals like a shroud: *a shroud of mystery.* **3** (in *plural*) a set of ropes supporting the mast or topmast of a sailing ship. • *verb* **1** clothe (a body) for burial. **2** cover, conceal.

Shrove Tuesday *noun* the day before Ash Wednesday.

shrub *noun* a woody plant smaller than a tree and having a very short stem with low branches.

shrubbery *noun* (*plural* **shrubberies**) **1** an area planted with shrubs. **2** shrubs collectively.

shrubby *adjective* **1** having the habit, growth, or size of a shrub. **2** of the nature of or consisting of shrubs.

shrug • *verb* (**shrugs, shrugged, shrugging**) slightly and momentarily raise the shoulders to express indifference, helplessness, contempt, etc. • *noun* an act of shrugging one's shoulders. PHRASES **shrug off** dismiss as unimportant etc. by or as if by shrugging.

shrunk *past participle of* SHRINK.

shrunken *adjective* (esp. of a face, person, etc.) having grown smaller esp. because of age, illness, etc.

shtetl *noun* *hist.* a small Jewish town or village in eastern Europe. [Say SHTET'll or SHTAIT'll]

shtick *noun* *slang* an attention-getting or theatrical routine, gimmick, or talent: *the same English butler shtick he always does.*

shuck • *noun* **1** a husk or pod, esp. the husk of an ear of corn. **2** the shell of an oyster or clam. • *verb* **1** remove the shucks of. **2** (often foll. by *off*) **a** remove, throw or strip off (clothes etc.). **b** get rid of. ▶ **shucker** *noun*

shucks *interjection* *informal* an expression of contempt or regret or self-deprecation in response to praise.

shudder • *verb* **1** shiver esp. convulsively from fear, cold, repugnance, etc. **2** feel strong repugnance etc.: *shudder to think of it.* **3** (of a machine etc.) vibrate or quiver. • *noun* an act of shuddering. ▶ **shudderingly** *adverb* **shuddery** *adjective*

shuffle • *verb* (**shuffles, shuffled, shuffling**) **1** move with a scraping, sliding, or dragging motion: *shuffles along* ◊ *shuffling his feet.* **2 a** rearrange (a pack of cards) by sliding them over each other quickly. **b** rearrange: *shuffled the documents.* **c** redistribute posts within (a cabinet, organization, etc.). **3** (usu. foll. by *on, off, into*) assume or remove (clothes, a burden, etc.) esp. clumsily or evasively: *shuffled off responsibility.* **4** continually shift one's position; fidget: *when given the chance to proclaim their aspirations, most Canadians would ponder and shuffle in embarrassment.* • *noun* **1** a shuffling movement. **2** an act of shuffling cards. **3** a general change of relative positions. **4** a rearrangement of ministerial posts within a government or cabinet. **5 a** a quick brushing movement of the feet in dancing. **b** a dance performed with such a step. PHRASES **lost in the shuffle** overlooked in a crowd, confusion, etc. ▶ **shuffler** *noun*

shuffleboard *noun* a game in which competitors use a long-handled implement to push discs into numbered scoring sections.

shul *noun* **1** a synagogue. **2** a service at a synagogue. [Say SHOOL]

shun *verb* (**shuns, shunned, shunning**) avoid; keep clear of.

shunt • *verb* **1** diverge or cause (a train) to be diverted esp. on to a siding. **2** *Electricity* provide (a current) with a shunt. **3 a** push aside or out of the way. **b** move (a person) to a different place, often a less important one: *she was shunted off to a regional office.* **4** pass (blood, fluid, etc.) through a shunt. • *noun* **1** a conductor joining two points of a circuit, through which more or less of a current may be diverted. **2** an alternative path for the circulation of blood or other fluid.

shush • *interjection* = HUSH *interjection*. • *verb* (**shushes, shushed, shushing**) **1** make or attempt to make silent: *shushed the baby.* **2** be silent. **3** make a soft, shushing sound; move with the sound of a rush of air. • *noun* an utterance of "shush".

Shuswap (*plural* **Shuswap** or **Shuswaps**) • *noun* **1** a member of an Aboriginal people living in the Thompson River area of BC. **2** the Salishan language of this people. • *adjective* of this people. [Say SHOO swop]

shut *verb* (**shuts, shut, shutting**) **1** close. **2** (usu. foll. by *in, out*) keep (a person, sound, etc.) in or out of a room etc. by shutting a door etc.: *shut out the noise* ◊ *shut them in.* PHRASES **be** (or **get**) **shut of** *slang* be (or get) rid of: *were glad to get shut of him.* **shut the door on** refuse to consider; make impossible. **shut down 1** stop (a factory, nuclear reactor, etc.) from operating. **2** (of a factory etc.) stop operating. **3** turn off (an engine, machine, etc.). **4** *Sport informal* render an opponent's offence ineffective: *shut down the Jays.* **shut one's eyes** (or **ears** or **heart** or **mind**) **to** pretend not, or refuse, to see (or hear or feel sympathy for or think about). **shut in** (of hills, houses, etc.) encircle, prevent access etc. to or escape from: *were shut in by the sea on three sides* (*see also* sense 4). **shut off 1 a** stop the flow of (water, gas, etc.) by shutting a valve. **b** switch off (a machine, light, etc.). **2** separate from society etc. **shut out 1** exclude (a person, light, etc.) from a place, situation, etc. **2** screen (landscape etc.) from view. **3** prevent (a possibility etc.). **4** block (a painful memory etc.) from the mind. **5** prevent (the opposing team) from scoring (*see also* sense 4). **shut up 1** close all doors and windows of (a house etc.); bolt and bar. **2** imprison (a person). **3** close (a box etc.) securely. **4** *informal* reduce to silence by rebuke etc. **5** put (a thing) away in a box etc. **6** *informal* stop talking. **shut up shop 1** close a business, shop, etc. **2** cease business etc. permanently. **shut your face** (or **mouth** or **trap**)! *slang* stop talking.

shutdown *noun* **1** the closure of a factory etc. **2** the turning off of a machine, computer, etc.

shut-eye *noun* *informal* sleep.

shut-in *noun* a person who is confined indoors because of ill health.

shut-off *noun* **1** something used for stopping an operation. **2** a cessation of flow, supply, or activity.

shut-off valve *noun* a valve used to cut off the flow of water esp. to a sink etc. when doing repairs etc.

shutout *noun* **1** the act of preventing an opposing team from scoring. **2** any game in which one side does not score.

shutter • *noun* **1 a** each of a pair or set of hinged panels fixed inside or outside a window for security or privacy or to keep the light in or out. **b** a structure of slats on rollers used for the same purpose. **2** a device on a camera that opens to allow light to pass through the lens. • *verb* **1** put up the shutters of. **2** close (a business etc.) permanently. **3** provide with shutters.

shutterbug *noun* an enthusiastic photographer.

shutter speed *noun* the nominal time for which a shutter on a camera is open at a given setting.

shuttle • *noun* **1 a** a bobbin with two pointed ends used for carrying the weft thread across between the warp threads in weaving. **b** a bobbin carrying the lower thread in a sewing machine. **2** a plane, bus, etc., going to and fro over a short route continuously. **3** = SPACE SHUTTLE. • *verb* (**shuttles, shuttled, shuttling**) **1** transport (a person) in a shuttle. **2** (of a person, train, etc.) travel backwards and forwards between places. **3** move or cause to move to and fro like a shuttle.

shuttlecock *noun* a small piece of cork, rubber, etc. fitted with a ring of feathers, or a similar device of plastic, used instead of a ball in badminton.

shy • *adjective* (**shyer, shyest**) **1** timid. **2** reluctant: *she's not shy about standing up for what she believes in* ◊ *customers are shy of patronizing small businesses.* **3** (in *combination*) showing fear of or distaste for: *gun-shy* ◊ *work-shy.* **4** (often foll. by *of*) *informal* short of (a stated amount, measurement, etc.). • *verb* (**shies, shied, shying**) **1** (usu. foll. by *at*) (esp. of a horse) start suddenly aside (at an object, noise, etc.) in fright. **2** (usu. foll. by *away from*) avoid doing or becoming involved in something

due to nervousness or lack of confidence: *honest people are shying away from running for public office.*

shyster *noun informal* a person, esp. a lawyer, who uses unscrupulous methods. [Say SHICE ter]

SI *abbreviation* INTERNATIONAL SYSTEM OF UNITS.

Si *symbol* silicon.

si *noun Music* = TI. [Say SEE]

Siamese • *noun* (*plural* **Siamese**) **1 a** a native of Siam (now Thailand) in Southeast Asia. **b** the language of Siam. **2** (also **Siamese cat**) a breed of cream-coloured, short-haired cat, with blue eyes and brown ears, face, paws, and tail. • *adjective* of or concerning Siam, its people, or language. [Say sigh a MEEZ]

Siamese twins *plural noun* = CONJOINED TWINS.

sib *noun* **1** esp. *Genetics* a sibling. **2** a blood relative.

Siberian • *noun* a native of Siberia, a vast region in the northeastern part of the Russian Federation. • *adjective* of or relating to Siberia. [Say sigh BEERY in]

Siberian husky *noun* (*plural* **Siberian huskies**) a hardy breed of husky, originally from Siberia, with a stocky body and blue eyes.

Siberian tiger *noun* a very large tiger of an endangered race occurring in southeastern Siberia and northeastern China.

sibilant • *adjective* **1** (of a letter or set of letters, as *s*, *sh*) articulated with a hissing sound. **2** hissing: *a sibilant whisper.* • *noun* a sibilant letter or letters. [Say SIBBLE int]

sibling *noun* each of two or more children having one or both parents in common; a brother or sister.

sibyl *noun* **1** any of the women in ancient times supposed to utter the oracles and prophecies of a god. **2** a prophetess, fortune teller, or witch. [Say SIBBLE]

sic[1] *adverb* (usu. in brackets) used, spelled, etc., as written (placed after a quoted word that appears odd or erroneous to show that the word is quoted exactly as it stands in the original): *he once wrote that "Nova Scotians [sic] are the friendliest people".* [Say SICK]

sic[2] *verb* (**sics**, **sicced**, **siccing**) **1** (esp. to a dog) attack (a person or animal): *sic 'em!* **2** (usu. foll. by *on*) **a** set (an animal) on another animal or person. **b** set (a person) to follow, harass, etc. another person. [Say SICK]

Sicilian • *noun* **1** a native of Sicily, an island off the southern coast of Italy. **2** a person of Sicilian descent. • *adjective* of or relating to Sicily. [Say si SILL yin]

sick[1] *adjective* **1** ill. **2** vomiting or tending to vomit. **3** mentally disturbed: *a sick mind.* **4** *informal* (of humour etc.) jeering at misfortune, illness, death, etc.; morbid: *sick joke.* **5 a** pining; longing: *lovesick.* **b** deeply affected by disappointment, fear, sorrow, grief, etc.: *worried sick.* **6** *informal* **a** disgusted by too much exposure: *sick of chocolates.* **b** angry, esp. because of surfeit: *am sick of being teased.* **7** of a sickly colour; pale, wan. PHRASES **sick to one's stomach** vomiting or nauseous.

sick[2] *verb* = SIC[2].

sick bay *noun* **1** part of a ship used as a hospital. **2** any room etc. for sick people.

sickbed *noun* **1** an invalid's bed. **2** the state of being an invalid.

sick building syndrome *noun* a high incidence of illness in office workers, attributed to pollutants etc. in the immediate working surroundings.

sick day *noun* a paid day off for a worker because of illness.

sicken *verb* **1** affect with loathing or disgust. **2** feel nausea or disgust: *he sickened at the sight.* **3** fall ill.

sickening *adjective* **1** causing or liable to cause sickness or nausea. **2** loathsome, disgusting.
▶ **sickeningly** *adverb*

sickie *noun informal* **1** a psychotic or perverted person. **2** a person who is unwell.

sickle *noun* **1** a short-handled farm tool with a semicircular blade, used esp. for cutting grass, grain, etc. **2** (also **sickle bar**) the cutting mechanism of a combine, mower, etc., consisting of a heavy bar with many blades. **3** anything sickle-shaped, esp. the moon.

sick leave *noun* leave of absence granted because of illness.

sickle cell *noun* a sickle-shaped blood cell, found in the blood of people with sickle-cell anemia.

sickle-cell anemia *noun* a severe hereditary form of anemia, in which a mutated form of hemoglobin distorts the red blood cells into a crescent shape.

sickly *adjective* (**sicklier**, **sickliest**) **1 a** of weak health; apt to be ill. **b** (of a person's complexion, look, etc.) languid, faint, or pale, suggesting sickness: *a sickly smile.* **c** (of light or colour) faint, pale, feeble. **2** causing ill health: *a sickly climate.* **3** (of a book etc.) sentimental or mawkish. **4** inducing or connected with nausea: *a sickly taste.* **5** (of a colour etc.) of an unpleasant shade inducing nausea: *a sickly green.*

sickness *noun* **1** the state of being ill. **2** a disease: *sleeping sickness.* **3** vomiting or a tendency to vomit.

sicko *noun* (*plural* **sickos**) *slang* a mentally ill or perverted person.

side • *noun* **1** a position to the left or right of an object, place, or central point. **2** either of the two halves of something regarded as divided by an imaginary central line. **3** an upright or sloping surface of a structure or object that is not the top or bottom and generally not the front or back. **4** each of the flat surfaces of a solid object. **5** each of the lines forming the boundary of a plane rectilinear figure. **6** each of the two surfaces of something flat and thin, e.g. paper. **7** each of the two faces of a record or of the two separate tracks on a cassette tape. **8** a part or region near the edge and away from the middle of something. **9** (as an *adjective*) subsidiary or less important: *a side issue.* **10** a person or group opposing another or others in a dispute or contest. **11** a particular aspect: *he had a disagreeable side.* **12** a person's kinship or line of descent as traced through either their father or mother. **13** a sports team. **14** *Baseball* a team's batters in one inning: *he struck out the side in the fifth.* • *verb* (**sides**, **sided**, **siding**) (usu. foll. by *with*) share an opinion, view, stance, etc. with (a person), esp. in a particular argument or dispute: *she sided with her father.* PHRASES **from side to side 1** across the whole width. **2** alternately each way from a central line: *staggered from side to side.* **let the side down** fail one's colleagues, esp. by frustrating their efforts or embarrassing them. **on the ... side** fairly, somewhat: *he's a little on the chubby side.* **on the side 1** in addition to one's regular work etc. **2** secretly or illicitly. **3** as a side dish. **side by side 1** standing close together. **2** in collaboration or solidarity. **take sides** favour or support one party in a dispute. **to one side** *she took me to one side.*

sidearm *Baseball* • *adjective* **1** (of a pitch or throw) performed or delivered with the arm swung or extended out to the side, parallel to the ground (compare OVERHAND 1). **2** (of a pitcher) that throws such a pitch. • *adverb* with the arm swung or extended out to the side: *he throws sidearm.* • *verb* throw (a pitch) sidearm.

sidebar *noun* **1** a short, usu. boxed, article in a newspaper etc. placed alongside a main article and containing additional information. **2** a secondary, additional, or incidental issue etc.: *he reduced war horrors to a sidebar in his inventory of personal anxieties* ◊ *one of the festival's sidebar events.*

sideboard *noun* a piece of dining room furniture used to store dishes, cutlery, table linen, etc., esp. one with a flat top, cupboards, and drawers.

S

sideburns *plural noun* hair grown by a man down the sides of his face beginning at the top of the ear and sometimes extending down as far as the cheek.

sidecar *noun* a small usu. open car with one wheel, attached to the side of a motorcycle, for one or more passengers.

side channel *noun Cdn* a shallow and narrow tributary running into a river.

sided *adjective* (usu. in *combination*) having a specified number or kind of sides: *double-sided tape ◊ cedar-sided*.

side dish *noun* an extra dish accompanying the main course but usu. served on a separate plate.

side effect *noun* **1** *Medical* a usu. adverse reaction caused by a drug in addition to the effect for which it is administered. **2** an unintended secondary result.

sidehill *noun US & Cdn* (esp. *BC*) a hillside.

sidekick *noun informal* **1** a close companion or partner, esp. in adventure. **2** the second member of a duo, subordinate and loyal to the first.

sidelight *noun* **1** a light coming from the side, esp. used in photography. **2** a piece of incidental information on a subject; an anecdote or item serving as a companion to the full account of an event etc.: *an interesting sidelight to the game emerged from a disputed call in the second half.* **3** a window by the side of a door or other window. ▶ **sidelighting** *noun*

sideline • *noun* **1** an activity pursued as a secondary job, interest, hobby, etc. **2 a** (in football, basketball, soccer, etc.) one of two lines running the length of a field or court to separate the part of the playing surface that is in bounds from that which is out of bounds. **b** (usu. in *plural*) the part of the playing surface out of bounds where coaches, players, and occasionally spectators sit. • *verb* (**sidelines**, **sidelined**, **sidelining**) **1** remove (a player) from participation in a game or games, esp. through injury or a suspension. **2** remove from action or consideration etc.: *they've sidelined their plans.* PHRASES **on** (or **from**) **the sidelines** in (or from) a position removed from the main action.

sidelock *noun* a long curly lock of hair falling from the side of the head down along the cheek, worn esp. by Orthodox Jews as a distinguishing mark.

sidelong *adjective & adverb* sideways: *looked sidelong at me ◊ a sidelong glance.*

sideman *noun* (*plural* **sidemen**) a supporting musician in a jazz etc. band.

side order *noun* a separate serving of food supplementing a meal ordered from a menu in a restaurant etc.

sidereal *adjective* **1** of or concerning the constellations or stars. **2** (of a period of time) determined or measured with reference to the apparent motion of the stars. [Say sigh DEERY ul]

side ribs *plural noun Cdn* a cut of pork from the belly including the ribs and adhering meat.

side road *noun* **1** a minor road, esp. joining or diverging from a main road. **2** *Cdn* (esp. *Ont.*) a rural road running perpendicular to a concession road.

sidesaddle • *noun* a saddle originally designed to allow a woman wearing a skirt to sit with both feet on one side of the horse, now usu. made with supports for the knees of the rider, who sits facing forward with the right knee raised. • *adverb* sitting in this position on a horse.

sideshow *noun* **1** a minor show or attraction in an exhibition, circus, etc. **2** a minor attraction, incident, or issue.

sideslip • *noun* **1** (esp. of a bicycle, car, etc.) a sideways skid or slip. **2** a sideways movement of an aircraft in flight, esp. downwards towards the inside of a turn.

3 *Skiing etc.* the action of travelling downwards at an angle. • *verb* (**sideslips**, **sideslipped**, **sideslipping**) **1** (of an aircraft) move sideways, esp. while turning. **2** *Skiing etc.* travel downwards at an angle.

sidesplit *noun Cdn* a house with floors raised half a level on one side, thus having an upper and lower basement and an upper and lower main floor.

sidestep • *verb* (**sidesteps**, **sidestepped**, **sidestepping**) **1** evade or dodge (an issue etc.) by refusing to address or confront it. **2** avoid someone or move by stepping to the side. • *noun* a step taken sideways.

side street *noun* a minor street usu. leading away from a main street.

side stroke *noun* a swimming stroke in which the swimmer lies on his or her side, drawing the arms through the water in opposite directions from the chest while using a scissor kick.

side-swipe • *noun* **1** a passing jibe or verbal attack; an indirect rebuke or criticism. **2** a glancing blow along the side of esp. a car or truck etc. • *verb* (**side-swipes**, **side-swiped**, **side-swiping**) **1** strike a glancing blow on the side of (esp. a car or truck etc.) in passing. **2** affect or attack indirectly.

sidetrack • *verb* **1 a** distract (a person) from an objective, issue, topic, etc. **b** divert (a plan etc.) from its intended purpose or aim. **2** run or shunt (a train) into a siding. • *noun* a railway siding.

sidewalk *noun* **1** a paved pedestrian path or walkway on either side of a street. **2** (as an *adjective*) designating things appearing or occurring on a sidewalk, esp. on the sidewalk in front of stores and other commercial buildings: *sidewalk vendor.*

side wall *noun* **1** a wall forming the side of a structure, room, or enclosure. **2 a** the side of a tire, usu. untreaded and distinctively marked or coloured. **b** (also **side wall tire**) a tire with distinctive side walls.

sideways • *adverb* **1** to or from a side. **2** with one side facing forward: *sat sideways.* **3** in an odd or unconventional manner: *the ability to look sideways at a situation.* • *adjective* **1** to or from a side. **2** odd or unconventional: *their priorities are completely sideways.*

sidewinder *noun* **1** a desert rattlesnake native to North America, which moves with a side-to-side slithering motion. **2** a punch delivered with a winding swing of the fist across the body. **3** (**Sidewinder**) a heat-seeking air-to-air missile.

siding *noun* **1** material used to cover the outside of a building, usu. made of wood, aluminum, or vinyl. **2** a short length of railway track connected to an adjacent line for storing and shunting trains and enabling trains on the same line to pass each other.

sidle *verb* (**sidles**, **sidled**, **sidling**) walk in a sly, sneaky, or timid manner: *he sidled up to me and asked if I was on my own ◊ Tim came to see me later, nervously sidling around the door.* [Say SIDE 'll]

SIDS *noun* = SUDDEN INFANT DEATH SYNDROME. [Say SIDZ]

siege *noun* **1** an operation in which an army, police force, etc. attempts to force the surrender of a fortified place, armed person, etc. by surrounding it or them and cutting off supplies and communication etc. **2** a prolonged and determined attack. PHRASES **lay siege to** esp. *Military* conduct the siege of. **under siege** the object of a fierce attack or criticism. [Say SEEDGE or SEEZH]

siemens *noun* the SI unit of conductance, equal to one reciprocal ohm. Abbreviation: **S**. [Say SEE mins]

sienna *noun* **1** a kind of iron-rich earth used as a pigment in oil and watercolour painting. **2 a** the natural colour of this earth, a yellowish brown. **b** (also

burnt sienna) the colour of this earth when roasted, a reddish brown. [Say see ENNA]

sierra *noun* (*plural* **sierras**) a long jagged mountain chain, esp. in Spain, the US, or Latin America. [Say see ERRA]

siesta *noun* (*plural* **siestas**) an afternoon nap or rest, esp. one taken during the hottest hours of the day in a country with a warm climate. [Say see ESTA]

sieur *noun hist.* a title for a member of the minor nobility, e.g. a seigneur, in France or New France. [Say SYER]

sieve • *noun* **1** a device consisting of a meshed or perforated surface enclosed in a frame, used to separate coarse particles from finer ones or from a liquid. **2** *slang Hockey* a goalie who lets in a large number of (esp. easily stopped) goals. • *verb* (**sieves**, **sieved**, **sieving**) esp. *Brit.* put through or sift with a sieve. PHRASES **memory** (or **head**) **like a sieve** *informal* a memory that retains little. [Say SIV]

SPELL CHECK	
seize	

Warning: **seize** is an exception to the "*i* before *e*" rule. In **seize** the *e* comes before the *i*.

sift *verb* **1** pass through a sieve or sifter, esp. in order to separate coarser from finer particles or to combine and aerate. **2** (usu. foll. by *out*, *from*) remove selectively: *read through these articles and sift out the better ones*. **3** subject (evidence, facts, etc.) to a close or thorough examination, esp. as part of a selection process; scrutinize. **4** (of snow, rain, sunlight, etc.) fall as if from a sieve. PHRASES **sift through** sort through or examine (evidence etc.) for specific details.

sifter *noun Cooking* **1** a metal or plastic cylinder, open at the top and having a meshed or perforated bottom through which dry ingredients are forced by means of a manual rotary blade in order to combine and aerate them. **2** a container with a perforated top used to sprinkle dry ingredients onto a surface.

SIG *abbreviation* SPECIAL INTEREST GROUP 2.

sigh • *verb* **1** emit a long deep audible breath as an expression of sadness, weariness, longing, relief, etc. **2** utter or express with sighs: "*I give up!*" *he sighed*. **3** (of the wind etc.) make a sound that resembles sighing. • *noun* a long and audible exhalation expressing sadness, weariness, etc. PHRASES **breathe a sigh of relief** become free of the anxiety or distress esp. caused by a particular situation.

SPELL CHECK	
sight, site	

A place where something is situated is a **site**. An Internet location is a *Web* **site**.

sight • *noun* **1** the ability to see. **2 a** a thing seen. **b** *informal* a person or thing having a ridiculous, repulsive, or dishevelled appearance. **3** (usu. in *plural*) the noteworthy features or attractions of a city, area, etc. **4** a range of space within which a person etc. can see or be seen. **5** a view of something. **6** (also in *plural*) a device on a gun or surveying instrument used to make one's aim or observation more precise. **7** *informal* a great quantity: *she's a sight better than she was.* **8** = SECOND SIGHT. **9** (as an *adjective*) designating a text previously unseen by students presented to them for commentary, translation, etc.: *sight passage.* • *verb* **1** note the presence of; observe, notice, or glimpse: *we have sighted the suspect.* **2** watch or locate (an object, target, etc.), esp. by viewing it through a sight. PHRASES **in** (or **within**) **sight 1** visible. **2** within reach, attainable:

the end is in sight. **lose sight of 1** no longer see or know the whereabouts of. **2** cease to be aware of. **lower one's sights** become less ambitious. **out of sight out of mind** it is easy to forget what is absent. **set one's sights on** strive for. **sight for sore eyes** a welcome person or thing, esp. a visitor.

sighted *adjective* **1** capable of seeing; not blind. **2** (in *combination*) having a specified kind of sight: *far-sighted*. ▶ **sightedness** *noun* (in sense 2)

sight gag *noun* a humorous effect produced by a visual action etc. as opposed to something spoken or written.

sighting *noun* **1** an occasion when something esp. unusual or fleeting is seen, esp. an observation reported or recorded formally: *there have been two sightings of the swift fox*. **2** the act or procedure of adjusting the aim or sights of a gun, bow, etc.

sightline *noun* a line of vision extending from a person's eye to what is seen, esp. one extending from the eye of a spectator in a theatre or sports venue to the stage or playing surface etc.

sight-read *verb* (**sight-reads**, **sight-read**, **sight-reading**) play or sing music that one has not seen or practised before. ▶ **sight-reading** *noun*

sightseeing *noun* the action of visiting places of interest in a particular location.

sightseer *noun* a person who visits places of interest; a tourist.

sight unseen *adverb* without a chance to look at or inspect a purchase etc. beforehand: *bought it sight unseen*.

sign • *noun* **1** a thing whose presence or occurrence indicates the probable presence, occurrence, or advent of something else. **2** a signal, gesture, or notice conveying information or an instruction. **3** a symbol or word used to represent something in algebra, music, or other subjects. **4** *Astrology* each of the twelve equal sections into which the zodiac is divided. • *verb* **1** write one's name on (something) for the purposes of identification or authorization. **2** engage for or commit oneself to work by signing a contract. **3** use gestures to convey information or instructions. PHRASES **make no sign** not react or protest. **signed, sealed, and delivered** properly settled or taken care of with all the necessary formalities having been completed. **sign in 1** sign a register upon arrival in a hotel etc. **2** authorize the admittance of (a person) by signing a register. **sign off** say or write one's name to mark the end of a letter, television or radio broadcast, etc. **sign on 1** agree to a contract, employment, etc. **2** begin work, broadcasting, etc., esp. by writing or announcing one's name. **sign over** (or **away**) surrender (one's right, property, etc.) by signing a document etc. **sign out 1** sign a register upon leaving a hotel etc. **2** authorize or record the release or departure of (a person or thing). **sign up 1** engage or employ (a person). **2** enlist in the armed forces. **3** enrol.

signage *noun* signs collectively, esp. those used commercially.

signal • *noun* **1** a sound, device, or gesture used to convey warning, direction, or information. **2** *Electricity* **a** a modulation of an electric current, electromagnetic wave, etc., by means of which information is conveyed from one place to another. **b** the current or wave itself, esp. regarded as conveying information. **3** an immediate occasion or cause of movement, action, etc.: *her entrance was the signal for cheering and applause*. **4** *Football* a series of letters and numbers called out by a player on offence or defence to indicate to teammates which play will be run on the next down. • *verb* (**signals**, **signalled**, **signalling**) **1** make a signal.

S

2 be a sign or indication of; mark: *their surrender signalled the end of the war*. • *adjective* remarkably good or bad; noteworthy: *a signal victory*.

signal fire *noun Cdn* a small fire or the remnant smoke of an extinguished fire serving to inform others of one's presence at a campsite etc.

signally *adverb* in a remarkably good or bad way: *I said I was sorry that I had so signally failed to make myself clear*.

signalman *noun* (*plural* **signalmen**) **1** a railway employee responsible for operating signals and switches. **2** (also **signaller**) a person employed to make or transmit signals, esp. in the army or navy.

signatory • *noun* (*plural* **signatories**) a person, party, or country that has signed a particular document, such as a treaty. • *adjective* (of a country etc.) that has signed a treaty or similar document. [Say SIG nuh tory]

signature *noun* **1 a** a person's name, initials, or distinctive mark used in signing a letter, document, etc. **b** the act of signing a document etc.: *this bill is ready for signature*. **2 a** a distinctive or identifying feature or characteristic: *the mountain has been carved and shaped by ice, which has left its signature in the form of deep gorges and jagged cliffs*. **b** (as an *adjective*) designating a characteristic or skill etc. that distinguishes or typifies a person, their work, etc.: *signature tune*. **3** *Music* **a** (also **key signature**) any of several combinations of sharps or flats after the clef at the beginning of each staff indicating the key of a piece of music. **b** (also **time signature**) an indication of tempo, expressed as a fraction with the numerator giving the number of beats in each bar and the denominator giving the basic note value of each beat.

signboard *noun* **1** a board displaying the name or logo of a business. **2** a board mounted on a signpost to direct travellers in a particular direction.

signee *noun* a person who has signed a contract, register, etc. [Say sigh NEE]

> **SPELL CHECK**
> **signet, cygnet**   ABC ✔
>
> A young swan is a **cygnet**.

signet *noun* **1** a small seal, usu. set in a ring, used with or instead of a signature to authenticate a document. **2** the stamp or impression of a seal. [Say SIG nit]

signet ring *noun* a ring worn on the finger usu. bearing the wearer's initials or an emblem etc.

significance *noun* **1** consequence, importance. **2** a concealed or real meaning. **3** the state of being significant.

significant *adjective* **1** of great importance or consequence: *a significant discovery*. **2** having or conveying an unstated meaning; having information that may be gathered: *I find it significant that he cannot talk to her*. **3** noteworthy, noticeable: *a significant drop in temperature*. ▶ **significantly** *adverb*

significant other *noun* often *jocular* a spouse, partner, or lover.

signification *noun* **1** the act of signifying. **2** the implication, sense, or meaning: *"sheep" and "mouton" have the same signification in English and French*.

signifier *noun* **1** *Linguistics* a physical medium (such as a sound, symbol, image, etc.) expressing meaning, as distinct from the meaning expressed. **2** a thing that signifies or conveys meaning.

signify *verb* (**signifies**, **signified**, **signifying**) **1 a** be a sign or symbol of; represent, denote. **b** offer a suggestion or hint of: *those clouds signify a storm*. **2** mean; have as its meaning: *"anorexia" signifies a type of eating disorder*. **3** communicate; announce, declare: *she signified her disappointment to me*. **4** be of importance; matter: *it signifies little*.

signing *noun* **1** the action of writing one's signature on an official document. **2** an act of signing a contract or signing a person to a contract. **3** sign language. **4** a session or period of time devoted to signing autographs: *a book signing*.

sign language *noun* a system of communication by visual gestures, used esp. by the hearing impaired.

sign law *noun Cdn* a Quebec provincial law regulating the use of languages other than French on signs.

sign-off *noun* the ending of a letter or broadcast etc.: *the CBC hopes to be Canadian from sign-on to sign-off*.

sign of the cross *noun* a Christian sign made in blessing or prayer, by tracing a cross from the forehead to the chest and to each shoulder, or in the air.

sign of the times *noun* an incident, event, person, etc. that typifies or foreshadows a trend developing or likely to develop in society.

signor *noun* (*plural* **signori**) **1** used as a title (preceding the surname or other designation) of, or as a respectful form of address to, an Italian or Italian-speaking man. **2** an Italian man of distinction, rank, or authority. [Say see NYOR for the singular, see NYORY for the plural]

signora *noun* (*plural* **signoras**) **1** used as a title (preceding the surname or other designation) of, or as a respectful form of address to, an Italian or Italian-speaking married woman. **2** a married Italian woman. [Say see NYORRA]

signpost • *noun* **1** a post with a sign giving directions or information. **2** a means of guidance; an indication or clue. • *verb* **1 a** provide with a signpost or signposts. **b** convey (information) by means of a signpost. **2** mark with indications, clues, or warnings about the content or nature etc. of something: *the way forward for him was signposted early on* ◊ *films where warnings of trouble ahead are conveniently signposted*.

Sikh • *noun* a member of a religion founded in Punjab in the 16th century, combining Hindu and Islamic elements and based on belief in one god. • *adjective* of Sikhs or Sikhism. ▶ **Sikhism** *noun* [Say SEEK, SEEK ism]

Siksika • *noun* (*plural* **Siksika** or **Siksikas**) **1** a member of an Aboriginal people, part of the Blackfoot, living in central Alberta. **2** the Algonquian language of this people. • *adjective* of this people. [Say sick SICKA]

silage *noun* grass or other fodder compacted and stored in airtight conditions, esp. in a silo, without first being dried, used as animal feed. [Say SIGH lidge]

silence • *noun* **1** absence of sound, noise, or speech. **2** the avoidance of mentioning or discussing a particular topic or thing; reticence: *silence is golden*. • *verb* (**silences**, **silenced**, **silencing**) **1** make quiet or silent: *silenced the alarm clock*. **2** defy (critics, detractors, arguments) by successfully defending one's position. **3** quell or disable (an esp. military opponent, their artillery, etc.). **4** prohibit or prevent (a person) from speaking, esp. to prevent the free expression of opinion. PHRASES **reduce** (or **put**) **to silence** overwhelm with superior argument.

silencer *noun* **1** a device used to reduce the sound of a gun as it is fired. **2** anything used to reduce the noise or sound of something.

silent *adjective* **1** characterized by an absence of sound or noise. **2** characterized by an absence of speech; not talking: *a silent greeting*. **3** (of a person) taciturn; speaking little. **4** (of a speaker, writer, book, etc.) omitting mention or discussion of a particular subject; offering no account or record. **5** (of a movie or film etc.) not having a recorded soundtrack or audible dialogue, but usu. having dialogue represented in printed form onscreen. **6** producing no detectable signs or

symptoms: *silent coronary*. **7** (of a letter) written but not pronounced, e.g. *b* in *doubt*. **8** inactive: *their guns were silent*.

silent auction *noun* an auction in which bids are submitted in writing during a specified period at the end of which the items are sold to the highest bidders.

silently *adverb* **1** without speaking: *they marched silently through the streets*. **2** without making any or much sound: *she crept silently out of the room*. **3** without using words or sounds to express something: *she prayed silently* ◊ *he silently agreed with much of what she had said*.

silent majority *noun* the presumed majority of people having moderate opinions but being too passive to assert them.

silent partner *noun* a person who has capital in a partnership but takes no part in its activities.

silhouette *noun* **1** a portrait or representation of a thing showing the outline only, usu. done in solid black and placed on a white or contrasting background. **2** the dark shadow or outline of a person or thing against a lighter background. **3** the contour or outline of a garment or a person's body. PHRASES **in silhouette** seen or placed in outline. [Say silla WET]

silhouetted *adjective* shown in silhouette.

silica *noun* a hard mineral substance, silicon dioxide, occurring in many rocks, soils, and sands as flint, opal, or quartz, etc., used in the manufacture of glass and ceramics. [Say SILLA kuh]

silicate *noun* any of the many insoluble compounds of a metal combined with silicon and oxygen, including mica, feldspar, etc. [Say SILLA kit]

siliceous *adjective* containing or consisting of silica. [Say suh LISH us]

silicon *noun* a non-metallic element occurring abundantly in oxides and silicates, used in electronic components for its semiconducting properties, as well as in the manufacture of glass. [Say SILLA con]

silicon chip *noun* a silicon microchip.

> **SPELL CHECK**
> **silicon, silicone**
>
> The element used in electronic components is **silicon**. The soft compound used in caulking, implants, etc. is **silicone**.

silicone *noun* any of the many polymeric organic compounds of silicon and oxygen used as electrical insulators, waterproofing agents, etc. [Say SILLA cone]

silicone implant *noun* = BREAST IMPLANT.

Silicon Valley *noun* an area with a high concentration of electronics industries, esp. the Santa Clara valley southeast of San Francisco.

> **SPELL CHECK**
> **soliloquy**
>
> Warning: the first part of **soliloquy** is spelled *sol-*, as in the word *solo*.

silk *noun* **1** a fine lustrous soft strong fibre produced by silkworms in making cocoons. **2** a similar fibre spun by some spiders. **3 a** a thread or cloth made from silk fibre. **b** a thread or fabric resembling silk. **4** (in *plural*) garments made of silk, esp. a jockey's cap and jacket bearing the colours of the horse's owner. **5** the long silky hairs forming in a tuft on an ear of corn.

silken *adjective* **1** made of silk. **2** resembling silk, esp. in texture, softness, or lustre.

silkscreen • *noun* **1** a screen of fine mesh used in screen printing. **2** the process of screen printing. **3** a print made by this process. • *verb* print, decorate, or reproduce using a silkscreen.

silkworm *noun* the commercially bred caterpillar of a domesticated moth, which spins a silk cocoon that is processed to yield silk fibre.

silky *adjective* (**silkier**, **silkiest**) **1** like silk in smoothness, softness, fineness, or lustre. **2** (of a person's manner, voice, etc.) suave, smooth.

sill *noun* **1** a strong horizontal beam forming the base or foundation of esp. a house. **2** (also **windowsill**) the bottom part of a window or door frame. **3** any of the lower horizontal pieces forming the frame of a car or truck etc.

silliness *noun* **1** the quality of being silly; foolishness. **2** something silly.

silly • *adjective* (**sillier**, **silliest**) **1** displaying a lack of judgment or common sense. **2** ridiculous: *she looked silly*. **3** stupefied: *we drank ourselves silly*. • *noun* (*plural* **sillies**) *informal* a foolish person.

silo *noun* (*plural* **silos**) **1** a tall cylinder or pit in which green corn or hay etc. is pressed and kept for fodder, undergoing fermentation. **2** a pit or tower for the storage of grain etc. **3** an underground chamber in which a missile is kept ready for firing. [Say SIGH lo]

> **SPELL CHECK**
> **silhouette**
>
> Warning: **silhouette** is spelled with an *h* between the *l* and the *o*.

silt • *noun* fine sand, clay, or other soil carried by moving water and deposited as sediment on the bottom or on the shore of a lake or stream etc. • *verb* **1** (often foll. by *up*) fill or block, or be filled or blocked, with silt. **2** flow, drift, or settle like silt; pass gradually. ▶ **siltation** *noun* **silty** *adjective*

Silurian • *adjective* of or relating to the third period of the Paleozoic era, lasting from about 438 to 408 million years BP, between the Ordovician and Devonian periods, when the first true fish and land plants appeared. • *noun* this period. [Say suh LOORY in]

silver • *noun* **1** a greyish-white precious metal. **2** the colour of silver. **3** coins collectively; change. **4** utensils and vessels made of or plated with silver collectively, esp. cutlery. **5** household cutlery of any material. **6** (in full **silver medal**) a medal of silver, usu. awarded as second prize. **7** = SILVER SALMON. • *adjective* **1** made wholly or chiefly of silver. **2** coloured like silver. **3** designating the twenty-fifth event of an esp. annual series: *silver wedding anniversary*. • *verb* **1** coat or plate with silver. **2** provide (mirror glass) with a backing of tin amalgam etc.

silver buffalo berry *noun* (*plural* **silver buffalo berries**) see BUFFALO BERRY.

silver bullet *noun* *informal* a cure-all or universal remedy, esp. any usu. undiscovered highly specific and highly successful drug: *there is no silver bullet in the treatment and control of malaria* ◊ *the fungus has been called the silver bullet in the war against marijuana cultivation*.

silverfish *noun* (*plural* **silverfish** or **silverfishes**) **1** a small silvery wingless insect often found living in houses. **2** a silver-coloured fish, esp. a colourless variety of goldfish.

silver fox *noun* (*plural* **silver foxes**) **1** a North American red fox at a time when its fur is black with white tips. **2** its fur or pelt.

silver-grey *noun & adjective* a pale or lustrous grey.

silver lining *noun* a consolation or hopeful prospect in misfortune.

silver plate *noun* **1** vessels or utensils made of or plated with silver or an alloy of silver. **2** the material of which these are made. ▶ **silver-plated** *adjective*

silver salmon *noun* a coho.

silver screen *noun* (usu. as **the silver screen**) the movie industry; motion pictures collectively.

silversmith *noun* a person who works with silver; a manufacturer of silver articles.

silver spoon *noun* **1** a spoon made of silver. **2** a sign of wealth or future prosperity: *she was born with a silver spoon in her mouth.*

silver thaw *noun* Cdn (Maritimes & Nfld) a slick coating of ice formed on the ground or an exposed surface, caused by freezing rain or a sudden light frost.

silvertip *noun* Cdn (West) a mature grizzly bear with white-tipped hairs, native esp. to the Rocky Mountains.

silverware *noun* tableware, esp. utensils used for eating and serving, made of silver or an alloy of silver, or of a metal coated with silver, stainless steel, etc.

silvery *adjective* **1** like silver in colour or appearance. **2** having a clear gentle ringing sound. **3** (of the hair) white and lustrous.

silvicultural *adjective* relating to the growing and cultivation of trees. [Say silva CULTURAL]

silviculture *noun* the branch of forestry concerned with the growing and cultivation of trees. ▶ **silviculturist** *noun* [Say SILVA culture]

sim *noun* simulation.

simcha *noun* (plural **simchas**) a Jewish party or celebration. [Say SIM chuh or SIM kuh]

Simcoe Day *noun* Cdn (S Ont.) (esp. in Toronto) a civic holiday celebrated on the first Monday in August.

simian • *adjective* **1** of or concerning the anthropoid apes. **2** characteristic of an ape or monkey: *a simian walk.* • *noun* an ape or monkey. [Say SIMMY in]

similar *adjective* **1** of the same nature or kind; alike. **2** (often foll. by to) having a resemblance. **3** Math (of two geometrical figures etc.) shaped alike; containing the same angles, having the same shape or proportions.

similarity *noun* (plural **similarities**) **1** the state or fact of being similar. **2** a point of resemblance.

similarly *adverb* **1** in almost the same way: *husband and wife were similarly successful.* **2** used to say that two facts, actions, statements, etc. are like each other.

simile *noun* **1** a figure of speech involving the explicit comparison of two different things, often using the words "like" or "as", e.g. *as brave as a lion*. **2** the use of such comparison. [Say SIMMA lee]

similitude *noun* the state of being similar to something; similarity or resemblance: *a similitude between things of natural and human creation ◊ an oil painting of his uncle, of remarkable similitude, stares out upon the dining room.* [Say suh MILLA tood or suh MILLA tyood]

simmer • *verb* **1** cook at or just below the boiling point; boil or bubble gently. **2** be in a state of suppressed anger or excitement. • *noun* a simmering condition. PHRASES **simmer down** become calm or less agitated.

simony *noun* hist. the buying or selling of ecclesiastical privileges, such as pardons or positions of authority within the Church. [Say SIMON ee or SIMMON ee]

simper • *verb* **1** smile in a silly or affected way. **2** express by or with simpering. • *noun* such a smile.

simple *adjective* **1** easily understood or done. **2** not complicated or elaborate; without luxury or sophistication. **3 a** not compound; consisting of or involving only one element or operation etc. **b** Grammar (of a tense) formed without an auxiliary verb. **4** unqualified: *the simple truth*. **5** foolish or ignorant. **6** plain in appearance or manner; unsophisticated, ingenuous, artless. **7** not of high social standing; ordinary: *simple people*. **8** Botany **a** consisting of one part. **b** (of fruit) formed from one pistil.

simple-minded *adjective* **1** feeble-minded.

2 unsophisticated. ▶ **simple-mindedly** *adverb* **simple-mindedness** *noun*

simple sentence *noun* a sentence with a single subject and predicate, e.g. *I went up the stairs* (compare COMPLEX SENTENCE, COMPOUND SENTENCE).

simpleton *noun* a foolish, gullible, or halfwitted person.

simplex *adjective* **1** simple; not compounded. **2** Computing (of a circuit) allowing transmission of signals in one direction only.

simplicity *noun* the fact or condition of being simple. PHRASES **be simplicity itself** be extremely easy.

simplification *noun* the act, process, or result of making something simple or of making something easy or easier to do or understand.

simplify *verb* (**simplifies**, **simplified**, **simplifying**) make simple; make easy or easier to do or understand.

simplistic *adjective* **1** excessively or affectedly simple. **2** oversimplified so as to conceal or distort difficulties: *to regard ourselves as nothing more than sophisticated computers is simplistic.* ▶ **simplistically** *adverb*

simply *adverb* **1** in a simple manner. **2** absolutely; without doubt: *simply astonishing.* **3** merely.

simulate *verb* (**simulates**, **simulated**, **simulating**) **1** pretend to have or feel: *it was impossible to force a smile, to simulate pleasure.* **2** imitate or counterfeit. **3 a** imitate the conditions of (a situation etc.), e.g. for training or amusement: *to simulate three years of normal use, we left them whirring for over 100 hours.* **b** produce a computer model of (a process etc.): *the programs can simulate how atmosphere and ground conditions change over time.* ▶ **simulated** *adjective* **simulation** *noun* **simulator** *noun*

simulcast • *noun* **1** a simultaneous transmission of the same program on radio and television, or on two or more channels, in two or more languages, etc. **2** a live transmission of a sports event, esp. a horse race, for usu. off-track betting purposes. • *verb* (**simulcasts**, **simulcast**, **simulcasting**) broadcast as a simulcast. ▶ **simulcasting** *noun* [Say SIGH mul kast or SIMMLE cast]

simultaneity *noun* the quality or fact of occurring or operating at the same time. [Say sigh mul tuh NAY uh tee or simmle tuh NAY uh tee]

simultaneous *adjective* occurring or operating at the same time: *a simultaneous withdrawal of troops*. ▶ **simultaneously** *adverb* [Say sigh mul TAY nee us or simmle TAY nee us]

SIN *abbreviation* Cdn SOCIAL INSURANCE NUMBER. [Say SIN]

sin¹ • *noun* **1** the breaking of divine or moral law, esp. by a conscious act. **2** an action regarded as a serious offence or fault: *it's a sin to stay inside on a nice day like this*. • *verb* (**sins**, **sinned**, **sinning**) **1** commit a sin. **2** (foll. by against) offend. PHRASES **as sin** informal extremely: *ugly as sin*. **cover** (or **hide** etc.) **a multitude of sins** conceal the real, usu. unpleasant, facts or situation. **do** (or **be**) **something for one's sins** jocular do (or be) something as a supposed punishment for something. **live in sin** jocular live together in a sexual relationship without being married.

sin² *abbreviation* sine. [Say SINE]

sin bin *noun* informal **1** Hockey the penalty box. **2** a place set aside for offenders of various kinds.

since • *preposition* throughout, or at a point in, the period between (a specified time, event, etc.) and the time present or being considered. • *conjunction* **1** during or in the time after. **2** because. • *adverb* **1** from that time or event until now or the time being considered. **2** ago, before now.

sincere *adjective* (**more sincere**, **sincerest**) **1** free

from pretense or deceit; the same in reality as in appearance. **2** genuine, honest, frank.

sincerely *adverb* in a sincere manner. PHRASES **(yours) sincerely** (also **sincerely yours**) a formula for ending a letter.

sincerity *noun* freedom from pretense or deceit; honesty, straightforwardness. [Say sin SERRA tee]

sine *noun* **1** the trigonometric function that is equal to the ratio of the side opposite a given angle (in a right-angled triangle) to the hypotenuse. **2** a function of the line drawn from one end of an arc perpendicularly to the radius through the other.

sinecure *noun* a position that requires little or no work but usu. yields profit or honour: *he hauled reservists from the comfort of their academic sinecures and ordered them to work*. [Say SINNA cure]

sine qua non *noun* an indispensable condition or qualification: *caribou, the sine qua non of traditional Chipewyan life*. [Say sin ay kwah NON]

sinew *noun* **1** tough fibrous tissue uniting muscle to bone; a tendon. **2** (in *plural*) muscles; bodily strength. **3** (in *plural*) something providing strength to an organization etc.: *the West built the sinews of a new world on the foundations of its technological, commercial and developmental prowess*. ▶ **sinewy** *adjective* [Say SIN you]

sinful *adjective* **1** (of a person) committing sin, esp. habitually. **2** (of an act) involving or characterized by sin. **3** *informal* self-indulgently delicious: *a sinful chocolate torte*. ▶ **sinfully** *adverb* **sinfulness** *noun*

WRITING TIP
sung, sang

Do not use **sung** for the past tense of **sing**, as in *She sung three songs* (the correct past tense is **sang**). **Sung** is only used as a past participle, as in *The song she had sung the evening before was still playing in their heads*.

---

sing *verb* (**sings**; *past* **sang**; *past participle* **sung**; **singing**) **1** utter musical sounds with the voice, esp. words with a set tune. **2** (of the wind, a kettle, etc.) make melodious, humming, buzzing, or whistling sounds. **3** *slang* turn informer; confess. PHRASES **sing out** call out loudly; shout.

sing. *abbreviation* singular.

singable *adjective* (of a song etc.) able to be sung; suitable for singing.

singalong *noun* an informal occasion when a group of people sing songs together.

Singaporean • *adjective* of or relating to Singapore, a country in SE Asia. • *noun* a native or inhabitant of Singapore. [Say sing a PORRY in]

singe • *verb* (**singes**, **singed**, **singeing**) burn superficially or lightly. • *noun* a superficial burn.

singer *noun* a person who sings, esp. professionally: *a pop singer*.

singing *noun & adjective* the activity of making musical sounds with one's voice.

single • *adjective* **1** one only, not double or multiple. **2** united or undivided. **3 a** designed or suitable for one person: *single bed*. **b** used or done by one person etc. or one set or pair. **4** one by itself; not one of several: *a single tree*. **5** regarded separately: *every single thing*. **6** not married; not involved in a romantic or sexual relationship. **7** even one; not to speak of more: *did not see a single person*. **8** (of a flower) having only one circle of petals. • *noun* **1** a single thing, or item in a series. **2 a** a record, compact disc, etc., containing only one or two songs or other short pieces of music. **b** one of these pieces of music. **3** *Baseball* a one-base hit. **4** (usu. *in plural*) a game with one player on each side. **5** an unmarried

person: *young singles*. • *verb* (**singles**, **singled**, **singling**) **1** select from a group as worthy of special attention, praise, etc.: *singled out for praise*. **2** *Baseball* **a** hit a single. **b** cause (a baserunner) to advance by hitting a single.

single-breasted *adjective* (of a coat etc.) having only one set of buttons and buttonholes, not overlapping.

single file • *noun* a line of people or things arranged one behind another. • *adverb* one behind another.

single-handed • *adverb* **1** without help from another. **2** with one hand. • *adjective* **1** done etc. single-handed. **2** for one hand. ▶ **single-handedly** *adverb*

single-issue *noun* (used as an *adjective*) designating a group, political platform, etc., characterized by an exclusive concern with one issue: *single-issue voters*.

single-minded *adjective* having or intent on only one purpose. ▶ **single-mindedly** *adverb* **single-mindedness** *noun*

singleness *noun* **1** the state of being unmarried. **2** the fact of being one in number or kind; oneness. **3** unity or concentration of purpose, mind, etc.: *a man of great singleness of mind*.

single parent *noun* a person bringing up a child or children without a partner. ▶ **single parenthood** *noun*

single point *noun* *Cdn Football* = ROUGE *noun* 3.

singles bar *noun* a bar frequented by esp. single people seeking a sexual partner, potential spouse, etc.

single space *verb* (**single spaces**, **single spaced**, **single spacing**) lay out or print (text) on consecutive lines. ▶ **single-spaced** *adjective*

singleton *noun* **1** the only card of a suit in a hand. **2 a** a single person or thing. **b** an only child. **3** a single child or animal born, not a twin etc.

single-user *adjective* **1** having one user. **2** (of a computer system, software, etc.) designed to be used by one person at a time.

singly *adverb* alone; one at a time; individually.

singsong • *adjective* characterized by or uttered with a monotonous or rising and falling rhythm, cadence, or intonation. • *noun* **1** a singsong manner. **2** *Cdn & Brit.* a singalong. ▶ **singsongy** *adjective*

singular • *adjective* **1** exceptionally good or great: *their singular achievement was that they elevated imaginative literature to a status far above other kinds of writing*. **2** eccentric or strange: *it centres on Miss Amelia, a singular woman who distills moonshine and practises rural medical arts*. **3** *Grammar* (of a word or form) denoting or referring to a single person or thing. **4** *Math* possessing unique properties. **5** single, individual. • *noun* *Grammar* **1** a singular word or form. **2** the singular number.

singularity *noun* (*plural* **singularities**) **1** the state or condition of being singular: *the point of these products is their singularity — they differ among themselves more than any other spirit*. **2** an odd trait or peculiarity: *the singularities with which his book is peppered are unlikely to attract doctors to the practice of acupuncture*. [Say sing gyoo LERRA tee]

singularly *adverb* very; in an unusual way: *singularly beautiful* ◊ *he chose a singularly inappropriate moment*.

Sinhalese • *noun* (*plural* **Sinhalese**) **1** a member of a people originally from northern India and now forming the majority of the population of Sri Lanka. **2** an Indic language spoken by this people. • *adjective* of this people or language. [Say sin huh LEEZ or sinna LEEZ]

sinister *adjective* **1** suggestive of evil; looking villainous. **2** wicked or criminal: *a sinister motive*. **3** of evil omen. ▶ **sinisterly** *adverb*

S

> **WRITING TIP**
> **sunk, sank**
>
> While it is not wrong to use **sunk** as the past tense of **sink**, as in *Our spirits sunk when we heard the news*, **sank** is by far more common in Canadian speech and writing and sounds much less informal. Note that the past participle is **sunk**, not **sunken**, which is used only as an adjective: *The ship had sunk more than three hundred years earlier, but the divers were still hoping to find sunken treasure*.

sink • *verb* (**sinks**; *past* **sank** *or sometimes* **sunk**; *past participle* **sunk**; **sinking**) **1** become submerged in liquid. **2** (with reference to a ship) go or cause to go to the bottom of the sea. **3** disappear and not be seen or heard of again. **4** drop downwards. **5** lower oneself or drop down gently. **6** insert beneath a surface. **7** cause (something sharp) to penetrate (a surface). **8** gradually decrease or decline in amount or intensity. **9** pass or fall into a particular state or condition: *she sank into sleep*. **10** (foll. by *in, into*) put (money or energy) into. **11** cause (a ball) to enter a pocket in billiards, a hole in golf, a basket in basketball, etc. • *noun* **1** a fixed basin with a water supply and outflow pipe. **2** a sinkhole. **3** a body or process by which energy or a component is removed from a system: *a heat sink*. PHRASES **sink in 1** penetrate or make its way in; be absorbed. **2** become gradually comprehended: *paused to let the words sink in*. **sink one's teeth into** take up (a challenge, cause, etc.) fervently or energetically. **sink or swim** fail totally or survive by one's own efforts. ▶ **sinkable** *adjective*

sinker *noun* **1** a person or thing which sinks. **2** a weight used to sink a fishing line etc. **3** *Baseball* **a** = SINKERBALL. **b** a hit in which the ball drops markedly.

sinkerball *noun Baseball* a pitch in which the ball drops markedly. ▶ **sinkerballer** *noun*

sinkhole *noun* **1 a** a large circular depression in the ground, occurring e.g. as a result of the collapse of a subterranean cave. **b** a cavity in limestone etc. into which a stream etc. disappears. **2** *informal* a place of vice or corruption: *an urban sinkhole, block after block of burned-out tenements, garbage-strewn streets and weed-choked lots*. **3** *informal* an enterprise etc. which seems to swallow all invested money to no effect.

sinless *adjective* free from sin. ▶ **sinlessness** *noun*

sinner *noun* a person who sins, esp. habitually.

Sinn Fein *noun* an Irish movement founded in 1905, originally aiming at the independence of Ireland and a revival of Irish culture and language, now dedicated, as the political wing of the IRA, to the political unification of Northern Ireland and the Republic of Ireland. ▶ **Sinn Feiner** *noun* [Say shin FAIN]

Sino- *combining form* Chinese; Chinese and: *Sino-American*. [Say SINE oh]

sinuous *adjective* **1** with many curves: *flamingos with their sinuous necks*. **2** moving in a smooth, flowing way: *the slow, sinuous dance*. ▶ **sinuously** *adverb* [Say SIN you us]

sinus *noun* (*plural* **sinuses**) **1** a cavity of bone or tissue, esp. in the skull connecting with the nostrils. **2** *Botany* the curve between the lobes of a leaf. [Say SIGH nus]

Sion = ZION. [Say SIGH un]

Siouan • *noun* an Aboriginal language family including Dakota, Sioux, and Omaha. • *adjective* of or designating this language family. [Say SOO in]

Sioux • *noun* (*plural* **Sioux**) **1** a member of a group of North American Aboriginal peoples chiefly inhabiting the upper Mississippi and Missouri river basins. **2** the language of this group. • *adjective* of or relating to these people or their language. [Say SOO]

sip • *verb* (**sips**, **sipped**, **sipping**) drink in one or more small amounts. • *noun* **1** a small mouthful of liquid: *a sip of brandy*. **2** the act of taking this.

siphon • *noun* **1** a pipe or tube used for conveying liquid from one level to a lower level, using the liquid pressure differential to force a column of the liquid up to a higher level before it falls to the outlet. **2** a bottle from which carbonated water is dispensed by allowing the gas pressure to force it out. **3** *Zoology* a tubular organ in an aquatic animal, esp. a mollusc, through which water is drawn in or expelled. • *verb* (often foll. by *off*) **1** conduct or flow through a siphon. **2** divert or set aside (funds etc.): *he had siphoned off $63,000 of the corporation's money, mostly by forging the signature of a former director*. [Say SIFE in]

sir *noun* **1** a polite, respectful, or formal form of address or mode of reference to a man. **2** (**Sir**) a titular prefix to the first name of a knight or baronet.

sire • *noun* **1** the male parent of an animal, esp. of a domestic quadruped. **2** *archaic* a respectful form of address, esp. to a king. • *verb* (**sires**, **sired**, **siring**) (esp. of a male domestic quadruped) be the father of: *this fox has sired at least three litters*.

siree *interjection* (also **sirree**) *informal* as an emphatic, esp. after *yes* or *no*. [Say sir EE]

siren • *noun* **1 a** a device for making a loud prolonged signal or warning sound, esp. by revolving a perforated disc over a jet of compressed air or steam. **b** the sound made by this. **2** (in Greek mythology) each of a number of women or winged creatures whose singing lured unwary sailors on to rocks. **3** a sweet singer. **4 a** a dangerously fascinating woman; a temptress. **b** a tempting pursuit etc. **5** an aquatic eel-like amphibian with external gills, no hind limbs, and tiny forelimbs, found in the southeastern US. • *adjective* irresistibly tempting: *the siren call of power*.

sirloin *noun* the choicer part of a loin of beef, from in front of the rump.

sis *noun informal* a sister.

sisal *noun* **1** a Mexican plant with large fleshy leaves, cultivated for fibre production. **2** the fibre made from this plant, used for making esp. rope. [Say SICE 'll]

siskin *noun* any of various small streaked yellowish-green finches, esp. the pine siskin of North American coniferous forests.

sissified *adjective* effeminate; cowardly.

sissy *informal* • *noun* (*plural* **sissies**) an effeminate or cowardly person. • *adjective* effeminate; cowardly.

sister *noun* **1** a woman or girl in relation to sons and other daughters of her parents. **2 a** (often as a form of address) a close female friend or associate. **b** a female fellow member of a trade union, class, sect, or the human race. **3** (often as a form of address) a member of a female religious order. **4** (as an *adjective*) of the same type or design or origin etc.: *sister ship*.

sister city *noun* (*plural* **sister cities**) **1** a city that is twinned with another. **2** a city linked to another by proximity, common interests, etc.: *Dartmouth, Halifax's sister city*.

sisterhood *noun* **1** the relationship between sisters. **2 a** a society or association of women, esp. when bound by monastic vows or devoting themselves to religious or charitable work or the feminist cause. **b** its members collectively. **3** community of feeling and mutual support between women.

sister-in-law *noun* (*plural* **sisters-in-law**) **1** the sister of one's wife or husband. **2** the wife of one's brother. **3** the wife of one's brother-in-law.

sisterly *adjective & adverb* having or showing the sort of mutual kindness and affection typically felt by sisters: *sisterly feelings* ◊ *sisterly advice*.

S

Sister of Charity noun (plural **Sisters of Charity**) = GREY NUN.

sit verb (**sits, sat, sitting**) **1** be or cause to be in a position in which one's weight is supported by one's buttocks and one's back is upright. **2** be or remain in a particular position or state: *the fridge was sitting in a pool of water*. **3** (of an animal) rest with the hind legs bent and the body close to the ground. **4** (of a parliament, committee, court, etc.) be engaged in its business. **5** serve as a member of a council, jury, or other official body. **6** (of a table or room) have enough seats for. **7** (foll. by *for*) pose for (an artist or photographer). **8** *Sport* **a** (often foll. by *out*) not participate in a game or games because of poor play, a suspension, etc. **b** (of a player) not participate in (a game) or for (a specified period); not play for the duration of (a suspension): *sat out half the season*. **c** (often foll. by *out*) (of a coach etc.) keep (a player) from participating because of poor play etc. PHRASES **be sitting pretty** be comfortably or advantageously placed. **make a person sit up** *informal* surprise or interest a person. **sit around** sit doing nothing, esp. while waiting. **sit back** relax one's efforts. **sit by** look on without interfering. **sit down 1** sit after standing. **2** cause to sit. **sit heavy on the stomach** take a long time to be digested. **sit in 1** occupy a place as a protest. **2** (foll. by *for*) take the place of. **3** (foll. by *on*) be present as a guest or observer at (a meeting etc.). **sit in judgment** assume the right of judging others; be censorious. **sit on 1** be a member of (a committee etc.). **2** hold a session or inquiry concerning. **3** *informal* delay action about. **sit on one's hands** take no action. **sit out 1** take no part in (a dance etc.). **2** stay till the end of (esp. an ordeal). **sit tight** *informal* **1** remain firmly in one's place. **2** not be shaken off or move away or yield to distractions. **sit up 1** rise from a lying to a sitting position. **2** sit firmly upright. **3** stay awake and later than usual, esp. while waiting for someone: *sat up watching TV*. **4** *informal* become interested or aroused etc. **sit up and take notice** *informal* have one's interest aroused, esp. suddenly. **sit well** (often foll. by *with*; usu. in *neg.*) be acceptable or undisturbing to: *their decision did not sit well with her*. **sit well on** suit or fit.

sitar noun a long-necked Indian guitar-like instrument with movable frets. [Say si TAR or SIT ar]

sitcom noun *informal* a situation comedy.

sit-down • adjective **1** (of a meal) eaten sitting at a table. **2** (of a protest etc.) in which demonstrators occupy their workplace or sit down on the ground in a public place. • noun **1** a period of sitting. **2** a sit-down protest etc.

site • noun **1** the ground chosen or used for a town or building. **2** a place where some activity is or has been conducted: *camping site*. **3** *Computing* a single source for files, services, etc. on the Internet: *visited several sites*. • verb (**sites, sited, siting**) **1** locate or place. **2** provide with a site.

sit-in noun a protest, strike, demonstration, etc. in which people occupy a workplace, public building, etc.

Sitka noun (plural **Sitkas**) a fast-growing spruce native to western North America and widely cultivated for its timber. [Say SIT kuh]

sitter noun **1** a person who sits, esp. for a portrait. **2 a** = BABYSITTER (see BABYSIT). **b** (esp. in *combination*) a

person who takes care of a house, pet, etc. while the owners are away: *house-sitter*.

sitting • noun **1** a continuous period of being seated, esp. engaged in an activity: *finished the book in one sitting*. **2** a time during which an assembly is engaged in business. **3** a session in which a meal is served: *dinner will be served in two sittings*. **4** a period during which a law court, legislature, etc. holds sessions. • adjective **1** having sat down. **2** (of a legislator, Member of Parliament, etc.) currently holding office. **3** (of an animal or bird) not running or flying. **4** (of a hen) engaged in hatching.

sitting duck noun (also **sitting target**) *informal* a person or thing that is very easy to attack.

sitting room noun a room in a house for relaxed sitting in.

situate verb (**situates, situated, situating**) **1** put in a certain position or circumstances: *is situated at the top of a hill*. **2** establish or indicate the place of; put in a context: *it's necessary to situate these ideas in the wider context of the class structure*.

situation noun **1** a place and its surroundings: *the house stands in a fine situation*. **2** a set of circumstances; a position in which one finds oneself; a state of affairs: *a difficult situation*. **3** an employee's position or job. **4** a critical point or complication in a drama. ▶ **situational** adjective

situation comedy noun (plural **situation comedies**) a comedy, esp. on TV, in which the humour derives from the situations the characters are placed in.

sit-up noun an exercise to strengthen the stomach muscles, in which a person lies with the back flat on the ground and lifts the torso into a sitting position.

sitz bath noun a bathtub formed like a chair for sitting in water up to the hips.

SIU abbreviation SPECIAL INVESTIGATIONS UNIT.

Siwash noun (plural **Siwashes**) *Cdn (West)* (also **Siwash sweater**) a thick woollen sweater decorated with symbols or animals from Aboriginal mythology. [Say SIGH wash]

six cardinal number (plural **sixes**) **1** one more than five. **2** *Cdn & Brit.* a group of six Brownies, Cubs, etc. **3** *informal* = SIX-PACK. PHRASES **at sixes and sevens** in confusion or disagreement. **six of one and half a dozen of the other** a situation of little real difference between the alternatives.

sixer noun *Cdn & Brit.* the leader of a group of six Brownies, Cubs, etc.

sixfold adjective & adverb **1** six times as much or as many. **2** consisting of six parts.

Six Nations noun the Iroquois confederacy after the Tuscarora joined in 1722.

six-pack noun a pack of six identical items, esp. cans or bottles of beer.

six-shooter noun (also **six-gun**) a revolver with six chambers.

sixteen cardinal number one more than fifteen. ▶ **sixteenth** ordinal number

sixteenth note noun *Music* a note having the time value of half an eighth note and represented by a large dot with a two-hooked stem.

sixth ordinal number **1** constituting number six in a sequence; 6th. **2** each of six equal parts into which something is or may be divided. **3** *Music* an interval spanning six consecutive notes in a diatonic scale. ▶ **sixthly** adverb

sixth sense noun **1** a supposed faculty giving intuitive or extrasensory knowledge. **2** such knowledge.

sixtieth ordinal number the ordinal number corresponding to sixty.

S

sixty *cardinal number* (*plural* **sixties**) **1** ten less than seventy. **2** (**Sixty**) *Cdn* the parallel of latitude 60° north of the equator as forming the boundary between the western provinces to the south and the territories to the north: *living North of Sixty.* PHRASES **sixty-first, -second,** etc. the ordinal numbers between sixtieth and seventieth. **sixty-one, -two,** etc. the cardinal numbers between sixty and seventy.

sizable *adjective* (also **sizeable**) large or fairly large. ▶ **sizably** *adverb*

size[1] • *noun* **1** the relative bigness or extent of a thing; dimensions, magnitude. **2** each of the classes, usu. numbered, into which things otherwise similar, esp. garments, are divided according to size: *three sizes too big.* • *verb* (**sizes, sized, sizing**) sort or group in sizes or according to size. PHRASES **of a size** having the same size. **of some size** fairly large. **the size of** as big as. **the size of it** *informal* a true account of the matter: *that is the size of it.* **size up 1** estimate the size of. **2** *informal* form a judgment of.

size[2] • *noun* a gelatinous solution used in glazing paper, stiffening textiles, etc. • *verb* (**sizes, sized, sizing**) glaze or stiffen with size.

sized *adjective* (also in *combination*) having a specified size: *comfortably sized rooms.*

sizzle • *verb* (**sizzles, sizzled, sizzling**) **1 a** make a sputtering or hissing sound when or as if frying. **b** fry or burn. **2** *informal* **a** be in a state of great heat or excitement. **b** be very exciting or passionate, esp. sexually: *sexual tension between the couple sizzled onscreen.* • *noun* **1** a sizzling sound. **2** *informal* intense heat or excitement. PHRASES **more sizzle than steak** *slang* more flash than substance. ▶ **sizzler** *noun* **sizzling** *adjective & adverb*

SK *abbreviation* Saskatchewan (in official postal use).

ska *noun* a style of popular music of Jamaican origin, with a fast tempo and strongly accentuated offbeat.

skag *noun slang* heroin.

skank • *noun* **1** a steady-paced dance performed to reggae music, characterized by rhythmically bending forward, raising the knees, and extending the hands palms downwards. **2** a piece of reggae music suitable for such dancing. • *verb* play reggae music or dance in this style.

skate[1] • *noun* **1** each of a pair of boots with steel blades fixed to the bottom for gliding on ice. **2** = ROLLER SKATE. **3** = IN-LINE SKATE. **4** an act or period of skating. **5** a device on which a heavy object moves. • *verb* (**skates, skated, skating**) **1 a** move on or as if on skates. **b** perform (a specified figure, a routine, etc.) on skates. **2** (foll. by *around, over*) refer fleetingly to, disregard. PHRASES **hang up one's skates** *Cdn informal* retire from professional life. **skate on thin ice** *informal* behave rashly, risk danger, esp. by dealing with a subject needing tactful treatment.

skate[2] *noun* (*plural* **skate** or **skates**) a large marine fish of the ray family, with a roughly diamond-shaped body and a long thin tail.

skate-a-thon *noun* esp. *Cdn* a prolonged period of skating as a fundraiser.

skateboard • *noun* a short narrow board mounted on roller skate wheels, used for riding on while standing, and propelled by one foot pushing occasionally against the ground. • *verb* ride on a skateboard. ▶ **skateboarder** *noun* **skateboarding** *noun*

skater *noun* **1** a person who skates. **2** *Hockey* a player other than the goalie. **3** a skateboarder.

skating *noun* the action or activity of skating on ice skates, roller skates, or a skateboard.

skating rink *noun* **1** an area of ice for skating. **2** a building containing a rink for skating.

skedaddle *informal* • *verb* (**skedaddles, skedaddled, skedaddling**) run away, depart quickly, flee. • *noun* a hurried departure or flight. [Say skuh DADDLE]

skeet *noun* (also **skeet shooting**) a shooting sport in which a clay target is thrown from a trap to simulate the flight of a bird.

skeeter *noun slang* a mosquito.

skeg *noun* **1** the after part of a vessel's keel or a projection from it. **2** a fin underneath the rear of a surfboard.

skein *noun* **1** a loosely coiled bundle of yarn or thread. **2** a cluster or arrangement resembling a skein. **3** a flock of wild geese etc. in flight. [Say SKAIN]

skeletal *adjective* **1** of, forming, or resembling a skeleton. **2** very thin, emaciated. **3** consisting of only a bare outline or minimum: *complex elaboration of skeletal melodies* ◊ *a skeletal overview of historical events.*

skeleton *noun* **1 a** a hard internal or external framework of bones, cartilage, shell, woody fibre, etc., supporting or containing the body of an animal or plant. **b** the dried bones of a human being or other animal fastened together in the same relative positions as in life. **2** the supporting framework or structure or essential part of a thing. **3** a very thin or emaciated person or animal. **4** the remaining part of anything after its life or usefulness is gone. **5** an outline sketch. **6** (as an *adjective*) having only the essential or minimum number of persons, parts, etc.: *skeleton staff.*

skeleton in the closet *noun* a discreditable or embarrassing fact kept secret.

skeptic *noun* **1** a person who doubts the validity of accepted beliefs in a particular subject. **2** a person who doubts the truth of Christianity and other religions. **3** a person who accepts the philosophy of skepticism.

skeptical *adjective* **1** inclined to question the truth or soundness of accepted ideas, facts, etc.: *experts are skeptical about postulated links between environmental conditions and the disease.* **2** *Philosophy* of or accepting skepticism; denying the possibility of knowledge. ▶ **skeptically** *adverb*

skepticism *noun* **1** a skeptical attitude in relation to accepted ideas, facts, etc.; doubt. **2** *Philosophy* the opinion that real knowledge is unattainable.

sketch • *noun* (*plural* **sketches**) **1** a rough, slight, merely outlined, or unfinished drawing or painting, often made to assist in making a more finished picture. **2** a brief account without many details conveying a general idea of something; a rough draft or general outline. **3** an item or scene in a comedy program. **4** a short descriptive piece of writing. • *verb* (**sketches, sketched, sketching**) **1** make or give a sketch of. **2** draw sketches esp. of landscape: *went out sketching.* **3** (often foll. by *in, out*) indicate briefly or in outline.

sketchbook *noun* **1** (also **sketch pad**) a book or pad of drawing paper for doing sketches on. **2** a notebook containing preliminary pictorial, verbal, or musical sketches or studies. **3** (usu. as a title) a book containing narrative or descriptive essays.

sketchily *adverb* in a sketchy way; roughly.

sketchiness *noun* the condition or quality of being sketchy.

sketchy *adjective* (**sketchier, sketchiest**) **1** not complete or thoroughly detailed: *a sketchy description of the event* ◊ *a sketchy knowledge of English.* **2** resembling a sketch; consisting of an outline without much detail: *she felt that leaving parts of the paper unpainted produced a sketchy and unfinished appearance.*

skew *verb* **1** make biased or distorted in a way that is considered inaccurate, unfair, or misleading: *distribution of power in the region was heavily skewed in*

favour of cities. **2** make crooked or set at an angle: *books are skewed on the messy shelves* ◊ *a skewed hut.* [Say SKYOO]

skewer • *noun* **1** a long metal or wooden pin for holding meat, vegetables, etc. compactly together while cooking. **2** any similar pin for fastening or securing something in place. • *verb* **1** fasten together or pierce with or as with a skewer. **2** criticize sharply. [Say SKYOO er]

ski • *noun* (*plural* **skis**) **1** each of a pair of long narrow pieces of wood etc., usu. pointed and turned up at the front, fastened under the feet for travelling over snow. **2** a similar device under a vehicle or aircraft. **3** = WATER SKI. **4** (as an *adjective*) of or pertaining to skis or skiing: *ski instructor* ◊ *ski boots.* • *verb* (**skis, skied, skiing**) **1** travel on skis. **2** ski at (a place). ▶ **skiable** *adjective*

ski bum *noun slang* an avid skier, esp. one who spends a great deal of time skiing.

skid • *verb* (**skids, skidded, skidding**) **1** (of a vehicle, wheel, or driver) slide on slippery ground, esp. sideways or obliquely. **2** cause (a vehicle etc.) to skid. **3** slip, slide. **4** *informal* decline or deteriorate: *the company's shares have skidded 29% since March.* **5** support or move or protect or check with a skid. **6** slide or haul (logs) down a prepared slide or along a skid trail or skid road. • *noun* **1** an act of skidding or sliding: *the car went into a skid.* **2 a** a plank or roller on which a heavy object may be placed to facilitate moving. **b** a pallet or portable platform for transporting and storing goods. **3** a piece of wood etc. serving as a support, ship's fender, ramp, etc. **4 a** each of a number of peeled and partially sunk logs or timbers forming a skid road (*see* SKID ROAD 1). **b** a skid road. **5** a braking device, esp. a wooden or metal shoe preventing a wheel from revolving or used as a drag. **6** a runner beneath an aircraft for use when landing on snow or grass. **7** *Sport informal* a losing streak. PHRASES **grease the skids** *informal* help make things run smoothly. **hit the skids** *informal* enter a rapid decline or deterioration. **on the skids** *informal* in a steadily worsening state.

skidder *noun* **1** a type of powerful four-wheel tractor used to haul logs from a cutting area. **2** a teamster who hauls logs from a cutting area.

skidding *noun* the process of hauling logs from a cutting area.

Ski-Doo • *noun proprietary* a snowmobile. • *verb* (**skidoo, skidoos, skidooed, skidooing**) **1** ride on a snowmobile. **2** *slang* go away; depart. ▶ **skidooer** *noun* **skidooing** *noun*

skid road *noun* **1** *hist.* a road formed of skids along which logs were hauled. **2** *hist.* a part of a town or city frequented by loggers. **3** = SKID ROW.

skid row *noun* a part of a town or city frequented by vagrants etc. PHRASES **on skid row** destitute.

skid trail *noun* a trail cut through the bush for hauling logs from a cutting area.

skidway *noun* **1** a (usu. inclined) platform for piling logs before transportation or sawing. **2** = SKID ROAD 1. **3** an inclined ramp of planks or logs used for sliding boats etc.

skier *noun* a person who skis.

skiff *noun* **1** any of various types of small light boat, esp. one adapted for rowing and sailing. **2** a light dusting of snow.

skiing *noun* the activity or sport of moving on skis.

ski jump *noun* **1** an artificial structure consisting of a steep ramp levelling off at the end to allow a skier to leap through the air. **2** a jump executed from this. **3** a competition in which such jumps are made. ▶ **ski jumper** *noun* **ski jumping** *noun*

skilful *adjective* (also **skillful**) having or showing skill. ▶ **skilfully** *adverb* **skilfulness** *noun*

ski lift *noun* a device for carrying skiers up a slope, usu. on seats hung from an overhead cable.

skill *noun* **1** (often foll. by *in*) expertness, practised ability, facility in an action. **2** (usu. in *plural*) a specific aptitude, esp. of a particular type: *management skills*.

skilled *adjective* **1** (often foll. by *in*) having or showing skill. **2** highly trained or experienced. **3** (of work) requiring skill or special training.

skillet *noun* a frying pan.

skim • *verb* (**skims, skimmed, skimming**) **1** take scum or cream or a floating layer from the surface of a liquid. **2 a** keep touching lightly or nearly touching (a surface) in passing over. **b** (or foll. by *over*) deal with or treat (a subject) superficially. **3** (often foll. by *over, along*) go lightly over a surface, glide along in the air. **4** throw (a flat stone) low over water so that it bounces on the surface several times. **5** read superficially, look over cursorily. **6** (often foll. by *off*) *slang* conceal or divert (earnings or takings, esp. from gambling) to avoid paying tax. • *noun* **1** an act of reading something quickly: *a quick skim through the brochure.* **2** a thin covering on the surface of something, esp. of a liquid: *skim of ice.* **3** = SKIM MILK. PHRASES **skim the cream off** take the best part of.

ski mask *noun* a protective, usu. knitted covering for the head and face, with holes for the eyes, mouth, and sometimes the nose, originally worn by skiers.

skimmer *noun* **1** a device for skimming liquids. **2** a person who skims. **3** a long-winged marine bird that feeds by skimming over water with its knifelike lower mandible immersed. **4** a hydroplane, hydrofoil, hovercraft, etc.

skim milk *noun* milk from which the cream has been skimmed.

skimp *verb* spend or use too little time, money, or material on something in an attempt to economize: *France skimped over the years on all the defences at Quebec.*

skimpy *adjective* (**skimpier, skimpiest**) **1** meagre; not ample or sufficient: *a skimpy budget.* **2** (of clothing) very short or revealing.

skin • *noun* **1** the flexible continuous covering of a human or other animal body. **2 a** the skin of a flayed animal with or without the hair etc. **b** esp. *hist.* this used as a unit of value. **c** a material prepared from skins esp. of smaller animals. **3** an outer layer or covering, esp. the coating of a plant, fruit, or sausage. **4** a film on the surface of a liquid etc. **5** a container for liquid, made of an animal's whole skin. **6 a** the planking or plating of a ship or boat, inside or outside the ribs. **b** the outer covering of any craft or vehicle, esp. an aircraft or spacecraft. **7** *slang* a skinhead. **8** (usu. in *plural*) a strip of sealskin or other material attached to the bottom of a ski to give traction when climbing slopes. **9** (usu. in *plural*) *slang* a drum. **10** *see* SKINS GAME. • *verb* (**skins, skinned, skinning**) **1 a** remove the skin from. **b** graze (a part of the body). **2** (often foll. by *over*) cover (a sore etc.) with or as with skin. **3** *slang* fleece or swindle. • *adjective* of, depicting, or presenting pornographic material. PHRASES **be skin and bone** be very thin. **by the skin of one's teeth** by a very narrow margin. **get under a person's skin** *informal* interest or annoy a person intensely. **have a thick** (or **thin**) **skin** be insensitive (or sensitive) to criticism etc. **no skin off one's nose** *informal* a matter of indifference or even benefit to one. **skin a person alive** used when threatening to punish someone severely.

skin deep *adjective* (of an emotion, an impression, a quality, etc.) superficial, not deep or lasting.

skin diver *noun* a person who swims underwater

skinflint *noun* a miserly person.

skinhead *noun* a person, esp. a youth, with shaven or close-cropped hair worn as a symbol of anarchy, racism, or nonconformity.

skink *noun* a smooth-bodied lizard with short or absent limbs, usu. burrowing in sandy ground and occurring throughout tropical and temperate regions.

skinless *adjective* lacking skin, or having had the skin removed: *boneless, skinless chicken breasts*.

skinned *adjective* having a skin of a specified type: *a fair-skinned woman*.

skinner *noun* a person who skins animals or prepares skins.

skinniness *noun* the quality or condition of being thin or emaciated.

skinny *adjective* (**skinnier**, **skinniest**) **1 a** (of a person) thin or emaciated. **b** (of an object) narrow, slim. **2** (of clothing) tight-fitting.

skinny-dip *informal* • *verb* (**skinny-dips**, **skinny-dipped**, **skinny-dipping**) swim nude. • *noun* (**skinny dip**) a swim in the nude. ▶ **skinny-dipper** *noun* **skinny-dipping** *noun*

skins game *noun Sport* a form of golf, curling, bowling, etc., in which the winner of each hole, end, or frame is awarded a financial prize, or "skin", with the value of the skin increasing as the game goes on.

skin test *noun* a test to determine whether an immune reaction is provoked when a substance is applied to or injected into the skin.

skin-tight *adjective* (of a garment) very close-fitting.

skip[1] • *verb* (**skips**, **skipped**, **skipping**) **1** move along lightly, stepping from one foot to the other with a hop or bounce. **2** jump repeatedly over a rope which is held at both ends and turned over the head and under the feet. **3** jump lightly over. **4** omit or move quickly over (a stage or point). **5** fail to attend or deal with; miss. **6** (of a record or compact disc) play erratically because of a defect in the playing surface. **7** (of a student) advance (two or more grades). • *noun* a skipping movement or action. PHRASES **skip it** *slang* abandon a topic etc. **skip off** *Cdn* (*S Ont.*) play truant from school. **skip out** *Cdn* (*West*) = SKIP OFF. **skip rope** play or exercise with a skipping rope.

skip[2] • *noun* the captain of a curling or bowling team. • *verb* (**skips**, **skipped**, **skipping**) be the skip of.

ski patrol *noun* a person or persons patrolling a ski area to check on the safety of skiers, monitor snow conditions, perform first aid, etc. ▶ **ski patroller** *noun*

skipjack *noun* (also **skipjack tuna**) a small striped Pacific tuna used as food.

skipper • *noun* **1** the captain of a ship, esp. of a small trading or fishing vessel. **2** the captain of an aircraft. **3** the captain of a side in a game or sport. • *verb* act as captain of.

skipping rope *noun Cdn & Brit.* a length of rope etc., usu. with handles at each end, revolved over the head and under the feet while jumping as a game or exercise.

skip rock *noun Curling* one of a rink's last two rocks of an end, usu. delivered by the skip.

skirl • *noun* the shrill sound characteristic of bagpipes. • *verb* make a skirl.

skirmish • *noun* **1** a piece of irregular or unpremeditated fighting esp. between small or outlying parts of armies or fleets; a slight engagement. **2** a short argument or contest of wit etc. • *verb* engage in a skirmish. ▶ **skirmisher** *noun*

skirt • *noun* **1** a woman's outer garment hanging from the waist. **2** the part of a dress, coat, etc. that hangs below the waist. **3** a piece of material fitting around the sides of a bed etc. to conceal the legs. **4** an edge, border, or extreme part: *the woods on either side of the road were dark and impenetrable behind a white skirt of snow*. **5** a surface that conceals or protects the wheels or underside of a vehicle etc. • *verb* **1** go along or around or past the edge of. **2** be situated along. **3** avoid dealing with (an issue etc.). **4** (foll. by *along*) go along the coast, a wall, etc. ▶ **skirted** *adjective*

ski run *noun* a slope, trail, etc. prepared for skiing.

skit *noun* a light, usu. short, piece of satire or comedy.

skitter *verb* **1 a** move lightly or hastily. **b** hurry about, dart off. **2** fish by drawing bait jerkily across the surface of the water.

skittery *adjective* skittish, restless.

skittish *adjective* **1** lively, playful. **2** (of a horse etc.) nervous, inclined to shy, fidgety. **3** fickle, changeable. ▶ **skittishly** *adverb* **skittishness** *noun*

skittle *noun* **1** a pin used in the game of skittles. **2** (in *plural*; usu. treated as *singular*) a game played with usu. nine wooden pins set up at the end of an alley to be bowled down usu. with wooden balls or a wooden disc.

skivvy • *noun* (*plural* **skivvies**) **1 a** esp. *Brit. informal* derogatory a female domestic servant. **b** a person doing work considered menial or poorly paid. **2** (in *plural*) underwear, esp. men's underwear. • *verb* (**skivvies**, **skivvied**, **skivvying**) *informal* work as a skivvy.

skookum esp. *Cdn* (*West*) • *adjective* strong, brave. • *noun* (esp. among Aboriginal peoples of the Northwest coast) an evil spirit. [Say SKOOK um (with OO as in COOK)]

skua *noun* a large seabird typically having brown or brown and white plumage and a strongly hooked bill, breeding in polar or cold regions, and with a habit of robbing other seabirds of food by forcing them to disgorge the fish they have caught. [Say SKYOO uh]

skulduggery *noun* trickery; unscrupulous behaviour.

skulk *verb* **1** move stealthily, lurk, or keep oneself concealed, esp. in a cowardly or sinister way. **2** stay or sneak away in time of danger. ▶ **skulker** *noun*

SPELL CHECK
skull, scull

A light narrow boat propelled with a pair of small oars is a **scull**. **Scull** is also the spelling for a migrating group of fish.

---

skull *noun* a bone framework enclosing the brain of a person or animal. PHRASES **out of one's skull** *slang* **1** out of one's mind, crazy. **2** very drunk.

skull and crossbones *plural noun* a representation of a skull with two thigh bones crossed below, used formerly on the flags of pirate ships and now to warn of danger, e.g. on bottles of poison.

skullcap *noun* a small close-fitting brimless cap.

skulled *adjective* having a specified kind of skull: *he was long-skulled and narrow-faced*.

skunk • *noun* **1** a cat-sized flesh-eating mammal with distinctive black and white striped fur, capable of emitting a powerful stench from a liquid secreted by its anal glands as a defence. **2** *informal* a thoroughly contemptible person. • *verb* **1** *slang* defeat soundly. **2** (in cribbage) defeat (one's opponent) by a margin of at least 31 points.

skunk cabbage *noun* a North American plant of the arum family, the flower of which has a distinctive and unpleasant smell.

skunky *adjective* (**skunkier**, **skunkiest**) *Cdn informal* (of beer) foul-tasting, esp. as a result of exposure to light.

sky • *noun* (*plural* **skies**) **1** the region of the atmosphere and outer space seen from the earth. **2** the weather or

---

without a diving suit, usu. in deep water with scuba equipment and flippers. ▶ **skin diving** *noun*

climate evidenced by this. • *verb* (**skies, skied, skying**) *Baseball etc.* hit (a ball) high into the air. **PHRASES** **the sky is the limit** there is practically no limit. **to the skies** very highly; without reserve: *praised to the skies*. **under the open sky** out of doors.

sky blue *noun & adjective* a bright clear blue.

skybox *noun* (*plural* **skyboxes**) a private box situated near the top of a sports stadium or arena, from where the game or event may be viewed.

skydive *verb* (**skydives, skydived, skydiving**) jump from an aircraft and fall for as long as possible before opening one's parachute, as a sport or recreational activity. ▶ **skydiver** *noun*

skydiving *noun* the sport of jumping from an aircraft and falling for as long as possible before opening one's parachute.

sky-high *adverb & adjective* very high: *sky-high interest rates*.

skyhook *noun* **1** *Basketball* a high-arcing throw, a lob. **2** a launching device for aircraft, satellites, etc. **3** an imaginary or fanciful device for suspension in or attachment to the sky.

skylark • *noun* a lark of Eurasia and North Africa, noted for singing while hovering in flight. • *verb* play tricks or practical jokes, indulge in horseplay, frolic.

skylight *noun* an opening in a roof or ceiling, covered with glass, Plexiglas, etc., for letting in daylight.

skyline *noun* **1** the outline of hills, buildings, etc., defined against the sky. **2** *Forestry* an overhead cable for transporting logs.

skylit *adjective* (of a room etc.) having a skylight: *a skylit atrium*.

skyrocket • *verb* (**skyrockets, skyrocketed, skyrocketing**) (esp. of prices etc.) rise very steeply or rapidly. • *noun* a firework exploding high in the air.

skyscraper *noun* a very tall building.

skyward • *adverb* (also **skywards**) towards the sky. • *adjective* moving skyward.

skyway *noun* **1** a route used by aircraft. **2** the sky as a medium of transport. **3** (also **skywalk**) a covered overhead walkway between buildings. **4** a long highly elevated section of highway, esp. one spanning water: *Burlington Skyway*.

skywriting *noun* legible smoke trails made by an airplane esp. for advertising.

slab *noun* **1** a flat broad fairly thick usu. square or rectangular piece of solid material, e.g. concrete or stone. **2** a large flat piece of cake, chocolate, etc. **3** an outer piece of wood sawn from a log. **4** a table in a margin.

slack • *adjective* **1** not taut; not held tensely: *slack rope* ◊ *slack-jawed*. **2** inactive or sluggish. **3** negligent or remiss. **4** (of tide etc.) neither ebbing nor flowing. **5** (of trade or business or a market) with little happening. **6** relaxed, languid. • *noun* **1** the slack part of a rope etc.: *haul in the slack*. **2** a slack time in trade etc. **3** *informal* a period of inactivity or laziness. • *verb* **1 a** slacken. **b** loosen (rope etc.). **2** *informal* be lazy; shirk. • *adverb* slackly. **PHRASES** **slack off 1** loosen. **2** reduce activity, effort, speed, etc. **slack up** reduce the speed of a train etc. before stopping. **take** (or **pick**) **up the slack** use up a surplus or make up a deficiency; avoid an undesirable lull.

slacken *verb* make or become slack. **PHRASES** **slacken off** = SLACK OFF (SEE SLACK).

slacker *noun* **1** a shirker; a lazy person. **2** such a person regarded as one of a subculture or generation of young people, esp. in the 1990s, characterized by apathy and aimlessness: *they never thought of themselves as slackers, the term used to describe adherents of grunge's "loser" ethos* ◊ *slacker culture*.

slackly *adverb* in a slack manner: *her arms hung slackly by her sides*.

slackness *noun* the quality of being slack.

slacks *plural noun* trousers, esp. for informal wear.

slag • *noun* **1** stony waste matter separated from metals during the smelting or refining of ore. **2** cellular lava, or fragments of it. • *verb* (**slags, slagged, slagging**) *informal* criticize someone in an abusive and insulting way: *hotel staff were slagging the rich and famous*.

slag heap *noun* a hill of refuse from a mine etc.

slain *past participle of* SLAY.

slake *verb* (**slakes, slaked, slaking**) **1** quench or satisfy (thirst, desire, etc.). **2** disintegrate (quicklime) by chemical combination with water.

slalom • *noun* **1** a downhill ski race on a zigzag course marked by artificial obstacles, usu. flags, and descended singly by each competitor in turn. **2** a similar obstacle race for canoeists, water skiers, skateboarders, etc. • *verb* (**slaloms, slalomed, slaloming**) **1** perform or compete in a slalom. **2** make frequent sharp turns in or as in a slalom. ▶ **slalomer** *noun* [Say SLAW lum]

slam • *verb* (**slams, slammed, slamming**) **1** shut forcefully and loudly. **2** put down (an object) with a similar sound. **3** move violently: *he slammed out of the room*. **4** put or come into sudden action: *slam the brakes on*. **5** *slang* criticize severely. **6** *slang* hit. **7** *slang* gain an easy victory over. • *noun* **1** a sound of or as of a slammed door. **2** the shutting of a door etc. with a loud bang. **3** a criticism or insult. **4** = SLAM DUNK 1. **5** the winning of every trick in a card game.

slam-bang • *adverb* with the sound of a slam. • *adjective* *informal* **1** impressive, exciting, or energetic. **2** noisy, violent.

slam-dance *noun & verb* (**slam-dances, slam-danced, slam-dancing**) dance to rock music (originally at punk rock concerts) in a form in which participants deliberately collide violently with one another. ▶ **slam-dancer** *noun*

slam-dancing *noun* a form of dancing to rock music (originally at punk rock concerts) in which participants deliberately collide violently with one another.

slam dunk • *noun* **1** *Basketball* a forceful and often dramatic dunk shot. **2** *informal* a sure thing; an easy victory. • *verb* (**slam-dunk**) **1** *Basketball* **a** dunk (the ball) in a forceful, often dramatic manner. **b** make a forceful, often dramatic dunk shot or shots. **2** *informal* easily defeat (a person or thing). **3** *informal* achieve (something) in a forceful, often dramatic way.

slammer *noun* *slang* **1** (usu. as **the slammer**) prison. **2** a slam-dancer.

slander • *noun* **1** a malicious, false, and injurious statement spoken about a person. **2** the uttering of such statements. • *verb* utter slander about; defame falsely. ▶ **slanderer** *noun* **slanderous** *adjective* **slanderously** *adverb*

slang *noun* words, phrases, and uses that are regarded as very informal and are often restricted to special contexts or are peculiar to a specified profession, class, geographic area, etc.: *street slang*.

slanging match *noun* a prolonged exchange of insults.

slangy *adjective* (**slangier, slangiest**) **1** of the character of slang. **2** fond of using slang. [Say SLANG ee]

slant • *verb* **1** lie or go obliquely to a vertical or horizontal line. **2** (often as **slanted** *adjective*) present (information) from a particular angle esp. in a biased or unfair way. • *noun* **1** a slope; an oblique position. **2** a way of regarding a thing; a point of view, esp. a biased

S

one. • *adjective* sloping, oblique. ▶ **slantwise** *adverb*
slanty *adjective*
slap • *verb* (**slaps**, **slapped**, **slapping**) **1** strike with
the palm of the hand or a flat object, or so as to make a
similar noise. **2** lay forcefully: *slapped the money on the
table*. **3** put hastily or carelessly: *slap some paint on the
walls*. **4** strike (a ball, puck, etc.) with a sharp slap.
5 *informal* punish with a fine, sentence, etc.: *slapped him
with a three-game suspension*. • *noun* **1** a blow with the
palm of the hand or a flat object. **2** a slapping sound.
• *adverb* with the suddenness or effectiveness or true
aim of a blow; suddenly, fully, directly: *ran slap into him*.
slapdash *adjective* hasty and careless.
slap-happy *adjective informal* **1** cheerfully casual or
flippant: *the movie is a slap-happy crime spoof*. **2** dazed or
disoriented; punch-drunk: *he settled for lager, which he
could drink all night without getting slap-happy*.
slap in the face *noun* a rebuff or affront.
slap on the wrist *noun* a mild rebuke or reprimand.
slapshot *noun* Hockey a hard shot taken by raising the
stick to waist height before striking the puck or ball.
slapstick *noun* **1** boisterous physical comedy,
characterized by pratfalls etc. **2** a device consisting of
two flexible pieces of wood joined together at one end,
designed to produce a loud slapping noise, used esp. by
a clown etc. to simulate the dealing of a hard blow.
slash • *verb* (**slashes**, **slashed**, **slashing**) **1** make a
sweeping or random cut or cuts with a knife, sword,
whip, etc. **2** make a long narrow gash or gashes in.
3 reduce (prices etc.) drastically. **4** Hockey strike or
swing at (an opponent) with the stick. **5** clear (land) of
vegetation; cut down (trees or undergrowth). • *noun*
(*plural* **slashes**) **1 a** a slashing cut or stroke. **b** a wound
or slit made by this. **2** an oblique stroke (/). **3** Forestry
a debris resulting from the felling or destruction of
trees. **b** an area in a forest strewn with such debris. **4** a
severe or drastic reduction. **5** Hockey an act of slashing.
slash-and-burn *adjective* **1** (of cultivation) in which
vegetation is cut down, allowed to dry, and then
burned off before seeds are planted. **2** aggressive or
ruthless: *businesspeople and politicians who prescribe social
spending cuts are fond of invoking the well-being of future
generations as an excuse for their slash-and-burn policies*.
slasher *noun* **1** a person or thing that slashes. **2** (also
slasher film, **slasher movie**) a film depicting violent
assault with a knife etc. **3** Cdn a form of circular saw
with several blades, used to cut logs into
predetermined lengths.
slashing • *noun* Hockey the infraction of striking or
swinging at an opponent with the stick. • *adjective*
vigorous: *a slashing approach to the drug problem* ◊ *a
slashing attack on her critics*.
slat *noun* **1** any thin narrow piece of wood, plastic, or
metal, such as one of those found on a fence or
Venetian blind. **2** (in *plural*) Cdn *informal* skis.
slate • *noun* **1** a fine-grained rock, typically dark grey,
green, or bluish-purple in colour, which splits readily
into flat smooth plates. **2** a piece of such a plate used as
a tile esp. to cover a roof or pave a walkway. **3** a piece of
such a plate, usu. framed in wood, formerly used for
writing on. **4** a bluish-grey or bluish-purple colour. **5** a
list of nominees for election or appointment to an
official post. **6** Film a board giving information about a
shot, held in front of the camera so that the film can be
identified later. **7** *informal* an agenda, schedule, or list:
what's on the slate for tonight? • *verb* (**slates**, **slated**,
slating) **1** (usu. foll. by *for*, *to*) make arrangements for
(an event etc.); plan. **2** propose or nominate (a candidate or
candidates) for a position, political office etc. **3** cover (a
roof etc.) with slates. • *adjective* **1** made of slate. **2** of

the colour of slate. PHRASES **wipe the slate clean**
forgive or cancel the record of past offences.
slather *verb informal* cover a surface with a large or
excessive portion of a substance: *way too much guck
slathered on the hamburgers*. [Rhymes with GATHER]
slatted *adjective* having slats: *a slatted bench*.
slattern *noun* an untidy and slovenly woman.
▶ **slatternly** *adjective*
slaty *adjective* **1** resembling slate in colour, texture, or
appearance. **2** characteristic of slate.
slaughter • *noun* **1** the killing of an animal or
animals for food. **2** the killing of a person or animal in
a brutal or ruthless manner. **3** the killing of many
people or animals at once or over a period of time, as in
a war; massacre. • *verb* **1** kill (an animal) for food;
butcher. **2** kill or murder (a person) in a ruthless or
brutal manner. **3** kill large numbers of people at once
or over a period of time. **4** *informal* defeat easily or by a
wide margin. ▶ **slaughterer** *noun* [Say SLOTTER]
slaughterhouse *noun* a place where animals are
butchered for food. [Say SLOTTER house]
Slav • *noun* a member of a group of peoples in central
and eastern Europe speaking Slavic languages.
• *adjective* of or relating to the Slavs or the Slavic
languages.
slave • *noun* **1** a person who is the legal property of
another or others and is bound to absolute obedience.
2 a person working very hard, esp. without appropriate
reward or appreciation. **3** a person completely under
the domination of or subject to a specified influence:
he's a slave to his passions. **4** a willing devotee to a
particular activity, cause, person, etc.: *a slave to fashion*.
5 a subsidiary part, esp. a device which is controlled by,
or which follows the movements of, another. • *verb*
(**slaves**, **slaved**, **slaving**) toil or work very hard.
slave-driver *noun* **1** a person who works others hard;
a demanding and unyielding supervisor, employer,
teacher, etc. **2** an overseer of slaves at work.
slaveholder *noun* a person who owns slaves.
▶ **slaveholding** *noun & adjective*
slave labour *noun* **1** arduous work assigned to slaves.
2 slaves collectively. **3** gruelling or forced labour for
which one receives little financial reward.
slaver[1] *noun hist.* **1** a ship used in the slave trade. **2** a
person dealing in or owning slaves. [Say SLAVE er]
slaver[2] • *noun* saliva running from the mouth. • *verb*
1 drool. **2** show excessive desire, eagerness, or
obsequiousness: *he's middle-class, and slavering to be
upper*. ▶ **slavering** *adjective* [Say SLAVVER]
slavery *noun* **1** the practice or institution of keeping
slaves. **2** the condition or fact of being a slave. **3** any
condition or practice similar to slavery, esp. involving
rigorous service or labour with little reward.
slave trade *noun hist.* the business of procuring,
transporting, and selling humans as slaves, esp. the
transporting of African blacks to the US to be sold into
slavery. ▶ **slave trader** *noun*
Slavey • *noun* (*plural* **Slavey** or **Slaveys**) **1** a member
of a number of Dene Aboriginal groups living between
Lake Athabasca and Great Slave Lake. **2** any of the
Athapaskan languages spoken by the Slavey. • *adjective*
of or relating to this people. [Say SLAY vee]
Slavic • *adjective* **1** of, pertaining to, or designating
the branch of Indo-European languages including
Russian, Polish, Ukrainian, and Czech. **2** pertaining to,
characteristic of, or designating the Slavs. • *noun* one of
the Slavic languages or the Slavic languages
collectively.
slavish *adjective* **1** befitting or characteristic of a slave.
2 showing no attempt at originality or development: *a
slavish reproduction*. ▶ **slavishly** *adverb*

S

Slavonic *adjective & noun* = SLAVIC. [Say sluh VON ick]
slaw *noun* coleslaw.

SPELL CHECK
slay, sleigh

A large sled is a **sleigh**.

---

slay *verb* (**slays**; *past* **slew**; *past participle* **slain**; **slaying**) **1** *literary or jocular* kill: *slay a dragon*. **2** (*in passive*) murder; kill (a person) in a ruthless or violent manner: *the victim was slain in the parking lot*. **3** *slang* overwhelm with amusement: *this joke will slay you*. **4** *jocular* defeat or overthrow (esp. a person or institution characterized as evil).

slayer *noun* **1** *literary* a person who kills or has killed mythological creatures, monsters, dragons, etc. **2** *jocular* a nemesis or conqueror, esp. of a person, institution, or thing portrayed as being evil.

slaying *noun* **1** a murder: *a gangland slaying*. **2** the killing of a mythical monster: *dragon-slaying*.

SLE *abbreviation* systemic lupus erythematosus.

sleaze *noun* *informal* **1** sleazy material, conditions, or behaviour: *the city's growing reputation for sleaze*. **2** a person who behaves in a sleazy way.

sleazebag *noun* (also **sleazeball**) *slang* a sordid, despicable, or shady person.

sleaziness *noun* the fact or quality of being sleazy, esp. sexually immoral or promiscuous.

sleazy *adjective* (**sleazier**, **sleaziest**) **1** disreputable or corrupt. **2** sexually immoral or promiscuous **3** filthy, grimy; dilapidated. **4 a** (of clothes, materials, etc.) thin or flimsy. **b** (of clothing) sexually revealing.

sled • *noun* **1** a low vehicle mounted on runners for transport over snow or ice. **2** a similar but usu. smaller vehicle, or any of various devices made of moulded plastic, used esp. by children to coast down hills. **3** a snowmobile. **4** *Cdn* (*North*) a covered vehicle mounted on runners used to carry freight or crew as part of a cat train. • *verb* (**sleds**, **sledded**, **sledding**) **1** ride or race on a sled. **2** convey or carry by sled.

sledder *noun* a person who races or rides a sled or snowmobile.

sledding *noun* **1** the activity or action of racing or riding a sled or snowmobile. **2** progress in any sphere of action: *tough sledding*.

sled dog *noun* a dog trained to pull a sled, esp. as part of a team.

sledge[1] • *noun* a sled. • *verb* travel or convey by sledge.

sledge[2] *noun* a sledgehammer.

sledgehammer • *noun* **1** a large heavy hammer with a long handle used to break stone etc. **2** (as an *adjective*) heavy-handed, unwieldy, excessive: *a sledgehammer approach*. • *verb* hit or break with or as if with a sledgehammer.

sleek *adjective* **1 a** (of hair, fur, or skin) having a smooth and shiny appearance. **b** (of a person or animal) having a shiny coat or hair. **c** having a well-groomed and healthy appearance. **2** smooth and polished in manners and behaviour; suave. **3 a** streamlined, smooth, aerodynamic: *a sleek car*. **b** contemporary, stylish: *a sleek interior*. ▶ **sleekly** *adverb* **sleekness** *noun*

sleep • *noun* **1** the naturally recurring condition of rest and inactivity assumed by people and many animals. **2** a period of sleep: *I need a sleep*. **3** *euphemism* a state resembling sleep, esp. death. **4** a condition assumed by many plants, esp. at night, marked by the closing of petals or folding of leaves. **5** a gummy secretion found in the corners of the eyes after sleep. • *verb* (**sleeps**, **slept**, **sleeping**) **1** be or fall asleep. **2** (foll. by *with*, *together*) **a** have or share a sexual

encounter. **b** have or share a sexual relationship. **3** (foll. by *on*) postpone a decision on (a matter or question) until the next day. **4** provide sleeping accommodation for: *sleeps six*. **5** be inactive or dormant: *trouble never sleeps*. **6** (of a plant) have its flowers or leaves folded over in sleep. **7** *euphemism* be at peace in death. **PHRASES** **go to sleep 1** achieve a state of sleep. **2** (of a limb) become numb as a result of prolonged pressure. **let sleeping dogs lie** avoid stirring up trouble. **lose sleep over something** lie awake worrying about something. **put to sleep 1** kill (an animal) in a humane manner. **2** anaesthetize. **sleep around** *informal* be sexually promiscuous. **sleep in 1** remain asleep later than usual in the morning. **2** (esp. of domestic help) sleep on the premises where one is employed. **sleep like a log** (or **a baby** or **the dead**) sleep soundly. **the sleep of the just** sound sleep. **sleep out 1** sleep out of doors. **2** sleep away from the premises where one is employed. **sleep over** spend the night at another's house. **sleep through 1** (esp. of a baby) sleep uninterruptedly through a period of time, usu. the night. **2** fail to be woken by: *slept through my alarm*. **sleep tight!** sleep well.

sleeper *noun* **1** a person that sleeps, esp. in a specified way. **2** a thing that is produced or introduced with little attention, fanfare, or promotion, but which turns out to be successful or popular (also as an *adjective*: *the sleeper hit of the summer*). **3** a sleeping car. **4** a berth in the cab of a truck or the sleeping car of a train etc. **5** (usu. in *plural*) one-piece pyjamas for infants or children. **6** a strong usu. horizontal beam or timber used to support a wall or floorboards. **7** a couch or chair that turns into a bed. **8** a spy or saboteur etc. who remains inactive while establishing a secure position.

sleepily *adverb* in a sleepy or drowsy manner.

sleepiness *noun* a sleepy or tired feeling; drowsiness.

sleeping bag *noun* a warm lined or padded body-length bag, usu. zippered, designed for sleeping in esp. outdoors or when camping etc.

sleeping car *noun* a railway car provided with beds or berths for passengers to sleep in on overnight trips.

sleeping pill *noun* a sedative taken to induce sleep.

sleeping platform *noun* *Cdn* (*North*) the bench or ledge for sleeping left around the inside of an igloo.

sleeping sickness *noun* **1** a tropical African disease caused by protozoans, which are transmitted by tsetse flies and proliferate in the blood vessels, ultimately affecting the central nervous system and leading to lethargy and death. **2** an infectious encephalitis caused by a virus, with headache and drowsiness leading to coma.

sleepless *adjective* **1** without sleep: *many sleepless nights*. **2** unable to sleep. **3** continually active or moving. ▶ **sleeplessly** *adverb* **sleeplessness** *noun*

sleepover *noun* an occasion of spending the night away from home, esp. (of children) at a friend's house.

sleepwalk *verb* walk or perform other actions in one's sleep, as if one were awake. ▶ **sleepwalker** *noun*

sleepy *adjective* (**sleepier**, **sleepiest**) **1** drowsy. **2** given to sleep; lazy. **3** lacking activity or bustle: *a sleepy little town*. **4** suggestive of or conducive to sleep: *her soft sleepy voice*.

sleepyhead *noun* (esp. as a form of address) a sleepy or inattentive person.

sleet *noun* precipitation in the form of melting snow, freezing rain, or a mixture of these. ▶ **sleety** *adjective*

sleeve *noun* **1** the part of a shirt or jacket etc. that wholly or partly covers the arm. **2** the paper or cardboard envelope used to protect a record. **3** any tubular piece of plastic or metal etc. resembling a sleeve, used esp. to cover or protect a rod or shaft etc. of

S

a similar shape and size. PHRASES **roll up one's sleeves** prepare to fight or work. **up one's sleeve** concealed but ready for use; in reserve. ▶ **sleeved** *adjective* **sleeveless** *adjective*

sleigh • *noun* a sled, esp. a large one drawn by horses and used to convey passengers over snow and ice. • *verb* travel on a sleigh. [Say SLAY]

sleigh bell *noun* any of a number of small bells attached to a sleigh or to the harness of a horse drawing a sleigh.

sleight of hand *noun* **1** skilful movements of the hand that other people cannot see, esp. in performing a trick or magic. **2** a particular display of this, esp. a magic trick. **3** a cunning manoeuvre, scheme, or deception: *their financial statements were largely sleight of hand.* [Say SLITE]

slender *adjective* (**more slender, slenderest**) **1** (of a person, a person's body, etc.) gracefully thin: *a slender waist.* **2** of small girth or width in proportion to length or height: *a slender post.* **3** relatively small; meagre: *slender resources.* ▶ **slenderness** *noun*

slept past and past participle of SLEEP.

sleuth *informal* • *noun* a detective or investigator. • *verb* act as a detective; investigate, research: *they'd been together just over a year, but they'd had a hand in sleuthing several difficult cases.* [Say SLOOTH]

slew[1] *verb* **1** (often foll. by *around*) turn or swing around, esp. without moving from a position. **2** skid or slide uncontrollably. **3** turn or swing (a thing) around; send toppling or spinning.

slew[2] past of SLAY.

slew[3] *noun informal* (usu. foll. by *of*) a large number or quantity.

slew[4] = SLOUGH[1].

slice • *noun* **1** a thin broad piece or wedge cut off or out of an item of food. **2** a share; a part taken, allotted, or gained: *a slice of the profits.* **3 a** the flight of a ball that has been struck from underneath producing a spin that causes it to drift or curve forward and away from the person hitting it. **b** a swing or stroke producing such an effect. **c** a ball hit in this way. **4** a dessert that is cut into small squares for serving. **5** a cut or incision: *the blade left a deep slice in my hand.* • *verb* (**slices, sliced, slicing**) **1** cut into slices. **2** cut (a piece) off. **3 a** make a cut or incision with a knife or other sharp object. **b** penetrate or cut through as if with something sharp; move quickly and effortlessly through: *the boat sliced through the water.* **4 a** strike (the ball) so that it deviates away from the person hitting it or (in baseball) into the opposite field. **b** (of a ball) drift or deviate away from the hitter. PHRASES **slice of life** (also **slice-of-life** as an adjective) a movie, play, incident, etc. that offers a realistic representation of everyday life.

sliced *adjective* **1** cut cleanly into slices. **2** (of food) sold already cut into slices. PHRASES **the best** (or **greatest**) **thing since sliced bread** *informal* the most wonderful thing to happen, be discovered, etc., in a long time.

slicer *noun* an implement or instrument for slicing: *an electric meat slicer.*

slick • *adjective* **1 a** (of a person) clever, crafty. **b** (of an action) deftly or skilfully executed: *a slick performance.* **2 a** (of a person) superficially smooth or suave; flattering and insincere. **b** shallow in spite of its appearance; plausible but insincere. **3 a** smooth and glossy; sleek: *a slick photo.* **b** (often foll. by *with*) slippery: *the road was slick with ice.* • *noun* **1 a** a patch or stretch of oil or ice etc., esp. slippery. **b** floating on a body of water. **b** a smooth patch on the surface of a fast-moving body of water. **2** a smooth tire having little or no tread, used for

racing. **3** *slang* a slick person, esp. a cheat or swindler. • *verb informal* **1** (often foll. by *up*) smarten or tidy up; make sleek. **2** (usu. foll. by *back, down*) flatten (one's hair etc.).

slicker *noun* **1** a raincoat of oilskin, rubber, plastic, etc., usu. in a bright colour. **2** *informal* = CITY SLICKER.

slickly *adverb* in a slick manner: *a slickly produced magazine.*

slickness *noun* the quality of being slick.

slide • *verb* (**slides, slid, sliding**) **1** move along a smooth surface while maintaining continuous contact with it. **2** move smoothly, quickly or unobtrusively. **3** change gradually to a worse condition or lower level. **4** *Baseball* dive headfirst or throw one's body feet first across the field, esp. in order to reach a base or make a catch. • *noun* **1** a structure with a smooth sloping surface for children to slide down. **2** a move along a smooth surface while maintaining continuous contact with it. **3** a rectangular piece of glass on which an object is mounted or placed for examination under a microscope. **4** a mounted transparency, esp. one placed in a projector for viewing on screen. **5** *Baseball* an act of sliding to reach a base or make a catch. **6** a landslide or avalanche. **7** *Cdn* a track or slope prepared with snow or ice for tobogganing. **8** (also **timber slide**) *Cdn* an artificial sluiceway made to assist the passage of logs downstream past obstructions such as rapids or falls. PHRASES **let things slide** be negligent; allow deterioration.

slide projector *noun* a projector used to display photographic slides on a screen.

slider *noun* **1** a part or device that slides. **2** *Baseball* a fast pitch that breaks sharply over the plate in front of the batter, curving away from the direction in which it was thrown.

sliding scale *noun* a scale of fees, taxes, etc., that varies in accordance with variation of some standard.

SPELL CHECK
slight, sleight

Magicians perform tricks using "**sleight** of hand".

---

slight • *adjective* **1** small in quantity, degree, or importance. **2** slender: *slight of build.* **3** any whatever: *wasn't the slightest bit interested.* • *verb* treat or speak of (a person etc.) with disrespect or a lack of courtesy. • *noun* a marked display of disregard or disrespect. ▶ **slightingly** *adverb* **slightly** *adverb*

slim • *adjective* (**slimmer, slimmest**) **1** of small girth or thickness. **2** (of a person) of thin or slender build. **3** poor, meagre: *a slim chance* ◊ *slim pickings.* **4** (of clothing) cut on slender lines: *a slim skirt.* **5** reduced to an economical or efficient size, level, etc.: *a slim budget.* • *verb* (**slims, slimmed, slimming**) (often foll. by *down*) make or become slim or slimmer; reduce in size or extent.

slime • *noun* **1** thick slippery mud or any soft substance of a similar consistency, esp. when considered noxious or unpleasant. **2** a viscous mucous secretion exuded by fish, snails, slugs, etc. **3** *slang* = SLIMEBALL. • *verb* (**slimes, slimed, sliming**) cover with or as if with slime.

slimeball *noun slang* a filthy, corrupt, morally degenerate, or despicable person; a sleaze.

slime mould *noun* a slime-like aggregate of small simple organisms that reproduce by means of spores, found esp. in damp habitats on land.

sliminess *noun* the quality of being slimy. [Say SLIME ee ness]

slimline *adjective* of sleek and slender design.

slimness *noun* the quality of being slim.

slimy *adjective* (**slimier**, **slimiest**) **1** of the consistency of slime. **2** covered, smeared with, or full of slime. **3** disgustingly or offensively foul or dishonest. **4** slippery; hard to hold.

sling • *noun* **1** a strap, rope, etc., in the form of a loop, in which an object may be raised, lowered, or suspended. **2** a bandage looped around the neck to support an injured arm. **3** a simple weapon for throwing stones etc. consisting of a loop of leather or other material in which a stone is whirled and then released. **4** a rope or net used to raise and lower cargo, esp. to or from a ship. **5** a pouch or frame supported by a strap around the neck or shoulders for carrying a young child. **6** a drink consisting usu. of gin diluted with water or soda and lemon juice and usu. sweetened. • *verb* (**slings**, **slung**, **slinging**) **1** hurl or cast from, or as if from, a sling. **2** *informal* speak or utter (insults, criticism, etc.). **3** hang or allow to hang, esp. loosely or sloppily; carry: *a bag slung over her shoulder.* **4** hoist or transfer (cargo etc.) with a sling. PHRASES **sling beer** *slang* work as a bartender. **sling hash** (or **plates**) *slang* work as a chef or server in a restaurant.

slingback *noun* a woman's shoe with an open back held in place by a strap above the heel.

slinger *noun* **1** *informal* a person who serves food or drinks in a bar or restaurant. **2** a person who operates a sling to hoist cargo. **3** a person who uses or carries etc. a specified thing: *gunslinger.*

slingshot *noun* a Y-shaped frame supporting an elastic which can be used to launch a small rock or projectile.

slink *verb* (**slinks**, **slunk**, **slinking**) (often foll. by *off*, *away*, *by*) **1** move or sneak away inconspicuously as if ashamed, embarrassed, timid, or guilty. **2** walk or move in a provocative, seductive, or alluring manner.

slinkiness *noun* the quality of being slinky.

slinky *adjective* (**slinkier**, **slinkiest**) **1** moving in an alluring or seductive manner. **2** (of clothes) close-fitting and provocative.

slip • *verb* (**slips**, **slipped**, **slipping**) **1** lose one's balance or footing and slide unintentionally for a short distance. **2** accidentally slide or move out of position or from someone's grasp. **3** fail to grip or make proper contact with a surface. **4** pass gradually to a worse condition. **5** (usu. foll. by *up*) make a careless error. **6** move or place quietly, quickly, or stealthily. **7** escape or get loose from. **8** fail to be remembered by. **9** release (the clutch of a motor vehicle) slightly or for a moment. **10** *Knitting* move (a stitch) to the other needle without knitting it. • *noun* **1** an act of sliding unintentionally for a short distance: *a single slip could send them plummeting down the mountainside.* **2** an accidental or slight error. **3** an article of lingerie usu. made of a slippery material, extending from the shoulder or the waist to the hemline of a dress or skirt. **4** a space at a dock or between two piers where a boat may be kept. **5** a pillowcase. **6** a small piece of paper. **7** a long and narrow piece; a strip: *a slip of land.* **8** an esp. young person of a small or slender build: *a slip of a girl.* **9** a cutting taken from a plant for grafting or planting. **10** a mixture of clay and water used to attach decorations etc. to pottery or to coat ceramics. PHRASES **give a person the slip** escape from or evade a person. **let slip 1** accidentally utter or reveal or disclose (information, a secret, the truth, etc.). **2** allow (an opportunity) to pass without taking advantage of it. **let slip through one's fingers 1** drop; lose hold of. **2** miss the opportunity of having. **slip away** (or **off**) depart without leave-taking etc. **slip of the tongue** (or **pen**) a small mistake in which something is said (or written) unintentionally.

slipcase *noun* a close-fitting case for a book or set of books that allows the spine or spines to remain visible.

slipcover *noun* a removable cover for a chair, couch, etc. or for a furniture cushion.

slip-on • *adjective* (of shoes or clothes) that can be easily slipped on and off. • *noun* a shoe without laces or straps etc.

slippage *noun* **1** the action or process of something slipping or subsiding: *slippage of even 2 cm will be enough to break the seal.* **2** failure to meet a standard or deadline. **3** a falling off or decline: *there had been some slippage in support for the NDP.* [Say SLIP idge]

slipped disc *noun* a disc between vertebrae that has become displaced, causing pain because of pressure on the nerves of the spine.

slipper *noun* **1** a light loose comfortable shoe meant to be worn indoors. **2** a light, slip-on, heelless shoe for dancing etc. ▶ **slippered** *adjective*

slipperiness *noun* the quality of being slippery.

slippery *adjective* (**slipperier**, **slipperiest**) **1** difficult to hold firmly or to stand or move on because of smoothness, wetness, sliminess, or elusive motion. **2** (of a subject) requiring tactful handling. **3** (of a concept etc.) difficult to grasp or comprehend due to its complexity. **4** unreliable, unscrupulous, shifty.

slippery slope *noun* an irreversible course leading to disaster.

slippy *adjective* (**slippier**, **slippiest**) *informal* slippery.

slipshod *adjective* **1** careless, esp. in working or in handling ideas or words. **2** shabby, untidy.

slipstream *noun* **1** a current of air or water driven back by a revolving propeller or a moving vehicle. **2** an assisting force regarded as drawing something along with or behind something else: *for the Ontario Liberal Party, the slipstream behind Prime Minister Chrétien's refurbished popularity must seem a pretty inviting place.*

slip-up *noun* *informal* a mistake or blunder.

slipway *noun* a slip for building ships or landing boats.

slit • *noun* **1** a long straight narrow incision. **2** a long narrow opening comparable to a cut. • *verb* (**slits**, **slit**, **slitting**) **1** make a slit in. **2** cut into strips. PHRASES **slit one's eyes** squint.

slither • *verb* **1** slide or slip with an unsteady movement, esp. from side to side or in different directions. **2** move along in a way similar to this, esp. with the body close to the ground. **3** move or go stealthily; sneak. • *noun* a slithering movement. ▶ **slithery** *adjective*

slitty *adjective* (**slittier**, **slittiest**) usu. *derogatory* (of the eyes) long and narrow.

sliver • *noun* **1** a usu. long thin piece that has been split, broken, or sliced off a larger one. **2** a sharp fragment of wood, glass, metal, etc. **3** (foll. by *of*) a small amount: *a sliver of reality.* • *verb* (esp. as **slivered** *adjective*) cut or break up into slivers: *slivered almonds.*

slob *noun* **1** *informal* an untidy, lazy, or fat person. **2** (also **slob ice**) *Cdn* sludgy masses of densely packed sea ice.

slobber • *verb* **1** let saliva or food run from the mouth, esp. while eating. **2** (foll. by *over*) **a** be too attentive or over-affectionate toward a person. **b** be excessively sentimental or enthusiastic about a thing. • *noun* saliva running from the mouth. ▶ **slobbery** *adjective*

slobbish *adjective* (also **slobby**) behaving like or having the qualities of a slob.

sloe *noun* **1** the fruit of the blackthorn, a small blue-black berry with a sharp sour taste. **2** the blackthorn shrub. [Say SLOW]

slog • *verb* (**slogs**, **slogged**, **slogging**) **1** (often foll. by *away*, *on*) work hard or steadily at something. **2** walk or move steadily with great effort or toil. **3** hit hard.

S

• *noun* **1 a** hard, steady work or effort. **b** a period of this. **2** a long, tiring walk or march. **3** a vigorous blow. PHRASES **slog it out** fight or struggle until a conclusion is reached.

slogan *noun* a word or phrase that is easy to remember, used by a political party or in advertising etc. to attract people's attention or suggest an idea quickly.

sloganeer *noun* one who devises or uses slogans. ▶ **sloganeering** *noun* [Say slogan EER]

slo-mo *noun informal* = SLOW MOTION.

sloop *noun* a small, one-masted, fore-and-aft-rigged vessel with mainsail and jib.

slop • *verb* (**slops, slopped, slopping**) **1** (often foll. by *over*) **a** (of a liquid) run, flow, or spill over the edge of a container, vessel, etc. **b** splash or spill (a liquid etc.). **2** walk or wander through a wet or muddy place. • *noun* **1** unappetizing or poorly cooked food. **2** (in *singular* or *plural*) semi-liquid food for pigs, esp. the remains of food intended for people. **3** (in *plural*) liquid household waste matter, such as the contents of a chamber pot or dirty dishwater. **4** *informal* weakly sentimental language. PHRASES **slop about** move about in a slovenly manner.

slope • *noun* **1** a piece of rising or falling ground. **2** a place for skiing on the side of a hill or mountain. **3** an upward or downward inclination; an inclined position or direction. **4 a** a difference in level between the two ends or sides of a thing: *a slope of 5 metres.* **b** the rate at which this increases with distance etc. • *verb* (**slopes, sloped, sloping**) **1** lie obliquely, esp. downwards; have or follow a slope; slant. **2** place or arrange or make in a sloping position. PHRASES **hit the slopes** go skiing. ▶ **sloped** *adjective*

slo-pitch *noun* a modified form of baseball in which the batter has three chances to hit a softball that is lobbed by the pitcher and must land within a circle encompassing the plate.

sloppily *adverb* in a sloppy manner.

sloppiness *noun* the quality of being sloppy.

sloppy *adjective* (**sloppier, sloppiest**) **1** careless, slipshod. **2** splashed with liquid. **3** untidy. **4** (of the ground, sidewalk, etc.) wet with rain or slush. **5** (of clothes) loose; baggy. **6** (of a substance) in a semi-liquid state, having a muddy consistency. **7** (of a thought or comment etc.) overly sentimental or emotional.

sloppy joe *noun* a sandwich consisting of a thick filling made with ground beef and tomato or barbecue sauce served on a bun.

slosh *verb* (**sloshes, sloshed, sloshing**) **1** move with a splashing sound. **2** make liquid move in a noisy way; use liquid carelessly: *the children were sloshing water everywhere ◊ the water sloshed onto the floor.*

sloshed *adjective slang* drunk.

slot • *noun* **1** a slit, groove, channel, or long opening into which something fits. **2** a slit or other opening in a machine for a coin or credit card etc. to be inserted. **3 a** a position to be filled in a schedule, order, or timetable. **b** an allotted place in a broadcasting schedule. **4** *Hockey* an unmarked area in front of the net considered an excellent shooting position for an offensive player. **5** (as an *adjective*) designating a screwdriver with a straight flat blade used for inserting and removing slotted screws. **6** *informal* = SLOT MACHINE. **7** *Computing* (in full **expansion slot**) a place in a computer where a circuit board can be inserted to give the machine more capabilities. • *verb* (**slots, slotted, slotting**) **1** place or be placed into or as if into a slot. **2** provide with a slot or slots.

slotback *noun Football* **1** either of two offensive players lining up in the backfield between the offensive

linemen and wide receivers, usu. to catch short passes. **2** this position.

sloth *noun* **1** laziness; reluctance to make an effort. **2** a slow-moving nocturnal mammal of South America, which has long limbs and hooked claws for hanging upside down from branches of trees. [Rhymes with *CLOTH*]

slot machine *noun* a coin-operated gambling machine, activated by a lever, that produces random combinations of symbols which must match for the player to win.

slotted *adjective* **1** having a slot or slots. **2** (of a screw) having a narrow slot on the head so that it may be turned with a slot screwdriver.

slouch • *verb* (**slouches, slouched, slouching**) **1** stand or sit with the back, shoulders, and neck bent or drooping forwards. **2** walk or move with a shuffling gait and slouching posture. **3** bend one side of the brim of (a hat) downwards. **4** droop or hang down loosely. • *noun* **1** a slouching posture or movement; a stoop. **2** a downward bend of a hat brim. PHRASES **no slouch** *informal* a competent person or performer: *she's no slouch at golf.* ▶ **slouchy** *adjective* (**slouchier, slouchiest**)

slough[1] *noun* **1** an area of soft miry ground; a swamp or quagmire. **2** *Cdn (West)* & *US Northwest* a small marshy pool or lake produced by rain or melting snow flooding a depression in the soil. **3** *Cdn (BC)* a shallow inlet or estuary lined with grass. [Say SLOO; for senses 1 and 3 you can also rhyme *SLOUGH* with *HOW*]

slough[2] • *noun* **1** a part that an animal sheds, esp. a snake's skin. **2** a layer of dead tissue, such as a scab, that will fall away from the skin. • *verb* **1** (often foll. by *off*) shed, remove, or cast off (skin, tissue, etc.). **2** (often foll. by *off*) (of skin, tissue, etc.) come away; drop or fall off. **3** (of a snake etc.) cast off or shed the skin. **4** (foll. by *off*) get rid of or abandon something: *sloughed off his complaints.* [Say SLUFF]

Slovak • *noun* **1** (also **Slovakian**) an inhabitant of Slovakia, a country in central Europe. **2** the official language of Slovakia. • *adjective* (also **Slovakian**) of or relating to Slovakia or Slovakians. [Say SLOE vack]

sloven *noun* **1** a person who is habitually untidy or careless. **2** *Cdn (Maritimes & Nfld)* a long low wagon esp. drawn by horses. [Say SLOV in or SLUV in]

Slovene *noun* & *adjective* = SLOVENIAN. [Say SLOE veen]

Slovenian • *noun* **1** an inhabitant of Slovenia, a country in southeast Europe. **2** the official language of Slovenia. • *adjective* of or relating to Slovenia, its language, or people. [Say sluh VEENY in]

slovenliness *noun* the quality or state of being habitually untidy or careless. [Say SLOV in lee ness or SLUV in lee ness]

slovenly *adjective* **1** (of a person, the appearance, habits, etc.) careless, untidy, negligent. **2** (of an action etc.) characterized by a lack of care or precision; unmethodical. [Say SLOV in lee or SLUV in lee]

GRAMMAR CHECK
slow, slowly   ⚠

The use of **slow** as an adverb instead of **slowly** is standard in compounds such as *slow-acting, slow-burning*; it is also established in short imperative expressions such as *go slow.* In sentences such as *he drives too slow* and *go as slow as you can*, however, **slowly** would be preferable, especially in formal contexts.

---

slow • *adjective* **1** moving or capable of moving only at a low speed. **2** lasting or taking a long time. **3** (of a clock or watch) showing a time earlier than the correct time. **4** not quick to understand, think, or learn.

5 uneventful; showing little activity. **6** *Photography* (of a film) needing long exposure. **7** (of a fire or oven) burning or giving off heat gently. • *adverb* **1** at a slow pace; slowly. **2** (in *combination*): *slow-moving traffic*. • *verb* (usu. foll. by *down*, *up*) **1** reduce one's speed or the speed of (a vehicle etc.). **2** reduce one's pace of life. **3** become or cause to be slow: *business is slowing down*. PHRASES **slow but** (or **and**) **sure** (or **steady**) achieving the required result eventually.

slow burn *noun* slowly mounting intensity, esp. of anger or annoyance. ▸ **slow-burning** *adjective*

slow cooker *noun* a large electric pot used for cooking stews etc. very slowly.

slow dance • *verb* (**slow dances**, **slow danced**, **slow dancing**) dance to soft music in the embrace of a partner. • *noun* a dance to soft music in the embrace of a partner.

slowdown *noun* **1** the action of slowing down. **2** a form of industrial action in which employees deliberately work slowly.

slowly *adverb* at a slow speed; not quickly.

slow motion *noun* **1** the technique of making or playing a film or video recording so that actions and movements appear to be slower than in real life. **2** the simulation of this in real action; motion of slower speed than normal.

slowness *noun* the quality of being slow.

slow-pitch *noun* = SLO-PITCH.

slowpoke *noun* a slow or lazy person, driver, etc.

slow-release *adjective* designating a drug, fertilizer, etc. that releases a substance slowly or intermittently so as to maintain a steady concentration.

slow-witted *adjective* slow to understand, learn, etc.

sludge *noun* **1** thick greasy mud, mire, ooze, etc. **2** muddy or slimy sediment, as in the bed of a river etc. **3** the sediment that settles out of waste in a sewage or septic tank. **4** an accumulation of dirty oil, esp. formed as waste in any of various industrial and mechanical processes. **5** sea ice newly formed in small pieces. ▸ **sludgy** *adjective* (**sludgier**, **sludgiest**)

sluff *noun & verb* = SLOUGH².

slug¹ • *noun* **1 a** a small shell-less mollusc that is often destructive to plants. **b** *informal* a slow or lazy person or thing. **2 a** a bullet esp. of irregular shape. **b** a missile for an air gun. **3** a drink, esp. of liquor; a swig. **4** a thick piece or lump of something. **5** a small circular piece of metal used as a counterfeit coin, esp. in machines. • *verb* (**slugs**, **slugged**, **slugging**) **1** (usu. foll. by *around*, *along*) move slowly or sluggishly; trudge: *the dogs and I would slug along*. **2** drink (esp. alcohol) quickly: *she picked up her drink and slugged it back*.

slug² *informal* • *verb* (**slugs**, **slugged**, **slugging**) **1** strike with a hard blow. **2** *Baseball* hit (esp. a home run). • *noun* a hard blow. PHRASES **slug it out 1** fight it out. **2** stick it out.

slugfest *noun informal* **1** a violent or intense fight or quarrel. **2 a** a boxing match in which the boxers throw many punches. **b** a baseball game in which many runs are scored, esp. many home runs.

sluggard *noun* a lazy sluggish person.

slugger *noun* **1** a person who delivers heavy blows, esp. a boxer. **2** a baseball player noted for hitting powerful home runs.

sluggish *adjective* slow-moving; lacking energy: *feel sluggish*. ▸ **sluggishly** *adverb* **sluggishness** *noun*

sluice • *noun* **1** (also **sluice gate**) a sliding gate or other device for controlling the volume or flow of water. **2** (also **sluiceway**) a channel or waterway controlled by means of a sluice or sluices. **3** (also **sluice box**) an artificial water channel fitted with grooves esp. for washing ore. • *verb* (**sluices**, **sluiced**,

sluicing) **1** wash or rinse abundantly with a stream or shower of water: *she sluiced her face in cold water* ◊ *crews sluiced down the deck of the ship*. **2** (of water) pour, flow, or shower abundantly: *the waves sluiced over them* ◊ *rain was sluicing down*. [Rhymes with *JUICE*]

slum • *noun* **1** an overcrowded and squalid district etc., usu. in a city and inhabited by very poor people. **2** a house or building unfit for human habitation. • *verb* (**slums**, **slummed**, **slumming**) **1** put up with less comfortable conditions, associate with persons of a lower social class, or frequent venues of a lower status etc. than one is used to. **2** live in slum-like conditions.

slumber • *verb* **1** sleep, esp. in a specified manner. **2** be idle, drowsy, or inactive. • *noun* a sleep, esp. a specified kind: *fell into a fitful slumber*.

slumlord *noun* a landlord who rents slum property to tenants.

slummy *adjective* (**slummier**, **slummiest**) like a slum in its poverty and squalor: *a slummy part of town*.

slump • *noun* **1** a sudden severe or prolonged fall in prices or values of commodities or securities. **2** a sharp or sudden decline in trade or business usu. bringing widespread unemployment. **3** a reduction in performance; a state of lessened productivity etc.: *the team has been in a slump*. • *verb* **1** undergo a slump; fail; fall in price. **2** (often foll. by *back*, *down*) sit or fall heavily or limply: *slumped into a chair*. **3** lean or subside.

slumped *adjective* hunched or slouched.

slung *past and past participle of* SLING.

slunk *past and past participle of* SLINK.

slur • *verb* (**slurs**, **slurred**, **slurring**) **1** pronounce or write indistinctly so that the sounds or letters run into one another. **2** *Music* perform (a group of two or more notes) legato. **3** (usu. foll. by *over*) pass over (a fact, fault, etc.) lightly. • *noun* **1** an unfair remark about someone that is likely to damage others' opinion of them: *a slur on my reputation* ◊ *racial slurs*. **2** an act of speaking indistinctly so that sounds or words are run together, or a tendency to speak in such a way: *his speech was a drunken slur*. **3** *Music* a curved line to show that two or more notes are to be sung to one syllable or played or sung legato.

slurp • *verb* drink or eat noisily, esp. producing a sucking or lapping noise. • *noun* **1** the sound of this. **2** a slurping gulp. ▸ **slurpy** *adjective*

slurry *noun* (*plural* **slurries**) **1** a semi-liquid mixture, esp. of fine particles of manure, mud, etc., and water. **2** thin liquid cement.

slush *noun* (*plural* **slushes**) **1** partially melted snow or ice. **2** watery mud. **3** silly sentiment. **4** a confection consisting of flavoured slushy ice.

slush fund *noun* a sum of money kept for illegal purposes, especially in politics: *he is accused of receiving millions from a slush fund run by his campaign manager*.

slushy • *adjective* (**slushier**, **slushiest**) **1** like slush; watery. **2** *informal* sentimental. • *noun* (*plural* **slushies**) = SLUSH 4.

slut *noun derogatory* a promiscuous woman. ▸ **sluttish** *adjective*

sly *adjective* (**slyer**, **slyest**) **1** cunning; crafty; wily. **2 a** (of a person) practising secrecy or stealth. **b** (of an action etc.) done etc. in secret. **3** playfully mischievous; roguish: *he gave her a sly grin*. PHRASES **on the sly** covertly: *it had to be done on the sly, of course, so that her mother would not know*. ▸ **slyly** *adverb* **slyness** *noun*

Sm *symbol* samarium.

smack • *noun* **1** a sharp slap or blow esp. with the palm of the hand or a flat object. **2** a hard hit in baseball etc. **3** a loud kiss. **4** a loud sharp sound. **5** a noisy parting of the lips in eager anticipation or enjoyment. **6** a single-masted sailboat for coasting or

fishing. **7** *slang* a hard drug, esp. heroin. • *verb* **1** strike sharply, as with an open hand, a bat, etc. **2** part (one's lips) noisily in eager anticipation or enjoyment of food or another delight. **3** (foll. by *of*) **a** have a flavour of; taste of: *smacked of garlic.* **b** suggest the presence or effects of (usu. something undesirable): *it smacks of nepotism.* • *adverb informal* **1** with a smack. **2** suddenly; directly; violently: *landed smack on my desk.* **3** exactly: *smack in the centre.*

smacker *noun* (also **smackeroo**) *slang* **1** a loud kiss. **2** one dollar.

small • *adjective* **1** of less than normal or usual size. **2** not great in amount, number, strength, or power. **3** not fully grown or developed; young. **4** insignificant; unimportant. **5** (of a business or its owner) operating on a modest scale. **6** lower case. • *noun* **1** the slenderest part of something. **2** a garment or food portion that is small in comparison to other available sizes. • *adverb* into small pieces: *chop it small.* PHRASES **be small potatoes** be insignificant. **feel** (or **look**) **small** be humiliated; appear mean or humiliated. **in a small way** not ambitiously; on a small scale. **no small** considerable; a good deal of: *that's no small accomplishment in the current market.* **small-a** (or **b**, **c**, etc.) designating a common noun or general term rather than a proper name: *small-l liberal who voted NDP.*

small-bore *adjective* **1** (of a firearm) with a narrow bore. **2** *informal* petty, insignificant, small-time: *this election won't turn on small-bore items.*

small calorie *noun see* CALORIE 2.

small-cap *adjective* designating or pertaining to a company with a relatively small market capitalization (few assets): *small-cap stocks.*

small change *noun* **1** money in the form of coins as opposed to bills. **2** a relatively insignificant amount of money. **3** a trivial thing.

small claims court *noun* a general name given to a court with jurisdiction over civil claims involving relatively small amounts of money, with trials conducted by judges alone.

small fry *plural noun* **1** young children or the young of various species. **2** small or insignificant things or people.

small hours *plural noun* the early hours of the morning after midnight.

small intestine *noun* the long and narrow part of the intestine that food first passes into from the stomach.

smallish *adjective* somewhat small.

small-minded *adjective* petty; of rigid opinions or narrow outlook. ▶ **small-mindedness** *noun*

smallmouth *noun* (*plural* **smallmouth** or **smallmouths**) (also **smallmouth bass**, *plural* **smallmouth bass**) a North American freshwater bass with a small mouth.

smallness *noun* the state of being small.

small of the back *noun* the part of the back below the waist.

smallpox *noun* an acute contagious viral disease, with fever and pustules usu. leaving permanent scars.

small print *noun* **1** printed matter in small type. **2** = FINE PRINT.

small-scale *adjective* made or occurring in small amounts, to a lesser degree, on a small scale, etc.

small screen *noun informal* television.

small talk *noun* light social conversation.

small-time *adjective informal* unimportant or petty.

small-town *adjective* relating to or characteristic of a small town; unsophisticated.

smarm *verb informal* behave in a way that is too polite and not sincere: *he smarmed his way to the top.*

smarmy *adjective* (**smarmier**, **smarmiest**) *informal* polite in a way that is not sincere: *a smarmy, flattering reply* ◊ *smarmy waiters do not necessarily mean good service.*

smart • *adjective* **1 a** intelligent. **b** impudent: *don't be smart.* **c** quick to take advantage; shrewd: *a smart businesswoman.* **2** well-groomed; neat; bright and fresh in appearance: *a smart suit.* **3** in good repair; showing bright colours, new paint, etc.: *a smart red bicycle.* **4** stylish; fashionable; prominent in society: *a smart restaurant.* **5** quick; brisk: *a smart pace.* **6** painfully severe; sharp; vigorous: *a smart blow.* **7 a** (of a device) capable of independent and seemingly intelligent action. **b** (of a powered missile, bomb, etc.) guided to a target by an optical system. • *verb* **1** (of a person or a part of the body) feel or give acute pain or distress: *smarting from the insult.* **2** (of an insult, grievance, etc.) rankle; cause bad or bitter feelings. • *noun* **1** a bodily or mental sharp pain; a stinging sensation. **2** (in *plural*) intelligence, esp. of a specified kind: *street smarts.*

smart aleck *noun* (also **smart alec**) *informal* a person displaying impudent or smug cleverness. ▶ **smart-alecky** *adjective*

smartass *noun* (*plural* **smartasses**) *slang* = SMART ALECK. ▶ **smartass** *adjective* **smartassed** *adjective*

smart card *noun* a plastic card with a built-in microprocessor, esp. as a credit or other bank card for the instant transfer of funds etc.

smart cookie *noun informal* a smart or shrewd person.

smart drug *noun* a drug which supposedly improves memory and mental acuteness.

smarten *verb* (usu. foll. by *up*) make or become smart or smarter.

smartly *adverb* **1** in a neat, well-groomed, visually appealing manner: *dressed smartly.* **2** quickly, briskly: *turned around smartly and trotted back to the car.* **3** in a clever or cheeky manner.

smart-mouth *verb informal* give a cheeky retort to someone.

smartness *noun* **1** the quality of being intelligent. **2** the quality of being neat or well-groomed. **3** a cheeky cleverness.

smarty *noun* (*plural* **smarties**) (also **smarty-pants**, *plural* **smarty-pants**) *informal* a know-it-all.

smash • *verb* (**smashes**, **smashed**, **smashing**) **1** (often foll. by *up*) **a** break. **b** bring or come to sudden or complete destruction, defeat, or disaster. **2** (foll. by *into*, *through*) (of a vehicle etc.) move with great force and impact. **3** hit (a ball etc.) with great force: *smashed it back over the net.* • *noun* (*plural* **smashes**) **1** an act or the sound of something smashing: *the cup hit the floor with a smash.* **2** (also **smash hit**) a very successful movie, song, performer, etc. **3 a** a stroke in tennis, squash, etc., in which the ball is hit esp. downwards with great force. **b** *Baseball* a powerful hit. **4** a violent blow with a fist etc. **5** bankruptcy; a series of commercial failures.

smash-and-grab *noun* (*plural* **smash-and-grabs**) (usu. as an *adjective*) a robbery in which the thief smashes a window and seizes goods quickly.

smashed *adjective* **1** broken into pieces. **2** *slang* drunk.

smasher *noun* **1** a person or thing that smashes. **2** *informal* a very beautiful or pleasing person or thing.

smashing *adjective informal* superlative; excellent; wonderful; beautiful. ▶ **smashingly** *adverb*

smash-up *noun* a violent collision; a complete smash.

smattering *noun* **1** a slight superficial knowledge of a language or subject: *had only a smattering of Inuktitut.* **2** a small amount: *top with lots of salsa, a smattering of chopped avocado, and a drizzle of sour cream.*

smear • *verb* **1** daub or mark with a greasy or sticky substance or with something that stains. **2** blot; smudge; obscure the outline of (writing, artwork, etc.).

3 defame the character of; slander; attempt to or succeed in discrediting (a person or his or her name) publicly. • *noun* **1** *Medical* **a** material smeared on a microscopic slide etc. for examination. **b** a specimen of this. **c** a procedure involving the removal of material to be examined in this way: *Pap smear*. **2** a mark or streak of a greasy or sticky substance. **3** a false accusation intended to damage someone's reputation: *the candidates promised not to use smear tactics*.

smear campaign *noun* a planned effort to slander and so discredit a public figure.

smeary *adjective* covered in greasy or sticky streaks or marks.

smell • *noun* **1** the faculty of perceiving odours or scents: *has a fine sense of smell*. **2** the quality in substances that is perceived by this: *the smell of oranges*. **3** an unpleasant odour. **4** the act of inhaling to ascertain smell. **5** a trace or suggestion of something; the special character of something: *the smell of success*. • *verb* (**smells, smelled, smelling**) **1** perceive the smell of; examine by smell. **2** emit odour. **3** seem by smell to be: *this milk smells sour*. **4** (foll. by *of*) **a** be redolent of: *smells of fish*. **b** be suggestive of: *smells of dishonesty*. **5** stink. **6** perceive as if by smell; detect, discern, suspect: *smell a bargain*. **7** have or use a sense of smell. **8** (foll. by *around, about*) sniff or search about. **9** (foll. by *up*) fill or affect with an esp. offensive odour. PHRASES **smell blood** (of an attacker or aggressor) be encouraged by the discernment of another's vulnerability. **smell a rat** begin to suspect trickery etc. **smell the roses** enjoy or appreciate what is often ignored.

smelliness *noun* the quality of being smelly.

smelling salts *plural noun* ammonium carbonate, a chemical with a very strong smell used to revive a person who has lost consciousness.

smelly *adjective* (**smellier, smelliest**) having a strong or unpleasant smell.

smelt[1] *verb* extract metal from ore by melting.

smelt[2] *noun* (*plural* **smelt** or **smelts**) any of various small silvery carnivorous fish of coastal sea waters and fresh waters near the coasts of the northern hemisphere, including the caplin.

smelter *noun* **1** a person engaged in smelting. **2** a place where ores are smelted.

smelting *noun* an act of extracting metal from ore by melting.

smidgen *noun* (also **smidge**) *informal* a small bit or amount.

smile • *verb* (**smiles, smiled, smiling**) **1** relax the features into a pleased or kind or gently skeptical expression or a forced imitation of these, usu. with the corners of the mouth turned up. **2** (foll. by *on, upon*) adopt a favourable attitude towards; encourage: *fortune smiled on me*. • *noun* an act of smiling: *gave a pleased smile*. PHRASES **be all smiles** (of a person) look very cheerful and pleased, esp. in contrast to a previous mood: *she was all smiles when the airline strike was called off*.

smiley • *adjective* displaying a smile or characterized by smiling. • *noun* **1** = EMOTICON. **2** (also **smiley face**) a schematic drawing of a face with two dots for eyes and an upturned curve for a mouth, usu. enclosed in a circle.

smiling *adjective* that smiles. ▶ **smilingly** *adverb*

smirk • *noun* a conceited, smug, scornful, or silly smile. • *verb* put on or wear a smirk. ▶ **smirky** *adjective*

smite *verb* (**smites**; *past* **smote**; *past participle* **smitten**; **smiting**) strike or hit forcefully: *he sighed, smiting his brow with his hand*.

smith *noun* **1** a worker in metal: *goldsmith*. **2** a blacksmith.

smithereens *plural noun* small fragments: *smashed to smithereens*. [SMITHER rhymes with WITHER]

smithy *noun* (*plural* **smithies**) a blacksmith's workshop; a forge.

smitten • *verb past participle of* SMITE. • *adjective* **1** affected with or by something specified: *he was suddenly smitten with remorse*. **2** in love; infatuated: *from the moment she first saw him, she was completely smitten*.

smock • *noun* **1** a loose garment, esp. as worn by artists etc. to protect their clothes. **2** a loose shirt-like garment for women and girls, with the upper part closely gathered in smocking. • *verb* (usu. as **smocked** *adjective*) adorn with smocking.

smocking *noun* an ornamental effect on cloth made by gathering the material tightly into pleats, often with stitches in a honeycomb pattern.

smog *noun* fog intensified by atmospheric pollutants, esp. smoke. ▶ **smoggy** *adjective* (**smoggier, smoggiest**)

smokable *adjective* able to be smoked.

smoke • *noun* **1 a** a visible suspension of carbon etc. in air, emitted from a burning substance. **b** vapour etc. resembling smoke. **2** an act or period of smoking tobacco: *had a quiet smoke*. **3** *informal* a cigarette or cigar. **4** *Baseball informal* a very effective fastball; a pitcher's arsenal of unhittable fastballs: *throws smoke*. **5** a clouding or obscuring medium or influence, esp. false information intended as a distraction. **6** a colour like that of smoke, esp. a bluish or brownish grey. • *verb* (**smokes, smoked, smoking**) **1** emit smoke or visible vapour: *the ruins continued to smoke*. **2** inhale and exhale the smoke of a cigarette, cigar, etc. **3** cure or darken by the action of smoke: *smoked salmon*. **4 a** rid of insects etc. by the action of smoke. **b** subdue (insects, esp. bees) in this way. **5** *informal* **a** shoot with a firearm. **b** defeat overwhelmingly. **6** esp. *Sport* hit and propel (a ball etc.) with great speed and force; make (a powerful shot, stroke, hit, etc.). PHRASES **go up in smoke** *informal* **1** be destroyed by fire. **2** (of a plan etc.) come to nothing. **where there's smoke there's fire** rumours are not entirely baseless. **smoke out 1** drive out by means of smoke. **2** drive out of hiding or secrecy etc. **smoke up** *Cdn informal* smoke a drug, esp. marijuana.

smoke and mirrors *plural noun* a thing or things intended to deceive or confuse; deceit.

smoke detector *noun* a device which warns of the presence of smoke.

smoked meat *noun* **1** meat that has been cured by smoking. **2** *Cdn* (esp. *Que. & Ont.*) cured beef similar to pastrami but more heavily smoked.

smoke-free *adjective* **1** free from smoke. **2** where smoking is not permitted.

smokehouse *noun* a house or room for curing meat, fish, etc. by exposure to smoke.

smokeless *adjective* having or producing little or no smoke.

smoker *noun* **1** a person or thing that smokes, esp. a person who habitually smokes tobacco. **2** a small box used for smoking fish or other meat.

smokescreen *noun* **1** a cloud of smoke diffused to conceal (esp. military) operations. **2** a ruse for disguising one's activities: *she tried to create a smokescreen by quibbling about the statistics*.

smoke shop *noun* **1** a store selling tobacco products. **2** a convenience store.

smoke signal *noun* a column of smoke used as a signal.

smokestack *noun* **1** a tall chimney, esp. of a factory. **2** a chimney or funnel for discharging the smoke of a locomotive or steamer. **3** (as an *adjective*) designating

S

heavy industry, typically associated with high pollution levels and outmoded technology: *smokestack economy*.

smokey • *adjective* (**smokier, smokiest**) = SMOKY. • *noun* (*plural* **smokeys** or **smokies**) *slang* a police officer or car, esp. patrolling a highway.

smokie *noun Cdn* a sausage or hot dog.

smokiness *noun* the quality of being smoky.

smoking • *noun* the act or habit of inhaling and exhaling the smoke from a burning cigarette etc. • *adjective* that is giving off smoke: *smoking embers*.

smoking gun *noun* a piece of evidence that proves something beyond doubt: *even though science has not found a smoking gun, the theory is gaining attention*.

smoky *adjective* (**smokier, smokiest**) **1** emitting, veiled or filled with, or obscured by, smoke. **2 a** stained with smoke. **b** (of a colour etc.) resembling smoke; of a bluish-grey tinge: *smoky grey*. **3** having the taste or flavour of smoked food. **4** (of a voice) having the slightly hoarse overtones characteristic of a heavy smoker.

smolder *verb & noun* = SMOULDER.

smolt *noun* (*plural* **smolts** or **smolt**) a young salmon migrating to the sea for the first time.

smooch *informal* • *verb* (**smooches, smooched, smooching**) **1** kiss. **2** cuddle. • *noun* (*plural* **smooches**) a kiss. ▶ **smoocher** *noun* **smoochy** *adjective*

GRAMMAR CHECK
smooth, smoothly

The use of **smooth** as an adverb is usually restricted to set phrases such as *goes down smooth*. Outside of such expressions, the adverb **smoothly** is more standard: write *the engine runs **smoothly***, not *the engine runs **smooth***.

---

smooth • *adjective* **1** having an even and regular surface; free from projections or indentations. **2** (of a liquid) having an even consistency; without lumps. **3** (of movement) without jerks. **4** without problems or difficulties. **5** charming in a suave or excessively ingratiating way. **6** (of a flavour) without harshness or bitterness. • *verb* (**smooths, smoothed, smoothing**) **1** make or become smooth. **2** reduce or get rid of (differences, faults, difficulties, etc.) in fact or appearance. • *noun* the easy part of life: *take the rough with the smooth*. • *adverb* smoothly: *goes down smooth*.

smoothbore *noun* a gun with a barrel that has no spiral grooves to make a bullet spin, unlike a rifle.

smoothie *noun* (*plural* **smoothies**) *informal* **1** a person who is suave, conciliatory, flattering, unruffled, or polite. **2** (also **smoothy**) a thick smooth drink of fresh fruit puréed with milk, yogourt, or ice cream.

smoothly *adverb* **1** in an even way, without suddenly stopping and starting again: *traffic is now flowing smoothly*. **2** without problems or difficulties: *the interview went smoothly*. **3** in a calm or confident way. **4** in a way that produces a smooth surface or mixture: *a smoothly polished table*.

smooth muscle *noun* a muscle without striations, usu. occurring in hollow organs and performing involuntary functions.

smoothness *noun* the quality of being smooth.

smooth sailing *noun* easy progress.

smooth talk *informal* • *noun* charming or flattering language, esp. when used to persuade. • *verb* (**smooth-talk**) address or persuade with this. ▶ **smooth talker** *noun* **smooth-talking** *adjective*

s'more *noun* a dessert made of a graham cracker topped with melted chocolate and marshmallow.

smorgasbord *noun* **1** a buffet offering a wide variety of dishes. **2** a wide range of something: *the album is a smorgasbord of different musical styles*. [Say SMORE gus bord]

smote *past of* SMITE.

smother *verb* **1** suffocate. **2** overwhelm with (kisses, gifts, kindness, etc.): *smothered with affection*. **3** cover entirely in or with: *chicken smothered in mayonnaise*. **4** extinguish or deaden (a fire or flame) by covering it or heaping it with ashes etc. **5 a** suppress or conceal; prevent from developing. **b** repress or refrain from displaying (feeling etc.) by self-control. **c** make (words etc.) indistinct or inaudible. **6** *Hockey* immobilize (the puck) on the ice by falling on top of it, covering it with a glove, etc.

smoulder *verb* **1** burn slowly with smoke but without a flame; slowly burn internally or invisibly. **2** (of emotions etc.) exist in a suppressed or concealed state. **3** (of a person) show silent or suppressed anger, hatred, passion, etc. ▶ **smouldering** *adjective*

smudge • *noun* **1** a blurred or smeared line or mark. **2 a** (also **smudge fire**) an outdoor fire with dense smoke made to keep off insects, protect plants against frost, etc. **b** dense smoke as produced by such a fire. • *verb* (**smudges, smudged, smudging**) **1** make a smudge on. **2** become smeared or blurred: *smudges easily*. **3** smear or blur the lines of (writing, drawing, etc.): *smudge the outline*.

smudgy *adjective* (**smudgier, smudgiest**) **1** dirty with smeared lines or blots. **2** (of an image etc.) with indistinct edges; blurred.

smug *adjective* (**smugger, smuggest**) self-satisfied; complacent.

smuggle *verb* (**smuggles, smuggled, smuggling**) **1** move (goods) illegally into or out of a country. **2** convey secretly: *Maggie smuggled some cookies into her room*. ▶ **smuggler** *noun* **smuggling** *noun*

smugly *adverb* in a self-satisfied manner: *"I am very good at what I do," he said smugly*.

smugness *noun* the quality of being smug or self-satisfied.

smush *verb* (**smushes, smushed, smushing**) *informal* mash, crush, smash.

smut *noun* **1** stories, pictures, or comments about sex that deal with it in a way that some people find offensive: *he can entertain audiences without resorting to smut*. **2 a** a fungous disease of cereals in which parts of the ear change to black powder. **b** a fungus causing this. **3** a small flake of soot etc. **4** a spot or smudge made by this. ▶ **smutty** *adjective* (**smuttier, smuttiest**) (esp. in sense 1)

Sn *symbol* the element tin.

snack • *noun* **1** a light, casual, or hurried meal. **2** a small amount or item of food eaten between meals. • *verb* (often foll. by *on*) eat a snack.

snack bar *noun* a usu. small store, kiosk, counter, etc. where snacks are sold.

snacker *noun* a person who eats snacks.

snaffle • *noun* (also **snaffle bit**) (on a bridle) a simple bit without a curb and usu. with a single rein. • *verb* (**snaffles, snaffled, snaffling**) **1** put a snaffle on. **2** *informal* take (something) for oneself, esp. quickly or without permission.

snafu *noun slang* (*plural* **snafus**) **1** a confused, muddled, or messed-up condition or state. **2** a mistake or blunder. [Say sna FOO]

snag • *noun* **1** an unexpected or hidden obstacle, drawback, or problem. **2 a** a jagged or projecting point. **b** a standing dead tree; a broken stump or branch. **c** a tree trunk or branch embedded under water, forming an obstruction to navigation. **3** a tear or pull in material etc. • *verb* (**snags, snagged,**

snagging) 1 catch or tear on or as if on a snag. **2** catch, seize, or obtain, esp. by quick action: *snagged a passing waiter*. **3** clear (land, a waterway, a tree trunk, etc.) of snags.

snaggletooth *noun* (*plural* **snaggleteeth**) one in a set of jagged, irregular or projecting teeth.

snaggle-toothed *adjective* having irregular or projecting teeth.

snail *noun* a slow-moving mollusc with a spiral shell into which the whole body can be withdrawn.

snail mail *noun slang* **1** the ordinary postal system as opposed to the e-mail system. **2** items sent using this.

snail's pace *noun* a very slow movement.

snake • *noun* **1 a** a long reptile with no limbs or eyelids and with jaws that are capable of considerable extension, including boas and pythons and poisonous varieties, such as cobras and vipers. **b** a limbless lizard or amphibian. **2** (also **snake in the grass**) a treacherous person or secret enemy. **3** (in full **plumber's snake**) a long flexible wire for clearing obstacles in pipes, toilets, etc. • *verb* (**snakes, snaked, snaking**) **1** move or twist or cause to move or twist like a snake. **2** make (one's way) by snaking.

snakebite *noun* a wound or condition resulting from being bitten by an esp. poisonous snake.

snake fence *noun* (also **snake-rail fence**) *Cdn* a fence of stacked roughly-split logs laid in a zigzag pattern with ends overlapping at an angle.

snakehead *noun* a member of an organized crime ring smuggling emigrants illegally from China.

snakelike *adjective* resembling a snake in shape or movement.

snake oil *noun informal* **1** quack medicine: *sellers of snake oil evolved into the pharmacists we have today*. **2** a fraudulent product: *the array of so-called natural fertilizers can be bewildering, but some could be snake oil*. **3** nonsense: *the president's foreign policy is snake oil*.

snakeskin • *noun* the skin of a snake. • *adjective* made of or resembling snakeskin.

snaky *adjective* (also **snakey**) **1** of or like a snake. **2** winding; sinuous. **3** showing coldness, ingratitude, venom, or guile. **4** infested with or composed of snakes. PHRASES **go** (or **drive someone**) **snaky** *Cdn* lose (or cause to lose) self-control.

snap • *verb* (**snaps, snapped, snapping**) **1** break suddenly or with a snap. **2** emit or cause to emit a sudden sharp sound or crack. **3** open or close, turn off or on, etc. with a snapping sound: *the bag snapped shut*. **4** speak to or say irritably or spitefully. **5** (esp. of a dog etc.) make a sudden audible bite. **6** move quickly: *snapped into action* ◊ *snap to it*. **7** take a snapshot of. **8** *Football* put (the ball) into play on the ground by a quick backward movement. **9** bring an end to (an esp. undecided condition, state of affairs, etc.): *snapped their losing streak*. **10** lose one's composure suddenly after having resisted increasing tension or pressure. • *noun* **1** an act or sound of snapping. **2** *slang* an easy task: *it was a snap*. **3** a crisp biscuit or cake: *gingersnap*. **4** a snapshot. **5** (also **cold snap**) a sudden brief spell of cold weather. **6** a card game in which players call "snap" when two similar cards are exposed. **7** crispness of style; fresh vigour or liveliness in action. **8** *Football* an act of snapping the ball. • *adjective* done or taken on the spur of the moment, unexpectedly, or without notice: *snap decision*. PHRASES **in a snap** with no hesitation or difficulty. **snap at** accept (bait, a chance, etc.) eagerly. **snap off** break off or bite off. **snap one's fingers** suddenly release a finger which has been bent and checked by another finger or thumb, producing an audible snap as the finger strikes the hand. **snap out** utter forcefully. **snap out of** *informal*

get rid of (a mood, habit, etc.) by a sudden effort. **snap up 1** accept (an offer, a bargain) quickly or eagerly. **2** pick up or catch hastily.

snapdragon *noun* any of several popular garden plants with bag-shaped flowers.

snapper *noun* **1** a person or thing that snaps. **2** a marine fish that is typically reddish and is valued as food. **3** a voracious blue-coloured marine food fish, inhabiting warmer waters of the Atlantic and Indian oceans. **4** a snapping turtle.

snappily *adverb* **1** in a way that is appealing because it is zestful or concise or fashionable. **2** in a curt, ill-tempered way.

snapping turtle *noun* a large aggressive Central and North American freshwater turtle with a large head and long tail, which seizes prey with a snap of the jaws.

snappish *adjective* **1** (of a person's) manner or a remark) curt; ill-tempered. **2** (of a dog etc.) inclined to snap. ▶ **snappishly** *adverb* **snappishness** *noun*

snappy *adjective* (**snappier, snappiest**) *informal* **1** brisk, full of zest. **2** fashionable, up-to-date: *a snappy red convertible*. **3** snappish. PHRASES **make it snappy** be quick about it.

snapshot *noun* **1** a casual photograph taken quickly with a small camera. **2** a description or profile of a thing or of one stage of a process etc. **3** (**snap shot**) a quick shot on goal, esp. (*Hockey*) a shot taken by lifting the stick a short distance off the ice before striking the puck quickly with a hard flicking motion.

snare • *noun* **1** a trap for catching birds or animals, esp. with a noose of wire or cord. **2** a thing that acts as a temptation. **3** a device for tempting an enemy etc. to expose himself or herself to danger, failure, loss, capture, defeat, etc. **4** (in *singular* or *plural*) twisted strings of gut, hide, or wire stretched across the lower head of a drum to produce a rattling sound. **5** (also **snare drum**) a drum fitted with snares. • *verb* (**snares, snared, snaring**) **1** catch (a bird etc.) in a snare. **2** lure or trap (a person) with a snare. **3** grab: *snared the ball*.

snarky *adjective* (**snarkier, snarkiest**) *informal* irritable; short-tempered.

snarl • *verb* **1** (of a dog) make an angry growl with bared teeth. **2** (of a person) make bad-tempered complaints or criticisms. **3** utter or express by snarling. **4** twist; entangle; confuse and hamper the movement of (traffic etc.). **5** become entangled, congested, or confused. • *noun* **1** the act or sound of snarling. **2** a knot or tangle.

snarl-up *noun Cdn & Brit. informal* a traffic jam.

snarly *adjective* irritable, ill-tempered.

snatch • *verb* (**snatches, snatched, snatching**) **1** take or seize something quickly or roughly. **2 a** steal (a wallet, purse, etc.). **b** kidnap (esp. a child). **3** take or get something quickly, esp. when a chance to do so occurs: *snatched a bite to eat*. **4** take away or from esp. suddenly: *snatched away my hand*. **5** rescue narrowly: *snatched from the jaws of death*. **6** (foll. by *at*) **a** try to take something with the hands. **b** take (an offer, opportunity, etc.) eagerly. • *noun* (*plural* **snatches**) **1** an act of snatching: *made a snatch at it*. **2 a** fragment of a song or talk etc.: *caught a snatch of their conversation*. **3** *slang* a kidnapping. **4** (in weightlifting) a movement in which a barbell is raised rapidly from the floor to above the head, followed by a straightening of the knees. **5** a short period of doing something: *slept in snatches*. ▶ **snatcher** *noun* (esp. in sense 2b of *verb*)

snazzily *adverb slang* in a smart and fashionable way.

snazziness *noun slang* the quality of being smart and fashionable.

snazzy *adjective* (**snazzier, snazziest**) *slang* smart or fashionable.

sneak • *verb* (**sneaks**; *past* and *past participle* **snuck** or **sneaked**; **sneaking**) **1** go quietly and secretly. **2** *informal* take or do something secretly, often without permission: *snuck a chocolate from the box.* • *noun* a cowardly deceitful person, esp. one who informs on others. • *adjective* acting or done without warning; secret: *a sneak attack.* PHRASES **sneak up** approach a person or thing quietly and stealthily.

sneaker *noun* = RUNNING SHOE. ▶ **sneakered** *adjective*

sneakily *adverb* in a sneaky or furtive manner.

sneakiness *noun* the quality of being sneaky or furtive.

sneaking *adjective* **1** undisclosed: *have a sneaking affection for her.* **2** = SNEAKY 2.

sneak preview *noun* a special showing of a new film, exhibition, etc. before it is shown to the public.

sneaky *adjective* (**sneakier**, **sneakiest**) **1** behaving in a secret and sometimes dishonest or unpleasant way: *the federal government is being sneaky, and no one will realize what's going on until it's too late.* **2** persistent in one's mind; nagging: *a sneaky feeling.*

sneer • *noun* a contemptuous smile or remark. • *verb* **1** smile contemptuously. **2** say sneeringly. **3** speak contemptuously esp. covertly or ironically: *sneered at her attempts.* ▶ **sneering** *adjective* **sneeringly** *adverb*

sneeze • *noun* a sudden involuntary expulsion of air from the nose and mouth caused by irritation of the nostrils. • *verb* (**sneezes**, **sneezed**, **sneezing**) make a sneeze. PHRASES **not to be sneezed at** regarded as of considerable value or importance; not insignificant. ▶ **sneezy** *adjective*

Sne Nay Muxw • *noun* (*plural* **Sne Nay Muxw**) **1** a member of an Aboriginal people inhabiting lower Vancouver Island and the mainland north of Vancouver and around the Fraser River delta. **2** the Salishan language of this people. • *adjective* of this people. [Say snuh NYE mo]

snicker • *noun* **1** a half-suppressed secretive laugh. **2** a whinny, a neigh. • *verb* **1** make such a laugh. **2** whinny.

snide *adjective* (of a person, remark, etc.) sneering; slyly derogatory; insinuating. ▶ **snidely** *adverb*

sniff • *verb* **1** draw up air audibly through the nose. **2** clear one's nose by sniffing. **3** express disdain, contempt, etc. by sniffing. **4** smell by sniffing. **5** *informal* take (a drug etc.) by breathing it in through the nose. **6** perceive as if by smell; discover, suspect. **7 a** say (something) in a complaining way. **b** say (something) in a proud or disdainful way. • *noun* **1** an act or sound of sniffing. **2** the amount of air etc. sniffed up. **3** a hint or intimation: *left at the first sniff of danger.* PHRASES **sniff around** search around, esp. in an underhanded way. **sniff at 1** try the smell of; show interest in. **2** show contempt for or discontent with. **sniff out** detect; discover by investigation.

sniffer *noun* **1** a person who sniffs esp. a drug or toxic substance: *glue sniffer.* **2** *informal* the nose. **3** *informal* any device for detecting gas, radiation, etc. **4** a dog trained to detect drugs or track missing people by using its sense of smell.

sniffily *adverb* in a disdainful or contemptuous manner.

sniffle • *verb* (**sniffles**, **sniffled**, **sniffling**) sniff slightly or repeatedly, esp. as a result of weeping or a cold. • *noun* **1** the act of sniffling. **2** (in *singular* or *plural*) a cold in the head causing a running nose and sniffling. ▶ **sniffly** *adjective*

sniffy *adjective* *informal* disdainful; contemptuous.

snifter *noun* **1** a short-stemmed glass with a large bowl tapering towards the top, used for drinking brandy. **2** *slang* a small drink of alcohol.

snigger • *noun* = SNICKER *noun* 1. • *verb* = SNICKER *verb* 1.

snip • *verb* (**snips**, **snipped**, **snipping**) cut with scissors or shears, esp. in small quick strokes. • *noun* **1** an act of snipping. **2** a piece of material etc. snipped off. **3** (in *plural*) hand shears for metal cutting. **4** *informal* **a** an insignificant person. **b** an irritating or impertinent person. PHRASES **snip at** make snipping strokes at.

snipe • *noun* **1** (*plural* **snipe** or **snipes**) a wading bird of marshes and wet meadows, with brown plumage and a long straight bill. **2** (*plural* **snipes**) a sly or petty criticism: *made a snipe at her.* • *verb* (**snipes**, **sniped**, **sniping**) **1** fire shots from hiding usu. at long range. **2** (foll. by *at*) make a sly critical attack. ▶ **sniper** *noun* **sniping** *noun*

snippet *noun* a small fragment or bit.

snippily *adverb* in an impertinently brusque manner.

snippy *adjective* (**snippier**, **snippiest**) *informal* impertinently brusque.

snit *noun* a state of agitation, irritation, pique, etc.: *she's always in a snit.*

snitch • *verb* (**snitches**, **snitched**, **snitching**) *slang* **1** steal. **2** (often foll. by *on*) inform on a person. • *noun* (*plural* **snitches**) an informer.

snivel *verb* (**snivels**, **snivelled**, **snivelling**) **1** cry and sniff in a miserable way. **2** complain, esp. in a miserable, crying voice. **3 a** have a runny nose. **b** make a repeated sniffing sound. ▶ **sniveller** *noun* **snivelling** *adjective*

snob *noun* **1 a** a person with an exaggerated respect for social position or wealth. **b** a person who seeks to cultivate people considered socially superior. **2** a person who is condescending to others whose (usu. specified) tastes or attainments are considered inferior: *a wine snob.* ▶ **snobbery** *noun* (*plural* **snobberies**) **snobbish** *adjective* **snobbishly** *adverb* **snobbishness** *noun* **snobbism** *noun* **snobby** *adjective* (**snobbier**, **snobbiest**)

sno-cone = SNOW CONE.

snooker • *noun* **1** a game played with cues on a rectangular table in which the players use a cue ball to pocket the other balls in a set order. **2** a position in this game in which a direct shot at a permitted ball is impossible. • *verb* **1** subject (oneself or another player) to a snooker. **2** *slang* (usu. in *passive*) **a** defeat; thwart. **b** trick; dupe. [SNOOK rhymes with *LOOK* or *LUKE*]

snoop *informal* • *verb* look around a place secretly in order to find something, obtain information, etc. • *noun* **1** an act of snooping. **2 a** a person who snoops. **b** a detective. ▶ **snooper** *noun* **snoopy** *adjective*

snoot *noun* *slang* the nose.

snootily *adverb* in a snobbish, conceited, or contemptuous manner.

snootiness *noun* the quality of being snobbish.

snooty *adjective* (**snootier**, **snootiest**) *informal* snobbish; conceited; contemptuous.

snooze *informal* • *noun* **1** a short sleep, esp. in the daytime. **2** *informal* something boring or tedious: *that meeting was a real snooze!* **3** (as an *adjective*) designating a function, button, etc. on an alarm clock or clock radio which turns off the alarm or radio for a short, fixed period of time, and then reactivates it. • *verb* (**snoozes**, **snoozed**, **snoozing**) take a snooze.

snoozer *noun* **1** a person who snoozes. **2** *informal* something boring or tedious.

snore • *noun* a snorting or grunting sound in breathing during sleep. • *verb* (**snores, snored, snoring**) make this sound. ▶ **snorer** *noun*

snorkel • *noun* a breathing tube for an underwater swimmer. • *verb* (**snorkels, snorkelled, snorkelling**) use a snorkel. ▶ **snorkeller** *noun*

snort • *noun* **1** an explosive sound made by the sudden forcing of breath through the nose, esp. expressing indignation or disbelief. **2** a similar sound made by an engine etc. **3** *informal* a small drink of liquor. **4** *slang* an inhaled dose of a (usu. illegal) powdered drug. • *verb* **1** make a snort. **2** (of an engine etc.) make a sound resembling this. **3** *slang* inhale (a usu. illegal narcotic drug). ▶ **snorter** *noun*

snot *noun* *slang* **1** nasal mucus. **2** a contemptible person.

snot-nosed *adjective* *slang* **1** (of a person) snotty. **2** conceited.

snotty *adjective* (**snottier, snottiest**) *slang* **1** producing or covered with snot. **2** showing a superior attitude toward others. **3** contemptible.

snout *noun* **1** the projecting nose and mouth of an animal. **2** *derogatory* a person's nose. **3** the pointed front of a thing; a nozzle. ▶ **snouted** *adjective*

snow • *noun* **1** atmospheric vapour frozen into ice crystals and falling to earth in light white flakes. **2** a fall of this, or a layer of it on the ground. **3** a thing resembling snow in whiteness or texture etc. **4** a mass of flickering white spots on a television or radar screen, caused by interference or a poor signal. **5** *slang* cocaine. **6** a dessert or other dish resembling snow. **7** frozen carbon dioxide. • *verb* **1** (of snow) fall. **2** (foll. by *in, over, up,* etc.) confine or block with large quantities of snow. **3** sprinkle or scatter or fall as or like snow. **4** *slang* deceive or charm with plausible words. PHRASES **be snowed under** be overwhelmed, esp. with work.

snow angel *noun* the outline of an angel made by a person lying on his or her back in the snow and moving the arms and legs.

snowball • *noun* **1** snow packed together or rolled into a ball, esp. for throwing. **2** any of various plants, esp. of the honeysuckle family, bearing rounded clusters of white flowers. • *verb* grow or increase rapidly: *the idea snowballed from there.* PHRASES **not a snowball's chance in hell** *informal* no chance at all.

snowbank *noun* a heap or mound of snow, esp. one caused by plowing or drifting.

snowbelt *noun* a region subject to heavy snowfalls.

snowbird *noun* **1** *informal* a person from Canada or the northern US who moves to a southern state in the winter. **2** any of various small birds resembling the finch, esp. the snow bunting or junco.

snow-blind *adjective* temporarily blinded by the glare of light reflected by large expanses of snow. ▶ **snow blindness** *noun*

snow blower *noun* a machine that clears snow by blowing it to one side.

snowboard *noun* a wide board like a ski, ridden in a standing position, used for sliding downhill on snow. ▶ **snowboarder** *noun* **snowboarding** *noun*

snowbound *adjective* prevented by snow from going out or travelling.

snow bunting *noun* a mainly white finch, which breeds in the Arctic and migrates further south in autumn.

snowcap *noun* the tip of a mountain when covered with snow. ▶ **snow-capped** *adjective*

snow cone *noun* a paper cone filled with crushed ice flavoured with fruit syrup.

snow crab *noun* an edible spider crab found off the eastern coast of Canada.

snowdrift *noun* a bank of snow heaped up by the wind.

snowdrop *noun* a bulbous plant with white drooping flowers in the early spring.

snowfall *noun* **1** a fall of snow. **2** the amount of snow that falls on one occasion or on a given area within a given time.

snow fence *noun* a usu. portable fence erected on the windward side of a road, building, etc., serving as a barrier to drifting snow. ▶ **snow fencing** *noun*

snowfield *noun* a permanent wide expanse of snow in mountainous or polar regions.

snowflake *noun* each of the small collections of crystals in which snow falls.

snow goggles *plural noun* (also **snow glasses**) slotted goggles of wood, bone, etc., worn as a protection against snow blindness.

snow goose *noun* (*plural* **snow geese**) a white Arctic goose with black-tipped wings.

snow job *noun* an attempt to deceive or persuade (a person), esp. through flattery.

snow leopard *noun* a large rare Asian cat with leopard-like markings on a cream coat.

snow line *noun* the level, e.g. on a mountain, above which snow never melts entirely.

snow machine *noun* a motor vehicle designed to travel over snow.

snow-making *noun* the production of artificial snow.

snowman *noun* (*plural* **snowmen**) a figure resembling a person, made of packed snow.

snowmelt *noun* **1** the melting of fallen snow, esp. in the spring. **2** the water that results from this.

snowmobile *noun* a motor vehicle equipped with runners and Caterpillar tracks for travelling over snow. ▶ **snowmobiler** *noun*

snowmobile suit *noun* a one-piece winter outer garment combining both coat and pants.

snowmobiling *noun* the act of riding a snowmobile.

snowpack *noun* the accumulation of winter snow, compressed and hardened by its own weight.

snow pea *noun* a variety of pea eaten whole including the pod.

snowplow (also **snowplough**) • *noun* **1** a device, or a vehicle equipped with one, for clearing roads etc. of snow by pushing it to one side. **2** *Skiing* a technique for slowing down or stopping in which the points of the skis are turned inwards. • *verb* **1** clear (a road etc.) of snow using a snowplow. **2** *Skiing* execute a snowplow.

snow route *noun* a major arterial road in a city which is designated for priority snow clearing.

snowshoe • *noun* a flat device like a racquet attached to a boot for walking on snow without sinking in. • *verb* (**snowshoes, snowshoed, snowshoeing**) travel on snowshoes.

snowshoe hare *noun* (also **snowshoe rabbit**) a North American hare with large hind feet and a white coat in winter.

snowshoer *noun* a person who travels on snowshoes.

snowstorm *noun* a heavy fall of snow, esp. with a high wind.

snowsuit *noun* a one- or two-piece winter outer garment combining both coat and pants.

snow tire *noun* a tire equipped with deep treads etc. to give increased traction on snow or ice.

snow-white *adjective* pure white.

snowy *adjective* (**snowier, snowiest**) **1 a** of or like snow. **b** pure white. **2** (of the weather etc.) with much snow. **3** covered with snow: *snowy fields*.

snowy owl *noun* a large white owl, native to the Arctic.

snub • *verb* (**snubs, snubbed, snubbing**) rebuff or humiliate with sharp words or a marked lack of cordiality. • *noun* an act of snubbing; a rebuff. • *adjective* short and blunt in shape.

snub nose *noun* a short turned-up nose. ▶ **snub-nosed** *adjective*

snuck *past and past participle of* SNEAK.

snuff • *noun* **1** the charred part of a candle wick. **2** powdered tobacco taken by sniffing it up the nostrils. • *verb* **1** smother the flame of (a candle). **2** trim the snuff from (a candle). **3** *slang* kill (a person). PHRASES **snuff out 1** extinguish by snuffing. **2** kill; put an end to. **up to snuff** *informal* up to standard.

snuffer *noun* **1** a small hollow cone with a handle used to extinguish a candle. **2** (in *plural*) an implement like scissors used to extinguish a candle or trim its wick.

snuffle • *verb* (**snuffles, snuffled, snuffling**) **1** make sniffing sounds. **2** speak or say nasally, whiningly, or like one with a cold. **3** breathe noisily as through a partially blocked nose. **4** sniff. • *noun* **1** a snuffling sound or tone. **2** (in *plural*) a partial blockage of the nose causing snuffling. **3** a sniff. ▶ **snuffly** *adjective*

snug • *adjective* (**snugger, snuggest**) **1** comfortably warm and cozy. **2** secure and sheltered: *a snug harbour*. **3** compact and well-organized. **4** (of clothing etc.) close-fitting. **5** fitting exactly: *make sure that the nuts are snug but not too tight*. **6** (of an income etc.) allowing comfort and comparative ease. • *verb* (**snugs, snugged, snugging**) make snug.

snuggle *verb* (**snuggles, snuggled, snuggling**) **1** (often foll. by *up, down*, etc.) lie or get close to a person or thing for warmth, comfort, or affection. **2** place something into a warm comfortable position.

snuggly *adjective* (**snugglier, snuggliest**) comfortably warm, cozy: *a snuggly blanket*. [Say SNUGGLE ee]

Snugli *noun* proprietary a pouch for carrying a baby.

> **SPELL CHECK** ABC✓
> **snuggly, snugly**
>
> Something cozy, soft, or comfortably warm is **snuggly**. Something that fits in a snug manner fits **snugly**: *it fits snugly in the box*.

snugly *adverb* in a snug manner; securely; comfortably: *it fits snugly in the box*.

snye *noun* Cdn **1** (*E Ont.*) a side channel, esp. one that bypasses a falls or rapids and rejoins the main river downstream, creating an island. **2** a narrow or meandering side channel, esp. one that comes to a dead end.

> **WRITING TIP**
> **SO**
>
> The use of **so** to mean "very" or "extremely", as in *It's so cold today*, is considered informal. In formal writing, whenever you have an adjective after **so** (e.g. *so severe*), there should eventually be a **that** as well, as in *The following winter was so severe on the prairie that many starved before spring*.

so[1] • *adverb* **1** to such a great extent. **2** extremely; very much. **3** to the same extent. **4** referring back to something previously mentioned. **5** similarly. **6** in the way described or demonstrated; thus. • *conjunction* **1** and for this reason; therefore. **2** (foll. by *that*) with the result or aim that. **3** and then. **4** introducing a question or concluding statement. **5** in the same way; correspondingly. • *pronoun* **1** something that is near to the number in question: *only six or so*. **2** used as a substitute for a clause or sentence: *you'll do it because I*

said so. PHRASES **and so on** (also **and so forth**) **1** and others of the same kind. **2** and in other similar ways. **so as** in order to: *so as to get it finished*. **so be it** an expression of acceptance or resignation. **so long!** *informal* goodbye till we meet again. **so much 1** a certain amount (of). **2** a great deal of: *is so much nonsense*. **3** (with *neg.*) **a** less than; to a lesser extent: *not so much forgotten as ignored*. **b** not even: *didn't give me so much as a penny*. **so much for** that is all that need be done or said about. **so to speak** (or **say**) an expression of reserve or apology for an exaggeration or neologism etc. **so what?** *informal* why should that be considered significant?

so[2] *noun* Music **1** (in tonic sol-fa) the fifth note of a major scale. **2** the note G in the fixed-do system.

soak • *verb* **1** make or become thoroughly wet. **2** (of rain etc.) drench. **3 soak oneself in** immerse oneself in (a subject of study etc.). **4** (foll. by *in, into, through*) **a** (of liquid) make its way or penetrate by saturation. **b** (of sunlight) penetrate thoroughly. **5** remove by soaking in water etc.: *soaked the label off the jar*. **6** *informal* extract money from by an extortionate charge, taxation, etc.: *soak the rich*. **7** *informal* drink persistently, booze. • *noun* **1** the act of soaking or the state of being soaked. **2** *informal* a hard drinker. PHRASES **soak up 1** absorb (liquid). **2** acquire (knowledge, experiences, etc.) copiously. **3** expose oneself to (the sun, heat, etc.) so as to absorb the maximum possible.

soaked *adjective* **1** thoroughly wet. **2** very drunk.

soaker *noun* a thing that soaks, esp. a hose with small holes along its length, used in gardening, or a heavy downpour of rain.

soaking • *adjective* (also **soaking wet**) very wet; wet through. • *noun* an act of wetting something thoroughly: *give the soil a good soaking*.

so-and-so *noun* (*plural* **so-and-sos**) **1** a particular person or thing not needing to be specified: *told me to do so-and-so*. **2** *informal* a person disliked or regarded with disfavour: *the so-and-so left me behind*.

soap • *noun* **1** a cleansing agent that is a compound of fatty acid with soda or potash which, when rubbed in water, yields a lather used in washing. **2** *informal* = SOAP OPERA (also as an *adjective*: *soap fan*). • *verb* **1** apply soap to. **2** scrub or rub with soap.

soapberry *noun* (*plural* **soapberries**) **1** = BUFFALO BERRY. **2** any of various tropical American shrubs with fruits yielding a substance that foams when shaken with water.

soapbox *noun* (*plural* **soapboxes**) **1** a makeshift stand for a public speaker. **2** something that provides an outlet for a person's opinions etc.: *her column is nothing but a soapbox*. **3** a child's homemade cart consisting of a wooden box mounted on wheels, and steerable at the front.

soap opera *noun* a television drama, esp. one broadcast every weekday, with continuous episodes about the events and problems in the daily lives of the same group of characters.

soapstone *noun* a soft metamorphic rock with a smooth greasy feel, readily sawn into slabs or carved.

soapsuds *plural noun* = SUDS 1.

soapy *adjective* (**soapier, soapiest**) **1** of or like soap. **2** containing or smeared with soap. **3** of or like a soap opera.

> **SPELL CHECK** ABC✓
> **soar, sore**
>
> Someone in pain or angry is **sore**.

soar *verb* **1** fly or rise high. **2** reach a high level or standard: *prices soared*. **3** maintain height in the air

without flapping the wings or using power. **4** sing or play esp. in the higher ranges in a particularly impressive or moving manner. ▶ **soaring** *adjective*

sob • *verb* (**sobs, sobbed, sobbing**) **1 a** draw breath in convulsive gasps usu. with weeping under mental distress or physical exhaustion. **b** weep in this way. **2** (usu. foll. by *out*) utter with sobs. • *noun* a convulsive drawing of breath, esp. in weeping.

soba *noun* (treated as *singular* or *plural*) Japanese noodles made from buckwheat flour. [Say SO buh]

sober • *adjective* (**soberer, soberest**) **1** not affected by alcohol. **2** not given to excessive drinking of alcohol. **3** moderate, well-balanced, tranquil, sedate. **4** not fanciful or exaggerated: *the sober truth*. **5** (of a colour etc.) quiet and inconspicuous. • *verb* (often foll. by *down*, *up*) make or become sober or less wild, reckless, enthusiastic, visionary, etc.: *a sobering thought*. PHRASES **sober as a judge** completely sober. ▶ **soberly** *adverb*

sober-sided *adjective* sedate, serious.

sober sides *noun* a sedate, serious person.

sobriety *noun* **1** the state of being sober. **2** moderation, esp. in the use of alcohol. **3** seriousness. [Say suh BRYE a tee]

sobriquet *noun* **1** a nickname. **2** an assumed name. [Say SO brick ay]

sob story *noun* (*plural* **sob stories**) *informal* a story or explanation intended to make the listener or reader feel sympathy or sadness, esp. one that fails to do so.

soc *noun informal* sociology. [Say SOASH]

soca *noun* a kind of calypso music with elements of soul, originally from Trinidad. [Say SO kuh]

so-called *adjective* commonly designated or known as, often incorrectly.

soccer *noun* a form of football played by two teams of 11, in which a round ball may be kicked or bounced off any part of the body except the arms and hands.

sociability *noun* the quality of being sociable; friendly disposition. [Say so shuh BILLA tee]

sociable *adjective* **1** fitted for or liking the society of other people; ready and willing to talk and act with others. **2** (of a person's manner or behaviour etc.) friendly. **3** (of a meeting etc.) marked by friendliness, not stiff or formal. ▶ **sociably** *adverb* [Say SO shuh bull]

social • *adjective* **1** of or relating to society or its organization. **2** concerned with the mutual relations of human beings or classes of human beings. **3** living in organized communities; not fitted for a solitary life: *humans are social animals*. **4** indicating activities in which people meet each other for pleasure: *social club ◊ social life*. **5 a** (of insects) living together in organized communities. **b** (of birds) nesting near each other in communities. **6** (of plants) growing thickly together and monopolizing the ground they grow on. • *noun* **1** a social gathering, esp. one organized by a club etc. **2** *Cdn* (*Prairies*) a public social gathering held before a wedding to raise money for the couple that is to be married.

social assistance *noun Cdn* = SOCIAL SECURITY.

social climber *noun derogatory* a person anxious to gain a higher social status. ▶ **social climbing** *noun* **social-climbing** *adjective*

social conscience *noun* a sense of responsibility or concern for the problems and injustices of society.

social contract *noun* (also **social compact**) an unspoken understanding among the members of a society (and between them and the state) that co-operation produces social benefits, e.g. sacrificing some individual freedoms for state protection.

social credit • *noun* **1** the economic theory that the purchasing power of consumers should be increased either by subsidizing producers so that they can reduce prices or by distributing the profits of industry to the general public. **2** (**Social Credit**) *Cdn* the Social Credit party, its supporters, etc. • *adjective* (**Social Credit**) *Cdn* of or relating to the Social Credit Party.

Social Crediter *noun Cdn* a member of the Social Credit Party.

Social Credit Party *noun Cdn* a political party formed in the 1930s espousing the economic theories of social credit, but soon evolving into a mainstream party with conservative financial and social policies.

social Darwinism *noun* a late 19th-century theory that individuals, groups, and peoples are subject to the same laws of natural selection as plants and animals, and that superior individuals or groups survived and succeeded while the weaker disappeared, to the benefit of society. ▶ **social Darwinist** *noun*

social democracy *noun* (*plural* **social democracies**) a socialist system achieved by democratic means. ▶ **social democrat** *noun*

social engineering *noun* the attempt to change society and to deal with social problems according to particular political beliefs, e.g. by changing laws: *some saw the government's enforced relocation of Aboriginal communities as a badly planned attempt at social engineering, while Ottawa saw it as a necessary step in the modernization of northern Aboriginal communities*.

social gospel *noun hist.* the gospel interpreted as having a social application, esp. as used to advocate social reform. ▶ **social gospeller** *noun*

social housing *noun Cdn & Brit.* = PUBLIC HOUSING.

social insurance number *noun Cdn* a nine-digit number by which the federal government identifies individuals for the purposes of taxation, employment insurance, pensions, etc. Abbreviation: **SIN**.

socialism *noun* **1** a political and economic theory of social organization which advocates that the community as a whole, and not private capitalists, should own and control the raw materials and tools used in producing goods and the means of selling them. **2** policy or practice based on this theory. **3** (in Marxist theory) a transitional social state between the overthrow of capitalism and the realization of communism. ▶ **socialist** *noun & adjective* **socialistic** *adjective*

socialite *noun* a person who is well-known in fashionable society and goes to a lot of fashionable parties. [Say SOCIAL ite]

socialization *noun* the process by which somebody, esp. a child, learns to behave in a way that is acceptable in their society.

socialize *verb* (**socializes, socialized, socializing**) **1** act in a sociable manner: *she didn't mind socializing with her staff*. **2** make (someone) behave in a way that is acceptable to their society: *nurses who were socialized in cultural settings where stoicism and a "stiff upper lip" are regarded as the intelligent response to illness*. **3** organize on socialistic principles: *argued for the need for a planned, socialized economic order*.

social justice *noun* the notion that society should be organized in a way that allows everyone equal opportunity for all its members: *social justice issues*.

social life *noun* leisure activities in which one associates with one's friends and acquaintances.

socially *adverb* **1** regarding one's position in society: *a socially disadvantaged family*. **2** having to do with society: *it's not socially acceptable*. **3** together in a society: *those birds live socially*. **4** as friends in social occasions: *we meet at work, but never socially*.

social order *noun* the network of human relationships in society.

social realism *noun* the realistic depiction of social

conditions or political views in art and literature. ▶ **social realist** *noun*

social science *noun* **1** the scientific study of human society and social relationships. **2** a branch of this (e.g. politics or economics). ▶ **social scientist** *noun*

social security *noun* state assistance to those lacking in economic security and welfare, e.g. the aged.

social service *noun* (usu. in *plural*) a service provided by the state or a charitable organization for the community, esp. education, health, and housing: *social service agency*.

social studies *plural noun* (treated as *singular*) a school course encompassing such subjects as geography, history, anthropology, sociology, etc.

social work *noun* work done to help people in the community with special needs. ▶ **social worker** *noun*

societal *adjective* having to do with society and the way it is organized: *societal structure*. [Say suh SIGH a tull]

society *noun* (*plural* **societies**) **1** the sum of human conditions and activity regarded as a whole functioning interdependently. **2** a social community: *all societies must have firm laws*. **3 a** a social mode of life. **b** the customs and organization of an ordered community. **4** *Ecology* a plant community. **5 a** the socially advantaged or prominent members of a community. **b** this, or a part of it, qualified in some way: *in polite society*. **6** participation in hospitality; other people's homes or company: *avoids society*. **7** companionship, company: *avoids the society of such people*. **8** an association of persons united by a common aim or interest or principle: *music society*.

Society of Friends *noun* a movement of Christians (called **Quakers**) devoted to peaceful principles and rejecting formal doctrine.

Society of Jesus *noun* a Catholic order of priests (also called **Jesuits**) founded in 1534 to do missionary work. The order was zealous in opposing the Protestant Reformation and has retained an important influence in Catholic thought and education.

socio- *combining form* **1** of society (and). **2** of or relating to sociology (and). [Say SO see oh or SO shee oh]

socio-cultural *adjective* combining social and cultural factors or elements. ▶ **socio-culturally** *adverb*

socio-economic *adjective* relating to or concerned with the interaction of social and economic factors. ▶ **socio-economically** *adverb*

sociolinguistic *adjective* having to do with the study of language in relation to social factors.

sociolinguistics *noun* the study of language in relation to social factors.

sociological *adjective* having to do with the development, structure, functioning, and problems of human society. ▶ **sociologically** *adverb* [Say so see a LOGICAL or so shee a LOGICAL]

sociologist *noun* a person who studies the development, structure, functioning, and problems of human society. [Say so see OLLA jist or so shee OLLA jist]

sociology *noun* **1** the study of the development, structure, and functioning of human society. **2** the study of social problems. [Say SO so see OLLA jee or so shee OLLA je]

sociopath *noun* a person with a personality disorder manifesting itself in extreme anti-social attitudes and behaviour, particularly a lack of moral responsibility or social conscience. ▶ **sociopathic** *adjective* [Say SO see oh path, so see oh PATH ick]

socio-political *adjective* combining social and political factors. [Say so see oh POLITICAL]

sock[1] *noun* **1** a short knitted covering for the foot, usu. not reaching the knee. **2** a removable inner sole put into a shoe for warmth etc. **3** = WINDSOCK. PHRASES **in one's sock feet** = IN ONE'S STOCKING FEET (*see* STOCKING).

knock (or **blow**) **one's socks off** astound, amaze. **pull up one's socks** *informal* make an effort to improve. **put a sock in it** *informal* be quiet.

sock[2] *informal* ● *verb* hit (esp. a person) forcefully. ● *noun* **1** a hard blow. **2** the power to deliver a blow. PHRASES **sock it to** attack or address (a person) vigorously.

socked in *adjective* (of an airport or aircraft) not operating because of snow, fog, etc.

socket *noun* **1** a natural or artificial hollow for something to fit into or stand firm or revolve in. **2** a device receiving a plug, light bulb, etc., to make an electrical connection.

sockeye *noun* (*plural* **sockeye**) a blue-backed salmon of the North American Pacific coast.

sock hop *noun* a social dance at which participants dance in their stocking feet.

Socratic ● *adjective* of or relating to the Greek philosopher Socrates (469–399 BC) or his philosophy, esp. the method associated with him of seeking the truth by a series of questions and answers. ● *noun* a follower of Socrates. [Say so CRAT ick]

Socred *Cdn* ● *adjective* = SOCIAL CREDIT *adjective*. ● *noun* = SOCIAL CREDITER. [Say SO cred]

sod ● *noun* the surface of the ground with grass, or a piece of this. ● *verb* (**sods**, **sodded**, **sodding**) cover (the ground) with sod.

soda *noun* **1** any of various compounds of sodium in common use: *baking soda*. **2** (also **soda water**) water made bubbly by the addition of carbon dioxide under pressure (originally made with sodium bicarbonate), and used alone or with an alcoholic beverage etc. as a drink. **3** (also **soda pop**) esp. *US* = POP[1] *noun* 2. **4** a sweet fizzy drink made with soda water, fruit juice and sometimes ice cream.

soda cracker *noun* a thin crisp cracker made with baking soda.

soda fountain *noun* **1** a shop or counter serving soft drinks, ice cream, etc. **2** a device dispensing soda water or soft drinks.

sodbuster *noun* *informal* a farmer who raises crops rather than livestock, esp. one of the early homesteaders on the Prairies.

sodden *adjective* **1** soaked through; saturated with liquid: *looked at the ruts the Cadillac had left in her sodden lawn*. **2** intoxicated; drunk: *snoring in a sodden stupor*.

SPELL CHECK **solder**	ABC ✓

The metallic substance that is melted and used to join pipes or wires is *solder*, spelled with an *l* and only one *d*.

sod house *noun* (also **sod hut**) a house with walls of sod and a canvas or sod roof supported by wooden rafters, built esp. by settlers on the Prairies.

sodium *noun* a soft silver-white reactive metallic element, occurring naturally in soda, salt, etc., which is an essential element in living organisms. [Say SO dee um]

sodium carbonate *noun* a white powder with many commercial applications including the manufacture of soap and glass.

sodium chloride *noun* a colourless crystalline compound occurring naturally in sea water and rock salt; salt.

sodium light *noun* (also **sodium vapour light**, **sodium lamp**) a street light using an electrical discharge in sodium vapour and giving a yellow light.

S

sodium nitrate *noun* a white powdery compound used mainly in the manufacture of fertilizers.

sodomite *noun* a person who engages in sodomy. [Say SOD um ite]

sodomize *verb* (**sodomizes**, **sodomized**, **sodomizing**) engage in anal intercourse with or force anal intercourse upon another person. [Say SODDA mize]

sodomy *noun* anal intercourse performed between two males or a male and a female [Say SODDA mee]

sod chack *noun* = SOD HOUSE.

sod-turning *noun* Cdn = GROUNDBREAKING *noun*.

sofa *noun* a long upholstered seat with a back and arms, for two or more people.

sofa bed *noun* a sofa that can be folded out to form a bed, usu. for occasional use.

soffit *noun* the undersurface of an arch, a balcony, overhanging eaves, etc.

soft • *adjective* **1** lacking hardness or firmness; yielding to pressure. **2** not rough or coarse in texture. **3** quiet and gentle. **4** (of light or colour) pleasingly subtle; not harsh. **5** sympathetic, lenient, or willing to compromise, esp. excessively so. **6** *informal* (of a job or way of life) requiring little effort. **7** *informal* foolish. **8** (of a drink) not alcoholic. **9** (of a drug) not likely to cause addiction. **10** (of water) free from mineral salts. **11** (also **soft-core**) (of pornography) suggestive but not explicit. **12** (of wheat) having a soft kernel rich in starch, used to make pastry flour (*compare* HARD *adjective* 13). **13 a** *Sport* (of a ball, puck, etc.) weakly or lightly hit. **b** *Hockey* (of a goal) that the goalie should have been able to stop. **14** (of support for a candidate etc.) not solid. • *adverb* softly: *play soft*. • *noun* a soft or yielding thing; the soft part of something. PHRASES **be soft on** *informal* **1** be lenient towards. **2** be infatuated with. **have a soft spot for** be fond of or affectionate towards (a person).

softball *noun* **1** a modified form of baseball played on a smaller diamond using a larger and softer ball that is pitched underarm. **2** the ball used in this sport.

soft-boiled *adjective* **1** (of an egg) lightly boiled leaving the yolk semi-liquid. **2** *informal* (of a person) mild, easygoing.

softcover *adjective & noun* = PAPERBACK.

soft drink *noun* a carbonated, non-alcoholic drink.

soften *verb* **1** make or become soft or softer. **2** make or become less severe: *his face softened and he almost smiled*. **3** modify, tone down; make less pronounced or prominent. **4** reduce the force of something: *soften the blow*. **5** (often foll. by *up*) **a** reduce the strength of (defences) by bombing or some other preliminary attack. **b** reduce the resistance of (a person). ▶ **softener** *noun* [Say SOFF'n]

soft-focus • *adjective* **1** characterized by or producing a deliberate slight blurring or lack of definition in a photograph: *soft-focus filter*. **2** deliberately unclear or imprecise: *soft-focus, unpolitical essays about life*. • *noun* (**soft focus**) **1** a deliberate slight blurring or lack of definition in a photograph. **2** deliberate lack of clarity or precision: *the subject was treated with verbal soft focus*.

soft-hearted *adjective* tender, compassionate.

softie *noun* (*plural* **softies**) *informal* **1** a kind, sympathetic, or sentimental person. **2** a weak or silly person. **3** *Hockey slang* a goal scored on a weak shot.

soft landing *noun* **1** a landing by a spacecraft during which no serious damage is incurred. **2** a slowing down of economic growth at an acceptable degree relative to inflation and unemployment.

softly *adverb* in a soft way.

softness *noun* the quality of being soft.

soft news *noun* news that focuses on personalities, provides background for hard news, or is not

immediately topical, e.g. entertainment and lifestyle reporting.

soft palate *noun* the rear part of the palate.

soft pedal • *noun* a pedal on a piano that makes the tone softer. • *verb* (**soft-pedal**, **soft-pedals**, **soft-pedalled**, **soft-pedalling**) refrain from emphasizing; be restrained (about): *event organizers soft-pedalled the host city's reputation as a major crime centre*.

soft return *noun* a line break inserted automatically by a word processor at the end of a line of text.

soft rock *noun* a type of rock music originating in the 1970s characterized by a pleasant, melodic sound and usu. romantic lyrics.

soft sell • *noun* restrained or subtly persuasive salesmanship. • *verb* (**soft-sell**, **soft-sells**, **soft-sold**, **soft-selling**) sell by this method.

soft-shoe • *noun* a kind of tap dance performed in soft-soled shoes. • *verb* (**soft-shoes**, **soft-shoed**, **soft-shoeing**) **1** perform this dance. **2** move quietly or lightly.

soft soap • *noun* **1** a semi-liquid soap, esp. one made with potassium not sodium salts. **2** *informal* persuasive flattery. • *verb* (**soft-soap**) *informal* persuade (a person) with flattery.

soft-spoken *adjective* speaking with a gentle quiet voice.

soft tissue *noun* body tissue other than bone or cartilage.

soft touch *noun* (*plural* **soft touches**) *slang* a person easily manipulated, esp. one easily induced to part with money.

software *noun* **1** the programs and other operating information used by a computer. **2** storage media such as video cassettes, audio tapes, etc. requiring playback on electronic equipment.

software engineer *noun* a person who develops, produces, or manages system software. ▶ **software engineering**

software package *noun* a set of computer programs directed at some application in general, e.g. computer graphics, word processing, etc.

softwood • *noun* **1** the wood of pine, spruce, or other conifers, easily sawn. **2** a tree producing such wood. • *adjective* **1** made of softwood: *softwood lumber*. **2** containing softwoods: *softwood forest*.

softy *noun* (*plural* **softies**) = SOFTIE.

soggy *adjective* (**soggier**, **soggiest**) **1** sodden, saturated. **2** (of weather) rainy, dank.

soh *noun* = SO².

soil • *noun* **1** the upper layer of earth in which plants grow, consisting of disintegrated rock usu. with an admixture of organic remains: *alluvial soil* ◊ *rich soil*. **2** the ground, the earth: *a tiller of the soil*. **3** ground belonging to a nation; territory: *on Canadian soil*. **4** a dirty mark; a stain or smear. **5** filth; refuse matter. • *verb* **1** make dirty; smear or stain with dirt. **2** dirty (diapers, clothes etc.) by involuntary defecation. **3** tarnish, defile; bring discredit to: *would not soil my hands with it*.

soil conservation *noun* protection of soil against erosion, loss of fertility, and damage.

soilless *adjective* containing no soil.

soil profile *noun* the arrangement of layers of soil from the earth's surface down to the bedrock, usu. displayed in a vertical cross-section.

soiree *noun* **1** a party in the evening. **2** Cdn (Nfld) **a** a social gathering held by an organization or service club. **b** a large party or community social with singing, dancing, and eating. [Say swah RAY for sense 1, suh REE for sense 2]

sojourn • *noun* a temporary stay: *a luxurious sojourn in*

the city's five-star hotel. • *verb* stay temporarily.
▶ **sojourner** *noun* [Say SO jurn]
sol *noun* **1** = SO². **2** *hist.* a former coin and monetary unit of France and New France etc., notionally equivalent to one-twentieth of a livre but varying in actual value. [Say SAUL]
solace • *noun* comfort in distress, disappointment, or tedium: *the church offered solace and peace to the faithful.* • *verb* (**solaces**, **solaced**, **solacing**) give solace to: *the art deco rooms of the hotel once solaced soldiers leaving for war.* [Say SAUL us]
solar *adjective* of, relating to, or reckoned by the sun: *solar eclipse* ◊ *solar time.*
solar cell *noun* a photoelectric device converting solar radiation into electricity.
solar eclipse *noun* an eclipse in which the sun is obscured by the moon.
solar energy *noun* **1** radiant energy emitted by the sun. **2** = SOLAR POWER.
solarium *noun* a room, balcony, etc. fitted with extensive areas of glass. [Say suh LARRY um]
solar panel *noun* (also **solar collector**) a panel that harnesses the energy in the sun's radiation, either to generate electricity using solar cells or to heat water.
solar plexus *noun* (*plural* **solar plexus** or **solar plexuses**) **1** a complex of radiating nerves at the pit of the stomach. **2** the region of the torso in front of this, esp. as regarded as vulnerable to a blow.
solar power *noun* power obtained by harnessing the energy of the sun's rays. ▶ **solar-powered** *adjective*
solar radiation *noun* electromagnetic radiated energy from the sun.
solar system *noun* the collection of nine planets and their moons in orbit around the sun, together with asteroids, meteoroids, and comets.
solar wind *noun* the continuous flow of charged particles from the sun into surrounding space.
solar year *noun* the time taken for the earth to travel once around the sun, measured from equinox to equinox.
sold *past and past participle* of SELL. PHRASES **sold on** *informal* enthusiastic about.
solder • *noun* a low-melting alloy, esp. one based on lead and tin, used to join less fusible metals in plumbing and electrical work or jewellery making etc. • *verb* join with solder. [Say SODDER]
soldering iron *noun* a tool used for applying solder. [Say SODDER ing]
solderless *adjective* made without soldering. [Say SODDER less]
soldier • *noun* **1** a person serving in or having served in an army. **2** a private or non-commissioned officer in an army. **3** a military commander of specified ability: *a great soldier.* **4** a person who fights for a cause. **5** (also **soldier ant**) a wingless ant or termite with a large head and jaws for fighting in defence of its colony. **6** (also **soldier beetle**) a carnivorous reddish beetle of the family Cantharidae. • *verb* serve as a soldier: *was off soldiering.* PHRASES **soldier on** *informal* persevere doggedly. ▶ **soldierly** *adjective*
soldier of fortune *noun* an adventurous person ready to take service under any state or person.
sold-out *adjective* having all tickets sold: *sold-out show.*

SPELL CHECK	
sole, soul	ABC ✓

A person's spirit is their **soul**.

sole¹ • *noun* **1 a** the undersurface of the foot. **b** the part of a shoe, sock, etc., corresponding to this (esp. excluding the heel). **c** the lower surface or base of an

implement, e.g. a plow. **2** (*plural* **sole** or **soles**) **a** a marine flatfish, important as a food fish. **b** the flesh of any flatfish prepared as food. • *verb* provide (a shoe etc.) with a sole; replace the sole of.
sole² *adjective* one and only: *the sole reason.*
solecism *noun* **1** a mistake of grammar or idiom; a blunder in the manner of speaking or writing: *"between you and I" and other solecisms.* **2** a piece of bad manners or incorrect behaviour: *most butlers were alert to every solecism* ◊ *Julian and Kate soon became disenchanted with each other's sartorial solecisms.* [Say SOLLA sism]
-soled *adjective* having soles of the specified kind: *rubber-soled shoes.*
solely *adverb* only; not involving anybody else: *she was motivated solely by self-interest* ◊ *he became solely responsible for the firm.*
solemn *adjective* **1** serious and dignified: *a solemn occasion.* **2** formal; accompanied by ceremony, esp. for religious purposes. **3** serious or cheerless in manner: *looks rather solemn.* **4** mysteriously impressive. **5** full of importance; weighty: *a solemn warning.* **6** grave, sober, deliberate; slow in movement or action: *solemn music.*
solemnity *noun* (*plural* **solemnities**) **1** the state of being solemn; a solemn character or feeling; solemn behaviour. **2** a rite or celebration. [Say suh LEM nuh tee]
solemnize *verb* (**solemnizes**, **solemnized**, **solemnizing**) **1** duly perform (a ceremony esp. of marriage). **2** celebrate or commemorate (an occasion etc.) by special observances or with special formality. [Say SOLEMN nize]
solemnly *adverb* in a serious, dignified, sober, or formal manner.
solenoid *noun* a cylindrical coil of wire acting as a magnet when carrying current. [Say SOLE annoyed]
sole practitioner *noun* *Cdn* a lawyer, accountant, etc. who is the sole member of a firm, rather than one who works in partnership with others.
solicit *verb* (**solicits**, **solicited**, **soliciting**) **1** ask for or try to obtain something from someone: *she called a meeting to solicit their views* ◊ *historians are solicited for their opinions.* **2** accost a person and offer one's services as a prostitute: *hookers were actively soliciting passersby.* ▶ **solicitation** *noun* [Say suh LISS it, suh lissa TAY sh'n]
solicitor *noun* **1** *Cdn* a lawyer. **2** a person who tries to obtain business orders, contributions, etc.: *we got an unlisted number to avoid calls from telephone solicitors.* **3** the chief law officer of a city, town, or government department. [Say suh LISSA tur]
Solicitor General *noun* (*plural* **Solicitors General**) (in Canada) a federal or provincial cabinet member who is responsible for correctional services, law enforcement, and some forms of licensing.
solicitous *adjective* showing interest or concern: *solicitous friends and well-meaning strangers ask if I'm okay.* ▶ **solicitously** *adverb* [Say suh LISSA tuss]
solicitude *noun* care or concern for someone or something: *I was touched by their solicitude for me.* [Say suh LISSA tood or suh LISSA tyood]
solid • *adjective* **1** firm and stable in shape; not liquid or fluid. **2** strongly built or made. **3** not hollow or having spaces or gaps. **4** consisting of the same substance throughout. **5** (of time) continuous. **6** able to be relied on; dependable or sound. **7** *Geometry* three-dimensional. • *noun* **1** a solid substance or object. **2** (in *plural*) food that is not liquid. **3** a three-dimensional body or geometric figure. **4** a solidly coloured garment or fabric: *mix stripes with solids.* • *adverb* so as to become solid; solidly: *booked solid* ◊ *frozen solid.*
solidarity *noun* (*plural* **solidarities**) **1** support or sympathy for the beliefs, actions, or plight of an individual or group: *organ donation is a sign of solidarity*

S

with people who need organ transplants to stay alive ◊ they wore red ribbons as a gesture of solidarity with AIDS sufferers. **2** agreement among individuals with a common interest; mutual support or cohesiveness within a group: herded together in the same deteriorated quarters, hirelings began to acquire a sense of common interest and a feeling of solidarity ◊ union solidarity. [Say solla DARE a tee]

solidification noun an act of solidifying. [Say suh lidda fuh KAY sh'n]

solidify verb (**solidifies**, **solidified**, **solidifying**) make or become solid. [Say suh LIDDA fie]

solidity noun the quality or state of being solid: the strength and solidity of Romanesque architecture ◊ her writings have extraordinary depth and solidity ◊ he could count on the solidity of their support. [Say suh LIDDA tee]

solidly adverb **1** in a firm and strong way: a large, solidly-built house. **2** continuously; without stopping: it rained solidly for three hours. **3** agreeing with or supporting somebody completely: her colleagues were solidly behind her.

solid state • noun the state of matter in which materials are not fluid but retain their boundaries without support, the atoms or molecules occupying fixed positions with respect to each other and unable to move freely. • adjective using the electronic properties of solids, e.g. a semiconductor, to replace those of valves.

soliloquize verb (**soliloquizes**, **soliloquized**, **soliloquizing**) talk alone or regardless of hearers, esp. in a drama: when emotional stress builds to its most profound intensity within one of Shakespeare's characters, that character tends to soliloquize. [Say suh LIL a kwize]

soliloquy noun (plural **soliloquies**) the act of talking when alone or regardless of any hearers, esp. in drama: Hamlet's "to be or not to be" soliloquy ◊ in a rambling soliloquy, Mr. Rollins spoke of his bewilderment over the controversy he had touched off. [Say suh LIL a kwee]

solipsism noun the view that the self is all that exists, or is all that can be known to exist: suburbanization nourished the solipsism of the middle class, which looked around its new environment and concluded, short-sightedly, that it was alone in America. ▶ **solipsistic** adjective [Say SOLLIP sism, sollip SIS tick]

solitaire noun **1** a diamond or other gem set by itself. **2** a ring having a single gem. **3** a game for one player in which cards taken in random order have to be arranged in certain groups or sequences. **4** a game for one player played by removing pegs etc. one at a time from a board by jumping others over them until only one is left. [Say SOLLA tare]

solitariness noun the condition of being solitary.

solitary • adjective **1** living alone; without companions: a solitary existence. **2** performed alone: a solitary expedition. **3** (of a place) secluded or not visited. **4** single or sole: a solitary instance. **5** (of an insect) not living in communities. **6** Botany growing singly, not in a cluster. • noun (plural **solitaries**) **1** a recluse or hermit. **2** informal = SOLITARY CONFINEMENT.

solitary confinement noun isolation of a prisoner in a separate cell as a punishment.

solitude noun the state or situation of being alone: on our vast northern lakes you'll find peace, solitude, and fish.

solo • noun (plural **solos**) **1 a** (plural **solos** or **soli**) a vocal or instrumental piece or passage performed by one person with or without accompaniment. **b** a dance performed by one person. **2 a** an unaccompanied flight by a pilot in an aircraft. **b** anything done by one person unaccompanied. **3** (as an adjective) Baseball designating a home run hit with no one on base. • verb (**soloes**, **soloed**, **soloing**) perform a solo, esp. a

musical solo or a solo flight. • adverb unaccompanied, alone: flew solo for the first time.

soloist noun **1** a performer of a solo, esp. in music or dance. **2** a ballet dancer of a rank between corps de ballet and principal, who performs some solo roles.

Solomon Gundy noun (also **Solomon Grundy**) Cdn (NS) a dish of salted herring marinated in vinegar, spices, sugar, and onions.

Solomon's seal noun **1** a figure like the Star of David. **2** a plant of the lily family, with arching stems and drooping green and white flowers.

solstice noun **1** either of the two times in the year when the sun reaches its highest or lowest point in the sky at noon, marked by the longest and shortest days. **2** the point in the ecliptic reached by the sun at a solstice. [Say SOLE stiss or SAUL stiss]

solubility noun the ability to be dissolved, esp. in water. [Say saul yoo BILLA tee]

soluble adjective that can be dissolved, esp. in water: cannabis is soluble in fats, oils, and alcohol, but not water. [Say SAUL yoo bull]

solute noun a dissolved substance: a solution in which more solute is present than the solvent can normally hold. [Say SAUL yoot]

solution noun **1 a** the act or a means of solving a problem or difficulty. **b** an explanation, answer, or decision. **2 a** the conversion of a solid or gas into a liquid by mixture with a liquid solvent. **b** the state resulting from this: held in solution. **c** a liquid, semi-liquid, or solid mixture produced by this process. **3** the act of dissolving or the state of being dissolved: the solution of glucose in water.

solvable adjective that can be solved.

solve verb (**solves**, **solved**, **solving**) find an answer to, or an action or course that removes or effectively deals with (a problem or difficulty).

solvency noun the state of not being in debt: doubts about the company's solvency. [Say SAUL vun see]

solvent • adjective **1** having enough money to meet one's liabilities: our bank is a solvent and profitable bank. **2** able to dissolve a substance: solvent additives. • noun **1** the liquid in which a solute is dissolved to form a solution: find the colour of iodine in solution in the solvents ethyl and ethanol. **2** a liquid used to dissolve other substances: paintbrushes can be cleaned with a solvent.

solvent abuse noun the use of volatile organic solvents as intoxicants by inhalation, e.g. glue sniffing.

solver noun a person who solves things: a good problem-solver.

SPELL CHECK
solely

Another word for only is **solely**: bonuses are based **solely** on performance.

Somali • noun **1** (plural **Somali** or **Somalis**) **a** a member of a Hamitic Muslim people of Somalia, a country in northeastern Africa. **b** a native or national of Somalia. **2** the language of this people. • adjective of Somalia, the Somalis, or their language. ▶ **Somalian** adjective & noun [Say suh MAWL ee or suh MAL ee]

somatic adjective of or relating to the body, esp. as distinct from the mind: sometimes we recall the traumatic event only at the somatic level, suffering stomach pain or headaches. [Say suh MAT ick]

somatic cell noun any cell of a living organism except the reproductive cells.

somatotropin noun (also **somatotrophin**) a growth hormone secreted by the pituitary gland. [Say so matto TRO pin, so matto TRO fin]

sombre adjective (also esp. US **somber**) **1** gloomy,

shadowy: *a sombre sky*. **2** dark in colour. **3** oppressively solemn or sober: *the sound had become too sombre for my taste, a little too bleak in character*. **4** dismal, foreboding: *a sombre prospect*. ▶ **sombrely** *adverb*

sombrero *noun* (*plural* **sombreros**) a broad-brimmed, flat-crowned felt or straw hat worn esp. in Mexico and the southwestern US. [Say som BRARE oh]

some • *adjective* **1** an unspecified amount or number of. **2** that is unknown or unnamed. **3** a considerable amount or number of: *went to some trouble*. **4** *informal* notably such: *that was some game*. • *pronoun* some people or things, some number or amount. • *adverb informal* **1** to some extent. **2** very; to a high degree: *we were some proud*. PHRASES **and then some** *informal* and plenty more than that.

-some *suffix* forming nouns from numerals, meaning "a group of (so many)": *foursome*.

somebody (also **someone**) • *pronoun* some person. • *noun* (*plural* **somebodies**) a person of importance.

someday *adverb* at some time in the future.

somehow *adverb* **1** in some way. **2** for some reason or other.

someplace *adverb & pronoun* = SOMEWHERE.

somersault • *noun* **1** an acrobatic movement in which a person turns head over heels in the air or on the ground. **2** a dramatic upset or reversal of policy or opinion: *what trust can I place in those who turn doctrinal somersaults overnight?* • *verb* perform a somersault. [Say SUMMER salt]

something • *noun & pronoun* **1 a** some unspecified or unknown thing. **b** (also **something or other**) as a substitute for an unknown or forgotten description: *she's a professor of something or other*. **2** a known or understood but unexpressed quantity, quality, or extent: *there's something in what she says*. **3** *informal* an important or notable person or thing: *the party was quite something*. **4** (in *combination*) used to denote a person's approximate age, esp. as being suggestive of the characteristic tastes and outlook of a particular generation: *thirtysomething*. • *adverb* **1** somewhat; in some degree. **2** *informal* to a high degree: *hurts something terrible*. PHRASES **something like 1** an amount in the region of: *something like a million dollars*. **2** somewhat like. **3** *informal* impressive; a fine specimen of. **something of** to some extent; in some sense: *something of an expert*.

sometime • *adverb* at some unspecified time. • *adjective* **1** former: *the sometime mayor*. **2** occasional: *a sometime contributor*.

sometimes *adverb* at some times; occasionally.

somewhat • *adverb* to some extent: *somewhat strange*. • *noun & pronoun* something: *loses somewhat of its force*.

somewhere • *adverb* in or to some place. • *pronoun* some unspecified place. PHRASES **get somewhere** *informal* achieve success. **somewhere around** approximately.

sommelier *noun* a waiter responsible for serving wine. [Say som'll YAY]

somnambulism *noun* sleepwalking. [Say som NAM byoo lism]

somnambulist *noun* a sleepwalker. [Say som NAM byoo list]

somnolence *noun* sleepiness, drowsiness: *symptoms include dizziness and somnolence*. [Say SOMNA lince]

somnolent *adjective* **1** sleepy, drowsy: *the city sleeps like somnolent cats*. **2** inducing drowsiness: *a somnolent summer day*. [Say SOMNA lint]

son *noun* **1** a boy or man in relation to either or both of his parents. **2 a** a male descendant. **b** (foll. by *of*) a male member of a family, nation, etc. **3** a person regarded as inheriting an occupation, quality, etc., or associated with a particular attribute: *sons of freedom*. **4** (also **my son**) a form of address esp. to a boy. **5** (**the Son**) (in Christian belief) Jesus Christ.

sonar *noun* **1** a system for the underwater detection of objects by reflected or emitted sound. **2** an apparatus for this. [Say SO nar]

sonata *noun* a composition for one instrument or two (one usu. being a piano accompaniment), usu. in several movements. [Say suh NOTTA or suh NATTA]

song *noun* **1** a musical composition comprising a short poem or other set of words set to music; a set of words meant to be sung. **2** singing or vocal music: *burst into song*. **3** a sound suggestive of singing. **4** the usu. repeated musical call of some birds. **5** a short poem in rhymed stanzas. PHRASES **for a song** *informal* very cheaply.

song and dance *noun* *informal* a fuss or commotion.

songbird *noun* **1** a bird with a musical call. **2** a perching bird of the group Oscines. **3** *informal* a superb female singer.

songbook *noun* a collection of songs with music.

song-like *adjective* like a song.

song sparrow *noun* a North American sparrow with a characteristic musical song.

songwriter *noun* a writer of songs or the music for them. ▶ **songwriting** *noun*

sonic *adjective* of or relating to or using sound or sound waves. ▶ **sonically** *adverb* [Say SAWN ick]

sonic boom *noun* a loud explosive noise caused by the shock wave from an aircraft breaking the sound barrier.

son-in-law *noun* (*plural* **sons-in-law**) the husband of one's daughter.

sonnet *noun* a lyric poem of 14 lines, usu. written in iambic pentameter, using any of a number of formal rhyme schemes and usu. having a single theme.

sonny *noun* *informal* often *derogatory* a familiar form of address to a young boy or man who is one's junior.

son of a gun *informal* • *noun* **1** a jocular or affectionate form of address or reference. **2** a rascal or rogue. • *interjection* an exclamation of shock or amazement.

son of God *noun* **1** (**Son of God**) Jesus Christ. **2** a person spiritually attached to God.

sonority *noun* (*plural* **sonorities**) the quality of having a loud, full, or deep sound: *the rich sonority of the bass*. [Say suh NOR a tee]

sonorous *adjective* **1** having a loud, full, or deep sound; resonant: *a sonorous voice*. **2** (of speech, style, etc.) imposing, grand: *the beautiful and sonorous language of the Bible of King James*. ▶ **sonorously** *adverb* [Say SAWN er us or SONE er us]

sook *noun* *Austral., NZ, & Cdn (Maritimes & Nfld) derogatory* a person acting childishly; a wimp or sissy. [Rhymes with BOOK]

sooky baby *noun* (*plural* **sooky babies**) *Cdn (Maritimes & Nfld)* = SOOK. [SOOKY rhymes with ROOKIE]

soon *adverb* **1** within a short period of time. **2** relatively early. **3** readily or willingly: *I would as soon stay behind*. PHRASES **as** (or **so**) **soon as** at the moment that; not later than. **how soon?** in what period of time; how early. **no sooner ... than** at the very moment that: *no sooner had we arrived than the rain stopped*. **sooner or later** at some time in the future; eventually.

soopollalie *noun* *Cdn (BC)* **1** = BUFFALO BERRY. **2** a thick drink made from crushed buffalo berries. [Say SOAP a lally]

soot *noun* a black substance rising in fine flakes in the smoke of wood, coal, oil, etc., and deposited on the sides of a chimney etc. [Rhymes with FOOT]

soothe *verb* (**soothes, soothed, soothing**) **1** bring or restore (a person or feelings etc.) to a peaceful or tranquil state; calm. **2** reduce the intensity of; soften, allay, or relieve (pain, an emotion, etc.). **3** provide relief or tranquility.

soother *noun* **1** *Cdn & Brit.* a ring or nipple made of rubber or plastic given to a baby to suck. **2** a thing that calms or comforts.

soothing *adjective* calming; pain-relieving: *a soothing bath.* ▶ **soothingly** *adverb*

soothsayer *noun* a person who predicts future events; a prophet. ▶ **soothsaying** *noun*

sooty *adjective* (**sootier, sootiest**) **1** covered with or full of soot. **2** (esp. of an animal or bird) of a dusky black or brownish black colour. [With OO as in *FOOT*]

sop • *noun* **1** a thing given or done to pacify or appease a person; a concession or bribe: *the proposed local councils were inadequate, a mere sop to demands for local democracy.* **2** a piece of bread etc. dipped in gravy or wine etc. • *verb* (**sops, sopped, sopping**) (foll. by *up*) absorb (liquid) in a sponge, towel, piece of bread, etc.

sophist *noun* (usu. **Sophist**) *Greek History* a paid teacher of philosophy and rhetoric, esp. one associated with moral skepticism and reasoning that is clever but false. [Say SOFF ist]

sophisticate *noun* a sophisticated person. [Say suh FISTA kit]

sophisticated *adjective* **1 a** (of a person) worldly, cultured, and refined; discriminating in taste and judgment. **b** showing awareness of the complexities of a subject; knowledgeable, experienced. **2** appealing to sophisticated people or sophisticated tastes. **3 a** (of a theory or idea etc.) based on or involving advanced concepts; complex, not plain or straightforward. **b** (of a piece of equipment etc.) highly developed. [Say suh FISTA kate id]

sophistication *noun* the quality of being sophisticated: *the increasing power and sophistication of computers.* [Say suh fista KAY sh'n]

sophistry *noun* (*plural* **sophistries**) **1** the use of clever but false arguments, esp. with the intention of deceiving: *they're more schooled in the saddle than in the subtlety and sophistry of high finance.* **2** such an argument: *few Canadians are seduced by such sophistries as "People kill, not guns".* [Say SOFF us tree]

sophomore *noun* **1** (esp. in the US) a student in his or her second year of high school, college, or university. **2** *Sport* an athlete in his or her second year at a particular level or in a particular league. **3** (as an *adjective*) designating the second work etc. of an artist or performer: *sophomore album.* [Say SOFFA more]

sophomoric *adjective* **1** of, relating to, or befitting a sophomore. **2** maintaining a pretentious demeanour of intellectual sophistication and maturity while immature, juvenile, or shallow: *their argumentation is specious and sophomoric, and their data are dubious when not obviously bogus.* [Say soffa MORE ick]

soporific • *adjective* **1 a** tending to induce or produce sleep. **b** tedious, boring. **2** (of a person) sleepy, drowsy: *she was asleep, or at least made soporific by the mantras of the commercials.* • *noun* a soporific drug or influence. [Say soppa RIFF ick]

sopping *adjective* (also **sopping wet**) soaked with liquid.

soppy *adjective* (**soppier, soppiest**) *informal* mawkishly sentimental; sappy, mushy.

soprano *noun* **1 a** the highest singing voice. **b** a female or boy singer with this voice. **c** a part written for it. **2** an instrument of a high or the highest pitch in its family: *soprano recorder.* [Say suh PRAN oh]

sorbet *noun* a soft water ice made with fruit juice or fruit purée served esp. between main courses to cleanse the palate and reinvigorate the appetite, or as a dessert. [Say sore BAY]

sorbitol *noun* a sweet crystalline alcohol found in some fruit, used as a substitute for sugar. [Say SORE bit awl]

sorcerer *noun* a person who claims to use magic powers; a wizard. [Say SORE sir ur]

sorceress *noun* (*plural* **sorceresses**) a woman who claims to use magic powers. [Say SORE sir ess]

sorcery *noun* (*plural* **sorceries**) magic that uses evil spirits. [Say SORE sir ee]

sordid *adjective* **1** immoral or dishonest: *it was a shock to discover the truth about his sordid past.* **2** dirty, filthy, squalid: *people living in sordid conditions.* ▶ **sordidly** *adverb* **sordidness** *noun*

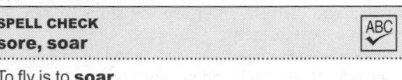

SPELL CHECK
sore, soar

To fly is to **soar**.

sore • *adjective* **1** (of a part of the body) painful from injury or disease. **2** (of a person) suffering bodily pain. **3** *informal* angry, irritated, or vexed. • *noun* **1** a raw or tender place on the body, such as a cut or wound. **2** a source of distress or annoyance: *reopen old sores.*

sore loser *noun* a person who cannot accept losing a game etc. graciously.

sorely *adverb* extremely, greatly, desperately: *Michael will be sorely missed.*

soreness *noun* pain.

sore point *noun* (also **sore spot**) a subject causing distress or annoyance; a contentious issue.

sorghum *noun* a tropical cereal grass that is a major source of grain and animal feed. [Say SORE gum]

sorority *noun* (*plural* **sororities**) a society for female students in a university or college. [Say suh ROAR a tee]

sorrel • *adjective* of a light reddish-brown or chestnut colour. • *noun* **1** this colour. **2** an animal of this colour, esp. a horse. **3** a meadow plant with triangular leaves that are used in salads and cooking for their acidic flavour. [Say SORE ul]

sorrow • *noun* **1** mental distress caused by bereavement, suffering, or disappointment; grief. **2** a cause of grief or sadness. • *verb* feel or express sorrow or sadness; grieve, mourn.

sorrowful *adjective* **1** feeling sorrow or grief. **2** characterized by or causing sorrow. **3** expressing sorrow: *a sorrowful expression.* ▶ **sorrowfully** *adverb* **sorrowfulness** *noun*

sorry • *adjective* (**sorrier, sorriest**) **1** feeling sadness or regret. **2** full of shame, guilt, and remorse, esp. about a past action. **3** used to express mild regret, disagreement, or refusal, and for making apologies and excuses. **4** pathetic: *the sorry state of our finances.* • *interjection* **1** used to express apology or regret. **2** (as a request for something to be repeated) I beg your pardon; what did you say? PHRASES **feel** (or **be**) **sorry for someone** feel sympathy or pity for. **feel** (or **be**) **sorry for oneself** bewail one's problems or plight; be self-indulgently depressed.

sort • *noun* **1** a group of things or people determined on the basis of common attributes; a type or kind. **2** (foll. by *of*) an unusual or uncertain example of a specified thing: *she is some sort of writer.* **3** *informal* a person of a specified character or kind: *a good sort.* • *verb* (often foll. by *out, through*) arrange systematically or according to type, class, etc.; separate and put into a different order or different groups. PHRASES **of sorts** (or **of a sort**) *informal* of an unusual kind; not fully deserving the name: *a holiday of sorts.* **out of sorts**

1 slightly irritable or grumpy. **2** slightly unwell. **sort of** informal to some extent; somewhat: *I sort of expected it.* **sort out 1** separate and arrange into groups according to kind or type. **2** separate (things of one type) from a miscellaneous group. **3** resolve (a problem or difficulty). **4** informal deal with or reprimand (a person). **sorter** noun a person who or thing which sorts, arranges, or classifies things.

sortie • noun **1** a sudden emergence, dash, or attack made by troops from a besieged garrison: *Superintendent Leif Crozier attempted a sortie from the fort with 100 Mounties and volunteers to seize a strategic supply point.* **2** an operational flight by a single military aircraft. **3** informal a jaunt or excursion. • verb (**sorties**, **sortied**, **sortieing**) make or go on a sortie. [Say SORE tee]

SOS noun (plural **SOS's**) **1** an international code signal of extreme distress, used esp. by ships at sea. **2** an urgent appeal for help.

so-so • adjective neither very good nor very bad. • adverb not very well and not very badly.

sot noun a habitual drunk.

sotto voce • adverb in a low voice so as not to be heard: *"Certainly," said Meighen, and sat down, adding, sotto voce, "You'll be sorry."* • adjective uttered or spoken etc. in a soft voice or undertone. [Say sotto VOE chay]

soubriquet noun = SOBRIQUET. [Say SO brick ay]

soufflé noun a light spongy dish usu. made by adding egg yolks and a sweet or savoury filling to stiffly beaten egg whites then baked until puffy. [Say soo FLAY]

sough • verb make a moaning, whistling, or rushing sound as of the wind in trees etc.: *the wind soughed in the corridors.* • noun a gentle rushing or murmuring sound: *a sough of wind whistled down Boulevard Saint-Laurent.* [Rhymes with COW]

sought past and past participle of SEEK.

sought-after adjective in high demand; generally desired.

soul noun **1** the spiritual or immaterial component or nature of a human being or animal, regarded as the seat of the emotions or intellect. **2 a** the spiritual part of a human being considered in its moral aspect or in relation to God, esp. regarded as immortal and being capable of redemption or damnation in a future state. **b** the disembodied spirit of a dead person, regarded as invested with some degree of personality and form. **3 a** a person regarded as the personification of a certain quality: *the very soul of discretion.* **b** a person regarded as embodying moral or intellectual qualities: *meaner souls.* **4** an individual: *not a soul in sight.* **5** a person regarded with familiarity, affection, pity, etc.: *the poor soul was utterly confused.* **6** (usu. foll. by *of*) **a** a person regarded as the inspirer or animating spirit of an activity or cause etc.: *she is the life and soul of the party.* **b** the essential quality or animating element of something: *honesty is the soul of this relationship.* **7** emotional or intellectual energy or intensity, esp. as revealed in a work of art. **8** (also as an adjective) the emotional or spiritual quality of black American life and culture, manifested in art, music, etc. **9** = SOUL MUSIC. **PHRASES** **upon my soul!** an exclamation of surprise. ▶ **-souled** adjective (in combination)

soul-destroying adjective **1** (of an activity etc.) excruciatingly monotonous, with no prospect of improvement. **2** capable of suppressing a person's emotional or intellectual spirit or faculties: *a soul-destroying drug.*

soul food noun food traditionally eaten by American blacks, esp. those dishes originating in the rural southern US.

soulful adjective full of soul or feeling; of a highly emotional or spiritual nature. ▶ **soulfully** adverb

soulfulness noun

soulless adjective **1** having no soul: *the soulless machine.* **2** dull, uninteresting. **3** (of a thing) made or done without imagination; lacking humanizing or distinguishing characteristics: *a soulless stretch of houses.*

soulmate noun a person with whom one shares an interest, passion, or bond, esp. a friend or spouse.

soul music noun a type of black American pop music which combines rhythm and blues with the emotional intensity and expressiveness of gospel, characterized by its emphasis on vocals.

soul-searching • noun a penetrating or critical examination of one's actions, beliefs, motives, or emotions. • adjective characterized by such analysis or scrutiny.

sound^1 • noun **1** a sensation caused in the ear by vibrations of waves of pressure passing through the surrounding air or other medium. **2 a** vibrations causing this sensation. **b** similar vibrations whether audible or not. **3** anything that can be heard; a noise. **4** an idea or impression conveyed by words: *don't like the sound of that.* **5** a distinctive or readily identifiable style of esp. pop music. **6 a** (also **sound crew**) the department of engineers responsible for producing or recording sound for a movie or concert etc. **b** = SOUND SYSTEM. **7** (also **speech sound**) any of a series of articulate utterances: *vowel and consonant sounds.* **8** (often as an adjective) broadcasting by radio as distinct from television. • verb **1** convey a specific impression when heard: *you sound like you know what you're doing.* **2** cause (an instrument etc.) to make a sound. **3** give an audible signal for (an alarm etc.): *sound the retreat.* **4** produce or emit sound: *the alarm clock sounded.* **5** pronounce or articulate (words) sound by sound. **PHRASES** **sound and fury** noisy or boisterous talk or activity, esp. without substance: *if we could get beyond the sound and fury, we might discover that a serious debate is trying to take place.* **sound off** talk loudly or express one's opinions vehemently; complain.

sound^2 • adjective **1** free from disease or injury. **2** undamaged, unbroken, in good condition. **3** (of advice, judgment, a policy, etc.) sensible, fair, correct. **4** financially secure: *a sound investment.* **5 a** (of sleep) undisturbed. **b** (of a person sleeping) tending to sleep deeply without being easily woken. **6** severe, hard, thorough: *a sound thrashing.* **7** (of theology) orthodox. **8** (of a person, character, etc.) honourable, honest, trustworthy. • adverb in a sound manner; soundly: *sound asleep.*

sound^3 verb **1 a** test the depth or quality of the bottom of (the sea or a river etc.). **b** measure (depth). **2 a** (often foll. by *out*) inquire (esp. cautiously or discreetly) into the opinions or feelings of (a person). **b** investigate, attempt to ascertain (a matter, a person's opinions, etc.). **3** get records of temperature, humidity, pressure, etc. from (the upper atmosphere).

sound^4 noun **1** a narrow channel or stretch of water, esp. one between the mainland and an island or connecting two large bodies of water. **2** an arm of the sea.

sound barrier noun **1** the increased drag, reduced controllability, etc. which occurs when an aircraft approaches the speed of sound. **2** a wall erected or insulated to prevent the passage of sound, as from one room to another. **PHRASES** **break the sound barrier** travel faster than or accelerate past the speed of sound.

sound bite noun a short extract from a recorded interview, speech, etc., chosen for its pungency or appropriateness and edited into a news broadcast.

soundboard noun **1** a thin resonating sheet of wood

in a piano or sound box of a stringed instrument, such as a violin or cello, over which the strings pass to increase the sound produced. **2** a sound card.

sound box *noun* (*plural* **sound boxes**) the hollow chamber providing resonance and forming the body of a stringed instrument.

sound card *noun* a device capable of converting digitized audio signals into an analog audio signal, inserted in a computer to allow the use of audio components for multimedia applications.

sound check *noun* a test of sound equipment before a concert or recording session to ensure that the desired sound is being produced.

sound effect *noun* a sound other than speech or music made artificially to evoke a particular atmosphere or produce a realistic effect in a movie or play etc.

sounder *noun* a person or machine that sounds the depth of water.

sounding^1 *noun* (usu. in *plural*) **1 a** the action or process of measuring the depth of water, now usu. by means of echo. **b** (in *plural*) the determination of any physical property at a depth in the sea or at a height in the atmosphere. **2** cautious investigation: *the initial soundings from provincial capitals were not promising*. **3** measurements taken by sounding.

sounding^2 *adjective* **1 a** having a specified sound. **b** giving a mental impression of a specified kind: *a funny-sounding idea*. **2** producing or capable of producing esp. loud or resonant sound: *sounding brass*.

sounding board *noun* **1** a canopy, screen, or board placed above or behind a stage or pulpit to direct sound towards the audience or congregation. **2** a means of making one's opinions, beliefs, etc. more widely known. **3** a person whose feedback will serve as an accurate assessment of how well a plan, idea, theory, etc. will succeed or be received. **4** = SOUNDBOARD 1.

soundless *adjective* quiet, without a sound. ▶ **soundlessly** *adverb*

soundly *adverb* **1** (of sleeping) deeply and well: *Iain is soundly asleep*. **2** in a way that is sensible or can be relied on: *your information is soundly based*. **3** completely and thoroughly: *the team was soundly defeated*. **4** strongly; firmly: *these houses are soundly built*. **5** very well, but not in an excellent way: *she played soundly*.

soundman *noun* (*plural* **soundmen**) an engineer responsible for producing sound for a concert, movie, etc.

soundness *noun* the quality of being sensible, reliable, or stable: *the soundness of his ideas* ◊ *the soundness of our financial situation*.

soundproof • *adjective* impervious to sound. • *verb* make soundproof. ▶ **soundproofing** *noun*

soundscape *noun* **1** a musical composition consisting of a texture of sounds. **2** the sounds which can be heard in a locale or environment: *a new addition to the New York soundscape: in Greenwich Village, a bell silent for nearly 135 years has been made to ring*.

sound stage *noun* an enclosed soundproof stage or studio with excellent acoustic properties, suitable for filming and recording concerts, movies, etc.

sound system *noun* a set of equipment used for the reproduction and amplification of sound, such as a stereo or public address system.

soundtrack • *noun* **1 a** the sound element of a film. **b** a narrow band on the edge of a strip of film containing this recording. **2** such a recording, or selected excerpts from it, made available for sale. **3** any constituent single track in a multi-track recording. • *verb* provide (a film) with a soundtrack: *it's soundtracked by the great Ennio Morricone*.

sound wave *noun* a vibration in the air, in water, etc. that is heard as sound.

soup • *noun* **1** a usu. savoury liquid dish made by boiling meat, fish, or vegetables etc. with seasoning in stock or water, and often served as a first course. **2** *informal* anything jumbled, blended, or mixed, or having a consistency resembling that of soup, usu. a dense fog. • *verb* (usu. foll. by *up*) *informal* **1** modify (an engine, car, etc.) so as to increase its power or efficiency. **2** revise (writing, music, etc.) so as to increase its power or impact; enhance. PHRASES **from soup to nuts** *informal* from beginning to end, completely. **in the soup** *informal* in trouble.

soupçon *noun* a very small amount: *a soupçon of balsamic vinegar adds zest*. [Say SOUP sawn]

soup du jour *noun* (*plural* **soups du jour**) the soup featured by a restaurant on a particular day.

soup kitchen *noun* a place where warm meals, usu. soup, are served to the needy for little or no charge.

soupy *adjective* (**soupier**, **soupiest**) **1** of the consistency of soup. **2 a** (of fog, mist, etc.) thick, dense. **b** (of the weather) foggy.

sour • *adjective* **1** having a tart or acid taste like that of lemon, vinegar, or unripe fruit. **2 a** (of food, esp. milk or cream) having gone bad because of fermentation. **b** smelling or tasting rancid or unpleasant. **3 a** (of a person, temper, etc.) angry, resentful, bitter, cranky. **b** (of a comment, facial expression, etc.) expressing discontent or irritation. **4** (of a thing) unpleasant; disagreeable: *a sour experience*. **5** (of a musical note) out of tune. **6** (of oil or gas etc.) containing a relatively high proportion of sulphur. • *noun* an alcoholic drink with lemon or lime juice and ice: *whisky sour*. • *verb* **1** make or become sour. **2** make or become unpleasant or strained. PHRASES **go** (or **turn**) **sour 1** (of food etc.) become bad because of fermentation. **2** turn out badly.

source • *noun* **1 a** a place, person, or thing from which something originates or may be obtained. **b** (foll. by *of*) a cause of or reason for: *my marks were a source of concern*. **2 a** a document from which original information or evidence in support of some fact or event may be obtained (also as an *adjective*: *source material*). **b** an esp. unnamed person who supplies information or gives statements to the media. **3** the beginning or origin of a river or stream. **4** *Computing* (as an *adjective*) denoting files, programs, software, etc. written using a source code rather than machine code. • *verb* (**sources**, **sourced**, **sourcing**) **1** contract a particular manufacturer or company to supply (a product, part, or materials). **2** have, cite, or identify (a book etc.) as a source of information. PHRASES **at source** at the point of origin or issue.

sourcebook *noun* **1** a collection of writings, articles, etc. on a particular subject used as a basic introduction to that subject. **2** a comprehensive directory or catalogue of a particular subject.

source code *noun* *Computing* the complex series of instructions supplied to a computer by a programmer using a compiler or interpreter which translates it into machine code.

sour cream *noun* cream soured by lactic acid bacteria, used esp. in dips, salads, and as a garnish.

sourdough *noun* **1** a mixture of flour and water left to ferment so that natural yeasts develop, then mixed with more flour to make bread dough, which has a slightly sour taste. **2** bread made from sourdough. **3** (*Yukon & Alaska*) **a** *hist.* an experienced prospector or miner. **b** an old-timer.

sour grapes *plural noun* (treated as *singular*) used to suggest that someone is pretending not to want what

they in fact do want: *he said he didn't want the job anyway, but that's just sour grapes*.

sourly *adverb* in a resentful or cranky manner.

sourness *noun* **1** ill temper. **2** the quality of tasting sour.

sourpuss *noun (plural* **sourpusses**) *informal* an irritable or sullen person.

soused *adjective informal* drunk.

south • *noun* **1** the point of the horizon 90° clockwise from east. **2** (usu. **the South**) **a** the part of the world or a country or a town lying to the south. **b** *Cdn* the ten provinces south of the Yukon, Nunavut, and the Northwest Territories. **c** the Southern States of the US, bounded on the north by Maryland, the Ohio River, and Missouri. **d** *hist.* the Confederate slaveholding States of the US south of the Pennsylvania-Maryland border. • *adjective* **1** toward, at, near, or facing the south. **2** coming from the south: *south wind*. • *adverb* **1** toward, at, or near the south: *they travelled south*. **2** (foll. by *of*) further south than. **3** *informal* into a sharp decline: *house prices went south this month*. PHRASES **south by east** (or **west**) between south and south-southeast (or south-southwest). **to the south** (often foll. by *of*) in a southerly direction.

South African • *adjective* of or relating to the republic of South Africa. • *noun* **1** a native or national of South Africa. **2** a person of South African descent.

South American • *adjective* of or relating to South America. • *noun* a native or citizen of South America.

South Asian • *noun* **1** a native or inhabitant of the Indian subcontinent, including India, Pakistan, Bangladesh, and Sri Lanka. **2** a South Asian emigrant or a descendant of a South Asian living outside of the Indian subcontinent. • *adjective* of or relating to the Indian subcontinent, South Asians, or their culture.

southbound *adjective & adverb* travelling or leading in a southward direction.

southeast • *noun* **1** the point of the horizon midway between south and east. **2** (**Southeast**) the part of a country or city lying to the southeast. • *adjective* of, toward, or coming from the southeast. • *adverb* toward, at, or near the southeast.

Southeast Asian • *noun* a native or inhabitant of Southeast Asia, a region including Brunei, Burma, Cambodia, Indonesia, Laos, Malaysia, the Philippines, Singapore, Thailand, and Vietnam. • *adjective* of or relating to Southeast Asia.

southeasterly • *adjective & adverb* = SOUTHEAST. • *noun (plural* **southeasterlies**) (also **southeaster**) a southeast wind or storm.

southeastern *adjective* located or existing in the southeast of a region. ▶ **southeasterner** *noun*

southeastward *adjective & adverb* (also **southeastwards**) toward the southeast.

southerly • *adjective & adverb* **1** in a southern position or direction. **2** (of a wind) blowing from the south. • *noun (plural* **southerlies**) a southerly wind. [Rhymes with MOTHERLY]

southern *adjective* **1 a** of or in the south; inhabiting the south. **b** (also **Southern**) of, relating to, or inhabiting the States of the US South. **2** lying or directed toward the south. **3** (of a wind) blowing from the south.

Southern Baptist *noun* **1** (also **Southern Baptist Convention**) a body of Baptist churches in the US, established in 1845. **2** a member of any of these churches.

southerner *noun* **1** a native or inhabitant of the south. **2** (also **Southerner**) **a** *Cdn* an inhabitant of any of the ten provinces. **b** an inhabitant of the southern US.

southern hemisphere *noun* the half of the earth below the equator.

southernmost *adjective* furthest to the south.

South Korean • *adjective* of or relating to South Korea (the Republic of Korea), a country in the Far East, occupying the southern part of the peninsula of Korea. • *noun* a native or inhabitant of South Korea.

south of 60 *noun* (also **south of sixty**) *Cdn* the areas of Canada south of 60 degrees latitude, esp. the ten provinces south of the Yukon, Nunavut, and the Northwest Territories.

southpaw *noun informal* **1** *Baseball* a pitcher who throws with his or her left hand. **2** *Boxing* a fighter who punches or leads with the left hand. **3** a left-handed person.

South Pole *noun see* POLE² 1.

south-southeast • *noun* the point or direction midway between south and southeast. • *adjective & adverb* from, toward, in, or facing this direction.

south-southwest • *noun* the point or direction midway between south and southwest. • *adjective & adverb* from, toward, in, or facing this direction.

southward • *adjective & adverb* (also **southwards**) toward the south. • *noun* a southward direction or region.

southwest • *noun* **1** the point of the horizon midway between south and west. **2** (**Southwest**) the part of a country etc. lying to the southwest. • *adjective* of, toward, or coming from the southwest. • *adverb* toward, at, or near the southwest.

southwesterly • *adjective & adverb* = SOUTHWEST. • *noun* (also **southwester**) a southwest wind or storm.

southwestern *adjective* located or existing in the southwest of a region. ▶ **southwesterner** *noun*

southwestward *adjective & adverb* (also **southwestwards**) toward the southwest.

souvenir *noun* a usu. inexpensive article given or purchased as a reminder of a place visited or an event witnessed etc.; a memento or keepsake. [Say soova NEAR]

souvlaki *noun* a Greek dish of pieces of marinated meat, esp. lamb or pork, grilled on a skewer. [Say soov LACKY]

sou'wester *noun* **1** a waterproof hat, usu. made of oilskin, with a broad flap covering the neck and flaps tied under the chin, worn esp. at sea. **2** a southwesterly wind. [Say sow WESTER (SOW rhymes with COW)]

sovereign • *noun* the recognized supreme ruler of a people or country under monarchical government; a monarch. • *adjective* **1** (of a thing, quality, power, etc.) supreme, greatest, absolute: *the absolute sovereign confidence that the future is ours to conquer*. **2 a** characterized by independence or autonomy, esp. having the rights and responsibilities of self-government: *a sovereign state*. **b** concerned with or pertaining to independence or autonomy: *sovereign ambitions*. **3 a** (of a person) having superior or supreme rank or power, esp. holding the position of ruler or monarch. **b** of or related to a monarch; royal. **4** excellent; effective: *a sovereign remedy*. [Say SOV rin]

sovereignist (also **sovereigntist**) *Cdn* • *noun* a supporter of Quebec's right to self-government; an adherent to the principle of sovereignty-association. • *adjective* concerned with or relating to the movement for Quebec independence. [Say SOV rin ist, SOV rin tist]

sovereignty *noun (plural* **sovereignties**) **1** the authority of a state to govern itself or another state: *proponents of Quebec sovereignty* ◊ *the country claimed sovereignty over the island*. **2** supremacy with respect to power and rank; supreme authority: *the sovereignty of our invincible monarch*. **3** a territory or community existing as a self-governing state. [Say SOV rin tee]

sovereignty-association *noun* Cdn a proposed arrangement whereby Quebec would achieve political independence while maintaining a formal esp. economic association with the rest of Canada.

Soviet *hist.* • *noun* **1** a citizen of the USSR, a former federation of Communist republics occupying northern Asia and part of eastern Europe. **2** (**soviet**) an elected local, district, or national council in the former USSR with legislative and executive functions. **3** (**soviet**) a revolutionary council of workers, peasants, etc. before 1917. • *adjective* of or concerning the former USSR or its people. [Say SO vee it]

SPELL CHECK
SOW, sew ABC ✓

To stitch is to **sew**.

---

sow[1] *verb* (**sows**; *past* **sowed**; *past participle* **sown** or **sowed**; **sowing**) **1 a** scatter, sprinkle, or deposit (seed) on or in the earth. **b** (often foll. by *with*) plant (a field etc.) with seed. **2** initiate; arouse or spread: *sowed doubt in her mind.* **PHRASES** **sow the seed** (or **seeds**) **of** instigate, introduce; implant (an idea etc.). [Say SO]

sow[2] *noun* **1** a female adult pig. **2** the full-grown female of certain other animals, e.g. the bear and guinea pig. [Rhymes with COW]

sowbug *noun* a small terrestrial crustacean that feeds on rotten wood, esp. in damp habitats, and is often able to roll into a ball. [SOW rhymes with COW]

soy *noun* (also **soya**) **1** *see* SOY SAUCE. **2** *see* SOYBEAN.

soya burger *noun* (also **soyburger**) a vegetarian hamburger made with tofu instead of ground beef.

soybean *noun* (also esp. *Brit.* **soya bean**) **1** a plant, originally of Southeast Asia, cultivated for the edible oil and flour it yields, and used as a replacement for animal protein in certain foods. **2** the seed of this.

soybean milk *noun* (also **soy milk**) a fat-free substitute for milk made by suspending soybean flour in water.

soy sauce *noun* (also **soya sauce**) a dark brown salty sauce made from pickled soybeans.

SP *abbreviation* standard play, a setting on a VCR allowing two hours of material to be recorded on a standard tape.

spa *noun* **1** a curative or medicinal mineral spring. **2** a commercial establishment offering health and beauty treatment through steam baths, exercise equipment, etc. **3** (also **spa bath**) = HOT TUB.

space • *noun* **1 a** a continuous unlimited area or expanse which may or may not contain objects. **b** an interval between one, two, or three-dimensional points or objects: *a space of 10 metres.* **c** an empty area; room. **2 a** area sufficient, required, or available for some purpose or thing: *parking space ◊ cargo space.* **b** any of a number of places or positions for a person or thing: *spaces are limited.* **3 a** the immense expanse of the physical universe beyond the earth's atmosphere. **b** the near vacuum occupying the regions between the planets and stars, containing small amounts of gas and dust. **4** an interval of time: *in the space of an hour.* **5 a** time spent alone and used to think, reflect, or relax: *give me some space.* **b** = PERSONAL SPACE. **6** a usu. designated place in a book, letter, form, etc. available for or occupied by written or printed matter: *sign your name in the space below.* **7 a** an interval or blank space between printed or written words or lines. **b** the width occupied by a single typed character. **8** (also **commercial space**) an area rented or sold as business premises. • *verb* (**spaces**, **spaced**, **spacing**) **1** set, place, or arrange at determinate intervals. **2 a** separate (words, letters, or lines) by means of a space or spaces. **b** make or insert more or wider spaces between (esp. words, letters, lines, etc. in printing, typing, or writing). **PHRASES** **space out 1** spread out with more or wider spaces or intervals between. **2** experience an esp. drug-induced stupor or daze.

space age • *noun* (also **Space Age**) the present period, in which human exploration of space has become possible. • *adjective* (**space-age**) **1** characteristic of the space age. **2** designed with the most sophisticated or advanced technology.

space bar *noun* **1** a long horizontal key on a typewriter used to make a space between characters or words etc. **2** a similar key on a computer keyboard which also moves the cursor and advances the text.

space cadet *noun informal* a person who seems out of touch with reality.

spacecraft *noun* any of various manned or unmanned vehicles designed to travel in outer space.

spaced *adjective slang* (also **spaced out**) in a dazed, disoriented, or confused state.

space heater *noun* a small portable esp. electrical appliance used to heat a contained space or room.

spaceman *noun* (*plural* **spacemen**) *dated* **1** = ASTRONAUT 1. **2** a visitor from outer space.

space probe *noun* = PROBE *noun* 4.

space program *noun* a program designed for the exploration of outer space and development of space technology.

spacer *noun* a device used to make or keep a space or gap in something.

space-saving *adjective* **1** designed to occupy little space. **2** that saves space.

spaceship *noun* a manned spacecraft.

space shuttle *noun* a spacecraft that is designed and built for repeated use carrying equipment and astronauts into orbit or to a space station.

space station *noun* a manned artificial satellite used as a long-term base for operations in space.

spacesuit *noun* a sealed and pressurized protective suit that allows an astronaut to survive in space.

space-time *noun* (also **space-time continuum**) time and three-dimensional space regarded as fused in a four-dimensional continuum containing all events.

spacewalk *noun* any operation or activity performed by an astronaut in space outside of a spacecraft.

spacey *adjective* (also **spacy**) (**spacier**, **spaciest**) **1** *slang* absent-minded or out of touch with reality. **2** (esp. of music) relating to or characteristic of supposed conditions in outer space.

spacing *noun* **1** the arrangement of typed or written text, esp. the precise amount of space inserted between each character, word, or line, used to make text legible. **2** the arrangement of objects at particular intervals.

spacious *adjective* **1** having ample space: *a spacious room.* **2** (of land etc.) of vast or indefinite extent; covering a wide area: *spacious gardens.* ▶ **spaciously** *adverb* **spaciousness** *noun* [Say SPAY shuss]

spade • *noun* **1** a tool resembling a shovel used for digging or cutting the ground, consisting of a long handle with a grip or crossbar at the top attached to a sharp-edged square metal blade that may be driven into the ground with the foot. **2** any tool resembling this in shape or function. **3** a black inverted heart-shaped figure with a small stalk used to denote a playing card of a particular suit. **4** (in *plural*) the suit denoted by this figure. **5** a playing card of this suit. • *verb* (**spades**, **spaded**, **spading**) dig up, work, or remove with or as if with a spade. **PHRASES** **call a spade a spade** speak plainly or bluntly. **in spades** *informal* with great or excessive force or persistence. ▶ **spadeful** *noun* (*plural* **spadefuls**)

S

spadix *noun* a spike of flowers closely arranged around a fleshy axis and usu. enclosed in a spathe, e.g. in a calla lily. [Say SPAY dix]

spaghetti *noun* **1** pasta made in solid thin strings, thicker than vermicelli. **2** a dish of this with a sauce.

spaghettini *noun* very thin spaghetti. [Say spag get TEENY]

spaghetti strap *noun* a thin string-like shoulder strap on a dress etc.

spall • *noun* a splinter or chip, esp. of rock. • *verb* **1** (of concrete, brick, etc.) flake away. **2** break up or cause (ore) to break up in preparation for sorting. ▶ **spalling** *noun* [Rhymes with MALL]

spam • *noun* **1** (**Spam**) *proprietary* a tinned meat product made mainly from ham. **2** *Computing slang* **a** an esp. advertising message sent indiscriminately to a large number of newsgroups, mailing lists, etc. **b** such messages collectively. • *verb* (**spams, spammed, spamming**) *Computing slang* **1** send spam. **2** send spam to (a person, newsgroup, etc.). ▶ **spammer** *noun* **spamming** *noun*

span • *noun* **1** the full extent from end to end in space or time: *the whole span of history*. **2** the length of time for which attention, concentration, etc. can be maintained. **3** each arch or part of a bridge between piers or supports. **4** the maximum lateral extent of an airplane, its wing, a bird's wing, etc. **5 a** the maximum distance between the tips of the thumb and little finger. **b** this as a measurement, equal to 23 cm (9 inches). **6** a short distance or time: *our life is but a span*. • *verb* (**spans, spanned, spanning**) **1 a** (of a bridge, arch, etc.) stretch from side to side of; extend across: *the bridge spanned the river*. **b** (of a builder etc.) bridge (a river etc.). **2** extend across (space or a period of time etc.). **3** measure or cover the extent of (a thing) with one's hand with the fingers stretched.

spanakopita *noun* an originally Greek phyllo pastry stuffed with spinach, feta, etc. [Say spanna co PEET uh]

spandex *noun* an elastic polyurethane fabric used in foundation garments, tights, bathing suits, and other tight-fitting, stretchy garments.

spangle • *noun* **1** a small thin piece of glittering material esp. used in quantity to ornament a dress etc.; a sequin. **2** a small sparkling object. • *verb* (**spangles, spangled, spangling**) (esp. as **spangled** *adjective*) cover with or as with spangles: *star-spangled*. ▶ **spangly** *adjective*

Spaniard *noun* a native or national of Spain. [Say SPAN yurd]

spaniel *noun* a dog of any of various breeds with a long silky coat and drooping ears. [Say SPAN yull]

Spanish • *adjective* of Spain or its people or language. • *noun* **1** the principal language of Spain and Spanish America. **2** (**the Spanish**; treated as *plural*) the people of Spain.

Spanish Inquisition *noun hist.* an ecclesiastical court established by the Spanish crown in 1478 for the detection of heretics and directed originally against converts from Judaism and Islam but later also against Protestants. It operated with great severity and was not suppressed until the early 19th century.

Spanish moss *noun* a tropical American plant that grows as silvery-green festoons on trees.

Spanish onion *noun* a large, mild variety of onion.

spank • *verb* slap esp. on the buttocks with the open hand, a slipper, etc. • *noun* a slap esp. with the open hand on the buttocks.

spanking • *adverb informal* very, exceedingly: *spanking new*. • *noun* an act of slapping on the buttocks, esp. as a punishment for children.

spanner *noun* esp. *Brit.* a wrench.

spar • *verb* (**spars, sparred, sparring**) **1** (often foll. by *at*) make the motions of boxing without landing heavy blows. **2** engage in argument. • *noun* **1 a** a sparring motion. **b** a boxing match. **2** an argument or dispute. **3** a stout pole esp. used for the mast, yard, etc. of a ship. **4** the main lengthwise beam of an airplane wing.

spare • *adjective* **1** not required for ordinary use; extra, available: *spare cash*. **2** lean; thin: *a tall, spare man in a faded brown jacket*. **3** scanty; frugal; not copious: *a spare prose style*. **4** not wanted or used by others: *a spare seat*. • *noun* **1** a spare part, esp. a spare tire. **2** *Bowling* the knocking down of all the pins with the first two balls. **3** *Cdn* a period in one's school day schedule in which one is not required to be in class. • *verb* (**spares, spared, sparing**) **1** afford to give or do without: *cannot spare him*. **2 a** abstain from killing, hurting, wounding, etc.: *spared his feelings*. **b** abstain from inflicting or causing; relieve from; refrain from troubling with: *spare me the details*. **3** be frugal or grudging of: *no expense spared*. PHRASES **not spare oneself** exert one's utmost efforts. **to spare** left over; extra.

spareribs *plural noun* a cut of meat, esp. pork, consisting of closely-trimmed ribs.

spare tire *noun* **1** an extra tire carried in a vehicle for emergencies. **2** *informal* a roll of fat around the waist.

sparing *adjective* moderate, restrained: *a sparing use of dramatic gestures* ◊ *she is sparing with embellishments*. ▶ **sparingly** *adverb*

spark • *noun* **1** a fiery particle thrown off from a fire etc. **2** a particle of a quality etc.: *a spark of interest*. **3** *Electricity* **a** a light produced by a sudden disruptive discharge through the air etc. **b** such a discharge serving to ignite the explosive mixture in an internal combustion engine. **4 a** anything acting as an incitement or inspiration to action, or which excites emotions. **b** energy or enthusiasm. **5** a small bright object or point, e.g. in a gem. **6** (**Spark**) *Cdn* a member of the branch of Girl Guides for 5- or 6-year-olds. • *verb* **1** emit sparks of fire or electricity. **2** (often foll. by *off*) stir into activity; initiate (a process) suddenly. **3** *Electricity* produce sparks at the point where a circuit is interrupted. PHRASES **sparks flew** (or **will fly** etc.) there was (or will be etc.) a heated confrontation, friction, etc.

sparkle • *verb* (**sparkles, sparkled, sparkling**) **1 a** emit or seem to emit sparks: *her eyes sparkled*. **b** be witty: *sparkling repartee*. **c** perform conspicuously well. **2** (of wine etc.) be bubbly. • *noun* **1** a flash of light. **2** a glittering particle. **3 a** glittering or flashing appearance or quality. **b** vivacity, liveliness of spirit.

sparkler *noun* **1** a person or thing that sparkles. **2** a hand-held firework that produces showers of sparks when lit. **3** *informal* a diamond or other gem. **4** a sparkling wine, mineral water, etc.

sparkling *adjective* **1** (of wine or other drinks) bubbly. **2** shining and flashing with light. **3** excellent, brilliant: *a sparkling performance*.

sparkly *adjective* glittering; covered in sparkles.

spark plug *noun* **1** a device fitted to the cylinder head of an internal combustion engine, used to ignite the explosive mixture by the discharge of a spark between two electrodes at its end. **2** *informal* a person or thing which initiates, inspires, or encourages an activity or undertaking: *the tiny centre has been a spark plug since joining the team in December*.

sparky *adjective* (**sparkier, sparkiest**) energetic, enthusiastic; full of life: *a sparky personality*.

sparrow *noun* **1** a small bird with brown and grey plumage, esp. the house sparrow. **2** any of various

small New World birds that resemble true sparrows in size or colour, e.g. a bunting.

sparrow hawk *noun* a small falcon that is capable of hovering while searching for prey on the ground.

sparse *adjective* (**sparser**, **sparsest**) **1** thinly dispersed or scattered; not dense: *sparse population* ◊ *sparse hair*. **2** scanty, meagre. ▶**sparsely** *adverb* **sparseness** *noun* **sparsity** *noun*

Spartan • *adjective* **1** of or relating to the city of Sparta in ancient Greece. **2** (**spartan**) **a** possessing the qualities of courage, endurance, stern frugality, etc., associated with Sparta: *the company was run in a notoriously spartan manner to conserve cash*. **b** (of a regime, conditions, etc.) lacking comfort; austere: *more than 100 transients now live in the spartan but functional rooms*. • *noun* **1** a citizen of Sparta. **2** *Cdn* a medium- or large-sized red eating or cooking apple with tiny white dots, bred to withstand relatively cold winters.

spar tree *noun* esp. *Cdn* a tree or other tall structure to which cables are attached for hauling logs.

spasm *noun* **1 a** a sudden involuntary muscular contraction: *back spasms*. **b** a condition or state characterized by a spasm or spasms: *in anaphylactic shock the lungs go into spasm*. **2** *informal* a moment or period of a feeling or activity: *a spasm of guilt* ◊ *a spasm of violence*.

spasmodic *adjective* **1** of, caused by, or subject to, a spasm or spasms: *spasmodic asthma*. **2** occurring or done by fits and starts: *spasmodic efforts*. ▶**spasmodically** *adverb* [Say spaz MOD ick]

spastic • *adjective* **1** *Medical* affected by or pertaining to a spasm or sudden involuntary movements, esp. as part of a muscular weakness typical of cerebral palsy. **2** *offensive* uncoordinated, incompetent, stupid. • *noun offensive* **1** a person with cerebral palsy. **2** an uncoordinated or incompetent person. [Say SPASS tick]

spat¹ *past and past participle of* SPIT¹.

spat² *noun* **1** (usu. in *plural*) *hist.* a short cloth covering to protect the ankle and instep from mud etc., formerly worn by men over the shoe and fastened with buttons at the side. **2** a cover for an aircraft wheel.

spat³ *informal* • *noun* a petty quarrel. • *verb* (**spats**, **spatted**, **spatting**) quarrel pettily.

spate *noun* **1** a situation in which the volume of water flowing through a river is much higher than normal, usu. temporarily as a result of heavy rains or melting snow. **2** a sudden outburst; a large or excessive amount: *a spate of inquiries*. PHRASES **in (full) spate 1** (of a river) flowing strongly at a much higher level than normal. **2** at the height of activity: *her greatest talents continued in spate into old age*.

spathe *noun Botany* a large bract or pair of bracts enclosing the flower cluster of certain plants, esp. the spadix of arums and palms. [Rhymes with BATHE]

spatial *adjective* **1** of or concerning space: *spatial extent*. **2** having extension in space; occupying space. ▶**spatially** *adverb* [Say SPAY shull]

spatter • *verb* **1 a** (often foll. by *with*) splash or stain (a person etc.) with spots of liquid etc.: *spattered him with mud*. **b** scatter or splash (liquid, mud, etc.), esp. in drops or small particles. **2** (of rain etc.) fall here and there. • *noun* **1** (usu. foll. by *of*) a splash: *a spatter of mud*. **2** a quick pattering sound.

spatula *noun* **1** any of various cooking utensils, esp.: **a** an implement with a broad flexible rubber blade, used to scrape the sides of a bowl etc. **b** a knifelike implement with a blunt blade, used to spread icing etc. **c** an implement with a rigid usu. square blade set at an angle, used to lift or flip pancakes, hamburgers, eggs, etc. **2** any of various broad-bladed implements for stirring, spreading, or technical uses.

spatulate *adjective* **1** having a broad rounded end.

2 (of a leaf) broad at the apex and tapering at the base. [Say SPATCH oo lut]

spawn • *verb* **1 a** (of a fish, frog, mollusc, or crustacean) produce or fertilize (eggs). **b** be produced as eggs or young. **2** *derogatory* (of people) produce (offspring). **3** produce or generate, esp. in large numbers: *the film spawned a large cult following*. • *noun* **1** the eggs of fish, frogs, etc. **2** *derogatory* human offspring: *the bejewelled Mrs. Scott-Baxter glowered at her former husband, sitting with the spawn of his most recent marriage*. **3** a product, result, or effect of something: *Garraveau examines nine cities and their architectural spawn, depicting a realm of malls, corporate parks, and artificial waterfalls*. **4** a white fibrous matter from which fungi are produced. ▶**spawner** *noun*

spay *verb* sterilize (a female animal) by removing the ovaries. ▶**spayed** *adjective*

spaz *noun* (*plural* **spazzes**) *slang* an uncoordinated, awkward, or disturbed person. PHRASES **spaz out** (**spazzes**, **spazzed**, **spazzing**) lose control; become frenetic, overly excited, emotional, etc.; freak out. **take** (or **have**) **a spaz** = SPAZ OUT.

SPCA *abbreviation* Society for the Prevention of Cruelty to Animals.

speak *verb* (**speaks**; *past* **spoke**; *past participle* **spoken**; **speaking**) **1** make articulate verbal utterances in an ordinary (not singing) voice. **2 a** (foll. by *of*) mention in writing etc.: *speaks of it in his novel*. **b** (foll. by *for*) articulate the feelings of (another person etc.) in speech or writing. **3** use or be able to use (a specified language): *cannot speak French*. **4** (usu. foll. by *to*) *literary* communicate feeling etc., affect, touch: *the sunset spoke to her*. PHRASES **nothing to speak of** nothing worth mentioning; practically nothing. **not to speak of** = NOT TO MENTION (see MENTION). **speak for itself** need no supporting evidence. **speak for oneself 1** give one's own opinions. **2** not presume to speak for others. **speaking of** used to introduce a statement etc. on a topic recently alluded to. **speak in tongues** *Christianity* speak or be able to speak in a language one does not know, identified as a gift of the Holy Spirit. **speak one's mind** speak bluntly or frankly. **speak out** speak loudly or freely, give one's opinion. **speak up** = SPEAK OUT. **speak volumes** (of a fact etc.) be very significant. **speak volumes** (or **well** etc.) **about** (or **for**) **1** be abundant evidence of. **2** place in a favourable light.

-speak *combining form* forming nouns denoting a particular variety of language or mode of speaking.

speakeasy *noun* (*plural* **speakeasies**) esp. *hist. slang* a bar etc. selling liquor illicitly.

speaker *noun* **1** a person who speaks, esp. in public. **2** a person who speaks a specified language: *a French-speaker*. **3** (**Speaker**) the presiding officer in a legislative assembly. **4** = LOUDSPEAKER.

speakerphone *noun* a telephone with a loudspeaker and microphone, which does not need to be held in the hand.

speaking • *noun* the action of uttering words etc., or of making speeches or lectures. • *adjective* **1** that speaks; capable of articulate speech. **2** (in *combination*) speaking or capable of speaking a specified language: *French-speaking*. **3** with a reference or from a point of view specified: *roughly speaking*. PHRASES **on speaking terms** (foll. by *with*) **1** slightly acquainted. **2** on friendly terms.

spear • *noun* **1** a thrusting or throwing weapon with a pointed tip and a long shaft. **2** a similar barbed instrument used for catching fish etc. **3** a pointed stem of asparagus etc. • *verb* **1** pierce or strike with or as if with a spear: *speared an olive*. **2** *Hockey* jab or poke (a player) with the blade of the stick.

spearfishing *noun* fishing using a spear.

spearhead • *noun* **1** (also **spear point**) the point of a spear. **2** an individual or group leading a campaign, attack, initiative, etc. • *verb* act as the spearhead of (an attack etc.).

spearing *noun* **1** *in senses of* SPEAR *verb*. **2** *Hockey* the illegal jabbing or poking of an opponent with the blade of one's stick.

spearmint *noun* a common garden mint, used in cooking and to flavour esp. chewing gum.

spec *noun* (usu. in *plural*) a detailed working description; a specification or specifications. PHRASES **on spec** *informal* without the assurance of success or reward; as a gamble: *bought the three properties on spec.*

special • *adjective* **1 a** particularly good; exceptional; out of the ordinary. **b** peculiar; specific; not general: *lacks the special qualities required.* **2** for a particular purpose: *sent on a special assignment.* **3** in which a person specializes: *statistics is her special field.* **4** denoting education for children with particular needs, e.g. the handicapped. • *noun* **1** a special person or thing, e.g. a special train, constable, dish on a menu, etc. **2** the offering of a product or service at a temporarily reduced price: *this week's specials.* **3** a program scheduled and aired in place of regular programming, usu. to mark an occasion, season, holiday, etc. **4** a newspaper article by a writer who is not a regular member of the newspaper's staff. PHRASES **on special** available for purchase at a temporarily reduced price.

special committee *noun* a committee, e.g. of a legislature, formed to examine one particular issue or piece of proposed legislation.

special constable *noun Cdn & Brit.* a police officer sworn in to assist in times of emergency etc. or having a limited range of responsibilities.

special edition *noun* **1** an extra edition of a newspaper etc. including later news than the ordinary edition. **2** a specially modified version of a product, esp. available in limited quantities: *special edition coupe.*

special education *noun* (also *informal* **special ed**) **1** the education of children with special needs arising from physical or mental disabilities. **2** a program providing such education.

special effects *plural noun* scenic or optical illusions for films, television, or the stage, created by computers, props, camera work, etc.

special interest group *noun* **1** (also **special interest**) a group of people or a corporation with a common political interest or purpose. **2** a computerized discussion group on a specific topic etc.

special investigations unit *noun* an independent police unit responsible for investigating the conduct of police officers of other forces. Abbreviation: **SIU**.

specialist *noun* **1** a person who is trained in a particular branch of a profession, esp. medicine. **2** a person who especially or exclusively studies a subject or a particular branch of a subject.

speciality (*plural* **specialities**) = SPECIALTY 1, 2. [Say speshy ALA tee]

specialization *noun* **1** an act of specializing. **2** an activity in which one specializes.

specialize *verb* (**specializes, specialized, specializing**) **1** (often foll. by *in*) **a** concentrate on and become an expert in a particular subject or skill: *he could specialize in mining law.* **b** limit oneself to providing a particular product or service: *they specialize in children's books.* **2** make a habit of engaging in a particular activity: *specializes in insulting people.* **3** *Biology* adapt or set apart an organ or part to serve a special function or to suit a particular way of life.

specialized *adjective* **1** requiring or involving detailed and specific knowledge or training: *film could reach a mass audience, whereas painting was so elitist and specialized.* **2** concentrating on a small area of a subject: *magazines have become more and more specialized.* **3** designed for a particular purpose: *specialized software.*

specially *adverb* for a particular purpose, person, etc.: *the ring was specially made for her ◊ a specially designed door frame.*

special needs *plural noun* **1** the special esp. educational requirements of people with disabilities. **2** (as an *adjective*) (**special-needs**) designating such people or their education: *special-needs children.*

specialness *noun* the quality of being special.

Special Olympics *plural noun* an international multi-event sporting competition (similar to the Olympic Games) for people with mental disabilities.

special team *noun* (also **specialty team**) a group of players on a team used especially or exclusively in certain well-defined circumstances, e.g. when killing penalties in hockey.

specialty *noun* (*plural* **specialties**) **1** a special pursuit, product, operation, etc., to which a company or a person gives special attention. **2** a special feature, characteristic, or skill. **3** (as an *adjective*) designating a product, store, etc. pertaining or devoted to a very specific interest: *a specialty bookstore.* [Say SPESH ul tee]

specie *noun* coin money as opposed to paper money: *Howe, as a believer in specie, tried to stem the flow of paper money.* [Say SPEE see]

species *noun* (*plural* **species**) **1** a group of living organisms consisting of related similar individuals capable of exchanging genes or interbreeding, classified as a rank below a genus and denoted by a Latin name with two parts: *a wolf of the species Canis lupus, commonly known as the grey wolf.* **2** a class of things having some common characteristic; a kind or sort: *that species of reflective thinker we call the philosopher ◊ molecular species.* [Say SPEE seez or SPEE sheez]

specific • *adjective* **1** clearly defined; definite; precise: *has no specific name.* **2** relating to one particular subject or thing; peculiar, particular: *music specific to the region ◊ culture-specific.* **3 a** of or concerning a species: *the generic name for a plant.* **b** possessing, or concerned with, the properties that characterize a species: *the specific forms of animals.* • *noun* (esp. in *plural*) a specific aspect or factor: *shall we discuss specifics?* ▶ **specifically** *adverb*

specification *noun* **1** an act of describing or identifying something precisely or of stating a precise requirement: *there was no clear specification of objectives.* **2 a** (esp. in *plural*) a detailed description of the construction, workmanship, materials, etc., of work done or to be done, prepared by an architect, engineer, etc. **b** (in *plural*) a detailed description of the components of an electronic system, e.g. a computer. **c** a specified standard of workmanship, materials, etc., to be achieved: *built to a high specification ◊ the house was built to our specifications.* [Say spess iffa KAY sh'n]

specific gravity *noun Chemistry* the ratio of the density of a substance to the density of a standard.

specificity *noun* the quality of being clearly defined or identified: *Quebec's cultural specificity within Canada.* [Say spess if ISSA tee]

specific land claim *noun Cdn* a land claim made against the federal government when specific treaty terms have not been met.

specify *verb* (**specifies, specified, specifying**) **1** name or mention expressly: *specified the type.* **2** name as a condition: *specified that he must be paid.* **3** include in specifications: *a French window was not specified.*

specimen *noun* **1** an individual or part taken as an example of a class or whole, esp. when used for investi-

gation or scientific examination: *a specimen of your handwriting*. **2** a sample of urine, blood, tissue, etc. for testing. **3** *informal* usu. *derogatory* a person of a specified sort.

specious *adjective* **1** seeming reasonable or believable but actually wrong or false: *he dismisses as specious a number of arguments* ◊ *a masterpiece of specious reasoning*. **2** misleadingly attractive in appearance: *depicted with specious picturesqueness*. ▶**speciously** *adverb* [Say SPEE shuss]

---

speck *noun* **1** a small spot, dot, or stain. **2** (foll. by *of*) a particle: *speck of dirt*.

specked *adjective* marked with small spots.

speckle *noun* a small spot, mark, or stain, esp. in quantity on the skin, a bird's egg, etc.

speckled *adjective* marked with small spots or patches: *speckled butterflies* ◊ *a sky speckled with stars*.

speckled trout *noun* = BROOK TROUT.

specs *plural noun informal* a pair of eyeglasses.

spec sheet *noun* a list of an item's specifications.

spectacle *noun* **1** a public show, ceremony, etc. **2** anything attracting public attention: *a disgusting spectacle*. **3** a ridiculous person or thing. PHRASES **make a spectacle of oneself** make oneself an object of ridicule.

spectacles *plural noun* a pair of eyeglasses.

spectacular • *adjective* **1** beautiful or impressive in a dramatic and eye-catching way. **2** strikingly large or obvious: *a spectacular increase*. • *noun* a spectacular thing or event, esp. a musical. ▶**spectacularly** *adverb*

spectate *verb* (**spectates, spectated, spectating**) be a spectator, esp. at a sporting event.

spectator *noun* a person who looks on at a show, game, incident, etc. ▶**spectatorship** *noun*

spectra *plural of* SPECTRUM.

spectral *adjective* **1 a** of or relating to spectres or ghosts: *spectral evidence became admissible in court, meaning that people could be accused if their ghost had been seen performing acts of witchcraft*. **b** ghostlike: *the spectral figure hanging from the attic window*. **2** of or concerning spectra or the spectrum: *spectral colours*.

spectral line *noun* each of a series of lines in a spectrum, associated with a characteristic wavelength of a particular frequency.

spectre *noun* **1** a ghost. **2** something widely feared as a possible unpleasant or dangerous occurrence: *the spectre of war*.

spectrograph *noun* an apparatus for photographing or otherwise recording spectra. ▶**spectrographic** *adjective* [Say SPECTRO graph, spectro GRAPHIC]

spectrometer *noun* an instrument used for the measurement of observed spectra. ▶**spectrometry** *noun* [Say speck TROMMA tur, speck TROMMA tree]

spectroscope *noun* an instrument for producing and recording spectra for examination. ▶**spectroscopic** *adjective* **spectroscopy** *noun* [Say SPECTRO scope, spectro SCOP ick, speck TROSS kuh pee]

spectrum *noun* (*plural* **spectra** or **spectrums**) **1** a band of colours, as seen in a rainbow etc., produced by separation of the components of light by their different degrees of refraction according to wavelength. **2** the entire range of wavelengths of electromagnetic radiation. **3 a** an image or distribution of components of any electromagnetic radiation arranged in a progressive series according to wavelength. **b** this as characteristic of a body or substance when emitting or absorbing radiation. **4** a similar image or distribution of components of sound, particles, etc., arranged according to frequency, charge, energy, etc. **5** the entire range or a wide range of anything arranged by degree or quality etc.: *political spectrum*.

speculate *verb* (**speculates, speculated, speculating**) **1** form a theory or opinion about a subject without firm evidence: *the coach refused to speculate on the trade rumours* ◊ *the author speculates about Shakespeare's views and feelings* ◊ *insiders have been speculating that an election call could come this week*. **2** invest in stocks, property, or other ventures in the hope of gain but with the possibility of loss: *speculating in gold futures*. ▶**speculation** *noun*

speculative *adjective* **1** of, based on, engaged in, or inclined to speculation: *a speculative analysis*. **2** (of a business investment) involving the risk of loss: *a speculative biotech stock*. ▶**speculatively** *adverb* [Say SPECK yoo luh tiv]

speculator *noun* a person who buys and sells goods or shares in a company in the hope of making a profit: *property speculators*.

speculum *noun* **1** an instrument to hold open or dilate a part of the body, esp. the vagina, for examination. **2** a lustrous coloured area on the wing of some birds, esp. ducks. [Say SPECK yoo lum]

sped *past and past participle of* SPEED.

speech *noun* (*plural* **speeches**) **1** the faculty or act of speaking. **2** a usu. formal address or discourse delivered to an audience or assembly. **3** a manner of speaking: *a man of blunt speech*. **4** a remark: *after this speech he was silent*. **5** the language of a nation, group, etc. **6** = SOUND[1] *noun* 7.

Speech from the Throne *noun Cdn* a statement summarizing the government's proposed measures, read by the sovereign, Governor General, or Lieutenant-Governor at the opening of a session of Parliament or a legislature.

speechify *verb* (**speechifies, speechified, speechifying**) *jocular* or *derogatory* make esp. boring or long speeches.

speech-language pathologist *noun* a specialist who treats disorders of speech and communication.

speech-language pathology *noun* (also **speech pathology**) the treatment of disorders of speech and communication.

speechless *adjective* **1** unable to speak, esp. temporarily because of emotion etc.: *speechless with rage*. **2** (of an emotion etc.) tending to deprive one temporarily of speech.

speech recognition *noun* the identification and interpretation or response by a computer to the sounds produced in human speech.

speech therapist *noun* = SPEECH-LANGUAGE PATHOLOGIST.

speech therapy *noun* esp. *Brit.* = SPEECH-LANGUAGE PATHOLOGY.

speed • *noun* **1** rapidity of movement: *at full speed*. **2** a rate of progress or motion over a distance in time: *attains a high speed*. **3** each of the possible gear ratios in a motor vehicle, bicycle, etc.: *a ten-speed bike*. **4** *Photography* **a** the sensitivity of film to light. **b** the light gathering power of a lens. **c** the duration of an exposure. **5** *slang* an amphetamine drug, esp. methamphetamine. **6** *informal* a person, activity, etc. that suits one's abilities or personality: *robbing banks is hardly his speed*. • *verb* (**speeds**; *past* and *past participle* **sped** or **speeded**; **speeding**) **1** go fast: *sped down the street*. **2** (of a motorist etc.) travel at an illegal or

dangerous speed. **3** send fast or on its way. PHRASES **at speed** moving quickly. **speed up** move or work at greater speed. **up to speed 1** operating at full speed. **2** operating or functioning at an anticipated level: *trying to get the company up to speed*. **3** fully informed.

speedball *noun* *slang* a mixture of cocaine with heroin or morphine.

speedboat *noun* a motorboat designed for high speed. ▶ **speedboater** *noun* **speedboating** *noun*

speed bump *noun* a ridge across a roadway requiring drivers to slow down to pass over it.

speed-dial *noun* a function on some telephones which allows frequently-called numbers to be entered into a memory for faster dialing. ▶ **speed-dialing** *noun*

speeder *noun* **1** a person who exceeds the speed limit while driving. **2** a small vehicle running on railway tracks for purposes of maintenance.

speedily *adverb* quickly; without delay.

speeding *noun* the traffic offence of driving at an illegal or dangerous speed.

speed limit *noun* the maximum speed at which a road vehicle may legally be driven in a particular area etc.

speed metal *noun* a variety of heavy metal music with a very fast tempo.

speedometer *noun* an instrument displaying the speed of motor vehicle etc. [Say spuh DOMMA tur]

speed-read *verb* (**speed-reads**, **speed-read**, **speed-reading**) read rapidly, e.g. by assimilating several phrases or sentences at once. ▶ **speed-reader** *noun*

speed skater *noun* a skater who races, esp. on an oval track.

speed skating *noun* racing performed on skates around a usu. oval track against other skaters or the clock.

speedster *noun* **1** a fast motor vehicle, esp. a sports car. **2** a person or animal that runs etc. quickly. **3** a person who drives too quickly.

speed trap *noun* a part of a highway etc. where police, usu. concealed, check the speed of passing vehicles.

speed-up *noun* an increase in the speed or rate of working.

speedway *noun* **1** a road or track used for motor racing. **2** a highway for fast motor traffic. **3 a** motor-cycle racing. **b** a stadium or track used for this.

speedy *adjective* (**speedier**, **speediest**) **1** moving quickly; rapid. **2** done without delay; prompt: *a speedy answer*.

spell¹ *verb* (**spells**; *past* and *past participle* **spelled** or **spelt**; **spelling**) **1** write or name the letters that form (a word etc.) in correct sequence. **2** (of letters) make up or form (a word etc.). **3** (of circumstances, a scheme, etc.) result in; involve: *this decision spells ruin for the project*. PHRASES **spell out 1** make out (words, writing, etc.) letter by letter. **2** explain in detail.

spell² *noun* **1 a** words which when spoken are thought to have magical power. **b** a state or condition caused by a person speaking such words: *put a spell on her*. **2** a fascinating or very attractive influence that a person or thing has. PHRASES **under a spell** mastered by or as if by a spell.

spell³ • *noun* **1** a period of time during which something lasts. **2** a period of a specified type of weather: *a hot spell*. **3** a bout or fit of something: *had a dizzy spell*. **4** a period of activity or duty, esp. one which two or more people share: *take a spell at the wheel*. • *verb* (**spells**, **spelled**, **spelling**) (often foll. by *off*) **1** relieve or take the place of (a person) in work etc. **2** allow to rest briefly.

spellbind *verb* (**spellbinds**, **spellbound**, **spellbinding**) hold the complete attention of

(someone) as though by magic; fascinate. ▶ **spellbinding** *adjective*

spellbound *adjective* entranced, fascinated, esp. by a speaker, activity, quality, etc.

spell check • *noun* a check of the spelling in a file of text using a spell checker. • *verb* check the spelling in (a text) using a spell checker.

spell checker *noun* (also **spelling checker**) a computer program which checks the spelling of words in files of text.

speller *noun* **1** a person who spells esp. in a specified way: *is a poor speller*. **2** a book for teaching spelling. **3** = SPELL CHECKER.

spelling *noun* **1** the process or activity of writing or naming the letters of a word etc. **2** the way a word is spelled. **3** the ability to spell: *her spelling is poor*.

spelling bee *noun* a competition in which competitors spell words orally and are eliminated for misspellings, until the competitor who spells the most words correctly is named the winner.

spelt¹ *past and past participle of* SPELL¹.

spelt² *noun* an older species of wheat, not widely grown but favoured as a health food.

spelunker *noun* a person who explores caves, esp. as a hobby. ▶ **spelunking** *noun* [Say spil LUNK er]

spend *verb* (**spends**, **spent**, **spending**) **1** pay out money. **2 a** use or consume (time or energy): *spent three hours fixing it*. **b** use up; exhaust; wear out: *his anger was soon spent*. **3** pass (time, one's life, etc.): *spent all our summers in Goderich*. ▶ **spender** *noun*

spendthrift • *noun* a person who spends money too freely or wastes money. • *adjective* extravagant.

spent • *verb* *past and past participle of* SPEND. • *adjective* having lost its original force or strength: *police found two bullet holes in the basement and a spent .22 bullet on the floor*.

sperm *noun* (*plural* **sperm** or **sperms**) **1** = SPERMATOZOON. **2** semen. **3** = SPERM WHALE. **4** = SPERMACETI.

spermaceti *noun* a white waxy substance produced by the sperm whale to help it float, formerly used in the manufacture of candles etc. [Say sperma SETTY]

spermatozoon *noun* (*plural* **spermatozoa**) a cell that is produced by the sex organs of a male and that can combine with a female egg to produce young. [Say sperm atto ZO un]

sperm bank *noun* a place where semen is stored for use in artificial insemination.

spermicidal *adjective* sperm-killing. [Say sperma SIDE ul]

spermicide *noun* a substance able to kill spermatozoa. [Say SPERMA side]

sperm whale *noun* a large toothed whale with a massive head, formerly hunted for the spermaceti and oil in its head and the ambergris in its intestines.

spew • *verb* **1** vomit. **2** (often foll. by *out*) **a** expel (contents) rapidly and forcibly. **b** (of contents) be expelled in this way. **3** (often foll. by *out*, *forth*) utter (language, esp. abusive or objectionable language): *was always spewing lies about us*. • *noun* vomited food etc.

SPF *abbreviation* sun protection factor (indicating the effectiveness of sunscreens etc.).

sphagnum *noun* (also **sphagnum moss**) a moss with spongy, absorbent leaves and stems, growing in bogs and used esp. as packing for plants and as a soil conditioner. [Say SFAG num or SPAG num]

sphere *noun* **1** a solid figure, or its surface, with every point on its surface equidistant from its centre. **2** an object having this shape; a ball or globe. **3 a** any celestial body. **b** a globe representing the earth. **c** the sky perceived as a vault upon or in which celestial bodies are represented as lying. **4 a** a field of action,

influence, or existence: *have done much within their own sphere*. **b** a (usu. specified) stratum of society or social class: *moves in quite another sphere*. PHRASES **sphere of influence** the claimed or recognized area of a state's interests, an individual's control, etc.

spherical *adjective* **1** shaped like a sphere; globular. **2 a** of or relating to the properties of spheres: *spherical geometry*. **b** formed inside or on the surface of a sphere: *spherical triangle*. [Say SFEER ick ul or SFAIR ick ul]

spheroid *noun* a body resembling or approximating to a sphere in shape, esp. one formed by the revolution of an ellipse about one of its axes. ▶ **spheroidal** *adjective* [Say SFEER oid, sfeer OID ul]

sphincter *noun* a ring of muscle surrounding and serving to guard or close an opening or tube, esp. the anus. [Say SFINK tur]

sphinx *noun* (*plural* **sphinxes**) **1** (**Sphinx**) (in Greek mythology) the winged monster of Thebes, having a woman's head and a lion's body, whose riddle Oedipus guessed and who consequently killed herself. **2 a** any of several ancient Egyptian stone figures having a lion's body and a human or animal head. **b** (**the Sphinx**) the huge sphinx near the Pyramids at Giza. **3** a mysterious person; a person that is difficult to understand or interpret: *he's still an enigma, a sphinx, a person we may never know the half of*. [Say SFINKS]

spic and span *adjective* (also **spick-and-span**) **1** smart and new. **2** neat and clean.

spice • *noun* **1** a strongly flavoured vegetable substance used to season food, e.g. ginger, pepper, or cinnamon. **2** spices collectively. **3** an interesting or piquant quality: *it could be time to put some spice and even a bit of adventure back in your holiday*. • *verb* (**spices, spiced, spicing**) **1** flavour with spice. **2** add an interesting or piquant quality to: *spiced with humour*.

spiciness *noun* the quality of being spicy.

spicule *noun* any small sharp-pointed body. [Say SPICK yule]

spicy *adjective* (**spicier, spiciest**) **1** of, flavoured with, or fragrant with spice. **2** sensational or improper: *a spicy story*.

spider *noun* **1** an eight-legged arthropod with a round unsegmented body, capable of spinning webs to capture insects as food. **2** any object comparable to a spider, esp. as having numerous or prominent legs or radiating spokes.

spider crab *noun* a crab with long thin legs and a compact pear-shaped body.

spider mite *noun* (also **red spider mite**) a plant-feeding mite that resembles a tiny spider and is often a garden pest.

spider monkey *noun* a monkey of Central and South America with long slender limbs and a long tail used for grasping.

spider plant *noun* a plant of the lily family, which has long narrow leaves with a central yellow stripe, native to southern Africa and popular as a houseplant.

spiderweb *noun* **1** a web spun by a spider. **2** something resembling this.

spidery *adjective* elongated and thin: *spidery handwriting*.

spiel[1] *slang* • *noun* a long or prepared speech or story, esp. a sales pitch. • *verb* (**spiels, spieled, spieling**) **1** speak in this style; hold forth. **2** reel off (a sales pitch etc.). [Say SHPEEL or SPEEL]

spiel[2] *noun informal* a bonspiel. [Say SPEEL]

spiff *verb* (foll. by *up*) *informal* make attractive or smart.

spiffily *adverb* in an excellent or elegantly fashionable manner.

spiffy *adjective* (**spiffier, spiffiest**) *informal* **1** excellent. **2** well-dressed. **3** elegant, fashionable.

spigot *noun* **1** a small peg or plug, esp. for insertion into the vent of a cask. **2 a** *US* a tap. **b** a device for controlling the flow of liquid in a tap. [Say SPIG ut]

spike[1] • *noun* **1 a** a sharp point. **b** a pointed piece of metal, esp. the top of an iron railing etc. **c** an upstanding pointed object. **2** a large nail, e.g. one used for railways or in eavestroughing. **3 a** any of several metal points set into the sole of a running shoe to prevent slipping. **b** (in *plural*) a pair of running shoes with spikes. **c** (in *plural*) spike heels. **4 a** a sharp increase. **b** *Electronics* a pulse of very short duration in which a rapid increase in voltage is followed by a rapid decrease. **5** (in volleyball) an act of spiking the ball. • *verb* (**spikes, spiked, spiking**) **1 a** fasten or provide with spikes. **b** fix on or pierce with spikes. **c** form into spikes. **2** *informal* **a** lace (a drink) with alcohol, a drug, etc. **b** contaminate (a substance) with something added. **c** flavour (a dish) with a strong herb, spice, condiment, etc. **3** (in volleyball) hit (the ball) forcefully from a position near the net so that it moves downward into the opposite court. **4** *Football* fling (the ball) forcefully to the ground, esp. in celebration of a touchdown or victory. **5** make useless, put an end to, thwart (an idea etc.). **6** *hist.* plug up the vent of (a gun) with a spike. **7** drive a long nail into (a tree) so as to make it dangerous to cut down the tree with a chainsaw. **8 a** experience (a rapidly rising fever). **b** (of a fever) rapidly rise to a high level.

spike[2] *noun* **1** a flower cluster formed of many flower heads attached closely on a long stem. **2** a separate sprig of any plant in which flowers form a spike-like cluster. ▶ **spikelet** *noun*

spike heel *noun* **1** a very slender high tapering heel of a shoe. **2** a shoe having this type of heel.

spiky *adjective* (**spikier, spikiest**) **1** resembling a spike. **2** having a spike or spikes.

spile *noun* **1** a small spout for tapping sap from a sugar maple. **2** a wooden peg or spigot. **3** a large timber or pile for driving into the ground.

spill • *verb* (**spills**; *past* and *past participle* **spilled** or **spilt**; **spilling**) **1 a** fall or run or cause (a liquid, powder, etc.) to fall or run out of a container, esp. unintentionally. **b** cast (light) or (of light) be cast into a darker area. **2** (esp. of a crowd) move out quickly from a place etc., esp. in great numbers: *spilled into the street*. **3** *slang* disclose (information etc.). **4** throw (a person etc.) from a vehicle, saddle, etc. • *noun* **1** an act of spilling a liquid; liquid that has been spilled: *an oil spill* ◊ *wipe up spills immediately*. **2** a tumble or fall, esp. from a horse etc.: *had a nasty spill*. PHRASES **spill the beans** *informal* reveal information etc., esp. unintentionally or indiscreetly. **spill blood** kill or wound people. **spill one's guts** reveal one's thoughts or feelings without restraint. **spill over 1** overflow. **2** (of a surplus population) encroach upon an area. ▶ **spillage** *noun*

spillover *noun* **1** something that has spread or overflowed into another area: *we catch the spillover from some of the more crowded centres*. **2** a consequence, repercussion, or by-product: *a casino in Windsor will have a spillover effect on surrounding communities*.

spillway *noun* a passage for surplus water from a dam, reservoir, etc.

spin • *verb* (**spins, spun, spinning**) **1** turn or cause (a person or thing) to turn or whirl round quickly. **2** make thread from wool, cotton, or a synthetic substance. **3** (of a spider, silkworm, etc.) make (a web, gossamer, a cocoon, etc.) by extruding a fine viscous thread. **4** tell or write (a story etc.): *spins a good tale*. **5** impart spin to

(a ball). **6** (of a person's head etc.) be dizzy. **7** (of a wheel or wheels) revolve rapidly without providing traction. **8** (of a ball) move through the air with spin. **9** *informal* play (records); act as a disc jockey: *she spins at a local dance club*. **10** (of a washing machine) rotate wet clothing rapidly to remove excess water. • *noun* **1** a spinning motion; a whirl. **2** = TAILSPIN *noun* 3. **3** a revolving motion through the air, esp. in a rifle bullet or ball. **4** *informal* **a** a brief excursion in a motor vehicle, airplane, etc., esp. for pleasure. **b** a rapid perusal: *a quick spin through her memoirs*. **5** a bias in information to give a favourable impression. **6** the cycle on a washing machine during which the clothing is spun. **7** *Figure Skating* any of a number of movements involving rotating rapidly in one spot. PHRASES **spin off 1** produce as a spinoff. **2 a** distribute (stock of a new company) to shareholders of a parent company. **b** create (a company) in this way. **3** throw off by centrifugal force in spinning. **spin out 1** prolong (a discussion etc.). **2** make (a story, money, etc.) last as long as possible. **3** spend or consume (time, one's life, etc., by discussion or in an occupation etc.). **4** (esp. of a driver or car) lose or go out of control, esp. in a skid. **spin one's wheels** waste one's time or efforts.

spina bifida *noun* a congenital defect of the spine, in which part of the spinal cord and meninges are exposed through a gap in the backbone. [Say spine a BIFFA duh]

spinach *noun* a green garden plant with succulent leaves that are eaten as a vegetable.

spinal • *adjective* of or relating to the spine. • *noun informal* an epidural anaesthetic, used esp. in childbirth to produce loss of sensation below the waist.

spinal column *noun* the spine.

spinal cord *noun* a cylindrical structure of the central nervous system enclosed in the spine, connecting all parts of the body with the brain.

spinal fluid *noun* a clear fluid surrounding the brain and spinal cord.

spinal tap *noun* the insertion of a needle into the spine, usu. in the lumbar region, so that spinal fluid may be withdrawn or something (such as an anesthetic) may be introduced.

spinarama *noun* *Cdn* an evasive move, esp. in hockey, consisting of an abrupt 360-degree turn.

spin control *noun slang* an attempt to give a particular slant to esp. political news coverage.

spindle • *noun* **1** a pin for twisting and winding thread. **2** a pin or axis that revolves or on which something revolves. **3** a turned piece of wood used as a banister, chair leg, etc. **4** *Biology* a spindle-shaped mass formed when a cell divides. • *verb* (**spindles, spindled, spindling**) impale (a piece of paper) on a spike.

spindly *adjective* (**spindlier, spindliest**) long or tall and thin; thin and weak.

spin doctor *noun informal* a political or corporate spokesperson employed to give a favourable interpretation of events to the media.

spindrift *noun* spray blown along the surface of the sea.

spine *noun* **1** the backbone. **2** *Zoology & Botany* any hard, pointed structure, e.g. a sharp-pointed ray on the fin of a fish. **3** a sharp ridge or projection, esp. of a mountain range or slope. **4** resolution, firmness of character: *he has no spine whatsoever*. **5** the part of a book's jacket or cover that encloses the part where the pages are stitched or glued. **6** a central feature, main support, or source of strength: *a long corridor along the building's spine provided access to the suites on either side*. ▶ **spined** *adjective*

spineless *adjective* **1** (of a person or action etc.) lacking energy or decisiveness; weak and purposeless. **2 a** having no spine. **b** (of a fish) having fins without spines. ▶ **spinelessly** *adverb* **spinelessness** *noun*

spine-tingling *adjective* thrilling or pleasurably frightening.

spinnaker *noun* a large triangular sail carried opposite the mainsail of a racing yacht running before the wind. [Say SPINNA cur]

spinner *noun* **1** a person or thing that spins. **2** (also **spinnerbait**) a fishing bait or lure fixed so as to revolve when pulled through the water.

spinneret *noun* **1** any of various organs through which the silk, gossamer, or thread of spiders, silkworms, etc. is produced. **2** a device for forming filaments of synthetic fibre. [Say SPINNER ett]

spinning *noun* the art or process of twisting wool etc. to make thread.

spinning wheel *noun* a device formerly used for spinning yarn or thread with a spindle driven by a wheel attached to a crank or treadle.

spinny *adjective* (**spinnier, spinniest**) *Cdn* crazy, foolish, ditzy.

spinoff *noun* **1** an incidental result or results. **2** something, e.g. a television program, book, etc., derived from another product of a similar type. **3** an incidental benefit arising from industrial or military technology. **4** a distribution of stock in a new company to shareholders of the parent company.

spinster *noun* **1** a woman, esp. an older one, thought unlikely to marry. **2** *Law* an unmarried woman. ▶ **spinsterhood** *noun*

spin the bottle *noun* a party game in which a bottle is spun and the person towards whom it points upon ceasing to spin kisses the spinner.

spiny *adjective* (**spinier, spiniest**) **1** full of spines; prickly. **2** difficult to understand or handle: *a spiny problem*. **3** having the form of a spine; sharp-pointed.

spiny lobster *noun* a large edible crustacean with a spiny shell and long antennae but no large anterior claws.

spiral • *adjective* **1** winding about a centre in an enlarging or decreasing continuous circular motion, either on a flat plane or rising in a cone; coiled. **2** winding continuously along or as if along a cylinder, like the thread of a screw. **3** spiral-bound: *a spiral workbook*. • *noun* **1** a spiral curve. **2** a spiral spring. **3** a spiral formation in a shell etc. **4** a progressive increase or deterioration, esp. one seen as being out of control: *a spiral of rising prices and wages*. **5** a continuous banking turn of an aircraft accompanying a descent or (rarely) ascent. • *verb* (**spirals, spiralled, spiralling**) **1** move in a spiral course, esp. upwards or downwards. **2** make spiral. **3** increase rapidly.

spiral binding *noun* a type of binding used esp. for notebooks in which the pages are held together by a spiral of wire that coils through holes punched into the side of each page. ▶ **spiral-bound** *adjective*

spiralling *adjective* rapidly increasing: *spiralling inflation rates*.

spirally *adverb* in a spiral course or form.

spire *noun* **1** a tapering cone- or pyramid-shaped structure built esp. on a church tower (*compare* STEEPLE).

2 any conical, pointed, or tapering thing, e.g. the spike of a flower.

spirea *noun* a shrub with clusters of small white or pink flowers, e.g. bridal wreath. [Say spy REE uh]

spirit • *noun* **1 a** the vital animating essence of a person or animal: *was sadly broken in spirit.* **b** the intelligent non-physical part of a person; the soul. **2 a** a rational or intelligent being without a material body. **b** a supernatural being such as a ghost, fairy, etc.: *haunted by spirits.* **c** (**the Spirit**) = HOLY SPIRIT. **3** a prevailing mental or moral condition or attitude; a mood; a tendency: *Christmas spirit.* **4 a** (usu. in *plural*) strong distilled liquor, e.g. brandy, whisky, gin, rum. **b** a distilled volatile liquid. **c** purified alcohol: *methylated spirits.* **d** a solution in alcohol of a specified substance: *spirit of ammonia.* **5 a** a person's mental or moral nature or qualities, usu. specified: *has an unbending spirit.* **b** a person viewed as possessing these: *is an ardent spirit.* **c** energy, vivacity, dash: *played with spirit.* **d** courage; assertiveness, determination: *argued her case with spirit.* **6** the general intent or true meaning of a statement etc. as opposed to its strict verbal interpretation: *the spirit of the law.* **7** feelings of loyalty to a team, group, organization, etc.: *team spirit.* **8** (in *plural*) a person's feelings or state of mind. • *verb* (**spirits, spirited, spiriting**) (usu. foll. by *away, off,* etc.) convey rapidly and secretly by or as if by spirits. • *adjective* of or relating to supernatural spirits: *the spirit world.* PHRASES **in spirit** in one's thoughts: *shall be with you in spirit.* **keep a person's spirits up** cheer a person up. **the spirit moves a person** he or she feels inclined (to do something). **the spirit is willing (but the flesh is weak)** one's intentions and wishes are good but weakness, love of pleasure, etc. prevent one from acting according to them.

spirit bear *noun Cdn* a white kermode bear.

spirited *adjective* **1** full of spirit; animated, lively, brisk, or courageous. **2** having a spirit or spirits of a specified kind: *mean-spirited.* ▶ **spiritedly** *adverb* **spiritedness** *noun*

spiritless *adjective* lacking courage or vigour.

spirit level *noun* a device containing a bent glass tube nearly filled with alcohol, used to test horizontality by the position of an air bubble.

spiritual • *adjective* **1** of or relating to the human spirit or soul. **2** concerned with sacred or religious things: *the spiritual life.* **3** of or relating to religion or religious belief: *Iran's spiritual leader.* • *noun* an emotional Christian song derived from the musical traditions of Blacks in the southern US.

spiritualism *noun* **1** the belief that the spirits of the dead can communicate with the living, esp. through mediums. **2** the practices associated with this. ▶ **spiritualist** *noun & adjective* [Say SPIRIT chew ull ism]

spirituality *noun* concern with spiritual or religious matters. [Say spirit chew ALA tee]

spiritually *adverb* in respect to spiritual things.

spirochete *noun* any of various flexible spirally twisted bacteria, esp. one that causes syphilis. [Say SPY ro keet]

spit¹ • *verb* (**spits;** *past* and *past participle* **spat** or **spit; spitting**) **1** eject saliva from the mouth. **2** (usu. foll. by *out*) **a** eject (saliva, blood, food, etc.) from the mouth: *spat the meat out.* **b** emit or throw forcefully in a manner resembling spitting. **c** utter (oaths, threats, etc.) vehemently. **3** (of a fire, pan, etc.) send out sparks, hot fat, etc. **4** (of rain) fall lightly: *it's only spitting.* **5** (esp. of a cat) make a spitting or hissing noise in anger or

hostility. • *noun* **1** saliva. **2** an act of spitting. **3** the foamy liquid secretion of some insects used to protect their young. **4** (usu. in *plural*) *Cdn (West) informal* a sunflower seed. PHRASES **spit it out** *informal* say what is on one's mind. **spit up** (esp. of a baby) vomit.

spit² • *noun* **1** a slender rod on which meat is skewered before being roasted on a fire etc. **2** a small point of land projecting into the water. • *verb* (**spits, spitted, spitting**) thrust a spit through meat in order to roast it over an open fire.

spitball *noun* **1** a ball of chewed paper etc. usu. blown through a straw at a person as a prank. **2** *Baseball* an illegal swerving pitch made with a ball moistened with saliva or sweat. ▶ **spitballer** *noun*

spite • *noun* ill will, malice towards a person. • *verb* (**spites, spited, spiting**) thwart, mortify, annoy: *does it to spite me.* PHRASES **in spite of** notwithstanding. **in spite of oneself** etc. though one would rather have done otherwise: *found himself smiling in spite of himself.*

spiteful *adjective* motivated by spite; malevolent. ▶ **spitefully** *adverb* **spitefulness** *noun*

spitter *noun* **1** *Baseball* a spitball. **2** a person who spits.

spitting distance *noun* a very short distance.

spitting image *noun* (foll. by *of*) *informal* the exact likeness of (another person or thing).

spittle *noun* **1** saliva, esp. as ejected from the mouth. **2** = SPIT¹ *noun* 3.

spittoon *noun* a metal or earthenware pot with csp. a funnel-shaped top, used for spitting into. [Say spit TOON]

splake *noun* a hybrid trout produced by crossing the North American lake trout and the brook trout.

splash • *verb* (**splashes, splashed, splashing**) **1** (with reference to a liquid) fall or cause to fall in scattered drops. **2** make wet or cover with scattered drops. **3** strike or move around in water, causing it to fly around. **4** (foll. by *down*) (of a spacecraft) land on water. **5** display (a story or photograph) in a prominent place in a newspaper or magazine. • *noun* (*plural* **splashes**) **1** an instance or sound of splashing. **2** a small quantity of liquid that has splashed on to a surface. **3** a small quantity of liquid added to a drink. **4** a bright patch of colour. **5** *informal* a prominent news feature or story. PHRASES **make a splash** attract much attention, esp. by extravagance.

splashguard *noun* **1** = MUD FLAP. **2** any protective guard against splashes, e.g. on a nozzle of a gas pump.

splashy *adjective* (**splashier, splashiest**) **1** attracting attention. **2** involving splashing.

splat *informal* • *noun* a slapping sound, as of something wet hitting a surface. • *adverb* with a splat: *the omelette fell splat on the floor.* • *verb* (**splats, splatted, splatting**) fall or hit with a splat.

splatter • *verb* **1** (often foll. by *with*) make wet or dirty by splashing, esp. in droplets. **2** splash, esp. with a continuous noisy action. **3** publish a newspaper story prominently: *the story was splattered over the front page.* • *noun* **1** a noisy splashing sound. **2** a quantity splattered. **3** a rough patch of colour etc., esp. splashed on a surface. **4** (as an *adjective*) *slang* designating or relating to films involving the depiction of many violent deaths.

splay • *verb* (**splays, splayed, splaying**) **1** (usu. foll. by *out*) spread (the fingers, legs, etc.) apart. **2** (of an opening or its sides) diverge in shape or position. **3** construct (a window, doorway, opening, etc.) so that it diverges or is wider at one side of the wall than the other. • *adjective* turned outward or widened: *splay feet.*

spleen noun **1** an abdominal organ involved in the production and removal of red blood cells in most vertebrates, forming part of the immune system. **2** lowness of spirits; ill temper, spite: *I'm not capable of spontaneous delight — my periods of spleen are more frequent*.

splendid adjective **1** magnificent, gorgeous, brilliant, sumptuous: *a splendid palace*. **2** dignified; impressive: *splendid isolation*. **3** excellent; fine: *a splendid chance*. ▶ **splendidly** adverb

splendour noun (also **splendor**) **1** magnificence; grandeur. **2** great or dazzling brightness. [Say SPLEN dur]

splice • verb (**splices, spliced, splicing**) **1** join the ends of (ropes) by interweaving strands. **2** join (pieces of film etc.) by sticking together the ends. **3** join (girders, beams, etc.) by partly overlapping the ends and fastening them together. **4** unite, join: *the author splices fictional and historical figures in her most recent novel*. **5** (esp. as **spliced** adjective) informal join in marriage. • noun a place in a film, tape, rope, etc. where it has been joined. ▶ **splicer** noun

spliff noun slang a marijuana cigarette.

splint • noun **1 a** a strip of rigid material used for holding a broken bone etc. when set. **b** a rigid device for maintaining a part of the body, e.g. the teeth, in a fixed position. **2 a** a tumour or bony growth on the inside of a horse's leg. **b** see also SHIN SPLINTS. **3** a thin strip of wood etc. used to light a fire, pipe, etc. • verb secure (a broken limb etc.) with a splint or splints.

splinter • noun **1** a small thin sharp piece broken off from wood, glass, stone, etc. **2** (also **splinter group**, **splinter party**) a group or party that has broken away from a larger one. • verb break into fragments or factions. ▶ **splintery** adjective

split • verb (**splits, split, splitting**) **1** break forcibly into parts. **2** divide into parts or groups. **3** (often foll. by *up*) end a marriage or other relationship. **4** slang leave, esp. suddenly. **5** (of a team) win half of the games in (a match or series): *split a doubleheader*. • noun **1** a tear, crack, or fissure. **2** a separation: *a damaging split within the party leadership*. **3** (in plural) the feat of leaping in the air or sitting down with the legs straight, spread apart, and at right angles to the body. **4** a formation of bowling pins left standing after the first bowl in which there is a large gap between two pins or two groups of pins, making a spare difficult. **5** a match or series that ends with both teams having won an equal number of games. • adjective **1** that has split or been split: *split logs*. **2** divided in opinion etc. PHRASES **split the difference** take the average of two proposed amounts. **split a gut** informal be convulsed with laughter. **split hairs** make small and insignificant distinctions. **split one's sides** be convulsed with laughter. **split the vote** Cdn & Brit. (of a candidate or minority party) attract votes from another so that both are defeated by a third.

split decision noun **1** a decision in a boxing match in which the judges and referee are not unanimous in their choice of a winner. **2** a court ruling etc. which is not unanimous.

split end noun **1** (usu. in plural) a hair which has split at the end from dryness etc. **2** Football a player at the end of and some distance from a line of players in formation.

split-finger adjective (also **split-fingered**) Baseball designating a pitch thrown with the index and middle fingers spread wide apart along the seams, so that it has little backspin and dips sharply and deceptively as it approaches the plate.

Whether or not infinitives can be split is a very controversial question. The rule against splitting infinitives is not well founded, being based not on the actual workings of English but on Latin, a very different language. Still, the rule has been trumpeted as absolute for generations, to the point where even today split infinitives just sound "wrong" to many people. It is certainly true that in many cases a split infinitive is less elegant, precise, or emphatic than an alternative wording, as in We wanted to *completely* give up the business, which is better rendered as We wanted to give up the business *completely*. But there are times when splitting an infinitive with an adverb in fact results in a clearer and more natural phrase than one with the adverb placed anywhere else, as in You have to listen *very closely* to actually notice the difference. Because of the controversy surrounding split infinitives, however, a prudent policy might be to split infinitives only when necessary for reasons of clarity, emphasis, or ease.

split infinitive noun a phrase consisting of an infinitive with an adverb etc. inserted between *to* and the verb, e.g. *seems to really like it*.

split-level • adjective (of a room or a building, esp. a house) having the floor level of one part about half a storey above or below the floor level of an adjacent part. • noun a split-level building.

split pea noun a pea dried and split in half for cooking.

split personality noun (plural **split personalities**) **1** the coexistence within one person, institution, etc. of seemingly contradictory or conflicting characteristics: *the daily had a split personality, being both a financial journal with a narrow focus and a broadly interesting newspaper for an intelligent general readership*. **2** informal schizophrenia or multiple personality disorder.

split-rail adjective designating a type of fence, corral, etc. made from split logs.

split-run noun a Canadian edition of a foreign magazine, with advertising aimed at the Canadian market but with little or no Canadian editorial content.

split-screen noun a screen on a computer etc. on which two or more separate images are displayed.

split second • noun a very brief moment. • adjective (**split-second**) **1** very rapid. **2** (of timing) very precise.

splitter noun **1** a person who splits, esp. someone employed in splitting fish. **2** any of various devices that send electrical current, a received or transmitted signal, etc. along two or more routes.

splitting adjective (of the head or a headache) very painful.

split-up noun **1** the act of splitting or dividing. **2** the termination of a relationship. **3** the division of a stock into two or more stocks of the same total value.

splotch • noun (plural **splotches**) a daub, blot, or smear. • verb (**splotches, splotched, splotching**) make a large, esp. irregular, spot or patch on. ▶ **splotchy** adjective (**splotchier, splotchiest**)

splurge informal • noun an act of spending money extravagantly or ostentatiously: *your trip should include a splurge at a three-star restaurant*. • verb (**splurges, splurged, splurging**) **1** (usu. foll. by *on*) spend large sums of money: *splurged on new furniture*. **2** spend (money etc.) extravagantly: *splurged $4,000 on a TV*.

splutter • verb **1 a** speak in a hurried, vehement, or choking manner. **b** make a series of spitting or choking sounds. **2 a** speak or utter (words) rapidly or

S

incoherently. **b** emit (food, sparks, hot oil, etc.) with a spitting sound. • *noun* spluttering speech or sound.

spoil • *verb* (**spoils**; *past and past participle* **spoiled** or esp. *Brit.* **spoilt**; **spoiling**) **1** damage, ruin; diminish the value of. **2 a** harm the character of (esp. a child, pet, etc.) by excessive indulgence. **b** pamper; pay attention to the comfort and wishes of (a person). **c** accustom (a person etc.) to ease, favourable conditions, etc. so as to be unsuited to adversity: *we have been spoiled by so much fine weather*. **3** (of food) go bad, decay. **4** render (a ballot) invalid by improper marking. • *noun* (usu. in *plural*) **1** plunder taken from an enemy in war, or seized by force. **2** esp. *jocular* profit or advantages gained by succeeding to public office, high position, etc. PHRASES **be spoiling for** aggressively seek (a fight etc.).

spoilage *noun* the deterioration or decay of food etc.

spoiler *noun* **1 a** a person or thing that spoils something. **b** a person who obstructs or prevents an opponent's success while not being a potential winner. **2 a** a flap projected from the upper surface of an aircraft wing to break up a smooth airflow and so reduce speed. **b** a similar device on a vehicle intended to reduce lift and so improve road-holding at high speed.

spoilsport *noun* a person who spoils others' pleasure or enjoyment.

spoke[1] • *noun* **1** each of the wire rods or bars running from the hub to the rim of a wheel. **2** a rung of a ladder. **3** each radial handle of the wheel of a ship etc. • *verb* (**spokes**, **spoked**, **spoking**) provide with spokes.

spoke[2] *past of* SPEAK.

spoked *adjective* (esp. of a wheel) having spokes.

spoken • *verb past participle of* SPEAK. • *adjective* **1** (in *combination*) speaking in a specified way: *soft-spoken*. **2** (of language, words, etc.) uttered in speech; oral as opposed to written. PHRASES **spoken for** claimed, requisitioned: *this seat is spoken for*.

spokes- *combining form informal* or *jocular* forming nouns denoting a person or animal appearing in advertising for a particular product: *spokesmodel*.

spokesman *noun* (*plural* **spokesmen**) **1** a person who speaks on behalf of others, esp. in public relations. **2** a person deputed to express the views of a group etc.

spokesperson *noun* (*plural* **spokespersons** or **spokespeople**) a spokesman or spokeswoman.

spokeswoman *noun* (*plural* **spokeswomen**) **1** a woman who speaks on behalf of others, esp. in public relations. **2** a woman deputed to express the views of a group etc.

sponge • *noun* **1** a primitive sea animal with a soft porous body supported by a rigid or elastic internal skeleton. **2 a** a piece of a soft, light, porous, and absorbent substance, originally the fibrous skeleton of such an invertebrate but now usu. a synthetic material, used in bathing, cleaning, painting, etc. **b** a similar material of porous rubber or plastic. **c** a piece of sponge or similar material (esp. one containing spermicide) inserted in the vagina as a contraceptive. **3** a thing of spongelike absorbency or consistency. **4** = SPONGER. **5** *informal* a person who drinks heavily. • *verb* (**sponges**; **sponged**; **sponging** or **spongeing**) **1** wipe or cleanse with a sponge. **2** (often foll. by *out*, *away*, etc.) wipe off or efface (writing, a memory, etc.) with or as with a sponge. **3** (often foll. by *on*, *off*) live at the expense of (another person) with no intention of reimbursement etc. **4** obtain (drink etc.) by sponging. **5** apply paint with a sponge to (walls, furniture, pottery, etc.) to achieve a mottled effect.

sponge cake *noun* a very light cake with a spongelike

consistency, made from beaten eggs, sugar, and flour, with little or no fat.

sponge hockey *noun Cdn* a form of hockey played on ice with rubber-soled boots and a sponge puck.

spongelike *adjective* resembling a sponge.

sponge puck *noun Cdn* a hockey puck made of hard sponge.

sponger *noun* a person who contrives to live at another's expense.

sponge rubber *noun* liquid rubber latex processed into a spongelike substance.

sponginess *noun* the quality of being like a sponge, esp. porous, squeezable, or absorbent.

spongy *adjective* (**spongier**, **spongiest**) like a sponge, esp. in being porous, compressible, elastic, or absorbent.

sponsor • *noun* **1** a person who supports an activity done for charity by pledging money in advance. **2 a** a person or organization that promotes or financially supports an artistic or sporting activity etc. in return for recognition. **b** a business organization that promotes a broadcast program in return for advertising time. **3** an organization lending support to an election candidate. **4** a person who introduces a proposal for legislation. **5 a** a godparent at baptism. **b** esp. *Catholicism* a person who presents a candidate for confirmation. **6** a person who makes himself or herself responsible for another: *she assists refugees with immigration by finding sponsors for them*. • *verb* be a sponsor for. ▶ **sponsorship** *noun*

spontancity *noun* the quality of being spontaneous. [Say sponta NAY a tee]

spontaneous *adjective* **1** acting or done or occurring because of a sudden impulse from within; not planned or caused or suggested by external forces: *spontaneous applause*. **2** voluntary: *a spontaneous offer*. **3** (of structural changes in plants and muscular activity esp. in young animals) instinctive, automatic, prompted by no motive. **4** (of bodily movement, literary style, etc.) gracefully natural and unconstrained. **5** (of sudden movement etc.) involuntary, not due to conscious volition. **6** growing naturally without cultivation. [Say spon TAINY us]

spontaneous combustion *noun* the ignition of a mineral or vegetable substance, e.g. a heap of rags soaked with oil, a mass of wet coal, etc., from heat engendered within itself, usu. by rapid oxidation.

spontaneously *adverb* in a spontaneous manner; without planning or incitement. [Say spon TAINY us lee]

spoof *informal* • *noun* a humorous imitation of something in which its characteristic features are exaggerated for comic effect. • *verb* parody.

spook • *noun* **1** *informal* a ghost. **2** *slang* a spy. • *verb slang* **1** frighten, unnerve, alarm. **2** take fright, become alarmed.

spookily *adverb* in a spooky manner.

spookiness *noun* the quality of being spooky; eeriness.

spooky *adjective* (**spookier**, **spookiest**) **1** *informal* ghostly, eerie. **2** *slang* nervous; easily frightened.

spool • *noun* **1 a** a reel for winding thread, yarn, or wire on. **b** a reel for winding magnetic tape, photographic film, etc., on. **c** a quantity of thread, tape, etc., wound on a spool. **2** the revolving cylinder of an angler's reel. • *verb* **1** wind on a spool. **2** *Computing* print out, read in, or otherwise process (data) on a peripheral device at the same time that an operating system is carrying out other processes. ▶ **spooler** *noun* **spooling** *noun*

spoon • *noun* **1 a** a utensil consisting of an oval or round bowl and a handle. **b** a spoonful, esp. of sugar.

c (in *plural*) *Music* a pair of spoons held in the hand and beaten together rhythmically as a percussion instrument. **2** a spoon-shaped thing, esp. (also **spoon bait**) a bright revolving piece of metal used as a lure in fishing. • *verb* **1** (often foll. by *up, out*) lift and move (food, liquid etc.) with a spoon. **2** *informal* behave in an amorous way, esp. foolishly. **3** lie close together or fit into each other in the manner of spoons. PHRASES **born with a silver spoon in one's mouth** born in wealthy circumstances.

spoonbill *noun* any of various wading birds that have a long spoon-shaped bill for feeding in water.

spoon-feed *verb* (**spoon-feeds, spoon-fed, spoon-feeding**) **1** feed (a baby etc.) with a spoon. **2** provide help etc., to (a person etc.) without requiring any effort on the recipient's part.

spoonful *noun* (*plural* **spoonfuls**) an amount that can be contained in a spoon.

spoor • *noun* the track or scent of a person or animal, esp. the footprints of a wild animal hunted as game. • *verb* follow by the spoor.

sporadic *adjective* occurring only here and there or occasionally: *for the next 25 years she made sporadic efforts to shape up.* ▶ **sporadically** *adverb* [Say spuh RAD ick]

spore *noun* **1** a specialized reproductive cell of many plants and micro-organisms. **2** these collectively.

sport • *noun* **1** a game or competitive activity, esp. one involving physical exertion. **2** (often as an *adjective*) recreation, amusement: *sport hunting.* **3** *informal* **a** a fair, cheerful, or generous person: *be a sport and lend me your bike.* **b** a person behaving in a specified way, esp. regarding games, rules, etc.: *a bad sport.* **4** an animal or plant deviating suddenly or strikingly from the normal type. **5** (as an *adjective*) designating a sports car: *sport coupe.* • *verb* wear, exhibit, or produce, esp. ostentatiously: *sported a pink tie.* PHRASES **make sport of** make fun of, ridicule.

sportcoat *noun* = SPORTS JACKET.

sport fish *noun* (*plural* **sport fish** or **sport fishes**) a kind of fish caught for sport. ▶ **sport fisherman** *noun* **sport fishing** *noun*

sporting *adjective* **1** connected with or interested in sports. **2** fair and generous, esp. in a game or contest: *fair play, honest competition, and good sporting behaviour.*

sporting chance *noun* a reasonable chance of success.

sports bar *noun* a bar where televised sports events are shown continuously.

sports car *noun* a low, fast car designed for superior acceleration and performance at high speed.

sportscast *noun* a broadcast of a sports event or information about sport. ▶ **sportscaster** *noun*

sports coat *noun* = SPORTS JACKET.

sports day *noun* *Cdn & Brit.* a day on which schoolchildren participate in games, races, etc.

sports jacket *noun* (also **sport jacket**) a man's jacket for informal wear, not part of a suit.

sportsman *noun* (*plural* **sportsmen**) **1** a person who takes part in sports, esp. professionally. **2** a person who behaves fairly and generously. ▶ **sportsmanlike** *adjective* **sportsmanship** *noun*

sportsperson *noun* (*plural* **sportspersons** or **sportspeople**) a sportsman or sportswoman.

sportsplex *noun* (*plural* **sportsplexes**) *Cdn* a building offering different sports facilities under one roof, e.g. a rink, pool, etc.

sports shirt *noun* (also **sport shirt**) a men's casual shirt with a squared-off shirt-tail.

sportswear *noun* **1** clothes worn for playing sports. **2** clothing of a somewhat informal type.

sportswoman *noun* (*plural* **sportswomen**) a woman who takes part in sports, esp. professionally.

sportswriter *noun* a journalist who writes on sports.

sport-utility *noun* (*plural* **sport-utilities**) (also **sport-utility vehicle**, **sport ute** *informal*) a hybrid between a Jeep and a minivan, used for everyday driving as well as driving over rough terrain.

sporty *adjective* (**sportier, sportiest**) *informal* **1** fond of sports. **2** (esp. of clothes) suitable for informal wear; designed in a casual style. **3** (of a car) resembling a sports car in appearance or performance.

spot • *noun* **1** a small round mark differing in colour or texture from the surface around it. **2** a particular place, point, or position. **3** a small circle or other shape used in various numbers on dice, cards, etc. **4** a moral blemish. **5** a particular part of one's body or aspect of one's character: *bald spot* ◊ *soft spot.* **6** an awkward or difficult situation: *in a tight spot.* **7** = SPOTLIGHT *noun* 1, 2. • *verb* (**spots, spotted, spotting**) **1** notice or recognize (someone or something) that is difficult to detect or that one is searching for. **2** mark with spots. **3** *informal* loan: *can you spot me ten bucks?* PHRASES **hit the spot** *informal* be exactly what is required. **on the spot 1** at the scene of an action or event. **2** *informal* in a position such that response or action is required. **3** without delay or change of place, then and there. **put on the spot** *informal* force to make a difficult decision, answer an awkward question, etc. **running on the spot** *Cdn & Brit.* raising the feet alternately as in running but without moving forwards or backwards.

spot check • *noun* a test made on the spot or on a randomly selected subject. • *verb* (**spot-check**) subject to a spot check.

spotless *adjective* immaculate; absolutely clean or pure. ▶ **spotlessly** *adverb* **spotlessness** *noun*

spotlight • *noun* **1** a beam of light directed on a small area, esp. on a particular part of a stage. **2** a lamp projecting this. **3** full attention or publicity. • *verb* (**spotlights**; *past* and *past participle* **spotlighted** or **spotlit**; **spotlighting**) **1** direct a spotlight on. **2** draw attention to.

spot market *noun* a market in which commodities etc. are traded for delivery within two days.

spotted *adjective* marked or decorated with spots.

spotted fever *noun* (also **Rocky Mountain spotted fever**) a rickettsial disease transmitted by ticks and characterized by fever and spots on the skin.

spotted owl *noun* a large, dark brown hornless owl of the west coast of North America.

spotter *noun* **1** (often in *combination*) a person who spots people or things: *trend spotter.* **2** an aviator or aircraft employed in locating enemy positions etc. **3** (in gymnastics etc.) a person stationed to prevent possible accident or otherwise to provide safety assistance to the performer.

spotting *noun* **1** in senses of SPOT *verb.* **2** a slight discharge of blood from the vagina.

spotty *adjective* (**spottier, spottiest**) **1** marked with spots. **2** patchy, irregular.

spousal *adjective* of or relating to marriage or a spouse. [Rhymes with AROUSAL]

spouse *noun* a husband or wife.

Spouse's Allowance *noun* *Cdn* a federal benefit paid to low-income 60–64-year-old spouses of Old Age Security pensioners.

spout • *noun* **1** a projecting tube or lip through which a liquid etc. is poured. **2** a jet or column of liquid, grain, etc. **3** a whale's blowhole. • *verb* **1** spray out in a steady flow or stream. **2** express one's views in a lengthy and tedious manner: *the arrant nonsense spouted*

by our in-house socialist ideologues ◊ *spouting off about novels he hasn't read*.

sprain • *verb* wrench (an ankle, wrist, etc.) violently so as to cause pain and swelling but not dislocation. • *noun* **1** such a wrench. **2** the resulting inflammation and swelling.

sprang *past of* SPRING.

sprawl • *verb* **1** sit or lie or fall with limbs flung out or in an ungainly way. **2 a** (of a building complex, a town, etc.) spread out irregularly to cover a large area. **b** (of a plant) be of irregular or straggling form. • *noun* **1** a sprawling movement or attitude. **2** a straggling group or mass. **3** the straggling expansion of an urban or industrial area. ▶ **sprawling** *adjective*

spray • *noun* **1 a** water or other liquid flying in small drops. **b** a quantity of small objects flying or propelled through the air. **c** a liquid preparation to be applied in this form: *hairspray*. **2 a** a sprig of flowers or leaves, or a branch of a tree with branchlets or flowers, esp. a slender or graceful one. **b** a bunch of flowers decoratively arranged. **c** an ornament in a similar form. • *verb* **1** throw (liquid) in the form of spray. **2** sprinkle (an object) with small drops or particles, esp. (a plant) with an insecticide. **3** (of a male animal, esp. a cat) mark its environment with the smell of its urine.

sprayer *noun* a piece of equipment used for spraying liquid, esp. paint or a substance used to kill insects.

spray-on *adjective* (of a product, esp. a liquid) applied in the form of a spray.

spray paint • *noun* paint packaged in an aerosol can for spraying upon a surface. • *verb* (**spray-paint**) paint (a surface) using spray paint.

spread • *verb* (**spreads**, **spread**, **spreading**) **1** open out so as to increase in surface area, width, or length. **2** stretch out (limbs, hands, fingers, or wings) so that they are far apart. **3** extend or distribute over a wide area or a specified period of time. **4** reach or cause to reach a larger area or more and more people: *the panic spread*. **5** apply (a substance) in an even layer. • *noun* **1** the fact or process of spreading over an area: *the spread of urbanization*. **2** the degree or extent of spreading: *this species has a broad geographical spread*. **3** diffusion or expansion: *the spread of knowledge*. **4** the distance between two points in space or time. **5** the difference between the buying and selling price of a commodity. **6** a garnish that is spread on bread or toast etc. **7** an article etc. displayed esp. on two facing pages or across more than one column. **8** *informal* an elaborate meal. **9** (in full **point spread**) the number of points constituting the margin by which a stronger team is expected to defeat a weaker one, for betting purposes. **10** a farm or ranch with extensive land. **11** a cover, such as a bedspread or tablecloth. PHRASES **spread oneself too thin** attempt to undertake too many projects at once so that none can be done properly. ▶ **spreadable** *adjective*

spread-eagle • *noun* **1** a representation of an eagle with legs and wings extended, used as an emblem. **2** *Figure Skating* a straight glide made with the feet a short distance apart and turned outwards in a straight line and the arms held out to either side. • *verb* (**spread-eagles**, **spread-eagled**, **spread-eagling**) **1 a** place (a person) in a position with arms and legs spread out. **b** assume the position of a spread-eagle. **2** *Figure Skating* perform a spread-eagle. • *adjective & adverb* in the position of a spread-eagle. ▶ **spread-eagled** *adjective*

spreader *noun* **1** a person or thing that spreads. **2** an implement used to spread manure, fertilizer, seed, etc. over a field or lawn. **3** a bar for stretching something out or keeping things apart.

spreadsheet *noun* a computer program allowing manipulation and flexible retrieval of esp. tabulated numerical data.

spree *noun* **1** a period or bout of extravagant indulgence: *a shopping spree*. **2** a period or outburst of a (usu. specified) activity: *a shooting spree*.

sprig *noun* **1** a small branch or shoot. **2** a representation of this used as an esp. fabric ornament.

sprightliness *noun* animation or cheerful vitality; briskness, liveliness.

sprightly *adjective* (**sprightlier**, **sprightliest**) characterized by animation or cheerful vitality; brisk, lively, spirited.

spring • *verb* (**springs**; *past* **sprang** or **sprung**; *past participle* **sprung**; **springing**) **1** move suddenly or rapidly upwards or forwards. **2** move suddenly by or as if by the action of a spring. **3** operate by or as if by means of a spring mechanism: *spring a trap*. **4** (foll. by *from*) originate or appear from. **5** (foll. by *up*) suddenly develop or appear. **6** (foll. by *on*) present (something) suddenly or unexpectedly to. **7** *informal* bring about the escape or release of (a prisoner). • *noun* **1** (also **Spring**) the season after winter and before summer. **2** a spiral metal coil that can be pressed or pulled but that returns to its former shape when released. **3** a sudden jump upwards or forwards. **4** a place where water wells up from an underground source. **5** elastic quality. **6** liveliness in a person or of a person's mind, faculties, etc.: *a spring in her step*. PHRASES **hope springs eternal** even in the worst situations, one tends to hope for improvement. **spring a leak** develop a leak.

springboard *noun* **1** a starting point or impetus for an activity, discussion, etc. **2** a springy board used in gymnastics to gain height or momentum in vaulting etc. **3** *Cdn & Austral.* a platform inserted into a notch cut in the side of a tree on which a lumberjack stands to chop at some height from the ground.

spring break *noun* an esp. college or university holiday of one or two weeks in February or March.

spring breakup *noun Cdn* = BREAKUP 3.

spring chicken *noun* PHRASES **no spring chicken** not a young person: *I'm no spring chicken*.

spring equinox *noun* (*plural* **spring equinoxes**) the date on which the sun crosses the celestial equator in a southerly direction (approx. Mar. 21) or, in the southern hemisphere, in a northerly direction (approx. Sept. 22).

springer spaniel *noun* either of two breeds of sturdy dog of medium height used esp. in hunting to rouse game, including the English springer spaniel and the Welsh springer spaniel.

spring fever *noun* a restless feeling sometimes associated with spring.

springform pan *noun* a round metal cake pan with sides that may be released from the bottom, allowing the cake to be easily removed when done.

springiness *noun* the quality of being springy, elastic, or bouncy.

spring-loaded *adjective* (of a device etc.) containing a spring that presses one part against another.

spring peeper *noun* a small brown tree frog that occurs throughout much of eastern North America and has a high-pitched piping call.

spring roll *noun* a deep-fried Oriental appetizer or snack, consisting of a very thin wrapper rolled around a mixture of chopped vegetables, usu. including bean sprouts, and sometimes meat.

spring salmon *noun Cdn* = CHINOOK 2.

spring tide *noun* a tide occurring just after the new and full moon, in which there is the greatest difference between high and low water.

springtime *noun* **1** the season of spring. **2** (often foll.

by *of*) the earliest and usu. most pleasant stage or period of something: *the springtime of their youth*.

spring training *noun Baseball* a pre-season period of practices and games during which managers decide on the roster.

spring wheat *noun* wheat that is planted in the spring (*compare* WINTER WHEAT).

springy *adjective* (**springier**, **springiest**) **1** springing back when compressed, squeezed, or stretched; elastic, resilient. **2** (of movement, music, etc.) buoyant and vigorous; bouncing.

sprinkle • *verb* (**sprinkles**, **sprinkled**, **sprinkling**) **1** scatter liquid, powder, etc. in small drops or particles. **2** distribute in small amounts. **3** (of precipitation, esp. rain) fall in a fine mist. • *noun* **1** the action or an act of sprinkling. **2** a dusting or light shower. **3** a small thinly distributed number or amount. **4** (usu. in *plural*) each of an assortment of tiny usu. multicoloured bits of candy used to decorate cookies, cupcakes, etc.

sprinkler *noun* **1** a device, machine, vehicle, etc. used to sprinkle esp. water. **2** an attachment for a garden hose used for watering flowers, a lawn, etc. **3** an overhead plumbing fixture for extinguishing fires.

sprinkling *noun* (usu. foll. by *of*) **1** a thinly distributed amount of a liquid or powder. **2** a relatively small number of things scattered over a broad area.

sprint • *verb* **1** run at a short distance at full speed. **2** cycle or drive etc. at full speed over a short distance, esp. in a race. **3** cover or traverse (a certain distance) by sprinting. • *noun* **1** a fast race in which the participants run, cycle, ride, etc. at full speed over a short distance. **2** a short burst of speed esp. to finish a longer race.
▶ **sprinter** *noun*

sprite *noun* **1** an elf or fairy, esp. a small mischievous or playful one. **2** a dainty or lively person.

spritz • *verb* (**spritzes**, **spritzed**, **spritzing**) **1** sprinkle, squirt, or spray (something) with a liquid: *spritzed her neck with perfume*. **2** apply (a liquid) by spraying. • *noun* (*plural* **spritzes**) a small spray.

spritzer *noun* a mixture of wine and soda water.

sprocket *noun* **1** each of several teeth on a wheel engaging with links of a chain on a bicycle or with holes in film etc. **2** a wheel with sprockets.

sprout • *verb* **1** put forth, produce, or develop (shoots, hair, etc.). **2** begin to grow, put forth shoots. **3** spring up or emerge, esp. suddenly: *new houses are sprouting up all over town*. **4** cause, produce, or seem to cause or produce; give rise to. • *noun* **1** a new growth developing from a bud, seed, or other part of a plant; a shoot. **2** (usu. in *plural*) a young tender shoot of a plant, esp. a bean or alfalfa, eaten as a vegetable. **3** (usu. in *plural*) = BRUSSELS SPROUTS. **4** a young person or child.

spruce¹ • *adjective* neat in dress and appearance. • *verb* (**spruces**, **spruced**, **sprucing**) (usu. foll. by *up*) make or become trim, neat, or smart.

spruce² *noun* **1** a coniferous evergreen tree of the pine family, which has a distinctive pyramid shape and hanging cones, widely grown for timber, pulp, and Christmas trees. **2** the wood of this tree used as timber.

spruce beer *noun* **1** a drink made by adding sugar or molasses to the water of boiled spruce twigs and needles, which is then fermented with yeast. **2** a similar non-alcoholic carbonated drink flavoured, usu. artificially, with spruce.

spruce budworm *noun* the brown larva of a North American moth, which is a serious pest of spruce and other conifers.

spruce grouse *noun* a grouse of North American coniferous forests.

sprung • *verb* past and past participle of SPRING. • *adjective*

1 fitted with springs. **2** that has been sprung. **3** (esp. of a dance floor) suspended above a subfloor in order to be resilient, flexible, or springy.

spry *adjective* (**spryer**, **spryest**) nimble, active, lively.

spud *noun slang* a potato.

spume • *noun* foam or froth on or from a liquid: *the rolling billows breaking in spumes of foam upon the shores*. • *verb* (**spumes**, **spumed**, **spuming**) froth, foam: *pop was spuming all over the place*. [Say SPYOOM]

spumoni *noun* a kind of rich layered ice cream with candied fruit and nuts. [Say spuh MOANY]

spun • *verb* past and past participle of SPIN. • *adjective* converted into threads: *spun glass*.

spunk *noun informal* energy, courage.

spunkily *adverb* in a spunky, energetic, courageous, or spirited manner.

spunkiness *noun* energy, courage, spirit.

spunky *adjective* (**spunkier**, **spunkiest**) *informal* full of energy, courage; spirited.

spur • *noun* **1** a small spike or a spiked wheel worn on a rider's heel for urging a horse forward. **2** a stimulus, incentive, or encouragement. **3** (also **spur line**) a short stretch of track branching off a railway line, esp. one making a connection to another line. **4** a mountain or hill etc., or a ridge that projects from a mountain or hill. **5** an abnormal growth or chalky deposit occurring esp. in the heel or elbow. **6** a sharp hard claw on the back foot or lower hind leg of a bird or animal, esp. a rooster. **7** *Botany* **a** a slender hollow projection from part of a flower. **b** a short lateral branch or shoot, esp. one bearing fruit. • *verb* (**spurs**, **spurred**, **spurring**) **1** prick (a horse) with spurs. **2 a** (often foll. by *on*) encourage or incite (a person). **b** be the cause of; stimulate (interest etc.). PHRASES **earn** (or **win**) **one's spurs** attain distinction, earn a high honour. **on the spur of the moment** on a sudden whim or impulse; without prior consideration or planning. **put** (or **set**) **spurs to 1** impel or urge (a horse or person). **2** stimulate (a resolution etc.).

spurge *noun* a plant or shrub that produces a bitter milky juice once used as a laxative, now having commercial importance as a source of latex.

spurious *adjective* **1** not proceeding from the reputed origin, source, or author; not genuine: *thousands taken in by the spurious diaries*. **2** based on false reasoning; not true or accurate: *a spurious argument*. **3** superficially resembling or simulating something, but lacking its genuine character or qualities: *spurious charm*. [Say SPUR ee us or SPYOOR ee us]

spurn *verb* reject or refuse (a person or thing) in a way that indicates contempt.

SPELL CHECK
spur-of-the-moment, spur of the moment [ABC✓]

Use hyphens when the phrase is used as an adjective, as in *it was a spur-of-the-moment decision*; otherwise do not: *we made the decision on the spur of the moment*.

---

spur-of-the-moment *adjective* impromptu, sudden; unplanned or unpremeditated.

spurred *adjective* (of a person, boots, etc.) fitted or provided with spurs.

spurt • *verb* **1 a** gush out in a jet or stream. **b** send out or expel (liquid, smoke, dust, etc.) in a jet or rapid stream; squirt. **2** move or act with a greater speed or exertion for a short time. **3** (of a stock, price, etc.) rise suddenly in price or value. • *noun* **1** a short stream of liquid etc. ejected or thrown up with some force and suddenness. **2** a marked or sudden increase of speed or exertion. **3** a sudden increase in speed, effort, activity

or emotion for a short period of time. **4** a marked increase or improvement, esp. in business, prices, etc.

Sputnik *noun* an unmanned Russian earth satellite, esp. each of a series of such satellites launched by the Soviet Union between 1957 and 1961. [Say SPUT nick]

sputter • *verb* **1 a** (esp. of a machine) emit a spitting, sizzling, or slight explosive sound or series of such sounds, often suggesting a struggling operation. **b** proceed with difficulty, struggle; show signs of fatigue or failure. **2** say or speak in a hurried, confused, or incoherent manner, esp. from anger or excitement. **3** emit (liquid, food, smoke, sparks, etc.) in small particles or puffs with a spitting sound. • *noun* a series of soft explosive sounds, typically produced by an engine or someone stammering.

sputum *noun* **1** saliva, spittle. **2** a mixture of saliva and mucus coughed up from the respiratory tract, usu. a sign of certain diseases. [Say SPEW tum]

spy • *noun* (*plural* **spies**) **1** a person employed by a country or organization to collect and report secret information on esp. the military activities of an enemy or hostile foreign state, or on the activities of a rival organization. **2** a person who keeps watch on others, esp. furtively. **3** (**Spy**) (also **Northern Spy**) a large bright red cooking apple streaked with green. • *verb* (**spies, spied, spying**) **1** catch sight of, discern, or make out, esp. by careful observation: *spied a house in the distance*. **2** work as a spy; be on the watch or lookout. ▨**PHRASES** **spy on** maintain a close and secret observation of a person or group.

spyglass *noun* (*plural* **spyglasses**) a small telescope.

spymaster *noun* *informal* the head of a spy organization.

SQ *abbreviation Cdn* (in Quebec) Sûreté du Québec (*see* SÛRETÉ).

sq. *abbreviation* square.

SQL *abbreviation Computing* structured query language.

squab *noun* a newly hatched or very young bird, esp. a pigeon not yet able to fly. [Say SKWOB]

squabble • *noun* a petty or noisy quarrel; a dispute. • *verb* (**squabbles, squabbled, squabbling**) engage in a petty quarrel or argument. ▶**squabbler** *noun*

squad *noun* **1** a small group of people sharing a task etc. **2** a small number of soldiers assembled for drill or assigned to some task. **3** *Sport informal* a team. **4** a specialized unit or division within a police force: *drug squad*.

squad car *noun* a police car.

squadron *noun* **1** a principal division of an armoured or cavalry regiment consisting of two or more troops. **2** the basic administrative unit of an air force, usu. consisting of two or more flights. **3** a formal unit in a navy consisting of a number of ships. **4** *informal* a large group of people or things.

squalid *adjective* **1** (of places and living conditions) very dirty and unpleasant: *squalid housing* ◊ *squalid, overcrowded refugee camps*. **2** involving low moral standards or dishonest behaviour; sordid: *it was a squalid affair involving prostitutes and drugs*. [Say SKWOL id]

squall • *noun* **1** a sudden and short-lived violent storm or gust of wind, esp. with rain, snow, or sleet. **2** a shrill cry or scream, as of a baby. • *verb* scream, cry out violently as in fear or pain. ▶**squally** *adjective*

squalor *noun* a filthy or squalid state: *the squalor that a social worker sees in a modern city*. [Say SKWOL er]

Squamish • *noun* (*plural* **Squamish**) **1** a member of an Aboriginal people living in southwestern BC. **2** the Salishan language of the Squamish. • *adjective* of this people or their culture or language. [Say SKWOM ish]

squamous *adjective* covered with, composed of, or

characterized by the development of scales. [Say SKWAY muss]

squander *verb* **1** spend (time, money, etc.) recklessly or lavishly; use or consume wastefully. **2** let (an opportunity) pass or be lost. [Say SKWON dur]

square • *noun* **1** a plane figure with four right angles and four equal straight sides. **2** an open usu. four-sided area enclosed by buildings. **3** an L-shaped or T-shaped instrument used esp. by a carpenter or architect to draw, obtain, or verify right angles. **4** the product of a number multiplied by itself: *81 is the square of 9*. **5** *slang* a conventional or old-fashioned person, esp. one ignorant of or opposed to current trends. **6** *slang* a square meal: *three squares a day*. **7 a** a dessert served cut into square pieces. **b** one of these pieces. • *adjective* (**squarer, squarest**) **1** having the shape of a square. **2** having or in the form of a right angle: *square corners*. **3 a** (of a person, animal, or body) having a width more nearly equal to the height or length than is usual; solid, stocky. **b** (of a feature, such as the jaw) having a square outline; not round. **4 a** (as an *adjective*) designating a unit of measure equal to the area of a square whose side is one of the unit specified: *one square metre*. **b** (of an area) being a square having four sides of the same specified length: *5 metres square*. **5 a** even, straight, level. **b** perpendicular; at right angles. **6** (also **all square**) **a** with all accounts settled, with no money owed. **b** (of teams or scores) tied. **7** fair and honest: *a square deal*. **8** *slang* out of touch with the ideas and conventions of a current trend. • *adverb* **1** *informal* exactly, directly: *hit him square on the nose*. **2** in a rectangular form or position; upright, straight. **3** in a straightforward manner; fairly, honestly: *won fair and square*. • *verb* (**squares, squared, squaring**) **1 a** make square or rectangular. **b** give a rectangular cross-section to (timber etc.). **2** multiply (a number) by itself: *3 squared is 9*. **3** (usu. foll. by *to, with*) correspond, harmonize, make or be consistent: *her conclusion doesn't square with her observations*. **4** (usu. foll. by *up*) settle (an account, debt, etc.) by means of payment. **5 a** place (one's shoulders) squarely facing forwards, esp. in a defensive position. **b** (often foll. by *up, around*) *Baseball* (of a batter) turn to face the pitcher with the bat held parallel to the ground while preparing to bunt. **6** (usu. in *passive*) mark out in squares: *she drew a graph on squared paper*. **7** *informal* satisfy or secure the compliance of (a person), esp. by bribery. **8** tie (a game or series); make scores square. ▨**PHRASES** **back to square one** *informal* back to the starting point with no progress made. **out of square** not at right angles. **squared away** taken care of, dealt with, put in proper order. **square the circle 1** construct a square equal in area to a given circle (a problem incapable of a purely geometrical solution). **2** do what is impossible. **square off 1** assume the stance or crouch of a boxer. **2** meet in competition or opposition. **3** mark out in squares.

square brackets *plural noun* brackets of the form [ ].

square dance • *noun* a type of dance which starts with four couples facing one another in a square, with steps shouted out by a caller. • *verb* (**square dances, square danced, square dancing**) participate in a square dance. ▶**square dancer** *noun* **square dancing** *noun*

square-flipper seal *noun Cdn* (*Nfld*) = BEARDED SEAL.

squarely *adverb* **1** directly; not at an angle or to one side: *she looked me squarely in the eye*. **2** directly or exactly; without any uncertainty: *the responsibility for the crisis rests squarely on the government*.

square meal *noun* a hearty and satisfying meal.

squareness *noun* the quality of containing right angles: *measured to ensure the squareness of the wall*.

square-rigged *adjective* (of a ship) with the principal sails at right angles to the length of the ship.

square root *noun* the number which produces a specified quantity when multiplied by itself.

square timber *noun* Cdn hist. logs cut into lengths with the round sides cut flat, ready to be shipped.

squarish *adjective* somewhat square-shaped.

squash • *verb* (**squashes**, **squashed**, **squashing**) **1** crush or squeeze into a pulp, flat mass, or distorted shape. **2** pack tightly, crowd together. **3** reject, dismiss, silence, or suppress. **4** flatten or be crushed under pressure. • *noun* **1** a game for two or four players with racquets and a small fairly soft ball that is struck against the walls of a closed court. **2** (*plural* **squash** or **squashes**) **a** an edible gourd, the flesh of which may be cooked and eaten as a vegetable, including **summer squash**, eaten before the seeds and rinds have hardened (e.g. zucchini), and **winter squash**, stored and eaten when mature (e.g. butternut squash, acorn squash). **b** the trailing plant of the gourd family that produces this fruit. ▶ **squashy** *adjective*

squat • *verb* (**squats**, **squatted**, **squatting**) **1** crouch on the balls of one's feet with the legs bent. **2** live without paying rent and without legal right on land or in premises otherwise unoccupied. **3** *Weightlifting* **a** perform a squat. **b** lift (a certain weight) while performing a squat. **4** (of an animal) crouch close to the ground. • *adjective* (**squatter**, **squattest**) disproportionately broad or wide; short and fat. • *noun* **1** *slang* = DIDDLY-SQUAT. **2** a property occupied by a squatter or squatters. **3** *Weightlifting* an exercise or lift in which a person squats down and rises again while carrying a barbell behind the neck. **4** a squatting posture.

squatter *noun* an unauthorized or illegal occupant of otherwise unoccupied land or premises.

squawfish *noun* (*plural* **squawfish** or **squawfishes**) a large predatory freshwater fish of the carp family of northwestern Canada and the US, formerly an important food fish for Aboriginal peoples.

squawk • *noun* **1** a loud harsh cry esp. of a bird. **2** a loud complaint or protest. • *verb* **1** utter a squawk. **2** utter with a squawk. **3** complain or protest loudly or vehemently. **4** (of an aircraft) transmit (a signal) as identification.

squawk box *noun* (*plural* **squawk boxes**) *informal* **1** an intercom. **2** the loudspeaker of a PA system.

squeak • *noun* **1** a sharp, shrill, high-pitched sound or cry. **2** (also **narrow squeak**) a narrow escape; a success barely attained. • *verb* **1** make or emit a thin high-pitched cry or squeak. **2** utter or sing in a shrill voice. **3** (usu. foll. by *by*, *through*) *informal* manage, succeed, or pass by only a narrow margin.

squeaker *noun* **1** a game etc. won by a narrow margin. **2** a person or thing that squeaks.

squeaky *adjective* (**squeakier**, **squeakiest**) tending to squeak.

squeaky clean *adjective* **1** above reproach; respectable, upstanding. **2** completely clean.

squeal • *noun* a long shrill sound, such as the cry of a pig or an exclamation of delight. • *verb* **1** make a squeal. **2** utter (words) with a squeal. **3** (often foll. by *on*) *slang* reveal confidential information about a person; turn informer against. **4** *slang* protest loudly or excitedly. ▶ **squealer** *noun*

squeamish *adjective* **1** easily turned sick, disgusted, or faint. **2** not wanting to do something that might be considered dishonest or immoral: *I'm too squeamish about making sharp judgments to be cut out for journalism*.

▶ **squeamishly** *adverb* **squeamishness** *noun*

squeegee • *noun* an implement with a handle joined to a wide rubber blade used to remove the excess liquid from glass when cleaning windows. • *verb* (**squeegees**, **squeegeed**, **squeegeeing**) clean or treat with a squeegee.

squeegee kid *noun* *informal* a youth who offers to clean the windows of cars stopped at traffic lights, esp. for money.

squeezable *adjective* able to be squeezed; that invites squeezing: *babies' squeezable cheeks*.

squeeze • *verb* (**squeezes**, **squeezed**, **squeezing**) **1** firmly press from opposite or all sides. **2** extract (liquid or a soft substance) from something by squeezing. **3** manage to get into or through (a restricted space). **4** (foll. by *in*) manage to find time for. **5** obtain from someone with difficulty. **6** hug or embrace (a person) firmly. • *noun* **1** an act of pressing or being pressed firmly from opposite or all sides. **2** a hug. **3** a small amount of liquid extracted by squeezing. **4** a strong financial demand or pressure. **5** *informal* a girlfriend or boyfriend: *my main squeeze*. **6** *Baseball* (also **squeeze play**) a play in which the batter attempts to bring a player home from third on a sacrifice bunt. **7** a difficult situation; a bind: *overenthusiastic expansion left the school in a squeeze*. PHRASES **put the squeeze on** *informal* coerce or pressure (a person).

squeezebox *noun* (*plural* **squeezeboxes**) *informal* an accordion or concertina.

squeeze bunt *noun* *Baseball* a sacrifice bunt attempted while executing a squeeze play.

squeezer *noun* a person or thing that squeezes.

squelch • *verb* (**squelches**, **squelched**, **squelching**) **1 a** walk or tread heavily in mud, on wet ground, or with water in the shoes, so as to make a sucking sound. **b** make a sucking sound. **2** crush, silence, suppress; put an end to (an idea, plan, rally, etc.). • *noun* a sucking sound as made by walking on wet muddy ground. ▶ **squelchy** *adjective*

squib • *noun* **1** a small firework burning with a hissing sound and usu. a final slight explosion. **2 a** a short piece of writing or written information, esp. a brief news item used as a filler in a newspaper. **b** a short satirical composition. **3** (also **squibber**) (esp. in baseball and football) a weakly hit or kicked ball. • *verb* (**squibs**, **squibbed**, **squibbing**) **1** (esp. in baseball and football) hit or kick (the ball) weakly so that it travels only a short distance. **2** (of a ball) travel a short distance after being hit or kicked weakly.

squid *noun* an elongated, fast-swimming marine mollusc related to the octopus, with eight arms in a ring around two longer tentacles, some varieties of which are used as food.

squidgy *adjective* (**squidgier**, **squidgiest**) *informal* soft, soggy, or moist.

squid jigger *noun* Cdn (Nfld) a weighted line with several tiny esp. unbaited hooks, used to catch small squid for bait. ▶ **squid jigging** *noun*

squiggle • *noun* a short curly or wavy line, esp. in handwriting or doodling. • *verb* (**squiggles**, **squiggled**, **squiggling**) **1** write in squiggles; scrawl. **2** wriggle, squirm. ▶ **squiggly** *adjective*

squinch *verb* (**squinches**, **squinched**, **squinching**) (usu. foll. by *up*) **1** screw up one's eyes, face, etc. **2** (of the eyes etc.) screw up, squint.

squint • *verb* **1** look obliquely or with the eyes partly closed, esp. in order to see something better or because of very bright light. **2** close (one's eyes) quickly; hold (one's eyes) half-shut. **3** suffer from a disorder of the eye muscles which causes each eye to look in a different direction. • *noun* **1** a permanent deviation or defective alignment of one or both eyes. **2** a stealthy or sidelong

glance through half-closed eyes. **3** *informal* a glance or look. ▶ **squinty** *adjective* (**squintier, squintiest**)

squire • *noun hist.* a young nobleman serving as a knight's attendant. • *verb* (**squires, squired, squiring**) (of a man) attend upon (a woman): *the spectacle of this dim-looking colonial squiring their princess*.

squirm *verb* **1** wriggle, writhe. **2** show embarrassment or shame. ▶ **squirmy** *adjective*

squirrel • *noun* **1 a** a slender agile tree-dwelling rodent with a long bushy tail, a furry coat, and pointy ears, usu. feeding on nuts and seeds. **b** any of various similar or related ground- or tree-dwelling rodents, e.g., a ground squirrel. **2** the fur of the squirrel. • *verb* (**squirrels, squirrelled, squirrelling**) **1** (usu. foll. by *away*) store or save; hoard (objects, food, time, etc.). **2** (often foll. by *around*) move about in an active or industrious manner; bustle, scurry.

squirrelly *adjective informal* **1** restless, fidgety, anxious. **2** eccentric, crazy.

squirt • *verb* **1** eject or propel (a liquid or semi-liquid substance) in a jet-like stream, esp. from a small opening. **2** (of liquid or a semi-liquid substance) be discharged in this way. **3** splash with liquid ejected by squirting. **4** (often foll. by *free* or *loose*) be lost or dropped; slip or fall, esp. from one's hand. • *noun* **1 a** a jet or stream of liquid. **b** a small quantity produced by squirting. **2** *informal* **a** a young person, esp. a meddlesome child. **b** an insignificant but presumptuous person. **3 a** an initiation level of sports for young children. **b** a player at this level.

squish *verb* (**squishes, squished, squishing**) **1** yield easily to pressure when walked upon, squeezed, or squashed, esp. making a gushing or squelching sound. **2** crush, squash, or squeeze. **3** force or be forced into a small space; pack or be packed tightly: *squished into the car*. **4** move with a squishing sound.

squishy *adjective* (**squishier, squishiest**) **1** a soft and wet. **2** lacking strength or substance; mushy: *all the premier's squishy promises* ◊ *squishy sentimental issues*.

Sr *symbol* strontium.

Sr. *abbreviation* **1** Senior. **2** Señor. **3** Signor. **4** *Christianity* Sister.

Sra. *abbreviation* Señora.

SRAM *abbreviation* (*plural* **SRAMs**) *Computing* static random access memory. [Say ESS ram]

Sri *noun* (in the Indian subcontinent) a title of respect preceding the name of a deity or distinguished person, or the title of a sacred book. [Say SHREE or SREE]

Sri Lankan • *noun* **1** a native or national of Sri Lanka (formerly Ceylon), an island country in the Indian Ocean. **2** a person of Sri Lankan descent. • *adjective* of Sri Lanka or its people. [Say shree LANK un or sree LANK un]

SRO *abbreviation* standing room only.

SS *abbreviation* **1** Saints. **2** steamship. **3** secondary school. **4** *Cdn* SCHOOL SECTION. **5** shortstop.

SSE *abbreviation* south-southeast.

SSW *abbreviation* south-southwest.

St. *abbreviation* **1** Street. **2** Saint.

stab • *verb* (**stabs, stabbed, stabbing**) **1** thrust a knife etc. into so as to wound or kill. **2** cause a feeling like being stabbed: *stabbing pain*. **3** make a thrusting gesture or movement at something with a pointed object: *the two players stab at a loose puck in the corner* ◊ *Kate stabbed a finger into the icing*. **4** pierce a hole in something. • *noun* **1 a** an instance of stabbing. **b** a blow or thrust with a knife etc.: *multiple stab wounds*. **2** a wound made in this way. **3** a sharply painful physical or mental sensation: *Katherine felt a stab of jealousy* ◊ *a sudden stab of pain in the chest*. **4** *informal* an attempt, a try: *I don't think I'll win, but I'll make a stab at it* ◊ *took a fourth stab at elected office*. **5** a vigorous thrust; a jabbing lunge

or gesture: *impatient stabs with his finger*. PHRASES **stab in the back 1** *noun* a treacherous or slanderous attack. **2** *verb* slander or betray. **stab in the dark** a blind attempt; an effort made without adequate information. ▶ **stabber** *noun* **stabbing** *noun*

stability *noun* the quality or state of being stable. [Say stuh BILLA tee]

stabilization *noun* an act of making stable: *budget stabilization* ◊ *slope stabilization*.

stabilization payment *noun Cdn* a payment made esp. by the federal government to a region or sector in order to stabilize a faltering economy.

stabilize *verb* (**stabilizes, stabilized, stabilizing**) make or become stable.

stabilizer *noun* a device or substance used to keep something stable, esp.: **1** the horizontal tailplane of an aircraft. **2** a gyroscopic device to prevent rolling of a ship. **3** a substance which prevents the breakdown of emulsions, esp. as a food additive maintaining texture.

stable • *adjective* (**stabler, stablest**) **1** firmly fixed or established; not easily adjusted, destroyed, disturbed or altered. **2 a** firm, resolute; not wavering or fickle. **b** mentally and emotionally sound; sane and sensible. **3** *Chemistry* (of a compound) not readily decomposing. **4** *Physics* (of an isotope) not subject to radioactive decay. **5** (of a patient or their medical condition) not deteriorating in health after an injury or operation. • *noun* **1** a building for keeping horses. **2** an establishment where racehorses are kept and trained. **3** the racehorses of a particular stable. **4 a** persons, products, etc., having a common origin or affiliation: *he'd retained a fat stable of lawyers who rarely lost a case*. **b** such an origin or affiliation: *a good addition to this year's fiction stable*. • *verb* (**stables, stabled, stabling**) keep (a horse) in a stable.

stablemate *noun* **1** a horse of the same stable. **2** a person, product, etc. from the same source; a member of the same organization etc.

stabling *noun* accommodation for horses.

stably *adverb* in a stable manner.

staccato • *adverb & adjective* **1** *Music* with each note sharply detached or separated from the others. **2** with short and sharp sounds: *a staccato burst of gunfire*. • *noun* (*plural* **staccatos**) **1** a staccato passage in music etc.: *the piece features an airy slowish staccato in a generally relaxed pace*. **2** staccato delivery: *the staccato of artillery fire*. [Say stuh KATTO or stuh KOTTO]

stack • *noun* **1** a pile or heap, esp. in orderly arrangement. **2** a circular or rectangular pile of hay etc. **3** *informal* a large quantity. **4** = SMOKESTACK. **5** a number of aircraft flying in circles at different altitudes around the same point while waiting for permission to land at an airport. **6** (in *plural*) a part of a library where most of the books are stored on shelving. **7** a vertical arrangement of stereo components, speakers, etc. **8** a vertical vent pipe or waste pipe. • *verb* **1** pile in a stack or stacks. **2** arrange (cards) secretly for cheating. **3** cause (aircraft) to fly around the same point at different levels while waiting to land at an airport. **4** create a disproportion in the representation on (a committee etc.) so that it will act in one's interests. PHRASES **stack the deck** (or **cards**) cause (circumstances etc.) to favour one person, group, etc. over another. **stack up** *informal* present oneself; measure up. ▶ **stackable** *adjective*

stacked *adjective* **1 a** put into a stack or stacks. **b** piled with goods etc. **2** (of odds, circumstances, etc.) biased. **3** *informal* (of a woman) having large breasts. **4** (of an aircraft) being one of a number of aircraft flying around the same point at different levels while waiting to land.

stacker *noun* a machine for raising things and depositing them in a stack or pile.

stadium *noun* (*plural* **stadiums**) an athletic or sports ground with tiers of seats for spectators.

stadium seating *noun* an arrangement of seats, esp. in a movie theatre, in which each row of seats is on a tier one step higher than the one in front of it.

staff • *noun* **1** (*plural* also **staves**) **a** a stick used as a support or weapon. **b** a rod held as a sign of office or authority. **c** a flagpole. **2 a** a group of people employed in a business etc. **b** a group of military officers assisting an officer in high command. **c** (also **pitching staff**) *Baseball* all of a team's pitchers. **3** *Music* a set of usu. five parallel lines on which a note is placed to indicate its pitch. • *verb* **1** provide (an institution etc.) with staff. **2** work as a member of staff in (an institution etc.). PHRASES **on staff** serving as a member of an organization's staff. ▶ **staffed** *adjective*

staffer *noun* a member of a staff, esp. of a newspaper.

staffing *noun* the provision of staff in a company, organization, etc.: *staffing levels*.

staff inspector *noun* (in some Canadian municipal police forces) an officer ranking above inspector and below superintendent.

staff officer *noun* an officer serving on the staff of an army etc.

staff room *noun* esp. *Cdn & Brit.* **1** a common room for staff, esp. in a school. **2** the staff themselves.

staff sergeant *noun* **1** (in some Canadian police forces) an officer ranking next above sergeant. **2** *hist.* (in the Canadian Army) a non-commissioned officer of a rank above sergeant.

stag • *noun* **1** an adult male deer, esp. one with a set of antlers. **2** an all-male celebration in honour of a man about to marry. **3** *informal* a man who attends a social gathering unaccompanied by a woman. • *adjective informal* **1** of, for, or composed of men only. **2** pornographic. • *adverb informal* without a date, unaccompanied: *went stag*.

stag and doe *noun* (*plural* **stag and does**) (also **stag and doe party**, *plural* **stag and doe parties**) *Cdn* (*Ont.*) a dance held in honour of an engaged couple, to whom the money raised from ticket sales is given.

stage • *noun* **1** a point or period in a process or development. **2 a** a raised floor or platform, esp. one on which plays etc. are performed before an audience. **b** (**the stage**) the acting or theatrical profession, esp. live theatre as opposed to film or television. **c** the art of writing or presenting plays. **d** the scene of action: *the stage of politics*. **e** = LANDING STAGE. **3** *Cdn* (*Nfld*) a shed near the shoreline for gutting, heading, salting, etc. fish before they are dried on flakes. **4 a** a regular stopping place on a route. **b** the distance between two stopping places. **5** a section of a rocket with a separate engine, jettisoned when its propellant is exhausted. **6** *Geology* a range of strata forming a subdivision of a series. **7** = STAGECOACH. • *verb* (**stages**, **staged**, **staging**) **1** present (a theatrical production) on stage. **2** arrange the occurrence of: *staged a comeback*. **3** (esp. as **staged** *adjective*) present or arrange a contrived or mock version of (an event). **4** (esp. of migrating animals) stop at a regular place on a route. PHRASES **by easy stages** gradually; without sudden changes. **go on the stage** become an actor. **on (the) stage** performing as an actor, dancer, singer, etc. **set the stage** (usu. foll. by *for*) prepare the way or conditions for (an event etc.).

stagecoach *noun* (*plural* **stagecoaches**) *hist.* a large closed horse-drawn coach running regularly by stages between two places.

stagecraft *noun* skill in mounting theatrical performances and creating theatrical effect.

stage direction *noun* an instruction in the text of a play as to the movement, position, tone, etc., of an actor, or sound effects etc.

stage door *noun* an entrance from the street to a theatre behind the stage, usu. reserved for performers and stage crew etc.

stage fright *noun* nervousness on facing an audience.

stagehand *noun* a person handling scenery etc. during a performance on stage.

stagehead *noun* *Cdn* (*Nfld*) the part of a fishing stage which extends over the water.

stage left *noun* the part of a stage which is to the left of a person facing the audience.

stage-manage *verb* (**stage-manages**, **stage-managed**, **stage-managing**) **1** be the stage manager of. **2** arrange and control for effect: *the entire party convention had been carefully stage-managed*.

stage management *noun* **1** the job or craft of overseeing the details of a stage performance. **2** stage managers collectively.

stage manager *noun* the person responsible for overseeing the details of a performance, giving cues to performers, stage hands, lighting crew, etc.

stage right *noun* the part of a stage which is to the right of a person facing the audience.

stage whisper • *noun* **1** a loud whisper addressed by one actor to another, meant to be heard by the audience. **2** any loud whisper meant to be heard by people other than the person addressed. • *verb* (**stage-whisper**) utter in a loud whisper.

stagey *adjective* (**stagier**, **stagiest**) = STAGY.

stagflation *noun* a state of inflation without a corresponding increase of demand and employment; inflation combined with economic stagnation.

stagger • *verb* **1** walk unsteadily, totter. **2 a** shock, confuse; cause to hesitate or waver. **b** continue in existence or operation in an uncertain or precarious manner: *raising interest rates will further hinder Canadian companies staggering under a burden of corporate debt*. **3** arrange (events, hours of work, etc.) so that they do not coincide. **4** arrange (objects, people, etc.) so that they are not in line. • *noun* **1** a tottering movement. **2** (in *plural*) **a** any of various parasitic or other diseases of farm animals marked by staggering or loss of balance. **b** giddiness. **3** an overhanging or slantwise or zigzag arrangement of similar parts in a structure etc.

staggering *adjective* **1** astonishing, bewildering. **2** that staggers. ▶ **staggeringly** *adverb*

staghorn *noun* (also **stag's horn**) **1** the horn of a stag, used to make knife handles etc. **2** any of various ferns with fronds resembling antlers. **3** a sumac of eastern North America with twigs covered with velvety hairs.

staging *noun* **1** an instance or method of presenting a play. **2** (as an *adjective*) referring to a stopping place or assembly point en route to an esp. military or migratory destination: *staging area*.

stagnant *adjective* **1** (of liquid) motionless, having no current. **2** (of the mind, business, a person, etc.) showing no activity, dull, sluggish. **3** stale or foul due to lack of motion or activity.

stagnate *verb* (**stagnates**, **stagnated**, **stagnating**) be or become stagnant. ▶ **stagnation** *noun*

stag party *noun* (*plural* **stag parties**) an all-male celebration in honour of a man about to marry.

stagy *adjective* (**stagier**, **stagiest**) theatrical; artificial, exaggerated: *stagy Italian "you-like-a-da-spicy-meatballs" accents*. [Say STAGE ee]

staid *adjective* usu. *derogatory* settled and dignified, esp. in a way that is considered dull or unadventurous: *the*

software industry cannot afford to become staid and set in its ways ◊ led the usually staid Toronto audience through a number of raucous and riotous singalongs.

stain • *verb* **1** discolour or be discoloured by the action of liquid sinking in. **2** spoil, damage (a reputation, character, etc.). **3** colour (wood, glass, etc.) by a process other than painting or covering the surface. **4** colour (a specimen) for microscopic examination. • *noun* **1** a discoloration, a spot or mark caused esp. by contact with foreign matter and not easily removed. **2 a** a blot or blemish. **b** damage to a reputation etc. **3** a substance used in staining. ▶ **stainable** *adjective*

stained glass *noun* dyed or coloured glass, esp. in a lead framework in a window.

stainless *adjective* **1** (esp. of a reputation) without stains. **2** not liable to stain.

stainless steel *noun* an iron alloy containing chromium and resistant to rust, used for cutlery etc.

stair *noun* **1** each of a set of fixed steps, esp. in a building. **2** (esp. in *plural*) a set of such steps.

staircase *noun* a flight or flights of stairs and the supporting structure.

stairway *noun* a flight of stairs, a staircase; a passageway with stairs.

stairwell *noun* the shaft in which a staircase is built.

stake¹ • *noun* **1** a stout stick or post sharpened at one end and driven into the ground. **2** *hist.* **a** the post to which a person was tied to be burned alive. **b (the stake)** death by burning as a punishment: *condemned to the stake*. • *verb* (**stakes, staked, staking**) **1** fasten, secure, or support with a stake or stakes. **2** (usu. foll. by *out*) mark off (an area) with stakes, esp. to claim a site for prospecting. **3** state or establish (a claim). PHRASES **pull** (or **pull up**) **stakes** depart; go to live elsewhere. **stake a** (or **one's**) **claim to** declare a special interest in; claim a right to. **stake out** *informal* **1** place under surveillance. **2** place (a person) to maintain surveillance. **3** declare a special interest in or right to e.g. a place or an area of study.

stake² • *noun* **1** a sum of money etc. wagered on an event. **2 a** (often foll. by *in*) an interest or concern, esp. financial. **b** (in *plural*) what is being risked; potential losses or consequences. **3** (in *plural*) **a** money offered as a prize esp. in a horse race. **b** a horse race in which all the owners of the horses contribute to the prize money. • *verb* (**stakes, staked, staking**) **1 a** wager. **b** risk: *staked everything on convincing him*. **2** *informal* give financial or other support to. PHRASES **at stake 1** risked, to be won or lost. **2** at issue, in question.

stakeholder *noun* **1** an independent party with whom each of those who make a wager deposits the money etc. wagered. **2** a person with an interest or concern in something.

stakeout *noun informal* a continuous secret watch by the police.

stalactite *noun* a tapering deposit of calcite hanging down like an icicle from the roof of a cave, cliff overhang, etc., formed by dripping water. [Say stuh LACK tite or STAL ack tite]

stalagmite *noun* a mound or tapering column of calcite rising from the floor of a cave etc., deposited by dripping water. [Say stuh LAG mite or STAL ag mite]

stale • *adjective* (**staler, stalest**) **1 a** not fresh, not quite new. **b** musty, insipid, or otherwise the worse for age or use. **2** lacking novelty or interest; trite or unoriginal. **3** (of an athlete or other performer) having

ability impaired by excessive exertion or practice. • *verb* (**stales, staled, staling**) make or become stale.

stalemate • *noun* **1** *Chess* a position counting as a draw, in which a player is not in check but cannot move except into check. **2** a deadlock or drawn contest. • *verb* (**stalemates, stalemated, stalemating**) **1** *Chess* bring (a player) to a stalemate. **2** bring to a standstill.

Stalinism *noun* **1** the policies followed by the Soviet dictator Joseph Stalin (1879–1953), esp. centralization, totalitarianism, and the pursuit of Communism. **2** any rigid centralized authoritarian form of socialism. ▶ **Stalinist** *noun* [Say STAL in ism or STOL in ism]

stalk¹ *noun* **1** the main stem of a herbaceous plant. **2** the slender attachment or support of a leaf, flower, fruit, etc. **3** a similar support for an organ etc. in an animal. **4** a slender support or linking shaft in a machine, object, etc., e.g. the stem of a wineglass.

stalk² *verb* **1** pursue or approach (game, prey, an enemy, etc.) stealthily. **2** stride, walk in a stately or haughty manner. **3** *formal* or *literary* move silently or threateningly through (a place): *fear stalked the streets*. **4** harass or persecute (a person) with unwanted and obsessive attention.

-stalked *combining form* (of a plant etc.) having a stalk of the kind specified: *thick-stalked*.

stalker *noun* **1** a person who stalks, hounds, or follows a particular person, esp. stealthily or obsessively. **2** a person who stalks game.

stalking *noun* the act of hounding or following a person stealthily or obsessively.

stalky *adjective* (**stalkier, stalkiest**) long and thin, suggestive of the stalk of a plant.

stall • *noun* **1** a trader's stand or booth in a market etc. **2 a** a stable. **b** a compartment for one animal in this. **c** a compartment for one horse at the start of a race. **3** a compartment or cubicle with a single shower or toilet, esp. in a public washroom. **4** a fixed seat in the choir or chancel of a church, more or less enclosed at the back and sides. **5** an area marked off for a single vehicle in a parking lot etc.; a parking space. **6 a** the stalling of an engine or aircraft. **b** the condition resulting from this. • *verb* **1 a** (of a motor vehicle or its engine) stop because of an overload on the engine or an inadequate supply of fuel to it. **b** (of an aircraft or its pilot) reach a condition where the speed is too low to allow effective operation of the controls. **c** cause (an engine or vehicle or aircraft) to stall. **2 a** (of a vehicle) stick fast as in mud or snow. **b** (of a process etc.) stop moving or progressing. **3** put or keep (cattle etc.) in a stall or stalls esp. for fattening. **4 a** play for time when being questioned etc.: *she was stalling for time*. **b** delay, obstruct: *the government was stalling the project* ◊ *stall him till I can get away*.

stallion *noun* an uncastrated adult male horse.

stalwart • *adjective* **1** strongly built: *stalwart brick chimneys*. **2** courageous, resolute, determined: *a stalwart member of the RCMP*. • *noun* a stalwart person, esp. a loyal uncompromising partisan: *a Liberal stalwart*. [Say STAWL wurt]

stamen *noun* the male fertilizing organ of a flowering plant. [Say STAY mun]

stamina *noun* the ability to endure prolonged physical or mental strain; staying power. [Say STAM uh]

stammer • *verb* **1** speak with halting articulation,

esp. with pauses or rapid repetitions of the same syllable. **2** (often foll. by *out*) utter (words) in this way. • *noun* a tendency to stammer.

stamp • *verb* **1** bring down (one's foot) heavily on the ground etc. **2** impress a pattern, mark, etc. on metal, paper, etc., with a die or similar instrument of metal, wood, rubber, etc. **3** affix a postage or other stamp to. **4 a** assign a specific character to; characterize; mark out: *this latest novel stamps her as a genius.* **b** (usu. in *passive*) mark or affect with a particular feeling or attitude: *reluctance was stamped all over their faces.* **5** crush or pulverize (ore etc.). • *noun* **1** an instrument for stamping a pattern or mark. **2 a** a mark or pattern made by this. **b** an official mark impressed on deeds, bills of exchange, etc., as evidence of payment of tax. **3 a** = POSTAGE STAMP 1. **b** a small adhesive piece of paper indicating that a price, fee, or tax has been paid. **4** *Cdn (Maritimes & Nfld)* **a** *hist.* an adhesive piece of paper affixed by an employer to an employee's record of employment, collected by the employee to prove eligibility for employment insurance. **b** (in *plural*) *slang* employment insurance benefits. **5** a mark impressed on or label etc. affixed to a commodity as evidence of quality etc. **6** a heavy downward blow with the foot. **7 a** a characteristic mark or impress. **b** character, kind: *avoid people of that stamp.* **c** a mark of authoritative approval. **8** an audio or digital mark made on a recorded message, data file, etc., e.g. to indicate the time the information was recorded. ▸ PHRASES **stamp out 1** produce by cutting out with a die etc. **2** put an end to, crush, destroy.

stampede • *noun* **1** a sudden flight and scattering of a number of horses, cattle, etc. **2** a sudden rapid movement or reaction of a mass of people in response to a particular circumstance or stimulus: *a stampede of last-minute Christmas shoppers.* **3** *hist.* a rush of prospectors to a newly-discovered deposit of esp. gold. **4** *Cdn & US West* an exhibition or fair involving rodeo events and other contests and entertainment. • *verb* (**stampedes, stampeded, stampeding**) **1** take part in a stampede. **2** cause to do this. **3** cause to act hurriedly or without thinking. ▸ **stampeder** *noun*

stamp pad *noun* an ink-soaked pad, usu. in a box, used for inking a rubber stamp etc.

stance *noun* **1** the way a person stands, esp. the position adopted for certain sports: *batting stance.* **2** a moral or intellectual attitude to something, esp. one expressed publicly: *the premier's stance on the drug issue.*

stanch *verb* = STAUNCH. [Rhymes with *RANCH*]

stanchion *noun* an upright bar, post, or frame forming a support or barrier: *the stern deck is protected by a safety rail on four stanchions that are slotted into the deck.* [Say STAN chun]

stand • *verb* (**stands, stood, standing**) **1** be in or rise to an upright position, supported by one's feet. **2** place or be situated in a particular position. **3** move in a standing position to a specified place: *stand aside.* **4** remain stationary or without disturbance. **5** be in a specified state or condition. **6** remain valid or unaltered. **7** adopt a particular attitude towards an issue. **8** be likely to do something: *investors stood to lose heavily.* **9** act in a specified capacity. **10** tolerate or withstand: *I can't stand it.* **11** be a candidate for (an office). **12** provide (food or drink) for (someone) at one's expense. • *noun* **1** an attitude towards a particular issue. **2** a determined effort to hold one's ground or resist something. **3** a stopping of motion or progress. **4 a** large raised tiered structure for spectators. **5** a raised platform for a band, orchestra, or speaker. **6** a rack, base, or item of furniture for holding or displaying something. **7** a small temporary stall or

booth from which promotional goods are sold or displayed. **8** a witness box. **9** a place where vehicles wait for passengers. **10** a group of trees or other plants. ▸ PHRASES **as it stands 1** in its present condition, unaltered. **2** (also **as things stand**) in the present circumstances. **stand alone** be unequalled; be without peers. **stand back 1** withdraw; take up a position further from the front. **2** withdraw emotionally in order to take an objective view. **stand by 1** stand nearby; look on without interfering: *will not stand by and see a cat ill-treated.* **2** uphold, support, side with (a person). **3** adhere to, abide by (terms or promises). **4** be ready to act or assist. **stand corrected** accept correction. **stand down 1** withdraw from a team, election, etc. **2** leave the witness box. **3** *Military* go off duty; relax after a state of alert. **stand firm** (or **fast**) be steadfast or unfaltering. **stand for 1** represent, signify, imply: *"BC" stands for "British Columbia".* **2** (often with *neg.*) *informal* endure, tolerate, acquiesce in. **3** espouse the cause of. **stand one's ground** maintain one's position, not yield. **stand high** be high in status, price, etc. **stand in** (usu. foll. by *for*) act in place of another. **stand off** move or keep away, keep one's distance. **stand on** insist on: *stand on ceremony.* **stand on one's own** not depend on an associated or related thing or person for legitimacy; be recognized for one's own merits: *the second movement stands on its own.* **stand on one's own two feet** (or **own feet**) be self-reliant or independent. **stand out 1** be prominent or conspicuous or outstanding. **2** (usu. foll. by *against, for*) hold out; persist in opposition or support or endurance. **stand over 1** stand close to (a person) to watch, control, threaten, etc. **2** be postponed, be left for later settlement etc. **stand to 1** *Military* stand ready for an attack (esp. before dawn or after dark). **2** abide by, adhere to (terms or promises). **3** be likely or certain to: *stands to lose everything.* **stand up 1 a** rise to one's feet from a sitting or other position. **b** come to or remain in or place in a standing position. **2** (of an argument etc.) be valid. **3** *informal* fail to keep an appointment with. **stand up for 1** support, side with, maintain, defend (a person or cause). **2** (also **stand up with**) act as best man or maid or matron of honour for (a bride or groom or both). **stand up to 1** meet or face (an opponent) courageously. **2** be resistant to the harmful effects of (wear, use, etc.). **stand well** (usu. foll. by *with*) be on good terms or in good repute. **take a** (or **one's**) **stand** commit to or declare a position in a debate etc. **where one stands 1** where one positions oneself in a debate, controversy, etc. **2** what one's situation, status, or condition is in a relationship etc.

stand-alone *adjective* **1** (of a computer) operating independently of a network or other system. **2** designed or intended not to rely on an external structure or system: *stand-alone copiers.*

standard • *noun* **1** a level of quality or attainment. **2** a required or agreed level of quality or attainment. **3** something used as a measure, norm, or model in comparative evaluations. **4** (in *plural*) principles of honourable, decent behaviour. **5** a military or ceremonial flag. **6** an upright water or glass pipe. **7** a tree that grows on an erect stem of full height. **8** a shrub grafted on an erect stem and trained in tree form. **9** a tune or song of established popularity. • *adjective* **1** used or accepted as normal or average. **2** (of a size, measure, etc.) regularly used or produced. **3** (of a work, writer, etc.) viewed as authoritative and so widely read. • *adverb* in its standard or normal state, form, etc.: *comes standard with racing stripes.* PHRASES

set the standard reach a level of excellence which others must try to match.

standard-bearer *noun* **1** a soldier who carries a standard. **2** a prominent leader in a cause.

standardbred *noun* a horse of a breed able to attain a specified speed, developed esp. for harness racing.

standard deviation *noun Statistics* a quantity indicating the extent of deviation for a group.

standard issue *noun* **1** that which is issued or supplied as a matter of course, esp. to military personnel. **2** (as an *adjective*) ordinary, undistinguished.

standardization *noun* the act of standardizing.

standardize *verb* (**standardizes, standardized, standardizing**) **1** cause to conform to a standard. **2** adopt as one's standard or model: *QR/z allows companies to standardize on one common system across all their diverse computing platforms*.

standard of living *noun* (*plural* **standards of living**) the degree of material comfort available to a person or class or community.

standard time *noun* a uniform time officially adopted for a country or region.

standby • *noun* (*plural* **standbys**) **1** a person or thing ready if needed in an emergency etc. **2** a thing which has proven to be reliable; a trusted or long-used resource etc.: *the café offers such calorie-rich standbys as cheesecake and chocolate torte*. **3** (also **standby time**) the maximum length of time the battery of a cellphone will remain charged while awaiting incoming calls (*compare* TALK TIME). • *adjective* **1** ready for immediate use, as in an emergency etc. **2** designating or pertaining to a system of air travel whereby seats are not booked in advance but allocated on the basis of availability just before departure. **3** *Cdn & Brit.* designating theatre tickets sold on the basis of availability on the day of performance, often at a reduced price. • *adverb* without having booked seats in advance: *fly standby*. PHRASES **on standby** prepared for immediate use or activity and awaiting instructions etc.

stand-in *noun* a substitute, esp. for an actor when the latter's acting ability is not needed.

standing • *noun* **1** esteem or repute, esp. high; status, position: *of high standing*. **2** duration: *of long standing*. **3** length of service, membership, etc. **4** (in *plural*) a ranking of teams or competitors in a league etc. esp. according to total points. **5** one's position in a classification or ranking. • *adjective* **1** that stands, upright. **2 a** established, permanent: *a standing rule*. **b** not made, raised, etc., for the occasion: *a standing army*. **3** (of a jump, start, etc.) performed from rest or from a standing position. **4** (of water) stagnant. **5** (of wheat etc.) not yet reaped. PHRASES **in good standing 1** fully paid-up as a member etc. **2** in favour.

standing committee *noun* a committee that is permanent during the existence of the appointing body.

standing joke *noun* something that regularly causes amusement or provokes ridicule: *that he ran over a tree in the Sahara remained a standing joke*.

standing order *noun* **1** (in *plural*) the rules governing the conduct of all business in a parliament, council, etc. **2** an esp. military order that remains valid and does not have to be repeated. **3** an order with a supplier to supply a product whenever it is available.

standing ovation *noun* prolonged applause during which the crowd or audience rises to its feet.

standing room *noun* **1** space to stand in. **2** accommodation in a theatre, arena, etc. where people must stand. **3** (**standing-room**; also **standing-room-only**) (as an *adjective*) designating an audience etc. filling all available seats and overflowing into standing room.

standoff *noun* **1** a deadlock. **2** a confrontation in which each side is entrenched and threatening.

standoffish *adjective* cold or distant in manner. ▶ **standoffishly** *adverb* **standoffishness** *noun*

standout *noun informal* (often as an *adjective*) a remarkable, notable, or outstanding person or thing.

standpoint *noun* **1** the position from which a thing is viewed. **2** a mental attitude.

standstill *noun* a stoppage; an inability to proceed.

stand-up • *adjective* **1** denoting a brand of comedy performed by standing before an audience and telling jokes. **2** that stands or is used upright, not turned down or on its side: *a stand-up collar*. **3** designating a bar, reception, meal, etc., at which people stand rather than sit. **4** (of a fight) violent, thorough, or fair and square. • *noun* **1** a stand-up comedian. **2** stand-up comedy.

Stanfields *plural noun Cdn* proprietary men's underwear, esp. long underwear.

stank *past of* STINK.

Stanley Cup *noun* a trophy awarded annually to the hockey team that wins the NHL championships.

stanza *noun* the basic metrical unit in a poem or verse, consisting of a recurring group of lines which may or may not rhyme. [Say STAN zuh]

stapes *noun* (*plural* **stapes**) a small stirrup-shaped bone in the ears of mammals. [Say STAY peez]

staph *noun informal* = STAPHYLOCOCCUS. [Sounds like *STAFF*]

staphylococcal *adjective* of, pertaining to, or produced by a staphylococcus. [Say staff illa COCKLE]

staphylococcus *noun* (*plural* **staphylococci**) any bacterium of the genus *Staphylococcus*, occurring in grape-like clusters, and sometimes causing pus formation usu. in the skin and mucous membranes of animals. [Say staff illa COCK us for the singular, staff illa COCK eye for the plural]

staple • *noun* **1 a** the principal or an important article of commerce. **b** the chief element or a main component, e.g. of a diet. **c** a raw material. **d** the fibre of cotton or wool etc. as determining its quality: *long-staple cotton*. **2** a small thin piece of U-shaped wire that is punched into wood, sheets of paper, etc., for fastening etc. • *verb* (**staples, stapled, stapling**) fasten or attach with a staple or staples. • *adjective* **1** main or principal: *staple commodities*. **2** important as a product or an export.

staple diet *noun* **1** the food that a person or animal normally eats: *Jerusalem artichokes have been a staple diet of native Americans for centuries*. **2** something that is used a lot: *sex and violence seem to be the staple diet of TV drama*.

stapler *noun* a small device for forcing staples into paper etc. or for stapling papers etc. together.

star • *noun* **1** a fixed luminous point in the night sky which is a large, remote incandescent body like the sun. **2** a stylized representation of a star, often used to indicate a category of excellence. **3** a famous or talented entertainer or sports player. **4** an outstanding person or thing in a group. **5** *Astrology* a planet, constellation, or configuration regarded as influencing one's fortunes or personality. • *verb* (**stars, starred, starring**) **1 a** (of a film etc.) feature as a principal performer. **b** (of a performer) be featured in a film etc. **2** (esp. as **starred** *adjective*) mark, set, or adorn with a star or stars. PHRASES **my stars!** *informal* an expression of surprise.

starboard • *noun* the right-hand side (looking forward) of a ship, boat, or aircraft (*compare* PORT³). • *adjective* on or turned towards the starboard side.

starburst *noun* **1** a pattern of radiating lines or rays

around a central object, light source, etc. **2** an explosion producing this effect.

starch • *noun* (*plural* **starches**) **1** an odourless tasteless carbohydrate obtained chiefly from cereals and potatoes, forming an important constituent of the human diet. **2** a preparation of this for stiffening fabric before ironing. **3** (in *plural*) foods containing much starch, e.g. potatoes, rice, pasta, etc. **4** strength, backbone; vigour: *she wondered if she would have the starch to break up with Tom the following morning.* • *verb* (**starches, starched, starching**) stiffen (clothing) with starch.

starchy *adjective* (**starchier, starchiest**) **1** (of food or diet) containing a lot of starch. **2** (of clothing) stiff with starch. **3** very stiff, formal, or prim in manner or character: *the manager is usually a bit starchy.*

stardom *noun* the state of being famous as an actor, a singer, etc.: *he shot to stardom in a Broadway musical.*

stardust *noun* a romantic mystical look or sensation: *stared at him with stardust in her eyes.*

stare • *verb* (**stares, stared, staring**) **1** look fixedly, esp. out of curiosity, surprise, bewilderment, admiration, horror, etc. **2** (of eyes) be wide open and fixed. **3** be unpleasantly prominent or striking. • *noun* a staring gaze. PHRASES **stare down** stare at someone until they feel embarrassed or defeated and are forced to look away. **stare one in the face** be evident or imminent.

starfish *noun* (*plural* **starfish** or **starfishes**) a marine creature with five or more radiating arms.

star fruit *noun* a juicy golden-yellow Southeast Asian fruit with a star-shaped cross-section.

stargazer *noun informal* **1** an astronomer or astrologer. **2** a daydreamer. ▶ **stargazing** *noun*

stark • *adjective* **1** desolate, bare. **2** sharply evident: *in stark contrast.* **3** downright, sheer. **4** devoid of any elaboration or adornment; brutally simple. **5** completely naked. • *adverb* completely, wholly: *stark naked.* ▶ **starkly** *adverb* **starkness** *noun*

starless *adjective* with no stars visible: *a starless night.*

starlet *noun* a promising young female performer.

starlight *noun* **1** the light of the stars. **2** (as an *adjective*) = STARLIT: *a starlight night.*

starlike *adjective* resembling a star.

starling *noun* **1** a small partly migratory bird with blackish-brown speckled lustrous plumage, chiefly inhabiting cultivated areas. **2** any of various similar or related birds.

starlit *adjective* **1** lighted by stars. **2** with stars visible.

Star of Courage *noun* Canada's second-highest award for bravery, given to civilians and military personnel. Abbreviation: **SC**.

Star of David *noun* a figure consisting of two interlaced triangles, used as a Jewish and Israeli symbol.

starry *adjective* (**starrier, starriest**) **1** covered with stars. **2** resembling a star.

starry-eyed *adjective informal* **1** visionary; enthusiastic but impractical. **2** euphoric.

starship *noun* (in science fiction) a large usu. manned spacecraft for interstellar space travel.

star-spangled *adjective* **1** covered or glittering with stars. **2** featuring many famous performers: *a star-spangled gala performance.*

star-struck *adjective* fascinated or greatly impressed by celebrities or stardom.

star-studded *noun* **1** containing or covered with many stars. **2** featuring many famous performers.

start • *verb* **1** begin to do, be, happen, or engage in. **2** begin to operate or work. **3** cause to happen or operate. **4** begin to move or travel. **5** jump or jerk from surprise. **6** *literary* move or appear suddenly. **7** rouse (game) from its lair. **8** (of eyes) bulge. **9 a** *Sport* be one of the players chosen to play at the outset of (a game). **b** *Baseball* be the starting pitcher of (a game). • *noun* **1** an act of beginning or the point at which something begins. **2** = HEAD START. **3** a sudden movement of surprise, pain, etc. **4** an intermittent or spasmodic effort or movement: *by fits and starts.* PHRASES **for a start** *informal* as a beginning; in the first place. **start in** *informal* **1** begin. **2** (foll. by *on*) make a beginning on. **start off 1** begin; commence. **2** begin to move. **start out 1** begin a journey. **2** *informal* proceed as intending (to do something): *started out to paint the bedroom.* **start over** begin again. **start something** *informal* cause trouble. **start up** arise; occur. **to start with 1** in the first place; before anything else is considered. **2** at the beginning.

starter • *noun* **1** a person or thing that starts. **2** an esp. automatic device for starting an engine. **3 a** a player who plays at the beginning of a game. **b** *Baseball* = STARTING PITCHER. **4** a person giving the signal for the start of a race. **5** a horse or competitor starting in a race. **6** the first course of a meal. **7** a culture used to initiate souring or fermentation in making yogourt, cheese, dough, etc. **8** the initial action etc. • *adjective* relating to or suitable for a start or beginning: *a starter home.* PHRASES **for starters** *informal* to start with.

starting block *noun* a shaped rigid block for bracing the feet of a runner at the start of a race.

starting gate *noun* a movable barrier for securing a fair start in horse races.

starting lineup *noun* a list of players chosen from a team's roster to start a game.

starting pitcher *noun Baseball* a pitcher who pitches the initial innings of a game.

starting point *noun* the point from which a journey, process, argument, etc. begins.

starting rotation *noun Baseball* the group of usu. four or five pitchers on a team that start games in succession.

startle *verb* (**startles, startled, startling**) give a shock or surprise to; cause (a person etc.) to start with surprise or sudden alarm. ▶ **startled** *adjective* **startling** *adjective* **startlingly** *adverb*

start-up *noun* the action or process of setting something in motion, esp. the starting up of a business, machine, or series of operations: *start-up costs.*

star turn *noun* the principal item in an entertainment or performance.

starvation • *noun* **1** the action of starving or depriving a person or animal of food. **2** the condition of having too little food to sustain life or health. • *adjective* **1** liable to cause starvation: *a starvation diet.* **2** seeming to cause starvation: *starvation wages.*

starve *verb* (**starves, starved, starving**) **1** (cause to) die of hunger or suffer from lack of food. **2** suffer from extreme poverty. **3** feel very hungry. **4 a** suffer from mental or spiritual want. **b** (foll. by *for*) feel a strong craving for (sympathy, amusement, knowledge, etc.). **5 a** (foll. by *of*) deprive of; keep scantily supplied with. **b** cause to suffer from mental or spiritual want. **6 a** (foll. by *into*) compel by starving: *starved into submission.* **b** (foll. by *out*) compel to surrender etc. by starving: *starved them out.* ▶ **-starved** *combining form*

stash *informal* • *verb* (**stashes, stashed, stashing**) (often foll. by *away*) **1** conceal; put in a safe or hidden place. **2** hoard, stow, store. • *noun* (*plural* **stashes**) **1** a hiding place or hideout. **2** a thing hidden; a cache. **3** a cache or quantity of an illegal drug.

stasis *noun* **1** a state of inactivity or equilibrium: *it is a*

document of both harrowing stasis and driving momentum. **2** a stoppage of circulation of any of the body fluids. [Say STAY sis or STASS iss]

stat • *noun informal* **1** a statistic. **2** *Cdn* a statutory holiday. • *adverb* esp. *Medical* immediately.

state • *noun* **1** the existing condition or position of a person or thing. **2** *informal* **a** an excited, anxious, or agitated mental condition: *was in a state.* **b** an untidy condition. **3 a** an organized political community under one government; a nation. **b** a political unit forming part of a federation, as in the US. **c (the States)** the US. **4** (as an adjective) **a** of, for, or concerned with the state: *state documents.* **b** reserved for or done on occasions of ceremony: *state visit.* **c** involving ceremony: *state opening of Parliament.* **5** (usu. **State**) civil government: *Church and State.* • *verb* (**states, stated, stating**) express, esp. fully or clearly, in speech or writing. PHRASES **of state** concerning politics or government.

statecraft *noun* the art of diplomacy and government.

stated *adjective* **1** fixed, established; regular: *at stated intervals.* **2** explicitly set forth.

State Department *noun* (in the US) the department of foreign affairs.

statehood *noun* **1** the fact of being an independent country and of having the rights and powers of a country. **2** the condition of being one of the states within a country such as the US: *West Virginia was granted statehood in 1863.*

stateless *adjective* **1** (of a person) having no nationality or citizenship. **2** without a state or states.

state line *noun* the boundary between two US states.

stateliness *noun* the quality of being dignified, imposing, or grand: *she glided around with that slowness of movement which to younger people looks like stateliness.*

stately *adjective* (**statelier, stateliest**) dignified; imposing; grand.

statement *noun* **1** a definite or clear expression of something in speech or writing. **2** an official account of facts, views, or plans, esp. one for release to the media: *the ministers issued a joint statement calling for negotiations.* **3** a formal account of events given by a witness, defendant, etc. to the police or in a court of law. **4** a record of transactions in a bank account etc. **5** an account containing a list of bills, invoices, or payments, and showing the total amount due or the balance owing. **6** the communication of a mood, idea, etc., through something other than words, e.g. clothing: *makes a fashion statement.*

statement of claim *noun* *Cdn* a legal document served in a civil suit which sets out the relief applied for by the plaintiff and the reasons for such relief.

state of affairs *noun* circumstances.

state of emergency *noun* a condition of danger or disaster affecting a country, esp. with normal constitutional procedures suspended.

state of the art • *noun* the current stage of development of a practical or technological subject. • *adjective* (usu. **state-of-the-art**) using the latest techniques or equipment: *state-of-the-art computers.*

stateroom *noun* a private compartment in a passenger ship, train, etc.

stateside esp. *US informal* • *adjective* of, in, or relating to the US. • *adverb* in or towards the continental US.

statesman *noun* (plural **statesmen**) **1** a person skilled in affairs of state, esp. one taking an active part in politics. **2** a distinguished politician. *See also* ELDER STATESMAN. ▶ **statesmanship** *noun*

statesperson *noun* a statesman or stateswoman.

stateswoman *noun* (plural **stateswomen**) **1** a woman skilled in affairs of state, esp. one taking an active part in politics. **2** a distinguished female politician.

state trooper *noun* US a member of a state police force.

statewide US • *adjective* extending over or affecting an entire state. • *adverb* so as to extend over or affect an entire state.

static • *adjective* **1** stationary; not acting or changing; passive. **2** of or relating to static electricity. **3** *Physics* **a** concerned with bodies at rest or forces in equilibrium (*opp.* DYNAMIC 3). **b** acting as weight but not moving: *static pressure.* • *noun* **1** static electricity. **2** electrical disturbances producing interference with the reception of telecommunications and broadcasts. **3** (also **static cling**) the adhering of a piece of clothing to a person's body or to other clothing etc., caused by a buildup of static electricity. **4** *slang* aggravation; criticism. ▶ **statically** *adverb*

static electricity *noun* a stationary electric charge, usu. produced by friction, which causes sparks or cracking, or the attraction of dust, hair, fabric, etc.

staticky *adjective* **1** producing static cling: *a staticky sweater.* **2** (of a radio broadcast etc.) crackling because of bad reception.

station • *noun* **1 a** a regular stopping place on a railway or subway line. **b** (also **bus station**) a place in a city or town where intercity buses depart and arrive. **2** a place or building etc. where a person or thing stands or is placed. **3 a** a designated point or establishment where a particular service or activity is based or organized: *police station.* **b** a subsidiary post office. **4 a** a studio or building used in making television or radio broadcasts. **b** an organization or establishment involved in radio or television broadcasting. **c** a specific frequency or band of frequencies assigned to a broadcaster. **5** a plant for generating electricity, esp. of a specified kind: *hydro station.* **6** a small military base. **7** position in life; rank or status. • *verb* **1** assign a station to. **2** put in position.

SPELL CHECK
stationary, stationery

Writing materials are **stationery**. An easy way to remember this is that stationery has an -*er*, like *paper* and *letter*.

---

stationary *adjective* **1** remaining in one place, not moving. **2** not meant to be moved; not portable. **3** not changing in magnitude, number, quality, efficiency, etc.: *population levels in this area are stationary.*

stationer *noun* a person who sells stationery.

SPELL CHECK
stationery, stationary

Something not moving is **stationary**.

---

stationery *noun* **1** writing paper. **2** writing materials, such as paper, envelopes, office supplies, etc.

station of the cross *noun* **1** each of a series of usu. 14 images representing the events in the last days of Christ's life, before which devotions are performed in some churches. **2** (**Stations of the Cross**) the act of performing such devotions.

station wagon *noun* a car with the passenger area extended and combined with space for luggage, usu. with an extra door at the rear.

statism *noun* centralized state administration and

S

control of social and economic affairs. ▶ **statist** *noun & adjective* [Say STATE ism]

statistic *noun* a statistical fact or item.

statistical *adjective* of or relating to statistics. ▶ **statistically** *adverb*

statistician *noun* a person who studies or works with statistics. [Say stat iss TISH'n]

statistics *plural noun* **1** (usu. treated as *singular*) the science of collecting and analyzing numerical data, esp. in or for large quantities, and usu. inferring proportions in a whole from proportions in a representative sample. **2** any systematic collection or presentation of such facts.

StatsCan *noun* *Cdn informal* Statistics Canada.

statuary • *adjective* of or for statues. • *noun* **1** statues collectively. **2** the art of making statues.

statue *noun* a sculptured, cast, carved, or moulded figure of a person or animal, esp. life-size or larger.

statuesque *adjective* **1** like a statue in size, dignity, or lack of movement. **2** (esp. of a woman) tall and graceful. [Say statue ESK]

statuette *noun* a small statue. [Say statue ETT]

stature *noun* **1** the natural height of the body: *small in stature*. **2** importance and reputation gained by ability or achievement: *her growing political stature*.

status *noun* (*plural* **statuses**) **1** the social or professional position of a person or thing in relation to others; relative importance. **2** high rank or social position. **3** *Law* a person's legal standing which determines his or her rights and duties, e.g. citizen, civilian, refugee, etc. (see also MARITAL STATUS). **4** *Cdn* (as an *adjective*) (of an Aboriginal person) registered as an Indian under the Indian Act. **5** the position of affairs at a particular time, esp. in political or commercial contexts. [Say STAT us or STATE us]

status quo *noun* the existing state of affairs: *they have a vested interest in maintaining the status quo*. [Say stat us KWO or state us KWO]

status symbol *noun* a possession that is thought to show a person's high social rank, wealth, etc.

statute *noun* **1 a** a law passed by a legislative body, and expressed in a formal document. **b** the document containing such an enactment. **2** any of the rules of an organization or institution.

statute law *noun* **1** the body of principles and rules of law laid down in statutes as distinct from rules formulated in practical application (*compare* COMMON LAW 1, CASE LAW). **2** a statute.

statute of limitations *noun* (*plural* **statutes of limitations**) a law that fixes the time within which criminal charges must be laid or legal action taken.

statutory *adjective* **1** required, permitted, or enacted by statute: *there is no statutory means by which such an assessment can be reopened*. **2** (of an offence) punishable under a statute: *insider trading is now a statutory offence*.

statutory holiday *noun* *Cdn* a public holiday established by federal or provincial statute.

statutory release *noun* *Cdn Law* parole as required by statute.

staunch • *adjective* **1** trustworthy, loyal. **2** (of a ship, joint, etc.) strong, watertight, etc. • *verb* (**staunches, staunched, staunching**) **1** restrain the flow of (esp. blood). **2** restrain the flow from (esp. a wound).

staunchly *adverb* in a strongly loyal manner: *she staunchly defended their policy*.

stave • *noun* **1** each of the curved pieces of wood forming the sides of a cask, pail, etc. **2** *Music* a set of usu. five parallel lines on which a note is placed to indicate its pitch. • *verb* (**staves**; *past* and *past participle* **stove** or **staved**; **staving**) **1** break a hole in: *the door was staved in*. **2** crush or knock out of shape. PHRASES **stave off**

(*past* and *past participle* **staved**) avert or defer (esp. danger or misfortune).

stay • *verb* (**stays, stayed, staying**) **1** remain. **2** have temporary residence as a visitor etc. **3** *archaic* or *literary* stop or check (progress, the inroads of a disease, etc.). **4** postpone (judgment, decision, etc.). **5** assuage (hunger etc.) esp. for a short time. **6 a** show endurance. **b** show endurance to the end of (a race etc.). **7** (foll. by *with*) (of food) give lasting satisfaction to hunger. **8** (in poker) raise one's ante sufficiently to remain in a round. **9** (foll. by *with*) **a** keep up with (a competitor etc.). **b** apply oneself to, continue with. • *noun* **1** a period of staying somewhere, in particular of living somewhere temporarily as a visitor or guest: *an overnight stay*. **2** a suspension or postponement of a sentence, judgment, etc.: *was granted a stay of execution*. **3** a rope or wire that supports a ship's mast, a pole, etc. **4** (in *plural*) *hist.* a corset esp. with whalebone etc. stiffening, and laced. PHRASES **has come** (or **is here**) **to stay** *informal* must be regarded as permanent. **stay the course** pursue a course of action or endure a struggle etc. to the end. **stay in** remain indoors, esp. at home or in school after hours as a punishment. **stay on** remain in a place or position. **stay put** remain where it is placed or where one is. **stay up** not go to bed (until late at night).

stay-at-home • *adjective* **1** remaining habitually at home. **2** (esp. of a parent) choosing to remain at home, esp. to care for children, rather than seeking outside employment. **3** *Hockey* (of a defenceman) conservative; unlikely to take risks or be caught out of position. • *noun* (*plural* **stay-at-homes**) a person who does this.

SPELL CHECK
stayed, staid

A dull or unchanging person or thing is **staid**.

---

staying power *noun* endurance, stamina.

staysail *noun* a triangular fore-and-aft sail extended on a stay. [Say STAY sail or STAY sull]

STD *abbreviation* SEXUALLY TRANSMITTED DISEASE.

stead *noun* PHRASES **in a person's** (or **thing's**) **stead** as a substitute; instead of him or her or it. **stand a person in good stead** be advantageous or serviceable to him or her: *your languages will stand you in good stead when it comes to finding a job*. [Say STED]

steadfast *adjective* **1** constant, firm, unwavering: *was known for her steadfast loyalty*. **2** (of a person's gaze etc.) fixed in intensity; steadily directed. ▶ **steadfastly** *adverb* **steadfastness** *noun* [Say STED fast]

steadily *adverb* in a uniform and regular manner.

steadiness *noun* the quality of being steady, unwavering, or unfaltering.

steady • *adjective* (**steadier, steadiest**) **1** firmly in place. **2** done or occurring in a uniform and regular manner: *a steady pace*. **3** not changeable or changing: *steady boyfriend* ◊ *a steady job*. **4** serious; cautious and dependable in behaviour. **5** not faltering: *a steady hand*. **6** steadily: *hold it steady*. • *verb* (**steadies, steadied, steadying**) make or become steady: *steady the boat*. • *interjection* as a command or warning to take care. • *noun* (*plural* **steadies**) **1** *informal* a regular boyfriend or girlfriend. **2** *Cdn* (*Nfld*) **a** a stretch of still water in a river or pond; a pool. **b** a small freshwater pond. PHRASES **go steady** (often foll. by *with*) *informal* have as a regular boyfriend or girlfriend.

steady state *noun* an unvarying condition, esp. in a physical process, e.g. of the universe theoretically having no beginning and no end.

steak *noun* **1** a slice of meat or fish, cut for frying or barbecuing. **2** beef cut for stewing or braising **steaklette** *noun* Cdn a thin patty of ground beef.

steak house *noun* a restaurant specializing in steaks.

steak tartare *noun* a dish of raw chopped steak mixed with raw egg, onion, and seasonings, shaped into small cakes or patties. [Say steak tar TAR]

steal • *verb* (**steals**; *past* **stole**; *past participle* **stolen**; **stealing**) **1** take illegally without right or permission. **2** obtain surreptitiously or by surprise: *stole a kiss.* **3** win or gain possession of, esp. insidiously or artfully: *stole her heart away* ◊ *stole the puck off the goalie.* **4 a** move, esp. silently or stealthily: *stole out of the room.* **b** (of a sound etc.) become gradually perceptible. **5** *Baseball* advance to (a base) while the ball is being pitched. • *noun* **1** *informal* an unexpectedly easy task or good bargain. **2** *Baseball* the act of advancing a base by stealing. PHRASES **steal a march on** gain an advantage over (someone), esp. by acting before they do: *the company will steal a march on the competition by introducing a downsized, cheaper laser printer.* **steal the show** outshine other performers. **steal a person's thunder 1** use another person's idea, policy, etc., and spoil the effect the originator hoped to achieve by expressing it or acting upon it first. **2** take the limelight or attention from another person. ▸ **stealer** *noun* (also in *combination*)

stealth *noun* **1** secrecy: *the government was accused of trying to introduce the tax by stealth* ◊ *lions rely on stealth when hunting.* **2** (as an *adjective*) designed in accordance with or designating the technology which makes detection by radar or sonar difficult: *stealth bomber.* [Rhymes with HEALTH]

stealthily *adverb* with stealth; without being noticed: *she crept stealthily along the corridor, then darted into the office to grab the fruitcakes.* [Rhymes with HEALTHILY]

stealthy *adjective* (**stealthier, stealthiest**) quiet or secret: *a stealthy movement.* [Rhymes with HEALTHY]

steam • *noun* **1 a** the gas into which water is changed by boiling. **b** a mist of liquid particles of water produced by the condensation of this gas. **2** any similar vapour. **3 a** energy or power provided by a steam engine or other machine. **b** *informal* power or energy generally. • *verb* **1 a** cook (food) in steam. **b** treat with steam, e.g. to remove wrinkles from garments or make timber pliable. **2** give off steam or other vapour. **3 a** move under the power of a steam engine: *steamed down the river.* **b** (foll. by *along, ahead,* etc.) *informal* proceed with speed or vigour. **4** cover or become covered with condensed water vapour. **5** *informal* be or cause to be angry or upset. **6** (foll. by *open* etc.) apply steam to the gum of (a sealed envelope) to open it. PHRASES **blow** (or **let**) **off steam** release one's pent-up feelings or energy. **full steam ahead** with as much speed and vigour as possible. **get up steam** work oneself into an energetic or angry state. **lose steam** slow down. **pick up steam** speed up. **run out of steam** lose one's impetus or energy. **under one's own steam** without help.

steam bath *noun* **1** a room etc. filled with steam for cleaning or refreshing oneself by sweating. **2** a bath taken in such a room.

steamboat *noun* a boat propelled by a steam engine.

steamed *adjective* **1** angry, upset. **2** (of food) cooked by steaming.

steamed up *adjective* **1** (of a surface) covered with condensed vapour. **2** *agitated or upset, angry.*

steam engine *noun* **1** an engine using the expansion or condensation of steam to generate power. **2** a locomotive powered by such an engine.

steamer *noun* **1** a thing that steams. **2** a ship etc. propelled by steam. **3** a usu. perforated container in which food is cooked by steam. **4** (also **steamer clam**) a marine bivalve mollusc with a thin shell, valued as food on the east coast of North America.

steamie *noun* Cdn (Que.) a steamed hot dog.

steam iron *noun* an electric iron that emits steam from its flat surface, to improve its pressing ability.

steamroller • *noun* **1** a heavy slow-moving vehicle with a roller, used for levelling roads. **2** a crushing power or force. • *verb* (also **steamroll**) **1** crush forcibly or indiscriminately: *some businesspeople think they've won negotiations because they've steamrollered the opposition and got what they wanted.* **2** force (a measure etc.) through a legislature by overriding opposition: *the minister was able to steamroller her bill through the House.*

steam room *noun* a room that may be filled with steam for taking steam baths.

steamship *noun* a ship propelled by a steam engine.

steamy *adjective* (**steamier, steamiest**) **1** like or full of steam. **2** *informal* erotic, passionate. **3** hot and humid.

steed *noun archaic* or *literary* a fast powerful horse.

steel • *noun* **1** a durable alloy of iron with carbon and usu. other elements, used as a structural and fabricating material. **2** toughness, strength: *nerves of steel.* **3 a** a steel rod for sharpening knives. **b** a piece of steel used with a flint to produce sparks. **4** Cdn a railway track or line. • *adjective* **1** made of steel. **2** like steel. • *verb* harden or make resolute: *steeled myself for a shock.*

steel band *noun* a group of musicians who play (chiefly calypso-style) music on steel drums.

steel blue *noun* & *adjective* a dark bluish-grey colour.

steel drum *noun* a percussion instrument made out of an oil drum with one end beaten down and divided into grooved sections to give different notes.

steel grey *noun* & *adjective* a dark metallic grey colour.

steel guitar *noun* **1** a type of acoustic guitar with steel resonating discs inside the body under the bridge. **2** (also called **Hawaiian guitar**) a steel-stringed instrument, usu. held horizontally, in which a characteristic glissando effect is produced by sliding a metal bar along the strings as they are plucked.

steelhead *noun* a large silvery North American rainbow trout, esp. after returning from the sea or when found in the Great Lakes and tributaries.

steelie *noun informal* **1** a steel ball bearing used as a marble. **2** a steelhead.

steelmaker *noun* a business that manufactures steel. ▸ **steelmaking** *noun* & *adjective*

steel wool *noun* an abrasive substance consisting of a mass of fine steel threads, used for cleaning metal, making a surface smooth, etc.

steelworker *noun* a person who works in a factory where steel is manufactured.

steelworks *plural noun* (usu. treated as *singular*) (also **steel mill**) a plant where steel is manufactured.

steely *adjective* (**steelier, steeliest**) **1** of, or hard as, steel. **2** inflexibly severe: *steely composure* ◊ *steely-eyed*.

steep • *adjective* **1** sloping sharply: *a steep hill*. **2** (of a rise or fall) rapid: *a steep drop in prices*. **3** *informal* (of a price etc.) exorbitant; unreasonable: *I would have bought it, but the price was too steep*. • *verb* **1** soak in liquid: *the tea is steeping*. **2** a surround or fill with a quality or influence: *a city steeped in history*. **b** make deeply acquainted with (a subject): *steeped in the classics*.

steepen *verb* become or make steeper.

steeple *noun* a tall tower, esp. one surmounted by a spire, above the roof of a church. ▶ **steepled** *adjective*

steeplechase *noun* **1** a horse race across the countryside or on a racecourse with ditches, hedges, etc., to jump. **2** a cross-country foot race. ▶ **steeplechaser** *noun* **steeplechasing** *noun*

steeply *adverb* **1** in a sharply sloping manner. **2** in a sudden or rapid way.

steepness *noun* the quality of something that rises or falls sharply.

steer • *verb* **1** direct or control the movement of. **2** guide (a person, action, etc.) by advice or instruction etc. **3** guide the movement or trend of: *steered the conversation away from that subject*. • *noun* **1** a piece of advice or information. **2** a castrated male of domestic cattle, esp. one raised for beef. PHRASES **steer clear of** take care to avoid.

steerable *adjective* that can be guided to move or point in a particular direction: *a steerable rocket*.

steerage *noun* esp. *hist.* the part of a ship allotted to passengers travelling at the cheapest rate.

steering *noun* **1** the action of steering a vehicle, vessel, or aircraft. **2** the mechanism in a vehicle, vessel, or aircraft that makes it possible to steer.

steering column *noun* the shaft or column which connects the steering wheel, handlebars, etc. of a vehicle to the rest of the steering gear.

steering committee *noun* (also **steering group**) a committee that decides the order of certain business activities and guides their general course.

steering wheel *noun* a wheel by which a vehicle etc. is steered.

steer wrestler *noun* a person who participates in the rodeo event of steer wrestling.

steer wrestling *noun* a rodeo event in which a contestant on a horse chases a steer, dismounts, and wrestles the steer to the ground.

stegosaurus *noun* (also **stegosaur**) a plant-eating dinosaur with a double row of large bony plates along the back. [Say stegga SORE us]

stein *noun* a large (usu. earthenware) mug, esp. for beer. [Say STINE]

stellar *adjective* **1** of or relating to a star or stars. **2** a having star performers: *a stellar cast*. **b** *informal* outstanding: *a stellar performance*.

Steller's jay *noun* a blue jay found in central and western North America.

Steller's sea lion *noun* a large red-brown sea lion of the northern Pacific.

stem • *noun* **1** the main body or stalk of a plant or shrub. **2** a the stalk supporting a fruit, flower, or leaf, and attaching it to a larger branch, twig, or stalk. **b** a stalk supporting or forming part of an organ or structure: *brain stem*. **3** a stem-shaped part of an object: **a** the slender part of a wineglass between the body and the base. **b** the tube of a tobacco pipe. **c** a vertical stroke in a letter or musical note. **d** the winding shaft of a watch. **4** the root or main part of a word. **5** the main upright timber or metal piece at the bow of a ship

to which the ship's sides are joined at the fore end. • *verb* (**stems, stemmed, stemming**) **1** (foll. by *from*) spring or originate from. **2** remove the stem or stems from (fruit, tobacco, etc.). **3** check or stop. **4** dam up (a stream etc.). **5** slide the tail of one ski or both skis outwards usu. in order to turn or slow down.

stem cell *noun* an undifferentiated cell from which specialized cells develop.

stemmed *adjective* **1** (of a plant) having the kind of stem described: *long-stemmed roses*. **2** (of a glass) having a base attached to the body by a slender part.

stemware *noun* crystal or glass vessels with rounded bowls on stems, used esp. for wine.

stench *noun* a foul smell.

stencil • *noun* **1** a thin sheet of plastic etc., in which a pattern or lettering is cut, used to produce a corresponding pattern on the surface beneath it by applying ink, paint, etc. to the cut-out areas. **2** the pattern, lettering, etc., produced by a stencil. • *verb* (**stencils, stencilled, stencilling**) produce (a pattern) or decorate (a surface) with a stencil.

stenographer *noun* a person whose job is to write down in shorthand what is said in a meeting, courtroom, etc. [Say sten OGGRA fur]

stenography *noun* the art of writing in shorthand and transcribing the shorthand on a typewriter. [Say sten OGGRA fee]

stentorian *adjective* (of a voice, sound, etc.) very loud and powerful: *the government made all sorts of commitments before its election, stentorian commitments shouted from the rooftops*. [Say sten TORY in]

step • *noun* **1** the complete movement of one leg in walking or running. **2** a unit of movement in dancing. **3** a measure taken, esp. one of several in a course of action, advancement, etc. **4** a flat-topped structure for passing from one level to another. **5** a short distance: *only a step from my door*. **6** the sound or mark made by a foot in walking etc.: *heard a step on the stairs*. • *verb* (**steps, stepped, stepping**) **1** lift and set down one's foot in walking. **2** come or go in a specified direction by stepping. **3** make progress in a specified way: *stepped into a new job*. **4** perform (a dance). PHRASES **in step** (often foll. by *with*) **1** stepping in time with music or other marchers. **2** conforming with others. **in a person's steps** following a person's example. **keep step** remain in step. **out of step** (often foll. by *with*) not in step. **step by step** gradually; cautiously; by stages or degrees. **step down 1** (also **step aside**) resign from a position etc. **2** *Electricity* decrease (voltage) by using a transformer. **step forward** offer one's help, services, etc. **step in 1** enter a room, house, etc.: *Jenn's eyes lit up as Frank stepped into the room*. **2** a intervene to help or hinder. **b** act as a substitute for an indisposed colleague etc. **step into a person's shoes** take control of a task or job from another person. **step on it** (or **on the gas**) *informal* **1** accelerate a motor vehicle. **2** hurry up. **step out 1** leave temporarily. **2** be active socially. **step out of line** behave inappropriately or disobediently. **step up 1** increase, intensify: *must step up production*. **2** come forward for some purpose. **watch one's step** be careful.

stepbrother *noun* a son of one's stepmother or stepfather by an earlier marriage.

step-by-step *adjective* (of an approach, guide, etc.) that proceeds through or involves a series of distinct stages or operations.

stepchild *noun* (*plural* **stepchildren**) a child of one's husband or wife by a previous marriage.

step dance • *noun* a dance intended to display special steps by an individual performer, esp. popular in Celtic cultures. • *verb* (**step-dance, step-dances, step-**

danced, **step-dancing**) perform a step dance. ▶ **step dancer** noun **step-dancing** noun

stepdaughter noun a female stepchild.

stepfather noun a male step-parent.

step-in • noun a garment or shoe put on by stepping into it. • adjective (of a garment or shoe) put on by being stepped into without unfastening.

stepladder noun a short folding ladder, used without being leaned against a surface.

stepmother noun a female step-parent.

step-parent noun a mother's or father's later spouse.

steppe noun a level grassy unforested plain, esp. in southeast Europe and Siberia. [Say STEP]

stepped adjective having or forming into a step or series of steps: *a stepped pathway up the hill*.

stepped-up adjective raised by degrees to a higher level; increased, intensified.

stepper noun **1** an exercise machine used to simulate the activity of climbing stairs. **2** informal a person who steps, esp. a dancer.

stepping stone noun **1** a raised stone, usu. one of a series, to facilitate crossing a stream, muddy ground, etc. on foot. **2** something used as a means of advancement in a career etc.

stepsister noun a daughter of one's stepmother or stepfather by an earlier marriage.

stepson noun a male stepchild.

stereo • noun (plural **stereos**) **1** a stereophonic CD player, tape deck, etc. **2** stereophonic sound: *broadcast in stereo*. • adjective **1** stereophonic. **2** stereoscopic.

stereophonic adjective (of sound reproduction) using two or more channels so that the sound has the effect of being distributed and of coming from more than one source. [Say stereo FON ick]

stereoscope noun a device by which two photographs of the same object taken at slightly different angles are viewed together, giving an impression of depth. ▶ **stereoscopic** adjective **stereoscopically** adverb

stereotype • noun **1** a widely held but fixed and oversimplified image of a particular type of person or thing. **2** a person or thing appearing to conform to such an image. • verb (**stereotypes**, **stereotyped**, **stereotyping**) (esp. as **stereotyped** adjective) view or represent as a stereotype. ▶ **stereotypic** adjective **stereotypical** adjective **stereotypically** adverb

sterile adjective **1** not able to produce children or young. **2** free from bacteria etc.: *sterile bandages*. **3** unproductive: *sterile discussions*. **4** lacking originality or emotive force: *the room felt cold and sterile*. **5** (of plants) not producing fruit or seeds. ▶ **sterility** noun [Say STARE ile or STARE ill, stuh RILLA tee]

sterilization noun **1** the action of making something free from bacteria or other living micro-organisms. **2** the action of depriving a person or animal of the ability to produce offspring. [Say stare uh lize AY sh'n]

sterilize verb (**sterilizes**, **sterilized**, **sterilizing**) **1** make something free from bacteria or other living micro-organisms: *the baby's bottle must be sterilized before it can be used*. **2** deprive a person or animal of the ability to produce offspring. ▶ **sterilizer** noun [Say STARE uh lize]

sterling • adjective **1** of or in British money: *pound sterling*. **2** denoting silver of $92\frac{1}{4}$% purity. **3** made of sterling silver. **4** (of a person or their work or qualities) excellent, valuable. • noun **1** British money. **2** sterling silver. **3** articles of sterling silver, esp. tableware. [Say STIR ling]

stern[1] adjective serious, severe, strict: *a stern expression*.

stern[2] noun the rear part, esp. of a boat.

sternly adverb in a strict or serious manner.

sternness noun a strict or serious manner.

sternum noun (plural **sternums** or **sterna**) the breastbone.

sternwheeler noun a steamer propelled by a paddlewheel positioned at the stern.

steroid noun any of a group of organic compounds with a structure of four rings of carbon atoms, including many hormones, alkaloids, and vitamins, used to treat various diseases and to increase muscle size. ▶ **steroidal** adjective [Say STARE oid, stare OID'll]

stethoscope noun an instrument used to listen to the action of the heart, lungs, etc., usu. consisting of a circular piece placed against the chest, with flexible tubes leading to earpieces. [Say STETH uh scope]

Stetson noun proprietary a soft hat with a very wide brim and a high crown, associated with cowboys.

stevedore • noun a person employed in loading and unloading ships. • verb (**stevedores**, **stevedored**, **stevedoring**) load or unload the cargo of (a ship). ▶ **stevedoring** noun & adjective [Say STEVE uh dor]

stew • verb **1** simmer in a pot, slow cooker, etc. **2** informal be oppressed by heat or humidity, esp. in a confined space. **3** informal **a** suffer prolonged embarrassment, anxiety, etc. **b** (foll. by *about*, *over*) fret or be anxious. • noun **1** a dish of stewed meat, fish, vegetables, etc. **2** informal an agitated or angry state. **3** a mixture: *a stew of different sounds*. PHRASES **stew in one's own juice** (or **juices**) be left to suffer the consequences of one's own actions.

steward • noun **1** a passengers' attendant on an aircraft, ship, or train. **2** an official appointed to keep order or supervise arrangements at a large public event. **3** = SHOP STEWARD. **4** a person responsible for supplies of food etc. for a college or club etc. **5 a** a person employed to manage another's property, esp. a large house or land. **b** (esp. in the United Church) a layperson appointed to manage the financial affairs of a congregation or circuit. • verb act as a steward of.

WRITING TIP
stewardess

Flight attendant is now usually preferred to **stewardess**.

---

stewardess noun a female flight attendant.

stewardship noun the action of managing or taking care of something, such as property, an organization, or money: *the organization flourished under his stewardship*.

stewed adjective **1** cooked by stewing. **2** informal drunk.

stewpot noun **1** a pot for cooking stew. **2** a mixture: *Boulevard Saint-Laurent, Montreal's ethnic stewpot*.

stick[1] noun **1** a slender branch broken or cut from a tree. **2** a thin wooden rod or branch for a particular purpose. **3** something resembling a stick: *stick of gum*. **4 a** = STICK SHIFT. **b** = JOYSTICK. **5** (**the sticks**) informal remote rural areas.

stick[2] verb (**sticks**; past and past participle **stuck**; **sticking**) **1** insert or thrust (a thing or its point). **2** insert a pointed thing into; stab. **3** (foll. by *in*, *into*, *on*, etc.) **a** fix or be fixed on a pointed thing. **b** fix or be fixed by or as by a pointed end. **4** fix or become or remain fixed by or as by adhesive. **5** endure; make a continued impression. **6** lose or be deprived of the power of motion or action. **7** informal **a** put in a specified position or place, esp. quickly or haphazardly: *stick it in your pocket*. **b** remain or be confined in a place: *stuck indoors*. **8** informal **a** (of an accusation etc.) be convincing or regarded as valid: *could not make the charges stick*. **b** (foll. by *on*) place the blame for (a thing)

on (a person). **9** (foll. by *at*) *informal* persevere with. **PHRASES** **stick around** *informal* linger; remain at the same place. **stick by** (or **with** or **to**) stay loyal or close to. **stick 'em up!** *informal* hands up! **stick fast** adhere or become firmly fixed or trapped in a position or place. **stick in one's throat** be against one's principles. **stick it out** *informal* persevere. **stick it to** (a **person**) *informal* **1** treat unfairly; cheat or take advantage of. **2** get even with; achieve revenge. **stick one's neck out** expose oneself to failure, criticism, etc. by acting or speaking boldly. **stick out** protrude or cause to protrude or project: *stuck his tongue out*. **stick out like a sore thumb** *informal* be very obvious or incongruous. **stick to 1** remain close to or fixed on or to. **2** remain faithful to. **3** keep to (a subject etc.): *stick to the point*. **stick together** *informal* remain united or mutually loyal. **stick to it** persevere. **stick to the ribs** (of food) be hearty and filling. **stick up 1** be or make erect or protruding upwards. **2** fasten to an upright surface. **3** *informal* rob or threaten with a gun. **stick up for** support or defend (a person or cause). **stick up to** be assertive in the face of; offer resistance to. **stick with** *informal* remain in touch with or faithful to; persevere with.

stickball *noun* a form of baseball using a rubber ball and a broomstick etc., usu. played by children.

sticker • *noun* **1** an adhesive label, price tag, picture, etc. **2** a person or thing that sticks. • *verb* **1** attach a sticker to. **2** attach a sticker to (a CD, tape, etc.) warning that the lyrics may be offensive.

sticker price *noun* the full asking price for an item, esp. a car, from which a discount may be deducted.

sticker shock *noun* *informal* shock experienced on discovering the high, or increased, price of a product, esp. a big-ticket item such as a car.

stick figure *noun* a figure drawn in thin simple lines.

stickhandle *verb* (**stickhandles, stickhandled, stickhandling**) **1** *Hockey* skilfully control the puck with the stick. **2** *Cdn* manoeuvre skilfully around (an issue etc.). ▶ **stickhandler** *noun* **stickhandling** *noun*

stickiness *noun* **1** the quality of something covered in a substance that sticks to things that touch it. **2** the adhesive property of something: *this tape loses its stickiness in the cold*.

sticking point *noun* the limit of progress, agreement, etc.

stick-in-the-mud *noun* (*plural* **stick-in-the-muds**) *informal* a person who refuses to try anything new or exciting.

stickleback *noun* a small fish with sharp spines along the back.

stickler *noun* **1** a person who insists on something: *a stickler for detail*. **2** a difficult problem or puzzle.

stick-on *adjective* adhesive: *stick-on address labels*.

stick shift *noun* **1** a manual transmission for a car etc. **2** a car etc. having a manual transmission. **3** a lever used to engage or change gear, esp. in a car etc.

stickup *noun* *informal* a robbery using a gun.

stickwork *noun* *Hockey* interference with the stick, e.g. butt-ending, slashing, etc.

sticky • *adjective* (**stickier, stickiest**) **1** tending or intended to stick. **2** glutinous, viscous. **3 a** (of the weather) humid. **b** damp with sweat. **4** *informal* awkward, uncooperative, difficult: *was sticky about giving me a day off* ◊ *a sticky problem*. • *noun* (*plural* **stickies**) *informal* = POST-IT.

sticky bun *noun* a sweet bread roll covered with a sticky glaze or icing or with a syrup-coated bottom.

sticky tape *noun* clear adhesive tape.

stiff • *adjective* **1** rigid; not flexible. **2** hard to move or turn etc.; not working freely. **3** thick; capable of retaining a definite shape: *beat egg whites until stiff*. **4** demanding strength or effort: *a stiff climb*. **5** severe or strong: *a stiff breeze* ◊ *stiff opposition* ◊ *a stiff drink*. **6** (of a person or manner) not relaxed. **7** aching due to previous exertion, injury, etc.: *stiff shoulder*. **8** (of a price, demand, etc.) exorbitant. **9** (foll. by *with*) *informal* full of: *stiff with tourists*. • *adverb* *informal* to an extreme degree: *bored stiff*. • *noun* *slang* **1** a corpse. **2 a** a foolish or useless person. **b** an ordinary person: *a working stiff*. • *verb* *slang* **1** cheat; refuse to pay or tip. **2** kill, murder. **3** fail to sell well or be popular: *his last album stiffed*.

stiffen *verb* make or become stiff. ▶ **stiffener** *noun* **stiffening** *noun*

stiffish *adjective* somewhat stiff.

stiffly *adverb* **1** in a way that is tense or formal, not relaxed or friendly. **2** in a way that is firm or rigid, not flexible or loose. **3** not (moving, acting, etc.) freely or with ease.

stiffness *noun* **1** soreness in the muscles resulting from physical activity, making movement difficult or painful. **2** the quality of something that is difficult to bend or move. **3** a tense or formal manner.

stiff upper lip *noun* control of one's feelings and emotions in the face of pain or disappointment.

stifle *verb* (**stifles, stifled, stifling**) **1** prevent or constrain (an activity or idea): *high taxes were stifling small businesses*. **2** suppress: *stifled a yawn*. **3** suffocate; stop or cause to stop breathing. [Say STIFE 'll]

stifling *adjective* **1** unbearably hot. **2** oppressive. ▶ **stiflingly** *adverb* [Say STIFE ling]

stigma *noun* (*plural* **stigmata** or **stigmas**) **1 a** a mark or sign of disgrace or discredit: *the stigma attached to his conviction*. **b** an unfavourable reputation. **2** the part of a pistil that receives the pollen in pollination. **3** (usu. as **stigmata** *plural*) (in Christian belief) marks corresponding to those left on Christ's body by the Crucifixion, said to have been impressed by divine favour on the bodies of others. **4** a mark or spot on the skin or on a butterfly's wing.

stigmatic • *adjective* denoting marks corresponding to the wounds of Christ, said to have been impressed by divine favour on the bodies of others. • *noun* *Christianity* a person bearing such marks. [Say stig MAT ick]

stigmatization *noun* the representation of someone or something as worthy of disgrace or disapproval: *women who choose to breast-feed in public are still often subjected to unfair stigmatization*. [Say stigma tize AY sh'n]

stigmatize *verb* (**stigmatizes, stigmatized, stigmatizing**) (often foll. by *as*) describe or regard someone or something as worthy of disgrace or great disapproval: *a stigmatized problem like alcoholism*. [Say STIGMA tize]

stile *noun* an arrangement of steps allowing people but not farm animals to climb over a fence or wall.

stiletto *noun* (*plural* **stilettos**) **1** a short dagger with a thick blade. **2** (also **stiletto heel**) **a** a very high slender heel on a women's shoe. **b** a shoe with such a heel. [Say still ETTO]

still • *adjective* **1** not or hardly moving. **2** quiet; calm and tranquil. • *noun* **1** deep silence and calm: *in the still of the night*. **2** an ordinary static photograph (as opposed to a motion picture), esp. a single shot from a cinema film. • *adverb* **1** without moving: *stand still*. **2** even now or at a particular time. **3** nevertheless. **4** increasingly: *still greater efforts*. **5** an apparatus for distilling alcoholic drinks. • *verb* make or become still; quieten. **PHRASES** **still and all** *informal* nevertheless. **still waters run deep** a quiet manner conceals depths of feeling or knowledge or cunning.

stillbirth *noun* the birth of a dead child.

stillborn *adjective* **1** (of a child) born dead. **2** (of an idea, plan, etc.) not able to succeed.

still life *noun* (*plural* **still lifes**) **1** a painting, drawing, or photograph of inanimate objects such as fruit or flowers. **2** this genre of art.

stillness *noun* the quality of being quiet and calm.

stilt *noun* **1** either of a pair of poles with supports for the feet enabling the user to walk at a distance above the ground. **2** each of a set of piles or posts supporting a building etc. **3** a long-billed wading bird with long slender legs.

stilted *adjective* **1** (of a literary style etc.) stiff and unnatural. **2** standing on stilts. ▶ **stiltedly** *adverb*

Stilton *noun* *proprietary* a kind of strong rich cheese, often with blue veins, originally made in southern England.

stimulant • *noun* **1** a substance that stimulates, esp. a drug or alcohol. **2** a stimulating influence. • *adjective* that stimulates, esp. bodily or mental activity.

stimulate *verb* (**stimulates, stimulated, stimulating**) **1** make something develop or become more active; encourage something: *the exhibition has stimulated interest in her work*. **2** make someone interested and excited about something: *parents should give children books that stimulate them*. **3** make a part of the body function: *some women were given fertility drugs to stimulate their ovaries*. ▶ **stimulating** *adjective* **stimulation** *noun* **stimulator** *noun*

stimulus *noun* (*plural* **stimuli**) **1** a thing that rouses to activity or energy. **2** a stimulating or rousing effect. **3** a thing that evokes a specific functional reaction in an organ or tissue. [Say STIM you lus]

sting • *noun* **1** a sharp painful wound inflicted by any of a number of insects, animals, and plants. **2** a sharp physical pain like that of a bee or wasp sting. **3** (often foll. by *of*) the painful or hurtful quality or effect of something: *the sting of poverty ◊ the sting of her satire*. **4** (also **sting operation**) an undercover operation in which police officers, attempting to implicate a presumed criminal, pose as buyers or sellers in an apparently illegal transaction. **5** *slang* a swindle or robbery. **6** = STINGER 1a. • *verb* (**stings**; *past* and *past participle* **stung**; **stinging**) **1 a** (of an insect etc.) prick or pierce with a sting. **b** be capable of stinging. **2** cause or be capable of causing a sharp physical or emotional pain or irritation, or emotional pain (in a person). **3** feel such pain: *my fingers are stinging from the cold*. **4** *informal* **a** cause to suffer a financial loss or hardship: *small businesses were stung by the recession*. **b** cheat.

stinger *noun* **1 a** a sharp organ in various insects and other animals capable of inflicting a dangerous and painful wound, esp. by injecting poison. **b** (in plants) a stiff sharp hair which emits an irritating fluid when touched. **c** a stinging insect, snake, nettle, etc. **2 a** sharp painful blow or comment. [Say STING er]

stinginess *noun* an ungenerous unwillingness to give or spend esp. money. [Say STIN jee ness]

stinging *adjective* **1** (of an animal or plant) that stings: *stinging insects ◊ stinging nettles*. **2** fiercely critical or hurtful: *a stinging attack on the prime minister*. **3** extremely painful. ▶ **stingingly** *adverb* [Say STING ing]

stinging nettle *noun* a nettle with stinging hairs, small green flowers, and strongly toothed oval leaves.

stingless *adjective* not capable of stinging.

stingray *noun* a broad flatfish with a flattened, roughly diamond-shaped body that tapers to a tail with a long poisonous serrated spine at its base.

stingy *adjective* (**stingier, stingiest**) **1** unwilling to give, spend, or use resources. **2** (of a portion, supply, etc.) given sparingly or grudgingly; meagre. **3** *Sport* (of a

team, goaltender, etc.) giving up few goals, points, or scoring opportunities. [Say STIN jee]

stink • *verb* (**stinks**; *past* **stank** or **stunk**; *past participle* **stunk**; **stinking**) **1** emit a strong offensive smell. **2** *informal* **a** be extremely or offensively bad or inept: *this team stinks*. **b** be unbearably unpleasant: *her job stinks*. **3** (foll. by *up*) fill (a place) with an offensive odour: *your perfume stinks the whole room up*. **4** *informal* have or be surrounded by an offensive amount of something: *the affair stinks of scandal*. • *noun* **1** a strong or offensive smell; a stench. **2** *informal* a fuss. **3** *informal* a scandal. PHRASES **like stink** *informal* extremely hard or fast etc.: *working like stink*.

stinker *noun* *slang* **1** a difficult or unpleasant person or thing. **2** something of inferior quality. **3** any person or thing that gives off a bad odour.

stinking • *adjective* **1** that gives off a foul or offensive odour. **2** *slang* despicable: *a stinking liar*. • *adverb* *slang* extremely and usu. to an objectionable degree: *stinking rich*. ▶ **stinkingly** *adverb*

stinko *adjective* *slang* drunk.

stinky *adjective* (**stinkier, stinkiest**) *informal* having a strong or unpleasant smell.

stint • *verb* **1** use, spend, offer, or distribute grudgingly or in small amounts: *she never stinted her praise for him*. **2** (often foll. by *on*) be sparing or cheap; economize. • *noun* **1** a short period of time. **2** a limitation of supply or effort: *without stint*.

stipe *noun* *Botany & Zoology* a stalk or stem, such as that which supports the cap of a mushroom or toadstool.

stipend *noun* **1** a salary or fixed regular sum paid for the services of a teacher, public official, or clergyman. **2** any fixed regular payment, such as an allowance or scholarship. [Say STIPE end]

stipple • *verb* (**stipples, stippled, stippling**) **1** mark (a surface) with small spots or flecks. **2** produce a roughened or gritty texture on (paint or cement etc.). • *noun* **1** (also **stippling**) the process or technique of providing a surface etc. with a dotted or textured appearance. **2** work that has been produced using this technique.

stipulate *verb* (**stipulates, stipulated, stipulating**) demand or specify as an essential part or condition of an agreement or contract etc.: *the British North America Act stipulated that law enforcement was a provincial responsibility*. ▶ **stipulation** *noun* [Say STIP yuh late]

stipulated *adjective* specified or set out in the terms of a contract or agreement. [Say STIP yuh late id]

stir • *verb* (**stirs, stirred, stirring**) **1** move a spoon or other utensil around and around in (a liquid or soft mass) in order to mix the ingredients. **2** cause to move or be disturbed, esp. slightly: *a breeze stirred the lake*. **3 a** move or begin to move slightly: *not a creature was stirring*. **b** rise from sleep. **4 a** arouse, inspire, or provoke (the emotions etc., or a person as regards these): *was stirred to anger*. **b** (of the emotions etc.) become active or excited: *anger stirred within my breast*. • *noun* **1** commotion or excitement: *caused quite a stir*. **2** an act of stirring: *give it a stir*. **3** the slightest movement. **4** *slang* prison: *in stir*. PHRASES **stir up** **1** cause, start, or instigate (trouble etc.). **2** provoke, excite, arouse (a person or emotion etc.).

stir-crazy *adjective* **1** restless, antsy, or fidgety, esp. from prolonged confinement indoors. **2** deranged from long imprisonment.

stir-fry • *noun* (*plural* **stir-fries**) a dish of assorted vegetables and sometimes meat fried rapidly at a high temperature, esp. in a wok. • *verb* (**stir-fries, stir-fried, stir-frying**) fry rapidly at high heat while stirring and tossing, esp. in a wok.

S

>
>
> **SPELL CHECK**
> **sterling**
>
> Note that **sterling** is spelled with an *e*, not an *i*:
> *sterling silver*, *pound sterling*, *a sterling reputation*.

stirrer *noun* an object or mechanical device used for stirring something.

stirring • *adjective* inspiring, exciting. • *noun* (usu. in *plural*) **1** initial stages of a particular activity: *stirrings of revolt*. **2** initial feelings: *stirrings of sympathy*.
▶ **stirringly** *adverb*

stirrup *noun* **1** either of a pair of supports for the foot of a person riding a horse, consisting of a flat-based metal loop attached by a leather strap to each side of a saddle. **2** a thing shaped like a stirrup. **3** either of a pair of stirrup-shaped supports at the end of a medical examination table, on which patients place their heels during a gynecological exam. **4 a** a loop attached to the bottom of a pant leg meant to pass beneath the foot in order to keep the pants from rising above the ankle. **b** (as an *adjective*) designating an article of clothing having such straps: *stirrup pants*. **5** (also **stirrup bone**) = STAPES. [Say STIR up]

stitch • *noun* (*plural* **stitches**) **1 a** (in sewing) a single pass of a threaded needle in and out of a fabric. **b** the resulting loop of thread left in the fabric between two successive needle holes. **c** (usu. with *neg.*) the least bit of fabric of an article of clothing: *hadn't a stitch on*. **2 a** a single complete movement of the needle used in knitting, crochet, embroidery, etc. **b** a particular method of knitting or crochet etc. **3** (usu. in *plural*) each of the loops of material used in sewing up a wound. **4** a painful cramp in the side of the body often resulting from vigorous exercise. • *verb* (**stitches, stitched, stitching**) join, fasten, attach, make, or decorate using stitches. PHRASES **in stitches** *informal* laughing uncontrollably. **stitch in time** a timely or preventative remedy. ▶ **stitcher** *noun* **stitching** *noun*

Stl'atl'imx • *noun* (*plural* **Stl'atl'imx**) **1** a member of an Aboriginal people living northeast of Vancouver. **2** the Salishan language of this people. • *adjective* of this people or their culture or language. [Say STAT lee um]

stn. *abbreviation* **1** station. **2 (Stn.)** *Cdn* Postal Station.

>
>
> **SPELL CHECK**
> **stock, stalk**
>
> A stem is a **stalk**; to pursue is to **stalk**.

stock • *noun* **1** a supply of merchandise etc. available for sale or distribution. **2** a supply of anything, esp. acquired or allowed to accumulate for future use: *cod stocks*. **3** the raw materials or equipment used in the manufacture of a particular product. **4** = LIVESTOCK. **5 a** capital raised by a business etc. through the issue and subscription of shares. **b** a quantity of shares represented by a certificate, the holder of which is considered one of the owners of the company, entitled to receive dividends of its profits. **c** a quantity of shares in a commodity or industry etc.: *gold stock*. **d** a security issued by the government or a company in fixed units with a fixed rate of interest. **6** one's reputation or popularity: *his stock is rising*. **7** liquid made by stewing bones, vegetables, etc., used as a basis for soup, gravy, etc. **8 a** one's ancestry or line of descent: *she is of Prairie stock*. **b** a family (of human beings, animals, plants, or languages). **9 a** a roll of film that has not been exposed or processed. **b** a selection of esp. outdoor scenes and cityscapes used to lend verisimilitude to a production shot on a set (also as an *adjective*: *stock footage*). **10 a** the trunk or stem of a tree or shrub, esp. one into which a graft is inserted. **b** a plant from which cuttings are taken. **11** a plant with fragrant white, pink, or lilac flowers. **12** (in *plural*) *hist.* a wooden structure with holes for securing a person's feet and hands, used for punishing criminals, usu. in public. **13 a** (also **stock company**) a repertory company performing esp. at a particular theatre. **b** the repertory of such a company. **14** the handle, support, or base of a tool or machine. **15 a** the usu. wooden part of a rifle to which the barrel is attached. **b** an analogous part of an automatic or semi-automatic weapon. **16** = ROLLING STOCK. • *adjective* **1** kept regularly in stock for sale, distribution, or use. **2 a** common or conventional: *a stock character*. **b** (of a theme, phrase, etc.) hackneyed, trite. • *verb* **1** have or keep (merchandise) available for sale or use. **2 a** furnish (a store or farm etc.) with goods, equipment, or livestock. **b** fill (a shelf) with merchandise. **c** fill (a pond etc.) with fish. **3** fit (a gun) with a stock. PHRASES **in stock** on the premises of a store or warehouse etc. and available for immediate sale. **out of stock** not available for immediate sale. **stock up 1** obtain or purchase stocks or supplies. **2** (foll. by *on* or *with*) obtain or purchase a supply of (food, fuel, etc.). **take stock 1** make an inventory of one's stock. **2** (often foll. by *of*) assess or review a situation etc.). **3** (foll. by *in*) concern oneself with; attach importance to.

stockade • *noun* **1** a barrier of upright stakes, erected for defensive purposes. **2** a prison, esp. a military one. • *verb* (**stockades, stockaded, stockading**) fortify with a stockade.

stockbroker *noun* a member of a stock exchange who deals in stocks and shares. ▶ **stockbrokerage** *noun* **stockbroking** *noun*

stock car *noun* **1** a car with the basic chassis of a commercially produced vehicle, modified for a form of racing in which collisions often occur. **2** a boxcar used to transport livestock.

stocked *adjective* having a full supply of something, esp. merchandise: *a well-stocked store*.

stock exchange *noun* **1** (also **Stock Exchange**) a building where stocks and shares are traded publicly. **2** the dealers working there. **3** the composite index of share prices or trading activity at a particular stock exchange.

stockholder *noun* an owner of stocks or shares. ▶ **stockholding** *noun*

stock index *noun* (also called **composite index**) a stock market index based on the performance of a selection of stocks.

stockiness *noun* the build of someone who is short and has a strong, sturdy body.

stocking *noun* **1 a** either of a pair of separate, close-fitting coverings for the feet and part or all of the leg worn by women, esp. one of diaphanous silk or nylon reaching the thigh and held up by a garter. **b** (in *plural*) = PANTYHOSE. **c** = SOCK[1] 1. **2** any close-fitting article of clothing resembling a stocking: *body stocking*. **3** (also **Christmas stocking**) a stocking hung esp. by children at Christmas to be filled with small gifts. **4** a cylindrical bandage for the leg, esp. one worn as a remedial support, such as for a leg affected with varicose veins. PHRASES **in one's stocking** (or **stockinged**) **feet** wearing socks but no shoes.

stocking cap *noun* a knitted toque with a long tapered end which hangs down.

stockinged *adjective* (often in *combination*) wearing stockings, esp. the kind of stockings described: *Julie came downstairs in her stockinged feet*.

S

stocking stuffer *noun* a small usu. inexpensive present suitable for putting in a Christmas stocking.

stock-in-trade *noun* **1 a** the equipment required for a particular business. **b** merchandise, esp. kept in sufficient supply by a dealer or shopkeeper to maintain business. **2 a** collection of attitudes, phrases, etc. characteristic of a person or group: *flippant remarks are part of his stock-in-trade*.

stockman *noun* (*plural* **stockmen**) **1** a person employed to look after livestock on a farm. **2** an owner of livestock.

stock market *noun* **1** a stock exchange. **2** the level of transactions or prices in the national or international market for stocks.

stock option *noun* the right, obtained by payment, to buy, sell, etc. specified stocks etc. at a specified price within a set time.

stockpile • *noun* an accumulated stock of goods, materials, weapons, etc., held in reserve and available for use esp. during a shortage or emergency. • *verb* (**stockpiles, stockpiled, stockpiling**) accumulate a stockpile of.

stockpot *noun* a large pot with handles, used for making soup, stews, sauces, etc. in large quantities.

stock-still *adverb* completely motionless.

stock-taking *noun* **1** the process of making an inventory of goods or merchandise in a store or factory etc. **2** an evaluation, assessment, or review of one's situation, prospects, and resources.

stocky *adjective* (**stockier, stockiest**) short and strongly built; thickset.

stockyard *noun* an enclosure with pens and sheds where livestock is temporarily confined and sorted, esp. prior to being sold, shipped, or slaughtered.

stodginess *noun* **1** the quality of a person or thing that is excessively conventional, uninspired, or dull. **2** the quality of food that is heavy, filling, and high in carbohydrates.

stodgy *adjective* (**stodgier, stodgiest**) **1** (of food) heavy, filling, and high in carbohydrates. **2** excessively conventional, uninspired, or dull: *the plot was stodgy and predictable*.

stogie *noun* (also **stogy**) (*plural* **stogies**) *informal* a cigar. [Say STOE ghee]

stoic • *noun* **1** (**Stoic**) a member of the ancient Greek school of philosophy which sought virtue as the greatest good and taught control of one's feelings and passions and indifference to pleasure and pain and to changes in fortune. **2** (**stoic**) a person who practises repression of emotion, indifference to pleasure and pain, and patient endurance in adversity. • *adjective* **1** (**stoic**; also **stoical**) indicating the ability to suffer pain or trouble without complaining or showing feelings. **2** (**Stoic**) of the school of the Stoics or its system of philosophy. ▶**stoically** *adverb* **Stoicism** *noun* (also **stoicism**). [Say STOE ick, STOE uh sizm]

stoke *verb* (**stokes, stoked, stoking**) **1** feed or tend (a fire, furnace, etc.) to maintain or increase the heat. **2** encourage, fuel: *her laughter stoked his anger*.

stoked *adjective informal* exhilarated, ecstatic.

stoker *noun* **1** a person who tends the furnace on a steamship. **2** a tool or esp. mechanical device used to feed or tend a fire.

stole[1] *noun* **1** a woman's long scarf or shawl made esp. of fur or wool and worn loosely over the shoulders. **2** an ecclesiastical vestment consisting of a long narrow strip of cloth, worn over one or both shoulders.

stole[2] *past of* STEAL.

stolen • *verb past participle of* STEAL. • *adjective* **1** obtained by theft: *stolen cars*. **2** accomplished or enjoyed by stealth or in secret: *enjoyed their stolen hours together*.

stolen base *noun Baseball* an act of advancing to the next base while a pitch is being thrown.

stolid *adjective* not feeling or expressing emotion or interest: *trying hard to inject her stolid audience with high energy*. ▶**stolidly** *adverb* **stolidness** *noun* [Rhymes with SOLID]

Sto:lo • *noun* (*plural* **Sto:lo**) **1** a member of an Aboriginal people living along the lower Fraser River, BC. **2** the Halkomelem language of this people. • *adjective* of this people or language. [Say STAW loe or STOE loe]

stomach • *noun* **1** the internal organ in which the first part of digestion occurs. **2** the belly or abdomen: *punched me in the stomach*. **3 a** (usu. foll. by *for*) an appetite. **b** the ability to digest food without becoming sick: *has a weak stomach*. **4 a** courage, inclination: *you haven't got the stomach to fight*. **b** tolerance, appreciation: *I have no stomach for bickering politicians*. • *verb* (**stomachs, stomached, stomaching**) **1** (usu. with *neg.*) tolerate, endure. **2** find sufficiently palatable to swallow or keep down: *can't stomach seafood*.

stomach-churning *adjective* causing or tending to cause nausea: *a stomach-churning ride*.

stomach upset *noun* indigestion or nausea.

stomp • *verb* **1** walk with loud, heavy, deliberate steps, often as a sign of anger. **2** stamp or trample on. **3** dance or play a stomp. • *noun* **1** any lively dance involving a heavy stamping step. **2** (also **stomper**) a tune or song with a percussive rhythm and upbeat tempo suitable for such a dance. **3** a heavy stamping step to the beat of such a dance. PHRASES **stomp one's foot** beat out a rhythm with one's foot. ▶**stomper** *noun*

stomping ground *noun* (usu. in *plural*) a favourite or familiar haunt or place of action.

stone • *noun* **1 a** a solid non-metallic mineral matter, of which rock is made. **b** a piece of this. **2 a** a piece of stone, usu. artificially shaped, used for some special purpose, such as building or paving. **b** = TOMBSTONE. **3 a** precious or semi-precious mineral or gemstone. **4** *Medical* (often in *plural*) a small piece of hard material that can form in the bladder or kidney and cause pain. **5** a hard shell containing the nut or seed in the middle of certain fruits, such as the peach, plum, or olive; a pit. **6** a shaped piece of stone used for grinding or sharpening something. **7** (also **curling stone**) = ROCK[1] 5. • *adverb* completely, totally: *stone cold*. • *verb* (**stones, stoned, stoning**) **1** pelt with stones. **2** remove the stones from (fruit). **3** pave, line, or build up with stones. **4** *Hockey informal* (esp. of a goaltender) thwart (an opponent). PHRASES **throw** (or **cast**) **stones** cast aspersions on a person's character etc. **throw** (or **cast**) **the first stone** be the first to make an accusation, esp. though guilty oneself. **a stone's throw** a short distance.

Stone Age *noun* **1** a prehistoric period characterized by the use of weapons and tools made of stone. **2** (as an *adjective*) (also **stone-age**) primitive, outmoded.

stoneboat *noun* a flat-bottomed sled used esp. for removing stones from fields.

stone circle *noun Archaeology* a group of (usu. large embedded) stones arranged in a circle.

stonecut *noun* **1** an Inuit printing technique in which an image engraved on the flat face of a stone that has been cut in half is impressed on paper with coloured inks. **2** a print made using this technique.

stonecutter *noun* a person or machine that cuts, shapes, or carves building or ornamental stone.

stoned *adjective slang* under the influence of drugs.

stonefly *noun* (*plural* **stoneflies**) **1** a slender insect

with transparent wings, the larvae of which live under stones in streams. **2** a fishing lure tied to resemble this.
stone-ground *adjective* **1** (of flour) ground using millstones rather than metal rollers. **2** (esp. of bread) made with stone-ground flour.
stonemason *noun* a person who cuts, prepares, and builds with stone.
Stone sheep *noun* (also **Stone's sheep**) a thinhorn sheep of the south central Yukon and northern BC.
stonewall *verb* **1** hold up (a discussion or interrogation etc.) by making lengthy speeches and vague or evasive answers: *opposition members of the committee were clearly frustrated that Lewis continued to stonewall*. **2** hinder or prevent (a person or thing): *she stonewalled their attempt to pass the legislation*. **3** *Sport* thwart (an opponent) with strong defence. ▶ **stonewalling** *noun*
stoneware *noun* a kind of dense, impermeable, usu. opaque pottery made from clay containing a high proportion of silica and partly vitrified during firing.
stonewash • *noun* a worn or faded appearance given to denim by washing it with abrasives (also as an *adjective*: *stonewash jeans*). • *verb* (**stonewashes, stonewashed, stonewashing**) wash (denim etc.) with abrasives. ▶ **stonewashed** *adjective*
stonework *noun* **1** masonry. **2** the parts of a building made of stone. **3** the art of working with stone.
Stoney • *noun* (*plural* **Stoneys** or **Stoney**) **1** a member of an Aboriginal people now living in southern Alberta, and formerly living in southern Manitoba and southern Saskatchewan. **2** any of the esp. Siouan languages spoken by this people. • *adjective* of this people or their languages.
stonily *adverb* in a cold or expressionless manner; without showing or feeling sympathy.
stony *adjective* (also **stoney**) (**stonier, stoniest**) **1** full of or covered with stones: *stony soil*. **2** lacking sensitivity or feeling; hardened. **3** (also **stony-faced**) cold, expressionless; not feeling or showing sympathy: *a stony gaze*. **4** (of silence, grief, fear, etc.) cold and harsh, grim. **5** having the hardness of stone; rigid.
stood *past and past participle of* STAND.
stooge *noun* **1** an unquestioningly loyal or fawning assistant. **2** a person of subordinate rank who performs esp. routine or unpleasant labour. **3** an entertainer who feeds lines to another comedian and serves as a butt of the other's jokes.
stook • *noun* **1** *Cdn & Brit.* a small stack of bales of hay or straw, or sheaves of grain, collected in a field, esp. to hasten drying. **2** *Cdn* (*West*) a card game similar to blackjack but which may be played by several players. • *verb* *Cdn & Brit.* arrange (bales or sheaves) in stooks. [Rhymes either with *BOOK* or with *SPOOK*]
stooking *noun* the activity of gathering hay into bales or grain into sheaves in order to hasten drying. [Rhymes either with *BOOKING* or with *SPOOKING*]
stool *noun* **1** a seat without a back or arms. **2** a short low bench on which to step or kneel, or for resting the foot. **3** (often in *plural*) = FECES. PHRASES **fall between two stools** fail to be or take either of two desirable alternatives: *the work falls between two stools, being neither genuinely popular nor truly scholarly*.
stool pigeon *noun* **1** a person, esp. a criminal, who helps the police catch other criminals by informing against them. **2** a person acting as a decoy.
stoop • *verb* **1** lower one's body by bending (the head and shoulders or trunk) forwards. **2** carry one's head and shoulders habitually bowed forward. **3** (foll. by *to*) lower oneself to conduct a course of action considered morally reprehensible or beneath oneself. • *noun* **1** a stooping posture. **2** a small raised platform

or set of steps at the entrance of a house. PHRASES **stoop and scoop** *Cdn* pick up the excrement of one's pet in parks and on streets and lawns.
stooped *adjective* having the head and shoulders habitually bent forward.
stop • *verb* (**stops, stopped, stopping**) **1** come or bring to an end. **2** prevent from happening or from doing something. **3** cease or cause to cease moving or operating. **4** (of a bus or train) call at a designated place to pick up or set down passengers. **5** *informal* stay somewhere for a short time. **6** withhold or deduct. **7** (also **stop payment on** or **of**) instruct a bank to withhold payment on (a cheque). **8** block or close up (a hole or leak). • *noun* **1** a cessation of movement or operation. **2 a** a place designated for a bus or subway etc. to stop. **b** a stay of considerable duration at a place, esp. during the course of a journey: *two refuelling stops along the way*. **3** an order stopping payment, esp. of a cheque. **4** the effective diameter of a lens as indicated by an f-number. **5** *Music* **a** a set of organ pipes producing tones of the same character. **b** the handle or knob which activates such a set. PHRASES **put a stop to** cause to end, esp. abruptly. **stop at nothing** do everything required to complete a task without being deterred by setbacks; be ruthless. **stop by** visit. **stop dead** (or **short**) cease abruptly. **stop in** = *stop by*. **stop over** rest or make a break in one's journey.
stop-and-go *adjective* alternately stopping and starting: *traffic is stop-and-go*.
stop-gap *noun* a temporary substitute or solution (also as an *adjective*: *stop-gap measures*).
stoplight *noun* a set of traffic lights.
stopover *noun* (also **stopoff**) **1** a brief stop in a journey. **2** such a stop made with the ability to proceed on the original ticket at a later time. **3** a city, hotel, etc. where one stops during a journey.
stoppage *noun* **1** an interruption of service, labour, a game, etc.: *a work stoppage*. **2** the condition of being blocked or plugged up. [Say STOP idge]
stop-payment *noun* an order stopping payment, esp. of a cheque.
stopper • *noun* **1** a plug for closing a bottle. **2** a plug used to close a drain. **3** *Baseball* a relief pitcher who enters the game in the late stages to preserve a lead. **4** a thing that attracts and holds attention. • *verb* close or plug (a bottle etc.) with a stopper.
stopping house *noun* *Cdn hist.* a modest house or inn offering accommodation to travellers.
stopping place *noun* **1** *Cdn hist.* **a** a settlement where groups of travellers customarily stop for food and lodging. **b** a stopping house. **2** a place at which a person, animal, or thing may stop.
stop sign *noun* a red octagonal sign at an intersection indicating that traffic should stop before proceeding.
stopwatch *noun* (*plural* **stopwatches**) a watch with a mechanism for recording elapsed time, used to time races etc.
storable *adjective* able to be kept or stored for use at a later date.
storage *noun* **1 a** the action of storing or keeping a thing or things in reserve; the condition of being stored. **b** space available or used for storing. **2** the cost of storing something. **3** *Computing* **a** the electronic retention of data in a device from which they can be retrieved. **b** (also **storage device**) = MEMORY 4b. [Say STOR idge]
store • *noun* **1** a retail establishment. **2** a quantity of something available for future use; a supply: *a store of wit*. **3** (in *plural*) articles such as food, clothing, weapons, etc., accumulated for a particular purpose, esp. to supply an army. **4** *Cdn* (*Nfld & Maritimes*) = FISH STORE 2.

• *verb* (**stores**, **stored**, **storing**) **1 a** accumulate a supply of (goods etc.), esp. for future use. **b** place or keep (possessions, merchandise, etc.) in a storage facility or warehouse. **2** retain (data) in some physical form that enables subsequent retrieval; transfer into a memory or storage device. **3** (of a receptacle) hold, keep, contain. **4** stock or provide with something useful: *a mind stored with facts*. PHRASES **in store 1** kept in readiness. **2** coming in the future; about to happen. **set** (or **put**) **store by** consider to be of importance, worth, or value.

store-bought *adjective* commercially manufactured and purchased in a store; not homemade.

storefront *noun* **1** the side of a store facing onto the street. **2** a commercial property with a window facing onto the street. **3** a room or rooms at the front of a commercial property or store, esp. as used for some other purpose, such as a small business, a centre for religious worship, etc. (also as an *adjective*: *storefront café*).

storehouse *noun* **1** a place where things are stored. **2** a person or thing considered to be a treasury or repository of something: *he is a storehouse of information*.

storekeeper *noun* **1** a store manager. **2** a store owner. **3** a person who looks after stored goods.

storeroom *noun* a room in a house or office etc. in which supplies and other items may be kept.

storey *noun* (*plural* **storeys**) **1** a single level of a house or building; a floor: *a ten-storey building*. **2** each of a number of rows of windows, columns, panels, etc. arranged horizontally on the facade of a building and dividing it into levels. **3** a rough estimate of height based on the approximate height of one storey of a building (about 3 metres).

storied *adjective* celebrated; legendary.

stork *noun* a large wading bird with long legs and a long heavy bill, sometimes portrayed as a deliverer of new babies.

storm • *noun* **1** a violent weather disturbance with high winds, heavy rain or snow, thunder and lightning, etc. **2** a wind classed as force 10 or 11 on the Beaufort scale (between a gale and a hurricane), having an average velocity of 48–63 knots (55–72 mph). **3 a** a violent outburst (of protest, controversy, etc.). **b** a violent shower of projectiles or blows. **4** *informal* a storm window. **5** a direct assault by troops on a stronghold. • *verb* **1 a** move violently or angrily: *stormed out of the meeting*. **b** say or shout in an angry or violent manner. **2** rush, attack; attempt to overwhelm or enter by force. **3** (of wind, rain, etc.) be violent or tempestuous. PHRASES **take by storm 1** capture by direct assault. **2** achieve sudden or overwhelming success with (an audience, city, etc.). **up a storm** with great enthusiasm and energy: *cook up a storm*.

storm cloud *noun* **1** a dark heavy cloud. **2** a threatening state of affairs.

storm petrel *noun* a small seabird of the open ocean, usu. with black plumage and a white rump.

storm sewer *noun* a drain built to carry away excess rainwater etc.

storm-stayed *adjective* *Cdn* (*Maritimes & Ont.*) stranded due to severe or inclement weather conditions.

storm trooper *noun* **1** *hist.* a member of the Nazi political militia. **2** a militant activist or member of any group of vigilantes or shock troops.

storm window *noun* a detachable outer window put up in winter as insulation and to protect an inner window from the effects of storms.

stormy *adjective* (**stormier**, **stormiest**) **1** (of the weather, sky, sea, etc.) disturbed by a storm; tempestuous. **2** (of a region) subject to or affected by storms. **3 a** (of an event, period, etc.) turbulent,

tempestuous: *a stormy meeting* ◊ *a stormy relationship*. **b** (of a person or their looks) angry.

story *noun* (*plural* **stories**) **1** an account of imaginary or real events told for entertainment. **2** an account of the life of a person or institution etc. **3** = STORYLINE. **4** a representation of facts, esp. given as evidence. **5** *informal* a fib or lie. **6** an item of news. **7** = STOREY. PHRASES **another story** a matter requiring separate treatment. **the same old story** the familiar or predictable course of events. **the story goes** it is said. **to make a long story short** a formula excusing the omission of details. **the story of my** (or **your, his, her** etc.) **life** an event, statement, or situation that supposedly epitomizes a person's life or experience.

storyboard *noun* a sequence of pictures etc. outlining the plan of a movie, TV commercial, etc.

storybook • *noun* a book of stories for children. • *adjective* denoting something that is as perfect as things typically are in storybooks: *it was a storybook finish to an illustrious career*.

storyline *noun* the plot of a novel, movie, etc.

storyteller *noun* **1** a person who tells stories. **2** *informal* a liar. ▶ **storytelling** *noun & adjective*

stout • *adjective* **1** rather fat. **2** thick or strong: *a stout stick*. **3** brave, vigorous: *put up stout resistance*. • *noun* a strong dark beer brewed with roasted malt or barley. ▶ **stoutly** *adverb*

stove¹ *noun* an apparatus burning fuel or using electricity for heating or cooking.

stove² *past and past participle of* STAVE *verb*.

stovepipe *noun* a pipe conducting smoke and gases from a stove to a chimney.

stovetop • *noun* the top surface of a stove, esp. the cooking elements. • *adjective* located on or cooked on a stovetop: *unsuitable for stovetop use*.

stow *verb* **1** pack (goods etc.) tidily and compactly. **2** place (a cargo or luggage) in its proper place. PHRASES **stow away 1** place (a thing) where it will not cause an obstruction. **2** be a stowaway on a ship etc.

stowage *noun* **1** the act of stowing. **2** a place for this. [Say STOE idge]

stowaway *noun* a person who hides on board a ship or aircraft etc. to get free passage. [Say STOE away]

straddle *verb* (**straddles**, **straddled**, **straddling**) **1 a** sit or stand with the legs one on either side of (a thing, person, horse, etc.). **b** be situated across or on both sides of: *the town straddles the border*. **2 a** (of the legs) be wide apart. **b** part (one's legs) widely. **3** participate in (two opposing or vastly different cultures etc.).

strafe • *verb* (**strafes**, **strafed**, **strafing**) attack repeatedly with bullets or bombs from low-flying aircraft. • *noun* an act of strafing.

straggle • *verb* (**straggles**, **straggled**, **straggling**) **1** trail behind others in a march or race etc. **2** grow, spread, or be laid out in an irregular, untidy way. • *noun* a group of straggling people or things. ▶ **straggler** *noun* **straggly** *adjective*

> **SPELL CHECK**
> **straight, strait**
>
> The spelling is **strait** for a narrow channel and in "dire straits".

straight • *adjective* **1 a** extending uniformly in the same direction; without a curve or bend etc. **b** *Math* (of a line) lying on the shortest path between any two of its points. **2** successive, uninterrupted: *three straight wins*. **3** arranged in proper order; level, symmetrical. **4** honest, candid; not evasive: *a straight answer*. **5** (of thinking etc.) logical, unemotional. **6** (of drama etc.)

serious, as opposed to popular or comic. **7** unmodified, undiluted. **8** *informal* **a** heterosexual. **b** (of a person etc.) conventional or respectable. **9** (of a person's back) not bowed. **10** (of the hair) not curly or wavy. **11** (of a garment) not flared. **12** coming direct from its source. • *noun* **1** the straight part of something, esp. the concluding stretch of a racecourse. **2** a straight condition. **3** a sequence of five cards in poker. **4** *informal* **a** a heterosexual. **b** a conventional person. • *adverb* **1** in a straight line; directly; without deviation, hesitation, or circumlocution. **2** continuously, without a break: *have been working for 16 hours straight.* **3** correctly: *can't see straight.* **4** honestly and directly; in a straightforward manner. **5** upright; in an erect posture: *stand straight!* **6** clearly and logically: *think straight.* PHRASES **go straight** live an honest life after being a criminal. **set** (or **put**) **a person straight** make sure that someone knows the correct facts etc. when they have the wrong idea or impression. **the straight and narrow** morally correct behaviour. **straight away** at once; immediately. **straight from the shoulder 1** (of a blow) well delivered. **2** (of a verbal attack) frank or direct. **straight off** *informal* without hesitation, deliberation, etc.: *cannot tell you straight off.* **straight up** *informal* **1** unmixed, undiluted. **2** truthfully, honestly.

straight-ahead *adjective* (esp. of popular music) straightforward, simple, or unadorned.

straight-arm • *verb* push away or deflect (an opponent or obstacle) with the arm outstretched. • *noun* an act of straight-arming an opponent or obstacle.

straight arrow *noun informal* a person who lives an honest, sober life. ▶ **straight-arrow** *adjective*

straightaway *noun* a straight course or section.

straightedge *noun* a bar with one edge accurately straight, used for testing.

straighten *verb* **1** make or become straight. **2** make neat, tidy, or orderly. PHRASES **straighten out 1** clear up (something that is confused or in disorder): *straighten out our finances.* **2** settle or resolve (a dispute etc.). **3** (of a person) improve in character or conduct. **straighten up 1** stand erect after bending. **2** reform or become reformed in character or conduct. ▶ **straightener** *noun*

straight face *noun* an intentionally expressionless face, esp. one that conceals an impulse to laugh or smile: *keep a straight face.* ▶ **straight-faced** *adjective*

straight flush *noun* (*plural* **straight flushes**) *Cards* a hand of cards that is a numerical sequence in a single suit, e.g. diamonds, clubs, etc.

straightforward *adjective* **1** honest or frank. **2** (of a task etc.) not complicated. ▶ **straightforwardly** *adverb* **straightforwardness** *noun*

straightjacket *noun* = STRAITJACKET.

straightlaced *adjective* = STRAITLACED.

straight man *noun* a member of a comedy team who makes remarks or creates situations for the main performer to make jokes about.

straightness *noun* **1** the quality of something that extends or moves uniformly in one direction only, without a curve or bend. **2** *informal* heterosexuality.

straight razor *noun* a razor having a long blade set in a handle and usu. folding like a penknife.

straight shooter *noun slang* a person who states bluntly what they think. ▶ **straight-shooting** *adjective*

straight-up *adjective informal* **1** true; trustworthy. **2** undiluted; unmodified.

strain¹ • *verb* **1** make or force to make a strenuous or unusually great effort. **2** (foll. by *at*) tug, pull: *the dog strained at the leash.* **3** stretch tightly. **4** make severe or excessive demands on: *strained her patience.* **5** injure (a muscle etc.) by overexerting it. **6 a** clear (a liquid) of solid matter by passing it through a sieve etc. **b** (foll. by *out*) filter (solids) out from a liquid. • *noun* **1** a force tending to pull or stretch something to an extreme or damaging degree. **2** an injury caused by straining a muscle etc. **3 a** a severe demand on physical or mental strength or resources. **b** a state of tension or exhaustion resulting from this: *suffering from strain.* **4** a short musical phrase. **5** a tone or tendency in speech or writing: *more in the same strain.* **6** *Physics* **a** the condition of a body subjected to stress. **b** a quantity measuring this. PHRASES **strain oneself 1** injure oneself by effort. **2** make undue efforts.

strain² *noun* **1** a breed or stock of animals, plants, etc. **2** a tendency, quality, or feature of a person's character: *a strain of aggression.* **3** a distinct (natural or cultured) variety of a micro-organism.

strained *adjective* **1** constrained, forced, artificial. **2** (of a relationship) mutually distrustful or tense. **3** (of an interpretation) far-fetched, laboured. **4** (of a liquid or semi-liquid, esp. a food) that has been passed through a strainer.

strainer *noun* a utensil or device made with tiny holes or a fine mesh for separating solid matter from liquid.

strait *noun* **1** a narrow passage of water connecting two seas or large bodies of water: *Queen Charlotte Strait.* **2** (usu. in *plural*) difficulty, trouble, or distress: *in dire straits.*

straitened *adjective* of or marked by a shortage of money: *spent much of our lives living in straitened circumstances.*

straitjacket • *noun* **1** a strong garment with long sleeves which are tied in the back to prevent the person wearing it from acting violently. **2** used in reference to something which restricts freedom of action, development, or expression: *the government is operating in an economic straitjacket.* • *verb* (**straitjackets**, **straitjacketed**, **straitjacketing**) **1** restrain with a straitjacket. **2** severely restrict: *the treaty should not be used as a tool to straitjacket international trade.*

straitlaced *adjective* having strict moral attitudes: *she thought of me as old-fashioned and straitlaced.*

Straits *noun* an Aboriginal language of BC, part of the Salishan language group.

strand¹ • *verb* **1** (esp. as **stranded** *adjective*) leave (a person) in a place where they are helpless or in a difficult situation. **2** run aground. • *noun literary* the margin of a sea, lake, or river, esp. the foreshore.

strand² *noun* **1** each of the threads or wires twisted round each other to make a rope or cable. **2 a** a single thread or strip of fibre. **b** a single linear polymer of a long-chain molecule, esp. DNA. **3** a lock of hair. **4** an element or strain in any composite whole.

strange *adjective* (**stranger**, **strangest**) **1** unusual, surprising; difficult to understand. **2** not previously visited, seen, or met; not familiar. **3** having unpleasant feelings; not well. **4** not at ease or comfortable in a situation; feeling that one does not fit in. **5** (foll. by *to*)

unaccustomed. **PHRASES make strange** *Cdn* (of a baby or child) fuss or be shy in company. **strange to say** it is surprising or unusual (that). ▶ **strangely** *adverb* **strangeness** *noun*

stranger *noun* **1** a person who does not know or is not known in a particular place or company. **2** (often foll. by *to*) a person one does not know: *was a complete stranger to me.* **3** (foll. by *to*) a person entirely unacquainted to (a feeling, experience, etc.): *no stranger to controversy.* **4** *Parliament* a person who is not a member or official of the House of Commons.

strangle *verb* (**strangles, strangled, strangling**) **1** kill (a person or animal) by squeezing or gripping their throat tightly. **2** restrict or prevent the proper growth, operation, or development of. **3** suppress (an utterance).

stranglehold *noun* **1** a wrestling hold that throttles an opponent. **2** a deadly grip. **3** complete and exclusive control.

strangler *noun* **1** a person who kills someone by squeezing their throat tightly. **2** a plant, esp. in a tropical rainforest, that smothers its host tree with twining branches or roots.

strangulate *verb* (**strangulates, strangulated, strangulating**) **1** constrict or compress (an organ, duct, hernia, etc.) so as to prevent circulation or the passage of a fluid. **2** strangle. ▶ **strangulation** *noun*

strap • *noun* **1** a strip of cloth, leather, or other flexible material, often with a buckle or other fastening, for keeping something in place or for fastening, carrying, or holding onto something. **2** a loop for grasping to steady oneself while standing in a moving vehicle. **3** (**the strap**) punishment by beating with a leather strap. **4** a strip of metal used to secure or connect. • *verb* (**straps, strapped, strapping**) **1** secure or bind with a strap. **2** beat with a strap.

strapless *adjective* (of a garment) without straps, esp. shoulder straps.

strapped *adjective* subject to a shortage (esp. of money): *I'm a bit strapped for cash.*

strapping • *adjective* (esp. of a person) large and sturdy. • *noun* **1** material for making straps. **2** a punishment by beating with a strap.

strata *noun* **1** plural of STRATUM. **2** a dish made of alternating layers of foods, esp. of bread with cheese etc., soaked in eggs and milk and baked. [Say STRATTA]

stratagem *noun* a cunning plan or scheme, esp. for deceiving an enemy: *a series of devious stratagems.* [Say STRATTA jem]

strategic *adjective* **1** of or serving the ends of strategy: *strategic considerations.* **2** (of materials) essential in fighting a war. **3** (of bombing or weapons) done or for use against an enemy's home territory as a longer-term military objective (*opp.* TACTICAL 1b). ▶ **strategically** *adverb*

strategist *noun* a person skilled in planning action or policy, esp. in war or politics. [Say STRATTA jist]

strategize *verb* (**strategizes, strategized, strategizing**) make strategy. [Say STRATTA jize]

strategy *noun* (plural **strategies**) **1** an esp. long-range policy designed for a particular purpose: *time to develop a coherent economic strategy.* **2** the process of planning something or carrying out a plan in a skilful way: *shifts in marketing strategy.* **3** a plan: *successful learning strategies.* **4 a** the art of planning and directing military activity in a battle or war (*compare* TACTICS 1). **b** a plan for such military operations and movements: *non-provocative defence strategies.* [Say STRATTA jee]

stratification *noun* **1** the natural formation of strata or layers, esp. in the earth's crust by successive deposits

of sediment. **2** the division of a population into distinct groups. [Say stratta fuh CAY sh'n]

stratify *verb* (**stratifies, stratified, stratifying**) **1** (esp. as **stratified** *adjective*) form or arrange into strata: *socially stratified cities* ◊ *the residues have begun to stratify.* **2** arrange or classify: *stratifying patients into well-defined risk groups.* [Say STRATTA fie]

stratigraphic *adjective* based on or having to do with the study of the order and relative position of strata: *stratigraphic analysis.* [Say stratta GRAPH ick]

stratigraphy *noun* *Geology & Archaeology* **1** the order and relative position of strata. **2** the study of this as a means of historical interpretation. [Say struh TIGGRA fee]

stratosphere *noun* **1** a layer of atmospheric air above the troposphere extending to about 50 km above the earth's surface. **2** a very high or the highest level on or as if on a stratified scale: *costs have hit the stratosphere.* ▶ **stratospheric** *adjective* [Say STRATTA sphere, stratta SFEER ick or stratta SFAIR ick]

stratum *noun* (plural **strata**) **1** esp. *Geology* a layer or set of successive layers of any deposited substance. **2** an atmospheric layer. **3** a layer of tissue etc. **4 a** a social grade, class, etc.: *the various strata of society.* **b** *Statistics* each of the groups into which a population is divided in stratified sampling. [Say STRAT um]

straw *noun* **1** dry cut stalks of grain, used esp. as bedding for animals. **2** a single stalk or piece of straw. **3** material made from straw and used for weaving hats, baskets, etc. **4** a hollow plastic or paper tube for sucking drink from a glass etc. **5** an insignificant thing; *not worth a straw.* **PHRASES draw the short straw** be chosen by lot, esp. for some disagreeable task. **grasp** (or **clutch**) **at straws** resort to an utterly inadequate expedient in desperation. **the last** (or **final**) **straw** a slight addition to a burden or difficulty that makes it finally unbearable. **straw in the wind** a slight hint of future developments.

strawberry • *noun* (plural **strawberries**) **1** an edible soft red fruit with very small seeds on its surface, which grows on a low plant with white flowers. **2** a deep pinkish-red colour. • *adjective* of a deep pinkish-red colour.

strawberry blond • *noun* **1** pinkish-blond hair. **2** a woman with such hair. • *adjective* of a pinkish-blond colour.

straw-colour *noun* pale yellow. ▶ **straw-coloured** *adjective*

straw man *noun* (plural **straw men**) a person or issue etc. set up as the object of an argument in order to be defeated: *he sets up the straw man that the Western family has always been nuclear in order to knock it down.*

straw poll *noun* (also **straw vote**) an unofficial ballot as a test of opinion: *I took a straw poll among my colleagues.*

stray • *verb* **1** wander from the right place; become separated from one's companions etc. **2** leave the subject one is supposed to be thinking about or discussing: *we seem to have strayed from the point.* **3** deviate morally, esp. be sexually unfaithful. **4** wander or roam around aimlessly. • *noun* **1** a domestic animal that has strayed from its home, owner, etc. **2** a homeless or friendless person or animal. • *adjective* **1** strayed or lost. **2** isolated; found or occurring occasionally: *a stray bullet.* **3** that is not in the normal or right place: *a few stray hairs.*

streak • *noun* **1** a long thin usu. irregular line or band, esp. distinguished by colour. **2** a strain or element in a person's character: *has a streak of mischief.* **3 a** a run or spell: *a streak of good luck.* **b** a continuous or uninterrupted series: *a 12-game losing streak.* **4** a flash of lightning. • *verb* **1** mark with streaks. **2** move very

rapidly, esp. in a straight line. **3** form streaks. **4** tint (the hair) with streaks.

streaking *noun* long, thin lines of a different colour from their surroundings.

streaky *adjective* (**streakier**, **streakiest**) **1** full of streaks. **2** changeable or variable; of uneven quality: *he's always been a notoriously streaky player*.

stream • *noun* **1** a flowing body of water, esp. a small river. **2 a** the flow of a fluid: *a stream of lava*. **b** (in *singular* or *plural*) a large quantity of something that flows or moves along. **c** an unbroken mass of people or things moving constantly in the same direction. **d** a continuous flow or series of words, time, events, etc.: *a stream of obscenities*. **e** *Computing* a continuous flow of data or instructions, esp. one having a constant or predictable rate. **3** a current or direction in which things are moving or tending: *against the stream*. **4** *Cdn & Brit.* a group of schoolchildren taught together as being of similar ability for a given age. • *verb* **1** flow or move as a stream. **2** run with liquid: *my eyes were streaming*. **3** (of a banner or hair etc.) float or wave in the wind. **4** emit a stream of (blood etc.). **5** (foll. by *in*, *out*, *down*, etc.) (of people or animals) move together continuously in an unbroken mass. **6** extend in rays or beams: *sunlight streaming through the windows*. **7** *Cdn & Brit.* arrange (schoolchildren) in streams. PHRASES **on stream** into operation or effect or participation.

streamer *noun* **1** a long narrow flag. **2** a long narrow strip of ribbon or paper, esp. in a coil that unrolls when thrown. **3** a fishing fly with feathers attached, resembling a small fish. **4** (in *plural*) the aurora borealis or australis. **5** *Cdn* an elongated band of clouds formed by convection around the Great Lakes, and generating large amounts of localized snow.

streamlet *noun* a small stream.

streamline *verb* (**streamlines**, **streamlined**, **streamlining**) **1** give (a vehicle etc.) the form which presents the least resistance to motion. **2** make (an organization, process, etc.) simple or more efficient or better organized. ▶ **streamlined** *adjective*

stream of consciousness *noun* **1** *Psychology* a person's thoughts and conscious reactions to events perceived as a continuous flow. **2** a literary style depicting events in such a flow in the mind of a character. ▶ **stream-of-consciousness** *adjective*

streamside *noun* the ground along the bank of a stream.

street • *noun* **1 a** a public road in a city, town, or village. **b** this including sidewalks. **c** this with the houses or other buildings on each side. **d** (in many North American cities with a grid layout) a road running perpendicular to an avenue, esp. north-south. **2** the persons who live or work on a particular street. **3** (**the Street**) **a** *Cdn* = BAY STREET. **b** *US* = WALL STREET. • *adjective* **1** of or adjoining the street: *use the street door*. **2** (of clothes etc.) suitable for everyday wear or use in public: *street clothes*. **3** occurring on a street: *a street party*. **4** appearing or performing on a street: *street performers*. **5** (of a person) homeless: *street people*. PHRASES **on the street** (or **streets**) **1** homeless. **2** out of prison; released from custody. **take to the streets** (of people) gather outdoors in a town or city in order to protest, celebrate, etc.

streetcar *noun* an electrically-powered passenger vehicle running on rails laid in an urban street.

street credibility *noun* (also **street cred**) *slang* acceptability among young fashionable urban people.

street hockey *noun Cdn* a version of hockey played on a street usu. by children using hockey sticks and a ball in place of a puck.

street legal *adjective* **1** (of a vehicle) legally

roadworthy. **2** *informal* above-board: *his business dealings are street legal, but perhaps morally questionable*.

street light *noun* (also **street lamp**) a light or lamp esp. on a lamppost, serving to illuminate a road etc.

street price *noun* the retail price, esp. of a piece of computer equipment.

streetproof *verb* train (children) to be wary of dangers outside the home or school.

streetscape *noun* a view or prospect provided by the design of a city street or streets.

street-smart *adjective* = STREETWISE.

street smarts *plural noun informal* **1** shrewd or cunning awareness of how to survive in an urban society or environment. **2** common sense.

street value *noun* the price for which something illegal or illegally obtained can be sold.

streetwalker *noun* a prostitute seeking customers in the street. ▶ **streetwalking** *noun & adjective*

streetwise *adjective* having the skills and knowledge necessary for dealing with modern urban life, esp. the difficult or criminal aspects of it.

strength *noun* **1** the state of being strong; the degree to which or respect in which a person or thing is strong. **2** the ability to resist force or support heavy objects without breaking or being damaged. **3 a** a person or thing affording strength or support. **b** an attribute making for strength of character: *patience is your great strength*. **4** a positive quality or attribute: *identified my strengths and weaknesses*. **5** the extent to which a feeling or opinion is strong: *the strength of public opinion*. **6** the potency or intensity of a drug, drink, active ingredient, etc. **7** a full complement: *below strength*. PHRASES **from strength** from a strong position. **from strength to strength** with ever-increasing success. **in strength** in large numbers. **on the strength of** on the basis of. **the strength of** the essence or main features of.

strengthen *verb* make or become stronger. PHRASES **strengthen a person's hand** enable a person to act with greater effect or vigour.

strenuous *adjective* **1** requiring or using great effort. **2** energetic; vigorously active. ▶ **strenuously** *adverb* **strenuousness** *noun* [Say STREN you us]

strep *informal* • *noun* **1** = STREPTOCOCCUS. **2** = STREP THROAT. • *adjective* STREPTOCOCCAL.

strep throat *noun* an acute sore throat with fever caused by streptococcal infection.

streptococcal *adjective* caused by or having to do with bacteria of the genus *Streptococcus*, some of which cause infectious diseases, the souring of milk, and tooth decay: *streptococcal infection*. [Say strep tuh COCKLE]

streptococcus *noun* (*plural* **streptococci**) any bacterium of the genus *Streptococcus*, some of which cause infectious diseases, the souring of milk, and tooth decay. [Say strep tuh COCK us for the singular, strep tuh COCK eye for the plural]

streptomycin *noun* an antibiotic produced by the bacterium *Streptomyces griseus*, effective against many disease-producing bacteria. [Say strep tuh MICE in]

stress • *noun* (*plural* **stresses**) **1** pressure or tension exerted on a material object. **2 a** a demand on physical or mental energy. **b** a condition or adverse circumstance that disturbs, or is likely to disturb, the normal physiological or psychological functioning of an individual. **c** distress caused by this: *suffering from stress*. **3 a** emphasis: *the stress was on the need for success*. **b** emphasis laid on a syllable or word. **c** an accent, esp. the principal one in a word. • *verb* (**stresses**, **stressed**, **stressing**) **1** emphasize. **2** subject to mechanical or physical or mental stress. **3** give extra force to (a word or syllable) when pronouncing it. **4** (usu. in *passive*) cause stress to. PHRASES **lay stress**

on indicate as important. **stress out** *informal* cause (a person) mental stress. ▶ **stressed** *adjective*
stressed out *adjective informal* debilitated or exhausted as a result of stress.
stress fracture *noun* a fracture of a bone caused by the repeated application of a high load.
stressful *adjective* causing stress; mentally tiring. ▶ **stressfully** *adverb* **stressfulness** *noun*
stressor *noun* a situation, experience, event, or other stimulus that causes stress. [Say STRESSER]
stretch • *verb* (**stretches, stretched, stretching**) **1** (of something soft or elastic) be made or be able to be made longer or wider without tearing or breaking. **2** pull (something) tightly from one point to another. **3 a** extend one's body or a part of it to its full length. **b** perform exercises to lengthen the muscles and improve flexibility, esp. before vigorous exercise. **4** last longer than expected. **5** extend over an area or period of time. **6** (of finances or resources) be sufficient for a particular purpose. **7** make demands on. • *noun (plural* **stretches**) **1** an act of stretching one's limbs or body. **2** the fact or condition of being stretched. **3** the capacity to stretch or be stretched; elasticity. **4** a continuous expanse or period. **5** (as an *adjective*) a motor vehicle modified with extended seating or storage capacity: *stretch limo.* **6** *informal* an exaggeration or distortion. **7** a straight part at the end of a racetrack. PHRASES **at a stretch 1** in one continuous period: *slept for two hours at a stretch.* **2** used to indicate that something is just possible but only with difficulty or in extreme circumstances: *it is aimed at university students, or, at a stretch, advanced high school students.* **by no** (or **not by any**) **stretch of the imagination** used to emphasize that something is definitely not the case: *by no stretch of the imagination could he ever be called good-looking.* **stretch one's legs** exercise oneself by walking, esp. after prolonged sitting. **stretch out 1** extend (a hand or foot etc.). **2** last for a longer period; prolong. **3** make (money etc.) last for a sufficient time. **4** relax by lying at full length. **stretch a point** agree to something not normally allowed. ▶ **stretchable** *adjective*
stretcher • *noun* **1** a framework of two poles with canvas etc. between, for carrying a sick, injured, or dead person in a lying position. **2** a brick or stone laid with its long side along the face of a wall (*compare* HEADER 4). • *verb* (often foll. by *off*) convey (a sick or injured person) on a stretcher.
stretch marks *plural noun* marks on the skin resulting from weight gain, or on the abdomen after pregnancy.
stretchy *adjective* (**stretchier, stretchiest**) able to stretch easily without tearing or breaking.
streusel *noun* a crumbly mixture of flour, butter, sugar, and usu. cinnamon, used as a topping or filling for cakes etc. [Say STROOSSLE or STROOZLE]
strew *verb* (**strews;** *past* **strewed;** *past participle* **strewn** or **strewed; strewing**) **1** scatter or spread or be scattered or spread over a surface. **2** (usu. foll. by *with*) spread (a surface) with scattered things.
striated *adjective* marked with linear marks or furrows; striped. [Say STRY ated]
striation *noun* a linear mark, ridge, or groove on a surface, often one of a number of similar parallel features: *a dark stain brings out the natural striations in the grain of the wood.* [Say stry AY sh'n]
stricken *adjective* affected or overcome with illness or misfortune etc.: *stricken with measles* ◊ *grief-stricken.*
strict *adjective* **1** (of a person) demanding that rules, esp. those concerning behaviour, are obeyed or observed. **2** following strict rules or beliefs exactly: *a strict*

Catholic. **3** precisely limited or defined. **4** without exception or deviation: *lives in strict seclusion.* **5** requiring complete compliance or exact performance: *gave strict orders.* **6** complete or absolute. ▶ **strictly** *adverb* **strictness** *noun*
stricture *noun* **1** (usu. in *plural*) a sternly critical remark or instruction: *his strictures on their lack of civic pride.* **2** (usu. in *plural*) rules that restrict behaviour or action: *the strictures imposed by the ministry.* **3** an abnormal narrowing of a canal or duct in the body.
stride • *verb* (**strides;** *past* **strode;** *past participle* **stridden; striding**) **1** walk with long firm steps. **2** cross with one step. • *noun* **1 a** a single long step. **b** the length of this. **2** a person's gait as determined by the length of stride. **3** (usu. in *plural*) progress: *has made great strides.* **4** the distance between the feet parted either laterally or as in walking. PHRASES **break stride 1** change one's gait. **2** slow down. **hit** (or **get into**) **one's stride** reach a settled or steady rate of progress or level of performance. **take in one's stride** manage without difficulty.
stridency *noun* an excessively urgent or aggressive manner, esp. in presenting a point of view. [Say STRIDE in see]
strident *adjective* **1** loud and harsh: *he could speak with indignation without sounding shrill or strident.* **2** urgent and aggressive: *strident demands.* ▶ **stridently** *adverb* [Say STRY dint]
strider *noun* = WATER STRIDER.
strife *noun* **1** conflict or struggle. **2** enmity or rivalry, esp. of a bitter kind.
strike • *verb* (**strikes, struck, striking**) **1** deliver a blow to; hit. **2** come into forcible contact with. **3** (in sport) hit or kick (a ball) so as to score a run, point, or goal. **4** ignite (a match) by rubbing it briskly against an abrasive surface. **5** (of a disaster, disease, etc.) occur suddenly and have harmful effects on. **6** attack suddenly. **7** (foll. by *into*) cause (a strong emotion) in. **8** cause to become suddenly: *she was struck dumb.* **9** suddenly come into the mind of. **10** (foll. by *on* or *upon*) discover or think of, esp. unexpectedly. **11** (esp. in *passive*) find particularly interesting or impressive. **12** (of employees) refuse to work as a form of organized protest. **13** cancel or remove by crossing out with a pen. **14** move or proceed vigorously or purposefully. **15** reach (an agreement, balance, or compromise). **16** (of a clock) indicate the time by sounding a chime or stroke. **17** make (a coin or medal) by stamping metal. **18** discover (gold, minerals, or oil) by drilling or mining. **19** take down or dismantle (a tent, camp, or theatrical scenery). **20** *Cdn* create (a committee). • *noun* **1** an organized refusal by employees to work. **2** a refusal to do something as an organized protest. **3** a sudden attack. **4** *Baseball* a batter's unsuccessful attempt to hit a pitched ball. **5** (in bowling) an act of knocking down all the pins with one's first ball. **6** (in sport) an act of striking a ball. **7** an act of striking gold, minerals, or oil. **8** a thing to one's discredit: *several strikes against him.* **9** a pull on a fishing line indicating that a fish has taken the bait. PHRASES **on strike** taking part in an industrial etc. strike. **strike down 1** knock down. **2** bring low; afflict: *struck down by a virus.* **strike home 1** deal an effective blow. **2** have an intended effect: *my words struck home.* **strike in 1** intervene in a conversation etc. **2** (of a disease) attack the interior of the body from the surface. **strike it rich** *informal* find a source of abundance or success. **strike a light** produce a light by striking a match. **strike it lucky** have a lucky success. **strike off 1** remove with a stroke. **2** delete (a name etc.) from a list. **strike oil 1** find petroleum by sinking a shaft. **2** attain

S

prosperity or success. **strike out 1** hit out. **2** act vigorously. **3** delete (an item or name etc.). **4** set off or begin: *struck out eastwards*. **5** use the arms and legs in swimming. **6** forge or devise (a plan etc.). **7** *Baseball* **a** dismiss (a batter) by means of three strikes. **b** be dismissed in this way. **8** be unsuccessful. **strike through** delete (a word etc.) with a stroke of one's pen. **strike up 1** start (an acquaintance, conversation, etc.) esp. casually. **2** begin playing (a tune etc.). **strike upon 1** have (an idea etc.) luckily occur to one. **2** (of light) illuminate. **strike while the iron is hot** act promptly at a good opportunity.

strikebound *adjective* immobilized or closed by a strike.

strikebreaker *noun* one working or employed in place of others who are on strike. ▶ **strikebreaking** *noun & adjective*

strike force *noun* **1** a military or police force ready for rapid effective action. **2** a similar group, e.g. of activists etc., organized to act quickly in a specific way.

strikeout *noun Baseball* an out called when a batter has had three strikes.

strike pay *noun* money paid to strikers by a union.

striker *noun* **1** a person or thing that strikes. **2** an employee on strike. **3** *Soccer* an attacking player positioned well forward in order to score goals.

strike zone *noun Baseball* an imaginary rectangle above home plate extending from the armpits to the knees of a batter.

striking ● *adjective* **1** impressive; attracting attention. **2** conspicuous: *a striking lack of effort*. **3** (of a person) on strike: *striking workers*. ● *noun* the act of striking: *announced the striking of a committee ◊ the striking of metal against stone*. PHRASES **within striking distance** near enough to hit or achieve. ▶ **strikingly** *adverb*

string ● *noun* **1** twine or narrow cord. **2** a length of catgut or wire etc. on a musical instrument, producing a note by vibration. **3 a** (in *plural*) stringed instruments (i.e. violin, cello, etc.) forming a section of an orchestra, group, etc. **b** (as an *adjective*) relating to or consisting of stringed instruments: *string quartet*. **4** (in *plural*) an awkward associated or consequent condition or complication: *no strings attached*. **5 a** a set of things strung together; a series or line of persons or things: *a string of beads ◊ a string of boyfriends*. **b** *Sport* a roster of players in order of selection or skill: *second string*. **6** a group of racehorses trained at one stable. **7** a piece of catgut etc. interwoven with others to form the head of a tennis etc. racquet. **8** = STRINGER 4. **9** *Computing* a linear sequence of characters, records, or data. **10** a continuous series of successes or failures: *a continuous sequence of games, turns at play, etc*. ● *verb* (**strings, strung, stringing**) **1** supply with a string or strings. **2 a** arrange in or as a string: *strung lights on the Christmas tree*. **b** put (esp. words, ideas, etc.) together in a connected sequence. **3** provide, equip, or adorn with something suspended or slung: *the backyard was strung with lanterns*. **4** thread (beads etc.) on a string. **5** tie with string. **6** place a string ready for use on (a musical instrument, racquet, bow, etc.). **7** *slang* deceive. **8** (often foll. by *out*) extend, stretch out. PHRASES **on a string** under one's control or influence. **string a person a line** *informal* purposely mislead a person. **string along** *informal* deceive, mislead (a person) about one's own intentions or beliefs. **string out** extend; prolong (esp. unduly). **string up 1** hang up on strings etc. **2** *informal* kill by hanging.

string bean *noun* **1** any of various beans eaten in their fibrous pods, esp. runner or French beans. **2** *informal* a tall thin person.

stringed *adjective* (of musical instruments) having strings: *twelve-stringed guitar*.

stringency *noun* **1** the quality of rules or conditions that are very strict and rigid: *the stringency of marriage laws*. **2** financial conditions that are very difficult and are strictly controlled: *the next four years will bring tough decisions and terrible stringency if we're to get a handle on the federal budget deficit*. [Say STRIN jin see]

stringent *adjective* (of rules etc.) strict, precise; requiring exact performance: *stringent environmental regulations ◊ their safety code is among the most stringent in the province*. ▶ **stringently** *adverb* [Say STRIN jint]

stringer *noun* **1** a horizontal member connecting uprights in a framework, supporting a floor, etc. **2** a longitudinal structural member in a framework, esp. of a ship or aircraft. **3** *informal* a newspaper correspondent not on the regular staff, esp. one retained on a freelance basis to report on events in a particular place. **4** a supporting timber or skirting in which the ends of a staircase steps are set. **5** (usu. in *combination*) an athlete, performer, etc. ranked according to ability: *first-stringer*. [Rhymes with *SINGER*]

stringy *adjective* (**stringier, stringiest**) **1** (of food etc.) fibrous, tough. **2** of or like string. **3** tall, wiry, and thin: *the family's newest acquisition is a stringy black poodle*. **4** (of a liquid) viscous; forming strings. [Say STRING ee]

strip ● *verb* (**strips, stripped, stripping**) **1 a** remove the clothes or covering from (a person or thing). **b** pull off or remove (a covering or property etc.): *strip away the pretense*. **2** undress oneself. **3** deprive (a person) of property, titles, etc. **4** leave bare of accessories or fittings. **5** remove bark and branches from (a tree). **6** (often foll. by *down*) remove the accessory fittings of or take apart (a machine etc.) to inspect or adjust it. **7** sell off (the assets of a company) for profit. **8** remove paint, wax, etc. from a surface: *strip a floor*. **9 a** tear the thread from (a screw). **b** (of a screw) lose its thread. **10** tear the teeth from (a gearwheel). ● *noun* **1** a long narrow piece: *a strip of land*. **2** a narrow flat bar of iron or steel. **3** (also **strip cartoon**) = COMIC STRIP. **4 a** an area of commercial development along a road in a town or city. **b** a part of a city street frequented by prostitutes, drug addicts, etc. **5** = AIRSTRIP. **6** = DRAG STRIP. **7** an act of stripping, esp. of performing a striptease. PHRASES **tear a strip off a person** *informal* angrily rebuke a person.

strip club *noun* (also **strip joint**) a club at which striptease performances are given.

stripe ● *noun* **1** a long narrow band or strip differing in colour or texture from the surface on either side of it. **2** *Military* a chevron etc. denoting military rank. **3** a category of character, opinion, etc.: *politicians of all stripes*. ● *verb* (**stripes, striped, striping**) mark with stripes. ▶ **striped** *adjective*

striped bass *noun* a large bass with dark horizontal stripes along the upper sides, inhabiting North American coastal waters.

striper *noun* **1** = STRIPED BASS. **2** (with specifying numeral) a member of the navy, army, etc. whose uniform carries a number of stripes denoting rank.

strip mall *noun* a shopping mall on a street, with the stores arranged in a row and accessed from outside.

strip mine ● *noun* a mine worked by removing surface material in successive parallel strips to expose the ore etc. ● *verb* (**strip-mine, strip-mines, strip-mined, strip-mining**) obtain or work by strip mining. ▶ **strip mining** *noun*

stripped-down *adjective* **1** (of a car, machine, etc.) that has had all superfluous or extraneous parts removed. **2** reduced to essentials; bare, lean: *a stripped-down musical style*.

stripper *noun* **1** a person who performs striptease. **2** a device or solvent for removing paint etc. **3** a person or thing that strips something.

striptease *noun* a form of erotic entertainment in which a performer removes his or her clothes in front of an audience, usu. to musical accompaniment.

stripy *adjective* having stripes: *a stripy T-shirt*.

strive verb (**strives**) *past* **strove** or **strived**, *past participle* **striven**; **striving**) **1** try hard, make efforts: *strive to succeed* ◊ *striving for the gold medal*. **2** (often foll. by *with*, *against*) struggle or contend.

strobe • *noun* (also **strobe light**) **1** a bright light that flashes on and off. **2** a stroboscope. • *verb* (**strobes**, **strobed**, **strobing**) **1** light as if with a strobe. **2** flash intermittently.

stroboscope *noun* **1** Physics an instrument for determining speeds of rotation etc. by shining a bright light at intervals so that a rotating object appears stationary. **2** = STROBE *noun* 1. ▶**stroboscopic** *adjective* [Say STROBE uh scope]

strode *past of* STRIDE.

stroganoff *noun* (also **beef stroganoff**) a dish of strips of beef cooked in a sauce containing mushrooms and sour cream. [Say STROE guh noff]

stroke • *noun* **1** an act of hitting. **2** Golf an act of hitting the ball with a club, as a unit of scoring. **3** a sound made by a striking clock. **4** an act of stroking with the hand. **5** a mark made by drawing a pen, pencil, or paintbrush once across paper or canvas. **6** a line forming part of a written or printed character. **7** a short diagonal line separating characters or figures. **8** one of a series of repeated movements. **9** a style of moving the arms and legs in swimming. **10 a** a specially successful or effective feat or event: *a stroke of diplomacy* ◊ *a stroke of genius*. **b** an unexpected piece of luck or misfortune. **11** the mode or action of moving the oar in rowing. **12** a sudden disabling attack or loss of consciousness caused by an interruption in the flow of blood to the brain. • *verb* (**strokes**, **stroked**, **stroking**) **1** move one's hand with gentle pressure over (hair or fur etc.). **2** *informal* manipulate (a person) by means of flattery, persuasion, etc. **3** hit (a ball) with a smooth, controlled movement. PHRASES **at a stroke** by a single action. **off one's stroke** not performing as well as usual. **on** (or **at**) **the stroke of one** etc. with the clock about to strike one etc. ▶**stroker** *noun* (also in *combination*).

stroll • *verb* **1** saunter or walk in a leisurely way. **2** walk in a leisurely fashion along (a street etc.). **3** achieve something easily, without effort: *strolled to victory*. • *noun* **1** a short leisurely walk: *go for a stroll*. **2** something easily achieved.

stroller *noun* **1** a folding chair on wheels in which a baby or small child can be pushed along from place to place. **2** a person who strolls.

strolling *adjective* itinerant: *strolling players*.

strong • *adjective* (**stronger**; **strongest**) **1** physically powerful. **2** done with or exerting great force. **3** able to withstand great force or pressure. **4** secure, stable, or firmly established. **5** great in power, influence, or ability. **6** great in intensity or degree. **7** (of language or actions) forceful and extreme. **8** (of something seen or heard) not soft or muted. **9** pungent and full-flavoured. **10** (of a drink) containing much alcohol. **11** used after a number to indicate the size of a group: *a large crowd, three thousand strong*. **12** Cdn slightly more than the stated measurement: *a strong quarter of an inch*. • *adverb* strongly. PHRASES **come on strong** behave aggressively or assertively. **going strong** *informal* continuing action vigorously; continuing to flourish; in good health or trim.

strong-arm • *adjective* using threats or force: *strong-arm tactics*. • *verb* threaten, intimidate.

strongbox *noun* (*plural* **strongboxes**) a strongly made, usu. metal chest for safeguarding valuables.

stronghold *noun* **1** a fortified place. **2** a secure refuge. **3** a centre of support for a cause etc.

strongly *adverb* to a great degree.

strongman *noun* (*plural* **strongmen**) **1** a forceful leader who exercises firm control over a state, group, etc.: *violent protests forced the country's long-time military strongman to resign*. **2** a performer (at a fair etc.) of feats of strength.

strong point *noun* **1 a** a thing at which one excels. **b** a feature of something that makes it attractive. **2** (**strongpoint**) a specially fortified defensive position.

strongroom *noun* a room designed to protect valuables against fire and theft.

strong suit *noun* **1** a suit at cards in which one can take tricks. **2** a thing at which one excels.

strong-willed *adjective* **1** determined, resolute. **2** stubborn, headstrong.

strontium *noun* a soft silver-white metallic element found in various minerals. [Say STRON shee um]

stroud *noun* Cdn a coarse woollen cloth used esp. in the North to make blankets, leggings, etc.

strove *past of* STRIVE.

struck • *verb* *past and past participle of* STRIKE. • *adjective* pertaining to or affected by an industrial strike: *a struck factory*.

structural *adjective* **1** affecting or having to do with the structure of a building: *the blast left ten buildings with major structural damage*. **2** having to do with the arrangement of and relations between the parts or elements of a complex whole: *structural changes in the industry*.

structuralism *noun* a method of analyzing and interpreting concepts in anthropology, linguistics, and other cognitive and social sciences in terms of contrasting relations among sets of items within conceptual systems that reflect patterns underlying a superficial diversity. ▶**structuralist** *noun & adjective*

structurally *adverb* in terms of the structure of something: *the two buildings are similar structurally*.

structure • *noun* **1 a** a whole constructed unit, esp. a building. **b** the way in which a building etc. is constructed: *has a flimsy structure*. **c** the state of being well planned or organized: *your essay lacks structure*. **2** a set of interconnecting parts of any complex thing; a framework: *sentence structure*. • *verb* (**structures**, **structured**, **structuring**) give structure to; organize. ▶**structured** *adjective* (also in *combination*)

strudel *noun* a dessert of thin pastry rolled up around a usu. fruit filling and baked: *apple strudel*. [Say STROODLE]

struggle • *verb* (**struggles**, **struggled**, **struggling**) **1** make forceful or violent efforts to get free of restraint or constriction. **2** make violent or determined efforts under difficulties; strive hard: *struggled to speak*. **3** contend; fight strenuously: *struggled with the disease*. **4** make one's way with difficulty: *struggled to my feet*. **5** (esp. as **struggling** *adjective*) have difficulty in gaining recognition or a living: *a struggling artist*. • *noun* **1** the act or a period of struggling. **2** a hard or confused contest. **3** a determined effort under difficulties. PHRASES **the struggle for existence** (or **life**) the competition between organisms esp. as an element in natural selection, or between persons seeking a livelihood.

strum *verb* (**strums**, **strummed**, **strumming**) **1** play a guitar, banjo, etc. by sweeping the thumb or a pick up

S

or down the strings. **2** play (a tune etc.) in this way. ▶ **strummer** *noun*

strung *past and past participle of* STRING.

strung out *adjective informal* **1** addicted to, using, or high on drugs. **2** in a state of extreme nervous tension.

strut • *noun* **1** a bar forming part of a framework and designed to resist compression. **2** a strutting gait. • *verb* (**struts, strutted, strutting**) walk in a proud upright way. PHRASES **strut one's stuff** *informal* display one's ability. ▶ **strutter** *noun*

strychnine *noun* a bitter and highly poisonous substance obtained from plants of the genus *Strychnos*. [Say STRICK nine or STRICK neen]

stub • *noun* **1** the remnant of a pencil or cigarette etc. after use. **2** the small part of a cheque, receipt, ticket etc. that remains, to be kept as a record, after the main part has been detached and given to someone. **3** a stunted tail etc. **4** the stump of a tree, tooth, etc. • *verb* (**stubs, stubbed, stubbing**) **1** strike (one's toe) against something. **2** extinguish (a lighted cigarette) by pressing the lighted end against something.

stubble *noun* **1** the cut stalks of cereal plants left sticking up after the harvest. **2** a short bristly growth of unshaven hair. ▶ **stubbled** *adjective*

stubble-jumper *noun Cdn slang* a prairie farmer.

stubbly *adjective* covered with stubble, esp. on the face: *Ed scratched his stubbly chin*.

stubborn *adjective* **1** unreasonably obstinate. **2** unyielding: *stubborn resistance*. **3** that will not respond to treatment: *a stubborn cough*. ▶ **stubbornly** *adjective* **stubbornness** *noun*

stubby • *adjective* (**stubbier, stubbiest**) short and thick. • *noun* (*plural* **stubbies**) *Cdn hist. informal* a small squat bottle of beer.

stucco • *noun* (*plural* **stuccoes**) plaster or cement used for coating wall surfaces or moulding into architectural decorations. • *verb* (**stuccoes, stuccoed, stuccoing**) coat with stucco.

stuck • *verb past and past participle of* STICK². • *adjective* **1** unable to progress. **2** confined in a place: *was stuck in the house*. **3** (of an animal) butchered by having its throat cut: *screaming like a stuck pig*. PHRASES **be stuck for** be at a loss for or in need of. **be stuck on** *informal* be infatuated with. **be stuck with** *informal* be unable to get rid of or escape from.

stuck-up *adjective informal* snobbish.

stud¹ • *noun* **1** a large-headed nail or knob, projecting from a surface esp. for ornament. **2** a small piece of jewellery for wearing in pierced ears or nostrils. **3** a small object like a button with two heads, used esp. formerly to fasten a collar or the front of a shirt. **4** a small object projecting slightly from a road surface as a marker etc. **5** a two-by-four to which drywall etc. is nailed. **6** any of a number of metal pieces set into the tire of a motor vehicle to improve roadholding in slippery conditions. • *verb* (**studs, studded, studding**) **1** set with or as with studs. **2** be scattered over or about (a surface).

stud² *noun* **1 a** a number of horses kept for breeding etc. **b** a place where these are kept. **2** (also **stud horse**) a stallion. **3** *informal* a man who has a reputation for being very sexually active. **4** (also **stud poker**) a form of poker with betting after the dealing of successive rounds of cards face up. PHRASES **at stud** (of a male horse or dog) publicly available for breeding on payment of a fee.

studded *adjective* thickly set or strewn: *diamond-studded*.

studding *noun* the wood framing of a wall in a house etc.

student *noun* **1 a** a person who is studying, esp. at

university, college, etc. **b** a school pupil. **2** (as an *adjective*) studying in order to become: *a student teacher*. **3** a person who observes or has a particular interest in something: *a student of current affairs*.

student-at-law *noun* (*plural* **students-at-law**) *Cdn* an articling student.

student loan *noun* a usu. government loan available to university and college students.

studied *adjective* deliberate, intentional: *with studied politeness*. ▶ **studiedly** *adverb*

studio *noun* (*plural* **studios**) **1** a place where films or recordings are made or where television or radio programs are made or produced. **2** a company which produces films: *works for a major studio*. **3** the workroom of a painter or photographer etc. **4** a large room where dancers rehearse. **5** (also **studio apartment**) an apartment with only one main room.

studious *adjective* **1** devoted to or assiduous in study or reading. **2** studied, deliberate, painstaking: *studious care*. ▶ **studiously** *adverb* **studiousness** *noun*

study • *noun* (*plural* **studies**) **1** the devotion of time and attention to acquiring information or knowledge, esp. of a specified subject. **2** (in *plural*) the pursuit of academic knowledge: *continued their studies abroad* ◊ *Native Studies*. **3 a** detailed consideration or investigation into a specified subject, phenomenon, etc.: *a study of child poverty*. **4** a room used for reading, writing, etc. • *verb* (**studies, studied, studying**) **1** make a study of; investigate or examine (a subject): *study law*. **2** (often foll. by *for*) apply oneself to study. **3** scrutinize or earnestly contemplate (a visible object): *studied their faces*. **4** try to learn (the words of one's role etc.). **5** read (a book) attentively.

stuff • *noun* **1** the material that a thing is made of; material that may be used for some purpose. **2** a substance or things or belongings of an indeterminate kind or a quality not needing to be specified: *leave your stuff in the hall*. **3** a particular knowledge or activity: *knows her stuff*. **4 a** what a person is perceived to be made of; a person's capabilities or inward character. **b** the makings of future attainment or excellence: *it was the stuff of legend*. **5** valueless matter, trash, nonsense: *take that stuff away*. **6** (**the stuff**) **a** *informal* an available supply of something, esp. drink or drugs. **b** *slang* money. **7** *informal* **a** (in baseball) a pitcher's repertoire of pitches and his or her skill in using it. **b** (in baseball, tennis, etc.) the spin given to a ball in order to make it vary its course. • *verb* **1 a** pack (a receptacle) tightly. **b** fill (a quantity of envelopes) with the same printed matter, as for a mass mailing. **2** (foll. by *in, into*) force or cram (a thing): *stuffed the socks in the drawer*. **3** fill out the skin of (an animal or bird etc.) with material to restore the original shape. **4** fill (poultry, vegetables, etc.) with a savoury or sweet mixture, esp. before cooking. **5** fill a person or oneself with food. **6** push, esp. hastily or clumsily: *stuffed the note behind the cushion*. **7** (usu. in *passive*; foll. by *up*) block up (a person's nose etc.). **8** *slang* (esp. as an expression of contemptuous dismissal) dispose of as unwanted: *you can stuff the job*. **9** place bogus votes in (a ballot box). PHRASES **do one's stuff** *informal* do what one has to. **get stuffed** *slang* an exclamation of dismissal, contempt, etc. **stuff it** *slang* an expression of rejection or disdain. **stuff one's face** eat a great deal.

stuffed shirt *noun informal* a pompous or prim person.

stuffer *noun* **1** a device used for stuffing something. **2** an item used to fill something.

stuffiness *noun* **1** the quality of a place that lacks fresh air or ventilation. **2** the condition of a person's nose when it is stuffed up. **3** the manner of a person who is too formal, boring, or old-fashioned.

stuffing *noun* **1** padding used to stuff cushions etc. **2** a savoury mixture, usu. of seasoned bread crumbs, put inside a chicken, turkey, etc. before it is cooked. PHRASES **knock** (or **take**) **the stuffing out of** *informal* make feeble or weak; defeat.

stuffy *adjective* (**stuffier, stuffiest**) **1** lacking fresh air or ventilation. **2** (of a person) dull, formal, and boring; old-fashioned. **3** (of a person's nose etc.) stuffed up.

stultifying *adjective* extremely tedious or boring: *the stultifying monotony of the suburb's residential architecture.* ▶ **stultifyingly** *adverb* [Say STUL tuh fie ing]

stumble • *verb* (**stumbles, stumbled, stumbling**) **1** lurch forward or have a partial fall from misplacing one's foot. **2** (often foll. by *along*) walk unsteadily with repeated stumbles. **3** act in a blundering or hesitating manner, esp. make a mistake or repeated mistakes in speaking etc. **4** (foll. by *on, upon, across*) find or encounter by chance. • *noun* an act of stumbling.

stumblebum *noun* *informal* a clumsy or inept person.

stumbling block *noun* an obstacle or circumstance causing difficulty or hesitation.

stump • *noun* **1** the projecting portion of the trunk of a cut or fallen tree that remains fixed in the ground. **2** the part remaining when a limb or other part of the body is amputated or severed. **3** the part of a broken tooth left in the gum. **4** a thing, e.g. a pencil or a candle, that has been worn down or reduced to a small part of its original length. **5** (in *plural*) *jocular* the legs. • *verb* **1** (of a question etc.) be too hard for; puzzle. **2** walk stiffly or noisily as if on a wooden leg. **3** traverse (a district) making speeches esp. for an election campaign. **4** remove the stumps from (land). PHRASES **on the stump** *informal* engaged in political speech making and campaigning.

stumpage *noun* **1** standing timber considered with reference to its quantity or marketable value. **2** (also **stumpage fee**) a tax charged for the cutting of timber on government-owned land. [Say STUMP idge]

stumped *adjective* at a loss; baffled.

stumpy *adjective* (**stumpier, stumpiest**) short and thick.

stun *verb* (**stuns, stunned, stunning**) **1** knock senseless. **2** bewilder or astound due to something shocking, unbelievable or unexpected. **3** (of a sound) deafen temporarily.

stung *past and past participle of* STING.

stun gun *noun* a gun which stuns a person or animal by means of an electric shock etc.

stunk *past and past participle of* STINK.

stunned *adjective* *Cdn informal* stupid; foolish.

stunner *noun* *informal* **1** a thing that stuns or dazes someone or something; an amazing or astounding thing. **2** a very attractive woman or girl.

stunning *adjective* *informal* **1** extremely impressive or attractive. **2** surprising or shocking. ▶ **stunningly** *adverb*

stunt[1] *verb* retard the growth or development of.

stunt[2] • *noun* **1** something unusual done to attract attention: *publicity stunt.* **2** an act notable or impressive on account of the skill, strength, or daring etc. required to perform it. • *verb* perform stunts, esp. aerobatics.

stuntman *noun* (*plural* **stuntmen**) a man employed to take an actor's place in performing dangerous stunts.

stupefaction *noun* **1** a state in which one is unable to think or function normally: *most of the guests were fortified to stupefaction with tankards of strong Turkish coffee.* **2** a state of shock or astonishment: *she gapes at me in stupefaction.* [Say stupe uh FACTION]

stupefy *verb* (**stupefies, stupefied, stupefying**) **1** make someone unable to think or feel properly:

stupefied with drink. **2** stun with astonishment: *the news was stupefying.* ▶ **stupefying** *adjective* **stupefyingly** *adverb* [Say STUPE uh fie]

stupendous *adjective* amazing or prodigious, esp. in terms of size or degree: *a stupendous achievement.* ▶ **stupendously** *adverb* [Say stew PEN dus]

stupid *adjective* (**stupider, stupidest**) **1** unintelligent: *a stupid man.* **2** showing lack of good judgment; foolish: *a stupid idea.* **3** uninteresting or boring. **4** obtuse; lacking in sensibility. **5** *informal* a general term of disparagement: *your stupid jokes.* ▶ **stupidity** *noun* (*plural* **stupidities**). **stupidly** *adverb*

stupor *noun* **1** a condition of near-unconsciousness characterized by great reduction in mental activity and responsiveness, caused by disease, narcotics, alcohol, etc. **2** a dazed, stunned, or torpid state. [Say STEW per]

sturdily *adverb* **1** strongly: *the fort was sturdily built.* **2** with confidence or determination: *went sturdily about their business.*

sturdiness *noun* **1** the quality of something that is strong and solid: *walls of closely related species can vary in the sturdiness of their construction.* **2** vigour, confidence, or determination: *the determination of his fiction takes on an even firmer sturdiness.*

sturdy *adjective* (**sturdier, sturdiest**) **1** robust; strongly built. **2** vigorous; determined: *sturdy resistance.*

sturgeon *noun* a large primitive shark-like fish covered with bony plates, which is of commercial importance for its caviar and flesh. [Say STIR gin]

stutter • *verb* **1** stammer, esp. by involuntarily repeating the first consonants of words. **2** (esp. of a vehicle or engine) move or start with difficulty, making short sharp noises or movements. • *noun* a tendency to stutter when speaking. ▶ **stutterer** *noun*

sty *noun* **1** (*plural* **sties**) **a** a pen or enclosure for pigs. **b** a filthy room or dwelling. **2** (*plural* **sties** or **styes**) an inflamed swelling on the edge of an eyelid.

-style *combining form* forming adjectives and adverbs with the sense "in a manner characteristic of".

style • *noun* **1** a kind or sort, esp. in regard to appearance and form. **2** a manner of writing or speaking or performing: *a florid style.* **3** a distinctive manner esp. in relation to painting, architecture, furniture, dress, etc. **4 a** a superior quality or manner: *do it in style.* **b** fashionableness or attractiveness of appearance or bearing: *she dresses with such style.* **5** a particular make, shape, or pattern: *in all sizes and styles.* **6** a method of reckoning dates: *Old Style.* **7** = STYLUS 1, 3. **8** *Botany* the narrow extension of the ovary supporting the stigma. **9** *Zoology* a small slender pointed appendage. • *verb* (**styles, styled, styling**) **1** design or make etc. in a particular (esp. fashionable) style. **2** give a person or thing a particular title, name, or description: *the foremost of the Metis captains was the hunt leader, variously styled as the "War Chief" and "le President"* ◊ *Clarence styled himself a rebel.*

stylish *adjective* **1** fashionable, chic. **2** having a superior quality, manner, etc. ▶ **stylishly** *adverb*

stylishness *noun*

stylist *noun* **1 a** a person employed by a firm to create, coordinate, or promote new styles or designs, esp. of clothes or cars. **b** a hairdresser. **2 a** a writer noted for or aspiring to good literary style. **b** (in sports or music) a person who performs with style.

stylistic *adjective* of or concerning esp. literary or artistic style. ▶ **stylistically** *adverb*

stylistics *noun* the study of literary or linguistic style.

stylization *noun* the depiction of something in a conventional and usu. artificial or unnatural way, esp. to achieve a particular artistic effect.

stylized *adjective* painted, drawn, etc. in a way that is

S

conventional and not natural or realistic, esp. to achieve a particular artistic effect: *the team's logo features a stylized image of a shark*.

stylus *noun* (*plural* **styli** or **styluses**) **1** any sharp instrument or point for engraving, tracing, etc., esp. an ancient implement for writing on wax. **2** *Computing* an electrical device shaped like a pen, used esp. to design graphical images on a computer screen. **3** a pointer for indicating a time, position, etc., esp. the gnomon of a sundial. **4** a tracing point used to produce a written record in a seismograph, telegraph receiver, etc. [Say STY lus for the singular; for *STYLI* say STY lie]

stymie • *verb* (**stymies**, **stymied**, **stymying** or **stymieing**) **1** obstruct or thwart (a person, project, process, etc.): *he found himself stymied by an old opponent* ◊ *financial difficulties have stymied the company's growth*. **2** puzzle or perplex (a person): *you'd be surprised how many men are stymied by that simple phrase, "black tie"*. **3** *Golf* block (an opponent, an opponent's ball, or oneself) with a stymie. • *noun* (*plural* **stymies**) *Golf* a situation on a green in which the path of a putt to the hole is obstructed by an opponent's ball. [Say STY mee]

styrene *noun* a liquid hydrocarbon, easily polymerized and used in making plastics etc. [Say STY reen]

Styrofoam *noun* *proprietary* a variety of expanded polystyrene often used in insulation, food containers, etc.

suasion *noun* *formal* persuasion as opposed to force: *moral suasion*. [Say SWAY zh'n]

suave *adjective* (especially of a man) confident, elegant and polite, sometimes in a way that seems insincere: *all the waiters were suave and deferential*. ▶ **suavely** *adverb*

suavity *noun* [Say SWOV, SWOVVA tee]

sub *informal* • *noun* **1** a submarine. **2** a sandwich made with a long roll or small loaf and filled with a variety of meats, cheeses, etc. **3 a** a substitute. **b** a substitute teacher. **4** a subscription. • *verb* (**subs**, **subbed**, **subbing**) (usu. foll. by *for*) act or work as a substitute for a person.

subalpine *adjective* **1** pertaining to or situated in the higher mountain slopes just below the timberline. **2** of or pertaining to the area at the foot of the Alps.

subarctic • *noun* (usu. **Subarctic**) the region immediately south of the Arctic Circle. • *adjective* characteristic of, pertaining to, or inhabiting this region.

subatomic *adjective* **1 a** (of a particle) existing in an atom. **b** (of a process etc.) occurring within an atom. **2 a** smaller than an atom. **b** *informal* extremely small.

subcategory *noun* (*plural* **subcategories**) a secondary category.

subclass *noun* (*plural* **subclasses**) **1 a** a secondary or inferior class. **b** each of the groups or categories that constitute a class. **2** a taxonomic category below a class.

subcommittee *noun* a body of people appointed by a committee, usu. composed of a selection of its own members, esp. to study or deal with a specific issue or an aspect of a larger matter.

subcompact • *adjective* designating a car that is smaller than a compact, usu. having a wheelbase of less than 85 inches, and a 1 litre engine. • *noun* a subcompact car.

subconscious • *noun* the part of the mind which influences actions etc. without one's full awareness. • *adjective* **1** of or existing in the subconscious. **2** operating or existing without one's full awareness: *subconscious impulses*. ▶ **subconsciously** *adverb*

subcontinent *noun* **1** a large section of a continent having a certain geographical or political identity or independence: *the Indian subcontinent*. **2** a large land

mass, smaller than a continent, e.g. Greenland. ▶ **subcontinental** *adjective*

subcontract • *verb* **1** hire a person, company, etc. to do (work) as part of a larger contract or project. **2** make or carry out a subcontract. • *noun* an agreement in which an individual or firm agrees to perform all or a portion of a previous contract, esp. to supply materials, labour, etc.

subcontractor *noun* an individual or company etc. to whom a principal contractor has sublet all or a portion of a contract.

subculture *noun* **1 a** a cultural group within a larger or predominant culture but distinguished from it by factors such as class, ethnic background, religion, or residence, unified by shared beliefs or interests which may be at variance with those of the larger culture. **b** the system of beliefs, customs, and behaviour etc. typical of such a group. **2** a culture of micro-organisms started from another culture.

subcutaneous *adjective* situated or introduced just under the skin. ▶ **subcutaneously** *adverb* [Say sub cue TAY nee us]

subdirectory *noun* (*plural* **subdirectories**) *Computing* a directory that is itself contained in another directory.

subdivide *verb* (**subdivides**, **subdivided**, **subdividing**) **1** divide into smaller parts, esp. after a previous division. **2** divide (a tract of land) into plots for sale or development.

subdivision *noun* **1** an area of land divided into plots for sale or development. **2** a housing development that has been built on such an area. **3** each of the parts into which a thing, esp. a previous division, is or may be divided; a secondary division. **4** the action of subdividing: *the subdivision of tasks within the industry*.

subduction zone *noun* a long narrow region containing a trench where two plates of the earth's crust collide, forcing one plate to plunge beneath the other, where it melts and is assimilated into the magma of the earth's mantle; subduction zones are associated with volcanoes and earthquakes, as well as with the formation of mountains.

subdue *verb* (**subdues**, **subdued**, **subduing**) **1** overcome or overpower (a person or animal etc.) by physical force or violence. **2** bring (a person etc.) under one's control by intimidation, persuasion, manipulation, etc. **3** check or restrain (an impulse, emotion, thought, etc.). **4** conquer and bring into subjection (an army, people, or country).

subdued *adjective* **1** (of a colour, light, or sound, etc.) reduced in or lacking intensity or force. **2** (of a person) not showing much excitement or activity.

subfamily *noun* (*plural* **subfamilies**) a subdivision of a family in a classification, e.g. biology or linguistics.

subfloor *noun* a rough floor serving as a foundation for a finished floor in a building. ▶ **subflooring** *noun*

subfreezing *adjective* below the freezing point.

sub-genre *noun* a secondary or subordinate style of esp. literature or art.

subgroup *noun* **1** a subordinate group; a subdivision of a group. **2** *Math* **a** a series of operations forming part of a larger group. **b** any group all of whose elements are elements of a larger group.

subheading *noun* (also **subhead**) **1** a subordinate heading, headline, caption, or title in a chapter, article, etc. **2** a subordinate division in a classification.

subhuman • *adjective* **1** (of an animal) closely related to, but of a lower order of being than, a human. **2** (of a person or behaviour) uncivilized, bestial; less than human. • *noun* a subhuman person or creature.

subject • *noun* **1** the focus of attention in a discussion, work of art, etc. **2** something studied or taught in an

academic institution: *math is her best subject*. **3** *Grammar* a word or phrase in a sentence indicating who or what performs the action of a verb or upon whom or which a verb is predicated, e.g. "we" in the sentence *we ate ice cream* or "my dog" in *my dog is clever*. **4** a person owing allegiance to and under the protection of a monarch or government. • *adjective* (usu. foll. by *to*) **1** (foll. by *to*) susceptible to some esp. harmful or medical condition, occurrence, etc. **2** liable: *prices are subject to change without notice*. **3** dependent or conditional upon; resting on the assumption of: *the arrangement is subject to your approval*. **4** bound by law or regulation: *subject to provincial sales tax*. **5** under the rule or domination of an individual or group, sovereign, country, etc.: *a subject nation*. • *adverb* (foll. by *to*) conditionally upon: *subject to your consent*. • *verb* (usu. foll. by *to*) **1** cause (a person or thing) to experience, undergo, or endure a specified treatment. **2** expose or make vulnerable to: *subjects herself to ridicule*. **3** extend one's influence over (a nation, person, etc.). PHRASES **on the subject of** concerning, about. ▶ **subjection** *noun*

subjective *adjective* **1** (of art, written history, a person's views, etc.) proceeding from, or influenced by, an individual's personal thoughts and opinions. **2** esp. *Philosophy* proceeding from or belonging to the individual consciousness or perception; partial, misconceived, or distorted. **3** (of a case or word) constructed as appropriate to the subject of a sentence or verb. **4** (of a symptom etc.) that is felt or is experienced only by a patient, and may not be diagnosed by someone else, such as a doctor. ▶ **subjectively** *adverb* **subjectivity** *noun*

subjugate *verb* (**subjugates**, **subjugated**, **subjugating**) **1** bring (a country, people, etc.) under one's control; conquer: *the Magyars were invited by the Carolingian emperor to cross the Carpathian mountains to help him subjugate the Moravian empire*. **2** make something subservient or dependent: *tell me, Stuart, do you still subjugate your art to your politics?* ▶ **subjugation** *noun* [Say SUB juh gate, sub juh GAY sh'n]

subjunctive *Grammar* • *noun* **1** (also **subjunctive mood**) a mood of verbs used to express a condition, wish, fear, possibility, command, suggestion or uncertainty, e.g. *if I were rich* or *I wish I were beautiful*. **2** a verb in this mood. • *adjective* (of a verb or phrase) expressed in the subjunctive. [Say sub JUNK tiv]

subkingdom *noun* a taxonomic category below a kingdom.

sublet • *verb* (**sublets**, **sublet**, **subletting**) **1** acquire a lease on (an apartment etc.) from a person who is leasing it from its owner. **2** rent out (an apartment etc.) that one is leasing from its owner. • *noun* an apartment etc. that is being sublet.

sub-lieutenant *noun* *Cdn & Brit.* a naval officer ranking next below lieutenant. Abbreviation: **SLt**.

sublimate *verb* (**sublimates**, **sublimated**, **sublimating**) **1** divert or channel the energy of (a primitive esp. sexual impulse) into a more highly valued or acceptable activity: *the tension between Monk and Davis is sublimated into music of unusual power*. **2 a** subject (a substance) to the action of heat to convert it into a vapour which, on cooling, is deposited in solid form. **b** (of a substance) pass from a solid state to a vapour, or from a gaseous state to a solid, without liquefaction: *as Halley's Comet approaches the sun a tenuous mist begins to envelop the body as some exposed ice sublimates*. ▶ **sublimation** *noun* [Say SUB luh mate]

sublime • *adjective* (**sublimer**, **sublimest**) **1** of the most exalted, grand, or noble kind; of a high intellectual, moral, or spiritual level: *sublime genius*. **2** (of nature, art, etc.) of such excellence, grandeur, or

beauty as to inspire great admiration or awe. **3** usu. ironic of the most extreme kind; supreme: *sublime indifference*. • *noun* a quality in art or nature etc. arousing or inspiring awe, reverence, terror, or high emotion in the person experiencing it. PHRASES **from the sublime to the ridiculous** moving or ranging from what is serious or important to what is trivial or laughable. ▶ **sublimely** *adverb* [Say sub LIME]

subliminal *adjective* perceived by or affecting someone's mind without their being aware of it: *subliminal advertising* ◊ *music containing subliminal messages*. ▶ **subliminally** *adverb* [Say sub LIMMA nul]

sublimity *noun* the excellence, grandeur, or beauty of something that inspires great admiration or awe: *the sublimity and beauty of the scene*. [Say sub LIMMA tee]

submachine gun *noun* a hand-held lightweight automatic or semi-automatic weapon designed to shoot small-calibre ammunition.

submarine • *noun* **1** a vessel capable of operating under water. **2** (also **submarine sandwich**) = SUB *noun* 2. • *adjective* living, occurring, or used under the surface of the sea.

submariner *noun* **1** a member of the navy who serves on submarines. **2** *Baseball* a pitcher who throws with the arm at or below shoulder level; a sidearm or underhand pitcher. [Say sub MERRA ner for sense 1, sub muh REEN er for sense 2]

submenu *noun* (*plural* **submenus**) *Computing* a secondary list of available commands, options, etc. displayed under a general heading listed in a menu.

submerge *verb* (**submerges**, **submerged**, **submerging**) **1** immerse, dip, or place in a liquid. **2** overwhelm or inundate (a person) with work, problems, etc. **3** conceal or suppress (an emotion etc.). **4** (of a submarine, a diver, etc.) dive below the surface of water.

submerged *adjective* **1** immersed, inundated, or buried in or beneath a liquid or substance. **2** suppressed, concealed, hidden. **3** growing entirely under water.

submergence *noun* the state of being covered with water, esp. the covering of an area of land with water or glacier ice.

submerse *verb* (**submerses**, **submersed**, **submersing**) submerge.

submersible • *noun* a submarine operating under water for short periods, used esp. for exploration. • *adjective* intended or designed to operate or be used under water.

submersion *noun* **1** the action of sinking or of setting something below the surface of water or another liquid. **2** a situation in which someone is placed in an environment whose culture and language is different from their own: *they feared submersion in the dominant English culture*.

submicroscopic *adjective* too small to be seen by an ordinary microscope.

submission *noun* **1** the action of submitting a proposal, document, etc. for consideration, evaluation, or judgment: *when is the last date for submission of proposals?* ◊ *we have made submissions to the court*. **2** the action of yielding to a superior force or the authority or will of another: *they were starved into submission*.

submissive *adjective* ready to conform to the authority or will of others; meekly obedient or passive: *she followed him like a submissive child*. ▶ **submissively** *adverb* **submissiveness** *noun*

submit *verb* (**submits**, **submitted**, **submitting**) **1 a** cease resistance; give way; yield. **b** consent to undergo a certain treatment or abide by a certain condition or limitation etc.; surrender (oneself) to.

S

2 present (an application, essay, etc.) for consideration or decision. **3** (usu. foll. by *to*) subject (a person or thing) to an operation, process, treatment, etc.: *submitted it to the flames.* **4** suggest or contend, esp. politely.

subnotebook *noun* a computer that is smaller than a notebook but larger than a palmtop or personal digital assistant.

suborder *noun* a taxonomic category below an order.

subordinate • *adjective* (often. foll. by *to*) **1** (of a person, position, etc.) of inferior rank; dependent upon the authority or power of another. **2** secondary, minor. **3** (of a thing) dependent upon or subservient to a principal thing of the same kind. • *noun* a subordinate person or thing, esp. a person working under another's control or orders. • *verb* (**subordinates, subordinated, subordinating**) (usu. foll. by *to*) **1** treat or consider something as being of lesser importance or value than something else. **2** bring into a subordinate or less important position; make dependent on something else. [Say sub ORDA nit for the adjective and noun, sub ORDA nate for the verb]

subordinate clause *noun* a clause, usu. introduced by a conjunction, that does not constitute a sentence itself but which depends on the principal clause that it modifies or in which it serves as a noun, e.g. "that she has come" in *I hope that she has come.*

subordinating conjunction *noun* a conjunction that joins a subordinate clause to a main clause, e.g. "because" in *I am happy because it is sunny.*

subordination *noun* **1** the treatment of something as being of lesser importance or value than something else: *coaches stressed the subordination of individual goals to team goals.* **2** the condition of being dependent upon or subservient to something or someone else: *social subordination.*

suborn *verb* pay or persuade someone to do something illegal, esp. to tell lies in a court of law: *accused of conspiring to suborn witnesses.* [Say suh BORN]

subphylum *noun* (*plural* **subphyla**) a taxonomic category below a phylum. [Say sub FIE lum for the singular, sub FIE luh for the plural]

subplot *noun* a secondary plot in a novel, play, etc.

subpoena • *noun* (*plural* **subpoenas**) a writ issued by a court or other authorized body requiring the attendance of a person at a stated time and place, usu. to testify or present evidence, subject to penalty for non-compliance. • *verb* (**subpoenas, subpoenaed, subpoenaing**) **1** summon (a person) to appear in court as a witness. **2** require (evidence etc.) to be brought by a witness so that it may be presented in court. [Say suh PEENA]

sub-post office *noun* **1** *Cdn & Brit.* a small local post office offering fewer services than a main post office. **2** *Cdn* a postal outlet located within a drugstore, convenience store, etc.

sub-region *noun* a subdivision of a geographical region, usu. considered in terms of the plant and animal life it sustains. ▶ **sub-regional** *adjective*

subroutine *noun* *Computing* (also **subprogram**) a routine designed to perform a frequently used operation within a program.

sub-Saharan *adjective* from or forming part of the African regions south of the Sahara desert.

subscribe *verb* (**subscribes, subscribed, subscribing**) **1** (often foll. by *to*) arrange to receive a periodical, service, or series of tickets in exchange for payment. **2** (usu. foll. by *to*) express or feel agreement with an idea or conclusion; hold as a belief or opinion: *Quebec chefs subscribe to the principles of classic French cuisine.* **3 a** (often foll. by *for*) pay or guarantee (a specified sum of money) for an issue of shares. **b** pledge

or contribute (a specified sum of money) to a fund or charity etc.

subscriber *noun* **1** a person who pays a fee to receive regular issues of a periodical etc. **2** a person who pays a regular fee in order to receive a particular service, such as telephone or cable television service. **3** a person who purchases advance tickets to a series of theatrical productions etc. **4** a person contributing money to a charity or toward the purchase of stock etc.

subscript • *noun* a character, number, or symbol written or printed below the line or below and usu. to the right of another symbol (*compare* SUPERSCRIPT *noun*). • *adjective* written or printed below the line or below and to the right of another symbol.

subscription *noun* **1** a fee paid usu. in advance to purchase tickets for a series of events, a number of issues of a periodical, etc. **2** an agreement to pay for and receive service from a cable television or telephone company etc. **3** an offer or agreement to purchase shares in a company. **4** a sum of money donated to or raised by a charity, fund, etc.

subsea *adjective* & *adverb* beneath the surface of the sea.

subsection *noun* a division of a section, esp. within a document or book.

subsequent *adjective* (usu. foll. by *to*) following a specified event etc. in time, esp. as a consequence. ▶ **subsequently** *adverb*

subservience *noun* the manner of someone who is too willing to obey or depend on other people: *Canada has managed to function as a close ally of the US without falling into subservience.* [Say sub SIR vee ince]

subservient *adjective* **1** too willing to obey other people: *the press was accused of being subservient to the government.* **2** less important than something else; subordinate: *the needs of individuals were subservient to those of the group as a whole.* ▶ **subserviently** *adverb* [Say sub SIR vee int]

subset *noun* **1** a secondary part of a set. **2** *Math* a set consisting of elements all of which are contained in another set.

subside *verb* (**subsides, subsided, subsiding**) **1** become calm or tranquil; die down; abate: *the excitement subsided.* **2** (of water) be reduced to a lower level. **3** (of the ground) cave in. **4** (of a building, ship, etc.) sink into the ground or water. **5** (of swelling etc.) be reduced, become less prominent. **6** (of a person) settle into a comfortable position.

subsidence *noun* the process by which an area of land sinks to a lower level than normal or by which a building sinks into the ground. [Say sub SIGH dince or SUB suh dince]

subsidiary • *adjective* **1** less important than but related to; secondary: *children are employed in many of the subsidiary workshops that support the main factory.* **2** designating a company whose controlling interest is owned by a parent company. • *noun* (*plural* **subsidiaries**) a company whose controlling interest is owned by a parent company. [Say sub SIDDY airy or sub SIDGE er ee]

subsidization *noun* **1** financial support of an organization or activity etc. **2** financial support of an industry, esp. by the government, designed to reduce prices for the consumer. [Say sub suh dize AY sh'n]

subsidize *verb* (**subsidizes, subsidized, subsidizing**) **1** pay part of the cost of producing something to reduce prices for the consumer: *government-subsidized housing.* **2** support (an organization, activity, person, etc.) by grants of money. **3** support financially in an indirect way: *our customers pay more to subsidize the*

high cost of rent here. ▶**subsidized** *adjective* **subsidizer** *noun* [Say SUB suh dize]

subsidy *noun* (*plural* **subsidies**) **1** money granted by the government to producers of certain goods to enable them to sell the goods to the public at a low price, to compete with foreign competition, or to avoid laying off employees. **2** money granted by the government to keep down the price of a service or commodity considered to be essential. **3** money granted to a charity, arts group, or other undertaking held to be in the public interest. **4** any grant or contribution of money. [Say SUB suh dee]

subsist *verb* **1** (often foll. by *on*) manage to stay alive, esp. with limited food or money: *the elderly often subsist on very small incomes.* **2** *formal* exist; be valid; remain in effect: *the terms of the contract subsist.* [Say sub SIST]

subsistence *noun* **1** the means of supporting life: *the garden provided not only subsistence but a little cash crop.* **2** the production of a sufficient quantity of goods required to sustain one's own existence or to support one's household, without producing a sufficient surplus for trade: *subsistence farming* ◊ *the industrializing nation is moving away from its subsistence economy to produce goods for the global market.* **3 a** a minimal standard of living: *the minimum income needed for subsistence.* **b** the income required to provide a minimal level of existence: *subsistence wages.* [Say sub SIST ince]

subsoil *noun* the layer of soil lying immediately under the topsoil.

subsonic *adjective* pertaining to, capable of, or designating speeds less than that of sound. ▶**subsonically** *adverb*

subspecies *noun* (*plural* **subspecies**) a distinct subdivision of a species, esp. one geographically or ecologically isolated from other such subdivisions.

substance *noun* **1** the essential esp. solid matter of which a physical thing consists. **2** a particular kind of material having a definite chemical composition and usu. uniform properties. **3** an intoxicating or narcotic chemical or drug, esp. an illegal one: *substance abuse.* **4 a** the content or inward nature of a thing as opposed to its superficial appearance or form. **b** steadiness or strength of character: *a man of substance.* **5 a** the essential point or theme conveyed. **b** concrete evidence. **6** wealth and possessions.

substandard *adjective* of less than the required or normal quality or size; inadequate, inferior.

substantial *adjective* **1** ample or considerable in size, amount, or importance: *a substantial price increase.* **2** of solid structure or build: *a substantial house.* **3** having substance or truth: *substantial evidence.* ▶**substantially** *adverb* [Say sub STAN shul]

substantiate *verb* (**substantiates, substantiated, substantiating**) prove the truth of (a charge, statement, claim, etc.): *we substantiate our claims by analyzing development patterns in Japan and Canada.* ▶**substantiation** *noun* [Say sub STAN shee ate]

substantive *adjective* **1** having a firm basis in reality and so important, meaningful, or considerable.: *Canadians want substantive change within the justice system.* **2** *Law* relating to rights and duties as opposed to forms of procedure. ▶**substantively** *adverb* [Say SUB stun tiv or sub STAN tiv]

substation *noun* **1** an outlet or establishment subordinate to a principal station: *postal substation.* **2** a station at which the high voltage of an electrical current from a generating station is reduced so that it is suitable for supply to consumers.

substituent • *adjective* (of a group of atoms) replacing another atom or group in a compound, esp. replacing

hydrogen in an organic compound. • *noun* such a group. [Say sub STITCH oo int]

substitute • *noun* **1** a thing that is or may be used in place of another. **2 a** a person who is available or is used to perform the duties of another, esp. temporarily, such as during a holiday or illness. **b** (also **substitute teacher**) a teacher who replaces another who is unable to teach because of illness etc. • *verb* (**substitutes, substituted, substituting**) **1 a** (often foll. by *for*) use or insert (a person or thing) in place of another. **b** act as a substitute. **2** *disputed* (usu. foll. by *with*, *by*) replace (a person or thing) with another. ▶**substitution** *noun*

substrate *noun* **1** a layer of earth or rock beneath the surface. **2 a** the surface or material on which any particular organism grows. **b** the substance upon which an enzyme acts. **3** an underlying surface or foundation of a structure or development: *improper construction of the roof's substrate was to blame.* [Say SUB strate]

substratum *noun* (*plural* **substrata**) **1** a foundation or basis: *but there remained a substratum of trust, and I liked to think I knew where Sarah usually was.* **2** = SUBSTRATE 1, 2. [Say sub strat um]

substructure *noun* an underlying or supporting structure.

subsume *verb* (**subsumes, subsumed, subsuming**) (often foll. by *in* or *under*) include something in a particular group or category and not consider it separately: *the original intent of the organization was subsumed under a larger national policy.* ▶**subsumption** *noun*

subsurface • *noun* that which lies immediately below the surface of something, esp. the stratum or strata below the earth's surface. • *adjective* existing, lying, or operating beneath the surface of earth, water, etc.

subsystem *noun* a self-contained system within a larger system.

subtend *verb* **1 a** (of a line, arc, figure, etc.) form (an angle) at a particular point when its extremities are joined at that point. **b** (of an angle or chord) have bounding lines or points that meet or coincide with those of (a line or arc). **2** *Botany* (of a bract etc.) extend under so as to embrace, support, or enfold.

subterfuge *noun* **1** a deceitful statement or action resorted to in an attempt to avoid blame, justify an argument, conceal something, etc.: *she could not lie and would not resort to subterfuge.* **2** the practice or policy of employing subterfuges. [Say SUB ter fuge (FUGE rhymes with *HUGE*)]

subterranean *adjective* existing, occurring, or done under the earth's surface. [Say sub tuh RAINY in]

subtext *noun* **1** an underlying, often distinct, theme in a text, conversation, etc.: *the film is a throwback to old-fashioned Hollywood romanticism, but its subtext of healing the inner child taps right into the zeitgeist of the '90s.* **2** the underlying theme of an event or period in history: *the sociological subtext of the Cold War.*

subtitle *noun* **1** a secondary or additional title. **2** a translation or transcription of the dialogue of a movie etc. printed at the bottom of the screen.

subtitled *adjective* having a subtitle or subtitles. ▶**subtitling** *noun*

S

subtle *adjective* (**subtler, subtlest**) **1 a** difficult to perceive or detect: *a subtle distinction*. **b** operating or performed imperceptibly or secretly: *we must try a subtle approach*. **2** (of scent, colour, etc.) faint: *subtle perfume*. **3 a** capable of making fine distinctions: *a subtle mind*. **b** organized in a clever way: *a subtle strategy*. ▶ **subtlety** *noun* (*plural* **subtleties**) **subtly** *adverb* [Say SUTTLE]

subtotal *noun* the total of one part of a group of figures to be added.

subtract *verb* **1** deduct (a quantity or number) from another. **2** perform the arithmetical operation of subtraction: *learn to add and subtract*. **3** remove (a portion or thing) from another. ▶ **subtraction** *noun*

subtropical *adjective* located in or having to do with the regions adjacent to or bordering on the tropics.

subtropics *plural noun* the regions adjacent to or bordering on the tropics.

subtype *noun* a subordinate type, esp. a type included within a broader or more general type.

subunit *noun* a distinct component, esp. each of two or more polypeptide chains in a large protein.

suburb *noun* **1** a residential district lying originally just beyond or now usu. within the boundaries of a city or town. **2** (in *plural*) the outlying part of a city or town composed of such districts.

suburban *adjective* **1** of, belonging to, situated in, or carried on in the suburbs. **2** *derogatory* having characteristics regarded as typical of the residents, architecture, or life of the suburbs; perceived as lacking the excitement, diversity, culture, or sophistication of residents or life in the city. ▶ **suburbanite** *noun* **suburbanization** *noun* **suburbanize** *verb* (**suburbanizes, suburbanized, suburbanizing**)

suburban sprawl *noun* the rapid and uncontrolled expansion of suburban areas.

suburbia *noun* **1** suburbs collectively. **2** *derogatory* the social and cultural aspects of suburban life or residents.

subversion *noun* the action of undermining the power and authority of an established system or institution, such as a government: *CSIS was to protect Canada from foreign espionage, subversion, and terrorism* ◊ *this kind of ending represents a subversion of the standard narrative structure*. [Say sub VERSION]

subversive • *adjective* seeking to subvert (esp. a government): *their school credentials provided a perfect camouflage for their subversive activities*. • *noun* a subversive person; a revolutionary: *political subversives*. ▶ **subversiveness** *noun* [Say sub VER siv]

subvert *verb* undermine the power and authority of an established system or institution, such as a government: *their goal is to create panic and subvert law and order* ◊ *attempts to subvert sexual stereotypes*. [Say sub VERT]

subway *noun* **1** an esp. urban railway most parts of which are underground. **2** a subway train or car. **3** a station on a subway line.

subwoofer *noun* a loudspeaker component designed to reproduce very low bass frequencies.

sub-zero *adjective* (esp. of temperature) lower than zero.

> **WRITING TIP**
> **succeed, secede**
>
> A country or nation that officially leaves an alliance or federal union in order to become independent is said to **secede**: *In 1860, South Carolina became the first state to secede from the United States*.

succeed *verb* **1 a** accomplish one's purpose. **b** (of a plan etc.) be successful. **2** come after and take the place of: *night succeeded day* ◊ *her embarrassment was succeeded by fear*. **3** take over a throne, inheritance, office, or other position from a person: *succeeded her father as owner* ◊ *succeeded to the throne*. PHRASES **nothing succeeds like success** one success leads to others.

success *noun* **1** the accomplishment of an aim. **2** the attainment of wealth, fame, or position. **3** a thing or person that turns out well.

successful *adjective* **1** having or resulting in success. **2** having wealth or status. ▶ **successfully** *adverb*

> **WRITING TIP**
> **succession, secession**
>
> The withdrawal of a country or nation from an alliance or federal union in order to become independent is **secession**: *Quebecers were urged to vote against secession*.

succession *noun* **1 a** the process of one thing following or replacing another in order: *shots were fired in rapid succession* ◊ *the succession of the seasons*. **b** a number of people or things following one after the other: *has been plagued by a succession of injuries* ◊ *played a succession of memorable screen villains*. **2 a** the action or process of inheriting a title, office, property, etc.: *the Queen was very young at the time of her succession*. **b** the right or sequence of inheriting a position: *succession to the throne was disputed*. **c** those having such a right: *Oxford was a notorious bastion for High Churchmen of questionable loyalty to the Hanoverian succession*. **3** the process by which a plant or animal community successively gives way to another until a stable climax community is reached: *scientists have observed the very beginnings of forest succession, as seeds from who knows where invade and colonize the fresh soil*. **4 a** the rotation of crops. **b** the continuous cultivation of a crop throughout a season by successive sowings or plantings. PHRASES **in quick succession** following one another at short intervals. **in succession** one after another. ▶ **successional** *adjective*

successive *adjective* following one after another. ▶ **successively** *adverb*

successor *noun* a person or thing following another in an office, function, or position.

success story *noun* (*plural* **success stories**) **1** a rise from poverty, insignificance, etc. to success. **2** such a successful person etc.

succinct *adjective* briefly expressed; concise: *a clear and succinct analysis*. ▶ **succinctly** *adverb* **succinctness** *noun* [Say suh SINCT or suck SINCT]

Succoth *noun* = SUKKOT. [Say SOO cot]

succour • *noun* assistance, esp. in time of need: *gospel music's imagery of salvation and succour* ◊ *medicine men give succour to Malays of all walks of life*. • *verb* assist (esp. a person in danger or distress): *succouring the poor*. [Say SUCKER]

succulence *noun* the quality of food that is tender, juicy, and tasty. [Say SUCK yuh lince]

succulent • *adjective* **1** (of food) tender, juicy, and tasty: *succulent strawberries* ◊ *a succulent roast*. **2** (of a plant) having thick, fleshy leaves or stems adapted to storing water: *geraniums are succulent and can withstand dry roots*. • *noun* a succulent plant, esp. a cactus. ▶ **succulently** *adverb* [Say SUCK yuh lint]

succumb *verb* **1** be overcome (by temptation etc.). **2** die as the result of a disease, wound, etc. [Say suh KUM]

S

WRITING TIP
such

The use of **such** merely to emphasize a quality, as in *It was such a beautiful coat* or *We've had such awful weather*, is considered informal. In formal writing, this kind of construction should only be used if it is followed by a clause starting with *that*, as in *It was such a beautiful coat that Lois wanted one for herself* or *We've had such awful weather that I've hardly left the house*.

---

such • *adjective* **1** of the kind or degree in question: *such a person* ◊ *people such as these*. **2** so great; in such high degree: *had such a fright that he fainted*. **3** of a more than normal kind or degree: *such foul language*. **4** of the kind or degree already indicated, or implied by the context: *there are no such things* ◊ *such is life*. • *pronoun* **1** the thing or action in question or referred to: *such were his words*. **2 a** *Commerce* the aforesaid thing or things; it, they, or them: *those without tickets should purchase such*. **b** similar things; suchlike: *sandwiches and such*. [PHRASES] **as such** as being what has been indicated or named: *there is no theatre as such*. **such as 1** of a kind that; like: *a person such as we all admire*. **2** for example: *insects, such as moths and bees*. **3** those who: *such as don't need help*. **such as it is** despite its shortcomings. **such a one** such a person or such a thing. **such that** in such a manner that.

such-and-such • *adjective* (often foll. by *a*) of a particular kind but not needing to be specified: *on such-and-such a day*. • *noun* a person or thing of this kind.

suchlike *informal* • *adjective* of such a kind. • *noun* things, people, etc. of such a kind.

suck • *verb* **1** draw (a fluid) into the mouth. **2** perform a sucking action on (the thumb, a candy, etc.). **3** *slang* be very bad, disagreeable, or disgusting. **4** make a sucking action or sound: *sucking at his pipe*. **5** (of a pump etc.) make a gurgling or drawing sound. **6** (usu. foll. by *down*, *in*) engulf, smother, or drown in a sucking movement. **7** draw in some direction, esp. by producing a vacuum. • *noun* **1** *Cdn informal* a crybaby or sore loser; a person who refuses to participate or go along, esp. out of spite; a feeble, self-pitying person. **2** *Cdn informal* a person who behaves obsequiously to those in authority, esp. a child. [PHRASES] **suck dry 1** exhaust the contents of (a bottle etc.) by sucking. **2** exhaust (a person's sympathy, resources, etc.) as if by sucking. **suck in 1** absorb. **2** = sense 6 of *v*. **3** draw in (the cheeks, the abdomen, etc.). **4** take in; cheat or deceive. **5** involve (a person) in an activity etc., esp. against his or her will. **suck up 1** (often foll. by *to*) *informal* behave obsequiously esp. for one's own advantage. **2** absorb.

sucker • *noun* **1** a person or thing that sucks. **2** *informal* **a** a gullible or easily deceived person. **b** (foll. by *for*) a person especially susceptible to. **3** *informal* a thing not specified by name: *I can't fix the sucker!* **4** *informal* a usu. round, flat hard candy on a small stick, held in the hand and sucked. **5 a** a rubber cup etc. that adheres to a surface by suction. **b** an organ enabling an organism to cling to a surface by suction. **6** a shoot springing from the root of a plant. **7** a North American freshwater fish related to the carp, which has thick lips used to suck up food. • *verb* *informal* fool, trick. [PHRASES] **there's a sucker born every minute** gullible people are not difficult to find.

sucker punch *noun* an unexpected punch or blow. ▶ **sucker-punch** *verb* (**sucker-punches, sucker-punched, sucker-punching**)

suckle *verb* (**suckles, suckled, suckling**) **1** feed (young) from the breast or udder. **2** feed by sucking the breast etc.

suckling *noun* a child or animal which has not yet been weaned.

sucky *adjective informal* **1** wimpy or childish. **2** trying too hard to impress someone important; obsequious. **3** unpleasant.

sucrose *noun* common sugar, a carbohydrate obtained from sugar cane, sugar beet, etc. [Say SUKE roace]

suction • *noun* **1** the process of removing air or liquid from a space or container. **2 a** the production of a partial vacuum by the removal of air etc. in order to force in liquid etc. or procure adhesion. **b** the force produced by this process. • *verb* draw etc. using suction; suck.

suction cup *noun* a usu. rubber concave disc which can be made to adhere to a smooth surface by suction.

Sudanese • *adjective* of Sudan, a republic in northeastern Africa, or the Sudan region south of the Sahara. • *noun* (*plural* **Sudanese**) **1** a native, national, or inhabitant of Sudan. **2** a person of Sudanese descent. [Say soo duh NEEZ]

sudden *adjective* occurring or done unexpectedly or without warning. [PHRASES] **all of a sudden** unexpectedly; suddenly. ▶ **suddenly** *adverb* **suddenness** *noun*

sudden death *noun* an extra period or session of play to break a tie, in which the winner is the first to take the lead.

sudden infant death syndrome *noun* the unexplained death of a baby while sleeping.

suds *plural noun* **1** froth of soap and water. **2** *informal* beer. ▶ **sudsy** *adjective*

sue *verb* (**sues, sued, suing**) **1** institute legal proceedings against. **2** make application to a law court for redress. **3** (often foll. by *for*) make entreaty for: *sued for peace*.

suede *noun* **1** soft leather with a velvety surface on one side, used esp. for making clothes and shoes. **2** a woven fabric resembling suede. [Sounds like SWAYED]

suet *noun* the hard white fat on the kidneys or loins of oxen, sheep, etc., used to make puddings etc. [Say SOO it]

WRITING TIP
suffer

Although in modern English **suffer** is used almost exclusively to mean "experience something unpleasant", it is important to be aware of the word's archaic sense, "tolerate or allow", which is heard in certain set phrases that survive from the Bible or from older literature. For example, someone who does not *suffer fools gladly* is unwilling to put up with foolish people, and *suffer the little children* is part of a longer phrase, *suffer the little children to come unto me*, meaning "let the children come to me". It does not mean "the children suffer", though it is much misused, especially as a journalistic cliché, in this way.

---

suffer *verb* **1** undergo (pain, grief, damage, etc.). **2** put up with. [PHRASES] **not suffer fools gladly** refuse to be patient with people one considers foolish, stupid, etc.

sufferance *noun* [PHRASES] **on sufferance** with someone's permission or consent, which may have been granted reluctantly: *Terri was there on sufferance, as was made clear by the cool reception she received from her co-workers*.

sufferer *noun* a person who suffers, esp. one affected by a particular disease or illness: *allergy sufferers*.

suffering *noun* experience of or subjection to something bad or unpleasant: *years of pain and suffering* ◊ *weapons that cause unnecessary suffering*.

suffice *verb* (**suffices, sufficed, sufficing**) be enough or adequate: *we would like a seven-foot tree, but a shorter one will suffice* ◊ *we could raise other objections but it suffices to mention this one*. PHRASES **suffice** (**it**) **to say** I shall content myself with saying. [Say suh FICE]

sufficiency *noun* **1** an adequate amount or adequate resources: *a sufficiency of materials*. **2** the condition or quality of being sufficient; adequacy: *the judge has heard the evidence and determined its sufficiency for extradition of the suspect*. [Say suh FISH'n see]

sufficient *adjective* adequate. ▶ **sufficiently** *adverb* [Say suh FISH'nt]

suffix • *noun* (*plural* **suffixes**) a verbal element added at the end of a word, e.g. *-ation*, *-fy*, *-ing*. • *verb* (**suffixes, suffixed, suffixing**) append, esp. as a suffix.

suffocate *verb* (**suffocates, suffocated, suffocating**) **1** choke or kill by stopping breathing, esp. by pressure, fumes, etc. **2** produce a choking or breathless sensation in, esp. by excitement, terror, etc. **3** be or feel suffocated or breathless. **4** *informal* restrict, stifle: *interest on the rising national debt will suffocate the very social programs her party stands for*. ▶ **suffocating** *adjective* **suffocatingly** *adverb* **suffocation** *noun*

suffrage *noun* the right of voting in political elections: *full adult suffrage*. [Say SUFF ridge]

suffragette *noun* *hist.* a woman engaged in esp. militant activity in favour of women's suffrage, esp. in the early 20th century. [Say suffra JET]

suffragist *noun* esp. *hist.* a person who advocates the extension of the suffrage, esp. to women. [Say SUFFRA jist]

suffuse *verb* (**suffuses, suffused, suffusing**) **1** (of colour, light, etc.) fill or spread through or over something: *a perfumy fragrance suffused the air*. **2** cover or fill something with colour, light, an emotion, etc.: *the artist suffuses her view of a Paris street in deep luminous blue*. ▶ **suffusion** *noun* [Say suh FUZE, suh FUSION]

Sufi *noun* (*plural* **Sufis**) a member of any of various spiritual orders within Islam based on mysticism and meditation and a simple lifestyle involving strict self-discipline. ▶ **Sufic** *adjective* **Sufism** *noun* [Say SOOF ee, SOOF ism]

sugar • *noun* **1 a** a sweet crystalline substance obtained from various plants, esp. the sugar cane and sugar beet; sucrose. **b** foods containing esp. refined sugar. **2** any of a group of soluble usu. sweet-tasting crystalline carbohydrates found esp. in plants, e.g. glucose, and also in milk and blood. **3** *informal* darling, dear. **4** = MAPLE SUGAR. • *interjection* expressing exasperation etc. • *verb* **1** sweeten with sugar. **2** coat with sugar: *sugared almond*. **3** (also **sugar off**) make maple syrup or maple sugar by collecting and boiling maple sap.

sugar beet *noun* a kind of beet from which sugar is extracted.

sugar bush *noun* (*plural* **sugar bushes**) a grove of sugar maples.

sugar cane *noun* a perennial tropical grass with tall, stout, jointed stems from which sugar is extracted.

sugar-coat *verb* (often as **sugar-coated** *adjective*) **1** cover or enclose (food) in sugar. **2** make superficially attractive: *sugar-coated the truth*. ▶ **sugar-coating** *noun*

sugar daddy *noun* (*plural* **sugar daddies**) *slang* an elderly man who lavishes gifts on a young person esp. in return for sex.

sugariness *noun* **1** sweetness. **2** the quality of something that is excessively emotional or sentimental.

sugaring *noun* **1** (also **sugaring off**) the making of maple syrup or maple sugar by collecting and boiling the sap from esp. the sugar maple. **2** a method of removing hair by applying to the skin a sticky sugar mixture, which is then peeled off together with the hair.

sugarless *adjective* containing no sugar.

sugar maple *noun* a North American maple that produces a sap from which maple sugar and maple syrup are made.

sugar pie *noun* *Cdn* esp. (*Que.*) an open-faced or lattice-topped pie with a filling of brown or maple sugar mixed with cream and baked.

sugar plum *noun* *archaic* a small round hard candy.

sugar shack *noun* *Cdn* **1** a building in which maple sap is boiled in making maple syrup or sugar. **2** esp. *Que.* a usu. small establishment in a sugar bush serving maple-flavoured dishes and other traditional fare.

sugary *adjective* **1 a** containing esp. a high proportion of sugar. **b** resembling sugar. **2** excessively sweet or esp. sentimental. **3** falsely sweet or pleasant: *sugary compliments*.

suggest *verb* **1** propose. **2 a** cause (an idea, memory, association, etc.) to present itself. **b** hint at: *his behaviour suggests guilt*. PHRASES **suggest itself** (of an idea etc.) come into the mind. [Say JEST or sug JEST]

suggestion *noun* **1** the action of putting forward a plan for consideration: *at my suggestion, the museum held an exhibition of her work*. **2 a** a theory, plan, etc., suggested: *made a helpful suggestion*. **b** something that implies or indicates a certain fact or situation: *there is no suggestion that he was involved in any wrongdoing*. **3** a slight hint: *a suggestion of garlic*. **4 a** the action or process of calling up an idea or thought in someone's mind by associating it with other things: *most advertising uses the power of suggestion*. **b** the influencing of a person to accept an idea, belief, or impulse uncritically, esp. as a technique in hypnosis or other therapies. [Say suh JESTION or sug JESTION]

suggestive *adjective* **1** causing someone to think of something: *music that is suggestive of warm summer days*. **2** (esp. of a remark, joke, etc.) making people think about sex. ▶ **suggestively** *adverb* **suggestiveness** *noun* [Say suh JESTIVE or sug JESTIVE]

suicidal *adjective* **1** deeply unhappy or depressed and likely to commit suicide: *far from being suicidal, he was clearly enjoying life*. **2** likely to lead to suicide: *I began to take his suicidal tendencies seriously*. **3** likely to have a disastrously damaging effect on oneself or one's interests: *a suicidal career move*. ▶ **suicidally** *adverb* [Say soo uh SIDE 'll]

suicide *noun* **1 a** the intentional killing of oneself. **b** a person who commits suicide. **2** a self-destructive action or course: *political suicide*. **3** (as an *adjective*) *Military* designating a highly dangerous or deliberately suicidal operation etc.: *a suicide mission*. [Say SOO uh side]

suicide squeeze *noun* a play designed to allow a baserunner to score from third base on a bunt, in which the runner breaks towards the plate just as the pitch has left the pitcher's hand, before the bunt has been successfully completed.

sui generis *adjective* of its own kind; unique: *nobody tried to imitate Paulson, who was regarded as sui generis*. [Say sooey JENNA riss]

suit • *noun* **1 a** a set of outer clothes of matching material, consisting usu. of a jacket, pants, and sometimes a waistcoat or a jacket and skirt. **b** a set of clothes worn for a particular activity or on a particular occasion: *bathing suit*. **2** any of the four sets (esp. spades, hearts, diamonds, clubs) into which a pack of cards is divided. **3** a lawsuit. **4** *slang* a business

executive. **5** (usu. foll. by *of*) a set of armour, sails, etc. **6** the process of trying to win a woman's affection, esp. with a view to marriage: *he could not compete with John's charms in Marian's eyes and his suit came to nothing*. • *verb* **1** go well with (a person's figure, features, character, etc.). **2** meet the demands or requirements of; satisfy; agree with: *can change the date if it doesn't suit*. **3** make fitting or appropriate; adapt: *suited her style to her audience*. PHRASES **suit the action to the word** carry out a promise or threat at once. **suit oneself 1** do as one chooses. **2** find something that satisfies one. **suit up** dress in clothing designed for a particular activity.

suitability *noun* the condition of being right or appropriate for a person, purpose, or situation: *Lena had to assess the suitability of candidates for the job*.

suitable *adjective* (usu. foll. by *to, for*) well fitted for the purpose; appropriate. ▶ **suitably** *adverb*

suitcase *noun* a usu. oblong case for carrying clothes etc., having a handle and a flat lid. PHRASES **live out of a suitcase** live temporarily with one's belongings still packed, esp. when travelling.

suite *noun* **1 a** a set of rooms in a hotel etc. for use by one person or group of people. **b** a set of furniture, usu. a sofa and armchairs etc., or table and chairs of the same design. **2** = APARTMENT 1a. **3 a** a set of instrumental compositions to be played in succession. **b** a set of selected pieces from an opera, musical, ballet, etc., arranged to be played as one instrumental work. **4** a set of people in attendance. [Say SWEET]

suited *adjective* appropriate; well fitted.

suitor *noun* **1** a man seeking to marry a specified woman. **2** a plaintiff or petitioner in a lawsuit. **3** a prospective buyer of a business or corporation. [Say SOOTER]

sukiyaki *noun* a Japanese dish of sliced meat simmered with vegetables and sauce. [Say soo kee OCKY]

Sukkot *noun* the Jewish autumn harvest and thanksgiving festival commemorating the sheltering of the Israelites in the wilderness. [Say SOO cot]

sulfate = SULPHATE.

sulfur etc. = SULPHUR etc.

sulk • *verb* indulge in a period of sullen esp. resentful silence or aloofness from others. • *noun* a period of sulking: *has been in a sulk* ◊ *got the sulks*.

sulkily *adverb* in a sullen or bad-tempered manner.

sulky • *adjective* (**sulkier, sulkiest**) sullen, morose, or silent, esp. from resentment or ill temper. • *noun* (*plural* **sulkies**) a light two-wheeled horse-drawn vehicle for one, esp. used in harness racing.

sullen *adjective* **1** morose, resentful, sulky. **2** (of a sky or the weather) dark and gloomy: *a sullen grey sky*. ▶ **sullenly** *adverb* **sullenness** *noun*

sully *verb* (**sullies, sullied, sullying**) **1** disgrace or tarnish (a person's reputation or character, a victory, etc.): *do not wish to sully the memory of the victims*. **2** dirty: *dust from surrounding hills sullied the ice surface*.

sulphate *noun* a salt or ester of sulphuric acid.

sulphide *noun* a binary compound of sulphur.

sulphite *noun* any of various substances containing sulphur, found typically in foods and wines.

sulphur *noun* **1 a** a pale yellow non-metallic element, burning with a blue flame and a suffocating smell, and used in making gunpowder, matches, and sulphuric acid, and in the treatment of skin diseases. **b** (as an *adjective*) like or containing sulphur. **2** the material of which hellfire and lightning were believed to consist. **3** a type of butterfly with predominantly yellow wings.

sulphur dioxide *noun* a colourless pungent gas formed by burning sulphur in air, used in making sulphuric acid and as a food preservative.

sulphuric *adjective* containing hexavalent sulphur. [Say sul FYOOR ick]

sulphuric acid *noun* a dense oily colourless highly acid and corrosive fluid much used in the chemical industry.

sulphurous *adjective* **1 a** relating to or suggestive of sulphur, esp. in colour: *a sulphurous yellow light*. **b** suggestive of burning sulphur, hellfire, etc.; fiery: *his sulphurous anger warmed the room*. **2** *Chemistry* containing tetravalent sulphur. [Say SUL fruss]

Sulpician *noun* a member of a Roman Catholic society of priests founded in Paris in 1641 and established in New France in 1657, concerned esp. with the training of priests. [Say sool PISH'n]

sultan *noun* **1 a** a Muslim sovereign. **b** (**the Sultan**) *hist.* the sultan of Turkey. **2** an absolute ruler. [Say SUL tin]

sultana *noun* (*plural* **sultanas**) **1** a seedless raisin used in puddings, cakes, etc. **2** the mother, wife, concubine, or daughter of a sultan. [Say sul TANA]

sultanate *noun* **1** the rank or position of a sultan. **2** an area of land that is ruled over by a sultan. **3** the period of time during which someone is a sultan. [Say SUL tuh nate]

sultry *adjective* (**sultrier, sultriest**) **1** (of the atmosphere or the weather) hot and humid. **2** (of a person, character, etc.) passionate; sensual. [Say SUL tree]

sum *noun* **1** the total amount resulting from the addition of two or more items, facts, ideas, feelings, etc.: *the sum of two and three is five* ◊ *the sum of their objections is this*. **2** a particular amount of money: *paid a large sum for it*. **3** an arithmetical problem. PHRASES **in sum** in brief. **sum up** (**sums up, summed up, summing up**) **1** (esp. of a judge) recapitulate or review the evidence in a case etc. **2** form or express an idea of the character of (a person, situation, etc.). **3** collect into or express as a total or whole.

sumac *noun* (also **sumach**) **1** a shrub or tree with cone-shaped clusters of reddish fruits. **2** the dried and ground leaves of this used in tanning and dyeing. [Say SOO mack]

Sumatran • *adjective* of Sumatra, a large island of Indonesia, or its people or language. • *noun* **1 a** a native or inhabitant of Sumatra. **b** a person of Sumatran descent. **2** the language of Sumatra. [Say soo MAW trin]

Sumerian • *adjective* of or relating to the early and non-Semitic element in ancient Babylonian civilization. • *noun* **1** a member of the early non-Semitic people of ancient Babylonia. **2** this language. [Say soo MERRY in]

summa cum laude *adverb & adjective* (of a degree, diploma, etc.) of the highest standard; with the highest distinction: *graduated summa cum laude from McGill*. [Say sooma koom LOUD ay]

summarily *adverb* briefly or suddenly, without spending time on formalities or needless details: *students caught vandalizing school property will be summarily suspended*. [Say suh MERRA lee]

summarize *verb* (**summarizes, summarized, summarizing**) make or be a summary of; sum up.

summary • *noun* (*plural* **summaries**) a brief account. • *adjective* **1** dispensing with needless details or formalities: *a summary report*. **2** (of a trial etc.) without the customary legal formalities: *summary justice*.

summary conviction *noun* a conviction made by a judge or magistrates without a jury.

summary conviction offence *noun* (also **summary offence**) *Cdn* a relatively minor criminal

S

offence tried by a magistrate and without a jury or preliminary hearing (compare INDICTABLE OFFENCE).

summation noun a summary of what has been done or said: *a summation of their activities*. [Say suh MAY sh'n]

summer • noun **1** the warmest season of the year, in the northern hemisphere from June to August and in the southern hemisphere from December to February. **2** the period from the summer solstice to the autumnal equinox. **3** the hot weather typical of summer. **4** (as an *adjective*) characteristic of or suitable for summer: *summer clothes*. • verb (usu. foll. by *at*, *in*) pass the summer.

summerfallow esp. *Cdn* • noun agricultural land left uncultivated in the summer to allow moisture and nutrient levels to recover. • verb lay (agricultural land) fallow during the summer.

summer house noun **1** a light building in a garden, park, etc. used for sitting in in fine weather. **2** a secondary residence occupied during the summer.

summer kitchen noun an extra kitchen adjoining or separate from a house, used for cooking in hot weather.

> **SPELL CHECK**
> **somersault** ✓ABC
>
> An acrobatic headfirst tumble is a **somersault**.

summer school noun **1** a course of remedial or accelerating classes held in the summer. **2** a course of classes etc. held during the summer.

summer solstice noun the solstice at midsummer, at the time of the longest day, about June 21 in the northern hemisphere and Dec. 22 in the southern hemisphere.

summer squash noun see SQUASH noun 2.

summer student noun *Cdn* an esp. university student working at a job for the summer.

summertime noun the season or period of summer.

> **SPELL CHECK**
> **summery, summary** ✓ABC
>
> A brief description of something is a **summary**.

summery adjective like or typical of summer.

summit noun **1** the highest point, esp. of a mountain; the apex. **2** the highest degree of power, ambition, success, etc. **3** (also **summit meeting, talks,** etc.) a discussion esp. between heads of government.

summiteer noun a participant in a summit meeting.

summon verb **1** call upon to appear, esp. as a defendant or witness in a law court. **2** call upon: *summoned her to assist*. **3** call together for a meeting or some other purpose: *summoned the members to attend*. **4** (often foll. by *up*) gather (courage, strength, energy, etc.): *summoned up her strength for the task*.

summons • noun (plural **summonses**) **1** an authoritative or urgent call to attend on some occasion or do something. **2 a** a call to appear before a judge or magistrate. **b** the writ containing such a summons. • verb (**summonses, summonsed, summonsing**) esp. *Law* serve with a summons.

sumo noun a Japanese form of wrestling in which wrestlers with immense bulky bodies try to force one another out of a ring (also as an *adjective: sumo wrestler*). [Say SOO moe]

sump noun a pit etc. in which superfluous liquid collects in a basement, mine, machine, etc.

sump pump noun a pump for removing waste water etc. from a sump.

sumptuous adjective lavish, magnificent: *we dined in sumptuous surroundings* ◊ *the interior is decorated in sumptuous reds and golds*. ▶ **sumptuously** adverb **sumptuousness** noun

sum total noun the total amount resulting from the addition of two or more items, facts, ideas, feelings, etc.

Sun. abbreviation Sunday.

sun • noun **1 a** the star around which the earth orbits and from which it receives light and warmth. **b** any similar star in the universe with or without planets. **2** the light or warmth received from the sun. **3** *literary* a person or thing regarded as a source of glory, radiance, etc. • verb (**suns, sunned, sunning**) **1** bask in the sun. **2** expose to the sun. PHRASES **beneath** (or **under**) **the sun** anywhere in the world. **in the sun** exposed to the sun's rays.

sun-baked adjective dried or hardened or baked from the heat of the sun.

sunbathe verb (**sunbathes, sunbathed, sunbathing**) bask in the sun, esp. to tan the body. ▶ **sunbather** noun

sunbeam noun a ray of sunlight.

sunbelt noun a strip of territory receiving a high amount of sunshine, esp. (**the Sunbelt**) the region stretching from California to Florida.

sunblock noun a cream or lotion for protecting the skin from the sun.

sunburn • noun inflammation of the skin caused by overexposure to the sun. • verb suffer from sunburn. ▶ **sunburned** adjective (also **sunburnt**)

sunburst • noun **1** something resembling the sun and its rays, e.g. an ornament, brooch, etc. **2** a sudden burst of sunshine, as from the sun appearing suddenly from behind clouds. **3** *Cdn* a trimming of fur around the hood of a parka. • adjective **1** *Cdn* (of a parka or parka hood) trimmed with a sunburst. **2** resembling a sunburst in design, colour, etc.

suncatcher noun an object made esp. of stained glass or coloured plastic hung in a window to sparkle in or reflect incoming sunlight.

sundae noun a dish of ice cream topped with sauce, fruit, whipped cream, nuts, etc.

sun dance noun an annual ceremony held at midsummer by some Plains Aboriginal peoples, marked by several days of fasting, dancing, and induced visions.

> **SPELL CHECK**
> **Sunday, sundae** ✓ABC
>
> The dessert is a **sundae**.

Sunday • noun the first day of the week, a Christian holiday and day of worship. • adverb **1** on Sunday. **2** (**Sundays**) on Sundays; each Sunday.

Sunday best noun a person's best clothes, kept for use on Sundays and special occasions.

Sunday school noun **1** a school for the religious instruction of children on Sundays. **2** the members of such a school.

sundeck noun a terrace or balcony positioned to catch the sun.

sunder verb *archaic* or *literary* separate: *such an action would split the party and sunder its links with its business supporters*.

sundew noun a small insect-consuming bog plant, which has rosettes of leaves covered with hairs that secrete a sticky fluid used to trap insects.

sundial noun an instrument showing time by the shadow of a pointer cast by the sun on to a graduated disc.

sun dog noun a bright spot, usu. one of two, on either side of the sun and coloured like the rainbow, caused by reflection of light by atmospheric ice crystals.

S

sundown *noun* sunset.

sun-drenched *adjective* **1** illuminated by sunshine. **2** (of a place) having very sunny weather.

sundress *noun* (*plural* **sundresses**) a sleeveless dress with a low neck and back, worn in hot weather.

sun-dried *adjective* dried by the sun, not by artificial heat.

sundry • *adjective* various; several: *sundry items.* • *noun* (*plural* **sundries**) (in *plural*) items or oddments not mentioned individually. PHRASES **all and sundry** everyone. [Say SUN dree]

sunfish *noun* (*plural* **sunfish** or **sunfishes**) **1** a large, almost spherical ocean fish with a tall dorsal fin and a very short tail. **2** any of various small, deep-bodied, North American freshwater fishes, including the largemouth and smallmouth bass and the pumpkinseed.

sunflower *noun* a very tall North American plant of the daisy family, bearing very large showy golden-rayed flowers and grown also for its edible seeds and oil.

sung *past participle of* SING.

sunglasses *plural noun* glasses tinted to protect the eyes from sunlight or glare.

sun god *noun* the sun worshipped as a deity.

sunk *past and past participle of* SINK.

sunken *adjective* **1** that has been sunk. **2** beneath the surface. **3** (of the eyes, cheeks, etc.) hollow. **4** (of a room) placed on a lower level than the surrounding area.

sunker *noun* Cdn (Nfld) a reef or rocky shoal.

sun-kissed *adjective* warmed or affected by the sun.

sun lamp *noun* a lamp giving ultraviolet rays for an artificial suntan, therapy, etc.

sunless *adjective* without any sun or sunlight: *a sunless sky ◊ three straight sunless days*.

sunlight *noun* light from the sun.

sunlike *adjective* resembling the sun.

sunlit *adjective* illuminated by sunlight: *the sunlit water*.

Sunna *noun* a traditional portion of Muslim law based on Muhammad's words or acts, accepted (with the Koran) as authoritative by Muslims. [Say SOON uh]

Sunni • *noun* **1** one of the two main branches of Islam, commonly described as orthodox, differing from the Shia in its understanding of the Sunna and in its rejection of Ali as Muhammad's first successor. **2** (*plural* **Sunni** or **Sunnis**) an adherent of this branch of Islam. • *adjective* of or relating to Sunni. [Say SOONY]

sunnily *adverb* in a bright, cheery, or optimistic way.

sunniness *noun* **1** a bright, cheery, or optimistic manner. **2** the state or condition of being exposed to or illuminated by sunshine.

sunny *adjective* (**sunnier, sunniest**) **1 a** bright with sunlight. **b** exposed to or warmed by the sun. **2** cheery, bright, and optimistic: *a sunny disposition*.

sun porch *noun* (*plural* **sun porches**) an enclosed porch with more windows than exterior walls, designed to receive sunlight.

sun protection factor *noun* a number indicating the effectiveness of sunscreens etc.

sunrise *noun* **1** the sun's rising at dawn. **2** the coloured sky associated with this. **3** the time at which sunrise occurs.

sunroof *noun* a sliding part of the roof of a car that can be opened to let in air and sunlight.

sunroom *noun* a room with large windows, designed to receive sunlight.

sunscreen *noun* a cream or lotion rubbed on to the skin to protect it from the sun.

sunset *noun* **1** the sun's setting in the evening. **2** the coloured sky associated with this. **3** the time at which

sunset occurs. **4** the declining period of something. **5** (as an *adjective*) designating a provision under which an agency or program is to be disbanded or terminated at the end of a fixed period unless formally renewed: *sunset clause*.

sunshade *noun* something that provides shade, as an awning or parasol.

sunshine *noun* **1 a** the light of the sun. **b** an area lit by the sun. **c** the warmth of the sun. **2** fine weather. **3** cheerfulness; joy. **4** informal a form of address. ▶ **sunshiny** *adjective*

sunspot *noun* one of the dark patches, changing in shape and size and lasting for varying periods, observed on the sun's surface.

sunstroke *noun* acute prostration or collapse from the excessive heat of the sun.

suntan *noun* a brown colour of the skin caused by exposure to the sun. ▶ **suntanned** *adjective*

suntanning *noun*

sun-up *noun* sunrise.

sunward *adjective* & *adverb* toward or facing the sun. ▶ **sunwards** *adverb*

sup • *verb* (**sups, supped, supping**) **1** take (soup, tea, etc.) by sips or spoonfuls. **2** (usu. foll. by *off, on*) archaic eat supper. • *noun* a sip of liquid.

super • *adjective* **1** informal exceptional; splendid. **2** of or to an extreme or the highest degree, power, etc. • *noun* informal **1** a superintendent. **2** an actor who appears on stage but does not speak. • *adverb* informal extremely; excessively.

super- *combining form* forming nouns, adjectives, and verbs, meaning: **1** above, beyond, or over in place or time or conceptually: *superstructure ◊ superimpose*. **2** to a great or extreme degree: *superhuman*. **3** extra good or large of its kind: *supertanker*. **4** of a higher kind, esp. in names of classificatory divisions: *superfamily*.

superannuated *adjective* **1** (of a person) retired with a pension. **2** dismissed or discarded as too old for use, work, etc. [Say super ANYOO ate id]

superannuation *noun* **1** a pension paid to a retired person. **2** a regular payment made towards this by an employed person. [Say super anyoo AY sh'n]

superb *adjective* **1** excellent; fine. **2** of the most impressive or majestic kind. ▶ **superbly** *adverb* [Say soo PERB]

Super Bowl *noun* proprietary the annual deciding game between the champions of the National Football Conference and of the American Football Conference.

SPELL CHECK **supersede**	
Warning: **supersede** is spelled with an *s*, not with a *c*.	

supercharge *verb* (**supercharges, supercharged, supercharging**) **1** charge (the atmosphere etc.) with energy, emotion, etc. **2** use a supercharger on (an engine). ▶ **supercharged** *adjective*

supercharger *noun* a device supplying air or fuel to an internal combustion engine at above normal pressure to increase efficiency.

supercilious *adjective* assuming an air of contemptuous indifference or superiority: *Henry was able to shrug off their supercilious comments about his heritage*. ▶ **superciliously** *adverb* **superciliousness** *noun* [Say super SILLY us]

supercomputer *noun* a powerful computer which can deal with complex problems. ▶ **supercomputing** *noun*

superconductivity *noun* the property of zero electrical resistance in some substances at very low

S

temperatures. ▶**superconducting** *adjective*
superconductor *noun*

supercontinent *noun* each of several large land masses thought to have divided to form the present continents in the geological past.

supercool • *verb* **1** cool (a liquid) below its freezing point without solidification or crystallization. **2** (of a liquid) be cooled in this way. • *adjective slang* very cool, relaxed, fine, etc.

supercritical *adjective* of or relating to a mass of radioactive material in which the rate of a chain reaction increases over time.

super-duper *adjective informal* exceptional, super.

superego *noun* (*plural* **superegos**) *Psychology* the part of the mind that acts as a conscience and responds to social rules. [Say SUPER ego]

superfamily *noun* (*plural* **superfamilies**) a taxonomic category between family and order.

superficial *adjective* **1** of or on the surface; lacking depth. **2** rapid; not in detail: *a superficial examination*. **3** apparent but not real: *a superficial resemblance*. **4** (esp. of a person) having no depth of character or knowledge. **5** lacking substance or profundity: *the show had a very superficial plot*. **6** not involving a profound or serious issue: *superficial differences*. ▶**superficiality** *noun* (*plural* **superficialities**). **superficially** *adverb* [Say super FISH'll, super fishy ALA tee]

superfine *adjective* **1** in very small granules etc.: *superfine sugar*. **2** *Commerce* of extra quality.

superfluous *adjective* more than is needed or wanted; unnecessary: *she gave him a look that made words superfluous*. [Say soo PUR flu us]

supergiant *noun* a very large and bright star.

super giant slalom *noun* *Skiing* (also *informal* **super G**) a downhill event with a longer course and wider turns than a giant slalom.

superglue • *noun* any of various adhesives with an exceptional bonding capability. • *verb* (**superglues**, **superglued**, **supergluing**) stick with superglue.

supergroup *noun* **1** a group made up of several related groups. **2 a** an exceptionally talented or successful rock group. **b** a rock group formed by star musicians from different groups.

superheat *verb* **1** heat (a liquid) above its boiling point without vaporization. **2** heat (a vapour) above its boiling point: *superheated steam*. **3** heat to a very high temperature. ▶**superheater** *noun*

superhero *noun* (*plural* **superheroes**) a person or fictional character with extraordinary heroic attributes.

superhighway *noun* a divided highway with two or more lanes in each direction.

superhuman *adjective* **1** beyond normal human capability: *required a superhuman effort*. **2** higher than human: *a superhuman being*. ▶**superhumanly** *adverb*

superimpose *verb* (**superimposes**, **superimposed**, **superimposing**) lay (a thing) on something else: *the number will appear on the screen, superimposed on a flashing button* ◊ *different stone tools were found in superimposed layers*. ▶**superimposition** *noun* [Say super im POZE, super im POSITION]

superintend *verb* **1** be responsible for the management or arrangement of (an activity etc.). **2** superintend (an institution, district, etc.). ▶**superintendence** *noun*

superintendent *noun* **1 a** a person who superintends. **b** a director of an institution etc. **2** (on some Canadian municipal police forces) an officer ranking above staff inspector. **3** (in the OPP, Royal Newfoundland Constabulary, and RCMP) an officer ranking above inspector. **4** a caretaker, esp. of an apartment building. **5** the chief administrator of a school division.

superior • *adjective* **1** in a higher position; of higher rank: *my superior officer* ◊ *a superior court of law*. **2 a** above the average in quality etc.: *superior apartments*. **b** having or showing a high opinion of oneself: *a superior smile* ◊ *he always looks so superior*. **3** better or greater in some respect: *superior intelligence* ◊ *this model is technically superior to its competitors* ◊ *the enemy won because of their superior numbers*. • *noun* **1** a person superior to another in rank, character, etc. **2** the head of a monastery or other religious institution: *Mother Superior*.

superior court *noun* (in Canada) the supreme court or courts of a province.

superiority *noun* the state of being superior.

superiority complex *noun* (*plural* **superiority complexes**) an undue conviction of one's own superiority to others.

superlative • *adjective* **1** of the highest quality or degree: *will bring his formidable retail knowledge and superlative marketing track record to bear on the topic*. **2** (of an adjective or adverb) expressing the highest or a very high degree of a quality (e.g. *bravest*, *most fiercely*). • *noun* **1** *Grammar* **a** the superlative expression or form of an adjective or adverb. **b** a word in the superlative. **2** (usu. in *plural*) an expression of abundant praise: *the critics ran out of superlatives to describe her*. ▶**superlatively** *adverb* [Say soo PUR luh tiv]

superman *noun* (*plural* **supermen**) **1** an ideal superior man of the future who achieves domination through integrity and creativity. **2** *informal* a man of exceptional strength or ability.

supermarket *noun* a large store selling foods, household goods, etc.

superminister *noun* *Cdn* a cabinet minister with responsibility for an important portfolio or a number of related portfolios.

supermodel *noun* a highly-paid model employed in high-profile glamour modelling.

supermom *noun informal* a mother who fulfills all the duties of motherhood superlatively, esp. one who is also employed outside of the home.

supernatural • *adjective* attributed to or thought to reveal some force above the laws of nature. • *noun* supernatural, occult, or magical forces, effects, etc. ▶**supernaturalism** *noun* **supernaturally** *adverb*

supernova *noun* (*plural* **supernovas** or **supernovae**) a star that suddenly increases very greatly in brightness because of an explosion ejecting most of its mass. [Say SUPER no vuh; for SUPERNOVAE say SUPER no vee]

supernumerary • *adjective* **1** in excess of the normal number: *supernumerary teeth*. **2** (of a person) engaged for extra work. **3** (of an actor) appearing on stage but not speaking. • *noun* (*plural* **supernumeraries**) **1** an extra or unwanted person or thing: *the person who had been the leader found himself a mere supernumerary*. **2** a supernumerary actor. **3** a person engaged for extra work. [Say super NUMER airy]

superpose *verb* (**superposes**, **superposed**, **superposing**) esp. *Math* place (a thing or a geometric figure) on or above something else, esp. so as to coincide. ▶**superposition** *noun*

superpower *noun* a state with supreme power and influence, esp. the US and, formerly, the USSR.

supersaturated *adjective* (of a solution) concentrated beyond saturation point. ▶**supersaturation** *noun*

superscript • *noun* a character, number, or symbol written or printed above the line and usu. to the right of another character (*compare* SUBSCRIPT *noun*). • *adjective*

S

written or printed above the line, esp. *Math* (of a symbol) written above and to the right of another.

supersede *verb* (**supersedes**, **superseded**, **superseding**) take the place of (a person or thing previously in authority or use): *the older models have now been superseded ◊ the rights of criminals supersede the rights of victims in this country.* [Say super SEED]

supersonic *adjective* designating or having a speed greater than that of sound. ▶ **supersonically** *adverb*

superstar *noun* an extremely famous or renowned actor, film star, musician, etc. ▶ **superstardom** *noun*

superstation *noun* a television station using satellite technology to broadcast over a very large area.

superstition *noun* **1** belief not based on reason, esp. as based on fear of or reverence for the supernatural. **2** an irrational fear of the unknown or mysterious. **3** a practice, opinion, or religion based on these. ▶ **superstitious** *adjective* **superstitiously** *adverb*

superstore *noun* **1** a large supermarket selling a wide range of goods. **2** a very large store selling a particular type of merchandise: *appliance superstore.*

superstructure *noun* **1** the part of a building above its foundations. **2** a structure built on top of something else. **3** the constructions above a ship's upper deck.

supertwist *adjective* designating varieties of liquid crystal display used in portable computers, in which, to change state, the plane of polarized light passing through the display is rotated by at least 180 degrees.

super VGA *abbreviation* see SVGA.

supervise *verb* (**supervises**, **supervised**, **supervising**) **1** superintend, oversee the execution of. **2** oversee the actions or work of. ▶ **supervision** *noun*

supervisor *noun* **supervisory** *adjective*

superwoman *noun* (*plural* **superwomen**) *informal* a woman of exceptional strength or ability.

supine *adjective* **1** lying face upwards (*compare* PRONE 1a). **2** having the front or ventral part upwards; (of the hand) with the palm upwards. [Say SOO pine]

supper *noun* **1** the evening meal, often the main meal of the day. **2** a light evening meal. **3** an evening social event, esp. one intended to raise money, at which a meal is served. PHRASES **sing for one's supper** do something in return for a benefit.

suppertime *noun* the time of day at which supper is, or is customarily, served.

supplant *verb* dispossess and take the place of, esp. by underhand means: *the socialist society which Marx believed would eventually supplant capitalism.* [Say suh PLANT]

supple *adjective* (**suppler**, **supplest**) **1** flexible, easily bent. **2** capable of or demonstrating easy or graceful movement. ▶ **suppleness** *noun*

supplement • *noun* **1** a thing or part added to remedy deficiencies: *dietary supplement.* **2** a part added to a book etc. to provide further information. **3** a separate section, esp. a colour magazine, added to a newspaper or periodical. **4** an additional charge payable for an extra service or facility. **5** *Math* the amount by which an angle is less than 180° (*compare* COMPLEMENT *noun* 4). • *verb* provide a supplement for. ▶ **supplemental** *adjective* **supplementation** *noun*

supplementary *adjective* forming or serving as a supplement; additional.

supplicant *noun* a person making a humble plea to someone in a position of power or authority: *lived as humbled supplicants among richer relatives ◊ supplicants for pardon.*

supplicate *verb* (**supplicates**, **supplicated**, **supplicating**) ask humbly. [Say SUP luh kate]

supplication *noun* the act of asking for something with a very humble request or prayer: *she knelt in supplication ◊ listened impatiently to their supplications.*

supplier *noun* a person or company that supplies goods: *a leading supplier of computers in Canada.*

supply[1] • *verb* (**supplies**, **supplied**, **supplying**) **1** provide. **2** meet or make up for (a deficiency or need etc.). **3** fill (a vacancy, place, etc.) as a substitute. • *noun* (*plural* **supplies**) **1** the action of providing what is needed: *a contract for the supply of steel.* **2** a stock, store, amount, etc., of something provided or obtainable. **3** (in *plural*) **a** food or other materials necessary for maintenance or for a specific activity. **b** the collected provisions and equipment for an army, expedition, etc. **c** a grant of money by Parliament for the costs of government (also as an *adjective*: *supply bill*). **4** (often as an *adjective*) a person, esp. a teacher or member of the clergy, acting as a temporary substitute for another: *supply teacher.* PHRASES **in short supply** available in limited quantity. [Say suh PLY]

supply[2] *adverb* in a supple manner. [Say SUPPLE ee]

supply and demand *noun* the amount of a product available and needed, as factors regulating its price.

supply line *noun* **1** a transportation or communication line along which necessary supplies are delivered. **2** a conduit etc. through which something is supplied.

supply-side *adjective* denoting a policy of low taxation and other incentives to produce goods and invest: *supply-side economics.* ▶ **supply-sider** *noun*

supply teacher *noun* *Cdn & Brit.* = SUBSTITUTE TEACHER (*see* SUBSTITUTE 2b).

support • *verb* **1** carry all or part of the weight of. **2** provide with a home and the necessities of life. **3** confirm or back up. **4** give assistance, encouragement, or approval to. **5** endure, tolerate: *can no longer support the noise.* **6** maintain or represent (a part or character) adequately. **7** contribute to the funds of (an institution). **8** (of a computer, operating system, etc.) allow the use or operation of (a program, device, etc.). **9** provide ongoing technical assistance for (a computer system etc.) once it is installed. • *noun* **1** the action of holding something firmly in position or preventing it from falling: *taped my ankle to give it some support ◊ clutched her arm for support.* **2** a person or thing that bears the weight of something or provides help in trouble: *make sure your shoes have arch supports ◊ she was a great support to me when my husband died.* **3** encouragement, sympathy, financial aid etc. given esp. to a person undergoing difficulties: *she's been through a bad time and needs our support ◊ their policies enjoy widespread support ◊ the ballet could not survive without the support of its donors.* **4** money paid to a divorced or separated person to his or her former spouse and/or their children. **5** technical help given to the user of a computer or other product. • *adjective* (of hosiery) reinforced with elastic fibres in order to support the muscles and veins of the legs. PHRASES **in support of** giving assistance to or showing approval of. ▶ **supportable** *adjective*

supporter *noun* **1** a person or thing that supports. **2** *Cdn* a person who pays education taxes to a usu. specified school system: *a separate school supporter.* **3** (also **athletic supporter**) = JOCKSTRAP.

support group *noun* a group of people who meet on a regular basis to provide mutual support by discussing a shared problem or experience.

supporting *adjective* **1** (of an actor etc.) having an important part but not the leading one: *the movie featured Kelly Baxter in a supporting role.* **2** helping to confirm: *there was a wealth of supporting evidence.* **3** carrying weight: *a supporting wall.*

supportive *adjective* providing support or encouragement. ▶ **supportiveness** *noun*

S

support staff *noun* employees providing esp. clerical and administrative assistance.

suppose *verb* (**supposes, supposed, supposing**) **1** assume, esp. in default of knowledge: *I suppose they will return.* **2** take as a possibility or hypothesis: *let's suppose you are right.* **3** as a formula of proposal: *suppose we go to the party.* **4** (of a theory or result etc.) require as a condition: *design in creation supposes a creator.* **5** in the circumstances that; if: *supposing we stay.* PHRASES **I suppose so** an expression of hesitant agreement.

supposed *adjective* **1** used to show doubt about a claim, statement, description etc. that may not be true or correct, though generally accepted as being so: *this is the opinion of the supposed experts ◊ when did this supposed accident happen?* **2** generally accepted or believed to be so: *is generally supposed to be wealthy.* **3 a** expected or required: *was supposed to write to you.* **b** allowed: *you are not supposed to go in there.* **4** intended: *what is that supposed to mean? ◊ we're not supposed to understand.*
▶ **supposedly** *adverb*

supposition *noun* an uncertain belief: *working on the supposition that his death was murder ◊ their outrage was based on supposition and hearsay.* [Say suppa ZISH'n]

suppository *noun* (*plural* **suppositories**) a medical preparation in the form of a cone, cylinder, etc., to be inserted into the rectum or vagina to melt. [Say suh POZZA tory or suh POZZA tree]

suppress *verb* (**suppresses, suppressed, suppressing**) **1** end the activity or existence of, esp. forcibly. **2** prevent (information, etc.) from being seen, heard, or known. **3** stop (a cough, sneeze, etc.). **4** prevent (a feeling, reaction, etc.) from being expressed. **5** *Psychology* keep out of one's consciousness.
▶ **suppression** *noun* **suppressive** *adjective*
suppressor *noun* [Say suh PRESS]

suppressant *noun* a suppressing or restraining substance: *cough suppressant.* [Say suh PRESS int]

suppurating *adjective* forming pus; festering: *bandaged the suppurating sores.* [Say SUP yuh rating]

supranational *adjective* involving more than one country. [Say soop ruh NATIONAL]

supremacist *noun* a person who believes in or advocates the supremacy of a particular group, esp. determined by race or sex. [Say soo PREMMA sist]

supremacy *noun* (*plural* **supremacies**) the state or condition of being superior to all others in authority, power, or status: *the supremacy of the king ◊ the battle for supremacy in the region.* [Say soo PREMMA see]

supreme *adjective* **1** highest in authority, rank, or power. **2** of the highest quality or importance: *supreme achievement.* **3** greatest in amount or degree: *supreme stupidity.* **4** (of a penalty or sacrifice etc.) ultimate; resulting in death. PHRASES **reign** (or **rule**) **supreme 1** be dominant; hold supreme power, authority, or popularity. **2** be widespread or pervasive; be a prevalent feature. [Say soo PREEM]

Supreme Being *noun* an all-powerful God.

Supreme Court *noun* the highest judicial court of appeal in a country, province, etc. hearing civil, criminal, and constitutional cases.

supremely *adverb* extremely: *her book has been supremely successful.* [Say soo PREEM ly]

surcharge *noun* **1** a fee charged in addition to the normal cost of something. **2** an overwhelming or excessive load or burden.

sure • *adjective* **1** certain. **2 a** reliable or unfailing: *a*

sure cure. **b** steady, secure: *a sure footing.* • *adverb informal* certainly, truly: *I'm sure glad.* • *interjection* yes; of course. PHRASES **be sure** do not fail, neglect, or forget to: *be sure to turn the lights out.* **for sure** *informal* without doubt. **make sure** (often foll. by *that*) make or become certain; ensure. **make sure of** establish the truth or ensure the existence or happening of. **sure enough** *informal* **1** in fact; certainly: *I asked him to leave and, sure enough, he did.* **2** almost certainly: *they will come sure enough.* **sure of oneself** self-confident; self-assured. **to be sure 1** it is undeniable or admitted. **2** it must be admitted.

surefire *adjective informal* reliable, guaranteed, assured.

sure-footed *adjective* **1** treading safely without slipping or stumbling. **2** not likely to fail or make a mistake. ▶ **sure-footedness** *noun*

surely *adverb* **1** indeed. **2** used to express a strong belief in the statement qualified, esp. in the face of possible dissent: *surely you don't believe it.* **3** inevitably, without fail: *improving slowly but surely.*

sureness *noun* the quality of being confident and steady, not hesitating or doubting.

Sûreté *noun* (also **Sûreté du Québec**) *Cdn* the provincial police force of Quebec. [Say soora TAY]

sure thing *informal* • *noun* a person or thing whose success is considered certain or guaranteed. • *interjection* used to express consent to a proposal, request, or order.

surety *noun* (*plural* **sureties**) **1** a person who assumes responsibility for the obligation of another, such as the payment of a debt or an appearance in court: *he has given his parents and children as sureties.* **2 a** (also **surety bond**) money given as a guarantee: *the judge took the unusual step of granting Lui bail with a $30,000 surety.* **b** a guarantee or assurance: *I'm taking your guards with me as surety in case your empire becomes recalcitrant.* **3** certainty: *I listened to these grim observations, antithetical to my idealistic surety that each child was a "blank slate".* PHRASES **stand surety** become a surety (for). [Say SHOORA tee]

surf • *noun* the swell of the sea breaking on the esp. shallow shore of a beach or a reef. • *verb* **1** ride the crest of a wave towards the shore, esp. on a surfboard or windsurfer. **2 a** flip from one television channel to another in rapid succession using a remote control. **b** search or scan (the Internet) in order to sample a selection of sites.

surface • *noun* **1** the upper or outside part of something: *the earth's surface.* **2 a** the superficial level or appearance of a person or thing as opposed to feelings, qualities, etc. which may not be apparent on a casual view or consideration: *seems quite happy on the surface.* **b** (as an *adjective*) superficial: *surface politeness.* **3** a relatively flat horizontal space or area used for some particular purpose or activity: *playing surface.* **4** *Geometry* a continuous extent having only two dimensions, length and width without thickness, whether plane or curved, finite or infinite. • *verb* (**surfaces, surfaced, surfacing**) **1** cover (a road etc.) with a particular type of surface. **2 a** rise to the surface of esp. water. **b** become visible, known, or apparent. PHRASES **come to the surface** become perceptible after being hidden.

surfaced *adjective* having or having been furnished with a surface of a specified kind.

surface temperature *noun* the temperature of a body of water or planet etc. taken at its surface.

surface tension *noun* the property causing the surface of a liquid to behave as if it were covered with a weak elastic skin, caused by the tendency of the exposed surface to contract to the smallest possible area.

surface-to-air *adjective* (of a missile) designed to be fired from the ground or sea towards a target in the air, such as an aircraft.

surface-to-surface *adjective* (of a missile) designed to be fired from a point on the ground or at sea and directed at a target elsewhere on the earth's surface.

surface water *noun* **1** water that collects on the surface of the ground. **2** the top layer of a body of water.

surfactant *noun* a substance which reduces surface tension of a liquid. [Say sir FACK tint]

surf and turf *noun* a restaurant meal combining seafood (esp. lobster) and steak.

surfboard *noun* a long narrow fibreglass board with a small fin on the underside, on which a surfer stands or lies while being carried on the crest of a breaking wave towards the shore.

surfeit *noun* a large or excessive amount: *it offers a surfeit of choices that tend to afflict visitors with indecision*. [Say SIR fit]

surfeited *adjective* filled to excess; wearied through excess: *Englishmen surfeited on Dickens*. [Say SIR fit id]

surfer *noun* **1 a** a person who participates in the sport of surfing. **b** (as an *adjective*) designating aspects or elements typical of the lifestyle, culture, language, etc. of a surfer: *surfer shorts*. **2** a person who surfs the Internet.

surfing *noun* **1** the sport or activity of riding waves on a surfboard or windsurfer etc. **2** = CHANNEL SURFING. **3** the activity of searching or scanning the Internet in order to sample a selection of sites.

surge • *noun* **1** a sudden or violent rush, onset, or burst. **2** a high rolling swell of water, esp. on the sea. **3** a rapid increase in price, activity, etc. over a short period. **4** a heavy forward or upward motion of a large or growing mass, volume, etc. **5** a sudden marked increase in voltage of an electric current. • *verb* (**surges, surged, surging**) **1** (of the sea etc.) rise and move forward in great waves; swell or heave with great force. **2** move forward suddenly or powerfully. **3** show a large, sudden, usu. brief increase in magnitude, power, growth, etc. **4** (of a feeling, activity, etc.) increase suddenly and dramatically.

surgeon *noun* a medical practitioner qualified to practise surgery. [Say SIR jin]

Surgeon General *noun* (*plural* **Surgeons General**) **1** (in the US) the senior medical officer of the Bureau of Public Health or (in some states) a similar state authority. **2** the senior officer in medical service of the armed forces.

surge protection *noun* = SURGE SUPPRESSION.

surgery *noun* (*plural* **surgeries**) **1** the branch of medicine concerned with treatment of injuries or disorders of the body by cutting, manipulation, or alteration of organs etc. **2** surgical treatment. **3** the part of or a room in a hospital where surgery is performed. **4** a detailed or extensive series of repairs, changes, or modifications made to something: *they hoped to perform major surgery on the new proposal before presenting it*. **5** *Brit.* a doctor's, dentist's, or vet's office.

surge suppression *noun* protection of an appliance, computer equipment, etc. from damage in the event of a sudden increase in the voltage of an electric current.

surge suppressor *noun* (also **surge protector**) a device used to protect an electrical appliance, computer equipment, etc. from damage in the event of a power surge.

surgical *adjective* **1** of, relating to, or performed by surgeons or surgery. **2** used or worn by surgeons or during surgery: *surgical gloves*. **3** designating a swift and precise military attack, esp. from the air: *surgical strike*. ▶ **surgically** *adverb*

surliness *noun* rudeness, hostility. [Say SIR lee niss]

surly *adjective* (**surlier, surliest**) **1** rude, ill-natured, unfriendly: *battered by surly service in state stores, Chinese consumers are putty in the hands of smooth-talking Avon ladies*. **2** hostile: *he has surely seen enough premiers who stayed past their prime, only to be chased out of office by a surly electorate*. [Say SIR lee]

surmise • *verb* (**surmises, surmised, surmising**) form an opinion that something may be true without sufficient evidence to be certain: *"I don't think they're locals," she surmised*. • *noun* a supposition that something may be true, even though there is no evidence to confirm it: *all that science has been able to provide so far are speculations and surmises, more or less plausible*.

surmount *verb* **1** overcome (an obstacle, difficulty, etc.). **2** rest on top of or be situated on or above: *a ring surmounted by a beautiful diamond*.

surname *noun* a hereditary name common to all members of a family, as distinct from a given name.

surpass *verb* (**surpasses, surpassed, surpassing**) **1** be greater, better than, or superior to. **2** outdo (another person or thing) in degree or prominence: *crime has surpassed unemployment as the key concern*. **3** go beyond, exceed (a certain limit etc.). **4** be beyond the range or capacity of; transcend: *surpasses description*.

surpassing *adjective* that surpasses what is ordinary; exceptional, matchless: *an area of surpassing natural beauty*. ▶ **surpassingly** *adverb*

surplice *noun* *Christianity* a loose white vestment with wide sleeves, worn usu. over a cassock by some clergy and choristers. [Say SIR pliss]

surplus • *noun* (*plural* **surpluses**) **1** an amount left over when requirements have been met. **2 a** an excess of revenue over expenditure in a given period (opp. DEFICIT 2). **b** the excess value of a company's assets over the face value of its stock. **3** military supplies, such as clothing and camping gear, exceeding the requirements of the forces and sold to the public (also as an *adjective*: *a surplus store*). • *adjective* exceeding what is needed or used; excess.

surprise • *noun* **1** an unexpected or astonishing event etc. **2** astonishment, shock, or amazement. **3** a gift. **4** a person or thing that achieves unexpected success. **5** an attack or approach made upon an unsuspecting victim. **6** (as an *adjective*) unexpected; made or done etc. without warning: *a surprise visit*. **7** often *jocular* or *informal* a dish, esp. a casserole, prepared with ingredients not made known to those to whom it is served: *tuna surprise*. • *verb* (**surprises, surprised, surprising**) **1** cause to feel astonishment, shock, or amazement. **2 a** startle with a sudden or unexpected approach. **b** capture or attack by surprise. • *interjection* used as an exclamation of triumph as a surprise is successfully revealed. PHRASES **should come as no surprise** (a piece of information) should have been anticipated, guessed, or previously known. **surprise, surprise** *ironic* just as one might expect. **take** (or **catch**) **by surprise** startle or astonish esp. with an unexpected encounter or statement.

surprised *adjective* **1** filled with mild astonishment or amazement. **2** shocked, scandalized.

surprising *adjective* that causes surprise. ▶ **surprisingly** *adverb*

surreal *adjective* very strange, bizarre; more like a

S

dream than reality, with ideas and images mixed together in a strange way: *surreal images*. [Say sir REAL]

surrealism *noun* **1** (**Surrealism**) a 20th-century movement in art and literature aiming to explore and express the subconscious and to move beyond the accepted conventions of reality by representing the irrational imagery of dreams using such techniques as automatism, the irrational juxtaposition of images, and the creation of mysterious symbols, as typified by Salvador Dali's painting *The Persistence of Memory* (1931), with its images of melting watches. **2** art or literature produced by or reminiscent of this movement. ▶ **surrealist** *noun & adjective* (also **Surrealist**) [Say sir REALISM]

surrealistic *adjective* **1** based on, influenced by, or pertaining to Surrealism or the Surrealists. **2** characteristic or suggestive of Surrealism. ▶ **surrealistically** *adverb* [Say sir REALISTIC]

surreally *adverb* in a strange or bizarre manner: *weepy landscapes surreally dotted with languorous women, stone tombs, and falling leaves*. [Say sir REALLY]

surrender • *verb* **1 a** cease resistance to an enemy or opponent and submit to their authority: *over 140 rebels surrendered to the authorities*. **b** give up possession or control of (something) to another, esp. on compulsion or demand: *they surrendered their guns to the police* ◊ *she had to surrender her passport*. **2** (also **surrender oneself**) submit or abandon oneself entirely to some influence, emotion, course of action, etc.; give in to: *he was surprised that Miriam would surrender to this sort of jealousy* ◊ *feeling he could no longer struggle, he surrendered himself to fate*. **3** *Sport* give up or allow one or a number of (goals, points, etc.). • *noun* the action of surrendering: *they demanded an unconditional surrender* ◊ *accused the NDP of a surrender to big business interests*.

surreptitious *adjective* obtained, done, etc. in secret or by stealth, in the hopes that people will not notice: *their surreptitious scheme to undermine Turner*. ▶ **surreptitiously** *adverb* [Say sir up TISH iss]

surrogacy *noun* the practice of surrogate motherhood. [Say SIR uh guh see]

surrogate *noun* **1** a person or thing taking the place of another, esp. a person appointed by authority to act in place of another in a specific role or office: *the first ministers are unlikely to meet face to face, so this political battle will be waged mostly through surrogates*. **2 a** a surrogate mother. **b** (as an *adjective*) relating to or involving surrogate motherhood: *surrogate parent*. **3** a person who fills the role of an absent or estranged relative, esp. a parent, in a child's upbringing. [Say SIR uh git]

surrogate mother *noun* **1** a woman who bears a child for another woman, either from her own egg fertilized by the other woman's partner or from the implantation in her uterus of a fertilized egg from the other woman. **2** a person or animal acting the role of mother.

surround • *verb* **1** stand or be situated around. **2 a** place a thing or things on all sides of or all around. **b** place people or things around (oneself); situate (oneself) among. **3** form the entourage of (a person). **4** exist as a predominant aspect of: *a mystery surrounds her disappearance*. • *noun* **1** a structure or border placed around something. **2** = SURROUND SOUND.

surrounding • *adjective* located or situated around. • *noun* (in *plural*) all the objects, conditions, etc. that are around and may affect a person or thing.

surround sound *noun* a system of sound reproduction in which three or more speakers create a sense of space and depth, and thus a more realistic effect.

surtax • *noun* (*plural* **surtaxes**) **1** a higher rate of tax

levied on personal incomes above a certain level. **2** any additional tax charged on something already taxed. • *verb* (**surtaxes**, **surtaxed**, **surtaxing**) impose a surtax on. [Say SIR tax]

surveillance *noun* **1** close observation or supervision, esp. of an enemy or suspected person: *an area of the city where police surveillance is heavy*. **2** a security device or system used to monitor premises and detect trespassers, thieves, etc. [Say sir VAIL ince]

survey • *noun* **1 a** a general and comprehensive discussion, treatment, etc. **b** (also **survey course**) an introductory academic course which gives a broad esp. historical overview of one subject. **2** a systematic collection and analysis of data relating to the opinions, habits, etc. of a population, usu. taken from a representative sample. **3 a** the process or an act of surveying land or property. **b** a map or plan based on the results obtained by surveying land. **c** a department carrying out the surveying of land. **4** a close inspection, investigation, or examination. • *verb* **1** make or present a general and comprehensive examination or assessment of. **2 a** record the views and opinions of (a person or group) in an opinion poll. **b** ascertain (the opinions etc.) of a person or group. **3** explore, measure, or determine the boundaries, extent, and ownership of (land etc.) in order to construct a map or detailed description.

surveying *noun* the examination and recording of the features of (an area of land) so as to construct a map, plan, or description.

surveyor *noun* **1** a person whose occupation is the surveying of land and property. **2** a person who conducts opinion polls or surveys.

survivability *noun* the ability to survive.

survivable *adjective* not fatal; able to be survived.

survival *noun* **1** the state of continuing to live or exist, esp. after some tragic or disastrous event: *the struggle for survival* ◊ *his only hope for survival is a heart transplant* ◊ *exports are necessary for our economic survival*. **2** the practice of coping with harsh or warlike conditions as a leisure activity or training exercise. **3** a person, thing, or practice that has remained from a former time: *the ceremony is a survival from pre-Christian times*. PHRASES **survival of the fittest** the continued existence of organisms which are best adapted to their environment, with the extinction of others, as a concept in the Darwinian theory of evolution.

survivalism *noun* **1** a policy of trying to ensure survival, esp. in the face of competition or a natural disaster, catastrophic event, or foreign invasion. **2** the practising of outdoor survival skills as a sport or hobby. ▶ **survivalist** *noun & adjective*

survival kit *noun* first aid supplies, emergency rations, and supplies for use when stranded or lost.

survive *verb* (**survives**, **survived**, **surviving**) **1** continue to live or exist, esp. after some event. **2** live or exist longer than: *she survived her husband*. **3** remain alive after going through, or continue to exist in spite of (a danger, accident, etc.): *he has survived two strokes*. **4** remain in use or existence. **5** *informal* or *jocular* endure a difficult situation.

survivor *noun* **1** a person who survives or has survived, esp. one remaining alive after an event in which others die. **2** *informal* a person who has a knack for overcoming difficulties or surviving afflictions unscathed.

susceptibility *noun* **1** the state of being very likely to be influenced, harmed, or affected by something: *exercise will help reduce a person's susceptibility to heart disease*. **2** (**susceptibilities**) a person's feelings, esp. considered as being easily hurt: *I was so careful not to offend their susceptibilities*. [Say suh septa BILLA tee]

S

susceptible *adjective* **1 a** (usu. foll. by *to*) likely to be affected by; prone or vulnerable to: *susceptible to pain*. **b** vulnerable, esp. lacking in defences against a disease: *the virus attacks susceptible children*. **2** impressionable, sensitive; easily moved by emotion: *being alone in the world puts this romantic and susceptible young woman in a vulnerable position*. [Say suh SEPTA bull]

sushi *noun* a Japanese snack of cold boiled rice flavoured with vinegar, salt, and sugar, and garnished with a variety of toppings, often raw fish or seaweed. [Say SOOSHY]

suspect • *verb* **1 a** imagine (something) to be possible or likely. **b** be inclined to think. **2** believe to be guilty with insufficient proof or knowledge; doubt the innocence of. **3** believe tentatively, without clear justification. **4** doubt the genuineness or truth of; mistrust. • *noun* a person suspected of an offence, evil intention, etc. • *adjective* subject to or deserving of suspicion or distrust; questionable. PHRASES **the usual suspects** *jocular* a group of people who are frequently and predictably present at events, called upon for comment, etc.

suspected *noun* **1** imagined to be. **2** that one suspects of something which is not certain. **3** (of an injury, ailment, etc.) believed to have been suffered although not yet diagnosed or confirmed.

suspend *verb* **1** attach (an object) to something above so that it hangs, usu. with free movement. **2** cause to remain in a floating or elevated position without attachment. **3** refrain from making, forming, or announcing (a judgment, opinion, etc.) until a later time. **4** cancel or halt, esp. temporarily: *the police suspended her driver's licence*. **5** forbid (a person) from performing a usual duty or participating in a usual activity for a temporary or indefinite period, esp. as a penalty. PHRASES **suspend disbelief** refrain from being skeptical about the believability of a work of fiction or its characters.

suspended animation *noun* a temporary cessation of the vital functions without death.

suspended sentence *noun* a judicial sentence imposed but unenforced as long as the offender commits no further offence within a specified period.

suspenders *plural noun* a pair of straps worn over the shoulder and fastened to the waistband of a pair of pants to hold them up.

suspense *noun* **1** a state of uncertainty or expectation, accompanied by anxiety or excitement, about an awaited outcome, decision, etc. **2 a** a quality in a work of fiction that arouses excited expectation about the outcome, culprit, etc. in the mind of the viewer or reader. **b** works having this quality. **3** the condition of something that is in doubt or undecided. PHRASES **keep in suspense** delay informing (a person) of important or useful information, thus heightening their excitement or anxiety. ▶ **suspenseful** *adjective*

suspension *noun* **1** the action of suspending or the condition of being suspended, esp. a temporary cessation or postponement. **2** a period during which one is prohibited from attending school or work, playing for a team, participating in an activity, etc. **b** temporary revocation of a licence, contract, etc. **3** (also **suspension system**) the system of springs and shocks that supports a vehicle on its axles. **4** a mixture in which small particles are distributed throughout a less dense liquid or gas.

suspension bridge *noun* a bridge with a deck suspended from cables supported by towers at each end.

suspicion *noun* **1** a feeling or belief that someone is guilty of an illegal, dishonest, or unpleasant action:

viewed him with suspicion ◊ *his actions raised suspicions*. **2** a faint belief: *a suspicion she's lying* ◊ *she had a sneaking suspicion he was laughing at her*. **3** a presumption of guilt based on evidence sufficient for arrest but not conviction: *arrested on suspicion of murder*. PHRASES **above suspicion** too obviously good etc. to be suspected. **under suspicion** thought to be guilty of wrongdoing.

suspicious *adjective* **1 a** prone to suspicion; mistrustful, esp. of something or someone in particular. **b** feeling suspicion; having one's suspicion aroused. **2** indicating suspicion: *a suspicious glance*. **3** inviting or justifying suspicion: *suspicious behaviour*. ▶ **suspiciously** *adverb* **suspiciousness** *noun*

suss *verb* (**susses**, **sussed**, **sussing**) *informal* (usu. foll. by *out*) **1** investigate, check out: *I'll suss out the restaurants*. **2** figure out.

sustain *verb* **1** provide with the basic necessities required to support or preserve life. **2** endure, stand; bear up against. **3** undergo or suffer (defeat or injury etc.). **4** maintain or keep (an action or process) going continuously. **5** (of a court etc.) uphold or decide in favour of (an objection etc.). **6** give strength to; encourage, support. **7** substantiate or corroborate (a statement or charge). **8** hold up or support the weight of, esp. for a long period. **9** hold (a note or chord) for an extended period.

sustainability *noun* **1** the ability of development to conserve an ecological balance by avoiding depletion of natural resources. **2** the ability of something to be maintained, esp. at a particular rate or level.

sustainable *adjective* **1** (esp. of development) that conserves an ecological balance by avoiding depletion of natural resources. **2** that may be maintained, esp. at a particular level. ▶ **sustainably** *adverb*

sustained *adjective* continued or prolonged over a long time, esp. without interruption or a change in rate: *the country hopes to achieve sustained economic growth*.

sustained yield *noun* the quantity of a crop that can be periodically harvested without long-term depletion.

sustenance *noun* **1** a means of sustaining life; nourishment: *Algonquian-speaking Indians north of the Great Lakes had to hunt big game, particularly caribou, for sustenance*. **2** the action or process of sustaining esp. life: *the goods purchased had to be essential for the sustenance of the family* ◊ *elections are essential for the sustenance of parliamentary democracy*. [Say SUSTA nince]

Sutra *noun* (*plural* **Sutras**) **1** a short phrase saying something wise, or collection of these, in Hindu literature. **2** a narrative part of Buddhist literature. **3** Jainist scripture. [Say SOOTRA]

suttee *noun* (*plural* **suttees**) esp. *hist.* **1** the Hindu practice of a widow committing suicide on her husband's funeral pyre. **2** a widow who undergoes or has undergone this. [Say suh TEE or SUT ee]

suture • *noun* **1 a** the joining of the edges of a wound or incision by stitching. **b** the material used to make surgical stitches. **2** the junction of two bones forming an immovable articulation, esp. each of the serrated borders between the bones of the skull. • *verb* (**sutures**, **sutured**, **suturing**) stitch up (a wound or incision) with a suture. ▶ **sutured** *adjective* [Say SOO chur]

SUV *abbreviation* (*plural* **SUVs**) = SPORT-UTILITY VEHICLE (see SPORT-UTILITY).

Suzuki *adjective* designating, pertaining to, or using a method of teaching the violin (esp. to young children), characterized by exercises involving large groups and parental participation. [Say soo ZOO kee]

svelte *adjective* slender: *a svelte beauty*. [Say SVELT]

Svengali *noun* (*plural* **Svengalis**) a person who

exercises a controlling or mesmeric influence on another, esp. for a sinister purpose: *the pop entrepreneur is often seen as a Svengali pulling all the strings.* [Say sven GALLEY]

SVGA *abbreviation* Computing a colour graphics adapter that is an upgrade of the VGA standard.

SW *abbreviation* **1** southwest. **2** southwestern. **3** short-wave.

swab • *noun* **1 a** an absorbent pad used in surgery for cleaning or applying medication to wounds. **b** a wad of cotton or other absorbent material fixed to the end of a rod and used for cleaning or applying medication. **c** a specimen of a possibly diseased secretion collected with a swab for examination. **2 a** mop or other absorbent device for cleaning or mopping up. • *verb* (**swabs, swabbed, swabbing**) **1** wipe or clean (a wound, ship's deck, etc.) with a swab. **2** absorb or apply (a substance) with a swab. [Say SWOB]

swaddle *verb* (**swaddles, swaddled, swaddling**) **1** wrap (oneself or another or part of the body) in bandages, clothes, a blanket, etc. **2** wrap (a newborn child) in a blanket or swaddling clothes. **3** surround (a person or thing) with: *this generation has grown up swaddled in consumer technology.* [Say SWODDLE]

swaddling clothes *plural noun* hist. narrow lengths of bandage wrapped around a newborn child to restrict its movements and quieten it. [Say SWODDLING]

swag *noun* **1** *slang* **a** the stolen goods carried off by a thief or burglar. **b** illicit gains. **2** a length of fabric or drapery fastened in such a way that it hangs loosely over a window, sagging in the middle. **3** an ornamental arrangement of flowers, leaves, or fruit.

swagger • *verb* **1** walk or behave with an air of confidence or toughness. **2** talk boastfully. • *noun* **1 a** an air or attitude of cockiness or toughness. **b** an air or attitude of smartness or flamboyance. **2 a** swaggering gait. **3** confident, boastful, or brash behaviour. ▶ **swaggering** *adjective* **swaggeringly** *adverb*

Swahili • *noun* (plural **Swahili**) **1** a member of a Bantu-speaking people of Zanzibar, an island off Tanzania in eastern Africa, and adjacent coasts. **2** their language, used as a common language among different peoples in eastern Africa. • *adjective* of or relating to the Swahili or their language. [Say swuh HEELY]

swain *noun* literary or jocular a young lover or suitor: *a Southern belle dressed in pink moved through the crowd surrounded by swains in black tie.*

swale *noun* a low or hollow place, esp. a marshy depression or hollow between ridges.

swallow¹ • *verb* **1** cause or allow (food etc.) to pass down the throat. **2** perform the muscular movement of the esophagus required to do this. **3** accept meekly, gullibly or unquestioningly. **4** repress; resist the expression of (a feeling etc.): *had to swallow my anger.* **5** (often foll. by *up*) engulf, absorb, or consume; cause to disappear. • *noun* **1** the act of swallowing. **2** an amount swallowed in one action. PHRASES **swallow one's pride** humble oneself in order to admit guilt or error or to ask for a favour.

swallow² *noun* a migratory swift-flying insect-eating bird with a forked tail and long pointed wings.

swallower *noun* a person who swallows something.

swallowtail *noun* **1** anything resembling the shape of a swallow's deeply forked tail. **2** a butterfly with wings extended at the back to this shape. ▶ **swallow-tailed** *adjective*

swam *past of* SWIM.

swami *noun* (plural **swamis**) **1** a Hindu male religious teacher. **2** informal an adviser or mentor. [Say SWOMMY]

swamp • *noun* a tract of low-lying ground in which

water collects; a bog or marsh. • *verb* **1 a** overwhelm, flood, or soak with water. **b** (of a boat) become filled with water and sink. **2** overwhelm with a large amount of something. **3** clear (a road) in a forest by felling trees, removing undergrowth, etc., esp. for hauling logs.

swamped *adjective* overwhelmed with work.

swamper *noun* **1** Cdn a person who clears logging roads through a forest by felling trees etc. **2** Cdn (BC) an assistant to a truck driver.

swampland *noun* land consisting of swamps.

swampy *adjective* (**swampier, swampiest**) consisting of, containing, or resembling a swamp; boggy, marshy: *swampy woods.*

Swampy Cree *noun* **1** a member of a Cree people living in northern Manitoba and in the area of western James Bay and Hudson Bay. **2** their Cree dialect.

swan *noun* a large web-footed swimming bird, with a long and gracefully curved neck and all white (or, in certain cases, black) feathers and black feet.

swan dive *noun* **1** a forward dive with the arms extended sideways until the diver is close to the surface of the water, at which point the arms are brought together over the head. **2** jocular a dramatic or spectacular fall, plunge, or dive.

swank informal • *noun* **1** style, elegance. **2** flashiness, swagger. • *adjective* posh, stylish: *Hong Kong's swank central business district.* ▶ **swanky** *adjective* (**swankier, swankiest**)

swan song *noun* the final work or performance of a writer, artist, etc. before retirement or death.

swap • *verb* (**swaps, swapped, swapping**) exchange or trade (one thing for another). • *noun* **1** an act of swapping one thing for another. **2** = SWAP MEET 1.

swap meet *noun* **1** a gathering at which enthusiasts or collectors trade or exchange items of a particular kind. **2** a flea market.

swapper *noun* a person who trades or exchanges collectibles, esp. at a swap meet. [Say SWOPPER]

swarm • *noun* **1** a cluster of bees leaving the hive with the queen to establish a new colony. **2** a large number of insects or birds moving in a cluster. **3** a large or dense group, esp. when active or moving. • *verb* **1** gather or proceed in a swarm or crowd. **2** (foll. by *with*) (of a place) be overrun, crowded, or infested: *the city swarms with tourists.* **3** (of a large group of people or things) fill (an area or space): *students swarmed the halls.* **4** gather around (a person), esp. in an aggressive or hostile manner. **5** climb up (a rope or tree etc.), esp. in a rush, by clasping or clinging with the hands and knees.

swarming *noun* an attack on an individual by a group of attackers who taunt, shove, etc. until the victim is too intimidated or confused to resist theft or assault.

swarthiness *noun* a dark colour or complexion. [Say SWOR thee niss]

swarthy *adjective* (**swarthier, swarthiest**) of a dark colour or complexion: *a swarthy, handsome, multilingual Arab.* [Say SWOR thee]

swashbuckler *noun* **1** a person who ostentatiously or flamboyantly engages in daring and romantic adventures. **2** a film etc. portraying such characters. ▶ **swashbuckling** *adjective & noun*

swastika *noun* (plural **swastikas**) **1** an ancient symbol in the form of a cross with each of its four arms of equal length bent at right angles at the end, all in the same direction and usu. clockwise. **2** this symbol with clockwise continuations used as the emblem of Nazi Germany and adopted subsequently as the emblem of anti-Semitic and other racially motivated hate groups. [Say swaw STEEKA or SWOSS tick uh]

SWAT *noun* (also **SWAT team**) a special detachment of

some US police forces trained to deal with terrorism, hostage-takings, etc. [Say SWOT]

swat • *verb* (**swats, swatted, swatting**) **1** crush (a fly etc.) with a sharp blow. **2** hit hard and abruptly; slap, smack. **3** direct a blow at a target, esp. without hitting it. • *noun* a sharp slap or hit.

swatch *noun* (*plural* **swatches**) **1 a** a sample, esp. of cloth, fabric, or paint colours. **b** a collection of samples. **2** a portion or section: *he appeals to a swatch of our listeners*. [Say SWOTCH]

swath • *noun* (*plural* **swaths**) **1** a strip in a field or lawn that has been left clear after the passage of a mower etc. **2** a row or line of grass, wheat, etc. as it falls or lies when mown or reaped. **3** a broad strip or long stretch of something: *a swath of rich blue carpet laid over a slate floor*. • *verb* = SWATHE. PHRASES **cut a wide swath** pass through causing great damage, destruction, or change: *crack has cut a wide swath through middle America*. [Say SWOTH]

swathe *verb* (**swathes, swathed, swathing**) **1** wrap (a person etc.) in bandages or clothes: *she was very allergic to sunshine and was always swathed in scarves and sunshade hats*. **2** cover in or under; envelop: *a vivid landscape of high red sandstone hills, each one swathed in green*. [Rhymes either with CLOTH or with BATHE]

swather *noun* a machine used to cut grain and deposit it in a row to dry and be collected. [Rhymes with FATHER, though it may have the TH of THIN]

swatter *noun* (in full **fly swatter**) a device for killing flies by hitting them, usu. a flat piece of plastic attached to a long handle. [Say SWOTTER]

sway • *verb* **1 a** move slowly and rhythmically back and forth or from side to side. **b** rock awkwardly or unsteadily as if about to fall. **2** waver between two options or opinions. **3 a** influence or direct the decision or opinion of. **b** control or direct the outcome of (an event). **4** cause to move or swing from side to side. **5** bend, lean, or incline to one side. • *noun* **1** a position of power, authority, or influence: *the part of the continent under Russia's sway* ◊ *rebel forces hold sway over much of the island*. **2** a to-and-fro movement: *the sway of the yacht was making her feel sick*.

Swazi • *noun* **1** (*plural* **Swazi** or **Swazis**) **a** a member of a people inhabiting Swaziland and parts of Eastern Transvaal in South Africa. **b** a native or national of Swaziland. **2** the Nguni language of this people. • *adjective* of or relating to Swaziland, the Swazi, or their language. [Say SWOZZY]

swear *verb* (**swears**; *past* **swore**; *past participle* **sworn**; **swearing**) **1 a** state or promise solemnly or on oath. **b** take (an oath). **2** *informal* state emphatically. **3** cause to take an oath: *sworn to secrecy*. **4** use profane or indecent language. **5** *informal* have or express great confidence or faith in: *I swear by my old typewriter*. **6** appeal to a sacred person or thing in confirmation of the truth of a solemn declaration: *I swear to God*. **7** admit the certainty of: *could not swear to it*. PHRASES **swear in** induct into office etc. by administering an oath. **swear off** *informal* promise or vow to abstain from (drink etc.). **swear out** obtain the issue of (a warrant for arrest) by making a charge on oath. ▶ **swearing** *noun*

swearing-in *noun* a ceremony at which a person formally accepts the conditions of an office, tenure, assignment, etc., by swearing an oath.

swear word *noun* a profanity.

sweat • *noun* **1** moisture exuded through the pores of the skin. **2** a state or period of sweating. **3** *informal* a state of anxiety. **4** *informal* a drudgery, effort. **b** a laborious task or undertaking. **5** condensed moisture on a surface. **6** (in *plural*) *informal* **a** = SWEATSUIT. **b** = SWEATPANTS. **c** = SWEATSHIRT. **7** (in full **sweat bath**) **a** a

structure filled with hot humid air to induce sweating. **b** the action of spending time in this with the intention of sweating profusely. • *verb* (**sweats**; *past* and *past participle* **sweated** or **sweat**; **sweating**) **1** exude sweat; perspire. **2** be terrified, suffering, etc. **3** (of a wall etc.) exhibit surface moisture. **4** drudge, toil. **5** *informal* worry about (something): *don't sweat the details*. PHRASES **by the sweat of one's brow** by one's own hard work. **no sweat** *informal* **1** there is no need to worry. **2** without any difficulty. **sweat blood** *informal* **1** work strenuously. **2** be extremely anxious. **sweat one's guts out** *informal* work extremely hard, esp. excessively in comparison to the reward or to other people's expectations. **sweat it out** *informal* endure a difficult experience to the end.

sweatband *noun* **1** a band of absorbent material worn around the head or wrist to soak up sweat. **2** a band of absorbent material lining a hat.

sweater *noun* **1** a knitted or crocheted garment covering the upper half of the body. **2** a sports jersey. ▶ **sweatered** *adjective*

sweatily *adverb* while sweating.

sweat lodge *noun* a structure heated by pouring water over hot stones, used by some Aboriginal groups to induce sweating, as for religious or medical purposes.

sweatpants *plural noun* loose fleece pants with a drawstring or elasticized waist and often with elasticized cuffs, worn as casual attire or for sports.

sweatshirt *noun* a loosely fitting long-sleeved fleece top, worn as casual attire or for sports.

sweatshop *noun* a factory etc., esp. in the garment industry, where workers work long hours in unpleasant conditions for low pay.

sweatsuit *noun* a suit of a sweatshirt and sweatpants, worn as casual attire or for sports.

sweaty *adjective* (**sweatier, sweatiest**) **1** covered, damp with, or smelling of sweat. **2** causing sweat.

Swede *noun* **1** a native or national of Sweden. **2** a person of Swedish descent.

swede saw *noun* *Cdn* a type of hand saw with a bow-like tubular frame and many cutting teeth.

Swedish • *adjective* of or relating to Sweden or its people or language. • *noun* the language of Sweden.

sweep • *verb* (**sweeps, swept, sweeping**) **1** clean or clear with or as with a broom. **2** (foll. by *aside, away,* etc.) **a** push with or as with a broom. **b** dismiss or reject abruptly: *their objections were swept aside*. **3** (foll. by *along, down,* etc.) carry or drive along with force. **4** (foll. by *off, away,* etc.) remove or clear forcefully. **5** cross swiftly or lightly: *the wind swept the hillside*. **6** impart a sweeping motion to: *swept his hand across*. **7** swiftly cover or affect. **8 a** glide swiftly; sweep along with unchecked motion. **b** go majestically. **c** move suddenly and with force over an area: *fire swept through the building*. **9 a** pass over (something) in order to examine it or search for something: *searchlights swept the sky*. **b** drag (a river bottom etc.) to search for something. **c** examine (a building, telephone line, etc.) for electronic listening or recording devices. **10** (of artillery etc.) include in the line of fire; cover the whole of. **11** win every event, award, or place in (a contest). • *noun* **1 a** a long, swift, curving movement: *a grandiose sweep of his hand*. **b** an act of sweeping something with a brush: *give the floor a quick sweep*. **2** a long, typically curved stretch of road, river, country, etc.: *we could see a wide sweep of country*. **3** range or scope: *the long sweep of history*. **4** (in *plural*) *informal* = SWEEPSTAKES 1, 2. **5** a long oar worked from a barge etc. **6** victory in all the games in a contest etc. by one team or competitor, or the winning of all the places in a single event. **7 a** a surprise raid by police through

a neighbourhood, building, etc., to arrest suspected persons or seize illicit goods. **b** a comprehensive search for electronic listening or recording devices. **8** a survey of an area, esp. the night sky, made in an arc or circle. **9** *Football* = END RUN 1. **10** = CHIMNEY SWEEP. **11** a piece of rubber affixed to the bottom of an exterior door to keep out drafts. PHRASES **make a clean sweep of 1** completely abolish or expel. **2** win all the prizes etc. in (a competition etc.). **sweep away 1** abolish swiftly. **2** (usu. in *passive*) powerfully affect, esp. emotionally. **sweep a person off his** (or **her**) **feet** affect a person with powerful emotion, esp. love.

sweeper *noun* **1** a person who cleans by sweeping. **2** a device for sweeping. **3** a person who or a vessel which sweeps for something under water. **4** *Cdn* **a** a tree overhanging a stream etc. **b** a drifting tree or log in a stream etc. **5** *Curling* a player who sweeps in front of a moving rock with a broom or brush.

sweeping • *adjective* **1** wide in range or effect. **2** taking no account of particular cases or exceptions. **3** complete, overwhelming. **4** passing over a wide area. • *noun* (in *plural*) dirt etc. collected by sweeping. ▶ **sweepingly** *adverb*

sweepstakes *noun* (also **sweepstake**) **1** a form of gambling in which all the money bet on the result of a contest is paid to the winner or winners. **2** a race with betting of this kind. **3** a prize or prizes won in a sweepstakes.

SPELL CHECK
sweet, suite

The spelling is **suite** for a set of furniture, a hotel room, an apartment, and for a musical composition.

---

sweet • *adjective* **1 a** having the pleasant taste characteristic of sugar. **b** (in the names of baked goods) sweet-tasting, esp. *Cdn* (*Nfld*) containing molasses and raisins, and prepared chiefly at Christmas: *sweet bread* ◊ *sweet loaf*. **2** smelling pleasant like roses or perfume etc. **3** (of sound etc.) melodious or harmonious. **4 a** not salty, sour, or bitter. **b** fresh and pure: *the sweet air of the countryside*. **c** (of food) fresh, with flavour unimpaired by rottenness. **d** (of water) fresh and readily drinkable. **5** highly gratifying or attractive: *the sweet feeling of success*. **6** amiable, pleasant: *has a sweet nature*. **7** *informal* (of a person or thing) pretty, charming, endearing. **8** (foll. by *on*) *informal* fond of; in love with. **9** esp. *ironic* one's own; particular, individual: *takes his own sweet time*. **10** *slang* as an intensifier in phrases meaning "nothing at all". **11** *informal* (of a deal etc.) with terms that are more lenient than deserved. • *noun* **1** (in *plural*) **a** sweet foods, such as pie, cake, chocolate, etc.: *doesn't like sweets*. **b** *Cdn* (*NB*) = DAINTY *noun* 2. **2** a sweet part of something; sweetness. **3** (esp. as a form of address) sweetheart etc.

sweet-and-sour *adjective* cooked in a sauce containing sugar and vinegar or lemon juice etc.

sweetbread *noun* the pancreas or thymus of an animal, used for food.

sweet chestnut *noun* a large European tree that produces edible chestnuts within bristly cases.

sweet corn *noun* **1** a kind of corn with kernels having a high sugar content. **2** these kernels, eaten as a vegetable when young.

sweeten *verb* **1** make or become sweet or sweeter in smell, taste, or sound. **2** make fresh or wholesome; purify: *use mouthwash to sweeten your breath*. **3** make agreeable or less painful. **4** increase the attractiveness or value of (a deal, proposal, etc.). **5** *Cards informal* increase the stakes in (a pot).

sweetener *noun* **1** a substance used to sweeten food

or drink, esp. any of various low-calorie sugar substitutes. **2** a thing that makes something more pleasant, agreeable, or tolerable. **3** *informal* a bribe or inducement.

sweet grass *noun* (*plural* **sweet grasses**) **1** any of several fragrant grasses used in basket making. **2** any of various grasses or other plants relished by cattle for their sweet succulent foliage.

sweetheart *noun* **1** a person with whom one is in love. **2** a term of endearment. **3** a lovable, amiable, or obliging person.

sweetheart deal *noun* (also **sweetheart contract**) *informal* an industrial agreement reached privately by employers and union leaders in their own interests.

sweetie *noun informal* **1** (also **sweetie pie**) a term of endearment (esp. as a form of address). **2** = SWEETHEART 3.

sweetish *adjective* somewhat sweet.

sweetly *adverb* **1** in a pleasant way: *she smiled sweetly*. **2** in a way that smells sweet: *sweetly smelling flowers*. **3** without difficulties or problems: *everything went sweetly according to plan*.

sweetmeat *noun* **1** a confectionery item, e.g. a preserved or candied fruit, a sugared nut, etc. **2** a small fancy cake.

sweetness *noun* the quality of being sweet. PHRASES **sweetness and light** a pleasant or enjoyable experience, situation, or person: *all was sweetness and light in the parish of Buckland before Cassie McChesney arrived on the scene* ◊ *we should like the old man — not that he's all sweetness and light*.

sweet pea *noun* a climbing plant of the pea family with colourful fragrant flowers.

sweet pepper *noun* a relatively mild-tasting pepper.

sweet potato *noun* (*plural* **sweet potatoes**) **1** an edible tuberous root with a slightly sweet white or orange flesh. **2** the Central American trailing plant that produces this root.

sweet spot *noun* the point on a bat, racquet, etc. at which it makes most effective contact with the ball.

sweet talk *informal* • *noun* flattery. • *verb* (**sweet-talk**) flatter in order to persuade. ▶ **sweet-talking** *adjective*

sweet tooth *noun* a liking for sweet-tasting things.

swell • *verb* (**swells**; *past* **swelled**; *past participle* **swollen** or **swelled**; **swelling**) **1** grow or cause to grow bigger or louder or more intense. **2** rise or raise up from the surrounding surface. **3** (foll. by *out*) bulge. **4** be intensely affected or filled with a particular emotion: *her heart swelled with pride*. • *noun* **1** an act or the state of swelling. **2** the heaving of the sea with waves that do not break. **3 a** a crescendo. **b** a mechanism in an organ etc. for obtaining a crescendo or diminuendo. **4** *informal* a person of distinction or of dashing or fashionable appearance. • *adjective* **1** *informal* fine, splendid, excellent. **2** *informal* smart, fashionable.

swelled head *noun informal* excessive pride or vanity.

swelling *noun* **1** an abnormal enlargement of a part of the body, typically as a result of an accumulation of fluid due to injury, disease, etc. **2** the process of swelling, becoming distended, or rising in intensity etc.

swelter • *verb* (usu. as **sweltering** *adjective*) be uncomfortably hot. • *noun* a sweltering atmosphere or condition. ▶ **swelteringly** *adverb*

swept *past and past participle of* SWEEP.

swerve • *verb* (**swerves**, **swerved**, **swerving**) change or cause to change direction, esp. abruptly. • *noun* **1** a swerving movement. **2** divergence from a course.

swift • *adjective* **1** soon coming or passing. **2** speedy, prompt. **3** *informal* smart, clever. • *adverb* (*archaic* except in *combination*) swiftly: *swift-moving*. • *noun* **1** a swift-

flying insect-eating bird with long wings that resembles a swallow. **2** *Cdn* an area of rapidly flowing current in a river.

swift fox *noun* (*plural* **swift foxes**) a small fox with a yellowish-buff coat and a black-tipped tail, living on the North American prairies.

swiftly *adverb* in a fast or speedy manner.

swiftness *noun* speed, quickness.

swig *informal* • *verb* (**swigs**, **swigged**, **swigging**) drink in large drafts. • *noun* a large swallow of a beverage, esp. of liquor.

swill • *verb* drink greedily. • *noun* **1** scraps of waste food, usu. mixed with water, for feeding pigs. **2** inferior liquor. **3** worthless matter; rubbish.

swim • *verb* (**swims**; *past* **swam**; *past participle* **swum**; **swimming**) **1** propel the body through water by working the arms and legs, or (of a fish) the fins and tail. **2** float on or at the surface of a liquid. **3** appear to undulate or reel or whirl. **4** have a dizzy effect or sensation: *my head swam*. **5** be flooded with liquid. **6** glide along, through, etc. • *noun* a period of or the act of swimming. PHRASES **in the swim** involved in or acquainted with what is going on. **swim against the tide** act against prevailing opinion or tendency.

swim bladder *noun* a gas-filled sac in fish used to maintain buoyancy.

swimmer *noun* a person who swims.

swimming *noun* the sport or activity of propelling the body through water by using the arms and legs.

swimmingly *adverb* with easy and unobstructed progress.

swimsuit *noun* an esp. one-piece bathing suit worn by women.

swim trunks *plural noun* (also **swimming trunks**) loose-fitting shorts worn by men for swimming.

swimwear *noun* clothing worn for swimming.

swindle • *verb* (**swindles**, **swindled**, **swindling**) cheat a person of money, possessions, etc. • *noun* **1** an act of swindling. **2** a person or thing represented as what it is not. **3** a fraudulent scheme. ▶**swindler** *noun*

swine *noun* **1** (*plural* **swine**) a pig. **2** (*plural* **swine** or **swines**) *informal* **a** a term of contempt for a person. **b** a very unpleasant or difficult thing.

swing • *verb* (**swings**, **swung**, **swinging**) **1** move or cause to move with a to-and-fro or curving motion. **2** revolve or cause to revolve. **3** go with a swinging gait. **4** (foll. by *around*) move around to the opposite direction. **5** change from one opinion or mood to another. **6** attempt to hit or punch. **7** *informal* **a** be lively, modern, or trendy. **b** be promiscuous. **8** *informal* (of a party etc.) be lively, successful, etc. **9** have a decisive influence on (esp. voting etc.). **10** *informal* deal with or achieve. **11** *informal* be executed by hanging. • *noun* **1** an act of swinging. **2** a swift tour involving a number of stops, esp. as part of a larger tour: *the ballet begins its western swing in Sault Ste. Marie on Friday*. **3** a swinging or smooth gait or rhythm or action. **4 a** a seat slung by ropes or chains etc. for swinging on or in. **b** a period of swinging on this. **5 a** jazz or dance music with an easy flowing but vigorous rhythm. **b** dance performed to this, esp. originally that popular in the late 1930s and early 1940s. **c** the rhythmic feeling or drive of this music. **6** a discernible change in opinion, esp. the amount by which votes or points scored etc. change from one side to another (often as an *adjective*: *swing riding* ◊ *swing voter*). **7** an attempted punch. PHRASES **get (back) into the swing of things** get used to (or return to) being easy and relaxed about an activity or routine one is engaged in. **swing the lead** *Brit. & Cdn informal* pretend to be sick in order to avoid

work or shirk one's duty. ▶**swinger** *noun* (esp. in sense 7 of *verb*)

swinging *adjective* **1** (of gait, melody, etc.) vigorously rhythmical. **2** *informal* **a** lively. **b** promiscuous.

swinging bridge *noun* a footbridge suspended from cables, which swings from side to side when walked on.

swinging door *noun* a door able to open in either direction and close itself when released.

swingman *noun* (*plural* **swingmen**) a versatile player who can play effectively in different positions, esp. both guard and forward in basketball.

swing set *noun* a fixture in a park, yard, etc. having one or more swings and sometimes a slide.

swingy *adjective* (**swingier**, **swingiest**) **1** (of music) characterized by swing (see SWING *noun* 5). **2** (of a dress etc.) designed to swing with body movement. **3** *Curling* (of ice) on which the lateral movement of a rock is greater than normal.

swinish *adjective* *informal* unpleasant: *aristocrats hated the idea of the swinish multitude having influence*. [Say SWINE ish]

swipe • *verb* (**swipes**, **swiped**, **swiping**) **1** hit hard and recklessly with a sweeping motion. **2** *informal* steal. **3** pass (a card) through an electronic device in order to read and process data magnetically encoded on it. • *noun* **1** a quick swinging blow, or attempt at this. **2** a sharp, antagonistic criticism, esp. made casually or in passing. ▶**swiper** *noun*

swirl • *verb* **1** move or flow or carry along with or as with a whirling motion. **2** give a twisted form to. • *noun* **1** a swirling motion of or in water, air, etc. **2** the act of swirling. **3** a twist or curl, esp. as part of a pattern or design. **4** commotion, disorder. ▶**swirly** *adjective*

swish • *verb* (**swishes**, **swished**, **swishing**) **1** move with or make a rustling or hissing sound. **2** cause to make such a sound. **3** swing (a stick etc.) audibly through the air, grass, etc. **4** *Basketball* sink (a shot) without the ball touching the backboard or rim. • *noun* **1** a swishing action or sound. **2** *Basketball informal* a shot that goes through the basket without touching the backboard or rim. **3** *Cdn* (*Nfld & Maritimes*) liquor made by filling a recently emptied rum barrel with boiling water and rotating it every few days for a couple of weeks. • *adjective* *slang* = SWISHY 2.

swishy *adjective* **1** making a swishing sound. **2** *slang* effeminate.

Swiss • *adjective* of or relating to Switzerland or its people. • *noun* (*plural* **Swiss**) **1** a native or national of Switzerland. **2** a person of Swiss descent.

Swiss Army knife *noun* (*plural* **Swiss Army knives**) a pocket knife incorporating multiple blades and other tools, such as a screwdriver, can opener, scissors, etc.

Swiss chard *noun* a kind of beet whose leaves have edible white stalks and green blades.

Swiss cheese • *noun* a mild hard yellow cheese with many large holes in it, originally made in Switzerland. • *adjective* (**Swiss-cheese**) characterized by large holes or spaces: *the goalie blamed his poor performance on the team's Swiss-cheese defence*.

switch • *noun* (*plural* **switches**) **1** a device for making and breaking the connection in an electric circuit. **2 a** a transfer, changeover, or deviation. **b** an exchange. **3** a slender flexible shoot cut from a tree. **4** a light tapering rod. **5** a device at the junction of railway tracks for transferring a train from one track to another. • *verb* (**switches**, **switched**, **switching**) **1 a** turn (an electrical device) on or off. **b** start or stop the flow or operation of (water, electricity, etc.) by means of a tap, switch, etc. **c** display or cease to display (a quality or emotion). **2** change or transfer position, subject, etc. **3** (often foll. by *over*) change or transfer.

S

4 reverse the positions of; exchange. **5 a** divert (a train etc.) on to another track by means of a switch. **b** (of a train) be diverted in this way. **6** move rapidly back and forth. PHRASES **switch off** *informal* cease to pay attention. ▶ **switchable** *adjective*

switchback *noun* a railway or road with 180° bends.

switchblade *noun* a pocket knife with the blade released by a spring.

switchboard *noun* a central panel in an office etc. for the manual control of telephone connections.

switcher *noun* a person or thing that switches, esp. a piece of electronic equipment used to select or combine different video and audio signals.

switcheroo *noun* (*plural* **switcheroos**) *slang* a change, reversal, or exchange, esp. if surprising or deceptive.

switch-hit *verb* (**switch-hits, switch-hit, switch-hitting**) *Baseball* bat or be able to bat either right- or left-handed.

switch hitter *noun Baseball* a hitter who can bat either right- or left-handed. ▶ **switch-hitting** *adjective*

switchover *noun* a change or exchange.

swivel • *noun* (often as an *adjective*) a fastening or coupling device between two parts enabling one to revolve without turning the other. • *verb* (**swivels, swivelled, swivelling**) turn on or as on a swivel. [Say SWIV'll]

swivel chair *noun* a chair with a seat able to be turned horizontally.

swizzle stick *noun* a stick used for stirring drinks.

swollen • *verb* past participle of SWELL. • *adjective* enlarged, expanded, or increased by or as if by swelling: *a swollen ankle* ◊ *the swollen river*.

swollen head = SWELLED HEAD.

swoon • *verb* **1** be emotionally overwhelmed or ecstatic at the sight of a person or thing one greatly admires: *his stretch black trousers made the ladies swoon in the front row* ◊ *swooned at the evening's first look at the Sicilian hills*. **2** experience a period of failure or poor performance: *biotech companies cannot swoon each spring and recover each fall*. **3** *literary* faint: *he handed her a bottle of ether and she swooned from the odour*. • *noun* **1** a state of being overwhelmed by rapture or emotion: *a fluff-filled swoon of sentimentality*. **2** a period of failure or poor performance: *the stock market fell by more than 5%, its worst swoon since the spring*. **3** an occurrence of fainting: *fell into a deep swoon, occasioned undoubtedly by the frigid water*. ▶ **swoony** *adjective*

swoop • *verb* **1** descend rapidly like a bird of prey. **2** make a sudden attack from a distance. **3** *informal* snatch the whole of at one swoop. • *noun* **1** a swooping or snatching movement or action. **2** a sudden and unexpected attack.

swoosh • *noun* (*plural* **swooshes**) the noise of a sudden rush of liquid, air, etc. • *verb* (**swooshes, swooshed, swooshing**) move or cause to move with this noise.

swop *verb & noun* = SWAP.

sword *noun* **1** a weapon usu. of metal with a long blade and hilt with a hand guard, used esp. for thrusting or striking. **2** (**the sword**) military power, violence, or destruction: *resistance to the bishops' spiritual authority was met with the sword*.

swordfish *noun* (*plural* **swordfish** or **swordfishes**) a large edible marine fish with a streamlined body and a flattened sword-like snout, popular as a game fish.

sword-like *adjective* resembling the long and pointy shape of a sword.

swordplay *noun* **1** fencing. **2** a conversation or debate characterized by quick, witty comments or replies: *I astounded the program's listeners with my devil-may-care swordplay*.

swordsman *noun* (*plural* **swordsmen**) a person of (usu. specified) skill with a sword. ▶ **swordsmanship** *noun*

swore past of SWEAR.

sworn • *verb* past participle of SWEAR. • *adjective* bound by or as by an oath: *sworn enemies*.

swum past participle of SWIM.

swung past and past participle of SWING.

sybarite *noun* a person who is self-indulgent or devoted to the pursuit of pleasure or luxury: *this is no resort for sybarites, for the rooms are basic and the pool has not enough water to fill it*. ▶ **sybaritic** *adjective* **sybaritism** *noun* [Say SIBBA rite, sibba RIT ick]

sycamore *noun* **1** an eastern North American plane tree (*see* PLANE³), which has greyish-brown peeling bark. **2** (also **sycamore maple**) a large maple of Eurasia, with winged seeds, grown for its shade and timber. **3** *Bible* a fig tree of the Middle East. [Say SICKA more]

sycophant *noun* a person who insincerely praises people in positions of importance or authority in order to win their favour or approval: *an entourage of hangers-on and sycophants who are constantly telling him how great he is*. ▶ **sycophantic** *adjective* **sycophantically** *adverb* [Say SICKA fant or SIKE uh fant]

syllabi *plural of* SYLLABUS. [Say SILLA bye]

syllabic • *adjective* **1** of, relating to, or based on syllables. **2** based on the number of syllables: *poetry written in alliterative and syllabic metres*. **3** (of a symbol) representing a whole syllable. **4** articulated with distinct separation of syllables: *a syllabic song with one note to each syllable*. • *noun* **1** a list of characters representing the syllables used in a language and sometimes serving the purpose of an alphabet: *one of the weekly papers is published in Inuktitut syllabics*. **2** a syllabic symbol. [Say suh LABBICK]

syllabication *noun* (also **syllabification**) division into or articulation by syllables. [Say suh labba CAY sh'n, suh labba fuh CAY sh'n]

syllable *noun* **1** a unit of pronunciation uttered without interruption, forming the whole or a part of a word and usu. having one vowel sound often with a consonant or consonants before or after. **2** a character or characters representing a syllable. **3** (usu. with *neg.*) the least amount of speech or writing: *did not utter a syllable*. PHRASES **in words of one syllable** expressed plainly or bluntly. [Say SILLA bull]

syllabus *noun* (*plural* **syllabuses** or **syllabi**) the program or outline of a course of study, teaching, etc. [Say SILLA bus for the singular; for *SYLLABI* say SILLA bye]

syllogism *noun* a form of reasoning in which a conclusion is drawn from two premises, e.g. seagulls are birds; all birds have wings; therefore, all seagulls have wings. ▶ **syllogistic** *adjective* [Say SILLA jism]

sylph *noun* **1** an elemental spirit of the air. **2** a slender graceful woman or girl. ▶ **sylphlike** *adjective* [Say SILF]

sylvan *adjective* esp. *literary* **1** having or associated with woods; wooded: *sylvan hills*. **2** pleasantly rural or pastoral: *the region has every manner of sylvan charm: deep primeval woodlands, wandering footpaths, and a deeply fetching lake*. [Say SILV'n]

symbiosis *noun* (*plural* **symbioses**) **1** an interaction between two different organisms living in close physical association, usu. to the advantage of both: *most reef-building corals live in symbiosis with microscopic algae*. **2** a mutually advantageous association or relationship between persons: *an ingrained symbiosis between mother and daughter*. [Say sim by OH sis or sim bee OH sis; for the plural say sim by OH seez or sim bee OH seez]

symbiotic *adjective* **1** denoting or having to do with the relationship between two different living creatures that live close together and depend on and benefit

from each other in particular ways: *certain fungi, in symbiotic association with the roots of higher plants, provide nutrients, moisture, or disease resistance to their hosts*. **2** denoting or having to do with a partnership or relationship that benefits both people or groups: *in a symbiotic partnership of politician and the press, Thompson made the scandal public by leaking it to the media, who gladly reported the salacious news item*. ▶ **symbiotically** *adverb* [Say sim by OT ick or sim bee OT ick]

SPELL CHECK
symbol, cymbal   ABC✓

The musical instrument is a **cymbal**.

---

symbol *noun* **1** a thing conventionally regarded as typifying, representing, or recalling something. **2** a mark or character taken as the conventional sign of some object, idea, function, or process. ▶ **symbolic** *adjective* **symbolically** *adverb*

symbolism *noun* **1 a** the use of symbols to represent ideas. **b** symbols collectively. **2** an artistic and poetic style using symbols and indirect suggestion rather than direct description to express ideas, emotions, etc. ▶ **symbolist** *noun*

symbolize *verb* (**symbolizes**, **symbolized**, **symbolizing**) **1** be a symbol of. **2** represent by means of symbols.

symbology *noun* (*plural* **symbologies**) **1** the use of symbols. **2** the branch of knowledge dealing with this. **3** symbols collectively. [Say sim BOLLA jee]

symmetric *adjective* = SYMMETRICAL. [Say suh METRIC]

symmetrical *adjective* (of a pattern, shape, object, etc.) made up of two halves, parts, or sides that are identical in size and shape facing each other: *the house features a symmetrical arrangement of rooms*. ▶ **symmetrically** *adverb* [Say suh METRIC'll]

symmetry *noun* (*plural* **symmetries**) **1** the quality of being made up of identical parts facing each other or around an axis: *the symmetry of a butterfly*. **2** correct or pleasing proportion of the parts of a thing: *the poem's overall symmetry*. **3** similarity or exact correspondence between different things: *there is a satisfying moral symmetry in cases where the traitor is himself betrayed*. [Say SIMMA tree]

sympathetic *adjective* **1** of, showing, or expressing sympathy. **2** due to sympathy. **3** likeable or capable of evoking sympathy. **4** (of a person) friendly and co-operative. **5** inclined to favour. **6** (of a pain etc.) caused by a pain or injury to someone else or in another part of the body. **7** sounding by a vibration communicated from another vibrating object. **8** designating the part of the autonomic nervous system consisting of nerves arising from ganglia near the middle of the spinal cord that supply the internal organs, blood vessels, and glands, and balance the action of the parasympathetic nerves. ▶ **sympathetically** *adverb*

sympathize *verb* (**sympathizes**, **sympathized**, **sympathizing**) (often foll. by *with*) **1** feel or express sympathy; share a feeling or opinion. **2** agree with a sentiment or opinion. ▶ **sympathizer** *noun*

sympathy *noun* (*plural* **sympathies**) **1 a** the act of sharing or tendency to share in an emotion or sensation or condition of another person or thing. **b** compassion; condolences. **2** a favourable attitude; approval. **3** agreement (with a person etc.) in opinion or desire. **4** (as an *adjective*) in support of another cause: *sympathy strike*. PHRASES **in sympathy** (often foll. by *with*) **1** having or showing or resulting from sympathy (with another). **2** by way of sympathetic action: *working to rule in sympathy*.

symphonic *adjective* of or having the form or character of a symphony: *symphonic music*. ▶ **symphonically** *adverb* [Say sim FONNICK]

symphony *noun* (*plural* **symphonies**) **1** an elaborate composition usu. for full orchestra, and in several movements. **2** an interlude for orchestra alone in a large-scale vocal work. **3** = SYMPHONY ORCHESTRA. **4** a harmoniously pleasing arrangement of colours, shapes, sounds, etc. [Say SIMFA nee]

symphony orchestra *noun* (*plural* **symphony orchestras**) a large orchestra suitable for playing symphonies etc.

symposium *noun* (*plural* **symposia**) **1** a conference or meeting to discuss a particular subject. **2** a collection of essays or papers for this purpose. [Say sim POZEY um for the singular, sim POZEY uh for the plural]

symptom *noun* **1** a change in the physical or mental condition of a person, regarded as evidence of a disorder. **2** a sign of the existence of something. ▶ **symptomatic** *adjective* **symptomless** *adjective* [Say SIMP tum, simp tuh MAT ick]

synagogue *noun* **1** the building where a Jewish assembly or congregation meets for religious observance and instruction. **2** the assembly itself. [Say SINNA gog]

synapse *noun* **1** a junction of two nerve cells, consisting of a minute gap across which impulses pass by diffusion of a neurotransmitter. **2** (in *plural*) the synapses in the brain, considered as an indicator of mental activity. ▶ **synaptic** *adjective* [Say SIN aps or suh NAPS, suh NAP tick]

sync (also **synch**) *informal* • *noun* synchronization. • *verb* (**synch**, **synchs**, **synched**, **synching**) (often foll. by *up*) synchronize. PHRASES **in** (or **out of**) **sync** (often foll. by *with*) working well (or badly) together; in (or out of) agreement. [Say SINK]

synchro *noun* (*plural* **synchros**) **1** a synchronizing device. **2** synchronized swimming. [Say SINK roe]

synchronicity *noun* the simultaneous occurrence of events which appear significantly related but have no discernible connection: *in 1989 a peculiar synchronicity of events occurred that was to bring the story to a much larger audience*. [Say sink ruh NISSA tee]

synchronization *noun* **1** the action of causing things to happen or operate at the same time or rate. **2** the occurrence of several things at the same time or rate: *the geese flew overhead in perfect synchronization*. PHRASES **in** (or **out of**) **synchronization** (often foll. by *with*) working well (or badly) together; in (or out of) agreement: *the dance team of Heddy and Schmidt appeared to be out of synchronization on some of their moves*. [Say sink ruh nize AY sh'n]

synchronize *verb* (**synchronizes**, **synchronized**, **synchronizing**) **1 a** cause to occur at the same time. **b** occur at the same time. **2** coordinate, combine: *we must synchronize our efforts*. **3 a** cause (clocks etc.) to show a standard or uniform time. **b** (of clocks etc.) be synchronized. **4** operate in unison. [Say SINK ruh nize]

synchronized swimmer *noun* an athlete who participates in the sport of synchronized swimming.

synchronized swimming *noun* a form of swimming in which participants perform coordinated dance-like leg and arm movements to music.

synchronous *adjective* **1** existing or occurring at the same time: *glaciations were approximately synchronous in both hemispheres*. **2** going at the same rate and exactly together: *synchronous motors*. ▶ **synchronously** *adverb* [Say SINK ruh nus]

synchrony *noun* simultaneous action, development, or occurrence: *the relative synchrony in the hatching of the first and second eggs*. [Say SINK ruh nee]

syncline *noun* a fold of layered rock in the earth's

S

crust, forming a trough-shaped depression in which the strata slope upwards from the middle. [Say SINK line]

syncopated *adjective* (of musical rhythm) having the strong accent shifted so that it falls on a beat that is normally not accented. ▶ **syncopation** *noun* [Say SINKA pate]

syncretic *adjective* attempting to combine or reconcile different cultures, religions, or schools of thought: *Latin America is a syncretic fusion of Europe, Amerindian and Afro-Caribbean culture*. [Say sin CRET ick]

syncretism *noun* the amalgamation or attempted amalgamation of different cultures, religions, or schools of thought: *it also demonstrates the syncretism of much Turkish popular music, in its combination of gypsy meter, modal melody, and ornamented vocal style*. ▶ **syncretistic** *adjective* [Say SINK ruh tism]

syndicate • *noun* **1** a combination of individuals or commercial firms to promote some common interest. **2** an association or agency supplying material simultaneously to a number of newspapers, periodicals, etc. **3** a group of people who combine to buy or rent property, gamble, organize crime, etc. • *verb* (**syndicates**, **syndicated**, **syndicating**) **1** form into a syndicate. **2 a** publish through a syndicate. **b** (esp. as **syndicated** *adjective*) publish the work of (a columnist, cartoonist, etc.) through a syndicate. **3** (esp. as **syndicated** *adjective*) make (a television or radio program) available to independent broadcasters. ▶ **syndication** *noun* **syndicator** *noun* [Say SIN duh kit for the noun, SIN duh kate for the verb]

syndrome *noun* **1 a** a group of symptoms or pathological signs which consistently occur together. **b** a condition characterized by such a set of associated symptoms. **2** a characteristic combination of opinions, emotions, behaviour, etc.: *the NIMBY syndrome now makes it almost impossible to build or locate vital facilities that the city needs to function*. [Say SIN drome or SIN drum]

synecdoche *noun* a figure of speech in which a part is made to represent the whole or vice versa, e.g. *new faces at the meeting*; *Italy won by two goals*. [Say suh NECK duh key]

synergistic *adjective* **1** involving the combination of substances, organizations, or other agents that produce a combined effect greater than the sum of their separate effects: *our operation is based on the synergistic integration of computers and communications*. **2** denoting one such substance, organization, or agent, which can be combined with others to produce an effect greater than the sum of their separate effects. ▶ **synergistically** *adverb* [Say sinner JISS tick]

synergy *noun* (plural **synergies**) the interaction or co-operation of two or more drugs, agents, organizations, etc., to produce an effect that exceeds or enhances the sum of their individual effects: *it was the kind of partnership where there's creative synergy and the total is more than the sum of its parts*. [Say SINNER jee]

synod *noun* **1** a church council attended by delegated clergy and sometimes laity. **2** a group of churches whose representatives meet regularly. **3** a Presbyterian church court above the presbyteries and subject to General Assembly. [Say SIN id]

synonym *noun* a word or phrase that means exactly or nearly the same as another in the same language, e.g. *shut* and *close*. [Say SINNA nim]

synonymous *adjective* **1** having the same meaning. **2** (of a name, idea, etc.) suggestive of or associated with another: *blackflies are synonymous with summer*. ▶ **synonymously** *adverb* [Say sin ONNA mus]

synopsis *noun* (plural **synopses**) **1** a summary or outline. **2** a brief general survey. ▶ **synopsize** *verb* (**synopsizes**, **synopsized**, **synopsizing**) [Say sin OP sis for the singular, sin OP seez for the plural]

synoptic *adjective* **1** of, forming, or giving a synopsis: *a synoptic outline of the contents*. **2** taking or affording a comprehensive mental view: *a synoptic model of higher education*. **3** (**Synoptic**) designating any of the Gospels of Matthew, Mark, and Luke, which describe events from a similar point of view. [Say sin OPTIC]

synovial *adjective* denoting or relating to a viscous fluid lubricating joints and tendon sheaths. [Say sigh NO vee ul]

syntactic *adjective* of or according to syntax. ▶ **syntactical** *adjective* **syntactically** *adverb* [Say sin TACTIC]

syntax *noun* the order of words in which they convey meaning collectively by their connection and relation; sentence structure.

synth *noun* *informal* = SYNTHESIZER. [Say SINTH]

synthase *noun* an enzyme which catalyzes the linking together of two molecules, esp. without the direct involvement of ATP. [Say SIN thace or SIN thaze]

synthesis *noun* (plural **syntheses**) **1** the process or result of building up separate elements, esp. ideas, into a connected whole, esp. into a theory or system. **2** a combination or composition. **3** *Chemistry* the formation of a compound by combination of its elements or constituents, esp. the artificial production of compounds from their constituents as distinct from extraction from plants etc. [Say SINTH uh sis for the singular, SINTH uh seez for the plural]

synthesist *noun* a person who synthesizes something, esp. a person who produces music or imitates sounds electronically using a synthesizer. [Say SINTH uh sist]

synthesize *verb* (**synthesizes**, **synthesized**, **synthesizing**) **1** make a synthesis of. **2** combine into a coherent whole. **3** (esp. as **synthesized** *adjective*) produce or imitate electronically using a synthesizer. [Say SINTH uh size]

synthesizer *noun* an electronic musical instrument, esp. operated by a music keyboard, producing a wide variety of sounds by generating and combining signals of different frequencies. [Say SINTH uh sizer]

synthetic • *adjective* **1 a** made by chemical synthesis, esp. to imitate a natural product: *synthetic rubber*. **b** artificial, imitation, invented. **2** (of emotions etc.) insincere. **3** of, pertaining to, involving, or using synthesis, or combination of parts into a whole. • *noun* a synthetic substance. ▶ **synthetically** *adverb*

syph *noun* *informal* syphilis. [Say SIFF]

syphilis *noun* a sexually transmitted disease progressing from infection of the genitals via the skin and mucous membrane to the bones, muscles, and brain. ▶ **syphilitic** *adjective & noun* [Say SIFFA liss, siffa LIT ick]

Syrah *noun* **1** a variety of black grape used in winemaking, grown originally in the Rhone valley of France, now also esp. in Australia and South Africa. **2** a red wine produced from these grapes. [Say SEERA]

Syrian • *noun* **1** a native or national of the modern state of Syria in the Middle East; a person of Syrian descent. **2** a native or inhabitant of the region of Syria in antiquity or later. • *adjective* of or relating to the region or state of Syria. [Say SEERY in]

syringe • *noun* **1** a tube with a nozzle and piston or bulb for sucking in and ejecting liquid in a fine stream. **2** (also **hypodermic syringe**) a similar device with a hollow needle for insertion under the skin. • *verb* (**syringes**, **syringed**, **syringing**) sluice or spray (the ear, a plant, etc.) with a syringe. [Say suh RINDGE]

syrup *noun* **1** any of various very sweet liquids used e.g. as a topping, to flavour a drink, to preserve canned fruit, as a medicine, etc. **2** *Cdn* (*Nfld*) a fruit-flavoured drink of water and syrup. ▶ **syrupy** *adjective*

S

sysadmin *noun* a system administrator. [Say SISS ad min]

sysop *noun* a system operator. [Say SISS op]

system *noun* **1** a complex whole; a set of connected things, parts, institutions, etc.; an organized body of material or immaterial things: *school system*. **2** a set of devices functioning together. **3 a** a set of organs in the body with a common structure or function: *the digestive system*. **b** the human or animal body as a whole. **4 a** a method; considered principles of procedure or classification. **b** a classification. **5 a** a body of theory or practice relating to or prescribing a particular form of government, religion, etc. **b (the system)** the prevailing political or social order, esp. regarded as oppressive and intransigent. **6** *Computing* a group of related hardware units or programs or both, esp. when dedicated to a single application. **7** a major group of geological strata: *the Devonian system*. **8** *Physics* a group of associated bodies moving under mutual gravitation etc. PHRASES **get a thing out of one's system** *informal* be rid of a preoccupation or anxiety.

system administrator *noun* a person who administers a computer system or network.

systematic *adjective* **1** done or conceived according to a plan or system, in a thorough, efficient or determined way. **2** (of a person etc.) acting according to a system; methodical. ▶ **systematically** *adverb*

systematize *verb* (**systematizes**, **systematized**, **systematizing**) arrange according to an organized system; make systematic: *Galen systematized medical thought*. [Say SYSTEM a tize]

systemic *adjective* **1 a** of or concerning the whole body, not confined to a particular part. **b** (of blood circulation) transporting oxygen to and carbon dioxide from the body in general, as opposed to transporting oxygen from and carbon dioxide to the lungs specifically. **2** (of an insecticide, fungicide, etc.) entering the plant via the roots or shoots and passing through the tissues. **3** of or pertaining to a system, esp. in its entirety: *by adopting a systemic approach it became possible to cover all aspects of heritage — genealogy, folklore, nature, history, and architecture — as parts of a whole*. ▶ **systemically** *adverb* [Say siss TEM ick]

system operator *noun* a person who manages the operation of an electronic bulletin board.

systems analysis *noun* the analysis of a complex process or operation in order to improve its efficiency, esp. by applying a computer system. ▶ **systems analyst** *noun*

systems operator *noun* a person who controls or monitors the operation of complex esp. electronic systems.

Szechuan *noun* (also **Szechwan**) (as an *adjective*) designating food cooked in the distinctively spicy style of cuisine originating in Sichuan, a province of west central China. [Say SETCH wahn or SESH wahn]

S

Tt

T¹ *noun* (also **t**) (*plural* **Ts** or **T's**) **1** the twentieth letter of the alphabet. **2** a T-shaped thing (esp. as an *adjective*: *T-joint*). **3** = T-SHIRT. PHRASES **to a T** exactly; to a nicety.

T² *symbol* **1** *Chemistry* the isotope tritium. **2** tesla. **3** temperature. **4** tenor. **5** thiamine. **6** the time at which an event, esp. the launch of a spacecraft, is scheduled to occur: *T minus three minutes*.

t. *abbreviation* **1** ton(s). **2** tonne(s).

T4 *noun* (*plural* **T4's**) (also **T4 slip**) *Cdn* an official statement issued by an employer, indicating one's earnings for the year as well as taxes and any deductions, used to calculate the amount of taxes owed, and submitted with one's tax return.

TA *informal* • *noun* (*plural* **TA's**) TEACHING ASSISTANT. • *verb* (**TA's, TA'd, TA'ing**) work as a teaching assistant.

Ta *symbol* tantalum.

tab • *noun* **1 a** a small flap or strip of material attached for grasping, fastening, or hanging up, or for identification. **b** a similar object as a decorative part of a garment etc. **2** *informal* a bill or price: *picked up the tab*. **3 a** a function on a typewriter or computer keyboard allowing the movement of the carriage, cursor, etc. to be pre-set. **b** the key used to advance the carriage or cursor this predetermined distance. **4** a tabloid. **5** *slang* a tablet, esp. containing an illicit drug. • *verb* (**tabs, tabbed, tabbing**) **1** provide with a tab or tabs. **2** designate, name, label: *was tabbed as her successor*. PHRASES **keep tabs on** *informal* **1** keep account of. **2** have under observation or in check.

Tabasco *noun* *proprietary* a hot pepper sauce. [Say tuh BAS co]

tabbouleh *noun* a Middle Eastern salad made with bulgur, parsley, onion, mint, lemon juice, oil, and spices. [Say tuh BOO lee]

tabby *noun* (*plural* **tabbies**) (also **tabby cat**) **1** a grey, orange, or brownish cat mottled or streaked with dark stripes. **2** any domestic cat, esp. female.

tabernacle *noun* **1** a tent used by the Israelites on their journey from Egypt to Canaan as a sanctuary for the Ark of the Covenant, the wooden chest which contained the tablets of the Law given to Moses by God. **2** *Christianity* a niche or receptacle esp. for the consecrated Eucharistic elements. **3** a place of worship.

tabla *noun* (*plural* **tablas**) (in Indian music) a pair of small drums played with the hands. [Say TAB luh or TOB luh]

> **WRITING TIP**
> **table**
>
> In Canada *to table a bill* usually means "to introduce a bill for discussion", especially in parliamentary contexts, while in the US it means "to set a bill aside indefinitely". Because of these contradictory senses, make sure your meaning is clear if you use the word, or use another word instead, e.g. **introduce** or **set aside**.

table • *noun* **1** a piece of furniture with a flat top and one or more legs. **2** a group seated at table for dinner etc. **3** a set of facts or figures systematically displayed, esp. in columns: *a table of contents*. **4** a flat surface for working on or for machinery to operate on. **5** a

tableland. **6** (**the table**) = BARGAINING TABLE: *sought to draw them back to the table*. **7** any plane or level area: *water table*. • *verb* (**tables, tabled, tabling**) **1** *Cdn* & *Brit.* bring forward for discussion or consideration at a meeting. **2** esp. *US* postpone consideration of (a matter). PHRASES **at table** taking a meal at a table. **lay on the table 1** submit for discussion. **2** esp. *US* postpone indefinitely. **on the table** offered for discussion. **turn the tables** (often foll. by *on*) reverse one's relations (with), esp. by turning an inferior into a superior position (originally in backgammon). **under the table** *informal* **1** (of a transaction etc., esp. payment) done surreptitiously esp. to avoid taxes or duties. **2** very drunk after a meal or drinking bout.

tableau *noun* (*plural* **tableaux**) a picturesque scene, either in real life or involving motionless actors, that reminds the viewer of a painting. [Say TAB loe for the singular, TAB loze for the plural]

tablecloth *noun* a cloth spread over the top of a table.

table d'hôte *noun* (*plural* **tables d'hôte**) a meal consisting of a set menu at a fixed price (*compare* À LA CARTE). [Say tab luh DOTE]

tableful *noun* (*plural* **tablefuls**) a number of people seated around a table.

table hockey *noun* = TABLETOP HOCKEY.

table lamp *noun* a small usu. decorative lamp designed to stand on a table etc.

tableland *noun* an area of fairly level high land; a plateau.

table linen *noun* tablecloths, napkins, etc.

table manners *plural noun* decorum or correct behaviour while eating at table.

table saw *noun* a power tool consisting of a fixed circular saw mounted beneath a metal table with the blade projecting up through a slot.

tablespoon *noun* **1** a large spoon used for eating soup, cereal, etc. or for serving food. **2** a measuring spoon used in cooking, equal to $^1/_2$ fluid ounce (approx. 15 ml). Abbreviation: **tbsp**. **3** the amount held by either of these. ▶**tablespoonful** *noun* (*plural* **tablespoonfuls**)

tablet *noun* **1** a small measured and compressed amount of a substance, esp. of a medicine or drug. **2** a flat slab of stone or wood, esp. for display or an inscription. **3** a writing pad.

table tennis *noun* an indoor game based on lawn tennis, played with small bats and a ball bounced on a table divided by a net.

tabletop *noun* **1** the top or surface of a table. **2** (as an *adjective*) that can be placed or used on a tabletop.

tabletop hockey *noun* a game played using a board or table resembling a miniature hockey rink, with players which can be made to move and shoot using connected rods running beneath the "ice" surface and projecting at either end.

tableware *noun* dishes, plates, etc., for use at meals.

table wine *noun* ordinary wine for a meal.

tabloid *noun* **1** a newspaper, usu. popular in style with bold headlines and large photographs, having pages half the size of those of the average broadsheet. **2** (as an

adjective) designating highly sensational or lurid journalism etc.: *tabloid TV.*

taboo • *noun* (*plural* **taboos**) **1** (also **tabu**; *plural* **tabus**) a system or the act of setting a person or thing apart as sacred or accursed. **2** a prohibition or restriction imposed by social custom: *taboos against marriage between members of different tribes.* **3** a thing, activity, word, etc. prohibited: *brewing your own coffee in your own office was a taboo.* • *adjective* avoided or prohibited, esp. by social custom: *taboo words.* • *verb* (**taboos, tabooed, tabooing**) **1** put (a thing, practice, etc.) under taboo: *the crime of touching tabooed objects.* **2** exclude or prohibit by authority or social influence.

tabular *adjective* **1** of or arranged in tables or lists: *the statistics were presented in tabular form.* **2** broad and flat like a table: *tabular icebergs can be colossal — one is recorded to have been 110 km long and 75 km wide.* **3** (of a crystal) having two broad flat faces. [Say TAB you ler]

tabula rasa *noun* the human mind (esp. at birth) viewed as a "blank slate", i.e. having no innate ideas. [Say tab you luh RAZZA]

tabulate *verb* (**tabulates, tabulated, tabulating**) arrange (figures or facts) in the form of a table. ▶ **tabulation** *noun*

tachometer *noun* an instrument for measuring the rate of rotation of a shaft and hence the speed or velocity of a vehicle. [Say tuh COMMA ter]

tachycardia *noun* an abnormally rapid heart rate. [Say tacky CARDY uh]

tacit *adjective* understood or implied without being stated: *tacit consent.* ▶ **tacitly** *adverb* [Say TASS it]

taciturn *adjective* reserved in speech; saying little; uncommunicative: *she was uneasy in a crowd, and taciturn with any but a small circle of friends.* ▶ **taciturnity** *noun* [Say TASSA turn, tassa TURN it ee]

tack¹ • *noun* **1 a** a small broad-headed sharp nail. **b** = THUMBTACK. **2** a long stitch used in fastening fabrics etc. lightly or temporarily together. **3 a** the direction in which a ship moves as determined by the position of its sails and regarded in terms of the direction of the wind: *starboard tack.* **b** a temporary change of direction in sailing made by turning the ship's head to the wind. **c** one of a consecutive series of such movements to port and starboard alternately, tracing a zigzag course, and made by a ship in order to reach a point to windward. **4** a course of action or policy: *try another tack.* **5** a sticky condition of varnish etc. • *verb* **1** fasten with or as if with tacks. **2** stitch (pieces of cloth etc.) lightly together. **3** (foll. by *to, on*) annex, append (a thing). **4 a** change a ship's course by turning its head to the wind. **b** make a series of tacks in order to progress to windward. **5** change one's conduct or policy etc.

tack² • *noun* the saddle, bridle, etc., of a horse. • *verb* (often foll. by *up*) put tack on (a horse).

tacker *noun* a tool for driving tacks or staples into wood.

tackiness *noun* **1** *informal* the quality of something that is poor in taste, quality, or style. **2** a slight stickiness of recently applied glue, paint, etc. that is not yet completely dry.

tackle • *noun* **1** equipment for a task or sport: *fishing tackle.* **2** a mechanism, esp. of ropes, pulleys, blocks, hooks, etc., for lifting weights, managing sails, etc.: *block and tackle.* **3** a windlass with its ropes and hooks. **4** an act of tackling in football etc. **5** *Football* **a** the position next to the end of either the offensive or defensive line. **b** the player in this position. • *verb* (**tackles, tackled, tackling**) **1** try to deal with (a problem or difficulty). **2 a** (esp. in football) seize forcefully or throw one's body at in order to stop or take down. **b** (in soccer etc.) obstruct, intercept, or stop (a

player running with the ball). **3** (often foll. by *on, about*) initiate discussion with (a person), esp. with regard to a disputed issue. **4** secure or lift by means of tackle.

tackle box *noun* a box with many compartments for storing and carrying fishing tackle.

tackler *noun* esp. *Football* a defensive player who makes or attempts a tackle.

tack room *noun* (also **tack shed** etc.) a room etc. in a stable where the saddles, bridles, etc. are kept.

tacky *adjective* (**tackier, tackiest**) **1** (of glue or paint etc.) still slightly sticky after application. **2** *informal* showing poor taste, quality, or style.

taco *noun* (*plural* **tacos**) a fried corn tortilla folded over and filled with ground meat, tomatoes, lettuce, shredded cheese, guacamole, etc. [Say TACKO or TOCKO]

taco shell *noun* a usu. crisp folded tortilla for tacos.

tact *noun* **1** skill in dealing with others or with difficulties arising from personal feeling. **2** intuitive perception of the right thing to do or say.

tactful *adjective* careful not to say or do anything that will annoy or upset other people. ▶ **tactfully** *adverb* **tactfulness** *noun*

tactic *noun* **1** a plan or method used to achieve something, esp. against an opponent. **2** = TACTICS 1.

tactical *adjective* **1 a** of, relating to, or constituting actions carefully planned to gain a specific military end: *a tactical retreat.* **b** (of bombing or weapons) done or for use in immediate support of military or naval operations (*opp.* STRATEGIC 3). **2** carefully planned in order to achieve a particular aim: *a tactical decision.* **3** (of voting) aimed at preventing the strongest candidate from winning by supporting the next strongest. ▶ **tactically** *adverb*

tactical team *noun* (also **tactical squad**) a unit in a police force trained to handle especially volatile situations.

tactician *noun* a person who is very clever at planning the best way to achieve something: *a fine political tactician.* [Say tack TISH'n]

tactics *plural noun* **1** (also treated as *singular*) the art of disposing armed forces esp. in contact with an enemy (*compare* STRATEGY 4a). **2** the esp. immediate or short-range plans and means adopted in carrying out a scheme or achieving some end.

tactile *adjective* **1** of the sense of touch: *the spider's tactile hairs.* **2** perceived by touch: *children need tactile objects to manipulate and visualize in order to think through an operation.* [Say TACK tile]

tactless *adjective* having or showing a lack of sensitivity in dealing with others or with difficult issues. ▶ **tactlessly** *adverb* **tactlessness** *noun*

tad *noun* *informal* a small amount (often used as an adverb: *a tad too salty*).

ta-dah *interjection* (also **ta-da**) expressing triumph, a dramatic revelation, etc.

tadpole *noun* the tailed aquatic larva of a frog, toad, or other amphibian from the time it leaves the egg until it loses its gills or tail and acquires legs.

Tadzhik *noun & adjective* = TAJIK. [Say tuh JEEK]

tae kwon do *noun* a modern Korean martial art similar to karate. [Say tie kwon DOE]

taffeta *noun* (*plural* **taffetas**) a fine lustrous silk or silk-like fabric. [Say TAFFA tuh]

taffy *noun* (*plural* **taffies**) **1** a chewy confection similar to toffee made from brown sugar or molasses boiled with butter and pulled until glossy. **2** *Cdn* a similar confection made by pouring hot maple syrup onto packed snow.

tag¹ • *noun* **1 a** a label attached to or worn by a person or thing, esp. to indicate price, ownership, identity, etc. **b** a metal clip used to identify an animal or bird, esp. in

order to trace its migratory patterns etc. **c** an electronic device that can be attached to a person or thing for monitoring purposes, e.g. to track offenders or to deter shoplifters. **2** informal a nickname or popular designation. **3** a trite quotation or stock phrase esp. used as a motto or slogan. **4 a** the refrain of a song. **b** a musical phrase added to the end of a piece. • *verb* (**tags, tagged, tagging**) **1** provide with a tag or tags. **2** (often foll. by *on*, *on to*) add, esp. as an afterthought; tack on. **3** informal follow closely or trail behind. **4** Computing label (an item of data) in order to identify it for subsequent processing or retrieval. **5** attach an identifying label to (an animal). PHRASES **tag along** (often foll. by *with*) go along with or accompany.

tag² • *noun* **1** a children's game in which one player chases the others, and anyone who is caught then becomes "it" and inherits the role of the pursuer. **2** = TELEPHONE TAG. **3** Baseball the act of tagging a runner. • *verb* (**tags, tagged, tagging**) **1** touch (a player) in a game of tag. **2** Baseball **a** touch (a runner) with the ball or a gloved hand holding the ball. **b** (foll. by *out*) put (a runner) out by doing this. **c** (usu. foll. by *up*) (of a runner) return to and touch a base before attempting to advance after a fly ball is caught. **d** score a hit or run off (a pitcher). **3** informal strike (a person) with a powerful punch or blow.

Tagalog • *noun* (plural **Tagalog** or **Tagalogs**) **1** a member of the principal people of the Philippines. **2** the language of this people, the vocabulary of which has been heavily influenced by Spanish with some adoptions from Chinese and Arabic. • *adjective* having to do with this people or language. [Say ta GAL og]

tagalong • *noun* a follower or companion, esp. one who is uninvited or unwelcome. • *adjective* **1** that is towed or trailed behind something else. **2** (of a follower or companion) uninvited or unwelcome.

tag end noun **1** a loose end of something, esp. a strand of tinsel etc. serving as the tail of an angler's fly. **2** = TAIL END.

tagged adjective that has been tagged; provided with a tag or tags.

tagine noun = TAJINE. [Say ta ZHEEN]

Tagish • *noun* (plural **Tagish**) **1** a member of an Aboriginal people living esp. in the southern Yukon. **2** the Athapaskan language of this people. • *adjective* of this people or their culture. [Say TAG ish]

tagliatelle noun **1** a type of pasta made in narrow ribbons. **2** a dish consisting of this pasta served with sauce etc. [Say tal yuh TELLY]

tag line noun a catchphrase or slogan, esp. one used in advertising or as the punchline of a joke.

tag team noun **1** a pair of wrestlers who fight as a team by alternately competing in the ring against one of another paired team of opponents. **2** two people completing a single task as a team.

tahini noun a paste or sauce made from ground sesame seeds. [Say tuh HEENY]

Tahitian • *noun* **1** a native or inhabitant of Tahiti, an island in the central South Pacific. **2** the Polynesian language of Tahiti. • *adjective* of or relating to Tahiti, its people, or language. [Say tuh HEE sh'n or tuh HEETY un]

Tahltan • *noun* (plural **Tahltan** or **Tahltans**) **1** a member of an Aboriginal people living in the area of the Stikine River, BC. **2** the Athapaskan language of this people. • *adjective* of or relating to this people. [Say TAWL tan]

Tai Chi noun (also **Tai Chi Chuan**) a Chinese martial art and system of exercises consisting of sequences of very slow controlled movements. [Say tie CHEE, tie chee CHWON]

taiga noun (plural **taigas**) any of the swampy coniferous

forests of subarctic North America, Europe, and Asia, usu. lying between Arctic tundra to the north and boreal forest or steppe to the south. [Say TIE guh]

taiko noun (plural **taikos**) any of a variety of Japanese two-headed drums made of a hollow wooden shell the opening of which is covered with cowhide. [Say TIKE oh]

tail • *noun* **1** the rear part of an animal, esp. an elongation of the vertebral column forming a flexible appendage that extends beyond the rest of the body. **2 a** a thing resembling an animal's tail in shape or position. **b** the rear end of anything, e.g. of a procession of people or vehicles. **c** the inferior or weaker part of anything, esp. in a sequence. **3** the rear part of an airplane, car, missile, etc. **4 a** a luminous trail of dust extending from the head of a comet and curving away from the sun. **b** a nearly straight trail of ionized atoms lying in the plane of a comet's orbit and blown away from the nucleus. **5 a** the hanging part of the back of a coat. **b** = SHIRT-TAIL noun. **6** (in plural) informal **a** a tailcoat. **b** a man's formal attire including tailcoat. **7** a twisted or braided tress of hair, such as a pigtail. **8 a** the image on the reverse of a coin. **b** (in plural) this side as a choice when tossing a coin. **9** an extra strip attached to the end of a kite. **10** Cdn the southeast portion of the Grand Banks of Newfoundland, lying outside Canada's 320-km (200-mile) fishing zone (compare NOSE 6). **11** informal a person who secretly watches or follows another, esp. as a detective or spy. **12** slang the buttocks: *had to work my tail off.* • *verb* **1** informal follow closely and secretly; spy on. **2** (often foll. by *away*) (of an object in flight) deviate; drift, carry, or curve away from a target. PHRASES **on a person's tail** closely following a person. **tail off** (or **away**) diminish gradually; decrease in intensity, output, production, etc. **with one's tail between one's legs** in a state of dejection or humiliation.

tailback noun Football the running back who lines up furthest from the line of scrimmage.

tailbone noun **1** each of the vertebrae in the tail of an animal. **2** the small triangular bone at the base of the spinal column in humans and some apes.

tailcoat noun a man's morning or evening coat with long tails at the back, worn as part of formal dress.

tailed adjective **1** having a tail of a specified type, shape, colour, size, etc. **2** having a tail.

tail end noun **1** the conclusion or final part: *the tail end of the movie.* **2** the back end of a thing; the part at the rear: *the tail end of the procession.*

tail fin noun **1** the rear fin of a fish. **2** an upswept projection on the rear of a car. **3** a small projecting surface on the tail of an aircraft to provide stability.

tailgate • *noun* the hinged door at the back of a pickup truck, station wagon, or hatchback, esp. one which drops down forming a shelf to facilitate loading and unloading. • *verb* (**tailgates, tailgated, tailgating**) informal follow (another vehicle) too closely. ▶ **tailgater** noun

tailings plural noun crushed stone and other waste produced in drilling, mining, or smelting ore.

tailings pond noun (also **tailing pond**) a large pool into which the tailings produced by mining and drilling etc. are drained.

tailless adjective without a tail: *a tailless cat.*

tail light noun (also **tail lamp**) a usu. red light on the back or at the rear of esp. a motor vehicle.

tailor • *noun* a person who alters men's clothing and makes suits and jackets etc. to measure. • *verb* **1** design and make (clothing) esp. to meet the size requirements of a particular customer. **2** design or adapt (something) to suit a specific need or purpose: *homes tailored to meet our needs.*

tailored *adjective* **1** made by a tailor, esp. in a specified way or style: *hand-tailored*. **2** (of clothing) well cut and closely fitted; having the appearance of custom-made or tailor-made clothes. **3** having a neat design or appearance; trim, sleek: *a tailored look*. **4** made to suit a specific purpose or need.

tailoring *noun* **1** the business or occupation of a tailor. **2** the skill or workmanship of a tailor.

tailor-made • *adjective* **1** (of clothing) made by a tailor to suit the needs of a particular customer. **2** altered or designed to meet a specific need, purpose, or requirement. **3** (of a person, situation, etc.) ideally suited; perfect. **4** (of a cigarette) made in a factory, not rolled by the smoker. • *noun* **1** a tailor-made article of clothing. **2** a tailor-made cigarette.

tailpiece *noun* **1** an appendage attached to a thing to extend or conclude it. **2** a tube that extends from the drain of a sink to a trap.

tailpipe *noun* the rear section of the exhaust pipe of a motor vehicle.

tailplane *noun* a horizontal airfoil at the tail of an aircraft.

tailrace *noun* a watercourse leading away from the turbine of a power station, a water wheel, a dam, etc.

tailspin • *noun* **1** a state of chaos, panic, or loss of control. **2 a** a sharp or rapid decline. **b** *Sport* a slump. **3** a nose-first spiralling descent of an aircraft. • *verb* (**tailspins, tailspun, tailspinning**) perform or fall into a tailspin.

tailwind *noun* a wind blowing in the direction of travel of an aircraft or vehicle.

taint • *noun* **1** a trace, suggestion, or connotation of some bad or undesirable quality. **2** a corrupting influence; a cause of corruption or decay: *the taint of racism*. **3** a trace of rot, decay, or putrefaction, esp. an unpleasant scent or smell. • *verb* **1** contaminate or pollute: *toxins have tainted the lake* ◊ *tainted blood*. **2** cause to turn foul or rotten: *tainted tuna*. **3** ruin, spoil: *tainted love*. **4** affect with a bad or undesirable quality: *this administration has been tainted by scandal* ◊ *ideologies tainted with fanaticism*.

Taiwanese • *noun* (*plural* **Taiwanese**) **1** a native or inhabitant of Taiwan (officially called the Republic of China), an island country off the southeastern coast of China. **2** a person of Taiwanese descent. • *adjective* of Taiwan or its people or culture. [Say tie wah NEEZ]

Tajik (*plural* **Tajiks** or **Tajik**) • *noun* **1** a native or inhabitant of the republic of Tajikistan, a mountainous country in central Asia. **2** the Iranian language of the Tajiks. • *adjective* of Tajikistan or its people. [Say taw JEEK]

tajine *noun* **1** a traditional shallow earthenware Moroccan cooking pot with a conical lid. **2** any of a variety of stews cooked in this pot. [Say ta ZHEEN]

take • *verb* (**takes**; *past* **took**; *past participle* **taken**; **taking**) **1** lay hold of with one's hands; reach for and hold. **2** occupy (a place or position). **3** capture or gain possession of by force. **4** carry or bring with one; convey. **5** remove from a place. **6** subtract. **7** consume as food, drink, medicine, or drugs. **8** bring into a specified state. **9** experience or be affected by. **10** use as a route or a means of transport. **11** accept or receive. **12** acquire or assume (a position, state, or form). **13** require or use up. **14** hold or accommodate. **15** act on (an opportunity). **16** regard, view, or deal with in a specified way: *he took it as an insult*. **17** submit to, tolerate, or endure. **18** make, undertake, or perform (an action or task). **19** be taught in (a subject). • *noun* **1** a sequence of sound or vision photographed or recorded continuously. **2** a particular version of or approach to something: *her whimsical take on life*. **3** an amount gained or acquired from one source or in one session. PHRASES **be taken ill** become ill, esp. suddenly. **have what it takes** *informal* have the necessary qualities etc. for success. **on the take** *slang* receiving bribes. **take after** resemble (a parent or relative etc.), esp. in behaviour or attitudes. **take apart 1** dismantle. **2** *informal* beat or defeat conclusively. **take away 1** (foll. by *from*) diminish; weaken; detract from. **2** subtract. **3** remove or carry elsewhere. **take back 1** retract (a statement). **2** convey (a person or thing) to his or her or its original position. **3** help (a person) recall or imagine an earlier time or incident. **4 a** return (merchandise) to a store. **b** (of a store) accept such merchandise for return. **5** accept (a person) back into one's affections, into employment, etc. **take the cake** (or **biscuit**) *informal* be the most remarkable, outrageous, amusing, annoying, etc. **take down 1** write down or record (spoken words, information, etc.). **2 a** disassemble (a structure) by dismantling. **b** remove (a fixture, decoration, etc.) from a hanging position. **3** (also **take down a peg**) humiliate. **4** *informal* **a** seize and wrestle to the ground; tackle. **b** defeat, subdue. **5** lower (one's pants or a similar article of clothing worn below the waist). **take heart** be encouraged. **take ill** (or **sick**) *informal* become ill or sick. **take in 1** draw or receive in (esp. air or moisture); absorb, swallow, inhale. **2** understand: *did you take that in?* **3** *informal* go out to see (a movie etc.). **4** offer hospitality or shelter to (a person or animal). **5** make (an article of clothing) smaller. **6** cheat: *take them all in*. **7** include or comprise. **take in hand 1** undertake; start doing or dealing with. **2** undertake the control or reform of (a person). **take it 1** (often foll. by *that* + clause) assume. **2** *informal* put up with or endure a difficult situation. **take it from me** (or **take my word for it**) I can assure you. **take it upon oneself** venture or presume: *She always took it upon herself to correct my "mistakes".* **take it or leave it** (esp. in *imper.*) an expression of indifference or impatience about another's decision after making an offer. **take it out on** relieve one's frustration or anger by attacking or treating harshly. **take a lot** (or **it**) **out of** exhaust the strength of. **take off 1** remove (clothing) from one's or another's body. **b** lose (weight). **2** remove. **3** deduct (part of an amount). **4** *informal* depart, esp. hastily: *took off in a fast car*. **5** *informal* mimic humorously. **6** jump from the ground. **7** become airborne. **8** (of a scheme, enterprise, etc.) become successful or popular. **9** have (a period) away from work. **take on 1** undertake (work etc.). **2** hire (an employee). **3** challenge or confront (an opponent or adversary). **4** acquire (a new meaning etc.). **take out 1** escort on a date or outing. **2** buy (food etc.) at a restaurant for eating elsewhere. **3 a** remove from within a place; extract. **b** carry (something) outside. **4** get (a licence or summons etc.) issued. **5** apply for and receive (a loan) from a bank. **6** borrow (a book etc.) from a library. **7** *slang* **a** *Sport* remove (a player) from play with a check, block, or tackle. **b** assassinate, murder. **take over 1** succeed to the management or ownership of. **2** take control (of). **take some** (or **a lot of**) **doing** be hard to do. **take that!** an exclamation accompanying a blow etc. **take one's time** not hurry. **take to 1** adopt as a habit, practice, pastime, hobby, etc. **2** form a liking for. **3** have recourse to: *took to drinking*. **4** escape to; seek refuge in. **take up 1** become interested or engaged in (an interest, pursuit, hobby, etc.). **2** adopt as a protege. **3** occupy (time or space). **4** begin (residence etc.). **5** resume after an interruption. **6** join in (a song, chorus, etc.). **7** accept (an offer etc.). **8** shorten (a garment). **9** go over the

correct answers to (homework, an assignment, a test, etc.). **10** lift up. **11** absorb: *sponges take up water.* **12** pursue (a matter etc.) further. **take a person up on** accept (a person's offer etc.). **take up the gauntlet** accept a challenge. **take up with** begin to associate with.

takeaway *noun* (*plural* **takeaways**) *Football* an interception made or fumble forced by the defence (*compare* GIVEAWAY 4).

take-charge *adjective* characterized by leadership or authority: *a take-charge attitude.*

takedown *noun* **1** a wrestling manoeuvre in which an opponent is swiftly brought to the mat from a standing position. **2** *informal* a police raid or arrest.

take-home *adjective* **1** that may be taken home. **2** (of pay etc.) remaining after taxes etc. have been deducted. **3** (of a test etc.) distributed to students to be written outside of class within a specified period of time.

take-it-or-leave-it *adjective* characterized by or involving indifference: *a take-it-or-leave-it attitude.*

take-no-prisoners *adjective* very aggressive or persistent; forceful: *a take-no-prisoners approach.*

takeoff *noun* **1** the action of an aircraft becoming airborne. **2 a** an act of mimicking, esp. a caricature or parody. **b** an imitation. **3 a** the moment of springing from the ground during a leap or jump. **b** a place from which one jumps. **4** the beginning of a new phase of accelerated or increased growth or development.

takeout *noun* **1 a** a food or a meal bought at a restaurant to be eaten off the premises. **b** a restaurant preparing food that may be bought and eaten elsewhere. **2** *Curling* a shot which removes an opponent's rock from play. **3** a pullout article in a newspaper or magazine.

takeover *noun* **1** the assumption of control or ownership of a business concern, esp. the buying out of one company by another. **2** a usu. hostile assumption of power or government; a military coup. **3** an act of taking over.

takeover bid *noun* an offer made to the shareholders of a company by an individual or organization to buy their shares at a specified price in order to gain control of that company.

taker *noun* **1** a person who takes a specified thing: *a drug-taker* ◊ *risk-takers.* **2** a person who takes a bet or accepts an offer or challenge: *there were plenty of takers when I offered a small wager.*

taking • *adjective* attractive or captivating. • *noun* **1** the action or process of TAKE *verb*: *mine for the taking.* **2** (in *plural*) the amount of money earned by a business from the sale of goods or services: *theatre owners keep, on average, 60% of box office takings.*

talc *noun* **1** a white, grey, or pale green soft mineral form of magnesium silicate with a greasy feel; consolidated fine-grained talc is known as soapstone, and in its powdered form it is used as a lubricant, as a filler in paper and paints, in ceramics, and in cosmetics. **2** talcum powder.

talcum *noun* (also **talcum powder**) a preparation of powdered talc, usu. scented or medicated for general cosmetic use.

tale *noun* **1 a** a story or narrative, true or fictitious, told for interest or entertainment. **b** a literary composition cast in narrative form. **2 a** a report of an alleged fact, often malicious or in breach of confidence. **b** (often in *plural*) a false or fanciful statement; a lie. **3** a true account of improbable or extraordinary events. PHRASES **live to tell the tale** survive an unpleasant or catastrophic event.

talent *noun* **1 a** a special skill or ability. **2 a** a person possessing exceptional skill or ability. **b** people of talent or ability collectively: *this team is loaded with*

talent. **3** an ancient unit of weight and currency, esp. among the Greeks. ▶ **talented** *adjective* **talentless** *adjective*

talent scout *noun* a person looking for talented performers, esp. in sport and entertainment.

talent show *noun* a show consisting of performances by promising amateur entertainers, esp. ones hoping to enter show business professionally.

talisman *noun* (*plural* **talismans**) **1** an object, esp. an inscribed ring or stone, supposed to be endowed with magic powers esp. of averting evil from or bringing good luck to its holder: *a gold ring in the shape of two snakes had been the countess's talisman.* **2** a thing supposed capable of working wonders: *among fitness mavens and longevity seekers, the favoured talismans are the antioxidant nutrients — vitamins E and C and beta carotene.* ▶ **talismanic** *adjective* [Say TAL iz mun, tal iz MANIC]

talk • *verb* **1** speak in order to give information or express ideas or feelings. **2** have the power of speech. **3** (foll. by *into, out of*) persuade (a person) to agree to do or not to do something: *he talked me into it.* **4** *informal* have in mind, think in terms of, envisage: *I'm talking six figures.* **5** gossip: *people are starting to talk.* • *noun* **1** conversation or talking. **2** a particular mode of speech: *baby talk.* **3** an informal address or lecture. **4** rumour or gossip: *there is talk of a merger.* **5** (often in *plural*) formal discussions or negotiations between conflicting parties etc. **6** empty promises or boasting. PHRASES **look who's talking** *informal* an expression of indignation or amusement at a person open to a criticism he or she has made of another. **now you're talking** *informal* now or at last you are saying, suggesting, etc. something that I agree with or approve of. **talk at** talk incessantly without consideration or concern for the thoughts and opinions of the person being addressed. **talk back** reply defiantly or with impudence. **talk big** *informal* talk boastfully. **talk is cheap** *informal* it is easier to announce one's intentions than to carry through with them. **talk down to** speak patronizingly or condescendingly to. **talk a person's ear off** *informal* talk incessantly. **talk a good game** *informal* talk convincingly yet fail to act effectively. **talk the hind leg off a donkey** *informal* talk incessantly. **talk of the town** a prominent topic of local interest and popular discussion. **talk out 1** *Cdn & Brit.* prevent the passage of (a bill in Parliament) by prolonging discussion until the time of adjournment. **2** attempt to resolve by discussing. **talk over** discuss at length. **talk shop** talk, esp. tediously, about one's occupation, business, etc. **talk the talk** say things and make promises that will please or impress others and not offend (*compare* WALK THE WALK, *see* WALK). **talk through** discuss thoroughly until a decision or resolution is reached. **talk through one's hat** *informal* **1** exaggerate, bluff. **2** talk wildly or nonsensically. **talk tough** (often foll. by *on* or *about*) speak in a brash, boastful, or menacing manner. **talk up** discuss (a subject) in order to arouse interest in it. **you should talk** *ironic* = LOOK WHO'S TALKING.

talkathon *noun* *informal* a prolonged conversation or discussion.

talkative *adjective* fond of or given to talking; chatty. ▶ **talkativeness** *noun*

talked-about *adjective* widely discussed.

talker *noun* **1** a person who talks. **2** a chatty or talkative person. **3** one who gives talks or lectures.

talkie *noun* *informal* a movie with a soundtrack, as distinct from a silent film.

talking • *adjective* **1** that talks or is capable of talking: *a talking doll.* **2** using a specified style or manner of

speaking: *smooth-talking*. **3** expressive: *talking eyes*. • *noun* in senses of TALK *verb*.

talking book *noun* a recorded reading of a book, esp. for the blind.

talking drum *noun* each of a set of drums of different pitch which are beaten to transmit words in a tonal language, originating in West Africa.

talking head *noun informal* **1** a close-up shot on a television news broadcast or documentary etc. in which a reporter or newscaster is shown only from the shoulders up. **2** a person featured in such a shot.

talking point *noun* **1** a topic suitable for or inviting discussion. **2** a fact supporting a decision, stance, or side in esp. a political debate.

talking stick *noun* a carved staff used in gatherings among some North American Aboriginal peoples, entitling the holder to speak to the rest of the group.

talking-to *noun* (plural **talking-tos**) *informal* a reproof, reprimand, or lecture.

talk radio *noun* a radio format that features interviews, listener phone-ins, and discussions.

talk show *noun* a TV or radio show in which people, esp. celebrities, are invited to talk informally about various topics.

talk time *noun* the length of time a cellular phone may be used before the battery will need to be recharged.

talky *adjective* (**talkier, talkiest**) **1** (of a book or theatrical production etc.) wordy or long-winded. **2** talkative.

tall • *adjective* **1** (of a person or animal) of greater than average height. **2** of a specified height: *two metres tall*. **3** high relative to width or surrounding objects: *tall mountains*. **4** *informal* (of a statement or story) exaggerated, extravagant, unlikely. • *adverb* straight and erect: *stand tall*.

tall grass prairie *noun* a prairie region characterized by certain tall moisture-favouring grasses.

tallis *noun* (plural **tallitim**) a shawl worn by Jewish men, esp. at prayer. [Say TAL iss for the singular, ta LEET im for the plural]

tall order *noun* an exorbitant or unreasonable demand.

tallow *noun* the harder kinds of esp. animal fat melted down for use in making candles, soap, etc.

tall ship *noun* a sailing ship with a high mast.

tally • *noun* (plural **tallies**) **1 a** a total score or amount. **b** the record of an amount, debt, score, etc. **2** *Sport* a goal or run scored. **3 a** a mark or number of marks used to represent a fixed number of things, e.g. a series of four vertical lines crossed by a diagonal line used to represent the number five. **b** a particular number, such as five, taken as a group or unit to facilitate counting. • *verb* (**tallies, tallied, tallying**) **1 a** set down or record (a number etc.). **b** calculate the total of. **2** achieve a total of. **3** agree or correspond; match. **4** *Sport* score (a run or goal etc.).

Talmud *noun* **1** the body of Jewish civil and ceremonial law and legend comprising the Mishnah and the Gemara. **2** either of two versions of the Gemara, containing the commentary of scholars and jurists on the administration of Jewish law, compiled AD *c.*200–500. ▶ **Talmudic** *adjective* **Talmudist** *noun* [MUD rhymes with HOOD]

talon *noun* **1 a** a claw of an animal, esp. a bird. **2 a** anything resembling this in form or appearance. **b** (often in *plural*) a grasping human finger or hand. ▶ **taloned** *adjective*

talus *noun* (plural **taluses**) **1** a scree slope at the base of a mountain etc. consisting of material which has fallen from the face of the cliff above. **2** the sloping side of a wall or earthwork. [Say TAY lus]

tam *noun* a round knitted or cloth cap of Scottish origin fitting closely around the brows but large and full above.

tamale *noun* a Mexican food of seasoned ground meat wrapped in cornmeal dough and steamed or baked in corn husks. [Say tuh MOLLY or tuh MALLY]

tamarack *noun* a slender North American larch, found in wet places across most of Canada. [Say TAMMA rack]

tamari *noun* a Japanese variety of rich, naturally fermented soy sauce. [Say tuh MAR ee]

tamarind *noun* **1** a brown pod containing one to twelve seeds embedded in a soft brown sticky acid pulp, which is valued for its laxative qualities and is also used to make esp. chutney and cold drinks. **2** the leguminous tree bearing this fruit, widely grown as a shade tree in tropical countries. [Say TAMMA rind]

tamarisk *noun* a shrub that produces long slender branches with small pink or white flowers, found by seashores and in mountainous areas from the Mediterranean region to central Asia and northern China. [Say TAMMA risk]

tambourine *noun* a musical instrument consisting of a hoop with a skin stretched over one side and pairs of small jingling discs in slots around the circumference, played by shaking, striking, etc. [Say tam buh REEN]

tame • *adjective* (**tamer, tamest**) **1** reclaimed by human management from a naturally wild condition to a domesticated state. **2** (of an animal) gentle, accustomed to people; not showing the natural shyness, fear, or fierceness of a wild animal. **3 a** unlikely to harm, frighten, or offend: *a tame ski run*. **b** lacking zest or vigour: *this sauce is pretty tame*. **4 a** (of land) cultivated. **b** (of a plant) produced by cultivation. **5** (of a person) co-operative, compliant, or servile. • *verb* (**tames, tamed, taming**) **1** bring (a wild animal) under the control or into the service of humans. **2** reduce the intensity of (a person, emotion, etc.); calm, temper. **3** control, subdue (a person etc.). **4** cultivate (land). ▶ **tamely** *adverb* **tamer** *noun*

Tamil • *noun* **1** a member of a Dravidian people inhabiting the southern Indian subcontinent and parts of Sri Lanka. **2** the language of this people. • *adjective* of this people or their language. [Say TAM ul]

tamoxifen *noun* a synthetic drug used to treat breast cancer and infertility in women. [Say tuh MOX if en]

tamp *verb* (often foll. by *down*) **1** pound down or pack (earth, gravel, asphalt, etc.) in order to produce a firm base or level surface. **2** stuff or consolidate tobacco in a pipe. **3** pack (a blasthole) full of clay, sand, etc., to concentrate the force of the explosion.

tamper *verb* (foll. by *with*) **1** meddle or interfere with something in order to cause damage or make unauthorized alterations: *tampering with the evidence* ◊ *the brakes have been tampered with*. **2** *Sport* negotiate with a player who is under contract to another team. ▶ **tampering** *noun*

tamper-proof *adjective* (also **tamper-resistant**) not readily susceptible to tampering.

tampon *noun* a soft plug of cotton or other material used to absorb secretions and stop the flow of blood etc. from an orifice or wound, esp. one inserted into the vagina during menstruation.

tan¹ • *noun* **1** a brown skin colour resulting from exposure to the sun or another source of ultraviolet light. **2** a yellowish-brown colour. • *adjective* **1** of a yellowish-brown colour. **2** (of a person, their body, or a part of the body) brown in colour due to exposure to ultraviolet light. • *verb* (**tans, tanned, tanning**) **1** make or become brown by exposure to ultraviolet light. **2** convert (rawhide) into leather by soaking in a

liquid containing tannic acid or by the use of mineral salts etc. **3** *slang* beat, thrash.

tan² *abbreviation* tangent.

tanager *noun* a small New World songbird of the bunting family, the male of which usu. has brightly coloured plumage. [Say TANNA jur]

tandem • *noun* **1** a team of two people or arrangement of two machines working together in conjunction. **2** a bicycle or tricycle equipped with seats and pedals for two riders, one in front of the other. • *adjective* **1** co-operative, joint, dual; involving two people, organizations, etc. **2** involving two similar things, one behind the other. **3** (of an articulated truck or trailer) supported at the rear by two axles. • *adverb* together, esp. one behind or after the other: *riding tandem*. PHRASES **in tandem 1** one behind another. **2** alongside each other, together, in conjunction.

tandoor *noun* **1** a clay oven of a kind used originally in northern India and Pakistan. **2** (as an *adjective*) designating food cooked in such an oven. [Say TAN dure]

tandoori *noun* (*plural* **tandooris**) **1** a style of Indian cooking based on the use of a tandoor. **2** food or a dish cooked in a tandoor (often as an *adjective*: *tandoori chicken*). [Say tan DURE ee]

tang *noun* **1** a sharp or penetrating taste, flavour, or smell. **2** a pointed projection on the blade of a knife etc., by which the blade is held in the handle. **3** a characteristic quality: *I tasted the tang of adventure ◊ their work has the tang of authentic life*.

tangent • *noun* Math **1** a straight line touching a curve or curved surface so that it meets it at a point but does not intersect it at that point. **2** a completely different line of thought or action: *Josh and I were discussing the election, and he went off on a tangent about the prime minister's hair*. **3** the ratio of the sides opposite and adjacent to an angle in a right-angled triangle. • *adjective* Math (of a line or surface) touching, but not normally intersecting, another line or surface; that is a tangent. [Say TAN junt]

tangential *adjective* **1** Math **a** of, pertaining to, or of the nature of a tangent. **b** acting or lying etc. in the direction of or along a tangent. **2** straying or digressing from the main topic: *Hetty has hardly been listening, off on her own tangential thoughts*. **3** of relatively minor importance: *tangential evidence ◊ with Britain no longer an imperial power, the army and navy seem increasingly tangential to national life*. ▶**tangentially** *adverb* [Say tan JEN shull]

tangerine *noun* **1** a mandarin orange, esp. one with a sweeter or tangier flavour and darker peel. **2** the tree bearing this fruit. [Say tan juh REEN]

tangible • *adjective* **1** that can be touched or felt: *tangible evidence*. **2** clear and definite; real: *tangible goals for the future ◊ tangible results*. • *noun* (usu. in *plural*) a tangible thing, esp. an asset: *the only safe haven for their wealth lay in tangibles, such as gold, art, and real estate*. ▶**tangibly** *adverb* [Say TAN juh bull]

tangle • *verb* (**tangles**, **tangled**, **tangling**) **1 a** twist, intertwine, or jumble (several strands of thread or string etc.) so that all the pieces are joined in a confused mass from which they may not be easily freed. **b** become twisted, intertwined, or jumbled. **2 a** become caught in a mess or tangle of rope, wires, etc.: *my foot is tangled in the cord*. **b** become embroiled in a difficult situation, controversy, affair, etc. **3** *informal* become involved with (a person, organization, etc.), esp. in conflict or disagreement. **4** complicate: *a tangled affair*. • *noun* **1** a confused mass of twisted or intertwined hairs, threads, etc. that may not be easily separated. **2** a single long thread, cord, etc. coiled or

knotted in a confusing manner. **3** a confused or complicated state or situation. ▶**tangled** *adjective*

tango • *noun* (*plural* **tangos**) **1** a syncopated ballroom dance of Argentinian origin, performed with long dramatic gliding movements and abrupt pauses and changes in direction in 2/4 or 4/4 time. **2** a piece of music in the rhythm of this dance and usu. used as an accompaniment. • *verb* (**tangoes**, **tangoed**, **tangoing**) dance the tango. PHRASES **it takes two to tango** both participants in a situation, esp. a dispute, must be held responsible.

tangy *adjective* (**tangier**, **tangiest**) having a strong, sharp flavour or scent.

tank • *noun* **1** a large receptacle or storage chamber usu. for liquid or gas. **2** a heavy armoured fighting vehicle carrying guns and moving on a tracked carriage. **3** a container for the fuel supply in a motor vehicle, aircraft, etc. **4** (also **tank top**) a sleeveless upper garment with a scoop neck. **5** a pond or reservoir. **6 a** *informal* a prison cell, esp. one for the temporary detention of more than one person: *drunk tank*. **b** *slang* prison: *was in the tank for 3 years*. • *verb* **1** (usu. foll. by *up*) fill the tank of (a vehicle etc.) with fuel. **2** *informal* **a** (foll. by *up*) drink heavily; become drunk. **b** (often as **tanked up** *adjective*) inebriate oneself with alcoholic drink or drugs. **3** *slang* defeat utterly or completely. **4** *Sport slang* lose or fail to finish (a game or match) deliberately. **5** *slang* (of prices, market values, etc.) decline or decrease.

tankard *noun* a tall mug with a handle and sometimes a hinged lid, esp. of silver or pewter for beer. [Say TANK urd]

tanker *noun* a ship, aircraft, or road vehicle for carrying liquids or gases in bulk.

tank farm *noun* an area of oil or gas storage tanks.

tanned *adjective* having a brown skin colour as a result of being in the sun: *he had a tanned face and clear eyes*.

tanner *noun* **1** a person who tans hides. **2** a person who sunbathes.

tannery *noun* (*plural* **tanneries**) a place where hides are tanned.

tannic *adjective* (of wine) having an astringent flavour due to the presence of tannin.

tannin *noun* (also **tannic acid**) a yellowish or brownish bitter-tasting organic substance present in tea, some galls, barks, and other plant tissues.

tanning *noun* the activity or process of making or becoming brown by exposure to ultraviolet light.

tansy *noun* (*plural* **tansies**) a plant with yellow button-like flowers and aromatic leaves.

tantalize *verb* (**tantalizes**, **tantalized**, **tantalizing**) **1** torment or tease by the sight or promise of something that is not obtainable: *for years the military has been tantalized by the concept of a weapon capable of travelling toward a target at the speed of light*. **2** tempt; excite the senses or desires of (someone): *the menu will further tantalize you with Greek specialities*. ▶**tantalizing** *adjective* **tantalizingly** *adverb* [Say TANTA lize]

tantalum *noun* a rare naturally occurring hard white metallic element, resistant to heat and the action of acids, used in surgery etc. [Say TANTA lum]

tantamount *adjective* (foll. by *to*) equivalent to: *the resignations were tantamount to an admission of guilt*.

Tantra *noun* (*plural* **Tantras**) any of a class of Hindu or Buddhist mystical and magical writings. ▶**Tantric** *adjective* **Tantrism** *noun*

tantrum *noun* an outburst of bad temper.

Tanzanian • *noun* a native or inhabitant of Tanzania, a country on the coast of east Africa. • *adjective* of or relating to Tanzania or Tanzanians. [Say tanza NEE un]

Tao *noun* **1** (in Taoism) the absolute being or principle

underlying the universe; ultimate reality. **2** (in Confucianism) the way, method, or norm to be followed, esp. in conduct. [Say TOW or DOW (TOW and DOW rhyme with COW)]

Taoism *noun* a Chinese philosophy based on the writings of Lao-tzu (6th century BC), advocating humility and religious piety. ▶**Taoist** *noun* [Say TOW ism or DOW ism (TOW and DOW rhyme with COW)]

tap¹ • *noun* **1** a device by which a flow of liquid or gas from a pipe or vessel can be controlled. **2** an act of tapping a telephone etc. **3** a tool for cutting the thread of a female screw. **4** the surgical withdrawal of fluid from a cavity etc.: *spinal tap*. • *verb* (**taps**, **tapped**, **tapping**) **1 a** provide (a cask) with a tap. **b** let out (a liquid) by means of, or as if by means of, a tap. **2** draw sap from (a tree) by cutting or drilling into it. **3 a** obtain information or supplies or resources from. **b** extract or obtain; discover and exploit: *tapping the skills of young people*. **4** connect a listening device to (a telephone or telegraph line etc.) to listen to a call or transmission. **5** cut a female screw thread in. **6** *Medical* drain (a cavity) of accumulated fluid. PHRASES **on tap 1** (of beer etc.) ready to be drawn from a keg; not bottled or canned. **2** *informal* ready for immediate use; freely available. **tap into** obtain something from.

tap² • *verb* (**taps**, **tapped**, **tapping**) **1** (foll. by *at*, *on*) strike a gentle but audible blow. **2** strike lightly: *tapped me on the shoulder*. **3** (foll. by *against* etc.) cause (a thing) to strike lightly: *tapped a stick against the window*. **4** = TAP DANCE *verb*. **5** (often foll. by *out*) **a** make a tap or taps: *tapped out the rhythm*. **b** write using a typewriter or computer keyboard. **6** walk with a tapping sound: *she tapped across the tiled floor*. • *noun* **1 a** a light blow; a rap. **b** the sound of this: *heard a tap at the door*. **2 a** = TAP DANCE *noun*. **b** a piece of metal attached to the toe and heel of a tap dancer's shoe to make the tapping sound. **3** (in *plural*, usu. treated as *singular*) *US* **a** a bugle call for lights to be put out in army quarters. **b** a similar signal at a military funeral. ▶**tapper** *noun*

tapas *plural noun* small savoury Spanish appetizers, esp. served with wine or beer. [Say TAP us]

tap dance • *noun* a form of display dance performed wearing shoes fitted with metal taps, with rhythmical tapping of the toes and heels. • *verb* (**tap dances**, **tap danced**, **tap dancing**) perform a tap dance. ▶**tap dancer** *noun* **tap dancing** *noun*

tape • *noun* **1** a narrow strip of woven material for tying up, fastening, etc. **2 a** a strip of material stretched across the finishing line of a race. **b** a similar strip for marking off an area or forming a notional barrier. **3** (also **adhesive tape**) a strip of opaque or transparent paper or plastic etc., esp. coated with adhesive for fastening, sticking, masking, insulating, etc. **4 a** = MAGNETIC TAPE. **b** a tape recording or tape cassette. **5** (also **tape measure**) a strip of tape or thin flexible metal marked for measuring lengths. • *verb* (**tapes**, **taped**, **taping**) **1 a** tie up or join etc. with tape. **b** apply tape to. **2** (foll. by *off*) seal or mark off an area or thing with tape. **3** record on magnetic tape. **4** wrap (a joint etc.) firmly with a bandage or tape to provide support.

tape deck *noun* a piece of equipment for playing audio tapes, esp. as part of a stereo system.

tape machine *noun* **1** = TAPE RECORDER. **2** = TICKER 2.

tapenade *noun* a Provençal dish, usu. served as an hors d'oeuvre, made mainly from puréed black olives, capers, and anchovies. [Say TAPPA nad]

tape player *noun* a tape recorder or tape deck.

taper • *noun* **1** a wick coated with wax etc. for conveying a flame. **2** a slender candle. **3** gradual diminution in width or thickness. • *verb* (often foll. by

off) **1** diminish or reduce in thickness towards one end. **2** make or become gradually less.

tape recorder *noun* a machine for recording sounds on magnetic tape and playing back the recording. ▶**tape recording** *noun*

tapering *adjective* diminishing gradually in breadth or thickness toward one end; becoming continuously narrower or more slender in one direction.

tapestry *noun* (*plural* **tapestries**) **1 a** a thick textile fabric in which coloured weft threads are woven to form pictures or designs. **b** embroidery imitating this, usu. in wools on canvas. **c** a piece of such embroidery. **2** events or circumstances etc. compared with a tapestry in being intricate, interwoven, etc.: *life's rich tapestry*. [Say TAP us tree]

tapeworm *noun* a flatworm with a segmented ribbon-like body and a small head with hooks and suckers, the adult of which lives as a parasite in the intestines.

tap-in *noun* (*plural* **tap-ins**) a close-range shot requiring little force, esp. into the goal in hockey.

taping *noun* **1** the act or an instance of recording something on magnetic tape, esp. a session where an item is taped for later broadcast. **2** the act of applying tape or bandages etc.

tapioca *noun* a starchy substance in hard white grains obtained from cassava and used for puddings etc. [Say tappy OAK uh]

tapir *noun* a nocturnal hoofed mammal with a short flexible protruding snout used for feeding on vegetation, native to Malaysia and Central and South America. [Sounds like TAPER]

taproom *noun* a room in which alcoholic drinks are available, esp. in a hotel.

taproot *noun* a tapering root growing vertically.

tar • *noun* **1 a** a dark thick inflammable liquid distilled from wood or coal etc. and used as a preservative of wood and iron, in making roads, as an antiseptic, etc. **b** a similar substance formed in the combustion of tobacco etc. **2** *informal* a sailor. • *verb* (**tars**, **tarred**, **tarring**) **1** cover with tar. **2** damage the appearance, image, or reputation of: *tarred the image of legitimate refugees*. PHRASES **beat** (or **kick** etc.) **the tar out of** *slang* beat or thrash severely. **tar and feather** smear with tar and then cover with feathers as a punishment. **tarred with the same brush** having the same faults.

tarabish *noun* *Cdn* (*Cape Breton*) a card game based on bridge. [Say TAR bish]

tarantula *noun* (*plural* **tarantulas**) a large hairy tropical spider, some kinds of which are venomous and are able to catch small lizards, frogs, and birds. [Say tuh RAN choo luh]

tardiness *noun* lateness in arriving, esp. at a meeting, work, a class or school, etc.

tardy *adjective* (**tardier**, **tardiest**) **1** late; unpunctual, esp. consistently. **2** slow to act or come or happen: *a tardy waiter*. **3** delaying or delayed beyond the right or expected time: *spring seemed to be tardy this past year*.

tare *noun* **1** the weight of a wrapping, container, or receptacle in which goods are packed. **2** an allowance made for this. **3** the weight of a motor vehicle without its fuel or load. [Rhymes with CARE]

target • *noun* **1** a mark or point fired or aimed at, esp. a round or rectangular object marked with concentric circles. **2 a** a person or thing aimed at, or exposed to gunfire etc.: *they were an easy target*. **b** a person, group, etc. which is the object of attention, a campaign, etc. (also as an *adjective*: *target audience*). **3** an objective or result aimed at (also as an *adjective*: *target date*). **4** a person or thing against whom criticism, abuse, etc., is or may be directed. • *verb* (**targets**, **targeted**, **targeting**) **1** identify or single out (a person or thing)

as an object of attention or attack. **2** aim or direct: *missiles targeted on major cities*. PHRASES **on target 1** on the correct course to meet an objective. **2** accurate; exactly right.

tariff *noun* **1 a** a duty on a particular class of imports or exports. **b** a list of duties or customs to be paid. **2** a table of fixed charges: *a hotel tariff*. [Say TARE iff]

tariff barrier *noun* a restrictive tax imposed on an imported product, designed to restrict the flow of certain goods into a country.

Tarmac *noun* **1** *proprietary* asphalt. **2** a surface made of this, e.g. a runway. [Say TAR mack]

tarnation *interjection* expressing exasperation. PHRASES **in tarnation** used as an intensifier.

tarnish • *verb* (**tarnishes, tarnished, tarnishing**) **1** lessen or destroy the lustre of (metal etc.). **2** impair (one's reputation etc.). **3** (of metal etc.) lose lustre. • *noun* **1** a loss of lustre. **2** a film of colour formed on an exposed surface of a mineral or metal.

taro *noun* (*plural* **taros**) a tropical plant of the arum family that has edible tuberous roots and edible fleshy leaves. [Say TARE oh]

tarot *noun* **1 a** any of several games played with a pack of cards having five suits, the last of which is a set of permanent trumps. **b** a similar pack used in fortune-telling. **2 a** any of the trump cards. **b** any of the cards from a fortune-telling pack. [Say TARE oh]

tarp *noun* *informal* a tarpaulin.

tarpaper *noun* paper coated with tar, often used as a building material (also as an *adjective*: *tarpaper shack*).

tarpaulin *noun* **1** heavy-duty waterproof cloth esp. of tarred canvas. **2** a sheet or covering of this. [Say tar POLLEN]

tarpon *noun* a large silvery herring-like fish of the tropical Atlantic or Pacific oceans. [Say TAR pon]

tarragon *noun* a bushy plant with narrow aromatic leaves that are used as a herb. [Say TARE a gone]

SPELL CHECK	
tariff	ABC ✓

Warning: **tariff** is spelled with two *f*'s but one *r*.

---

tarry¹ *adjective* (**tarrier, tarriest**) of or like or smeared with tar.

tarry² *verb* (**tarries, tarried, tarrying**) *archaic* or *literary* stay longer than intended; delay leaving a place: *she could tarry a bit and not get home until four*.

tarsal • *adjective* of or relating to the bones in the ankle. • *noun* a tarsal bone. [Say TAR sull]

tar sand *noun* a deposit of sand containing bitumen.

tarsus *noun* **1 a** the group of bones forming the ankle and upper foot. **b** the shank of a bird's leg. **c** the terminal segment of a limb in insects. **2** the fibrous connective tissue of the eyelid.

tart • *noun* **1** a small, usu. open pie containing a fruit or sweet filling. **2** *slang* a prostitute or promiscuous woman. • *verb* (foll. by *up*) *informal* smarten (oneself or a thing) up, esp. flashily or gaudily: *she'll tart herself up, and maybe get her hair done*. • *adjective* **1** sharp or acid in taste. **2** (of a remark etc.) cutting, bitter.

tartan *noun* **1** a pattern of coloured stripes crossing at right angles, esp. a distinctive plaid of a sort originally worn by the Scottish Highlanders to denote their clan. **2** woollen cloth woven in this pattern: *a tartan scarf*.

Tartar (also **Tatar** except in sense 3 of *noun*) • *noun* **1 a** a member of a group of Turkic peoples inhabiting parts of European and Asiatic Russia. **b** *hist.* a member of the combined forces of central Asian peoples, including Mongols and Turks, who overran and devastated much of Asia and eastern Europe in the early 13th century, and established a large empire in central Europe in the 14th century. **2** the Turkic language of these peoples. **3** (**tartar**) a person in a position of authority who has a very bad temper: *her supervisor is a terrible tartar*. • *adjective* of or relating to the Tartars. [Say TAR tur]

tartar *noun* **1** a hard deposit of saliva, calcium phosphate, etc., that forms on the teeth. **2** a hard crust that forms on the inside of a cask during the fermentation of wine. [Say TAR tur]

tartar sauce *noun* a sauce of mayonnaise and chopped pickles, capers, etc.

tartlet *noun* a small tart, usu. containing a fruit or sweet filling.

tartly *adverb* **1** with a slight sourness: *tartly sweet cream cheese inside a tender crepe*. **2** sharply; with sharpness or bitterness of tone: *spoke to her husband tartly*.

tartness *noun* **1** sourness; bitterness: *enjoyed the tartness of the apples*. **2** sharpness or bitterness of tone: *there was a tartness in her voice*.

tartufo *noun* (*plural* **tartufos**) a ball of ice cream with one flavour in the centre surrounded by another flavour, the whole often coated in cocoa etc. [Say tar TOO foe]

tarty *adjective* (**tartier, tartiest**) *informal* **1** (esp. of a woman) promiscuous; sleazy. **2** (of clothing, makeup, etc.) typical of that worn by prostitutes; immodest.

task • *noun* **1** a piece of work to be done or undertaken. **2** a difficult or unpleasant piece of work. • *verb* **1** make great demands on (a person's powers etc.): *it tasked her diplomatic skills to arrange their departure in safety*. **2** assign a task to: *wrote a letter to the chief of review services tasking him to begin an internal inquiry*. PHRASES **put to the task** begin or cause to actively working on or doing something: *I put myself to the task of composing a speech*. **take to task** rebuke, scold.

task force *noun* (also **task group**) **1** *Military* an armed force organized for a special operation. **2** a unit specially organized for a task.

taskmaster *noun* a person who imposes a task or burden, esp. regularly or severely.

Tasmanian • *noun* **1** a native of Tasmania, an island state of Australia. **2** a person of Tasmanian descent. • *adjective* of or relating to Tasmania. [Say taz MAINY un]

Tasmanian devil *noun* a bearlike nocturnal flesh-eating marsupial with a large head and powerful jaws, now found only in Tasmania.

tassel • *noun* **1** a tuft of loosely hanging threads or cords etc. attached for decoration to a cushion, scarf, cap, etc. **2** a tassel-like head of some plants, esp. a flower head with prominent stamens at the top of a corn stalk. • *verb* (**tassels, tasselled, tasselling**) **1** provide with a tassel or tassels. **2** (of corn) form tassels. ▶ **tasselled** *adjective* [Rhymes with HASSLE]

taste • *noun* **1 a** the flavour of something, causing a particular sensation when it comes into contact with the tongue. **b** the sense by which a flavour is recognized: *was bitter to the taste*. **2** a small portion of food or drink taken as a sample. **3** a slight experience: *a taste of success*. **4** a liking or predilection: *has expensive tastes*. **5** aesthetic discernment in art, literature, fashion, etc., esp. of a specified kind: *dresses in poor taste*. **6** a sense of what is tactful or polite etc. in a given situation. • *verb* (**tastes, tasted, tasting**) **1** sample or test the flavour of (food etc.) by taking it into the mouth. **2** perceive the flavour of: *could taste the lemon*. **3** eat or drink a small portion of: *had not tasted food for days*. **4** have experience of: *tasted failure*. **5** (often foll. by *of*) have a specified flavour. PHRASES **a bad** (or **bitter** etc.) **taste** *informal* a strong feeling of regret or unease. **to taste** in the amount needed for a pleasing result.

T

taste bud *noun* any of the cells or nerve endings on the surface of the tongue by which things are tasted.

tasteful *adjective* having, or done in, good taste. ▶ **tastefully** *adverb* **tastefulness** *noun*

tasteless *adjective* **1** lacking flavour. **2** having, or done in, bad taste. ▶ **tastelessly** *adverb* **tastelessness** *noun*

tastemaker *noun* a person or institution that determines or influences what is or will become stylish or fashionable.

taster *noun* **1** a person employed to test food or drink by tasting it, esp. for quality. **2** an instrument etc. used in sampling or tasting. **3** a sample or foretaste.

taste test *noun* a usu. blind comparison of the flavours of two or more similar products. ▶ **taste-test** *verb*

tasting *noun* a gathering at which food or drink (esp. wine) is tasted and evaluated.

tasty *adjective* (**tastier, tastiest**) (of food) pleasing in flavour; appetizing.

tatami *noun* (*plural* **tatamis** or **tatami**) a rush-covered straw mat forming a traditional Japanese floor covering. [Say tuh TOMMY]

Tatar *see* TARTAR. [Say TAW tur]

tater *noun slang* = POTATO. [Say TAY tur]

tatter *noun* (usu. in *plural*) a rag; an irregularly torn piece of cloth or paper etc. PHRASES **in tatters** *informal* **1** torn to shreds. **2** (of a negotiation, argument, etc.) ruined, demolished. ▶ **tattered** *adjective*

tattle *verb* (**tattles, tattled, tattling**) (often foll. by *on*) inform against a person; tell tales; *she's always tattling on her brother*. ▶ **tattler** *noun*

tattle-tale *noun* a telltale, esp. a child.

tattoo[1] *noun* (*plural* **tattoos**) **1** an evening drum or bugle signal recalling soldiers to their quarters. **2** an elaboration of this with music and marching, presented as an entertainment. **3** a rhythmic tapping or drumming.

tattoo[2] • *verb* (**tattoos, tattooed, tattooing**) **1** mark (the skin) with an indelible design by puncturing it and inserting pigment. **2** make (a design) in this way. • *noun* (*plural* **tattoos**) a design made by tattooing. ▶ **tattooist** *noun*

tatty *adjective* (**tattier, tattiest**) *informal* **1** tattered; worn and shabby: *the room was furnished with slightly tatty upholstered chairs and a couch*. **2** of poor quality: *the high, but generally tatty, output of the current Celtic revival*.

SPELL CHECK
taught, taut

The word for "tight" or "tense" is **taut**.

taught *past and past participle of* TEACH.

taunt • *noun* a thing said in order to anger or wound a person. • *verb* **1** assail with taunts. **2** reproach (a person) contemptuously. ▶ **taunter** *noun* **tauntingly** *adverb*

taupe *noun & adjective* a grey with a tinge of another colour, usu. brown. [Say TOPE]

Taurus *noun* **1** a constellation between Gemini and Aries, traditionally regarded as contained in the figure of a bull. **2 a** the second sign of the zodiac. **b** a person born when the sun is in this sign, usu. between Apr. 20 and May 20. ▶ **Taurean** *adjective & noun*

SPELL CHECK
taut, taught

The past tense of *teach* is **taught**.

taut *adjective* **1** (of a rope, muscles, etc.) tight; not slack. **2** (of nerves) tense. ▶ **tautly** *adverb* **tautness** *noun*

tautological *adjective* pertaining to, characterized by, involving, or using tautology; repeating the same word, or the same notion in different words. [Say totta LOGICAL]

tautology *noun* (*plural* **tautologies**) **1** the saying of the same thing twice over in different words, esp. as a fault of style, e.g. *arrived one after the other in succession*. **2** a statement that is necessarily true, e.g. *boys will be boys*. [Say taw TOLLA jee]

tavern *noun* **1** a drinking establishment, esp. one serving beer and wine but not hard liquor. **2** *hist.* an inn or pub.

taverna *noun* a Greek café or restaurant. [Say tuh VARE nuh]

tawdriness *noun* the quality of being showy, gaudy, or vulgar.

tawdry *adjective* (**tawdrier, tawdriest**) **1** showy but cheap and of poor quality. **2** involving low moral standards; extremely unpleasant or offensive: *a tawdry affair* ◊ *the tawdry business of politics*.

tawny • *adjective* (**tawnier, tawniest**) of an orange- or yellow-brown colour. • *noun* this colour.

tawny owl *noun* **1** a reddish-brown European owl. **2** (**Tawny Owl**) *Cdn* an assistant adult leader of a Brownie pack.

tax • *noun* (*plural* **taxes**) **1** a compulsory contribution to government revenue levied on individuals, property, or businesses. **2** (usu. foll. by *on, upon*) a strain or heavy demand; an oppressive or burdensome obligation. • *verb* (**taxes, taxed, taxing**) **1** impose a tax on (persons or goods etc.). **2** deduct tax from (income etc.). **3** make heavy demands on (a person's powers or resources etc.): *you tax my patience*. **4** confront (a person) with a fault or wrongdoing: *why are you taxing me with these preposterous allegations?*

taxa *plural of* TAXON.

taxable *adjective* (of money) that one has to pay tax on: *taxable income* ◊ *a taxable benefit*.

tax-and-spend *adjective* (of a government policy or its proponents) advocating high taxes and government spending on programs beyond the basic responsibilities of government, esp. as a spur to the economy.

taxation *noun* **1** the fact or condition of being taxed. **2** the act of taxing. **3** revenue raised by taxes.

tax bracket *noun* a range of incomes taxed at a given rate.

tax break *noun informal* a tax concession or advantage allowed by government.

tax credit *noun* a sum that may be deducted from the amount of tax owing. ▶ **tax-creditable** *adjective Cdn*

tax-deductible *adjective* (of expenses) that may be deducted from income before the amount of tax to be paid is calculated.

tax dollar *noun* a dollar paid as tax.

tax evasion *noun* the illegal nonpayment or underpayment of income tax.

tax-exempt *adjective* **1** (of income) not subject to taxation. **2** (of a security etc.) earning income that is not subject to taxation.

tax-free *adjective* exempt from taxes.

tax grab *noun* an excessive or unjustified tax demand by a government, esp. when disguised as other forms of payment, e.g. licence fees etc.

taxi • *noun* (*plural* **taxis**) **1** (also **taxicab**) a car with a driver that may be hired for journeys, esp. one with a meter that records the fare to be paid. **2** a boat, airplane, etc. similarly used. • *verb* (**taxis, taxied, taxiing**) **1 a** (of an aircraft or pilot) move along the ground under the machine's own power before takeoff or after landing. **b** cause (an aircraft) to taxi. **2** go in a taxi.

taxidermist *noun* a person who practises the art of preparing, stuffing, and mounting the skins of animals etc. in lifelike poses. [Say TAXA dur mist]

taxidermy *noun* the art of preparing, stuffing, and mounting the skins of animals etc. in lifelike poses. [Say TAXA durmy]

taxing *adjective* tiring or demanding; requiring great physical or mental effort.

taxiway *noun* a route along which an aircraft can taxi when moving to or from a runway.

taxman *noun* (*plural* **taxmen**) *informal* **1** an inspector or collector of taxes. **2** the personification of the government department dealing with taxes.

Taxol *noun* *proprietary* a compound obtained from the bark of certain yews, which inhibits the growth of some tumours. [Say TAX awl]

taxon *noun* (*plural* **taxa**) a taxonomic group of any rank, such as a species, family, or class. [Say TAX un]

taxonomic *adjective* pertaining or relating to taxonomy or classification. [Say taxa NOM ick]

taxonomist *noun* an expert in the science of the classification of living and extinct organisms. [Say tax ONNA mist]

taxonomy *noun* (*plural* **taxonomies**) the science of the classification of living and extinct organisms into orders, families, genera, species, etc. [Say tax ONNA mee]

taxpayer *noun* a person who pays taxes. ▶ **taxpaying** *adjective*

tax return *noun* a declaration of income for taxation purposes.

tax shelter *noun* a financial arrangement, such as an investment, intended to minimize payment of tax. ▶ **tax-sheltered** *adjective*

TB *abbreviation* **1** tubercle bacillus. **2** tuberculosis.

Tb *symbol* terbium.

t.b.a. *abbreviation* to be announced.

T-ball *noun* a form of baseball for young children, in which the ball is placed on a stand in front of the batter instead of being thrown by the pitcher.

T-bar *noun* **1** (also **T-bar lift**) a type of ski lift in the form of a series of inverted T-shaped metal bars for towing skiers. **2** a metal bar with a T-shaped cross section. **3** a T-shaped fastening on a shoe etc.

T-bill *noun* a bill of exchange issued by the government to raise money for temporary needs; a treasury bill.

T-bone • *noun* a T-shaped bone, esp. in steak from the thin end of a loin. • *verb* (**T-bones, T-boned, T-boning**) (usu. in *passive*) *informal* (of a car or truck) run into or collide with (another vehicle) on the side.

tbsp *abbreviation* = TABLESPOON 2.

Tc *symbol* technetium.

T-cell *noun* = T-LYMPHOCYTE.

tchotchke *noun* *informal* a knick-knack. [Say CHOTCH kee]

TCP *abbreviation* *proprietary* a disinfectant and germicide.

TCP/IP *abbreviation* *proprietary* Transmission Control Protocol/Internet Protocol, the obligatory standard to be used by any system connecting to the Internet.

TD *abbreviation* (*plural* **TDs**) touchdown.

TDD *abbreviation* (*plural* **TDDs**) Telephone Device for the Deaf.

Te *symbol* tellurium.

te (*plural* **tes**) = TI. [Say TEE]

tea *noun* (*plural* **teas**) **1 a** a drink made by infusing the crushed, dried leaves of a tea plant in boiling water. **b** a cup of this. **c** the dried leaves used to make such a drink. **d** the evergreen shrub or small tree, native to South and East Asia, that produces these leaves. **2** a similar drink made from the leaves of other plants or from another substance: *camomile tea* ◊ *beef tea*. **3 a** esp.

Brit. a light afternoon meal consisting of tea, bread, cakes, etc. **b** esp. Brit. a cooked (esp. early) evening meal. **c** an afternoon reception at which tea is served. **d** Cdn (Nfld) an afternoon or early evening social gathering in a church hall etc. at which a light meal is sold.

tea bag *noun* a small perforated paper or cloth bag containing tea leaves for infusion.

tea biscuit *noun* Cdn a small baked food, leavened with baking powder or soda, often containing raisins.

tea caddy *noun* (*plural* **tea caddies**) a small container for tea leaves.

tea ceremony *noun* (*plural* **tea ceremonies**) an elaborate Japanese ritual of serving and drinking tea, as an expression of Zen Buddhist philosophy.

teach *verb* (**teaches, taught, teaching**) **1** impart knowledge to or instruct in how to do something, esp. in a school or as part of a recognized programme. **2** give instruction in (a subject or skill). **3** cause to learn by example or experience. **4** advocate as a practice or principle. PHRASES (**one can't**) **teach an old dog new tricks** (one cannot) successfully make old people change their ideas, methods of work, etc.

teachable *adjective* **1** (of a subject) that can be taught or imparted by instruction, training, etc. **2** apt at learning.

teacher *noun* a person who teaches, esp. in a school.

teacherly *adjective* of or like a teacher.

teacher's pet *noun* the favourite or a favoured student of a teacher.

teach-in *noun* (*plural* **teach-ins**) an informal lecture and discussion or series of lectures on a subject of public interest.

teaching *noun* **1** the profession of a teacher. **2** (often in *plural*) what is taught; a doctrine.

teaching assistant *noun* a graduate student hired to assist a professor, esp. by marking assignments and teaching seminars.

teaching hospital *noun* a hospital associated with a university, where medical students receive practical training.

tea cozy *noun* (*plural* **tea cozies**) a cover placed over a teapot to keep the contents hot.

teacup *noun* a cup from which tea is drunk, usu. with a matching saucer.

tea dance *noun* an afternoon tea with dancing.

tea house *noun* a restaurant, esp. in China or Japan, where tea and other refreshments are served.

teak *noun* **1** a large deciduous tree native to India and Southeast Asia. **2** (also **teakwood**) its hard lightweight durable timber, used esp. in shipbuilding and furniture.

teakettle *noun* = KETTLE 1.

teal *noun* (*plural* **teal** or **teals**) **1** either of two small freshwater ducks, the green-winged teal, the male of which has a chestnut head and a green stripe, and the blue-winged teal, which has a chalky blue forewing with a lustrous green patch. **2** *noun* & *adjective* (also **teal blue**) a dark greenish-blue colour.

tea leaf *noun* **1** a dried leaf of tea. **2** (esp. in *plural*) these after infusion or as dregs, the patterns formed by which are interpreted by fortune tellers.

SPELL CHECK **team, team**	
The spelling is **teem** in "teeming with fish" etc.	

team • *noun* **1** a set of players forming one side in a game or contest: *a hockey team*. **2** two or more persons working together. **3 a** a set of draft animals. **b** one animal or more in harness with a vehicle. • *verb* **1** (usu. foll. by *up*) join in a team or in common action: *decided to*

team up with them. **2** harness (horses etc.) in a team. **3** match or coordinate (clothes): *teamed a collared cashmere sweater with a lace-trimmed silk skirt*.

teammate *noun* a fellow member of a team or group.

team player *noun* a person who plays or works well as a member of a team.

teamster *noun* **1** (also **Teamster**) a truck driver, esp. a member of the Teamsters Union. **2** a driver of a team of animals.

teamwork *noun* the combined action of a team, group, etc., esp. when effective and efficient.

teapot *noun* a pot with a handle, spout, and lid, in which tea is brewed and from which it is poured.

tear¹ • *verb* (**tears**; *past* **tore**; *past participle* **torn**; **tearing**) **1** pull apart or to pieces with some force. **2** make a hole or rent in by tearing: *have torn my coat*. **3** pull violently or with some force: *tore a page out*. **4** violently disrupt or divide: *the country was torn by civil war* ◊ *torn by conflicting emotions*. **5** *informal* go or travel hurriedly or impetuously. **6** undergo tearing. **7** (foll. by *at* etc.) pull violently or with some force. • *noun* **1** a hole or other damage caused by tearing. **2** a torn part of cloth etc. **3 a** a spree. **b** *Sport* a winning streak; a successful run. PHRASES **be torn between** have difficulty in choosing between. **tear apart 1** destroy, divide utterly. **2** search (a place) exhaustively. **3** criticize forcefully. **4** distress greatly. **tear down** demolish. **tear one's hair out** behave with extreme desperation or anger. **tear into 1** attack verbally; reprimand. **2** make a vigorous start on (an activity). **tear oneself away** leave despite a strong desire to stay. **tear to shreds** *informal* refute or criticize thoroughly.

tear² • *noun* **1** a drop of clear salty liquid appearing in or flowing from the eyes, as a result of emotion, physical irritation, pain, etc. **2** a drop. • *verb* (**tears**, **teared**, **tearing**) (of the eyes) fill with tears.

teardrop *noun* **1** a single tear. **2** a thing resembling a teardrop in shape, esp. a jewel.

tearful *adjective* **1** crying or inclined to cry. **2** causing or accompanied by tears; sad: *a tearful goodbye*. ▶ **tearfully** *adverb* **tearfulness** *noun*

tear gas • *noun* a gas that causes severe irritation to the eyes, used in warfare or riot control to disable opponents or make crowds disperse. • *verb* (**tear-gas**, **tear-gases**, **tear-gassed**, **tear-gassing**) attack with tear gas.

tearing *adjective* *informal* extreme, overwhelming, violent: *in a tearing hurry*. [Say TARE ing]

tearjerker *noun* *informal* a sentimental story, film, etc., calculated to evoke sadness or sympathy. ▶ **tearjerking** *noun & adjective*

tea room *noun* a small restaurant or café where tea and other refreshments are served.

tea rose *noun* a hybrid rose bush bearing flowers with a scent resembling that of tea.

teary *adjective* tearful; sad: *a teary farewell*.

tease • *verb* (**teases**, **teased**, **teasing**) **1 a** make fun of or attempt to provoke a person or animal in a playful or unkind way. **b** say something ironically to provoke a reaction. **2** tempt someone sexually with no intention of satisfying the desire aroused. **3** comb (the hair) from the ends towards the scalp to make it look thicker. **4** pick (wool etc.) into separate fibres. • *noun* **1** *informal* a person fond of teasing. **2** an act of making fun of or tempting someone: *it was only a gentle tease, nothing malicious*. PHRASES **tease out 1** separate by disentangling. **2** extract, obtain or ascertain, esp. by painstaking effort: *to tease out the truth*.

teaser *noun* **1** *informal* a hard question or task. **2** a teasing person. **3** a short introductory advertisement,

esp. an excerpt or sample designed to stimulate interest or curiosity.

tea service *noun* (also **tea set**) a matching teapot, milk jug, and sugar bowl (often also including a matching coffee pot and tray), for serving tea.

teasingly *adverb* **1** in a playful way that is intended to provoke a person: *their friends teasingly call them "pickles" for the olive drab uniforms they wear*. **2** in a way that suggests something and makes someone want to know more: *the author's intentions are revealed teasingly only in the last chapter*. **3** in a way that is intended to make someone sexually excited.

teaspoon *noun* **1** a small spoon for stirring coffee, tea, etc. **2** an amount held by this, esp. as a unit of measure in cooking, equal to $\frac{1}{3}$ tablespoon (approx. 5 ml). Abbreviation: **tsp.** ▶ **teaspoonful** *noun* (*plural* **teaspoonfuls**)

teat *noun* a mammary nipple, esp. of an animal. [Say TEET or TIT]

tea towel *noun* a thin linen or cotton towel for drying washed dishes etc.

tech (*plural* **techs**) *informal* • *noun* **1** technology. **2** a technician. **3** a technical college or school. • *adjective* technical.

techie *noun* (*plural* **techies**) *informal* an expert in or enthusiast for technology, esp. computers. [Say TECKY]

technetium *noun* an artificially produced radioactive metallic element. [Say teck NEE shee um or teck NEE shum]

technical *adjective* **1** of or involving or concerned with the mechanical arts and applied sciences: *a technical school*. **2** of or relating to a particular subject or craft etc.: *technical terms*. **3** (of a book or discourse etc.) requiring special knowledge to be understood. **4** due to mechanical failure: *technical difficulties*. **5** legally such; such in strict interpretation: *technical assault*. **6** of or relating to the technique of an art form, esp. as contrasted to the emotional, lyrical etc. aspects. **7** of or relating to technological equipment: *technical support*.

technicality *noun* (*plural* **technicalities**) **1** the state of being technical. **2** a technical expression. **3** a technical point or detail: *was acquitted on a technicality*.

technical knockout *noun* Boxing a termination of a fight by the referee on the grounds of a contestant's inability to continue, the opponent being declared the winner. Abbreviation: **TKO**.

technically *adverb* **1** with reference to the technique displayed. **2** according to the facts of a case, the exact meaning of words, etc.; strictly.

technician *noun* **1** a person employed to look after technical equipment and do practical work in a laboratory etc. **2** an expert in the practical application of a science. **3** a person skilled in the technique of an art or craft.

Technicolor *noun* (often as an *adjective*) **1** *proprietary* a process of colour cinematography using synchronized monochrome films, each of a different colour, to produce a colour print. **2** (usu. **technicolor** or **technicolour**) *informal* **a** vivid colour. **b** artificial brilliance. [Say TECKNA colour]

technique *noun* **1 a** a particular method of doing something, such as the execution or performance of an artistic work, usu. involving a set special skills: *he is one of the game's best, despite his unorthodox technique*. **b** skill or ability in a particular field: *her technique has improved a great deal over the summer*. **2** a skilful or efficient way of doing or achieving something: *a simple technique for painting window frames*.

techno • *noun* a style of popular dance music making extensive use of electronic instruments and synthesized sound (also in *combination*: *techno-rock*).

• adjective of, pertaining to, or characterized by technology; technologically advanced: *techno trends*.

techno- *combining form* relating to or using technology.

technobabble *noun informal* incomprehensible technical jargon.

technocracy *noun* **1** the government or control of society or industry by technical experts. **2** a society governed in this way. [Say teck NOCKRA see]

technocrat *noun* an expert in science, technology, engineering, etc. having political power. ▶ **technocratic** *adjective*

technological *adjective* of, relating to, or using technology: *the quickening pace of technological change*. ▶ **technologically** *adverb*

technology *noun* (*plural* **technologies**) **1** the study or use of the mechanical arts and applied sciences. **2** the application of this to practical tasks in industry. **3** a tool etc. used for this. ▶ **technologist** *noun* [Say teck NOLLA jee]

technology transfer *noun* the transfer of new technology or advanced technological information from developed to underdeveloped countries.

technophile *noun* an enthusiast about new technology. [Say TECHNO file]

technophobe *noun* a person who fears, dislikes, or avoids new technology. ▶ **technophobia** *noun* **technophobic** *adjective* [Say TECHNO fobe, techno FOE bee uh, techno FOE bick]

techy *adjective informal* technical: *a techy gizmo ◊ explaining techy stuff*. [Say TECKY]

tectonic *adjective* relating to the deformation of the earth's crust or to the structural changes caused by this. [Say teck TONIC]

tectonic plate *noun* each of a number of solid plates forming the earth's surface, which move slowly over the underlying mantle and occasionally break apart or collide; the interaction of tectonic plates is responsible for earthquakes, volcanoes, and the formation of mountains.

tectonics *plural noun* (usu. treated as *singular*) processes involving large-scale structural features of the earth's surface: *plate tectonics*. [Say teck TONICS]

teddy *noun* (*plural* **teddies**) **1** (also **teddy bear**) a soft toy bear. **2** a woman's undergarment combining camisole and panties.

tedious *adjective* tiresomely long or boring. ▶ **tediously** *adverb* **tediousness** *noun* [Say TEEDY us]

tedium *noun* the state of being tedious; boredom. [Say TEEDY um]

tee¹ *noun* (*plural* **tees**) = T¹.

tee² **• noun 1 a** a cleared space from which a golf ball is struck at the beginning of play for each hole. **b** a small support of wood or plastic from which a ball is struck at a tee. **2** a mark aimed at in curling etc. **3** *Football* a stand on which the ball is placed for a kickoff. **• verb** (**tees**, **teed**, **teeing**) (often foll. by *up*) place (a ball) on a tee ready to strike it. **PHRASES** **tee off** **1** play a ball from a tee. **2** *informal* start, begin. **3** *informal* make angry; annoy.

tee-hee **• noun** a titter or giggle, esp. one that expresses smugness or mockery. **• verb** (**tee-hees**, **tee-heed**, **tee-heeing**) titter or laugh in this way.

teem *verb* **1** be abundant: *fish teem in these waters*. **2** (foll. by *with*) be full of or swarming with: *teeming with ideas*. **3** (of rain) fall heavily: *rain was teeming down ◊ it's teeming with rain*.

teeming *adjective* present in large numbers; full of people, animals, etc. that are moving around: *teeming insects ◊ the teeming streets of the city*.

teen **• adjective** = TEENAGE. **• noun** = TEENAGER.

teenage *adjective* relating to or characteristic of teenagers. ▶ **teenaged** *adjective*

teenager *noun* a person from 13 to 19 years of age.

teens *plural noun* the years of one's life, the years of a century, or the units of a scale of temperature from 13 to 19.

teeny *adjective* (**teenier**, **teeniest**) (also **teensy**, **teensier**, **teensiest**) *informal* tiny.

teenybopper *noun informal* a young teenager, usu. a girl, who keenly follows the latest fashions in clothes, pop music, etc.

teeny-weeny *adjective* (also **teensy-weensy**) *informal* very tiny.

teepee *noun* (*plural* **teepees**) a conical tent formerly used by Plains Aboriginal peoples, made of skins, cloth, etc. on a frame of poles.

tee-shirt *noun* = T-SHIRT.

teeter *verb* **1** totter; stand or move unsteadily. **2** hesitate; be indecisive. **PHRASES** **teeter on the brink** (or **edge**) be in imminent danger (of disaster etc.).

teeter-totter *noun* = SEE-SAW.

teeth *plural of* TOOTH.

teethe *verb* (**teethes**, **teethed**, **teething**) grow baby teeth. ▶ **teething** *noun* [Rhymes with *BREATHE*]

teetotal *adjective* choosing or advocating to drink no alcohol. [Say tee TOTAL]

teetotaller *noun* a person advocating or practising abstinence from alcoholic drink. ▶ **teetotalling** *noun* & *adjective* [Say tee TOTAL er]

tefillin *plural noun* the two small leather boxes containing Biblical texts in Hebrew, worn by Jewish men during morning prayer on all days except the Sabbath as a reminder to keep the law. [Say tuh FILL in]

TEFL *abbreviation* teaching of English as a foreign language. [Say TEFF ul]

Teflon *noun* **1** *proprietary* polytetrafluoroethylene, a tough chemical-resistant polymer, esp. used as a non-stick coating for kitchen utensils. **2** (as an *adjective*) (of a politician etc.) having an undamaged reputation, in spite of scandal or misjudgment; able to deflect criticism on to others: *the Teflon defendant has been acquitted in three previous trials*. [Say TEFF lawn]

tekkie *noun* = TECHIE.

tel. *abbreviation* (also **Tel.**) telephone.

telco *noun* (*plural* **telcos**) esp. *US* a telecommunications company.

telebanking *noun* a method of banking in which the customer conducts transactions by telephone, esp. by means of a computerized system using touch-tone dialing or voice-recognition technology.

telecast **• noun** a television broadcast. **• verb** (**telecasts**, **telecast**, **telecasting**) transmit by television. ▶ **telecaster** *noun*

telecom *noun* telecommunications.

telecommunication *noun* **1** communication over a distance by telephone, radio, television, etc. **2** (usu. in *plural*) the branch of technology concerned with this.

telecommute *verb* (**telecommutes**,

telecommuted, telecommuting) work from home, communicating by modem, telephone, fax, etc. ▶ **telecommuter** *noun* **telecommuting** *noun*
teleconference *noun* a conference with participants in different locations linked by telecommunication devices. ▶ **teleconferencing** *noun*
telegenic *adjective* having an appearance or manner that looks pleasing on television. [Say tella JEN ick]
telegram *noun* a message sent by telegraph and then usu. delivered in written or printed form.
telegraph • *noun* a system of or device for transmitting messages or signals to a distant place esp. by making and breaking an electrical connection. • *verb* **1** send a message by telegraph. **2** give an advance indication of: *during a recent slump the struggling centre asked if he was telegraphing his shots.* **3** make signals: *telegraphed to me to come up.*
telegraphic *adjective* **1** of or by telegraphs or telegrams. **2** very concise and omitting unimportant or inessential words: *their only communication consisted of postcards written in a telegraphic style.* ▶ **telegraphically** *adverb*
telegraphy *noun* the science or practice of using or constructing telegraphs. [Say luh LEGRA fee]
telekinesis *noun* movement of objects at a distance supposedly by mental power or other non-physical means. ▶ **telekinetic** *adjective* [Say tele kin EE sis, tele kin ETT ick]
telemark *Skiing* • *noun* a swing turn with one ski advanced and the knee bent, used to change direction or stop short. • *verb* perform this turn.
telemarketer *noun* a person who markets goods etc. by means of usu. unsolicited telephone calls.
telemarketing *noun* the marketing of goods etc. by means of usu. unsolicited telephone calls.
telemedicine *noun* the practice of remote medical diagnosis and treatment of patients by means of the transmission of information by telecommunications.
teleological *adjective* **1** based on or having to do with the theory that events and developments are meant to achieve a purpose and happen because of that purpose: *classical music has been intensely teleological: we feel strongly how the end of a movement is implied in the beginning, and how we are led to it step by step.* **2** (in Christian theology) of or involving an argument for the existence of God from the evidence of design and purpose in the material world: *at the root of Norman's belief is teleological thinking: God created nothing in vain without purpose* ◊ *Darwin shattered the teleological conception of nature as reflecting an intelligent purpose.* [Say telly a LOGICAL or teely a LOGICAL]
teleology *noun* **1** the explanation of phenomena by the purpose they serve rather than by postulated causes, e.g. that there is a natural purpose or goal to the evolutionary changes of animals. **2** (in Christian theology) the doctrine of design and purpose in the material world. [Say telly OLLA jee or teely OLLA jee]
telepath *noun* a person with the ability to communicate or perceive thoughts or ideas without speech or writing or by any of the known senses.
telepathic *adjective* **1** communicating or perceiving thoughts or ideas without speech or writing or by any of the known senses: *telepathic intuition.* **2** (of a person) able to communicate or perceive thoughts or ideas without speech or writing or by any of the known senses. ▶ **telepathically** *adverb*
telepathy *noun* the supposed communication or perception of thoughts or ideas without speech or writing or by any of the known senses. [Say tuh LEPPA thee]
telephone • *noun* **1** an apparatus for transmitting

sound (esp. speech) over a distance, esp. by converting acoustic vibrations to electrical signals. **2** a transmitting and receiving instrument used in this. **3** a system of communication using a network of telephones. • *verb* (**telephones**, **telephoned**, **telephoning**) = PHONE *verb*.
telephone booth *noun* a public booth or enclosure from which telephone calls can be made.
telephone tag *noun* a situation in which two people try repeatedly to return each other's telephone calls but fail to make contact because when either calls the other cannot answer.
telephonic *adjective* pertaining to telephones: *telephonic communications.* [Say tele FON ick]
telephony *noun* the use or a system of telephones. [Say tel EFFA nee]
telephoto • *noun* (*plural* **telephotos**) (also **telephoto lens**, *plural* **telephoto lenses**) a lens with a longer focal length than standard, giving a narrow field of view and a magnified image. • *adjective* of or using such a lens: *a telephoto shot.*
teleport *verb* move objects at a distance by mental power or other non-physical means. ▶ **teleportation** *noun*
telepresence *noun* **1** the use of virtual reality technology esp. for remote control of machinery or for apparent participation in distant events. **2** a sensation of being elsewhere created in this way.
teleprinter *noun* a device for transmitting telegraph messages as they are keyed, and for printing messages received.
teleprompter *noun* a device, unseen by the audience, displaying a magnified television script to a speaker or performer.
telesales *plural noun* selling by telephone.
telescope • *noun* **1** an optical instrument using lenses or mirrors or both to make distant objects appear nearer and larger. **2** = RADIO TELESCOPE. • *verb* (**telescopes**, **telescoped**, **telescoping**) **1** press or drive (sections of a tube, colliding vehicles, etc.) together so that one slides into another like the sections of a folding telescope. **2** close or be driven or be capable of closing in this way. **3** compress so as to occupy less space or time.
telescopic *adjective* **1 a** of, relating to, or made with a telescope. **b** visible only through a telescope: *telescopic stars.* **2** (esp. of a lens) able to focus on and magnify distant objects. **3** consisting of sections that telescope. ▶ **telescopically** *adverb* [Say tele SCOP ick]
teletheatre *noun* an off-track betting facility where horse races are shown on television.
telethon *noun* an exceptionally long television program, esp. one featuring live performers, broadcast to raise money for a charity.
Teletype • *noun* *proprietary* a kind of teleprinter. • *verb* (**teletype**, **teletypes**, **teletyped**, **teletyping**) **1** operate a teleprinter. **2** send by means of a teleprinter.
televangelist *noun* an evangelical preacher who appears regularly on television. [Say tele VAN jell ist]
televise *verb* (**televises**, **televised**, **televising**) transmit by television.
television *noun* **1** a system for reproducing on a screen visual images converted (usu. with sound) into electrical signals and transmitted esp. by radio waves. **2** (also **television set**) a device with a screen for receiving these signals. **3** the medium, art form, or occupation of broadcasting on television. **4** the programs broadcast on television: *watched television.*
televisual *adjective* relating to or suitable for television. ▶ **televisually** *adverb*

telework *verb* = TELECOMMUTE. ▶**teleworker** *noun* **teleworking** *noun*

telex • *noun* (*plural* **telexes**) **1** an international system of telegraphy with printed messages transmitted and received by teleprinters using the public telecommunications network. **2** a message sent this way. • *verb* (**telexes, telexed, telexing**) send or communicate with by telex.

tell¹ *verb* (**tells, told, telling**) **1** express in words. **2** reveal or signify to (a person): *your face tells me everything*. **3** (foll. by *on*) informal inform against (a person). **4** explain in writing; instruct: *this book tells you how to cook*. **5** decide, determine, distinguish: *cannot tell which button to press*. **6 a** (often foll. by *on*) produce a noticeable effect: *the strain was beginning to tell on me*. **b** reveal the truth: *time will tell*. **c** have an influence: *the evidence tells against you*. **7** count (votes) at a meeting, election, etc. PHRASES **as far as one can tell** judging from the available information. **tell apart** distinguish between: *could not tell them apart*. **tell it like it is** informal relate the facts of a matter realistically or honestly, holding nothing back. **tell me another** informal an expression of disbelief. **tell off 1** informal reprimand, scold. **2** count off or detach for duty. **tell on** tattle on; reveal a person's activities, esp. to a person in authority. **tell a tale** be significant or revealing. **tell tales** report a discreditable fact about another. **tell (the) time** determine the time from the face of a clock or watch. **there is no telling** it is impossible to know. **you're telling me** informal I agree wholeheartedly.

tell² *noun* an artificial mound in the Middle East etc. formed by the accumulated remains of ancient settlements.

tell-all *adjective* designating books etc. in which a person reveals all about their life, esp. the most sordid details.

teller *noun* **1** a person employed to receive and pay out money in a bank etc. **2** a person who tells esp. stories: *a teller of tales*. **3** a person who counts (votes).

telling *adjective* **1** having a marked effect; striking. **2** significant. ▶**tellingly** *adverb*

telltale *adjective* that reveals or betrays: *a telltale smile*.

tellurium *noun* a rare brittle lustrous silver-white element occurring naturally in ores of gold and silver, used in semiconductors. [Say tel LURE ee um]

telnet • *noun* **1** a network protocol that allows a user on one computer to log in to another computer that is part of the same network. **2** a program that establishes a connection from one computer to another by means of such a protocol. **3** a link thus established. • *verb* (**telnets, telnetted, telnetting**) log in or connect to a remote computer using a telnet program. [Say TELL net]

temerity *noun* excessive confidence or boldness; audacity: *had the temerity to call me a liar in public*. [Say tuh MARE a tee]

temp. *abbreviation* temperature.

temp *informal* • *noun* **1** a temporary employee, esp. a secretary. **2** a temperature. • *verb* work as a temp.

tempeh *noun* a fermented soybean product, usu. eaten fried. [Say TEM puh]

temper • *noun* **1** habitual or temporary disposition of mind esp. as regards composure. **2** irritation or anger: *in a fit of temper*. **3** a tendency to have fits of anger: *have a temper*. **4** composure or calmness: *lose one's temper*. **5** the condition of metal as regards hardness and elasticity. • *verb* **1** bring (metal or clay) to a proper hardness or consistency. **2** (foll. by *with*) moderate: *temper justice with mercy*.

tempera *noun* (*plural* **temperas**) **1** a method of painting using a kind of paint consisting of powdered pigment typically held together with egg yolk and water. **2** this type of paint. [Say TEMPER uh]

temperament *noun* **1** a person's distinct nature and character, esp. as permanently affecting behaviour; natural disposition, personality: *a nervous temperament*. **2** a creative or spirited personality: *was full of temperament*. [Say TEMPRA m'nt or TEMPER m'nt]

temperamental *adjective* **1** of or having temperament: *a temperamental aversion to hard work*. **2 a** (of a person) liable to erratic or moody behaviour. **b** (of a thing, e.g. a machine) working unpredictably; unreliable. ▶**temperamentally** *adverb* [Say tempra MENTAL or temper MENTAL]

temperance *noun* **1** total or partial abstinence from alcoholic drink: *was convinced to abandon his strict temperance and agree that alcohol can in some circumstances be quite pleasant*. **2** (as an *adjective*) advocating or concerned with abstinence from alcohol: *the temperance movement*. [Say TEMPER ince]

temperate *adjective* **1** showing moderation or self-restraint: *a temperate and balanced study* ◊ *was temperate in her consumption of food and drink*. **2 a** (of a region or climate) characterized by mild temperatures. **b** (of a plant, tree, etc.) growing in a region characterized by mild temperatures: *temperate and tropical species of plants*. [Say TEMPER it]

temperate zone *noun* the belt of the earth between the frigid and the torrid zones.

temperature *noun* **1** the degree or intensity of heat of a substance, the air, etc. in relation to others, esp. as shown by a thermometer or perceived by touch etc. **2** the degree of internal heat of the body. **3** informal a body temperature above the normal: *have a temperature*. PHRASES **take a person's temperature** ascertain a person's body temperature.

-tempered *combining form* **1** having a specified temper or disposition. **2** (of a piano or other instrument) tuned so as to adjust the note intervals correctly: *a well-tempered keyboard*.

tempest *noun* **1** a violent windy storm. **2** activity or an incident involving strong and often conflicting emotions, agitation, violence, etc.: *a media tempest* ◊ *her resignation set off a political tempest*. PHRASES **tempest in a teapot** great agitation over a trivial matter.

tempestuous *adjective* **1** stormy. **2** (of a person, relationship, etc.) turbulent, violent, passionate. ▶**tempestuously** *adverb* **tempestuousness** *noun* [Say tem PESS chew us]

template *noun* **1 a** a pattern or gauge, usu. a piece of thin board or metal plate, used as a guide in cutting or drilling metal, stone, wood, etc. **b** a flat card or plastic pattern esp. for cutting cloth for patchwork etc. **2 a** timber or plate used to distribute the weight in a wall or under a beam etc. **3** Computing a stored pattern for a document or part of a document from which new documents or parts of documents may be made. [Say TEM plate or TEM plit]

temple *noun* **1** a building devoted to the worship, or regarded as the dwelling place, of a god or gods or other objects of religious reverence. **2** hist. any of three successive religious buildings of the Jews in Jerusalem. **3** a synagogue. **4** a place of Christian public worship, esp. a Mormon church. **5** a place in which God is regarded as residing, esp. a Christian's person or body. **6** any large imposing building devoted to a particular interest etc.: *a temple of the arts*. **7 a** the flat part of either side of the head between the forehead and the ear. **b** either of the two side pieces on a pair of glasses extending from the frame toward the ear.

tempo *noun* **1** (*plural* **tempos** or **tempi**) *Music* the speed at which music is or should be played, esp. as

characteristic: *waltz tempo*. **2** (*plural* **tempos**) the rate of motion or activity: *the tempo of the war is quickening*.

temporal *adjective* **1** of worldly as opposed to spiritual affairs: *an elected council was organized to administer the parish's temporal affairs*. **2** of or relating to time: *temporal changes in migration*. **3** of the temples of the head. [Say TEMPER ul]

temporal bone *noun* either of two bones forming part of the side of the skull on each side and enclosing the middle and inner ear.

temporality *noun* (*plural* **temporalities**) the state of existing within or having some relationship to time. [Say temper ALA tee]

temporal lobe *noun* each of the paired lobes of the brain lying beneath the temples, including areas concerned with the understanding of speech.

temporally *adverb* **1** in regard to worldly as opposed to spiritual affairs; in, or with respect to, this life: *under whose roof did I feel temporally and spiritually more at ease?* **2** with regard to time: *Christianity and Islam developed in close proximity, both spatially and temporally*.

temporarily *adverb* during a limited time.

temporary *adjective* lasting or meant to last only for a limited time.

temporize *verb* (**temporizes**, **temporized**, **temporizing**) avoid committing oneself so as to gain time: *he's been temporizing for months now, hoping that if the problem could be ignored long enough, it might somehow go away*. [Say TEMPER ize]

tempt *verb* **1** entice or incite (a person) to do a wrong or forbidden thing. **2** allure, attract. **3** risk provoking (esp. an abstract force or power): *would be tempting fate to try it*. **PHRASES** **be tempted to** be strongly disposed to: *I am tempted to go*.

temptation *noun* **1** a desire to do something, esp. something wrong, unwise, or self-indulgent: *he yielded to the temptation to call Lauren at work ◊ Katherine can resist anything but temptation ◊ baking brownies is putting temptation in her way*. **2** an attractive thing or course of action: *an expensive bike is a temptation to thieves*.

tempter *noun* **1** a person who tempts. **2** (**the Tempter**) the Devil.

tempting *adjective* **1** attractive, inviting. **2** enticing to evil, wrongdoing, etc. ▶ **temptingly** *adverb*

temptress *noun* (*plural* **temptresses**) a woman who tempts.

tempura *noun* (in Japanese cuisine) fish, shellfish, or vegetables, fried in batter. [Say tem POO ruh]

ten *cardinal number* **1** one more than nine. **2** (in *plural*) the digit second from the right of a whole number in decimal notation, representing a multiple of ten less than a hundred: *numbered in the tens of thousands*.

tenable *adjective* that can be maintained or defended against attack or objection: *a tenable position ◊ a tenable theory*. [Say TEN a bull]

tenacious *adjective* **1** that does not stop holding something or give up something easily: *a tenacious grip ◊ the party has kept its tenacious hold on power for more than twenty years ◊ a tenacious memory*. **2** continuing to exist, have influence, etc. for longer than one might expect; persistent: *tenacious traditions*. ▶ **tenaciously** *adverb* [Say ten AY shuss]

tenacity *noun* the quality of not giving up easily, of holding on stubbornly. [Say ten ASS it ee]

tenancy *noun* (*plural* **tenancies**) **1** the status of a tenant; possession as a tenant. **2** the duration or period of this. [Say TEN un see]

tenant • *noun* **1** a person, business, etc. who rents a residence, premises, etc. from the owner. **2** (often foll. by *of*) the occupant of a place. • *verb* occupy as a tenant.

tenant farmer *noun* a person who farms rented land.

Ten Commandments *plural noun* (usu. as **the Ten Commandments**) *Bible* the divine rules of conduct given by God to Moses.

tend *verb* **1 a** (usu. foll. by *to*) be apt or inclined. **b** (usu. foll. by *toward*) suggest or exhibit a tendency towards (a quality etc.). **c** be moving; be directed: *tends to the same conclusion*. **2 a** take care of, look after, be responsible for. **b** (foll. by *to*) give attention to.

tendency *noun* (*plural* **tendencies**) **1** (often foll. by *to, toward*) a leaning or inclination; a way in which a person or thing is likely to behave: *an agreeable tendency to avoid confrontation and seek consensus*. **2** a direction in which something moves or changes: *the tendency since the turn of the century has been towards a simplification of capital structures*.

tendentious *adjective* *derogatory* (of writing etc.) calculated to promote a particular cause or viewpoint; having an underlying purpose: *we'll report all the significant events of the day, factually, without bias or tendentious comment*. ▶ **tendentiously** *adverb* **tendentiousness** *noun* [Say ten DEN shuss]

tender • *adjective* (**tenderer**, **tenderest**) **1** easily cut or chewed, not tough: *tender steak*. **2 a** easily touched or wounded, susceptible to pain or grief: *a tender heart*. **b** easily damaged; delicate: *tender plants*. **c** somewhat painful: *her ankle's still tender from the sprain*. **3** loving, affectionate, fond: *wrote tender verses*. **4** (of age) early, immature: *of tender years*. • *verb* **1 a** offer, present (one's services, apologies, resignation, etc.). **b** offer (money etc.) as payment: *they tendered the full sum in cash*. **2** (often foll. by *for*) make a tender for the supply of a thing or the execution of work: *local firms were invited to tender for the building contract*. **3** invite bids for (a contract): *the contract wasn't tendered until March; six bids were subsequently received*. • *noun* **1** an offer, esp. an offer in writing to execute work or supply goods at a fixed price. **2** the auctioning of an item of value, e.g. a contract, to bidders. **3** money or other commodities that may be legally tendered or offered in payment (see LEGAL TENDER). **4** a person who looks after people or things. **5** a ship attending a larger one to supply stores, convey passengers or orders, etc. **6** a special railway car closely coupled to a steam locomotive to carry fuel, water, etc. **PHRASES** **put out to tender** seek tenders with respect to (work etc.).

tenderer *noun* a person who tenders or makes a formal offer, esp. for a proposed contract.

tenderfoot *noun* (*plural* **tenderfoots** or **tenderfeet**) a newcomer or novice, esp. in the bush or in the Scouts or Guides.

tender-hearted *adjective* having a tender heart, easily moved by pity etc. ▶ **tender-heartedness** *noun*

tenderize *verb* (**tenderizes**, **tenderized**, **tenderizing**) make tender, esp. make (meat) tender by pounding, marinating, etc. ▶ **tenderizer** *noun*

tenderloin *noun* **1** a tender cut of meat from the inside of a loin of beef or pork. **2** *slang* a district of a city where vice and corruption are prominent.

tenderly *adverb* in a tender way; with tenderness.

tenderness *noun* **1** the quality or condition of being easily cut or chewed. **2** the quality or condition of being easily hurt or wounded. **3** the quality or condition of being loving or affectionate; kindness.

tendinitis *noun* (also **tendonitis**) inflammation of a tendon, most commonly from overuse but also from infection or rheumatic disease. [Say tendon ITE iss]

tendon *noun* **1** a cord or strand of strong fibrous tissue attaching a muscle to a bone etc. **2** (in a quadruped) = HAMSTRING *noun* 2.

tendril *noun* **1** each of the slender leafless shoots, often growing in a spiral form, by which some climbing plants cling for support. **2 a** a slender curl, e.g. of hair. **b** something which curls or clings like a plant tendril: *tendrils of smoke*.

tenement *noun* a building with apartments or rooms rented cheaply, esp. in a poor area of a city.

tenet *noun* a belief or principle held by a group or person: *one of the basic tenets of Christianity*.

tenfold *adjective & adverb* **1** ten times as much or as many. **2** consisting of ten parts.

10-gallon hat *noun* = COWBOY HAT.

Tenn. *abbreviation* Tennessee.

tenner *noun informal* a ten-dollar bill or ten-pound note.

Tennessean *noun* a native or inhabitant of Tennessee. [Say tenna SEE un]

tennis *noun* either of two games in which two or four players strike a ball with racquets over a net stretched across a court.

tennis elbow *noun* a painful inflammation of the tendons in the elbow caused by playing tennis or engaging in other activities involving repetitious movement of the elbow joint.

tennis shoe *noun* **1** a light canvas or leather soft-soled shoe used in tennis. **2** esp. *US* a running shoe.

tenon *noun* a projecting piece of wood made for insertion into a corresponding cavity (esp. a mortise) in another piece. ▶ **tenoned** *adjective*

tenor *noun* **1 a** a singing voice between baritone and alto or counter-tenor, the highest of the ordinary adult male range. **b** a singer with this voice. **c** a part written for it. **2** an instrument, esp. a saxophone or viola, of which the range is roughly that of a tenor voice. **3** the general meaning, sense, or content of a document, talk, etc.: *I am disturbed by the tenor of the discussion in council*. **4** a settled or prevailing course or direction, esp. the course of a person's life or habits: *you're disturbing the even tenor of our home*.

tenpin *noun* **1** (often in *plural*) (also **10-pin bowling**) a variety of bowling in which players have two chances to knock down sets of ten pins using a large hard rubber ball. **2** a pin used in this game.

tense¹ • *adjective* **1** stretched tight, strained: *tense muscles*. **2** in a state of, causing, or characterized by nervous strain or tension: *tense nerves ◊ a tense moment*. • *verb* (**tenses**, **tensed**, **tensing**) make or become tense. • *noun* *Grammar* a form taken by a verb to indicate whether the action takes place in the past, present, or future, and whether it is completed or ongoing: *present tense ◊ imperfect tense*. PHRASES **tense up** become tense.

tensely *adverb* in a tense manner: *the swans were tensely wary*.

tensile *adjective* **1** of or relating to tension. **2** that can be drawn out or stretched: *tensile steel*. [Say TENSE ile]

tensile strength *noun* resistance to breaking under forces acting in opposite directions.

tension *noun* **1 a** the state of being stretched tight: *the parachute keeps the cable under tension as it drops*. **b** the state of having the muscles stretched tight, esp. as causing strain or discomfort: *the elimination of neck tension can relieve headaches*. **2** mental strain or excitement: *we laughed and that helped ease the tension ◊ as the movie progresses the tension builds*. **3 a** a strained (political, social, etc.) state or relationship: *the coup followed months of tension between the military and the government ◊ racial tensions*. **b** a relationship between ideas or qualities with conflicting demands or implications: *the basic tension between freedom and control*. **4** *Mechanics* the strained condition resulting from forces acting in opposite directions. **5** electromagnetic force.

tensor *noun* **1** a muscle that tightens or stretches a part of the body. **2** *Math* a generalized form of vector involving an arbitrary number of indices.

Tensor bandage *noun* *Cdn proprietary* a wide elasticized bandage used to provide support to injured joints.

ten-spot *noun informal* **1** a ten-dollar bill or ten-pound note. **2** a playing card with ten pips.

tent • *noun* **1** a portable shelter or dwelling of canvas, cloth, etc., supported by a pole or poles and stretched by cords or loops attached to pegs driven into the ground. **2** (as an *adjective*) composed of or occurring in or under a tent or tents: *tent show*. **3** (in full **oxygen tent**) a tent-like enclosure containing air enriched with oxygen, placed over a patient to aid breathing. • *verb* **1 a** cover with or as with a tent. **b** cover (a dish) with a tent-like lid of foil etc. **2** camp in a tent. **3** form into a tent-like shape, esp. with sides etc. meeting at a top point or ridge.

tentacle *noun* **1** a long slender flexible appendage of an (esp. invertebrate) animal, used for feeling, grasping, or moving. **2** *Botany* a sensitive hair or filament. **3** (usu. in *plural*) a sinister influence that reaches to all parts of something: *the spreading tentacles of the Mafia*. ▶ **tentacled** *adjective* **tentacular** *adjective* [Say TENT cull, ten TACK yoo lur]

tentative *adjective* **1** done by way of trial, experimental, provisional: *management and the union have reached a tentative agreement*. **2** hesitant, not definite: *a tentative suggestion*. ▶ **tentatively** *adverb* **tentativeness** *noun*

tent caterpillar *noun* a moth larva that lives in groups inside tent-like silken webs in a tree, which it often strips of leaves.

tent city *noun* (*plural* **tent cities**) a very large collection of tents, esp. erected in an emergency or in protest.

tented *adjective* composed of or provided with tents.

tenterhook *noun* PHRASES **on tenterhooks** in suspense or mentally agitated due to uncertainty.

tenth *ordinal number* the position in a sequence corresponding to the number 10 in the sequence 1-10. ▶ **tenthly** *adverb*

tent pole *noun* a pole supporting a tent.

tent ring *noun* *Cdn* a ring of stones for holding down a tent, teepee, etc., esp. as indicating a past campsite.

tenuous *adjective* **1** very weak or slight: *his links with the organization turned out to be, at best, tenuous*. **2** very slender or fine; insubstantial: *the tenuous threads of a spider's web*. ▶ **tenuously** *adverb* [Say TEN yoo us]

tenure *noun* **1** a condition, or form of right or title, under which (esp. real) property is held: *land tenure*. **2 a** the holding or possession of an office or property. **b** the period of this: *during his tenure of office*. **3** guaranteed permanent employment, esp. as a teacher or lecturer after a probationary period: *a faculty*

job at $20,000 a year, with every second year a sabbatical, and tenure after six months. [Say TEN yur]

tenured *adjective* **1** (of an official position) carrying a guarantee of permanent employment. **2** (of a teacher etc.) having permanent employment guaranteed. [Say TEN yurd]

tepee *noun* (*plural* **tepees**) = TEEPEE.

tepid *adjective* **1** slightly warm: *tepid water*. **2** unenthusiastic: *the audience's tepid applause*. ▶ **tepidly** *adverb* [Say TEP id]

tequila *noun* a Mexican alcoholic liquor made by distilling the fermented sap of an agave, a plant with succulent spiny leaves. [Say tuh KEY luh]

tera- *combining form* **1** denoting a factor of 10^{12}: *terawatt*. **2** *Computing* (in the binary system) denoting a factor of 2^{40} (i.e. 1 099 511 627 776): *terabyte*.

terbium *noun* a silvery metallic element. [Say TURBY um]

teriyaki *noun* **1** (in Japanese cuisine) fish or meat marinated in soy sauce etc. and grilled. **2** this sauce. [Say terry YACKY or terry YOCKY]

term • *noun* **1** a word used to express a definite concept, esp. in a particular branch of study etc. **2** (in *plural*) mode of expression: *answered in no uncertain terms*. **3** (in *plural*) a relation or footing: *we are on familiar terms*. **4** (in *plural*) **a** conditions or stipulations: *do it on your own terms*. **b** financial charges: *my terms are very reasonable*. **5 a** a limited period of some state or activity: *for a term of five years*. **b** a period over which operations are conducted or results contemplated: *in the short term*. **c** a period of some weeks, alternating with holiday or vacation, during which instruction is given in a school etc. or during which a law court holds sessions. **d** a period of imprisonment. **e** a period of tenure. **6** *Math* **a** each of the two quantities in a ratio. **b** each quantity in a series. **c** a part of an expression joined to the rest by + or −, e.g. *a*, *b*, *c* in *a* + *b* − *c*. **7** the completion of a normal length of pregnancy. **8** an appointed day, esp. for payment of money due. • *verb* give a name to, call; assign a term to: *the music termed classical*. **PHRASES** **bring to terms** cause to accept conditions. **come to terms** agree on conditions; come to an agreement. **come to terms with 1** reconcile oneself to (a difficulty etc.). **2** conclude an agreement with. **in terms of** as regards, with reference to. **make terms** conclude an agreement. **be on good** (or **friendly** etc.) **terms with** have a good relationship with.

term deposit *noun* Cdn an amount of money, usu. between $1,000 and $5,000, deposited with a financial institution for a fixed term, usu. between 30 days and a year, at a fixed interest rate, which can be withdrawn before term on payment of a penalty.

terminal • *adjective* **1** relating to an illness or disease leading to death: *terminal cases ◊ terminal illness*. **2** of or forming a limit or terminus: *terminal station*. **3 a** *Zoology* etc. ending a series: *terminal joints*. **b** *Botany* at the end of a stem etc. **4** *informal* very great; irreparable: *terminal laziness*. • *noun* **1** a terminus for trains or long-distance buses. **2** a departure and arrival building for air passengers at an airport. **3** a device for entering data in to a computer or receiving its output, esp. one that can be used by a person as a means of two-way communication with a computer, e.g. a keyboard and monitor. **4** an installation where grain, oil, etc. is stored at the end of a rail line or pipeline, or at a port.

terminal elevator *noun* a large grain elevator to which grain is shipped from country elevators for accumulation before onward shipment, usu. by water.

terminally *adverb* **1** in a way that will be fatal: *a terminally ill patient*. **2** *informal* extremely; irreparably: *a terminally boring movie*.

terminate *verb* (**terminates**, **terminated**, **terminating**) **1** bring or come to an end. **2** end (a pregnancy) by artificial means before the fetus is viable. **3** fire (an employee).

termination *noun* **1** the action of bringing something or coming to an end: *the termination of a contract*. **2** an induced abortion. **3** dismissal from employment. **4** the point or part in which something ends.

terminator *noun* a person or thing that terminates something.

terminology *noun* (*plural* **terminologies**) **1** the system of terms used in a particular subject. **2** the science of the proper use of terms.

terminus *noun* (*plural* **termini** or **terminuses**) **1 a** the end of a railway, bus route, etc. **b** a station at this point. **2** a point at the end of a pipeline etc. **3** *Math* the end point of a vector etc. [Say TERM in us for the singular, TERM in eye or TERM in us iz for the plural]

termite *noun* a small antlike insect that lives in large colonies and feeds on wood and can be highly destructive to trees and timber.

term of endearment *noun* a pet name or other term used to convey love or fondness.

term paper *noun* an essay or dissertation representative of the work done during a term.

terms of reference *noun* the limits that are set on what an official committee or report has been asked to do: *the matter, they decided, lay outside the commission's terms of reference*.

tern *noun* a seabird related to the gulls, usu. smaller with long pointed wings and a forked tail.

terrace • *noun* **1 a** each of a series of flat areas formed on a slope and used for cultivation. **b** a similar levelled top of a natural slope. **2** a level paved area next to a house. **3** the flat roof of a house, esp. in warm climates, where the roof is used as a cool resting area. **4** a row of houses on a raised level or along the top or face of a slope. **5** a natural horizontal shelf-like formation on a slope leading to a river, sea, etc. • *verb* (**terraces**, **terraced**, **terracing**) (esp. as **terraced** *adjective*) form into or provide with a terrace or terraces. ▶ **terracing** *noun*

terra cotta • *noun* **1** usu. brownish-red earthenware that has not been glazed, used chiefly as an ornamental building material, in flowerpots etc., and in modelling. **2** the brownish-red colour of terra cotta. • *adjective* of a brownish-red colour.

terraform *verb* (esp. in science fiction) transform (a planet) so as to resemble the earth.

terrain *noun* ground, a tract of land, esp. with regard to its physical characteristics or their capacity for use by a military tactician, traveller, etc.

terrapin *noun* an edible North American freshwater turtle. [Say TERRA pin]

terrarium *noun* (*plural* **terrariums** or **terraria**) **1** a place or container artificially prepared for keeping very small land animals such as newts and snakes in (nearly) their natural state. **2** a sealed transparent globe etc. containing growing plants. [Say tuh RARE ee um]

terrazzo *noun* (*plural* **terrazzos**) a flooring material of stone chips set in concrete and given a smooth surface. [Say tuh RAT so or tuh RAZ oh]

terrestrial • *adjective* **1** (of animals and plants) living on the land or on the ground, rather than in water, in trees, or in the air: *terrestrial species ◊ a terrestrial habitat*. **2** (of a planet) similar in size or composition to the earth: *some of Jupiter's moons are similar in size to the smaller terrestrial planets, e.g. Mercury*. **3** of or on or relating to the earth. • *noun* an inhabitant of the earth.

terrible *adjective* **1** *informal* **a** dreadful, awful: *the accident was terrible*. **b** very bad: *terrible cigars ◊ a terrible*

bore. **2** *informal* very incompetent: *terrible at tennis.* **3** *informal* ill: *Tristan ate too much and feels terrible.* **4** *informal* full of remorse: *I feel terrible about it.* **5** causing or fit to cause terror: *he fell to his death, releasing a terrible cry that echoed from the mountain far out across the land.*

terrible two *noun* (*plural* **terrible twos**) *informal* **1** a two-year-old child regarded as typically troublesome. **2** (*in plural*) this age.

terribly *adverb* **1** *informal* very, extremely: *terribly nice.* **2** in a terrible manner.

terrier *noun* any of various breeds of dog originally used for turning out foxes etc. from their earths, known for their eagerness and tenacity.

terrific *adjective informal* **1** excellent: *did a terrific job.* **2** of great size or intensity. **3** excessive: *a terrific noise.* ▶ **terrifically** *adverb*

terrify *verb* (**terrifies, terrified, terrifying**) fill with terror; frighten severely. ▶ **terrifying** *adjective* **terrifyingly** *adverb*

terrine *noun* **1** a kind of pâté, usu. coarse textured. **2** a usu. oval earthenware vessel, esp. one in which pâté is cooked, served, or sold. [Say tuh REEN]

territorial *adjective* **1** of land: *territorial conquests.* **2** having to do with a particular district or locality: *American territorial waters ◊ he has territorial responsibility for the eastern hemisphere.* **3** (of a person or animal etc.) inclined to claim and become especially defensive of an area. **4** (usu. **Territorial**) of or relating to any of the Territories of Canada or other countries.

Territorial Court *noun Cdn* a court established in a Territory by territorial legislation, usu. having both criminal and civil divisions, which conducts hearings by judge alone on offences of a relatively minor nature.

territoriality *noun* a pattern of behaviour in which an animal or group of animals defends an area against others of the same species.

territorial waters *plural noun* the waters under the jurisdiction of a country, esp. the part of the sea within a stated distance of the shore, traditionally three miles from low-water mark.

territory *noun* (*plural* **territories**) **1** the extent of the land under the jurisdiction of a ruler, country, city, etc. **2** (**Territory**) **a** (in Canada) a region which has not been admitted as a province and which is governed by a federally appointed commissioner and an elected legislative assembly. **b** a region administered by the US federal government without the full rights of a state. **c** any similar division of other countries. **3 a** an area of knowledge, activity, or experience: *much of her writing remains fairly unfamiliar territory ◊ dancers are hardly ever not in pain — it goes with the territory.* **b** an area for which one has responsibility with regard to a particular type of activity: *hardware issues are Owen's territory.* **4** the district over which a sales representative or agent operates. **5** *Zoology* **a** an area defended by an animal or group of animals against others of the same species. **b** the part of a city a person or group of people is associated with. **6** *Sport* an area of a playing surface, esp. one defended by a team or player. **7** an area of land, esp. with a specified characteristic: *steep-sloped and bear-prowled territory high up in the mountain valleys.*

terror *noun* **1** extreme fear or dread. **2 a** a person or thing that causes terror. **b** *informal* or *jocular* an exasperating or troublesome person, esp. a child: *the twins are holy terrors.* **c** *Sport* a dreaded or formidable opponent. **3** the use of organized intimidation; terrorism. **4** (**the Terror**; also **the Reign of Terror**) the period (1793–4) of the French Revolution when the ruling Jacobin faction attempted to eliminate domestic

and foreign opposition to the radical Revolution through a series of extreme political, economic, and military reforms. During the course of the Terror, 40,000 French citizens were executed, 1,300 in its last six weeks in Paris alone. It ended with the fall and execution of Robespierre.

terrorism *noun* the systematic employment of violence and intimidation to coerce a government or community, esp. into agreeing to specific political demands. ▶ **terrorist** *noun*

terrorize *verb* (**terrorizes, terrorized, terrorizing**) **1** fill with terror. **2** coerce by terror; use terrorism against. **3** bully, harass, persecute.

terry cloth *noun* (also **terry**) an absorbent cotton pile fabric with the loops uncut, used for making esp. towels and bathrobes.

terse *adjective* (**terser, tersest**) (of a person or their language) using few words, esp. in a manner that seems rude or unfriendly; curt, abrupt: *issued a terse statement announcing that the concert was cancelled.* ▶ **tersely** *adverb* **terseness** *noun*

tertiary • *adjective* **1** third in order or rank etc. **2** (**Tertiary**) of or relating to the first period in the Cenozoic era, lasting from about 65 to 2 million years ago, during which mammals evolved rapidly. **3** (of an industry or type of economic activity) concerned with the provision of services, such as transportation and leisure etc. • *noun* the Tertiary period. [Say TUR shur ee]

TESL *abbreviation* teaching of English as a second language. [Say TESS ul]

tesla *noun* (*plural* **teslas**) the SI unit of density of magnetic flux, equal to one weber per square metre or 10,000 gauss. [Say TESS luh]

TESOL *abbreviation* teaching (or teachers) of English to speakers of other languages. [Say TESS awl]

test • *noun* **1** a critical examination or trial of the qualities, genuineness, or suitability of a person or thing. **2 a** a procedure for assessing a person's aptitude, competence, skill, or intelligence. **b** a set of questions on an academic subject to be answered without assistance: *spelling test.* **3** a procedure performed in order to determine a person's physical or psychological condition: *pregnancy test.* **4** a situation requiring a person to demonstrate a particular ability or strength: *talking to her is a real test of your patience.* **5** a standard for comparison or trial: *it does not stand up to our test.* **6** *Chemistry* **a** a procedure for examining a substance under known conditions or with a specific reagent to determine its identity or the presence or absence of some constituent, activity, etc. **b** a substance by means of which this may be done. **7** (as an *adjective*) designating esp. fishing line having a strength or capacity of a specified weight: *20-pound test line.* • *verb* **1** subject (a person or thing) to a close or critical examination; evaluate by experiment. **2** subject (a substance) to a chemical test: *tested his blood for alcohol.* **3 a** apply or carry out a test on a person or thing: *they're testing for HIV.* **b** achieve or receive a specific result: *tested positive for banned substances.* **4** try the patience or endurance of (a person). PHRASES **put to the test** cause to undergo a test. **stand** (or **withstand**) **the test of time** be or remain popular after the passage of a long period of time. **test out** subject (a theory etc.) to a practical test; try out. **test whether** perform a test to see; check. ▶ **testable** *adjective*

testament *noun* **1** *Bible* **a** (**Testament**) either of the main divisions of the Christian Bible. **b** (**Testament**) a copy of the New Testament. **c** an agreement between God and a person, nation, etc. **2** evidence, proof; a

tribute: *it is a testament to your loyalty*. **3** a will: *last will and testament*.

test ban *noun* an agreement among several countries to discontinue the testing of nuclear weapons.

test bed *noun* **1** a testing site. **2** equipment for testing machines before acceptance for general use.

test case *noun* **1** *Law* a case that sets a precedent for other cases involving the same legal principle: *the company was sued last year in a test case involving discrimination against pregnant employees*. **2** a person, thing, or set of circumstances used to test something: *biologists see reintroduction of the flying squirrel to the park as an important test case*.

test drive • *verb* (**test drives**, **test drove**, **test driving**) **1** drive (a car or truck etc.) in order to assess its quality and performance before buying it. **2** run (software) to sample its features and assess its suitability. **3** *informal* sample (a product) prior to purchase. • *noun* **1** a drive taken to assess the performance of a car or truck etc. one is thinking of buying. **2** a test of a product, such as computer software, prior to purchase.

tester *noun* **1** a device or instrument used to test something: *circuit tester*. **2** a person who conducts a test of esp. a product. **3 a** a small amount of a perfume or cosmetic for a customer to sample before purchase. **b** the bottle from which this is dispensed.

testes *plural of* TESTIS. [Say TESS teez]

test flight *noun* a flight during which the performance of an aircraft is tested. ▶ **test-fly** *verb* (**test-flies**; *past* **test-flew**; *past participle* **test-flown**; **test-flying**)

testicle *noun* either of the two oval organs that produce sperm in male mammals, enclosed in the scrotum behind the penis. ▶ **testicular** *adjective* [Say TESTA cull, tess TICK yoo lur]

testify *verb* (**testifies**, **testified**, **testifying**) **1 a** appear as a witness to give evidence in a court of law. **b** state under oath in a court of law. **2** affirm or declare, esp. based on first-hand knowledge or prior experience. **3** bear witness; attest: *I can testify to the quality of her work*. **4** (of a thing) serve as proof or evidence of: *his poetry testifies to his torment*. PHRASES **testify against** give testimony that may help to convict (a defendant).

testily *adverb* in an irritable or touchy manner.

testimonial *noun* **1 a** a written or oral statement attesting to the quality of esp. a product or service and recommending it to others. **b** a certificate of a person's character, conduct, or qualifications. **2** a gift presented to a person, esp. in public, as a mark of esteem, in acknowledgement of services, etc.; a tribute (also as an *adjective*: *testimonial dinner*. [Say testa MOANY ul]

testimony *noun* (*plural* **testimonies**) **1** evidence presented under oath in a court of law by one or more witnesses. **2** a declaration or statement of fact. **3** (usu. foll. by *to*) proof; a demonstration: *the pyramids are testimony to the engineering skills of the ancient Egyptians*. [Say TESTA moany]

testiness *noun* the quality or condition of being irritable or touchy.

testing • *noun* the activity of testing someone or something in order to find something out, see if it works, etc.: *nuclear testing ◊ testing and assessment in education*. • *adjective* (of a problem or situation) difficult to deal with and needing particular strength or abilities: *this has been a testing time for us all*.

testing ground *noun* a place or situation where something may be tried out to assess its suitability or acceptability before being used, implemented, or adopted on a larger scale.

testis *noun* (*plural* **testes**) a testicle. [Say TESS tiss for the singular, TESS teez for the plural]

test-market • *verb* introduce (a new product or service) in a limited region in order to assess consumer response. • *noun* (usu. **test market**) a limited area that serves as the market for a new product.

testosterone *noun* **1** a steroid hormone that stimulates the development of male secondary sexual characteristics, produced in the testicles and, in much smaller quantities, in the ovaries and adrenal cortex. **2** *informal* stereotypical male aggressiveness, pride, or sexuality: *testosterone-charged lyrics ◊ the presidential campaign turned into a testosterone contest*. [Say tess TOSS tur own]

test pilot *noun* a pilot who test-flies aircraft. ▶ **test-pilot** *verb* (**test-pilots**, **test-piloted**, **test-piloting**)

test spin *noun informal* = TEST DRIVE *noun* 1.

test tube *noun* **1** a cylindrical vessel of thin transparent glass, having a closed rounded bottom at one end, used in laboratories etc. to hold small amounts of liquid for analysis and experimentation. **2** (as an *adjective*, usu. **test-tube**) designating procedures and operations carried out artificially or under laboratory conditions: *test-tube fertilization*.

test-tube baby *noun* (*plural* **test-tube babies**) *informal* a baby that grows from an egg that is fertilized outside the mother's body and then reinserted in the uterus to continue developing normally.

testy *adjective* (**testier**, **testiest**) irritable, touchy.

tetanus *noun* a disease marked by rigidity and spasms of the voluntary muscles, caused by bacteria entering the body through cuts or wounds. [Say TET nuss or TET a nuss]

tetchily *adverb* in an annoyed, peevish, or irritable way.

tetchiness *noun* the quality or condition of being annoyed, peevish, or irritable.

tetchy *adjective* (**tetchier**, **tetchiest**) easily angered or annoyed; peevish, irritable.

tête-à-tête (*plural* **tête-à-têtes**) • *noun* a conversation between two people. • *adverb* **1** together in private: *they spoke tête-à-tête*. **2** face to face: *we were seated tête-à-tête*. • *adjective* involving or attended by only two people; private. [Say tet a TET]

tether • *noun* a rope etc. by which an animal is tied to confine it to the spot. • *verb* **1** tie or confine (an animal etc.) with a tether. **2** bind by circumstances or conditions: *she was drifting beyond his influence and reach, the only things that tethered her to her tiny hometown*.

tetracycline *noun* any of a large group of antibiotics used in the treatment of acne and various kinds of infection. [Say tetra SIKE lean or tetra SIKE lin]

tetraethyl lead *noun* a colourless oily toxic liquid formerly added to gasoline as an anti-knock agent. [Say tetra ETH ul]

Tetragrammaton *noun* the Hebrew name of God transliterated in four letters as YHVH or JHVH and articulated as *Yahweh* or *Jehovah*. [Say tetra GRAMMA tawn]

tetrahedral *adjective* having the form of a tetrahedron. [Say tetra HEE drul]

tetrahedron *noun* (*plural* **tetrahedrons** or **tetrahedra**) a solid figure or object with four plane faces, esp. (also **regular tetrahedron**) one with four equal equilateral triangular faces. [Say tetra HEE drun for the singular, tetra HEE druh or tetra HEE druns for the plural]

tetrahydrocannabinol *noun* a crystalline compound that is the main active ingredient of cannabis. [Say tetra hydro kuh NAB in awl]

tetravalent *adjective Chemistry* having a valence of four. [Say tetra VAY lunt]

Teuton *noun* a member of a Teutonic nation, esp. a German. [Say TOO tun or TYOO tun]

Teutonic *adjective* **1** German. **2** displaying characteristics stereotypically attributed to Germans. [Say too TONIC or tyoo TONIC]

Texan • *adjective* of or relating to Texas. • *noun* a native or inhabitant of Texas.

Texas gate *noun Cdn* (*West*) a ditch covered by metal bars spaced so as to allow vehicles and pedestrians to pass over but not cattle or other animals.

Texas leaguer *noun Baseball* a shallow fly ball or pop-up that falls between the infield and outfield.

Texas mickey *noun Cdn informal* a 130-ounce bottle of rye whisky.

Tex-Mex • *noun* **1** a Texan style of cooking characterized by the adaptation of Mexican ingredients and influences with more moderate use of hot flavourings such as chilies. **2** the variety of Mexican Spanish spoken in Texas. • *adjective* of or relating to the blend of Texan and Mexican cooking, music, language, or culture, existing or originating in the southwestern US.

text *noun* **1** the wording of something written or printed. **2** the main written or printed part of a book as distinct from notes, illustrations, appendices, etc. **3** the original words of an author or document, esp. in the original language, form, and order as opposed to a translation, revision, paraphrase, or commentary. **4** data in textual form, esp. as stored, processed, or displayed in a word processor or text editor. **5 a** a textbook. **b** (in *plural*) books prescribed for study. **6** a short passage from the Scriptures, esp. one quoted as illustrative of a belief, doctrine, or moral, or chosen as the subject or starting point for a sermon. **7** a subject or theme.

textbook • *noun* a book giving instruction in a particular, esp. academic, subject. • *adjective* conforming to a standard or model, esp. one widely recognized by experts or specialists in a particular field: *a textbook interrogation technique* ◊ *a textbook example of how not to build a dock*.

text file *noun Computing* a file used to store data in textual form.

textile • *noun* fabric; cloth. • *adjective* used in or relating to the production of textiles: *textile mill*.

textual *adjective* **1** of, concerning, or contained in a text: *textual errors*. **2** based on, following, or conforming to the text of a work: *textual analysis*. ▶**textually** *adverb*

textural *adjective* relating to texture: *the textural characteristics of the rocks*. ▶**texturally** *adverb*

texture • *noun* **1 a** the surface of a thing assessed in terms of its roughness, smoothness, softness, etc. by the senses of esp. sight and touch. **b** the feel of food or wine in the mouth: *a light creamy texture*. **2** a discernible roughness or bumpiness on a surface. **3** the physical or perceived structure and composition of the constituent parts or formative elements of something, such as soil or rock. **4** *Music* the quality of sound created by the combination of the different elements of a work or passage. • *verb* (**textures**, **textured**, **texturing**) provide with a texture.

textured *adjective* **1** having a discernible texture; not smooth or flat. **2** having a specified kind of texture: *coarse-textured*. **3** having a distinctive or characteristic texture: *textured harmonies*.

textured vegetable protein *noun* spun or extruded vegetable protein, usu. made to simulate the texture, taste, and appearance of meat. Abbreviation: **TVP**.

TGV *noun* a type of high-speed French passenger train.

Th *symbol* thorium.

Th. *abbreviation* Thursday.

Thai • *noun* (*plural* **Thai** or **Thais**) **1 a** a native or inhabitant of Thailand, a kingdom in Southeast Asia. **b** a member of the people forming the largest ethnic group in Thailand and also inhabiting neighbouring regions. **2** the language of Thailand. • *adjective* of Thailand or its people or language. [Sounds like TIE]

thalamus *noun* (*plural* **thalami**) either of two masses of grey matter lying between the hemispheres of the brain on either side of the third ventricle, which relay sensory information and act as a centre for pain perception. [Say THALLA muss, THALLA my]

thalassemia *noun* (*plural* **thalassemias**) any of a group of hereditary diseases caused by faulty hemoglobin synthesis and widespread in Mediterranean, African, and Asian countries. [Say thalla SEEMY uh]

thalidomide *noun* **1** a drug formerly used as a sedative but found in 1961 to cause fetal malformation when taken by a mother early in pregnancy. **2** (as an *adjective*) designating a baby or child etc. born with a congenital abnormality due to the effects of thalidomide. [Say thuh LIDDA mide]

thallium *noun* a rare soft white metallic element, occurring naturally in zinc blende and some iron ores. [Say THALLY um]

GRAMMAR CHECK
than ⚠️

She's older than me (or *her* or *us*) is much more natural than *She's older than I* (or *she* or *we*), which can sound too formal. Because some people object to the common usage, however, consider adding a verb after **than**, e.g. *she's older than I am*, which nobody would criticize. Some circumstances require a distinction between **I** and **me** after **than**: *they like you better than I* means "they like you better than I (do)", whereas *they like you better than me* means "they like you better than (they like) me".

---

than *conjunction* **1** introducing the second element in a comparison. **2** introducing the second element in a statement of difference. **3** in a statement expressing hypothesis or consequence. **4** when.

thank • *verb* **1** express gratitude to: *thanked her for the present*. **2** hold responsible: *if you are late, you have no one to thank but yourself*. • *noun* (in *plural*) **1** gratitude. **2** an expression of gratitude: *give thanks to Heaven*. • *interjection* (in *plural*) (also **thanks a lot**) **1** used as an expression of gratitude; thank you: *thanks for your help*. **2** *ironic* used to express disappointment, anger, etc. at the action of another. PHRASES **give thanks** say grace at a meal. **I will thank you to** *ironic* (implying reproach) I'd rather you would; I would ask you to: *I'll thank you to mind your own business!* **no thanks to** despite. **thank goodness** (or **God** or **heavens** etc.) **1** *informal* an expression of relief or pleasure. **2** an expression of pious gratitude. **thanks to** as a (good or bad) result of: *thanks to my quick thinking* ◊ *thanks to your stupid idea*.

thankful *adjective* **1** grateful, appreciative, pleased, relieved. **2** (of words or acts) expressive of thanks.

thankfully *adverb* **1** *disputed* let us be thankful; fortunately: *thankfully, prices are dropping*. **2** in a thankful manner.

thankless *adjective* **1** not expressing or feeling gratitude. **2** (of a task etc.) giving no pleasure or profit; not likely to win or receive thanks. ▶ **thanklessly** *adverb*

Thanksgiving *noun* **1** *Cdn* **a** (also **Thanksgiving Day**) an annual holiday, originally for giving thanks to God for the success of the harvest, celebrated on the second Monday in October. **b** (also **Thanksgiving weekend**) the long weekend ending with Thanksgiving Day. **2** *US* **a** (also **Thanksgiving Day**) a similar holiday observed annually on the fourth Thursday in November. **b** (also **Thanksgiving weekend**) the long weekend beginning with Thanksgiving Day and usu. lasting until Sunday. **3** (**thanksgiving**) **a** the expression of thanks or gratitude, esp. to God. **b** a form of words used for this. **4** (**thanksgiving**) a public celebration, marked with religious services, held as an expression of gratitude for divine favour.

thank you • *interjection* **1** a polite formula acknowledging and expressing gratitude for a gift, service, inquiry into one's health, etc. **2** used to emphasize a preceding statement, esp. one implying refusal or denial: *I said no, thank you*. • *noun informal* **1** an act of expressing gratitude or appreciation: *took the money without so much as a thank you*. **2** (as an *adjective*) (usu. **thank-you**) designating a gesture etc. intended as a way of expressing appreciation or gratitude: *thank-you gift*.

that • *pronoun & demonstrative adjective* (*plural* **those**) **1** used to identify a specific person or thing observed or heard by the speaker. **2** referring to the more distant of two things near to the speaker. **3** referring to a specific thing previously mentioned or known. **4** used in singling out someone or something with a particular feature. **5** (as a *pronoun*) (*plural* **that**) used instead of *which* or *whom* to introduce a defining clause: *the book that you sent me*. • *adverb* **1** to such a degree. **2** *informal* very. • *conjunction* **1** introducing a subordinate clause.

2 *literary* expressing a wish or regret. PHRASES **all that** very: *I'm not all that tired*. **and all that** (or **and that**) *informal* and all or various things associated with or similar to what has been mentioned. **like that 1** of that kind. **2** in that manner. **3** *informal* without effort. **4** of that character. **that is** (or **that is to say**) a formula introducing or following an explanation of a preceding word or words. **that's that** a formula concluding a narrative or discussion or indicating completion of a task. **that there** *slang* = sense 1 of *adjective*. **that will do** no more is needed or desirable.

thataway *adverb informal* or *jocular* **1** (esp. with reference to the route taken by an object of pursuit) in that direction: *he went thataway*. **2** in that manner.

thatch • *noun* (*plural* **thatches**) **1 a** a covering for a roof made of straw, reeds, palm leaves, or similar material. **b** the material used to make such a covering. **c** (as an *adjective*) designating a hut, cottage, roof, etc. having such a covering. **2 a** a matted layer of plant debris etc. on a lawn. **b** material forming such a layer. **3** *informal* a covering of some material, such as the hair of the head. • *verb* (**thatches**, **thatched**, **thatching**) **1** cover (a roof or a building) with thatch. **2** remove (thatch) from a lawn.

thatched *adjective* **1** made of, covered, or roofed with thatch: *thatched hut*. **2 a** covered with something resembling thatch. **b** arranged in a manner similar to thatch: *thatched hair*.

thaw • *verb* **1** (often foll. by *out*) **a** (of ice, snow, or something that is frozen) pass into a liquid or unfrozen state. **b** (of a person or part of the body) warm up after being very cold. **2** (of the weather) become warm enough to melt snow and ice etc.: *it began to thaw*. **3** (often foll. by *out*) cause (something frozen or very cold) to melt or warm up; defrost. **4** make or become animated or amicable after a period of hostility or animosity: *the stiff-necked admiral, reputed to eat an ensign or two each day for breakfast, thawed as Low talked*. • *noun* **1** a period of warmer weather marked by the rise of temperature above the freezing point and the melting of snow and ice. **2** *Politics* a reduction in the hostility or formality of relations; an increase in friendliness or cordiality: *a thaw in relations between the two countries*.

THC *abbreviation* tetrahydrocannabinol, a crystalline compound that is the main active ingredient of cannabis.

the • *definite article* **1** denoting one or more people or things already mentioned, under discussion, implied, or familiar. **2** serving to describe as unique. **3 a** which is, who are, etc. **b** denoting a class described. **4** best known or best entitled to the name (with *the* stressed). **5** used to indicate a following defining clause or phrase. **6 a** used to indicate that a singular noun represents a species, class, etc. **b** used with a noun which figuratively represents an occupation, pursuit, etc. **c** a, per. **d** designating a disease, affliction, etc. **7** (foll. by a unit of time) the present, the past. • *adverb* in or by that (or such a) degree; on that account. PHRASES **all the** in the full degree to be expected. **so much the** so much, in that degree.

theatre *noun* (also **theater**) **1 a** a building or facility in which plays etc. are performed in front of an audience. **b** a movie theatre. **2 a** forms of entertainment performed in theatres, such as plays, opera, dance, or music. **b** theatrical or dramatic entertainment of a specified quality: *makes good theatre*. **c** in names of theatrical companies: *Toronto Dance Theatre*. **3 a** the writing, production, and performance

of plays. **b** the drama of a particular author, period, or place: *Restoration theatre*. **4 a** a place where action takes place in public view; a scene or field of action: *the theatre of war*. **b** (as an *adjective*) designating weapons for use in a region in which active combat operations are conducted: *theatre nuclear missiles*. **5** (also **operating theatre**) a room for surgical operations. **6** a room or hall for lectures etc. with seats in tiers.

theatre-goer *noun* a person who often attends theatres. ▶ **theatre-going** *noun & adjective*

theatre of the absurd *noun* drama portraying the futility and anguish of human struggle in a senseless and inexplicable world.

theatrical • *adjective* **1** of or for the theatre; of acting or actors. **2 a** (of a manner, speech, or gesture) calculated for effect; showy. **b** (of a person) artificial, affected. **•** *noun* **1** (usu. in *plural*) a dramatic performance: *amateur theatricals*. **2** (in *plural*) theatrics. ▶ **theatricality** *noun* **theatrically** *adverb*

theatrics *plural noun* **1** showy dramatic gestures, exaggerated behaviour and display of emotion: *courtroom theatrics*. **2** the art of staging or performing plays.

thee *pronoun* archaic objective case of THOU[1].

theft *noun* the action or crime of stealing: *convicted of theft ◊ a recent rash of car thefts*.

their *possessive adjective* **1** of or belonging to them or themselves: *their house ◊ their own business*. **2** (**Their**) (in titles) that they are: *Their Majesties*. **3** *disputed* his or her: *has anyone lost their keys?*

theirs *possessive pronoun* **1** the one or ones belonging to or associated with them: *it is theirs ◊ theirs are over here*. **2** *disputed* the one or ones belonging to an indefinite singular antecedent: *each of them brought theirs*. **PHRASES of theirs** of or belonging to them: *a friend of theirs*.

theism *noun* belief in the existence of gods or a god, esp. one God supernaturally revealed ◊ man (compare DEISM), who created and intervenes in the universe. ▶ **theist** *noun* **theistic** *adjective* [Say THEE ism, THEE ist, thee ISS tick (with TH as in *THIEF*)]

them *pronoun* **1** *objective case of* THEY: *I saw them*. **2** *informal* they: *it's them again*. **3** *disputed* him or her; used in relation to a singular noun or pronoun of undetermined gender: *if anyone comes, ask them to wait*.

thematic *adjective* of or relating to subjects or topics: *the arrangement is thematic*. ▶ **thematically** *adverb* [Say theme ATTIC]

theme • *noun* **1 a** a subject or topic on which a person speaks, writes, or thinks; a topic of discussion etc. **b** a dominant subject or motif in work of art; a topic of composition. **2** a prominent or frequently recurring melody or group of notes in a composition. **3** = THEME SONG 1. **•** *verb* (**themes**, **themed**, **theming**) (esp. a park, restaurant, etc.) around a theme to unify ambience, decor, etc.

theme park *noun* an amusement park organized around a unifying idea.

theme song *noun* **1** a distinctive tune used to introduce a particular program or performer on television or radio. **2** a recurrent melody in a musical.

themselves *pronoun* **1 a** *emphatic form of* THEY or THEM. **b** *reflexive form of* THEM (compare HERSELF). **2** in their normal state of body or mind: *are quite themselves again*. **3** *disputed* (referring back to an indefinite pronoun) himself, herself; himself or herself: *everyone kept it to themselves*. **PHRASES be themselves** act in their normal, unconstrained manner.

then • *adverb* **1** at that time. **2 a** next. **b** and also.

c after all. **3 a** in that case. **b** used parenthetically to resume a narrative etc. • *adjective* that or who was such at the time in question: *the then artistic director*. • *noun* that time: *until then*. PHRASES **but then** but, that being so; but on the other hand. **then again** on the other hand. **then and there** immediately and on the spot.

thence *adverb* (also **from thence**) archaic or *literary* **1** from that place or source: *a route across the northern prairies through Battleford and Edmonton and thence by the Yellowhead Pass to the Pacific*. **2** for that reason; as a consequence: *they could present to parliament everything which favoured their purposes, and thence more effectively deceive the nation*. **3** = THENCEFORTH.

thenceforth *adverb* (also **from thenceforth**) archaic or *literary* from that time onward: *I had decided thenceforth to be more cautious with expenditures*.

theocracy *noun* (*plural* **theocracies**) **1** a form of government by God or a god directly or by a priestly order etc. which rules in the name of God or a god. **2** a state so governed. ▶ **theocratic** *adjective* [Say thee OCKRA see, thee uh CRAT ick (with TH as in *THIEF*)]

theologian *noun* a person who studies theology. [Say thee uh LOW jun (with TH as in *THIEF*)]

theological *adjective* of or relating to theology or theologians: *a theological college* ◊ *theological beliefs*. ▶ **theologically** *adverb* [Say thee uh LOGICAL (with TH as in *THIEF*)]

theology *noun* (*plural* **theologies**) **1** the study of the nature of God and religious belief. **2** religious beliefs and theory when systematically developed: *in Christian theology, God came to be viewed as the Father, Son, and Holy Spirit* ◊ *demonstrates a willingness to tolerate new theologies*. [Say thee OLLA jee (with TH as in *THIEF*)]

theorem *noun* esp. *Math* **1** a general proposition not self-evident but proved by a chain of reasoning; a truth established by means of accepted truths (*compare* PROBLEM 4b). **2** a rule in algebra etc., esp. one expressed by symbols or formulas. [Say THEER um]

theoretical *adjective* (also **theoretic**) **1** concerned with knowledge but not with its practical application. **2** based on theory rather than experience or practice. **3** existing only in theory; ideal, hypothetical. ▶ **theoretically** *adverb* [Say thee uh RET ick ul (with TH as in *THIEF*)]

theoretician *noun* a person concerned with the theoretical aspects of a subject. [Say theer a TISH'n]

theorist *noun* a holder or inventor of a theory or theories. [Say THEER ist]

theorize *verb* (**theorizes, theorized, theorizing**) **1** form or construct theories; indulge in theories. **2** consider or devise in theory. [Say THEER ize]

theory *noun* (*plural* **theories**) **1** a supposition or system of ideas explaining something, esp. one based on general principles independent of the particular things to be explained: *atomic theory* ◊ *theory of evolution*. **2** a speculative (esp. fanciful) view: *one of my pet theories*. **3** (the sphere of) abstract knowledge or speculative thought: *this is all very well in theory* ◊ *has been studying theory*. **4** the principles on which a subject of study is based: *music theory*. **5** *Math* a collection of propositions to illustrate the principles of a subject: *probability theory*.

theosophy *noun* a philosophy professing to achieve a knowledge of God by spiritual ecstasy, direct intuition, or special individual relations, esp. a modern movement following Hindu and Buddhist teachings and seeking universal fellowship. [Say thee OSSA fee (with TH as in *THIEF*)]

therapeutic *adjective* **1** of, for, or contributing to the cure of disease. **2** contributing to general, esp. mental,

well-being: *Elizabeth finds walking therapeutic*. ▶ **therapeutically** *adverb* [Say therra PYOOT ick]

therapeutics *plural noun* (usu. treated as *singular*) the branch of medicine concerned with the treatment of disease. [Say therra PYOOT icks]

therapist *noun* a person who practises or administers therapy, esp. a psychotherapist. [Say THERRA pist]

therapy *noun* (*plural* **therapies**) **1** the treatment of physical or mental disorders, other than by surgery. **2** a particular type of such treatment. [Say THERRA pee]

there • *adverb* **1** in, at, or to that place or position. **2** at that point (in speech, performance, writing, etc.). **3** in that respect. **4** used for emphasis in calling attention. **5** used to indicate the fact or existence of something. • *interjection* **1** expressing confirmation, triumph, satisfaction, etc. **2** used to soothe. PHRASES **be there for someone** be ready to give support etc. **have been there before** *slang* know all about it. **so there** *informal* expressing defiance or defiant triumph. **there and then** immediately and on the spot. **there it is** that is the situation; nothing can be done about it. **there you are** (or **go**) *informal* **1** this is what you wanted etc. **2** expressing confirmation, triumph, resignation, etc.

thereabouts *adverb* (also **thereabout**) **1** near that place: *ought to be somewhere thereabouts*. **2** near that number, quantity, etc.: *two litres or thereabouts*.

thereafter *adverb* formal after that.

thereby *adverb* by that means, as a result of that: *regular exercise strengthens the heart, thereby reducing the risk of heart attack*. PHRASES **thereby hangs a tale** much could be said about that.

therefore *adverb* for that reason; accordingly.

therein *adverb* formal **1** in or into that place etc.: *the answer to this question can be found therein*. **2** in that respect; in that matter: *the costs incurred therein shall be charged to the owner*.

thereof *adverb formal* of that or it.
thereon *adverb formal* on that or it (of motion or position).

there's *contraction* there is.
thereto *adverb formal* that or it.
thereupon *adverb* immediately or shortly after that: *King thereupon resigned and Meighen became prime minister.*
thermal • *adjective* **1** of, for, or producing heat. **2** promoting the retention of heat: *thermal underwear.* • *noun* **1** a rising current of heated air. **2** (in *plural*) thermal underwear. ▶ **thermally** *adverb*
thermidor *see* LOBSTER THERMIDOR. [Say THERMA dore]
thermodynamic *adjective* of or relating to the science of the relations between heat and other (mechanical, electrical, etc.) forms of energy.
thermodynamics *plural noun* (usu. treated as *singular*) the science of the relations between heat and other (mechanical, electrical, etc.) forms of energy.
thermometer *noun* an instrument for measuring temperature.
thermonuclear *adjective* **1** relating to or using nuclear reactions that occur only at very high temperatures. **2** relating to or characterized by weapons using thermonuclear reactions.
thermoplastic • *adjective* (of a substance) that becomes soft and plastic on heating and hard and rigid on cooling, and is able to repeat these processes. • *noun* a thermoplastic substance.
Thermos *noun* (*plural* **Thermoses**) *proprietary* an insulated flask for keeping a liquid hot or cold, esp. with a double lining enclosing a vacuum.
thermostat *noun* a device that automatically regulates temperature, or that activates a device when the temperature reaches a certain point. ▶ **thermostatic** *adjective* **thermostatically** *adverb*
thesaurus *noun* (*plural* **thesauruses** or **thesauri**) a book that lists words in groups of synonyms and related concepts. [Say thuh SORE us for the singular, thuh SORE iz or thuh SORE eye for the plural]
these *plural of* THIS.
thesis *noun* (*plural* **theses**) **1** a proposition to be maintained or proved: *her central thesis is that psychological life is not part of the material world.* **2** a dissertation, esp. by a candidate for a degree: *he never managed to finish his master's thesis.* [Say THEE sis for the singular, THEE seez for the plural (with TH as in THIEF)]
thespian • *adjective* of or relating to tragedy or drama. • *noun* an actor or actress: *the supporting cast included the cream of Canadian thespians.* [Say THESPY un]

they *pronoun* **1** the people, animals, or things previously named or in question. **2** people in general. **3** those in authority. **4** *disputed* as a third person singular indefinite pronoun meaning "he or she": *anyone can come if they want to.*
they'd *contraction* **1** they had. **2** they would.
they'll *contraction* **1** they will. **2** they shall.

they're *contraction* they are.
they've *contraction* they have.
thiamine *noun* a vitamin of the vitamin B complex, naturally occurring in unrefined cereals, beans, and liver, a deficiency of which causes beriberi. [Say THIGH a min]
thick • *adjective* **1** of great or specified extent between opposite surfaces: *a thick wall* ◊ *a wall two metres thick.* **2 a** arranged closely; crowded together; dense. **b** numerous. **3** (usu. foll. by *with*) densely covered or filled: *air thick with snow.* **4** firm in consistency: *thick soup.* **5** impenetrable by sight: *thick darkness.* **6** *informal* (of a person) stupid, dull. **7** (of an accent) very marked. **8** *informal* intimate or very friendly: *thick as thieves.* **9** (of one's head) suffering from a headache, hangover, etc. • *noun* a thick or dense part of anything. PHRASES **in the thick of 1** at the busiest or most intense part of. **2** heavily occupied with. **lay it** (or **something**) **on thick** exaggerate. **thick and fast** in great quantity or large numbers, and rapidly or in quick succession: *plaudits arrived thick and fast.* **thick on the ground** abundant; in great quantity. **through thick and thin** under all conditions; in spite of all difficulties.
thicken *verb* **1** make or become thick or thicker. **2** become more complicated: *the plot thickens.* ▶ **thickener** *noun*
thickening *noun* **1** the process of becoming thick or thicker. **2** a substance used to thicken liquid. **3** a thickened part.
thicket *noun* a tangle of shrubs or trees.
thick-headed *adjective informal* stupid.
thickly *adverb* **1** in a way that produces a wide piece or deep layer of something: *thickly sliced bread.* **2** having a lot of trees, people, etc. close together: *thickly populated.* **3** in a deep voice that is not as clear as normal, esp. because of illness or emotion.
thickness *noun* (*plural* **thicknesses**) **1** the state of being thick. **2** the extent to which a thing is thick. **3** a layer of material of a certain thickness. **4** a part that is thick or lies between opposite surfaces: *steps cut in the thickness of the wall.*
thickset *adjective* **1** heavily or solidly built. **2** set or growing close together.
thick skin *noun* **1** a thick or hard skin or outer layer. **2** *informal* insensitivity to reproach or criticism. ▶ **thick-skinned** *adjective*
thief *noun* (*plural* **thieves**) a person who steals esp. secretly and without violence.
thieve *verb* (**thieves, thieved, thieving**) **1** (esp. as **thieving** *adjective*) be a thief. **2** steal (a thing).
thievery *noun* the act or practice of stealing; theft.
thievish *adjective* **1** given to stealing. **2** of, pertaining to, or characteristic of a thief or thieves.
thigh *noun* the part of the leg between the hip and the knee.
thigh bone *noun* = FEMUR.
thigh-high • *adjective* reaching to the thighs: *thigh-high boots.* • *noun* (in *plural*) thigh-high stockings etc.
thimble *noun* **1** a metal or plastic cap, usu. with a

closed end, worn to protect the finger and push the needle in sewing. **2** = THIMBLEFUL.

thimbleberry *noun* (*plural* **thimbleberries**) any of several North American raspberries with thimble-shaped fruit.

thimbleful *noun* (*plural* **thimblefuls**) a small quantity, esp. of liquid to drink.

thin • *adjective* (**thinner**, **thinnest**) **1** having the opposite surfaces close together; of small thickness or diameter. **2** made of thin material: *a thin dress.* **3** lean; not plump. **4 a** not dense or copious: *a thin audience.* **5** of slight consistency: *a thin paste.* • *adverb* thinly: *slice it as thin as silk and serve on toasted country bread.* • *verb* (**thins**, **thinned**, **thinning**) **1** make or become thin or thinner. **2** (often foll. by *out*) reduce; make or become less dense or crowded or numerous. **3** (often foll. by *out*) remove some of a crop of (seedlings, saplings, etc.) or some young fruit from (a vine or tree) to improve the growth of the rest. PHRASES **thin on top** balding.

thin air *noun* a state of invisibility or non-existence: *vanished into thin air.*

thin blue line *noun* the police or military seen as the only defence against invasion etc.

thine *possessive pronoun* archaic **1** the one or ones belonging to thee. **2** (before a vowel) = THY.

WRITING TIP
thing

Instead of using the word **thing**, use more precise and interesting words:

*She is known for many remarkable **accomplishments**.*
*That was the most puzzling **aspect** of the situation.*
*What is this bird's most distinctive **characteristic**?*
*I want to know every **detail** of what happened.*
*Smog is a **feature** of city life.*
*She has campaigned on many controversial **issues**.*
*We have several important **matters** to go over.*
*The main **objective** is to save the money you make.*
*She has a **penchant** for champagne and chocolate.*
*You made an interesting **point**.*
*Agility is an essential **quality** for a goalie.*
*We discussed a number of **subjects**.*
*The book covers a wide range of **topics**.*
*Her generosity is one of her most attractive **traits**.*

To avoid wordiness, don't use **thing** after an adjective when the adjective can be used on its own:
Having your own computer is very useful (not *Having your own computer is a very useful thing*).

---

thing *noun* **1** an inanimate material object. **2** an unspecified object. **3** (**things**) personal belongings or clothing. **4** an action, activity, concept, or thought. **5** (**things**) unspecified circumstances or matters: *how are things?* **6** (**the thing**) *informal* what is needed, required, acceptable, or fashionable. PHRASES **do one's own thing** *informal* pursue one's own interests or inclinations. **do things to** *informal* affect remarkably. **have a thing about** (or **for**, **with**) *informal* be obsessed about; be peculiarly interested in, repulsed by, etc. **make a thing of** *informal* **1** regard as essential. **2** cause a fuss about. **one** (or **just one**) **of those things** *informal* something unavoidable or to be accepted.

thingamajig *noun* (also **thingamabob**) *informal* = THINGY.

thingummy *noun* (*plural* **thingummies**) *informal* = THINGY.

thingy *noun* (*plural* **thingies**) *informal* a person or thing

whose name one has forgotten or does not know or does not wish or care to mention.

thinhorn sheep *noun* a mountain sheep with long, slender, pointed horns flaring away from the head.

think • *verb* (**thinks**, **thought**, **thinking**) **1** have a particular opinion, belief, or idea about someone or something. **2** direct one's mind toward someone or something; use one's mind actively to form connected ideas. **3** (foll. *by of* or *about*) take into account or consideration. **4** (foll. *by of* or *about*) consider the possibility or advantages of. **5** (foll. *by of*) have a particular opinion of. **6** call something to mind; remember. • *noun* *informal* an act of thinking. PHRASES **have another think coming** be greatly mistaken. **think again** revise one's plans or opinions. **think aloud** utter one's thoughts as soon as they occur. **think back** to recall (a past event or time). **think better of** change one's mind about (an intention) after reconsideration. **think for oneself** have an independent mind or attitude. **think little** (or **nothing**) **of** consider to be insignificant or unremarkable. **think much** (or **highly**) **of** have a high opinion of. **think out 1** consider carefully. **2** produce (an idea etc.) by thinking. **think over** reflect upon in order to reach a decision. **think through** reflect fully upon (a problem etc.). **think twice** use careful consideration, avoid hasty action, etc. **think up** *informal* devise.

thinkable *adjective* conceivable.

thinker *noun* **1** a person who thinks, esp. in a specified way. **2** a person with a skilled or powerful mind.

thinking • *adjective* **1** using thought or rational judgment. **2** thoughtful, reflective, intellectual. • *noun* opinion or judgment. PHRASES **a thinking person's** (or **man's**, **woman's**) designed for intelligent people; designating an intellectual version of a designated thing etc.: *a thinking person's sitcom.* **put on one's thinking cap** *informal* meditate on a problem.

think piece *noun* an article containing discussion, analysis, opinion, etc., rather than facts or news.

think-tank *noun* a body of experts, as a research organization, providing advice and ideas on specific national or commercial problems.

thinly *adverb* **1** in a way that produces a thin piece or layer of something. **2** with very few things or people close together in one place. **3** in a way that is not sincere or enthusiastic. **4** in a way that does not hide the truth very well.

thinner *noun* a liquid used to dilute paint etc.

thinness *noun* **1** the state of being thin. **2** the extent to which a thing is thin.

thinnings *plural noun* plants, trees, etc. which have been removed to improve the growth of those remaining.

thin red line *noun* the military seen as the only defence against lawlessness, invasion, etc.

thin-skinned *adjective* **1** (esp. of fruit) having a thin skin or outer layer. **2** sensitive to reproach or criticism.

Thinsulate *noun* *proprietary* a thin batting made from very fine propylene fibres trapping tiny pockets of air to provide high insulation with little bulk or weight. [Say THINSA late]

third *ordinal number* **1** constituting number three in a sequence; 3rd. **2** each of three equal parts into which something is or may be divided. **3** *Music* an interval spanning three consecutive notes in a diatonic scale, e.g. C to E.

third base *noun* *Baseball* **1** the third of the bases that must be touched to score a run. **2** the position of the player covering this base and the area of the infield surrounding it. ▶ **third baseman** *noun*

third-best • *adjective* of third quality. • *noun* a thing in this category.

third degree • *noun* long and severe questioning esp. by police to obtain information or a confession: *gave her the third degree for a bit, but her answers measured up.* • *adjective* (**third-degree**) denoting burns of the most severe kind, affecting lower layers of tissue.

third eye *noun* **1** *Hinduism & Buddhism* the "eye of insight" in the forehead of an image of a deity, esp. the god Siva. **2** the faculty of intuitive insight; the ability to foresee the future. **3** the pineal gland in certain vertebrates.

third force *noun* a group, as a political party, acting as a check on conflict between two opposing groups.

third-generation *adjective* designating computer technology distinguished by the introduction of integrated circuits and operating systems and belonging essentially to the period 1960–70.

thirdly *adverb* used to introduce the third of a list of points mentioned in a speech or piece of writing.

third party • *noun* (*plural* **third parties**) **1** a party or person besides the two primarily concerned: *you think a third party could spill the beans to your boyfriend.* **2** a person involved incidentally. **3** a political party other than the two (or more) most important. **4** *Law* a person against whom a defendant commences a claim for all or part of the plaintiff's claim. • *adjective* *Cdn & Brit.* (of insurance) covering damage or injury suffered by a person other than the insured.

third-rate *adjective* inferior; very poor in quality.

third reading *noun* a third presentation of a bill to a legislative assembly, in Canada to debate it for the last time in the House of Commons.

Third Reich *noun* the Nazi regime, 1933–45.

third-string *adjective* (esp. of an athlete) inferior. ▶ **third-stringer** *noun*

Third Wave *noun* the current phase of economic, social, and cultural change (following the agrarian and industrial waves), in which knowledge is the primary productive force.

third way *noun* any option regarded as an alternative to two extremes.

Third World *noun* (usu. as **the Third World**) the developing countries of Asia, Africa, and Latin America.

thirst • *noun* **1** an intense physical need or craving to drink something. **2** a strong desire or craving: *a thirst for power.* • *verb* (usu. foll. by *for*) **1** feel thirst. **2** have a strong desire.

thirstily *adverb* in a thirsty manner.

thirst-quencher *noun* a drink that satisfies or is capable of satisfying thirst.

thirst-quenching *adjective* that satisfies or is capable of satisfying thirst.

thirsty *adjective* (**thirstier**, **thirstiest**) **1** having a need or desire to drink. **2** (of land, a crop, etc.) dry; needing moisture. **3** (often foll. by *for*) eager. **4** *informal* causing thirst: *thirsty work*.

thirteen *cardinal number* one more than twelve. ▶ **thirteenth** *ordinal number*

thirtieth *ordinal number* corresponding to thirty.

thirty *cardinal number* (*plural* **thirties**) ten more than twenty. PHRASES **thirty-first, -second**, etc. the ordinal numbers between thirtieth and fortieth. **thirty-one, -two**, etc. the cardinal numbers between thirty and forty.

thirtyish *adjective* *informal* about thirty, esp. in age.

thirty-second note *noun* *Music* a note having the time value of half a sixteenth note and represented by a large dot with a three-hooked stem.

thirtysomething *informal* • *noun* **1** an undetermined age between thirty and forty. **2** a person of this age. • *adjective* **1** characteristic of the tastes and lifestyle of this group. **2** between thirty and forty years of age.

this • *demonstrative pronoun & demonstrative adjective* (*plural* **these**) **1** used to identify a specific person or thing close at hand or being indicated or experienced. **2** referring to the nearer of two things close to the speaker. **3** referring to a specific thing or situation just mentioned. **4** used with periods of time related to the present. • *adverb* to the degree or extent indicated: *knew Kyle when he was this high.* PHRASES **these days** nowadays. **this and that** *informal* various unspecified things. **this here** *slang* this particular (person or thing). **this much** the amount or extent about to be stated: *I know this much, she's not here.*

thistle *noun* **1** a prickly plant with tubular, chiefly purple flowers in globular heads, often occurring as a weed. **2** any of several prickly plants of other families. **3** one of these plants as the national emblem of Scotland. [With TH as in *THIN*]

thistledown *noun* **1** the light feathery down of a thistle seed. **2** thistle seeds collectively, esp. as carried along by the wind. [With TH as in *THIN*]

thither *adverb* *archaic* or *formal* to or towards that place.

Thompson *noun* = NLAKA'PAMUX. [Say TOM sun]

thong *noun* **1** a narrow strip of hide or leather used esp. as a lace, cord, strap, rein, or as the lash of a whip. **2** = FLIP-FLOP 2. **3** a skimpy undergarment that covers the genitals but not the buttocks. ▶ **thonged** *adjective*

thoracic *adjective* of or relating to the thorax. [Say thor ASS ick]

thorax *noun* **1 a** the part of the body of a mammal between the neck and the abdomen, including the cavity enclosed by the ribs, breastbone, and dorsal vertebrae, and containing the chief organs of circulation and respiration. **b** the corresponding part of a bird, reptile, amphibian, or fish. **2** the middle section of the body of an arthropod, between the head and abdomen. [Say THOR axe]

thorium *noun* a radioactive metallic element occurring naturally and used in electronic equipment and as a source of nuclear energy. [Say THORRY um]

thorn *noun* **1** a stiff sharp projection on a plant. **2** a thorn-bearing bush, shrub, or tree, such as the hawthorn. **3** a cause of pain, grief, irritation, or trouble. PHRASES **a thorn in one's side** (or **flesh**) a constant annoyance. ▶ **thornless** *adjective*

thorny *adjective* (**thornier**, **thorniest**) **1** having many thorns. **2** (of a subject, issue, problem, etc.) difficult to handle or resolve; delicate.

thorough *adjective* **1** applied to or affecting every part or detail. **2** done with great care and completeness. **3** (of a person) taking pains to do something carefully and completely. **4** absolute, utter.

thoroughbred • *noun* **1** a purebred animal, esp. a horse. **2** (**Thoroughbred**) a racehorse of a breed originating from English mares and Arab stallions, whose ancestry for several generations is fully documented. **3** a distinguished or first-rate person or thing: *it's a thoroughbred fishing machine that will likely set the standard for comfort and efficiency.* • *adjective* **1** of pure breed. **2** of outstanding quality; remarkable: *a thoroughbred car*.

thoroughfare *noun* **1 a** a road or path open at both ends through which esp. traffic may pass. **b** a main road or highway. **2** a navigable waterway, esp. a channel for shipping.

thoroughgoing *adjective* **1** extremely thorough; not superficial: *a thoroughgoing attack.* **2** absolute; out-and-out: *a thoroughgoing idiot*.

thoroughly *adverb* **1** very much; completely. **2** completely and with great attention to detail.

thoroughness *noun* **1** the quality or condition of being thorough or of doing things thoroughly. **2** the condition of being done thoroughly.

those *plural of* THAT.

thou¹ *pronoun* second person singular pronoun, now replaced by *you* except in some formal, liturgical, dialect, and poetic uses. [With TH as in *THAT*]

thou² *noun* (*plural* **thou** or **thous**) *informal* a thousand, esp. a thousand dollars: *she makes 50 thou a year*. [With TH as in *THOUSAND*]

though • *conjunction* **1** despite the fact that: *even though it was early we went to bed*. **2** even if: *ask him though he may well refuse*. **3** nevertheless: *she read on, though not to the very end*. **4** in spite of being: *the portions were small though expensive*. • *adverb* **1** however; all the same: *I wish you had told me, though*. **2** (used as an intensifier after a question or emphatic statement) indeed, truly: *"She's awfully smart." "Isn't she, though?"* PHRASES **as though** = AS IF (*see* AS¹).

thought • *noun* **1** the process or power of thinking; the faculty of reason. **2** the intellectual activity or way of thinking characteristic of or associated with a particular time, people, group, etc. **3 a** sober reflection or consideration. **b** deep meditation or contemplation. **4** a piece of reasoning produced by thinking; an idea. **5** (often in *plural*) attention: *turn our thoughts to summer*. **6 a** regard, concern, consideration: *did it without any thought of the consequences*. **b** (in *plural*) sympathy: *our thoughts are with you*. **7** a hope, intention, or expectation; a notion: *gave up all thoughts of winning*. **8** the mere contemplation: *the thought of it makes me nervous*. **9** the subject of one's thinking: *my one thought was to get away*. • *verb* *past and past participle of* THINK. PHRASES **give thought to** consider. **on second thought** contrary to what one originally decided or announced. **without a second thought** without giving a matter full or proper consideration.

thoughtful *adjective* **1** (often foll. by *of*) showing thought or consideration for others; considerate, kind. **2** showing signs of careful thought or consideration: *thoughtful gifts*. **3 a** absorbed in meditation; deep in thought. **b** given to contemplation; prudent, reflective. ▶ **thoughtfully** *adverb* **thoughtfulness** *noun*

thoughtless *adjective* **1** lacking in consideration for others; inconsiderate. **2** showing a lack of concern for the possible consequences of one's actions; careless. **3** resulting from a lack of thought. ▶ **thoughtlessly** *adverb* **thoughtlessness** *noun*

SPELL CHECK
thought out, thought-out

Note the difference in spelling between *the strategy was clearly* **thought out** *and a clearly* **thought-out** *strategy*. There is a hyphen when the latter kind of structure is used.

---

thought out *adjective* produced by mental effort: *the plan was carefully thought out*.

thought police *noun informal* an authoritarian special interest group that monitors others for signs of behaviour or views it considers deviant, inappropriate, or politically incorrect.

thought-provoking *adjective* (of an article, question, etc.) that prompts others to further contemplation of matters or issues raised.

thousand *cardinal number* **1** the number equivalent to the product of a hundred and ten; 1,000. **2** (**thousands**) *informal* an unspecified large number. ▶ **thousandfold** *adjective & adverb*

Thousand Island *noun* designating a mayonnaise salad dressing made with tomatoes, chili sauce, finely

chopped boiled egg, onion, green pepper, and occasionally celery or pickle.

thousandth *ordinal number* corresponding to one thousand.

thrall *noun literary* a condition of or like slavery; subjection to a person, power, or influence: *in thrall to the needs of her aging mother* ◊ *his critics accused him of being a dupe in the thrall of atheist Marxists*. ▶ **thralldom** *noun* [Rhymes with MALL]

thrash • *verb* (**thrashes**, **thrashed**, **thrashing**) **1** beat severely with a stick or whip, esp. as a punishment. **2 a** *informal* defeat (an opponent) convincingly. **b** criticize or scold severely: *was thrashed by the critics*. **3** move or fling the body, limbs, etc., about violently, esp. in panic or helplessness; flail: *thrashed around in the water*. **4** lash about like a flail or whip: *the branches thrashed in the wind*. **5** = THRESH 1. • *noun* (also **thrash metal**) a style of fast loud heavy metal rock music similar to speed metal but with a greater presence of punk elements. PHRASES **thrash out 1** discuss (a matter etc.) at length in order to reach a solution or consensus. **2** establish (a plan, solution, etc.) after discussing a matter thoroughly.

thrasher *noun* **1** a person that plays or listens to thrash music. **2** a person or thing that thrashes. **3** = THRESHER 2. **4** a North American songbird with greyish or brownish plumage and a slightly down-curved bill.

thrashing *noun* **1** an act of hitting someone very hard, esp. with a stick. **2** *informal* a severe defeat in a game.

thread • *noun* **1** a long, thin strand of cotton, nylon, or other fibres used in sewing or weaving. **2** a long thin line or piece of something. **3** (also **screw thread**) a spiral ridge on the outside of a screw, bolt, etc., or on the inside of a cylindrical hole, to allow two parts to be screwed together. **4** a theme or characteristic running throughout a situation or piece of writing. **5** (**threads**) *informal* clothes. • *verb* **1** pass a thread through. **2** move or weave in and out of obstacles. **3** *Sport* (esp. in hockey and football) complete (a pass) to a teammate through a crowd of players. PHRASES **hang by a thread** be in a precarious state, position, etc.

threadbare *adjective* **1** (of fabric, carpeting, etc.) so worn that the nap is lost and the thread visible. **2 a** having lost effect, freshness, or force through overuse: *a threadbare plot*. **b** weak or insubstantial: *a threadbare excuse*. **3** (of a person) wearing threadbare clothing.

threaded *adjective* that has been threaded; provided with a thread or threads: *a threaded rod*.

threadlike *adjective* resembling a thread or threads.

threat *noun* **1** an expression of an intention to inflict pain, injury, damage, etc. unless a particular demand or set of demands is met. **2** an indication of the approach or imminent occurrence of something unwelcome or undesirable: *the threat of rain*. **3** a person or thing regarded as a likely cause of harm or damage etc.: *she's a security threat*.

threaten *verb* **1** (often foll. by *with*) make a threat or threats against (a person): *threatened him with a knife*. **2 a** declare one's intention of inflicting (punishment, injury, etc.), esp. in retaliation for something done or not done: *she is threatening legal action*. **b** express an intention or promise: *they threatened to quit*. **3** appear likely or certain to cause or do (something undesirable): *the epidemic threatens to kill thousands*. **4** jeopardize or endanger: *pollution is threatening our water supply*. **5** be a sign or indication of the approach or imminent occurrence of (something undesirable): *those clouds threaten rain*. **6** intimidate or frighten.

threatened *adjective* **1** (of a species etc.) in danger of becoming rare or extinct; at risk of becoming en-

dangered: *threatened species*. **2** vulnerable, intimidated: *the bear cub felt threatened by my presence*. **3** having been vowed, predicted, or foreshadowed: *the threatened destruction of European forests*. **4** in jeopardy or danger: *rejects the notion that their language is threatened*.

threatening *adjective* **1** designed or tending to menace or intimidate: *a threatening letter*. **2** foreboding: *threatening clouds*. ▶ **threateningly** *adverb*

three *cardinal number* (*plural* **threes**) one more than two.

three-and-a-half *noun* (*plural* **three-and-a-halfs**) *Cdn* (*Que.*) an apartment having a kitchen, living room, bedroom, and bathroom.

3-D • *adjective* **1** having or presenting a three-dimensional image or appearance: *a 3-D movie*. **2** used to produce a three-dimensional image or appearance: *3-D glasses*. • *noun* a format that presents three-dimensional images: *the movie is in 3-D*.

three-dimensional *adjective* **1 a** having or appearing to have length, width, and depth. **b** producing the appearance of having length, width, and depth: *three-dimensional effects*. **2** (of literature etc.) vivid, realistic. ▶ **three-dimensionality** *noun*

threefold • *adjective* **1** three times as much or as many. **2** consisting of three parts. • *adverb* to or by three times the number.

three-legged *adjective* having or supported by three legs.

three-on-one *noun* (*plural* **three-on-ones**) *Sport* a rush led by three players against one defender or against one defender and a goalie.

three-on-three *noun* a scaled-down game of basketball involving two teams of three players playing on a schoolyard court or half court and usu. shooting at only one basket.

three-peat *Sport informal* • *noun* a third consecutive win of a particular championship by one player or team. • *verb* win a particular championship for a third consecutive time.

three-piece • *adjective* **1** consisting of three matching or related parts: *a three-piece band* ◊ *a three-piece furniture suite*. **2** (of a suit) consisting of matching pants, jacket, and vest. • *noun* (also **three-piecer**) an ensemble or group consisting of three matching or related components, members, etc.

three-pitch *noun Cdn* a variety of softball in which the batter cannot draw a walk, having only three chances to hit a ball delivered underhand by a teammate.

three-point *adjective Basketball* **1** worth three points: *three-point basket*. **2** relating to the shooting of three-point field goals: *a shot from three-point range*.

three-pointer *noun Basketball* a three-point basket.

three-point turn *noun* a method of turning a vehicle around in a narrow space by moving in three arcs, forwards, backwards, and forwards again.

three-pronged *adjective* having three aspects, stages, aims, or lines of attack: *three-pronged attack*.

three-ring circus *noun* **1** a circus with three rings for simultaneous performances. **2** a public spectacle, esp. one with little substance: *the art world is a three-ring circus, full of glamour and glitz and sideshow hucksterism*.

three-sixty *noun* (*plural* **three-sixties**) *informal* a spin of 360°; a complete turn or revolution.

threesome *noun* **1** a group of three people. **2** an activity or game in which three people participate.

three-star *adjective* **1** (of a hotel, restaurant, etc.) given three stars in a grading in which this denotes a high quality, usu. one or two grades below the highest. **2** having or designating a military rank distinguished by three stars on the epaulette of the uniform.

three-way *adjective* **1** involving three participants: *a*

three-way tie. **2** designating or relating to a trilight bulb: *three-way bulb*. **3** (of a loudspeaker) having three separate drive units for different frequency ranges.

three-wheeler *noun* a vehicle with three wheels, esp. a kind of small all-terrain vehicle.

thresh *verb* (**threshes**, **threshed**, **threshing**) **1** shake, beat, or mechanically treat (wheat etc.) to separate the grain from the husk and straw, esp. by the action of a revolving mechanism. **2** = THRASH *verb* 1, 3. [Rhymes with MESH or MASH]

thresher *noun* **1 a** a person that threshes grain. **b** a threshing machine. **2** (also **thresher shark**) a shark with a long upper lobe to its tail, which it uses when hunting, usu. in pairs, to lash the water and herd its prey into tightly packed schools. [THRESH rhymes with MESH or MASH]

thresherman *noun* (*plural* **threshermen**) *hist.* a person who participates in the annual threshing of grain. [THRESH rhymes with MESH or MASH]

threshing machine *noun hist.* a machine for separating grain from the straw or husk. [THRESH rhymes with MESH or MASH]

threshold *noun* **1 a** a strip of wood or stone forming the bottom of a doorway and crossed upon entering a house or room. **b** the entrance to a house or building etc. **c** the boundary of a region. **2** the point just before a new situation, period of life, etc. begins: *on the threshold of victory*. **3** a limit below which a stimulus causes no reaction: *pain threshold*. **4** a level that must be exceeded for a certain reaction, phenomenon, result, or condition to take place: *the dividend payout represents profits that exceed a threshold established by an internal formula*. **5** a step in a scale of wages or taxation at which increases become due or mandatory, usu. operative in specified conditions, such as a rise in the cost of living.

threw *past of* THROW.

thrice *adverb archaic* or *literary* three times.

thrift *noun* **1** prudent financial management; the habit of saving money and spending it carefully; frugality. **2** a European plant with dense heads of small pink flowers, leafless stems, and dense rosettes of linear leaves.

thriftiness *noun* the quality or state of being careful about spending money and not wasting things.

thrift shop *noun* (also **thrift store**) a store that sells second-hand merchandise, esp. clothing, with proceeds often going to charity.

thrifty *adjective* (**thriftier**, **thriftiest**) careful about spending money and not wasting things: *he was brought up to be thrifty and never to get into debt*.

thrill • *noun* **1** a powerful and often sudden feeling of excitement, exhilaration, or emotion. **2 a** a thing that causes such a feeling of excitement or exhilaration: *his new book was a real thrill*. **b** an exciting or exhilarating event or experience: *it was a thrill to meet her*. **3** intense excitement: *the thrill has gone out of our marriage*. • *verb* **1** cause (a person) to feel intense excitement. **2** thoroughly please or delight. **3** (usu. foll. by *at* or *to*) feel or become excited. **4** quiver or throb with or as if with emotion. ▶ **thrilled** *adjective*

thriller *noun* **1** an exciting or sensational movie or novel etc., esp. a suspenseful one involving mystery, crime, or espionage. **2** a person or thing that thrills or excites.

thrilling *adjective* exciting and enjoyable: *a thrilling experience*. ▶ **thrillingly** *adverb*

thrill-seeker *noun* **1** a person who enjoys the excitement of participating in dangerous activities. **2** usu. *derogatory* a person seeking thrills. ▶ **thrill-seeking** *adjective & noun*

thrips *noun* (*plural* **thrips**) a minute dark-coloured

insect, usu. having a slender body and four fringed wings, which sucks plant sap and can be a pest of ornamental and food plants.

thrive *verb* (**thrives**; *past* **thrived** or **throve**; *past participle* **thrived**; **thriving**) **1** grow vigorously, flourish. **2** be or become successful or prosperous: *the tourist industry thrives during the summer.* PHRASES **thrive on 1** (of an animal etc.) depend upon for growth or sustenance. **2** (of a person) depend upon for the strength or motivation required to succeed; be driven or encouraged by: *thrives on pressure.*

thriving *adjective* **1** prospering; doing well: *a thriving business.* **2** growing vigorously; flourishing: *thriving potato gardens.* [Say THRIVE ing]

throat *noun* **1** the front part of the neck beneath the chin and above the collarbone. **2** the windpipe or gullet. **3** anything resembling or compared to a throat, such as a narrow passage or entranceway. **4** the part of a chimney or furnace etc. immediately above the fireplace, which narrows down to the neck. PHRASES **be at each other's** (or **one another's**) **throats** quarrel violently. **cut one's own throat** bring about one's own downfall. **ram** (or **thrust** etc.) **down a person's throat** force a person to accept (a thing). ▶-**throated** *adjective* (*in combination*)

throaty *adjective* **1** (of a voice) rough, husky. **2** produced or modified in the throat; deep, guttural: *a throaty laugh.*

throb • *verb* (**throbs**, **throbbed**, **throbbing**) **1** (of the heart or pulse) beat or palpitate, esp. with more than usual force or rapidity. **2** pulsate or vibrate, esp. with a deep audible rhythm. **3** ache with a recurrent or pulsating pain: *my head is throbbing.* • *noun* **1** a palpitation or (esp. violent) pulsation. **2** a rhythmic esp. audible beat or vibration.

throes *plural noun* intense or violent pains or struggles, esp. accompanying death, birth, or great change: *the animal cast about the ground in its death throes.* PHRASES **in the throes of** in the midst of a difficult or emotional situation: *in the throes of a bitter divorce* ◊ *in the throes of passion.*

thrombosis *noun* a local clotting of the blood in a part of the circulatory system. [Say throm BO sis]

throne • *noun* **1** an ornate, elaborate, and usu. raised chair occupied by a monarch etc., esp. on ceremonial occasions. **2 a** the position, office, power, or dignity of a sovereign: *a claim to the throne.* **b** the occupant of a throne; a monarch or ruler. **3** *informal* a toilet. • *verb* (**thrones**, **throned**, **throning**) place on or as if on a throne.

throne room *noun* **1** a room containing a throne, esp. one used for audiences with a monarch. **2** *informal* a bathroom.

Throne Speech *noun* (*plural* **Throne Speeches**) *Cdn* = SPEECH FROM THE THRONE.

throng • *noun* a crowd or multitude of esp. people. • *verb* **1** gather or assemble in or around: *crowds thronged the streets.* **2** travel in large numbers: *thronged to the malls.*

throttle • *noun* **1** (also **throttle valve**) a valve controlling the flow of fuel or steam etc. in an engine. **2** (also **throttle control** or **throttle lever**) a lever or pedal operating this valve. • *verb* (**throttles**, **throttled**, **throttling**) **1** choke or strangle. **2** stifle or suppress (words, a rumour, etc.). **3** control the flow of gas or steam (to an engine etc.). PHRASES **throttle back** (or **down**) close the throttle of (an engine or vehicle) in order to slow down or stop.

through • *preposition* **1 a** from one end to the other of. **b** going in one side or end and out the other of. **c** beyond; past. **2** between or among. **3** from

beginning to end of. **4 a** by means of. **b** due to; because of. **5** up to and including. • *adverb* **1 a** from side to side, end to end, or beginning to end of a body or space. **b** all the way; to the end of a journey. **2** past or across a barrier or space. **3** successfully past a particular stage or test. **4** so as to be connected by telephone. • *adjective* **1** (of a flight etc.) that travels the whole distance or journey without interruption or change. **2** (of traffic) going through a place to a destination. **3** (of a road, route, etc.) open at both ends, allowing a continuous journey. PHRASES **be through** *informal* **1** have finished. **2** cease to have dealings. **3** have no further prospects. **through and through 1** thoroughly; in every respect. **2** repeatedly through; through again and again.

throughout • *preposition* **1** through all of; in or to every part of; everywhere in. **2** during the whole time, extent, or length of; from beginning to end. • *adverb* **1** in every part or respect. **2** during the whole time.

throughput *noun* **1** the amount of material put through a process, esp. in manufacturing or computing. **2** processing or handling capacity.

throve *past of* THRIVE.

throw • *verb* (**throws**; *past* **threw**; *past participle* **thrown**; **throwing**) **1** propel with force through the air by a rapid movement of the arm and hand. **2** move or put into place quickly, hurriedly, or roughly. **3** project, direct, or cast (light, an expression, etc.) in a particular direction. **4** send suddenly into a particular position or condition: *the country was thrown into chaos.* **5** disconcert or confuse. **6** have (a fit or tantrum). **7** *informal* give or hold (a party). **8** form (ceramic ware) on a potter's wheel. **9** (of a horse) unseat its rider. **10** project (one's voice) so that it appears to come from somewhere else. • *noun* **1** an act of throwing. **2** a small rug or light cover for furniture. **3** (preceded by *a*) *informal* a single turn, round, or item. PHRASES **throw around** (or **about**) **1** throw in various directions. **2** spend (one's money) in a reckless or ostentatious manner. **throw away 1** dispose of or discard (something no longer wanted), esp. by putting it in the garbage. **2 a** waste or fail to make use of (an opportunity etc.). **b** (often foll. by *on*) waste (money, one's life, etc.) in foolish ventures, on undeserving people, etc. **3** discard (a card). **4** *Theatre* speak (lines) with deliberate underemphasis. **throw back 1** (usu. in *passive*; foll. by *on*) force (a person) to rely on something: *was thrown back on his savings.* **2** pull aside (curtains, bedclothes, etc.), esp. with a sharp movement. **3** swallow (a drink) quickly and in one gulp. **throw a person a curve** confuse someone by doing or saying something unexpected. **throw down** fling, hurl, or bring to the ground or floor. **throw down the gauntlet** (or **glove**) issue a challenge. **throw for** *Football* (of a quarterback) amass (a specified number of yards, interceptions, etc.) by passing the ball. **throw good money after bad** incur further loss in a hopeless attempt to recoup a previous loss. **throw one's hand in 1** *Cards* fold. **2** give up; withdraw from a contest. **throw in 1** include at no extra cost. **2** add or make (a remark) casually. **3 a** (in basketball or soccer) throw (the ball) in bounds. **b** (in baseball) return (the ball) from the outfield. **throw in the towel** (or **sponge**) **1** admit defeat. **2** (of a boxer or a boxer's attendant) throw the towel or sponge used between rounds into the air as a token of defeat. **throw off**

1 confuse or distract (a person speaking, thinking, or acting) from the matter in hand. **2** discard; contrive to get rid of. **3** write or utter in an offhand manner. **throw oneself at** make eager or overt advances upon (someone) regarded as a potential romantic partner or spouse. **throw oneself into** engage vigorously in. **throw oneself on** (or **upon**) **1** rely completely on. **2** attack. **throw open 1** open (a window or door etc.) wide and usu. suddenly. **2** (often foll. by *to*) make vulnerable or accessible. **throw out 1** discard or dispose of (something no longer wanted), esp. by putting it in the garbage. **2 a** force (a troublemaker, trespasser, unruly patron, etc.) to leave the premises. **b** evict (a tenant etc.) from a house or apartment. **c** *Sport* (of an official) eject (a player, manager, or coach) from a game as a disciplinary measure. **3** wrench or dislocate (one's back, shoulder, hip, etc.). **4** put forward tentatively. **5 a** reject (a proposal or bill) in Parliament. **b** dismiss (a case or charges) in a court of law. **6** *Baseball* put (a runner) out by throwing the ball to the base before he or she reaches it. **throw over** desert or abandon. **throw together 1** prepare or assemble hastily. **2** introduce; cause to meet. **throw up 1** vomit. **2** abandon. **3** resign from. **4** erect hastily. **5** bring to notice. **6** lift (a sash window) quickly. **throw one's weight around** (or **about**) *informal* act with unpleasant self-assertiveness.

throwaway • *adjective* **1** disposable: *throwaway diapers*. **2** (of a line, word, etc.) deliberately underemphasized for effect. **3** disposed to throwing things away; wasteful: *throwaway society*. • *noun* **1** something that is meant to be discarded after esp. one use. **2** printed material meant to be discarded once read, such as a flyer or advertising supplement. **3** a child or youth who has been cast out or rejected by family or society (also as an *adjective*: *throwaway children*).

throwback *noun* (often foll. by *to*) **1** a person who embodies the principles, views, and characteristics of an earlier era. **2** a thing, such as a song, that recalls a similar thing of a previous era.

throw cushion *noun* (also **throw pillow**) one of usu. several small cushions placed on a chair.

thrower *noun* a person who throws something.

throw-in *noun* (*plural* **throw-ins**) (in basketball and soccer) the act of throwing the ball in bounds from the sidelines during play.

throw rug *noun* a light rug used as a casual covering for furniture.

thrum[1] • *verb* (**thrums**, **thrummed**, **thrumming**) **1** play (a stringed instrument) monotonously or unskilfully. **2** (often foll. by *on*) drum idly: *rain thrummed on the roof*. **3** produce or emit a low hum or thrumming sound, esp. monotonously or continuously. • *noun* **1** a low monotonous hum or drone, such as that of a car or machinery operating. **2 a** music consisting of the unskilled or monotonous playing of a guitar or other stringed instrument. **b** the sound of a guitar being thrummed.

thrum[2] • *noun* loose strands or wisps of unspun wool or raw fleece etc. twisted and knitted into a toque or mitten etc. • *verb* (**thrums**, **thrummed**, **thrumming**) knit thrums into a mitten or toque etc. at regular intervals. ▶ **thrummed** *adjective* **thrumming** *noun*

thrush *noun* (*plural* **thrushes**) **1** any small or medium-sized songbird, usu. having a brown back, a spotted breast, and a loud song. **2** a fungal disease, candidiasis, characterized by white patches on the inside of the mouth and throat and on the tongue. **3** this disease affecting any other part of the body, esp. the vagina, and characterized by pain and severe itching; a yeast infection.

thrust • *verb* (**thrusts**, **thrust**, **thrusting**) **1** push or shove with a sudden force or impulse. **2 a** (foll. by *on*) impose (a thing) forcibly on a person; enforce acceptance of (a thing): *had this task thrust on me at the last minute*. **b** (usu. foll. by *into*) force (a person) into some condition or course of action: *the scandal has thrust him into the limelight*. **3 a** make (one's way) forcibly; advance through a crowd or past an obstacle etc.: *she thrust past me abruptly*. **b** make a sudden lunge forward. **c** lunge forward with a pointed weapon; stab. • *noun* **1** a sudden or forcible push or lunge. **2** the propulsive force exerted by the propeller of a ship or aircraft, or developed by a jet or rocket engine. **3** (often foll. by *of*) **a** the principal theme or gist of remarks, an argument, etc. **b** the aim or underlying principle of an undertaking, movement, etc. **4** a caustic, critical, or witty remark aimed at a person. **5 a** a lunge or attack with a pointed weapon. **b** a strong attempt to penetrate an enemy's line or territory. **6** the sideways pressure exerted by an arch or other structure against an abutment or support.

thruster *noun* **1** a small rocket engine on a spacecraft, used to make alterations in its flight path or altitude. **2 a** (also **bow thruster**) a propeller located on the bow of a ship, used esp. when docking. **b** each of several jets or propellers on an offshore rig etc., used for accurate manoeuvring and maintenance of position.

thud • *noun* a dull low sound like that of a blow on something soft. • *verb* (**thuds**, **thudded**, **thudding**) produce or fall with a thud.

thug *noun* **1** a vicious ruffian; a violent criminal or gangster. **2** *derogatory* a person regarded as a threat or menace; a punk or bully. ▶ **thuggery** *noun* **thuggish** *adjective*

thulium *noun* a soft metallic element occurring naturally in apatite. [Say THOOLY um]

thumb • *noun* **1 a** the short thick first digit of the human hand. **b** a corresponding digit of the hand or foot of other animals. **2** the part of a glove meant for a thumb. • *verb* **1** turn the pages of a book with or as if with a thumb. **2** make (a book or its pages etc.) dirty or worn by or as if by repeated handling with the thumb: *a well-thumbed book*. **3** solicit or obtain (a ride etc.) by signalling with a closed fist and raised thumb to passing vehicles while standing at the side of a road or highway. PHRASES **be all thumbs** be clumsy; lack manual dexterity. **thumb one's nose** (usu. foll. by *at*) **1** hold one's thumb to the bottom of the nose with the hand open and fingers spread out as a gesture of derision or contempt. **2** mock, deride, or scorn. **thumbs-down** an indication of rejection or failure. **thumbs-up** an indication of success or approval. **under a person's thumb** completely under a person's influence or sway. ▶ **thumbed** *adjective* (also in *combination*)

thumb index *noun* (*plural* **thumb indexes**) a set of labelled notches cut into the side of a dictionary etc. for easy reference. ▶ **thumb-indexed** *adjective*

thumbnail • *noun* **1** the nail of a thumb. **2** a very small or concise account, summary, or representation: *most programs allow you to browse a group of images called thumbnails*. • *adjective* (of a description, summary, or representation) very small or concise: *a thumbnail account of the events*.

thumbprint *noun* **1** an impression of a thumb used esp. for identification. **2** a distinguishing trait etc.: *risk-taking abandon became Quebec modernism's thumbprint*.

thumbscrew *noun* **1** an instrument of torture for crushing the thumbs. **2** a screw with a flattened head for turning with the thumb and forefinger.

thumbtack • *noun* a pin with a flat head that may be

pushed into a bulletin board for fastening a notice or message etc. • *verb* fasten (a note, message, artwork, etc.) to a wall or bulletin board etc. using a thumbtack or thumbtacks.

thump • *verb* **1** beat or strike heavily, esp. with the fist. **2** throb or pulsate strongly: *my heart was thumping.* **3** step or tread heavily; stomp. **4** (usu. foll. by *on*) pound with the hand, esp. to attract attention. **5** *informal* achieve a resounding victory over. **6** play (a tune etc.) with a heavy touch. • *noun* **1** a dull heavy blow, as with the fist or a blunt instrument. **2** the sound of this. ▶ **thumper** *noun*

thumping • *adjective* **1** *informal* exceptionally large: *a thumping lie.* **2** that thumps. • *noun* **1** a series of repeated thumps or the sound of this. **2** *informal* a thorough beating. ▶ **thumpingly** *adverb*

thunder • *noun* **1** a loud rumbling or crashing noise accompanying a flash of lightning, caused by the sudden heating and expansion of gases along the channel of the discharge. **2** a resounding loud deep noise: *the thunder of applause.* • *verb* **1** (of thunder) sound. **2** make or proceed with a noise suggestive of thunder: *bison thundered across the prairie.* **3** utter or communicate in a loud voice or forceful manner; shout, roar. **4** criticize or denounce something loudly or vehemently: *the government thunders against the practice, but it persists.* PHRASES **steal a person's thunder** spoil the effect of another's idea, action, etc. by expressing or doing it first.

thunderbird *noun* a mythical bird which, according to the legends of many North American Aboriginal peoples, created the thunder with its beating wings and the lightning with its flashing eyes.

thunderbolt *noun* **1** a flash of lightning with a simultaneous crash of thunder. **2** a bolt of lightning believed to be used as an agent of divine punishment or destruction. **3** a sudden and unexpected occurrence or item of news.

thunderclap *noun* **1** a crash of thunder. **2** a very loud, sudden noise. **3** something that happens quickly or unexpectedly: *the couple may meet in a thunderclap of passion.*

thundercloud *noun* **1** a cumulonimbus cloud with a towering or spreading top, which is charged with electricity and produces thunder and lightning. **2** something threatening or dreadful: *he managed to ignore the thundercloud of scandal hanging over her head.*

thunderhead *noun* a tall cumulonimbus cloud with an anvil-shaped top extending horizontally, usu. indicating an approaching thunderstorm.

thundering *adjective informal* **1** very great or excessive; immense: *a thundering nuisance.* **2** as loud as thunder. ▶ **thunderingly** *adverb*

thunderous *adjective* **1** powerful, violent, very hard or heavy: *a thunderous collision.* **2** very loud; rumbling or resounding like thunder. ▶ **thunderously** *adverb*

thundershower *noun* a rain shower accompanied by thunder and lightning.

thunderstorm *noun* a storm with thunder and lightning, and usu. heavy rain or hail.

thunderstruck *adjective* amazed, astonished.

thunk *noun & verb informal* = THUD.

Thurs. *abbreviation* (also **Thur.**) Thursday.

Thursday • *noun* the fifth day of the week, following Wednesday. • *adverb* **1** on Thursday. **2** (**Thursdays**) on Thursdays; each Thursday.

thus *adverb formal* **1 a** in this way; in the manner that has been shown or indicated. **b** as follows; in the manner about to be shown or indicated. **2** therefore, consequently; as a result. **3** so; to the degree or extent indicated: *thus far.*

thusly *adverb* thus.

thwack • *noun* **1** a sharp resonant sound as produced esp. by one flat surface striking another. **2** a heavy blow producing such a sound. • *verb* lash, slap, or whack (a person or thing), esp. with something flat, such as the palm of one's hand.

thwart • *verb* successfully oppose (a person or thing). • *noun* a structural member extending across a boat, esp. a seat in a canoe etc.

thy *possessive pronoun* (also **thine** before a vowel) of or belonging to thee: now replaced by *your* except in some formal, liturgical, dialect, and poetic uses.

thyme *noun* a low-growing aromatic plant of the mint family, grown for use as a herb. [Sounds like *TIME*]

thymine *noun* a compound found in all living tissue as a component base of DNA. [Say THIGH mean]

thymus *noun* (also **thymus gland**) an organ situated near the base of the neck of vertebrates which is the site of maturation of T-lymphocytes, in humans becoming much smaller at the approach of puberty. [Say THIGH muss]

thyroid *noun* **1 a** (also **thyroid gland**) a large ductless gland in the neck of vertebrates which secretes hormones regulating growth and development through control of the rate of metabolism. **b** an extract prepared from the thyroid gland of animals and used to treat conditions resulting from abnormal thyroid activity, such as goitre and cretinism. **2** (also **thyroid cartilage**) the largest of the cartilages of the larynx, consisting of two broad four-sided plates joined in front at an angle, enclosing the vocal cords and, in men, forming the Adam's apple. [Say THIGH roid]

thyself *pronoun archaic emphatic & reflexive form of* THOU[1], THEE; = YOURSELF.

Ti *symbol* titanium.

ti *noun* (*plural* **tis**) **1** (in tonic sol-fa) the seventh note of a major scale. **2** the note B in the fixed-do system. [Say TEE]

tiara *noun* (*plural* **tiaras**) a woman's jewelled ornamental coronet or headband worn on the front of the hair. [Say tee AIR uh or tee ARR uh]

Tibetan • *noun* **1 a** a native or inhabitant of Tibet, a mountainous country in Asia (an autonomous region of China). **b** a person of Tibetan descent. **2** the language of Tibet. • *adjective* of or relating to Tibet or its language. [Say tib BET un]

tibia *noun* (*plural* **tibiae** or **tibias**) **1** the inner and larger of the two bones of the lower leg extending from the knee to the ankle, articulating at its upper end with the fibula. **2** the corresponding part in other four-legged animals. **3** the fourth segment of the leg in insects. ▶ **tibial** *adjective* [Say TIBBY uh for the singular, TIBBY ee for the plural, TIBBY ul]

tic *noun* **1** a disorder characterized by a repeated habitual twitching of one or more muscles, esp. of the face, largely involuntary and accentuated under stress. **2** a habitual mannerism or idiosyncrasy; a habit or quirk: *I began the description with just the kind of generalization that was one of my primary tics as a writer.*

tick • *noun* **1 a** the regular slight click made by a watch or clock. **b** the short soft metallic sound of two things clicking together. **2** a mark (√) made with a pen or pencil to check off items on a list, indicate the correctness of an answer, etc. **3** *Stock Market* the smallest recognized amount by which the price of a commodity

or stock etc. may fluctuate. **4** a tiny spider-like bloodsucking animal that attaches itself to the skin of dogs, cattle, and other mammals, and may transmit disease to humans. **5** any of various parasitic flies infesting birds, sheep, and bats. **6** *Cdn & Brit. informal* credit: *buy it on tick.* **7** a case or cover filled with feathers etc. to form a mattress or pillow. **8** = TICKING. • *verb* **1 a** (of a clock etc.) operate with or make a tick. **b** (foll. by *away, down*) (of time) pass. **2** (of a mechanism) operate, function, work. **3** (often foll. by *off*) mark (an item on a list, a box or option on an application form, a written answer, etc.) with a tick. PHRASES **tick off** *informal* annoy, irritate. **tick over** (of a person, project, etc.) be working or functioning at a basic or minimum level. **what makes a person tick** *informal* what makes a person behave in a certain way; a person's motivation.

tick-borne *adjective* (of a disease) transmitted by ticks.

ticked *adjective* (also **ticked off**) *informal* angry.

ticker *noun* **1** *informal* **a** the heart. **b** a watch. **2** an electronic instrument for receiving and recording telegraph messages, esp. one that prints out stock prices or news stories.

tickertape *noun* **1** a long narrow strip of paper on which a ticker prints esp. stock prices. **2** this or similar material, such as streamers, ribbon, or confetti, thrown from windows to greet a celebrity in a motorcade (also as an *adjective*: *tickertape parade*).

ticket • *noun* **1 a** a written or printed piece of paper or card entitling the holder to enter a place, watch or participate in an event, travel by public transport, etc. **b** a similar printed card making the bearer eligible for a raffle, draw, etc. **c** a receipt for an item left temporarily for safe keeping, such as at a coat check. **2** an official notification of a traffic violation: *speeding ticket.* **3 a** a list of candidates for election nominated by a political party or group. **b** the declared principles or policies of a political party or group. **4** a tag or label attached to an item and giving its name, price, or other details. **5** *Cdn* a negotiable cash receipt issued to a farmer by the manager of a grain elevator for grain received. **6 a** (foll. by *to*) a means of reaching or achieving: *this promotion is my ticket to upper management.* **b** (foll. by *out*) something enabling a person to leave an unfavourable location or situation: *his ticket out of unemployment.* **7** (**the ticket**) *informal* the ideal, correct, or required thing: *that's just the ticket.* **8** a person or thing, esp. a performer or performance, the popularity of which is judged according to its availability or accessibility: *this band's the hottest ticket in town!* **9** a certificate of qualification as a ship's officer, pilot, etc. **10** *Cdn hist.* = LOCATION TICKET. • *verb* (**tickets, ticketed, ticketing**) **1** issue a ticket to (the driver of a vehicle). **2** attach a ticket to; label. **3 a** issue (a person) with a ticket for a trip. **b** *informal* designate (a person) for a particular role or destiny: *is ticketed to be the starting goalie.* PHRASES **write one's own ticket** dictate one's own terms.

ticket holder *noun* a person who has purchased a ticket for a sporting or theatrical event, concert, etc.

ticking *noun* a strong durable usu. striped linen or cotton fabric used esp. to cover pillows.

tickle[1] • *verb* (**tickles, tickled, tickling**) **1 a** lightly touch, stroke, or poke (a person or part of a person's body) in such a way that the nerves are excited, producing a reflex spasmodic movement and usu. laughter. **b** (of a part of the body) be affected by this sensation: *my throat tickles.* **c** cause this sensation: *this sweater tickles.* **2** amuse, delight, or excite (a person, curiosity, a sense of humour, etc.): *I was tickled by the thought of it.* • *noun* **1** an act of tickling. **2** a tickling

sensation: *a tickle in my throat.* PHRASES **tickled pink** (or **to death**) *informal* extremely amused or pleased.

tickle[2] *noun* *Cdn* (*Nfld & Maritimes*) **1** a narrow strait or channel between islands or between an island and the mainland, esp. one that is difficult to navigate. **2** an entrance to a harbour that is narrow and difficult to navigate.

tickler *noun* a thing that tickles.

ticklish *adjective* **1** sensitive to tickling. **2** (of a matter to be dealt with etc.) requiring careful treatment or handling; tricky, delicate. **3** (of a person) touchy; easily offended, irritated, or upset. ▶ **ticklishness** *noun*

tick-tock *noun* the ticking sound of esp. a large clock.

tic-tac-toe (also **tick-tack-toe**) • *noun* a children's game in which players attempt to complete a row of three Xs or three Os marked alternately on a square grid of nine squares drawn on paper etc. • *adjective* *Hockey* designating skilful play involving quick accurate passes: *a beautiful tic-tac-toe goal.*

tidal *adjective* of, related to, or affected by the tides: *tidal basin.* ▶ **tidally** *adverb*

tidal pool *noun* (also **tide pool**) a usu. large pool of water that remains on a shore or beach etc. after the tide has receded.

tidal wave *noun* **1** (not in technical use) an exceptionally large ocean wave, esp. one caused by an underwater earthquake or volcanic eruption; a tsunami. **2 a** a widespread manifestation of feeling, opinion, etc. **b** a large or overwhelming quantity or amount of something.

tidbit *noun* **1** a small piece of food; a dainty morsel or delicacy. **2** an interesting or piquant item of news or information.

tiddlywink *noun* **1** a small plastic counter flicked into a cup by being pressed on its edge by a larger one. **2** (in *plural*) this game.

tide *noun* **1 a** the alternate rising and falling of the sea, usu. twice each lunar day in a given place, due to the attraction of the moon and sun. **b** the alternate inflow and outflow of water on a shore or coast produced by this (see EBB *noun* 1, FLOOD *noun* 3). **c** the water as affected by this. **2** the course or trend of opinion, luck, or events: *turned the tide in our favour.* **3** the flow or movement of a large amount of something: *the tide of illegal drugs.* **4** (in *combination*) a particular time or season: *Eastertide.* PHRASES **tide over** (**tides over, tided over, tiding over**) enable or help (a person) to get through esp. a difficult period: *the money will tide me over.*

tide line *noun* **1** the level reached by the sea water at high tide. **2** a mark left on the shore by the water at this level.

tidewater *noun* **1** water carried or affected by tides. **2** a region situated on tidewater (also as an *adjective*: *tidewater port*).

tidily *adverb* in a tidy manner.

tidiness *noun* the quality or condition of being tidy or neat.

tidings *plural noun* *literary* news, information.

tidy • *adjective* (**tidier, tidiest**) **1** neat, orderly; methodically arranged. **2** (of a person) **a** having a clean and neat appearance. **b** inclined to keep things neat. **3** free of complications; convenient: *a tidy ending.* **4** *informal* considerable: *it cost a tidy sum.* • *verb* (**tidies, tidied, tidying**) (often foll. by *up*) **1** make (a room, oneself, etc.) neat; put or arrange in good order. **2** (also foll. by *away*) put (things) away for the sake of tidiness: *tidy up the mess on the floor.* • *noun* (*plural* **tidies**) an act or period of tidying: *give the place a quick tidy.*

tie • *verb* (**ties, tied, tying**) **1** bind or fasten with rope or string etc. **2 a** form a string, ribbon, shoelace, etc.

into a knot or bow. **b** secure (an article of clothing, esp. a shoe or boot) by tying a lace, belt, etc. **3** (usu. in *passive*) **a** be closely or inextricably linked to (a person or thing). **b** bind or restrict (a person) with an obligation or responsibility etc. **4 a** (often foll. by *for*, *at*) finish a game, event, or competition with the same score or standing as (an opponent or opponents). **b** make (a game or score) even: *the goal tied the game*. **c** match or equal (a record). **5** *Fishing* make (an artificial fly) by dressing a hook with strands of silk and feathers etc. • *noun* **1** a rope, cord, or chain, etc. used for fastening or tying something: *a twist-tie*. **2** a strip of material worn around the neck under the collar and tied with a knot in front. **3** (often in *plural*) something uniting or restricting people or things; a link or connection, esp. a bond or obligation: *all economic ties have been severed*. **4** a game or competition etc. in which two or more opponents have or finish with the same score. **5** a wooden or concrete beam laid horizontally to support the rails of a train track. PHRASES **fit to be tied** *informal* very angry. **tie down 1** fasten or secure with rope to a fixed point. **2** limit or restrict (a person), esp. with responsibility or commitment. **tie in** (foll. by *with*) make or be relevant to or consistent with; fit. **tie one on** get drunk. **tie up 1** bind or fasten securely with cord etc. **2** (usu. in *passive*) fully occupy or engage (a person), esp. in business or a meeting etc. **3** hinder or obstruct; prevent from acting freely. **4 a** complete (an undertaking etc.). **b** take care of (loose ends). **5** invest or reserve (capital etc.) so that it is not immediately available for use. **6** moor (a boat). **7** secure or tether (an animal).

tie-back *noun* a decorative strip of fabric or cord for holding a curtain back from the window.

tiebreaker *noun* (also **tiebreak**) esp. *Sport* **1** a means of determining the winner when two competitors are tied. **2** a goal or point etc. that gives a person or team the lead in a tie game. ▶ **tiebreaking** *adjective*

tied *adjective* **1** fastened or attached with string etc.: *a neatly tied package*. **2** (of a game or contest) with both or more competitors or teams achieving the same score or level of success: *the first tied game this season* ◊ *a tied vote*. **3** *Music* (of two or more notes) united by a tie and performed as one unbroken note.

tie-down *noun* a device, esp. a cord or strap, used to secure or fasten something.

tie-dye • *noun* **1** a method of producing coloured patterns on fabric or a garment by tying parts of it so that they receive less dye than other parts when the fabric is dyed. **2** a garment etc. dyed in this way (also as an *adjective*: *tie-dye T-shirt*). • *verb* (**tie-dyes**, **tie-dyed**, **tie-dying**) dye (fabric or a garment) using this method. ▶ **tie-dyed** *adjective*

tie-in *noun* **1** a connection or association; a link. **2 a** a joint promotion of related items esp. featuring promotional merchandise produced to take advantage of the success of a movie or television series etc. **b** an item marketed in such a promotion.

tier¹ *noun* **1** each of a series of rows or horizontal units placed one above another in a structure, such as in theatre seating. **2** a rank, grade, or stratum: *fears about a two-tier health system that would see the rich get the best care*. [Rhymes with PIER]

tier² *noun* a person who ties something, esp. a person who ties artificial flies for fishing. [Say TIRE]

tiered *adjective* **1** arranged in tiers: *tiered seating* ◊ *a tiered wedding cake* ◊ *a tiered interest rate structure*. **2** having the number of tiers mentioned: *a two-tiered system*. [Rhymes with WEIRD]

tie-up *noun* **1** a stoppage, esp. of labour or business. **2** a traffic jam.

TIFF *noun* a file format used widely in desktop publishing for representing colour or grey-scale images.

tiff *noun* a petty quarrel; a minor argument, disagreement, or rift.

tiffany *noun* (*plural* **tiffanies**) (also **tiffany lamp**) any of various lamps with stained glass shades, esp. a suspended ceiling lamp with a polygonal shade scalloped around the bottom edge.

tiger *noun* **1** a large powerful carnivorous feline, tawny yellow in colour with blackish stripes and a white belly, found in several races in parts of Asia. **2** a person of great energy, strength, or courage: *despite his wounds, he still fought like a tiger*. PHRASES **have a tiger by the tail** be engaged in an undertaking etc. which proves unexpectedly difficult but cannot easily or safely be abandoned.

tiger cat *noun* any moderate-sized feline resembling the tiger, e.g. the ocelot or margay.

tigerish *adjective* like a tiger, esp. in being fierce or energetic: *she continued her tigerish pacing of the room*.

tiger lily *noun* (*plural* **tiger lilies**) a tall lily with flowers of dull orange spotted with black or purple.

tiger shrimp *noun* (*plural* **tiger shrimp**) a large shrimp marked with dark bands.

tight • *adjective* **1** not loose. **2** (of money etc.) scarce; not easily obtainable. **3** dense, compact: *a tight ball*. **4 a** (of control etc.) strictly imposed. **b** (of a deadline, budget, etc.) allowing no leeway. **c** (of a schedule) having no free time. **5** difficult to deal with or manage; resolved or achieved by a narrow margin: *a tight situation*. **6** of such close texture as to be impervious to a specified thing: *airtight*. **7** (of a corner or curve) having a short radius. **8** (of a game, competition, etc.) close. **9** *informal* on terms of close friendship; intimate. **10** *informal* drunk. **11** *informal* (of a person) cheap, stingy. • *adverb* tightly: *hold on tight!* PHRASES **run a tight ship** maintain the efficiency of an organization etc. with strict management. **sit tight 1** remain in one's seat. **2** do nothing, either as a safeguard against making a mistake or so as to wait for an opportunity to get what one wants.

tighten *verb* make or become tight or tighter.

tight end *noun* *Football* **1** an offensive end who lines up next to the tackle and may be used either as a blocker or to receive passes. **2** this position.

tight-fisted *adjective* stingy. ▶ **tight-fistedness** *noun*

tight-fitting *adjective* **1** (of clothing) fitting very close to the body. **2** that fits snugly or securely: *tight-fitting lid*.

tight-lipped *adjective* **1** refusing to discuss esp. a particular matter; secretive. **2** with the lips pursed, esp. in anger.

tightly *adverb* closely and firmly; in a tight manner.

tightly knit *adjective* (also **tight-knit**) = CLOSE-KNIT.

tightness *noun* the quality or condition of being tight.

tightrope *noun* **1** a rope or wire stretched tightly high above the ground, on which acrobats perform. **2** a delicate or risky situation.

tights *plural noun* a one-piece article of clothing made usu. of knitted nylon, designed to cover the hips and each of the legs and feet, worn by women, dancers, etc.

tightwad *noun* *slang* a cheap or miserly person.

tigress *noun* (*plural* **tigresses**) **1** a female tiger. **2** a fierce or passionate woman: *even the mildest of mothers can turn into a tigress when defending her young*.

tikka *noun* an Indian dish of marinated meat, esp. chicken or lamb, threaded on skewers and grilled. [Say TICK uh or TEAK uh]

tilde *noun* a mark (˜), placed over a letter, e.g. over a

Spanish *n* when pronounced *ny* (as in *señor*) or a Portuguese nasal *a* or *o* (as in *São Paulo*). [Say TIL duh]

tile • *noun* **1** a thin slab of baked clay, usu. of a regular shape, used in series for paving a floor, lining a wall or fireplace, covering a roof, etc. **2** a piece of glazed ceramic, cork, linoleum, slate, etc., used for similar purposes. **3** tiles collectively. **4** a hollow pipe used for draining land, roads, etc. **5** a thin flat piece used in a game, such as in Scrabble or mah-jong. • *verb* (**tiles, tiled, tiling**) **1** cover with tiles. **2** lay drainage tile in. • PHRASES **on the tiles** *informal* enjoying a night out in a wild or reckless manner, esp. drinking.

tiling *noun* **1** the action of covering a surface with tiles: *this adhesive is for tiling on fairly flat surfaces.* **2** an area covered with tiles: *an area of plain tiling.*

WRITING TIP
till, until
Both **till** and **until** are perfectly acceptable, though only **until** is used at the beginning of a sentence.

till[1] *preposition & conjunction* = UNTIL.

till[2] *noun* a drawer for money in a store etc., esp. with a device recording the amount of each purchase.

till[3] *verb* **1** prepare and use (land, soil, etc.) for growing crops. **2** plow (land, a field, etc.).

till[4] *noun* stiff clay containing boulders, sand, etc. deposited by melting glaciers and ice sheets.

tillage *noun* **1** the action or process of tilling land. **2** tilled land.

tiller *noun* **1** a horizontal bar fitted to the head of a boat's rudder to turn it in steering. **2** a machine or implement used for breaking up or cultivating soil. **3** a person who tills soil or cultivates a crop.

tilt[1] • *verb* **1 a** lean from the vertical or incline from the horizontal. **b** cause to lean, slant, or slope. **2** (often foll. by *towards*) incline towards a particular opinion. **3 a** bias or influence (a decision, verdict, etc.) in favour of a particular person or thing. **b** aim or direct (something) towards a particular audience or objective: *their advertising is tilted at middle-aged men.* **4** *hist.* rush or charge at in a joust. • *noun* **1** a slanting or sloping position; a lean. **2** an inclination or bias. **3 a** an encounter between opponents: *the two teams engaged in an entertaining tilt.* **b** *hist.* a joust between two knights on horseback with lances, each attempting to throw the other from the saddle. **4** (also **pelvic tilt**) an exercise designed to relieve back ailments by flattening the small of the back. **5** on a pinball machine, a device that stops the game if the game is jarred or lifted. • PHRASES **full** (or **at full**) **tilt 1** at full speed. **2** with the utmost force or energy. **tilt at windmills** attack an imaginary enemy or grievance.

tilt[2] *noun* *Cdn* (*Nfld*) **1** a small shack, cabin, or hut characterized by a sloping roof, used seasonally by fishermen and trappers. **2** a rudimentary tent or shelter consisting of a sealskin or canvas covering.

tilth *noun* **1** the condition of cultivated soil: *a fine tilth.* **2** tillage.

SPELL CHECK
timber, timbre
The quality of a sound is its **timbre**.

timber • *noun* **1** wood that has been prepared for use as building material, in carpentry, etc. **2 a** a beam or piece of wood forming or capable of forming part of a building or structure. **b** (usu. in *plural*) the pieces of wood forming the ribs, bends, or frames of a ship's hull. **3** large standing trees, esp. when considered as

building material. • *interjection* a warning cry that a tree is about to fall.

timbered *adjective* **1** (esp. of a building) made wholly or partly of timber. **2** (of land, a region, etc.) covered with trees; wooded: *timbered mountains.*

timber frame • *noun* **1 a** usu. factory-prepared section of timber framework used in the construction of houses and barns etc. **2** a house or barn etc. built using a timber framework. • *adjective* **1** (usu. **timber-framed**) having a frame of esp. large timbers. **2** (of a house) built using usu. factory-prepared sections of timber framework.

timberland *noun* land covered with forest yielding timber.

timber licence *noun* *Cdn* a licence to cut timber from a berth conditional upon payment of dues to the government.

timberline *noun* **1** the level on a mountain above which no trees grow. **2** (in the northern hemisphere) the latitudinal limit north of which no trees grow.

timber rights *plural noun* *Cdn* the rights to cut timber of a certain diameter in a specified region, which are controlled by the provincial government and may be obtained in exchange for payment.

timber wolf *noun* = WOLF 1.

timbre *noun* the distinctive character or quality of a sound, esp. that of a musical voice or instrument, apart from its pitch and intensity: *his voice had the strength and timbre of a young man's.* [Say TAM bur or TAM bruh]

Timbuktu (also **Timbuctoo**) any remote or outlandish place in a faraway country. [Say tim buck TOO]

SPELL CHECK
time, thyme
The herb is **thyme**.

time • *noun* **1** the indefinite continued progress of existence and events in the past, present, and future, regarded as a whole. **2** a point of time as measured in hours and minutes past midnight or noon. **3** the favourable or appropriate moment to do something. **4** (**a time**) an indefinite period. **5** (also **times**) a portion of time characterized by particular events or circumstances: *Victorian times.* **6** (**one's time**) a period regarded as characteristic of a particular stage in one's life. **7** the length of time taken to complete an activity. **8** time as allotted, available, or used. **9** an instance of something happening or being done. **10** *informal* a prison sentence. **11** an apprenticeship. **12** the normal rate of pay for time spent working. **13** the rhythmic pattern or tempo of a piece of music. • *verb* (**times, timed, timing**) **1** arrange a time for. **2** perform at a particular time. **3** measure the time taken by. **4** (foll. by *out*) (of a computer or program) cancel (an operation) automatically because a predefined interval of time has passed. • PHRASES **against time** with utmost speed, in order to finish by a certain time: *working against time.* **ahead of one's time** having ideas too enlightened or advanced to be accepted by one's contemporaries. **ahead of time** in advance of an event or occurrence; earlier, beforehand. **all the time 1** constantly: *nags all the time.* **2** at all times: *leaves a light on all the time.* **3** during the whole of the time referred to (often despite some contrary expectation etc.): *he was there all the time.* **at one time 1** in or during a known but unspecified past period. **2** simultaneously. **at the same time 1** simultaneously; at a time that is the same for all. **2** nevertheless. **at a time** separately or in successive groups of a specified number each: *one at a time.* **at times** occasionally, periodically. **before one's time 1** prematurely: *old before her time.* **2** before

one was born or present etc.: *that was before my time*. **call time** *Sport* ask an official for a time out. **find the time** make arrangements to one's schedule so that there is enough time for a particular activity. **for the time being** for the present; until some other arrangement is made. **give a person the time of day 1** tell a person what time it is. **2** (with *neg.*) *slang* refuse to help or talk or pay attention to a person; snub, ignore. **half the time** *informal* **1** very often, esp. too often: *I couldn't tell if he was being serious half the time*. **2** in a relatively short period: *she did the job in half the time*. **have no time for 1** be unable or unwilling to spend time on. **2** dislike. **have the time 1** be able to spend the time needed. **2** know what time it is. **have a time of it** undergo trouble or difficulty. **in no** (or **less than no**) **time 1** very soon. **2** very quickly. **in one's own good** (or **sweet**) **time** at a pace decided by oneself. **in one's own time** outside working hours. **in time 1** not late, punctual: *was in time to catch the bus*. **2** eventually: *in time you may agree*. **in one's time** in one's heyday. **keep good** (or **bad**) **time 1** (of a clock etc.) record time accurately (or inaccurately). **2** be habitually punctual (or not punctual). **keep time** move or sing etc. in time. **know the time of day** be well informed. **lose no time** (often foll. by *in* + verbal noun) act immediately: *lost no time in cashing the cheque*. **make time** find an opportunity to spend time with a person or participate in some activity, esp. while one is already very busy: *made time for baseball ◊ I've been trying to make time to come and see you*. **no time** *informal* a very short interval: *came in no time*. **pass the time of day** *informal* exchange a greeting or casual remarks. **time after time 1** repeatedly, on many occasions. **2** in many instances. **time and** (or **time and time**) **again** on many occasions. **time and motion** concerned with measuring the efficiency of industrial and other operations: *time and motion studies*. **the time of day** the hour by the clock. **the time of one's life** a thrilling, exciting, or extremely enjoyable occasion or moment. **time of the month** *informal* or *euphemism* a woman's menstrual period. **time was** there was a time.

time and a half *noun* an increased amount of money paid to an employee for overtime work, equal to one and a half times the pay the employee would normally earn for working the same number of hours.

time bomb *noun* **1** a bomb designed to explode at a pre-set time. **2 a** a situation on the verge of becoming a crisis or disaster if not defused in time. **b** an unpredictable or moody person, esp. one whose psychological stability is questioned.

time capsule *noun* a sealed box etc. containing objects chosen as representative of life at a particular time, buried for discovery in the future.

time-consuming *adjective* (of a process, activity, etc.) that requires a large or inconvenient amount of time.

time exposure *noun* **1** a method of taking a photograph in which the film is exposed for longer than the maximum normal shutter setting. **2** a picture taken using this method.

time frame *noun* a specific period in which something occurs, has occurred, or is planned to occur.

time-honoured *adjective* (also **time-honored**) (of a custom, tradition, etc.) that is revered as a result of having been observed etc. for many years.

time immemorial *noun* a longer time than anyone can remember or trace: *we have maintained our freedom, our languages, and our traditions from time immemorial*.

timekeeper *noun* **1** an official responsible for recording time, esp. at a competition or game. **2 a** a device that records time, such as a watch or clock, esp. regarded in terms of its accuracy: *a good timekeeper*. **b** a

person regarded in terms of punctuality. ▶ **timekeeping** *noun*

time lag *noun* an interval of time between related events, esp. a cause and its effect.

time-lapse *adjective* pertaining to a method of taking a sequence of photographs at long intervals to photograph a slow process, and showing them at a faster speed.

timeless *adjective* not affected by the passage of time; remaining popular, effective, significant, etc., over time: *a timeless truth*. ▶ **timelessly** *adverb* **timelessness** *noun*

timeline *noun* **1** a line graduated in years on which esp. historical events are marked, used to teach or learn the dates and order of important events in history. **2** a schedule for a project etc. showing the dates by which certain stages must be completed in order for the project to be ready on time.

timely *adjective* (**timelier**, **timeliest**) opportune; occurring, done, or made at a suitable or appropriate time. ▶ **timeliness** *noun*

time machine *noun* an imaginary machine capable of transporting a person backwards or forwards in time.

time off *noun* a period of time spent away from work, esp. taken for rest or recreation.

time out *noun* **1** *Sport* a short stoppage in play requested so that a team can consider or discuss strategy, attend to an injured player, etc. **2** a short break or period away from an activity.

timepiece *noun* an instrument, such as a clock or watch, for measuring the passage of time.

timer *noun* **1** a device that measures elapsed time, esp. one that sounds to indicate that a certain amount of time has passed. **2** a device that can be set to turn an appliance etc. on or off at a pre-set time. **3** a person responsible for keeping track of time.

times • *noun* used following a number to express multiplication of what follows: *two times six is twelve ◊ ten times better*. • *adverb* multiplied by: *the party will cost $10 times the number of people coming*.

time saver *noun* an activity, method, tool, etc., that reduces the amount of time required to do something. ▶ **time-saving** *adjective*

time scale *noun* the time allowed for or taken by a sequence of events.

time-sensitive *adjective* that must be completed, performed, arranged, etc. at or by a certain time.

time-share *noun* **1** a property that is owned jointly by several people under a time-sharing arrangement (also as an *adjective*: *time-share condos*). **2** a share in a property owned jointly under a time-sharing arrangement.

time-sharing *noun* **1** an arrangement in which a vacation home is jointly owned or rented by several people, each of whom is entitled to use it for a fixed limited period of time each year. **2** the simultaneous use of a single computer system by several users stationed at different terminals and performing different operations.

time signature *noun* *Music* an indication of tempo, expressed as a fraction with the numerator giving the number of beats in each bar and the denominator giving the basic note value of each beat.

time slot *noun* an allotted place in a broadcasting schedule.

time span *noun* a period of time, usu. of a specified length: *during a five-week time span*.

times table *noun* **1** a chart showing the products of a number when multiplied by each of the numbers from one to twelve, learned and often memorized by children in school. **2** (in *plural*) the times tables for each

T

of a range of numbers, esp. those from one to twelve: *do you know your times tables?*

timetable • *noun* **1** a list or plan of the times or dates when successive things are to occur or be done; a schedule or timeline. **2 a** a student's schedule indicating the days and times of classes. **b** a schedule of departure and arrival times of buses, trains, airplanes, etc. • *verb* (**timetables, timetabled, timetabling**) outline or arrange (events etc.) in a timetable; schedule.

time-tested *adjective* that has, over time, been proven or shown to be effective, useful, or accurate; reliable.

time travel *noun* travel through time into the past or the future, esp. as a feature of science fiction. ▶ **time traveller** *noun*

time trial *noun* a race in which participants are individually timed, often used to determine qualifiers and their starting positions for a later race.

time warp *noun* **1** (in science fiction) an imaginary or hypothetical distortion of space in relation to time that causes or enables a person to remain stationary in time or to travel backwards or forwards in time. **2** a state in which the styles, attitudes, etc. of a past period are retained: *stuck in a 1950s time warp*.

time-worn *adjective* **1** antiquated. **2** adversely affected by age or time. **3** trite; hackneyed.

time zone *noun* each of the longitudinal divisions of the globe throughout which a standard time is used.

timid *adjective* **1** easily frightened; meek, shy. **2** characterized by or indicating a fear or shyness: *a timid handshake.* ▶ **timidity** *noun* **timidly** *adverb*

timing *noun* **1** the ability to act or speak at the right time in order to achieve the greatest effect. **2** the time or period of time chosen for an event etc. **3** the act of recording time. **4** the regulation of the opening and closing of valves in an internal combustion engine.

Timorese • *noun* (*plural* **Timorese**) a member of the indigenous people of Timor, a large island in the southern Malay Archipelago. • *adjective* of this island or these people. [Say tee more EEZ]

timorous *adjective* nervous and easily frightened: *"Who's that?" asked a timorous voice.* ▶ **timorously** *adverb* **timorousness** *noun* [Say TIMMER us]

timothy *noun* a Eurasian grass, naturalized in North America, widely grown for grazing and hay.

timpani *plural noun* a set of large drums, each shaped like a bowl with a membrane adjustable for tension (and so pitch) stretched across; kettledrums. ▶ **timpanist** *noun* [Say TIMPA nee]

tin • *noun* **1** a silvery-white metallic element resisting corrosion, used esp. in alloys and for plating thin iron or steel sheets to form tin plate. **2 a** a container made of tin: *a cookie tin.* **b** esp. *Brit.* a hermetically sealed container made of tin, tin plate, or aluminum, in which food is preserved and sold; a can. **3** = TIN PLATE. • *verb* (**tins, tinned, tinning**) **1** seal (food) in an airtight tin for preservation. **2** cover or coat with tin. ▶ **tinned** *adjective*

tincture *noun* **1** (often foll. by *of*) a tinge, trace, or hint: *she could not keep a tincture of bitterness out of her voice.* **2** a substance dissolved in alcohol for use as a medicine: *a tincture of morphine.* [Say TINK chur]

tinder *noun* a dry substance, such as bits of wood, that readily catches fire, used to start a fire from a spark struck with a flint. [Say TIN dur]

tinderbox *noun* (*plural* **tinderboxes**) **1** *hist.* a box containing tinder, flint, and steel, formerly used for kindling fires. **2** a situation or thing that may erupt into violence, confusion, etc.: *the troubles in Kosovo, Northern Ireland and a dozen other tinderboxes continue to smoulder and burst into destructive flame.* [Say TIN dur box]

tine *noun* any of a series of projecting points or prongs,

such as on a fork, comb, cultivating tool, the antler of a deer, etc. ▶ **tined** *adjective*

tinfoil *noun* aluminum foil.

ting *noun* a thin clear high-pitched sound made by a small bell or glass etc. when struck.

tinge *noun* **1** a trace of some colour: *the light takes on an eerie tinge of blue.* **2** a touch or trace of something: *a tinge of regret.*

tinged *adjective* **1** having a slight shade of a usu. specified colour: *white walls tinged with pink.* **2** affected slightly with the addition of a small amount of a characteristic or quality: *sadness tinged with anger.*

tingle • *noun* **1** a slight prickling or stinging sensation, usu. felt in a limb that has been exposed to cold or which has fallen asleep. **2** a slight tickling sensation or goosebumps as a result of stimulation or excitement. • *verb* (**tingles, tingled, tingling**) experience or cause this sensation. ▶ **tingly** *adjective* (**tinglier, tingliest**)

tinker • *verb* **1** (foll. by *with, at*) **a** work in an amateurish or desultory way, esp. to adjust or mend machinery etc. **b** meddle, tamper. **2** (usu. foll. by *with*) make minor adjustments to; refine. • *noun* **1** a mender of kettles and pans etc. who wanders from place to place to seek work. **2** a period of tinkering. PHRASES **not give a tinker's damn** not care at all. ▶ **tinkerer** *noun* **tinkering** *noun*

Tinkertoy *noun proprietary* a type of building toy consisting of short coloured dowels that may be inserted into round connecting blocks.

tinkle • *verb* (**tinkles, tinkled, tinkling**) **1** make or cause to make a succession of short light ringing sounds. **2** *informal* urinate. • *noun* **1** a tinkling sound. **2** *informal* or *euphemism* an act of urinating. ▶ **tinkly** *adjective*

tinnitus *noun* a ringing in the ears. [Say tin ITE us]

tinny *adjective* (**tinnier, tinniest**) **1 a** having a sound like that of tin being struck. **b** (of music, esp. on a recording) thin and metallic, missing the lower frequencies. **2** (of a metal object) flimsy, insubstantial.

tin plate *noun* sheet iron or sheet steel coated with tin.

tin-plated *adjective* coated with tin.

tinpot *adjective* second-rate, inferior: *a tinpot dictator.*

tinsel • *noun* **1** glittering metallic strands or threads used for decoration, esp. on a Christmas tree. **2** cheap or superficial brilliance or splendour; showiness, glitz: *the visitor who sees beyond the thin layer of tinsel trappings enters a wasteland.* ▶ **tinselly** *adjective*

tinsmith *noun* a person who manufactures or repairs items of tin and tin plate. ▶ **tinsmithing** *noun*

tinsnips *noun* a pair of hand-held shears used to cut sheet metal.

tint • *noun* **1** a shade, colour, or hue. **2** a faint colour spread over the surface of something to give a specified tone to a different colour. **3** a semi-permanent hair dye. • *verb* **1** apply a tint to (hair, paint, a picture, etc.); colour. **2** give (glass) a darker tone or colour in order to decrease the strength of light passing through.

tiny *adjective* (**tinier, tiniest**) very small; minuscule.

tip[1] • *noun* **1** an extremity or end, esp. of a small or tapering thing. **2** a small piece or part attached to or over the end of something. **3** (usu. in *plural*) a leaf bud of tea. • *verb* (**tips, tipped, tipping**) **1** provide or adorn with a tip. **2** colour or mark the tip of. PHRASES **on the tip of one's tongue** about to be remembered. **the tip of the iceberg** a small evident part of something much larger or more significant.

tip[2] • *verb* (**tips, tipped, tipping**) **1** (often foll. by *up*) (cause to) assume a slanting position. **2** (usu. foll. by *over*) overturn. **3 a** tilt (a container) in order to empty its contents. **b** (usu. foll. by *into*) pour out or spill (the contents of a container). **4** strike or touch lightly.

5 a *Hockey* deflect (a shot or the puck) toward the net. **b** *Baseball* (of a batter) barely hit (a pitch or the ball) foul or into the catcher's glove. **c** *Basketball* tap (a rebound) lightly toward the basket. • *noun* **1** a gentle push or slight tilt. **2** *Hockey* an act of deflecting the puck. **3** *Baseball* an act of tipping a pitch or ball. **4** *Basketball* **a** the act of tapping a ball towards the basket. **b** = TIPOFF 3. PHRASES **tip the scales 1** (also **tip the balance**) (of a circumstance or event) be the deciding factor; settle a matter that was previously undetermined: *the opponents are well matched, but Kurashiki's experience tips the scales in her favour*. **2** (foll. by *at*) weigh: *tips the scales at 215 lb*. **tip one's hand** unintentionally reveal one's intentions. **tip one's hat** (or **cap**) **1** raise or touch one's hat or cap in greeting or acknowledgement. **2** (usu. foll. by *to*) acknowledge or thank. **tip off** *Basketball* (of two teams) begin a game with a jump ball.

tip³ • *noun* **1** a small sum of money given in appreciation for a service given. **2** a useful suggestion or piece of advice. **3** a piece of private or special information, esp. regarding an investment or bet. • *verb* (**tips, tipped, tipping**) give a small sum of money to (a person) in appreciation for a service given. PHRASES **tip off** *informal* give advance warning or confidential information, esp. discreetly or covertly.

tipi *noun* (*plural* **tipis**) = TEEPEE. [Say TEE pee]

tip-in *noun* (*plural* **tip-ins**) *Hockey & Basketball* a shot that is tipped in.

tipoff *noun* **1** a warning or piece of information etc. given discreetly or confidentially. **2** something that serves as a warning; a sign or indication. **3** *Basketball* a jump ball at the start of a game.

tipper *noun* a person who leaves a specified sort of tip as a reward for services received: *he's a big tipper*.

tippet *noun* *Fishing* a length of twisted nylon or hair to which a hook is attached.

tipple • *verb* (**tipples, tippled, tippling**) **1** drink liquor habitually. **2** drink (liquor) repeatedly in small amounts. • *noun informal* an alcoholic drink. ▶ **tippler** *noun*

tippy *adjective* (**tippier, tippiest**) *informal* unstable; liable to tip over.

tippytoe *noun, verb, adjective, & adverb informal* = TIPTOE.

tipsheet *noun* a publication offering readers information, advice, and predictions, esp. on wagering or the stock market.

tipster *noun* a person who provides tips or confidential information, esp. about betting at horse races.

tipsy *adjective* (**tipsier, tipsiest**) **1** slightly drunk. **2** caused by or showing intoxication: *a tipsy grin*. **3** = TIPPY.

tiptoe • *noun* the tips of the toes. • *verb* (**tiptoes, tiptoed, tiptoeing**) **1** walk gently with the heels raised and one's weight supported by the toes and balls of the feet. **2** (usu. foll. by *around*) cautiously avoid. • *adjective* **1** characterized by standing or walking on tiptoe. **2** extremely cautious or careful. • *adverb* (also **on tiptoe**) (stand etc.) on the toes and balls of the feet with the heels raised.

tip-top *adjective* excellent.

tip-up • *noun* (*plural* **tip-ups**) (in ice fishing) a rod or arm that supports the line and tilts up when a fish has been hooked. • *adjective* that may be tipped or folded up: *tip-up seats*.

tirade *noun* a long vehement rant or outburst, esp. in denunciation of a particular thing: *launched into a tirade about cars running red lights*. [Say TIE raid]

tiramisù *noun* an Italian dessert consisting of layers of sponge cake or biscuit soaked in coffee and brandy or liqueur, filled with mascarpone cheese and topped with cocoa powder. [Say teera mee SOO or teera MEE soo]

tire¹ *verb* (**tires, tired, tiring**) **1** make or become weak or exhausted through exertion. **2** (usu. foll. by *of*) **a** (in *passive*) exhaust the patience or interest of: *I am tired of their excuses*. **b** have one's interest or patience exhausted by.

tire² *noun* a rubber covering placed around each of the wheels of a vehicle to give a soft contact with the road.

tired *adjective* **1** (often foll. by *out*) weak, exhausted, or fatigued from exercise or exertion. **2** (of an idea etc.) overused; trite. **3** (of vegetables, flowers, etc.) limp, no longer fresh. ▶ **tiredly** *adverb* **tiredness** *noun*

tireless *adjective* showing or characterized by inexhaustible energy. ▶ **tirelessly** *adverb*

tiresome *adjective* **1** wearisome, tedious. **2** annoying. ▶ **tiresomely** *adverb*

tiring *adjective* making one feel the need to sleep or rest: *it had been a long tiring day*.

'tis *archaic* it is.

tissue *noun* **1** the material of which an animal or plant body, or any of its parts or organs, is composed, consisting of an aggregation of specialized cells. **2 a** (also **facial tissue**) a disposable piece of thin soft absorbent paper for blowing one's nose, drying one's eyes, etc. **b** (also **toilet tissue**) = TOILET PAPER. **3** (also **tissue paper**) thin translucent paper, often coloured, used esp. for wrapping fragile articles or gifts. **4** (foll. by *of*) an intricate mass, series, or network of things: *a tissue of lies*. **5** any of various rich or fine materials of a delicate or gauzy texture.

tit *noun* **1** a small songbird that searches acrobatically in trees for insects. **2** *informal* a nipple; a teat. **3** *coarse slang* a woman's breast.

Titan *noun* **1** (usu. **titan**) a person or organization of very great power, importance, or strength: *this playoff matchup is being hyped as a clash of the titans*. **2** *Greek Myth* a member of a family of early gigantic gods, the offspring of Heaven and Earth. [Say TITE un]

titanic *adjective* of exceptional strength, size, or power: *a titanic change in Canadian business practice*. [Say tie TAN ick]

titanium *noun* a grey metallic element occurring in many clays etc., and used to make strong light alloys that are resistant to corrosion. [Say tie TAINY um]

titanium dioxide *noun* (also **titanium oxide**) a naturally occurring inert compound of titanium and oxygen, used esp. as a white pigment in the production of paints and plastics.

tit-for-tat *noun* a situation in which a blow, injury, insult, etc. is given in retaliation for one received.

tithe • *noun* **1** *hist.* one-tenth of the annual produce of agriculture, formerly taken as a tax for the support of the Church and clergy. **2 a** a tenth of an individual's income, pledged or donated to a church. **b** any tax or donation, usu. of one-tenth of a person's income. • *verb* (**tithes, tithed, tithing**) **1** pay one-tenth of (one's earnings etc.), esp. towards the support of a church and clergy. **2** impose the payment of a tithe on (a person). ▶ **tithing** *noun* [Rhymes with WRITHE]

titillate *verb* (**titillates, titillated, titillating**) excite or delight a person, esp. with pictures, stories, etc. of a sexual nature: *titillated viewers with steamy scenes of lambada dancers* ◊ *titillating Hollywood gossip* ◊ *although silk and tea were prized, English ladies were most titillated by the blue and white porcelain*. ▶ **titillating** *adjective* **titillation** *noun* [Say TITTLE ate, tittle AY sh'n]

title • *noun* **1** the name given to a book, work of art, piece of music, etc. **2** the formal heading of each section of a legal document, statute, book, etc. **3** a publication: *published 20 new titles*. **4** a caption or credit

in a movie etc. **5 a** a form of nomenclature indicating a person's status or rank, either appended to a person's name, e.g. *Dr.*, *Mrs.*, or used as a form of address or reference, e.g. *Your Majesty*. **b** a description indicating a person's role, job, or function, e.g. *Queen*, *Editor-in-Chief*, *Assistant Coach*. **6** *Sport* a championship. **7** *Law* **a** the right to the possession of land or property. **b** the evidence of such a right. **c** (foll. by *to*) a just or recognized claim. **8** (as an *adjective*) **a** designating a song featured on an album of the same name: *title track*. **b** designating the role or part in a play etc. from which the title of the piece is taken: *title role*. • verb (**titles**, **titled**, **titling**) give a title to.

titled *adjective* having a title of nobility or rank.

title page *noun* a page at the beginning of a book giving the title, author, and usu. the publisher.

titmouse *noun* (*plural* **titmice**) a small songbird that searches acrobatically in trees for insects.

titter • verb laugh or giggle, esp. nervously. • noun a restrained or nervous giggle.

tittle *noun* the smallest part of something; an insignificant amount: *knew every jot and tittle of his background*.

tittle-tattle *noun* petty gossip.

titular *adjective* **1** being what is specified in name or title only without having the attributes or exercising the functions implied by it: *titular ruler*. **2** from whom or which a title or name is taken: *the book's titular hero*. **3** of or relating to a title. [Say TIT yoo lur]

tizzy *noun* (*plural* **tizzies**) (also **tizz**; *plural* **tizzes**) *informal* a flustered, agitated, or hysterical state; a panic of excitement or nervousness.

TKO • noun (*plural* **TKOs**) *Boxing* a technical knockout. • verb (**TKO's**, **TKO'd**, **TKO'ing**) **1** *Boxing* defeat (an opponent) by technical knockout. **2** *informal* thwart (a person), esp. at the last minute to prevent completion of a task: *I got TKO'd by a subway delay*.

Tl *symbol* thallium.

TLC *abbreviation* *informal* tender loving care.

Tlingit • noun (*plural* **Tlingit** or **Tlingits**) **1** a member of an Aboriginal people living on the islands and coast of southeastern Alaska and northern BC. **2** the language of this people. • adjective of or relating to this people or their culture or language. [Say TLING git]

T-lymphocyte *noun* a type of white blood cell produced by the thymus gland and active in the body's immune response. [Say tee LIM foe site]

TM *abbreviation* **1** trademark. **2** transcendental meditation.

Tm *symbol* thulium.

TNT *abbreviation* trinitrotoluene, a high explosive that is relatively insensitive to shock.

SPELL CHECK
to, too, two   ABC ✓

The spelling is **too** in "too much" and "I like it too".
The number is spelled **two**.

---

to • preposition **1** introducing a noun: **a** expressing what is reached, approached, or touched. **b** expressing what is aimed at: often introducing the indirect object of a verb. **c** as far as; until. **d** to the extent of. **e** expressing what is followed. **f** expressing what is considered or affected. **g** expressing what is caused or produced. **h** expressing what is compared. **i** expressing what is increased. **j** expressing what is involved or composed as specified. **2** introducing the infinitive. **3** as a substitute for *to* + infinitive. • adverb **1** in the normal or required position or condition. **2** in a nearly closed position.

toad *noun* **1** any frog-like tailless amphibian that

breeds in water but lives chiefly on land, usu. having dry skin and walking rather than leaping. **2** a repulsive or loathsome person.

toadstool *noun* a non-technical name for the spore-bearing structure of various fungi, usu. poisonous or inedible, consisting of a round flat cap that surmounts a slender stalk or stipe.

toady • noun (*plural* **toadies**) a person who treats someone in a position of importance or authority with insincere kindness or respect in order to win their favour or approval: *he was a junior, to be sure, but not a toady who lets the boss win*. • verb (**toadies**, **toadied**, **toadying**) treat someone in a position of importance or authority with insincere kindness or respect in order to win their favour or approval: *if he invited the Americans, other Arab leaders would denounce him for toadying to the West*. ▶ **toadying** *adjective*

to and fro • adverb **1** backwards and forwards. **2** repeatedly between the same points. • noun (usu. **to-and-fro**) **1** movement to and fro. **2** vacillation, indecision, or debate on an issue. PHRASES **toing and froing** constant bustling movement or travelling back and forth or here and there.

toast • noun **1** sliced bread browned on both sides by exposure to dry heat. **2 a** a very brief speech or tribute offered in honour of a person, occasion, institution, etc., before drinking, esp. at a formal dinner or celebration. **b** a call by the speaker to other guests to endorse this tribute by raising their glasses before drinking. **3 a** a person, institution, etc. in whose honour a company is asked to drink. **b** (foll. by *of*) a person or thing that is extremely popular or celebrated among a specified group of people or in a specified place etc.: *the toast of the town*. **4** *informal* a person or thing that is or is about to be in severe difficulty: *if I don't get this done on time I'm toast*. • verb **1** cook or brown by exposure to a source of radiating heat. **2** (of bread etc.) become brown in this way. **3** warm (one's feet, oneself, etc.) at a fire etc. **4** drink to the health of or in honour of (a person or thing).

toaster *noun* a device used to toast bread etc..

toasty *adjective* (**toastier**, **toastiest**) **1** comfortably warm. **2** like or resembling toast.

tobacco *noun* (*plural* **tobaccos**) **1** a narcotic and addictive preparation of the dried leaves esp. of a plant of the nightshade family, which is smoked or chewed for pleasure, and used for ceremonial and religious purposes among some North American Aboriginal groups. **2** (also **tobacco plant**) the plant of the nightshade family producing these leaves.

Tobacco Nation *noun* = PETUN.

tobacconist *noun* a person who deals in tobacco, esp. the owner of a store selling tobacco, pipes, cigars, cigarettes, and other assorted items. [Say tuh BACKA nist]

-to-be *adjective* (usu. in *combination*) that will soon become what is specified; future: *bride-to-be*.

toboggan • noun a long narrow sled without runners, bent or curled upwards at the front, which may be drawn by a rope over compacted snow or ice or used to coast down hills. • verb coast down hills or ride on a toboggan. ▶ **tobogganing** *noun*

toboggan slide *noun* Cdn **1** = SLIDE *noun* 7. **2** *informal* a rapid and usu. irreversible decline: *one might assume that Canada is on a toboggan slide of discord, hell-bent to balkanization province by province*.

toccata *noun* (*plural* **toccatas**) a brisk musical composition for a keyboard instrument, having the air of an improvisation and designed to demonstrate the performer's touch and technique. [Say tuh CATTA]

tock • noun a short, hollow sound, deeper and more resonant than a tick. • verb make this sound.

tocopherol *noun* any of several closely related alcohols occurring in plant oils, wheat germ, egg yolk, and leafy vegetables, and which are antioxidants essential in the diets of animals and humans. *Also called* VITAMIN E. [Say toe COFFER awl]

today • *adverb* **1** on or in the course of this present day. **2** nowadays, in modern times. • *noun* **1** this present day. **2** modern times. PHRASES **a week today** one week from today.

toddle *verb* (**toddles, toddled, toddling**) **1** walk with short unsteady steps like those of a small child. **2** *informal* **a** take a casual or leisurely walk. **b** (usu. foll. by *off, along*) depart.

toddler *noun* a child who has just recently learned to walk, usu. between the ages of a year and a half and three years. ▶ **toddlerhood** *noun*

toddy *noun* (*plural* **toddies**) an alcoholic drink made with esp. rum or whisky and hot water, usu. flavoured with lemon juice and sweetened with sugar or honey.

to-do *noun* (*plural* **to-dos**) a commotion or fuss.

to-do list *noun* a list of chores, projects, assignments, etc. that one must or hopes to complete.

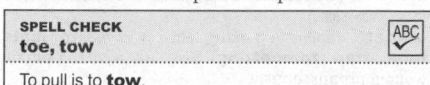

SPELL CHECK
toe, tow
To pull is to **tow**.

toe • *noun* **1** any of the five terminal projections of the foot. **2** the corresponding part of an animal. **3** the part of an item of footwear that covers the toes. **4** *Figure Skating* **a** = TOE PICK. **b** = TOE LOOP. **5** a part resembling a toe or the toes in shape or position, esp. the lower end, tip, or point of something. • *verb* (**toes, toed, toeing**) touch with one's toe. PHRASES **make a person's toes curl** excite or thrill a person. **on one's toes** alert, ready. **step** (or **tread**) **on a person's toes** offend or threaten a person by encroaching upon their privileges or responsibilities, esp. unintentionally. **toe the line** conform to a general policy or principle, esp. unwillingly or under pressure. **toe to toe 1** directly in front of and facing (another or each other). **2** (of adversaries, rivals, opponents, etc.) in competition or conflict.

toecap *noun* the reinforced outer covering of the toe of a boot or shoe.

toed *adjective* **1** (of an animal) having toes of a specified number or kind. **2** (of a shoe, boot, etc.) having a toe of a specified kind: *steel-toed boots*.

toehold *noun* **1** a small foothold. **2** a favourable position from which a minor advantage may be gained or influence or support increased minimally.

toe loop *noun Figure Skating* a loop jump in which the toe of the free skate is dug into the ice to assist the takeoff from the opposite foot.

toenail *noun* the nail at the tip of each toe.

toe pick *noun* a jagged toothed edge on the front tip of a skate blade, used to dig into the ice when completing various technical manoeuvres, esp. jumps.

toffee *noun* a hard and often brittle candy that softens in the mouth, made by boiling sugar and butter.

tofu *noun* a pale curd of varying consistency made from soybean milk and used as a source of protein esp. in vegetarian recipes and Asian cuisine. [Say TOE foo]

togged *adjective informal* (foll. by *out, up*) dressed up, esp. elaborately or stylishly.

togs *plural noun informal* clothes, esp. several articles of clothing constituting a single outfit: *ski togs*.

toga *noun* (*plural* **togas**) *Roman History* a loose flowing outer garment made of a single piece of cloth and covering the whole body apart from the right arm. [Say TOE guh]

together • *adverb* **1** in company. **2** at the same time. **3** collectively. **4** so as to form a connected, united, or coherent whole. **5** *informal* **a** into an organized state. **b** into a rational state of mind. • *adjective informal* composed, self-assured, well-organized; free of emotional difficulties or inhibitions. PHRASES **together with** as well as; in addition to.

togetherness *noun* **1** a feeling of comfort proceeding from a close and harmonious association with others. **2** the condition of being together.

toggle • *noun* **1** a short decorative crosspiece sewn on one side of a garment, fastened by being pushed through a loop or hole on the other side. **2** *Computing* a key or command that is always operated in the same way but has opposite effects on successive occasions. **3** a pin or other crosspiece put through the eye of a rope, a link of a chain, etc., to keep it in place. • *verb* (**toggles, toggled, toggling**) **1** *Computing* **a** (often foll. by *between*) switch from one function or state of operation to another by using a toggle. **b** (usu. foll. by *on* or *off*) activate or deactivate (a feature or function etc.) using a toggle. **2** provide or fasten with a toggle.

toggle switch *noun* (*plural* **toggle switches**) **1** an electric switch operated by means of a short projecting lever that is moved usu. up and down. **2** *Computing* = TOGGLE *noun* 2.

toil • *verb* **1** work laboriously or incessantly. **2** make slow painful progress: *toiled along the path*. • *noun* prolonged or intensive labour. ▶ **toiler** *noun*

toilet *noun* **1 a** a bathroom fixture for defecation and urination, consisting of a large basin usu. with a hinged lid and seat and a flushing mechanism. **b** a room containing such a fixture. **2** (*also* **toilette**) the process of washing, dressing, arranging one's hair, etc.: *make one's toilet*. PHRASES **go into** (or **down**) **the toilet** *informal* **1** go into sharp decline, esp. in quality. **2** become irrecoverably lost. [For TOILETTE say way LET]

toilet paper *noun* (*also* **toilet tissue**) soft absorbent paper used for cleaning oneself after defecating or urinating.

toiletry *noun* (*plural* **toiletries**) (usu. in *plural*) any of various articles or cosmetics used in washing and dressing, such as soap, shampoo, deodorant, etc.

toilet train *verb* teach (a young child) to use the toilet.

toilet training *noun* the process of teaching a young child to use the toilet.

toke *slang* • *noun* **1** a drag on a cigarette containing a narcotic substance, esp. marijuana. **2** a marijuana cigarette. • *verb* (**tokes, toked, toking**) (often foll. by *up*) smoke or take a drag on a marijuana cigarette.

token • *noun* **1 a** a thing used to represent or symbolize something abstract or immaterial: *wore black as a token of mourning for her people suffering the humiliation of foreign rule*. **b** a thing given as an expression of affection, or to be kept as a memento. **2** a coin-like object, used as a limited medium of exchange, such as on public transit, in a casino, etc. **3** a person chosen as a nominal representative of an under-represented group, usu. in order to pre-empt charges of discrimination: *I felt like a token at work, somebody who was needed for what he is instead of what he knows*. • *adjective* **1** chosen out of tokenism as a nominal representative of a minority group: *the token woman*. **2** done or made as a matter of form; nominal: *token effort*. **3** conducted briefly to demonstrate strength of feeling: *token resistance*. **4** serving to acknowledge a principle only: *a token payment*. PHRASES **by the same token 1** in the same way; similarly. **2** moreover. **in token of** as a symbol of.

tokenism *noun* the principle or practice of granting minimum concessions, esp. to minority or under-

represented groups, as a token gesture to appease public pressure, comply with legal requirements, etc.: *the public service is staffed by skilled, competent women who deserve to be rewarded for their excellence, not out of tokenism*. ▶ **tokenistic** *adjective*

told *past and past participle of* TELL[1].

tolerable *adjective* **1** able to be endured; bearable. **2** reasonably good. ▶ **tolerably** *adverb* [Say TOLLER a bull]

tolerance *noun* **1** a willingness or ability to accept or allow something without protest or irritation, esp. the existence of opinions and behaviour that one does not necessarily agree with: *tolerance of corruption* ◊ *religious tolerance*. **2** the ability of an organism to endure and withstand subjection to something, e.g. a transplant or particular environmental condition, without adverse reaction: *the camel shows great tolerance to dehydration* ◊ *increase a child's tolerance to bee stings* ◊ *species are grouped according to pollution tolerance*. **3** a decrease in the body's response to a drug after prolonged use. [Say TOLLER ince]

tolerant *adjective* **1** tending to adopt a liberal attitude towards the beliefs and opinions of others. **2** (usu. foll. by *of*) patient, forgiving; willing to allow or put up with. **3** able to withstand the action of a drug, toxin, etc. **4** able to withstand a (usu. specified) environmental condition: *drought-tolerant plants*. ▶ **tolerantly** *adverb* [Say TOLLER unt]

tolerate *verb* (**tolerates**, **tolerated**, **tolerating**) **1** allow the existence, practice, or occurrence of. **2** endure or allow with patience, leniency, or understanding. **3** sustain or endure (pain, suffering, etc.). **4** be capable of continued subjection to (a drug, radiation, etc.) without harm. [Say TOLLER ate]

toleration *noun* **1** sanction for the practice of forms of religion at variance with those officially accepted or recognized by a country or state. **2** = TOLERANCE. [Say toller AY sh'n]

toll[1] *noun* **1** a sum of money charged for permission to travel along a road or highway etc. (also as an *adjective*: *toll bridge*). **2** the loss or damage caused by a disaster etc.: *death toll*. **3** a charge for a long-distance telephone call. **PHRASES** **take its toll** cause or be accompanied by loss, damage, injury, etc.

toll[2] *verb* **1** ring with a slow succession of uniform strokes. **2** announce or mark (the time, a death etc.) by this kind of bell-ringing. • *noun* the action or sound of a bell as it tolls or is struck.

toll booth *noun* a booth at a bridge or highway etc. where tolls are collected.

toll-free • *adjective* (esp. of a telephone call, number, or service) that can be made, used, or accessed without charge. • *adverb* without charge.

tollgate • *noun* **1** a gate preventing passage until a toll is paid. **2** *Cdn* a barrier imposed illegally on business or trade etc. pending payment of a bribe or tribute: *critics charged that the $750 fee is nothing more than a political tollgate*. • *verb* (**tollgates**, **tollgated**, **tollgating**) *Cdn* block or hinder (a business contract etc.) pending payment of a bribe or tribute: *was accused of tollgating contracts and orders*.

tollgating *noun* *Cdn* the illegal practice of paying or extorting a bribe or tribute for the right to do business with or within a province, country, etc.

toluene *noun* (also **toluol**) a colourless liquid hydrocarbon obtained from coal tar and petroleum, and used esp. as a solvent as well as in the manufacture of explosives. [Say TOL yoo een, TOL yoo awl]

tom *noun* **1** a tomcat. **2** a male of various other animals, such as a turkey. **3** = TOM-TOM 2.

tomahawk *noun* a hatchet-like tool or weapon with a handle and a sharp stone or iron cutting head, formerly used by some North American Indians.

tomatillo *noun* (*plural* **tomatillos**) esp. *US* **1** a purplish edible fruit used esp. for sauces and preserves. **2** a Mexican plant that bears this. [Say tomma TILLO]

tomato *noun* (*plural* **tomatoes**) **1** a glossy, usu. bright red and pulpy edible fruit, eaten raw or cooked as a vegetable. **2** the plant that bears this fruit. [Say tuh MAY toe or tuh MAT oh]

tomato clam cocktail *noun* a drink consisting of tomato juice mixed with clam juice.

tomatoey *adjective* tasting of tomatoes: *a very tomatoey barbecue sauce*. [Say tuh MAY toe ee or tuh MAT oh ee]

tomb *noun* **1** a large esp. underground vault for the burial of the dead. **2** an excavation in the earth etc. to receive a corpse. **3** a monument erected over a person's grave. **4** (**the tomb**) *literary* death. [Say TOOM]

tomboy *noun* a girl whose behaviour, pastimes, and style of dress are considered typical of those of a young boy. ▶ **tomboyish** *adjective*

tombstone *noun* a usu. engraved stone slab placed upright or laid flat over a person's grave as a memorial. [Say TOOM stone]

tomcat • *noun* a male cat. • *verb* (**tomcats**, **tomcatted**, **tomcatting**) *slang* (of a man) pursue women promiscuously.

Tom, Dick, and Harry *noun* (usu. preceded by *any*, *every*) usu. *derogatory* ordinary people taken at random: *every Tom, Dick, and Harry was there!*

tome *noun* **1** a large, heavy, learned book or volume of a work. **2** *informal* or *jocular* a book, esp. one that is excessively long or dull. [Rhymes with *HOME*]

tomfoolery *noun* foolish or silly behaviour.

tommycod *noun* (*plural* **tommycod**) (also **tomcod**) a small edible greenish-brown North American fish of the cod family, popular with anglers.

tomography *noun* any of various techniques which provide images of successive plane sections of the human body or other solid objects using X-rays or ultrasound, now usu. processed by computer to give a three-dimensional image. [Say tuh MOGRA fee]

tomorrow • *noun* **1** the day after today. **2** the future, esp. the near future. • *adverb* **1** on the day after today. **2** at some future time. **PHRASES** **like** (or **as if**) **there is no tomorrow** with no regard for the future; recklessly.

tom-tom *noun* **1** a simple hand-beaten drum associated with North American Aboriginal, African, or Eastern cultures. **2** a small to medium-sized drum used esp. as part of a set of drums and cymbals in popular music and jazz.

SPELL CHECK
ton, tonne

Ton is used for various units of weight or volume, most commonly for a unit of 2,000 pounds. A **metric ton** is equivalent to 1,000 kg, and is also referred to as a **tonne**.

---

ton • *noun* **1** (also **short ton**) a unit of weight equal to 2,000 lb. avoirdupois (907.19 kg). **2** (also **long ton**) *Brit.* a unit of weight equal to 2,240 lb. avoirdupois (1016 kg). **3** = METRIC TON. **4 a** (also **displacement ton**) a unit of measurement of a ship's weight or volume in terms of its displacement of water, equal to 2,240 lb. (1016 kg) or 35 cu. ft. (0.99 cubic metres). **b** (also **freight ton**) a unit of weight or volume of cargo, equal to a metric ton (1 000 kg) or 40 cu. ft. **5 a** (also **gross ton**) a unit of gross internal capacity, equal to 100 cu. ft. (2.83 cubic metres). **b** (also **net** or **register ton**) an equivalent unit of net internal capacity. **6** a measure of capacity

for various materials, esp. 40 cu. ft. of timber. **7** (usu. in *plural*) *informal* a large number or amount: *tons of things to do ◊ has a ton of stuff to learn.* • *adverb* (usu. in *plural*) *informal* much, a lot: *am feeling tons better.* PHRASES **weigh a ton** *informal* be very heavy.

tonal *adjective* **1** of or relating to tone or tonality. **2** designating or pertaining to music written in a definite key or keys. [Say TONE ul]

tonality *noun* (*plural* **tonalities**) **1** *Music* **a** the relationship between the tones of a musical scale. **b** the observance of a single tonic key as the basis of a composition. **2** the colour scheme of a picture. [Say toe NALA tee]

tone • *noun* **1** a musical or vocal sound, esp. with reference to its pitch, quality, and strength. **2** (often in *plural*) modulation of the voice expressing a particular feeling or mood: *a cheerful tone ◊ suspicious tones.* **3** a manner of expression in writing. **4** *Music* an interval of a major second, e.g. C–D or do–re. **5 a** the general effect of colour or of light and shade in a photograph, painting, etc. **b** the tint or shade of a colour. **6 a** the general spirit or character of something. **b** an attitude or sentiment expressed in a letter, speech, etc. **7** (of the body) the state of being firm and strong. **8** a state of good or specified health or quality. • *verb* (**tones, toned, toning**) **1** give the desired tone to. **2** modify the tone of. **3** strengthen, firm: *tone the skin.* PHRASES **tone down 1** make or become softer in tone of sound or colour. **2** make less strong or extreme. **tone up 1** make or become stronger in tone of sound or colour. **2** strengthen (muscles etc.).

tone-deaf *adjective* unable to perceive differences of musical pitch accurately. ▶ **tone-deafness** *noun*

tone poem *noun* an extended orchestral composition, usu. in one movement and freer in form than a symphony, on a descriptive theme.

toner *noun* **1** a powder used in photocopiers, laser printers, etc. **2** an astringent applied to the face to control oiliness and tighten pores.

Tongan • *adjective* of or relating to the island group of Tonga in the South Pacific or its people or language. • *noun* **1** a native or national of Tonga. **2** the Polynesian language spoken in Tonga. [Say TONG gun]

tongs *plural noun* (also **pair of tongs** *singular*) an instrument with two hinged arms for grasping etc.

tongue *noun* **1** the fleshy muscular organ in the mouth used in tasting, licking, and swallowing, and (in humans) for speech. **2** the tongue of an ox etc. as food. **3** the faculty of or a tendency in speech: *a sharp tongue.* **4** a particular language. **5** a thing like a tongue in shape or position, esp.: **a** a long low promontory. **b** a strip of leather etc., attached at one end only, under the laces in a shoe. **c** the clapper of a bell. **d** the pin of a buckle. **e** the projecting strip on a wooden etc. board fitting into the groove of another. **f** a vibrating slip in the reed of some musical instruments. **g** a jet of flame. PHRASES **find** (or **lose**) **one's tongue** be able (or unable) to express oneself after a shock etc. **the gift of tongues** the power of speaking in unknown languages, regarded as one of the gifts of the Holy Spirit. **give tongue** speak one's thoughts. **with one's tongue hanging out** eagerly or expectantly. **with tongue in cheek** insincerely or ironically.

tongue-and-groove *noun* (usu. as an *adjective*) panelling etc. with a projecting strip down one side and a groove down the other.

tongued *adjective* **1** having a specified kind of tongue: *the blue-tongued lizard.* **2** (in carpentry) constructed using or fitted with a tongue. **3** (of a musical note) played by tonguing.

tongue depressor *noun* a flat wooden stick for pressing down the tongue, esp. to allow examination of the mouth or throat.

tongue-in-cheek • *adjective* ironic; slyly humorous. • *adverb* insincerely or ironically.

tongue-lashing *noun* a severe scolding or reprimand.

tongue-tied *adjective* too shy or embarrassed to speak.

tongue trooper *noun* *Cdn slang* (in Quebec) a member of the language police.

tongue twister *noun* a sequence of words difficult to pronounce quickly and correctly.

tonguing *noun* the technique of playing a wind instrument using the tongue to articulate notes.

tonic • *noun* **1** an invigorating medicine. **2** anything serving to invigorate: *the whole trip was a tonic, exactly what I needed to fortify me for whatever lay ahead.* **3** = TONIC WATER. **4** *Music* the first degree of a scale, forming the keynote of a piece (see KEYNOTE 3). • *adjective* **1** serving as a tonic; invigorating: *enjoyed the superb golf and the tonic sun.* **2** *Music* denoting the first degree of a scale.

tonic sol-fa *noun* a system of notation used esp. in teaching singing, with do as the keynote of all major keys and la as the keynote of all minor keys.

tonic water *noun* a carbonated drink containing quinine, often used as a mix with gin.

tonight • *noun* the evening or night of the present day. • *adverb* on the present or coming evening or night.

tonnage *noun* **1** a ship's internal cubic capacity or freight-carrying capacity measured in tons. **2** the total carrying capacity esp. of a country's mercantile marine. **3** a charge per ton on freight or cargo. [Say TUN idge]

WRITING TIP
tonne
Tonne can only refer to 1,000 kilograms, or a *metric ton*. It is therefore redundant to say "metric tonne".

tonne *noun* = METRIC TON. [Say TUN]

tonsil *noun* either of two small masses of lymphoid tissue on each side of the root of the tongue.

tonsillectomy *noun* (*plural* **tonsillectomies**) the surgical removal of the tonsils. [Say tonsil ECKTA me]

tonsillitis *noun* tonsil inflammation. [Say tonsil ITE us]

tonsure • *noun* **1** the shaving of the crown of the head or the entire head, esp. of a monk. **2** a bare patch made in this way. • *verb* (**tonsures, tonsured, tonsuring**) give a tonsure to. ▶ **tonsured** *adjective* [Say TAWN sure]

tony *adjective* (**tonier, toniest**) *informal* stylish, fashionable, high-class: *a tony neighbourhood.*

SPELL CHECK
too, to, two
The spelling is **to** in "go to bed", "come to" (i.e. regain consciousness), and before a verb ("to dream"). The number is spelled **two**.

too *adverb* **1** to a greater extent than is desirable, permissible, or possible for a specified or understood purpose: *too large.* **2** in addition, also: *them too?* **3** *informal* very; extremely: *you're too kind.* **4** moreover: *we must consider, too, the time of year.* PHRASES **none too 1** rather less than: *feeling none too good.* **2** barely.

toodle-oo *interjection* *informal* goodbye.

took *past of* TAKE.

SPELL CHECK
tool, tulle
A soft fine net for veils and tutus is **tulle**.

tool • *noun* **1 a** any device or implement used to carry out mechanical functions whether manually or by a

machine. **b** an item of software for interactive applications. **2** a thing used in an occupation or pursuit: *reference tools*. **3** a person used as a mere instrument by another. • *verb* **1** work or shape (stone, wood, etc.) with a tool. **2** impress a design on (leather). **3** (foll. by *along, around*, etc.) *slang* drive or ride, esp. in a casual or leisurely manner. **4** (often foll. by *up*) equip with tools.

toolbar *noun* a row of computer icons which can be clicked on to execute frequently used commands.

tool box *noun* (*plural* **tool boxes**) **1** (also **tool chest**) a box or container for keeping tools in. **2 a** a set of software tools. **b** the set of programs or functions accessible from a single menu.

tooling *noun* **1** the process of dressing stone or wood with a chisel etc. **2** the impressing of ornamental designs on leather with heated tools. **3** these designs.

tool kit *noun* **1** a set of tools. **2** a set of software tools, usu. designed for a specific application. **3** a repertoire of techniques used to solve problems, make decisions, etc.

tool shed *noun* a shed in which tools etc. are stored.

toon *noun informal* **1** = CARTOON *noun* 1, 2, 3. **2** a cartoon character.

toonie *noun Cdn informal* the Canadian two-dollar coin.

toot • *noun* **1** a short sharp sound as made by a horn. **2** *slang* cocaine or a snort of cocaine. **3** *slang* a drinking spree. • *verb* **1** sound (a horn etc.) with a short sharp sound. **2** give out such a sound. **3** *slang* break wind. □ PHRASES **toot one's own horn** praise oneself; boast.

tooth *noun* (*plural* **teeth**) **1** each of a set of hard bony enamel-coated structures in the jaws of most vertebrates, used for biting and chewing. **2** a toothlike part or projection, e.g. the cog of a gearwheel, the point of a saw or comb, etc. **3** (in *plural*) force or effectiveness: *the penalties give the contract teeth*. □ PHRASES **armed to the teeth** completely and elaborately armed or equipped. **fight tooth and nail** fight very fiercely. **get one's teeth into** devote oneself seriously to. **in the teeth of 1** in spite of (opposition or difficulty etc.). **2** contrary to (instructions etc.).

toothache *noun* a (usu. prolonged) pain in a tooth.

toothbrush *noun* (*plural* **toothbrushes**) a small brush with a long narrow handle, for cleaning the teeth.

toothed *adjective* **1** having teeth. **2** having the type of teeth mentioned: *a gap-toothed smile*.

toothed whale *noun* any of a number of whales that have teeth rather than baleen plates, including sperm whales, killer whales, dolphins, and porpoises.

tooth fairy *noun* (*plural* **tooth fairies**) (in folk legend) a fairy who leaves a small amount of money for a child in exchange for a baby tooth placed under the child's pillow at night.

toothless *adjective* **1** having no teeth. **2** lacking genuine force or effectiveness: *laws that are well-intentioned but toothless*.

toothlike *adjective* resembling or like a tooth.

toothpaste *noun* a usu. minty-tasting paste for cleaning the teeth, applied with a toothbrush.

toothpick *noun* a small pointed stick for removing bits of food stuck between the teeth.

toothsome *adjective* **1** (of food) delicious, appetizing. **2** alluring; sexy.

toothy *adjective* (**toothier, toothiest**) having or showing large, numerous, or prominent teeth.

tootle *verb* (**tootles, tootled, tootling**) **1** *informal* move casually or aimlessly. **2** toot gently or repeatedly. **3** play (a wind instrument).

toots *noun slang* used as a very familiar form of address, esp. to a woman or girl. [With OO as in *FOOT*]

tootsie *noun* (*plural* **tootsies**) **1** (usu. in *plural*) *informal*

usu. *jocular* a foot; a toe. **2** *slang* **a** a woman; a female lover. **b** a prostitute. [Rhymes with *FOOTSIE*]

top[1] • *noun* **1** the highest point or part. **2** the highest rank or place: *at the top of her profession*. **3** the upper surface of a thing. **4** the upper part of a thing, esp.: **a** a garment covering the upper part of the body. **b** the upper part of a shoe or boot. **c** the stopper of a bottle. **d** the lid of a jar, pot, or other container. **e** the folding roof of a car, baby carriage, etc. **5** the utmost degree; height: *shouted at the top of his voice*. **6** *Baseball* the first half of an inning, in which the visiting team bats. **7** the beginning (of a piece of music, scene in a play, etc.): *start again from the top*. **8** (in *plural*) *informal* a person or thing of the best quality: *he's tops at golf*. **9** (esp. in *plural*) the leaves etc. of a plant grown esp. for its root: *turnip tops*. **10** = TOPSPIN. • *adjective* **1** highest in position. **2** highest in degree, importance, or skill. • *verb* (**tops, topped, topping**) **1** provide with a top, cap, etc. **2** remove the top of (a tree, plant, fruit, etc.). **3 a** be higher or better than; surpass. **b** be at the top of: *topped the list*. **4** reach the top of (a hill etc.). □ PHRASES **at the top** in the highest rank of a profession etc. (**at**) **tops** at the most. **come to the top** win distinction. **from top to toe** from head to foot; completely. **on top 1** in a superior position; above. **2** on the upper part of the head. **on top of 1** fully in command of. **2** in close proximity to. **3** in addition to. **on top of the world** *informal* exuberant. **over the top 1** *esp. hist.* over the parapet of a trench (and into battle); into action. **2** to excess, beyond reasonable limits: *that joke was over the top*. **top off 1** put an end or the finishing touch to (a thing). **2** = TOP UP 1b. **top out 1** reach a peak; stop rising: *prices topped out at around $200*. **2** put the highest stone on (a building). **top up 1 a** add to; bring up to a certain level: *topped up EI benefits*. **b** fill up (a glass or other partly full container). **2** top up something for (a person): *your glass is empty — may I top you up?*

top[2] *noun* a toy spinning on a point when set in motion.

Top 40 *noun* (also **Top Forty**) the forty most popular songs in the music charts at a given time.

topaz *noun* (*plural* **topazes**) a transparent or translucent aluminum silicate mineral, usu. yellow, used as a gem. [Say TOE paz]

top banana *noun* (*plural* **top bananas**) *slang* **1** a leader of an organization etc. **2** a comedian topping the bill.

top brass *noun informal* persons in authority or of high (esp. military) rank: *the government cannot afford updated equipment and new military hardware but still has money for fancy office furniture for the top brass*.

top-class *adjective* of the best quality or highest order.

topcoat *noun* **1** an overcoat. **2** an outer coat of paint, nail polish, etc.

top dog *noun informal* a victor or master.

top dollar *noun* a high or the highest price.

top-down *adjective* **1** proceeding from general to particular, or from the top downwards. **2** hierarchical.

top drawer • *noun* **1** the uppermost drawer in a chest etc. **2** *informal* high social position or origin. • *adjective* (**top-drawer**) *informal* of the highest quality or esp. social level.

top-dress *verb* (**top-dresses, top-dressed, top-dressing**) apply (manure or fertilizer) to the top of the earth around a plant or plants.

top dressing *noun* **1** the application of manure or fertilizer to the top of the earth around a plant or plants. **2** manure so applied.

top-end *adjective* of, relating to, or associated with the most expensive section of the market.

top-flight *adjective* in the highest rank of achievement.

top gun *noun informal* **1** an ace fighter pilot. **2** an important person, company, etc.

top hat *noun* a man's tall hat, worn esp. on formal occasions. ▶ **top-hatted** *adjective*

top-heavy *adjective* **1** disproportionately heavy at the top so as to be in danger of toppling. **2 a** (of an organization etc.) having a disproportionately large number of people in senior administrative positions. **b** (of a company) having had its capital overestimated. **3** *informal* (of a woman) having a disproportionately large bust.

topiary • *adjective* concerned with or formed by clipping shrubs, trees, etc. into ornamental or animal forms. • *noun* (*plural* **topiaries**) **1** topiary art. **2** a piece or example of topiary work. [Say TOPE ee airy]

topic *noun* **1** a theme for a book, discourse, etc. **2** the subject of a conversation or argument.

topical *adjective* **1** of or pertaining to current affairs or a subject in the news etc. **2** relating to a particular subject; classified according to subject: *the book contains a topical bibliography.* **3** (of an ailment, medicine, etc.) affecting or applied externally to a part of the body. ▶ **topicality** *noun* **topically** *adverb*

topknot *noun* **1** a bun or tuft of hair worn on the crown of the head. **2** a tuft or crest growing on the head.

topless *adjective* **1** without or seeming to be without a top. **2 a** (of clothes) having no upper part. **b** (of a person) bare-breasted. **c** (of a place, esp. a beach) where women go topless. ▶ **toplessness** *noun*

top-level *adjective* of the highest level of importance, prestige, etc.

top-line *adjective* **1** of the highest quality. **2** (esp. of an entertainment act) considered worthy of top billing.

topmast *noun* the mast next above the lower mast on a sailing ship.

topmost *adjective* uppermost.

top-notch *adjective* *informal* first-rate.

topo (*plural* **topos**) • *noun* **1** topography. **2** a topographical map. • *adjective* topographical. [Say TOP oh]

top-of-the-line *adjective* the most expensive (and usu. highest quality) of a group of similar products.

topographical *adjective* **1** of or relating to the arrangement or accurate representation of the physical features of an area: *the topographical features of the river valley.* **2** (of a work of art or an artist) dealing with or depicting places (esp. towns), buildings, and natural prospects in a realistic and detailed manner. ▶ **topographic** *adjective* **topographically** *adverb* [Say toppa GRAPHIC]

topography *noun* (*plural* **topographies**) **1** a detailed description, representation on a map, etc., of the natural and artificial features of an area. **2** such features. [Say tuh POGRA fee]

topology *noun* (*plural* **topologies**) *Math* **1** the study of geometrical properties and spatial relations unaffected by the continuous change of shape or size of figures. **2** the way in which constituent parts are interrelated or arranged: *the topology you use in a computer system depends on the nature of the application.* [Say tuh POLLA jee]

topper *noun* **1** a thing that tops. **2** *informal* = TOP HAT. **3** a woman's short loose jacket or coat. **4** *Cdn* a short curtain, often ruffled or gathered, hung at the top of a window.

topping *noun* a garnish, sauce, etc. put on top of food.

topple *verb* (**topples**, **toppled**, **toppling**) **1** totter and fall (over), or cause to do so. **2** overthrow or be overthrown.

topsail *noun* **1** the rectangular sail, or each of two such sails, next above the lowest on a sailing ship. **2** a fore-and-aft sail above the gaff. [Say TOP sail or TOP sull]

top secret *adjective* of the highest secrecy.

top seed *noun* the top-ranked competitor or team in a tournament etc. ▶ **top-seeded** *adjective*

top shelf *Hockey informal* • *noun* the highest part of the net, just beneath the crossbar. • *adverb* at or into this part of the net.

topside • *noun* the side of a ship above the waterline. • *adverb* on or to the upper deck of a ship.

topsoil *noun* the surface layer of soil (*opp.* SUBSOIL).

topspin *noun* a fast forward spin imparted to a ball in tennis etc. by hitting it forward and upward.

topstitch *verb* (**topstitches**, **topstitched**, **topstitching**) make a row of neat, esp. decorative, stitches on the right side of (fabric). ▶ **topstitching** *noun*

topsy-turvy • *adverb* & *adjective* **1** upside down. **2** in utter confusion. • *noun* utter confusion.

toque *noun* **1** *Cdn* **a** a close-fitting knitted hat, often with a tassel or pompom on the crown. **b** a long knitted stocking cap. **2** a tall white hat with a full pouched crown, worn by chefs. [Sense 1 rhymes with *FLUKE*; sense 2 rhymes with *POKE*]

Torah *noun* the law of God as revealed to Moses and recorded in the first five books of the Hebrew scriptures (Genesis, Exodus, Leviticus, Numbers, and Deuteronomy). [Say TORE uh]

torch • *noun* (*plural* **torches**) **1 a** a piece of wood, cloth, etc., soaked in a flammable substance and lighted. **b** any similar lamp, e.g. an oil lamp on a pole. **2** used to refer to a valuable or important quality, principle, or cause, which needs to be protected or maintained: *mountain warlords carried the torch of Greek independence.* **3** a blowtorch. • *verb* (**torches**, **torched**, **torching**) *slang* set fire to, esp. as an act of arson. PHRASES **carry a torch for** suffer from unrequited love for. **put to the torch** destroy by burning.

torchbearer *noun* **1** a person who leads the way in an attempt to reform, inspire, etc.: *his success as a musical torchbearer of a new world order makes him one of the most performed living composers.* **2** a person who carries a usu. ceremonial torch.

torchlight • *noun* the light of a torch or torches. • *adjective* done or accompanied by torchlight. ▶ **torchlit** *adjective*

torch singer *noun* a person who sings torch songs.

torch song *noun* a melancholy or sentimental romantic song with a slow tempo.

tore *past of* TEAR[1].

torment • *noun* **1** severe physical or mental suffering. **2** a cause of this: *public speaking was a torment.* • *verb* **1** subject to torment. **2** tease or worry excessively. ▶ **tormentor** *noun*

torn • *verb* past participle of TEAR[1]. • *adjective* **1** that has been torn or violently pulled apart. **2** anxious because having to make a painful choice between two options.

tornado *noun* (*plural* **tornadoes**) a violent storm with very strong circular winds over a small area, often accompanied by a funnel-shaped cloud.

Torontonian *noun* a native or inhabitant of Toronto. [Say tuh ron TONY un]

torpedo • *noun* (*plural* **torpedoes**) **1 a** a self-propelled underwater missile, usu. cylindrical with a pointed or tapered nose, fired at a ship and exploding on impact. **b** (also **aerial torpedo**) a similar device dropped from an aircraft. **2** a sluggish bottom-dwelling marine ray that typically lives in shallow water and can produce an electric shock for the capture of prey and for defence. • *verb* (**torpedoes**, **torpedoed**, **torpedoing**)

1 destroy or attack with a torpedo. **2** make ineffective or inoperative: *saw a chance to torpedo that deal and replace it with another, larger one.* PHRASES **damn the torpedoes** *slang* let us proceed aggressively without fear of the danger or concern for consequences.

torpedo boat *noun* a small fast lightly armed warship for carrying or discharging torpedoes.

torpid *adjective* **1** mentally or physically inactive; lethargic: *he was praised for his efforts to awaken a torpid Soviet society.* **2** (of a part of the body etc.) numb. **3** (of a hibernating animal) dormant. ▶ **torpidity** *noun*

torpor *noun* a state of physical or mental inactivity; lethargy: *they veered between apathetic torpor and hysterical fanaticism.* [Say TORE pur]

torque • *noun* a twisting or rotating force, esp. in a mechanism. • *verb* (**torques, torqued, torquing**) **1** apply torque or a twisting force to. **2** (often foll. by *up*) *informal* heighten; increase (sound, intensity, etc.). [Say TORK]

torrent *noun* **1** a rushing stream of water, lava, etc. **2** (in *plural*) a great downpour of rain. **3** a violent or copious flow. ▶ **torrential** *adjective* [Say TORE unt, tuh REN shull]

torrid *adjective* **1** very hot and dry: *the torrid heat of the afternoon.* **2** (of language or actions) emotionally charged; passionate: *a torrid love affair.* **3** hard to contain or stop: *a torrid economy.* [Say TORE id]

torrid zone *noun* the central belt of the earth between the Tropics of Cancer and Capricorn.

torsion *noun* **1** twisting, esp. of one end of a body while the other is held fixed. **2** the extent to which a curve departs from being planar. **3** the state of being twisted into a spiral. ▶ **torsional** *adjective* **torsionally** *adverb* [Say TORE shun]

torso *noun* (*plural* **torsos**) **1 a** the trunk of the human body. **b** the part of the human body between the pelvis or waist and the shoulders. **2** a statue of a human consisting of the trunk alone, without head or limbs.

tort *noun* *Law* a breach of duty (other than under contract) for which damages can be obtained in a civil court by the person wronged.

torte *noun* an elaborate rich cake, esp. one with ground nuts as an ingredient and having multiple layers.

tortellini *noun* small crescent-shaped pasta pouches stuffed with meat, cheese, etc. [Say torta LEENY]

tortilla *noun* (*plural* **tortillas**) (esp. in Mexican cooking) a thin round bread made with either cornmeal or wheat flour and usu. filled with meat, cheese, beans, etc. [Say tore TEE uh]

tortilla chip *noun* (usu. in *plural*) a fried segment of a corn tortilla, often covered with a cheesy or spicy powdered coating, eaten cold like a potato chip.

tortoise *noun* **1** any slow-moving land or freshwater reptile encased in a scaly or leathery domed shell, with a head that can be retracted into the shell. **2** a slow-moving person or thing. **3** tortoiseshell; tortoiseshell colour. [Say TORE tuss]

tortoiseshell • *noun* **1** the yellowish-brown mottled or clouded outer shell of some turtles, used for decorative combs, jewellery, etc. **2 a** (also **tortoiseshell cat**) a domestic cat with a mottled black, orange, and cream or white coat. **b** (also **tortoiseshell butterfly**) any of various butterflies with wings mottled like tortoiseshell. • *adjective* **1** having the colouring or appearance of tortoiseshell. **2** made of tortoiseshell or a synthetic substitute. [Say TORE tuss shell]

---

tortuous *adjective* **1** full of twists and turns: *the route is remote and tortuous.* **2** not direct or straightforward; unnecessarily complex: *a tortuous argument.* ▶ **tortuously** *adverb* [Say TORE chew us]

torture • *noun* **1** the infliction of severe bodily pain esp. as a punishment or a means of interrogation or intimidation. **2** severe physical or mental suffering. • *verb* (**tortures, tortured, torturing**) subject to physical or mental torture. ▶ **torturer** *noun* [Say TORCHER]

torturous *adjective* characterized by, involving, or causing pain or suffering: *a torturous five days of fitness training.* [Say TORCHER us]

Tory *informal* • *noun* (*plural* **Tories**) a member or supporter of a Conservative party, esp. (in Canada) the Progressive Conservative Party. • *adjective* of or relating to a Conservative party. ▶ **Toryism** *noun*

toss • *verb* (**tosses, tossed, tossing**) **1** throw lightly or carelessly or easily. **2** roll about, throw, or be thrown, restlessly or from side to side. **3 a** throw (a coin) into the air to decide a choice etc. by the side on which it lands. **b** settle a question or dispute in this way. **c** settle a dispute with (a person) in this way: *will toss you for it.* **4 a** (of a horse etc.) throw (a rider) off its back. **b** (of a bull etc.) throw (a person) up with the horns. **c** throw (a pancake) up so that it flips on to the other side in the frying pan. **5** coat (food) with dressing etc. by stirring with a light up-and-down motion. **6** debate; discuss: *tossed the question back and forth.* • *noun* (*plural* **tosses**) **1** the act or an instance of tossing (a coin, the head, etc.). **2** a game or competition in which something is tossed: *ring toss.* PHRASES **toss in** add (an ingredient or element) to a mixture, concoction, etc., esp. casually. **toss off 1** dispatch (work) rapidly or without effort. **2** drink in one gulp. **3** utter in an offhand manner.

toss-up *noun* **1** a situation in which either of two alternatives is equally possible. **2** the tossing of a coin.

tot¹ *noun* **1** a small child: *a tiny tot.* **2** a dram of liquor.

tot² *verb* (**tots, totted, totting**) **1** (usu. foll. by *up*) add (figures etc.). **2** (foll. by *up*) (of times) mount up.

total • *adjective* **1** complete, comprising the whole or all. **2** absolute, unqualified. **3** (of an eclipse) in which the whole disc (of the sun, moon, etc.) is obscured. • *noun* a total number or amount. • *verb* (**totals, totalled, totalling**) **1 a** amount in number to. **b** find the total of (things, a set of figures, etc.). **2** amount to, mount up to. **3** *slang* wreck (a car etc.) completely. • *adverb* in total.

totalitarian • *adjective* (of a country or system of government) in which there is only one political party that has complete power and control over the people: *a totalitarian state.* • *noun* a person advocating such a system. ▶ **totalitarianism** *noun* [Say toe tala TERRY in]

totality *noun* **1** the complete amount or sum: *the totality of their current policies.* **2** the quality of being total; entirety: *it did not resolve the architectural problem in its totality.* [Say toe TALA tee]

totalize *verb* (**totalizes, totalized, totalizing**) (usu. as **totalizing** *adjective*) (of an institution) bring all other institutions under its control or influence: *the state has become a totalizing instrument in the lives of Aboriginal peoples.*

totally • *adverb* completely: *they come from totally different cultures* ◊ *I'm still not totally convinced that he knows what he's doing* ◊ *this behaviour is totally unacceptable.* • *interjection* I agree; yes it is.

total war *noun* a war in which all available weapons and resources are employed.

tote *informal* • *verb* (**totes, toted, toting**) **1** carry: *toting a gun.* **2** find the total of (things, a set of figures, etc.): *toted up the cost.* • *noun* **1** (also **tote bag**) a large open bag with handles, usu. made of fabric, esp. canvas. **2** *Cdn* any large container for storage or transportation. **3** *slang* (also **tote board**) a device showing the number and amount of bets staked on a race, to facilitate the division of the total among those backing the winner.

totem *noun* **1 a** (among some North American Aboriginal peoples) the emblem or symbol of a clan or family, usually the animal or plant that the family claims as its mythical ancestor. **b** an image of this. **2** an emblem or symbol: *the Pacific salmon is as valued a totem in the Northwest as the bald eagle is in the rest of the US.* ▶**totemic** *adjective* **totemism** *noun* [Say TOE tum, toe TEM ick, TOE tum ism]

totem pole *noun* **1** a pole on which family crests or totems are carved or hung. **2** a grouping of people or things in order of their status or importance: *in this city there's nothing higher on the totem pole than a room with a view.*

tote road *noun* a rough temporary road used esp. to convey provisions to a work camp.

-toting *combining form* carrying the object specified: *a gun-toting security guard.*

totter • *verb* **1** stand or walk unsteadily or feebly. **2 a** shake or rock as if about to collapse. **b** (of an institution, government, etc.) be about to fall. • *noun* an unsteady or shaky movement or gait. ▶**tottering** *adjective* **tottery** *adjective*

toucan *noun* a brightly coloured tropical American fruit-eating bird, with a huge beak. [Say TOO can]

touch • *verb* (**touches, touched, touching**) **1** come into or be in physical contact with at one or more points. **2** bring esp. the hand into contact with something; handle. **3 a** (of two things etc.) be in or come into contact with one another. **b** bring (two things) into mutual contact. **4** rouse tender or painful feelings in. **5** strike lightly. **6** (usu. with *neg.*) **a** disturb or interfere with. **b** have any dealings with. **c** consume; use up; make use of. **7 a** deal with (a subject) lightly or in passing. **b** concern. **8 a** reach or rise as far as, esp. momentarily. **b** (usu. with *neg.*) approach in excellence etc. **9** affect slightly; modify: *pity touched with fear.* **10** affect in a way specified or implied by the context; transform: *has touched many lives.* **11** strike (the keys, strings, etc. of a musical instrument). **12** (usu. foll. by *for*) *slang* ask for and get money etc. from (a person) as a loan or gift: *touched him for $5.* • *noun* (*plural* **touches**) **1** the act or an instance of touching, esp. with the body or hand: *her touch on his shoulder was hesitant.* **2 a** the faculty of perception through physical contact, esp. with the fingers: *soft to the touch.* **b** the qualities of an object etc. as perceived in this way. **3** a small amount; a slight trace. **4 a** a musician's manner of playing keys or strings. **b** the manner in which the keys or strings respond to touch. **c** an artist's or writer's style of workmanship, writing, etc. **5 a** a distinguishing quality or trait. **b** a special skill or proficiency. **6** (esp. in *plural*) **a** a light stroke with a pen, pencil, etc. **b** a slight alteration or improvement. **7** (preceded by *a*) slightly. **8** *slang* **a** the act of asking for and getting money etc. from a person. **b** a person from whom money etc. is so obtained. **9** *Soccer & Rugby* the part of the field outside the sidelines. PHRASES **get** (or

put) **in** (or **into**) **touch with** come or cause to come into communication with; contact. **in touch** (often foll. by *with*) **1** in communication: *still in touch after all these years.* **2** up to date, esp. regarding news etc. **3** aware, conscious, empathetic: *not in touch with her own feelings.* **lose touch** (often foll. by *with*) **1** cease to be informed. **2** cease to correspond with or be in contact with another person. **lose one's touch** not show one's customary skill. **out of touch 1** not in correspondence. **2** not up to date or modern. **3** lacking in awareness or sympathy: *out of touch with her son's beliefs.* **touch bottom 1** reach the bottom of water with one's feet. **2** be at the lowest or worst point. **touch down 1** (of an aircraft or spacecraft) make contact with the ground in landing. **2** *Rugby* touch the ground with the ball behind one's own or esp. the opponent's goal line. **touch off 1** explode by touching with a match etc. **2** initiate (a process, incident, etc.) suddenly. **touch on** (or **upon**) **1** treat (a subject) briefly, refer to or mention casually. **2** verge on. **touch the spot** *informal* find out or do exactly what was needed. **touch up** give finishing touches to or retouch (a picture, writing, etc.). **touch wood** touch something wooden with the hand to avert ill luck. **would not touch with a 10-foot** (or **barge**) **pole** refuse to be associated or concerned with (a person or thing). ▶**touchable** *adjective*

touch and go *adjective* uncertain regarding the outcome.

touchdown *noun* **1 a** *Football* the act of scoring six points by being in possession of the ball in the opposing side's end zone. **b** *Rugby* an act of touching the ground behind the opposing side's goal with the ball held in the hands, to score points. **2** the moment at which an aircraft's wheels or part of a spacecraft make contact with the ground during landing.

touché *interjection* **1** the acknowledgement of a hit by a fencing opponent. **2** the acknowledgement of a justified accusation, a witticism, or a point made in reply to one's own: *"Sorry I didn't call — I was busy last night." "Busy watching sitcoms?" "Touché".* [Say too SHAY]

touched *adjective* **1** in senses of TOUCH verb. **2** (also in phr. **touched in the head**) *informal* slightly mad.

touch football *noun* a form of football in which the ball carrier need only be touched to be stopped.

touchily *adverb* in an overly sensitive manner.

touchiness *noun* the quality of being overly sensitive.

touching *adjective* exciting tender feeling or sympathy; moving. ▶**touchingly** *adverb*

touchless *adjective* (of an automatic car wash) operating with sprays and jets only, without brushes etc. that touch the car.

touchpad *noun* **1** a usu. square area on a flat panel that needs only to be touched to activate an electrical device. **2** a panel including these.

touch screen *noun* a computer screen that responds to the touch of a finger or stylus by transmitting the coordinates of the touched area to the computer.

touch-sensitive *adjective* **1** operated by the touch of a finger, stylus, etc. **2** designating an electronic musical keyboard which responds dynamically to the varying force of a player's touch.

touchstone *noun* **1** a fine-grained dark schist or jasper used for testing alloys of gold etc. by observing the colour of the mark which they make on it. **2** a thing which serves to test the genuineness or value of anything; a standard or criterion: *they tend to regard grammar as the touchstone of all language performance.*

Touch-Tone *adjective* *proprietary* designating a telephone system in which a different single tone is

generated by each of the numbered buttons pushed to make a call.

touch type *verb* (**touch types, touch typed, touch typing**) type without looking at the keys. ▶ **touch typing** *noun* **touch typist** *noun*

touch-up *noun* a quick restoration or improvement (of paintwork, a piece of writing, etc.).

touchy *adjective* (**touchier, touchiest**) **1** apt to take offence; over-sensitive. **2** delicate; requiring careful handling: *a touchy subject*.

touchy-feely *adjective* displaying, encouraging, or relating to an uninhibited sharing of thoughts and emotions, often associated with physical touching, hugging, etc., as the basis of relationships.

tough • *adjective* **1** hard to break, cut, tear, or chew; durable; strong. **2** (of a person) able to endure hardship. **3** unyielding, stubborn; difficult. **4** *informal* **a** acting sternly. **b** (of circumstances, luck, etc.) severe, unpleasant, unjust. **5** (of a law, policy, etc.) demanding; strictly enforced. **6** *informal* rough, aggressive, or violent. • *noun* a tough person, esp. a ruffian or criminal. • *interjection ironic* that is unfortunate (used unsympathetically or defiantly to underscore an unfortunate condition or circumstance which another must face). **PHRASES** **be a tough sell** be difficult to convince others about. **have it tough** be hard-pressed or in difficulty. **tough as nails** extremely tough. **tough (it) out** *informal* endure or withstand (difficult conditions).

toughen *verb* make or become tough.

toughie *noun* (also **toughy**) (*plural* **toughies**) *informal* a tough person or problem.

toughish *adjective* somewhat tough.

tough love *noun* the withholding of assistance from a person or the placing of strict constraints on him or her, undertaken for the person's own good.

toughly *adverb* in a tough manner.

tough-minded *adjective* **1** realistic, not sentimental. **2** determined. ▶ **tough-mindedness** *noun*

toughness *noun* the quality of being tough: strength, durability, the ability to endure hardship.

toupée *noun* a wig or artificial hairpiece to cover a bald spot. [Say too PAY]

tour • *noun* **1 a** a journey from place to place as a holiday. **b** an excursion, ramble, or walk: *made a tour of the garden*. **c** an organized and guided trip, excursion, or visit. **2 a** a period of duty on military or diplomatic service. **b** the time to be spent at a particular post. **3** a series of performances, matches, etc., at different places on a route through a country etc. • *verb* **1** make a tour. **2** make a tour of (a country etc.). **PHRASES** **on tour** (esp. of a musical or theatrical performer, sports team, etc.) touring.

tour de force *noun* (*plural* **tours de force** *pronunc.* same) a feat of skill or strength; an impressive performance, achievement, or creation: *a pianistic tour de force, and very well recorded too.*

Tourette's syndrome *noun* (also **Tourette Syndrome**) a neurological disorder characterized by involuntary tics and utterances and the compulsive use of obscene language. [Say too RET]

tourism *noun* the business or industry of attracting and providing accommodation and services for visitors and travellers on holiday.

tourist *noun* a person making a visit or tour as a holiday; a person travelling for pleasure.

tourist trap *noun* a place where tourists are exploited, e.g. where everything is excessively expensive.

touristy *adjective* usu. *derogatory* appealing to or visited by many tourists.

tourmaline *noun* a boron aluminum silicate mineral of various colours, possessing unusual electrical properties, and used in electrical and optical instruments and as a gemstone. [Say TOOR muh leen]

tournament *noun* **1** any contest of skill or series of contests involving a number of competitors: *tennis tournament*. **2** *hist.* **a** a pageant in which jousting with blunted weapons took place. **b** a meeting for jousting between single knights for a prize etc.

tournedos *noun* (*plural* **tournedos**) a small round thick cut of beef tenderloin. [Say TOOR nuh doe]

tourney *noun* (*plural* **tourneys**) a tournament. [Rhymes with JOURNEY]

tourniquet *noun* a device for stopping the flow of blood through an artery by twisting a bar etc. in a ligature or bandage so as to tighten it. [Say TURN a kay]

tour of duty *noun* (*plural* **tours of duty**) = TOUR *noun* 2.

tourtière *noun* a French-Canadian meat pie consisting esp. of ground pork and spices with a flaky double crust, traditionally served at Christmas. [Say tor TYAIR]

tousle • *verb* (**tousles, tousled, tousling**) make (esp. the hair) untidy; rumple. • *noun* a tousled mass of hair etc. [Say TOUSE'll (with TOUSE rhyming either with HOUSE or with PLOWS)]

tout • *verb* **1** attempt to persuade people of the merits of someone or something: *she was touted as a potential prime minister*. **2** attempt to sell something, typically by pestering people in an aggressive or bold manner: *Sanjay was touting his wares ◊ shop managers would stand in the street touting for business*. • *noun* a person soliciting business aggressively. ▶ **touted** *adjective*

touton *noun* *Cdn* (*Nfld*) a deep-fried flat round of bread dough, eaten with molasses. [Say TOUT'n]

SPELL CHECK
tow, toe

The spelling is **toe** in "toe the line".

---

tow • *verb* **1** pull (a boat, motor vehicle, etc.) along by a rope, chain, etc. **2** pull (a person or thing) along behind one. **3** remove (a motor vehicle) to a pound, garage, etc. • *noun* **1** an act of towing a boat or vehicle. **2** *Forestry* a set of boomed logs gathered to be towed. **3** a mechanism for pulling skiers up a hill. **PHRASES** **in tow 1** (also **under tow**) being towed. **2** accompanying, often as a charge or as an admirer etc. ▶ **towable** *adjective*

WRITING TIP
toward, towards

Toward and **towards** are equally common in Canada — you can use them interchangeably.

---

toward *preposition* (also **towards**) **1** in the direction of. **2** as regards; in relation to. **3** as a contribution to. **4** near.

towboat *noun* a boat used to tow other boats etc.

towel • *noun* **1** a piece of rough-surfaced absorbent, usu. terry cloth, used for drying oneself or a thing after washing. **2** absorbent paper used for this. • *verb* (**towels, towelled, towelling**) (also foll. by *off*) wipe or dry (oneself, a thing, etc.) with a towel.

towelette *noun* a small moistened tissue for wiping esp. the hands or face, often individually wrapped.

towelling *noun* **1** *in senses of* TOWEL *verb*. **2** absorbent cloth, esp. cotton with uncut loops, used as material for towels.

tower • *noun* **1 a** a tall narrow building or structure, either standing alone or forming part of a castle, church, etc. **b** a fortress etc. comprising or including a tower. **c** a tall structure housing machinery, apparatus, operators, etc.: *control tower*. **d** a tall building

containing offices or apartments. **2** a lofty pile or mass. **3** a casing for computer components which stands upright, either alone or on a desk etc. • *verb* reach or be high or above; be superior. ▶ **towered** *adjective*

towering *adjective* **1** high, lofty. **2** of exceptional importance or influence. **3** of great intensity: *towering rage.*

towhead *noun* a person with very light-coloured or unkempt hair.

towheaded *adjective* having very light-coloured or unkempt hair.

towhee *noun* a North American bunting of brush and woodland, usu. having a black back, rust sides, and a white breast. [Say TOW hee (TOW rhymes either with *PLOW* or with *GROW*)]

town *noun* **1 a** an urban area with a name, defined boundaries, and local government, usu. larger than a village and smaller than a city. **b** any densely populated area, esp. as opposed to the country or suburbs. **c** the people of a town. **d** the government, administration, or employees of a town. **2** the central business or shopping area. PHRASES **go to town** *informal* act or work with energy or enthusiasm. **on the town** *informal* enjoying the entertainments, esp. the nightlife, of a town; celebrating.

town hall *noun* **1** a building for the administration of local government, having public meeting rooms etc. **2** (also **town hall meeting**) a meeting or television broadcast allowing people to express their opinions on political issues to political leaders.

townhouse *noun* **1** (also **townhome**) any of a row of usu. similar joined houses, two or three storeys high, along a street; a row house. **2** an urban residence, esp. of a person with a house in the country.

townie *noun* (also **townee**) *derogatory* a person living in a town, esp. as opposed to those living in the country or (in a university town) a student etc.

town line *noun Cdn* (*Ont.*) a road separating two municipalities, esp. townships.

townscape *noun* the visual appearance of a town; an urban landscape: *watercolours of the Moose Jaw townscape.*

townsfolk *noun* the inhabitants of a particular town.

township *noun* **1** a division of a county with some corporate powers. **2** (in areas of western Canada and the US surveyed into ranges and townships) a district six miles square, containing thirty-six sections. **3** *hist.* an urban area in South Africa set aside for black occupation.

Townshipper *noun Cdn* a resident of the Eastern Townships.

townsite *noun* esp. *Cdn* **1** the site of a town, esp. a tract of land set apart by legal authority to be occupied by a town, and usu. surveyed and laid out with streets etc. **2** an unincorporated town in a national park etc.

townsman *noun* (*plural* **townsmen**) an inhabitant of a town.

townspeople *plural noun* the people of a town.

towpath *noun* a path beside a river or canal, originally used for towing barges by horse.

tow truck *noun* a truck used to tow away motor vehicles.

toxemia *noun* **1** blood poisoning. **2** a condition in pregnancy characterized by increased blood pressure. ▶ **toxemic** *adjective* [Say tox EEMY uh]

toxic **1** of or relating to poison: *toxic symptoms.* **2** poisonous: *toxic gas.* **3** caused by poison: *toxic anemia.* ▶ **toxically** *adverb*

toxicity *noun* (*plural* **toxicities**) **1** the quality of being poisonous; the extent to which something is poisonous: *substances with high levels of toxicity.* **2** the

state of being poisoned: *showed some of the signs of amphetamine toxicity.* [Say tox ISSA tee]

toxicological *adjective* having to do with poisons. [Say toxa kuh LOGICAL]

toxicologist *noun* a scientist who studies poisons. [Say toxa COLLA jist]

toxicology *noun* the scientific study of poisons. [Say toxa COLLA jee]

toxic shock syndrome *noun* acute blood poisoning in women, typically caused by bacterial infection from a retained tampon, IUD, etc. Abbreviation: **TSS**.

toxin *noun* a poison produced by a living organism, esp. one formed in the body and stimulating the production of antibodies.

toxoplasmosis *noun* a disease caused by infection with the protozoan *Toxoplasma gondii*, transmitted esp. through poorly prepared food or in cat feces and dangerous in unborn children. [Say toxo plaz MOE sis]

toy • *noun* **1 a** a plaything, esp. for a child. **b** a model or miniature replica of a thing, esp. as a plaything: *Aidan likes to play with his toy fire trucks.* **2 a** a thing, esp. a gadget or instrument, regarded as providing amusement or pleasure. **b** a task or undertaking regarded in an unserious way. **3** (usu. as an *adjective*) a small breed or variety of dog etc. • *verb* (usu. foll. by *with*) **1 a** consider something casually or without serious intent. **b** deal with something or someone thoughtlessly. **2 a** move a material object idly. **b** nibble at food etc. without enthusiasm.

toy boy *noun informal* a much younger male lover.

toylike *adjective* like a toy, esp. in smallness or triviality.

trace¹ • *verb* (**traces, traced, tracing**) **1 a** observe, discover, or find vestiges or signs of by investigation. **b** follow or mark the track or position of. **c** follow to its origins. **2** copy (a drawing etc.) by drawing over its lines on a superimposed piece of translucent paper, or by using carbon paper. **3** mark out, sketch, or write esp. laboriously. **4** pursue one's way along (a path etc.). • *noun* **1 a** a sign or mark or other indication of something having existed. **b** a very small quantity. **2** a track or footprint left by a person or animal. **3** a track left by the moving pen of an instrument etc. **4** a line on the screen of a cathode ray tube showing the path of a moving spot. **5** a curve's projection on or intersection with a plane etc. **6** the track made by the passage of a person or thing.

trace² *noun* each of the two side straps, chains, or ropes by which a horse draws a vehicle. PHRASES **kick over the traces** become insubordinate or reckless.

traceable *adjective* able to be traced: *the firearms were traceable to a dealer on the outskirts of town.* [Say TRACE a bull]

trace element *noun* **1** a chemical element occurring in minute amounts. **2** (also **trace mineral**) a chemical element needed only in minute amounts by living organisms for normal growth.

tracer *noun* **1** a person or thing that traces. **2** a bullet etc. visible in flight because of flames etc. emitted. **3** an artificially produced radioactive isotope capable of being followed through the body by the radiation it produces. **4** a person whose business is the tracing of missing persons, property, etc.

tracery *noun* (*plural* **traceries**) **1** ornamental stone openwork esp. in the upper part of a Gothic window. **2** a fine or delicate decorative pattern.

trachea *noun* the passage reinforced by rings of cartilage, through which air reaches the bronchial tubes from the larynx; the windpipe. ▶ **tracheal** *adjective* [Say TRAKE ee uh or TRACK ee uh]

tracheotomy *noun* (*plural* **tracheotomies**) a surgical

T

operation to make an opening in the trachea, esp. so that the patient can breathe through it via a curved tube. [Say trake ee OTTA mee]

tracing *noun* **1** a copy of a drawing etc. made by tracing. **2** = TRACE[1] *noun* 3.

track • *noun* **1** a mark or marks left by a person, animal, or thing in passing. **2** a rough path, esp. one beaten by use. **3** a continuous railway line. **4 a** a racecourse for horses etc. **b** *Sport* a prepared course for runners etc. **c** *Sport* the athletic events, esp. running, which take place on a track. **d** = WARNING TRACK. **5 a** a section of a phonograph record, cassette tape, compact disc, etc., containing one song etc. **b** one of several lengthwise divisions of a strip of magnetic tape, containing one sequence of signals; a channel. **c** that which is recorded on such a strip: *laugh track* ◊ *drum track*. **6 a** a line of travel, passage, or motion. **b** the path travelled by a ship, aircraft, etc. **7** a continuous band around the wheels of a tank, tractor, etc. **8 a** a course of action or conduct; a way of proceeding. **b** a line of reasoning or thought: *this track proved fruitless*. **9** (also **track mark**) (usu. in *plural*) *slang* a line on the skin made by repeated injections of an addictive drug. • *verb* **1 a** follow the track of (an animal, person, spacecraft, etc.). **b** trace the movements of. **2 a** follow (a course, development, etc.). **b** follow the course or development of. **3** (of a film or television camera) move in relation to the subject being filmed. **4** make a track with (dirt etc.) from the feet. PHRASES **in one's tracks** *informal* where one stands, there and then: *stopped him in his tracks*. **keep** (or **lose**) **track of** follow (or fail to follow) the course or development of. **make tracks** *informal* go or run away. **make tracks for** *informal* go in pursuit of or toward. **off the track** away from the subject. **on a person's track 1** in pursuit of him or her. **2** in possession of a clue to a person's conduct, plans, etc. **on the right** (or **wrong**) **track** following the right (or wrong) line of inquiry. **on** (or **off**) **track** following (or deviating from) the desired direction or goal. **on the wrong side of the tracks** *informal* in a poor or less prestigious part of town. **track down** reach or capture by tracking.

track and field *noun* athletic events comprising track events (such as sprints, hurdles, etc.) and field events (such as throwing and jumping).

trackball *noun* Computing a small ball that is rotated in a holder to move a cursor on a screen.

tracked *adjective* (of a wheeled vehicle) equipped with tracks (see TRACK *noun* 7).

tracker *noun* **1** a person or thing that tracks. **2** a police dog tracking by scent.

tracking *noun* **1** *in senses of* TRACK *verb*. **2** the formation of a conducting path over the surface of an insulating material. **3** in a VCR, the alignment of the tape with the tape head, which may need to be adjusted for tapes recorded on another machine.

trackless *adjective* **1** without a track or tracks. **2** leaving no track or trace. **3** (esp. of a vehicle) not running on a track.

track light *noun* (usu. in *plural*) one of a line of lights fitted on a metal or plastic strip, each of which can be positioned individually. ▶ **track lighting** *noun*

track pants *plural noun* loose pants, usu. with elasticized cuffs, worn casually or by an athlete etc. for exercising or jogging.

track record *noun* the past achievements of a person or an organization.

trackside *noun* the area beside a railway line or racetrack.

track suit *noun* a loose warm two-piece suit worn by an athlete etc. for exercising or jogging.

tract *noun* **1** a region or area of indefinite, esp. large, extent. **2** an area of an organ or system: *digestive tract*. **3** a short treatise in pamphlet form esp. on a religious or political subject. **4** an anthem replacing the alleluia in some Masses.

tractability *noun* the quality of being easily handled or docile: *the Italian greyhounds were chosen for their diminutive size and tractability*.

tractable *adjective* easy to deal with or control: *this approach helps to make the issues more tractable* ◊ *Marie is childlike, docile, tractable*.

tract house *noun* (also **tract home**) one of a number of similar houses built as part of a real estate development. ▶ **tract housing** *noun*

traction *noun* **1** the grip of a tire, footwear, etc. on the ground. **2** the act of drawing or pulling a thing over a surface, esp. a road or track. **3 a** a sustained pulling on a limb, muscle, etc., by means of pulleys, weights, etc. to maintain the positions of fractured bones, correct deformity, etc. **b** the state of being subjected to such a pull. **c** contraction, e.g. of a muscle.

tractor *noun* a powerful motor vehicle used for hauling etc., esp. one with large treaded rear wheels used to haul farm machinery.

tractor pull *noun* a competition in which tractors pull increasingly heavy loads.

tractor-trailer *noun* an articulated truck consisting of a powerful cab pulling a large detachable trailer.

tractor train *noun* Cdn (North) a train of sleds pulled by a tractor etc.

trad *adjective* *informal* traditional.

tradable *adjective* (also **tradeable**) able to be traded: *tradable shares in the company*.

trade • *noun* **1 a** buying and selling. **b** buying and selling conducted between nations etc.; the exchange of goods between peoples. **c** business conducted for profit (esp. as distinct from a profession). **d** business of a specified nature or time: *tourist trade*. **2 a** skilled handicraft esp. requiring an apprenticeship. **3** (usu. as **the trade**) the people engaged in a specific trade. **4 a** a transaction, esp. a swap. **b** *Sport* an exchange of players between two or more franchises or teams. • *verb* (**trades, traded, trading**) **1** (often foll. by *in, with*) buy and sell. **2 a** exchange in commerce; barter (goods). **b** exchange (insults, blows, etc.). **c** (foll. by *for*) swap, exchange. **d** exchange products or commodities with (a person). **e** *Sport* (of a franchise or team) relinquish the rights to (a player) to another team in exchange for the rights to one or more of theirs or for other considerations. **3** have a transaction with a person for a thing. **4** (of shares, currency, etc.) be bought and sold. PHRASES **trade in** exchange (esp. a used car etc.) in part payment for another. **trade off** exchange, esp. as a compromise. **trade on** take advantage of (a person's credulity, one's reputation, etc.). **trade up** sell something in order to buy a better or more expensive replacement.

trade barrier *noun* a policy or regulation that restricts trade between countries, provinces, etc.

tradecraft *noun* **1** skill or art in connection with a trade or calling. **2** skill in espionage and intelligence.

trade deficit *noun* (also **trade gap**) the extent by which a country's imports exceed its exports.

trade fair *noun* = TRADE SHOW.

trade-in *noun* a thing, esp. a car, exchanged in part payment for another.

trade journal *noun* (also **trade paper**) a periodical containing news etc. concerning a particular trade.

trademark • *noun* **1** a logo, word, or words, secured by legal registration or established by use as representing a company, product, etc. **2** a distinctive

characteristic etc. • *adjective* characteristic or distinctive: *wearing his trademark cap*. • *verb* (usu. as **trademarked** *adjective*) **1** provide with a trademark. **2** register as a trademark.

trade name *noun* **1** a name by which a thing is called in a trade. **2** a name given to a product; a brand name. **3** a name under which a business operates.

trade-off *noun* a balance achieved between two desirable but incompatible features; a compromise.

trader *noun* **1** a person engaged in trading. **2** a person who trades stocks.

trade show *noun* a gathering of members of a trade or industry for the exhibition of the latest technology, products, developments, etc.

tradesman *noun* (*plural* **tradesmen**) a person engaged in a trade, esp. a skilled craftsman.

tradespeople *plural noun* people engaged in trade.

tradeswoman *noun* (*plural* **tradeswomen**) a woman engaged in a trade.

trade union *noun* an organized association of workers formed to protect and further their rights and interests and to bargain collectively with employers. ▶ **trade unionism** *noun* **trade unionist** *noun*

trade war *noun* a situation in which governments act aggressively in international markets to promote their own countries' trading interests.

trade wind *noun* a wind blowing continually towards the equator and deflected westward.

trading *noun* the act of engaging in trade.

trading card *noun* a small card depicting a figure or figures from popular culture, esp. sports, for collecting or trading.

trading post *noun* a store or other place for conducting trade, usu. in remote areas, esp. originally established by colonial powers to trade with Aboriginal peoples.

tradition *noun* **1 a** a custom, opinion, or belief handed down to posterity esp. orally or by practice. **b** this process of handing down. **2** an established practice or custom. ▶ **traditional** *adjective*

traditionalism *noun* respect or support for tradition, esp. in contrast with modern practices or styles.

traditionalist *noun* a person who prefers tradition to modern ideas or ways of doing things.

traditionally *adverb* from a traditional point of view or in keeping with tradition.

traffic • *noun* **1 a** vehicles moving on a public road or highway, esp. of a specified kind, density, etc. **b** such movement in the air, at sea, or by rail. **c** people moving, esp. on foot. **2** trade, esp. illegal. **3 a** the transportation of goods, the coming and going of people or goods by road, rail, air, sea, etc. **b** the persons or goods so transported. **4** dealings or communication between people etc. **5** the messages, signals, etc., transmitted through a communications system; the flow or volume of such signals. • *verb* (**traffics, trafficked, trafficking**) **1** deal or trade in something, esp. something illegal: *cracking down on those responsible for trafficking drugs* ◊ *the fisheries inspector was charged with trafficking in sea cucumbers during the ban*. **2** offer for consumption or use: *she traffics in sardonic humour* ◊ *movies that trafficked in themes of alienation and despair*.

traffic calming *noun* the deliberate slowing of traffic, esp. along residential streets, by building speed bumps, obstructions, etc.

traffic circle *noun* a road junction at which traffic moves in one direction around a central island.

traffic island *noun* a paved or grassed area in a road to divert traffic, provide a refuge for pedestrians, etc.

traffic jam *noun* traffic at a standstill because of volume, construction, an accident, etc.

trafficked *adjective* (of a roadway, route, etc.) used by an esp. specified amount of traffic.

trafficker *noun* a person who deals in something esp. illegally.

traffic light *noun* (usu. in *plural*) each of a set of automatic lights, usu. red, amber, and green, for controlling road traffic, esp. at intersections.

tragedy *noun* (*plural* **tragedies**) **1** an event causing great suffering, destruction, and distress, such as a serious accident, crime, or natural catastrophe. **2** the tragic element or circumstances surrounding a person or event: *found both humour and tragedy in the situation*. **3 a** a dramatic representation dealing with tragic events and with an unhappy ending, esp. concerning the downfall of the main character because of a fatal flaw. **b** the tragic genre.

tragic *adjective* **1** greatly distressing: *a tragic tale*. **2** of, or in the style of, tragedy: *a tragic actor*. ▶ **tragically** *adverb*

tragicomedy *noun* (*plural* **tragicomedies**) **1 a** a play having a mixture of comedy and tragedy. **b** plays of this kind as a genre. **2** an event etc. having tragic and comic elements. ▶ **tragicomic** *adjective*

trail • *noun* **1 a** a track left by a thing, person, etc., moving over a surface. **b** a track, scent, or other trace followed in hunting, seeking, etc. **2 a** a beaten or maintained path or track, esp. through a park, wild region, etc., often for a specified traffic: *ski trail*. **b** a route into or through wild territory, followed by a wave of migrants, prospectors, etc. **c** a highway route designated for its interest to tourists: *the Cabot Trail*. **d** *Cdn* (in Alberta) a major arterial road through a city. **e** a tour or series of performances, shows, etc.: *on the festival trail*. **3** a part dragging behind a thing or person: *a trail of smoke*. • *verb* **1** draw, be drawn, or appear to draw along behind. **2** (often foll. by *behind*) walk wearily. **3** follow the trail of. **4** a be losing in a game or other contest. **b** have fewer points in a game, series, etc. than (one's opponent). **5** (usu. foll. by *away, off*) peter out. **6 a** (of a plant etc.) grow or hang over a wall, along the ground etc. **b** (of a garment etc.) hang loosely.

trailblazer *noun* **1** a person who marks a new track through wild country. **2** an innovator. ▶ **trailblazing** *noun & adjective*

trail-breaker *noun* a person who clears a path through rough terrain, deep snow, etc. ▶ **trail-breaking** *noun*

trailer • *noun* **1** a vehicle towed by another, esp.: **a** the rear section of a tractor-trailer. **b** an open cart. **c** a platform for transporting a boat etc. **d** a camper, mobile home, house trailer, or other towed vehicle with living accommodations. **2** a series of brief extracts from a film etc., used to advertise it in advance; a preview. **3** a person or thing that trails. **4** a trailing plant. • *verb* transport or travel by trailer.

trailer park *noun* (also **trailer court**) a place where mobile homes or other trailers may be parked for holiday or more permanent accommodation.

trailhead *noun* the starting point of a trail.

trail mix *noun* a mixture of nuts, dried fruit, chocolate chips, etc., esp. as a snack eaten by hikers.

trail ride *noun* a ride on horseback along a trail esp. through rugged country. ▶ **trail riding** *noun*

train • *verb* **1 a** teach (a person, animal, oneself, etc.) a specified skill esp. by practice. **b** undergo this process. **2** bring or come into a state of physical efficiency by exercise, diet, etc.; undergo physical exercise, esp. for a specific purpose: *trains every day*. **3** cause (a plant) to grow in a required shape. **4** (usu. as **trained** *adjective*) improve the abilities of (the mind, eye, voice, etc.) as a result of instruction, practice, etc. **5** point or aim (a

gun, camera, etc.) at an object etc. • *noun* **1 a** a series of railway cars drawn by a locomotive. **b** *Cdn* (*North*) = TRACTOR TRAIN. **2** something dragged along behind or forming the back part of a dress, robe, etc. **3** a succession or series of people, things, events, etc.: *train of thought*. **4** a body of followers. **5** a succession of military vehicles etc., including artillery, supplies, etc.: *baggage train*. **6** a series of connected wheels or parts in machinery. PHRASES **in train** properly arranged or directed. **in a person's train** following behind a person. ▶ **trainable** *adjective*

trainee *noun* a person undergoing training.

trainer *noun* **1** a person who trains. **2 a** a person who trains athletes, horses, etc., as a profession. **b** a person who attends to the medical and physical well-being of athletes, esp. on a team. **3** an aircraft or device simulating it used to train pilots. **4** a piece of equipment used for training; an exercise machine.

training *noun* **1** the act or process of teaching or learning a skill, discipline, etc. **2** the process of developing physical fitness and efficiency by diet and exercise. **3** (as an *adjective*) designating a thing designed or modified to facilitate the learning of a skill etc.

training camp *noun* **1** the gathering of members of a sports team for organized physical training before the start of a season. **2** any camp where training occurs.

training ground *noun* any setting where one learns or develops specific skills, attributes, etc.

training school *noun* **1** (also **training college**) a college or school where students are trained in a particular profession or occupation. **2** a vocational institution for juvenile delinquents.

training wheel *noun* a small wheel fitted to each side of the rear wheel of a bicycle to stabilize it for a child learning to ride.

trainload *noun* a number of people, or quantity of goods etc., transported by train.

traipse *informal* • *verb* (**traipses**, **traipsed**, **traipsing**) **1** walk or move wearily or reluctantly: *students had to traipse all over campus to attend lectures*. **2** walk about casually or needlessly: *traipsed giddily through the fields collecting wildflowers*. • *noun* a tedious journey on foot. [Rhymes with GRAPES]

trait *noun* **1** a distinguishing feature or characteristic esp. of a person. **2** a characteristic that is or can be inherited.

traitor *noun* a person who is treacherous or disloyal, esp. to his or her country. ▶ **traitorous** *adjective* **traitorously** *adverb* [Say TRAY ter]

trajectory *noun* (*plural* **trajectories**) **1** the path of an object that has been fired, launched, thrown, or hit into the air: *the trajectory of an artillery shell*. **2** a path or course of action: *every interview follows its own trajectory*. [Say truh JECKTER ee]

tram *noun* **1** esp. *Brit.* = STREETCAR. **2** each of a series of small enclosed passenger cabins suspended from a cable and drawn up and down a mountainside by an engine at one end. **3** a four-wheeled vehicle used in coal mines.

tramp • *verb* **1 a** walk heavily and firmly. **b** go on foot, esp. a distance. **2 a** cross on foot, esp. wearily or reluctantly. **b** cover (a distance) in this way. **3** tread on; trample. • *noun* **1** a person who travels from place to place on foot in search of work or as a vagrant or beggar. **2** *slang derogatory* a promiscuous woman. **3** the sound of a person, or esp. people, walking, marching, etc., or of horses' hooves. **4** an esp. long journey on foot. **5** a merchant ship running on no regular line or route: *a tramp steamer*.

trample • *verb* (**tramples**, **trampled**, **trampling**) **1** tread under foot. **2** press down or crush in this way.

3 disregard with contempt; put down. • *noun* the sound or act of trampling. PHRASES **trample on** (or **over**) **1** tread heavily on. **2** treat roughly or with contempt; disregard (a person's feelings etc.).

trampoline • *noun* a strong fabric sheet connected by springs to a horizontal frame, used by gymnasts etc. for somersaults, as a springboard, etc. • *verb* use a trampoline.

trampy *adjective* (of a woman) dressed or made up in a way that suggests promiscuity.

tramway *noun* **1** a crude road with wooden, stone, or metal tracks for wheels, used in mining etc. **2 a** rails for a streetcar. **b** a streetcar system.

trance *noun* **1** a sleeplike or half-conscious state in which a person is unable to respond to stimuli, e.g. after being hypnotized: *the medium puts himself into a trance state and give permission for the spiritual entity to overshadow him*. **2** a state of extreme exaltation or rapture; ecstasy. **3** a stunned or dazed state. **4** a state of mental absorption or abstraction from external things. ▶ **trancelike** *adjective*

tranche *noun* a portion, esp. of income, or of a block of shares. [Say TRANSH]

tranny *noun* (*plural* **trannies**) *Mechanics slang* a transmission.

tranquil *adjective* calm, serene: *the lake is tranquil*.

tranquility *noun* the quality or state of being tranquil; calmness, serenity. [Say tran KWILLA tee]

tranquilize *verb* (**tranquilizes**, **tranquilized**, **tranquilizing**) make tranquil, esp. by a drug etc.

tranquilizer *noun* a person or thing which tranquilizes, esp. a drug used to diminish tension or anxiety.

tranquilizing *adjective* (of a drug) that makes one tranquil or calm.

tranquilly *adverb* calmly.

trans- *prefix* across: *transcontinental*.

transact *verb* perform or carry through (business): *manufacturers typically transact up to 60 percent of their business at trade shows*.

transaction *noun* **1 a** a piece of esp. commercial business done. **b** an exchange of players between two or more franchises or teams; a trade: *reads the sports section to keep track of player transactions*. **c** the management of business etc. **2** (in *plural*) published reports of discussions, papers read, etc., at the meetings of a learned society.

transactional *adjective* **1** in senses of TRANSACTION. **2** *Psychology* of, pertaining to, or involving interpersonal communication viewed as transactions of attitude between participants.

transatlantic *adjective* **1** crossing or spanning the Atlantic. **2** beyond the Atlantic, esp.: **a** *Brit.* North American. **b** European.

transborder *adjective* that crosses, is situated on, or pertains to both sides of a border.

Trans-Canada • *noun* (in full **the Trans-Canada Highway**) a highway spanning Canada from St. John's to Victoria. • *adjective* (**trans-Canada**) spanning, including, or involving all of Canada: *a trans-Canada journey*.

transceiver *noun* any device which is both a transmitter and receiver of signals. [Say tran SEEVER]

transcend *verb* be or go beyond the range or limits of something abstract: *the issue of human rights should transcend party lines* ◊ *a vast global economy that transcends national boundaries*. [Say tran SEND]

transcendence *noun* **1** the quality of something that goes beyond or above the range of normal or merely physical human experience: *transcendence of the ordinary categories of human experience*. **2** the quality of

something that surpasses what is ordinary: *the goal of surrealist activity is the transcendence of this bankrupt culture and its barbaric economic/political system*. **3** existence apart from and beyond the limitations of the physical universe: *strove to preserve the transcendence and freedom of God from any attempt to tie God down to our human categories and wishes*. [Say tran SEN dince]

transcendent *adjective* **1** beyond or above the range of normal or merely physical human experience: *Henry sees theatre as a potentially transcendent experience, which can not only take those involved out of themselves, but transform them*. **2** surpassing the ordinary; exceptional: *transcendent beauty*. **3** (esp. of God) existing apart from, not subject to the limitations of, the physical universe: *the belief that a transcendent authority exists to which humankind is accountable for its actions*. ▶ **transcendently** *adverb* [Say tran SEN dint]

transcendental *adjective* going beyond the limits of human knowledge, experience, or reason, esp. in a religious or spiritual way; transcendent: *religious activity is predicated on transcendental concepts*. ▶ **transcendentally** *adverb* [Say tran sin DENTAL]

transcendental meditation *noun* a technique for detaching oneself from anxiety and promoting harmony and self-realization by various yogic practices, including meditation and the use of a repeated word or speech sound to aid concentration.

transcontinental ● *adjective* extending across a continent. ● *noun* a transcontinental railway or train.

transcribe *verb* (**transcribes, transcribed, transcribing**) **1** put thoughts, speech, or data into written or printed form: *each interview was taped and transcribed*. **2** write or print a letter or word using the closest corresponding letters of a different alphabet or language: *transcribed Chinese characters into English*. **3** write out (shorthand, notes, etc.) in ordinary characters or continuous prose. **4** arrange (music) for a different instrument etc. **5** represent (a speech sound or spoken word) in a written form using phonetic characters. ▶ **transcriber** *noun*

transcript *noun* **1 a** a written or recorded copy. **b** something transcribed. **2** any copy. **3** a written record of public proceedings etc. **4** an official record of a student's grades etc.

transcription *noun* **1 a** the action or process of transcribing something: *the funding covers the transcription of nearly illegible photocopies*. **b** a written or printed representation of something: *phonetic transcriptions of the words*. **2** an arrangement of a piece of music for a different instrument, voice, or number of these: *a transcription for voice and lute*.

transcultural *adjective* pertaining to or involving more than one culture; cross-cultural.

transduce *verb* (**transduces, transduced, transducing**) convert (energy, esp. in the form of a signal) into a different medium or form of energy: *electrical instruments transduce mechanical phenomena such as a vibrating string into an electric signal via a pickup*.

transducer *noun* any device for converting a signal from one medium of transmission to another, esp. a non-electrical signal into an electrical one, e.g. pressure into voltage.

transduction *noun* an act of converting energy, esp. in the form of a signal, into a different medium or form of energy.

transect ● *verb* cut across or transversely: *the surgical procedure involved transecting the massive fibre bundle connecting the two halves of the brain*. ● *noun* a line or strip across the earth's surface or through any object, along which a survey or observations are made. ▶ **transection** *noun*

transept *noun* **1** either arm of the part of a cross-shaped church at right angles to the nave: *north transept* ◊ *south transept*. **2** this part as a whole. [Say TRAN sept]

transexual *adjective & noun* = TRANSSEXUAL.

trans fat *noun* (also **trans fatty acid**) any unsaturated fatty acid with the same atoms on opposite sides of its double bonds, found frequently in margarines and cooking oils as a result of hydrogenation during processing.

transfer ● *verb* (**transfers, transferred, transferring**) **1** (often foll. by *to*) **a** move from one place to another. **b** hand over the possession of to a person. **2** move or change to another department, school, group, etc. **3** change from one route, airport, station, etc., to another on a journey. **4** reroute (a telephone connection or caller) to another line, department, etc. **5** convey or apply (a drawing or design) from one surface to another, esp. from a prepared sheet. **6** change (the sense of a word etc.) by extension or metaphor. ● *noun* **1** an act of moving someone or something to another place, group, job, etc.: *asked for a transfer to Winnipeg* ◊ *the transfer of currency from one country to another* ◊ *after the election there was a swift transfer of power*. **2** a ticket allowing a journey to be continued on another route etc. **3 a** a design etc. conveyed or to be conveyed from one surface to another. **b** a small usu. coloured picture or design on paper, which is transferable to another surface. **4** a person who is or is to be transferred. **5 a** the conveyance of property, a right, etc. **b** a document effecting this. **6** = TRANSFER PAYMENT.

transferability *noun* the ability to be transferred. [Say transfer a BILLA tee]

transferable *adjective* that can be transferred. [Say trans FUR a bull]

transferee *noun* the person to whom something is transferred. [Say transfer EE]

transference *noun* **1** the action of transferring something: *transference of ownership*. **2** *Psychology* the redirection of childhood emotions to a new object, esp. to a psychoanalyst. [Say TRANSFER ince]

transfer payment *noun* a direct payment from a government not made in exchange for goods or services, e.g. to an individual or family in the form of an employment insurance payment or family allowance, or (in Canada) esp. to another level of government.

transfer station *noun* a facility where garbage is collected for compression etc. before being trucked to a landfill.

transfiguration *noun* **1** a change of form or appearance: *describes the transfiguration of a prostitute from Down East into some kind of pure, clean, saint-like virgin*. **2** (**Transfiguration**) **a** Christ's appearance in radiant glory to three of his disciples. **b** the festival of Christ's transfiguration. [Say trans figure AY sh'n]

transfigure *verb* (**transfigures, transfigured, transfiguring**) change in form or appearance, esp. so as to elevate or idealize: *she is a woman transfigured into a hero*. [Say trans FIGURE]

transfix *verb* (**transfixes, transfixed, transfixing**) **1** pierce with a sharp implement or weapon: *a white cockatoo, its breast transfixed by an arrow, swoons in death*. **2** root (a person) to the spot with fascination, astonishment, fear, etc.: *Charlap riveted his listener with glittering blue eyes, much as cobras are said to transfix their prey*.

transform *verb* **1 a** make a thorough or dramatic change in the form, outward appearance, character, etc., of. **b** (often foll. by *into*, etc.) undergo such a change. **2** change the voltage etc. of (a current). ▶ **transformable** *adjective*

transformation *noun* **1** a thorough or dramatic change in form or appearance: *Quebec society underwent a radical transformation in the sixties*. **2** a complete change of form at metamorphosis, esp. of insects, amphibians, etc. ▶ **transformational** *adjective*

transformative *adjective* causing change or able to cause change: *a transformative experience*.

transformer *noun* **1** an apparatus for reducing or increasing the voltage of an alternating current. **2** a person or thing that transforms.

transfuse *verb* (**transfuses**, **transfused**, **transfusing**) **1** transfer blood from one person or animal to another. **2** inject liquid into a blood vessel to replace lost fluid. ▶ **transfusion** *noun*

transgenic *adjective* having genetic material introduced from another species: *by injecting fertilized mouse eggs with human genes, the research group has created strains of transgenic mice*. [Say trans JEN ick]

transgress *verb* (**transgresses**, **transgressed**, **transgressing**) go beyond the limit of what is morally, legally, or socially acceptable: *she had transgressed an unwritten social law* ◊ *they had transgressed the bounds of decency*.

transgression *noun* the breaking of a moral law or rule of behaviour: *forgiven for her youthful transgressions*.

transgressor *noun* a person who violates a rule or law: *leaders must define the behaviour that is unacceptable and publicize their commitment to punish the transgressors*.

tranship *verb* = TRANSSHIP.

transience *noun* the quality of being momentary or passing; impermanence: *withering flowers symbolized life's transience*. [Say TRANZY ince]

transient ● *adjective* of short duration; momentary; passing; impermanent: *transient cough and chest pain*. ● *noun* **1 a** a temporary visitor, worker, etc.: *forty-three of the region's bird species are spring migrants or summer transients*. **b** a vagrant; a tramp: *no identification is found on the body and it is concluded that he is a transient*. **2** *Electricity* a momentary variation in current, voltage, or frequency: *data line protectors provide effective protection from high-energy transients, such as those produced by lightning strikes*. ▶ **transiently** *adverb* [Say TRANZY int]

transistor *noun* **1** a small electronic device made of semiconductor material, such as silicon or germanium, and used esp. in satellites, computers, televisions, and portable radios for controlling an electric current as it passes along a circuit; transistors may be used as amplifiers, photoelectric cells, or switches. **2** (also **transistor radio**) a portable radio with transistors. [Say tran ZIST er]

transit ● *noun* **1** the act or process of going, conveying, or being conveyed, esp. over a distance. **2** a passage or route. **3** the local conveyance of passengers on public routes. **4 a** the apparent passage of a celestial body across the meridian of a place. **b** the passage of an inferior planet across the face of the sun, or of a moon etc. across the face of a planet. **5** a surveying instrument for measuring horizontal angles. ● *verb* (**transits**, **transited**, **transiting**) pass across or through an area: *years ago I transited Tokyo's Narita airport*. PHRASES **in transit** while going or being conveyed.

transition *noun* **1** a passing or change from one place, condition, etc., to another: *the transition from an agricultural economy to an industrial economy* ◊ *her contact with the church was limited to the major transitions in her life — birth, marriage, and death*. **2** a passage in thought, speech, writing, or music from one subject or section to another: *the transition to the chapter on the seas of Norden is rather too abrupt*. ▶ **transitional** *adjective*

transition house *noun* (also **transition home**) *Cdn* a home operated by a social service agency, esp. for abused women.

transitive *Grammar* ● *adjective* (of a verb or sense of a verb) that takes a direct object (whether expressed or implied). ● *noun* a transitive verb. ▶ **transitively** *adverb* **transitivity** *noun* [Say TRANZA tiv, tranza TIVVA tee]

transitoriness *noun* the quality of not being permanent: *human transitoriness*. [Say TRANZA tory niss]

transitory *adjective* not permanent; brief, passing: *this is more than a transitory problem*. [Say TRANZA tory]

translatable *adjective* able to be translated.

translate *verb* (**translates**, **translated**, **translating**) **1** express the sense of in another language. **2** (of a literary work etc.) be translatable. **3** express (an idea, book, etc.) in another, esp. simpler, form. **4** interpret the significance of. **5** (foll. by *into*) express something or be expressed in a different, esp. a more practical form: *it's time to translate our ideas into action*. **6** *Christianity* **a** remove (a bishop) to another see. **b** remove (a saint's relics etc.) to another place. **7** *Bible* convey to heaven without death; transform.

translation *noun* **1** the process of translating words or text from one language into another: *the book loses something in translation*. **2** a written or spoken rendering of the meaning of a text in another language. **3** the process of changing something into a different form: *the translation of ideology into practice*.

translator *noun* **1** a person who translates from one language into another. **2** a program that translates from one (esp. programming) language into another.

transliterate *verb* (**transliterates**, **transliterated**, **transliterating**) represent (a word etc.) in the closest corresponding letters of a different alphabet or language: *Romans called the town Eboracum, which was transliterated into Old English as Eoforwic and eventually became, in Modern English, York*. ▶ **transliteration** *noun* [Say trans LITTER ate]

translocate *verb* (**translocates**, **translocated**, **translocating**) move from one place to another: *nutrients are taken in through the stomata on the leaf surface and are then translocated throughout the plant*. ▶ **translocation** *noun*

translucence *noun* (also **translucency**) the quality of something that allows light but not detailed shapes to pass through it: *grey translucence was spreading across the sky, gradually driving out the fainter stars*.

translucent *adjective* allowing light, but not detailed shapes, to pass through: *they put a sheet of translucent glass in the window to brighten the room while maintaining privacy*. ▶ **translucently** *adverb* [Say trans LOO sint]

transmigration *noun* **1** the passage of the soul into a different body after death: *their belief in transmigration eliminates the need for a concept of heaven*. **2** migration: *the transmigration of people from the densely populated island of Java to the country's outer islands*. [Say trans MIGRATE]

transmissible *adjective* (esp. of a disease) able to be transmitted from one person to another. [Say trans MISSA bull]

transmission *noun* **1** the action or process of transmitting something or the state of being transmitted: *transmission of the HIV virus*. **2** a broadcast radio or television program. **3** the mechanism by which power is transmitted from an engine to the axle in a motor vehicle. [Say trans MISSION]

transmission line *noun* a conductor or conductors, esp. a cable, carrying electricity over large distances.

transmit *verb* (**transmits**, **transmitted**, **transmitting**) **1 a** pass or hand on; transfer. **b** communicate (ideas, emotions, etc.). **2 a** allow (heat, light, sound, electricity, etc.) to pass through. **b** be a

medium for (ideas, emotions, etc.): *his message transmits hope*. **3** broadcast (a radio or TV signal, message, etc.). ▶ **transmittable** *adjective* **transmittal** *noun* **transmitter** *noun* **1** a person or thing that transmits. **2** a set of equipment used to generate and transmit electromagnetic waves carrying messages, signals, etc., esp. those of radio or TV. **3** = NEUROTRANSMITTER.

transmogrification *noun jocular* an esp. magical or surprising transformation: *the absurd transmogrification of a marine mollusc into an extraterrestrial marauder*. [Say trans mogra fi CAY sh'n]

transmogrify *verb* (**transmogrifies**, **transmogrified**, **transmogrifying**) *jocular* transform, esp. in a magical or surprising manner: *alchemists strove to transmogrify base metals into gold*. [Say trans MOGRA fie]

transmutation *noun* **1** the action of changing or the state of being changed into another form etc.: *the transmutation of the political economy of the post-war years was complete*. **2** the supposed process of changing base metals into gold by alchemy. **3** the changing of one element into another by nuclear bombardment etc.

transmute *verb* (**transmutes**, **transmuted**, **transmuting**) **1** change the form, nature, or substance of: *she would somehow transmute his anguish to publishable prose*. **2** subject (base metals) to transmutation: *humanists were always seeking the mineral that, by its merest touch, could transmute base metals such as lead into gold*.

transnational • *adjective* extending beyond national boundaries: *transnational crime was identified as a growing threat to the security of nations*. • *noun* a transnational company. ▶ **transnationally** *adverb*

transoceanic *adjective* **1** situated beyond the ocean. **2** concerned with crossing the ocean: *transoceanic flight*. [Say trans oh see ANN ick]

transom *noun* **1** a horizontal bar of wood or stone across a window or the top of a door. **2** a strengthening crossbar. **3** a window divided by or placed above a transom. PHRASES **over the transom** offered or sent without the prior agreement of the recipient; (esp. of a manuscript etc.) unsolicited. [Say TRAN sum]

trans-Pacific *adjective* **1** on the other side of the Pacific Ocean. **2** crossing the Pacific Ocean.

transparency *noun* (*plural* **transparencies**) **1** the condition of being transparent. **2** a positive transparent photograph mounted between glass plates or in a frame to be viewed using a slide projector. **3** a clear plastic page containing usu. written information, projected on a wall or screen using an overhead projector.

transparent *adjective* **1** allowing light to pass through so that bodies can be distinctly seen (*compare* TRANSLUCENT). **2 a** (of a disguise, pretext, etc.) easily seen through. **b** (of a motive, quality, meaning, etc.) easily discerned; evident; obvious. **3** (of a person etc.) having motives that are easily understood. **4** *Computing* (of a program, process, etc.) operating in a manner which the general user does not perceive, or such that other software does not need to take account of it. ▶ **transparently** *adverb*

transpiration *noun* the loss of moisture by evaporation from the surface of a plant.

transpire *verb* (**transpires**, **transpired**, **transpiring**) **1 a** (preceded by *it* as subject) turn out; prove to be the case: *it transpired he knew nothing about it*. **b** (of a secret or something unknown) leak out; come to be known: *it transpired that he had been under surveillance for quite some time*. **2** occur; happen: *nobody knows what transpired between them*. **3** (of a plant or leaf) release water vapour.

transplant • *verb* **1 a** plant in another place. **b** move

to another place: *a Winnipegger transplanted to Toronto*. **2** transfer (living tissue or an organ) and implant in another part of the body or in another body. • *noun* **1 a** the transplanting of an organ or tissue. **b** such an organ etc. **2 a** a thing, esp. a plant, transplanted. **3** *informal* a person not native to his or her place of residence. ▶ **transplantable** *adjective* **transplantation** *noun* **transplanter** *noun*

transponder *noun* a device for receiving a radio signal and automatically transmitting a different signal.

transport • *verb* **1** take or carry (a person, goods, etc.) from one place to another. **2** *hist.* take (a criminal) to a penal colony. • *noun* **1** the action of transporting something or the state of being transported: *the transport of nuclear waste* ◊ *the goods were damaged during transport*. **2** a system or way of moving people, goods, etc., from place to place: *air transport* ◊ *her bike was her only means of transport*. **3 a** a ship, aircraft, etc. used to carry soldiers, supplies, etc. **b** = TRANSPORT TRUCK. **4** (esp. in *plural*) an overwhelmingly strong emotion: *art can send people into transports of delight*. ▶ **transportable** *adjective*

transportation *noun* **1** the act or process of transporting something; conveyance of people, goods, etc.: *the era of global mass transportation*. **2** a way by which something is transported: *transportation at the site includes a monorail*. **3** *hist.* the act of transporting convicts to a penal colony.

transported *adjective* affected with strong emotion, esp. joy: *Karen was transported with pleasure*.

transporter *noun* **1 a** a person or device that transports. **2** a vehicle used to transport other vehicles or large pieces of machinery etc. by road.

transport truck *noun* a large, long truck, used esp. for conveying goods long distances.

transpose *verb* (**transposes**, **transposed**, **transposing**) **1** cause (two or more things) to change places: *two letters were accidentally transposed and "gun" got printed as "gnu"*. **2** change the order or position of (words or a word) in a sentence. **3** (often foll. by *up*, *down*) *Music* write or perform in a different key from the original. **4** *Algebra* transfer (a term) with a changed sign to the other side of an equation. ▶ **transposable** *adjective* **transposition** *noun*

transsexual • *adjective* having the physical characteristics of one sex and the supposed psychological characteristics of the other. • *noun* **1** a transsexual person. **2** a person whose sex has been changed by surgery.

transship *verb* (**transships**, **transshipped**, **transshipping**) transfer from one ship or form of transport to another. ▶ **transshipment** *noun*

transubstantiation *noun* (in Catholic and Orthodox belief) the conversion in the Eucharist, after consecration, of the whole substance of the bread and wine into the body and blood of Christ, only the appearances of bread and wine remaining. [Say tran sub stanshy AY sh'n]

transverse *adjective* situated, arranged, or acting in a crosswise direction. ▶ **transversely** *adverb* [Say TRANS vers]

transvestism *noun* the practice of wearing or desire to wear the clothes of the opposite sex. [Say trans VEST ism]

transvestite *noun* a person, esp. a man, who dresses in the clothes of the opposite sex, esp. as a sexual stimulus. [Say trans VEST ite]

trap • *noun* **1 a** an enclosure or device, often baited, for catching animals, usu. by affording a way in but not a way out. **b** *Cdn* (*Nfld*) a large box-shaped fishing net used in inshore waters to catch migrating cod and salmon.

c a device with bait for killing vermin, esp. mice. **2 a** a trick betraying a person into speech or an act: *is this question a trap?* **b** an unpleasant situation from which escape is difficult. **3** an arrangement to catch an unsuspecting person, e.g. a speeding motorist. **4** a device for hurling an object such as a clay pigeon into the air to be shot at. **5 a** a curve in a drainpipe etc. that fills with liquid and forms a seal against the upward passage of gases. **b** a device for preventing the passage of steam etc. **6** *slang* the mouth: *shut your trap!* **7** *Golf* a bunker. **8** *Hockey* a conservative, defensive strategy in which a team positions all its skaters in the neutral zone to challenge their opponents' rush, rather than send players into the opponents' end to forecheck. **9** *Football* a tactical play in which an attacking team permits a defensive player to cross the line of scrimmage in order to block him from the side, so enabling the ball carrier to move unopposed through the gap created. **10** a two-wheeled carriage: *a pony and trap*. **11** = TRAP DOOR. **12** (esp. in *plural*) *informal* a percussion instrument esp. in a jazz band. **13** (usu. in *plural*) *slang* a trapezius muscle. • *verb* (**traps, trapped, trapping**) **1** catch (an animal or fish) in a trap. **2 a** catch wild animals in traps for their fur. **b** set traps for game. **3** catch or catch out (a person) by means of a trick, plan, etc. **4 a** stop and retain in a trap. **b** cause a person to be unable to leave a location: *trapped on the ice*. **5** provide (a place) with traps. **6** keep (something) in a particular place and prevent it from escaping: *trapped the puck*. **7** *Baseball* catch (a ball) just after it has hit the ground. ▶ PHRASES **trap out** deplete the supply of fur-bearing animals in a region through trapping.

trap door *noun* a door or hatch in a floor, ceiling, or roof, usu. made even with the surface.

trapeze *noun* a crossbar or set of crossbars suspended by ropes used as a swing for acrobatics etc. [Say tra PEEZ]

trapezium *noun* (*plural* **trapezia** or **trapeziums**) a quadrilateral with no two sides parallel. [Say truh PEEZY um for the singular; for TRAPEZIA say truh PEEZY uh]

trapezius *noun* (*plural* **trapezii**) either of a pair of large triangular muscles extending over the back of the neck and shoulders. [Say truh PEEZY us for the singular, truh PEEZY eye for the plural]

trapezoid *noun* a quadrilateral with only one pair of sides parallel. ▶ **trapezoidal** *adjective* [Say TRAPPA zoid]

trapline *noun* **1** a series of traps set outdoors for catching animals. **2** the trail along which a trapper walks to check his or her traplines. **3** the general area in which a trapper has traplines set up.

trapper *noun* **1** a person who traps wild animals esp. to obtain furs. **2** *Hockey* a goalie's catching glove.

trappings *plural noun* **1** outward signs, objects, ceremonies, etc. esp. as an indication of status: *she was familiar with all the trappings of success such as contracts and corporate sponsorships*. **2** the harness of a horse esp. when ornamental.

Trappist • *noun* a member of a branch of the Cistercian order of monks founded in 1664 and noted for an austere way of life including a vow of silence. • *adjective* of or relating to this order.

trap shooter *noun* a person who shoots at clay pigeons launched into the air from a trap.

trap shooting *noun* the sport of shooting at clay pigeons launched into the air from a trap.

trash • *noun* **1** garbage, refuse. **2 a** things of poor workmanship, quality, or material; worthless stuff. **b** literary or artistic work of an inferior quality. **3** nonsense; foolish talk. **4** a worthless person or persons. • *verb* (**trashes, trashed, trashing**) *informal* **1** wreck, destroy. **2** expose the worthless nature of; criticize harshly.

trashed *adjective* **1** *informal* very drunk. **2** destroyed.

trash fish *noun* (*plural* **trash fish**) a fish sold for animal feed etc. rather than human consumption.

trashily *adverb* in a trashy way.

trashiness *noun* the quality of being of poor quality or worthless.

trash talk esp. *US informal* • *noun* **1** *Sport* insulting or boastful talk delivered with the intention of demoralizing, intimidating, or humiliating an opponent. **2** any contemptuous or boastful statement. • *verb* (**trash-talk**) **1** deliver trash talk; bad-mouth an opponent. **2** demoralize or attempt to demoralize (an opponent) with trash talk. ▶ **trash-talker** *noun* **trash-talking** *noun & adjective*

trashy *adjective* (**trashier, trashiest**) **1** of poor quality; cheap, inferior. **2** (of a person) worthless, disreputable.

trattoria *noun* an Italian restaurant. [Say tratta REE uh]

trauma *noun* (*plural* **traumas**) **1 a** *Psychology* emotional shock following a stressful event, sometimes leading to long-term neurosis. **b** (in general use) a distressing or emotionally disturbing experience etc. **2** any physical wound or injury. **3** physical shock following this, characterized by a drop in body temperature, mental confusion, etc. [Say TROMMA]

traumatic *adjective* **1** of or causing trauma. **2** (in general use) distressing; emotionally disturbing. [Say truh MAT ick]

traumatize *verb* (**traumatizes, traumatized, traumatizing**) shock and upset somebody very much, often making them unable to think or work normally. [Say TROMMA tize]

travail *noun* *literary* painful or laborious effort: *the country was deep in the travails of adjusting to independence*. [Say truh VAIL or TRAV ail]

travel • *verb* (**travels, travelled, travelling**) **1** go from one place to another; make a journey esp. of some length or abroad. **2 a** journey along or through (a country). **b** cover (a distance) in travelling. **3** withstand a long journey: *not all wines travel*. **4** go from place to place as a salesperson. **5** move or proceed in a specified manner or at a specified rate: *light travels faster than sound*. **6** *informal* move quickly. **7** pass esp. in a deliberate or systematic manner from point to point: *his eye travelled over the scene*. **8** *Basketball* make two or more steps' progress in any direction while carrying (esp. instead of dribbling) the ball, in violation of the rules. **9** (of a machine or part) move or operate in a specified way. • *noun* **1 a** the act of travelling, esp. in foreign countries. **b** (often in *plural*) a period of this. **2** (as an *adjective*) suitable for use when travelling because of size, portability, dual voltage, etc.: *travel alarm*.

travel agency *noun* (*plural* **travel agencies**) a company which makes transportation, accommodation, etc. arrangements for travellers. ▶ **travel agent** *noun*

travelled *adjective* experienced in travelling: *many of them were urbane, well-travelled, and widely read*.

traveller *noun* **1** a person who travels or is travelling. **2** (also **New Age traveller**) a person who embraces New Age values and leads an unconventional lifestyle involving movement from place to place.

traveller's cheque *noun* a cheque for a fixed amount that may be cashed on signature, usu. internationally.

travelling *noun* *Basketball* the taking of two or more steps while carrying the ball without dribbling, in violation of the rules.

travelogue *noun* a film, book, or illustrated lecture about travel. [Say TRAVEL og]

traverse • *verb* (**traverses, traversed, traversing**) travel or lie across: *traversed the country*. • *noun* **1** a sideways movement, e.g. while ascending or descending a mountain: *a solo geological traverse is never boring*. **2** an act of crossing something: *because Steger purposely chose the longest possible traverse, he has already mushed more than 1,000 miles further than Amundsen*. [Say truh VERSE]

travertine *noun* a white or light-coloured chalky rock deposited from springs. [Say TRAVER teen]

travesty • *noun* (*plural* **travesties**) a grotesque misrepresentation or imitation: *a travesty of justice*. • *verb* (**travesties, travestied, travestying**) make or be a travesty of: *my reasons for choosing to travesty the work of dear old Frances*. [Say TRAVA stee]

travois *noun* (*plural* **travois**) *hist.* a V-shaped frame of teepee poles pulled by dogs or horses, used by Plains Aboriginal peoples to carry teepee covers and other possessions. [Say TRAV wah for the singular, TRAV wahs for the plural]

trawl • *verb* (often foll. by *through, for*) **1** fish by dragging either a large wide-mouthed net or a long buoyed line supporting baited hooks. **2** search thoroughly: *trawled the schools for new trainees*. • *noun* **1** an act of trawling. **2** (also **trawl net**) a large wide-mouthed fishing net dragged by a boat along the sea floor. **3** (also **trawl line**) a long buoyed sea-fishing line supporting short lines with baited hooks.

trawler *noun* **1** a boat used for trawling. **2** a person who trawls.

tray *noun* **1 a** a flat shallow vessel usu. with a raised rim for carrying, storing, or collecting items. **b** something carried on a tray: *a tray of drinks* ◊ *cheese tray*. **2** a shallow lidless box forming a compartment of a cabinet, trunk, etc.

treacherous *adjective* **1** guilty of or involving betrayal; disloyal; deceiving. **2** (of ice, conditions, etc.) dangerous, hazardous. ▶**treacherously** *adverb* **treacherousness** *noun* [Say TRETCHER us]

treachery *noun* (*plural* **treacheries**) betrayal of trust: *his resignation was perceived as an act of treachery* ◊ *the committee is like a medieval court: snits, treacheries, and umbrage*. [Say TRETCHER ee]

treacle *noun* esp. *Brit.* **1** a syrup produced in refining sugar. **2** molasses. ▶**treacly** *adjective* [Say TREEKLE]

tread • *verb* (**treads**; *past* **trod**; *past participle* **trodden** or **trod**; *treading*) **1** (often foll. by *on*) **a** set down one's foot; walk or step. **b** (of the foot) be set down. **2 a** walk on. **b** (often foll. by *down*) press or crush with the feet. **3** perform (steps etc.) by walking: *trod a few paces*. **4** make (a hole etc.) by treading. **5** (foll. by *on*) suppress; subdue mercilessly. **6** make a track with (dirt etc.) from the feet. **7** (often foll. by *in, into*) press down into the ground with the feet: *trod dirt into the carpet*. • *noun* **1** a manner or sound of walking: *recognized the heavy tread*. **2** the top surface of a step or stair. **3** the thick moulded part of a vehicle tire for gripping the road. **4 a** the part of a wheel that touches the ground or rail. **b** the part of a rail that the wheels touch. **5** the part of the sole of a shoe that rests on the ground. PHRASES **tread water 1** maintain an upright position in the water by moving the feet with a walking movement and the hands with a sideways circular motion. **2** fail to advance. ▶**treader** *noun* [Say TRED]

treadle • *noun* a lever worked by the foot and imparting motion to a machine. • *verb* (**treadles, treadled, treadling**) work a treadle. [Say TREDDLE]

treadmill *noun* **1** a device for producing motion by the weight of persons or animals stepping on steps on the inner surface of a revolving upright wheel. **2** an exercise machine consisting of a continuous moving belt on which a person walks or jogs. **3** monotonous routine work. [Say TRED mill]

treason *noun* **1** (also **high treason**) violation by a subject of loyalty to the sovereign or to the state, esp. by attempting to kill or overthrow the sovereign or to overthrow the government. **2** any betrayal of trust; treachery.

treasonable *adjective* involving or guilty of treason.

treasonous *adjective* involving or guilty of treason. [Say TREASON us]

treasure • *noun* **1 a** wealth or riches stored or accumulated, esp. in the form of gems, precious metals, etc. **b** a hoard of such wealth. **2** a thing valued for its rarity, workmanship, associations, etc.: *art treasures*. **3** *informal* a much loved or highly valued person. • *verb* (**treasures, treasured, treasuring**) value highly; cherish.

treasure chest *noun* **1** a chest for holding or storing treasure. **2** a collection of valuable or delightful things.

treasure house *noun* **1** a building or room in which treasure is kept. **2** an abundant source of something valuable: *a treasure house of information*.

treasure hunt *noun* **1** a search for treasure. **2** a game in which players seek a hidden object from a series of clues.

treasurer *noun* **1** a person appointed to administer the funds of a society, corporation, etc. **2** an officer authorized to receive and disburse public revenues.

treasure trove *noun* **1** *Law* treasure of unknown ownership which is found hidden in the ground etc. and is declared the property of the Crown. **2** a collection of valuable or delightful things.

treasury *noun* (*plural* **treasuries**) **1** a place or building where treasure is stored. **2** the funds or revenue of a state, institution, or society. **3** (**Treasury**) **a** the department managing the public revenue of a country. **b** the offices and officers of this. **c** the place where the public revenues are kept. **4** = TREASURY BILL.

treasury bill *noun* a bill of exchange issued by the government to raise money for temporary needs.

Treasury Board *noun* *Cdn* a committee of the Privy Council responsible for reviewing and prioritizing planned government expenditures and programs etc.

treasury bond *noun* a government bond issued by the Treasury.

Treasury Branch *noun* (*plural* **Treasury Branches**) *Cdn* (in Alberta) one of a network of savings banks operated by the government of Alberta.

treat • *verb* **1** act or behave towards or deal with (a person or thing) in a certain way: *treated me kindly* ◊ *treat it as a joke*. **2** deal with or apply a process to: *treat it with acid*. **3** apply medical care or attention to. **4** present or deal with (a subject) in literature or art. **5** (often foll. by *to*) **a** provide with food or drink or entertainment at one's own expense: *treated us to dinner*. **b** provide with a special gift or indulgence. **6** (often foll. by *with*) negotiate terms (with a person). **7** (often foll. by *of*) give a spoken or written exposition. • *noun* **1** an event or circumstance (esp. when unexpected or unusual) that gives great pleasure. **2** a meal, entertainment, etc., provided by one person for the enjoyment of another or others. **3** a candy, cookie, or other small sweet food item. ▶**treatable** *adjective* **treater** *noun* **treating** *noun*

treatise *noun* a written work dealing formally and systematically with a subject: *a treatise on the theory and practice of landscape gardening*. [Say TREE tiss]

treatment *noun* **1** a process or manner of behaving towards or dealing with a person or thing. **2** the application of medical care or attention to a patient. **3 a** a manner of treating a subject in literature or art.

b a preparatory version of a screenplay, including descriptions of sets and of the camera work required. **4** subjection to the action of a chemical, physical, or biological agent. **5 (the treatment)** *informal* the customary way of dealing with a person, situation, etc.: *got the full treatment.*

treaty *noun* (*plural* **treaties**) **1 a** a formally concluded and ratified agreement between states. **b** the document embodying such an agreement. **2** an agreement between individuals or parties, esp. for the purchase of property.

treaty band *noun* *Cdn* an Aboriginal band that has signed a treaty with the federal government.

treaty Indian *noun* *Cdn* a status Indian who is a member of a treaty band.

treaty rights *plural noun* *Cdn* the rights, e.g. that of holding land on a reserve, granted to a group of Aboriginal people under the terms of a treaty.

treble • *adjective* **1** (of a voice) high-pitched. **2** *Music* soprano (esp. of an instrument or boy's voice). **3** esp. *Brit.* **a** threefold. **b** triple. **c** three times as much or many: *treble the amount.* • *noun* **1 a** *Music* soprano (esp. a boy's voice or part, or an instrument). **b** a high-pitched voice. **2** the high-frequency output of a radio, record player, etc., corresponding to the treble in music. [Say TREBBLE]

treble clef *noun* *Music* a sign that indicates that the second lowest line of the staff represents the G above middle C.

tree • *noun* **1 a** a perennial plant with a woody self-supporting main stem or trunk when mature and usu. without branches for some distance above the ground (*compare* SHRUB). **b** any similar plant having a tall erect usu. single stem, e.g. a palm tree. **2** a piece or frame of wood etc. for various purposes. **3** *archaic* or *literary* a cross, esp. the one used for Christ's crucifixion. **4** (also **tree diagram**) *Math*, *Computing*, etc. a branching figure or graph in which processes, relationships, etc., are represented by points or nodes joined by lines. **5** a family tree. **6** a Christmas tree. • *verb* (**trees, treed, treeing**) force to take refuge in a tree. **PHRASES grow on trees** (usu. with *neg.*) be plentiful. **out of one's tree** *informal* crazy.

treed *adjective* (of a tract of land) containing trees.

tree farm *noun* an area of land where trees are grown for commercial purposes.

tree fern *noun* a large fern with an upright trunklike stem.

tree frog *noun* a tree-dwelling tailless amphibian that climbs by means of adhesive discs on its digits.

tree house *noun* a structure built in the branches of a tree for children to play in.

tree hugger *noun* *informal* a person who cares for trees or the environment; an environmentalist.

treeless *adjective* (of a tract of land) without trees.

treelike *adjective* resembling a tree, esp. in having a branching form.

treeline *noun* **1** (in the northern hemisphere) the latitudinal limit north of which no trees grow. **2** the level on a mountain above which no trees grow.

tree ring *noun* a ring in a cross-section of a tree, produced by one year's growth.

tree surgeon *noun* a person who treats decayed trees in order to preserve them.

treetop *noun* the topmost part of a tree.

trefoil • *noun* **1** a plant of the pea family with yellow flowers and three-lobed leaves, resembling clover. **2** any similar or related plant with three-lobed leaves. **3** a thing arranged in or with three lobes. • *adjective* of or concerning a three-lobed plant etc. [Say TREFF oil or TREE foil]

trek • *verb* (**treks, trekked, trekking**) travel or make one's way arduously. • *noun* a journey or walk made by trekking: *it was a trek to the nearest laundromat.* ▶ **trekker** *noun*

Trekkie *noun* (also **Trekker**) *slang* a fan of *Star Trek*, a TV science fiction drama series.

trellis • *noun* (*plural* **trellises**) a lattice or grating of light wooden or metal bars used esp. as a support for fruit trees or creepers and often fastened against a wall. • *verb* (**trellises, trellised, trellising**) **1** provide with a trellis. **2** support (a vine etc.) with a trellis.

tremble • *verb* (**trembles, trembled, trembling**) **1** shake involuntarily from fear, excitement, weakness, etc. **2** be in a state of extreme apprehension: *trembled at the very thought of it.* **3** move in a quivering manner: *leaves trembled in the breeze.* • *noun* a trembling state or movement; a quiver: *couldn't speak without a tremble.*

trembling aspen *noun* (also **trembling poplar**) a poplar found across Canada, with leaves that tremble in a slight breeze.

tremblingly *adverb* in a trembling manner.

trembly *adjective* *informal* trembling; agitated.

tremendous *adjective* remarkable, considerable, excellent. ▶ **tremendously** *adverb* **tremendousness** *noun*

tremolo *noun* (*plural* **tremolos**) **1** a shaky effect produced on musical instruments or in singing: **a** by rapid repetition of a note, esp. on bowed stringed instruments or on an organ. **b** by rapid alternation between two notes. **c** by rapid repeated slight variation in the pitch of a note, e.g. on an electric guitar. **2** a device in an organ producing a tremolo. [Say TREMMA loe]

tremor • *noun* **1** a shaking or quivering. **2** a thrill (of fear or exultation etc.). **3** a slight earthquake. • *verb* undergo a tremor or tremors. [Say TREMMER]

tremulous *adjective* **1** trembling or quivering, esp. from nervousness: *in a tremulous voice.* **2** (of a line etc.) drawn by a shaky hand. ▶ **tremulously** *adverb* **tremulousness** *noun* [Say TREM yuh lus]

trench • *noun* (*plural* **trenches**) **1** a long narrow usu. deep depression or ditch. **2** *Military* **a** this dug by troops to stand in and be sheltered from enemy fire. **b** (in *plural*) a defensive system of these, as used in World War I. **3** a long narrow deep depression in the ocean bed. **4** *informal* = TRENCH COAT. • *verb* (**trenches, trenched, trenching**) **1** dig a trench or trenches in (the ground). **2** turn over the earth of (a field, garden, etc.) by digging a succession of adjoining ditches. **PHRASES in the trenches** actively involved in the practical details or hard work connected with a project.

trenchancy *noun* the quality of being strongly and effectively expressed: *I dealt with the criticisms with a trenchancy that I think even Meighen himself could hardly have bettered.* [Say TREN chun see]

trenchant *adjective* (of a style or language etc.) expressed strongly and effectively, in a clear way: *a very trenchant observation.* ▶ **trenchantly** *adverb* [Say TREN chunt]

trench coat *noun* a loose belted double-breasted raincoat.

trencher *noun* a machine, usu. self-propelled, used in digging trenches.

trench warfare *noun* **1** hostilities carried on from more or less permanent trenches. **2** a protracted dispute in which the parties maintain entrenched positions while persistently attacking their opponents.

trend • *noun* a general direction and tendency (esp. of events, fashion, or opinion etc.). • *verb* (esp. of a geographical feature) bend or turn away in a specified direction: *the Richelieu River trending southward to Lake*

Champlain. **2** change or develop in a general direction: *unemployment has been trending upwards.*

trendily *adverb* in a way that is fashionable: *trendily torn jeans.*

trendiness *noun* the quality of being trendy.

trendoid *informal* often *derogatory* • *adjective* trendy; self-consciously or extravagantly fashionable. • *noun* a person who sets or follows fashions; a trendy.

trend-setter *noun* a person who leads the way in fashion etc. ▶ **trend-setting** *adjective*

trendy *informal* • *adjective* (**trendier**, **trendiest**) often *derogatory* fashionable; following fashionable trends. • *noun* (*plural* **trendies**) a fashionable person.

trepidation *noun* a feeling of fear or agitation about something that may happen: *with a mix of anticipation and trepidation, we separate into groups and slip gently into the water.* [Say treppa DAY sh'n]

très *adverb* very. [Say TRAY]

trespass • *verb* (**trespasses**, **trespassed**, **trespassing**) **1** (usu. foll. by *on*, *upon*) make an unlawful or unjustifiable intrusion (esp. on land or property). **2** (foll. by *on*) make unjustifiable claims: *shall not trespass on your hospitality.* **3** (foll. by *against*) *literary* or *archaic* offend. • *noun* (*plural* **trespasses**) **1** *Law* a voluntary wrongful act against the person or property of another, esp. unlawful entry to a person's land or property. **2** *archaic* a sin or offence. ▶ **trespasser** *noun*

tress *noun* (*plural* **tresses**) **1** a long lock of human (esp. female) hair. **2** (in *plural*) a woman's or girl's head of hair. ▶ **tressed** *adjective*

trestle *noun* **1** a supporting structure for a table etc., consisting of two frames fixed at an angle or hinged or of a bar supported by two divergent pairs of legs. **2** (also **trestle table**) a table consisting of a board or boards laid on trestles or other supports. **3** (also **trestlework**) an open braced framework to support a bridge etc. **4** (also **trestle bridge**) a bridge supported on trestles. [Rhymes with WRESTLE]

T. Rex *noun* (*plural* **T. Rexes**) *Tyrannosaurus rex* (see TYRANNOSAUR).

trey *noun* (*plural* **treys**) **1** Basketball *informal* a three-point field goal. **2** a three in dice or cards. [Say TRAY]

tri- *combining form* **1** forming nouns and adjectives meaning three or three times. **2** *Chemistry* containing three atoms or groups of a specified kind.

triactor *noun* Cdn a bet on the first three finishers in a horse race, specifying the order of finish. [Say TRY actor]

triad *noun* **1** a group of three people or things: *by the sixteenth century the triad — corn, beans, and squash — was being grown throughout agricultural North America.* **2** *Music* a chord of three notes, consisting of a given note with the third and fifth above it. **3** (usu. **Triad**) any of several Chinese secret societies in various countries, usu. involved in criminal activities. ▶ **triadic** *adjective* [Say TRY ad, try AD ick]

triage *noun* **1** the process of determining the order in which a large number of injured or ill patients will receive medical treatment, with priority usu. given to those patients with the most severe ailments or the greatest chance of survival: *battlefield surgeons must perform triage at the front.* **2** the process of prioritizing a large number of people or things requiring attention: *all of this information will help you understand exactly what you're paying for, and if you do go over budget, it can come in handy for triage as well.* [Say TREE azh or TREE ozh]

trial *noun* **1** a formal examination of evidence by a judge and often a jury, in order to decide guilt in a case of criminal or civil proceedings: *stood trial for fraud* ◊ *is on trial for murder.* **2** a test of the qualities, performance, or suitability of someone or something: *the drug has undergone rigorous clinical trials* ◊ *the system*

was introduced on a trial basis ◊ *the two of them got back together after a trial separation.* **3 a** a frustrating or exasperating experience, thing, or person. **b** (in *plural*; usu. foll. by *of*) the frustrating aspects of something: *the trials of being an artist.* **4** any of various races or competitions to evaluate the speed and overall abilities of athletes, vehicles, or animals: *sheepdog trials.* ■ PHRASES ■ **on trial 1** being tried in a court of law. **2** being tested; to be chosen or retained only if found suitable or satisfactory.

trial and error *noun* a method of finding the most effective way of completing a task, resolving a situation, etc., by experimenting with various unsuccessful approaches until a suitable one is found.

trial balloon *noun* an announcement or experiment made in order to see how a new policy will be received: *a trial balloon on raising the retirement age to 67 was floated last winter.*

Trial Division *noun* Cdn (in Newfoundland and PEI) a division of the Supreme Court, with judges appointed federally, which has jurisdiction over a wide range of civil and criminal cases, and hears appeals from lower provincial courts.

trial run *noun* **1** a preliminary test of the performance of a new procedure etc. **2** a drive taken to assess the performance of a car or truck etc. one is thinking of buying.

triangle *noun* **1** a plane closed figure with three sides and angles. **2** a three-sided object, area, etc. having this shape: *fold the napkins into triangles.* **3** any three things not in a straight line, with imaginary lines joining them: *the Toronto-Ottawa-Montreal triangle.* **4** a percussion instrument consisting of a steel rod bent into the shape of a triangle and sounded by striking it with a small thin rod. **5** a situation or relationship involving three people: *love triangle.* **6** a flat wooden or plastic instrument in the form of a right-angled triangle used for drawing lines and square angles.

triangular *adjective* **1** arranged in the form or shape of a triangle; having three corners or sides. **2** (of a pyramid) having a three-sided base. **3** involving three people or parties: *a triangular relationship.*

triangulation *noun* (**triangulates**, **triangulated**, **triangulating**) a method of finding out distance and position, usually on a map, by measuring the distance between two fixed points and then measuring the angle from each of these to the third point.

Triassic • *adjective* of or relating to the earliest period of the Mesozoic era, which lasted from about 248 to 213 million years ago. Many new organisms appeared following the mass extinctions of the end of the Paleozoic era, including the earliest dinosaurs and the first primitive mammals. • *noun* this period. [Say try ASSICK]

triathlete *noun* an athlete who competes in three different events in one competition, usu. swimming, cycling, and long-distance running. [Say try ATHLETE]

triathlon *noun* an athletic contest in which competitors engage in three different events, usu. swimming, cycling, and long-distance running. [Say try ATH lon]

tribal *adjective* of, relating to, or characteristic of a tribe or tribes.

tribal council *noun* an organization encompassing a number of Aboriginal communities that have grouped together for social, political, and sometimes economic strength.

tribalism *noun* **1** the condition of existing as a separate tribe or tribes; tribal organization. **2** loyalty to one's tribe or social group.

tribally *adverb* by a tribe or suggestive of a tribe: *tribally controlled schools*.

tribe *noun* **1 a** a group of families claiming descent from a common ancestor, sharing a common culture, religion, dialect, etc., and usu. occupying a specific geographical area and having a recognized leader. **b** a group of Aboriginal peoples sharing a common ancestry, language, culture and name. **2** *Jewish Hist.* each of the twelve divisions of the Israelites claiming descent from the twelve sons of Jacob. **3 a** a group or community of people united by a shared profession or hobby etc.: *the whole tribe of actors*. **b** a large family. **4** *Biology* a group of related animals or plants, esp. one ranking between genus and the subfamily.

tribesman *noun* (*plural* **tribesmen**) a member of a tribe or of one's own tribe, esp. one who is male.

tribesperson *noun* (*plural* **tribespeople**) a member of a tribe.

tribeswoman *noun* (*plural* **tribeswomen**) a female member of a tribe.

tribulation *noun* great trouble or suffering: *his time of tribulation was just beginning* ◊ *the tribulations of being a megastar*. [Say trib yuh LAY sh'n]

tribunal *noun* **1** a board established to settle certain types of dispute, esp. one appointed by a government to investigate a matter of public concern: *appeared before the human rights tribunal*. **2** a court of justice. [Say try BYOO nul or trib YOO nul]

tribune *noun* **1** a popular leader who attempts to protect the rights and interests of the people: *a candidate who claims to be the tribune of the working stiff*. **2** *Roman History* **a** (also **tribune of the people**) an official appointed to protect the rights and interests of the plebeians. **b** (also **military tribune**) a legionary officer. [Say TRIB yoon or truh BYOON]

tributary • *noun* (*plural* **tributaries**) **1** a stream etc. flowing into a larger river or lake. **2** *hist.* a person or nation required to pay a tax or tribute to another. • *adjective* **1** (of a river etc.) that flows into a larger river or lake. **2** *hist.* required to pay or paying a tribute or tax. [Say TRIB yuh terry]

tribute *noun* **1 a** an act, statement, or gift made or given as a gesture of respect, admiration, or affection for a person: *paid tribute to her achievements* ◊ *a floral tribute*. **b** a show, concert, album, etc., produced to honour the life, career, or work of esp. an artist or entertainer: *tribute album*. **2** (foll. by *to*) a thing attributable to or indicative of a praiseworthy quality or act: *his recovery is a tribute to the skill of his doctors*. **3** *hist.* a payment made periodically by one nation or ruler to another as a sign of dependence or submission or to ensure peace and protection. **4** any donation of esp. money exacted or extorted.

trice *noun* PHRASES **in a trice** in a moment; instantly.

tricep *noun* *informal* a triceps muscle. [Say TRY sep]

WRITING TIP
tricep, triceps

Although **tricep** is becoming more common, it is still considered informal. **Triceps** remains the standard form for both the singular noun and its plural.

---

triceps *noun* (*plural* **triceps**) any muscle having three heads or points of attachment at one end, esp. the large extensor muscle at the back of the upper arm. [Say TRY seps]

triceratops *noun* (*plural* **triceratopses**) a plant-eating dinosaur with a bony horn on the snout, two longer ones above the eyes, and a bony frill around the neck. [Say try SERRA tops]

trick • *noun* **1** an action or scheme used to fool, outwit, or deceive. **2** an optical illusion or figment of the imagination: *a trick of the light*. **3** a special technique; a knack or special way of doing something. **4 a** a feat of skill or dexterity: *the magician performed several tricks*. **b** an unusual action learned by an animal, e.g. shaking a paw or rolling over and playing dead. **5 a** mischievous or underhanded act; a prank, a practical joke. **6** a peculiar or characteristic habit or mannerism: *has a trick of repeating himself*. **7** (as an *adjective*) done to deceive, mystify, or to create an illusion: *trick photography* ◊ *trick question*. **8** *slang* **a** a prostitute's client. **b** a prostitute's session with a client. **9 a** the cards played in a single round of a card game, usu. one from each player. **b** such a round of play. **c** a point gained as a result of this. **10** (as an *adjective*) designating a limb or joint that is unsound and liable to weaken suddenly and without warning: *a trick knee*. • *verb* **1** deceive by a trick; outwit. **2 a** (usu. foll. by *into* + verbal noun) lure or induce by trickery; fool. **b** (foll. by *out of*) cheat, defraud; cause (a person) to relinquish or lose something by deceitful means. PHRASES **up to one's old tricks** *informal* involved in a former bad habit or reprehensible pattern of behaviour. **do the trick** *informal* accomplish one's purpose; achieve the required result. **how's tricks?** *informal* how are you? **try every trick in the book** attempt every method or technique that can be used to achieve what one wants. **turn a trick** *slang* (of a prostitute) have a session with a client. **up to a person's tricks** aware of the mischief a person is likely to attempt.

trickery *noun* the use of tricks or deception.

trickiness *noun* the quality of being tricky.

trickle • *verb* (**trickles**, **trickled**, **trickling**) **1** (esp. of a liquid) flow in a thin stream or drops. **2** come, go, or pass gradually: *the news has trickled out*. **3** (foll. by *down*) (esp. of wealth or information) be dispersed or distributed among recipients at various levels in diminishing amounts. • *noun* **1** a thin or dripping stream of liquid. **2** a slow passage or flow: *traffic slows to a trickle*.

trickle-down *noun* **1** the spread of wealth, information, etc., from concentrated levels at a limited number of sources through or among many recipients in ever smaller amounts. **2** (as an *adjective*) relating to the economic theory that government benefits favouring large companies will result in increased profits for smaller companies and their suppliers etc., and improvements in the economy at all levels.

trick of the trade *noun* (*plural* **tricks of the trade**) a clever way of doing a job, known and used by experienced members of a particular industry or profession.

trick-or-treat • *noun* a Halloween custom in which children, dressed in costumes, knock on the doors of neighbours soliciting a treat of esp. candy, threatening to commit a prank if denied. • *interjection* (usu. **trick or treat!**) shouted by children while trick-or-treating. ▶ **trick-or-treater** *noun*

trick-or-treating *noun* the custom of calling on neighbours on Halloween, asking for candy or other treats.

trickster *noun* **1** a person who enjoys playing pranks and practical jokes on others; a joker. **2** a person who deceives others for esp. financial or political gain.

tricky *adjective* (**trickier**, **trickiest**) **1** difficult, challenging; requiring care and adroitness: *the driving was tricky*. **2** awkward; difficult to manage or operate: *this lock is quite tricky*. **3** (of a person) deceitful, crafty, or skilful: *he's a tricky guy — he'll manage it somehow*.

tricolour • *noun* a flag of three colours, esp. the French national flag of blue, white, and red. • *adjective* (also

tricoloured) having three colours. [Say TRY colour; for the noun you can also say TRICKA ler]

tricycle *noun* a vehicle, esp. ridden by children, having three wheels, two on an axle at the back and one at the front, driven by pedals in the same way as a bicycle.

tricyclic • *adjective* having three rings or circles. • *noun* any of a number of antidepressant drugs having molecules with three fused rings. [Say try SIKE lick or try SICK lick]

trident *noun* **1** a three-pronged spear. **2 (Trident) a** any of a class of US nuclear-powered submarines designed to carry ballistic missiles. **b** a ballistic missile designed to be carried by such a submarine.

tried • *verb* past and past participle of TRY. • *adjective* proven or tested by experience or examination.

tried-and-true *adjective* proven reliable by experience.

trifecta *noun* **1** Horse Racing = TRIACTOR. **2** a group of three related events or people: *the track athlete will attempt a trifecta of the long jump, triple jump, and 110-metre hurdles*. [Say try FECKTA]

trifle • *noun* **1** a dessert consisting of sponge cake soaked in liquor, esp. sherry, covered with custard, jam, whipped cream, and fruit, and served from a large bowl. **2 a** a small amount of money: *it sold for a trifle*. **b** (preceded by *a*) somewhat: *she was a trifle annoyed*. **3** a thing of little value or importance. • *verb* (**trifles, trifled, trifling**) (foll. by *with*) treat someone or something with a lack of seriousness or respect. ▶ **trifler** *noun*

trifling *adjective* **1** of little importance or significance; petty, trivial. **2** frivolous, not serious. ▶ **triflingly** *adverb*

trifocal • *noun* (in *plural*) a pair of eyeglasses having lenses with three parts, each with a different focal length. • *adjective* having three focuses. [Say TRY focal]

trig *noun* informal trigonometry.

trigger • *noun* **1 a** a movable lever for releasing a spring or catch and so setting off a mechanism. **b** a catch that may be depressed by the finger in order to fire a gun. **2** an event or occurrence etc. that sets off a reaction or chain reaction. • *verb* **1** set (an action or process) in motion; initiate, precipitate. **2** fire (a gun) by the use of a trigger. PHRASES **quick on the trigger** quick to react or respond. ▶ **triggered** *adjective*

trigger finger *noun* the finger with which one pulls the trigger of a gun, usu. the forefinger of the right hand.

trigger-happy *adjective* **1** apt to shoot with little or no provocation. **2** liable to act or react rashly and heedless of possible consequences.

triglyceride *noun* Chemistry any ester formed from glycerol and three acid radicals, including the main constituents of fats and oils. [Say try GLISSER ide]

trigonometric *adjective* having to do with trigonometry. [Say trigga nuh METRIC]

trigonometry *noun* the branch of mathematics dealing with the relations between the sides and angles of triangles and with the relevant functions of any angles. [Say trigga NOMMA tree]

trike *noun* informal a tricycle.

trilateral *adjective* **1** of, on, or with three sides. **2** involving or shared by three countries, esp. as parties to an agreement concerning trade and finance. [Say try LATTER ul]

tri-level *adjective* having three levels, storeys, or floors.

trilight *noun* Cdn **1** a light bulb that can be adjusted to shine at any of three degrees of brightness. **2** (as an *adjective*) designating a lamp, socket, switch, etc., used with or using such a bulb.

trilingual *adjective* **1** able to speak three languages,

esp. fluently. **2** spoken or written in three languages. [Say try LING gwul or try LING gyoo ul]

trill • *noun* **1** a musical effect produced with the voice or an instrument, in which a quavering or tremulous sound is produced by a rapid alternation of two notes a tone or semitone apart. **2** a usu. high-pitched sound resembling this, such as the warbling song of a bird. **3** the pronunciation of *r* with a vibration of the tongue. • *verb* **1** produce a trill. **2 a** sing or play (a song etc.) with a trill. **b** pronounce (the letter *r*) with a trill.

trillion *noun* **1** a million million (1,000,000,000,000 or 10^{12}). **2** (in *plural*) informal a very large number. ▶ **trillionth** *adjective & noun*

trillium *noun* any of various esp. North American plants of the lily family, bearing a whorl of three leaves at the summit of the stem and in the middle a solitary flower with three white or brightly coloured petals; it is the floral emblem of Ontario.

trilobite *noun* any of numerous extinct marine arthropods which had a body divided into an anterior solid head, a segmented thorax or trunk, and a posterior tail, and which are found abundantly as fossils. [Say TRY luh bite]

trilogy *noun* (*plural* **trilogies**) a group or series of three related novels, theatrical works, etc., often produced by a single author and unified by a common theme or set of characters. [Say TRILLA jee]

trim • *verb* (**trims, trimmed, trimming**) **1** make (something) neat or of regular size or shape, esp. by cutting away irregular or unwanted parts. **2** (foll. by *off*, *away*) remove or cut away (irregular, uneven, or unwanted parts). **3 a** reduce the size, amount, or number of (a budget, payroll, costs, etc.). **b** eliminate (superfluous costs, jobs, etc.): *they trimmed six jobs*. **4 a** decorate, finish, or adorn with ornaments etc.: *trim the Christmas tree*. **b** (often foll. by *up*) make (a person) neat in dress and appearance. **5** adjust the balance of (a ship or aircraft) by distributing its cargo evenly. **6** arrange (a ship's sails) to suit the wind. • *noun* **1** a haircut to shorten a person's hair without changing the hairstyle. **2** decorative material or other ornamentation, usu. of a contrasting design or colour, added to clothing or upholstery. **3** decorative wood mouldings used esp. as a border around the windows, doorways, and walls of a house. **4** ornamental finishing pieces mounted on the outside of a car or truck etc. **5** a person's clothing or outfit: *jogging trim*. **6** the balance or inclination of an aircraft. • *adjective* **1** neat, tidy. **2** in proper order; well arranged or equipped. **3** slender, slim, esp. as a sign of physical fitness. PHRASES **in trim** having a neat or healthy appearance.

trimester *noun* **1** a period of three months. **2** one third of the length of human pregnancy. **3** each of three terms of an academic year at some universities and high schools. [Say TRY mester or try MESTER]

trimethoprim *noun* an antibiotic often used to treat respiratory and urinary tract infections. [Say try METHA prim]

trimmer *noun* **1** a device or instrument, esp. an electric one, for trimming (esp. hair, grass, hedges, etc.). **2** a person who trims something.

trimming *noun* **1** ornamentation or decoration, esp. for a hat or other articles of clothing. **2** (in *plural*) informal accessories, the usual accompaniments, esp. the garnishes and side dishes traditionally served with the main course of a particular meal. **3** (in *plural*) pieces cut off in trimming.

Trinidadian • *noun* a native or inhabitant of Trinidad, an island in the West Indies. • *adjective* of or relating to

Trinidad or its people. [Say trinna DADDY in or trinna DAY dee in]

Trinitarian • *noun* Christianity a person who believes in the doctrine of the Trinity, the three modes of being of God: the Father, Son, and Holy Spirit. • *adjective* of or believing in the doctrine of the Trinity. [Say trinna TERRY in]

trinitrotoluene *noun* = TNT. [Say try nite ruh TOL you een]

Trinity *noun* (*plural* **Trinities**) **1** Theology **a** the three modes of being of the Christian God as conceived in orthodox Christian belief; the Father, Son, and Holy Spirit as one God. **b** the existence of God in three persons. **2** (often foll. by *of*) a group of three people or things.

trinket *noun* a small ornament or piece of jewellery etc., esp. one having little worth or value.

trio *noun* (*plural* **trios**) **1** a set or group of three. **2** Music **a** a composition for three performers. **b** a group of three performers. **c** the alternative section in a minuet, scherzo, march, etc., usu. in a different key or style from the preceding and following passages.

trioxide *noun* Chemistry an oxide containing three oxygen atoms. [Say try OXIDE]

trip • *verb* (**trips, tripped, tripping**) **1 a** (often foll. by *up*) cause (a person) to stumble or fall by entangling the feet. **b** (often foll. by *over*) stumble or fall, esp. by suddenly catching the foot against an obstacle. **2** (usu. foll. by *up*) **a** cause (a person) to make a mistake or blunder. **b** expose the error of (a person), esp. by detecting an inconsistency in their facts or calculations. **3** make an error, esp. in calculation or articulation. **4 a** run or dance with quick light steps. **b** (of a rhythm, words, etc.) flow lightly and gracefully. **5 a** esp. Cdn make a journey or expedition through rough country, esp. in a canoe: *we went canoe tripping in Algonquin Park*. **b** make an excursion to a place. **6 a** release or depress (a catch or lever etc.) in order to activate a mechanism. **b** activate (a mechanism) in this way: *she tripped the lights*. **7** (often foll. by *out*) informal undergo a hallucinatory experience induced by drugs. • *noun* **1** a journey or excursion, either one made repeatedly on a particular usu. short route or one taken for pleasure. **2 a** an act of causing a person to stumble or blunder. **b** a stumble or blunder. **3** an illusory or self-indulgent activity or attitude; an intense and usu. temporary enthusiasm or preoccupation: *power trip ◊ guilt trip*. **4** informal a hallucinatory experience caused by a drug. **5 a** an intense or exhilarating experience. **b** an exciting or stimulating person. **6** a contrivance for a tripping mechanism etc. PHRASES **trip the light fantastic** jocular dance.

tripartite *adjective* **1** divided into or consisting of three parts: *originally a public school, this building features tripartite dormer windows*. **2** shared by or involving three parties: *a tripartite agreement between the federal government and the provinces of Ontario and British Columbia*. [Say try PAR tite]

tripe *noun* **1** the first or second stomach of a ruminant, esp. an ox or cow, prepared as food. **2** informal something considered worthless or foolish.

triple • *adjective* **1** consisting of three usu. equal parts or things; threefold. **2** involving three parties. **3** three times as much or many: *triple the amount ◊ triple thickness*. **4** Figure Skating, Dance, etc. (of a jump, pirouette, etc.) involving three revolutions: *triple lutz*. • *adverb* to three times the amount or extent: *the cars were triple parked*. • *noun* **1** a threefold number or amount. **2** a set of three. **3** Baseball a hit that enables the batter to reach third base. **4** Figure Skating, Dance, etc. a jump, spin, etc. involving three revolutions. • *verb* (**triples, tripled, tripling**) **1** multiply or increase by three. **2** Baseball

a hit a triple. **b** (foll. by *in* or *home*) drive (a baserunner) in by hitting a triple.

Triple A *noun* = AAA 1, 2, 3.

triple crown *noun* the title awarded to the winner of three important events, esp. to the horse that wins the Preakness, Belmont Stakes, and Kentucky Derby, or to the baseball player who finishes the year leading the league in batting average, home runs, and runs batted in.

triple-decker *noun* something with three decks, layers, or levels, e.g. a sandwich made with three pieces of bread and two layers of filling, or a three-storey building.

Triple-E Senate *noun* Cdn a proposed senate that would have more effective powers than the existing Senate and which would consist of elected members equally representing the provinces.

triple jump *noun* a sport in which athletes attempt to achieve the greatest distance on a jump that involves a hop followed by a long step and a leap. ▶ **triple jumper** *noun*

triple play *noun* Baseball a play in which three players, usu. the batter and two baserunners, are put out.

triplet *noun* **1** (usu. in *plural*) each of three children or animals born at one birth. **2 a** a group of three equal notes played in the time of two. **b** a group of three successive lines of verse, esp. when rhyming and of the same length. **3** a set of three people or things.

triple time *noun* musical time with three beats to the bar; waltz time.

triple whammy *noun* (*plural* **triple whammies**) informal a threefold blow or setback.

triplex • *noun* (*plural* **triplexes**) a residential building divided into three apartments, esp. a three-storey dwelling with a separate apartment on each floor. • *adjective* triple or threefold. [Say TRY plex or TRIP lex]

triplicate • *adjective* **1** existing in three examples or copies. **2** having three corresponding parts. • *noun* each of a set of three copies or corresponding parts. • *verb* (**triplicates, triplicated, triplicating**) **1** make in three copies. **2** multiply by three. PHRASES **in triplicate** (written, printed, produced, etc.) in three identical or exactly corresponding copies. [Say TRIPLA kit for the adjective and noun, TRIPLA kate for the verb]

triploid • *noun* an organism or cell having three times the haploid set of chromosomes. • *adjective* of or being a triploid. [Say TRIP loyd]

triply *adverb* in a triple manner; three times: *with his bad hair as well as his ripped pants and broken shoe, Austin was triply embarrassed*.

tripman *noun* (*plural* **tripmen**) Cdn hist. a man hired for temporary duty on a fur brigade, paid by the trip.

tripod *noun* **1** a stand with three usu. adjustable and collapsible legs for supporting a camera or telescope etc. **2** a three-legged stool, seat, or table, etc. [Say TRY pod]

tripper *noun* **1** esp. Cdn (North) a person who makes an expedition through rough country, esp. by canoe. **2** a person who goes on a journey or short trip, esp. for pleasure: *day tripper*.

tripping *noun* **1** esp. Cdn (North) the activity of travelling through rough country, esp. by canoe. **2** Hockey **a** an illegal act of causing an opponent to fall by obstructing him or her with one's stick, leg, or foot etc. **b** a minor penalty assessed for this.

trippingly *adverb* with great ease and rapidity: *medicinal names now began to roll trippingly off her tongue*.

trippy *adjective* (**trippier, trippiest**) informal (of music etc.) producing an effect resembling that of a psychedelic drug.

triptych *noun* **1** a picture or relief carving on three

panels, usu. hinged vertically together and often used as an altarpiece. **2** a set of three artistic works, usu. meant to be viewed or performed together. [Say TRIP tick]

tripwire *noun* a wire stretched close to the ground in order to trip up trespassers, enemies, etc., or to activate an alarm when disturbed.

trisodium phosphate *noun* a water-soluble compound, occurring as crystals, used esp. as a detergent for removing grease stains from asphalt, washing walls prior to painting, etc. Abbreviation: **TSP**. [Say try SODIUM]

trite *adjective* (**triter, tritest**) **1** (of a phrase, opinion, etc.) stale through constant use or repetition; hackneyed, commonplace, worn out; lacking originality: *her character's philosophical speculations seem trite and offhand*. **2** (of a work, novel, etc.) containing or characterized by stale or commonplace ideas, subjects, etc. ▶ **triteness** *noun*

triticale *noun* a high-protein hybrid between wheat and rye. [Say tritta KAY lee]

tritium *noun* a radioactive isotope of hydrogen with a mass about three times that of hydrogen, which occurs naturally in minute amounts and is produced artificially, esp. for use in fusion reactors. [Say TRITTY um]

triumph • *noun* **1** a great success, achievement, or victory; a major accomplishment: *a triumph of engineering*. **2** the state of being successful or victorious: *raised her fist in triumph*. **3** the thrill, joy, or satisfaction of success or victory. • *verb* (often foll. by *over*) **1** be successful or victorious; prevail. **2** rejoice at victory or success; exult.

triumphal *adjective* done, used, or made to celebrate or commemorate a success or victory: *triumphal arch*.

triumphalism *noun* extreme or ostentatious pride or excessive exultation over one's achievements or those of one's country, party, etc.: *extreme distaste for the triumphalism of Mussolini's regime*. ▶ **triumphalist** *adjective & noun* [Say try UMF ul ism]

triumphant *adjective* **1** victorious or successful. **2** exultant. ▶ **triumphantly** *adverb*

triumvirate *noun* **1** a group of three people in a joint position of power or authority: *power passed to a series of triumvirates, one of which—Khrushchev, Bulganin, and Zhukov—eventually gained control*. **2** *informal* any set of three people or things: *that triumvirate of policies dear to modern politicians—namely, austerity, deregulation, and privatization*. [Say try UM ver it]

trivalent *adjective* Chemistry **1** having a valence of three. **2** (of a vaccine) providing immunity against three strains of an infective agent. [Say try VAIL int]

trivet *noun* **1** a low, flat, usu. three-legged cast iron or ceramic stand placed under a hot kettle, pot, or serving dish to protect the surface of a table. **2** a similar stand with three or more legs used to keep something raised while being heated or cooked. [Say TRIVVIT]

trivia *noun* **1** unimportant but interesting or amusing tidbits of factual information, esp. on a particular subject, often used as the basis for quizzes or games: *hockey trivia*. **2** unimportant or inconsequential matters or details.

trivial *adjective* of little importance or consequence. ▶ **triviality** *noun* (*plural* **trivialities**)

trivialization *noun* the act of diminishing or downplaying the importance, significance, or value of.

trivialize *verb* (**trivializes, trivialized, trivializing**) diminish or downplay the importance, significance, or value of; minimize, belittle: *the magazine has been accused of trivializing serious issues*.

trivially *adverb* in a trivial manner: *she trivially*

compared the Fascist European parties of the 1930 with contemporary Canadian political parties.

trod *past and past participle of* TREAD.

trodden *past participle of* TREAD.

troglodyte • *noun* **1** a cave dweller, esp. of prehistoric times. **2** *derogatory* a person regarded as living in wilful ignorance, esp. of current trends and subjects; a conservative or old-fashioned person: *a troglodyte who refuses to acknowledge that a new era has dawned*. **3** a person living in seclusion; a hermit. • *adjective* **1** dwelling in caves. **2** ignorant; old-fashioned, unmannerly, or uncouth. ▶ **troglodytic** *adjective* [Say TROGLA dite, trogla DIT ick]

troika *noun* **1 a** a Russian carriage or sleigh drawn by a team of three horses. **b** this team of horses. **2** a group of three people working together, esp. in an administrative or managerial capacity: *the three men formed a troika, which would appeal to their countrymen until more of their people could be brought in*. [Say TROY kuh]

Trojan • *adjective* of the ancient city of Troy on the coast of Turkey or its inhabitants. • *noun* **1** a native or inhabitant of Troy. **2** a person of great energy, courage, or endurance: *works like a Trojan*. [Say TRO jin]

Trojan Horse *noun* **1** a seemingly harmless person or device that eludes a person's defences to bring about his or her downfall: *let us not use this bill as a Trojan Horse to undermine the family*. **2** *Computing* a program that breaches the security of a computer system, esp. by apparently functioning as part of a legitimate program, in order to erase, corrupt, or remove data.

troll¹ *noun* *Scandinavian Myth* a member of a race of grotesque dwarfs (or, formerly, giants) usu. dwelling in caves or under bridges. [Rhymes with ROLL]

troll² • *verb* **1 a** fish by drawing bait along in the water behind a moving boat. **b** draw (a lure or baited line) behind a boat. **c** practise this method of fishing in (a particular stretch of water). **2** (foll. by *for*) **a** attempt to catch a particular type of fish using this method. **b** pursue, seek; go looking or searching: *a group of companies trolling for partnership opportunities*. • *noun* **1** an act or method of trolling for fish. **2** a baited line or lure used in this. [Rhymes with ROLL]

troller *noun* **1** a person who trolls for fish. **2** a fishing boat used for trolling. [Rhymes with ROLLER]

trolley *noun* (*plural* **trolleys**) **1 a** a small cart on wheels or casters used for serving food. **b** a small wheeled cart for other purposes, e.g. carrying luggage. **2** a grooved metal pulley receiving current from an overhead electric wire and conveying this by a pole etc. to the motor of a trolley bus or streetcar. **3** (also **trolley bus**, *plural* **trolley buses**) a bus powered by electricity from an overhead cable. [Rhymes with DOLLY]

trombone *noun* **1** a large brass wind instrument with a sliding tube used to increase and decrease its length, thereby varying its pitch. **2** a person who plays or is playing a trombone. ▶ **trombonist** *noun*

tromp *verb* *informal* **1** march with a heavy step; trudge, stomp. **2** trample.

trompe l'oeil *noun* an optical illusion, esp. a still-life painting designed to deceive the spectator by giving an illusion of reality: *if I had possessed the skill, I would have painted a trompe l'oeil mural on the inside of the blinds depicting all that they hid*. [Say tromp LOY]

SPELL CHECK
troop, troupe

A company of actors or dancers is a **troupe**.

---

troop • *noun* **1** an assembled company of people or animals. **2 a** a detachment of police officers or soldiers etc., esp. a unit of artillery and armoured formation.

b (in *plural*) soldiers or armed forces. **3** a cavalry unit commanded by a captain. **4** a group of Scouts or Girl Guides usu. consisting of three or more patrols. • *verb* (foll. by *in*, *out*, *off*, etc.) walk, march, or proceed in large numbers, in or as if in a troop.

SPELL CHECK	ABC
trooper, trouper	

A performer in a theatre troupe is a **trouper**.

trooper *noun* **1** (also **Trooper**) a private in an armoured or cavalry unit. **2** *US* = STATE TROOPER. **3** *informal* a hard-working, reliable, or uncomplaining person: *most gave up long ago, but not Yuri — a real trooper*. PHRASES **like a trooper** constantly: *swears like a trooper*.

troopship *noun* a ship used for transporting troops.

trope *noun* a word or phrase that is used in a way that is different from its usual meaning in order to create a particular mental image or effect, e.g. a metaphor or simile. [Rhymes with ROPE]

trophy *noun* (*plural* **trophies**) **1** an ornamental commemorative object awarded as a prize for excellence or an outstanding achievement, e.g. in sports or academics. **2** an animal or part of an animal captured in hunting and displayed as a memorial, e.g. a deer's antlers. **3** an animal that is hunted and usu. kept to prove the skill of the hunter: *trophy fish*. **4** *derogatory* a person or thing regarded as having been obtained to enhance a person's status by association: *trophy wife*.

tropic • *noun* **1** (**Tropic**) either of two parallels of latitude 23°26′ north (**Tropic of Cancer**) or south (**Tropic of Capricorn**) of the equator, defining the torrid zone and representing, respectively, the northernmost and southernmost limits at which the sun can be directly overhead. **2** (**Tropic**) each of two corresponding circles on the celestial sphere where the sun appears to turn after reaching its greatest declination. **3** (in *plural*) the torrid zone and parts immediately adjacent. • *adjective* = TROPICAL 1.

tropical *adjective* **1** pertaining to, occurring in, or characteristic of the tropics. **2** resembling the tropics in climate; very hot and humid. **3** (esp. of clothing) suitable for wearing or using in the tropics.

tropical cyclone *noun* **1** a system of winds rotating inwards to an area of low barometric pressure, formed in localized areas over tropical oceans, sometimes developing into a hurricane or typhoon. **2** such a wind system having hurricane-force winds, originating in the Indian Ocean.

tropical storm *noun* a tropical cyclone with winds ranging from 30 to 64 knots (63–118 km/h), often associated with heavy rain.

tropism *noun* *Biology* the turning of all or part of an organism in a particular direction by growth, bending, or locomotion, in response to an external stimulus. [Say TROPE ism]

troposphere *noun* the lowest region of the atmosphere, extending to a height of between 8 and 18 km and marked by convection and a general decrease of temperature with height. ▶ **tropospheric** *adjective* [Say TROPPA sfeer or TROPE a sfeer, troppa SFAIR ick or trope a SFAIR ick]

trot • *verb* (**trots**, **trotted**, **trotting**) **1** (of a person) run with short strides at a moderate pace. **2** (of a horse) proceed at a pace faster than a walk in which the legs move in diagonal pairs almost together. **3** *informal* walk, go. **4** cause (esp. a horse) to proceed at a trot. • *noun* **1** a trotting pace or gait: *proceed at a trot*. **2** a run at this pace. **3** (**the trots**) *slang* an attack of diarrhea. PHRASES **hot to trot** *informal* **1** eager, enthusiastic.

2 sexually active or excited. **on the trot** *informal* continually busy: *kept them on the trot*. **trot out 1** lead out and show off the paces of (a horse). **2** produce or introduce (as if) for inspection and approval, esp. tediously or predictably.

troth *noun* *archaic* PHRASES **plight** (or **pledge**) **one's troth** pledge one's word esp. in marriage or betrothal. [Rhymes with BOTH]

trotter *noun* **1** a horse bred or trained for harness racing. **2** (usu. in *plural*) **a** the foot of certain animals, esp. the pig, eaten as food. **b** *jocular* a human foot.

trotting *noun* = HARNESS RACING.

troubadour *noun* **1** any of a number of French medieval lyric poets composing and singing in Provençal esp. on the themes of chivalry and courtly love, living in southern France, eastern Spain, and northern Italy between the 11th and 13th centuries. **2** a singer or poet. [Say TROOBA dor]

trouble • *noun* **1 a** difficulty, problems, complications; a hard time. **b** disturbance of the mind or feelings; worry, distress. **2 a** inconvenience, bother; unpleasant or unnecessary exertion: *he went to a lot of trouble*. **b** a cause of this: *she was no trouble*. **3** (usu. foll. by *with*) an annoying, disconcerting, or problematic feature or aspect: *the trouble with you is your attitude*. **4** a faulty condition or operation: *engine trouble*. **5 a** fighting, disturbance: *we don't want any trouble*. **b** (in *plural*) political or social unrest, public disturbances. **6** disagreement, strife: *he and his wife are having trouble*. • *verb* (**troubles**, **troubled**, **troubling**) **1** cause distress or anxiety to; disturb, worry: *we were troubled by the news*. **2** subject or be subjected to inconvenience, bother, or unpleasant exertion: *sorry to trouble you*. **3** afflict; cause pain etc. to: *she is troubled with arthritis*. **4** be disturbed or worried: *don't trouble about it*. PHRASES **ask for trouble** *informal* invite danger or difficulty by rash or indiscreet behaviour. **be no trouble** cause no inconvenience or nuisance. **go to the** (or **some**) **trouble** devote one's time or energy to do something. **in trouble 1** involved in a matter likely to bring criticism or punishment. **2** *euphemism* pregnant while unmarried. **look for trouble** *informal* **1** aggressively seek to cause trouble. **2** invite trouble. **take the trouble** = GO TO THE TROUBLE.

troubled *adjective* **1 a** feeling worry, distress, anxiety, or apprehension. **b** indicating worry or distress: *a troubled look*. **2** fraught with trouble, problems, unrest, turmoil, etc.: *a financially troubled company*. **3** physically unsettled or disturbed; not calm: *troubled waters*.

trouble-free *adjective* **1** free of problems, complications, or difficulties: *a trouble-free journey*. **2** that is unlikely to malfunction or require maintenance: *a trouble-free car*.

troublemaker *noun* a person who habitually causes trouble. ▶ **troublemaking** *noun* & *adjective*

troubleshoot *verb* (**troubleshoots**, **troubleshot**, **troubleshooting**) detect and correct faults in machinery, computer equipment, etc.

troubleshooter *noun* **1** a person who detects and corrects faults in machinery, computer equipment, etc. **2** a mediator who specializes in resolving esp. industrial or diplomatic disputes. ▶ **troubleshooting** *noun*

troublesome *adjective* **1** that causes problems or difficulty. **2** distressing, worrisome, disconcerting: *troublesome news*. **3** fraught with problems, complications, or turmoil: *a troublesome period*.

trough *noun* **1 a** a long narrow open receptacle for water, animal feed, etc. **b** *jocular* a source of wealth or prosperity: *the trough of political patronage*. **2 a** a narrow channel or conduit for conveying a liquid. **b** =

EAVESTROUGH. **3** *Meteorology* an elongated region of low barometric pressure (*compare* RIDGE 4). **4** a hollow between two wave crests. **5** the lowest point of something, esp. the lowest level of economic activity or prosperity. **6 a** a broad elongated depression or valley: *Labrador Trough.* **b** an elongated depression of the sea floor. [Say TROFF]

trounce *verb* (**trounces, trounced, trouncing**) **1** defeat decisively or convincingly. **2** beat, thrash. ▶ **trouncing** *noun*

SPELL CHECK
troupe, troop

A group of soldiers or scouts (or of people generally) is a **troop**.

---

troupe *noun* a company of actors or dancers etc. [Say TROOP]

SPELL CHECK
trouper, trooper

The spelling is **trooper** for a soldier, a police officer, and in "a real trooper".

---

trouper *noun* **1** a member of esp. a theatrical troupe; a performer, esp. an experienced one. **2** = TROOPER 3. [Say TROOPER]

trousers *plural noun* **1** an outer garment reaching from the waist usu. to the ankles, divided into two parts to cover the legs. **2** (**trouser**) (as an *adjective*) designating a part or parts of such a garment: *trouser leg.*

trousseau *noun* (*plural* **trousseaux** or **trousseaus**) the clothes collected by a bride for her marriage. [Say TROO so or troo SO for the singular, TROO soze or troo SOZE for either plural]

trout *noun* (*plural* **trout** or **trouts**) **1** a chiefly freshwater fish of the salmon family, found in both Eurasia and North America and highly valued for food and game. **2** *slang derogatory* a woman, esp. an old or ill-tempered one. **3** *Cdn* (*Nfld*) *informal* a term of affectionate address: *me old trout.*

trove *noun* = TREASURE TROVE.

trowel • *noun* **1** a small hand-held tool with a flat metal blade, used to apply and spread mortar, cement, plaster, etc. **2** a hand-held gardening tool resembling a small shovel, consisting of a pointed scoop-like blade attached to a handle, used for lifting plants or earth. • *verb* (**trowels, trowelled, trowelling**) **1** dig, move, or apply with a trowel. **2** apply plaster etc. to (a wall etc.) with a trowel. [Rhymes with *TOWEL*]

troy *noun* (also **troy weight**) a system of weights used for precious metals and gems, based on a pound of 12 ounces or 5,760 grains (often as an *adjective*: *troy ounce*).

truancy *noun* (*plural* **truancies**) unjustified absence from school or work. [Say TROO in see]

truant *noun* **1** a student who stays away from school without leave or explanation. **2** a person absent from work. [Say TROO int]

truce *noun* **1** a temporary suspension of hostilities, usu. for a limited period, between warring armies or factions or between individuals in a private feud or quarrel. **2** an agreement or treaty achieving this.

truck • *noun* **1** any of various kinds of large sturdy road vehicle used for a variety of purposes. **2 a** any of a variety of wheeled carts and platforms used to transport goods. **b** (also **hand truck**) a sturdy upright metal frame with two wheels and a short perpendicular shelf used to move large appliances, boxes, etc. **3** a pivoted undercarriage with two or more

pairs of wheels, mounted to the underside of a railway car. **4** each of two axle units on a skateboard or roller skate, to which the wheels are attached. • *verb* **1** deliver or convey by truck. **2** drive a truck, esp. for a living. **3** *informal* go or proceed at a casual pace. PHRASES **have no truck with** avoid dealing, interacting, or associating with.

trucker *noun* **1** a person who drives a truck, esp. a person who drives a transport truck or tractor-trailer etc. for a living. **2** a company dealing in long-distance transportation of goods.

truck farm *noun* esp. *US* = MARKET GARDEN. ▶ **truck farmer** *noun* **truck farming** *noun*

trucking *noun* the action or business of transporting goods by truck.

truckload *noun* **1** the quantity of goods that is or can be transported in a truck. **2** (usu. foll. by *of*) *informal* a large quantity or amount. PHRASES **by the truckload** in large quantities or amounts.

truck stop *noun* a roadside restaurant or diner, often having a gas station on the premises, catering esp. to truckers.

truculence *noun* the quality of being bad-tempered or touchy: *he reminded me, with his truculence, of some of the younger girls at the school, trying to pick a quarrel so that they would have attention.* [Say TRUCK yuh lince]

truculent *adjective* tending to argue or be bad-tempered; somewhat aggressively defiant; touchy: *he was quiet, reflective, a little drunk, maybe, a little truculent, but nothing wild.* ▶ **truculently** *adverb* [Say TRUCK yuh lint]

Trudeaumania *noun* *Cdn* widespread popularity of, and fascination with, Prime Minister Pierre Elliott Trudeau (1919–2000) among the Canadian public, esp. during the election campaign of 1968. [Say troo doe MANIA]

trudge • *verb* (**trudges, trudged, trudging**) **1** walk laboriously, or without energy or spirit, but steadily and persistently. **2** travel (a road or specified distance etc.) in this way. • *noun* a steady laborious walk.

true • *adjective* (**truer, truest**) **1** in accordance with or consistent with fact or reality: *a true story*. **2** genuine, authentic; rightly or strictly so called; not spurious or counterfeit: *a true friend*. **3** (often foll. by *to*) loyal or faithful: *true to one's word*. **4** (foll. by *to*) closely conforming (to a standard or expectation etc.): *true to form*. **5** correctly positioned, fitted, balanced, or aligned; level, square. **6** exact, accurate, precise: *a true copy*. **7** (also **it is true**) certainly, admittedly: *true, it would cost more*. **8** (of a compass bearing) measured relative to true north. **9** reliable, trusty, sure: *a true sign*. • *adverb* **1** in a sincere or genuine manner; truly: *tell me true*. **2** accurately: *aim true*. **3** conforming with the ancestral type; without variation: *breed true*. • *verb* (**trues, trued, truing** or **trueing**) (often foll. by *up*) bring into the correct, exact, or required form, position, alignment, shape, etc. PHRASES **come true** actually happen or transpire; be realized. **out of true** not in the correct or exact position. **too good to be true** better than one could have hoped for or imagined. **true to form** (or **type**) being or behaving as expected. **true to life** accurately representing or consistent with real life.

true believer *noun* **1** a person who trusts or sincerely believes: *she is a true believer in homeopathy*. **2** an ardent or fanatical supporter of esp. a political or religious movement or cause; a zealot: *a core of true believers remains, suspicious of all compromise, suspecting their leader has sold them out.*

true-blue *adjective* steadfastly loyal or devoted.

true-false *adjective* (also **true and false**)

1 designating a type of test question consisting of a statement designed to elicit either the response "true" or "false". 2 designating a test consisting of such questions.
true life *noun* 1 reality; actual life or existence. 2 (as an *adjective*; usu. **true-life**) designating things resembling or occurring in reality: *a true-life story*.

> **SPELL CHECK**
> **truly**
> Note that there is no *e* in **truly**.

trueness *noun* 1 the quality of being exact or correctly balanced or aligned. 2 truth.
true north *noun* 1 north according to the earth's axis, not magnetic north. 2 (**the True North**) *Cdn informal or jocular* Canada.
truffle *noun* 1 a strong-smelling underground fungus regarded as a gourmet food item, collected in France and northern Italy with the help of trained dogs or pigs. 2 a round soft chocolate, often flavoured with alcohol. ▶ **truffled** *adjective*
truism *noun* a self-evident or indisputable truth, esp. a trivial or hackneyed one, e.g. *nothing lasts forever*. [Say TROO ism]
truly *adverb* 1 a sincerely, genuinely: *truly grieved*. b (used as an emphatic affirmative) very, really: *truly frustrated*. 2 really, indeed: *truly, I do not know*. 3 faithfully, loyally: *served them truly*. 4 accurately, truthfully: *has been truly stated*. 5 rightly, properly: *well and truly*. 6 used in formulaic closings of letters: *yours truly*.
trump • *noun* 1 (in *plural*) *Cards* the suit determined, usu. by cutting or bidding, to rank above the other three during a deal or game: *hearts are trumps*. 2 (also **trump card**) a a playing card of this suit. b a card cut or turned up to determine this suit. 3 (also **trump card**) an important resource available to a person but held, usu. secretly, in reserve until an opportune moment when it may be used or revealed to gain a decisive advantage: *in this month General Haig decided to play his trump card: the tank*. 4 *informal* an admirable, helpful, or reliable person. • *verb* 1 a defeat (a card or its player) with a trump. b play a trump card when another suit has been led. 2 *informal* a foil or thwart (a person, proposal, etc.), esp. with an unexpected move at the last minute or by means of a previously secret resource. b surpass; gain an unexpected advantage over. PHRASES **trump up** fabricate or invent (an accusation, excuse, etc.).
trumped-up *adjective* fabricated, invented.
trumpet • *noun* 1 a any of a family of brass wind instruments with a bright, penetrating tone, consisting of a straight or curved tube with a flared bell and most commonly three valves. b a person who plays or is playing a trumpet. 2 anything resembling a trumpet in shape, such as the tubular corona of a daffodil. 3 anything resembling the sound of a trumpet. • *verb* (**trumpets, trumpeted, trumpeting**) 1 herald, announce, celebrate, or proclaim loudly. 2 a blow or play a trumpet. b make a loud sound like that of a trumpet: *elephants trumpeting in the jungle*.
trumpeter *noun* 1 a person who plays a trumpet. 2 any of various birds having a loud cry resembling the sound of a trumpet.
trumpeter swan *noun* a large North American wild swan with a black bill and a loud, trumpet-like, guttural call.
truncate *verb* (**truncates, truncated, truncating**) shorten or diminish, e.g. by cutting off the top or end

part of: *they had to truncate the article for publication*. [Say TRUN kate or trun KATE]
truncated *adjective* 1 having been shortened or reduced by or as if by cutting: *a truncated pyramid*. 2 limited in depth or scope; narrow: *a truncated view*. [Say TRUN kated or trun KATED]
truncation *noun* an act of truncating. [Say trun KAY sh'n]
truncheon *noun* a short club or cudgel, esp. carried by a police officer. [Say TRUN chin]
trundle *verb* (**trundles, trundled, trundling**) 1 move or roll on a wheel or wheels, esp. heavily or noisily. 2 go or move, esp. heavily, noisily, or at a steady pace. 3 push (a wheeled vehicle) along.
trunk *noun* 1 the main stem of a tree as distinct from its branches and roots. 2 the human body, or that of an animal, considered apart from the limbs and head. 3 the mobile elongated prehensile snout of an elephant, containing the passages to the nostrils and also used to draw in and spray water for cooling. 4 a large box with a hinged lid for transporting luggage, clothes, etc. 5 a compartment at the rear of most cars, used to transport luggage etc. 6 (in *plural*) a man's garment worn for swimming, boxing, etc., either loose-fitting shorts or close-fitting briefs. 7 the main part of any structure, esp. one that branches off into smaller parts. 8 the main body of a blood vessel, artery, or nerve etc. 9 an enclosed duct or conduit for cables, ventilation, etc.
trunk line *noun* 1 a main railway line or route. 2 a large or main pipeline for oil or gas, esp. one from a production field to a refinery or terminal. 3 a telephone line running between exchanges.
trunk road *noun* *Cdn* an access road, esp. for logging.
truss • *noun* (*plural* **trusses**) 1 a metal or wooden structural framework, esp. consisting of rafters, posts, and struts, supporting a roof or bridge etc. 2 a medical device used to provide even pressure on a hernia, usu. consisting of a padded belt fitted with straps. • *verb* (**trusses, trussed, trussing**) 1 tie or skewer the wings and legs of (a fowl etc.) to the body for cooking. 2 (often foll. by *up*) tie up (a person) by binding the arms close to the body. 3 support (a roof or bridge etc.) with a truss or trusses.
trust • *noun* 1 a faith or confidence in the loyalty, veracity, reliability, strength, etc., of a person or thing. b the state or condition of being trusted or relied on. 2 the obligation or responsibility placed in a person who is trusted or relied on: *she is in a position of trust*. 3 reliance on the truth of a statement etc. without examination. 4 a confident expectation. 5 a person or thing upon whom one relies or depends: *God is our sole trust*. 6 a thing or person committed to one's care; a charge. 7 *Law* the confidence placed on a person by making that person the nominal owner of property to be used for the enjoyment and benefit of another. b the property or estate held in this way. c the legal relationship between the nominal owner and the property. 8 a a body of trustees. b an organization managed by trustees. 9 a group of associated companies in a particular area of business, organized to reduce or defeat competition, lessen mutual expenses, etc., esp. one in which a central committee of trustees holds a majority or all of the stock and has a controlling vote in each company, prohibited by law in some jurisdictions, including the US. • *verb* 1 a have or place faith or confidence in the loyalty, veracity, reliability, honour, etc. of (a person or thing). b rely upon; have confidence in the ability of (a person or thing): *I trust our dog to come when called*. 2 (foll. by *with*) allow (a person) to have, use, or be responsible for something with confidence that it will be properly

used or cared for: *would trust him with my life*. **3** believe the veracity of (a person or statement etc.): *I seldom trust what I read in that newspaper*. **4** have faith, confidence, or hope that a thing is occurring or will occur: *I trust that she is recovering*. **5** (foll. by *in*) place reliance on: *we trust in you*. **6** (foll. by *to*) place (esp. undue) reliance on: *shall have to trust to luck*. **7** (foll. by *for*) allow credit to (a customer) for goods. PHRASES **in trust** *Law* held by one person for the enjoyment and benefit of another. **on trust 1** on credit. **2** on the basis of trust or confidence. **take on trust** accept (an assertion, claim, etc.) without evidence or investigation. **not trust a person as far as one can throw him or her** not trust a person at all. **trust a person to do something!** it is characteristic or predictable for a person to act in such a way: *trust her to be late!* ▶ **trustable** *adjective*

trust company *noun* (*plural* **trust companies**) a company formed to act as a trustee or to deal with trusts, esp. one that offers banking services.

trusted *adjective* in which or in whom trust has been placed: *a trusted friend*.

trustee *noun* **1** *Law* a person given control or powers of administration of property held in trust with a legal obligation to administer it solely for the purposes specified. **2** any of a group of people appointed to manage the affairs of an institution etc. **3** *Cdn* an elected member of a school board. **4** a state made responsible for the government of an area. ▶ **trusteeship** *noun*

trustful *adjective* inclined to trust; not feeling or showing suspicion. ▶ **trustfully** *adverb*

trust fund *noun* a fund of money etc. held in trust: *a trust fund has been started to take donations for victims' families*.

trusting *adjective* inclined to trust others, esp. characteristically. ▶ **trustingly** *adverb*

trustworthiness *noun* the quality of being trustworthy; reliability, dependability.

trustworthy *adjective* reliable, dependable.

trusty *adjective* (**trustier, trustiest**) *archaic* or *jocular* trustworthy: *a trusty steed*.

truth *noun* (*plural* **truths**) **1** the quality or a state of being true; conformity to fact or reality; genuineness, authenticity. **2 a** what is true; the matter or circumstance as it really is. **b** a true statement; a report or account consistent with fact or reality. **3** something held or accepted as true; a fixed or established principle: *fundamental truths*. **4** accuracy of delineation or representation, esp. in art or literature; lifelike quality. **5** ideal or spiritual reality as a subject of revelation or an object of esp. philosophical or religious interpretation or quest. PHRASES **in truth** *literary* truly, really. **to tell the truth** (also **if truth be told** or **truth to tell**) to be honest; frankly.

truthful *adjective* **1** habitually speaking the truth; sincere, honest. **2** (of an artistic or literary representation etc.) accurate, realistic, true to life. **3** (of a story etc.) true. ▶ **truthfully** *adverb* **truthfulness** *noun*

truth serum *noun* (also **truth drug**) any of various drugs supposedly able to induce a person to tell the truth.

try • *verb* (**tries, tried, trying**) **1** make an effort with a view to success: *tried to be on time* ◊ *try and be early*. **2** make an effort to achieve: *had better try something easier*. **3 a** test (the quality of a thing) by use or experiment. **b** test the qualities of (a person or thing): *have you tried the salad?* **4** make severe demands on (a person, quality, etc.): *my patience has been sorely tried*. **5** examine the effectiveness or usefulness of for a purpose: *have you tried kicking it?* **6** ascertain the state of

fastening of (a door, window, etc.). **7 a** investigate and decide (a case or issue) judicially. **b** subject (a person) to trial: *will be tried for murder*. **8** make an experiment in order to find out: *let us try which takes longest*. **9** (foll. by *for*) **a** apply or compete for. **b** seek to reach or attain: *am going to try for a gold medal*. **10** (often foll. by *out*) **a** extract (oil) from fat by heating. **b** treat (fat) in this way. • *noun* (*plural* **tries**) **1** an effort to accomplish something; an attempt: *give it a try*. **2** *Rugby* the act of touching the ball down behind the opposing goal line, scoring points and entitling the scoring side to a kick at goal. PHRASES **try (on) for size** try out or test for suitability. **try one's hand** see how skilful one is, esp. at the first attempt. **try on** put on (clothes etc.) to see if they fit or suit the wearer. **try out 1 a** put to the test. **b** test thoroughly. **2** (often foll. by *for*) undergo a test in the hope of being selected for a role, a position on a sports team, etc.

trying *adjective* annoying; hard to endure.

tryout *noun* (often in *plural*) **1** a test of the qualities or performance of a person or thing. **2** a gathering of prospective members of a team, troupe, etc. for such testing.

trypsin *noun* a digestive enzyme which hydrolyzes proteins, secreted by the pancreas. [Say TRIP sin]

tryst • *noun* an esp. secret meeting between lovers. • *verb* keep a tryst. [Say TRIST]

tsar *noun* = CZAR. [Say ZAR]

TSE *abbreviation* Toronto Stock Exchange.

tsetse *noun* an African fly that feeds on human and animal blood and transmits sleeping sickness. [Say TSEET see or SEET see]

T-shirt *noun* a short-sleeved casual top, usu. of a cotton knit fabric and having the form of a T when spread out. ▶ **T-shirted** *adjective*

Tsilhqot'in • *noun* (*plural* **Tsilhqot'in**) **1** a member of an Athapaskan people inhabiting the basin of the Chilcotin River valley, between the Coast Mountains and the Fraser River in BC. **2** the Athapaskan language of this people. • *adjective* of or relating to this people. [Say tsill COAT in]

Tsimshian • *noun* (*plural* **Tsimshian** or **Tsimshians**) **1** a member of a group of Aboriginal peoples living in coastal and interior northern BC. **2** the group of languages spoken by the Tsimshian and related Aboriginal peoples. • *adjective* of or relating to this people. [Say TSIMSHY in or TSIM shin]

tsk *interjection, noun, & verb* (also **tsk tsk**; *verb* **tsk-tsk**) = TUT (*see* TUT-TUT). [Say TISK]

TSP *abbreviation* TRISODIUM PHOSPHATE.

tsp. *abbreviation* teaspoonful.

T-square *noun* a T-shaped instrument for drawing parallel lines or right angles.

TSR *noun* (*plural* **TSRs**) a program that stays in a computer's memory once it has been executed and remains ready to be reactivated instantly, without subsequently activated programs needing to be terminated.

TSS *abbreviation* TOXIC SHOCK SYNDROME.

tsunami *noun* (*plural* **tsunamis**) a long high sea wave caused by underwater earthquakes etc. [Say tsoo NOMMY]

Tsuu T'ina *noun & adjective* (*plural* **Tsuu T'ina**) = SARCEE. [Say tsoo TINNA]

tub • *noun* **1** an open flat-bottomed usu. round container for various purposes. **2** a bathtub. **3** a tub-shaped (usu. plastic) carton. **4** the amount a tub will hold. **5** *informal* a clumsy slow boat. **6** *informal* (usu. derogatory) a fat person. • *verb* (**tubs, tubbed, tubbing**) plant, place, bathe, or wash in a tub.

tuba *noun* (*plural* **tubas**) **1** a large, very low-pitched valved brass wind instrument. **2** a tuba player.

tubal *adjective* of or relating to a tube, esp. the Fallopian or bronchial tubes. [Say TUBE ul]

tubal ligation *noun* a surgical procedure for making a female incapable of bearing offspring, which involves cutting and tying the Fallopian tubes.

tubbiness *noun* fatness.

tubby *adjective* (**tubbier**, **tubbiest**) fat.

tube *noun* **1** a long hollow rigid or flexible cylinder, esp. for holding or carrying air, liquids, etc. **2** a soft metal or plastic cylinder sealed at one end and having a screw cap at the other, for holding a semi-liquid substance ready for use: *a tube of toothpaste*. **3 a** *Anatomy & Zoology* a hollow cylindrical organ in the body: *Fallopian tubes*. **b** *Botany* a hollow cylindrical structure in a plant. **4 a** a cathode ray tube esp. in a television set. **b** (**the tube**) *informal* television. **5** = INNER TUBE. **6** (as an *adjective*) designating a close-fitting skirt or sleeveless cylindrical dress or top, esp. of elasticized fabric: *tube top*. **7** the cylindrical body of a wind instrument. ▪ PHRASES **down the tube** (or **tubes**) lost, wasted; in or into a state of failure: *another trip to the mechanic means more money down the tube* ◊ *felt his life was going down the tube*.

tuber *noun* **1** the short thick rounded part of a stem or rhizome, usu. found underground and covered with modified buds, e.g. in a potato. **2** the similar root of a dahlia etc. [Say TUBE er]

tubercle *noun* **1** a small rounded bump esp. on a bone. **2** a small rounded swelling on the body or in an organ, esp. a node-like lesion characteristic of tuberculosis in the lungs etc. [Say TUBE er cul]

tubercle bacillus *noun* a bacterium causing tuberculosis.

tubercular ▪ *adjective* (also **tuberculous**) of or having tubercles or tuberculosis. ▪ *noun* a person with tuberculosis. [Say too BERK yuh ler]

tuberculosis *noun* an infectious disease caused by the bacillus *Mycobacterium tuberculosis*, characterized by the growth of small rounded swellings or tubercles in the tissues, esp. in the lungs, and causing inflammation of the membranes around the lungs (pleurisy), fever, weight loss, etc. [Say too berk yuh LOE sis]

tuberose *noun* a Mexican plant with heavily scented white waxy flowers, strap-shaped leaves, and a bulb-like base. [Say TUBA roze or TUBE roze]

tuberous *adjective* **1** having or consisting of a tuber or tubers: *tuberous begonias* ◊ *a tuberous root*. **2** characterized or affected by rounded swellings: *tuberous sclerosis*. [Say TUBE er us]

tube skate *noun* *Cdn* an ice skate with the blade running along a hollow metal tube.

tubing *noun* **1 a** a length of tube. **b** a quantity of tubes; tubes collectively. **2** a recreational activity in which one sits in an inflated oversized inner tube and floats down a river, is pulled by a boat, or slides down a snow-covered hill.

tub-thumper *noun* *informal* a ranting preacher or orator. ▶ **tub-thumping** *adjective* & *noun*

tubular *adjective* **1** tube-shaped. **2** having or consisting of tubes. **3** (of furniture etc.) made of tubular pieces. [Say TUBE yuh ler]

tuck ▪ *verb* **1** (often foll. by *in*, *up*) **a** draw, fold, or turn the outer or end parts of (cloth or clothes etc.) close together so as to be held; thrust in the edge of (a thing) so as to confine it: *tucked his shirt into his pants*. **b** thrust in the edges of bedclothes around (a person): *tuck me in*. **2** draw together into a small space: *the bird tucked its head under its wing*. **3 a** stow (a thing) away in a specified place or way: *tucked it out of sight*. **b** (usu. in

passive) hide away, seclude: *a town tucked away in the foothills*. **4** (often foll. by *down*) bring one's knees to one's chest; curl oneself into a ball. **5 a** make a stitched fold in (material, a garment, etc.). **b** shorten, tighten, or ornament with stitched folds. ▪ *noun* **1** a flattened usu. stitched fold in material, a garment, etc., often one of several parallel folds for shortening, tightening, or ornament. **2** (also **tuck position**) **a** (in diving, gymnastics, etc.) a position with the knees bent upwards into the chest and the hands clasped round the shins. **b** (in skiing) a tight crouched position, with the chest bent down to the knees and the arms close by the sides; a squatting position. **3** *informal* a cosmetic surgical operation: *tummy tuck*. ▪ PHRASES **tuck in** *informal* eat food heartily. **tuck into** (or **away**) *informal* eat (food) heartily: *tucked into their dinner*.

tuckamore *noun* *Cdn* (*Nfld*) **1** a stunted tree or bush, esp. a spruce or juniper, with creeping roots and interlacing branches. **2** dense scrub formed by such trees or bushes. [Say TUCKA mor]

tuckered out *adjective* tired out; exhausted: *he was tuckered out from all that yardwork*.

tucking *noun* a series of usu. stitched tucks in material or a garment.

tuck shop *noun* *Cdn* a small store within a hospital, hotel, apartment block, etc., selling snacks and daily necessities to residents or guests.

'tude *noun* = ATTITUDE 3.

Tudor *hist.* ▪ *adjective* **1** of, characteristic of, or associated with the royal family of England that ruled from 1485 to 1603, or with the English monarchs of this period, Henry VII, Henry VIII, Edward VI, Mary I, and Elizabeth I. **2** of or relating to the architectural style of this period, or one in imitation of it, esp. with half-timbering and elaborately decorated houses. ▪ *noun* **1** a member of the Tudor royal family. **2** a house with Tudor architecture. [Say TOO der or TYOO der]

Tues. *abbreviation* (also **Tue.**) Tuesday.

Tuesday ▪ *noun* the third day of the week, following Monday. ▪ *adverb* **1** on Tuesday. **2** (**Tuesdays**) on Tuesdays; each Tuesday.

tufa *noun* **1** a porous rock composed of calcium carbonate and formed around mineral springs. **2** = TUFF. [Say TOO fuh or TYOO fuh]

tuff *noun* rock formed by consolidation of volcanic ash.

tuffet *noun* **1** a low seat. **2** a clump or tuft of something: *there were butterflies in the grass tuffets*. [Say TUFFIT]

tuft ▪ *noun* a bunch or collection of threads, grass, feathers, hair, etc., held or growing together at the base. ▪ *verb* **1** provide with a tuft or tufts. **2** make depressions at regular intervals in (upholstery etc.) by passing a thread through. **3** grow in tufts.

tufted *adjective* **1** having or growing in a tuft or tufts. **2** (of a bird) having a tuft of feathers on the head.

tufting *noun* **1** in senses of TUFT *verb*. **2** (in northern Canada) **a** a handicraft in which plucked moosehair or caribou hair is dyed, gathered in tufts, stitched in patterns on a background of fabric or leather, and finally contoured or sculpted with clippers. **b** a product of such handiwork.

tug ▪ *verb* (**tugs**, **tugged**, **tugging**) **1** pull hard or violently; jerk. **2** tow (a ship etc.) by means of a tugboat. ▪ *noun* **1** a hard, violent, or jerky pull. **2** a sudden strong emotional feeling: *felt a tug as I watched them go*. **3** (also **tugboat**) a small powerful boat for towing larger boats and ships. **4** an aircraft towing a glider. ▶ **tugger** *noun*

tug-of-war *noun* **1** a contest in which two teams pull at opposite ends of a rope until one drags the other over

a central line. **2** an intense struggle between two opponents.

tuition *noun* **1** a fee paid for education or instruction. **2** teaching or instruction, esp. if paid for. [Say too ISH'n]

tulip *noun* **1** a bulbous spring-flowering plant with many cultivated forms that bear showy cup-shaped flowers of various colours and markings. **2** a flower of this plant.

tulip tree *noun* a tree of eastern North America, with tulip-like flowers.

tulle *noun* a soft fine net used in veils, tutus, etc. [Say TOOL]

tum *noun informal* the stomach.

tumble • *verb* (**tumbles, tumbled, tumbling**) **1** fall or cause to fall suddenly, clumsily, or headlong. **2 a** fall rapidly in amount etc.: *prices tumbled*. **b** fall in ruins; collapse, topple. **3** (often foll. by *around*, *about*) roll or toss erratically or helplessly to and fro. **4** move or rush in a headlong or blundering manner: *children tumbled out of the car*. **5** (often foll. by *to*) *informal* understand the meaning or hidden implication of a situation: *I finally tumbled to the fact that they were seeing one another outside the office*. **6** overturn; fling or push roughly or carelessly. **7** perform gymnastic or acrobatic feats, esp. somersaults. **8** rumple or disarrange; pull about; disorder. • *noun* **1** a sudden or headlong fall. **2 a** somersault or other acrobatic feat. **3** an untidy or confused state.

tumbledown *adjective* falling or fallen into ruin.

tumble dry *verb* (**tumble dries, tumble dried, tumble drying**) dry (clothing etc.) in a clothes dryer with a heated rotating drum.

tumbler *noun* **1** a drinking glass with no handle or foot, with a thick heavy base. **2** an acrobat or gymnast, esp. one performing somersaults. **3** a pivoted piece in a lock that holds the bolt until lifted by a key. **4** (also **tumbling box** *plural* **tumbling boxes, tumbling barrel**) a revolving drum or barrel containing an abrasive substance, in which castings, gemstones, etc., are cleaned by friction. ▶ **tumblerful** *noun* (*plural* **tumblerfuls**)

tumbleweed *noun* any of various plants, esp. of arid regions, that form a globular bush that breaks off in late summer and is tumbled about by the wind.

tumescence *noun* the action of swelling, esp. as a response to sexual stimulation. [Say too MESS ince or tyoo MESS ince]

tumescent *adjective* **1** swollen or swelling. **2** (of a man) sexually aroused. [Say too MESS'nt or tyoo MESS'nt]

tummy *noun* (*plural* **tummies**) *informal* the stomach.

tummy tuck *noun informal* cosmetic surgery in which excess abdominal fat and skin is removed.

tumorous *adjective* having to do with or affected by tumours. [Say TUMOUR us]

tumour *noun* (also **tumor**) an abnormal swelling or enlargement in any part of the body, esp. a permanent swelling without inflammation, caused by excessive continued growth and proliferation of cells in a tissue, which may be either benign or malignant.

tumpline *noun* a sling for carrying a load on the back, with a strap which passes around the forehead.

tumult *noun* **1 a** a loud, confused noise, esp. one caused by a large crowd of people: *"Move it!" is the cry heard above the tumult*. **b** a large crowd, esp. involved in a demonstration or public disturbance: *they rushed to the balcony to watch the growing tumult*. **2** confusion or disorder: *her time at university was one of tumult and frustration*. [Say TOO mult or TUM ult]

tumultuous *adjective* **1** very loud or noisy: *tumultuous applause*. **2** characterized by confusion, disorder, or intense conflicting emotions: *a bitter and tumultuous*

campaign ◊ *the tumultuous period in her private life began with a letter bomb from a deranged fan*. **3** agitated. ▶ **tumultuously** *adverb* **tumultuousness** *noun* [Say tuh MUL choo us or too MUL choo us or tyoo MUL choo us]

tun *noun* **1** a large beer or wine cask. **2** a brewer's fermenting vat. **3** a measure of capacity, equal to 210 imperial gallons or 252 US gallons (about 955 litres).

tuna *noun* (*plural* **tuna** or **tunas**) **1** a large marine food and game fish of the mackerel family, which has a rounded body and a pointed snout and is found in warm seas worldwide. **2** (also **tuna fish**) the flesh of the tuna, often tinned in oil or water.

tundra *noun* a vast level treeless Arctic region usu. with a marshy surface and underlying permafrost.

Tundra Buggy *noun* (*plural* **Tundra Buggies**) *Cdn proprietary* a large-wheeled sightseeing bus used to take tourists into polar bear country.

tundra tire *noun Cdn* a wide airplane tire inflated to low pressure, used to operate from rough terrain.

tune • *noun* **1** a melody with or without harmony. **2** a song. **3** the proper musical pitch or intonation; harmony: *out of tune*. • *verb* (**tunes, tuned, tuning**) **1** put (a musical instrument) in tune. **2 a** adjust (a radio receiver, television, etc.) to a particular frequency, channel, etc.: *the TV was tuned to a basketball game*. **b** (usu. foll. by *in*) adjust a radio receiver, television, etc. to the required signal or channel: *tuned in to their favourite station*. **c** (in *passive*) cause to be interested in, watching, or listening to a broadcast etc.: *troops tuned to Army radio heard the DJ rejoice that she was pregnant*. **3** adjust (an engine etc.) to run smoothly and efficiently. **4** (foll. by *to*) adjust or adapt to a required or different purpose, situation, etc. PHRASES **in tune 1** having the correct pitch or intonation: *sings in tune*. **2** (usu. foll. by *with*) in agreement or harmony with a situation, person, idea, etc.: *she's in tune with a younger generation of Liberals*. **out of tune 1** not having the correct pitch or intonation. **2** (usu. foll. by *with*) not in agreement or harmony with a situation, person, idea, etc.: *they're out of tune with our changing interests*. **stay tuned 1** continue to watch or listen to a broadcast etc. **2** *informal* more news or information is forthcoming. **to the tune of** *informal* to the considerable sum or amount of. **tune in** (often foll. by *to*) *informal* become acquainted with or aware of. **tune out 1** stop tuning in to a broadcast etc. **2** become oblivious to (something) or to one's surroundings. **tune up 1** (of a musician) bring one's instrument to the proper or uniform pitch. **2** bring to the most efficient condition.

tuneful *adjective* melodious, musical. ▶ **tunefully** *adverb* **tunefulness** *noun*

tuneless *adjective* **1** not melodious; unmusical. **2** out of tune. ▶ **tunelessly** *adverb*

tuner *noun* **1** a person who tunes musical instruments, esp. pianos. **2 a** a device for tuning a radio receiver. **b** a radio receiver. **3** an electronic device for tuning a musical instrument.

tunesmith *noun informal* a songwriter.

tune-up *noun* **1** an act of making esp. minor adjustments to a motor vehicle etc. to ensure optimum performance. **2** *Sport* (often foll. by *for*) an event that serves as a practice for a subsequent event.

tung *noun* a tree, native to China, bearing poisonous fruits that contain seeds yielding an oil used in paints and varnishes.

tungsten *noun* a steel-grey dense metallic element with a very high melting point, occurring naturally and used for the filaments of electric lamps and for alloying steel etc. [Say TUNG stin]

tunic *noun* **1** a close-fitting short coat of police or

military etc. uniform. **2** a loose often sleeveless garment usu. reaching to about the knees, as worn in ancient Greece and Rome. **3** a loose, knitted, women's upper garment reaching to mid-thigh, usu. worn over leggings, a skirt, blouse, or pants. **4** a loose sleeveless usu. belted dress worn over a blouse, esp. as part of a girl's school uniform. **5** any of various loose, pleated dresses gathered at the waist with a belt or cord.

tuning *noun* **1** *in senses of* TUNE *verb.* **2** the process or a system of putting a musical instrument in tune. **b** the state of being in tune.

tuning fork *noun* a two-pronged steel fork that gives a particular note when struck, used in tuning musical instruments etc.

Tunisian • *adjective* of or relating to the North African country of Tunisia. • *noun* a native or inhabitant of Tunisia. [Say tuh NEEZH in or tuh NEEZY in]

tunnel • *noun* **1** an artificial underground passage through a hill or under a road or river etc., esp. for a railway or road to pass through, or in a mine. **2** an underground passage dug by a burrowing animal. **3** a long enclosed passageway or corridor through a building etc., e.g. from the dressing room to the playing area in a sports stadium. **4** (esp. in metaphors) a prolonged period of difficulty or suffering: *a light at the end of the tunnel.* **5** a canal or hollow groove in the body: *carpal tunnel.* • *verb* (**tunnels, tunnelled, tunnelling**) **1** (foll. by *through, into*, etc.) make a tunnel through (a hill etc.). **2** make (one's way) by tunnelling. ▶ **tunneller** *noun*

tunnel vision *noun* **1** vision that is defective in not adequately including objects away from the centre of the field of view. **2** *informal* the tendency to focus exclusively on a single objective or a limited aspect of an argument or situation: *they approach everything with tunnel vision, thinking only about discharging their obligation to you, not the substance of the task ◊ he demonstrated an ability to decide what he wanted and pursue it with tunnel vision.*

tupelo *noun* (*plural* **tupelos**) **1** an Asian and North American deciduous tree with colourful foliage, which grows in swampy conditions. **2** the wood of this tree. [Say TOOPA loe or TYOOPA loe]

tupik *noun* a traditional skin tent used by Inuit groups during the summer. [Say TOO pick]

Tupperware *noun* *proprietary* a range of plastic containers for storing food.

tuque *noun* = TOQUE 1.

turban *noun* **1** a man's headdress, consisting of a length of cotton or silk wound around a cap or the head, worn esp. by Muslims and Sikhs. **2** a woman's headdress or hat resembling this. ▶ **turbaned** *adjective*

turbid *adjective* (of a liquid or colour) muddy, thick; not clear: *heavily shaded or turbid rivers tend to be devoid of higher plants.* ▶ **turbidity** *noun*

turbine *noun* a rotary motor or engine driven by a flow of water, steam, gas, wind, etc., esp. to produce electrical power.

turbo *noun* (*plural* **turbos**) **1 a** = TURBOCHARGER. **b** a motor vehicle equipped with this. **2** (also in *combination*) = TURBINE.

turbocharged *adjective* **1** (of a car or engine etc.) equipped with a turbocharger for increased power. **2** *informal* featuring a high or higher than usual level of energy, intensity, power, or speed: *a turbocharged microprocessor ◊ she's a turbocharged social butterfly.*

turbocharger *noun* a system driven by a turbine that gets its power from an engine's exhaust gases. It sends the mixture of gasoline and air into the engine at high pressure, making it more powerful.

turboprop *noun* **1** a jet engine in which a turbine is used to drive a propeller. **2** an aircraft powered by this.

turbot *noun* (*plural* **turbot**) **1** a large speckled European flatfish with a broad scaleless diamond-shaped body covered with bony bumps, valued for food. **2** any of various similar fishes, including halibut. [Say TUR bit]

turbulence *noun* **1 a** an irregularly fluctuating flow of air or fluid. **b** a disturbed state caused by this. **2** stormy conditions as a result of atmospheric disturbance. **3** a disturbance, commotion, or tumult: *minor economic turbulence.* [Say TUR byoo lince]

turbulent *adjective* **1** characterized by conflict, disorder, or confusion; not controlled or calm: *the turbulent and unpredictable events of the late twentieth century.* **2** (of a flow of air or water) moving unsteadily or violently: *the plane encountered turbulent air currents.* [Say TUR byoo lint]

turd *noun* *coarse slang* **1** a lump of excrement. **2** a term of contempt for a person.

tureen *noun* a deep covered dish for serving soup etc. [Say toor EEN]

turf • *noun* (*plural* **turfs** or **turves**) **1 a** a layer of grass etc. with earth and matted roots as the surface of grassland. **b** a piece of this cut from the ground. **c** *informal* artificial turf. **2** a slab of peat for fuel. **3** (**the turf**) **a** a horse racing generally. **b** a general term for racecourses. **4 a** an area regarded as being under the control of a particular person or group; one's personal territory. **b** one's sphere of influence or activity. • *verb* **1** (often as **turfed** *adjective*) cover (ground) with turf. **2** (esp. foll. by *out*) *informal* expel or eject (a person or thing).

turf war *noun* (also **turf battle**) a fight or struggle over spheres of influence or control.

turgid *adjective* **1** swollen, inflated, enlarged: *turgid blossoms.* **2** (of language) tediously pompous: *the book is couched in the turgid academic style of French deconstructionism.* [Say TUR jid]

Turing test *noun* *Computing* a test for intelligence in a computer, which requires that a human should be unable to distinguish it from another human by the replies to questions put to both. [Say TYUR ing]

Turk *noun* **1 a** a native or national of Turkey, a country in western Asia and southeastern Europe. **b** a person of Turkish descent. **2** a member of a Central Asian people from whom the Ottomans derived, speaking Turkic languages.

turkey *noun* (*plural* **turkeys**) **1** a large chiefly domesticated game bird, originally of North America, having dark feathers with a green or bronze sheen, prized as food esp. on festive occasions including Christmas and Thanksgiving. **2** the flesh of the turkey as food. **3** *slang* **a** a theatrical failure; a flop. **b** a stupid or inept person. PHRASES **talk turkey** *informal* talk frankly and straightforwardly; get down to business.

turkey vulture *noun* (also **turkey buzzard**) a North American vulture with dark feathers, a white beak and legs, and a bare red head.

Turkic • *adjective* of or relating to a large group of Altaic languages including Turkish and Azerbaijani or the peoples speaking them. • *noun* the Turkic languages collectively. [Say TURK ick]

Turkish • *adjective* of or relating to Turkey or to the Turks or their language. • *noun* this language.

Turkish bath *noun* **1** a hot-air or steam bath followed by washing, massage, etc. **2** (in *singular* or *plural*) a building for this.

turmeric *noun* **1** a tropical Asian plant of the ginger family, yielding aromatic roots. **2** this root powdered and used as a spice esp. in curry powder. [Say TUR mur ick]

turmoil *noun* a state of great disturbance, confusion, or uncertainty: *the country was in turmoil ◊ endured years of inner turmoil*.

turn • *verb* **1** move around a fixed point or central axis; rotate, revolve. **2** reverse the position of so that the back faces forward, the bottom faces up, or the inside faces out. **3 a** take a new direction: *turn left*. **b** (of a road) bend, curve. **4** go around (a corner). **5** change the course or direction of; aim, direct: *she turned her eyes away*. **6** (usu. foll. by *to* or *from*) focus or conclude focusing (one's thoughts or attention) on a particular subject etc. **7** (foll. by *to*) **a** apply oneself to; set about: *turned to doing the ironing*. **b** have recourse to: *turned to her for help*. **8** (foll. by *into*) change in nature, form, or condition; transform. **9** cause to become or become: *they have turned crazy*. **10** (foll. by *against*) make or become hostile to: *our actions have turned them against us*. **11** (foll. by *on*) become hostile towards; attack: *the dog turned on its owner*. **12 a** (of hair or leaves) change colour. **b** cause (the hair) to change colour. **13** make or become sour: *the milk has turned*. **14 a** (of the stomach) be nauseated. **b** cause (the stomach) to become nauseated. **15** reach the age of: *turned 40*. **16 a** flip (a page of a book) in order to read or write on the other side. **b** (foll. by *to*) go to (a particular page or passage). **17** become an informer. **18** (of the head) become giddy. **19** twist or sprain (an ankle). **20** (foll. by *on*) depend on; be determined by: *it all turns on the weather tomorrow*. **21** *Baseball* execute (a double play). **22** perform (a somersault etc.). **23** make or earn (a profit etc.): *she turned a quick buck*. **24** (often foll. by *aside*) divert (a bullet). **25** shape (an object) on a lathe. **26** (of the tide) change from flood to ebb or vice versa. • *noun* **1** an act of turning around on an axis; a total or partial revolution. **2 a** an act of turning or facing another way; a change of direction. **b** a point at which a turning or change occurs. **3 a** a place where a road turns off or branches onto another: *took a wrong turn*. **b** a place where a road, river, etc., changes direction; a bend. **4** a change of the tide from ebb to flow or from flow to ebb. **5** a change in circumstances or in the course of events, esp. for better or worse. **6** the transition from one period of time to the next: *the turn of the century*. **7** an opportunity or obligation etc. that comes successively to each of several people. **8** a period of work done by a group of people in succession; a shift. **9** a short walk or ride: *a turn in the garden*. **10** the halfway point in a round of golf. **11** an act or deed, esp. one that does good or harm to another: *one good turn deserves another*. **12** *informal* a momentary shock or feeling of concern: *the news gave me quite a turn*. **13** a variation or particular manner of linguistic expression, esp. for effect: *turn of phrase*. **14** a tendency or disposition: *is of a mechanical turn of mind*. PHRASES **at every turn** at every change of circumstance, at each new stage; continually. **by turns** one after the other in regular succession; alternately. **in turn** in succession; one by one. **in one's turn** when one's turn or opportunity comes. **not know which way** (or **where**) **to turn** be unsure how to act, whom to trust, etc.; be completely at a loss. **out of turn 1** at a time when it is not one's turn. **2** inappropriately; tactlessly: *did I speak out of turn?* **take turns** act or work alternately or in succession. **to a turn** (esp. cooked) to exactly the right degree etc. **turn around 1** (also **turn about**) turn and face the opposite direction. **2** adopt an opposite course or policy. **3** begin to show an opposite trend or movement. **4** receive, process, and send (passengers, goods, etc.) out again. **turn away 1** turn and face another direction; avert one's eyes. **2** refuse to accept or admit; reject, send away. **turn**

back 1 return, go back the way one has come. **2** fold back. **turn the corner 1** make a turn at an intersection onto a perpendicular street. **2** pass the critical point in an illness, difficulty, etc.; begin to make noticeable improvement. **turn a person's crank** *slang* (usu. with *neg.*) amuse, thrill, or excite a person. **turn down 1** reject (a proposal, application, etc.). **2** reduce the volume or strength of (sound, heat, etc.) by turning a knob etc. **3** fold down (bedsheets etc.). **turn an honest penny** earn money fairly. **turn in 1** hand in, submit. **2** achieve or register (a performance, score, etc.). **3** *informal* go to bed. **4** fold inwards. **5** incline inwards: *his toes turn in*. **6** hand over (a suspect etc.) to the authorities. **turn loose 1** release and set free (an animal). **2** allow (a person) to go where, or do as, he or she pleases. **turn off 1 a** stop the flow or operation of (water, electricity, etc.) by means of a tap, switch, etc. **b** operate (a tap, switch, etc.) to achieve this. **2 a** enter a side road. **b** (of a side road) lead off from another road. **3** *informal* cause to lose interest. **turn on 1 a** start the flow or operation of (water, electricity, etc.) by means of a tap, switch, etc. **b** operate (a tap, switch, etc.) to achieve this. **c** activate, begin to use (charm, genius, etc.). **2** *informal* excite, arouse; stimulate the interest of, esp. sexually. **3** *informal* introduce to or make aware of: *she turned me on to classical music*. **turn out 1** prove to be the case; result: *we shall see how things turn out ◊ it turned out that she was right ◊ turned out to be the thief*. **2** extinguish (a light etc.). **3** *informal* assemble; attend a meeting etc. **4** expel. **5** produce (manufactured goods etc.). **6** dress or equip: *well turned out*. **7** empty (a pocket) to see the contents. **8** empty or clean out (a room etc.). **9** *informal* a get out of bed. **b** go out of doors. **turn over 1** turn from one side onto another; bring the reverse or underside into view: *turn over the page*. **2** upset; cause to fall over. **3 a** cause (an engine) to run. **b** (of an engine) start running. **4** consider thoroughly. **5** (foll. by *to*) **a** transfer the care or conduct of (a person or thing) to (a person). **b** = TURN IN 6. **6** *Sport* lose possession of (the ball or puck) to the opposing team. **7** do business to the amount of: *turns over $5000 a week*. **turn round** esp. *Brit.* = TURN AROUND. **turn tail** run away from something feared; flee. **turn the tide** reverse the trend of events. **turn up 1** increase the volume or strength of (sound, heat, etc.) by turning a knob etc. **2** place upwards. **3** discover or reveal. **4** be found, esp. by chance: *it turned up in a bus depot*. **5** happen or present itself; (of a person) put in an appearance: *turned up late*.

turnabout *noun* **1** a change or reversal of direction. **2** an abrupt change of opinion or policy etc. PHRASES **turnabout is fair play** committing an action against someone else is fair if that person has already committed the same action against you.

turnaround *noun* **1 a** an abrupt or unexpected reversal of a trend, attitude, opinion, fortune, etc. **b** an improvement or recovery, esp. in business. **2 a** the process of receiving, processing, and sending out again. **b** the process of unloading and reloading an airplane, ship, etc. **c** the amount of time required for such processes. **3** esp. *US* a place where vehicles can turn around, such as at the end of a street.

turncoat *noun* a person who changes sides in a conflict, dispute, etc.; a traitor.

turndown • *noun* **1** a rejection or refusal. **2** an act of turning down the sheets of a bed, esp. as a courtesy performed in a hotel: *turndown service*. **3** a downturn. • *adjective* (esp. of a collar) that is or may be turned down.

turner *noun* **1** a thing that turns or is used for turning, e.g. a spatula. **2** a person who turns wood on a lathe.

turning *noun* **1** the act or practice of using a lathe. **2** work or an article produced on a lathe.

turning point *noun* **1** a moment at which a decisive change occurs in one's life, a process, etc. **2** an incident that causes or results in decisive change.

turnip *noun* **1** = RUTABAGA. **2 a** a plant of the cabbage family with a large white globular root and sprouting edible leaves. **b** this root used as a vegetable.

turnkey *adjective* **1** (of a contract, solution, etc.) providing for a supply of equipment in a state ready for operation: *we offer a complete turnkey service for dynamic flexible bakery production systems.* **2** (of a computer system etc.) assembled ahead of time and complete with all the parts and equipment necessary for immediate use.

turnoff *noun* **1** a road that leads away from a larger or more important one. **2** *informal* something that causes disgust or a loss of interest.

turn of the century • *noun* the period at the end of one century and beginning of the next, esp. around 1900. • *adjective* (usu. **turn-of-the-century**) used, manufactured, or existing around 1900.

turn-on *noun informal* a thing or person that thrills, excites, or causes esp. sexual stimulation or arousal.

turnout *noun* **1** the number of people attending or participating in an event, such as a meeting or a vote: *low voter turnout.* **2** the quantity of goods produced in a given time. **3** a place where animals may be turned out to graze. **4** *Dance* the outward rotation of the leg in the hip socket.

turnover *noun* **1** the amount of money made in a business in a given time. **2** the rate at which a particular asset or product is sold and replaced. **3** the rate at which employees join and leave a company, tenants move into and out of housing, etc. **4** a small usu. triangular or semicircular pie, made by folding a piece of pastry over onto itself to enclose a usu. sweet filling. **5** *Sport* a loss of possession of the ball or puck to the opposing team.

turnpike *noun* **1** *US* a toll highway. **2** a tollgate.

turn signal *noun* each of a pair of flashing lights on either side of a motor vehicle used to indicate turns or lane changes.

turnstile *noun* a mechanical gate consisting of usu. four revolving arms fixed to a vertical post allowing people through singly, and usu. functioning in one direction only.

turntable *noun* **1** a circular revolving platform spinning a phonograph record that is being played. **2** the unit housing this; a record player. **3** a circular revolving platform for turning a railway locomotive or other vehicle.

turpentine *noun* **1** (also **oil of turpentine**) a volatile essential oil with a pungent odour, obtained by distilling gum turpentine or pine wood, used esp. as a solvent and thinner for paints and stains, and in medical liniments. **2** (also **crude turpentine** or **gum turpentine**) any of various sticky substances which exude from coniferous trees, esp. pines, and can be distilled to yield gum rosin and oil of turpentine.

turpitude *noun formal* wickedness: *conviction for a crime, especially when it involves moral turpitude such as stealing or embezzlement, may be grounds for summary dismissal.* [Say TERPA tude]

turquoise *noun* **1** a semi-precious stone, usu. opaque and of a sky-blue to blue-green colour, consisting of hydrated copper aluminum phosphate. **2** *noun & adjective* the colour of this mineral, usu. a greenish-blue. [Say TUR koyz or TUR kwoyz]

turr *noun Cdn (Nfld)* = MURRE.

turret *noun* **1** a small tower, usu. projecting from the wall of a building, such as a castle. **2** a low flat usu. revolving armoured tower or enclosure for a gun and gunners in a ship, aircraft, fort, or tank. **3** an attachment for a lathe, drill, etc. that holds various tools or bits and may be rotated to access the one required to do a particular job. ▶ **turreted** *adjective*

turtle *noun* **1** any of various marine or freshwater reptiles encased in a shell of bony plates, and having flippers or webbed toes used for swimming. **2** the flesh of the turtle, esp. used for soup. PHRASES **turn turtle** turn over, capsize.

turtledove *noun* a wild dove noted for its soft cooing and its affection for its mate and young.

turtleneck *noun* **1** a high round turned-over collar, esp. on a knitted garment. **2** a garment having this type of neck.

turtle shell • *noun* the yellowish-brown mottled or clouded outer shell of some turtles, used for decorative combs, jewellery, etc. • *adjective* (**turtleshell**) **1** having the colouring or appearance of turtle shell. **2** made of turtle shell or a synthetic substitute.

Tuscan • *noun* **1** an inhabitant of Tuscany (the area around Florence) in central Italy. **2** the classical Italian language of Tuscany. • *adjective* of or relating to Tuscany or the Tuscans. [Say TUS kin]

Tuscarora • *noun* (*plural* **Tuscarora** or **Tuscaroras**) **1** a member of an Iroquois people living in southern Ontario and western New York, the last member to join the Iroquoian confederacy. **2** the Iroquoian language of this people. • *adjective* of or relating to this people. [Say TUSKA rora]

tush *noun slang* the buttocks. [Rhymes with *PUSH*]

tusk *noun* a long pointed tooth, esp. protruding from a closed mouth, as in the elephant, walrus, etc. ▶ **tusked** *adjective* (also in *combination*)

tussle • *noun* a struggle, scuffle, or conflict, esp. a minor or playful one. • *verb* (**tussles, tussled, tussling**) engage in a tussle.

tussock *noun* a tuft or clump of grass etc. forming a small hill. ▶ **tussocky** *adjective* [Say TUSS uck]

tut *interjection, noun, & verb* (**tuts, tutted, tutting**) = TUT-TUT.

Tutchone • *noun* (*plural* **Tutchone** or **Tutchones**) **1** a member of an Aboriginal people living in the area of the Yukon River. **2** the Athapaskan language of this people. • *adjective* of or relating to this people. [Say too CHONEY]

tutelage *noun* **1** instruction: *he has made excellent progress under her tutelage.* **2** protection, care, guardianship: *under his able tutelage the NDP won 12% of the vote in Quebec.* [Say TOOTA lidge or TYOOTA lidge]

tutelary *adjective* **1** serving as a guardian, protector, or patron: *when a tutelary spirit like myself is given a life to watch over, pity merely makes a mess of things.* **2** of or relating to a guardian: *the state maintained a tutelary relation with the secret police.* [Say TOOTA lerry or TYOOTA lerry]

tutor • *noun* **1** a private teacher, either one in general charge of a person's education or employed to give a student additional instruction in a particular subject or subjects. **2** esp. *Brit.* a university teacher supervising the studies of assigned undergraduates. • *verb* **1** act as a tutor to; teach or assist (a student) privately, esp. in a particular subject. **2** work as a tutor.

tutorial • *adjective* of or relating to a tutor or tuition: *arts professors taught summer school and performed tutorial duties for extramural students throughout the year.* • *noun* **1** a period of instruction given by a teaching assistant at a university to a small group of students. **2** a period of instruction given privately by a tutor, to either a single pupil or small group. **3** any training session or

seminar. **4** a program that enables a user to learn how to use a type of software by offering onscreen instruction interspersed with practice exercises. [Say too TORY ul]

Tutsi *noun* (*plural* **Tutsi** or **Tutsis**) a member of a Bantu-speaking people forming a minority of the population of Rwanda. [Sounds like *TOOTSIE*]

tutti-frutti *noun* (*plural* **tutti-fruttis**) **1** a candy or dessert, esp. ice cream, consisting of or flavoured with a mixture of chopped preserved fruits and nuts. **2** an artificial flavour combining the tastes of several fruits. [Say tooty FROOTY]

tut-tut • *interjection* expressing rebuke, impatience, or contempt. • *noun* an exclamation of "tut-tut" or the sound of consecutive clicks of the tongue against the alveolar ridge. • *verb* (**tut-tuts, tut-tutted, tut-tutting**) **1** exclaim "tut-tut". **2** express disapproval.

tutu *noun* (*plural* **tutus**) a female ballet dancer's costume with a long, flowing bell-shaped skirt of layered tulle or a short, stiff skirt of layered net standing out from the hips.

tux *noun* (*plural* **tuxes**) *informal* = TUXEDO.

tuxedo *noun* (*plural* **tuxedos**) **1** a suit worn esp. by men on formal occasions, consisting of a usu. black jacket and matching pants, often trimmed in silk, traditionally worn with a black tie, cummerbund, and white dress shirt. **2** the formal coat or jacket worn as part of this suit.

TV *noun* (*plural* **TVs**) television.

TV dinner *noun* a prepared frozen single-serving meal packaged in a compartmentalized tray in which it is heated.

TVP *abbreviation proprietary* = TEXTURED VEGETABLE PROTEIN.

TV table *noun* (also **TV tray**) one of usu. a set of small portable folding tables with a detachable tray forming the tabletop, from which a person sitting in an easy chair etc. may eat, as while watching TV.

twaddle *noun* useless, senseless, silly, or dull talk, ideas, or writing.

twang • *noun* **1 a** a strong ringing sound made by the plucked string of a musical instrument or bow. **b** any sound resembling this. **2 a** a nasal quality of pronunciation or intonation characteristic of the speech of an individual, area, country, etc. **b** an accent having such a quality. • *verb* **1 a** ring, resound, or resonate with a sound like that of a plucked string. **b** cause (a bow, arrow, etc.) to produce this sound. **2** usu. *derogatory* play (a tune or instrument) in this way. **3** utter with a nasal twang. ▶ **twangy** *adjective* (**twangier, twangiest**)

'twas *archaic* it was.

tweak • *verb* **1** pinch and twist sharply; pull with a sharp jerk; twitch. **2** make fine adjustments to: *tweak the program a little so that it works with your printer*. • *noun* **1** a sharp twist or pull: *she gave his ear a tweak*. **2** a slight change made to improve something.

twee *adjective* usu. *derogatory* affectedly dainty, quaint, or sentimental: *it seems more than a little twee to sit down at a formal coffee tasting and begin sniffing, slurping and spitting as if it were fine Burgundy*.

tweed *noun* **1** a rough-surfaced woollen cloth of varying texture, usu. of mixed flecked colours. **2** (in *plural*) clothes made of tweed.

tweedy *adjective* (**tweedier, tweediest**) **1** of or relating to tweed cloth. **2** often dressed in tweed cloth (usu. with connotations of dowdiness, heartiness, or professorial demeanour): *they arrive in buses, stolid tweedy folks, wholesomely smelling of tobacco, pine needles, and sausages*.

tween • *noun* a tween-ager. • *adjective* tween-age.

tween-age *adjective* (of a person) between 8 and 14 years of age.

tween-ager *noun* (also **tweenie**) a person who has not yet, or has only recently, become a teenager, usu. between the ages of 8 and 14.

tweet • *noun* the chirp of a small bird. • *verb* make a chirping noise.

tweeter *noun* a loudspeaker designed to reproduce high frequencies (*compare* WOOFER).

tweeze *verb* (**tweezes, tweezed, tweezing**) **1** pinch or grab with or as if with tweezers. **2** pluck (the eyebrows) with tweezers.

tweezers *plural noun* a small pair of pincers used for picking up tiny objects, plucking eyebrows, etc.

twelfth *ordinal number* constituting number 12 in a series.

twelve *cardinal number* one more than eleven.

twelve-pack *noun* a case of twelve items sold together, esp. bottles or cans of beer.

12-step *adjective* designating or pertaining to a program designed to help addicts overcome esp. a drug or alcohol dependency, based on progressing through twelve stages towards recovery. ▶ **12-stepper** *noun*

twentieth *ordinal number* constituting number 20 in a series.

twenty *cardinal number* (*plural* **twenties**) ten less than thirty. PHRASES **twenty-first, -second**, etc. the ordinal numbers between twentieth and thirtieth. **twenty-one, -two**, etc. the cardinal numbers between twenty and thirty. ▶ **twentyfold** *adjective & adverb*

twenty-one *noun* a card game in which players try to acquire cards with a face value exceeding the dealer's but no more than 21.

twenty-six *noun* (*plural* **twenty-sixes**) *Cdn* a 26-ounce (or 750-ml) bottle of liquor.

twentysomething • *noun* **1** an undetermined age between twenty and thirty. **2** a person of this age or generation. • *adjective* **1** characteristic of the tastes and lifestyle of this group. **2** between twenty and thirty years of age.

20/20 *adjective* (also **twenty-twenty**) denoting vision of normal sharpness. PHRASES **hindsight is 20/20** it is much easier to understand and criticize events, decisions, etc. after the fact than while they are occurring or being made.

twenty-two *noun* a .22-calibre gun or cartridge.

twerp *noun* slang a foolish, pathetic, or insignificant person.

twice *adverb* **1** on two successive occasions; two times. **2** in double degree or quantity: *twice as good*.

twiddle *verb* (**twiddles, twiddled, twiddling**) **1 a** cause to rotate lightly or delicately with the fingers; twirl; adjust. **b** (often foll. by *with*) play idly; fiddle, tinker. **2** move twirlingly. PHRASES **twiddle one's thumbs** **1** move one's thumbs around each other with the fingers linked together, esp. as a sign of boredom or impatience. **2** have nothing to do. ▶ **twiddly** *adjective*

twig¹ *noun* **1** a small branch or shoot of a tree or shrub. **2** *Anatomy* a small branch of an artery etc.

twig² *verb* (**twigs, twigged, twigging**) *informal* **1 a** understand; grasp the meaning or nature of. **b** (often foll. by *to*) become conscious or aware of; catch on. **2** recognize, perceive, observe.

twiggy *adjective* **1** resembling a twig; long and slender. **2** containing twigs: *twiggy ground*.

twilight *noun* **1 a** the soft glowing light from the sky when the sun is below the horizon, esp. in the evening. **b** any faint light resembling this. **2** the period or time of day when this occurs, esp. in the evening. **3** an intermediate condition or period, esp. one of decline or

destruction (also as an *adjective*: *twilight years*). [Say TWY lite]

twilight zone *noun* any physical or conceptual area lying undefined or intermediate between two distinct fields or regions, having characteristics of both but belonging to neither.

twilit *adjective* dimly illuminated by or as if by twilight. [Say TWY lit]

twill *noun* 1 a woven fabric with a surface of diagonal parallel ridges, produced by passing the weft threads over one and under two or more threads of the warp, instead of over and under in regular succession. 2 the method of weaving this fabric. ▶ **twilled** *adjective*

twin • *noun* 1 each of two children or animals born at the same time to the same mother, having developed from the same ovum (**identical twins**) or two separately fertilized ova (**fraternal twins**) (also as an *adjective*: *twin sisters*). 2 either of two closely related or similar things; a counterpart (also as an *adjective*: *twin houses*). 3 either of two parts, usu. identical, working in unison (also as an *adjective*: *twin cylinder engine*). 4 a (as an *adjective*) denoting a twin-size mattress, bed, etc. (see TWIN-SIZE). b such a bed or mattress. 5 a twin-engined aircraft. • *verb* (**twins**, **twinned**, **twinning**) 1 a join, unite (two people or things) closely or intimately. b (often foll. by *with*) be or become coupled or joined; pair. 2 (usu. in *passive*) establish official links between (two cities or towns, esp. in different countries) for the purposes of friendship and cultural exchange.

twin bill *noun* informal 1 Baseball two games in succession between the same or different opponents on the same day. 2 two films, plays, etc. presented to an audience one after the other in the same program.

twin city *noun* 1 (**Twin Cities**) two neighbouring cities situated close together, such as St. Paul and Minneapolis, Minnesota or (formerly) Fort William and Port Arthur, Ontario (now Thunder Bay). 2 each of a pair of usu. international cities with official ties for the purposes of friendship and cultural exchange.

twine • *noun* a strong cord or string made of the twisted strands of hemp, cotton, sisal, etc. • *verb* (**twines**, **twined**, **twining**) 1 a join together (two or more strands etc.) by twisting: *she twined her hair into a braid*. b (often foll. by *with*) twist or join (one thing, strand, etc.) with another: *I twined my arm with hers*. 2 (of two things) become joined, linked, or tangled: *their lives twined inextricably the moment they met*. 3 (often foll. by *around*) wind or wrap (one or more strands etc.): *twined the rope around a tree*. 4 form (a garland or wreath etc.) by twisting or weaving flowers, leaves, etc. 5 (of a plant) grow in a twisting or winding manner.

twin-engined *adjective* (also **twin-engine**) (of an aircraft etc.) having two engines.

twinge • *noun* 1 (often foll. by *in*) a sudden sharp physical pain: *she felt a twinge in her shoulder*. 2 (usu. foll. by *of*) a sudden emotional pang: *a twinge of guilt*. • *verb* (**twinges**, **twinged**, **twinging**) cause or experience a twinge.

twinkle • *verb* (**twinkles**, **twinkled**, **twinkling**) 1 (of a star or light etc.) shine with rapid alternation between brightness and faintness. 2 (of the eyes) have a bright lively expression, esp. of amusement. 3 (of the feet in dancing) move lightly and rapidly. • *noun* 1 a sparkle or gleam of the eyes, esp. as a reflection of liveliness, youthfulness, or mischievousness. 2 a brief or intermittent flash, flicker, or gleam of light; a glimmer. ▶ **twinkler** *noun*

twinkling • *noun* the action of twinkling. • *adjective* that twinkles. PHRASES **in a twinkling** (or **the twinkling of an eye**) in an instant.

twinkly *adjective* that twinkles; twinkling.

twinning *noun* the uniting of two things, e.g. the establishment of official links between two distant cities.

twinship *noun* the condition of being twin or a twin.

twin-size *adjective* (also **twin-sized**) designating the smallest standard size of mattress, usu. 98 by 191 cm (38.5 by 75 in.), or of the bed frame, sheets, etc. designed for such a mattress.

twirl • *verb* 1 spin, turn, or rotate rapidly or quickly. 2 roll or twist between the thumb and forefinger: *he twirled his moustache*. • *noun* 1 a twirling motion. 2 a twirling object or shape, such as a flourish made with a pen. ▶ **twirler** *noun* **twirly** *adjective*

twist • *verb* 1 a distort the shape of (something usu. long and thin) by turning two ends in opposite directions or by turning one end while the other remains fixed. b cause (something long and thin, such as a string, wire, or strand of hair) to coil around an axis, thus imparting a spiral shape to it. c assume a spiral or twisted form by being distorted in this way. 2 a wind (strands of hemp etc.) together to form a rope. b form (a rope etc.) by winding strands of hemp or cotton etc. 3 (often foll. by *around*) wind or coil (a thread etc.) around something. 4 turn (oneself or a part of one's body) around partly or completely in order to face another direction. 5 a accidentally turn (one's ankle, knee, etc.) sharply, so as to strain and injure the ligaments or tendons. b deliberately turn (a person's arm etc.) around violently in order to cause pain or injury. c screw up or contort (one's face or features), esp. in pain, anger, or contempt. d (of the face or features) be contorted. 6 distort or misrepresent (facts or someone's meaning, intentions, etc.). 7 a apply a rotating movement to. b (foll. by *off*) remove by twisting: *twist the top off the jar*. 8 rotate or turn, or be capable of this: *falling leaves twisted in the air*. 9 (of a road, river, person, etc.) follow a very winding path. 10 dance the twist. • *noun* 1 an act or an instance of twisting: *give the lid a sharp twist*. 2 a thing formed by or as by twisting; a twisted form or shape, such as a spiral ornamentation in the stem of a wineglass. 3 a bend or curve in a road or path, esp. one followed immediately by a curve in the opposite direction. 4 a a complication, esp. an unexpected or ironic development in a story or in a person's life. b a slight change made to an existing model, usu. to add interest or flair: *the classic old story with a modern twist*. 5 usu. derogatory an eccentric inclination or attitude, esp. a peculiar mental bent. 6 a a curled piece of lemon peel to flavour a drink. b an item of food having a spiral or twisted shape: *cinnamon twists*. 7 (**the twist**) a dance in which the upper and lower body are swivelled back and forth in opposite directions, popular in the early 1960s. 8 a sprain or strain of a limb. 9 Physics a a twisting strain or force; torque. b forward motion combined with rotation about an axis, e.g. the movement of a screw. PHRASES **twist a person's arm** *informal* apply coercion to a person to overcome their reluctance to do something. **twist of fate** an ironic reversal of fortune. **twist the knife** cause further damage or mental pain, in addition to some previously inflicted. **twist in the wind** be left in a state of painful suspense or uncertainty.

twisted *adjective* 1 (of a person, their mind, etc.) morally warped; perverted. 2 (of a story) having many complications and unexpected changes of plot. 3 misshapen, mangled. 4 (of an ankle etc.) sprained. 5 entwined. 6 (of the face or features) contorted.

twister *noun* 1 a tornado. 2 a person or thing that twists.

twist-tie • *noun* a small strip of plastic-covered wire

which can be looped around something, typically the neck of a plastic bag, and fastened by twisting the two ends together. • *verb* (**twist-ties, twist-tied, twist-tying**) fasten with a twist-tie.

twisty *adjective* (**twistier, twistiest**) (esp. of a road) having many bends or turns.

twit • *noun slang* a silly or foolish person. • *verb* (**twits, twitted, twitting**) reproach or scold, esp. in a good-humoured or teasing manner.

twitch • *verb* (**twitches, twitched, twitching**) **1 a** (of the features, muscles, etc.) move or contract spasmodically. **b** move (part of the body) spasmodically. **2** give a short sharp pull at; jerk, tug. • *noun* **1 a** a sudden involuntary contraction or movement of a muscle etc. **b** a pang; a twinge: *a twitch of irritation*. **2** a sudden sharp pull or jerk.

twitchy *adjective* (**twitchier, twitchiest**) **1** having a tendency to twitch. **2** nervous, fidgety.

twitter • *verb* **1** (of a bird) chirp with a succession of light tremulous sounds. **2** talk or say rapidly in a high tremulous voice; chatter. • *noun* **1** a light tremulous chirping. **2** *informal* a state of excitement. ▶ **twitterer** *noun* **twittery** *adjective*

SPELL CHECK
two, too, to

The spelling is **too** in "too much" and "I like it too".
The spelling is **to** in "go to bed", "come to" (i.e. regain consciousness), and before a verb ("to dream").

---

two *cardinal number* one more than one. **PHRASES in two** in or into two pieces. **or two** denoting several: *a thing or two*. **put two and two together** make (esp. an obvious) inference from what is known or evident. **that makes two of us** *informal* I am in the same position or am of the same opinion. **two by two** in pairs. **two can play at that game** *informal* I am equally capable of using a person's strategy, to their disadvantage.

two-and-a-half *noun* (*plural* **two-and-a-halfs**) *Cdn* (*Que.*) an apartment having two rooms, typically a combined kitchen/living room and a bedroom, plus a bathroom.

two-bagger *noun informal* (also **two-base hit**) *Baseball* a successful hit which allows a player to get to second base safely; a double.

two-bit *adjective informal* cheap, worthless, minor, small-time.

two bits *noun informal* twenty-five cents.

two-by-four *noun* a length of timber that has a rectangular cross-section of $1^1/_2$ inches by $3^1/_2$ inches (3.8 cm by 8.9 cm) when trimmed, or 2 inches by 4 inches (5.1 cm by 10.2 cm) when not trimmed.

two cents *plural noun* (also **two cents' worth**) *informal* an unsolicited opinion.

two-cycle *adjective* (of an internal combustion engine) having its power cycle completed in one up-and-down movement of the piston.

2-D • *adjective* having or portraying a two-dimensional appearance. • *noun* a format that presents two-dimensional images.

two-dimensional *adjective* **1** having or appearing to have length and width but no depth. **2** lacking depth or substance; superficial: *it's easy to lament the way their enemies are callously reduced to two-dimensional bad guys*.

two-faced *adjective* insincere, deceitful.

two-fisted *adjective* tough, aggressive, vigorous: *a two-fisted average Joe with the guts to look them in the eye*.

twofold *adjective & adverb* **1** twice as much or as many. **2** consisting of two parts.

two-four *noun Cdn informal* a case of twenty-four bottles of beer.

2,4-D *noun* a partially soluble white to yellow crystalline powder, the active ingredient in many herbicides.

two-handed *adjective* using or requiring two hands.

two-on-one *noun* (*plural* **two-on-ones**) **1** *Hockey* a rush led by two players against one defender and a goalie. **2** *Basketball* a rush led by two players against one defender.

two percent *noun* (also **2 percent, 2%**) partly skimmed milk containing two percent milk fat.

two-piece • *adjective* (esp. of a suit, snowsuit, bathing suit, etc.) consisting of two matching items. • *noun* (also **two-piecer**) a two-piece suit or bathing suit etc.

two-ply • *adjective* consisting of two strands or thicknesses. • *noun* two-ply wool or wood etc.

two-pronged *adjective* having two aspects, stages, aims, or lines of attack: *many saw Meech and free trade as a two-pronged attack on the power of the federal government*.

two-seater *noun* a vehicle or aircraft with two seats.

two-sided *adjective* **1** having two sides. **2** having two aspects; controversial: *the two-sided nature of the debate*.

two solitudes *plural noun Cdn* the anglophone and francophone populations of Canada, portrayed as two cultures coexisting independent of and isolated from each other.

twosome *noun* **1** two people together. **2** a game, dance, etc., for two people.

two-step • *noun* a ballroom dance for couples involving a sliding step in march or polka time. • *verb* (**two-steps, two-stepped, two-stepping**) dance the two-step. • *adjective* involving two successive actions or stages.

two-stroke *adjective* **1** (of an internal combustion engine) having its power cycle completed in one up-and-down movement of the piston. **2** (of a vehicle) having a two-stroke engine.

two-time *informal* • *verb* (**two-times, two-timed, two-timing**) **1** be unfaithful to (esp. a lover or spouse). **2** swindle, double-cross. • *adjective* having achieved a specified distinction twice: *two-time champion*. ▶ **two-timer** *noun*

two-tone *adjective* having two colours or two shades of the same colour.

two-way *adjective* **1** involving two participants. **2** (of a radio) capable of transmitting and receiving signals. **3** (of a loudspeaker) having two separate drive units for different frequency ranges, a woofer and a tweeter. **4** (of traffic etc.) moving in opposite directions.

two-way mirror *noun* a panel of glass that is transparent from one side but reflects light and images from the other.

two-wheeled *adjective* having two wheels.

two-wheeler *noun* a vehicle with two wheels.

Twp. *abbreviation* Township.

tycoon *noun* a business magnate.

tyee *noun Cdn* (*BC*) a chinook salmon, esp. one weighing more than 13.6 kg (30 lb.). [Say TIE ee]

tying *pres. part. of* TIE.

tyke *noun* **1** *informal* a small child. **2** *Cdn* **a** an initiation level of sports competition for young children. **b** a player at this level.

Tylenol *noun proprietary* acetaminophen.

tympani = TIMPANI. [Say TIMPA nee]

tympanic membrane *noun Anatomy* = EARDRUM. [Say tim PANIC]

tympanum *noun* (*plural* **tympana** or **tympanums**) **1** *Anatomy* **a** = MIDDLE EAR. **b** = EARDRUM. **2** the membrane covering the hearing organ on the leg of an

insect. [Say TIMPA num for the singular; for *TYMPANA* say TIMPA nuh]

Tyndall stone *noun* (also **Tyndall limestone**) *Cdn* a variety of mottled dolomitic limestone quarried near Winnipeg, noted for the presence of a large number of fossils. [Say TINDLE]

type • *noun* **1 a** a class of people or things distinguished by common essential characteristics. **b** a kind or sort: *a new type of coffee*. **2** a person, thing, or event serving as an illustration, symbol, or characteristic specimen of another, or of a class. **3** (in *combination*) made of, resembling, or functioning as. **4 a** a person of a particular specified or contextually implied character: *she's not the type to pick a fight*. **b** the kind of person to whom one is attracted: *he's not my type*. **5 a** the general form, structure, or character distinguishing a particular group or class of things. **b** an object, conception, or work of art serving as a model for subsequent artists. **6** *Printing* **a** a character for printing, originally a metal casting from a matrix, reproducing a punch on which a letter or other character was engraved. **b** such pieces collectively, esp. with reference to size or font. **c** printed characters collectively: *printed in large type*. • *verb* (**types, typed, typing**) **1 a** write with a typewriter. **b** use a computer keyboard. **2 a** assign to a type; classify. **b** *Biology & Medical* determine the type to which (blood, tissue, etc.) belongs. **3** = TYPECAST.

Type A *noun* (*plural* **Type A's**) **1** a personality type characterized by ambition, impatience, and aggressive competitiveness, thought to be particularly susceptible to stress. **2** a person of this type.

Type B *noun* (*plural* **Type B's**) **1** a personality type characterized as easygoing and thought to have low susceptibility to stress. **2** a person of this type.

typecast *verb* (**typecasts, typecast, typecasting**) **1** assign (an actor) repeatedly to the same type of role which he or she has often played successfully in previous productions or which seems to fit his or her personality: *his brawny build and gruff voice typecast him as Hollywood's tough GI*. **2** consider (a person) as fitting a stereotype: *I had an inclination to typecast students as either sixties activists or seventies overachievers*. ▶ **typecasting** *noun*

typed *adjective* **1** classified as or having a certain character or type: *they had him firmly typed as the same sort of self-satisfied prig as the platoon commander*. **2** = TYPEWRITTEN.

typeface *noun* **1** the particular style, appearance, size, etc. of a type or set of types. **2** *Computing* the design of a particular font.

typescript *noun* a typewritten document.

typeset *verb* (**typesets, typeset, typesetting**) prepare a book for printing by arranging the characters etc. on the page. [Say TYPE set]

typesetter *noun* a person, machine or company that prepares a book for printing by arranging the characters etc. on the page. ▶ **typesetting** *noun*

typewriter *noun* a machine for producing characters like those used in printing by means of keys which, when pressed one at a time, cause a type mounted on a bar or ball to strike a sheet of paper inserted around a roller, through an inked ribbon. ▶ **typewriting** *noun*

typewritten *adjective* produced with a typewriter.

typhoid *noun* (also **typhoid fever**) a severe infectious fever involving a rash, muscle pain, and in some cases delirium and intestinal inflammation. [Say TIE foid]

typhoon *noun* a violent storm occurring in or around the Indian subcontinent, esp. a tropical cyclone occurring in the region of the Indian or western Pacific Oceans. [Say tie FOON]

typhus *noun* any of a group of acute infectious fevers, often transmitted by lice or fleas, and characterized by a purple rash, headaches, fever, and usu. delirium. [Say TIFE us]

typical *adjective* **1** serving as a characteristic example; representative: *a typical student*. **2** characteristic of or serving to distinguish a type: *a typical feature of Maritime architecture*. **3** (often foll. by *of*) conforming to expected esp. undesirable behaviour, attitudes, etc.: *it's typical of them to forget*. ▶ **typically** *adverb*

typify *verb* (**typifies, typified, typifying**) **1** be a typical example of something: *clothes that typify the 1960s* ◊ *the new style of politician, typified by the prime minister*. **2** be a typical feature of something: *the haunting guitar melodies that typify the band's music*. [Say TIPPA fie]

typist *noun* a person who types or uses a typewriter, esp. professionally.

typo *noun* (*plural* **typos**) *informal* an error in typed or printed material, esp. resulting from a mistake in typing.

typographic *adjective* having to do with the art, practice, or process of printing, or with the style and appearance of printed matter. ▶ **typographical** *adjective* **typographically** *adverb* [Say type a GRAPHIC]

typography *noun* the art or work of designing how text will appear when it is printed. [Say type OGGRA fee]

typological *adjective* having to do with or from the point of view of typology. ▶ **typologically** *adverb* [Say type a LOGICAL]

typologist *noun* a specialist in typology. [Say type OLLA jist]

typology *noun* (*plural* **typologies**) **1 a** the branch of knowledge that deals with classes with common characteristics. **b** a classification of esp. human behaviour or characteristics according to type. **2** the branch of religion that deals with esp. Biblical symbolic representation. [Say type OLLA jee]

tyrannical *adjective* using power or authority over people in an unfair and cruel way: *tyrannical power* ◊ *a tyrannical government* ◊ *he was brought up by a cruel and tyrannical father*. ▶ **tyrannically** *adverb* [Say ti RANNA cull]

tyrannize *verb* (**tyrannizes, tyrannized, tyrannizing**) **1** rule, control, or behave oppressively or cruelly towards: *she tyrannized her family and used her rage to manipulate and get her own way*. **2** (usu. foll. by *over*) exercise power or control oppressively or cruelly: *Colin is portrayed as spoiled and selfish, tyrannizing over his servants*. [Say TEERA nize]

tyrannosaur *noun* (also **tyrannosaurus**, *plural* **tyrannosauruses**) a huge bipedal carnivorous dinosaur, with powerful hind legs and jaws, a large well-developed tail, and small claw-like front legs. [Say tuh RANNA sore, tuh ranna SORE us]

tyranny *noun* (*plural* **tyrannies**) **1 a** the arbitrary, cruel, and excessive exercise of power, control, or authority. **b** (often foll. by *of*) an unduly oppressive influence: *the tyranny of public opinion*. **2** a tyrannical act; tyrannical behaviour: *she resented his rages and his tyrannies*. **3** *Greek History* **a** absolute rule by someone who seizes power without legal right. **b** a period of this. **c** a state ruled by a such a leader. ▶ **tyrannous** *adjective* **tyrannously** *adverb* [Say TEERA nee]

tyrant *noun* **1** an oppressive or cruel ruler. **2** any person exercising power oppressively or cruelly. **3** *Greek History* an absolute ruler who seizes power without legal right. [Say TIE runt]

tyrant flycatcher *noun* a small New World bird that catches insects by a short flight from a perch.

tyro *noun* (*plural* **tyros**) a beginner or novice: *his first*

novel is filled with shrewdness and wit, an astonishing feat for a 29-year-old tyro. [Say TIE roe]

tzatziki *noun* a Greek side dish of yogourt with cucumber, garlic, and sometimes mint. [Say tsat SEEKY]

T

Uu

U¹ *noun* (also **u**) (*plural* **Us** or **U's**) **1** the twenty-first letter of the alphabet. **2** (usu. in *combination*) a U-shaped object or curve: *U bolt*.

U² *abbreviation* (also **U.**) university.

U³ *symbol* uranium.

U⁴ *pronoun* informal you: *While-U-Wait* ◊ *U-pick*.

u *symbol* = MICRO- 2.

UAW *abbreviation* United Auto Workers.

ubiquitous *adjective* seeming to be everywhere or in several places at the same time; very common: *the main difficulty for most observers trying to sort one Northerner from another in winter is the ubiquitous beige (or navy blue) parka* ◊ *among the performers was the ubiquitous Stella Duane, who was performing her fourth show in three days*. ▶ **ubiquitously** *adverb* **ubiquity** *noun* [Say you BICK wi tus, you BICK wi tee]

U-boat *noun* hist. a German submarine.

u.c. *abbreviation* upper case.

udder *noun* the mammary gland of cattle, sheep, etc., hanging as a bag-like organ with several teats.

UFA *abbreviation* Cdn United Farmers of Alberta.

UFFI *noun* Cdn urea formaldehyde foam insulation. [Say UFFY]

UFO *noun* (*plural* **UFOs**) (*plural* **UFOs**) an unidentified flying object, esp. one supposed to have come from outer space.

Ugandan • *adjective* of or relating to Uganda, a landlocked country in East Africa. • *noun* a native or inhabitant of Uganda. [Say you GAN din]

ugh *interjection* **1** expressing disgust or horror. **2** the sound of a cough or grunt.

Ugli *noun* (*plural* **Uglies**) proprietary a mottled green and yellow citrus fruit, a hybrid of a grapefruit and tangerine.

ugliness *noun* **1** the state of being ugly to look at; repulsiveness or marked unpleasantness of appearance. **2** moral repulsiveness; disgusting wickedness.

ugly • *adjective* (**uglier**, **ugliest**) **1** unpleasing or repulsive to see or hear: *an ugly scar*. **2** unpleasantly suggestive; discreditable: *ugly rumours*. **3** threatening, dangerous: *the sky has an ugly look*. **4** morally repulsive; vile: *ugly vices*. **5** characterized by violence or hostility: *an ugly confrontation*. • *noun* (*plural* **uglies**) (in *plural*) slang ugly or unpleasant things: *the uglies he hasn't done personally he's paid to have done*.

ugly duckling *noun* a person who turns out to be beautiful or talented etc. against all expectations.

uh *interjection* expressing the sound made by a speaker who hesitates or is uncertain what to say.

UHF *abbreviation* ultra-high frequency.

uh-huh *interjection* informal expressing assent or a noncommittal response to a question or remark.

uh-oh *interjection* expressing sudden concern, worry, etc.

UHT *abbreviation* ultra-high-temperature sterilization (used to designate esp. dairy products sterilized at very high temperatures so that they can be kept without refrigeration).

uh-uh *interjection* expressing a negative response to a question or remark; no.

UI *abbreviation* (in Canada) unemployment insurance.

UIC *abbreviation* Cdn **1** hist. Unemployment Insurance Commission. **2** informal unemployment insurance: *has been living on UIC*.

UK *abbreviation* United Kingdom.

Uke *noun* (also **Ukie**) Cdn dated informal a Ukrainian.

Ukrainian • *noun* **1** a native of Ukraine, a country in eastern Europe. **2** the Slavic language of Ukraine. • *adjective* of or relating to Ukraine or its people or language. [Say you CRAY nee in]

Ukrainian Catholic • *adjective* of or pertaining to an Eastern Church of the Catholic communion under the jurisdiction of the Metropolitan of Lviv, including large communities in Canada and the US. • *noun* a member of this Church.

Ukrainian Christmas *noun* Christmas as celebrated by Ukrainian Christians on 7 January.

Ukrainian Easter egg *noun* = PYSANKA.

Ukrainian Orthodox *adjective* (also **Ukrainian Greek Orthodox**) of or pertaining to an Eastern Orthodox Church under the Patriarch of Kiev or the Patriarch of Moscow, including large communities in Canada and the US.

ukulele *noun* a small four-stringed Hawaiian guitar. [Say yooka LAY lee]

ulcer *noun* an open sore on an external or internal surface of the body, caused by a break in the skin or mucous membrane that fails to heal. Ulcers range from small, painful sores in the mouth to serious lesions of the stomach or intestine.

ulcerate *verb* (**ulcerates**, **ulcerated**, **ulcerating**) (often as **ulcerated** *adjective*) develop into or affect with an ulcer: *when these lesions become malignant they enlarge and ulcerate* ◊ *an ulcerated stomach*. ▶ **ulceration** *noun* **ulcerative** *adjective* [Say ULCER ate, ULCER a tiv]

ulcerous *adjective* having to do with ulcers. [Say ULCER us]

ulna *noun* (*plural* **ulnae**) **1** the thinner and longer bone in the forearm, on the side opposite to the thumb (compare RADIUS 3). **2** a corresponding bone in an animal's foreleg or a bird's wing. ▶ **ulnar** *adjective* [Say ULL nuh for the singular, ULL nee for the plural]

ulterior *adjective* existing in the background, or beyond what is evident or admitted; hidden, secret: *she must have an ulterior motive for being so nice to me*. [Say ul TEERY ur]

ultimate • *adjective* **1** last, final. **2** beyond which no other exists or is possible: *the ultimate analysis*. **3** fundamental, primary: *ultimate truths*. **4** maximum: *ultimate tensile strength*. **5** informal unsurpassed, best: *the ultimate car wash*. • *noun* **1** (**the ultimate**) the best achievable or imaginable. **2** a final or fundamental fact or principle. **3** a non-contact field sport resembling football but using a Frisbee, in which passes may be made in any direction, but running with the Frisbee is prohibited. ▶ **ultimately** *adjective*

ultimatum *noun* (*plural* **ultimatums**) a final demand or statement of terms by one party, the rejection of which by another could cause a breakdown in relations, war, or an end of co-operation etc. [Say ulta MAY tum]

ultra • *adjective* **1** favouring extreme views or measures, esp. in religion or politics: *her politics have swung from the ultra left to the extreme right.* **2** going beyond what is usual or ordinary; extreme: *on the weekends they run ultra marathons.* • *adverb* very, extremely; excessively: *the picture is so ultra clear, ultra bright, and ultra sharp it looks like real life.* • *noun* (plural **ultras**) an extremist: *the cover shows four photogenic ultras grinning insolently at a riot policeman.*

ultra- *combining form* extreme(ly), excessive(ly).

ultra-high *adjective* **1** extremely high. **2** (of a frequency) in the range 300 to 3000 megahertz.

ultralight • *noun* a very small, light, low-speed, one- or two-seater aircraft with an open frame. • *adjective* extremely light.

ultramarine *noun* **1 a** a brilliant blue pigment originally obtained from lapis lazuli. **b** an imitation of this. **2** *noun* & *adjective* the colour of this. [Say ultra MARINE]

ultramontane • *adjective* **1** situated on the other side of the Alps from the point of view of the speaker. **2 a** advocating supreme papal authority in matters of faith and discipline. **b** *Cdn hist.* (in Quebec) advocating the subordination of the state to the Catholic Church. • *noun* **1** a person living on the other side of the Alps. **2 a** person advocating ultramontane views. ▶ **ultramontanism** *noun* **ultramontanist** *noun* [Say ultra MON tane, ultra MON tuh nism]

ultrasonic *adjective* of or involving sound waves with a frequency above the upper limit of human hearing. ▶ **ultrasonically** *adverb*

ultrasonics *plural noun* (usu. treated as *singular*) the science and application of ultrasonic waves.

ultrasound *noun* **1** sound having an ultrasonic frequency. **2** ultrasonic waves. **3 a** an esp. diagnostic procedure using echoes of ultrasonic pulses to delineate objects or areas of different density in the body. **b** an image produced by such a procedure.

ultraviolet *adjective* of or using electromagnetic radiation having a wavelength shorter than that of the violet end of the visible spectrum but longer than that of X-rays.

ultra vires *adverb* & *adjective* beyond one's legal power or authority: *the bylaws were ultra vires the province* ◊ *an ultra vires contract.* [Say ultra VIE reez or ultra VEE rays]

ulu *noun* an Inuit knife consisting of a crescent-shaped blade and a handle centred behind the non-cutting edge, traditionally used by women. [Say OO loo]

ululate *verb* (**ululates, ululated, ululating**) howl, wail: *the lead singer ululated over the guitar riffs* ◊ *no one can ever forget the ululating sound of the loons.* ▶ **ululation** *noun* [Say ULL yuh late or YOOL yuh late]

um *interjection* expressing hesitation or a pause in speech.

umbel *noun* a flower cluster in which stalks nearly equal in length spring from a common centre and form a flat or curved surface, as in parsley. ▶ **umbelliferous** *adjective* [Rhymes with HUMBLE]

umber *noun* **1** a natural pigment like ochre but darker and browner. **2** *noun* & *adjective* the colour of this.

umbilical • *adjective* **1** affecting or having to do with the navel or umbilical cord. **2** (of a pipe or cable) connecting someone or something to a source of essential supplies: *an umbilical hose.* **3** inseparably linked: *the view of modern science with its umbilical connection to ancient Greece.* • *noun* a flexible cable, pipe, or other line carrying essential supplies from a main source to a site otherwise difficult to access: *umbilicals for seabed crawlers and towed vehicles.* [Say um BILLA cull]

umbilical cord *noun* **1** a flexible cord-like structure containing blood vessels and attaching a fetus to the

placenta. **2** a supply cable linking a missile to its launcher, or an astronaut in space to a spacecraft. **3** a close link or connection, esp. one that represents the dependency of one person or thing on another: *true innovators of hard rock finally cut the umbilical cord to traditional rock 'n' roll.*

umbra *noun* (*plural* **umbras** or **umbrae**) **1** the fully shaded inner region of a shadow cast by an opaque object, esp. the area on the earth or moon experiencing the total phase of an eclipse (compare PENUMBRA 1). **2** the dark central part of a sunspot. [Say UM bruh for the singular; for *UMBRAE* say UM bree]

umbrage *noun* offence; a sense of slight or injury: *took umbrage at the suggestion.* [Say UM bridge]

umbrella *noun* **1** a light portable device for protection against rain, strong sun, etc., consisting of a usu. circular canopy of cloth mounted by means of a collapsible metal frame on a central stick. **2** protection or patronage. **3** (often as an *adjective*) a coordinating or unifying agency: *umbrella organization.* **4** a screen of fighter aircraft or a curtain of fire put up as a protection against enemy aircraft. **5** the gelatinous disc of a jellyfish etc., which it contracts and expands to move through the water.

umiak *noun* a large, open, flat-bottomed boat made by stretching an animal hide over a wooden frame, traditionally used by Inuit women. [Say OOMY ack]

umlaut *noun* a mark (¨) used over a vowel, esp. in Germanic languages, to indicate a vowel change, as in Möbius strip. [Say OOM lout]

ump *informal* • *noun* an umpire, esp. in baseball. • *verb* **1** act as umpire. **2** act as umpire in (a game).

umph *noun* = OOMPH 1.

umpire • *noun* **1** a person chosen to enforce the rules and settle disputes in various sports, e.g. baseball. **2** a person chosen to arbitrate between parties in a dispute, or to ensure fair play. • *verb* (**umpires, umpired, umpiring**) **1** (usu. foll. by *for, in*, etc.) act as umpire. **2** act as umpire in (a game etc.).

umpteen *slang* • *adjective* indefinitely many; a lot of. • *pronoun* indefinitely many. ▶ **umpteenth** *adjective*

un- *prefix* **1** added to adjectives and participles and their derivative nouns and adverbs, meaning: **a** not: denoting the absence of a quality or state: *unusable* ◊ *unhappiness.* **b** the reverse of, usu. with an implication of approval or disapproval, or with some other special connotation: *unselfish* ◊ *unsociable* ◊ *unscientific.* **2** (less often) added to nouns, meaning "a lack of": *unrest* ◊ *untruth.* **3** added to verbs and (less often) nouns, forming verbs denoting: **a** the reversal or cancellation of an action or state: *undress* ◊ *unlock* ◊ *unsettle.* **b** deprivation or separation: *unmask.* **c** release from: *unburden* ◊ *uncage.* **d** causing to be no longer: *unman.*

'un *pronoun informal* one: *young 'uns* ◊ *a good 'un.*

unabashed *adjective* not ashamed, embarrassed, or discouraged in circumstances in which others might be: *his unabashed approach to sexually explicit subjects.* ▶ **unabashedly** *adverb* [Say un uh BASHED, un uh BASH id lee]

unabated *adjective* without any reduction in intensity or strength: *her fascination with dinosaurs continues unabated.* ▶ **unabatedly** *adverb*

unable *adjective* not able; lacking ability.

unabridged *adjective* (of a text etc.) not shortened; complete.

unaccented *adjective* not accented; not emphasized.

unacceptability *noun* the quality of being unacceptable.

unacceptable *adjective* not acceptable. ▶ **unacceptably** *adverb*

U

unaccompanied *adjective* **1** not accompanied, alone. **2** *Music* without accompaniment.

unaccountable *adjective* **1** (of a person or organization) not required or expected to justify actions or decisions; not responsible for results or consequences: *how can an unelected, unaccountable public body not justify its expenses to the public?* **2** unable to be explained: *unaccountable coincidences*. ▶ **unaccountably** *adverb*

unaccounted for *adjective* **1** (esp. of a person) missing: *had no way of knowing whether the one man still unaccounted for had survived or not*. **2** unexplained; not included in an account: *the MP resigned after it was revealed that much of his travel allowance was unaccounted for*.

unaccustomed *adjective* **1** (usu. foll. by *to*) not accustomed. **2** not customary; unusual: *his unaccustomed silence*.

unacknowledged *adjective* not acknowledged. [Say un ack KNOWLEDGED]

unadorned *adjective* not adorned; plain.

unadulterated *adjective* **1** absolute, total, utter: *unadulterated nonsense*. **2** not mixed or diluted with any different or extra elements: *wholesome and unadulterated foods*.

unaffected *adjective* **1** not affected: *unaffected groundwater supplies ◊ were unaffected by the changes*. **2** free from affectation: *unaffected good manners*. ▶ **unaffectedly** *adverb* **unaffectedness** *noun*

unaffiliated *adjective* not affiliated. [Say un a FILLY ated]

unaided *adjective* not aided; without help.

unalloyed *adjective* not mixed with anything else; pure, total: *unalloyed pleasure ◊ unalloyed goodness*. [Say un a LOID]

unambiguous *adjective* not ambiguous; clear or definite in meaning. ▶ **unambiguously** *adverb* [Say un am BIG you us]

un-American *adjective* **1** not in accordance with American characteristics etc. **2** contrary to the interests of the US; (in the US) treasonable.

unanimity *noun* complete agreement about something among a group of people. [Say yoona NIMMA tee]

unanimous *adjective* **1** all in agreement: *the committee was unanimous*. **2** (of an opinion, vote, etc.) held or given by general consent: *the unanimous choice*. ▶ **unanimously** *adverb* [Say you NANNA muss]

unannounced *adjective* not announced; without warning (of arrival etc.).

unanswerable *adjective* **1** unable to be answered: *an unanswerable question*. **2** unable to be refuted: *has an unanswerable case*. ▶ **unanswerably** *adverb*

unanticipated *adjective* not anticipated. [Say un ANTICIPATED]

unapologetic *adjective* not apologetic or sorry. ▶ **unapologetically** *adverb* [Say un a pollo JET ick]

unapproachable *adjective* **1** not friendly or inviting: *he was cold and unapproachable ◊ most of his work remains unapproachable to the general public*. **2 a** faraway, distant, remote: *an unapproachable mountainous area*. **b** that cannot be matched or equalled: *he is only 40 goals away from a record that was believed to be unapproachable*.

unarguable *adjective* not arguable; certain. ▶ **unarguably** *adverb*

unarmed *adjective* not armed; without weapons.

unashamed *adjective* **1** feeling no guilt, shameless. **2** blatant; bold. ▶ **unashamedly** *adverb* [Say un a SHAMED, un a SHAME id lee]

unassailable *adjective* unable to be attacked or questioned: *an unassailable humanitarian cause*.

unassertive *adjective* (of a person) not assertive or forthcoming.

unassisted *adjective* **1** not assisted. **2** *Hockey* (of a goal) scored by a player who takes possession of the puck from the opposing team rather than receiving it from a teammate.

unassuageable *adjective* (of something unpleasant) that cannot be made less severe: *unassuageable sadness and rage*. [Say un a SWAGE a bull]

unassumed *adjective Cdn* (of a road) not taken over for maintenance by a local authority; privately owned.

unassuming *adjective* not pretentious or arrogant; modest. ▶ **unassumingly** *adverb*

unattached *adjective* **1** (often foll. by *to*) not attached, esp. to a particular organization etc. **2** not engaged or married; not having a boyfriend or girlfriend.

unattainable *adjective* not attainable.

unattended *adjective* **1 a** not supervised; alone: *don't leave your child unattended*. **b** with the owner not present: *unattended cars will be towed*. **2** (usu. foll. by *to*) not made the object of one's attention, concern, etc.; not dealt with: *letters unattended to*.

unauthorized *adjective* **1** not authorized. **2** (of a biography) written without the consent and co-operation of the subject.

unaware • *adjective* not aware: *unaware of her presence*. • *adverb* = UNAWARES. ▶ **unawareness** *noun*

unawares *adverb* **1** unexpectedly: *met them unawares*. **2** inadvertently: *dropped it unawares*.

unbalance • *verb* (**unbalances**, **unbalanced**, **unbalancing**) upset the physical or mental balance of. • *noun* lack of balance; instability, esp. mental.

unbalanced *adjective* **1** not balanced. **2** (of a mind or a person) unstable or deranged.

unban *verb* (**unbans**, **unbanned**, **unbanning**) remove a ban or prohibition from (a publication, person, group, etc.); lift official restrictions on. ▶ **unbanning** *noun*

unbearable *adjective* not bearable. ▶ **unbearableness** *noun* **unbearably** *adverb*

unbeatable *adjective* **1** not beatable; unable to be defeated. **2** superlative, excellent; that cannot be improved: *unbeatable prices*.

unbeaten *adjective* **1** not beaten. **2** (of a record etc.) not surpassed.

unbecoming *adjective* **1** (esp. of clothing) not flattering or suiting a person. **2** unsuitable, inappropriate: *since our grandparents' generation had it so much worse it seemed unbecoming of us to complain about our lot in life*. ▶ **unbecomingly** *adverb*

unbeknownst *adjective* (also **unbeknown**) (foll. by *to*) without the knowledge of: *was there all the time unbeknownst to us*. [Say un bee NOANST]

unbelief *noun* lack of belief, esp. in religious matters.

unbelievable *adjective* not believable; incredible. ▶ **unbelievably** *adverb*

unbeliever *noun* a person who does not believe, esp. in God, a religion, etc.

unbelieving *adjective* feeling or showing that one does not believe somebody or something: *she stared at us with unbelieving eyes ◊ he gazed at the letter, unbelieving*. ▶ **unbelievingly** *adverb*

unbend *verb* (**unbends**, **unbent**, **unbending**) **1** change from a bent position. **2** relax from strain or severity. ▶ **unbendable** *adjective*

unbending *adjective* **1** not bending; inflexible: *unbending in their demands*. **2** reserved, formal, or strict in behaviour or attitudes: *portrayed my aunt as rather stern and unbending*.

unbiased *adjective* not biased; impartial.

unbidden *adjective* **1** not commanded or invited: *arrived unbidden*. **2** without conscious effort; spontaneous.

unblemished *adjective* not blemished.

unblinking *adjective* **1** not blinking. **2** steadfast; not hesitating. **3** stolid; cool. ▶ **unblinkingly** *adverb*

unborn *adjective* **1** not yet born: *an unborn child*. **2** never to be brought into being: *unborn hopes*.

unbound *adjective* **1** not bound or tied up. **2** unconstrained. **3 a** (of a book) not having a binding. **b** having paper covers.

unbounded *adjective* not bounded; infinite: *unbounded optimism*.

unbowed *adjective* undaunted: *they remain defiantly unbowed despite the criticism*. [Say un BOWED (BOWED rhymes with PLOWED)]

unbreathable *adjective* not fit or pleasant to breathe: *unbreathable air*.

unbridgeable *adjective* unable to be bridged.

unbridled *adjective* unconstrained: *unbridled insolence*.

unbroken *adjective* **1** not broken. **2** not tamed: *an unbroken horse*. **3** not crushed in health or spirit; not subdued or weakened. **4** (of ground) not broken up by digging etc. **5** not interrupted or disturbed: *unbroken sleep*. **6** not surpassed: *an unbroken record*.

unbudgeable *adjective* *informal* that cannot be moved. [Say un BUDGE a bull]

unbuilt *adjective* not yet built or (of land) not yet built on.

unbundle *verb* (**unbundles**, **unbundled**, **unbundling**) **1** unpack; remove from a bundle. **2** market or price (goods or services) as individual items rather than as part of a package. **3** split (a company) into separate businesses.

unburden *verb* **1** relieve of a burden. **2** relieve (oneself, one's conscience, etc.) by confession etc.: *work with a therapist to unburden yourself of old emotional baggage*. ▶ **unburdened** *adjective*

unburned *adjective* (also **unburnt**) **1** not consumed by fire. **2** not scorched; not damaged by fire etc.

uncalled *adjective* not summoned or invited. PHRASES **uncalled for** (of an opinion, action, etc.) impertinent or unnecessary: *that remark was uncalled for*.

un-Canadian *adjective* not in accordance with Canadian characteristics, practices, etc.

uncannily *adverb* in an uncanny way: *he looked uncannily like someone I knew*. [Say un CANNA lee]

uncanniness *noun* the quality of being uncanny. [Say un CANNY ness]

uncanny *adjective* (**uncannier**, **uncanniest**) **1** seemingly supernatural; mysterious. **2** of an unsettling accuracy, intensity, etc.: *an uncanny resemblance*. [Say un CANNY]

uncaring *adjective* **1** neglectful. **2** lacking compassion.

uncastrated *adjective* not castrated.

unceasing *adjective* continuous: *unceasing effort*. ▶ **unceasingly** *adverb*

uncensored *adjective* not censored.

unceremonious *adjective* **1** lacking ceremony or formality. **2** abrupt; discourteous: *an unceremonious interruption*. ▶ **unceremoniously** *adverb* [Say un serra MOANY us]

uncertain *adjective* **1** not certainly knowing or known: *the result is uncertain*. **2** unreliable: *his aim is uncertain*. **3** changeable; erratic: *uncertain weather*. **4** not confident; hesitant. PHRASES **in no uncertain terms** clearly and forcefully. ▶ **uncertainly** *adverb*

uncertainty *noun* (*plural* **uncertainties**) **1** the fact or condition of being uncertain. **2** an uncertain matter or circumstance.

uncertified *adjective* **1** not attested as certain. **2** not guaranteed by a certificate of competence etc. **3** not certified as insane.

unchallenged *adjective* not challenged.

unchangeable *adjective* not changeable; immutable, invariable. ▶ **unchangeably** *adverb*

unchanged *adjective* not changed; unaltered.

unchanging *adjective* not changing; remaining the same. ▶ **unchangingly** *adverb*

uncharacteristic *adjective* not characteristic. ▶ **uncharacteristically** *adverb*

uncharitable *adjective* unkind, harsh, and unsympathetic. ▶ **uncharitably** *adverb*

uncharted *adjective* not charted, mapped, or surveyed.

unchecked *adjective* **1** not checked. **2** freely allowed; unrestrained: *unchecked violence*.

unchristian *adjective* **1** contrary to Christian principles, esp. uncaring or selfish. **2** not Christian.

unchurched *adjective* not associated with a church; not churchgoing.

uncivil *adjective* ill-mannered; impolite.

uncivilized *adjective* **1** not civilized. **2** rough; uncultured.

unclasp *verb* **1** loosen the clasp or clasps of. **2** release the grip of (a hand etc.).

unclassified *adjective* **1** not classified. **2** (of state information) not secret.

uncle *noun* **1 a** the brother of one's father or mother. **b** an aunt's husband. **2** *informal* a name given by children to a male family friend. **3** *Cdn* (*Nfld*) a term of respectful address to an older man. PHRASES **cry** (or **say** or **yell**) **uncle** *informal* surrender; admit defeat; yell for mercy.

unclean *adjective* **1** not clean. **2** morally wrong: *unclean thoughts*. **3** (of food) regarded by a particular religion as impure and not fit to be eaten: *Ethiopian Christians scrupulously avoided the flesh of unclean birds and mammals*. **4** *Bible* (of a spirit) wicked.

unclear *adjective* **1** not clear or easy to understand; obscure, uncertain. **2** (of a person) doubtful, uncertain: *I'm unclear as to what you mean*.

uncleared *adjective* **1** (of land) not cleared of trees etc. **2** not cleared away or up.

unclench *verb* (**unclenches**, **unclenched**, **unclenching**) **1** release (clenched hands, features, teeth, etc.). **2** (of clenched hands etc.) become relaxed or open.

Uncle Sam *noun* *informal* a personification of the federal government or citizens of the US.

unclog *verb* (**unclogs**, **unclogged**, **unclogging**) unblock (a drain, pipe, etc.).

unclothed *adjective* not covered or clothed.

unclouded *adjective* **1** not clouded; clear; bright. **2** untroubled: *unclouded serenity*.

uncollected *adjective* **1** left awaiting collection. **2** (of money) not collected or claimed. **3** (of literary work) not gathered into a collection for publication.

uncomfortable *adjective* **1** not comfortable. **2** uneasy; causing or feeling disquiet: *an uncomfortable silence*. ▶ **uncomfortably** *adverb*

uncommitted *adjective* **1** not committed. **2** unattached to any specific political cause or group.

uncommon *adjective* **1** not common; unusual. **2** remarkably great etc.: *an uncommon fear of spiders*. ▶ **uncommonly** *adverb*

uncommunicative *adjective* not wanting to communicate; taciturn. [Say un kuh MYOONA kay tiv]

U

uncomplaining *adjective* not complaining; resigned.
▶ **uncomplainingly** *adverb*

uncomplimentary *adjective* not complimentary; insulting.

uncomprehending *adjective* not comprehending.
▶ **uncomprehendingly** *adverb*

uncompromising *adjective* unwilling to compromise; stubborn; unyielding.
▶ **uncompromisingly** *adverb*

unconcern *noun* indifference; apathy.
▶ **unconcerned** *adjective* **unconcernedly** *adverb* [Say un CONCERN, un CONCERN id lee]

unconditional *adjective* not subject to conditions: *unconditional surrender*. ▶ **unconditionally** *adverb*

uncongenial *adjective* **1** not friendly, pleasant, or agreeable: *uncongenial dining companions* ◊ *uncongenial surroundings*. **2** not suitable: *planetary environments that are uncongenial to human life*. [Say un k'n JEENY ul]

unconnected *adjective* **1** not physically joined. **2** not connected or associated. **3** (of speech etc.) disconnected; not joined in order or sequence: *unconnected ideas*. ▶ **unconnectedly** *adverb*

unconscionable *adjective* **1** (of an action or behaviour) shamefully wrong or immoral: *the unconscionable destruction of a rainforest for industrial development* ◊ *to target the weakest and most vulnerable segment of society with their false and manipulative advertising is unconscionable*. **2** unreasonably excessive: *an unconscionable length of time*. ▶ **unconscionably** *adverb* [Say un CONSH'n a bull]

unconscious • *adjective* not conscious. • *noun* that part of the mind which is inaccessible to the conscious mind but which affects behaviour, emotions, etc. (compare COLLECTIVE UNCONSCIOUS): *the unconscious reveals itself to us through the imagination*. ▶ **unconsciously** *adverb* **unconsciousness** *noun*

unconstitutional *adjective* not in accordance with the political constitution or with procedural rules.
▶ **unconstitutionality** *noun* **unconstitutionally** *adverb*

unconstrained *adjective* not constrained or compelled.

uncontaminated *adjective* not contaminated; pure, unpolluted.

uncontested *adjective* not contested.
▶ **uncontestedly** *adverb*

unconventional *adjective* not bound by convention or custom; unusual; unorthodox.
▶ **unconventionality** *noun* **unconventionally** *adverb*

uncool *adjective* slang not stylish or fashionable; not having street credibility.

uncooperative *adjective* not co-operative.

uncoordinated *adjective* **1** not coordinated. **2** (of a person, a person's movements etc.) clumsy.

uncork *verb* draw the cork from (a bottle etc.).

uncorrupted *adjective* not corrupted.

uncountable *adjective* inestimable, immense.

uncountable noun *noun* a noun that cannot form a plural or be used with the indefinite article, e.g. *happiness*.

uncounted *adjective* **1** not counted. **2** very many; innumerable.

uncouple *verb* (**uncouples, uncoupled, uncoupling**) **1** unfasten, disconnect, detach. **2** release (railway cars) from couplings. **3** (of a couple) break up.

uncouth *adjective* (of a person, manners, appearance, etc.) lacking in ease and polish; uncultured, rough.
▶ **uncouthly** *adverb* **uncouthness** *noun* [Say un COOTH]

uncover *verb* **1** remove a cover or covering from. **2** make known; disclose: *uncovered the truth at last*.

uncovered *adjective* **1** not covered by a roof, clothing, etc. **2** not wearing a hat.

uncredited *adjective* not acknowledged as the author, actor, etc.

uncritical *adjective* **1** not critical; complacently accepting. **2** not in accordance with the principles of criticism. ▶ **uncritically** *adverb*

unction *noun* **1 a** a solemn or fervent manner of expression arising or apparently arising from deep emotion: *"Those unmentionable desires —"* he spoke the last two words with unction. **b** excessive or insincere flattery: *the poet who heaps invective upon an enemy today can ooze unction tomorrow*. **2 a** the action of anointing someone with oil or ointment, e.g. as a religious rite or for medical purposes. **b** the oil or ointment used for this: *she sent for one of the backstreet healers whose concoctions and plant unctions purported to cure the most stubborn ills*. [Say UNK shin]

unctuous *adjective* **1** (of behaviour, speech, etc.) unpleasantly or excessively flattering: *a voice as false and unctuous as that of an insurance salesman*. **2** having a greasy or oily feel: *an unctuous basil sauce*.
▶ **unctuously** *adverb* **unctuousness** *noun* [Say UNK choo us]

uncultured *adjective* not cultured, unrefined.

uncut *adjective* **1** not cut. **2** (of a book, film, etc.) complete; uncensored. **3** (of a stone, esp. a diamond) not shaped by cutting. **4** (of alcohol or a drug) not diluted or mixed with inferior elements; pure.

undaunted *adjective* not daunted. [Say un DON tid]

undead • *adjective* (esp. of a vampire etc. in fiction) technically dead but still animate. • *noun* (preceded by *the*; treated as *plural*) those who are undead.

undecided • *adjective* **1** not settled or certain: *the question is undecided*. **2** hesitating; irresolute: *undecided about their relative merits*. • *noun* a person who is undecided, esp. as regards a vote. ▶ **undecidedly** *adverb*

undecipherable *adjective* that cannot be read or understood. [Say un dee CIPHER a bull]

undeclared *adjective* not declared.

undecorated *adjective* **1** not adorned; plain. **2** not honoured with an award.

undefiled *adjective* not defiled; pure.

undefinable *adjective* not definable.

undefined *adjective* **1** not defined. **2** not clearly marked; vague.

undemanding *adjective* not demanding.

undemocratic *adjective* not democratic.
▶ **undemocratically** *adverb*

undeniable *adjective* **1** unable to be denied or disputed; certain. **2** excellent: *was of undeniable character*. ▶ **undeniably** *adverb*

undependable *adjective* not to be depended upon; unreliable.

under • *preposition* **1 a** in or to a position lower than; below; beneath: *fell under the table* ◊ *under the left eye*. **b** within, on the inside of (a surface etc.): *wore a vest under his shirt*. **2 a** inferior to; less than: *is under 18*. **b** at or for a lower cost than: *was under $20*. **3 a** subject to or liable to; controlled or bound by: *lives under oppression* ◊ *the country prospered under him*. **b** undergoing: *is under repair*. **c** classified or subsumed in: *that book goes under biology*. **4** at the foot of or sheltered by: *hid under the wall* ◊ *under the cliff*. • *adverb* **1** in or to a lower position or condition: *kept him under*. **2** *informal* in or into a state of unconsciousness: *put him under for the operation*. • *adjective* lower: *the under jaw*. ▐PHRASES▌ **under separate cover** in another envelope. **under the sun**

anywhere in the world. **under water** in and covered by water.

under- *prefix in senses of* UNDER: **1** below, beneath: *undercarriage* ◊ *underground.* **2** lower in status; subordinate: *undersecretary.* **3** insufficiently, incompletely: *undercook* ◊ *underdeveloped.*

underachieve verb (**underachieves**, **underachieved**, **underachieving**) do less well than might be expected (esp. scholastically). ▶ **underachievement** noun **underachiever** noun

underage adjective **1** not old enough, esp. not yet of adult status. **2** (of an activity) carried on by a person below the legal age for the activity: *underage drinking.*

underarm • adjective **1** (of a throw, pitch, etc.) performed with the hand lower than the level of the shoulders. **2** in, of, or for the armpit: *underarm deodorant.* • adverb (throw or pitch a ball etc.) with the hand below the level of the shoulder. • noun the armpit.

underbelly noun (plural **underbellies**) **1** the undersurface of an animal etc. **2** an area etc. vulnerable to attack: *no one wants to reveal their underbelly to a pack of fang-toothed potential rivals.* **3** a hidden, unpleasant, or criminal part of society: *a renewed interest in Victorian society and its values brought in turn a sharpened awareness of that society's underbelly.*

underbid verb (**underbids**, **underbid**, **underbidding**) make a lower bid than (a person).

underbrush noun undergrowth in a forest.

undercapitalize verb (**undercapitalizes**, **undercapitalized**, **undercapitalizing**) (esp. as **undercapitalized** adjective) provide (a business etc.) with insufficient capital to achieve a desired result.

undercarriage noun **1** the supporting frame of a vehicle. **2** a structure of wheels or floats beneath an aircraft to receive the impact on landing and support the aircraft on the ground, water, etc.

underclass noun (plural **underclasses**) a subordinate social class.

underclothes plural noun clothes worn under others, esp. next to the skin; underwear.

underclothing noun underclothes collectively.

undercoat noun **1 a** a preliminary layer of paint under the finishing coat. **b** the paint used for this. **2** an animal's under layer of hair or down. **3** a coat worn under another. ▶ **undercoating** noun

undercook verb cook insufficiently. ▶ **undercooked** adjective

undercover • adjective involved in or involving spying, typically by working with or among those whose activities one is secretly observing, esp. as part of a police investigation: *an undercover narcotics officer* ◊ *an undercover journalist.* • adverb as an undercover agent: *in the movie, a tough cop is forced to go undercover as a kindergarten teacher.*

undercurrent noun **1** a current below the surface. **2** an underlying often contrary feeling, activity, or influence: *an undercurrent of protest.*

undercut • verb (**undercuts**, **undercut**, **undercutting**) **1** sell or work at a lower price or lower wages than. **2** Golf etc. strike (a ball) so as to make it rise high. **3 a** cut away the part below or under (a thing). **b** cut away material to show (a carved design etc.) in relief. **4** render unstable or less firm; undermine. • noun **1** a notch cut in a tree trunk to guide its fall when felled. **2** any space formed by the removal or absence of material from the lower part of something.

underdeveloped adjective **1** not fully developed; immature. **2** (of a country etc.) below its potential economic level. **3** Photography not developed sufficiently to give a normal image. ▶ **underdevelopment** noun

underdog noun **1** a person, team, etc. thought to be in

a weaker position, and therefore not likely to win a competition, fight, etc. **2** a person who is in a state of inferiority or subjection.

underdress verb (**underdresses**, **underdressed**, **underdressing**) dress too plainly or too lightly.

undereducated adjective poorly educated.

underemphasize verb (**underemphasizes**, **underemphasized**, **underemphasizing**) place an insufficient degree of emphasis on.

underemployed adjective **1** employed at a task that uses less than one's full talents or abilities. **2** employed less than full-time. **3** (of a facility etc.) used less than it could be. ▶ **underemployment** noun

underestimate • verb (**underestimates**, **underestimated**, **underestimating**) **1** fail to recognize the strength, skill, etc. of a person, esp. an opponent. **2** form too low an opinion or estimate of. • noun an estimate that is too low. ▶ **underestimation** noun

underexpose verb (**underexposes**, **underexposed**, **underexposing**) **1** use too short an exposure or too narrow an aperture with (a film) or when photographing (a subject), resulting in a darkened picture. **2** expose (a person etc.) too little to the public eye. ▶ **underexposure** noun

underfed adjective insufficiently fed.

underfoot adverb **1** beneath one's feet; on the ground. **2** sitting, lying, etc. right at or around one's feet so as to obstruct or inconvenience; in the way.

underfund verb provide insufficient funding for: *complaints that the government is underfunding health care.*

underfunded adjective not having sufficient funding. ▶ **underfunding** noun

undergarment noun an article of underclothing.

undergird verb provide support or a firm basis for: *trust undergirds love* ◊ *discovered the ice that undergirds the earth here.*

undergo verb (**undergoes**; past **underwent**; past participle **undergone**; **undergoing**) experience.

undergrad noun & adjective informal = UNDERGRADUATE.

undergraduate • noun a student at a university who has not yet completed a bachelor's degree. • adjective **1** of or related to an undergraduate or undergraduates. **2** of or related to the course of study of a student completing a bachelor's degree.

underground • adverb **1** beneath the surface of the ground. **2** into hiding or some secret activity. • adjective **1** situated beneath the surface of the ground. **2 a** secret, hidden, not open to the public. **b** designating a secret group, movement, or activity, esp. one aiming to subvert an established order or a ruling power. **3 a** of or pertaining to a subculture seeking to provide alternatives to the socially accepted or established mode. **b** unconventional, experimental: *underground press.* • noun **1** a secret group or activity, esp. aiming to challenge or subvert a ruling power. **2** a subculture seeking to provide radical alternatives to the socially accepted or established mode. **3** a place below the surface of the earth.

underground economy noun financial transactions not officially declared or recorded.

Underground Railroad noun (also Cdn **Underground Railway**) hist. a secret network of safe houses and transportation established to help fugitive slaves escape from the southern US to Canada and the Free States of the American North in the years before the Civil War.

undergrowth noun a dense growth of shrubs etc., esp. under large trees.

underhand • adjective **1** Sport (of a throw, pitch, serve, etc.) performed with the hand lower than the level of

U

the shoulders. **2** = UNDERHANDED 1, 2. • *adverb* (throw or pitch etc.) with the hand lower than the level of the shoulder. • *verb* throw (a ball etc.) with the hand below the level of the shoulder.

underhanded • *adjective* **1** deceptive, crafty. **2** secret, clandestine, surreptitious. **3** = UNDERHAND 1. • *adverb* = UNDERHAND.

underlay • *verb* (**underlays**, **underlaid**, **underlaying**) lay something under (a thing) to support or raise it: *the green fields are underlaid with limestone*. • *noun* a thing laid under another, esp. material laid under a carpet or mattress as protection or support.

underlie *verb* (**underlies**; *past* **underlay**; *past participle* **underlain**; **underlying**) **1** (esp. of a layer of rock or soil) lie or be situated under something. **2** be the cause or basis of (something): *the fundamental issue which underlies the conflict*.

underline • *verb* (**underlines**, **underlined**, **underlining**) **1** draw a line under (a word etc.) to give emphasis or draw attention or indicate italic or other special type. **2** emphasize, stress. • *noun* a line drawn under a word etc. ▶ **underlining** *noun*

underling *noun* usu. *derogatory* a subordinate.

underlying • *verb pres. part. of* UNDERLIE. • *adjective* **1** lying under or beneath the surface. **2 a** having a visible effect though not immediately obvious or openly present: *an underlying cause*. **b** fundamental, basic: *underlying principle*.

undermanned *adjective* having too few people such as crew or staff.

undermine *verb* (**undermines**, **undermined**, **undermining**) **1** weaken, injure, destroy, ruin (a person, reputation, health, etc.) by secret or insidious means. **2** wear away the base or foundation of: *rivers undermine their banks*. **3** dig a tunnel or excavate beneath (a wall etc.).

undermost *adjective* holding the lowest place or position; lowest.

underneath • *preposition* **1** at or to a lower place than: directly below. **2** below or behind a covering of: *she wore a shirt underneath her sweater*. • *adverb* **1** at or to a lower place. **2** directly beneath or covered by something. • *noun* the lower surface or part. • *adjective* lower.

undernourished *adjective* insufficiently nourished. ▶ **undernourishment** *noun*

underpaid *adjective* paid too little.

underpants *plural noun* an article of underclothing worn to cover the hips, crotch, and sometimes the thighs.

underpart *noun* the lower part or underside of anything, esp. an animal.

underpass *noun* (*plural* **underpasses**) a section of road etc. providing a passage beneath another road, railway, etc.

underpay *verb* (**underpays**, **underpaid**, **underpaying**) pay (an employee etc.) too little. ▶ **underpayment** *noun*

underperform *verb* **1** perform less well or be less profitable than expected. **2** perform less well or be less profitable than (something or someone else). ▶ **underperformance** *noun*

underpin *verb* (**underpins**, **underpinned**, **underpinning**) **1** form the basis for; support, strengthen. **2** support or strengthen (a building etc.) from below, esp. by laying a solid foundation.

underpinning *noun* **1** a thing or structure that supports or strengthens. **2** (in *plural*) a basis, foundation, or underlying principle.

underplay *verb* **1** play down the importance of.

2 *Theatre* **a** perform with deliberate restraint. **b** act a part etc. with insufficient force.

underpowered *adjective* **1 a** lacking full electrical, mechanical, etc. power. **b** lacking sufficient amplification. **2** with insufficient authority.

underprice *verb* (**underprices**, **underpriced**, **underpricing**) **1** price lower than what is usual or appropriate. **2** undercut (a competitor) in price.

SPELL CHECK
underprivileged

Warning: there is no *d* before the *g* in **underprivileged**; do not forget the *i* before the *l*.

---

underprivileged *adjective* **1** less privileged than others; deprived. **2** not enjoying the normal standard of living or rights in a society.

underrate *verb* (**underrates**, **underrated**, **underrating**) have too low an opinion of; underestimate. ▶ **underrated** *adjective* [Say under RATE]

under-report *verb* fail to report fully.

under-represent *verb* provide with inadequate or insufficient representation.

underscore • *verb* (**underscores**, **underscored**, **underscoring**) = UNDERLINE. • *noun* **1** = UNDERLINE. **2** the character _, used in e-mail addresses etc. to represent a word break or blank space.

undersea *adjective* below the sea or the surface of the sea.

undersecretary *noun* (*plural* **undersecretaries**) a subordinate official, esp. a junior minister or senior civil servant.

undersell *verb* (**undersells**, **undersold**, **underselling**) **1** sell at a lower price than (another seller). **2** sell at less than the true value.

undershirt *noun* a light usu. cotton knitted short-sleeved or sleeveless shirt with no collar worn as an article of underclothing.

undershorts *plural noun* men's underpants.

underside *noun* (also in *plural*) the lower side or bottom; the surface underneath.

undersigned *adjective* whose signature is appended below: *we, the undersigned, wish to state...*

undersized *adjective* (also **undersize**) of less than the usual size.

undersold *past and past participle of* UNDERSELL.

understaffed *adjective* having too few staff. ▶ **understaffing** *noun*

understand *verb* (**understands**, **understood**, **understanding**) **1** perceive the meaning of (words, a person, etc.). **2** perceive the significance, explanation, or cause of: *I don't understand why he came*. **3 a** have a sympathetic awareness of the character or nature of; know how to deal with, be sympathetic to: *nobody really understands me*. **b** accept without anger or resentment: *if you can't come, I'll understand*. **4 a** be conversant or familiar with, have a mastery of (a subject, skill, etc.): *she understands hockey*. **b** be sufficiently acquainted with (a language) to be able to interpret the meaning of the words employed. **5** accept as true without positive knowledge or certainty; learn, gather, infer: *am I to understand that you refuse?* **6** supply (a word) mentally: *the verb may be either expressed or understood*. **7** have understanding (in general or in particular): *you don't have to explain, I understand perfectly*. PHRASES **understand each other 1** know each other's views or feelings. **2** be in agreement or collusion.

understandability *noun* the quality of being understandable.

understandable *adjective* **1** that one might expect;

natural or reasonable: *it is an understandable mistake.*
2 comprehensible: *very understandable instructions.*
▶ **understandably** *adverb*

understanding • *noun* **1** the ability to reason and comprehend; intellect. **2 a** an individual's perception or interpretation of a situation etc. **b** a person's knowledge of a subject. **3** an agreement; a thing agreed upon, esp. informally: *had an understanding with the company.* **4** harmony in opinion or feeling. **5** sympathetic awareness or tolerance; empathy. • *adjective* **1 a** sympathetic to others' feelings. **b** of a forgiving nature. **2** having understanding, insight, or good judgment. ▶ **understandingly** *adverb*

understate *verb* (**understates, understated, understating**) **1** express in greatly or unduly restrained terms. **2** represent (a thing) as being less than it actually is.

understated *adjective* **1** (of fashion, architecture, appearance, etc.) restrained in style or colour; not showy, simple: *the decor is refreshingly understated.* **2** stated or expressed in unduly restrained terms: *understated irony.* ▶ **understatedly** *adverb*

understatement *noun* **1** a statement that expresses an idea etc. in mild or restrained terms. **2** the quality of being understated or restrained in style or appearance. **3** the action or practice of understating.

understeer • *noun* a tendency of a car or truck etc. to turn less sharply than was intended. • *verb* (of a vehicle) have such a tendency.

understood • *verb past and past participle of* UNDERSTAND. • *adjective* **1** inferred or implied without being explicitly stated. **2** accepted or agreed upon. **3 a** properly interpreted or perceived. **b** capable of being properly interpreted or perceived: *he could not make himself understood.*

understorey *noun* (*plural* **understoreys**) (also **understory** *plural* **understories**) **1** a layer of vegetation beneath the main canopy of a forest. **2** the plants forming this.

understudy esp. *Theatre* • *noun* (*plural* **understudies**) a person who studies another's role or duties in order to perform at short notice in the absence of the other. • *verb* (**understudies, understudied, understudying**) **1** study (a role etc.) as an understudy. **2** act as an understudy to (a person).

undersurface *noun* the lower surface or surface underneath; the underside.

undertake *verb* (**undertakes**; *past* **undertook**; *past participle* **undertaken**; *present participle* **undertaking**) **1** take on (an obligation, task, etc.); commit oneself to perform. **2** accept an obligation; promise: *undertook to be present.*

undertaker *noun* a person whose business is to make arrangements for funerals; a funeral director.

undertaking *noun* **1** work etc. undertaken: *a serious undertaking.* **2** a pledge or promise. **3** the management of funerals as a profession.

under-the-counter *adjective* (of merchandise) not available in stores without a licence, prescription, or special permission, and thus often purchased and sold illegally.

undertone *noun* **1** a subdued tone of sound or colour. **2** an underlying quality. **3** an undercurrent of feeling.

undertook *past of* UNDERTAKE.

undertow *noun* a current below the surface of the sea moving in the opposite direction to the surface current. [Say UNDER toe]

underuse • *verb* (**underuses, underused, underusing**) use below the optimum level. • *noun* insufficient use.

underutilization *noun* the fact of underusing. [Say under UTILIZATION]

underutilize *verb* (**underutilizes, underutilized, underutilizing**) underuse. [Say under UTILIZE]

underutilized *adjective* underused. [Say under UTILIZED]

undervalue *verb* (**undervalues, undervalued, undervaluing**) **1** value insufficiently. **2** underestimate.

underwater • *adjective* **1** living or situated below the surface of the water. **2** designed to be used or done under the surface of the water. • *adverb* under water.

underway *adjective* **1** (of a process, project, activity, etc.) having been instigated; in progress. **2** (of a person) having begun an activity etc. **3** *Nautical* (of a ship) in motion.

underwear *noun* **1** underclothing. **2** underpants.

underweight *adjective* weighing less than is normal or desirable.

underwent *past of* UNDERGO.

underwhelm *verb jocular* fail to impress.

underwire *noun* **1** a thin semicircular support of wire stitched into the underside of each cup of a bra. **2** a bra with such a support.

underworld *noun* **1** the part of society comprising those who live by organized crime and immorality. **2** the mythical abode of the dead under the earth.

underwrite *verb* (**underwrites**; *past* **underwrote**; *past participle* **underwritten**; **underwriting**) **1 a** sign, issue, and accept liability under (an insurance policy). **b** insure (a person, property, etc.). **c** assume liability up to (a certain amount). **2 a** guarantee (an undertaking or venture etc.) by assuming responsibility for any losses or debts incurred. **b** pay for or contribute financially towards. **3** guarantee the sale of (shares in a new company) by agreeing to purchase a certain percentage of shares not bought by the public.

underwriter *noun* **1** a person who examines a risk, decides whether or not it can be insured, and if it can, works out a premium to be charged, usu. on the basis of the frequency of past claims for similar risks. **2** a financial institution that guarantees to buy a certain proportion of any unsold shares when a new investment security is offered to the public. **3** a person, company, etc. that pays for or contributes to the cost of something.

undeserved *adjective* (of a reward or punishment) not deserved. ▶ **undeservedly** *adverb* [Say un DESERVED, un DESERVE id lee]

undesirability *noun* the quality of being undesirable or objectionable.

undesirable • *adjective* not desirable; objectionable, unpleasant. • *noun* (usu. in *plural*) an objectionable or unpleasant person, animal, insect, etc. ▶ **undesirably** *adverb*

undetected *adjective* not detected; unobserved, unnoticed.

undetermined *adjective* = UNDECIDED *adjective*.

undeterred *adjective* not deterred. [Say un dee TURD]

undid *past of* UNDO.

undies *plural noun informal* (esp. women's) underclothes.

undifferentiated *adjective* not differentiated.

undigested *adjective* **1** not digested. **2** (esp. of information, facts, etc.) not properly arranged or considered.

undiluted *adjective* **1** not diluted. **2** complete, utter: *it's just sheer undiluted stupidity!*

undirected *adjective* aimless; lacking direction.

undisciplined *adjective* lacking discipline; not disciplined.

undisclosed *adjective* not revealed or made known.

U

undiscriminating *adjective* **1** lacking taste or good judgment. **2** not selective, indiscriminate.

undisguised *adjective* not disguised or concealed; open, candid. ▶**undisguisedly** *adverb* [Say un DISGUISED, un DISGUISE id lee]

undisputed *adjective* **1** not disputed or called into question. **2** universally acknowledged; generally recognized as being: *the undisputed champion*.

undistinguished *adjective* **1** lacking any distinguishing characteristic or feature: *an undistinguished square building*. **2** unremarkable, mediocre: *an undistinguished author*.

undivided *adjective* not divided or shared; whole, entire: *gave him my undivided attention*.

undo • *verb* (**undoes**; *past* **undid**; *past participle* **undone**; **undoing**) **1 a** unfasten or untie (a coat, button, knot, etc.). **b** become unfastened: *how does this necklace undo?* **c** unfasten the clothing of (a person). **2** restore to the original form or condition; annul, cancel: *cannot undo the past*. **3** ruin the prospects, reputation, or morals of. • *noun* Computing **1** a feature of some programs that allows the user to reverse the effect of the last action or actions, including restoring deletions. **2** the key on some keyboards that controls this feature.

undocumented *adjective* **1** not having the appropriate legal document or licence. **2** not proved by or recorded in documents.

undoing *noun* **1 a** ruin, downfall, destruction. **b** the cause of this. **2** the process of reversing what has been done. **3** the action of opening or unfastening.

undone *adjective* **1** not done; incomplete: *left the job undone*. **2** not fastened or tied: *undone shoelaces*.

undoubtedly *adverb* beyond doubt; without question; certainly.

undreamed of *adjective* (also **undreamt of**) not considered or imagined; completely unexpected and usu. very pleasing.

undress • *verb* (**undresses**, **undressed**, **undressing**) **1** take off one's clothes. **2** take the clothes off (a person). • *noun* **1 a** Military a uniform or clothing worn on ordinary rather than ceremonial occasions (also as an adjective: *undress cap*) (opp. FULL DRESS). **b** casual or informal clothing. **2** the state of being naked or only partially clothed.

undressed *adjective* **1** not or no longer dressed; partly or wholly naked. **2** (of leather etc.) not treated. **3** (of food) not having a dressing.

undue *adjective* **1** excessive, disproportionate; unwarranted. **2** inappropriate, improper, unjust.

undulate *verb* (**undulates**, **undulated**, **undulating**) **1** have a wavy or rippling outline or appearance: *40 kilometres of trails undulate gently through woodsy countryside*. **2** have a wavelike motion; move with a smooth regular rising and falling or rippling back and forth: *her body undulated to the thumping rhythm of the music*. [Say UN dyoo late or UN joo late]

undulation *noun* a smooth curving shape or movement like a series of waves: *the road followed the undulations of the landscape*.

unduly *adverb* more than is reasonable or necessary; excessively: *he did not sound unduly worried at the prospect* ◊ *the levels of pollution in this area are unduly high* ◊ *the thought did not disturb her unduly* ◊ *the sentence was criticized as being unduly lenient*. [Say un DUE lee]

undying *adjective* eternal, never-ending: *undying love*.

unearned *adjective* **1** not earned. **2** Baseball (of a run) resulting from an error or passed ball.

unearth *verb* **1** discover by investigation, searching, or while rummaging; bring to light. **2** uncover by the removal of earth; dig up.

unearthly *adjective* **1 a** not of this world: *unearthly creature*. **b** eerie, supernatural, mysterious. **2** not typical of this world; rare, uncommon: *unearthly beauty*. **3** *informal* absurdly early or inconvenient: *an unearthly hour*.

unease *noun* lack of ease, anxiety, discomfort, distress.

uneasily *adverb* in an uneasy manner: *I wondered uneasily what he was thinking* ◊ *she shifted uneasily in her chair* ◊ *his socialist views sit uneasily with his huge fortune*.

uneasiness *noun* the state of being uneasy; anxiety, discomfort.

uneasy *adjective* (**uneasier**, **uneasiest**) **1** (of a person) apprehensive; uncomfortable in mind or body. **2** characterized by or causing nervousness or restlessness; disturbing: *an uneasy silence*. **3** tenuous, shaky: *an uneasy alliance*.

uneatable *adjective* that is not in a condition to be eaten (compare INEDIBLE).

uneconomic *adjective* not economic; incapable of being profitably operated etc.

uneducated *adjective* not educated.

unemployable • *adjective* not qualified or suitable for paid employment. • *noun* **1** (often in plural) an unemployable person. **2** (preceded by *the*; treated as plural) unemployable people collectively.

unemployed • *adjective* **1** not having paid employment; out of work. **2** not in use. • *noun* (preceded by *the*; treated as plural) unemployed people.

unemployment *noun* **1** the state of being unemployed. **2** the condition or extent of this in a country or region etc., esp. the number or percentage of unemployed people: *unemployment is down*. **3** Cdn informal = UNEMPLOYMENT INSURANCE: *I'm on unemployment*.

unemployment benefit *noun* a regular payment made by a local government or, in the US, a trade union, to an unemployed person.

unemployment insurance *noun* Cdn the former name for EMPLOYMENT INSURANCE. Abbreviation: **UI**.

unencumbered *adjective* **1** not having any burden or impediment: *he needed to travel light and unencumbered*. **2** free of debt or other financial liability.

unending *adjective* having or apparently having no end. ▶**unendingly** *adverb*

unenforceable *adjective* (of a contract, law, etc.) impossible to enforce.

un-English *adjective* **1** not characteristic of the English language. **2** not characteristic of or derived from the culture or inhabitants of England.

unenlightened *adjective* not enlightened. ▶**unenlightening** *adjective*

unenterprising *adjective* not enterprising.

unenviable *adjective* unpleasant, undesirable. ▶**unenviably** *adverb* [Say un ENVY a bull]

unequal *adjective* **1** not equal in amount, size, value, etc. **2** (usu. foll. by *to*) inadequate in ability or resources etc.: *unequal to the task*. **3 a** (of a contest, conflict, treaty, etc.) not evenly balanced; favouring one side: *an unequal bargain*. **b** inconsistent; varying or variable: *unequal distribution*.

unequalled *adjective* **1** superior to all others. **2** (foll. by *by*) not matched or surpassed.

unequally *adverb* in an unequal manner; not equally.

unequipped *adjective* not equipped.

unequivocal *adjective* not ambiguous; plain, unmistakable: *as a statement of policy, Davis's words are clear and unequivocal*. ▶**unequivocally** *adverb* [Say un ee KWIVVA cull]

unerring *adjective* always right or accurate: *an unerring sense of direction*. ▶**unerringly** *adverb*

UNESCO *abbreviation* (also **Unesco**) United Nations

Educational, Scientific, and Cultural Organization. [Say you NESS co]

unethical *adjective* not ethical, esp. unscrupulous in business or professional conduct. ▶**unethically** *adverb*

uneven *adjective* **1** not level or smooth. **2** not consistent, regular, or uniform. **3** (of a competition) unequal. ▶**unevenly** *adverb* **unevenness** *noun*

unexceptionable *adjective* to whom or to which no exception can be taken; perfectly satisfactory or adequate.

WRITING TIP
unexceptional, unexceptionable

Do not confuse **unexceptionable** and **unexceptional**: *Her new book is unexceptionable* means it contains nothing that would cause objections, while *Her new book is unexceptional* means it is mediocre.

---

unexceptional *adjective* not out of the ordinary; usual, normal.

unexpected • *adjective* not expected; surprising. • *noun* (preceded by *the*; usu. treated as *singular*) an unexpected thing or unexpected things collectively. ▶**unexpectedly** *adverb* **unexpectedness** *noun*

unexplainable *adjective* that cannot be explained. ▶**unexplainably** *adverb*

unexplained *adjective* not explained.

unexplored *adjective* not explored.

unfailing *adjective* **1** unlimited, inexhaustible: *an unfailing source of comfort*. **2** unceasing, constant: *unfailing devotion*. **3** certain, reliable: *unfailing accuracy*. ▶**unfailingly** *adverb*

unfair *adjective* **1** not just, reasonable, or objective: *unfair criticism*. **2** not according to the rules: *unfair play*. **3** dishonest: *obtained by unfair means*. ▶**unfairly** *adverb* **unfairness** *noun*

unfaithful *adjective* **1** (of a person) not faithful, esp. to a sexual partner. **2** (of behaviour) disloyal. ▶**unfaithfulness** *noun*

unfaltering *adjective* not faltering; steady, resolute.

unfasten *verb* **1** loosen. **2** open the fastening or fastenings of. **3** detach.

unfastened *adjective* **1** that has not been fastened. **2** that has been loosened, opened, or detached.

unfathomable *adjective* incapable of being fathomed. ▶**unfathomably** *adverb* [Say un FATHOM a bull]

unfavourable *adjective* (also **unfavorable**) not favourable or beneficial; adverse. ▶**unfavourably** *adverb*

unfazed *adjective* *informal* untroubled; not disconcerted.

unfeasible *adjective* not feasible; impractical.

unfeeling *adjective* **1** unsympathetic, harsh, not caring about others' feelings. **2** lacking sensation or sensitivity: *my unfeeling hands*. ▶**unfeelingly** *adverb*

unfeminine *adjective* **1** not characteristically or stereotypically feminine. **2** not regarded as suitable or appropriate for a woman.

unfenced *adjective* not provided with fences.

unfermented *adjective* not fermented.

unfettered *adjective* unrestrained, unrestricted: *the sensation that a man feels when he is stark naked — a fine sense of unfettered freedom*.

unfiltered *adjective* **1** not filtered. **2** (of a cigarette) not provided with a filter.

unfinished *adjective* **1** not finished; incomplete. **2** (of wood furniture etc.) not painted or stained etc.

unfinished business *noun* **1** a task or tasks that must be completed. **2** *Psychology informal* unresolved issues.

unfit *adjective* **1 a** (of a thing) not fit, proper, or suitable: *unfit for human consumption* ◊ *unfit to be used*. **b** (of a person) not qualified or worthy: *an unfit parent* ◊ *unfit to stand trial*. **2** in poor physical shape. ▶**unfitness** *noun*

unflagging *adjective* tireless, persistent: *her unflagging efforts on behalf of marine conservation*. ▶**unflaggingly** *adverb*

unflappability *noun* the quality of being able to remain calm in a crisis.

unflappable *adjective* *informal* remaining calm in a crisis. ▶**unflappably** *adverb*

unflinching *adjective* not showing reluctance, hesitation, indecision, or fear. ▶**unflinchingly** *adverb*

unfold *verb* **1** open the fold or folds of, spread out. **2** develop, become clear: *the plot begins to unfold*. **3** become opened out. **4** reveal, explain, or make clear (a thought, idea, mystery, etc.).

unforced *adjective* **1** not produced by effort; easy, natural. **2** not compelled or constrained.

unforeseeable *adjective* not foreseeable.

unforeseen *adjective* not foreseen.

unforgettable *adjective* that cannot be forgotten; memorable, wonderful. ▶**unforgettably** *adverb*

unforgivable *adjective* without any justifiable motive; inexcusable, disgraceful. ▶**unforgivably** *adverb*

unforgiving *adjective* not forgiving.

unformed *adjective* **1** not formed. **2** shapeless. **3** not developed.

unfortunate • *adjective* **1 a** having bad fortune; unlucky. **b** unhappy. **2** regrettable. **3** unsuitable, inappropriate, or inauspicious: *a most unfortunate choice of words*. • *noun* (usu. in *plural*) an unfortunate person.

unfortunately *adverb* **1** (qualifying a whole sentence) it is unfortunate that. **2** in an unfortunate manner.

unfounded *adjective* having no basis in fact; unsubstantiated, not valid: *the rumour was unfounded*.

unfreeze *verb* (**unfreezes**; *past* **unfroze**; *past participle* **unfrozen**; **unfreezing**) **1** cause to thaw. **2** thaw. **3** remove restrictions from, make (assets, credits, etc.) convertible into cash.

unfriendly *adjective* (**unfriendlier, unfriendliest**) **1** not friendly. **2** (in *combination*) *informal* not helpful or beneficial to: *ozone-unfriendly*. ▶**unfriendliness** *noun*

unfrozen • *verb* *past participle of* UNFREEZE. • *adjective* not frozen.

unfulfillable *adjective* (of dreams, goals, etc.) that cannot be fulfilled.

unfulfilled *adjective* not fulfilled. ▶**unfulfilling** *adjective* **unfulfillment** *noun*

unfunny *adjective* (**unfunnier, unfunniest**) not amusing, although meant to be.

unfurl *verb* **1** spread or open out (a sail, flag, etc.) to its greatest length or width. **2** become spread out or fully extended.

unfurnished *adjective* **1** (of an apartment etc.) without furniture. **2** (often foll. by *with*) not provided or supplied.

ungainliness *noun* awkwardness, clumsiness.

ungainly *adjective* awkward, clumsy, not graceful: *he walks in long ungainly strides*.

unglamorous *adjective* **1** lacking glamour or appeal. **2** mundane.

unglued *adjective* having no glue, unstuck. PHRASES **come** (or **become**) **unglued 1 a** fall apart, lose one's composure. **b** become crazy. **2** fall into a state of chaos or disarray.

ungodliness *noun* the quality of being ungodly.

ungodly *adjective* **1** impious, wicked. **2** *informal* outrageous: *an ungodly hour to arrive*.

ungracious *adjective* not cordial, courteous, or polite; rude or unkind to others. ▶ **ungraciously** *adverb*

ungrammatical *adjective* contrary to the rules of grammar. ▶ **ungrammatically** *adverb*

ungraspable *adjective* **1** that cannot be grasped or seized. **2** that cannot be comprehended.

ungrateful *adjective* **1** not feeling or showing gratitude. **2** not pleasant or acceptable. ▶ **ungratefully** *adverb* **ungratefulness** *noun*

unguarded *adjective* **1 a** (of a person) not on one's guard; candid, open. **b** resulting from such candidness: *she told me so in an unguarded moment*. **2** careless, thoughtless, not cautious: *an unguarded remark*. **3** not guarded; vulnerable. ▶ **unguardedly** *adverb*

unguent *noun* a soft substance, such as a perfumed oil, used esp. as an ointment. [Say UNG gwint]

ungulate ● *adjective* hoofed. ● *noun* a hoofed mammal. [Say UNG gyoo lit or UNG gyoo late]

unhappily *adverb* **1** in an unhappy way: *he sighed unhappily* ◊ *"I've made a big mistake," she said unhappily*. **2** used to say that a particular situation or fact is sad or disappointing; unfortunately: *unhappily, such good luck is rare* ◊ *his wife, unhappily, died five years ago*.

unhappiness *noun* the state or condition of being unhappy; discontent.

unhappy *adjective* (**unhappier**, **unhappiest**) **1 a** not happy, miserable. **b** (often foll. by *with*, *about*) displeased, dissatisfied, upset. **2** unsuccessful, unfortunate, regrettable. **3** inauspicious: *an unhappy omen*.

unhealthily *adverb* in an unhealthy manner: *she's unhealthily obsessed with the issue* ◊ *unhealthily thin models*.

unhealthiness *noun* the quality of being unhealthy.

unhealthy *adjective* (**unhealthier**, **unhealthiest**) **1** not in good health. **2** not conducive to good physical, mental, or emotional health or well-being: *an unhealthy diet*. **3** not indicative of good health; unwholesome: *an unhealthy complexion*. **4** inappropriate, perverse: *he maintains an unhealthy attachment to her*.

unheard of *adjective* **1** unknown, unfamiliar. **2** unprecedented, not previously attempted or considered. **3** outrageous, preposterous.

unheeded *adjective* not heeded; disregarded.

unheralded *adjective* not heralded; unannounced.

unhesitating *adjective* **1** without pause, uncertainty, or hesitation: *an unhesitating reply*. **2** without interruption; relentless, constant: *her unhesitating generosity and kindness*. ▶ **unhesitatingly** *adverb*

unhinge *verb* (**unhinges**, **unhinged**, **unhinging**) **1** take (a door etc.) off its hinges. **2 a** unsettle or unbalance (a person); make crazy. **b** throw (a situation etc.) into chaos or confusion. **3** detach, separate, or dislodge.

unhinged *adjective* unsettled, unbalanced, disordered, confused.

unhip *adjective* *informal* not hip; not aware of or consistent with the latest trends or styles.

unhitch *verb* (**unhitches**, **unhitched**, **unhitching**) **1** release from a hitched state. **2** unhook, unfasten.

unhittable *adjective* (esp. of a pitched baseball) that cannot be hit.

unholy *adjective* (**unholier**, **unholiest**) **1** evil, wicked. **2** *informal* dreadful, terrible: *this room is an unholy mess!* **3** not holy.

unhook *verb* **1** remove from a hook or hooks. **2** unfasten by releasing a hook or hooks.

unhoped for *adjective* not hoped for or expected.

unhuman *adjective* **1** not human. **2** superhuman. **3** inhuman, brutal.

unhyphenated *adjective* not hyphenated.

uni- *combining form* one; having or consisting of one.

unicameral *adjective* with a single legislative chamber. [Say yoona CAMMER ul]

UNICEF *abbreviation* United Nations Children's Fund. [Say YOONA seff]

unicellular *adjective* (of an organism, organ, tissue, etc.) consisting of a single cell. [Say yoona CELL yuh ler]

unicorn *noun* **1** a legendary animal usu. represented as a horse with a single straight horn projecting from its forehead. **2** a heraldic representation of this.

unicycle *noun* a single-wheeled cycle, esp. as used by acrobats. ▶ **unicyclist** *noun*

unidealized *adjective* not represented as perfect or ideal; not embellished. [Say un IDEAL ized]

unidirectional *adjective* having only one direction of motion, operation, etc. [Say yoona DIRECTION ul]

unification *noun* **1** the process of being united or made into a whole: *Garibaldi was the father of Italian unification*. **2** *Cdn* the action or policy of merging the traditional army, navy, and air force into a single combined force. [Say yoona fuh KAY sh'n]

unified *adjective* joined together to form a single unit: *a unified system of national education*. [Say YOONA fide]

uniform ● *adjective* **1** not changing in form or character; the same, unvarying: *all of uniform size and shape*. **2** conforming to the same standard, rules, or pattern. **3** constant in the course of time: *uniform acceleration*. ● *noun* **1** uniform distinctive clothing worn by members of the same body, e.g. by soldiers, members of a sports team, etc. **2** clothing, usu. white or in pastel colours, worn by nurses and other members of medical professions. **3** a style of dress typical of a certain group.

uniformed *adjective* wearing an esp. military uniform: *a uniformed officer*.

uniformity *noun* (*plural* **uniformities**) the state of being uniform; sameness, consistency: *the drab uniformity of the houses*. [Say yoona FORMA tee]

uniformly *adverb* in an even or consistent manner: *the principles were applied uniformly across all the departments* ◊ *pressure must be uniformly distributed over the whole surface*.

unify *verb* (**unifies**, **unified**, **unifying**) make united or uniform. ▶ **unifying** *adjective* [Say YOONA fie]

unilateral *adjective* performed by or affecting only one person or party: *unilateral disarmament* ◊ *unilateral declaration of independence*. ▶ **unilaterally** *adverb* [Say yoona LATTER ul]

unilingual *esp. Cdn* ● *adjective* **1** able to speak only one language. **2** spoken or written in or involving only one language. ● *noun* a unilingual person. [Say yoona LING gwul or yoona LING gyoo ul]

unimaginable *adjective* impossible to imagine. ▶ **unimaginably** *adverb*

unimagined *adjective* not imagined.

unimpaired *adjective* not impaired.

unimpeachable *adjective* giving no opportunity for criticism; beyond reproach: *he replied with unimpeachable documentary evidence*. ▶ **unimpeachably** *adverb*

unimpeded *adjective* not impeded. [Say un im PEED id]

unimportance *noun* lack of importance.

unimportant *adjective* not important.

unimproved *adjective* **1** not made better or improved. **2** (of land) not used for agriculture or building; not developed.

unincorporated *adjective* not formed into a corporation: *in most cases, unincorporated groups are not recognized by the courts and may not sue or be sued.* [Say un in CORE pur ate id]

uninformed *adjective* **1** not informed or instructed. **2** ignorant, uneducated.

uninhabitable *adjective* that cannot be inhabited.

uninhibited *adjective* not inhibited. ▶ **uninhibitedly** *adverb*

uninitiated *adjective* not initiated; not admitted or instructed. [Say un in ISHY ate id]

uninspired *adjective* not imaginative or inspiring; dull.

unintelligible *adjective* not intelligible. [Say un in TELLA juh bull]

uninterested *adjective* **1** not interested. **2** unconcerned.

uninviting *adjective* not inviting; unattractive, repellent. ▶ **uninvitingly** *adverb*

union *noun* **1 a** the action or fact of joining together or being joined together, esp. in a political context: *Joey Smallwood promoted Newfoundland's union with Canada.* **b (the Union)** *hist.* the uniting of the English and Scottish crowns in 1603, of the English and Scottish parliaments in 1707, or of Great Britain and Ireland in 1801. **2 a** a whole resulting from the combination of parts or members. **b** a political unit formed in this way, esp. the US, the UK, the USSR, or South Africa. **3 a** = LABOUR UNION. **b** a group of people united for a common cause. **4** a marriage: *their union was blessed with four children.* **5** a state of harmony or agreement: *lived together in perfect union.* **6** *Math* the totality of the members of two or more sets. **7 (the Union)** *US hist.* the body of northern states in the American Civil War. **8** a joint or coupling for pipes etc.

Union Government *noun Cdn hist.* the coalition government that governed Canada from 1917–1920.

unionism *noun* membership in or advocacy of an organized association of workers formed to protect and further their rights and interests.

unionist *noun* **1 a** a member of a labour union. **b** an advocate of labour unions. **2** (usu. **Unionist**) an advocate of union, esp.: **a** a person opposed to the rupture of the parliamentary union between Great Britain and Northern Ireland (formerly between Great Britain and Ireland). **b** a member of a party having these aims. **c** *hist.* a person who opposed secession during the US Civil War.

unionization *noun* the action of bringing a company or industry or its employees under the organization or rules of a labour union.

unionize *verb* (**unionizes, unionized, unionizing**) bring or come under the organization or rules of a labour union.

Union Jack *noun* the national flag of the United Kingdom, formed by the union of the crosses of St. George, St. Andrew, and St. Patrick.

Union Nationale *noun Cdn* (in Quebec) a provincial party identified with conservative French-Canadian nationalism which held power 1944–60 under Maurice Duplessis (1890–1959). [Say oon yon nass yuh NAL (with on as in French)]

unique *adjective* **1** of which there is only one; unequalled; having no like, equal, or parallel. **2** *disputed* unusual, remarkable: *the most unique person I ever met.* **3** (foll. by *to*) limited in occurrence to a particular area, situation, etc.: *that species is unique to this part of Canada.* ▶ **uniquely** *adverb* **uniqueness** *noun* [Say yoo NEEK]

unisex *adjective* (of clothing, hairstyles, etc.) designed to be suitable for both sexes. [Say YOONA sex]

unison ● *noun* **1** *Music* **a** identity in pitch of two or more sounds or notes. **b** the sounding of notes or melodies at the same pitch, or at pitches one or more octaves apart, by different voices or instruments together. **2** agreement, concord: *acted in perfect unison.* ● *adjective* *Music* coinciding in pitch. ▰PHRASES▰ **in unison** together; as one: *read the poem in unison.* [Say YOONA sun]

unit *noun* **1 a** an individual thing, person, or group regarded as single and complete, esp. for purposes of calculation. **b** each of the (smallest) separate individuals or groups into which a complex whole may be analyzed: *the family as the unit of society.* **2** a quantity chosen as a standard in terms of which other quantities may be expressed: *SI unit.* **3** a private residence forming one of several in a large building or group of buildings; an apartment etc. **4** a device with a specified function forming part of a complex mechanism. **5** a piece of furniture for fitting with others like it or made of complementary parts. **6 a** a group with a special function in an organization. **b** a subdivision of a larger military grouping. **7** a group of buildings, wards, etc., in a hospital. **8** a portion of a school course centring on a particular theme: *a unit on insects.* **9** *Cdn (PEI)* = SCHOOL UNIT. **10** the number "one".

unitard *noun* a tight-fitting one-piece garment of stretchable fabric which covers the body from the shoulders to the toes or ankles. [Say YOONA tard]

Unitarian ● *noun* **1** a person who believes that God is not a Trinity but one person. **2** a member of a religious body maintaining this and advocating freedom from formal dogma or doctrine. ● *adjective* of or relating to the Unitarians. ▶ **Unitarianism** *noun* [Say yoona TERRY un]

unitary *adjective* **1** marked by unity or uniformity: *the Oblates in Canada abandoned their unitary structure and organized themselves in two linguistic sections.* **2** of or relating to a system of government in which the powers of the separate constituent parts are vested in one central body, rather than in separate levels of jurisdiction such as provincial and federal. [Say YOONA terry]

unite *verb* (**unites, united, uniting**) **1** join together; make or become one; combine. **2** join together for a common purpose or action: *united in their struggle for justice.* **3** join in marriage. **4** possess (qualities, features, etc.) in combination: *united anger with mercy.* **5** form or cause to form a physical or chemical whole: *oil will not unite with water.*

U

united • *adjective* **1** joined together for a common purpose. **2** joined politically. **3** joined together by love or sympathy. **4** in agreement. **5** (**United**) *Cdn* of, relating to, or belonging to the United Church. • *noun* (**United**) *Cdn* a member of the United Church.

United Church *noun* (also **United Church of Canada**) (in Canada) a Protestant denomination formed in 1925 by the merger of the Methodist and Congregationalist Churches together with the majority of Presbyterians.

United Empire Loyalist *noun Cdn* **1** any of the colonists of the American revolutionary period who supported the British cause, many of whom afterwards migrated to Canada. **2** *Cdn* a descendant of such a person.

United Farmers *noun Cdn* any of various political groups growing out of provincial farmers' organizations.

United Nations *noun* an international organization of countries set up in 1945, in succession to the League of Nations, to promote international peace, security, and co-operation. Abbreviation: **UN**.

unity *noun* (*plural* **unities**) **1** oneness; being one, single, or individual; being formed of parts that constitute a whole: *the pictures lack unity ◊ national unity*. **2** harmony or concord between persons etc.: *lived together in unity*. **3** a thing forming a complex whole: *a person regarded as a unity*. **4** *Math* the number "one".

Univ. *abbreviation* University.

universal • *adjective* of, belonging to, or done etc. by all persons or things in the world or in the class concerned; applicable to all cases: *the feeling was universal ◊ universal approval*. • *noun Philosophy* a quality that particular things may have in common, signified by a general term, e.g. redness.

universalism *noun* **1** *Theology* the belief that all humankind will eventually be saved. **2** loyalty to and concern for others without regard to national or other allegiances.

universalist *noun* **1** a person advocating loyalty to and concern for others without regard to national allegiance. **2** *Theology* a person who believes that all mankind will eventually be saved. **3** a person who is learned in many subjects or who has a wide range of interests etc. ▶**universalistic** *adjective* [Say UNIVERSAL ist, universal ISS tick]

universality *noun* the quality of something that affects or is done or shared by all people or things in the world or in a particular group: *universality is one of the most important aspects of our health care system*. [Say yoona vur SALLA tee]

universalize *verb* (**universalizes**, **universalized**, **universalizing**) **1** apply universally; give a universal character to: *we universalize our own references and images into a language and format that people all around the world can relate to*. **2** bring into universal use; make available for all: *bold attempts to universalize health care*. [Say UNIVERSAL ize]

universally *adverb* **1** by everyone: *the theory is universally accepted*. **2** everywhere or in every situation: *the treatment is not universally available*.

Universal Product Code *noun* a bar code printed on the packaging of many consumer goods and used esp. in retail sales and inventory control. Abbreviation: **UPC**.

universe *noun* **1** all existing things; the cosmos. **2** all of humanity. **3** a sphere of activity, existence, interest, etc.: *he is the centre of her universe*.

university *noun* (*plural* **universities**) **1** an educational institution designed for instruction of students in many branches of advanced learning, conferring

degrees in various faculties, and often embodying colleges and similar institutions. **2** the members of this collectively.

Unix *noun Computing proprietary* a multi-user operating system. [Say YOO nix]

unjust *adjective* not just, contrary to justice or fairness. ▶**unjustly** *adverb*

unkempt *adjective* **1** untidy, of neglected appearance. **2** not combed; dishevelled.

unknowable • *adjective* that cannot be known. • *noun* **1** an unknowable thing. **2** (**the Unknowable**) the postulated absolute or ultimate reality.

unknowing *adjective* not knowing; ignorant, unconscious. ▶**unknowingly** *adverb*

unknown • *adjective* not known. • *noun* **1** an unknown thing or person. **2** an unknown quantity: *equation in two unknowns*. PHRASES **unknown to** without the knowledge of: *did it unknown to me*.

unlawful *adjective* not lawful; illegal, not permissible. ▶**unlawfully** *adverb* **unlawfulness** *noun*

unleaded • *adjective* **1** (of gasoline etc.) without added lead. **2** not covered, weighted, or framed with lead. • *noun* unleaded gasoline etc. [Say un LED id]

unlearn *verb* (**unlearns**; *past* and *past participle* **unlearned** or **unlearnt**; **unlearning**) **1** discard from one's memory. **2** rid oneself of (a habit, false information, etc.).

unleash *verb* (**unleashes**, **unleashed**, **unleashing**) **1** release (something powerful or destructive). **2** set free to engage in pursuit or attack.

unleavened *adjective* not leavened; made without yeast or other raising agent. [Say un LEV ind]

unless *conjunction* if not; except when: *shall go unless I hear from you ◊ will make it home by 8 unless the train is late*.

unlettered *adjective* **1** illiterate. **2** not well educated.

unlicensed *adjective* (also **unlicenced**) not licensed, esp. without a licence to sell alcoholic drink.

unlighted *adjective* **1** not provided with light. **2** not set burning.

unlike • *preposition* **1** different from; not similar to: *they were unlike anything ever seen before*. **2** in contrast to; differently from: *unlike Elena he was not superstitious*. **3** uncharacteristic of: *he sounded irritable, which was unlike him*. • *adjective* not alike: *though twins, they seemed utterly unlike*.

unlikely *adjective* (**unlikelier**, **unlikeliest**) **1** improbable: *an unlikely story*. **2** not to be expected to do something: *she's unlikely to be available*. **3** unpromising: *an unlikely candidate*.

unlimited *adjective* without limit; unrestricted; very great in number or quantity.

unlined *adjective* **1** (of paper etc.) without lines. **2** (of a face etc.) without wrinkles. **3** (of a garment etc.) without lining.

unlisted *adjective* **1** (of a telephone number) not listed in a telephone directory. **2** not included in a published list, esp. (of a security) not eligible for trading on an exchange.

unload *verb* **1** remove a load from (a vehicle etc.). **2** remove (a load) from a vehicle etc. **3** remove the charge from (a firearm etc.). **4** *informal* get rid of. **5** (often foll. by *on*) *informal* **a** divulge (information). **b** give vent to (feelings). ▶**unloader** *noun*

unlock *verb* **1 a** release the lock of (a door, box, etc.). **b** release or disclose by unlocking. **2** release thoughts, feelings, etc., from (one's mind etc.). **3** become unlocked.

unloved *adjective* not loved.

unlucky *adjective* (**unluckier**, **unluckiest**) **1** not

fortunate or successful. **2** wretched. **3** bringing bad luck. **4** unwise; badly considered.

unmade *adjective* not made.

unmake *verb* (**unmakes**; *past* and *past participle* **unmade**; **unmaking**) undo the making of.

unman *verb* (**unmans**, **unmanned**, **unmanning**) deprive of supposed manly qualities (e.g. self-control, courage); cause to weep etc.; discourage.

unmanageable *adjective* not (easily) managed, manipulated, or controlled. ▶ **unmanageably** *adverb*

unmanned *adjective* **1** not manned. **2** overcome by emotion etc.

unmannerly *adjective* **1** without good manners. **2** (of actions, speech, etc.) showing a lack of good manners.

unmapped *adjective* **1** not represented on a map. **2** unexplored.

unmarked *adjective* **1** not marked. **2** not noticed.

unmask *verb* **1 a** remove the mask from. **b** expose the true character of. **2** remove one's mask.

unmatched *adjective* not matched or equalled.

unmediated *adjective* with no intervention; directly perceived: *the essence of the new media is that it is unmediated – there is no filtering by professional journalists*. [Say un MEEDY ate id]

unmentionable • *adjective* that cannot (properly) be mentioned. • *noun* **1** (in *plural*) *jocular* undergarments. **2** a person or thing not to be mentioned.

unmerciful *adjective* merciless. ▶ **unmercifully** *adverb*

unmet *adjective* (of a quota, demand, goal, etc.) not achieved or fulfilled.

unmindful *adjective* (often foll. by *of*) not mindful; unaware.

unmissable *adjective* that cannot or should not be missed.

unmistakable *adjective* that cannot be mistaken or doubted, clear. ▶ **unmistakably** *adverb*

unmitigated *adjective* **1** (of something bad) not made less severe, not moderated; pure, complete: *it was an unmitigated disaster*. **2** absolute, unqualified: *the changeover to agriculture was not an unmitigated blessing*. [Say un MITTA gate id]

unmolested *adjective* not molested. [Say un muh LEST id]

unmotivated *adjective* without motivation; without a motive.

unmoved *adjective* **1** not moved. **2** not changed in one's purpose. **3** not affected by emotion.

unmoving *adjective* **1** not moving; still. **2** not emotive.

unmusical *adjective* **1** not pleasing to the ear. **2** unskilled in or indifferent to music.

unnameable *adjective* that cannot be named, esp. too bad to be named.

unnatural *adjective* **1** contrary to nature or the usual course of nature; not normal. **2 a** lacking natural feelings. **b** extremely cruel or wicked. **3** artificial. **4** affected. ▶ **unnaturally** *adverb*

unnecessarily *adverb* in a way that is not necessary or called for; in a way that could be avoided; needlessly: *the wording of this definition is unnecessarily long* ◊ *there is no need to alarm the employees unnecessarily*. [Say un nessa SARE uh lee]

unnecessary • *adjective* **1** not necessary. **2** more than is necessary: *with unnecessary care*. • *noun* (*plural* **unnecessaries**) (usu. in *plural*) an unnecessary thing. [Say un NESSA sare ee]

unnerve *verb* (**unnerves**, **unnerved**, **unnerving**) deprive of strength or resolution. ▶ **unnerving** *adjective* **unnervingly** *adverb*

unobtrusive *adjective* not making oneself or itself noticed. ▶ **unobtrusively** *adverb* **unobtrusiveness** *noun* [Say un ub TRUCE iv]

unofficial *adjective* **1** not officially authorized or confirmed. **2** not characteristic of officials. ▶ **unofficially** *adverb*

unoriginal *adjective* lacking originality.

unorthodox *adjective* not orthodox. ▶ **unorthodoxy** *noun* [Say un ORTHA docks, un ORTHA docksy]

unpack *verb* **1** open and remove the contents of (a package, luggage, etc.). **2** take (a thing) out from a package etc. **3** unload (a vehicle etc.).

unpaid *adjective* (of a debt or a person) not paid.

unpaired *adjective* **1** not arranged in pairs. **2** not forming one of a pair.

unpalatable *adjective* **1** not pleasant to taste. **2** (of an idea, suggestion, etc.) disagreeable, distasteful. [Say un PALA tuh bull]

unparalleled *adjective* having no parallel or equal.

unpardonable *adjective* that cannot be pardoned. ▶ **unpardonably** *adverb*

unparliamentary *adjective* contrary to proper parliamentary usage. [Say un parla MENTA ree]

unperceptive *adjective* not perceptive.

unperturbed *adjective* not perturbed.

unplayable *adjective* **1** *Sport* (of a ball) that cannot be struck or returned. **2** that cannot be played.

unpleasant *adjective* not pleasant; displeasing; disagreeable. ▶ **unpleasantly** *adverb* **unpleasantness** *noun*

unplug *verb* (**unplugs**, **unplugged**, **unplugging**) **1** disconnect an electrical device by removing its plug from the socket. **2** unclog. **3** remove a stopper or plug from.

unplugged *adjective* **1** that has been unplugged. **2** (of rock music, etc.) performed or played on instruments without electric amplification.

unpolished *adjective* **1** not polished; rough. **2** without refinement; crude.

unpopular *adjective* not popular; not liked by the public or by people in general. ▶ **unpopularity** *noun*

unpowered *adjective* (of a boat, vehicle, etc.) propelled other than by fuel.

unprecedented *adjective* **1** having no precedent; unparalleled. **2** new. ▶ **unprecedentedly** *adverb* [Say un PRESSA dent id]

unpredictability *noun* the condition of a person or thing that cannot be predicted.

unpredictable *adjective* that cannot be predicted. ▶ **unpredictably** *adverb*

unprejudiced *adjective* not prejudiced. [Say un PREDGE uh dist]

unpremeditated *adjective* not previously thought over, not deliberately planned; unintentional. [Say un pre MEDITATE id]

unprepossessing *adjective* not attractive: *the towns are mostly unprepossessing collections of wooden structures*. [Say un pre POSSESSING]

unpretentious *adjective* not making a great display; simple, modest. [Say un pre TEN shuss]

unprincipled *adjective* lacking or not based on good moral principles. [Say un PRIN sip pulled]

unprintable *adjective* that cannot be printed, esp. because too indecent or libellous or blasphemous.

unproductive *adjective* not productive. ▶ **unproductively** *adverb*

unprofessional *adjective* **1** contrary to professional standards of behaviour etc. **2** not belonging to a profession; amateur. ▶ **unprofessionally** *adverb*

UNPROFOR *abbreviation* United Nations Protection Force. [Say UN pruh fore]

U

unpromising *adjective* not likely to turn out well.

unprotected *adjective* **1** not protected. **2** (of sexual intercourse) performed without a condom or other contraceptive.

unproven *adjective* (also **unproved**) not proven.

unprovoked *adjective* (of a person or act) without provocation.

unpublished *adjective* not published.

unqualified *adjective* **1 a** not having the necessary qualifications. **b** not competent: *unqualified to give an answer*. **2** not legally or officially qualified: *an unqualified practitioner*. **3** not modified or restricted; complete: *an unqualified success*.

unquenchable *adjective* that cannot be quenched.

unquestionable *adjective* that cannot be disputed or doubted. ▶ **unquestionably** *adverb*

unquestioned *adjective* **1** not disputed or doubted; definite, certain. **2** not interrogated or investigated.

unquestioning *adjective* **1** asking no questions. **2** done without asking questions. ▶ **unquestioningly** *adverb*

unquiet *adjective* **1** restless, agitated, stirring. **2** perturbed, anxious.

unquote *adverb* (in speech, reading aloud, etc.) indicating the presence of closing quotation marks.

unquoted *adjective* not quoted, esp. on the Stock Exchange.

unranked *adjective* (in sports etc.) that has not been ranked or considered a contender.

unravel *verb* (**unravels, unravelled, unravelling**) **1** cause to be no longer ravelled, tangled, or intertwined. **2** probe and solve (a mystery etc.). **3** undo (a fabric, esp. a knitted one). **4** become disentangled or unknitted. **5** come apart, collapse: *our plans have unravelled*.

unread *adjective* **1** not read. **2** (of a person) not well-read. [Say un RED]

unreadable *adjective* **1** too dull or too difficult to be worth reading. **2** illegible.

unreal *adjective* **1** not real. **2** imaginary, illusory. **3** *slang* incredible, amazing. ▶ **unreality** *noun*

unrealized *adjective* not realized, not achieved.

unreason *noun* lack of reasonable thought or action.

unreasonable *adjective* **1** going beyond the limits of what is reasonable or equitable: *unreasonable demands*. **2** not guided by or listening to reason. ▶ **unreasonableness** *noun* **unreasonably** *adverb*

unrecognized *adjective* not recognized.

unreconstructed *adjective* not reconciled or converted to the current political orthodoxy: *her unreconstructed belief in a tax-till-they-drop agenda* ◊ *an unreconstructed flower child, still living in a commune*.

unrefined *adjective* not refined.

unregenerate • *adjective* not reforming or showing repentance; obstinately wrong or bad: *she didn't allow smoking in the house, but she did provide a "smokers' porch" for unregenerate puffers*. • *noun* an unregenerate person. [Say un re JENNER it]

unreleased *adjective* not released, esp. (of a recording, film, etc.) to the public.

unrelenting *adjective* **1** not relenting or yielding. **2** unmerciful. **3** not abating or relaxing. ▶ **unrelentingly** *adverb*

unreliability *noun* the quality of a person or thing that is erratic and cannot be trusted or depended upon: *Danilo's long history of unreliability made him an unlikely choice for the job*.

unreliable *adjective* not reliable; erratic. ▶ **unreliably** *adverb*

unrelieved *adjective* **1** lacking the relief given by contrast or variation. **2** not aided or assisted.

unremitting *adjective* never relaxing or slackening, incessant: *in the unremitting cold of March*. ▶ **unremittingly** *adverb*

unrepeatable *adjective* **1** that cannot be done, made, or said again. **2** too indecent to be said again.

unrepentant *adjective* not repentant. ▶ **unrepentantly** *adverb*

unrepresentative *adjective* not representative.

unrequited *adjective* **1** (of love etc.) not reciprocated or returned: *one of the story's most powerful passages is a description of Lucy in the throes of unrequited love*. **2** (of a yearning etc.) not satisfied or rewarded: *our unrequited pursuit of capital*. [Say un re QUITE id]

unreserved *adjective* **1** not reserved: *unreserved seats*. **2** without reservations; absolute: *unreserved confidence*. **3** free from reserve: *an unreserved nature*. ▶ **unreservedly** *adverb* [Say un re ZURVD, un re ZURV id lee]

unresolved *adjective* (of a problem, dispute, emotion, etc.) not yet settled or resolved: *unresolved conflicts* ◊ *unresolved anger*.

unrest *noun* a state of disturbance and dissatisfaction accompanied by angry protest, violence, etc.

unrestrained *adjective* not restrained.

unrestricted *adjective* not restricted.

unrivalled *adjective* having no equal; peerless. [Say un RYE vuld]

unroll *verb* **1** open out from a rolled-up state. **2** (of a landscape) appear stretched out before the viewer. **3** (of events) happen one after the other.

unruffled *adjective* **1** not agitated or disturbed; calm. **2** not physically ruffled or made rough.

unruliness *noun* behaviour that is disruptive and not easily controlled: *the unruliness continued until Mrs. Bukowski returned to the classroom*. [Say un RUE lee ness]

unruly *adjective* (**unrulier, unruliest**) not easily controlled or disciplined, disorderly. [Say un RUE lee]

unsaddle *verb* (**unsaddles, unsaddled, unsaddling**) **1** remove the saddle from (a horse etc.). **2** dislodge from a saddle.

unsaid *adjective* not said or uttered.

unsaleable *adjective* (also **unsalable**) not saleable.

unsatisfactory *adjective* not satisfactory; poor, unacceptable.

unsaturated *adjective* **1** (of a compound, esp. a fat or oil) having double or triple bonds in its molecule and therefore capable of further reaction. **2** not saturated. [Say un SATCH a rate id]

unsavoury *adjective* (also **unsavory**) **1** morally offensive and objectionable; disagreeable, unpleasant: *a more unsavoury crew would have been hard to round up*. **2** (esp. of a taste or smell) foul, unpleasant: *gave off an unsavoury odour*.

unsayable *adjective* not able to be said, esp. because considered too controversial or offensive to mention.

unscathed *adjective* without suffering any injury: *despite the heavy snow, we all arrived at work unscathed* ◊ *her company emerged from the recession relatively unscathed*. [SCATHE rhymes with BATHE]

unschooled *adjective* **1** uneducated, untaught. **2** not sent to school. **3** untrained, undisciplined.

unscientific *adjective* **1** not in accordance with scientific principles. **2** not familiar with science. ▶ **unscientifically** *adverb*

unscramble *verb* (**unscrambles, unscrambled, unscrambling**) restore from a scrambled state, esp. interpret (a scrambled transmission etc.).

unscrew *verb* **1** unfasten or be unfastened by turning

or removing a screw or screws or by twisting like a screw. **2** loosen (a screw, lid, etc.).

unscrupulous *adjective* having no scruples, unprincipled. ▶ **unscrupulously** *adverb* [Say un SCREW pyoo lus]

unseasonable *adjective* (esp. of weather) not appropriate to the season: *the unseasonable spring frost killed most of my spring plants ◊ buried among the Christmas cards is the unseasonable notice notifying parents that it's time once again to sign up the kids for Little League baseball*. ▶ **unseasonably** *adverb*

unseasonal *adjective* not typical of, or appropriate to, the time or season.

unseasoned *adjective* **1** not flavoured with salt, herbs, etc. **2** (esp. of timber) not matured. **3** inexperienced.

unseat *verb* **1** remove from power or office, esp. in an election. **2** dislodge from a seat, esp. on horseback.

unseeing *adjective* **1** not seeing; not observant. **2** blind. ▶ **unseeingly** *adverb*

unseemly *adjective* (**unseemlier, unseemliest**) **1** indecent. **2** unbecoming.

unseen *adjective* **1** not seen. **2** invisible. **3** (of a passage for translation) not previously read or prepared.

unselfconscious *adjective* not worried about or aware of what other people think of what one's actions or opinions: *she found him sitting half-naked but unselfconscious in the leather chair*. ▶ **unselfconsciously** *adverb*

unserviceable *adjective* not serviceable; unfit for use.

unserviced *adjective* Cdn (esp. of a campsite) not serviced with electricity etc.

unsettle *verb* (**unsettles, unsettled, unsettling**) cause to feel anxious or uneasy; disturb: *Kafka has the ability to confuse, unsettle, and obsess his readers*.

unsettled *adjective* **1** worried or uneasy; disturbed: *Pete's indifference left her unsettled*. **2** lacking stability or calm; changing or liable to change: *his health was unsettled ◊ unsettled weather*. **3** unresolved: *an unsettled dispute*. **4** (of a region) having no settlers or inhabitants: *early days in the unsettled West*.

unsettling *adjective* causing a person to feel anxious or uneasy; disturbing: *the presentation left us with some rather unsettling questions*.

unsex *verb* (**unsexes, unsexed, unsexing**) **1** deprive (a person) of the qualities of her or his sex. **2** castrate or spay. ▶ **unsexed** *adjective*

unsexy *adjective* (**unsexier, unsexiest**) **1** not sexually attractive or stimulating. **2** unfashionable or unexciting.

unshakeable *adjective* (also **unshakable**) that cannot be shaken; firm.

unsheathe *verb* (**unsheathes, unsheathed, unsheathing**) remove (a knife etc.) from a sheath.

unsightly *adjective* unpleasant to look at, ugly.

unsigned *adjective* **1** not signed. **2** not having signed a contract.

unskilled *adjective* lacking or not needing special skill or training.

unsociable *adjective* not sociable, disliking the company of others. [Say un SO shuh bull]

unsocial *adjective* **1** not social; not suitable for, seeking, or conforming to society. **2** outside the normal working day: *unsocial hours*. **3** anti-social. ▶ **unsocially** *adverb*

unsolicited *adjective* not asked for. [Say un suh LISS it id]

unsophisticated *adjective* **1** not having or showing much experience of the world and social situations.

2 not complicated or refined; basic: *unsophisticated equipment*. [Say un suh FISTA kate id]

unsought *adjective* **1** not searched out or sought for. **2** not having been asked; without being requested. [Say un SOT]

unsound *adjective* **1** unhealthy, diseased. **2** rotten, weak, unsafe: *the building is structurally unsound*. **0 a** not based on sound evidence or reasoning and therefore unreliable or unacceptable. **b** unorthodox, heretical. PHRASES **of unsound mind** insane.

unsparing *adjective* **1** giving freely and generously. **2** severe; not caring about people's feelings.

unspeakable *adjective* **1** that cannot be expressed in words. **2** indescribably bad or objectionable. ▶ **unspeakably** *adverb*

unspecified *adjective* not specified.

unspoiled *adjective* (also esp. *Brit.* **unspoilt**) not ruined or spoiled, esp. (of a place) not marred by development.

unspoken *adjective* **1** understood without being expressed verbally. **2** not uttered as or expressed in speech.

unsportsmanlike *adjective* (of behaviour, an act, etc.) dishonourable, unseemly; unfair.

unsportsmanlike conduct *noun* a penalty imposed in various sports for unprofessional or unseemly conduct, e.g. pulling the hair of one's opponent.

unstable *adjective* **1** not stable. **2** changeable. **3** showing a tendency to sudden mental or emotional changes. **4** (of weather, an air mass, etc.) likely to produce precipitation.

unsteadily *adverb* in an awkward or unstable manner, as if one is about to fall: *Rory walked unsteadily out of the bar*.

unsteadiness *noun* **1** an unstable feeling, as if one is about to fall. **2** the condition of something that changes or may change.

unsteady *adjective* (**unsteadier, unsteadiest**) **1** not steady or firm. **2** changeable; not uniform or regular.

unstick *verb* (**unsticks, unstuck, unsticking**) separate (a thing stuck to another). PHRASES **come unstuck** *informal* come to grief, fail.

unstinting *adjective* lavish: *unstinting hospitality ◊ unstinting in her praise of the event*. ▶ **unstintingly** *adverb*

unstoppable *adjective* that cannot be stopped or prevented. ▶ **unstoppably** *adverb*

unstressed *adjective* **1** (of a word, syllable, etc.) not pronounced with stress. **2** not subjected to stress.

unstring *verb* (**unstrings, unstrung, unstringing**) **1** remove or relax the string or strings of (a bow, guitar, etc.). **2** remove from a string. **3** (esp. as **unstrung** *adjective*) unnerve.

unstructured *adjective* **1** not structured. **2** informal.

unsubstantiated *adjective* not substantiated: *the company has been accused of making unsubstantiated claims about its product*. [Say un sub STAN shee ate id]

unsuited *adjective* (usu. foll. by *for*, *to*) not suited (to); inappropriate; not fit (for).

unsung *adjective* **1** unrecognized, unknown. **2** not sung.

unsure *adjective* not sure.

unsurpassed *adjective* not surpassed.

unsuspecting *adjective* not suspecting.

unsustainable *adjective* not sustainable.

unswerving *adjective* **1** steady, constant. **2** not turning aside. ▶ **unswervingly** *adverb*

unsympathetic *adjective* not sympathetic. ▶ **unsympathetically** *adverb*

untainted *adjective* not tainted.

U

untangle *verb* (**untangles, untangled, untangling**) **1** free from a tangled state. **2** free from entanglement.

untapped *adjective* not (yet) tapped: *untapped resources*.

untaught *adjective* **1** not instructed by teaching; ignorant. **2** not acquired by teaching; natural.

untaxed *adjective* not required to pay or not attracting taxes.

untenable *adjective* (of an argument, position, etc.) not tenable; that cannot be defended. [Say un TEN a bull]

untended *adjective* not tended; neglected.

untestable *adjective* that cannot be tested or proved: *his theory was untestable and therefore useless*.

untested *adjective* not tested or proved.

unthinkable *adjective* **1** that cannot be imagined or grasped by the mind. **2** *informal* highly unlikely or undesirable.

unthinking *adjective* **1** not thinking. **2** characterized by thoughtlessness or absence of thought. ▶ **unthinkingly** *adverb*

untie *verb* (**unties, untied, untying**) **1** undo (a knot etc.). **2** unfasten the cords etc. of (a package etc.). **3** release from bonds or attachment.

until • *preposition* **1** up to or as late as: *wait until six o'clock* ◊ *did not return until night*. **2** up to the time of: *faithful until death*. • *conjunction* **1** up to the time when: *wait until I return*. **2** so long that: *laughed until I cried*.

untimeliness *noun* the nature of something that happens too soon or at an unsuitable time.

untimely *adjective* **1** (of an event or act) happening or done at an unsuitable or inconvenient time: *an untimely remark*. **2** (esp. of death) happening too soon or sooner than normal or expected.

unto *preposition archaic* to: *do unto others*.

untold *adjective* **1** not told. **2** not (able to be) counted or measured: *untold misery*.

untouchability *noun* **1** the condition of something that cannot be touched, harmed, or affected: *outrage over the two murders and the seeming untouchability of those who committed them*. **2** the condition of belonging to the lowest hereditary caste of Hindus, believed to defile members of higher castes on contact.

untouchable • *adjective* **1** that may not be harmed, criticized, disrupted, etc. **2** that cannot be matched or rivalled. • *noun* **1** a member of a hereditary Hindu group, believed to defile members of higher castes on contact. **2** an untouchable person or thing.

untouched *adjective* **1** not touched. **2** not affected physically; not harmed, modified, used, or tasted. **3** not affected by emotion. **4** not discussed.

untoward *adjective* **1** unseemly, improper, inappropriate: *there was something untoward about Fifi taking all the blame* ◊ *there was nothing untoward about the letters* ◊ *untoward behaviour*. **2** unexpected, inconvenient, or awkward: *exposure triggers an untoward event like an allergic reaction*.

untracked *adjective* **1** not marked with tracks from skis etc. **2** having no previously-trodden track; unexplored. **3** not traced or followed.

untrammelled *adjective* not impeded, hindered or constrained: *a strong sense of purpose untrammelled by conventional restraint*.

untranslatable *adjective* that cannot be translated (satisfactorily). ▶ **untranslated** *adjective*

untreated *adjective* not treated.

untried *adjective* **1** not tried or tested. **2** inexperienced. **3** not yet tried by a judge.

untrue *adjective* **1** not true, contrary to what is the fact. **2** (often foll. by *to*) not faithful or loyal.

untruth *noun* **1** the state of being untrue, falsehood. **2** a false statement: *told me an untruth*.

unturned *adjective* not turned over, around, away, etc.

PHRASES **leave no stone unturned** explore every possibility.

untutored *adjective* **1** uneducated, untaught. **2** simple, unsophisticated.

untying *pres. part. of* UNTIE.

unused *adjective* **1 a** not in use. **b** never having been used. **2** (foll. by *to*) not accustomed.

unusual *adjective* **1** not usual. **2** exceptional, remarkable, strange. ▶ **unusually** *adverb* **unusualness** *noun*

unutterable *adjective* inexpressible; beyond description. ▶ **unutterably** *adverb*

unvarnished *adjective* **1** not varnished. **2** (of a statement or person) plain and straightforward: *the unvarnished truth*.

unvarying *adjective* not varying.

unveil *verb* **1** remove a veil from. **2** remove a covering from (a statue, plaque, etc.) as part of the ceremony of the first public display. **3** disclose, reveal, make publicly known. ▶ **unveiling** *noun*

unvoiced *adjective* **1** not spoken or expressed. **2** *Phonetics* (of a vocal sound) uttered without vibration of the vocal cords.

SPELL CHECK
unwanted, unwonted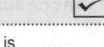

Something that is not usual or expected is **unwonted**: *She spoke with unwonted enthusiasm*.

---

unwanted *adjective* not or no longer desired: *a safe and easy way to remove unwanted hair*.

unwarranted *adjective* **1** unauthorized. **2** not justified.

unwary *adjective* **1** not cautious. **2** (often foll. by *of*) not aware of possible danger etc. [Say un WARE ee]

unwashed *adjective* **1** not washed. **2** not usually washed or clean. *See also* GREAT UNWASHED.

unwavering *adjective* not wavering. ▶ **unwaveringly** *adverb*

unwelcome *adjective* not welcome or acceptable; displeasing.

unwell *adjective* not in good health; (somewhat) ill.

unwholesome *adjective* **1** not promoting, or detrimental to, physical or moral health; unhealthy. **2** unhealthy-looking.

unwieldy *adjective* (**unwieldier, unwieldiest**) cumbersome, clumsy, or hard to manage, owing to size, shape, weight, etc.: *procedures to streamline the organization's unwieldy bureaucracy* ◊ *long and unwieldy e-mail addresses*. [Say un WHEEL dee]

unwilling *adjective* not willing or inclined; reluctant. ▶ **unwillingly** *adverb* **unwillingness** *noun*

unwind *verb* (**unwinds, unwound, unwinding**) **1 a** draw out (a thing that has been wound). **b** become drawn out after having been wound. **2** *informal* relax.

unwise *adjective* (of a person or action) not wise or sensible; foolish: *unwise policies* ◊ *thought it was unwise for their mother to continue living alone*. ▶ **unwisely** *adverb*

unwitting *adjective* **1 a** not aware of being or intending to be the thing described: *an unwitting contributor to her tragic fate*. **b** unaware: *the house's unwitting inhabitants*. **2** not done on purpose; unintentional, inadvertent: *unwitting sins*. ▶ **unwittingly** *adverb*

unwonted *adjective* not customary or usual: *"a great cynic is a great fool," she said, with unwonted severity*. [Sounds like UNWANTED]

unworkable *adjective* not workable; impracticable.

unworldly *adjective* **1** spiritually-minded. **2** spiritual.

unworthiness *noun* the condition of a person or

thing that lacks value and does not deserve attention or respect.

unworthy *adjective* (**unworthier, unworthiest**) **1** (often foll. by *of*) not worthy or befitting the character of a person etc.: *conduct unworthy of a judge*. **2** having or possessing insufficient merit, excellence, or worth: *have proven themselves unworthy members of their university*.

unwound[1] *adjective* not wound or wound up.

unwound[2] *past and past participle of* UNWIND.

unwrap *verb* (**unwraps, unwrapped, unwrapping**) **1** remove the wrapping from. **2** open or unfold. **3** unfold, reveal, disclose. **4** become unwrapped.

unwritten *adjective* **1** not written. **2** (of a law etc.) resting originally on custom or judicial decision, not on statute. **3** (of a convention etc.) not expressed in words, implicit.

unyielding *adjective* **1** not yielding to pressure etc. **2** firm, obstinate.

unzip *verb* (**unzips, unzipped, unzipping**) **1** unfasten the zipper of. **2** unfasten a zipper (esp. in undressing). **3** *Computing* decompress (a compressed file).

up • *adverb* **1** at, in, or towards a higher place or position: *jumped up in the air* ◊ *what are they doing up there?* **2** to or in a place regarded as higher, esp. northwards: *up in Yellowknife*. **3** *informal* ahead etc. as indicated: *went up front*. **4 a** to or in an erect position or condition: *stood it up*. **b** to or in a prepared or required position: *wound up the watch*. **c** in or into a condition of efficiency, activity, or progress: *stirred up trouble* ◊ *the house is up for sale*. **5** in a stronger or winning position or condition: *up three goals* ◊ *am $10 up*. **6** (of a computer) running and available for use. **7** to the place or time in question or where the speaker etc. is: *a child came up to me* ◊ *has been fine up till now*. **8** at or to a higher price or value: *costs are up*. **9 a** completely: *eat up* ◊ *use up*. **b** more loudly or clearly: *speak up*. **10** in a state of completion; denoting the end of availability, supply, etc.: *time is up*. **11** into a compact, accumulated, or secure state: *pack up* ◊ *save up*. **12** out of bed: *are you up yet?* **13** (of the sun etc.) having risen. **14** happening, esp. unusually or unexpectedly: *something is up*. **15 a** *Baseball* at bat. **b** next in line or in order of business. **16** taught or informed: *is well up in French*. **17** (usu. foll. by *before*) appearing for trial etc.: *was up before the parole board*. **19** (of a jockey) in the saddle. **20** towards the source of a river. **21** inland. **22** (of the points etc. in a game): **a** registered on the scoreboard. **b** forming the final score for the time being. **23** upstairs, esp. to bed: *are you going up yet?* **24** (of a theatre curtain) raised etc. to reveal the stage. **25** (as *interjection*) get up. • *preposition* **1** upward along, through, or into. **2** from the bottom to the top of. **3** along: *walked up the road*. **4 a** at or in a higher part of: *is situated up the street*. **b** towards the source of (a river). • *adjective* directed upward. • *noun* a period of good fortune: *we've had our ups and downs*. • *verb* (**ups, upped, upping**) **1** *informal* begin abruptly to say or do something: *upped and hit him*. **2** increase or raise, esp. abruptly: *upped all their prices*. **PHRASES** **be all up with** (with *it* as subject) be disastrous or hopeless for (a person). **on the up and up** *informal* honest(ly); on the level. **something is up** *informal* something unusual or undesirable is afoot or happening. **up against 1** in or into contact with. **2** *informal* confronted with: *up against a problem*. **up against it** *informal* in great difficulties. **up and around** (or **about, doing**) having risen from bed; active. **up close** very close(ly). **up and down 1** back and forth (along): *have been up and down the road four times*. **2** in every direction. **3** *informal* in varying health or spirits. **up for** available for or being considered for (office etc.). **up hill and down dale** up and down hills,

or confronting many obstacles, on an arduous journey or in the fulfillment of an arduous task. **up on** informed about (a matter or subject). **up to 1** until: *up to the present*. **2** not more than: *you can have up to five*. **3** less than or equal to: *sums up to $100*. **4 a** incumbent on: *it is up to you to tell them*. **b** to be decided by: *I'll leave it up to you*. **5** capable of or fit for: *am not up to a long walk*. **6** occupied or busy with: *what have you been up to?* **up with** *interjection* expressing support for a stated person or thing. **what's up?** *informal* **1** what is going on? **2** what is the matter?

upalong *Cdn* (*Nfld*) • *adverb* to or on a location away from a person or place, esp. to or on mainland Canada. • *noun* such a location: *from upalong*.

up-and-comer *noun* a person who is making good progress in a new job or activity and is likely to become successful.

up-and-coming *adjective* *informal* (of a person, esp. one beginning a new job or activity) making good progress and likely to succeed.

up and running *adjective & adverb* functioning; in operation.

upbeat • *noun* an unaccented beat in music. • *adjective* *informal* optimistic or cheerful.

upbraid *verb* (often foll. by *with*, *for*) chide or reproach (a person): *upbraided him for arriving late at their wedding*.

upbringing *noun* **1** the bringing up of a child; education. **2** the manner of this.

UPC *noun* (*plural* **UPCs**) UNIVERSAL PRODUCT CODE.

upchuck *verb & noun* *slang* vomit.

up-close-and-personal *adjective* *informal* intimate, cozy.

upcoming *adjective* forthcoming; about to happen.

upcountry *adverb & adjective* inland.

update • *verb* (**updates, updated, updating**) **1** make more modern or up-to-date, esp. by replacing old material, methods, etc. or including new material. **2** provide (a person) with the latest information about something. • *noun* **1** an act of bringing someone or something up to date: *Dave asked for an update on the investigation*. **2** an updated version; a set of updated information. ▶ **updated** *adjective*

updraft *noun* (also **updraught**) an upward draft.

upend *verb* **1** set or become upside down or so that one end is at the top. **2** knock over; cause to fall down. **3** (of a duck etc.) dip the head below water and raise the tail into the air, when feeding in shallow water. **4** *Sport* defeat.

upfront *informal* • *adverb* (usu. **up front**) **1** at the front; in front: *sitting up front helped Shari see the movie better*. **2** (of payments) in advance: *we paid the clown up front, before the party*. • *adjective* **1** honest, open, frank: *Oliver is upfront about his problems*. **2** (of payments) made or required in advance: *an upfront cash outlay for the franchise*. **3** at the front or most prominent: *an attractive cooktop with upfront controls*.

upgrade • *verb* (**upgrades, upgraded, upgrading**) **1** raise in rank etc. **2** improve (equipment etc.) esp. by replacing components. **3** replace (components of) one's equipment, software, etc. with improved versions. **4** move to a higher category in a hierarchy; choose something of better quality than the standard offered: *upgraded to business class*. • *noun* **1** an act of upgrading something. **2** an upgraded piece of equipment etc. ▶ **upgradeable** *adjective* **upgrader** *noun*

upheaval *noun* **1** a violent or sudden change or disruption. **2** *Geology* an upward displacement of part of the earth's crust.

uphill • *adverb* in an ascending direction up a hill, slope, etc. • *adjective* **1** sloping up. **2** arduous, difficult: *an uphill struggle*. • *noun* an upward slope.

uphold *verb* (**upholds**, **upheld**, **upholding**) **1** confirm or maintain (a decision etc., esp. of another). **2** give support or approval to (a person, practice, etc.). **3** maintain unimpaired and intact. ▶ **upholder** *noun*

upholster *verb* provide (furniture) with upholstery. ▶ **upholsterer** *noun* [Say up HOLE stir]

upholstery *noun* **1** textile covering, padding, springs, etc., for furniture. **2** an upholsterer's work. [Say up HOLE stir ee]

U-pick • *adjective* designating an orchard or farm where customers pick produce directly from the fields etc. • *noun* such a farm or orchard.

up-island *adverb* & *adjective* *Cdn* towards or of the northern or more remote parts of Vancouver Island.

upkeep *noun* **1** maintenance in good condition. **2** the cost or means of this.

upland • *noun* high or hilly country. • *adjective* of or relating to this.

uplift • *verb* **1** raise; lift up. **2** elevate or stimulate morally or spiritually. • *noun* **1** an act of raising something: *increased consumer spending provided the economy with a significant uplift.* **2** the raising of part of the earth's surface: *the landscape will change as erosion and tectonic uplift occur.* **3** *informal* a morally or spiritually elevating influence: *reading was meant to provide moral uplift.* **4** support for the bust etc. from a garment: *an uplift bra.* ▶ **uplifting** *adjective* (esp. in sense 2 of v.).

uplink • *noun* a communications link to a satellite. • *verb* (esp. as **uplinked** *adjective*) provide with or send by an uplink.

upload *Computing* • *verb* transfer (data) to a larger storage device or to a central system. • *noun* (usu. as an *adjective*) a transfer of this type: *upload feature.*

upmarket *adjective* & *adverb* = UPSCALE.

upon *preposition* = ON.

upper • *adjective* **1** situated above another part: *the upper atmosphere ◊ the upper lip.* **2** higher in position or status: *the upper class.* **3** (**Upper**) **a** situated on higher ground: *Upper Egypt.* **b** situated to the north: *Upper California.* **4** (often **Upper**) *Geology* & *Archaeology* designating a younger, and hence usu. shallower, stratum or layer of rock, archaeological deposit, etc., or the period in which it was formed or deposited. • *noun* **1** the part of a boot or shoe above the sole. **2** *slang* a stimulant drug, esp. an amphetamine.

Upper Canadian *Cdn* • *noun* **1** *hist.* a native or inhabitant of the former British colony of Upper Canada (1791–1841), now the southern part of Ontario. **2** esp. *Maritimes* a native or inhabitant of Ontario. • *adjective* **1** *hist.* of or relating to the colony of Upper Canada. **2** esp. *Maritimes* of or relating to Ontario.

upper case • *adjective* designating the larger characters used in printing and writing, often differing in shape and size from the minuscule forms. • *noun* an upper case letter.

upper class • *noun* (*plural* **upper classes**) the highest class of society. • *adjective* (**upper-class**) of the upper class.

upper crust *noun* *informal* the upper class.

uppercut • *noun* an upward blow delivered with the arm bent. • *verb* (**uppercuts**, **uppercut**, **uppercutting**) hit with an uppercut.

upper hand *noun* dominance or control; an advantage.

upper house *noun* (also **upper chamber**) the usu. smaller body in a bicameral legislature, often representing regional or sectional interests, esp. (in Canada) the Senate.

upper middle class • *noun* the class of society between the middle and upper classes. • *adjective* (**upper-middle-class**) of the upper middle class.

uppermost • *adjective* **1** highest in place or rank. **2** predominant. • *adverb* at or to the highest or most prominent position.

uppitiness *noun* *informal* the manner or behaviour of someone who is arrogant, snobbish, and rude.

uppity *adjective* *informal* arrogant, snobbish, rude.

uppityness *noun* = UPPITINESS.

upraise *verb* (**upraises**, **upraised**, **upraising**) (esp. as **upraised** *adjective*) raise to a higher level.

upright • *adjective* **1** erect, vertical: *an upright posture ◊ stood upright.* **2** (of a piano) with vertical strings. **3** (of a person or behaviour) righteous; strictly honourable or honest. • *noun* **1** a post or rod fixed upright esp. as a structural support. **2** (usu. in *plural*) a goalpost, esp. in football. **3** an upright piano. • *verb* raise or restore to an upright or vertical position.

uprising *noun* **1** a rebellion or revolt. **2** the action or an act of rising or uprising.

upriver • *adverb* at or towards a point nearer the source of a river. • *adjective* situated or occurring upriver.

uproar *noun* a loud and noisy disturbance, esp. as an expression of protest or anger.

uproarious *adjective* **1** very noisy. **2** provoking loud laughter. ▶ **uproariously** *adverb* [Say up ROAR ee us]

uproot *verb* **1** pull (a plant etc.) up from the ground. **2** displace (a person) from an accustomed location. **3** destroy. **4** move away from one's accustomed location or home.

upsadaisy *interjection* = UPSY-DAISY.

upscale *adjective* & *adverb* toward or relating to the more expensive or affluent sector of the market.

upset • *verb* (**upsets**, **upset**, **upsetting**) **1** overturn or be overturned. **2** disturb the composure of: *was very upset by the news.* **3** disturb (the digestion): *may upset the stomach.* **4** disrupt: *upset all their plans.* **5** defeat (a favoured opponent). • *noun* **1** a condition of upsetting or being upset: *a stomach upset.* **2** a surprising victory over a favoured opponent. • *adjective* **1** disturbed, esp. temporarily: *an upset stomach.* **2** distressed, esp. emotionally. ▶ **upsetting** *adjective*

upshot *noun* (usu. as **the upshot**) the final or eventual outcome or conclusion.

upside • *noun* **1** the upper side or surface of something. **2** *informal* the positive aspect of something; an advantage. **3** an upward movement of share prices etc. • *preposition* *slang* on or against: *slapped him upside the head.*

upside down • *adverb* **1** with the upper part where the lower part should be; in an inverted position. **2** in or into total disorder: *everything was turned upside down.* • *adjective* that is positioned upside down; inverted.

upstage • *adjective* & *adverb* nearer the back of a theatre stage. • *verb* (**upstages**, **upstaged**, **upstaging**) **1** (of an actor) move upstage to make (another actor) face away from the audience. **2** divert attention from (a person) to oneself.

upstairs • *adverb* **1** to or on an upper floor. **2** to or in a more influential position or higher authority. **3** *informal* mentally, in the head: *doesn't have much upstairs.* • *adjective* situated upstairs. • *noun* an upper floor.

upstanding *adjective* **1** standing up. **2** honest or straightforward.

upstart • *noun* a person who has risen suddenly to prominence, esp. one who behaves arrogantly. • *adjective* **1** that is an upstart. **2** of or like an upstart.

upstate *US* • *noun* part of a state remote from its large cities, esp. the northern part of New York State. • *adjective* of or relating to this part. • *adverb* in or to this part.

upstream • *adverb* against the flow of a stream etc. • *adjective* moving upstream.

upsurge *noun* **1** an upward surge; a rise (as in feelings etc.). **2** a rapid growth in number or size.

upswept *adjective* **1** (of the hair) combed to the top of the head. **2** curved or sloped upward.

upswing *noun* an upward movement or trend.

upsy-daisy *interjection* expressing encouragement to a child who is being lifted or has fallen.

uptake *noun* **1** *informal* understanding; comprehension: *slow on the uptake*. **2** absorption or incorporation of something by a living system: *oxygen uptake*.

uptempo *adjective & adverb* at a fast or an increased tempo.

uptick *noun* an increase, esp. a small one.

uptight *adjective* *informal* **1** nervously tense or angry. **2** rigidly conventional.

SPELL CHECK
up-to-date, up to date

Note the difference in spelling between *up-to-date technology* and *the technology is up to date*. There is no hyphen when the latter kind of structure is used.

---

up-to-date *adjective* meeting, according to, or familiar with the latest requirements, knowledge, or fashion: *claims to provide the most up-to-date information*.

up-to-the-minute *adjective* latest; most modern.

uptown • *adjective* of or in the esp. more affluent part of a city between downtown and the outer suburbs. • *adverb* in or into this part. • *noun* this part.

upturn • *noun* **1** an upward trend; an improvement. **2** an upheaval. • *verb* turn up or upside down.

upward • *adverb* (also **upwards**) towards what is higher, superior, larger in amount, more important, or earlier. • *adjective* moving, extending, pointing, or leading upward. **PHRASES** **upwards of** more than: *found upwards of forty*. ▶ **upwardly** *adverb*

upwardly mobile *adjective* able or aspiring to advance socially or professionally. ▶ **upward mobility** *noun*

upwelling *noun* **1** a welling upward, esp. the rising of cold water from the bottom of the sea, often bringing with it a renewed source of nutrients. **2** the water that has risen in this way.

upwind *adjective & adverb* against the direction of the wind.

uranium *noun* a heavy radioactive metallic element occurring naturally in pitchblende and other ores, which is capable of nuclear fission and used as a source of nuclear energy. [Say yoor AINY um]

urban *adjective* of, living in, or situated in a town or city: *an urban population* (opp. RURAL).

urbane *adjective* elegant and refined in manner and style; courteous, sophisticated: *an urbane and charming gentleman* ◊ *the building exhibited an urbane elegance*. [Say er BANE]

urbanism *noun* **1** the development of an urban community; urbanization. **2** the character or way of life of a city. **3** a study of the development or way of life of a city. ▶ **urbanist** *noun* (in sense 3)

urbanite *noun* a resident of a city.

urbanity *noun* (*plural* **urbanities**) **1** suavity, courteousness, and refinement of manner: *speaks English with an urbanity of accent that makes the premiers of other provinces sound like clodhoppers*. **2** the state, condition, or character of a city; urban life: *yet all this variety, density, and urbanity has been achieved without New Jersey's having even one major city*.

urbanization *noun* the process of making a rural area more like a city.

urbanize *verb* (**urbanizes, urbanized, urbanizing**) make a mainly rural area more like a city.

urban myth *noun* (also **urban legend**) a story, not verifiable and usu. untrue, widely recounted as if true, which typically depicts outlandish or sensational happenings in a plausible contemporary setting.

urban planner *noun* a person who plans the construction, growth, and development of urban communities as a profession. ▶ **urban planning** *noun*

urban renewal *noun* the process of rejuvenating derelict or dilapidated districts of a city through demolition of slums and redevelopment.

urban sprawl *noun* the uncontrolled expansion of urban areas.

urchin *noun* **1** a poor, dirty, and ill-clothed child, esp. in an urban area. **2** = SEA URCHIN.

Urdu *noun* a language closely related to Hindi with an admixture of Persian and Arabic words, now the official language of Pakistan and also used in India. [Say ER doo]

urea *noun* a waste product of mammals formed during the metabolic breakdown of nitrogen compounds in the liver and excreted in urine; the purified form of this, a white soluble crystalline solid, is used esp. in fertilizers and de-icing agents and in the manufacture of synthetic resins. [Say yoo REE uh]

urea formaldehyde *noun* a plastic, resin, or foam made by condensation of urea with formaldehyde, used esp. for insulation. [Say yoo REE uh for MALDA hide]

urethane • *noun* **1** a synthetic resin used esp. as an ingredient in paints, varnishes, adhesives, and foams. **2** a paint or varnish etc. containing this resin. • *verb* (**urethanes, urethaned, urethaning**) cover a surface with a paint or varnish containing urethane. [Say YOORA thane]

urethra *noun* the tube or canal through which urine is carried out of the body from the bladder, and which in the male also conveys semen. ▶ **urethral** *adjective* [Say yoo REETH ruh, yoo REETH rull]

urge • *verb* (**urges, urged, urging**) **1** (often foll. by *on*) drive, hasten, or impel with force or encouragement: *she urged her teammates on*. **2** encourage or entreat earnestly or persistently: *urged them to go*. **3** advocate or recommend eagerly or insistently: *we urge caution* ◊ *we urge that they should be cautious*. • *noun* a strong impulse, desire, or tendency.

urgency *noun* (*plural* **urgencies**) **1** the state, condition, or fact of being urgent. **2** a pressing or urgent need.

urgent *adjective* **1** demanding or requiring immediate action or attention; pressing: *an urgent need for help*. **2** expressing a need for prompt action or attention; insistent: *an urgent call for help*. ▶ **urgently** *adverb*

urging *noun* an attempt to encourage or persuade someone to do something: *he moved here at the urging of his friends*.

uric acid *noun* an almost insoluble crystalline acid, formed as a waste product during the metabolic breakdown of food and body protein; it is the main excretory product in birds, reptiles, and insects. [Say YOOR ick]

urinal *noun* **1** a ceramic plumbing fixture for men to urinate into, usu. equipped with a flushing mechanism. **2** any receptacle for urination, such as a chamber pot.

urinalysis *noun* (*plural* **urinalyses**) the analysis of urine to test for the presence of disease or drugs etc. [Say urine ALA sis for the singular, urine ALA seez for the plural]

urinary *adjective* **1** of or relating to urine. **2** affecting or occurring in the urinary system: *urinary diseases*.

U

urinate *verb* (**urinates**, **urinated**, **urinating**) discharge urine. ▶ **urination** *noun*

urine *noun* the pale yellow fluid containing waste products filtered from the blood by the kidneys, stored in the bladder, and discharged at intervals through the urethra.

URL *noun* Computing the address used to specify the location of a Web site on the Internet.

urn *noun* **1** a large decorative vase or container with a rounded usu. egg-shaped body and a pedestal. **2** any usu. ornamental vessel, vase, or container used to store or bury the ashes of the cremated dead. **3** a large metal container with a tap, in which coffee or tea is made and kept hot.

urologist *noun* a doctor who studies and treats disorders of the kidney and urinary tract. [Say yoor OLLA jist]

urology *noun* the branch of medicine that deals with disorders of the kidney and urinary tract. [Say yoor OLLA jee]

Ursuline • *noun* a nun of an Augustinian order founded in 1535 for nursing the sick and teaching girls. • *adjective* of this order. [Say URSE yoo lin or URSE yoo line]

Uruguayan • *noun* a native or inhabitant of Uruguay, a country on the Atlantic coast of South America. • *adjective* of or relating to Uruguay or its people or culture. [Say yoora GWAY un]

US *abbreviation* **1** United States. **2** Undersecretary. **3** unserviceable.

> **GRAMMAR CHECK**
> **us, we**
>
> The use of **us** instead of **we** after the verb "to be", as in *It's us again*, is now considered acceptable in writing as well as speech. In sentences like *It is we who know you best*, however, **we** must be used instead of **us**. To avoid sounding excessively formal, such a sentence could be reworded *We're the ones who know you best*, which is much more natural. *See also usage note at* THAN.

us *pronoun* **1** *objective case of* WE: *they saw us*. **2** *informal* = WE: *it's us again*. **3** *informal* ourselves, to or for ourselves: *we've got to get us one of those!* **4** *informal* = ME[1]: *give us a kiss*.

USA *abbreviation* **1** United States of America. **2** United States Army.

usability *noun* the quality of something that is able to be used easily.

usable *adjective* (also **useable**) that can be used.

USAF *abbreviation* United States Air Force.

usage *noun* **1** the action or an instance of using something or of being used: *a survey of water usage*. **2 a** habitual or customary practice, esp. as creating a right, obligation, or standard. **b** established or customary use of words, expressions, constructions, etc. in a language, esp. as opposed to what is prescribed. **3** a manner of using or treating; treatment: *damaged by rough usage*.

use • *verb* (**uses**, **used**, **using**) **1 a** employ (something) for a particular purpose: *can I use the phone?* ◊ *use your discretion*. **b** employ or avail oneself of (something) regularly: *uses the subway to get to work*. **2 a** (in *past*) did, was, or had in the past as a customary practice or continuous state: *I used to be a dancer* ◊ *it didn't use to rain so often*. **b** (usu. in *passive*) familiar by habit; accustomed: *not used to hard work*. **3** exploit (a person or thing) for one's own ends: *he's just using you to make his girlfriend jealous*. **4** treat (a person) in a specified manner: *they used him shamefully*. **5** take (drugs, alcohol, etc.) regularly. • *noun* **1** the act of using or the state of being used; application to a purpose: the

use of force. **2** the manner or mode of using, employing, or utilizing something: *she put it to good use*. **3** the right or power of using: *lost the use of my right arm*. **4** advantage, value, usefulness: *a flashlight would be of some use right now*. **5** need or occasion for employing something; necessity, demand, call: *would you have any use for this radio?* **6** habitual, usual, or common practice: *long use has accustomed me to it*. PHRASES **could use** *informal* **1** would like to have; want. **2** would be in a position to benefit from; need. **have no use for 1** do not need. **2** dislike or be impatient with. **It's (or there's) no use** it would be pointless to; it will not help to: *there's no use trying to talk to her when she's like this*. **make use of 1** employ, apply. **2** benefit from. **use it or lose it 1** an opportunity etc., if not taken advantage of, may not be made available again. **2** something, e.g. a skill, may become lost or unusable through neglect. **use a person's name** quote a person as an authority or reference etc. **use up 1** consume completely, use all of. **2** find a use for (something remaining). **3** exhaust or wear out e.g. with overwork.

used *adjective* having been previously owned; second-hand.

useful *adjective* **1** that can be used for a practical purpose; beneficial. **2** of use or value to someone: *he's useful around the house*. **3** *informal* reasonably effective or successful: *their most useful player*. PHRASES **make oneself useful** be helpful. ▶ **usefully** *adverb* **usefulness** *noun*

useless *adjective* **1** failing to fulfill the intended purpose or produce the desired results: *this knife is useless*. **2** serving no purpose: *useless information*. **3** *informal* incompetent, ineffectual: *I'm useless at swimming*. ▶ **uselessly** *adverb* **uselessness** *noun*

Usenet *noun* any of a number of services designed to help users access information on a network, usu. consisting of an index of newsgroups arranged according to subject matter. [Say YOOZ net]

user *noun* **1** a person who uses or operates something, esp. a computer. **2** *informal* a drug addict. **3** a person who manipulates others for personal advantage.

user-defined *adjective* Computing that has been specified or varied by a user.

user fee *noun* a fee charged for a service, esp. an additional amount of money or tax charged for a service that is paid for or subsidized by the government.

user-friendliness *noun* the quality of something that is easy to use or understand.

user-friendly *adjective* **1** (of a system, program, software, etc.) designed to make the user's task as easy as possible, esp. by offering onscreen instructions, prompts, and feedback. **2** *informal* or *jocular* easy to read, use, or understand.

user group *noun* Computing a newsgroup exchanging technical information, advice, and services.

user interface *noun* Computing the means of communication between a user and a system, referring esp. to the use of input/output devices with supporting software (compare GRAPHICAL USER INTERFACE).

usher • *noun* **1** a person who shows people to their seats in a theatre, stadium, church, etc. **2** an attendant of the groom at a wedding, responsible for greeting guests at the church and showing them to their seats. • *verb* **1** (usu. foll. by *into*) show or guide (a person) into a room, to a seat, etc.: *ushered us into the room*. **2** (foll. by *in*) be the forerunner of (an era, age, movement, etc.). **3** act as usher to.

usherette *noun* a woman who shows people to their seats, esp. in a theatre or stadium etc.

Usher of the Black Rod *noun* *Cdn* = BLACK ROD 1.

USS *abbreviation* United States Ship.

USSR *abbreviation* *hist.* Union of Soviet Socialist Republics.

usu. *abbreviation* usually.

usual • *adjective* such as commonly occurs, or is observed or done; customary, habitual, regular. • *noun informal* **1 (the usual)** what is commonly said or done etc.; what is customary or habitual: *"What did you talk about?" "Oh, the usual."* **2** (preceded by *the*, *my*, etc.) the drink or meal a person habitually orders in a bar or restaurant. PHRASES **as usual** as is or was commonly the case: *they were late, as usual.* **than usual** than is or was customary or habitual: *I ate less than usual today.*

usually *adverb* **1** as a rule; generally speaking; normally. **2** in a usual or customary manner.

usurer *noun* a person who practises usury. [Say YOO zer er or YOO zher er]

usurious *adjective* **1** of, involving, or practising usury. **2** (of interest) taken or charged by usury; exorbitant, excessive. ▶ **usuriously** *adverb* [Say yoo ZUR ee us or yoo ZHUR ee us]

usurp *verb* **1** seize or assume (another's position or authority) by force. **2** take possession of (land etc.) unlawfully. ▶ **usurpation** *noun* **usurper** *noun* [Say yoo SURP or yoo ZURP, yoo sur PAY sh'n or yoo zur PAY sh'n]

usury *noun* **1** the act or practice of lending money at interest, esp. at an exorbitant, excessive, or illegal rate. **2** interest on money lent at such a rate. [Say YOO zur ee or YOO zhur ee]

utensil *noun* a tool or implement for domestic use, esp. any of those objects found in a kitchen and used for eating or preparing food: *cooking utensils.*

uterine *adjective* having to do with the uterus or womb. [Say YOO tur in]

uterus *noun* (*plural* **uteruses** or **uteri**) the womb. [Say YOO tur us for the singular, YOO tur eye for the plural]

utilidor *noun* *Cdn* (*North*) an enclosed insulated conduit running above ground and carrying water, sewerage, and electricity between houses in settlements built on permafrost. [Say yoo TILLA dore]

utilitarian • *adjective* **1** designed to be practically useful rather than attractive; functional. **2** of or pertaining to the doctrine of utilitarianism. • *noun* a person who believes that the guiding principle of conduct should be to achieve the greatest benefit or happiness for the greatest number of people. [Say yoo tilla TERRY un]

utilitarianism *noun* the doctrine that an action is right in so far as it promotes happiness, and that the guiding principle of conduct should be to achieve the greatest benefit or happiness for the greatest number of people. [Say yoo tilla TERRY un ism]

utility • *noun* (*plural* **utilities**) **1** the condition or quality of being useful or beneficial: *a small story to illustrate the utility of dry, academic knowledge about science.* **2 a** (often in *plural*) = PUBLIC UTILITY. **b** (in *plural*) shares in a public utility. **c** (in *plural*) electricity, natural gas, etc. as provided by a public utility. **3** *Computing* (also **utility program**) a program for carrying out a routine function. • *adjective* **1** designating things made for utility; useful, functional rather than attractive: *utility furniture.* **2** *Baseball* designating a substitute player, esp. an infielder, who is capable of playing several different positions. **3** designating the lowest grade of domestic meat, e.g. of a chicken that is missing a part.

utilization *noun* the action of making practical and effective use of something.

utilize *verb* (**utilizes**, **utilized**, **utilizing**) make practical and effective use of something.

utmost 1 greatest in amount or degree; most extreme, ultimate: *of the utmost importance.* **2** furthest, most remote; outermost: *the utmost limits.* • *noun* (**the utmost**) **1** that which is greatest in degree, amount, or extent: *these shoes offer the utmost in durability.* **2** the extreme limit, the ultimate degree: *my patience was tested to the utmost.* **3** the greatest or best of one's ability or power: *we performed to our utmost.* PHRASES **do one's utmost** do all that one can.

utopia *noun* (*plural* **utopias**) **1** an imaginary or hypothetical place or state of things considered to be perfect; a condition of social or political perfection: *the utopia envisioned in their literature was a material world where all would live prosperous, contented, and comfortable lives* ◊ *the Canadian West was the utopia for which people had searched for centuries.* **2** an impossibly ideal scheme, esp. for social or political improvement, or a literary work based on this: *has written several utopias.* [Say yoo TOPE ee uh]

utopian • *adjective* **1** of, pertaining to, or characteristic of an ideal society or utopia: *utopian communities.* **2** impossibly ideal or perfect; idealistic: *utopian hopes for the possibilities of virtual reality* ◊ *his proposal for a four-hour workday seems hopelessly utopian now.* • *noun* an idealistic reformer. ▶ **utopianism** *noun* [Say yoo TOPE ee un]

utter[1] *adjective* complete, total: *utter misery* ◊ *an utter fool.*

utter[2] *verb* **1** emit audibly: *uttered a startled cry.* **2** speak or say (words, a phrase, a prayer, etc.). **3** *Law* issue or circulate (a forged document, counterfeit money or cheques, etc.).

utterance *noun* **1** the action of saying or expressing something aloud: *the simple utterance of a few platitudes.* **2** a spoken word, statement, or vocal sound: *meaningless utterances.*

utterly *adverb* completely, absolutely: *he looked utterly ridiculous.*

uttermost *adjective & noun* = UTMOST.

U-turn • *noun* **1** an act of driving a vehicle in a U-shaped course in order to turn around and travel in the opposite direction. **2** a reversal of policy. • *verb* perform a U-turn.

UV *abbreviation* **1** ultraviolet. **2** ultraviolet radiation: *UV protection.*

UVA *abbreviation* ultraviolet radiation of relatively long wavelengths.

UVB *abbreviation* ultraviolet radiation of relatively short wavelengths.

UVC *abbreviation* ultraviolet radiation of very short wavelengths, which does not penetrate the earth's ozone layer.

UV Index *noun* an index used to represent the intensity of the sun's ultraviolet rays, ranging from "low" (less than 4) to "extreme" (more than 9).

uvula *noun* (*plural* **uvulae**) a fleshy extension of the soft

U

palate hanging above the throat. [Say YOO view luh or UV yoo luh for the singular, YOO view lee for the plural]

Uzbek *noun* **1** a member of a Turkic people living mainly in Uzbekistan, an independent republic in central Asia. **2** the language of this people. [Say OOZ beck (with OO as in *FOOT*)]

Uzi *noun* a type of submachine gun. [Sounds like *OOZY*]

Vv

V¹ *noun* (also **v**) (*plural* **Vs** or **V's**) **1** the twenty-second letter of the alphabet. **2** a V-shaped thing. **3** (as a Roman numeral) five.

V² *symbol* **1** vanadium. **2 a** volt(s). **b** voltage, potential difference. **3** volume.

v. *abbreviation* **1** verse. **2** verso. **3** versus. **4** very.

V6 *noun* (*plural* **V6's**) **1** an engine with six cylinders forming a V shape. **2** a vehicle with such an engine.

V8 *noun* (*plural* **V8's**) **1** an engine with eight cylinders forming a V shape. **2** a vehicle with such an engine.

Va. *abbreviation* Virginia.

vac *noun informal* a vacuum cleaner.

vacancy *noun* (*plural* **vacancies**) **1** the state of being vacant or empty. **2** an available room in a hotel, apartment building, etc. **3** an unoccupied position; a job opening. **4** emptiness of mind; lack of intelligence. [Say VAY kun see]

vacant *adjective* **1** containing no objects; empty. **2** (of land, a building, etc.) uninhabited: *a vacant lot*. **3** (of a place, room, etc.) unoccupied; not in use: *a vacant seat*. **4** (of a post or position) available. **5** characterized by or exhibiting a lack of attention or thought: *a vacant stare*. ▶ **vacantly** *adverb* [Say VAY k'nt]

vacate *verb* (**vacates**, **vacated**, **vacating**) **1** leave or cease to occupy (a place). **2** give up tenure of (a post etc.). [Say VAY kate or vuh KATE]

vacation • *noun* **1** a period of several days or weeks spent away from work or school etc., used esp. for recreation and travel; a holiday. **2** the act of vacating a house or position etc. • *verb* take or spend a vacation. ▶ **vacationer** *noun*

vacation pay *noun Cdn* the wages which an employee is entitled, under federal law, to receive either as paid vacation, or in lieu of paid vacation, amounting to four percent of the year's salary or six percent for an employee who has worked for a single employer for six or more consecutive years.

vaccinate *verb* (**vaccinates**, **vaccinated**, **vaccinating**) immunize. ▶ **vaccination** *noun* [Say VAC sin ate, vac sin AY sh'n]

vaccine *noun* **1** a substance used to stimulate the production of antibodies and procure immunity from one or several diseases, prepared from the infective agent causing the disease or a synthetic substitute. **2** *Computing* a program designed to protect a computer system from the effect of destructive software such as a virus. [Say vac SEEN or VAC seen]

vacillate *verb* (**vacillates**, **vacillated**, **vacillating**) waver between different opinions, options, actions, etc.: *Canadian English speakers vacillate between standards of American and British usage*. ▶ **vacillating** *adjective* **vacillation** *noun* [Say VASS ill ate, vass ill AY sh'n]

vacuity *noun* (*plural* **vacuities**) a lack of intelligence or thought; mindlessness: *it's easy to attack his work for its vacuity*. [Say vuh CUE it ee]

vacuole *noun* a small cavity or vesicle in organic tissue, esp. a tiny space within the cytoplasm of a cell containing air, fluid, food particles, etc. [Say VAC yoo ul]

vacuous *adjective* **1** unintelligent, expressionless: *a vacuous stare*. **2** lacking substance or content;

meaningless: *a vacuous criticism*. ▶ **vacuousness** *noun* [Say VAC yoo us]

vacuum • *noun* **1** a space entirely devoid of matter. **2** a space or vessel from which the air has been completely or partly removed by a pump etc. **3 a** a place or situation etc., marked by an absence of the usual, former, or expected contents: *the vacuum created by the death of his wife*. **b** a place or situation etc. in which one is insulated from external influences; a state of isolation. **4** (*plural* **vacuums**) a vacuum cleaner. **5** a decrease of pressure below the normal atmospheric value. • *verb informal* **1** clean (a room or carpet etc.) with a vacuum cleaner. **2** remove (dust etc.) with or as if with a vacuum cleaner.

vacuum cleaner *noun* an electrical appliance for removing dust from carpets etc., by suction.

vacuum packed *adjective* **1** (esp. of food) sealed in an airtight package or container from which some or all of the air has been removed, usu. in order to preserve freshness. **2** (of a package or container etc.) sealed and made airtight after some or all of the air has been removed.

vacuum tube *noun* a sealed glass tube containing a near-vacuum for the free passage of electric current.

vagabond • *noun* a person who roams or wanders from place to place with no settled habitation and no visible means of support; a tramp or hobo, esp. an idle or dishonest one. • *adjective* roving or wandering: *his vagabond companions*.

vagaries *plural noun* unexpected and inexplicable changes in a situation or in someone's behaviour: *has found time to adjust to the joys and vagaries of fatherhood* ◊ *the vagaries of the weather*. [Say VAY guh reez]

vagina *noun* the canal leading from the vulva to the cervix of the uterus in women and most female mammals. ▶ **vaginal** *adjective* [Say vuh JIE nuh, VAJ in ul]

vagrancy *noun* the crime of living on the streets and begging. [Say VAY grun see]

vagrant • *noun* **1** a person with no settled home or regular work. **2** a person who roams or wanders. • *adjective* **1** characteristic of or relating to a vagrant or vagrancy. **2** wandering or roving: *a vagrant musician*. [Say VAY grunt]

vague *adjective* **1** (of a statement etc.) couched in general, indefinite, or imprecise terms; lacking in details or particulars: *a vague answer*. **2** (of an idea, notion, feeling, etc.) not definite, clear, or fully established. **3** lacking physical definiteness of form or outline; indistinctly seen or perceived. **4** (of a person or mind) inexact in thought, expression, or understanding. ▶ **vaguely** *adverb* **vagueness** *noun*

SPELL CHECK
vain, vein, vane　　　　ABC

A blood vessel or a streak in a rock is a **vein**. The spelling is **vane** in "weather vane".

---

vain *adjective* **1** having an excessively high opinion of one's own appearance, abilities, worth, etc.; conceited. **2** useless, ineffectual, futile: *a vain hope*. **3** empty, trivial, unsubstantial: *vain boasts*. PHRASES **in vain** without success; ineffectually, uselessly: *it was in vain*

that we protested. **take a person's name in vain** mention a person's name (formerly esp. that of God) casually or irreverently, such as when swearing.

vainglorious *adjective* excessively proud of one's achievements or abilities: *the expedition was nothing more than a vainglorious attempt to recapture old feelings of leadership and adventure*. [Say vain GLORIOUS]

vainglory *noun literary* excessive pride in oneself or one's achievements; extreme vanity. [Say VAIN glory]

vainly *adverb* **1** without success: *I tried vainly to fix the faucet*. **2** in a way that shows excessive pride in one's appearance, abilities, or worth: *he declaimed proudly and vainly the words he had written*.

SPELL CHECK
valance, valence

The chemistry term is **valence**.

---

valance *noun* a short ornamental curtain hung around a bedstead or above a window etc. in order to conceal the frame or supporting hardware. [Say VAL ince or VALE ince]

SPELL CHECK
vale, veil

A piece of light material worn to cover the head or face is a **veil**.

---

vale *noun archaic* or *literary* a valley.

valedictorian *noun* a person who gives a valedictory. [Say valla dick TORY un]

valedictory • *noun* (*plural* **valedictories**) **1** a speech or address given by a student of a graduating class at a school or university as a part of the graduation exercises. **2** any statement or address made upon leaving or bidding farewell. • *adjective* of, pertaining to, or performed as a valedictory: *valedictory address*. [Say valla DICK tuh ree]

SPELL CHECK
valence, valance

A short curtain is a **valance**.

---

valence *noun* the power or capacity of an atom or group to combine with or displace other atoms or groups in the formation of compounds, equivalent to the number of hydrogen atoms that it could combine with or displace. [Say VALE ince]

valentine *noun* **1** a note, card, or gift given as a token of love or affection on Valentine's Day. **2** a person courted as a sweetheart on Valentine's Day.

Valentine's Day *noun* (also **St. Valentine's Day**) Feb. 14, celebrated with the courting of sweethearts and the exchange of valentines etc.

valerian *noun* **1** a Eurasian plant that typically bears clusters of small pink or white flowers. **2** a bitter-tasting drug derived from the rootstock of this plant, used as a stimulant etc. [Say vuh LEERY un]

valet *noun* **1** a male servant who attends to a gentleman's clothes etc. **2** a hotel employee with similar duties for guests. **3** an attendant responsible for parking the cars of patrons of a restaurant etc.: *valet parking*. **4** a rack on which clothing may be hung. [Say val AY or VAL ay]

Valhalla *noun* **1** *Scandinavian Myth* the hall in which the souls of those who have died in battle feast with Odin, the supreme god and creator, for eternity. **2** *informal* or *jocular* a situation or place representing a state of perfection or bliss: *the Newark Watershed is an outdoor enthusiast's Valhalla*. [Say val HAL uh]

valiant *adjective* (of a person or conduct) brave, courageous, heroic. ▶ **valiantly** *adverb* [Say VALLEY unt]

valid *adjective* **1** (of an argument, assertion, etc.) well-founded and defensible; sound. **2 a** legally binding and acceptable: *a valid contract*. **b** not having reached its expiry date: *this credit card is no longer valid*. **3** having legitimacy, authenticity, or authority: *valid information*.

validate *verb* (**validates**, **validated**, **validating**) **1** check or prove the validity or accuracy of something: *the congruence of the two lowest curves validates the data in each survey*. **2** demonstrate or support the truth or value of; lend force or validity to: *black feminist filmmakers were the first to use film to validate their experience and history*. ▶ **validation** *noun*

validity *noun* **1** the state of being legally or officially acceptable: *the validity of the contract has been disputed*. **2** the state of being logical and true; legitimacy, credibility: *we doubt the validity of his argument*. [Say vuh LID it ee]

validly *adverb* **1** in a way that is legally or officially acceptable: *the vehicle was validly transferred into my possession*. **2** in a way that is logical or well founded: *the theory can validly be attacked on these two points*.

valise *noun* a small piece of luggage similar to a suitcase or portmanteau. [Say vuh LEEZ]

Valium *noun proprietary* the drug diazepam used as a tranquilizer and relaxant. [Say VALLEY um]

Valkyrie *noun Scandinavian Myth* each of the twelve handmaidens who hovered over battlefields and conducted the fallen warriors to Valhalla. [Say VAL keery]

valley *noun* (*plural* **valleys**) **1 a** a low usu. elongated area more or less enclosed by hills and typically having a stream flowing through it. **b** the extensive tract of land drained by a single large river system. **2** any depression or hollow resembling or compared to this. **3** an internal angle formed by the junction of two sloping sides of a roof etc.

valorization *noun* the action of giving something value or validity: *the movie's nostalgic valorization of the 1960s becomes tiresome after a while*.

valorize *verb* (**valorizes**, **valorized**, **valorizing**) give or ascribe value or validity to something: *her book was influential in valorizing the role of women in the colonial era*.

valorous *adjective* brave, courageous.

valour *noun* personal courage, esp. in battle.

valuable • *adjective* **1** of material or monetary value; precious. **2** of great use or benefit; having considerable importance or worth. • *noun* (usu. in *plural*) a valuable thing, esp. a small article of personal property such as jewellery. ▶ **valuably** *adverb*

valuation *noun* **1 a** an estimation of a thing's monetary value, esp. by a professional appraiser. **b** the estimated monetary value. **2** an appraisal of something with respect to excellence or merit: *his high valuation of friendship and loyalty*.

value • *noun* **1** the worth, usefulness, or importance of a thing. **2** the worth of something measured according to the amount of money or goods for which it can be traded or exchanged. **3** the worth or quality of something compared to the price paid for it: *for $22.50 the book is good value*. **4** the ability of a thing to serve a specified purpose or cause a specified effect: *shock value* ◊ *R-value*. **5** (in *plural*) the principles or moral standards of a person or social group. **6** *Music* the length or duration of a sound signified by a note. **7 a** *Math* the amount represented by an algebraic term or expression. **b** *Physics & Chemistry* the numerical measure of a quantity or a number denoting magnitude on some conventional scale: *the value of gravity at the equator*. **8** (foll. by *of*) **a** the meaning (of a word etc.).

b the quality of a spoken sound; the sound represented by a letter. **9** the relative rank or importance of a playing card, chess piece, etc., according to the rules of the game. • *verb* (**values, valued, valuing**) **1** (often in *passive*, foll. by *at*) estimate the value of; appraise (esp. professionally): *their house is valued at $400,000*. **2** consider of worth or importance; have a high opinion of: *I value his friendship*.

value added • *noun* the amount by which the value of an article is increased at each stage of its production, exclusive of initial costs. • *adjective* (**value-added**) **1** (of food, goods, etc.) having features or ingredients added to the basic line or model to justify an increase in price and thereby enhance the profit margin for the producer and retailer. **2** (of a company) offering specialized or extended services in a commercial area.

value-added tax *noun* a tax on the amount by which the value of an article has been increased at each stage of its production or distribution.

value-free *adjective* free from criteria imposed by subjective values or standards.

value judgment *noun* an estimate of esp. moral or artistic merit based on personal opinion rather than facts.

valueless *adjective* having no value.

value system *noun* the set of connected or interdependent values of a person or social group.

valve *noun* **1** a device for controlling the passage of air, steam, water, etc. through a pipe, esp. an automatic device allowing movement in one direction only. **2** *Anatomy & Zoology* a membranous fold in a hollow organ or tubular structure of the circulatory system, digestive tract, etc. which automatically closes to prevent the reflux of blood or other contents. **3** *Music* a device for extending the range of pitch of a brass instrument by increasing or decreasing the effective length of the tube. **4** each of the two shells of an oyster, mussel, etc. ▶ **valved** *adjective*

vamoose *verb* (**vamooses, vamoosed, vamoosing**) (often in *imper.*) *slang* leave, disappear, take off. [Say va MOOSE]

vamp¹ • *noun* **1** the part of a boot or shoe covering the front of the foot. **2** *Music* a short simple introductory passage or accompaniment, sometimes improvised and usu. repeated several times until otherwise instructed. • *verb Music* play (a passage or accompaniment etc.) as a vamp: *the guitarist vamped the intro*.

vamp² *informal* • *noun* a woman who uses sexual attraction to exploit men. • *verb* **1** behave as a vamp. **2** act as a vamp towards (usu. a man).

vampire *noun* **1** a ghost or reanimated corpse supposed to leave its grave at night to suck the blood of sleeping people, often represented as a human figure with long pointed canine teeth. **2** a person who preys ruthlessly on others: *there are many who view true-crime writers as vampires out to capitalize on the misfortunes of others*.

vampire bat *noun* a small bat, found esp. in tropical South America, that feeds on the blood of mammals or birds using its two sharp incisor teeth and anticoagulant saliva.

vampiric *adjective* **1** having the manner or appearance of a vampire: *vampiric demons ◊ the pale and vampiric Evadne de Gauss welcomed us coldly into her home*. **2** ruthless: *vampiric hustlers preying on the naive*. [Say vam PEER ick]

vampish *adjective* = VAMPY.

vampy *adjective* sexually attractive in a way that is intended to seduce or manipulate men: *Lucinda emerges in a vampy, low-cut black dress and stiletto heels*.

van¹ *noun* **1** any of a range of covered vehicles, usu.

smaller than a truck, with space in the back for cargo and usu. enclosed with no side windows. **2** a similar vehicle for carrying passengers.

van² *noun* = VANGUARD.

vanadium *noun* a hard grey metallic element occurring naturally in several ores, used in small quantities to strengthen some steels. [Say vuh NAY dee um]

Vancouverite *noun* a resident or native of Vancouver.

vandal • *noun* **1** a person who wilfully or maliciously destroys or damages property. **2** (**Vandal**) a member of a Germanic people that ravaged Gaul, Spain, northern Africa, and Rome in the 4th–5th centuries, destroying many books and works of art. • *adjective* of or relating to the Vandals. ▶ **vandalism** *noun* **vandalize** *verb* (**vandalizes, vandalized, vandalizing**)

Van Doos *plural noun Cdn informal* the Royal 22e Régiment (the Royal 22nd Regiment), a French-speaking Canadian infantry regiment. [Say van DOOZ]

SPELL CHECK
vane, vain, vein

A conceited person is **vain**; a futile attempt is **vain** or made in **vain**; the spelling is **vein** for a blood vessel or a streak in a rock.

---

vane *noun* **1** = WEATHER VANE. **2** a blade of a screw propeller or a windmill etc. **3** the sight of surveying instruments, a quadrant, etc. **4** the flat part of a bird's feather formed by the barbs. **5** a broad flat projecting surface designed to guide the motion of a projectile, e.g. an arrow. ▶ **vaned** *adjective*

vanguard *noun* **1** the foremost part of an army or fleet advancing or ready to advance. **2** the leaders of a movement or of opinion etc.: *the experimental spirit of the modernist vanguard*. **3** a position at the forefront of a movement, field of activity, etc.: *Canada is in the vanguard of new information technologies*. [Say VAN gard]

Vanier Cup *noun Cdn* a trophy awarded annually to the winner of the Canadian inter-university football championship. [Say VAN yay]

vanilla • *noun* **1 a** a tropical climbing orchid with fragrant flowers. **b** (also **vanilla bean**) the fruit of these. **2** a substance obtained from the vanilla bean or synthesized and used to flavour ice cream and other foods. • *adjective* = PLAIN-VANILLA.

vanish *verb* (**vanishes, vanished, vanishing**) **1 a** disappear suddenly. **b** disappear gradually; fade away. **2** cease to exist. **3** go away.

vanity *noun* (*plural* **vanities**) **1 a** a conceit and desire for admiration of one's personal attainments or attractions. **b** excessive concern with one's physical appearance. **c** something about which one is vain. **2** the quality of being unimportant or futile, especially compared with other things that are important: *the vanity of human ambition in the face of death*. **3** a unit consisting of a sink set into a flat top with cupboards beneath, esp. in a bathroom. **4** a dressing table.

vanquish *verb* (**vanquishes, vanquished, vanquishing**) *literary* conquer or overcome. [Say VANG kwish]

vantage *noun* (also **vantage point**) a place affording a good view or prospect. [Say VAN tidge]

vapid *adjective* insipid; lacking interest: *tuneful but vapid musicals filling the theatres of Toronto*. ▶ **vapidity** *noun* [Say VAP id, vuh PIDDA tee]

vaporization *noun* the action of converting something into vapour.

vaporize *verb* (**vaporizes, vaporized, vaporizing**) convert or be converted into vapour.

vaporizer *noun* a device that vaporizes substances, esp. for medicinal inhalation.

vaporous *adjective* **1** full of or consisting of vapour: *vaporous clouds*. **2** resembling vapour in lack of substance: *John gets to deliver the vaporous blank-verse soliloquies*.

vapour (also **vapor**) • *noun* **1** moisture or another substance diffused or suspended in air, e.g. mist or smoke. **2** *Physics* a gaseous form of a normally liquid or solid substance (*compare* GAS 1). **3** a medicinal agent for inhaling. • *verb* make idle boasts or empty talk: *perhaps he wasn't just vapouring when he used the word totalitarian to stigmatize the main tendencies in contemporary architecture*.

vapour trail *noun* = CONTRAIL.

vapourware *noun* *Computing slang* software that as yet exists only in the plans or publicity of its developers.

vaquero *noun* (*plural* **vaqueros**) (esp. in Spanish-speaking areas) a cattle driver. [Say vuh CARE oh]

var. *abbreviation* variant.

variability *noun* the condition of something that varies or is likely to vary.

variable • *adjective* **1 a** that can be varied or adapted: *a rod of variable length*. **b** (of a gear) designed to give varying speeds. **2** apt to vary; not constant: *variable fortunes*. **3** *Math* (of a quantity) indeterminate. **4** (of wind or currents) tending to change direction. **5** (of a star) periodically varying in brightness. **6** *Botany & Zoology* (of a species) including individuals or groups that depart from the type. **7** *Biology* (of an organism or part of it) tending to vary in structure or function. • *noun* **1** a variable thing or quantity. **2** *Math* **a** a variable quantity. **b** a symbol, such as x, y, or z, that represents this. ▶ **variably** *adverb*

variance *noun* **1** difference of opinion; dispute, disagreement: *a theory at variance with all known facts*. **2** a discrepancy between statements or documents. **3** an official dispensation, esp. from a building regulation or zoning bylaw.

variant • *adjective* **1** differing in form or details from the main one: *a variant spelling*. **2** having different forms: *forty variant types of pigeon*. **3** variable or changing. • *noun* a variant form, spelling, type, reading, etc.

variation *noun* **1** a change or slight difference in condition, amount, or level, typically with certain limits: *regional variations in house prices* ◊ *the figures showed marked variation from year to year*. **2** a different or distinct form or version of something: *ringette is a variation of hockey*. **3** *Music* a repetition (usu. one of several) of a theme in a changed or elaborated form: *variations on a theme by Mozart*. **4** a deviation of a heavenly body from its mean orbit or motion. **5** *Math* a change in a function etc. due to small changes in the values of constants etc. **6** a solo that is part of a full-length ballet etc. PHRASES **variations on a theme** a variety of things that differ slightly but have a strong common element: *these dog breeds are all variations on a theme*.

varicose *adjective* (esp. of the veins of the legs) affected by a condition causing them to become dilated and swollen. [Say VARE a cose (COSE rhymes with DOSE)]

varied *adjective* showing variety; diverse.

variegated *adjective* **1** (of plants) having leaves containing two or more colours. **2** marked or characterized by variety or diversity: *a variegated assortment of folk attended the convention*. [Say VARY a gate id]

varietal • *adjective* **1** esp. *Botany & Zoology* of, forming, or designating a variety. **2** (of wine) made from a single

designated variety of grape. • *noun* a wine made from a single, designated variety of grape. [Say va RIOT'll]

variety *noun* (*plural* **varieties**) **1** diversity; absence of uniformity; many-sidedness: *not enough variety in our lives*. **2** a quantity or collection of different things: *for a variety of reasons*. **3 a** a class of things different in some common qualities from the rest of a larger class to which they belong. **b** a specimen or member of such a class. **4** (foll. by *of*) a different form of a thing, quality, etc. **5** *Biology* **a** a subspecies. **b** a cultivar **c** an individual or group usually fertile within the species to which it belongs but differing from the species type in some qualities capable of perpetuation. **6** a mixed sequence of dances, songs, comedy acts, etc. (usu. as an *adjective*: *a variety show*).

variety store *noun* = CONVENIENCE STORE.

various *adjective* **1** different, diverse: *too various to form a group*. **2** more than one, several: *for various reasons*. **3** individual or separate: *the various members of the staff*. ▶ **variously** *adverb*

varmint *noun* *informal jocular* **1** a destructive or undesirable wild animal. **2** a troublesome or objectionable person.

varnish • *noun* **1** a resinous solution used to give a hard shiny transparent coating to wood, metal, paintings, etc. **2** any other preparation for a similar purpose. **3** a superficial polish of manner. • *verb* (**varnishes, varnished, varnishing**) apply varnish to.

varsity *adjective* **1** designating sports played at the university or college level. **2** designating the most advanced level of athletic competition in a high school etc.

Varsol *noun* *Cdn proprietary* a liquid distilled from petroleum and used esp. as a paint thinner.

vary *verb* (**varies, varied, varying**) **1** make different; modify, diversify: *seldom varies the routine*. **2 a** undergo change; become or be different: *the temperature varies from 20° to 30°*. **b** be of different kinds: *her mood varies*. **3** (foll. by *as*) be in proportion to. ▶ **varying** *adjective*

varying hare *noun* = ARCTIC HARE.

vascular *adjective* of, made up of, or containing vessels for conveying blood or sap etc.: *vascular functions* ◊ *vascular tissue*. [Say VASS cue lur]

vas deferens *noun* the duct carrying sperm from the testicle to the urethra. [Say vass DEFFA renz]

vase *noun* a vessel, usu. tall and circular, used as an ornament or container, esp. for flowers. [Say VOZ or VAZE]

vasectomy *noun* (*plural* **vasectomies**) the surgical removal of part of each vas deferens esp. as a means of sterilization. [Say vuh SEKTA me]

Vaseline *noun* *proprietary* a type of petroleum jelly used as an ointment, lubricant, etc.

vassal *noun* **1** *hist.* a man in the Middle Ages who promised to fight for and be loyal to a king or other powerful owner of land, in return for being given land to live on. **2** a dependent person or country: *a vassal state of the Chinese empire*. ▶ **vassalage** *noun* [Rhymes with *HASSLE*]

vast *adjective* **1** immense, huge; very great: *a vast expanse of water*. **2** *informal* great, considerable: *makes a vast difference*. ▶ **vastly** *adverb* **vastness** *noun*

vat *noun* a large tank or other vessel, esp. for holding liquids or something in liquid in the process of brewing, tanning, dyeing, etc.

Vatican *noun* (**the Vatican**) **1** the palace and official residence of the Pope in Rome. **2** papal government.

Vatican Council *noun* each of two general councils of the Roman Catholic Church, held in 1869–70 and 1962–65. The second of these (**Vatican II**) reformed

the liturgy, encouraged dialogue with other religions and churches, and emphasized the role of lay people.

vaudeville *noun* **1** a form of variety entertainment popular esp. in the US from about 1880 until the early 1930s. **2** a stage play on a trivial theme with interspersed songs: *vaudeville act*. ▶**vaudevillian** *adjective & noun* [Say VOD vill, vod VILLY un]

vault • *noun* **1 a** an arched roof. **b** a continuous arch. **c** a set or series of arches whose joints radiate from a central point or line. **2** a vault-like covering: *the vault of heaven*. **3** an underground chamber, esp. as a place of interment beneath a church or in a cemetery etc.: *family vault*. **4** a place of storage, esp. for valuables: *bank vault*. **5** an act of vaulting. • *verb* **1** leap or spring, esp. while resting on one or both hands or with the help of a pole. **2** spring over (a gate etc.) in this way. **3** (esp. as **vaulted**) **a** make in the form of a vault. **b** provide with a vault or vaults.

vaulting *noun* **1** arched work in a vaulted roof or ceiling. **2** a gymnastic or athletic exercise in which participants vault over obstacles. • *adjective* **1** excessively confident or presumptuous: *vaulting ambition*. **2** used to vault or in vaulting: *a vaulting pole*.

vaunt *verb literary* boast about or praise (something), esp. excessively: *vaunting the joys of being a club member*.

vaunted *adjective* highly praised, esp. to excess: *their much vaunted reforms did not materialize*.

v-chip *noun* a device that, when installed in a TV set or receiver, can be programmed by the user to block or scramble any TV program that contains violence, sex, or bad language (as indicated by a code inserted into the signal by the broadcaster).

VCR *noun* (*plural* **VCRs**) an electrical apparatus used in conjunction with a television for recording broadcast material onto videotape and for playing back video cassettes.

VD *abbreviation* VENEREAL DISEASE.

VDT *abbreviation* VIDEO DISPLAY TERMINAL.

VE *abbreviation* Victory in Europe (in 1945).

veal *noun* **1** calf's flesh. **2** a calf raised for veal.

vector • *noun* **1** *Math & Physics* a quantity having direction as well as magnitude, esp. as determining the position of one point in space relative to another. **2** a carrier of disease. **3** a course to be taken by an aircraft. • *verb* **1** direct (an aircraft in flight) to a desired point. **2** change or alter the direction of (the thrust of a jet engine) in order to steer an aircraft etc.

Veda *noun* (in *singular* or *plural*) the most ancient Hindu scriptures, esp. four collections called Rig-Veda, Sāma-Veda, Yajur-Veda, and Atharva-Veda. [Say VAY duh or VEE duh]

VE day *noun* May 8, the day marking the Allied victory in Europe in 1945.

Vedic • *adjective* of or relating to the Veda or Vedas. • *noun* the language of the Vedas, an older form of Sanskrit. [Say VAY dick or VEE dick]

vee *noun* (*plural* **vees**) **1** the letter V. **2** a thing shaped like a V.

veejay *noun informal* = VJ.

veep *noun informal* a vice-president.

veer • *verb* **1 a** change direction or course, esp. suddenly. **b** (of a conversation, or a person's behaviour or opinions) change suddenly. **2** (of the wind) change direction clockwise (*compare* BACK *verb* 5). • *noun* a change of course or direction.

veg¹ *noun informal* a vegetable or vegetables.

veg² *verb* (**vegges**, **vegged**, **vegging**) (often foll. by *out*) relax in a mindless manner.

vegan • *noun* a person who does not eat or use animal products. • *adjective* using or containing no animal products. ▶**veganism** *noun* [Say VEE gun or VAY gun or VEDGE un]

vegetable • *noun* **1** any plant or edible fungus whose leaves, roots, tubers, fruit, seeds, or flowers are used for food, e.g. lettuce, potatoes, carrots, tomatoes, and mushrooms. **2** *informal* **a** a person who is incapable of normal intellectual activity, esp. through brain injury etc. **b** a person lacking in animation or living a monotonous life. • *adjective* **1** of, derived from, relating to, or comprising plants or plant life, esp. as distinct from animal life or mineral substances. **2** of or relating to vegetables as food. **3 a** not responsive to stimulus: *vegetable behaviour*. **b** uneventful, monotonous: *a vegetable existence*.

vegetable oil *noun* an oil derived from plants, e.g. canola oil, olive oil, corn oil.

vegetal *adjective* of or having the nature of plants: *vegetal growth*. [Say VEDGE a tul]

vegetarian • *noun* a person who does not eat animal food, esp. that from slaughtered animals, though often not eggs and dairy products. • *adjective* **1** of or relating to vegetarians or vegetarianism. **2 a** containing no meat. **b** containing no animal products. ▶**vegetarianism** *noun*

vegetate *verb* (**vegetates**, **vegetated**, **vegetating**) **1** live an uneventful or monotonous life. **2** relax in a mindless or passive manner: *went home and spent the evening vegetating*. **3** cover with vegetation or plant life: *sparsely vegetated beaches of gravel, cobbles, and slabs*.

vegetation *noun* **1** plants collectively; plant life: *luxuriant vegetation*. **2** the process of vegetating.

vegetative *adjective* **1** of, relating to, or concerned with growth and development as distinct from reproduction. **2** of or relating to vegetation or plant life. **3** (of a person or way of life) unthinking or inactive. ▶**vegetatively** *adverb*

veggie *informal* • *noun* **1** a vegetable. **2** a vegetarian. • *adjective* made of vegetables; vegetarian: *veggie burger*.

vehemence *noun* strong and forceful feeling; intense passion or anger: *she slammed the door with such vehemence that the house seemed to shake*. [Say VEE a munce]

vehement *adjective* showing or caused by strong feeling; forceful: *a vehement protest*. ▶**vehemently** *adverb* [Say VEE a m'nt]

vehicle *noun* **1** any conveyance for transporting people, goods, etc., esp. on land. **2** a medium for thought, feeling, etc. **3** a liquid etc. as a medium for suspending pigments, drugs, etc. ▶**vehicular** *adjective* [Say VEE a cull, vuh HICK yoo lur]

SPELL CHECK
veil, vale

A literary term for a valley is **vale**, which is used in the phrase "vale of tears".

veil • *noun* **1** a piece of fabric worn, esp. by women, over the head or face for concealment, to protect the face from the sun, dust, etc., or traditionally as part of a bride's attire. **2** a piece of fabric as part of a nun's headdress, resting on the head and shoulders. **3** a curtain, esp. that separating the sanctuary in the Jewish Temple. **4** something that conceals, covers, or disguises: *a veil of mist*. • *verb* cover or conceal with or as if with a veil. **PHRASES** **draw a veil over** avoid discussing or calling attention to. **take the veil** become a nun.

veiled *adjective* **1** (of a person) wearing a veil. **2** partially concealed or disguised: *veiled threats*.

vein • *noun* **1 a** any of the anatomical tubes by which
blood is conveyed to the heart (*compare* ARTERY 1). **b** (in
general use) any blood vessel: *has German blood in her
veins*. **2** a slender bundle of tissue forming a rib in the
framework of a leaf. **3** a streak or stripe of a different
colour in wood, marble, cheese, etc. **4** a fissure in rock
filled with ore or other deposited material. **5** a source
of a particular characteristic: *a rich vein of humour*. **6** a
distinctive feature or quality: *a vein of humour in her
work*. **7** a manner, style, or mood: *in a more serious vein*.
• *verb* fill or cover with or as with veins. ▶**veined**
adjective

veining *noun* a pattern of streaks or veins.

veiny *adjective* (**veinier, veiniest**) having prominent
veins or streaks: *veiny forearms ◊ veiny marble*.

Velcro *proprietary* • *noun* a fastener for clothes etc.
consisting of two strips of nylon fabric, one looped and
one burred, which adhere when pressed together.
• *verb* (**Velcroes, Velcroed, Velcroing**) fasten with
Velcro. ▶**Velcroed** *adjective*

veld *noun* (also **veldt**) *South Africa* grassland. [Say VELT]

vellum *noun* **1 a** fine parchment originally from the
skin of a calf. **b** a manuscript written on this. **2** smooth
writing paper imitating vellum.

velociraptor *noun* a small bipedal carnivorous
dinosaur of the Cretaceous period, with an enlarged
curved claw on each hind foot. [Say vuh LOSSA raptor]

velocity *noun* (*plural* **velocities**) **1** the measure of the
rate of movement of a usu. inanimate object in a given
direction. **2** speed in a given direction. **3** (in general
use) speed. [Say vuh LOSSA tee]

velour *noun* any of various fabrics with a velvet-like
finish, used for clothing, upholstery, etc. [Say vuh LOOR]

velvet • *noun* **1** a closely woven fabric of silk, cotton,
etc., with a thick short pile on one side. **2** the furry skin
on a deer's growing antler. **3** anything smooth and soft
like velvet. • *adjective* of, like, or soft as velvet.

velveteen *noun* a cotton fabric with a pile like velvet
but not as thick.

velvet revolution *noun* a non-violent political
revolution, esp. (**Velvet Revolution**) the sequence of
events in Czechoslovakia which led to the ending of
Communist rule in late 1989.

velvety *adjective* **1** having the appearance, texture, or
softness of velvet: *the leaves are shiny on one side, velvety on
the other*. **2** pleasantly smooth or soft: *a velvety red wine ◊
a velvety singing voice*.

venal *adjective* **1** (of a person) willing to act dishonestly
or immorally, or to sacrifice principles, for money: *a
small coterie of venal politicians made a decision in a hotel
room whose ramifications could threaten the republic*. **2**
characterized by or associated with corruption or
bribery: *the public tended to associate lobbying with the
corrupt and venal side of politics*. ▶**venality** *noun* [Say
VEEN ul, vee NALLA tee]

vend *verb* **1** offer (merchandise) for sale. **2** *Law* sell.

vendetta *noun* (*plural* **vendettas**) **1** a blood feud in
which the family of a murdered person seeks
vengeance on the murderer or the murderer's family.
2 a prolonged bitter quarrel. [Say ven DETTA]

vending machine *noun* a coin-operated machine for
the sale of small items, e.g. pop, snacks, etc.

vendor *noun* **1** *Law* the seller in a sale, esp. of property.
2 a person who sells, esp. at an outdoor stand, in a
stadium, etc.: *hot dog vendors*. **3** = VENDING MACHINE.

vendu *noun* (*plural* **vendus**) *Cdn derogatory* a Québécois
who is viewed as having sold out or become assimilated
to English-Canadian society. [Say von DOO]

veneer • *noun* **1 a** a thin covering of fine wood or
other surface material applied to a coarser wood. **b** a
layer in plywood. **2** (often foll. by *of*) a deceptive
outward appearance of a good quality etc.: *behind the
veneer of stylish modernity, powerful macho traditions remain
in force*. • *verb* apply a veneer to (wood, furniture, etc.).

venerable *adjective* **1** entitled to veneration on
account of character, age, associations, etc.: *venerable
relics*. **2** *Catholicism* as the title of a deceased person who
has attained a certain degree of sanctity but has not
been fully beatified or canonized. **3** as the title of an
archdeacon in the Anglican Church. [Say VENNER a bull]

venerate *verb* (**venerates, venerated, venerating**)
1 regard with deep respect. **2** revere on account of
sanctity etc. ▶**veneration** *noun* [Say VENNER ate,
venner AY sh'n]

venereal *adjective* relating to diseases spread by
sexual contact: *a venereal infection*. [Say ven EERIE ul]

venereal disease *noun* any of various diseases
contracted chiefly by sexual intercourse with a person
already infected. Abbreviation: **VD**.

Venetian • *noun* **1** a native or citizen of Venice in
northeast Italy. **2** the Italian dialect of Venice.
3 (**venetian**) (also **venetian blind**) a window blind
consisting of a number of adjustable horizontal slats to
control the light. • *adjective* of Venice. [Say ven EESH un]

Venezuelan • *noun* a native or inhabitant of
Venezuela, a republic on the north coast of South
America. • *adjective* of or relating to Venezuela or its
people or culture. [Say ven iz WAIL un]

vengeance *noun* **1** punishment inflicted or
retribution exacted for wrong to oneself or to a person
etc. whose cause one supports. **2** the desire for revenge.
PHRASES **with a vengeance** in a higher degree than
was expected or desired; in the fullest sense: *punctuality
with a vengeance*. [Say VEN jince]

vengeful *adjective* **1** vindictive; seeking vengeance.
2 characterized by or demonstrating a desire for
revenge. ▶**vengefulness** *noun*

venial *adjective* (of a sin or fault) not very serious and
therefore able to be forgiven; not mortal. [Say VEENY ul]

venison *noun* a deer's flesh as food. [Say VEN iss un or
VEN iz un]

Venn diagram *noun* a diagram representing
mathematical sets as intersecting circles, with the
intersections representing common elements of the
sets.

venom *noun* **1** a poisonous fluid secreted by snakes,
scorpions, etc., usu. transmitted by a bite or sting.
2 strong, bitter feeling or language; malice, spite.

venomous *adjective* **1 a** containing, secreting, or
injecting venom. **b** (of a snake etc.) inflicting poisonous
wounds by this means. **2** (of a person etc.) malicious,
spiteful. ▶**venomously** *adverb*

venous *adjective* **1** of or full of veins. **2** (of blood)
deoxygenated and of a dusky red colour (*opp.* ARTERIAL
1b). [Sounds like VENUS]

vent • *noun* **1** (also **vent hole**) a hole or opening
allowing motion of air etc. out of or into a confined
space. **2** an outlet; free passage or play: *gave vent to their
indignation*. **3** the anus esp. of a lower animal, serving
for both excretion and reproduction. **4** an aperture or
outlet through which volcanic products are discharged
at the earth's surface. **5** a slit in a garment, esp. in the
lower edge of the back of a coat. **6** a flue of a chimney.
• *verb* **1 a** make a vent in (a cask etc.). **b** (often as

vented *adjective*) provide (a machine, space, etc.) with a vent. **2** give vent or free expression to: *vented my anger*. **PHRASES** **vent one's spleen on** scold or ill-treat without cause.

ventilate *verb* (**ventilates, ventilated, ventilating**) **1 a** cause air to circulate freely in (a room etc.). **b** provide with a vent or vents. **c** (of wind etc.) blow upon or through so as to purify or freshen. **2** submit (a question, grievance, etc.) to public consideration and discussion: *the Senate is more aptly designed than the House of Commons to ventilate regional grievances*. **3** *Medical* **a** oxygenate (the blood). **b** admit or force air into (the lungs). ▶ **ventilation** *noun*

ventilator *noun* **1** an appliance or aperture for ventilating a room etc. **2** *Medical* an apparatus for maintaining artificial breathing.

ventral *adjective* **1** *Anatomy & Zoology* of or on the abdomen (compare DORSAL). **2** *Botany* of the front or lower surface. ▶ **ventrally** *adverb*

ventricle *noun* **1** either of the two muscular lower chambers of the heart (in some animals, a single chamber), which pump the blood to the arteries and through the body. **2** each of four fluid-filled cavities in the brain, formed by enlargements of the spinal cord. ▶ **ventricular** *adjective* [Say VEN trickle, ven TRICK yoo lur]

ventriloquism *noun* the skill of speaking or uttering sounds so that they seem to come from the speaker's dummy or a source other than the speaker. ▶ **ventriloquist** *noun* [Say ven TRILLA quiz um, ven TRILLA quist]

venture • *noun* **1 a** an undertaking of a risk. **b** a risky enterprise. **2** a business enterprise involving risk. • *verb* (**ventures, ventured, venturing**) **1** dare; not be afraid: *did not venture to stop them*. **2** (usu. foll. by *out* etc.) dare to go somewhere dangerous or unpleasant. **3** dare to put forward (an opinion, suggestion, etc.). **4 a** expose to risk; stake (a bet etc.). **b** take risks. **5** (foll. by *on, upon*) dare to engage in etc.: *ventured on a journey*. **PHRASES** **nothing ventured, nothing gained** one cannot expect to achieve anything without taking risks.

venture capital *noun* **1** money invested in a project in which there is a substantial element of risk, esp. money invested in a new venture or an expanding business in exchange for shares in the business. **2** (as an *adjective*) designating a company investing in such ventures.

venture capitalist *noun* a supplier of venture capital for investment.

venturer *noun* **1** *hist.* a person who undertakes or shares in a trading venture. **2** (**Venturer**) *Cdn* a member of a level (ages 14–17) in Scouting.

venturesome *adjective* **1** disposed to take risks. **2** risky.

venturi *noun* (*plural* **venturis**) (also **venturi tube**) a tube with a narrower middle section for measuring flow rate or exerting suction. [Say ven CHOORY]

venue *noun* **1 a** an appointed site or meeting place, as for a sports event, meeting, concert, etc. **b** a building for such a meeting or event: *downtown's newest venue*. **2** *Law* the location of a trial.

Venus flytrap *noun* a small bog plant with hinged leaves that spring shut on and digest insects that land on them, native to the southeastern US and occasionally kept as a houseplant.

veracity *noun* **1** truthfulness, honesty: *voters should be concerned about his veracity and character*. **2** accuracy (of a statement etc.): *officials expressed doubts about the veracity of the story*. [Say vuh RASSA tee]

veranda *noun* (also **verandah**) a usu. roofed porch or external gallery along one or more sides of a house.

verb *noun* a word used to indicate an action, state, or occurrence, and forming the main part of the predicate of a sentence, e.g. *hear, become, happen*.

> **WRITING TIP**
> **verbal**
>
> Because **verbal** can refer either to words generally (whether written or spoken), or to spoken words in particular, it may be better to use phrases like **oral statement** instead of **verbal statement** to avoid ambiguity or perceived redundancy. There are some expressions, however, in which the use of **verbal** to mean "oral" is well established and perfectly acceptable, e.g. *verbal agreement*. Words derived from **verbal** (like **verbally**) should be used with the same care.

verbal *adjective* **1** of or concerned with words: *made a verbal distinction*. **2** oral, not written: *gave a verbal statement*. **3** of or in the nature of a verb: *verbal inflections*. **4** talkative, articulate.

verbalization *noun* **1** the action of verbalizing something. **2** a verbal expression or statement.

verbalize *verb* (**verbalizes, verbalized, verbalizing**) **1** express in words. **2** make (a noun) into a verb.

verbally *adverb* in spoken words and not in writing or actions: *the company had received complaints both verbally and in writing* ◊ *the player was banned for verbally abusing the referee*.

verbal noun *noun* *Grammar* a noun formed as an inflection of a verb and partly sharing its constructions, e.g. *smoking* in *smoking is forbidden*.

verbatim *adverb & adjective* in exactly the same words; word for word: *copied it verbatim*. [Say vur BATE um]

verbena *noun* a herbaceous plant that bears clusters of fragrant showy flowers, widely cultivated as a garden ornamental. [Say vur BEENA]

verbiage *noun* needless accumulation of words; verbosity: *don't hesitate to slash unnecessary verbiage, alter sentences, or restructure paragraphs*. [Say VURBY idge]

verbose *adjective* using or expressed in more words than are needed: *much academic language is obscure and verbose*. ▶ **verbosity** *noun* [Say vur BOSE, vur BOSSA tee (BOSE rhymes with *DOSE*)]

verboten *adjective* forbidden, esp. by an authority: *what can be said out loud these days and what's verboten*. [Say vur BO tun]

verdant *adjective* **1** of the bright green colour of fresh grass: *a deep, verdant green*. **2** (of countryside) green with grass or other rich plant growth: *surrounded by verdant round hills on three sides*. [Say VUR dunt]

verdict *noun* **1** a decision on an issue of fact in a civil or criminal cause or an inquest. **2** a decision or an opinion given after testing, examining, or experiencing something.

verdigris *noun* **1 a** a green crystallized substance formed on copper by the action of acetic acid. **b** this used as a medicine or pigment. **2** green rust on copper or brass. [Say VUR degrees]

verge • *noun* **1** an edge or border. **2** an extreme limit beyond which something happens: *on the verge of tears*. • *verb* (**verges, verged, verging**) (foll. by *on*) border on; approach closely: *verging on the ridiculous*.

verifiable *adjective* able to be verified: *a verifiable statement*.

verification *noun* **1** the process of establishing the truth, accuracy, or validity of something: *verification of official documents*. **2** the process of verifying procedures laid down in weapons agreements.

verify *verb* (**verifies, verified, verifying**) make sure

V

or demonstrate that something is true, accurate, or justified: *her conclusions have been verified by later experiments* ◊ *we have no way of verifying his story*.

verisimilitude *noun* the appearance or semblance of being true or real: *the details give the novel some verisimilitude*. [Say vare uh suh MILLA tood or vare uh suh MILLA tyood]

veritable *adjective* real; rightly so called: *a veritable feast*. ▶ **veritably** *adverb* [Say VARE it a bull]

vérité *noun* (esp. in *combination*) realism or naturalism in the arts, esp. in film: *cinéma-vérité*. [Say very TAY]

verity *noun* (*plural* **verities**) **1** a true principle or belief, esp. one of fundamental importance: *the eternal verities*. **2** truth: *irrefutable, objective verity*. [Say VARE it ee]

vermicelli *noun* pasta made in long slender threads. [Say vurma CHELLY]

vermiculite *noun* a yellow or brown mineral found as a natural product of mica and other minerals, used for insulation or as a medium for growing plants. [Say vur MICK yoo lite]

vermilion *noun* **1** a bright red mineral form of mercuric sulphide from which mercury is obtained. **2** a brilliant red pigment made by grinding this or artificially. • *noun & adjective* the colour of this. [Say vur MILLION]

vermin *noun* (usu. treated as *plural*) **1** mammals and birds injurious to crops, etc., e.g. rodents and noxious insects: *garbage can encourage vermin such as rats*. **2** parasitic worms or insects: *she shook the blankets outside to get rid of the vermin that infested them*. **3** vile or contemptible persons: *the vermin who ransacked her house*.

Vermonter *noun* a native or inhabitant of Vermont. [Say vur MONT er]

vermouth *noun* a fortified wine flavoured with aromatic herbs. [Say vur MOOTH]

vernacular • *noun* **1** the language or dialect of a particular country: *Latin gave place to the vernacular*. **2** the language used by people belonging to a specified group or engaged in a specialized activity: *gardening vernacular*. **3** informal speech: *I don't wish to engage in ego-tripping, as they say in the vernacular, but I do think I've achieved a few things as editor of this journal*. • *adjective* (of language) of one's native country; not of foreign origin or of learned formation. [Say vur NACK yoo lur]

vernal *adjective* of, in, or appropriate to spring: *the vernal equinox*.

vernal equinox *noun* = SPRING EQUINOX.

versatile *adjective* **1** turning easily or readily from one subject or occupation to another: *a versatile mind*. **2** (of a device etc.) having many uses. ▶ **versatility** *noun* [Say VERSE a tile, versa TILLA tee]

verse *noun* **1** writing arranged with a metrical rhythm, typically having a rhyme (also as an *adjective*: *verse drama*). **2 a** a metrical line in accordance with the rules of prosody. **b** a group of a definite number of such lines. **c** a stanza of a poem or song with or without refrain. **d** a poem. **3** each of the short numbered divisions of a chapter in the Bible etc. **4** each of the short sentences in a liturgy said or sung by a priest etc. and alternating with responses.

versed *adjective* (foll. by *in*) experienced or skilled in; knowledgeable about.

versify *verb* (**versifies**, **versified**, **versifying**) **1** turn into or express in verse. **2** compose verses.

version *noun* **1** an account of a matter from a particular person's point of view: *told them my version of the incident*. **2** a book or work etc. in a particular edition or translation: *the Revised Standard Version of the Bible*. **3** a form or variant of a thing as adapted, performed, etc.

verso *noun* (*plural* **versos**) **1 a** the left-hand page of an open book. **b** the back of a printed leaf of paper or manuscript (opp. RECTO 2). **2** the reverse of a coin. [Say VERSE oh]

versus *preposition* **1** against (esp. in legal and sports use). *Abbreviation:* **v.**, **vs**. **2** as opposed to; in contrast with.

vertebra *noun* (*plural* **vertebrae**) **1** each segment of the backbone. **2** (in *plural*) the backbone. ▶ **vertebral** *adjective* [Say VURTA bruh for the singular, VURTA bray for the plural, VURTA brul]

vertebrate • *noun* any animal having a spinal column, including mammals, birds, reptiles, amphibians, and fishes. • *adjective* of or relating to the vertebrates. [Say VURTA brate or VURTA brut]

vertex *noun* (*plural* **vertices**) **1** the highest point; the top or apex. **2** *Math* **a** each angular point of a polygon, polyhedron, etc. **b** a meeting point of two lines that form an angle. **c** the point at which an axis meets a curve or surface. [Say VUR tex for the singular, VUR tuh seez for the plural]

vertical • *adjective* **1** at right angles to a horizontal plane, perpendicular. **2** in a direction from top to bottom of a picture etc. **3** of or at the vertex or highest point. **4** at, or passing through, the zenith. **5** involving all the levels in an organizational hierarchy or stages in the production of a class of goods: *vertical integration*. • *noun* **1** a vertical line or plane. **2** (in *plural*) (also **vertical blinds**) a window blind consisting of a number of adjustable vertical slats to control the light. **3** (also **vertical drop**) the difference in elevation between the top and bottom of a mountain, ski run, etc. ▶ **verticality** *noun* **vertically** *adverb*

vertically challenged *adjective jocular* short.

vertically integrated *adjective* denoting a company that controls all aspects of production, including those normally operated by separate firms, from harvesting raw materials to manufacturing finished goods.

vertiginous *adjective* of, causing, or affected by vertigo; dizzying: *seemed to enjoy their vertiginous perch above Niagara Falls*. ▶ **vertiginously** *adverb* [Say vur TIDGE in us]

vertigo *noun* a condition with a sensation of whirling and a tendency to lose balance; dizziness. [Say VUR tig oh]

verve *noun* enthusiasm, vigour, spirit, esp. in artistic or literary work.

very • *adverb* **1** in a high degree: *did it very easily* ◊ *a very bad cough*. **2** in the fullest sense: *at the very latest* ◊ *my very own room*. • *adjective* real, true, actual; truly such: *the very thing we need* ◊ *her very words*. PHRASES **not very 1** in a low degree. **2** far from being. **very good** (or **well**) a formula of consent or approval.

Very Reverend *noun* **1** (in Canada) the title of the moderator or a former moderator of the United Church. **2** the title of a dean etc.

vesicle *noun* **1 a** *Anatomy & Biology* a small fluid-filled bladder, sac, or vacuole. **b** *Botany* an air-filled swelling in a seaweed etc. **2** *Geology* a small cavity in volcanic rock produced by gas bubbles. **3** *Medical* a blister. ▶ **vesicular** *adjective* [Say VESS ick ul, vuh SICK yoo lur]

vespers *plural noun* the service of evening prayer in some Christian churches.

vessel *noun* **1** a hollow receptacle esp. for liquid, e.g. a cask, cup, pot, bottle, or dish. **2** a ship or boat, esp. a large one. **3 a** *Anatomy* a duct or canal etc. holding or conveying blood or other fluid, esp. = BLOOD VESSEL. **b** *Botany* a woody duct carrying or containing sap etc.

vest • *noun* **1** a sleeveless and collarless, usu. V-necked garment covering the shoulders and reaching the waist or hip, often with a buttoned front, worn over a shirt. **2** any sleeveless garment worn for a specified purpose:

bulletproof vest. • *verb* **1** bestow or confer (powers, authority, etc.) on (a person): *the executive power is vested in the President.* **2** (foll. by *in*) confer (property or power) on (a person) with an immediate fixed right of immediate or future possession: *players are fully vested in their pension plan the first day they get to the major leagues.* **3** put on vestments. PHRASES **close to the vest** cautious(ly), careful(ly), guarded(ly).

vestal virgin *noun* (in ancient Rome) a virgin consecrated to Vesta, the goddess of the hearth and household, and vowed to chastity, sharing the task of maintaining the sacred fire burning on the goddess's altar.

vested interest *noun* **1** *Law* an interest (usu. in land or money held in trust) recognized as belonging to a person. **2 a** a personal interest in a state of affairs, usu. with an expectation of gain: *since Biff is a shareholder as well as an employee, he has a vested interest in the success of the company.* **b** (usu. in *plural*) a person or group with such an interest.

vestibule *noun* **1 a** a hall or lobby just inside the outer door of a building, e.g. where coats may be left. **b** the area between two sets of doorways at the main entrance of a church etc. **2** an enclosed space between railway passenger cars. **3** *Anatomy* **a** a chamber or channel connected with others. **b** the central cavity of the labyrinth of the inner ear. ▶ **vestibular** *adjective* [Say VESTA byool, vess TIB yoo lur]

vestige *noun* **1** a trace or piece of evidence; a sign: *vestiges of an earlier civilization.* **2** a slight amount; a particle: *without a vestige of clothing.* **3** *Biology* a part or organ of an organism that is reduced or functionless but was well developed in its ancestors. [Say VESS tidge]

vestigial *adjective* **1** being a vestige or trace: *he felt a vestigial flicker of anger from last night.* **2** *Biology* (of an organ) atrophied or functionless from the process of evolution: *a vestigial wing.* [Say ves TIDGE ee ul]

vestment *noun* **1** (usu. in *plural*) any of the official robes of clergy, choristers, etc., worn during a service. **2** a garment, esp. an official or state robe.

vestry *noun* (*plural* **vestries**) **1** a room or building attached to a church for keeping vestments in. **2 a** esp. *Anglicanism* a meeting of the members of a parish. **b** a body of parishioners meeting in this way. [Say VESS tree]

vet¹ • *noun* *informal* a veterinarian. • *verb* (**vets, vetted, vetting**) **1** make a careful and critical examination of (a scheme, work, candidate, etc.). **2** examine or treat (an animal).

vet² *noun* *informal* an esp. military veteran.

vetch *noun* (*plural* **vetches**) a widely distributed plant of the pea family, which is cultivated as a silage or fodder crop.

veteran *noun* **1** a person who has grown old in or had long experience of esp. military service or an occupation: *a veteran goalie.* **2** an ex-serviceman or servicewoman.

veterinarian *noun* a person qualified to treat diseased or injured animals.

veterinary • *adjective* of or for diseases and injuries of esp. farm and domestic animals, or their treatment. • *noun* (*plural* **veterinaries**) a veterinarian.

veto • *noun* (*plural* **vetoes**) **1 a** a constitutional right to reject a legislative enactment. **b** the right of a permanent member of the UN Security Council to reject a resolution. **c** such a rejection. **d** an official message conveying this. **2** a prohibition: *put one's veto on a proposal.* • *verb* (**vetoes, vetoed, vetoing**) **1** exercise a veto against (a measure etc.). **2** forbid authoritatively: *the proposal for a longer lunch hour was vetoed by the company's directors.*

 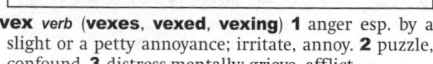
vex *verb* (**vexes, vexed, vexing**) **1** anger esp. by a slight or a petty annoyance; irritate, annoy. **2** puzzle, confound. **3** distress mentally; grieve, afflict.

vexation *noun* **1** the state of being annoyed, frustrated, or worried: *Carol bit her lip in vexation.* **2** an annoying or distressing thing.

vexatious *adjective* **1** causing or tending to cause frustration, annoyance, or worry: *as his employers found out, he could be vexatious and difficult to control.* **2** *Law* not having sufficient grounds for action and seeking only to annoy the defendant: *if the claim is deemed to be frivolous or vexatious, it is denied.* [Say vex AY shuss]

vexed *adjective* **1** irritated, angered. **2** (of a problem, issue, etc.) difficult; problematic.

vexing *adjective* annoying, troubling, distressing, irritating.

V-formation *noun* a formation, esp. of flying geese, airplanes, etc., resembling the letter V.

VGA *abbreviation* *Computing* video graphics array, a standard for graphics adapters originally capable of generating a 640 by 480 pixel 16-colour screen.

VHF *abbreviation* very high frequency (designating radio waves of frequency *c.* 30–*c.*300 MHz and wavelength *c.*1–10 metres).

VHS *abbreviation* *proprietary* Video Home System (one of the standard formats for video cassettes).

via *preposition* **1** by way of; through: *Montreal to Rome via Paris* ◊ *via satellite.* **2** by means of; with the aid of: *tried to improve the economy via fiscal restraint.* [Say VEE uh or VIE uh]

viability *noun* the quality of being esp. economically or practicably viable: *gave the community a solid base for future viability and prosperity.* [Say vie ABILITY]

viable *adjective* **1** (of a plan etc.) feasible; practicable, esp. from an economic standpoint. **2 a** (of a seed or spore) able to germinate. **b** (of a plant, animal, etc.) capable of living or developing normally under particular environmental conditions. **3** *Medical* (of a fetus or unborn child) able to live after birth. ▶ **viably** *adverb* [Say VIE a bull]

viaduct *noun* **1** a long bridge-like structure, esp. a series of arches, carrying a road or railway across a valley, low-lying ground, etc. **2** such a road or railway. [Say VIE a duct]

Viagra *noun* *proprietary* the drug sidenafil citrate, taken orally as a tablet in the treatment of male impotence. [Say vie AGRA]

vial *noun* a small (usu. cylindrical glass) vessel esp. for holding liquid medicines.

vibe *noun* *informal* **1** (often in *plural*) vibration, esp. in the sense of feelings or atmosphere communicated: *the house had bad vibes.* **2** (in *plural*) = VIBRAPHONE.

vibrancy *noun* the quality of being vibrant; excitement; brightness.

vibrant *adjective* **1** full of life and energy; exciting. **2** (of colours etc.) bright and striking. **3** vibrating. **4** (often foll. by *with*) (of a person or thing) quivering; pulsating: *he seemed vibrant with energy and self-confidence.* **5** (of sound) resonant. ▶ **vibrantly** *adverb*

vibraphone *noun* a percussion instrument of tuned metal bars with motor-driven resonators and metal

V

tubes giving a vibrato effect. ▶**vibraphonist** *noun* [Say VIE bruh phone, VIE bruh phone ist]

vibrate *verb* (**vibrates, vibrated, vibrating**) **1** move or cause to move continuously and rapidly to and fro. **2** *Physics* move unceasingly to and fro, esp. rapidly. **3** (of a sound) throb; continue to be heard. **4** (foll. by *with*) quiver, thrill: *vibrating with passion*. **5** (of a pendulum) swing to and fro.

vibration *noun* **1** a continuous rapid shaking movement or sensation: *powerful vibrations from the earthquake* ◊ *this motor generates less vibration*. **2** *Physics* (esp. rapid) motion to and fro esp. of the parts of a fluid or an elastic solid whose equilibrium has been disturbed or of an electromagnetic wave. **3** (**vibrations**) a person's emotional state, the atmosphere of a place, or the associations of an object, as communicated to and felt by others. ▶**vibrational** *adjective*

vibrato *noun* (*plural* **vibratos**) a rapid slight variation in pitch in singing or playing a stringed or wind instrument, producing a tremulous effect (*compare* TREMOLO). [Say vib ROT oh]

vibrator *noun* a device that vibrates or causes vibration, esp. an electric or other instrument used in massage or for sexual stimulation. [Say VIE brate er]

vibratory *adjective* of, relating to, or causing vibration: *vibratory signals*. [Say VIBE ruh tory]

viburnum *noun* a shrub or small tree that typically bears flat or rounded clusters of white flowers. [Say vie BURN um]

vicar *noun* **1 a** (in the Church of England) a clergyman appointed to act as priest of a parish, who, formerly, received only a salary or stipend but not the tithes of the parish (*compare* RECTOR). **b** (in other Anglican churches) a member of the clergy who acts as a substitute for or assistant to the rector of a parish or a bishop (*compare* RECTOR). **2** *Catholicism* a representative or deputy of a bishop. [Say VICKER]

vicarious *adjective* **1** experienced, enjoyed, or undergone second-hand by imagining one's own participation in the experiences of another: *the movie offers the vicarious delight that one may find oneself taking in wholesale destruction* ◊ *the game show has had audiences squealing with vicarious greed*. **2** performed, accomplished, or undergone on behalf of another: *Don Quixote goes mad as vicarious atonement for our drabness, our ungenerous dearth of imagination*. ▶**vicariously** *adverb* [Say vick AIRY us or vie CARE ee us]

SPELL CHECK
vice, vise

Canadians usually spell the clamp **vise**.

---

vice[1] *noun* **1 a** illegal or grossly immoral conduct; extreme corruption or depravity. **b** a particular form of this, esp. involving prostitution or drugs etc. **c** an immoral, dissolute, or illegal habit or practice. **2 a** personal flaw or bad habit: *drunkenness was not among his vices*.

vice[2] esp. *Brit.* = VISE.

vice- *combining form* forming nouns meaning "next in rank or authority to" or "acting as a substitute or deputy for": *vice-chairperson* ◊ *vice-governor*.

vice admiral *noun* (also **Vice Admiral**) a naval officer ranking below admiral and above rear admiral.

vice-chancellor *noun* **1** the deputy of a chancellor. **2** *Cdn & Brit.* the acting representative of the chancellor of a university, discharging most of the administrative duties.

vice-presidency *noun* (*plural* **vice-presidencies**) **1** the office of a vice-president. **2** the period of this.

vice-president *noun* **1** a government official who ranks immediately below the president and assumes the role and responsibilities of the president in the event of his or her inability to govern due to absence, illness, or death. **2** an executive officer deputizing for a president and often overseeing a division of a corporation etc. ▶**vice-presidential** *adjective*

vice-principal *noun* the assistant to a principal, esp. in a school, college, or university.

viceregal *adjective* of or relating to a Governor General or viceroy: *has held the viceregal post since 1996*. ▶**viceregally** *adverb* [Say vice REE gull]

viceroy *noun* a person who exercises authority over a colony or province etc. on behalf of a sovereign. [Say VICE roy]

vice squad *noun* a special unit of a police force for the enforcement of laws related to prostitution, drug trafficking, illegal gambling, etc.

vice versa *adverb* with the order of the terms or conditions changed; the other way around: *I'll help you and vice versa*. [Say vice VERSE uh]

vichyssoise *noun* a thick soup made of puréed leeks and potatoes with cream, usu. served chilled. [Say VEESHY swoz]

vicinity *noun* (*plural* **vicinities**) the area near or surrounding a particular place: *a mob of songbirds storms the saw-whet owl in an effort to drive this predator from the immediate vicinity*. PHRASES **in the vicinity of 1** near: *in the vicinity of the park*. **2** approximately: *in the vicinity of $300,000*.

vicious *adjective* **1** malevolent, spiteful, wicked: *vicious sarcasm*. **2** savage, brutal: *a vicious dog* ◊ *a vicious slaying*. **3** fierce, intense, severe: *a vicious storm*. ▶**viciously** *adverb* **viciousness** *noun*

vicious circle *noun* (also **vicious cycle**) an unbroken sequence of reciprocal cause and effect in which two or more elements intensify each other, leading to a worsening of the situation: *a vicious circle of drought, reduced vegetation, higher evaporation rates, and more drought*.

vicissitudes *plural noun* changes in circumstance; uncertainties or variations of fortune or outcome: *the vicissitudes of a harsh climate* ◊ *has managed to remain invulnerable to the vicissitudes of the stock market*. [Say viss ISSA toodz or viss ISSA tyoodz]

victim *noun* **1** a person who suffers or dies as a result of an event or circumstance. **2** a person fooled or taken advantage of; a dupe: *fell victim to a hoax*. PHRASES **fall victim to** succumb to or suffer as a result of. **a victim of one's own success** a person for whom success results in unexpected problems: *some companies become victims of their own success, expanding too quickly to meet growing consumer needs, then running into financial difficulty*. ▶**victimhood** *noun*

victimization *noun* the act of victimizing someone; the fact of being victimized.

victimize *verb* (**victimizes, victimized, victimizing**) **1** make a victim of; cause (a person etc.) to suffer harm, inconvenience, discomfort, etc. **2** single out (a person) for punishment or unfair treatment. ▶**victimizer** *noun*

victimology *noun* the study of the victims of crime or discrimination, the psychological effects on them of their experience, and methods of recovery.

victor *noun* a person or country etc. that succeeds in overcoming or defeating an adversary or opponent.

Victoria Cross *noun* (*plural* **Victoria Crosses**) a medal awarded to members of the Commonwealth armed forces for conspicuous acts of bravery, instituted by Queen Victoria in 1856.

V

Victoria Day *noun Cdn* a holiday falling on the Monday immediately preceding May 25.

Victorian • *adjective* **1** of or characteristic of the reign of Queen Victoria (reigned 1837–1901). **2** associated with attitudes attributed to this time, esp. of prudery and moral strictness. **3** resembling or typical of the architectural style of this time, characterized by lavish ornamentation set in neoclassical or neo-Gothic forms. • *noun* **1** a person of this time. **2** a resident of a place called Victoria.

Victoriana *plural noun* **1** articles, esp. collectors' items and furniture, of the Victorian period. **2** attitudes characteristic of this period. [Say vick tory ANNA]

Victorian Order of Nurses *noun Cdn* a non-profit community-based health organization that provides home care for the elderly and chronically ill.

victorious *adjective* **1** having won a victory; conquering, triumphant. **2** of or characterized by victory: *a victorious cheer*. ▶ **victoriously** *adverb*

victory *noun (plural* **victories)** **1** an act of defeating an enemy or opponent in a battle, game, or other competition: *an election victory ◊ Carolyn is confident of victory in Saturday's final*. **2** a success in some endeavour or in overcoming an obstacle or difficulty.

victual • *noun* (usu. in *plural*) food, provisions: *they could only sell ale and victuals if they had obtained a licence*. • *verb* (**victuals, victualled, victualling**) supply or feed (a person) with victuals: *they shall be humanely treated, lodged, and victualled*. [Say VICK chew ul or VITTLE]

vid *noun informal* a video.

video • *noun (plural* **videos) 1** the process of recording, reproducing, or broadcasting visual images on magnetic tape (also as an *adjective*: *video equipment*). **2** the visual element of television broadcasts. **3 a** a recording made on videotape, esp. one commercially produced and available for sale or rent on video cassette. **b** = MUSIC VIDEO. **4 a** = VIDEO CASSETTE: *available on video this fall*. **b** = VIDEOTAPE 1. • *verb* (**videoes, videoed, videoing**) record on videotape.

video arcade *noun* = ARCADE 3.

video camera *noun* (also **videocam**) a camera used to record images on videotape or to transmit images to a monitor screen.

video card *noun* the circuit board that enables a computer monitor to display graphics.

video cassette *noun* a length of videotape enclosed in a sealed plastic casing, suitable for use in a video camera or VCR.

video cassette recorder *noun* = VCR.

video conference *noun* an arrangement in which television sets linked by telephone lines are used to enable a group of people in different places to communicate with each other in sound and vision. ▶ **video conferencing** *noun*

videodisc *noun* an optical disk on which material is recorded for reproduction on a television screen.

video display terminal *noun* (also **video display unit**) a device for displaying on a screen data stored in a computer, usu. incorporating a keyboard for manipulating the data.

video game *noun* any of a variety of games that can be played by using a joystick to manipulate computer-generated images displayed on a television screen, computer monitor, or the screen of an arcade game.

videographer *noun* a person who videotapes events. [Say viddy OGRA fur]

videography *noun* the process or art of making videos. [Say viddy OGRA fee]

video lottery terminal *noun* a government-regulated gambling machine, operated by coin, that offers a selection of esp. card games on a video screen and rewards a winner in credit rather than coin, usu. located in a bar, restaurant, casino, or racetrack.

video-on-demand *noun* a pay-per-view television service that allows a customer to select from a list of programs, which may be accessed from a server through a telephone line at any time.

videophone *noun* a telephone incorporating a television screen allowing communication in both sound and vision.

video recorder *noun* = VCR.

video signal *noun* a signal that contains all the information required for producing a television image.

videotape • *noun* **1** magnetic tape for recording television pictures and sound. **2 a** a length of this. **b** a video cassette, esp. one on which nothing has been recorded. **3** a recording made on videotape. • *verb* (**videotapes, videotaped, videotaping**) make a recording of (a person, an event, etc.) on videotape.

videotape recorder *noun* **1** a device used to record images and sound onto an open spool of videotape, used esp. in television broadcasting. **2** = VCR.

vie *verb* (**vies, vied, vying**) compete, contend: *the two teams vying for the Cup ◊ modern motels vie with historic inns to tempt overnighters*.

Viennese • *adjective* of, relating to, or associated with Vienna, Austria. • *noun (plural* **Viennese)** a native or citizen of Vienna. [Say vee en EEZ]

Viet Cong *noun (plural* **Viet Cong)** a member of the Communist guerrilla movement in Vietnam which fought the South Vietnamese government forces 1954–75 with the support of the North Vietnamese army and opposed the South Vietnam and US forces in the Vietnam War. [Say vee et KONG]

Vietnamese • *adjective* of or relating to Vietnam, a country in Southeast Asia, or its inhabitants or language. • *noun (plural* **Vietnamese) 1** a native or national of Vietnam. **2** the language of Vietnam. [Say vee etna MEEZ]

view • *noun* **1** range of vision; extent of visibility. **2 a** what is seen from a particular point; a scene or prospect. **b** a picture etc. representing this. **3 a** an opinion or belief concerning a particular subject or thing. **b** a mental attitude; an outlook: *took a favourable view of the matter*. **c** a manner of considering a thing: *took a long-term view of the situation*. **4** a visual examination, inspection, or survey. **5** an opportunity for a formal visual inspection: *a private view of the exhibition*. **6** an instance of viewing, esp. a television program: *pay-per-view*. • *verb* **1** inspect or examine in a formal or official manner: *we are going to view the house*. **2** catch sight of; spy, see. **3** regard or approach in a particular manner; consider: *they viewed her with suspicion*. **4** *Computing* read or examine (a document or the contents of a file) in a window in which changes and corrections cannot be made. **5** watch (television or a program on television). **PHRASES have in view 1** have as one's object. **2** bear (a circumstance) in mind in forming a judgment etc. **in view of 1** considering; on account of. **2** so as to be seen by; within the visible range of. **on view** being shown (for observation or inspection); being displayed or exhibited. **with a view to 1** with the hope or intention of. **2** with the aim of attaining or achieving. ▶ **viewable** *adjective*

viewer *noun* **1** a person who views, watches, or looks at something; an observer, a spectator. **2** a person watching television. **3** a device for looking at photographic slides or transparencies etc.

viewership *noun* **1** the audience for a television

V

program or channel etc. **2** the number of viewers comprising this audience.

viewfinder *noun* a device on a camera showing the field of view of the lens, used in framing and focusing a picture.

viewing *noun* **1** an opportunity or occasion to view. **2** the activity or a period of watching television. **3** an opportunity for mourners to see the body of a deceased person for a final time prior to a funeral.

viewpoint *noun* **1** a point of view; a mental standpoint from which a matter is considered. **2** a place or position from which a view or prospect may be seen.

vigil *noun* **1** a stationary and peaceful demonstration in support of a particular cause, usu. without speeches or other explicit advocacy of the cause, and often with some suggestion of mourning. **2** an occasion or period of keeping awake for any reason during a time usually devoted to sleep, esp. to keep watch or pray. **3** *Christianity* the eve of a festival or holy day as an occasion for religious observance. [Say VIDGE ul]

vigilance *noun* the quality of being alert to harm, danger, or difficulties: *its vigilance with regard to safety is one reason why the safety of Canada's nuclear sector is second to none*. [Say VIDGE a lunce]

vigilant *adjective* keeping careful watch for signs of harm, danger, or difficulty: *the regional director in charge of railway safety said the public was not at risk as long as the company inspectors remain vigilant ◊ mining companies must be vigilant about preventing unnecessary damage to the environment.* ▶ **vigilantly** *adverb* [Say VIDGE a lunt]

vigilante *noun* a person, often a member of a group, who attempts to prevent crime or punish criminals without the legal authority to do so, usu. because proper law enforcement organizations do not exist or are perceived to be inadequate. ▶ **vigilantism** *noun* [Say vidge a LANTY]

vignette *noun* **1 a** a brief descriptive account, anecdote, essay, or character sketch: *specialized in charming or odd vignettes of hometown boys designed for hometown consumption.* **b** a short evocative usu. self-contained episode in a play, novel, movie, etc.: *the movie is a series of vignettes that take place in and around an old-fashioned Brooklyn cigar store.* **2** an illustration or decorative design on a blank space in a book. **3** an evocative image or photograph: *the interior is a vignette of old Quebec charm, with fieldstone fireplaces and low wood-beamed ceilings.* [Say vin YET]

vigorous *adjective* **1 a** (of a person, animal, etc.) physically strong, healthy and robust. **b** (of a plant) growing actively; flourishing. **2** characterized by, requiring, or involving physical force or energy. **3** (of language etc.) powerful, vehement, rousing. ▶ **vigorously** *adverb* **vigorousness** *noun*

SPELL CHECK   ABC ✓
vigour, invigorate, reinvigorate

Note that while **vigour** is spelled with a *u*, **invigorate** and **reinvigorate** are not.

vigour *noun* (also **vigor**) **1** active physical strength or energy. **2** a flourishing physical condition. **3** intensity of effect or operation: *the storm's vigour.* **4** mental or emotional strength, intensity, or vitality as shown in thought or speech or in literary style.

Viking • *noun* any of the Scandinavian seafaring pirates and traders who raided and settled in parts of northwestern Europe in the 8th–11th centuries. • *adjective* of or relating to the Vikings or their time.

SPELL CHECK
vile, vial

A small vessel for medicine is a **vial**.

vile *adjective* **1 a** disgusting: *all Dora could smell was his vile aftershave.* **b** abominably bad: *followed with a vile rendition of "O sole mio".* **2** shameful, wicked: *her attack on Dr. Green is uncalled for and vile.* ▶ **vileness** *noun*

vilification *noun* an act of speaking or writing about someone in an abusively critical or disapproving manner: *the military authorities began a campaign of personal vilification against the opposition leader.* [Say villa fuh KAY sh'n]

vilify *verb* (**vilifies**, **vilified**, **vilifying**) speak or write about someone in an abusively critical or disapproving manner: *critics have vilified him as a pro-business toady.* [Say VILLA fie]

villa *noun* (*plural* **villas**) **1** a luxurious country residence, esp. in continental Europe. **2** *Roman History* a large country house with an estate.

village *noun* **1 a** a group of houses and associated buildings, larger than a hamlet and smaller than a town, esp. in a rural area. **b** the inhabitants of a village regarded as a community. **2** a self-contained district or community within a city or town, regarded as having features characteristic of a village. **3** a small municipality with limited corporate powers. ▶ **villager** *noun*

villain *noun* **1** a person guilty or capable of great wickedness. **2** the character in a play, novel, etc., whose evil actions or motives are important in the plot. **3** *informal usu. jocular* a rascal or rogue. PHRASES **villain of the piece** the person responsible for mishandling or interfering with a situation, esp. in business or politics.

villainous *adjective* characteristic of a villain: *a villainous plot.* ▶ **villainously** *adverb*

villainy *noun* wicked or criminal behaviour: *intelligent criminals hide their villainy well.*

-ville *combining form informal* forming words designating a place, situation, etc. having a specified quality: *hicksville ◊ dullsville.*

villein *noun hist.* a feudal tenant entirely subject to a lord or attached to a manor. [Sounds like *VILLAIN*]

vim *noun informal* vigour, energy.

vinaigrette *noun* a dressing served with salads and cold meats, made with oil, vinegar, and various seasonings. [Say vinna GRETT]

vindaloo *noun* (*plural* **vindaloos**) a heavily spiced Indian curry dish made with meat, fish, or poultry. [Say vin duh LOO]

vindicate *verb* (**vindicates**, **vindicated**, **vindicating**) **1** clear someone of blame or suspicion: *hospital staff were vindicated by the inquest verdict.* **2** show or prove to be right, reasonable, or justified: *scientific observation will vindicate her theories.* ▶ **vindication** *noun* [Say VINDA kate]

vindictive *adjective* having or showing a strong or unreasonable desire for revenge: *his public criticism of her suggestion was cruel, petty, and vindictive.* ▶ **vindictiveness** *noun* [Say vin DICK tiv]

vine *noun* **1** a climbing or trailing woody-stemmed plant that bears grapes. **2** the slender stem of a trailing or climbing plant.

vinegar *noun* **1** a sour liquid consisting mainly of dilute acetic acid, produced by the oxidation of the alcohol in wine or cider etc., and used as a condiment or food preservative. **2** energy, vitality: *three major surgeries for cancer had taken a lot of zip and vinegar out of me.* ▶ **vinegared** *adjective* **vinegary** *adjective*

vineyard *noun* a plantation of grapevines, esp. one cultivated for winemaking. [Say VIN yurd]

vinifera • *adjective* of, derived from, or designating the vine *Vitis vinifera* or its grape, native to Europe and also widely cultivated in North America. • *noun* (*plural* **vinifera** or **viniferas**) the vinifera wine or grape. [Say vie NIFFER uh]

vinification *noun* the conversion of grape juice etc. into wine by fermentation. ▶ **vinify** *verb* (**vinifies**, **vinified**, **vinifying**) [Say vin iffa KAY sh'n, VIN if eye]

vino *noun* informal or jocular wine. [Say VEE no]

vintage • *noun* **1 a** the year in which the grapes are picked for the production of a particular wine. **b** the wine made from these grapes. **2** a wine of high quality from a single identified year and district. **3** the process of gathering grapes for winemaking. **4** the year or period when a thing was made or produced: *a car of pre-war vintage*. • *adjective* **1** being of high quality and earlier time: *a vintage house*. **2** characteristic of the best period of a person's work or career. **3** (of wine) produced in an exceptional or outstanding year.

vintner *noun* a person who makes or sells wine.

vinyl *noun* **1** Chemistry the radical –CH:CH$_2$, derived from ethylene by removal of a hydrogen atom: *vinyl group*. **2** any plastic made by polymerizing a compound containing the vinyl group, esp. polyvinyl chloride. **3 a** a phonograph record. **b** phonograph records collectively, esp. as opposed to audio tapes and compact discs.

viol *noun* a musical instrument of the Renaissance and Baroque periods, having five, six, or seven strings, often with frets, played with a bow and held vertically on the knees or between the legs. [Sounds like *VIAL*]

viola[1] *noun* (*plural* **violas**) **1 a** a four-stringed musical instrument of the violin family, larger than the violin and of lower pitch. **b** a person who plays or is playing a viola. **2** a viol. [Say vee OH luh]

viola[2] *noun* (*plural* **violas**) **1** any plant of a genus that includes the pansy and violet. **2** a cultivated hybrid of this genus. [Say vee OH luh or vee OH luh]

viola da gamba *noun* a viol held between the player's legs, esp. one corresponding to the modern cello. [Say vee OH luh da GAMBA]

violate *verb* (**violates**, **violated**, **violating**) **1** fail to observe or comply with: *violated the agreement*. **2 a** treat irreverently; desecrate, defile (a sanctuary etc.). **b** fail to respect; disregard: *violate tradition*. **3** break in or intrude upon, disturb (a person's privacy etc.). **4** assault sexually; rape. ▶ **violation** *noun* **violator** *noun*

violence *noun* **1** the esp. illegal exercise of physical force to cause injury or damage to a person or property; violent behaviour. **2** strength or intensity of emotion; fervour, passion. PHRASES **do violence to 1** misinterpret, misapply, or distort. **2** cause harm or injury to.

violent *adjective* **1 a** involving or characterized by the use of great physical force, esp. in order to cause injury: *a violent game*. **b** involving an unlawful use of force: *violent crime*. **2** (of a person) tending to use aggressive physical force, esp. to injure or intimidate others. **3** operating with great and usu. destructive physical force: *a violent storm*. **4** passionate, intense, extreme: *violent dislike*. **5** (of death) resulting from external force or from poison. ▶ **violently** *adverb*

violet • *noun* **1** a plant of temperate regions, usu. having purple, blue, yellow, or white five-petalled flowers. **2** the bluish-purple colour seen at the end of the spectrum opposite red. • *adjective* of a bluish-purple colour.

violin *noun* **1** a musical instrument with four strings, rested on the shoulder beneath the chin and played with a bow, having about the same range as a soprano singer. **2** a violin player. ▶ **violinist** *noun*

violist *noun* a person who plays a viola. [Say vee OLE ist]

violoncello *noun* (*plural* **violoncellos**) formal = CELLO. [Say vee uh lun CHELL oh or vie uh lun CHELL oh]

VIP *noun* (*plural* **VIPs**) a very important person, esp. a high-ranking official or guest.

viper *noun* **1** a venomous snake with large hinged fangs, usu. having a broad head and a stout body, with dark patterns on a lighter background. **2** a spiteful or treacherous person.

viral *adjective* of or caused by a virus. [Say VIE rull]

vireo *noun* (*plural* **vireos**) a small plain songbird inhabiting woodlands throughout the western hemisphere. [Say VEERY oh]

virgin • *noun* **1** a person who has never had sexual intercourse. **2 a** (**the Virgin**) the Virgin Mary. **b** a picture or statue etc. representing the Virgin Mary. **3** informal a naive, innocent, or inexperienced person: *a political virgin*. **4** a member of any order of women under a vow of chastity. • *adjective* **1 a** being a virgin. **b** of or befitting a virgin: *virgin modesty*. **2** not yet used, explored, or exploited: *virgin prairie*. **3** undefiled, spotless: *stepped out into a thick blanket of virgin snow*. **4** (of olive oil) obtained from the first pressing of olives; unrefined. **5** (of wool) that has never, or only once, been spun or woven.

virginal *adjective* **1** that is a virgin. **2** that belongs or relates to a virgin. **3** that befits, resembles, or is characteristic of a virgin.

Virginia creeper *noun* a North American vine that is cultivated esp. for its red autumn foliage.

Virginian • *adjective* of or relating to the US state of Virginia. • *noun* a native or inhabitant of Virginia.

virginity *noun* **1** the state of being a virgin. **2** a naive, innocent, or inexperienced state: *the lawsuit will be remembered as the moment when the computer industry lost its political virginity*.

Virgo *noun* (*plural* **Virgos**) **1** a constellation on the celestial equator between Leo and Libra, containing several bright stars and a dense cluster of galaxies, which is traditionally regarded as representing a maiden or goddess associated with the harvest. **2 a** the sixth sign of the zodiac. **b** a person born when the sun is in this sign, usu. between Aug. 23 and Sept. 22. ▶ **Virgoan** *noun & adjective*

virile *adjective* **1** (of a man) having strength, energy, and a strong sex drive: *with 100,000 bachelors on the prairies, most of them young and virile, the bawdy houses did not lack customers*. **2** having or characterized by strength and energy: *his playing is elegant, virile, and sensitive* ◊ *a virile economy*. ▶ **virility** *noun* [Say VEER ile, vuh RILLA tee]

virologist *noun* a scientist who studies viruses. [Say vie RAWLA jist]

virology *noun* the branch of science that deals with the study of viruses. [Say vie RAWLA jee]

virtual *adjective* **1** that is such in essence or effect, though not recognized as such in name or according to strict definition: *she married a virtual stranger*. **2 a** not physically existing but made by software to appear to do so from the point of view of the program or user: *virtual memory*. **b** designating or existing or experienced in an environment created by virtual reality. **3** Physics designating particles and processes that cannot be directly detected and occur over very short intervals of time and space with correspondingly indefinite energy and momenta. **4** Optics designating the apparent focus or image resulting from the effect of reflection or refraction upon rays of light.

V

virtual community *noun Computing* a group of users who communicate regularly in cyberspace.

virtuality *noun* virtual reality.

virtually *adverb* **1** in effect; practically. **2** nearly, almost.

virtual memory *noun Computing* an apparent increase in the amount of available RAM, which is actually supported by data held in secondary storage, e.g. a hard disk, transfer between the two being made automatically as required.

virtual reality *noun* **1** a notional image or environment generated by computer software with which a user can interact realistically by using gloves fitted with sensors and a helmet containing a screen. **2** the software or technology used to generate this environment.

virtue *noun* **1** conformity of life and conduct with moral principles; voluntary adherence to recognized laws or standards of conduct; moral excellence. **2** a particular form of moral excellence; a manifestation of the influence of moral principles in life or conduct: *patience is a virtue*. **3** chastity or sexual purity, traditionally esp. of women. **4** a particular beneficial quality or feature inherent in or pertaining to something: *the virtues of the legislation*. PHRASES **by** (or **in**) **virtue of** on the strength or basis of; due to. **make a virtue of necessity** derive some credit or benefit from an unwelcome obligation.

virtuosic *adjective* having or displaying the skills of a virtuoso. [Say virtue OSS ick]

virtuosity *noun* a very high degree of skill in performing or playing: *technical virtuosity* ◊ *a performance of breathtaking virtuosity*. [Say virtue OSSA tee]

virtuoso • *noun* (*plural* **virtuosi** or **virtuosos**) **1** a person who has mastered the technique of a fine art, esp. music. **2** a person with outstanding technical skill in any sphere. • *adjective* requiring or displaying the skills of a virtuoso: *a virtuoso piece*. [Say virtue OH so for the singular, virtue OH see or virtue OH soze for the plural]

virtuous *adjective* **1** having or showing high moral standards. **2** chaste.

virulence *noun* **1** violent hostility: *the virulence of some of the attacks was disturbing*. **2** (in diseases or micro-organisms) the quality of being virulent. [Say VEER oo l'nt or VEER yoo l'nt]

virulent *adjective* **1** violently bitter; full of hostility: *virulent abuse*. **2 a** (of a disease) malignant or severe. **b** (of micro-organisms) capable of producing disease. **3** possessing venomous or poisonous qualities. ▶ **virulently** *adverb* [Say VEER oo l'nt or VEER yoo l'nt]

virus *noun* (*plural* **viruses**) **1 a** a submicroscopic organism that can multiply only inside living host cells, has a non-cellular structure lacking any intrinsic metabolism and usu. comprising a single DNA or RNA molecule inside a protein coat, and is usu. pathogenic. **b** an infection with such an organism. **2** = COMPUTER VIRUS. **3** a harmful, corrupting, or malignant influence: *the virus of corruption endemic to Africa*.

visa *noun* (*plural* **visas**) **1** an endorsement on a passport etc. showing that it has been found correct, esp. as allowing the holder to enter or leave a country. **2** the term for which such an endorsement remains valid: *overstayed their visa*.

visage *noun literary* a face, a countenance. [Say VIZ idge]

vis-à-vis • *preposition* **1** in relation to; with regard to: *many agencies now have a unit to deal with women's needs vis-à-vis employment*. **2** as compared with; as opposed to: *the advantage for US exports is the value of the American dollar vis-à-vis other currencies*. • *noun* (*plural* **vis-à-vis**) a person occupying a corresponding position in another group: *his admiration for the US armed services extends to their vis-à-vis, the Russian military*. [Say veez a VEE]

viscera *plural noun* the internal organs in the main cavities of the body, esp. those in the abdomen, e.g. the intestines. [Say VISSER uh]

visceral *adjective* **1** of the viscera. **2** relating to inward feelings or instinct rather than conscious reasoning: *the voters' visceral fear of change*. ▶ **viscerally** *adverb* [Say VISSER ul]

viscid *adjective* glutinous, sticky: *a thick black viscid liquid distilled from coal*. [Say VISS id]

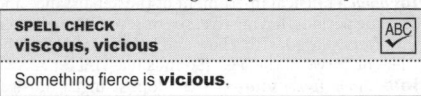

> **SPELL CHECK** ABC
> **viscose, viscous**
>
> Something sticky is **viscous**.

viscose *noun* **1** a form of cellulose in a highly viscous state suitable for drawing into yarn. **2** rayon made from this. [Say VISS kose (KOSE rhymes with DOSE or DOZE)]

viscosity *noun* (*plural* **viscosities**) **1** the quality or degree of being viscous. **2** *Physics* **a** (of a fluid) internal friction, the resistance to flow. **b** a quantity expressing this. [Say viss KOSSA tee]

viscount *noun* a nobleman ranking between an earl or count and a baron. [Say VIE count]

viscountess *noun* (*plural* **viscountesses**) **1** a viscount's wife or widow. **2** a woman holding the rank of viscount in her own right. [Say VIE countess]

> **SPELL CHECK** ABC
> **viscous, vicious**
>
> Something fierce is **vicious**.

viscous *adjective* **1** glutinous, sticky. **2** semi-liquid. **3** *Physics* having a high viscosity. [Say VISS cuss]

> **SPELL CHECK** ABC
> **vise, vice**
>
> The spelling is **vice** for a bad habit and in *vice squad* and *vice-president* etc.

vise • *noun* an instrument, esp. attached to a workbench, with two movable jaws between which an object may be clamped so as to leave the hands free to work on it. • *verb* (**vises, vised, vising**) secure in a vise. ▶ **viselike** *adjective*

visibility *noun* (*plural* **visibilities**) **1** the state of being visible; ability to be seen. **2** the range or possibility of vision as determined by the conditions of light and atmosphere: *visibility was down to 50 metres*. **3** the degree to which something impinges on public awareness or attracts attention: *product visibility*.

visible *adjective* **1 a** that can be seen by the eye. **b** (of light) within the range of wavelengths to which the eye is sensitive. **2** that can be perceived or ascertained; apparent, open: *has no visible means of support*. **3** in a position of public prominence; attracting attention.

visible minority *noun* (*plural* **visible minorities**) esp. *Cdn* **1** an ethnic group whose members are clearly racially distinct from those of the predominant race in a society. **2** a member of such an ethnic group.

visible spectrum *noun* the range of wavelengths of electromagnetic radiation to which the human eye is normally sensitive.

visibly *adverb* in a way that is easily noticeable: *he was visibly shocked* ◊ *she paled visibly at the news*.

Visigoth *noun* **1** a West Goth, a member of the branch of the Goths who settled in France and Spain in the 5th century and ruled much of Spain until 711. **2** *informal* an

uncivilized or barbarous person: *a number of beery Visigoths hung out of their car windows*. [Say VIZ a goth]

vision *noun* **1** the act or faculty of seeing. **2 a** a thing or person seen in a dream or trance. **b** a supernatural or prophetic apparition. **3** a thing or idea perceived vividly in the imagination: *had visions of sandy beaches*. **4** imaginative insight. **5** ability to plan or form policy in a far-sighted way, e.g. in politics. **6** a person etc. of unusual beauty.

visionary • *adjective* **1** (esp. of a person) thinking about or planning the future with imagination or wisdom: *a visionary leader*. **2** of, relating to, or able to see visions in a dream or trance, or as a supernatural apparition: *a visionary experience*. • *noun* (*plural* **visionaries**) a visionary person.

vision quest *noun* (among some North American Aboriginal peoples) a sacred ceremony in which an individual, often a teenage boy, goes to a secluded place to fast and communicate with the spiritual world, often through visions.

visit • *verb* (**visits**, **visited**, **visiting**) **1 a** go or come to see (a person, place, etc.) as an act of friendship or ceremony, on business or for a purpose, or from interest. **b** go or come to see for the purpose of official inspection, supervision, consultation, or correction. **2** reside temporarily with (a person) or at (a place). **3** access and view a site on the World Wide Web. **4** (of a disease, calamity, etc.) come upon, attack. **5** *Bible* **a** (foll. by *with*) punish (a person). **b** (often foll. by *upon*) inflict punishment for (a sin). **6 a** (foll. by *with*) go to see (a person) esp. socially. **b** (usu. foll. by *with*) converse, chat. • *noun* **1 a** an act of visiting, a call on a person or at a place. **b** temporary residence with a person or at a place. **2** (foll. by *to*) an occasion of going to a doctor, dentist, etc. **3** a formal or official call for the purpose of inspection etc. **4** a chat.

visitation *noun* **1** a visit, esp. a formal one. **2 a** divorced person's visit with his or her child in the custody of a former spouse, granted as a right by a court. **3** a visit with a sick person in a hospital, a prison inmate, etc. **4** (**Visitation**) **a** the visit of the Virgin Mary to Elizabeth related in Luke 1:39-56. **b** the feast commemorating this on May 31 or July 2. **5** an official visit of inspection. **6** *informal* an unduly protracted visit or social call. **7** trouble or difficulty regarded as a divine punishment.

visiting • *noun* paying a visit or visits. • *adjective* **1** that visits: *visiting nurse*. **2** (of an academic etc.) having been invited from one institution to spend some time at another: *a visiting professor*. **3** pertaining to visits: *visiting hours*.

visitor *noun* **1** a person who visits a person or place. **2** *Sport* a team competing in the opposing side's home stadium, rink, etc. **3** a person who views or has viewed a site on the World Wide Web.

visor *noun* **1 a** a movable part of a helmet covering the face. **b** the projecting front part of a cap. **c** a half-moon shaped shade on an adjustable or elasticized headband, worn to protect the eyes from strong light. **2** a movable flap at the top of a windshield inside a car to protect the eyes from glare. ▶ **visored** *adjective*

vista *noun* (*plural* **vistas**) **1** a long narrow view as between rows of trees. **2** a scenic wide view; a panorama. **3** a mental view of a long succession of remembered or anticipated events: *opened up new vistas to her ambition*.

visual • *adjective* of, concerned with, or used in seeing. • *noun* (usu. in *plural*) **1** a visual image or display, a picture. **2** the visual element of a film or television broadcast.

visual art *noun* (often in *plural*) any art meant to be appreciated mainly or exclusively through sight, e.g. graphic art, sculpture, etc. ▶ **visual artist** *noun*

visualization *noun* an act of visualizing.

visualize *verb* (**visualizes**, **visualized**, **visualizing**) **1** make visible esp. to one's mind (a thing not visible to the eye). **2** make visible to the eye.

visually *adverb* of or pertaining to vision: *visually stunning*.

vital • *adjective* **1 a** essential to the existence or functioning of a thing or to the matter in hand; extremely important: *secrecy is vital*. **b** paramount, very great: *of vital importance*. **2** of, concerned with, or essential to organic life: *vital functions*. **3** full of life or activity; lively. • *noun* (in *plural*) the body's vital organs, e.g. the heart and brain.

vitality *noun* **1** liveliness, animation. **2** the ability to sustain life, vital power. **3** (of an institution etc.) the ability to endure and perform its functions.

vitalize *verb* (**vitalizes**, **vitalized**, **vitalizing**) **1** endow with life. **2** infuse with vigour.

vitally *adverb* extremely; in an essential way: *careful planning is vitally important*.

vital signs *plural noun* clinical measurements that indicate the state of a person's essential body functions, esp. pulse rate, temperature, respiration rate, and blood pressure.

vital statistics *plural noun* **1** the number of births, marriages, deaths, etc. **2** *jocular* the measurements of a woman's bust, waist, and hips.

vitamin *noun* **1** any of a group of organic compounds essential in small amounts for many living organisms to maintain normal health and development. **2** (often in *plural*) a pill providing any of these as a dietary supplement.

vitamin A *noun* = RETINOL.

vitamin B$_1$ *noun* = THIAMINE.

vitamin B$_2$ *noun* = RIBOFLAVIN.

vitamin B$_3$ *noun* = NIACIN.

vitamin B$_{12}$ *noun* a vitamin of the B complex, found in foods of animal origin such as liver, fish, and eggs.

vitamin B complex *noun* a group of vitamins which, although not chemically related, are often found together in the same foods.

vitamin C *noun* = ASCORBIC ACID.

vitamin D *noun* any of a group of vitamins found in liver and fish oils and sunlight, essential for the absorption of calcium and the prevention of rickets.

vitamin D$_3$ *noun* = CHOLECALCIFEROL.

vitamin E *noun* = TOCOPHEROL.

vitamin K *noun* any of a group of vitamins found esp. in green leaves, essential for blood clotting.

vitiate *verb* (**vitiates**, **vitiated**, **vitiating**) **1** spoil or impair the quality or efficiency of: *development programs have been vitiated by the increase in population*. **2** destroy or impair the legal validity of. [Say VISHY ate]

viticultural *adjective* having to do with the cultivation of grapevines. [Say vitta CULTURAL]

viticulture *noun* the cultivation of grapevines; the science or study of this. [Say VITTA culture]

vitreous *adjective* **1** of, or of the nature of, glass. **2** like glass in hardness, brittleness, transparency, structure, etc.: *vitreous enamel*. [Say VITRY us]

vitrify *verb* (**vitrifies**, **vitrified**, **vitrifying**) convert or be converted into glass or a glasslike substance esp. by heat. [Say VITRA fie]

vitriol *noun* **1** sulphuric acid or a sulphate. **2** cruel and bitter criticism: *her mother's sudden rush of fury and vitriol*. [Say VITRY ul]

vitriolic *adjective* (of speech or criticism) cruel or

bitter: *Stella Duane's critics launched a bitter and vitriolic attack against her*. [Say vitry AWL ick]

vittle *informal* = VICTUAL *noun*.

vituperation *noun* bitter and abusive language: *no one else attracted such vituperation from him*. [Say vit tooper AY sh'n]

vituperative *verb* bitter and abusive: *the criticism soon turned into a vituperative attack*. [Say vit TOOPER a tiv]

vivacious *adjective* (esp. of a woman) attractively lively and animated: *a smart, pretty, and vivacious girl*.
▶ **vivaciously** *adverb* **vivacity** *noun* [Say viv AY shuss or vive AY shuss, viv ASSA tee or vive ASSA tee]

vivid *adjective* **1 a** (of light or colour) strong, intense, glaring: *a vivid green*. **b** brilliantly coloured or lit. **2 a** (of an impression, description, etc.) clear, striking, graphic. **b** (of a mental faculty) capable of strong and distinct impressions, producing clear images; active: *has a vivid imagination*. ▶ **vividly** *adverb* **vividness** *noun*

vivify *verb* (**vivifies**, **vivified**, **vivifying**) enliven or animate: *field trips vivify education*. [Say VIV a fie]

vivisect *verb* perform experiments on live animals for medical or scientific research. [Say VIV a sect]

vivisection *noun* the practice of doing experiments on live animals for medical or scientific research. [Say VIV a section]

vixen *noun* **1** a female fox. **2** a spiteful or quarrelsome woman.

viz. *adverb* namely; that is to say; in other words: *came to a firm conclusion, viz. that we were right*.

vizier *noun hist.* a high official in some Muslim countries, esp. in Turkey under Ottoman rule. [Say VIZZY ur or viz EAR]

VJ *noun* (*plural* **VJs**) video jockey, a person who introduces music videos on television etc.

VLSI *abbreviation* very large-scale integration, the technology integrating over 100,000 transistors on a single chip.

VLT *noun* (*plural* **VLTs**) VIDEO LOTTERY TERMINAL.

V-neck *noun* (often as an *adjective*) **1** (also **V-neckline**) a neck of a pullover etc. with straight sides meeting at an angle in the front to form a V. **2** a garment with this.
▶ **V-necked** *adjective*

vocab *noun informal* vocabulary. [Say VO cab]

vocabulary *noun* (*plural* **vocabularies**) **1** the (principal) words used in a language or a particular book or branch of science etc. or by a particular author. **2 a** list of these, arranged alphabetically with definitions or translations. **3** the range of words known to an individual: *his vocabulary is limited*.

vocal • *adjective* **1** of or concerned with or uttered by the voice: *a vocal communication*. **2** expressing one's feelings freely in speech: *was very vocal about his rights*. **3** (of music) written for or produced by the voice with or without accompaniment (*compare* INSTRUMENTAL *adjective* 2). • *noun* (in *singular* or *plural*) the sung part of a musical composition.

vocal cords *plural noun* (also **vocal folds**) folds of the lining membrane of the larynx near the opening of the glottis, which vibrate in the airstream when close together to produce voiced sounds.

vocalic *adjective* of or consisting of a vowel or vowels. [Say vo KAL ick]

vocalist *noun* a singer, esp. of jazz or popular songs.

vocalization *noun* **1** a word or sound that is produced by the voice: *the vocalizations of animals*. **2** the process of producing a word or sound with the voice.

vocalize *verb* (**vocalizes**, **vocalized**, **vocalizing**) **1 a** form (a sound) or utter (a word) with the voice. **b** make voiced: *f is vocalized into v*. **2** utter a vocal sound: *babies with this condition often vocalize spontaneously*.

3 articulate, express: *Gillie could scarcely vocalize her responses*. **4** *Music* sing with several notes to one vowel.

vocally *adverb* **1** in a way that uses the voice: *to communicate vocally*. **2** by speaking in a loud and confident way: *they protested vocally*.

vocation *noun* **1 a** a strong feeling of suitability for a particular career or occupation. **b** a divine call to the religious life. **2 a** a person's employment, esp. regarded as requiring dedication. **b** a trade or profession.

vocational *adjective* **1** of or relating to an occupation or employment. **2** (of education or training) directed at a particular esp. manual or technical occupation and its skills: *vocational school*.

vocative *Grammar* • *noun* the case of nouns, pronouns, and adjectives used in addressing or invoking a person or thing. • *adjective* of or in this case. [Say VOKKA tiv]

vociferous *adjective* **1** noisy, clamorous: *engaged in a vociferous debate*. **2** insistently and forcibly expressing one's views: *became a vociferous critic of the oil companies*.
▶ **vociferously** *adverb* **vociferousness** *noun* [Say vo SIFFER us]

vodka *noun* (*plural* **vodkas**) **1** a colourless alcoholic liquor made by distillation of rye etc. **2** a drink of this.

vogue *noun* **1** (**the vogue**) the prevailing fashion. **2** popular use or currency: *has had a great vogue*. ▐PHRASES▌ **in vogue** in fashion, generally current. [Say VOAG]

voguing *noun* solo dancing with movements reminiscent of a fashion model's posing. [Say VOAG ing]

voguish *adjective* in vogue, fashionable. [Say VOAG ish]

voice • *noun* **1 a** a sound formed in the larynx etc. and uttered by the mouth, esp. human utterance in speaking, shouting, singing, etc.: *heard a voice*. **b** the ability to produce this: *has lost her voice*. **c** this regarded as characteristic of an individual. **2 a** the use of the voice; utterance, esp. in spoken or written words: *give voice*. **b** an opinion so expressed; the expressed will of the people, a group, etc. **c** the right to express an opinion: *I have no voice in the matter*. **3** *Grammar* a form or set of forms of a verb showing the relation of the subject to the action: *passive voice*. **4** *Music* **a** a vocal part in a composition. **b** a constituent part in a fugue. **5** *Phonetics* sound uttered with resonance of the vocal cords, not with mere breath. **6** (usu. in *plural*) the supposed utterance of an invisible guiding or directing spirit. • *verb* (**voices**, **voiced**, **voicing**) **1** give utterance to; express: *the letter voices our opinion*. **2** (esp. as **voiced** *adjective*) *Phonetics* utter with vibration of the vocal cords, e.g. *b, d, g, v, z*. ▐PHRASES▌ **in voice** (or **good voice**) in proper vocal condition for singing or speaking. **with one voice** unanimously.

voice box *noun* (*plural* **voice boxes**) the larynx.

-voiced *combining form* having a voice of the kind indicated: *a squeaky-voiced kid*.

voiceless *adjective* **1** dumb, mute, speechless. **2** *Phonetics* uttered without vibration of the vocal cords, e.g. *f, k, p, s, t*.

voice mail *noun* a system for electronically storing, processing, and reproducing verbal messages left through the conventional telephone network.

voice-over *noun* narration in a film etc. not accompanied by a picture of the speaker.

voice print *noun* a visual record of speech, analyzed with respect to frequency, duration, and amplitude.

voicing *noun* **1** the act of uttering with the voice. **2** the tonal quality of a group of jazz instruments etc.

void • *adjective* **1 a** empty, vacant. **b** (foll. by *of*) lacking; free from. **2** esp. *Law* (of a contract, deed, promise, etc.) invalid, not binding: *null and void*. **3** useless, ineffectual: *recent challenges to this form of thinking may*

render many of the arguments void. • *noun* **1** an empty space, a vacuum: *cannot fill the void made by his death.* **2** an unfilled space in a wall or building. • *verb* **1** render invalid. **2** empty the contents of esp. the bowels or bladder; excrete.

voila *interjection* expressing satisfaction or ease of accomplishment. [Say wah LAH]

voile *noun* a thin semi transparent material. [Say VOIL or VWOL]

vol. *abbreviation* volume.

volatile • *adjective* **1** evaporating rapidly: *volatile salts.* **2** liable to change rapidly and unpredictably, esp. for the worse: *the political situation was becoming more volatile.* **3** (of a person or their moods) liable to display rapid changes of emotion: *she is a highly volatile person.* **4** *Computing* designating memory whose contents are destroyed on the removal of power to the memory. • *noun* a volatile substance. ▶**volatility** *noun* [Say VOLLA tile, volla TILLA tee]

volcanic • *adjective* of, like, or produced by a volcano. • *noun* (usu. in *plural*) a rock etc. formed by volcanic action. ▶**volcanically** *adverb*

volcanism *noun* volcanic activity.

volcano *noun* (*plural* **volcanoes**) **1** a mountain or hill having an opening or openings in the earth's crust through which lava, cinders, steam, gases, etc., are or have been expelled continuously or at intervals. **2** a state of affairs likely to cause a violent outburst.

volcanologist *noun* a scientist who studies volcanoes. [Say vol can OLLA jist]

volcanology *noun* the scientific study of volcanoes. [Say vol can OLLA jee]

vole *noun* a small rat-like or mouselike burrowing plant-eating rodent.

volition *noun* the faculty or power of using one's will: *without conscious volition she backed into her office.* PHRASES **of** (or **by**) **one's own volition** voluntarily. [Say vuh LISH un]

volley • *noun* (*plural* **volleys**) **1 a** the simultaneous discharge of a number of weapons. **b** the bullets etc. discharged in a volley. **2** (usu. foll. by *of*) a rapid emission of many things at once in quick succession: *a volley of insults.* **3 a** the return of a ball, shuttlecock, etc. in play in tennis etc. before it touches the ground. **b** a series of these. **4** *Soccer* the kicking of a ball in play before it touches the ground. **5** *Volleyball* a pass etc. made with the fingertips. • *verb* (**volleys, volleyed, volleying**) **1** *Sport* return or send (a ball) by a volley. **2** discharge (bullets, abuse, etc.) in a volley. **3** (of bullets etc.) fly in a volley. **4** (of guns etc.) sound together.

volleyball *noun* **1** a game for two usu. six-player teams in which a large inflated ball is hit back and forth over a net with the fingers, fist, or forearm. **2** the ball used in this game.

vols. *abbreviation* volumes.

> SPELL CHECK
> **volt, vault** ABC✔
>
> An arch, chamber, or leap is a **vault**.

volt *noun* the SI unit of electromotive force, the difference of potential that would carry one ampere of current against one ohm resistance. Abbreviation: **V.**

voltage *noun* electromotive force or potential difference expressed in volts.

volte-face *noun* a complete reversal of position in argument or opinion: *a remarkable volte-face on taxes.* [Say volta FASS]

volubility *noun* the state of being voluble in speech; talkativeness: *provided a contrast to the noisy volubility of Paris.* [Say vol yoo BILLA tee]

voluble *adjective* **1** talking a lot, and with enthusiasm, about a subject: *Evelyn was very voluble on the subject of women's rights.* **2** expressed in many words and spoken quickly: *voluble protests.* ▶**volubly** *adverb* [Say VOL yoo bull]

volume *noun* **1 a** a set of sheets of paper, usu. printed, and bound together; a book, esp. one of a matching set or series: *issued in three volumes* ◊ *a library of 12,000 volumes.* **b** several consecutive issues of a magazine etc. esp. designed to be bound together as a book. **2 a** solid content, bulk. **b** the space occupied by a substance. **c** (usu. foll. by *of*) an amount or quantity: *large volume of business.* **d** the amount of space in a container. **3 a** quantity or power of sound. **b** a knob etc. controlling this, as on stereo equipment. **c** fullness of tone. **4** (foll. by *of*) **a** a moving mass of water etc. **b** (usu. in *plural*) a wreath or coil or rounded mass of smoke etc. ▶**volumed** *adjective* (also in *combination*)

volumetric *adjective* of or relating to measurement by volume. ▶**volumetrically** *adverb* [Say vol yoo METRIC]

voluminous *adjective* **1** large in volume; bulky: *a voluminous backpack.* **2** (of drapery, a skirt, etc.) loose and ample: *she was suddenly in the room, wearing one of her voluminous caftans.* **3** (of writing) very lengthy and full: *she seems to have read the entirety of their voluminous correspondence.* ▶**voluminously** *adverb* [Say vuh LOO min us]

voluntarily *adverb* **1** willingly; without being forced: *he was not asked to leave — he went voluntarily.* **2** without payment: *the fund is voluntarily administered.* [Say vol un TARE a lee]

voluntarism *noun* **1** the principle of relying on voluntary action rather than compulsion, esp. as regards social welfare. **2** *Philosophy* the doctrine that will is a fundamental or dominant factor in the individual or the universe. ▶**voluntarist** *noun* [Say VOL un tuh rism]

voluntary • *adjective* **1** done, acting, or able to act of one's own free will: *a voluntary donation.* **2** unpaid: *voluntary work.* **3** (of an institution) **a** supported by voluntary contributions. **b** staffed by volunteers. **4** brought about, produced, etc., by voluntary action. **5** (of a movement, muscle, or limb) controlled by the will. **6** (of a confession by a criminal) not prompted by a promise or threat. **7** not accidental; intentional: *voluntary manslaughter.* • *noun* (*plural* **voluntaries**) **1** an organ solo played before, during, or after a church service. **2** the music for this. [Say VOL un terry]

volunteer • *noun* **1** a person who voluntarily takes part in an enterprise or offers to undertake a task. **2** a person who enrols voluntarily for military service. **3** a person who works for an organization voluntarily and without pay. **4** (as an *adjective*) designating an organization etc. composed of volunteers: *volunteer fire department.* • *verb* **1** undertake or offer (one's services, a remark or explanation, etc.) voluntarily: *she volunteered to stay late.* **2** (often foll. by *for*) make a voluntary offer of one's services; be a volunteer. **3** (usu. in *passive*) often *ironic* assign or commit (a person) to a particular esp. "voluntary" undertaking, esp. without consultation: *my boss volunteered me to go to the conference.* ▶**volunteering** *noun*

volunteerism *noun* the involvement of volunteers, esp. in community service.

voluptuous *adjective* **1** (of a woman) curvaceous and sexually desirable: *a voluptuous redhead.* **2** of, relating to, or characterized by luxury or sensual pleasure: *long curtains in voluptuous crimson velvet.* ▶**voluptuously** *adverb* **voluptuousness** *noun* [Say vuh LUP chew us or vuh LUP tyoo us]

vomit • *verb* (**vomits, vomited, vomiting**) **1** eject

(matter) from the stomach through the mouth. **2** (of a volcano, chimney, etc.) eject violently, belch forth. • *noun* matter vomited from the stomach.

VON *Cdn* • *abbreviation* VICTORIAN ORDER OF NURSES. • *noun* (*plural* **VONs**) a nurse belonging to this organization.

voodoo *noun* **1** a religion practised in the West Indies and the southern US, characterized by sorcery and spirit possession, and combining elements of traditional African religious rites with Catholic ritual. **2** a person skilled in this. **3** a voodoo spell.

voodoo doll *noun* a small figure in the likeness of a real person, the tormenting or hexing of which supposedly affects the person.

voracious *adjective* **1** greedy in eating. **2** insatiable: *a voracious reader.* ▶**voraciously** *adverb* [Say vuh RAY shuss]

voracity *noun* the quality of being voracious: *ate with a voracity known only to the starving.* [Say vuh RASSA tee]

vortex *noun* (*plural* **vortices** or **vortexes**) **1** a mass of whirling fluid, esp. a whirlpool or whirlwind. **2** any whirling motion or mass. **3** a system, occupation, pursuit, etc., viewed as swallowing up or engrossing those who approach it: *the vortex of society.* [Say VORE tex for the singular, VORE tuh seez for the plural]

votary *noun* (*plural* **votaries**) **1** a devoted follower of a religion, deity, or cult, esp. one who is bound, by vow, to the worship of God: *the installation of members of the royal families as priests and votaries.* **2** (often foll. by *of*) a devoted follower, adherent, or advocate of a person, cause, occupation, or pursuit: *a votary of human rights.* [Say VOTE a ree]

vote • *noun* **1 a** a formal expression of choice or opinion by means of a ballot, show of hands, etc., concerning esp. a choice of candidate or approval or rejection of a motion or resolution. **b** a ballot or ticket used for recording one's choice: *still counting the votes.* **2** the collective votes that are or may be given by or for a particular group: *we hope to win the francophone vote.* **3** (usu. as **the vote**) the right to vote, esp. in general elections. **4 a** an opinion expressed or decision reached by a majority of votes: *a vote of confidence.* **b** a resolution passed or grant of appropriation authorized by Parliament. • *verb* (**votes**, **voted**, **voting**) **1 a** express a choice or preference by casting a vote. **b** (foll. by *on*) register or express one's opinion regarding: *they vote on the proposal today.* **2** decide by a majority of votes: *striking workers have voted to accept the latest proposal.* **3** support (a candidate, party, side, etc.) habitually or in a particular election: *I vote Liberal.* **4** pronounce or declare by formal ballot or general consent: *he was voted the league's MVP.* **5** *informal* announce one's proposal: *I vote that we all go home.* PHRASES **put to a** (or **the**) **vote** submit to a decision by voting. **vote down** defeat (a proposal etc.) in a vote. **vote in** elect (a candidate) by votes. **vote out** dismiss (an incumbent) from office etc. by voting. **vote with one's feet** *informal* indicate an opinion by one's presence or absence.

vote of confidence *noun* (*plural* **votes of confidence**) **1** a vote showing that the majority support the policy of the governing body etc. **2** an indication from a person of his or her support for or approval of another, their work, etc.

vote of non-confidence *noun* (*plural* **votes of non-confidence**) *Cdn* a vote indicating that the majority does not support a policy of the governing party, as a result of which the governing party is usu. forced to resign.

voter *noun* **1** a person eligible to vote in an election. **2** a person voting.

voting shares *plural noun* (also **voting stock** *noun*) shares in a company that entitle the holder to vote at any meetings of the company.

votive *adjective* **1** offered or undertaken in fulfillment of a vow or as a thanksgiving: *votive offering.* **2** expressive of a vow or wish: *votive prayer.* [Say VO tiv]

votive candle *noun* **1** (in some Christian denominations) a candle, often contained in a glass vase, that may be lit as a symbol of prayer, usu. in front of a religious image. **2** a type of squat household candle, usu. tapering at the top and often scented, used for decoration.

vouch *verb* (foll. by *for*) **1** assert or confirm as a result of one's own experience the truth or accuracy of (something): *the explosive used is of my own making, and I can vouch for its efficiency.* **2** confirm the identity or good character of (someone): *she was refused entry until someone could vouch for her.*

voucher *noun* **1** a document which can be exchanged for goods or services, or which entitles the holder to a reduction in the price of something. **2** a person who vouches for a person, statement, etc.

vouchsafe *verb* *formal* **1** give as a gift or privilege: *she would not vouchsafe me a reply.* **2** permit or agree.

vow • *noun* **1** a solemn promise made to God, another deity, or a saint, to perform an action or adopt a particular way of life. **2 a** a solemn undertaking or resolve: *I made a vow never to speak to her again.* **b** (foll. by *of*) a solemn promise to observe a specified state or condition: *a vow of silence.* **3** (in *plural*) **a** the promises by which a monk or nun is bound to poverty, chastity, and obedience. **b** the promises of fidelity made during a marriage ceremony. **4** (usu. as **baptismal vows**) the promises given at baptism by the baptized person or by sponsors. • *verb* **1** promise or undertake solemnly: *she vowed that she would never return.* **2** make a solemn resolve or threat to inflict (injury) or exact (revenge). PHRASES **under a vow** bound by a vow one has made.

vowel *noun* **1** a speech sound made with vibration of the vocal cords but without audible friction, more open than a consonant and capable of forming a syllable. **2** a letter of the alphabet representing such a sound, such as *a, e, i, o, u.*

vox pop *noun* *informal* **1** popular opinion as represented by informal comments from members of the public. **2** statements or interviews of this kind.

voyage • *noun* a journey, esp. a long one by water, air, or in space. • *verb* (**voyages**, **voyaged**, **voyaging**) make a voyage.

voyager *noun* **1** a person who makes a voyage; a traveller. **2** *Cdn* = VOYAGEUR.

voyageur *noun* **1** esp. Cdn hist. a usu. French-speaking or Metis canoeman employed by merchants in Montreal to transport goods to and from trading posts in the interior. **2** an outdoorsman or adventurer, esp. one who goes canoe tripping through rough country. [Say voy a ZHUR or vwah ya ZHUR]

voyageur canoe *noun* *Cdn hist.* a birchbark canoe of the fur trade, about 9 m (30 ft.) long, used on the rivers and lakes northwest of Lake Superior.

voyeur *noun* **1** a person who derives sexual gratification from the covert observation of others as they undress or engage in sexual activities. **2** a powerless or passive observer, esp. one who derives an inordinate amount of enjoyment from observing a situation without participating in it: *voyeurs watched TV pictures of US marines landing on the Somali beaches.* ▶**voyeurism** *noun* **voyeuristic** *adjective* [Say voy YUR, VOY er ism, voy er ISS tick]

VP *abbreviation* Vice-President.

VQA *abbreviation* *Cdn* (as an *adjective*) designating a

Canadian wine certified by the Vintners Quality Alliance, a body of winemakers, wine merchants, and federal government officials, as meeting certain standards of taste and conforming to statutory regulations.

VR *abbreviation* virtual reality.

vroom • *verb* **1** (esp. of a car or engine) make a roaring or revving noise, suggestive of great speed. **2** (of a car or truck etc.) travel at high speed. • *noun* the roaring sound of an engine. • *interjection* an imitation of such a sound.

vs. *abbreviation* versus.

V-shaped *adjective* having a shape or a cross-section resembling the letter V.

Vt. *abbreviation* Vermont.

vulcanize *verb* (**vulcanizes**, **vulcanized**, **vulcanizing**) treat (rubber or rubber-like material) with sulphur at a high temperature to increase its durability and elasticity.

vulcanology *noun* = VOLCANOLOGY. [Say vulcan OLLA jee]

vulgar *adjective* **1** likely to offend; indecent, rude, obscene: *a vulgar joke*. **2** displaying or proceeding from ignorance or a lack of refinement, manners, or taste. **3 a** popular, common. **b** of or characteristic of the common people, plebeian.

vulgarity *noun* (*plural* **vulgarities**) **1** the fact of lacking refinement or manners: *she was offended by the vulgarity of their jokes*. **2** an object etc. that is offensive or lacking in taste: *the vulgarities of theme parks*. [Say vull GARE it ee]

vulgarize *verb* (**vulgarizes**, **vulgarized**, **vulgarizing**)

1 make (a person, manners, etc.) less refined: *her voice was vulgarized by its accent*. **2** make widely known or accessible to the public; make less complex: *an attempt to vulgarize the argument*.

vulgarly *adverb* in a vulgar or offensive manner.

Vulgate *noun* **1** the Latin version of the Bible prepared mainly by St. Jerome in the late 4th century. **2** the official Catholic Latin text of the Bible as revised in 1592. [Say VULL gate or VULL gut]

vulnerability *noun* (*plural* **vulnerabilities**) the state of being vulnerable: *I'm concerned about the plant's vulnerability to cold*.

vulnerable *adjective* **1** able to be physically or emotionally hurt. **2** liable to damage or harm, esp. from aggression or attack: *a vulnerable position*. **3** (foll. by *to*) exposed or susceptible to a destructive agent or influence etc.: *vulnerable to criticism*. ▶ **vulnerably** *adverb*

vulture *noun* **1** a large bird of prey with a mainly bald head and neck, which feeds chiefly on carrion and is reputed to gather with others in anticipation of a death. **2** a ruthless or greedy person, esp. one who preys upon those who are vulnerable or weak: *the vultures waited for the company to falter*.

vulva *noun* (*plural* **vulvas**) the external female genitals, consisting (in women) of the labia, clitoris, and vaginal opening. ▶ **vulval** *adjective*

vying *pres. part. of* VIE.

V

Ww

W¹ *noun* (also **w**) (*plural* **Ws** or **W's**) the twenty-third letter of the alphabet.

W² *abbreviation* (also **W.**) **1** watt(s). **2** West(ern). **3** women's (size).

W³ *symbol* tungsten.

w *abbreviation* (also **w.**) **1** with. **2** wife. **3** weight. **4** width.

wacked *adjective* = WHACKED.

wackiness *noun* the quality of being wacky; goofiness.

wacko *slang* • *adjective* crazy, insane. • *noun* (*plural* **wackos** or **wackoes**) a crazy person.

wacky *adjective* (**wackier, wackiest**) *informal* crazy, madcap, goofy.

wad • *noun* **1 a** a small mass of soft material: *a wad of bubble gum*. **b** a compact bundle of material for stuffing or packing. **2 a** a number of banknotes or papers etc. stacked or rolled together. **b** (in *singular* or *plural*) a large quantity of esp. money. **3** a disc or plug of paper, cloth, or felt retaining the powder and shot in position in a gun or cartridge. • *verb* (**wads, wadded, wadding**) **1** press, crumple, or arrange (soft material). **2** plug (the barrel of a gun) with a wad. [Say WOD]

wadding *noun* **1** any soft, loose, or pliable material used to line, stuff, or pad garments, quilts, etc., or to pack fragile articles. **2** any material from which the wads for guns are made. [Say WODDING]

waddle • *verb* (**waddles, waddled, waddling**) walk with short steps and a clumsy rocking or swaying motion, like a stout short-legged person or a bird with short legs set far apart. • *noun* a waddling gait. ▶ **waddler** *noun*

wade • *verb* (**wades, waded, wading**) **1** walk through a deep liquid or soft substance that impedes motion, such as water, mud, or snow. **2** (often foll. by *through*) go laboriously or doggedly through a tedious task, a long or uninteresting novel, etc. **3** walk through (water etc.). PHRASES **wade in** (or **into**) *informal* involve oneself energetically.

wader *noun* **1** (in *plural*) high waterproof boots, or a waterproof garment for the legs and body, worn esp. for fishing. **2 a** any large, long-necked, long-legged wading bird, as a heron, stork, or crane. **b** a wading bird, esp. any of various birds of the order Charadriiformes. **3** a person who wades.

wading bird *noun* any usu. long-legged wader that finds its food in shallow waters or along the shore.

wafer *noun* **1** a very thin light crisp cookie. **2** a thin disc of unleavened bread used in the Eucharist. **3** *Electronics* a very thin slice of a semiconductor crystal used as the substrate for solid state circuitry. **4** a disc of red paper stuck on a legal document instead of a seal.

waferboard *noun* esp. *Cdn* a rigid sheet or panel ranging in thickness from 6.5 mm (¹/₄ inch) to 19 mm (³/₄ inch), of randomly arranged chips of wood, larger than those of particleboard, bonded with resin.

wafer-thin • *adjective* very thin. • *adverb* very thinly.

waffle¹ • *verb* (**waffles, waffled, waffling**) **1** waver in opinion or resolve. **2** (often foll. by *on*) indulge in rambling aimless speech or writing. • *noun* **1** verbose but aimless talk or writing. **2** (**Waffle**) *Cdn hist.* a caucus of NDP members organized in 1969 to promote a socialist and nationalist agenda, which included the replacement of US private ownership of Canadian industry with Canadian public ownership, the establishment of an independent Canadian labour movement, the right of Quebec to self-determination, and the advancement of the feminist movement.

waffle² *noun* **1** a crisp pancake with a grid-like pattern of indentations on each side. **2** (as an *adjective* or in *combination*) designating esp. fabrics with a texture resembling that of a waffle: *waffle-knit sweater*.

waffle iron *noun* an appliance used to bake waffles, consisting of two hinged metal pans with a grid pattern, which forms indentations on the waffle.

waffler *noun* **1** a person who wavers in opinion or resolve. **2** (**Waffler**) *Cdn hist.* a member of the Waffle caucus of the NDP.

waft • *verb* **1** float or glide gently through or as if through the air or over water. **2** carry or send gently through or as if through the air. • *noun* (usu. foll. by *of*) a scent passing through the air or carried by a breeze; a whiff. [Rhymes with *LOFT* or *RAFT*]

wag¹ • *verb* (**wags, wagged, wagging**) shake, wave, or sway to and fro or from side to side, esp. in a rapid energetic manner: *wagged her finger at me*. • *noun* a single wagging motion: *with a wag of his tail*. PHRASES **the tail that wags the dog** a subordinate or unimportant person who controls the organization etc. of which he or she is a member. **tongues** (or **chins** or **jaws**) **wag** there is talk or gossip.

wag² *noun* a humorist; a joker or wit.

wage • *noun* **1** (in *singular* or *plural*) **a** a payment made by an employer to an employee in exchange for work or service rendered. **b** a fixed regular payment, usu. daily or weekly, made by an employer to a manual or unskilled worker (*compare* SALARY). **2** (in *plural*) *Economics* the part of total production that is the return to labour as earned income as distinct from the remuneration received by capital as unearned income. **3** (in *singular* or *plural*) *literary* reward, recompense: *the wage of sin is death*. • *verb* (**wages, waged, waging**) conduct, carry on (a war, campaign, etc.).

wager • *verb* **1** stake (esp. a sum of money) on the outcome of an uncertain event or on an undecided or unresolved matter. **2 a** make a bet that (a certain outcome, result, etc.) will occur: *I'll wager that my team beats yours*. **b** *informal* confidently assert; be certain: *I'll wager they've left by now*. • *noun* **1** a betting transaction: *for those fond of a wager or two, Sydney now has a casino* ◊ *won it on a wager*. **2** a thing, esp. a sum of money, laid down as a bet: *a $5 wager*. ▶ **wagering** *noun*

waggish *adjective* amusing, witty, tongue-in-cheek: *a waggish riposte*.

waggle *informal* • *verb* (**waggles, waggled, waggling**) **1** move with short movements from side to side or up and down. **2** *Golf* swing the head of one's club back and forth over the ball before playing a shot. • *noun* a waggling motion. ▶ **waggly** *adjective*

Wagnerian • *adjective* **1** of, relating to, or characteristic of the German composer Richard Wagner (1813–83) or his music and theories of musical and dramatic composition. **2** grandiose, highly

dramatic. • *noun* an admirer of Wagner or his music. [Say vog NAIRY un]

wagon *noun* **1** a large sturdy four-wheeled vehicle, usu. drawn by horse or tractor, for transporting heavy or bulky loads, esp. an open cart for carrying hay etc. with an elongated body and extended framework attached to the sides. **2** *hist.* a covered horse-drawn vehicle used for conveying goods and passengers by road. **3** a child's small four-wheeled cart, drawn by hand and used for carrying light loads or passengers. **4 a** = STATION WAGON. **b** = PADDY WAGON. **5** a cart or trolley for serving tea or meals. PHRASES **fix a person's wagon** *slang* get even with a person: *I didn't care how she fixed Uncle Cecil's wagon, as long as it got done soon so that things could return to normal.* **off the wagon** *informal* indulging in alcoholic drinks after a period of temperance. **on the wagon** *informal* abstaining from alcoholic drinks.

wagon train *noun* esp. *hist.* a succession of wagons, esp. a train of covered wagons and horses used by migrating pioneers or settlers.

Wahhabi *noun* (also **Wahabi**) (*plural* **Wahhabis**) a member of a strictly orthodox Sunni Muslim sect founded in the 18th century by Muhammad ibn Abd al-Wahhab, who called for a return to the earliest doctrines and practices of Islam as embodied in the Koran and Sunna. [Say wuh HOBBY]

wahoo[1] *noun* (*plural* **wahoo** or **wahoos**) a large fast-swimming streamlined predatory fish found in all tropical seas. [Say wuh HOO]

wahoo[2] *interjection* = YAHOO[2]. [Say wuh HOO]

wah-wah *noun* **1** an effect achieved on brass instruments by alternately applying and removing a mute, or on an electric guitar by using a pedal to control the output from the amplifier. **2** a device for producing this effect on an electric guitar, consisting of a pedal and circuit box.

waif *noun* **1** a homeless and helpless person, esp. a neglected, abandoned, or starved child. **2** a lost or ownerless article. ▶**waifish** *adjective* **waiflike** *adjective*

wail • *noun* **1** a long loud inarticulate high-pitched cry of pain, grief, or despair. **2** a sound resembling or suggestive of this. • *verb* **1** utter a wail or wails. **2** (of the wind, a siren, etc.) produce a sound like that of a person wailing. **3** complain or lament persistently and bitterly. **4** (often foll. by *away*) (of esp. a rock or jazz musician) play with great intensity or emotion. ▶**wailer** *noun*

Wailing Wall *noun* the remaining part of the wall of Herod's temple in Jerusalem destroyed in AD 70, where Jews traditionally pray and lament on Fridays.

wainscot • *noun* panelling of oak or other wood lining, esp. covering the lower part of a wall of a room. • *verb* (**wainscots**, **wainscotted**, **wainscotting**) line (a wall or room etc.) with wainscot. [Say WAYNE scott]

wainscotting *noun* **1** wooden panelling that lines the lower part of a walls of a room. **2** the material used for this. [Say WAYNE scott ing]

SPELL CHECK
waist, waste

Garbage is **waste**. If you use more of something than you need, you **waste** it. Someone or something that gets smaller **wastes away**.

---

waist *noun* **1 a** the part of the human body below the

ribs and above the hips, usu. of smaller circumference than these. **b** the circumference of this part of the body. **2 a** the part of a garment encircling or covering the waist. **b** the horizontal seam joining the upper and lower parts of a dress, often encircling the waist but sometimes raised to below the bust or lowered to the hips. **3** the narrow middle part of a violin, hourglass, etc. **4** the constriction between the thorax and abdomen of a wasp or ant etc.

waistband *noun* a band of material fitting around the waist and forming the upper part of a garment.

waistcoat *noun* a man's formal vest, usu. buttoned and worn over a shirt and under a jacket.

waist-deep • *adjective* **1** (of water, snow, etc.) so deep as to reach the waist. **2** submerged to the waist. • *adverb* immersed up to the waist.

waisted *combining form* having the type of waist indicated: *a slim-waisted suit.*

waist-high • *adjective* as tall or high as one's waist. • *adverb* at or up to the level of one's waist.

waistline *noun* **1** a person's waist, usu. with reference to its circumference: *chocolate is bad for the waistline.* **2** = WAIST 2.

wait • *verb* **1** remain inactive for a specified period of time or until some expected event occurs: *wait for the signal* ◊ *wait while I put on my shoes.* **2** (usu. foll. by *for*) remain for a time without something promised or expected: *waited for the bus* ◊ *the chance I've been waiting for.* **3** (foll. by *for*) stop or slow down so that a person catches up: *wait for me!* **4** = AWAIT: *wait your turn.* **5** be ready or available: *exotic islands waiting to be discovered.* **6 a** (of a matter, work, etc.) be neglected or unresolved for some time. **b** be delayed or postponed: *our trip will have to wait until I've finished my work.* **7** defer (a meal etc.) until a person's arrival: *waited supper for me.* • *noun* **1** a period of waiting: *had a long wait for the train.* **2** the action or process of watching out for an enemy or lurking in ambush: *lie in wait.* PHRASES **can't wait** is very impatient: *I can't wait to see what she bought me.* **wait a minute** (or **second**) used when one has just noticed something or had a sudden idea or inspiration. **wait and see** await the progress of events before acting. **wait for it!** *informal* **1** do not begin before the proper moment. **2** used to create an interval of suspense before saying something unexpected or amusing. **waiting to happen** likely to happen imminently: *a disaster waiting to happen.* **wait on 1 a** attend to the needs of. **b** take orders from and serve meals to. **c** serve (a customer in a store). **2** remain in expectation of; wait for. **3** pay a respectful visit to. **wait out** *informal* remain inactive during; wait for the end of: *wait out the rain.* **wait tables** (or **on tables**) work in a restaurant taking orders from patrons and serving their meals. **wait up 1** (often foll. by *for*) not go to bed until a person arrives or an event happens. **2** used to urge a person to stop or slow down so that one can catch up. **you wait!** used to imply a threat, warning, or promise.

waiter *noun* **1** a person, esp. a man, who works in a restaurant waiting tables. **2** a tray or salver. **3** a person who waits for a time, event, or opportunity.

waiting list *noun* a list of people waiting for something not immediately available.

waiting room *noun* a room where one may wait for an appointment, train, etc.

wait-list • *noun* a waiting list. • *verb* (usu. in *passive*) place the name of (a person) on a waiting list.

waitperson *noun* (*plural* **waitpersons** or **waitpeople**) a waiter or waitress.

Server is now usually preferred to the noun **waitress**.

waitress • *noun* (*plural* **waitresses**) a woman who works in a restaurant waiting tables. • *verb* (**waitresses, waitressed, waitressing**) work as a waitress. ▶ **waitressing** *noun*

wait staff *noun* the waiters and waitresses of a restaurant collectively.

SPELL CHECK
waive, wave

The spelling is **wave** in "wave goodbye", "wave aside objections", and "wave off a goal".

waive *verb* (**waives, waived, waiving**) **1** decline to take advantage of (a right, claim, opportunity, etc.): *he will waive all rights to the money*. **2** refrain from insisting upon (a rule, requirement, etc.): *the team waived the age requirement and let her play*. **3** refrain from charging or imposing (a penalty, cost, fee, etc.): *the lawyers waived their fees for the case*. **4** *Sport* **a** (of a team) give up the rights to (a player) for the purposes of a trade, demotion, or unconditional release. **b** (of a team) refrain from exercising the right to sign (a player) from another team in the same league.

SPELL CHECK
waiver, waver

To be unsteady or undecided is to **waver**.

waiver *noun* **1** the act or an instance of declining to take advantage of a right, claim, etc. **2** a formal document recording this, e.g. one guaranteeing that a party will not be held responsible for damage or injury sustained in the course of an activity. **3** *Sport* **a** a team's waiving of the right to sign a player from another team in the same league before he or she is demoted, traded, or unconditionally released. **b** (in *plural*) the process in which teams waive the right to sign or claim such a player: *he was picked up on waivers*.

Wakashan *noun* an Aboriginal language family of the west coast of North America, including Haisla, Heiltsuk, Kwa-kwa-la, and Nuu-chah-nulth. [Say WOKKA shan]

wake¹ • *verb* (**wakes**; *past* **woke** or **waked**; *past participle* **woken** or **waked**; **waking**) **1** (often foll. by *up*) **a** come out of the state of sleep or unconsciousness. **b** rouse from sleep or unconsciousness. **2** (often foll. by *up*) become or cause to become alert, attentive, or aware. **3** (usu. foll. by *up*) disturb (a place) with noise: *he woke up the whole house with his music*. **4** stir or evoke (an emotion, memory, etc.). **5** rise or raise from the dead. • *noun* **1** a watch or vigil held by relatives and friends beside the body of a dead person before burial. **2** a gathering of friends and relatives to celebrate and remember the life of a person who has died, usu. over food and drink.

wake² *noun* **1** the track left on the water's surface by a moving vessel. **2** turbulent air left behind a moving aircraft. **3** the trail left by anything that has passed: *the storm left a path of destruction in its wake*. PHRASES **in the wake of 1** behind, following. **2** in the aftermath of; as a result or consequence of.

wakeboard *noun* a surfboard-like board used in wakeboarding.

wakeboarding *noun* a water sport in which

participants ride on a short, wide board resembling a surfboard, towed by a motorboat.

wakeful *adjective* **1** unable to sleep. **2** (of a night etc.) passed with little or no sleep. ▶ **wakefulness** *noun*

waken *verb* make or become awake.

wake-up call *noun* **1** a telephone call made to wake a person up, esp. one requested from a hotel employee by a guest. **2 a** an act of drawing attention to a problem or concern. **b** a surprising and esp. distressing incident etc. symptomatic of and drawing attention to a larger problem or concern requiring immediate action.

wakey-wakey *interjection* used to wake a person up.

waking *adjective* being or occurring while one is awake: *in her waking hours*.

Waldorf salad *noun* a salad of diced apples, walnuts, and usu. celery, with mayonnaise. [Say WOL dorf]

Waldorf school *noun* a private school based on the ideas of the Austrian philosopher Rudolf Steiner (1861–1925), such as the belief that the human consciousness can and must be trained to rise above attention to material things. [Say WOL dorf]

walk • *verb* **1 a** move along at a slow or moderate pace by lifting up and putting down each foot in turn. **b** progress with similar movements: *walked on his hands* ◊ *walked on stilts*. **2 a** travel or go on foot: *she walks to work*. **b** exercise in this way: *he walks for two hours each day*. **3** travel on foot over or through: *walking the halls*. **4 a** escort or accompany on foot: *he walked me home*. **b** lead (a dog or horse etc.) at a walking pace. **5** move (a large heavy object) by rocking it on alternate edges in a manner suggestive of walking. **6** (of a ghost) roam or appear. **7** *Baseball* **a** (of a batter) reach first base by taking four balls from the pitcher. **b** (of a pitcher) allow (a batter) to go to first base by throwing four balls. **c** (foll. by *in* or *home*) force in (a run) by issuing a walk to a batter with the bases loaded. **8** *Basketball* take two or more steps with the ball without dribbling. **9** *slang* **a** be released from suspicion or from a charge. **b** = WALK OUT 2. • *noun* **1** a short journey on foot for exercise or pleasure: *we went for a walk*. **2 a** the slowest gait or pace of a person or animal: *go at a walk*. **b** the particular manner of walking of a person or animal: *I recognized her by her walk*. **3** a place intended or suitable for walking. **4** a sidewalk or the paved path leading from this to a house or building: *shovelled the front walk*. **5** a distance to be walked usu. defined by a specified amount of time required to traverse it on foot: *it's quite a walk to the store*. **6** a sponsored event in which participants walk a certain distance for charity. **7** *Baseball* a free pass to first base awarded to a batter who has taken four balls from a pitcher. PHRASES **in a walk** *Sport* easily; without effort: *they won the game in a walk*. **walk around** (or **about**) stroll. **walk all over** *informal* **1** defeat easily. **2** take advantage of. **walk away (from) 1** refuse to confront or become involved with. **2** survive (an accident etc.) without serious injury. **3** easily outdistance (an opponent) in a race. **walk away with** *informal* = WALK OUT WITH. **walk in** (often foll. by *on*) enter or arrive, esp. unexpectedly or with surprising ease. **walk in the park** (often with *neg.*) a feat or accomplishment achieved with ease. **walk into** *informal* encounter through unwariness: *walked into the trap*. **walk off 1** depart (esp. abruptly). **2** ease the effects of (a meal, injury, etc.) by walking: *walked off his anger*. **walk a person off his** (or **her**) **feet** (or **legs**) exhaust a person with walking. **walk off the job** go on strike. **walk off with** *informal* **1** steal. **2** win easily. **walk out 1** depart suddenly in anger or protest. **2** go on strike. **walk out on** desert, abandon. **walk over 1** *informal* = WALK ALL OVER. **2** traverse (a racecourse) at a walking pace to win a race with little or

no opposition. **walk the streets 1** be a prostitute. **2** traverse the streets esp. in search of work etc. **walk tall** *informal* feel justifiable pride. **walk through 1** rehearse (a scene in a play or movie etc.). **2** guide (a person) carefully through each stage of a procedure. **walk the walk** carry through on promises made (*compare* TALK THE TALK, *see* TALK).

walkable *adjective* (of a distance or area) capable of being walked; not too large to be walked.

walkathon *noun* = WALK 6.

walker *noun* **1** a person who walks, esp. for exercise or recreation. **2** a wheeled framework with a sling or seat that supports a baby within reaching distance of the ground so that he or she can learn to walk. **3** a usu. tubular metal frame used by injured, disabled, or old people to help them walk.

walkie-talkie *noun* a small portable radio transmitter and receiver that provides two-way communication.

walk-in • *adjective* **1** (of a storage area) large enough to walk into: *walk-in closet*. **2** designating a commercial establishment or medical facility etc. that serves customers and patients without appointments: *a walk-in clinic*. **3** designating the clientele of such an establishment or facility: *walk-in customers*. • *noun* (*plural* **walk-ins**) **1** a business or medical facility that serves customers without appointments. **2** a client of such an establishment or facility.

walking • *noun* the action of taking a walk, esp. for recreation or exercise. • *adjective* **1** that can, does, or appears to walk. **2** used or worn for walking: *walking stick ◊ walking boots*. **3** done on foot: *a walking tour of the city*. **4** a person regarded as embodying the qualities of a specified thing: *he's a walking disaster ◊ she's a walking encyclopedia*.

walking wounded *plural noun* **1** war casualties capable of walking despite their injuries. **2** *informal* a group of people suffering from illnesses, injuries, or mental or emotional difficulties.

Walkman *noun* (*plural* **Walkmans**) *proprietary* a type of personal stereo consisting of a radio or cassette or compact disc player and lightweight headphones.

walk of life *noun* (*plural* **walks of life**) a person's profession or social rank: *its supporters have included Prime Ministers and Canadians from every walk of life*.

walk-on *noun* **1** a small role with no or little speaking in a dramatic production. **2** an actor who plays such a role. **3** a player who tries out for a team despite not having been drafted or officially invited.

walkout • *noun* **1** a sudden angry departure, esp. in protest. **2** a strike called by workers (*compare* LOCKOUT). **3** a doorway or passageway providing access to the outside or another room. • *adjective* designating a room or building etc. with access to the outside: *a walkout basement*.

walkover *noun* **1** a horse race in which the eventual winner is unchallenged, having merely to walk over the finish line in order to record the victory. **2** an easy victory or achievement.

walk-through • *noun* **1** a rough rehearsal of a theatrical production or film. **2** an unchallenging role in a theatrical production or film. **3** a performance (of a play etc.) that lacks enthusiasm or vitality. • *adjective* designating a building etc. permitting access from either end: *a walk-through garden*.

walk-up *noun* **1** a building with no elevator, in which access to the upper floors is possible only by stairs. **2** an apartment or office etc. located in such a building.

walkway *noun* any passage or path designed for or used by pedestrians.

wall • *noun* **1** a continuous and usu. vertical structure of little thickness in proportion to its length and

height, enclosing, protecting, or dividing a space or supporting a roof. **2** a vertical rock face, such as one that lies exposed on the steep side of a mountain, or one excavated in a quarry or mine. **3** *Anatomy* the outermost layer or enclosing membrane etc. of an organ or hollow structure etc.: *stomach wall*. **4** *Baseball* the barrier enclosing the playing field at its outermost limit, extending along the curved perimeter of the outfield from one foul line to the other. **5** a thing or group of things serving as an obstacle or barrier: *a wall of security guards*. **6** an immaterial thing resembling a wall in terms of its imposing nature or in its ability to isolate or protect: *a wall of secrecy*. • *verb* **1** (usu. foll. by *off*, *in*) surround, fortify, or enclose with or as if with a wall or walls. **2** (usu. foll. by *off*, *up*) block, seal, or close (a space etc.) with a wall. **3** (foll. by *up*) confine or enclose within a sealed space. **PHRASES between you and me and the wall** *informal* in strict confidence. **go to the wall** (usu. foll. by *for*) do everything in one's power to help another, often putting oneself at risk in the process. **hit the wall 1** (of a long-distance or marathon runner) reach the point of onset of extreme fatigue at which the body's stores of energy are virtually exhausted. **2** reach a point at which one can proceed no further. **off the wall** *informal* unorthodox, unconventional. **up the wall** *informal* crazy or furious: *this song drives me up the wall*. **walls have ears** one should be cautious about what one says lest it be overheard.

wallaby *noun* (*plural* **wallabies**) a kind of marsupial that is similar to, but smaller than, a kangaroo, having large hind feet and a long tail. [Say WOLLA bee]

wallboard *noun* = DRYWALL.

wallcovering *noun* any of various materials used to cover and decorate interior walls, such as a tapestry or wallpaper.

walled *adjective* having, surrounded by, or fortified by a wall or walls, or by the type of wall indicated: *a walled town ◊ a glass-walled balcony*.

wallet *noun* **1** a flat pocket-sized folding case, usu. of leather, for keeping money, credit, identification, etc. on one's person. **2** a person's financial resources.

walleye *noun* **1** a large North American freshwater fish that has large prominent eyes and is valued as a food and sport fish. **2 a** an eye with a streaked, white, or parti-coloured iris. **b** an eye with an opaque cornea. **3** an eye squinting outwards.

walleyed *adjective* **1** having one or both eyes with a streaked or whitish iris or opaque cornea. **2** having a divergent squint. **3** having wide and glaring eyes, as if from anger or excitement.

wallflower *noun* **1 a** a fragrant spring garden plant, with esp. brown, yellow, or dark red clustered flowers. **b** any of various flowering plants growing wild on old walls or stony ground. **2** *informal* a shy or socially awkward person. **3** a person sitting out at a dance for lack of partners.

wall hanging *noun* a usu. large decorative tapestry etc. hung for display on an interior wall.

wall-mounted *adjective* that is or may be attached by a bracket or other support to a wall.

Walloon • *noun* **1** a member of a French-speaking people inhabiting southern and eastern Belgium and neighbouring parts of France (*compare* FLEMING 2). **2** the French dialect spoken by this people. • *adjective* of or concerning the Walloons or their language. [Say wuh LOON]

wallop *informal* • *verb* (**wallops**, **walloped**, **walloping**) **1 a** pound or strike with great force. **b** spank; beat. **2** esp. *Sport* defeat decisively. • *noun* **1** a heavy or resounding blow. **2 a** the ability to deliver

such a blow. **b** the capacity to create a powerful impact or impression: *this film packs quite an emotional wallop*.

walloping • *noun* **1** a sound thrashing. **2** a decisive victory. • *adjective* **1** huge: *a walloping profit*. **2** powerful.

wallow • *verb* **1** (esp. of an animal) lie or roll around in mud, water, etc. **2** indulge in unrestrained self-pity, misery, sensuality, pleasure, etc.: *wallows in nostalgia*. • *noun* **1** an act of wallowing: *the movie is a wretched wallow in misogyny and violence*. **2** a place used by buffalo, rhinoceros, etc., for wallowing. **3** a depression in the ground caused by this.

wallpaper • *noun* **1** decorative paper printed or embossed with designs, usu. sold in a roll and cut into strips to be pasted on interior walls as decoration. **2** *Computing* an optional background pattern or picture displayed onscreen. **3** usu. *derogatory* a plain or common thing or collection of these regarded as constituting an unobtrusive atmosphere or backdrop etc.: *whether as stories, novels, movies, or television shows, Westerns were basic cultural wallpaper for most of the century*. • *verb* decorate with wallpaper.

Wall Street *noun* the American money market or financial interests. ▶ **Wall Streeter** *noun*

wall-to-wall *adjective* **1** (of carpeting) covering the entire floor area; extending from one wall to another. **2** filling a space entirely: *wall-to-wall restaurants*. **3** exclusive of all else: *wall-to-wall sports coverage*.

walnut *noun* **1** a tall tree with aromatic compound leaves and drooping catkins, valued for its edible nuts and its ornamental timber, which is used esp. in cabinetmaking. **2** the nut of this tree, consisting of a wrinkled edible kernel in a ridged shell covered with a thick green husk. **3** the wood of the walnut tree.

walrus *noun* (*plural* **walrus** or **walruses**) a large amphibious long-tusked Arctic mammal, related to the seal and sea lion.

waltz • *noun* (*plural* **waltzes**) **1** a dance in triple time performed by couples who rotate and progress around the floor. **2** the usu. flowing and melodious music for this. • *verb* (**waltzes**, **waltzed**, **waltzing**) **1** dance a waltz. **2** (often foll. by *in*, *out*, *around*, etc.) *informal* move lightly, casually, with deceptive ease, etc.: *waltzed in and took first prize*. **3 a** move (a person) in a waltz. **b** cause a person to move rapidly or easily: *was waltzed off to Paris*.

wampum *noun hist.* small, cylindrical, blue and white beads cut from a quahog shell and woven into strings or belts by Aboriginal peoples of eastern North America to be used as a form of money or to record treaties. [Say WOM pum]

WAN *noun* WIDE-AREA NETWORK. [Rhymes with *PAN*]

wan *adjective* (**wanner**, **wannest**) **1** (of a person's complexion or appearance) pale, sickly; exhausted. **2** (of a star etc. or its light) partly obscured; faint. [Rhymes with *PAWN*]

wand *noun* **1 a** a supposedly magic stick used in casting spells by a fairy, magician, etc. **b** a stick used by a conjuror for effect. **2** a slender rod carried or used as a marker in the ground. **3** a small applicator for mascara etc., usu. with a brush at one end. **4** a hand-held electronic device which can be passed over a bar code to read the data this represents.

wander • *verb* **1** (often foll. by *in*, *off*, etc.) go about from place to place aimlessly. **2 a** (of a person, river, road, etc.) wind about; meander. **b** (of esp. a person) get lost; leave home; stray from a path etc. **3 a** talk or think incoherently; be inattentive or delirious. **b** (of a talk, words, thoughts, etc.) be incoherent; lack focus. **4** cover while wandering: *wanders the world*. • *noun* an act of wandering: *went for a wander around the garden*. ▶ **wanderer** *noun* **wandering** *noun* (esp. in *plural*)

wanderlust *noun* a desire to travel or wander.

wane *verb* (**wanes**, **waned**, **waning**) **1** (of the moon) decrease in apparent size after the full moon (compare WAX[2] 1). **2** decrease in power, vigour, importance, brilliance, size, etc.; decline: *in response to the city's waning economic fortunes, I left to go west*. PHRASES **on the wane** waning; declining.

wangle *verb informal* (**wangles**, **wangled**, **wangling**) obtain (a favour etc.) by scheming etc.; *managed to wangle a $100,000 government contract* ◊ *can I wangle a couple of free tickets?* ◊ *wangled his way backstage*.

wanly *adverb* **1** with a wan or pale look. **2** dejectedly: *she smiled wanly*. [WAN rhymes with *PAWN*]

wannabe *noun slang* often *derogatory* a person who tries to emulate a particular celebrity, follow the lifestyle of a particular group, etc. (also as an *adjective*: *all those wannabe guitar heroes*).

want • *verb* **1 a** desire; wish for possession of; need: *wants a bike* ◊ *wanted to leave*. **b** need or desire (a person, esp. sexually). **c** require to be attended to in esp. a specified way: *the garden wants weeding*. **d** *informal* ought; should; need: *you want to pull yourself together*. **2** (usu. foll. by *for*) lack; be deficient: *wants for nothing*. **3** (foll. by *in*, *out*) *informal* desire to be in, out, etc.: *wants in on the deal*. • *noun* **1** (often foll. by *of*) **a** a lack, absence, or deficiency: *could not go for want of time*. **b** poverty; need: *living in great want*. **2 a** a desire for a thing etc.: *meets a long-felt want*. **b** a thing so desired: *can supply your wants*.

want ad *noun* a classified advertisement, esp. seeking employees.

wanted *adjective* (of a suspected criminal etc.) sought by the police.

wanting *adjective* **1** lacking (in quality or quantity). **2** absent, not supplied or provided. PHRASES **be found wanting** fail to meet requirements.

> **SPELL CHECK**
> **wanton, won ton**
>
> A Chinese dumpling is a **won ton**: *won ton soup*.

wanton *adjective* **1** random; motiveless: *wanton destruction*. **2** sexually promiscuous. ▶ **wantonly** *adverb* **wantonness** *noun*

wapiti *noun* (*plural* **wapitis**) a North American deer, *Cervus canadensis*. [Say WOP it ee]

war • *noun* **1 a** armed hostilities between esp. nations. **b** a specific conflict or the period of time during which such conflict exists: *was before the war*. **2** the operations by which armed hostilities are carried out; warfare as a profession or art. **3 a** hostility or contention between people, groups, etc.: *war of words*. **b** (often foll. by *on*) a sustained campaign against crime, disease, poverty, etc. **c** sustained rivalry or competition, e.g. between companies: *the cola war*. See also PRICE WAR. • *verb* (**wars**, **warred**, **warring**) make war. PHRASES **at war** (often foll. by *with*) engaged in a war. **go to war 1** declare or begin a war. **2** (of a soldier etc.) see active service.

warbird *noun informal* a fighter aircraft.

warble *verb* (**warbles**, **warbled**, **warbling**) sing in a gentle trilling bird-like manner.

warbler *noun* **1** a person, bird, etc. that warbles. **2** a small insect-eating bird with a warbling song.

war bonnet *noun* a headdress worn as traditional garb by some North American Indian peoples, esp. one with feathers attached to a headband and extending down the back, typical of some Plains peoples.

war chest *noun* a store of funds for a war or any other esp. political campaign.

war crime *noun* a crime violating the international laws of war, including, e.g. the murdering of civilians. ▶ **war criminal** *noun*

war cry *noun* (*plural* **war cries**) **1** a phrase or name shouted to rally one's troops. **2** a party slogan etc.

ward *noun* **1** a separate room or division of a hospital etc. **2** an esp. municipal administrative or electoral division. **3 a** a minor under the care of a guardian appointed by the parents or a court. **b** (also **ward of the government**) a minor or mentally deficient person placed under the protection of a government or children's aid society. PHRASES **ward off 1** parry (a blow). **2** avert, turn away (danger, poverty, etc.).

warden *noun* **1** a supervising official: *game warden*. **2** *Cdn* the head of a county council. **3 a** a prison governor. **b** the governor of an institution at a university or college: *warden of residences*. **4** *Anglicanism* either of two elected lay representatives of a parish.

warder *noun* a person who guards prisoners in a prison: *we had to talk very loudly, with the warder standing alongside us listening to every word*.

wardrobe *noun* **1** a large movable or built-in cupboard for storing clothes. **2** a person's entire stock of clothes. **3** the costume department or costumes of a performing arts company etc.

wardroom *noun* **1** a room in a warship for the use of commissioned officers. **2** these officers collectively.

SPELL CHECK
ware, wear   ABC ✓

The spelling is **wear** in "wear a hat" and "wear away the paint". Shoes etc. are **footwear**.

---

ware *noun* **1** things of the same kind, esp. ceramics or cutlery: *silverware ◊ hardware*. **2** (usu. in *plural*) **a** articles for sale: *displayed his wares*. **b** a person's skills, talents, etc. **3** ceramics etc. of a specified material, factory, or kind.

warehouse • *noun* **1** a building in which esp. retail goods are stored and from which they are distributed to retailers etc. **2** (in proper names) a wholesale or large retail store. • *verb* (**warehouses, warehoused, warehousing**) **1** deposit or store (goods) temporarily in a warehouse. **2** *informal* shut up (esp. a person) in a prison or hospital etc. and forget about or ignore.

warfare *noun* **1** the activity of fighting a war, esp. of a particular type: *chemical warfare*. **2** an aggressive or violent conflict or struggle.

warfarin *noun* a water-soluble anticoagulant used esp. as a rat poison and treating thrombosis. [Say WORF er in]

war game *noun* **1** a military exercise testing or improving tactical knowledge etc. **2** a battle etc. conducted with counters representing military units. ▶ **war-gaming** *noun*

warhead *noun* the explosive head of a missile, torpedo, or similar weapon.

warhorse *noun* **1** *hist.* a knight's or trooper's powerful horse. **2** *informal* a veteran of any activity, esp. a soldier, politician, etc.; a dependable or stalwart person or thing: *aging party warhorses put to pasture on a board or commission*. **3** a frequently used or very familiar thing, esp. a work of art which is frequently performed: *a standard operatic warhorse, most productions of which come and go without leaving behind so much as a ripple*.

warily *adverb* in a wary manner; cautiously, suspiciously. [Say WARE a lee]

wariness *noun* the state of being wary or on one's guard; caution. [Say WARE ee ness]

warlike *adjective* **1** threatening war; hostile: *a warlike nation*. **2** of or like warfare: *warlike conditions*.

warlock *noun* a sorcerer or wizard; a man who practises witchcraft.

warlord *noun* the leader of a military group that is not official and that fights against other groups within a country or an area: *rival warlords*.

warm • *adjective* **1** of or at a fairly or comfortably high temperature. **2** (of clothes etc.) providing warmth. **3 a** (of a person, action, feelings, etc.) sympathetic; friendly; loving: *a warm welcome*. **b** enthusiastic: *was warm in her praise*. **4** animated, excited: *a warm exchange of views*. **5** *informal* **a** (of a participant in esp. a children's game of seeking) close to the object etc. sought. **b** near to guessing or finding out a secret. **6** (of a colour, light, etc.) reddish, pink, or yellowish, etc., suggestive of warmth. **7** *Hunting* (of a scent) fresh and strong. • *verb* **1 a** make warm. **b** excite; make cheerful: *warms the heart*. **2 a** (often foll. by *up*) become warm. **b** (often foll. by *to*) become animated, enthusiastic, or sympathetic: *warmed to his subject*. • *noun* **1** the act of warming; the state of being warmed. **2** the warmth of the atmosphere etc. PHRASES **warm the bench** (or **pine**) *Sport* be made to sit inactively and not participate in a game etc. **warm up 1** (of an athlete, performer, etc.) prepare oneself by preliminary light exercise or practice. **2** become or cause to become warmer. **3** (often foll. by *to*) (of a person) become enthusiastic etc. (about). **4** (of an engine, electrical equipment, etc.) reach a temperature for efficient working. **5** reheat (food).

warm-blooded *adjective* **1** having warm blood; mammalian. **2** ardent, passionate. ▶ **warm-bloodedness** *noun*

warmed-over *adjective* **1** (of food etc.) reheated or stale. **2** stale; second-hand: *a defensive rehash of warmed-over ideas*.

war memorial *noun* a monument etc. commemorating those killed in a war.

warmer *noun* a thing which warms something specified: *leg warmer*.

warm front *noun* the leading edge of an advancing mass of warm air.

warm fuzzy *informal* • *noun* (*plural* **warm fuzzies**) a gut feeling of emotional warmth or pleasant satisfaction in reaction to something: *donating to environmental causes always gave them the warm fuzzies*. • *adjective* (also **warm and fuzzy**) pertaining to, evoking, or evoked by such a reaction: *a warm fuzzy feeling*.

warm-hearted *adjective* kind, friendly. ▶ **warm-heartedly** *adverb* **warm-heartedness** *noun*

warming *noun* the process of making something, or of becoming, warm or warmer: *global warming ◊ the seasonal warming of the Pacific*.

warmly *adverb* in a warm manner.

warmonger *noun* a person who seeks to bring about war: *Franklin Delano Roosevelt was regarded as a warmonger and almost a traitor by many Americans because of his eagerness to oppose Hitler*. ▶ **warmongering** *noun* & *adjective* [Say WAR mong gur or WAR mung gur]

warmth *noun* **1 a** the state of being warm. **b** moderate heat. **2** a friendly or loving attitude, personality, etc.

warm-up *noun* **1** a session of preparatory exercise or practice for a contest, performance, etc. **2** (as an *adjective*) **a** designating clothing worn during an esp. athletic warm-up: *warm-up suit*. **b** designating an act that performs prior to the main attraction at a concert etc.: *warm-up band*. **3** (often in *plural*) an esp. knitted or fleece garment worn over other clothing to provide warmth during warm-up exercises.

warn *verb* **1 a** inform of danger, unknown circumstances, etc.: *warned them of the danger ◊ warned her that she was being watched*. **b** (often foll. by *against*) inform (a person etc.) about a specific danger, hostile person, etc.: *warned her against trusting him*. **2** (usu. with *neg.*) admonish; tell forcefully: *has been warned not to go*.

W

3 give (a person) cautionary notice regarding conduct etc.: *I've warned you many times*. PHRASES **warn off** warn (a person) to keep away (from).

warning • *noun* **1** *in senses of* WARN *verb*. **2** anything that serves to warn; a hint or indication of difficulty, danger, etc. **3** an indication of any impending event: *without warning*. • *adjective* serving to warn or indicate. PHRASES **take warning** take heed; beware; recognize the danger.

warning track *noun* Baseball a strip of gravel etc. around a baseball field which warns fielders of the proximity of the wall, stands, etc., esp. that portion along the farthest perimeter of the outfield.

war of attrition *noun* a prolonged war in which military strategy is based on the calculation that the enemy's manpower and material resources will be exhausted before one's own as a result of numerous battles, usu. involving massive losses on both sides, e.g. the First World War.

warp • *verb* **1** make or become bent or twisted out of shape, esp. by the action of heat, damp, etc. **2** make or become perverted, bitter, or strange: *too much TV warps the mind*. • *noun* **1** a state of being warped, esp. of shrunken or expanded timber. **2** the threads stretched lengthwise in a loom to be crossed by the weft. **3** (in science fiction) an imaginary or hypothetical distortion in space in relation to time: *time warp ◊ space warp*. **4** (as an *adjective*) of or pertaining to warp speed: *warp drive*.

warpath *noun* **1** hist. the path or route taken on a warlike expedition by North American Indians. **2** informal any hostile course or attitude: *is on the warpath again*.

warped *adjective* **1** in senses of WARP *verb*. **2** (of a person, mind, attitude, etc.) perverted, twisted, sick; bizarre.

warplane *noun* a military aircraft, esp. one equipped for fighting, bombing, etc.

warp speed *noun* **1** (in science fiction) travelling speed faster than that of light. **2** informal an extraordinarily high speed.

warrant • *noun* **1** a written authorization allowing police to search premises, arrest a suspect, etc. **2** an acceptable reason for doing something: *there is no warrant for such speculations about her character*. **3** a written authorization, money voucher, travel document, etc.: *travel warrant*. **4** a certificate entitling the holder to subscribe for shares of a company. • *verb* **1** justify; make necessary or appropriate in the circumstances: *nothing can warrant his behaviour*. **2** guarantee or attest to esp. the genuineness of an article, the worth of a person, etc.: *the vendor warrants the accuracy of the report*.

warrant officer *noun* **1** (also **Warrant Officer**) (in the Canadian Army and Air Force) a non-commissioned officer of a rank above sergeant. Abbreviation: **WO**. **2** an officer of a similar rank in other armies.

warranty *noun* (plural **warranties**) a manufacturer's written promise as to the extent to which defective goods will be repaired, replaced, etc.

warren *noun* **1 a** a network of interconnecting rabbit burrows. **b** a piece of ground occupied by this. **2** a densely populated or maze-like building etc.: *a warren of alleys off the main streets*.

warring *adjective* **1** fighting: *warring factions*. **2** conflicting: *warring principles*.

warrior *noun* **1** a person experienced or distinguished in fighting in an armed force, tribe, etc. **2** (as an *adjective*) **a** of or relating to a warrior. **b** martial: *a warrior nation*.

warship *noun* an armoured ship used in war.

wart *noun* **1** a small benign growth on the skin, usu.

hard and rounded, caused by a virus-induced abnormal growth of skin cells and thickening of the epidermis. **2** any protuberance, as on the skin of an animal, surface of a plant, etc. PHRASES **warts and all** informal with no attempt to conceal blemishes or inadequacies.

warthog *noun* an African wild pig with a large head and warty lumps on its face, and large curved tusks.

wartime *noun* the period during which a war is waged.

war-torn *adjective* racked or devastated by war.

warty *adjective* (**wartier, wartiest**) covered in warts.

war-weary *adjective* (esp. of a population) exhausted and dispirited by war.

wary *adjective* (**warier, wariest**) **1** on one's guard. **2** (foll. by of) cautious, suspicious: *am wary of buying used cars*. **3** showing or done with caution or suspicion: *a wary expression*. [Say WARE ee]

was 1st & 3rd singular past of BE.

wasabi *noun* a plant whose root (resembling horseradish) is used in Japanese cooking, usu. ground as an accompaniment to raw fish. [Say wuh SOBBY]

wash • *verb* (**washes, washed, washing**) **1** cleanse with liquid, esp. water and usu. soap or detergent. **2** (foll. by out, off, away, etc.) remove (a stain or dirt) in this way. **3** wash oneself or esp. one's hands and face. **4** wash clothes etc. **5** (of fabric or dye) bear washing without damage. **6** (foll. by off, out) (of a stain etc.) be removed by washing. **7** (of a river, sea, etc.) touch (a country, coast, etc.) with its waters. **8 a** (of moving liquid) carry along in a specified direction: *a wave washed him overboard*. **b** be carried in this way: *shells wash up on the beaches*. **9** scoop out: *the water had washed a channel*. **10** (foll. by over, along, etc.) sweep, move, or splash. **11** sift (ore) by the action of water. **12** brush a thin coat of watery paint or ink over (paper in watercolour painting etc., or a wall). • *noun* (plural **washes**) **1** the act of washing; the process of being washed: *shrank after only two washes*. **2** a quantity of clothes for washing or just washed: *your pants are in the wash*. **3** the visible or audible motion of agitated water or air, esp. due to the passage of a ship etc. or aircraft: *the canoe was rocked by the wash of a passing ferry*. **4** a liquid to spread over a surface to cleanse, heal, or colour. **5** an expanse of colour appearing to have been washed on: *a wash of cool orange twilight*. **6** a situation or result which is of no net benefit to either of two opposing sides, values, etc. PHRASES **come out in the wash** informal be clarified, or (of difficulties) be resolved or removed, in the course of time. **wash down 1** wash completely (esp. a large surface or object). **2** (usu. foll. by with) accompany or follow (food) with a drink. **wash one's hands of** renounce responsibility for. **wash out 1** clean the inside of (a thing) by washing. **2** clean (a garment etc.) by brief washing. **3 a** rain out (an event etc.). **b** informal cancel. **4** (of a flood, downpour, etc.) make a breach in (a road etc.). **5** informal fail, drop out: *washed out of med school*. **6** = sense 2 of *verb*. **wash up 1** wash (dishes, cutlery, etc.) after use. **2** wash one's face and hands. **won't wash** informal (of an argument etc.) will not be believed or accepted.

washable *adjective* that can be washed, esp. without damage.

wash-and-wear *adjective* **1** (of a fabric) easily washed, drying readily, and not needing ironing. **2** (of a haircut) requiring little or no styling after washing.

wash basin *noun* a basin for washing the hands, face, etc.

washboard *noun* **1 a** a board of ribbed wood or a sheet of corrugated zinc on which clothes are scrubbed in washing. **b** this used as a percussion instrument, played with the fingers. **2** a dirt or gravel road whose surface has become corrugated by weather and use.

W

3 (as an *adjective*) designating any corrugated surface: *a washboard stomach*.

washcloth *noun* = FACE CLOTH.

washed out *adjective* **1** faded by washing. **2** pale. **3** *informal* limp, enfeebled.

washed up *adjective slang* having failed.

washer *noun* **1 a** a person or thing that washes. **b** a washing machine. **2** a flat ring of rubber, metal, etc., to tighten or prevent leakage at a joint. **3** a similar ring placed under a nut or the head of a screw, etc., to disperse its pressure. ▶ **washerless** *adjective*

washerwoman *noun* (*plural* **washerwomen**) a woman whose occupation is washing clothes, linen, etc.

washing *noun* **1** a quantity of clothes for washing or just washed. **2** the act of washing clothes.

washing machine *noun* a machine for washing clothes and linen etc.

Washingtonian • *adjective* **1** of or relating to the US state of Washington. **2** of or relating to Washington, DC. • *noun* a native or inhabitant of the state of Washington or of Washington, DC. [Say washing TONY un]

washout *noun* **1** a narrow river channel that cuts into pre-existing sediments. **2** a breach in a road etc., caused by flooding. **3** *informal* **a** a fiasco; a complete failure. **b** a person who has failed or dropped out.

washroom *noun* **1** esp. *Cdn* a room with toilet facilities. **2** a room with facilities for washing oneself. PHRASES **go to the washroom** esp. *Cdn euphemism* defecate or urinate.

washstand *noun* a piece of furniture to hold a basin, jug of water, soap, etc. for washing oneself with.

washtub *noun* a tub or vessel for washing clothes etc.

wasn't *contraction* was not.

WASP usu. *derogatory* • *noun* **1** a white Protestant of Anglo-Saxon descent. **2** a middle-class North American white Protestant. • *adjective* of, pertaining to, being, or typical of a WASP or WASPs.

wasp *noun* a stinging often flesh-eating insect, with black and yellow stripes and a very thin waist.

waspish *adjective* bad-tempered and unpleasant; irritable: *she sounded waspish and impatient*. ▶ **waspishly** *adverb*

WASPy *adjective* usu. *derogatory* characteristic of middle-class North American white Protestants.

wastage *noun* **1** an amount wasted. **2** loss or destruction of something, esp. something valuable that has not been used or kept carefully. [Say WASTE idge]

SPELL CHECK

waste, waist

The middle part of the body is the **waist**.

---

waste • *verb* (**wastes, wasted, wasting**) **1** use to no purpose or for inadequate result or extravagantly: *waste time*. **2** fail to use (esp. an opportunity). **3** (often foll. by *on*) **a** give (advice etc.), utter (words etc.), without effect. **b** (often in *passive*) fail to be appreciated or used properly: *I feel wasted in this job*. **4** (often foll. by *away*) wear gradually away; make or become weak; wither. **5** treat as wasted or valueless. **6** be expended without useful effect. **7** *slang* **a** beat up. **b** kill, murder. • *adjective* **1** superfluous; no longer serving a purpose. **2** (of a district etc.) not inhabited or cultivated: *waste ground*. • *noun* **1** the act or an instance of using or expending something carelessly, extravagantly, or to no purpose: *it's a waste of time trying to argue with him* ◊ *it's a shocking waste to throw out good food*. **2 a** a waste material or food; refuse; useless remains or by-products: *nuclear waste*. **b** excrement. **3** a waste region;

a desert etc.: *the icy wastes of Antarctica*. PHRASES **go to waste** be wasted. **lay waste** ravage, devastate. **waste not, want not** extravagance leads to poverty.

wastebasket *noun* a receptacle for waste paper.

wasted *adjective* **1** *in sense of* WASTE *verb*. **2** *slang* **a** very tired. **b** intoxicated by alcohol or drugs.

wasteful *adjective* **1** extravagant. **2** causing or showing waste. ▶ **wastefully** *adjective* **wastefulness** *noun*

wasteland *noun* **1** an unproductive, useless, or devastated area of land. **2** a place or time considered spiritually or intellectually barren: *he underestimated the nature of the wasteland of modernity; he did not sense the void*.

waste management *noun* the collection, disposal, treatment, or recycling of waste.

wastepaper basket *noun* = WASTEBASKET.

waste product *noun* (esp. in *plural*) a useless by-product of manufacture or of an organism or organisms.

waster *noun* a wasteful person.

waste stream *noun* the mass of waste generated e.g. by a city for disposal etc.

waste water *noun* **1** water that has served an esp. industrial purpose, allowed to run away. **2** sewage.

wastrel *noun* a wasteful or good-for-nothing person. [Say WASTE rull]

watch • *verb* (**watches, watched, watching**) **1** keep the eyes fixed on; look at. **2 a** keep under observation; follow observantly. **b** monitor or consider carefully; pay attention to: *have to watch my weight*. **c** be careful to prevent damage or harm to: *watch your head*. **3** (often foll. by *for*) be in an alert state; be vigilant; take heed: *watch for an opportunity*. **4** (foll. by *over*) look after; take care of. • *noun* (*plural* **watches**) **1** a small timepiece worn on one's person. **2** a state of alert or constant observation or attention. **3** *Nautical* **a** a usu. four-hour spell of duty. **b** each of the halves into which a ship's crew is divided to take alternate watches. **4** *hist.* a watchman or group of watchmen, esp. patrolling the streets at night. **5** a former division of the night: *the watches of the night*. PHRASES **on the watch** waiting for an expected or feared occurrence. **on watch** on lookout duty. **watch one's back** be alert to danger. **watch it** (or **oneself**) *informal* be careful. **watch out 1** (often foll. by *for*) be on one's guard. **2** as a warning of immediate danger. **watch one's step** proceed cautiously. ▶ **watchable** *adjective*

watchdog *noun* **1** a dog kept to guard property etc. **2** a person or body monitoring others' rights, behaviour, etc.

watcher *noun* a person who watches or observes or follows something closely (often in *combination*: *birdwatcher*).

watchful *adjective* watching or observing closely; alert; on the watch. ▶ **watchfully** *adverb* **watchfulness** *noun*

watchmaker *noun* a person who makes and repairs watches and clocks. ▶ **watchmaking** *noun*

watchman *noun* (*plural* **watchmen**) a man employed to look after an empty building etc. at night.

watchtower *noun* a tower from which observation can be kept.

watchword *noun* a phrase summarizing a guiding principle; a slogan: *the baby boomers made social justice a watchword of the era*.

water • *noun* **1** a colourless transparent odourless tasteless liquid compound of oxygen and hydrogen (*see also* HEAVY WATER). **2** a liquid consisting chiefly of this and found in seas, lakes, and rivers, in rain, and in secretions of organisms. **3** an expanse of water; a sea,

lake, river, etc. **4** (in *plural*) part of a sea or river: *in Canadian waters*. **5** (often as **the waters**) mineral water at a spa etc. **6** the state of a tide: *high water*. **7** a solution of a specified substance in water: *lavender water*. **8** (as an *adjective*) **a** found in or near water. **b** of, for, or worked by water. **c** involving, using, or yielding water. **9 a** urine. **b** (usu. in *plural*) the amniotic fluid discharged from the womb before childbirth. • *verb* **1** sprinkle or soak with water. **2** give water to (an animal) to drink. **3** (of the mouth or eyes) secrete saliva or tears. **4** (usu. as **watered** *adjective*) (of silk etc.) having irregular wavy glossy markings. **5** (usu. foll. by *down*) dilute. **6** (of a river etc.) supply (a place) with water. **7** (of an animal) go to a pool etc. to drink. **PHRASES** **by water** using a ship etc. for travel or transport. **in deep water** (or **waters**) in serious trouble or difficulty. **like water** lavishly, profusely. **make one's mouth water** cause one's saliva to flow, stimulate one's appetite or anticipation. **make water 1** urinate. **2** (of a ship) take in water. **of the first water 1** (of a diamond) of the greatest brilliance and transparency. **2** of the finest quality or extreme degree. **on the water** on a ship etc. **water down 1** dilute with water. **2** (often as **watered down** *adjective*) make less vivid, forceful, or horrifying. **water under the bridge** past events accepted as past and irrevocable.

water-based *adjective* (of a solution, substance, etc.) having water as the main ingredient.

waterbed *noun* a bed with a mattress of rubber or plastic etc. filled with water.

water bomber *noun Cdn* an aircraft used to drop water on forest fires, esp. one which takes on water by skimming the surface of a lake etc. ▶ **water bombing** *noun*

water-borne *adjective* **1** (of goods etc.) conveyed by or travelling on water. **2** (of a disease) communicated or propagated by contaminated water.

water buffalo *noun* (*plural* **water buffalo** or **water buffaloes**) a large black domesticated buffalo with heavy swept-back horns, used as a beast of burden throughout the tropics.

water chestnut *noun* **1** an aquatic plant with small white flowers, producing an edible rounded seed. **2 a** the tuber of a tropical sedge that is widely used in Asian cuisine, its white flesh remaining crisp after cooking. **b** the sedge that yields this tuber, cultivated in flooded fields of Southeast Asia.

watercolour *noun* (also **watercolor**) **1** artists' paint made of pigment to be diluted with water and not oil. **2** a picture painted with this. **3** the art of painting with watercolours. ▶ **watercolourist** *noun*

water cooler *noun* a vessel in which water is cooled and kept cool, esp. a tank of cooled drinking water in a workplace as a setting for informal conversation or gossip.

watercourse *noun* **1** a brook, stream, or artificial water channel. **2** the bed along which this flows.

watercraft *noun* (*plural* **watercraft**) any boat.

watercress *noun* a hardy perennial cress that grows in flowing water, with strong-flavoured leaves used in salads etc.

water cycle *noun* the circulation of water from the atmosphere, where water vapour condenses and falls as precipitation, to the earth where it collects as liquid or ice, and back to the atmosphere through evaporation or transpiration.

waterfall *noun* a stream, river, or artificial watercourse flowing over a precipice or down a steep hillside.

waterfowl *noun* birds frequenting water, esp. swimming game birds.

waterfront *noun* esp. urban land adjoining a river, lake, harbour, etc.

water garden *noun* a garden with pools or a stream, for growing aquatic plants.

water hazard *noun* a pond or stream on a golf course that acts as an obstruction to playing a shot.

water hole *noun* a shallow depression in which water collects; a pond, a pool.

water ice *noun* a confection of flavoured and frozen water and sugar etc.; a sorbet, slush, etc.

watering can *noun* a portable container with a long spout usu. ending in a perforated sprinkler, for watering plants.

watering hole *noun* **1** a pool of water from which animals regularly drink; a water hole. **2** *slang* a bar.

water lily *noun* (*plural* **water lilies**) an aquatic plant with broad flat floating leaves and large cup-shaped flowers.

waterline *noun* **1 a** the line along which the surface of water touches the side of something. **b** such a line marked on a ship for use in loading. **2** a pipe etc. used to convey water.

waterlogged *adjective* **1** saturated with water. **2** (of a boat etc.) hardly able to float from being saturated or filled with water. **3** (of ground) made useless by being saturated with water.

Waterloo *noun* (*plural* **Waterloos**) a decisive defeat; an irrevocable end: *Krystal had to fish her golf ball out of the water on 15, a hole that proved to be her Waterloo at the annual company mini-putt tournament.* [Say water LOO]

water main *noun* a water supply system's main pipe.

watermark • *noun* a faint identifying design made in some paper during manufacture, when held against the light. • *verb* mark with this.

watermelon *noun* a large smooth green melon with sweet edible red pulp and watery juice.

water meter *noun* a device which measures and records the amount of water supplied to a house etc.

water park *noun* a public recreation area with water slides, swimming pools, etc.

water pipe *noun* **1** a pipe that conveys water. **2** an oriental tobacco pipe with a long tube passing through water for cooling the smoke as it is drawn through.

water pistol *noun* a toy pistol shooting a jet of water.

water polo *noun* a game played in a swimming pool, in which teams of seven swimmers attempt to throw an inflated ball into the other team's goal.

water power *noun* **1** mechanical force derived from the weight or motion of water. **2** a fall in the level of a river, as a source of this force.

waterproof • *adjective* impervious to water. • *verb* make waterproof.

water repellent *adjective* not easily penetrated by water.

water-resistant *adjective* (of a fabric, wristwatch, etc.) able to resist, but not entirely prevent, the penetration of water.

watershed *noun* **1** a line of separation between waters flowing to different rivers, basins, or seas. **2** a turning point in affairs. **3** the area drained by a single lake or river and its tributaries.

waterside *noun* the margin of a sea, lake, or river.

water ski • *noun* each of a pair of long thin boards, or a single board, strapped to the feet to enable a person pulled by a motorboat to skim over the surface of the water. • *verb* (**water-ski**, **water-skis**, **water-skied**, **water-skiing**) be pulled along the water's surface while on a water ski or skis. ▶ **water skier** *noun* **water skiing** *noun*

W

waterslide *noun* a usu. high or long slide down which water cascades, esp. into a swimming pool.

water snake *noun* any of various snakes frequenting fresh water, esp. harmless snakes of the genus *Nerodia*.

water-soluble *adjective* that can be dissolved in water.

waterspout *noun* a rotating column of water and spray formed by a whirlwind between sea and cloud.

water strider *noun* a slender predatory bug that moves quickly across the surface of water, using its front legs for catching prey.

water table *noun* a level below which the ground is saturated with water.

water taxi *noun* (*plural* **water taxis**) a small boat for hire for transporting passengers, usu. over short distances.

watertight *adjective* **1** (of a joint, container, vessel, etc.) fastened or fitted or made so as to prevent the passage of water. **2** (of an argument etc.) unassailable.

water torture *noun* a form of torture in which the victim is exposed to the incessant dripping of water on the head, or the sound of dripping.

water tower *noun* a tower with an elevated tank to give pressure for distributing water.

waterway *noun* **1** a navigable channel. **2** a route for travel by water.

water wheel *noun* a wheel driven by water to work machinery, or to raise water.

waterworks *noun* **1** an establishment for managing the water supply of a city etc. **2** *informal* the shedding of tears: *turn on the waterworks.* **3** *informal* the urinary system.

watery *adjective* **1** containing too much water. **2** too thin in consistency. **3** of, consisting of, or of the consistency of water. **4** (of the eyes) suffused or running with water. **5** (of colour) pale. **6** (of the sun, moon, or sky) rainy-looking.

watt *noun* the SI unit of power, equivalent to one joule per second, corresponding to the rate of energy in an electric circuit where the potential difference is one volt and the current one ampere. Symbol: **W**.

wattage *noun* an amount of electrical power expressed in watts, esp. the operating power of an appliance etc.

watt-hour *noun* the energy used when one watt is applied for one hour.

wattle[1] *noun* **1** interlaced rods and split rods as a material for making fences, walls, etc. **2** (in *singular* or *plural*) rods and twigs for this use. [Rhymes with *BOTTLE*]

wattle[2] *noun* a loose fleshy appendage on the head or throat of a turkey or other birds. ▶ **wattled** *adjective* [Rhymes with *BOTTLE*]

> **SPELL CHECK**
> **wave, waive**
>
> If you choose not to exercise your rights, you **waive** them.

wave • *verb* (**waves, waved, waving**) **1** move a hand etc. to and fro in greeting or as a signal: *Zoe waves goodbye to us daintily, like the Queen.* **2 a** show a motion as of a flag, tree, or a field of wheat etc., in the wind. **b** impart a waving motion to. **3** brandish (a sword etc.) as an encouragement to followers etc. **4** tell or direct (a person) by waving: *waved them away.* **5** express (a greeting etc.) by waving: *waved goodbye to them.* **6** give an undulating form to (hair, drawn lines, etc.); make wavy. **7** (of hair etc.) have such a form; be wavy. • *noun* **1** a moving ridge of water caused by the wind or tide. **2** a long body of water curling into an arched form and breaking on the shore. **3 a** a thing compared to this,

e.g. a body of persons in one of successive advancing groups. **b** (usu. as **the wave**) a wavelike effect produced by a crowd at a sporting event etc., whereby adjoining sections successively stand or raise hands momentarily. **4** a gesture of waving. **5 a** the process of waving the hair. **b** a slight curl in the hair. **6 a** a temporary occurrence or increase of a condition, emotion, or influence: *a wave of enthusiasm.* **b** a specified period of widespread weather: *heat wave.* **7** *Physics* **a** a periodic disturbance of the particles of a substance which may be propagated without net movement of the particles, as in the passage of undulating motion, heat, sound, etc. **b** a single curve in the course of this motion. **8** *Electricity* a similar variation of an electromagnetic field in the propagation of light or other radiation through a medium or vacuum. PHRASES **make waves** *informal* **1** cause trouble. **2** create a significant impression. **wave aside** dismiss as intrusive or irrelevant. **wave down** wave to (a vehicle or its driver) as a signal to stop. **wave off 1** signal an approaching person or thing to stop approaching. **2** (in hockey etc.) disallow (a goal).

waveband *noun* a range of (esp. radio) wavelengths between certain limits.

wavelength *noun* **1** the distance between successive crests of a wave, esp. points in a sound wave or electromagnetic wave. **2** this as a distinctive feature of radio waves from a transmitter. **3** *informal* a particular mode or range of thinking and communicating: *we don't seem to be on the same wavelength.*

wavelet *noun* a small wave on water.

wavelike *adjective* resembling the up-and-down motion of a wave.

> **SPELL CHECK**
> **waver, waiver**
>
> A document that clears someone of responsibility is a **waiver**. Athletes are put on **waivers**.

waver *verb* **1** be or become unsteady; falter; begin to give way: *her voice wavered.* **2** be undecided between different courses or opinions; be shaken in resolution or belief: *she supported the accord in a Commons vote last fall but has since been wavering and has not said how she will vote when the deal comes before the House a second time.* **3** (of a light) flicker: *the flame was pale, wavering, almost dying out.* ▶ **wavery** *adjective*

waviness *noun* the condition of something that is not straight, but has waves or curves.

wavy *adjective* (**wavier, waviest**) (of a line or surface) having waves or curves: *her hair looks pretty either wavy or straight.*

wax[1] • *noun* (*plural* **waxes**) **1** a sticky mouldable yellowish substance secreted by bees as the material of honeycomb cells. **2** a white translucent material obtained from this and used for candles, as a basis of polishes, and for other purposes. **3** any similar substance, typically a lipid or hydrocarbon: *earwax* ◊ *paraffin wax.* **4** a session of waxing to remove hair. • *verb* (**waxes, waxed, waxing**) **1** cover, polish, or treat with wax. **2** remove unwanted hair by applying wax and peeling off the wax and hairs together. **3** *informal* defeat resoundingly. PHRASES **the whole ball of wax** the full complement of related or necessary things.

wax[2] *verb* (**waxes, waxed, waxing**) **1** (of the moon) have an ever larger part of its visible surface illuminated, increasing in apparent size. **2** become philosophical, eloquent, poetic, etc. while speaking or writing: *seeing the old photograph prompted her to wax*

W

nostalgic about her childhood. PHRASES **wax and wane** undergo alternate increases and decreases.

wax bean *noun* a yellow-podded bean.

waxbill *noun* a small finch-like songbird, usu. brightly coloured with a red bill that resembles sealing wax in colour.

waxed paper *noun* (also **wax paper**) waterproof or greaseproof paper coated with wax.

waxen *adjective* having a smooth pale translucent surface as of wax.

waxwing *noun* a crested songbird with small tips like red sealing wax to some wing feathers.

waxwork *noun* **1 a** an object, esp. a lifelike dummy, modelled in wax. **b** the making of waxworks. **2** (in *plural*) an exhibition of wax dummies.

waxy *adjective* (**waxier**, **waxiest**) resembling wax in consistency or in its surface.

SPELL CHECK
way, whey `[ABC✓]`

Little Miss Muffet ate curds and **whey**.

---

way • *noun* **1** a road etc., for passing along. **2** a route for reaching a place, esp. the best one: *asked the way to Sherbrooke*. **3** a place of passage into a building etc.: *could not find the way out*. **4 a** a method or plan for achieving something: *that is not the way to do it*. **b** the ability to obtain one's object: *has a way with him*. **5 a** a person's desired or chosen course of action. **b** a custom or manner of behaving; a personal peculiarity: *that's just her way* ◊ *things had a way of going badly*. **6** a specific manner of life or procedure: *soon got into the way of it*. **7** the normal course of events: *that is always the way*. **8** (also *informal* **ways**) a travelling distance; a length traversed or to be traversed: *is a long way away* ◊ *a good ways down the road*. **9 a** an unimpeded opportunity of advance. **b** a space free of obstacles. **10** a region or ground over which advance is desired or natural. **11** advance in some direction; impetus, progress: *pushed my way through*. **12** movement of a ship etc.: *gather way*. **13** the state of being engaged in movement from place to place; time spent in this: *on the way home*. **14** a specified direction: *step this way* ◊ *one-way traffic*. **15** (in *plural*) parts into which a thing is divided: *split it three ways*. **16** *informal* the scope or range of something: *want a few things in the stationery way*. **17** a specified condition or state: *things are in a bad way*. **18** a respect: *is useful in some ways*. • *adverb informal* to a considerable extent; very much: *you're way off the mark*. PHRASES **across the way** facing or opposite. **be on one's way 1** set off; depart. **2** be in the course of a journey etc. **by the way** incidentally; as a more or less irrelevant comment. **by way of 1** through; by means of. **2** as a substitute for or as a form of: *did it by way of apology*. **3** with the intention of: *asked by way of discovering the truth*. **come one's way** become available to one. **find a way** discover a means of obtaining one's object. **get** (or **have**) **one's way** (or **have it one's own way** etc.) get what one wants; ensure one's wishes are met. **give way 1 a** make concessions. **b** fail to resist; yield. **2** (often foll. by *to*) concede precedence (to). **3** (of a structure etc.) be dislodged or broken under a load; collapse. **4** (foll. by *to*) be superseded by. **5** (foll. by *to*) be overcome by (an emotion etc.). **go all the way 1** go the whole distance. **2** do something wholeheartedly or completely. **3** *informal* engage in sexual intercourse. **go out of one's way** make a special effort: *went out of their way to help*. **go one's own way** act independently, esp. against contrary advice. **go one's way 1** leave, depart. **2** (of events, circumstances, etc.) be favourable to one. **go a person's way** accompany a person: *are you going*

my way? **in its way** if regarded from a particular standpoint appropriate to it. **in no way** not at all; by no means. **in a way** in a certain respect but not altogether or completely. **in the** (or **one's**) **way** forming an obstacle or hindrance. **lead the way 1** act as guide or leader. **2** show how to do something. **look the other way 1** ignore what one should notice. **2** disregard an acquaintance etc. whom one sees. **make way 1** (often foll. by *for*) allow room for others to proceed. **2** achieve progress. **make one's way** proceed. **one way or another** by some means. **on the** (or **one's**) **way 1** in the course of a journey etc. **2** having progressed: *is well on the way to completion*. **3** *informal* (of a child) conceived but not yet born. **on the way out** *informal* going down in status, estimation, or favour; going out of fashion. **the other way around** (or **about**) in an inverted or reversed position or direction. **out of the way 1** no longer an obstacle or hindrance. **2** disposed of; settled. **3** (of a person) imprisoned or killed. **4** (with *neg.*) common or unremarkable: *nothing out of the way*. **5** (of a place) remote, inaccessible. **out of one's way** not on one's intended route. **put a person in the way of** give a person the opportunity of. **way back** *informal* long ago.

waybill *noun* **1** a document on which a shipper, courier, etc. records details of the sender, recipient, weight, etc. of an item to be transported. **2** a list of passengers or parcels on a vehicle.

wayfarer *noun* a traveller, esp. on foot. ▶**wayfaring** *noun* [Say WAY fare er]

waylay *verb* (**waylays**, **waylaid**, **waylaying**) **1** lie in wait for. **2** stop to rob or talk to.

way of life *noun* (*plural* **ways of life**) the principles or habits governing all one's actions etc.

way-out *adjective informal* **1** unusual, eccentric. **2** avant-garde, progressive. **3** excellent, exciting.

waypoint *noun* **1** a stopping place, esp. on a journey. **2** the computer-checked coordinates of each stage of a flight etc.

ways and means *plural noun* **1** methods of achieving something. **2** methods of raising government revenue.

wayside *noun* **1** the side or margin of a road. **2** the land at the side of a road. PHRASES **fall by the wayside 1** fail to continue in an endeavour etc. **2** be discarded.

way station *noun* **1** a minor station on a railway. **2** a point marking progress in a certain course of action etc.

wayward *adjective* difficult to control or predict because of perverse, disobedient, or erratic behaviour: *the old couple hoped that marriage would reform their wayward son* ◊ *an organic fungicide can help wayward spores from beginning to grow*. ▶**waywardly** *adverb* **waywardness** *noun*

Wb *abbreviation* weber(s).

WCB *abbreviation Cdn* Workers' Compensation Board.

WCTU *abbreviation* Woman's Christian Temperance Union.

we *pronoun* **1** used by and with reference to more than one person speaking or writing, or one such person and one or more associated persons. **2** used for or by a royal person in a proclamation etc. and by a writer or editor in a formal context. **3** people in general (*compare* ONE *pronoun* 3). **4** *informal* = I². **5** *informal* (often implying condescension) you: *how are we feeling today?*

weak *adjective* **1** deficient in strength, power, or number; fragile; easily broken or bent or defeated. **2** deficient in vigour; sickly, feeble. **3 a** deficient in resolution; easily led: *a weak character*. **b** (of an action or features) indicating a lack of resolution: *a weak chin*. **4** not convincing; logically deficient: *a weak argument*.

W

5 (of a mixed liquid or solution) watery: *weak tea*. **6** (of a syllable etc.) unstressed.

weaken *verb* make or become weak or weaker.

weakfish *noun* (*plural* **weakfish** or **weakfishes**) a large slender marine fish living along the east coast of North America, popular as a food and sport fish.

weak-kneed *noun informal* lacking resolution.

weakling *noun* a feeble person or animal.

weak link *noun* a weak or defective element which renders the whole vulnerable.

weakly • *adverb* in a weak manner. • *adjective* (**weaklier**, **weakliest**) sickly, not robust.

weakness *noun* (*plural* **weaknesses**) **1** the state or condition of being weak. **2** a weak point; a defect. **3** the inability to resist a particular temptation. **4** a self-indulgent liking: *have a weakness for chocolate*.

weal¹ *noun* = WELT 1. [Sounds like *WHEEL*]

weal² *noun literary* welfare, prosperity; good fortune: *the myth of the brave common soldier, whose commitment to the common weal overrides his desire to save his own neck ◊ a tale of weal and woe*. [Sounds like *WHEEL*]

wealth *noun* **1** riches. **2** the state of being rich. **3** (foll. by *of*) an abundance or profusion: *a wealth of new material*.

wealthy *adjective* (**wealthier**, **wealthiest**) having an abundance esp. of money.

wean *verb* **1** accustom (an infant or other young mammal) to food other than (esp. its mother's) milk. **2** disengage (from a habit etc.) esp. gradually. **3** (foll. by *on*) nourish with or expose to from an early age: *was weaned on talk shows and sitcoms*.

weanling *noun* a newly-weaned animal etc.

weapon *noun* **1** a thing designed or used or usable for inflicting bodily harm, e.g. a gun or knife. **2** a means used to gain an advantage: *irony is a double-edged weapon ◊ new weapons against disease*. ▶ **weaponless** *adjective*

weaponry *noun* weapons collectively.

weapons-grade *adjective* designating fissile material of a suitable quality for making nuclear weapons.

SPELL CHECK
wear, ware

Articles for sale are **wares**. China, cutlery etc. are **tableware**.

---

wear • *verb* (**wears**; *past* **wore**; *past participle* **worn**; **wearing**) **1** have on one's person as clothing or an ornament etc. **2** be dressed habitually in: *I don't wear black*. **3** exhibit or present (a facial expression or appearance): *wore a frown*. **4** (often foll. by *away*, *down*) **a** injure the surface of, or partly obliterate or alter, by rubbing, stress, or use. **b** undergo such injury or change. **5** (foll. by *off*, *away*) rub or be rubbed off. **6 a** make (a hole etc.) by constant rubbing or dripping etc. **b** make (a path etc.) by repeated travel along the same route. **7** (often foll. by *out*) exhaust, tire or be tired. **8** (foll. by *down*) overcome by persistence. **9 a** remain for a specified time in working order or a presentable state; last long. **b** (foll. by *well*, *badly*, etc.) endure continued use or life. **10 a** (of time) pass, esp. tediously. **b** (usu. foll. by *on*) pass (time) gradually away. • *noun* **1** the act of wearing or the state of being worn: *suitable for informal wear*. **2** things worn; clothing suitable for a specified purpose or part of the body (esp. in *combination*: *sportswear ◊ footwear*). **3** (also **wear and tear**) damage sustained from continuous use. **4** the capacity for resisting wear and tear: *still a great deal of wear left in it*. PHRASES **in wear** being regularly worn. **wear off** lose effectiveness or intensity. **wear out** **1** use or be used until no longer usable. **2** tire or be

tired out. **wear thin 1** (of patience, excuses, etc.) begin to fail. **2** tax one's patience or interest. **wear the pants** (or **trousers**) be the dominant partner in a marriage or relationship. **wear** (or **wear one's years**) **well** *informal* remain young-looking. ▶ **wearable** *adjective* & *noun* **wearer** *noun*

wearily *adverb* in a tired manner: *I wearily climbed the steps to the porch*. [Say WEER a lee]

weariness *noun* the condition of someone who is tired or no longer interested in something: *she got off the bike with a sense of weariness ◊ his weariness with urban life led him to buy a farm*. [Say WEERY ness]

wearing *adjective* **1** tiring; stressful; frustrating: *in theory Rob got on fine with Karen's folks, but these days he was tending to find them wearing*. **2** tedious: *this radical polemic becomes wearing after a while*. [Say WARE ing]

wearisome *adjective* tedious: *the ordinary, wearisome world of work*. [Say WEER ee sum]

weary • *adjective* (**wearier**, **weariest**) **1** tired. **2** (foll. by *of*) no longer interested in; bored or tired of: *she was weary of their arguments*. **3** tiring or tedious. • *verb* (**wearies**, **wearied**, **wearying**) make or grow weary. [Say WEER ee]

weasel • *noun* **1** any of various small carnivorous mammals including ermines, minks, and ferrets, and noted for their ferocity, esp. the long-tailed weasel of North America, having a brown and yellow coat, or the least weasel of North America and Eurasia, with a very short tail and brown and white coat. **2** *informal* a deceitful, sneaky, or treacherous person. • *verb* (**weasels**, **weaseled**, **weaseling**) default on an obligation: *Canada is accused of trying to weasel out of the treaty*. PHRASES **weasel one's way into** obtain by cunning, sneakiness, etc.: *weaseled his way into their affection*. ▶ **weaselly** *adjective*

weather • *noun* **1** the state of the atmosphere at a place and time as regards temperature, cloudiness, dryness, sunshine, wind, precipitation, etc. **2** a news report concerning the weather: *listened to the weather*. **3** bad weather; destructive rain, frost, wind, etc.: *had not been expecting weather*. • *verb* **1** expose to or affect by atmospheric changes, esp. deliberately to dry, season, etc.: *weathered timber*. **2 a** (usu. in *passive*) discolour or partly disintegrate (rock or stones) by exposure to air. **b** be discoloured or worn in this way. **3 a** come safely through (a storm). **b** survive (a difficult period etc.). PHRASES **keep a** (or **one's**) **weather eye on** (or **open**) be watchful. **make heavy weather of** *informal* exaggerate the difficulty or burden presented by (a problem, course of action, etc.). **under the weather** *informal* **1** slightly unwell. **2** in low spirits.

weather-beaten *adjective* worn, damaged, or discoloured by exposure to wind, rain, etc.

weatherboard • *noun* **1** (also **weatherboarding**) **a** a siding material consisting of a series of horizontal boards with edges overlapping to keep out the rain etc. **b** one of these boards. **2** a sloping board attached to the bottom of an outside door to keep out the rain etc. • *verb* fit or supply with weatherboards.

weathering *noun* the action of the weather on materials etc. exposed to it.

weatherman *noun* (*plural* **weathermen**) **1** a man who broadcasts a forecast of the weather. **2** a meteorologist.

weatherproof • *adjective* resistant to the effects of bad weather, esp. rain. • *verb* make weatherproof.

weather station *noun* an observation post for recording meteorological data.

weatherstrip • *noun* a piece of material used to make a door or window proof against rain or wind. • *verb* (**weatherstrips**, **weatherstripped**,

W

weatherstripping) apply a weatherstrip to. ▶ **weatherstripping** *noun*

weathertight *adjective* (of a dwelling) proof against bad weather.

weather vane *noun* a revolving pointer mounted on a spire or other high place to show wind direction.

weather-worn *adjective* weather-beaten.

weave[1] • *verb* (**weaves**; *past* **wove**; *past participle* **woven** or **wove**; **weaving**) **1 a** form (fabric) by interlacing long threads in two directions. **b** form (thread) into fabric in this way. **2 a** make fabric in this way. **b** work at a loom. **3** make (a basket or wreath etc.) by interlacing rods or flowers etc. **4 a** contrive, devise, or construct (a poem, spell, narrative, etc.), esp. skilfully. **b** intermingle or blend in closely as if by weaving; work up (separate elements) into an intricate and connected whole. • *noun* a style of weaving.

weave[2] *verb* (**weaves**; *past* **weaved** or **wove**; *past participle* **weaved** or **woven**; **weaving**) move repeatedly from side to side; take an intricate course to avoid obstructions.

weaver *noun* **1** a person who weaves. **2** (also **weaver bird**) a tropical finch-like bird that builds elaborately woven nests.

weaving *noun* **1** the action of creating woven materials. **2** something woven, esp. a decorative hanging.

web *noun* **1** a network of fine threads constructed by a spider to catch its prey, from fluid secreted from its spinnerets. **2 a** a complete network or connected series: *a web of social problems.* **b** = **Web**) = WORLD WIDE WEB. **c** a snare or trap: *a web of deceit.* **3** a membrane between the toes of a swimming animal or bird.

webbed *adjective* **1 a** (of a bird's foot etc.) having the digits connected by a membrane or fold of skin. **b** (of fingers or toes) united by a fold of skin. **2** covered with or as if with a web.

webbing *noun* a web or woven fabric, esp. strong narrow closely-woven fabric used for supporting upholstery, for belts, etc.

 Web browser *noun* a program used to locate and access hypertext documents on the World Wide Web.

weber *noun* the SI unit of magnetic flux, causing the electromotive force of one volt in a circuit of one turn when generated or removed in one second. Abbreviation: **Wb**. [Say VAY bur]

web-footed *adjective* having the toes connected by webs.

Web page *noun* a hypertext document that is accessible via the World Wide Web.

Web server *noun* **1** a program providing access to World Wide Web documents, which accepts requests from Web browsers, and delivers the required hypertext documents. **2** the computer or system on which such a program runs, and on which the documents are stored.

Web site *noun* **1** a hypertext document or a set of linked documents, usually associated with a particular person, organization, or topic, that is held on a computer system and can be accessed via the World Wide Web. **2** the computer system that holds such a hypertext document or documents.

Wed. *abbreviation* Wednesday.

wed *verb* (**weds**; *past* and *past participle* **wedded** or **wed**; **wedding**) **1** usu. *formal* or *literary* **a** marry. **b** join in marriage. **2** unite: *wed efficiency to economy.*

we'd *contraction* **1** we had. **2** we should; we would.

wedded *adjective* **1** of or in marriage: *wedded bliss.* **2** obstinately attached or devoted (to a pursuit etc.): *scholars, like artists, should be wedded to their work.*

wedding *noun* **1** a marriage ceremony (considered by itself or with the associated celebrations). **2** an act of uniting or joining: *the wedding of the past with the present.*

wedding band *noun* = WEDDING RING.

wedding cake *noun* a cake served at a wedding reception, esp. a multi-tiered fruitcake with white icing.

wedding party *noun* (*plural* **wedding parties**) the principal figures at a wedding, including the bride, groom, maid or matron of honour, best man, and often including bridesmaids, ushers, a flower girl, etc.

wedding ring *noun* (also **wedding band**) a ring given during a wedding ceremony and worn afterwards to show that the person wearing it is married.

wedge • *noun* **1** a piece of wood or metal etc. tapering to a sharp edge, that is driven between two objects or parts of an object to secure or separate them. **2** anything resembling or acting as a wedge: *a wedge of cheese* ◊ *drove an emotional wedge between them.* **3** a golf club with a wedge-shaped head. **4 a** a women's shoe with a solid wedge-shaped sole which is higher at the heel and lower towards the front of the foot. **b** such a sole. • *verb* (**wedges**, **wedged**, **wedging**) **1** tighten, secure, or fasten by means of a wedge: *wedged the door open.* **2** force open or apart with a wedge. **3** (foll. by *in*, *into*) pack or thrust (a thing or oneself) tightly in or into. ❑ PHRASES **thin edge** (or **end**) **of the wedge** *informal* an action or procedure of little importance in itself, but likely to lead to more serious developments.

wedge-shaped *adjective* **1** shaped like a solid wedge. **2** V-shaped.

wedgie *noun informal* **1** a woman's shoe with a wedge sole. **2** a practical joke in which the victim's underpants are pulled up tightly between the buttocks.

Wedgwood *noun proprietary* **1** ceramics made by the English potter Josiah Wedgwood (1730–95) and his successors, esp. a kind of fine stoneware with a white cameo design. **2** the characteristic blue colour of this stoneware.

wedlock *noun* the married state. ❑ PHRASES **born in** (or **out of**) **wedlock** born of married (or unmarried) parents.

Wednesday • *noun* the fourth day of the week, following Tuesday. • *adverb* **1** on Wednesday. **2** (**Wednesdays**) on Wednesdays; each Wednesday.

wee[1] *adjective* (**weer**; **weest**) **1** *informal* very small in amount or extent: *a wee bit late.* **2** esp. *Scot.* small in size or stature.

wee[2] *verb* (**wees**, **weed**, **weeing**) esp. *Brit. slang* urinate.

weed • *noun* **1** a wild plant growing where it is not wanted. **2** *slang* **a** marijuana. **b** tobacco. • *verb* **1 a** clear (an area) of weeds. **b** remove unwanted parts from. **2** (foll. by *out*) **a** sort out (inferior or unwanted parts, elements, etc.) for removal. **b** rid (a quantity or company) of inferior or unwanted members etc. **3** cut off or uproot weeds.

weedbed *noun* an area of a lake etc. with many weeds, esp. as frequented by fish.

weeder *noun* a small tool used to remove weeds.

weedless *adjective* **1** having no weeds: *a weedless garden.* **2** *Fishing* (of a lure) designed not to become caught in weeds and other underwater vegetation.

weedy *adjective* (**weedier**, **weediest**) **1** having many weeds. **2** (esp. of a person) having a weak or feeble appearance: *there are men with receding hair who, in defence, grow an informal rat-tail at the back, oblivious to how weedy and wasted this makes them look.*

week *noun* **1** a period of seven consecutive days starting on Sunday or Monday. **2** a period of seven days counted from or beginning with a usu. specified point: *three weeks since we were there*. **3** one week of the year devoted to a specific event, holiday, cause, or activity: *Grey Cup week ◊ reading week*. **4** the period of five days from Monday through Friday. **5** the period during which one works in a week: *a 35-hour week*. **6** (in *plural*) *informal* a long time: *I haven't seen you in weeks*.

weekday *noun* any of the days from Monday to Friday.

weekend • *noun* **1** the period from Friday evening to Sunday evening. **2** this period extended slightly: *a three-day weekend*. • *adjective* **1** held on or over a weekend. **2** carrying out a specific activity or hobby, or fulfilling a particular role, only on weekends. **3** for use on weekends. • *verb* spend a weekend.

weekender *noun* a person who spends weekends away from home.

weekend warrior *noun informal* or *jocular* a person who participates in an activity only in his or her spare time, esp. on weekends.

week-long *adjective* lasting for a week: *a week-long festival*.

weekly • *adjective* **1** done, produced, or occurring once a week. **2** calculated or determined by the week: *a weekly salary*. • *adverb* once a week; from week to week. • *noun* (*plural* **weeklies**) a weekly newspaper etc.

weeknight *noun* each of the nights of a week not falling on a weekend, i.e. from Monday to Thursday.

weenie *noun* **1** a frankfurter. **2** *derogatory* (as a term of contempt) an objectionable, feeble, or insignificant person. **3** *slang* the penis.

weeny *adjective* (**weenier**, **weeniest**) (also **weensy**, **weensier**,**weensiest**) *informal* tiny.

weep • *verb* (**weeps**, **wept**, **weeping**) **1** express grief or misery etc. by tears usu. accompanied by sobs and moans. **2** (foll. by *for*) shed tears for; bewail. **3** shed or exude (liquid etc.). • *noun* a fit or period of weeping.

weeper *noun* **1** a person who weeps esp. habitually. **2** an emotional or sentimental ballad, song, movie, etc.

weepie *noun* (*plural* **weepies**) *informal* a sentimental or emotional movie, novel, etc.; a tearjerker.

weeping • *adjective* **1** (of a tree) having drooping branches. **2** that cries or weeps. • *noun* the act of shedding tears.

weeping willow *noun* any of several ornamental willows with drooping branches and slender yellowish-green leaves.

weepy *adjective* (**weepier**, **weepiest**) *informal* **1** inclined to cry or weep. **2** (of a movie, novel, etc.) intended to evoke tears.

weevil *noun* **1** a small destructive beetle with a head that extends into a beak, the larvae of which typically develop inside seeds, stems, or other plant parts. **2** any insect damaging stored grain. [Rhymes with *EVIL*]

wee-wee *noun informal* = PEE-PEE 1.

weft *noun* **1 a** the threads woven across a warp to make fabric. **b** yarn used for this. **2** strips of cane, straw, etc. used as filling in weaving baskets or mats etc.

weigh *verb* **1** determine the heaviness of (a body or substance), esp. by placing it on a scale or balancing it against something of known heaviness. **2** (often foll. by *out*) **a** use scales to measure and remove a definite quantity of (a substance) from a larger supply. **b** distribute in exact amounts by weight. **3 a** consider the relative value, importance, or desirability of: *weighed the options*. **b** (foll. by *against*, *with*) compare (one consideration) with another. **4** have or be equal to a specified degree of heaviness: *this weighs three kilograms ◊ he weighs more than I do*. **5** have a usu. specified degree of importance: *this issue will weigh heavily on the outcome*. **6** (usu. foll. by *on*) be a source of worry or concern (to): *it's been weighing on her mind for some time*. ■PHRASES■ **weigh anchor** take the anchor up. **weigh down 1** bring or keep down by exerting weight. **2** be oppressive or burdensome to: *weighed down with worries*. **weigh in 1** (of a boxer, jockey, etc.) have one's weight checked officially. **2** (foll. by *at*) have a specified weight officially recorded at a weigh-in: *the prizewinning salmon weighed in at 39.2 lb*. **3 a** bring one's weight or influence to bear; contribute to a discussion, undertaking, etc. **b** (foll. by *with*) introduce or contribute (something) to an undertaking etc.: *the whole family weighed in with offers of help*. **weigh into** *informal* attack (physically or verbally). **weigh up** *informal* consider carefully; evaluate (a person, situation, etc.). **weigh with** be of importance to. **weigh one's words** carefully choose a sensitive or tactful way of expressing something.

weigh-in *noun* an official weighing of a person or thing, such as a boxer prior to a bout or an angler's catch at the end of a competition.

weigh scale *noun* (also **weigh station**) a large metal platform at the side of a highway where trucks are required to have their cargo weighed to ensure that it does not exceed the legal limit for that road.

weight • *noun* **1** *Physics* **a** the force experienced by a body as a result of the earth's gravitational pull (compare MASS *noun* 8). **b** any similar force with which a body tends to a centre of attraction. **2** the heaviness of a body regarded as a property of it: *it's held in position by its weight*. **3 a** the quantitative expression of a body's weight: *it has a weight of three pounds*. **b** a unit or system of units used for measuring or expressing how much a body weighs: *troy weight*. **4** a body of a known weight for use in weighing. **5** a heavy body used to hold something down, to drive the mechanism of a clock, as a sinker in fishing, etc. **6 a** a heavy mass or load. **b** an emotional burden: *a weight off my mind*. **7 a** a power to persuade, convince, or impress; influence, sway: *carried weight with the public*. **b** preponderance: *the weight of evidence was against them*. **8** *Statistics* a relative value assigned to a factor or observation, esp. a multiplier associated with any of a set of numerical quantities that are added together. **9 a** (in *plural*) heavy blocks or discs of metal, barbells, etc. designed to be used in lifting and other exercises to improve or demonstrate physical strength and fitness. **b** = SHOT[1] 7. **10** (also **weight class**) each of a series of divisions to which an athlete in some sports, e.g. boxing, may be assigned, according to how much he or she weighs. **11** (usu. in *combination*) the relative weight of a fabric or garment as a measure of its quality or suitability for a particular use or season: *a lightweight spring jacket*. • *verb* **1 a** supply with an additional weight. **b** (usu. foll. by *down*) hold down with a weight or weights. **2** devise or manipulate (a rule or law etc.) so that it favours a particular individual, group, or goal over others: *legislation weighted in favour of the working class*. **3** *Statistics* multiply (the components of an average) by factors reflecting their relative importance. **4** (foll. by *with*) impede or burden. **5** assign a handicap weight to (a horse). ■PHRASES■ **worth one's** (or **its**) **weight in gold** extremely valuable, useful, or helpful. ▶ **weighted** *adjective*

weightiness *noun* the quality of being weighty; heaviness; importance.

weightless *adjective* **1** lacking or apparently lacking

W

weight. **2** (of an orbiting satellite etc.) not apparently acted on by gravity, either due to a locally weak gravitational field, or because both the body and its surroundings are freely and equally accelerating under the influence of the field. ▶ **weightlessly** *adverb* **weightlessness** *noun*

weightlifter *noun* a person who lifts heavy weights for exercise or in competitions.

weightlifting *noun* the sport or exercise of lifting heavy weights.

weight room *noun* a room where weights and related equipment are kept and used for physical training.

weighty *adjective* (**weightier**, **weightiest**) **1** of considerable weight; heavy. **2** of great importance or significance. **3** (of an argument, speech, etc.) producing a powerful effect; convincing, persuasive. **4** (of a person) having great authority; influential.

weir *noun* **1** a dam built across a river to raise the level of water upstream or regulate its flow. **2** an enclosure of stakes and netting set in a stream or river etc., used for trapping fish. [Say WEER]

weird *adjective* **1** strange, unusual, bizarre. **2** suggestive of fate or the supernatural. PHRASES **weird out** *slang* **1** make or become uncharacteristically depressed or upset. **2** induce a sense of disbelief or alienation in (a person). ▶ **weirdly** *adverb* **weirdness** *noun*

weirdo *noun* (*plural* **weirdos**) (also **weirdy**) (*plural* **weirdies**) *informal* a strange or abnormal person.

welch *verb* = WELSH.

welcome • *noun* **1** a kind or hospitable reception given to a visitor or stranger upon arriving. **2** a greeting or reception of a specified (usu. friendly or unfriendly) kind: *gave them a warm welcome*. • *interjection* used to greet a visitor or guest, esp. expressing pleasure at the arrival: *welcome home!* • *verb* (**welcomes**, **welcomed**, **welcoming**) **1 a** greet or receive with pleasure; give a friendly reception to: *welcomed them home*. **b** (foll. by *with*) greet or receive with something of a specified kind: *the audience welcomed him with boos*. **2** be pleased at or receptive to the prospect of (something): *we welcome your comments*. • *adjective* **1** that one receives with pleasure: *welcome news*. **2** freely allowed or cordially invited: *you are welcome to anything in the fridge* ◊ *you are welcome to bring a friend along*. PHRASES **make welcome** receive hospitably. **wear out** (or **overstay** or **outstay**) **one's welcome** inconvenience one's host by staying longer than is reasonable or expected. **welcome aboard!** *jocular* a greeting to a person joining a particular group, starting a job, etc. **you're** (or **you are**) **welcome** a polite response to an expression of thanks, signifying that the recipient of a favour is without obligation to the giver.

welcome mat *noun* **1** a doormat typically bearing some message of greeting, such as *Welcome*. **2** anything used to invite, entice, or solicit investors, customers, etc.: *the company has thrown down the welcome mat to potential investors*.

welcomer *noun* a person who welcomes others, e.g. to a hospital.

welcome tax *noun Cdn* (*Que.*) a municipal tax levied on all house purchases in the Province of Quebec.

welcoming *adjective* **1** (of a person) friendly towards somebody who is visiting or arriving. **2** (of a place) attractive and looking comfortable to be in: *his home was quiet, warm and welcoming*.

weld • *verb* **1 a** hammer or press (pieces of heated iron or steel) into one piece. **b** join (pieces of metal or plastic etc.) by melting, using heat provided by an electric arc, acetylene torch, or laser. **c** form or repair by welding.

2 bring together (arguments, members of a group, etc.) into an effectual or homogeneous whole. • *noun* a welded joint.

welder *noun* **1** a person who welds, esp. as a profession. **2** a torch etc. used in welding.

welfare *noun* **1** well-being, happiness; health and prosperity of a person or a community etc. **2 a** the organized provision for the basic esp. physical and economic well-being of needy members of a community by legislation or social effort. **b** financial support given for this purpose. PHRASES **on welfare** receiving financial assistance from the government for basic living needs.

welfare state *noun* **1** a system whereby the government of a country etc. undertakes to protect the health and well-being of its citizens, esp. those in financial or social need, by means of pensions, allowances, etc. **2** a country practising this system.

welfarism *noun* the principles or policies associated with a welfare state. ▶ **welfarist** *noun*

> **SPELL CHECK**
> **well**
>
> Combinations beginning with **well**, such as **well aimed**, are written as two separate words when following a verb, as in *That shot was well aimed*, but with a hyphen when they come before a noun, as in *That was a well-aimed shot*.

well¹ • *adverb* (**better**, **best**) **1** in an acceptable or satisfactory manner. **2** with some talent or distinction. **3** in a way appropriate to the facts or circumstances: *you did well to tell me*. **4** in a kind way. **5** thoroughly, carefully. **6** favourably. **7** with equanimity or good nature: *he took it well*. **8** probably: *you may well be right*. **9** to a considerable extent: *she is well over forty*. **10** intimately; closely, in detail. **11** successfully, fortunately. **12** with a fortunate outcome; without disaster: *were well rid of them*. **13** profitably: *did well for themselves*. **14** comfortably: *we live well*. **15** *informal* used with preceding adverb to form intensive phrases: *I should bloody well hope so!* • *adjective* (**better**, **best**) **1** in good health; free or recovered from illness. **2 a** in a satisfactory state or position: *all is well*. **b** proper, advisable: *it would be well to inquire*. • *interjection* **1** expressing surprise, insistence, resignation, etc.: *well I never!* ◊ *oh well, at least we tried*. **2** used to resume or continue speaking, esp. after a pause: *well...who was it?* ◊ *well anyway, as I was saying*. PHRASES **all's well that ends well** the inconvenience of a problem or matter is negligible as long as it is resolved satisfactorily. **as well 1** also, in addition; to an equal extent. **2** (also **just as well**) with equal reason or result; with no loss of advantage or need for regret: *we might as well go home*. **as well as** in addition to. **leave** (or **let**) **well enough alone** refrain from trying to improve something that is already satisfactory. **well and good** expressing dispassionate acceptance of a statement or decision etc. **well and truly** decisively, completely. **well worth** certainly worth: *well worth a visit*.

well² • *noun* **1** a shaft sunk into the ground to obtain water, oil, natural gas, etc. **2** a natural source or spring of water. **3 a** the open space or shaft in a building enclosing a staircase or housing an elevator. **b** a deep narrow space in the middle of a building or group of buildings, to provide light and ventilation. **4** a receptacle, reservoir, or depression designed to hold liquid, such as one in a dish for gravy or in a desk for ink. **5** a deep receptacle, compartment, or recess, such as that in the trunk of a car in which a spare tire is kept. **6** a source, esp. a copious one: *a well of information*.

W

• **verb 1** (foll. by *up, out*) gather, gush, or spring as in or from a fountain: *anger welled up inside her*. **2** (foll. by *up*) be filled with tears.

we'll *contraction* we shall; we will.

well-acquainted *adjective* (usu. foll. by *with*) familiar.

well-adjusted *adjective* **1** *Psychology* mentally and emotionally stable. **2** in a state of proper adjustment.

well-advised *adjective* **1** (of a person) prudent, wise: *would be well-advised to wait*. **2** (of an action etc.) carefully thought out.

well-aimed *adjective* **1** (of a jibe or criticism) unkind and hurtful. **2** precisely directed; accurate.

well-appointed *adjective* furnished with all of the necessary equipment, accessories, or desirable features: *a well-appointed kitchen*.

well-attended *adjective* (of a meeting etc.) attended by a large number of people.

well aware *adjective* certainly aware.

well-balanced *adjective* **1** having no constituent lacking or in excess; regulated to ensure a proper balance: *a well-balanced diet*. **2** sane, sensible.

well-behaved *adjective* having or demonstrating good manners or conduct.

well-being *noun* a happy, healthy, and prosperous state or condition; moral or physical welfare.

well-bred *adjective* **1** demonstrating qualities indicative of a good upbringing, such as refined speech, courteous behaviour, and excellent manners. **2** (of an animal) of good or pure stock.

well-built *adjective* **1** of solid and reliable construction. **2** (of a person) well-proportioned with a strong, sturdy, or muscular build.

well-chosen *adjective* (of words etc.) carefully selected for effect.

well-connected *adjective* having powerful or influential relatives, friends, associates, contacts, etc.

well-defined *adjective* clearly marked, outlined, or indicated; having definite shape, structure, or guidelines.

well-deserved *adjective* rightfully merited or earned.

well-developed *adjective* **1** fully developed or grown; mature. **2** of generous size.

well-documented *adjective* supported or attested by much documentary evidence.

well done • *adjective* **1** (of meat) thoroughly cooked. **2** (of a task etc.) performed or executed skilfully or effectively. • *interjection* expressing approval of a person's actions.

well-endowed *adjective* **1** well provided with talent or resources. **2** *euphemism* **a** (of a woman) having large breasts. **b** (of a man) = WELL-HUNG.

well equipped *adjective* **1** having a plentiful supply of equipment. **2** having the necessary requirements or resources: *well equipped to deal with the situation*.

well-established *adjective* **1** (of a custom, rule, etc.) long-standing. **2** firmly entrenched in a profession, role, or position; proven: *a well-established artist*.

well-fed *adjective* **1** having had plenty to eat. **2** *euphemism* plump, overweight.

well-formed *adjective* correctly or attractively proportioned or shaped.

well-founded *adjective* (of a belief, statement, etc.) having a foundation in fact or reason; based on strong evidence.

well-groomed *adjective* **1** (of a person) looking clean and neat with carefully tended hair, clothes, etc. **2** (of an animal) having a clean and brushed coat. **3** (of ski trails etc.) properly maintained or looked after.

well-grounded *adjective* **1** = WELL-FOUNDED. **2** (often

foll. by *in*) having a good training in or knowledge of the basic principles of a subject.

wellhead *noun* **1** a structure built over an oil or gas well. **2** = WELLSPRING.

well-heeled *adjective* *informal* wealthy.

well-hung *adjective* *slang* (of a man) having large genitals.

well-informed *adjective* possessing or communicating much knowledge in general or of a specified subject.

wellington *noun* (also **wellington boot**) (usu. in *plural*) esp. *Brit.* a waterproof rubber or plastic boot usu. reaching the knee, worn in wet or muddy conditions.

well-intentioned *adjective* having or showing good intentions.

well-kept *adjective* **1** kept in good order or condition. **2** carefully preserved; not revealed: *a well-kept secret*.

well-known *adjective* **1** known to many; widely known, famous. **2** thoroughly known.

well-maintained *adjective* **1** kept in good repair. **2** kept up to date: *well-maintained inventory*.

well-mannered *adjective* having or demonstrating good manners; courteous, polite.

well-marked *adjective* clearly defined, distinct; easy to distinguish or recognize.

well-matched *adjective* **1** compatible, suited; fit to be a pair. **2** (of opponents or adversaries) evenly matched; having similar or offsetting strengths and weakness.

well-meaning *adjective* **1** having or demonstrating good intentions, esp. despite being misguided or unhelpful. **2** (also **well-meant**) (of advice etc.) based on good intentions but usu. ineffective or ill-advised.

wellness *noun* the state of being well or in good health.

well-nigh *adverb* very nearly; almost: *well-nigh impossible*.

well off *adjective* **1** having plenty of money. **2** in a fortunate situation or position.

well-oiled *adjective* *informal* **1 a** sufficiently or generously lubricated. **b** (of an organization, operation, etc.) running smoothly. **2** drunk.

well-ordered *adjective* neatly, carefully, or properly composed or arranged.

well-paid *adjective* **1** (of a person) amply rewarded for a job. **2** (also **well-paying**) (of a job) that pays well.

well placed *adjective* **1** set in a good place or position; properly, conveniently, or judiciously placed. **2** holding a position of influence, authority, or high social standing. **3** in a suitable position; easily able: *you are well placed to know*.

well-preserved *adjective* **1** having remained in good condition over time: *a well-preserved artifact*. **2** (of an elderly person) showing little sign of aging.

well-proportioned *noun* having good, graceful, or correct proportions.

well-read *adjective* knowledgeable from much reading.

well-received *adjective* favourably received or reviewed.

well-rounded *adjective* **1** (of a person) having or showing a fully developed personality combined with a wide range of knowledge and interests. **2** well-balanced, full, and varied: *a well-rounded team*.

well-spent *adjective* (esp. of money or time) used profitably or judiciously.

well-spoken *adjective* (of a person) speaking articulately and grammatically or with an accent considered to be refined.

wellspring *noun* **1** the place where a spring breaks out of the ground; the source of a stream or river. **2** an

W

esp. abundant source: *melancholy is the wellspring of creativity*.

well-stocked *adjective* having an abundant supply.

well-suited *adjective* (usu. foll. by *to*, *for*) suitable.

well-supported *adjective* **1** attended by many. **2** supported by much evidence.

well-taken *adjective* (of an argument) accepted as valid.

well-thought-of *adjective* having a good reputation; esteemed, respected.

well-thought-out *adjective* carefully planned or devised in advance.

well-thumbed *adjective* (of a book or page etc.) bearing marks of frequent handling.

well-to-do *adjective* comfortably wealthy or prosperous.

well-travelled *adjective* **1** having travelled extensively. **2** (of a path etc.) much frequented.

well-used *adjective* **1 a** used properly or frequently. **b** worn from frequent handling or use. **2** (of a road or path etc.) frequently travelled.

well versed *adjective* very learned, experienced, or skilled in (a subject, art, etc.); knowledgeable about.

well-wisher *noun* a person conveying his or her congratulations, wishes of luck, etc. to another.

well-worn *adjective* **1** decrepit, shabby, or worn out from extensive use or handling. **2** (of a phrase or idea etc.) trite, hackneyed.

Welsh • *adjective* of or relating to Wales, a principality of the United Kingdom, to the west of central England, or its people or language. • *noun* **1** the Celtic language of Wales. **2** (**the Welsh**; treated as *plural*) the people of Wales.

welsh *verb* (**welshes, welshed, welshing**) (usu. foll. by *on*) **1** fail or refuse to pay or repay money owed: *he welshes on gambling debts*. **2** fail or refuse to honour or fulfill a promise or obligation: *she welshed on our agreement*.

Welshman *noun* (*plural* **Welshmen**) a man who is Welsh by birth or descent.

Welshwoman *noun* (*plural* **Welshwomen**) a woman who is Welsh by birth or descent.

welt *noun* a ridge raised on the flesh by the impact of a rod, whip, etc., or by an allergic reaction.

welter *noun* a confused mixture of things or people.

welterweight *noun* **1** a weight class in certain sports between lightweight and middleweight, in the amateur boxing scale 63.5-67 kg but differing for professionals and wrestlers. **2** a boxer etc. of this weight.

wench *noun* (*plural* **wenches**) **1** *jocular* a girl or young woman. **2** *archaic* a prostitute or mistress.

wend *verb* PHRASES **wend one's way** make one's way.

Wen-Do *noun* *Cdn* *proprietary* a program of self-defence for women, emphasizing awareness and avoidance of potentially dangerous situations as well as appropriate reactions, including, as a last resort, physical attacks directed against the particularly vulnerable areas of an assailant's body. [Say wen DOE]

GRAMMAR CHECK
went, gone ⚠
Never say *I should have went*. The correct form is *I should have gone*.

went past of GO.

wept past of WEEP.

were 2nd singular past, plural past, and past subjunctive of BE.

we're *contraction* we are.

weren't *contraction* were not.

werewolf *noun* (*plural* **werewolves**) a mythical being who at times changes from a person to a wolf. [Say WARE wolf or WEER wolf]

Wesleyan • *adjective* of or relating to a Protestant denomination founded by the English evangelist John Wesley (1703–91) (*see also* METHODISM). • *noun* a member of this denomination. ▶**Wesleyanism** *noun* [Say WEZZLY un or WESSLY un]

west • *noun* **1** the point of the horizon where the sun sets at the equinoxes (cardinal point 90° to the left of north). **2** the compass point corresponding to this. **3** the direction in which this lies. **4** (usu. **the West**) **a** Europe and the countries of the western hemisphere as distinguished from those of the regions or countries lying to the east of the Mediterranean, esp. China, Japan, and other East Asian countries. **b** *hist.* the non-Communist countries of Europe and North America. **5** (usu. **the West**) **a** the western part of a country or city etc. **b** *Cdn* the part of the country west of the Ontario-Manitoba border. **c** *US* the states lying to the west of the Mississippi. • *adjective* **1** towards, at, near, or facing west. **2** coming from the west: *west wind*. • *adverb* **1** towards, at, or near the west. **2** (foll. by *of*) further west than.

westbound *adjective* travelling or leading westwards.

westerly • *adjective & adverb* **1** in a western position or direction. **2** (of a wind) blowing from the west. • *noun* (*plural* **westerlies**) a wind blowing from the west.

western • *adjective* **1** of or in the west; inhabiting the west. **2** lying or directed towards the west. **3** (esp. of a wind) blowing from the west. **4** (**Western**) **a** of or relating to the Occident or (formerly) the non-Communist countries of Europe and North America. **b** of or related to the Canadian or American West. • *noun* **1** a film or novel of a genre depicting life in the North American West in the 19th and early 20th centuries, usu. featuring cowboys in heroic roles, gunfights, etc. **2 a** = WESTERN SANDWICH. **b** = WESTERN OMELETTE. • *adverb* (ride etc.) in the manner of a cowboy, in a relaxed style with a deep-seated saddle and almost straight legs.

Western Church *noun* the part of the Christian Church including the Catholic and Protestant Churches, as distinct from the Orthodox or Eastern Churches.

westerner *noun* (also **Westerner**) a native or inhabitant of the western part of any country or of any country of the western hemisphere.

western hemisphere *noun* the half of the earth containing North and South America and the surrounding waters.

westernization *noun* the process of becoming westernized.

westernize *verb* (**westernizes, westernized, westernizing**) influence with or convert to Western ideas and customs etc., esp. the ideas and customs of Occidental countries.

westernmost *adjective* furthest to the west.

western omelette *noun* an omelette made with diced onion, ham, and often green peppers.

Western provinces *plural noun* Manitoba, Alberta, Saskatchewan, and British Columbia.

western sandwich *noun* (*plural* **western sandwiches**) a toasted sandwich with a western omelette as filling.

Western Wall *noun* the remaining part of the wall of Herod's temple in Jerusalem destroyed in AD 70, where Jews traditionally pray and lament on Fridays.

West Indian *noun* **1** a native or national of any island of the West Indies, a chain of islands extending from

the Florida peninsula to the coast of Venezuela, lying between the Caribbean and the Atlantic. **2** a person of West Indian descent.

west-northwest *noun* the direction or compass point midway between west and northwest.

west-southwest *noun* the direction or compass point midway between west and southwest.

westward • *adjective & adverb* (also **westwards**) towards the west. • *noun* a westward direction or region.

SPELL CHECK
wet, whet

If you make someone hungry or eager for something, you **whet** their appetite.

---

wet • *adjective* (**wetter**, **wettest**) **1** covered, dampened, or soaked with water or another liquid. **2** (of the weather etc.) rainy. **3** (of paint, ink, etc.) not yet dried. **4** used or done with water: *a wet shave*. **5** (of ingredients in a recipe) liquid, such as water, oil, eggs, etc. **6** (of a baby) having urinated; having a diaper that needs changing. **7** *informal* **a** of or pertaining to alcohol, esp. as drunk in substantial quantities: *a wet lunch*. **b** (of a country, of legislation, etc.) favouring or permitting the sale of alcohol. • *verb* (**wets**; **wet** or **wetted**; **wetting**) **1** dampen, make wet. **2 a** urinate in or on: *wet the bed*. **b** urinate involuntarily: *I laughed so hard I nearly wet myself*. • *noun* **1** moisture; liquid that makes something wet. **2** precipitation or a period of this: *come in out of the wet*. PHRASES **all wet** *informal* completely wrong or mistaken. **wet the baby's head** *informal* celebrate the birth of a baby with a drink. **wet behind the ears** immature, inexperienced. **wet through** (or **to the skin**) with one's clothes soaked. **wet one's whistle** *informal* drink.

wet bar *noun* a bar or counter in the home equipped with a sink and running water, from which drinks are served.

wet dream *noun* an erotic dream with involuntary ejaculation of semen.

wetland *noun* (often in *plural*) a marsh, swamp, or other stretch of land that is frequently saturated with water (also as an *adjective*: *wetland vegetation*).

wetly *adverb* while wet; moistly.

wetness *noun* **1** the state or condition of being wet. **2** moisture.

wet nurse *noun* a woman employed to breast-feed another's baby.

wet snow *noun* large cohesive flakes of snow that fall when the temperature is above or slightly below the freezing point, accumulating in dense heavy masses.

wetsuit *noun* a close-fitting one-piece rubber garment worn by scuba divers, surfers, etc., to protect them from the cold.

Wet'suwet'en • *noun* (*plural* **Wet'suwet'en**) **1** a member of an Aboriginal people living in north-central BC, along the Skeena River. **2** the Tsimshian language of this people. • *adjective* of or relating to this people or their language or culture. [Say wut SOO wuh tun]

wettable *adjective* able to be wetted.

wetting *noun* an act of soaking or dampening.

we've *contraction* we have.

whack *informal* • *verb* **1** strike or beat forcefully with a sharp slap or blow. **2** *slang* kill. • *noun* **1** a sharp or resounding blow. **2** *slang* a large number or amount: *a whole whack of people*. PHRASES **have** (or **take**) **a whack at** *slang* attempt. **out of whack** *slang* **1** out of order; malfunctioning. **2** (of calculations, figures, etc.) maladjusted, skewed.

whacked *adjective informal* **1** (usu. foll. by *out*) **a** mad,

crazy, wild. **b** high or intoxicated on drugs or alcohol. **2** (sometimes foll. by *out*) tired out; exhausted.

whacko *adjective and noun* = WACKO.

whacky *adjective* = WACKY.

whale[1] *noun* (*plural* **whales** or **whale**) a large marine mammal with a streamlined fishlike body, forelimbs modified as fins, and a tail with horizontal flukes, which breathes through a nasal opening on top of its head. PHRASES **a whale of a** *informal* an exceptionally good or large etc.

whale[2] *verb informal* beat, thrash.

whaleboat *noun* a long narrow double-bowed boat formerly used for whaling, now used esp. as a lifeboat.

whalebone *noun* **1** an elastic horny substance which grows in a series of thin parallel plates in the upper jaw of baleen whales, serving to strain plankton from the sea water. **2** a strip of this esp. used as a stiffening in stays and dresses etc.

whale-watch • *noun* (*plural* **whale-watches**) an excursion made by boat to observe whales in their natural habitat. • *verb* (**whale-watches**, **whale-watched**, **whale-watching**) go on an excursion to observe whales.

whaling *noun* the hunting and killing of whales, esp. for their oil, meat, or whalebone.

wham *informal* • *noun* the sound of forcible impact. • *interjection* expressing such a sound. • *verb* (**whams**, **whammed**, **whamming**) **1** make such a sound or impact. **2** strike with force.

whammy *noun* (*plural* **whammies**) esp. *US informal* **1** an evil or unlucky influence; a hex or curse. **2** (esp. in phr. **double whammy**) a powerful or unpleasant effect or a problematic situation.

whang *informal* • *verb* **1** produce a loud resonating or ringing sound under or as if under a forceful blow. **2** strike heavily and loudly. • *noun* a loud resonating or ringing sound or blow.

whap • *noun* **1** a hard slap as if with a flat object or the palm of the hand. **2** the sound of this. • *verb* (**whaps**, **whapped**, **whapping**) strike or slap forcefully, esp. with or as if with a flat object or the palm of the hand. [Say WOP or WAP]

wharf • *noun* (*plural* **wharves** or **wharfs**) a level quayside structure to which a ship may be moored to load and unload. • *verb* **1** moor (a ship) at a wharf. **2** unload and store (goods) on a wharf. [Say WORF]

what • *interrogative adjective* used in asking the identity of a choice made from a set of alternatives: *what books have you read?* • *adjective* (usu. in exclamation) how great or remarkable: *what luck!* • *relative adjective* the or any...that: *will give you what help I can*. • *pronoun* **1 a** used in asking the identity or name of a thing or things specified, indicated, or understood: *I don't know what you mean*. **b** used in asking the character, function, occupation, etc. of a person or persons specified, indicated, or understood: *what are you going to be when you grow up?* **2** (asking for a remark to be repeated) = what did you say? **3** asking for repetition, clarification, or confirmation of something disputed or not completely understood: *you did what?* ◊ *what, you want me to do it?* **4 a** how much: *what is it going to cost?* **b** how great: *what a save!* **5** (preceded by *or*) *informal* representing the unknown final alternative in a set of proposed options: *I didn't know if she was scared, nervous, or what*. • *relative pronoun* that or those which: *tell me what you think*. • *adverb* to what extent: *what does it matter?* • *interjection* **1** expressing surprise or astonishment: *what, that's it?* **2** expressing disbelief and inviting repetition or confirmation of a previous remark. PHRASES **what about** what is your position on or opinion of: *what about me?* ◊ *what about a game of*

W

tennis? **what for** *informal* **1** why? for what reason? **2** a severe reprimand: *gave her what for*. **what have you** *informal* (preceded by *or*) anything else similar. **what if? 1** what would result etc. if. **2** what would it matter if. **what is more** and as an additional point; moreover. **what next?** *informal* what more absurd, shocking, or surprising thing is possible? **what of?** what is the news concerning? **what of it?** why should that be considered significant? **what's his** (or **her**) **name** (also **what's his** (or **her**) **face**) *informal* a person whose name one cannot recall, does not know, or does not wish to specify. **what's what** *informal* what things are useful or important. **what's with** *informal* what is the matter with? what has happened to? what is the reason for? **what with** *informal* on account of; because of (usu. several things).

whatchamacallit (also **whatchacallit**, **what-d'you-call-it**) *noun informal* a thing the proper name of which one cannot recall, does not know, or does not wish to mention.

whatever • *pronoun* **1** anything or everything that: *do whatever it takes*. **2** no matter what: *whatever it is, it's coming this way*. **3** representing an unknown final alternative, usu. in a set of proposed options: *he'll drink wine, beer, whatever*. **4** what in any way: *whatever can you mean?* • *adjective* **1** any...that: *whatever money you can lend me will help*. **2** any; no matter what: *whatever garbage he writes sells*. **3** (used as a perfunctory designation of anything a speaker is reluctant or unable to describe specifically) denoting an unnamed person or thing: *for whatever reason, she left early*. **4** = WHATSOEVER.

whatnot *noun* **1** (usu. preceded by *and*) other similar items: *a drawer full of paper, pens, and whatnot*. **2** an unspecified or trivial thing. **3** a stand with shelves used for keeping or displaying small objects.

what say • *interjection* pardon? what did you say? • *adverb* indicating a suggestion or proposition to which a reply is expected: *what say we go to a movie?*

whatsit *noun* **1** = WHATCHAMACALLIT. **2** a person whose name one cannot recall, does not know, or does not wish to specify.

whatsoever *adjective* (with *neg.*) at all; of any kind: *there is no doubt whatsoever*.

wheat *noun* **1** a cereal plant bearing dense four-sided seed spikes. **2** its grain, used in making flour etc.

Wheat Board *noun Cdn* a Crown corporation responsible for the sale of all wheat and barley produced in western Canada and destined for export or for domestic human consumption.

wheaten *adjective* **1** made of the grain or flour of wheat. **2** of the colour of ripe wheat, usu. a pale gold.

wheat germ *noun* the embryo of the wheat grain.

wheat grass *noun* (*plural* **wheat grasses**) a North American grass grown for fodder.

wheat pool *noun Cdn* a grain farmers' co-operative in Western Canada for the sale of wheat and other cereal crops.

whee *interjection* expressing delight or excitement.

wheedle *verb* (**wheedles**, **wheedled**, **wheedling**) **1** attempt to coax or persuade (a person) by flattery or endearments. **2** (often foll. by *out*) talk or coax a person into giving up possession of (something); obtain or acquire by wheedling. ▶ **wheedler** *noun* **wheedling** *adjective*

wheel • *noun* **1** a solid disc or circular frame with spokes radiating from the centre, attached or able to be attached at its centre to an axle around which it revolves, used to facilitate the motion of a vehicle or for various mechanical purposes. **2** anything resembling a wheel in function or appearance: *roulette wheel ◊ a wheel* *of brie*. **3** a machine etc. of which a wheel is an essential part: *spinning wheel*. **4** (in *plural*) *slang* a car. **5** = STEERING WHEEL. **6** a recurring course of actions or events; an endless cycle: *wheel of life*. **7** (in *plural*, usu. foll. by *of*) the driving or animating force: *wheels of industry*. **8** a motion like that of a wheel, esp. the movement of a line of people with one end as a pivot. **9** *hist.* a large wheel used in various ways as an instrument of torture. • *verb* **1** turn or rotate on an axis or pivot. **2 a** change direction or face another way, esp. quickly or suddenly. **b** cause to do this. **3** push or pull (a wheeled thing, esp. a bicycle, or stroller, or its load or occupant). **4** move in circles or curves: *seagulls wheeled overhead*. **5** (of a line of people) swing around in line with one end as a pivot. PHRASES **at the wheel 1** (also **behind the wheel**) driving a car or truck etc. **2** directing a ship. **3** in control of affairs. **wheel and deal** engage in political or commercial scheming. **wheels within wheels 1** intricate machinery. **2** *informal* used to indicate that a situation is complicated and affected by secret or indirect influences. ▶ **wheeled** *adjective* (also in *combination*)

wheelbarrow *noun* a shallow open container for moving small loads, with a wheel at one end and two legs and two handles at the other.

wheelbase *noun* the distance between the front and rear axles of a vehicle.

wheelchair *noun* a chair on wheels for an invalid or a disabled person.

wheeler *noun* (in *combination*) a vehicle having a specified number of wheels: *an 18-wheeler*.

wheeler-dealer *noun* a person who engages in political or commercial scheming. ▶ **wheeler-dealing** *noun*

wheelhouse *noun* **1** the structure on a ship containing the steering wheel. **2** *Baseball slang* the area over the plate where a pitch is most likely to be hit by a particular batter.

wheelie *noun slang* the stunt of riding a bicycle or motorcycle for a short distance with the front wheel off the ground. PHRASES **pop a wheelie** perform this stunt.

wheel of Fortune *noun* **1** a notional wheel which the goddess Fortune is said to turn in order to determine the fates of humans. **2** a gambling game in which an upright wheel bearing symbols, such as the four suits of a deck of cards, is spun, and points are won depending on where the wheel stops spinning.

wheeze • *verb* (**wheezes**, **wheezed**, **wheezing**) **1** breathe with an audible chesty whistling sound, due to dryness or obstruction of the air passages. **2** make a similar whistling or rasping sound: *the bus wheezed to a stop*. • *noun* **1** a sound of or resembling wheezing. **2** *informal* a hackneyed running joke or comic phrase. ▶ **wheezy** *adjective*

whelk *noun* a shellfish with a spiral shell, some kinds of which are edible.

whelp • *noun* a young dog, seal, or mink. • *verb* (of a female animal, esp. a bitch or seal) give birth to (a whelp or whelps). PHRASES **in whelp** (of a female animal) pregnant.

when • *interrogative adverb* **1** at what time? **2** how soon? **3** how long ago? **4** on what occasion? under what circumstances?: *when is it best to ask?* • *adverb informal* in the past: *I can say I knew her when*. • *relative adverb* (preceded by *time* etc.) at or on which: *there are times when I could cry*. • *conjunction* **1 a** at the time that, on the occasion that: *come when it is convenient ◊ when I was your age*. **b** at any time that: *I smile when I hear her voice*. **2** although; considering that: *why stand when you could sit?* **3** at which time; after which; but just then:

was nearly asleep when the phone rang. **4** while on the contrary, whereas: *gave me $2.00 when she meant to give me $5.00*. • *pronoun* what time?: *till when can you stay?* ◊ *since when have you been married?* • *noun* time, occasion, date: *fixed the where and when*.

WRITING TIP
whence, from whence

The expression **from whence** is considered redundant by many people on the grounds that **whence** already implies **from**. It's safer to say *they returned whence they came* than to say *they returned from whence they came*.

---

whence *formal* • *adverb* from what place?: *whence did they come?* • *conjunction* **1** to the place from which: *return whence you came*. **2** (often preceded by *place* etc.) from which: *the source whence these errors arise*. **3** and thence: *whence it follows that*.

whenever *conjunction & adverb* **1** at whatever time. **2** every time that. PHRASES **or whenever** *informal* or at any similar time.

where • *interrogative adverb* **1** in or at what place or position? **2** to what place? **3 a** in what book or passage of a book? **b** from whom? from what source? **4** in what direction or respect?: *where are you going with this argument?* **5** in what situation or condition?: *where does that leave us?* **6** at what point or stage?: *where did we go wrong?* • *relative adverb* in or to which: *places where they meet.* • *conjunction* **1** in, at, or to the place in which: *put it where we can all see it.* **2** in the situation or circumstances in which: *give credit where credit is due.* **3** *informal* that: *I see where the jewellery store was robbed again.* • *pronoun* what place?: *where do you come from?* • *noun* a place, esp. the or a place at which something happens, has happened, or will happen.

GRAMMAR CHECK ⚠
whereabouts

While **whereabouts** most commonly takes a plural verb, as in *her whereabouts are not known*, it may also be used correctly with a singular verb: *the whereabouts of the purse and its contents remains a mystery*.

---

whereabouts • *adverb* where or approximately where? • *noun* the place in or near which a person or thing is; the approximate location.

whereas *conjunction* **1** in contrast or comparison with the fact that: *at Halifax the British had to build a defensive system from scratch, whereas at Quebec they inherited what was left of the French defences after the Seven Years' War*. **2** (esp. in legal preambles) taking into consideration the fact that; since.

whereby *conjunction* **1** by means of which; in which: *a process whereby public concerns may be expressed*. **2** according to which; under the terms of which: *a deal whereby she will receive a royalty*.

WRITING TIP
wherefore

The sentence "Wherefore art thou Romeo?" does not mean, "Where are you, Romeo?" but "Why are you Romeo?", i.e. "Why are you who you are, the son of a family my family hates?"

---

wherefore • *adverb* archaic **1** for what cause, purpose, or reason? why? **2** on account of which; as a result of which. • *noun* a reason: *the whys and wherefores*.

wherein *formal* • *conjunction* in which thing, matter, place, etc. • *adverb* in what place or respect?

whereof *formal* • *conjunction* of which or whom: *the person whereof she writes*. • *adverb* of what? PHRASES **know whereof one speaks** recognize or understand what one is talking about.

whereupon *conjunction* upon the occurrence of which; immediately after and as a consequence of which: *he got a US visa in June, whereupon he and his family immediately left Canada*.

wherever • *adverb* in or to whatever place. • *conjunction* in every place that. PHRASES **or wherever** *informal* or in any similar place.

wherewithal *noun* the means by which to do something: *the US will have the political and military wherewithal to counter aggression effectively*. [Say WHERE with all]

whet *verb* (**whets, whetted, whetting**) **1** sharpen (a tool or weapon) by grinding it on a stone. **2** stimulate (the appetite, a desire, interest, etc.): *each chapter brings with it a new surprise and whets your appetite for more*.

whether *conjunction* **1** introducing an indirect question or an expression of doubt or choice between alternatives, in which the final alternative is introduced by *or* or *or whether*: *I'm not sure whether it's Monday or Tuesday*. **2** introducing an indirect question, simple inquiry, or opinion, in which the second alternative is implied only: *I wonder whether we should go* ◊ *I doubt whether it matters*. **3** introducing a statement that is applicable whichever of the possibilities given is true: *whether he likes it or not, he has to do it*.

whetstone *noun* a shaped fine-grained stone used to sharpen tools and cutlery etc. by grinding.

whew *interjection* expressing relief, surprise, or exhaustion as from heat or exertion.

whey *noun* the watery liquid that remains when milk forms curds. [Sounds like WAY]

SPELL CHECK
which, witch

A sorceress or adherent of the Wiccan religion is a **witch**.

---

which • *interrogative adjective* used in asking the identity of a choice from a set of alternatives: *which Robert are you talking about?* ◊ *tell me which book you prefer*. • *relative adjective* being the thing or things just referred to, usu. introducing a clause not essential for identification: *the newspaper comes at 6:00, by which time I am usually up* ◊ *he might not come tonight, in which case I won't see him until tomorrow*. • *interrogative pronoun* **1** which person or persons: *which of you is responsible?* **2** which thing or things: *tell me which you prefer*. • *relative pronoun* (*possessive* **of which, whose**) **1** introducing a clause that describes or states something additional about the antecedent but which is not essential for identification (*compare* THAT *pronoun*): *this house, which happens to be for sale, was built in the 1880s*. **2** used in place of *that* after *in* or *that*: *there is the house in which I was born* ◊ *that which you have just seen*. PHRASES **which is which** a phrase used when two or more people or things are difficult to distinguish from each other.

whichever *adjective & pronoun* **1** either or any of a definite set of people or things that: *take whichever one you like*. **2** no matter which: *whichever one wins, they both get a prize*.

whiff • *noun* **1** a puff or breath of air, smoke, etc. **2** a smell or odour. **3** a trace or suggestion: *a whiff of danger*. **4** *Baseball informal* a strikeout. • *verb* **1** sniff, get a slight smell of. **2** blow or puff lightly. **3** *Baseball informal* **a** (of a batter) strike out. **b** (of a pitcher) strike (a batter) out.

whiffle • *verb* (**whiffles, whiffled, whiffling**) **1** (of

W

the wind) blow gently. **2** make the sound of or like wind blowing gently. **3** flutter: *leaves whiffled in the wind*. • *noun* a slight movement of air.

Whig *noun hist.* **1** a member of the English, later British, reforming and constitutional party that after 1688 sought the supremacy of Parliament and was eventually succeeded in the 19th century by the Liberal Party. **2 a** a member of a 19th-century US political party established in 1834 in opposition to the Democratic Party, favouring a protective tariff and strong central government, succeeded by the Republican Party. **b** a colonist who supported the American Revolution.

> **SPELL CHECK**
> **while, wile**
>
> A trick or lure is a **wile**.

while • *noun* a period of time considered with respect to its duration, usu. a relatively short one. • *conjunction* **1** during the time that. **2** in spite of the fact that. **3** when on the contrary; whereas. • *verb* (**whiles**, **whiled**, **whiling**) (foll. by *away*) pass (a period of time) in a leisurely or pleasant manner. ▶PHRASES **all the while** during the whole time (that). **worth while** (or **one's while**) worth the time or effort spent; worth doing, beneficial, profitable, advantageous.

whilst *adverb & conjunction* esp. *Brit.* while. [With I as in WHILE]

whim *noun* **1** a spontaneous and unaccountable idea or decision; a fanciful notion. **2** capriciousness.

whimbrel *noun* a small curlew with a striped head and a trilling call. [Say WIM brull]

whimper • *verb* **1** make feeble, or plaintive sounds expressive of fear, pain, or distress. **2** say in a whimpering voice. • *noun* **1** a feeble intermittent cry; a whimpering sound. **2** a dull, disappointing, or anticlimactic note or tone: *the conference ended on a whimper*.

whimsical *adjective* **1** spontaneous; inspired by whim. **2 a** imaginative or playful: *a whimsical sense of humour*. **b** unconventional, fanciful, or quaint: *a whimsical set of furnishings*. ▶**whimsicality** *noun* **whimsically** *adverb* [Say WIMZA cull, wimza KALLA tee]

whimsy *noun* (*plural* **whimsies**) **1** an unpredictable, fanciful, or playful quality or condition. **2** a spontaneous or capricious notion or fancy; a whim.

whine • *noun* **1** a prolonged cry or wail suggesting pain, distress, or complaint. **2** a shrill prolonged sound resembling this: *the whine of the engine*. **3 a** a complaining tone of voice. **b** a feeble or undignified complaint: *a constant whine about the quality of public services*. • *verb* (**whines**, **whined**, **whining**) **1** emit or utter a whine. **2** complain in a querulous tone, esp. about unimportant things. **3** say or express in a whining tone. ▶ **whiner** *noun* **whiningly** *adverb*

whinny • *noun* (*plural* **whinnies**) **1** a gentle high-pitched neigh, usu. expressing pleasure. **2** a sound resembling this. • *verb* (**whinnies**, **whinnied**, **whinnying**) give a whinny. [Say WIN ee]

whiny *adjective* (**whinier**, **whiniest**) **1** tending to complain in a feeble, undignified, and irritating manner: *I had to spend a day at the zoo with the whiny little brat*. **2** resembling a high-pitched plaintive wail in sound: *one whiny tenor spoiled the whole performance*. [Say WHINE ee]

whip • *noun* **1** a flexible switch or a rod with a leather lash attached, used for urging animals on or flogging. **2** a member of a political party appointed to monitor and control its conduct and tactics and to ensure the attendance and voting of its members in debates. **3** a

light fluffy dessert made with whipped cream or beaten eggs. **4** a slender shoot without branches. • *verb* (**whips**, **whipped**, **whipping**) **1** beat or urge with a whip. **2** (usu. foll. by *into*) bring (a person) into a usu. specified condition or state: *she whipped us into shape*. **3** beat (cream or eggs etc.) into a froth. **4** move suddenly or quickly. **5** *informal* throw or propel with great force or speed. **6** *slang* defeat convincingly. **7** *Fishing* cast a line over (a stretch of water) repeatedly. **8** wind rope or twine around (something) to bind it. ▶PHRASES **whip off 1** remove (an article of clothing) hurriedly. **2** produce or complete in a short amount of time. **whip on** urge into action. **whip out** draw out or remove suddenly: *whipped out a knife*. **whip up 1** prepare in a short amount of time or with ease: *whipped up a meal*. **2** excite or stir up (feeling etc.).

whiplash • *noun* damage to the neck or spine caused by a severe jerk of the head, esp. as in a car accident. • *verb* (**whiplashes**, **whiplashed**, **whiplashing**) **1** shake or jerk violently causing a whiplash effect. **2** move suddenly and forcefully like the lash of a whip.

whipped *adjective* **1** that has been whipped. **2** *informal* tired, exhausted.

whipped cream *noun* heavy cream beaten until stiff and used as a topping or filling for desserts.

whipper *noun* a person or thing that whips.

whipper-snapper *noun* **1** a presumptuous or intrusive young person. **2** a child.

whippet *noun* a dog of a breed that is a cross between a greyhound and a terrier or spaniel, used for racing. [Say WIP it]

whipping *noun* **1** a beating or flogging with a whip. **2** *Sport* a sound defeat.

whipping boy *noun* a person who is blamed for the wrongdoings, mistakes, or faults of others; a scapegoat: *they seem to be everyone's whipping boy — people blame them just for being coyotes*.

whipping cream *noun* heavy cream, usu. with 35% milk fat, often with stabilizers and thickeners added so as to be suitable for whipping.

whippoorwill *noun* a North American bird with a loud cry uttered repeatedly at dusk and during the night. [Say WIPPER will]

whippy *adjective* (**whippier**, **whippiest**) flexible, springy: *sticks could be built with a shaft that is most whippy in just the area that optimizes energy load for a successful slapshot*.

whipsaw • *noun* **1** a saw with a narrow blade usu. operated by two people pulling at either end of its frame. **2** something that is disadvantageous in two ways: *the whipsaw of inflation and recession*. • *verb* (**whipsaws**; *past* **whipsawed**; *past participle* **whipsawed** or **whipsawn**; **whipsawing**) **1** cut with a whipsaw. **2** (usu. in *passive*) *slang* subject to two opposing and usu. harmful influences or forces: *when prices started falling, we put protection on, but then they'd rally and we'd take it off — we got whipsawed by the market*.

whir *noun & verb* = WHIRR.

whirl • *verb* **1** turn around rapidly, esp. repeatedly. **2** (often foll. by *away*) convey or travel swiftly, esp. in a vehicle. **3 a** (of the brain, senses, etc.) seem to spin; be dizzy or confused. **b** (of thoughts etc.) follow each other in bewildering succession. • *noun* **1** a swift circling or whirling movement: *she vanished in a whirl of dust*. **2** *informal* an attempt: *give it a whirl*. **3** a state of intense activity: *the political whirl*. **4** a state of confusion: *my mind is in a whirl*.

whirligig *noun* **1** anything having a rapid circling movement. **2** any of various toys that are whirled or spun around, such as a toy with four arms like miniature windmill sails which whirl around when it

is moved through the air. **3** anything characterized by constant frantic activity or change: *the whirligig of time*. **4** (also **whirligig beetle**) a freshwater beetle with paddle-like legs, found in large numbers circling rapidly over the surface of still water.

whirling *adjective* **1** moving around and around rapidly; spinning: *a whirling tornado*. **2** moving frantically or rapidly: *whirling onstage confusion*.

whirling dervish *noun* a member of any of various Muslim religious fraternities who has taken vows of poverty and austerity and whose order includes the practice of dancing or howling as a spiritual exercise.

whirlpool *noun* **1 a** a powerful circular eddy in a body of water that draws or sucks objects to its centre, usu. caused by the meeting of adverse currents. **b** a turbulent situation from which it is hard to escape: *Natalie was being dragged into a whirlpool of problems*. **2** a large bathtub with underwater jets of hot usu. aerated water, used for physiotherapy or relaxation.

whirlwind *noun* **1** a small rotating storm of wind in which a vertical usu. funnel-shaped column of air whirls rapidly around a core of low pressure and moves progressively over land or water. **2** (as an *adjective*) very rapid or hasty: *a whirlwind romance*. **3** a confused tumultuous process. **4** an active, impetuous, or reckless person. PHRASES **reap the whirlwind** suffer the consequences of one's own offence: *this time NATO is trapped, reaping the whirlwind that it sowed in March*.

whirr • *noun* a continuous droning, humming, or buzzing sound like that of machinery or the fluttering of a bird's wings. • *verb* (**whirrs, whirred, whirring**) **1** make this sound. **2** move swiftly with such a sound: *the cyclists whirred away*.

whisk • *verb* **1** brush lightly with a sweeping movement: *she whisked the hair from her face*. **2** (usu. foll. by *away, off*) **a** take, seize, or remove with a sudden sweeping motion. **b** convey quickly. **3 a** whip (cream, eggs, etc.) with a whisk. **b** (foll. by *in, together*) add or combine (ingredients) with a whisk. **4** go quickly; rush, dart: *a car whisked past*. • *noun* **1** a whisking action or motion. **2** a utensil consisting of wire hoops attached to a handle, used for beating eggs or cream etc. lightly. **3** (also **whisk broom**) a bundle of straw, or bristles bound at one end around a usu. short handle, used to sweep dust or debris from a surface.

whisker *noun* **1 a** any of the hairs growing on a person's face. **b** (in *plural*) these hairs collectively growing on esp. a man's chin, upper lip, or cheek; a moustache or beard. **2** each of a number of long projecting hairs growing on the face of many mammals, such as dogs, cats, and seals. **3** *informal* a small distance or amount; a narrow margin: *won by a whisker*. ▶ **whiskered** *adjective* **whiskery** *adjective*

SPELL CHECK
whisky, whiskey
Whisky is the standard spelling used in Canada unless the drink being referred to is **Irish whiskey**; in the US the word is generally spelled **whiskey** except in **Scotch whisky**.

whisky *noun* (*plural* **whiskies**) (also **whiskey**, *plural* **whiskeys**) **1** an alcoholic liquor distilled esp. from rye, malted barley, or corn. **2** a drink of this.

whisky blanc *noun* Cdn (Que.) a type of colourless whisky made by distilling the alcohol fermented from grain. [Say whisky BLONK]

whisky-jack *noun* Cdn = GREY JAY.

whisper • *verb* **1** say or speak in a soft breathy voice without vibration of the vocal cords. **2 a** speak or converse in private, esp. to conspire or to exchange

rumours about a person or thing. **b** (in *passive*) be rumoured. **3** (of leaves, wind, water, etc.) make a soft rustling or murmuring sound that resembles whispering. • *noun* **1** whispering speech: *talking in whispers*. **2** something whispered. **3 a** a rumour or piece of gossip. **b** (usu. with *neg.*) a suggestion or hint. **4** a soft rustling or whispering sound. ▶ **whisperer** *noun* **whispering** *noun*

whist *noun* a card game for four players grouped into pairs, in which points are scored according to the number of tricks won and, in some forms, by the highest trumps or honours held by each pair. [Rhymes with LIST]

whistle • *noun* **1** a clear shrill sound made by forcing breath through the narrow opening made by contracting the lips or through a space between the teeth constricted by the tip of the tongue. **2** a similar sound made by a bird, the wind, a projectile, etc. **3 a** a small device that produces such a sound when blown, used esp. as a signal. **b** a simple musical instrument resembling a pipe or recorder. • *verb* (**whistles, whistled, whistling**) **1** sound or emit a whistle. **2** give a signal or call for attention or express surprise, approval, or derision by whistling. **3** produce (a tune etc.) consisting of a series of whistled sounds of various pitch. **4** summon, announce, or signal by whistling or blowing a whistle: *the referee whistled the play dead*. **5** (of a kettle, train, etc.) emit a clear shrill sound produced by the passage of steam through a small opening. **6** (of the wind, a projectile, etc.) move or fly past with a whistle. PHRASES **as clean** (or **clear** or **dry**) **as a whistle** very clean or clear or dry. **blow the whistle on** *informal* **1** call attention to (a questionable or illicit activity) in order to have it brought to an end. **2** inform on (those responsible) for such an activity. **whistle Dixie** be overly optimistic. **whistle in the dark** pretend to be unafraid.

whistle-blower *noun* a person who calls attention to a questionable or illicit activity in an attempt to have it brought to an end. ▶ **whistle-blowing** *adjective* & *noun*

whistle stop *noun* **1 a** the train station of a small town at which trains stop only when given a particular signal indicating that a passenger is waiting to board. **b** a small or unimportant town. **2** a politician's brief stop in a town to give an electioneering speech during a campaign tour. **3** (as an *adjective*) designating a journey or tour with brief stops made at many of the small towns along the way.

SPELL CHECK
whit, to wit
Note that there is no *h* in **to wit**, meaning "namely", as in *the attitudes of grunge, to wit: angst, apathy, and boredom*.

whit *noun* (usu. with *neg.*) the least possible amount: *not a whit better*.

white • *adjective* **1** having a colour like that of fresh snow or milk. **2** (esp. of the skin) approaching such a colour; pale, esp. in the face. **3 a** designating or belonging to any of various peoples having light-coloured skin, usu. of European origin. **b** of, relating to, or characteristic of white people or their culture. **c** predominantly inhabited by or consisting of white people: *a white neighbourhood*. **4 a** (of hair) having lost its colour, esp. in old age. **b** (of a person) white-haired. **5** (of wine) made from white grapes or dark grapes with the skins removed, and of an amber, golden, or pale yellow colour. **6** (of coffee) having milk or cream added. **7** (of metal or an object made of metal) silvery grey and

 W

lustrous. • *noun* **1** a white colour. **2** the white or light-coloured part of anything. **3** the translucent viscous fluid surrounding the yolk of an egg, which turns white when cooked; albumen. **4** the visible part of the eyeball around the iris. **5 a** white clothing or material: *dressed in white.* **b** (in *plural*) white clothes as worn in tennis, as a naval uniform, etc. **c** (in *plural*) white linen or clothing etc. separated from coloured laundry for washing. **6** a member of a light-skinned race. PHRASES **white out 1** make or become white. **2** (often in *passive*) obliterate or conceal with whiteness, as with snow. **3** cover (a typewritten or printed error) with correction fluid.

white blood cell *noun* (also **white cell**) any of various colourless nucleated cells found in the blood, lymph, and connective tissue, which produce antibodies and which migrate through the walls of vessels to the sites of injuries, where they surround and isolate dead tissue, foreign bodies, and bacteria.

whiteboard *noun* a board with a white surface, which can be written on with a marker and wiped clean.

white bread • *noun* bread of a light colour, made from usu. bleached wheat flour from which the bran and germ have been removed. • *adjective* (**white-bread**) **1** of, belonging to, or representative of the white middle class. **2** conventional, inoffensive; bland.

whitecap *noun* (usu. in *plural*) a wave or breaker with a foamy white crest.

whitecoat *noun* **1** a young seal, having a coat of white fur. **2** the fur or skin of this seal. **3** (**white coat**) a white lab coat, worn by doctors, scientists, laboratory workers, etc. PHRASES **men in white coats** *jocular* attendants in a mental asylum. ▶ **white-coated** *adjective* (in sense 3)

white-collar *adjective* **1** designating, pertaining to, or performing non-manual, esp. clerical, administrative, or professional, work. **2 a** (of a crime) non-violent, esp. involving fraud, embezzlement, income tax evasion, etc. **b** (of a person) guilty of such a crime.

white elephant *noun* an item etc. that is no longer useful or wanted, esp. one that is difficult to maintain or dispose of.

white-faced *adjective* **1** (of an animal etc.) having white facial markings or a naturally white face. **2** having a face that is or has become pale, as with fear. **3** having a face that has been made white with makeup.

whitefish *noun* (*plural* **whitefish** or **whitefishes**) **1** a mainly freshwater fish of the trout family, used esp. for food. **2** (**white fish**) any fish with pale flesh, such as cod, haddock, plaice, etc.

white flag *noun* the flag traditionally used to signal surrender or a truce. PHRASES **raise** (or **wave** or **run up**) **the white flag** admit defeat in an argument, contest, etc.

whitefly *noun* (*plural* **whiteflies**) a small insect with wings covered with powdery white wax, which damages plants by feeding on the sap of shrubs and coating them with honeydew.

white goods *plural noun* **1** household linen such as bedding, tablecloths, etc. **2** large domestic electrical equipment, such as refrigerators, washing machines, and other appliances.

whitehead *noun* a white or white-topped pimple.

white heat *noun* the very high temperature at which metal radiates a white light.

white-hot *adjective* **1** (of metal) at white heat. **2** (of an emotion, esp. anger) passionate, ardent: *a white-hot rage*.

White House *noun* **1 a** the official residence of the US President in Washington, DC. **b** the US President or the executive branch of the US government. **2** the Russian parliament building.

white knight *noun* **1** a person who comes to the aid of someone: *he'll try using the referendum to leap into an election as the white knight who saved Canada*. **2** a welcome company bidding for a company facing an unwelcome takeover bid: *as ACME's prices started to tumble, rumours came out about their looking for a white knight*.

white-knuckle *adjective* **1** (esp. of a flight or amusement park ride) causing fear or terror. **2** (of a participant) feeling fear or terror.

white lie *noun* a harmless or trivial untruth, esp. one told in order to avoid hurting someone's feelings.

white light *noun* colourless light, e.g. sunlight.

whitely *adverb* so as to appear white: *his teeth flashed whitely in the dim light*.

white meat *noun* **1** any meat that is pale when cooked, such as veal or poultry. **2** the breast meat of poultry.

whiten *verb* make or become white.

whitener *noun* **1** a thing that whitens, such as a bleaching agent for clothes or a toothpaste. **2** a soluble powder added to coffee as a substitute for cream.

whiteness *noun* the state or quality of being white; a white part or colour.

white noise *noun* noise having nearly equal intensities at all the frequencies of its range.

whiteout *noun* **1 a** a weather condition in which the horizon and physical features of snow-covered country are indistinguishable due to uniform light diffusion. **b** a dense blizzard that reduces visibility. **2** a usu. white liquid that is painted over a typed or written error leaving a blank space for typing or writing afresh.

white pages *plural noun* (usu. treated as *singular*) a telephone directory or section of this containing the phone numbers and addresses of residential and business subscribers listed alphabetically.

whitepainting *noun* *Cdn* the renovation or reclamation of a house, building, or neighbourhood in a derelict part of a city's urban core: *the whitepainting trend of downtown Toronto*.

white paper *noun* **1** (also **White Paper**) an official report summarizing the results of an investigation into an issue, policy, or proposed legislation, and outlining the government's intention regarding it. **2** an authoritative report on an item of particular interest issued by any organization.

White Russian • *noun* **1** a native or national of Belarus in Eastern Europe; a Belarusian. **2** a drink made with vodka, cream, and chocolate- or coffee-flavoured liqueur. • *adjective* of or relating to Belarus, its people, or language; Belarusian.

white sale *noun* a sale of household linen.

white sauce *noun* a sauce made with flour, melted butter, and milk or cream.

white supremacist *noun* a person who believes that whites are innately superior to non-whites.

white supremacy *noun* a belief that whites are innately superior to non-whites.

white-tailed deer *noun* (also **whitetail**, **whitetail deer**) a deer that has a white underside to the tail and is found from Canada to northern South America.

white tie *noun* **1** a man's white bow tie worn as part of full evening dress. **2** full formal evening dress (also **white-tie** as an *adjective*: *white-tie affair*).

white trash *noun* *derogatory* lower-class white people lacking culture or refinement.

whitewall *noun* (also **whitewall tire**) an automotive tire with a white side wall.

whitewash • *noun* (*plural* **whitewashes**) **1** a

W

solution, e.g. of chalk and water, used for painting houses and walls white. **2** something that conceals faults or mistakes in order to clear or uphold the reputation of a person or institution: *the committee's conclusion was criticized as a whitewash because it didn't say anything negative.* **3** a victory in which the opponent fails to score or is defeated by a lopsided margin. • *verb* (**whitewashes**, **whitewashed**, **whitewashing**) **1** cover with whitewash. **2** attempt to clear or uphold the reputation of a person, institution, etc. by concealment of faults or mistakes: *the government is desperate to whitewash its broken promise on the GST.* **3** *Sport* defeat convincingly, esp. in a shutout.

whitewater • *noun* **1** a stretch of turbulent foamy water in a river caused by a steep drop or by large rocks in the riverbed. **2** the surf or a stretch of clear or frothy sea water, esp. on a beach or shoal. • *adjective* **1** designating a river or stretch of a river where there is whitewater. **2** designating an activity or event that takes place on such a river: *whitewater rafting.* **3** designating a person who participates in such an activity or event.

white whale *noun* = BELUGA 1.

whither *adverb & conjunction archaic* **1** to what place? **2** to what result?

whiting *noun* **1** any of various fishes of the cod family with pearly-white flesh and white coloration. **2** ground chalk used to make whitewash, metal polish, putty, etc. [Say WHITE ing]

whitish *adjective* somewhat white.

whittle *verb* (**whittles**, **whittled**, **whittling**) **1** cut or shape (wood etc.) by carving thin shavings from the surface with a knife. **2 a** (often foll. by *away*) make repeated reductions to: *whittled away at the deficit.* **b** (often foll. by *down*) reduce or diminish by repeated subtractions: *whittled down the waiting list.*

whiz *informal* • *noun* (*plural* **whizzes**) **1** the humming or buzzing sound made by the friction of a body moving quickly through the air. **2** *informal* a person who is remarkable or skilful in some usu. specified respect: *is a whiz at chess.* **3** *slang* an act of urinating. • *verb* (**whizzes**, **whizzed**, **whizzing**) **1** make or emit a sibilant humming or buzzing sound. **2** move with or as if with such a sound. **3** cause to make such a sound, esp. by rotating rapidly in a blender or food processor etc. **4** *slang* urinate.

whiz-bang *adjective informal* **1** fast-paced, lively. **2** technologically innovative or advanced: *whiz-bang computer graphics.*

whiz kid *noun informal* an exceptionally bright or successful young person.

WHO *abbreviation* World Health Organization.

> **WRITING TIP**
> **who, whom**
>
> While it may be acceptable in informal speech to use **who** for the object of a verb, as in *Who did you see?* and *the teacher who I saw*, you should always use the more standard **whom** in essays, formal speeches, etc. (*Whom did you see?*; *the teacher whom I saw*), especially after a preposition (*For whom will you vote?*).

who *pronoun* (*obj.* **whom** or *informal* **who**; *possessive* **whose**) **1 a** what or which person or persons?: *who called?* ◊ *you know who it was* ◊ *whom or who did you see?* **b** what sort of person or persons?: *who am I to object?* **2** (a person) that: *anyone who wishes can come* ◊ *the woman whom you met* ◊ *the man who you saw.*

whoa *interjection* **1** commanding a horse etc. to stop.

2 *jocular* demanding a person to stop or slow down. [Sounds like WOE]

who'd *contraction* **1** who had. **2** who would.

whodunit *noun informal* a crime story or murder mystery. [Say who DUN it]

whoever *pronoun* (*obj.* **whomever** or *informal* **whoever**; *possessive* **whosever**) **1** the or any person or persons who: *whoever comes is welcome.* **2** *informal* any or some similar person: *"Who's going to man the booth?" "Brent or whoever.".*

whole • *adjective* **1** not less than; entire: *waited a whole year* ◊ *the whole school knows.* **2** unbroken, intact: *swallowed it whole.* **3** containing all the proper or essential constituents. • *noun* **1** a thing complete in itself. **2** all there is of a thing: *spent the whole of the summer by the sea.* • *adverb* in every way; entirely: *that's a whole different matter.* PHRASES **as a whole** in its entirety. **on the whole** taking everything relevant into account; in general: *it was, on the whole, a good report.* **a whole new** (or **different**) **ball game** *informal* **1** a separate issue or matter very different from the one currently under discussion or consideration. **2** a new situation very different from the present one. **the whole nine yards** *slang* everything.

whole blood *noun* blood as taken from donors, altered only by the addition of a substance that stops it from clotting, used for transfusions.

whole cloth • *noun* cloth of the full size as manufactured, as opposed to a cut piece used to make a garment. • *adjective* (usu. **whole-cloth**) not based on fact: *the supposed romance was a whole-cloth fabrication.* PHRASES **out of whole cloth** with no basis in fact or reality: *he invents rumours out of whole cloth.*

whole food *noun* food that has not been unnecessarily processed or refined, such as brown rice.

whole-grain *adjective* (of cereal products) containing the whole grain, including the bran and the germ.

wholehearted *adjective* **1** (of a person) completely devoted or committed. **2** (of an action etc.) done with all possible effort, attention, or sincerity. ▶ **wholeheartedly** *adverb*

> **SPELL CHECK**
> **wholly**
>
> Something that is owned completely or entirely is **wholly** owned.

whole milk *noun* milk which has not been skimmed.

wholeness *noun* **1** the condition of being whole, unbroken, or complete. **2** a state of psychological or physical health and well-being.

whole note *noun Music* a note having the time value of four quarter notes, represented by a hollow ring.

whole number *noun* a number without fractions.

whole rest *noun Music* a rest having the time value of a whole note.

wholesale • *noun* the selling of goods in large quantities to be retailed by others. • *adjective* **1** of, pertaining to, or involved in wholesale: *a wholesale distributor.* **2** extensive: *wholesale changes.* • *adverb* **1** at a wholesale price: *I can get it for you wholesale.* **2** on a large scale. • *verb* **1** sell (goods) wholesale. **2** be sold wholesale, esp. for a specified price. ▶ **wholesaler** *noun*

wholesome *adjective* **1** promoting physical health or well-being: *wholesome food.* **2** promoting mental or moral health: *wholesome pursuits.* **3** indicative of good health: *wholesome appearance.* ▶ **wholesomely** *adverb* **wholesomeness** *noun*

whole wheat *noun* wheat with none of the bran or germ removed: *whole wheat flour.*

W

wholly *adverb* entirely, completely.

whom *objective case of* WHO.

whomever *objective case of* WHOEVER.

whomp *informal* • *noun* a loud dull heavy sound. • *verb* **1** bang or strike heavily with such a sound. **2** make such a sound.

whoop • *noun* **1** a loud excited cry. **2** a long rasping intake of air in whooping cough. • *verb* utter a whoop. **PHRASES no big whoop** *slang* no big deal. **whoop it up** *informal* engage in revelry. [Say WOOP or HOOP (with OO as in HOOT or HOOD)]

whoop-de-do *slang* • *noun* (*plural* **whoop-de-dos**) **1** a fuss, a commotion. **2** a party or other festive event. • *interjection* used to express exultation or, with irony, indifference. [Say woop dee DOO (with OO in WOOP sounding like that in HOOT or HOOD)]

whoopee *informal* • *interjection* expressing exuberant joy. • *noun* exuberant enjoyment or revelry. **PHRASES make whoopee** *informal* **1** rejoice noisily or hilariously. **2** make love. [Say woo PEE for the interjection, WOOP ee for the noun (with OO as in HOOT or HOOD)]

whoopee cushion *noun* a rubber cushion used in a practical joke, that when sat on makes a sound like the breaking of wind. [Say WOOP ee (with OO as in HOOT or HOOD)]

whooper *noun* a whooping crane or swan. [Say WOOP er or HOOP er (with OO as in LOOP)]

whooping cough *noun* an infectious bacterial disease, esp. of children, with a series of short violent coughs followed by a whoop. [Say WOOP ing or HOOP ing (with OO as in LOOP)]

whooping crane *noun* a large endangered mainly white North American crane, which passes through the prairies in migration between northern Alberta and Texas. [Say WOOP ing or HOOP ing (with OO as in LOOP)]

whooping swan *noun* a swan that makes a characteristic whooping sound in flight. [Say WOOP ing or HOOP ing (with OO as in LOOP)]

whoops *interjection* *informal* expressing surprise or apology, esp. on making an obvious mistake. [Say WOOPS (with OO as in HOOD)]

whoop-up *noun* *Cdn informal* a noisy celebration or party.

whoosh • *verb* (**whooshes**, **whooshed**, **whooshing**) (cause to) move with a rushing sound. • *noun* (*plural* **whooshes**) a sudden movement with a rushing sound. • *interjection* an exclamation imitating this. [Rhymes with SPLOOSH or PUSH]

whop *noun & verb* = WHAP.

whopper *noun* *slang* **1** something big. **2** a blatant or gross lie.

whopping *adjective* *slang* very big.

whore • *noun* **1** a prostitute. **2** *derogatory* a promiscuous woman. • *verb* (**whores**, **whored**, **whoring**) **1** use the services of prostitutes. **2** act as a whore. [Rhymes with LORE or LURE]

whorehouse *noun* a brothel. [WHORE rhymes with LORE or LURE]

whorl *noun* **1** a ring of leaves etc. around a stem of a plant. **2** one turn of a spiral, esp. on a shell. **3** a coil. **4** a complete circle in a fingerprint. ▶ **whorled** *adjective* [Say WORL or WURL]

who's *contraction* **1** who is. **2** who has.

whose • *pronoun* of or belonging to which person: *whose is this book?* • *adjective* of whom or which: *whose book is this?* ◊ *the house whose roof was damaged*.

whosever *possessive of* WHOEVER.

who's who *noun* **1** the significant people in a given field. **2** a list with facts about notable persons.

whump • *noun* a dull thudding sound, as of a body landing heavily. • *verb* **1** make or move or knock with such a sound. **2** strike heavily or with such a sound.

whup *verb* (**whups**, **whupped**, **whupping**) esp. *US informal* **1** whip or beat a person. **2** defeat soundly.

why • *adverb* **1 a** for what reason or purpose: *why did you do it?* **b** on what grounds: *why do you say that?* **2** for which: *the reasons why I did it*. • *interjection* expressing: **1** surprised discovery or recognition: *why, it's you!* **2** impatience: *why, of course I do!* **3** reflection: *why, yes, I think so*. **4** objection: *why, what is wrong with it?* • *noun* (*plural* **whys**) a reason or explanation: *whys and wherefores*. **PHRASES why so?** on what grounds?; for what reason or purpose?

Wicca *noun* the religious cult of modern witchcraft, a benevolent nature-oriented goddess-worshipping religion founded in England in the mid-20th century and claiming its origins in pre-Christian pagan religions. ▶ **Wiccan** *adjective & noun* [Say WICK uh]

wick • *noun* a strip or thread of fibrous or spongy material feeding a flame with fuel in a candle, lamp, etc. • *verb* absorb or draw up moisture through narrow openings in a fabric or other material: *long johns made of polypropylene are best because they wick moisture away from the body*.

wicked *adjective* (**wickeder**, **wickedest**) **1** sinful; given to or involving immorality. **2** spiteful, ill-tempered; intending or intended to give pain. **3** playfully malicious. **4** *informal* foul; very bad: *wicked weather*. **5** *slang* excellent. ▶ **wickedly** *adverb* **wickedness** *noun*

wicker *noun* braided twigs or osiers etc. as material for chairs, baskets, mats, etc.

wicket *noun* **1** a station for an employee in a ticket office, bank, etc., often closed by a window. **2** (also **wicket door** or **wicket gate**) a small door or gate esp. beside or in a larger one or closing the lower part only of a doorway. **3** *Cricket* a set of three stumps with the bails in position defended by a batsman. **4** a croquet hoop.

wickiup *noun* a hut formerly used by some North American Indians, consisting of a domed oval frame covered with grass and broken twigs etc. [Say WICKY up]

wide *adjective* (**wider**, **widest**) **1 a** measuring much or more than other things of the same kind across or from side to side. **b** more than is needed: *a wide margin*. **2** (following a measurement) in width: *a metre wide*. **3** extensive: *has wide experience*. **4** not tight or close or restricted; loose. **5** not specialized. **6** open to the full extent: *wide eyes*. **7 a** (foll. by *of*) not within a reasonable

distance of. **b** at a considerable distance from a point or mark. **8** (in *combination*) extending over the whole of: *nationwide*.

wide-angle *adjective* (of a lens) having a short focal length and hence a field covering a wide angle.

wide-area network *noun* *Computing* a communications network, typically between buildings or different sites. Abbreviation: **WAN**.

wide-band *adjective* having a wide band of frequencies or wavelengths.

wide-bodied *adjective* (of a jet) having a cabin divided by two aisles.

wide-body *noun* (*plural* **wide-bodies**) (often as an *adjective*) a large jet with a cabin divided by two aisles.

wide-eyed *adjective* **1** having one's eyes wide open in surprise, amazement, or excitement: *wide-eyed customers press their noses against the glass of the store window*. **2** naive, innocent: *even through the rose-coloured glasses of wide-eyed 1960s optimism, this Broadway musical must have seemed hopelessly idealized*.

widely *adverb* **1** far apart: *widely spaced*. **2** extensively: *widely read*. **3** by many people: *widely accepted*. **4** to a large degree: *holds a widely different view*.

widen *verb* make or become wider.

wide open *adjective* **1** fully open. **2** stretching over an outdoor expanse: *wide open spaces*. **3** (esp. of a contest) having an unpredictable outcome. **4** (often foll. by *to*) exposed or vulnerable (esp. to attack): *their careless work left them wide open to criticism*.

wide-ranging *adjective* covering an extensive range.

wide receiver *noun* (also **wideout**) *Football* a player positioned on the wide side of the offensive line used mainly to receive passes.

wide-screen *adjective* designed with or for a screen presenting a wide field of vision relative to its height.

widespread *adjective* widely distributed or disseminated.

widget *noun* *informal* any gadget or device.

widow *noun* **1** a woman whose husband has died and who has not remarried. **2** *informal* a woman whose husband is often away on a specified activity: *golf widow*. **3** the short last line of a paragraph at the top of a page or column (*compare* ORPHAN *noun* 2).

widowed *adjective* bereft by the death of a spouse: *my widowed mother*.

widower *noun* a man who has lost his wife by death and has not married again.

widowhood *noun* the state or period of being a widow or widower.

widow-maker *noun* *slang* **1** a dead branch caught high in a tree which may fall on a person below. **2** any dangerous thing usu. operated by people, e.g. an aircraft, piece of equipment, etc.

widow's walk *noun* a railed platform built on the roof, originally in New England houses, esp. for giving a good view of the sea.

width *noun* **1** measurement or distance from side to side. **2** a large extent. **3** a strip of material of a particular width: *you'll need two widths of fabric for each curtain*. **4** the distance between the long sides of a swimming pool. ▶ **widthways** *adverb* **widthwise** *adverb*

wield *verb* **1** hold and use (a weapon or tool). **2** exert or command (power or authority etc.). ▶ **wielder** *noun* [Rhymes with FIELD]

wiener *noun* **1** a frankfurter. **2** *slang* the penis.

Wiener schnitzel *noun* a breaded and fried pork or veal cutlet. [Say VEEN er shnit zul]

wienie *noun* = WEENIE.

---

wife *noun* (*plural* **wives**) a married woman esp. in relation to her husband. ▶ **wifely** *adjective*

wig *noun* **1** an artificial head of hair esp. to conceal baldness or as a disguise or part of a costume, or worn by a judge or lawyer. **2** a hairpiece. PHRASES **wig out** (**wigs**, **wigged**, **wigging**) *slang* lose control of one's emotions. ▶ **wigged** *adjective* (also in *combination*)

wiggle *informal* • *verb* (**wiggles**, **wiggled**, **wiggling**) move irregularly and quickly from side to side etc. • *noun* an act of wiggling. ▶ **wiggler** *noun*

wiggly *adjective* (**wigglier**, **wiggliest**) *informal* **1** moving with a wiggle. **2** having small irregular bends: *a wiggly line*.

wigwam *noun* (among some North American Aboriginal peoples) a dome-shaped house consisting of bent saplings stuck in the ground and covered with birch bark. [Say WIG wom]

wild • *adjective* **1** (of an animal or plant) in its original natural state; not domesticated or cultivated. **2** not civilized. **3** (of an area of land etc.) not cultivated or settled by people. **4** unrestrained, disorderly: *a wild youth* ◊ *wild hair*. **5** tempestuous: *a wild night*. **6 a** intensely eager; excited, frantic: *wild with excitement* ◊ *wild delight*. **b** (of looks, appearance, etc.) indicating distraction. **c** (foll. by *about*) *informal* enthusiastically devoted to. **7** *informal* infuriated, angry. **8** haphazard, ill-aimed, rash: *a wild guess* ◊ *a wild shot*. **9** (of a horse etc.) shy; easily startled. **10** *informal* exciting, delightful. **11** *informal* amazing, incredible: *a wild story*. **12** (of a card) having any rank chosen by the player holding it: *the joker is wild*. • *adverb* in a wild manner: *shooting wild*. • *noun* (usu. in *plural*) a wilderness. PHRASES **in the wild** in an uncultivated etc. state. **in** (or **out in**) **the wilds** *informal* far from normal habitation. **run wild** grow or stray unchecked or undisciplined. **wild and woolly** uncouth; lacking refinement.

wild card *noun* **1** a playing card having any rank chosen by the player holding it. **2** *Computing* a character that will match any character or sequence of characters in the name of a computer file etc. **3** an extra player or team chosen for a competition at the organizers' discretion after the regular places have been taken. **4** an unpredictable person or thing.

wildcat • *noun* **1** a smallish cat of a non-domesticated kind; esp. *Felis sylvestris* of Eurasia and Africa, with a grey and black coat and bushy tail, or, in North America, a bobcat. **2** a hot-tempered or violent person. **3** an exploratory oil well. **4** a sudden and unofficial strike. • *adjective* **1** having to do with prospecting for oil: *wildcat oil wells*. **2** (of a strike) called at short notice, usu. without union backing.

wildcatter *noun* **1** a prospector who sinks wildcat oil wells. **2** a person who promotes or engages in risky business enterprises. **3** a wildcat striker.

wildebeest *noun* a large antelope native to southern Africa, with a large erect head and brown stripes on the neck and shoulders. [Say WILL duh beast *or* VILL duh beast]

wilderness *noun* **1** a wild, uncultivated, and uninhabited region (often as an *adjective*: *wilderness area*). **2** a confused assemblage of things: *a wilderness of anecdotes* ◊ *a wilderness of boxes, suitcases, and trunks*. PHRASES **voice in the wilderness** an unheeded advocate of reform.

wildfire *noun* a destructive or uncontrollable fire, esp.

in a forest. PHRASES **spread like wildfire** spread quickly.

wildflower *noun* a flowering plant growing in a natural state without human intervention.

wildfowl *noun* (*plural* **wildfowl**) a game bird, esp. an aquatic one.

wild goose chase *noun* a foolish or hopeless and unproductive quest.

wild horse *noun* **1** a horse not domesticated or broken in. **2** (in *plural*) *informal* even the most powerful influence etc.: *wild horses couldn't keep me away!*

wilding *noun* *US* the activity or an instance of a gang of youths rampaging violently through the streets, parks, etc., attacking or mugging people at random along the way.

wildlife *noun* wild animals.

wildly *adverb* **1** in a way that is not controlled: *she looked wildly around for an escape ◊ his heart was beating wildly ◊ interest rates have been fluctuating wildly.* **2** extremely; very: *the story had been wildly exaggerated ◊ it is not a wildly funny play.*

wildness *noun* the quality or condition of being wild.

wild oat *noun* a European grass, naturalized in North America, similar to the cultivated oat and often found as a weed of other cereals.

wild pitch *noun* (*plural* **wild pitches**) *Baseball* a pitch not hit by the batter and not stopped by the catcher, enabling a baserunner to advance.

wild rice *noun* a tall aquatic grass related to rice, yielding edible grains.

wild rose *noun* any of several species of uncultivated rose, e.g. *Rosa acicularis*, the floral emblem of Alberta.

Wild West *noun* the western regions of the US in the 19th century, when they were lawless frontier districts.

wildwood *noun* woodland that is not cultivated or not visited.

SPELL CHECK
wile, while ✓ABC

The spelling is **while** in "while away the time", as well as in "a short while" and "while that may be true".

---

wiles *plural noun* clever tricks used to manipulate someone or persuade someone to do what one wants: *once she was ensconced as leader, she discovered that she had to resort to many tricks and wiles to get men to deliver the goods as subordinates.*

wilful *adjective* **1** (of an action or state) intentional, deliberate: *wilful disobedience.* **2** headstrong. ▶ **wilfully** *adverb* **wilfulness** *noun*

will[1] *verb* **1** expressing the future tense in statements, commands, or questions: *you will regret this.* **2** expressing a wish or intention: *I will return soon.* **3** expressing desire, consent, or inclination: *will you have a sandwich? ◊ the door will not open.* **4** expressing ability or capacity: *the jar will hold 2 litres.* **5** expressing habitual or inevitable tendency: *accidents will happen ◊ will sit there for hours.* **6** expressing probability or expectation: *that will be my wife.* PHRASES **will do** *informal* expressing willingness to carry out a request.

will[2] • *noun* **1** the faculty by which a person decides or is regarded as deciding on and initiating action. **2** (also **willpower**) control exercised by deliberate purpose over impulse; self-control. **3** a deliberate or fixed desire or intention: *a will to live.* **4** the power of effecting one's intentions or dominating others. **5** directions (usu. written) in legal form for the disposition of one's property after death: *make one's will.* **6** disposition toward others: *good will.* **7** what one desires or ordains: *thy will be done.* • *verb* **1** intend: *what God wills.* **2** cause

by the exercise of willpower: *will it to happen.* **3** bequeath by the terms of a will: *shall will my money to charity.* PHRASES **at will** whenever one pleases. **have one's will** obtain what one wants. **what is your will?** what do you wish done? **where there's a will there's a way** determination will overcome any obstacle. **a will of one's own** obstinacy; wilfulness of character. **with the best will in the world** however good one's intentions. **with a will** energetically or resolutely. ▶ **willed** *adjective* (also in *combination*)

willet *noun* (*plural* **willet**) a large grey and white North American shorebird with a loud call.

willful = WILFUL.

willies *plural noun* *informal* nervous discomfort: *gives me the willies.*

willing *adjective* **1** ready to consent or undertake: *a willing ally ◊ am willing to help.* **2** given, done, etc. by a willing person: *willing help.* ▶ **willingly** *adverb* **willingness** *noun*

will-o'-the-wisp *noun* **1** a bluish light seen hovering or floating at night on marshy ground, thought to result from the combustion of natural gases. **2** a person or thing that is difficult or impossible to find, reach, or catch: *we will explore the forests in pursuit of our will-o'-the-wisp, the rare Adonis blue butterfly.*

willow *noun* a tree or shrub with small flowers borne on catkins and flexible branches yielding osiers used for weaving baskets etc.

willow herb *noun* a plant with narrow willow-like leaves and pink or purple flowers.

willowy *adjective* **1** tall, slender, and graceful. **2** having or bordered by willows.

willpower *noun* = WILL[2] *noun* 2.

willy *noun* (*plural* **willies**) *slang* the penis.

willy-nilly • *adverb* **1** whether one likes it or not: *he would be forced to collaborate willy-nilly in the dominance of human intention over the world.* **2** haphazardly, at random: *the posting had been spammed willy-nilly to many different newsgroups.* • *adjective* existing or occurring willy-nilly: *down in the basement there was an equally willy-nilly placement of tools, garden machines, and old knick-knacks.*

wilt • *verb* **1** (of a plant etc.) wither, droop. **2** (of a person) lose one's energy. **3** cause to wilt. • *noun* **1** the action or an act of wilting. **2** a plant disease causing wilting.

wily *adjective* (**wilier**, **wiliest**) crafty, cunning.

wimp *noun* *informal* a feeble or ineffectual person. PHRASES **wimp out** demonstrate one's feebleness by failing to act or by avoiding an undertaking; chicken out. ▶ **wimpish** *adjective* **wimpishness** *noun*

wimple *noun* a linen or silk headdress covering the neck and the sides of the face, formerly worn by women and still worn by some nuns.

wimpy *adjective* (**wimpier**, **wimpiest**) characteristic of a wimp; feeble, ineffectual.

win • *verb* (**wins**; *past* and *past participle* **won**; **winning**) **1** acquire or secure as a result of a fight, contest, bet, litigation, or some other effort: *won my admiration.* **2** be victorious in (a fight, game, race, etc.). **3 a** be the victor; win a race or contest etc. **b** make one's way or become by successful effort. **4** reach by effort: *win the summit.* • *noun* a victory in a game or bet etc. PHRASES **win the day** be victorious. **win out** overcome obstacles. **win over** persuade, gain the support of. **you can't win** *informal* there is no way to succeed. **you can't win them all** *informal* a resigned expression of consolation on failure.

wince • *verb* (**winces**, **winced**, **wincing**) grimace, tense, or shrink away involuntarily in pain,

W

embarrassment, or distress. • *noun* a wincing movement.

winch • *noun* (*plural* **winches**) a hauling or lifting device consisting of a rope or chain winding around a horizontal axle, turned manually by a crank or by a motor or other power source. • *verb* (**winches**, **winched**, **winching**) lift with a winch.

wind¹ • *noun* **1 a** air in more or less rapid natural motion, esp. from an area of high pressure to one of low pressure. **b** a current of wind blowing from a specified direction or otherwise defined: *north wind* ◊ *bitter wind*. **2** breath as needed in physical exertion or in speech. **3** mere empty words; meaningless rhetoric. **4** gas generated in the bowels etc. by indigestion. **5 a** an artificially produced current of air, esp. for sounding an organ or other wind instrument. **b** air stored for use or used as a current. **c** (usu. in *plural*) (a player of) a wind instrument. • *verb* **1** cause someone to have difficulty breathing because of exertion or a punch to the stomach. **2** renew the wind of by rest: *stopped to wind the horses*. PHRASES **before the wind** helped by the wind's force. **sail close to the wind 1** sail as nearly against the wind as is consistent with using its force. **2** *informal* verge on indecency, dishonesty, or disaster: *most universities live chancily from year to year, depending heavily on contributions from their alumni and philanthropic friends, sailing close to the wind*. **get wind of 1** detect by smell. **2** begin to suspect; hear a rumour of. **get** (or **have**) **the wind up** *informal* be alarmed or frightened. **how** (or **which way**) **the wind blows** (or **lies**) **1** what is the state of opinion. **2** what developments are likely. **in the wind** happening or about to happen. **like the wind** swiftly. **on the wind** (of a sound or scent) carried by the wind. **put the wind up** *informal* alarm or frighten. **take the wind out of a person's sails** frustrate a person by anticipating an action or remark etc. **to the winds** (or **four winds**) **1** in all directions. **2** into a state of abandonment or neglect. **wind and weather** exposure to the effects of the elements. **wind** (or **winds**) **of change** a force or influence for reform.

wind² • *verb* (**winds**, **wound**, **winding**) **1** go in a circular, spiral, curved, or crooked course: *the path winds up the hill*. **2** make (one's way) in such a course: *wound their way into our affections*. **3** wrap closely; surround with or as with a coil. **4** coil. **5** wind up (a clock etc.). **6** hoist or draw with a windlass etc.: *wound the cable car up the mountain*. • *noun* **1** a bend or turn in a course. **2** a single turn when winding. PHRASES **wind down 1** lower by winding. **2** (of a mechanism) unwind. **3** (of a person) relax. **4** draw gradually to a close. **wind off** unwind (string, wool, etc.). **wind up 1** coil the whole of (a piece of string etc.). **2** esp. *Brit.* tighten the coiling or coiled spring of (esp. a clock etc.). **3 a** *informal* increase the tension or intensity of: *wound myself up to fever pitch*. **b** irritate or provoke (a person) to the point of anger. **4** bring to a conclusion: *wound up his speech*. **5** *informal* end in a specified state or circumstance: *wound up owing $100*. **6** draw back the arm in preparation for a throw, shot, etc. **wound up** *adjective* (of a person) excited or tense or angry.

windbag *noun informal* a person who talks a lot but says little of any value.

windblown *adjective* **1** carried or made untidy by the wind: *windblown snow*. **2** (of trees) made to grow in a certain shape by strong prevailing winds.

windbreak *noun* an obstacle, such as a row of trees, a fence, etc., which breaks the wind's force and shelters houses, crops, or animals.

windbreaker *noun* a wind-resistant outer jacket with close-fitting neck, cuffs, and hip band.

windburn *noun* inflammation of the skin caused by exposure to wind. ▶ **windburned** *adjective* (also **windburnt**)

wind chill *noun* the cooling effect of wind blowing on a person or surface.

wind chill factor *noun* a measure or scale of the combined effect of low temperature and wind speed on body temperature.

wind chimes *plural noun* small pieces of glass, metal, etc. suspended from a frame so as to tinkle against one another in the wind.

windfall *noun* **1** an unexpected gift of money, piece of good luck, etc. **2** an apple or other fruit blown to the ground by the wind. **3 a** a branch or tree blown down by the wind. **b** timber blown down by the wind.

wind farm *noun* a group of energy-producing windmills or wind turbines.

winding • *noun* **1** the action of winding something or of moving in a twisting or spiral course. **2** (**windings**) twisting movements: *followed the windings of the creek*. • *adjective* following a twisting or spiral course: *our bedroom was at the top of a winding staircase*.

wind instrument *noun* a musical instrument in which sound is produced by the player blowing a current of air through or across a mouthpiece.

windjammer *noun* a merchant sailing ship.

windlass *noun* (*plural* **windlasses**) a hauling or lifting device, esp. on a ship or in a harbour, consisting of a rope or chain winding around a horizontal axle, turned manually by a crank or by a motor or power source; a winch. [Sounds like *WINDLESS*]

windless *adjective* without wind: *a perfect, windless day*.

windmill • *noun* a mill, pump, or generator driven by the action of the wind on its rotating sails or blades. • *verb* whirl or fling (one's limbs) around in a manner suggestive of a windmill. PHRASES **tilt at windmills** attack an imaginary enemy or grievance: *in fact, Siegfried was tilting at windmills: the "inaccuracies" he detected were caused by the weather, not human error*.

window *noun* **1 a** an opening in a wall, door, etc., usu. with glass, to admit light or air etc. and allow the occupants to see out. **b** the glass filling this opening: *have broken the window*. **2** a space for display behind the front window of a store. **3** an aperture in a wall etc. through which customers are served in a bank, ticket office, etc. **4** an opportunity to observe or learn. **5** an opening or transparent part in an envelope to show an address. **6** *Computing* a defined area on a display screen in which a part of a file or image can be displayed. **7 a** an interval during which atmospheric and astronomical circumstances are suitable for the launch of a spacecraft. **b** any interval or opportunity for action.

window box *noun* a long narrow box placed on an outside windowsill, used for growing flowers.

window dressing *noun* **1** the art of arranging a display in a store window etc. **2** a skilful presentation of facts etc. to give a deceptively favourable impression.

windowed *adjective* (also in *combination*) **1** having a window or windows for admitting light or air: *a row of bay-windowed houses*. **2** *Computing* having or using framed areas on a display screen for viewing information.

windowing *noun Computing* the use of windows for the simultaneous display of parts of different files, images, etc.

window ledge *noun* = WINDOWSILL.

windowless *adjective* without windows: *a tiny, windowless cell*.

windowpane *noun* a pane of glass in a window.

window shop *verb* (**window shops**, **window shopped**, **window shopping**) look at goods

W

displayed in store windows, usu. without buying.
▶ **window shopper** *noun*

windowsill *noun* a sill below a window.

window treatment *noun* a blind, curtain, or other drapery for a window.

windpipe *noun* the air passage from the throat to the lungs; the trachea.

windproof *adjective* (esp. of a garment) impervious to wind.

windrow *noun* **1** a line of raked hay, sheaves, etc., laid out for drying by the wind. **2** a long pile or row of leaves, dust, etc. heaped up by or as if by the wind. **3** *Cdn* a ridge of snow, gravel, etc. heaped along the side of a road by a snowplow, grader, etc. [Say WIN droe]

wind shear *noun* a variation in wind velocity at right angles to the wind's direction.

windshield *noun* a glass window across the front of a motor vehicle or aircraft.

windsock *noun* a nylon cylinder or cone on a mast to show the direction of the wind at an airfield etc.

windstorm *noun* a storm with very strong wind but little or no rain, snow, etc.

windsurf *verb* ride on the water on a sailboard.
▶ **windsurfer** *noun* **windsurfing** *noun*

windswept *adjective* exposed to or swept back by wind.

wind tunnel *noun* a tunnel-like device for producing an airstream of known velocity past models of aircraft, buildings, etc., in the study of wind flow or wind effects on the full-size object.

windup • *noun* **1** a conclusion. **2** *Baseball & Hockey* the drawing back of the arm or stick as part of the throwing or shooting motion. **3** a device operated by being wound up, as a toy. • *adjective* operated by being wound up.

windward • *adjective & adverb* on the side from which the wind is blowing (*opp.* LEEWARD). • *noun* the windward region, side, or direction: *to windward* ◊ *on the windward of*.

windy[1] *adjective* (**windier**, **windiest**) **1** stormy with wind. **2** exposed to the wind; windswept. **3** *informal* wordy.

windy[2] *adjective* (**windier**, **windiest**) that winds, winding: *a narrow windy path*.

SPELL CHECK
wine, whine

When someone complains in an annoying voice they **whine**.

---

wine *noun* **1** fermented grape juice as an alcoholic drink. **2** a fermented drink resembling this made from other fruits: *elderberry wine*. **3** the dark red colour of red wine. PHRASES **wine and dine** (**wines and dines**, **wined and dined**, **wining and dining**) entertain or be entertained with food and drink.

wine cellar *noun* **1** a cellar for storing wine. **2** the contents of this.

wine cooler *noun* **1** a drink of wine, soda water, and fruit flavours. **2** a usu. insulated bucket-like container for holding ice to chill a bottle of wine.

wineglass *noun* (*plural* **wineglasses**) **1** a glass for wine, usu. with a stem and foot. **2** the contents of this.

wine grower *noun* a cultivator of grapes for wine.
▶ **wine-growing** *noun & adjective*

winemaker *noun* a producer of wine; a wine grower.

winemaking *noun* the production of wine, either commercially or as a hobby.

winery *noun* (*plural* **wineries**) an establishment where wine is made.

SPELL CHECK
winey, whiny

The voice of someone who is complaining is **whiny**.

winey *adjective* (**winier**, **winiest**) resembling wine in taste or appearance.

SPELL CHECK
windfall

Warning: do not forget the *d* in **windfall**.

---

wing • *noun* **1** each of the limbs or organs by which a bird, bat, or insect is able to fly. **2** anything resembling or analogous to a wing in form or function. **3** either of a pair of rigid horizontal structures extending on either side of an aircraft that support it in the air. **4** (in *plural*) a badge depicting a pair of wings to symbolize that the holder is a certified pilot. **5** part of a building which projects or is extended in a certain direction from the main or central part: *lived in the north wing*. **6** a section of a political party or group holding more progressive or reactionary views than those of the more moderate centre (see RIGHT WING, LEFT WING). **7** esp. *Hockey & Soccer* **a** the area along the side of a playing surface: *he skated down the wing and fired a shot on goal*. **b** the position of the forward player who covers this area. **c** a player at this position; a winger. **8 a** either of the flanks on the right or left side of the main body of an army or fleet in battle array. **b** an operational unit of some air forces consisting of two or more squadrons. **9** (in *plural*) the sides of a theatre stage out of view of the audience. **10** a cut of beef including the thirteenth rib (also as an *adjective*: *wing steak*). • *verb* **1 a** fly through the air, on wings or in an aircraft or as if so: *the ball came winging through the air*. **b** make (one's way) through the air. **2** cause to sail or soar through the air; throw. PHRASES **give** (or **lend**) **wings to** speed up (a person or a thing). **on the wing** flying or in flight. **on a wing and a prayer** with only the slightest chance of success. **spread** (or **stretch**) **one's wings** test or develop one's abilities. **take under one's wing** treat as a protege. **take wing** fly away. **waiting in the wings** awaiting one's opportunity to fill a position expected to become available. **wing it** *informal* improvise; speak or act without preparation.

wingback *noun* **1** *Football* **a** an offensive back who lines up next to an end. **b** the position of this player. **2** (also **wingback chair**, **wing chair**) a high-backed armchair with side pieces projecting forward at the top of a high back.

wingbeat *noun* one complete cycle of movements made by the wing of a bird etc. in flying.

wingding *noun* *informal* a wild party; a festive social gathering or celebration.

winged *adjective* having wings, esp. of the kind indicated.

winger *noun* **1** esp. *Hockey & Soccer* a forward who plays on the wing. **2** (in *combination*) a person affiliated with a specified political wing: *left winger*.

wingless *adjective* without wings.

wing-like *adjective* resembling a wing.

wingman *noun* (*plural* **wingmen**) the pilot of an aircraft which is positioned behind and to one side of the leading aircraft, as in attack formation.

wing nut *noun* **1** a threaded nut with flat projections so that it may be tightened or loosened by hand with the thumb and forefinger, without the aid of a wrench. **2** *slang* a stupid or inept person.

wingspan *noun* (also **wingspread**) the maximum extent from tip to tip of the wings of a bird or aircraft.

wing tip *noun* **1** the tip of the wing of an aircraft, bird, bat, or insect. **2 a** a usu. perforated toecap on a shoe with a backward extending point and curved sides. **b** (usu. **wingtip**, in full **wingtip shoe**) a shoe having such a toecap.

wingy *adjective* (**wingier**, **wingiest**) *Cdn informal* crazy. [Say WING ee]

wink • *verb* **1** close and open one eye to convey a message to a person, or as a signal of friendliness. **2** (of a light etc.) twinkle; shine or flash intermittently. **3** (usu. foll. by *out*) disappear or go out suddenly. • *noun* **1** an act of closing and opening the eye, esp. as a signal. **2** a brief moment; an instant: *was done in a wink*. **3** (usu. with *neg.*) *informal* a very brief or the shortest possible period of sleep: *I didn't sleep a wink*. PHRASES **as easy as winking** *informal* very easy. **wink at** purposely avoid seeing (an offence, impropriety, etc.); pretend not to notice.

winkle • *noun* a small, edible, plant-eating shore-dwelling mollusc with a spiral shell. • *verb* (**winkles**, **winkled**, **winkling**) (foll. by *out*) extract: *winkled the information out of them*.

winless *adjective* characterized by an absence of victories.

winnable *adjective* able to be won: *the party focused its energies on winnable ridings*.

Winnebago *noun* (*plural* **Winnebagos**) *proprietary* a van or camper used for recreational purposes, such as touring and camping, esp. a large motorhome. [Say winna BAY go]

winner *noun* **1** a person etc. who is victorious in a competition. **2** a goal etc. that decides the outcome of a game or competition. **3** *informal* a successful or highly promising idea, enterprise, etc.

winner-take-all *adjective* **1** denoting a conflict in which victory is outright or the winner alone is rewarded. **2** denoting the attitude of a person whose sole goal is outright victory.

winning • *adjective* **1** victorious, successful. **2** that determines the outcome of a game or competition. **3** denoting a streak of consecutive victories uninterrupted by losses or ties: *a winning streak*. **4** attractive, persuasive: *a winning smile*. • *noun* **1** the action of being victorious: *winning isn't everything*. **2** (in *plural*) money won esp. in gambling.

winningest *adjective Sport informal* that has won the most often. [Say WINNING est]

winningly *adverb* attractively, persuasively: *smiled winningly*.

Winnipeg couch *noun* (*plural* **Winnipeg couches**) *Cdn* a couch with no arms or back that converts into a double bed.

Winnipegger *noun* a native or inhabitant of Winnipeg.

Winnipeg goldeye *noun Cdn* = GOLDEYE.

winnow *verb* **1** expose (grain) to the wind or to a current of air so that unwanted lighter particles of chaff are separated or blown away. **2** (foll. by *out, from*) separate (chaff) from grain by exposing it to a current of air. **3** (often foll. by *down*) subject to a process which separates esp. the good from the bad: *winnow down the number of candidates*. **4** (often foll. by *out, from*) **a** extract or obtain (something valuable or desirable) by separating it from something undesirable: *winnow out the best players from a group of prospects*. **b** eliminate or clear away (something undesirable) by separating it from something useful: *winnow the lies from the truth*.

wino *noun* (*plural* **winos**) *slang* a habitual excessive drinker of cheap wine; an alcoholic, esp. one who is destitute. [Say WINE oh]

winsome *adjective* (of a person) attractive or appealing in appearance or character: *a winsome smile*. ▶ **winsomely** *adverb* **winsomeness** *noun* [Say WIN sum]

winter • *noun* **1 a** the fourth and coldest season of the year, beginning at the end of fall and lasting until the start of spring. **b** the period from the winter solstice to the spring equinox. **2** cold or wintry weather typical of this season. • *adjective* **1** characteristic of, done or occurring in, or suitable for use in winter: *winter weather* ◊ *winter sports* ◊ *winter coat*. **2 a** (of plants or animals) active or flourishing in winter. **b** (of crops) sown in fall for harvesting the following year. • *verb* **1** (usu. foll. by *in*) spend the winter: *her family winters in Florida*. **2** (often foll. by *over*) **a** (of animals) find or be provided with food and shelter in the winter. **b** keep or maintain (animals or plants) during the winter.

winter aconite *noun* a plant with buttercup-like flowers blooming in early spring.

winterberry *noun* (*plural* **winterberries**) any of several deciduous North American hollies with non-prickly leaves and berries that last through the winter.

winter club *noun Cdn* an organization that offers access to various recreational facilities for activities such as skating and curling throughout the winter.

winterer *noun Cdn hist.* = WINTERING PARTNER.

wintergreen *noun* **1** any of several North American evergreen plants that yield a pungent oil containing methyl salicylate, which is used medicinally in lotions and creams and as a flavouring. **2** (also **wintergreen oil**) this oil, now often produced synthetically.

winter ice road *noun Cdn* = WINTER ROAD.

wintering ground *noun* (usu. in *plural*) the region to which animals, esp. birds, migrate in the winter.

wintering partner *noun Cdn hist.* a stock-holding member and representative of a fur trading company stationed year-round at a trading post in the northern interior to negotiate the acquisition of furs.

winterization *noun* an act of winterizing.

winterize *verb* (**winterizes**, **winterized**, **winterizing**) adapt or prepare (a home, cottage, car, etc.) for use in cold weather. ▶ **winterized** *adjective*

winterkill • *noun* **1** the death of plants or animals by exposure to frost, snow, and extreme cold. **2** a plant, part of a plant, or animal that has died in this way. • *verb* **1** (usu. in *passive*) kill (plants or animals) by exposure to frost, snow, and extreme cold. **2** (of a plant or animal) die from exposure to cold etc.

winter road *noun Cdn* (*North*) a secondary road made of compact snow or ice, often plowed over a frozen lake or ground impassable in the summer.

winter solstice *noun* the time of year when the sun appears at its lowest altitude above the horizon at noon and daylight is at a minimum, occurring in the northern hemisphere when the sun reaches its southernmost point in the sky on about Dec. 22, or in the southern hemisphere when it reaches its northernmost point on about June 21.

winter squash *noun* an edible gourd, the flesh of which may be cooked and eaten as a vegetable, usu. stored and eaten when mature (e.g. butternut squash, acorn squash).

wintertime *noun* the season of winter.

winter wheat *noun* wheat that is planted in the fall and harvested the following summer.

wintry *adjective* (also **wintery**) (**wintrier**, **wintriest**) **1** characteristic of or affected by winter: *wintry weather* ◊ *a wintry landscape*. **2** (of a smile, greeting, etc.) lacking warmth or enthusiasm.

win-win *adjective* designating or pertaining to a situation which is beneficial to both parties involved.

W

winy = WINEY. [Say WINE ee]

wipe • *verb* (**wipes**, **wiped**, **wiping**) **1** clean or dry the surface of by rubbing with a cloth or towel etc. **2** spread or apply (a soft or liquid substance) over a surface by rubbing with a soft cloth or the hand etc. **3** (often foll. by *away*, *off*) **a** clear or remove (moisture, dirt, etc.) from something. **b** remove or eliminate completely: *the village was wiped off the map.* **4** (often foll. by *from*) remove or erase (a thought, memory, etc.) from one's mind. **5 a** erase (data, a recording, etc.) from a computer disk, videotape, etc. **b** erase data from (a medium). • *noun* **1** an act of wiping. **2** a disposable piece of absorbent paper or cloth, usu. treated with a cleaning agent, for wiping something clean. PHRASES **wipe down** clean (esp. a vertical surface) by wiping. **wipe the floor with** *informal* inflict a humiliating defeat on. **wipe off** annul (a debt etc.). **wipe out 1 a** greatly or completely reduce the strength or significance of: *the whole population was wiped out.* **b** efface, obliterate: *wiped it out of my memory.* **2** *slang* murder. **3** *informal* **a** (of a surfer) fall or be knocked from one's surfboard. **b** fall, skid, or crash. **4** clean the inside of. **5** avenge (an insult etc.). **wipe up** clear or remove (a liquid etc.) by wiping or absorbing it with a cloth. ▶ **wipeable** *adjective*

wiped out *adjective* **1** destroyed. **2** financially ruined. **3** *informal* tired out.

wipeout *noun* **1** a fall, crash, or accident, esp. while surfing, skiing, skating, etc. **2** *informal* a dismal failure. **3** an instance of complete destruction: *a nuclear wipeout.*

wiper *noun* **1** (in full **windshield wiper**) a rubber blade on an arm which moves in an arc to keep a windshield clear of rain etc. **2** *Electricity* a moving component that rotates or slides to make electrical contact with one or more terminals.

wire • *noun* **1 a** metal drawn out into the form of a fine thread or thin flexible rod. **b** a piece of this. **2** a single line of esp. copper wire, or several of these braided or twisted together, usu. insulated and used as a conductor of electrical current. **3 a** *dated* a telegram. **b** a service transmitting the latest news stories, e.g. via teleprinter, satellite, or the Internet. **4** an electronic listening device, esp. one which can be concealed on a person. **5 a** a line or cable made of several strands of wire twisted or braided together for strength. **b** several strands of wire woven or arranged into a mesh: *chicken wire.* **6** a wire stretched across and above a racetrack at the starting and finish line. • *verb* (**wires**, **wired**, **wiring**) **1** fit, fasten, strengthen, or secure with a wire: *wired my jaw shut.* **2** (often foll. by *up*) furnish (a building etc.) with electrical circuits, fibre optic cabling, telephone lines, etc. **3** fit (a person) with a concealed listening device. **4** *informal* arrange to have (money) sent, formerly by telegraph, now usu. by some other means. PHRASES **by wire** by telegraph. **get one's wires crossed** become confused or misunderstood. **under the wire** just in time. **wire-to-wire** from start to finish.

wire brush *noun* (*plural* **wire brushes**) **1** a brush with stiff wire bristles used for removing rust, paint, or dirt from hard surfaces, esp. metal. **2** either of a pair of thin sticks with long wire bristles for striking cymbals to produce a soft metallic sound.

wired *adjective* **1** *slang* hyper, strung out, or antsy, esp. due to the effects of a drug or stimulant, such as

caffeine. **2 a** fitted with electrical connections or electric or fibre optic cables. **b** *informal* having access to the Internet. **3** supported, strengthened, or stiffened with wire. PHRASES **wired for sound** fitted with or wearing an electronic listening device.

wireless • *adjective* designating or pertaining to any of various devices, communication systems, etc. not requiring wires, esp. employing radio transmission. • *noun* (also **wireless telegraphy**) radio transmission.

wire-rimmed *adjective* (of a pair of eyeglasses) having a frame made of wire.

wire rims *plural noun* a pair of wire-rimmed eyeglasses.

wire service *noun* a news agency that supplies syndicated news stories to its subscribers, e.g. media outlets, by electronic means.

wiretap • *noun* **1** an act of tapping a telephone line, esp. as a means of surveillance. **2** a device used to do this. • *verb* (**wiretaps**, **wiretapped**, **wiretapping**) **1** tap the telephone lines of (a house etc.). **2** monitor (a conversation etc.) by means of a wiretap. ▶ **wiretapper** *noun* **wiretapping** *noun*

wiring *noun* **1** a system of electrical wires in an apparatus or building. **2** the installation of these.

wiry *adjective* (**wirier**, **wiriest**) **1** resembling wire in texture or appearance, esp. stiff and flexible: *wiry hair.* **2** (of a person) thin and sinewy. **3** made of wire.

wisdom *noun* **1** the state of being wise. **2** experience and knowledge together with the power of applying them critically or practically. **3** prudence; common sense. **4** wise sayings, thoughts, etc., regarded collectively. PHRASES **in his** (or **her** etc.) **wisdom** usu. *ironic* in the belief that it would be best: *the committee in its wisdom decided to abandon the project.*

wisdom tooth *noun* (*plural* **wisdom teeth**) each of four hindmost teeth on either side of the jaws, which usu. break through the gums around the age of 20, often removed if painful.

wise¹ *adjective* (**wiser**, **wisest**) **1 a** having experience and knowledge and the ability to apply them sensibly. **b** (of an action, behaviour, etc.) demonstrating knowledge and judgment. **2** prudent, sensible. **3** having knowledge; learned. **4** suggestive of wisdom: *a wise nod.* **5** *informal* **a** alert, crafty. **b** impudent, cocky. PHRASES **wise to** *informal* aware of, esp. so as to know what to do or how to act. **none the** (or **no**) **wiser** knowing no more than before. **put a person wise** (often foll. by *to*) *informal* inform a person (about). **wise after the event** able to understand and assess an event or circumstance after its implications have become obvious. **wise up** become informed, aware, or enlightened. **without anyone's being the wiser** undetected.

wise² *noun* *archaic* way, manner. PHRASES **in no wise** not at all.

-wise¹ *suffix* *informal* forming adverbs meaning "in terms of, regarding": *music-wise they're a success but they need to improve image-wise.*

-wise² *suffix* forming adjectives meaning "mindful and careful of, having or showing common sense regarding": *a media-wise celebrity ◊ a penny-wise investor.*

wiseacre *noun* **1** a person with an affectation of wisdom or knowledge, regarded with scorn or irritation by others; a know-it-all. **2** = WISE GUY.

wiseass *noun* (*plural* **wiseasses**) *slang* = WISE GUY.

wisecrack *informal* • *noun* a witty or sarcastic remark. • *verb* **1** make a wisecrack. **2** say in a sarcastic manner. ▶ **wisecracker** *noun* **wisecracking** *noun & adjective*

wise guy *noun informal* a smug or cocky person who makes sarcastic quips or comments, esp. in order to display cleverness.

wisely *adverb* in a way suggesting or indicating wisdom.

wish • *verb* (**wishes, wished, wishing**) **1** desire or aspire to (esp. something that cannot or is unlikely to occur): *I wish I were you* ◊ *I wish I played in the NHL.* **2** intend or hope: *I wish to travel.* **3** demand or request: *I wish you to go.* **4** (often foll. by *for*) have or express a desire or yearning for (esp. something not easily or likely to be obtained): *I wish for a million dollars.* **5** have or express one's hopes for (the success or well-being etc. of another): *I wish you no harm* ◊ *she wished me a happy birthday.* **6** (usu. with *neg.*, foll. by *on, upon*) foist on a person: *I wouldn't wish that on anyone.* • *noun* (*plural* **wishes**) **1 a** a desire, request, or aspiration. **b** an expression of this. **2** a thing desired: *got my wish.* PHRASES **best** (or **good**) **wishes** hopes felt or expressed for another's happiness etc. **the wish is father to the thought** we believe a thing because we wish it true.

wishbone *noun* **1** a forked bone between the neck and breastbone of a bird, traditionally removed from the carcass of cooked fowl and broken between two people, the longer portion entitling the holder to make a wish. **2** an object of similar shape. **3** a wishbone-shaped element in the independent suspension of a vehicle, having two arms which are hinged to the chassis at their ends and to the wheel at their joint.

wishful *adjective* full of yearning; having or expressing a wish. ▶ **wishfully** *adverb* **wishfulness** *noun*

wishful thinking *noun* belief or expectation founded on wishes rather than on what one has reason to think is true.

wish list *noun* a list of wishes, desires, aspirations, or objectives.

wishy-washy *adjective* **1** (of a person) indecisive. **2** lacking strength or substance: *a wishy-washy article.*

wisp *noun* **1** several strands of hair, pieces of grass, etc. **2** a thin faint diffuse trace or streak of smoke etc.: *wisps of cloud.* **3** a person or thing that is slender or delicate: *a wisp of a child.* **4** (usu. foll. by *of*) a hint or suggestion: *a wisp of hope.* ▶ **wispy** *adjective* (**wispier, wispiest**)

wisteria *noun* a climbing plant with hanging bunches of blue, purple, or white flowers. [Say wis TEERY uh]

wistful *adjective* (of a person, looks, etc.) yearningly or mournfully expectant or wishful. ▶ **wistfully** *adverb* **wistfulness** *noun*

SPELL CHECK
wit, whit

A small amount is a **whit**.

---

wit¹ *noun* **1** the apt, clever, and funny expression of thought or juxtaposition of contrasting ideas and expressions, calculated to delight an audience: *conversation sparkling with wit.* **2** a person possessing such an ability; a cleverly humorous person. **3** (often in *plural*) mental or intellectual power; intelligence, quick understanding: *a battle of wits.* PHRASES **at one's wits'** (or **wit's**) **end** in a state of utter perplexity or despair. **have** (or **keep**) **one's wits about one** be vigilant or mentally alert. **live by one's wits** live by ingenious or crafty expedients, without a settled occupation. **match wits with** contend with someone

intellectually. **scare** (or **frighten**) **the wits out of** frighten severely.

wit² *verb* PHRASES **to wit** that is to say; namely.

SPELL CHECK　　　　　　　　　　　　
witch, which

The spelling is **which** in "Which one?" and "your letter, which I read twice".

---

witch *noun* (*plural* **witches**) **1** a person, usu. a woman, who practises magic, esp. one supposed to consort with evil spirits and perform supernatural acts with their help. **2** a follower or practitioner of the religious cult of modern witchcraft; a Wiccan. **3** an ugly or malevolent old woman; a hag.

witchcraft *noun* **1 a** the practices of a witch, esp. the use of magic and sorcery. **b** the use of supernatural power supposed to be possessed by a person in league with the devil or evil spirits. **2** the practices and beliefs of the Wiccans.

witch doctor *noun* one who claims to cure disease and counteract witchcraft by magic, esp. a tribal magician.

witches' brew *noun* (also **witch's brew**) **1** a magic brew prepared by witches. **2** any harmful, suspicious, or disgusting concoction or mixture: *people are applying to their skin a witches' brew of chemicals, many of which contain cancer-causing ingredients.*

witch hazel *noun* **1** a North American shrub with fragrant yellow flowers, widely grown as an ornamental. **2** an astringent lotion made from the bark and leaves of this plant.

witch hunt *noun* **1** *hist.* a search for and persecution of people suspected of witchcraft. **2 a** malicious campaign directed against a group of people with unpopular or unorthodox views or behaviour, formerly esp. communists. ▶ **witch-hunting** *noun*

witching hour *noun* midnight, when witches are supposedly active.

witchlike *adjective* characteristic of a witch.

witchy *adjective* characteristic of or resembling a witch.

with *preposition* expressing: **1** an instrument or means used: *cut with a knife* ◊ *can walk with assistance.* **2** association or company: *works with IBM* ◊ *beef with gravy.* **3** separation or release: *break with tradition.* **4** cause or origin: *shiver with fear* ◊ *in bed with measles.* **5** possession, attribution: *a vase with handles.* **6** circumstances: *a holiday with all expenses paid.* **7** manner adopted or displayed: *spoke with vehemence* ◊ *handle with care.* **8** agreement: *sympathize with.* **9** antagonism, competition: *incompatible with* ◊ *stop arguing with me.* **10** responsibility or care for: *the decision rests with you.* **11** material: *made with gold.* **12** addition or supply; possession of as a material, attribute, circumstance, etc.: *threaten with dismissal* ◊ *spread with jam.* **13** reference or regard: *how are things with you?* **14** relation or causative association: *keeps pace with the cost of living.* **15** an accepted circumstance or consideration: *with all your faults, we like you.* PHRASES **away** (or **in** or **out** etc.) **with** (as *interjection*) take, send, or put (a person or thing) away, in, out, etc. **be with a person 1** agree with and support a person. **2** *informal* follow a person's meaning: *are you with me?* **one with** part of the same whole as. **with child** (or **young**) *literary* pregnant. **with it** *informal* **1 a** up to date; conversant with modern or fashionable trends or ideas. **b** (**with-it**) fashionable: *with-it clothes.* **2** alert, attentive, with that thereupon.

withdraw *verb* (**withdraws;** *past* **withdrew;** *past participle* **withdrawn; withdrawing**) **1** pull or draw

aside or back. **2** discontinue, cancel: *withdrew my support*. **3 a** remove (a person etc.) from a position, situation, competition, etc. **b** remove oneself from a position or situation etc. **4** take (money) out of an account. **5 a** retire from a society or community, from public life, etc. **b** become reserved or uncommunicative. **6** retract (an unparliamentary remark) made during a parliamentary debate.

withdrawal *noun* **1 a** the action of withdrawing something: *the withdrawal of troops*. **b** the removal of money from a place of deposit. **2** the process of ceasing to take an addictive drug, often associated with unpleasant and sometimes life-threatening physical reactions. **3** a state of apathy, depression, or retreat from objective reality, usu. as a response to severe stress or physical danger. [Say with DRAWL]

withdrawn *adjective* **1** abnormally shy and unsociable. **2** (of a place) private, secluded.

wither *verb* **1** (of a plant) become or cause to become dry and shrivelled. **2** (often foll. by *away*) lose or deprive of vigour or freshness. **3** (often foll. by *away*) cease to flourish. **4** mortify (a person) with a look of extreme contempt.

withering *adjective* **1** scornful, scathing: *a withering glare*. **2** fading, decaying. ▶ **witheringly** *adverb*

withers *plural noun* the highest part of the back of a horse, sheep, ox, etc., lying between the shoulder blades.

withhold *verb* (**withholds**, **withheld**, **withholding**) **1** restrain or hold back from action. **2** keep back (what belongs to, is due to, or is desired by another); refuse to give: *withhold one's consent ◊ withhold the truth*.

within *preposition* **1** inside; enclosed or contained by. **2 a** not beyond or exceeding: *within one's means*. **b** not transgressing: *within the law ◊ within reason*. **3** not further off than: *within three miles of a station ◊ within shouting distance*. **4** before the end of (a period of time). ▬PHRASES▬ **within reach** (or **sight**) **of** near enough to be reached or seen.

without • *preposition* **1** not having, feeling, or showing. **2** with freedom from. **3** in the absence of. **4** with neglect or avoidance of. • *adverb* archaic or literary **1** outside: *seen from without*. **2** out of doors: *remained shivering without*. **3** in outward appearance: *rough without but kind within*. ▬PHRASES▬ **without end** infinite, eternal.

withstand *verb* (**withstands**, **withstood**, **withstanding**) **1** maintain one's position against; resist, oppose: *withstood the attack*. **2** tolerate, endure, bear: *this plant will withstand the harsh climate*. **3** offer resistance.

witless *adjective* **1** lacking wisdom or sense; stupid. **2** crazy, out of one's mind. ▶ **witlessly** *adverb* **witlessness** *noun*

witness • *noun* (*plural* **witnesses**) **1** a person present at some event or occurrence and able to give information about it from observation. **2 a** a person giving testimony under oath in a court of law. **b** testimony, evidence, confirmation: *he was bribed to give false witness*. **3 a** a person selected or appointed to be present at a transaction etc. in order to testify to its having taken place. **b** a person who signs a document attesting to its proper execution. **4** a person or thing whose existence, condition, etc., attests or proves something: *this village is a witness to the ravages of war*. **5** (**Witness**) = JEHOVAH'S WITNESS. • *verb* (**witnesses**, **witnessed**, **witnessing**) **1** be a witness of (an event etc.): *did you witness the accident?* **2 a** sign (a document) as a witness of its authenticity. **b** formally be present as a witness of (a transaction etc.). **3** (of a place, time, etc.) be associated with (a fact or event); be the scene or

setting of: *Europe witnessed massive political change in the late 1980s*. **4** introducing an illustration of the preceding statement: *he is an accomplished musician: witness his performance last week*. **5** (foll. by *to*, *against*) give or serve as evidence. **6** publicly assert one's religious convictions, esp. in an attempt to convert others. ▬PHRASES▬ **bear witness to 1** attest the truth of. **2** state one's belief in. **call to witness** appeal to for confirmation etc.

> **WRITING TIP**
> **witness box, witness stand**
>
> The official Canadian term is **witness box**.

witness box *noun* (*plural* **witness boxes**) *Cdn & Brit.* (also **witness stand**) an enclosure in a court of law from which witnesses give evidence.

-witted *combining form* having or showing intelligence of the kind described: *quick-witted*.

witticism *noun* a witty remark. [Say WITTA sism]

wittily *adverb* in a witty manner.

wittiness *noun* the quality of being witty.

witting *adjective* **1** (of a person) conscious or aware of the full facts of a situation: *there is no evidence to suggest that the Chinese were witting accomplices*. **2** done in full awareness and consciousness; deliberate, intentional: *his errors are the witting distortions of someone who will say whatever suits his purpose at the moment*. ▶ **wittingly** *adverb*

witty *adjective* (**wittier**, **wittiest**) **1** capable of or given to saying or writing clever and amusing things. **2** (of speech, writing, etc.) characterized by wit or humour.

wives *plural of* WIFE.

wizard *noun* **1** a man who practises magic; a sorcerer. **2** a person noted for remarkable ability: *she's a financial wizard*. ▶ **wizardly** *adjective*

wizardry *noun* **1** the art or practice of a wizard. **2** remarkable skill in a particular field or activity.

wizened *adjective* shrivelled or wrinkled, esp. with age: *his wizened old face was contorted into an irregular smile*. [Say WIZZ'nd]

wk. *abbreviation* **1** week. **2** work.

w/o *abbreviation* without.

wobble • *verb* (**wobbles**, **wobbled**, **wobbling**) **1 a** sway or rock erratically from side to side. **b** cause to do this. **2** stand or proceed unsteadily; stagger. **3** (of the voice or a sound) quaver. **4** hesitate or waver between different opinions or actions. • *noun* **1** an unsteady movement from side to side. **2** a tremble or quaver in the voice. **3** a moment of hesitation or vacillation.

wobbliness *noun* the quality of being wobbly.

wobbly *adjective* (**wobblier**, **wobbliest**) **1** wobbling or tending to wobble. **2** (of a line, handwriting, etc.) not straight or regular; shaky, wavy, undulating. **3** wavering, uncertain.

woe *noun* **1** bitter grief. **2** (in *plural*) troubles, misfortunes. ▬PHRASES▬ **woe betide** (or **to**) there will be unfortunate consequences for. **woe is me** an exclamation of distress.

woebegone *adjective* sad, miserable, or dismal in appearance: *she sits wrapped in a blanket and wearing a woebegone expression*. [Say WOE be gon]

woeful *adjective* **1** afflicted with sorrow or misfortune. **2** causing sorrow or affliction. **3** very bad or poor; dreadful: *woeful ignorance*. ▶ **woefully** *adverb* **woefulness** *noun*

wok *noun* a large bowl-shaped frying pan used in esp. Chinese cooking.

woke *past of* WAKE[1].

woken *past participle of* WAKE[1].

wolf • *noun* (*plural* **wolves**) **1** a wild flesh-eating tawny-grey mammal related to the dog, living and hunting in packs. **2** the skin, hide, or fur of this animal. **3** *slang* **a** a ferocious or rapacious person. **b** a womanizer. • *verb* (**wolfs, wolfed, wolfing**) (often foll. by *down*) devour (food) ravenously. PHRASES **cry wolf** raise repeated false alarms (so that a genuine one is disregarded). **keep the wolf from the door** have enough money to provide for oneself or one's family. **throw to the wolves** sacrifice (a friend or colleague) in order to avert danger or difficulties for oneself. **wolf in sheep's clothing** a person whose hostile intentions are concealed by a pretense of friendliness.

wolfhound *noun* a dog of any of several large breeds, e.g. a borzoi, originally kept for hunting wolves.

wolfish *adjective* resembling or characteristic of a wolf. ▶**wolfishly** *adverb*

wolflike *adjective & adverb* characteristic of a wolf.

wolf pack *noun* **1** any group which operates as a hunting and attacking pack, such as a group of submarines or aircraft. **2** a number of wolves naturally associating as a group, esp. for hunting.

wolf whistle • *noun* a rising and falling whistle imitating the howl of a wolf, made esp. by a man to express his admiration of a woman's appearance. • *verb* (**wolf-whistle, wolf-whistles, wolf-whistled, wolf-whistling**) make such a whistling sound.

wolf willow *noun* Cdn a North American tree with pinkish bark, silvery leaves, yellow musky-smelling flowers, and large dry silvery berries.

wolverine *noun* **1** a carnivorous animal of the weasel family, resembling a small bear, with dark brown fur and a long bushy tail, native to the tundra and forests of Arctic and subarctic regions. **2** wolverine fur. [Say wool ver EEN]

wolves *plural of* WOLF.

woman *noun* (*plural* **women**) **1** an adult female person (also in *combination*: *businesswoman* ◊ *Frenchwoman*). **2** (as an *adjective*) female: *women friends*. **3** *informal* a wife or female sexual partner. **4** the female human person, esp. viewed as a type: *how does woman differ from man?* **5** (**the woman**) the character or qualities traditionally associated with women: *brought out the woman in me*.

womanhood *noun* **1 a** the state or condition of being a woman. **b** the state of being a grown woman; female maturity. **2** the character or qualities traditionally attributed to women. **3** women collectively.

womanish *adjective* **1** usu. derogatory (of a man) effeminate. **2** suitable to or characteristic of a woman.

womanize *verb* (**womanizes, womanized, womanizing**) (of a man) pursue or engage in casual sexual encounters with women. ▶**womanizer** *noun*

womankind *noun* women collectively.

womanless *adjective* without a woman or women.

womanlike *adjective* resembling or characteristic of a woman or women.

womanliness *noun* the quality of being womanly.

womanly *adjective* (of a woman) having or showing qualities traditionally associated with women; not masculine or girlish.

womb *noun* **1** the organ in the body of a woman or female mammal in which offspring are carried, protected, and nourished before birth; the uterus. **2** a place of origin, development, or growth. [Say WOOM]

wombat *noun* a burrowing plant-eating Australian marsupial that resembles a small bear with short legs. [Say WOM bat]

womblike *adjective* like a womb, esp. in providing comfort or isolation. [Say WOOM like]

women *plural of* WOMAN.

womenfolk *plural noun* **1** women collectively. **2** the women of a particular family, household, etc.

women's lib *noun* (also **Women's Lib**) *informal* = WOMEN'S LIBERATION.

women's libber *noun informal* a supporter of women's liberation.

women's liberation *noun* **1** the liberation of women from inequalities and subordinate status in relation to men, and from sexist attitudes. **2** (also **Women's Liberation**, in full **Women's Liberation Movement**) = WOMEN'S MOVEMENT.

women's movement *noun* a movement campaigning for women's liberation and for the recognition and extension of women's rights.

women's room *noun* a women's washroom.

women's shelter *noun* an establishment offering refuge and counselling to women who are victims of esp. domestic abuse, and their children.

women's studies *plural noun* (usu. treated as *singular*) a course of academic studies focusing on women and their role in society, as well as their history and literature.

womenswear *noun* clothes for women.

won *past and past participle of* WIN.

wonder • *noun* **1** the emotion excited by the perception of something unexpected, unfamiliar, or inexplicable, esp. surprise or astonishment mingled with admiration, perplexity, or curiosity. **2** an amazing or remarkable person or thing. **3** (as an *adjective*) having marvellous or amazing properties or qualities: *a wonder drug* ◊ *Sleuth the wonder dog*. **4** a miraculous or surprising thing: *it is a wonder you were not hurt*. • *verb* **1** desire or be curious to know: *I wonder what time it is*. **2** speculate with curiosity or doubt: *I wonder about him sometimes*. **3** used to express a tentative inquiry or polite request: *I was wondering if you might be free tomorrow night?* **4** be filled with wonder or great surprise. PHRASES **I shouldn't wonder** *informal* it would not surprise me. **no** (or **small**) **wonder** it is natural or hardly surprising; one might have guessed. **wonders will never cease** an exclamation of extreme (usu. delightful) surprise. **work** (or **do**) **wonders 1** perform miracles. **2** achieve remarkable success.

wonderful *adjective* **1** very remarkable or admirable: *a wonderful meal*. **2** marvellous, terrific: *I feel wonderful*. **3** that arouses wonder or astonishment. ▶**wonderfully** *adverb* **wonderfulness** *noun*

wondering *adjective* filled with wonder; marvelling: *their wondering gaze*. ▶**wonderingly** *adverb*

wonderland *noun* **1** an imaginary world of marvels. **2** an actual place of remarkable beauty: *a winter wonderland*.

wonderment *noun* a state of surprise or awe.

wonder-struck *adjective* reduced to silence by wonder.

wondrous *adjective* literary wonderful: *twenty years later, it was still a wondrous place*. ▶**wondrously** *adverb* [Say WUN drus]

wonk *noun* slang usu. derogatory **1** a studious or hard-working person, esp. one obsessively devoted to academic studies at the expense of social activities. **2** (also **policy wonk**) esp. US a person who takes an unnecessary interest in minor details of policy. ▶**wonkery** *noun*

wonkiness *noun* the state of being wonky.

wonky *adjective* (**wonkier, wonkiest**) *informal* **1** crooked, loose. **2** faulty, unreliable, askew.

wont • *adjective* accustomed: *as we were wont to say*. • *noun* what is customary, one's habit: *as is my wont*. [Sounds like WANT]

won't *contraction* will not.

wonted *adjective* habitual, accustomed, usual: *looked up with his wonted patience*. [Sounds like *WANTED*]

won ton *noun* (in Chinese cooking) a small round dumpling containing a savoury filling, sometimes deep-fried and served as an accompaniment to a meal, but more commonly boiled and served in a broth. [Say WON ton (both parts of this word rhyme with *DAWN*)]

woo *verb* (**woos**, **wooed**, **wooing**) **1** court; seek the hand or love of (esp. a woman). **2** seek the favour or support of: *trying to woo voters*. **3** try to win (fame, fortune, etc.). **4** coax, entreat, or importune. ▶ **wooer** *noun*

wood *noun* **1 a** a hard fibrous material that forms the main substance of the trunk or branches of a tree etc. **b** this cut for timber or for fuel, or for use in crafts, manufacture, etc. **2** trees densely occupying a tract of land. **3** (**the wood**) wooden storage, esp. a cask, for wine etc.: *poured straight from the wood*. **4** a wooden-headed golf club, or any club with a head relatively broad from face to back.

wood bison *noun* (*plural* **wood bison**) (also **wood buffalo**, *plural* **wood buffalo** or **wood buffaloes**) a subspecies of North American bison found in wooded parts of western Canada, somewhat larger than the plains bison.

woodblock *noun* **1** a block from which woodcuts are made. **2** each of the small pieces of wood used in making a parquet floor, often arranged in a pattern.

wood-burning *adjective* using wood as fuel.

woodcarver *noun* **1** a person who carves designs in relief on wood. **2** a tool for carving wood.

woodcarving *noun* **1** the act, process, or art of carving wood. **2** a design in wood produced by this art.

woodchuck *noun* a reddish-brown and grey North American marmot.

woodcock *noun* (*plural* **woodcock**) a woodland game bird of the sandpiper family, with a long bill and brown camouflaged plumage.

woodcut *noun* **1** a relief cut on a block of wood sawn along the grain. **2** a print made from this, esp. as an illustration in a book. **3** the technique of making such reliefs and prints.

woodcutter *noun* **1** a person who cuts wood, esp. one who fells trees. **2** a woodcut maker. ▶ **woodcutting** *adjective & noun*

wood duck *noun* a North American wild duck, the male of which has an iridescent green and blue head with white stripes.

wooded *adjective* having woods or many trees.

wooden *adjective* **1** made of wood. **2** like wood. **3 a** stiff, clumsy, or stilted; without animation or flexibility: *a wooden performance*. **b** expressionless: *a wooden stare*. ▶ **woodenly** *adverb* **woodenness** *noun*

wood fibre *noun* fibre obtained from wood esp. as material for paper.

wood grain *noun* **1** the grain of wood. **2** a surface or finish imitating this.

woodiness *noun* **1** the condition of something that resembles wood, esp. in texture or appearance. **2** the condition of a plant that has become hard like wood.

woodland *noun* wooded country, woods. ▶ **woodlander** *noun*

woodland caribou *noun* (*plural* **woodland caribou**) a caribou found in wooded areas of Canada, larger than the barren ground caribou.

Woodland Cree *noun* (*plural* **Woodland Cree** or **Woodland Crees**) **1** a member of any of the Cree peoples who live in forested areas (as opposed to the Plains). **2** the dialect of Cree spoken by this people.

woodlot *noun* a treed plot of land, esp. on a farm, from which firewood may be obtained.

woodpecker *noun* a bird with a stiff tail and a strong bill, which climbs and taps tree trunks in search of insects.

woodpile *noun* a pile of wood, esp. for fuel.

wood pulp *noun* wood fibre reduced chemically or mechanically to pulp as raw material for paper.

woodruff *noun* a white-flowered plant grown for the fragrance of its whorled leaves when dried or crushed.

woods *plural noun* trees densely occupying a tract of land. **PHRASES** **out of the woods** out of danger or difficulty.

woodshed *noun* a shed where wood for fuel is stored.

woodsman *noun* (*plural* **woodsmen**) **1** a person who lives or frequents the woods for hunting, camping, etc. **2** a person skilled in woodworking.

woodsmoke *noun* the smoke from a wood fire.

wood stain *noun* a commercially-produced substance for colouring wood.

wood stove *noun* a wood-burning stove.

woodsy *adjective* (**woodsier**, **woodsiest**) like or characteristic of woods.

woodwind *noun* (usu. in *plural*) the wind instruments of the orchestra that were (mostly) originally made of wood, e.g. the flute and clarinet: *the woodwinds are out of tune* ◊ *woodwind instruments*.

woodwork *noun* **1** the making of things in wood. **2** things made of wood, esp. the wooden parts of a building. **PHRASES** **crawl** (or **come**) **out of the woodwork** *informal* (of something unwelcome) emerge from obscurity into prominence. ▶ **woodworker** *noun* **woodworking** *noun*

woodworm *noun* **1** the larva of a small brown beetle, which bores holes in dead wood and causes considerable damage to old furniture and building timbers. **2** damaged wood affected by this.

woody • *adjective* (**woodier**, **woodiest**) **1** (of a region) abounding in woods. **2** like or of wood: *a woody stem*. • *noun* (*plural* **woodies**) *informal* a wood duck.

woof[1] • *noun* the gruff bark of a dog. • *verb* **1** give a woof. **2** (often foll. by *down*) *informal* consume ravenously. [With OO as in *WOOL*]

woof[2] *noun* **1** the threads woven across a warp to make fabric. **2** yarn used for this. [With OO as in either *WOOL* or *PROOF*]

woofer *noun* a loudspeaker designed to reproduce low frequencies (compare TWEETER). [With OO as in *WOOL*]

wool *noun* **1** fine soft wavy hair from the fleece of sheep, goats, etc. **2 a** yarn produced from this hair. **b** cloth or clothing made from it. **3** any of various wool-like substances: *steel wool*. **4** *informal* a person's hair, esp. when short and curly. **PHRASES** **pull the wool over a person's eyes** deceive a person.

woolgather *verb* be absent-minded or inattentively dreamy. ▶ **woolgathering** *noun*

woollen (also **woolen**) • *adjective* made wholly or partly of wool, esp. from short fibres. • *noun* (in *plural*) woollen garments.

woolliness *noun* **1** the quality of something that is covered with wool or that resembles wool in softness or appearance. **2** the quality of sound, thought, etc. that is vague, distorted, or confused.

woolly • *adjective* (**woollier**, **woolliest**) **1** bearing or naturally covered with wool or wool-like hair; downy. **2** resembling or suggesting wool: *woolly clouds*. **3** made of (esp. knitted) wool. **4** (of a sound) indistinct. **5** (of thought) vague or confused. **6** lacking in definition or incisiveness. • *noun* (*plural* **woollies**) *informal* a woollen garment, esp. a sweater.

woosh *verb, noun, & interjection* (**wooshes, wooshed, wooshing**) = WHOOSH.

woozily *adverb* in a dizzy, unsteady, or dazed way: *Tammy woozily aimed the camera and took pictures of our feet.*

wooziness *noun* a dizzy, unsteady, or dazed manner or feeling.

woozy *adjective* (**woozier, wooziest**) *informal* dizzy, unsteady, or dazed.

Worcestershire sauce *noun* a pungent sauce containing soy, vinegar, and seasoning. [Say WUSS tuh sher or WURST er sher]

word • *noun* **1** a sound or combination of sounds forming a meaningful element of speech, usu. written with a space on either side of it. **2** speech, esp. as distinct from action: *bold in word only*. **3** one's promise: *gave us their word*. **4** (in *singular* or *plural*) a thing said, a remark or conversation. **5** (in *plural*) the text of a song or an actor's part. **6** (in *plural*) angry talk: *they had words*. **7 a** news; a message: *send word*. **b** a rumour: *word is she's left town*. **8** a command, password, or motto: *gave the word to begin*. **9** (**the Word**) **a** any divine message. **b** the Gospel. **c** Jesus. **d** the Bible. • *verb* put into words; select words to express: *how shall we word that?* PHRASES **be as good as one's word** fulfill (or exceed) what one has promised. **break one's word** fail to do what one has promised. **have no words for** be unable to express. **have a word** (often foll. by *with*) speak briefly (to). **in other words** expressing the same thing differently. **in so many words** explicitly or bluntly. **in a** (or **one**) **word** briefly. **keep one's word** do what one has promised. **my** (or **upon my**) **word** an exclamation of surprise or consternation. **not the word for it** not an adequate or appropriate description. **of few words** taciturn. **of one's word** reliable in keeping promises: *a woman of her word*. **on** (or **upon**) **my word** a form of asseveration. **put into words** express in speech or writing. **take a person at his** or **her word** interpret a person's words literally or exactly. **take a person's word for it** believe a person's statement without investigation etc. **too ... for words** too ... to be adequately described: *was too funny for words*. **waste words** talk in vain. **word for word** in exactly the same or (of translation) corresponding words. **words fail me** an expression of disbelief, dismay, etc. **a word to the wise** a piece of advice etc. given in the hope that it will be sufficient to change a person's behaviour etc.

wordiness *noun* a tendency to use too many words to express an idea.

wording *noun* **1** a form of words used. **2** the way in which something is expressed.

wordless *adjective* **1** without any words spoken or used; silent: *a wordless prayer*. **2** (of people) not saying anything. ▶ **wordlessly** *adverb* **wordlessness** *noun*

word of mouth *noun* spoken communication between people as a means of transmitting information.

wordplay *noun* witty use of words, esp. by punning.

word-processed *adjective* (of text) created, stored, and formatted using a computer.

word processing *noun* the production, storage, manipulation, and formatting of text using a computer.

word processor *noun* a computer system for storing, manipulating, editing, and usu. displaying and printing text entered from a keyboard.

wordsmith *noun* a skilled user or maker of words.

word wrap *noun* (in word processing) the automatic shifting of a word too long to fit on a line to the beginning of the next line.

wordy *adjective* (**wordier, wordiest**) using many or too many words.

wore *past of* WEAR.

work • *noun* **1** the application of mental or physical effort to a purpose. **2 a** a task to be undertaken. **b** the materials for this. **3** a thing done or made by work; the result of an action; an achievement; a thing made. **4** a person's employment or occupation etc., esp. as a means of earning income. **5 a** a literary or musical composition. **b** (in *plural*) all such by an author or composer etc. **6** actions or experiences of a specified kind: *good work!* ◊ *this is thirsty work*. **7** (in *combination*) things or parts made of a specified material or with specified tools etc.: *needlework*. **8** (in *plural*) the operative part of a clock or machine. **9** *Physics* the exertion of force overcoming resistance or producing molecular change: *convert heat into work*. **10** (in *plural*) *informal* all that is available; everything needed. **11** (usu. in *plural*) *Theology* a meritorious act. **12** (usu. in *plural* or in *combination*) a defensive structure: *earthworks*. **13** (in *combination*) **a** ornamentation of a specified kind: *latticework*. **b** articles having this. • *verb* **1** do work; be engaged in bodily or mental activity. **2** be employed in certain work: *works in industry* ◊ *works as a secretary*. **3** make efforts; conduct a campaign: *works for peace*. **4** (foll. by *in*) be a craftsman (in a material). **5** operate or function, esp. effectively: *your idea will not work*. **6** (of a part of a machine) run, revolve. **7** carry on, manage, or control: *cannot work the machine*. **8 a** put or keep in operation or at work; cause to toil: *works the staff very hard*. **b** cultivate (land). **9 a** bring about: *worked miracles*. **b** *informal* arrange (matters): *worked it so that we could go*. **10** knead, hammer; bring to a desired shape or consistency. **11** (cause to) progress or penetrate, or make (one's way), gradually or with difficulty in a specified way: *worked our way through the crowd*. **12** gradually become (loose etc.) by constant movement. **13** artificially excite: *worked themselves into a rage*. **14 a** purchase with one's labour instead of money: *work one's passage*. **b** obtain by labour the money for (one's way through university etc.). **15** (foll. by *on*, *upon*) have influence. PHRASES **at work** in action or engaged in work. **get worked up** become angry, excited, or tense. **give a person the works** **1** *informal* give or tell a person everything. **2** *informal* treat a person harshly. **have one's work cut out** be faced with a hard task. **in the works** being planned, worked on, or produced. **set to work** begin or cause to begin operations. **work away** (or **on**) continue to work. **work in** find a place for. **work it** *informal* bring it about; achieve a desired result. **work off** get rid of by work or activity. **work out** **1** solve or find out by calculation. **2** be calculated: *the total works out to 230*. **3** give a definite result. **4** have a specified result: *the plan worked out well*. **5** provide for the details of: *work out a scheme*. **6** accomplish or attain with difficulty. **7** exhaust with work: *the mine is worked out*. **8** engage in physical exercise or training. **work over** **1** examine thoroughly. **2** *informal* treat with violence. **work a** (or **the**) **room** *informal* make the rounds of people in a room, in order to impress favourably. **work to rule** (esp. as a form of industrial action) follow official working rules exactly so as to reduce output and efficiency. **work up** **1** bring gradually to an efficient state. **2** (foll. by *to*) advance gradually to a climax. **3** elaborate or excite by degrees. **4** learn (a subject) by study.

workability *noun* the ability of something to be worked or manipulated to achieve a desired effect.

workable *adjective* **1** that can be worked or will work. **2** practicable, feasible: *a workable scheme*.

W

workaday *adjective* **1** ordinary, everyday, practical. **2** fit for, used, or seen on workdays.

workaholic *noun informal* a person who willingly works too hard, esp. for too long. ▶ **workaholism** *noun*

workbench *noun* (*plural* **workbenches**) a bench for doing mechanical or practical work, esp. carpentry.

workbook *noun* **1** a student's book giving information on a subject and exercises. **2** a student's notebook.

workboot *noun* a sturdy leather boot worn esp. by people engaged in manual labour.

work camp *noun* **1** a prison camp enforcing a regime of hard labour. **2** a camp at which community work is done esp. by young volunteers.

workday *noun* **1** a day on which work is usually done. **2** the part of the day devoted to work: *a shorter workday*.

worker *noun* **1** one who works, esp. one who does a particular type of work: *factory workers* ◊ *rescue worker*. **2 a** one who works in a specified way: *a slow worker*. **b** one who works hard: *she's quite the worker!* **3** a neuter or undeveloped female of various social insects, esp. a bee or ant, that does the basic work of its colony.

workers' compensation *noun* money paid to a person to compensate for injury suffered on the job.

work ethic *noun* the principle that hard work is intrinsically virtuous or worthy of reward.

workfare *noun* a welfare system which requires some work or training from those receiving benefits.

workforce *noun* **1** the workers engaged or available in an industry etc. **2** the number of such workers.

workgroup *noun* a group of people who have simultaneous access via a network to shared software and data, enabling them to work together on projects.

workhorse *noun* **1** a horse used for heavy work, e.g. plowing, hauling, etc., rather than riding or racing. **2** a person, machine, etc. that does much work.

workhouse *noun Brit. hist.* an institution where poor people used to have to live if they couldn't afford living anywhere else, with the requirement that they perform tedious manual labour in return.

working • *adjective* **1 a** having a job; employed. **b** having a job that involves physical labour. **c** spent in work or employment. **2** functioning or able to function: *a working model*. **3** that is good enough as a basis for work, argument, etc. and may be improved later: *the book's working title*. • *noun* **1** the activity of work. **2** (often in *plural*) the act or manner of functioning of a thing: *the workings of the human mind*. **3** (usu. in *plural*) **a** a mine or quarry. **b** the part of this in which work is being or has been done: *disused mine workings*.

working capital *noun* capital needed and used in running a business and not invested in buildings, equipment, etc.

working class • *noun* (*plural* **working classes**) the class of people employed for wages, esp. in manual or industrial work. • *adjective* (**working-class**) of or relating to this class.

working group *noun* a group appointed to study a particular problem or advise on some question.

working order *noun* the condition in which a machine works (satisfactorily or as specified).

work-in-progress *noun* (*plural* **works-in-progress**) work undertaken but not yet completed.

workload *noun* the amount of work to be done by an individual etc.

workman *noun* (*plural* **workmen**) **1** a man employed to do manual labour. **2** a person considered with regard to skill in a job: *a good workman*.

workmanlike *adjective* characteristic of a good workman; showing practised skill.

workmanship *noun* **1** the degree of skill in doing a task or of quality in the product made. **2** a thing made or created by a specified person etc.

workmate *noun* a person with whom one works.

work of art *noun* (*plural* **works of art**) a fine picture, poem, or building etc.

workout *noun* a session of physical exercise or training.

workplace *noun* a place at which a person works.

workroom *noun* a room for working in, esp. one equipped for a certain kind of work.

worksheet *noun* **1** a paper for recording work done or in progress. **2** a paper listing questions or activities for students etc. to work through.

workshop • *noun* **1** a room or building in which goods are made. **2 a** a meeting for concerted discussion and practical work on a particular subject, in which knowledge and experience are shared: *a writing workshop*. **b** the members of such a group. • *verb* (**workshops**, **workshopped**, **workshopping**) present a workshop performance of (a dramatic work), esp. in order to explore aspects of the production before it is staged formally.

workspace *noun* **1** space in which to work. **2** an area rented or sold for commercial purposes. **3** *Computing* a memory storage facility for temporary use.

workstation *noun* **1** a computer terminal or the desk etc. where this is located. **2** a location on an assembly line at which a manufacturing operation is carried out.

work-to-rule *noun* the act of following official working rules exactly so as to reduce output and efficiency, esp. as a kind of industrial action.

workup *noun* a diagnostic examination of a patient.

workweek *noun* the number of days or hours per week devoted or allotted to work.

world *noun* **1 a** the earth, or a planetary body like it. **b** its countries and their inhabitants. **c** the earth as known or in some particular respect. **2 a** the universe or all that exists; everything. **b** everything that exists outside oneself: *dead to the world*. **3 a** the time, state, or scene of human existence. **b** (preceded by *the*, *this*) mortal life. **4** secular interests and affairs. **5** active life: *how goes the world with you?* **6** average, respectable, or fashionable people or their customs or opinions. **7** all that concerns or all who belong to a specified class, time, domain, etc.: *the medieval world* ◊ *the sports world*. **8** a vast amount: *that makes a world of difference*. **9** (as an *adjective*) affecting many nations, of all nations: *world politics* ◊ *world record*. ▪ PHRASES ▪ **be worlds apart** be completely different in attitudes etc. **bring into the world** give birth to or attend at the birth of. **come into the world** be born. **for all the world** precisely: *looked for all the world as if they were real*. **in the world** of all; at all (used as an intensifier in questions): *what in the world is it?* **man** (or **woman**) **of the world** a person experienced and practical in human affairs. **out of this world** *informal* extremely good etc. **see the world** travel widely. **think the world of** have a very high regard for. **the** (or **all the**) **world over** throughout the world. **the world to come** supposed life after death. **world without end** forever.

World Bank *noun* the International Bank for Reconstruction and Development, which administers economic aid between member nations.

world beat *noun* = WORLD MUSIC.

world-class *adjective* of a quality or standard regarded as high throughout the world.

world-famous *adjective* known throughout the world.

World Health Organization *noun* an agency of the

United Nations, which promotes health and controls communicable diseases. Abbreviation: **WHO**.

World Heritage Site *noun* a natural or man-made site of outstanding international importance and deserving special protection.

worldliness *noun* **1** concern with or relation to material values or ordinary life rather than a spiritual existence. **2** experience, sophistication: *the children were impressed by the worldliness of their visitor from the big city, since most of them had never travelled further than the neighbouring town of Pouce Coupe.*

worldly *adjective* (**worldlier, worldliest**) **1** of or concerned with material values or ordinary life rather than a spiritual existence. **2** experienced and sophisticated.

world music *noun* **1** traditional local or ethnic music, esp. from the developing world. **2** a style of pop music incorporating elements of such traditions.

world power *noun* a nation having power and influence in world affairs.

World Series *noun* a North American professional baseball championship played between the champions of the American League and the National League.

world's fair *noun* an international exhibition of the industrial, scientific, technological, and artistic achievements of the participating nations.

world view *noun* a comprehensive view or philosophy of life, the world, and the universe.

world war *noun* a war between many important nations.

world-weariness *noun* feelings of weariness, boredom, or cynicism as a result of long experience of life.

world-weary *adjective* feeling or indicating weariness, boredom, or cynicism as a result of long experience of life.

worldwide • *adjective* affecting, occurring in, or known throughout the world. • *adverb* throughout the world.

World Wide Web *noun* an international computer network incorporating multimedia and using hypertext links to access and retrieve information.

worm • *noun* **1** any of various types of creeping or burrowing invertebrate animals with long slender bodies and no limbs, esp. segmented in rings or parasitic in the intestines or tissues. **2** the long slender larva of an insect, esp. in fruit or wood. **3** (in *plural*) intestinal or other internal parasites. **4** a maggot supposed to eat dead bodies in the grave. **5** an insignificant or contemptible person. • *verb* **1** move with a crawling motion. **2** (foll. by *into*) insinuate oneself into a person's favour etc.: *is trying to worm his way back into the life of his ex-wife.* **3** (foll. by *out*) obtain (a secret etc.) by cunning persistence: *managed to worm the truth out of them.* **4** rid (a plant or dog etc.) of worms. PHRASES **the worm turns** a meek person retaliates after being pushed too far. ▶ **wormer** *noun*

wormlike *adjective* resembling a worm in appearance.

wormwood *noun* **1** a woody shrub with a bitter taste used in vermouth, absinthe, and medicine. **2** a state or source of bitterness, grief, or sadness: *all this is wormwood to scientists like myself, who think that the task of science is to bring us closer and closer to objective truth.*

wormy *adjective* (**wormier, wormiest**) **1** infested with or eaten into by worms: *no one likes a wormy apple.* **2** (of wood or wooden articles) full of holes made by woodworms. **3** (of a person) weak, abject, or revolting: *a spiteful, wormy little man.*

worn • *verb* past participle of WEAR. • *adjective* **1** damaged by use or wear. **2** looking tired and exhausted. **3** (also **well-worn**) (of a joke etc.) stale; often heard.

worn out *adjective* **1** exhausted. **2** worn, esp. so as to be no longer usable.

worried *adjective* **1** uneasy, troubled in the mind. **2** suggesting worry: *a worried look.*

worriedly *adverb* in a worried or anxious manner.

worrier *noun* a person who worries habitually about unpleasant things that have happened or that might happen.

worrisome *adjective* causing or apt to cause worry.

worry • *verb* (**worries, worried, worrying**) **1** give way to anxiety or unease; allow one's mind to dwell on difficulty or troubles. **2** be a trouble or anxiety to. **3 a** (of a dog etc.) shake or pull repeatedly with the teeth. **b** attack repeatedly. • *noun* (*plural* **worries**) **1** a thing that causes anxiety. **2** anxiety; a worried state. PHRASES **not to worry** *informal* there is no need to worry. **worry along** (or **through**) manage to advance by persistence in spite of obstacles. **worry oneself** (usu. in *neg.*) take needless trouble. ▶ **worrying** *adjective* **worryingly** *adverb*

worrywart *noun* *informal* a person who tends to worry unduly.

worse • *adjective* **1** bad to a greater degree or on a greater scale. **2** in or into worse health or a worse condition: *is getting worse.* • *adverb* more badly or more ill. • *noun* **1** a worse thing or things: *you might do worse than accept.* **2** (**the worse**) a worse condition: *a turn for the worse.* PHRASES **none the worse** (often foll. by *for*) not adversely affected (by). **or worse** or as an even worse alternative. **the worse for wear 1** damaged by use. **2** injured. **3** drunk. **worse off** in a worse (esp. financial) position.

worsen *verb* make or become worse.

worship • *noun* **1 a** reverence paid to a deity, esp. in a formal service. **b** the acts, rites, or ceremonies of worship. **2** quasi-religious adoration or devotion to a person or principle: *the worship of wealth.* • *verb* (**worships, worshipped, worshipping**) **1** adore as divine; honour with religious rites. **2** idolize or regard with adoration: *worships the ground she walks on.* **3** attend public worship. PHRASES **Your** (or **His** or **Her**) **Worship** esp. *Cdn & Brit.* a title of respect used to or of a mayor, certain magistrates, etc.

worshipful *adjective* **1** (usu. **Worshipful**) a title given to officers of certain organizations. **2** full of worship; adoring: *worshipful fans.* ▶ **worshipfully** *adverb*

worshipper *noun* **1** a person who worships a god or attends a religious ceremony. **2** a person who treats someone or something with adoration or reverence: *a beach full of sun worshippers.*

worst • *adjective* most bad. • *adverb* most badly. • *noun* the worst part, possibility, etc.: *the worst of the storm is over* ◊ *prepare for the worst.* • *verb* get the better of. PHRASES **at its** etc. **worst** in the worst state. **at worst** (or **the worst**) in the worst possible case. **get** (or **have**) **the worst of it** be defeated. **if** (**the**) **worst comes to** (**the**) **worst** if the worst happens. **in the worst way** to an extreme degree.

worst-case *adjective* pertaining to the worst of the possible foreseeable outcomes, scenarios, etc.

worsted *noun* **1** a fine smooth yarn spun from combed long staple wool. **2** fabric made from this. [Say WORSE tid]

worth • *adjective* **1** of a value equivalent to: *is worth $50.* **2** such as to justify; deserving: *not worth the trouble.* **3** possessing or having property amounting to: *is worth a million dollars.* • *noun* **1** what a person or thing is worth; the (usu. specified) merit of. **2** the equivalent of money in a commodity: *ten dollars' worth of gas.*

....

for all one is worth *informal* with one's utmost efforts; without reserve. **for what it is worth** without a guarantee of its truth or value. **worth it** *informal* worth the time or effort spent.

worthily *adverb* in a way that deserves respect or recognition.

worthiness *noun* **1** the quality of someone or something that deserves respect or recognition. **2 a** the condition of being deserving of something: *creditworthiness* ◊ *we discussed my worthiness for the promotion*. **b** suitability for something: *roadworthiness* ◊ *seaworthiness*.

worthless *adjective* without value or merit. ▶ **worthlessly** *adverb* **worthlessness** *noun*

worthwhile *adjective* that is worth the time or effort spent; of value or importance.

worthy • *adjective* (**worthier, worthiest**) **1** having some moral worth; deserving respect: *lived a worthy life*. **2** esp. *jocular* (of a person) entitled to recognition: *the worthy citizens of the town*. **3 a** deserving: *worthy of mention*. **b** adequate or suitable to the dignity etc. of: *worthy of the occasion*. • *noun* (*plural* **worthies**) **1** a worthy person. **2** a person of some distinction. **3** *jocular* a person.

> **GRAMMAR CHECK**
> **would**   ⚠
>
> Do not say *If I would have been there I would have spoken my mind*. Use **would** only once, with the verb that is *not* introduced by "if": *If I had been there I would have spoken my mind*.

would *auxiliary verb* used esp.: **1 a** in reported speech: *he said he would be home by evening*. **b** to express the conditional mood: *they would have been killed if they had gone*. **2** to express habitual action: *would wait for her every evening*. **3** to express a question or polite request: *would they like it?* ◊ *would you come in, please?* **4** to express probability: *I guess she would be over fifty by now*. **5** (foll. by *that* + clause) *literary* to express a wish: *would that you were here*. **6** to express consent: *they would not help*.

would-be *adjective* often *derogatory* desiring or aspiring to be: *a would-be politician*.

wouldn't *contraction* would not. **I wouldn't know** *informal* (as is to be expected) I do not know.

wound[1] • *noun* **1** an injury done to living tissue by a cut or blow etc., esp. beyond the cutting or piercing of the skin. **2** an injury to a person's reputation or a pain inflicted on a person's feelings. • *verb* inflict a wound on. [Say WOOND]

wound[2] *past and past participle of* WIND[2]. [Rhymes with SOUND]

wounded *noun* suffering from or damaged by a wound or wounds: *wounded soldiers* ◊ *wounded feelings*.

wove *past of* WEAVE[1].

woven *past participle of* WEAVE[1].

wow • *interjection* expressing astonishment or admiration. • *verb slang* impress or excite greatly.

WP *abbreviation* word processor or processing.

Wpg. *abbreviation* Winnipeg.

w.p.m. *abbreviation* words per minute.

> **SPELL CHECK**
> **wrack, rack**   [ABC ✓]
>
> The spelling is **rack** for "storage rack", "rack up points", "rack your brains", and "rack and ruin".

wrack[1] *noun* **1** seaweed cast up or growing on the shore. **2** a wreck or wreckage.

wrack[2] *var. of.* RACK *verb*.

wraith *noun* **1** a ghost or apparition. **2** the spectral appearance of a living person supposed to portend that person's death. ▶ **wraithlike** *adjective* [Say RAITH]

wrangle • *noun* a heated or prolonged dispute. • *verb* (**wrangles, wrangled, wrangling**) **1** engage in a wrangle. **2** get (a thing) from a person by argument or persuasion. **3** herd (horses, cattle, etc.).

wrangler *noun* **1** a cowboy. **2** a person who wrangles. **3** a person who supervises and handles animals used on a film set.

wrangling *noun* prolonged argument, debate, or dispute: *there has been considerable political wrangling over the site of the proposed new arena*.

wrap • *verb* (**wraps, wrapped, wrapping**) **1** envelop in folded or soft encircling material. **2 a** arrange or draw (a pliant covering) around (a person). **b** use (oneself or a part of one's body) to embrace a person: *wrapped her arms around his neck*. **3** (foll. by *around*) *slang* crash (a vehicle) into a stationary object. **4** finish filming (a movie etc.). **5** *Computing* **a** cause (a word or other unit of text) to be carried over to a new line automatically as the right margin is reached. **b** (of a word etc.) be so carried over. • *noun* **1** a shawl or scarf or other such addition to clothing. **2** material used for wrapping. **3** the completion of the filming of a movie etc. **take the wraps off** disclose. **under wraps** in secrecy. **wrapped up in** engrossed or absorbed in. **wrap up 1** finish off, bring to completion: *wrapped up the deal in two days*. **2** put on warm clothes: *wrap up well*.

wraparound • *adjective* **1** (of a garment, esp. a woman's skirt or top) designed to wrap around the body. **2** curving or extending around at the edges. • *noun* anything that wraps around.

wrapper *noun* **1** a thing in which something is wrapped, esp. a flexible piece of paper etc. forming a protective covering for a product: *candy wrappers*. **2** a cover enclosing a newspaper or similar packet for mailing. **3** a paper cover of a book or magazine, usu. detachable.

wrapping *noun* (often in *plural*) material used to wrap; wrappers, wrapping paper, etc.

wrapping paper *noun* strong or decorative paper for wrapping gifts etc.

wrap-up • *noun* a summary, esp. of news; a conclusion: *a wrap-up of the day's events*. • *adjective* that concludes or sums up a program, book, etc.

wrath *noun literary* extreme anger: *the government felt the wrath of the electorate*. ▶ **wrathful** *adjective* **wrathfully** *adverb* [Say RATH]

wreak *verb* (**wreaks, wreaked, wreaking**) **1** give expression or vent to (vengeance, anger etc.): *he was determined to wreak vengeance on those who had betrayed him*. **2** cause (damage etc.): *their policies would wreak havoc on the economy*. [Say REEK]

wreath *noun* (*plural* **wreaths**) **1** flowers or leaves fastened in a ring esp. as an ornament for a person's head or a building or for laying on a grave etc. as a mark of honour or respect. **2** (foll. by *of*) something shaped like a wreath: *wreaths of cloud*. [Say REETH]

wreathe *verb* (**wreathes, wreathed, wreathing**) encircle as, with, or like a wreath. [Say REETHE (with the TH of *BATHE*)]

wreck • *noun* **1 a** the destruction or disablement esp. of a ship. **b** a ship that has suffered a wreck: *the shores are strewn with wrecks*. **2** a greatly damaged or disabled building, vehicle, aircraft, etc. **3** a person whose health, esp. mental health, has been damaged or destroyed. **4** a crash or collision on a road, railway, etc. **5** (foll. by *of*) a wretched remnant or disorganized set of remains. • *verb* **1** cause the wreck of (a ship etc.);

W

damage or destroy. **2** completely ruin (hopes, chances, etc.). **3** suffer a wreck. **4** deal with wrecked vehicles etc.

wreckage *noun* **1** wrecked material. **2** the remnants of a wreck. **3** the action or process of wrecking.

wrecked *adjective* **1** involved in a shipwreck: *wrecked sailors*. **2** *informal* intoxicated by alcohol or drugs.

wrecker *noun* **1** a person or thing that wrecks or destroys. **2** a person employed in demolition, or in recovering a wrecked ship or its contents. **3** a person who breaks up damaged vehicles for spare parts and scrap.

wrecking ball *noun* (also **wrecker's ball**) a heavy metal ball which may be swung from a crane into a building to demolish it.

wrecking bar *noun* a steel bar with one end chisel-shaped for prying and the other end bent and split to form a claw.

wren *noun* **1** a small usu. brown short-winged songbird with an erect tail, of North America and Eurasia. **2** (**Wren**) *hist.* (in Canada) a member of the Women's Royal Canadian Naval Service.

wrench • *noun* (*plural* **wrenches**) **1** a violent twist or oblique pull or act of tearing off. **2** a tool for gripping and turning a nut on a bolt etc. **3** a painful uprooting or parting: *it will be a real wrench to leave after eight years*. • *verb* (**wrenches, wrenched, wrenching**) **1** twist or pull violently around or sideways. **2** pull off with a wrench. **3** injure (a limb, etc.) by undue twisting or stretching.

wrest *verb* **1** force or wrench away from a person's grasp. **2** obtain by effort or with difficulty: *the Liberals' inability to wrest Prairie seats away from Diefenbaker's Conservatives cost Pearson majority governments in 1963 and 1965*.

wrestle • *noun* **1** a contest in which two opponents grapple and try to throw each other to the ground esp. as an athletic sport under a code of rules. **2** a hard struggle. • *verb* (**wrestles, wrestled, wrestling**) **1** take part in a wrestle. **2** fight (a person) in a wrestle: *wrestled his opponent to the ground*. **3 a** struggle, contend. **b** do one's utmost to deal with (a task, difficulty, etc.). ▶ **wrestler** *noun* **wrestling** *noun*

wretch *noun* (*plural* **wretches**) **1** an unfortunate or unhappy person. **2** often *jocular* an evil or wicked person.

wretched *adjective* **1** unhappy or miserable. **2** of very poor quality. **3** ill or unwell. **4** despicable. **5** used to express annoyance: *this wretched car refuses to start*. ▶ **wretchedly** *adverb* **wretchedness** *noun* [Say RETCH id]

wriggle • *verb* (**wriggles, wriggled, wriggling**) **1** twist or turn with short writhing movements. **2** move or go in this way: *wriggled into the corner*. **3** make (one's way) by wriggling. • *noun* an act of wriggling. PHRASES **wriggle out of** *informal* avoid on a contrived pretext. ▶ **wriggler** *noun* **wriggly** *adjective*

wring *verb* (**wrings, wrung, wringing**) **1** squeeze and twist something to force liquid from it: *she wrung the cloth out in the sink* ◊ *I wrung out the excess water*. **2** break something by twisting it forcibly. **3** squeeze tightly, esp. with sincere emotion: *he wrung my hand*. **4** obtain with difficulty or effort: *few concessions were wrung from the government*. **5** cause pain or distress to: *the letter must have wrung her heart*. PHRASES **wring one's hands** clasp them as a gesture of great distress. **wring the neck of** kill (a chicken etc.) by twisting its neck.

wringer *noun* a device for wringing water from washed clothes etc. PHRASES **put through the wringer** *informal* subject to a very stressful experience.

wrinkle • *noun* **1** a slight crease or depression in the skin such as is produced by age. **2** a similar mark in another flexible surface. **3** *informal* a minor difficulty; a snag. **4** a clever innovation in technique etc.: *a new marketing wrinkle in automobile dealers' never-ending quest to find better ways to sell cars*. • *verb* (**wrinkles, wrinkled, wrinkling**) **1** make wrinkles in. **2** form wrinkles; become marked with wrinkles. ▶ **wrinkled** *adjective*

wrinkly *adjective* (**wrinklier, wrinkliest**) having many wrinkles.

wrist *noun* **1** the joint connecting the hand with the forearm. **2** the part of a garment covering the wrist. PHRASES **slap on the wrist** a mild rebuke or reprimand.

wristband *noun* **1** a band forming or concealing the end of a shirt sleeve; a cuff. **2** a strip of material worn around the wrist to absorb sweat. **3** a strap or band attached to a watch worn around the wrist. **4** a bracelet used for identification, e.g. while in hospital or as admission to an event etc.

wrist shot *noun Hockey* a shot taken by sweeping the puck along the ice before releasing it.

wristwatch *noun* a watch worn on a strap around the wrist.

writ¹ *noun* **1** a form of written command in the name of a sovereign, court, government, etc., to act or abstain from acting in some way. **2** a government document ordering an election. PHRASES **serve a writ on** deliver a writ to (a person).

writ² PHRASES **writ large** in magnified or emphasized form: *this form of anglophone nationalism was in fact Ontario regionalism writ large*.

W

write *verb* (**writes**; *past* **wrote**; *past participle* **written**; **writing**) **1** mark paper or some other surface by means of a pen, pencil, etc., with symbols, letters, or words. **2** form (such symbols etc.). **3** form the symbols that represent or constitute (a word or sentence, or a document etc.). **4** fill or complete (a sheet, cheque, etc.) with writing. **5** record (data) in a computer memory. **6** indicate (a quality or condition) by one's or its appearance: *guilt was written on his face*. **7** compose (a text, article, novel, etc.) for written or printed reproduction or publication; put into literary etc. form and set down in writing. **8** be engaged in composing a text, article, etc.: *writes for the local newspaper*. **9 a** (foll. by *to*) write and send a letter (to a recipient). **b** communicate by writing: *she hardly ever writes*. **10** write and send a letter to (a person): *wrote him last week*. **11** convey (news, information, etc.) by letter: *wrote that they would arrive next Friday*. **12** *Cdn & South Africa* take (an exam or test). **13** write in a cursive hand, as opposed to printing individual letters. **14** state in written or printed form: *it is written that*. **15** cause to be recorded. **16** (foll. by *into, out of*) include or exclude (a character or episode) in a story by suitable changes of the text. PHRASES **nothing to write home about**

informal of little interest or value. **write down 1** record or take note of in writing. **2** write as if for those considered inferior. **3** reduce the nominal value of (stock, goods, etc.). **write in** send a suggestion, query, etc., in writing to an organization, esp. a broadcasting station. **write off 1** write and send a letter. **2** cancel the record of (a bad debt etc.); acknowledge the loss of or failure to recover (an asset). **3** damage (a vehicle etc.) so badly that it cannot be repaired. **4** dismiss as insignificant. **write out 1** write in full or in finished form. **2** exhaust (oneself) by writing. **write up 1** write a full account of. **2** praise or bring to public attention in writing: *the concert was written up in the newspapers*.

writedown *noun* a reduction in the estimated or nominal value of stock, assets, etc.

write-off *noun* **1** a thing written off, esp. a vehicle too badly damaged to be repaired. **2** a person or thing that is given up as being hopeless etc.: *the entire weekend was a write-off*. **3** an act of cancelling a debt because there is no chance that it will be paid.

writer *noun* **1** one who writes or has written something. **2** one who writes professionally, esp. books or screenplays.

writer-in-residence *noun* a writer holding a usu. temporary residential post in a university etc. in order to share his or her professional insights with students and faculty.

writerly *adjective* **1** characteristic of a professional author. **2** consciously literary.

writer's block *noun* a (usu. temporary) inability to express thoughts in writing due to lack of inspiration.

writer's cramp *noun* a muscular spasm in the hands due to excessive writing.

write-up *noun informal* a written account, a review.

writhe *verb* (**writhes, writhed, writhing**) **1** twist or roll oneself about in or as if suffer in acute pain. **2** suffer severe mental discomfort or embarrassment: *writhed with shame*. [Say RITHE (with the I of *RIDE* and the TH of *BATHE*)]

writing *noun* **1** a group or sequence of letters or symbols. **2** = HANDWRITING. **3** (usu. in *plural*) a piece of literary work done; a book, article, etc. **4** the work or profession of a writer. **PHRASES in writing** in written form: *give me your request in writing*. **the writing is on the wall** *see* HANDWRITING.

writing desk *noun* a desk for writing at, esp. with compartments for papers etc.

written • *verb* past participle of WRITE. • *adjective* that has been or is to be done in writing: *a written agreement*.

wrong • *adjective* **1** mistaken; not true. **2** unsuitable; less or least desirable. **3** contrary to law or morality. **4** out of order, in or into a bad or abnormal condition. • *adverb* in a wrong manner or direction; with an incorrect result: *guessed wrong*. • *noun* **1** what is morally wrong; a wrong action. **2** injustice; unjust action or treatment: *suffer wrong*. • *verb* **1** treat unjustly; do wrong to. **2** mistakenly attribute bad motives to; discredit. **PHRASES do wrong** commit sin; transgress, offend. **do wrong to** malign or mistreat (a person). **get in wrong with** incur the dislike or

disapproval of (a person). **get off on the wrong foot** begin badly; make a bad start. **get wrong 1** misunderstand (a person, statement, etc.). **2** obtain an incorrect answer to. **get** (or **get hold of**) **the wrong end of the stick** misunderstand completely. **go down the wrong way** (of food) enter the windpipe instead of the gullet. **go wrong 1** take the wrong path. **2** stop functioning properly. **3** depart from virtuous or suitable behaviour. **in the wrong** responsible for a quarrel, mistake, or offence. **on the wrong side of 1** out of favour with (a person). **2** somewhat more than (a stated age). **wrong side out** inside out. **wrong way round** in the opposite or reverse of the normal or desirable orientation or sequence etc.

wrongdoer *noun* a person who behaves immorally or illegally. ▶ **wrongdoing** *noun*

wrongful *adjective* **1** characterized by unfairness or injustice. **2** contrary to law. **3** not entitled to the position etc. occupied. ▶ **wrongfully** *adverb*

wrong-headed *adjective* perverse and obstinate. ▶ **wrong-headedness** *noun*

wrongly *adverb* in a way that is unfair, immoral or not correct: *she was wrongly accused of stealing* ◊ *he assumed, wrongly, that she did not care* ◊ *the sentence had been wrongly translated* ◊ *they knew they had acted wrongly*.

wrongness *noun* the quality or state of being wrong or incorrect: *the wrongness of racism and colonialism is taken to be self-evident*.

wrote *past of* WRITE. **PHRASES that's all she wrote** *informal* that's it; that's the end.

wrought *adjective* **1** (of metals) beaten out or shaped by hammering. **2** made, crafted: *a well-wrought composition*. [Say ROT]

wrought iron *noun* a tough form of iron suitable for forging, hammering, or rolling, not for casting.

wrung *past and past participle of* WRING. **PHRASES wrung out** exhausted.

wry *adjective* (**wryer, wryest** or **wrier, wriest**) **1** (of humour) dry and mocking. **2** (of a face or smile etc.) contorted in disappointment, mockery, etc. ▶ **wryly** *adverb* **wryness** *noun* [Say RYE]

wt. *abbreviation* weight.

WTO *abbreviation* World Trade Organization.

wunderkind *noun informal* a person who achieves great success while relatively young. [Say VOONDER kint]

wuss *noun* (*plural* **wusses**) (also **wussy** *plural* **wussies**) *slang* an inept, feeble, or cowardly person. ▶ **wussy** *adjective* [Say WOOSS (with OO as in *WOOL*)]

WW I *abbreviation* World War I.

WW II *abbreviation* World War II.

WWW *abbreviation* World Wide Web.

Wyandot (also **Wyandotte** esp. in sense 2 of *noun*) • *noun* **1 a** a member of a North American Aboriginal people originally of Ontario, now living esp. in Oklahoma. **b** the Iroquoian language of this people. **2** a breed of medium-sized domestic fowl. • *adjective* of or relating to the Wyandots or their language or culture. [Say WHY in dot]

WYSIWYG *adjective* (also **wysiwyg**) *Computing* denoting the representation of text onscreen in a form looking exactly like the printout. [Say WIZZY wig]

W

Xx

X *noun* (also **x**) (*plural* **Xs** or **X's**) **1** the twenty-fourth letter of the alphabet. **2** (as a Roman numeral) ten. **3** (usu. **x**) *Algebra* the first unknown quantity. **4** *Math* the first coordinate. **5** an unknown or unspecified number or person etc. **6** a cross-shaped symbol esp. used: **a** to indicate position: *X marks the spot.* **b** to indicate incorrectness. **c** to symbolize a kiss. **d** to symbolize a vote. **e** as the signature of a person who cannot write.

X-C *abbreviation* (also **XC**, **X-country**) cross-country.

X chromosome *noun* a sex chromosome of which the number in female cells is twice that in male cells.

Xe *symbol* xenon.

xeno- *combining form* **1 a** foreign. **b** a foreigner. **2** other. [Say ZENNO or ZEENO]

xenon *noun* a heavy colourless odourless inert gaseous element occurring in traces in the atmosphere and used in fluorescent lamps. [Say ZEN on]

xenophobe *noun* a person who dislikes foreigners. ▶ **xenophobia** *noun* **xenophobic** *adjective* [Say ZENNA fobe, zenna FOE bee uh]

Xer *noun* *informal* a member of Generation X. [Say ECKS er]

xeriscape *noun* **1** a style of landscape design requiring little or no irrigation or other maintenance, used in arid regions. **2** a garden or landscape created in such a style. [Say ZERRA scape]

xeriscaping *noun* a landscaping method requiring little or no irrigation or other maintenance, used in arid regions. [Say ZERRA scape ing]

xerographic *adjective* of or using a dry copying process in which black or coloured powder adheres to parts of a surface remaining electrically charged after exposure of the surface to light from an image of the document to be copied. [Say zeera GRAPHIC]

xerography *noun* a dry copying process in which black or coloured powder adheres to parts of a surface remaining electrically charged after exposure of the surface to light from an image of the document to be copied. [Say zee ROGRA fee]

Xerox ● *noun* (*plural* **Xeroxes**) *proprietary* **1** a photocopier. **2** a photocopy. ● *verb* (**xerox**, **xeroxes**, **xeroxed**, **xeroxing**) photocopy. [Say ZEE rocks]

Xhosa ● *noun* **1** (*plural* **Xhosa** or **Xhosas**) a member of a Bantu-speaking people forming the second largest ethnic group in South Africa after the Zulus. **2** the language of this people, forming part of the Nguni language group. ● *adjective* of this people or language. [Say CO suh or COSSA]

XL *abbreviation* (esp. of clothing) extra large.

Xmas *noun* *informal* = CHRISTMAS. [Say CHRISTMAS or ECKS mus]

X-rated *adjective* indecent, pornographic.

X-ray (also **x-ray**) ● *noun* **1** (in *plural*) electromagnetic radiation of short wavelength, able to pass through opaque bodies. **2** an image made by passing X-rays through something onto a photographic plate. ● *verb* photograph, examine, or treat with X-rays.

XS *abbreviation* (esp. of clothing) extra small.

X's and O's *noun* = TIC-TAC-TOE.

Xwe Nal Mewx *noun & adjective* = SNE NAY MUXW.

XXL *abbreviation* (esp. of clothing) extra, extra large.

xylem *noun* *Botany* the woody tissue in the stem of a plant (*compare* PHLOEM). [Say ZYE lem]

xylene *noun* a volatile liquid hydrocarbon obtained from wood etc., used in fuels and solvents and in chemical synthesis. [Say ZYE leen]

xylophone *noun* a musical instrument of wooden or metal bars of increasing length struck with a small hammer. ▶ **xylophonist** *noun* [Say ZYE luh phone]

Yy

Y¹ *noun* (also **y**) (*plural* **Ys** or **Y's**) **1** the twenty-fifth letter of the alphabet. **2** (usu. **y**) *Algebra* the second unknown quantity. **3** *Math* the second coordinate. **4 a** a Y-shaped thing. **b** a forked clamp or support.

Y² *abbreviation* (also **Y.**) **1** yen. **2 a** = YMCA. **b** = YWCA. **c** = YMHA. **d** = YWHA.

Y³ *symbol* yttrium.

y. *abbreviation* year(s).

yacht • *noun* **1** a light sailing vessel, esp. equipped for racing. **2** a larger usu. power-driven vessel equipped for cruising. • *verb* race or cruise in a yacht. ▶ **yachting** *noun* [Say YOT]

yachtsman *noun* (*plural* **yachtsmen**) a person who sails yachts. [Say YOTS m'n]

yack *noun & verb* (also **yackety-yack**) *informal* = YAK *noun 2, verb.*

yaffle *noun* Cdn (Nfld) an armful or small load, esp. of cod.

yahoo¹ • *noun* (*plural* **yahoos**) a coarse, brutish, or uncivilized person. • *adjective* characteristic of a yahoo.

yahoo² *interjection* an exclamation of excitement.

Yahweh *noun* (also **Yahveh**) a form of the Hebrew name of God in the Bible. [Say YAW way or YAW vay]

Yajur-Veda one of the four Hindu Vedas, a collection of sacrificial formulas in early Sanskrit used in the Vedic religion by the priest in charge of sacrificial ritual. [Say yuh joor VAY duh or yuh joor VEEDA]

yak • *noun* **1** a large domesticated ox with shaggy hair, humped shoulders, and large horns, used in Tibet as a pack animal and for its milk, meat, and hide. **2** *informal* often *derogatory* trivial or unduly persistent talk. • *verb* (**yaks**, **yakked**, **yakking**) *informal* often *derogatory* chatter.

yakuza *noun* (*plural* **yakuza**) **1** a member of a Japanese organized crime gang. **2** (in *plural*) Japanese organized crime gangs. [Say yuh COOZA]

yam *noun* **1** a tropical or subtropical climbing plant bearing edible starchy tubers. **2** esp. *US* a sweet potato.

yammer *verb* *informal* **1** grumble. **2 a** make a loud noise. **b** talk incessantly with little substance. **3** utter complainingly. **4** (esp. of an animal) howl or wail.

yang *noun* (in Chinese philosophy) the active male principle of the universe (*compare* YIN).

Yank *noun* *informal* often *derogatory* a resident of the US.

yank *informal* • *verb* **1** pull sharply or with a jerk. **2** remove, withdraw, or cancel abruptly. • *noun* a sudden hard pull.

Yankee *informal* • *noun* **1** often *derogatory* = YANK. **2** *US* an inhabitant of New England or one of the northern States. **3** *hist.* a Federal soldier in the American Civil War. • *adjective* of or characteristic of a Yankee.

yap • *verb* (**yaps**, **yapped**, **yapping**) **1** bark shrilly or fussily. **2** *informal* talk noisily or complainingly. • *noun* **1** a shrill bark; a yelp. **2** idle or tiresome chatter. **3** *slang* the mouth: *shut your yap!* ▶ **yapper** *noun*

yappy *adjective* (**yappier**, **yappiest**) (of a dog) inclined to yap.

yard¹ *noun* **1** a unit of linear measure equal to 3 feet (0.9144 metre). **2** a square or cubic yard, esp. of sand, topsoil, etc. **3** a cylindrical spar tapering to each end slung across a mast for a sail to hang from. **4** (in *plural*; foll. by *of*) *informal* a great length or amount.

yard² • *noun* **1** a piece of enclosed ground, esp. attached to a building. **2** the area at the front or back of a house, usu. including a lawn and sometimes a garden. **3** an enclosed area used for a particular business or purpose: *lumberyard.* **4** = RAILWAY YARD. **5** a place where deer or moose etc. congregate, esp. during the winter months. **6** *Forestry* = LANDING 3. • *verb* **1** put (cattle) into a stockyard. **2** *Forestry* move (felled trees) from the felling site to the landing.

yardage *noun* **1** a number of yards of material etc. **2** a distance measured in yards. [Say YARD idge]

yarder *noun* an engine or vehicle used to move logs from the bush to a yard, landing, etc.

yard sale *noun* a sale of used household items, held in the front yard of a house.

yardstick *noun* **1** a measuring rod a yard long, usu. divided into inches etc. **2** a standard used for comparison.

yardwork *noun* gardening and other maintenance work required in the yard of a residence.

yarmulke *noun* (also **yarmulka**) a skullcap worn by Jewish men. [Say YAR mull kuh]

yarn • *noun* **1** any spun thread, esp. for knitting, weaving, rope making, etc. **2** *informal* a long or rambling story or discourse. • *verb* *informal* tell yarns.

yarrow *noun* a perennial plant with feathery leaves and heads of small white or pale pink aromatic flowers.

yaw • *verb* **1** (of a ship) deviate temporarily from its course, esp. through faulty steering or adverse weather conditions. **2** (of an aircraft, missile, etc.) rotate about a vertical axis. • *noun* the yawing of a ship etc. from its course. [Rhymes with *SAW*]

yawn • *verb* **1** open the mouth wide and inhale esp. when sleepy or bored. **2** (of a chasm etc.) gape, be wide open. **3** utter or say with a yawn. • *noun* **1** an act of yawning. **2** *informal* a boring or tedious idea, activity, etc.

yawp • *noun* a harsh or hoarse cry. • *verb* make a yawp.

yaws *plural noun* (usu. treated as *singular*) a contagious tropical skin disease with large red swellings.

yay • *interjection* *slang* (also **yea**, **yeah**) expressing triumph, approval, or encouragement. • *adverb* *informal* (with adjectives of size, height, etc.) so, this: *about yay big.*

Yb *symbol* ytterbium.

Y chromosome *noun* a sex chromosome occurring only in male cells.

yd. *abbreviation* yard (measure).

ye¹ *pronoun* archaic plural of THOU¹.

ye² *adjective* pseudo-archaic = THE: *Ye Olde Book Shoppe.*

yea • *interjection* **1** yes. **2** = YAY *interjection.* • *adverb* indeed, even: *ready, yea eager.* • *noun* (*plural* **yeas**) **1** the word "yea". **2** an affirmative answer or assent, esp. in voting. **PHRASES** **the yeas have it** the affirmative votes are in the majority. [Say YAY]

yeah *adverb* *informal* **1** yes. **2** = YAY *interjection.* **PHRASES** **oh yeah?** expressing incredulity.

year *noun* **1** (also **solar year**) the time occupied by the earth in one revolution around the sun, 365 days, 5 hours, 48 minutes, and 46 seconds in length. **2** (also

calendar year) the period of 365 or 366 days from Jan. 1 to Dec. 31. **3 a** a period of the same length as this starting at any point: *four years ago today*. **b** such a period in terms of a particular activity etc. occupying its duration: *school year*. **4** (in *plural*) age: *young for his years*. **5** (usu. in *plural*) *informal* a very long time. **6** a group of students entering university etc. in the same academic year. PHRASES **in the year of Our Lord** (foll. by the year) in a specified year AD. **year in, year out** continually over a period of years.

yearbook *noun* **1** an annual publication dealing with events or aspects of the (usu. preceding) year. **2** a book published by the graduating class of a school etc., commemorating the events of the past year with stories and photographs.

year-end *noun* the end of esp. the financial year.

yearling • *noun* **1** an animal between one and two years old. **2** a racehorse in the calendar year after the year of foaling. • *adjective* a year old: *a yearling heifer*.

year-long *adjective* lasting a year or the whole year.

yearly • *adjective* **1** done or occurring once a year. **2** lasting a year. • *adverb* once a year; from year to year.

yearn *verb* have a strong emotional longing: *yearned to be with her again* ◊ *yearning for a vacation*. ▶ **yearner** *noun* **yearning** *noun & adjective* **yearningly** *adverb*

year-round • *adjective* existing etc. throughout the year. • *adverb* throughout the year.

yeast *noun* **1** a fungous substance obtained esp. from fermenting malt liquors and used to raise bread etc. **2** any of various single-celled fungi in which vegetative reproduction takes place by budding or fission.

yeast infection *noun* a fungal disease, candidiasis, esp. affecting the vagina and characterized by pain and severe itching.

yeasty *adjective* (**yeastier**, **yeastiest**) **1** of, resembling, or containing yeast. **2** in a ferment; characterized by upheaval or agitation: *their status quo was threatened by the yeasty combination of events arising out of Confederation*. **3** (of talk etc.) light and superficial: *he talked on and on in a yeasty gush*.

yech *interjection* expressing disgust.

yee-haw *interjection* expressing enthusiasm.

yeesh *interjection* *informal* expressing frustration, exasperation, etc.

yell • *noun* a loud sharp cry. • *verb* make or utter with a yell. ▶ **yelling** *noun*

yellow • *adjective* **1** of the colour between green and orange in the spectrum, of lemons, egg yolks, or gold. **2** usu. *offensive* designating or pertaining to Oriental people. **3** *informal* cowardly. **4** (of newspapers etc.) unscrupulously sensational: *in the heyday of yellow journalism, publishing moguls didn't think twice about making up "facts" if they thought it would mean a few thousand new readers*. • *noun* **1** a yellow colour or pigment. **2** a yellow light as part of a set of traffic lights, indicating that the intersection should be cleared. • *verb* make or become yellow.

yellow-bellied *adjective* cowardly.

yellow-belly *noun* (*plural* **yellow-bellies**) **1** *informal* a coward. **2** any of various fish with yellow underparts.

yellow-billed loon *noun* a loon that breeds in the Arctic and resembles the common loon but with a whitish-yellow bill.

yellow fever *noun* an often fatal tropical virus disease characterized by fever and jaundice.

yellowhammer *noun* a flicker with yellow plumage.

yellowish *adjective* somewhat yellow.

yellow jacket *noun* a wasp of the genus *Vespula*, with black and yellow markings.

Yellowknife *noun* (*plural* **Yellowknife** or **Yellowknives**) a member of an Aboriginal people

formerly living around the Coppermine River; they are now absorbed into the Chipewyan.

Yellowknifer *noun* a native of Yellowknife, NWT.

yellowlegs *noun* (*plural* **yellowlegs**) a migratory sandpiper with yellow legs.

Yellow Pages *noun* *proprietary* a telephone book or section of one printed on yellow paper, listing businesses according to the goods or services they offer.

yellowy *adjective* yellowish.

yelp • *noun* a sharp shrill cry of or as of a dog in pain or excitement. • *verb* utter a yelp.

Yemeni (*plural* **Yemenis**) • *noun* a native or inhabitant of Yemen, a country in the southern Arabian peninsula. • *adjective* of Yemen or its people. [Say YEMMA nee]

yen[1] *noun* (*plural* **yen**) the chief monetary unit of Japan.

yen[2] *noun* (*plural* **yens**) *informal* a longing or yearning.

yenta *noun* (also **yente**) *slang* a gossip or busybody.

yeoman *noun* (*plural* **yeomen**) **1** *Brit.* esp. *hist.* a man holding and cultivating a small landed estate. **2** (**Yeoman**) (also **Chief Yeoman of Signals**) a signaller in the Canadian Navy or the Royal Navy, responsible for transmitting both visual and radio signals. [Say YO min]

Yeoman of the Guard *noun* **1** a member of the British sovereign's bodyguard, wearing Tudor dress as uniform and now having only ceremonial duties. **2** (in general use) a warder in the Tower of London.

yeoman service *noun* (also **yeoman work**) efficient or useful help in need: *now late in her second term in Ottawa, the MP has performed yeoman service for the PM*.

yep *adverb & noun* *informal* = YES.

yes • *adverb* **1** used to give an affirmative response. **2** (in answer to a summons or address) an acknowledgement of one's presence. • *noun* (*plural* **yeses**) **1** an utterance of the word *yes*. **2** an affirmation or assent. **3** a vote in favour of a proposition.

yeshiva *noun* (also **yeshivah**) **1** an Orthodox Jewish college or seminary. **2** an Orthodox Jewish elementary school, teaching both religious and secular subjects. [Say yuh SHEEVA]

yes-man *noun* (*plural* **yes-men**) *informal* a weak person who always agrees with people in authority in order to gain their approval.

yesterday • *adverb* **1** on the day before today. **2** in the recent past. • *noun* **1** the day before today. **2** the recent past.

yesteryear *noun* *literary* the past: *paid tribute to movie stars of yesteryear*.

yet • *adverb* **1** as late as, or until, now or then. **2** so soon as, or by, now or then. **3** again; in addition. **4** in the remaining time available; before all is over. **5** nevertheless. **6** (as an ironic intensive at the end of a sentence) too; what's more. • *conjunction* but at the same time; but nevertheless. ■ PHRASES **nor yet** and also not: *won't listen to me nor yet to you*.

yeti *noun* (*plural* **yetis**) = ABOMINABLE SNOWMAN.

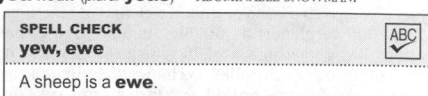

SPELL CHECK	
yew, ewe	ABC ✓

A sheep is a **ewe**.

yew *noun* **1** a dark-leaved evergreen coniferous tree or shrub, historically planted in churchyards. **2** its wood, used in cabinetmaking.

Yiddish • *noun* a language used by Jews in or from central and eastern Europe before the Holocaust, originally a German dialect with words from Hebrew and several modern languages, and written using Hebrew characters. • *adjective* of or relating to this language.

Y

yield • *verb* **1** produce. **2** give up: *yielded the fortress.* **3** (often foll. by *to*) **a** surrender. **b** give consent or change one's course of action in deference to. **4** (foll. by *to*) be inferior or confess inferiority to: *I yield to none in understanding the problem.* **5** give right-of-way to other traffic. • *noun* **1** an amount yielded or produced; an output. **2** the income produced by an investment.

yielding *adjective* **1** compliant, submissive. **2** (of a substance) able to bend; not stiff or rigid.

yikes *interjection slang* an expression of surprise or alarm.

yin *noun* (in Chinese philosophy) the passive female principle of the universe (*compare* YANG).

yin-yang *noun* the harmonious interaction of the female and male forces of the universe.

yin-yang symbol *noun* a circle divided by an S-shaped line into a dark and a light segment, representing respectively yin and yang.

yip *verb & noun* (**yips, yipped, yipping**) = YELP.

yippee *interjection* expressing delight or excitement.

yippie *noun* (also **Yippie**) a member of a group of politically active hippies, esp. in the 1960s.

YMCA *abbreviation* (*plural* **YMCAs**) Young Men's Christian Association.

YMHA *abbreviation* (*plural* **YMHAs**) Young Men's Hebrew Association.

yo *interjection slang* used to greet someone or get their attention.

yodel • *verb* (**yodels, yodelled, yodelling**) sing with melodious inarticulate sounds and frequent changes between falsetto and the normal voice, in the manner of Swiss and Austrian mountaineers. • *noun* a yodelling cry. ▶ **yodeller** *noun* [Say YODE 'll]

yoga *noun* **1** a Hindu system of philosophic meditation and asceticism designed to effect reunion with the universal spirit. **2** a system of esp. posture and breathing exercises used to attain control of the body and mind.

yogi *noun* (*plural* **yogis**) a person proficient in yoga.

yogic *adjective* of or pertaining to yoga: *yogic breathing.*

yogourt *noun* (also **yoghurt, yogurt**) a semi-solid slightly tart food prepared from milk fermented with added bacteria, usu. flavoured with fruit.

SPELL CHECK
yoke, yolk

The centre of an egg is a **yolk**.

yoke • *noun* **1** a wooden crosspiece fastened over the necks of two oxen etc. and attached to the plow or wagon to be drawn. **2** (*plural* **yoke** or **yokes**) a pair (of oxen etc.). **3** an object like a yoke in form or function, e.g. a wooden bar held across the shoulders for carrying a pair of pails. **4** a fitted part of a garment, usu. placed across the shoulders or around the hips, from which the rest hangs. **5** something that exercises control in an oppressive or burdensome manner: *throwing off the yoke of tyranny.* **6** a bond or union, esp. that of marriage. **7** (in an airplane) a double handle somewhat resembling a steering wheel, by which the elevators of the tailplane are controlled to change the pitch of the plane. • *verb* (**yokes, yoked, yoking**) **1** put a yoke on. **2** couple or unite (a pair). **3** (foll. by *to*) link (one thing) to (another). **4** match or work together.

yokel *noun* a country bumpkin. [Say YOKE 'll]

SPELL CHECK
yolk, yoke

A harness or a burden is a **yoke**.

yolk *noun* **1** the yellow inner part of an egg that

nourishes the young before it hatches. **2** *Biology* the corresponding part of any animal ovum. ▶ **yolked** *adjective* (also in *combination*) **yolky** *adjective*

Yom Kippur *noun* the most solemn Jewish religious holiday, eight days after the Jewish New Year, marked by fasting and repentance. [Say yom ki POOR]

yon *adjective & adverb* yonder.

yonder • *adverb* over there; at some distance in that direction. • *adjective* situated yonder. • *noun* the distance; a remote place: *the wild blue yonder.*

yoo-hoo *interjection* used to attract a person's attention.

yore *noun* PHRASES **of yore** formerly; in or of old days: *mermaids sighted by seamen in days of yore may have been small aquatic mammals known as manatees.*

York boat *noun Cdn hist.* a large, shallow-draft inland cargo boat used esp. in the Prairies for the fur trade.

Yorkshire pudding *noun* a puffy baked mixture of flour, eggs, and milk, usu. eaten with roast beef. [Say YORK sher]

Yoruba • *noun* **1** (*plural* **Yorubas** or **Yoruba**) a member of a people inhabiting the west coast of Africa, esp. Nigeria. **2** the language of this people. • *adjective* of the Yorubas or their language. [Say YORRA buh]

SPELL CHECK
you, ewe, yew

A female sheep is a **ewe**. The tree is a **yew**.

you • *pronoun* **1** used with reference to the person or persons addressed or one such person and one or more associated persons. **2** (with a noun) in an exclamatory statement: *you fools!* **3** (in general statements) one, a person, anyone, or everyone. • *noun* the personality or essential nature of the person or persons being addressed: *that dress just isn't you.* PHRASES **you and yours** you together with your family, property, etc.

you-all *pronoun US informal* you; all of you.

you'd *contraction* **1** you had. **2** you would.

you-know-what *noun* (also **you-know-who**) a thing or person unspecified but understood.

you'll *contraction* you will; you shall.

young • *adjective* (**younger, youngest**) **1** not far advanced in life, development, or existence; not yet old. **2 a** immature or inexperienced. **b** youthful. **3** felt in or characteristic of youth: *young love.* **4** representing young people: *Young Liberals.* **5** distinguishing a son from his father: *young Jones.* **6** (**younger**) distinguishing one person from another of the same name: *the younger Pitt.* • *noun* offspring, esp. of animals before or soon after birth. PHRASES **with young** (of an animal) pregnant.

young blood *noun* a younger member or members of a group, esp. representing an invigorating force with fresh new ideas.

youngish *adjective* somewhat young.

young offender *noun* a young criminal, esp. (in Canada) one older than 12 and younger than 18.

youngster *noun* a child or young person.

Young Turk *noun* **1** a member of a group of reformers in the Ottoman Empire who carried out the revolution of 1908. **2** a young person eager for radical change to the established order: *Simon was a Young Turk and social radical who, by temperament and ideology, would try to overturn established truth.*

young 'un *noun informal* a youngster.

your *possessive adjective* **1** of or belonging to you or yourself or yourselves: *your house.* **2** (**Your**) (in titles) that you are: *Your Majesty.* **3** *informal* usu. *derogatory* much talked of; well known: *why not ask your self-styled "expert".*

Y

4 belonging to or associated with an unspecified person: *the second door on your left*.

you're *contraction* you are.

yours *possessive pronoun* **1** the one or ones belonging to or associated with you: *it is yours* ◊ *yours are over there*. **2** your letter: *yours of the 10th*. **3** introducing a formula ending a letter: *yours sincerely*. PHRASES **of yours** of or belonging to you: *a friend of yours*.

GRAMMAR CHECK
yourself

Do not misuse **yourself** or **yourselves**. Sentences like *The team and yourself will have a tough game tonight* and *There will be an assembly for your teachers and yourselves* are not recommended. It is better to say *You and the team will have a tough game tonight* and *There will be an assembly for you and your teachers*. Reserve **yourself** for reflexive uses like *You can help yourself to a drink* or emphatic ones like *You yourself had problems when you were her age*.

---

yourself *pronoun (plural* **yourselves**) **1 a** *emphatic form* of YOU. **b** *reflexive form* of YOU. **2** in your normal state of body or mind: *are quite yourself again*. PHRASES **be yourself** act in your normal, unconstrained manner.

yours truly *noun informal* myself, me; I: *has a picture of yours truly on the cover*. PHRASES **yours truly** used as a conventional formula preceding a signature.

youse *pronoun* (also **yous**) *non-standard* you (usu. more than one person).

youth *noun (plural* **youths**) **1** the state of being young; the period between childhood and adult age. **2** the vigour or enthusiasm, inexperience, or other characteristic of this period. **3** an early stage of development etc. **4** a young person. **5** (treated as *plural*) young people collectively.

youth court *noun* a court which has jurisdiction over all cases involving young offenders or youths.

youthful *adjective* **1** young, esp. in appearance or manner. **2** having the characteristics of youth: *youthful impatience*. **3** having the freshness of youth: *a youthful complexion*. ▶ **youthfully** *adverb* **youthfulness** *noun*

youth hostel *noun* a place where (esp. young) travellers can stay cheaply for the night.

you've *contraction* you have.

yowl • *noun* a loud wailing cry of or as of a cat or dog in pain or distress. • *verb* utter a yowl.

yo-yo • *noun (plural* **yo-yos**) **1** a toy consisting of a pair of discs with a deep groove between them in which string is attached and wound, and which can be spun alternately downward and upward by its weight and momentum as the string unwinds and rewinds. **2** a thing that repeatedly falls and rises again. **3** *slang* a stupid or incompetent person. • *adjective* characterized by repeated upward and downward movement, fluctuation, etc.: *yo-yo dieting*. • *verb* (**yo-yoes**, **yo-yoed**, **yo-yoing**) alternate between two positions or situations, esp. move up and down: *stock prices have yo-yoed* ◊ *she is constantly on the move, yo-yoing from one part of the airport to another*.

yr. *abbreviation* **1** year(s). **2** your.

yrs. *abbreviation* **1** years. **2** yours.

YST *abbreviation* Yukon Standard Time.

YT *abbreviation* **1** Yukon Territory. **2** YUKON TIME.

YTD *abbreviation* year to date.

ytterbium *noun* a silvery metallic element occurring naturally as various isotopes. [Say it TERBY um]

yttrium *noun* a greyish metallic element resembling the lanthanides, occurring naturally in uranium ores and used in making superconductors. [Say ITTRY um]

yuan *noun (plural* **yuan**) the chief monetary unit of China. [Say yoo ON]

yucca *noun (plural* **yuccas**) a North American plant with white flowers and sword-like leaves. [Say YUCKA]

yuck[1] *interjection slang* an expression of strong distaste or disgust.

yuck[2] *verb & noun* = YUK[1].

yucky *adjective* (**yuckier**, **yuckiest**) *slang* **1** messy, repellent. **2** sickly, sentimental. **3** distasteful, contemptible.

Yugoslav (also **Yugoslavian**) • *noun* **1** a native or national of Yugoslavia, a country in southeastern Europe. **2** a person of Yugoslav descent. • *adjective* of or relating to Yugoslavia or its people. [Say YOOGA slov or YOOGA slav]

yuk[1] *informal* • *verb* (**yuks**, **yukked**, **yukking**) **1** laugh heartily. **2** fool around: *yuk it up*. • *noun* **1** a hearty laugh. **2** something, such as a joke, that causes hearty laughter.

yuk[2] = YUCK[1].

yukky (**yukkier**, **yukkiest**) = YUCKY.

Yukoner *noun* a native or inhabitant of the Yukon Territory.

Yukon Gold *noun* a large, yellow-fleshed, smooth-skinned, early-maturing variety of potato.

Yukon stove *noun Cdn* (*North*) a simple stove for cooking and heating, esp. an oil drum on legs.

Yukon Time *noun* = PACIFIC TIME.

yule *noun* (also **yuletide**) *archaic* or *literary* the Christmas festival.

yule log *noun* **1** a large log burned in the hearth on Christmas Eve. **2** a log-shaped rolled cake eaten at Christmas, usu. with icing resembling bark.

yum *interjection* (also **yum-yum**) expressing pleasure from eating or the prospect of eating.

yummy *adjective* (**yummier**, **yummiest**) *informal* tasty, delicious.

yup *noun* = YUPPIE.

Yupik • *noun* **1** a member of a group of Aboriginal peoples living in coastal areas of Alaska and northeastern Siberia. **2** any of the languages spoken by the Yupik. • *adjective* of or relating to this people or their culture or language. [Say YOU pick]

yuppie *noun (plural* **yuppies**) *informal*, usu. *derogatory* a young, affluent, middle-class professional person, esp. one working in a city and characterized by careerism and desire for trendy status symbols. ▶ **yuppiedom** *noun*

yuppification *noun* the act of yuppifying: *disappointed by the yuppification of the old neighbourhood*. [Say yup i fi CAY sh'n]

yuppify *verb* (**yuppifies**, **yuppified**, **yuppifying**) (esp. as **yuppified** *adjective*) *informal* make characteristic of yuppies. [Say YUPPA fie]

yurt *noun* a circular tent of felt, skins, etc., on a collapsible framework, used by nomads in Mongolia and Siberia.

YWCA *abbreviation* (*plural* **YWCAs**) Young Women's Christian Association.

YWHA *abbreviation* (*plural* **YWHAs**) Young Women's Hebrew Association.

Zz

Z *noun* (also **z**) (*plural* **Zs** or **Z's**) **1** the twenty-sixth letter of the alphabet. **2** (usu. **z**) *Algebra* the third unknown quantity. **3** *Math* the third coordinate. **4** *Chemistry* atomic number. [Say ZED or ZEE]

zabaglione *noun* (*plural* **zabagliones**) a dessert consisting of egg yolks, sugar, and (esp. Marsala) wine whipped to a frothy texture over low heat, served warm or cold. [Say za BA lee oh nay]

zaftig *adjective informal* (of a woman) plump; having a full, rounded figure. [Say ZAFF tig]

zag • *noun* a sharp change of direction in a zigzag course. • *verb* (**zags, zagged, zagging**) perform a zag.

Zairean (also **Zairian**) • *noun* a native or inhabitant of Zaire (now Congo) in central Africa. • *adjective* of or relating to Zaire (now Congo) or its people. [Say za EERY in]

Zambian • *noun* a native or inhabitant of Zambia in central Africa. • *adjective* of or relating to Zambia or its people. [Say ZAMBY in]

Zamboni *noun* (*plural* **Zambonis**) *proprietary* a tractor-like machine for shaving the ice of a rink and spraying water on it to provide a clean smooth surface. [Say zam BONEY]

zanily *adverb* in a zany or ridiculous way. [Say ZANE uh lee]

zaniness *noun* the quality of being zany. [Say ZANY niss]

zany • *adjective* (**zanier, zaniest**) comically idiotic; crazily ridiculous. • *noun* (*plural* **zanies**) a foolish or eccentric person; a buffoon.

zap *slang* • *verb* (**zaps, zapped, zapping**) **1 a** kill or destroy; deal a sudden blow to. **b** hit forcibly. **2 a** move quickly and vigorously. **b** use a remote control to move rapidly between television channels. **3** overwhelm emotionally. **4** *Computing* erase or change (a file etc.). **5 a** (foll. by *through*) fast-forward or rewind a videotape to skip a section. **b** delete or skip over (a television commercial or commercials), e.g. by fast-forwarding a videotape. **6** *informal* cook (food) in a microwave. • *noun* **1** energy, vigour. **2 a** strong emotional effect. • *interjection* expressing the sound or impact of a bullet, ray gun, etc., or any sudden event.

zappable *adjective informal* microwaveable.

zapper *noun slang* **1** a remote control for a television, VCR, etc. **2** a device, person, or technique that kills or does away with something, esp. insects.

zeal *noun* **1** earnestness or fervour in advancing a cause: *has suggested that Lutheran zeal in 16th-century Germany was most concentrated in areas of Catholic strength.* **2** great energy and enthusiasm in the pursuit of a goal or objective: *MaryLynne possesses a ferocious drive and competitive zeal that intimidate industry foes and adversaries.*

zealot *noun* **1** an uncompromising or extreme partisan; a fanatic: *one auto zealot summed up the great possibilities for the entire economy in expanding automobile production.* **2** (**Zealot**) *hist.* a member of a Jewish sect in Palestine during the 1st century AD that advocated overthrowing the Romans. ▶**zealotry** *noun* [Say ZELLIT, ZELLA tree]

zealous *adjective* full of zeal; enthusiastic. ▶**zealously** *adverb* **zealousness** *noun* [Say ZELLIS]

zebra *noun* (*plural* **zebras** or **zebra**) **1** an African quadruped, related to the ass and horse, with black and white stripes and an erect mane. **2** (as an *adjective*) with alternate dark and pale stripes.

zebra mussel *noun* a tiny freshwater mussel that proliferates rapidly and adheres in large numbers to any surface, thus becoming a pest by clogging water intake pipes etc.

zed *noun* *Cdn & Brit.* the letter Z.

zeda *noun* (*plural* **zedas**) (among Jewish people) grandfather. [Say ZAY duh]

zee *noun* the letter Z. **PHRASES catch** (or **bag**) **some zees** *slang* get some sleep.

Zeitgeist *noun* the defining spirit or mood of a particular period in history as shown by the ideas and beliefs of the time: *while the style of the movie is a throwback to old-fashioned Hollywood romanticism, its subtext of healing the inner child taps right into the zeitgeist of the '90s.* [Say ZITE geist (GEIST rhymes with PRICED)]

Zen *noun* a form of Buddhism emphasizing the value of meditation and intuition.

zenith *noun* **1** the part of the celestial sphere directly above an observer (*opp.* NADIR): *the sun crept up to the zenith.* **2** the highest or culminating point, e.g. of power: *during the early decades of the 20th century, the era of the great ocean liner was at its zenith.* [Say ZEE nith or ZEN ith]

Zenlike *adjective* suggestive of Zen Buddhism: *her Zenlike concentration.*

zeolite *noun* any one of a number of natural or synthetic minerals consisting mainly of silicates of calcium, sodium, and aluminum, which are characterized by the ability to lose or gain water without undergoing any change in crystal structure, making them useful for separating mixtures by selective absorption and for ion exchange (e.g. in water-softening). [Say ZEE uh lite]

zephyr *noun literary* a mild gentle wind or breeze. [Say ZEFFER]

Zeppelin *noun hist.* a large dirigible airship of the early 20th century, originally for military use. [Say ZEP lin]

zero • *noun* (*plural* **zeros**) **1 a** the figure 0. **b** no quantity or number; nil. **2** a point on a scale from which a positive or negative quantity is reckoned. **3** (also **zero hour**) **a** the hour at which a planned, esp. military, operation is timed to begin. **b** a crucial moment. **4** the lowest point; a nullity or nonentity. • *adjective* that amounts to zero; no, not any: *zero tolerance.* • *verb* (**zeroes, zeroed, zeroing**) **1** adjust (an instrument etc.) to zero point. **2** set the sights of (a gun) for firing. **PHRASES zero in on 1** take aim at. **2** focus one's attention on.

zero-emission *adjective* designating a motor vehicle which does not emit pollutant gases: *zero-emission vehicles*.

zero gravity *noun* the state or condition in which there is no apparent force of gravity acting on a body.

zero-sum *adjective* (of a game, political situation, etc.) in which whatever is gained by one side is lost by the other so that the net change is always zero: *life, in Greta's opinion, was a zero-sum game, in which any improvement of an individual's lot came from the deterioration of another's*.

zero tolerance *noun* a policy of rigorously punishing all infractions against a law, behavioural code, etc., no matter how minor.

zest *noun* **1** an exciting or stimulating flavour or quality: *cornices add zest to bland walls and ceilings*. **2** great enthusiasm or energy: *Biff attacked life with boundless zest and an unremitting playfulness ◊ Biff had a zest for life*. **3** the outer, coloured, covering of the peel of a citrus fruit, grated and used as flavouring: *Da Vanda's specialty is tortellini stuffed with turbot in a cream sauce with lemon zest*.

zester *noun* a kitchen utensil for obtaining zest from citrus fruit by scraping or peeling.

zestful *adjective* full of zest, piquancy, or enjoyment. ▶ **zestfully** *adverb*

zesty *adjective* (**zestier**, **zestiest**). **1** (of food) piquant, agreeably sharp. **2** energetic, stimulating.

zidovudine *noun* = AZT. [Say zye DOV you deen]

zig • *noun* an abrupt angled movement, esp. in a zigzag course. • *verb* (**zigs**, **zigged**, **zigging**) perform a zig.

ziggurat *noun* **1** a rectangular stepped tower in ancient Mesopotamia, surmounted by a temple. **2** something having this shape. [Say ZIGGA rat]

zigzag • *noun* **1** a line or course having abrupt alternate right and left turns. **2** (often in *plural*) each of these turns. • *adjective* **1** having the form of a zigzag; alternating right and left. **2** (of sewing machine stitches) produced in a zigzag, used on unfinished edges etc. • *adverb* with a zigzag course. • *verb* (**zigzags**, **zigzagged**, **zigzagging**) move in a zigzag course.

zilch *noun slang* nothing.

zillion *noun informal* an indefinite large number.

zillionaire *noun informal* a very rich person.

zillionth *informal* • *adjective* following very many others; umpteenth: *you're the zillionth person who's asked me today*. • *noun* a tiny fraction of something: *you only beat me by a zillionth of a second*.

Zimbabwean • *noun* a native or inhabitant of Zimbabwe, a landlocked country in southeastern Africa. • *adjective* of or relating to Zimbabwe or its people. [Say zim BOB wee in or zim BOB way in]

zinc *noun* a white metallic element used as a component of brass, in galvanizing sheet iron, and in electric batteries.

zinc oxide *noun* a powder used as a white pigment and in medicinal ointments.

zine *noun informal* a magazine, esp. a fanzine. [Say ZEEN]

Zinfandel *noun* **1** a red, white, or rosé wine made esp. in California. **2** the black grape from which this is made. [Say ZIN fan dell]

zing *informal* • *noun* **1** vigour, energy. **2** a short, high-pitched buzzing or ringing sound, as of a bullet moving through the air. **3** zest, liveliness: *lemon juice adds zing to this cheesecake*. • *verb* **1** move swiftly or with a shrill sound. **2** criticize or rebuke (a person) severely.

zinger *noun slang* **1** a witty or pointed remark. **2** an unexpected turn of events or piece of news. **3** an outstanding person or thing.

zingy *adjective* (**zingier**, **zingiest**) energetic, exciting, lively.

zinnia *noun* (*plural* **zinnias**) a plant of the daisy family, which is widely cultivated for its bright showy flowers. [Say ZIN yuh]

Zion *noun* **1** Jerusalem; allegorically, the heavenly city or kingdom of heaven. **2** the Jewish religion or people. **3** the region of Palestine as the Jewish homeland and as the symbol of Judaism. **4** the Christian Church. [Say ZYE in]

Zionism *noun* a movement originally for the re-establishment and now the development of a Jewish nation in what is now Israel. ▶ **Zionist** *noun* [Say ZYE in ism]

zip • *noun* **1** a light fast sound, as of a bullet passing through air. **2** energy, vigour. **3** zest: *these chili peppers have a lot of zip!* **4** *informal* nothing, zero; zilch. **5** esp. *Brit.* **a** (also **zip fastener**) = ZIPPER *noun*. **b** (as an *adjective*) having a zipper: *zip bag*. • *verb* (**zips**, **zipped**, **zipping**) **1** (often foll. by *up*) fasten with a zipper. **2** move with zip or at high speed. **3** *Computing* compress (a file or files).

Zip code *noun US proprietary* a system of postal codes consisting of five- or nine-digit numbers.

zip-lock *adjective* designating a plastic bag with a special strip along the open edges that can be sealed shut by pressing and readily reopened or resealed.

zipper *noun* a fastening device of two flexible strips with interlocking projections closed or opened by pulling a slide along them.

zippered *adjective* **1** having a zipper: *a handbag with two zippered compartments*. **2** fastened with a zipper: *wore his blue track suit zippered up tight around his neck*.

zippily *adverb* in a lively or speedy manner.

zippiness *noun* the quality of being lively or speedy.

zippo *noun informal* nothing.

zippy *adjective* (**zippier**, **zippiest**) *informal* **1** bright, fresh, lively. **2** fast, speedy.

zip-up *adjective* able to be fastened with a zip fastener.

zircon *noun* a zirconium silicate of which some translucent varieties are cut into gems. [Say ZER con]

zirconia *noun* zirconium dioxide, a white solid with a high melting point used in ceramics and fuel cells, and as a synthetic substitute for diamonds in jewellery. [Say zer CONEY uh]

zirconium *noun* a grey metallic element occurring in zircon and used in various industrial applications. [Say zer CONEY um]

zit *noun slang* a pimple.

zither *noun* a musical instrument consisting of a flat wooden sound box with numerous strings stretched across it, placed horizontally. [Rhymes with HITHER]

Zn *symbol* zinc.

zodiac *noun* **1 a** a belt of the heavens within about 8° of the ecliptic, including all apparent positions of the sun, moon, and most familiar planets, and divided into twelve parts (signs) named after constellations and used in astrology. **b** a diagram of these signs. **2** (**Zodiac**) *proprietary* a kind of inflatable rubber dinghy, esp. one powered by an outboard motor. [Say ZOE dee ack]

zodiacal *adjective* of or in the zodiac. [Say zuh DIE a cull]

zombie *noun* **1** *informal* a dull, apathetic, or exceedingly tired person. **2** a corpse said to be revived by witchcraft. **3** *Cdn slang* (during World War II) a conscript, originally for national defence as opposed to overseas service. **4** a drink consisting of several kinds of rum mixed with fruit juice and sugar. ▶ **zombielike** *adjective*

zombified *adjective* **zombify** *verb* (**zombifies**, **zombified**, **zombifying**)

zonal *adjective* arranged in zones: *a zonal pattern*.

zone • *noun* **1** an area having particular features, properties, purpose, or use. **2 a** an area between two

exact or approximate concentric circles. **b** a part of the surface of a sphere enclosed between two parallel planes, or of a cone or cylinder etc., between such planes cutting it perpendicularly to the axis. **3** (also **time zone**) a range of longitudes where a common standard time is used. **4** *Geology etc.* a range between specified limits of depth, height, etc., esp. a section of strata distinguished by characteristic fossils. **5** *Geography* any of five divisions of the earth bounded by circles parallel to the equator. **6** an encircling band or stripe distinguishable in colour, texture, or character from the rest of the object encircled. • *verb* (**zones**, **zoned**, **zoning**) **1** encircle as or with a zone. **2** arrange or distribute by zones. **3 a** divide (a city, land, etc.) into areas subject to particular planning restrictions. **b** designate (a specific area) for use or development in this manner. PHRASES **zone out** *slang* lose concentration; cease paying attention. ▶ **zoning** *noun* (in sense 3 of *verb*)

zonk *verb* *slang* **1** hit or strike. **2** (foll. by *out*) **a** overcome, knock out. **b** fall heavily asleep.

zoo *noun* **1** a place where wild animals are kept for exhibition to the public, breeding, study, etc. **2** any busy, noisy place: *it's a zoo in the lobby*. **3** a diverse or motley collection of people or things.

zookeeper *noun* a person employed in a zoo to care for the animals.

zoological *adjective* of or relating to the scientific study of animals, esp. with reference to their structure, physiology, classification, and distribution. [Say zoo a LOGICAL or zo a LOGICAL]

zoologist *noun* a scientist who specializes in the scientific study of animals, esp. with reference to their structure, physiology, classification, and distribution. [Say zoo OLLA jist or zo OLLA jist]

zoology *noun* the scientific study of animals, esp. with reference to their structure, physiology, classification, and distribution. [Say zoo OLLA jee or zo OLLA jee]

zoom • *verb* **1** move quickly, esp. with a low-pitched humming or buzzing sound. **2** cause (an airplane) to mount at high speed and a steep angle. **3** alter the field of view of a camera by varying the focal length of a zoom lens, esp. so as to close up on a subject without losing focus. **4** (of prices, costs, etc.) rise sharply. • *noun* **1** a zooming camera shot. **2** (also **zoom lens**) a lens with a variable focal length.

zooplankton *noun* the animal component of plankton, consisting of small animals and the immature stages of larger animals. [Say zoo a PLANK tun or zo a PLANK tun]

zoot suit *noun* *informal* a man's suit of an exaggerated style popular in the 1940s, characterized by a long draped jacket with padded shoulders and high-waisted tapering trousers.

Zoroastrian • *adjective* of or relating to the Persian prophet Zoroaster (or Zarathustra; *c.*628–*c.*551 BC) or the religious system taught by him or his followers, based on the concept of a conflict between a spirit of good and a spirit of evil. • *noun* a follower of Zoroaster. ▶ **Zoroastrianism** *noun* [Say zoro ASTRY un]

zouk *noun* an exuberant style of popular music, originating in the Antilles, combining Caribbean and Western elements and characterized by a strong fast beat derived from Antillean drumming. [Rhymes with FLUKE]

zowie *interjection* expressing astonishment, admiration, or delight.

Zr *symbol* zirconium.

zucchini *noun* (*plural* **zucchini** or **zucchinis**) a green-skinned summer squash, similar in appearance to a cucumber. [Say zoo KEENY]

Zulu • *noun* (*plural* **Zulus** or **Zulu**) **1** a member of a Bantu-speaking people forming the largest ethnic group in South Africa. **2** the language of this people. • *adjective* of or relating to the Zulus or their language. [Say ZOO loo]

Zuni (*plural* **Zuni** or **Zunis**) • *noun* **1** a member of a Pueblo people of New Mexico. **2** the language of this people. • *adjective* of or relating to the Zuni or their language. [Say ZOO nee or ZOON yee]

Zyban *noun* *proprietary* an antidepressant drug, bupropion, used as an aid in quitting smoking. [Say ZYE ban]

zygote *noun* a cell formed by the union of two gametes; a fertilized ovum. [Say ZYE goat]

zzz *interjection* imitating the sound of snoring.

Z

Appendices

Irregular Verbs

This appendix lists all the verbs with irregular forms that are included in the dictionary, except for those formed with a hyphenated prefix (e.g. *pre-qualify, re-edit*) and the modal verbs (e.g. *can, must*). If more than one form is given for a tense, check the entry in the dictionary to see whether the second form applies to particular senses or is a general variant. Full information on usage, pronunciation, etc. is given at the entry.

Infinitive	Third Person Singular Present	Past Tense	Past Participle	Present Participle
abide	abides	abided	abided	abiding
arise	arises	arose	arisen	arising
awake	awakes	awoke	awoken	awaking
babysit	babysits	babysat	babysat	babysitting
backlight	backlights	backlit, backlighted	backlit, backlighted	backlighting
backslide	backslides	backslid	backslid	backsliding
be	is	was [s]/were [pl]	been	being
bear	bears	bore	borne	bearing
beat	beats	beat	beaten	beating
become	becomes	became	become	becoming
befall	befalls	befell	befallen	befalling
beget	begets	begat, begot	begotten	begetting
begin	begins	began	begun	beginning
behold	beholds	beheld	beheld	beholding
bend	bends	bent	bent	bending
beseech	beseeches	beseeched, besought	beseeched, besought	beseeching
beset	besets	beset	beset	besetting
bespeak	bespeaks	bespoke	bespoken	bespeaking
bestride	bestrides	bestrode	bestridden	bestriding
bet	bets	bet, betted	bet, betted	betting
bid	bids	bid, bade	bid, bidden	bidding
bind	binds	bound	bound	binding
bite	bites	bit	bitten	biting
bivouac	bivouacs	bivouacked	bivouacked	bivouacking
bleed	bleeds	bled	bled	bleeding
blow	blows	blew	blown	blowing
break	breaks	broke	broken	breaking
breed	breeds	bred	bred	breeding
bring	brings	brought	brought	bringing
broadcast	broadcasts	broadcast	broadcast	broadcasting
browbeat	browbeats	browbeat	browbeaten	browbeating
build	builds	built	built	building
burn	burns	burned, burnt	burned, burnt	burning
burst	bursts	burst	burst	bursting
bust	busts	busteds, bust	busted, bust	busting
buy	buys	bought	bought	buying
cast	casts	cast	cast	casting
catch	catches	caught	caught	catching
cha-cha	cha-chas	cha-chaed	cha-chaed	cha-chaing
choose	chooses	chose	chosen	choosing
cleave[1]	cleaves	cleaved, clove, cleft	cloven, cleft, cleaved	cleaving
cling	clings	clung	clung	clinging
come	comes	came	come	coming

Infinitive	Third Person Singular Present	Past Tense	Past Participle	Present Participle
cost	costs	cost, costed	cost, costed	costing
creep	creeps	crept	crept	creeping
crossbreed	crossbreeds	crossbred	crossbred	crossbreeding
crosscut	crosscuts	crosscut	crosscut	crosscutting
crow	crows	crowed, crew	crowed, crew	crowing
cut	cuts	cut	cut	cutting
deal	deals	dealt	dealt	dealing
DH	DH's	DH'd	DH'd	DH'ing
dig	digs	dug	dug	digging
dive	dives	dived, dove	dived	diving
do	does	did	done	doing
draw	draws	drew	drawn	drawing
dream	dreams	dreamt, dreamed	dreamt, dreamed	dreaming
drink	drinks	drank	drunk	drinking
drive	drives	drove	driven	driving
dwell	dwells	dwelt, dwelled	dwelt, dwelled	dwelling
eat	eats	ate	eaten	eating
fall	falls	fell	fallen	falling
feed	feeds	fed	fed	feeding
feel	feels	felt	felt	feeling
fight	fights	fought	fought	fighting
find	finds	found	found	finding
fit	fits	fitted, fit	fitted, fit	fitting
flee	flees	fled	fled	fleeing
fling	flings	flung	flung	flinging
floodlight	floodlights	floodlit	floodlit	floodlighting
fly	flies	flew, flied	flew, flied	flying
forbear	forbears	forbore	forborne	forbearing
forbid	forbids	forbade, forbad	forbidden	forbidding
forecast	forecasts	forecast, forecasted	forecast, forecasted	forecasting
foreknow	foreknows	foreknew	foreknown	foreknowing
foresee	foresees	foresaw	foreseen	foreseeing
foretell	foretells	foretold	foretold	foretelling
forget	forgets	forgot	forgotten	forgetting
forgive	forgives	forgave	forgiven	forgiving
forgo	forgoes	forwent	forgone	forgoing
forsake	forsakes	forsook	forsaken	forsaking
freeze	freezes	froze	frozen	freezing
frolic	frolics	frolicked	frolicked	frolicking
FTP	FTP's	FTP'd	FTP'd	FTP'ing
gainsay	gainsays	gainsaid	gainsaid	gainsaying
get	gets	got	got, gotten	getting
give	gives	gave	given	giving
go	goes	went	gone	going
grind	grinds	ground	ground	grinding
grow	grows	grew	grown	growing
hamstring	hamstrings	hamstrung	hamstringing	hamstringing
hang	hangs	hung, hanged	hung, hanged	hanging
have	haves	had	had	having
hear	hears	heard	heard	hearing
heave	heaves	heaved, hove	heaved, hove	heaving
hew	hews	hewed	hewn, hewed	hewing
hide[1]	hides	hid	hidden	hiding
hit	hits	hit	hit	hitting
hold	holds	held	held	holding

Infinitive	Third Person Singular Present	Past Tense	Past Participle	Present Participle
hurt	hurts	hurt	hurt	hurting
inbreed	inbreeds	inbred	inbred	inbreeding
inlay	inlays	inlaid	inlaid	inlaying
input	inputs	input, inputted	input, inputted	inputting
inset	insets	inset	inset	insetting
intercut	intercuts	intercut	intercut	intercutting
interweave	interweaves	interwove	interwoven	interweaving
keep	keeps	kept	kept	keeping
kneel	kneels	knelt, kneeled	knelt, kneeled	kneeling
knit	knits	knitted, knit	knitted, knit	knitting
know	knows	knew	known	knowing
KO	KO's	KO'd	KO'd	KO'ing
lade	lades	laded	laden	lading
lay	lays	laid	laid	laying
lead	leads	led	led	leading
lean	leans	leaned, leant	leaned, leant	leaning
leap	leaps	leaped, leapt	leaped, leapt	leaping
learn	learns	learned, learnt	learned, learnt	learning
leave	leaves	left	left	leaving
lend	lends	lent	lent	lending
let	lets	let	let	letting
lie¹	lies	lay	lain	lying
light¹	lights	lit	lit, lighted	lighting
light²	lights	lit, lighted	lit, lighted	lighting
lose	loses	lost	lost	losing
magic	magics	magicked	magicked	magicking
make	makes	made	made	making
MC	MC's	MC'd	MC'd	MC'ing
mean	means	meant	meant	meaning
medevac	medevacs	medevacked	medevacked	medevacking
meet	meets	met	met	meeting
mimic	mimics	mimicked	mimicked	mimicking
miscast	miscasts	miscast	miscast	miscasting
misdeal	misdeals	misdealt	misdealt	misdealing
mishear	mishears	misheard	misheard	mishearing
mislay	mislays	mislaid	mislaid	mislaying
mislead	misleads	misled	misled	misleading
misread	misreads	misread	misread	misreading
misspell	misspells	misspelled, misspelt	misspelled, misspelt	misspelling
misspend	misspends	misspent	misspent	misspending
mistake	mistakes	mistook	mistaken	mistaking
misunderstand	misunderstands	misunderstood	misunderstood	misunderstanding
mow	mows	mowed	mowed, mown	mowing
narrowcast	narrowcasts	narrowcast, narrowcasted	narrowcast, narrowcasted	narrowcasting
OD	OD's	OD'd	OD'd	OD'ing
offset	offsets	offset	offset	offsetting
OK	OK's	OK'd	OK'd	OK'ing
outbid	outbids	outbid	outbid	outbidding
outdo	outdoes	outdid	outdone	outdoing
outgrow	outgrows	outgrew	outgrown	outgrowing
output	outputs	output	output	outputting
outrun	outruns	outran	outrun	outrunning
outsell	outsells	outsold	outsold	outselling
outshine	outshines	outshone	outshone	outshining

Infinitive	Third Person Singular Present	Past Tense	Past Participle	Present Participle
outshoot	outshoots	outshot	outshot	outshooting
outspend	outspends	outspent	outspent	outspending
outspread	outspreads	outspread	outspread	outspreading
overcome	overcomes	overcame	overcome	overcoming
overcut	overcuts	overcut	overcut	overcutting
overdo	overdoes	overdid	overdone	overdoing
overdraw	overdraws	overdrew	overdrawn	overdrawing
overeat	overeats	overate	overeaten	overeating
overfeed	overfeeds	overfed	overfed	overfeeding
overfly	overflies	overflew	overflown	overflying
overhang	overhangs	overhung	overhung	overhanging
overhear	overhears	overheard	overheard	overhearing
overlay	overlays	overlaid	overlaid	overlaying
overlie	overlies	overlay	overlain	overlying
overpay	overpays	overpaid	overpaid	overpaying
override	overrides	overrode	overridden	overriding
overrun	overruns	overran	overrun	overrunning
oversee	oversees	oversaw	overseen	overseeing
oversell	oversells	oversold	oversold	overselling
overshoot	overshoots	overshot	overshot	overshooting
oversleep	oversleeps	overslept	overslept	oversleeping
overspend	overspends	overspent	overspent	overspending
overtake	overtakes	overtook	overtaken	overtaking
overthrow	overthrows	overthrew	overthrown	overthrowing
overwind	overwinds	overwound	overwound	overwinding
overwrite	overwrites	overwrote	overwritten	overwriting
panic	panics	panicked	panicked	panicking
partake	partakes	partook	partaken	partaking
pay	pays	paid	paid	paying
picnic	picnics	picnicked	picnicked	picnicking
plead	pleads	pleaded, pled	pleaded, pled	pleading
politic	politics	politicked	politicked	politicking
prepay	prepays	prepaid	prepaid	prepaying
preset	presets	preset	preset	presetting
proofread	proofreads	proofread	proofread	proofreading
prove	proves	proved	proven, proved	proving
put	puts	put	put	putting
quit	quits	quit	quit	quitting
read	reads	read	read	reading
rebroadcast	rebroadcasts	rebroadcast, rebroadcasted	rebroadcast, rebroadcasted	rebroadcasting
rebuild	rebuilds	rebuilt	rebuilt	rebuilding
recast	recasts	recast	recast	recasting
recut	recuts	recut	recut	recutting
redo	redoes	redid	redone	redoing
redraw	redraws	redrew	redrawn	redrawing
refreeze	refreezes	refroze	refrozen	refreezing
regrow	regrows	regrew	regrown	regrowing
relight	relights	relit	relit	relighting
remake	remakes	remade	remade	remaking
rend	rends	rent	rent	rending
repay	repays	repaid	repaid	repaying
reread	rereads	reread	reread	rereading
rerun	reruns	reran	rerun	rerunning
resell	resells	resold	resold	reselling
reset	resets	reset	reset	resetting

Infinitive	Third Person Singular Present	Past Tense	Past Participle	Present Participle
reshoot	reshoots	reshot	reshot	reshooting
respell	respells	respelled, respelt	respelled, respelt	respelling
restring	restrings	restrung	restrung	restringing
retake	retakes	retook	retaken	retaking
retell	retells	retold	retold	retelling
rethink	rethinks	rethought	rethought	rethinking
rewind	rewinds	rewound	rewound	rewinding
rewrite	rewrites	rewritten	rewritten	rewriting
rid	rids	rid	rid	ridding
ride	rides	rode	ridden	riding
ring²	rings	rang	rung	ringing
rise	rises	rose	risen	rising
RSVP	RSVP's	RSVP'd	RSVP'd	RSVP'ing
rumba	rumbas	rumbaed, rumba'd	rumbaed, rumba'd	rumbaing
run	runs	ran	run	running
samba	sambas	sambaed, samba'd	sambaed, samba'd	sambaing
saw	saws	sawed	sawn, sawed	sawing
say	says	said	said	saying
see	sees	saw	seen	seeing
seek	seeks	sought	sought	seeking
sell	sells	sold	sold	selling
send	sends	sent	sent	sending
set	sets	set	set	setting
sew	sews	sewed	sewn, sewed	sewing
shake	shakes	shook	shaken	shaking
shave	shaves	shaved	shaved, shaven	shaving
shear	shears	sheared	shorn, sheared	shearing
shed	sheds	shed	shed	shedding
shellac	shellacs	shellacked	shellacked	shellacking
shine	shines	shone, shined	shone, shined	shining
shoe	shoes	shod, shoed	shod, shoed	shoing
shoot	shoots	shot	shot	shooting
show	shows	showed	shown	showing
shrink	shrinks	shrank, shrunk	shrunk	shrinking
shut	shuts	shut	shut	shutting
simulcast	simulcasts	simulcast	simulcast	simulcasting
sing	sings	sang	sung	singing
sink	sinks	sank, sunk	sunk	sinking
sit	sits	sat	sat	sitting
slay	slays	slew	slain	slaying
sleep	sleeps	slept	slept	sleeping
slide	slides	slid	slid	sliding
sling	slings	slung	slung	slinging
slink	slinks	slunk	slunk	slinking
slit	slits	slit	slit	slitting
smite	smites	smote	smitten	smiting
sneak	sneaks	snuck, sneaked	snuck, sneaked	sneaking
sow	sows	sowed	sown, sowed	sowing
speak	speaks	spoke	spoken	speaking
speed	speeds	sped, speeded	sped, speeded	speeding
spell¹	spells	spelled, spelt	spelled, spelt	spelling
spellbind	spellbinds	spellbound	spellbound	spellbinding
spend	spends	spent	spent	spending
spill	spills	spilled, spilt	spilled, spilt	spilling
spin	spins	spun	spun	spinning

Infinitive	Third Person Singular Present	Past Tense	Past Participle	Present Participle
spit[1]	spits	spat, spit	spat, spit	spitting
split	splits	split	split	splitting
spoil	spoils	spoiled, spoilt	spoiled, spoilt	spoiling
spotlight	spotlights	spotlighted, spotlit	spotlighted, spotlit	spotlighting
spread	spreads	spread	spread	spreading
spring	springs	sprang, sprung	sprung	springing
stand	stands	stood	stood	standing
stave	staves	stove, staved	stove, staved	staving
steal	steals	stole	stolen	stealing
stick	sticks	stuck	stuck	sticking
sting	stings	stung	stung	stinging
stink	stinks	stank, stunk	stunk	stinking
strew	strews	strewed	strewn, strewed	strewing
stride	strides	strode	stridden	striding
strike	strikes	struck	struck	striking
string	strings	strung	strung	stringing
strive	strives	strove, strived	striven	striving
sublet	sublets	sublet	sublet	subletting
swear	swears	swore	sworn	swearing
sweat	sweats	sweated, sweat	sweated, sweat	sweating
sweep	sweeps	swept	swept	sweeping
swell	swells	swelled	swollen, swelled	swelling
swim	swims	swam	swum	swimming
swing	swings	swung	swung	swinging
TA	TA's	TA'd	TA'd	TA'ing
tailspin	tailspins	tailspun	tailspun	tailspinning
take	takes	took	taken	taking
tarmac	tarmacs	tarmacked	tarmacked	tarmacking
teach	teaches	taught	taught	teaching
tear[1]	tears	tore	torn	tearing
telecast	telecasts	telecast	telecast	telecasting
tell	tells	told	told	telling
think	thinks	thought	thought	thinking
thrive	thrives	thrived, throve	thrived	thriving
throw	throws	threw	thrown	throwing
thrust	thrusts	thrust	thrust	thrusting
TKO	TKO's	TKO'd	TKO'd	TKO'ing
traffic	traffics	trafficked	trafficked	trafficking
tread	treads	trod	trodden, trod	treading
troubleshoot	troubleshoots	troubleshot	troubleshot	troubleshooting
typecast	typecasts	typecast	typecast	typecasting
typeset	typesets	typeset	typeset	typesetting
unbend	unbends	unbent	unbent	unbending
underbid	underbids	underbid	underbid	underbidding
undercut	undercuts	undercut	undercut	undercutting
undergo	undergoes	underwent	undergone	undergoing
underlay	underlays	underlaid	underlaid	underlaying
underlie	underlies	underlay	underlain	underlying
underpay	underpays	underpaid	underpaid	underpaying
undersell	undersells	undersold	undersold	underselling
understand	understands	understood	understood	understanding
undertake	undertakes	undertook	undertaken	undertaking
underwrite	underwrites	underwrote	underwritten	underwriting
undo	undoes	undid	undone	undoing
unfreeze	unfreezes	unfroze	unfrozen	unfreezing

Infinitive	Third Person Singular Present	Past Tense	Past Participle	Present Participle
unlearn	unlearns	unlearned, unlearnt	unlearned, unlearnt	unlearning
unmake	unmakes	unmade	unmade	unmaking
unstick	unsticks	unstuck	unstuck	unsticking
unstring	unstrings	unstrung	unstrung	unstringing
unwind	unwinds	unwound	unwound	unwinding
uphold	upholds	upheld	upheld	upholding
uppercut	uppercuts	uppercut	uppercut	uppercutting
upset	upsets	upset	upset	upsetting
wake[1]	wakes	woke, waked	woken, waked	waking
waylay	waylays	waylaid	waylaid	waylaying
wear	wears	wore	worn	wearing
weave[1]	weaves	wove	woven, wove	weaving
weave[2]	weaves	weaved, wove	weaved, woven	weaving
wed	weds	wedded, wed	wedded, wed	wedding
weep	weeps	wept	wept	weeping
wet	wets	wet, wetted	wet, wetted	wetting
whipsaw	whipsaws	whipsawed	whipsawed, whipsawn	whipsawing
win	wins	won	won	winning
wind	winds	wound	wound	winding
withdraw	withdraws	withdrew	withdrawn	withdrawing
withhold	withholds	withheld	withheld	withholding
withstand	withstands	withstood	withstood	withstanding
wring	wrings	wrung	wrung	wringing
write	writes	wrote	written	writing

Punctuation and Capitalization

Punctuation is used to separate strings of words into manageable groups and help clarify their meaning. The marks most commonly used to divide a piece of prose or other writing are the period, the semicolon, and the comma, with the strength of the dividing or separating role diminishing from the period to the comma. The period marks the main division into sentences; the semicolon joins sentences (as in this sentence); and the comma (which is the most flexible in use and causes the most problems) separates smaller elements with the least loss of continuity. Brackets and dashes also serve as separators — often more strikingly than commas, as in this sentence.

period .

■ A period is used to mark the end of a sentence that is not a question or exclamation. In prose, sentences marked by periods normally represent an independent or distinct statement; more closely connected or complementary statements are joined by a semicolon (as here).

■ Periods are used to mark abbreviations (*Wed., Gen., p.m.*). They are often omitted in abbreviations that consist entirely of capital letters (*CBC*, *EDT*, *RRSP*), and in acronyms that are pronounced as a word rather than a sequence of letters (*Intelsat*), and should be omitted in abbreviations for SI units (*Hz, kg, cm*).

■ If an abbreviation with a period comes at the end of a sentence, another period is not added:

They have a collection of many animals, including dogs, cats, tortoises, snakes, etc.

but

They have a collection of many animals (dogs, cats, tortoises, snakes, etc.).

■ A period is used as a decimal point (*10.5%*; *$1.65*), and to separate the domains of an e-mail or Web address (*www.oupcan.com*). It is commonly used in British practice to divide hours and minutes in giving time (*6.15 p.m.*), where a colon is standard in North American use.

semicolon ;

■ The main role of the semicolon is to join sentences that are closely related or that parallel each other in some way, as in the following:

Many new houses are being built north of the city; areas to the south are still largely industrial.

To err is human; to forgive, divine.

■ It is often used as a stronger division in a sentence that already includes several commas:

Joanne and Emily went out for dinner, as they usually did on Wednesday; but when, upon arriving at the restaurant, they were told they would have to wait for a table, they went home and ordered Chinese.

■ It is used in a similar way in lists of names or other items, to indicate a stronger division:

I would like to thank the managing director, Jennifer Dunbar; my secretary, Raymond Martin; and my assistant, David Singh.

comma ,

Use of the comma is more difficult to describe than other punctuation marks, and there is considerable variation in practice. Essentially, it is used to give structure to sentences, especially longer ones, and make their meaning clear. Too many commas can be distracting; too few can make a piece of writing difficult to read or, worse, difficult to understand.

■ A comma is used to separate the main clauses of a sentence, often followed by a conjunction, such as *and*, *but*, or *yet*:

Mario cooked a roast, and Jan baked a pie for dessert.

A comma is not used when the subject of the first clause is understood to be the subject of the second clause:

Mario cooked a roast and baked a pie for dessert.

■ It is considered incorrect to join the clauses of a compound sentence without a conjunction. The following sentence:

I like skating very much, I go to the local rink every day after school.

should be rewritten as

I like skating very much; I go to the local rink every day after school.

or as

I like skating very much and I go to the local rink every day after school.

■ It is also considered incorrect to separate a subject from its verb with a comma:

Those with the smallest incomes and no other means, should get more support.

should be rewritten as

Those with the smallest incomes and no other means should get more support.

■ Commas are usually inserted between adjectives coming before a noun:

An enterprising, ambitious person.

A cold, damp, poorly heated room.

But the comma is omitted when the last adjective has a closer relation to the noun than the others:

A distinguished foreign politician.

A noisy blue jay.

■ An important role of the comma is to prevent ambiguity. Imagine how the following sentences might be interpreted without the comma:

With the police pursuing, the people shouted loudly.

She did not want to leave, from a feeling of loyalty.

In the valley below, the houses appeared very small.

■ Commas are used in pairs to separate elements in a sentence that are not part of the main statement:

I would like you all, ladies and gentlemen, to raise your glasses.

There is no truth, as far as I can see, to this rumour.

It appears, however, that we were wrong.

■ A comma is also used to separate a relative clause from a noun when the clause is used to provide additional information about the noun but is not essential in identifying it:

The picture, which was hanging above the fireplace, was a present.

In the above sentence, the information in the *which* clause is incidental to the main statement; without the comma, it would form an essential part of it in identifying which picture is being referred to (and could be replaced by *that*):

The picture which/that was hanging above the fireplace was a present.

■ Commas are used to separate items in a list or sequence:

Emma, Sheilah, and Dorcas went out for lunch.

The doctor told me to go home, get some rest, and drink plenty of fluids.

It is acceptable to omit the final comma before *and*; however, the final comma has the advantage of clarifying the grouping at a composite name occurring at the end of a list:

I buy my art supplies at Midoco, Loomis and Toles, and Grand and Toy.

■ A comma is often used in numbers of four or more digits, to separate each group of three consecutive digits starting from the right (e.g. *10,135,793*). In metric practice, a space is used instead of a comma to separate each group of three consecutive figures (*10 135 793*).

■ A comma is used to introduce a quotation of a complete sentence:

Joan exclaimed, "Isn't he fabulous!".

and substitutes for a period at the end of a quotation if this is followed by a continuation of the sentence:

"I've never seen such a fabulous dancer," said Joan.

colon :

■ The main role of the colon is to separate main clauses when there is a step forward from the first to the second, especially from introduction to main point, from general statement to example, from cause to effect, and from premise to conclusion:

There is something I forgot to tell you: your mother called earlier.

It was not easy: to begin with, we had to raise the necessary capital.

■ It also introduces a list of items:

This recipe requires the following: semi-sweet chocolate, cream, egg whites, and sugar.

■ It is used to introduce, more formally

and emphatically than a comma would, speech or quoted material:

I told them last week: "Do not under any circumstances open this box."

■ It is used to divide hours and minutes in giving time (6:30 *p.m.*; 18:30).

question mark   ?

■ A question mark is used in place of a period to show that the preceding sentence is a question:

She actually volunteered to do it?

Would you like another cup of coffee?

It is not used when the question is implied by indirect speech:

I asked you if you would like another cup of coffee.

■ It is used (often in brackets) to express doubt or uncertainty about a word or phrase immediately following or preceding it:

Jean Talon, born (?) 1625.

They were then seen boarding a bus (to Kingston?).

exclamation mark   !

An exclamation mark is used after an exclamatory word, phrase, or sentence expressing any of the following:

■ Absurdity:

That's preposterous!

■ Command or warning:

Watch out!

■ Contempt or disgust:

Your hands are filthy!

■ Emotion or pain:

I love this song!

Ouch! That hurts!

■ Enthusiasm:

I can't wait to see you!

■ Wish or regret:

If only I could fly!

■ Wonder, admiration, or surprise:

Isn't that beautiful!

apostrophe   '

■ The main use of an apostrophe is to indicate the possessive case, as in *Julie's*

book or *the boys' mother*. It comes before the *s* in singular and plural nouns not ending in *s*, as in *the girl's costumes* and *the women's costumes*. It comes after the *s* in plural nouns ending in *s*, as in *the girls' costumes*.

■ In singular nouns ending in *s* practice differs between (for example) *Charles'* and *Charles's*; in some cases the shorter form is preferable for reasons of sound, as in *Xerxes' fleet* or *in Jesus' name*.

■ It is also used to indicate a place or business, e.g. *the butcher's*. In this use it is often omitted in some names, e.g. *Tim Hortons*, *Shoppers Drug Mart*, *Smiths Falls*.

■ It is used to indicate that a letter or series of letters has been removed to form a contraction, e.g. *we're, mustn't, Hallowe'en, o'clock*.

■ It is sometimes used to form a plural of individual letters or numbers, although this use is diminishing. It is helpful in *dot your i's and cross your t's*, but unnecessary in *MPs* and *1940s*.

quotation marks   " "

■ The main use of quotation marks is to indicate direct speech and quotations. Quotation marks are used at the beginning and end of quoted material:

She said, "I have something to tell you."

The closing quotation marks should come after any punctuation mark which is part of the quoted matter, but before any mark which is not:

They shouted, "Watch out!".

They were described as "an unruly bunch".

Punctuation dividing a sentence of quoted speech is put inside the quotation marks:

"Go away," he said, "and don't ever come back."

■ Quotation marks are also placed around cited words and phrases:

What does "integrated circuit" mean?

■ A quotation within a quotation is put in single quotation marks:

"Have you any idea," he asked, "what 'integrated circuit' means?"

This is the practice followed by most North American publishers. British publishers use single quotation marks

for a first quotation and double quotation marks for a quotation within:

'Have you any idea,' he asked, 'what "integrated circuit" means?'

brackets

- The types of brackets used in normal punctuation are round brackets (), also known as parentheses, and square brackets [ ]. The main use of round brackets is to enclose explanations and extra information or comment:

  He was (and still is) a rebel.

  Congo (formerly Zaire).

  He spoke at length about his Weltanschauung (world view).

- They are used to give references and citations:

  Wilfrid Laurier (1841–1919).

  A discussion of integrated circuits (see p. 38).

- They are used to enclose optional words:

  There are many (apparent) difficulties.

  (In this example, the difficulties may or may not be only apparent.)

- Square brackets are used less often. The main use is to enclose extra information added by someone (normally an editor) other than the writer of the surrounding text:

  Robert walked in, and his sister [Sara] greeted him.

- They are sometimes used to enclose extra information within text that is already in round brackets:

  Robert and Rebecca entered the room, and Sara greeted them. (Robert and Rebecca had concluded a three-week driving adventure [through Quebec] and had not seen Sara in some time.)

dash

- A single dash is used to indicate a pause, either to represent a hesitation in speech or to introduce an explanation of what comes before it:

  We must try to help — before it's too late.

  We then saw the reptiles — snakes, crocodiles, that sort of thing.

- A pair of dashes is used to enclose an aside or additional piece of information, like the use of commas as explained

above, but forming a more distinct break:

  He refused to tell anyone — least of all his wife — about that embarrassing moment during the medical exam.

- It is sometimes used to indicate an omitted word or a portion of an omitted word, for example a coarse or offensive word in reported speech:

  "They were p—off," he said.

- It is also used to sum up a list before carrying on with a sentence:

  Chocolates, flowers, champagne — any of these would be appreciated.

- Because many keyboards do not have a dash, two hyphens, with no space before or after, can be used to make a dash.

hyphen

- The hyphen has two main functions: to link words to form longer words and compounds, and to mark the division of a word at the end of a line in print or writing.

- The use of the hyphen to connect words to form compound words is diminishing in English. It is often retained to avoid awkward collisions of letters (as in *twist-tie*, *re-emerge*, or *mis-hit*) or to distinguish a word like *re-sign* from *resign*.

- The hyphen serves to connect words that have a syntactic link, as in *soft-centred candies* and *French-speaking people*, where the reference is to candies with soft centres and people who speak French, rather than soft candies with centres and French people who can speak (which would be the sense conveyed if the hyphens were omitted). It is also used to avoid more extreme kinds of ambiguity, as in *twenty-odd people*.

- A particularly important use of the hyphen is to link compounds and phrases used attributively, as in *a well-known man* (but *the man is well known*), *water-cooler gossip* (but *gossip around the water cooler*), and *a sold-out show* (but *the show is sold out*).

- A hyphen is often used to turn a phrasal verb into a noun:

  She injured her shoulder in the warm-up before the game.

■ Notice however that while a hyphen is used in the noun, the verb is still spelled without a hyphen:

Stretching is a good way to warm up before a game.

■ It is used to indicate a common second element in all but the last of a list, e.g. *two-, three-, or fourfold*.

■ The hyphen used to divide a word at the end of a line is a different matter, because it is not a permanent feature of the spelling. The general principle to follow is to insert the hyphen where it will least distract the reader, usually at a syllable break.

ellipsis

■ A sequence of three periods is used to mark an ellipsis or omission in a sequence of words, especially when forming an incomplete quotation. When the omission occurs at the end of a sentence, a fourth point is added as the period of the whole sentence:

He left the room, slammed the door...and went out.

The report said: "There are many issues to be considered, of which the most important are money, time, and personnel....Let us consider personnel first."

capital letter

■ A capital letter is used for the first letter of the word beginning a sentence:

She decided not to come. Later she changed her mind.

■ A sentence contained in brackets within a larger sentence does not normally begin with a capital letter:

I have written several letters (there are many to be written) and hope to finish them tomorrow.

In the following, however, the sentence is a separate one and therefore it does begin with a capital letter:

We have more than one option. (You have said this often before.) So we should think carefully before acting.

■ A capital letter also begins sentences that form quoted speech:

The assistant turned and replied, "We think it works."

■ The use of capital letters to distinguish proper nouns or names from ordinary words is subject to wide variation in practice. Some guidelines are offered here, but the most important criterion is consistency within a single piece of writing.

Capital letters are used for:

the names of people and places (*Terry Fox, Prince Edward Island, Robson Street*)

the names of languages, peoples, and words derived from these (*Inuktitut, Vietnamese, Quebecer, Englishwoman, Americanism*)

the names of institutions and organizations (*the Crown, the Senate, the Department of Health, the National Museum of Natural Sciences, the Law Society of Upper Canada*)

the names of religions and their adherents (*Judaism, Muslim, the United Church*)

the names of months and days (*June, Monday, New Year's Day*)

nouns or abstract qualities personified (*a victim of Fate*)

■ Note that *the Anglican Church* is an institution, but *the Anglican church* is a building; a *Democrat* belongs to a political party, but a *democrat* simply supports democracy; *Northern Ireland* is a name with recognized status, but *northern England* is not.

■ A capital letter is used by convention in many names that are trademarks (*Xerox, Cineplex, Arborite*) or are otherwise associated with a particular manufacturer. Some proprietary terms are now conventionally spelled with a lower case initial (*aspirin, pablum, jeep*), and this is generally true of established verbs derived from proprietary terms (to *xerox*, to *skidoo*).

■ Capital letters are used in titles of courtesy or rank, including compound titles, when these directly precede a name (*the Right Honourable Lester B. Pearson, Dame Emma Albani, Brigadier General Daigle, Prime Minister Jean Chrétien*).

It is not necessary to capitalize a title when it is not placed directly before a name or when it is set off by commas (*an interview with Jean Chrétien, prime minister of Canada; an interview with the prime minister, Jean Chrétien*).

- A capital letter is used for the name of a deity (*God, Father, Allah, Great Spirit*). However, the use of capitals in possessive determiners and possessive pronouns (*in His name*) is now generally considered old-fashioned.

- Capital letters are used for the first and other important words in titles of books, newspapers, plays, movies, and television programs (*The Merchant of Venice*, *Who Has Seen the Wind*, *Guide to the Use of the Dictionary*, *Hockey Night in Canada*).

- Capital letters are used for historical events and periods (*the Dark Ages, the Renaissance, the First World War*); also for geological time divisions, but not for certain archaeological periods (*Devonian, Paleozoic,* but *neolithic*).

- Capital letters are frequently used in abbreviations, with or without periods (*CTV, M.B.A.*).

- A capital letter is used for a compass direction when abbreviated (*N, NE, NNE*) or when denoting a region (*cold weather in the North*).

Prime Ministers and Governors General of Canada

Prime Ministers of Canada

John A. Macdonald	1867-73	Conservative
Alexander Mackenzie	1873-78	Liberal
John A. Macdonald	1878-91	Conservative
John J.C. Abbott	1891-92	Conservative
John S.D. Thompson	1892-94	Conservative
Mackenzie Bowell	1894-96	Conservative
Charles Tupper	1896	Conservative
Wilfrid Laurier	1896-1911	Liberal
Robert L. Borden	1911-20	Conservative
Arthur Meighen	1920-21	Conservative
William Lyon Mackenzie King	1921-26	Liberal
Arthur Meighen	1926	Conservative
William Lyon Mackenzie King	1926-30	Liberal
Richard B. Bennett	1930-35	Conservative
William Lyon Mackenzie King	1935-48	Liberal
Louis S. St. Laurent	1948-57	Liberal
John G. Diefenbaker	1957-63	Progressive Conservative
Lester B. Pearson	1963-68	Liberal
Pierre Elliott Trudeau	1968-79	Liberal
Joseph Clark	1979-80	Progressive Conservative
Pierre Elliott Trudeau	1980-84	Liberal
John Turner	1984	Liberal
Brian Mulroney	1984-93	Progressive Conservative
Kim Campbell	1993	Progressive Conservative
Jean Chrétien	1993-2004	Liberal
Paul Martin	2004-	Liberal

Governors General of Canada

Viscount Monck of Ballytrammon	1867-69
Baron Lisgar of Lisgar and Bailieborough	1869-72
The Marquess of Dufferin and Ava	1872-78
The Marquess of Lorne	1878-83
The Marquess of Lansdowne	1883-88
Baron Stanley of Preston	1888-93
The Earl of Aberdeen	1893-98
The Earl of Minto	1898-1904
Earl Grey	1904-11
The Duke of Connaught and Strathearn	1911-16
The Duke of Devonshire	1916-21
Viscount Byng of Vimy	1921-26
Viscount Willingdon of Ratton	1926-31
The Earl of Bessborough	1931-35
Baron Tweedsmuir of Elsfield	1935-40
The Earl of Athlone	1940-46
Earl Alexander of Tunis	1946-52
Vincent Massey	1952-59
Georges Vanier	1959-67
Roland Michener	1967-74
Jules Léger	1974-79
Edward Schreyer	1979-84
Jeanne Sauvé	1984-90
Ramon Hnatyshyn	1990-95
Roméo LeBlanc	1995-99
Adrienne Clarkson	1999-

Provinces and Territories of Canada

Provinces

Alberta	Edmonton
British Columbia	Victoria
Manitoba	Winnipeg
New Brunswick	Fredericton
Newfoundland and Labrador	St. John's
Nova Scotia	Halifax
Ontario	Toronto
Prince Edward Island	Charlottetown
Quebec	Québec
Saskatchewan	Regina

Territories

Northwest Territories	Yellowknife
Nunavut	Iqaluit
Yukon Territory	Whitehorse

Weights, Measures, and Notation

The conversion factors are not exact unless so marked. They are given only to the accuracy likely to be needed in everyday calculations.

1. Metric, with Imperial Equivalents

Linear measure

1 millimetre		= 0.039 inch
1 centimetre	= 10 millimetres	= 0.394 inch
1 decimetre	= 10 centimetres	= 3.94 inches
1 metre	= 100 centimetres	= 1.094 yards
1 decametre	= 10 metres	= 10.94 yards
1 hectometre	= 100 metres	= 109.4 yards
1 kilometre	= 1000 metres	= 0.6214 mile

Square measure

1 square centimetre		= 0.155 square inch
1 square metre	= 10 000 square centimetres	= 1.196 square yards
1 are	= 100 square metres	= 119.6 square yards
1 hectare	= 100 ares	= 2.471 acres
1 square kilometre	= 100 hectares	= 0.386 square mile

Cubic measure

1 cubic centimetre		= 0.061 cubic inch
1 cubic metre	= one million cubic centimetres	= 1.308 cubic yards

Capacity measure

1 millilitre		= 0.002 pint (imperial)
1 centilitre	= 10 millilitres	= 0.018 pint
1 decilitre	= 100 millilitres	= 0.176 pint
1 litre	= 1000 millilitres	= 1.76 pints
1 decalitre	= 10 litres	= 2.20 gallons (imperial)
1 hectolitre	= 100 litres	= 2.75 bushels (imperial)

Weight

1 milligram		= 0.015 grain
1 centigram	= 10 milligrams	= 0.154 grain
1 decigram	= 100 milligrams	= 1.543 grains
1 gram	= 1000 milligrams	= 15.43 grains
1 decagram	= 10 grams	= 154.3 grains
1 hectogram	= 100 grams	= 3.527 ounces
1 kilogram	= 1000 grams	= 2.205 pounds
1 tonne (metric ton)	= 1000 kilograms	= 0.984 (long) ton

2. Imperial and American, with Metric Equivalents

Linear measure

1 inch		= 25.4 millimetres exactly
1 foot	= 12 inches	= 0.3048 metre exactly
1 yard	= 3 feet	= 0.9144 metre exactly
1 (statute) mile	= 1,760 yards	= 1.609 kilometres
1 international nautical mile	= 1.150779 miles	= 1.852 kilometres exactly

Square measure

1 square inch		= 6.45 square centimetres
1 square foot	= 144 square inches	= 9.29 square decimetres
1 square yard	= 9 square feet	= 0.836 square metre
1 acre	= 4,840 square yards	= 0.405 hectare
1 square mile	= 640 acres	= 259 hectares

Cubic measure

1 cubic inch		= 16.4 cubic centimetres
1 cubic foot	= 1,728 cubic inches	= 0.0283 cubic metre
1 cubic yard	= 27 cubic feet	= 0.765 cubic metre

Capacity measure

Name	System	Equal to	Metric
fluid ounce	imperial	1/20 imperial pint	28.41 millilitres
	US (liquid)	1/16 US fluid pint	29.57 millilitres
pint	imperial	20 imperial fluid ounces	568.26 millilitres
	US (liquid)	16 US fluid ounces	473.18 millilitres
	US (dry)		550.61 millilitres
quart	imperial	2 imperial pints	1.1365 litres
	US (liquid)	2 US fluid pints	0.9464 litre
	US (dry)	2 US dry pints	1.1012 litres
gallon	imperial	4 imperial quarts	4.546 litres
	US (liquid)	4 US fluid quarts	3.785 litres
peck	imperial	2 imperial gallons	9.092 litres
	US (dry)	8 US dry quarts	8.810 litres
bushel	imperial	4 imperial pecks	36.369 litres
	US (dry)	4 US dry pecks	35.239 litres

Avoirdupois weight

1 grain		= 0.065 gram
1 ounce	= 437.5 grains	= 28.35 grams
1 pound	= 16 ounces = 7,000 grains	= 0.45359237 kilogram exactly
1 stone	= 14 pounds	= 6.35 kilograms
1 (long) ton	= 2,240 pounds	= 1.016 tonnes
1 short ton	= 2,000 pounds	= 0.907 tonne

3. SI Units

Base units

Physical quantity	Name	Abbr. or symbol
length	metre	m
mass	kilogram	kg
time	second	s
electric current	ampere	A
temperature	kelvin	K
amount of substance	mole	mol
luminous intensity	candela	cd

Derived units with special names

Physical quantity	Name	Abbr. or symbol
frequency	hertz	Hz
energy	joule	J
force	newton	N
power	watt	W
pressure	pascal	Pa
electric charge	coulomb	C
electromotive force	volt	V
electric resistance	ohm	Ω
electric conductance	siemens	S
magnetic flux	weber	Wb
inductance	henry	H
magnetic flux density	tesla	T
illumination	lux	lx

4. Temperature

Celsius (or Centigrade): Water boils (under standard conditions) at 100° and freezes at 0°.
Fahrenheit: Water boils at 212° and freezes at 32°.
Kelvin: Water boils at 373.15 kelvins and freezes at 273.15 kelvins.

Celsius	Fahrenheit
-50°	-58°
-40°	-40°
-30°	-22°
-20°	-4°
-17.8°	0°
-10°	14°
0°	32°
10°	50°
20°	68°
30°	86°
40°	104°
50°	122°
60°	140°
70°	158°
80°	176°
90°	194°
100°	212°

To convert Celsius into Fahrenheit: multiply by 9, divide by 5, and add 32.
To convert Fahrenheit to Celsius: subtract 32, multiply by 5, and divide by 9.

5. Metric Prefixes

	Abbr. or symbol	Factor
deca-	da	10
hecto-	h	10^2
kilo-	k	10^3
mega-	M	10^6
giga-	G	10^9
tera-	T	10^{12}
deci-	d	10^{-1}
centi-	c	10^{-2}
milli-	m	10^{-3}
micro-	μ	10^{-6}
nano-	n	10^{-9}
pico-	p	10^{-12}

6. Binary system

Only two units (O and 1) are used, and the position of each unit indicates a power of two.

One to ten written in binary form:

	eights (2^3)	fours (2^2)	twos (2^1)	one
1				1
2			1	0
3			1	1
4		1	0	0
5		1	0	1
6		1	1	0
7		1	1	1
8	1	0	0	0
9	1	0	0	1
10	1	0	1	0

Ten is written as 1010 ($2^3 + 0 + 2^1 + 0$); one hundred is written as 1100100 ($2^6 + 2^5 + 0 + 0 + 2^2 + 0 + 0$).